INTERNATIONAL
WHO'S WHO
IN MEDICINE

INTERNATIONAL WHO'S WHO IN MEDICINE

EDITORIAL DIRECTOR

Ernest Kay, D.Litt., F.R.S.A., F.R.G.S

Sales Director:

Roger W. G. Curtis M.A. (Cantab.)

Production Director:

Nicholas S. Law

Assistant Editors:

Diane Butcher

Angela Bridgeman

Deborah Fitchett

Researcher:

Joy Dean

All communications to: International Biographical Centre,
Cambridge CB2 3QP, England

INTERNATIONAL WHO'S WHO IN MEDICINE

FIRST EDITION

EDITORIAL DIRECTOR
ERNEST KAY

International Biographical Centre
Cambridge England

First Edition 1987

ISBN 0900332 86 7

Computer typesetting by D and S Graphics, Sucklings Yard, Church Street, Ware, Hertfordshire, England.

Printed and bound in Great Britain by: The Bath Press, Lower Bristol Road, Bath BA2 3BL

FOREWORD BY THE HON. GENERAL EDITOR

After more than a year of research, a great deal of correspondence and detailed editorial work the International Biographical Centre is proud to publish this First Edition of the INTERNTIONAL WHO'S WHO IN MEDICINE. It is hoped that further editions will appear before too long.

All the biographical and career information published herein has been acquired from those who are listed, in response to worldwide questionnaire mailing. Once our editorial team had written entries, proofs were made available for checking, prior to publication, to ensure accuracy.

Doctors in general practice, surgeons, consultants, administrators and senior teaching staff are included together with nurses, dentists, pharmacologists and those concerned with public health and rehabilitation, mental health and research.

No work, however large, can include all the world's senior medical professionals and staff. Our editors have attempted to include biographies in this First Edition from as many different countries and fields of medicine as possible in order to reflect the work being done by as wide a variety of individuals as possible; future editions will offer relatively few up-dated entries, space being given instead to additional individuals. Selection has, for this edition, been made on the grounds of interest to the general reader as well as to those within the profession, the amount of information offered, and the status of each person within a section or level of the medical and allied professions, and within the country in which they work.

While each international reference book published by the IBC is in itself a tribute to the lives and careers of those listed, it was decided during 1985, our Silver Jubilee Year celebrating 25 years of publishing Who's Whos, to Dedicate a number of volumes to a selected few individuals who represent the diversity of nations, skills and achievements represented in the main sections of each book. It is therefore my pleasure to Dedicate this First Edition of the INTERNATIONAL WHO'S WHO IN MEDICINE to the following and to congratulate them on their particular professional accomplishments.

Dr. Richard Ackerman (USA)
Maj. Gen. M. Arshad Mirza (Pakistan)
Dr. Steven K. H. Aung (Canada)
Dr. James E. Bates (USA)
Dr. Carlos Bedrossian (USA)
Prof. Syeda F. Begum (Bangladesh)
Mr. Pedro A. Garcia Calderon (Spain)
Dr. Chin-Hong Chan (Taiwan)
Dr. Harold T. Conrad (USA)
Dr. James M. Croker (Australia)
Dr. Ahmed D. Faheem (USA)
Dr. Charles M. French (Kenya)
Dr. Michael J. Gentlesk (USA)
Mr. Drago Ikic (Yugoslavia)
Dr. Asoka W. Jayasinghe (USA)
Prof. Barbro Johansson (Sweden)
Dr. Irving Kaufman (USA)
Dr. Yong-Kook A. Kim (USA)

Dr. A. Gurney Kimberley (USA)
Mr. Israel Kleinberg (USA)
Dr. Fouad E. Lajam (USA)
Dr. Sewa Singh Legha (USA)
Dr. V. B. Mahesh (USA)
Dr. Howard G. Malin (USA)
Prof. Dr. A. A. Mallick (India)
Dr. Thomas H. Mallory (USA)
Dr. Ronald J. Malpiede (USA)
Mr. Charles Marks (USA)
Mr. Gosaku Naruse (Japan)
Dr. Vickie L. M. Newcomb (USA)
Dr. Howard J. Peak (Australia)
Mr. Alphonse Salerno (USA)
Dr. Kathleen Sandman (USA)
Dr. Diane W. Schuller (USA)
Dr. Kayode A. Shenkoya (Nigeria)

Dr. Emmanuel H. Tadross F.R.C.P. (Canada)

Dr. Albert Y. M. Tsai (Hong Kong)

Mr. A. Villeneuve (Canada)

Dr. Pei-yen Wang (Taiwan)

Dr. Thomas A. Williams P.A. (USA)

Mr. Vern A. Wolfley (USA)

The co-operation of thousands of individuals and hundreds of health authorities and professional societies, institutes and associations is gratefully acknowledge by the International Biographical Centre, its researchers and editors.

Readers are encouraged to propose the names and addresses of those they feel have been omitted from this edition; these will be invited to submit material for future publication.

It must be emphasized that no charge or fee is made for inclusion in the INTERNATIONAL WHO'S WHO IN MEDICINE.

Whilst every effort has been made to ensure a high standard of accuracy in editing and publishing this edition, it is possible that occasional errors may occur in a work of this nature. In this event we apologize in advance.

Cambridge,
England.

November 1986

INTERNATIONAL BIOGRAPHICAL CENTRE

The IBC group publishes one of the widest ranges of contemporary biographical reference works under any one imprint; some titles date back to the 1930's.

Current titles include:
Dictionary of International Biography
Men of Achievement (Illustrated)
The World Who's Who of Women (Illustrated)
International Authors and Writers Who's Who*
International Businessmen's Who's Who
International Who's Who in Art and Antiques
International Who's Who in Community Service
International Who's Who in Education
International Who's Who in Engineering
International Who's Who in Medicine
International Who's Who in Music
International Who's Who in Poetry*
International Youth in Achievement
The World Who's Who of Women in Education
Who's Who in the Commonwealth
Who's Who in Western Europe
Dictionary of Latin American and Caribbean Biography
Dictionary of Scandinavian Biography
Foremost Women of the Twentieth Century

*recently published in combined volumes

All enquiries to:
International Biographical Centre
Cambridge CB2 3QP
England

Dedications

Dr. Richard C. Ackerman

"For an Outstanding Contribution as Physician, Author and Clinical Professor of Orthopaedics".

DR. R. C. ACKERMAN

"Gross Anatomy of the Extremities', 1974, "An In Depth Study of Neuro-Anatomy -Part 1 The Spinal Cord", 1975, "Part II The Brain", 1975, "Illustrated Manual of Extra Vertebral Technics - Supplement Number One: Shoulder and Knee", 1977; "A Chiropractic Guide to Clinical History and Physical Examination", 1977, and author of numerous articles to professional journals including, 'Pathfinder Press Inc', 'RCA Publications', and 'NCC'. Dr Richard Ackerman is an Orthopaedist, Professor, and Author.

Born on 27 September 1949 in New York, USA, Richard Ackerman gained his BA in Clinical Psychology in 1973, his BS in Human Anatomy in 1975, his DC in 1976, is a Diplomate of the American Board of Chiropractic Orthopaedists, and a Fellow of the Academy of Chiropractic Orthopaedists. From 1974-1975 he was an Anatomy Lab Assistant at the National College of Chiropractic, a Lab Instructor, Clinicopathologic Conference, 1974-77, Lab Instructor, Clinical Neurology, 1977, Physical Diagnosis, 1974-77. His Faculty positions include, National College of Chiropractic, Lombard, 1974-78, and one academic year residency programme in Orthopaedics.

Dr Ackerman is a member of the American Chiropractic Association, American College of Chiropractic Orthopaedics, American Medical Writers Association, American Heart Association Teaching Staff, American National Red Cross and is a Council Member, Neurology, Diagnosis & Internal Disorders. A Graduate of the National College of Chiropractic with Honours, he received the Bovenaan Outstanding Junior Senior Award from Hofstra University in 1972 and was on the Honour Roll and Deans List on numerous occasions at the National College of Chiropractic. In 1976, Richard Ackerman received the Outstanding Senior Award from the American Chiropractic Association, and in the same year was the recipient of the Springwall Residency Grant for Orthopaedic Residency.

In 1984 on the 7 December he married Marylynn Moore, in Albuquerque, and has 1 son and 2 daughters.

A biography of Dr. Richard C. Ackerman appears in the main section of this Volume/Edition.

Dr. Steven K. H. Aung

"For An Outstanding Contribution to Medicina Alternativa - Natural Medicine - Acupuncture & Traditional Chinese Medicine".

S.K.H. AUNG

Family and Geriatric Physician, Medical Acupuncture Consultant, and Visiting Professor, Alternative Medicine, Steven Kyaw Htut Aung gained his MBBS from Rangoon University, Burma, his MD in Canada, and his D.Ac., from the Acupuncture Research Institute, Steven Aung also has a PhD in Alternative Medicine, and is an FICAN Nutrition, California, and an FACA, Fellow Acupuncture.

From 1973 to 1976 he was an Assistant Surgeon at North Oklahoma General Hospital, USA, becoming a Medical Resident, at St Vincent's Hospital, in Vancouver, Canada, 1976-78, and a Rotating Intern at McGill University, 1978-79. From 1979 to 1980 he was the Family Medicine Resident at the Memorial University, Newfoundland, becoming Family Physician at the Health Sciences Centre, 1982-83. In 1980 until 1982 Dr Aung was the District Medical Officer at the Jeffreys Medical Centre, Newfoundland. In 1983 until 1984 he was the Geriatric Clinical Assistant at the Edmonton General Hospital, and since 1984 has been the Acupuncture (Medical) Consultant, at the Edmonton General Hosptial, Cross Cancer Institute, Misericordia Hospital, and Director of the Edmonton Medical Acupuncture Centre. Dr Aung has been visiting Professor in Alternative Medicine since 1985.

Steven Aung has written "Obesity", 1973, "Pain and Acupuncture", 1973, and "Acupuncture for Cancer Pain", 1984. He is a Member and Fellow of several professional organisations including the American and Canadian Medical Association, and the American Academy of Acupuncture. In 1962 he received the Aung-San UNISCEF Literature Gold Medal, his MD in 1973, his PhD, 1985, and his MD in Acupuncture in 1977.

Dr Aung enjoys Sports, Arts, Writing, and Outdoor Nature, He married Debbie on the 8 February 1974 and has 1 son and 3 daughters.

A biography of Dr. Steven K. H. Aung appears in the main section of this Volume/Edition.

James Earl Bates

"For An Outstanding Contribution to Podiatric Medical Education".

DR. J. E. BATES

James Earl Bates is married to Lauralou Courtney Bates, and has 2 sons and 2 daughters.

He gained a DSC at Temple University School of Chiropody in 1946, and a DPM from the Pennsylvania College of Podiatric Medicine in 1970, and an EdD, from Franklin Pierce in 1972. From 1948 to 1960 Dr Bates was an Associate Professor of Roentgenology, at Temple University, and since 1962 has been President of the Pennsylvania College of Podiatric Medicine, PCPM, and Professor Podiatric Medicine at the same College, A Fellow of the Royal Society of Health, England, and a Fellow of the College of Physicians of Philadelphia, Dr Bates is also a member of the American College of Foot Roentgenologysts, 1958-59, Greater Philadelphia Podiatry Society, Pennsylvania Podiatry Association of which he was President 1959-60, and a member of numerous other professional organisations. Since 1975 Dr Bates has been General Chairman of the American Podiatry Association Region Three Annual Convention, and Chairman of the International Committee of the American Podiatry Association. A member and past President of the Board of Managers, Germantown YWCA, James Bates is also a Past member of the Board of Trustees of the First United Methodist Church of Germantown and Past Chairman of the Finance Commission of the First United Methodist Church of Germantown. Chairman of the 277th and 278th Annual Germantown Week, Dr Bates is a past Deputy Service Director of the Philadelphia Civil Defence Council.

His contributions to professional journals includes: 'Journal of the American Podiatry Association'; 'Journal of Podiatric Medical Education'; 'Current Podiatry Journal'; 'British Journal of Chiropody'. In 1961, James Bates, received the Man of the Year Award from the Pennsylvania Podiatry Association, and in 1962 was the recipient of a merit award from the American Podiatry Association, Region Three. Germantown Businessmen's Association awarded Dr Bates their distinguished service award in 1964, and in 1970 he received a special citation from the Board of Trustees of the Pennsylvania College of Podiatric Medicine, and this was followed in 1973 by a recognition award for Service to Principles and Purposes of the American Podiatry Students' Association, from that Association. In the same year the Pennsylvania Podiatry Students Association gave him an Appreciation Award for Contributions to the Student Government and to the Advancement of Podiatric Medicine, and he was the Recipient of the Milton J. Shapp, Governor of the Commonwealth of Pennsylvania Citation. Also in 1973 he received the Special Citation from the Pennsylvania Podiatry Association, and in 1974 was the recipient of a Fellowship Award from the International Academy of Preventive Medicine.

A biography of James Earl Bates appears in the main section of this Volume/Edition.

Carlos Bedrossian MD

"For An Outstanding Contribution as Practitioner, Teacher, Researcher and Leader in the field of Pathology".

DR. C. BEDROSSIAN

Professor of Pathology at St Louis University School of Medicine, Carlos W.M. Bedrossian, gained his BS in 1962 from Movra Lacerda College in Brazil, and his MD from the University of Sao Paulo, Brazil in 1967. Born on the 1 May 1944 in Brazil, he married Ursuala Kay Kennedy on 8 August 1970 in Jacksonville, Florida, USA, and has 2 sons and 1 daughter.

A Fellow of the American Pathologists Association, Dr Bedrossian is President of the Latin American Pathology Foundation, a member of the International Academy of Pathology, International Academy of Cytology, American Society of Clinical Pathology, and the American Society of Cytology. Dr Bedrossian is also a member of the American College of Chest Physicians, American Thoracic Society, and the Latin American Society of Pathology. From 1973 to 1975 he was an Assistant Professor at the University of Oklahoma, and in 1975 joined the University of Texas as an Assistant Professor, becoming an Associate Professor in 1977 until 1981. Dr Bedrossian became Chief of the Laboratory, and Professor, at the Vanderbilt University, Nashville, 1981-84, and since 1984 has been Professor and Director of the Cytopathology & Immunocytochemistry Department at the St Louis University School of Medicine.

In 1967 he was awarded the Best Student Basic Sciences, and in 1972 the MD Anderson Award in Clinical Research. Dr Bedrossian, was the Editor in Chief of 'Diagnostic Cytopathology', 1984. He has written numerous articles in professional journals and these include, 'American Journal Clinical Pathology'; 'Cancer'; 'American Surgery'; 'Journal Experimental and Molecular Pathology'; 'Human Pathology'; 'Chest'; 'Southern Medical Journal'; 'Laboratory Medicine', etc. His most recent include: Co-author, "Analysis of Pleural Effusions by Pulse Cytophotometry", 'Cancer', 1983; Co-Author, "Flow Cytometry in Cancer Diagnosis", in 'Stefanini's Progress in Clinical Pathology', 1983; Co-Author, "Azathioprine-associated interstitial pneumonitis", 'American Journal Clinical Pathology', 1983; and "Immunoperoxidase method to detect herpes virus in cytologic specimens", 'Labroatry Medicine', number 15.

Listed in Who's Who in the South, Who's Who in Cancer Research, Dr Bedrossian enjoys Stamp Collecting, Soccer Coaching and Travel in his leisure hours.

A biography of Dr Carlos Bedrossian appears in the main section of this Volume/Edition.

Dr. Ching-Hong Chan

"For An Outstanding Contribution as A Pioneer in Adolescent Psychiatry in the Republic of China".

DR. CHIN-HONG CHAN

Chin-Hong Chan was born on 26 June 1951 in Macau, Portuguese Colony, near Hong Kong, and married Rhumn-Hwa Fu on 4 June 1978 and has 2 sons.

He gained his Bachelor of Medicine, from the National Defence Medical Centre, Taipei, Taiwan, and Chinese Specialist Certificate in Psychiatry from the Chinese Society of Neurology & Psychiatry, Taiwan, Republic of China. He gained a Diploma in Professional Counselling, International Academy of Professional Counselling & Psychotherapy, and is a Member of the Council of Delegates, International Society of Adolescent Psychiatry.

Clinical Supervisor, Department of Psychiatry, Yu-Li Veterans (Mental) Hospital, Yu-Li, Hua Lian, Taiwan, 1982-84, Dr Chan is currently, Clinical Lecturer, Psychiatry at the National Defence Medical Centre, Taipei, Attending Psychiatrist of Inpatient Service and Child and Adolescent Mental Health Clinic, Department of Psychiatry, Veterans General Hospital, Taipei; Clinical Lecturer, Psychiatry, National Yang Ming Medical College, Taipei. Dr Chan is a Member of the American Group Psychotherapy Association, Corresponding Member of the Canadian Psychiatric Association, member of the Canadian Academy of Child Psychiatry, Canadian Society for Youth Psychiatry and Canadian Group Psychotherapy Association.

He is the author of "Emergency Pharmacological Management of Agitated Patients", in Chinese, 'Clinical Medicine', 1979; "Drug Treatment of Anxiety State: A Double Blind Crossover Trial of Clobazasm", 'Bulletin of Chinese Society of Neurology & Psychiatry', in Chinese, 1980; "Borderline State, Clinical Medicine", in Chinese, 1980; "The Epidemiological Study on the Death from Suicide and Self-inflicted Injury in Taiwan", 'Bulletin of Chinese Society of Neurology & Psychiatry', in Chinese, 1981; "The Survey of Psychiatric Symptoms Among the Mentally Ill Inpatients", 'Bulletin of Chinese Society of Neurology & Psychiatry', in Chinese, 1982; "The Common Psychiatric Problems in the Intensive Care Unit", 'Clinical Medicine', 1984.

Dr Chan was the Recipient of Doctor of the Year, Veterans General Hospital, Taipei, in 1981, and his hobbies and recreations include Taekwon-Do of which he is a 3rd degree Black Belt, International Taekwon-Do Federation & World Taekwon-Do Association, Soccer and Jogging.

A biography of Dr Chin-Hong Chan appears in the main section of this Volume/Edition.

Harold T. Conrad, MD

"For An Outstanding Contribution to Clinical Psychiatry, Medical Education and Hospital Administration".

DR. H. T. CONRAD

Harold Theodore Conrad obtained an AB in Liberal Arts, 1954, and SB in Anatomy in 1955, and an MD in 1958, from the University of Chicago, becoming a Rotating Intern at the US Public Health Service Hospital in San Francisco from 1958-59. From 1959-1962 he was a Resident in Psychiatry in the US Public Health Service Hospital, Lexington, Kentucky. In 1962-1967 he was a Clinical Instructor in Psychiatry at the L.S.U. Medical School, joining the University of Kentucky Medical School in 1969 until 1973 as a Clinical Assistant Professor of Psychiatry. In 1981 he joined the University of Washington Medical School, as a Clinical Assistant Professor, of Psychiatry, a position he held until 1984. Dr. Conrad has been Clinical Associate Professor of Psychiatry at the University of Washington, since 1985. From 1962-67 he was Chief of Psychiatry at the US Public Health Service Hospital, New Orleans, and in 1967-1968 he appointed Clinical Director. Dr Conrad became Deputy Director, Division of Field Investigations, National Institute of Mental Health, 1968-69, and Chief of the NIMH Clinical Research Centre at Lexington in 1969 until 1973. A Consultant in Psychiatry, Division of Alcohol Drug Abuse and Mental Health Programmes, US Public Health Service Regional Office IX, San Francisco, 1973-79, Director, Adolescent Unit, Alaska Psychiatric Institute, 1979-81, Director, Alaska Psychiatric Institute, 1981-85, Dr Conrad is Medical Director, HSA Bayou Oaks Hospital, Houma, 1985-. Harold Conrad was born on 25 January 1934 in Milwaukee, Wisconsin, USA, and married Elaine Marie Blaine on 1 September 1962, in New Orleans, and has 4 sons and 1 daughter. He is a Member of the American Medical Association, Alaska Psychiatric Association, Alaska State Medical Association, American Academy of Medical Directors, American College of Physician Executives, Anchorage Medical Society, and Association of Military Surgeons of the United States. A Fellow of the American Psychiatric Association, he is also a member of the Retired Officers' Association, American Geriatrics Society, American Association for Geriatric Psychiatry, and is a Fellow of the Royal Society of Health, London, England. Dr Conrad's Special National Responsibilities include: Consultant to Surgeon General, USPHS, 1968-73, Delegate to the White House Conference on Youth, 1971, Consultant to the National Commission of Marijuana and Drug Abuse, 1973, Consultant to the Social Security Administration, 1983-, and he has many local special responsibilities. Harold Conrad's articles in professional journals, include, "New Directions in treating Narcotic Addicts", 'Mental Health Digest', 1970; "Rehabilitation of the Narcotic Addict", 'Archivos de investigacion Medica', 1974; "Psychiatric Treatment of Narcotic Addiction", 'Handbuch der experimentellen Pharmakologie', 1977, and "Orthomolecular psychiatry, A Report to the Alaska State Legislature", 1985. Dr Conrad has been a member of the Alpha Omega Alpha Medical Society since 1958, and is the recipient of the Commendation Medal from the US Public Health Service in 1970. In 1971 he received the Omega Psi Phi National Award for Studies in Drug Abuse, and recieved the Resolution of Commendation from Guam Legislature in 1977.

A biography of Dr Harlold Conrad appears in the main section of this Volume/Edition.

James Meyrick Croker

"For An Outstanding Contribution to the Dental Profession, other Professions and the Community".

J. M. CROKER, ESQ

Lawn Bowls, Stamp Collecting, and Fishing are the hobbies of James Meyrick Croker, President of the 24th Australian Dental Asssociation Congress. Born on the 17 May 1927 in Mackay, Queensland, Australia, he married Joan Catherine Morris on 22 February 1952, in Brisbane, and has 4 daughters.

Chairman of numerous committees of the Queensland Branch of the Australian Dental Association, and an Executive Member, and President of the Queensland Branch of that association, Mr Croker is a member of the Federation Dentaire International, Dental Circle Post Graduate Study Club, Delta Sigma Delta, and is a Member, President, of the Queensland Council of Professions, Australian Council of Professions.

A Consultant of the Dental Health, International College of Dentists, Mr Croker was awarded Life Membership of the Queensland Branch of the Australian Dental Association, in December 1985. The Recipient of a Distinguished Service Award, Queensland Branch of the Australian Dental Association Mr Croker also recieved the Paul Harris Fellowship from the Rotary Club in 1981.

On 26 January 1986, James Croker was awarded the AM, in the General Division of the Order of Australia for his services to the profession of dentistry.
A biography of Mr James Croker appears in the main section of this Volume/Edition.

Ahmed Daver Faheem, MD

"For An Outstanding Contribution to Clinical Psychiatry, Education and Community Work".

DR. AHMED D. FAHEEM

Clinical Associate Professor of Psychiatry, Ahmed Daver Faheem, was elected Giant in Medicine by the University of Missouri Medical School Graduating Class in 1981, and was the Recipient of the Best Teacher Award, Residents in Psychiatry, at the University of Missouri in 1979, 1980, 1981.

Born in Nizamabad, India on 7 March 1948, Dr Faheem married Najama on 4 June 1972 in Hyderbad, India and has 2 daughters. His qualifications include an MD, MRC Psychiatry from the United Kingdom, and a DPM from the United Kingdom, and he is Certified by the American Board of Psychiatry and Neurology.

A Senior House Officer at the Walsgrove Hospital, Coventry, England, in 1973-74, he was appointed Registrar at the Central Hospital, Warwick in 1974-76. In 1976 he received a Fellowship in Psychosomatic Medicine, and in 1978-1982 was an Assistant Professor at the University of Missouri, Columbia, Missouri, USA. Dr Faheem was appointed Clinical Associate Professor at the University of West Virginia, Morgantown, in 1983, and has been in Private Practice in General and Adolescent Psychiatry, in Beckley, since 1982.

A member of the American Psychiatric Association, and the American Society of Clinical Hypnosis, Dr Faheem also belongs to the West Virginia State Medical Association, and the Raleigh County Medical Society in West Virginia, and is an Examiner of the American Board of Psychiatry and Neurology. Theatre, Public Speaking, Jogging and Films are the interests of Ahmed Faheenm in his leisure hours, and his biography appears in Who's Who, Directory of Medical Specialists, USA. He is the author of "Indiginous Healing Groups", in Kaplan and Sadock's 'Comprehensive Group Psychotherapy', 1983, and "Themes in Cultural Psychiatry: An Annotated Bibliography 1975-1980", 1982.

He is the Author of several articles to professional journals and these include: "Commitment of the Mentally Ill in Missouri", co-author, 'Missouri Medicine', 1979; "The Heavenly Vision of a Poor Woman", 'Journal of Operational Psychiatry', 1979; "Respiratory Dyskinesia and Dysarthria from prolonged Neuroleptic Use: Tardive Dyskinesia?", 'American Journal of Psychiatry', 1982; and "Long-term Care of Older People: A Practical Guide", Book Review, 'Journal of Biological Psychology', 1978.

A biography of Dr Ahmed Faheem appears in the main section of this Volume/Edition.

Syed Firoza Begum

"For An Outstanding Contribution as a Leader in Maternal & Child Health, Physician, Teacher, Public Servant".

PROFESSOR S. FIROZA BEGUM

Member and Fellow of the Royal College of Obstetrics & Gynaecologists, England, Syeda Firoza Begum was born on 1 April 1930, in Comilla, Bangladesh. She married Professor M.A. Jalil in 1953 and has 1 son and 1 daughter.

She gained her MB BS in Dhaka, and was Senior House Officer at the Hammersmith Post Graduate Medical Institute, 1962, and served for six months as Registrar at the Welsh National School of Medicine in the Department of Obstetrics and Gynaecology, Cardiff, 1962. In 1964, Professor Begum gained her MRCOG and became a member of the Royal College of Obstetricians and Gynaecologists of London. She joined Dhaka Medical College and Hospital in 1964 as an Associate Professor of Obstetrics and Gynaecology, and was appointed Professor in 1967, and since 1971 has been Professor and Head of the Obstetrics and Gynaecology Department at that college.

Professor Begum is the Author of various articles in professional journals including 'Pakistan Medical Review', 'Proceedings of Asia and Oceania Federation of Obstetricians and Gynaecologists Conference in Bankok', 1972, and is the author of a book, "Medical Problems in Obstetrics Practice", in 1974, Her most recent articles include: "Risks and Costs of Illegally Induced Abortion in Bangladesh", 'International Fertility Research Programme', 1981, "Patient Treatment of Pregnancy Wastage", 1983, "Clinical Trial of Neo Sampon Vaginal Contraceptive Tablets", 'International Fertility Research Programme', 1980; "Smoking and Fetal Growth", in 'Intra Uterine Growth Retardation', 1981.

A member of the Medical Protection Society of London, the Education Committee of Asia, and Oceania Federation of Obstetrics and Gynaecologists, Population Crisis Committee, American Asssociation of Laperocopist, Professor Begum is President of the Teachers Association of Bangladesh, a Member of the Voluntary Health Services Society, International Women's Health Coalition, Washington DC, and a Member of the Bangladesh Family Planning Clinic. Professor Begum is also the President of the Bangladesh Medical Association, President of the Bangladesh Association for Prevention of Septic Abortion and President of the Bangladesh Association for Maternal and Neonatal Health.

A Recipient of an Award by the Path Finder Fund for Outstanding activities on Research, Teaching and Population Control Activities, in Briston, USA, in 1983, Professor Begum enjoys music.

A biography of Professor Syeda Firoza Begum appears in the main section of this Volume/Edition.

Dr Charles Marcus French

"For An Outstanding Contribution in promoting the development of health care and research services in remote, inaccessible underdeveloped places".

DR. C. M. FRENCH

Born of English parents in Dar-es-Salaam in 1938 when hs father was working for the British Colonial service in Tanganyika (now Tanzania), Charles Marcus French, studied at St Catharine's College, Cambridge University, England, gaining a BA in 1959, and qualified as a Medical Practitioner in 1962 at the London Hospital Medical School. Dr French was appointed Junior Lecturer in Physiology at the London Hospital Medical School in 1963 until 1966, and in 1967 was commissioned into the Regular Army, and seconded to the South Arabian Army. He returned to the United Kingdom when Aden achieved independence and served in Western Germany and West Berlin, 1968-69 as a Family Doctor. In 1969 to 1970 he was Garrison Medical Officer in British Honduras, returning to England in 1970 to undertake a Senior Officer's course, during which he was appointed Specialist in Physiology. After completing the course in August 1972, Dr French was appointed to a Research Post with the Army Personnel Research Establishment in England until 1974. He was promoted to the rank of Major in 1972, and Senior Specialist in 1973. The last year of his army service was spent as Assistant Director of Army Health. In 1976 he took up an appointment with the African Medical and Research Foundation in June 1976, and is an Honorary Lecturer in Parasitology at the Liverpool School of Tropical Medicine. A Fellow of the Royal Society of Medicine, Dr French is a member of the British Medical Assocition, the Kenya Medical Association and Life Member of the Aero Club of East Africa. Charles French is the Author of "Guidelines for the Surviellance, Prevention and Control of Echinococcosis/Hydahdosis", in 1981 and a contributor to "Treatment of Human Echinococcosis", for the WHO in 1981. He is the author of numerous articles to professional journals and these include: "Hydatid Disease in the Turkana District of Kenya I - The Background to the Problem with Hypotheses to Account for the Remarkably High Prevalence of the Disease in Man", 'Annals of Tropical Medicine and Parasitology', co-author, 1982, "Hydatid Disease in the Turkana District of Kenya II - A Study in Medical Geography", 'Annals of Tropical Medicine and Parasitology', co-author; "Hydatid Disease in the Turkana District of Kenya IV - The Prevalance of Echinococcus Granulosus infections in dogs and observations on the role of the dog in the lifestyle of the Turkana", 'Annals of Tropical Medicine and Parasitology', 1985; "Hydatid Disease in the Turkana District of Kenya V - Problems of Interpretation of data from a mass Serological Survey", 'Annals of Tropical Medicine and Parasitology', 1984. Dr French is the Recipient of the Kenya Open Scholarship in 1955, the Andrew Elliot Prize, London Hospital, England in 1962, and the De Chanmont Prize in 1967. In 1971 he recieved the Parks Medal, the Katherine Webb Medal, The Montetiore Medal, and the Leishaman Medal, 1st Order of Merit, from the Royal Army Medical Corps in London. His leisure interests include, Private Pilot and Aircraft Operator, Classical Music, and Dr French is a Life Member of the International Wine and Food Society.

A biography of Dr Charles French appears in the main section of this Volume/Edition.

Pedro A. Garcia-Calderon

"For An Outstanding Contribution to Allergy and Ocular Immunology".

DR. P. A. GARCIA CALDERON

Pedro Antonio Garcia-Calderon was born on 13 June 1945, in Cartagena, Spain, and is a Consultant in Immunology, and a Director of the Immunolab Centre. He married Ma Jose Muriel Villoria, on 29 July 1969 in Cartagena and has 1 son.

Dr Garcia-Calderon gained his BMed, 1968, MMed, 1970, from Salamanca University and his PhD in Medicine, from the Autonoma University, Barcelona, in 1972. In 1968-70, he was Resident Doctor at St Cruz and San Pablo Hospitals, and was appointed an Assistant Lecturer at the Autonoma University, Barcelona, 1970-72. A Consultant at the Immunological Unit, St Cruz and San Pablo Hospital, Barcelona, 1972-75, a Lecturer in Immunology, Autonoma University, 1972-75, Dr Garcia-Calderon has been Consultant Immunologist, Spanish Social Security Service, 1976-, and Director of the Immunolab, Immunology and Allergy Research Centre, Barcelona, 1980-.

A Member of the Spanish Immunology Society, Spanish Society of Allergy and Immunology, Spanish Society of Biopathology, Association of Medical Dominicana, Catalana Society of Allergy and Clinical Immunology, Catalana Society of Immunology, European Academy for Allergy and Clinical Immunology, Dr Garcia-Calderon is also a member of the European Committee for Clinical Laboratory Standards.

He is the Author of "A New Rapid and More Sensitive Microcytotox Text", 1971, "Lymph. transform test in fixed drug eruption", 1975, "Immune regulators in transfer factor" 1979, "An in vitro study of lymph. in pat. with atopia", 1983, "Cell Mediated immun. in perenn. allergic rhinitis", 1984, and "Immune Complexes in retinitis pigmentosa", 1984.

Dr Garcia-Calderon is an Honorary Member, of the Dominican Academy of Medicine, and enjoys reading, philosophy and classical music and the cinema in his leisure time.

A biography of Dr Pedro Garcia-Calderon appears in the main section of this Volume/Edition.

Michael J. Gentlesk, MD

"For An Outstanding Contribution as a Practicing Physician in the Research and Development of newer treatments and approaches to Allergic/Immunologic Diseases (esp. Asthma & Hymenoptera Hypersensitivity)".

DR. M. J. GENTLESK

Michael John Gentlesk, was born on 23 May 1938, Haddon Heights, New Jersey, USA, and married Jurate Elizabeth Pauliukonis on 5 October 1963 at the Holy Maternity Church, has 4 sons and 3 daughters.

Dr Gentlesk gained his BS in 1960, and his MD in 1964, both from Georgetown University, Washington. Director of Paediatrics and Patient Services, at the Childrens Heart Hospital, in 1972-73, he was appointed Chief, of the Department of Allergy and Immunology, Paediatrics, Our Lady of Lourdes Medical Centre, in 1982, and is currently, Associate Professor of Paediatrics at the Thomas Jefferson University, Philadelphia, Pennsylvania, Clinical Associate Professor, Paediatrics at Rutgers University, and Adjunct Clinical Assistant Professor of Paediatrics at Temple University, St Christophers Hospital.

Michael Gentlesk is a member of the American College of Allergists, American Academy of Allergy and Clinical Immunology, American College of Chest Physicians, American Medical Association, and is a Fellow of the American Academy of Paediatrics.

He is the Author or Co-author of articles in professional journals and these include: "The Comparison of Zaditen Syrup and Placebo in the Prophylaxis of Bronchial Asthma in Children,", co-author, "Home Peak Flow Monitoring in Asthmatic Children", co-author, "Airways Obstruction During Sleep in Hypertrophy of the Tonsils and Adenoids", co-author, 'American Journal of Nursing'; "The Clinical Usefulness of Amphetamine-like Drugs in the Treatment of Chronic Urticaria and Angio-Edema", co-author, 'Journal of Allergy and Immunology', 'Archives of Dermatology'; and "Use of Cromolyn in Allergic Ocular Disease", co-author.

Dr Gentlesk is an Elected Delegate of the New Jersey Medical Society to American Medical Association Meetings for the period 1983 to 1986. His hobbies include, Fishing, Tennis, Golf, Stamp Collecting, Antique Car Collecting.

A biography of Dr Michael Gentlesk appears in the main section of this Volume/Edition.

Mr Drago Ikic

"For An Outstanding Contribution in the field of Science".

ACADEMICAN DRAGO IKIC

Drago Ikic was born on 2 July 1917, in Foca, Yugoslavia, and married Smiljka, now deceased, on 10 May 1948 in Zagreb, and has one daughter.

He gained a Diploma from the Medical Faculty, in Hygiene and Social Medicine, Bacteriology, Virology, Parasitology and Immunology, and an ScD in Immunology. Currently Director of the Institute for Research and Standardization of Immunologic Substances of the Yugoslav Academy of Science and Arts, Dr Ikic has also been Director of the Institute for Control and Research Vaccines in Zagreb, Director of the Serovaccinal Institute in Zagreb, and Director of the Institute of Immunology in Zagreb.

Dr Ikic is a member of the Panel for the Biological Standardization of the WHO, 1957-82, a Director of Interregional Courses for the Biological Standardization of the WHO, 1967, 1968, 1973, 1976, Head and Principal Investigator of the Collaborating Laboratory for Scientific Research and Establishment of the Reference Preparations and Methods of the WHO, 1971-81, and Head of the International Reference Centre for Bacteriological Vaccines for the WHO, 1973-81. He has been a Member of the British Royal Society of Medicine since 1961, a Life Member of the New York Academy of Sciences since 1964, and an Honorary Member of the All-Union Scientific Society of Microbiologists and Epidemiologists, "I.I. Mecnikov", in the USSR.

Dr Ikic is the Editor of, "Clinical Use of Interferon", 1975; "Preparation, Standardization and Clinical Use of Interferon", 1977; "Interferon", 1979; "Stability and Effectiveness of Measles, Poliomyelitis and Pertussis Vaccines", 1976. He is the author of numerous articles in professional journals including: "The Safety of Human Diploid Cell Strains for Man", 'American Journal Epidemiology', 1968; "Vaccines produced in Diploid Cell Lines. Cell Culture for Virus Vaccine Production", 'National Cancer Insitute Monograph', 1968, "Attenuation of Characterization of Edmonston-Zagreb Measles Virus", 'Annals Immunolog. Hung.', 1972, "Application of Human Leucocyte Interferon in Patients with Urinary Bladder Papillomatosis, Breast Cancer and Melanoma: Application of Human Leucocyte Interferon in Patients with Tumors of the Head and Neck: Application of the Human Leucocyte Interferon in Patients with Carcinoma of the Uterine Cervix", 'The Lancet', 1981.

Dr Ikic is the recipient of the Ruder Boskovic Prize in 1972, The Life Achievement Prize in 1980, both awarded by the Socialist Republic of Croatian.

A biography of Dr Drago Ikic appears in the main section of this Volume/Edition.

Dr Asoka W. Jayasinghe

"For An Outstanding Contribution to Private Practice of Psychiatry".

A. W. JAYASINGHE

Asoka Wimalananda Jayasinghe was born on 7 April 1945 in Kandy, Sri Lanka. Since 1977 he has been in Private Practice in the Field of Psychiatry. A Member of the American Psychiatric Association, the Southern California Psychiatric Society, Asoka Jayasinghe is a Fellow of the American Association for Social Psychiatry. Mr Jayasinghe is a Medical Director with the Advanced Mental Health Services of Los Angeles, California, and an Assistant Clinical Professor of Psychiatry at the University of California Los Angeles School of Medicine. An MD, he is also a Diplomate of the American Board of Psychiatry and Neurology.

A biography of Asoka Jayasinghe appears in the main section of this Volume/Edition.

Professor Barbro Johansson

"For An Outstanding Contribution to the effect on the brain of acute and chronic hypertension".

DR. B. B. JOHANSSON

Underwater Archaeology is one of the interests of Barbro Birgitta Johansson, the Professor and Chairman of the Department of Neurology at the University of Lund, Sweden. She is also a member of the International Society of Microcirculation, International Society of Hypertension, the Stroke Council of the American Heart Association.

Born on the 23 December 1933 in Falkenberg, Sweden, she gained her MD in 1959, and her PhD in 1974 both from the University of Goteborg, and a DTM&H from the London School of Hygiene and Tropical Medicine, England in 1964. Her appointments include: Associate Professor, Department of Neurology, University of Goteborg, Consultant to Occupational Neurology, Department of Occupational Health, Goteborg University, and Visiting Scientist, National Institutes of Health, Betheda, Maryland, USA, 1967-68.

Dr Johansson is a Member of the World Federation of Neurology, International Society for Cerebral Circulation, European Neuroscience Association, Royal Society of Medicine, and is a Member of the Committee for Medical Disaster, Swedish Defence Department.

The Author of about 200 Medical Articles in International Journals, and 10-15 book chapters, Dr Johansson's other interests include: Music, Ethnographic Art, Anthropology, International Literature and Languages.

A biography of Dr Barbro Johansson appears in the main section of this Volume/Edition.

Irving Kaufman, MD

"For An Outstanding Contribution as Psychiatrist, Author and Teacher".

DR. I. KAUFMAN

Consultant Psychiatrist, Instructor in Psychiatry, Irving Kaufman is the Editor of 3 books, contributor of 11 book chapters, 29 papers in professional journals and 7 book reviews and a monograph. Born on 16 September 1917 in Orange, New Jersey, USA, he has 3 sons and 1 daughter. After gaining an AB at New York University in 1939, Dr Kaufman studied at the George Washington University School of Medicine, obtaining his MD in 1943. From January to October 1944 he was a Rotating Intern at Newark City Hospital, and from October 1944 to March 1946 was Resident in Pathology at the Sibley Memorial Hospital, Washington DC. Dr Kaufman became a Resident in Psychiatry, at the Taunton State Hospital, 1946-48, and Staff Psychiatrist at Valleyhead Hospital, May 1948 to August 1948. A Training Programme in Child Psychiatry, combined two years at the Judge Baker Guidance Centre, Boston, and James Jackson Putnam Children's Centre, Roxbury, 1948-50, and Dr Kaufman also attended Boston Psychoanalytic Society and Institute Inc. He joined the Judge Baker Guidance Centre in 1950 as a Staff Psychiatrist, becoming Chief Psychiatrist 1953-57, and was the Principal Investigator in Studies in Childhood Schizophrenia, 1952-59, Research in Juvenile Delinquency, 1954-59, and the Pilot Programme for Training Personnel to work in the field of Juvenile Delinquency from 1955-58, and was appointed Research Psychiatrist, 1957-59 before becoming Chief Research Psychiatrist, in 1959. In September 1959, Dr Kaufman joined the Metropolitan State Hospital as Clinical Director, Day Care Programme for Schizophrenic Children and Their Families until 1960. From 1959 to 1979 he was a Staff Member of the Adult Unit, Supervision and Teaching, and since 1959 to date has been a Staff Member of Supervision, Teaching and Research, Gaebler Childrens Hospital. Dr Kaufman was the Staff Psychiatrist, Medical Department, Massachusetts Institute of Technology, 1959-67, and a Director of the Centre of Child and Family Study Inc., Newtonville, 1961-66. He joined the McLean Hospital, Belmont, as an Attending Psychiatrist in 1964, and has been a Member of the Consulting Staff since 1979. Since 1949 he has been on the Visiting Staff, Bournewood Hospital, Brookline, Mass. Dr Kaufman's Teaching Appointments include: Instructor, in Psychiatry, Harvard University School of Medicine, 1956 to 1959, 1965-, Lecturer, Social Psychology 1951 to 1953, 1966 to 1967, Simmons College School of Social Work, and Faculty Member, Smith College School for Social Work, Northampton, 1951-. He has been Consulted and is a Consultant to numerous social agencies, clinics and schools. A Fellow of the American Medical Association, Dr Kaufman is a Life Fellow of the American Psychiatric Association, and American Orthopsychiatric Association, and is a member of the Boston Psychoanalytic Society and Institute, American Psychoanalytic Society and Institute, and International Psychoanalytic Association. A Fellow of the Academy of Phsychosomatic Medicine, American Geriatric Society, Dr Kaufman is a Life Member of the Pan American Medical Association, and the Royal Society of Health, London, England, as well as numerous other professional organisations. The Author of "Character Disorders in Parents of Delinquents", 1959, and Editor of "Normal Psychology of the Aging Process", 1963, "Normal Psychology of the Aging Process," Spanish Edition, 1976, he is the recipient of numerous honours and awards. Dr Kaufman enjoys Cello, Chamber Music, Folk and Square Dancing, and is a Black Belt in Karate.

A biography of Dr Irving Kaufman appears in the main section of this Volume/Edition.

Yong-Kook A. Kim, MD

"For An Outstanding Contribution to the Delivery of Psychiatric Care to the Community".

DR. Y-K. A. KIM

Yong-Kook Augustine Kim was born on 15 August 1939 in Korea and gained his MD in 1964 from the School of Medicine at the Seoul National University, in Korea. In 1981 he was Board Certified by the American Board of Psychiatry and Neurology.

Dr Kim was appointed Director of Development Disability at the Albert Einstein Community Mental Health Centre in Philadelphia, USA, and subsequently became Director of the Older Adult Unit, at the Horsham Clinic, Ambler and a Director of the ADAPT (Substance Abuse Programme) at the Eugenia Hospital. Dr Kim is currently Clinical Director, and Chief of the Psychiatry Department at the Warminster General Hospital, in Warminster, Pennsylvania.

A Recipient of the Legion of Honour from the Chapel of Four Chaplains in July 1982, Dr Kim is a Member of the American Medical Association, Pennyslvania Medical Association, American Psychiatric Association, and the Pennsylvania Psychiatric Society. He is also a Member of the Southern Medical Association, Philadelphia Psychiatric Society and the Philadelphia Medical Association,.

On the 5 April 1967 he married Theresa Kwang-Oak in Korea and has 4 daughters. Dr Kim's hobbies include Golf, Listening to Classical Music, and he is listed in the Directory of Medical Specialties.

A biography of Dr Yong-Kook Kim appears in the main section of this Volume/Edition.

A. Gurney Kimberley

"For An Outstanding Contribution to the study of Low Back and Sciatic Pain, the cause and the treatment thereof".

DR. A. G. KIMBERLEY

Associate Editor of 'Western Journal of Surgery', for 20 years, A. Gurney Kimberley is a Life Member of the Academy of Orthopaedic Surgery, American Medical Association, Pan American Medical Society and the Pan Pacific Surgical Society. A Founding Partner of Orthopaedic Consultants PC, Dr Kimberley is Emeritus Professor of Ortho-paedics at the University of Oregon Medical School, and has been Visiting Professor of Autonomous University of Guadalajara, Mexico, retiring from active practice in 1982.

During World War II, Dr Kimberley was Senior Surgeon for the US Public Health Service, and Consultant for the Selective Service in Oregon. Dr. Kimberley's pre-medical studies were undertaken at Reed College, and he gained his MD from the University of Oregon in 1930. An Internship was taken at St Luke's Hospital, Spokane, Washington and from 1931 to 1937 he was first a resident, then a Kane Fellow in Orthopaedic Surgery at the New York Orthopaedic Hospital. For the last four years of that period he was also Instructor in Orthopaedics at Columbia University Medical School where he gained a DMSc., in 1937. In 1937, Dr Kimberley started private practice in Portland, Oregon, making a sub-specialty of spinal disorders, and became Board Certified and a Diplomate in Orthpaedics, in 1938.

A Charter Member and the first President of the Portland Orthopaedic Club, in 1938, Dr Kimberley is a past President of the North Pacific Orthopaedic Society, 1952-53, Oregon Chapter of the Western Orthopaedic Society, Northwestern Medical Association, The Staff of the Good Samaritan Hosptial, Portland, Oregon, 1970. In 1938 Dr Kimberley was chosen by the National Junior Chamber of Commerce as one of the 100 outstanding Americans below the age of 35.

Born on 14 February 1905 in Northfield Vermont, USA, , Dr Kimberley enjoys skiing, and was a former President of the American Society of Skiing Doctors, and also enjoys Mountain Climbing, Hiking and Gardening. He married Marjorie A Smith in Portland, Oregon on 14 February 1943 and has 4 sons and 3 daughters.

A biography of Dr Kimberley appears in the main section of this Volume/Edition.

Israel Kleinberg

"For An Outstanding Cointribution as a pioneer and innovator of teaching and research programmes in Oral Biology that have helped significantly to establiah Oral Biology as a major health science".

DR. I. KLEINBERG

Professor and Chairman of the Department of Oral Biology and Pathology, at the School of Dental Medicine, State University of New York, Stony Brook, USA, since 1973, Dr Israel Kleinberg is a Member of the International American Associations for Dental Research, American Society of Microbiology and the Royal College of Dentists of Canada. He is the author of numerous original scientific papers contributed to professional journals and his books include: "Caries Research", and "Calcified Tissue Research". His articles appear in 'British Dentist'; 'Journal Dental Research'; 'British Dentist Journal'; 'Archives Oral Biology'; 'Journal Periodontic Research'; and is the inventor of several patents.

Israel Kleinberg was born on 1 May 1930 in Toronto, Canada, and married Louise Sfreddo on 19 September 1955 in Dryden, Ontario, and has 3 sons and 1 daughter.

He obtained his DDS from the University of Toronto in 1952, his PhD from the University of Durham, England in 1958, and is a Fellow of the Royal College of Dentists, Canada. An Assistant Professor, Biochemistry, Faculty of Medicine, 1958-59, Associate Professor, Biochemistry, 1959-61, Associate Professor, Oral Biology, Head, Biochemistry, Faculty of Dentistry, 1961-65, Professor, Oral Biology, Head, Oral Biology and Biochemstry, 1965-73, at the University of Manitoba, Canada, he joined the State University of New York, USA in 1973.

Dr Kleinburg is the co-author, with S.A. Ellison and I.D. Mandel, of "Saliva and Dental Caries", in 1979. He is the recipient of the Canada Centennial Medal, from the Government of Canada, 1967, and an Honorary DSc, from the University of Manitoba, 1983. Israel Kleinberg's most recent journal articles include, "Urea Enhancement of the pH-rise Activities of Arginine and Arginine Peptide", 1983; "Further Comparison of the Microbial Compositions of Salivary Sediment and Pooled Dental Plaque"; 1984; "Relation between Sugar Clearance and Salivary Flow Rate", 1984; 'Effect of Saliva on the pH-fall Activity of Salivary Sediment", 1984; "Ability of Differnt Oral Micro-organisms to produce Base from Urea and Arginine", all co-authored and all in 'Journal Dental Research'. His main interest is Gardening.

A biography of Dr. Israel Kleinberg appears in the main section of this Volume/Edition.

Fouad E. Lajam, MD

"For An Outstanding Contribution to Thoracic Surgery".

DR. F. E. LAJAM

A Diplomat of the American Board of Surgery and a Diplomat of the American Board of Thoracic Surgery, Fouad Elias A. Lajam was born in Israel on the 4 November 1937. He married Joanne Termine in New York City, USA on 27 November 1965 and has 1 son and 2 daughters.

An MD, DFACS, FACC, FCCP, Dr Lajam studied at the University of Santo Domingo, joining the Mount Sinai School of Medicine, New York, USA, in 1968 as an Instructor in Surgery. From 1971-1972 he was an Instructor in Cardio Thoracic Surgery 1972-75 an Associate in Surgery, and since 1975 has been an Assistant Professor of Cardio Thoracic Surgery. From 1972-1975 he was Attending, Cardio Thoracic Surgery, and since 1975 has been Chief of Cardio Thoracic Surgery at the Mount Sinai Hospital Services, Elmhurst, New York. In 1972 until 1975 Dr Lajam was Clinical Assistant in Surgery, and since 1975 has been Assistant Attending, in Cardio-Thoracic Surgery at Mount Sinai Medical Centre, New York, and since 1973 has been Chief of Cardio-Thoracic Surgery at the Bronx Vereran's Administration Hospital, Mount Sinai Hospital Services, New York.

A Member of the Society of Thoracic Surgeons, New York Society of Thoracic Surgery, Dr Lajam is a Fellow of the American College of Surgeons, American College of Cardiology and American College of Chest Physicians. Dr Lajam is the author or co-author of numerous articles in professional journals and the most recent include: "Pulsus Paradoxus: A Manifestation of a Marked Reduction of Left Ventricular End-Diastolic Volume in Cardiac Volume in Cardia Tamponade", 'The Journal of Thoracic and Cardiovascular Surgery', 1980, Co-author, "One State Surgery for Bilateral Bullous Emphysema via Median Sternotomy: Report of Three Cases", 'The Mount Sinai Journal of Medicine', 1983.

A biography of Dr Fouad Lajam appears in the main section of this Volume/Edition.

Sewa Singh Legha, MD

"For An Outstanding Contribution to the Development of Cancer-Chemotherapy".

DR. SEWA S. LEGHA

Associate Professor of Medicine, Sewa Singh Legha's hobby is reading. Educated in India he obtained his Pre-Medical Diploma from DAV College, Punjab University in 1965, and his MBBS, in 1970 from Christian Medical College, at Punjab University. He joined the Medical College, Wisconsin, Milwaukee, USA, as an Assistant Clinical Instructor, 1972-74, becoming a Specialist Assistant in Cancer Therapy Evaluation Programme at Bethesda, Maryland, 1974-76.

From 1977-78 Dr Legha was a Faculty Associate at the UTMD Anderson Hospital and Tumor Institute, Houston, and in 1978 was appointed Assistant Professor, Medicine, Assistant Internist, and in 1980 became, Associate Professor, Medicine, Associate Internist, and since 1983 Associate Professor, Medicine, Chemotherapy Research, UTMDAH, Houston. In 1985 he was appointed Associate Professor of Medical Oncology at the UTMD Anderson Hospital and Tumor Institute, Houston. A Member of the American Federation Clinical Research, American Association of Cancer Research, American Society of Clinical Oncology, American Medical Association, American Society of Cancer Chemotherapy, Dr Legha is also a member of the American Society of Internal Medicine, Harris County Medical Society, Texas Medical Association, American Association for Advancement of Science, European Association of Cancer, Indian Society Clinical Oncology, International Society Chemotherapy and the International Medical Science Academy.

Dr Legha is the author of 83 articles, and his chapters in books include: "New Drugs in the Treatment of Cancer", 1984; "Doxorubicin Administration by Continuous Venous Infusion"; "Clinical Trials of Infusion Chemotherapy in Breast Cancer" and his articles appear in National and International journals including: 'Cancer'; 'Cancer Treatment'; 'Journal of the American Medical Assocition'; 'Ultrastructural Pathology'; 'European Journal Cancer Clinical Oncology'; 'American Journal of Clinical Oncology'; 'Cancer Research'; and 'Cancer Therapy Update'

A Fellow of the American College of Physicians, 1977, Dr Legha received the Junior Faculty Clinical Fellowship from the American Cancer Society in 1978-81. Sewa Singh Legha was born on 17 December 1946 in the Punjab, India, and married Kuldip Gill on 12 October 1975 in Washington DC, USA, and has 1 son and 2 daughters.

A biography of Dr Sewa Legha appears in the main section of this Volume/Edition.

Dr V. B. Mahesh

"For An Outstanding Contribution to Medical and graduate education and research in the area of reproductive biology and hormone action".

DR. V. B. MAHESH

Regents Professor, Robert B. Greenblatt Professor, Chairman of the Department of Endocrinology at the Medical College of Georgia, 1970-, Dr Mahesh joined the Medical College of Georgia, in 1959 as an Assistant Research Professor of Endocrinology. Born on 25 April 1932 in Khanki, Punjab, India, Dr Virendra B. Mahesh is a Citizen of the USA. He gained BSc with Honours from Patna University, India, in 1951, an MSc., in Chemistry, in 1953, and a PhD in Organic Chemistry in 1955, both from Delhi University, and in 1958 received a D.Phil., in Biological Sciences from Oxford University, England. From 1953-56 he was a Research Fellow of the Council of Scientific and Industrial Research, India, and in 1956 joined the Department of the Regius Professor of Medicine at Oxford University, England as Assam Oil Company Fellow. In 1958, Dr Mahesh was Travelling Fellow of the Welcome Foundation at the Organisch-Chemische Anstalt der Universitat Basel, Switzerland, and in 1958-59 was James Hudson Brown Memorial Fellow, at Yale University, USA. An Editorial Board Member of the 'Journal of Clinical Endocrinology and Metabolism', 1976-81, Dr Mahesh has been on the Editorial Board of 'Steroids' since 1963, and was on the Advisory Board of 'Maturitas', 1977-81, and 'Journal of Endocrinological Investigations'. A Referee for papers in: American Journal of Gerontology, American Journal of Obstetrics and Gynaecology, Biology of Reproduction, Endocrinology, Fertility and Sterility, Journal of Clinical Endocrinology and Metabolism, Obstetric and Gynaecology, Proceedings of the Society of Experimental Biology and Medicine, Science and Steroids, Dr Mahesh is a Review for Grants for the National Science Foundation. The Recipient of the Rubin Award from the American Society for the Study of Sterility for his work on Polycystic Overies in 1963, Dr Mahesh received the Billings Silver Medal for his work on Gonadeal Dysgenesis in 1965, the Best Teacher Award, School of Medicine Class of 1972, and Outstanding Faculty Award, School of Graduate Studies, 1981. A Member of the American Association for Laboratory Animal Science, American Association for University Professor American Fertility Society, American Physiological Society; Biochemical Society, England, Chemical Society, Endocrine Society, Sigma Xi, International Society for Neuroendocrinology, New York Academy of Science and Society of Biological Chemists. President, 1980-82, of the International Society of Reproductive Medicine, Dr Mahesh also belongs to the Society for Gynaecologic Investigations and Society for the Study of Reproduction. Dr Mahesh has been an invited speaker to numerous symposia and lectures, has organised NIH Workshops, and NIH Study Sections. He is the Editor of "The Menopausal Syndrome", 1974, and co-editor of "The Pituitary - A Current Review", 1977, "Functional Correlates of Hormone Receptors in Reproduction", 1981, "Recent Advances in Fertility Research, Part A & B", 1982, "Hirsutism and Virilism", 1983, "Unwanted Hair - Its Cause and Treatment", 1985. Dr Mahesh has written numerous articles in professional journals including: 'Journal Pharmacology Experimental Theory'; 'Journal of Theoretical Biology', 'Neuroendocrinology'. Virendra Bushan Mahesh married Sushila Aggarwal on 29 June 1955 and has 1 son and 1 daughter.

A biography of Dr Virendra Mahesh appears in the main section of this Volume/Edition.

Howard Gerald Malin, D. P. M.

"For An Outstanding Contribution to the Profession of Podiatric Medicine".

DR. H. G. MALIN

Podiatrist, Journalist, Educator, National and International Lecturer, Howard Gerald Malin was born on 2 December 1941 in Providence, Rhode Island, USA. A Member of the American Public Health Association, 1972-81, American Podiatric Medical Association, 1973-, New York Academy of Science, and Academy of Podiatric Medicine and an Associate Member of the American Academy of Podiatric Sports Medicine. Dr Malin received an AB from the University of Rhode Island in Biology in 1964, and a Certificate in Cytotechnology in 1965. In 1965 he gained a Certificate d'Etudes Françaises from the Université de Poitiers, Institute d'Etudes Françaises de Touraine, France, and an SH, from the Université de Tours, France, 1965-67. In 1969 he received a BSc, and in 1972 a DPM, from the California College of Podiatric Medicine, San Francisco, and in 1969 an MA from Brigham Young University, Provo. Dr Malin studied at the New York College of Podiatric Medicine, New York, 1972-74, and holds a Certificate, Instructors Advanced Cardiac Life Support, from the American Heart Association and David Grant USAF Medical Centre, 1978. From Pepperdine University in 1978 he was awarded an MSc. An Instructor in Advanced Cardiac Life Support, 1978-80, and a Member of the Hospital Staff (Podiatrist), 1977-80, at the David Grant USAF Medical Centre, Travis Air Force Base, California, Dr Malin has been Chief of the Podiatric Section of the Veterans Administration Medical Centre, Martinsburg, West Virginia, since 1980, and for the same period Reserve Staff Podiatrist at Malcolm Grown USAF Medical Centre, Andrews Air Force Base, Maryland. Author of "The Asclepiadian-Hermian Dilemma", 'Archives of Podiatric Medicine and Foot Surgery', 1977, "Atlante: The First Generation Greek Mythological Female Sports Runner", 1979, "Pheidippides: The First Marathon Runner", 1979, "The Aeneid: Vergil's Contribution to the Heritage of Podiatry", 1980, all in 'Sports Medicine', he is the author of an English Translation of Maurice Ledos' book, "Architecture and Geometry of the Foot: Collapse, Deformities, Eversions of Mechanical Origin, and Their Repercussions on the Skeleton Orthopedics and Shoe Apparel" and Paul-Victor Dupuis' book, "Tibial Torsion: Its Management - Its Clinical, Radiological and Surgical Interests". His most recent articles are in 'Current Podiatric Medicine', and are "The 'Anacharsis': Lucianus' Contribution to the Heritage of Podiatric Sports Medicine", 1984, and the "Gymasticus: Philostratus' Contribution to the Heritage of Podiatric Sports Medicine", 1984. Howard Malin is the Recipient of the Toastmasters Well-Informed Speaker's Awards in Literature/Philosophy, 1971, History/Law, 1972, California College of Podiatric Medicine, The Continual Higher Education Award, 1972, Basic Sciences Award, 1972, Pi Omega Delta's Clemenson Award, 1972, California College of Podiatric Medicine, and the Podiatry Toastmasters Club Service Award, in 1972 from the same college. In 1972, Dr Malin was presented with the Key to the City of Marseilles, France, and in 1973 and 1974 recieved the Dr Marvin D. Steinberg Book Award, New York College of Podiatric Medicine. In 1974-75 he was Outstanding Professional in Human Services, American Academy of Human Services, and received several awards from the Davis Grant USAF Air Force Base. In his spare time, Dr Malin visits the Legitimate Theatre, enjoys writing, numismatics, clarinet, oil painting, philately, travel, and the classics.

A biography of Dr Howard Malin appears in the main section of this Volume/Edition.

Professor Dr. A. A. Mallick

"For An Outstanding Contribution to 'Defeat TB - Now and Forever' and service of the suffering humanity".

PROFESSOR DR. A. A. MALLICK

"Study of Tuberculin Reaction in the Contacts and the General Population", 1964, "Hospital and Home-in The Treatment of Pulmonary Tuberculosis", 1967, "Isorian Therapy in Tuberculosis", 1975, "Short Course Chemotherapy", 1982-83, and "Tuberculosis Control in India with Particular Reference to Bihar", 1984, are the works of Asrar Ahmad Mallick, Professor of T.B. and Chest Diseases at Patna University, India.

A Life Member of the Indian Medical Association, and Tuberculosis Assocation of India, Dr Mallick is a Founder Member of the Indian Society of Chest, a Member of the International Union Against Tuberculosis, General Secretary of Bihar T.B. Association, and is Vice President of Bihar State Health Services Association. His qualifications include, an MB.BS, DTD, PhD, FNCCP, FCCP (USA) and FAMS

He joined the TBD & TC at Patna as a Resident Junior House Surgeon, becoming a Senior House Surgeon, then Honorary Clinical Assistant, Medical Officer, Epidemiologist and is currently Director of the State TB and Demonstration and Training Centre in Patna, India. Dr Mallick is also Director of the TB Control Programme at Bihar.

On 17 June 1957 he married I.N. Mallick in Patna and they have 3 sons and 1 daughter. In his leisure hours Dr Mallick enjoys Gardening and Reading.

A biography of Professor Dr. Asrar Mallick appears in the main section of this Volume/Edition.

Thomas H. Mallory, MD

"For An Outstanding Contribution in Surgery of the Hip".

T. H. MALLORY, ESQ

A Diplomate of the American Board of Orthopaedic Surgery, and Contributor of numerous papers and articles to professional journals, Thomas Howard Mallory is a member of the American Academy of Orthopaedic Surgeons, American College of Surgeons, American Medical Association, Association of Bone and Joint Surgeons, Sir John Charnley Society, Ohio State Medical Society, Columbus Orthopaedic Society, Hip Society, Knee Society, Columbus Surgical Society, Ohio Orthopaedic Society, American Rheumatism Society, and Mid American Orthopaedic Society.

Born on 10 January 1939 in Columbus, Ohio, USA, Thomas Howard Mallory married Kelly Lynn Smith on 31 December 1964 in Columbus and has 3 sons. He gained his AB from Miami University, Oxford, Ohio and his MD from the Ohio State University at Columbus. Dr Mallory received his MA (Fellowship, Hip Surgery) from the Harvard Medical School, in Boston, and became a Teaching Fellow at the Harvard Medical School/Tufts University, Boston in 1970.

Dr Mallory is currently Clinical Instructor in Orthopaedic Surgery at the Ohio State University Hospitals and Riverside Methodist Hospital, Columbus, Ohio, and is a Member of Joint Implant Surgeons Inc., in Columbus. His Medical Staff Appointments include: St Anthony's Hospital, St Ann's Hospital, Grant Hospital, Mt. Carmel Medical Centre, all in Columbus, and the Highland District Hospital in Hillsboro. A Member of the Executive Committee, Medical Society, Ohio State University Hospital, Dr Mallory is also on the Editorial Advisory Board of the Professional Education Programs Inc., and is a member of the Orthopaedic Advisory Panel of Richards Medical Company.

A Trustee of Columbus Academy he is also on the Editorial Board of "Clinical Ortho-paedic and Related Research", Thomas Mallory's most recent presentations include: "Revision Total Knee Replacement", Knee Society, Las Vegas, 1985; "Femoral Endo-prosthetic Replacement in Younger Patients", Discussion of Paper, 52nd Annual Meet-ing, American Academy of Orthopaedic Surgeons, Las Vegas, 1985; "Revision of Failed Cemented Total Hip Replacements", 52nd Annual Meeting, American Academy of Orthopaedic Surgeons, 1985, "Infected Total Hip Arthroplasty", Panel, City Wide Orthopaedic Grand Rounds, Mount Carmel Medical Centre, 1985, and "Porus Coated Anatomical Total Hip Replacement - An Early Experience", 'Association of Bone & Joint Surgeons' Annual Meeting, 1985. In his leisure time Dr Mallory enjoys Polo, Jogging and Riding.

A biography of Thomas Howard Mallory appears in the main section of this Volume/Edition.

Dr Ronald J. Malpiede, DC

"For An Outstanding Contribution as Chiropractic Physician - Orthopaedics".

DR. R. J. MALPIEDE

Golf and travel are the interests of Dr Ronald Joseph Malpiede, a Chiropractic Orthopaedic Practioner, who has been in private practice since 1976.

The Recipient of the Outstanding Student Award from Cleveland Chiropractic College of Kansas City in 1973, he also received the Distinguished Service Award from Colorado Chiropractic Association in 1978. A Member of the American Chiropractic Association, Dr Malpiede is on the Board of Directors of the Colorado Chiropractic Association, and is also a Member of the American College of Chiropractic Orthopaedists, and American College of Sports Medicine. In 1984 he received the Board of Directors Award from the Colarado Chiropractic Society.

He is the Author of "Chiropractic Podiatric Biomechanical Inter-relationships - (Pelvic-podiatric Biomechanical Inter-relationships)", 1978, his biographical details appear in 'International Who's Who of Intellectuals'; 'Men of Achievement'; 'Youth in Achievement'; 'Community Leaders of America'; and 'Directory of Distinguished Americans'.

Dr Malpiede married Evelyn Rimbey on the 3 December 1971 at St John's the Episcopal Church, and has 2 daughters.

A biography of Dr Ronald Joseph Malpiede appears in the main section of this Volume/Edition.

Charles Marks

"For An Outstanding Contribution as Surgeon, Educator, Author and Clinician".

PROFESSOR C. MARKS

Professor of Surgery, Charles Marks was born on 28 January 1922 in the Ukraine. He gained his MB ChB from the University of Cape Town in South Africa, his MD MS from the University of Wisconsin in the USA, and his PhD, from Tulane University.

From 1953 to 1963 he was a Consultant Surgeon at Salisbury General Hospital, in Rhodesia, and from 1963 to 1967 was an Associate Professor of Surgery at the Marquette University Medical School in the USA. During the same period he was also Attending Surgeon at the Milwaukee General Hospital and Veterans Administration Hospital. An Associate Clinical Professor of Surgery at the Case Western Reserve Medical School in Clevelend, Ohio, a Director of the Department of Surgery, at Mount Sinai Hospital, he was Attending Surgeon at the University Hospital and Veterans Administration Hospital, Cleveland, 1967-71.

Since 1971, Dr Marks has been Professor of Surgery at the Louisiana State University Medical School, New Orleans, and Senior Surgeon of the Charity Hospital and Veterans Administration Hospital, New Orleans. A member of the British and American Medical Association, Professor Marks is also a member of the Royal Society of Medicine, Royal (England) and American College of Surgeons; Society International de Chirug, American College of Cardiology, American College of Chest Physicians, and American Association of Anatomists.

Charles Marks is the author of "Atlas of Techniques in Surgery", 1965, "Applied Surgical Anatomy", 1972; "The Portal Venus System", 1973; "A Surgeon's World", 1973; "Carcinoid Tumors", 1979, and "The Zimbabwe Story: A Sequence of Events", 1981. The Hunterian Professor at the Royal College of Surgeons, England in 1956, Dr Marks was awarded Clinical Teacher of the Year, by the Aesculapian Honour Society of Louisiana State University Medical School in 1972, 1974, and 1979, and is also President of the New Orleans Surgical Society in 1981.

His hobbies include, Travel, Tennis and Writing. Dr Marks is listed in 'American Men of Science', 'Men of Achievement', 'Who's Who in America' and 'Who's Who in the World'. Charles Marks married Joyce Wernick on 11 December 1949 in Salisbury, Rhodesia and they have 4 sons.

A biography of Professor Charles Marks appears in the main section of this Volume/Edition.

Maj. Gen. M. Arshad Mirza

"For an Outstanding Contribution to the service of ailing humanity, particularly victims of Cardiovascular Diseases, through original research, sincere practice and teaching of medicine".

DR. M. A. MIRZA

Mohammad Arshad Mirza was born on 7 May 1928 in Punjab, India, and is married to Hamida Bano, and has 2 sons and 2 daughters. Mohammad Mirza gained an MD in Cardiology from the Punjab University in 1955, and was a House Physician at the Mayo Hospital, Lahore, 1950-51. From 1952-54 he attended a Medicine Speciality Course at the Military Hospital, Rawalpindi, and was a Graded Specialist in Medicine, 1955-57, a Classified Specialist in Medicine in 1957. Dr Mirza has attended numerous other courses and in 1971, was a Fellowship and British Council Bursor in Cardiology at the Royal Postgraduate Medical School in London. From 1954 to 1978 he was a Specialist in Medicine at various Defence Hospitals, and from 1965-1972 was an Instructor in Aerospace Medicine at the Aero Medical Institute of Pakistan Air Force. In 1972 until 1975 he was Chief Physician, and Director of the Eastern Province Armed Forces Hospital in Saudi Arabia, and from 1965-1972 was Visiting Instructor, at the Pakistan Armed Forces Medical College, Rawalpindi. Since 1979 Dr Mirza has been Professor, and Head of Medicine, at the Army Medical College, Rawalpindi, is Senior Instructor in medicine at the Armed Forces Medical College, Rawalpindi, and is Senior Visiting Physician to Military Hospitals in Rawalpindi. A Past Vice-President, and Founder Member of the Pakistan Cardiac Society, Mohammad Mirza is a Fellow of the College of Physicians and Surgeons of Pakistan. A Fellow of the American College of Chest Physicians, and is a Founder Member of the Pakistan Cardiac Society. He is the author of "Constitution -Study of 5202 Males in Northern Areas of Pakistan", 'Journal of Pakistan Army Medical College', 1956, "Innocent Cardiac Murmurs - Study of Young Healthy Males", 'Pakistan Armed Forces Medical Journal', 1973; "Prevalence of Hypertension also Comparison with Western Data and Suggestion of a New Classification of Hypertension", 'Pakistan Armed Forces Medical Journal', 1976; "Hypertension in the Elderly", in 'Proceedings 16th Annual National Health Conference', in 1983. A Captain of the University of Punjab Football Team in 1948, Dr Mirza was a member of the North West India Football Team in 1945, and now enjoys playing Tennis, Reading, Gardening and Architecture. A Major General in the Pakistan Army, Dr Mirza is also the Author of 2 sections in a book on "Anaesthesia and Patient Care", by Anis and Salim, and has written "Non Tuberculous Bacterial Infections and Antibiotic Selection", a study based on culture reports is under publication. The Recipient of the Neil Memorial Silver Medal for standing first in surgery in the final professional MB BS Examination at the Punjab University in 1950, Dr Mirza was awarded the Colonel Bakhle Memorial Silver Medal, and the Burton Brown Memorial Silver Medal, and was selected for the award of Rhodes Scholarship, by the Rhodes Selection Committee in Pakistan in 1951. An Honorary Phsycian to the President of Pakiston, Major General Mirza is also listed in 'Men of Achievement'.

A biography of Dr Mohammad Mirza appears in the main section of this Volume/Edition.

Gosaku Naruse

"For An Outstanding Contribution to Hypnotherapy, Self-therapy and Psychological Rehabilitation.

DR. G. NARUSE

Recipient of the Hayami Award from the Japanese Association of Psychology in 1952, and the Memorial Award from the Tokyo Bunrika University, 1953.

Dr Gosaku Naruse, was born on 5 June 1924 in Japan, and is the assistant in the Psychology Department at Tokyo Bunrika University in 1951, he was Chairman of Psychological Clinic at the Tokyo University of Education in 1953. In 1962 he joined the Psychology Department at the Faculty of Education at Kyushu University as an Assistant Professor, being appointed Professor in 1969, a position he holds to this day. He gained his MR in Literature from Tokyo Bunrika University in 1950, and his Doctor of Medical Science from Niigate University in 1959, and received a Diploma in Clinical Hypnosis in the USA in 1962.

Gosaku Naruse is the author of "Techniques of Hypno-interview", 1959; "Hypnosis", 1960; "Self Hypnosis", with J. H. Schultz, 1963; "Jiko-Control", 1969; "Psychological Rehabilitation", 1973; "Theory of Motor Action Training", in 1985. In his free time enjoys Utai (Noh Song), Skiing and Windsurfing. He married Meikei Kaikan on 17 December 1952, and has 2 sons.

A biography of Dr Gosaku Naruse appears in the main section of this Volume/Edition.

Dr Vickie Lee McFall Newcomb

"For An Outstanding Contribution in the field of Chiropractic Paediatrics".

DR. V. NEWCOMB

Doctor of Chiropractic, Vickie Lee McFall Newcomb, has an Associates Degree in Secretarial Sciences gained in 1977, a BS in Health and Biological Science, received in 1980, and was awarded her DC in 1983.

Born on the 17th October 1957 in Tennessee, USA, she married Thomas Harrison Newcomb, also a Doctor of Chiropractic, at the Baptist Church in Buffalo Trail on the 3 January 1982.

A Member of the International Chiropractic Association, Tennessee Chiropractic Association, Dr Newcomb is the Youngest Female Chiropractor in the State of Tennessee. The Author of "What Chiropractic Really Is", in 'Voice for Health', 1984; and "Candida Albicans", in 'Today's Chiropractic', 1985. Dr Newcomb has been a Doctor of Chiropractic since 23 March 1983, and since 1 April 1983 has been Secretary of the Morristown Chiropractic Clinic Inc.

In her spare time Dr Newcomb enjoys her Paediatric Chiropractic Practice, Modelling, Showing Tennessee Walking Horses, Aerobics, Boating, Reading, Broadway Shows and Travel.

A biography of Dr Vickie Newcomb appears in the main section of this Volume/Edition.

Howard John Peak

"For An Outstanding Contribution to the Development of Cardiology in Canberra".

DR. H. PEAK

Howard John Peak was born on 17 May 1926, in Sydney, Australia, and married Judith Peak, 29 November 1969, in Sydney, Australia, and has 2 sons and 1 daughter.

A Cardiologist, he gained his MB BS, Sydney, FRACP, 1972, FACC, 1975, DDU, 1977, and from 1965-66 was a Fellow in Medicine at the John Hopkins Hospital, Baltimore, USA. An Honorary Assistant Physician, in 1966 to 1970, an Honorary Assistant Cardiologist, 1970-71, at the Royal Prince Alfred Hospital, Sydney, Dr Peak was appointed Consulting Cardiologist at the National Heart Foundation of Australia, 1966-70, and at the Royal Canberra Hospital, 1971-75. He was appointed Director of Cardiology at the Royal Canberra Hospital, 1975-.

Howard Peak was President of the ACT Division of the National Heart Foundation of Australia, 1980-85, and is a member of the Cardiac Society of Australia & New Zealand. A Fellow of the Royal Society of Medicine, New York Academy of Sciences, Dr Peak is a Corresponding Member of the British Cardiac Society, and a Member of the Australian Institute for Ultrasound in Medicine.

Co-Author of "The Treatment of Hypercholesterolaemia by MER 29", 'Medical Journal of Australia', 1961; "Two Year Evaluation of 'Atromid', for the Control of Abnormal Blood Lipid Levels", 1965, 'Medical Journal of Australia', "A Brief Review for the General Practitioner", 1975, and "Clinical Profile for Hypertrophic Cardiomyopathy", 1977, Dr Peak is interested in Music, Languages, Walking, and Fishing in his spare time.

A biography of Dr Howard Peak appears in the main section of this Volume/Edition.

Alphonse Salerno

"For An Outstanding Contribution as General Surgeon/Family Practitioner dedicated to the Holistic Approach".

A. SALERNO, ESQ.

Alphonse Salerno was born on 4 March 1923 in Newark, New Jersey, USA, and is separated with 1 son and 1 daughter. He gained his BS in 1944 and his DO in 1948, from Louisiana State University, New York University, Seton Hall University, and Philadelphia College of Osteopathic Medicine. Chief of Surgery at the West Essex General Hospital since 1975, he was Chief of Staff at the hospital in 1967.

Mr Salerno is on the Board of Governors of the American Academy of Osteopathic Surgeons and was President of Essex County Osteopathic Society in 1966. He is a Member of the Essex County, New Jersey State and National Osteopathic Societies, and Life Member of the American Medical Society of Vienna, and the New York Academy of Sciences. In 1975, he was President of the American Academy of Surgeons, and in 1985 was on the Certifying Committee of the Board of Surgery, and in 1980 was Vice President of the Hospital Staff, and in 1983, Secretary Treasurer of Staff at the West Essex General Hospital.

Alphonse Salerno is the Author of "Pseudo-Hermaphroditism", in the 'Journal of A.O.A.', in 1967, and of "Different Phases of Placenta Accreta", in 1981, in 'New Jersey O.P.S. ', He also belongs to the International College of General Practice, American College of General Practice, American Academy of Osteopathic Surgeons, American Academy of Osteopathic Specialists, and was awarded Fellowships in General Surgery in 1966 and Surgery in 1967.

His hobbies include Music, Opera, Renaissance Art, Tennis, Reading Biographies and Classics.

A biography of Alphonse Salerno appears in the main section of this Volume/Edition.

Dr Kathleen Sandman

"For An Outstanding Contribution to biomedical communication as a chiropractic physician".

DR. K. SANDMAN

"Myofacial Pain Syndromes: Their Mechanism, Diagnosis and Treatment", 1981, "Rheumatoid Arthritis of the Cervical Spine: Examination Prior to Chiropractise Manipulative Therapy Procedure", 1981, and "Psychophysiological Aspects of Myofacial Pain", 1984, all in 'Journal of Manipulative Physiological Therapy', were written by Kathleen B. Sandman, Medical Writer, Chiropractor and Owner of Sandman Clinics. Born on the 4 June 1949 in Warren, Ohio, USA, she has 1 son and 2 daughters.

Dr Sandman gained her DC from the Chiropractic National College in 1977, and her BS in Human Biology in 1973. She studied Journalism at Geneva College and gained her Private Pilot's Licence in 1981. An Associate Chiropractic Physician, 1978-79, at Rehabilitation Associates in Denver, Colorado, Kathleen Sandman joined the Faculty in the Department of Diagnosis at the National College of Chiropractic in Lombard, becoming a Medical Writer there in 1982.

Since 1982, Kathleen Sandman has been the Director and Owner of the Sandman Chiropractic Clinics. A Member of the American Medical Writers Association; American Chiropractic Association; Delta Tau Alpha; National College Chiropractic Alumni, Reunion Chairman, 1983, Dr Sandman is also a member of the American Council of Women Chiropractors, and was President of the Student Chapter, 1976-77.

In her spare time Dr Sandman enjoys Flying and Sailing.

A biography of Dr Kathleen Sandman appears in the main section of this Volume / Edition.

Dr Diane E. Schuller

"For An Outstanding Contribution to Paediatric Allergy, Immunology and Pulmonary Medicine".

DR. D. E. SCHULLER

Director of the Department of Paediatric Allergy, Immunology and Pulmonary Disease, and Associate Clinical Profesor of Paediatrics, Diane Ethel Schuller was born on 27 November 1943 in New York, New York, USA.

She studied at Bryn Mawr College gaining an AB cum laude with honours in Biology, and gained an MD from the State University of New York, Downstate Medical College, and was Certified by the National Board of Medical Examiners in 1971, and the American Board of Paediatrics in 1975 and 1981, American Board of Allergy and Immunology.

An Associate, Department of Paediatics, 1974-78, Director, Paediatric Cardiopulmonary, Allergic and Infectious Diseases, 1979-84, Director, Paediatric Allergy Immunology and Pulmonary Disease, 1985-, Geisinger Medical Centre, Danville, Pennsylvania, Dr Schuuller was Assistant Professor, 1975-81, Associate Professor, 1981-, Clinical Professor of Paediatrics at Pennsylvania State University, Milton S. Hersey Medical College. Diane Schuller is a Fellow of the American Academy of Allergy and Immunology, American College of Allergy, and is a Fellow and Regional Director (Northeast), of the American Academy of Paediatrics. A Member of the American Medical Association, New York Academy of Sciences, American Association for the Advancement of Science Association for the Care of Asthma, Dr Schuller is on the Board of Directors, of the Pennsylvania State Lung Association, and on the Executive Committee of the American Lung Association of Pennsylvania.

The Author of 19 articles and 33 presentations including, "Acute Urticaria with Streptococcal Infection", 1980, "Prophylaxis of Otitis Media in Asthmatic Children", 1983, "Adverse Effects of Brompheniramine on Pulmonary Function in a Subset of Asthmatic Children", 1983, "Skin Tests at Cessation of Immunotherapy", 1985, and "Remission of Hereditary Angioedema at Puberty", 1985. Dr Schuller is a Member of the Drug Committee of the American Academy of Allergy and Immunology, a Reviewer for 'Paediatrics', 1982, Reviewer for 'Clinical Paediatrics' 1984, and is an Elected Regional Director, Northeastern Region, American Association for Clinical Immunology and Allergy. Medical Director for Camp Breathe Easy, a camp for asthmatic children sponsored by the Central Pennsylvania Lung Association for 1983, 1984, and 1985, Dr Schuller's hobbies include Numismatics and Travel. She is listed in 'Who's Who in the World'; 'Who's Who of American Women'; 'World Who's Who of Women'; 'Who's Who in the East'; 'Who's Who of America'.

A biography of Dr Diane Schuller appears in the main section of this Volume/Edition.

Dr Kayode Adeley Shenkoya F.C.C.P.

"For An Outstanding Contribution to Effective Health Care in the Nigerian Oil Industry".

DR. K. A. SHENKOYA

Kayode Adeleye Shenkoya was born on 29 November 1943 in Lagos, Nigeria. Director of Medical Services he married Folashade Adetoun Neye on 29 November 1971 in Lagos, and has 1 son and 3 daughters.

He gained his MB BS in Lagos in 1969 with distinctions in Pathology, Physiology and Medicine, and was appointed Fellow of the American College of Chest Physicians in 1980, and Fellow of the International Academy of Chest Physicians & Surgeons in 1982. A House Officer (Professional Units), 1960-70, Senior House Officer in Medicine, 1970-71, at Lagos University Teaching Hosptial, Dr Shenkoya was appointed Resident in Internal Medicine, 1971-73, Fellow in Cardiology, 1973-75, Clinical Instructor in Medicine (Faculty), 1975, at the University of Chicago in the USA.

From 1976 to 1978 he was a Supernumerary Registrar in Cardio Pulmonary Unit, at the Lagos University Teaching Hospital, 1976-1978, and during the same period was a part time Consultant Physician, Cardiologist at the Central Bank of Nigeria. In 1978, Dr Shenkoya was appointed Head of the Health Department, Chief Medical Officer, Chief Consultant Physician in 1982 of the Nigerian National Petroleum Corporation.

Kayode Shenkoya was the first President of the Federation of African Medical Student Association, 1967-68, and Executive Council Member of the Nigerian Medical Association, 1976-79, and a Member of the American Heat Association American Thoracic Society, International Society of Occupational Health Physicians. The Author of "Mitral Valve Prolapse in Sacoid Heart Disease", 'Illinois Medical Journal', 1976, Dr Shenkoya has also written "Aortic Arch Dissection - Medical v Surgical Therapy", 'American Journal of Cardiology', 1977, "Medical Hazzards of Oil Pollution", 'Nigerian Medical Journal', 1983, and "Tetra-Ethyl Lead in Nigerian Oil Industry Workers - Clinical & Laboratory Studies' in press.

The Recipient of the Provost's Award for Best Student in Medicine, College of Medicine, University of Lagos, 1969, Dr Shenkoya enjoys Classical Music, Light Reading, and Lawn Tennis.

A biography of Dr Kayode Shenkoya appears in the main section of this Volume/Edition.

Emmanuel H. Tadross

"For An Outstanding Contribution to Academic Teaching, Clinical Practice and Advancement of Modern Psychiatry".

PROFESSOR E. H. TADROSS

Photography, Music, and Electronics are the hobbies of Emmanuel H. Tadross, Consultant Psychiatrist and Adjunct Professor of Clinical Psychology.

The Recipient of a Diploma in Psychological Medicine, London, a Member of the Royal College of Psychiatrists, Fellow, Royal College of Physicians, Canada; DPM&N, DABP&N, CRCP(C), IAPC, Dr Tadross is also a member of the Canadian Psychiatric Association, American Psychiatric Association, Canadian Medical Association, Ontario Medical Association, International Academy of Psychotherapy, and the Association for Academic Psychiatry, USA. A Registrar in Psychiatry at the Warley Hospital, Essex, England, then at the Central Middlesex Hospital, London, Dr Tadross became Senior Registrar at the Cell Barnes Hospital, St Albans, Hertfordshire. Staff Psychiatrist at Queen Street Mental Health Centre, Toronto, Canada, and Lecturer, Psychiatry, at the University of Toronto, Dr Tadross is Consultant Psychiatrist at the Kitchener-Waterloo & St Mary's Hospitals, and Adjunct Professor of Clinical Psychology at the University of Waterloo, and Consultant Psychiatrist, Psychiatrist in Chief, Kitchener-Waterloo Hospital.

Emmanuel H. Tadross was born on 28 Octorber 1940 in Cairo, Egypt, and married Mary E. Aldridge, at Hornchurch, London, England and has 1 son and 1 daughter.

A biography of Professor Emmanuel Tadross appears in the main section of this Volume/Edition.

Dr Albert Y. M. Tsai

"For An Outstanding Contribution to Health Care, Research and Education".

PROFESSOR DR. A. Y. M. TSAI

The Author of 12 learned articles in the field of Obstetrics & Gynaecology, 1966-78, Professor Doctor Albert Y. M. Tsai was born on 3 April 1941 in China, and is a Consultant Obstetrician & Gynaecologist.

He recieved his MD from the University of Chicago, USA, in 1968, and is a Diplomate of the American Board of Obstetrics & Gynaecology, 1974. He also received a Diploma of Special Competence in Reproductive Endocrinology from the American Board of Obstetrics & Gynaecology. Dr Tsai was an Assistant Professor at the School of Medicine, University of Chicago, 1973-75, and an Associate Professor, Abraham Lincoln School of Medicine, University of Illinois, 1975-78.

A Fellow of the American College of Obstetricians & Gynacologists, 1974, Dr Tsai is also a Fellow of the American College of Surgeons, a Member of the American Diabetes Association, College of Physicians and Surgeons, Manitoba, Canada, American Medical Association, Illinois State Medical Association, Chicago Medical Society, Chicago Gynaecological Society, and the Chicago Endorine Club. Dr Tsai married Suzanna on 16 July 1968 in Chicago, Illinois, and has 1 son and 1 daughter. In his spare time he enjoys swimming, Chinese art and antiques.

A biography of Professor Dr Albert Tsai appears in the main section of this Volume/Edition.

André Villenueve

"For An Outstanding Contribution in the Field Biological Psychiatry, particularly Neuropsychopharmacology".

A. VILLENEUVE, ESQ

André Villeneuve was born on 17 September 1932 in Chicoutimi, Canada and is a Professor at the Department of Psychiatry, Laval University, Quebec, Psychiatrist in Chief, Clinique Roy-Rousseau, and Consultant Emeritus at the Neuropsychopharmacology Unit, Centre Hospitalier Robert Giffard, Quebec, Canada.

He married Gisela Bellefeuille on 16 June 1958 and has 1 daughter. André Villeneuve gained his MD from Laval University, Quebec, and he is a Graduate of the New York School of Psychiatry, USA and received his MSc., from McGill University, Montreal.

A Fellow of the Royal College of Physicians and Surgeons of Canada, Dr Villeneuve is a Member of the American Psychiatric Association, a Fellow of the Canadian Psychiatric Association, Member of the Royal College of Psychiatrists, and is a Fellow of the Collegium Internationale Neuropsycholopharmacologiucum. He is a Fellow of the American College of Forensic Psychiatry, and a Fellow of several other professional organisations.

He is the author of 150 various scientific publications, 5 books including: Editor, 'Lithium in Psychiatry', 1976, Co-Editor, 'Neuro-Psychopharmacology', 1978, Editor, 'Brain Neurotransmitters and Psychiatry' 1985. He enjoys Tennis and Alpine Skiing.

A biography of André Villeneuve appears in the main section of this Volume/Edition.

Pei-yen Wang

"For An Outstanding Contribution to Surgical Management for Carcinoma of Esophagus and Cardia".

MR P. WANG

Chief of Surgery at the Veterans General Hospital, Taichung, Pei-yen Wang is the Author of, "Vascular Implantation of the Liver", "Total Parenteral Ailmentation with a Combination of Carbohydrates in Surgical Patients with Carcinoma of the Esophagus", "Surgical Treatment of the Esophagus and Cardia Among the Chinese", and "A Spiral Grooved Endoesophageal Tube for Management of Malignant Esophageal Obstruction", 1985.

Surgical Resident of Thoracic Surgery, First Army General Hospital, China, 1952-65, Dr Wang was appointed Surgical Resident at the Memorial Cancer Centre in New York, 1965-68, and then Instructor, Assistant Professor, Professor of Surgery at the National Defence Medical Centre, 1970-1984. In 1968, he was appointed Chief of Thoracic Surgery, in 1974 Chief of Experimental Surgery at the Veterans General Hospital, Taipei. Mr Wang is currently Chief of Surgery at the Veterans General Hospital, Taichung.

A Member of the Chinese Medical Association, and the Surgical Association of China, Pei-yen Wang is also a Member of the Association of Surgeons of South East Asia, Association of Thoracic and Cardiovascular Surgeons of Asia and a Fellow of the International College of Surgeons, and International College of Chest Physicians.

Born on the 1 February 1926, in Honan, China, he married Chu Shu-Mei on 8 October 1954 in Taichung, and has 2 sons and 1 daughter. Go Go Chess, Mountain-Climbing, and Tennis are the main interests in Mr Wang's leisure time.

A biography of Pei-yen Wang appears in the main section of this Volume/Edition.

Thomas Arthur Williams, M.D., P.A.

"For An Outstanding Contribution as an Academic Practioner of Psychiatric Medicine".

DR. THOMAS A. WILLIAMS

Clinical Professor, Private Practitioner of Psychiatric Medicine, Thomas Arthur Williams was born on 11 May 1936 at Kenosha, Wisconsin, USA. He gained a BA from Harvard University in 1958, an MD from Columbia University in 1963, and was an Intern and Resident in Psychiatry at the Presbyterian Hospital and New York State Psychiatric Institute, 1963-67. Dr Williams had various Clinical and Administrative appointments from 1968 to 1983, and various positions at the Universities of Pittsburgh, Utah, Columbia University, Veterans Administration Hospitals, 1959-.

A Reviewer for the American Journal of Psychiatry, since 1979, Dr Williams is Chief of Psychiatry Service, James A. Haley Veterans Hospital in Tampa, Florida, 1981 to 1983, and since 1983 has been in private practice in Tampa. A Clinical Professor of Psychiatry at the University of South Florida College of Medicine, Tampa, 1983-, Dr Williams is Editorial Reviewer of 'Archives of Internal Medicine', 1983-. A Member of the American Medical Association, American Psychiatric Association, American Psychopathological Association, Society for Psychophysiological Research, Hillsborough County Medical Society, and Tampa Florida Medical Association, and Tampa Psychiatric Society.

Thomas Williams is the author or co-author of numerous papers contributed to professional journals including: 'American Journal of Psychiatry', 'Psychophysiology', 'Archives of General Psychiatry', 'American Psychologist', 'Behaviour Research Methods and Instrumentation'. He is contributing Editor to "Recent Advances in the Psychobiology of the Depressive Illnesses", and 'Psychobiology of Convulsive Therapy".

The Recipient of a Predoctorial Fellowship from the National Institute of Mental Health, Columbia University, 1960-61, Resident Research Prize, from the Alumni Association of New York State Psychiatric Institute, 1965, Dr Thomas Williams is a Member of the Veterans Administration Mental Health Mission to the USSR in 1974, and the Recipient of various awards from the American Psychiatric Association, 1975, and an Examiner for the American Board of Psychiatry and Neurology.

A biography of Dr Thomas Williams appears in the main section of this Volume/Edition.

Vern A. Wolfley

"For An Outstanding Contribution to the study of Malocclusion, it's prevention and correction with Functional appliances".

DR. V. A. WOLFLEY

Born in Etna, Wyoming, USA, Vern A Wolfely is a Life Member of the American Dental Association and Arizona State Dental Association. He married Bernice Michaelson on 12 June 1936 in Salt Lake City, Utah, and has 2 sons and 2 daughters. He studied at the University of Wyoming from which he gained a BS in 1934, and the Univeristy of Nebraska from which he gained a BSD in 1947, and a DDS also in 1947.

President of the Idaho Falls Dental Society, The Upper Snake River District Dental Society, and Arizona State Childrens Dental Society, Vern Wolfley is also a member of the Central Arizona District Society, Academy of General Dentistry, International Association of Orthodontics, American Association of Functional Orthodontists, Federation Dentaire International, American Society of Dentistry for Children.

Dr Wolfley is the recipient of the Woodbury Study Club Award, Scholastic Proficiency in Gold Foil 1947, was admitted to the Omicron Kappa Upsilon Honorary Dental Society also in 1947, and the University of Nebraska Nineteenth Annual Honours Convocation High Scholastic Achievement Award, 1947.

In his leisure time Dr Wolfley enjoys Deep Sea Fishing, Painting, Jewelry Casting and Design and Computer Science.

A biography of Dr Vern Wolfley appears in the main section of this Volume/Edition.

A

AARLI, Johan Arild, b. 1 May 1936, Kvinesdal, Norway. Professor of Neurology. m. Gullborg Gullestad, 9 June 1962, Kvinesdal, 2 sons, 3 daughters. *Education;* MD, University of Bergen, 1961; Specialist in Neurology, 1969; EEG Competence, 1970; Dr med, Bergen, 1972. *Appointments:* Assistant Head of Department 1970-77, Head of Department of Neurology 1977 -, University Clinic of Bergen; Assistant Professor of Neurology 1974-77, Professor of Neurolgoy 1977 -, Dean, Faculty of Medicine 1985-, University of Bergen. *Memberships:* Chairman 1984-, Norwegian Neurological Association; Scandinavian Society for Immunology; International Society for Immunopharmacology; American Neurological Association. *Publications include:* "Immunological Aspects of Neurological Diseases" (with O Tönder), 1980: 130 publications on neuroimmunology and clinical neurology. *Honours:* Doctor Ragnar Forsbergs Prize, 1971; Sören Falch's Award, 1973; Monrad Krohn Award for Neurological Research, 1976; Norwegian Hospital Association Medal, 1982. *Hobbies:* History of Neurolgoy; The 1890's. *Address:* Department of Neurolgoy, 5016 Haukeland Sykehus, Bergen, Norway.

ABADIR, Rushdy, b. 1 Aug. 1929, Cairo, Egypt. Clinical Professor, Radiation Oncology, University of Missouri, USA. m. Janeva E. Abadir, London, 5 sons. *Education;* MB, B.Ch., Cairo University; FRCR, 1966; ABR. *Appointments:* Assistant Professor, Cancer Clinic, Saskatoon, Canada, 1969-71, Albert Einstein College of Medicine, New York, USA, 1971-74; Professor, Chief Radiation Oncology, University of Missouri, Columbia, 1974- . *Memberships:* Royal College of Radiologists; Canadian Association of Radiologists; American College of Radiology. *Publications:* "Hyperthemia", 1978, 1979, 1980; "Cancer of Prostate", 1978, 1980, 1983, 1984, 1985; "Cancer of the Lung", 1975, 1978, 1979; "Cancer of Head and Neck", 1972, 1973, 1985. *Hobby:* Egyptology. *Address:* Regional Radiation Therapy Centre, 500 Keene Street, Columbia, MO 65201, USA.

ABBOTT, Leal M, b. 16 Aug. 1940, St. Joseph, Missouri, USA. Transitional Care Co-ordinator. m. 1 son, 2 dauthters. *Education:* BA (Psychology), Hofstra University, New York; Masters degree, social work, Adelphi University, New York. *Appointments:* Programme Co-ordinator, South East Nassau Guidance Centre, 1976-78; Clinic Co-ordinator, Mohave County Mental Health Clinic, Lake Havasu City, Arizona, 1978-80; Director of Social Services, Mohave General Hospital, Kingman, 1980-81; Transitional Care Co-ordinator, Yolo County Mental Health Services, 1981-present. *Memberships:* Board of Directors, Yolo County Sexual Assault /Battered Women Centre; Academy of Clinical Social Workers; National Association of Social Workers; Expert Examiner, Board of Behavioural Health and Sciences; Commissioner, Yolo County Commission to Prevent Violence against women. *Honours:* Certificate of Excellence, Yolo Community Care Continum, 1982; Mental Health Practitioner of the Year Award, Yolo County Mental Health Association, 1983. *Hobbies:* Flying; Home computer; Writing. *Address:* 2657 Harkness Street, Sacramento, CA 95818, USA.

ABBOTT, Paul Vincent, b. 18 June 1957, New South Wales, Australia. Endodontist. m. Meredith Allan, 15 May 1982, Perth, 2 sons. *Education:* BD Sc (W.A.); M.DS (Adel.). *Appointments:* Area Dental Officer, Western Australia State Health; Private General Dental Practice; Visiting Dental Officer, Adelaide Dental Hospital; Part-time Tutor, University of Adelaide; Private Practice limited to Endodontics; Part-time Endodontist, Perth Dental Hospital; Visiting Lecturer, University of Western Australia. *Memberships:* Australian Dental Association; Australian Society of Endodontology; International Association for Dental Research; Australian Society of Hypnosis. *Honours include:* Convocation Prize, 1976; Australian Dental Association, Western Australia Branch, Prize, 1977; G.D. Henderson Prize, 1979; Commonwealth Post-Graduate Course Award, 1985. *Hobbies:* Rowing; Cricket; Waterskiing. *Address:* 69 Woodlands Street, Woodlands, Western Australia, Australia.

ABBOUD, Francois Mitry, b. 5 Jan. 1931, Cairo, Egypt. Professor of Medicine. m. Doris Evelyn Khal, 5 June 1955, Cairo, 1 son, 3 daughters. *Education:* MB.BCh., Ain Chams University, Cairo, 1955; Residency, medicine, Milwaukee County Hospital, USA, 1955-58; Fellow, Cardiology, Marquette University School of Medicine, USA, 1958-60. *Appointments:* Instructor, 1960-61, Assistant Professor, 1961-65, Associate Professor, 1965-68, Professor, 1968-, Medicine, Director, 1970-76, Cardiovascular Division, Director, Cardiovascular Centre, 1974-, Professor, Physiology & Biophysics, 1975-, Head, Internal Medicine, 1976-, University of Iowa College of Medicine, Iowa City, USA. *Memberships:* American Heart Association; American Federation for Clinical Research; American Association of University Professors; Sigma Xi; Central Society for Clinical Research; American Society for Experimental Biology and Medicine; American Physiological Society; American Society for Clinical Investigation; etc. *Publications:* Numerous articles in professional journals including: 'American Journal Physiology'; 'Circulation'; 'Hypertension'; etc. *Honours include:* President, American federation for Clinical research, 1971; ASPET Award for Experimental Therapeutics, American Society for Pharmacology and Experimental Therapeutics, 1972; Award of Merit, American Heart Association, 1982; President, Central Society for Clinical Research, 1986; National Institutes of Health, Principal Investigator programme Project Grant, 1971-; Editor, Circulation Research, 1981-86. *Address:* Department of Internal Medicine, University of Iowa Hospitals and Clinics, Iowa City, IA 52242, USA.

ABDULLA, Mundel, b. 8 Sep. 1941, Thekkil, India. Principal Medical Officer, University Teaching Hospital. m. Vilasini, 23 Oct. 1968, Calicut, India, 2 sons. *Education;* MB, BS, University of Kerala, India, 1967; DTM&H, University of Liverpool, England, 1977; DTCD, University of Vienna, Austria, 1981. *Appointments:* Tutor in Microbiology, Medical College, Trivandrum, India; Medical Officer, Indian Medical Mission, Jeddah; Medical Officer, Central Relief Committee, New Delhi; Private Practitioner of Medicine, Kasaragod; General Duty Medical Officer, Central Leprosy Teaching and Research Institute, Madras, India; Medical Officer, Silver Jubilee Childrens' Clinic, Madras; General Practitioner, Ministry of Social Security, Libya; Senior Medical Officer, Out Patients' Department, University Teaching Hospital, Benin City, Nigeria, West Africa. *Memberships:* Fellow of Royal Institute of Health; Royal Society of Tropical Medicine; Royal Society of Medicine; Royal Institute of Public Health; International Academy of Chest Physicians; American College of Tropical Medicine; College of Hansenology for Endemic Countries. *Publications:* "Towards Understanding Diabetes", 1969; "Medicine in the Middle East", 1980. *Hobbies:* Photography; Reading. *Address:* Thekkil-670541, India.

ABDUL WAHAB Mohamed Abdul Wahab, b. 26 June 1946, State of Bahrain, Consultant and Chairman, Surgical Department, Salmaniya Medical Center; Assistant Professor, Arabian Gulf University, College of Medicine and Medical Sciences, State of Bahrain. m. Dr A El-Shafei, 19 July 1969, Cairo, 1 son, 3 daughters. *Education:* M.B.Ch.B, College of Medicine, AinShams University, Cairo, FRCS (Glasgow), FACS. After graduation from Medical School in Cairo proceeded for higher surgical training in Dublin, Ireland, London, England,

Glasgow and Edinburgh in Scotland where the surgical training programme was completed. *Appointments:* Consultant Surgeon, Chairman, A & E Department, Chief of Medical Staff and Chairman, Surgical Department, Assistant Professor, College of Medicine and Medical sciences, Arabian Gulf University, State of Bahrain. *Membership:* Bahrain Medical Society; Amiri Academy of Medical Specialists in Bahrain; New York Academy of Sciences; Founder, Bahrain Philanthropic Society; International Society of Surgery. *Bibliography:* The use of fine needle percutaneous transhepatic cholangiogram in the Diagnosis of Jaundince, Bahrain Medical Bulletin 1979, Management of Spinal Injuries, Emergency Medical Services, Economic impact of Traffic Accidents, Rehabilitation and Social Services for victims of traffic accidents. Member of several Hospital, Ministerial, National and Regional Professional Academic and Advisory Committees. *Honours:* Scholarship, Government of Bahrain 1963-69; Ministry of Education, Arab Republic of Egypt 1963-69 and Scholarship post graduate training in Surgery, UK and Ireland 1972-78. *Main area of Interest:* Thyroid Surgery, Peptic and Biliary diseases in addition to surgical endoscopy. *Hobbies:* Tennis; Travel; Photography. *Address:* P.O.Box 26875, Adliya, State of Bahrain.

ABELA, Anthony, b. 16 Oct. 1943, Aleppo, Syria. Assistant Clinical Professor of Surgery. m. Denise Sikias, 8 Mar. 1969, Beirut, Lebanon, 1 son, 1 daughter. *Education:* French Baccalaureat, 1961; MD, French Faculty of Medicine, Beirut, 1969; LMCC; CSPQ; Fellow in Otolaryngology, Royal College of Surgery of Canada, Montreal University of Medicine, Montreal, Quebec, Canada, 1974. *Appointments:* Attending Otalaryngologist, St-Charles Boromée Hospital, Beirut, Lebanon, 1975-76; Attending Otolaryngologist, Centre Hospitalier de Jonquière, Jonquière, Quebec, Canada, 1976-78; Attending Otolaryngologist, Ste-Justine Hospital and St-Luc Hospital, Montreal, Quebec, 1980-. *Memberships:* American Academy of Otolaryngology, Head and Neck Surgery; Corporation Professionelle des Mèdecins du Quèbec; Ordre des Mèdecins du Liban; Association of Otolaryngologists of the Province of Quebec; Canadian Otolaryngological Society; Royal College of Surgery of Canada. *Publications:* 'Rèticulose maligne de la ligne mèdiane', 1974; 'Post-myringotomy car: A preopsective study'; 'Dermoid cyst of the Eustachian tube'. *Honour:* First Prize, MED-CHI Meeting, Montreal, 1972. *Hobbies:* Tennis; Backgammon. *Address:* 65 Avenue Springgrove, Outremont, Quebec H2V 3J1, Canada.

ABELA, George Samih, b. 1 Jan. 1950, Tripoli, Lebanon. Doctor of Medicine Cardiology; Assistant Professor of Medicine. m. Sonia Zablit, 14 May, 1977, Beirut, Lebanon, 2 sons. *Education:* BSc, American University Beirut, Lebanon, 1971, MSc, 1974, MD, 1976. *Appointments:* Pathology Intern, Medical Intrern, Resident in Internal Medicine: Emory University Hospital, USA; Fellow in Cardiology, University of Florida; Instructor of Medicine, Cardiology. *Memberships:* Associate Fellow, American College of Cardiology; Member, American Heart Association; Fellow, American Society of Laser Medicine and Surgery. *Publications:* Author Circulation 71(2), 1985: 403-411, 'American Journal of Cardiology', 50, 1199-1205 1982; Author chapter 119 in "The Heart: Arteries and Veins", 6th Edition 1986: 1422-24. *Honours:* Merck Fellow, American College of Cardiology, 1982-83; Research Fellow, Florida Affiliate, American Heart Association, 1983-84; NIH New Investigator Research Award, 1983-86. *Hobbies:* History; Jogging. *Address:* University of Florida, Medicine/Cardiology, Box J-277, JHMHC, Gainesville, FL 32610, USA.

ABER, Geoffrey Michael, b. 19 Feb 1928, Leeds, England, Professor of Renal Medicine, Head of Department of Postgraduate Medicine, University of Keele; Consultant Physician, m. Eleanor Maureen, 27 June 1964, Birmingham, England, 1 son, 1 daughter. *Education:* MB, ChB, MD (with Distinction), University of Leeds; MRCP, FRCP, London; PhD, University of Birmingham. *Appointments:* House Physician, 1952-53, Medical Registrar, 1953-54, Leeds General Infirmary; Senior House Officer, Medicine, Bradford Royal Infirmary, 1953; Senior House Officer, Clinical Pathology, 1956-57, Registrar, 1958-59, Senior Registrar, 1959-64, Queen Elizabeth Hospital, Birmingham; House Physician, Brompton Hospital, London, 1957-58; Wellcome Senior Research Fellow, Honorary Senior Lecturer, University of Birmingham, 1964-65; Professor, Adviser in Clinical Research, 1979-82, Professor of Renal Medicine, Head of Department, 1982-, University of Keele; Consultant Physician, North Staffs Hospital Centre, 1965-. *Memberships:* Editorial Board, Journal Clinical Experimental Hypertension; Research Committee, National Kidney Research Fund; Research Committee, West Midlands Regional Health Authority; Vice Chairman, Scientific Committee of the WMRHA; Council, Royal College of Physicians, London; Research Programme Committee, International Society of Nephrology; Research Programme Committee, International Society for the Study of Hypertension in Pregnancy. *Publications include:* "Recent Advances in Renal Medicine", (Contributor), 1983; "Postgraduate Nephrology", (Contributor), 1985; "Textbook of Genitourinary Surgery", (Contributor), 1985; 'The extra cellular acid base state and metabolism of ammonium in respiratory failure', 1964; 'Renal fubction in ventilatory failure', 1964; 'The renal response to chronic hypercarbia and hypoxaemia in man', 1966; 'Quantative measurement of plasminogen activator activity in rat renal cortical tissue', (with E H F McGale, M Euden, P F Naish), 1985; Author of over 100 scientific papers in learned journals. *Hobbies:* Music; Sport; Motor cars. *Address:* University of Keele, Department of Postgraduate Medicine, North Staffordshire Medical Institute, Hartshill Road, Hartshill, Stoke-on-Trent, Staffordshire ST4 7NY, England.

ABERDOUR, Kenneth Robert, b. 9 Mar. 1927, Surrey, England. Consultant Radiologist, Mid Essex District Health Authority. m. Jean Rosemary Hardy, 17 Sep. 1960, Wimbledon, 1 son, 1 daughter. *Education:* St. George's Hospital London: LRVP MRCS, 1950; MB BS, London, 1951; AKC; MRCP, 1958; DMRD, 1959; FFR, 1961; FRCP, 1976. *Appointments:* Various house officer posts at St. Georges Hospital, Whittington Hospital, Central Middlesex Hospital, London Chest Hospital and National Heart Hospital, 1950-54; Registrar, Infectious Diseases, St. Georges Hospital, 1954-56; Registrar, Radiology, St. Georges Hospital, 1956-60; Senior Registrar, Radiology, St. Georges Hospital, 1960-62; Consultant Radiologist, Mid Essex District Hospitals, 1962-. *Memberships:* British Institute of Radiology; British Medical Association; Royal Society of Medicine. *Hobbies:* Gardening; Reading. *Address:* The Old Rectory, Wickham Bishops, Witham, Essex CM8 3LA, England.

ABIDOR, Gerard, b. 6 Mar. 1947, New York City, USA. Doctor of Chiropractic. *Education:* BSc, University of Rhode Island; BSc, Doctor of Chiropractic, National College of Chiropractic. *Appointments:* Director, Abidor Chiropractic Center. *Memberships:* International Chiropractic Association; American Chiropractic Association; Connecticut Chriopractic Association; International Academy for Chiropractic Study of the Lunber spine; New York Academy of Sciences. *Honours:* Teaching Fellowships: University of Connecticut School of Medicine, July 1974, Medical College of Georgia, June 1975. *Hobbies:* Electronics; Computer Science; Aerobics; Cycling. *Address:* 17 Brookpine Drive, Shelton, CT 06484, USA.

ABRAHAMS, Lawrence Michael, b. 17 Oct 1934,

Asheville, North Carolina, USA. Chief of Drug Dependence Treatment Unit. m. Hanna Elisabeth Den Hartog, 5 July 1969, Concord, Massachusetts. *Education:* AB, cum laude, Harvard University, 1956; MD, Vanderbilt University, 1961. *Appointments;* Research Fellow in Psychiatry, Harvard Medical School, 1965-66; Senior Psychiatrist, 1967-69, Clinical Director, 1969-71, Director of Psychiatry, 1971-73, Taunton State Hospital, Massachusetts; Director, Mental Health Center, Touro, 1973; Chief, Drug Dependence Treatment Unit, VA medical Center, New Orleans, Louisiana 1973-. *Memberships:* Massachusetts Medical Society; Orleans parish Medical Society; Louisiana Psychiatric Association; American Psychiatric Association; Reserve Officers Association. *Publications:* 'Multicenter Double-Blind Comparison of Nomifensine and Impramine for Efficacy and Safety in Depressed Outpatients' Journal of Clinical Psychiatry, 1984. *Honour:* Detur Prize, Harvard University, 1953. *Hobbies:* Walking; Reading. *Address:* VA Medical Center, 1601 Perdido Street, New Orleans, LA 70146, USA.

ABRAHAMSON, Dale Raymond, b. 18 June 1949, Washington, District of Columbia, USA. Assistant Professor of Cell Biology & Anatomy. m. Susan K.Spell, 14 Aug. 1971, Fairfax, Virginia, 1 daughter. *Education:* BA, University of Virginia, 1971; BA, George Mason University, 1976; PhD, University of Virginia, 1981. *Appointments include:* Research Fellow, Department of Medicine, Harvard Medical School /Department of Rheumatology & Immunology, Brigham & Women's Hospital, Boston, Massachusetts. *Memberships:* American Association of Anatomists; American Society for Cell Biology; American Association for the Advancement of Science. *Publications include:* Research contributions to various professional journals such as 'Science', 'Journal of Cell Biology', 'Journal of Experimental Medicine', etc. *Honours:* Baccalaureate High Distinction, 1976; Individual National Research Service Award, US Public Health Service, 1980-83. *Hobbies:* Tennis; Music; Gardening; Photography. *Address:* Department of Cell Biology & Anatomy, University of Alabama at Birmingham, University Station, Birmingham, AL 35294, USA.

ABRUZZO, John, b. 27 Apr. 1931, USA. Director, Arthritis Clinical Research Centre, Professor of Medicine. m. Elaine Alpisa, 13 Sep. 1958, Paterson, New Jersey, 6 sons, 2 daughters. *Education:* BS, St Peter's College, Jersey City, New Jersey; MD, Georgetown University Medical School, Washington DC. *Appointments:* Assistant in Medicine, Seton Hall College of Medicine, 1958-60; Fellow in Medicine, Columbia-Presbyterian Medical Centre, 1960-61; Instructor in medicine, Seton Hall College of Medicine, 1963-64; Assistant Professor of Medicine, New Jersey College of Medicine, 1964-67; Assistant Professor, 1967-69, Associate Professor, 1969-74, Professor of Medicine, 1974-, Thomas Jefferson University, Philadelphia, Pennsylvania; Director, Division of Rheumatology, ibid. *Memberships:* American Federation for Clinical research (National); Philadelphia Rheumatism Society; American Rheumatism Association; The Arthritis Foundation; American College of Physicians. *Publications:* Author & Co-author of some 70 articles in medical journals. *Honours:* Gold Key Society (National Jesuit Honour Society), 1953; Alpha Omega Alpha (National Honour Medical Society); Fellow, American College of Physicians. *Address:* Jefferson Medical College of Thomas Jefferson University, 1015 Walnut Street Rm 613, Philadelphia, PA 19107, USA.

ABU-SAIF, Adel-Nessim, b. 9 Nov. 1947, Cairo, Egypt. Lecturer, Radio-Diagnosis, Suez Canal University Ismalia. m. Hoda-Said, 8 Jan. 1982, 2 daughters. *Education:* MB.BCh.; DMRD; FRCR; FICA. *Appointments:* Registrar, Radio Diagnosis,

Cairo University, 1972-73; Registrar, Radio Diagnosis, St Mary's Hospital, London, England, 1974-75; Locum Consultant, Radio Diagnosis, Lewisham General Hospital, 1976-79; Lecturer, Radiology, Suez Canal University, 1981-. *Memberships:* Fellow, Royal College of Radiologists; Fellow, International College of Angiology. *Publications:* Articles in 'Ultrasound of Liver-Disease and Masses', 1985; "Ultrasound of Female Pelvis Lesions and in Obstetrics", 'Angiography of Splenic Artery After Ligation', 1982. *Hobbies:* Cinema; History; Karate – Black Belt; Food; Politics. *Address:* 78 El Gom Horeya St., Cairo, Egypt.

ABYHOLM, Frank Ellof, b. 9 Apr. 1939, Oslo, Norway, Professor, Head of Department of Plastic Surgery, m. Kari Sveinar, 29 June 1962, 2 sons, 1 daughter. *Education:* Cand odont, 1962; Cand med, 1967; Specialist in general surgery, 1974; Specialist in Plastic surgery 1978; Dr med, 1981. *Appointments:* Consultant Plastic surgeon, University Hospital, Rikshospitalet, Oslo, Norway, 1980-85. *Memberships:* The Norwegian Medical Association; The Norwegian Dental Association; The Norwegian Association of Plastic Surgeons; The Scandinavian Association of Plastic Surgeons. *Publications:* 'Cleft Lip and Palate in Norway', 1981. *Address:* Department of Plastic Surgery, Haükeland University Hospital, 5000 Bergen, Norway.

ACKERMAN, Richard, b. 27 Sep. 1949, New York, USA. Orthopaedist; Professor; Author. m. Marylynn Moore, 7 Dec. 1984, Albuquerque, New Mexico. 1 son, 2 daughters. *Education:* BA, Clinical Psychology, 1973; BS, Human Anatomy, 1975; DC, 1976; Diplomate, American Board of Chiropractic Orthopaedist, 1981; Fellow, Academy of Chiropractic Orthopaedists, 1984. *Appointments:* Anatomy Lab Assistant, National College of Chiropractic, 1974-75; Lab Assistant, Obstetrics and Gynecology, 1974-75; Lab Assistant, Clinical Cardiology, Chiropractic Orthopedics, 1974-77; Lab Instructor, Clinicopathologic Conference, 1974-77; Lab Instructor, Clinical Neurology, 12977, Physical Diagnosis, 1974-77; Faculty Position, National College of Chiropractic, Lombard, 1974-78; etc. *Memberships:* American Chiropractic Association; American College of Chiropractic Orthopaedics, Council Member, Neurology, Diagnosis & Internal Disorders; American Medical Writers Association; American Heart Association Teaching Staff; American National Red Cross. *Publications Include:* "Gross Anatomy of the Extremities", 1974; "An In Depth Study of Neuro-Anatomy – Part 1 The Spinal Cord", 1975; "Part II The Brain", 1975; "Illustrated Manual of Extra Vertebral Technics – Supplement Number One: Shoulder and Knee", 1977; "A"A Chriopractic Guide to Clinical History and Physical Examination", 1977; Author, numerous articles to professional journals including: 'Pathfinder Press Inc'; 'RCA Publications'; NCC. *Honours:* Recipient, numerous honours and awards including: Bovenaan, Outstanding Junior-Senior Award, Hofstra University, 1972; Honour Roll, Deans List, numerous times, National College of Chiropractic; Outstanding Senior Award, American Chiropractic Association, 1976; Outstanding Educator, College of DuPage, 1975; Centurion, National College of Chiropractic, 1978; etc. *Address:* 8900Robin NE, Albuquerque, NM 87121, USA.

ACKERMAN, Robert Carl, b. 30 May 1944, Los Angeles, California, USA. Executive Director, AMI Valley Medical Centre. m. 23 May 1971, Los Angeles, 1 son, 1 daughter. *Education:* BA, History, Loma Linda University, 1966; MPH, University of California, Los Angeles, 1971. *Appointments:* Administration Resident, Orange County Medical Centre, 1970-71; Administrative Assistant, St Luke's Hospital, Pasadena, 1971-72; Administrative Director, Ambulatory & Special Services, Children's Hospital of Los Angeles, 1972-76; Assistant Administrator, Intercommunity Hospital, Covina, 1976-77; Senior

Provider Representative, Orange county, Long Beach and Los Angeles County, Blue Cross of Southern California, Woodland Hills, 1977-80; Director, Provider Services, Health Maintenance Network of Southern California, 1980-81; Associate Executive Director, Medical Centre of North Hollywood, 1981-83; Operations Assistant, 1983, Executive Director, 1983-, AMI Valley Medical Centre. *Memberships:* American College of Hosptial Administrators; Secretary, Board of Directors, AMI Valley Medical Centre; Charter Review commission of San Diego County; Health Advisory Committee, Greater San Diego Chamber of Commerce; Director, El Cajon Valley Chamber of Commerce; Director, El Cajon Valley Boys Club; Past Chief Financial Officer, North Hollywood Chamber of Commerce; Health care Advisory Committee to Congressman Duncan Hunter. *Honours:* Citizen of the Year, North Hollywood Chamber of Commerce, 1983; Honoured Guest to review Recruits and Graduation, San Diego Naval Training Centre, 1984. *Hobbies:* Tennis; Swimming; Bicycling; Fine Art Collecting; Travel. *Address:* 13871 Durango Drive, Del Mar, CA 92014, USA.

ADAMS, Aileen Kirkpatrick, b. 5 Sep. 1923, Sheffield, England. Dean, Faculty of Anaesthetists, Royal College of Surgeons, England. *Education:* MA (Cantab), 1977; MB ChB, (Sheffield), 1945; FFARCS(Eng.), 1954. *Appointments:* Consultant Anaesthetist, Addenbrooke's Hospital, Cambridge, 1960-84; Associate Lecturer, University of Cambridge. *Memberships:* Association of Anaethetists Great Britain and Ireland, Past Hon. Sec., Vice-President; Fellow, Royal Society of Medicine, President, Section of Anaesthetics, 1985-86; British Medical Association. *Publications:* Chapter 'Premedication' in "General Anaesthesia", 1980; Papers on cardiovascular effect of Suxamethonium, Anaesthesia for Ophthalmic Surgery, Management of Head Injuries, 1964-84. *Honours:* Queen's Jubilee Medal, 1977. *Hobbies:* Choral Singing; Birdwatching; Mountain Walking; Skiing. *Address:* 90 High Street, Great Abington, Cambridge CB1 6AE, England.

ADAMS, Duncan Dartrey, b. 18 Apr. 1925, Hamilton, New Zealand. Director, Autoimmunity Research Unit, Medical Research Council of New Zealand. m. Yvonne Joan Macfarlane, 2 Apr. 1958, Dunedin, 1 son, 1 daughter. *Education:* MB, ChB, University of New Zealand, 1949; MRC NZ Research Fellow, 1951-53; MD, 1962, D.Sc., 1962, University of Otago; MRACP, 1973; FRACP, 1977. *Appointments:* House Surgeon, House Physician, Wellington Hospital, 1950; Research Fellow, MRCNZ Endocrinology Research Dept., 1951-53; Clinical Endocrinologist, Dunedin Hospital, 1951-; Lecturer, University of Western Ontario, Canada, 1954-55; Research Officer, MRCNZ Endocrinology Research Dept., 1955-70; Visiting Professor, Sheffield, Engla·,d, 1964; Visiting Scientist, MRCUK, Clinical Research Centre, London, 1974-75; Director, MRCNZ, Autoimmunity Research Unit, Medical School, Dunedin. *Memberships include:* New Zealand Medicla Association; Royal Australasian College of Physicians; American Academy of Microbiology; New Zealand Society of Endocrinology; New Zealand Society of Immunology. *Publications include:* 109 Scientific papers in professioanl journals. *Honours:* Van Meter Prize of American Goiter Association, 1958; Commonwealth Visiting Fellow, 1964; Organon Senior Endocrine Research Award, 1976; Mallinkrodt Prize VIIIth International Thyroid Congress, 1980; Fellow, American Academy of Microbiology, 1985. *Hobbies:* Russian Language; Bridge; Chess; Horse Riding; Skiing; Swimming. *Address:* Medical School, Dunedin, New Zealand.

ADAMSON, Geoffrey David, b. 16 Sep. 1946, Ottawa, Ontario, Canada. Clinical Assistant Professor. m. Rosemary Chilton Oddie, 28 Apr. 1973 Perth, Western Australia, 1 son, 2 daughters. *Education:* BSc Honours, Trinity College, University of Toronto, 1969; MD, School of Medicine, University of Toronto, 1973; Resident, 1974-77, Fellow, 1977, 78, Obstetrics and Gynecology, Toronto General Hospital; Fellow, Reproductive Endocrinology, Stanford University School of Medicine, USA, 1978-80. *Appointments;* Clinical Assistant Professor, University School of Medicine, Stanford University, 1980-. *Hobbies:* Computers; Running. *Address:* 540 University Avenue, Suite 200, Palo Alto, CA 94301, USA.

ADAMSKI, Stanislaw, b. 7 Oct. 1915, Walsnow, Poland. Surgeon /Professor. m. Halina Lisiecka, 24 Apr. 1947, 1 son, 1 daughter. *Education:* Graduated, Medical Faculty, University of Warsaw, 1945; Doctor of Surgery, Medical Faculty Lodz, 1948; Habilitated Docent Surgery, University Lodz, 1961; Professor of Surgery, Medical Academy Bailystok, 1971. *Appointments:* Senior Assistant to Docent Surgery, 1945-65, Master Surgery 1952, Master Thorax Surgery 1960, Master Heart Surgery, 1976, Medical Academy, Lodz, Surgery Department; Head of Surgery Department, 1965-70, Head, Thorax-Cardiovascular Surgery, 1970-73; Member, Faculty Medical Academy Bialystok; Vice Rector, Medical Academy Bialystok 1973-75; Member, Faculty Medical Academy Lodz 1961-65 and Bialystok 1965-. *Memberships:* International College of Surgeons, 1968-; Polish Society of Surgeons 1947-; European Society of Cardiovascular Surgery, 1975-; Polish Society of Cardiology, 1969-; Chairman, Thorax-Cardiovascular Section 1967-69, and Bialystok's Section 1983-85, Polish Society of Surgeons; Polish Medical Society 1947-. *Publications:* Contributor of numerous articles to medical journals. Author: "Tetniaki /aneurisms" edited by PZWL, Warsaw 1978; 'Direct myocardial revascularisation' in Handbook of Microsurgery, Vol II 1984. *Honours:* Scientific Prize 1st Degree, Ministry of Health and Social Welfare, 1973, 1973-75, 1985; Medal of National Education, Ministry of Education, 1975. *Hobbies:* Skiing; Yachting; Tourism. *Address:* 35 /A /1 Szpitalna, Bialystok 15-295, Poland.

ADDANTE, Joseph B, b. 25 Aug. 1926, Fitchburg, Massachusetts, USA. Podiatric Surgeon. m. Alice Baldarelli, 21 Nov. 1951, 2 sons, 1 daughter. *Education:* DSC, Temple University 1953; DPM, Pennsylvania College of Podiatric Medicine, 1970; MEd, Administration, State College of Fitchburg, 1976; Board Certification: American Board of Podiatric Surgery, 1975; American Board of Podiatric Orthopedics, 1982. *Appointments:* Private Practice, Fitchburg, Massachusetts, 1954-; Staff Appointments: Matthew Thornton Health Plan Incorporated, Medfield State Hospital, New England Deaconess Hospital, University of Massachusetts Medical Center, West Roxbury-Brockton VA Hospital, Mary Lane Hospital, Burbank Hospital, Leominster Hospital, Fairlawn Hospital; Clinical Adjunct Professor: California College of Podiatric Medicine, Dr. William School College of Podiatric Medicine 1978, Ohio College of Podiatric Medicine, 1972, Pennsylavania College of Podiatric Medicine, 1978; Distinguished Visiting Professor, NY College of Podiatric Medicine, 1978-80, 1982-; Orthopedic Associate, University of Massachusetts Medical School, 1981; Clincial Professor, College of Podiatric Medicine, University of Osteopathic Medicine and Health Sciences, 1984. *Memberships:* Fellow and Member of numerous professional organizations. Participant in community activities and member of social organizations. *Publications:* contributor to professional journals, etc. *Honours include:* Distinguished Practitioner of Podiatry, National Academy of Practice, 1982. *Address:* 32 Adams Street, Fitchburg, MA 01420, USA.

ADDISON, Robert G., b. 11 Dec. 1921, USA. Director, Centre for Pain Studies, Rehabilitation Institute of Chicago; Clinical Associate Professor, Department of Orthopaedic Surgery & Department of Rehabilitation Medicine, Northwestern University

Medical School. m. Beverly Minkin, 3 Apr. 1955, 4 daughters. *Education:* BS 1946, MD 1949, Northwestern University. *Appointments:* Senior attending staff, Northwestern Memorial Hospital, 1953; Acting Medical Director, Rehabilitation Institute of Chicago, 1961; Chief of Staff 1963, 1977, ibid; Chief, division of Orthopaedic Surger , St. Joseph Hospital, Chicago, 1968; Director, Low Back & pain Clinic, Rehabilitation Institute of Chicago, 1974. *Memberships:* American Academy of Orthopaedic Surgeons; American College of Surgeons; American Congress of Rehabilitation Medicine; American Medical Association; American Pain Society; American Academy of of Algology; International Society for Study of Lumbar Spine; State & Local medical societies. *Publications include:* "Living With Your Bad Back", with T. Berland, 1972; Contributions to 'Cancer Focus', 'American Journal of Medicine', 'Clinical Journal of Pain', etc. *Honours:* Board, Rehabilitation Institute of Chicago, 1977-79; President-elect, American Academy of Algology, 1986; 1st President, Midwest Pain Society, 1979. *Hobbies:* Sculpture; Writing; Tennis; Racquetball. *Address:* Rehabilitation Institute of Chicago, 345 E.Superior Street, Chicago, IL 60611, USA.

ADEKUNLE, Opeoluwa Oladeinde, b. 20 Nov. 1940. Professor of Surgery, Consultant Surgeon, University of Ibadan and University College Hospital. m. 2 sons, 2 daughters. *Education:* MBBS, 1966; FRCS Edinburgh, 1970; FRCS England, 1970; FWACS, 1970; FMCS Nigeria, 1976; SM, Epidemiology, Harvard, 1985. *Appointments:* Clinical Teacher, University of Edinburgh, Scotland, 1970-71; Part-time Demonstrator, Anatomy, Royal College of Surgeons, Edinburgh, 1971; Professor, University of Ibadan, 1983-. *Memberships:* Secretary, Nigerian Medical Association, Oyo State Branch, 1975-80; Executive Council, Nigerian Medical Association, 1975-84; Secretary, Africa Region, World Medical Association, 1979-81; Vice President, West Africa, Commonwealth Medical Association, 1982-84; Secretary General, Confederation of African Medical Associations and Societies, 1982-. *Publications:* 39 scientific articles; contributed chapters, 2 books. *Address:* Dept. of Surgery, University College Hospital, Ibadan, Nigeria.

ADELSTZIN, S(tanley) James, b. 24 Jan. 1928, New York City, USA. Professor of Radiology, Dean, Academic Programmes, Harvard Medical School. m. Mary Charlesworth Taylor, 20 Sep. 1957, Lincoln, 1 son, 1 daughter. *Education:* BS, MS, PhD, Biophysics, M.I.T., Cambridge; MD, Harvard Medical School; House Officer, Senior Assistant Resident, Chief Resident Physician, Peter Bent Brigham Hospital, Boston; Hoseley Travelling Fellow, Cambridge University; Fellow, Nuclear Medicine, Johns Hopkins Medical School. *Appointments:* Instructor, Associate, Assistant Professor, Anatomy, Associate Professor, Professor Radiology, Harvard Medical School. *Memberships:* Association for Radiation Research; Radiation Research Society; Society for Nuclear Medicine; American College of Nuclear Physicians; National Council for Radiation Protection and Measurements; Association of University Radiologists; Institute of Medicine. *Publications:* Contributor to books and journals on nuclear medicine and radiation biophysics. *Honours:* Quitman Lecturer, Haifa University, 1980; Blumgart Award, New England Chapter, Society Nuclear Medicine, 1982; Fellow, American College Nuclear Physicians, 1983; Aebersold Award, Society Nuclear Medicine, 1986. *Address:* 25 Shattuck Street, Boston, MA 02115, USA.

ADELUSI, Babatunde, b.30 June 1941, Ifaki-Ekiti. University Professor of Obstetrics and Gynaecology. m. Iyabode Oluremi Adeyemi, 30 Jan 1966, Ibadan, 3 sons, 1 daughter. *Education:* MBBS, University of Ibadan, 1967; MRCOG, Royal College of Obstetri-

cians and Gynaecologists, London, 1972; PhD, University of Ibadan, 1976; Emory University School of Medicine, Atlanta, Georgia, USA, 1979-80; MD, University of Ibadan, 1982. *Appointments:* Rotating Internship, 1967-68, Post Registration (SHO) 1968-69, University College Hospital Ibadan; Residency Training in Obstetrics and Gynaecology in various hospitals in UK, 1969-72; Senior Resident in Obstetrics and Gynaecology, University College Hospital, Ibadan, 1972-74; Rockefeller Medical Research Training Fellow, University of Ibadan, 1974-75; Lecturer/Consultant, Obstetrics and Gynaecology, 1975-76, Senior Lecturer/Consultant, Obstetrics and Gynaecology, 1976-80, Professor of Obstetrics and Gynaecology/Consultant 1980-, College of Medicine, University College Hospital, Ibadan; Head of Department of Obstetrics and Gynaecology, College of Medicine, University College Hospital, Ibadan. *Memberships:* Society for Gynaecology and Obstetrics of Nigeria; The Nigeria Medical Association; The Nigerian Society for Immunology; The Nigerian Society for Endoscopy; The New York Academy of Sciences; The Royal College of Obstetricians and Gynaecologists. *Publications:* Over seventy published articles in learned journals. *Honours:* Federal Republic of Germany Undergraduate Scholarships for Medicine, 1964-67; Rockefeller Medical Research Training Fellowship, 1973-74; Forgarty International Research Fellowship of the National Institutes of Health, USA, 1979-80. *Hobbies:* Table Tennis;Lawn Tennis; Swimming; Squash. *Address:* Department of Obstetrics and Gynaecology, College of Medicine, University College Hospital, Ibadan, Nigeria.

ADENDORFF, Christiaan Paulus, b. 29 Dec. 1950, Dalmas. Private Practice in Pretoria, South Africa. m. Wilna Swart, 21 June 1973, Pretoria, 2 daughters. *Education:* B.Ch.D., Pretoria. *Appointments:* Member, Executive Committee, Northern Transvaal Branch of DASA: President of N.Tvl. Branch of DASA; Member of Federal Council, DASA; Member of Committee of Preliminary Enquiry, Medical and Dental Council, RSA: Editor of Newsletter NTVL, DASA. *Memberships:* Dental Association of South Africa; Vryburgers of South Africa; Management of Art. Lure Angling in N.TVL. *Honour:* Past Presidential Medal, NTVL DASA. *Hobby:* Artifical Lure Angling. *Address:* P.O. Box 27323, Sunnyside 0132, Republic of South Africa.

ADER, Robert, b. 20 Feb. 1932, New York, USA. Psychologist; Divisional Director, University Medical School. m. Gayle Simon, 2 June, 1957, New York, USA, 4 daughters. *Education:* BS, Tulane University, New Orleans, USA, 1953; PhD, Cornell University, USA, 1957. *Appointments:* Research Instructor, Department of Psychiatry, University of Rochester School of Medicine and Dentistry, Professor of Psychiatry, 1957-68; Visiting Professor, Rudolf Magnus Institute for Pharmacology, University of Utrecht Medical Faculty, Utrecht, The Netherlands, 1970-71; Director, Division of Behavioural and Psychosocial Medicine, Department of Psychiatry, University of Rochester School of Medicine and Dentistry, Rochester, New York-. *Memberships:* Academy of Behavioural Medicine Research; American Association of University Professors; American Psychosomatic Society; Eastern Psychological Association; International Society for Developmental Psychobiology; Psychonomic Society; Society of Behavioural Medicine. *Publications:* Editor, "Psychoneuroimmunology", 1981; Approximately 150 papers in scientific journals. *Honours:* President, American Psychosomatic Society, 1979-80; President, International Society for Developmental Psychobiology, 1981-82; President, Academy of Behavioural Medicine Research, 1984-85; Research Career Development Award; Research Scientist Award, NIMH; George L. Engel Professor of Psychosocial Medicine, 1983-. *Hobbies:* Photography; Travel; Fishing; Gardening; Tennis. *Address:* Department of Psychiatry, University of Rochester Medical Centre, Rochester, NY 14642,

ADLER, Barry Lloyd, b. 21 Feb. 1956, Brooklyn, New York, USA. Director, Adler Chiropractic Health Center. m. Rebecca Adler, 1982. *Education:* ASc.,Pensacola Junior College; BSc., Human Biology, DC, Logan College of Chiropractic; Certified Acupuncturist, National College of Chiropractic. *Appointments:* United States Naval Hospital Corps, 1974-76; Ferguson Chiropractic Clinic, 1980; Adler Chiropractic Health Center, 1981-85. *Memberships:* American & Florida Chiropractic Associations; Broward County Chiropractic Society; ACA Council on Roentgenology and Nutrition; Diplomat, National Board of Chiropractic Examiners; Parker Chiropractic Research Foundation; Foundation for Chiropractic Education and Research. *Honour:* Clinican of the Year Award. *Hobbies:* Computers; Travel; Backgammon; Chess. *Address:* 660N St. Rd. 7, Suite 15, Plantation, FL 33317, USA.

ADLER, Charles Spencer, b. 27 Nov. 1941, New York City, USA. Private Practice, Psychiatry and Psychosomatic Medicine; Chief, Psychiatry, Rose Medical Centre. m. Shelia Noel Morrissey Adler, PhD, 8 Oct. 1966, Tucson. *Education:* BA, Cornell University, 1962; MD, Duke University Medical School, 1966; Internship, Medical-Surgical, Tucson Hospitals Medical Education Programme, 1966-67; Psychiatric Residency, University of Colorado Medical Centre, 1967-70. *Appointments:* Private Practice, 1970-; Staff Psychiatrist, part time, Bethesda Community Mental Health Centre, 1970-773; Co-Founder, Applied Biofeedback Institute, part time, 1972-75; Professor, Pro Tempore, Cleveland Clinic Educational Foundation, 1977; Editorial Board, 'Cephalalgia', 1985; Consultant, Rose Medical Centre Cardiac Rehabilitation Programme, 1982-; Advisory Board, Duke University Centre for Aging and Human Development, 1983-. *Memberships:* American Academy of Psychoanalysis; American Association for the Study of Headache; International Headache Society; American Psychiatric Association; Colorado Psychiatric Society; American Medical Association; many other professional organisations. *Publications:* "E.M.G. Feedback Applied to Tension Headache : A Controlled Outcome Study", co-author, 'Psychosomatic Medicine', 1973; "We are But a Moments Sunlight", 1976; "Existential Deterrents to Headache Relief Past Mid-Life", 'Advances in Neurology', Volume 33, 1982; "Psychiatric Treatment of Headache", 'Paniminerva Medica', 1982; Section of Biofeedback in The American Psychiatrist Association Textbook 'The Psychiatric Therapies', 1984; "Psychiatric Aspects of Headache", in press; Section on Biofeedback, 'Encyclopedia Britannica Medical and Health Annual', 1980. *Honours:* American Medical Association Physician Recognition Award, 1969, 1979, 1982, 1985; Elected Fellow; American Psychiatric Association, 1983; Elected Scientific Associate, American Academy of Psychoanalysis, 1982; Award of Recognition, National Migraine Foundation, 1981. *Hobbies:* Writing and Reading Poetry; Travel; Skiing. *Address:* 955 Eudora Street, Suite 1605, Denver, CO 80220, USA.

ADLER, David Avram, b. 25 Aug. 1947, New York City, USA. Professor of Psychiatry. m. Jill, 5 Oct. 1975, Waltham, Massachussetts, USA, 1 son, 1 daughter. *Education:* BA, University of Rochester, 1969; MD, Yale University, School of Medicine, 1973. *Appointments:* Assistant Professor of Psychiatry, Tufts University School of Medicine, 1976-83; Director, Partial Hospitalization Service, New England Medical Center, 1979-82; Director of Aftercare Services, Bay Cove Medical Health Center, 1979-; Adjunct Assistant Professor, Simmons College School of Social Work, 1980-; Assistant Chief, Division of Adult Psychiatry, NEMC, 1982-83, Associate Chief, 1983-84, Chief, 1984-; Associate Professor of Psychiatry TUSM, 1984-. *Memberships:* American Psychiatric Association; Massachussetts Psychiatric Society; Group for Advancement of Psychiatry. *Publications include:* Numerous Monographs, Book reviews, Abstracts and articles in professional journals including: 'The Medical Model and Psychiatry's Task' in 'Hospital and Community Psychiatry', 1981; 'Perspectives on Rehabilitative and Educative Developmental Psychotherapy' in 'American Journal of Psychotherapy', 1984; 'Framework for the Analysis of Psychotherapeutic Approaches to Schizophrenia' in the Yale 'Journal of Biology and Medicine', 1985; Book Chapter: 'Shelter is Not Enough: Clinical Work with the Homeless Mentally Ill' in "The Homeless Mentally Ill", 1984. *Honours:* Phi Beta Kappa, University of Rochester, 1969; Alpha Omega Alpha, Yale University School of Medicine, 1973; Harry C Solomon Research Award, 1975; Fellow, American Psychiatric Association, 1985. *Hobbies:* Family; Reading. *Address:* 20 Sylvan Avenue, Newton, MA 02165, USA.

ADLER, Gerald, b. 1 July 1930, New York, USA. Director of Medical Student Education in Psychiatry. m. Corinne Borman, 15 Sept 1984, Boston, Massachusetts, 1 son, 1 daughter. *Education:* AB, Columbia College, 1951; MD, Columbia College of Physicians and Surgeons, 1957; Fellow in Child Psychiatry, James Jackson Putnam Children's Center, Boston, 1962-63; Candidate, Boston Psychiatric Society and Institute, Boston, 1961-67, Graduated 1967. *Appointments:* Assistant Professor of Psychiatry, 1965-70, Associate Professor of Psychiatry, 1970-74, Professor of Psychiatry, 1974-79, Tufts University School of Medicine; Lecturer on Psychiatry, Harvard Medical School, 1979-; Director of Medical Student Education in Psychiatry, Massachusetts General Hospital; Training and Supervising Analyst, Boston Psychoanalytic Society and Institute. *Memberships:* American Psychiatric Association; American Psychoanalytic Association. *Publications:* "Borderline Psychopathology and Its Treatment" 1985; "Confrontation in Psychotherapy" editor with P G Myerson, 1973; 'Aloneness and Borderline Psychopathology: The Possible Relevance of Child Development Issues' in "International Journal of Psycho-analysis" 1979, with D H Buie. *Honour:* Alpha Omega Alpha, 1956. *Address:* Massachusetts General Hospital, 16 Blossom Street, Boston, MA 02114, USA.

ADLER, Solomon Stanley, b. 26 May 1945, New York, USA, Associate Professor of Medicine, m. Rochelle Steinlauf, 27 Aug. 1967, New York, 2 sons, 3 daughters. *Education:* MD. *Appointments:* Instructor in Medicine, 1973-75, Assistant Professor of Medicine, 1975-78, Associate Professor of Medicine, 1978-, Chief, Special Haematology Laboratory, 1974-76, Chief, Special Morphology Laboratory, 1976-, Adjunct Attending Physician, 1974-75, Assistant Attending Physician, 1975-78, Associate Attending Physician, 1978-82, Senior Attending Physician, 1982-, Rush-Presbyterian-St Lukes Medical Centre, Chicago, Illinois. *Memberships:* Fellow, American College of Physicians; American Federation of Clinical Research; American Society of Clinical Oncology; American Society of Haematology; Central Society for Clincial Research; Member, Editorial Board, Experimental Haematology. *Publications:* "Advances in Biosciences 16", (with R Burkhardt, C L Conley, K Lennert and T Pincus), 1974; Contributor to numerous articles to professional journals. *Honours:* New York State Regents Scholarship, 1962-66; Alpha Sigma Lambda, 1963-66; Phi Beta Kappa, 1964; Graduate, Summa cum Laude, 1966; Jonas Salk Scholarship, New York, 1970. *Address:* Department of Medicine, Rush-Presbyterian-St Lukes Medical Centre, 1753 West Congress Parkway, Chicago, IL 60612, USA.

ADMANI, Abdul Karim, b. 19 Sep. 1934, Palitana, India. Consultant Physician; Clinical Lecturer; m. Seema Robson, 23 Mar. 1968, South Shields, England, 1 son, 1 daughter. *Education:* BSc, Hons. Gujrat University, India; MB, BS, Dow Medical

College, Karachi University, Pakistan; DTM&H, London University, England; MRCP, FRCP, Edinburgh, Scotland. *Appointments include:* Senior House Officer, Sunderland General Hospital, England, 1964, Junior Registrar, 1965; Registrar Physician, Darlington Memorial Hospital, 1965-66, Registrar Physician, St. Catherine's Hospital, Birkenhead, 1966-68; Senior Registrar, Neurology, Civil Hospital, Karachi, Pakistan, 1968-69; Senior Registrar, Medicine for the Elderly, Sheffield Teaching Hospital, England, 1969-70, Consultant Physician, 1970-present, Clinical Lecturer, Medical School, 1972-present. *Memberships:* British Medical Association; Chairman, Overseas Doctors Association in UK; British Geriatric Society; Medico-Chirurgical Society in Sheffield; Affiliated member Royal College of Physicians, London; Pakistan Medical Society; President, British Red Cross Society, South Yorkshire Region; General Medical Council; Central Committee for Hospital Medical Services nationally. *Publications:* Editor of "Guidance for Overseas Doctors in NHS", 1982; contributions to medical journals include: 'Postural Hypertension and Electrolytesian Elderly' in 'Age and Ageing', 1972 (co-author); 'New Approach in the Treatment of Acute Stroke' in 'British Medical Journal', 1977; 'Vasolastine in the Treatment of Stroke' in 'Current Medical Research', 1982; 'Management of Elderly Patients with Acute Lower Respiratory Tract Infection' in 'Current Medical Research', 1985. *Honour:* Justice of the Peace, City of Sheffield, since 1974. *Hobbies:* Tennis; Snooker; Table Tennis; Community and Race Relations; Social Work. *Address:* 1 Derriman Glen, Silverdale Road, Sheffield S11 9LQ, England.

ADRIAN, Richard Hume (Lord), b. 16 Oct. 1927, Cambridge, England. Professor of Cell Physiology. m. Lucy Caroe, 1967. *Education:* Swarthmore High School, USA; Westminster School; MA, Trinity College, University of Cambridge; MB, BChir, Cantab; MD, University College Hospital, 1951; National Service, Royal Army Medical Corps, 1952-54; G H Lewes Student, University of Cambridge Physiology Laboratory, 1954. *Appointments:* University Demonstrator, 1956; Fellow, Corpus Christi College, 1956; University Lecturer, 1961-68; Reader in Experimental Biophysics, 1968-78; Professor of Cell Physiology, University of Cambridge, 1978-; Fellow, Churchill College, 1961-81; Master of Pembroke College, 1981-; Vice-Chancellor, University of Cambridge, 1985-87. *Memberships:* Fellow of the Royal Society, 1977; Trustee, British Museum, 1979-, British Museum (Natural History), 1984; Member of Council, Royal Society, 1984-. *Publications:* Numerous articles in 'Journal of Physiology'. *Honours:* Honorary Doctorate, University of Poitiers, France, 1975. *Hobbies:* Sailing; Skiing. *Address:* The Master's Lodge, Pembroke College, Cambridge, CB2 1RF, England.

ADUM, Ognjan, b. 11 Feb. 1924, Sibenik, Yugoslavia. Professor, Occupational Health, University of Belgrade. m. Professor Stojanka Unkovic, 3 Aug. 1980, Belgrade, 1 son. *Education:* MD, Medical Faculty, University of Belgrade, 1954; Diploma, Specialist Occupational Health, 1962; Diploma DSc., Belgrade, 1975; PhD (habil.), Belgrade, 1967; Postgraduate Fellow, Institut fur Arbeitsphysiologie an der Universitat, Dortmund, Federal Republic of Germany, 1977. *Appointments:* General Practitioner 1955-57; Chief Phsyician, Factory Medical Service, 1957-61; Institute for Occupational Health, Belgrade, 1961-62; Medical Faculty, Assistant 1962-78, Assistant Professor, 1979-84, Associate Professor 1984-, University of Belgrade; Professor, Occupational Hygiene, Higher Medical School, Belgrade, 1966-. *Memberships:* International Union for Health Education; Association of Occupational Health of Yugoslavia; Association of Traffic Medicine of Yugoslavia; Society of Psychologists of Serbia. *Publications:* "Occupational Medicine", 2nd Edition 1966; "Accidents at Work and their Prevention", 1964; "Ele-

ments of Occupational Medicine", 1981, 2nd Edition 1983; "Occupational Hygiene with Occupational Diseases", 1985; "Experiment. Studies of Shiftwork", 1975. *Honours:* Silver Decoration, from President of the Republic of Yugoslavia, 1972; Diploma, Association of Occupational Health of Yugoslavia, 1983. *Hobbies:* Classical Music; Sport; Travel. *Address:* 27 Marta 4/11, 11000 Belgrade, Yugoslavia.

AGARWAL, Kailash Nath, b. 5 July 1937, Pilibhit, India. Professor of Paediatrics, Professor-in-charge Reorientation of Medical Education Programme. m. D K Agarwal, 27 Apr. 1967, Delhi, 2 daughters. *Education:* MBBS, King George's Medical College, Lucknow, 1959; DCH 1961, MD 1969, University of Delhi; MD honours, University of Uppsala, Sweden, 1964. *Appointments:* Lecturer in Paediatrics 1964, Reader in Paediatrics 1971-73, Professor and Head of Paediatrics 1973-83, Professor of Paediatrics and Professor-in-charge Reorientation of Medical Education Programme 1983-, Institute of Medical Sciences, Banaras Hindu University, Varansi. *Memberships:* International College of Pediatrics; Indian Academy of Pediatrics; Nutritional Society of India; Indian Hematology Society. *Publications include:* Over 200 publications including: 'Corticosteroids and erythrocytes', 1964; 'Current Status National goitre Control Programme 1982'; 'Current status of infant and early childhood'. *Honours:* S T Achar Gold Medal, 1969; Applied Research Award, MCI, 1974-76; Heinz 50th Anniversary British Paediatric Association Award, 1978; Shri Amrut Mody Research Foundation Award, 1979. *Address:* Department of Paediatrics, Institute of Medical Sciences, Banaras Hindu University, Varanasi, India.

AGBAYEWA, M Olu-wafemi, b. 2 Feb. 1950, Nigeria, Assistant Professor; Consultant, Psychiatrist, Deer Lodge Geriatric Centre, Beacon Hill Lodge, Tuxedo Villa, Oakview Place. *Education:* MBBS, University of Ibadan, Nigeria, 1974; Dip Psych, University of Ottawa, Canada, 1980; MRCPsych, London, England; FRCP(C). *Appointments:* Senior Psychiatrist, Saskatchewan Health Moose Jaw Psychiatric Centre, Canada, 1981-82; Staff Psychiatrist, Health Sciences Centre, Winnipeg, Manitoba, 1982-; Consultant Psychiatrist, Deer Lodge Geriatric Centre, Winnipeg, 1985-; Assistant Professor of Psychiatry, University of Manitoba, 1982-; Consultant to other nursing homes in Winnipeg. *Memberships:* Canadian and Manitoba Medical and Psychiatric Associations; American Psychiatric Association; American Orthopsychiatric Association; International Psychogeriatric Association; Geriatric Psychiatry Section of World Psychiatric Association. *Publications:* Author of over 12 publications. *Hobbies:* Jazz music; Jazz dancing; Movies; Reading. *Address:* Department of Psychiatry, University of Manitoba, 75 Emily Street, Winnipeg, Manitoba, Canada R3E OR3.

AGGARWAL, Darshan C., b. 2 Jan. 1945, India. Neurologist. m. Santosh Zutshi, 6 Aug. 1976, 1 son, 1 daughter. *Education:* MD, Medical College, Amritsar, India, 1970; Residency, Internal Medicine, 1970-74, Postgraduate Institute of Medical Education & Research. *Appointments:* Chief Resident, Medicine, Postgraduate Institue Medical Education and Research, Chandigarh, 1974-76; Senior Resident, Geriatric & Internal Medicine, 1976-77; Chief Resident, Medicine, 1977-78, St Catherine Hospital, Liverpool, England; Neurology Resident, University of Alabama Medical Centre, USA, 1978-81. *Memberships:* American Medical Association; American Academy of Neurology; Florida State Medical Society; St Lucie Okeechobee County Medical Society. *Publications:* "Systolic Time Intervals in Normals"; "Systolic Time Intervals in Preoperative Patients with Constrictive Pericarditis"; "Systolic time Intervals in Postoperative Pericardectomy Patients". *Honours:*

Valedictorian Licentiate, 1967; Distinction in Forensic Medicine, 1967; Silver Medal, Pathology, 1969; Valedictorian Graduating Class, 1970. *Hobby:* Photography. *Address:* 2215 Nebraska Avenue, Fort Pierce, FL 33450, USA.

AGORI-IWE, Cornelius Ouigho, b. 6 Jan. 1942, Nigeria. Senior Consultant, Obstetrics and Gynaecology; Medical Director. m. Elizabeth Ogbon, 1 Sep. 1984, Warri, 2 sons, 6 daughters. *Education:* BA, Hope College, Michigan, USA, 1967; MD, Howard University, 1971; Montefiore Hospital and Medical Centre, New York, 1972-76; Diplomate of American Board of Obstetrics and Gynaecology. *Appointments:* Assistant Attendant, Montefiore Hospital and Medical Centre, 1976-78; Consultant Gynaecologist, Specialist Hospital, Benin City, Nigeria, 1978-79; Senior Consultant Gynaecologist, Mariere Hospital, Ughelli, 1980-84; Zonal Medical Director, Ughelli Medical Zone, 1970-84; Medical Director, Osalees International Women and Children's Hospital, Ughelli, 1985-. *Memberships:* Fellow, American College of Obstetrics and Gynaecology; Society of Gynaecology and Obstetrics of Nigeria; Nigerian Medical Association. *Hobbies:* Table Tennis; Listening to Music. *Address:* Osalees International Women and Children's Clinic, P.O. Box 193, Ughelli, Bendel State, Nigeria.

AGRAWAL, S.R., b. 1 Apr. 1941, Sagar, India. Reader in ENT. m. Veena Agrawal, 21 Nov. 1972, Bareilly, 2 sons, 1 daughter. *Education:* MS; DLO; MBBS. *Appointments:* RMO, ENT; Lecturer, ENT. *Memberships:* Association of Otolaryngologists of India; Indian Medical Association. *Publications:* Numerous articles in professional journals including: 'Antiseptic'; 'Indian Journal of Otolaryngology'; 'Indian Medical Journal'; 'Indian Medical Gazette'; "A Histological Study in Atrophic Rhinitis'', Paper presented, 22nd Annual Conference, Association of Otolaryngologists of India, Varanasi, 1970. *Honour:* Certificate of Honour, DLO, 1967. *Hobbies:* Cultural and Service Activities. *Address:* 12 J.A. Hospital Campus, Gwalior (MP), India 474-009.

AGUILAR, Carlos, b. 30 Nov. 1927, Chihuahua, Mexico. Cardiologist, Private Practice; Professor of Cardiology, University Autonoma de Chihuahua. m. Beatriz Silva, 30 May 1955, Juárez, Mexico, 2 sons, 1 daughter. *Education:* BSc, Institute Scientific and Literary in Chihuahua, Mexico, 1945; MD, National University Autonoma de Mexico, 1953. *Appointments:* Internship, Hotel Dieu, Sisters Hospital, El Paso, Texas; Residency, Scott & White Memorial Hospital, Temple, Texas, USA - Dec. 1957; Director, Cardiovascular Research, central Hospital, Chiuaua, 1961-; Founder and Director, 2nd Coronary Care Unit in Mexico, Palmore Hospital, Chikuahua, 1969; Director, Cardiology, ISSSTE Hospital, Chihuahua, 1964-71; Professor, Clinical Cardiology, University of Chihuahua, 1961-; Private Practice to date. *Memberships:* Fellow, American College of Cardiology; Fellow, American College of Physicians; Miembre Titular, Sociedad Mexicana de Cariologia; Fellow, Concilii Scientiarum Collegii Internationalis Angiologie; Founder, State Medical Pensiones, 1969; President, State Basketball Association, 1968; Founder, Executive Director and Honorary Life President, Mexican National Universities Athletic Organization, 1971. *Publications:* "Reflexions about Tarahumara Indian", 1953; "Effects of 'Peyote' in Tarahumara Indians", 1953; "Actual Considerations About Rheumatic Fever", 1962; "Profilactic results for Rheumatic Fever in 'Teaching the Teachers Program' in 5,000 Grammar School Boys", 1962; "Essential Hypertension and Alpha Methyl Dopa", 1964; "Experimental Study about Essential Hypertension and alfametyl-dopa'', 1964; "Hiposodic Diet in Hypertension", 1966; "Essential Hypertension", 1968; "Treatment, Cardiac Arrest", 1968; "Emergencies in Coronary Care Unit, 1969; "Management Cardiogenic Shock", 1970. *Honour:* Best Career Professor 6 consecutive generations

University Autonoma of Chihuahua. *Hobby:* Basketball. *Address:* Presa Granero 2000, Lomas del Santuario, Chihuahua, Chih, Mexico.

AGUIRRE BIANCHI, Renato, b. 10 Nov. 1943, Santiago, Chile. Director, Clinica Lautaro; Chief of Staff, Clinica Mutual de Seguridad. m. Sara Aguirre Troncoso, 30 Nov. 1968, Santiago, 1 son, 1 daughter. *Education:* Medico-Cirujano, Medical School, Universidad de Chile, Santiago, 1969; Specialist in General Surgery, Postgraduate School, Universidad de Chile, Hospital del Salvador, Santiago and Hospital Juan Noe, Arica, 1969-73. *Appointments:* Docent on Human Anatomy, Nurse School, Universidad de Chile, Santiago, 1966-68; Student Resident, Chilean Air Force, 1967-69; Resident in General Surgery, Hospital del Salvador, Santiago, 1969-72; Post-Resident, Hospital Juan Noe, Arica, 1972-73; Associate Instructor in Surgery, Medical School of University of Chile, 1971-72; Chief of Surgery, Hospital Juan Noe, Arica, 1973-83; Director, Department of Medical Sciences, Universidad del Norte, Arica, 1975-76; Director, Clinica Lautaro, 1981-; Chief of Staff, Clinica Mutual de Seguridad, 1983-. *Memberships:* Sociedad de Cirujanos de Chile: Fellow, American College of Surgeons; International Cardiovascular Society; New York Academy of Sciences; Founder Fellow, Sociadad Medica del Norta, Chile. *Publications:* Co-author, "Tratado de Cirugia", Dr. Raul Romero Torres, Editor, 1984. Over 40 published articles in medical journals. *Honours:* David Benavente Award, Chilean Society of Surgeons, 1976; Juan Gandulfo Award, Chilean Society of Surgeons, 1978. *Hobbies:* Sports; Sky Diving; Airplane Flying; Skin Diving; Cross-Country Bicycle Riding; Competitive Sailing in cruisers and windsurf; Swimming. *Address:* Lautaro 487, Arica, Chile

AHLGREN, Johan G A, b. 24 Sep. 1926, Linkoping, Sweden. Professor and Chairman of Orthodontics Department of Orthodontics, School of Dentistry, Malmö, Sweden. m. 25 May 1958, Lund, 3 daughters. *Education:* DDS; Odont.Dr.; Diploma, Swedish Board of Orthodontics. *Appointments:* Assistant Professor, School of Dentistry, Malmö, Sweden; Assistant Professor, School of Dentistry, Ann Arbor, Michigan, USA; Associate Professor, School of Dentistry, Göteborg, Sweden; Professor, School of Dentistry, Malmö, Sweden. *Memberships:* Swedish Orthodontic Society; British Orthodontic Society; European Orthodontic Society. *Publications:* "Mechanism of Mastication", 1966; "Mastication", 1976; "Oral Physiology and Occlusion'', 1978; "25 Years of Activator Treatment", 1984. *Honour:* Certificate in Orthodontics, University of Michigan, Ann Arbor, USA. *Hobby:* Golf. *Address:* School of Dentistry, 21421 Malmö, Sweden.

AHLIN, Jeffrey Haynes, b.9 June 1943, Boston, Massachusetts, USA. Clinical Instructor, Harvard School of Dental Medicine. *Education:* BA, Tulane University, 1965; DDS, Temple University, 1969; Certificate Pedodontics, Boston University, 1973; Diplomate, American Board of Pedodontics; Fellow, American Academy of Pediatric Dentistry. *Appointment:* Dental Officer, USNR. *Memberships:* International Association of Orthodontics; American Dental Association; American Society of Dentistry for Children; American Academy of Gnathological Orthopedics; American Academy of Pedondontics; American Board of Pediatric Dentistry. *Publications:* Co-author: Maxillofacial Orthopedics: AClinical Approach for the Growing Child, 1984; Co-author: A Screening procedure for differentiation temporomandibular joint related headache, 1984. *Hobbies:* Research; Skiing. *Address:* 198 Ash Street, Reading, MA 01867-3680, USA.

AHLSTEN, Stig Åke Gustaf, b. 15 Feb. 1913, Linkoping, Sweden. Dental Surgeon. m. Ann-Mari Helsinger, 16 Aug. 1941, 4 sons, 1 daughter. *Education:* DDS 1935; Master Examination, 1949, Licence in Dental Surgery, Sweden, 1935; Special

Certificate in Oral Surgery, 1968 and in Oral Prosthetics, 1984. *Appointments:* Assistant and Associate Professor, Dental High School, Stockholm, 1935-43; Consultant, Dental Surgeon, St. Gorans Hospital, Stockholm, 1936-46; Chief Dental Surgeon and Head, Oral Surgery Department, University Hospital, Uppsala, 1944-79; Dental Director, Public Dental Service, Uppsala County, 1943-79; Master in Odontology for Medical Students, Faculty of Medicine, Uppsala University, 1949-80; Representative Dental Surgeon, Dental Care Insurance, Uppsala County, 1973-; Publishing Company Executive of Tandlakarforlaget, Stockholm, 1982-. *Memberships:* Swedish Dental Federation; Swedish Oral Surgery Association; Odontological Society, Stockholm, Honor. Member, 1950; Uppsala Medical Society; Swedish Society for Dental Directors, Honor. Member 1979. *Publications:* Author of 2 books and numerous papers in Dentistry; Editor, 'Journal Odontological Society', 1939-56. *Honours:* Medal of Merit, Swedish Red Cross, 1940; Cross of Liberty, Order of Finland, 1942; Knight, 1959 Knight Commander, 1975, Royal Northern Star Order of Sweden. *Hobbies:* Philately; Flowers. *Address:* Borgvägen 1, 752 36 Uppsala, Sweden.

AHMAD, Kamaluddin, b. 1 Sep. 1923, Bangladesh. Professor of Biochemistry; Director, Institute of Nutrition and Food Science. m. Nahar K Ahmad, 19 Aug. 1951, Dhaka, 5 sons, 2 daughters. *Education:* MSc, Dhaka University, 1944; PhD, University of Wisconsin, USA, 1949; 1st Nuffield Foundation Fellow, Natural Science, 1951; SEATO Research Fellow, 1950; Diploma in Isotope Research, 1956; BSc Honours. *Appointments:* Reader (Associate Professor), Department of Biochemistry, Professor, 1st Head of Department of Biochemistry, 1st Head, Department of Pharmacy, Founder-Director, Institute of Nutrition and Food Science, Dean, Faculty of Science, University of Dhaka; Vice-Chancellor, Bangladesh Agricultural University. *Memberships:* Fellow, Bangladesh Academy of Sciences. President: Nutrition Society of Bangladesh; Biochemical Society of Bangladesh; American Universities Alumni Association of Bangladesh. Member: Bangladesh Medical Research Council; Executive Committee and Chairman, Research Review Committee; American Institute of Nutrition. *Publication:* "Lectures on Nutrition and Related Problems"; "Khadya-O-Pushti" Food and Nutrition; "Pushti Bidya, Nutrition Education; Author over 150 research articles on nutrition and related fields. *Honours:* Gold Medal, Pakistan Academy of Sciences, 1967; Prize of Performance, President of Pakistan; Sonali Bank Gold Medal, Bangladesh Academy of Science, 1984. *Hobby:* Research. *Address:* Institute of Nutrition and Food Science, University of Dhaka, Dhaka 2 Bangladesh.

AHMED, Iqbal, b. 23 Aug. 1951, India. Assistant Professor; Director. m. Lisa Suzanne Rose Ahmed, 9 Oct. 1983, Boston. *Education:* MB, BS, St Johns Medical College, India, 1974; MRC Psychiatry, 1981. *Appointments:* Staff Psychiatrist Consultation, Liason Psychiatry, 1981-, Staff Psychiatrist, Geriatric Nemopsychiatry Unit, Boston City Hospital, 1982-84. *Memberships:* American Medical Association; American Psychiatric Association; Royal College of Psychiatrists, UK; American Psychomosomatic Society; Transcultural Psychiatry Society, UK. *Publications:* 'Anti-psychotic drugs: Problems and guidelines', (co-author), 1979; 'Treatment of Sleepwalking: A Controlled Study', 1981. *Honours:* Gov't of India, National Ment Scholarship for Medical Education, 1968-74; Honorary Assistant Instuctor, Psychiatry, Nebraska Psychiatric Institute, 1978-79. *Hobbies:* Philately; Numismatics; Theatre. *Address:* 818 Harrison Avenue, Acc 4S-25, Boston, MA. 02118, USA.

AHMED, Nahaluddin, b. 19 Jan. 1932, Puraini, Pakistan. Consultant Chest Phsyician. m. Shamshum Nehar, 21 nov. 1957, Amrath, 1 son, 4 daughters. *Education:* MB BS; ACCME; FCCP, USA; Post Graduate Fellow, USA. *Appointments:* Researcher, Tuberculosis, Central TB Sanatorium, Karachi; currently, Consultant Chest Physician, Nehal Hospital, Karachi; currently, Consultant Chest Physician, Nehal Hospital, Karachi. *Memberships:* International Academy of American College of Chest Physicians and Surgeons. *Honours:* Stood 1st in Pharmacology and 2nd in Surgery in professional examinations; Fellowship, American College of Chest Physicians. *Hobby:* Reading. *Address:* Nehal Hospital, 26 Kala Board, Malir Township, Karachi 37, Pakistan.

AHO, Allan Johannes, b. 3 July 1931, Viborg, Finland. Acting Professor (Chairman). m. Sirkka-Liisa Lehtikanto, 7 Aug. 1955, Vaasa, 3 sons. *Education:* MD, 1957; Competency of Surgery, 1964; D.Med.Sci, 1966; Competency of traumatology and orthopaedics, 1979. *Appointments:* Rural Practitioner, 1958-59; Resident in Pathology Anatomy, 1959-60; Resident in Surgery, 1961-64; Surgeon, 1965-67; Assistant Professor (docent) and Assistant Chief Surgeon, 1968-71; Associate Professor, 1972-. *Memberships:* Association Finnish Physicians; Society of Finnish Surgeons and Orthopaedics; Nordic Society of Surgery; Nordic Society of Orthopaedics; International College of Surgeons; Society Inter. Chir. Orthop. Traumatol. *Publications:* Thesis: "Electron microscopic and histologic observations on fracture repair in young and old rats", Acta Pathol. Micro-biol. Scand. Suppl. 184, 1966; Articles on traumatology, bone tumors and allografts, pancreatitis and ultrastructure. *Honour:* Silver Medal of Finnish Sports Union. *Address:* The University Central Hospital of Turku, SF-20520 Turku, Finland.

AKAMAGUNA, Anthony Ifechukude, b. 5 Aug. 1949, Ubulo-Uno, Nigeria. Lecturer & Consultant Radiologist, University of Benin & University Teaching Hospital. m. Camille Lena Smith, 20 Dec. 1980, Cardiff, 1 son, 1 daughter. *Education:* MB,BS, University of Lagos, Nigeria, 1974; DMRD, University of Wales, Cardiff, UK, 1979. *Appointments include:* Registrar, Radiology, University of Wales, 1977-80; Locum consultant radiologist, Royal Gwent Hospital, Newport, UK, 1980; Senior Registrar, University of Benin Teaching Hospital, 1980-81; Lecturer /Consultant Radiologist, 1981-. *Memberships:* British Institute of Radiology; Association of Radiologist of West Africa; West African College of Surgeons. *Publications include:* Contributions to 'Annals of Tropical Paediatrics', 'Urologic Radiology', 'European Journal of Paediatrics', 'European Journal of Radiology', 'Tropical & Georgraphic Medicine', 'Paediatric Radiology', 'Gastrointestinal Radiology', etc. *Honours:* Elected Fellow, West African College of Surgeons 1983, International College of Angiology 1985. *Hobbies:* Travel; Lawn tennis; Photography. *Address:* Department of Radiology, University of Benin, PMB 1154, Benin City, Nigeria.

AKBAR, Modammad Rahim, b. 26 Dec. 1941, Iran. Assistant Professor of Obstetrics and Gynaecology. m. Z Akbar, 17 Aug. 1970, 3 sons. *Education:* MD; Obstetrics and Gynaecology speciality with oncology. *Appointments:* Medical Director, Kashani Hospital; Chairman, Department of Obstetrics and Gynaecology, Medical School, Director of Amin Hospital, Isfahan University; Examiner of Obstetrics and Gynaecology Speciality Boards, Iran. *Memberships:* Tulanes Ex-Residents Society; American College of Obstetrics and Gynaecology; Iran Obstetrics and Gynecology Society; Iran Medical Society; Isfahan Medical Society. *Publications:* Contributor of papers to professional journals including: 'Drug Development and Research'; 'Journal of Abdominal Surgery'; 'Journal of Isfahan Medical School'. *Hobbies:*

Greenhouse and garden. *Address:* PO Box 32, Isfahan University, Isfahan, Iran.

AKERT, Konrad Hans, b. 21 May 1919, Zürich, Switzerland. University Rector. m. Ruth Giger, 1947, 3 sons, 1 daughter. *Education Includes:* MD, Medical School, University of Zurich, 1949; Assistant, Institute of Physiology, University of Zurich, 1946-51; Research Fellow, Swiss Academy of Medical Sciences, Johns Hopkins University, Maryland, USA, 1951-52. *Appointments:* Instructor, Physiology, Johns Hopkins University, USA, 1952; Assistant Professor, Physiology, 1953, Associate Professor, 1955, University of Wisconsin; Professor of Anatomy and Physiology, University of Wisconsin, 1960; Professor, Neurophysiology and Director, Brain Research Institute, 1961, Dean, Medical Faculty, 1974-76, Director, Physiology Institute, 1979-, Member Board of Directors, Brain Research Institute, 1984, 1984-, University of Zurich, Switzerland. *Memberships include:* Swiss Societies of Anatomy, Physiology, Neurology and Molecularbiology; Union Schweiz. Gesegg. exp. Biologie; American Association of Anatomists; International Brain Research Organisation; European Brain and Behavioral Society; European Training Programme in Brain and Behavioral Research; European Neuroscience Association; Japanese Society of Anatomists. *Publications:* Author of about 330 scientific publications. Founder and Editor in Chief, 'Journal of Brain Research', 1966-76. *Honours:* Robert Bing Prize, Swiss Academy of Medical Sciences; Otto Naegeli Prize for Medical Research; Honorary Doctorate, University of Geneva, 1976; Member of Scholars, Johns Hopkins University, 1978; Honorary Research Professor, Academia Sinica Peking, 1980; Emeritus Professor of Brain Research and Physiology, 1984. *Address:* University of Zürich, President's Office, Rämistrasse 71, CH-8006 Zürich, Switzerland.

AKHTAR, Muhammad, b. 23 Feb. 1933, Pakistan. Professor, Biochemistry. m. Monika E. Schurmann, 3 Aug. 1963, 2 sons. *Education:* BSc., Government College, University of Punjab, Lahore, 1952; MSc., University of Punjab, Pakistan, 1954; PhD, DIC, Imperial College, University of London, England, 1959. *Appointments:* Research Scientist, Research Institute for Medicine & Chemistry, Cambridge, USA, 1959-63; Lecturer, 1963-66, Senior Lecturer, 1966-68, Reader, 1968-73, Professor, 1973, Head, 1978, Biochemistry, Chairman, School of Biochemical and Physiological Sciences, 1983-, University of Southampton, England. *Memberships:* Biochemical Society Committee; American Chemical Society; Chemical Society. *Publications:* Numerous articles in professional journals. *Honours:* Fellow, Royal Society, 1980; Award, Sitara-I-Imtiaz, Government of Pakistan; Founding Fellow, Third World Academy of Sciences. *Address:* Dept. Biochemistry, University of Southampton, Southampton S09 3TU, England.

AKHTAR, Tasleem, b. 1 Sep. 1944, North West Frontier Province, Pakistan. Research Director. m. Fazal Mohammad, 19 Mar. 1969, Jhanda, North West Frontier Province, 1 son, 1 daughter. *Education:* MBBS, Peshawar; DCH, London, England; MRCP (Paed), England. *Appointments:* Registrar, Department of Neonatal Paediatrics, Royal Maternity Hospital, Glasgow, Scotland, 1975-76; Senior Registrar, Department of Paediatrics, Khyber Hospital, Peshawar, Pakistan, 1977-78; Senior Medical Officer 1979-80, Research Director 1980-, PMRC Research Centre, Khyber Medical College, Peshawar; Co-Investigator, Community Health Study, Tehkal Bala, Mathra and Chaparisa. *Memberships:* General Secretary, Pakistan Paediatric Association, North West Frontier Province Branch, Executive Committee Member, Pakistan Paediatric Association; Editorial Board, 'Journal of Pakistan Medical Association'. *Publications:* 'Proceedings of Medical Research

Congress', (editor), Peshawar 1982 and Islamabad 1984. *Hobbies:* Reading; Collector of handicrafts. *Address:* PMRC Research Center, Khyber Medical College, Peshawar, Pakistan.

AKINKUGBE, Oladipo Olujimi, b. 17 July 1933, Ondo, Nigeria. Professor of Medicine. m. Folasade Modupeore Dina, 8 May 1965, Ibadan, 2 sons. *Education:* MB BS, London, England, 1958; DTM&H, Liverpool, 1960, D Phil, Oxford, 1964; MD, London, 1968. *Appointments:* Clinical Assistant, Medical Unit, London Hospital; Lecturer 1964, Senior Lecturer 1966, Professor of Medicine 1968-, University of Ibadan, Nigeria; Dean of the Medical School 1970-74, Head of Medicine 1972, Principal /Vice-Chancellor 1975-78, University of Ilorin; Visiting Professor of Medicine, Harvard University, Massachusetts, USA, 1974-75, and Oxford University, England, 1981-82; Chairman, Joint Admissions and Matriculation Board, 1977; Vice-Chancellor, Ahmadu Bello University, 1978-79. *Memberships:* Member 1961, Fellow 1968, Royal College of Physcians of Edinburgh; Fellow 1976, West African College of Physcians; Fellow 1977, Nigerian Medical Council; Fellow 1979, Nigeria Academy of Science; Council member, International Society of Hypertension; International Society of Nephrology; Scientific Advisory Council, CIBA Foundation; Medical Research Society of Great Britain. *Publications include:* 'Priorities in National Health Planning' (symposium proceedings), 1973; "High Blood Pressure in the African", 1972; "Cardiovascular Disease in Africa" (editor), 1976; Publications on hypertension and renal disease in Africa. *Honours:* Commander of the Order of the Niger, 1977; Officer de l'Ordre National de la Republique de Côte d'Ivoire, 1981; Honorary DSc, University of Ilorin, 1982. *Hobbies:* Music; Gardening. *Address:* Summit, Olubadan Aleshinloye Way, Iyaganku, Ibadan, Nigeria.

ALAJMO, Ettore, b. 7 Dec 1924, Palermo, Italy. Professor of Otolaryngology. m. 11 Feb 1950, Florence, 2 sons. *Education:* Medical School, University of Florence, Board in Otorynolaryngology. *Appointments:* Assistant Professor, Associate Professor then Professor of Otolaryngology; Director of School of Specialization in Otolaryngology; Director of Institute of Otolaryngology, University of Florence. *Memberships:* Società Italiana di O.R.L.; Société Française d'O.R.L.; Società Italiana di Foniatria; American Society for Head and Neck Surgery. *Publications:* 98 papers on ORL topics, most of them concerning Head and Neck Cancer surgery in Italian, French, English and American journals. 'Nose and Sinus Diseases' in "Trattato Italiano di Medicina Interna"; Editor, "Handbook of Oto-Rhino-Laryngology", 1986. *Honours:* Fulbright Scholarship 1961-62; Presidente Onorario dell-Associazione Italiana tra Foniatri e Logopedisti. *Hobby:* Tennis. *Address:* Via Jacopo Nardi, 17 – 50132 Firenze, Italy.

ALAVEZ, Ernesto Cesar, b. 7 Oct. 1933, Cuba. Professor of Medicine. m. Maria Vidal, 20 Aug. 1980, 2 sons, 1 daughter. *Education:* MD, School of Medicine, University of Havana, Cuba, 1959; Postgraduate Studies in Endocrinology, C I Parham Institute of Endocrinology, Romania, 1964; Research Fellow, Aberdeen Royal Infirmary, Scotland, 1968; Endocrinologist, 2nd degree, National Institute of Endocrinology, Cuba, 1984. *Appointments:* General Practitioner in the country, 1960-61; Resident, Internal Medicine, 1961-63; Resident in Endocrinology, 1964-65, Specialist in Endocrinology, 1965-85; Scientific Committee, National Institute of Endocrinology, 1970-85; Adviser to Ministry of Health, 1972-85; Deputy Director, National Institute of Endocrinology, 1972-85, Chief of Scientific Group (thyroid disease), 1975-85; Member, National Commission for Health Research, 1976-78; National Commission for Pacific Atomic Energy.

Memberships: Cuban Society of Endocrinology; Latin-American Thyroid Society; Honorary Member, Colombian Society for Diabetes; Corresponding Member, Venezuelan Society for Diabetes. *Publications:* "Textbook of Surgery" (co-author), 1971; "Diagnostic & Therapeutic Guide on Endocrinology" (co-author), 1981; 65 articles in national & international journals. *Honours:* Mention in 1976 for Endemic Goitre in Cuba (Study in Baracoa Region); Scientific Council, Ministry of Public Health, Cuba; Medal for 25 years as Medical Doctor. *Hobby:* Philately. *Address:* National Institute of Endocrinology, Zapata y D Vedado, Habana 4, Cuba.

ALBERT, David Stuart, b. 20 Oct. 1948, Abington, Pennsylvania, USA. Director; Chiropractic Physician. m. Helene Feuerstein, 7 Sep. 1969, Irvington, New Jersey, 1 daughter. *Education:* BA, Fairleigh Dickenson University; MA, Montclair State College; Graduate Studies; Fordham University; University of Waterloo, Ontario, Canada; New York Chiropractic College, State University of New York. *Memberships:* Parker Chiropractic Research Foundation, New Jersey, Former Vice-President; New Jersey Chiropractic Association; National Chiropractic Foundation; Board Member, Free Chiropractic Advisory Board, Bloomfield College, New Jersey. *Publications:* Several small articles in various Chiropractic Journals. *Honour:* New York Chiropractic College Ambassador Club, Meritorious Service Outstanding Intern. *Hobbies:* Automobiles; Jogging; Tennis; Weight Lifting. *Address:* 1505 Alps Road, Wayne, NJ 07470, USA.

ALBRITTON, William Lennard, b. 1 Dec. 1941, USA. Head, Microbiology. m. Elizabeth Renfroe, 22 Dec. 1963, Andalusia, 1 son, 1 daughter. *Education:* BSc., University of Alabama, 1964; PhD, University of Tennessee, 1968; MD, Medical College of Alabama, 1970. *Appointments:* Assistant /Associate Professor, Paediatrics and Medical Microbiology, Head, Paediatric Infectious Diseases, University of Manitoba, 1976-82; Director, STD Laboratory Programme, Centre for Disease Control, Atlanta, Georgia, 1982-84; Head, Microbiology, University of Saskatchewan, 1984-. *Memberships:* American Academy of Paediatrics; American Academy of Microbiology; Infectious Diseases Society of America; American Society for Microbiology; Canadian Society of Microbiologists; Royal College of Physicians and Surgeons of Canada; Canadian Infectious Disease Society; Canadian Public Health Association. *Hobbies:* Hunting; Fishing. *Address:* Dept. of Microbiology, University of Saskatchewan, Saskatoon, S7N 0W0, Canada.

AL-DABBAGH, Asma Abdallah, b. 26 July 1950, Jedda, Saudi Arabia. Assistant Professor; Consultant Radiologist. m. Dr. Tarik Mohsen Al-Baghdadi, 27 July 1978, 1 son. *Education:* BSc.; MBBS; DMRD; FRCR; Diploma, Medical Radio Diagnosis, Middlesex Hospital, London, England; Fellowship, Royal College of Radiologists. *Appointments:* House Surgeon, Mayo Hospital; House Physician, General Medicine, Royal Salop Infirmary, Shrewsbury, England; Senior House Officer, Accident and Emergency, Old Church Hospital, Romford; Senior House Surgeon, Neurosurgery; Registrar, Radiology, Middlesex Hospital, London. *Memberships:* Royal College Radiologists, London; British Institute of Radiologists; Royal Society of Medicine, London. *Publications:* "Flowoscopic Assessment of Bilharzial wreters", 'Clinical Radiology' 1985. *Hobbies:* Cookery; Swimming; Photography. *Address:* Dept. of Diagnostic Imaging, King Abdul Aziz University Hospital, PO Box 6615, Jaddah 21431 Saudi Arabia.

ALEKSANDROWICZ, Ryszard, b. 1 Sep. 1926, Cmielów, Poland. Professor of Medicine. m. Barbara Maniecka, 21 Jan. 1967, Warsaw, Poland, 1 son. *Education:* MD, MS, Faculty of Medicine, Warsaw Academy of Medicine, 1953, Doctoral Thesis 1963; Habitation Thesis 1968. *Appointments:* Lecturer, 1953, Senior Lecturer, 1955, Assistant Professor, 1970, Head of Department, 1978-, Department of Normal Anatomy, Faculty of Medicine, Silesian Medical Academy, Katowice, Poland, Dean, Faculty of Nursing, 1980-81, Dean, Faculty of Medicine, 1982-84, Academy of Medicine, Katowice. *Memberships:* Polish Medical Society; Vice-President, Polish Anatomical Society; Foreign Member, Anatomische Gesellschaft. *Publications:* "On the Vascular Segments of the Liver", 1963; "On the Vascular Segments of Kidneys and Spleen", 1968; "Functional Anatomy & Bioengineering of the Third Finger of the Human Hand", 1981; "On Valves of Reproductive Organ Veins in Women", 1980; Set of slides for "Respiratory System", 1977. *Honour:* Cross of Order of "Polonia Restituta", 1978. *Hobbies:* Walking; Tourism; Mountains; Relief in Roots. *Address:* Department of Anatomy; Silesian Academy of Medicine, 20 Medyków, 40-752 Katowice, Poland.

ALEKSIC, Ivan, b. 5 Dec. 1927, Zrenjanin, Yugoslavia. University Professor m. Desanka Momirov, 16 Dec 1971, Belgrade, 1 son, 1 daughter. *Education;* MD, Faculty of Medicine, 1955 Habilitation, Faculty of Physical Education, 1961, DSc, Faculty of Physical Education, 1973, Speciality in Hygiene and Public Health, Faulty of Medicine, 1962, University of Belgrade; Diploma, Doctor of Sportsmedicine, Society of Doctors of Sportsmedicine of Yugoslavia, 1973. *Appointments:* General practitioner, Sportsmedicine Department, Faculty of Physical Education, Belgrade, 1956-58; Assistant for Course in Hygiene (Chair of Sportsmedicine, Faculty of Physical Education, Belgrade, 1958-61; Assistant Professor (Docent), 1961-66, Associate Professor 1966-74, Full Professor, 1974-, University of Belgrade. *Memberships:* Serbian Medical Association, Section of Sportsmedicine (Former Vice President); Association of Nutritionists of Serbia. *Publications:* "Hygiene Textbook" Faculty of Physical Education, Belgrade, 1962, 5th edition 1980; "Contribution to the hygiene problems of school gymnasiums" Habilitation 1961, Annals, Advanced School of Physical Education, Belgrade, 1963; "Theory and praxis of defining the notion of the hygiene minimum of school building for physical culture" Doctoral dissertation, Faculty of Physical Education, Belgrade, 1973; "Postgraduate Studies on F Ph E" Monograph, Faculty of Physical Education, Belgrade, 1978. Contributor of articles to scientific journals, presenter of Papers and contributor of chapters to edited volumes in the field of Sports Medicine and Physical Education, especialy concerning the Problems of Human Nutrition. *Honours:* May Award for scientific work, Union of organizations for physical culture of Serbia, 1974; L'Ordre du Merite Agricole (Grade de chevalier) Republique Francaise, 1981. *Hobbies:* Drawing; Writing. *Address:* 43 Ognjena Price, 11000 Beograd, Yugoslavia.

ALEXANDER, Albert Geoffrey, b. 22 Sep. 1932, Hull, England. Professor. m. Dorothy Constance Johnson, 2 June 1956, Orpington, 1 daughter. *Education:* BDS (London), 1956, LDS RCS (Eng), 1955, FDS RCS (Eng) 1961, MDS (London), 1968, University College London Dental School, University of London. *Appointments:* Dental House Surgeon, UCH London; House Surgeon, Dental Unit, UCH London; National Service, RADC; Clinical Assistant, UCH London; Private Practice; Lecturer, Conservation, UCL Dental School; Senior Lecturer, Conservation & Periodontics, UCL Dental School; Reader, Conservative Dentistry, University of London; Professor, Conservative Dentistry, Dean, dental studies, University College, London Dental School. *Memberships:* British Dental Association; British Soceity for Dental Research; British Society for Restorative Dentistry; Federation Dentaire Internationale; Fellow, International College of

Dentists; Fellow, University College, London. *Publications:* Articles in professional journals including: 'British dental Journal; 'Journal Periodontics''; "The Prevention of Periodontal Disease", 1971; "Self Assessment Manual No. 3", 1978. *Honours:* Editorial Board, Companion to Dental Studies. *Hobby:* Photography. *Address:* 18 Masefield View, Orpington, Kent BR6 8PH, England.

ALEXANDER, Joseph F Jr., b. 16 Feb. 1950, Ohio, USA. Medical Practitioner; Allergy specialist. *Education:* BS; MD; Fellow, American College of Allergists; Certified American Board of Internal Medicine; Certified American Board of Allergy and Immunology. *Appointments:* Private medical practitioner-; Chief, Allergy Service, Akron City Hospital, Ohio, USA-. *Memberships:* American Academy of Allergy and Immunology; American College of Allergists; Ohio State Medical Association; American College of Physicians. *Publications:* Articles – 'Basidiospore Sensitivity and Asthma'; 'Responses to Conjugated Age in Ragweed Hay Fever'; 'Boosting of Patients with High and Low Doses of Allergoid'; 'Immunologic Responses to Conjugates of Antigen E in Patients with Eagweed Hay Fever' in 'The Journal of Allergy and Clinical Immunology' vol. 73, No. 6, June 1984. *Address:* 550 East Market Street, Ste 306, Akron, OH 44303, USA.

ALEXANDER, Margo, b. 10 May 1952, New York, USA. Director of Hospital Nutrition and Food Service. m. Robert Robinson, 7 Dec 1984. *Education:* BA, Foods and Nutrition, Brooklyn College, 1974; MA, Food Service Management, New York University, 1977; Postgraduate coursework, Pace University, 1980-81. *Appointments:* Clinical Dietitian, Brookdale Medical Center, Brooklyn, New York, 1974-77; Supervising Dietition, Beth Israel Medical Center, New York City, 1977-78; Assistant Director of Food Service, 1978-82, Associate Director of Food Service, 1982 (5 months), Director of Nutrition and Food Service, 1982-, The Long Island College Hospital, Brooklyn, New York. *Memberships:* The American Dietetic Association; The American Hospital Association- American Society for Health Care Food Administrators; The Hospital Food Administrators Associaiton of Greater New York, Inc. *Honours:* Recognized Young Dietitian of the Year, American Dietetic Association, 1982; Accomplished Health Care Food Administrator, The American Hospital Association, 1985. *Hobbies:* Travel; Physical exercies (aerobic and callisthenics); Reading; Watersports. *Address:* The Long Island College Hospital, Brooklyn, NY 11201, USA.

ALFONSO CESPEDES, Gabriel Miguel, b. 21 Aug. 1922, Havana, Cuba. Physician Specialist. m. Otilia Perez Arias, 17 May 1953, Corpus Christi Church, 2 sons. *Education:* MD, Havana University, 1948; Educational Council for Foreign Medical; Florida License, USA, 1973; Resident in Psychiatry, Department of Human Resources, 1972-74; Medical College of Georgia, 1970-75. *Appointments:* Medical Doctor: Marianao Municipal; Asociacion Cubana de Beneficencia; Asilo Caravajal; Asilo Santa Marta; Private practitioner. Larned State Hospital, Kansas, USA; Western State Hospital, Virginia; Central State Hospital, Georgia. *Memberships:* American Medical Association; Medical Association of Georgia; Baldwin Medical Society; American and Georgia Psychiatric Associations; Cuban Medical; Association in Exile. *Honours:* Several Diplomas, Havana and Marianao; Awards, American Medical Association, 1975, 78, 81, 85; Awards American Psychiatric Association, 1978, 81, 85; *Hobbies:* Philately; Classical music. *Address:* 12 Broad Street, CSH Box 85, Milledgeville, GA 31062, USA.

ALFORD, Bobby Ray, b. 30 May 1932, Dallas, Texas, USA. Vice President and Dean, Academic and Clinical affairs; Olga Keith Wiess Professor; Chairman, Department of Otorhinolaryngology and Communicative Sciences. m. Othelia Dorn, 28 Aug. 1953, 2 sons, 1 daughter. *Education:* As cum laude, Tyler Junior College, Texas, 1951; University of Texas, 1951-52; MD with honours, Baylor college of Medicine, Houston, 1956; Intern, Jefferson Davis Hospital, Houston, 1956-57; Otolaryngology Resident, Baylor Affiliated Hospital Programme, 1957-60. *Appointments:* Instructor Fellowship in Otology, University of Texas Medical Branch, 1960-61; Special Fellow, National Institute of Health, Neurophysiology, John Hopkins Hospital, 1961-62; currently, Vice President and Dean, Academic and Clinical Affairs, Olga Keith Wiess Professor and Chairman, Department of Otorhinolaryngology and Communicative Sciences, Baylor College of Medicine, Houston. *Memberships:* American Academy of Otolaryngology – Head and Neck Surgery; Association of Academic Departments of Otolaryngology – Head and Neck Surgery; President, American Board of Otolaryngology; Fellow, American College of Surgeons; Collegium Oto-Rhino-Laryngologicum Amicitiae Sacrum. *Publicaitons:* "Neurological Aspects of Audiotory and Vestibular Disorders'', Co-Editor, 1964; 'Idiopathic Facial Paralysis' in "Current Therapy in Otlolaryngology – Head and Neck Surgery'', 1984. *Honours:* Outstanding Student, Herman Johnson Award, 1956; Outstanding Senior Student, Phi Chi Award, 1956; Physician Recognition Award, American Medical Association, 1979, 82. *Hobby:* Sailing. *Address:* Baylor College of Medicine, 1 Baylor Plaza, Houston, TX 77030, USA.

ALFSEN, Annette, b. 4 Apr. 1928, Paris, France. Research Director. m. Erik Alfsen, 6 Sep. 1952, Paris, 1 son, 1 daughter. *Education:* MD, 1950; Doctor of Physical Sciences, 1958. *Appointments:* Medical Practitioner, 1950-51; Research Staff 1951-, Research Assistant, Assistant Professor, Professor, Director of Research 1981-, Centre National Recherche Scientifique. *Memberships:* Société Chimie Biologieque, France; Société Biophysique, France; Biochemical Society, United Kingdom; Biophysical Society, United Kingdom; New York Academy of Sciences. *Publications include:* Over 80 articles including: 'Relationship between active structure of a membraneous enzyme in a proteolipidic subunit and ionic perturbation of aqueous solvent' (with J Gallay, M Vincent and C de Paillerets), 1975; 'Biophysical aspect of the mechanism of action of steroid hormone', 1983; 'Organization and dynamics of lipids in Bovien brain coated and uncoated vesicles' (with C de Paillerets, K Prasad, F K Nandi, R E Lippoldt and H Edelhoch), 1984; 'Structural characterization of labeled clathrina and coated vesicles' (with K Prasas, R E Lippoldt, P K Nandi and H Edelhoch), 1984. *Hobbies:* Music; Archaeology. *Address:* VER Biomédicale des Saints-Péres, 45 Rue des Saints-Péres, 75270 Paris 6, France.

ALGOM, Moshe, b. 23 Mar. 1939, Bulgaria. Senior Cardiologist. m. Lea Arditti, 12 Oct. 1966, 2 sons. *Education:* MD, Hadassa Medical School, Hebrew University 1968; Specialist Cardiology, 1977, Specialist Internal Medicine, 1974, Tel Aviv University. *Appointments:* Intern, Beilinson Medical Center, 1968; Resident in Internal Medicine, Hasharon Hospital and Heart Institute, Beilinson Medical Center, 1969-74; Resident in Cardiolgoy, heart Institute, Chaim Sheba Medical center and Beilinson Medical Center; Senior Cardiologist, Heart-Institute, Assaf Harofeh Medical Center, Zerifin, Israel, 1977-. *Memberships:* Israel Heart Society; Israel Medical Association; Israel Painters and Sculpture Association; Israel Numismatic Society. *Publications:* Contributor to: 'Heart and Lung', 'British Heart Journal', 'Journal of Medical Genetics', 'Harefuah', 'Obstetrics and Gynaecology', 'Cardiology', 'Journal of Cardiovascular Ultrasonography', 'Chest', 'Clinical Cardiology'. *Hobby:* Painting (Completed studies in painting at

Avni Institute of Fine Arts, 1977). *Address:* 6 Hazamir Street, Ramat-Gan 52596, Israel.

ALHO, Antti Viljo, b. 13 May 1935, Kotka, Finland. Professor, Chief Surgeon. m. Seija Kyllikki Leirisara, 6 Feb. 1954, Kotka, 3 sons, 1 daughter. *Education:* MD 1959 MSc 1961, University of Helsinki; USPHS International Postdoctoral Research Fellow, University of Minnesota, Minneapolis, Minnesota, USA, 1969-70; Orthopaedic Research Fellow, Harvard University, Massachusetts General Hospital. 1982. *Appointments:* Resident, Surgical Department 1962-68, Assistant Chief Surgeon, Department of Orthopaedics and Traumatology 1968-74, Clinical Instructor, Assistant Professor, Department of Orthopaedics and Traumatology 1974-76, University of Helsinki, Finland; Chief Surgeon, Central Hospital, Lahti, 1976; Professor of Orthopaedics and Traumatology, University of Bergen, Norway, 1976-83; Chief Surgeon, Orthopaedic Division, Ullevaal Hospital, Oslo,1983-; Professor, University of Oslo, 1983-. *Memberships:* Société Internationale de Chirurgie Orthopédique et de Traumatologie; Internaional Orthopaedic Association; International College of Surgeons; Finnish and Norwegian Medical Associations; Finnish and Norwegian Surgical Associations; Finnish and Norwegian Orthopaedic Association. *Publications:* "Traumatologia" (co-editor), 1972, 4th edition 1980; "Katastrofemedisin" (co-editor), 1984; 'Clinical manifestations of fat embolism syndrome', 1978; 'Assessment of malignancy of cartilage tumors using flow cytometry' (co-authro), 1983; 'Mechanical factors in loosening of Christiansen and Charnely arthroplasties' (co-author), 1984. *Hobby:* Sauna. *Address:* Orthopaedic Division, Ullevaal Hospital, N-0407 Oslo 4, Norway.

ALIAS, Susy, b. 2 June 1944, Kerala, India. Associate Physiatrist. m. A.G.Alias, 1 son. *Education:* MD. *Appointments:* Rotating internship, 1969-70; Physician I, Midimo Mental Health Centre, Columbia, Missouri, 1975; Residency, PM&R, 1976-78; Board certified in PM&R, 1981; Associate Physiatrist, Jewish Hospital, St.Louis, Missouri. *Memberships:* American Academy of PM&R; Association of Academic Physiatrist; Central Society of Rehabilitation; American Spinal Cord Injury Association; American Academy of Electromyography & Electrodiagnosis. *Publications:* 'Management & outcome in rehabilitation of patients with acute intermittent porphyria', 1983; 'CPR in patients with halo traction of unstable spine', 1983. *Hobby:* Swimming. *Address:* 15 Maryhill, St.Louis, MO 63124, USA.

ALI, Mirghani Yousif, b. 18 June 1925, Khartoum, Sudan. Director, Educational Resources in Medical Sciences, Canberra, Australia. m. Irena Malgorzata, 10 Aug. 1979, Sydney. *Education:* DKSM, University of Khartoum, 1952; DTM & H, DAP&E, DCP, University of London, 1958; D. Path, 1958; MD, University of Singapore, 1967; Teaching Fellow, University of Pittsburgh, USA, 1954-55. *Appointments:* Specialist, Pathology, Sudan Ministry of Health, 1959-62; Senior Lecturer, Pathology, University of Singapore, 1962-67; Foundation Professor, Pathology, University of Papua New Guinea, 1971-75; Assocaite Head, School of Life Sciences, New South Wales Institute of Technology, Sydney, 1975-79; Foundation Professor, Pathology, University of Kuwait, 1979-82; Visiting Professor, Pathology, University of Singapore, 1982-84; Director, Educational Resources in Medical Sciences, Canberra, Australia, 1984-. *Memberships:* Fellow: Royal College of Pathologists, London; Royal College of Pathologists of Australia; College of American Pathologists; International Academy of Cytology; Australian Institute of Management. *Major Publications:* "Malignant Renal Neoplasms in Singapore", 'British Journal of Urology', 1964; "Histology of Human Nasopharyngeal Mucose", 'Journal of Anatomy',

1965; "Cytodiagnosis of Nasopharyneal Carcinoma", 'Acta Cytol.', 1967; "Textbook of Diagnostic Cytology", 1978. *Hobbies:* Computing; Photography; Graphic Art. *Address:* Educational Resources in Medical Sciences, GPO Box 430 Canberra, ACT 2601, Australia.

ALLEN, David Franklyn, b. 21 Aug. 1943, Nassau, Bahamas. Consultant, Psychiatry, Ministry of Health, Bahamas. m. Victoria Stevens, 27 Apr. 1972, Cambridge, 1 son, 1 daughter. *Education:* MB.Ch.B, MPH: FAPA: Diplomate, American Board of Psychiatry and Neurology. *Appointments:* Fellow, Joseph P. Kennedy, Medical Ethics, Harvard School of Public Health, 1973-74; Research Fellow, Psychiatry, Harvard Medical School, Massachusetts General Hospital,1973-76; Assistant Professor, Psychiatry, Yale Medical School, 1976-80; Lecturer, Public Health, Yale School of Public Health, 1981-. *Memberships:* Fellow, American Psychiatric Association; Medical Association of the Bahamas; Massachusetts Medical Society. *Publications:* "Ethical Issues in Mental Retardation", 1978; "Trends in Mental Health Evaluation", 'Encyclopedia of Bioethics', 1981. *Honours:* Joseph P. Kennedy Junior Fellowship, Bioethics, Harvard School of Public Health. *Hobby:* Jogging. *Address:* PO Box N 1023, Nassau, Bahamas.

ALLEN, George Sewell, b. 10 Jan. 1942, St.Louis, Missouri, USA. Professor & Chairman, Department of Neurological Surgery, Vanderbilt University. m. Shannon Hershey, 1 daughter. *Education:* BA, Wesleyan University, Middletown Connecticut, 1963; MD, Washington University, St.Louis, Missouri, 1967; PhD, University of Minnesota, 1975. *Appointments include:* Assistant Professor 1975-79, Associate Professor 1979-83, Professor of Neurological Surgery, Johns Hopkins University & Hospital, 1984-; Medical staff, Vanderbilt University Hospital, 1984-. *Memberships include:* American College of Surgeons; American Association of Neurological Surgeons; Congress of Neurological Surgeons; Brain Surgery Society; H.William Scott, Jr., Society; Offices, Maryland Neurological Society; Society of Neurosurgical Anaesthesia & Neurological Supportive Care. *Publications include:* Numerous book chapters, contributions to professianl journals, conference papers, etc. Editorial boards, 'Contemporary Neurosurgery', 'Bi-Weekly Review of Clinical Neurosurgical Practice'. *Hobbies:* Tennis; Fishing. *Address:* Vanderbilt University Medical Centre, Department of Neurological Surgery, T-4224, Medical Centre North, Nashville, TN 37232, USA.

ALLEN, John Glyn, b. 31 Dec. 1939, Hull, England. Head of Drug Metabolism, Roche Products Limited. m. Celia Lois Layzell, 31 Mar. 1964, Cheltenham, 1 son. *Education:* BSc Chemistry 1961, PhD Organic Flourine Chemistry 1964, Birmingham University. *Appointments:* Research Fellow, Department of Anatomy, Birmingham University, 1964-67; Senior Biochemist, Nicholas Research Institute, Slough, 1967-68; Senior Biochemist 1968-80, Head of Drug Metabolism 1980-, Roche Products Limited, Welwyn Garden City. *Memberships:* Society for Drug Research; United Kingdom Drug Metabolism Group; ISSX. *Publications:* 'Acidic Urinary Metabolites of Progesterone', 1968; 'Plasma Levodopa and Its Metabolites', 1973; 'Metabolism of Detrisoquine', 1975; 'Metabolic Deacctylation', 1976; 'Phosphonopeptics of a new radiosensitiser in Human', 1984. *Hobbies:* Politics; Youth work; Hill walking. *Address:* Roche Products Limited, Broadwater Road, Welwyn Garden City, Hertfordshire, England.

ALLEN, Philip Wesley, b. 15 Mar. 1937, London, England. Director, Histopathology Department, Queen Elizabeth Hospital, Woodville, South Australia. m. R.Valmai Mogg, 4 Feb. 1961, Adelaide, 2 sons, 3 daughters. *Education:* MB,BS; FRCPA. *Appointments include:* Registrar, Institute of

Medical & Veterinary Science, Adelaide, South Australia; Trainee, Queen Elizabeth Hospital; Assistant pathologist, Armed Forces Institute of Pathology, Washington DC, USA. Pathologist, Institute of Medical Veterinary Science, Adelaide; Chairman, Histopathology Division, ibid; Director, Institute of Medical & Veterinary Science, Mount Gambier, South Australia. *Memberships:* Fellow, Royal Australasian College of Pathologists; Australian Division, International Academy of Pathology. *Publications include:* "Tumours & Proliferations of Adipose Tissue", 1981. *Address:* Histopathology Department, Queen Elizabeth Hospital, Woodville, SA 5011, Australia.

ALLEN, William Corwin, b. 30 Sep. 1934, Geneva, Ohio, USA. Professor and Chief, Division of Orthopaedic Surgery, University of Missouri. m. Kathryn Engelhard, 22 June 1957, Owego, New York, 2 sons, 1 daughter. *Education:* BA, Hiram College, 1956; MD, University of Chicago, 1960; Internship, Surgery, Philadelphia General Hospital, 1960-66; Orthopaedic Residency, Stanford University, 1965-66; Chief Resident, Orthopaedic Surgery, Stanford University, 1965-66. *Appointments:* Instructor, University of Florida, 1966-67; Public Health Fellow in Biomechanics, 1967-68, Instructor, Department of Orthopaedic Surgery, 1967-68, Case-Western Research University and Clinic; Assistant Professor, Department of Surgery, 1968-71, Assistant Professor, Department of Mechanical Engineering, 1968-71, University of Florida; Team Physician, University of Florida, 1970-76; Associate Professor, Department of Surgery, 1971-76, Associate Professor, Department of Mechanical Engineering, 1971-76, Director of Orthopaedic Clinics, 1973-76, Director of Orthopaedic Residency Program, 1973-76, Professor, Department of Orthopaedics, 1976, Professor, Department of Mechanical Engineering, 1976, University of Florida; Professor and Chief, Division of Orthopaedic Surgery, 1976, Co-Director of Sports Medicine, 1984-, University of Missouri. *Memberships:* Academy of Orthopaedic Surgeons, Member of Board of Directors, 1979-80; American Orthopaedic Society for Sports Medicine, various offices including President, 1984-85; Mid-America Orthopaedic Association, Treasurer; Member of Board of Director, 1982-; Member various other organizations. *Publications:* Contributor of papers and articles to professional journals, etc; Associate Editor, 'Clinical Orthopaedics', 1979-82; Associate Editor, "Journal of Sports Medicine', 1980-83; Consultant Reviewer, 'Journal of Bone and Joint Surgery', 1982-. *Honour:* Member of Black Key, Men's honorary society at Hiram College. *Hobbies:* Hiking; Fishing; The out-of-doors. *Address:* Division of Orthopaedic Surgery, University of Missouri Health Sciences Center, Columbia, MO 65212, USA.

ALLISON, David John, b. 21 Mar. 1941, Leeds, England. Professor of Diagnostic Radiology. m. Deirdre Mary, 16 Apr. 1966, London, 1 son 2 daughters. *Education:* BSc, Physiology, King's College, London, 1961; MB, BS (Hons) MRCS, LRCP, King's College, Hospital, London, 1961-65; MD, St. Bartholomew's Hospital Medical School, 1970; DMRD, DRCR, Royal Postgraduate Medical School, Hammersmith Hospital, 1970-86. *Appointments include:* Registrar in Diagnostic Radiology, 1970-73, Senior Registrar in Diagnostic Radiology, 1973-75, Consultant in Diagnostic Radiology, 1975-83, Hammersmith Hospital, London; Professor of Diagnostic Radiology, Royal Postgraduate Medical School, University of London and Director of Department of Diagnostic Radiology, Hammersmith Hospital, 1983-. *Memberships:* Harveian Society of London; Fleischer Society; Royal College of Radiologists; European College of Angiography; European Scoiety of cardiovasculr and Internventional Radiology; British Institute of Radiology. *Publications:* Co-editor: "Diagnostic Radiology: An Anglo-American Textbook of

Imaging" 1985; Over 200 chapters, papers and review articles on cardiovascular and respiratory physiology, angiography, internventional radiology and general clinical topics. *Honours:* Inchley's Prize, King's College, London, 1961; Hughes Prize, King's College, Hospital, London, 1965; Wellcome Senior Research Fellowship in Clinical Science, 1975; George Simon Memorial Award of Fleischer Society for cardiovascular research, 1979; Oliphant Lecturer, Flinders University, Adelaide, Australia, 1985. *Hobbies:* Gardening; Do-it-Yourself; Food and Wine. *Address:* Department of Diagnostic Radiology, Royal Postgraduate Medical School, Hammersmith Hospital, Du Cane Road, London W12 0HS, England.

ALLISON, John Graham, b. 11 Oct. 1941, Pretoria, South Africa. Chief of Surgical Service, VA Medical Center, Charleston, South Carolina, USA; Associate Professor of Surgery. m. Wendy Lee Meaker, 12 Mar. 1966, Cape Town, South Africa, 1 son, 2 daughters. *Education:* MD Ch.B, University of Cape Town Medical School, 1964; FRCS (Edinburgh), 1973 FCS (South Africa), 1974; Intern, Groote Schuur Hospital, Cape Town, 1965-66; Resident, Surgery, Groote Schuur Hospital, 1970-74; Research Fellow, University of Cape Town, 1974-75; Research Fellow, Surgery, Harvard Medical School and Beth Israel Hospital, USA, 1977-78. *Appointments:* Consultant Surgeon and Lecturer in Surgery, University of Stellenbosch Medical School and Tygerberg Hospital, Cape Town, 1975-77; Assistant Professor, Surgery, University of Iowa Hospitals and Clinics, USA, 1978-83; Staff Physician, VA Medical Center, Iowa City, 1978-83; Associate Professor, Surgery, Medical University of South Carolina, 1983; Chief, Surgical Services, VA Medical Center, Charleston, 1983-. *Memberships:* Fellow, American College of Surgeons and Member of professional organizations in South Africa, UK and USA. *Publications:* Contributor to professional journals, etc; Abstracts; Presentations and Books and/or Chapters. *Honours:* American Medical Association Physicians Recognition Awards, 1980, 1983, 1986. *Hobbies:* Golf; Fly Fishing; Sailing; Reading. *Address:* Department of Surgical Service, VA Medical Center, 109 Bee Street, Charleston, SC 29403, USA.

ALMANSA PASTOR, Angel F, b.12 Sep. 1934, Malaga, Spain. Medical Director. m. Isabel Mendez Peña, 16 May 1970, Malaga, 1 son, 2 daughters. *Education:* Medical Diploma, Hons, Granada University, 1957; Medical Diploma Thoracic Surgery, 1965; Medical Diploma, Pneumology, 1980; Medical Diploma, Cardiology, 1980. *Appointments:* Assistant, Hospital Princesa, Madrid, 1958-59; Assistant, Speziallungenklinik Hemer, Westfalem, West Germany, 1959-61; Assistant, University Chirurg Klinik, Dusseldorf, 1961-65; Chief, Pneumology, Hospital Civil Provincial, Malaga, 1966-75; Medical Director, Hospital Thorax, Malaga, 1975-. *Memberships:* Fellow, American College of Chest Physicians; College Intern, Angyologiae; Society Espania Patolog. A. Respiaratorio; Society Espania Cardiologia; Society Espania Geriatria; Associacion Medicos Naturistas. *Publications:* Mechanismos de Autoperfusion, Fundamentos, Indicaciones Generales, Enf Del Torax, 1984; Rigidez de Hemidiafragma, Signo Guia de Tromboembolia Pulmonar, Actualida Medica, 1979; Hemangioma Costal, Enf Torax, 1975 Fibrosarcoma Pulmonar, Enf Torax, 1981; Tumorraciones Primarias Pared Costales, Rev Esp Tubercolosis, 1976. *Honours:* Premio Paso, F A C Medicine, Granada, 1957; Internat Univ Menendez Pelayo, Santander, 1957; Deutscher Akademischer Austauschdienst, Dusseldorf, 1961. *Hobbies:* Golf; Tennis. *Address:* Alameda Principal 45, San Lorenzo 2, Malaga 29001, Spain.

ALMOND, Carl Herman, b. 1 Apr. 1926, Latour, Missouri, USA. Professor, Surgery, Associate Dean for Research and Development, University of South Carolina. m. Nancy Bewick Ginn Almond, 2 sons. *Education:* BS, Chemistry, 1949, MD, 1953,

Washington University; FACS. *Appointments:* Assistant Professor, Surgery, University of Missouri School of Medicine, 1959-64; Staff Surgeon, University Hospital, Columbia, 1959-78; House Surgeon, Thoracic & Cardiovascular Surgery, Brompton Hospital, London, England, 1961; House Surgeon, Thoracic & Cardiovascular Surgery, Children's Hospital, University of Southern California Service, Los Angeles, 1962, Good Samaritan Hospital, 1962; Staff Surgeon, University Hospital, Columbia, 1962-78; Associate Professor, Surgery, Thoracic and Cardiovascualr Surgery, 1964-68, Professor, Surgery, Chief, Thoracic and Cardiovascular Surgery, 1968-77, University of Missouri; Director, University Hospital, Columbia, 1968-77; Director, VA Dean's Hospital, Columbia, 1972-77; Invited Visiting Professor, Cardiovascular Surgery, University of Geneva Hospitals, Switzerland, 1973-74; Consultant, Thoracic & Cardiovascular Surgery, Elles Fischel Cancer Hospital, Columbia, 1976-78; Professor, Chairman, Surgery, 1978-85, Programme Director, General Surgery Residency Training Programme, Richland Memorial Hospital, 1979-85, South Carolina School of Medicine. *Memberships include:* International Association for Cardiac biolgical Implants; International Cardiovascular Society; Surgical Advisory Group to Air Force; United States Commission, UNESCO, 1983-85; American Assocation for Medical Colleges; American Association for Throacic Surgery; American College of Cariology; American College of Chest Physicians; Fellow, American College of Surgeons; American Heart Association; American Medical Association; etc. *Publications:* Author numerous articles in professional journals. *Honours:* Recipient, various honours and awards. *Address:* Two Richland Park, Suite 300, Columbia, SC 29203, USA.

ALPERT, Martin Jeffrey, b. 22 Apr 1951, New York City, USA. Chiropractor. m. Elyse S Sherman, 26 Dec. 1976, Spring Valley, New York. *Education:* BS, Syracuse University, 1972; MSc, University of Bridgeport, 1979; DC, New York Chiropractic College, 1976. *Appointments:* Director, Sadore Lane Chiropractic Office, Yonkers, New York, 1977-84; Chiropractor, Broward Chiropractic Associates, Fort Lauderdale, Florida, currently. *Memberships:* American Chiropractic Association; International ChiropracticAssociation; New Jersey Chiropractic Society; International Academy of Preventive Medicine; International College of Applied Nutrition; American College of Sports Medicine; New York Academy of Sciences; Councils on Nutrition, Technic and Roentgenology, American Chiropractic Association; KiwanisInternational, Rotary International. *Hobbies:* Chess; Swimming; Jogging; Basketball; Football; Coin and stamp collecting. *Address:* 357 Lakeview Drive, Fort Lauderdale, FL 33326, USA.

AL-SHAIBI, Faisal Ameen, b. Dec. 1936, Chief of Professional Services. m. Oct, 1960, 2 sons, 2 daughters. *Education:* MB BcH, Diploma in Child Health; Diploma in General Medicine. *Appointments:* Deputy Chief of Emergency and Ambulatory Services; Chief of Emergency and Ambulatory Services; Deputy Chief of Professional Services: currently Chief of Professional Services. *Honours:* Physician of the Year, Asir Region, 1984. *Hobbies:* Gardening; Driving. *Address:* King Faisal Military Hospital, PO Box 101, Khamis Mushayt, Kingdom of Saudi Arabia.

ALTEKRUSE, Joan Morrissey, b. 15 Nov. 1928, Cohoes, New York, USA. Professor. m. Ernest Brenton Altekruse, 17 Dec. 1950, 6 sons, 2 daughters. *Education:* AB; MD; MPH; DrPH. *Appointments:* Professor, Chairman, Preventive Medicine & Community Health, University of South Carolina School of Medicine; US Public Health Service, Medical Officer; Chronic Disease Consultant, California Department of Public Health; Office of Health Planning, University of California;

Faculty, Community Psychiatry, University of Heidelberg, West Germany; District Health Officer, Florida. *Memberships:* Fellow: American Public Health association, American College of Preventive Medicine. *Hobbies:* Travel; Church Watching. *Address:* Department of Preventive Medicine & Community Health, School of Medicine, University of South Carolina, Columbia SC 29208, USA.

ALTMAN, Sheldon, b. 15 May 1937, Denver, Colorado, USA, Veterinarian, Veterinary Acupuncturist. m. Arlene B Heller, 23 Aug. 1959, Denver, 1 son, 2 daughters. *Education:* BS high distinction Biological Science 1959, DVM 1961, Colorado State University. *Appointments Include:* Commanding Officer, 3rd United States Army Element 3197, Veterinary Detachment, Memphis, Tennessee, 1962-64; Veterinarian: Mewmark Animal Hospital, Compton, California 1961-62, Lockhart Animal Hospital, Hollywood, California 1964, Universal City Pet Clinic, North Hollywood, California 1965-70, M S Animal Hospitals Incorporated, Burbank, California 1970-. *Memberships Include:* Phi Sigma Delta; Beta Beta Beta; Phi Kappa Phi; Phi Zeta; Chairman Acupuncture Committee 1976-83, California Veterinary Medical Association; American Veterinary Medical Association (Committee on alternative Therapies); President 1973, California Chapter, American Veterinarians for Israel; Academy of Veterinary Cardiology; Board of Directors, International Veterinary Acupuncture Society; Center for Chinese Acupuncture; Acupuncture Research Institute; Association of Orthodox Jewish Scientists. *Publications:* "An Introduction to Acupuncture for Animals"; various articles on Veterinary Acupuncture. *Honours Include:* Honorary Professor of Chinese Medicine, University of Oriental Studies, School of Chinese Medicine, Los Angeles, California; Commendation, Los Angeles City Council, 1973. *Address:* 2723 West Olive Avenue, Burbank, CA 91505, USA.

ALTNER, Peter Christian, b. 19 Apr. 1932, Starnberg, Germany. Professor of Orthopaedic Surgery. m. Louise Ruth Bonney, 7 Feb. 1959, 1 son, 2 daughters. *Education:* Physics degree, University of Würzburg, Federal Republic of Germany, 1954; MD, University of Kiel, 1957; Internship, University of Kiel, 1957-58; American Internship, Muhlenberg Hospital, Plainfield, New Jersey, 1958-59; Surgical Residency, Evangelical Lutheran Diaconate Centre, Flensburg, Germany, 1960-61, Borgess Hospital, Kalamazoo, Michigan, USA, 1961-62; Orthopaedic Residency, University of Chicago Hospitals & Clinics, 1962-66. *Appointments:* Instructor of Orthopaedic Surgery, University of Chicago, 1966-67; Associate, Department of Orthopaedic Surgery, Northwestern University, 1967-68; Assistant Professor, Department of Orthopaedic Surgery, University of Illinois, 1967-71; Associate Professor, Chief, Division of Orthopaedic Surgery, Chicago Medical School, Mount Sinai Hospital Medical Centre, 1971-73; Acting Chairman, Department of Surgery, University of Health Sciences, Chicago Medical School, 1974-75; Current Main Appointment, Professor & Chief, Division of Orthopaedic Surgery, ibid, VA Medical Centre, North Chicago. *Memberships include:* American Academy of Orthopaedic Surgery; American College of Surgeons; American Medical Association; International College of Surgeons; Association of Orthopaedic Chairmen. *Publications:* Translation of "The Callus Problem" by G Kuntscher, 1974; "Treatment of Fractures & Dislocations" in series on Critical Care Medicine (edited M H Weil & R J Henning; Some 30 articles, abstracts & recordings. *Honours:* Various awards & recognitions, including Physicians Recognition Award, American Medical Association, 1970; Visiting Professorship, Orlando, Florida, 1978; Leadership VA, Washington DC, 1979. *Hobbies:* Board Sailing; Carpentry. *Address:* 290 Lee Road, Northbrook, IL 60062, USA.

ALVES, José Gabriel C. S. M. Rocha, b. 30 Sep.

1932, Portugal. Director, Radiotherapy Service. m. Maria Luisa, 20 Dec. 1958, Coimbra, 3 sons, 3 daughters. *Education:* MD, University of Coimbra; Speciality of Radiotherapy and Nuclear Medicine (Portugal). *Appointments:* Clinical Assistant, Radio-Isotopes Laboratory, Faculty of Medicine, Coimbra; Radiotherapist, IPOFG, Centre of Oncology, Coimbra; Radiotherapist, University of Coimbra Hospitals; Chief Radiotherapist, IPOFG, Centre of Oncology. *Memberships:* British Institute of Radiology; Sociedade Portugesa De Radiologia E, Medicina Nuclear; European Society for Therapeutic Radiology and Oncology; Sociedade Portuguesa De Oncologia. *Publications:* "Topical Iodine as a Low Thyroid 1131 Upptake Factor", 'Gaz.Med.Port', 1962; "Vitamin B4 in Radiotherapy", 'Coimbra Med', 1967; and many other articles in professional journals. *Address:* Servico De Radioterapia, Centro De Oncologia De Coimbra DO IPOFG, Av. Bissaia Barreto, 3000 Coimbra, Portugal.

AMATAYAKUL, Kosin, b. 2 Oct. 1933, Bangkok, Thailand. Research Institute Director. m. Valai Amatayakul, 28 Dec. 1958, Edinburgh, Scotland, 2 daughters. *Education:* MB ChB, Edinburgh University, Scotland; FRCOG. *Appointments:* Associate Professor, Obstetrics and Gynaecology, Fauclty of Medicine, currently Director of Research Institute for Health Sciences, Chiang Mai University, Thailand. *Memberships:* Science Society of Thailand; Royal College of Obstetricians and Gynaecologists, England; Obstetrical and Gynaecological Society of Thailand; External Examiner, Membership Examination of the Royal College of Obstetricians & Gynaecologists, London, Jan 1979. *Publications:* Author or Co-Author of numeorus papers contributed to: "Protein-Calorie Malnutrition", 1974; 'British Medical Journal'; 'Chiang Mai Medical Bulletin'; 'Far East Medical Journal'; 'Journal of Medical Association of Thailand'; 'Endocrinology'; 'American Journal of Dis Child'; 'Contraception'; 'Journal of Steroid biochemistry'; 'Oral Contraceptives', Health Research Monograph, 1980. Participant in numerous international congresses and symposium with papers being reproduced in conference records. *Honours:* Temporary Consultant and Steering Committee Member, World Health Organisation; HRP. *Address:* Research Institute for Health Sciences, PO Box CMU, Chiang Mai University, Chiang Mai, Thailand.

AMBACH, Walter, b. 13 Jan. 1929, Innsbruck, Austria. Head, Medical Physics, Innsbruck University. m. Eva Prey, 13 Aug. 1955, 1 daughter. *Education:* Magister rer.nat., 1951, PhD, Physics, 1954, Habilitation, 1962, University of Innsbruck. *Appointments:* Head, Physics of Snow and Ice, 1974-76, Head, Medical Physics, 1976-, University of Innsbruck. *Memberships:* Austrian and German Societies of Medical Physics; several national societies. *Publications:* 180 articles in professional journals. *Honours:* Felix-Kuschenitz Award, Austrian Academy of Sciences, Vienna, 1965. *Hobbies:* Skiing; Mountaineering. *Address:* Institute of Medical Physics, Muellerstrasse 44, A-6020 Innsbruck, Austria.

AMBROSE, Edmund Jack, b. 2 Mar. 1914, Cambridge, England. Adviser in Cancer and Leprosy Research in India. m. Andrée Huck, 31 July 1943, Cambridge, 1 son, 1 daughter. *Education:* MA (Cantab); DSc (London). *Appointments:* Admiralty Research, 1940-45; Research Scientist, Protein Structure, Courtauld Basic Research Laboratories, 1946-52; Research Scientist, Cancer, Chester Beatty Research Institute, London, 1952-61; Reader, 1961-67; Professor of Cell Biology, Head of Department, 1967-76; Adviser in Leprosy and Cancer, India, 1976-; Emeritus Professor, University of London. *Memberships:* Honorary President, International Cell, Tissue and Organ Culture Group for Human Cancer Studies; Emeritus Member,

International Society for Differentiation and Neoplasia; British Society for Cell Biology; Founder. *Publications:* Co-author of Books; "Cell Electrophonesis", 1965; "Biology and Cancer", 1966, New Edition, 1975; "Cancer Cell Invitra", 1967; "Cell Biology", 1970, Revised Edition, 1976; Research Papers. *Honour:* St. Elizabeth Memorial Medal for Leprosy Order of St. John, Paris, 1981. *Hobbies:* Sailing; Pastel Sketching. *Address:* Institute of Cancer Research, Fulham Road, London SW3, England.

AMDRUP, Erik, b. 21 Feb. 1923, Visby, Denmark. Professor of Surgery. m. Bente Amdrup. *Education:* MD, 1950, DMSc, 1960, Copenhagen, Denmark; Copenhagen Municipal Hospitals, 1950-65. *Appointments:* Chief Surgeon, Reader in Surgery, Dpt 1, Municipal Hospital, Copenhagen, 1965-71; Chief Surgeon, University Clinic, Aarhus; Surgical Gastroenterology; Professor of Surgery; Director, Institute of Experimental Clinical Research, Aarhus University. *Memberships:* General Secretary, Nordic Surgical Society; Danish Representative, Société Internationale de Chirurgie. *Publications:* Papers in journals, book chapters, in field of gastroenterology. *Honours:* Honorary Member, Royal College of Surgeons, England; Hon. Member, Association of Surgeons in Great Britain & Ireland. *Hobby:* Author of Suspense novels. *Address:* Afd d4, Kommunehospitalet, Aarhus 8000, Denmark.

AMER, Magid Hashim, b. 5 June 1941, Cairo, Egypt. Head of Division of Medical Oncology. m. Sabah El-Sayed Shehata, 3 Dec 1973, Paris, France, 3 daughters. *Education:* MBBCh, Hons, Diploma of Surgery, Cairo University; Diploma of Surgery, Royal College of Surgeons of Edinburgh; Diploma of American Board of Internal Medicine, Diploma of American Board of Medical Oncology, American College of Physicians. *Appointments:* Resident, General Surgery and Medicine, Cairo University; Resident, Surgery, Northampton General Hospital, England; Resident, Internal Medicine, Worcester General Hospital, Worcester, Massachusetts, USA; Resident, Internal Medicine, Lemuel Shattuck Hospital, Boston, Massachusetts; Fellow, Medical Oncology, Assistant Professor of Medical Oncology, Wayne State University, Detroit, Michigan; Head, Division of Medical Oncology, King Faisal Specialist Hospital, PO Box 3354, Riyadh 11211, Saudi Arabia. *Memberships:* Fellow, Royal College of Surgeons, Edinburgh; Fellow, Royal college of Physicians of Canada; Fellow, The American College of Physicians; American Society of Clinical Oncology; American Association of Cancer Research; the New York Acadmey of Sciences; American Association for the Advancement of Sciences. *Publications:* Over 60 publications including: "Chemotherapy and Pattern of Metasteses in Breast Cancer Patients" 'Journal of Surgical Oncology' 1982; "Bullous Pemphigoid" 'International Journal of Dermatology' 1982; "Pattern of Cancer of Saudi Arabia" 'UICC Technical Report Series' 1983; "Cancer Therapy: Past Present and Future" 'Ann. Saudi Medicine' 1986. *Hobbies:* Photography; Computers. *Address:* King Faisal Specialist Hospital, PO Box 3354, Riyadh 11211, Saudi Arabia.

AMES, Lousie Bates, b. 29 Oct. 1908, Portland, USA. Associate Director. m. Smith Whittier Ames, 22 May 1930, Bangor, Maine, 1 daughter. *Education:* MA, University of Maine, 1933; PhD, Yale University, 1936; ScD, University of Main; ScD, Wheaton College. *Appointments:* Research Assistant, 1933-38, Instructor, then Assistant Professor, 1938-50, Yale Medical School; Curator, Yale Films of Child Development, 1944-50; Co-Founder, 1950, Director of Research, 1950-60, Co-Cirector, 1960-70, Acting Director, 1980, Associate Director, 1980-, President, 1975-, Gesell Institute. *Memberships:* Sigma Xi; American Psychological Association; Connecticut Psychological Association; Society for Research in Child Development; Society for

Projective Techniques and Rorschach Institute, Secretary 1963-65, President, 1969-71; International Society for Study of Behavioral Development; many editorial boards. *Publications:* 30 books; 300 articles; daily syndicated newspaper column, 1952-75; several TV series. *Honours:* Bruno Klopfer Distinguished Contribution Award, 1974; University of Maine Alumni Career Award, 1974; Selected by 'Ladies Home Journal', as one of America's 100 Most Important, Newsworth and Noteworth Women, 1983. *Hobbies:* Reading; Writing; Gardening; Travel. *Address:* 310 Prospect Street, New Haven, CT 06511, USA.

AMES, Richard Arthur, b. 1 Apr. 1954, Los Angeles, California, USA. Lecturer; Chiropractor. *Educations:* BSc., Biology, Loyola University, Los Angeles, USA; DC, Los Angeles College of Chiropractic. *Appointments:* Private Practice, Anaheim, California; Consultant, West Heidelberg Community Health and Welfare Centre, Victoria, Australia; Lecturer, Phillip Institute of Technology, Melbourne; Private Practice, Bundoora, Victoria, Australia. *Memberships:* Australian Chiropractors' Association; American Chiropractic Association; California Chiropractic Association; Australian Sports Medicine Federation; Australian Spinal Research Foundation. *Publications:* "The Fundamentals of Palpation", 1985; "Correlative Chiropractic Technique", co-author, 1983; "Posture in the Assessment, Diagnosis & Treatment of Chronic Low Back Pain", 'Journal Australian Chiropractors Association', 1985. *Honours:* Dean's List, Delta Sigma Honorary Scholastic Society, Los Angeles College of Chiropractic, 1980. *Hobbies:* Fishing; Hiking; Weightlifting; Racquetball; Squash. *Address:* School of Chiropractic, Phillip Institute of Technology, Bundoora, Victoria 3083, Australia.

AMIDON, Gordon Lewis, b. 27 Apr. 1944, Seneca Falls, New York, USA. Professor of Pharmaceutics, Research Director. m. Pamela J Aruri, 27 Aug. 1966, Freeport, New Jersey, 4 sons. *Education:* BS Pharmacy, State University of New York, Buffalo, New York; MA Mathematics, PhD Pharmaceutics, The University of Michigan, Ann Arbor, Michigan. *Appointments:* Assistant Professor 1971-76, Associate Professor 1976-81, University of Wisconsin, Madison, Wisconsin; Adjunct Professor, University of Kansas, Lawrence, Kansas, 1981-83; Director of Pharmaceutical and Chemical Research, INTERx Research Corporation, Lawrence, Kansas, 1981-83; Director of Research, Smith Kline Consumer Products, Philadelphia, Pennsylvania, 1983-; Professor of Pharmaceutics, The University of Michigan, Ann Arbor, Michigan, 1983-. *Memberships:* Fellow, Academy of Pharmaceutical Sciences, Basic Pharmaceutics Section; American Pharmaceutical Association; Fellow, American Association for the Advancement of Science. *Publications include:* "The Chemical Stability of Pharmaceuticals" (with K A Conners and V J Stella), 2nd edition 1985; Over 30 articles and book chapters including: 'Design of prodrugs based on enzyme-substrate specificity' (with P K Banerjee) in "Prodrugs" (editor: H Bundgaard), 1985; 'Intestinal aminopeptidase distribution and specificity: bases for a prodrug strategy' (with K C Johnson) in "Theory and Application on Bioreversible Carriers in Drug Design" (editor: E B Roche), 1985; 'Absorption potential: estimating the fraction absorbed after an oral dose' (with J B Dressman and D Fleisher), 1985. *Honours:* Ebert Prize, American Pharmaceutical Association, 1974 and 1981, co-recipient 1984. *Address:* College of Pharmacy, The University of Michigan, Ann Arbor, MI 48109-1065, USA.

AMIN, Nagin C, b. 25 July 1920, Virsad, India. Consultant Physician. m. Usha 16 Feb. 1959, Bombay, 2 sons. *Education:* MB,BS, Bombay University, 1946; DCG, College of Physicians and Surgeons, Bombay, 1949; MD, Bombay University, 1952; Elected Fellow of American College of Chest Physicians, 1966. *Appointments:* Honorary Professor of Medicine,

Topiwala National Medical College and Honorary Physician, B Y L Nair Hospital, 1952-78; Currently Honorary Consultant Physician, J R Hospital, Western Railway, Honorary Consultant Physician, Bhatia General Hospital and Medical Research Centre and Chief Medical Referee, New India Assurance Co Ltd, Medical Consultant to Tata Institute of Fundamental Research. *Memberships:* Life Member, Association of Physicians of India; Life Member, Indian Rheumatism Association; Indian Medical Association, Bombay West Sub. Branch; Founder Member, Yusuf Meherally Centre, Tara, Raighad District. *Publications:* 'Diphtheria Immunisation' The Licentiate, 1955; 'Vitamin A in Acne Vulgaris' Current Medical Practice, 1958; 'Clinical Trials with Reverin' Current Medical Practice, 1958. *Honour:* Sanman Patra (Freedom Fighter's Certificate) awarded by Chief Minister, Government of Maharashtra, Bombay, 1978. *Hobbies:* Motoring in the country; Reading Medical Journals. *Address:* 534, Sandhurst Bridge, Bombay-400 007, India.

AMIN, Rajni Shivabhai, b. 29 June 1936, Nairobi. Consultant Radiation Oncologist. m. Bhanu U. Patel, 9 Sep. 1973, London, 1 son. *Education:* MB BS, University of Calcutta, India, 1962; MRCP, Royal College of Physicians of UK, 1970; LRCP (London); MRCS (England), 1973; DMRT (England), 1973; FFR, Faculty of Radiology, 1974; FRCR, Royal College of Radiologists, 1975. *Appointments:* House Surgeon, Makerere University, Uganda, 1963-64; House Physician, Maidenhead General Hospital, 1964; Senior House Officer, Thoracic Medicine, Tindal General Hospital, Aylesbury, 1964-65; Senior House Officer, General Medicine, Leicester General Hospital, 1966; Registrar, Thoracic Medicine, Clare Hall Hospital, South Mimms, 1966-68; Registrar, Radiation Oncology, University College Hospital, London, 1968-74; Senior Registrar, Radiation Oncology, University College Hospital, London, 1974-75. *Memberships:* British Institute of Radiology; Fellow, Royal College of Radiologists; Royal Society of Medicine; British Medical Association; Hospital Consultants and Specialists Association. *Publications:* "Extramedullary Plasmacytoma of the Lung Cancer", 1985; "Hypertrophic Osteoarthropathy in association with metastases from carcinoma of the bladder", 'Urology', 1985; Contributor to professional journals including British Journal of Radiology; Postgraduate Medical Journal. *Honour:* Second Certificate of Honours in Anatomy (1958-59), Calcutta National Medical Institute, Calcutta. *Hobbies:* Golf; Tennis; Philately; Collecting Miniatures; Table-Tennis. *Address:* Four Acres, Exton, Near Exeter, Devon, England.

AMMONS, Daryl L, b. 26 July 1955, Sanford, North Carolina, USA, Doctor of Chiropractic. m. Terry Lee Fletcher, 26 Nov 1983, 1 daughter. *Education:* Associate of Science, Sandhills Community College; BA, University of North Carolina; Doctor of Chiropractic, Life Chiropractic College; Atlas Orthogonist, Post graduate studies. *Memberships:* American Chiropractic Association; North Carolina Chiropractic Association; Parker Chiropractic Research Foundation; R W Sweat Research Foundation; Chairman, Health and Happiness Committee, Jonesboro Rotary Club; Member, Flat Springs Baptist Church. *Honours:* Cum Laude, Life Chiropractic College, 1980. *Hobbies:* Fishing; Hunting; Boating; Water-skiing; Snow-skiing; Horse riding. *Address:* 3828 Farrell Road, Sanford, NC 27330, USA.

AMPRINO, Rodolfo, b. 5 Jan 1912, Turin, Italy. *Education:* MD, Faculty of Medicine, Turin, Italy, 1934. *Appointments:* Professor of Histology and General Embryology, 1945; Director, Institute of Normal Human Anatomy, University of Bari, Italy, 1955-82; Director, Retired, Anatomical Institute. *Memberships:* Honorary Member, European Society of Osteoarthrology; Honorary memberships of numerous scientific institutions. *Publications:* Author of over 190 scientific and professional papers. *Honours:* Recipient of numerous honours. *Address:* European Society of Osteoarthrology, Prague, Czechoslovakia.

ANANDKUMAR, Trichynopoly Chelvaraj, b. 18 June 1936, Bangalore, India. Director, Institute for Research in Reproduction. m. Karpagam, 21 Oct. 1963, India, 1 son, 1 daughter. *Education:* BSc., Honours; MSc.; PhD. *Appointments:* UGC Research Fellow, University of Rajasthan, 1960-64; Postdoctoral Fellow, Medical School, University of Birmingham, England, 1964-68; Assistant Professor, 1968-76, Associate Professor, 1976-82, All India Institute of Medical Science, New Delhi; Director, Institute for Research in Reproduction, Bombay, 1982-. *Memberships:* International Primatological Society; European Society of Comparative Endocrinology; President, Primatological Society of India; Fellow, Indian Academy of Science. *Publications:* Numerous articles in professional journals: Editor: "Neuroendocrine Regulation of Fertility", 1975, "Non-humane Primate Models for Study of Reproduction", 1980; Co-editor: "Use of Non-human Primates in Biomedical Research", 1977, "Methods for Regulation of Male Fertility", 1984. *Honours:* S.S. Bhatnagar Award, 1977; Jawaharlal Nehru Fellow, 1980-82; Sanjay Gandhi Award, Family Planning, 1983. *Hobbies:* Photography; Music; Travel. *Address:* Institute for Research in Reproduction, ICMR, Jehangir Mehrwanji Street, Parel, Bombay 400012, India.

ANASTASATU, Constantin, b. 2 Sep. 1917, Corabia, Romania. Professor. m. Lia Pascu, 14 July 1950. *Education:* MD, Faculty Medicine, Bucharest, 1944; DMS 1956; Docent 1964. *Appointments:* Assistant Lecturer, 1945-48, Lecturer, Faculty of Medicine, Cluj, 1948-56; Associate Professor, Faculty of Medicine, Timisoara, 1956-62; Professor, Phthisiology, 1962, Member, University Senate, Prorector, Rector, Institute Medicine and Pharmacy, Bucharest, 1964-74; Head, Phthisiology Clinic, 1962-; Director 1970-, Chairman, TB Specialsit Committee, Tuberculosis, Research Institute, Bucharest, 1983-. *Memberships:* Regular Member, Academy Medical Sciences, Romania; Corresponding Member, Academy Romania; President, Society Pneumology and Phthisiolgoy, Romania; Member, Society of Pneumo-Phthisiology in France, FRG, GDR, Portugal, Bulgaria, Czechoslovakia; Former President, Councillor, IUAT Managing Board and IUAT Europe Region. *Publications:* "Pneumology", 1965; "Lung Scanning", 1970; "Tuberculosis Therapy", 1973; "Clinical Phthisiology";' 4 volumes, 1972-81; "Lung Diseases", 1983; Editor in Chief, "Problems of Tuberculosis", 1970; More than 800 titles on diagnosis, pathogenesis, treatment of tuberculosis and other lung diseases, tb control organization, tb epidemiology. *Honours:* Romanian Orders, Scientific Merit, 1966; Health Merit, 1972; Honoured Physician, 1973; Distringuished Professor, 1984; Differnt Medals of Romania, 1960-85; Carlo Forlanini, (Italy), 1967; Robert Koch, 1982; Purkinje Medal of Honour, 1978. *Hobbies:* Violin; Chess. *Address:* Tuberculosis Research Institute, sos. Viilor 90, sect. 4, 75239 Bucharest, Romania.

ANASTASSIADES, Pantelis, C., b. 30 Aug. 1943, Kyrenia, Cyprus. Director, Cardiovascular Diagnostic Centre, Nicosia, Cyprus. m. Anita Patsalidou, 4 Mar. 1978, Nicosia, 1 son, 1 daughter. *Education:* MD, Hebrew University, Hadassah Medical School, Jerusalem, Israel; Diplomate, American Board of Internal Medicine; Fellow, American College of Physicians; Research Fellow, Cardiology, Baylor College of Medicine, Houston, USA, 1973-75. *Appointments include:* Assistant Instructor, Medicine, Baylor College of Medicine, 1972-75; Resident, Internal Medicine, Mount Sinai Medical Centre, Chicago, 1971, Baylor College 1972-73; Fellow /Research Fellow, Cardiology, Baylor, 1973-75. *Memberships:* Fellow, American College of Physicians; Associate Fellow, American College of Cardiology; American Society of Echocadiography; Fellow, International College of Angiology. *Publications include:* Contributions to various professional journals, national & international. *Honours:* Fellowship throughout medical studies, World Health Organisation, 1962-68; Recognition awards, American Medical Association, 1974-77; British Council, Edinburgh, UK, 1985. *Hobbies:* Hunting; Swimming; Journalism. *Address:* Corner Kennedy Avenue & 1 Thassos Street, Nicosia 138, Cyprus.

ANBAR, Michael, b. 29 June 1927, Danzig, Professor and Chairman of Biophysics, 1977-, m. Ada Anbar, 2 sons. *Education:* MSc, 1950, PhD, 1953, Hebrew University, Jerusalem, Israel. *Appointments:* Research Associate, Department of Chemistry, University of Chicago, USA, 1954-55; Senior Research Scientist, 1956-67, Associate Professor, 1961-67, Weizmann Institute of Science; Head, Chemical Division, Soreq Research Establishment, 1965-67; Senior Research Associate, Senior Scientific Director, Stanford Research Institute, 1968-77; Chairman and Professor, Biophysical Sciences, State University of New York at Buffalo, 1977-83; Associate Dean for Applied Research, School Medical Executive Director, Health care Instrument and Device Institute, 1983-85. *Memberships:* American Chemical Society; Biophysical Society; American Association Mass Spectrometry; American Association for Advancement of Science; American Association Clinical Chemistry; American Association Dental Research; Association American Medical Colleges; IEEE; Association Advanced Medical Institutes; American Institute Ultrasound in Medicine. *Publications:* Contributor of over 213 professional articles for medical and scientific journals. *Honours:* Sigma Xi, 1954; UNESCO Research Scholarship; Israeli Delegate, 2nd UN Conference on Peaceful Use of Atomic Energy, 1956; Meir Award, 1959; Herman Zonelek Award, 1962; NAS, NRC Fellowship, 1962. *Hobbies:* Photography; Computer Programming. *Address:* Department of Biophysical Sciences, State University of New York /Buffalo, 120 Cary Hall, Buffalo, NY 14214, USA.

ANDERER, Friedrich Alfred, b. 4 June 1926, Ravensburg, Federal Republic of Germany. Professor of Biochemistry; Laboratory Director. m. Johanna Aust, 16 Mar. 1956, Lübeck, Germany, 1 son, 1 daughter. *Education:* Student of Chemistry, 1948-54; Diploma in Chemistry, 1953; Dr rer nat, 1957. *Appointments:* Scientific Assistant, 1957-67; Scientific Staff 1967-69, Director Friedrich-Miescher-Laboratorium 1972-, Max-Planck-Gesellschaft, Tüebingen; Head of Department, Max-Planck-Institut für Virusforschung, 1969-72. *Memberships:* Gesellschaft für Biologische Chemie; Gesellschaft für Immunologie; Gesellschaft Deutscher Naturforscher und Ärtze. *Publications:* Numerous publications in international journals of biochemistry, biology, virology, immunology and medicine. *Honours:* Fritz Merck Prize, 1967; Feliz Haffner Prize, 1969; E K Frey Prize, 1973. *Hobby:* Painting. *Address:* Friedrich-Miescher-Laboratorium der Max-Planck-Gesellschaft, Spemannstrasse 37-39, D 7400 Tüebingen, Federal Republic of Germany.

ANDERSON, Helge A, b. 27 Aug. 1939, Copenhagen, Denmark. Researcher. m. Charlotte Hald, 5 May 1963, 3 sons, 1 daughter. *Education:* Magister scientarum, 1964; D.Sc, University of Copenhagen, 1977. *Appointments:* Research Associate, Biochemistry, Veterinary University, 1965-68; Research Associate, University of Copenhagen, 1968-71; Research Associate, The Biological Institute of Carlsberg Foundation, 1971-79; Acting Director, Biological Institute, 1980-82; Researcher, Carlsberg Foundation, associated with Department of Biochemistry B, University of Copenhagen 1983-.

Memberships: Nordic Society for Cell Biology; British Society for Cell Biology. *Publications:* Co-author and Author of some 50 published articles. *Address:* Department of Biochemistry B, Panum Institute, University of Copenhagen, DK-2200, Copenhagen N, Denmark.

ANDERSEN, Ib Harald Peder, b. 19 July 1936, Denmark. Director. *Education:* MD; PhD; MPH. *Appointments:* Assistant Professor, 1963-68, Associate Professor, Institute of Hygiene, University of Aarhus, Denmark, 1968-79; Director, Danish National Institute of Occupational Health, 1979-. *Memberships:* Danish Academy of Technical Sciences (ATV). *Publications:* Several books including "The Nose", (with D F Proctor), 1982; 75 scientific papers. *Honours:* Gold Medal in otorhino-laryngology and hygiene, University of Aarhus, 1966; Rockwool Research Award, Copenhagen 1985. *Hobby:* Yachting. *Address:* Danish National Institute of Occupational Health, Baunegårdsvei 75, DK 2900, Hellerup, Denmark.

ANDERSON, John Allan Dalrymple, b. 16 June 1926, Edinburgh, Scotland, Professor of Community Medicine, Honorary Consultant, Guy's Hospital, London, m. Mairead Mary MacLaren, 3 Apr. 1965, Edinburgh, 3 daughters. *Education:* MB, ChB, 1949, MD, 1964, Edinburgh; BA, 1946, MA, 1954, Oxford; DPH, London, 1960; TD; DI; FFCM; FRCGP; MROM; DRCOG. *Appointments:* Lecturer General practice, 1954-59, Director, Industrial Survey Unit, 1960-63, University of Edinburgh; Senior Lecturer, Social Medicine, London School of Hygiene and Tropical Medicine, 1963-69; Senior Lecturer, Reader, 1970-75, Professor Community Medicine, 1975-83, Guy's Hospital Medical School, London, England. *Memberships:* British Rheumatological Society; Society for Social Medicine; Society of Occupational Medicine. *Publications:* "New Look at Social Medicine", 1965; "Self Medication", (Editor), 1979; "Low Back Pain", (Co-Editor), 1980; 'Occupational Aspects of Low Back Pain', 1980; 'Osteoarthritis, Shoulder Pain and Tension Neck and their relation to Work', 1984. *Honours:* TD, 1964; DL, 1985. *Hobbies:* Hill walking; Golf; Bridge. *Address:* 24 Lytton Grove, Putney, London SW15 2HB, England.

ANDERSON, Kenneth Ritchie, b. 6 July 1944, Christchurch, New Zealand. Pathologist. m. Fern Annette, 20 Nov. 1967, Christchurch, 2 sons, 2 daughters. *Education:* MB ChB, University of Otago; DCP, Otago; Fellow, Royal College of Pathologists of Australasia. *Appointments:* Lecturer in Pathology, University of Otago; Special Fellow in Cardiovascular Pathology, Mayo Clinic; Research Assistant, Cardiothoracic Institute, London; Senior Lecturer in Pathology; Consultant Pathologist. *Memberships:* College of Pathologists of Australasia; New Zealand Medical Association; New Zealand Federation of Sports Medicine. *Publications:* Approx. 30 book chapters & learned articles on sudden death, cardiovascular diseases & other pathology topics. *Hobbies:* Rugby; Skiing; Tramping. *Address:* 119 Don Street, Invercargill, New Zealand.

ANDERSON, Page Albert Willis, b. 12 Jan 1942, California, USA, Professor of Paediatrics; Assistant Professor of Physiology, m. Nadia Najla Malouf, 31 Dec 1968, Los Angeles, California, 1 son, 1 daughter. *Education:* AA, 1957, BA, 1960, University of California, Berkeley; MD, Duke University Medical Centre, Durham, North Carolina, 1963. *Appointments:* Associate in Paediatrics, 1972, Associate in Physiology, 1972, Assistant Professor of Paediatrics, 1973, Associate Professor of Paediatrics, 1977, Assistant Professor of Physiology, 1978, Professor of Paediatrics, 1983, Duke Medical Centre, Durham, North Carolina. *Memberships:* American Academy of Paediatrics; American College of Cardiology; Past President, American Heart Association; North Carolina Affiliate, North Carolina Executive Board of Directors; Chairman,

North Carolina Medical and Community Program Committee; Cripple Children's Advisory Committee, North Carolina Medical Society; Southeastern Paediatric Cardiology Society, past president. *Publications:* 'The force-frequency relationship: A new basis for an index of cardiac contractility', (with A Manring, E A Joghnson), 1973; 'Evaluation of the force-frequency relationship as a descriptor of the inotropic of canine left ventricular myocardium', (co-author), 1976; 'Developmental changes in cardiac contractility in fetal and postnatal sheep', (Co-author), 1984. *Honours:* Recipient, Young Investigators Award, Cardiology Section, AAP, 1972; Special Research Fellowship, NIH, 1974-75; Research Career Development Award, NIH, 1978; Alpha Omega Alpha, 1976; NC Heart Association, Founder's Day Award, 1976; Silver Service recognition Award, 1984. *Hobbies:* Enjoying the company of his family. *Address:* Duke University Medical Centre, Box 3218, Division of Paediatric Cardiology, Durham, NC 27710, USA.

ANDERSON, Richard Elliott, b. 28 Dec. 1946, New York City, USA. Medical Oncologist; Chairman, Department of Medicine, Scripps Memorial Hospital, La Jolla, California. m. Patricia W. Anderson, 12 Sep. 1970, Santa Paula, California, 2 daughters. *Education:* BA, magna cum laude, Yale University, 1968; MD, Stanford Medical School, 1973; FACP. American College of Physicians, 1983. *Appointments:* Clinical Assistant Professor, University of California, San Diego, 1977-; Private practice, medical oncology, 1977-; Senior staff physician, Scripps Memorial Hospital, 1981-; Chairman, Department of Medicine, ibid, 1985-. *Memberships:* American College of Physicians; American Society of Clinical Oncology; Alpha Omega Alpha; National Board of Medical Examiners; San Diego County Medical Society; California Medical Association. *Honours:* Honours with exceptional distinction, Department of Psychology, Yale University, 1968; Fellow, American Cancer Society, 1971; Alpha Omega Alpha, Stanford Medical School, 1973; Fellow, American College of Physicians, 1983. *Hobbies:* Photography; White-water rafting. *Address:* 9834 Genesee Avenue, Suite 311, La Jolla, CA 92037, USA.

ANDERSON, Robert Henry, b. 4 Apr. 1942, Wellington, Shropshire, England. Doctor of Medicine. m. Christine Ibbotson, 9 July 1966, Grantham, Lincolnshire, 1 son, 1 daughter. *Education:* BSc 1963, MB ChB 1966, MD 1970, University of Manchester. *Appointments:* House Physician and Surgeon, Manchester Royal Infirmary, 1966-67; Assistant Lecturer 1967-69, Lecturer 1968-73, Anatomy Department, University of Manchester; Senior Lecturer 1973-77, Reader in Paediatric Cardiac Morphology 1977-79, Joseph Levy Professor in Paediatric Cardiac Morphology 1979-, Brompton Hospital, Cardiothoracic Institute, University of London. *Memberships:* Royal College of Pathologists; Anatomy Society of Great Britain; Pathology Society of Great Britain; Royal Society of Medicine; British Cardiac Society; Honorary member, Brazilian Society of Paediatric Cardiology. *Publications include:* "Cardiac Anatomy" (with A Becker), 1980I; "Pathology of Congenital Heart Disease" (with A Becker), 1981; "Pathology of Conduction System" (with M Davies and A Becker), 1983; "Cardiac Pathology" (with A Becker), 1983; "Cardiac Anatomy for the Surgeon" (with B Wilcox), 1985; 7 other books; Over 250 learned articles; Over 125 chapters in edited books. *Honours:* Medical Research Council Travelling Fellowship, University of Amsterdam, The Netherlands, 1973-74; Excerpta Medica Travel Award and Gold Medal, 1977; Thomas Lewis Lecturer and Gold Medallist, 1979; British Heart Foundation Prize for Cardiovascular Research, 1985. *Hobbies:* Music; Golf; Wine. *Address:* Department of Paediatrics, Cardiothoracic Institute, Brompton Hospital, Fulham Road, London SW3 6HP, England.

ANDERSON, William Ferguson (Sir) b. 8 Apr. 1914, Glasgow, Scotland. Emeritus Professor of Geriatric Medicine. m. Margaret Gebbie, 25 Sep. 1940, Glasgow, 1 son, 2 daughters. *Education:* MB ChB, Hons, Glasgow; MD, Hons, Glasgow; FRCP Glasgow, Edinburgh, London; HON. FRCPI, FRCP(C), FACP. *Appointments:* Major, RAMC; Lecturer, Materia Medica; Senior Lecturer, Medicine, Welsh National School of Medicine; Consultant Physician, Cardiff Royal Infirmary; Physicians, Geriatric Medicine, Stobhill General Hospital, Glasgow; Advisor, Diseases in Old Age and Chronic Sickness, West Regional Hospital Board, Scotland; Professor of Geriatric Medicine, University of Glasgow. *Memberships:* Past President, Royal college of Physicians, Glasgow; Association of Physicians of Great Britain and Ireland; Scottish Society for Experimental Medicine; Past President, Honorary Vice President, British Geriatric Society; Fellow, Past President, British Medical Association. *Publications:* "The Practical Management of the Elderly" with Dr B Williams, 4th edition 1983; Numerous papers on Geriatric Medicine 1971-. *Honours:* Kt. OBE, K St., Bellahouston Gold Medal, University of Glasgow, 1942; St Mungo's Prize, Glasgow, 1968; Edward Henderson Gold Medal, American Geriatric Society, 1974; Brookdale Award, American Society of Gerontology, 1984. *Hobbies:* Walking; Golf. *Address:* 'Rodel', Moor Road, Strathblane, Glasgow G63 9EX, Scotland.

ANDERSSON, George Erik, b. 12 Oct. 1946, Walla Walla, Washington, USA. Controller, School of Medicine. m. Lorna Rosalyn Maxwell, 5 Sep. 1967, Loma Linda, California, 1 son. *Education:* BA, University of California, Riverside, 1972. *Appointments:* Accountant, 1968-71, Administrative Assistant, Financial Analysis and Planning, Medical Centre, 1971-73, Assistant to the Dean, School of Medicine, 1973-77, Loma Linda University, California; Director of Finance, College of Medicine, University of Kentucky, Lexington, Kentucky, 1977; Controller, School of Medicine, Georgetown University,Washington, District of Columbia, 1978-. *Memberships:* Group on Business Affairs and Group on Institutional Planning, Association of American Medical Colleges; National Association of College and University Business Officers; Medical Group Management Association. *Honours:* Omicron Delta Epsilon, 1970. *Hobbies:* Music, violin; Orchid culture; Bicycling. *Address:* 6801 Rock Creek Court, Alexandria, VA 22306, USA.

ANDREWS, Mason Cooke, b.20 Apr. 1919, Norfolk, Virginia, USA. Professor, Chairman, Obstetrics, Gynaecology, Eastern Virginia Medical School. m. Sabine Alston Goodman, 24 Sep. 1949, Jacksonville, Florida, 2 daughters. *Education:* AB, Princeton University, 1940; MD, Johns Hopkins University School of Medicine, 1943. *Appointments:* Resident, Johns Hopkins Hospital, 1944, 1946-50; Assistant Lecturer, 1948-50, Lecturer, 1971-72, Johns Hopkins University School of Medicine; Chairman, Eastern Virginia Medical Authority, 1964-70; Councilman, 1974-, Vice-Mayor, 1978-82, City of Norfolk. *Memberships:* American Gynaecological & Obstetrical Society; American Fertility Society; South Atlantic Association of Obstetrics and Gynaecologists, President, 1972. *Publications:* Numerous articles in professional journals including:'Fertil.Steril'; 'Journal Modern Medicine'; 'American Journal Obstetrics & Gynaecology'; 'Virginia Medical Monthly'; 'Southern Medical Journal'; 'Medical Times'; etc. *Honours:* Citation, Outstanding Service, City of Norfolk, 1961. *Hobby:* Boating. *Address:* Eastern Virginia Medical School, Obstetrics and Gynaecology, Hofheimer Hall, 825 Fairfax Avenue, 6th Floor, Norfolk, VA 23507, USA.

ANDREWS, J. Robert, b. 10 June 1906, Kent, Ohio, USA. University Professor; Medical Research Associate. m. Anne Cosgrove, 2 sons, 1 daughter. *Education:* PhB, Brown University, Providence, Rhode Island, USA; MD, Western Reserve University, Cleveland, Ohio; DSc, University of Pennysylvania, Philadelphia. *Appointments:* Chief, Radiation Branch, National Cancer Institute, National Institutes of Health; Chief, Radiotherapy Section, Washington Veterans Administration Hospital; Professor and Director, Department of Radiation Therapy, Georgetown University Medical Centre, Professor Emeritus and Research Associate-. *Memberships:* American Medical Association; American Radium Society; American Society of Therapeutic Radiologists and Oncologist; American Society for Cancer Research; American Roentgen Ray Society; Radiological Society of North America; Radiation Research Society. *Publications:* "The Radiobiology of Human Cancer Radiotherapy", 1968, 2nd edition, 1978; 75 research communications on radiobiology, cancer radiotherapy and risk analysis. *Hobbies:* Photography; Art; White water canoeing; Sailing. *Address:* Bles Building Lower Level, Georgetown University Medical Centre, 3800 Reservoir Road NW, Washington, DC 20007, USA.

ANDREWS, Niel Corbly, b. 31 Mar. 1916, Spokane, USA. Professor, Surgery, University of California, Davis. m. Carla Virginia Foster, 14 Nov. 1970, Santa Monica, 1 son, 1 daughter. *Education:* BA, University of Oregon, 1940; MD, University of Oregon School of Medicine, 1943; MMSc., Ohio State University, 1950; Certification, various other Universities. *Appointments include:* Captain, US Army, 1945-47; Resident, Surgery, 1947-50, Instructor, Anatomy, 1947-52, Instructor, Thoracic Surgery, 1950-52, Assistant Professor, 1952-57, Associate Professor, 1957-67, Professor, 1967-70, Throacic Surgery, Ohio State University, Columbus; Chief of Surgery, Supervisor of Surgical Residency Training Programme, Ohio Tuberculosis Hospital, 1950-66; Private Practice, Thoracic Surgery, Active Staff, Ohio State University Hospitals, 1961-70; Consultant, VA Hospital, Chillicothe, 1953-70, VA Hospital Dayton, 1954-70, VA Area Consultant, 1960-70; Assistant Dean, Research & Training, 1966-70, Programme Director, 1966-67, Co-ordinatior, Regional Medical Programme, 1967-70, Ohio State University; Consultant, 1969-70, Co-ordinator, Regional Medical Programme, 1970-73, Professor, Surgery, (in residence) 1970-71, Professor, Surgery, 1971-, Chairman, Community & Postgraduate Medicine, 1971-79, Chairman, Postgraduate Medicine, 1973-81, University of California, Davis. *Memberships include:* American Medical Society; Ohio State Medical Association; Academy of Medicine, Columbus and Franklin County, various committees; Columbus Surgical Society; National Tuberculosis Association; Fellow, American College of Chest Physicians; American Association for Thoracic Surgery; numerous other professional organisations. *Publications include:* Author, more than 50 articles in professional journals; Editorial, 'Yolo County medical Society Bulletin', April, May June, Sep,. Nov., 1985; Editor, 'Yearbook of Cancer', Section on Chest, 1965-79; etc. *Honours:* Recipient, various honours and awards including: Sigma Xi; Asculapius Honorary Society; Service Awards, Central Ohio Heart Association, 1963, 1968; Service Awards, American Cancer Society, California Division, 1980, 1981, 1982, 1983, 1984. *Address:* Box 3007, El Macero, CA 95618, USA.

ANDREY-KRONSTEIN, Line Nathalie Elvina, b. 29 Oct. 1934, Geneva, Switzerland. Physician; Artist. Painter. m. Pierre-Francois Andrey, 22 Apr. 1971, Venice, Italy. *Education:* Letters a Philosophy, University of Rome; Medicine, University of Geneva. *Appointments:* Classical Ballet Dancer; Sculptor, Sketcher and Painter, jointly with medicine. *Honours:* Federal Diploma of Medicine, 1963; Sculpture Diploma, Superior Visual Arts School of Geneva, 1981. *Creative Works:* Paintings (Portraits, a Human figure). *Hobbies:* Painting on ivory and enamel of Geneva; Reading Philosophia Perennis. *Address:* 17

Rue Toepffer, 1206 Geneva, Switzerland.

ANDRONESCU-GHIKA, Serban, b. 8 Nov. 1931, Paris, France. Senior Research Worker; Head of Research Department. m. Maria Andronescu-Ghika, 5 Jan. 1955, Bucharest. *Education:* Graduate, Medical School of Bucharest, Romania; Doctorate degree in Medical Sciences; Specialist in Anaesthesia and Intensive Care. *Appointments:* Head of Medical Dispensary, 1960; Head of Anaesthesia and Intensive Care Department of a Hospital; Scientific Research Worker, 1965-75; Senior Scientist in Haematological Research, 1975-83; Head of Research Department, The Centre of Haematology and Blood Transfusion, Bucharest, 1983-. *Memberships:* Romanian Society of Haematology; Romanian Union of Scientific Medical Societies. *Publications include:* ''The Haemophilliac'', 1986; Over 200 articles and communications. *Honours:* The Red Cross Merit Medal; The Sanitary Merit Medal. *Hobbies:* Touring; Photography; Literature. *Address:* The Centre of Haematology and Blood Transfusion, Str Dr Felix Nr 89, Section 1, Bucharest, Romania.

ANG, Ah Hoo, b. 23 Feb. 1938, Malaysia. Consultant Radiologist. m. Mok Sek Kua, 27 Mar 1965, Malaysia, 1 son, 1 daughter. *Education:* MBBs, Singapore, 1963; DMRD, England, 1968; FRCR, London 1973; FRACR, Australia, 1979. *Appointments:* Medical Officer, Ministry of Health, Malaysia, 1963-66; Lecturer in Radiology, 1966-72 Associate Professor of Radiology, 1972-77, University of Malaya; Staff Radiologist, Royal Newcastle Hospital, Newcastle, Australia, 1977-82; Consultant Radiologist, Private Radiology Practice, 1982-. *Memberships:* British Institute of Radiology; Royal College of Radiologists, London; Royal Australasian College of Radiologists; Australian Medical Association. *Publications:* 'Ectopic Thoracic Kidney' Journal of Urology, 1972; 'Extradural Haematoma of the Anterior Fossa' International Surgery, 1972; 'Amniography in the Early Diagnosis of Hydatidiform Mole' British Journal of Radiology, 1975; 'Radiological Changes in the Chest in Malignant Trophoblastic Disease' Australasian Radiology, 1976. *Hobbies:* Music; Reading. *Address:* 48 Thomas Street, Cardiff, New South Wales 2285, Australia.

ANG, Özdem, b. 13 Dec. 1933, Izmir, Turkey. Microbiologist. m. Tüten Ayla, 25 July 1957, Eskisehir, Turkey, 1 son, 1 daughter. *Education:* MD, Medical Faculty, Istanbul University, 1956. *Appointments:* Assistant, 1957-59, Specialist, 1959-64, Assistant Professor, 1964-70, Professor of Microbiology, Department of Microbiology, Medical Faculty, Istanbul University, Turkey, 1970-. *Memberships:* Turkish Microbiological Society; Turkish Society of Parasitology; American Society of Microbiology; British Society for Antimicrobial Chemotherapy; European Society of Clinical Microbiology. *Publications:* ''Infekesiyon Hastaliklari'', 1979; ''Tibbi Parazitoloji'', 1985. *Hobby:* Volleyball. *Address:* Department of Microbiology, Istanbul Medical Faculty, Gapa – Istanbul, Turkey.

ANGE, Constance Elizabeth, b. 24 Sep. 1949, North Carolina, USA. Psychiatrist (Adult and Child). m. Richard Fryman, 9 Sep. 1978. *Education:* Doctor of Osteopathy, 1974. *Appointments:* General Practice, 1975-77; Visiting Clinical Faculty, Ohio University at Athens, 1982, 83; Clinical Staff, Grandview Hospital, 1982, 83, 84; Consultant, Montgomery Development Centre, 1983; Consultant, Dunn Mental Health Center, 1983, 84, 85. *Memberships:* American Osteopathic Association; Dayton Osteopathic Association; Dayton District Academy; American College of Neuropsychiatry; American Psychiatric Association; Ohio Psychiatric Association; Cincinnati Council of Child Psychiatry; American Academy of Child Psychiatry; Dayton Psychiatric Association; Clinical Sleep Society; National Association of Female Executives. *Publication:*

Group Consultation with Highly Stressed Medical Personnel to Avoid Burn Out, Journal of American Academy of Child Psychiatry, 1982. *Honours:* Robert Wood Johnson Scholarship; Sigma Sigma Phi Fraternity, 1975. *Hobby:* Reading. *Address:* 1410 Talbott Tower, Dayton, OH 45405, USA.

ANKKURINIEMI, Olavi, b. 9 Jan. 1934, Kuusamo, Finland. Surgeon General for Dental Services, Finnish Defence Forces. m. Marjukka Toivonen, 1969, Helsinki, 1 son, 2 daughters. *Education:* Candidate 1956, Licentiate 1958, Doctor 1979, all of Odontology, University of Helsinki; Specialist, Oral Surgery, 1975; Colonel, MC, 1980. *Appointments:* Assistant, Department of Oral Surgery, University of Helsinki, 1959-61; Dental Officer, Helsinki Garrison (Guards Battalion), 1959-64; Dental Officer, Central Military Hospital, 1964-65; Dental Officer-in-Chief, Central Military Hospital, 1965-; Surgeon General for Dental Services, Finnish Defence Forces, 1983-. *Memberships:* Finnish Dental Association; Finnish Dental Society; Finnish Association of Oral & Maxillofacial Surgeons; Scandinavian Association of Oral & Maxillofacial Surgeons; International Association of Oral & Maxillofacial Surgeons; Consultant, FDI Committee of Defence Forces Dental Services. *Publications:* Numerous publications in military dentistry, epidemiology & oral surgery. *Honours:* Medal for Military Merit, 1979; Knight 1st Class, Order of the White Rose of Finland, 1980. *Hobby:* Fly-fishing. *Address:* General Headquarters, P.O. Box 919, SF-00101 Helsinki 10, Finland.

ANSELL, Ian David, b. 15 Feb. 1938, Chichester, Sussex, England. Consultant Histopathologist. m. Jacqueline Alysia Dolan, 4 Apr. 1975, London, England, 1 son, 1 daughter. *Education:* BA, MB, B.Chi., Cambridge, England, 1963; MRC(Path.); FRC(Path). *Appointments:* Senior House Officer and Registrar, Pathology Department, St. Bartholomew's Hospital, London, England; Lecturer in Morbid Anatomy, Kings college, Hospital, London; Research Fellow in electron Microscopy, St. Paul's Hospital, London; Lecturer and Honorary Consultant in Histopathology, Royal Postgradute Medical School, London. *Memberships:* British Medical Association; Association of Clinical Pathologists; International academy of Pathology, British Division; Pathological Society of Great Britain; British Society of Gastroenterology. *Publications:* Chapter 'Histopathology of the Prostate' in ''Scientific Foundations of Urology'', 1982; ''Atlas of Male Reproductive System Pathology'', 1985. *Hobbies:* Opera; Cooking; Walking. *Address:* Department of Histopathology, City Hospital, Huchral Road, Nottingham NG5 1PB, England.

ANSELL, George, b. 11 Dec. 1921, Liverpool, England. Senior Consultant Radiologist, Whiston Hospital; Lecturer in Radiodiagnosis, Liverpool University. m. Vera Wolfe, 5 Nov. 1961, Southend. *Education:* MD; DMRD; FRCP; FRCR: Liverpool University. *Appointments:* Medical Registrar, United Liverpool Hospitals; Squadron Leader (Medical Specialist), RAF; Greaves Research Fellow, Sheffield University; Radiological Registrar, Liverpool Royal Infirmary; Assistant Radiologist, Broadgreen Hospital, Liverpool. *Memberships:* British Medical Association; British Institute of Radiology; Royal College of Radiologists; Liverpool Medical Institution. *Publications:* ''Radiology of Adverse Reactions to Drugs and Toxic Hazards'', 1985; ''Complications in Diagnostic Radiology'', 1976 and 1986; Numerous Papers and Chapters on radiological contrast media, etc. *Address:* 101 Childwall Park Avenue, Liverpool LI6 0JF, England.

ANSFORD, Anthony Joseph, b. 14 Apr. 1940, Temuka, New Zealand. Director, Laboratory of Microbiology & Pathology. m. Susan Maryann, 18 June 1984, Brisbane, 2 sons. *Education:* MB; ChB; DCP; FRACP; FRCPA. *Appointments include:* Resident House Officer, Timaru Hospital, 1966-76;

Local Medical Officer, Middlemarch, New Zealand, 1968; Cardiological, Renal and General Medical Registrar, Assistant Lecturer, Medicine, Professiorial Unit, Dunedin Hospital, & Otago University, 1969; Registrar, Assistant Lecturer, Pathology, Dunedin Hospital, & Otago University, 1970; Registrar, Histopathology, Fairfax Institute of Pathology, Australia, 1972-74; Patholgist, Laboratory of Microbiology & Pathology, 1974-, Institute of Forensic Pathology, Brisbane; Tutor, part-time, Pathology, University of Queensland, 1975-; Visiting Lecturer, Forensic Pathology, University of Quennsland, 1976-; Deputy Director, 1980-82, Director, 1983-, Laboratrory of Microbiology & Pathology, Institute of Forensic Pathology, Brisbane. *Memberships include:* Associate Member, New Zealand Society of Pathologists; Royal Australasian College of Physicians; Foundation Member, Australasian Division, International Academy of Pathology; etc. *Publications include:* Numerous articles in professional journals including: 'Lancet'; 'Medical Journal of Australia'; 'British medical Journal'; etc. *Honours:* Scott Memorial Prize, 1962; William Ledingham Christie Prize, Surgical Anatomy, 1964; Fowler Scholarship in Medicine, 1965; James Boyd Prize in Clinical Medicine, Wellington Hospital, New Zealand, 1965, Smith, Kline and French Prize in Clinical Psychiatry, 1965. *Hobby:* Organ Playing. *Address:* 8 /49 Maryvale Street, Toowong, Queensland 4066, Australia.

ANSORGE, Wilhelm, b. 14 July 1944, Jablonec, Czechoslovakia. Applied Physicist. m. Petruska Sula, 25 June 1976, Geneva, Switzerland, 3 daughters. *Education:* MS Physics, Mathematics, 1966; Doctor (Natural Sciences) Experimental Physics, 1968. *Appointments:* Assistant to Professor, 1967-69; Applied Physicist, Texas Instruments Inc, Dallas, Texas, USA, 1969-73; Applied Physicist, CERN, Geneva, Switzerland, 1973-79; Group Leader, Biochemical Instrumentation, European Molecualr Biology Laboratory, Heidelberg, Federal Republic of Germany, 1979-. *Memberships:* Electrophoresis Society. *Publications:* Numerous articles in biochemical journals, 14 patents in experimental cell research. *Hobbies:* Music; Tennis; Chess. *Address:* European Molecular Biology Laboratory, Postfach 10.2209, D-6900 Heidelberg, Federal Republic of Germany.

ANTALOCZY, Zoltán, b. 22 Mar. 1923, Tolcsva, Hungary. Director of Medical Department, Budapest. m. Edit Juhász, 2 Dec. 1957, 2 sons. *Education:* MD, Budapesti Pázmány Péter Tudományegyetem Orvostudomány Kara. *Appointments:* Assistant Professor, Medical school, 2nd Medical Department, University of Budapest, 1947-57; Head, State Hospital for Cardiology, Balatonfürred, 1957-75; Professor, Postgraduate Medical School, 1975-79, Director, 2nd Medical Department of Postgraduate Medical School, Budapest, Hungary,1 979-. *Memberships:* Presidium, Hungarian Society on Cardioloyg; Collegium Cardiologicum of Ministry of Health; Scientific Committee, Postgraduate Medical School. *Publications:* "Investigation on Electric Function of the Heart", 1972; "Electrocardiology in Medical Praxis", 1976; "Myocardial Infarction", 1977;' "Rehabilitation of Myocardial Infarction", 1981; "Cardiology", 1983; "About Heart & Vascular Diseases for Everybody", 1984. *Honours:* Award of Hungarian Academy of Sciences for Excellent Research Work, 1968; Award, Best Hungarian Medical Book of the Year, 1972, 1984, 1985. *Hobby:* Study of Fine Arts. *Address:* 2nd Medical Department, Postgraduate Medical School, Pf 112, 1389 Budapest, Hungary.

ANTHONY, Peter Paul, b. 22 June 1933, Nemesnad-udvar, Hungary. Consultant Pathologist, Royal Devon & Exeter Hospitals; Reader, Histopathology, University of Exeter. m. Mary Capsticks, 27 May 1961, Anston, 1 son, 1 daughter. *Education:* MBBS, St Bartholomews Hospital, University of London, England; MRCS LRCP, London; FRCPath, England. *Appointments:* Senior Lecturer, University of East Africa, 1969; Senior Lecturer, Middlesex Hospital Medical School, London, 1971-77. *Memberships:* Council Member, Royal College of Pathologists; Association of Clinical Pathologists, Education Secretary, Council Member; International Academy of Pathologists, Past Council Member; Member, Secretary, Chairman, WHO Committees; British Scoiety of Gastroenterology; European Association for the Study of the Liver; other professional organisations. *Publications:* Co-Editor, "Recent Advances in Histopathology", 1978, 1981, 1984, 1986; "Pathology of Liver", 1978, 1986; Author, approximately 100 original articles, reviews and chapter in books on cancer, Liver and gastrointestinal disease. *Honour:* Dyke Memorial Lecturer, 1982. *Hobbies:* Sailing; Photography; Walking. *Address:* Area Department of Pathology and Postgraduate Medical School, University of Exeter, Exeter, Devon, England.

APPENZELLER, Otto, b. 11 Dec. 1927, Czernowitz, Romania. Professor of Neurology and Medicine. m. Judity Bryce, 11 Dec. 1956, Sydney, Australia, 3 sons. *Education:* MB; BS; MD, Sydney; PhD, London. *Appointments include:* Registrar 1959-60, Professorial Medical Registrar 1960, Royal Prince Alfred Hospital, Sydney; Lecturer in Clinical Neurology and Neurophysiology, Queen Square Research Society, 1961-62; Assistant Professor of Neurology, University of Cincinnati College of Medicine, Cincinnati, Ohio, USA, 1965-67; Chief, Neurology Service, Veterans Administration Hospital, 1965-67; Associate Professor 1967-70, Professor of Neurology and Medicine 1970-, University of New Mexico School of Medicine, Albuquerque, New Mexico; Consultant Neurologist, Veterans Administration Hospital, Albuquerque, 1968-; Visiting Professor, Division of Neurology, McGill University, Montreal, Canada, 1977; Honorary Research Fellow, Centre for Neurosciences, Department of Anatomy and Embryology, University College, London, England, 1983-84. *Memberships:* Fellow, Royal Australasian College of Physicians; Fellow, American College of Physicians; Fellow, American Academy of Neurology; American College of Sports Physicians; New York Academy of Sciences; Clinical Autonomic Research Society. *Publications:* 'An Introduction to Basic and Clinical Concepts' in "The Autonomic Nervous System", 1970, 3rd edition 1982; "Headache", 1980; 'Fitness Training Injuries' in "Sports Medicine", 1981, 2nd edition 1984; "Kopfschmerz", 1982; "Le Cephalee", 1984; "Neurologic Differential Diagnosis", 1985. *Honours:* Hinder Prize, Clinical Surgery, University of Sydney, 1957; Honorable mention, Rolex Awards for Enterprise, 1984. *Hobbies:* Sculpture; Long distance running. *Address:* University of New Mexico School of Medicine, Department of Neurology, Albuquerque, NM 87131, USA.

APESOS, James, b. 16 Mar. 1948, Philadelphia, Pennsylvania, USA. Program Director, Plastic and Reconstructive Surgery. m. Elizabeth, 2 sons, 1 daughter. *Education:* BA, University of Pennsylvania, Philadelphia, 1970; MD, Georgetown University School of Medicine, Washington DC, 1974. *Appointments:* 1981-84: Assistant Professor of Plastic Surgery, Division of Plastic Surgery, University of Kentucky, Lexington; Attending Surgeon, Division of Plastic Surgery, Veterans Administration Hospital, Lexington, Kentucky; Associate Staff Physician, Cardinal Hill Hospital and Rehabilitation Center, Lexington, Kentucky; Attending Physicians, Shriner's Hospital for Crippled Children, Lexington; Staff Plastic Surgeon, Kentucky Crippled Children's Services, Lexington; Active Staff Central Baptist Hospital Lexington, Saint Joseph Hospital, Lexington and Lexington Community Hospital, 1984-, Associate Clinical Professor, Division of Plastics and Reconstructive Surgery, Wright State University /Kettering Medical Center,

Dayton, Ohio; 1984- (Pending) Active Staff Kettering Medical Center, Kettering, Ohio, Saint Elizabth Medical center, Dayton, Children's Medical Center, Dayton, Miami Valley Hospital, Dayton, Good Samaritan Hospital, Dayton, Sycamore Hospital, Miamisburg, Ohio, 1984-, Director, Plastic and Reconstructive Surgery Residency, Kettering Medical Center, Wright State University Affiliated Hospitals, Dayton, Ohio; 1984-, Director, Plastic Surgery Laboratories, Cox Heart Institute, Kettering, Ohio; 1984-, Affiliated Member, Biomedical Sciences Doctoral Program Faculty, Wright State University School of Graduate Studies, Dayton, Ohio. *Memberships include:* American Medical Association; American Association for the Advancement of Science; American Burn Association; American Society for Plastic and Reconstructive Surgery; American Association of Tissue Banks. *Publications:* Presenter of numerous papers to medical conferences and contibutor of articles to medical journals in the field of Plastic and Reconstructive Surgery. *Honours:* Honorable Order of Kentucky Colonels; Fellow, University of Kentucky; Physician's Recognition Award, American Medical Association; Alpha Epsilon Delta. *Address:* 7030 Winter Hill Court, Dayton, OH 45459, USA.

APIRION, David, b. 17 July 1935, Palestine, Professor, m. Mary R Mckinley, 10 Sep. 1963, Glasgow, Scotland, 2 sons, 1 daughter. *Education:* MSc, Hebrew University, Jerusalem, Israel 1960; PhD, Glasgow University, Glasgow, Scotland, 1963. *Appointments:* Research and Teaching Assistant, Hebrew University, Jerusalem, Israel, 1959-60; Research Student, 1960-62, Assistant Lecturer, 1962-63, Glasgow University, Glasgow, Scotland; Research Fellow, Harvard University, Cambridge, Massachusetts, USA, 1963-65; Assistant Professor, Department of Microbiology, 1965-70, Associate Professor, department of Microbiology and Immunology, 1975-78, Professor, Department of Microbiology and Immunology, 1978-, Washington University School of Medicine, St Louis, Missouri, USA. *Memberships:* Genetics Society of America; The American Society for Microbiology; The American Association for the Advancement of Science; Sigma Xi; The Royal Society of Medicine, United Kingdom; The American Society of Biological Chemists; The Biophysical Society; The American Society for Cell Biology. *Publications:* "Processing of RNA", (Editor), 1984; Contributor of 167 articles in professional journals. *Honours:* The Tuvia Kushnir Prize, 1960; The Alexander Milman Prize, 1961; The Sir Maurice Bloch Award, 1962; Visiting Scholar, Cambridge University, England, 1973; Visiting Professor, Tel-Aviv University, Israel, 1974; Lady Davis Visiting Professor, Hebrew University, 1980; National Academy of Science Exchange in Hungary and USSR, 1980; National Science Foundation Visiting Scientist in India, 1985. *Hobbies:* Photography; Swimming; Reading political science; Volleyball; Mountaineering. *Address:* 408 South Hanley, Clayton, MO 63105, USA.

APPLETON, Derek Sidney, b. 16 June 1946, Epsom, England. Consultant Radiologist. m. Susan R.K. Blyth, 8 Aug. 1970, Cambridge, 2 daughters. *Education:* MA, 1971, MB BChir, 1971, Cambridge University; D.Obst.RCOG, 1974; FRCR, 1979. *Appointment:* Consultant Radiologist, Addenbrookes and Papworth Hospitals, Cambridge. *Memberships:* Royal College of Radiologists; British Institute of Radiology. *Address:* Four Winds, 39 Fox Road, Balsham, Cambridge CB1 6EZ, England.

APPLEYARD, William James, b. 25 Oct. 1935. Consultant Paediatrician. m. Elizabeth Anne Ward, 25 Jan. 1964, 1 son, 2 daughters. *Education:* MA, (Oxon), BM BCh, DRCOG, FRCP, Oxford University and Guy's Hospital. *Appointments:* Resident, Paediatrics, Junior Medical Registrar, Senior Registrar, Paediatrics, Guy's Hospital; Senior House Officer, Hospital for Sick Children, Great Ormond Street; Dyers Company Research Registrar, St Thomas's Hospital; Consultant Paediatrician for Canterbury and Thanet Health District. *Memberships:* General Medical Council; British Paediatric Association; Neonatal Society; British Medical Association. *Publications:* "The Review of Medical, Educational and Social Needs of 207 Handicapped Children", with Dr. G. Blair, 'Child Health and Development', Volume 13, 1975; "A Child with Parital Trasiomy of Chromosome 17 and Partial Monasamy of Chromosome 3", with Drs Shawe and Fear, 'Journal of Medical Genetics', Volume 20, 1983. *Honours:* Alumnus Award for Paediatric Research, University of Louisville, USA, 1965. *Hobbies:* Lawn Tennis; Former Allotment Holder. *Address:* 20 St Stephen's Road, Canterbury, Kent, England.

APUZZIO, Joseph, b. 10 June 1947, USA. Associate Professor, Obstetrics & Gynaecology, University of Medicine & Dentistry of New Jersey, New Jersey Medical School. *Education:* MD; BA, Rutgers University, 1969. *Memberships:* American College of Obstetrics & Gynaecology; American College of Surgeons. *Publications:* Over 35 articles. *Honours:* Phi Beta Kappa, Rutgers University, 1969. *Hobby:* Jogging. *Address:* Dept. of Ob-Gyn, 100 Bergen St., Newark NJ 07103, USA.

ARAI, Tadashi, b. 2 Jan. 1923, Toyama, Japan, Professor of Chiba University, Research Institute for Chemobiodynamics, Chiba University, m. Yuko Arai, 27 Dec. 1982, Tokyo, Japna, 1 son, 2 daughters. *Education:* MD; DMS. *Appointments:* Research Associate, Institute of Food Microbiology, 1947; Associate professor, 1951; Visiting Research Fellow, Instructor, University of Pennsylvania, USA, 1957-59; Professor, Insitute of Food Microbiology, 1959, Professor, Departemnt of Antibiotics, Research Institute of Chemobiodynamics, 1973, Director, Research Institute for Chemobiodynamics, 1974-86, Chiba University. *Memberships:* President, Society of Actinomycetes, Japan, 1967-75; President, Japan National Committee on Microbiology; Japanese Society for Medical Mycology; Japanese Society for Bacteriology; Japan Society for Chemotherapy; Japanese Cancer Association; Japan Antibiotics Research Association; Science Council of Japan; American Society for Microbiology, New York Academy of Science; International Society for Human and Animal Mycology. *Publications:* "Actinomycetes-The boundary Micro-organisms", 1976; 'Isoquinolinequinones from Actinomycetes and Sponges', (Ed. A Brossi), 1983; 'Filamentous Micro organisms-Biomedical Aspects', 1985. *Honorus:* Prize of the Japanese Society for Medical Mycology, 1984. *Address:* Research Institute for Chemobiodynamics, Chiba University, 1-8-1, Inohana, Chiba, 280 Japan.

ARAN, Jean-Marie, b. 15 Sep. 1939, Montpelier, France, Director, INSERM Research No 229; Director of Research INSERM, m. Anne-Marie Ploux, 2 sons, 2 daughters. *Education:* MSc, 1963, Engineering Degree, 1963, DSc, 1973, Bordeaux. *Appointments:* Research Assistant in basic sciences, 1963-64; Research Fellow, 1964-65, Visiting Professor, 1982-83, Kresge Hearing Research Institute, University of Michigan, USA; Research Associate, 1965-66, 1967-71, Group Scientific Engineer, 1966-67, Research Deputy, 1971-74, Master of Research, 1974-82, Director of Research, 19832-, National Institute of Health and Medical Research, (INSERM). *Memberships:* Speech and Hearing Association of Bordeaux and Southwestern France, 1965-; Society of French Acousticians, 1979-; Acoustical Society of America, 1966-; International Society of Audiology, 1970; Member, Executive Committee International Electric Response Audiomentry Study Group, 1970-; Member of Council, 1972, Collegium ORLAS, 1972-; Portmann Foundation, 1973-. *Honours:* Prize of the Society of

French Acousticians, 1975; Chelalier of the National Order of Merit, France, 1978; Amplifon International Prize, 1981. *Address:* INSERM U 229, Laboratoire d'Audiologie Experimentale, Hopital Pellegrin, 33076 Bordeaux, France.

ARAVANIS, Christos Ioannis, b. 30 Nov., 1923, Lefkas, Greece. Professor of Cardiology. m. Tula Theodos, 12 June 1958, Athens, 1 son, 1 daughter. *Education:* MD, 1948, PhD, 1958, As. Professor 1962, University of Athens Medical School. *Appointments:* Associate, Chicago Medical School, Illinois, USA, 1957-60; Attending Physician, Hipocrates University Hospital, Athens, Greece, 1960-74; Programme Director, Epidemiology Cardiovascular Diseases in Greece, USPHS, 1960-70; Visiting Professor, Chicago Medical School, Illinois, USA, 1969-71; Professor of Physiology and Biophysics, 1972; Director, Department of Cardiology, Evangelismos Hospital Medical Centre, Athens, Greece, 1975-. *Memberships:* Fellow: American College of Cardiology; American College of Chest Physicians; International College of Angiology; Royal Medical Society, England. Member: New York Academy of Sciences; American Gerontological Society; American Heart Association; European Society of Cardiology; American Association for Advancement of Sciences; Consultant, World Health Organisation; International Society of Thrombosis; Regent for Greece ACCP; Investigator for Heart Diseases EEC 1982-86. *Publications:* "Digitalis", 1957; "Diseasesof the Chest", 1960; "Encyclopedia of Cardiology", 1960; "American Heart Association Monograph", 1970; "Acta Med. Scand.", Monograph, 1967; "Seven Countries", 1980; "Nutritional Prev. Cardiov. Dis.", 1983. Contributor of numerous articles on cardiovascular subjects. *Hobbies:* Art; Painting; Writing. *Address:* Queen Sofia's Avenue, 47, Athens, Greece.

ARBEIT, Byron Sheldon, b. 14 Dec. 1950, New Orleans, Louisiana, USA. Executive Director; President; Instructor. 1 son, 2 daughters. *Education:* BA, Philosophy and Political Science, Tulane University, USA, 1972; MA, University of Iowa, 1974; NHA Licensed Nursing Home Administrator. *Appointments:* Senior Assistant Administrator, Biscayne Medical Centre, Miami, Florida, USA, 1974-76; Associate Administrator, Community Hospital of South Broward, Hollywood, Florida, 1976-78; Executive Director, Mid-County Medical Centre, West Palm Beach, Florida, 1978-82; Executive Director, Willow Wood Home for Jewish Aged, New Orleans-; President, Arbeit and Arbeit Consultants Inc.-; Instructor, Tulane University School of Medicine and Tulane School of Public Health-. *Memberships:* American College of Hospital Administrators; Gerontological Society; American Association of Homes for the Aging; National Association on Aging; National Association of Day Care Centres; National Association of Jewish Homes and Housing for Aged. *Publications:* 'Employee Rating Techniques and a Proposed Program of Employemnt Standards' in 'Public Personnel Management', 1975; 'Mid-County Medical Centre Research Project: Community Health Centres in Action' in 'Primary Care Focus', 1981 Convention Edition. *Hobbies:* Fishing; Golf; Jogging. *Address:* Willow Wood Home for Jewish Aged, 3701 Behrman Place, New Orleans, LA 70114, USA.

ARDILA, Alfredo, b. 4 Sep. 1946, Colombia, South America. Psychologist; Chief, Neuropsychology, Neurological Institute of Colombia. m. Monica Rosselli, 17 May 1985, 2 daughters. *Education:* PhD, Neuropsychology. *Appointments:* Director, Psychology, National University of Colombia, 1976-78; Director, Laboratory of Psychology, Institute of Research, Caracas, Venezuela, 1978-79; Visiting Professor, Researcher, National Autonomous University of Mexico, 1979-80; Chief,m Neuropsychology, Neurological Institute of Colombia, 1980-. *Memberships:* International Neuropsychological Society; Colombian Association of Neuropsychology; Colombian

Society of Neurobiology; Colombian Association of Neurology; American Psychological Association; Colombian Association for Development of Science. *Publications:* "Psychophysiology of Complex Processess", 1979; "Neuropsychological Assessment", 1981; "Psychobiology of Language", 1983; "The Right Hemisphere ; Neurology and Neuropsychology", 1984; 'Neurolinguistics", 1984; "Neuropsychology of Memory", 1985. *Honour:* National Award of Psychology, 1980. *Hobby:* Literature. *Address:* PO Box 17021, Bogota, Colombia, South America.

AREEKUL, Suvit, b. 17 Nov. 1935, Suradhani, Thailand. Professor and Chairman, Department of Tropical Radioisotopes, Faculty of Tropical Medicine. m. Saiehai Swasdirurk, 22 Aug. 1967, Suradhani, 1 son, 2 daughters. *Education:* MD, Siriraj Hospital, Thailand, 1961; MD, (Medicine Doctor), Uppsala, Sweden, 1969; DTM & H, Mahidol University, Thailand, 1970. *Appointments:* Lecturer, Department of Tropical Radioisotopes, Faculty of Tropical Medicine, Mahidol University, Thailand, 1963; Acting Head of Department, 1971-75; Assistant Professor and Head of the Department, 1975; Associate Professor, 1977; Professor, 1983; Assistant Dean for Academic Affairs, 1985. *Memberships:* Medical Association of Thailand; Radiological Society of Thailand; Science Society of Thailand; Parasitology and Tropical Medicine Association of Thailand; Radioisotope Society of the Philippines; New York Academy of Sciences; American Society of Primatologists; Academie Universelle de Lausanne; International Biographical Association. *Publications:* Two books on Research Methodology and Application of Radioisotopes in Medical Diagnosis and Research. Over 100 research publications in professional journals of medical and biological fields. *Honour:* First Prize for best research work in field of Medical Sciences from National Research Council of Thailand, 1976. *Hobbies:* Travel; Collecting stamps. *Address:* 39/75 Soi Lad Prao 23, Lad Prao Road, Bangkok 10900, Thailand.

ARIAS, Maria E Villalaz de, b. 11 Feb. 1930, Panama. Physician (Otolaryngology). m. Rogelio E Arias, 10 June 1961, Panama, 2 sons. *Education:* MD, Faculty of Medicine, University of Buenos Aires, Argentina, 1954; Revalidation of Doctor's qualification, University of Panama, 1958. *Appointments:* House Doctor, Otolaryngology, Santo Tomas Hospital, Panama City, 1957-60; Specialist, Social Security Hospital, 1960; Head of Service, Othorhinolaryngology, Social Security Hospital, 1979; Professor (Ear, Nose & Throat), University of Panama. *Memberships:* Panamenian Medical Association (President since 1983); Panamenian ENT Society; Panamenian Association of ENT & BE; World Association of ENT. *Publications:* Over 30 learned articles in medical journals. *Hobbies:* Music; Poetry (writing). *Address:* P.O. Box 4682, Panama 5, Republic of Panama.

ARIS, Alejandro, b. 27 Apr. 1943, Barcelona, Spain. Chief of Cardiac Surgery Unit. m. Montse Casas, 10 Dec. 1966, Barcelona, 3 daughters. *Education:* MD, Medicine and Surgery, University of Barcelona Medical School, 1966; Diplomate, American Board of Surgery; Specialist in Cardiovascular and Thoracic Surgery, Spain; FACS; FACP. *Appointments:* Intern, Washington Hospital Center; Surgical Resident, Maimonides Hospital, Brooklyn and Sinai Hospital of Detroit, USA; Resident in Thoracic and Cardiovascular Surgery, Medical College of Wisconsin, USA; Attending Surgeon, Hospital Sta. Creu i Sant Pau, Barcelona, Spain. *Memberships:* American College of Surgeons; Society of Thoracic Surgeons; International Society for Cardiovascular Surgery; American College of Chest Physicians; Spanish Society of Cardiovascular Surgery; Spanish Society of Cardiology; Catalanian Society of Cardiac Surgery; Catalonian Society of Cardiology. *Publications:* More then 100 papers in journals related to Cardiovascular Surgery; Two chapters in books of Cardiology. *Hobbies:* Travel;

Photography. *Address:* Capitan Arenas 48-50, 08034 Barcelona, Spain.

ARMAND, Jean Pierre, b. 14 Oct 1943, Constantine, Medical Oncology Service, Institut Gustave Roussy, Villejuif, France. *Education:* MD, Universite Paul Sabathier, Toulouse, France Master, Hematology; Master, Oncology; Master, Immunology. *Appointments:* Assistant Professor, University Paul Sabathier, Toulouse, France, 1973-74; Head, Department of Medical Oncology, Cancer Institute, Toulouse, France, 1976-84. *Memberships:* Member, ASCO; Member, ESMO; Chairman, Clinical Screening Group, EORTC. *Address:* Department Medical Oncology, Institut Gustave Roussy, 36 Av Camille Desmoulins, Villejuif, 94805 France.

ARMENIAN, Haroutune Krikor, b. 18 June 1942, Lebanon. Dean, Faculty of Health Sciences. m. Sona Terzian, 20 June 1971, Beirut, 1 son, 1 daughter. *Education:* BS, MD, American University of Beirut (AUB), 1968; MPH, Dr.P.H., Johns Hopkins University, USA. *Appointments include:* Assistant Professor, Epidemiology, AUB, 1974-79; Coordinator, Office of Professional Standards & Systems Analysis, Ministry of Health, Bahrain, 1976-81; Associate Professor, Epidemiology, AUB, 1979-84; Senior Associate in Epidemiology, Johns Hopkins University, 1980-; Professor of Epidemiology, AUB, 1984-. *Memberships:* Fellow, American College of Epidemiology; International Epidemiological Association; Lebanese Order of Physicians; American Public Health Association. *Publications include:* Numerous contributions to professional journals, conference proceedings, etc. *Honours:* Alpha Omega Alpha, 1979; Delta Omega, Alpha Chapter, 1985. *Hobbies:* Watercolour painting; Tennis. *Address:* Dean, Faculty of Health Sciences, American University of Beirut, Beirut, Lebanon.

ARNESJØ, Bo Anders, b. 21 Mar. 1934, Gothenborg, Sweden. Professor of Surgery. m. Bodil Anita Arnesjø, 21 Aug. 1959. *Education:* Candidate in Medicine, 1955, Licentiate in medicine, 1961, University of Stockholm; MD, University of Lund, 1968. *Appointments:* Surgical Training, Departments of Surgery, Seraphimerlasarettet, Stockholm, Krisianstad Central Hospital, University Hospital, Lund, in Sweden; Assistant Professor, Department of Surgery, University Hospital, Lund, 1969-75; Medical Director, Head, Department of Surgery, Central Hospital, Karlskrona, 1975-80; Professor of Surgery, Head, Department of Surgery, Chairman, Surgical Institute, Haukeland University Hospital, Bergen, Norway, 1981-. *Memberships:* Medical Advisory Board, Health Directorate, Norway; Co-editor, European Journal of Surgical Oncology; Executive Committee, European Society of Surgical Oncology; Member of Several editorial Boards. *Publications:* Numerous publications within Gastroenterology, Oncology, Surgical & Hospital administration. *Honours:* Sailing; Tennis. *Address:* Department of Surgery, 5016 Haukeland University Hospital, Bergen, Norway.

ARNOLD, Gayle Gardner, b. 5 Oct. 1920, Kentucky, USA. Professor of Paediatrics. m. Elizabeth Key Boyle, 17 Nov. 1945, Washington, District of Columbia, 2 sons, 1 daughter. *Education:* AB, Johns Hopkins University, 1938-42; MD, University of Maryland School of Medicine, 1942-45; Rotating Interne, Union Memorial Hospital, Baltimore, 1945-46; Assistant Resident (Medicine), University Hospital, Baltimore, 1948-49, with Baltimore city TB Hosptial, Sydenham Infectious Diseases Hospital & Shepherd-Pratt Psychiatric Hospital; Assistant Resident (Paediatrics), Duke Hospital, Durham, North Carolina, 1949-50, with Watts Hospital, Durham, Charity Hospital, New Orleans, Louisiana; Chief Resident, Children's Memorial Hospital, Montreal, Canada, 1950-51. *Appointments:* Teaching Fellow, McGill University, Montreal,

Canada, 1950-51; Instructor, Associate, Associate Clinical Professor of Paediatrics, 1980-. *Memberships:* American Board of Paediatrics; American Academy of Paediatrics; American Academy for Cerebral Palsy; Board of Directors, 1977-. *Publications:* Various articles & book chapters in field of paediatrics. *Hobbies:* Music; Travel. *Address:* 3603 Grove Avenue, Richmond, VA 23221, USA.

ARNOLD, Lawrence Eugene, b. 16 Feb. 1936, Zanesville, Ohio, USA. Professor of Psychiatry and Paediatrics. m. Billie Marie Crowley, 26 Dec. 1961, Zanesville, Ohio, 3 sons, 2 daughters. *Education:* BS, University of Dayton, Ohio, USA, 1959; MD, Ohio State University, 1963; M.Ed. Johns Hopkins University, 1969. *Appointments:* Rotating Internship, University of Oregon, USA, 1963-64; Psychiatry Residency, Johns Hopkins University, 1964-66; Staff Psychiatrist, St. Elizabeth's Hospital, Washington DC, 1966-68; Child Psychiatry Residency, Johns Hopkins University, 1968-70; Professor of Psychiatry and Paediatrics, Director, Division of Child Psychiatry, Ohio State University, 1973-85; Vice Chairman, Department of Psychiatry, 1985-. *Memberships:* Fellow, American Academy of Child Psychiatry; Fellow, American Psycahiatric Association; Society of Professors of Child Psychiatry; American Orthopsychiatric Association; American Medical Association. *Publications:* "Helping Parents to Help Their Children", 1978; "Preventing Adolescent Alienation", 1983; "Parents' Survival Handbook", 1983; "Parents, Children and Change", 1985; "Parent-Child Group Therapy", 1985. *Honours:* Nu Sigma Nu Award, 1962; C.V. Mosby Book Award, 1963. *Hobbies:* Bridge; Gardening; Writing. *Address:* Department of Psychiatry, Ohio State University, Columbus, OH 43210, USA.

ARNOLD, Philip Bruno, b. 14 Aug. 1941, New Haven, Connecticut, USA. Director, Department of Physical Medicine and Rehabilitation. m. Alison Richter, 17 July 1965, White Plains, New York, 2 sons. *Education:* BA, Yale University, 1963; MD, Tufts Medical School, 1967; Internship, Maine Medical Center, 1968; Residency, Letterman Army Medical Center, 1971; Board Certified PM & R, 1973. *Appointments:* Assistant Chief, PM&R, US Army Letterman Medical Center; Director, PM&R, Gaylord Hospital, Wallingford, Connecticut; Director, PM&R, Danbury Hospital, Danbury, Connecticut; Director, department of PM&R, Newington Children's Hospital, Newington, Connecticut. *Memberships:* American Academy of Physical Medicine and Rehabilitation; American Congress of Rehabilitation Medicine; American association of electromyography, electrodiagnosis; American Medical Association; Connecticut Medical Society; National Spinal Injury Association; American Spinal Injury Association. *Publications:* 'Rehabilitation in Acute Hospital', 'Connecticut Medicine', 1984; 'Prevention of TBI and Spinal Injuries', 'Emergency Medical Quarterly', 1985. *Honours:* American Medical Association Physician Recognition Award, 1972; Certificate of Achievement, US Army, 1973; Special Award for Recognition of Service to Spinal People, Connecticut Spinal Cord Injury Association, 1982; The James Schemittkamp Award for Service to Spinal Cord Injured People and the National Spinal Cord Injury Association, 1984. *Hobbies:* Racquet Ball; Minerals; Gems; Wood Working. *Address:* Newington Children's Hospital, Newington, CT 06111, USA.

ARNOLD, Richard Byron, b. 27 Aug. 1937, West Virginia, USA. Epidemiologist, Immunization Programme, Ministry of Health, Jakarta, Indonesia. m. Suzanne Abrahamson, 13 Apr. 1968, 3 sons. *Education:* MD, West Virginia University, School of Medicine, 1962; DTPH, University of London, School of Hygiene and Tropical Medicine, England, 1966. *Appointments:* Epidemiologist: Smallpox Eradication Programme, Centres for Disease Control, Atlanta, Georgia, assigned to Kaduna, Nigeria, 1968-71: Director, Cochise County Health Department, Bisbee, Arizona, 1973-78; Deputy Health Officer, Santa Barbara County, 1978-80; Epidemiologist, Immunization Programme, Ministry of Health, Republic of Indonesia, Jakarta, 1980-85. *Memberships:* Royal Society of Tropical Medicine & Hygiene; American Public Health Association; American Medical Association; American Society of Tropical Medicine & Hygiene. *Publications:* "A Neutralization Test Survey for Lassa Fever Activity in Lass, Nigeria", 'Royal Society of Tropical Medicine & Hygiene', Volume 71, 1977. *Hobbies:* Swimming; Tennis; Microcomputer; History. *Address:* c/O USAID, Box 4, APO San Francisco, CA 96356, USA.

ARNOLD, William Wright III, b. 10 Dec. 1948, Long Beach, California, USA. Deputy Hospital Director. m. Joan Doell, 18 Dec 1971, San Gabriel, California, 2 sons. *Education:* BA, University of Washington, 1972; MPH, UCLA, 1974. *Appointments include:* Hospital Administration Resident, 1974; Administrative Assistant to Administrator 1974, Assistant Administrator, 1975-79, Santa Barbara Cottage Hospital, Santa Barbara, California; Assistant Director, 1982-83, Senior Associate Director, 1982-84, Deputy Director, 1984 – Stanford University Hospital, Stanford, California. *Memberships:* American College of Hospital Administrators; Health Care Executives of Northern California; Advisory Council of College of Notre Dame. *Honour:* W Glenn Ebersole Merit Award, 1974. *Hobbies:* Hiking; Backpacking; Sailing; Running. *Address:* 2609 Alpine Road, Menlo Park, CA 94025, USA.

ARNOLD, Wolfgang, b. 22 Nov. 1941, Munich, Germany. Head, Department of Otolaryngology, Head and Neck Surgery. m. Dr Christa Möhler, 5 Dec. 1970, Munich, 2 sons. *Education:* MD, University of Munich, 1967; Dr med habil, University of Frankfurt, 1973; Associate Professor, University of Dusseldorf, 1977, University of Munich, 1981. *Appointments:* Scientific Assistant, Max Planck Institute of Psychiatry, Munich, 1969-70; ENT Resident, 1970-73, Chief Resident, 1973-77, University of Frankfurt; Associate Professor, University of Dusseldorf, 1977-81, University of Munich, 1981; Head, Department of Otolaryngology, Head and Neck Surgery, Kantonsspital Lucerne, Lucerne, Switzerland, currently. *Memberships:* German, Austrian and Swiss Societies of Otolaryngology Head and Neck Surgery; German Society of Laser Surgery. *Publications:* Author of over 130 scientific publications in German, Swedish and American journals and 2 handbook chapters; Chief Editor 'Journal ofOtolaryngology' and 'Diseases of the Head and Neck Atlas of Histopathology'. *Honours:* Corresponding Member: French Society of Otolaryngology, 1975; American Association of Research in ORL, 1977. Honorary Member, Greek Society ORL, 1979; Member, Collegium Otorhinolaryngologicum Amicitiae, 1978. *Hobbies:* Classical Music; String quartets; Sailing. *Address:* Breitenstrasse, CH-6047 Kastanienbaum, Switzerland.

ARNTZENIUS, Alexander Cornelis, b. 15 Juen 1922, Den Haag, The Netherlands. Emeritus Professor of Cardiology. m. Mary Rose Burnet, 18 Aug. 1951, Kilmacolm, Scotland, 2 sons. *Education:* MD, Leiden University, Leiden, The Netherlands, 1951. *Appointments:* General Practitioner, 1952-58; Senior Registrar in Cardiology 1963-69, Professor of Cardiology 1972-84, Emeritus Professor of Cardiology 1984-, Leiden University; Lecturer in Cardiology, Rotterdam University, 1969-72. *Memberships:* Dutch Society of Cardiology; American College of Cardiology; Fellow, Royal College of Physicians and Surgeons of Glasgow. *Publications include:* "Praktische elektrocardiografée" (with A A H Meurs), 1984; 128 medical publications including; 'Reduced HDL in women aged 40-41 using oral contraceptives' 'Diet,

lipoproteins and the progression of coronary atherosleroisis: The Leiden Intervention Trial' (with D Kromhout, J D Barth and others); Contribution to 'The New England Journal of Medicine', 1985. *Hobby:* Playing the viola. *Address:* Van Voorschotenlaan 24, 2597 PB, Den Haag, The Netherlands.

ARNY, Richard Andrew, b. 24 July 1947, Akron, Ohio, USA. Doctor of Chiropractic. m. Billie Jean Miller, 6 Mar. 1971, Barberton, 2 sons, 1 daughter. *Education:* BA, Anderson College: RT, USAMC; BS, DC, National College. *Appointments:* Secretary, TCC.A, 1981-85; Key Man, OSCA, 1983-85. *Memberships:* American Chiropractic Association; Ohio State Chiropractic Association; Tricounty Chiropractic Association; Parker Chiropractic Research Foundation; Ohio Kinesiology Association; Acupuncture Society of America. *Hobbies:* Tennis; Swimming. *Address:* 2830 Copley Road, Akron, OH 44321, USA.

ARORA, Tejinder Singh, b. 7 Aug. 1939, Murree, India. Internist. m. Baljit Kaur, 6 June 1978, New Delhi, 1 son, 2 daughters. *Education:* MB BS; FICA; FCCP; FRCP; FACP; FISCD; FIAMS; FRSM. *Appointments:* Research Fellow, Internal Medicine, Irwin Hospital, New Delhi, 1963-65; Intern, Iocum, London, England, 1965; Residencies, Wales, England, 1965-67; Chief Resident, Withington and Wythenshawe Hospitals, 1967-69; Junior Attending Physician, Withington Hospital, 1972; Internist, Family Practice, New Delhi, India, 1970-73; Internist, Family Practice and Clinical Cardiology, Kuwait, 1973-. *Memberships:* Fellow, Royal Society of Medicine; International College of Angiology; Indian Academy of Medical Specialists; American College of Chest Physicians. *Publications:* Contributions to 'British Journal of Clinical Practice'; 'British Medical Journal'; 'Journal of Association of Physicians of India'; 'American Review of Respiratory Diseases'; 'Postgraduate Medical Journal'; 'Case Report and Review'; 'Diabetes Care'. *Hobbies:* Walking; Jogging; Music. *Address:* PO Box 18049, Farwania, Kuwait.

ARROYAVE, Fernando, b. 21 Mar. 1934, Colombia, South America. Medical Director, Regional Alcoholism Unit, Oxford. m. Doris Arroyave /Jaramillo, 8 June 1966, Bogota, 1 son, 2 daughters. *Education:* Medico Cirujano, Salamanca University, Spain; MA Oxon; FRC.Psych.; M.Inst.G.A.; Assoc.M.SAP; Honorary Clinical Lecturer, Psychiatry, University of Oxford. *Appointments:* Neurologist, Red Cross Hopital, Madrid, Spain, 1962-64; Psychiatrist, Littlemore Hospital, Oxford, England, 1964-67; Research Psychiatrist, Littlemore Hospital, Oxford, 1967-; Consultant Psychiatrist, Oxford Regional Health Authority, 1975-; Medical Director, Oxford Regional Alcoholism Unit, 1979-. *Memberships:* Fellow, Royal College of Psychiatrists, London; Institute of Group analysis, London; Associate Member, Society of Analytical Psychology; International Association for Analytical Psychology. *Publications:* Articles on Alcohol and Drug Dependence, 1973-; Book Chapter, on Alcohol and Drug Dependence. *Honour:* MA, Oxon, 1984. *Hobbies:* Theatre; Reading; Travel. *Address:* Foxcombe Field, Fox Lane, Boars Hill, Oxford OX1 5DR, England.

ARSAC, Michel Louis Paul, b. 7 Oct. 1923, Paris, France. Professor of Clinical Surgery. m. Ghislaine Candeliez, 22 Nov. 1956, Paris, 2 sons. *Education:* Lycee Janson de Sailly; Baccalaureat in Classics. *Appointments:* Intern, Paris Hospitals; Surgeon, Paris Hospitals, 1966; Certified Professor, Faculty of Paris, 1966; Professor of Clinical Surgery, 1978. *Memberships:* Academy of Surgery, France; International Society of Surgery. *Publications:* Serveral publications about gastro-intestinal, biliary and pancreatic surgery. *Address:* Hopital Laennec, 42 rue de Sèvres, Paris, §eme, France.

ARSENOVIC, Alexander, b. 19 Dec. 1928, Beograd.

Geriatrician-Internist. m. Vukosava, 1 son, 1 daughter. *Education:* MD, University of Beograd Medical School, 1953; Specialty Board, Internist-Infectologist, 1958; ECMFG Exam, Nostrification (USA), 1968; Diploma, American Board of Family Practice, 1979; Diploma American Board of Quality Assurance, 1979. *Appointments:* Practicing Internist, Chief of Clinical Laboratory, Polyclinic Vracar, Belgrade, 1958-68; Practicing General Internist, Williamsport, Pennsylvania, USA, 1974-76; Kansas City Medical Center, Chief of Medical Department, Downtown Hospital, Kansas City, Missouri, 1977-80; Practicing Internist and Geriatrician, VA Hospital, Topeka, Kansas, 1980-86. *Memberships:* American Medical Association; Fellow, American Academy of Family Practice; Fellow, American Geriatrics Society; Fellow, American College of Uticis Physicians; Associate Member, Federation of State Medical Boards, USA; American Society of Law and Medicine, etc. *Publication:* "Viral Cause of Neoplasms (Theory)", 1966. *Honours Include:* Awards American Medical Association, 1974, 77, 80, 85. *Address:* 1820 West 32 Street, Topeka, KS 66611, USA.

ARTIS, Daphne Maria Jones, b. 31 Mar. 1956, New Jersey, USA. Licensed Clinical Psychologist, Private Practice. m. Ronald E. Artis, 16 Oct 1982, Orange. *Education:* BA, Princeton University, 1977; Psy.D., Rutgers University Graduate School of Applied & Professional Psychology, 1982. *Appointments:* Volunteer, Trenton Psychiatric Hospital, 1975-77; Programme Coordinator, Young Womens Christian Association, 1977-78; Director, Professor, Psychology Trainee, Rutgers University, 1978-80; Programme Consultant, College of Medicine & Dentistry, New Jersey, 1979-80; Predoctoral Psychology, Intern-Family & Child Guidance Centre, N.Orange County, 1980-81; Psychological Assistant, Ronald W. Jue Inc., Fullerton, 1982-85. *Memberships:* American Psychological Association; Association of Black Psychologists; Child Sexual Abuse Network of Orange County. *Honours:* Family and Child Guidance Centre Recognition of Performance, 1981; Afro-American Studies Certificate, 1977; Student Volunteer Committee Certificate of Outstanding Work, 1976; Bambergers Award of Scholarship, 1973; National Honour Society, 1972; many other awards and recognitions. *Address:* 11872 Melody Park Drive, Garden Grove, CA 92640, USA.

ARULKUMARAN, Sabaratnam, b. 17 Jan. 1948, Jaffna, Sri Lanka. Senior Lecturer and Consultant, National University of Singapore. m. Gayathri Muthuthamby, 9 Nov. 1975, Colombo, 1 son, 1 daughter. *Education:* MB BS, DCH, University of Ceylon, 1972, 78; FRCS, Edinburgh, 1979; LRCP & MRCS, London, 1979; MRCOG, UK, 1980; AM, Academy of Medicine, Singapore, 1980; FICS, International College of Surgeons, USA, 1984. *Appointments:* House Officer, Castle Street Hospital, 1972; Registrar, Paediatrics, Colombo North Hospital, 1974; Registrar, Obstetrics and Gynaecology, Castle Street Hospital, 1975-77; Registrar, Accident and Emergency Department, Colombo, 1978; Registrar, Obstetrics and Gynaecology, Maelor General Hospital, Wrexham, Wales, 1978-81; Lecturer, Senior Lecturer, Department of Obstetrics and Gynaecology, National University of Singapore, 1982-85. *Memberships:* Medical Protection Society, UK; General Medical Council, UK; Academy of Medicine, Singapore; International College of Surgeons, USA. *Publications:* Contributor of papers, articles, etc. to professional journals including: 'British Journal of Obstetrics and Gynaecology'; 'American Journal of Obstetrics and Gynaecology'; 'International Journal of Obstetrics and Gynaecology'; 'Singapore Journal of Obstetrics and Gynaecology', etc. Papers presented to Congresses worldwide. *Honours Include:* Gold Award for contribution to teamwork and improvements in the public service, Public Sector WITs convention, Singapore, 1983. *Hobbies:* Sports including Basketball and Hockey. *Address:* Department of Obstetrics and Gynaecology, National University Hospital, Lower Kent Ridge Road, Singapore 0511.

ARVILOMMI, Heikki Sakari, b. 18 Oct. 1939, Kotka, Finland. Professor. m. Pirjo Riitta Santalahti, 25 May 1962, 2 sons, 1 daughter. *Education:* Licentiate in Medicine, 1965; MD, 1973; Reader in Immunology, 1983. *Appointments:* Assistant Professor of Bacteriology & Serology, Turku University, 1969-71; Head of National Public Health Institute, Jyväskylä. *Memberships:* British Society of Immunology; American Society for Microbiology; Scandinavian Society of Immunology; several Finnish professional societies. *Publications:* Various publications in field of Immunology & Microbiology. *Hobby:* Music. *Address:* Hannikaisenkatu 11-13 B29, SF-40620 Jyväskylä, Finland.

ARYASINGHA, Chand Jasen, b. 21 Feb. 1936, Sri Lanka, Physician. m. Luxshimi Aryasingha, 12 May 1972, Colombo. *Education:* MD; Diplomate, American Board of Obstetrics and Gynecology. *Appointments:* Associate Professor in Anatomy, University of Ceylon, Colombo; Chief Resident, Obstetrics and Gynaecology, De Soysa Hospital for Women, Colombo, and Saint James Hospital, London, England; Chief Resident, Obstetrics and Gynecology, Attending Physician, California Hospital, Los Angeles, California, USA. *Memberships:* Fellow, American College of Obstetrics and Gynecology; Fellow, Los Angeles Obstetrics and Gynecology Society; Royal College of Obstetricians and Gynaecologists; American Association of Sex Education. *Publications:* 2 articles in medical journals on obstetrics and gynaecology, 1971 and 1983. *Hobbies:* Tennis; Skiing; Swimming; Dancing; Music. *Address:* 3120 Kingridge Way, Glendale, CA 91206, USA.

ASHDEN, Richard Neil, b. 21 Dec. 1942, Binghamton, New York, USA. Doctor of Chiropractic. m. Laura Carol Correale, 15 May 1978, Fort Lee, New Jersey. *Education:* BA, University of City of New York, 1971; Doctor of Chiropractic, New York Chiropractic College, 1979; International College of Kinesiology, 1981; Certificate, Graduate Division, Texas Chiropractic College, 1983; Independent Medical Examiner, Los Angeles Chiropractic College Graduate Division, 1985; PhD Candidate, Donsbach University; Fellow, International Academy of Clinical Acupuncture. *Appointments:* Analytical Chemist, New York; Associate Faculty Member, 1983-84, Reserve Faculty List, 1984-85, Cochise College, Sierra Vista, Arizona; Vice President, Cochise County Counselling Services Advisory Council, 1985-. *Memberships:* Council Member, American Chiropractic Association; Fellow, International Academy of Clinical Acupuncture; Occidental Institute of Chinese Studies; Diplomate, National Board of Chiropractic Examiners; Flower Essence Homeopathic Society. *Publications:* "Nutrition's Dynamic Role in Wholistic Therapy", PhD thesis and book. *Honours:* Arista Honour Society, 1960; Political Science National Honour Society, 1971; Phi Chi Omega, 1979; Nationai Deans List, 1978. *Hobbies:* Hiking; Swimming; Toastmasters International; Contract bridge; Chess. *Address:* Route 2 Box 550C, Sierra Vista, AZ 85635, USA.

ASHERSON, Geoffrey Lister, b. 21 Oct. 1929, London, England. Head, Division of Immunological Medicine, Clinical Research Centre, Harrow. m. Barbara Ann Armstrong, 6 Apr. 1952, London, 2 sons, 1 daughter. *Education:* BA, Physiology, Oxford; MA (Oxon) 1953, BM, 1953, Oxford & University College Hospital Medical School; DCH (London) 1957; DM (Oxon) 1963; FRCP (Edinburgh) 1971; FRCP 1973; FRCPath 19073; MSc, Synthetic Organic Chemistry, National Council for Academic Awards; BM, Jesus College, Oxford and UCH, London. *Memberships:* British Society of Immunology (International Secretary, Past General Secretary); Pathology Society; Biochemical Association; American Immunological Association; Royal Society of Medicine (Former President, Section of Immunology and Allergy); Royal Institution (Former Visitor). *Publication:* Co-author: "Diagnosis and Treatment of Immune Deficiency

Diseases", 1981; contributor to scientific journals. *Hobbies:* Walking; Theatre; Italian. *Address:* Division of Immunological Medicine, Clinical Reasearch Centre, Watford Road, Harrow HA1 3UJ, England.

ASHLEY, Mark James, b. 9 Aug. 1956, Ogdensburg, New York, USA. Executive Director, Centre for Neuro Skills. m. Susan Marie Hess, 12 Sep. 1975, 2 sons. *Education:* BSc, Speech Pathology, State University College of Arts and Sciences, Geneseo, New York, 1977; MSc, Speech Pathology, Southern Illinois University, Carbondale, Illinois, USA, 1978. *Appointments:* Rehabilitation Assistant, Centre for Comprehensive Services, Carbondale, Illinois, 1977-78; Research Assistant, Southern Illinois University, Carbondale, Illinois, 1977-78; Clinical Supervisor, Speech Pathology Inc., Bakersfield, California, 1979-80; Executive Director, Centre for Neuro Skills, Bakersfield, California, 1980-. *Memberships:* National Student Speech and Hearing Association, 1977-78; President, 1978; American Speech and Hearing Association; California Speech and Hearing Association; National Rehabilitation Association; National Rehabilitation Counselors; National Rehabilitation Administration Association; National Association for Independent Living; American Congress of Physical Medicine and Rehabilitation; National Head Injury Foundation; Traumatic Head Injury Professional Association of California; Advisory Board, Kern County Head Injury Support Group. *Publications:* Co-Author: "A Descriptive Study of the Relationship of Introral Air Pressure to EMG Activity of the Levator palatini during CV Syllables", Folia phoniat, in press, 1985. *Honours:* New York State Regents Scholarship, 1974-77; Research Assistantship, Jan.-Dec. 1978; Adjunct Professor, Department of Communication Disorders and Sciences, Southern Illinois University, Carbondale, Illinois, 1985. *Hobbies:* Vocal Music; Guitar; Piano; Golf; Salt water Aquaria; Raquetball; Antique clock collecting. *Address:* 2658 Mount Vernon, Bakersfield, CA 93306, USA.

ASHTON, Geoffrey C, b. 5 July 1925, Croydon, England. Chairman and Professor, University Department of Genetics. m. Joyce K Stanley, 17 Feb. 1951, Birmingham, 1 son, 3 daughters. *Education:* BSc honours, PhD, DSc, University of Liverpool. *Appointments:* Glaxo Laboratories Limited, 1950-56; Farm Livestock Research Centre, 1956-58; Division of Animal Genetics, Commonwealth Scientific and Industrial Research Organisation, Australia, 1958-64; Chairman and Professor, Department of Genetics, School of Medicine, University of Hawaii, Honolulu, Hawaii, USA, 1965-. *Memberships:* Behavior Genetics Association; American Society for Human Genetics; Society for Applied Learning Technology. *Publications include:* Over 80 publications including: 'Handedness: an alternative hypothesis', 1982; 'Mental abilities of children of incross and outcross matings in Hawaii', 1983; 'Segregation analysis of ocular refraction and myopia', 1985. *Honours:* Junior 1936, Senior 1942 and Research 1945, Scholarships, City of Liverpool; Highly cited article, Science Citation Index, 1984. *Hobby:* Travel. *Address:* Department of Genetics, School of Medicine, 1960 East-West Road, Honolulu, HI 96821, USA.

ASKENASI, Robert Samy, b. 11 Aug. 1939, Brussels, Belgium. Professor of Internal Medicine. m. Anne Neuckens, 15 July 1963, La Hulpe, Belgium, 2 daughters. *Education:* MD, Université Libre de Bruxelles, 1965; Specialist in Internal Medicine, 1970. *Appointments:* Head of Emergency Department, Brugmann Hospital, University of Brussels, 1974-77; Associate Professor of Internal Medicine. *Memberships:* Sociètè Belge de Soins Intensifs; University Association for Emergency Medicine. *Publications:* "Manuel de Medecine d'Urgence", 2nd edition 1985; "Manuel d'formation médicale de l'Infirmière d'Urgence", 1985. *Hobbies:* Classical Guitar; Photography. *Address:* Service des Urgences, Hôpital Erasme, route de Lennik, B-1070 Brussels, Belgium.

ASOKAN, Nedumgayil Narayanan, b. 24 May, 1935, Cochin, India. Clinical Cardiologist; Medical Superintendent; Chief Consultant Physician. m. Smt Soudamini, 28 August, 1966, Cochin, India, 2 sons. *Education:* BSc; MBBS; MD; FCCP: FICA: FCGP(I). *Appointments:* Tutor, Jawaharlal Institute of Psot Graduate Medical Education and Research, Pondicherry, India, 1962-65; Clinical Cardiologist, Medical Superintendent, Chief Consultant Physician, Shantinikethan Hospital, Muvattupuzha-686 673, Kerala State, India –. *Memberships include:* Indian Society for Clinical Pharmacology and Therapeutics; Obstetric and Gynaecological Society of India; Indian Medical Association; Association of Physicians of India; Diabetic Association of India; Cardiological Society of India; Indian Chest Society; National Council on Hypertension; Indian Society of Electro Cardiology; Nutrition Society of India. *Publications include:* 'Primary Pulmonary Tuberculosis in Adolescents and Adults' in the 'Indian Practitioner', 1982; 'Dopamine in Shock – a Preliminary Report on its Uses in Few Cases' in 'Kerala Medical Journal', 1982; 'Febrile Convulsion in Children (A Critical Evaluation of Prognosis and Drug Therapy' in 'The Antiseptic' 1983; 'Comparative Study of Serum Cholesterol Triglycerides and Impaired Glucose Tolerance in Obese and Non Obese Subjects' in Kerala Medical Journal', 1983. *Hobby:* Reading. *Address:* Shantinikethan Hospital, Muvattupuzha-686 673, Kerala State, India.

ASSEF, Abraham, b. 17 Apr. 1928, Australia. Senior Partner, Abesway Medical Practice. m. Olga Voloshin, 31 Dec. 1955, London, 1 son. *Education:* MBBS, Sydney University, 1953; Dip.Obst.RCOG, London University, 1957; FRACGP, 1974; Diploma, Practice Management; Fellow, Australian Association Practice Managers, 1982. *Appointments:* RMO, Tamworth Base Hospital, 1953-54; SHO, Prince of Wales' Hospital, London, 1955-56; Chairman, Canterbury-Bankstown Branch, AMA, 1962; Trainer for Family Medicine Programme, RACGP, 1974-; College Representative, ACOSH, 1977; NSW Faculty Treasurer, 1980-84; Faculty Board, 1979-; Chairman, Practice Management Committee, NSW Faculty, 1978-81; Chairman, Computer Sub-Committee PMC, 1979-84; Practice Management Committee of Council, 1981-; President, NSW Branch, AAPM, 1981-83; National President, AAPM, 1985-; Managing Editor, 'Practice Computing', 1984-. *Memberships:* Australian Medical Association; Sydney University Union; Royal Australian College of General Practitioners; Australian Association of Practice Managers; Affiliate, Australian Computer Society. *Publications:* "How to Succeed in Practice by Really Trying", 'Australian Family Physician', 1982; "Smoking Cessation in General Practice", 'Australian Alcohol /Drug Review', 1984; "The Practice Computer – How Long Before You Leap?", 'Practice Computing', 1984; "Online Support for Medical Practitioners", 'Practice Computing', 1986. *Hobbies:* Walking; Music; Art; Food & Wine; Literature. *Address:* 229 The River Road, Revesby, NSW 2212, Australia.

ASTACIO SORIA, Jose Nicolas, b. 22 Oct. 1928, El Salvador, Central America. Chief, Department of Pathology, Instituto Salvadoreno del Seguro Social Medical Center. m. Maria Flora Garcia Prieto, 26 July 1967, El Salvador. *Education:* MD; Training in Pathology, Massachusetts General Hospital Department of Pathology, Boston, Massachusetts, USA (Harvard Medical School). *Appointments:* Asociate Professor, Department of Pathology, University of El Salvador Medical School; Director, Teaching Department, Instituto Salvadoreno del

Seguro Social Medical Center. *Memberships:* Colegio Medico de El Salvador; Associacion Salvadorena de Patologia; Sociedad de Medicina Interna de El Salvador; Associacion Centro Americana de Patologia; Associacion Mexicana de Patologos, Sociedad Latino Americana de Patologia; International Academy of Pathology; International Society of Gynecological Pathologist. *Publications:* Patologia de la Sangre y los Organos Hematopoyeticos en Texto de Patologia; La prensa Medica Mexicana, 1970 and 1975; Escleroma: Experiencias en El Salvador, 1971; Patologia Oncologica del sistema Oseo, 1980. *Honours:* 7 Diplomas, Colegio Medico de El Salvador, 1962, /64, 70, 74, 75, 77; 3 Diplomas, Inst. Salvador Seg. Social, 1977, 79, 80; 6 Diplomas and 1 silver plate, 1977. *Hobbies:* Music; Beach Exercises. *Address:* Department of Pathology, Medical Center, Instituto Salvadoreno Del Seguro Social, San Salvador, El Salvador, Central America.

ASTRAND, Irma Linnéa, b. 13 Mar. 1927, Falköping, Sweden. Professor of Work Physiology. m. Per-Olof Astrand, 14 July 1956, Bredaryd, 1 son, 1 daughter. *Education:* MD, Karolinska Institute, Stockholm, 1960. *Appointments:* Physician, medicine 1960-62, clinical physiology 1962-66, Serafimer Hospital; Assistant Professor, Institute Occupational Medicine, 1966; Professor of Work Physiology, Head of Section for Work Physiology, 1974, Head of Research Department 1981-, National Board of Occupational Safety and Health, Solna. *Memberships:* Royal Swedish Academy of Engineering Sciences; Member of the Board, Swedish Society of Medical Sciences; Member of the Board, Swedish Medical Research Council. *Publications:* Approximately 175 publications in exercise physiology and in toxicology including: "Exercise Physiology", in Swedish, textbook, 1977; "Effect of Physical Exercise on Uptake, Distribution and Elimination of Vapors in Man", 1983. *Hobbies:* Botany; Ornithology. *Address:* Research Department, National Board of Occupational Safety and Health, 17184 Solna, Sweden.

ATCHISON, Beth Elaine, b. 2 Dec. 1955, Saskatchewan, Canada. Medical Director, Geropsychiatry. *Education:* MD, University of Saskatchewan, Licentiate, Medical Council of Canada; Member, College of Family Physicians of Canada; Fellow, Royal College of Physicians of Canada. *Appointments:* Currently, Medical Director, Geropsychiatry, St Boniface General Hospital, Winnipeg, Manitoba, Canada. *Memberships:* College of Physicians and Surgeons of Manitoba; Canadian Psychiatric Association: Geriatric Psychiatry Section, World Psychiatric Association; Canadian Association of Gerontology; International Psychogeriatric Association. *Publications:* 'The Joint Mature Women's Clinic or Menopause Revisited' in 'Canadian Journal of Psychiatry', 1st author, 1983; 'The Menopause - Stressors and Facilitators' in 'Canadian Medical Association Journal', 1984. *Hobbies:* Sewing; Needlework; Painting; Furniture finishing. *Address:* Department of Psychiatry, M5 McEwen Building, St Boniface General Hospital, 409 Tache Avenue, Winnipeg, Canada R2H 2A6

ATERMAN, Kurt, b. 9 Sep. 1913, Bielitz. Director of Laboratories. m. Rita Lawrence, Birmingham, England, 3 sons. *Education:* M U DR, Charles University, Prague, Czechoslovakia; MB ChB BAO Hons, Queens University, Belfast. DCH, London; MRCP, London; PhD, University of Birmingham; DSc, Queens University, Belfast. *Appointments include:* Senior Lecturer, University of Birmingham, and University of London 1950-58; Associate Professor, Department of Pathology, Dalhousie University, Halifax, Canada 1958-61; Professor, Department of Pathology, Woman's Medical College, Pennsylvania, 1961-63; Professor, Department of Pathology, State University New York at Buffalo, 1963-67; Professor, Department of Pathology, Dalhousie University, Halifax 1963-79.

Memberships: Pathology Society, Great Britain; Deutsche Gesellschaft fur Pathologie; Histochemical Society; American Society of Experimental Pathology; American Society of Pathologists and Bacteriologists; Internal Academy of Pathology, CAP, ASCP. *Publications:* 'The development of the concept of lysosomes. A historical survey with particular reference to the liver' "Histochemical Journal, 1979; 'Connective tissue an eclectic historical review with particular reference to the liver' Histochemical Journal 1981, etc. *Honours:* Commonwealth Fund Fellowship, Harvard University, 1948-50; May Cave Willet Fellowship, University of Chicago Hospital, 1956-57; Visiting Professor of Pathology, University of Wurzburg, Wuarzburg, Germany; Honorary Research Associate, Department of Biology, University of New Brunswick, Fredericton, New Brunswick. *Address:* 1722 Robie Street, Halifax, Nova Scotia, Canada B3H 3E8.

ATHANASOPOULOS, Constantin, b. 27 June 1935, Athens, Greece. Associate in Cardiology. m. Sophie Papanconstantinou, 1 Dec. 1973, Athens, 1 son, 1 daughter. *Education:* University of Athens Medical School, 1954-60, DSc, 1968; Resident in Internal Medicine, 1963-66, Fellow in Cardiology, 1966-68, General Hospital, Athens; Rotating Intern, Swedish Covenant Hospital, Chicago, Illinois, USA, 1968-69; Resident, Internal Medicine, University of Illinois, 1969-70; Fellow in Cardiology, University of Chicago, 1970-72; Fellow, Michael Reese Hospital and Medical Centre, Chicago, 1972; Greek Board of Internal Medicine, 1966, Cardiology, 1967; Boards of Education Council for Foreign Medical Graduates, 1967; American Boards of Internal Medicine, 1972; Licenced Physician and Surgeon, Illinois, USA, 1973. *Appointments:* Associate in Cardiology, Columbus-Cuneo Medical Centre, Chicago, Illinois, USA, 1972-73; Instructor in Cardiology, General Hospital, Athens, Greece, 1973-76; Director Department of Cardiology, General Hospital, Athens, 1976-78; Associate in Cardiology, Evangelismos Medical Centre, Athens, 1979-; Adjunct Professor of Cardiology, University of Athens, 1984; Professor of Medicine-Cardiology, State University of New York, 1985. *Memberships include:* Fellow: International Academy of Chest Physicians; American College of Chest Physicians. New York Academy of Sciences; American Medical Association; Panamerican Medical Association; International Society and Federation of Cardiology; European Heart Association. *Publications:* Contributor over 60 articles in English, French and Greek medical journals including: 'Journal of Nuclear Medicine'; 'British Heart Journal';'Acta Cardiologica'; 'Epidemiology Newsletter'. *Honours:* Fellowships of International and American organisations for Chest physicians. *Hobbies:* Sea Sports; Classical Music. *Address:* 23 Ypsilantou Street, Athens, 106-75, Greece.

ATHEY, Geoffrey Norman, b. 2 Sep. 1943, Rotherham, England. Consultant Radiologist, East Cumbria. m. Sheila Rosemary Court, 20 Sep. 1969, Tarleton, Lancashire, 2 sons. *Education:* MB, ChB, Manchester, 1967; DMRD 1973; FFR 1974; FRCR 1975. *Appointments include:* House surgeon, house physician, Manchester Royal Infirmary, 1967-68; Assistant Lecturer, Anatomy, University of Manchester, 1968-69; Senior house officer, surgery, 1969-70; Registrar, Radiology, Manchester Royal Infirmary, 1971-73; Senior registrar, radiology, 1973-76; Consultant radiologist, East Cumbria, 1976-. *Memberships:* British Institute of Radiology; Royal College of Radiologists; British Medical Ultrasound Society. *Publications include:* 'Unusual demonstration of a mecitel's diverticulum containing enterolitis', in 'British Journal of Radiology', 1980; 'Gastric ulcer, is endoscopy always necessary?', BMJ, 1981; 'Hepatic haematoma following blunt injury: non-operative management', 1982; etc. *Hobbies:* Walking; Birdwatching; Sailing; Gardening. *Address:* 36

Greenacres, Wetheral, Cumbria, CA4 8LD, England.

ATKINS, Joseph Preston, b. 1 May 1940, Red Lion, Pennsylvania, USA. Head, Section of Otorhinolaryngology and Human Communication. m. Maureen, 7 Aug. 1965, 2 sons, 2 daughters. *Education:* St. Joseph's College, Philadelphia, 1958-59; BS, Biology, Mount St. Mary's College, 1962; University of Pennsylvania School of Medicine, 1962-66; Internship, Pennsylvania Hospital, Philadelphia, 1966-67; Residency: Otolaryngology, 1967-68; General Surgery, 1968-69; Otolaryngology, 1969-71; Chief Residency, 1971-72. *Appointments:* Research Assistant, Graduate Hospital, University of Pennsylvania, 1964-65; Fellow in Laryngology and Otology, The Johns Hopkins University School of Medicine, 1967-72; Assistant Chief, Department of Otolaryngology, US Naval Hospital, Bethesda, 1972-74; Consultant, National Institute of Allergy and Infectious Diseases, 1972-74; Chief, Department of Otorhinolaryngology and Human Communication, Pennsylvania Hospital, Philadelphia, 1974-; Assistant Clinical Professor, Otorhinolaryngology and Human Consumption, University of Pennsylvania School of Medicine, Philadelphia, 1974-; Surgeon and Attending several hospitals. *Memberships include:* Fellow, American Academy of Ophthalmology and Otolaryngology; Fellow, American Academy of Facial Plastic and Reconstructive Surgery; Fellow, American Society for Head and Neck Surgery; Fellow, Society of Head and Neck Surgeons; Fellow, American College of Surgeons; American Medical Association. *Publications:* Contributor to Professional Journals, etc.; Presentations; Abstracts. *Honours include:* American Academy of Otolaryngology, Head and Neck Surgery Honor Award to acknowledge contributions to the Academy Education Programs, 1983. *Hobby:* Golf. *Address:* Pennsylvania Hospital, 8th & Spruce Streets, Philadelphia, PA 19107, USA.

ATTAH, Edward B., b. 23 Dec. 1937, Nigeria. Professor; Provost. m. Hyacinth M. Douglas, 13 June 1980, Kadune, 1 son, 5 daughters. *Education:* MB, BS, University College, Ibadan, Nigeria, 1963; FRCP(C), McMaster University Residency Programme, Hamilton, Canada, 1970; FMCPath; FICS; FWACP. *Appointments:* Consultant Pathologist, Sarnia General Hospital, Sarnia, Ontario, Canada, 1971-72; Senior Lecturer, Department of Pathology, University of Ibadan, Nigeria, 1972-78; Professor of Pathology, Ahmadu Bello University, Laria, Nigeria, 1978-82. *Memberships:* Nigerian Medical Association; Royal Society of Medicine (UK); President, Association of Pathologists of Nigeria; President, Nigerian Cancer Society, etc. *Publications:* "Cancer in Five Continents", 1976; "Cancer in Nigeria", 1982; "Sickle Cell Disease", 1981; "Global Geocancerology", 1985; Numerous articles in medical and science journals on pathology and tropical medicine. *Hobbies:* Walking; Reading. *Address:* College of Medical Sciences, University of Calabar, Calabar, Nigeria.

ATTALLAH, Abdelfattah M, b. 2 Feb 1944. Immunologist. *Education:* BS, Alexandria University, Egypt, 1967; DEA, University of Paris, France, 1971; PhD, George Washington University, USA, 1974. *Appointments include:* Research Assistant 1972-74, Research Associate 1974-76, Research Foundation of Children's National Medical Center, Washington, DC, USA; Research Scientist, Cellular Immunology Division, Clinical and Experimental Immunology Department, Naval Medical Research Institute, Bethesda, Maryland, USA, 1976-78; Chief of Immunology Section, Office of biologics Research and Review, National Center for Drugs and Biologics, National Institutes of Health Campus, Bethesda, Maryland, 1978-; Professor (Adjunct) Georgetown University, Washington DC, 1982-; Professor (Adjunct) Genetics Department, George Washington University, Washington, DC,

1982-; Professor of Immunology (Visiting) Alexandria University, Alexandria, Egypt, 1982-. *Memberships:* American Association of Immunologists; Tissue Culture Association; The New York Academy of Sciences; American Association for the Advancement of Science; The American Society for Microbiology; Association of Egyptian-American Scholars; International Society for Interferon Research. *Publications:* Contributor of numerous articles to medical journals and chapters to edited medical publications, also presenter of many papers to medical conferences. *Honours:* Young Investigators Competition Award, Southern Society for Pediatric Research, USA; Postdoctoral Research Associate, National Research Council, National Academy of Sciences, USA, Sigma XI. *Hobbies:* Classical music; Sport; Photography; Travel. *Address:* 5919 Beech Avenue, Bethesda, MD 20817, USA.

ATTWOOD, Harold Dallas, b. 1 July 1928, Dundee, Scotland. Professor of Pathology; Curator, Medical History Unit, University of Melbourne, Australia. m. Isobel Jean Dobbie Butters, 20 Mar. 1954, Dundee, 2 sons, 1 daughter. *Education:* MB, ChB 1951, MD 1957, University of St. Andrews, Scotland; MD, University of Melbourne, Australia, 1964; Fellow, Royal College of Pathologists, Australia 1962, UK 1964; Fellow, Royal Australasian College of Physicians, 1970. *Appointments include:* Lecturer, Pathology, University of St. Andrews, Dundee, 1953-59; James Hudson Brown Senior Research Fellow, Pathology, Yale University, USA, 1957-58; Senior Pathologist, Pfizer Ltd., UK, 1959-61; Assistant Director, Director, Pathology, Royal Women's Hospital, Melbourne, Australia, 1961-66; Professor of Pathology, University of Melbourne, 1966-, Curator 1980-. *Publications include:* Papers, medical journals, 1956-85; Co-editor, "Festschrift for Kenneth Fitzpatrick Russell", 1978, "Medical History Australia", newsletter, 1981-; "Occasional Papers on Medical History Australia", 1984, "Patients, Practitioners & Techniques", 1985. *Honours:* Orator, 17th Tracy-Maund Memorial Lecturer, 1981; Orator, Langford Oration, 1983. *Hobbies:* Photography; Painting. *Address:* 7 Chelmsford Street, North Balwyn, Victoria 3104, Australia.

ATWELL, John David, b. 17 May 1929, Maracaibo, Venezuela. Consultant Paediatric Surgeon, Wessex Centre for Paediatric Surgery, General Hospital, Southampton, England. m. Susan Nightingale, 30 Apr. 1960, 2 sons, 1 daughter. *Education:* MB, ChB (Leeds); FRCS (Eng). *Appointments:* Demonstrator in Anatomy, University of Leeds; House Officer, Leeds General Infirmary, & St James Hospital; Senior House Officer, Surgery, Leeds General Infirmary; House Officer, Postgraduate Medical School, Hammersmith; Senior House Officer, Hospital for Sick Children, London; Surgical Registrar, Radcliffe Infirmary, Oxford; Senior Registrar, Paediatric Surgery, Hospital for Sick Children, London; Lecturer in Surgery, University of Leeds; Senior Lecturer in Paediatric Surgery, Institute of Child Health, University of London; Paediatric Surgeon, Westminster Children's Hospital; Neonatal Surgeon, St Thomas' Hospital, London. *Memberships include:* British Association of Paediatric Surgeons; British Association of Urological Surgeons; Royal Society of Medicine; British Paediatric Association; Society of Paediatric Urological Surgeons; Paediatric Visiting Club; English Paediatric Surgical Club; Court of Examiners, Royal College of Surgeons, England; External Examiner, Medicine and Surgery in Childhood, Royal College of Surgeons in Ireland. *Publications:* Numerous articles in professional journals; Book Chapters in 'Operative Surgery and Management'; 'Primary Reflux and Renal Growth', 1984; "Everyday Paediatric Surgery", in 'Current Surgical Practice', Volume 3; etc. Previously, External Examiner, Surgical Paediatrics, University of Glasgow, Examiner, General Nursing Council.

Hobbies: Sailing; Antique Glass. *Address:* The Dolphin, High Street, Old Bursledon, Nr. Southampton, SO3 8DJ, England.

AUBRY, Jean Robert, b. 17 Oct. 1948, Hawksbury, Ontario, Canada. Family Physician. m. Marie-Luce Lafontaine, 30 Aug. 1969, Pointe Gatineau, 1 son, 2 daughters. *Education:* BA 1970, MD 1975, University of Ottawa; CCFP, Ottawa General Hospital, 1977. *Appointments:* Chief Resident Family Medicine, Ottawa General Hospital, 1976-77; Active Staff, General Hospital, Sturgeon Falls, Ontario, 1977-; Private practice in Family Medicine, Sturgeon Falls, 1977-. *Memberships:* Associate, American Osteopathic Academy of Sclerotherapy; Charter member, American Association of Orthopedic Medicine; Founding member, Canadian Association of Orthopedic Medicine; North American Academy of Manipulative Medicine; Acupuncture Foundation of Canada; College of Family Physicians of Canada; College of Physicians and Surgeons of Ontario. *Hobbies:* Research and clinical practice of acupuncture, orthopedic medicine and application of low power soft laser therapy; Photography; Sports; Boating. *Address:* 65 B Queen Street, Sturgeon Falls, Ontario POH 2G0, Canada.

AUGTER, Gary Keith, b. 30 July, 1955, Kansas City, Missouri, USA. Emergency Medicine, Trauma, Orthopaedic Consultant. *Education:* BS, University of Oregon, USA; MS, University of Oregon Graduate School; DO, Philadelphia, USA. *Appointments:* Director, Animal Research Facility, Good Samaritan Hospital, Neurological Institute, Oregon, USA; Representative, AOA Research Conference for Philadelphia College; Director of Emergency Medicine, Parker Hospital, Parker, Arisona; Chief Orthopaedic Resident, North Eastern Community Hospital, Dallas, Texas. *Memberships:* American Association of Osteopathic Specialists; American Osteopathic Association; American Osteopathic Association of Sports Medicine; Physicians Martial Arts Association of America; Pennsylvania Osteopathic Medical Association; Texas Osteopathic Medical Association; Phi Sigma Gamma Medical Society. *Publications include:* Co-author: 'Hormones from the Eye of Pplysia? Effect of Cutting the Optic Nerve on the Circadian Rhythm of Behavioural Activity', 1974 (presentation to Society for Neuroscience); Co-Author: 'Climbing Fiber Responses of Cerebellar Purkinje Cells to Passive Movement of the Cat Forepaw', in 'Brain Research', 1976; Co-author: 'The Consequences of Eye Removal for the Circadian Rhythm of Behavioral Activity in Aplysia', in 'Journal of Comparative Physiology', 1977; co-author: 'Analysis of Local Excitatory Mechanisms in the Hippocampus', presented to the American Osteopathic Association Research Conference, 1978. *Honour:* The American College of Osteopathic Surgeons First Neurological Award, Transsphenoidal Operations of Pituitary Adenomas, 1979, with Dr. Clark Okulski. *Hobbies:* Computers; Scuba Diving; Ski-ing; Martial Arts. *Address:* Parker Hospital, PO Box 1149, Mohave Road, Parker, AZ 85344, USA.

AUNG, Steven Kyaw Htut, b. 8 Feb. 1948, Pyinmana, Burma. Family and Geriatric Physician; Medical Acupuncture Consultant; Visiting Professor; Medicina Alternativa. m. Debbie, 8 Feb. 1974, 1 son, 3 daughters. *Education:* MBBS Rangoon University, Burma; MD, Canada; D.Ac, Acupuncture Research Institute; PhD, Alternative Medicine; FICAN Nutrition, California; FACA, Fellow Acupuncture. *Appointments:* Assistant Surgeon, North Oklahoma General Hospital, 1973-76; Medical Resident, St. Vincent's Hospital, Vancouver, 1976-78; Rotating Intern, McGill University, 1978-79; Family Medicine Resident, Memorial University, Newfoundland, 1979-80; District Medical Officer, Jeffreys Medical Center, Newfoundland, 1980-82; Family Physician, Health Sciences Center, Memorial University, 1982-83; Geriatric Clinical Assistant, Edmonton General Hospital, 1983-84; Acupuncture (Medical) Consultant, Edmon-

ton General Hospital, Cross Cancer Institute, Misericordia Hospital, 1984-; Director, Edmonton Medical Acupuncture Center, 1984-; Visiting Professor, Alternative Medicine, 1985-. *Memberships:* Member and Fellow of several professional organizations, including: American and Canadian Medical Associations; Fellow, American Academy of Acupuncture. *Publications:* Obesity, 1973; Pain and Acupuncture, 1973; Acupuncture for Cancer Pain, 1984. *Honours:* Aung-San UNISCEF Literature Gold Medal, 1962; MD Award, 1973; PhD Award, 1985; MD (Acupuncture), 1977; Visiting Professor (Alternative Medicine) 1985. *Hobbies:* Sports; Arts; Writing; Outdoor-Nature. *Address:* 10815 - 37 Avenue, Edmonton, Alberta, Canada T6J OG6.

AURELL, Nils Mattias, b. 5 Aug. 1934, Sweden. Professor of Nephrology. m. Elisabeth, 26 Feb. 1960, Göteborg, 2 sons. *Education:* MD 1963, PhD 1969, University of Göteborg, Göteborg. *Appointments:* Associate Professor of Clinical Physiology 1970-75, Associate Professor of Nephrology 1975-82, Professor of Nephrology 1982-, Medical Faculty, University of Göteborg. *Memberships:* Swedish Association of Physicians; International Society of Nephrology; International Society of Hypertension; European Dialysis and Transplant Association. *Publications include:* 200 in Renal Physiology, Essential and Renovascular Hypertension and Clinical Naphrology; 'Renal Response in Man to Plasma Volume Expansion and Angiotension', thesis, 1969. *Hobbies:* Travelling; Golf. *Address:* Department of Nephrology, Sahlgrenska Sjukhuset, S 413 45 Göteborg, Sweden.

AUROUSSEAU, Michel Emile, b. 26 Mar. 1926, France. Professor of Pharmacology. m. Marie-Louise Carrot, 25 July 1953, Melun. *Education:* Doctorate, Faculty of Medicine, Faculty of Pharmacy and Faculty of Sciences; PhD; MD; DSc. *Appointments:* Head, Pharmacological Department: Clin Byla Lab; Ish Roussel Lab. Director of Biological Research, Bellon Laboratory; Counsellor in Pharmacology, Innothera Laboratory; currently, Professor of Pharmacology, University of Reims. *Memberships:* New York Academy of Sciences; Academy National Pharmacie; European Society of Medical Chemistry; European Society of Toxicology; Societe Francaise de Pharmacie Clinique; Society of Biochemical Pharmacy; Associacion Francaise de Psych Biologie; Societe de Circ Metab Cerveau; Associacion Pharmacologistes. *Publications:* "Medicaments organiques de synthese", VII, 1974; author of over 200 articles in pharmacological publications including 'European Journal of Medical Chemistry'; 'Cell and Molecular Biology'; 'International Journal of Clinical Pharmacology'; 'Arzneimittel Forsch'; 'Journal de Pharmacologie' and others. *Address:* Laboratoire de Pharmacologie, Faculte de Pharmacie, 51096 Reims Cedex, France.

AUVERGNAT, Jean-Charles, b. 1 Oct. 1944, Toulouse, France. Professor of Infectious and Tropical Diseases. m. Arielle Costes-Azeret, 4 Sep, 1970, Morlhon, 2 sons, 1 daughter. *Education:* MD; Diplomas in Tropical Diseases and Internal Medicine. *Appointments:* Chief of Clinic, 1972; Assistant in Infectious Diseases, 1972; Professosr in Infectious Diseases, 1977-. *Publications:* "Antibiotics into SCF", 1972-; 'Experimental Meningitis', 1979-; 'Labelled Granulocytes', 1975-76. *Honour:* Ordre National du Merite. *Hobbies:* Riding; GOLf; Tennis. *Address:* Infectious and Tropical Diseases Department, CHU Toulouse, Purpan, 31059 Toulouse Cedex, France.

AUZEPY, Philippe, b. 3 Jan 1931, Paris, France, m. 1956, 2 sons, 2 daughters. *Education:* MD. *Appointments:* Professor, Faculty of Medicine, Paris Sud, France; Chief of Intensive Care, Hospital of Bicetre, Paris, France. *Memberships:* Societe de reamimation de lougue francoise; French Society of Cardiology; Medical Society of the Hospital of Paris. *Publications:* 'Experimental intoxication with diethylene-glycol', 1976; 'Aortic atherosclerosis in Laennec's cirrhosis', 1978; "Risques et accidents des medicaments", Maloine edit, Paris, 1979. *Address:* Intensive Care Unit, Bicetre Hospital, F94275, Le Kremlin-Bicêtre, France.

AVELLAN, Lars Eitel, b. 9 Mar. 1923, Helsingfors, Finland. Associate Professor. m. Inger, 3 Sep. 1955, Helsingfors, 1 son, 2 daughters. *Education:* MD, University of Helsingfors, 1952; Specialist in General Surgery, 1957, Plastic Surgery, 1964, Maxillofacial Surgery, 1967; PhD, University of Gothenburg, 1980. *Appointments:* Assistant Surgeon, Municipal Hospital, Vasa, 1954-55; Surgical Residencies, Provinicial Hospital, Kuopio, 1955; Department of Surgery, University of Helsingfors, 1956-59; Maria Hospital, Helsingfors, 1960-61; Resident Physician, Department of Plastic Surgery, Sahlgrenska Sjukhuset, Gothenburg, 1962-68; Assistant Chief Surgeon, Department of Plastic Surgery, 1968-; Associate Professor, Plastic Surgery, University of Gothenburg, 1981-. *Memberships:* Past Board Member, Younger Doctors Association of Finland; Past Vice President, currently President, Swedish Association for Plastic Surgery; Scandinavian Orthopaedic Association; Scandinavian Association of Surgeons; Past President, Swedish-Finnish Society, Gothenburg. *Publications:* Contributing Author: "Plastic and Reconstructive Surgery of the Genital Area", 1973; "Long Term Results in Plastic and Reconstructive Surgery", 1980. Monograph: "Hypospadias Studies on Incidence, Aetiology, Morphology and Results of Surgical Treatment in a Clinical Material", thesis, 1980. *Honours:* Service with Medical Corps, Finnish Army, 1941-44; Awarded Medal and Cross of War, 1941-44; Honour Member, Swedish-Finnish Society, Gothenburg. *Hobbies:* Walking and Marching; Awarded the Silver Cross, Royal Netherlands League for Physical Culture, 1985. *Address:* Doktor Lindhs gata 1, S-413 25 Gothenburg, Sweden.

AVERILL, Stuart Carson, b. 31 May 1924, Sacramento, California, USA. Director, C.F. Menninger Memorial Hospital. m. Elizabeth Walter, 10 Aug. 1946, Dixon, California, 3 sons, 1 daughter. *Education:* BA, Pre-Medicine; MA, Anatomy, University of California, Berkeley, 1950; MD, University of California, San Francisco, 1952; Psychiatric Residency, Menninger School of Psychiatry, 1958; American Board of Psychiatry and Neurology, 1959; Topeka Institute for Psychoanalysts, Adult 1973, Child, 1975. *Appointments:* Rotating Internship, San Francisco County Hospital, 1952-53; Resident, Topeka State Hospital, Menninger School of Psychiatry, Topeka, 1953-54; Staff Psychiatrist, 1954-56, Clinical Director, 1958-72, Boys Industrial School, Topeka; Faculty, Menninger School of Psychiatry, Adult and Child Training Programs, 1958-; Staff Psychiatrist, Adult Outpatient Clinic, 1972-76; Director, Diagnostic and Consultation Service, Adult Outpatient Department, 1976-84, The Menninger Foundation; Training and Supervising Analyst, Topeka Institute of Psychoanalysis, 1982-; Director, C.F. Menninger Memorial Hospital, The Menninger Foundation, 1984-. *Memberships:* Shawnee County Medical Society, Past President; Kansas Medical Society, Delegate; American Medical Association; Kansas Psychiatric Society, President; American Psychiatric Association, Fellow, 1964-; Kansas Group Psychotherapy Society; Past President; American Group Psychotherapy Association; Topeka Psychoanalytic Society, Past President; American Psychoanalytic Association; Association for Child Psychoanalysis. *Publications:* Contributor to professional journals including 'Crime and Delinquency', 'Journal of Kansas Medical Society', 'Bulletin of Menninger Clinic'. *Honour:* Fellow, American Psychiatric Association, 1964. *Hobbies:* Bicycling; Bagpipes; Fishing; Family. *Address:* Box 829, Topeka, KS 66601, USA.

AVETISOV, Eduard Sergeevich, b. 21 Dec 1921,

Samarkand, Deputy Director, Moscow Helmholtz Institute of Eye Diseases, USSR, 2 sons. *Education:* DMS, 1963; Samarkand Medical Institute, 1951; Candidate of Medical Sciences, 1956; Professor, 1965. *Appointments:* Ophthalmologist, Catta-Curgan, Usbekssr, 1951; Assistant, Samarkand Medical Institute, 1953; Research Assistant, 1957, Chief of Department, 1961, Deputy Director, 1966, Helmholtz Institute of Eye Diseases, Moscow, USSR. *Memberships:* President, National Ophthalmological Society of USSR, 1979-; Member, International Ophthalmological Academy. *Publications:* 'Disbinocular Amblyopia and its treatment', 1967; 'Children Vision Care', 1975; 'Problems of Ophthalmology', 1973; 'Concomitant Squint', 1977; 'Optical Correction of Vision', 1981. *Honours:* Averbach Award and Diploma, Academy of Medical Sciences of USSR, 1977. *Address:* Sadovaya-Chernogriasskaya, 14 /19 Helmholtz Institute of Eye Diseases, Moscow 103064, USSR.

AWON, Maxwell Philip, b. 10 Mar. 1920, Port-of-Spain, Trinidad and Tobago. Specialist Obstetrician and Gynaecologist in Private Practice. m. Dr. Sylvia Hawthorne, 18 July 1956, 2 sons, 2 daughters. *Education:* BSc, Economics Part 1, London (External), 1941; BSc (Special), Physiology, London (External), 1950; BSc (Hons.), 1950; MSc, 1952, National University of Ireland; LAH, University College, Dublin, 1953; MB, BCh, BAO, National University of Ireland, 1953; LM (Rotunda), 1953; MRCP (Ireland); FRCS (Ireland); MRCOG, 1960; FRCS (Edinburgh), 1960; FRCP (Ireland), 1970; FRCOG, 1970; FACOG, 1974. *Appointments include:* Major (Honorary Commission), Trinidad and Tobago Regiment, 1981-; Lecturer, various hospitals and universities nationally and internationally; Various hospital appointments; Specialist Medical Officer, Government of Trinidad and Tobago; Government appointments include: Member of House of Representatives, Arima Constituency, 1966-71, 1971-76; Member of Cabinet of Government of Trinidad and Tobago: Minister of Health, 1967-71; Minister of Local Government, 1969-71; Chairman and Director of several companies. *Memberships include:* Family Planning Association of Trinidad and Tobago; American Association of Gynaecological Laparoscopists; The St. John's Ambulance Association; Trinidad and Tobago Chamber of Commerce. *Publications:* Author of several scientific publications. *Honours:* Recipient of several honours and awards. *Hobbies:* Sailing (Skipper of Sloop 'Hooligan' Racer-Cruiser); Windsurfer Sailing; Dinghy Sailing; Keep Fit Exercises. *Address:* 1 Alexandra Street, St. Clair, Port-of-Spain, Republic of Trinidad and Tobago.

AXELROD, David, b. 7 Jan. 1935, Great Barrington, Massachusetts, USA. Commissioner, New York State Department of Health. m. Janet Claire Ross, 30 Aug. 1964, 1 son. *Education:* AB, MD. *Appointments:* Intern, 1960-61, Medical Resident, 1961-62, Strong Memorial Hospital, Rochester, New York; Research Associate, 1962-65, Virologist, 1965-68, US Public Health Service, Washington DC; Director, Infectious Disease Centre, 1968-77, Director, 1977-79, Division of Labs & Research, New York State Department of Health; Commissioner, 1979-. *Memberships:* Institute of Medicine; National Research Council. *Honours:* National Governor's Association Award for Distinguished Service to State Government, 1984; Nelso A Rockefeller Award, New York State Academy of Public Administration, 1985. *Address:* Empire State Plaza, Corning Tower Building Rm 1408, Albany, NY 12237, USA.

AYARS, Garrison Hubert, b. 18 Apr. 1950, Sunnyside, Washington, USA. Clinical Assistant Professor, Allergy and Infectious Diseases. m. Wendy A Westland, 28 Dec. 1974, Seattle, Washington, 1 son, 1 daughter. *Education:* BS, University of Washington, 1972; MD, University of

Washington Medical School, 1976; Medical Residency, 1976-79, Chief Medical Resident, 1979-80, University of Utah Affiliated Hospitals; Fellowship in Infectious Disease and Allergy, University of Seattle, 1980-84. *Appointments:* Acting Instructor, University of Washington Medical School, 1983-84; Clinical Assistant Professor, Infectious Diseases & Allergy, 1984-; Allergist, Pacific Medical Center, Seattle, 1984-; Part-time Private Practice in Allergy and Infectious Diseases, 1984-. *Memberships:* American Academy of Allergy and Immunology; American College of Physicians; American Society of Internal Medicine; Phi Beta Kappa; Alpha Epsilon Delta. *Publications:* Contributor of learned papers and abstracts to professional journals, etc. including: American Heart Journal; Journal of American Thoracic Society. *Honour:* Magnum cum laude, University of Washington. *Hobbies:* Snow Skiing; Jogging. *Address:* 901 Boren, Seattle, WA 98104, USA.

AYMARD, Michèle Andrée Mariette, b. 11 Nov. 1933, Champforgeuil, France. Professor, Biologist, Lyons University Hospital Centre. *Education:* MD; Certificates of Special Studies in: Medical & Technical Parasitology, Haematology, Applied Serology in diagnostics of Venereal Diseases; Medical & Technical Biochemistry; Medical & Technical Bacteriology; Certification as Graduate-Teacher Lecturer; University Professor. *Appointments:* Assistant; Head of Department; Senior Lecturer; Professor. *Memberships:* Expert at OMS on virus diseases, 1972; Director, WHO Collaborating Centre for Virus Reference & Researach, 1973; Expert, specialist pharmacologist-toxicologist, 1981; Ministry of Health registration no. 51, 1982; Director, National Reference Centre on Influenza France-Sud and on Entérviruses. *Publications:* "Infections: à Myxovirus Influenza: grippe, à Paramyxovirus, à Coronavirus" in 'Diagnostic des Maladies à Virus', 1975-81; 'Les Orthomyxoviridae' in 'Virologie Médicale', 1985; 'Swine Influenza', 1980, 1985 in two journals; 'Human Influenza', 1979, 1982 in 'Journal of Biological Standards'. *Honours:* Chevalier, French Order of Merit, 1977; Chevalier, French Order of Academic Palms, 1985. *Hobbies:* Reading; Listening to Music; Walking; Swimming. *Address:* Laboratoire de Bacteriologie-Virologie, Université Calude-Bernard Lyon 1, 8 avenue Rockefeller, 69373 Lyon Cedex 08, France.

AYYAR, Krishna Subramoni, b. 10 Oct. 1953, India. Consulting Psychiatrist; Honorary Assistant Psychiatrist. m. Lalitha K. Ayyar, 5 July 1984, Bombay. *Education:* MD, University of Bombay, 1980; MBBS; MCPS. *Appointments:* House Officer, Psychiatry, K.E.M. Hospital, Bombay, 1977-78; Registrar, Psychiatry, K.E.M. Hospital, 1978-81; Senior Research Fellow, WHO Collaborating Centre in Psychopharmacology in India, 1981-. *Membership:* Fellow, Indian Psychiatric Society. *Publications:* "Male, Homosexuality"; "Treatment of Homosexuality"; "Treatment of Sexual Dysfunction"; "Drug Surveillance in Psychiatry"; "Behaviour Therapy of Obsessive Compulsive Neurosis", (Indian Journal of Psychiatry); "Haemodialysis and Peritoneal Dialysis in chronic Schizophrenia", (Psycopharmacology Bulletin), 1984. *Hobbies:* Chess; Bridge; Literature. *Address:* H. Bhagwati Municipal General Hospital, S.V.P. Road, Borivli, Bombay 400 103, India.

AZAMI, Mohammad Bashir, b. 1 Aug. 1922, Daska. Registrar, College of Physicians & Surgeons, Pakistan; Consulting Physician, PIA Hospital. m. Iffat Ara Azami, 9 Aug. 1947, Lahore, 2 sons, 4 daughters. *Education:* MBBS (Pb), 1944; FRCP Edinburgh; MRCP Edinburgh; FCPS Pakistan; Postgraduate training, medicine, various hospitals, UK. *Appointments:* Medical Officer, Graded Medical Specialist, IMS /IAMC; Senior Physician, Army, 9 years; Instructor, medicine, AFM College, Rawalpindi, 3 years; Associate Physician, Jinnah

Postgraduate Medical Centre, Karachi; Honorary Professor, JPMC Karachi, 6 years; Part-time Teacher, Pathology & medicine, College of Physicians & Surgeons, Pakistan, 1974-; Examiner, medicine & Pathology, for various Diplomas, College of Physicians & Surgeons, Pakistan; WHO Scholar and Advisor, Continuing Education, Postgraduate Medical Education & Medical Writing, PG Training, 6 occasions. *Memberships:* British Medical Association; Founder Member, Pakistan Academy of Medicine, Society of Physicians, Pakistan, Neurological Society of Pakistan; Pakistan Cardiac Society; Pakistan Medical and Dental Council; Pakistan Medical Research Council. *Publications:* Articles in Armed Forces Medical Journals; various other articles in professional journals. *Hobbies:* Photography; Reading, English and Urdu; Literature. *Address:* Registrar, College of Physicians & Surgeons, Pakistan, 7th Central Street, Defence Housing Authority, Karachi 46, Pakistan.

AZIM, Hassan F.A., b. 1 Feb. 1932, Cairo, Egypt. Clinical Professor of Psychiatry and Family Medicine; Director, Division of External Psychiatric Services. m. Norma, 22 Dec. 1966, Montreal, Quebec, Canada, 3 sons. *Education:* BA, American University, Cairo, 1955; MB BCh, Cairo University, 1955; Diploma in General Medicine, Cairo, 1958; Diploma in Psychiatry, McGill University, Montreal, Quebec, Canada, 1962; Psychoanalytic training, Canadian Psychoanalytic Institute, 1968; FRCP(C); FAPA; FAGPA. *Appointments:* Assistant Professor, Psychiatry, McGill University, Montreal, Quebec, Canada, 1968-73; Associate Psychiatrist, Royal Victoria Hospital, Montreal, 1970-73; Director of External Services, Allan Memorial Institute of Psychiatry, Montreal, 1970-73; Clinical Professor of Psychiatry and Family Medicine, Director of Division of External Psychiatric Services, University of Alberta Hospitals, Edmonton, currently. *Memberships Include:* Canadian Psychoanalytic Society; Canadian Psychiatric Association; Fellow, American Psychiatric Association, Royal College of Physicians and Surgeons of Canada and American Group Psychotherapy Association. *Publications:* Co-Authorcontributions to: 'Canadian Psychiatric Association Journal'; "Community Psychiatry: Review and Preview", 1978; 'Canadian Journal of Psychiatry'. *Honours:* First President; Western Branch, Canadian Pschoanalytic Society, 1978-81; Alberta Psychiatric Association, 1981-82. Fellowships: American Psychiatric Association, 1972; American Group Psychotherapy Association, 1976. *Hobbies:* Travelling; Photography. *Address:* Department of Psychiatry, University of Alberta Hospitals, Edmonton, Alberta, Canada T6G 2B7

AZIZ, Khwaja Muhammed Sultanul, b. 28 Feb. 1936, Comilla, Bangladesh. Associate Director, Training, Extension and Communication. m. Mrs Saiyada Ashrafunnessa Sabera Begum, 24 Mar. 1967, Dhaka, 1 son, 1 daughter. *Education:* BSc Honours, 1956, MSc, 1957, Dhaka University; PhD, Duke University, USA, 1964. *Appointments:* Associate Professor, Biology, North Carolina College, North Carolina Central University, covered by Parentheses, Durham, North Carolina, USA, 1964-65; Senior Investigator, 1966-75, Head, Laboratory Division, 1975-77, Cholera Research Laboratory, Dhaka, Bangladesh; Associate Director, Training, Extension and Communication, International Centre for Diarrhoeal Disease Research, Dhaka, 1977-. *Memberships:* Past President, Bangladesh Society of Microbiologists; Past Vice President, Bangladesh Association for the Advancement of Science; Past Sectional Council for Bacteriology; Member, International Association for Microbiological Societies. *Publications:* Author or co-author of 35 papers in professional journals including: 'Journal of Infectious Disease'; 'Science'; 'South East Asian Journal of Tropical Medicine and Public Health'; 'Bangladesh Pharmaceutical Journal'; 'Bangladesh Medical Research Council Bulletin'; 'The Lancet'. Contributor of chapter in "Proceedings of the 5th International Seaweed Symposium", 1965. *Honours:* Award for 1st in MSc, 1957,

Blue in Swimming, 1957, Dhaka University; Fulbright Scholarship, USA, 1959-60; Fellow, American Association for the Advancement of Science. *Hobbies:* Swimming; Reading. *Address:* C-109 Banani, Road 13A, Dhaka 13, Bangladesh.

AZZI, Angelo Manfredo, b. 26 Oct 1939, Modena, Italy, Director of Institute, m. Margherita Visentini, 30 May 1965, 3 daughters. *Education:* MD, 1963; Libera Docenza in General Pathology, 1969; Libera Docenza in Biochemistry, 1970; Professor. *Appointments:* Assistant Professor, 1963-66, Associate Professor, 1970-75, Full Professor, 1976-77, Padova, Italy; Research Fellow, Bristol, England and Philadelphia, USA, 1967-69; Professor and Head of Section, 1977-84, Professor and Director of Institute für Biochemie und Mole Kularbiologie Universität Bern, Switzerland. *Memberships:* British Biochemical Society; American Association of the Advancement of Science; New York Academy of Sciences; Italian Society of Biochemistry; Biophysical Society; Italian Group of Bioenergetics; Italian Society of Biophysics and Molecular Biology; Swiss Biomembrane Group; Swiss Biochemical Society. *Publications:* "Membrane Proteins. A Laboratory Manual", 1981; "Enzymes, Receptors and Carriers of Biological Membranes", 1984. *Hobbies:* Classical music; Photograpyy. *Address:* Institut für Biochemie und Molekularbiologie Universität Bern, Bühltrasse 28, CH-3012 Bern, Switzerland.

B

BABIGIAN, Haroutun Melkon b, 3 May 1935 Jerusalem, Professor & Chairman Department of Psychiatry, m. Alice 2 Dec, 1961, Syracuse New York, 1 son 1 daughter. *Education:* BSc 1956, MD 1960, American University of Beirut, Lebanon; Internship, American University Hospital, Beirut 1959-60; Psychiatric Residency Rochester New York 1960-63. *Appointments:* Instructor & Fellow inPsychiatry 1963-64, Senior Instructor in Psychiatry & Preventive Medicine & Community Health 1964-65, Assistant Professor 1965-69 Associate professor 1969-75 Professor of Psychiatry 1975-, all University of Rochester Medical Centre, Rochester NY. *Memberships:* American Public Health Association; Fellow American Psychiatric Association; American Association of Suicidology; Society for Life History Research in Psychopathology; Psychiatric Research Society; Fellow American Psychiatric Association; American Association of Suicidology; Society for Life History Research in Psychopathology; Psychiatric Research Society; Fellow, American Psychopathological Association; Sigma Xi; American Association for the Advancement of Science. *Publication:* Author & Co-author of over 50 articles in medical journals; "The Origins & Course of Psychopathology Methods of Longitudinal Research" (with J S Strauss & M Roff). *Address:* Department of Psychiatry, School of Medicine & Dentistry University of Rochester 300 Crittenden Boulevard, Rochester, NY 14642 USA.

BACHE, Robert James, b. 8 Sep. 1938, Minnesota, USA, Professor, Medicine, Cardiovascular Division, University of Minnesota. m. Elaine Mary Anderson, 5 Nov. 1966, 2 sons, 1 daughter. *Education:* BA, 1960, MS, Physiology, 1961, University of North Dakota; MD, Harvard University Medical School, 1964, *Appointments:* Assistant Professor, 1971-75, Associate, 1975-76, Duke University Medical Centre; Associate Professor, 1976-79, Professor, 1979-, University of Minnesota Medical School. *Memberships:* Phi Eta Sigma; Phi Beta Kapparivestigation; American Society for Clinical Investigation; Central Society for Clinical Research; Fellow, Council on Clinical Cardiology and Council of Circulation; Association of University Cardiologists, *Publications:* Author, 90 scientific articles. *Honours:* Phi Beta Kappa, 1969; Research Career Development Award, US Public Health Service, 1975-80; Research Grant Awards, National Heart, Lung and Blood Institutes, National Institutes of Health, 1974-. *Address:* University of Minnesota Medical School, Dept, of Medicine, Box 338 Mayo Memorial Bldg., Minneapolis, MN 55455, USA.

BACHRACH, Uriel, b. 9 Sep. 1926, Germany. Professor of Molecular Biology. m. Esther Zacharin, 26 Sep. 1954, 1 son, 2 daughters. *Education:* MSc, PhD, Hebrew University, Jerusalem, Israel, *Appointments:* Lecturer 1957, Senior Lecturer 1960, Associate Professor 1965, Professor 1971, Department of Molecular Biology, Hebrew University-Hadassah Medical School, Jerusalem. *Memberships:* New York Academy of Sciences; President 1978-81, Israel Biochemical Society; Israel Society for Microbiology. *Publications:* "Function of Naturally Ocurring Polyamines", 1973; Co-Editor: "Advances in Polyamine Research" volume 3 1981, volume 4 1983; "Polyamines: Basic and Clinical Aspects", 1985. *Hobbies:* Natural History; Archaeology; Camping. *Address:* Department of Molecular Biology, Hebrew University-Hadassah Medical School, Jerusalem, Israel.

BACH-Y-RITA, Paul, b. 24 Apr. 1934, New York City, USA. Professor, Chairman, Rehabilitation medicine, University of Wisconsin School of Medicine. m. 2 July 1977, San Francisco, 4 daughters. *Education:* MD, Escuela Nacional de Medicina, 1959; Internships, Residencies, various Hospitals, 1958-79. *Appointments Include:* Rural Public Health Physician, Tilzapotla, Mexico, 1958-59; Post-doctoral Mental Health Trainee, 1959-60, Junior Research Pharmacologist, 1960, University of California, Los Angeles; Various Fellowships, 1961-63; Senior Research Member, 1963-79, Acting Director, 1969, Smith-Kettlewell Institute of Visual Sciences; Director, San Francisco Rehabilitation Engineering Centre, 1974-77; Chief, Rehabilitation Medicine Service, Martinez Veterans Administration Medical Centre, California, 1979-83; Professor, Human Physiology, University of California, Davis, 1979-83; Professor, Chairman, Rehabilitation medicine, University of Wisconsin, 1983-. *Memberships Include:* American Physiological Society; American Association for the Advancement of Science; Society for Neurosciences; etc. *Publications Include:* "The Control of Eye Movements", co-editor, 1971; "Brain Mechanisms in Sensory Substitution", 1972; "Basic Mechanisms of Ocular Motility and their Clinical Implications", co-editor, 1975; "Vitamins, Their Use and Abuse", co-author, 1976; "Symposium on Sensory Substitution", Co-editor, 1983; 'Symposium of Rehabilitation Following Brain Damage: Some Neurophysiological mechanisms', editor, 1982; 'Symposium on Visual Rehabilitation', Co-editor, 1983; numerous articles in professional journals, book chapters, book reviews, etc. *Honours:* Recipient, numerous honours and awards most recent include: Inaugural Speaker, 1st Martin Kaplan Lecture in Rehabilitation, Moss Rehabilitation Hospital, 1984; Karl Harpuder Memorial Lecturer, New York Academy of Medicine, 1984. *Address:* 3532 Blackhawk Drive, Madison, WI 53705, USA.

BACIA, Tadeusz, b. 25 Dec. 1926, Zychcice, Poland. Professor. m. Christine Klamczynska, 10 Nov. 1962, Warsaw. *Education:* Physician, Medical Faculty, Wroclaw University, 1950; MD, neurology, medical Institute, Moscow, 1955; PhD, Medical Academy, Warsaw, 1969. *Appointments:* Resident, Neurology, Wroclaw, 1950-51; Resident, Medical Institute, Moscow, 1951-55; Assistant Professor, 1956-72, Associate Professor, 1972-77, Professor, 1977-, Medical Academy, Warsaw. *Memberships:* Polish medical Association; Polish Society of Neurosurgery; Polish Neurological Association; Polish Society of EEG and Clinical Neurophysiology, President, 1985-; International League Againt Epilepsy. *Publications:* "Vasomotor distrubances in cerebral Atherosclerosis", 1955; "Neurophysilolgical investigations in psychomotor epilepsy", 1969; "Epileptice focus and surgical treatment of epilepsy", 1974; "Clinical Electroencephalography", 1979; "Ultrasonography in Medicine", 1980. *Honours:* Golden Cross of Merit, 1969; Knight of Order Polonia Restituta, 1979. *Hobbies:* Growing Plants & Trees; Food and Good Wine in the Company of Wise Friends. *Address:* Central Clinical Hospital, Dept. of EEG and Clinical Neurophysiology, ul. Banacha 1A, 02097 Warsaw, Poland.

BACIU, Clement, b. 2 Sep. 1922, Bucharest, Romania. Chief of Orthopaedic Department, Colentina Clinical Hospital, Bucharest. m. Ecaterina Duta, 26 June 1978, 2 sons. *Education:* Faculty of Human Medicine, Bucharest, 1942-48; Academy Physical Education, 1941-47; MD, 1958, MDD, 1971; Specialization in Wien, 1967; Specialization in Rehabilitation, Konstantin, 1972. *Appointments:* Second Orthopaedic Surgeon, 1948-58, First Orthopaedic Surgeon, 1958-66, Brincovenesc Clinic and Hospital; Gastartz Unfallkrankenhaus XX, Vienna, Austria, 1967; First Surgeon, Queen Elizabeth Hospital, Aden, Southern Yemen, 1968-69; Assistant Professor, Functional Anatomy and Biomechanics, Parhon University, Bucharest, 1970-72; Chief, Orthopaedic Department, Clinical Hospital, Colentina, 1970-. *Memberships:* Societate Ortop. si Traum, USSM, Bucharest; Societe Belde d'Orthopaedie et Traumatologie, Brussels, Belgium; Société Francaise d'Orthopaedie et Traumatologie, Paris, France; Ostereichische Gesellschaft Unfallchirurgie, Vienna, Austria; Deutsche

Gesselschaft fur Orthopaedie, Munich. *Publications:* Author of 22 books including: "The Knee", 1963; "Treatise for Osteo-articular Traumatology", 2 volumes, 1967-68; "Functional Anatomy and Biomechanics of Locomotor System", 3 Editions, 1968, 72, 77; "Semiology of Locomotor System"; "The Locomotor Systems", 1981, etc. 1981, etc. 192 written papers in journals worldwide. *Honours:* Evidentiat Munca Medico-Sanitara, Bucharest, 1956, 77; Diploma Comite International Red Cross, Geneva, 1969; Ordinul Munca Medico Sanitara, Bucharest, 1972. *Address:* str. Ronda nr. 2 bis, Bucharest 73.221, Romania.

BACKMAN, Zoe-Marcia, b. 25 Dec. 1950, Brooklyn, New York, USA. Doctor of Chiropractic. Single, 1 daughter. *Education:* PhD Program in Neuropharmacology, New York University School of Medicine, 1975-80; BA, MA, Hofstra University; DC, New York Chiropractic College, 1981. *Appointments:* Research Scientist, Department of Research Biochemistry, Edno Labs, Division of DuPont Industries, Garden City, New York, 1972-75; Instructor of Chemistry and Laboratory Diagnosis, New York Chiropractic College, 1976-77; Team Physician Trainer, America de Quito, 1982, 83, 84; Private Practice of Chiropractic, Merrick New York, 1981-. *Memberships:* New York State, American and International Chiropractic Associations; US Homeopathy Association; ACA Council on Nutrition; New York State Nutrition Committee; International Platform Association; Association for Commerce and Industry, Association for Children with Learning Disabilities. *Publications:* Contributor to : 'New England Quarterly'; 'New Voices in American Poetry'; 'The Advertiser'; 'Digest of Chriropractic Economics'; 'ACA Journal'; 'Upper Cervical Monograph'; 'Our World's Most Cherished Poems'. *Honours:* Honorable Mention, Greatest Poems Contest, 1985; Certificate of Merit, Poetry Contest, N A Mentor Magazine, 1984; Alternate Delegate, New York State Chiropractic Association, 1984; 2nd, ACA Scientific Paper Awards, 1983; Spotlighted, Suffolk County Orten Society, 1982-83; NUCCA Paper Award, 1979; Board of Director, 1976-84, Recording Seceretary, 1980-84, Nassau Association for Children with Learning Disabilities; LPA Conference Paper Presentation, 1977; Quoted as Medical Authority, Dear Meg, New York Post Magazine, 1982; Green Angel Award, Girl Scouts of America, 1980. *Hobbies:* Science fiction; Swimming; Dancing Ballet. *Address:* 3069 Wynsum Avenue, Merrick, NY 11566-5415, USA.

BACON, Paul Anthony, b. 3 May 1938, London, England. Professor of Rheumatology. m. 1 son, 2 daughters. *Education:* BA, MA, MB BChir, Cambridge University; FRCP. *Appointments:* Research Registrar, Kennedy Institute, London, 1965-67; Senior Registrar, St Bartholomew's Hospital, London, 1967-71; Research Fellow, University of California, Los Angeles, California, USA, 1971; Consultant Physician, Royal National Hospital for Rheumatic Diseases, Bath, Avon, England, 1972-81; Honorary Senior Lecturer, University of Bath, 1972-81; Professor of Rheumatology, University of Birmingham, 1981-. *Memberships:* Council Member, British Society for Rheumatology; Overseas Member, American Rheumatism Association; British Society for Immunology; Education Committee Chairman, British Society for Rheumatology. *Publications:* Co-Author over 100 papers on clinical and immunological aspects of rheumatology and vasculitis. *Hobbies:* Gardening; Music. *Address:* Rheumatism Research Wing, The Medical School, Birmingham University, Birmingham B15 2TJ, England.

BACOVSKY, Rosemary Ann, b. 25 Aug. 1953, Coleman, Alberta, Canada. Acting Director of Pharmacy, Cross Cancer Institute. m. William Trefanenko, 24 June 1978, Edmonton. *Education:* Master of Pharmacy, University of Alberta, 1985; Hospital Pharmacy Residency Certificate, Royal Alexandra Hospital, Edmonton, 1978; BSc, Pharmacy with distinction, 1977; BSc, 1974, University of Alberta. *Appointments:* Pharmacist, Cross Cancer Institute, 1978-81; Assistant Director of Pharmacy, Cross Cancer Institute, 1981-85. *Memberships:* Canadian Society of Hospital Pharmacists, President, 1985-86; Canadian Pharmaceutical Association; Alberta Pharmaceutical Association; American Society of Hospital Pharmacists; Federation Internationale Pharmaceutique; American College of Clinical Pharmacy. *Publication:* Disposal of Hazardous; Pharmaceuticals, Canadian Journal of Hospital Pharmacy, 1981. *Honours:* CSHP Winthrop Award, 1985; CSHP Smith Kline & French Award, 1984; Province of Alberta Graduate Scholarship, 1983; Canadian Foundation for the Advancement of Pharmacy Fellowship in Hospital Pharmacy, 1977. *Hobbies:* Alpine Hiking; Gourmet Cooking. *Address:* 11602 74 Avenue, Edmonton, Alberta T6G 0G2, Canada.

BADAKERE, Suresh Shanker, b. 13 May 1944, Bombay, India. Senior Research Officer. m. Jyoti Anant Swamirao Belligund, 21 Aug. 1971, Bombay, 2 daughters. *Education:* MSc, Seth G S Medical College, Bombay, PhD; Commonwealth Medical Fellowship, London Hospital, England. *Appointments:* Research Assistant, Assistant Research Officer, Research Officer, currently Senior Research Officer, Institute of Immunohaematology, Bombay, India. *Memberships:* Life Member, Bombay Haematology Group; Indian Society of Haematology and Blood Transfusion. *Publications:* Author or Co-Author of 24 papers contributed to: "Techniques in Blood Banking", 1985; 'Indian Journal of Haematology'; 'Indian Journal of Medical Research'; 'Trends in Immunohaematology'; 'Clinical Experimental Immunology'; 'Collegium Anthropologicum'; 'Indian Journal of Medical Science'; contributions to various conferences. *Honours:* Kishor Udani Gold Medal, Indian Society of Haematology and Blood Transfusion, 1974; Dr S V Gharpure Award for Studies in new blood group antigen, Teaching Pathologist Association, Bombay, 1974; Dr J C Patel Award (Special Prize Co-Winner), 7th Annual Conference of Bombay Haematology Group, 1983; Commonwealth Medical Fellowship, London Hospital and Medical College, University of London, England, 1980-81. *Hobbies:* Ancient History; Hiking. *Address:* Nirvan 651-A, 17th Road, Khar, Bombay 52, India.

BADDILEY, James (Sir), b. 15 May 1918, Manchester, England. Retired Professor. m. Hazel Mary Townsend, 20 Sep. 1944, Manchester, 1 son. *Education:* BSc Chemistry 1st Class Honours 1941, PhD 1944, DSc 1953, Manchester University: MA, Cambridge University, 1981. *Appointments:* ICI Research Fellow, Pembroke College, Cambridge; Swedish Medical Research Council Fellow, Wenner-Grens Institute, Stockholm, Sweden; Rockefeller Fellow, Massachusetts General Hospital, Harvard Medical School, USA; Staff member, Lister Institute of Preventive Medicine, London, England; Professor of Organic Chemistry, University of Durham, King's College, Newcastle upon Tyne; Professor of Chemical Microbiology, University of Newcastle Science and Engineering Research Council Senior Fellow, University of Cambridge; Fellow, now Emeritus, Pembroke College, Cambridge. *Memberships:* Council 1962-65, Chemical Society Committee 1964-67, Biochemical Society; Council 1973-75, Society of General Microbiology; Royal Society of Medicine; Council 1977-79, Royal Society; Council, SERC, 1979-81. *Publications:* Many research kpapers in chemical microbiology, biochemistry and chemistry, mainly concerning bacteria; Review articles. *Honours:* Meldotla Medal, Royal Institute of Chemistry, 1947; Tilden Medal 1959, Pedler lecturer 1978, Chemical Society; Fellow 1961, Leeuwenhoek Lecturer 1967, Davy Medal 1974, Royal Society; Fellow, Royal Society of Edinburgh, 1962; Honorary DSc,

Heriot-Watt University, 1979, University of Bath, 1986; Honorary member, American Society of Biological Chemists. *Hobbies:* Music; Photography. *Address:* Department of Biochemistry, University of Cambridge, Tennis Court Road, Cambridge DCB2 1GW, England.

BADDOURA, Rachid Joseph, b. 4 Aug. 1947, Lebanon. Clinical Faculty, Georgetown University, Washington, DC, USA: Director, Department of Emergency Medicine, The Memorial Hospital, Danville, Virginia. *Education:* BS, American University of Beirut, 1970; MD, American University of Beirut, 1974; Resident, Internal Medicine, St. Joseph's Medical Center, Paterson, New Jersey, 1974-76; Fellow, Pulmonary Medicine and Critical Care Medicine, Duke University, 1976-78; Diplomate: American Board Internal Medicine, American Board Pulmonary Disease, American Board Emergency Medicine. *Appointments:* Staff Physician, Wake Memorial Hospital, Raleigh, North Carolina; Staff Physician, Randolph Hospital, Asheboro, North Carolina. *Memberships:* Fellow, American College of Emergency Medicine; American Thoracic Society; American College of Chest Physicians; American College of Sports Medicne; American Society of Clinical Hypnosis. *Publication:* Co-author: Effects of Anemia, Hypo and Hyperthermia on Cerebral Oxygen Sufficiency, Federation Proceedings Abstract, 1978. *Hobbies:* Fishing; Hunting; Scuba Diving; Philosophy. *Address:* 212-3 Pinegate Circle, Chapel Hill, NC 27514, USA.

BADUI, Elias, b. 24 July 1942, Mexico City, Mexico. Chief Cardiology Service. m. Adela Tame, 28 May 1977, Mexico City, 2 sons. *Education:* MD; Medical Intern, 1969-70, Resident in Internal Medicine, 1970-72, Chief Medical Resident, 1972-72, Resident in Cardiology, 1972-74, Chief Cardiology Resident, 1973-74, Teaching Fellow, 1974-75, Mount sinai Hospital Services, New York, USA. *Appointments:* Full Time Cardiologist, 1975-77; Chief Cardiology Service, General Hospital, National Medical Center, Mexican Institute of Social Security, 1977-; Professor, Nursing School, 1976; Professor, National University of Mexico, 1983-; Associate Professor, Cardiovascular and Renal, National Institute of Politecnology, 1984-. *Memberships:* Member of 19 medical societies including: Fellow: American College of Physician; American College of Cardiology; American College of Aniology; American College of Chest Psysicians; New York Cardiological Society; Titular Member: Asociacion de Medicina Interna de Mexico; Sociedad Mexicana de Cardiologia; Fellow, American Heart Association. Senior member, American Federation for Clinical Research. *Publication:* Author of some 40 papers contributed to professional journals including: 'Chest'; 'Archivos del Instituto de Cardiologia de Mexico'; 'Clinical Research'; 'American Journal of Cardiology'; 'Prensa Medica Mexicana'; 'Neurosurgery'; 'American Heart Journal'; 'Gaceta Medica de Mexico'; 'Revista Medica'; 'Angiology'. *Honour:* MD summa cum laude, 1968. *Hobbies:* Snow Skiing; Architectural reading. *Address:* Bosque de Granados, 521, Bosques de las Lomas, ¹1700 Mexico DF, Mexico.

BAERGER, Paul Joseph, b. 18 Jan. 1934, New York, USA. Private Dental Practice. m. Carol Smith, 31 Aug. 1980, West Orange. *Education:* BS, Magna cum Laude, City College of New York, 1954; DDS, 1958, MSD, 1964, Honours, New York University. *Appointments:* Chairman, Dentistry and Oral Surgery, Park East Hospital, 1970-77; Lecturer, New York University Dental Centre; Professor, Kean College, Dept. of Health; Medical Director, Vice Chairman, Board of Directors, Dental Transplants Inc. *Memberships:* Fellow, Academy of Preventive Medicine, 1968-74; Member, Council on Dental Health; Fellow, United States Public Health Service; Fellow, Guggenheim Foundation, Institute for Dental

Research; Chairman, Municipal Environmental Protection Authority; American Academy of Oral Medicine; Founding Member, American Academy of Psychodentistry; many other professional organisations. *Publications:* Numerous articles in professional journals including: 'Annals of Dentistry'; 'Journal Dental Research'; etc. *Honours Include:* Discoverer, Kreb's Cycle Acids in Saliva; Former Visiting Professor, Perio-Prosthetics, Universities of Madrid, Milan and Naples. *Address:* 57 West 57th Street, New York, NY 10019, USA.

BAGG, Charles Ernest, b. 7 May 1920, London, England. Honorary Adviser, Research Board of Advisers, International Division, American Biographical Institute. m. Diana Patricia Ovenden, 21 Sep. 1955, Newdigate, 2 daughters. *Education:* MA; MRCS; LRCP; FRCPsych.; DPM; Cambridge University; Westminster Hospital Medical School; Postgraduate Courses, Neurology, National Hospital, Queen Square; Electroencephalography, Maida Vale Hospital for Nervous Diseases; Child Psychiatry, Hill End Child Guidance Clinic. *Appointments:* House Appointments, Windsor EMS Hospital, 1946; Senior Medical Officer, Central Signals Area, England, RAF, 1946-48; various Psychiatric Hospitals, Junior Appointments; Senior Hospital Medical Officer, Three Counties Hospital; Consultant Psychiatrist, Oxford Regional Health Authority; Medical Director, Amersham Child & Family Guidance Clinic; Consultant, Preventive Psychiatry, Bucks Area Health Authority; Consultant Psychiatrist, Chilterns Samaritans. *Memberships:* MBA; Fellow, International Biographical Association; Fellow, World Literary Academy. *Publications Include:* (Books) "Depression". in "The Samaritans in the 70's", 1973; "Handbook of Psychiatry for Social Workers & Health Visitors", 1977; numerous articles in professional journals; Book REviews include: "Current Themes in Psychiatry", 1980, "Community Care for the Mentally Disablewd", 1981, 'British Journal of Occupational Therapy'. *Honours:* Mitchel Memorial Prize, Council for Music in Hospitals, 1956; Silver Medal, International Biographical Centre, 1985. *Hobbies:* Music; Walking; Poetry; Reading; Writing Plays. *Address:* Little Broomfield, Broomfield Hill, Great Missenden, Buckinghamshire, England.

BAGGISH, Micheal Simeon, b. 22 July 1936, Hartford, Connecticut, USA. Professor of Obstetrics and Gynaecology, 2 sons, 2 daughters. *Education:* BS 1957, MD high honours Medicine 1961, University of Louisville, Kentucky. *Appointments Include:* Assistant Chief Gynaecology and Obstetrics, Sinai Hospital of Baltimore Incorporated, Baltimore, Maryland, 1970-72; Assistant Professor, Obstetrics, Gynaecology, 1970-72, Fellow Gynaecologic Pathology, 1970-72. The John Hopkins Hospital, Baltimore, Maryland; Chairman, Department of Obstetrics and Gynecology, Mount Sinai Hospital, Hartford, Connecticut, 1972-73; Associate Professor Gynaecology and Obstetrics 1972-77, Associate Professor Pathology 1976-83, Professor Obstetrics and Gynaecology 1978-83, University of Connecticut School of Medicine, Farmington, Connecticut; Professor, Chairman, Obstetrics and Gynaecology, State University of New York, Upstate Medical Center, Syracuse, New York, 1983-; Chief, Crouse-Irving Memorial Hospital, Syracuse, New York; Editor, various scientific journals. *Memberships Include:* Alan Barnes Society; President and Co-Founder of Gynaecologic Laser Society; Fellow, American College of Obstetricians and Gynaecologists; Fellow, American College of Surgeons; American Medical Association; American Society for Colposcopy and Colpomicroscopy; Board of Directors, American Laser Society. *Publications:* Over 90 contributions to books and scientific journals, including: 'Status of the Carbon Dioxide Laser for Infertility Surgery', 1983; 'Lasers in Gynaecology' in "Obstetrics and Gynaecology" (editor: J Sciarra), 1984; 'Use of

Hysteroscopy in Gynaecology' in "Progess in Gynecology" (editors: M Taymor, J Nelson), 1984. *Hobbies:* Boating; Shooting; Collector of Winston Churchill, History. *Address:* Department of Obstetrics and Gynaecology, SUNY, Health Sciences Center, 736 Irving Avenue, Syracuse, NY 13210, USA.

BAGLEY, James Edward, b. 21 Sept 1930, Waterloo, Iowa, USA. Hospital Administrator. m. Kathie Rebeca Smith, 29 November, 1968, Rockford, Illinois, 6 daughters. *Education:* BA, Public Administration; Masters Hospital and Health Administration (MHA); Credentials of Advanced Studies in Hospital and Health Care Administration. *Appointments:* USVA Hospital, Knoxville, Iowa 1952-63; State of Iowa, Department of Public Safety, 1965-63; Administrator, Ellsworth municipal Hospital, Iowa Falls, Iowa, 1963-68; 1956-68; President, Greene County Medical Center,Jefferson, Iowa, 1968-83; Executive Vice President, Phoenix Baptist Hosptial and Medical Center 1983-. *Memberships:* Fellow (Past Chairman) American Academy of Medical Administrators; American College of Hospital Administrators; Fellow, American College of Health Care Administrators. *Honours:* Medical Administrator of the Year, AAMA, 1977; Boss of the Year, Jefferson Jaycees, 1978; Regional Director of the Year, AAMA, 1980; James B Seaman Award, Iowa Hospital Association Planning 1980. *Hobbies:* Reading; Coin Collecting; Travelling. *Address:* 6025 North 46th Street, Phoenix, AZ 85015, USA.

BAHADORI, Reza, b. 22 May 1934, Iran. Chairman, Department of Obstetrics and Gynaecology. m. Vahideh Mohajer, 26 Jan. 1972, 2 sons. *Education:* MD, Tabriz Medical School, 1961. *Appointments Include:* 2nd Lieutenant, VA Physican, Army, Iran, 1962-64; Iran Health Service Phsycian, Trabriz, Iran, 1964-68; Rotating Intern, Luteran Hospital, Baltimore, Maryland, USA, 1968-69; Chief Resident in Obstetrics and Gynaecology, Luterhan Hospital, Maryland, 1971-72, Prince George General Hospital, Cleverland, 1972-73; Resident Instructor, Crownsville Hospital Medical Center, Maryland, 1973-74; Assistant Professor, 1974-78, Head of Gynaecology, 1978-84, Medical Director, Department of Obstetrics and Gynaecology, 1981-84, University of Tabriz, Iran; Visiting Professor, 1984-, Fellow in Reproductive Biology, 1984-, Case Western Reserve University, Cleveland, Ohio, USA. *Memberships:* Fellow, American College of Obstetrics and Gynaecology; Iranian Obstetrics and Gynaecology Board Examiner. *Publications:* "TBC in Tabriz"; "Practical Endocrinology of Dr Leon Speroff"; "Prolactor 4- Intersox". *Honours:* Fellow, American College of Obstetrics and Gynaecology. *Hobby:* History. *Address:* Khiaban Chaharom Ordibehsht, Koche Savam Ordibehsht, Tabriz, Iran.

BAHL, Amrit Lal, b. 26 Sep. 1937, Jhelum, India. Consultant Physician; Cardiologist. m. Usha Bahl, 28 Feb. 1962, New Delhi, 1 son, 1 daughter. *Education:* MBBS; MD; FCCP; FICA; FNCCP. *Appointments:* Assistant Physician, Willingdon Hospital, New Delhi; Lecturer in Medicine, Jawahar Lal Institute of Medicine and Educational Research, Pondicherry (India); Physician to the President of India. *Memberships:* British Medical Association; Indian Medical Association; Cardiological Society of India; Association of Physicians of India; Indian Association of Chest Diseases. *Publications:* 'Serum Lipids in Diabetes Mellitus', 1966; 'Peripheral Vascular Disease in Diabetes Mellitus', 1966; 'Precocious Ischemic Heart Disease', 1967 'Treatment of Myocardial Infarction with Phenothiazine Derivatives', 1967; 'Preclinical Diabetes Mellitus in Precocious Myocardial Infarcion', 1967. *Honour:* Honorary Physician to the President of India. *Hobbies:* Reading; Chess. *Address:* A-10/15, Vasant Vihar, New Delhi 110057, India.

BAILEY, Alison George Selborne (Joe), b. 19 July 1915, Bourne End, Bucks, England. General Practitioner/Consulting Manipulative Surgeon. m. Christine Delfosse, 15 May 1947, Wooburn, Bucks, England, 2 sons 2 daughters. *Education:* MA (Cantab); LMSSA: FRCGP. *Appointments:* House Surgeon, St Bartholomews Hospital; General Practioner/Consulting Manipulative Surgeon/Council Member, Royal College of Surgeons. *Memberships:* 'Crohns Disease' in 'Encyclopaedia of General Practice'. *Hobbies:* Rowing; Riding; Gardening; Fishing. *Address:* Clayfield House, Woburn, High Wycombe, Bucks, HP10 0HR, England.

BAILEY, Christian Martin, b. 4 Aug. 1949, London, England. Consultant Otolaryngologist, Royal National Throat, Nose & Ear Hospital, London, & The Hospital for Sick Children, Great Ormond Street, London; Hon. Senior Lecturer, Institute of Laryngology & Otology, London; Hon. Consultant Otolaryngologist, St Luke's Hospital for the Clergy, London. m. Jane Nicola Rotha Barnfield, 24 Apr. 1971, Checkendon, 1 son, 1 daughter. *Education:* BSc., London, 1970; LRCP, MRCS, England, MB.BS, London, 1973; FRCS England, 1978. *Appointments:* House Surgeon, House Physician, Senior House Officer, Accident & Emergency, The Royal Free Hospital, London; Senior House Officer, Otol., Royal National Throat, Nose & Ear Hospital, London; Senior House Officer, General Surgery, Royal Northern Hospital, London; Registrar, Senior Registrar, Otol., Royal National Throat Nose & Ear Hospital, London & Sussex Throat & Ear Hospital, Brighton; TWJ Clinical & Research Fellow, University of Michigan, USA. *Membership:* Fellow, Royal Society of Medicine; British Association of Otolaryngologists; European Academy of Facial Surgery; British Medical Association. *Publications:* "Tuberculous laryngitis", jointly, 'Laryngoscope', 1981; "Recovery from prolonged sensorineural hearing loss", jointly 'American Journal of Otology', 1982; "Intratemporal facial nerve neuroma", jointly, 'Journal of Laryngology & Otology', 1983-1985; "Treatment of the drooling child by submandibular duct transposition", jointly, '1985; etc. *Hobbies:* Walking; Sailing. *Address:* 55 Harley Street, London W1N 1DD, England.

BAILEY, Jack Bennett, b. 29 Aug. 1940, Celina, Tennessee, USA. President and Chief Operating Officer, International Healthcare Management Inc., m. Lyla E French, 19 Oct. 1968, New Castle, Pennsylvania, 1 son, 1 daughter. *Education:* BS, Business Administration, Tennessee Technological University; Certified Public Accountant. *Appointments:* Audit Staff, Ernst & Whinney, Nashville, Tennessee; Controller, Coliseum Park Hospital, Macon, Georgia; Internal Audit Manager and Assistant Controller, Hospital Corporation of America, Nashville, Tennessee; Executive Director, Humana Hospital/Southwest, Louisville Kentucky; Assistant Regional Manager, Humana Inc., Mobile, Alabama; General Director, Hopital de la Tour et Pavillon Gourgas, Geneva, Switzerland; Executive Director, Humana Hospital Florence, Alabama; Administrator, Springhill Hospital, Mobile; President, Spectra Professional Search, Atlanta, Georgia. *Memberships:* American College of Hospital Administrators; American Istitute of Certified Public Accountants; Healthcare Financial Management Association. *Honour:* Kentucky Colonel, 1978. *Hobbies:* Snow Skiing; Camping; Travel. *Address:* 140 Valley Cove, Atlanta, GA 30338, USA.

BAILEY, James Paul, b. 20 Nov. 1937, St. Louis, Missouri, USA. Hospital Administrator. Divorced, 1 son, 1 daughter. *Education:* BS, The George Washington University; MS, Health Care Administration, Trinity University, San Antonio, Texas. *Appointments:* Assistant Administrator, Administrator, Wysong Memorial Hospital, McKinsey, Texas; Health Administrator, State of

Oklahoma, Oklahoma City; Administrator, US Coast Guard Academy Hospital, New London, Connecticut; Medical Administrator, Assistant to Assistant Surgeon General, US (US Coast Guard), Washington, DC.; Chief of Health Services, US Coast Guard, Boston, Massachusetts. *Memberships:* Affiliate American College of Hospital Administration. *Publications:* "Penicillin Testing" (with R. Marvit), 1967; "Nursing Shortage A Fallacy or Poor Management", 1977. *Hobbies:* Travel; Hunting; Gardening. *Address:* PO Box 1886, Plano, TX 75074, USA.

BAIN, John, b. 18 Aug. 1940, Aberdeen Scotland. Professor, Primary Medical Care, University of Southampton. m. Sandra, 2 sons, 1 daughter. *Education:* MB., CHB, 1964, MD, 1974, University of Aberdeen; D.OBST.R.COG., Royal/College of Obstetricians, 1966; DCH, Royal College of Physicians, 1968; MRCGP, Royal College of General Practitioners, 1969. *Appointments:* Principal, General Practice, Livingston New Town, Scotland; Visiting Fellow, College of Medicine, University of Florida, USA; Senior Lecturer, University Department of General Practice, Aberdeen. *Memberships:* British medical Association; Royal College of General Practitioners; (Royal Society of Medicine. *Publications:* "General Practitioners) in a District Hospital", 1972, "Paediatrics in Livingston New Town", 1975, "Developmental Screening of Pre-School Children", 1977, "Referral to ENT Specialists", 1981, "Clinical Trials in the Treatment of Otitis Media", 1983, 1985, all in British Medical Journal'; "Doctor-Patient Communication", 'Medical Education', 1977' "Colour Atlas of Mouth Throat and Ear Disorders", MTP Press Ltd, 1985. *Hobbies:* Golf; Photography; Travel; Exploring Book Shops; Watching Cricket. *Address:* Dept. of Primary Medical Care, Aldermoor Health Centre, Southampton S01 6ST, England.

BAIRD, Patricia Ann, b. 11 Oct. 1937, Rochdale, Lancashire, England. Professor of Medical Genetics. m. Robert Merrifield Baird, 22 Feb. 1964, Montreal, Canada, 2 sons, 1 daughter. *Education:* BSc Biological Sciences, 1959, MD, CM, 1963, McGill University, Montreal; Fellow, Royal College of Physicians of Canada, 1968; Fellow Canadian College of Medical Geneticists, 1976. *Appointments:* Intern, Royal Victoria Hospital, Montreal, 1963-64; Resident Fellow, Vancouver General Hospital, 1964-68; Instructor in Paediatrics, 1968-72, Assistant Professor, 1972-77, Associate Professor, 1977-79, Head of Department of Medical Genetics, 1979-, Professor of Medical Genetics, 1982-, University of British Columbia, Vancouver. *Memberships:* Board of Governors, University of British Columbia; Chairman, Genetics Grants Committee, Medical Research Council of Canada, 1983-; Vice-President, Canadian College of Medical Geneticists, 1984-86; National Working Group on Epidemiology of Mental Retardation (Health & Welfare Canada), 1984-; Deputy Chairman, Scholarships & Fellowships Committee, British Columbia Health Care Research Foundation; Research Advisory Committee of Children's Research Foundation. *Publications:* Over 100 papers & abstracts in scientific & medical journals. *Hobbies:* Skiing; Music; Gardening. *Address:* Department of Medical Genetics, Rm 226, 6174 University Boulevard, University of British columbia, Vancouver BC, V6T 1W5, Canada.

BAIRD, William Hennings, b. 3 Nov. 1928, Bridgeport, Connecticut, USA. Director, Hospital Rehabilitation Unit. m. Clare Griffin Baird, 23 Aug. 1952, Chelsea, Massachusetts, USA, 3 sons, 3 daughters. *Education:* BA, Brown University, 1949; MD, Tufts Medical College, 1952. *Appointments:* Chief, Intermediate Service, USVAH, West Haven, Connecticut, 1958-69; Chief, Medical Services, Gaylord Hospital, Wallingford, Connecticut, 1969-72; Adjunct Professor, Allied Health Sciences, Quinnipiac College, 1972-; Director, Rehabilitation Unit, Bridgeport Hospital, 1972-. *Memberships:*

Connecticut State Medical Society; American Society of Internal Medicine; American Congress of Rehabilitation Medicine; American Rheumatology Association; Brown Medical Alumni Association. *Publications:* Contributing Author: "Care of the Nursing Home Patient" 1968. *Honour:* American Board of Internal Medicine, 1960. *Address:* 226 Mill Hill Avenue, Bridgeport, CT 06610, USA.

BAJAJ, Jasbir Singh, b. 26 Sep. 1936, Lahore, W. Punjab. Professor, Medicine, All India Institute of Medical Sciences. m. Avninder, 18 Jan. 1964, New Delhi, 1 son, 1 daughter. *Education:* MB BS, Punjab, 1958; MD (AIIMS), 1962; MRCPE, 1967; FRCP, 1973; MD, Honoris Causa, Karolinska, Stockholm, 1985; Fellow, national academy of Medical Sciences, 1980. *Appointments Include:* Commonwealth Scholar, UK, 1965-66; Assistant Professor, 1967-72, Associate Professor, 1972-79, Professor, 1979-, Medicine, Sub-Dean, 1972-74, All India Institute of Medical Sciences, New Delhi; Visiting Professorships: Queens University of Belfast, UK, 1970, New York Medical College, USA, 1973, Kuwait University, 1983, Karolinska Institute, Stockholm, 1984; WHO Assignments: Short Term Consultant to Government of Bangladesh, 1977-78; Temporary advisor, Member, Several Task Forces and Steering Committees, 1975-; WHO Expert Advisory Panel on Chronic Degenerative Diseases, Diabetes, 1979-; Vice Chairman, WHO Expert Committee on Diabetes, 1979; Co-Chairman, WHO Study Group on Diabetes, 1985; etc. *Memberships:* President Elect, International Diabetes Federation, 1982-85; Association of Physicians of India; Endocrine Society of India, Past President; Diabetic Association of India, President, research Section; Indian Association for the Advancement of Medical Education. *Publications:* Numerous articles in professional journals including: 'Excerpta Medica'. Amsterdam, 1977; Editor, Indian Journal of Medical Education; Member, Advisory editorial Boards, several National & International Journals; Author: "Glucogon: Its Role in Physiology and Clinical Medicine", 1977; "Diabetes Mellitus in Developing Countries", 1984. *Honours:* Padma Bhushan, 1982; Padma Shri, 1981; Banting and Best Oration, 1971; Arasthur Memorial Oration, 1972; etc. *Hobbies:* Music; Urdu Poetry. *Address:* All India Institute of Medical Sciences, Ansari Nagar, New Delhi 110 029, India.

BAJAS, Teresita Awa, b. 12 Jan 1942, Philippines. Child Psychiatrist. m. Edgardo P Bajas MD, 25 Nov 1967, 1 daughter. *Education:* Pre Med (Hons) Xavier University, Philippines, 1961; MD, University of Sto Tomas, Philippines, 1966; New York School of Psychiatry, 1973. *Appointments include:* Child Psychiatry Fellow, Staten Island Mental Health Society, New York, 1973-75; Co-ordinator of Psychiatry, Bushwick-Ridgewood Mental Health Clinic, New York, 1976-77; Supervising Psychiatrist, East Flatbush Mental Health Clinic, New York, 1977-78; Staff Child Psychiatrist, Staten Island Mental Health Clinic, New York, 1978-79; Consultant Child Psychiatrist, Children's Aid Society, Goodhue Center, 1979-; Consultant Psychiatrist, Richmond Memorial Hospital, Doctors Hospital of Staten Island; Golden Gate Nursing Home; Associate Staff Psychiatrist, St Vincents Hospital and Medical Center of Richmond, 1979-, Bayley Seton Hospital of Staten Island, 1983-85. *Memberships:* American Psychiatric Association; New York Council on Child Psychiatry; American Womens Medical Association; Brooklyn Psychiatric Society; Philippine Medical Association in America, Secretary 1975-76, Board of Directors, 1976-77. *Publications:* Participant in publication of "Diagnostic and Statistical Manual of Mental Disorders" 3rd edition. *Honour:* Voted OUtstanding Alumni in Medicine, Lourdes College, 1983. *Hobbies:* Playing piano; Collecting antique porcelain; Travel; Gardening. *Address:* 11 Ralph Place, Staten Island, NY 10304, USA.

BAKARANIA, Magan L, b. 20 Apr. 1948, India

Physician. m. Rekha Gopaldas Khambhayata, 29 Jan. 1974, Bombay, India, 1 son, 1 daughter. *Education:* MB, MD, BJ Medical College. *Appointments:* Clinical Assistant Instructor of Medicine, State University of New York at Buffalo, 1979-1980. *Memberships:* Hillsborough Medical Association; Florida Medical Association; American Medical Association; West Coast Academy of Cardiology. *Honours:* American Boards of Internal Medicine 1980, Cardiology 1981, Chest Physicians 1983. *Address:* 500 Vonderburg Drive, Suite 212W, Brandon, FL 33511, USA.

BAKER, Arthur Barrington, b. 24 June 1939, Brisbane, Australia, Professor of Anaesthesia and of Intensive Care. m. Jane Elizabeth Colliss, 29 July 1981, Oxford, England, 2 sons, 1 daughter. *Education:* MB, BS, Queensland, Australia, 1963; FFARACS, 1968, FFARCS, 1968; D Phil, Oxford University, England, 1971; DHMSA, 1982. *Appointments:* Resident 1964-65, Registrar in Anaesthesia 1966-67, Resuscitation Officer 1968, Royal Brisbane Hospital, Brisbane, Australia; Research Senior Registrar, Oxford University. England, 1968-71; Reader in Anaesthesia, Queensland University, Australia, 1972-75; Professor of Anaesthesia and of Intensive Care, Otago University, Dunedin, New Zealand, 1975-. *Memberships:* Australian Medical Association; New Zealand Medical Association; ASA; NZSA; AA GB & I; RSM; ANZICS; NZPS. *Publications:* Numerous journal articles including 'Physiology of Artificial Ventilation', 1971. *Hobbies:* Chess; Mountaineering; Reading. *Address:* Department of Anaesthesia and Intensive Care, Otago University, Dunedin, New Zealand.

BAKER, Carl Gwin, b. 27 Nov. 1930, Louisville, Kentucky, USA. Consultant and Emeritus Medical Director. m. Catherine Valerie Smith, 23 May 1975, Rockville, Maryland, USA, 2 daughters, 3 step-sons, 1 step-daughter. *Education:* AB, Zoology, University of Louisville, 1942; MD, University of Louisville School of Medicine, 1944; MA, Biochemistry, University of California (Berkeley), 1949; Diploma, Federal Executive Development, University of Chicago, 1957; DSc, honorary, university of Louisville, 1980. *Appointments Include:* Director, National Cancer Institutes, National Instutute of Health, USA, 1969-72; Assistant Surgeon General, USA Public Health Service, 1970-; Special Assistant to Director, National Institutes of Health, 1972; President and Scientific Director, Hazleton Laboratories, Vienna, Virginia, USA, 1972-73; Private Consultant, Medical Research Administration, USA, 1973-75; Director, Program Policy Staff, Health REsources Administration, Department of Health,Education and Welfare, USA, 1975-76; Medical Director, 1977-82, Member Scientific Advisory Committee, 1971-85, Consultant and Medical Director Emeritus, 1985-, Ludwig Institute for Cancer Research, Zurich, Switzerland. *Memberships:* American Association for Cancer Research (Director 1973-76; American Society of Biological Chemists; American Chemical Society, Division of Biological Chemistry, Secretary, 1955-57, Councillor 1958-61; Society of Experimental Biology and Medicine; Sigma Xi; Washington Society for the History of Medicine. *Publications Include:* "The Convergence Technique: A Method for the Planning and Programming of Research Efforts" in Management Science, 1967; "Assessments of New Methods of Therapy" in Postgraduate Medicine, 1970; "Cancer' Encyclopaedia Brittannica, 1972 edition; "Cancer Research Program Strategy and Planning" Journal of National Cancer Institute, 1977. *Honours:* Jane Coffin Childs Fellowship, 1946-48; Honorary Order of Kentucky Colonels, 1964; US Public Health Service meritorious Medal, 1966; Vice-President, Tenth International Cancer Congress, 1970; Cosmos Club of Washington; Board of Directors, American Association for Cancer Research, 1973-76; DSC (h.c.) University of

Louisville, 1980. *Hobbies:* Classical music; Photography; Computers; History and Philosophy of Science. *Address:* 19408 Charline Manor Road, Olney, MD 20832, USA.

BAKER, David Walter, b. 2 June, 1916, Illinois, USA. General Practitioner of Electro-Acupuncture. m. Alberta Hensel Pew, 29 Sep. 1951, Bryn Mawr, Pennysylvania, USA, 2 sons, 4 daughters. *Education:* AB, Coe College, USA, 1936; ThB, Princeton Theological Seminary, 1939; MD, University of Pennysylvania, 1950. *Appointments:* Urologist, Lahey Clinic, Boston, Massachussetts, 1955-56; Urologist, Lankenau Hospital, Philadelphia, 1957-70; General Practice of Electro-acupuncture EAV, Chester, Nova Scotia, Canada, 1978-present. *Memberships:* Canadian Medical Association; Canadian Pain Society; Nova Scotia Medical Society; Occidental Research Foundation. *Publication:* 'An Introduction to the Theory and Practice of German Elecroacupuncture (EAV) and Accompanying Medications' published in the 'American Journal of Acupuncture', volume 12, No. 4, October-December, 1984, pp 327-332. *Honour:* DD, Eastern Baptist College, 1963. *Hobbies:* Lapidary; Genealogical Research. *Address:* 295 Queen Street, Chester, Nova Scotia, Canada, BOJ 1JO.

BAKER, Eric Anthony, b. 3 Sep. 1920, Birmingham, England, Retired in 1985, m. Margaret Newton, 28 Aug. 1943, Birmingham. *Education:* MD; FRCP; FRCS. *Appointments:* Consultant in Accident and Emergency; Medical Superintendent, Charles Johnson Memorial Hospital, Nqutu, Zululand, Republic of South Africa, 1945-75. *Memberships:* Member of local Medical societies. *Publications:* "The Man Next To Me", 1958; Contributor to various journals. *Honours:* Honorary PhD, Natal, 1974; LLD, Birmingham, 1975; CBE, 1975. *Hobbies:* Cycling; Woodwork. *Address:* 14A Lansdowne Road, Wimbledon, London SW20 8AN, England.

BAKER, Gordon Fred, b. 3 Apr. 1941, Pennsylvania, USA. Vice President, Schick Shadel Hospital, Santa Barbara. m. Sandra J. Stevens, 25 Mar. 1967, Meadville, 2 sons. *Education:* BA, Psychology, University of Maryland; MA, Health Care Administration, George Washington University. *Appointments:* Administrative Resident, Medical Centre, Princeton; Assistant Administrator, Pascack Valley Hospital; Associate Director, Bellevue Hospital Centre, New York City; Vice President, Frederick Memorial Hospital; Administrator, Vice President, Chief Executive Officer, Schick Shadel Hospital of Santa Barbara. *Memberships:* Member, American College of Hospital Administrators; American College of Alcoholism Treatment Adminstrators, Fellow; American Hosptial Association; California Hospital Association; Hospital Council of Southern Caiifornia. *Hobby:* Running. *Address:* Schick Shadel Hospital of Santa Barbara, 45E Alamar Ave., Santa Barbara, CA 93105, USA.

BAKER, Herman, b. 22 Jan. 1926, New York City, USA. Professor. m. Shirley Levitz, 15 Nov. 1952, New York City, 2 sons. *Education:* BS, City College of New York, 1946; MS Emory University, 1948; PhD, New York University, 1956. *Appointments:* Research Assistant, Columbia University Medical School, 1948-50; Research Associate, Chemistry, Mount Sinai Hospital, New York, 1950-60; Associate Professor, Medicine, New Jersey College Medicine, 1960-70; Professor, Medicine, Preventive Medicine, New Jersey Medical School, 1970-. *Memberships:* American Society Clinical Nutrition; Society, Experimental Biology & Medicine; Fellow, American College of Nutrition; Pan American Medical Association; President, Society of Preventive Medicine. *Publications:* "Clinical Vitaminolgoy", 1968; over 260 articles in professional journals. *Honours:* Specialist, human Nutrition, American

Board of Nutrition, 1968. *Hobbies:* Music. *Address:* New Jersey Medical School, 100 Bergen St., Martland GB 159, Newark, NJ 07103, USA.

BAKER, John Garrett, b. 20 July 1946, Gary, Indiana, USA. Supervisor of Mycology and Mycobacteriology. *Education:* BS, University of Vermont, 1968; MACT, University of North Carolina, 1976. *Appointments:* Assistant Supervisor, Mycology and Mycobacteriology, North Carolina Memorial Hospital, Chapel Hill, North Carolina; Supervisor, Mycology Diagnostic Laborator, Analytab Products, Plainview, New York; Currently, Supervisor, Mycology and Mycobacteriology, Lahey Clinic, Burlington, Massachusetts. *Memberships:* Mycological Society of America; Medical Mycological Society of the Americas; International Society for Human and Animal Mycology; American Society for Microbiology; Northeast Association for Infectious Disease and Microbiology. *Publications:* Co-author of articles contributed to : 'Mycotaxon'; 'Journal of Clinical Microbiology'; 'Archives of Pathology and Laboratory Medicine'; Journal of Elisha Mitchell Science Society' and others. Participant in interviews on radio and contributed to 'Urology Times' and 'Mycology Observer'. *Hobbies:* Jazz; Biking; Running; Swimming. *Address:* 1 Pembroke Drive, Unit 19, Derry, NH 03038, USA.

BAKER, Philip Alan, b. 16 Oct. 1929, Whitstable, England, Professor of Psychiatry and Paediatrics, m. Heather Ferguson, 7 Sept.1957, Alnwick, Northumberland, England, 1 son, 2 daughters. *Education:* MRCP (Edinburgh), 1960; FRCP (Edinburgh), 1976; MRCPsych, 1971; FRCPsych, 1980; FRCP(C), 1980; DCH, 1958; DPM, 1960; MB, BS, (London), 1953. *Appointments:* Consultant Children's Psychiatrist, Dundee Child Psychiatry Service, Scotland, 1962-67; Consultant in Clinical Charge of the Charles Burns Clinic, Birmingham, England, 1967-75; Part-time Lecturer, Postgraduate Tutor in Child Psychiatry, University of Birmingham, 1968-75; Director of Inpatient Services, 1975-79, Director of Psychiatric Education, 1979-80, Thistletown Regional Centre, Toronto, Canada; Professor of Psychiatry, University of Toronto, Canada, 1979-80; Professor of Psychiatry and Paediatrics, University of Calgary, Alberta Childrens Hospital, Alberta, Canada. *Memberships:* Fellow, American Orthopsychiatric Association; American Society of Clinical Hypnosis; Alberta Medical Association; Association for Child Psychology and Psychiatry; Association for Family Therapy; Canadian Academy of Child Psychiatry; Canadian Medical Association. *Publications:* "Basic Family Therapy", 1971, 4th edition, 1983; "Basic Child Psychiatry", 1981; "Care Can Prevent", 1973; "Using Metaphors in Psychotherapy", 1985; "The Residential Psychiatric Treatment of Childlren", 1974; Author of numerous professional articles on psychiatry. *Hobbies:* Photography; Jazz and blues music. *Address:* 1820 Richmond Road SW, Calgary, Alberta T2T 5C7, Canada.

BAKER, Terry George, b. 27 May 1936, Brighton, England. Professor of Medical Sciences. m. Pauline Archer, 21 Aug. 1958, Conventry, 3 sons. *Education:* BSc (Hon) Zoology, University of Wales, 1959; PhD, Birmingham University, 1964; DSc, Edinburgh University, 1975; MRCPath; FIMLS; FIBiol; FRSE. *Appointments:* Lecturer in Anatomy, University of Birmingham, 1961-68; Leturer, Obstetrics and Gynaecology, University of Edinburgh, 1968-74; Senior Lecturer, Obstetrics and Gynaecology, University of Edinburgh, 1974- 79. *Memberships:* Royal Society of Edinburgh; Royal College of Parthologists; Institute of Biology; Institute of Medical Laboratory Sciences; Society for Study of Fertility; Society for Study of Reproduction; British Society for Developmental Biology. *Publications:* "Effects of Ionizing Radiation on the Ovary", "The Development of the Ovary and the Process of Dogenesis", both in "The Ovary", (ed Zuckerman S

& Weir BJ), 1976. *Hobbies:* Sculpture; Music; Photography. *Address:* School of Biomedical Sciences, University of Bradford,Bradford BD7 1DP, West Yorkshire, England.

BAKER, Theresa Suzanne, b. 10 Mar. 1952, Bremerton, Washington, USA, Chief, Basic Sciences Division, Department of Military Medicine, Uniformed Services University of Health Sciences, m. Patrick J Pound, 4 Aug 1979, Burton, Washington, USA. *Education:* Certificate, Executive Management, Claremont Graduate School, Claremont, Calif, 1982; Masters, Hospital Health Administration, Xavier University, Cincinnati, Ohio, 1980; BA, Park College, MO, 1975; AA Business Administration, Highline Community College, Wash, 1972. *Appointments:* Assistant Administrator, Adminstrator, Resource Management, Commander Medical Squadron Section, USAF Hospital, Vandenberg AFB, Calif, 1976-78; Director, Medical Logistics Management, USAF Regional Hospital, March AFB, Calif, 1980-82; Active Duty Member, United States Air Force, 1973-; Assistant Professor, Department of Military Medicine, 1982-. *Memberships:* American College of Hospital Administrators, 1984-; American Business Women's Association, 1977-; Toastmasters International, 1977-. *Publications:* 'ABC Analysis An Executive's Approach to Inventory Control', 1980. *Honours:* Outstanding Young Women in America, 1984; Joint Service Commendation Medal, 1983; Meritorious Service Medal, 1978, 1982. *Hobbies:* Fishing; Needlework, Carpentry. *Address:* USUHS-MIM, 4301 Jones Bridge Road, Bethesda, MD 20814-4799, USA.

BALAZS, Robert, b. 8 Nov. 1923, Budapest, Hungary. Director. m. 25 Feb. 1958, Cardiff, Wales, *Education:* MD, Summa cum Laude, Eotvos Lorant Egyetem Orvostudomanyi Kar, Budapest; Candidate of Medical Sciences, Magyar Tudomanyos Akademia, Budapest. *Appointments:* Research Assistant, Lecturer, Department of Medical Chemistry, University Medical School, Budapest, 1948-55; Biochemist, Biological Research Laboratory, Hungarian Air Force, Budapest, 1955-56; Rockefeller Grant, Whitechurch Hospital, Cardiff, Wales, 1957; Scientist, 1958-72, Acting Director, Medical Research Council Neuropsychiatry Unit, Cardiff and Carshalton, England, 1972-75; Director, Medical Research Council Developmental Neurobiology Unit, Institute of Neurology, London, 1975-; Honorary Lecturer, London University, 1978-; Honorary Consultant, National Hospital, Queen Square, London, 1978-. *Memberships:* International Brain Research Organisation; International Society for Developmental Neuroscience; International Society for Neurochemistry; The Biochemical Society; The British Neuropatholigocal Society; Brain Research Assn.; European Society for Neuro-chemistry; The Royal Society of Medicine. *Publications:* "Metabolic Compartmentation in the Brain", (Co-editor)m, 1980. *Hobbies:* Travel; Photography. *Address:* MRC Developmental Neurobiology Unit, Institute of Neurology, 33 John's Mews, London, WC1N 2NS.

BALE, Patricia Marea, b. 20 May 1931, Melbourne, Australia. Head of Department of Histopathology. m. Edmond Hirst, 30 May 1962, Sydney. *Education:* MB BS, University of Melbourne, 1955. *Appointments:* Resident in Pathology, Beth-El Hospital, New York, USA, 1958-59; Resident and Teaching Fellow in Pathology, Bellevue Hospital Center, New York, 1960; Teaching Fellow in Pathology, Bellevue Hospital Center, New York, 1960; Teaching Fellow in Pathology, Sydney University Medical School, Sydney, Australia, 1961; Registrar in Pathology 1962-63, Assistant Director of Morbid Anatomy 1964-68, Sydney Hospital; Staff Histopathologist 1969-77, Head of Histopathology Department, Royal Alexandra Hospital for Children, Sydney. *Memberships:* Royal College of Pathologists of Australasia; Royal College of Pathologists UK;

International Academy of Pathology; Australian and New Zealand Paediatric Pathology Group; Australian College of Paediatrics. *Publications;* 'Teratomas in childhood', (with D M Painter and D Cohen), 1975; 'Congenital cystic malformation of the lung', 1979; 'Diagnosis and behaviour of juvenile rhabdomyosarcoma',(with R E Parsons and M H Stevens), 1983; 'Sacrococcygeal developmental abnormalities and tumours in children', 1984. *Honour:* Member of the Order of Australia, Queen's Birthday, 1985. *Hobbies:* Oil painting; Writing; Swimming. *Address:* Histopathology Department, Royal Alexandra Hospital for Children, Camperdown, New South Wales 2050 Australia.

BALIM, Ali Ihsan, b. 1 Sep. 1923, Isparta. Physician, Outpatient Dept; IBM, Ankara. m. Mukaddes, 7 Sep. 1951, 1 son, 1 daughter. *Education:* MD; Internist; FCCP. *Appointments:* Resident, Municipal Hospitals: Seton Hospital, Bronx Municipal Hospital Centres, 1953-54, Albert Einstein College of Medicine, 1955; Specialist Physician, Sumlu Army Hospital, Erzurum, 1952; Internist, Medical Director, Local State Hospitals, Yalvac, 1953; Senirkent, 1955-60; Specialist Resident, Lecturer, Nontuber-Culous Chest Diseases, Chest Clinic, Faculty of Medicine, Ege University, 1960-61. *Memberships:* FCCP; Turkish Medical Association, Ankara Section. *Publications:* "Typhoid Fever Epidemic involving immunized Soldiers", 'US Armed Forces Medical Journal', 1954; "A Report on Antibacterial Treatment of 103 Cases (Among Children) with special reference to Bronchial Involvement", 'International Congress of American College of Chest Physicians, 1956; "Mediastinal Liposaroma", 'Diseases of the Chest', 1963. *Honours:* Honorary Membership, Turkish red Crescent Society, 1965. *Hobbies:* Mountaineering; Writing Short Stories; Reading History & Memoirs. *Address:* Dostlar Sitesi, C Blok No. 125, Ziyabey Cad. - Balgat, Ankara, Turkey.

BALL, David Lee, b. 6 July 1947, Adelaide, South Australia. Deputy Head, Department of Cancer Medicine and Consultant Radiotherapist, Peter MacCallum Hospital, The Cancer Institute, Melbourne. m. Mary Elezabeth Regan, 20 Feb. 1971, Adelaide, 2 sons, 2 daughters. *Education:* MB BS, Adelaide, 1970; FRACR, 1976. *Appointments:* Resident Medical Officer, Royal Adelaide Hospital, 1971; Radiotherapy Registrar, Peter MacCallum Hospital, 1973-76; Locum Radiotherapy Registrar, Royal Marsden Hospital, London, 1979-80; Consultant Radiotherapist, Peter MacCullum Hospital, 1983-; Deputy Head, Department of Cancer Medicine, Peter MacCallum Hospital, 1985. *Memberships:* Australian Medical Association; Clinical Oncological Society of Australia; Royal Asutralasian College of Radiologists. *Publications:* Co-author, 'The Management of Metastatic Seminoma Testis' in 'Cancer', 1982; 'The Late Effect of Radical Radiotherapy for Lung Cancer on Pulmonary Function', 'Australian Radiology', 1985. *Hobbies:* Wine; Gardens; Music. *Address:* Peter MacCallum Hospital, 481 Little Lonsdale Street, Melbourne, Victoria 3000, Australia.

BALSAM, Rosemary Marshall, b. 31 Dec. 1939, Northern Ireland. Staff Psychiatrist and University Associate Clinical Professor; Psychoanalyst. m. 1) Alan Balsam, 18 Dec. 1968, dec. 1972, Bangor, Northern Ireland, 1 daughter. 2) Paul Schwaber, 9 Aug. 1979, Middletown, Connecticut, USA. *Education:* MB BCh, BAO, Queens University, Belfast, Northern Ireland; DPM, London University; MRCP, Edinburgh, Scotland; MRCPsy, London, England; Graduate, Western New England Institute for Psychoanalysis; Member, American Psychoanalytic Association. *Appointments:* Houseman, Royal Victoria Hospital, Belfast, Northern Ireland; Registrar, Department of Mental Health, Queen University, Belfast; Clinical Instructor, Connecticut Mental Health Center; Clinical

Instructor, Fellow and Assistant Clinical Professor, currently Staff and Associate Clinical Professor; Department of Student Mental Health, Yale University. *Memberships:* Royal College of Psychiatrists, London, England; Royal College of Physicians, Edinburgh, Scotland; American Psychoanalytic Association. *Publications:* "Becoming a Psychotherapist –A Clinical Primer", 2nd edition, 1984; contributor to "Fathers and Their Families", 1986; 'Psychoanalytic Study of the Child', 1984. *Honour:* Book of the Year, American Journal of Nursing, 1975. *Hobbies:* Music; Literature. *Address:* 80 Underhill Road, Hawden, CT 06517, USA.

BAMFORD, Frank Noel, b. 25 Dec. 1927, Stockport, Cheshire, England. Reader in Developmental Paediatrics. m. Marian Ruth Green, 21 Mar. 1953, Stockport, 4 sons. *Education:* MB, ChB, University of Manchester, 1945-51; DPH, University of Leeds, 1957-59. *Appointments:* House Surgeon, Hospital for Sick Children, London; Resident Medical Officer, Duchess of York Hospital, Manchester; Principal Medical Officer in Child Health, Bradford; Reader, Honorary Consultant in Developmental Paediatrics. *Memberships:* British Medical Association (Former Divisional Chairman); Academic Board, British Paediatric Association; Former Chairman, Medical Group, British Agencies for Adoption & Fostering. *Publications:* 'Social Paediatrics' – chapter in Textbook of Paediatrics edited by Forfar & Ameil (3rd edition); 'School Health Services' – chapter in Child Health & the Community, edited Mitchell (1st & 2nd editions); Sundry articles on adoption, Child Abuse, Immigration. *Hobby:* Walking. *Address:* Dolphin's Green, 8 Broughton Road, Adlington, Macclesfield, Cheshire, SK10 4ND, England.

BANERJEE, Rabindra Nath, b. 1 Apr. 1935, Laokhowa, Nowgong, Assam, India. Consultant Cardiologist; Medical Specialist. m. Krishna Ganguh, 4 Mar. 1971, Calcutta, 1 son. *Education:* BSc, 1956, MB, Surgery, 1962, MD, 1975, Calcutta University; FCCP, American College of Chest Physicians, 1983. *Appointments:* Pre-Registration Clinical Assistant, 1962-63, Junior, Intermediate and Senior Hosue Staff, 1963-67, N R S Medical College, Calcutta; Research Fellow in Cardiovascular diseases, ICMR, 1967-69; RMO, Clinical Tutor, SSKM Hospital, Calcutta, 1969-71; Medical Officer, State Bank of India, Consultant Cardiologist, Oil and National Gas Commissions, India, 1975-. *Memberships:* Indian Medical Association; American College of Chest Physician. *Publications:* "Studies on Cardiomegaly with Special Reference to Idiopathic Variety", Doctoral Dissertation, 1970; contributions to 'Indian Medical Forum'. *Honurs:* Fellowship, American College of Chest Physicians, 1983. *Hobbies:* Music, Vocal and instrumental; Sports. *Address:* 123 Jodhpur Park, Calcutta 700068, India.

BANEZ Y VIRATA, Armin, b. 30 June 1925, Manila, Philippines. Associate Professor of Surgery. m. Grace, 14 Mar., 1971, New Castle, Pennysylvania, USA, 2 sons, 2 daughters. *Education:* Associate in Arts, Doctor of Medicine, University of Santo Tomas, Manila, Philippines. *Appointments:* Attending Surgeon, Youngstown Hospital Association, 1960 – present; Attending Surgeon, St. Elizabeth Hospital, 1960 – present. Director of Colo-Rectal Surgery, Youngstown Hospital Association, 1965 – present; Director of Enterostomal Rehabilitation Service, Youngstown Hospital Association; Assistant Professor of Surgery, Northeastern Ohio University College of Medicine; Attending Surgeon, Northern Columbiana County Community Hospital, Associate Professor of Surgery, Northeastern Ohio University College of Medicine, USA. *Memberships Include:* American Medical Association; World Medical Association; International College of Surgeons, Fellow; Americaan Society of Abdominal Surgeons, Fellow;

American Society of Contemporary Medicine and Surgery. *Publications:* Contributions to: 'American Journal of Proctology', 1974, 1980, 1981; 'Gastrointestinal Endoscopy', 1976; "Colonoscopy, Diagnosis and Treatment of Colonic Diseases" by Hiromi Shinya; "Atlas of Coloscopy", by F.P. Rossini. *Honours:* Recipient of numerous awards and certificates from various bodies including: American Medical Association Physician's Recognition Award, 1973-76; Certificates of appreciation from the American Cancer Society, 1973, 1975, 1978 (outstanding service) 1982; American Cancer Society Highest Award for Symposium on Cancer and colon-Rectal Cancer Screening. *Hobbies:* Gardening; Scuba Diving; Trout Fishing; Painting. *Address:* 3034 Frederick Drive, Youngstown, OH 44505, USA.

BANKIER, Robert Gordon, b. 1 June, 1926, Scotland. Professor; Head, Forensic Psychiatry, University of Manitoba, Canada. *Education:* MB, ChB, University of Glasgow, Scotland, 1949; Dip. Psychiatry, University of Manitoba, Canada, 1965; Certified Specialist, Psychiatry, Royal College of Physicians of Canada, 1965; MSc., University of Manitoba, 1968, PhD, Neuroanatomy, 1983. *Appointments Include:* General Practice, England, 1953-56; General Practice, Alberta, Canada, 1956-61; Assistant Resident, Psychiatry, Winnipeg General Hospital, Canada, 1962-63; Resident in Psychiatry, Children's Hospital and Child Guidance Clinic, Winnipeg, 1963-64; Senior Resident in Psychiatry, Psychiatric Institute, Winnipeg, 1964-65; Assistant Research Psychiatrist, University of Manitoba, 1965-66; Director of Research and Residency Training, Hospital for Mental Diseases, Selkirk, Manitoba, 1966-72; Director, Forensic Services, Province of Manitoba, Professor and Head, Forensic Psychiatry, University of Manitoba, 1972-. *Memberships Include:* Canadian Medical Association; Canadian Psychiatric Association; American Psychiatric Association; Royal College of Psychiatrists; Royal Society of Medicine, etc. *Publications Include:* Author and co-author of articles in professional journals; conference papers; 4 book reviews including "Criminality and Psychiatric Disorders", 1977; "The Psychopath", 1981. *Honours:* Research Grants from E R Squibb & Sons Ltd., 1966, Sandoz Pharmaceutical Co., 1970, McNeil Laboratories, Canada Ltd., 1972 and 1974, Department of Public Health. *Hobbies:* Reading; Golf; Gardening; Singing. *Address:* PN 141 Health Sciences Centre, 7700 William Avenue, Winnipeg R3E 0Z3, Canada.

BANKOWSKI, Edward, b. 29 May 1942, Lomazy, Poland. Head, Biochemistry, Medical Academy, Bialystok, Poland. m. Janina Cymbor, 2 Jan. 1965, Bialystok, 3 daughters. *Education:* D.Med.Sc., Medical Academy of Bialystok, 1965. *Appointments:* Intern, District Hospital, Bialystok, 1965-67; Research Assistant, Biochemistry, 1967-71, Lecturer, 1972-78, Docent, 1978-80, Biochemistry, Medical Academy, Bialystok; Postdoctoral Fellow, Microbiology, Vanderbilt University, Nashville, USA, 1971-72. *Memberships:* Polish Medical Society; Polish Biochemical Society. *Publications:* Author, 50 papers in professional journals. *Honours:* Awards, Ministry of Health, 1968, 1975. *Hobbies:* Tourism; Literature. *Address:* Dept. of Biochemistry, Medical Academy, Ul. Mickiewicza 2, 15-230 Bialystok, Poland.

BANKS, Elisabeth Ann (Cooper), b. 21 Nov. 1938, Adelaide, Australia. State Director, Family Medicine Programme, Victoria. m. Garnet James Banks, 19 Dec. 1961, Adelaide, 2 daughters. *Education:* MB, BS, University of Adelaide, 1962; Planning Methodologies & Educational Methodologies, Chicago, USA, 1970-72; FRAGP; 1980; Dip.Obst., Royal College of Obstetricians & Gynaecologists, 1979. *Appointments Include:* General practice, 1964-70; Associate professor, Medical Education, Department of Community Medicine, University of

Illinois USA, 1972; Consultant, planning methods, Institute of Cultural Affairs International, 1973-85; General practice, Canberra, 1974-80; Consultant, Primary Health Care, European Office, World Health Organisation (Denmark), 1980-83; Anaesthesia & Intensive Care, Kommune Hospital, Copenhagen, Denmark, 1980-83; Assistant Director (National Office), Family Medicine Programme, 1983-85; Tutor, Department of Community Medicine, Monash University, 1984-85. *Memberships:* Royal Australian College of General Practitioners; WHO Consultant; Associate, Royal Australian College of Medical Administrators; GP member, Royal Australian College of Obstetricians & Gynaecologists. *Publications:* Various articles, professional journals. *Hobbies:* Travel; Reading; Gardening. *Address:* 'Trawalla', 22 Lascelles Avenue, Toorak, Victoria 3142, Australia.

BANOCZY, Jolán, b. 2 Mar. 1929, Budapest, Hungary. Dean, Dental Faculty; Professor and Chairperson, Department of Conservative Dentistry. m. László Pál, 11 Oct. 1962, Budapest, 1 son. *Education:* MD, Semmelweis Medical University, 1953; DDS, Specialisation in Dentistry, 1956; Candidate of Medical Sciences, 1968; DMS, 1977. *Appointments:* Assistant, 1953-71, Assistant Professor, 1971-74, Director, Department of Conservative Dentistry, 1974-, Dean, Faculty of Dentistry, Semmelweis Medical University, Budapest, Hungary, 1980. *Memberships Include:* Advisory Expert, Head of Collaborating Center for Oral Precancerous Lesions, World Health Organisation; Board Member, ORCA; Honory Member, German and Cuban Dental Associations; Corresponding Member, Finnish Dental Association; Vice President, International Documentation Center for Preventive Dentistry; Directory Member, Hungarian Dental Association. *Publications:* Author of 9 scientific books and book chapters., 180 scientific papers in English, German, French and Spanish including: "Oral Leukoplakia', 1982; 'Oral Oncology', 1984. *Honours:* Award, Hungarian Academy of Sciences, 1972; Arkovy Award, 1979. *Hobbies:* Swimming; Music, *Address:* Mikszáth Kálmán tér 5, Budapest, Hungary 1088.

BAPTIST, Jeremy Eduard, b. 22 Mar. 1940, Chicago, Illinois, USA. Allergist. m. Sylvia Evelyn Bonin, 21 July 1962, Chicago, 3 daughters. *Education:* BS 1960, PhD 1966, University of Chicago; MD, University of Missouri, 1978. *Appointments Include:* Assistant Professor of Radiation Biophysics, University of Kansas, Lawrence, 1966-73. *Memberships Include:* International Correspondence Society of Allergists; American Association for Clinical Immunology & Allergy; American College of Allergists; American Medical Association; International Association for Aerobiology; American Association for the Advancement of Science; New York Academy of Sciences; Various local & state medical societies. *Publications Include:* Contributions to "Britannica Year Book of Science & the Future", 1973; "Encyclopaedia Britannica", 1972, 1973; Co-author, "Handbook of Clinical Allergy", 1982; Assistant, associate editor, 'The Allergy Letters', 1984-; Editorial board, 'Topics in Allergy & Clinical Immunology', 1982-83. *Honour:* Sigma Xi, 1964-. *Hobby:* Scandinavian folk dancing. *Address:* Speer Allergy Clinic, 5811 Outlook Drive, Shawnee Mission, KS 66202, USA.

BARAC, Boško, b. 11 Sep. 1930, Zagreb, Yugoslavia. Head, Neurology and Neuropathology, Clinical Medical Centre; Chairman, Neurology and Neuropathology. m. Dragica Sokačić, 21 Sep. 1963, Zagreb, 3 daughters. *Education:* MD, 1956, Dr.Med.Sc., 1965, University of Zagreb; Specialist, Neurology, Psychiatry, Zagreb, 1962. *Appointments:* Clinical Assistant, Nurology, 1865-68, Assistant Professor, 1968-75, Associate Professor, 1975-77,

Professor, 1977-, Neurology, Medical Faculty, Clinical Medical Centre, Zagreb. *Memberships:* Medical Association of Croatia; Association for Neurology and Psychiatry of Yugoslavia, Secretary General 1965-68; Society for EEG and Clinical Neurophysiology; Medical Association of Croatia, President, 1972-81; Association of EEG and Clinical Neurophysiology of Yugoslavia, Vice President 1976-80; American Neurological Association, 1985-; many other professional organisations. *Publications:* (Books) ''Post-traumatic encephalopathy'', in Croatian, 1975; ''Fundamentals of Neurology'', in Croatian, series of Textbooks, University of Zagreb, 1979; Contributor of more than 180 papers in Yugoslav and International journals including ''Vestibular influences upon the EEG of epileptics'', 'EEG & Clin. Neurophys.', 1967; ''Analysis of the Epileptic Seizures appearing in the acute Phase of Cerebrovascular Disease'', 'Neuropsihijatrija', 1976; ''A neurologic Intensive Care Unit'', 'Acta Med.lug', 1977; ''Effects of Mental Activation on Regional Cerebral Blood Flow in Patients with Cerebrovascular Disease'', 'Neurologija', 1983; etc. *Hobbies:* Music, Theatre. *Address:* Pantovčak 102, 41000 Zagreb, Yugoslavia.

BARADNAY, Gyula Julius, b. 3 Nov. 1931, Miskolc, Hungary. Professor, Surgery. m. Martha Szilagyi, 26 Dec. 1966, Szeged, 1 son, 1 daughter. *Education:* MD, 1956; Qualified as Pathologist, 1960; Qualified as Surgeon General, 1963; Candidate of Surgery, Hungarian Academy of Sciences, 1975. *Appointments:* Fellow, I. Surgical Clinic, Medical University, X Szeged, 1960-75; Assistant Professor, 1977, Professor, Surgery, 1985, Head, Surgery, 1984-, Municipal Hospital of Szeged. *Memberships:* Hungarian Pathological, Surgical, Gastroenterological Societies; Societe Internationale de Chirurgie, 1983. *Publications:* 87 publications on surgical pathology, clinical oncology, breast cancer, colo-rectal cancer, proctology. *Hobbies:* Music; Swimming. *Address:* Municipal Hospital, Department of Surgery, 6701, Szeged, P0B 455, Hungary.

BARBENEL, Joseph Cyril, b. 2 Jan. 1937, London, England. Professor in Bioengineering. m. Lesley Mary Hyde Jowett, 6 Aug. 1964, Bournemouth, 2 sons, 1 daughter. *Education:* BDS, LDS, RCS (Eng), London Hospital Medical School, University of London, 1955-60; BSc, Queen's College, Dundee, University of St Andrews, Scotland, 1963-66; MSc, University of Strathclyde, Glasgow, Scotland, 1966-67. *Appointments:* Dental House Surgeon, London Hospital, 1960; Lieutenant, Later Captain, Royal Army Dental Corps, Malaya, 1960-62; General Dental Practice, London, 1963; Lecturer, Dundee Dental School Hospital, University of Dundee, Scotland, 1967-69; Senior Lecturer, Later Professor, Bioengineering Unit, University of Strathclyde, 1970-. *Memberships:* Member of Council, Biological Engineering Society; Chairman, Professional Committee, International Society for Bioengineering & the Skin; Member of Committee & Sci. for Standardisation, Royal Society of Medicine Forum on Haemorheology; Member of Steering Committee, Society for Tissue Viability; Member of Council, Hospital Physicists Association; British Society for the Study of Prosthetic Dentisty. *Publications:* ''Clinical Aspects of Blood Rheology'' (co-author with G Lowe & C Forbes), 1981; ''Pressure Sores'' (co-author with G Lowe & C Forbes), 1983; 'Effects of time varying, magnetic fields on fibroblast growth' (co-author with P Schuetz & J Paul) 1985; 'Haemocrit, bleeding time & platelet aggregation' (co-author with A Saniabadi & G Lowe) in 'The Lancet', 1984. *Hobbies:* Music; Theatre; Reading; Work. *Address:* Bioengineering Unit, University of Strathclyde, Wolfson Centre, Glasgow, G4 0NW, Scotland.

BARBERA, Guillermina, b. 11 Sep. 1944, Barcelona, Spain. Clinical Analyst. m. Javier de Hendoza Sans,

22 Jan. 1970. Barcelona, 2 sons, 2 daughters. *Education:* Pharmacy degree, 1968, PhD Pharmacy, 1972, School of Pharmacy, Barcelona; Diploma in Statistics applied to Medical Sciences, 1974, Diploma in Supervision of RIA Laboratories, Barcelona, 1976; MD, School of Medicine, Barcelona, 1980. *Appointments:* Biochemistry Medical Position in PPEE Hospital, Barcelona, 1974-82; Assistant Professor in Animal Physiology, School of Pharmacy, Barcelona, 1978-82; Head of Department of Clinical Analysis, National health Institute, Madrid, 1982-. *Memberships:* Spanish Immunology Society; Spanish Society of Allergy & Clinical Immunology; Spanish Society of Clinical Chemistry; Spanish Society of Biopathology; European Society of Allergy & Clinical Immunology; New York Academy of Sciences, USA. *Publications:* Various articles in professional & medical journals. *Honours:* Special Award in Pharmacy degree, Barcelona, 1969. *Hobbies:* Music; Sport. *Address:* Maestro Chapi 35, 28015, Madrid, Spain.

BARET, Trevor John, b. 19 Oct. 1953, Sydney, New South Wales, Australia. General Dental Practitioner. *Education:* Bachelor of Dental Surgery. *Appointments:* General Dental Practitioner, Woollahra, Sydney. *Memberships:* Australian Society of Prosthodontists; Australian Society of Periodontists; Australian Society of Occlusal Studies; Eastern Suburbs Dental Group; Australian Dental Association; Dental Aesthetics and Ceramics Society; Clinical Dental Study Group; Continuing Dental Education Committee. *Hobbies:* Skiing; Surfing; Squash; Swimming; Boating; Classic sports cars. *Address:* 27 Grosvenor Street, Woollahra, Sydney, NSW 2025, Australia.

BARKIN, Penny Anne, b. 1 Mar. 1945, San Francisco, California, USA. Tumor Registrar, Seton Medical Centre. *Education:* BA, American University, Washington DC, 1967; AS, medical Records Technology, West Valley College, Saratoga, 1982. *Appointments:* Journalist, editor, 1968-80; Consultant, Medical (Records, Nursing Home Ombudsman, Program of Monterey County, california, 1982-893. *Memberships:* American Medical Record Association; American Medical) Writers Association; Tumor Registrars Association of California, North; California Medical Record Association; San Francisco Medical Record Association. *Publications:* Author, several newspaper articles on alcoholism, environmental health problems, etc., 1968-76; Author, ''1983 Annual Report of the Tumor Registry'', 1984; Pamphlets; ''Confidential Services for Physicians with Substance Abuse-Related Problems''; ''Obtaining Your Medical Records''. *Honours:* Phi Alpha Theta; Pi Gamma Mu; Departmental Honours, American University, 1967; Outstanding Student, Medical Records Major, West Valley College, 1982; Distinguished Student, of the Year, California MedicalRecord Association, 1982; Distinguished Student, Journal of the American Medical Record Association, 1982. *Hobbies:* Photographer; Near East Studies; Cooking Middle Eastern and North African Foods; Racquetball; Swimming. *Address:* Seton Medical Centre, 1900 Sullivan Avenue, Daly City, CA 94015, USA.

BARKER, Clyde, Frederick, b. 16 Aug. 1932, Salt Lake City, Utah, USA, Chief of Surgery, Hospital of the University of Pennsylvania; Chairman, Department of Surgery, University of Pennsylvania, m. Dorothy Joan Bieler, 11 Aug. 1956, Western Springs, Iowa. *Education:* BA, 1954, MD, 1958, Cornell University. *Appointments Include:* Attending Surgeon, Hospital, 1966-, Chief, Division of Transplantation, School of Medicine, Department of Surgery, 1968-, Assistant Professor of Surgery, School of Medicine, 1968-69, Associate Professor of Surgery, 1969-73, Professor of Surgery, 1973-, J William White Professor of Surgical Research, 1978-82, Chief, Division of Vascular Surgery, School of Medicine, Department of Surgery, 1982-, Guthrie Professor of Surgery, School of Medicine, 1982-, John Rhea Barton Professor of Surgery, School of Medicine, 1983-, Chairman, Department of Surgery, School of Medicine, 1983-, Chief of Surgery, Hospital, 1983-, University of Pennsylvania, Philadelphia, Pennsylvania. *Memberships Include:* Fellow, American College of Surgeons; Fellow, College of Physicians of Philadelphia; Member, Society of University Surgeons; International Cardiovascular Society; International Surgical Group; Councilman, 1978-84, Transplantation Society; Membership Chairman, 1980-81, American Society of Transplant Surgeons; Member, Society for Vascular Surgery; Member, Association for Academic Surgery; American Diabetes Association; American Society of Artificial Internal Organs; American Surgical Association. *Publications:* Contributor of over 178 articles to medical textbooks and journals; Author of over 25 abstracts on professional and medical subjects. *Honours:* Markle Scholar in Academic Medicine, 1968-74; Forum committee of American College of Surgeons Immunobiology Study Section. *Hobby:* Competitive tennis. *Address:* Department of Surgery, Hospital of the University of Pennsylvania, 3400 Spruce Street, Fourth Floor Silverstein, Philadelphia, PA 19104, USA.

BARKER, David Nicholson, b. 7 Mar. 1933, Derby, England, District Superintendent Radiographer, Southampton & Southwest Hampshire Health Authority. m. Brenda Mary Dunmore, 4 May 1957, Derby, 1 daughter. *Education:* Diploma, College of Radiographers; Higher Diploma, Teachers' Diploma, ibid. *Appointments Include:* Radiographer, Burton-on-Trent General Hospital; Deputy Superintendent Radiographer, ibid; Superintendent Radiographer /teacher, North Staffordshire Hospital Centre, Stoke-on-Trent. *Memberships:* College of Radiographers; Institute of Radiological Protection; British Institute of Radiology. *Honour:* Election, Fellow of the Society of Radiographers, 1972. *Hobbies:* Local history & genealogy. *Address:* 29 Brook Way, Romsey, Hampshire, SO51 7JZ, England.

BARNARD, Ernest Edward Peter, b. 22 Feb. 1927, Highbury, London, England. Acting Executive Director, Medical Council on Alcoholism. m. Joan Marion Gunn,12 Mar. 1955, Grays, Essex, 1 son, 1 daughter. *Education:* MB, BS, MRCS, LRCP, St. Mary's Hospital Medical School, 1955; DPhil, St. John's College, Oxford, 1969; MFCM, 1974; MFOM, 1979; FFCM, 1980. *Appointments Include:* House Surgeon Physician, King Edward Memorial Hospital, Ealing, 1955-56; Acting Surgeon Lieutenant, Royal Navy, 1956; Retired, Royal Navy, Surgeon Rear Admiral, 1984. *Memberships:* Fellow, Royal Society of Medicine; Honorary life member, Undersea Medical Society, European Undersea Biomedical Society. *Publications Include:* Numerous articles & reports, various medical journals and /or Underwater Physiology Sub-Committee, Royal Naval Personnel Research Committee of the Medical Research Council; Director of Naval Physical Research, Royal Naval Physiological Laboratory. *Honours:* Erroll-Eldridge Prize, 1971; Albert Behnke Award, 1982; Order of St.John, 1982; Honorary Physician to HM the Queen, 1980-84. *Hobbies:* Gardening; Literature; Furniture making; Photography. *Address:* Chesilcote Chapel Road, Swanmore, Southampton, SO3 2QA, England.

BARNARD, Robin Osler, b. 21 Oct. 1932, London, England. Neuropathologist, The National Hospitals for Nervous Diseases, Maida Vale Hospital, London. *Education:* MBBS, London, St Thomas's, 1956; Trainee in Pathology, St Thomas's Hospital Medical School, 1957; Registrar, Senior Registrar, Neuropathology, Maida Vale Hospital, 1960. *Memberships:* British Neuropathological Society, Secretary 1980-85; Association of British Neurologists; Royal Society of Medicine; Pathological Society. *Publications:* "An Atlas of Tumours Involving the Central Nervous System", 1976; "Tumour Biopsy in Brain Tumour in Handbook of ClinicalNeurology", Volume 16, 1974. *Hobby:* Motoring History. *Address:* Maida Vale Hospital, London W9 1TL, England.

BARNESS, Lewis A, b. 31 July 1921, New Jersey, USA. Professor and Chairman, Department of Paediatrics. m. Elaine Berger, 14 June 1953 Philadelphia, Pennsylvania, (div.) 1 son, 2 daughters. *Education:* BA, 1941, MD, 1944, Harvard University; MA Honours, University of Pennsylvania, 1971. *Appointments:* Intern, Philadelphia General Hospital, 1944; Medical Corps, US Army 1945-46; Resident, Fellow, Boston Childrens Hospital and Massachusetts Institute of Technology, 1947-51; Instructor, Professor, University of Pennsylvania College of Medicine, 1951-72; Chief of Paediatrics, Philadelphia General Hospital, 1951-57; Hospital of University of Pennsylvania, 1957-72; Professor and Chairman, Department of Paediatrics, University of South Florida Medical College, Tampa, Florida, 1972-. *Memberships:* President, Past Recorder, American Paediatric Society; Sigma Xi; Alpha Omega Alpha; Past Committee Chairman, American Academy of Paediatrics; American Institue of Nutrition; American Society of Clinical Nutrition; American College of Nutrition; Society for Paediatric Research; American Association for Advancement of Science; American Medical Association. *Publications:* "Paediatric Physical Diagnosis", 1957, 5th edition, 1981; "Core Textbook of Paediatrics", with R Kaye and F A Oski, 1978, 82; Nutrition in Medical Practice", Editor, 1981; "Advances in Paediatrics", Editor, 1976, 10th Edition, 1985. *Honours:* Lindback Award for Teaching, 1963; MA University of Pennsylvania, 1971; Borden Award, American Academy of Paediatrics, 1972; Noer Distinguished Professor, USAF, 1980; Goldberger Award, American Medical Association, 1984. *Hobby:* Music. *Address:* University of South Florida, College of Medicine, Box 15, Tampa, FL 33612, USA.

BARNETT, Crawford Fannin, Junior, b. 11 May 1938, Atlanta, Georgia, USA. Physician. m. Elizabeth McCarthy Hale, 6 June 1964, 2 sons. *Education:* University of Minnesota, 1957; AB, magna cum laude, Yale University, 1960; Postgraduate (Davison Scholar), Oxford University, England, 1963; MD (Trent Scholar), Duke University Medical Centre, 1964-65; Resident, 1965; Resident, Internal Medicine, Duke University Medical Centre, 1964-66; Director, Tennessee Heart Disease Control Program, Nashville, 1966-68; Practice Medicine specializing in internal medicine, Atlanta, 1968-; Member of Staff, Crawford Long, Northside, Grady Memorial, Doctors Memorial, West Paces Ferry, Piedmont, Hospitals, Atlanta; Member, Teaching Staff, Vanderbilt, Medical Center, Nashville, 1966-68; Crawford Long Memorial Hospital, 1969-; Clinical Instructor, internal medicine, Department of Medicine, Emory University Medical School, Atlanta, 1969-; Vice-President, Director, Preferred Equities Corporation, 1970-; Board of Governors, Doctors Memorial Hospital, 1971-80; Board of Directors, Atlanta Speech School, 1976-80; Historic Oakland Cemetery, 1976-; South Turf Nuseries, 1977-; Tech. Industries, 1978-; Served as Surgeon USPHS, 1966-68. *Memberships:* Fellow, American Geographic Society; American Federation Clinical Research; Council Clinical Cardiology; American, Georgia and Atlanta Medical Associations; America and Georgia Heart Associations; American and Georgia Societies of Internal Medicine; American Association History of Medicine, Georgia, Atlanta, Director, 1976-; Historical Societies of Georgia; National Trust for Historic Preservation; International Hippocratic Foundation Society, Greece; Worshipful Society of Apothecaries of London; Phi Beta Kappa and several other organizations. *Publications:* Contributor of articles to professional journals. *Address:* 3250 Howell Mill Road NW /STE 205, Atlanta, GA 30327-4187, USA.

BARNETT, Margaret Edwina, b. 28 July 1949, Fort Benning, Georgia, USA. Assistant Professor, Medicine/Nephrology. *Education:* MD, Johns Hopkins University School of Medicine, 1973; Intern, Medicine, Greater Baltimore Medical Centre, Towson, 1973-74; Residencies: Cleveland Clinic Educational Foundation, 1974-75, University Hospitals of Cleveland, Lakeside and Cleveland VA Hospital, 1975-76; Phd, Case Western Reserve University, 1984; Fellowship, Nephrology University Hospitals of Cleveland Lakeside, 1976-78. *Appointments:* Senior Research Associate, Nephrology, University Hospital of Cleveland, 1978-79; Dialysis Rounding Physician, Community Dialysis Centre Inc., Ohio, 1978-83; Teaching Fellow, Medicine, University Hospitals of Cleveland/Lakeside, 1978-84; Instructor, Anatomy, 1979-80, Preceptor, Renal Correlation Conference, 1980-81, Instructor, Anatomy & Histology, 1980-83, Research Associate, Anatomy, Case Western Reserve University, 1983-84, Physician, Huron Regional Urgent Care Centres, Inc., Cleveland, 1983-84; Assistant Professor, Pennsylvania State University, 1984-; Acting Chief, Renal & Electrolyte Director, Pennsylvania State University, 1985. *Memberships Include:* National Association of Residents and Interns; Johns Hopkins Medical & Surgical Society; Associate, American College of Physicians; American Association for the Advancement of Science; National Kidney Foundation; etc. *Honours:* Recipient, various honours, awards and grants including: Ohio Kidney Foundation: Gentamicin Nephrotoxicity, 1977-78; NIH National Research Award, 1979-82; Ohio American Heart Association, 1980-81; MENSA; Alpha Kappa Alpha. *Hobbies:* Video Electronics; Downhill Skiing; Tae Kwon Do. *Address:* 107 Heather Drive, Harrisburg, PA 17112, USA.

BARON, Denis Neville, b. 3 Oct. 1924, London, England. Professor of Chemical Pathology. m. Yvonne Stern, 6 Dec. 1951, London, 1 son, 3 daughters. *Education:* MB, BS, Middlesex Hospital Medical School, University of London, 1945; MD; DSc; Fellow, Royal College of Physicians; Fellow, Royal College of Pathologists. *Appointments:* Senior Lecturer in Clinical Biochemistry, Middlesex Hospital Medical School, 1951-54; Reader in Chemical Pathology, Royal Free Hospital School of Medicine, 1954-63; Professor of Chemical Pathology, Royal Free Hospital School of Medicine, London. *Memberships:* Medicines Commission; Member of Senate, University of London; Numerous medical & scientific societies. *Publications:* "Short Textbook of Chemical Pathology", 4th edition, 1982; "Units, Symbols & Abbreviations", 3rd edition, 1977; Numerous articles in medical & scientific journals, book chapters. *Honour:* Rockefeller Travelling Fellowship in Medicine, 1960-61. *Hobbies:* Gardening; Opera. *Address:* 47, Holne Chase, London, NW2 0QG, England.

BARRACLOUGH, Geoffrey, b. 20 July 1924, London, England Medical Superintendent of Kobe International Hospital and Medical Services Association. *Education:* Christ Church, Oxford.Matoribanks Scholarship, 1942; BM, BCH, 1956; MA, 1965. *Appointments:* Registrar in Pathology, London Hospital, 1960-61; Hospital for Sick Children, Great Ormond Street, 1961-64. *Honour:* OBE, Dec. 1976. *Address:* Ninomiya-cho, 4 chome 23-11, Chuo-ku, Kobe.

BARRETT, John Anthony, b. 17 Apr 1945, Cork, Ireland. Director, Hospital Trauma Unit. m. Kathleen Mary Curzon, 2 May 1981, Chicago, Illinois, USA. 1 son, 1 daughter. *Education:* MB, BCh, Hons Medicine and Surgery, 1963-69; MCh, 1975, National University of Ireland, University College, Cork. *Appointments:* Intern North Charitable Infirmary, Cork, 1969-70; Intern, Norfolk General Hospital, Virginia, USA, 1970-71; Senior House Officer, 1971-72, Registrar, Department of Surgery, 1972-73, St Finbarrs Hospital, Cork; Research Fellow, Tulane University, New Orleans, 1973-75; Surgical Resident, Cook County Hospital, Chicago, 1975-80; Director, Trauma Unit, Cook County Hospital, Chicago, 1980-. *Memberships:* American Trauma Society; American College of Surgeons; Royal College of Surgeons in Ireland; Association for Academic Surgery; Association for Surgical Education; Chicago Surgical Society. *Publications:* "Trauma Management for Civilian and Military Physicians" Wienen and Barrett, 1986; "Treatment of shock" 2nd edition, edited by Barrett and Nyhus, in press. Contributor of chapters edited volumes and articles to medical journals. *Honour:* Ainsworth Research Fellow, 1973-75. *Hobbies:* Mountain climbing; Sky diving. *Address:* Trauma Office M-7, Department of Surgery, Cook County Hospital, 1825 West Harrison Street, Chicago, IL 60612, USA.

BARROWMAN, James Adam, b. 4 June 1936, Edinburgh, Scotland. Assistant Dean for Research and Graduate Studies; Professor of Medicine, Gastroenterology. m. Gwynedd Price, 28 Nov. 1964, Mapledurham, 2 sons, 1 daughter. *Education:* BSc Honours, 1958, MB, ChB, Medalist in Surgery, Edinburgh University; MRCP, London, England, 1964; PhD, London University, 1966; FRCP in Gastroenterology, 1977, in Internal Medicine, 1978, Canada; FACP, 1980; FRCP (London), 1982. *Appointments:* Lecturer, Physiology, Senior Lecturer, Physiology, Senior Lecturer, Medicine, London Hospital Medical College; Wellcome-Swedish Travelling Research Fellow, University of Lund, Sweden; Associate Professor, Professor, Medicine (Gastroenterology), currently Assistant Dean for Research and Graduate Studies, Faculty of Medicine, Memorial University of Newfoundland, Canada. *Memberships:* Royal College of Physicians and Surgeons of Canada; Royal College of Physicians, England; American College of Physicians; American Society of Gastroenterology; American Gastroenterological Association; Physiological Society; Canadian Association of Gastroenterology; Canadian Physiological Society; International Society of Lymphology. *Publications:* "Physiology of the Gastrointestinal Lymphatic System", Monograph, 1978; "Clinical Gastrointestinal Physiology", with D N Granger and P R Kvietys, 1985. *Hobbies:* Swimming; Piano playing; Philately. *Address:* Faculty of Medicine, Memorial University of Newfoundland, St John's, Newfoundland, Canada A1B 3V6.

BARRY, Peter Hosford, b. 24 Aug. 1941, England. University Lecturer. m. C. Elizabeth Schuyler, 27 June, 1970, California, USA, 2 sons, 1 daughter. *Education:* BSc (Hons.), University of Sydney, Australia, 1963, PhD, 1968. *Appointments:* Post Doctoral Research Physiologist, UCLA, 1967-68, Assistant Research Physiologist, 1968-70, Post Doctoral Fellow, Wellcome Trust, University of Cambridge, England, 1970-71; Post Doctoral Fellow, Queen Elizabeth II, University of New South Wales, Australia, 1972-73, Lecturer, School of Physiology and Pharmacology, 1974-75, Senior Lecturer, 1976-82, Associate Director, Nerve-Muscle Research Centre, 1982-83, Senior Lecturer, School of Physiology and Pharmacology, 1984-. *Memberships:* USA Biophysical Society; Society of General Physiologists, USA; Australian Physiological and Pharmacological Society; Australian Society for Biophysics. *Publications Include:* Co-author of articles in 'Journal of Membrane Biology, 1970, 1971, 1977, 1979, 1984; Contributions to 'Biophysics', 1969; 'Physiological Review', Biophysical Journal, 1984; Conference presentations to Alfred Benzon Symposium, 1981; Proc. Roy. Society, 1982. *Hobbies:* Church and family activities; Computer programming; Carpentry; Reading. *Address:* School of Physiology and Pharmacology, University of New South Wales, PO Box 1 Kensington, New South Wales, Australia.

BARTON, Nelda Ann Lambert. Nursing Home

Administrator. m. Harold Bryan Barton, 11 May 1951 (deceased 1977), 3 sons (1 deceased), 2 daughters. *Education:* Western Kentucky University, USA 1947-49; Graduate, Norton Memorial Infirmary School of Medical Technology, 1959. *Appointments:* Registered Medical Technologist, ASCP, 1950-52; Licensed Nursing Home Administrator, 1979-; Director, Corbin Deposit Bank Board, 1980-84; Federal Council on Aging, 1982,-; Chairman of the Board, Tri-County National Bank, 1985-; President and Chairman of the Board: Health Systems Inc; Barton and Associates Inc; Hazard Nursing Home Inc; Barbourville Nursing Home Inc; Key Distributing Inc; 'The Whitl;ey Whiz' Inc. *Memberships Include:* Board Director, Leadership Kentucky, 1984-; Board Director, Kentucky Chamber of Commerce, 1983-; Vice-President 1983-84, Business and Professional Women's Club; American College of Nursing Home Administrators; Legislative Committee, Kentucky Association on Health Care Facilities, 1980-; American Health Care Association; American and Kentucky Educational, Medical and Political Action Committee. *Honours include:* The Dwight David Eisenhower Award, 1970; Recognition Award, Joint Republican Leadership of the United States Congress. *Hobbies:* Fishing; Painting with Oils. *Address:* 1311 Seventh Street Road, Corbin, KY 40701, USA.

BARTON, Walter Earl, b. 29 July 1906, Oak Park, Illinois, USA. Professor of Psychiatry (Active Emeritus); m. Elsa V Benson, 2 July 1932, Worcester, Massachusetts, 2 sons, 1 daughter. BS. MD, Hon DSc, University of Illinois. *Appointments:* Assistant Superintendent, Worcester State Hospital, Worcester, Massachusetts; Lt Col AUS Surgeon Generals Office and CO, 116th Station Hospital, Philippines; Superintendent, Boston State Hospital, Boston, Massachusetts; Medical Director, American Psychiatric Association, Washington; Senior Physician, VA Hospital White River Junction, VT; Professor of Psychiatry Dartmouth Medical School, Hanover, New Hampshire. *Memberships:* American Medical Association; American Psychiatric Association; President; Medical Director, Group for the Advancement of Psychiatry, President; American Board of Neurology and Psychiatry, Director; American College of Physicians; American College of Mental Health Administration, President; Royal College of Psychiatrists. *Publications:* Over 160 publications; 10 books including "Ethics and Law in Mental Health Administration" 1984; "Mental Health Administration" 2 vols, 1983 with Gail Barton; "Law and the Mental Health Profession" 1978. *Honours:* Nolan D C Lewis Award, 1960; E V Bowis Award, 1970; Thomas W Salmon Medal, 1974; Distinguished Service Award, 1975; Administrative Psychiatry Award, 1983. *Hobbies:* Gardening; Swimming; Canoeing; Music; Travel. *Address:* RFD 1 Box 188, Hartland, UT 05048, USA.

BARTOSEK, Ivan, b. 29 Oct. 1934, Vlachovo Brêzi, Czechoslovakia. Head of Toxicology Laboratory. m. Anna Schröpferová, 26 July 1960, 1 son, 1 daughter. *Education:* MSc Biology, Charles University, Prague, 1957; PhD Biochemistry, 1st Organic Chemsitry & Biochemistry, Czechoslovak Academy of Science, Prague, 1964. *Appointments:* Researcher, Institute of Natural Drugs, Prague, 1957-60; Researcher, Czechoslovak Academy of Science, Prague, 1960-64; Researcher, Institute for Pharmacy & Biochemistry, Prague, 1964-68; Instituto di Ricerche Farmacologiche "Mario Negri", Milan, Italy, 1968, Head of Toxicology Laboratory. *Memberships:* Italian Society of Toxicology; ItalianSociety of Biochemistry; New York Academy of Sciences; European Association for Cancer Research. *Publications:* "Isolated Liver Perfusion & its Applications" (with Buaitani & Miller), 1973; "Animals in Toxicological Research" (with Guaitani & Pacei), 1982; Over 70 scientific papers in different journals, 1960-. *Honour:* Gold Medal "Ambrogino d'Oro", City of Milan, 1971. *Hobby:* Photography.

Address: Istituto di Ricerche Farmacologiche "Mario Negri", via Eritrea 62, 20157 Milan, Italy.

BARTSCHT, Karl G, b. 19 June 1936, Detroit, Michigan, USA. Chief Executive Officer. m. Karen Davis Nothoff, MD, 12 Nov. 1982, 3 sons, 1 daughter. *Education:* MSE, University of Michigan. *Appointments:* Teacher, University of Michigan, 1961; Director, Hospital Systems Research Group, 1961; Director, Chairman of the Board, Director of Research and Development, Community Systems Foundation, 1962; Chief Executive Officer, Chi Systems Inc; Chief Executive Officer, Michigan Health Systems Inc. *Memberships:* Fellow, Chairman of the Board, American Association of Healthcare Consultants; Board member, American Association for Hospital Planning; Society for Hospital Planning; Hospital Management Systems Society; Foundation for Health Education and Applied Research; American Health Planning Association; American Hospital Association . *Publications:* Publisher: 'Health Care Strategic Management'; 'Hospital Purchasing Management'. *Hobbies:* Running; Skiing; Travel. *Address:* 130 S First, Ann Arbor, MI 48104, USA.

BASHLINE, Tina Louise, b. 6 May 1954, San Francisco, California, USA. Copy Supervisor, Windermere Communications Inc; Part-time Instructor, Charles Morris Price School of Advertising and Journalism. m. Robert Maxwell Brownell, 6 May 1984, Radnor, Pa. *Education:* BA, Communications, Journalism, Shippensburg State College, 1976. *Appointments:* Editorial Assistant, Clemprint, Concordville; Copy Editor, House Plants & Porch Gardens; Editor, Writer, Mel Richman Inc.; Pharmaceutical Copywriter, Wyeth International Ltd; Copy Supervisor, Windermere Communications Inc. *Memberships:* American Medical Writers Association; Philadelphia Club of Advertising Women; American Advertising Federation; Laubach Literacy Action; Delaware County literacy Council. *Hobbies:* Tutor Adults in Reading Skills/Literacy; Horticulture. *Address:* Windermere Communications Inc., 44 West Lancaster Avenue, Ardmore, Pa 19003, USA.

BASHOUR, Fouad Anis, b. 3 Jan. 1924, Tripoli, Lebanon. University Professor. m. Valeria Imm, 29 Sep. 1978, Dallas, Texas, USA. *Education:* MD, American University of Beirut, Lebanon, 1949; PhD, University of Minnesota, Minneapolis, USA, 1957. *Appointments Include:* Research Associate, American University Medical School, Beirut, Lebanon, 1957, Assistant Professor of Medicine, 1957-59; Instructor in Internal Medicine, University of Texas Southwestern Medical School, Dallas, Texas, USA, 1959-60, Assistant Professor, 1960-63, Associate Professor, 1963-71, Professor, 1971-present. *Memberships Include:* American Federation of Clinical Research; Fellow of the American College of Chest Physicians; American Physiological Society; Sigma XI; American Heart Association; American Medical Association; Texas Medical Association; Association for the Advancement of Medical Instrumentation, etc. *Publications Include:* Over 200 contributions to medical journals and publications including 'New England Journal of Medicine'; 'Surgical Gynaecology and Obstetrics'; 'Journal of Laboratory and Clinical Medicine'; 'Texas Medical Journal'; 'American Heart Journal'; 'Diseases of the Chest'; 'Physiology'; 'Clinical Research', etc.' 'Circulation'. etc. *Honours Include:* The Two Thousand Men of Achievement Award, 1970 and 1971; Consultant to National Heart and Lung Insitute; Listed in 'American Men of Science', 11th Edition, 'Personalities of the South', Community Leaders and Noteworthy Americans', 1977, 'Men of Achievement', etc; Eminent Scholar, State of Texas; Chancellor Advisory Council of the University of Texas System, 1982- (member); Fouad Bashour Chair in Cardiovascular Physiology, 1984. *Hobbies:*

Gardening; Reading. *Address:* 5140 Seneca Drive, Dallas, TX 75209, USA.

BASILOTTA, Carmelo S, b. 21 Mar. 1925, Italy. Doctor of Chiropractic. m. Josephine Buscemi, 9 July 1949, Nissoria, Italy, 1 daughter. *Education:* BA, N Spadeliere, Catania, 1945; Medical School, University of Catania, 1945-51; DC, Chiropractic Institute of New York USA, 1966. *Appointments:* Assistant to Surgeon, Garibaldi Hospital, Catania, Italy, 1945-51; Inventor and Importer, 1951-; Doctor of Chiropractic, USA, 1966-. *Memberships:* American Chiropractic Association; Pennsylvania Chiropractic Association; New York Academy of Sciences. *Honours:* Patents: Italy, 1963; USA, 1963, 65. Award Winner, Inventor's Show, New York, USA, 1965; Picture on Front cover of Clipper Cargo Horizons Magazine 1965; Honour Award of X-Ray Technology, Chiropractic Institute of New York, 1965. *Hobbies:* Gardening; Fishing. *Address:* 1008 West Main Street, Norristown, PA 19401, USA.

BASLER, Donald Steven, b. 17 Nov. 1946, Cleveland, Ohio, USA. President, The Health Executive Advisory. m. Sarah J. Fansher, 21 Dec. 1967, Dayton, 1 son, 1 daughter. *Education:* BBA, Ohio University, Athens, 1968; MHA, Duke University, 1970; Special Education, Case Western Reserve University, Cleveland, John Carroll University, Cleveland. *Appointments:* Consultant, James A. Hamilton Associates, 1970-73; Editor, Hospital Administration Currents, 1974-83; Consultant, Abbott Hospital Planning Consultants, 1973-76; Director, Ross Planning Associates, 1973-83. *Memberships:* Fellow, American College of Healthcare Executives, National Perinatal Association. *Publications:* "The Nurse Staffing Pattern of a Small Community Hospital - An In-Depth Analysis", 1970; "Planning and Design for Perinatal and Pediatric Facilities", 1977; "1979 Guide to Referral Centers Providing Perinatal and Neonatal Care", 1977; "Alternatives in obstetric Design", 1980; "The New Regulators", 1981; "1982 Guide to Centers Providing Perinatal and Neonatal Special Care", 1982; "A Dissertation on the Demise of Standard Planning Ratios Which Use Beds as the Denominator, and the development of More Applicable Planning Ratios for a Changing Health Delivery System", 1983; "Hospital Material Management Quarterly", 1983; Contributor of numerous articles to professional journals. *Hobbies:* Travel; Golf; Financial Planning. *Address:* 2641 Woodley Road, Columbus, OH 43229, USA.

BASMAJIAN, John V, b. 21 June 1921, Constantinople, Turkey. Professor of Medicine. m. Dora Lucas, 4 Oct. 1947, Toronto, Canada, 1 son, 2 daughters. *Education:* MD University of Toronto, 1945; Fellow, American College of Angioloy, 1974; Fellow, Royal College of Physicians of Canada, 1979. *Appointments:* Lecturer, Professor, University of Toronto, 1949-57; Research & Clinical Fellow, Hospital for Sick Children, Toronto, 1950-57; Research & Clinical Fellow, Hospital for Sick Children, Toronto, 1950-57; Professor & Head, Department of Anatomy, Queen's University, Kingston, Ontario, Canada, 1957-69; Professor of Rehabilitative Medicine, Anatomy & Psychiatry, Emory University, Atlanta, Georgia, USA, Director, Regional Research & Training Centre, 1969-77; Professor of Medicine, Director, Rehabilitation Centre, McMaster University & Chedoke-McMaster Hospitals, Hamilton, Canada, 1977-86; Medical Consultant, Office of VP Research, Georgia, Institute of Technology, Atlanta. *Memberships:* . American Orthopaedic Foot Society; Australian & Venezuelan Biofeedback Societies; Mexican Society of Anatomy; Colombian Association of Physical Medicine; Past President, Co-Founder, International Society of Electromyographic Kinesiology; President, American Association of Anatomists, 1986. *Publications:* More than 300 scientific articles, 15 books, Series Editor, 22-volume "Rehabilitation Medicine Library", Various editorial responsibilities

for medical journals. *Honours Include:* Gold Key Recipient, Congress of Rehabilitative Medicine, 1977; Starr Gold Medal for Medical Research, Toronto, 1967; Kabakjian Award, New York, 1967; J C B Grant Award, Canadian Association of Anatomists, 1985. *Hobbies:* Travel; Gardening; Music. *Address:* 106 Forsyth Avenue North, Hamilton, Ontario, L8S 4E4, Canada.

BASOEKI, Wirjowidjojo, b. 20 June 1922, Lumajang, Indonesia. Head, Department of Surgery-Neurosurgery, Faculty of Medicine, Airlangga University, Surabaya. m. Soediani, 28 Mar. 1954, Bandung, 2 sons, 1 daughter. *Education:* MD, Faculty of Medicine, University of Indonesia, Jakarta. *Appointment:* Neurosurgeon, St. Elisabeth Hospital, Tilburg, Holland. *Memberships:* Indonesian Asscociation of Surgery; Indonesian Association of Neurosurgery. *Honour:* Chevalier l'Ordre National du Merite, Republic of France, 1985. *Hobbies:* Painting; Sports (Tennis, Soccer). *Address:* Jalan Sri Ikana 61, Surabaya 60286, Indonesia.

BASORA SALDANA, Graciela Eloisa, b. 26 Nov. 1931, Arroyo, Puerto Rico. Private Practice; Chief Pathologist, Ponce Oncologic Hospital. m. Lucio Garcia-Moliner, 20 June 1956, Madrid, Spain, 3 daughters. *Education:* BA, Barnard College, Columbia University, 1951; MD, Universidad Central de Madrid, Spain, 1956. *Appointments:* Assistant Head, Pathology & Cytopathology, Ponce General Hospital, 1962-75; Pathologist, Lafayette Hospital, Arroyo, 1967-82, Aguirre Hospital, 1967-81; Lecturer, Pathology, School of Medicine, Catholic University, Ponce, 1978-79. *Memberships:* American Medical Association; PR.MA; Academia Medica del Sur; American Cytology Association; Sociedad de Patologos de Puerto Rico. *Honours:* Premio Quevedo Baez, 1960; Cytology Association of Puerto Rico, 1972; SSS, 1984. *Hobbies:* Boating; Fishing; Photography; Music. *Address:* 310 San Vicente, Concordia Street 143, Ponce, PR 00731, USA.

BASSON, Johan Kristof, b. 21 Feb. 1928, Stellenbosch, South Africa. General Manager, Atomic Energy Corporation. m. Helga Lotz, 30 Dec. 1963, Pretoria, 2 sons, 1 daughter. *Education:* BSc, 1945, MSc., 1947, University of Stellenbosch; DSc., Nuclear Physics, University of Pretoria, 1953. *Appointments:* Head, Biophysics & Applied Radioactivity, National Physical Research Laboratory, 1947-58; Medical Physicist, Royal Marsden Hospital, London, England, 1955-56; Medical Scientist, Brookhaven National Lab, USA, 1955; Senior Lecturer, University of Stelllenbosch, 1958-59; Director, Isotopes and Radiation, Atomic Energy Board, 1960-79; Health Physicist, AERE, Harwell, 1960-61; Group General Manager, Nuclear Development Corp, AEC, 1982-85; Member, International Atomic Energy Agency Panels, 1965-78. *Memberships:* Numerous professional organisations including: Foundation Member, South African Institute of Physics; South African Association of Physicists in Medicine and Biology, President, 1969. *Publications:* 77 Scientific and research articles in professional journals. *Honours:* Medical Physicist, Atomic Energy Board, 1956; Health Physics Journal Advisory Board, 1971; etc. *Hobbies:* Tennis; Jogging; Scientific Societies. *Address:* Atomic Energy Corporation, Private Bag, X256, Pretoria 0001, South Africa.

BASTIAN, Bruce Charles, b. 2 Nov. 1948, Hamilton, New South Wales, Australia. Director of Cardiology. m. Carol Margaret Kiefel, 30 June 1973, Newcastle, 2 sons, 1 daughter. *Education:* MB BS, University of Sydney; FRACP; DDU. *Appointments:* Registrar: Sydney Hospital; Royal Newcastle Hospital; Glasgow Royal Infirmary. Research Associate; University of Texas, USA; Health Science Centre of Dallas. Staff Cardiologist, currently Director of Cardiology, Royal Newcastle Hospital New South

Wales, Australia. *Memberships:* Secretary, Medical Staff Council, Royal Newcastle Hospital; Cardiac Society of Australia dn new Zealand. *Hobby:* Fishing. *Address:* Department of Cardiology, Royal Newcastle Hospital, Newcastle, NSW 2300, Australia.

BASU, A.K., b. 15 Apr. 1935, India. Associate Professor, Head, Nuclear Medicine. m. Jessie Basu, 28 Feb. 1962, 1 son, 1 daughter. *Education:* MB, BS; DRM; MAMS; FIMSA. *Appointments:* Senior Scientific Officer, Institute of Nuclear Medicine; Lecturer, Nuclear Medicine, Institute of Medical Science, B.H.U. *Memberships:* Society of Nuclear Medicine, India; Endocrine Society of India; Indian Association of Radiation Protection; Indian Society of Clinical Oncology; Indian Hospital Association. *Publications:* Over 50 scientific articles including: "Hepatobiliary scintigraphy in congenital cystic dilation of biliary tract", 'Clinical Nuclear Medicine', 1985; "Red Blood cell survival in patients with ventricular septal defect and patent ductus arterisus", 'American Journal of Clinical Paediatrics", 1981; Textbook: "Textbook in Nuclear Medicine", In Preparation: "Thyroid Hormones in Starvation", in press; "Scintigraphic findings in a case of hydatid cyst of liver communicating with biliary system", 'Clinical Nuclear Medicine, 1986. *Honours:* Korary Club Award, 1982; S.S. Misra Oration Lecture, 1984. *Hobbies:* Coin Collection; Reading. *Address:* All-India Institute of Medical Science, Ansari Nagar, New Delhi 110029, India.

BATES, James Earl. Chiropodist; Podiatrist. m. Lauralou Courtney Bates, 2 sons, 2 daughters. *Education:* DSC, Temple University School of Chiropody, 1946; DPM, Pennsylvania College of Podiatric Medicine, 1970; EdD, Franklin Pierce, 1972. *Appointments:* Associate Professor, Roentgenology, Temple University, 1948-60; President, Pennsylvania College of Podiatric Medicine, 1962-; Professor, Podiatric Medicine, PCPM, 1962-. *Memberships:* Fellow, Royal Society of Health, England; Fellow, College of Physicians of Philadelphia; American Association of Colleges of Podiatric Medicine, President, 1969-72; American College of Foot Roentgenologists, 1958-59; Greater Philadelphia Podiatry Society, 1955-56; Pensylvania Podiatry Association. President, 1959-60; numerous other professional organisations. *Contributor to:* 'Journal of the American Podiatry Association'; 'Journal of Podiatric Medical Education'; 'Current Podiatry Journal'; 'British Journal of Chiropody'. *Honours:* Pi Epsilon Delta; Pi Delta National Podiatry Honour Society; Milton J. Shapp, Governor of the Commonwealth of Pennsyulvania Citation, 1973; Special Citation, Pennsylvania Podiatry Association, 1973; Fellowship Award, International Academy of Preventive medicine, 1974; Recipient, numerous other honours and awards. *Address:* 314 South Lawrence Court, Philadelphia, PA 19106, USA.

BATES, Thelma Dorothy, b. 18 Aug. 1929, Staffordshire, England. Consultant Radiotherapist and Oncologist, St. Thomas' Hospital, London. m. Sidney Edward Mills Bates, 23 July 1960, Christchurch, New Zealand, 2 sons, 1 daughter. *Education:* NB, ChB, Birmingham; MRCS (London); LRCP (England); DCRA (Australasia); FRCR (London). *Appointments:* General Practice, Australia and New Zealand; Radiotherapist-in-Training, Peter MacCallum Clinic, Launceston, Tasmania. *Memberships:* Fellow of the Royal Society of Medicine; Royal College of Radiologists; British Institute of Radiology; Fellow, Royal Society of Arts. *Publications:* Editor'High Dose-Rate afterloading in the Treatment of Cancer of the Uterus", 1980; 'Combination Chemotherapy in Advanced Breast Cancer', 1980; 'The St Thomas Hospital Terminal CAre Support Team – A New Concept of Hospice Care', 1981. *Hobbies:* Interior Design: Travel. *Address:* "Saxonwood", Albany Close, Esher, Surrey, KT10 9JR, England.

BATT, Ronald Elmer, b. 24 Sep. 1933, Buffalo, USA. Clinical Associate Professor, Gynaecology. m. (1) Carol Mary Schaab, 28 Dec. 1957, Buffalo, 4 sons, 2 daughters; (2) Kathleen May Over, 19 May 1982, 5 stepsons, 1 stepdaughter. *Education:* MD, University of Buffalo Medical School, 1958; Residency, State University of New York, 1959-60, 1962-66; US Navy, 1960-62. *Appointments:* Fellowship, Reproductive Endocrinology, Harvard Medical School, 1963-64; Summer Fellowship, Reproductive Surgery, Mayo Clinic, 1965; Clinical Instructor, Gynaecology, 1966-70, Clinical Assistant Professor, 1970-79, Clinical Associate Professor, 1979-, State University of New York, Buffalo; President, Batt & Naples Professional Corporation, 1972-. *Memberships:* ACOG; ACS; American Fertility Society; Society of Reproductive Surgeons; AAGL; Fellow, Royal College of Surgeons, Canada; Royal Society Medicine, England; American Association History Medicine; International Society History of Medicine; Epigraphic Society. *Publications Include:* Co-Author, "The Chapel", 1979; Articles in professional journals including 'Obstetric and Gynecology', 1977; Monograph Series, "Conservative Surgery for Endometriosis in the Infertile Couple", 1982. *Address:* 1000 Youngs Road, Buffalo, NU 14221, USA.

BATTISTA, O. A., b. 20 June 1917, Cornwall, Canada. Chairman: President; Chief Executive Officer. m. Helen Battista, 1 son, 1 daughter. *Education:* Degree in Chemistry, 1st class honours, McGill University, 1940; DS, h.c., St Vincent College, 1955; ScD, h.c., Clarkson University, 1985. *Appointments Include:* Chairman, President and Chief Executive Officer, Research Services Corporation, Consultants to Research Management; Founder-President, World Olympiads of Knowledge; Chairman, President and Chief Executive Officer, The O. A. Battista Research Institute; President, American Institute of Chemists, 1977-79; Adnunnct Professor of Chemistry; Director, Center for Microcrystal Polymer Science, UT-Arlington, 1975-76; Special Consultant to Bausch and Lomb, Capsugel, Chemtree, Essilor, Microtech Industries, etc. *Memberships Include:* Chairman of Division, 1959-60, American Chemical Society; President, Chief Executive Officer, 1977-79, Past President, Director, 1980-81, American Institute of Chemists; Lifetime Fellow, 1955; AIC Honor Scroll, NJ Chapter, 1965; AIC Honor Scroll, Philadelphia Chapter, 1967; Elected Fellow, NY Academy of Sciences, 1969; Elected Fellow, 1955, Lifetime Fellow, 1981, National Assn of Science Writers. *Publications:* (books) 20 including treatise on "Micro-crystal Polymer Science", 1975; "Quotoons", 1981; "Olympiad of Knowledge 1984", 1981; "Research for Profit", 1985; "Knowledge Power", 1985; "Gods's World and You", 1985; "How to Enjoy Life 365 Days a Year", 1986; Over 1,000 articles in National Magazines; Author of over 60,000 Quotoons; 80 Scientific papers; Contributing Editor, Quote Magazine. *Honours:* James T Grady Award, 1973; Gold Medal, Creative Invention Award, 1983; Captain of Achievement Award, American Academy of Achievement, 1971; Boss of the Year Award, National Secretaries Assn., 1972. *Address:* World Headquarters, Olympiads of Knowledge, 3863 Southwest Loop 820, Suite 100, Fort Worth, TX 76133 USA.

BATTY, Vincent Bernard, b. 8 June 1951, London, England. Consultant, Radiology & Nuclear Medicine, Southampton General Hospital. 1 son, 1 daughter. *Education:* BSc., 1973, MBBS, 1976, DMRD, 1981, FRCR, 1983, MSc., 1985, Middlesex Hospital Medical School. *Appointments:* House Physician, Watford General Hospital; House Surgeon, Middlesex Hospital; Senior House Officer, Casualty, Middlesex Hospital; General Practitioner, Hythe, Hants; Registrar, Radiology, Senior Registrar, Radiology, Southampton General Hospital; Senior Registrar, Radiology & Ultrasound, Royal Marsden Hospital. *Memberships:* Fellow, Royal College of

Radiologists; British Institute of Radiology. *Publications:* Various papers on radiological and nuclear medicine topics; Co-Editor, "Clinics in Oncology", 1986. *Hobbies:* Music; Squash; Sailing; Chess. *Address:* 5 Fir Close, Cedar Mount, Lyndhurst, Hants. SO4 7EE, England.

BAUER, Gaston Egon, b. 7 May 1923, Vienna, Austria. Cardiologist. m. Phyllis Smith, 7 Jan. 1946, 3 sons. *Education:* MB BS, Hons, Sydney University, 1946, MRCP, London, 1951; MRACP, 1952; FRACP, 1963; FRCP (London) 1972; FACC, 1972. *Appointments:* Medical Officer, Royal Prince Alfred Hospital, 1946-48; Postgraduate Medical School of London, Hammersmith Hospital, 1950-51; Physician, Sydney Hospital, 1955-76; Consultant Physician, Hornsby District Hosptial, 1964-79; Cardiologist, Royal North Shore Hospital. *Memberships:* Fellow, Royal Australasian College of Physicians; Fellow, Royal College of Physicians, London; Member, International Society of Hypertension; Member Cardiac Society of Australia and New Zealand. *Publications:* 120 scientific papers and 9 chapters in medical textbooks dealing with heart disease and hypertension. *Honours:* University Medal, University of Sydney, 1946; Arthur E Mills Graduation Prize, 1946; Archie Telfer Prize, Sydney Hospitallers, 1963. *Hobbies:* Music, Chairman, Musica Viva Australia, 1974-81; Sport, Vice President N S W Federation of Soccer Clubs, 1967-70. *Address:* 115 Shirley Road, Roseville, New South Wales 2069, Australia.

BAUER, A (August) Robert, b. 23 Dec. 192 Philadelphia, USA. Surgeon, Private Practice. m. Charmaine Louise Studer, 28 June 1957, 5 sons, 1 daughter. *Education:* BS, Chemistry, 1949, MS, Physiology, 1950, MD, 1954, University of Michigan; M.Med.S., Surgery, Ohio State University, 1960. *Appointments:* Intern, Walter Reed Army Medical Centre, 1954-55; Active Duty, US Army, 1955-57; Residency, General Surgery, University Hospital, Ohio State University, 1957-61; Private Practice, Surgery, 1962-74, St Mark's Hospital, Salt Lake City, 1974-; Clinical Instructor, Ohio State University, 1960-61, Michigan State College of Human Medicine, 1974, University of Utah, 1975-. *Memberships:* Salt Lake County Medical Society; Utah State, and American Medical Associations; Salt Lake Surgical Society; Utah Society of Certified Surgeons; Fellow, Southwestern Surgical Congress; Fellow, American College of Surgeons; etc. *Publications:* "The Effects of Prolonged Coffee Intake on Genetically Identical Mice", 'Life Sciences', 1977; "The Depression of T Lymphocytes After Trauma", 'American Journal of Surgery', 1978; "Computed Tomographic Localization of Wooden Foreign Bodies in Children's Extremities", 'Archives of Surgery', 1983. *Honours:* Service on numerous committees & councils with active involvement. *Hobby:* Reading History. *Address:* Suite 3B, 1220 East 3900 South, PO Box 17533, Salt Lake City, UT 84117, USA.

BAYLISS, (Sir) Richard (Ian Samuel), b. 2 Jan. 1917, Tettenhall, England. Consultant Physician. m. Marina Rankin de Borchgrave, 24 Feb. 1979, London. 1 son, 3 daughters (from previous marriage). *Education:* MB, B.Chir, Cambridge, 1941; MRCS, LRCP, 1941; MRCP, 1942; MD, Cambridge, 1946; FRCP, 1956. *Appointments:* Casualty Officer, House Physician, Registrar, Resident Assistant Physician, St. Thomas' Hospital, London; Officer-in-Charge Medical Division, RAMC, India; Senior Medical Registrar and Tutor, Hammersmith Hosptial; Rockefeller Fellow in Medicine, Columbia University, New York, USA; Lecturer in Medicine and Physician, Postgraduate Medical School, London; Dean, Westminster Medical School 1960-64; Physician to H.M. Household, 1964-70; Consultant Physician, Westminster Hospital, 1954-81; Physician to H.M. The Queen, 1970-82; Head of H.M. Medical Household, 1973-82. *Memberships:* Fellow, Royal Society of Medicine;

Association of Physicians of Great Britain and Ireland; London Thyroid Club; British Cardiac Society; Member of Council, British Heart Foundation. *Publications:* "Practical Procedures in Clinical Medicine", 3rd edition, 1960; Various papers in medical journals and textbooks on endocrine, metabolic and cardiac diseases. *Honours:* Croonian Lecturer, R.C.P. 1974; KCVO, 1978; Harveian Lecturer, RCP, 1983; Honorary Fellow, Clare College, Cambridge, 1983; Honorary Member, Sec. of Endocrinology, RSM, 1983; Second Vice-President, RCP, 1983. *Hobbies:* Skiing; Music. *Address:* 6 Harley Street, London, WiN 1AA, England.

BEARD, Bruce H., b. 15 May 1921, Fort Worth, Texas, USA. Private Practice of Psychiatry. m. Barbara A Beard, 23 July 1971, Dallas, 2 sons. *Education:* BA ,. Texas Tech University, 1940; MD, University of Texas Medical Branch, 1944; Certified, American Board of Psychiatry and Neurology, 1951. *Appointments:* Private Practice, Psychiatry, Forth Worth, Texas, 1948-66; Major, US Air Force, 1955-57; Associate Professor of Psychiatry; University of Oklahoma School of Medicine, 1966-69; University of Texas Health Science Centre, Dallas, Texas, 1969-74. Professor of Psychiatry: Texas Tech University School of Medicine, 1974-77; University of Texas Health Science Center, 1977-81. Private Practice, Psychiatry, Dallas, 1981-; Clinical Professor of Psychiatry, University of Texas Health Science Centre, Dallas, 1981-. *Memberships:* American and Texas Medical Associations; Dallas County Medical Society; Life Fellow,(American Psychiatric Association; Central neuropsychiatric Association; Texas Psychiatric Association.) *Publications:* Contributions of papers to professional journals: 'Archives of General Psychiatry'; 'Diseases of the Nervous System'; 'International Journal of Artificial Organs'. Book chapter in "The Systemic Consequences of Renal Failure", 1984. *Honours:* Honorary Member, South Central Section, American Urological Association, 1972; Signa Xi, 1975. *Hobbies:* Breeding and training labrador Retrievers; Hunting; Amateur radio operator. *Address:* 10199 Vistadale Drive, Dallas, TX 75238, USA.

BEARDMORE, John Alec, b. 1 May 1930, Burton-on-Trent, England. University Professor; Head, Department of Genetics; Director, Institute of Marine Studies. m. Anne Patricia Wallace, 26 Dec. 1953, Sheffield, 3 sons, 1 daughter. *Education:* BSc, Botany, 1st Class Honours, 1953, PhD, Genetics, 1956, University of Sheffield; F.I.Biol., 1967. *Appointments:* Research Demonstrator, University of Sheffield, 1954-56; Commonwealth Fund (Harkness) Fellow, Columbia University, USA, 1956-58; Lecturer, University of Sheffield, 1958-61; Professor of Genetics Director of Institute, University of Groningen, Netherlands, 1961-66; University of Wales, 1966-. *Memberships:* Royal Society of Arts; Genetical Society; Linnean Society; Eugenics Society; Society for the Study of Evolution; Squatic Life Sciences Committee NERC, Chairman 1984-. *Publications Include:* "Marine Organisms: Genetics, Ecology & Evolution", ed. with β. Battaglia, 1977; Numerous articles, evolutionary genetics, human genetics, biological education. *Honours:* Medal, University of Helsinki, 1980; Darwin Lecturer, 1984. *Hobbies:* Bridge; Walking. *Address:* Department of Genetics, University College of Swansea, Singleton Park, Swansea SA2 8PP, Wales.

BECK, Felix, b. 13 Dec. 1931, Opava. Professor, Anatomy, Head of Department. m. Anne Josephine Morgan, 14 Oct. 1961, Newport, 2 daughters. *Education:* MB.Ch.B., 1954, MD, 1963, DSc, 1978, University of Birmingham, England. *Appointments:* Lecturer, Senior Lecturer, Anatomy, University College, Cardiff, 1957-58; Reader, Anatomy, 1968-71, Professor, 1971-72, Embryology, University of London; Foundation Professor, Anatomy, University of Leicester, 1972-. *Memberships:* Royal

Society of Medicine; British Medical Association; Anatomical Society of Great Britain & Ireland. *Publications:* "Human Embryology", co-author, 2nd edition 1985; many articles in professional journals. *Honours:* Fulbright Scholar, Carnegie Institute of Washington, USA, 1963-64. *Hobbies:* Travel; Collecting. *Address:* Dept. of Anatomy, University of Leicester Medical School, University Road, Leicester LE1 7RH, England.

BECK, John Swanson, b. 22 Aug. 1928, Glasgow, Scotland. Professor, Pathology, University of Dundee, 1971-. m. Marion Tudhope Paterson, 10 June 1960, Glasgow, 1 son, 1 daughter. *Education:* BSc., Honours, 1950, MBChB, Honours, 1953, MD, Honours, 1963, University of Glasgow; FRCPath; FRCPG; FRCPEd. *Appointments:* House Officer, Western Infirmary, and Royal Hospital for Sick Children, Glasgow, 1953-54; Senior House Officer, 1954-56, Registrar, 1955-58, Pathology, Western Infirmary; Lecturer, Pathology, University of Glasgow, 1958-63; Senior Lecturer, pathology University of Aberdeen, 1963-71. *Memberships:* Pathological Society of Great Britain and Ireland; British Society for Cell Biology; Chairman, Biomedical Research Committee; Chairman, Breast Tumour Panel, MRC; Chief Scientist Committee, SHHD; Tayside Health Board. *Publications:* Numerous papers in scientific journals. *Honours:* FRS Edinburgh, 1983. *Hobbies:* Walking; DIY. *Address:* 598 Perth Road, Dundee DD2 1QA, Scotland.

BECKER, Bruce Carl, b. 8 Sept. 1948, Chicago, USA. Director of Family Practice Residency. *Education:* BS, Aero and Astro Engineering, University of Illinois, USA, 1970; MS, Colorado State University, 1972; MD, Chicago Medical School, 1978; MS, Health Service Administration, 1984. *Appointments:* Assistant Director, St. Mary of Nazareth Hospital Centre, Chicago, USA, 1981-82; Clinical Instructor, Chicago Medical School, 1982, Affiliate Instructor, 1982-83, Assistant Professor and Vice Chairman, Department of Family Medicine, 1983-; Director, Family Practice Residency, St. Mary of Nazareth Hospital Centre, Chicago, 1983-; Chairman, Department of Family Practice, 1985-. *Memberships:* Fellow, American Academy of Family Physicians; Illinois Academy of Family Physicians; Society of Teachers of Family Medicine; Association of American Medical Colleges; American College of Hospital Administrators; American Medical Association; Illinois Medical Association; Chicago Medical Association. 6 conference presentations; Articles: 'Gastric Leimyoma' in 'Medical/Dental Journal' of St. Mary of Nazareth Hospital Centre; 'St. Francis Answering Needs of Administrators' in 'Chicago Crain's Business' (Co-author), 1984. *Honours:* Literary Key Award, 1981, 1984. *Hobbies:* Gourmet Cooking; Gardening; Fine Arts; Hunting; Isometric Weight Training. *Address:* 7107 West Belmont, Suite 7, Chicago, IL 60634, USA.

BECKER, Yechiel, b. 29 June 1931, Tel Aviv, Israel, Professor. m. June 1955, 2 sons, 1 daughter. *Education:* The Hebrew University, Jerusalem, 1951-56; MSc, 1957; PhD, 1960. *Appointments:* Research Associate, department of Biology, Massachusetts Institute of technology, Cambridge, Massachusetts, USA, 1962-63; Research Associate, Departemnt of Cell Biology, Einstein College of Medicine, New York, 1963-64; Visiting Professor, Department of Microbiology, University of Chicago, Illinois, 1969-70; Visiting Professor, Cancer Biological Research Laboratory, Department of Radiology, Stanford University School of Medicine, Stanford, California, 1983-84; Senior Lecturer, Department ofVirology, 1965-68, Associate Professor, Department of Virology, 1968-71, Professor, Department of Molecular Virology, 1972-, Chairman, Department of Molecular Virology, 1973-83, Hebrew University, Jerusalem, Israel. Memberships: International Comm Nomenclature of Viruses; International Association Microbiological

Society; Editorial Board, Interviriology; Comite de Lecture Contre la Trachome; Editorial board, Chemioterapia, International Journal Mediterranean Society of Chemotherapy; Editorial Board, Arch Virology. *Publications:* "Viruses as Molecules", 1970; "The Agent of Trachoma", 1974; "Antiviral Drugs: Mode of Action and Chemotherapy of Virul Infections of Man", 1976; "Chapters on Viruses", 1982; "Molecular Virology. Molecular and medical aspects of disease-causing viruses of man and animals", 1983; "Developments in Molecula. Virology", (Series Editor); "Developments in Veterinary Virology" (Series Editor); "Developments in Medical Virology", (Series Editor). *Honours:* Gold Headed Cane Award, College of Medicine, University of Arizona, 1980; Incumbent, Carolyn Jane Bendheim Chair in Molecular Virology, Hebrew University, 1981. *Hobbies:* Gardening. *Address:* Department of Molecular Virology, The Hebrew University-Hadassa Medical School, PO Box 1172, 91 010 Jerusalem, Israel.

BECKMAN, George Claus Jr. b. 16 Aug. 1922, Savannah, Georgia USA. Hospital Administrator. m. Mary Helen Scranton, 19 Sept. 1944, Independence, Kansas, USA, 2 daughters. *Education:* BS, Industrial Management, Georgia Institute of Technology, Atlanta, Georgia, USA, 1951. *Appointments:* Assistant to Executive Director, Elks Aidmore Inc., Children's Hospital, 1947-50; Assistant Administrator, Emory University Hospital, Atlanta, Georgia, 1951-53; Administrator, Georgia Warm Springs Foundation, Warm Springs, Georgia, 1953-73; Vice President, Candler General Hospital, Savannah, Georgia, 1973-78; Vice President, St. Joseph's Hospital, Savannah, Georgia, 1978-present. *Memberships:* American College of Hospital Administrators; American Hospital Association; Delegate at Large, House of Delegates, 1973-74; Georgia Hospital Association; West Central Georgia Hospital Council, President 1958; Georgia Gerontology Society, Vice President, 1965-66; Georgia Hospital Service Association (Blue Cross); Association of Rehabilitation Centres; National Rehabilitation Association; Georgia Rehabilitation Association; American Academy of Health Administration; Governor's Conference on Arthritis; Governor's Committee on Employment of the Handicapped; American Red Cross; National Amputee Golf Association. *Honour:* Joe Avans Amputee Golf Service Award, 1975. *Hobbies:* Golf; Directing Amputee Sports Programmes. *Address:* 13108 Spanish Moss Road, Savannah, GA 31419, USA.

BECKWITH, J. Bruce, b. 18 Sep. 1933, Spolkane, Washington, USA. Chairman of Pathology, The Children's Hospital Denver. m. (1) Lorna Glen Gourlay, 10 Sep. 1954 (deceased 1983); (2) Nancy Gay Browning, 21 June 1984, Seattle, Washington, 3 daughters. *Education:* BA (Hons.), Whitman College, Walla Walla, Washington, 1954; MD (Hons.), Universtiy of Washington School of Medicine, Seattle, 1958. *Appointments:* Director of Laboratories, Children's Orthopaedic Hospital and Medical Ceneter, Seattle, Washington, 1964-84; Assistant Professor, 1964, Associate Professor, 1968, Professor, 1974, Pathology and Paediatrics, University of Washington School of Medicine (1964-84); Chairman of Pathology, The Children's Hospital, Denver, Colorado; Clinical Professor, Pathology and Paediatrics, University of Colorado School of Medicine, 1985-.*Memberships:* Phi Beta Kappa; Alpha Omega Alpha; Society for Paediatric Pathology; International Society for Paediatric Oncology; College of American Pathologists; Teratology Society. *Publications:* Books: "Sudden Infant Death Syndrome", Co-Editor, 1970; "Tumours of the Kidney, Ureters and Bladder", Co-author, 1972; "Anancephaly", Co-author, 1980; Approximately 85 articles 1963-85. *Honours:* Distinguished Alumnus Award, University of Washinton School of Medicine, 1980; Honorary Doctor of Science, Whitman College, 1980. *Hobbies:*

Antiquarian Books (Teratology); Collecting Christmas seals; Distance Running. *Address:* The Children's Hospital 1056 E. 19th Avenue, Denver, CO 80218, USA.

BEDBROOK, (Sir) George Montario, b. 8 Nov. 1921, Melbourne, Australia. Orthopaedic Surgeon in Private Practice; Senior Surgeon, Spinal Injuries Service, Royal Perth Hosptial and Royal Perth Rehabilitation Hospital. m. Jessie Violet Page, 23 Feb. 1946, Melbourne, 2 sons, 3 daughters. *Education:* MB BS, 1944; MS, 1950, University of Melbourne; FRACS (Melbourne), 1950; FRCS (England), 1951; Diploma in Physical Rehabilitation Medicine, 1970. *Appointments:* Resident Medical Officer, Royal Melbourne Hospital, 1944-45, Lecturer in Anatomy, University of Melbourne, 1946-50; Resident Medical Officer, National Orthopaedic Hosptial, England, 1951; Registrar, Croydon Group Hospitals, 1951-53; Private Practice, Perth, 1953-; Paraplegic Service with Royal Perth Hospital, 1954; Head, Department of Paraplegia, Royal Perth Hospital, Royal Perth Rehabilitation Hospital, 1954-72; Senior Surgeon, 1972; Head, Departemnt of Orthopaedic Surgery, 1965-75; Chairman, Department of Orthopaedic Surgery, 1975-79; Senior Surgeon, 1979-81; Senior Surgeon, Spinal Unit (currently). *Memberships Include:* National Advisory Council for the Handicapped, Vice-Chairman, 1975-83; Australian Orthopaedic Association, President, 1977; Royal Australian College of Surgeons; Court of Examiners, Orthopaedic Surgery, Royal Australasian College of Surgeons, 1973-83; Australian Council for Rehabilitation of the Disabled, Vice-President, 1970-80; Life Member, Paraplegic Quadriplegic Association of Western Australia Incorporated; International Medical Society Paraplegia, President, 1981-84; Chairman, Western Australian Committee, 1981 International Year of the Disabled Persons; Chairman, Organising Committee, 7th Western Pacific Orthopaedic Association Congress, Perth, 1982. *Publications:* Over 114 Scientific Papers and Publications; Books: "The Care and Management of Spinal Cord Injuries"; "Lifetime Care of the Paraplegic Patient". *Honours Include:* Betts' Medallist of Australian Orthopaedic Association, 1972; Medal of Honour from International Medical Society of Paraplegia, 1978. *Hobbies:* Reading; Music; Walking; Travel. *Address:* 13 Colin Grove, West Perth 6005, Western Australia.

BEDELL, John Francis, b. 14 Nov. 1931, Lahore, Pakistan, Family physician; Active Staff Queensway Hospital and George McCall Chronic Care Hospital, Toronto, Canada. m. Elsa Doreen Clarke, 12 Aug 1961, Grenada, 1 son, 2 daughters. *Education:* LRCP, London; MRCS, England, 1959; LMCC, Canada, 1972. *Appointments:* Medical Officer, Government of Trinidad and Tobago, 1960-65; Medical Officer, Shell Trinidad Ltd, 1965-71; Family Practice Toronto, Ontario, Canada, 1971-. *Memberships:* College of Physicians and Surgeons of Ontario; Canadian College of Family Practice; Ontario Medical Association., *Hobby:* Golf. *Address:* 441 Targa Road, Mississauga, Ontario, Canada L5A 1S7.

BEDI, Ashok Ramprakash, b. 10 Feb. 1948. Associate Clinical Professor of Psychiatry and Clinical Director, Psychiatric Hospital. m. Usha Bedi, 26 July 1972, India, 1 son 1 daughter. *Education:* Graduated as Physician, B J Medical College and Gujarat University, Ahmedeked, India, 1970. *Education:* Council for Foreign Medical Graduates Examination, 1973; Certified as Diplomat in Psychiatry, Royal College of Physicians and Surgeons of England, 1975; Certified Member, Royal College of Psychiatrists, United Kingdom, 1975; Federal Licensing Examiniation, 1976; Certified as Diplomat, American Board of Psychiatry and Neurology; 1979. *Appointments Include:* Internship, B J Medical College and Affiliated Hospitals, Gujarat, India, 1970-71; Resident in Psychiatry, BJ Medical College,

Gujarat, Feb - July 1972; Resident in Psychiatry, North Wales Psychiatric Hospital Denbigh, Wales, UK, 1972-73; House Surgeon, Maelor General Hospital, Wrexham, Powys, North Wales and Mawddach Hospital Mangement Committee, 1973-74; Resident in Psychiatry, St. Crispin Hospital, Northampton, Oxford Regional Hospital Board, England, 1974-76; Senior Fellowship in Community Psychiatry Medical College of Wisconsin, 1976-77; Staff Psychiatrist, Milwaukee County Mental Health Center, 1977-79; Catchment Area Director, Westside Community Mental Health Center, Milwaukee, 1979-80; Full time Assistant Professor in Psychiatry and Mental Health Sciences, Medical College of Wisconsin, 1977-80; Assistant Clinical Professor of Psychiatry, Medical College of Wisconsin, 1980-82; Attending Psychiatrist, 1980-, Clinical Director, 1983-, Milwaukee Psychiatric Hospital; Associate Clinical Professor in Psychiatry, Medical College of Wisconsin, 1982-. *Memberships Include:* Diplomat, American Board of Psychaitry and Neurology; British Medical Association (eligible for Membership); General Medical Council, London; Royal College of Psychiatrists, UK; Royal College of Physicians and Surgeons, England, Diplomat in Psychiatry; Full member, American Group Psychotherapy Asociation; American and Wisconsin Psychiatric Association; American Medical Association (eligible for Membership). *Publications:* Contributor of articles to medical journals and chapters to edited medical publications. *Honour:* Governemnt of India National Merit Scholarship. *Address:* c /o Milwaukee Psychiatric Hospital, 1220 Dewey Avenue, Wauwatosa, WI 53213, USA.

BEDROSSIAN, Carlos W M, b. 1 May 1944, Brazil, Professor. m. Ursula Kay Kennedy, 8 Aug. 1970, Jacksonville, Florida, USA, 2 sons, 1 daughter. *Education:* BS, Moura Lacerda College, Brazil, 1962; MD, V. Sao Paulo (Rib. Preto) Brazil, 1967. *Appointments:* Assistant Professor, University of Oklahoma, 1973-75; Assistant Professor, 1975-77, Associate Professor, 1977-81, University of Texas, Houston; Professor of Pathology, Chief of Laboratory, Vanderbilt University, Nashville, 1981-84; Professor of Pathology, Director, Cytopathology & Immunocytochemistry, St Louis University, 1984-. *Memberships:* President, Latin-American Pathological Foundation; international Academy of Pathology; International Academy of Cytology; American Society of Clinical Pathology; American Society of Cytology; American College of Chest Physicians; American Thoracic Society; Latin-American Society of Pathology. *Publications:* Some 50 papers in professional & medical journals. *Honours:* Best Student, Basic Sciences, 1967; MD Anderson Award in Clinical Research, 1972; Editor-ibn-Chief, 'Diagnostic cytopathology', 1984. *Hobbies:* Stamp-collecting; Soccer Coaching; Travel. *Address:* 1402 South Grand Boulevard, St Louis, MO 63104, USA.

BEDWELL, Stephen Frederick, b. 14 June 1931, Toronto, Canada. Professor, Neurologist. m. Ruth Sylvia Arthur, 14 Feb. 1966, Liverpool, Nova Scotia, Canada, 1 son. *Education:* MD, Faculty of Medicine, University of Toronto, 1955; Certification, Royal College of Physicians & Surgeons of Canada, 1962; Fellowship, RCP(C) in Neurology, 1964. *Appointments:* Internship, Toronto Western Hospital 1955-56; Assistant Resident (Neurology), Baltimore City Hospitals 1956-58, Johns Hopkins Hospital 1958-59, Baltimore, Maryland, USA; Assistant Resident (Medicine), Sunnybrook Hospital, Toronto, 1959-60; Research Assistant Resident (Neurology) Neurophysiology Best Institute, Toronto 1961, Victoria General Hospital, Halifax NS, 1962; Assistant in Neurological Medicine, Johns Hopkins University, 1956-59; Demonstrator in Clinical Techniques, University of Toronto, 1960-61; Demonstrator, 1962, Lecturer in Medicine 1963-67, Assistant Professor of Medical Neurology, Dalhousie University, 1967-85. *Memberships:*

Fellow of: Royal College of Physicians & Surgeons of Canada; Academy of Medicine (Toronto); American Academy of Neurology; Member of: Canadian Medical Association; Medical Society of Nova Scotia; Halifax Medical Society; Canadian Congress of Neurological Sciences; Canadian Society of Clinical Neurophysiology; Atlantic Neurosciences Association. *Publications:* Various articles in 'Canadian Medical Acotiation Journal', 'Neurology', 'Canadian Journal of Neurological Sciences', and others. *Hobbies:* Collecting phonograph records; Photography, Sound Reproduction; Travel. *Address:* Suite 1030, 5991 Spring Garden Road, Halifax, Nova Scotia. B3H 1Y6, Canada.

BEECH, James Wilson, b. 16 June 1952, Marshall County, Lewisburg, Tennessee, USA. Corporation Director. *Education:* Pre-professional, Memphis State University; DC, Palmer College; Diplomate, National Board of Chiropractic Examiner; Postgraduate work, National College of Chiropractic. *Appointments:* Commercial Pilot, Flight Instructor, Memphis International Airport, 1971-73; Director of Ground Schools, 1973-75; Professional College, 1975-80; President and Director, Beech Chiropractic Corporation, Columbia and Lewisburg, 1980-. *Memberships:* American and Tennessee Chiropractic Associatiions; International Academy of Preventive medicine; American Public Health Association. *Publications:* 'The American Chiropractor'. *Honours:* Delta Delta Pi; Certificate of merit, Intern, Palmer College of Chiropractic, Judiciary Committee, Palmer College; Outstanding Young Man of America, National Jaycees, 1982; Decorations, Search and Rescue, CAP-USAF, 1973. *Hobbies:* Flying; Radio communications; Fishing. *Address:* 1404 Hatcher Lane, Columbia, TN 38401, USA.

BEERING, Steven Claus, b. 20 Aug. 1932, Berlin, Germany. President, Purdue University, USA. m. Catherine Jane Pickering, 26 Dec. 1956, Pittsburgh, 3 sons. *Education:* BSc., 1954, MD, 1958, University of Pittsburgh; Honorary DSc., Indiana Central University, 1983, University of Evansville, 1984. *Appointments:* Professor of Medicine, 1969-; Assistant Dean, 1969-70, Associate Dean, 1970-74, Dean, 1974-83, Indiana University School of Medicine. *Memberships:* National Academy of Sciences Institute of Medicine; Association of American Medical Colleges; American College of Physicians; American Medical Association; Endocrine Society. *Publications:* Numerous articles. *Honours:* Steven C. Beering Professorship in Medicine, Indiana University School of Medicine, 1983-; Convocation Medal, American College of Cardiology, 1983; University of Pittsburgh Distinguished Medical Alumnus Award (Philip Hench Medal), 1983. *Hobbies:* Music; Photography; Reading; Travel. *Address:* Purdue University, West Lafayette, IN 47907, USA.

BEGG, Adrian Campbell, b. 12 Feb. 1946, London, England. Senior Research Scientist, Netherlands Cancer Institute. *Education:* BSc., Honours, Physics, University of Sussex; MSc., Biophysics, University of East Anglia; PhD, Royal Postgraduate Medical School, London. *Appointments:* Scientific Officer: Royal Postgraduate Medical School, London. *Appointments:* Scientific Officer: Royal Postgraduate Medical School, 1968-70, Gray Laboratory, Mount Vernon Hospital, 1970-75; Postdoctoral Fellow, University of California, San Francisco, USA, 1975-78; Research Scientist, Grey Laboratory, Mount Vernon Hospital, 1979-83; Research Scientist, Netherlands Cancer Institute, Amsterdam, 1984-. *Memberships:* Association for Radiation Research; British Institute of Radiology; Radiation Research Society, USA; European Society for Therapeutic Radiology and Oncology; Society for Analytical Cytology; Netherlands Society for Radiobiology. *Publications:* Articles in various journals including 'British Journal Radiology';

'Radiotherapy Oncology'. *Honours:* Postdoctoral Fellowship, 1975-78; Invited keynote Speaker, Rodent Tumour Research Conference, Munich, 1984. *Hobbies:* Squash; Windsurfing; Skiing; Guitar & Piano Playing; Chess; Reading. *Address:* The Netherlands Cancer Institute, HG, Plesmanlaan 121, 1066 CX Amsterdam, The Netherlands.

BEHNKE, Olav, b. 3 May 1929, Graasten, Denmark. Professor of Medical Cytology. m. Lis Roland Behnke, 13 Sept. 1952, Hellerup, 2 sons, 1 daughter. *Education:* MD, 1955; DMS, 1972. *Appointments:* Clinical Training, Surgery, 1955-60; Assistant Professor, Anatomy, 1960-62, Associate Professor, 1962-68, Royal Dental College, Copenhagen; Associate Professor, Institute of Anatomy, 1968-74, Professor, 1974, Dean, Medical Faculty, 1977-82, Copenhagen University. *Membership:* Executive Board, NOVO Foundation. *Publications:* Author of about 75 learned articles, 1957-. *Honour:* Electred Member, Royal Danish Academy of Sciences and Letters, 1974; EMBO, 1976. *Address:* Institute of Anatomy C, The Panum Institute, Blegdamsvej 3C, DK-2200 Copenhagen, Denmark.

BEIGHTON, Peter Herbert, b, 28 June 1934, Bolton, England, Professor of Human Genetics, m, Greta Janet Winch, 5 May 1970, 1 son, 1 daughter. *Education:* MB, BS, St Mary's Hospital Medical School, University of London, 1957, *Appointments:* Resident posts, St Mary's Hospital. 1957-60; Captain, Royal Army Medical Corps, United Nations, Congo, 1960-62; Training in Internal medicine, St Thomas's Hospital, London, England, 1966-69; Professor of Human Genetics, University of Cape Town, Republic of South Africa, 1972; Director, South African Medical Research Unit for Inherited Skeletal Disorders, 1983. *Memberships:* Fellow, Royal Society of South Africa; Fellow, Royal Geographic Society; International Skeletal Society; Clinical Genetics Society UK; British Orthopaedic Association. *Publications:* Monographs: 'The Ehlers-Danlos Syndrome', 1970; 'Inherited Disorders of the Skeleton', 1978; 'Bone Dysplasias of Infancy', (with B Cremin), 1978; 'Sclerosing Bone Dysplasias', (with B Cremin), 1980; 'Inherited Orthopaedic Disorders', (with F Horan), 1982; 'Genetics and Otology', (with S Sellars), 1982; 'Hypermobility of Joints', (with R Grahame and H Bird), 1983; 'Gamut Index of Skeletal Dysplasias'; (with K Kozlowski), 1984; More than 200 medical articles. *Honours:* British Orthopaedic Association Robert Jones Medal, 1975; South African Orthopaedic Aociation President's Medallion, 1978; Smith and Nephew Literary award, 1979; Andries Blignault Memorial Medal (jointly), 1980. *Hobbies:* Mountaineering; Cross-country running; Rugby; Military History. *Address:* Department of Human Genetics, UCT Medical School, Observatory, Cape Town 7925, Republic of South Africa.

BEILIN, Lawrence Joseph, b. 6 Aug. 1936, London, England. Professor of Medicine and Department Head. m. Brenda, 3 sons. *Education:* MB BS, 1959, MRCP, 1961, MD Thesis, 1965, London; MA, Pemb, 1968; FRCP, England, 1975; FRACP, 1977. *Appointments:* House Surgeon and House Physician, Kings College Hospital, London, England, 1959; Senior House Officer, Hammersmith Hospital, 1960-61; Senior House Officer, Great Ormond Street Hospital for Sick Children, 1962; Lecturer in Medicine, Kings College Hospital Medaical School, 1962-65; MRC Travelling Fellow-ship, Metabolic Unit, University of Southern California, USA, 1965-66; Senior Registar, Hammersmith Hospital, London, England, 1966-68; Tutor in Medicine, Royal Postgraduate Medical School; First Assistant and Honoury Consultnt Physician, Department of Regius Professor of Medicine, OxfordUniversity, 1968-77; Professor of Medicine, Honorary Physician, 1977-81, Professor and Head, Department of Medicine, 1982-, Honorary Physician, Royal Perth Hospital, Perth, Western Australia. *Memberships Include:* Executive Member, Australian Council for High Blood Pressure

Research; Australian Society of Clinical and Experimental Pharmacology; Australian Society for Medical Research; Australian Society of Nephrology; British Pharmacology SocietyInternational Hypertension Society; Medical Research Society, UK; International Society for Hypertension in Pregnancy; Association of Clinical Professors of Australia. *Honours:* State Scholarship, Kings College, London, England, 1954; Entrance Scholarship in Anatomy and Physiology, 1956; Prizes in Medicine, Surgery and others, MRCS,LRCP, 1959. *Hobbies:* Cycling; Sailing; Music. *Address:* University Department of Medicine, 35 Victoria Square, Royal Perth Hospital, Perth, WA 6000, Australia.

BEKS, Johannes Waltherus Franciscus, b. 27 Sept. 1928, Eindhoven, Netherlands. Professor of Neurosurgery. m. Maria Metzemaekers, 6 May 1957, Eindhoven, Holland, 1 son, 1 daughter. *Education:* MD, University of Utrecht. *Appointments* Professor of Neurosurgery, State University , Gronigen, Holland, 1966-. *Memberships:* Dutch Society of Neurosurgeons; Concilium Neurochirurgicum; Royal Dutch Academy of Sciences; Many Foreign Neurosurgical Societies. *Publications:* 130 articles in all international neurosurgical journals. *Honour:* Member of the Royal Dutch Society of Arts & Science. *Address:* Esserweg 16, SN 9722 Groningen, Holland.

BELCOURT, Alain Bernard Cyrille, b. 10 Apr. 1943, Aix-les-Bains, France. Doctor of Sciences; Director of Research INSERM. m. Nicole Grimm, 19 Dec. 1970, Strasbourg, 3 sons. *Education:* Master of Sciences in Chemistry; Diploma of Advanced Studies in Biochemistry; State Doctorate of Sciences. *Appointments:* INSERM, French National Institute of Health and Medical Research, 1972; Visiting Scientist, National Institute of Health, Bethesda, Maryland, USA, 1978-81. *Memberships:* Society for Biochemistry, France; International Association for Dental Research; European Calcified Tissue Society; French College for Mouth Biology; French National Association of Doctors of Science. *Publications:* Contributions to books including: "Experimental Approaches to the Study of Enamel Matrix" in "Experimental Dentistry", 1983; "Le Fluor" in "Nutrition et Sante Publique. Approche Epidemiologique"; Numerous articles and papers in professional journals. *Honour:* Gibbs Prize, Signal Special, 1976. *Hobbies:* Duplicate Bridge; Skiing; Travel. *Address:* 16 Avenue de la Paix, 67000 Strasbourg, France.

BELCOURT, Christian Louis, b. 26 Feb. 1926, Mauritius. Assistant Professor. m. Teresita Curran, Wellington, Massachusetts, USA, 2 sons 1 daughter. *Education:* MB, BS, London, England, 1952; LRCP, MRCS, England, 1952; LMCC Canada, 1963; Certificate in Diagnostic Radiology, 1965. *Appointments:* Medical Officer, Mauritius, 1956-59; Medical Officer, Newfoundland, 1959-62; Fellow in Radiology, Harvard Medical School, Mount Auburn, Cambridge, Massachusetts, 1965-66; Resident and Chief Resident, Children's Hospital Medical Centre, Boston, Massachusetts, 1966-68; Staff Radiologist, IWK Hospital Halifax, 1968-; Assistant Professor, Dalhousie Universtiy (currently). *Memberships:* Canadian Medical Association; Canadian Association of Radiologists; Royal College of Physicians and Surgeons of Canada; Nova Scotia Association of Radiologists; Fellow of American College of Cardiology. *Publications:* Co-author of articles in medical journals and contributions to edited scientific volumes. *Hobbies:* Alpine Skiing; Sailing. *Address:* 6 Homecrest Terrace, Halifax Nova Scotia, Canada B3N 1Y4.

BELESLIN, Dusan, b. 26 Mar. 1931, Senta, Yugoslavia. Professor of Pharmacology, Vice-Dean of Medical Faculty, Belgrade, Yugoslavia; President of MRC of the SR of Serbia. m. Tomic Nevenka, 25 Feb. 1961, Belgrade, 1 son. *Education:* MD, 1955;

Doctor of Medical Sciences, 1968. *Appointments:* Assistant Professor of Pharmacology, 1964, Associate Professor of Pharmacology, 1970, Professor of Pharmacology, 1976, Vice Dean, 1976-78, 1984, Medical Faculty, Belgrade; President of Medical Research Council of the SR of Serbia; Visiting Associate Professor, Department of Psychology, Purdue University, Lafayette, Indiana, USA, 1968-70; Visiting Associate Professor, Department of Pharmacology, University of Illinois, Medical Center, Chicago, USA, 1976. *Memberships:* Yugoslav Physiological Society; Yugoslav Pharmacological Society; Yugoslav Society of Biophysics; Sigma XI; New York Academy of Sciences. *Publications:* 'The Neurobiology Assay; in 'Methods in Psychobiology', Volume 2. Editor, R D Myers, 1972; '6-Hydroxydopamine and Aggression in Cats', 1981; 'Central effects of calcium, magnesium and lithium ions: Differetiation of muscarinic cholinoceptors by calcium and magnesium ions', *Address:* Department of Pharmacology, Medical Faculty, P.). Box 662, 11000 Belgrade, Yugoslavia.

BELL, Christopher, b. 30 Sep. 1941, Australia. *Education:* BSc, 1962, MSc., 1964, PhD, 1967, University of Melbourne. *Appointments:* Fellow, National Heart Foundation of Australia, 1967-68; Overseas Fellow, National Heart Foundation of Australia, 1969-73; Lecturer, 1973-75, Senior lecturer, 1976-79, Reader, Physiology, University of Melbourne. *Memberships:* Australian Physiological & Pharmacological Society, Treasurer, 1981-86; Australian Society of Clinical and Experimental Pharmacologists; Physiological Society; British Pharmacological Society; Zoological Society of London; International Brain Research Organisation. *Publications:* Lecture 8, IUPHAR 9th International Congress of Pharmacology, 1984; *Review Articles:* "Medical Biology", 1974 and "Neuroscience", 1982 in cited journals. *Honours:* 1st Sandoz Prize, British Pharmacological Society, 1972; DSc., University of Melbourne, 1980. *Hobbies:* Opera; Georgian England; Building Conservation. *Address:* Dept. of Physiology, University of MelbourneMedical Centre, Parkvilel, Victoria 3052, Australia.

BELL, Kenneth, E, b. 2 July 1936, New York, New York, USA. Chief of Obstetrics and Gynaecology. m. Robert Lynn Bell, 28 June 1959, New York, 3 daughters. *Education:* BS Honours History, Washington and Jefferson College, 1956; MD with Honours, University of Buffalo School of Medicine, 1961; Junior Assistant Resident 1962-63, Assistant Resident 1963-65, Chief Resident 1965-66, Kings County Hospital. *Appointments:* Chief, Obstetrics-Gynecology Service, Hill Air Force Base, Utah, 1966-68; Attending Physician, Kaiser Foundation Hospital, Bellflower, California, 1968-; Attending Physician 1968-78, Executive Committee Professional Staff Association 1976-78, Hasrbor General Hospital, Torrance; Attending Physician, Los Angeles County, University of Southern California Medical Center, Los Angeles, 1970-80; Attending Physician, University of California at Los Angeles University Hospital, 1968-78; Director Obstetrics-Gynaecology Allied Health Personnel Training 1971-, Board of Directors 1975-77 and 1981-, Chief of Department of Obstetrics-Gynaecology -, Southern California Permanente Medical Group; Advisory Committee, Department of Nursing, California State University, Los Angeles, 1977-; Kaiser Permanente Medical Center, Anaheim , 1979 -. *Memberships Include:* American College of Obstetrics-Gynaecology; American Fertility Society; Association of Professors of Gynaecology and Obstetrics; International Family Planning Research Association; Pacific Coast Fertility Society; The Cybele Society. *Publications:* 'Planning For Family-Centered Maternity Care', 1984; 'Obstetric Care - The HMO Perspective', 1984; 'Modern OB Care', 1985; 'Family-Centered Care; Patient Pleasing, Provider Satisfying and Cost Effective', 1985; 'Team Obstethics: Nurse

Midwife/Obstetrician Combined Practice in a Large HMO'. *Address:* 1188 N Euclid Street 401 , Anaheim, CA 92805, USA.

BELL, Jonathan Martin, b. 26 May 1954, London, England. Senior Registrar in Radiodiagnosis. *Education:* BSc, Hons, Physiology, 1975, MB, ChB, 1978, University of Bristol. *Appointments:* House Physician, 1978-79, House Surgeon, Feb - July 1979, Bristol Royal Infirmary; Senior House Officer in Thoracic Medicine, Ham Green Hospital, Pill, Bristol, 1979-80; Senior House Officer in Geriatric Medicine, Dudley Road Hospital, Birmingham, 1980-81; Registrar in Geriatric Medicine, Dudley Road Hospital, Birmingham, March - Sept 1981; Registrar in Radiodiagnosis, 1981-84, Senior Registrar in Radiodiagnosis, 1984-, Bristol Royal Infirmary. *Memberships:* British Medical Association; Member of Royal College of Physicians of London; Fellow, Royal College of Radiologists; Member, British Institute of Radiology. *Publications Include:* 'The Effect of Left Atrial Size on the Oesophageal Transit of Capsules' with KS Channer and J Virjee in "British Heart Journal" 1984; 'The Swollen Leg: The Sonographic Appearances of Non-thrombotic Causes' with FGM Ross, S Mackenzie and P Goddard and H Andrews in "Respiratory Disease in Practice" 1985. *Hobbies:* Speleology; Squash. *Address:* 13 Carnarvon Road, Redland, Bristol BS6 7DP, Avon, England.

BELL, Pete Robert Frank, b. 12 June 1938, Bangalore, India. Professor of Surgery. m. Anne Jennings, 25 Aug. 1961, 1 son, 2 daughters. *Education:* MDChB, University of Sheffield, England, 1961; FRCS, England, 1965; MD, University of Sheffield, 1970; FRCSG, Scotland, 1971. *Appointments:* Registrar, Surgery, Sheffield Health Board, Sheffield, Yorkshire,1963-65; Lecturer, Surgery, University of Glasgow, Scotland, 1965-68; Sir Henry Wellcome Travelling Fellow, Wellcome Foundation, Denver, Colorado, USA, 1968-69; Senior Lecturer in Surgery, University of Glasgow, Scotland, 1969-74; Foundation Professor of Surgery, University of Leicester, 1974-. *Memberships:* Fellow: Royal College of Surgeons, England; Royal College of Physicians and Surgeons, Glasgow, Scotland. Past Secretary, President, Surgical Research Society; Vascular Societry of Great Britain and Northern Ireland; Secretary, Transplantation Society. *Publications:* 'Operative Arterial Surgery', 1983: 'Surgical Aspects of Haemodialysis', 1985. Editor and Contributor, 'Vascular Surgery', 1985. Author of artciles in transplantation and vascular surgery, 1968-. *Honours:* Invited Speaker, Australian College of Surgeons, New Zealand, 1984; Invited Lecuter, Surgical Research Society, Southern Africa, 1984; Mark Sharp and Dohme Invited Lecturer, Australian Nephrological Society, 1987. *Hobbies:* Horticulture; Oil painting; Tennis. *Address:* Department of Surgery, Clinical Sciences Building, Leicester Royal Infirmary, Leicester LE2 7LX, England.

BELL, Randall William, b. 28 Jan. 1938, New York, USA. Senior Partner, Main Line Eye Care Inc; Chief, Opthalmology. m. Carole Anne Gilligan, 6 June 1959, 4 sons, 1 daughter. *Education:* BSc., US Military academy, West Point, 1959; Columbia University Pre-Med and Advanced Chemistry, 1961; MD, Cornell University Medical College, 1966; Intern, Walter Reed General Hospital, 1966-67; Residence, Ophtalmology, Walter Reed General Hospital, 1967-70; Courses in Ophtalmology, 1968-72. *Appointments:* Commander, 2290th Hospital, Walter Reed Army Medical Centre; Chief, Opthalmology, Valley Forge General Hospital, Phoenixville; Senior Partner, Main Line Eye Care Inc; Chief, Opthalmology, Sacred Heart Hospital, Norristown. *Memberships Include:* Fellow, American Academy of Opthalmology & Otolaryngology; Fellow, American College of Surgeons; American Medical Association; Fellow, College of physicians of Philadelphia; Royal Society

of Medicine, London, England; Society of Military Ophthalmologists. *Publications:* Articles in professional journals. *Hobies:* Cricket; Squash. *Address:* 124 Bloomingdale Ave., Wayne, PA 19087, USA.

BELLACK, Alan S, b. 27 Nov. 1944, New York, New York, USA. Professor of Psychiatry. m. Barbara Bartlett, 16 Nov. 1969, East Orange, New Jersey, 2 sons. *Education:* BS, City College of New York, 1965; MA, St John's University, 1967; PhD, Pennsylvania State University, 1970. *Appointments:* Assistant Professor, Pennsylvania State University, 1971; Assistant-Full Professor, Udniversity of Pittsburgh, 1972-82; Professor, Medical College of Pennsylvania, 1982-. *Memberships:* Fellow, American Psychological Association; President 1985, Association for Advancement of Behavior Therapy. *Publications:* "International Handbook of Behavior Modification and Therapy", 1982; "The Clinical Psychology Handbook'', 1983; "Schizophrenia: Treatment, Management and Rehabilitation", 1984; "Handbook of Clinical Behavior with Adults", 1985. *Hobbies:* Sailing; Jogging. *Address:* Medical College of Pennsylvania /EPP1, 3200 Henry Avenue, Philadelphia, PA 19129, USA.

BELLINGHAM, Francis Richard, b. 6 Feb. 1940, Sydney, Australia. Specialist Obstetrician and Gynaecologist, Westmead Hospital. m. Mary Angela Borthwick, 15 May 1965, Sydney, 1 son, 1 daughter. *Education:* MBBS (Hons), Sydney Undiversity, 1963; MRCOG (London), 1970; FRCOG, 1983; FFRACOG, 1979; Diploma in Venereology, Liverpool, 1972. *Appointemnts:* Resident Staff, St. Vincent's Hospital, 1964-65; Registrar, The Women's Hospital Crown Street, 1966-69; Registrar, Royal Victoria Hospital, Bournemouth England, 1970-71; Medical Officer, Kabalushi, Zambia, 6 Months 1971; Specialist Visiting Medical Officer. The Women's Hosptial, Crown Street, Sydney, until the hospital closed. *Memberships:* MSSVD; Member, AVDA; Current President, Venereology Society of New South Wales. *Address:* 29 / 1A Ashely Lane, Westmead 2145, Australia.

BELLO, Cornelius Sunday Saliu, b. 2 Feb. 1947, Adum-Woiwo, Nigeria. Senior Lecturer; Consultant Microbiologist. m. Hannah Hajara, 26 Dec. 1974, Lokoja, Nigeria, 1 son, 2 daughters. *Education:* MBBS; Lagos; Dip, Ven., London, England; DP, Bact., Manchester England; MD, ANU, Zaria, Nigeria; FMC, Path; FRSH. *Appointments:* House Officer through to Consultant in Medical Mjicrobiology, Abu Hospital, Zaria, Nigeria, 1974 -. Venereologist to Abu Hospital, 1977 -. *Memberships:* Nigeria Medical Association; Nigeria Society for Microbiology; African Venereal Disease Association; British Venereal Disease Association; American Venereal Disease Association; British Royal Society of Health. *Publications:* 'Sex and VD', 1984; 'Sexually Transmissible Diseases: Management Guide for the General Practitioners', 1985; 25 articles in International Journals. *Honours:* Kwara Scholar, 1969-74; Benue Scholar, 1978-79; Federal Scholar, 1980-83; Fellow, West African College of Physicians; Fellow, Royal Society of Health. *Hobbies:* Photography; Lawn Tennis. *Address:* Special Treatment Clinic Department of Medical Microbiology, ABU Hospital, Zaria, Nigeria.

BELLO-REUSS, Elsa, b. 12 May 1939, La Plata, Argentina, Associate Professor of Cell Biology and Physiology. m. Luis Reuss, 15 Apr. 1965, Santiago, Chile, 2 sons. *Education:* BA, 1957, MD, 1964, University of Chile, Santiago, Chile. *Appointments:* Instructor, Pathophysiology, University of Chile, Santiago, Chile, 1966-72; International NIH Fellow, 1972-74, Career Investi Visiting Scientist, 1974-75, Louis Welt Fellow, 1975-76, University of North Carolina, USA; Assistant Professor, Medicine and Physiology, 1976-85. *Memberships:* International Society Nephrology; American Society of

Nephrology; American Federation for Clinical Research; American Heart Association, Kideny Council; The New York Academy of Sciences; American Association for the Advancement of Science; Society of General Physiology; The American Physiological Society; The Mathematical Association of America. *Publications:* Contributor of over 40 articles, reviews, book chapters and abstracts on professional and scientific subjects. *Honours:* Fogarty Fellow, 1972-74; Louis Welt Fellow, 1975-76. *Hobby:* Creative Writing. *Address:* Washington University School of Medicine, Department of Cell Biology and Physiology, 660 South Euclid, Box 8101, St Louis, MO 63110, USA.

BELLOWS-BLAKELY, David Sewell, b. 13 Aug. 1951, Topeka, Kansas, USA. Staff Psychiatrist. m. Karen F Bellows-Blakely, 5 July 1976, Topeka, 1 son. *Education:* BA, Stanford University, 1973; Pre-Medicine course, 1974-75, MD, School of Medicine, 1977, Kansas University; Intern and Resident, Stanford University Medical Centre, 1977-81; Fellow and Advanced Fellow, Austen Rigss Centre Inc., 1981-85. *Appointments:* Intern Resident and Chief Resident, Stanford University Medical Centre, 1977-81; Extra Help Psychiatrist, Emergency Psychiatry Services, Santa Clara Valey Medical Centre and Santa Clara Valley Jail, 1980-81. Consulting Psychiatrist; Westfield Area Mental Health Centre, 1981-82; Westfield Community Support Services, 1983-85; Massachusetts Society for Prevention of Cruelty to Children, 1984-85. Honorary Staff, Berkshire Medical Centre, Massachusetts, 1982-85; Part-time private practice, Stockbridge, Massachusetts, 1981-85; Staff Psychiatrist, Prairie View Incorporated, Newton, Kansas, 1985-. *Memberships:* American Medical Association; American Psychiatric Association; Massachusetts and Berkshire District Medical Societies; Massachusetts Psychiatric Society; American Association for the Advancement of Science. *Publications:* 'Coercian and Countertransference', 1985. *Honours:* Scholar of the Year, Alpha Sigma Phi, 1973; BA with Distinction, Department of Human Biology, Stanford University, 1973; Board Certified, American Board of Psychiatry and Neurology, 1984. *Hobbies:* Backpacking; Bicycling; Canoeing; Hunting; Fishing; Tennis, Multiple team sports; Skiing; Gardening. *Address:* Prairie View Incorporated, 1901 East 1st Street, Box 467, Newton, KS 67114-0467, USA.

BELLWARD, Gail Dianne, b. 27 May 1939, Brock, Canada. Assistant Dean, graduate studies and research, Faculty of Pharmaceutical Sciences, University of British Columbia. *Education:* BSc. (Pharm) 1960; MSc., 1963, Phd, 1966, University of British Columbia; Fellow, Clinical Pharmacology, Emory University, Atlanta, Georgia USA, 1968-69. *Appointments:* Assistant Professor, Pharmacology and Toxicology, Associate Professor, 1973-79, Professor, 1979- Chairman, 1981-85, Assistant Dean, Graduate Sudies and Research, 1985, University of British Columbia; Visiting Professor, Clinical Pharmacology, Royal Postgraduate Medical School, London, England, 1975. *Memberships:* Pharmacological Society of Canada, Secretary, 1977-80, Nominating Committee, 1983-85, Vice President, 1985-87;IUPHAR Committee, 1985-87; Canadian Federation of Biological Societies, Board Member, 1977-80, Board Member, 1985-87; Society of Toxicology of Canada; American Society for Pharmacology ;and Experimental Therapeutics; Federation of American Societies of Experimental Biology; Lambda Kappa Sigma. *Publications:* Numerous articles in professional journals *Honours:* MRC Visiting Professor, University of Toronto, 1971-72, University of Saskatchewan, 1975-76, Dalhousie University, 1975-76, Award of Merit, Lambda Kappa Sigma, 1980. *Hobbies:* Music; Gardening; Cross-Country Skiing; Bicycling. *Address:* Faculty of Pharmaceutical Sciences, University of British Columbia, 2146 East Mall, Vancouver, BC V6T 1W5, Canada.

BELMONTE-CUYUGAN, Carmelita, b. 26 Aug. 1921, Manila, Philippines. Professor of Paediatrics; Paediatric Consultant. m. Dr Angel Cuyugan, 22 Sep. 1965, Hancock, New York, USA, 3 sons, 3 daughters. *Education:* AA, 1940, BSc, 1942, BSc Magna cum laude, 1946, BA, magna cum laude, 1947, MD, Summa cum laude, 1948, University of Santo Tomas, Philippines; Residency, Childrens Hospital and General Hospital, Louisville, Kentucky, USA, 1950-52; Clinical Fellow, Boston, 1952. *Appointments Include:* Head, Division of Paediatrics, 1981-84, Chairman, 1981-84, Professor, Faculty of Medicine and Surgery, University of Santo Tomas; Paediatric Consultant and Medical Staff Member, University of Santo Tomas Hospital, Makati Medical Center, Metro Manila; Paediatric Visiting Consultant and Medical Staff Member, Lungsod Ng Kabataan Children's Hospital, Quezon City; Visiting Consultant, St Luke's Hospital, Quezon City; Paediatric Consultant, Santa Teresita Hospital. *Memberships Include:* Chairman, Council of Health Agencies of the Philippines; Adviser, Philippine Medical Womens Association; Fellow, Philippine Pediatric Society; Association of Philippine Medical Colleges; Philippine Medical Association; Maniala Medical Society; International College of Paediatrics; Medical Womens International Association. *Publications:* Author or co-author of some 81 papers contributed to professional jounals including: 'Philippine Journal of Paediatrics:Journal of the Philippine Medical Association'; 'Filipino Family Physician'; 'Journal of PMWA; 'Santo Thomas Journal of Medicine'' 'The Pulse'' 'Philippine Medical World'. Numerous invited conference participations. *Honours Include:* Outstanding Pediatrician Award of 1978 By The Philipine Paediatric Society; Plaques of Appreciation: Philippine Paediatric Society, 1982; Philippine Medical Association, 1982; Philippine Paediatric Society Research Foundation, 1984. Certificates of Appreciation from various national and international organisations. *Hobbies:* Reading; Dancing; Swimming. *Address:* PO Box 3060, Manila, Philippines.

BELTRAMI, Vanni A., b. 5 June 1932, Turin, Italy, Professor of Surgery. m. Cecilia Banardi-Prosperi, 12 Apr. 1958, Rome, 1 son, 1 daughter. *Education:* MD, University of Rome, 1956; Specialist, Surgery, University of Rome, 1961; Specialist, Thoracic Surgery, 19064. *Appointments:* Resident Assistant Surgeon, University of Rome, 1966-68; Resident Surgeon, Hospital of Nettuno, Rome, 1968-73; Professor, Surgery, University of Chicti, 1973-. *Memberships:* Italian General Surgical Society; Italian Thoracic Surgical Faculty; American College of Chest Physicians. *Publications:* "Emergency in Thoracic Surgery", 1967, 1984; "Tumours of the Chest Wal", 1973: "Cancer of the Lung", 1982; "Surgery of the Chest Wall", 1984. *Hobbies:* African History and Archaelogy. *Address:* Clinica Chirurgica, Generale Universita, c/o Osp.Riuniti, 66100 Chleti, Italy.

BENAGIANO, Giuseppe Pino, b. 15 Oct. 1937, Rome, Italy. Professor of Gynaecological Endocrinolgoy. m. Orietta Bianchini, 4 Oct. 1965, Rome, 1 son, 1 daughter. *Education:* MD Medicine & Surgery; PhD Obstetrics & Gynaecology; PhD Human Reproduction; Specialist in Obstetrics & Gynaecology. *Appointments:* Acting Assistant Professor, Institute of Obstetrics & Gynaecology, University of Rome, 1961-64; Ford Foundation Fellow in Reproductive Endocrinology, Karolinska Institute, Stockholm; 1964-67; Research Associate, Population Council, Rockefeller University, New York, 1967; Assistant Professor, Institute of Obstetrics & Gynaecology, University of Rome, 1967-73; Scientist & Medical Officer, Special Programme of Research in Human Reproduction, World Health Organisation, Geneva, 1973-81; Professor of Gynaecology, 1981-, University of Rome La Sapienza, Rome, Italy. *Memberships:* Vice-President, Italian Society of Clinical Sexology;

Board Member, Society for the Advancement of Contraception; Italian Society of Obstetrics & Gynaecology. *Publications:* Editor, "Progestogens in Therapy", 1983; "Endocrine Mechanisms in Fertility Regulation" (editor), 1984; "Long-acting Injectable Contraceptive Drugs", 1984. *Hobby:* Gardening. *Address:* Via Savoia 29, Rome, Italy.

BENDALL, Michael Geoffrey, b. 24 May 1946, Johannesburg, South Africa. Head of Department of Obstetrics and Gynaecology, Whitehorse General Hospital, Yukon. m. Pamela Carson, 15 July 1981, Whitehorse, 2 sons. *Education:* MB ChB (Pretoria), 1971; FRCSC, 1980; ACOE Board Certified, 1985. *Appointments:* Intern, Natalspoint, South Africa, 1972; Registrar, Edendale Hospital, South Africa, 1973; General Practitioner, Frobisher Bay, NWT, Canada, 1974-75; Resident, Obstetrics and Gynaecology, Ottawa, 1976-80; Consultant, Obstetrics and Gynaecology, Whitehorse, Yukon, 1980-85. *Memberships:* Yukon Medical Association; British Columbia Medical Association; Society of Obstetricians and Gynaecologists, Canada; American College of Obstetrics and Gynaecology. *Hobbies:* Sailing (Costal, Offshore); Cross Country Skiing; Hiking; Fishing. *Address:* 27 Juniper Drive, Whitehorse, Yukon, Canada Y1A 4W8.

BENDECK-NIHER, Alberto Costa, b. 7 Feb. 1936, Tegucigalpa D.C., Honduras, Central Africa. Professor of Paediatrics. m. Isabel Widad, 8 Jan. 1961, Tegucigalpa, 3 sons, 2 daughters. *Education:* BS, San Miguel College, 1952; MD, School of Medicine, University of Chile, 1960; Internship, St. Mary's Hospital, West Palm Beach, USA, 1961-62; Paediatric Residency, Miami Children's Hospital, Florida, USA, 1962-64. *Appointments:* Paediatrician, San Felipe Hospital, 1964-67; Chief, Emergency Ward (Paediatrics), 1967-69; Chief, Infants Ward, Hospital Materno-Infantel, 1969-79; Chief, Paediatric Department, Hospital Materno-Infantel, 1972-77; Chief, Paediatric Department, Social Security Hospital, 1977-84; Professor of Paediatrics, School of Medicine, University of Honduras. *Memberships:* Honduran Medical Association; Honduran Paediatric Association; American Academy of Paediatrics; International College of Paediatrics; Honorary Dominican Representative, Paediatric Association; Columbia Paediatric Association. *Publications:* Several articles in Professional journals in field of paediatrics. *Honours:* Honours, Paediatrics Association, 1970, 74, 82, 84; Honour Al Merito, School of Medicine, University of Honduras, 1981. *Address:* Clinicas Medicas, Boulevard Moirazan, Colonia San Carlos, Tegucigalpa D.C, Honduras, Central Africa.

BENDIKS, Jean-Scott, b. 20 Feb. 1958, Anaco, Venezuela. Doctor of Chiropractic. *Education:* Texas Christian University; Texas Chiropractic College. *Memberships:* Texas Chiropractic Association; Dallas ChiropracticAssociation; American Chiropractic Association; Colorado Chiropractic Association. *Hobbies:* Fencing; Fly-fishing; Sailing; Skiing. *Address:* 3730 Spring Valley Road, Dallas, TX 75244, USA.

BENESON, David Elliot b. 5 Nov. 1957, Michigan, USA. Podiatric Physician & Surgeon. m. Marci Beneson , 24 Dec. 1978, 1 son. *Education:* Wayne State University, Detroit, Michigan; DPM, Ohio College of Podiatric Medicine, Cleveland, Ohio. *Memberships:* Academy of Ambulatory Foot Surgery; American Running & Fitness Association; American College of Foot Surgeons; American College of Podiatric Dermatology. *Publications:* Various articles in professional journals. *Honours:* Award of Merit, The Dean's List, 1979-80; International Youth in Achievement, 1980-83; Dr A Weissfeld Memorial Award for Excellence in Podopaediatraics, 1982; Member of Delegation, Lecturer, Academy of Ambultory Foot Surgery to People's Republic of China, 1983. *Hobbies:*

Photography; Needlepoint. *Address:* 3349 Woodward Avenue, Berkley, M1 48072, USA.

BENFIELD, John Richard, b. 24 June 1931, Vienna, Austria. Professor of Surgery. m. Joyce Arlene Cohler, 22 Dec. 1963, Chicago. Illinois, 2 sons, 1 daughter. *Education:* AB, Columbia University, 1952; MD, Universtiy of Chicago, 1955; Intern, Columbia-Presbyterian Hospital, New York, 1956; Residency, University of Chicago clinics, 1956-57, 1959-63, Chief Resident, 1963-64; Military Service, US Army, Korea, 1957-59. *Appointments:* Instructor in Surgery, University of Chicago, 1961-63; Assistant Professor, Universtiy of Wisconsin, 1963-67; Assistant Professor, University of California at Los Angeles, 1967-69; Associate Professor, 1969-71, Professor of Surgery, 1971-76; James Utley Professor & Chariman of Surgery, Boston University, 1977; Chairman, Division of Surgery, City of Hope Medical Centre, Clinical Professor of Surgery, University of California at Los Angeles School of Medicine, 1978-. *Memberships:* Director, American Board of Thoracic Surgery; Governor, American College of Surgeons; Fellow, American Surgical Association; American Association of Thoracic Surgery; Society for Thoracic Surgery; Society of University Surgeons; Pacific Coats Surgeical Society; Central Surgical Society; Société Internationale de Chirurgie. *Publications:* Over 160 articles & books in field. *Honours:* Distinguished Service Alumnus Award, University of Chicago, 1985; Scientific Gallery of Achievement, City of Hope, 1985. *Hobbies;* Aquatics; Art. *Address:* City of Hope National Medical Centre, Duarte, CA 91010, USA.

BENGMARK, Stig Bertil Samuel, b. 10 Apr. 1929, Östervåla, Sweden . Surgeon. *Education:* Medical School 1949-56, MD Licensed doctor 1956, PhD 1958, University of Lund. *Appointments:* Resident in Surgery,1959-62, Associate Head of Department and Leader of Liver Surgery Unit 1962-70, Sahlgren Hospital, Gothenburg;Instructor and Assistant Professor of Surgery 1959-62, Associate Professor and Vice-Chairman of Department of Surgery II 1962-70,University of Gothenburg; Intern 1958-59, Professor and Chairman and Surgeon-in-Chief 1970-, Department of Surgery, University of Lund. *Memberships:* Vice-Chairman 1965-66, Swedish Young Doctors' Association; Official representative 1966-67, Gothenburg Medical Association; President 1971-72, European Society for Experimental Surgery; Founder member, Executive Committee 1970-75, Collegium Internationale Chirurgiae Digestivae; Executive Committee 1972-76, Societe Internationale de Chirurgie; Scandinavian Association of Surgery; Swedish Medical Association; Swedish Association of Surgery; Swedish Association of Gastroenterology; International Biliary Association; Editorial Consultant, Surgical Gastroenterology', 1981; Editorial Board Member: ;Digestion;, 1967 -; 'European Surgical Research';, 1968-; 'Leber,Magen,Darm', 1971-; 'Acta Chirurgica Scandinavica'; 1972-; 'British Journal of Surgery'; 1976 -; 'Annales Chirurgie; et Gynecologiae Fennae'; 1976 'Scandinavian Journal of Gastroenterology', 1976 -; 'Zeitschrift fur Chirurgie', 1977 -; 'Excerpta Medica Surgery'; 1977 -; 'World Journal of Surgery'; 1978-; 'Surgical Gastroenterology', 1981 -. *Address:* Barytongranden 17, S 223 68 Lund, Sweden.

BENHAMOU, Jean-Pierre, b. 13 July 1927, Algiers, Professor of Medicine. m. Francoise Teissier, 3 July 1952, Paris, France, 1 son, 2 daughters. *Education:* MD, Paris, 1957. *Appointments:* Resident, Hospitals of Paris, 1952-57; Research Fellow, Institut National d'Hygiene, 1957-61; Associate Professor of Medicine, University of Paris, France, 1961-72. *Memberships:* European Association for the Study of the Liver; Association Francaise pour I'for the Etude du Foi. *Publications:* 'Foie, voies Biliaires Pancreas', 1972, 3rd Edition, 1980. *Honour:* Legion d'Honneur, 1980. *Address:* 26 Rue Chardon-Lagache, 75016 Paris, France.

BEN-PORATH, Rivka, b. 1 Feb. 1943, Israel. Chairman, Occupational Therapy. m. Gavriel Ben-Porath, 20 Feb. 1964, Israel. *Education:* Institute for Crippled & Disabled, New York, USA, 1973; Diploma, Advanced Occupational Therapy. *Appointments:* Occupational Therapy Service, Physical Medicine & Rehabilitation, Hadassah University Hospital, Jerusalem, 1967-76; Evaluation Committee, Mentally Retarded Children in Jersulaem and Southern Region, Israel,1970-71; Initiated Home Care Programme, Chronic Patients, Tel Hai, Jerusalem, 1971-76; Research Project, 1972-75; Fellowship, Special Training I.C.D. New York, 1973; Brrok Army Burn Unit, San Antonio, Texas, 1973; Burn Unit, Hand Clinic, Hadassah University Hospital, 1973-76; Instructor, Splinting, School of Occupational Therapy, 1974-76; WHO Consultant, Rangoon, Burma, 1976; Chairman, Occupational Therapy, Shaare Zedek Hospital, Jerusalem, 1976-; Taught handtreatment and splinting to occupational therapy students. Tel Aviv Universtiy, 1977-79; Teacher, Special Education Students, David Yellis Teachers Institute, 1978-81; Teacher, Splinting and hand treatment, Physiotherapy School, Assaf Harofeh, Tel Aviv, 1979-81; LIFE Program, New York, USA, Rose Fitzgerald Kennedy Center for Research in Mental Retardation and Human Development, Albert Einstein College of Medicine, Yeshiva Universtiy, 1985. *Memberships:* American Society of Hand Therapists, Affiliate Member, 1980; Israeli Organization for Occupational Therapy. *Hobby:* Writer, Childrens Stories. *Address:* 4 Zur Hadassah, Doar Na HaEla, Jerusalem, Israel.

BENNETT, Maxwell Richard, b. 19 Feb. 1939, Melbourne, Australia. Professor of Physiology; Director, Neurobiology Research Center. m. Gillian Rosemary Bennett, 2 Mar. 1965, Perth, 1 son, 1 daughter. *Education:* Beng; MSc; PhD; DSc; Fellow, Australian Academy of Science. *Appointments:* Lecturer; Senior Lecturer; Reader; Personal Chair, Sydney. *Honour:* Australian Academy of Science, 1982. *Hobby:* Science. *Adderess:* University of Sydney, Sydney, NSW, Australia.

BENNETT, Ronald, b. 1 Aug. 1933, New York, USA. Consulting Physician. m. dissolved, 2 daughters. *Education:* PhD Biochemistry, Pontzen Academy, Naples, Italy, 1968; Honorary PhD Science, Brantridge Forest School, Haywards Heath, England, 1968; Medical Degree, Univerisdad del Caribe, Caracas, Venezuela, 1971. *Appointments:* US Navy, Korea, 1950; TV & film producer, 1952-60; Founder & Publisher, Aloha TV Guide, Hawaii, 1961-64; Founder & Franchiser , 'Ever Young Way' company (non-surgical face-lifts), 1964-68; Medical stus dies, 1968-72; Consulting Physician in Cosmetic Surgery, esp. Exodermology treatments, 1973-; Host, syndicated TV show 'Young Again' (with P Presley), 1976; Licenced State Investigator in Forensic Medicine, California, 1979 . *Membership:* New York Academy of sciences; American Association of Criminology; Pontzen Academy of Arts & Sciences; Knights of Malta; International Society of Gerontology; Military Order of St Bridgette of Sweden; Cancer Society of Austria; Professor, Metropolitan University of Mexico. *Publications:* 'Young Again', 1975; 'Aging - Just One More Challenge' (booklet), 1978; 'The Medical Outrage - Health Care Revolt' (booklet), 1979; 'The Conquest of Aging', 1985. *Honours:* Purple Heart (Korea), 1950; Grand Officer, Knights of Malta, 1968; Gold Medal, Pontzen Academy of Arts & Sciences (for research in Biochemistry), 1968; Named :Leader in Law'by American Association of Criminology for work in forensic medicine, 1973; 10 letters of Commendation for anti-aging research & preventive health care, 1979. *Hobby:* Medical Research in Gerontology. *Address:* 660 South Federal Highway, Pompano Beach, FL 33062, USA.

BENNETT, Winfield Robert Curtis, b. 22 July 1927, Reigate, England. Director, Radiology, Preston & Northcote Community Hospital. m. Elmira Murray, 17 Mar. 1951, Camberwell, 4 daughters. *Education:* MB, BS, Melbourne University, 1950; FRCR; FRACR. *Appointments:* Resident Medical Officer, Alfred Hospital, Melbourne, 1951, Repatriation Dept., Melbourne, 1952-54; Registrar, Radiology, 1954-56; Specialist Radiology, 1957, Repatriation Dept., Melbourne; Assistant Radiologist, Perth Radiological Clinic, 1957-59; Assistant Radiologist , Royal Melbourne Hospital, 1959-60; Director, Radiology, Preston & Northcote Comunity Hospital, 1960-; Senior Associate, Melbourne University, Department of Radiology. *Memberships:* Royal College of Radiologists; Fellow, Royal Australasian College of Radiologists; British Institute of Radiology; Australian Medical Association; Australian Society for Ultrasound in Medicine; Museums Association of Australia; President, Australian Medical Association Arts Group, Victoria; Custodian, Museum of the Royal Australasian College of Radiologists. *Publicatiions:* 'Gas in the Foetal Vertebral Canal : A Further Sign of Intra Uterine Death'. 'Journal of the college of Radiologists of Australasia', 1965; 'The Value of Radiology in Teaching Anatomy to Medical Students';'Australasian Radiology'; 1968; 'The Museum of ;the College of Radiologists of Australasia', 1965; 'The Value of Radiology in Teaching Anatomy to Medical Students', 'Australasian Radiology', 1968; 'The Museum of the College of Radiologists of Australasia - A Beginning', 'Australasian Radiology', 1970. *Hobbies:* Painting; Photography; Gardening; Collecting Old X-Ray Equipment; Medical History. *Address:* Preston & Northcote Community Hospital, 205 Bell St., Preston 3072, Victoria, Australia.

BENNISON, Robert John, b. 4 Feb. 1928, Rangoon, Burma. Principal in General Medical Practice, Hatfield Broad Oak, Essex 1959-. m. Kathleen Mary Underwood, MA, MBB-Chir. 19 July 1952, London, 2 sons, 3 daughters. *Education:* BA, 1948, MA, 1953, Corpus Christi College, Cambridge; MB.B.Chir., London Hospital Medical College, 1951. *Appointments:* House Officer, London Hospital and Poplar Hospital, 1951-52; RAF Medical Branch, 1952-54; Junior Registrar, Obstetrics, Middlesborough Maternity Hospital, 1956-57; Associate Adviser in General Practice, 1975-79; Medical Editor, Well-Being (Channel 4 TV), 1982-84; Temporary Adviser WHO, Europe, 1983, 84. *Memberships:* Royal College of General Practitioners (Member, 1961; Fellow, 1972; Council, 1975-84; Vice-Chairman, 1982-83; Chairman, Education Commitee, 1978-81); English National Board; Royal Society of Medicine; British Medical Association; Societas Internationalis Medicinae Generalis (SIMG). *Publications:* Author of several articles, etc. *Hobbies:* Music; Drama; Wine; Making Things; france. *Address:* Eden End, Hatfield Broad Oak, Near Bishop's Stortford, Hertfordshire CM22 7HD, England.

BENSON, Lawrence Paul, b. 25 Jan 1942, Duluth, Minnesota, USA. President/Chief Executive Officer, Gerimed of America. m. Donita Gay Buck, 23 Apr 1972, Crystal Lake, Illiois, 1 son 1 daughter. *Education:* BScEngineering,US Naval Academy, 1964; Master in Business Administration, 1972, Master in Health Administration, 1975, University of Chicago. *Appointments Include:* Instructor, Duke University Medical Center,Durham, North Carolina, 1973-74; Executive Assistant, Duke University Hospital, Durham, North Carolina, 1974-75; Chief Executive Officer, Toledo Mental Health Center, Toledo, Ohio, 1976-79; Preceptor in Health Administration, University of Minnesota, 1976-80; President, The Benson Group, Toledo, 1978-83; Regional Director, Strategic Planning and Organisation Services, Arthur Young and Co, Detroit, 1983-; President and Chief Executive Officer,

Gerimed of America Inc. *Memberships:* Fellow, Healthcare Financial Management Association; American College of Healthcare Executives American Hospital Association; Federation of American Hospitals; Board nominee, US Naval Academy Alumni Association; Commander US Naval Reserve. *Publications:* Several Published works between 1970-84. *Hobbies:* Sailing; Scuba; Flying; Skiining; Tennis. *Address:* 1400 One Denver Place, Denver, CO 80202, USA.

BENTLEY, George, b. 19 Jan. 1936, England. Professor of Orthopaedic Surgery. m. Ann Gillian Hutchings, 4 June 1960, Wickersley, 2 sons, 1 daughter. *Education:* MB ChB 1959, Master of Surgery 1972, University of Sheffield; Fellow, Royal College of Surgeons of England, 1964. *Appointments:* House Surgeon and House Physician, Sheffield Royal Infirmary; Registrar in Orthopaedics, Sheffield Royal Infirmary and Orthopaedic Hospital, Oswestry; Senior Registrar and Lecturer in Orthopaedics, Oxford University Hospitals; Senior Lecturer and Clinical Reader in Orthopaedics, University of Oxford; Porfessor of Orthopaedics and Accident Surgery, Universtiy of Liverpool; Currently Professor of Orthopaedic Surgery, University of London. *Memberships:* British Medical Association; British Orthopaedic Association; President 1984-86, British Orthopaedic Research Society; Royal College of Surgeons of England; British Association of Professors of Orthopaedic Surgery; British Scoliosis Society. *Publications:* "Operative Surgery - Orthopaedics", 3rd edition 1979; "Mercer's Orthopaedic Surgery", (with R B Duthie), 8th edition 1979; Publications on scoliosis, knee disorders and the surgery of arthritis in major medical journals. *Honours:* Visiting Professor, Universities of Pittsburgh 1974, Johns Hopkins, Baltimore 1977, Minneapolis 1978, Kuala Lumpur 1979, Winnipeg 1982, Hong Kong 1982, Toronto 1983, Singapore 1983, Lisbon 1984, Perth 1984, Dunedin 1984. *Hobbies:* Tennis; Music; Horology. *Address:* 120 Fishpool Street, St Albans, Hertfordshire AL3 4RX, England.

BEREGI, Edit, b. 3 Mar. 1926, Brasşo, Hungary. Professor; Medical Doctor. m. István Foldes, 21 Dec. 1947, Budapest, 1 son, 1 daughter. *Education:* CMSc., Hungarian Acadmey of Sciences, 1956; DMSc., Hungarian Academy of Sciences, 1969; MD, 1950. *Appointments:* Assistant, Pathology, Medical School, 1950-53; Academic Scholar, Hungarian Academy Science, 1953-56; ASsistant, Pathology, medical School, 1956-60; Director, Research Department, Gerontology, 1961-78; Professor, Director, Gerontogy Centre Medical School, 1978-; Head, Physician, pathology, Semmel. Hospital., 1960-76. *Memberships:* Honorary Secretary: International Association of Gerontology, 1975-81, European Clinical Section; Chairman, International Association of Gerontology, European Clinical Section, 1981-85; Consultant on Aging, United Nations Network on Aging, 1983-. *Publications:* Author 5 books including, "Malignant Tumors of the Thyroid Gland", 1967 "Renal Biopsy in Glomerular Diseases", 1978; 15 book chapters; 164 articles in professional journals. *Honours:* Board of Directors, International Centre, Society of Gerontology, Paris, 1976-; Verzar Award Committee, 1974-. *Hobby:* Writing. *Address:* Németovolgyi ut 69b, Budapest 1124, Hungary.

BEREGOFF-GILLOW, Pauline, b. 22 May 1902, Kiev, Russia. Director, Institute of Scientific Investigations and Preventive Medicine. m. Arthur Stanley Gillow. *Education:* PhG Pharmacology Biochemistry, Temple University, 1918; Bacteriology, Parasitology, University of Pennsylvania, USA, 1918; MSc 1920, MD 1925, University of Cartegena, Colombia. *Appointments:* Director, Clinical Laboratories 1925, Professor of Bacteriology & Parasitology 1926, Head of Department of Pathology, Professor of Pathology 1930-33, University of Cartegena, Colombia; Leprosy Director, Cano de Loro, 1923-26; Directorof

Pathology, Traverse City State & General Hospitals, Michigan, USA, 1929-30; Litaur Fellow in Cancer Research, New York University, New York City Cancer Institute, 1930-35; Director, Institute Scientific Laboratories, Internal Medicine & Pathology, Montreal, Canada, 1940-65; Director, Instituto de Investigaciones Cientificas y Medicina Preventiva A S Gillow, Bogota, Colombia, 1965-85; Conferences around the world on Health and Prevention of Diseases. *Memberships:* Canadian Medical Association; Honorary Member, Colegio Colombiano de Ciruganos; Federacion Medica; Soc. Medico Guirurgica de Cartegena; Alumni Association, Temple University; Associacion Colombiana de Medicos; Academi de Medicino de Cartegena; Life Member, Womens' Medical Association; and others. *Publications:* "A Doctor Dares to Tell", 1957; "El Amor Unico", 1970; "Mi vida en Colombia", 1972; "Quienes y Como Somos", 1980; "Classification of Diseases of the Breast", 1984; over 80 scientific papers. *Honour:* Honorary Professor, Habei University, Peoples Republic of China, 1980-82. *Hobbies:* Music; Piano; Chess; Research. *Address:* Instituto de Investigaciones Cientificas y Medicina Preventiva A S Gillow, Calle § 12-02, Bogota, Colombia, South America.

BERENCSI, George, senior, b. 3 June 1913, Budapest, Hungary. Retired Director & Professor . m. Clare Matthes, 30 Dec. 1940, Budapest, 1 son, 1 daughter. *Education:* MD; Various Specialities.*Appointments:* Assistant Professor, Institute for Bacteriology, University of Budapest, 1935-50; Head of the Central Laboratory of Tuberculosis Clinic, Debrecen, 1951-65; Director, Professor, Institute for Hygiene & Epidemiology, University of Medicine, Szeged, 1966-83; Consultant, ibid, 1984-. *Memberships:* Hungarian Association for Hygiene; Hungarian Association of Natural Sciences; European Association for Cancer Research; Honorary Member, Association for Hygiene, German Democratic Republic; Hungarian Representative, Medichem. *Publications:* Some 476 scientific publications in numerous special periodicals. 1937-85; Member, Editorial Board, 'Handbuch der Antiseptik'(in 6 volumes); Member, Foreign Advisory Board of IC American. *Honours:* Honorary Doctorate, Martin-Luther University, Halle-Wittenberg, German Democratic Republic; Gold Decoration,. Komensk University, Bratislava, Czechoslovakia; Many Hungarian Decorations. *Hobby:* Tourism. *Address :* Dom ter 10, H-6720 Szeged, Hungary.

BERENCSI, György, b. 4 Dec. 1941, Budapest, Hungary. Senior Lecurer in Microbiology. m. Éva Horvath, 19 Nov. 1964, 3 sons. 1 daughter. *Education:* MD, University Medical School of Debrecen, Hungary, 1965; Graduate, Specialist Faculty of Philosophy, Budapest, 1968; Spedialisation in Virology, 1975; Scientific degree, Hungarian Academy of Sciences, 1980. *Appointments:* Laboratory for Diagnostic Virology, Public Health Station of Debrecen, Hungary, 1965-67; Department of Virus Research, National Institute of Public Health, Budapest, 1967-73; Fellow-ship, Institute for Virus Research, Cancer Research Centre, Heidelberg, Federal Republic of Germany, 1973-74; Senior Lecturer, Institute of Microbiology, Semmelweis University Medical School, Budapest, 1974-. *Memberships:* Hungarian Microbiological Societies; Programme Committee of the International Congress for Virology, 1975-; European Group for Rapid Viral Diagnosis. *Publications:* (with G Nagy) 'Intracellular Neutralization of polivirus by type-specific antiserum' in 'Arch. Virol., 1973; 'The Length of repetitive sequences of monkey cell and salmon sperm DNA' in BBRC, 1974; (with A Lengyel & L Nasz) 'Taxonomic definition of viruses as autonomous extrachromosomal elements' in Problems of Virology (in Russian), 1981. *Hobbies:*

Singing; Philosophy. *Address:* Institute of Microbiology, Semmelweis University Medical School, P.O. Box 370, Budapest 1445, Hungary.

BEREND, Norbert, b. 5 Mar. 1947, Nuremberg, Federal Republic of Germany. Associate Professor, Respiratory Medicine, Unviersity of Sydney Australia;; Head, Thoracic Medicine, Royal North Shore Hospital. m. Bronwyn Lorraine Lees, 21 June 1972, Hobart, 2 daughters. *Education:* MD, BM.BS, University of Sydney; FRACP; FCCP. *Appointments:* Research Fellow, Respiratory Medicine, Concord Hospital, Sydney, 1976(-78; Research Fellow, Pulmonary Pathology, University of Manitoba, Canada, 1978-)79; Assistant Professor, Medicine, University of Colorado/National Jewish Hospital and Research Centre, Denver, USA, 1980-82; Senior Lecturer, 1982-83, Associate Professor, 1984, Medicine, Associate Professor, Respiratory Medicine, 1985- , University of Sydney; head, Thoracis Medicine, Royal North Shore Hospital, 1985- . *Memberships:* Royal (Australasian College of Physicians; Thoracis Society of Australia; American) Thoracic Society; International Academy of Chest Physicians; Australian Society of Medical Research. *Publications:* Author of 52 articles in professional journals. *Hobbies:* Swimming; Squash; Hiking; Music. *Address:* Dept. of Thoracic Medicine, Royal North Shore Hospital, St Leonards 2065, NSW, Australia.

BEREZIN, Martin Arthur, b. 14 Sept 1912, USA. Emeritus Professor of Psychiatry. m. Evelyn Polan, 14 Jan 1942, Boston, Massachusetts, 2 sons 1 daughter. *Education:* BS, Boston University, 1944; MD, Boston University School of Medicine,1937. *Appointments:* Chief, Psychiatric Service, Camp Polk, Louisiana; Staff Physician, Massachusetts General Hospital. *Memberships:* President, Massachusetts Psychiatric Society; Massachusetts Medical Society; American Psychiatric Association; Secretary, American Psychoanalytic Association. *Publications:* 'Geriatric Psychiatry' 1965; over 60 articles and book chapters. *Honours:* Phi Beta Kappa, 1934; Collegium Distinguished Alumni, Boston University, 1979. *Hobbies:* Music; Tennis. *Address:* 90 Forest Avenue, West Newton, MA 02165, USA

BERGER, Leslie Alexander, b. 29 Mar. 1942, Melbourne, Australia. Consultant Radiologist. divorced. *Education:* MB BS, Sydney University, 1965; FRACP, 1969; DMRD; RACP; RCS, England 1971; FRCR, 1973. *Appointments:* Junior Medical Officer, St Vincents Hospital, Sydney, Australia, 1965-66; Senior Medical Officer, The Prince Henry Hospital, Sydney, 1966-67; Senior Resident Medical Officer, Medical Registrar, The Royal Perth Hospital, Western Australia, 1967-69; Registrar in Radiology, St. Bartholomew's Hospital, London, England, 1969-72; Senior Registrar in Radiology, St. Bartholomew's Hospital and The hospital for Sick Children, Great Ormond Street, London, 1972-75; Consultant Radiologist, The Royal Free Hospital, 1975-. *Memberships:* British Institute of Radiology. *Publications:* Numerous Papers and Chapters on Diagnostic Ultrasound. *Hobbies:* Music; theatre; cycling; yoga. *Address:* Department of Diagnostic Radiology, The Royal Free Hospital, Pond Street, London, NW3 2QG, England.

BERGOLD, Orm, b. 30 Apr. 1925, Nuremberg. Medical Educator. m. Sylvia Patricia Sanchez. *Education:* MD, Chicago Medical College, 1974; D.Chem., Benjamin Franklin Institute, New York, 1976; Master of Acupuncture, Old Chinese Acupuncture Academy, Hong Kong, 1978. *Appointments:* President, Institue of Medical Biophysics and Biochemistry, Campione; Professor, Cybernetic Medicine, Akademic Gentiu, p.P, Rome; Professor Extraordinary, University Fancisco Marroquin, Guatemala City; President, Institute of Medical Biophysics and Biochemistry, San Jose.

Memberships: Academia Gentium p.P., Rome (Senator); Universidad Francisco Marroquin, Guatemala City (Senator h.c.), Colegio de Medicos y Cirujanos de Costa Rica. *Publications:* "Kybernetische Medizin", 1977; Cancer Prophylaxis: A Problem of Early Recognition and Treatment", 1980; "Cancer Treatment with Human Fibroblast Interferon", 1982; "Cancer Treatment of Natural Remedies"f, 1983; "Biocybernetic Harmonization of Cells", 1985. *Honours:* Honorary DSc, St Andrew's College, London, 1965; Grand Cross, Ordre Equestre de la Sainte Croix de Jerusalem, 1977; Community Leaders of the World Award, 1984. *Address:* P.O. Box 359, CR-1250 Escazu, Costa Rica.

BERGMANN,Fred H., b. 26 Jan. 1928, Germany. Programme Director, Genetics, National Institute of General Medical Science. m. Barbara Berman, 20 July 1965, New York, USA, 1 son, 1 daughter. *Education:* BS, MS, MIT, 1951; PhD, University of Wisconsin, 1957. *Appointments:* Research Chemist, Ethicon Inture Laboratories, 1951-53; USPHS Fellow, Microbiology, Medical School, Washington University, 1957-59; Fellow, Biology, Brandeis University, 1959-61; Research Biochemist, NIH, 1961-66; Scientist Administrator, 1966-72, Director, Genetics Programme, 1972- , NIGMS, NIH. *Memberships:* American Society Human Genetics; Sigma Xi; American Chemical Society. *Honours:* US Public Health Superior Service Award, 1974. *Hobbies:* Music; Instruments. *Address:* Genetics Programme, Room 910, Westwood Bldg., National Institute of General Medical Sciences, NIH, Bethesda, MD 20205, USA.

BERITIC, Tihomil, b. 24 June 1919, Hercegnovi, Yugoslavia. University Professor Emeritus. m. Dr Dunja Beritic-Stahuljak, 23 June 1962, Zagreb, 1 son, 2 daughters. *Education:* MD, PhD, Specialisation in Internal Medicine, University of Zagreb; Postgraduate study, Prague, Czechoslovakia, 1947; Toronto, Canada, 1949-50; Study tours, London, England, Stockholm Sweden, Paris, France, Copenhagen, Denmark and Hammn, Germany. *Appointments:* Physician-in-Charge, Outpatient Department of Occupational Health, Social Insurance Services of Croatia, Zagreb, 1945-49; Staff member, 1949-, Head, Department of Occupational Diseases, Assistant Professor, 1956-61, Full Professor, 1961-, Institute for Medical Research and Occupational Health, Zagreb; Lecturer on Occupational Health and Toxicology, Andrija Stampar School of Public Health, Medical Faculty, University of Zagreb, 1956- . *Memberships:* Medical Association of Croatia; Yugoslav Association of Toxicology, 1st President: European Association of Poison Control Centres; MEDICHEM, Occupational Health in the Chemical Industry. *Publications:* "Occupational Diseases in Croatia", 1981; Co-author of 7 books on occupational health; numerous contributions to professional journals. Editor in Chief: 'Medical Journal of Croatia', 1958-74; 'Archives of Occupational Health and Toxicology', 1972-79. *Honours:* Medal for Work merit, 1965; Honorary President, European Association of Poison control Centres, 1969-. *Hobbies:* Fishing; Sailing. *Address:* Mlinarska 51, 41000 Zagreb, Yugoslavia.

BERK, Karen Melanie, b. 11 Dec. 1950, Chicago, Illinois, USA. Chiropractic Physician, Private Practice; Professional Staff Member. *Education:* BA, Northeastern Illinois University, 1974; BS, 1977, DC, 1979, National College of Chiropractic. *Appointments:* Lecturer, Workshop Leader: Association for Humanistic Psychology, 1976-80; OASIS Center for Human Potential, 1976- . Faculty member, College of Du Page, 1976-79; Conference originator, National Conference on Healing, OASIS Center for Human Potential, 1980, 81; Chiropractic Physician in private practice. *Memberships:* Professional Staff Member, OASIS Centre for Human Potential. International College of Applied Kinesiology: American Holistic Medical Foundation:

American Chiropractic Association: Illinois Chiropractic Society: International Academy for Preventive Medicine. *Hobbies:* Canoeing: Hiking: Modern Dance. *Address:* 6450 North California, Chicago, IL 60645, USA.

BERK, Steven, b. 12 Mar. 1949, USA. University Professor and Associate Departmental Chairman. m. Shirley Anne Holksclaw, 10 Oct. 1981, Johnson City, Tennessee, 1 son. *Education:* BA Degree, Brandeis University, 1971; MD, Boston University School of Medicine, 1975. *Appointments:* Medical Intern, Boston City Hospital, USA, 1975-76; Medical Resident, 1976-77, Senior Medical Resident, 1977-78, Research and Clinical Fellow, 1977-79; Chief, Infectious Disease Division, VA Medical Centre, Johnson City, Tennessee; Associate Chairman, Department of Internal Medicine, Associate Professor and Chief, Infectious Disease, East Tennessee State University, 1983- present. *Memberships:* American College of Chest Physicians; Association of Programme Directors in Internal Medicine; Association of Veterans Administration Chiefs of Medicine; American Geriatric Society (Fellow); American Federation for Clinical Research; The Gerontological Society of America; Infectious Disease Society of America (Fellow). *Publications:* Contributions to:'Annals of Internal Medicine'; 'American Journal of Medicine'; 'Medical Clinics of North America'; Chapter 'Bacterial Meningitis' in 'Infections in the Elderly', 1983: Co-Author of article: 'Bacterial Pneumonia in the Elderly' published in 'Medicine', 1983. *Honours:* Distinguished Faculty Award, ETSU College of Medicine, 1982, 1983, 1984; Teacher of the Year, ETSU College of Medicine, 1984; Teacher of the Year, Int. Med. Resid. ETSU College of Medicine, 1984. *Hobby:* Tennis. *Address:* East Tennessee State University, College of Medicine, Johnson City, TN 37614, USA.

BERKSON, D.L., b. 24 Dec. 1948, Chicago, Illinois, USA. Director of Berkson Health Clinic; Chiropractor; Nutritionist; Lecturer; Author. *Education:* Doctor of Chiropractic, Western States Chiropractic College, 1979; Masters in Nutrition, Goddard College; Double BA, Psychology, Theatre, University of Michigan, 1969. *Appointments:* Professor of Nutrition, Western States Chiropractic College; Professor of Nutrition, Pacific College of Naturopathy. *Memberships:* American Chiropractic Association; Price-Pottenger Association; National Federation for Nutritional Information; California Chiropractic Association; National Federation for Nutritional Information; California Chiropractic Association; Orthomolecular Medical Society; American Bach Society. *Publications:* "Foot Book", 1977; "Body, Mind and Spirit", 1981. *Honours:* Botherman, Most Distinguished Award in Chiropractic, 1983; American Poetry Award, 1979. *Hobbies:* Tennis; Writing. *Address:* 4600 El Camino 213, Los Altos, CA 94022, USA.

BERLIN, Herman, b. 20 Nov. 1921, Chicago, Illinois, USA. Physician, Gynaecologist. m. Arnoldine, 30 Dec. 1951, Brussels, Belgium, 1 son, 1 daughter. *Education:* BA Zoology, University of California at Los Angeles, USA, 1948; MD, University of Lausanne Medical School, Switzerland, 1954. *Appointments:* Staff Physician, Obstetrics-Gynaecology, Kaiser Foundation Hospital/Permanente Medical Group, California, USA, 1960- . *Memberships:* Fellow, American College of Obstetrics-Gynecology; San Francisco Academy of Hypnosis; American Medical Association; California Medical Association; American Society for Psychosomatic Obstetrics and Gynaecology; The New York Academy of Sciences; American Society for Psychoprophylaxis in obstetrics; Sex Information and Education Council of the USA. *Publication:* 'Effects of Human Sexuality on Well-Being from Birth to Aging', 1976. *Hobbies:* Photography; Sculpture. *Address:* 280 West

MacArthur Boulevard, Oakland, CA 94611, USA.

BERMAN, Michael Leonard, b. 11 Mar. 1942, Washington, District of Columbia, USA. Associate Professor & Director of Gynaecologic Oncology, University of California Irvine Medical Centre (UCIMC). m. Marlene J. Rosenberg, 21 June 1964, Washington, District of Columbia, 4 daughters. *Education:* BS, University of Maryland, 1963; MD, George Washington University, 1967; Intern, resident, Colorado & Washington DC; Fellow, Gynaecologic Oncology, University of California Los Angeles (UCLA), 1974-76. *Appointemnts Include:* Associate, National Institutes of Health, Bethesda, Maryland, 1969-71; Acting Assistant Professor 1974-75, Assistant Professor 1975-77, Obstetrics & Gynaecology, UCLA School of Medicine; Assistant Professor/Director, Division of Gynaecologic Oncology, University of Pittsburgh School of Medicine/Magee Women's Hospital, 1977-81. *Memberships:* Alpha Omega Alpha; Fellow, American College of Obstetrics & Gynaecology; Western Association of Gynaecologic Oncology; Gynaecologic Oncology Group; Society of Gynaecologic Oncologists; American Radium Society. *Publications Include:* Co-author, 10 books, eg "Cancer Treatment", ed.C.C. Haskell, 1984; "Gynaecologic Controversies in Cancer Treatment", ed.S.C. Ballon, 1981; "Lymphatic System Metastasis", ed.Weiss, gilbert & Ballon, 1980; etc. Co-author, 4 abstracts, numerous contributions to professional journals. *Honours:* 1st year Fellow 1974-75, 2nd year Fellow 1975-76, 1st year Faculty Clinical Fellow 1976-77, American Cancer Society; Physician's award, Harbor General Hospital Department OB/GYN, 1977; 2nd year Faculty Clinical Fellow, American Cancer Society, 1977-78; Certification, Continuing Medical Education, California Medical Associates, 1975-78. *Address:* Department of OB/GYN, UCI Medical Centre, 101 City Drive, Orange, CA 92668, USA.

BERNAL-VILLEGAS, Jaime Eduardo, b. 11 Apr. 1950, Bogota, Colombia. Assistant Professor of Pathology; Head, Medical Genetics Unit. m. Maria Mercedes Rueda, 16 Dec. 1979, Newcastle, England, 1 son, 1 daughter. *Education:* MD, Universidad Javeriana, Bogota, 1974; PhD, University of Newcastle Upon Tyne, England, 1980. *Appointments:* Head, Medical Service, Colombian Civil Defence; Consultant, Genetics, Military Hospital, Bogota; Consultant, Centro Medico de los Andes, Bogota; Editor in Chief, Universitas Medica, Bogota; currently Assistant Professor of Pathology and Head, Medical Genetics Unit, Medical School, Universidad Javeriana, Bogota. *Memberships:* International Association of Human Biologists; Honorary member, various Latin-American and Colombian scientific societies; Past President, Colombian Society of Immunology; Jansenn Research Council. *Publications:* "Genetica Inmunologica", 1981; "Genetica Clinica Simplificada", 1982; "Human Immunogenetics",1986; author of over 20 papers contributed to international journals on human genetics. *Honours:* Plaque, Civil Defence (for distinguished service to country), 1979; Honorary Mention, Colombian Academy of Medicine, 1981. *Hobbies:* Painting; Writing. *Address:* The Medical School, Universidad Javeriana, Carrera 7a No 40-62. Bogota,. Colombia, South America.

BERNATH, Gábor, b. 19 Sep. 1933, Kunszentmiklós, m. Róza Balogh, 22 Dec. 1962, Szeged, Hungary, 1 son, 1 daughter. *Education:* PhD, University Szeged, 1962; CSc, 1967, DSc, 1974, Academy of Science, Budapest, Hungary. Appointemnts: Assistant, 1957, Lecturer, 1963, Reader, 1974, Full Professor, 1977, Institute of Organic Chemistry, József Attila University, Szeged; Professor, Head of Institute of Pharmaceutical Chemistry, University Medical School, Szeged, 1979-. *Memberships:* Member, Commitee of Theoretical Organic Chemistry; Member, Alkaloid Chemistry committee of Hungarian Academy Science; Member, Committee,

Pharmaceutical Sciences and Pharmacopoeia of Hungarian Academy Sciences and Ministry of Health; President, Hungarian Chemical Society Group Csongrad; Member, Presidium, Hungarian Chemical Society; Member, Editorial Board 'Acta Pharmaceutica Hungarica Magyar Kemiai Folyoirat'. *Publications:* Author of over 150 scientific papers, 130 lectures and 18 drug patents. *Honours:* Postdoctoral Fellow, Institute of Organic Chemistry and Biochemistry, Czechoslovakian Academy of Science, Prague, 1963-64; National Research Council, Division of Biological Science, Ottawa, Ontario, Canada, 1968-69. *Hobbies:* Philately; Gardening. Address: Institute of Pharmaceutical Chemistry, University Medical School Szeged, Eotvos u 6, H-6720 Szeged, Hungary.

BERNER, Jan, b. 2 Mar. 1932, Pabianice, Poland. Head, Surgical Oncology; Dean, Medical School. m. 28 Apr. 1956, 1 son, 1 daughter. *Education:* MD, 1955, PhD, 1965; Specialisation, Surgery, 1966. *Appointments:* Assistnat, Municipal Hospital, 1955-62; Adiunkt, 1962-73, Assistant Professor, 1973-78, Head, Surgical Oncology, 1978-85, Professor, 1985-, School of Medicine. *Memberships:* Association of Polish Surgeons; Polish Oncological Society. *Publications:* Articles in professional journals; "Sympozjum Med.", 1968; "Acta Physiol. Polon", 1973; "Wiad Lek", 1977; "Nowotwory", 1980; etc. *Hobbies:* Sport; Motor Sport; Skiing; Music; Travel. *Address:* Warszawska 95C, 95-200 Pabianice, Poland.

BERNIER, George M, Jr, b. 29 June 1934, Portland, Maine, USA. Professor of Medicine. m. Mary Jane Marron, 6 June 1963, Windber, Pennsylvania, USA, 1 son, 1 daughter. *Education:* AB, Boston College; MD, Harvard Medical School; MA, Dartmouth College. *Appointemnts:* Intern, Resident in Medicine, University Hospitals of Cleveland, 1960-62, 1966; Research Associate, Department of Biochemistry, 1962-64; Resident in Medicine, University of Florida, 1964-65; Instructor to Professor of Medicine, School of Medicine, Case Western Reserve University, 1967-68; Research Haematologist, Walter Reed Army Institute of Research, 1967-70; Joseph M Huber Professor & Chairman of Medicine, Darmouth-Hitchcock Medical Centre, Hanover, New Hampshire, USA, 1978-. *Memberships:* American Society of Haematology; American Society of Clinical Oncology; American Federation for Clinical Research; American Society for Clinical Investigation; Association of American Physicians; American Clinical & Climatological Association; Association of Professors of Medicine. *Publications:* 75 Publications in areas of Haematology, Oncology, Immunology. *Honours:* Fellow, Leukemia Society of America, 1970-75; Fellow, American College of Physicians, 1973; Alpha Omega Alpha, 1975. *Hobbies:* Fly-Fishing; Swimming; Painting. *Address:* Department of Medicine, Dartmouth-Hitchcock Medical Centre, Hanover, NH 03756, USA.

BERNHEIM, Alain, b. 7 Dec. 1947, Paris, France. Master of Research. INSERM. *Education:* Medical Studies in Paris with MD Thesis in 1976; Scientific Studies: Master's Degree in Human Genetics; DEA Diploma of Advanced Studies in Embryology. *Appointments:* Hospital Assistant, Faculty Assistant, Hopital St Louis, Paris, 19767-80; Research, cytogenetic laboratory, Centre Hayem, Hopital St Louis, 1980-81; Charge de Recherche (in charge of research project), INSERM, 1981-84; Master of Research, INSERM, 1985. *Publications:* Over 70 publications in scientific journals; contributions to several books in the field of cytogenetics in malignancy & gene mapping. *Honour:* Prix Paris, 1981. *Hobby:* Reading. *Address:* Laboratoire de Cytogenetique, Centre Hayem, Hopital St Louis, 75475 Paris Cedex 10, France.

BERRY, Buford Eugene, b. 14 June 1940, Mississippi, USA. Clinical Associate Professor of Surgery, Louisiana State University Medical School. m. Johanna Louise Wamble, 7 Nov. 1964, Jackson, Mississippi, 1 son, 1 daughter. *Education:* BS, 1961, MD, 1964, Tulane University. *Appointments:* Intern, Southern Pacific Memorial Hospital, San Francisco, 1964-65; General Surgery Felow, Ochsner Clinic, New Orleans, 1968-72; Thoracic Surgery Fellow, Mayo Clinic, Rochester, Minnesota, 1972-74; Private Practice Thoracic and Cardiovascular Surgery, Baton Rouge, Louisiana; Clinical Associate Professor of Surgery, Louisiana State University Medical School; Hospitals Appointments; Baton Rouge General Medical Center, Our Lady of the Lake Regional Medical Center, Medical Center of Baton Rouge, Woman's Hospital, Baton Rouge. *Memberships:* American College of Surgeons; American College of Chest Physicians; American College of Cardiology; Alton Ochsner Surgical Society; American Association for Thoracic Surgery; American Heart Association; Southern Thoracic Surgical Association; International Society for Cardiovascular Surgery; Surgical Association of Louisiana; Society of Thoracic Surgeons; Alpha Omega Alpha. *Publications:* Contributor to professional journals; Presentations. *Hobbies:* Fishing; Skiing; Texas Longhorn Cattle Breeder. *Address:* 2717 E Lakeshore Drive, Baton Rouge, LA 70808, USA.

BERRY , Roger Julian, b. 6 Apr. 1935, New York, USA. Professor of Oncology. m. Joseline Valerie Joan Butler, 25 Sep. 1960, New York. *Education:* BSc Medicine 1957, MD 1958, Duke University, Durham, North Carolina; MA, DPhil 1967, Magdalen College, University of Oxford, England; Member 1971, Fellow 1978, Royal College of Physicians, London;Fellow 1979, Royal College of Radiologists; Honorary Fellow 1983; American College of Radiology. *Appointments:* Senior Investigator, Radiation Branch, National Cancer Institute, USA, 1960-62; Head of Radiobiology Laboratory, Radiotherapy Department, Churchill Hospital, Oxford, England, 1962-74; Medical Research Council External Scientific Staff, 1969-74; Honorary Consultant Medical Radiobiologist, United Oxford Hospitals, 1970-76; Clinical Lecturer in Radiotherapy, University of Oxford, 1969-76; Head of Neutrons and Therapy-Related Effects Laboratory, Medical Research Council Radiobiology Unit, Harwell, 1974-76; Professor of Oncology, Middlesex Hospital Medical School, London. *Memberships:* International Commission on Radiological Protection; British Institute of Radiology; National Radiological Protection Board; Radioactive Waste Management Advisory Committee; British Commission on Radiological Units and Measurements; Medical Research Council Committee on Effects on Ionising Radiations. *Publications:* 'Manual on Radiation Dosimetry', (with N W Holm)1970; Chapters in Florey's 'Textbook of Pathology' 1070, 'Oxford Textbook of Medicine' 1983; 'Cell and Tissue Kinetics', (editor), 1976-80; Over 150 papers in journals. *Honours:* Borden Award for Medical Research, 1958; Röntgen Prize, British Institute of Radiology, 1970; Knox lecture, Royal College of Radiologists, 1981; Florence Blair-Bell Lecture, Liverpool Medical Institution, 1982. *Hobbies:* Royal Naval Reserve (Currently Surgeon-Commander): Sailing; Music. *Address:* 13 Tamar House, 12 Tavistock Place, London WC1H 9RA, England.

BERTOLINI, Alfio, b. 3 Dec. 1937, Bibbiano, Italy. Institute Director. m. Laura Lasagni, 30 Aug. 1964. Reggio Emilia. *Education:* MD, 1962; Professor of Pharmacology, 1968. *Appointments:* Assistant Professor of Pharmacology 1962, Professor of Chemotherapy 1970, Professor of Pharmacology 1970, Director, Institute of Pharmacology 1980-, University of Modena. *Memberships:* Società Italiana di Farmacologia; Società Italiana di Chemioterapia; Società di Medicina Sperimentale. *Publications:* 'Induction of sexual excitement by the action of adrenocorticotrophic hormone in the brain', 1969; 'ATCH-induced hyperalgesia in rats', 1979; 'Chloramphenicol administration during brain development: impairment of avoidance learning in adulthood', 1981; 'ATCH-(1-24) antagonizes the contractile effect of morphine on the isolated rat colon', 1985. *Address:* Via V Veneto 8, Scandiano, Reggio Emilia, Italy.

BESTERMAN, Edwin Melville Mack, b. 4 May 1924, USA. Honorary Consultant Cardiologist, Department of Medicine, University of West Indies and St. Mary's Hospital, London, England. m. Perri Marjorie Burrowes, 9 July 1978, London, 4 sons (by 2 previous marriages). *Education:* BA, Physiology, Pathology, Biochemistry, 1943; MB,B.Chir (Cantab) 1947; MA (Cantab), 1948; MRCP (London), 1949, MD (Cantab), 1955; FRCP (London), 1967; FACC (USA), 1985. *Appointments:* Guy's Hospital, London, England, 1947; House Physician, Lambeth Hospital, London, 1947; House Physician, Postgraduate Medical School, London, 1948; House Physician and Registrar, Canadian Red Cross Memorial Hospital, Juvenile Rheumatism Research Unit, 1949-52; Lecturer, First Assistant, Institute of Cardiology, National Heart Hospital, London, 1953-55; Senior Medical Cardiac Registrar, Middlesex Hospital, London, 1956-62; Consultant Cardiologist, St Mary's Hospital and Paddington Green Children's Hospital, London, 1962-84; Honorary Consultant Cardiologist, Royal Postgraduate Medical School, Hammersmith Hospital, London, 1982-. *Memberships:* British Cardiac Society; British medical Association; American College of Cardiology; etc. *Publications:* 120 articles on phonocardiography, pulmonary hypertension, arterioschlerosis, lipid fractions, etc., 1947-85; 2 chaptersin Diseases of Heart and Circulation, by Paul Wood, 3rd Edition, 1968. *Hobbies:* Photography; History; Gardening; Tennis; Dogs. *Address:* P.O. Box 340, Stony Hill, Kingston, 9 Jamaica, West Indies.

BETTLES, Roger Haywood, b. 18 May 1938, Leicester, England. Regional Dental Officer, Trent RHA; Specialist, Community Dental Health, Leicestershire HA; Unit General Manager, Central Community Unit, Leicestershire. m. 16 Dec. 1961, Leicester, 2 sons, 2 daughters. *Education:* BDS, University of Birmingham, 1961; Licentiate, Dental Surgery, Royal College of Surgeons, 1962; Diploma, Dental Public Health, ibid, 1971; Diploma, Dental Health, University of Birmingham, 1971. *Appointments Include:* Dental Officer, senior dental officer, area dental officer, chief dental officer, Leicester City Health Department, 1962-74; Administrative Dental Officer, Leicestershire Health Authority, 1974-83; Regional Dental Officer, Trent RHA, 1983-; Specialist, Community Dental Health, 1984-. *Memberships:* British Dental Association; British Association for the Study of Community Dentistry; Midland Society for the Study of Childrens Dentistry (affil., British Paedodontic Society); British Institute of Management. *Publications:* "The Dental Health of 12-year Old Children in 2 Areas of Leicester", DDH dissertation, 1971; 'Hospital & Community Orthodontic Services in Leicestershire', British Dental Journal, 1975. *Honour:* Cale Matthews Prize, Orthodontics, University of Birmingham, 1961. *Hobbies:* Music; Fly fishing; Food & wine; Badminton; Campanology; Tennis; Amateur photography; Theatre. *Address:* Department of Community Dental Health, 140 Regent Road, Leicester, LE1 7PA, England.

BETTS, Thomas John, b. 16 Sept. 1931, London, England. Head, School of Pharmacy. m. 2 Apr. 1960, Mansfield, England, 1 son, 2 daughters. *Education:* B.Pharm, 1949-52, PhD, 1961, School of Pharmacy, University of London; Diploma in Management. *Appointments:* Assistant Lecturer, 1952-58, Lecturer, 1958-68, School of Pharmacy, University of London; Head, School of Pharmacy, Western Australian

Institute of Technology. *Memberships:* Fellow, Royal Society of Chemistry; Member, Pharmaceutical Societies of Great Britain, Western Australia. *Publications:* 'Pharmacy & Chromatography', 1978,'Official Surgical Dressings', 1981, in 'Australian Journal of Pharmaceutical Science'; 'Detection of Possible Toxic Constituents in Plant Material' in'Toxicon Supplement 3', 1983. *Honour:* President, Pharmaceutical Sciences Section, Australian & New Zealand Association for the Advancement of Science, Melbourne, 1977. *Hobbies:* Breeding Louisiana Iris; Collecting Conus seashells. *Address:* School of Pharmacy, W. Australian Institute of Technology, Kent Street, Bentley, Western Australia, 6102.

BETZ, Eberhard Ludwig, b.10 June 1926, Holzhausen, Germany. Director, Institute of Physiology, Tübingen. m. Margarete Gebhardt, 7 May 1955, Giessen, Federal Republic of Germany, 1 son, 2 daughters. *Education:* MD, 1953; Docent, Physiology, 1964; Assistant, Internal Medicine, 1953-59, Assistant, Institute of Physiology, 1959-61, University of Marburg/Hahn. *Appointments:* Medical Practitioner, 1961-62; Assistant, Institute of Physiology, Marburag, 1962-64, Docent, 1962-64, Docent, 1964-67; Professor of Applied Physiology, 1967-69, Chairman, Institute of Physiology, 1970-,University of Tübingen. *Memberships:* International Society of Angiology; German Society of Angiology; German Physiological Society; German Society for Circulatory Research. *Publications:* 'Biologie des Menschen' (11 editions, last edition 1981); 'Vascular Smooth Muscle', 1971; Editor, Publications for Tübinger Arbeitskreis für GefsaBerkrankungen; More than 300 publications on problems of peripheral circulation, cerebral blood flow, vessel walls, atherosclerosis. *Honour:* Honorary Member, International Society of Angiology. *Address:* Physiologisches Institut (I), GmelinstraBe 5, D-7400 Tubingen, Federal Republic of Germany.

BEVAN, Peter Gilroy, b. 13 Dec. 1922, Birmingham, England. Consultant Surgeon, Dudley Road Hospital, Birmingham (1958); Postgraduate Director, University of Birmingham, (1978); Professor of Surgery and Postgraduate Medical Education (1982). m. Patricia Joan Laurie, 14 Apr. 1949, Hamburg, 1 son, 1 daughter. *Education:* ChM (Birmingham), 1958; FRCS, 1952; FRCS (Ireland) Hon. 1984. *Appointments:* Lecturer in Anatomy, University of Birmingham, 1950; Casualty Officer, General Hospital, Birminghanm, 1951; Resident Surgical Officer, Birmingham General Hospital, 1952-54; lecturer in Surgery and Senior Surgical Registrar, Queen Elizabeth Hospital, Birmingham, 1954-58; UK Representative on Monospecialist Section of Surgery, WEMS, 1974-84; UK Representative on Advisory Committee for Medical Training, European Commission, 1980-85. *Memberships:* Member of Council, Royal College of Surgeons of England, 1971-83; Vice-President, 1980-81; Fellow, Association of Surgeons of Great Britain and Ireland, 1960-, President, 1984-85; Vice-President, British Association of Surgical Oncology, 1975-78; President, Pancreatic Society of Great Britain, 1977. *Publications:* "Reconstructive Procedures in Surgery", 1981; 'Efficiency in the Operating Theatre' Chapter in "Operating Theatre Desiogn", 1984; various papers on surgical topics and surgical training. *Honour:* CBE, 1983., *Hobbies:* Inland Waterways; Golf; Photography. *Address:* 10 Russell Road, Moseley, Birmingham B13 8RD, England.

BEVER, Christopher T., b. 12 Mar. 1919, Munich, Germany. Private Practice, Psychiatry, Psychoanalysis; Director, Washington Psychoanalytic Clinic. m. Josephine J. Morton, 12 Mar. 1944, Cambridge, Massachusetts, 2 sons, 2 daughters. *Education:* MD, Harvard Medical School, USA, 1943; Diploma, Washington School of Psychiatry, 1952; Washington Psychoanalytic Institute, 1953. *Appointments:* Intern, Hartford

Hospital, 1944; US Army Captain, 1944-46; Research Staff Psychiatrist, St Elisabet HS Hospital, Washington DC, 1947-50; Psychiatrist, Washington Institue Mental Hygiene, 1950-51; Director, Montgomery County Mental Hygiene Clinic, 1951-54; Clinical Instructor, Georgetown University Medical School, 1949-51; Associate Professor, University North Carolina, 1954-56; School Social Work, 1955-56; George Washington University School of Medicine, 1957- ; Clinical Professor, Psychiatry, Washington School of Psychiatry, 1956- ; Washington Psychoanalytic Institute 1954- ; Teaching Analyst, 1961- ; Director, Washington Psychoanalytic Clinic, 1982- . *Memberships:* American Psychiatric Association, Life Fellow; American Psychoanalytic Association, life member; American Academy of Psychoanalysis, Fellow; American Orthopsychiatric Association, Life Fellow; American Medical Association; Medical and Chirugical Faculty, Maryland. *Hobbies:* Travel; Photography; Sailing. *Address:* 6812 Connecticut Avenue, Chevy Chase, MD 20815, USA.

BEWLEY, David Kevin, b. 21 May 1923, London, England. Assistant Director, Research, MRC Cyclotron Unit. m. Christina Mary Erskine Muir, 13 May 1956, Southwold, 2 daughters. *Education:* BA, 1947, MA, 1953, Cambridge NaturalSciences; PhD, London, 1961; DSc, London 1982. *Appointments:* Ministry of Supply RRDE Assistant Experimental Officer, 1943-46; London County Council Hammersmith Hospital, 1947-, later Department of Health Assistant Physciist, 1957-;Medical Research Council, Cylotron Unit, 1957-, Assistant Director, 1975-; Royal Postgraduate Medical School, Honorary Lecturer, 1962-75, Honorary Sec. Lecturer, 1975-. *Memberships:* Hospital Physicists Association, Treasurer, 1961-64; British Institute of Radiology, Council Member, 1975-81;Institute of Physicist C0-author, 'Fast Neutrons in the Treatment of Cancer', 1979; Articles in professional journals including: 'British Medical Journal'; :British Journal Radiology'; 'Medical Uses of Cyuclotrons: Treatment and Diagnosis', 9th International Conference on Cyclotrons and their Applications, Caen, France, 1981. *Honours:* Roentzen Prize. BIR, 1968; Barclay Medal 1986, *Address:* 44 Addison Avenue, London W11, England.

BEWLEY, Thomas Henry, b. 8 July 1926, Dublin, Ireland. Consultant. Psychiatrist. m. Beulah Knox, 20 Apr. 1955, Dublin, 1 son, 4 daughters. *Education:* MA, MD, Trinity College, Dublin University; FRCPI; DPM; PRC. Psych. *Appointments:* Various hospital posts in Ireland, England and USA; Consultant Psychiatrist, Tooting Bec Hospital, 1961-; St. George's Hospital, St. Thomas' Hospital, 1968-; Clinical Tutor, Tooting Bec Hospital, 1968-73; Consultant Psychiatrist, West Lambeth Health District (Teaching) 1974-; Consultant, St. George's Hospital, London, (Honorary since 1974). *Memberships Include:* Royal College of Psychiatrists, President, 1984-; Conference of Presidents of Royal Colleges; Joint Co-founder and Council Member, Institute for the Study of Drug Dependence; Sub-Dean, Royal College of Psychiatrists, 1972-77, Dean, 1977-82. *Publications Include:* "Effects of Certain, Social and Cultural Factors on the Progress and Development of Alcholism", MD thesis, Trinity College, Dublin, 1958; Chapters in Books: 'Drug Dependence in the USA', Bulletin on Nacrotics, 21 No. 2, 1969; 'Treatment of Opiate Addiction in Great Britain' (Abridged), Psychopharmacology Bulletin, Vol. 9/3, July 1973. "Prescribing — World Medicine", 1975; "Handbook for Inceptors and Trainees in Psychiatry", Royal College of Psychiatrists, 1976; "Cannabis: Options for Control" (with F.Logan), 1979; Presentations. *Hobby:* Member, London Chapter Irish Georgian Society. *Address:* 11 Garrad's Road, London, SW16 1JU, England.

BHAGAVAN, Nadhipuram V, b. 5 Oct. 1931, India.

Professor and Chairman, Department of Biochemistry/Biophysics, University of Hawaii. m. Betty, 2 daughters. *Education:* BSc, Physics, Chemistry, Math., University of Mysore, India, 1951; MSc, Chemistry, University of Bombay, 1955; PhD, Pharmaceutical Chemistry, Universtiy of California, Berkeley/San Francisco, USA, 1960. *Appointments:* Research Associate, Biochemistry, University of California, San Francisco, 1960-64; Assistant Biochemist/Assistant Professor, Anatomy, University of Hawaii, 1965-67; Associate Professor, Hawaii Loa College, 1967-70; Associate Professor, Biochemistry/Medical Technology, University of Hawaii, 1970-72; Professor Biochemistry and Medical Technology, University of Hawaii; Consultant Biochemist, Kaiser Foundation Hospital, 1972-79; Professor and Chairman, Department of Biochemistry and Biophysics, Universityof Hawaii, 1982-. *Memberships:* American Chemical Society; Sigma Xi. *Publications:* 44 publications including: "Biochemistry: A Text for students in various heatlh related fields" 2nd Edition, 1978; Co-author: "A sixth lacate dehydrogenase isoenzyme (LD6) and its significance', 'Arch. Pathol. and Lab. Medicine', 1982. *Honours:* Lunsford Richardson Award, 1961; Outstanding Professor, University of Hawaii School of Medicine, 1970, 72, 81; Excellence in Teaching Award, University of Hawaii Monoa Campus, 1973; Faculty Merit and Chancellors's Distinction Award, 1982. *Address:* Department of Bio-chemistry and Biophysics, John A. Burns School of Medicine, University of Hawaii at Manoa, Honolulu, HI 96822, USA.

BHALA, Ram P, b. 6 May 1935, India, Associate Clinical Professor, Medical College of Wisconsin; W1 and Physiatrist, St Luke's Hospital, Milwaukee, USA, m. 20 Dec 1975, Madison, Wisconsin, USA, 1 son, 1 daughter. *Education:* MBBS, Punjab University, India, 1959;FRCP (Canada), 1972; FACP, 1975; Diplomate, American Board of PM & R, 1967. *Appointments:* Staff Physiatrist, Associate Director, Department of Rehabilitation Medicine, Glenrose Hospital, 1967-72, Assistant Clinical Professor, Department Community Medicine, Faculty of Medicine, 1967-72, University of Alberta, Edmonton, Alberta, Canada; Clinical Director, Department of Rehabilitation Medicine, University of Wisconsin, Madison,Wis, USA, 1972-76. *Memberships:* American Academy of Physical Medicine and Rehabilitation, 1967-. American Association of Electromyography and Electrodiagnosis, 1967-; Association of Academic Physiatrists, USA, 1972; International Society for Prosthetics and Orthotics, 1982-; International Rehabilitation Medicine Association, 1983-. *Publications:* 'Motor Concuction in the Deep Palmar Branch of the Ulnar Nedave', (with J Goodgold), 1968; 'Electrodiagnosis of Ulnar Nerve Lesons at the Elbow', 1976; 'Early Detection of Carpal Tunnel Syndrome by Sensory Nerve Conduction', (with E Thoppil), 1981; 'Photophobia - Phobia Fear of Falling and Its Clinical Management', (with J O'Donnell, E Thoppil), 1982; Gold Club Holding Device for Upper Limb Amputees;(with C F Schultz), 1982-83. *Honours:* Bronze Medal for Scientific Exhibit, American Congress of Rehabilitation Medicine, Atlanta,Ga, 1975. *Hobbies:* Tennis; Photography; Travel. *Address:* 2900 West Oklahoma Avenue, Milwaukee, WI 53215, USA.

BHAMBER, Avtar Singh, b. 11 Oct. 1957, Eldoret, Kenya. Doctor of Chiropractic; Ilford Chiropractic Clinic. m. Satwinder Kaur, 27 Oct. 1983, Redbridge, 1 son. *Education:* DC, Anglo-European College of Chiropractic; Diploma, Reentgenology; Advanced Certificate in Acupuncture, Zlongshan Medical College, China. *Appointments:* Assistant Clinic Director, Aldershot Chiropractic Clinic, 1983-85; Clinic Director, Ilford Chiropractic Clinic, 1985-. *Memberships:* British and American Chiropractic Associations; Life Member, International Acupuncture Society, Hong Kong. *Honours:* Best Thesis Award, European Chiropractors Union,

British Chiropractors Association. *Hobbies:* Hockey; Motor Rallying; Reading Science Books. *Address:* 38 Richmond Road, Ilford, Essex IG1 1JY, England.

BHARDAWAJ, Ved Prakash, b. 25 Feb. 1935, Agra, India. Deputy Director, Head, Laboratory Research, Central Jalma Institute for Leprosy. m. Dr Madhu Bharadwaj, 23 Apr. 1985. *Education:* MSC., Chemistry, PhD, Biochemistry, Agra University; Postdoctoral training, as Visiting Professor, Cancer Institute, Tokyo, Japan, National Institute for Medical Research, London & Japan. *Appointments:* Research Fellow, medical Research Council, U.P, 1963-65; Assistant Research Officer, 1965-69, Research Officer, 1969-76, IMCR, S.N. Medical College, Agra; Senior Research Officer, 1976-81, Assistant Director, 1981-82, Deputy Director, 1982-, Central JALMA Institute for Leprosy, Agra. *Memberships:* Founder Member, Indian Academy of Cytologists; Japanese Leprosy Association; Indian Association of Leprologists, Honorary Secretary. *Publications:* Author, 45 scientific articles in Indian, Japanese, European and American Medical Journals. *Honours:* Cancer Research 1st prize, Indian Council of Medical Research, 1972; Shankuntala Amirchand Prize, 1972. *Hobbies:* Sports; Photography; Travel; Social Work. *Address:* Central Jalma Institute for Leprosy, Agra 282 001, India.

BHARADWAJ, Vinod Kumar, b. 15 May 1949, India, Otolaryngologist. m. Rusum Rani, 26 Apr. 1978, Guna, 1 son. *Education:* MBBS, 1973; MS Otolaryngology, 1977; MD, 1983. *Appointments:* Demonstrator in Otolaryngology, Gajara Raja Medical College, 1975-77; Senior Resident Chief Resident 1984-85; Dalhousie University, Halifax, Nova Scotia, Canada. *Memberships:* Canadian Society of Otolaryngologists; American Academy of Otolaryngology; Fellow, Royal College of Surgeons, Canada. *Publications:* 'Hair Patterns on Pinna in Central Indians', 1977; 'Necrosis of the Tympanic Bone', 1984. *Hobbies:* Urdu and English Poetry; Hindi Music; Squash; Tennis; Chess. *Address:* 3623-105 Street, Edmonton, Alberta T6J 2K4, Canada.

BHATT, Arvind Paramanand, b. 26 Feb. 1936, Washim Maharashtra, India. Professor and Head, Department of Oral Pathology. m. Dr Jyotsna Champaklal Trivedi, 18 Feb. 1968, Bhavnagar, 2 daughters. *Education:* BSc, Honours, BDS, University of Bombay; MDS, Oral Pathology, Bombay. *Appointments:* Lecturer, Oral Pathology and Microbiology, Government Dental College and Hospital, Bombay, 1966-71; Assistant Professor, 1971-82, Professor and Head, Department of Oral Pathology and Microbiology, 1982-, Nair Hospital Dental College, Bombay. *Memberships:* Indian Dental Association; International Association of Oral Pathologists . *Publications:* Contributor to: "Compendium of Oral Diseases", 1981; 'Oral Diseases in the Tropics', 1987. Author of numerous papers in professional journals. *Honours:* President's Plaque for Best Scientific paper, 30th Indian Dental Conference, 1975; Alarsin Award, International College of Dentists, New Delhi, 1978. *Hobbies:* Cricket; Yoga; Visiting historical places. *Address:* Department of Oral Pathology and Microbiology, Nair Hospital Dental College, Dr A L Nair Road, Bombay 8, India.

BHATTI, Rashid, b. 7 July 1939, Karachi, Pakistan, Director. m. Angela, 30 Oct. 1969, Chicago, USA, 1 daughter. *Education:* MSc., Universtiy of Karachi; MS, Eastern Illinois University; Diploma, Tumor Biology, Harvard Medical School, Boston. *Appointments:* Scientific Officer, Pakistan Council of Scientific & Industrial Research, 1963-66; Research Assistant, Rush Prebyterian St Luke Medical Centre, Chicago, 1971-73; Senior Scientific Officer, Hektoln Institute for Medical Research, Chicago, 1973-; Director, Urology Research Labs, Cook County Hospital, and University of Ilinois, College of

Medicine. *Memberships:* American Association for Cancer Research; European Association for Cancer Research; New York Academy of Science; Association of Pakistan Scientists and Engineers of North America. *Publications:* Articles in professional journals including: 'Journal Reticuloendothelial. Society'; 'Journal of Urology'; 'European Journal of Cancer'; 'Journal of American Medical Association'; 'Urology'; etc. *Honours:* Fulbright Scholarship, 1967; Fellow, Pakistan Academy of Medical Sciences; Recipient, 2 International Awards, Amateur Photography. *Hobby:* Photography. *Address:* 8927 Chestnut Drive, Tinley Park, IL 60477, USA.

BHELLA, Surjit K, b. 13 Dec. 1939, Punjab, India. Mental Health Centre Executive Director. m. Harbans S Bhella, 17 May 1964, Nabha, 2 sons. *Education:* BEd; BA; MS Education; PhD Education. *Appointments:* Graduate Assistant, Oregon State University, Corvallis, Oregon, USA, 1971-75; Psychology Instructor, Linn-Benton Community College, Corvallis, 1973; Assistant Professor of Psychology, College of Lake County, Grayslake, Illinois, 1976-77; Coordinator, Financial Aid and Student Employment, Iowa State University, Ames, Iowa, 1977-82; Mental Health Therapist 1983-84, Currently Executive Director, Southeastern Illinois Mental Health Center Inc, Olney. *Memberships:* National Association of Community Mental Health; Illionois Association of Community Mental Health Agencies; Psychiatric Outpatient Centers of America; National Alliance for Family Life Inc; Phi Kappa Phi *Publications:* :'Principals' Leadership Style:Does it Affect Teacher Morale?'; 'Student Part-time Jobs: The Relationship Between Type of Job and Academic Performance'; 'Student Expense Survey and its Ramifications for Budget Construction'; 1979. *Honour:* Honoured by Phi Kapa Phi Society, 1973. *Hobbies:* Reading; Painting; Flower Arranging; Boating; Camping; Swimming. *Address:* 1580 Seawind Drive, Charleston, SC 29407, USA.

BIASSEY, Earle Lambert, b. 20 Oct. 1920, New Brunswick, USA. Private Practice; Consultant. m. Marie Davis, 20 Sep. 1946, Jersey City, 2 sons, 2 daughters. *Education:* BS, Upsala College, 1943; MD, Howard University School of Medicine, 1947; MS, University of Michigan. *Appointments:* Chief, Mental Health Consultant, US Army, 1953-55; Chief, Member Hygien Clinic, U.A. Offices, Bridgeport, 1955-60; Chief, Psychiatric, Bridgeport Hospital, 1975-78. *Memberships:* American Psychiatric Association; Fellow, American Academy of Psychoanalytical; etc. *Publications:* Article in 'Journal of NMA', 1971. *Address:* 3200 Main St., Stratford, CT 06497, USA.

BIERING, Kerstin, b. 29 May 1939, Stockholm, Sweden. President, Norwegian Association of Occupational Therapists. m. Finn C. Biering, 25 Aug. 1962, Stockholm, 3 daughters. *Education:* Diploma 1962, Master's degree 1981, Occupational Therapy. *Appointments:* Occupational therapist: Nursing home, 1962-63; Community health care, 1974-79; Research team, 1979-81. *Membership:* Norsk Ergoterapeut Forbund. *Publication:* "Ergoterapi hos hjemme-boende eldre", 1981. *Hobbies:* Classical music; Crosscountry skiing. *Address:* Arnulf Ø Overlands vei 200, 0764 Oslo 7, Norway.

BIGGIN, Paul Andrew, b. 6 Mar. 1951, Toronto, Canada. Hospital Vice President. *Education:* BA, Hon., York University, Canada; MA, University of Ottawa, Canada. *Appointment:* Vice President, Doctors Hospital, Toronto, Canada-. *Membership:* American College of Hospital Administrators. *Publications:* Co-author 'The Least Purity Difference Near Spectrum Locus as a Function of Wavelength' in 'Journal of the Optical Society of America, 1974; Co-author 'Comparison of Rehospitalised and Non Rehospitalised Psychiatric Patients on Community

Adjustment! The Self Assessment Guide' in 'Psychiatry', 1976; 'What Can One Expect When he Dons the Hat of the Programme Evaluator?' in 'Ontario Psychologist', 1977; 'Utilisation of Mental Retardation Services', technical report to the Ontario Ministry of Community and Social Services, 1978; 'Costs and Benefits of Automated Word Processing Equipment' in 'Health Care in Canada', 1983; Several papers and conference presentations. *Honours;* Philip Roth Bursary, 1974; Dr Paul Christie Memorial Bursary, 1974; National Institute Mental Retardation Award for Research, 1976; Ontario Graduate Scholar, 1978; Robert Wood Johnson Award, 1980. *Hobbies:* Music performance, study and composition; Keyboards. *Address:* Doctors Hospital, 45 Brunswick Avenue, Toronto, Ontario M5S 2M1, Canada.

BIGIERI, Edward George, b. 17 Jan. 1925, San Francisco, California, USA. Professor of Medicine. m. Beverly Ann, 16 May 1953, San Francisco, 3 sons. *Education:* BS, Chemistry, summa cum laude, University of San Francisco, 1948; MD, University fo California, San Francisco; Honorary DSc, University of San San Francisco, 1985. *Appointments:* Intern, University of California, San Francisco, 1952; Resident: University of California and VA Hospital San Francisco, 1953-56; Clinical Associate, National Institutes of Health, 1956-58; Research Physician, Endocrine Unit, University of California, 1958-61; University of California, San Francisco: Assistant Professor, Medicine, 1962-65, Associate Professor, 1965-71; Professor, 1971-; Program Director, Clinical Study Center, San Francisco General Hospital, 1962-; Chief, Endocrinology Service, San Francisco General Hospital, 1962-; Visiting Scientist, Monash University, Australia, 1968. *Memberships:* Endocrinology Society, USA; Council of High Blood Pressure Research; Association of American Physicians; American Society of Clinical Investigation; Fellow, American Society of Physicians; International Society of Hypertension. *Publications:* Over 200 articles on Endocrinology, Endocrine Hypertension and Regulation of Minerald Cortoid Hormones; Over 50 chapters in texts of endocrine; Editor of 6 books on Endocrinology. *Honour:* NATO Visiting Professor of Medicine, 1983. *Hobby:* Cooking (own style of Italian Cooking). *Address:* Clinical Study Center, San Francisco General Hospital, 1001 Potrero Avenue, San Francisco, CA 94110, USA.

BIRKINSHAW, John Howard, b. 8 Oct. 1894, Kippax, Yorkshire, England. Professor Emeritus. m. Elizabeth Goodwin Guthrie, 18 Apr. 1929, Ardrossan, 1 son, 1 daughter. *Education:* BSc (Hons) Chemistry; DSc, Leeds University. *Appointments:* Research Biochemist (ICI); Senior Lecturer, Reader, Professor, London School of Hygiene and Tropical Medicine. *Memberships:* FRSC; Society of Chemical Ind.; Biochemical Society; British Mycological Society. *Publications:* Author or Joint Author of about 70 papers in biochemical Journal, etc. *Hobby:* Photography. *Address:* 87 Barrow Point Avenue, Pinner, Middlesex HA5 3HE, England.

BILLING, Donal Michael, b. 19 Feb. 1931, New York City, USA. Medical Officer, Naval Medical Command, Washington, District of Columbia, m. Bonny Brown, 19 Jan. 1985, Bethesda, 2 daughters by prior marriage. *Education:* AB, University of Louisville, 1952; MD, University of Louisville School of Medicine, 1956. *Appointments:* Internship, 1956-57, Residency, 1957-58, Bellevue Hospital, New York City; Fellow, Columbia Presbyterian Medical Centre, New York City; 1958-59; Resident, 1960-66, Instructor, 1966-68, Surgery & Thoracic Surgery, Baylor Hospitals, Houston; Assistant Professor, Tufts University Medical School, 1968-72; Associate Professor, 1972-73, Professor, Chairman, Cardio Thoracic Surgery, Hahenan Medical College, Professor, Surgery, 1973-81; Professor, Surgery, Uniformed Services Medical College, Bethesda,

1983-85. *Memberships include:* Society of Thoracic Surgeons; Society for Vascular Surgery International Society for Cardiovascular Surgery; Council on Cardiovascular Surgery of American heart Association; Royal Society of Health; American College of Surgeons; etc. *Publications:* 'Management of neonates & Infants with Congenital Heart Disease', co-author, 1973; numerous articles in professional journals; book reviews; etc. *Honours:* Woodcock Society 1952; Baylor College of Medicine Teaching Award, 1968; Senior Editor, 'Chest', 1974-79; many other honours and awards. *Hobbies:* English; History; Tennis. *Address:* Naval Medical Command, Washington DC, 20372,USA.

BILLINGY, Zelda Eva Ruth, b. 8 June 1950, Trinidad. Chairwoman, Obstetrics & Gynaecology, Monterey Park Hospital California, USA. *Education:* BA, French, Loma Linda University, 1977; MD, Loma Linda University, 1981. *Appointments:* Director, Health Dept., Smyrna SDA Church, 1981; Associate, White Memorial Medical Centre, 1982; Chairwoman, Obstetrics & Gynaecology, Monterey Park Hospital, 1984- . *Memberships:* Board, Directors, Monterey Park Boys & Girls Club; Doctors Advisery Committee, State of California; Ambassador, Chamber of Commerce, Monterey Park; Founder, Director, Centre for Prenatal Fitness & Education etc. *Publications:* Various articles in professional journals. *Honours:* Best All-Round Athlete, St Augustin Girls High School, 1967, 1968. *Hobbies:* Opera; Singing; Tennis; Racquetball. *Address:* 850 S. Atlantic Blvd §304, Monterey Park, CA 91754, USA.

BILODEAU, Rolland, b. 19 June 1932, Montreal, Canada. Obstetrician. m. Monique Desnommee, 28 Dec. 1980, Valleyfield, 1 daughter. *Education:* BA, College, Jean de Brebeuf, Montreal, 1953; MD, University of Montreal, 1960; CSPQ - FRCS(C) Obstetrics, 1964; FACOG, 1974, FSOGC, 1985. *Appointments:* Active Member, Obstetrics Departments of Maisonneuve Hospital, Misericorde Hospital, Ste Justine Hospital, 1964-72; Active Member, Obstetrics Department, Notre Dame Hospital, 1972-85; Honorary Member, Obstetrics Departments, Maisonneuve Hospital, Ste Justine Hospital, 1972-85; Associate Professor of Clinics, 1972-77, Aggregate Professor of Clinics, 1972-77, Aggregate Professor of Clinics, 1977-85, University of Montreal. *Memberships:* Corporation de Medecins et Chirurgiens du Quebec; Association des Obstetriciens et Gynecologies du Quebec; Association des Medecins de langue francaise du Canada; American College of Obstetricians and Gynecologists; Society of Obstetricians and Gynecologists of Canada. *Publications:* 122 Publications including: 'Breech presenatation at term' in 'American Journal of Obstetricians and Gynecology, 1978; 'Predictions of preeclampsia' in 'American Journal of Obstetrics and Gynecology, 1985. *Hobbies:* Gentleman farmer; Angora goat breeder; Tennis. *Address:* 532 Cherrier, Montreal, Quebec, Canada H2L IH3.

BILOWIT, David S, b. 6 Feb. 1921, New York City, New York, USA. College Professor. m. Shoshana Walder, 3 Mar. 1945, New York, New York, 1 son, 2 daughters. *Education:* BS, MA, Columbia University; PhD, New York University; Fellow, American College of Sports Medicine, Royal Society of Health and American Association of Mental Deficiency. *Appointments:* Physical Therapist, Kabat-Kaiser Institute of Neuromuscular Rehabilitation, Washington, 1947-53; Supervisor, Neurological Section, C T Clinic, Veterans Administration Hospital, East Orange, New Jersey 1953-58; Private Practice, Physical Therapy, 1958-; Consultant, Rehabilitation Medicine, Veterans Administration Medical Center, East Orange, 1967-84; Professor, Kean College of New Jersey, Union, 1967-. *Memberships:* American College of Sports Medicine; American Association on Mental

Deficiency. *Publications:* "Physical Activities for the Handicapped; Theory Through Practice", 1980; contribution to 'Paraplegia', co-author, 1980; author of 20 other publications, 1956-. *Honours:* Annual American Corrective Therapy Award, 1958. Fellow: American College of Sports Medicine, 1969; Royal Society of Health, 1974; American Association on Mental Deficiency, 1976. *Hobbies:* Bicycling; Racquetball; Writing short stories. *Address:* Child Study Center, Kean College of New Jersey, Union, NJ 07083, USA.

BINDER, Fred C, b. 16 Oct. 1954, New York, USA, Director, Binder Chiropractic Office. *Education:* BA; DC; Diplomate, National Board of Chiropractic Examiners. *Appointments:* Assistant Tax Manager; Staff Doctor, Long Island Chiropractic Office; Director, Binder Chiropractic Office. *Memberships:* American Chiropractic Association; New York ChiropracticAssociation. *Honour:* International Chiropractic Honor Society, 1982. *Hobies:* Swimming; Health lectures; Composing music; Painting; Tennis; Paddleball. *Address:* 115-10 Queens Boulevard, Forest Hills, NY 11375, USA.

BIORCK, Gunnar Carl Wilhelm, b. 4 Apr. 1916, Gothenburg, Sweden. Physician. m. Margareta Lundberg, 26 May 1944, 2 sons, 3 daughters. *Education:* B.Med., Licentiate, Karolinska Institute, Stockholm, 1942; MD, 1949; MD Honours, University of Helsinki, 1981. *Appointments:* Assistant Professor, Cardiology, Karolinska Institute, 1949; Professor, Medicine, 1958-82; Emeritus, 1982-, Internal Medicine, University Lund, Sweden; Head, Medicine, Sera Hospital, Stockholm, 1958-80; Physician in Chief, 1961-68; Senior Physician, Karol Hospital, 1980-81; Physician to Royal Family, 1965-85, 1st Physician to King Gustaf VI Adolf of Sweden, 1968-73, to Crown Prince Carl Gustaf of Sweden, 1970-73, to King Carl XVI Gustaf, 1973-85, to Queen Silvia and Princess Lilian, 1976-85, to Prince Bertil, 1984-85; Member, Parliament, 1976- ; Scientific Adviser, Royal Medical Board, 1960-81; etc. *Memberships:* Military Medical Board, 1960- ; WHO Expert Advisory Panel, 1960-68; Chairman, Nobel Assembly, Karolinska Institute, 1981; Ethical Delegation, Swedish Society of Medical Sciences, 1969-84; Governments Medical Ethical Council, 1985- ; etc. *Publications:* Research, numerous publications on biochemistry, physiology, clinical manifestations, epidemiology and rehabilitation of heart disease; "Our People and its Future", 1940; "Myoglobin in Man", 1949; "If Your Heart Troubles You", 1953; "Medicine for Politicians", 1953; "Man's Possibilities", 1956; "Conditions of Medical Care", 1966; "Soul and Heart", 1967; "The Physician in Modern Society;", 1968; "At the Other Side of the Corridor", 1970; "Honestly Said", 1972; "To the Defence of Serafimer Hospital", 1974; "Concepts of Sschaemic Heart Disease", 1974; Lilly lectures,1975; speeches at closing of Serafimer Hospital, 1980. *Honours:* Recipient, numerous honours and awards including FRCP, 1967; Grand Cross, Royal Order Polar Star, 1973; King's Gold Medal, 1981; Knight Commander Royal Victoria Order, 1983; etc. *Address:* Vaestra Ekedal, 13200 Saltsjoe-Boo, Sweden.

BIRCH, Rolfe, b. 18 Feb 1944, London, England, Orthopaedic Department, St Mary's Hospital, London; Director, Peripheral Nerve Injury Unit, Royal National Orthopaedic Hospital, London; Honorary Civilian Consultant Orthopaedic Surgeon, Royal Navy. m. Frances, 1 July 1970, Oxford, 1 son, 1 daughter. *Education:* BA, Cambridge University, 1966; MB BChir, St George's Hospital. Medical School, London, 1969; FRCS. *Appointments:* Orthopaedic Senior Registrar St George's Hospital. *Memberships:* British Orthopaedic Association; British Hand Society. *Publications:* 'The Hand', (with Donal Brooke, Rob Smith), 4th Edition, 1984; Papers on, 'Brachial Plexy and Peripheral nerve surgery'. *Hobby:* Mountaineering. *Address:* Orthopaedic Department, Winston Churchill Wing, St Mary's Hospital, Praed Street, London W2, England.

BIRD, Charles K, b. 5 Oct. 1948, Riverside, California, USA. Naval Medical Equipment Manager, m. Catherine L Jones, 4 Sep. 1971, Los Angeles, California, 2 sons, 2 daughters. *Education:* BS Business Administration, Brigham Young University, Provo, utah, 1972; MBA, California State College, San Bernardino, California; Lieutenant Commander, United States Navy Medical Services Corp. *Appointments:* Convalescent Hospital Administration, Beverly Enterprises Incorporated 1976, Edward Shea Enterprises 1977; United States Navy Administrator, Chief of Branch Clinics for Naval Hospital, Camp Lejeune, North Carolina, 1980; United States Navy Program Manager, Capital Equipment, Naval Medical Command, Washington, District of Columbia, 1982; Equipment Manager, NAVMEDCOM NATCAPREG, Bethesda, Maryland, 1985. *Membership:* Affiliation, American College of Hospital Administration. *Publication:* 'Patient Perceptions of a Branch Clinic Ambulance Service', 1981. *Honour:* United States Navy Commendation Medal, 1985. *Hobby:* Cub Scout Leader. *Address:* 3109 Calloway Court, Woodbridge, VA 22192, USA.

BIRKBECK, John Addison, b. 24 Jan. 1933, Scotland. Director, New Zealand Nutrition Foundation; Professor, Human Nutrition, University of Otago; Clinical Reader, Medicine, University of Auckland. m. Adele Cholmondeley Smith, 23 Jan. 1959, Edmonton, Canada, 3 sons, 1 daughter. *Education:* MB, ChB, Edinburgh; Cert. American Board of Paediatrics; FRCPC. *Appointments:* Fellow, Paediatrics, State University of Iowa, 1960-62; Assistant Professor, Paediatrics, University of British Columbia, 1962-67; Associate Professor, Paediatrics and Human Nutrition, UBC, 1968-72; Visiting Scientist, MRC Reproduction and Growth Unit, Newcastle Upon Tyne,1972-73; Senior Lecturer, Paediatrics, University of Southampton, 1973-75; Foundation Professor, Chairman,Human Nutrition, University of Otago, Dunedin, New Zealand, 1975-84. *Memberships:* Nutrition Society of England; Human Biology Council; American Society Clinical Nutrition; Nutrition Society New Zealand; etc. *Publications: 'New Zealanders and their Diet', 1979, 2nd edition, 1983;* Various papers on Fetal and Child growth and Nutrition. *Honours:* Queen Elizabeth II Fellow, Paediatrics, 1960-61; US Public Health Service Fellow, 1961-62; Markle Scholar in Academic Medicine, 1964-69. *Hobbies:* Tramping; Music; Films. *Address:* Nutrition Foundation of New Zealand, PO Box 3358, Auckland, New Zealnd.

BIRN, Herluf, b. 14 July 1939, Aarhus, Denmark. Associate Professor. m. Bodil Birn, 27 July 1963, Skive, 1 son, 1 daughter. *Education:* DDS; Dr.Odont. *Appointemnts:* Dentist (Lieutenant) Royal Danish Navy; Associate Professor. *Memberships:* Scandinavian Association for Dental Research; IADR; Community Dentistry Group; Danish Association Social Medicine; Danish Dental Association. *Publications:* "Manual of Minor Oral Surgery", 1975, also in Spanish, Italian, Greek, Japanese, Portuguese; ''Community Dentistry'',1980; Articles in professional journals. *Honours:* Danish Fluo-Calcin Award, 1981; FDI Award, Dental Health, 1984. *Hobbies:* Badminton; Skiing; Painting; Reading; Philosophy; Psychology; Education. *Address:* Royal Dental College, Vennelyst Boulevard, DK 8000 Århus C, Denmark.

BISASE, Arnold Spero, b. 3 May 1936, Mengo, Kampala. Consultant Private Oral Surgeon; Specialist Dental Surgeon. m. Constance Mary Sebana, 30 Sep. 1967, Kampala, 4 sons, 2 daughters. *Education: BDS., London, 1962; LDS, RCS, 1966;FDS, RCS, 1967. Appointments:* Assistant Dental Surgeon, Philip Domb Ltd., 1963; Government Dental Surgeon , Mulago Hospital, Uganda, 1963-65; Senior House Officer, King College Hospital, London, 1965-66; Honorary registrar, Royal Dental School & Hospital, London, 1966-67; Consultant Oral Surgeon, Oral Surgery, Mulago Hospital, Kampala, 1967; Consultant Oral Surgeon, Oral Surgery Mulago Hospital Kampala, 1967; Lecturer, Makerere University; Private Specialist, Dental & Consultant Oral Surgeon, Private Practice, Mengo Hospital, Rubaga & Nsambya Hospitals, 1968-74; Specialist Dental Consultant, Oral Surgeon, Private Practice, 1975-. *Memberships:* Kenya Medical Association; Kenya Dental Association, Fellow, Association of Surgeons of East Africa; International Dental Federation; Council Member, International Association of Dentistry for the Handicapped; Fellow, International Association of Oral Surgeons. *Honours Include:* Minister of Health, Uganda Goverment, 1979; Chairman, Board of Directors, Uganda Pharmaceutical Ltd; Board Member, Advisory Board of Trade, Uganda Government, 1974-75; etc. *Hobbies include:* Art; Travel; Reading; Writing Letters; Poems; Sport. *Address:* Ambalal House, 1st Floor, Nkrumah Road, PO Box 86071, Mombasa, Kenya.

BISHOP, Harry Craden, b. 1 Apr. 1921, New York, USA. Professor of Paediatric Surgery. m. 3 sons, 1 daughter. *Education:* AB, Dartmouth College; MD, Harvard Medical School. *Appointments:* Instructor in Surgery, Harvard Medical School, 1945; At University of Pennsylvania School of Medicine: Instructor in Paediatric Surgery, 1955-57, Associate in Paediatraic Surgery, 1957-62, Clinical Assitant Professor, 1962-67, Associate Professor, 1967-72,(Clinical Paediatric Surgery); Associate Professor, 1972-79, Professor of Paediataric Surgery, 1979-, Senior Surgeon, Children's Hospital of Philadelphia. *Memberships:* American Medical Association; Diplomate, American Board of Surgery; American Association of paediatrics; American College of Surgeons; British Association of Paediatric Surgeons; German Society for Paediatric Surgery; Lilliputian Surgical Society; American Paediatric Surgical Association. *Publications:* Over 60 articles in medical journals. *Honours:* Phi Beta Kappa, 1943; Magna cum Laude, Dartmouth, 1943; Boylston Medical Society, Harvard, 1945. *Hobby:* Sailing. *Address:* Children's Hospital of Philadelphia, One Children's Centre 34th Street & Civic Centre Boulevard, Philadelphia, PA 19104, USA.

BISHOP, James Frank, b. 31 Oct. 1948, Australia. First Clinical AssistantCancer Institute. m. Dr Michelle Bishop, 3 Mar. 1973, Melbourne, 1 son, 2 daughters. *Education:* MB BS, Melbourne; Fellow, Royal Australian College of Physicians; Fellow, Royal College of Pathologists of Australasia. *Appointments:* Resident, 1973, Senior Resident 1974, Medical Registrar 1975, Royal Melbourne Hospital; Haematology Registrar, Alfred Hospital, Melbourne, 1976, Royal Melbourne Hosptial, 1977, Peter MaCullum Hospital & Cancer Institute, Melbourne, 1978; Clinical Associate, Baltimore Cancer Research Programe, National Cancer Research Incstitute, USA, 1979-81; Assistant Professor, University of Maryland, USA, 1980-81; Medical Oncologist, Peter MacCullum Hospital & Cancer Institute, Melbourne, 1981-85; Visiting Haematologist, Alfred Hospital, Melbourne, 1981-85; First Clinical Assistant, Department of Cancer Medicine, Cancer Institute & University of Melbourne, 1985-. *Memberships:* American Society of Clinical Oncology; Clinical Oncology Society of Australia; Haematology Society of Australia; Thoracic Society of Australia; Transplatation Society of Australia & New Zealand. *Publications:* Various articles & books in field (with others). *Honours;* J F Ryan Prize for Anatomy, 1969; Post-doctoral Fulbright Fellow, 1979-81; K F Sprague Research Award, Anti-Cancer Council of Victoria. *Hobbies:* Sailing; Gardening. *Address:* Cancer Institute, 481 Little Lonsdale Street, Melbourne 3000, Victoria, Australia.

BISQUERRA, Jose, b. 12 May 1927, Spain. Chief, Mental Health Clinic, VA Medical Centre, Shreveport, USA. m. Amalia C. Riaza, 5 July 1956, Cadiz, Spain, 1 son, 1 daughter. *Education:* MD, PhD, Seville Medical School. *Appointments:* Clinical Director, NHMR, 1965; Medical Director, Surgeon, Reynolds Metals Co., Guyana, South America, 1960; Medical Director, Bisquerra Clinic, 1978; Professor, LSUMC, Louisiana, 1981; Chief, MHC, VA Medical Centre, Shreveport, USA, 1981. *Hobbies:* Music; Sports. *Address:* 220 Norcross, Bossier City, LA 71111, USA.

BISS, David James, b. 28 Nov. 1944, Spangler, Pennsylvania, USA. Accident Research Scientist. m. Caroline Goering, 6 Sep. 1969, State College, Pennsylvania, USA, 1 daughter. *Education:* BS Mechanical Engineering 1969, MEng, Civil Engineering 1972, Pennsylvania State University; BS Communications, University of Maryland, 1981. *Appointments:* Transportation Research Center, Pennsylvania State University, 1968-72; Cornell Aeronautical Laboratory, Buffalo, New York, 1972-76; National Highway Safety Administration, US Department of Transportation, 1976-82; President, David James Ltd. (accident research), 1982- ; Resident Research Engineer, Biomechanics, Volvo Car Corporation Advanced Engineering Department, Goteborg, Sweden, 1983-84. *Memberships:* American Association for Automotive Medicine; American Association for the Advancement of Science; Society of Automotive Engineers; American Society of Mechanical Engineers. *Publications:* 'A SystemsApproach to Quantifying Airbag - Thoracic Interaction', 1981; 'A Systems Approach to Airbag Design & Development', 1980; 'Citation Crash Test with Airbags', 1980; 'A Field Accident Investigation of an Out-of-position Driver in an ACRS-equipped Oldsmobile', 1977; 'Use of the CRACR Airbag Model', 1985. *Honours:* Tau Beta Pi (Engineering), 1967; Administrator's Award for Merit, US Department of Transportation, 1978. *Hobbies:* Sailing; Skiing; Historical Geography; Languages. *Address:* David James Ltd., 10600 Kenilworth Avenue apt 1, Bethesda, MD0814, USA.

BITRAN, Jacob D, b. 23 Sept 1947, Thessaloniki, Greece. Physician Director of Clinical Cancer Research. m. 26 Dec 1971, Chicago, 2 daughters. *Education:* BS, 1968, MD, 1971, University of Illinois. *Appointments:* University of Chicago, Michael Reese Medical Center, 1977-84; Associate Professor of Medicine, University of Chicago, 1984 -. *Memberships:* Fellow, American College of Physicians; American Society of Hematology; American Association for Cancer Research; American Society of Clinical Oncology. *Publications:* More than 100 publications since 1973. *Address:* Michael Reese Medical Center, 31st and Lakeshore Drive, Chicago, IL 60616, USA.

BJELLE, Anders Otto, b. 3 May 1931, Stockholom, Sweden. Professor, Rheumatology, Gothenburg University; Head, Rheumatology, Sahlgren University Hospital. *Education:* MD; PhD. *Appointments:* Head, WHO collaborating Centre for Education and Community-based programmes in Rheumatology, Gothenburg University: Assistant Head, Rheumatology, Lund University Hospital, 1972-73: Head, Rheumatology, Umea University Hospital, 1973-82. *Memberships:* Swedish Medical Society: American Rheumatism Association: British Society for Rheumatology: Societe Francaise de Rhumatologie. *Publications:* Scientific Papers, Reviews, Chapters in Rheumatology Journals and Textbooks. *Address:* Dept. Rheumatology, Sahlgren University Hospital, S-413 45 Gothenburg, Sweden.

BJORNSSON, Sigurdur, b. 5 June 1942, Princeton, New Jersey, USA, Consultant in Internal Medicine and Medical Oncology. m. Gudny Kristjansdottir, 11

June 1966, Reykjavik, Iceland, 1 son, 2 daughters. *Education:* MD, University of Iceland School of Medicine, 1968; American Board of Internal Medicine, USA, 1973; Federal Licensure Examination, USA, 1974; Aemrican Board of Internal Medicine, Medical Oncology, 1975. *Appointments:* Clinician I, 1974-77, Clinician II, 1977-78, Roswel Park Memorial Institute, Buffalo, NY, USA; Clinical Instructor in Medicine, 1974-77, Research Assistant Professor of Medicine, 1977-78, State University of New York, Buffalo, USA; Attending Physician, Department of Medicine, St Joseph's Hospital, Reykjavik, Iceland, 1978-; Attending Physician, Department of Neoplastic Diseases National Hospitals, Reykjavik, 1978-; Lecturer in Medicine and Oncology, University of Iceland School of Medicine, Reykjavik, 1978-. *Memberships:* Icelandic Medical Society; Icelandic Cancer Society; The New York Academy of Sciences; Americann Association for Cancer Research; Americanm Society for Clinical Oncology; World Medical Association; The Icelandic Internal Medicine Society; The Icelandic Association of Medical Specialists; Icelandic Physicians for the Prevention of Nuclear War. *Publications:* Author of numerous articles including 'Major Surgery in Acute Leukemia', (with J W Yates, A Mittelman, J F Holland), 1974; 'Centrl Nervous System Leukemia and Studies on Cerebrospinal Fluids from Patients with Acute Myelocytic Leukemia', 1974; 'Blindness in a patient with Malignant Histiocytosis', (with H Sperry, M Barcos, Y Satchidanand, D Klein, E S Henderson, H D Preisler), 1977; 'Inducers of Friend Leukaemic Cell Differentiation in Vitro - Effects of in vivo Administration', (with H D Preisler, M Morid, G Lyman), 1976; 'A Study of Antibiotic Therapy in Fever of Unknown Origin in Neutropenic Cancer Patients', (with H D Preisler, E S Hernderson), 1977; 'Periodic Mass Screening for Breast Cancer', 1984. *Address:* St Joseph's Hospital, Landakoti, Reykjavik, Iceland.

BJORNTORP, Per Arvid, b. 25 May 1931, Jonkoping, Sweden. Professor of Medicine. m. Marianne B., 3 Apr. 1958, 1 son, 3 daughters. *Education:* MD, 1952, PhD, 1960, University of Goteborg, Sweden. *Appointments:* Assistant, 1957-70, Associate Professor, 1970-76, Professor of medicine 1977-, University Goteborg. *Memberships:* American Diabetes Association; European Society Clinical Investigation; New York Academy of Sciences; American College Sports Medicine. *Publications:* Scientific articles in professional journals. *Honours:* Editor-in-chief, 'International Journal Obesity'; President, 3rd International Congress on Obesity, Rome, 1980. *Hobbies:* Sailing; Chamber Music. *Address:* Dept. Medicine I, Sahlgren's Hospital, 41345 Goteborg, Sweden.

BLACK, Robin Charles, b. 12 Nov 1946, Toronto, Ontario, Canada. Adjunct Professor/Research Officer. m. Mary Anderson-Black. *Education:* BSc, McMaster University, Hamilton, 1968; BASc, Queens Universtiy, Kingston, 1971; P Eng, APEO, Ontario, 1973; PhD, University of Strathclyde, Glasgow, 1984. *Appointemnts:* Research Assistant Banting Institute, University of Toronto, 1970-73; Project Engineer, Ontario Crippled Children's Centre, 1973-80; Research Officer, National Research Council Canada 1980-. *Memberships:* Association of Professors of Engineering of Ontario; Canadian Medical and Biological Engineering Society; International Federation of Medical and Biological Engineers. *Publications:* with C McLaurin: 'Transportation for the Handicapped and the Elderly' in "Human Rights for the Physically Handicapped and Aged" 1974; 'Supension Seating' in "Bedsore Biomechanics" 1978; with L D Reed. 'The use of thermography in the prevention of pressure sores' in "Pressure Sores" 1982. *Address:* National Research Council of Canada, Division of Electrical Engineering, M-50 rm 178, Ottawa, Ontario, Canada K1A OR6.

BLACKLOCK, Hilary Anne, b. 16 Nov. 1948, New Zealand. Senior Lecturer, Haematology, Institute of Child Health; Honorary Consultant, Hospital for Sick Children, Great Ormond Street. m. Michael Venter, Auckland. *Education:* MB,ChB, School of Medicine, University of Otago, New Zealand, 1971; Fellow, Royal Australasian College of Physicians, 1979;

Fellow, Royal College of Pathologists of Australasia, 1980. *Appointments:* Registrar, 1975-76, Senior Registrar, 1977-78, Haematology, Auckland Hospital; Lecturer, Haematology, Auckland University School of Medicine, 1978-80; Research Fellow, Honorary Senior Registrar, Coordinator of Bone Marrow Transplant Unit, Royal Free Hospital School of Medicine, 1980-84. *Memberships:* British Transplantation Society; European Bone Marrow Transplant Group; Amnesty International. *Hobbies:* Films; Friends; Tennis; Reading; Fine Food and Wine; Collecting Antique Maps; Scrabble; Crossword Puzzles. *Address:* 18 St Marks Crescent, Primrose Hill, London NW1 7TU, England.

BLACKWELL, Barry, b. 5 July 1934, Birmingham, England. Professor, Chairman, Psychiatry, Milwaukee Clinical Campus, University of Wisconsin, USA. m. Mary Kathleen Eilers, 7 Jan. 1977, Dayton, 3 sons, 1 daughter. *Education:* MA, MB, B.Chir., Cambridge University; MD, Guys Hospital; Maudsley and Bethlem Royal Hospitals. *Appointments:* Professor, psychiatry, Associate Professor, Pharmacology, University of Cincinnati, 1972-75; Professor, Chairman, Psychiatry, Professor, Pharmacology, Professor, Applied Behavioural Sciences Programme, Wright State University School of Medicine, Dayton, 1975. *Memberships:* American Medical Association; American Psychosomatic Society; American Psychiatric Association, Fellow; Society for Behavioural Medicine; American College of Neuropsychopharmacology, Fellow. *Publications:* "Hypertensive Crisis due to MAOI", 'Lancet', 1963; "Drug Therapy: Patient Compliance", 'New England Journal Medicine', 1973; "Chronic Pain Management", co-author, 'Hospital and Community Psychiatry', 1984; "Discoveries in Biological Psychiatry",. co-editor, 1970 *Honours:* Whittington Hospital Research Prize, 1962; Mental Health Research Fund Fellowship, 1965; Taylor Manor Award for Discoveries in Biological Psychiatry, 1970; Golden Apple Award for Undergraduate Medical Student Teaching, 1975; Psychiatric Residents Teacher of the Year Award, 975. *Hobbies:* Racquet Ball, Creative Writing - Poetry and Short Fiction. *Address:* Mt. Sinai Medical Centre, 950 N 12th Street, PO Box 342, Milwaukee, WI 53201, USA.

BLAHD, William Henry, b. 21 May 1921, Cleveland, Ohio, USA. Chief of Nuclear Medicine Ultrasound Service. m. Miriam Weiss, 29 Jan. 1971, Los Angeles, 1 son, 2 daughters. *Education:* MD, Tulane Universtiy Medical School, Louisiana, 1945; Diplomate, American Board of Internal Medicine, 1953; Diplomate, American Board of Nuclear Medicine, 1972. *Appointments:* Ward Officer, Metabolic Research Ward, Veterans Administration Center, Lost Angeles, California, 1951-52; Assistant Chief, Radioisotope Service, VA Wadsworth Hospital Center, Los Angeles, 1952-56; Chief, Nuclear Medicine Ultrasound Service, Veterans Administration Medical Center, West Los Angeles 1956-; Clinical Instructor in Medicine 1953, Assistant Clinical Professor of Medicine 1959, Professor of Medicine 1966-, University of California, Los Angeles. *Memberships:* Chairman 1982, American Board of Nuclear Medicine; American Board of Internal Medicine; President 1977-78, Society of Nuclear Medicine; American Colege of Nuclear Physicians; American Medical Association; American Thyroid Association. *Publications:* "The Practice of Nuclear Medicine", (editor), 1958; "Nuclear Medicine", (editor), 1965-1971; 145 scientific articles. *Honours:* Fellow, American College of Physicians, 1959; Distinguished Scientist

Award, Southern-Northern California chapters, Society of Nuclear Medicine, 1975. *Hobbies:* Photography; Golf. *Address:* Nuclea' Medicine Ultrasound Service, Wadsworth Divisio'n 691/W115, VA Medical Center West Los Angeles, Los Angeles, CA 90073, USA.

BLAICH, Robert Merrill, b. 12 Mar. 1951, Buffalo, New York, USA. Chiropractic Physician; Lecturer; Consultant; Researcher, Chairman, International College of Applied Kinesiology. *Education:* BA, Biology, Ithaca College, 1973; BS, 1976, DC 1977, National College of Chiropractic, Lombard. *Appointments:* Chiropractic Physician, private practice, Pueblo, Colorado, 1978-84; International lecturer, 19789- ; Chiropractic Physician, private practice, Los Angeles, 1985-. *Memberships:* American Chiropractic Association; California Chiropractic Association; International Academy of Preventive Medicine; Federation for Chiropractic Education and Research; International College of Applied Kinesiology; Organization for Progressive Health Concepts. *Publication:* Numerous scientific papers in Collected Papers and Selected Papers of the International College of Applied Kinesiology, 1980-845; Haldeman Interprofessional Conference on the Spine, 1981. *Honours:* Diplomate, 1980, Chairman, 1985, International College of Applied Kinesiology *Hobbies:* Tennis; Skiing; Bicycling; Jazz Trumpet; Windsurfing; Travel; Writing. *Address:* 12301 Wilshire §416, Los Angeles, CA 90025, USA.

BLAIR, James Bryan, b. 26 May 1944, Waynesburg, Pennsylvania, USA. Professor of Biochemistry. m. Daphna Killen, 1 son, 1 daughter. *Education:* BS Chemistry cum laude, West Virginia University, 1966; PhD Biochemistry, University of Virginia, 1969. *Appointments:* Postdoctoral Fellow, Institute for Enzyme Research, University of Wisconsin, Madison, 1969-72; Assistant Profesor 1972-76, Associate Professor 1976-81, Professor 1981-, Acting Chairman 1984-85, Department of Biochemsitry, West Virginia University Medical Center, Morgantown, West Virg'nia. *Memberships:* American Chemical Society; American Association for the Advancement of Science; American Society of Biological Chemists; Biophysical Society; Sigma Xi. *Publications:* 38 research articles and chapters in books. *Honours:* NSF Research Career Development Award, 1974-75. *Hobbies:* Skiing; Painting; Woodworking. *Address:* Department of Biochemsitry, West Virginia University Medical Center, Morgantown, WV 24506, USA.

BLAIR, Frank Michael, b. 18 Apr. 1948, Boston, Massachusetts, USA. Chiropractic Physician. m. Mary Ann Girard, 24 June 1973, Quincy. *Education:* BA, Psychology, Boston University; DC, Palmer College of Chiropractic. *Memberships:* American Chiropractic Association; Massachusetts Chiropractic Society; International Chiropractic Society; Sacro-Occipital Research Society International; Council on Roentgenology of the American Chiropractic Association. *Publications:* "A Spinal Specialist's Guide to Exercise, Fitness & Health", 1985; "A Spinal Specialist's Guide to Low Back Pain", 1986. *Hobbies:* Writing; Painting; Sculpture, Tennis; Skiing. *Address:* 73 Summer Street, Hingham, MA 02043, USA.

BLAIR-WEST, John Reginald, b. 7 Aug. 1929, Adelaide, Australia. Research Scientist, Howard Florey Institute. m. Esme Margaret Feltscheer, 16 June 1950, Melbourne, 2 sons, 1 daughter. *Education:* BSc., MSc (honours), PhD, Melbourne. *Appointments:* Research Fellow, Harvard University; ResearchFellow, National Health and Medical Research Council of Australia; Visiting Professor: University of California, San Francisco, USA, University of Mississippi, USA; Principal Research Fellow, National Health & Medical Research Council of Australia. *Memberships:* International Society of Hypertension; International

Study Group for Steroid Hormones; Society for Protection of Old Fish; Australian Physiological and Pharmacological Society; Endocrine Society of Australia; Australasian Society of Nephrology; High Blood Pressure Research Council of Australia. *Publications:* Chapters in Books: "Renin-angiotensin system and sodium metabolism", 'International Review of Physiology', Volume 11, 1976; (with others) "The Control of aldosterone secretion", 'Rec. Progress Horm Research', 1963; etc. *Honours:* Shared International Society of Hypertension, merck, Sharp and Dohme Award, 1976. *Hobbies:* Sailing; Golf. *Address:* Howard Florey Institute of Experimental Physiology & Medicine, University of Melbourne, Parkville, Victoria 3052, Australia.

BLAKEMORE, Colin Brian, b. 1 June 1944, Stratford-on-Avon, England. Waynflete Professor of Physiology and Fellow of Magdalen College, Oxford. m. Andree Elizabeth Washbourne, 11 Aug. 1965, 3 daughters. *Education:* BA, Natural Sciences (Medicine), 1965, MA, 1969, Corpus Christi College, Cambridge; PhD, Physiological Optics, University of California,Berkeley, 1968; MA, Magdalen College, Oxford, 1979. *Appointments:* Harkness Fellowship, University of California, Berkeley, 1965-67; University Demonstrator, Physiological Laboratory, University of Cambridge, 1968-72; University Lecturer; Fellow of Downing College, Cambridge, 1972-79; Royal Society Locke Research Fellow, Physiological Laboratory, Cambridge, 1976-79; Visiting Professor, New York University, 1970; Massachusetts Institute of Technology, 1971; Salk Institute, San Diego, 1982, 83. *Memberships:* Physiological Society; Experimental Psychology Society International Brain Research Organization, Executive Committee and Governing Council, European Brain and Behaviour Society; Society for Neuroscience; Member, BBC Science Consultative Group, 1975-79. *Publications:* "Handbook of Psychobiology", 1975; "Mechanics of the Mind", 1977; "Mind Waves", 1986; Articles in professional journals; Numerous broadcasts for BBC Radio and TV. *Honours Include:* Phi Beta Kappa Award in Science, USA, 1978; John Locke Medal, Worshipful Society of Apothecaries, London, 1983; several Fellowships, awards, etc. *Hobbies:* Running; Broadcasting. *Address:* University Laboratory of Physiology, Parks Road, Oxford OX1 3PT, England.

BLANCO-BENAVIDES, Roberto, b. 20 Jan. 1942, Mexico City. Professor of Surgery. m. Celia Escandon, 14 Dec. 1964, 1 son, 2 daughters. *Education:* MD, Universidad Nacional Autonoma de Mexico; Residencies, Internal Medicine, Surgery, Instituto Nal Nutricion, Mexico; Residencies, Internal Medicine, Surgery, Instituto Nal Nutricion, Mexico; Residency in Surgery, Mayo Graduate School of Medicne, Rochester, Minnesota, USA. *Appointments:* Surgeon, Chief of General Surgery, Hospital General Centro Medico NAL, IMSS, Hospital Gabriel Moncera, IMSS; Assistant Professor of Surgery, Universidad Nal Mexico. *Memberships:* Asociacion Mexicana Cirugia general; Asociacion Mexicana Gastroenterologia; American College of Surgeons; Mayo Alumni; Priestley Society. *Publications:* 'A Simple Modification of the Child intestinal Plication Method', 1977, 'External Bypass Operation for Biliary Tract Obstruction', 1981 (in Archives of Surgery); 'Esophagocardioplasty with Gastric Pouch; & An Experimental Study with Dogs', 1982,'Treatment of Bleeding Esophageal Varices: A New Technique', 1983 (in American Journal of Surgery). *Hobby:* Reading. *Address:* Apartado Postal 85004, Mexico City DF 10200, Mexico.

BLAND,Calvin, b. 17 Nov. 1943, Philadelphia, USA. Executive Director. m. Jeanette Carter, 24 Aug. 1968, Philadelphia, USA, 1 daughter. *Education:* MS, Columbia University , 1974; BS, 1972, University of Pennsylvania. *Appointments:* Programme Officer, Robert Wood Johnson Foundation, Princeton,

1974-77; Associate Vice President, St Christopher's Hospital for Children, Philadelphia, 1977-80, Executive Director, 1980-. *Membership:* American College of Hospital Administrators. *Honours:* BS, Cum Laude; Outstanding Young Men of America, 1976; Community Leaders and Noteworth Americans. *Hobbies:* Reading; Jogging. *Address:* 5th and Lehigh Ave., Philadelphia, PA 19133, USA.

BLANDY, John Peter, b. 11 Sept.1927, Calcutta, India. Professor of Urology. m. Anne Mathias, 6 Aug. 1953, Tenby, England, 4 daughters. *Education:* BA, 1948, BM BCh, 1951, MA, 1953, MCh, DM, 1963, Balliol College, Oxford University, England; FRCS, England, 1956. FACS. *Appointments:* House Surgeon and Physician, 1952-53, Registrar, Lecturer and Senior Lecturer, 1955-63, Consultant General Surgeon, 1964, The London Hospital, London, England; Captain, RAMC, 1953-55; Robinson Fellow, Presbyterian St Luke's Hospital, Chicago, Illinois, USA, 1960-61; RSO, Institute of Urology, 1963, Consultant Urological Surgeon, 1968, St Peters Hospitals; Professor of Urology, University of London, 1969-. *Memberships:* Royal College of Surgeons of England; Royal Society of Medicine; Society of Paediatric Urological Surgeons; Mexican Academy of Urology; Australasian Urological Association;International Continence Society; International Transplantation Society; British Transplantation Society and others. *Publications:* 'Tumours of the Testicle', 1970; 'Transurethral Resection' 1970,78; 'Lecture Notes on Urology', 1976, 3 editions and foreign translations; 'Urology',2 volumes, Editor, 1976; 'Operative Urology', 1978,85. Author of numerous papers contributed to professional journals. *Honours:* Hitchinson Prize, 1956; Hunterian Professor, 1964; Davidson Award, 1980. *Hobbies: Painting; Sculpture. Address:* The London Hospital, London, England.

BLAQUIERE, Richard Murray, b. 2 Oct. 1950, England. Consultant Radiologist. m. Stephanie Van Beek, 10 May 1975, 2 daughters. *Education:* BSc, University of St Andrews, 1971; MB ChB, University of Manchester, 1974; Fellow, Royal College of Radiologists, 1981. *Appointments:* House Physican & Surgeon, Manchester Royal Infirmary; Resident, University Hospital, Kingston, Jamaica; Registrar & Senior Registrar, Southampton University Hospitals; Research Fellow & Lecturer, Institute of Cancer Research & Royal Marsden Hospital, London; Consultant Radiologist, University of Southampton; Consultant-in-Charge, Wessex Body Scanner Unit. *Memberships:* British Institute of Radiology. *Publications:* Various articles on diagnostic Radiology, mainly computed Tomography. *Address:* 10 Portswood Park, Portswood, Southampton, S02 1EW, England.

BLASCHKE, Gottfried, b. 3 Feb. 1937, Loschitz, Germany. Professor; Director; Vice-Dean. m. 20 Jan. 1964, 2 sons, 1 daughter. *Education:* Diploma Organic Chemistry; PhD, Pharmaceutical Chemistry. *Appointments:* Dozent, Kiel University, 1972; Professor, Bonn University, 1975-. *Memberships:* Gesellshaft Deutscher Chemiker; Deutsche Pharmazeutische Gesellshaft; American Chemical Society. *Publications:* "Pharmazeutische Analytic", 1977; "Chromatographic Resolution" 1980. *Address:* Vredenweg 18, D-4400 Münster, Federal Republic of Germany.

BLAU, Joseph Norman, b. 5 Oct. 1928, Berlin, Germany. Consultant Neurologist. m. Jill Seligman, 19 Dec. 1968, 2 sons, 1 daughter. *Education:* MB, BS, St. Bartholomew's Hospital Medical College, London; MD; FRCP; FRCPath. *Appointments include:* Medical Officer, Royal Army Medical Corps Wheatley Neurological Hospital; Registrar Neurology/Senior Registrar, London & Maida Vale Hospitals; Research Fellow, Neurology, Massachusetts General Hosptial, Boston, USA. *Memberships:* Association of British Neurologists;

Royal Society of Medicine; London Jewish Medical Society. *Publications Include:* Contributions to; 'Brain', 1958, 1978; 'Headache', 1980-85; 'Nature', 1965, 1967; 'Cephalgia', 1981; 'Lancet', 1955-; 'Migraine: Update', 1982; 'British Medical Journal', 1966-; 'New England Journal of Medicine', 1969. *Honours:* Open Science Scholarship, St.Bartholomew's 1947; Nuffield Medical Scholarship, 1962. *Hobby:* Music (cellist, London Medical Orchestra). *Address:* National Hospital, Queen's Square, London WC1N 3BG, England.

BLAUER, Joanne, b. 13 Feb. 1950, Portland, Oregon, USA, Special Assistant to the Dean for Legal Affairs; Secretary of the Medical College, Cornell University. m. Floyd J Weintraub, 28 Nov. 1981, Portland, Oregon, 1 daughter. *Education:* BA, Philosophy and Religion, Scripps College, 1972; JD, Law, University of Washington, 1975. *Appointments:* Special Assistant to the President, Skidmore College, 1976-78; Deputy Assistant to the President, Barnard College, 1978-80. *Memberships:* ABA; NACUA. *Address:* 300 York Avenue, New York, NY 10021, USA.

BLAYNEY, Keith Dale, b. 8 Feb. 1937, Anamosa, Iowa, USA. University Dean. 2 sons. *Education:* BS Labour Management 1959, MA Hospital Administration 1961, PhD Hospital and Health Administration 1966, University of Iowa. *Appointments:* Director of Bureau of Research and Community Services 1966-67, Director 1967-69, School of Health Services Administration, Administrator of University of Alabama Hospitals 1969-71, Dean of School of Community and Allied Health 1971-, University of Alabama, Birmingham; Past Chairman, American Medical Association's Committee on Allied Health Education and Accreditation. *Memberships:* American College of Hospital Administrators; American Society of Allied Health Professions: Association of University Programs in Health Administration; American Public Health Association; American Association of Community and Junior Colleges. *Publications:* Contributor, 'Webster's Medical Office Handbook', (Editor A H Soukhanov), 1979; 'Improving Health Services in Developing Countries with New Types of Public and Allied Health Personnel', 1982. *Honours:* 1of 50 Outstanding Contributors to Allied Health Education in USA, American Medical Association, 1979; Honorary Director, Xian Medical College, Shaanxi, The People's Republic of China 1985. *Hobbies:* Hunting; Fishing. *Address:* School of Community and Allied Health, University Station, Birmingham, AL 35294, USA

BLECHER, Stan Ronald, b. 27 Apr. 1935, Johannesburg, Republic of South Africa. University Professor and Director. m. Hanne Ostergaard, 4 Apr. 1964, Johannesburg, 2 sons. *Education:* MB BCh, University of the Witwatersrand Johannesburg, 1958; Studies in Medical Genetics, Johannesburg, Copenhagen in Denamrk and Canada; Fellow, Canadian College of Medical Geneticists, 1982. *Appointments:* Intern, Department of Surgery, Coronation Hospital, Johannesburg, Republic of South Africa, 1959; Intern, Department of Medicine, Johannesburg General Hospital, 1959; Lecturer, Department of Anatomy, University of Witwatersrand, Johannesburg, 1960-65; Associate Professor and Reader, Department of Anatomy, Royal Dental College, Copenhagen, Denmark, 1965-78; External Examiner in Medical Genetics, Institute of Human Genetics, University of Copenhagen, 1967-78; Professor of Anatomy, Dalhousie University, Halifax, Nova Scotia, Canada, 1978-84; Director, School of Human Biology, University of Guelph, Ontario, 1984-. *Memberships Include:* British, Danish and Canadian Medical Associations; Cell Biology Society of Copenhagen; cell Biology Society of Canada; Scandinavian Society for Electron Microscopy; Canadian Association of Anatomists; American Association of Anatomists. *Publications Include:* 'Microscopical epididymides in testicular ·feminization', 1978; 'Pleiotropic effect of Tabby gene on epidermal growth factor - containing cells of mouse submandibular gland' (with M Debertin and J S Murphy), 1983. *Honours:* Fellowship in Human Genetics, World Health Fellowhsip, 1972; Fulbright-Hayes Travel Fellowship, 1972. *Hobbies:* Music; Sport. *Address:* School of Human Biology, University of Guelph, Ontario N1G 2W1, Canada.

BLEDSOE, (Ellen) Alene, b. 5 May 1914, Texas, USA. Physician. *Education:* MD; EFCAP; EFASCP. *Appointments:* Intern, Bridgeport (CT) Hospital, 1949-50; General Practice, Skagway, 1951; Pathologist, 2 hospitals, Hutchinson, Kansas, 1958; Pathologist, Fort Bragg, California 1961-69; Director, Pathology, Cumberland Region, Nova Scotia, 5 Hospitals, 1970-72; Quality Control Physician, Cutters Intake Labs, Stockton, California 1974-75; Medical Director, Administrator, Clinica de Salud para Familias, Hollister, 1975-76; Family Practice, Fort Bragg, 1978-84. *Memberships:* Diplomate: National Board of medical Examiners; Pan American Medical Association; CMA; Emeritus Fellow, College of American Pathologists and American Society Clinical Pathology Life member, New York Academy of sciences; Cancer Society; Lung Association; Heart Association. *Publications:* 'Resident's Manual of clinical Pathology', 1955; Co-Author, 'Path. Anat. Coronary Heart Disease', 'American Archives of Pathology', 1963; numerous articles in professionaljournals. *Honours:* Birtcher Prize for Project & Paper 'Heliotherapy' 1947; Fellowship, Clinical Cancer, University Southern California, 1969. *Hobbies Include:* Music; Paintings & Sculpture; Gardening; Writing Poetry; etc. *Address:* 33201 Jefferson Way, Fort Bragg, CA 95437.

BLEEHEN, Norman Montague, b. 24 Feb. 1930, Manchester, England. Professor, Clinical Oncology, Cambridge University, Radiotherapeutic Centre, Addenbrooke's Hospital; Honorary Director, MRC Clinical Oncology & Radiotherapeutics Unit. m. Tirza Loeb, 14 Feb. 1969, London. *Education:* MA; BSc; MB DCH, Oxford University; DMRT London; FRCP; FRCR: Hon. FACR. *Appointments:* Research Fellow, Radiography, Stanford University, 1966-67; Locum Consultant Radiotherapist, Middlesex Hospital London, 1967-69; Professor, Clinical Oncology, Cambridge University, 1975-;Hon. Director,MRC Clinical Oncology & Radiotherapeutics Unit, 1975-; Director Radiotherapeutic Centre, Addenbrooke's Hospital, Cambridge, 1984-. *Memberships:* British Institute of Radiology; Royal Society of Medicine; International Association for the Studyof Lung pCancer; International Society of Radiation for Oncology. *Publications:* Over 200 articles in scientific journals; Editor: 'Radiation Therapy Planning', jointly, 1983; 'Ovarian Cancer', 1985; 'Tumours of the Brain'in press. *Honours:* Gotch Medal, Oxford University, 1953; Hon. FACR, 1984. *Hobbies:* Gardening; Television. *Address:* Radiotherapeutic Centre, Addenbrooke's Hospital, Hills Road, Cambridge CB2 2QQ, England.

BLEUMINK, Eric, b. 19 May 1935, Dieren, Netherlands, Professor Dermatology, Head Dept., Vice Chancellor, State University of Groningen. m. Berendina Tijssen, 30 May 1963, 1 son, 1 daughter. *Education:* PhD, Biochemistry, 1967. *Appointments:* Research Assistant, State University of Utrecht; Junior Scientist, Central Institute for Food and Nutrition Research TNO Zeist; Senior Scientist, Medical Faculty, State University of Utrecht; Head, Biochemistry of the Skin, Groningen; Lecturer, Biochemistry of the Skin; Professor, Dermatology. *Publications:* "The Chemistry of Atopic Food Allergies", 1967;; "Contact Eczeem", 1974; "Antihistamines in 'Side Effects of Drug Annual', 1977-81; "Food Allergy", 1979; "Protesese Inhibitor Deficiencies in Patients with Urticaria", 1975, 1985. *Hobbies:* Gardening; Mountaineering. *Address:*

Dept. of Dermatology, Academisch Ziekenhuis, Oostersingel 59, 9713 EZ Groningen, The Netherlands.

BLICHERT-TOFT, Morgens, b. 9 Sept. 1936, Spoettrup Castle, Denmark. Professor of Surgery. m. Birthe Justelin, 23 Jan 1960, Copenhagen, 1 daughter. *Education:* MD, 1964, Doctor Medicine, Thesis, 1975, University of Copenhagen; Qualified Surgeon in Surgical Gastroenterology, 1978, in Endocrine Surgery, 1979. *Appointments:* Senior Surgeon: Rigshospitalet, Copenhagen University, 1970-74,Glostrup Hospital, Copenhagen University, 1974-77, Herlev Hospital, Copenhagen University, 1977-79; Chief Surgeon & Professor of Surgery, University Hospital, Odense Medical School, 1979-. *Memberships:* President, Nordic Association of Endocrine Surgeons; Danish Delegate, European Society of Surgical Oncology; Fellow, International Association of Endocrine Surgeons; Executive Member, Danish Thyroid Association; Executive Member, Danish Breast Cancer Cooperative Group (DBCG);Nordic Surgical Society; Societe Internationale de Chirurgie. *Publications:* Thesis on 'ACTH Reserve in the Aged', 1975; 'Geriatric Endocrinology' (co-author), 1978; 'Breast Cancer',1985 Some 150 papers in international journals, mainly in field of endocrinology & Breast cancer. *Honours:* B C Nielsen Prize, 1978; Danish Cancer Society Prize, 1984. *Address:* Department of Surgery, Odense University Hospital, 5000 Odense, C, Denmark.

BLOCH, Antoine, b. 9 Aug. 1938, Lausanne, Switzerland. Chief, Cardiac Unit, Hospital de la Tour, Switzerland. m. Josee Sanchez, 25 Aug. 1973, Geneva. *Education:* MD; FACC; Intern, University Hospital, Lausanne, 1964-66; Resident, Cardiac Unit, St Antonius Hospital, utrecht, The Netherlands, 1966-67; Resident, University Hospital of Lausanne and Geneva, 1967-70; Chief Resident, University Cardiac Centre of Geneva, 1970-73; Cardiac Fellow, Massachusetts General Hospital, Boston, 1973-75. *Appointments:* Cardiologist, University Cardiac Centre of Geneva, 1975-80; Swiss National Fund Grantee, 1977-79; Privat-Docent, Charge de Coure, University Medical School of Geneva, 1975-. *Memberships:* Fellow, American College Cardiology; American Society Echocardiography; Swiss Society Cardiology Swiss Society Intensive Care; European Society of Intensive Care; Swiss Society Ultrasound; Medical Society, Geneva; Presiden, Echocardiographic Society of La Tour. *Publications:* 'L'echocardiographie', 1978; L'infarctus du myocarde', 1979, 1985; over 150 articles in professional journals. *Hobbies:* Reading; Sport; Art; Travel. *Address:* Cardiac Unit, Hospital de la Tour, CH 1217 Meyrin-Geneva, Switzerland.

BLOCH, Patrick Harry, b. 6 Nov. 1942, Paris, France. Professor of Surgery. American Hospital, Paris. m. Any Edery, 13 Mar. 1972, Paris, 2 sons, 1 daughter. *Education:* Professor of Surgery; Expert, Paris Court of Appeal; Clinical Expert, French Health Ministry. *Appointments:* Assistant Professor, St Antoine Hospital, Paris; Associate Professor, Chief of Surgery, University Hospital, Paris. *Memberships:* New York Academy of Sciences; European Society for Surgical Research; Association for Academic Surgery; European Association of Surgical Oncology; Euyropean Society for the Study of the Liver. *Publications:* More than 150 papers in the medical and surgical journals; more than 100 presentations at Congresses. *Address:* American Hospital in Paris, 63 Bvd. Victor Hugo, 92200 Neuilly, France.

BLOCK, Pierre J C F,. b. 30 Aug. 1940, Antwerp. University Professor/Head of Department of Cardiology. m. Chr Pestiau, 6 Mar. 1967, Brussels, 1 son 1 daughter. *Education:* MD, 1965, Licentiate in Cardiology, 1967, Licentiate in Industrial Health, 1975, PhD, Free University of Brussels. *Appointments:* Assistant, Department of Int

Medicine, University Institute Bordet, Brussels and Assistant Laboratory of Physiology, ULB; 1965-70; Assistant, Department of Cardiology, University Hospital, St Pierre, ULB and Assistant, Laboratory of Pathological Chemistry, ULB, 1970-76; Assistant Head, Department of Cardiology, Hospital St Pierre, ULB, 1976-79; Head, Department of Cardiology, University Hospital, VUB, Professor of Cardiology, Medical School of VUB, Head, Unit of Cardiovascular Research, Medical School of VUB, 1979- . *Memberships:* Vice President, Belgian Heart Society, 1981-85; Director and Scientific Commitee Member, Belgian Heart Foundation; Commitee for recognition of Postgraduate Medical Doctors, Belgium Ministry of Public Health; member of Working Group on Exercise Physiology and Physiopathology, European Society of Cardiology; Fellow of different Belgian and International Scientific Societies. *Publications:* 113 publications in Belgian and international reviews of Cardiology, Physiology, Bio Medicine, Engineering and Industrial Medicine and chapters in books on Cardiology. *Hobbies:* Tennis, Sailing, Skiing. *Address:* Res. Brussels 27-9, Provincienlaan, 1, 1080 Brussels, Belgium.

BLOOM, Samuel William, b. 18 Sep. 1921, Reading, Pennsylvania, USA, Professor of Sociology and Community Medicine; Director, Division of Behavioural Sciences, Department of Community Medicine, Mount Sinai School of Medicine, New York; Professor of Sociology, CUNY Graduate School. m. 11 Jan 1948, New York, 1 son, 1 daughter. *Education:* BA, University of Pennsylvania, 1943; MA, New School for Social Research, 1950; PhD, University of Wisconsin. *Appointments:* Instructor, Bennington College, Vermont, 1951-53; Research Associate, Columbia University and Field Representative, University of Pennnsylvania College of Medicine, 1953-56; Assistant Professor of Sociology, Baylor University College of Medicine, 1956-62; Visiting Associate Professor of Sociology, Bryn Mawr College, 1961-62; Professor of Sociology in Psychiatry, 1965-68, Associate Professor of Sociology in Administration, 1962-65, Professor of Sociology and Community Medicine, 1968-, Mount Sinai School of Medicine, Professor of Sociology, Graduate School, 1968-, City University of New York. *Memberships:* American Public Health Association; American Sociological Association; Eastern Sociological Society; Association of American Medical Colleges; American Association for the Advancement of Science; Association for the Behavioral Sciences and Medical Education; Alpha Kappa Delta. *Publications:* "Power and Dissent in the Medical School", 1973; "The Sociology of Medicine, 1947-1972: A Report of Trends and Developments", 1972; "The Doctor and His Patient: A Sociological Interpretation", 1963, 2nd Edition, 1965; "The Preclinical Teaching of Psychiatry", (co-author), 1962; "The Medical School as a Social System: A Case Study of Faculty-Student Relationships", 1971; Contributor of numerous articles in professional and medical journals and book chapters. *Hobby:* Racquet ball. *Address:* 1212 Fifth Avenue, New York, NY 10029. USA.

BLUGLASS, Robert Saul, b. 22 Sep. 1930, London, England. Professor of Forensic Psychiatry, University of Birmingham; Consultant in Forensic Psychiatry, West Midlands, Regional Health Authority and the Home Office. m. Dr. Kerry Montgomery, 24 Aug. 1962, St. Andrews, Scotland, 1 son, 1 daughter. *Education:* MB, ChB, 1957, MD, 1967, University of St. Andrews; DDP, Joint Board of Royal colleges, 1961; MRCPsych, 1971; FRCPsych, 1976; Postgraduate Education in Dundee. *Appointments:* House Officer posts in Dundee, Edinburgh and Ipswich 1957-59; Senior House Officer, Registrar, Dundee, 1959-62; Senior Registrar to Professor Sir Ivor Batchelor, Dundee, 1962-67; Senior Clinical Lecturer in Forensic Psychiatry,

previously Clinical Lecturer, 1975-79; Joint Director, Midland Institute of Forensic Medicine, 1975-; Postgraduate Clinical Tutor, University of Birmingham, 1967-; Consultant in Charge, Midland Centre for Forensic Psychiatry, 1967-; Deputy Regional Advisor in Psychiatry (NHRHA), 1982-. *Memberships:* Royal College of Psychiatrists, Vice-President, 1983-85; Fellow, Royal Society of Medicne; British Medical Association; Birmingham Medical Institute, Sec. of Psych., Past President. *Publications:* "Psychiatry, The Law and the Offender", 1980, "A Guide to the Mental Health Act, 1983", 1983; Co-author, "Psychiatry, Human Rights and the Law", 1985; Approximately 50 papers on related topics. *Honours:* Council of Europe Travelling Fellowship, 1971; Denis Carroll Memorial Lecture, ISTD, 1980; Baron C. Ver Heyen De Lancey Prize, Royal Society of Medicine, 1983. *Hobbies;* Water Colour Painting; France; Music. *Address:* Midland Centre for Forensic Psychiatry, All Saints Hospital, Birmingham B18 55D, England.

BLUM, Lionel, b. 17 Nov. 1918, Johannesburg, South Africa, Dentist; Private Practice; Part-time Teacher. m. Joan, 7 Feb. 1945, deceased, 1 son, 2 daughters. *Education:* BDS, H.Dip.Dent., Witwatersrand University; *Appointments:* Part-time, Conversation & Orthodontics, University Witwarterstrand, 1947-65; Part-time, Dental Research Unit, 1965-68; Part-time Lecturer, Dental Ethic & Jurisprudence, University of Witwaterstand, 1968-; Member, Faculty of Dentistry, College of Medicine of South Africa, 1973-;. *Memberships:* Elected Member, South African Medical & Dental Council, 1968-; Board Member, Professional Provident Society of South Africa, 1969-; College of Medicine of South Africa; Dental Association of South Africa; Prosthodontic Society of South Africa; Institute for the Study of Man in Africa; Federation Dentaise Internationale; South African Division, International Association for Dental Research. *Publications:* 'The Odontological South Africa'; Graduation Address, 'Gazette of the University of Witwatersrand', 1971. *Honours:* Robert Vincent Bird Gold Medal, 1969, Honorary Life Member, 1972, Dental Association of South Africa; Silver Jubilee Award, College of Medicine of South Africa, 1981. *Hobbies:* Walking; Sculpture. *Address:* 701 Medical City Building, 106 Eloff Str., Johannesburg, South Africa 2001.

BLUMGART, Leslie Harold, b. 7 Dec. 1931, South Africa. Director and Professor of Surgery, Royal Postgraduate Medical School, London, England. m. 20 Apr. 1968, Wales, 2 sons, 2 daughters. *Education:* BDS, Witwatersrand, 1954; MB ChB, 1962, MD, 1969, University of Sheffield, 1969; FRCS (England), 1966; FRCS (Glasgow), 1973; FRCS (Edinburgh), 1976. *Appointments:* Senior Lecturer and Deputy Director, University Department of Surgery, Welsh National School of Medicine, Cardiff, 1970-72; St. Mungo Professor of Surgery, University of Glasgow; Honorary Consultant Surgeon, Glasgow Royal Infirmary, 1972-79; Director and Professor of Surgery, Royal Postgraduate Medical School; Honorary Consultant Surgeon, Hammersmith Hospital, 1979-. *Memberships:* Association of Surgeons of Great Britain and Ireland; Surgical Research Society; British Society of Gastroenterology; International Biliary Association; Collegium Internationale Chirurgiae Digestivae; Honorary Member: Society for Surgery and Alimentary Tract, USA; Los Angeles Surgical Society. *Publications:* Editor, 'The Bilary Tract', 'Clinical Surgery International', 1983; Editor, 'Surgery of the Liver and Biliary Tract' (in preparation); 'Benign bile duct stricture following cholecystectomy', 'British Journal of Surgery', Nov. 1984; 'Pre-operative cholangiography and post-cholecystectomy biliary strictures', Annals of Royal College of Surgeons of England, 1985. *Honour:* Moynihan Fellowship of Association of Surgeons of Great Britain and Ireland, 1972. *Hobbies:* Water Colour Painting; Wood Carving.

Address: Department of Surgery, Royal Postgraduate Medical School, Hammersmith Hospital, Ducane Road, London W12 OHS, England.

BLUST, Jeanne Elizabeth, b. 10 Jan. 1943, Somerville, New Jersey, USA. Administrator, Quality Care Homecare Service, Louisville, Kentucky. *Education:* RN, 1964; BA 1979; MA 1983; Certified, Nursing Administration, Amercan Nurses Association, 1984. *Appointments Include:* Director, Educational Services, American Red Cross, Louisville; Clinical Supervisor, Cardiothoracic Surgery, Mount Sinai Medical Centre, New York; Clinical Supervisor, Intravenous Therapy/Blood Bank, ibid. *Memberships:* Board, Kentucky division American Cancer Society; American Nurses Association; National Intravenous Therapy Association; American Association of Blood Banks. *Publications Inlcude:* Book chapter, 'Nursing Intervention in Haemapheresis', 1985; Numerous articles, various nursing publications, intravenous therapy, blood transfusion, critical care nursing. *Honour:* CNA, American Nurses Association, 1984. *Hobbies:* Shell collecting; Reading; Handmade quilts. *Address:* 208 Hopkins Lane, Jeffersonville, IN 47103, USA.

BOAKE, William Charles, b. 27 Jan. 1922, Melbourne, Australia. Cardiologist, Arizona Heart Institute, Sun City. m. Frances Elise Gillespie, 29 Jan. 1949, Melbourne, 1 son, 1 daughter. *Education:* MSc., 1954, MB.BS, 1948, Melbourne; MRCP, London 1955. *Appointments:* Research Assistant, Walter and Eliza Hall Institute, Melbourne, 1944-45, House Physician, Royal Melbourne Hospital, 1949; Nuffield Dominion Demonstrator, Sir William Dunn School of Pathology, Oxford, England, 1950-52; Assistant, Medical Unit, St Mary's Hospital, London, 1953-54; Instructor, Medicine, Western Reserve University, Ohio, USA, 1955-56; Assistant, Cardial Dept., St Thomas's Hospital, London, 1956-57; Assistant, Medicine, University of Melbourne, 1958-61; Assistant Professor to Professor, Medicine, University of Wisconsin, USA, 19061-81; Cardiologist, Arizona Heart Institute, Phoenix, 1981-85. *Memberships:* Fellow, Royal College of Physicians; Fellow, Royal Australasian College of Physicians; Fellow, American College of Physicians; Fellow, American College Cardiology and American College of Angiology; Transplant Society; etc. *Publications:* Numerous in International Literature, 1945-85. *Hobbies:* Photography; Painting; Travel; Fly Fishing. *Address:* 10512 Mountain View Road, Sun City, AZ 85351, USA.

BOAYKE-YIADOM, Kwabena, b. 29 Dec. 1938, Koforidua, Ghana. Vice-Chancellor and Dean, Faculty of Pharmacy. m. Beatrice Frempong, Koforidua, Ghana, 3 sons, 3 daughters. *Education:* B. Pharm., Faculty of Pharmacy, University of Science and Technology, Kumasi, Ghana, 1964; PhD, Biological Institute, Czechoslovak Academy of Sciences, Bratislava, Czechoslovakia, 1969. *Appointments:* Research Assistant, National Institute of Health and Medical Research, Accra, Ghana, 1964-65; Junior Fellow, Ghana Academy of Arts and Science, 1964-9; Lecturer, Department of Pharmaceutics, University of Science and Technology, Kumasi, Ghana, 1969, Senior Lecturer, Associate Professor, ViceChancellor and Dean, Faculty of pharmacy,-. *Memberships:* Pharmaceutical Society of Ghana; Ghana Science Association; University Teachers Association of Ghana; West African Pharmaceutical Federation. *Publications:* Co-author 'Incidence of Antibacterial Activity in the Connaraceae' in 'Plant Medica', 1975; Co-author 'Antimicrobial activity of Xylopic Acid and Other Constituents of the Fruits of Xylopia Aethiopica Dunal. A. Rich (Annonacae)' in 'Lloydia', 1977; Co-author 'Cryptolepine Hydrochloride Effect on Staphylococcus Sureus' in 'Journal of Pharm. Sci.' 1979; Co-author 'Comparison of Antimicrobial Action of Cryptolepine Alkaloid on Staphylococcus Aureus and Escheridia Coli' in 'Lloydia', 1979.

Honours: Fulbright Hays, Senior Fellow, 1977-78; Travelling Fellowship, Association of Commonwealth Universities, 1985. *Hobbies:* Sports; Classical and traditional music. *Address:* Faculty of Pharmacy, University of Science and Technology, Kumasi, Ghana.

BOCCABELLA, Anthony Vincent, b. 12 June 1929, Brooklyn, New York, USA, Professor and Chairman of Anatomy, 1 son, 1 daughter. *Education:* MS, 1956; PhD, 1958; JD, 1984. *Appointments:* Instructor, State University of Iowa, 1958-59; Instructor, Seton Hall College of Medicine and Dentistry, 1959-60; Assistant Professor, Seton Hall College of Medicine and Dentistry, 1953-67; Professor, 1967-, Chairman, Department of Anatomy, 1971-, UMDMJ-New Jersey Medical SChool, Newark, New Jersey. *Memberships:* American Association of Anatomists Charter Member, American Society of Andrology; American Society of Law and Medicine; Association of Anatomy Chairmen; Association for Development of Computer-Based Instructor Systems; Endocrine Society; Sigma Xi; Experimental Aircraft Association; New York Society of Electron Microscopists; Charter Member, Society for the Study of reproduction. *Publications:* contributor of numerous articles in professional and medical journals; "A Visual Approach to Radiographic Anatomy", (with T Pearlman and E A Alger), 1976; "A Computer-Based Self-Assessment Program on the Gross Anatomy of the Head and Neck", (with E A Alger and J Glassman), 1973, 1976; "Laboratory Guide to Microscopic Anatomy: Cells and Tissues", 1974. *Honours:* Alumni Award, New Jersey Medical School, 1981; Travel Award, Society of the Study of Reproduction, 1968; Travel Award, American Association of Anatomists, 1965; Travel award Society of Animal Science, 1964; Squibb Travel Grant, Endocrine Society, 1964. *Hobbies:* Private pilot's licence, 1965; Sailing. *Address:* UMDNJ-New Jersey Medical School, Department of Anatomy, 100 Bergen Street, Newark, NJ 07103, USA.

BOCHNER, Felix, b. 22 Apr. 1939, Brno, Czechoslovakia. Professor of Clinical Pharmacology. m. Dianne Sheliah Russell, 21 Dec. 1963, Coffs Harbour, New South Wales, 1 son, 2 daughters. *Education:* MB BS, University of Queensland, 1963; Royal Australasian College of Physicians, 1969; Fellow 1974; MD, University of Queensland, 1974. *Appointments:* Resident Medical Officer, Royal Brisbane Hospital, 1964-65; Registrar, 1966-70; Visiting Physician, Princess Alexandra Hospital, Brisbane, 1971-73, Royal Brisbane Hospital 1973-75; Clinical Fellow in Clinical Pharmacology, National Health & Medical Research Council of Australia, 1975-77; Fellow in Clinical Pharamcology, University of Kansas Medical centre, USA, 1975-76; Fellow in Clinical Pharmacology, University of Manchester, England, 1976-77; Senior Lecturer in Medicine, 1977-79, Reader in Medicine, 1980, University of Queensland; Professor of Clinical Pharmacology, University of Adelaide, Head of Clinical Pharmacology, Royal Adelaide Hospital. *Memberships:* Royal Australasian College of Physiciasn; Australasian Society of Clinical & Experimental Pharmacologists; British Pharmacological Society. *Publications:* "Handbook of Clinical Pharmacology", (with S G Carruthers, J P K Kampmann, J A Steiner), 1978, translated into Spanish 1980, Dutch 1980, Japanese 1981, 1985); 2nd edition, 1983; "Introduction to Clinical Pharmacology" (with Eadie M J, Tyrer J H), 1981. *Honours:* Lithgow Scholarship, University of Sydney, 1957; Clinical Fellowship in Clincial Pharmacology, National Health & Medical Research Council of Australia, 1975-77. *Hobbies:* Music; Reading. *Address:* Department of Clinical & Experimental Pharmacology, University of Adelaide, Adelaide, South Australia 5000, Australia.

BOODY, Keith, b. 1 Nov. 1937, Stockton-on-Tees,

England. Professor and Head, Regional Medical Physics Department. m. Sylvia Goodier, 20 Aug. 1960, Stockton-on-Tees, 2 sons. *Education:* BSc, University of Liverpool; MSc, University of London; PhD, University of Glasgow, Scotland; DSc, University of Strathclyde; Fellow, Institute of Physics:FRSE. *Appointments:* Radiation Protection Officer, Research Laboratory, Associated Electrical Industries Limited, Aldermaston Court, 1959-63; Head, Health Physics and Nuclear Medicine Unit, Scottish Universities Research and Reactor Centre, East Kilbride, Scotland, 1963-78; Head, Regional Medical Physics Department, North Regional Health Authority and Professor of Medical Physics, Department Head, University of Newcastle-upon-Tyne, 1978-. *Memberships:* Hospital Physicists Association; Institute of Physical Sciences in Medicine; British Institute of Radiology; Institute of Physics; Society of Radiological Protection; British Nuclear Medicine Society. *Publications:* Author of more than 200 papers in medical and scientific journals and books. Editor, 'Proceedings of the Second East Kilbride Conference on Progress and Problems of IN VIVO Activation Analysis'; 1976. *Honours:* Fellow: Royal Society of Edinburgh, 1980; Institute of Physics, 1969. Honorary Member,British Nuclear Medicine Society; Calderwood Award, Postgraduate Medical Institute, Isle of Man, 1980. *Hobbies:* Work; Walking; Gardening; Music; Generating Perspectives on Sellafield and public health. *Address:* Regional Medical Physics Department, Newcastle General Hospital, Westgate Road, Newcastle upon Tyne NE4 6BE, England.

BODEY, Alan Stewart, b. 19 Sept. 1928, Melbourne, Australia. Proprietor, Unipath Laboratories. m. Diana Wendy Carson Hill (deceased), 23 Jan. 1960, Hampton, 3 daughters. *Education:* BSc, MB, BS, University of Melbourne, 1958; Fellow, Royal College of Pathologists of Australasia, 1965; MC Pathology, 1966; Fellow, Royal College of Pathologists, 1978; MD, University of Melbourne, 1979. *Appointments:* Junior RMO, Alfred Hospital, 1959; Registrar, Geelong Hospital, 1960; Medical Royal Melbourne Hospital, 1962; Trainee in Pathology, Royal Melbourne & Royal Women's Hospitals, 1963-65; Regional Pathologist, North-West Victoria, Mildura, 1966-69; Medical Officer, Antarctic Division, 1969-71; Specialist Medical Officer, (Pathology), Prince Henry's Hospital, 1972; Assistant Pathologist, Mercy Maternity Hospital, 1972-78; Proprietor, Unipath Laboratories, 1977-. *Membership:* American Association for Clinical Chemistry. *Publications:* Various articles in field of Antarctic experience & fertility. *Hobbies:* Skiing; Railways. *Address:* Unipath Laboratories.

BODFISH, Ralph Elwin, b. 24 Jan. 1922, Denver, Colorado, USA. Associate Chief of Staff, VA Medical Centre, Long Beach; Clinical Professor, Radiological Science, University of California, Irvine. m. Mildred Ethridge Mann, 12 Dec. 1952, Atlanta, divorced 1968, 2 sons. *Education:* BA, Duke University, 1949; MD, Emory University School of Medicine, 1954; Internship, Internal Medicine Residency, Long Beach California VA Medical Centre, 1954-58; Flight Surgeon Rating, School of Aerospace Medicine, Brook Air Force Base, San Antonio, 1970. *Appointments:* Chief, Nuclear Medicine, 1956-72; Deputy Chief of Staff, 1968-71; VA medical Centre; Chief, Aeromedical Services, March Air Force Base, 1968-72; Consultant, Nuclear Medicine and Research, VA Medical Centre, 1971-74; Chief, Medicine, Rancho Campus, University of Southern California, 1971-74; Professor, Medicine, Radiology, University of Southern California School of Medicine, 1971-74. *Memberships:* Society of Nuclear Medicine; American College of Physicians; American Federation for Clinical Research; Aerospace Medical Association; Inter-Agency Institute for Health Care Executives. *Publications:* Articles in 'Clinical Research'; 'American Journal

Roentgenography'; 'Modern Medicine'; etc. *Honours:* Fellow, American College of Physicians, 1966' Physicians Recognition Awards, 1969, 1972, 1976; Golden Eagle, Paral. Veterans Association, 1977. *Hobbies:* English & Scottish Genealogy; Amateur Archaeology; Classic Cars; Music; Painting; Flying. *Address:* 2686 Copa de Oro Drive, Rossmoor, Los Alamitos, CA 90720, USA.

BODMER, Walter Fred, b. 10 Jan. 1936, Frankfurt-am-Main, Germany. Director. m. Julia G Pilkington, 11 Aug. 1956, Manchester, England. 2 sons, 1 daughter. *Education:* BA, 1956, PhD, Cambridge University, 1959. *Appointments:* Research Fellow, 1958-60, Official Fellow, 1961; Fellow, Visiting Assistant Professor, 1961-62, Assistant Professor, 1962-66, Professor, Department of Genetics, Stanford University, 1968-70; Professor of Genetics, Oxford University, 1970-79; Director, Research Imperial Cancer Research Fund, 1979-. *Memberships:* Fellow, Royal Society; Fellow, Royal College of Pathologists; Honorary Fellow, Royal college Physicians; Foreighn Honorary Member, American Academy Arts and Sciences; Foreign Associate US National Academy Sciences;Honorary Member, American Assn. Immunologists; President, Royal Statistical Society, 1984-85; Vice President, Royal Institution, 1981-82. *Publications:* 'The Genetics of Human Populations', (with L Cavalli-Sforza), 1971; 'Our Future Inheritance: Choice or Chance?', (with A Jones), 1974; 'Genetics, Evolution and Man', (with L Cavalli-Sforza), 1976. *Honours:* William Allan Memorial Award, 1980; Conway Evans Prize, 1982; Rabbi Shai Shacnai Memorial Prize Lectureship in Immunology and Cancer Research, 1982; John Alexander Memorial Prize, 1984. *Hobbies:* Playing Piano; Riding; Swimming. *Address:* Imperial Cancer Research Fund, PO Box 123, Lincoln's Inn Fields, london WC2A 3PX, England.

BOEDHI-DARMOJO, Raden, b. 31 Mar. 1929, Madiun, Indonesia, Professor and Head of Department Internal Medicine, Diponegoro University, m. Siti Soehardinah, 17 Sep. 1961, Malang, 1 son, 2 daughters. *Education:* MD, 1958, Specialist brevet in internal medicine, 1963, Specialist brevet in cardiology, 1971, faculty of Medicine, University of Indonesia, Jakarta.; Postgraduate Training, Internal medicine and geriatrics, Amsterdam, The Netherlands, 1966-67; Cardiology, London, England, 1970. *Appointments:* Lecturer in Internal Medicine, University of Indonesia, 1959-63; Lecturer in Internal Medicine, 1963; Senior Lecturer in internal medicine, 1965-72, Professor of Internal Medicine, 1972-, Dean, Medical Faculty, 1964-65, Chairman, Research Institute, 1982-, Diponegoro University; Chairman, Cardiac Team, 1978-, Supervisor, ICU/CCU, 1976, Dr Kariadi Hospital. *Memberships:* Chairman, Scientific Council, Indonesian Heart Association, 1978-; Member, Advisory Committee on Medical Research, WHO/SEA, 1983-; Chairman, Ethical Code Commission (Medicine) Central Java, 1978-83; Member, research Group, National Consortium on Medical Science, 1977-; Member, research Council, Asian-Pacific Society of Cardiology, 1984-; Research Coordinator on Hypertension, ASEAN Federation of Cardiology, 1978-. *Publications:* Contributor to the National Symposium on Geriatrics, 1977; "Diseases of the Heart", (Editor and Contributor), 1979; 'A report on Ischemic Heart Disease and its risk factors in Indoneasia', 1985; Author of numerous other publications. *Honours:* MEDIKA Journal Awards, 1979, 1980, 1981; Order of Faithful Service 1st Class, Republic of Indonesia, 1983; Recipient of 7 other medals. *Hobbies:* Photography; Traditional and classical music. *Address:* 24 Sisingamngaraja Street, Semarang, Indonesia.

BOERI, Renato Raimondo, b. 15 May 1972, Milano, Italy. Neurologist. m. Cini Mariani, 14 Sep. 1950, divorced 1969, 3 sons, m. Maria Grazia Casiraghi, 15 Sep. 1978, Liceo. *Education:* MD, University of

Milano, 1947; Diplomate Neurology and Psychiatry, University of Milan, 1951. *Appointments:* Intern, Resident, Istituo Nerologico C. Besta, Milano; Clin. and Scientific Director, Istituto Neurologico Caro Besta, Milan, 1977-. *Memberships:* Italian Society Neurology, Vice President, 1982; American Acdemy Neurology; Societe Francaise de Neurologie; New York Academy of Sciences. *Publications:* Editor, Italian Jouranl Neurological Sciences, 1980-. *Address:* Instituto Neurologico Carlo Besta, Via Celoria 11, Milan, Italy, 20133.

BOHACEK, Nenad,, b. 20 Nov. 1920, Zagreb, Yugoslavia. Professor, Psychiatry, Medical School, University of Zagreb. m. Dr Maja Mihovilović, 25 Dec. 1983, Yugoslavia, 1 son. *Education:* MD, 1947; MDSc, 1966; Specialist, Neurology, Psychiatry, 1952. *Appointments:* Assistant Professor 1952-66, Associate Professor 1966-72, Professor 1972- , Psychiatry, Medical School, University of Zagreb; Head, WHO Collaborating Centre for Study of Psychotropic Drugs for Yugoslavia, 1970-84; Head, WHO Collaborating Centre for Research and Training in Mental Health for Yugoslavia, 1984- . *Memberships:* Zbor liječnika Hrvatke; Society of Yugoslav Psychiatrists, 1952; Societe International de Psychopathologie de l'Expression, Vice President, 1962-82; International Association of Suicide Prevention, various offices; Collegium Internationale Neuro-Psychopharmacologium (CINP), 1966; Arbeitsgemeinschaft fuŕ Methodik und Dokumentation in der Psychiatrie (AMDP), 1966. *Publications:* "Psihijatrijska farmakoterapija manicnih i depresivnih stanja", 1966; "Psihofarmakologija I", 1968, II, 1970, III, 1974; "Suvremeni pristup farmakoterapiji depresija", 1981; "Pharmakogene depressive Verschiebung", 1964, 1967. *Honours:* Honorary Member: Societa Italiana di Psicofarmacologia, 1970; Associacion Argentina di Psichiatria Biolgica, 1974; Honorary Vice President, Societe International de Psychopathologie de l'Expression, 1982; Honorary member, Czechoslovak medical Association, 1980; Permanent Council Member; Yugoslav-Czechoslovakian Psychiatric Congresses, 1968 and Danubian Psychiatric Symposia, 1984. *Hobbies:* Philately; Collecting Bells; Hiking. *Address:* Department of Psychiatry, Medical School, University of Zagreb, 41000 Zagreb, Rebro, Yugoslavia.

BOHINJEC, Jože, b. 31 May 1923, Ljubljana, Yugoslavia, Professor and Head of Department, m. Mateja Plavsak, 5 Feb. 1970, 1 daughter. *Education:* MD, University of Ljubljana, 1949; Specialist in Internal Medicine Degree, 1954; PhD, 1972. *Appointments:* Assistant in Internal Medicine, Professor of Internal Medicine, Head of Department of Hematology, Clinical Centre, University of Ljubljana; Consultant Physician, Department of Internal Medicine, Imperial Army Hospital, Addis Ababa, Ethiopia. *Memberships:* Slovenian Medical Association. *Publications:* "Fundamentals of Clincial Hematology", 1976, 2nd Edition, 1983; Author of numerous articles to Professional journals. *Honours:* Yugoslave Order of Work with Golden Wreath, 1985. *Hobbies:* Skiing; Hunting; History. *Address:* Hematoloska Klinika, Univerzitetni Klinicni Centre, Zaloška 7, 61000 Ljubljana, Yugoslavia.

BOHNEN, Robert F, b. 3 Jan. 1941, Huntington, New York, USA. Oncologist/Hematologist, Private Practice. m. Mollyn Villareal, 20 June 1965, 2 sons, 1 daughter. *Education:* BS, Zoology, Syracuse University, New York, 1961; MD, Columbia University, New York, 1965. *Appointments:* Intern, Straight Medicine, Buffalo General Hospital, New York, 1965-66; Resident, Medicine, State University of New York at Buffalo, 1968-69; Resident, Medicine, 1969-70, Fellow, Clinical Hematology, 1970-71, Fellow, Medical Oncology, 1971-72, University of Utah. *Memberships:* Phi Beta Kappa; American Society of Clinical Oncology. *Publications:* Co-author, 'The Direct Coombs' Test: Its Clinical

Significance' in 'Annals of Internal Medicine', 1968; Co-author, 'Sardoidosis and autonomous parathyroid hyperplasia' in 'Journal of American Medical Association', 1971; Co-author, 'Effective participation in cooperative clinical trials by an independent community organization. An NCOG model' in 'American Journal Clinical Oncology', 1983; Co-author, 'Chemotherapy of small-cell carcinoma of lung: a randomized comparison of alternating and sequential combination chemotherapy programs', in 'Journal of Clinical Oncology', 1984. *Honour:* Clinical Trainee Fellowship, American Cancer Society, 1971-72. *Hobbies:* Choral and solo singing; Amateur theatrical productions. *Address:* Consultants Medical Group, 406 Sunrise Avenue, Roseville, CA 95678, USA.

BOISSONEAU, Robert Allen, b. 23 Sept 1937 Detroit, Michigan, USA, Professor, Centre for Health Services Administration, Arizona State University, m. Jo Ellen Marie Fitzgerald, 15 Oct 1960, San Antonio, Texas, 2 sons, 1 daughter. *Education:* PhD, Ohio State University, 1974; MHA, Virginia Commonwealth University, 1965; BA, Eastern Michigan University, 1960. *Appointments:* Administrator of Means Hall, Ohio State Universtiy Hospitals, Instructor, OSU College of Medicine, 1967-72; Associate Director, Assistant Professor, Graduate Studies in Health Services Management, School of Medicine, University of Missouri, Columbus, 1972-75; Dean, Professor, College of Human Services, Eastern Michigan University, Ypsilanti, 1975-80. *Memberships:* The Academy of Managerment; American College of Hospital Administrators; American Hospital Association; American Public Health Association; American Society of Allied Health Professions. *Publications:* 'Health Care Organization and Development', 1985; 'Continuing Education in the Health Professions', 1980. *Honours:* Recognition Award for Dedicated Community Service, Desert Samaritan hospital, Mesa, Ariz, 1983; Honorary DSc, Indiana Northern Graduate School of Professional Management, 1979. *Hobbies:* Running; Tennis; Reading. *Address:* 2113 S Paseo Loma, Mesa, AZ 85202, USA.

BOITANO, Marilyn Ann, b. 9 Aug. 1944, Livermore, California, USA. Staff Surgeon, Commander USA Navy. *Education:* BS Biology, University of Santa Clara, California, 1962-66; MD, St Louis University School of Medicine, Missouri, 1966-70; Fellowships; Accident Surgery, Birmingham Accident Hospital, Birmingham, England, 1972; Pathokinesiology, Rancho Los Amigos Hospital, California, USA 1976-77; A-O Osteosynthesis, Regionalspital Sta, Maria, Visp, Switzerland, 1983. *Appointments:* Staff Orthopedic Surgeon, Naval Regional Medical Center, Camp Lejeune, North Carolina, USA, 1979-81; Department of Orthopedic Surgery, National Naval Medical Center, Bethesda, Maryland, 1982-85; Assistant Professor, Department of Surgery, Uniformed Services University of the Health Sciences, Bethesda, Maryland, 1982-85; Staff Surgeon, United States Naval Hospital, Okinawa Japan, 1985-. *Memberships:* American College of Sports Medicine; American Association for Automotive Medicine; Association of Military Surgeons of USA; USA Amateur Boxing Federation, *Publications include:* 'Surgical Treatment of Low Velocity Gunshot Wounds of the Extremities', (with M E Ashby), 1976, 'Principles and management of Penetrating Vascular Injuries Secondary to Gunshot Wounds', (with A K Mandal), 1978; 'Gunhot Wounds of the Aorta and Inferior Vena Cava in Civilian Practice', (with A K Mandal, L J Lundy and J L Alexander), 1979; 'Functional Evaluation of the Pes Anserinus Transfer by Electromyography and Gait Analysis', (with J Perry, J M Fox, S R Skinner, L A Barnes and K Cerny), 1980; 'Amateur Boxing Injuries at the 1981 and 1982 USA/ABF National Championships', (with J J Estwanik), 1984; 'Driver

Injuries in Auto Road Racing', 1985. *Honours:* Life member, California Scholarship Federation, 1962; Honorary Member, Egyptian Orthopedic Association; Physician of the Year Award, USA/Amateur Boxing Federation, 1984. *Hobies:* Running; Auto Road Racing; Gardening. *Address:* USNH-Box 141, FPO Seattle, WA 98778, USA.

BOJAR, Samuel, b. 23 Jan. 1915, New York City, USA. Associate Clincial Professor of Psychiatry, Harvard Medical School. m. Leah S. Cohen, 1 July 1947, Boston, Massachusetts, 1 son, 1 daughter. *Education:* AB, summa cum laude, Brown University, 1936; MA, University of Rochester, 1937; MD, Johns Hopkins University School of Medicine, 1941. *Appointments:* Assistant in Psychiatry, 1948-50, Junior Associate in Psychiatry, 1950-51, Associate in Medicine (Psychiatry), 1951-58; Senior Associate in Medicine (Psychiatry), 1958-83; Physician, 1983-, Peter Bent Brigham Hospital (now Brigham and Women's Hopsital); Assistant in Psychiatry, 1947, Instructor in Psychiatry, 1951-61, Clinical Associate in Psychiatry, 1961-67, Assistant Clinical Professor of Psychiatry, 1967-73, Associate Clinical Professor of Psychiatry, 1973-85; Harvard University; Psychiatrist, Medical Area Health Service, 1953-79; Lecturer on Psychiatry, Divinity School, Harvard University, 1963-81. *Memberships:* Life Fellow, American Psychiatric Association; American Psychoanalytic Association; Boston Psychoanalytic Society; Massachusetts Psychiatric Society; American Medical Association; Massachusetts Medical Society; Norfolk District Medical Society; Phi Beta Kappa; Sigma Xi. *Publications:* 'Psychiatric Problems of Medical Students' in "Emotional Problems of the Students", Edited by Blaine and McArthur, 1961; Second edition, 1972; "The Science of Health", (co-authors: Guild, W.R. and Fuisz, R.E.), 1969; "Physiology of Medical Practice" co-authors Guild, W R and Fuisz, R E, 1972; 'Psychosomatic Aspects of Urology' (co-author Reich, P) in "Campbell's Textbook of Urology", 1979. *Honour:* William James Lecturer, Harvard Divinity School, 1971-72. *Hobbies:* Gardening; Silversmithing; Rare Coin Collecting; International Travel. *Address:* 10 Aston Road, Chestnut Hill, MA 02167, USA.

BOKHOUT, Maarten, b. 9 Mar. 1952, The Netherlands. Medical Officer of Health. m. Helena Jocelyn McShane, 13 Dec. 1975, Toronto, Ontario, Canada, 3 daughters. *Education:* MD, 1977, MHSc, 1985, University of Toronto, Canada; Certificant college of Family Practice of Canada, 1979. *Appointments:* Medical Officer, 1980-83, currently, Medical Officer of Health, Grenfell Regional Health Services, Newfoundland, Canada; Chief Resident, Community Medicine, University of Toronto, 1984-85. *Memberships:* Canadian Medical Association; College of Family Practice of Canada. *Hobbies:* Philately; Violist; Choral singing. *Address:* Department of Public Health, Grenfell Regional Health Services, St Anthony, Newfoundland, Canada AOK 4SO.

BOLAN, William Thomas, b. 13 Feb. 1958, Wichita, Kansas, USA. Doctor of Chiroporactic; Masters in Clinical Nutrition. m. Louanne Stringfield, 16 Aug. 1980, Manhattan, Kansas, 2 sons, 1 daughter. *Education:* BS, Biology, Logan College of Chiropractic, & Kansas State University; DC, Logan College of Chirpractic *Memberships:* Foundation of Chiropractic Education and Research; American Chiropractic Association; International Chiropractic Association; American Academy of Research Biochemists; Kansas Chiropractic Association; International Academy of Acupuncture; Midwest Academy of Preventative Medicine. *Honours:* Valedictorian of Graduating Class, 1982; Outstanding Clinician Award, 1982. *Hobbies:* Golf; Basketball; Volleyball. *Address:* 2940 South Seneca, Wichita, KS 67217, USA.

BOLIN, Darald E. b. 15 May 1930, Eugene, Oregon, USA. Instructor; Lecturer; Inventor: Author. m. Dona Lee Bennett, 14 Jan. 1951, 1 son, 1 daughter. *Education:* DC, Western States Chiropractic College, Portland, 1961. *Appointments:* Private Practice, Chiropractic, Salem, 26 years; Past Instructor, Western States Chiropractic College; Lecturer, High Schools, Service Clubs, etc. *Memberships:* President, Oregon Association of Chiropractic Physicians, 1975; Former Member, Board of Trustees, Western States Chiropractic College; Board of Chiropractic Examiners, 1979; Board of Directors, Gonstead Clinical Studies Society; Statutory Advisory Committee, Medical Care, Oregon Workers Compensation Department, State of Oregon. *Publications:* "Philosophy of Chiropractic", 1974; Co-Inventor, Developer, X-Ray Filters and Shields, known as Bolin X-Ray Equipment. *Honours:* Recipient, Good Citizen Award, United Good Neighbours, 1974. *Hobbies:* Motorhoming; Model Railroad; Anthropology; Archaeology. *Address:* 1803 Lansing Avenue NE, Salem, OR 97303, USA.

BOLTON, Thomas B, b. 14 Nov 1941, England, Professor of Pharmacology. *Education:* BSc, 1964, PhD, 1967, B Vet Med, 1969, London; MA, Oxford, 1975; MRCVS. *Memberships:* British Biophysical Society; The Physiological Society; The British Pharmacological Society; Research Defence Society; University Federation of Animal Welfare. *Publication:* 'Smooth Muscle', 1979. *Address:* Department Pharmacology, St George's Hospital Medical School, London SW17 ORE England.

BONDONNA,Gianni, b. 28 July 1934, Milan, Italy, Director, Division of Medical Oncology, m. Noemi Candini, 13 Oct 1966, Milan, 1 son, 1 daughter. *Education:* Diploma of Liceo Classico, Instituto Zaccaria, Milan, 1953; MD, University of Milan School of Medicine 1959; Board of Hematology, 1964; Board in Oncology. *Appointments:* Research Fellow, Division of Clinical Chemotherapy, Memorial Sloan-Kettering Cancer Centre, NY, USA, 1961-64; Clinical Assistant, 1964-69, Clinical Associate, 1969-75, Director, Division of Medical Oncology, 1975-, Istituto Nazionale Tumori, Milan, Italy; Professor of Hematology, University of Milan, 1984-. *Memberships:* American Society of Clinical Oncology; American Association of Cancer Research; Associazione Italiana di Cancerolgia. *Publications:* 'Manuale di Oncologia Medica', (Editor), 1981, 1983, 1986; 'Breast Cancer: Diagnosis and Management', 1984;'Advances in Anthracyline Chemotherapy: Epirubicin', 1984; 'Clinical Trials in Cancer Medicine', 1985; 'Malignant Lymphomas and Hodgkin's Disease', 1985. *Honours:* Richard and Hinda Rosenthal Foundation Award, 1982; Jeffrey A Gottlieg Memorial Award, 1982; RBS Pharma Award, 1985. *Hobbies:* Music; Archaeology; History. *Address:* Istituto Nazionale Tumori, Via Venezian 1, Milan 20133, Italy.

BONDY, Philip K, b. 15 Dec. 1917, New York, USA. Professor of Medicine. m. Sarah B Ernst, 18 Mar. 1949, Scarsdale, New York, 2 sons, 1 daughter. *Education:* BA; MD. *Appointments:* Associate in Medicine, Assistant Professor, Emory University; Assistant Professor, Associate Professor, Chairman, Department of Medicine, Yale University; Professor, Institute of Cancer research, Post-Graduate Medical Foundation, University of London, England; Honorary Consultant, Royal Marsden Hospital, London; Associate, Chief of Staff Research, West Haven VA Medical Centre. *Memberships:* Master, American College of Physicians; Fellow, Royal College of Physicians; Fellow, Royal Society of Medicine; American Society for Clinical InvestigationsAssociation of American Physicians; Association of Physicians of Great Britain & Ireland; American Federation for Clinical Research; Interurban Clinical Club; Endocrine Society; Society for Experimental Biology & Medicine; Fellow,

American Association for the Advancement of Science. *Publications:* 85 research papers on Endocrinology & Biochemistry, 1942-85; 'Diseases of Metabolism '6th edition 1969, 7th, 1974, 8th, 1980; Section on Metabolic Diseases annually 1954-84 in 'Year book of Medicine', also some 20 additional chapters 1954-85. *Honours:* Brainard Prize, Columbia University, 1938; Phi Beta Kappa, ibid.; Sigma Xi Award, Emory University, 1949; Alpha Omega Alpha, Harvard University, 1942; Several Honorary Memberships & Fellowships. *Hobbies* Playing the 'cello'; Sailing small boats. *Address:* 9 Chestnut Lane, Woodbridge, CT 06525, USA.

BONILLA Romero, Ernesto, b. 16 June 1941, Marcaibo, Venezuela. Head, Neurochemistry, Instituto de Investigaciones Clinicas. m. Lenor Chacin, 14 Jan. 1967, Maracaibo, 1 son, 3 daughters. *Education:* MD, Universidad del Zulia, 1966; MS, 1969, PhD, 1971, Tulane University, USA; MD, Universidad del Zulia, 1974. *Appointments:* Head, Neurochemistry, Instituto de Investigaciones Clinicas, Maracaibo, 1971-; Director Postgraduate Studies, Medicine, 1981-84, Council member, 1984-88,Head, Neurobiology, Fundacite, 1981-, Universidad del Zulia; Associate. Instituto Internacional de Estudios Avanzados, Caracas, 1980-. *Memberships:* Asociacion Venezolana para el Avance de las Cirencias; International Society for Neurochemistry; American Society for Neurosciences; International Brain Research Organization. *Publications:* Co-Author: 'Neurochemical research', 1982; 'Experientia', 1982; 'Brain research', 1982; 'Nature', 1983. *Honours:* Magna Cum Ladum, Universidad del Zulia, 1966; Member Committee, Development of Medical Research in venezuela. *Hobby:* Philosophy. *Address:* Instituto de Investigaciones Clinicas, Apartado 1151, Maracaibo, Venezuela.

BONNAR, John, b. 12 July 1934, Scotland. Dean of Faculty of Health Sciences, Professor, Trinity College, Dublin, Ireland. m. Dr Elizabeth Murray, 17 Sep. 1960, 3 sons, 1 daughter. *Education:* MA, MB, ChB, University of Glasgow, 1952-58; Member, Royal College of Obstetricians & Gynaecologists, 1963; MD (Hons), University of Glasgow, Scotland; Fellow, RCOG, 1971; Fellow, Trinity College, University of Dublin, Republic of Ireland, 1976. *Appointments:* House Surgeon, Southern General Hospital, Glasgow, House Physician, Glasgow Royal Infirmary, 1958-59; Senior House Officer, Bellshill Maternity Hospital & Mairmyres Hospital, Lanarkshire, 1960-61; Registrar, Falkirk Royal Infirmary, Glasgow Victoria Infirmary & Robroyston Hospitals, 1962-64; Senior Registrar, Glasgow Royal Maternity Hospital & Victoria Infirmary, 1965-69; Samuel Research Scholar, Royal College of Obstetricians & Gynaecologists, 1968; First Assistant, Reader in Obstetrics & Gynaecology, Nuffield Department of Obstetrics & Gynaecology, Radcliffe Infirmary, John Radcliffe Hospital, Oxford, 1969; Professor, Head of Obstetrics & Gynaecology, University of Dublin, Trinity College, St James Hospital and Adelaide Hospital, Dublin, Republic of Ireland, 1975- . *Memberships:* Irish Medical Organisations; Royal Society of Medicine; International Society for the Study of Thrombosis & Haemostasis; British Fertility Society; Gynaecological Visiting Society of Great Britain & Ireland; Medical Council of Ireland; Americal Fertility Society. *Publications:* (co-author with W Hathaway) "Perinatal Coagulation", 1980; (editor) "Recent Advances in Obstetrics & Gynaecology", 1983, 1986; Numerous publications on Haemostasis & Thrombosis in relation to Obstetrics & Gynaecology. *Hobbies:* Fishing; Gardening. *Address:* Trinity College Department of Obstetrics & Gynaecology, St James' Hospital, Dublin 8, Republic of Ireland.

BONNELL, John Aubrey Luther, b. 2 Mar. 1924, Cymmer, South Wales, Medical Adviser, Electricity Council and Central Electricity Generating Board. m. 24 Mar. 1966, Epsom, 2 daughters. *Education:* Kings College, London; Kings College Hospital; MB BS; MRCS; LRCP, 1948. *Appointments:* House Surgeon, Casualty Officer, Metropolitan Hospital, London, 1948; House Physician, Oldchurch Hospital, Romford, 1949; Assistant Physician, Department for Research in Industrial Medicine (Medical Research Council), London Hospital; Honorary Clincial Assistant, London Hospital, 1950; Senior Medical Officer, Central Electricity Authority, 1957; Deputy Chief Nuclear Health and Safety Officer, Central Electricity Generating Board, 1959; Medical Adviser, CEGB, 1975; Medical Adviser, Electricity Council, 1978; Regional Speciality Adviser, Occupational Medicine, South West Thames Regional Health Authority, 1980. *Memberships:* International Commission on Occupational Health, Member of Board; Royal Society of Medicine, Past President, Occupational Medicine Section; Society of Occupational Medicine, Past President; Worshipful Society of Apothecaries, London; Society for Radiological Protection, Past President. *Publications:* Various Papers, Cadmium Poisoning, 1950-60; "Radiation Protection 1960-85"; "Studies on Health Effects Electro Magnetic Fields 1980-85"; Contributions on various aspects of occupational health 1950-85. *Hobbies:* Music; Bridge; Gardening. *Address:* 71 The Green, Ewell, Surrey KT17 3JX, England.

BOODOOSINGH, Lal Andrew, b. 13 June 1940, Trinidad. Director, Day and Evening Treatment Programme. m. Artje P de Jong, 30 Aug. 1959, Vancouver, Canada, 1 son, 1 daughter. *Education:* BSc, University of British Columbia, Canada; MD, Ottawa; FRCP, Canada. *Appointments:* Chief Resident Psychiatrist, University of Ottawa, 1970-72; Staff Psychiatrist, Child and Adolescent Psychiatry, Royal Ottawa Hospital; Director, Day and Evening Treatment Programme, Royal Ottawa Hospital, currently; Assistant Clinical Professor, Health Sciences Faculty, University of Ottawa. *Memberships:* Canadian Medical Association; American and Canadian Psychiatric Associations; American Association of Child and Adolescent Psychiatry. *Hobbies:* Tennis; Parapsychology. *Address:* 1145 Carling Avenue, Ottawa, Ontario, Canada K1Z 7K4.

BOOR, Myron Vernon, b. 21 Dec 1942, Wadena, Minnesota, USA. Clinical Psychologist. *Education:* BS, Psychology, University of Iowa, 1965; MA, Clinical Psychology, 1967, PhD, Clinical Psychology, 1970, Southern Illionois University; MS, Hygiene, University of Pittsburgh, 1981. *Appointments:* Researach Psychologist, Milwaukee County Mental Health Center, Milwaukee, Wisconsin, 1970-72; Assistant to Associate Professor, Fort Hays State University, Hays, Kansas, 1972-79; National Institute of Mental Health Postdoctoral Fellow, in Psychiatric Epidemiology, University of Pittsburgh and Western Psychiatric Institute and Clinic, 1979-81; Research Psychologist, Rhode Island Hospital and Assistant Professor of Psychiatry and Human Behaviour, Brown University, 1981-83; Clinical Psychologist, Northern Kentucky Comprehensive Care Center, Florence, Kentucky, 1984; Clinical Psychologist, Mental Health Management Inc, Newman Memorial County Hospital, Emporia, Kansas, 1984 -. *Memberships:* American Psychological Association; International Society for the Study of Multiple Personality. *Publications:* 'Effects of United States Presidential elections on suicide and other causes of death' 'American Sociological review' 1981; 'The multiple personality epidemic' 'Journal of Nervous and Mental Disease' 1982; 'Psychiatric aspects of traffic accidents' with, MT Tsuang and JA Fleming 'American Journal of Psychiatry' 1985. *Honours:* National Institute of Mental Health Postdoctoral Fellowship (Natinal Research Service Award) in Psychiatric Epidemiology at University of Pittsburgh and the Western Psychiatric Institute and Clinic,

1979-81. *Address:* 2225 Prairie, Emporia, KS 66801, USA.

BORCHGREVINK, Hans Henrik Christian, b. 20 June 1926, Röyken, Norway. Consultant Plastic Surgeon. m. Björg Rönneberg, 5 Nov. 1948, Hof, Vestfold, Norway, 1 son, 2 daughters. *Education:* MD, University of Oslo, 1952; Authorised Specialist in Plastic Surgery, 1967. *Appointments:* Senior House Officer, Red Cross Hospital, Oslo, 1953; Medical Officer, Norwegian Army, 1953-54; SHO, Röros General Hospital, 1954-56; General Practice, Horten, 1956-558; SHO, Oslo City Hospital, Surgery/Pathology, 1958-60; Registrar, Plastic Surgery (with Prof H Schjelderup), Bergen 1961-62; SHO, Plastic Surgery, Odstock, Salisbury, England, 1962-63; SHO Plastic Surgery, Frenchay,Bristol, England, 1963; Registrar, Plastic Surgery, Rikshospitalet, University Hospital, Oslo, 1963-66; Locum Head of this Department, 1965-66, 1967-68; Registrar (General Surgery), Rikshospitalet, Oslo, 1966-67; Consultant Plastic Surgeon, Rikshospitalet, University Hospital, Department of Plastic Surgery, 1967-. *Memberships:* Norwegian Medical Association; Norwegian Society of Medicine; Norwegian Association of Surgeons; Norwegian Association of Plastic Surgeons; Scandinavian Association of Plastic Surgeons (Honorary Secretary); British Association of Plastic Surgeons (Royal College of Surgeons); International Confederation of Plastic & Rec. Surgery; Fellow, Royal Society of Medicine, England. *Publications:* "Cleft Lip & Palate" (with Bergland & Böhn), 1968; 'The Rotation-Advancement Operation of Millard as applied to Secondary Cleft Lip Deformities', in Cleft Palate Journal, 1969; 'Cleft Palate Repair' in 'Current Operative Surgery', (editor I.F.K. Muir); 1985; Numerous articles. *Hobbies:* Photography; Drawing; Wood-carving. *Address:* Bleikerhaugen 66, N-1370 Asker, Norway.

BORDEN, Ernest Carleton, b. 12 July 1939, Norwalk, Connecticut, USA. Professor, Departments of Human Oncology & Medicine, University of Wisconsin. m. Louise Dise, 24 June 1967, 2 daughters. *Education:* AB, Harvard University, 1961; MD, Duke University, 1966. *Appointments include:* Medical Officer, US Public Health Service, Viropathology Laboratory, National Communicable Disease Centre/Clinical instructor, Emory University & Grady Memorial Hospital, 1968-70; Postdoctoral Fellow, Oncology Division, Department of Medicine, Johns Hopkins University, 1970-73; Assistant Professor, Associate Professor, Professor, Divison of Clinical & Departments of Human Oncology & Medicine, Wisconsin Clincial Cancer Centre, University Hospitals & School of Medicine, University of Wisconsin, 1973-; Chief, Division of Clinical Oncology, William S. Middleton Memorial Veterans Hospital, Madison, 1977-81. *Memberships include:* Diplomate, 1973, American Board of Internal Medicine; Diplomate, 1975, Medical Oncology, ibid; American Association for the Advancement of Science; Aemrican Society for Microbiology; Fellow, American College of Physicians; American Association for Cancer Research; International Society for Interferon Research; etc. *Publications:* Over 120 learned articles on host response to virus & tumour & therapeutic stimulation of immunity. *Honours include:* Davison Scholar, Oxford University, 1966; Junior Faculty Fellow, American Cancer Society, 1975-78; Wisconsin State Medical Society; Elvehjem Memorial Lecture, 1983; American Cancer Society Professor of Clincial Oncology, 1984-; Award of Merit, Eastern Cooperative Oncology Group, 1984. *Address:* Department of Human Oncology, Wisconsin Clinical Cancer Centre, University of Wisconsin Clinical Sciences Centre, 600 Highland Avenue. Madison, WI 53792, USA.

BOREL, Jacques Paul, b. 27 Apr. 1931, Le Pouget, France. University Professor. m. Baschet Nadine

Rahaele, 9 July 1960, Paris, 2 sons, 2 daughters. *Education:* Professor of Biochemistry; PhD; MD. *Appointments:* Assistant Professor, University of Nantes, 1957-61; Associate Professor, Biochemistry, 1962-67, Professor, 1967-85, University of Reims; visiting Professor, University of Pennsylvania, USA , 1975-76. *Memberships:* American Association for Advancement of Science; European College Tissue Culture Association; American College Tissue Culture Association; Societe Chimie Biologique; Societe Francaise Chimie; Societe Francaise du Tissue Conjontif; Societe de Biologie clinique. *Publications:* Author of many papers on biochemistry, biophysics in professional journals. Books including: 'Comment Prescrire un Examen de Biochimi', 1983-85; 'Textbook of Biochemistry', 1986. *Address:* Lab Biochemistry, Faculty of Medicine, 51 rue Cognacq, Jay Reims, France 51095.

BORKOWSKI, Tomasz, b. 1 Mar. 1925, Labunie, Poland. Professor; Doctor of Medicine. m. Madecka Irena, 21 July 1949, Lublin, 1 daughter. *Education:* MD. *Appointments:* Assistant, 1948-61, Junior Lecturer, 1962-70, Professor, 1970-, Head, Biochemistry, 1965-, Vice Rector, 1972-81, Medical Academy, Lublin. *Memberships Polish Biochemical Society, President, 1971-74; International Society for Neurochemistry; Societe de Chimie Biologique,. Publications:* 'Nucleic Acids in the Central Nervous System', Monograph in Polish, 1962; Articles: 'Fractionation of Specific Mitochondrial and Cytoplasmic tRNAs Obtained from Calf Brain', 'Journal Neurochemistry', 1975; 'Occurence of Amionacyl-tRNA Synthetase Complexes in Calf Brain', 'Archives Biochemistry, Biophysics', 1981. *Hobbies:* Tennis; Skiing. *Address:* Dept. Biochemistry, Medical Academy, Lubartowska 85, 20-123 Lublin, Poland.

BORN, Gustav Victor Rudolf, b. 29 July 1921, Göttingen. Professor, Pharmacology, King's College, University of London. m. Faith Elisabeth Maurice-Williams, 3 sons, 2 daughters. *Education:* MB, ChB, Edinburgh; MA, D.Phil, Oxon; FRCP; FRS; Various hospital appointments, 1943-52. *Appointments:* Scientific Staff, Medical Research Council, Toxicology Research Unit, 1952-53; Research Officer, Senior Research Officer, University of Oxford, 1953-60; Shield Professor, Pharmacology, University of Cambridge, 1973-78; Fellow, Gonville and Caius College, Cambridge, 1973-78; various Visiting Professorships and Consultanships; etc. *Memberships Include:* Committee Member, British Pharmacological Society; Chairman, Government Grant Board H, Royal Society; Examiner, Pharmacology, Universities of Edinburgh, Cambridge, Oxford; Scientific Committee, Nufflied Institute of Comparative Medicine, Zoological Society of London; Research Grants Committee, British Heart Foundation; Council, International Society of Thrombosis and Haemostasis; Trustee, Heineman Research Center. *Publications:* Numerous articles in professional journals; various lectures including: Beyer Lectures, University of Wisconsin, 1969; Lo Yuk Tong Foundation Lecture, University of Hong Kong, 1978; Sir Henry Dale Lecture, London, 1981; Rokitansky memorial Lecture, Vienna, 1983; Annual Oration, Medical Society, London, 1983; etc. *Honours:* Recipient, numerous honours and awards including:Fellow, Royal Society, Royal College of Physicians; Dr. Hon. Causa, Universities of Bordeaux, Munster, Leuven and Edinburgh; Albrecht-von-Haller Medallist, University of Gottingen; Ratschow Memorial Medal, International Angiology Curatorium; Auenbrugger Medal, University of Graz, 1984; President, VIIth International Congress on Thrombosis and Haemostatis, 1979; Foundation President, British Society for Thrombosis and Haemostasis; Professor, Foundation de France, Paris, 1982-84; etc. *Address:* Dept. of Pharmacology, King's College, Strand, London WC2R 2LS, England.

BORRAJO, Emilio, b. 15 Aug. 1932, Logrono, Spain. Professor of Paediatrics & Child Welfare. m. 4 Apr. 1960, 2 sons, 2 daughters. *Education:* MD, Specialist in Paediatrics & Paediatric Endocrinology. *Appointments:* Assistant Professor, Department of Paediatrics, Valencia; Associate Professor of Paediatrics, Murcia. *Memberships:* Paediatrics Society of South-Eastern Spain; Valencian Society of Paediatrics; Endocrinology Section, Spanish Paediatrics, Society. *Hobbies:* Golf; Tennis; Music; Reading. *Address:* Department of Paediatrics, Faculty of Medicine, Espinardo - Murcia, Spain.

BORSOS, Tibor, b. 12 Mar. 1927, Budapest, Romania. Chief of Laboratory of Immunobiology. m. Ruth Moser, 17 July 1950, Washington, District of Columbia, USA, 2 sons. *Education:* BA, Catholic University of America, 1954; ScD, Johns Hopkins University, 1958. *Appointments:* Research Associate 1958-60, Assistant Professor 1960-62, Johns Hopkins School of Medicine; Senior Scientist 1962-66, Section Chief 1966-85, Associate Chief of Laboratory 1971-85, Chief of Laboratory of Immunobiology 1985-, National Cancer Institute. *Membership:* American Association of Immunologists. *Publications:* "Molecular Basis of Complement Action", (with H J Rapp), 1970; 200 scientific articles. *Honour:* NIH Director's Award, 1976. *Hobbies:* Music; Hiking. *Address:* NCI-FCRF, Building 560 room 1271, Frederick, Md 21701, USA.

BORST, Hans Georg, b. 17 Oct. 1927, Munich, Germany. Chairman, Surgical Centre. m. Petra A. Borst, 4 Apr. 1968, Munich, 1 son, 3 daughters. *Education:* MD, Harvard Medical School, USA, 1953; D.Med., Marburg University, 1955; Dozent, Munich University, 1962; Full Professor, Hannover, 1968. *Appointments:* Resident, Senior Resident, Surgery, Marburg and Munich Univerisities, 1956-68; Chairman, Surgical Centre, Hannover Medical school, 1968-. *Memberships include:* Bayrische Chirurgenvereinigung; Deutsch Gesellschaft für Chirurgie; Deutsch Gesellschaft für Thorax; International Society for Cardiovascular Surgery; American Society of Thoracic Surgeons; Cardio Thoracic Society; Cardiac Surgeons Club; Honorary Member, American Association for Thoracic Surgery; European Society for Experimental Surgery; Corresponding Member, British Cardiac Society; International Society for Heart Transplantation. *Publications:* 315 in Thoracic and Cardiovascular Surgery, 25 Monographs or articles in Monographies, 1955-; Editor, 'The Thoracic and Cardiovascular Surgeon', 1968-. *Honour:* Langenbeck Prize for Surgical Research, 1968. *Hobbies:* Alpinism; Music; Painting. *Address:* Medizinische Hochschule Hannover, Klinik für Thorax, Herz und Gefässchirurgie, Konstanty-Gutschow Str, 8, D-3000 Hannover 61, Federal Republic of Germany.

BORVENDEG, János, b. 25 June 1935, Budapest, Hungary, Head, Biomedical Division, National Institute of Pharmacy, Budapest, Hungary, m. 12 July 1962, 1 son. *Education:* Semmelweis Medical School, Budapest, 1959; Specialist for Medical laboratory Examinations, 1965; Specialist for Internal Diseases, 1968; Specialist for Clinicopharmacology, 1981; MD; PhD. *Appointments:* Assistant Doctor, Department for Internal Diseases, Municipal Hospital, Oze, Hungary; Scienctific co-worker, Department of Pharmacology, Head of Medical Department, Institute of Drug Research, Budapest; Professor's Assistant, Department of Endocrinology, University Medical Clinic, Szeged; Head of Biomedical Division, National Institute of Pharmacy, Budapest. *Memberships:* Member, Steroid Committee, Hungarian Academy of Science; Member, Committee of Drug. *Publications:* Author of over 50 publications including, 'Studies on the structure-activity relationships of synthetic LHRH analogs', (with others), 1974; 'Radioimmunoassay

of beta-endorphin: Immunoreactive substances in the brain and the pituitary', (co-author), 1978; 'Drugs of Future', 1985. *Hobbies:* Music; Qualified organist. *Address:* National Institute of Pharmacy, PO Box 450, H-1051 Budapest, Hungary.

BOSCH, Leendert, b. 13 Nov. 1924, Appingedam, Netherlands. Professor, Biochemistry. m. 1950. *Education:* PhD. *Appointments:* Research associate, Netherlands Cancer Institute; Extra Ordinarius Free University Amsterdam; Professor,Biochemistry, University of Leiden, Netherlands. *Membership:* Royal Dutch Academy of Arts and Sciences. *Publications:* 'Protein Synthesis', Editor, 1972. *Address:* Dept. of Biochemistry, Wassenaaresweg 64, Leiden-Neth, Netherlands.

BOSSIE, Norman L., b. 2 July 1940, Lincoln, New Hampshire, USA. Assistant Vice President, Medical Imaging Services, Holy Cross Hospital. m. Marie Lorraine Interbartolo, 21 Nov. 1961, Boston, 2 sons, 2 daughters. *Education:* ASC., Northeastern University, 1971; BSc., Manhattan College, 1975; MPA, New York University, 1978. *Appointments:* Chief Technologist, Peter Bent Brigham Hospital, 1966-71; Radiology Administrator, Greenwich Hospital Association, 1971-76; Administrative Assistant, Newark Beth Israel Medical Centre, Newark, 1976-80; Administrator, Radiology Services, University of Michigan Hospital, 1980-81. *Publication:* "Capital Equipment Acquisition, Strategies for Survival", 1985. *Honours:* Nominee, American College of Hospital Administrators. *Hobbies:* Sailing; Reading. *Address:* 14821 Perrywood Drive, Burtonsville, MD 20866, USA.1950,

BOTHS, Marthinus Christoffel, b. 10 Apr. 1922, Cape Town, Republic of South Africa. Professor and Head, Department of Haematology. m. 4 Dec. 1956, White River, 2 daughters. *Education:* MB ChB, Cape Town; DCP, London, England; FRCPath. *Appointments:* Senior Government Pathologist, Durban, Republic of South Africa, 1952-53; Director, Provincial Blood Grouping Laboratory, Cape Town; Honorary Senior Lecturer, Pathology and Human Genetics, University of Cape Town; Honorary Senior Lecturer, Pathology, University of Stellenbosch 1953-79;Director of Pathology Department of Health, 1981-82; Professor of Haematology, Medical University of Southern Africa, 1982-. *Memberships:* South African Society for Pathology; Southern African Society for Haematology; Royal Society of South Africa; Transplantation Society of SouthAfrica. *Publications:* Author of numerous contributions to books and national and International medical journals. *Honours:* Oppenheimer Memorial Travelling Fellowship, 1967; Gold Medal, South African Technological Societies, 1969; Visiting Professor, Department of surgery, Gothenburg University, 1970. *hobbies:* Chairman, Board, Committee for Research and Education, Nationale Botanic Gardens of South Africa; Club Captain, Pretoria Harlequins Rugby Club. *Address:* Department of Haematology, Medunsa 0204, Republic of South Africa.

BOTTINI, Egidio, b. 10 Mar. 1931, Italy. Professor. m. Gloria Fulvia, 16 Oct. 1971, 2 sons. *Education:* MD. *Appointments:* Assistant Professor, Paediatrics; Chief Investigator, National Research Council; Associate Professor, Population Genetics; Professor of Genetics; Professor, Interdisciplinary Centre of Pure & Applied Mathematics of Lincei National Academy; Professor, Human Development, 2nd University of Rome. *Memberships:* Ordine Dei Meici; European Society for Paediatric Research; Associazione Genetica Italiana. *Publications:* Articles in numerous professioanl journals including: 'Science'; 'American Journal Human Genetics'; 'Vox Sang.'; 'The Lancet'; 'Journal of Paediatrics'; 'Journal of Medical Genetics'; 'Experientia'; etc. *Hobbies:* Gardening; Agriculture. *Address:* Largo Olgiata 15, Rome, Italy.

BOTWIN, Clifford Alan, b. 17 May 1942, Elizabeth, New Jersey, USA. Orthopaedic Surgeon. m. Linda, 26 Dec. 1979, Edison, New Jersey, 3 sons, 2 daughters. *Education:* Rutgers University, 1965; BS, Newark College of Arts & Sciences, 1965; B.Ph, Rutgers College of Pharmacy, 1965; DO, Kansas City College of Osteopathic Medicine, 1971; Internship, Union Memorial General Hospital, New Jersey, 1971-72; Residency, Orthopaedic Surgery, Delaware Valley Hospital, Bristol, Pennsylvania, 1972-76; Medical Licensure, Missouri 1971, New Jersey, Pennsyulvania, Florida, 1972. Board Certification, Orthopaedic Surgery, American Academy of Osteopathic Surgeons, 1982, American Osteopathic Board of Orthopaedic Surgery, 1985. *Appointments:* Clinical Instructor, Department of Surgery, College of Osteopathic Medicine of New Jersey, 1978; Adjunct Clinical Associate, New York College of Osteopathic Medicine, 1978; Secretary, Medical Staff, Union Memorial General Hospital, 1980-84; Osteopathic Orthopaedic Surgeon. *Memberships include:* Lambda Omicron Gamma Osteopathic Fraternity, 1971; American Osteopathic Academy of Sports Medicine, 1975 (Founder Member); International Arthroscopy Association (Founder Member), 1974; Director, New Jersey Association of Osteopathic Physicians & Surgeons, 1981-85, Secretary, 1985-. *Publications:* Various lectures & Scientific papers. *Honours:* Psi Sigma Alpha, 1971; Sigma Sigma Phi, 1971; Ethicon Writing Award, 1974; Mead Johnson Award, 1975; Fellow, American Academy of Osteopathic Physicians & Surgeons, 1971. *Address:* 900 Stuyvesant Avenue, Union, NJ 07083USA.

BOUDOULAS, Harisios, b. 3 Nov. 1935, Greece. m. Olga Paspati, 27 Feb. 1971, 1 son, 1 daughter. *Education:* MD, University of Salonica, 1959; Licenced to Practice Medicine, Greece, 1960; Doctorate Diploma, University of Salonica, 1967; Board of Internal Medicine, 1967; Board of Cardiology, 1967; various other Diplomas etc. *Appointments Include:* Resident, Internal Medicine, Red Cross Hospital, Athens, 1960-61; Resident, Internal Medicine, 1962-64, Resident Cardiology, 1964-66, Attending Physician, Renal unit, 1966-67, Attending Physician,Coronary Care Unit, 1967-69, Lecturer, medicine, 1969-70, First Medical Clinic, University of Salonica, Greece; Postdoctoral Fellow, Instructor, Ohio State University, USA, 1970-73; Senior Lecturer, medicine, head, Coronary Care, 1st Medical Clinic, University of Salonica, 1973-75; Assistant Professor, medicine, Division of Cardiology, 1975-78, Director, Cardiovascular Non-Invasive Research Laboratories, 1978-80, Associate Professor, medicine, Cardiology, 1978-80, Ohio State University; Professor, medicine, 1980-82, Director, Clinical Cardiovascular Research, 1980-82, Wayne State University, USA; Acting Director, Caridology, Wayne State University, 1982; Professor of Medicine, Cardiology, Ohio State University college of Medicine, 1982-; Professor, College of Pharmacy, Ohio State University, 1983-. *Memberships:* Numerous professional organisations including Medical Association of Salonica, Greece; Greek Society of Biochemistry; Affiliate, Royal Society of Medicine; Greek Renal Association; American Heart Association; Fellow, American College of Cardiology; Greek Heart Association; etc. *Publications:* Over 160 articles in scientific journals and books; over 130 presentaitons at national and international meetings. *Honours Include:* Distinguished Research Investigator, Central Ohio Heart Chapter, American Heart Association, Columbus, 1983. *Address:* 4185 Mumford Ct., Columbus, OH 43220, USA

BOUDREAU, Robert James, b. 27 Dec. 1950. Lethbridge, Canada. Assistant Professor. m. Francine Archambault, 16 Jan. 1982, Montreal. *Education:* Diplomate, American Board of Nuclear Medicine; BSc Honours Biochemistry, University of Saskatchewan; PhD Pharmacology, University of British Columbia; MD, LMCC, University of Calgary.

Appointments: Residency training in Diagnostic Radiology and Nuclear Medicine, McGill University Affiliated Hospitals; Assistant Professor (part-time), Division of Pharmacology, University of Calgary; Assistant Professor, Division of Nuclear Medicine, Department of Radioloogy, University of Minnesota Hospitals, Minneapolis, Minnesota, USA. *Memberships:* Academic Council, Society of Nuclear Medicine; Radiological Society of North America; Royal College of Physicians and Surgeons; Canadian Medical Association; Fellow, Royal College of Physicians, Canada. *Publications:* 16 publications and book chapters; 11 abstracts. *Honours:* Society of Chemical Industry Gold Key Award, 1972; Medical Research Council Studentship, 1972-75; Canadian Heart Foundation Medical Scientist Fellow, 1976-78; Society for Clinical Investigation Young Investigator Award, 1978. *Hobbies:* Sailing; Skiing; Gardening; Computers.*Address:* University of Minnesota Hospitals, Box 382 Mayo, 420 Delaware Street, South East, Minneapolis, MN 85455, USA.

BOULANGER, Jean Baptiste, b. 24 Aug. 1922, Edmonton, Canada. Professor, Psychiatry, University of Montreal; Training, Suepervisor, Anly Canadian Institute of Psychiatry; Consultant Child Psychiatrist, Ste Justine Hospital; Training Staff, Lafontaine Hospital; Neurological Psychiatrist, (Adult & Child). *Education:* BA, University of Montreal, 1941; Faculty of Law, 1941-42, Faculty Science, PCB, 1943; MD, LMCC, 1948; MA, French, Language, literature, McGill University, 1950; Studied, Harvard University Institute of Medicine, University of Paris, Sorbonne; Certificate, Specialist Province of Quebec; FRCP (C), 1955. *Appointments:* Lecturer, 1953, Professor, 1954, Associate Professor, 1959, Coord Behavioural Science Course, 1968-77; Professor, 1970- , Psychiatry, Medical University of Montreal; Staff Neurologist, Psychiatric Hospital, Notre Dame, 1953-61; Staff Child Psychiatrist, 1958- , Director Group Psychotherapist, 1959-76, Hospital St Justine; Consultant, Institute Prevost, 1969-73; Consultant, Lakeshore General Hospital, 1965-78; Consultant, Hospital General Verdun, 1965-70; Consultant, Hospital L.H. Lafontaine, 1971-77; 1981- ; Senior Research Bioethics, Clinical Research Isntitute, Montreal, 1977-78; Consultant, Institute Pinel, 1978-81. *Memberships:* Numerous professional organisations including: International Psychoanlis Association; Founder Member, Training & Supervisory Psychoanlys; President, Canadian Psychiatric Association, 1975-76; etc. *Publications:* "Psychol d'amour & drame intime M Proust", 'Amer Franc', 1951; "Methodes psychanal collect enfants", 3rd World Cong Psychiatry', 1961; Articles in Canadian Journal Psychiatry'; 'Psychoanal Psychdr'; etc. *Honours:* Prix de la Langue Francaise, Medaille de vermeil, Academie Francaise, Paris, 1935. *Hobbies:* Philosophy of Mind; Art Collection; Aerobic Dancing. *Address:* 3610 Avenue Atwater, Montreal H3H 1Y6, Canada.

BOULTON, Alan A, b. 14 Mar. 1936, Cheshire, England. Director of Psychiatric Research Division, Department of Health; Professor, Department of Psychiatry, University of Saskatchewan m. Anne McCall, 28 Mar. 1959, Poynton, Cheshire, 2 sons, 2 daughters. *Education:* BSc, 1958; PhD, 1962; DSc, 1976; University of Manchester. *Appointments:* Research Assistant, Biochemistry, University of Manchester, 1960-62; Honorary Research Fellow, Physiology, University of Birmingham, 1962-68; Member, MRC Unit, Research Chemical PathologyMental Disorders, University of Birmingham, 1962-68; Chief Research Biochemist, sDepartment of Health, Psychiatric Research Division, Saskatoon, 1968-69; Director, Biochemical Research, 1969-71; Director, Psychiatric Research Division, 1971-; Associate Professor, Department of Psychiatry, University of Saskatchewan, 1971-75; Professor, 1975-. *Memberships:* Member several professional organizations. *Publications:*

'Neurobiology of the Trace Amines: Analytical, Physiological, Pharmacological, Behavioural and Clinical Aspects'; 1984; 'Neuropsychopharmacology of the Trace Amines: Experimental and Clinical Aspects', 1984; 1985; Co-editor: 'Neuromathods', a major series in the Neurosciences; 180 papers in International Journals. *Honours:* Clark Institute of Psychiatry, University of Toronto, Prize, 1970; Grass Visiting Scientist, Mayo Clinic, 1977, Central Savannah River Area, 1981; DSc, Manchester University,1976; President Canadian College of Neuropsychophasmacology 1984-86; Chairman, International Society for Neurochemistry, 1984-87; *Hobbies:* Reading Biographies; Piano; Politics. *Address:* Psychiatric Research Division, A114 Cancer and Medical Research Building, University of Saskatchewan, Saskatoon, Saskatchewan, Canada 57N DWO.

BOULTON, Thomas Babington, b. 6 Nov. 1925, Bishop Auckland, England, Consultant Anaesthetist Nuffield Department of Anaesthetics, University of Oxford and Royal Berkshire Hospital, m. Helen Currey Brown, 30 Aug. 1952, Cumberland, 2 sons, 1 daughter. *Education:* MA, MB, BChir, University of Cambridge, St Bartholemew's Hospital, London; FFARCS; FDSRCS; TD; MA, University of Oxford. *Appointments:* House Srugeon, Junior Resident Anaesthetist, 1949-50, Registrar, Senior Registrar, 1952-58, Consultant Anaesthetist, Consultant in Charge of Intensive Care, 1961-73, St Bartholemew's Hospital London; Graded Specialist (Captain), Royal Army Medical Corps, 1950-52; Registrar, Senior Registrar, General Hospital Southend on Sea, 1952-58; Instructor in Anaesthesia, University of Michigan, USA, 1956-57; Consultant Anaesthetist, Royal Berkshire Hospital, Reading, Berkshire, England, 1958-61; Seconded to childrens Medical Relief Internation, Vietnam, 1969; Editor of 'anaesthesia', 1972-83; Territorial Army Volunteer Reserve, 1952-86. *Memberships:* President, 1984-86, Association of Anaesthetists of Great Britain and Ireland; President, Section of Anaesthetics, 1983-84, Royal Society of Medicine; Member of the Board, Faculty of Anaesthetists of the Royal College of Surgeons of England. *Publications:* 'Anaesthesia for Diagnostic Procedures', 1962; ''Progress in Anaesthesiology'', (Editor), 1970; 'Anaesthesia and Resuscitation in Difficult Environments', 1973; ''Anaesthesia Beyond the Major Medical Centre'', (Editor), 1985; Author of various professional articles. *Honours:* Mentioned in Despatches, Malaya, 1952; Emergency Reserve Decoration, 1968; Territorial Army Decoration, 1979. *Hobbies:* Gardening; Household carpentry. *Address:* Townsend Farm, Streatley, Berkshire RG8 9JX, England.

BOULUKOS, Peter Nicholas, b. 25 Jan. 1937 Amityville, New York, USA, Chiropractic Physician. *Education:* DC, Columbia Institute of Chiropractic; St Vladimirs Orthodox Theological Seminary; Diploma, Rizareios Therological School, Athens, Greece; Holy Cross Orthodox Theological School. *Appointments:* Executive Secretary, 7th Archdiocesan District, Detroit, USA, 1963-64; Youth Director, St Mary's Greek Orthodox Church, Minneapolis, Minn, 1964-65; Lay Assistant Administrator, Holy Trinity Greek Orthodox Church, New Rochelle, NY, 1965-68. *Memberships:* American Chiropractic Association; NY Chapter Parker Chiropractic Research Foundation; NY Chapter, Sacral Occipital Technique Society; Bergen Passaic Counties Chiropractic Society; International Systemic Health Organisation. *Hobbies:* Skiing; Sailing; Stained glass; Singing in choral groups; Hiking; Travel. *Address:* 175 Cedar Lane, Teaneck, NJ 07666, USA.

BOURDEAU, (Joseph Paul Lionel) Yvon, b. 30 Nov. 1938, Montreal, Canada. Orthopaedic Medicine. m. Yvonne Seguin, 5 June 1961, Williamstown, 1 son, 4 daughters. *Education:* Ba Pre-medicine 1960, MD 1964, University of Ottawa; Junior Rotating Internship, St Mary's Hospital, Montreal, Quebec,1964-65; Licenciate, Medical Council of Canada, 1965; Certificate, College of Family Physicians of Canada, 1973; Yearly refresher courses in general medicine, 1982. *Appointments:* General solo practice, Alexandria, Ontario, 1965-77; Active member 1965-77, Chief of Medical staff 1966-69, Glengary Memorial Hospital; Courtesy Staff, Hotel Dieu Hospital, Cornwall General Hospital, Cornwall; Coroner, United Counties of Stormont, Dundas and Glengarry, 1967-72; Casualty Officer, Centre Hospitalier Regional de l'Outaouais, Hull, Quebec, 1977-83; Part-time Orthopaedic Medicine, 1977-83; Executive Administrator, Service d'Urgence de l'Outaouais, 1978-80; Orthopaedic Medicine, 1983-. *Memberships:* Canadian Medical Association; Ontario Medical Association; College of Family Physicians of Canada; Federation des Medicins Omnipraticiens du Quebec; Canadian Medical Protective Association; Society of Orthopaedic Medicine; North American Academy of Manipulative Medicine; American Association of Orthopaedic Medicine; Canadian Association of Orthopaedic Medicine. *Address:* 45 East Park Drive, Gloucester, Ontario K1B 3Z6, Canada.

BOURNE, Geoffrey, b. 17 Nov. 1909, Perth Australia. Vice Chancellor Professor, Nutrition, St George's University School of Medicine, Grenada. m. Maria Nelly Golarz, 31 Oct. 1959, Freeport, 2 sons, by previous marriage. *Education:* BSc., MS., DSc., University of Western Australia; P.Phil., University of Oxford, England. *Appointments:* Biologist, Australian Institute of Anatomy, 1934; Biochemist, Commonwealth of Australia Advisory Council, 1936; Demonstrator, Physiology, University of Oxford, 1938; Reader, Histology, University of London, 1949; Professor, Chairman, Anatomy, Emory University, 1956; Director, Yerkes Primate Research Center, University, 1962; Vice Chancellor, Professor, Nutrition, St Georges University School of Medicine, Grenada, West Indies, 1978-. *Memberships:* Fellow: Royal Society of Medicine, Institute of Biology, Zoological Society of London, American Ageing Society; American Association Anatomists; Aerospace Medical Association; Intercontinental Institute of Astronautics. *Publications:* Over 600 articles in professional journals;100 volumes (edited) International review of Cytology; 50 volumes (edited) World Review Nutrition & Dietetics; etc. *Honours:* Recipient, various honours and awards including Beif Memorial Fellowship for Medical Research, 1938-41. *Hobbies:* Surfing; Gem Cutting; Writing. *Address:* St Georges University School of Medicine, Grenada, West Indies.

BOURRIER-REYNAUD, Colette Simone, b. 18 Apr. 1930, Lantosque, France. Paediatrician; Allergologist; Consultant Physician Attache. m. Michel Bourrier, 24 Dec. 1958, Nice, 1 son. *Education:* Certificates in Physics, Chemistry, Biology, Physical Chemistry and Natural Sciences, 1949; MD, University of Paris; Diploma in Occupational Medicine, Faculty of Medicine, Paris, 1959; Specialist Certification in Paediatrics, University of Paris, 1960; Qualified Doctor in Allergology; Non-resident medical student, Paris Hospitals, 1952. *Appointments:* Occupational Physician, Compagnie Industrialle des telephones, Paris, 1957-62; Physician in Mother and Child Care, Public Assistance of the Seine area; Social Security of Paris region; Town Hall of Vieux Saint Ouen; City of Nice; Specialist Physician in Nice, 1962- (Paediatrics, Infantile Allergology); Physician attached to Regional Hospital Centre of Nice, 1965-; Currently Consultant Attaché. *Memberships:* Titular Member, French Allergy Society; Council of Administration ANAFORCAL; European Academy of Allergy; Secretary-General, Immuno-Allergological Study Circle of Côte d'Azur, 1981; Nice Medical Society; European Academy of Allergology and Clinical Immunology, 1971-; Founder Member, Nice

Paediatrics Study Circle, 1971. *Publications:* Contributor to professional journals, books, etc; Author of several non-medical publications. *Hobbies:* Public Life (Municipal Councillor); Historical and Ethno-sociological Research in local area. *Address:* 9 Boulevard Gorbella, 06100, France.

BOVORNKITTI, Somchai, b. 26 Feb. 1929, Chantaburi, Thailand. Professor of Medicine; Chief, Division of Respiratory Disease and Tuberculosis. m. 22 Dec. 1974, Bangkok, 2 sons, 2 daughters. *Education:* MD, 1952; Diploma in Tropical Medicine and Hygiene Liverpool, England, 1953; Tuberculosis Diseases diploma, Wales, 1954; DSc, Bangkok, Thailand, 1963. *Appointments Include:* House Officer, England and Wales, 1953-54; Registrar, 1954-55; Resident, Childrens Chest Service, Bellevue Hospital, New York, USA, 1955-56; Lecturer, 1956-62, Senior Lecturer, 1963-70, Department of Medicine, University of Medical Sciences, Bangkok, Thailand; Assistant Professor, 1971-75, Associate Professor, 1975-76, Professor, Medicine, 1976-, Chief, Division of Respiratory Disease and Tuberculosis, 1983-, Department of Medicine, Mahidol University, Bangkok. *Memberships include:* Medical Association of Thailand; American Thoracic Society; American College of Chest Physicians; Thoracic Society of Thailand; International College of Angiology; Radiological Society of Thailand; Royal College of Physians of London; Allergy and Immunology Society of Thailand. *Publications:* 'Physical examination of the Respiratory System and Palpatation of Lumph Nodes', co-author, 1966; 'Symtomatology and Physical Examination in Respiratory Diseases', 1971; Author and co-author of 464 papers contributed to professional journals including numerous to Siriraj Hospital Gazette'. *Honours:* Knight Grand Cross, 1st class, Most Noble Order of the Crown of Thailand, 1981 and other Most Exalted Order of the White Elephant, 1984. *Hobby:* Gardening. *Address:* 69-41 Tivanond Road, Nontaburi, Thailand.

BOWDEN, Boyd W., b. 20 May 1940, Wheeling, West Virginia, USA. Chairman, Orthopaedic Surgery. m. Ellen Gorman, 3 daughters. *Education:* BS, Denison University, 1962; DO, Kirksville College of Osteopathic Medicine, 1968; Intern, Doctors Hospital, Colubus, Ohio; Hand Surgery Fellowship, University of New Mexico, 1973. *Appointments:* Orthopaedic and Hand Surgery, Doctors Hospital and Children's Hospital, Columbus, Ohio, 1973-. *Memberships:* Board of Trustees, AOAO; President, American Osteopathic Hand Society, 1974, 1983-84; Physical Fitness & Sports Medicine Board, State of Ohio, 1984-; American Academy of Osteopathy; American Osteopathic Hand Society; American and Ohio Osteopathic Associations; etc. *Publications:* Articles in numerous professioanl journals including: "Tennis Elbow – A Surgical Approach". *Hobbies:* Hunting; Fishing; Water Sports. *Address:* 1313 Olentangy River Road, Columbus, OH 43212, USA.

BOWEN, David Aubrey Llewellyn, b. 31 Jan. 1924, Pontycymmer, Wales. Professor of Forensic Medicine, Charing Cross Hospital Medical School, London. m. Helen Landcastle, 18 Jan. 1975, London, 2 sons, 1 daughter (by previous marriage). *Education:* MA, MB.B.Chir, (Cambridge); FRCP (London); FRCP (Edinburgh); FRC.Path. *Appointments:* Assistant Pathologist Senior Registrar, National Hospital for Nervous Diseases, London and Royal Marsden Hospital, London, 1952-56; lecturer, Forensic Medicine, St. George's Hospital Medical School, London, 1956-66; Lecturer, Reader, Charing Cross Hospital Medical School, London, 1966-78. *Memberships:* British Association Forensic Medicine; British Academy of Forensic Sciences; Medico-Legal Society; Forensic Science Society; International Academy of Legal and Social Medicine. *Publications:* Numerous articles on Medico-Legal subjects in forensic journals; Taylor's

Principles and Practice of Medical Jurisprudence, 1985. *Hobbies:* Jogging; Hockey. *Address:* Department of Forensic Medicine, Charing Cross Hospital Medical School, London, England.

BOWEN, (Major General), Esmond John, b. 6 dec. 1922, Lyndford, England. Retired. m. Elsie Midgley, 24 July 1948, Acocks Green, 2 sons, 3 daughters, 1 deceased. *Education:* LDS, University of Birmingham. *Appointments:* Commissioned into Royal Army Dental Corps, 1947, Dental Hygienist Instructor, Training Establishment, RADC, 1956-59, Senior Dental Officer, East Africa Command, 1959-62, Chief Instructor, Depot & TE RADC, 1966-69, CO, 2 Dental Group RADC, 1968-72, 3 Dental Group RADC, 1972-74; Assistant Director Army Dental Service, Ministry of Defence, 1974-76, Commandant, HQ & Training Centre RADC, 1967-77, Deputy Director, Dental Service, HQ BAOR, 1977-78, Director Army Dental Service, MOD, 1978-82, Colonel Commandant, RADC, 1982. *Membership:* British Dental Association. *Honours:* Officer (Brother) Order of St John, 1976; Queen's Honorary Dental Surgeon, 1976-82; Companion of the Bath, 1981. *Hobbies:* Muzzle Loading Shooting; Motor Caravanning; Parochial Church Council. *Address:* 72 Winchester Road, Andover, Hampshire SP10 2ER, England

BOWEN, Peter, b. 6 May 1932, Toronto, Canada. Director, Division of Medical Genetics. m. Catherine Shiao-Ning Lee, 15 May 1965, Baltimore, Maryland, USA, 1 son, 1 daughter. *Education:* MD; Fellow, Royal College of Physicians of Canada; CCMG. *Appointments:* Instructor in Medicine, Johns Hopkins University & Hospital, Baltimore, Maryland, 1963-64; Director, Division of Medical Genetics, Department of Paediatrics, University of Alberta. *Memberships:* American Society of Human Genetics; Canadian Society for Clinical Investigation; Western Society for Paediatric Research; International Dermatoglyphics Society. *Publications:* Various articles in medical journals. *Hobbies:* Music; Gardening; Skiing; Windsurfing. *Address:* 2C3.53 WC Mackenzie Health Sciences Centre, Edmonton, Alberta, T6G 2R7, Canada.

BOWEN, William Henry, b. 11 Dec. 1933, Enniscorthy, Ireland. Chairman, Department of Dental Research; Acting Chairman, Department of Microbiology, University of Rochester, New York, USA. m. Carole Barnes, 9 Aug. 1958, 3 sons, 2 daughters. *Education:* BDS, National University, Ireland 1955; MSC, University of Rochester, USA, 1959; PhD, University of London, UK, 1965; DSc. University of Ireland, 1974. *Appointments include:* Research Fellow, Eastman Dental Centre, Rochester, New York, USA, 1956-59. Royal College of Surgeons, UK: Quninten Hogg Fellow, 1959-62; Nuffield Foundation Fellow, 1962-65; Senior Research Fellow, 1965-69; Sir Wilfred Fish Fellow, Odontology, London, 1969-73. Acting Chief, Caries Prevention & Research Branch, National Caries Programme 1973-79, Chief 1979-82, National Institute of Dental Research, USA; Chairman, Department of Dental Research, University of Rochester, New York, USA, 1982-. *Memberships:* International Association for Dental Research; European Organisation for Caries Research, Scientific Council; Federation Dentaire Internationale; Laboratory, Animal Science Association; Zoological Society; American Society of Microbiology. *Publications:* Numerous contribution, professional journals; Research interests: Oral microbiology, Immunology of dental caries, Preventive methods; Oral Disease in primates. *Honours include:* Numerous prizes, awards; Fellowships; Editorial appointments; Consultancies; Keynote speaker; Association appointments; Honorary degrees; etc. *Hobbies:* Sports; Reading. *Address:* University of Rochester Department of Dental Research, PO Box 611, 601 Elmwood Avenue, Rochester, NY 14620, USA.

BOWIE, Malcolm David, b. 20 Apr. 1929, Scotland. Associate Professor; Chief Specialist in Paediatrics. m. Elaine Phyllis Allan, 30 Mar. 1967, Cape Town, South Africa, 2 sons, 1 daughter. *Education:* BSc, University of Natal, 1949; MB ChB, 1954, MD,1971, University of Cape Town; Member, 1960, Fellow, 1973, Royal College of Physicians, Scotland; DCH, Royal College of Physicians, London, and Surgeons, England. *Appointments:* Registrar, Red Cross War Memorial Childrens Hospital, Cape Town, Republic of South Africa, 1957-60; Senior Resident Officer, Bristol Royal Infirmary, Bristol, England, 1960-61; Chief Resident and Teaching Fellow, Cleveland Metropolitan General Hospital, Ohio, USA, 1961-62; Senior Research Fellow Department of Child Health, University of Cape Town, South Africa, 1962-64; Visiting Research Fellow, Department of Paediatrics, Kinderspital, Zurich, Switzerland, 1964; Lecturer, Consultant Paediatrician Institute of Child Health, University of Birmingham and Birmingham Childrens Hospital, England, 1971-72; Senior Lecturer, Chief Paediatrician, 1964-74, currently, Associate Professor and Chief Specialist Paediatrician, Institute of Child Health, University of Cape Town, *Memberships Include;* Medical Association of South Africa; Executive Committee, South African Paediatric Association; Past President, South African Nutrition Society; South African Gastroenterological Society. *Publications:* Contributor to: 'Paediatrics and Child Health' 1984; 'Paediatric Handbook'; 4th edition, 1982; 'American Journal of Clinical Nutrition', 1967. *Honours:* Certificate of Merit, University of Natal, 1949; Dowie Dunne Prize, University of Cape Town, 1954; Research Prize for Residents, Western Reserve University, 1962; Associate Professor, Ad Hominem Promotion, University of Cape Town, 1974. *Hobbies:* Golf; Gardening. *Address:* Institute of Child Health, University of Cape Town, Red Cross War Memorial Childrens Hospital, Rondebosch 7700, Republic of South Africa.

BOWLAN, Walter Lewis, b. 4 Aug 1932, Norwood, Missouri, USA, President, Northwest Medical Clinic Incorporated, Medical Hypnosis Clinic Incorporated, Oklahoma City, Oklahoma, m. Vallie Marshall, 7 Feb. 1956, Las Vegas, Nevada, 2 sons, 1 daughter. *Education:* BS, Central State University, Edmond, Oklahoma, 1958; MD, University of Oklahoma School of Medicine, 1961; Diplomate, American Board of Family Practice 1977, American Board of Examiners in Psychology. *Appointments:* Affiliate Faculty, University of Oklahoma School of Medicine, Oklahoma Heart Association; President, Northwest Medical Clinic Incorporated, Medical Hypnosis Clinic Incorporated, Oklahoma City, Oklahoma. *Memberships Include:* American Academy of Family Physicians American Medical Association; Fellow, International Academy of Forensic Psychology; Fellow, American Academy of Behavoiral Sciences; Oklahoma State Mental Health Committee, American Academy of Family Practice; Fellow, Oklahoma Representative, Board of Governors, American Society of Clinical Hypnosis; American Scientific Affiliation; American Institute of Hypnosis; Charter member, American Holistic Medical Association. *Publications:* 'Sub Conscious – Hypnosis and Dream Analysis'; 'Pain and Hypnosis', 1975. *Honours:* 12 Distinguished Physicians Awards, American Medical Association, 1973-85. *Hobbies:* Golf; Music; Reading. *Address:* 3124 Quail Creek Road, Oklahoma City, OK 73120, USA.

BOWLING, Ann Patricia, b. 7 May 1951, Surrey, England, Senior Research Fellow, Department Clinical Epidemiology, The London Hospital Medical College, London. *Education:* BSc, 1973, MSc, 1976, University of London; PhD, University of Wales, 1981. *Appointments:* Research Assistant, Royal Postgraduate Medical School, London, 1976-77; Research Officer, Institute for Social Studies in Medical Care, London, 1978-81; Research Officer, Ealing, Hammersmith and Hounslow Health Authority, London, 1981-82; Research Officer, National Children's Bureau, London, 1982-83. *Memberships:* Medical Sociology Group of British Sociological Association; Society for Social Medicine. *Publications Include:* 'Delegation in General Practice: A Study of Doctors and Nurses', 1981; 'Life After a Death: a study of the elderly widowed', (with A Cartwright), 1982; 'A Nurse Practioner in Britain', 1982; 'The Elderly widowed', (with A Cartwright), 1984; 'Doctors and Nurses: Delegation and Substition', 1985; 'Delegation to nurses in general practice', 1981; 'Primary Health care in residential homes for the elderly', 1982; 'Nurses for residentialhomes', 1982; 'The hospitalisation of death', 1983; 'Caring for the elderly widowed the burden on their supporters;, 1984; Contributor to numerous Conferences and professional journals; Book reviewer. *Hobbies:* Ballet; Dance. *Address:* Department of Clinical Epidemiology, The London Hospital Medical College, Turner Street, London E1, England.

BOYD, E (Edwin) Forrest, Junior, b. 5 July 1920, Los Angeles, California, USA. Clincial Professor, Obstetrics and Gynaecology, University of Southern California Medical School; Senior Attending, Kaiser Foundation Hospital, Los Angeles. m. Frances Elizabeth Ross, 21 Dec. 1942, Los Angeles, 3 sons, 1 daughter *Education:* AB, 1942;' MD, 1945; Leland Stanford Jr. University; Internship, Hollywood Presbyterian Hospital, 1946. *Appointments include:* Family Practice, Hollywood, 1949; Resident Obstetrician-Gynaecologist, Elizabeth Steel Magee, University of Pittsburgh, 1949-52; Private practice, hollywood, 1952-70; Southern California Permanente Medical Group, 1970-; Clinical Professor, Obstetrics and Gynaecology, University of Southern California Medical School, 1953-; Senior Attending, Kaiser Foundation Hospital, Los Angeles, 1970-, President of Staff, 1985; Clin. Attending, Los Angeles County/USC Medical Center, 1953-; Emeritus, Hollywood Pres. Medical Center, 1944-. *Memberships include:* Diplomate, American Board Obstetrics and Gynaecology; Fellow, American College of Surgeons; Fellow, International College of Surgeons; Life Fellow, Pacific Coast Obstetrics and Gynaecology Society; Delta Tau Delta; Nu Sigma Nu, several other professional and civic organisations. *Publications:* Contributor to professional journals. *Hobbies:* Amateur Radio; Stain Glass Crafting; Swimming; Music; Golf;. Trap and Pistol Shooting. *Address:* 4815 Alta Canyada Road, La Canada, CA 91011, USA.

BOYD, Hamish William, b. 3 July, 1925, Glasgow, Scotland. Consultant Physician. m. Fiona Jean Murray, 19 May, 1960,, Gartocharn, Scotland, 2 daughters. *Education:* MB. Ch. B; FRCP (Glasgow); FF.Hom. DCH. *Appointments:* House Physician, Royal Hospital for Sick Children, Glasgow, Scotland; House Officer, Aldrrhey Children's Hospital, Liverpool, England; House Officer, Southern General Hospital, Glasgow, Scotland; Junior House Medical Officer, Ruchill Hospital, for Chest Diseases, Glasgow, Scotland; Principal in General Practice; Assistant Physician, Glasgow Homeopathic Hospital. *Memberships:* British Medical Association; Royal Medicohirurgical Society, Glasgow; Fellow, Royal Society of Medicine. *Publications:* 'Alternative Therapies,' 1985. *Hobbies:* Gardening; Singing; Sailing; Skiing; Walking. *Address:* Bencreuch, Fintry, Stirlingshire, G6OLW, Scotland.

BOYD, James Ferguson, b. 6 May 1925, Kilbirnie, Ayrshire, Scotland. Senior Lecturer Pathology of Infectious Diseases. m. Christina Maggie Macleod, 5 Jan. 1951, Glasgow, 2 sons, 2 daughters. *Education:* MB ChB 1948, MD Commendation 1960, University of Glasgow. *Appointments Include:* Resident House Physician, Hairmyres Hospital, East Kilbride, Lanarkshire, 1948-49; Resident House Surgeon, Royal Alexanra, Infirmary, Paisley, Renfrewshire, 1949; Royal Army Medical Corps, 1949-51; Resident

Casualty Officer 1951-52, Senior House Officer 1952-53, Registrar 1953-54, Senior Registrar 1954-56, Temporary Lecturer 1957-61, Pathology Department, Western Infirmary, Glasgow; Currently Senior Lecture in Pathology of Infectious Diseases, University of Glasgow. *Memberships Include:* British Medical Association; Pathological Society of Great Britain and Ireland; Association of Clinical Pathologist; Royal Medico-Chirurgical Society of Glasgow; Research Defence Society; European Society of Patholgy; International Federation for the Study of Infectious andParasitic Diseases; British Society for the Study of Infection; Fellow, Royal College Physicians, Edinburgh: Fellow, Royal College of Pathologists; Fellow, Royal College of Physicians, Surgeons Glasgow. *Publications Include:* 'A 14 Year Study to Identify Measles antigen in Urine Specimens by Fluorescent Antibody Methods',1983; 'Fetal Damage After Accidental Polio Vaccination of an Immune Mother', (co-author), 1984; 'The Histopathology and Electron Microscopy of a human Monkeypox Lesion', (co-author), 1985; 'The Pathology of the Alimentary Tract in Salmonella Typohimrium Infection', 1985. *Honours:* Dr David Foulis Memorial Scholarship, Andrew H Arnott Prize (shared), McCunn Research Scholarship, University of Glasgow. *Hobbies:* Golf; Walking. *Address:* 44 Woodend Drive, Jordanhill, Glasgow G13 1TQ, Scotland.

BOYD, Margaret Louise, b. 4 Jan. 1930, Saskatchewan, Canada. Health Services Consultant. m. William Boyd, 12 Jan. 1954, Prince Albert, 1 son, 1 daughter. *Education:* BSc.N., University of Saskatchewan, 1951; Nursing Unit Administration Diploma, Canadian Hospital Association, Canadian Nurses Association; Masters in Health Services Administration, University of Alberta, 1974; Law Student, 1975-76.*Appointments:* Numerous appointments including: Research Co-ordinator, Programme Planning Branch, Senior Administration Consultant, Alberta Hospitals & Medical Care; Co-ordinator, Functional Planning,Alberta Hospital Services Commission; Director of Nursing, Provincial Cancer Hospitals Board; Surgical Supervisor, University of Alberta Hospital; Clinical Supervisor, Co-Director, Registered Nursing Assistant Programme, Ottawa Civic Hospital; Physicians Office Assistant, Pediatrics, Ottawa; Head Nurse, Womens' General Surgery, Ottawa Civic Hospital, Medicine & Pediatrics, Vernon Jubilee Hospital; S.R. Nurse, Indian Health Services, Northern Saskatchewan; Sciences Instructor, Victoria Hospital, Prince Albert. *Memberships:* Numerous professional organisations. *Publications:* "Prosthetic Services in Alberta",. 1973; "Medical Terminology - Cancer Records Officers' Manual",1975; "Ostomy Manual", 1970; "SI - What is It?", 1981; "Space Programming Methodology Manual", 1981; "The Planning Process for Capital Projects - Long Term Care", in press. *Honours:* Prize, Surgical Nursing, Saskatchewan City Hospital, 1951; Nominee, Nurse of the Year Award, Alberta, 1970. *Hobbies:* Sewing; Knitting; Crochet; Gardening; Houseplants; Collecting - Books, Stamps, Antiques; Farming with Husband. *Address:* General Delivery, Darwell, Alberta, Canada T0E 0L0.

BOYD, Robert David Hugh, b. 14 May 1938, Professor of Paediatrics, Honorary Consultant Paediatrician, University of Manchester. m. Meriel Cornelia Talbot, 1 May 1966, 1 son, 2 daughters. *Education:* Clare College, Cambridge University; University College Hospital, London; MA; MB; MSc; FRCP., *Appointments:* Previously, Senior Lecturer, honorary Consultant, University College Hospital, Whittington Hospital, Brompton, Gt Ormond Street Hospital, London. MRC Travelling Fellow, University of Colorado, USA: Assistant Registrar, Royal College of Physicians of London; Secretary, Academic Board, British Paediatric Association. *Memberships:* BPA; Physiological Society; Neonatal Society. *Publications:* 'Paediatric Problems in General Practice',(with M Modell), 1982; 'Perinatal Medicine', (editor with F C Battaglia), 1983; Author of various medical papers. *Address:* Department of Child Health, St Mary's Hospital, Manchester M13 0JH, England.

BOYS, Christopher Lovett, b. 23 Mar. 1940, Ann Arbor, Michigan, USA. Vice-President, Barger and Sargeant Inc., Concord, New Hampshire. m. Claudia E. Vookles, 13 June 1970, Memphis, Tennessee, 2 sons. *Education:* BA, Albion College, 1963; MHA, Graduate School of Business, University of Michigan, 1966. *Appointments:* Assistant to Administrator, St Joseph Mercy Hospital, Ann Arbor, 1963; Administrative Resident, 1964-65, Administrative Assistant, 1965-66, Wm. Beaumont Hospital, Royal Oak, Michigan; US Navy Medical Service Corps, 1966-69; Assistant Director, 1969-71, Associate Director, 1971-75, Maine Hospital Association; Founder & Vice President, Research & Education Trust of Maine Hospital Association, 1972-75; Assistant Director, Central Maine Medical Centre, 1975-80; Senior Vice President, Portsmouth Hospital, 1980; President, Chief Executive Officer, Portsmouth Hospital, 1980-83; Administrator, Chief Executive Officer, Hospital Corporation of America/Portsmouth Hospital, 1983-84; Executive Director, Hospital Corporation of America/Ohio Valley General Hospital, 1984; Interim Administrator, Hospital Corporation of America/Brownsville General Hospital, 1984; Vice President, Barger and Sargeant Inc., 1985- . *Memberships include:* New England Hospital Assembly, Connecticut and New Hampshire Hospital Associations; Association of Executive Search Consultants; Business and Industry Association of New Hampshire; American College of Healthcare Executives. *Publications:* "Reference Guide for Hospital Governance", 1983. *Honours:* Award of Merit, American Red Cross, Lewiston, Maine, 1979; Service Excellence Award, School of Health Studies Visitng Committee, University of New Hampshire, 1984. *Hobbies include:* Sailing; Tennis; Skiing; Working with Youth Groups. *Address:* Barger and Sargeant Inc., One Bicentennial Square, Concord, NH 03301, USA.

BRACK, Ronald Peter, b. 23 Mar. 1956, New York, USA. Doctor of Chiropractic. m. Debra Ann Miller, 4 July 1976, Harrison, New York, 2 sons. *Education:* Diplomate, National Board of Chiropractic Examiners, 1979; DC, New York Chiropractic College, 1980; BS, Biological Science, SUNY at Stony Brook, 1980. *Appointments:* Practising Chiropractor, East Hampton, New York, 1980-84; Director, East Hampton Chiropractic and Wellness Center, 1985- . *Memberships:* American Chiropractic Association; New York State Chiropractic Association; Member of Council on Roentgenology, American Chiropractic Association. *Honour:* Deans List, New York Chiropractic College, 1977. *Hobbies:* Endurance athlete; Marathon runner, Triathlete. *Address:* 53, The Circle, East Hampton, NY 11937, USA.

BRADFORD, Henry Francis, b. 9 Mar. 1938, London, England, Professor of Neurochemistry, m. Helen Caplan, 1 son, 1 daughter. *Education:* BSc, Birmingham University; PhD, DSc, London University; MRC Path. *Appointments:* MRC Scientific Staff, 1965-71, Lecturer in Biochemistry, 1971-74, Senior Lecturer in Biochemistry, 1974-76, Reader in Neurochemistry, 1976-79, Imperial College, London Honorary Secretary, The Biochemical Society, 1973-81; Member, MRC Grants Committees and Boards, 1973-82. *Memberships:* Royal College of Pathologists; the UK Biochemical Society; The International society for Neurochemistry. *Publications:* 'Biochemistry and Neurology', 1976; 'Neurotransmitter Interaction and Compartmentation', 1982; 'Chemical Neurobiology', 1985; Author of 200 papers in scientific journals. *Hobbies:* Reading; Theatre; Natural History.

Address: Department Biochemistry, Imperial College, London SW7 2AZ, England.

BRADLEY, John, b. 9 July 1933, Nr Bangor, North Wales. Head, Department of Clinical Immunology, Flinders Medical Centre, Adelaide, Australia. m. Brenda Mary Whitehouse, 27 Apr. 1961, Sutton Coldfield, 2 sons, 2 daughters. *Education:* BSc., Birmingham, 1954; MB, ChB, Birmingham, 1957; MD, Birmingham. 1967; MRCP (Ed), 1962; MRCP (London), 1964; FRCPEd, 1973; FRCP London, 1975; FRCPA, 1977; FRACP, 1977. *Appointments:* Captain, RAMC, 1960-62; Medical Registrar, Warwick & Stratford Hospital, 1962-64; Sheldon Research Fellow, University of Birmingham, 1964-67; International Fellow, USPH, Medicine, University of Texas, USA, 1967-68; Lecturer, Senior Lecturer, 1968-73, Director, Immunology, 1973-75, University of Liverpool; Consultant, Liverpool Royal Infirmary, 1973-75. *Memberships:* Australian & British Societies for Immunology; Australian Society for Medical Research; transplantation society; Australian Rheumatism Association. *Publications:* Scientific papers in a number of journals. *Honours:* USPHS International Fellowship, 1967-1968; Wellcome Travelling Fellowship, 1970. *Hobbies:* Music; Gardening. *Address:* 12 Balham Avenue, Kingswood, Adelaide,SA 5062Australia.

BRADLEY, Myra James, b. 1 Feb. 1924, Cincinnati, Ohio, USA. Hospital President. *Education:* BS, Education, Atheneum of Ohio, Cincinnati, USA; RN, Nursing, Good Samaritan Hospital, Dayton, Ohio; MHA, St. Louis University, Missouri, USA. *Appointments:* Faculty, University of Dayton, Ohio, 1955-57; Faculty, Good Samaritan Hospital, Dayton, Ohio, 1955-57; Assistant Administrator, St Mary-Corwin Hospital, Pueblo, Colorado, 1960; Administrator, St. Joseph Hospital, Mount Clemens, Michigan, 1960-65; President, Penrose Hospitals, Colorado Springs, Colorado -. *Memberships:* American Hospital Association; Aemrican College of Hospital Administrators; Colorado Hospital Association; National Council of Community Hospitals; Colorado Foundation for Medical Care Regional Council; Colorado Springs Chamber of Commerce. *Honours:* Distinguished Service Award, University of Colorado at Colorado Springs, 1983; Civis Princips, Regis College, Colorado Springs, 1984. *Hobbies:* Painting; Cross Country Ski-ing. *Address:* 2215 North Cascade, Colorado Springs, CO 80907, USA.

BRADY, Luther W, b. 20 Oct. 1925, Rocky Mount, North Carolina, USA. Professor and Chairman of University Department of Radiation Oncology. *Education:* AA 1944, AB 1946, MD 1948M, George Washington University, Washington, District of Columbia. *Appointments:* Associate in Radiology, George Washington University, 1952-53; Assistant Instructor in Radiology, Thomas Jefferson, 1954-55; Assistant Instructor 1955-56, Instructor 1956-57, Associate 1957-59, Radiology, University of Pennsylvania; Assistant Professor of Radiology, Columbia University, New York, 1959; Associate Professor of Radiology, Hahnemann Medical College, 1959-62; Assistant Professor of Radiology, Harvard Medical school, 1962-63; Currently Professor and Chairman, Department of Radiation Oncology, Hahnemann University, Philadelphia, Pennsylvania. *Memberships:* Past President, American Radium Society; Past President, American Society of Therapeutic Radiology and Oncology; Past President, Radiological Society of North America; President, American Board of Radiology. *Publications:* Textbooks; More than 325 publications in professional journals. *Honorus:* Gold Medal, American Radium Society, 1981; Gold Medal, Gilbert H Fletcher Society, 1984; Honorary Fellowship, Royal College of Radiologists, 1985. *Hobbies:* Board of Trustees, Philadelphia Museum of Art; Board of Trustees, Opera Company of Philadelphia. *Address:* Department of Radiation

Oncology, Hahnemann University MS 200, Broad and Vine, Philadelphia, PA 19102, USA.

BRAIN, Peter, b. 13 Nov 1922, Pretoria, RSA, Medical Director,Natal Blood Transfusion Service; Director, Natal Institute of Immunology; Medical Director, National Blood Fractionation Centre, m. Joy Blundell Brown, 29 Dec 1948, Johannesburg, RSA, 2 sons, 3 daughters. *Education:* BSc, 1942, MB, 1949, MD, 1953, DSc, 1980, Cape Town; MA,1978, PhD, 1983, Natal; FRCPA. *Appointments:* Medical Officer, Rhodesian and General Asbestos Corporation, 1950-53; Pathologist, East London and Border Labortatory, South Africa, 1957-58; Director, Red Cross Blood Transfusion Service, Western Australia, 1958-65; Pathologist, Natal Blood Transfusion Service, RSA, 1965-74; Deputy Director, Natal Institute of Immunology, 1968-74. *Publications:* 'Galen on Blood letting', 1986; Author of over 60 papers in scientific journals. *Hobbies:* Classical Literature; History of Medicine; Natural Histrory; Building harpsichords. *Address:* Natal Institute of Immunology, P O Box 2356, Durban 4000, Republic of South Africa.

BRAMLEY, Paul Anthony, (Sir), b. 24 May, 1923, England. Professor of Dental Surgery, University of Sheffield. m. Hazel Morag Boyd, 16 Feb. 1952, Glasgow, Scotland, 1 son, 3 daughters. *Education:* MB, ChB, BDS; FRCS; FDS; FRACDS (Honorary); University of Birmingham Medical & Dental Schools. *Appointments:* House Surgeon, Queen Elizabeth's Hospital, Birmingham, 1945; Captain, RAC, 224 Para FDAMB, 1945-48; Medical Officer, Church of Scotland, Kenya, 1952; Registrar, Rooksdown House, Basingstoke, Hampshire; Consultant Oral Surgeon, South West Regional Hospital Board, 1954-69; Civilian Consultant, Royal Navy, 1959-; Professor of Dental Surgery, University of Sheffield, 1969-; Honorary Consultant Oral Surgery, Trent RHA, 1969-; Dean, School of Clinical Dentistry, 1972-75; Dean, Faculty of Dental Surgery, Royal College of Surgeons, England, 1980-83. *Memberships:* General Dental Council; Medical Protection Society Council; Chairman, Standing Dental Advisory Committee, DHSS; Consultant Adviser, Prince of Songkla University, Thailand; British Association of Oral & Maxillofacial Surgeons, Secretary 1968-72, President, 1975-76; President - Designate, British Dental Association, 1988; Formrely Member of Royal Commission on NHS. *Publications:* Various Papers & Chapters on Oral Surgery Topics. *Honours:* Knight Bachelor, 1984; Honorary Fellow, RACDS, 1982. *Address:* Greenhills, Back Lane, Hathersage, S30 1AR, England.

BRAND, Karl Albert, b. 22 Apr. 1931, Beilngries, Bavaria, Federal Republic of Germany. University Professor, Director of the Institute of Physiological Chemistry. m. Ilse Ruda, 16 May 1959, Heidelberg, 1 son. *Education:* Degree in Pharmacy, University of Freiburg; Degree in Medicine, Medical Doctor; University of Heidelberg. *Appointments:* Postdoctoral Fellow, University of Heidelberg, 1961-66; Research Associate, Department of Molecular Biology, Albert Einstein College of Medicine, New York City, USA, 1966-68; Senior Research Scientist, Max-Planck-Institut, Dortmund, Federal Republic of Germany, 1968-72; Professor of Biochemistry 1972 - , Director of the Institute of Physiological Chemistry, University of Erlangen-Nuremberg. *Memberships:* Gesellschaft Deutscher Naturforscher und Aerzte; Gesellschaft Fuer Biologische Chemie; Gesellschaft Fuer Klinische Chemie. *Publications:* 'Evidence for a Specific Function for Histidine Residues in Transaldolase', (with O Tsolas and B L Horecker), 1969; 'Energy Metabolism of Various Substrates and the 2,3-Bisphosphoglycerate Bypass in Human Erythrocytes', (with K-H Quadflieg), 1978; 'Glutamine and Glucose Metabolism During Thymocyte Proliferation', 1985; 'Hormones' chapter in'Kurzgefasstes Lehrbuch der Physiologie' 6th edition (editor W-D Keidel), 1985. *Honour:* Dr Fritz-Merck Award for Biochemistry, Justus Liebig University Giessen, 1969. *Hobbies:* Classical Music; Sailing; Climbing; Skiing. *Address:* Institute of Physiological Chemistry, University of Erlangen-Nuremberg,Fahrstrasse 17, D8520 Erlangen, Federal Republic of Germany.

BRANDIS, Henning, b. 17 July 1916, Elberfeld, Germany. Professor Emeritus. m. Dr. Ursula Becker, 24 Aug. 1959, Frankfurt. *Education:* MD, 1942. *Appointments:* Professor and Director, Institute of Hygiene, University of Göttingen, 1957-67; Professor and Director, Institute of Medical Microbiology and Immunology, University of Bonn, 1967-84. *Memberships:* American Society of Microbiology; Deutsche Gesellschaft für Hygiene and Mikrobiologia. *Publications:* Contributor to professional journals; Books, etc. *Honours:* Bundesverdienstkreuz 1 Klasse; Member Deutsche der Naturforscher, Leopoldina, Halle, 1974. *Hobby:* Botany. *Address:* Zedernweg 3, D-5300 Bonn 1, Federal Republic of Germany.

BRANDON, Milan Louis, b. 28 Nov. 1927, Oakland, California, USA. Private Practitioner, Allergy & Internal Medicine. m. Mary Elizabeth Brown, 9 June 1954, Los Angeles, California, 3 sons. *Education:* BA, University of California at Berkeley, 1949; Postgraduate Study of Genetics, ibid, 1949-50; MD, University of Southern California School of Medicine, Los Angeles, 1950-54; Rotating Interne, Los Angeles County General Hospital, 1954-55; Resident, Internal Medicine, Henry Ford Hospital,Detroit, Michigan, 1955-56; Resident, Allergy & Immunology, ibid, 1957-58. *Appointments:* Head, Allergy Clinic, US Naval Hospital, San Diego, 1958-59; Head, Allergy Clinic, Mercy Hospital, San Diego, 1959-75; Diplomate, American Board of Allergy & Immunology,Fellow American College of Allergy and Immunology; speciality Internal Medicine & Paediatrics, 1975-. *Memberships:* American Society of Internal Medicine; American Academy of Allergy & Immunology;American Association of Certified Allergy; Fellow, American Association of Allergy & Immunology; American Rheumatism Association; American Association for the Study of Headaches; and others. *Publications:* 'Corticosteroids in Medical Practice', 1960; Numerous articles on allergy & immunology, arthritis, numerous clinical investigative studies. *Honour:* Diplomate, American Board of Allergy & Immunology, 1975. *Hobbies:* Hunting, Fishing, Writing, Research, Reading, Sports. *Address:* 2800 Third Avenue, San Diego, CA 92103, USA.

BRAWN, William James, b. 22 May 1946, Buckingham, England. Paediatric Cardiovascular Surgeon. m. Carolyn Mary Topham, 29 Aug. 1970, Portsmouth, England, 1 son, 2 daughters. *Education:* MB,BS, The London Hospital, 1970; Fellow, Royal College of Surgeons, 1975; Fellow, Royal Australasian College of Surgeons, 1981. *Appointments:* House Officer, The London Hospital, London, England, 1970; Senior House Officer, (General Surgery), Exeter, 1971; Junior Lecturer in Anatomy, The London Hospital, 1972; Senior House Officer, Accident & Emergency, Reading, 1973; Surgical Registrar, Southampton, 1974-75; Surgical Registrar, Wessex Cardiothoracic Unit, 1976-77; Registrar in Cardiothoracic & Vascular Surgery, Green Lane Hospital, Auckland, New Zealand, 1978-79: Pediatric Cardiovascular Surgeon, Royal Children's Hospital, Melbourne, Australia, 1980-. *Memberships:* Cardiac Society of Australia & New Zealand. *Publications:* Various papers on congenital heart disease. *Hobbies:* Gardening; Good Food (Italian & Indian); Home renovation; Classical Music. *Address:* 42 Stawell Street, Kew, Melbourne, Victoria 3101, Australia.

BRAY, David Noel, b. 14 Feb. 1941, Sheffield,

England. Private Practice. m. Monica Shears, 10 Dec. 1966, Johannesburg, South Africa, 1 son, 1 daughter. *Education:* Science Laboratory Technicians Certificate, City & Guilds, London; Doctor of Chiropractic, Magna Cum Laude; Open University, 2 credits, Arts, Social Sciences. *Appointments:* Consultant, Enton Hal Residential Clinic, 2 years; Associate, Leeds Chiropractic Centre, 6 years. *Memberships:* British Chiropractic Association, Past Treasurer; International Stress & Tension Control Society, Founder Member, Executive Committee Information Officer Back Pain Association; Institute of Complementary Medicine. *Publications:* 'Mid-Laser - A Brief Encounter', 'European Journal of Chiropractic', 1985. *Honours:* Student Academic Achievement Award, 1971; Student Service Award, 1971. *Hobbies:* Music Performance; Drama; Judo; Squash; Hiking; Camping. *Address:* 25 Sutherland Ave., Leeds, W. Yorkshire LS8 1BY, England.

BRAZEU-LAMONTAGNE, Lucie, b. 13 Nov. 1949, Sherbrooke, Quebec, Canada, Dean of Admission, Medicine, University of Sherbrooke. m. Albert Lamontagne, 12 Sep. 1973, Sherbrooke, 1 son, 1 daughter. *Education:* BA, 1969, MD, 1973, Sherbrooke University, Quebec; LMCC, 1974; CSPQ Radiologie, 1977; FRCP(C), 1977. *Appointments:* Assistant Professor of Radiology, 1977-82, Associate Professor of Radiology, 1982-, University of Sherbrooke. *Memberships:* Canadian Association of Radiologists; Societe Canadienne Francaise de Radiologie. *Publications:* 'High resolution CT of the Temporal bone', 1983; 'CT Assessment of Cricoarytenoiditis in Rheumatoid Arthritis', 1985. *Honours:* Congress Award, Canadian Association of Radiology, 1977; Boutsiere des echanges France, Quebec, 1981; Examiner for the Royal College (Canada), 1983-. *Hobbies:* Classic singing; Travel. *Address:* 63 Laurier, Bromptonville, Quebec, Canada JOB 1HO.

BREATHNACH, Caoimhghin Seosamh, b. 13 Oct 1923, Dublin, Republic of Ireland, Associate Professor of Applied Physiology. *Education:* MD, 1960, PhD, 1962, NUI. *Appointments:* House Physician, Mater Hospital, Dublin; Assistant Medical Officer, Rialto Chest Hospital, Dublin; Lecturer in Pharmacology, University College, Cork. *Memberships:* Physiological Society; Royal Academy of Medicine in Ireland; Irish Medical Organisation. *Publications:* 'Foetal Neonatal and Adult Haemoglobins', 1964; 'The Hierarchy in Homeostatis', 1971; 'The Development of Blood Gas Analysis', 1972. *Hobbies:* Medical history; Gardening; Ambling. *Address:* Department of Physiology and Histology, University College, Earlsfort Terrace, Dublin 2, Republic of Ireland.

BREDA, Raffaello Vittorio F, b. 18 Oct. 1914, Alzano Lombardo, Bergamo, Italy. Professor of Internal Medicine and Haematology in Postgraduate Schools; Consultant Physician. m. Morvillo Vincenzina, 15 July 1952, Milan, 1 son, 4 daughters. *Education:* MD, Milan University, 1939; Professor of Medical Pathology, 1951; Medical clinic, 1955. *Appointments:* Assistant Professor, Medical Pathology, 1940-49, Assistant Professor, Medical Clinic, 1950-55, Milan University; Professor Head, Medical Clinic, Sassari, Sardinia, 1955-65; Professor Head, Medical Pathology, 1965-71, Professor Head, Medical Clinic, 1971-84, Catholic University, Rome. *Memberships:* Italian Societies of Internal Medicine, Haematology, Cardiology, Angiology, Infectious Diseases, Endocrinology; International Society of Haematology; Swiss Society of Haematology, Medical Academy of Rome, Lancisiana Academy, Rome. *Publications:* Over 160 publications on Internal Medicine, Thrombotic and Haemorrhegic Diseases, Cardiology, Angiology, 1940-84. *Honour:* Commander of Order of St. Gregory the Great. *Hobby:* Artistic Tourism. *Address:* Via Luigi Arbib Pascusci 64, 00168, Rome, Italy.

BRENNER, Sydney, b. 13 Jan. 1927, Germiston, Republic of South Africa, Director, MRC Laboratory of Molecular Biology, Cambridge, England, m. May Woolf Balkind, 1 son, 1 stepson, 2 daughters. *Education:* MSc, 1947, MB, BCh, 1951, University of Witwatersrand, Republic of South Africa; DPhil, Oxford University, England, 1954. *Appointments:* Carnegie Corporation Fellow, USA, 1954; Virus Laboratory, University of California at Berkeley, 1954; Lecturer in Physiology, University of Witwatersrand, Republic of South Africa, 1955-57; Member, of Scientific Staff, 1957-, Director, 1979-, Medical Research Council Laboratory of Molecular Biology, Cambridge, England. *Memberships:* Fellow of the Royal Society; Fellow, Royal College of Physicians; Honorary Member, Deutsche Akademie der Natursforscher Leopoldina; Society for Biological Chemists; Honorary Fellow, Royal Society of Edinburgh, Exeter College, Oxford; Foreign Associate, US National Academy of Sciences; Royal Society of South Africa; Foreign Honorary Member, American Academy of Arts and Sciences; Foreign member, American Philosophical Society. *Publications:* Author of over 120 publications including, 'Genes and development', 1981; 'Summary to Nucleic Acid Research', 1983; 'Recombinants that are the same but different', 1982; 'Nematode research', 1984. *Honours include:* Honorary DSc, Trinity College, Dublin, Republic of Ireland, 1967; Honorary DSc, University of Witwatersrand, Republic of South Africa, 1972; Honorary DSc, University of Chicago, USA, 1976; Honorary LLD, University of Glasgow, Scotland, 1981; Honorary DSc, University of London, 1982; Honorary DSc, University of Leicester, 1983; Foreign Associate, Royal Society of South Africa, 1983; Honorary DSc, University of Oxford, 1985; Foreign Member, Real Academia de Ciencias, 1985; Fellow of King's College, Cambridge, 1959-. *Address:* MRC Laboratory of Molecular Biology, Hills Road, Cambridge CB2 2QH, England.

BRESSON, Gilbert, b. 9 Nov. 1920, Alger. General Secretary, International Centre of Radiopathology. *Education:* PhD. *Appointments:* (Simultaneously) Protection Deputy Director, CEA;President CEDHYS; President; AFTIM; Executive Officer, IRPA; General Secretary, ICR. *Memberships:* French Radiation Protection Society; Association of Environment Technicians and Engineers; American Nuclear Society. *Publications:* "Training in Radiological Protection for Nuclear Programmes",1964; "La Protection Radiologique",1965; "Radioactive Du Rhin",1969; "Les Effects de la Pollution de l'Environment sur la Sante",1974; "Applications Sanitaires De La Production D'Energie Nucleaire",1975; 'La Protection Des Travailleurs Dans L'Industrie Nucleaire', 1979; 'L'Accident Radiologique",1981; " Prospective en Matiere de Securite'', 1982; ''Organisation de la Radioprotection'' 1983; "Analyse Globale De La Securite'', 1984; etc. *Honours:* Legion D'Honneur, 1971; Merite National, 1968. *Address:* 18 Rue Le Courte, 75015 Paris, France.

BRETON, Jacques D. b. 16 Sep. 1950, Ottawa, Canada. President of the College of Chiropractic Sports Sciences of Canada. m. Montreal, Canada, 1 son, 1 daughter. *Education:* BSc; DC; FCCSS (C); from Ottawa University, Canada, Palmer College of Chiropractic and Canadian College of Sports Sciences. *Appointments:* Faculty Member at Palmer College of Chiropractic; Chairman of the Commission on Industrial Relations of the Quebec Chiropractic Association; Chairman of the Council on Sports Injuries of the Quebec Chiropractic Association; Vice President of the Quebec ChiropracticAssociation; Member of the Advisory Committee on Post-Graduate Education at Canadian Memorial Chiropractic College; Member of the Commission on Continuing Education of the Quebec Order of Chiropractic Physicians. *Memberships:* Faculty Member, Post-Graduate Division, CMCC;

American Chiropractic Association; Canadian Chiropractic Association; Quebec Chiropractic Association; Quebec Order of Chiropractic Physicians; Canadian Council on Chiropractic Sports Sciences. *Publications:* 'Comprehensive Examination and Therapentic Approaches to Shoulder Injuries', 1980; 'The Concept of Biomechanical Stress Index Measurement of the Low Back', 1981; 'Comprehensive Evaluation of the Shoulder', 1984; 'Comprehensive Evaluation of the Elbow, Wrist and Hand', 1984; 'Comprehensive Evaluation of Hip, Thorax and Abdomen',1985; 'Comprehensive Evaluation of the Knee', 1985; 'Comprehensive Evaluation of the Lower Leg, the Foot and the Ankle', 1985; 'Computerized Clinical Profilig; The Low Back Model', 1986. *Address:* 193 La Savane, Gatineau, Quebec, Canada J8T 1R3.

BREWER, Lyman Augustus, III b. 28 July 1907, Toledo, Ohio, USA. Distinguished Physician, EM. US Veterans Administration. m. Jane Lippitt, 17 Oct. 1942, Toledo, 3 sons. *Education:* BA, Amherst College, 1928; MD, 1932, MS Surgery, 1945, University of Michigan School for Medicine; PhD, Golden State University California, 1984; ScD, Honoris Causae, Amherst College, 1978. *Appointments:* Assistant, Surgery, Washington University School of Medicine, 1937-38; Instructor, Surgery, University of Michigan School of Medicine, 1938-40; Assistant Clinical Professor, Surgery, 1942-46, Associate Professor, 1956-61, Clinical Professor, Surgery, 1961-64, Professor, Surgery, 1965-, Loma Linda University School of Medicine; Professor, 1965-, Honorary Clinical Professor, Medicine, 1984, University of California, Irvine; Clinical Professor, Surgery, University Southern California School of Medicine, 1966-. *Memberships Include:* American Association for Thoracic Surgery, President, 1973; Society of Thoracic Surgery, President, 1968; Pacific Coast Surgical Association, President, 1968; Trudeau Society, President, 1948; Excelsior Surgical Society, President, 1965; John Alexander Surgical Society, President, 1967; American College of Surgeons, Vice President, 1968. *Publications:* "Routine Practics 4th Med. Service",1934; "History Thoracic Surgery WWII" 'US Army Med. Corp.' Volume I 1961, Volume II, 1963; "Prosthetic Heart Valves" 1969;'National Thoracic Surgery Manpower Study', 1974; 'Cameron Haight, Personal Recollections',1972; 132 Scientific Articles in leading surgical journals. *Honours:* Honorary Member: Chilian Surgical Society, 1974, Chicago Surgical Society, 1977, Chicago Surgical Society, 1977, Society International de Cardio, Nephro.Ped.Soc., 1979; Gold Medal, American Lung Association, 1980; Founded, LA Brewer III International Surgical Society, 1981; etc. *Hobbies:* Medical History; Camping; Travel. *Address:* 225 Grand Ave., South Pasadena, CA 91030, USA.

BRIAND, Claudette, b. 11 Mar. 1942, Nice, France. Head, Pharmaceutical Physics Laboratory. *Education:* Licence, Physical Sciences; Doctor, Pharmaceutical Scineces. *Appointments:* Assistant, Assistant Professor, Professor, University of Aix Marseille II. *Membership:* Bodie of Hospital Chemists. *Publications:* Articles in: 'Mol.Pharmacol'; 'Biochemical Pharmacology'; 'Cancer Treatment Reports'; 'Therm. Chemica Acta'. *Address:* Laboratory of Pharmaceutical Physics, Faculty of Pharmacy, 27 Bd Jean Moulin, 13005 Marseille, France.

BRICK, John, b. 18 Mar. 1950, New York City, USA. Laboratory Director, Alcohol Behavior Research Laboratory. m. Laurie Stockton, 1 May 1976. *Education:* BA; MA; PhD. *Appointments:* Research Associate, Assistant Research Professor, Assistant Research Specialist, Rutgers Center of Alcohol Studies; Laboratory Director, Alcohol Behavior Research Laboratory, Rutgers University, New Brunswick, New Jersey. *Memberships:* Research

Society on Alcoholism; Society for Neuroscience; Eastern Psychological Association. *Publications:* Over 20 articles, books, etc. including the following: "Stress and Alcohol Use", 1983; "Role of Monoamines in Ethanol-induced Changes in Corticosterone and Non-Esterified Fatty Acids", 'Alcohol', 1985; 'Biochemcial and Behavioral Responses to Ethanol: Effect of Circadian Cycle Phase', 'Alcoholism: Clin. Exp. Res.', 1984. *Hobbies:* Bicycling; Gunning; Computing. *Address:* Alcohol Behaviour Research Laboratory, Building 3530, Rutgers University, Piscataway, NJ 08854, USA.

BRIDGEO, William Alphonsus, b. 15 Dec. 1927, Saint John, New Brunswick Canada. Professor, St Mary's University, Halifax; President, Bridco ValuesLtd. m. Margaret C. Campbell, 8 Oct. 1955, Ottawa, 1 son, 3 daughters. *Education:* BSc., St Francis Xavier University; PhD, University of Laval, University of Ottawa; Postgraduate, Notre Dame University, New York State, USA. *Appointments:* Director, Technical Services, Director, Chemistry Division, NS Research Foundation; Dean of Science, St Mary's University. *Memberships:* Chemical Institute of Canada; American Institute of Chemists; International Association on Water Pollution Research and Control. *Publications:* "Cyanoacetic esters, amino acids and pyrazolones", 'Canadian Journal of Chemistry', 1952; "Synthesis of Stable Strontium Compounds for Dietary Supplementation", in preparation. *Honours:* Fellow, Chemical Institute of Canada, American Institute of Chemists; Centennial Medal, Canada. *Hobbies:* Camping; Forestry; Walking. *Address:* 82 Stoneybrook Court, Halifax, Canada B3M 3J7.

BRIDGES, Bryn A., b. 24 July 1936, London, England. Director, MRC Cell Mutation Unit, University of Sussex. m. Jennifer E. Wilkins, 2 Apr. 1960, 1 son, 1 daughter. *Education:* BSc., PhD, University of Reading. *Appointments:* UKAEA (Wantage-Harwell), 1957-62; MRC Radiobiology Unit, Harwell, 1962-70. *Memberships:* Fellow, Institute of Biology; UK Enviromental Mutagen Society, Honorary Life Member; Genetical Society, Vice President, 1985; Association for Radiation Research; Chairman, International Commission, Protection Against Enviromental mutagens and Carcinogens. *Publications:* 'Ataxia-telangiectasia', co-editor, 1982; 'Proceedings National Academy of Science, US', 1985; 'Cellular Responses to DNA Damage', co-editor, 1983. *Honours:* Weiss Medal, Association for Radiation Researach. *Hobbies:* Music; Skiing; Windsurfing. *Address:* MRC Cell Mutation Unit, University of Sussex, Falmer, Brighton BN7 9RR, England.

BRIDGES, Charles Hubert, b. 23 Feb. 1921, Shreveport, Louisiana. USA. Professor of Veterinary Pathology, Texas A & M University. m. Mildred L Kruse, 14 Oct. 1945, Brenham, Texas, 2 sons, 1 daughter. *Education:* DVM, Texas A & M University, 1945; MS, Texas A & M University, 1954; PhD, Texas A & M University, 1957; Certified Veterinary Pathologist, American College of Veterinary Pathology, 1956; Fellow, Veterinary Pathology, Armed Force Institute of Pathology, 1955; Special Studies in Microbiology, Louisiana State University, 1949-51. *Appointments:* Practice of Veterinary Medicine, 1945-49; Research Associate, Louisiana Agricultural Experimental Station, 1949-51; Captain, Veterinary Service, US Air Force, 1951-53; Retired major, US Air Force Reserve; Associate Professor, Professor, Department of Veterinary Pathology, College of Veterinary Medicine, Texas A & M University, 1955-; Chairman, Department of Veterinary Pathology, 1960-78; Adjunct Professor, Department of Pathology, Baylor College of Medicine, Houston, 1978- . *Memberships:* American College of Veterinary Pthologists; International Academy of Pathology; American & Texas Veterinary Medical Associations; Society of Human and Animal Mycology; Conference of Research Workers in Animal Diseases. *Publications:* More than 50 publications in scientific and professional journals. *Honours:* Sigma Xi; Phi Zeta; Phi Kappa; Gamma Sigma Delta. *Hobbies:* Fishing; Hunting; Camping. *Address:* Department of Veterinary Pathology, College of Veterinary Medicine, Texas A & M University, College Station, TX 77843, USA.

BRIDGES, James Wilfrid, b. 9 Aug. 1938, Orpington, Kent, England. Director of Robens Institute of Industrial and Environmental Health and Safety, Professor of Toxicology. m. Daphne Hammond, 2 Feb. 1963, Eastcote, Middlesex, 1 son, 1 daughter. *Education:* BSc, Queen Elizabeth College, London University; 1962-68; Senior Lecturer Reader in Department of Biochemistry 1968-78, Director of Robens Institute and Professor of Toxicology 1979-, University of Surrey; Visiting Professor, University of Texas, Dallas, Texas, USA, 1973 and 1979; Visiting Professor, University of Rochester, New York, 1974; Senior Scientist, National Institute of Environmental Health Sciences, North Carolina, 1976. *Memberships:* Chairman 1980-81, British Toxicology Society; 1st President, Federation of European Societies of Toxicology, 1985-; Secretary Pharmacological Biochemistry Group 1974-77, Biochemical Society; Royal Society of Chemistry; Institute of Biology; Royal College of Pathology; Institute of Environmental Sciences; Society of Toxicology USA; ASPET USA, Europe; President-elect, Society of Biochemical Pharmacology; Vice-Chairman; UV Group, 1979 -; National Committee of Pharmacology, 1983 -; MRC System Disorders Board Grand Committee, 1983 -. *Publications:* Over 250 research papers and reviews in scientific journals; Joint editor of 11 books including 9 volumes of 'Progress in Drug Metabolism' series. *Hobbies:* Theatre-going; Sports. *Address:* 3 Chatsworth Close, Caversham Park Village, Reading, Berkshire RG4 ORS, England.

BRIDGES, Trevor Edwin, b. 20 Sep. 1942, Isle of Wight, England. Senior Lecturer, in Charge, Pharmacology & Therapeutics, Dept. of Dentistry, University of Adelaide, Australia. m. Diana Christine McLeod Day, 26 Aug. 1967, Ramsgate, 1 daughter. *Education:* B.Pharm., Honours, 1966, PhD, Pharmacology, 1970, London University; MPS; ClBiol; MlBiol. *Appointments:* Visiting Scientist, Institute of Medical Physiology, University of Copenhagen, Denmark, 1969-78; Research Fellow, Pharmacology & Therapeutics, University of Calgary, Canada, 1970-71; Lecturer, Pharmacology, St Thomas's Hospital Medical School, London, 1971-75; Lecturer, Pharmacology & Therapeutics, 1977-83, Senior Lecturer in Charge, 1984- , University of Adelaide. Visiting Professor, Pharmacology, Health Sciences Centre, University of Calgary 1984. *Memberships:* Pharmaceutical Society of Great Britain; Institute of Biology; Society of Endocrinology; British Pharmacological Society; Endocrine Society of Australia; Australian Physiological & Pharmacological Society; Australian Society for Medical Research; Australian Neuroscience Society; Australasian Society of Clinical and Experimental Pharmacologists; Royal Zoological Society of South Australia; etc. *Publications:* "Pain Control", Undergraduate Teaching Text, 1982; "Pharmacology for Dental Students", Undergraduate Handbook, 1984; numerous articles in professional journals. *Honours:* Visiting Scientist, University of Copenhagem, 1969; Research Fellowship, 1970, Visiting Professorship, 1984, University of Calgary. *Hobbies:* Local Apex Service Club and 41 Club; Home Improvements; Woodwork; Wood Carving; Classical Music; Walking. *Address:* Pharmacology Research Laboratory, Dept. of Dentistry, University of Adelaide, GPO Box 498, Adelaide, Australia 5001.

BRIDGES-WEBB, Charles, b. 15 Oct. 1934, Victoria, Australia. Professor, Head, Community Medicine, University of Sydney. m. Anne Margetts, 5 Mar.

1960, Melbourne, 3 sons, 1 daughter. *Education:* MB BS, Melbourne, 1957; MD, Monash, 1971; FRACGP, 1971. *Appointments:* JRMO, Royal Melbourne Hospital, 1958; GP, Locums, Britain & Australia, 1959; GP, Deakin Street Clinic, Traralgon, 1960-75; Visiting Medical Officer, Central Gippsland Hospital, Traralgon, 1960-75; Hon. Clinical Assistant, Royal Children's Hospital, Melbourne, 1965. *Memberships:* Australian Medical Association; Royal Australian College of General Practitioners; Australian and New Zealand Society for Epidemiology and Researach in Community Health; International Epidemiological Association; many other professional organisations. *Publications Include:* Chapters, various books; articles in professional journals including 'Family Practice', 'International Journal of Epidemiology'. *Honour:* Faulding Prize, RACGP, 1967. *Hobbies:* Reading; Literature; Gardening; Cricket; Soccer; Australian History; Food. *Address:* Dept. of Community Medicine, University of Sydney, 11 Croydon Avenue, Croydon, NSW 2132, Australia.

BRIGDEN, Wallace William, b. 8 June 1916, London, England. Consulting Cardiologist. *Education:* MA, MD, Cambridge University; Henry Fellow, Yale University, USA; Kings College Hospital Medical School. *Appointments:* House Physicians and Sambrook Registrar, Kings College Hospital; Medical Specialist, Hon. Rank Major, R.A.M.C; Lecturer, Royal Postgraduate Medical School; Consultant Physician and Consultant Cardiology, The London Hospital; Consultant Physician, National Heart Hospital; Civil Consultat Cardiologist, Royal Navy; Chief Medical Officer, · Munich Reinsurance, London. *Memberships:* Association of Physicians; British Cardiology Society; Council, Clinical Cardiology; Honorary Member, Cardiology Society of Australia and New Zealand; Fellow, Royal College of Physicians. *Publications:* Papers on various cardiological subjects; Chapter 'Cardio-Vascular Medicine' "Price Textbook of Medicine"; Chapter 'Cardiomyopathy', Beeson and McDermott "Textbook of Medicine". *Hobbies:* Food; Wine; Gardening; Painting. *Address:* 45 Wimpole Street, London, W.1, England.

BRIGG, David John, b. 27 Oct. 1953, Nelson, Lancashire, England. Consultant Radiologist. *Education:* BSc (1st class hons.), Physiology, Manchester University, 1974; MB ChB, 1977, DCH, 1979, DMRD, 1981, FRCR, 1982, Manchester University. *Appointments:* House Surgeon, House Physician, Steppinghill Hospital, Stockport; Senior House Officer, Paediarics, South Manchester; Registrar, Diagnostic Radiology, Senior Registrar, Manchester Rotation. *Memberships:* British Institute of Radiology; British Medical Association; Fellow, Royal College of Radiologists. *Publications:* Co-author, "Lung Uptake of Technetium 99 m Diphosphonate due to Focal Matastatic Callification', 'British Journal of Radiology', 1984; Co-author, 'The Prognostic Significance of Mediastinal Bulk in Patients with Stage 1A-IVB Hodgkins Disease', 'Clinical Radiology', 1985. *Address:* Department of Radiology, Bury General Hospital, Walmersley Road, Bury, Lancashire, England.

BRIGHT, Thomas Peter, b. 4 Feb. 1946, Covington, Kentucky, USA. Private Practice, Diseases of the Chest. m. Mary Anne Woltermann, 10 June 1967, Bellevue, Kentucky, 1 son, 1 daughter. *Education:* MD, University of Kentucky College of Medicine, 1970; Fellow, Pulmonary Diseases, Indiana University Medical Centre, Indianapolis, 1972-74. *Appointments:* Consultant in Pulmonary Physiology, Division of Toxicology, 1973-74, Clinical Assistant Professor of Medicine, 1976, Assistant Professor of Toxicology, 1976, Indiana University Medical Centre; Chief, Respiratory Research Laboratory, Dow Pharmaceuticals, Dow Chemicals Co., Indianapolis, 1976-83; Staff andConsultant Physician, presently Director, Indiana Poison Centre,

1979-0; Assistant Clinical Professor, Indiana University Medical Centre, 1985-. *Memberships:* American Medical Association; American Geriatric Society; American Thoracic Society; American Federation for Clinical Research; American College of Chest Phsyicians; American Occupational Medical Association; Central States Occupational Medical Association; Indiana State Medical Association; Indiana Thoracic Society; Sigma Xi; Society of Toxicology *Publications:* Various articles & scientific papers in 'Life Sciences', 'Applied Pharmacology', 'Clinical Pharmaceutical Therapy', and others. *Address:* Suite 110, St John's Medical Arts, 2101 Jackson Street, Anderson, IN 46014, USA.

BRILLIANDE, Timothy Wayne, b. 25 July 1948, Honolulu, Hawaii, USA. Registered Respiratory Therapist, ICU Care. m. K. Storrs, 5 Aug. 1972, 1 son. *Education:* BA, Botanical Sciences, 1971, MS Mycology-Microbiology, 1973, University of Hawaii; Advanced Graduate Work: University of Oklahoma, 1976-78: AS, Respiratory Therapy, 1981-83. *Appointments:* U.D. Clinician, State of Hawaii Department of Health, 1979-81. *Memberships:* Sigma Xi; American Society for Microbiologists; Mycological Society of America; Honolulu Association of Artists; Stain Glass Association of Hawaii. *Publications:* Articles in professional journals including: 'Streptococcus bovis'; 'American Journal Clinical Pathology';etc. *Honours:* Outstanding Botany Graduate, University of Hawaii, 1971. *Hobbies:* Writing Children's Literature; Stained Glass Art. *Address:* 7269 Nuulolo St., Honolulu, HI 96825, USA.

BRINDLEY, Giles Skey, b. 30 Apr. 1926, Woking, Surrey, England. Professor of Physiology. m. Hilary Richards, 25 Nov. 1964, Cambridge, 1 son, 1 daughter. *Education:* BA Natural Sciences, Downing College, University of Cambridge, 1944-47; MB, B.Chir, MD, 1956, London Hospital Medical College; Fellow of the Royal Society, 1965; Fellow, Royal College of Physicians, 1973. *Appointments:* Junior medical & research posts, 1950-54; Demonstrator, Lecturer, Reader in Physiology, University of Cambridge, 1954-68; Visiting Associate Professor, Johns Hopkins Medical School, Baltimore, USA, 1962; Visiting Professor, University of California at Berkeley, USA, 1968; Professor of Physiology, Institute of Psychiatry, University of London, 1968-; Honorary Director, Medical research Council Neurological Prostheses Unit, 1968-. *Memberships:* Physiological Society; Association of British Neurologists; International Medical Society of Paraplegia. *Publications:* 'Sacral anterior root stimulators for bladder control in Paraplegia', in 'Paraplegia', 1982; 'Effects of electrical stimulation of the visual cortex', in'Human Neurobiology', 1982; 'Cavernosal alpha-blockade: a new method for treating erectile impotence' in 'British Journal of Psychiatry', 1983; 'New Treatment for Priapism', in 'The Lancet', 1984; 'The Fertility of men with spinal injuries', in 'Paraplegia', 1984. *Honours:* Liebrecht-Franceschetti Prize, German Ophthalmological Society, 1971. *Hobbies:* Music; Skiing; Running(UK Over-55 age best holder, 3000m steeplechase). *Address:* 102 Ferndale Road, London SE24 OAA, England.

BRINK, Hilla-Ilse Luise, b. 17 Aug. 1933, Glencoe, Natal, Republic of South Africa. Professor in Nursing Education. m. Daniel Johannes de Villiers Brink, 11 May 1972, Glencoe, Natal, 1 son. *Education:* BA; BA Honours Psychology; MA; D.Litt. et Phil. Nursing Science; Diplomas in General Nursing, Midwifery, Nursing Education, Nursing Administration; Registered Nurse and Midwife. *Appointments:* Ward Sister; Sister Tutor; Senior Matron; Principal of Nursing College; Lecturer; Senior Lecturer; Associate Professor; Professor in Nursing Education. *Memberships:* The South African Nursing Association; Society for Research in Nursing Education; Association for the Study of

Evaluation in Education in Southern Africa; Society for Oncological Nursing in South Africa. *Publications:* "Introductory Statistics for Nurses", 1978; co-editor and author of 5 chapters in "Aspects of Community Health", 1982. *Honours:* Honours Exhibition, University of South Africa, 1972; Doctoral Bursary, Human Science Research Council. *Hobby:* Reading. *Address:* PO Box 905-400, Garsfontein, Pretoria 0042, Republic of South Africa.

BRINGHURST, John F, b. Nov. 1943, Ogden, Utah, USA, Assistant Administrator, m. Jeanne Taylor, 19 Dec. 1969, Logan, Utah, 4 sons, 3 daughters. *Education:* MBA, Northwestern University, Evanston, I11, 1973; BA, Utah State University, Logan, Utah, 1969. *Appointments:* Administrative Assistant, 1973-74, Assistant Adminitrator, 1974-76, Vice President, 1976-82, Valley Presbyterian Hospital, Van Nuys, Calif; Assistant Administrator, Rogue Valley Medical Centre, Medford, ORE, 1982-. *Memberships:* Member, American college of Hospital Administrators; Fellow, Hospital Financial Managemnt Association; Member, American Society of Hospital Planners; Member, Western Gerontological Society. *Honorus:* 1st Lieutenant, US Army, 1969-71. *Address:* 2825 Barnett Road, Medford, OR 97504, USA.

BRISSON, Marcelle Liliane, b. 18 Dec. 1931, Canada. Clinical Social Worker, Regional Palliative Care Unit. 4 sons, 1 daughter. *Education:* BA, Liberal Arts, University of Ottawa, Canada; MSW, University of California, Los Angeles, USA. *Appointments:* Clinical Social Worker, Neurophyciatric Institute, Los Angeles, California: Social Work Supervisor, Regional Center for Developmentally Disaabled, Orange County, California; Senior Social Worker, US Department of Defence, Athens, Greece; Social Work Supervisor, Department of Psychiatry, Ottawa General Hospital, Canada; Director of Social Work, St. Paul's Hospital, Vancouver, British Columbia; Clinical Social Worker, Regional Palliative Care Unit, Elizabeth Bruyers Health Center, Ottawa, Ontario; Secretary-General, International Social Service, Geneva, Switzerland, 1986. *Memberships:* Academy of Certified Social Workers, USA; Licensed Clinical Social Worker, California; Marriage, Family and Child Counselor, California; Ontario Association of Professional Social Workers, Canada. Extensive lecturing (conference and workshops) in the field of Palliative Care. *Hobbies:* Needlework; Reading; Skiing; Swimming; Long Walks. *Address:* Elizabeth Bruyere Health Center, 43 Bruyers Street, Ottawa, Ontario, Canada.

BRITO, Gilberto Ney Ottoni, b. 24 May 1951, Brazil. Associate Professor, Universidade Federal Fluminense. m. Linda Christine Stopp, 15 July 1984, Rochester, USA, 1 son, 1 daughter. *Education:* MD, State University of Rio de Janeiro, 1974; MA, Carleton University, 1977; MSc., 1980, PhD, 1981, University of Rochester, USA. *Appointmetns:* Postdoctoral fellow, 1981, Assistant Professor, 1982, University of Rochester. *Memberships:* Rio de Janeiro Medical Council; American Association for the Advancement of Science; Society for Neuroscience; New York Academy of Sciences; Association for Child Psychology and Psychiatry; International Neuropsychological Society. *Publications:* Articles in various journals including: 'Brain researach'; 'Journal Comparative Physiological Psychology'; 'Brain Researach Bulletin'; 'Percep. Mot. Skills'. *Honour:* Reviewer, Articles for Journals in Neuroscience. *Hobbies:* Karate; Soccer; Swimming. *Address:* Rua Rego Lopes, 30 casa 12. Rio de Janeiro, RJ 20520, Brazil.

BROCH, Johan Anthony Zincke, b. 22 June 1920, Fana, Norway. Senior Radiologist. m. Helene Runeberg, 22 Sept. 1955 (deceased 1960), 1 son, 1 daughter. *Education:* Medical Degree, Oslo University, 1948; Authorised Norwegian Radiologist, 1958. *Appointments:* Medical Officer,

Norwegian Ind. Brigade Gp, Germany, 1948-49; Assistant Physician, Det Norsk Radium Hospital, Oslo, 1949-51; Assistant Physician, Vestfold Sentralsykehus, 1951-55; Medical Officer (Radiologist), Norwegian MASH, Korea, 1952; Assistant Physician, Ulleval Sykehus (Oslo City Hospital), 1955-56; Assistant Physician, Stavanger Hospital, 1956-57; General practitioner (Deputy) in Stokke, 1957-58; Assistant physician and Deputy, Superior Oslo University Hospital, 1958-67; Senior Radiologist, Diagnostic Dept 12 Hospital Lovisenberg, Rontgen, Oslo-. *Memberships:* The Norwegian Association of Physicians; Norwegian Association of Medical Radiology; European Association of Radiology; British Institute of Radiology. *Publications:* Papers in Norwegian on Oncology and Diagnostic Radiology; Co-author: 'Morbus Meniere - Cerebral Atrophy' in'Acta Otolaryng.', 1967; 'Respiration and Cerebral Blood Flow in Metabolic Acidosis and Alcalosis in Humans' in 'Journal of Applied Physiology', 1969; 'Occipital Steal with Symtoms of Meniere's Syndrome' in 'European Neurology', 1970; 'Studies on Cerebral Ocular Circulation in a Patient with a Cluster Headache' in'Headache', 1970. *Hobbies:* Opean air activities; Touring; Book-binding; Stone polishing and jewellery. *Address:* Diakonisschusets sykehus, Lovisenberg, N 0456 Oslo 4, Norway.

BROCKETT, Margaret Marion, b. 10 Aug. 1942, Republic of South Africa, Executive Director, m. Andrew Brockett, 19 Sep. 1964, Edinburgh, Scotland, 1 son, 1 daughter. *Education:* BSR(OT), University British Columbia, Canada; Diploma in Occupational Therapy, Edinburgh, Scotland; OT(C). *Appointments:* Occupational Therapist in Charge, Barnsley Hall Hospital, Bromsgrove, England, 1963; Domiciliary Occupational Therapist, Oxford City Council, Oxford, 1964-66; Occupational Therapist, London Borough of Sutton, 1972-75; Staff Occupational Therapist, 1975-76, Director of Occuptional Therapy, 1976-84, Pearson Hospital, Vancouver, British Columbia, Canada; Senior Occupational Therapist, Vancouver General Hospital, 1984-85; Executive Director, Canadian Association of Occupational Therapists, 1985-. *Memberships:* Canadian Association of Occupational Therapists; World Federation of Occupational Therapists; President, 1984-85, British Columbia Society of Occupational Therapists; Directors of Occupational Therapy of British Columbia. *Publications:* 'Professionalism or Unionism – The Therapists Dilemma?', 1985. *Honours:* Occupational Therapist of the Year, BCSOT, 1982; Honorary Clincial Assistant Professor, UBC, 1983-85. *Hobbies:* Calligraphy; Reading; Walking; Singing; Cooking. *Address:* Canadian Association of Occupational Therapists 110 Eglinton Avenue West, 3rd Floor, Toronto, Ontario, Canada M4R 1A3.

BRODD, Debra Anne, b. 6 July 1955, Evanston, Illinois, USA. Chiropractic Physician; Senior Staff Physician. *Education:* BS, Biology, University of Notre Dames; BS, DC, National College of Chiropractic. *Appointments:* Senior Staff Physician, National College of Chiropractic. *Memberships:* American and Illinois Chiropractic Associations; FCA; President Elect, Polk County Chiropractic Society; Council of Sport and Athletic Injuries, American Chiropractic Association. *Honour:* National Honour Society, 1973. *Hobbies:* Athletics; Racketball; Swimming; Equestrian events; Wind surfing; Horticulture; Painting. *Address:* 62 South Meyer Court, Des Plaines, IL 60016, USA.

BRODERSEN, Rolf, b. 28 Mar. 1921, Skovshoved, Denmark. Professor. m. Grethe Larsen, 5 May 1951, Sollerod, 2 sons, 1 daughter. *Education:* MA, Biochemistry, University of Copenhagen, 1944; 1949; Studies at Billings Hospital, University of Chicago,USA, 1947-48; Institute Pasteur, Paris, 1950; Brown University, Rhode Island, USA, 1977;

University of San Francisco, USA,1977. *Appointments:* Institute General Pathology, University of Copenhagen, 1944-47; State Serum Institute, Copenhagen, 1947; Leo Pharm. Products, 1949-54; Ndolage Mission Hospital, Tanganyika, 1954-61; Institute of Biochemistry, University of Copenhagen, 1961-69; Institute of Medical Biochemistry, University of Aarhus, 1969-. *Memberships:* The Biochemical Society, Denmark; The Learned Society Aarhus; Society Experimental Biological Medicine, New York, etc. *Publications:* Thesis: 'Inactivation of Penicillin in Aqueous Solution: A Reaction-Kinetic Study,' Munksgaard, Copenhagen, 1949; About 120 papers in Scandinavian and International journals on buffers, pencillin, chemotherapy of Tuberculosis, bilirubin in relation to prevention of brain damage in the newborn, serum albumin'. *Honour:* Knight of the Dannebroge, 1977. *Hobby:* Sailing. *Address:* Ny Moesgaardvej 33, DK-8270 Hojbjerg, Denmark.

BRODIE, Brian Sidney, b. 27 May 1943, Enfield, Middlesex, England. Chiropodist. m. Gillian Mary Taylor, 21 Sep. 1968, Enfield. *Education:* Qualifying Examination, London Foot Hospital, 1968; BA, Open University, 1977. *Appointments:* Senior Chiropodist, Chief Chiropodist, Bournemouth, Dorset, 1968-76; Area Chiropodist, Berkshire, 1976-79; Area Chiropodist, Hampshire, then District Chiropodist, Southampton & Southwest Hampshire, 1979-84; Coordinator, Chiropody Programme, George Brown College, Toronto, Canada, 1982-83; Regional Chiropodist, Saskatchewan Health, 1984-. *Memberships:* Society of Chiropodists, 1968-; Royal Society for the Promotion of Health, 1969-76; Association of Chief Chiropody Officers, 1972-; American College of Podopaediatrics, 1981-. *Publications:* 'A Survey of Children's Feet', 1974, 'Aspects of Pain', 1976 (in 'The Chiropodist'); Editor, 'NHS Chiropody Services', 1977; 'Wessex Feet – A Regional Foot Health Survey', 1984. *Honour:* Crowther Award, Open University, 1979. *Hobbies:* Collecting; Walking; Running; Amateur Radio (G4LUU). *Address:* 6th Floor Humford House, 1855 Victoria Avenue, Regina S4P 3V5, Canada.

BRODIE, Elizabeth, b. 4 Sep. 1923, Budapest, Hungary. Psychiatrist. Private Practice. m. Tom Philbrook, 1 son. *Education:* MD, University of Vienna, Austria, 1957; LMCC, Medical Council of Canada, 1959; D.Psych., University of Toronto, 1963; CRCP (C), 1963, FRCP (C), 1973, Royal College of Physicians & Surgeons of Canada. *Appointments:* Intern, McKellar General Hospital, Thunder Bay, 1958; Resident, Internal Medicine, Women's College Hospital, Toronto, 1959; Resident, Psychiatry, Ontario Hospital, 1960; Resident, Psychiatry, Addiction Research Foundation, Toronto, 1961-63; Fellow, Psychiatric Addiction Research Foundation, Toronto, 1964; Director, Day Hospital for Alcoholics, 1965-69; Psychiatrist, Private practice, Toronto, 1969-77; Adjunct Associate Professor, Faculty of Environmental Studies, York University, Toronto, 1973-76; Psychiatrist, Private Practice, Houston, Texas, USA, 1978- . *Memberships:* American Psychiatric Association; Texas Medical Association; Houston Psychiatric Society. *Publications:* Contributor to'McLeans'; 'Chatelaine'; 'Association for Planned Parenthood'; "Exerpta Medica", IV World Congress of Psychiatrists, Madrid, 1966. *Honours:* Rockefeller Fellowship, Vinna, 1956. *Hobbies:* Piano; Gourmet Cooking; Tennis; Travel. *Address:* 9055 Katy Frwy., Ste. 210, Houston, TX 77024, USA.

BROGARD, Jean-Marie, b. 26 Dec. 1935, Strasbourg, France. Professor of Internal Medicine. m. Christiane Meyer, 7 July 1960, Strasbourg, 2 sons, 2 daughters. *Education:* Medicine studies at Faculty of Medicine of Strasbourg, 1958-65. *Appointments:* Internship, Strasbourg Hospitals; Clinical Chief, CHU, Strasbourg; Head, Department of Experimental Medicine, CHU, Strasbourg; Certified Professor, CHU, Strasbourg, 1975. *Memberships:* European Association for Study of Diabetes; French Association for Study of Diabetes; American Society of Microbiology; French Society of Infectious Pathology; French National Society of Internal Medicine; European Association of Internal Medicine. *Publications:* "Antibiotics and Chemotherpay"; "Pharmacokinetics" I and II, volume 25 et 31, 1978, 82, S Karger, Basel. *Honour:* General Secretary of European Association of Internal Medicine since 1977. *Address:* Clinique Medicale B, Centre Hospitalo-Universitaire de Strasbourg, Hospices Civils de Strasbourg, 67091, France.

BROITMAN, Selwyn Arthur, b. 20 Aug. 1931, Boston, Massachusetts, USA, Assistant Dean, Professor of Pathology and Microbiology, m. Barbara Merle Schwartz, 13 June 1953, Boston, Massachusetts, 1 son, 1 daughter. *Education:* BS, University of Massachusetts, 1952; Ms, 1953, PhD, 1956, Michigan State University. *Appointments:* Research Associate, Malory Institute, Pathology, Boston City Hospital Gastro Intestinal Research Laboratory, 1956-71; Associate in Medicine, Thorndike Memorial Laboratory, 1969-74; Director, Biotech Associates, 1959-62; Research Instructor, Department of Pathology, Boston University School of Medicine, 1963-64; Assistant Professor, Department of Microbiology, 1965-69, Associate Professor, Department of Microbiolgoy, 1969-75, Professor, 1975-, Associate Professor, Nutritional Sciences, School of Grad Dentistry, 1974-, Professor of Pathology, 1982-, Assistant Dean, 1981-, Boston University School of Medicine, Boston, Massachusetts; Associate, Medicine, Department of Medicine, Harvard University Medical School, 1969-74. *Memberships:* Founding Member, Digestive Disease Foundation; Member, Committee on Diet, Nutrition and Cancer, National Academy of Science/NRC, 1980-83; AAAS; Society of Experimental Pathology; American Institute Nutrition; Federation for Clinical Research; American Society for Applied Bacteriology; Society of Experimental biology and Medicine; Founding Member, Nutrition Today Society; American Gastroenterology Association; Boston Gastroenterology Society; New York Academy of Sciences; President, 1976, Boston Bug Club; Sigma Xi. *Publications:* Contributor of articles to professioal journals. *Honours:* Served with AUS, 1952-66; Recipient Outstanding Teaching Award, Boston University School of Medicine 1st Year Class, 1976. *Address:* Boston University School of Medicine, Department of Microbiolgoy, 80 East Concord Street, Boston, MA 02118, USA.

BROOK, John Roger, b. 15 Mar. 1924, London, England. Family Practitioner. m. Joan Margaret Clucas, 23 July 1949, Liverpool, 1 son, 2 daughters. *Education:* MB BS; CCFP, Canada. *Appointments:* General Practice, Portsmouth, England; General Practice, Hearts Content, Newfoundland, Canada; Family Practice, St Catherines, Ontario; Chief of Staff, Hotel Dieu Hospital, St Catherines, 1978-82. *Memberships:* Ontario Medical Association; Canadian Medical Association. *Honours:* CD and Bar, 1973, 83. *Hobby:* Cross country skiing. *Address:* 156 St Paul Crescent, St Catherines, Ontario, Canada L25 1N3.

BROOKE, Nevill Hamilton, b. 4 Apr. 1925, Blenheim, New Zealand. Consulting Physician; Visiting Specialist Physician,. m. Janet Ramsay Low, 9 Feb. 1952, Nelson, 3 sons, 2 daughters. *Education:* MB.CH.B. Otago, New Zealand; FRCP (Edinburgh); MRACP. *Appointments:* President, Medical Officer, Wellington Hospital, 1950-52; Medical Registrar, Edinburgh, Scotland, 1953-55; Consulting Physician, Palmerston North N2, and Visiting Specialist Physician, Palmerston North Hospital, New Zealand, 1956-; Consultant Physician to New Zealand Army; Patron, Manawatu Diabetic Society, New Zealand.

Memberships: Cardiac Society of Australia & New Zealand; New Zealand Medical Association; Aviation Medical Society of Australia & New Zealand. *Hobbies:* Golf; Gardening; Walking; Swimming. *Address:* PO Box 8044, 59 Te Awe Awe St., Palmerston North, New Zealand.

BROOKE, Ralph Ian, b. 25 Apr. 1934, England. Dean, University Faculty of Dentistry. m. Lorna Ruth Shields, 21 apr. 1963, Liverpool, England, 2 sons. *Education:* BCh.D; LDS; MRCS: LRCP; FDSRCS (Oral Surgery); FRCD (Canada); FICD. *Appointments:* Dental House Surgeon, Leeds University Dental School and St. George's Hospital, London, England, 1957-58; Lecturer in Clinical Dental surgery, Leeds University, 1963-69, Senior Lecturer in Oral Medicine, 1969-72; Professor and Chairman, Department of Oral Medicine, University of Western Ontario, Canada, 1972-82, Dean, Faculty of Dentistry, 1982-. *Memberships:* Numerous. *Publications:* Numerous. *Address:* Faculty of Dentistry, University of Western Ontario, London, Ontario, Canada N6A 5C1.

BROOKES, Gerald Barry, b. 15 Jan. 1950, London, England. Consultant Otolaryngologist. m. Christine Raywood, 17 Jan. 1975, Sheffield, 2 sons. *Education:* MB; Ch.B; FRCS, Distinction in Paediatrics. *Appointments:* House Officer, Royal Infirmary, Shefield, 1974, Royal Hospital, Sheffield, 1975; Senior House Officer: Casulty/Orthopaedics, Northern General Hospital, Sheffield, 1975, General Surgery, Royal Infirmary, Hull, 1976, Neurosurgery, Frenchay Hospital, Bristol, 1976, Otolaryngology, Royal Infirmary, Bristol, 1977; Registrar, Otolaryngology, Plastic Surgery, King's College Hospital, London, 1978-79; Senior Registrar, Otolaryngology, London Hospital, 1980-84; Clincial & Research Fellow, Otology, University of Michigan, USA, 1982; Consultant Otolaryngologist, Royal National Throat Nose & Ear Hospital, & National Hospitals for Nervous Diseases, Queen Square & Maida Vale; Honorary Senior Lecturer, Otolaryngology, University of London and Institute of Laryngology & Otology. *Memberships:* British Medical Association; Royal Society of Medicine; ENT Research Society. *Publications:* Articles in professional journals including: 'Drugs'; 'Journal Royal Society of Medicine'; 'Journal Laryngology & Otology'; 'Acta Otolaryngology' "Systemic Diseases Affecting the Temporal Bone", Chapter in 'Diseases of the Ear, Nose & Throat', 5th edition 1986; "Nutritional Problems in Head and Neck Cancer Patients", Chapter in 'Otalryngology', 1986. *Honours:* Down's Travelling Scholarship, Royal Society of Medicine, 1981; Runner-up, BUPA Doctor of the Year Awards, 1981; TWJ Travelling Fellowship, Otology, University of Michigan, 1982. *Hobbies:* Chess; Jogging. *Address:* 66 New Cavendish Street, London W1M7 LD, England.

BROOKES, Peter, b. 16 June 1928, Coventry, England. Professor of Chemical Carcinogenesis. m. Vera Sutton, 26 Mar. 1951, Stoke-on-Trent, 2 son, 1 daughter. *Education:* BSc Chemistry, University of Birmingham; PhD, DSc, University of London. *Appointments:* Research Scientist, Glaxo Laboratories Ltd, 1952-53, National Institute for Medical Research, Mill Hill, London, 1954-56; Professor of Chemical Carcinogenesis, University of London; Chairman; Chemical Carcinogenesis Section, Institute of Cancer Research, London, 1957-. *Memberships:* Biochemical Society; British Association for Cancer Research; American Association for Cancer Research. *Publications:* Over 100 publications in scientific journals, 1961-85. *Honours:* Karl-August-Forster Prize, Academy of Science & Literature,Mainz, Federal Republic of Germany. *Hobbies:* Bridge; Golf; Reading Scientific papers. *Address:* Institute of Cancer Research, Fulham Road, London SW3 6JB, England.

BROOKS, Ethel Audrey Victoria, b. 24 May 1924,

London, England. Sessional Cytopatholgoist, Fremantle Hospital, Australia. m. John Leicester Holme, 10 Sep. 1960, Perth, Australia, 1 son, 1 daughter. *Education:* MB,BS, London; Diploma, Clinical Pathology, London, 1955; Felow, Royal College of Pahologists of Australia, 1956. *Appointments include:* House Officer, various London hospitals, 1948-51; Pathology Registrar, Princess Margaret Hospital, Perth, West Australia, 1952-54; Assistant, Acting Pathologist, ibid, 1955-60; Cytopathologist, Fremantle hospital, 1963-. *Memberships:* Royal College of Pathologists of Australasia; Australian Society of Cytology. *Hobbies:* Gardening; Sewing; Painting. *Address:* 75 Mountjoy Road, Nedlands, West Australia, 6009.

BROWN, Carl Dee, b. 8 Dec. 1939, Lead Hill, Arkansas, USA. Health Care Logistics Administrator. m. Nancy Carol Smith, 18 Feb. 1967, Gainesville, Georgia, 1 son, 1 daughter. *Education:* BS; MA, MHA. *Appointments:* Hospital Supply Officer; Medical Plans Officer; Commander, Medical Battalion; Health Care Administrator; Health Care Logistics Administrator. *Memberships:* American Hospital Association; American College of Hospital Administrators Association of United States; National Geographic Society; Sigma Xi; Euromed Medical Commitee Observer; Military Honour Society; US-German Combat Logistics Support System Committee. *Honours:* Bronze Star, 1970; Meritorious Service Awards, 1970-084; Commendation Medal, 3 awards, 1965-69; Certificate of Achievement, 1964. *Hobbies:* Travel; Water Sports; Botany. *Address:* 667 Crestway Drive, San Antonio, TX 78239, USA.

BROWN, David, 27 Dec 1940, Southport, England, Senior Lecturer in Dental Materials Science; Sub-Dean of Admissions (Dental), UMDS. *Education:* BSc, MSc, PhD, University of Manchester; C Eng; MIM. *Appointments:* Post Doctoral Researach Fellow, Department of Metallurgy, 1966-69, Assistant Lecturer, 1969-70, Lecturer, 1970-72, Dental Materials Science, Sub-Warden, St Anselm Hall, 1967-72, University of Manchester; Lecturer, 1972-77, Senior Lecturer, Dental School, 1977-. Sub-Dean for Admissions (Dental), Materials Science, Guy's Hospital Dental School, 183-86; Sub-Dean of Dental Studies, 1979-83, Guys Hospital Dental School; Vice Warden, Hughs Parry Hall, University of London, 1972-. *Memberships:* Institute of Metals; Chartered Engineer; Member, British society for Dental Research; member, American Institute of Mining, Metallurgy and Petroleum Engineers; Member, BSSPD. *Publications:* 'The detection of mecury vapour in the dental surgergy', 1983; "The Clinical Handling of Dental Materials", (with B G N Smith, P S Wright), 1986; Contributor of various chapters to professional books. *Honours:* Reckitt Prize, British Society for the Study of Prosthetic Dentistry (BSSPD), 1973. *Address:* Department of Dental Materials Science, United Medical and Dental Schools of Guy's and St Thomas' Hospitals, London Bridge, London SE1 9RT, England.

BROWN, David Lee, b. 28 Aug. 1932, St Paul, Minnesota, USA. Director of Management Services, Lutheran Health Systems. m. Norma Kay Vik, 8 Jan. 1956, Oakland, Nebraska, 2 sons, 1 foster-daughter. *Education:* BBA, University of Minnesota, 1954; M A Hospital Administration, University of Iowa, 1959. *Appointments:* Business Manager,Iowa Annie Wittenmeyer Home, Davenport, Iowa, 1959-61; Associate Administrator, Iowa Lutheran Hospital, Des Moines, Iowa, 1961-74; Executive Director,Des Moines General Hospital, Des Moines, Iowa, 1974-76; Administrator, Bishop Randall Hospital, Lander, Wyoming, 1976-81; Director of Management Services,Lutheran Health Systems, 1981- Administrator, Mandan Hospital. *Memberships:* Fellow, American College of Hospital Administrators; Member, Certified Professional

(CPQA), National Association of Quality Assurance Professionals; American Society for Hospital Risk Management. *Publications:* 'Fire Protections Systems Tested', in 'Hospital', 1973; 'System wide Quality Assurance leans heavily on Board Talk', in 'Multis', 1984; 'Guidelines can resolve Turf Battles between local & coporate Boards', in 'Trustee', 1983. *Honours:* Past President, Midwest Health Congress, 1982-83; Regent, State of Wyoming, American College of Hospital Administrators, 1980-82, also Oral Examiner 1972-; Past President, Polk County Association for Mental Health, Iowa, 1974-76. *Hobbies:* Running; Golf; Canoeing; Backpacking; Photography; Bird-watching. *Address:* Mandan Hospital, 1000-18th Street NW, Mandan, ND-58554, USA.

BROWN, Douglas C. S., b. 29 Dec. 1930, Canada. Orthopaedic Surgeon. m. Pamela M Mylward, 2 July 1960, Holybourne, Hampshire, 3 daughters. *Education:* BSc, MDCM, Dalhousie University; FRCS(C). *Appointments:* Assistant Professor, Surgery, Dalhousie University, Halifax, NA, Canada. *Memberships:* Canadian Medical Assn.; Canadian Orthopaedic Assn. *Honour:* Mclaughlin Travelling Fellow, 1967. *Hobbies:* Sailing; Skiing; Stamp Collecting. *Address:* 5991 Spring Garden Road, Halifax, NS B3H 8Y6, Canada.

BROWN, Eric Gradwell, b. 8 Sept 1930, Liverpool, England, Professor of Biochemistry, Head of Department, m. Muriel Owen, 6 Dec 1955, Liverpool. *Education:* BSc (Hons), 1953, PhD, 1956, University of Liverpool, 1953-56; ICI Research Fellow, University College Hospital Medical School, University of London, 1956-59; Lecturer in Biochemistry, 1959, Senior Lecturer in Biochemistry, 1962, Reader in Biochemistry, 1965, Appointed to new chair of Biochemistry, 1972, University College of Swansea, Wales. *Memberships:* Biochemical Society; Royal Society of Chemistry; Former Chairman, Phytochemical Society of Europe. *Publications:* Author of numerous articles in professional journals including 'Metabolism of the amino acid BETA-pyrazol I-ylalanine and its parent base pyrazole', 1984; 'Analysis of free nucleotide pools by HPLC', 1982. *Honours:* DSc, University of Liverpool, 1971; Elected Honorary Member, Phytochemical Society of Europe. *Hobbies:* Languages; Gardening. *Address:* Department of Biochemistry, University College of Swansea, Swansea SA2 8PP, Wales.

BROWN, Eugene Richard, b. 17 Feb. 1942, Plainfield, New Jersey, USA. Associate Professor. m. Marianne Parker, 19 June 1966, Berkeley, California, 2 sons. *Education:* BA, 1966, MA, 1968, PhD, 1975, University of California. *Appointments:* Visiting Assistant Professor, Sociology, Antioch College, Yellow Springs, 1972; Co-ordinator, Theme House in Community Health, University of California, Berkeley, 1972-76; Health Planner, Alameda County Department of Health, 1977-78; Assistant Professor, 1979-84, Associate Professor, 1984-, University of Californian School of Public Health, Los Angeles. *Memberships:* American Public Health Association; Society for Public Health Education; National Association for Public Health Policy; International Group for Study of Political Economy of Health; Delta Omega. *Publications:* "Rockefeller Medicine Men: medicine and Capitalism in America", 1979; "Public Medicine in Crisis: Public Hospitals in California", 1981; Numerous articles in professioal journals. *Honours:* Outstanding Achievement Award, American Cancer Society Los Angeles Coastal Cities Unit, 1980; Career Development Award, University of California, Los Angeles, 1982. *Address:* School of Public Health, University of California, Los Angeles, CA 90024, USA.

BROWN, Fred, b. 31 Jan. 1925, Clayton-le-Moors, Lancashire, England. Head of Virology Research & Development, Wellcome Biochemistry Ltd. m.

Audrey Alice Doherty, 1 May 1948, Sale Moor, 2 sons. *Education:* BSc, MSc. PhD Chemistry, University of Manchester. *Appointments:* Assistant Lecturer in Chemistry, University of Manchester; Senior Scientific Officer, Hannah Dairy Researach Institute; Senior Research Assistant, Christie Hospital & Holt Radium Institute, Manchester; Senior Scientific Officer, Principal Scientific Officer, Senior Principal Scientific Officer, Deputy Chief Scientific Officer, Deputy Director, Animal Virus Research Institute, Pirbright. *Memberships:* Fellow of the Royal Society; Society for General Microbiology. *Publications:* Numerous papers on Virology during the last 30 years in scientific journals and books. *Hobbies:* Watching Cricket & Soccer; Fell-Walking. *Address:* 'Syndal', Glaziers Lane, Normandy, Surrey, England.

BROWN, Forst E, b. 24 July 1933, Louisville, Kentucky, USA. Chairman, Section Plastic and Reconstructive Surgery; Clinical Professor, Plastic Surgery, Dartmouth-Hitchcock Medical Center. m. Jean Sandmann, 29 June 1957, Louisville, Kentucky, 1 son, 1 daughter. *Education:* BS, University of Notre Dame, 1955; MD, Harvard University, 1959. *Appointments:* Intern and Resident, University Hospitals, Cleveland, Ohio, 1959-67 (exclusive of 2-year Army stint, 1961-63). *Memberships:* American Society of Plastic and Reconstructive Surgeons; American Association of Plastic and Reconstructive Surgeons; Northeastern Society of Plastic and Reconstructive Surgeons; New England Society of Plastic and Reconstructive Surgeons; New England Surgical Society; American College of Surgeons; American Medical Association; American Society of Surgery of the Hand; American Association for Hand Surgery. *Publications:* Author of 17 articles; "Hypovolemia following Intraperitoneal Nitrogen Mustard Therapy", SG&D, 1965; 'Current Embryology and Treatment of Gastrochisis and Omphalocele', 'Arch. Surgery', 1966; 'Collagenase Systems in Rheumatoid Arthritis', 'Clinical Ortho.', 1975; 'Compression Neuropathies', 'Hand Surgery', 1981; 'Wrist Deformity in Rheumatoid Arthritis Extensor Carpi Ulnaris Tendon Transfer', 'Annals of Plastic Surgery', 1984; 'Induce Vasodilation in the treatment of Post-Traumatic Digital Cold Intolerance', 'Journal of Hand Surgery'. *Hobbies:* Music; Golf; Marathon Running. *Address:* Dartmouth-Hitchcock Medical Center, Section of Plastic and Reconstructive Surgery, Hanover, NH 03756, USA.

BROWN, Gregory Michael, b. 27 Mar. 1934, Toronto, Canada. Professor and Chairman, Department of Neurosciences, McMaster University, Hamilton. m. Audrey Christina Shute, 18 June 1960, Toronto, 2 sons, 6 daughters. *Education:* BA, 1955, Md, 1959, University of Toronto; PhD, University of Rochester, USA, 1971; FRCP(Canada), 1971. *Appointments:* Assistant Professor, Psychiatry, 1969; Associate Professor, Psychiatry, 1971; Professor of Psychiatry, 1973, University of Toronto; Professor, Psychiatry and Neurosciences, 1977-; Chairman, Department of Neurosciences, 1977- McMaster University. *Memberships:* American and Canadian Medical Associations; American and Canadian Psychiatric Associations; Endocrine Society; International Society of Psychoneuroendocrinology; Canadian College of Neuropsychopharmacology; American Psychosomatic Society. *Publications:* Co-author: "Neuroendocrinology and Psychiatric Disorder", 1984; 'Scheduled feeding and 24 hour rhythms of Nacetylserotonin and Melatonin in rats', 'Endocrinology', 1985. *Honours:* John Dewan Award, Ontario Mental Health Foundation, 1980; Heinz Lehmann Award, Canadian College of Psychopharmaoclogy, 1983; MRC Visiting Scientist Award, 1984-85. *Hobbies:* Singing; Performing in Operas and Musical Comedies. *Address:* Department of Neurosciences, McMaster University, 1200 Main Street West, Hamilton, Ontario, Canada L8N 2Z5.

BROWN, Kenneth Aylesbury, b. 14 Feb. 1926, Adelaide, South Australia. Senior Lecturer in Forensic Odontology and Head, Forensic Odontology Unit, University of Adelaide. m. Daphne May Reeves, 6 Oct. 1953, Sydney, 2 sons, 1 daughter. *Education:* BDS, University of Adelaide, 1950; FICD. *Appointments:* Private Dental Practice, 1951-80; Honorary Assistant Dental Surgeon, Adelaide Children's Hospital, 1952-55; Tutor in Dental Anatomy, Department of Oral Biology, University of Adelaide, 1959-80; Honorary Consultant in Dentistry to South Australian Dental Service, 1983-; Consultant odontologist, Department of Aviation (Bureau opf Air Safety), 1975-; Consultant in Forensic Odontology to: S.A. Police Department, 1972-; State Coroner's Office, 1972-, Australian Federal Police, 1980- , Royal Australian Air Force Reserve, Flight Lieutenant (retired); Working Group on Forensic Odontology, Federation Dentaire Internationale Australian Representative, 1980-; Editorial Board, Journal of Forensic Odonto-Stomatology, 1982-; International Editor, Journal of Medicine and Law, 1977-; Honorary Visiting Lecturer in Forensic Odontology, Tokyo Dental College, 1985- . *Memberships:* Australian Dental Association, S.A. branch (Conduct Committee, 1978-); Federation Dentaire Internationale; Forensic Science Society, S.A. branch; Australian Forensic Science Society; International Society for Forensic Odonto-Stomatology; Australian Society of Forensic Dentistry (Foundation President, 1982-). *Publications include:* Books and articles in professional publications. *Honours include:* Distinguished Services Award, Australian Dental Association, 1984. *Hobbies:* Oil Painting: Wood/Metal Craft Work. *Address:* Forensic Odontology Unit, Department of Dentistry, University of Adelaide, GPO Box 498, Adelaide, South Australia.

BROWN, Kenneth Marc, b. 25 Feb. 1948, New York, USA. Director of Health Care Facility. m. Cheryl Kawaler, 29 Dec. 1974, New York, USA, 2 daughters. *Education:* Masters Degree in Hospital Administration, Long Island University, New York, USA; Bachelor Degree in Psychology, University of Miami. *Appointments:* Unit Service Co-ordinator, Mount Sinai Medical Centre, Miami Beach, Florida; Centre; Director of Personnel, Margaret Tietz Centre for nursing Care, Queens, New York; Assistant Administrator, Margaret Tietz Centre; Adjunct Assistant Professor, Health Care Administration, St. John's University, Jamaica, New York. *Memberships:* North American Association of Jewish Homes and Housing for the Aged; New York Association of Homes and Services for the Aging; American Geriatric Society; American College of HealthCare Administrators. *Honours:* Member, Board of Directors, New York Association of Homes and Services for the Aging; Member, Board of Directors, North American Association of Homes and Housing; Advisory Council on Urban Health Management at St John's University, Jamaica, New York, 1982-85; Chairman of New York Association Downstate Administrators Regional Council, 1983-85; Member, Advisory Council of Aging Holocaust Survivors in America, Tate University, Detroit, Michigan, 1984-present. *Hobbies:* Writing; Poetry; Teaching; Tennis; Golf. *Address: 5 Lantern Lane, Nesconset, NY, 11767, USA.*

BROWN, Marvin Wayne, b. 10 Sep. 1917, Artesia, New Mexico, USA. Doctor of Chiropractic; Instructor, Psychiatry, Pasadena College of Chiropractic. m. Vera Covello, 13 Nov. 1982, Las Vegas. *Education:* AB, PhD, DC, Graduate Orthopedics Certificate; Diversified Technique Certificate. *Appointments:* Methodist Minister, 1940-47; Consulting Psychologist, Instructor, Psychology, Woodbury College, Vice President, Glo-Vita Corp, Owner, Career Engineering, Aptitude Testing Co., 1947-59; Doctor, Chiropractic, 1962-85;

Head, Psychiatry, Los Angeles College of Chiropractic, 1973-83; Psychiatry, Pasadena College of Chiropractic, 1983-85. *Memberships:* American Chiropractic Association; California Chiropractic Association, President, ACA Council on Mental Health, 1979-83; American Academy of Holistic Chiropractic, President; Fellow, Meninger Foundation. *Publications:* 5 Articles in 'Journal of the American Chiropractic Association' on Holism and Chiropractic. *Honours:* Oratory Championships: Rocky Mt. Tournament, 1938; Mid West Tournament, 1939; Southern California 1938; Outstanding speaker, College Seniors, 1940. *Hobbies:* Piano, Organ. *Address:* 2008 N. Glenoaks Blvd., Burbank, CA 91504, USA.

BROWN, Michael Nelson, b. 10 Aug. 1958, Madera, California, USA. Doctor of Chiropractic. m. 26 May 1979, Fresno. *Education:* DC, Palmer College of Chiropractic; American College of Chiropractic Orthopedics, Los Angeles; Diplomate, American Board of Chiropractic Orthopedics. *Appointments:* Associate Doctor, Schroeder's Chiropractic Inc., 1983-84; Associate Director, Chiropractic Health Clinic, Fresno, 1984-85; Associate Director, Chiropractic Health Centre, Director, Central California Sports Clinic, 1985- . *Memberships:* American Chiropractic Association; California Chiropractic Association; Council on Roentgenology, American Chiropractic Association; Council, Orthopedics, Council, Physical Therapy, American Chiropractic Association; Palmer College Alumni Association; Roentgenology Technological Society. *Publications:* "Lateral Patella Femoral Compression Syndromes", (publication pending). *Honours:* Magna cum laude Graduate, Palmer College of Chiropractic, 1982; Certificate of Merit, Palmer College of Chiropractic Student Council Award; National Board of Chiropractic Examiners Diplomat. *Address:* 3120 Willow Avenue, Clovis, CA 93612, USA.

BROWN, Monica Julienne, b. 3 July 1938, Colon, Panama. Head Hospital Endocrine Unit and Diabetes Clinic. *Education:* MD, University of Panama, 1964; APMC. *Appointments:* Assistant Professor of Propedeutics and Physiopathology, University of Panama, 1966-68, Assistant Professor of Medicine, 1970-74, Clinical Professor of Medicine, 1975-86; Head of Diabetic Clinic, Hospital Santo Tomas, Panama, 1977-86, Head of Endocrine Unit, 1978-86, Deputy Head of Nuclear Medicine Laboratory, 1984. *Memberships:* Medical Association of the Panama Canal Area; Honorary President, Panamanian Diabetic Association; National Medical Association; Panamanian Academy of Medicine and Surgery, elected to Board of Directors for period 1986-1992; Hospital Santo Toma Specialists Association; American Diabetes Association; Panamanian Society of Internal Medicine; Latin American Diabetes Association; Central American and Carribbean Association of Endricronology and Metabolism; Pan American Medical Womens' Alliance. *Publications Include:* Contributions to Panamanian and international medical journals including 'Verlag der Wiener Medizinischer Akademie'; 'Revista Medica de Panama, columes 1, 2, 8 and 10. *Honours:* First Place Honours, Sigma Lambda Chapter, 1964; Honorary Citizen of Colon, Panama, 1976; Latin American Diabetes federation Award, 1980; Plaque of Honour for contribution to social and economic development, Professional and Commercial Women's Club of Panama, 1982. *Hobbies:* Classical Music; Jazz; reading. *Address: PO Box 4968, Panama 5, Republic of Panama.*

BROWN, Oliver Wellington Jr., b. 14 Sep. 1926, Pittsburgh, Pennsylvania, USA. Manager, Media Relations, Therapeutics, SmithKline Beckman Corp. m. Majorie Lou Clarke, 1 Oct. 1955, Dayton, Ohio, 2 daughters. *Education:* AB, English, Washington & Jefferson College, 1949. *Appointments:* Staff writer, Washington PA, reporter, 1951-53; Advertising

Production, Copperweld Steel, Pittsburgh, 1953-54; Copy Editor, Knoxville News Sentinel, 1954; MedicalEditor, Dayton Daily News, 1954-64; Medical Relations, SmithKline Beckman Corp., 1964- ; Freelance Writer, 1960-64. *Memberships:* American Medical Writers Association; National Association of Science Writers; American Association for the Advancement of Science; International Public Relations Association; Overseas Press Club. *Honours:* Science Writing Fellowship, Council for Advancement of Science Writing, 1963. *Hobbies:* Watercolour Painting; History, Genealogy. *Address:* 600 Mount View Road, Berwyn, PA 19312, USA.

BROWN, Rennie, b. 3 Nov. 1926, Newcastle. Medical Director, Leamington Medical Centre, Ontario, Canada; Coroner. m. Leslie Ann Prudhoe, 19 Jan. 1957, Newcastle, 1 son, 1 daughter. *Education:* MB, BS, Dunelm, 1953; D(Obst)FCOG; LMCC; CCFP(C). *Appointments include:* 4 years' rotating internship, UK; General practitioner, Guyana 1957-60, East Suffolk, UK 1961-66; Newfoundland, Canada 1966-67. *Memberships:* Ontario Medical Association; Canadian Medical Association; Essex County Medical Society. *Hobbies:* Sailing; Running; Reading; Painting. *Address:* Medical Centre, 106 Talbot Street West, Leamington, Ontario, Canada N8H 1N1.

BROWN, Robert John, b. 31 Aug. 1949, Winnipeg, Canada. Chief Forensic Psychologist; Chairman of Board, Health and Law Foundation. m. Betsy Mae Ramsay, 19 May 1973, CutKnife, Saskatchewan, 1 son, 1 daughter. *Education:* BA, MA, PhD; American Board of Professional Neuropsychology Diplomate. *Appointments:* Lecturer, University of Guelph, 1975-76; Associate Professor, Wilfred Laurier University, 1976-77; Assistant Professor, University of Toronto, 1977-79; currently, Chief Forensic Psychologist, Calgary General Hospital; Chairman of Board, Health and Law Foundation. *Memberships:* Psychologist Association of Alberta; Canadian Psychological Association; American Society of Clinical Hypnosis; National Academy of Neuropsychologists; International Society of Hypnosis. *Publications:* Author or co-author of articles contributed to: 'American Journal of Clinical Hypnopsis'; 'Bio. chem. Med.'; 'Clinical Neuropsychology'; 'Physiological Behaviour'. *Honours:* Diploma, American Board of Professional Neuropsychology, 1985. *Hobbies:* Philately; Ledgerdemainb/Necromancy; Photography; Private aviation; Downhill skiing; Swimming; Camping. *Address:* Forensic Services, Calgary General Hospital, 841 Center Avenue East, Calgary, Alberta, Canada T2E 0A1.

BROWN, Stephen Joseph, b. 8 Apr. 1944, Tiffin, Ohio, USA. Senior Vice-President and Chief Operating Officer. m. Marilyn Ann Distel, 3 Sep. 1966, Tiffin, Ohio, 3 sons, 1 daughter. *Education:* BA; MA. *Appointments:* Assistant Administrator, USAF Regional Hospital, Minot, North Dakota, 1969-73; Assistant Administrator, USAF Regional Hospital, Torrejon Air Base, Spain, 1973-76; Review Associate, Metropolitan Health Planning Assocition, Cleveland, Ohio, 1976-78; Assistant Administrator, 1978-84, Senior Vice-President and Chief Operating Officer, 1984-, St. Gabriel's Hospital, Little Falls, Minnesota. *Memberships:* American college of Hospital Administrators; Association of Military Surgeons of the United States. *Address:* 815 2nd Street, S.E., Little Falls, MN 56345, USA.

BROWN, Thomas Christopher Kenneth, b. 9 Dec. 1935, Kenya. Director of Anaesthesia, Royal Children's Hospital, Melbourne, Australia. m. Janet Patricia Penfold, 8 July 1961, Melbourne, 3 sons, 2 daughters. *Education:* MB ChB, St. Andrews University, Scotland, 1960; FFARACS, 1967; MD, University of Melbourne, 1980. *Appointments:* Intern, Victoria Hospital, London, Ontario, Canada, 1960-61; GP, Yellowknife, NWT, Canada, 1961-62,

Resident, Anaesthesia and Medicine, Vancouver General and Children;s Hospital; Research Fellow, Department of Medicine, University of British Columbia, 1963-65; Anaesthesia Resident, Hospital for Sick Children, Toronto, 1965; Anaesthetic Registrar, Royal Melbourne Hospital, Australia, 1966; Medical Officer, 1967, Fellow, 1968-69, Intensive Care, Royal Children's Hospital, Melbourne; Special Anaesthetist, Perfusionist, 1970-74, Director of Anaesthesia 1974-, Chairman, Division of Specialist Services, 1980-, Royal Children's Hospital, Melbourne. *Memberships:* Australian Society of Anaesthetists; Faculty of Anaesthetists, RACS; Australian College of Paediatrics. *Publications:* "Anaesthesia For Children" (co-author), 1979 (English), 1981 (Spanish), 1985 (German); "Anaesthesia and Patient Care", 1983; "Tricyclic Antidepressant Overdosage in Children", MD Thesis, 1980; 50 scientific papers; Films include: "Practical Aspects of Paediatric Anaesthesia", 1975; "Lives Can Be Saved", 1982; Videos: 5 on anatomy related to nerve blocks, 1983-85. *Honours:* Gilbert Brown Prize, Faculty of anaesthetists, 1977; Lennard Travers Professor, Faculty of Anaesthetists, 1985; Memorial Lectures: John MacLeod, 1978, E.H. Embley, 1985, L. Travers, 1986. *Hobbies:* Photography; Painting; Tennis; Hockey. *Address:* Royal Children's Hospital, Parkville, Victoria, Australia 3052.

BROWN, Valerie Anne, b. 28 Feb. 1951, Elizabeth, New Jersey, USA. Psychotherapist; Senior Psychiatric Social Worker; Supervisor, Family Therapy. *Education:* BA, summa cum laude, Long Island University, New York; MSW, Hunter College School of Social Work, New York City. *Appointments:* Intern, Greenwich House Counseling Center, New York City, 1973-74; Intern, Metropolitan Consultation Center, New York City, 1974-75; Senior Psychiatric Social Worker, Essex County Guidance Center, New Jersey, 1975-80; Substnace House Consultant, Passaic Drug Clinic, New Jersey, 1976-80; Therapist, Women's Growth Center, Co-founder, New Jersey, 1979-81; Private Psychotherapy Practice, Cranford, New Jersey, 1979-; Assistant Professor, New York University School of Social Work, New York City, 1980-84; Family Alcohol Therapist, Family Service of Princeton, New Jersey, 1982-83. *Memberships:* National Association of Social Workers; Pi Gamma Mu; Psi Chi; Sigma Tau Delta. *Honours:* Fellowship, Long Island University, 1972; Silberman Scholar, Hunter College, 1973-75. *Hobbies:* Christian Service Work; Evangelism; Crocheting; Canoeing; Weight Training. *Address:* 1250 N. 19th Street, Kenilworth, NJ 0733, USA.

BROWNE, Orla Mairead, b. 5 July 1933, Dublin, Ireland. Consultant Immunologist, Charitable Infirmary, Dublin; Lecturer, Research, Pathology, Royal College of Surgeons in Ireland. m. 1959, Dublin, 3 sons, 1 daughter. *Memberships:* Founder Member, Irish Society for Immunology; Institute of Clinical Science and Research of the Royal College of Surgeons in Ireland, Founder Member; Irish Nephrology Association, Founder Member; Irish Institute for Neurosciences, Founder Member; British Society for Immunology; Renal Association; Association of Clinical Pathologists. *Publications:* "Autoantibodies in Rheumatoid Arthritis", 'Irish Journal of Medical Science', 1972; "DNA Antibodies in Systemic Lupus Erythematosis", 'Irish Medical Journal', 1981; "Plasmapheresis and Immunostimulation", 'Lancet' 1976; "Goodpastures syndrome with normal renal function", 'Irish Journal Medical Science', 1980; "Godpastures syndrome: Reappearance of circulating glomerular basement membrane antibodies after transplantation", 'Dialysis Transplant', 1983. *Hobbies:* Art; Music; Fishing. *Address:* Pathology Dept., Royal College of Surgeons in Ireland, St Stephen's Green, Dublin 2, Republic of Ireland.

BROWNE, Roger Michael, b. 19 June 1934,

Birmingham, England. Professor of Oral Pathology, m. Lilah Hilda Manning, 31 May 1958, Leek, Staffordshire, 1 son, 1 daughter. *Education:* BSC Honours Physiological Studies, BDS Honours, PhD, DDS, University of Birmingham; FDS, Royal College of Surgeons, England Fellow, Royal College of Pathologists. *Appointments:* Lecturer in Dental Surgery 1960-64, Lecturer in Dental Pathology 1964-67, Senior Lecturer in Oral Pathology 1967-77, Postgraduate Adviser in Dentistry 1977-82, Professor of Oral Pathology 1982 -, University of Birmingham. *Memberships:* Fellow, Royal College of Pathologists; Fellow, Royal College of Surgeons, England British Dental Association; British Society for Dental Research; International Association of Dental Research; Association of Clinical Pathologists; British Society for Oral Pathology. *Publications:* "Colour Atlas of Oral Histopathology", (with E Marsland), 1975; 'Peridontal Features in Blood and Lymphoreticular Disorders' in "The Peridontal Ligament in Health and Disease' (Editors B K Berkovitz, B J Moxham and H N Newman), 1982; "Radiological Atlas of Diseases of the Teeth and Jaws", (with H D Edmondson and P J Rout', 1983. *Address:* Department of Oral Pathology, Dental School, St Chad's Queensway, Birmingham, B4 6NN, England.

BROWNLEE, George Gow, b. 13 Jan. 1942. E.P. Abraham Professor of Chemical Pathology. m. Margaret Susan Kemp, 1966, 1 son, 1 daughter. *Education:* Dulwich College, England; MA, PhD, Emmanuel College, Cambridge. *Appointmetns:* Fellow, Emmanuel College, Cambridge, 1965-69; Scientific Staff of MRC at Laboraotry of Molecular Biology, Cambridge, 1966-80; E.P. Abraham Professor of Chemical Pathology, Sir William Dun School of Pathology, University of Oxford, 1981-. *Memberships:* Biochemical Society; Cambridge Philosophical Society. *Publications:* Various learned articles in 'Nature', 'Cell', 'Lancet', etc. *Honours:* Colworth Medal, Biochemical Society, 1977; Wellcome Trust Award, Biochemical Society, 1985. *Hobbies:* Gardening; Cricket. *Address:* Sir William Dunn School of Pathology, University of Oxford, South Parks Road, Oxford OX1 3RE, England.

BROWSE, Norman Leslie, b. 1 Dec. 1931, London, England, Professor of Surgery. University of London. m. Joan A. Menage, 6 May 1957, London, 1 son, 1 daughter. *Education:* MB BS, London, 1955; MD, Bristol, 1961; FRCS, England, 1959. *Appointments:* Lecturer in Surgery, Westminster Hospital, 1962; Tarkness Fellow, Research Associate, Mayo Clinic, USA, 1964; Senior Lecturer in Surgery, St. Thomas' Hospital, London, 1965; Professor of Vascular Surgery, St. Thomas' Hospital, 1972- . *Memberships:* European Society for Cardiovascular Surgery, (Past-President): Vascular Society of Great Britain and Ireland; Surgical Research Society; Association of Surgeons; Honorary Member, American Society for Vascular Surgery; Association of Professors of Surgery (Chairman). *Publications:* 160 original publications: books: "Physiology and Pathology of Bed Rest", 1964; "Symptoms and Signs of Surgical Disease", 1978; "Diseases of the Veins", 1987. *Hobby:* Marine Art. *Address:* Department of Surgery, St. Thomas' Hospital, London SE1, England.

BROXMEYER, Hal Edward, b. 27 Nov. 1944, Brooklyn, New York, USA. Associate Professor. m. C. Beth Biller, 27 July 1969, Brooklyn, 2 sons. *Education:* BS, Brooklyn College, 1966; MS, Long Island University, 1969; PhD, New York University, 1973. *Appointments:* Laboratory Specialist, Physical Science, Midwood High School, Brooklyn 1966-71; Laboratory Instructor, Cell Biology, Queens University, Kingston, Ontario, Canada, 1973-74; Research Associate, Medicine, Queen's University, 1973-75; Associate Researcher, Sloan Kettering Institute for Cancer Research, New York, 1975-76; Research Associate, 1976-78; Associate, SKI, 1978-83; Associate Professor, Biology, SKI Division,

Cornell University Graduate School of Medical Sciences, New York, 1980-83; Associate Member, SKI, 1983; Associate Professor to Professor, Medicine, Director, Cancer Research, Regenstrief Foundation, Indiana University school for Medicine. *Memberships include:* American Society of Haematology; International Society of Experimental Haematology; American Association of Immunologists; American Association for Cancer Research; Reticuloendothelial Society; Cell Kinetics Society; New York Academy of Sciences; New York Society for the Study of Food; American Federation for Clinical Research, Midwestern Section; Southeastern Cancer Study Group. *Publications:* Reviewer for: 'Blood'; 'Experimental Haematology'; 'Journal of Clinical Investigation'; 'British Journal of Haematology'; 'Journal of Immunology'; 'Leukemia Research'; 'Cancer Research'; 'Journal of Leukocyte Biology' and many others; numerous articles in professional journals including: "Identification of lactoferrin as the granulocyte-derived inhibitor of colony stimulating activity (CSA) production', co-author, 'Journal of Experimental Medicine', 1978; "Release from mouse macrophages of acidic isoferritins that suppress hematopoietic progenitor cells is induced by purified L-cell colony stimulating factors and suppressed by human lactoferrin', Co-author, 'Journal Immunology', 1985. *Honours:* Recipient, various honours & awards. *Hobbies:* Weight Lifting; Track & Field. *Address:* Dept. of Medicine, Indiana University School of Medicine, Clinical Building, Room 379, 541 Clinical Drive, Indianapolis, IN 46223, USA.

BRUCE-BELLIN, Susan Elizabeth, b. 10 July 1954, Fort Worth, Texas, USA. Administrator. m. Harvey Bellin, 23 Apr 1983, Moorestown, New Jersey. *Education:* BBA, Southern Methodist University; MS (Master of Science), Trinity University. *Appointments:* Assistant Administrator, Tri County Hospital, Springfield, Pennsylvania; Project Director - MEDIQ, Pennsauken, New Jersey; Director, Ambulatory Services. *Membership:* American College of Hospital Administrators. *Address:* 213 Demorest Road, Moorestown, NJ 08057, USA.

BRUCK, Kurt, b. 6 Nov 1925 Koln, Federal Republic of Germany. Professor of Physiology. m. Monika Bruck, 28 July 1956, Berlin, 2 daughters. *Education:* Dr Med, Rupprecht-Karl-Universitat, Heidelberg, 1951; Habilitation 1959, Professor 1966, Department of Physiology, Philipps University, Marburg. *Appointments:* Research Fellow in Physiology, University of Heidelberg, 1951-53; Resident Physician in Pediatrics, University of Hamburg, 1953-55; Research Fellow 1956-59, Reader 1961-66, Professor 1966-70, Physiology, University of Marburg; Research Fellow in Pediatrics, University of California at Los Angeles, California, USA, 1960-61; Professor of Physiology, University of Giessen, 1970-; Acting Director, Physiological Institute, Justus-Liebig-University, Giessen. *Memberships:* President 1981-82, German Physiological Society; Internatonal Society of Biometerology; German Society for Perinatal Medicine; Honorary member, Hungarian Physiological Society. *Publications Include:* Numerous scientific articles to textbooks, review editions and journals. *Honour:* Honorary membership, Hungarian Physiological Society, 1984. *Address:* Physiologisches Institut, Aulweg 129, D 6300 Giessen, Federal Republic of Germanys

BRUCKHEIM, Allan Herbert, b. 11 Nov 1928, Brooklyn, New York, USA. Director of Family Medicine. m. Joyce Sandra Lieblin, 15 Jan 1955, New York, 3 daughters. *Education:* BA, Transylvanis University, Lexington, Kentucky, 1950; Doctor of Optometry, Chicago College of Optometry, Chicago, Illinois, 1954; Doctor of Medicine, University of Lausanne, Switzerland, 1961. *Appointments include:* Associate Professor of Family Medicine, SUNY Stony Brook, New York, 1979-82; Acting Director,

Family Practitioner Res. Program, Nassau County Medical Center, New York, 1979; Associate Professor of Clinical Medicine, SUNY Stony Brook,New York, 1982-85; Director, Family Pract. Res. Program, South Nassau Community Hospital, Oceanside, New York, 1979-82; Director, Family pract. Res. Program, 1982 -, Director, Department of Family Medicine, 1982 -, St Mary Hospital, Hoboken, New York; Clinical Associate Professor, Department of Family Medicine, Rutgers Medical School, UMDNJ, New Jersey. *Memberships:* Fellow, American Academy of Family Physicians; Delegate, Congress of Delegates, AAFP, 1978; Society of Teachers of Family Medicine; Board of Directors, National Council on Patient Information and Education, 1982. *Publications:* "Government and Third Party Payers", 'Family Medicine Principles and Practice' 1978; "Critical Care" 'Family Medicine Principles and Practice' 2nd Edition 1983; "Mediquiz" 2nd Edition; "Patient care flow Chart Mannual" Review Board, 2nd Edition Patient care Publications 1980; "Drug Abuse" Monograph, AAFP, 1981. *Honours:* President, New York State Academy of Family Practice, 1979-80; President, Society of Directors of Academic Family Practice Programs of New York, 1981-82. *Hobby:* Computers. *Address:* 264 North Street, Harrison, NY 10528, USA.

BRUECK, Robert Paul, b. 8 Apr 1928, Cincinnati, Ohio, USA. Consultant. m. Norene L. Blacketer, 30 Jan 1954, Nashville, Tennessee, USA. *Education:* BA, Vanderbilt University, 1950. *Appointments:* Laboratory Assistant, West End Laboratory, 1945-49; Research Assistant, Vanderbilt University, 1949-50; Senior Bacteriologist, Tennessee Department of Public Health, 1950-51; Senior Assistant Administrator, Baptist Hospital, Nashville, Tennessee, 1952-62; Administrator, Henry Co General Hospital, Paris, Tennessee, 1962-65; Executive Director, Health and Hospital Planning Council, 1965-68; Vice President, Senior Executive Vice President, Domestic and International Operations, Hospital Corporation of America, 1968-81; President, Center for Health Studies, 1981-83; Director, Hospital Corporation of America 1983- . *Memberships:* Director, Tennessee Hospital Association, 1963-65; Consultant, Department HEW, US Public Health Service, 1967. *Publications:* Contributor of articles to professional journals. *Honour:* Fellow, American College of Hospital Administrators. *Hobbies:* Yachting; Photography. *Address:* 469 Yacht Harbor Drive, Osprey, FL 33559, USA.

BRUFMAN, George Albert, b. 21 July. 1943, Argentina. Chief Physician. m. Aida Goldstein, 3 Mar. 1973, Cordoba, Argentina, 1 son, 1 daughter. *Education:* MD, University of Cordoba, Argentina, 1968. *Appointments:* House Physician, Department of Oncology, Hadassah University Hospital, Jerusalem, Israel, 1970, Chief Physician, 1976. *Memberships:* Israel Medical Association; American Society of Clinical Oncology; European Association of Cancer Research; European Society of Therapeutic Radiation and Oncology; European Society for Medical Oncology; Mediterranean Society of Chemotherapy; International Society of Chemotherapy. *Publications:* Co-author: 'The treatment of locally advanced breast carcinoma with high dose external beam supervoltage radiotherpay' in'Israel Journal of Medical Sciences', 1981; Co-author: 'Treatment of metastatic breast cancer with aminoglutethimide after progression on chemotherapy and or hormonal therapy with tamoxifen' in 'European Journal of Surgical Oncology',1985. *Honours:* Lecturer in Onçology, the Hebrew University, Hadassah Medical School, 1977. *Hobbies:* Piano playing (formerly professional concert player); Cooking. *Address:* PO Box 12025, Jerusalem 91120, Israel.

BRUHN, John Glyndon, b. 27 Apr. 1934, Norfolk,

Nebraska, USA. Dean, School of Allied Health Sciences. *Education:* BA, University of Nebraska, USA, USA, 1956, MA, 1958; PhD, Medical Sociology, Yale University, 1961. *Appointments Include:* Research Sociologist, (Fulbright Fellow), Department of Psychological Medicine, University of Edinburgh, Scotland, 1961-62; Instructor in Medical Centre, Oklahoma city, 1962-63, Assistant Professor, 1963-64, Assistant Professor of Preventive Medicine and Public Health, 1964-67, Associate Professor of Sociology in Medicine, 1967-72, Professor and Chairman, Department of Human Ecology, 1969-72; Associate Dean for Community Affairs University of Texas Medical Branch, Galveston, Texas, 1972-81, Dean, School of Allied Health Sciences and Special Assistant to the President for Community Affairs, 1981-. *Memberships Include:* American Heart Association, Fellow; American Public Health Association, Fellow; Royal Society of Health, Fellow; American Psychosomatic Society; American Association of University Professors; Clinical Sociology Association; Alpha Kappa Delta; Sigma XI. *Publications include:* Author and Co-author of 128 articles in professional journals; 45 invited conference papers; 13 book reviews; Author and co-author of 15 book chapters; Co-author of 5 books including:"The Roseto Story: An Anatomy of Health", 1979; "Medical Sociology: An Annotated Bibliography, 1972-82", 1985. *Honours Include:* Career Development Award, National Heart Institute, 1968-69; Danforth Foundation Associate, 1973; Katherine and Nicholas C Leone Award for Administrative Excellence, 1983; J. Warren Perry Distinguished Author Award, Journal of Allied Health, 1984. *Hobbies:* Stamp and coin collecting; Travel; Theatre. *Address:* University of Texas Medical Branch, School of Allied Health Sciences, Galveston, TX 77550, USA.

BRUMFIELD, Shannon Maureen, b. 14 Sep. 1946, New Orleans, Louisiana, USA. Speech and Language Pathologist, Private Practice. *Education:* BA, Speech Therapy; MA, Speech Pathology; PhD, Speech Pathology, Linguistics/Psychology. *Appointments:* Hilda Knoff School for the Deaf and Hard of Hearing; Instructor, Holy Cross College; Instructor, University of Florida; Volunteer at Veterans Administration Hosptial, Gainesville, Florida; Volunteer Instructor, Louisiana State University Medical Center; Participated in professional workshops and service activities. *Memberships:* American Speech Language Hearing Association; Louisiana Speech and Hearing Association; American Educators of the Deaf; International Association of Logopedics and Phoniatrics; American Society of Clinical Hypnosis; Greater New Orleans Speech Forum. *Publications:* Contributor to 'Journal of Speech and Hearing Disorders' and 'American Annals of the Deaf'. *Hobbies:* Music; Theatre; Tennis. *Address:* 4333 Loveland Street, Metaire, LA 70006, USA.

BRUNE, Kay, b. 30 Jan. 1941, Freital, Germany. Professor of Pharmacology. m. L Brune, 23 Feb. 1967, 1 son, 1 daughter. *Education:* MD. *Appointments:* Resident, Northeim; Research Assistant, University of Basle, Switzerland; Visiting Scientist, University of North Carolina, USA; Associate Professor, University of Basle; Professor & Chairman, Department of Pharmacology, University of Erlangen, Federal Republic of Germany. *Memberships:* German, Swiss Pharmacological Societies; American Association for the Advancement of Science. *Publications:* Book chapters in "Handbook of Experimental Pharmacology" 1979; "Handbook of Inflammation", 1985. *Honour:* Pappenheim Prize, German Society for Haematology, 1972. *Address:* Pharmakologisches Institut, UniversitätsstraBe 22, D-8520 Erlangen, Federal Republic of Germany.

BRUNK, James R., b. 5 May 1926, Harrisonburg, Virginia, USA. Staff Physician, Rockingham

Memorial Hospital; Clinical Assistant Professor, Internal Medicine, Visiting Physician, Outpatients, University of Virginia School of Medicine. m. Thelma Grace Ketterman, 10 July 1948; Harrisonburg, 3 sons, 1 daughter. *Education:* BS, Eastern Mennonite College, 1950; MD, University of Virginia, 1954; Intern, Medicine, University of Virginia, 1954-5; Staff Physician, Blue Ridge Sanatorium, 1955-62; Fellowships, Internal Medicine, University of Virginia Hospital, 1962-64; Instructor, Internal Medicine, University of Virginia, 1964-65. *Appointments:* Private Practice, Internal Medicine, 1965; Visiting Physician, Outpatients Dept, University of Virginia Hospital, 1965; Staff Physician, Rockingham Memorial Hospital, 1966; Co-Director, Respiratory Therapy and Pulmonary Function, Rockingham Memorial Hospital, 1970; Clinical Assistant Professor, Internal Medicine, University of Virginia School of Medicine, 1971. *Memberships include:* Albemarle and Rockingham County Medical Societies; American and Virginia Thoracis Societies; American and Virginia Society of Internal Medicine; Virginia and American College of Physicians; Southeastern Allergy Association; Board Member, Shenandoah Chapter, American Lung Association of Virginia; American Academy of Allergy; Medical Society of Virginia; American Medical Associations; Mennonite Medical Association; Virginia and American Heart Associations; etc. *Publications:* "Rheumatoid Pleuritis Successfully Treated with Decorticetion", Report of A Case and Review of the Literature, 'American Journal of the Medical Sciences', Volume 251, 1966. *Honours:* Physicians' Recognition Award, 1969- . *Hobbies:* Watercolour painting; Skiing; Stamp Collecting. *Address:* Medical Arts Building, Suite 28, 1031 S. Main St., Harrisonburg, VA 22801, USA.

BRUNNER, Sam Aage, b. 18 Feb. 1920, Copenhagen, Denmark, Chairman, Department of Diagnostic Radiology. m. Kirsten Randbol, 5 Nov. 1948, 2 sons, 1 daughter. *Education:* MD, PhD, University of Copenhagen; Specialisation in Diagnostic Radiology, Sweden, 1955, Denmark, 1959. *Appointments:* Various departments in Diagnostic Radiology, Sweden and Denmark, 1949-64; Chief Radiologist, 1964, currently Chairman, Department of Diagnostic Radiology, Gentofte University Hospital, Guest professor, Chicago, Illinois, USA, 1962, New York, 1964, 69, Tel Aviv, Israel, 1968. *Memberships:* Secretary General, Scandinavian Association of Radiology; President, International Society of Radiology in ORL, 1976-79: Past President, Danish Society of Diagnostic Radiology. President: Scandinavian Society of Nammography; Danish Radiological Association. *Publications:* "Lung Cyst", 1964; "Modern Thin-Section Tomography", 1973; "Advances in ORL", 1974: "Modern Methods in Radiology in ORL", 1977; "X-Ray Techniques", 1971; "Diagnostic Radiology", 1983. *Honours:* Flemming Møller Prize, 1965.Corresponding Member: American Society of Pediatric Radiology, 1960; Swedish Society of Radiology, 1974; Norwegian Society of Radiology, 1974; Finnish Society of Radiology, 1975; Honorary member, Danish Society of Diagnostic Radiology, 1986. *Hobbies:* Golf, Hunting. *Address:* 79 Kvaedevej, Virum, Copenhagen, Denmark.

BRUNO, J Joan, b. 13 Feb. 1951, New Jersey, USA. Director, Communication Technology Center; Chief Speech Language Pathologist. *Education:* AB, Speech Therapy, Marywood College, Scranton, Pennsylvania; MS, Speech Pathology, Pennsylvania State University. *Appointment:* Speech-Language Pathologist, Home of the Mericful Savior, Philadelphia, Pennsylvania. *Memberships:* American Speech and Hearing Association; International Soceity for Augmentative and Alternative Communication; Pennsylvania Speech and Hearing Association; New Jersey Speech and Hearing Association. *Publications:* Co-author,

'Computer Aided Development of Phonetic Skills in Non-Vocal Pre-Reading Children', 'Journal of Special Education Technology', 1983; Co-author, 'A Computer-Aided Communication Aid for a Cerebral Palsey Child', 'Archives of Physical Medicine and Rehabilitation', Oct. 1984. *Honours:* Award for Continuing Education, American Speech and Hearing Association, 1984; Distinguished Alumna, Maryland College, 1984. *Hobby:* Travel. *Address:* Communication Technology Center, Children's Seashore House, 4100 Atlantic Avenue, Atlantic City, NJ 08404, USA.

BRUNT, Peter William, b. 18 Jan. 1936, Prestatyn, North Wales. Consultant Physician and Gastroenterologist, Aberdeen Royal Infirmary; Clinical Senior Lecturer, University of Aberdeen; Physician to H.M. The Queen in Scotland. m. Dr. M.E. Anne Mewis, 27 May 1961, Liverpool, 3 daughters. *Education:* MB ChB, 1959, MD, Liverpool University; FRCP (London); FRCP (Edinburgh). *Appointments:* House Physician; House Surgeon, Liverpool Royal Infirmary; Medical Registrar, Liverpool Hospitals; Research Fellow, Medical Genetics Deparmtent, Johns Hopkins School of Medicine, Baltimore, USA; Lecturer in Medicine, University of Edinburgh; Honorary Lecturer in Medicine, Royal Free Hospital School of Medicine, London. *Membership:* Association of Physicians of Great Britain and Ireland. *Publications:* Co-author, "Diseases of the Liver and Biliary System", 1985; Co-author, "Gastroenterology", 1985; Papers in various journals and chapters in books especially in field of alcohol and liver disease. *Hobbies:* Mountaineering; Music. *Address:* 17 Kingshill Road, Aberdeen AB2 4JY, Scotland.

BRUTSAERT, Dirk Lodewijk, b. 28 Feb 1937, Ghent, Belgium, Professor of Physiology and Medicine,m. Gerda De Wilde, Mar. 1961, 2 sons. *Education:* MD; PhD Physiology, 1967-72, Professor of Physiology and Medicine, 1972-, Head, Non-Invasive cardiology, University Hospital, University of Antwerp. *Memberships:* Belgian societies of Physiology, Pharmacology and Cardiology. *Publications:* 'Circulation Research', 1980; 'Circulation',1984; 'Cardiovascular Disease', 1985. *Honours:* Member, Royal Academy of Medicine of Belgium; Tri-annual RIT Award, 1971-73. *Hobbies:* Tennis; Skiing; English and French Literature; classical music. *Address:* University of Antwerp, Groenenborgerlaan 171, Antwerp, Belgium.

BRYAN, Katherine, b. Kansas, USA. National Sales Vice-President, TSG. m. John Shelby Bryan, 12 Mar. 1982, New York, 3 sons. *Education:* BA, University of Missouri, 1969; PhD, Counselling Psychology, 1979. *Appointments:* Associate Psychologist, Vice-President, Marketing, Corporate Health Examiners, 1978-82. *Membership:* American Psychological Association. *Publications:* "Application of the Trail Making Test as a Measure of Organicity in the Alcoholic Patient"; articles in professional journals. *Address:* 220 East 63rd Street, New York, NY 10021, USA

BRYANT, Stewart James, b. 3 June 1939, Australia. Director of Hospital Pathology Services. m. Lynette June Maskell, 7 Sep. 1963, Brisbane, Queensland, 3 sons. *Education:* MBBS, University of Queensland, 1963; Fellow, Royal College of Pathologists of Australasia, 1969; Member, Australian Association of Clinical Biochemists, 1971. *Appointments:* Resident Medical Officer 1963-64, Registrar in Pathology 1965-69, Staff Chemical Pathologist 1968-72, Director of Chemical Pathology 1972-79, Director of Pathology Service 1979-, Royal Brisbane Hospital. *Memberships:* Royal College of Pathologists of Australasia; Australian Association of Clincial Biochemists; Gastroenterological Society of Queensland. *Publciations:* 'Neonatal meningitis due to mima polymorpha var. oxidans', 1968; 'Phenformin-induced lactic acidosis in diabetes mellitus', 1972; 'Hyalin droplet formation in the renal epithelium of patients with haemoglobinuria', 1973; 'The effect of multiphasic screening on the diagnosis of primary hyperparathyroidism', 1975; 'A study of the use of serum protein electrophoretic patterns', 1980; 'Precision requirements in a study of computer-aided diagnosis of jaundice', 1980; 'S I units in medicine' in "Clinical Sciences for Surgeons"; (editor W Burnett), 1981; "Differential diagnosis of jaundice: a pocket diagnostic chart', 1984; 'Development and maintenance of a laboratory computer system: resource considerations' in "Medical Laboratory Computing", (editor R J Collins), 1985. *Honour:* Research and Education Travel Grant, Royal College of Pathologists of Australasia, 1979. *Hobby:* Sailing. *Address:* Department of Pathology, Royal Brisbane Hospital, Herston, Queensland 4029, Australia.

BRYCE-SMITH, Derek, b. 29 Apr 1926, London, England, Professor of Organic chemistry,m. (1) Marjorie Anne Stewart, Dec 26 May 1966, 2 sons, 2 daughters, (2) Pamela Joyce Morgan, 21 June 1969, Henley on Thames, 2 stepdaughters. *Education:* BSc, 1948, PhD, 1951-55, Assistant lecturer in Chemistry, 1955-56,Kings College, London; Lecturer in chemistry, 1956-63, Reader in Chemistry, 1963-65, Professor of Organic Chemistry, 1965-, University of Reading. *Memberships:* Royal Society of Chemistry; American Chemical Society. *Publications:* "Lead or Health",(with R Stephens), 1980; 'Case of Anorexia Nervosa responding to Zinc Sulphate', (with R I D Simpson), 1984; author of numerous research articles in scientific journals. *Honours:* ICI Postdoctoral Fellowship, University of London, 1951; John Jeyes Silver Medal and Endowed Lectureship, 1984-85. *Hobbies:* Singing; Playing Piano; Gardening. *Address:* Chemistry Department, University of Reading, Whiteknights, Reading, Berks, England.

BRYNER, Peter, b. 16 Dec. 1955, Auckland, New Zealand. Lecturer, Chiropractic Science, School of Chiropractic, Phillip Institute of Technology, Bundoora, Australia. m. Janice Helen Kitchen, 1 Sep. 1978, Auckland. *Education:* Diploma, Applied Science, Bachelor Applied Science, Chiropractic, Phillip Institute of Technology. *Memberships:* Australian Chiropractors Association; Chiropractic Alumni Association of Phillip Institute of Technology; American Chiropractic Association (Member Council on Technic). *Honours:* Award for Excellence, Chiropractic Science, Phillip Institute of Technology, 1981. *Hobbies:* Tennis; Sailing; Reading; Computer Science. *Address:* School of Chiropractic, Phillip Institute of Technology, Plenty Road, Bundoora, Victoria, Australia 3083.

BRYNES, Russell K. b. 7 May 1945, New York, USA. University Professor. m. Angelita S. Cordero, MD, 31 May 1970, Salem, Massachussetts, 2 daughters. *Education:* BA, University, of Massachussetts, USA, 1967; MD, Tufts University, Boston, Massachussetts, 1971. *Appointments:* Intern, Resident, Fellow, Haematopathology, University of Chicago, USA, 1971-75; Fellow, Haematopathology, University of Minnesota, Minneapolis, 1975-77; Chief, Clinical Pathology Service, Madigan Army Medical Centre, Tacoma, Washington, 1977-79; Associate Professor, Department of Pathology and Laboratory Medicine, Emory University, Atlanta, Georgia, -. *Memberships:* American Medical Association; American Society of Clinical Pathologists; American Society of Haematology; College of American Pathologists; Society for Haematopathology; International Academy of Pathology. *Publications:* 'Mesocolic Lymph Node Histology is a Prognostic Indicator for Patients with Carcinoma of the Siginoid Colon' in 'Cancer', 1975; 'Bone Marrow Aspiration and Tryphine Biopsy: an Approach to a Thorough Study' in 'American Journal of Clinical Pathology', 1978; 'Morphologic Features of the Unexplained Lymphadenopathy of Homosexual Men' in 'Journal

of the American Medical Association', 1983; 'Histopathology of AIDS in "Making the AIDS Diagnosis", 1986. *Honour:* Hectoen Award, Chicago Pathological Society, 1974. *Hobbies:* Swimming; Scuba Diving. *Address:* Clinical Laboratory, Emory University Hospital, Atlanta, GA, 30322, USA.

BRZOZOWSKE, Walter Travis, b. 2 July 1941, Victoria, USA. Chiropractic Orthopedist. m. Sharon Vitopil, 17 July 1965, Texas, 2 daughters. *Education:* DC, DABCO, FACO, Texas Chiropractic College, 1967. *Appointments:* Surgical Technicial, Darnall Army Hospital, Ft. Hood, 1960; Surgical Technician, Brooke General Hospital, San Antonio, 1961-62; Surgical Technician, Baptist Memorial Hospital, San Antonio, 1963-64. *Memberships:* American Board of Chiropractic Orthopedists; American College of Chiropractic Orthopedists; Academy of Chiropractic Orethopedists; International Academy of Preventive Medicine; Texas Chiropractic College Alumni Association, various offices; Texas Chiropractic College Board of Regents, 1981-85; etc. *Publications:* "Costosternal Neuropathy", 'American Chiropractic Association Journal', 1968; "The Effect of Chiropractic Treatment on Students with Learning and Behavioral Impairments Resulting from Neurological Dysfunction", 1977; "Persistent Postnatal Malposture and Consequential Pathologies", 'American Chiropractic Association Journal', 1983; Numerous other professional articles for 'Texas Chiropractic Association Journal'. *Honours:* Recipient, Numerous honours and awards including Lanier Fellowship, Texas Chiropractic College, 1966. *Address:* 205 Whispering Creek, Victoria, TX 77904, USA.

BUBLITZ, Karl Adolf, b. 22 Aug. 1923, Hagenow, Germany. Dentist. m. Käthe Peters, 16 Sep. 1949, 3 sons. *Education:* Doctor of Dental Medicine. *Appointments:* President, Dental Chamber of Hamburg; Past Vice-President, Federal Dental Chamber; Chairman, German Society for Diseases of Teeth, Mouth & Jaw; Chairman, State Working Party for Promotion of Youth Dental Care; Chairman, German Association for Dentistry on Young People. *Memberships:* International Federation of Dentists; European Sub-division; Past President, Dental Communication Commitee to the European Community. *Publications:* Various articles in specialist dental literature on professional policies and science. *Honours:* Various awards. *Hobbies:* Sailing; Flying *Address:* Glissmannweg 9, D-2000 Hamburg 61, Federal Republic of Germany.

BUCHANAN, Douglas James, b. 28 Sept 1942, Manchester, England, Medical Services Adviser and Surgeon, m. Geneve Krikor Buchanan, 18 Jan 1969, Edinburgh, Scotland, 2 sons. *Education:* MBChB, University of Edinburgh, Scotland, 1966; DTM &H, University of Liverpool, England, 1969; DRCOG, 1969; FRCS, Edinburgh and London, 1975. *Appointments:* Houseman, Surgery, Royal Infirmary, Edinburgh, Scotland; Houseman, Medicine, Peel Hospital, Galashiels, Scotland; Assistant Lecturer, Anatomy, University of Glasgow; Senior House Officer, Obstetrics, Maternity Hospital, Dunfermline; Senior House Officer, Accident and Emergency Department, Royal Infirmary, Edinburgh; GDMO, Ministry of Health, Ndola Central Hospital, Zambia; Surgical Registrar, Dumfries and Galloway Royal Infirmary, Scotland; Surgical Specialist, RCM Luanshya Division, Zambia; Chief Medical Officer, RCM/Zambia Consolidated Copper Mines, Kalushi Division, Zambia; Medical Services Adviser, Zambia Consolidated Copper Mines, Surgeon, Kalululshi Division, Zambia; Medical Adviser, The British Council. *Memberships:* British Medical Association; Zambia Medical Association; Association of Surgeons of East Africa; British Association of Sport and Medicine; British Society of Nutritional Medicine. *Publications:* 'Fourniers Gangrene, Case Reports', 1971; 'Acute Pancreatitis 1st Cases in

Zambia', 1970; 'A Trauma Survey at Ndola Central Hospital', 1971; 'The Middle Pole of the Kidney', 1972; 'Penile Burns due to Roots', 1975; 'A Double Blind Controlled Trial of Ben card HDM, 1980; 'Housemite Allergy and asthma in Zambia', 1974; 'Accident Prevention in the Mining Industry'. *Hobbies:* Squash; Ornithology; Wildlife conservation. *Address:* Glenholm, Kirkbean, Dumfries DG2 8DW, Scotland.

BUCHANAN, John Gordon, b. 27 Dec. 1932, Auckland, New Zealand, Associate Professor of Haematology, University of Auckland School of Medicine, 1971-; Director of Continuing Education Programmes for New Zealand, Royal Australasian College of Physicians. m. Noeline Chamberlin, 5 May 1962, London, England, 2 sons, 2 daughters. *Education:* BMedSc, 1955, MB, ChB, 1957, University of New Zealand; MA, Michigan State University, USA. *Appointments:* House Surgeon, Auckland Hospital Board, 1958-59; Assistant Lecturer in Pathology, University of Otago, 1960; Junior Assistant Pathologist and Nuffield Foundation Fellow, St Thomas' Hospital Medical School, London, England, 1961-63; Assistant Haematologist, Auckland Hospital, New Zealand, 1964-65; Lecturer in Medicine, University of Melbourne, Australia, 1966; Haematologist-in-charge, Auckland Hospital, New Zealand, 1967-70. *Memberships:* Fellow, Royal College of Physicians, Edinburgh, Scotland; Fellow of the Royal Australasian College of Physicians; Fellow of the Royal College of Pathologists; Fellow of the Royal College of Pathologists of Australasia. *Publications:* Author of numerous medical and scientific papers. *Hobby:* Gardening. *Address:* 82 Mountain Road, Epsom, Auckland 3, New Zealand.

BUCHANAN, Geneve Krikor, b. 7 Nov 1941, Baghdad, Iraq, Consultant obstetrician, m. Douglas James Buchanan, 18 Jan 1969, Edinburgh, Scotland, 2 sons. *Education:* MBChB, Baghdad; FRCS, Edinburgh, Scotland, 1969; LMSSA, 1969. *Appointments:* House Surgeon, Senior House Officer, Registrar, Obstetrics Medical City, Baghdad, Iraq; Senior House Officer, Simpson Memorial Maternity Pavilion, Edinburgh, Scotland; General Practice, Scotland; General Practice, Zambia; Graded Specialist, Zambia Consolidated Copper Mines, Luanshya and Kalulushi, 1976-79; Consultant Obstetrician, Kalulushi Division ZCCM. *Memberships:* ambia Medical Association; South African Medical Ultrasound Society. *Publications:* 'Experience with diagnoistic ultrasound in a Zambian Obstetrical Practice'. *Hobbies:* Golf; Domestic crafts. *Address:* Glenholm, Kirkbean, Dumfries DG2 8DU, Scotland.

BUCHANAN, Keith Deans, b. 24 June 1934, Glasgow, Scotland. Professor. m. Maureen Bryans, 21 Mar. 1961, Glasgow, 2 sons, 2 daughters. *Education:* MB ChB, Glasgow University, 1958; MRCP, Edinburgh, 1961; MRCP, Glasgow, 1962; MRCP, London, 1964; MD, Glasgow, 1969; FRCP, Glasgow, 1971; PhD, Belfast, 1973; FRCP, Edinburgh, 1973; FRCP, London, 1977; MRCPI, 1985. *Appointments:* Hall Tutorial Fellow In Medicine, 1959-62, Senior Registrar in Medicine, Royal Infirmary Glasgow, 1966-68; Senior Research Fellow, Instructor in Medicine, Division of Endocrinology and Metabolism, Department of Medicine, University of Washington, Seattle, 1966-68 Senior Lecturer in Medicine, Consultant Status, 1968-76, Professor of Metabolic Medicine, (Personal Chair), Department of Medicine, The Queen's University of Belfast, 1976-. *Memberships:* Scientific Section of the British Diabetic Assn.; European Assn. for the Study of Diabetes; Medical Research Society; European Society for Clinical Investigation; Ulster Medical Society; Association of Physicians of GB and Ireland; British Society of Gastroenterology; Royal Academy of Medicine(Ireland); Irish Society of Gastroenterology. *Publications:* Approx- 200 publications in sientific

and medical journals mainly on aspects of gastrointestinal hormones, diabetes mellitus. Editor of "Clinics in Endocrinology and Metabolism, GI Hormones", 1979. *Honours:* McFarland Prize in Medicine, Royal Infirmary, Glasgow, 1956; R D Lawrence Lecturer, British Diabetic Assn., 1972; Grave's Lecturer, Royal Academy of Medicine, Ireland, 1975; Burn's Lecturer,Royal College of Physicians, Glasgow, 1977; Conway Review Lecturer, Royal Academy of Medicine, Ireland, 1980. *Hobbies:* Golf; Fishing; Gardening; Swimming. *Address:* Department of Medicine, Wellcome Research Laboratories, The Queen's University of Belfast, Grosvenor Road, Belfast BT12 6BJ.

BUCHBERGER, Josef F, b. 14 May 1930, Prague. Scientific Adviser; Deputy Medical Director. m. Marie Cucova, 18 Oct. 1961, Prague, 2 sons. *Education:* MD, Charles University Prague, 1955; Eng.C., Chemistry, College of Technology, Prague; PhD, & University of Fribourgh, & Charles University, Prague, 1974; Academy of Occupational Medicine, Berlin, 1976; Certificate, Bavarian Academy of Occupational& Social Medicine, 1977. *Appointments:* Physician, Institut of National Health, CSSR, 1955-59; Scientist, Institut of Hygiene and Epidemiology, 1959-60; Special Lecturer, Charles University, Prague, 1961-69; Assistant Lecturer, University of Bern, 1969-76; Scientific Adviser, Federal Office for Industry & Labour, 1976-. *Memberships:* Swiss Society for Anthropology; International Committee for Physical Fitness Research; Swiss Academy of Sciences; Swiss Society for Social and Preventive Medicine; International Organisation of Human Ecology; New York Academy of Sciences. *Publication:* Editor, Principal Author, Swiss Periodical, 'Occupational Medicine Information'; Numerous articles in professional journals; etc. *Hobbies:* Globe Trotting; Alpine Tours; Nature; Art History; Opera. *Address:* Federal Office for Industry & Labour, Division of Occupational Medicine, Bundesgasse 8, CH 3003 Bern, Switzerland.

BUCHBINDER, Richard, b. 23 Nov. 1945, New Jersey, USA. Medical Practitioner. *Education:* BS, Transylvania College, Lexington, Kentucky, USA, 1967; DPM, Ohio College of Podiatric Medicine, 1974. *Appointments:* Surgical Preceptor, Philadelphia Podiatry Association, 1975; Surgical Resident, Cleveland Foot Clinic, 1977; Podiatry Staff of Scottsdale Memorial Hospital, Phoenix General Hospital, Mesa General Hospital, Scottsdale Community Hospital-. *Memberships:* American Podiatry Association; Arizona Podiatry Association; Fellow, American College of Foot Surgeons, American College of Foot Orthopedists, American Academy of Podiatric Sports Medicine. *Publications:* Contributions to professional journals and publications, 1978-82, including 'Journal of the American Podiatry Association'; 'The New Times Weekly Running Supplement'; 'Arizona Marathon Society' (now 'Body and Sole'); 'The Jogger'; 'Runners World Magazine'; 'The Fore Runner' magazine; Co-author: chapter 'Triple Arthrodesis and Subsequent Distance Running' in "Sports Medicine '80'' Part II, 1980; Columnist for 'Footnotes' and 'East Valley Runner's Newsletter'. *Honours:* Diplomate, American Board of Podiatric Surgery; Diplomate, American Board of Podiatric Orthopedists. *Hobbies:* Hiking; Marathon Running; Cycling. *Address:* 4602 North 16th Street, Phoenix, AZ 85016, USA.

BUCKLEY, Louis Anthony, b. 14 Oct. 1934, Cork, Ireland. Associate Professor of Conservative Dentistry; Head of Periodontology; Consultant. m. Sheila Waters, 26 Oct. 1960-, Cork, 4 sons, 3 daughters. *Education:* BDS, NUI, 1957; FDSRCS (Edinburgh), 1963; D.Orth.RCS (Eng.), 1968; FFDRCSI, 1974; PhD, NUI, 1977; Fellow, Harvard University, 1974; Fellow, International College of Dentistry, 1980; Clinical Fellow in Dentistry, Harvard School of Dental Medicine. *Appointments:* Clincial

Assistant, Eastman Dental Hospital, London; Consultant, Chalmsford and Essex Hospital Group; Lecturer in Conservative Dentistry, University College, Cork; Fellow, Harvard School of Dental Medicine, 1974; Associate Professor, University College, Cork. *Memberships:* Irish Dental Association; Irish Society of Periodontology; British Society of Periodontology; Irish Society of Orthodontics; Irish Society of Dentistry for Children. *Publications:* Book: "The Treatment of Periodontal Disease and the Ecology of Dental Plaque", 1978; "Malocclusion and Periodontal Disease'', PhD Thesis, National University of Ireland, 1977; 'A Longitudinal Study of Untreated Periodontal Disease', 'Journal of Clinical Periodontology', 1984. *Honours:* Scholarship, Irish Scholarship Board, 1973; Fellowship, Harvard School of Dental Medicine, 1974; Medal of Royal Academy of Medicine in Ireland, 1976-77. *Hobbies:* Golf; Tennis; Fishing. *Address:* Maryland, Wilton Road, Cork, Republic of Ireland.

BUCHOK, Roman W, b. 12 June 1924, Ukraine. Physician-in-Chief, McGregor Medical Center, Winnipeg. m. Maria Cruz Mayo, 2 Apr. 1950, Madrid, 3 sons, 2 daughters. *Education:* MD; PhD; LMCC. *Appointments:* Active Staff: Grace Hospital, Children's Hospital, Victoria Hospital; Courtesy Staff, Health Science Center; Active Staff, Misericordia Hospital, Seven Oaks Hospital; President, Medical Staff, Seven Oaks Hospital. *Memberships:* Manitoba Medical Association; Canadian Medical Association; Association of Christian Therapists; Christian Medical Foundation. *Publication:* "Classification and Causes of Asthenia" 1952. *Hobby:* Jogging. *Address:* 527 Ladlaw Boulevard, Winnipeg, Manitoba, Canada R3P OL2.

BUDD, Richard Donald, b. 21 Sep. 1923, Detroit, Michigan, USA. Chairman,Dept. Psychiatry, Providence Hospital, Michigan. m. Barbara Jean Renton, 21 Jan. 1950, Topeka, 4 daughters. *Education:* MD, Wayne University College of Medicine, 1948; Diplomate, American Board of Psychiatry, 1957. *Appointments:* Assistant, Section Chief, Topeka State Hospital, 1952-53; Chief of Female Service, Assistant Clinical Director, Northville State Hospital, 1953-57; Private practice, Psychiatry, 1957-68; Superintendent, Northville State Hospital, 1968-75; Clinical Director, Mental Health Clinic and Day Hospital, Providence Hospital, Southfield, 1975-76; Chairman, Psychiatry, Providence Hospital, Southfield, 1976- ; Assistant Clinical Professor, Psychiatry, College of Medicine, Michigan State University, 1977-82. *Memberships:* American Psychiatric Association; Michigan Psychiatric Society; American Phobia Society *Publications:* "MAOI's in the Treatment of Phobias" presented at 3rd Annual Phobia Society Meeting 1982; "Psychodynamic Psychopharmacology", presented to Northville Psychiatric Association, 1982. *Honour:* Commendation, Wayne State University College of Medicine, 1973. *Hobbies:* Reading; Research; Fishing. *Address:* 17730 Fairfield, Livonia, MI 48152, USA.

BUERK, Charles Adolphus, b. 8 Feb. 1937, Chicago, Illinois, USA. Professor, Chairman, Dept. of Surgery. m. Marsha Gardner, 15 Sep. 1973, Denver , 2 sons, 2 daughters. *Education:* AB, University of Rochester, 1959; MD, Western Researve University School of Medicine, 1963. *Appointments:* Director, University of Colorado Medical Centre Burn Unit, 1977-80; Medical Director, Burn Care Unit, Southern Nevada Memorial Hospital, Las Vegas, 1980-; Vice Chairman, Surgery, University of Nevada School of Medicine, 1980-82; Director, Surgical Resident Education, Southern Nevada Memorial Hosptial, 1981-; Chairman, Surgery, University of Nevada School of Medicine, 1984-. *Memberships:* Society for Surgery of the Alimentary Tract; International Society for Burn Injuries; American Society of Parenteral and Enteral Nutrition; American Burn

Association; Society of Academic Surgeons; Western Surgical Association. *Publications:* "Surgical Techniques in Patient Care", Co-author, 1978; articles in professional journals. *Address:* 2040 W. Charleston §503, Las Vegas, NV 89102, USA.

BUHRING, Malte, b. 8 Jan. 1939, Münster, Federal Republic of Germany. Senior Consultant. m. Dorothea Wischeropp, 13 May 1966, 1 son, 3 daughters. *Education:* MD, Berlin, Tubingen, Munchen; Habilitation for Internal Medicine, Physical Therapy and Rehabilitation, 1982; Prov. Doz. *Appointments:* Assistant: Institut fur Arbeitsphysiologie und Rehabilitationsforschung, University of Marburg, 1967-69; L R Grote Institut fur Physiotherapie und Rehabilitation, Bad Berleburg, 1969-72;currently, Senior Consultant, Klinikum der Johann Wolfgang Goethe University, Frankfurt. *Memberships:* Deutsche Gesellschaft fur Physikalische Medizin und Rehabilitation; Deutsche Gesellschaft fur Innere Medizine; Deutsche Gesellschaft fur Rheumatologie; Mitteleuropaische Gesellschaft fur Chronobiologie. *Publications:* "Klinik der Hyperthermie", 1984. *Address:* Klinikum der Johann Wolfgang Goethe Universität, Zentrum der Inneren Medizin, Abteilung für Physikalisch-Diätetische Therapie, Theodor Stern Kai 7, D-600 Frankfurt am Main, Federal Republic of Germany.

BULINSKI, Romuald Zdzislaw, b. 5 Feb. 1929, Tyszowce, Poland, Bromatologist, Food Science, m. 1 Jan. 1955, 1 daughter. *Education:* Faculty of Pharmacy, Medical Academy, Lublin, Poland, 1952. *Appointments:* M Pharmacy, 1952, Doctor, 1963-74, Assistant Professor, 1974-83, Professor, 1984-, Head, Bromatology Department, Faculty of Pharmacy, 1970-, Medical Academy, Lublin. *Memberships:* Member, Polish Society of Pharmacists, 1952-; Scientific Society of Lublin, 1975-. *Publications:* Contributor of numerous articles on scientific subjects. *Hobbies:* Philately; Tourist hiking. *Address:* ul Szczerbowskiego 13/14, 20-012 Lublin, Poland.

BULLARD, Ray Elva, b. 25 Jan. 1927, Dallas, Texas, m. Jennie Knepp, 27 June 1979, Hollidaysburg, Pennsylvania, 1 son, 2 daughters. *Education:* BS Zoology, University of Washington, Seattle, Washington, 1948; MD, University of Texas Medical Branch, Galveston, Texas, 1953; BA Psychology, University of Texas, Austin, Texas, 1957; Board Certified in Psychiatry, American Board of Psychiatry and Neurology, 1981. *Appointments:* Private General Practice, 1955-63; Section Chief, Veterans Administration Hospital, Topeka, Kansas, 1966-71; Chief of Psychiatry, Veterans Administration Hospital, Oklahoma City, Oklahoma, 1971-73; Assistant Professor of Psychiatry, University of Oklahoma, 1971-73; Superintendent, Hollidaysburg State Hospital, Hollidaysburg, Pennsylvania 1973-76, Torrance State Hospital, Torrance, Pennsylvania 1976- ; Adjunct Professor of Psychiatry, University of Pittsburg, Pittsburg, Pennsylvania, 1973- . *Memberships:* American Medical Association; American Academy of General Practice; American Psychiatric Association; Pennsylvania Medical Society. *Honour:* Mead-Johnson Scholarship, 1954-55. *Address:* PO Box 10, Torrance, PA 15779, USA.

BULLOCK, John David, b. 31 July 1943, Cincinnati, Ohio, USA. University Professor and Department Chairman. m. Gretchen H. Bullock, 26 June 1966, New Canaan, Connecticut, USA, 2 sons, 1 daughter. *Education:* AB, Dartmouth College, Hanover, New Hampshire, 1965; BMS, Dartmouth Medical School 1966, MD, Harvard Medical School, 1968; MS, Wright State University, Dayton, Ohio, 1982. *Appointments:* Teaching Appointments include: Assistant Clinical Professor of Ophthalmology, Ohio State University, Columbus, 1981-; Lecturer in Law and Medicine, University of Dayton Law School,

Dayton, Ohio, 1981-; Voluntary Associate Professor, Department of Microbiology and Immunology, 1982-84, Associate Professor of Ophthalmology, 1984-, Associate Professor of Microbiology and Immunology, 1984-85, Chairman, Department of Ophthalmology, 1984-, Associate Professor of Surgery (Plastic) 1985-, Wright State University, School of Medicine, Dayton, Ohio. Hospital Appointments: Miami Valley Hospital, Dayton, Ohio, 1975-, Kettering Medical Center, Kettering, Ohio, 1975-, Children's Medical Center, Dayton, Ohio, 1975-, St. Elizabeth Medical Center, Dayton, Ohio, 1976-, Good Samaritan Hospital, Dayton, Ohio, 1979-, Sycamore Medical Center, Miamisburg, Ohio, 1979-. Memberships include: American Association of Ophthalmology; American Academy of Ophthalmology; American Ophthalmologic Society; Society of Heed Fellows; Orbital Society; Fellow, American College of Surgeons; American Association for Pediatric Ophthalmology and Strabismus; American Society of Ophthalmic Plastic and Reconstructive Surgery; American Academy of Facial Plastic and Reconstructive Surgery. Publications: Contributor of numerous articles to medical journals and chapters to edited medical textbooks. Honours: Merrill J Reeh Ophthalmic Pathology Award, 1985; Honor Award, American Academy of Ophthalmology, 1983; Teacher of the Year, Miami Valley Hospital, Dayton, Ohio, 1978; Marvin H Quickert Award, 1975. Hobby: Golf. Address: 1520 South Main Street, 230 Intermed Building, dayton, OH 45409, USA.

BULLOCK, Joseph Daniel, b. 23 Jan.1 942, Cincinnati, Ohio, USA. Assistant Professor of Paediatrics. m. Martha Foss, 20 June, 1964, Cleveland, Ohio, USA, 2 sons. Education: BA, Wittenberg University, 1963; MD, Ohio State University School of Medicine, 1967. Appointments: Residency in Paediatrics, Ohio State University, 1967-69; Fellowship, Allergy-Immunology, University of California, 1969-71; Assistant Professor, Ohio State University, 1971-75, Associate Professor of Paediatrics, 1975-. Memberships: Fellow, American Academy of Allergy; Fellow, American Acadmey of Paediatrics; Fellow, American College of Allergists; American Thoracic Society; Interasma. Publications: 23 Book Reviews and abstracts; 9 conference presentations; 10 articles in learned journals including: 'The Skin Window as a Diagnostic Tool in Paediatric Allergy' in 'Annals of Allergy', 1968; 'Inflammatory Response in Neonate Re-Examined' in 'Paediatrics', 1969; 'Skin Window Eosinophil Response in House Dust Allergy' in'Journal of Allergy and Clinical Immunology', 1971; 'Mite Sensitivity in House Dust - Allergic Children' in 'American Journal of Diseases of Children', 1972; 'An Immunological Approach to the Diagnosis of Food Sensitivity' in 'Clinical Allergy', 1973; 'Children with Allergic Rhinitis and/or Bronchial Asthma Treated with Elimination Diet: 5 year follow up' in 'Annals of Allergy', 1980. Honours: Allergy Foundation of American Fellowship, 1965; Mead Johnson Felowship, 1966; Clemens von Pirquet Award, 1968, 1969, 1970, 1971. Hobby: Golf. Address: 85 East Wilson Bridge Road, Worthington, OH 43085, USA.

BUNNER, David Leslie, b. 18 Sep. 1940, Columbus, Ohio, USA. Chief, Division of Pathophysiology, Army Institute of Infectious Disease; Clinical Associate Professor, Walter Reed Medical Center. m. Bobbie Lou Baesman, 9 Sep. 1961, Columbus, 1 son, 1 daughter. Education: BS, 1961; MD, 1965; Ohio State University; Boards: Internal Medicine, 1972; Endocrinology and Metabolism, 1972. Appointments: Assistant Professor in Ambulatory Medicine, Ohio State University, 1972-73; Staff Member, Scripps Clinic, 1973-79; Acting Chief Endocrinology, Scripps Clinic and Research Foundation, 1978-79; Principal Investigator in Metabolism, Army Institute of Infectious Disease. Memberships: Endocrine Society; Sigma Xi; Phi

Beta Kappa; Phi Eta Sigma. Publications: Contributor to professional journals; Abstracts. Honour: Outstanding Student, Medicinal and Surgery, 1965. Address: Division of Pathophysiology, US Army Institute of Infectious

BUNNEY, William Edward, b. 27 June. 1930, Boston, Massachusetts, USA. Chairman and Distinguished Professor of Psychiatry. m. Blynn Linda Garland, 1 daughter, 2 sons. Education: BA, Oberlin College, Ohio; MD, University of Pennsylvania Medical School; Diploma, Washington Psychoanalytic Institute. Appointments Include: Intern, Henry Ford Hospital, Detroit, Michigan, 1956-57; Yale Psychiatric Residency, Connecticut, 1957-60; Clinical Associate, Project Chief, Chief, Sections of Psychosomatic Medicine and Psychiatry, 1960-71, Director, Division of Narcotic Addiction and Drug Abuse, 1971-73, Chief, Adult Psychiatry Branch, 1973-77, Chief Biological Psychiatry Branch, 1977-82, Deputy Clinical Director, Division of Clinical and Behavioral Research, 1977-81, National Institute of Mental Health, Bethesda, Maryland; Professor and Chairman, Department of Psychiatry, California College of Medicine, University of California, 1982-. Memberships Include: Past President, American College of Neuropsychopharamcology; President Elect, Collegium Internationale Neuropsychopharmacologicaum; Past President Psychiatric Research Society; fellow, American Psychiatric Association; Society for Neuroscience. Publications: Author of over 300 papers contributed as book chapters, journal articles. Participant in numerous invited lectures, Nationally and Internationally. Member and Past Member of various editorial boards including: 'American Journal of Psychiatry'; 'Psychiatric Annals'; 'Psychiatry Research'; 'Substance and Alcohol Action Misuse'; 'Human Neurobiology'; 'Journal of Nerual Transmission'. Honours Include: Honorable mention, 1969, 1st place 1971, APA Hofheimer Research Award; Member, Mental Health Advisory Council, World Health Organisation, 1984; Committee member, World Psychiatric Association. Hobbies: Sailing; Skiing. Address: Department of Psychiatry, California College of Medicine, University of California, Irvine, CA 92717, USA.

BUNTING, Edward Davidson, b. 22 Aug. 1925, Belfast, Ireland. Medical Administrator. m. Anne Evelyn Bolton, 26 Mar. 1951, Maghera, Co. Derry, Ireland, 2 sons, 1 daughter. Education: Member, Certificate, Institute of Personnel Management, London; Licentiate, Institute of Health services Management, London. England; Diploma Social Studies, Queen's University, Belfast; BA Business Administration, Upper Iowa University; LLB, La Salle University, Chicago. Appointments: Hughs Tool Co., Belfast, 1952-59; Labour Relations Director, 1960-62, Senior Employee Relations Manager, 1962-65, Assistant Business Manager & Controller, 1965-70, Medical Administrator, 1970-86, Kaiser Permanente Medical Care Programme, Los Angeles, California, USA. Memberships: Medical Group Management Association; American Society of Law & Medicine; American Association of Hospital Personnel Directors, Publications: Articles in the 1970's in 'Inquiry', journal of the Blue Cross Society. Honours: Certificates of Appreciation, American Red Cross 1970, Volunteers of America, 1975. Hobbies: Sailing; Fishing. Address: 1512 Rose Villa, Pasadena, CA 91106, USA.

BUNTING, John Stanton, b. 27 Nov. 1924, London, England. Consultant Radiotherapist and Oncologist. m. 24 Nov. 1949, 2 sons. Education: MB BS, London, 1953; DMRT, England, 1956; FFR, 1961; Fellow, Royal College of Radiologists. Appointments: House Physician, Addenbrooke's Hospital, Cambridge; Registrar, Guys Hospital, London; Registrar, Senior Registrar, Chief Asistant, Department of Radiotherapy, St Bartholomews Hospital, London; Consultant Radiotherapist, Colchester, Essex; Consultant Radiotherapist, Reading Hospitals,

Oxford Regional Health Authority; Honorary Consultant, Sue Ryder Foundation. *Memberships:* Fellow, Royal Society of Medicine; Liveryman, Society of Apothecaries of London; European Society of Radiation Oncologists. *Publications:* ''Anatomical influence in megavoltage radiotherapy of carcinoma of maxillary antrum', 1965; 'Pattern of survival and spread in 596 cases of breast cancer related to clinical staging and histological grade', (co-author), 1976. *Hobbies:* Painting; Art appreciation. *Address:* 1 Kennet Place, Chilton Foliat, Hungerford, Berkshire, RG17 0TB, England.

BURASTERO, Robert John, b. 15 June 1931, California, USA. Vice President, Applied Health Services, Inc. m. Lillian Katherine Arbini, 24 July 1955, San Rafael, California. *Education:* BA, San Francisco State University, 1956; MBA, Golden Gate University, 1965; Certificates: Comprehensive Health Planning, 1974, Medical Care Administration, 1960, Computer Applications for Business, 1958. *Appointments:* Administrator, Valco Hospital, Tema, Ghana, 1965-68; Vice President, Kaiser Foundation International, 1968-80; General Manager, Khobar Cooperative Clinic, Alkhobar, Saudi Arabia, 1980-81; Project Director, As Salaam Hospital, Sadah, Yemen Arab Republic, 1982-83; Deputy Project Director, Tawam Hospital, Al Ain Abu Dhabi, United Arab Emirates, 1984-85. *Memberships:* American College of Hospital Administrators; Hospital Financial Management Association; International Hospital Federation. *Publications:* ''American Style Hospital for Ghana'', 'Hospitals', Volume 43, 1969; Keynote Speech International Hospital Federation Regional Meeting, ''The Education and Training of Health and Hospital Personnel in Developing Countries'', Manila 1978. *Honours:* Preceptor in Hospital Administration; University of Minnesota - Programme in Hospital Administration, School of Public Health, 1973-80. *Hobbies:* Swimming; Jogging. *Address:* PO Box 485, Moraga, CA 94556, USA.

BURCHARTH, Flemming, b. 15 Oct. 1938, Copenhagen, Denmark. Surgical Gastroenterologist. *Education:* MD, Medical Faculty, University of Copenhagen, 1965; Specialist in General Surgery, 1974, Specialist in Surgical Gastroenterology Surgery, 1976, PhD Doctor of Medicine, 1981, University of Copenhagen. *Appointments:* Resident in Medicine (General Surgery) Gynaecology & Anaesthesiology), 1965-72, Senior Resident in Thoracis Surgery, Orthopaedic surgery, Urology and Gastoenterology, 1968-72, First Resident (consultant) in surgical gastroenterology, 1972-83, Chief of Surgery, Head of Department of Surgical Gastroenterology, 1983-, Lecturer in Surgery (Professor), pre- and postgraduate study, 1972-, Herlev and University Hospitals in Copenhagen. *Memberships:* Danish Surgical Society; Danish Medical Society (Committee Member); Danish Society of Gastroenterology (Committee Member); Danish Association for the Study of the Liver (Committee member). *Publications:* Author & Editor, 10 textbooks (Liver, Pancreas, Surgery), 1979-85; 116 papers in international medical journals 1966-85; 170 lectures in Medical Societies, Meetings & Congresses, 1967-85; Doctoral Thesis: 'Transhepatic pontography', 1981; 'Inventions': transhepatic endoprosthesis', 1972; 'Continent Colostomy Device', 1984. *Honours:* Danish Surgical Society Prize, 1981; University of Copenhagen Prize, 1984; Collegium Chirurgorum Honour Prize, 1985; several grants for scientific work. *Hobby:* Travel. *Address:* Department of Surgical Gastroenterology, Herlev Hospital, University of Copenhagen, DK-2730, Denmark.

BURCKHARDT, Peter, b14 Feb. 1939, Basle, Switzerland. Professor of Medicine; Chairman of Department. m. Ismene Panagopoulos, Athens, 2 sons. *Education:* Medical School of University of Basle, Switzerland. *Appointments:* Fellow, Endocrine University, Massachusetts General Hospital, Boston, USA; Resident, Chief, University Hospital, Lausanne, (CHUV), Switzerland. *Memberships:* Swiss Society Internal Medicine; Swiss Society Endocrinology; European Society Calcified Tissues; American Society Bone Min. Res. *Publications:* 'Parathyroid function in Patients with Paget's', 1973; 'Preop. Localization of hyperfonct. parathyr. tissue', 1976; 'Parathyoid response to EDTA', 1980; 'Sec. hyperparathyr. in renal IHC', 1981; 'The fate of PTH during hemodialysis', 1985. *Address:* Department of Internal Medicine CHUV, 1011 Lausanne, Switzerland.

BURDON, Jonathan Gareth William, b. 3 Sept. 1946, Simla, India. Respiratory Physician. m. Marilyn June Woodruff, 30 Dec, 1970, South Yarra, Australia, 1 son, 2 daughters. *Education:* MBBS, Melbourne, Australia, 1971, FRACP, 1979, MD, 1980, FCCP, 1980. *Appointments:* Resident Medical Officer and Medical Registrar, Royal Melbourne Hospital, Australia, 1972-77, Research Fellow, Department of Thoracic Medicine, 1978-79; Research Fellow, Cardio-Respiratory Unit, McMaster University, Hamilton, Ontario, Canada, 1980-82; Respiratory Physician St. Vincent's Hospital, Melbourne, Australia -. *Memberships:* Royal Australasian College of Physicians; Thoracic Society of Australia; American College of Chest Physicians; American Thoracic Society; Society of Critical Care Medicine; Australian Medical Association; Australian Society for Medical Research; Society of Critical Care Medicine; Australian and New Zealand Intensive Care Society. *Publications:* 31 articles, abstracts and letters published in professional journals including 'Medical Journal of Australia'; Archives of Surgery'; 'Chest'; 'Clinical Science'; 'Journal of Applied Physiology'; 'American Review of Respiratory Diseases'; 'Australian and New Zealand Medical Journal'. *Honours:* A.H. Wall Prize, Royal Melbourne Hospital, 1972; Travelling Fellow in Applied Health Sciences, NH and MRC, Australia, 1980-83. *Address:* Respiratory Function Laboratory, St. Vincent's Hospital, Victoria Parade, Fitzroy 3065, Australia.

BURG, Robert Jules, b. 7 Jan. 1956, New Jersey, USA. Medical Administrator. *Education:* Administrative Resident, Jackson Memorial Hospital; Assistant Head, Operations Management, US Naval Hospital, Oakland, California; Head, Operations Management, US Naval Hospital, Okinawa, Japan; Officer in Charge, Branch Clinic, Treasure Island, San Francisco, California. *Memberships:* American College of Health Care Executives; Health Care Executives of Northern California; Association of Western Hospitals; Instructor, Columbia College, San Francisco, California; University of Maryland Far East Division. *Honours:* Navy Achievement Medal, 1982; Navy Commendation Medal, 1985. *Hobbies:* Boating; Skiing; Tennis. *Address:* Naval Station Treasure Island Branch Clinic, Bldg 257, San Francisco, CA 94130, USA.

BURGER, Charles Nelson, b. 29 Oct. 1940, Cincinnati, Ohio, USA. Executive Director. m. Charlene Ann Young, 14 Sep. 1963, Fort Mitchell, Kentucky, 1 son, 2 daughters. *Education:* BS Zoology, University of Cincinnati, Ohio, 1963; MBA Hospital Administration, Xavier University, 1970. *Appointments:* Assistant Administrator, Central Baptist Hospital, Lexington, Kentucky, 1970-74; Administrator, County Hospital, Paris, Kentucky 1974-76; West Shoshone General Hospital, Kellogg, Idaho 1976-79, Carroll County Memorial Hospital, Carrollton, Kentucky 1979-81, Hickory Memorial Hospital, Hickory, North Carolina 1981-83; Executive Director, Uniform Business Medical Coalition, Hickory, North Carolina, 1983- . *Membership:* American College of Hospital Administrators. *Hobbies:* Hiking; Swimming; Snorkeling; Gardening. *Address:* PO Box 3584, Hickory, NC 28603, USA.

BURGER, June Mary, b. 28 Nov. 1927, Liverpool, England. Private Homoeopathic Practice; Paediatrician, Royal London Homoeopathic Hospital. m. Peter Burger, 3 Sep. 1952, Woolton, Liverpool, 1 son, 3 daughters. *Education:* MRCS; LRCP; DCH; MFHom. *Appointments:* Secretary, Faculty of Homoeopathy, 1974-81; Vice-President, 1981-84. *Memberships:* British Medical Association; Faculty of Homoeopathy. *Hobbies:* Music; Painting; Gardening. *Address:* 6 St. Peters Close, St. Albans, Hertfordshire AL1 3ES, England.

BURGER, Kálmán, b. 19 Oct. 1929, Aszód, Hungary. University Head of Department of Inorganic and Analytical Chemistry. m. Dr Anna Gimes, 24 Nov 1953, 1 son, 1 daughter. *Education:* PhD, L Eotvos University, Budapest, 1958; D Sc, Hungarian Academy of Sciences, Budapest, 1966. *Appointments:* Assistant Professor, L. Eotvos University Budapest, 1953-62; Research Fellow, Royal Institute of Technology, Stockholm, 1962-63; Reader, 1963-68, Professor, 1968-83, L Eotvos University; Head of Department of Inorganic and Analytical Chemistry, A Jozsef University, Szeged, 1983-; Visiting Professor, Chemistry Department, Princeton University, New Jersey, USA, 1981. *Memberships:* Head of Working Group for Co-ordination Chemistry of Hungarian Academy of Sciences; Member of Committee for Pharmaceutical Sciences at Hungarian Academy of Sciences; Member of Advisory Board of following international journals: Inorganica Chimica Acta; ICA Bioinorganic Articles and Letters; Journal of Crystallorgraphic and Spectroscopic Research. *Publications:* "Co-ordination Chemistry: Experimental Methods" 1973; "Organic Reagents in Metal Analysis" 1973; "Mossbauer Spectroscopty" with A Vertes, L Korecz, 1979; "Solvation, Ionic and Complex Formation in Non-aqueous Solutions" 1983; Over 100 research papers in international journals. *Hobbies:* Travel; Excursions; Classical music. *Address:* A József University, Department of Inorganic and Analytical Chemistry, H-6701 Szeged, P O Box 440, Hungary.

BURGESS, Warren Gilbert, b. 10 Jan. 1930, Sanford, Maine, USA. Controller. m. (2) Judith L Wibel, 12 July 1974, Warner, New Hampshire, 8 sons, 4 daughters. *Education:* Diplima, Bentley College; BS, Suffolk University. *Appointments:* Administrator, Read Memorial Hospital; Director, Fiscal Services; Consultant, Private Practice. *Memberships:* ACHA; HFMA; AHA. *Hobby:* Bible Teacher. *Address:* Rte. 2 Box 17A, Boonville, NC 27011, USA.

BURGHARDT, Erich, b. 20 July 1921, Almaspuszta. Head of Department. m. Brigitte Wolfgang, 4 June 1964. *Education: MD, Medical School University, Graz. Memberships:* International Federation for Cervical Pathology and Colposcopy; Austrian Society of Applied Cytology; Austrian Society of Gynecology and Obstetrics; International Academy of Cytology; International society for the Study of Vulvar Disease; society of Pelvic Surgeons; Cancer Committee FIGO; Deutsche Akademie d. Naturforscher Leopoldina; Austrian Society of in vitro-fertilisation. *Publications:* More than 100 publications; 14 book contributions; (textbooks) "Early Histological Diagnosis of Cervical Cancer", 1973; German Japanese, Spanish translations; "Proceedings of the Second World Congress of Cervical Pathology and Colposcopy", 1978; "Minimal Invasive Cancer", 1982; "Colposcopy, Cervical Pathology", 1984, German,Spanish, Japanese, French, Italian Translations; Editor, "Spezielle Gynakologie und Gevurtshilfe", 1985. *Honours:* Hoechst-Prize, 1967; Honorary Member, Italian Society of Gynaecology and Obstetrics; Society of Gynaecology and Obstetrics of GDR; Society Francaise de Colposcopie et de Pathologie Cervico-Vaginale; Felix Rutledge Society; Indian Academy of Cytology. *Address:* University Clinic of Obstetrics and Gynaecology, Auenbruggerplatz 14, A-8036, Graz, Austria.

BURGOYNE, David Sidney (Senior), b. 28 Mar. 1923, Idaho, USA. Psychiatrist, Private Practice. m. Helen Louise Seewer, 15 Nov. 1945, Logan, 2 sons, 1 daughter. *Education:* MD, Cornell University Medical College, 1951. *Appointments:* Private General Practice, Medicine, 1952-59; Residency, Psychiatry, US Naval Hospital, Oakland, 1960-63; Chief, Neuropsychiatry, US Naval Dispensory, US Naval Ship Yard, Pearl Harbor, Hawaii, 1963-65; Chief, Neuropsychiatry, US Naval Hospital, Camp Pendelton, California, 1966; Private Practice, Psychiatry, Phoenix, 1967- . *Memberships:* Phoenix Psychiatric Council; Arizona Psychiatric Society; American Psychiatric Association; Central Neuropsychiatric Association; American Association for Social Psychiatry, various offices. *Publications:* "Psychiatric Emergencies Aboard Submarines", 1964; "What's Psychotherapy and Who needs It", ; etc. *Honours:* Fellow, American Psychiatric Association, 1975. *Hobbies:* Snow Skiing; Long Distance Running; Tennis; Trap Shooting; Photography; Travel. *Address:* 4630 E. Indian School Road, Phoenix, AZ 85018, USA.

BURISH, Thomas G, b. 4 May 1950, Menominee, Minnesota, USA. Associate Professor of Psychology and Assistant Professor, Department of Medicine; Chairman, Department of Psychology. m. Pamela Zebrasky 19 June 1976, Peshtigo, Wisconsin, 2 sons. *Education:* AB, Psychology, University of Notre Dame; MA, Psychology, University of Kansas; PhD, Clincial Psychology, University of Kansas. *Appointments:* Assistant Instructor, Department of Psychology, University of Kansas, 1975-76I; Assistant Professor, 1976-80, Director of Clinical Training, 1980-84, Department of Psychology, Vanderbilt University. *Memberships:* American Psychological Association, Divson 12 (member) and 38 (Fellow); Biofeedback Society of America; Biofeedback Society of Tennessee. *Publications:* Contributor to professioanl journals including: 'Journal of Behavior Therapy and Experimental Psyciatry', 'Psychophysiology', 'Science', 'Journal of Personality and Social Psychology', 'Biofeedback and Self-Regulation', etc.; Abstracts; Presentations. *Honours:* David Shulman Memorial Award for Excellence in Clinical Psychology, University of Kansas, 1975; Madison Sarratt Award of Excellence in Undergraduate Teaching, Vanderbilt, University, 1980. *Hobby:* Jogging. *Address:* Department of Psychology, 134 Wesley Hall, Vanderbilt University, Nashville, TN 37240, USA.

BURKHOLDER, Peter Miller, b. 7 May 1933, Cambridge, Massachusetts, USA, Staff Pathologist, m. Barbara Beers, 3 June 1956, South Hadley, Massachusetts, 2 daughters. *Education:* BS, Yale University, 1955; MD, Cornell University Medical College, 1959. *Appointments:* Assistant Professor, Pathology, Cornell University Medical College, New York, 1964-65; Associate Professor, Pathology, Duke University, North Carolina, 1965-70; Professor and Chairman, Pathology, University of Wisconsin, Madison, 1971-79; Director, Kidney Disease Institute and Deputy Director, Division of Laboratories and Research, New York State Department of Health, 1979-82; Chief of Staff, VA Medical Centre, Ann Arbor, Michigan, 1982-84. *Memberships:* American Association Pathologists; Sigma Xi; International Academy of Pathology; American Society Nephrology; International Society of Nephrology; American Association Immunologists; International Society of Nephrology. *Publications:* "Atlas of Human Glomerular Pathology", 1974; Author of 76 orignal manuscripts, 15 chapters in books and 74 abstracts and presentations. *Honours:* Polk Prize for graduate research, 1959. *Hobbies:* Carpentry; Landscape gardening; Canoeing. *Address:* 2023 Devonshire Road, Ann Arbor, MI 48104, USA.

BURKI, Nausherwan Khan, b. 25 Sep. 1940, Assam, India. Professor and Chief of Pulmonary Division, University Department of Medicine. *Education:* MB BS, Punjab University, Pakistan, 1962; PhD,

Medicine, London University, England, 1969; MRCP (UK) Royal College of Physicians, London, 1970. *Appointments:* Assistant Professor, Experimental Medicine, KE Medical College, Lahore, Pakistan, 1971-74; Assistant Professor, Department of Medicine, University of Kentucky, USA, 1974-77; Associate Professor 1977-82, Professor and Chief Pulmonary Division, 1982-. *Memberships:* Medical Research Society, England, 1968; American Thoracic Society, 1974; American Physiological Society, 1976; Central Society of Clinical Research, 1977. *Publications:* Textbook: "Pulmonary Diseases" 1982; Numerous articles in medical journals and chapters in medical volumes; many papers presented to medical conferences. *Honours:* Fellow, American College of Chest Physicians; Fellow, American College of Physicians. *Hobbies:* Squash; Water sports. *Address:* Pulmonary Division, Department of Medicine, MN-578, 800 Rose Street, University of Kentucky Medical Center, Lexington, KY 40536-0084, USA.

BURKOWSKY, Mitchell Roy, b. 11 Aug. 1931, Cooperstown, New York, USA. Professor. m. Diane F. Benowitz, 24 June 1956, Newark, 1 son, 2 daughters. *Education:* AB, State University of New York, 1952; 3 Certificates, University of Paris, Sorbonne, 1955; PhD, Wayne State University, 1960; Post Doctural Residency, University of Florida College of Health Related Professions, 1965-66. *Appointments:* Assistant Professor, Detroit Institute of Technology, 1959-61; Assistant Professor, Clinic Director, University of North Dakota, 1961-65; Assistant Professor, Syracuse University, 1966-72; Associate to Full Professor, State University of New York, Clinic Director, Department Chairman,1972-. *Memberships:* American Speech Language Hearing Association; Council on Exceptional Children, New York State Speech Language Hearing Association; etc. *Publications:* "Teaching American Pronunciation to Foreign Students", 1969; "Parents' and Teachers' Guide to the Care of Autistic Children", 1972; "Orientation to Language and Learning Disorders", 1973; Films: "English as a Second Language", 1972, "Voice, Articulation and Resonance", 1984; several articles in professional journals. *Honours:* Commendations, Adjutant General, US Army, New York State Speach & Hearing Association; Appointed 3 times by 2 New York State Governors to Board of Visitors of J N Adam Developmental Centre. *Hobbies:* Barbershop Singing; Swimming/Diving Officiating; Gardening; Cooking. *Address:* 164 Temple St., Fredonia, NY 14063, USA.

BURLEY, Denis Michael, b. 16 Mar 1927, Croydon, Surrey, England, Head of International Medical Liaison Ciba-Geigy Pharmaceuticals, m. Dorothy Mary Wyndham, 8 Sept 1951, Chelsea, London, England. *Education:* LRCP MRCS (Eng), King's College/Westminster Hospital Medical School, MB BS (Lond); MRCP, 1976, FRCP, 1980, Royal College of Physicians. *Appointments:* Casualty Officer, 1950-51, Clinical Assistant, Rheumatism Unit, 1958-75, Westminster Hospital; House Physician, St Marys Hospital, Isle of Wight, 1951; Military Service, RAMC, 1951-53; House Physician, 1953-54, Senior House Officer,1954, St Stephen's Hospital; Registrar, St Stephen's and Westminster Hospitals, 1954-58; Medical Adviser, Distiller's Company(Biochemicals) Ltd, 1958-62; Medical Adviser, 1963-69, Head of Medical Services, 1969-79, CIBA Laboratories; Head of Medical Services, 1979-81, Head of International Medical Liason, 1981-, Ciba-Geigy Pharmaceuticals Division. *Memberships:* British Medical Association; The British society for Rheumatology; british Thoracic Society; Treasurer, Association of Medical Advisers in the Pharmaceutical Industry; Treasurer, Trust for Education and Research in Therapeutics; Chairman, Medico-Pharmaceutical Forum; President, International Federation of Associations of Pharmaceutical Physicians; Examiner, Diploma of

Pharmaceutical Medicine. *Publications:* 'Designing the correct protocol', 1976; 'Rifampicin, enzyme induction, oestrogens and the 'pill', 1977; 'Data Handling and statistics', 1981; 'Therapeutic progress - review III. Can drugs prevent recurrent mycarial infarction?, 1982; 'Pharmaceutical Medicine', (co-editor T B Binns), 1985. *Hobbies:* Contract bridge; Chess; Stock market. *Address:* "Kumalo", Farm Lane, Ashtead,Surrey KT21 1LJ, England.

BURMAN, Neil Timothy Charles, b. 22 Nov. 1947, Manchester, England. Dental Surgeon. Private Practice. Divorced, 3 sons, 1 daughter. *Education:* BDS, London, 1970; Licentiate of Dental Surgery, Royal College of Surgeons, England, 1970; BA, Open University, 1976; Fellow, Royal Australasian College of Dental Surgeons, 1980; Graduate Diploma in Business and Administration, Western Australian Institute of Technology, 1984; MDSc, University of Western Australia, 1986. *Appointments:* Secretary and Treasurer, Royal Australasian College of Dental Surgeons, Western Australia, 1980-81; Councillor, 1980-81, Executive Officer, 1982, Vice President, 1983, President, 1984, Australian Dental Association (WA), Chairman, Royal Australasian College of Dental Surgeons (WA), 1982-85. *Memberships:* Australian Dental Association; Royal Australasian College of Dental Surgeons. *Publications:* Contributions to 'Australian Dental Journal', 1983, 84; "Epidemiology of Cleft Lip and Palate: A Case Control Study in Western Australia", Thesis, 1985. *Honour:* Commissioner for Declarations, 1981. *Hobbies:* Blondes, Avoiding insurance salesmen, Contemplating physical exercise. *Address:* 157 Duffy Road, Carine, WA 6020, Australia.

BURNETT, Syringa A Marshall, b. 11 May 1935, Jamaica, University Lecturerm. Jasper N Burnett, 2 Feb. 1974, Half Way Tree, Jamaica, 1 daughter. *Education:* Registered Nurse; Registered Midwife; Diploma in Public Health Nursing; BScN, University of Toronto, Canada; MA Nursing, New York University, USA. *Appointments:* Staff Nurse, Tower Isle and Arawak Hotels, Jamaica, 1957-58; Staff Nurse, Head Nurse, Assistant Evening Supervisor, Administrative Nursing Supervisor, Clinical coordinator, Doctors Hospital, Toronto, Ontario, Canada, 1959-67; Assistant Director of Nursing, North York General Hospital, Willowdale, Ontario, 1967-68; Head Nurse, Nursing Instructor, New York State Department of Mental Hygiene, 1969-72; Lecturer, University of the West Indies, 1972- ; Short term Consultant, World Health Organisation and Pan American/World Health Organisation; Assistant Editor 1973-76; Editor 1976- , The Jamaican Nurse. *Memberships:* President 1984-86, Commonwealth Nurses Federation; Board 1977-85, International Council of Nurses; Society for International Development; Sigma Theta Tau; Canadian Psychiatric Association; Life Member, Nurses Association of Jamaica; Jamaica Society of Scientists and Technologists; Jamaica Council for Adult Education. *Honour:* Caribbean Nurses Organization Mavis Harney Award, 1984. *Hobbies:* Visual and performing art; Cricket; Cooking; Gardening; Dogrearing. *Address:* P O Box 361, Kingston 8, Jamaica.

BURNS, Carol Ann Morris, b. 11 June 1945, New Jersey, USA. Director, Medical Libraries. m. Dr Thomas S. Burns, 29 June 1968, Livingston, 1 daughter. *Education:* BA, Wittenberg University, 1963; MA, History, Eastern Michigan University, 1972;' AMLS, Medical librarianship, University of Michigan, Ann Arbor, 1974. *Appointments:* Audiovisual Librarian, 1974-79, Assistant Director, Services to the Public, 1979-83, Acting Director, 1983-84, Director, 1984-, Medical Libraries, Emory University. *Memberships:* Medical Library Association; Association of Academic Health Sciences Library Directors; Consortium of Southern Biomedical Libraries; George Health Sciences

Libraries Association; Research Libraries Group. *Honours:* Beta Phi Mu. *Hobbies:* Hiking; Wilderness Canoeing; Camping; Tennis; Softball. *Address:* A.W. Calhoun Medical Library, Emory University, Atlanta, GA 30322, USA.

BURNS, Johnny L, b. 23 June 1949, Fayetteville, North Carolina, USA. President, InterHealth Corporation. m. Cheryl Ann Greenburg, 26 May 1973, Fort Knox, Kentucky, 1 son, 1 daughter. *Education:* BA, Psychology and French, Tulane University, 1971; MA, Hospital Administration, 1979. *Appointments:* US Army Captain, Test Pilot, 1971-76; Sales Representative, American Hospital Supply Corporation, 1976-78; Assistant Administrator, Lakeside Hospital, Hospital Corporation of America, 1978-80; Administrator, Lee Memorial Hospital, Giddings, Texas, 1980-82; Adminsitrator, Odessa Women and Children's Hospital, Texas, 1982-83; President, InterHealth Corporation, Giddings, 1983-. *Memberships:* American College of Hospital Administrators; American Academy of Medical Administrators; American Public Health Association; Texas Hospital Association; American Academy of Political Science; Civic Bodies; President, Giddings Lions; Vice-President, Giddings Chapter, American Cancer Society; Board of Directors, American Heart Association, Board of Directors, Giddings Chamber of Commerce; Area Coordinator, Boy Scouts of America Fund Drive; Emergency Medical Services Advisory Council, Austin; Advisory Board Texas Youth Council, Giddings State Home and School. *Honours:* Outstanding Junior Officer, US Army, 1975; Outstanding Young Man of America, 1984; Army Commendation Medal *Hobbies:* Tennis; Golf; Reading; Skiing. *Address:* 891 East Industry, Giddings, TX 78942, USA.

BURNS, Paul David, b. 20 Aug. 1956, Kansas City, Missouri, USA. Doctor of Chiropractic. m. Gail Ann Ruhl, 6 Oct. 1984, 1 son, 1 daughter. *Education:* BA, Biology & Political Science, Drury College, Springfield, Missouri; BSc Human Physiology, Logan College, St. Louis, Missouri; Doctor of Chiropractic, Logan College of Chiropractic Medicine. *Memberships:* American Chiropractic Association, Council on Orthopaedics, Sports Medicine, Radiology; Colorado Chiropractic Association. *Publications:* "Biomechanical Aspects of Orthopaedics", 1983; "Chiropractic Neurology", 1984. *Honours:* Team Physician to the World Professional Skiers' Council, 1983- ; Graduate School Faculty, Sports Medicine, Logan College of Chiromedicine, 1984-. *Hobbies:* Tennis; Skiing; Racquetball. *Address:* 7936 East Arapahoe Court, Suite 2200,. Englewood, CO 80112, USA.

BURRELL, Christopher John, b. 8 Nov. 1941, Sydney, Australia. Senior Director, Medical Virology, Institute of Medical & Veterinary Science. m. Margaret Eileen Cobb, 23 Dec. 1970, Canberra, 2 sons. *Eduacation:* BSc.(Med), 1964, MB, BS, 1965, University of Sydney; PhD, Australian National University of Sydney; PhD, Australian National University, 1971; MRCPath (UK), 1977; FRCPA (Aust) 1980. *Appointments:* Lecturer, Bacteriology, Edinburgh University Medical School, 1971-79; Hon. Registrar, Bacteriology, Royal Infirmary, Edinburgh, 1973-79; Medical Specialist, IMVS, Adelaide, 1979-85; Clinical Senior Lecturer, University of Adelaide, 1980-83; Associate Specialist, Virology, Adelaide Childrens' Hospital, 1983-; Senior Consultant Specialist, Virology, Royal Adelaide Hospital, 1982-; Clinical Reader, Virology, University of Adelaide, 1984-. *Memberships:* Society for General Microbiology, UK; American Socity for Microbiology;Australian Society for Microbiology; Australasian Society for Infectious Diseases. *Publications:* "Carbohydrate in hepatitis B antigen", co-author, "Nature New Biology", 1973; "The expression in Escherichia coli of hepatitis B DNA sequences cloned in the plasmid pBR322", co-author, "Nature", 1979; over 50 research papers.

Honours: Wellcome australia Medal and awarad for distinguished scientific achievement, 1984. *Hobbies:* Family; Music; Tennis. *Addres:* Division of Medical Virology, Institute of Medical and Veterinary Science, Frome Road, Adelaide, South Australia, 5000

BURRY, Alastair Fleet, b. 8 Dec. 1926, Christchurch, New Zealand, Consultant Anatomical Pathologist, m. Jill Helen Leech, 22 Nov 1958, Rangiora, 1 son, 3 daughters. *Education:* MB, ChB, 1951; MD, 1956; FRCPA, 1964. *Appointments:* House Srugeon, 1951, Registrar, Pathology, 1952-56, Junior Pathologist, 1956-59, Anatomical Pathologist, 1977-85, Christchurch Hospital; Pathologist in Charge, Princess Margaret Hospital, Christchurch, 1959-62; Anatomical Pathologist, Princess Alexandra Hospital, Brisbane, Australia, 1963-67; Director of Pathology, Royal Brisbane Hospital, 1967-76; Visiting Consultant Pathologist, Christchurch Hospital, 1976-. *Memberships:* Fellow, Royal College of Pathologists of Australasia, State Councillor, 1975-76; New Zealand Society of Pathologists; New Zealand Medical Society; Pathological Society of Great Britain and Ireland. *Publications:* 'Endocardial thrombosis', 1956; 'Staphlococcal Pneumonia in the Newborn', (with D W Beaver), 1956; 'A Profile of renal disease in Queensland', 1966; 'The Evaluation of analgesic nephropathy', 1967; 'Analgesic nephropathy and the renal concentrating mechanism', (Co-author), 1977; 'Cerebeller calcification: A Possible marker of head nephropathy', 1977. *Hobbies:* Angling; Golf; Gardening. *Address:* Whincops Road, Halswell, Christchurch 3, New Zealand.

BURTON-BRADLEY, Burton Gyrth, b. 18 Nov. 1914, Sydney, Australia. Psychiatrist; Author. m. Ingeborg Roeser, 7 Oct. 1950 (deceased 1972). *Education:* DPM, University of Melbourne, Australia, 1956; DTM & H, 1963, Dip. Anth. 1964, University of Sydney, Australia; FRACMA, Royal Australian College of Medical Administrators, 1967; MD, University of New South Wales, 1969; FRANZCP, Royal Australian and New Zealand College of Psychiatrists, 1970, FRCPsych, Royal College of Psychiatarists, England, 1972; MD (Hon) UPNG,1986;Medical Officer, Psychiatric Services, Queensland, 1951-57; Lecturer in Psychological Medicine, University of Malaya, 1957-59; Chief Mental Health PNG, 1959-75; Associate Professor of Psychiatry, University of Papua New Guinea, 1972-75; Clinical Associate Professor of Psychiatry, University of Hawaii, 1976-present; Professor of Psychiatry, (Hon.), University of Papua New Guinea, 1978-present; Counsellor, Societe Internationale de Psychopathologoie de l'Expression, 1982-present. *Memberships:* Wenner-Gren Foundation Research Fellow, 1970; Abraham Flexner Lecturer, Vanderbilt University, USA, 1973; Advisory Panel on Mental Health of World Health Organisation, 1977; Vice-President, International College of Psychosomatic Medicine, 1977; Regional Counsellor, World Association for Social Psychiatry, 1977; President, Papua New Guinea Psychiatric Association, 1978; WHO Adviser, Solomon Islands, 1979; Fellow l'Organisation Internationale de Psychophysiologie, Montreal, 1981; Hon. Member, Sociedad International de Nuavas Ciencias de la Conducta, Argentina, 1982. *Publications:* "South Pacific Ethnopsychiatry"; 1967; "Mixed Race Society in Port Moresby", 1968; "Psychiatry and the Law in the Developing country", 1970; "Longlong",1973; "Stone Age Crisis", 1975; 200 scientific papers in professional journals. *Honours:* Wenner Gren Research Award, 1970; Benjamin Rush Bronze Medal, 1974; Yale-Based Foundations Fund for Research, 1975; OBE, 1982. *Hobbies:* Historical Research in Medicine & Psychiatry. *Address:* PO Box 111, Port Moresby, Papua New Guinea.

BUSAT, William, Executive Director, St Mary's McGill University Hospital, Canada. m. Clara Ebertz,

5 June 1952, Wuerzburg, 2 sons, 3 daughters. *Education:* MBA, FACHE (USA); FRSH (England); Dipl. HOM, University Manitoba, 1963-65; PhD (prep) Germany; MCCHSE, Canada. *Appointments:* Officer, Post Exchanges, US Army EUCOM, 1946-512; Assistant Comptroller, Bronx Hospital, New York, 1952-57; Director, Finance & Assist? Administrator, St Mary's Hospital Centre, Montreز Canada, 1957-67; Director, Administration, 1967-75, CEO, Executive Director, 1975- , St Mary's Hospital, Montreal; Special Advisor, Ministry of Social Affairs, Quebec, 1969-77. *Memberships:* American College of Health Care Executives (Repent of Province Quebec 1977-85); International Hospital Association; American Hospital Association; Combined Council CA Institute & Ministry of Social Affairs, Quebec; Quebec Hospital Association; Association of Teaching Hospitals of Canada; Board of Directors: Montreal Joint Hospital Institute of Mcgill University; American Association of Hospital Presidents; International Health Economics and Management Institute; OPRON Sante International du Canada Corp. *Publications:* Task Force Book, "Operational Efficiency in Hospitals", 1968; "Global Budget and Prospective Reimbursement System in Quebec", 1970; Review of Memoire "Resolving Quebec's Healthcare Dilemma through Colaborative Action", 1976; Research Contribution to "Alternative Cost - Reimbursement System"; Preparation of a Draft Law for Puerto Rican Health Insurance Plan, 1975. *Honours:* Distinguished Service Award letter, Minister of Health and Welfare, Canada, 1969, Distinguished Service Award, ACHE. *Hobbies:* Oil & Watercolour Painting. *Address:* 4870 Cote des Neiges, Penthouse 1503, Montreal, Quebec Canada H3V 1H3.

BUSHELL-GUTHRIE, Phillip, b. 27 July 1940, Brisbane, Australia. Plastic Surgeon. m. Vicki Trapp, 1 son, 1 daughter. *Education:* MBBS, BDSc, (Hons) University of Queensland,Australia; FRACDS, Royal Australasian College of Dental Surgeons; Diploma in Oral Surgery; FRCS, Glasgow, Scotland, Fellow International College of Surgeons. *Appointments:* Dental Research Fellow, Department of Health Medical Research Council of Australia, 1963; Resident Medical Officer, Princess Alexandra Hospital, Brisbane, Australia, 1969; Senior Resident Medical Officer, Repat, General Hospital, Greenslopes, 1970; Registrar, Oral and mazillo-facial surgery, the London Hospital, London, England, 1972; Senior House Officer in Plastic Surgery, Frenchay Hospital, Bristol, England, 1973; Registrar in Plastic Surgery, Royal Prince Alfred Hospital, Sydney, Australia, 1974-76; Private Practice of Plastic Surgery, 1977-. *Memberships:* Australian Medical Association; Australian Dental Association; Australian and New Zealand Association for Oral and Maxillo-facial Surgeons. *Honour:* National Medal, Reserve forces. Decoration. *Hobby:* Army Reserve. *Address:* 225 Wickham Terrace, Brisbane, Queensland 4000, Australia.

BUSTAMANTE, Jose Angel, b. 8 Jan. 1911, Havana, Cuba. Professor of Psychiatry. m. Maria Luisa Rodriguez, Mar. 1940, 1 son, 1 daughter. *Education:* MD, University of Havana, 1939; specialist in Psychiatry, Ministry of Health, 1950; Professor Psychiatry, Faculty of Medicine, Havana, 1961; DSc, National Board of Degrees, 1980; Postgraduate Psychotherapy, 1945-50. *Appointments:* Resident and Instructor of Psychiatry, Havana Faculty of Medicine, 1939-61; Chief, Clinical Psychiatry, Psychiatric Hospital, 1943-61; Director, Department of Medical Psyuchology, Havana Faculty of Medicine, 1961-68; Director, Institute of Brain Research, Cuban Academy of Sciences, 1961-83; Professor of Psychiatry, Havana Faculty of Medicine, 1961-; Vice-President, Cuban Academy of Sciences, 1976-83; Director, Official Course of Psychotherapy for Specialists, 1984-; Chief, Post-graduate Teaching and Research on Psychiatry, Havana Faculty of Medicine, 1983-; Member, Advisory Group,

Diagnosis and Classification of Mental Disorders WHO, 1981-. *Memberships:* Member and Officer of numerous professional organizations. *Publications:* Author of 15 books, 24 monographies, 103 articles and contributor or editor of 6 journals. *Honours:* Many honours and awards from Spain, USA, Venezuela, Cuba and Peru. *Hobbies:* Baseball; Theatre. *Address:* Facultad de Ciencias Medicas, Hospital Calixto Garcia, La Habana, Cuba.

BUTCHER, Brian Thomas, b. 28 Dec. 1940, Guildford, Surrey, England. Professor of Medicine. m. Carol Ann Mudie, 27 Oct, 1962, Witley, Surrey, 1 son. *Education:* AIMLT (Haematology), 1960-62, FIMLT (Bacteriology), 1962-64, Ewell College, Surrey, England; MS (Bacteriology & Immunology), University of North Carolina, 1965-68; Continuing Studies, Tulane University, New Orleans, LA, 1968-70; PhD (Microbiology & Immunology), LSU Medical School, New Orleans, 1971-73. *Appointments:* Laboratory Technician, King George V Hospital, Godalming, Surrey, England, 1957-63; Laboratory Supervisor, St Thomas' Hospital, Godalming, 1963-64; Laboratory Supervisor, Epidemiology Department, University of North Carolina, 1964-68; Instructor, Epidemiology Department, Tulane University, 1968-71; Research Associate, Department of Medicine, LSU Medical centre, New Orleans, 1973-75; Assistant Professor of Medicine, 1975-79, Associate Professor, 1979-83, Professor, 1983-, Tulane University, New Orleans. *Memberships:* American Society for Microbiology; American Association for the Advancement of Science; American Association of University Professors; American Thoracic Society; American Academy of Allergy; Society for Experimental Biology & Medicine. *Publications:* Over 70 contributions to books & medical and scientific journals; Over 40 abstracts. *Honour:* NIH Pre-Doctoral Fellowship, 1971-73. *Hobbies:* Sailing; Youth Soccer; Carpentry; Music; Chess; Reading; Painting; Computers. *Address:* Section of Clinical Immunology, Department of Medicine, 1700 Perdido Street, New Orleans, LA 70112, USA.

BUTENANDT, Adolf Friedrich Johann, b. 24 Mar. 1903, Bremerhaven-Lehe, Germany. Honorary President of the Max-Planck Society. m. 28 Feb. 1931, Göttingen, 2 sons, 5 daughters. *Education:* Diplo. Chem, University of Göttingen, 1925; Promotion Dr Phil, 1927. *Appointments:* Bozent in Organic and Biological Chemistry, University Gottingen, 1931-33; Professor of Chemistry; Director, Organic Chemistry, Institute, Danzig Institute of Technology, 1933-36; Director, Kaiser-Wilhelm Institute of Biochemistry, Berlin-Dahlem (later at Tubingen), now Max Planck Institute of Biochemistry, Munich, 1936-72; Professor of Physiological Chemistry, University Tubingen, 1945-56l; Professor of Physiological Chemistry, University Munich, 1956-72; President, 1960-72; Honorary President, 1972-, Max Planck Society. *Memberships:* Gottingen Akademie der Wissenschaften; Preussische Akademie der Wissenschaften, Berlin, jetzt Akademie der DDR; Bayerische Akademie der Wissenschaften; Société d'Endocrinologie, Paris; New York Academy of Sciences; Japanische biochemische Gesellschaft; Chemische Gesellschaft Japan; Leopoldian Akademie der Naturforscher, Halle (Mitglied seit 1943); Osterreichische Akademie der Wissenchaften; Akdmie der bildenden Kunste, Munchen; Consejo Superior de Investigaciones Cientificas, Madrid; Gesellschaft der Arzte in Wien; Japan Akademie, Tokyo; Foreign Member, Royal Society, London and several other organizations. *Publications:* Biochemistry Hormones and Pheromones "Das Werk eines Lebens", 1981. *Honours include:* Nobel Prize for Chemistry, 1939; Paul Ehrlich Prize, Frankfurt, 1953; Dale-Medaille, Society for Endocrinology, London, 1962; Medaille Munchen leuchtet in Gold, 1978; Bayerischer Maximiliansorden fur Wissenschaft und Kunst,

1981; Goldene Ehrenmunze der Stadt Munchen, 1983. *Address:* Marsopstr. 5, D-8000 Munich 60, Democratic Republic of Germany.

BUTT, Wilfrid Roger, b. 2 May 1922, Southampton, England, Head of Department of Clinical Endocrinology, Professor of Endocrinology, Birmingham University, Honorary Professor of Clinical Endocrinology, Nottingham University, m. Patricia Doreen Sharp, 2 Apr 1951, Wanstead, London, 1 son, 1 daughter. *Education:* BSc, London University, 1944; PhD, 1954, DSc, 1968, Birmingham University; CChem, 1945; FRSC, 1966. *Appointments:* Experimental Officer, Chemical Inspection Department, Royal Arsenal, Woolwich, London, 1939-46; Research Assistant, Endocrine Unit, London Hospital, Whitechapel, London, 1946-49. *Memberships:* Member of Council, 1977-80, Society for Endocrinology; Past Chairman, Midland Section, Association of Clinical Biochemsits; Biochemical Society; Royal Society of Chemistry; Blair Bell Research Society; Midlands Gynaecological and Obstetrical Society; Midlands Endocrine Club. *Publications:* "Chemistry of Gonadotrophins", 1967; "Hormone Chemistry", 2nd Edition, Volumes 1 and 2, 1976, 1978; "Clinics in Endocrinology and Metabolism: the Testis", (Co-editor, DR R London), 1975; "Topics in Hormnone Chemistry",(Editor), 1978; "Practical Immunossay", (Editor), 1984. *Honours:* Wellcome Prize, Clinical Chemistry, 1978. *Hobbies:* Oil painting; Chess. *Address:* Department of Clinical Endocrinology, Birmingham and Midland Hospital for Women, Showell Green Lane, Sparkhill, Birmingham B11 4HL, England.

BUTZLER, Jean-Paul-Louis, b. 25 Feb, Brussels, Belgium. Professor. m. Rolande Van Den Herrweghen, 15 July 1967, Brussels. *Education:* MD, PhD, Free University of Brussels. *Appointments:* Director, Department of clinical Microbiology, St Pierre University Hospital, Brussels, 1974; Director, Infectious Diseases Unit, Free University, Brussels, 1975; Director , WHO Collaborating Centre for Camplyobascter jejuni, 1980; Director, Department of Clinical Pathology, St Pierre University Hospital. *Memberships:* National commission of Hospitals; National Commission for Child Health; Aids Commission, Dutch Health Council. *Publications:* Various articles in medical journals. *Honours:* Van Beneden Prize in Epidemiology, 1976; Prize in Infectious Diseases, Belgian Academy of Medicine, 1977; Brohee Prize in Gastroenterology, 1979. *Hobbies:* Tennis; Fishing. *Address:* St Pierre University Hospital, 322, Rue Haute, 1000 Brussels, Belgium.

BUYSE, Marylou, b. 27 June 1946, New York City, USA. Pediatrician; Clinical Geneticist. m. Carl N. Edwards, 22 Jan. 1982. *Education:* AB, Hunter College, 1966; MD, Medical College, Pennsylvania, 1970. *Appointments:* Intern, University of Michigan, 1970-071; Resident, Pediatrics, Los Angeles County-University Southern California Medical Centre, 1971-73; Fellow, 1973-75; Instructor, Boston University, 1975; Assistant Professor, Pediatrics, University of Southern California, 1973-75, Tufts University, 1976-; Coordinator, Myelodysplasia Clinic, Tufts-New England Medical Centre, Boston, 1976-79; Director, Cystic Fibrosis Clinic, Staff Pediatrician, Centre for Genetic Counselling and Birth Defects Evaluation, 1975-82; Medical Director, 1982- ; Member, Medical Advisory Board, Massachusetts Cystic Fibrosis Foundation; Consultant in Field. *Memberships:* Diplomate, American Board Clinical Genetics; Fellow, American Academy Pediatrics; Massachusetts Medical Society; American Association Mental Deficiency; American Medical Woman's Association; American Society Human Genetics; AAAS; New York Academy of Sciences; Society Medical Decision Making; American Cleft Palate Association; Teratology Society; Common Cause Association;

Vice President, Cranial Facial Genetics Society, 1984-85; Chair, Public Relations Committee, AMWA, Branch 39, 1982- ; Chairman, Information Science Committee, Tufts University School ofMedicine, 1982-84; Medical Education Committee, Massachusetts Medical School, 1984. *Publications:* Editor, "Birth Defects Compendium", 2nd Edition, 1979; Associate Editor, "Syndrome Identification Journal', 1977-82; Editor, 1982- ; Editor, 'Journal Clinical Dysmophology', 1982. *Honours:* Recipient, Physicians Recognition Award, AMA, 1975. *Hobbies:* Equestrian Sports; Racket Sports. *Address:* PO Box 1776, Dover, MA 02030, USA.

BUZINA, Ratko. b. 27 Nov. 1920, Samobor. Professor, Nutrition, medical Faculty, Zagreb. m. Kornelia Suboticanec, 26 Nov. 1981, Zagreb. *Education:* MD, Medical Faculty, Zagreb, 1944; Biochemical Institute, University of Basle, Switzerland, Postgraduate Training, 1950-51;MPH, School of Public Health, Zagreb, 1953; Research fellow, Laboratory of Physiological Hygiene, University of Minnesota USA, 1955-56; Sc.D., University of Zagreb, 1963. *Appointments:* Chief, Community Health Services, P. Slatina, 1947-50; Assistant Professor, Nutrition, Institute of Public Health, Zagreb, 1950-56; Nutritional Advisor, WHO, Regional Office, SE Asia, New Delhi,1959-62; Associate Professor, Nutrition, Institute of Public Health, Zagreb, 1956-63; Professor, Nutrition, Medical Faculty, Zagreb, 1963-. *Memberships:* Croatian Medical Association; New York Academy of Sciences; American Society of Clinical; Nutrition; International Society and Federation of Cardiology; Expert Panel on Nutrition, World Health Organization; American Public Health Association; International Union of Nutritional Sciences, President, 1982-85. *Publicataioans:* More than 130 scientific papers in field of nutrition, cardiovascular disease, goitre, growth & development, nutrition and physical performance, nutrition and immunity, nutritional biochemistry, etc. *Hobbies:* Reading; Music; Tennis; Skiing. *Address:* Medical Faculty, University of Zagreb, Rockefellerova 4, Yugoslavia.

BYERS, G. Harold Jr. b. 23 Mar 1954, Louisville, Kentucky, USA. Doctor of Chiropractic. m. Christy Lynn, 2 Mar. 1984, Duncan Memorial. *Education:* BA, Psychology/Biology, Morehead St University; Experimental Psychology, Morehead St University Graduate School; Doctor of Chiropractic, Palmer College of Chiropractic. *Appointment:* Graduate Assistant, Morehead St University. *Membership:* Kentucky Chiropractic Society. *Address:* 4001 Preston Highway, Louisville, KY 40213, USA.

BYRNE, William Joseph, b. 30 Apr. 1937, Dundalk, Republic of Ireland, Managing Director, Byrne Chemists Limited, m. Ann Machale, 10 July 1972, Ballina, 1 son, 1 daugher. *Education:* Fellowship Association of Opticians Ireland (FAOI); Member, Pharmaceutical Society of Ireland, (MPSI). *Memberships:* Pharmaceutical Society of Ireland; Irish Pharmaceutical Union; Dundalk Pharmacists Association; Association of Ophthalmic Opticians Ireland. *Hobbies:* History and old photgraphs of County Louth; Shooting; Coin collecting; DIY; Gardening. *Address:* 1 Church Street, Dundalk, County Louth, Republic of Ireland.

BYUN, Chong-Soo, b. 25 June 1924, Korea. Professor, m. 8 Mar. 1943, 1 son, 3 daughters. *Education:* Graduate: Dental School, National Seoul University; Law School, Yongnam University; Graduate School, Medicine, University of Pennsylvania, USA; LLB; DDS; PhD, National Seoul University; FICD. *Appointments:* Chief, Dental Department, Presbyterian Mission Hospital, Taegu; Clinical Professor, Yonsae University School of Dentistry and Medical School; Professor and Dean, Kyung-Buk National University, School of Dentistry. *Memberships:* Korean Academy of Maxillofacial Oral Surgery. *Publications:* "Condylectomy of TMJ

Ankylosis'', 1952; ''Tic Douloureaux in Oral Surgery'', 1961; ''A Study of the Perlesh in Korea'', 1962. *Hobbies:* Sports; Calligraphy. *Address:* 1307 Sangkyuk-Dong, Buk-Ku Taegu, Korea.

C

CABANAC, Michel, b. 8 Aug 1934, Montpellier, France. University Professor. m. Marie-Claude Bonniot, 1 June 1963, 4 sons 1 daughter. *Education:* MD, University of Lyon; Lices. Sc. University of Paris; Agregation, National competition examination. *Appointments:* Assistant, University of Grenoble, 1956-57; Chef de Travaux, University Claude Bernard Lyon, 1966; Maitre de Conférence Agrégé, University Claude Bernard Lyon, 1966-80; Visiting Professor, University Laval, Quebec, 1980-83; Professor, University Claude Bernard Lyon, 1983-. *Memberships:* Chairman, Commission on thermal physiology at International Union of Physiological Society, 1977-83; Association des Physiologistes; American Association for the Advancement of Science; European Brain and Behaviour Society; Intern. Society of Biometeorology; European Neuroscience Association; European Chemor. Res. Organisation; Corresponding Member, American Physiological Society. *Publications:* "Régulation et contrôle en biologie" 1982; Review articles in 'Science'; 'Journal of Physiology Paris'; 'Quarterly Review of Biology'; 'Annual Review of Physiology'. *Honours:* Thesis Prize 1961; Fellow, Japan Society for the Promotion of Science, 1985. *Address:* Physiology Laboratory, Faculty of Medicine Lyon-Sud, Claude Bernard University, 69921 Oullins Cedex, B P 12, France.

CABANILLAS, Fernando, b. 20 Nov. 1945, San Juan, Puerto Rico, USA. Associate Professor of Medicine. m. Myrta Narvaez-Ochoa, 14 July 1967, 2 daughters. *Education:* BS Biology, University of Puerto Rico, 1966; MD, University of Puerto Rico School of Medicine, San Juan, 1970; Internship & Residency (Medicine), University District Hospital, Puerto Rico, 1970-73, Fellow in Haematology 1973-74; Fellow in Medical Oncology, M D Anderson Hospital, University of Texas, 1974-76. *Appointments:* Clincial Instructor, University of Puerto Rico School of Medicine, 1973-74; At M D Aderson Hospital, Houston, Texas: Faculty Associate 1976-77, Assistant Professor of Medicine 1977-78, Associate Intern, Assistant Professor 1978-80, Associate Professor of Medicine 1980-, Chief, Section of Lymphoma, 1984-. *Memberships:* American College of Physicians; American Association for Cancer Research; American Association for the Advancement of Science; American Society for Clinical Oncology;' Texas Medical Association. *Publications:* More than 110 articles, book chapters, abstracts in field. *Honours:* Pfizer Scholarship, 1968-69; 2nd Prize Research Award, Puerto Rico Medical Association, 1973; 2nd Prize, Annual Clinical Training Research Project Competition, M D Anderson Hospital, 1976; Fellow, American College of Physicians, 1981. *Address:* University of Texas, M D Anderson Hospital & Tumour Institute, 6723 Bertner, Department of Hematology (Section Lymphoma), Houston, TX 77030, USA.

CACHERA, Jean-Paul, b. 8 Dec. 1930, Billancourt, France. Cardio-Vascular Surgeon. m. Marie-Claire Carn, 28 June, 1958, Quimper, 2 sons, 2 daughters. *Education:* BA, Literature and Philosophy, 1948, MD, University of Paris. *Appointments:* Assistant, Cardio-Vascular Clinic, Hopital Broussais, 1962-66; Associate Professor, 1972-84, Professor and Chief, 1984, Division of Thoracic and Cardio-Vascular Surgery, Henri-Mondor Hospital, Paris; Director of Centre of Surgical Research, University of Paris XII. *Memberships:* Academie de Chirurgie; Societe Francaise de Cardiologie; International Society of Cardiovascular Surgery; International Society of Transplantation; Past-President, European Society for Surgical Research; Editorial Board, Journal de Chirurgie; Editorial Board of Medicine Science. *Publications:* Editor of Abstract Book of The Xth Congress of the European Society of Surgical Research; Editor of French-Canadian book "La

Maladie Coronarienne" 1980. *Honours:* Chevalier de L'Ordre du Merite, 1969; Palmes Academiques, 1977; Chevalier de la Legion D'Honneur, 1980. *Hobbies:* French Literature and History; Sail Boarding; Jogging. *Address:* Hospital Henri-Mondor, 51 Ave. Marechal Delattre, Creteil 94, France.

CADSAWAN, Maria Teresa Martinez de Luciano, b. 1 Jan, 1917, Laguna, Philippines. Private Medical Practitioner; Police Surgeon; Chief Medical Officer. m. Rudolph Luciano, 3 Dec. 1960, Chicago, USA, 1 daughter. *Education:* AA, University of the Philippines, 1933, BS, 1935, MD, 1939; Aviation Medicine, 1972, Fellow of American Academy of Family Physicians, 1979. *Appointments include:* Assistant Medical Director, Woodrow Wilson Rehabilitation Centre, Virginia, USA; Senior Physician, United States Psychiatric Veterens Hospital, Illinois; Medical Director, United States Naval Ordnance, Illinois; Chief Medical Officer, National Transportation Safety Board and St. Lawrence Seaway; Aviation Medical Examiner, Chief Washington DC Medical Clinic, Federal Aviation Administration; Medical Advisor, Department Motor Carrier Safety; Chief Medical Officer, Department of Transportation; Private Medical Practice. *Memberships include:* Royal Society of Medicine, London; World Medical Association; New York Academy of Sciences; American Academy of Family Physicians; International Academy of Geriatrics; American Medical Association; American Association for the United Nations; Illinois Alumni Association; American Academy for Family Physicians; American Association for Automotive Medicine; Illinois Association of General Practice; Civil Aviation Medical Association, etc. *Honours:* Medal of Leadership, courage, service and patriotism, Daughters of the American Revolution, 1966; Citizen of the Year Award, 1966; Women of Achievement Award, 1967; Professional Service Citation, 1975; Gold Medal of Merit, Presidential Task Force, 1982-84. *Hobbies:* Music; Ballet; Theatre; Tennis; Swimming; Reading; Cooking. *Address:* 2611 South Grant Street, Arlington, VA 22202, USA.

CAGUIAT, Carlos, J., b. 23 Jan. 1937, New York City, USA. Administrator. m. Julianna Skomsky, 29 Aug. 1958, New York City, 2 sons, 1 daughter. *Education:* BA, City College of NY; General Theological Seminary; MPA, NY University. *Appointments:* Project Manager, Community Relations, Ambulatory Care, 1973, Operations Co-ordinator, NYC, Health and Hospitals Corporation, 1975; Associate Direcotr, 1976, Administrator, Morrisania Neighborhood Family Care Center, 1978; Administrator, MI State University Clinical Center, 1981-. *Memberships:* American College of Health Executives; American Association of Academic Health Centers; American Medical Group Management Assn.; American Hospital Assn.; MI Hospital Assn.; Mid-MI South Health Systems Agency; South Centre MI Hospital Council. *Hobbies:* Jogging; Softball; Swimming; Skiing. *Address:* Michigan State University Clinical Center, Room A 201, 138 Service Road, East Lansing, MI 48824, USA.

CAIRNS, Barry John, b. 30 Aug. 1941, Geelong, Australia. Hospital Director of Pathology. m. Mary Farley, 8 Jan. 1982. *Education:* MB BS, Melbourne, 1964; Fellow, Royal College of Pathologists of Australasia, 1979. *Appointments:* Resident Medical Officer 1965-66, Trainee in Pathology 1967-68, The Geelong Hospital; Trainee in Pathology, Royal Melbourne Hospital, 1969-71; Pathologist, Australian Army, South Vietnam, 1971; Director of Pathology, Latrobe Valley Hospital, Moe, Victoria, Australia, 1971-. *Memberships:* Australian Medical Association; Royal College of Pathologists of Australasia; Australian Association of Clinical Biochemists; AACC; ISBT; RSTM&H. *Honour:* RFD, 1983. *Hobby:* Model trains. *Address:* Moe South Road, Moe South, Victoria, Australia.

CAJAL, Nicolae, b. 1 Oct. 1919, Bucharest, Romania.

Professor of Virology; Institute Director. m. Berthin Berman, 23 Dec. 1942, Bucharest, 1 son, 1 daughter. *Education:* MD Medicine and Surgery 1945, PhD 1946, Dr dozent in Medical Sciences 1963, Professor 1966, Bucharest Faculty of Medicine. *Appointments:* Assistant 1946-50, Senior Lecturer 1950-58, Associate Professor 1958-66, Professor at the Chair of Virology 1966-, Bucharest Faculty of Medicine; Head of Laboratory 1951-54, Chief of Department 1954-55, Scientific Manager 1955-67, Director 1967-, Stefan S Nicolau Institute of Virology, Bucharest. *Memberships:* Corresponding member, Romanian Academy; Romanian Academy of Medical Sciences; European Association for Poliomyelitis and other Virus Diseases; Royal Society of Medicine, London; International Society of Infectious Pathology; New York Academy of Sciences; Virology Expert, World Health Organisation. *Publications:* Numerous papers, monographs, treatises and handbooks in virology. *Honours:* Order of Labour, 3rd class 1956, 2nd class 1962; Sanitary Merit, 3rd class, 1971. *Address:* Institute of Virology, 285 Sos Mihai Bravu, R-79650 Bucharest 77, Romania.

CALAME, Kathryn Lee, b. 23 Apr. 1940, Leavenworth, Kansas, USA. Associate Professor. m. Byron Calame, 9 June 1962, Kansas City, 1 son, 1 daughter. *Education:* BS, Honours, University of Missouri, 1962; MS, 1965, PhD, 1975, Biochemistry, George Washington University. *Appointments:* Post-doctoral Fellow, University of Pittsburgh, 1975-78; Research Associate, California Institute of Technology, 1978-80; Assistant Professor, 1980-85, Associate Professor, 1985-, Biological Chemistry, University of California, Los Angeles. *Memberships:* Phi Beta Kappa; Sigma Xi; American Association for Advancement of Science; American Society of Biological Chemists. *Publications:* Articles in professional journals including: 'Cell'; 'Science'; 'Ann.Rev.Immunology'; etc. *Honours:* Merck Award for Achievement in Chemistry, 1962; Public Health Service Postdoctoral Fellow Award, 1975; Leukemia Society Scholar Award, 1984-89; Dwyer Award for Cancer Research. *Hobbies:* Hiking; Gourmet Cooking. *Address:* 302 Molecular Biology Institute, UCLA, Los Angeles, CA 90024, USA.

CALDWELL, Charles A (Chip), b. 19 Apr. 1952, London, Tennessee, USA. Administrator, Putnam Community Hospital. m. Donna Patterson, 15 Sept 1973, Knoxville, Tennessee, USA, 2 daughters. *Education:* MA, Hospital Administration, Central Michigan University; BA, Clinical Psychology, University of Tennessee. *Appointments:* Assistant Administrator, North Florida Regional Hospital; Chief Operating Officer, Ambulatory Services Management Corp; Assistant Administrator, US Army Hospital, Fort Campbell, KY. *Memberships:* American College of Hospital Administrators; Florida Hospital Association; Florida League of Hospitals; Federation of American Hospitals; American Hospital Association. *Address:* PO Drawer 778, Palatka, FL 32078, USA.

CALDWELL, John Mars, b. 29 Nov. 1904, Augusta, Georgia, USA. Psychiatrist. m. Dorothy Driskell, 8 Oct. 1932, Rochester, Minnesosta, 1 son, 1 daughter. *Education:* BS, University of Georgia, 1925; MD, University of Georgia School of Medicine, 1928; MS, Medicine, University of Minnesota, 1932. *Appointments Include:* US Army, 1932-; Chief, Neuropsychiatry Consultants Division, 1946-52; Chief, Department of Psychiatry, Letterman Army Hospital, 1953-55; Clinical Professor of Psychiatry, Georgetown University, 1946-52; Professor and Chairman, Department of Psychiatry and Neurology, Medical College of Georgia, 1955-57; Professor and Chairman, Department of Psychiatry, University of Miami School of Medicine, 1957-70; Professor Emeritus, 1970-; Psychiatrist: Georgia, Minnesota, California and Florida. *Memberships Include:* Alpha Omega Alpha; Alpha Kappa Kappa; Delta Tau Delta; Life Fellow or Life Member: American Psychiatric Association; American and International

Psychoanalytic Associations; American and Florida Medical Associations; American College of Psychiatrists; American Academy of Neurology; American College of Physicians; American College of Psychoanalysts. *Publications:* Contributor to professional journals; Military Psychiatry in the Comprehensive Textbook of Psychiatry, Editors Alfred M Freedman and Harold I Kaplan, 1967. *Honours Include:* Bronze Star and Commendation Ribbon, 1945-46. *Address:* 4421 Santa Maria, Coral Gable, FL 33146, USA.

CALHOUN, Kevin Paul, b. 22 Aug. 1951, Huntington, West Virginia, USA. Associate Administrator. m. Gloria L Aleutz, 21 Apr. 1974, Granville, Ohio, 2 sons. *Education:* BSc, Wright State University, Dayton, Ohio, 1974; MHA, Xavier University, Cincinnati, 1979. *Appointments:* Deputy Director, Comprehensive Drug Dependency Treatment Programme, Dayton, Ohio, 1976-77; Vice President, Greene Memorial Hospital, Xenia, 1979-84; Associate Administrator, W A Foote Memorial Hospital, Jackson, Michigan, 1984-. *Memberships:* American College of Hospital Administrators; Past Member, American Hospital Association. *Publications:* 'Building Blocks to Comprehensive Quality Assurance' in 'The Hospital Medical Staff', 1980. *Hobby:* Private pilot. *Address:* 506 West High Street, Jackson, MI 49203, USA.

CALLEJA, Homobono B, b. Philippines. Head, Echocardiography Laboratory; Consultant Cardiologist. m. Alma Maceda, 8 Oct. 1964, 2 sons, 3 daughters. *Education:* BSc, Zoology, 1954; MD, 1954; Fellow in Internal Medicine, Cleveland Clinic Foundation, 1956-58; Fellow in Clinical Cardiology, Ohio State Medical Center, Central Ohio Heart Association, White Cross Hospital, Childrens Hospital, Columbus, Ohio, USA, 1959-60. *Appointments:* Consultant Cardiology, St James Hospital, Columbus, Ohio, USA, 1959-60; Visiting Professor, Cardiology, University of Istanbul, Turkey, 1963; Head, Section of Cardiology, GSIS Hospital, 1970-71; Head, Department of Adult Cardiology, Philippine Heart Center of Asia, 1975-82; Visiting Professor, Cardiology, Martin Luther King General Hospital, Los Angeles, California, USA, 1982; Head, Echocardiography Laboratory, Philippine; Consultant Cardiologist, St Luke's Medical Center and Makati Medical Center. *Memberships:* Fellow, Philippine College of Physicians; Philippine College of Cardiology; American College of Chest Physicians; American College of Cardiology; American College of Angiology. American Society of Echocardiography. *Publications:* "Initial Orders in Cardiology", 1977; "Electrocardiography and Vectorcardiography", 1978; "Romance of the Heart", 1979; "Frontiers in Philippine Cardiology", 1981; "Two Dimensional Echocardiography", 1983; "Ischemic Heart Disease", 1984; "Strokes and Periphal Vascular Diseases", 1985; author of over 115 scientific papers in professional journals. *Honours:* Governor, Philippine District, Kiwanis International, 1973; Representative, Kiwanis International Southeast Asia-Pacific Region, 1974; Secretary General, 2nd ASEAN Congress of Cardiology, 1977; President, Philippine Heart Association, 1977. *Address:* American Heart Clinic, St Luke's Medical Centre, E Rodriquez Avenue, Quezon City, Philippines.

CALLIAUW, Luc, b. 25 Aug. 1928, Brugge, Belgium. Neurosurgeon/University Professor of Neurosurgery. m. Dora Hoeksema, 3 Sep. 1960, Zeist, 1 son, 2 daughters. *Education:* PhD, MD, Professor of Neurosurgery. *Appointments:* Director of Neurosurgical Department, St John Hospital, Brugge; Currently:Director, Neurosurgical Department, Academic Hospital, Ghent and Professor of Neurosurgery, University of Ghent. *Memberships:* Belgian, Dutch, German and Italian Societies of Neurosurgery; American Congress of Neurological Surgeons; Societe Internationale pour l'histoire de la medecine. *Publications:* Contributor of numerous articles in scientific journals and magazines in German, French and English. *Hobbies:* Music; History. *Address:* Bisschopsdreef 53, 8310 Brugge III, Belgium.

CALLIHAN, Harriet K, b. 8 Feb. 1930, USA. Executive Director, Medical Institute. m. 17 Dec. 1955, Chicago, Illinois, 1 daughter. *Education:* BA; MBA. *Appointments:* Acccount Executive, Leo Burnett Company; Office Manager, Needham, Harper and Steers; Personnel Director, Follett Publishing Company; Office Manager, Bell, Boyd and Lloyd with Hume, Clement, Hume and Lee; Owner, Recruiting Agency; Executive Director, Institute of Medicine, Chicago, Illinois, 1975-. *Memberships:* Past President, American Medical Writers Association; Committee Chairman, Chicago Society of Association Executives; Past President, Conference on Medical Society Executives; Secretary and Treasurer, Illinois Interagency Council on Smoking and Disease; National Association of Science Writers; Board Member and Committee Chairman, Publicity Club; Women in Health Care; Women in Management; National Society of Fund Raising Executives; Professional Convention Managers Association; Midwest Pharmaceutical Advertising Club; Metropolitan Council on Aging; Chicago Council on Foreign Relations; Chicago Communications. *Publications:* Editor, 'The Proceedings of the Institute of Medicine', 10 years. *Hobbies:* Travel; Theatre; Collecting dolls, miniatures and coins; Swimming; Tennis; Bicycling. *Address:* 422 Central Avenue, Wilmette, IL 60091, USA.

CALVERT, Alan Hilary, b. 18 Feb 1947, Cheshire, England, Reader in Clinical Pharmacology, Institute of Cancer Research, Honorary Consultant in Medicine, Royal Marsden Hospital, m. Drusilla M E Dean, 22 Nov 1969, Cambridge, 3 daughters. *Education:* BA, University of Cambridge, 1966-69; University College Hospital, 1969-72; MSc, University of London, 1975-77; MRCP, 1975; MD 1981. *Appointments:* Registrar, Renal Unit, Royal Free Hospital, 1974; Research Fellow, 1975-77, Royal Marsden Hospital; Lecturer in Clinical Pharmacology, 1977-80, Senior Lecturer in Clinical Pharmacology, 1981-85, Institute of Cancer Research. *Memberships:* American Association of Cancer Research; British Association of Cancer Research; European Organisation for Research and Treatment of Cancer; American Society for Clinical Oncology. *Publications:* 'Early Clinical Studies with cisdiammine1, 1-cyclobutaned icarbozylateplatinum (II)', (Co-author), 1982; 'Cytotoxic drugs in the treatment of oral cancer', 1985; 'JM8 Development and Clinical Projects', (Co-author), 1983. *Hobbies:* Skiing; Mathematics. *Address:* Department Biochemical Pharmacology, Block E, Clifton Avenue, Belmont, Sutton, Surrey MS2 5PX, England.

CALVERT, Allan Frederick, b. 2 Feb. 1941, Canberra, Australia. Senior Salaried Specialist in Medicine (Cardiology), Department of Veterans Affairs. m. Christine Gillan, Melbourne, 3 sons. *Education:* MB, BS; FRACP; FACRM. *Appointments:* Resident Medical Officer, 1965-66; Medical Registrar, 1967-69, Fellow in Cardiology, 1970, Sydney Hospital; Registrar in Cardiology, Royal Prince Alfred Hospital, Sydney, 1971. Research Fellow in Cardiology: Harvard University, Boston, Massachusette, USA, 1972-74; Royal Prince Alfred Hospital, Sydney, Australia, 1975. Senior Specialist in Cardiology, Repatriation General Hospital, Department of Veterans Affairs, Daw Park, South Australia, 1976-; Clinical Senior Lecturer in Medicine, Flinders University and Medical Center, 1976-. *Memberships:* Fellow, Royal Australian College of Physicians; Australian College of Rehabilitation Medicine. Cardiac Society of Australia and New Zealand; Chairman of Research

Committee, Institute of Fitness Research and Training, Adelaide. *Publications:* Contributions to: 'Australia and New Zealand Medical Journal'; 'Medical Journal of Australia'. *Hobbies:* Reading; Computing; Gardening. *Address:* Department of Cardiology, Repatriation General Hospital, Adelaide, SA 5041, Australia.

CALVERT, Rosemary Anne, b. 30 Aug. 1935, Ballymena, County Antrim, Northern Ireland. Secretary, Northern Ireland Board, Royal College of Nursing. *Education:* SRN; SCM; HV Certificate; NA(H) Certificate. *Appointments:* Student Nurse, Midwifery and Health Visitor Training, 1953-60; Health Visitor, 1960-63; Voluntary Service, Algeria, 1963-65; Health Visitor, 1965-69; Administrative Sister, 1969-70; Administrative Course, Royal College of Nursing, Edinburgh, Scotland, 1970-71; Principal Nursing Officer, Fermanagh, Northern Ireland, 1971-73; District Administrative Nursing Officer, Eastern Health and Social Services Board, 1973-76; Secretary, Northern Ireland Board, Royal College of Nursing, 1976-. *Memberships:* Royal College of Nursing; Northern Ireland Hospice Council; Past Chairman, Northern Ireland Council Branch, British Red Cross Society; Vice Chairman, Board of Governors, Voluntary Grammar School; Soroptimist International of Bangor. *Hobbies:* Gardening; Classical Music; Reading. *Address:* Royal College of Nursing, 17 Windsor Avenue, Belfast BT6 6EE, Northern Ireland.

CAMENGA, David LeRoy, b. 26 Aug. 1938, New Berlin, New York, USA. Associate Professor of Neurology, University of Maryland School of Medicine. *Education:* BS, Quantitative Biology, Massachusetts Institute of Technology, 1960; MS, Neurophysiology, 1964, MD, 1965, University of Wisconsin School of Medicine; Board Certified in Neurology by American Board of Psychology and Neurology. *Appointments:* Neurologist, USPHS Hospital, 1969-79; Fellowship, Johns Hopkins University, 1971-73; Assistant Professor of Neurology, Emory University, 1973-77; Assistant Professor of Neurology, 1977-83; Assistant Professor of Microbiology, 1977-, Associate Faculty, Graduate School, 1977-, Associate Professor of Neurology, 1983-, University of Maryland. *Memberships:* American Academy of Neurology, Fellow; American Association for the Advancement of Science; American Society for Microbiology; Rehabilitation Engineering Society of North America; New York Academy of Science. *Honours:* NINCDS Special Fellowship in Neurovirology, Johns Hopkins University, 1971-73. *Hobbies:* Swimming; Canoeing. *Address:* Department of Neurology, University of Maryland Medical System, Baltimore, MD 21201, USA.

CAMERON, James Malcolm, b. 29 Apr. 1930. Professor, Forensic Medicine, University of London, London Hospital Medical College, 1973, Director, Forensic Medicine; Ver Heyden De Lancey Readership, Forensic Medicine, Council of Legal Education, 1978-; Honorary Consultant to: The London Hospital, 1967-; the Army at Home, in Forensic Medicine, 1971-; Royal Navy, Forensic Medicine, 1972-; Secretary General, British Academy of Forensic Sciences, 1969-85; Editor, 'Medicine, Science & Law'. m. Primrose Agnes Miller McKerrell, MCST, 1956, 1 daughter. *Education:* MB, ChB, MD, PhD, University of Glasgow; Senior House Officer, Pathology, Southern General Hospital, Glasgow, 1955-56; Registrar, various Hospitals, 1957-62; Lecturer, Pathology, University of Glasgow, 1962; Lecturer, Forensic Medicine, 1963-65, Senior Lecturer, 1965-70, Reader, Forensic Medicine, 1970-72, London Hospital Medical College; Lecturer, Forensic Medicine, St Bartholomew's Hospital Medical College and University College Hospital Medical School; Lecturer, Metropolitan Police Detective Training School, SW Detective Training School,

Bristol, and Special Investigation Branch of RMP; etc. *Memberships include:* British Medical Association; Council, British Association in Forensic Medicine, President 1985-; British Academy of Forensic Sciences, Secretary General, 1969-85, President, 1978-79; Medico-Legal Society, past Vice President; Association of Police Surgeons of Great Britain, Honorary Fellow; Forensic Science Society; Association of Clinical Pathologists; Pathological Society of Great Britain and Ireland; etc. *Publications:* Scientific papers in numerous learned journals, both medical and forensic. *Hobbies:* Sports Medicine; Legal Medicine. *Address:* Dept. of Forensic Medicine, The London Hospital Medical College, Turner Street, London E1 2AD, England.

CAMERON, John Clifford, b. 17 Sep. 1946, Philadelphia, Pennsylvania, USA. Hospital Vice-President and House Counsel. m. Eileen Duffy, 12 July 1975, New Jersey, 1 son, 1 daughter. *Education:* BA, University of Pittsburgh; MBA Hospital Administration, Temple University; JD, Delaware Law School-Widener University; LLM, New York University School of Law. *Appointments* Assistant Administrator, Philadelphia Psychiatric Center, 1972-76; Judicial Law Clerk, Superior Court of New Jersey, 1977; Assistant Administrator, St Elizabeth Hospital, New Jersey, 1977 Administrative Resident 1971, Vice President and House Counsel 1978-85, Methodist Hospital, Pennsylvania. *Memberships:* American, Pennsylvania, New Jersey and Philadelphia Bar Associations;American Hospital Association; American College of Hospital Administrators; American Corporate Counsel Association. *Publications Include:* 'Pre-Accreditation Review of Hospital Policy and Procedure Manuals', 1974; 'Using a Computer Profile to Assess Quality of Care in a Hospital', 1976; 'An Attorney's Potential Role in a Health Care Organization', 1977; Trial Court Not Transfer Products Case to Malpractice Panel', 1978; 'Change Challenges Traditional Hospital/Medical Staff Relationship', 1981; 'Issues for Hospital Medical Staffs', 1981. *Honour:* Moot Court Honor Society, 1976. *Hobbies:* Swimming; Music. *Address:* 1410 Church Road, Malvern, PA 19355, USA.

CAMERON, Karl William Friday, b. 25 Jan. 1954, Spokane, Washington, USA. Managing Director, Procare Pty. Ltd. m. Deanna Saxby, 29 Dec. 1977, Brisbane, Australia. *Education:* Dip. App. Sc., Chiropractic; Dip.App. Sc., Human Biology; B.App.Sc., Chiropractic; Diplomat, National Board of Chiropractic Examiners, USA. *Appointments:* Associate, Cameron Chiropractic Clinic, Ballina, New South Wales; Clinic Director, Lalor Chiropractic Clinic; Consultant, Adelaide Chiropractic Clinic. *Memberships:* Australian Chiropractors' Association; Australian Spinal Research Foundation; American Chiropractic Association; Council on Roentgenology to the American Chiropractic Assocation; University of Melbourne Medical Society; Chiropractic and Osteopathic College of South Australia; Company Directors Association of Australia. *Publications:* Submission to the Task Force on Repetition Strain Injury in the Australian Public Service, 'Hyperbolic Keyboard', 1984; Videotape: "Body Bio-Mecahnics", 'Archery Association of South Australia', 1985. *Hobbies:* Golf; Marlin Fishing; Fishing; Target Shooting; Stamp Collecting; Study of Unique Weapons; Archery. *Address:* Narooma Chiropractic Centre, No. 12, Southfield Mall, Narooma, NSW 2546, Australia.

CAMIEL, Edwin Peter, b. 24 June 1950, Philadelphia, Pennsylvania, USA. Private Practitioner; Consultant; Educator. m. Judith Anne Gervasi, 17 Sep. 1983, Philadelphia, 1 daughter. *Education Includes:* BA, Franklin and Marshall College, 1972; MD, University of Pennsylvania, 1976; Intern, 1976-77, Resident, 1977-79, Pennsylvania Hospital; Naval Aerospace Medical Institute, 1980; Fellow, Temple University Institute of Law and the Health Sciences, 1979-80.

Appointments Include: Physician, City of Philadelphia, 1977-82; Consultant, Commonwealth of Pennsylvania Office of Mental Health, 1980-81, Police and Fire Medical Association, 1981-, Philadelphia Court of Common Pleas, 1980-; Staff Member, 1980-, Supervisor of Forensic Training, 1984-, Temple University Institute of Law and the Health Sciences; Private Practice, various fields, primarily Forensic Psychiatry, 1979-; Instructor in Psychiatry and Human Behaviour, Thomas Jefferson University, Jefferson Medical College, 1980-. *Memberships Include:* American Psychiatric Assocation; Committee member, Pennsylvania and Philadelphia Psychiatric Societies; Committees, American Academy of Psychiatry and the Law; American College of Forensic Psychiatry; Association of Military Surgeons of USA; Mental Health Association of South East Pennsylvania; Aerospace Medical Association; Naval Reserve Association. *Publications:* Numerous presentations at conferences and educational institutions; Guest panelist, WHYY Public Televisi n, 1984. *Honours:* Diplomate, National Board of Medical Examiners; Pennyslvania License to practice medicine and surgery; Certified Aerospace Medical Officer. *Hobbies:* Chess; Racquetball. *Address:* 7233 Mallard Place, Philadelphia, PA 19153, USA.

CAMMACK, Thomas N, Junior, b. 13 June 1944, Lubbock, Texas, USA. Senior Vice-President, All Saints Episcopal Hospital. m. Joyce A. Larson, 3 July 1980, Houston, Texas. *Education:* MSc, Health Care Administration, Trinity University; MSci. Pharmacy; BSci, Pharmacy, University of Houston. *Appointments:* Administrative Resident, Presbyterian Hospital of Dallas, Texas, 1975-76; Assistant Hospital Director, 1977-79, Associate Hospital Director, 1980-82, Hermann Hospital, Houston, Texas; Associate Director, 1982-84; Senior Vice-President, 1985-; All Saints Episcopal Hospital, Fort Worth. *Membereships:* American College of Hospital Administrators; American Hospital Association; Texas Hospital Association; American College of Apothecaries, Associate Fellow. *Hobbies:* Hunting; Fishing; Camping; Jogging; Gardening. *Address:* All Saints Episcopal Hospital, 1400 Eighth Avenue, Fort Worth, TX 76104, USA.

CAMM, Alan John, b. 11 Jan. 1947, England. Professor of Cardiovascular Medicine. *Education:* BSc, St. Bartholomew's Medical College, London, England, 1968, MRCS, LRCP, MBBS, 1971, MRCP, 1974; MD, London University, 1981. *Appointments:* House Physician, Registrar in Medicine, Guy's Hospital, London, England, 1971-75; Travelling Fellow, Burlington, USA, 1975-76; Fellow in Cardiology, St. Bartholomew's Hospital, London, 1976-82, Wellcome Senior Lecturer, 1982-83; Professor of Cardiology, British Heart Foundation, 1983-present. *Memberships:* Royal College of Physicians; British Cardiac Society; British Pacing and Electrophysiology Group; American College of Cardiology; New York Academy of Sciences. *Publications include:* Over 200 major research papers. *Hobby:* Collecting Watercolours and Prints. *Address:* Cardiology Department, St. Bartholomew's Hospital, London EC1A 7BE, England.

CAMPBELL, Jerry, b. 13 Aug. 1946, New York, USA. Hospital Management Consultant; Government Advisor. m. Polly Foster, 27 May 1973, Corpus Christi, Texas, 1 son, 1 daughter. *Education:* BSc, MSc, Texas A&M University; MHA, University of Minnesota; FBIM. *Appointments:* USPHS Fellow, University of Minnesota, 1974-75; Resident, Baylor University Medical Center, 1975-76; Administrator, Midland Memorial Hospital, 1976-79; Administrator, Preceptor, Salmaniya Medical Center, 1980-83; Assistant Director, Texas Tech University School of Medicine; Advisor to Minister of Health, State of Bahrain, 1980-85. *Memberships:* American College of Hospital Administrators; American Hospital

Association; American Association for World Health; Hospital Financial Management Association; British Institute of Management; World Health Organisation; Texas Hospital Association; International Hospital Federation. *Publications:* 'Healthcare Development in Bahrain' in 'Texas Hospitals', 1984. *Honours:* ACHA Examination, 1980; Fellowship, British Institute of Managaement, 1985. *Hobbies:* Water sports; Travel; Gardening; Photography. *Address:* 3515 Tanglewood Drive, Bryan TX 77802, USA.

CAMPBELL, Melanie C W b. 21 Mar. 1953, Enfield, England. Assistant Professor. m. Alan Murray Campbell, 23 Aug. 1975, Toronto, Ontario, Canada, 1 daughter. *Education:* BSc Chemical Physics, Victoria College University of Waterloo, Ontario, 1977; PhD, Institute of Advanced Studies, Australian National University, Australia, 1982. *Appointments:* CSIRO Postdoctoral Fellow, Australian National University, 1982-84; Research Assistant Professor, School of Optometry, University of Waterloo, Ontario. *Memberships:* Association for Research in Vision and Opthalmology; Optical Society of America; Australian Physiological and Pharmacological Society. *Publications:* Contributions to books and scientific journals, including 'Measurement of the refractive index distribution of an intact crystalline lens', 1984; 'Optical quality during crystalline lens growth' (co-author; P J Sands), 1984; 'A wavelength dependent gradient index model of the rat eye predicts chromatic aberration' in 'Modelling the eye with gradient index optics' (editor: A Hughes), 1986. *Honours:* Auger Alumni Scholarship, Victoria College, 1971-75; NSERC Postgraduate Scholarship, 1975-77; PhD Scholarship, Australian National University, 1977-81; CSIRO Postdoctoral Fellow, 1982-84; NSERC University Research Fellow, 1984-87. *Hobbies:* Sailing; Hiking. *Address:* School of Optometry, University of Waterloo, Waterloo, Ontario N2L 3G1, Canada.

CAMPBELL, Thomas Way, b. 10 Aug. 1942, Waynesville, North Carolina, USA. University Professor of Psychiatry. m. Sarah Elizabeth Gates, 2 Jan. 1981, Nashville, Tennessee, 1 son, 1 daughter. *Education:* BA, 1964, MD, 1968, Vanderbilt University; Psychiatry Residency, Yale Unviersity, 1973-74; Candidate, St. Louis Psychoanalytical Institute, 1980-. *Appointments:* Assistant Director, Consult Liaison Service, Department of Psychiatry, Vanderbilt University, Nashville, Tennessee, 1977-81; Private Practice, Psychiatry and Psychoanalysis, 1981-. *Memberships:* American Psychiatric Association; American Psychoanalytic Association; Tennessee Medical Association; Southern Medical Association. *Publications:* 'Death Anxiety on a CCU' Psychosomatics, 1980; 'Use of a Multiple Family Group for Crisis Intervention' General Hospital Psychiatry, 1980; 'Do Death Attitudes of Nurses and Phsyicians Differ?' Omega, 1983-84. *Honours:* Beauchamp Prize for Outstanding Student in Psychiatry, 1968; Fellowship in Biomedical Ethics, National Endowment for the Humanities, 1979. *Hobbies:* Fly-fishing; Canoeing; Computers. *Address:* Suite 206, 1916 Patterson Street, Nashville, TN 37203, USA.

CAMPBELL-MACDONALD, John, b. 30 June 1941, Harrow on the Hill, England. Cardiologist. m. Marilyne Wilson, 6 Dec. 1975, Chichester, 2 sons, 2 daughters. *Education:* MA, 1968, BM BCh, 1968, Oxford University; MRCP, UK, 1974. *Appointments:* Registrar: Harefield Hospital; Chichester Hospital; National Heart Hospital. Physician, Hawera Hospital, New Zealand; Cardiologist, Palmerston North Hospital. *Memberships:* International Physicians for the Prevention of Nuclear War, New Zealand; Cardiac Society of Australia and New Zealand. *Hobbies:* Prevention of nuclear war; Bricklaying. *Address:* 145 Ruahine Street, Palmerston North, New Zealand.

CAMPBELL-SMITH, Rosemary, b. 16 Mar. 1939, Rapid City, South Dakota, USA. Consultant, m. Richard L Smith, 1 daughter. *Education:* Diploma, Dental Hygiene, Eastman School of Dental Hygiene and University of Rochester, NY; Associate of Arts degree, Palm Beach Junior College, Fla; BSc, University of Florida; MSc, DA, School of Medicine, University of Miami, Fla. *Appointments:* Dental Assistant, Private Practice of Dental Hygiene; Chief Laboratory Technician in Physiology; Health Educator and Public Relations Officer; Instructor, College Biology; Coordinator, College Biology Laboratories; Illustrator, Coordinator, College Freshman Biology Manal Development; Instructor, Medical Student Anatomy and Physiology Laboratories; Assistant Professor of Dental Hygiene; Clinic Supervisor in Dental Hygiene; Lead Instructor, Dental Hygiene, Chairman of Curriculum Committee; Dental Consultant, Office Administrator; Editor; Freelance writer. *Memberships:* American Association for the Advancement of Science; American Association for Dental Research; American Dental Hygienists' Association; Florida Dental Hygienists' Association; International Platform Association; International Association for Dental Research; Society of Sigma Xi. *Publications:* "Head and Neck: What's It All About", 1976, 1980. *Honours:* Science Award, 1960; Albert E Stevenson Award for Art, Science and Service, 1960; J Hillis Award, 1964; Cancer Association Award, 1964; Elected to Phi Kappa Phi, 1964; Phi Lambda Pi, 1968; Society of Sigma Xi, 1973; Merit Citation for Course Development, 1979. *Hobbies:* Reading; Swimming; Tennis; Jogging. *Address:* 3609 NW 30 Boulevard, Gainesville, FL 32605, USA.

CAMU, Frederic, b. 19 May 1942, Uccle, Belgium. Chairman, Department of Anaesthesia. m. Van Mol Lieve, 21 May 1968, Aalst, 1 son, *Education :*BA, 1962, MD, 1966, University of Brussels. *Appointments:* Fellow, Anaesthesia, University of Stanford, USA, 1970; Assistant Professor, Pathological Physiology, University of Brussels, Belgium, 1974; Assistant Professor, Department of Anaesthesia, 1976 Associate Professor, 1978, Professor of Anaesthesia, 1980-, University of Brussels. *Memberships:* Belgian Society of Physiology and Pharmacology; European Association for the Study of Diabetes; Belgian Society of Anaesthesia and Reanimation; Alumnus, University Foundation; International Anaesthesia Research Society, USA; European Society of Biochemical Pharmacology; European Academy of Anaesthesiology. *Publications:* Author of some 63 papers contributed to professional publications including: "Cardiovascular Measurements in Anaesthesiology", 1982; 'Acta Anesthesiologica Belgica'; 'Postgraduate Medical Journal'; 'Intensive Care Medicine'; 'Archives of International Physiology'; 'Diabetologia'; 'European Journal of Clinical Investigation'; 'British Journal of Anaesthesiology'; contributions to numerous international conferences. *Honours:* CRB Graduate Fellow, Belgian American Educational Foundation, New York, USA, 1970; C F Aaron Endowment Fund, Stanford University, 1971; Certified, Belgian Board of Anesthesiology, 1970, Educational Council for Foreign Medical Graduates, USA, 1966. *Hobbies:* Photography; Computer science; Swimming; Gardening. *Address:* Academisch Ziekenhuis, Vrye Universitet Brussels, Dept Anaesthesia, Laarbeeklaan 101, B-1090 Brussels, Belgium.

CANAL, Nicola, b. 21 July 1931, Farra di Soligo, Italy. Doctor in Medicine; m. Maria S. Clementi, 1 Sep. 1958, Verona, 3 sons, 2 daughters. *Education:* MD; PhD, Pharmacology. *Appointment:* Professor, neurology, University of Milan. *Memberships:* Italian Society of Neurogloy; Italian Society of Neuropathology; Foreign Member, German Society for Muscle Diseases, Member, Research Committee on Muscle Diseases of the World Federation of Neurology.. *Publications:* Co-Editor, "Biochemical and Neurophysiological Correlations of Centrally Acting Drugs", 1964; Co-Editor, "Muscle Diseases", 'Excerpta Medica', 1970; "Peripheral Neuropathies", 1978. *Honours:* Premio Bertarelli, 1960; Premio Ganassini, 1964. *Hobbies:* Chess; Collecting Ancient Engravures. *Address:* Via L. Papi, 15, 20135 Milan, Italy.

CANALA-ECHEVARRIA, Ramon, b. 4 Dec. 1942, Rancagua, Chile. Medical Doctor; Chest Physician; Professor of Pathophysiology; Medical Center Chief Doctor. m. Cecilia Sagre, 7 Dec. 1968, Vina del Mar, 2 sons, 1 daughter. *Education:* MD, University of Chile; Chest Physician, Chilean Society of Thorax Diseases; Respiratory Allergist, Chilean Society of Allergy and Immunology; Professor of Pathophysiology, University of Valparaiso. *Appointments:* Scholarship in Respiratory Diseases, Santiago; Attending Physician and 2nd Chief Doctor, Hospital Valparaiso Neumologic Service; Chief Doctor, Respiratory Intensive Care Unit, Valparaiso Hospital; Medical Director, Centre for Broncho-Pulmonary Diseases, Valparaiso; Chief Doctor, Internal Medicine Department, Respiratory Section, Hospital Gustavo Fricke, Vina del Mar; Professor of Pathophysiology, Medical School, University of Valparaiso. *Memberships:* Sociedad Medica de Valparaiso; Chilean Society of Thorax Diseases and TBC; Chilean Society of Allergy and Immunology; Latin American Society of Allergy and Immunology; American College of Chest Physicians. *Publications:* Contributor: "Bronchial Asthma, Clinical and Immunological Aspects", 1976; 'Revista Medica Chile'; 'Revista Medica Valparaiso'; 'Bol. Hospital'; 'Acta Med Fab'. *Hobbies:* Chess; History; Good music. *Address:* 7 Norte 744, Vina del Mar, Chile, South America.

CANE, Roy Douglas, b. 29 Jan. 1945, South Africa. Associate Professor of Anaesthesia. *Education:* MB BCh, University of Witwatersrand School of Medicine, South Africa, 1969; Intern, Medicine and Surgery, Coronation Hospital, Johannesburg, 1970; Registrar, Anaesthesia, Baragwanath Hospital and University of Witwatersrand Medical School, 1971-73; Resident, Northwestern University Medical School, Chicago, Illinois, USA, 1974. *Appointments include:* Senior Medical Officer, 1974, Anaesthetist and Director of Intensive care, 1975, Principal Anesthetist and Director of Intensive Care, 1976-77, Baragwanath Hospital and University of Witwatersrand, Medical School, Johannesburg, South Africa; Assistant Medical Director, Department of Respiratory Therapy, 1978-85, Associate Attending Staff, 1979-83, Attending Staff, 1984-, Associate Medical Director, Repiratory Therapy, 1985-, Northwestern Memorial Hospital; Assistant Professor, Clinical Anesthesia, 1978-81, Associate Professor, 1981-, Associate Director, Respiratory and Critical Care, 1985-, Northwestern University Medical School; Lecturer, Cook County Graduate School of Medicine, 1980-. *Memberships include:* American Association of Respiratory Therapy; Illinois Society of Respiratory Therapy; American Society of Anesthesiologists; Founder Member, South African Critical Care Medicine Society; Association of University Anesthetists; Sigma Xi. *Publications:* "Clinical Application of Respiratory Care", Co-author, 3rd edition, 1985; "Case Studies in Critical Care Medicine", Co-Editor, 1985. Author of some 50 original contributions to professional journals, 6 abstracts. Assistant Editor, "The Year Book of Anesthesia", 1980; Consultant, Year Book Medical Publishers Incorporated, Illinois, 1981-; Reviewer several professional journals. *Honours:* Atherstone Prize, South African Society of Anesthetists, 1972; Biographee in various USA and UK texts. *Address:* 250 East Superior, Suite 678, Chicago, IL 60611, USA.

CANETE, Danelo R, b. 15 Apr. 1937, Philippines. Cardiologist. m. dissolved, 1 son, 1 daughter. *Education:* MD, University of Santo Tomas, Manila, Philippines, 1960. *Appointments:* Chief, Cardiac Catheterization Laboratory, Edgewater Hospital, Chicago, Illinois, USA, 1966-68; Cardiologist, US Naval Hospital, Guam, 1968-70; Assistant Clinical Professor, University of Hawaii School of Medicine; Scientific Chairman, 6th Asian Pacific Congress of Cardiology, 1976; Medical Director, Fronk Clinic, Honolulu, 1974-76; Medical Director, Pearlridge Hospital, Hawaii, 1976-82; Member, International Advisory Board, 1st Asian Pacific International Pacemaker Conference, Jerusalem, Israel, 1980; Cardiologist to Open Heart Surgery Team invited by Chinese Government to Hanzhou, 1985; Captain, US Naval Reserve. *Memberships:* Past President, Hawaii Heart Association, Vice President Health Affairs, Naval Reserve Association, Pearl Harbor Chapter; Chairman, TV & Radio Committee, Hawaii Medical Association; Medical Advisor to "Body Talk", weekly TV Health series. *Publications:* Author of several publications. *Hobby:* Tennis. *Address:* 839 S Beretania Street, Honolulu, HI 96813, USA.

CANGIALOSI, Charles Philip. *Education:* BSc., John Carroll University, 1970; DPM, Academic Honours, Ohio College of Podiatric Medicine, 1975; Residency, Foot Clinic of Youngstown, 1975-76. *Appointments:* Podiatric Medicine and Surgery, Community Hospital of Warren; Podiatry Section, Barnet Memorial Hospital Medical Center, Paterson; Bergen Pines Hospital, Ridgewood, etc. *Memberships:* American Society of Podiatric Medicine; American Association of Hospital Podiatrists; American Society of Podiatric Dermatology; Alpha Epsilon Delta; Academy of Ambulatory Foot Surgery; Fellow, American College of Foot Surgeons; Fellow, American Academy of Podiatric Microsurgery, Charter Member; Diplomate, International College of Podiatric Laser Surgery; Fellow, International Biographical Association, Cambridge, England; FellowAmerican Academy of Podiatric Laser Surgery; many other professional organisations. *Publications:* Textbooks: Contributing Editor, "Yearbook of Podiatric Medicine and Surgery", 1984; "Clinics in Podiatry, Minimal Incision Surgery", 1986; Articles in professional journals include 'Current Podiatry'; 'Journal of American Podiatry Association'; 'Skin Diver Magazine'; 'Journal of Foot Surgery'; 'Ohio Academy of Science Journal'; 'Journal of the Academy of Ambulatory Foot Surgery'; etc. *Honours Include:* Past President, Phi Delta National Podiatry Honor Society; Distinguished Lecture Series, New York College of Podiatric Medicine, 1984-85; Associate Editor, 'Hospital Podiatrist', 1983; Vice President, American Society of Podiatric Medicine, 1984-85; numerous other honours and awards. *Address:* Waldwick Podiatry Centre, 22 Wyckoff Avenue, Waldwick, NJ 07483, USA.

CANTAFORA, Alfredo, b. 21 July 1946, Crotone, Italy. Senior Researcher, Director, Biochemistry of Metabolic Disorders, Institute Superiore di Sanita. m. Ida Blotta, 9 May 1971, Sorrento, 1 son, 2 daughters. *Education:* Degree, Chemistry, University of Rome. *Appointments:* Researcher, Defence Administration; Researcher, Senior Researcher, Instituto Superiore di Sanita. *Memberships:* American Oil Chemist's Society; Association of Official Analytical Chemists; International Union of Pure and Applied Chemistry; Societa Italiana Biologia Sperimentale; Associazione Italiana Analisti Chimici. *Publications:* "Gas-chromatographic method for the determination of sulfated and unsulfated bile acids in serum", 'Clinica Chimica Acta', 1979; "HPLC Analysis of molecular species of PC", 'Clinica Chimica Acta', 1984; "Free Fatty Acids in Liver Cirrhosis", 'Metabolism', 1984. *Honours:* Professsor, Applied Biochemistry, University Marsilio Ficino, Venice, 1983. *Hobbies:* Electronic Devices; Stamp Collection; Wood Carving. *Address:* Istituto Superiore de Sanita, Lab. Metabolism & Biochemistry, Viale Regina Elena 299, 00161 Rome, Italy.

CANTIN, Pierre Francois Roland, b. 1 Aug. 1928, Mauritius. General Practitioner. m. Hilary Ingrid Chandler, 15 Dec. 1956, London, England, 1 son, 2 daughters. *Education:* MBBS, LRCP, London, 1955; MRCS, England, 1955; LMCC, 1967; CCFP, Canada, 1971; FCFP, Canada, 1980. *Appointments:* House Surgeon and Physician, The London Hospital, England, 1955-56; Junior Registrar, The Whitechapel Clinic, The London Hospital, 1957; Resident Medical Officer, the Civil and Victoria Hospitals, Mauritius, 1957-60; Senior Medical Officer, The Princess Elizabeth Hospital, Rodrigues, 1960-62; Senior Resident in General Practice, The Misericordia General Hospital, Winnipeg, Manitoba, 1962; Family Physician, St. Pierre, Manitoba, Canada, 1963-present. *Memberships:* British Medical Association; Canadian Medical Association; Member of College of Family Physicians of Canada. *Hobbies:* Reading; Painting; Tennis; Swimming. *Address:* 535 Cote Street, St. Pierre, Manitoba, Canada R0A IV0.

CANTONI, Carlo Alessandro, b. 30 Oct. 1936, Milan. Professor of Food Hygiene. m. Anna Maria, Fabbris, 1 daughter. *Education:* PhD in Food Hygiene. *Appointments:* Assistant Professor, 1961-68, Professor of Food Hygiene, 1968-, Istituto Ispezione Alimenti, Milan. *Memberships:* Societa Italiana Scienze Veterinarie; Societa Italiana Nutrizione Umana; Societa Italiana Microbiologia Applicata; Association A Tessier. *Publications:* About 500 publications and articles in the field of Food Hygiene. *Hobbies:* Rugby football; Rowing. ress: Istituto Ispezione Alimenti, Via Celoria 10, 20133, Milan, Italy.

CANTORE, Giampaolo, b. 22 Apr. 1931, Orbetello, Italy, Professor, Chair of Neurotraumatology, m. Giuliana Menichini, 14 Apr. 1958, Rome, Italy, 3 sons, 1 daughter. *Education:* Medical degree, University La Sapienza, Rome; Degree in Surgery; Professor of Neurosurgery. *Appointments:* Head, Institute of Neurosurgery, University of Siena, 1973-77; Chair of Neurotraumatology, University La Sapienza, Rome, 1997-. *Memberships:* Congress of Neurological Surgeons; Italian Society of Neurology; Italian Society of Neurosurgery;' Corresponding Member, British, Argentinian and Belgian-Dutch Neurosurgical Societies; Sectretary, 1978-82, Italian Neurosurgical Society. *Publications:* Author of over 160 publications including, 'Oral glycerol for the reduction of intracranial pressure', 1964; 'Dura mater treated with gamma rays for dural plastic surgery', 1969; 'Surgery of arteries in the neck', 1981; 'Diagnosis and surgical indications for obstructive cerebral vasculopathies', 1984. *Honours:* Marco Besso Prize and 1st Lepetit prize for experimental thesis, 1956. *Hobbies:* Gentleman rider in obstacle races until 1959; Rider in competitions of highest national category, 1966. *Address:* Via Cassia 837, Rome, Italy.

CANUT, Jose-Antonio, b. 28 Aug. 1938, Salamanca, Spain. Orthodontist; Stomatologist. m. Mercedes Barona, 27 Dec. 1964, Valencia, Spain, 4 sons, 1 daughter. *Education:* Doctor of Medicine. *Appointments:* Director of Spanish Journal of Orthodontics; President of Spanish Society of Orthodontics (1985). *Memberships:* European Orthodontics Society; Spanish Society of Orthodontics; American Association of Orthodontists; European Angle Society of Orthodontics. *Publications:* 'Clinical Management of the Mandibular Molars' in the 'American Journal of Orthodontics', 1975; "Clinische Anwendung des Mandibularen Nackenmandzuges", Munich, 1980; 'Morphological Analyses of Cases with Ectopic Eruption of the Maxillary First Permanent Molar', E Journal of Orthodontics', 1983. *Honours:* International College of Dentistry Pierre Fauchard Academy. *Hobby:* Jogging. *Address:* Escuela de Estomatologia, Facultad de Medicina, Avda. Blasco Ibanez 17, 46010 Valencia, Spain.

CAPLAN, Bruce, b. 17 May 1950, USA. Associate Professor/Chief Psychologist, Rehabilitation, Thomas Jefferson University Hospital, Philadelphia. m. Joan Mayer, 2 Apr. 1978, 1 son, 1 daughter. *Education:* PhD, New York University, 1977. *Appointments include:* Assistant Professor, University of Rochester School of Medicine, New York. *Memberships:* American Psychological Association; International Neuropsychological Scoiety; American Congress of Rehabilitation Medicine; British Psychological Society. *Publications include:* Contributions to: 'Brain & Language', 'Cortex', 'Archives of Physical Medicine & Rehabilitation', 'Rehabilitation Psychology', 'Journal of Clinical Neuropsychology', 'Perceptual & Motor Skills', 'Neuropsychologia', etc. *Address:* Department of Rehabilitation Medicine, Thomas Jefferson University, 11th & Walnut Streets, Philadelphia, PA 19107, USA.

CAPLAN, Yale H., b. 27 Dec. 1941, Baltimore, Maryland, USA. Chief Toxicologist, Office of Chief Medical Examiner, State of Maryland. m. 4 Feb. 1965, Baltimore, 1 son, 2 daughters. *Education:* BS, Pharmacy, 1963, PhD, Medicinal Chemistry, 1968, University of Maryland, Baltimore; Diplomate, American board of Forensic Toxicology. *Appointments:* Graduate Assistant, 1964-65, Adjunct Assistant Professor, 1977-79, Adjunct Associate Professor, 19790-, Medicinal Chemistry/Pharmacognosy, Instructor, Toxicology, 1972-73, Clincial Assistant Professor, 1973-79, Director, Graduate Programme, Forensic Toxicology, 1974-, Clinical Associate Professor, 1979-85, Clinical Professor, 1985-, Forensic Pathology, University of Maryland; Assistant in Surgery, 1969-70, Surgery, Lecturer, 1973-, Forensic Pathology, Johns Hopkins University; Professorial Lecturer, Forensic Sciences, George Washington University, 1975-76; Various Consulting Positions, 1970-. *Memberships include:* American Academy of Forensic Science, Fellow, various committees; American Association for the advancement of Sciences; American Association for Clinical Chemistry; American Board of Forensic Toxicology, Director, 1984-, Secretary-Treasurer, 1984-; American Chemical Society, various offices; American Institute of Chemists; California Association of Toxicologists; International Association of Forensic Toxicologists; Society of Forensic Toxicologists; etc. *Publications:* Editorial Advisory Board: 'Journal of Analytical Toxicology'; 'Journal of Forensic Sciences'; Co-Author, "Review Questions in Analytical Toxicology", 1982; Author, Chapters in various books; numerous articles in professional journals. *Honours:* Rho Chi; Phi Kappa Phi; Society of Sigma Xi. *Hobbies:* Racquetball; Jogging. *Address:* 3411 Philips Drive, Baltimore, MD 21208, USA.

CAPON, Andre Paul, b. 7 May 1930, Virton, Belgium. Head of Neurological Rehabilitation Department, University of Brussels, div. 1 son, 1 daughter. *Education:* MD, University of Brussels, 1955; Postgraduate in Neurology, Queen Square, London, 1961; Agrégé de l'Enseignement supérieur, 1971. *Appointments:* Research worker, 1952-60, Assistant, Internal Medicine, 1957-63, Adjoint in Neurology, 1963-67, Neurologist, Neurology Department, 1967-76, Neurological Rehabilitation Department, 1976-, Head of Department, 1983-, Professor of EEG, University of Brussels. *Memberships:* Belgian Neurological Society; Belgian Physiological Society; French EEG Society; Editor in chief, 'Acta neurologica Belgica'. *Hobbies:* Gardening; Golf. *Address:* Service de Revalidation neurologigue, Hôpital Brugmann, 1020 Brussels, Belgium.

CARAFOLI, Ernesto, b. 14 Oct. 1932, Sedegliano, Italy. Professor of Biochemistry. m. Annamaria Benucci, 14 July 1963, Modena, Italy, 2 sons. *Education:* BSc, Udine, Italy, 1951; MD, University of Modena, Italy, 1957; Habilitation (General

Pathology) 1964, (Biochemistry) 1968, University of Modena. *Appointments:* Research Associate, Institute of General Pathology, 1957, Assistant Professor, Department of Neurophsychiatry, 1958-59, Assistant Professor, Department of General Pathology, 1959-63, University of Modena; Fogarty International Postdoctoral Fellow, Johns Hopkins University, Baltimore, USA, 1963-65; Associate Professor, Department of General Pathology, University of Modena, 1965-73; Professor of General Pathology, University of Padua, Italy, 1973; Professor of Biochemistry, Swiss Federal Institute of Technology (ETH) Zürich, Switzerland, 1973-. *Publications:* Some 300 articles on topics of Membrane Biochemistry since 1955, especially on calcium biochemistry; Editor or Co-editor of 13 books on various topics of membrane biochemistry and bioenergetics. *Honours:* Prize Fondazione Giacomozzi, Modena 1957; Award & Medal for Outstanding Research, International Society for Heart Research, 1984; Fogarty Scholar-in-residence, Bethesda, USA, 1985-86. *Hobbies:* Mountaineering; Classical Music; Philosophy of Science. *Address:* Laboratory of Biochemistry, Swiss Federal Institute of Technology (ETH), Universitätstrasse 16, 8092 Zürich, Switzerland.

CARAYON, Pierre, b. 11 Apr. 1945, Conakry, Guinea. University Professor. Divorced, 1 son. *Education:* Master of Sciences, University of Aix-Marseille II, France, 1974, Medical Doctor, 1974, Doctor ot Sciences, 1983. *Appointments:* Research Associate, University of Paris, France, 1971-72; Research Associate, University of Aix-Marseille, 1972-74, Assistant, Biochemistry, 1974-78, Assistant Professor, 1978-79; Visiting Scientist, Developmental Endocrinology Branch, NIH, Bethesda, 1979-80; since 1980- Assistant Professor of Cellular Biology, University of Aix-Marseille, Chief Hormone Laboratory, Centre Hospitalier de Marseille; Professor of Mollecular and Cellular Endocrinology, University of Pisa, Italy, 1985-present. *Memberships:* American, French and Italian Endocrine Societies; European and Latino-American Thyroid Societies; French Society of Biological Chemistry; French Society of Paediatric Research. *Publications:* Articles related to biochemistry, theoretical biology, Endocrinology, Cell Biology, Immunology. *Honours:* Thesis Prize for Medicine, 1974; Thesis Prize for Sciences, 1983. *Hobbies:* Swimming; Skiing; Travel; Art Collecting. *Address:* Laboratoire des Hormones Proteiques, Faculté de Médecine, F-13385 Marseille Cedex 5, France.

CARBONE, Paul Peter, b. 2 May 1931, White Plains, New York, USA. Director, Wisconsin Clinical Cancer Centre; Professor, Chairman, Human Oncology. m. Mary Iamurri, 21 Aug. 1954, 3 sons, 4 daughters. *Education:* MD, Albany Medical College; Intern, Resident, US Public Health Service Hospital, Baltimore. *Appointments:* Senior Investigator, 1960-65, Head, Solid Tumor Service, 1965-69, Chief, 1968-72, Medicine, Associate Director, Medical Oncology, 1972-74, Special Assistant to Director, Cancer Biology and Diagnosis, 1975-76, NCI; Consultant, Medicine, VA Hospital, Washington DC, 1970-76. *Memberships:* American Association for Cancer Research; American Society of Clinical Oncology; American College of Physicians; Association of American Physicians; American Society of Clinical Investigation; etc. *Publications:* Associate Editor: "Estrogen Receptors in Human Breast Cancer", 1975, "Perspectives on Prevention and Treatment of Cancer in the Elderly", 1983, "Current Therapy in Hematology/Oncology 1984-85", 1985. *Honours:* American Cancer Society Professor of Clinical Oncology, 1976-81; Richard & Hinda Rosenthal Foundation Award, 1977; Clowes Lecture, 1979; Albert Lasker Award for Clinical Cancer Chemotherapy, 1972. *Hobbies:* Bicycling; Gardening. *Address:* K4/614 CSC, Wisconsin Clinical Cancer Centre, 600 Highland Avenue, Madison, WI 53792, USA.

CARDENAS, Diana D, b. 10 Apr. 1947, San Antonio, Texas, USA. Associate Professor, University of Washington. m. Thomas M. Hooton, MD, Mineola, Texas, 2 daughters. *Education:* BA, University of Texas, Austin; MD, University of Texas Southwestern Medical School, Dallas; MS, University of Washington, Seattle. *Appointments:* Staff Physician, Rehabilitation Medicine, VAH, Atlanta, Georgia, 1976-77; Assistant Professor, 1976-81, Associate Chief, 1978-81, Director, Amputee Clinic, 1979-81, Rehabilitation Medicine, Emory University; Assistant Professor, 1982-86, Director, 1982-, Associate Professor, 1986-,. Rehabilitation Medicine Clinic, University of Washington, Seattle. *Memberships:* Phi Beta Kappa; International Rehabilitation Medicine Association; American Academy of Physical Medicine and Rehabilitation; American Congress of Rehabilitation Medicine; American Spinal Injury Association; American Medical Association; Association of Academic Psychiatrists; National Association of Physical Medicine and Rehabilitation; International Rehabilitation Medicine Assocition; Pan American Medical Association. *Publications:* Contributor of articles and papers to professional journals; monographs and presentations. *Honours:* Winner of 1976 Annual essay Contest sponsored by ACRM; Recognition Award, American Medical Association, 1980. *Hobbies:* Art Collecting; Knitting; Needlepoint; Painting. *Address:* Department of Rehabilitation Medicine, RJ 30, University of Washington School of Medicine, Seattle, WA 98195, USA.

CARDENAS, Manuel, b. 13 Dec. 1928, Mexico. Chief, Coronary Care Unit; Professor of Cardiology. m. Rosa Maria Lang, 3 Jan. 1957, Mexico, 1 son. *Education:* MD; Mexican Cardiology Speciality Board; FACP; FACC. *Appointments:* Associate Cardiologist, currently Chief, Coronary Care Unit, Instituto Nacional de Cardiologia; Professor in Cardiology, Faculty National of Medicine. *Memberships:* Mexican, Spanish, Peruvian and Chilean Societies of Cardiology; National Academy of Medicine; American Heart Association; American College of Cardiology. *Publications:* "La clinica de las Arritmias", 1976; "Manual de Servicio de Urgencias y Unidad Coronaria", 1977; "Urgancias Cardiovasculares", 1985. *Address:* Instituto Nacional de Cardiologia, Juan Badiano 1, Mexico DF 14080, Mexico.

CARLON, Graziano C, b. 18 Dec. 1945, Padova, Italy. Chief, Department of Critical Care. m. Anne T Corsa, 7 Sep. 1985, New York, 1 son. *Education:* Classical Maturity, Udine, Italy, 1963; MD, University of Padova, 1969; Diplomate, American Board of Anesthesiology, 1978; Specialist in Anesthesiology, Intensive Care, University of Padova, 1972. *Appointments:* Assistant Professor, Anesthesiology, University of Padova, Italy, 1972-75; Assistant Professor, 1978-81, Associate Professor, 1981-, Cornell University, New York, USA; Director, Department of Respiration Therapy, Memorial Sloan-Kettering Cancer Center, New York, 1984-. *Memberships:* American Society of Anesthesiology; Society of Critical Care Medicine; International Anesthesia Research Society; American College of Chest Physicians. *Publications:* Co-author: "Critical Care of Cancer Patient", 1985; "High Frequency Ventilation", 1985. Contributor over 200 articles on respiratory failure and mechanical ventilation. Consultant Editor, 'Chest'. Co-author, "International Symposium on High Frequency Ventilation", 1984. *Honours:* Grant, Society of Memorial Hospital, 1981; Grant, National Institutes of Health, 1982-85; Editorial Board Member, Critical Care Medicine, International Journal of Monitoring and Computing, Hospital Physician. *Hobbies:* Tennis; Travelling; Computers. *Address:* 1275 York Avenue, New York, NY 10021, USA.

CARLSON, Curtis Harvey, b. 31 Dec. 1926, Minneapolis, Minnesota, USA. University Professor,

m. Reverend Edna Mae Carlson, 1 July 1949. *Education:* MD; PhD; Fellow, American College of Forensic Psychiatrists; Senior Investigator, National Institutes of Health. *Appointments:* Professor, University of Minnesota, Minneapolis Veterans Administration Medical College;Colonel, US Army Reserve. *Memberships:* American College of Forensic Psychiatrists; American Psychiatric Association; American Medical Association; Minnesota State Medical Association; Minnesota Psychiatric Association; Hennepin County Medical Association. *Publications:* "Radiofluoride Metabolism", 1960; "Depression in Chemical Dependents", 1984; "Forensic Psychiatry", 1985. *Honours:* Bausch and Lomb Award, 1945; Phi Beta Kappa, 1952. *Hobbies:* Travel; Gardening. *Address:* 6029 Pine Grove Road, Minneapolis, MN 55436, USA.

CARLSON, Robert Gabriel, b. 18 Sep. 1915, Minneapolis, Minnesota, USA. Consultant; Private Practice; Assistant Clinical Professor. m. Jean Caverhill Hogarth, 12 Aug. 1939, Denver, Colorado, 3 sons, 1 daughter. *Education Includes;* Graduate, Menninger School of Psychiatry, Topeka, Kansas; BA, University of Denver, 1937; Graduate School, Physiology, 1937-39, MD, 1943, University of Colorado. *Appointments Include:* Medical Director, Mount Airy Psychiatric Sanitarium, Denver, Colorado, 1947-53; Clinical Lecturer, University of Colorado, 1948-52; Chief, NP Section, USAH, Fort McClellan, Alabama, 1953-55; Director, Diagnostic and Inpatient Services, Kansas Treatment Center for Children, 1957-58; Director, Boulder County Child Guidance Clinic, Colorado, 1958-62; Consultant, Fort Logan Mental Health Center, 1967-69, Wallace Village for Children 1967-75; Medical Director, Wallace Village for Children, 1975-77; Clinical Director, Adolescent Treatment Programme, Mount Airy Psychiatric Center, Denver, 1978-84. *Memberships:* Life Fellow, Amercian Psychiatric Association; Colorado Psychiatric Society; American Medical Association; Denver and Colorado Medical Societies; Life Fellow, American Orthopsychiatric Association; American Academy of Pediatrics; various others. *Honours Include:* Honorary Member: Alpha Omega Alpha, 1941; Sigma Xi, 1941, Diplomate, American Board of Psychiatry and Neurology: Psychiatry 1958; Child Psychiatry 1961. Chairman, Colorado Community Mental Health Advisory Council, 1960-70; Member, State Health Facilities Advisory Council, 1965-74; Member State Advisory Council on Mental Health, 1968-69. *Hobbies:* Philately; Photography; Woodwork; Sports; Music. *Address:* 1175 South Williams Street, Denver, CO 80210, USA.

CARLSSON, Gunnar Erik Helmer, b. 8 Aug. 1930, Umeå, Sweden. Professor and Chairman of University Department of Stomatognathic Physiology. m. Anita Wedel, 30 Jan. 1972, 3 sons. *Education:* Dentistry, Royal Dental School, Stockholm, 1950-54; Dr Odontology (PhD), University of Umeå, 1967. *Appointments:* Dentist, National Dental Service, Lycksele, 1955; Assistant Professor, Dental School, Umeå, 1957; Associate Professor, Faculty of Odontology, University of Umeå, 1967; Professor and Chairman of Department of Stomatognathic Physiology 1969-, Dean 1974-77, Vice-Dean 1984-, Faculty of Odontology, University of Göteborg. *Memberships:* International Association of Dental Reasearch; American Equilibration Society; Society of Oral Physiology; President 1980-84, Swedish Society of Prosthetic Dentistry and Stomatognathic Physiology. *Publications:* "Temporomandibular Joint. Function and Dysfunction", (eidotr with G A Zarb), 1979; "Klinisk Bettfysiologo för Allmäntandläkaren", 1982; About 200 scientific articles on prosthetic dentistry and stomatognathic physiology. *Honours:* Elander Prize, Göteborg Dental Society, 1972; Prosthodontic Award, International Association of Dental Research, 1975. *Address:* Faculty of Odontology,

University of Göteborg, Box 33070, S 40033 Göteborg, Sweden.

CARMEL, Peter Wagner, b. 12 Jan. 1937, Brooklyn, New York, USA. Professor of Neurological Surgery. m. Ann Ardmann, 1968, 3 sons. *Education:* AB, Hons, College of the University of Chicago, 1956; MD, New York University – Bellevue College of Medicine, 1960; D Med S, Neuroanatomy, Columbia University College of Physicians and Surgeons, 1970. *Appointments include:* Academic: Assistant Professor of Clinical Neurological Surgery, 1971-76, Associate Professor of Clinical Neurological Surgery, 1976-, College of Physicians and Surgeons, Columbia University, New York; Chief, Division of Pediatric Neurosurgery, Columbia Presbyterian Medical Center, 1985-. Hospital: Consultant, in Neurological Surgery, Blythedale Children's Hospital, Valhalla, New York, 1971-; Associate Attending Neurological Surgeon, Columbia Presbyterian Hospital, New York, 1976-; Associate Attending Surgeon (Neurological Surgery) St. Likes/Roosevelt Hospital Center, New York, 1981-; Professor of Clinical Neurological Surgery, 1986. *Memberships include:* New York County Medical Society; New York State Medical Society; American Medical Association; Fellow, American College of Surgeons; American Association of Neurological Surgeons etc. *Publications:* Numerous articles published in medical journals and papers presented to medical conferences. *Honours include:* First prize, Residents Night – New York Neurological and Neurosurgical Societies, 1965; The Allen Fellow, College of Physicians and Surgeons, Columbia University, New York, 1967-68; Sigma Xi; Society of Research Neurosurgeons, 1974. *Address:* 710 West 168th Street, New York, NY 10032, USA.

CARMICHAEL, Robert John, b. 14 June 1933, Sussex, England. Surgeon Captain, Royal Navy; Head, Defence Radiological Protection Service. m. Josephine Mary Vagg, 2 Aug. 1957, Oldland, 1 son, 2 daughters. *Education:* MSc., Radiation Biology; MB; BS; M.Fom. *Appointments Include:* Familes and Dockyard MO, Gibraltar, 1960-62; Medical Officer, HMS Woodbridge Haven/Manxman, 1962-65; Medical Officer, HMS Resolution, 1966-68; Principal Medical Officer, HMS Forth and SM7, 1969-71; Base Health and Safety Officer, Clyde Submarine Base, 1972-73; Deputy Chairman Naval Nuclear Technical Safety Panel, 1973-76; Head, Naval Radiological Protection Service, 1976-81; Head, Defence Radiological Protection Service, 1981-. *Memberships:* British Medical Association; Society for Radiological Protection; Society of OccupationalMedicine; Faculty of Occupational Medicine, Royal College of Physicians. *Publications:* Various papers, radiation matter. *Hobbies:* Golf; France and the French; Diving and Underwater Photography. *Address:* Netherton, 25 Catisfield Lane, Fareham, Hants PO15 5NW, England.

CARMODY, John Joseph, b. 23 Apr. 1940, Brisbane, Australia. University Lecturer. m. Diana Mary Booth, 4 Dec. 1967, 4 sons (1 deceased), 1 daughter. *Education:* MB, BS, 1963, MD, 1977, University of Queensland. *Appointments:* Resident Medical Officer, Mater Misericordiae Hospital, Brisbane, 1964; Tutor, School of Physiology, University of New South Wales, 1965, 1967; Research Fellow, Life Insurance Medical Research Fund of Australia, 1966; Senior Tutor, 1968-73, Lecturer, 1974-79, Senior Lecturer, 1979-, School of Physiology & Pharmacology, University of New South Wales. *Memberships:* Australian Physiology & Pharmacological Society; Medical Science Club of Sydney; Musicological Society of Australia. *Publications:* Various articles in 'Journal of Physiology'; 'European Journal of Pharmacology'; 'Neuroscience Letters'; 'Medical Journal of Australia'; on neurophysiological and neuropharmacolgical topics. *Hobbies:* Music Critic of 'The National Times' (important Australian

Weekly). *Address:* School of Physiology & Pharmacology, University of New South Wales, Kensington, NSW 2033, Australia.

CARPENTER, David Arthur, b. 22 Aug. 1944, Sydney, Australia. Head, Engineering Research, Ultransonics Institute. m. Lynette Mary Yeats, 4 Dec. 1971, Sydney, 2 sons. *Education:* BEng., Electronics, 1966; M.Eng.Sc., 1971. *Appointments:* Engineer, Class I, PMG Dept., 1966-67; Engineer, Class II, Commonwealth Acoustic Laboratory, Ultrasound Section, 1968-71; Senior Hospital Physicist, Institute of Cancer Research, London, 1972-73; Engineer Class III, National Acoustics, 1974-78; Engineer IV, Ultrasonics Institute, 1979-. *Membership:* Past President, Australian Society for Ultrasound in Medicine. *Publications include:* Numerous articles in professional journals; "Handbook of Clinical Ultrasound", 1978; "Ultrasonic Transducers: New Techniques and Instrumentation in Ultrasonography", 1980; "Instrumentation: Ultrasonic Differential Diagnosis of Tumours", 1983; Co-Patentee, 3 patents. *Honours:* Honorary Biomedical Engineer, Royal Hospital for Women, Paddington, New South Wales, 1974-85. *Hobbies:* Motoring; HiFi; Astronomy. *Address:* 5 Hickson Road, Millers Point, 2000, Australia.

CARR, John Edward, b. 6 Feb. 1934, Carthage, Indiana, USA. Professor of Psychiatry & Behavioural Science, University of Washington School of Medicine. m. Danielle Joan Fleischner, 14 June 1959, New York, 2 sons, 2 daughters. *Education:* BA, Earlham College, 1956, MA 1958, PhD 1963, Syracuse University. *Appointments include:* Associate Professor, University of Washington School of Medicine, 1970-76; Visiting Professor, Psychology, University of Malaya, 1974-75; Director, Division of Psychology 1970-77, Professor & Director, Medical Education 1976-81, Professor & Acting Chairman 1981-85, Department of Psychiatry & Behavioural Science, University of Washington School of Medicine. Various committees, 1981-85. *Memberships include:* President 1984-86, Association of Medical School Professors of Psychology. *Publications include:* "Behavioural Sciences in the Practice of Medicine", with H.A. Dengerink, 1984; 50 journal articles on Cross-cultural medicine & epidemiology, therapy outcome, behavioural treatments, cognition, stress, etc. *Honour:* National Board of Medical Examiners in Behavioural Sciences, 1985-87. *Hobbies:* Hiking; Skiing; Cross-cultural & medical history research. *Address:* Department of Psychiatry & Behavioural Sciences, University of Washington School of Medicine, Seattle, WA 98195, USA.

CARSTAIRS, Lindsay Steven, b. 10 July 1919, Glasgow, Scotland. Curator of Film Library Royal College of Radiologists (Retired). m. Margaret Harrington, 12 Oct. 1946, Okayama, Japan, 1 son, 2 daughters. *Education:* MRCS LRCP, 1941; MD BS 1949; ADMR (London) 1942; FRCR, 1975. *Appointments:* House Surgeon, Radiological House Officer then Assistant Radiotherapist, St. George's Hospital, London SW1; Army Radiologist 81 (BR) General Hospital, 18 (BR) General Hospital, 80 (BR) General Hospital, OC 80 (BR) General Hospital, DADMS, BRITCOM, BASE, Japan; Senior Registrar, St George's Hospital; Consultant Radiologist, Royal Northern Hospital, London N7; Consultant Radiologist, Royal Chest Hospital; City of London Maternity Hospital. *Memberships:* Royal Society of Medicine, Past President, Section of Radiology; British Institute of Radiology; Thoracic Society; Past Vice-Chairman, Fellowship for Freedom in Medicine; Past Vice-President, Metropolitan Branch Council, BMA. *Publications include:* "Military Diseases of the Lungs" co-author 1962; "Chickenpox Virus Pneumonia" Proceedings of RSM 1963; 'The Hospital Plan' chapter in "Trends in the NHS" 1964; "Skeletal Maturation in Under-sized Children Treated with Anabolic Steroids" 1965; "Sarcoidosis of Bone" co-author Qu. J of Med 1977.

Honours: Honorary Lieutenant Colonel RAMC, 1957; Brackenbury Prize in Medicine, 1941. *Hobby:* Gardening. *Address:* Windmill House, Hadley Green, Barnet, Hertfordshire, England.

CARTER, Walter Hansbrough, b. 20 Mar. 1941, Winchester, Virginia, USA. Chairman of University Department of Biostatistics. m. Judith P Gott, 15 June 1963, Front Royal, Virginia, 2 sons, 1 daughter. *Education:* BS Physics and Mathematics, 1963; MS Mathematics 1966, PhD Statistics 1968, Virginia Polytechnic Institute and State University. *Appointments:* Assistant Professor of Biometry 1968, Associate Professor of Biostatistics 1972, Professor of Biostatistics 1979, Professor of Medicine 1981, Professor of Pharmacology and Toxicology 1984, Chairman of Department of Biostastics 1984-, Virginia Commowealth University. *Memberships:* American Statistical Association; Biometric Society; Phi Beta Kappa; Phi Kappa Phi; Sigma Xi. *Publications include:* 'Regression methods in the analysis of survival data in cancer combination chemotherapy', (with G L Wamples nd E M Stablein), 1983; 'Confidence internal about the response at the stationary point of a response surface with an application to pre clinical cancer therapy', (co-author), 1984; 'Response surface methodology and the design of clinical trials for evaluation of cancer chemotherapy', 1985. *Hobbies:* Tennis; Hunting. *Address:* Box 32, MCV Station, Richmond, VA 23298, USA.

CARTMILL, Timothy Boyd, b. 10 May 1933, S Grafton, Australia. Staff Cardiac Surgeon and Chairman, Division of Surgery. m. Marilyn May McKenzie, 2 Feb. 1957, Sydney, 1 son, 1 daughter. *Education:* MB BS, University of Sydney Medical School, 1955; Fellow, Royal Australian College of Surgeons, 1961. *Appointments:* Staff Specialsit in Cardiac Surgery, 1966-69, Part-time Staff Specialist in Cardiac Surgery 1969-81, Royal Prince Alfred Hospital, Sydney; Staff Cardiac Surgeon (part-time) 1969-, Chairman, Division of Surgery, 1985-, Royal Alexandra Hospital for Children, Sydney; Visiting Cardiothoracic Surgeon 1979-84, Consultant Cardiothoracic Surgeon 1985-. *Memberships:* Fellow, Royal Australasian College of Surgeons; Cardiac Society of Australia and New Zealand; Australian Association of Surgeons; International Society of Surgery; Pan Pacific Surgical Association. *Publications:* 31 publications in various scientific journals including: 'Results of repair in ventricular septal defeat' 1966; 'Cardiothoracic Surgery in Australia: future manpower needs' 1977; 'Profound hypothermia with circulatory arrest – nine years clincial experience' 1982. *Honours:* Fullbright Scholarship, 1963; National Heart Foundation Travelling Fellowship, 1964. *Hobbies:* Reading; Sailing. *Address:* Wade House Consulting Rooms, Royal Alexandra Hospital for Children, Camperdown, New South Wales 2050, Australia.

CARUSO, Vincent, b. 21 Apr. 1946, Italy. Pathologist. m. Yolande Carol Kozel, 23 May 1970, Perth, Australia, 3 daughters. *Education:* MB BS, University of Western Australia, 1973; FRCPA, Sydney, 1980; MRCPath., London, 1980; MBA, University of Western Australia. *Appointments:* Residential Medical Officer, Royal Perth and Princess Margaret Hospital, Western Australia; Surgical Registrar, Royal Perth Hospital, Western Australia; Pathology Registrar, SCGH, Western Australia; Lecturer in Histopathology, Charing Cross Hospital Medical School, University of London; Consultant Pathologist, State Health Laboratories, Western Australia; Consultant Pathologist, Western Pathology Services and Princess Margaret Hospital, Western Australia. *Memberships:* Australian Medical Association; International Dermatopathology Society; International Academy of Pathology, Australian Division; Royal College of Pathologists, UK; Royal College of Pathologists, UK; Royal College of Pathologists of Australia;

Australian Society of Cytology. *Address:* 8 Corbusier Place, Balcatta 6021, Western Australia, Australia.

CARVALHO, Angelina De Chaves America De Sousa, b. 26 Sep. 1938, Portugal. Chief, Haematology Section, Veterans Administration Medical Centre; Associate Professor of Medicine, Brown University, USA. m. Jaime S. Carvalho, MD, 18 July 1966, 1 daughter. *Education:* BS, University of Coimbra, Portugal; MD, Honours, Lisbon Medical School. *Appointments include:* Research Associate, Massachusetts Institute of Technology/Instructor in Medicine, Harvard Medical School, USA, 1972-73; Head, Special Coagulation Laboratory, Massachusetts General Hospital/Instructor, Medicine, Harvard/Principal Investigator, MIT Arteriosclerosis Centre, 1973-77; Head, Haemostasis Laboratory & Associate Haematologist, Memorial Hospital, Pawtucket, Rhode Island/Assistant Professor, Medicine, Brown University/Principal investigator, American Cancer Society Research Grant, 1977-78; Chief, Haematology Section, VA Medical Centre, Providence/Associate Professor, Brown University/Principal investigator SCOR in acute respiratory failure, NHLBi Grant 1979-. *Memberships include:* New York Academy of Science; American Federation for Clinical Research; American Heart Association; International Society for Thrombosis & Haematosis; American Thoracic society; etc. *Publications include:* 65 research papers & 42 abstracts: 'Blood alterations in the adult respiratory distress syndrome', book chapter, 1985; 'Acquired disorders of platelet function', book chapter, co-author, 2nd edition 1986; etc. *Honours:* Scholarship, Calouse Gulbenkian Foundation, Lisbon, 1962-65; Physicians Recognition Award, American Medical Association, 1980-88; Citation, outstanding service to disabled American veterans,

CASELLA, Charles Wilkersham, b. 28 July, 1940, USA. Psychiatrist; Associate Professor. *Education:* BA, Harvard College, USA, 1961; MD, Harvard Medical School, 1965. *Appointments:* Chief, Psychiatry Service, USPHS Hospital, New Orleans, USA, 1969-71; Director, In-Patient Psychiatric Services, Stanford University Hospital, California, 1971-73; Consultant, Substance Abuse Unit, VA Hospital, Menlo Park, California, 1973-75; Forensic Evaluter, San Mateo/Santa Clara Area, 1974-; Consultant, California Division of Vocational Rehabilitation, 1979-82; Deputy Chief, Psychiatry Service, Stanford University Hospital, 1982-83. *Memberships:* Mid-Peninsula Psychiatric Society; Southern California Psychiatric Association; American Psychiatric Association. *Hobbies:* Swimming; Tennis; Ski-ing. *Address:* 701 Welch Road, Palo Alto, CA 94304, USA.

CASHMAN, Timothy Terence, b. 21 July 1936, Dublin, Republic of Ireland. Ophthalmic Optician. m. Anne Monaghan, 28 Mar. 1980, Mount Charles, Co. Donegal, 1 son. *Appointments:* Employee Pharmacist in General Practice, 1962-67; Medical representative, Burroughs Wellcome & Co; Optician & Manager, McGivney's Ltd Opticians & Berlin Optical Institute; Assistant Editor, Irish Pharmacy Journal; Owner Optician, Berlin Opticians, Dublin, 1976-. *Memberships:* Pharmaceutical Society of Ireland; Irish Pharmaceutical Union; Association of Ophthalmic Opticians, Ireland. *Honour:* Honorary Vice-President, International Pharmaceutical Students' Federation, 1965. *Hobbies:* Mountaineering; Gardening; Aikido; Classical Guitar; Member of Irish Greenland Mountaineering Expedition, 1971. *Address:* 25 Laurel Road, Churchtown, Dublin 14, Republic of Ireland.

1982. *Hobbies:* Painting; Reading; Music. *Address:* 263 Powell Street, Stoughton, MA 02072, USA.

CASPERS, Heinz J, b. 22 Sep. 1921, Federal Republic of Germany. University Professor of Physiology and Institute Director. m. Margaret Freimuth, 1949. *Education:* Study of Medicine, Universities of Marburg and Muenster; Dr med. *Appointments:* Docent in Physiology 1955-61, Professor of Physiology, 1961-66, Professor and Director of the Institute of Physiology 1966-, University of Muenster. *Memberships:* German Physiological Society; German EEG Society; Affiliate, Royal Society of Medicine; New York Academy of Sciences. *Publications include:* Co-editor of EEG Handbook, monographs and Z EEG-EMG; Contributions to handbooks and textbooks; About 250 papers in scientific journals mainly in the field of neurophysiology. *Honours:* Hans Berger prize, German EEG Society, 1960; Michael Prize, Michael Foundation, 1974. *Address:* Robert-Koch-Strasse 27a, 4400 Müenster, Federal Republic of Germany.

CASSIERS, Léon J M G, b. 23 May 1930, Brussels, Belgium. Professor of Psychiatry. m. Francoise Delwart, 14 Sep. 1954, 3 sons, 4 daughters. *Education:* MD 1954, Psychiatrist 1958, Doctor of Criminology 1967. *Appointments:* Adjunct Psychiatrist, Clinic 'La Ramée', Brussels; Teacher in Criminology; Adjunct Psychiatrist, Chief of Service of Psychiatry, University Clinic, Brussels; Professor of Psychiatry, Catholic University, Louvain. *Memberships:* Société Royale de Médicine Mentale (Past President); AIEMPR, (Past President); Ecole Belge de Psychoanalyse; Board Member, Thérapie Familiale, Geneva, Switzerland; European Association of Psychiatry. *Publications:* "Le Psychopathe délinquant", 1968; "Les premiers rendex-vous" (editor), 1982; Various articles in field of criminology, psychoanalysis & Family Therapy; "Nos illusions de Psychoanalystes" (editor), 1984; "Ethique de l'Hospitalisation", (editor), 1985. *Hobbies:* Fishing; Computers. *Address:* Centre de Guidance, 30 Clos Chapelle aux Champs, B-1200 Brussels, Belgium.

CASSILL, Kay, b. Iowa, USA. Medical Correspondent. m. R V Cassill, 2 sons, 1 daughter. *Education:* BA English, University of Iowa, 1953; Graduate study in communications management, photojournalism, feature writing, printmaking, drawing, painting. *Appointments:* Research Assistant, Ford Foundation, Education & Arts Division, New York; Executive Secretary, Member, Board of Directors, Associated Writing Program; Founding President, The Twins Foundation; Lecturer, Providence College, University of Rhode Island; Correspondent, People Weekly, New York Times Syndicate, FAN, NANA, TWINS. *Memberships:* Iowa Writers' Workshop; American Society of Journalists & Authors; Authors' Guild; Associated Writing Programs; Women in Communications Inc; Overseas Press Club. *Publications:* "Twins: Nature's Amazing Mystery", 1982; "The Complete Handbook for Freelance Writers", 1981. *Honours:* Distinctive Short Stories, 1976 (Martha Foley annual collection); Penney-Missouri Journalism Award, 1975; Radcliffe Institute; Merit Scholarship. *Address:* 22 Boylston Avenue, Providence, RI 02906, USA.

CASTEJON SANDOVAL, Orlando Jose, b. 26 Feb. 1937, Maparai, Venezuela. Director, Facultad de Medicina, Unidad de Investigaciones Biologicas, Universidad del Zulaa. m. Haydéa V Castejón, 19 Aug. 1960, Maracaibo, Venezuela, 1 son, 3 daughters. *Education:* Medical Surgeon, 1961; Graduated Student: Venezuelan Scientific Research Institue, 1961-62; Postdoctoral Research Fellow, University of California, Los Angeles, USA, 1963; MD, Faculty of Medicine, Luz, 1968. *Appointments:* Head, Electron Microscopy Section, Clinical Research Institute, Luz, 1964; Director, Biological Research Institute, 1972; President, Latin American Society of Electron Microscopy, 1972; President, Ibere-american Society of Cell Biology, 1976; Minister of Environment and Natural Renewable Resources, 1984; President, Latin American Society of Electron Microscopy, 1984; Member, Directive National research Council, CONICIT, Venezuela, 1972-82. *Memberships:* New York Society of

Electron Microscopists, New York; Societe Francaise de Microscopie Electonique, Paris, France; International Academy of Pathology, Washington; Fellow, Royal Microscopical Society, London. *Publications:* "Manual of Basic techniques for Electron Microscopy", 1976; "Electron Microscopy of Human Cerebral Edema", 1976; "Scientific Policy in Venezuela", 1983; "Electron Microscopy and Histochemistry of Central Nervous System", 1984. *Honours include:* National Prize in Biology, National Research Council CONICIT, Venezuela, 1980. *Hobbies:* Guitar; Tennis. *Address:* Instituto de Investigaciones Biologicas, Facultad de Medicina, Universidad del Zulia, Apdo 526, Maracaibo, Venezuela.

CASTELLINO, Ronald Augustus Dietrich, b. 18 Feb. 1938, New York City, USA. Professor. m. Joyce Cuneo, 26 Jan. 1963, San Francisco, California, 3 sons. *Education:* MD, Greighton University School of Medicine, 1962. *Appointments:* Intern, Highland Alaineda County Hospital, 1962-63; Peace Corps Physicians, (USPHS), Brazil, 1963-65; Resident, Diagnositc Radiology, Stanford Medical School, 1965-68; Assistant Professor, 1968-74, Associate Professor, 1974-81, professor, 1981-, Director, Diagnostic Radiology, Associate Chairman, Department of Radiologic, Stanford University School of Medicine, 1986. *Memberships:* Radiologic Society of North American; American College Radiology; Association of University Radiologists; California Radiology Society; International Society Lymophology; American Roentgen Ray Society. *Publciations:* Over 125 scientific papers and book chapters; Co-editor, "Pediatric Oncologic Radiology". *Honours:* Alpha Omega Alpha Honer Medical Society, 1962; John Guggenheim Fellowship, 1974-75. *Hobbies:* Tennis; Gardening; Travel. *Address:* Stanford Medical School, Stanford, CA 94305, USA.

CASTON, John Christopher, b. 23 Aug. 1946, Spartanburg, South Carolina, USA. Psychiatrist, Private Practice. m. Carol Lee Sanborn, 11 Sep. 1977, Spartanburg, 1 son, 2 dauthers. *Education:* BS, Clemson University, 1974; MD, 1971, Psychiatric Resident, 1974, Medical University of South Carolina. *Appointments:* Associate, Department of Psychiatry, Medical University of South Carolina, 1974-76; Assistant Professor in Psychiatry, Family Practice Residency, Spartanburg General Hospital, 1976-77. Private Practice, Psychiatry, Spartanburg, 1977-. *Memberships:* American Psychiatric Association; American Psychosomatic Society; South Medical Association; American Medical Association. *Publications:* Contributions to: 'Journal of South Carolina Medical Association'; 'Southern Medical Journal'; 'Diseases of the Nervous System'; "Psychic and Neurologic Dysfunctions After Open-Heart Surgery", 1980. *Honours:* Outstanding Young Men of America, 1972; Phi Kappa Phi, 1967. *Hobby:* Field trial beagles, AKC. *Address:* 370-A Serpentine Drive, Spartanburg, SC 29303, USA.

CASTRIOTTA, Richard J, b. 21 Dec. 1945, Winchester, Massachusetts, USA. Director, Pulmonary Medicine, Mount Sinai Hospital. m. Laura Gillespie, 19 Feb. 1983, Canton, 1 daughter. *Education:* AB, College of the Holy Cross, 1967; MD, University of Bologna, Italy, 1974; University of Freiburg, Federal Republic of Germany, Summer, 1964. *Appointments:* Research Assistant, Massachusetts General Hospital, Summers 1965-68; Medical Resident, 1974-77, Chief Medical Resident, 1977-78, Hospital of St Raphael, New Haven; Fellow, Pulmonary Disease, 1978-80, Research Fellow, Immunopathology, 1980, Instructor, Medicine, 1980, Assistant Professor, Medicine & Pathology, 1981-, University of Connecticut School of Medicine. *Memberships:* Society of Critical Care Medicine; American College of Chest Physicians, Council on Critical Care; American College of Physicians; American Medical Association; American Thoracic Society; Clinical Sleep Society; New York Academy

of Sciences. *Publications:* Co-Author, "Strain Variation of Bacillus Calmette-Guerin-Induced Pulmonary Granuloma Formation is Correlated with Anergy and the Local Production of Migration Inhibition Factor and Interleukin 1", 'American Journal Pathology', 1985. *Honours:* Certified: American Board of Internal Medicine, 1978, ABIM, Pulmonary Subspeciality, 1980. *Address:* Mount Sinai Hospital, 500 Blue Hills Ave., Hartford, CT 06112, USA.

CASTREN , Olli Mikko, b. 13 Sep. 1929, Pielavesi, Finland. Professor of Obstetrics and Gynaecology, University of Kuopio; Medical Director of University Central Hospital of Kuopio. m. Liisa Sippola, 15 Dec. 1954, Helsinki, 3 sons, 1 daughter. *Education:* MD, University of Turku, 1963. *Appointments:* Assistant Doctor, Department of Pharmacology, University of Turku, 1956-57; Asistant Doctor, Department of Social Medicine, 1957-59, Assistant Doctor Obstetrics and Gynaecology, 1959-63; Assistant Professor, 1963-69; Professor in Obstetrics and Gynaecology, 1969, University of Kupio; Rector of University of Kuopio, 1969-73; Medical Director of University Central Hospital of Kuopio, 1974-81, 1984-. *Memberships:* Finnish Association of Gynaecology, President, 1980-83; Nordic Association Obstetrics and Gynaecology; College International des Chiruriens; German Association Obstetricians and Gynaecologists. *Publications:* "Urinary Excretion of Adrenaline and Noradrenaline in Normal and Toxaemic Pregnancy" (Dissertation), 1963. *Honour:* Decorated Commander of Order of Finnish Lion, 1979. *Address:* Ahmantie 8, 70400 Kuopio, Finland.

CASTRO, Joseph Ronald, b. 9 Apr. 1934, Chicago, Illinois, USA. Professor, Vice-Chairman. m. Barbara Ann Kauth, 12 Oct. 1957, Chicago, 2 sons, 4 daughters. *Education:* BS, Natural Science, 1956, MD, 1958, Loyola University. *Appointments:* Assistant Professor, Associate Professor, Radiotherapy, University of Texas MD Anderson Hospital & Tumor Institute, 1966-71; Associate Professor, Professor, Radiation Oncology, 1971-, University of California School of Medicine; Director, Radiotherapy, University of California Lawrence Berkeley Laboratory 1975-. *Memberships:* American Society of Therapeutic Radiology & Oncology; Radiation Research Society; American Radium Society; Groupe European de Curietherapie. *Publications:* Over 100 published articles, book chapters and abstracts. *Honours:* Honorary Member, Rocky Mountain Radiological Society, 1970; Distinguished Teaching Award, Mount Zion Hospital Medical Centre, 1972; Special Award, University of Tokyo, 1982. *Hobbies:* Equitation; Gardening. *Address:* Radiotherapy Department, Bldg. 55, University of California Berkeley, Lawrence Laboratory, Berkeley, CA 94720, USA.

CASTRO-CARRO, Teresa, b. 1 June 1927, San Juan, Puerto Rico, USA. Private Practice in Psychoanalysis, Child, Adolescent and Adult Psychiatry. divorced, 2 sons, 2 daughters. *Education:* MD. *Appointments:* Resident, Psychology, EPI, Philadelphia, Pennsylvania; Researcher, Temple School of Medicine, 1960-64; Consultant, Mental Health Clinic, Veterans Administration, Philadelphia, 1960-64; Instructor, Department of Psychology, University of Pennsylvania Medical School, 1962-64; Professor of Psychology, College of the Sacred Heart, San Juan, Puerto Rico; Researcher on Modern Child Relations,EPPI, Philadelphia, Pennsylvania; currently in Private Practice, San Juan, Puerto Rico. *Memberships:* Past Delegate, American Academy of Child Psychology; Government Commission on Drugs Prevention, Puerto Rico, 1970-73; Institute of Philadelphia Psychoanalysts, 1971-74, *Hobbies:* Sailing; Yachting; Golf; Fishing; Collections and Original paintings. *Address:* Condominio del Mar

Apt 403, 20 Delcasse St., Condado, San Juan, PR 00907, USA.

CATTAFI, Albert Frank, b. 22 Nov. 1941, New Jersey, USA. Private Practitioner; Doctor of Chiropractic, Specialist in Sports Injury. m. Geraldine Marie Consolvo, 8 Oct, 1978, Fair Lawn, 1 son, 1 daughter. *Education:* BA, Bloomfield College, 1970; DC, Columbia Institute of Chiropractic, New York, 1976; Professional Licences, New Jersey, Florida: Diplomate, National Board of Chiropractic Examiners. *Appointmnets:* Certified Athletic Trainer, American Athletic Trainers Association; Certified Chiropractic Team Physician. *Memberships:* New Jersey Chiropractic Society; American and International Chiropractic Associations; New York Chiropractic Alumni Association; Foundation for Chiroporactic Education and Research; American College of Sports Medicine; Florida Chiropractic Association; American Academy of Nutritional Consultants. *Publications:* "Chiropractic in New Jersey, 1978. *Honours:* President, Inter County Council on Drug and Alcohol Abuse, 1982-83; Master, Triune Lodge, F&AM, 1977; President, Kearny Rotary Club, 1980-81; Board Member, West Hudson Council for Handicapped, 1980-84. *Hobbies:* Golf; Reading; Photography. *Address:* 655 Kearny Avenue, Kearny, NJ 07032, USA.

CATANE, Raphael, b. 27 Oct. 1942, France. Professor, Oncology. m. Haya, 20 Sep. 1965, Jerusalem, 4 sons, 1 daughter. *Education:* Hebrew University, Hadassah Medical School. *Appointments:* Resident, Brazilian Medical Centre, Ashkelon, 1972-75; Fellow, Roswell Park Memorial Institute, Buffalo, New York, USA, 1975-77; Visiting Scientist, NCI, NIH, Bethesda, USA, 1977-79; Professor, Oncology, Hadassah University Hospital, Jerusalem. *Memberships:* Israel Medical Associaiton; Israel Oncology Society; American Society Clinical Oncology; European Society Medical Oncology; European Society Cancer Research. *Publications:* 70 papers in medical journals. *Honour:* Awardee, Israel Cancer Research Fund, 1982-84. *Address:* Dept. of Oncology, Hadassah University Hospital, Jerusalem, Israel 91120.

CATE, Hendrik Janten, b. 13 Jan. 1921, Oosterhesselen, Netherlands. Specialist in Allergic Diseases. m. Shirley J Oxby, 6 Oct. 1978, Barston, Birmingham, 1 son, 2 daughters. *Education:* MD, University of Groningen, 1948; Specialist in Internal Medicine, 1953; Doctorate, Thesis, University of Groningen, 1954. *Appointments:* General Practitioner, 1948-49; Medical Assistant, Department of Internal Medicine, Berweg Hospital, Rotterdam, 1949-50; Medical Assistant, Department of Internal Medicine and Allergy Departments, NTE Department and Dermatology Department, University of Groningen, 1950-55; Practice in Allergic Diseases, Rotterdam, 1955-. *Memberships:* Dutch Association for Allergy; Dutch Professional Body for Allergy; European Acadmey of Allergy; Royal Society of Medicine. *Publications:* Author of several published papers and doctoral thesis. *Honours:* Token of Honour, Academia Europea, Stockholm, Sweden, 1965. *Hobbies:* Photography; Studies of Modern and Biblical Hebrew and theology. *Address:* G W Burgerplein 19, 3021 AT Rotterdam, Netherlands.

CATOVSKY, Daniel, b. 19 Sept. 1937, Buenos Aires, Argentina. Senior Lecturer in Haematology & Medicine. m. Julia M Pola, 11 Feb. 1960, Buenos Aires, 2 sons, 1 daughter. *Education:* MD, Faculty of Medicine, University of Buenos Aires, 1961. *Appointments:* Honorary Lecturer in Haematology & Medicine, Royal Postgraduate Medical School, London, 1974-76; Honorary Consultant Physician, Hammersmith Hospital, London, 1976-; Honorary Senior Lecturer in Haematology & medicine, Royal Postgraduate Medical School, 1976-; Senior Staff, Medical Research Council Leukaemia Unit, Hammersmith Hospital, 1974-79. *Memberships:* Royal College of Pathologists; Royal College of Physicians. *Publications:* Some 300 publications by 1985; "The Leukaemic Cell", 1981. *Honour:* Travelling Fellowship, National Research Council, Argentina, 1967-69; DSc (Med), London University, 1985. *Hobbies:* Squash; Films. *Address:* MRC Leukaemia Unit, Hammersmith Hospital, London W12 OHS, England.

CAUCHI, Maurice Nicholas, b. 6 Dec 1936, Malta. Director, Section of Haematology and Immunology. m. Agnes, 23 Sep 1962, Malta, 2 daughters. *Education:* MSC, PhD, London University; MD, Royal University of Malta. *Appointments:* Research Fellow, Institute of Cancer Research, London; Lecturer, Royal University of Malta; Senior Lecturer, Monash University, Melbourne; Director, Section of Haematology and Immunology, The Royal Women's Hospital, Melbourne, Australia. *Memberships:* Australian Medical Association; Royal College of Pathology of Australia and London; Australian Immunology Society; Australian Haematology Society. *Publications:* "Obstetric and Perinatal Immunology", 1981; "Health" 1982 (in Maltese); "The Clinical Pathology of Pregnancy and the Newborn Infant", 1984. *Honour:* Gordon Jacobs Research Award, 1964. *Hobbies:* Music; Gardening. *Address:* 88 Canberra Grove, Brighton 3187, Victoria, Australia.

CAVANAGH, Harrison Dwight, b. 22 July 1940, Atlanta, Georgia, USA. F. Phimizy Calhoun Senior Professor, Chairman, Ophthalmology, Emory University School of Medicine; Director, Emory Eye Centre, Atlanta. m. Lynn Ayres Gantt, 24 Dec. 1964, Gloucester County, 1 daughter. *Education:* AB, 1962, MD, 1965, Johns Hopkins University; PhD, Harvard University, 1972. *Appointments:* Teaching Assistant, Biology, 1966-69, Assistant Professor, Ophthalmology, 1976-76, Harvard University; Instructor, Ophthalmology, Johns Hopkins University, 1969-73; Associate Professor, 1976-78, F. Phinizy Calhoun Senior Distinguished Professsor, Chairman, 1978-, Ophthalmology, Emory University; Director, Emory Eye Centre, 1984-. *Memberships:* Fellow, Diplomate, American Academy of Ophthalmoloy; Fellow, American College of Surgeons; Fellow, International College of Surgeons; Secretary-Treasurer, Association for Research on Vision and Ophthalomology; Fellow, Castrovrejo Society; Pan American Ophthal Association; New England Ophthalmology Society; Georgia Ophthalmology Society; etc. *Publications:* 75 publications, distinguished lectureships including: Jean Lacerte Distinguished Lecturer, Royal College of Surgeons, Laval University, Canada, 1982; M K Bochner Lecture, University of Toronto, Canada, 1983; 2nd Joseph E. Koplowitz Lecture, Georgetown University, 1984. *Honours:* Phi Beta Kappa, Johns Hopkins, 1962; The Heed Award, 1982. *Hobbies:* Tennis; Genealogy; Reading; History. *Address:* 327 Clifton Road Northeast, Atlanta, GA 30322, USA

CAVIN, Elmo, M, b. 21 Oct. 1945, San Antonio, Texas, USA. Associate Dean, Finance & Administration, East Tennessee State University; Executive Director, Medical Education Assistance Corporation. m. Janis Ivie, 29 Mar. 1980, El Paso, Texas, 1 son. *Education:* MBA, Financial Management, BBA, Accounting, St Mary's University, San Antonio. *Appointments:* Director, Accounting, 1968-74, Director, Budget & Payroll Services, 1974-79, University of Texas Health Science Centre, San Antonio; Business Manager, 1979-80, Assistant Vice President, Business Affairs, 1980-82, University of Texas, El Paso, Texas; Associate Dean, Finance & Administration, East Tennessee State University, Quillen-Dishner College of Medicine, 1982-; Executive Director, Medical Education Assistance Corporation, Johnson City, Tennessee, 1984-. *Memberships:* Texas Association of State and Senior College and University Business

Officers; National Association of College and University Business Officers; Association American Medical Colleges; Medical Group Management Association; Southern Association of College and University Business Officers. *Hobbies:* Sports; Boating. *Address:* Quillen-Dishner College of Medicine, East Tennessee State University, PO Box 15100A, Johnson City, TN 37614, USA

CAYOLLA DA MOTTA, Luis A C R , b. 24 Nov. 1923, Lisbon, Portugal. Professor of Epidemiology, National School of Public Health, Lisbon; Consultant, Ministry of Health, Lisbon. m. Maria Angela Paes Gomes, 23 Sep. 1950, Lisbon, 2 daughters. *Education:* MD, Faculty of Medicine, Lisbon, 1947; Diploma, Tropical Medicine, Institute of Hygiene, Lisbon, 1950; Diploma, Public Health, London School of Hygiene and Tropical Medicine, University of London, 1958; Certificate, Epidemiology and Medical Statistics, Same School, 1964; Certificate, Health Programme Planning, CDC Atlanta, 1972. *Appointments:* Intern, Civilian Hospitals of Lisbon, 1948-49, 1950-51; Medical Officer, Directorate General of Health, 1950-66; Director, Quarantine Health Services and Port and Airport Health Authority, 1967-71; Superior Inspector of Health, Public Health Services, 1970-71; Deputy Director of Health Studies and Planning, 1971-76; Director, 1977-83; Consultant, Ministry of Health,1 984-; Full Professor of Epidemiology, National School of Public Health, Lisbon, Portugal; Several times Consultant, World Health Organization; Chairman, Public Health Committee, Council of Europe, 1980-81. *Memberships:* International Epidemiological Association. *Publications:* About 150 papers mainly on communicable diseases, health statistics and epidemiology. *Honours:* Award, Best Student Superior Hygiene Course, Lisbon, 1950; Ministry of Interior Award, 1955; Portugal Red Cross Award, 1982. *Address:* Rua Dinis Dias 12 1400 Lisbon, Portugal.

CENDROWSKI, Wojciech, b. 11 Nov. 1928, Warsaw, Poland. Clinical Neurologist. m. Hanna Grzeda, 10 Nov, 1961, Warsaw, 2 sons. *Education:* Physician, Medical Academy, Warsaw, 1952; MD, Medical Academy, Warsaw, 1964; Dr.hab.med.science, Medical Academy, Poznan, Poland, 1977. *Appointments:* Assistant, Department of Neurology, District Hospital, Bydgoszcz; Assistant, Neurological Clinic, Psychoneurological Institute,ruszkow; Research Fellow, Department of Neurology, Royal Victoria Infirmary, Newcastle-upon-Tyne, England; Visiting Research Associate, Neurological Clinic, Turku, Finland; Visiting Research Fellow, Department of Neurology, University of Göttingen, Federal Republic of Germany, also Department of Neurology, VA Hospital, Minneapolis, USA; Adjunct, Department of Neurology, Psychoneurological Institute, Warsaw. *Memberships:* MS Section of the Polish Neurological Society; MS Research Committee, WFN; IMAB of the IF MSS; Neuroepidemiological Section, American Academy of Neurology. *Publications:* More than 200 papers, articles, reviews, on "Multiple Sclerosis", PZWL Warsaw, 1966; "Demyelinating Diseases", 1986. *Honours:* Secretary of the MS Section, Polish Neurological Society, 1967-77; Golden Badge, Polish Society for Fighting the Disability, 1985. *Hobbies:* Tourism; Sightseeing. *Address:* Karlowicz Street 1-116, 02501, Warsaw, Poland

CEPPELLINI, Ruggero, b. 19 Jan. 1917, Milan, Italy. Director, CNR Centre for Immunology & Histocompatibility. m. Ruth Steinbrecher, 16 Dec. 1944, Milan, 3 daughters. *Education:* Laurea in Medicina e Chirurgia, Milan, 1944; Libera Docenza in Genetica, 1960. *Appointments:* Assistant Professor, Internal Medicine, Assistant Professor, Genetics, Professor, Human Genetics, University of Milan; Visiting Professor, Human Genetics, Columbia University, New York, USA. Professor, Medical Genetics, University of Torino; Permanent Member, Basel Institute of Immunology, Basel. *Memberships:* Ordine dei Medici; Histocompatibility Workshops; Associazione Italina Genetica medica. *Publications:* "La Malattia Emolitica del neonato", 1952; "I meccanismi evolutivi delle popolazioni umane", 1952; "Physiological Genetics of Blood Group Factors", 1956; etc. *Honours:* Karl Landsteiner Memorial Award, 1963; John E. Fogarty Scholar in Residence, USA, NIH, 1971; Premio Feltrinelli, Academia dei Lincei, 1984. *Hobbies:* Skiing; Swimming. *Address:* Centro Studio Immunogenetica ed Istocompatibilita CNR, Via Santena 19, 10126 Torino, Italy.

CERILLI, G. James, b. 23 June 1933, Providence, Rhode Island, USA. Professor of Surgery. m. Barbara Schaefer, 7 Feb. 1976, Columbus, Ohio, 2 sons 1 daughter. *Education:* AB, Brown University, 1954 Magna Cum Laude; MD, Johns Hopkins Unviersity, 1958. *Appointments:* Professor of Surgery 1973-82, Director, Renal Transplant Program, 1967-82, Program Director, Clinical Cancer Education Program, 1967-82, Ohio State University; Professor and Chairman, Department of Surgery, 1982-85, Professor of Surgery, 1985-, Albany Medical College, Albany, New York. *Memberships:* American College of Surgeons; American Surgical Association; Society of University Surgeons; Association for Academic Surgery; Central Surgical Association; American Society of Transplant Surgeons. *Publications:* Articles in 'Surgical Gynecology and Obstetrics', 'Surgery', 'Human Immunology' and 'Transplantation'. *Honours:* James Manning Scholarship, 1954, 1954; Magna Cum Laude, Brown University, 1954; Sigma Xi Scientific Honor Society, 1954; Phi Beta Kappa Honor Society, 1954; Alpha Omega Alpha, 1958; Fulbright Scholarship, 1963; Distinguished Service Award, Association for Academic Surgery, 1976. *Hobby:* Sailing. *Address:* Department of Surgery, Albany Medical College, Albany, NY 12208, USA.

CESARENI, Giovanni, b. 1 Sept. 1949, Bergamo, Italy. Group Leader. m. Luisa Castagnoci, 31 July 1977, Rome, 2 daughters. *Education:* Maturita Classica, Liceum Tito Lucrezio Caro, Rome, 1968; Doctor of Physics, University of Rome, 1973. *Appointments:* Post Doctoral Training, Laboratory of Molecular Biology, MRC, Cambridge, England, 1976-79; Group Leader, European Molecular Biology Laboratory, Heidelberg, Federal Republic of Germany, currently. *Publications:* Author or Co-Author of 28 papers contributed to: "The Initiation of DNA Replication", 1981; "DNA Cloning Techniques, A Practical Approach", 1984; "Proteins Involved in DMA Replication", 1984; 'Nature'; 'Proceedings of National Academy of Science'; 'Journal of Molecular Biology'; 'Genetics Research'; 'Nucleic Acid Research'; 'UCLA Symposium'; 'Cell' and others. *Address:* European Molecular Biology Laboratory, Postfach 10.2203, 6900 Heidelberg, Federal Republic of Germany.

CHADLI, Amor, b. 14 May 1925, Tunis, Tunisia. Director, Institut Pasteur. m. 15 October 1958, Hale Esh-Chadli, 2 sons 3 daughters. *Education:* Professor, Faculty of Medicine, Tunis; Doctor of Medicine; Professeur Agrege. *Memberships:* Titular of Academie Nationale de Medicine of France. *Publications:* Over 150 papers in professional journals in Tunisia & Europe. *Honours:* Decorations & Honours of Tunisia, Arab States and European Countries. *Address:* Institut Pasteur de Tunis, BP, 74, 1002 Tunis-Belvedere, Tunisia.

CHAITCHIK, Samario, b. 19 June, 1936, Sao Paulo, Brazil. Head, Department of Oncology. m. Rina Birk, 3 Mar. 1963, Tel-Aviv, Israel, 2 sons 1 daughter. *Education:* MD, University of Brazil, Rio de Janeiro, 1960. *Appointments:* Resident, Internal Medicine, Municipal Hospital, Tel-Aviv Medical Center, 1962-63; Senior Resident, Department of Nuclear Medicine and Radiotherapy, Chalm Sheba Medical Center, Tel-Hashomer, 1963-64; Senior Staff and

Deputy Director, Department of Oncology and Radiotherapy, The Chalm Sheba Hospital, Tel-Hasomer; 1968-81; Head, The Tel-Aviv University Institute of Oncology, the Tel-Aviv Medical Center, 1981-. *Memberships include:* American Nuclear Medicine Society The Brazilian Medical Association; The Nuclear Medicine Society, Isreal; The Israel Medical Association; The Israel Physical Health Society; The Israel Clinical Oncology and Radiotherapy Society; General Director; The Latin American Association on Radiotherapy; The American Society of Clinical Oncology; The European Society of Therapeutic Radiation and Oncology. *Publications:* Contributor of numerous articles to medical journals and presenter of many papers at scientific meetings. *Honours:* Special Award for Cultural Contribution from Government of Sao Paulo, Brazil, 1972; Special Award, Officer of the Order of Rio Branco from the President of the United States of Brazil for Cultural Contribution Brazil-Izrael, 1974; Avenue in Brazilia named "Dr Samario Chaitchik Avenue" by Senate of Brazil, 1984; Bar Lemmensdorf Award for Study of Receptors of Hormones in Human Breast Tumors, 1973 and 1976; Sapir Grant for Research on Breast Cancer Pathology, 1980. *Address:* Department of Oncology, Tel-Aviv Medical Center, 6 Weizman Street, 64239 Tel-Aviv, Israel.

CHAITIN, Raymond M, b. 27 July 1915, New York City, USA, Physician, Psychiatrist, Legal Scholar, m. Jeannette Weisburg, 7 Apr 1940, Brooklyn, New York, 1 son, 1 daughter. *Education:* MD, Medical School; DO, Osteopathic Medical School; LLB, JD, Law School; BS. *Appointments:* Epidermologist, 1940-46; Medico-Legal Consultant, 1940-; Assistant Professor of Psychiatry, Downstate Medical School, New York State University, 1971-78; Psychiatric Consultant, Social security; Pasnel Arbitrator, American Arbitration Association; Psychiatric Consultant, State of California Medical Agency; Forensic Psychiatrist to New York City, State and Federal Courts; Advisor to Courts. *Memberships:* American Psychiatric Association; Fellow, American Association of Psychoanalytical Physicians; Fellow, International Academy of Geriatrics; Diplomate American Board of Psychiatric Medicine. *Publications:* "Crime and Violence"; "Hypnosis for Alcoholism and Drug Abuse"; "The Criminal Mind". *Honours:* American Arbitration Association, 25 years Service. *Hobbies:* Economics; Political Science; Forensic Psychiatry. *Address:* 2159 Glastonbury Road, Westlake Village, CA 91361, USA.

CHAKRABORTY, Ajita, b. 31 Oct. 1926, Calcutta, India. Professor of Psychiatry. *Education:* MBBS, DPM, FRCPE, FRCPsych., London, England. *Appointments:* Registrar, Senior Hospital Medical Officer, various hospitals in the United Kingdom; Teaching posts, Postgraduate Institute, Calcutta, India; Director, Institute of Postgraduate Medical Education and Research, Calcutta. *Memberships:* Past President, General Secretary, Honorary Treasurer, Indian Psychiatric Society; Committee, Transcultural Section World Psychiatric Association; Fellow, Royal College of Physicians; Fellow, Royal College of Psychiatrists. *Publications:* numerous articles on transcultural psychiatry. *Hobbies:* Growing cacti; Golf. *Address:* 84 NE, Block 'E', New Alipore, Calcutta 700053, India.

CHAMBERLAIN, Geoffrey Victor Price, b. 21 Apr. 1930, Hove, Sussex, England. Professor, Chairman, Obstetrics & Gynaecology, St George's Hospital Medical School, London. m. Jocelyn Oliver Kerley, 23 June 1956, 3 sons, 2 daughters. *Education:* MB, 1954; D(Obst) RCOG, 1956; MD, 1968; FRCS, 1960; MRCOG, 1963; FRCOG, 1978; University College, London; University College Hospital Medical School. *Appointments:* Residencies, Royal Postgraduate Medical school, Great Ormond St.,

Queen Charlotte's & Chelsea Hospitals & King's College Hospital, 1955-69; Tutor, George Washington Medical School, USA, 1965-66; Consultant Obstetrician & Gynaecologist, Queen Charlotte's and Chelsea Hospitals, 1970-82. *Memerhips:* Council, Royal College of Obstetricians and Gynaecologists, 1971-77, 1982-; Vice President, 1984-; Royal Navy reserve, 1955-74; Council, Royal Society of Medicine, 1977-84, Treasurer, 1982-84; Council, Obstetrical Section, Royal Society of Medicine, 1970-; Chairman, Medical Committee, National Birthday Trust, 1982-; Chairman, Blair Bell Research Society, 1977-80. *Publications:* "Safety of Unborn Child", 1969; "Lecture Notes in Obstetrics", 1975, 3rd edition, 1985; "Obstetrics by Ten Teachers", 11th Edition, 1980, 12th edition 1985; "Gynaecology by Ten Teachers", 11th Edition 1980, 12th edition 1985; "British Births 1970", Volume I 1975, Volume II 1977; "Placental Transfer", 1979; "Clinical Physiology in Obstetrics", 1980; "Tubal Infertility", 1982; "Pregnant Women at Work", 1984; "Prepregnancy Care", 1985. *Honours:* Goldsmith Scholarship, 1948; Fulbright Fellowship, ROCG, 1966; Thomas Eden Fellowship, ROCG, 1966; Foundation Prize, American Association Obstetricians, 1967; Visiting Professor: Beckman, USA, 1984, Daphne Chun, Hong Kong, 1985. *Hobbies:* Travel; Viniculture and Wine. *Address:* 10 Burghley Road, Wimbledon, London SW19, England.

CHAMBERLAIN, Jocelyn, b. 4 Jan. 1932, London, England. Specialist, Community medicine; Senior Lecturer, Epidemiology; Medical Director, Thames Cancer Registry. m. Geoffrey Chamberlain, 23 June 1956, London, 3 sons, 2 daughters. *Education:* MBBS, St George's Hospital Medical School, 1955; Diploma in Child Health, 1957; Member, 1972, Fellow, 1976, Faculty of Community Medicine; Felow, Royal College of Physicians of London, 1985. *Appointments:* Clinical Medical Officer, London County Council, 1958-61; Research fellow, Guy's Hospital Medical School, 1961-66; Lecturer, Johns Hopkins School of Hygiene & Public Health, 1966-67; Research Fellow, London School of Hygiene & Tropical Medicine, 1968-73; Senior Lecturer, Community Medicine, University College Hospital Medical School, 1973-78; Senior Lecturer, Epidemiology, Institue of Cancer Research, 1978-81. *Memberships:* Royal College of Physicians, London; Faculty of Community Medicine; Royal Society of Medicine; International Epidemiology Association; Society for Social Medicine. *Publications:* "Evaluation of Screening Procedures", "The Theory & Practice of Public Health", 1979; "Screening for Cancer", "Prevention of Cancer", 1982. *Hobbies:* Walking; Gardening. *Address:* S.W. Thames Regional Cancer Organisation, Royal Marsden Hospital, Sutton, Surrey, England.

CHAMPION, Howard Randall, b. 10 Oct. 1944, Leeds, England. Medical Director. m. Maria Clara, 11 Jan. 1985, Bogota, Colombia. *Education:* MRCS, LRCP, 1967; FRCS, Edinburgh, Scotland, 1972; FACS, USA, 1983. *Appointments:* Assistant Clinical Director, University of Maryland, USA, 1974-75; Chief, Trauma Service, Washington Hospital Centre, USA, 1976-, Senior Attending Surgeon, 1979-present; Chief, Division of Trauma, Uniformed Services University of Health Sciences, Bethesda, 1985-; Medical Director, International Health Affairs, Washington 1985-. *Memberships Include:* American Public Health Association; American College of Surgeons; American Trauma Society; American Association for Automotive Medicine; American College of Emergency Medicine; American Association for the Surgery of Trauma; American Federation for Clinical Research. *Publications Include:* 70 articles in medical journals inclduing: 'British Journal of Cancer'; 'Journal of the Royal College of Surgeons'; 'The Lancet'; 'British Journal of Surgery'; Chapters in: "Textbook of Critical Care", 1983; "Emergency Medicine Annual", 1984;

"Current Emergency Therapy", 1985; "Trauma Systems", 1985; numerous abstracts and conference papers. *Honour:* Honorary Consultant, Alfred Hospital Monash University, Melbourne, Australia. *Hobbies:* Skiing - Water and Snow. *Address:* Washington Hospital Center, 110 Irving Street, NW Washington, DC 20010, USA

CHAMPION, Robert Harold, b. 21 Mar. 1929, Sevenoaks, Kent, England. Consultant Dermatologist. m. Phyllis Laura Gaddum, 21 Apr. 1965, Cambridge, 1 son, 1 daughter. *Education:* MA; MB; Member, 1957, Fellow, 1974, Royal College of Physicians. *Appointments:* Registrar and Senior Registrar, Addenbrooke's Hospital, Cambridge, 1957-60; Senior Registrar, St Thomas's Hospital, London, 1960-61; currently, Consultant Dermatologist, Addenbrooke's Hospital, Cambridge. *Memberships:* Journal Editor, 1974-81, British Association of Dermatologist; Royal Society of Medicine; British Medical Association. *Publications:* "Recent Advances in Dermatology"; Co-Editory contributor to "Text Book of Dermatology", 4th edition and others. *Honours:* Honorary Member, Corresponding Member, Bulgarian, Netherlands and Swedish Dermatology Societies. *Hobbies:* Music; Postal history; Bird watching. *Address:* Addenbrooke's Hospital, Hills Road, Cambridge, England.

CHAN, Anthony Quan, b. 8 Jan. 1944, Philippines. Cardiologist. m. Dr. Estrillita Chan, 27 May 1972, 4 sons, 2 daughters. *Education:* Doctor of Medicine and Surgery, University of Santo Tomas, Milan, Philippines, 1968. *Appointments:* Rotating Intern, Union Memorial Hospital, Baltimore, Maryland, USA, 1968-69; Medical Resident and Cardiac Fellow, Michael Reese Hospital, Chicago, Illinois, 1969-73. *Memberships:* Fellow, Council on Clinical Cardiology, American Heart Association; American College of Cardiology; American College of Chest Physicians; American college of Angiology. *Publications include:* Articles in 'Circulation', 1974; American Heart Journal', 1979. *Honour:* Most Outstanding Medical Intern, 1968. *Hobbies:* Reading; Music; Financial Investments; Chess. *Address:* 14 Heather Lane, Oak Brook, IL 60521, USA.

CHAN, Chin-Hong, b. 26 June 1951, Macau, China. m. Rhumn-Hwa Fu, 4 June 1978, 2 sons. *Education:* Bachelor of Medicine, National Defense Medical Center, Taipei, Taiwan, Republic of China, 1969-75; Chinese Specialist Certificate in Psychiatry, Chinese Society of Neurology and Psychiatry, Republic of China; Diplomas, International Academy of Professional Counselling and Psycotherapy. *Appointments Include;* Clinical Supervisor, Department of Psychiatry, Yu-Li Veterans (Mental) Hospital, Yu-Li, Hua-Lia, Taiwan, 1982-84; Currently: Clinical Lecturer, Department of Psychiatry, National Defense Medical Center, Taipei; Attending Psychiatrtist of In-patient Service and Child and Adolescent Mental Health Clinic, Department of Psychiatry, Veterans General Hospital, Taipei; Clinical Lecturer, Department of Psychiatry, National Yang Ming Medical College, Taipei. *Memberships Include:* International Society for Adolescent Psychiatry; World Psychiatric Association; World Association for Infant Psychiatry and Allied Disciplines; International Association of Group Psychotherapy; Chinese Medical Association: Chinese Society of Neurology and Psychiatry; Chinese National Association for Mental Hygiene; American Orthopsychiatric Association; American & Canadian Psychiatric Associations; American & Canadian Academies of Child Psychiatry; American & Canadian Societies for Adolescent Psychiatry; American and Canadian Group Psychotherapy Association. *Publications:* In Chinese: 'Emergency Pharmacological Management of Agitated Patients', 1979; 'Drug Treatment of Anxiety State: A Double Blind Crossover Trial of Clobazam', 1980; 'Borderline State', 1980; 'The Epidemiological Study

on the Death from Suicide and Self-Inflicted Injuryin Taiwan', 1981; 'Delirium - The Psychiatric Problem Primary Care Physician Frequently Encounters', 1982; 'The Survey of Psychiatric Symptoms Among the Medically Ill Inpatients', 1982; 'The Common Psychiatirc Problems in the Intensive Care Unit', 1984. *Hobbies Include:* Taekwon-Do; Soccer. *Address:* Department of Psychiatry, Veterans General Hospital, 201 Shih-Pai Road, Section 2, Taipei, Taiwan 11217, Republic of China.

CHAN, Ming Chit, b. 5 May 1935, China. Deputy Chief, Department of Medicine; Associate Professor of Medicine; Co-Director; Cardiovascular Research Fellow. m. King Yuk Wu, 19 Jan. 1961, Beijing, 1 son, 1 daughter. *Education:* MD, Beijing Medical College, 1959, Natonal Board of Medical Examainers, USA, 1980; Beijing Traditional Chinese Medical College, 1975; Federation Licensing Examination, 1981; Cardiovascular Fellow, Cedar's Medical Center, Miami, Florida, USA, 1983. *Appointments Include:* Resident, 3rd Hospital, 1959-64, Chief Resident, Department of Medicine, 1964-65, Attending Doctor of Medicine, 1965-, Chief, Division of Pulmonary Diseases, 1973-79, Vice Chairman, Medicine, 3rd Hospital, 1973-84, Assistant Professor, Medicine, 1978-83, Beijing Medical College; Co-Director, Cardiovascular Laser Research Laboratory, 1984-; Cardiovascular Research Fellow, Western Heart Institute, St Mary's Hospital and Medical Center, California, USA, 1984-; Deputy Chief, Department of Medicine, 3rd Hospital, Beijing Medical Center, China, 1985-; Associate Professor of Medicine, Medical Sciences University of Beijing, 1985-. *Memberships:* Fellow American Society for Laser Medicine and Surgery; New York Academy of Sciences; American Federation for Clinical Research; Midwest Bio-Laser Institute. *Publications:* Co-Author of some 5 books, 6 abstracts and 25 journal publications, including: 'The Chinese Journal of Tuberculosis and Respiratory Disease'; 'American Journal of Cardiology'; 'American Heart Journal'; 'Chest'; numerous international symposiums, seminars and conferences. *Hobby:* Swimming. *Address:* Western Heart Institute, St Mary's Hospital and Medical Center, 450 Stanyan Street, San Francisco, CA 94117, USA.

CHAN, Wai-Yee, b. 28 Apr. 1950, Canton, China. Molecular Geneticist; Associate Professor. m. May-Fong, 23 Sep. 1976, Hong Kong, 1 son, 2 daughters. *Education:* BSc, First Class Honours The Chinese Unviersity of Hong Kong, 1970-74; PhD, University of Florida, Gainesville, 1977. *Appointments:* Teaching Assistant, Department of Biochemisty and Molecular Biology, University of Florida, Gainesville, 1974-77; Research Associate, 1978-79, Assistant Professor, Department of Paediatrics, 1979-82; Associate Professor, Department of Biochemistry and Molecular Biology, 1979-82, University of Oklahoma; Staff Affiliate, Paediatric Endocrine, Metabolism and Genetic Service, Oklahoma Children's Memorial Hospital, 1979-; Assistant Scientific Director, Biochemical Genetics Laboratory, Oklahoma Children's Memorial Hospital, 1980-; Consultant, Medical Service, Veterans Administration Medical Center, Oklahoma City, 1981-; Visiting Scientist, Department of Biochemistry, University of Washington, Seattle, 1982; Associate Professor, Department of Paediatrics, 1982-, Associate Professor, Department of Biochemistry and Molecular Biology, 1982-, Co-Scientific Director, Clinical Chemistry, State of Oklahoma Teaching Hospitals, Oklahoma City, 1982-; Affilate Associate Member, Oklahoma Medical Reserch Foundation, Oklahoma City, 1984-. *Memberships:* American Society of Biological Chemists; Nutrition Society, UK; American Genetic Association; American Society for Cell Biology; American Society of Microbiology; American Institute of Nutrition; American Society of Human Genetics; American Chemical Society; The Biochemical Society, UK; International Association of Biolnorganic Scientists; New York Academy of Science; Society for Experimental Biology and Medicine; Society for Paediatric Research; Southern Society for Paediatric Research; Tissue Culture Association; Sigma Xi, Treasurer, 1985-87; Oklahoma Endocrine Society; American Federation for Clincial Research; Association of Clinical Scientists. *Publications:* Co-Editor, "Metabolism of Trace Metals in Man", Volumes I and II, 1984; Contributions of chapters in books and articles in referred scientific journals. *Honours:* Scholarship for Chemsitry, The Chinese University of Hong Kong, 1972-74; Scholarship for Biochemistry, The Chinese University of Hong Kong, 1973-74; Fellowship to Advance Study Institute, North Atlantic Treaty Organization, 1979; Research Grants, National Institutes of Health, USA. *Hobbies:* Music; Stamp Collecting. *Address:* 8725 Raven Avenue, Oklahoma City, OK 73132, USA.

CHAN, Wan Hor, b. 13 Dec. 1939, Batu Gajah, Malaysia. Obstetrician, Gynaecologist, Private Practice. m. Dr Amy Chan, 1967, 1 son, 2 daughters. *Education:* Diplomate: Royal College of Obstetricians & Gynaecologists, England, Royal College of Physicians & Surgeons, Canada, American Board of Obstetrics & Gynaecology; MBBS; FRCOG; FRCSC; FACOG; FICS. *Appointments:* Resident, Obstetrics & Gynecology, University of Singapore, 1966, Queen's University, Belfast, Ireland, 1967-69; Blair-Bell memorial Research Fellow, Royal College of Obstetricians & Gynaecologists, England, 1970-71; Assistant Professor, Charles Drew Postgraduate Medical School, University of Southern California, USA, 1972-74; Attending Obstetrician, Gynaecologists, Los Angeles County Martin Luther King Hospital, 1972-74; Attending Staff, Los Banos Community Hospital, 1974-. *Memberships:* American Medical Association; New York Academy of Science; American Fertility Society; etc. *Publications:* "Outlines of Obstetrics-Gynaecology", 1971; scientific articles in 'Singapore Medical Journal'; 'British medical Journal'; 'American Journal of Obstetrics-Gynaecology'; "Journal of Obstetrics-Gynaecology of the British Commonwealth". *Hobbies:* Music; Golf; Chess; Philately. *Address:* 600 West 1 Street, Los Banos, CA 93635, USA.

CHANARD, Jacques Michel, b. 6 Feb 1939, Meknes, Morocco, Professor of Nephrology, Chief of Nephrology Unit, m. Elisabeth Pinaud, 30 June 1967, Paris France, 3 sons. *Education:* MD; BSc. *Appointments:* Chef de Clinique, University of Paris, France, 1969-74; Research Fellow, 1975, visiting Professor, 1976, Washington University, St Louise, Mo, USA; Professor of Nephrology, University of Reims, France. *Memberships:* Société de Néprologie; International Society of Nephrology; American Society for Artificial Internal Organs; International Society of Artificial Organs; American Society for Bone and Mineral Research. *Publications:* Author of numerous articles in international medical journals. *Address:* Centre Hospitalier et Universitaire, 45 rue Cognacq Jay, 51092 Reims Cedex, France.

CHAND, Deep, b. 10 Sep. 1945, Sardarshahr, India. Consultant Radiologist; Chairman, Division of Radiclogy. m. Sushma Vashishtha, 21 Jan. 1975, New Delhi, 2 sons. *Education:* MB BS; MD, 1976; DMRD, 1980; FFR RCSI, 1981; Senior Member, American Institute of Ultrasound Medicine, 1984. *Appointments:* House Officer, P B M Hospital, Bikaner, 1972-73; Senior House Officer, All India Institute of Medical Sciences, New Delhi, 1973; Senior House Officer in Medicine and Surgery, Sajdarjang Hospital, New Delhi, 1974; Registrar in Radiology, Post Graduate Institute, Chandiharh, 1975-76; North Staffs Hospital Centre, England, 1977-79; Senior Registrar, Radiology, North Staffs Hospital Centre, 1979-81; currently, Consultant Radiologist, Chairman of Division of Radiology,

Sandwell District General Hospital, West Bromwich, West Midlands. *Memberships:* Royal College of Radiologists, England; British Institute of Radiology; British Medical Association; British Medical Ultrasound Society; American Institute of Ultrasound Medicine; Fellow, Faculty of Radiologists, Royal College of Surgeons, Ireland. *Publications:* Contributor to 'International Congress of Radiology', Hawaii, USA, 1985; 'Role of Ultrasound & ERCP in Management of Biliary and Pancreatic Disease'; Radiolgoical Contribution for Small Bowel Cancer Book. *Honours:* Merit Scholarship, Medical School; Winner, Quiz Competition, College of Radiologist, Royal Society of Medicine and British Institute of Radiology, 1984. *Hobbies:* Swimming; Jogging; Snooker; Social and community work. *Address:* Sandwell District General Hospital, West Bromwich, West Midlands, England.

CHANDLER, Harold Mullins, b. 13 July 1935, Broken Bow, Oklahoma, USA. Private Practice, Psychiatry. m. Clema Jo Bruton, 3 Sep. 1957, Broken Bow, 1 son, 3 daughters. *Education:* MD, University of Oklahoma Medical School, 1956-60. *Appointments:* Director, Gynaecology Obstetrics Liaison Service, Oklahoma University, Health Sciences Centre, 1971-74; Medical Director, VA Drug Treatment Unit, Oklahoma City, 1971-74; Board of Directors, Contact, Oklahoma City, 1971-74; Chairman, Community & Mental Health Committee, 1981-83, Chairman, Public & Mental Health Committee, 1982-84, Oklahoma County Medical Society; Advisory Council, Oklahoma Board of Nurse Administration, Registration & Nursing Education, 1981-85. *Memberships:* American Psychiatric Association; Vice President, Oklahoma Psychiatric Association; American Medical Association; Oklahoma State Medical Association; Director of Clinics, Oklahoma City Clinical Society; Oklahoma County Medical Society; Medical Staff, Baptist Medical Centre: etc. *Publications:* "Crisis Intervention : Plan for Therapy and Family Followup", 'Roche Report : Frontiers of Hospital Psychiatry', 1969; "The Mobile Crisis Unity", 'Journal Georgia Psychiatric Association', 1971; "Family Crisis Intervention", 'Journal National Medical Association', 1972; "Nuclear Neurosis", 'Private Practice', 1979. *Hobbies:* Music; Writing; Athletics; Travel. *Address:* 3201 N.W. 63rd Street, Oklahoma City, OK 73116, USA.

CHANDRA, Benjamin, b 5 Oct. 1930, Surbaya, Indonesia. Professor and Head, Department of Neurology. m. Rita Wanamarta, 2 May 1958, Jember, 1 son, 1 daughter. *Education:* MD, 1956; PhD, 1960; Specialist in Neurology, 1960; Certificate in Clinical Electroencephalography, University of California, USA, 1963. *Appointments:* Lecturer, 1964, Senior Lecturer, 1971,Head of Department, 1973-, Professor, 1978-, Neurology, Airlangga University. *Memberships:* American Academy of Neurology; Vice President, Indonesian Association of Neurologists, 1971; American Medical Electroencephalographic Association; Fellow, Stroke Council, American Heart Association. *Publications:* Contributions to: "Textbook of Epilepsy", 1982; "Advances in Epileptology", 1978, 82. *Honour:* Honorary Award of President of Republic of Indonesia, 1983. *Hobbies:* Chess; Reading. 2Address: Diponegoro 100, Surabaya, Indonesia.

CHANG, Alexander Russell, b. 12 Aug. 1941, Dunedin, New Zealand. Senior Lecturer, Pathology, University of Otago; Consultant Pathologist, Dunedin Hospital; Head, Cytology Department. m. Andrina Lim, 11 Feb. 1966, Dunedin, 1 son, 2 daughters. *Education:* MB, ChB, Diploma in Clinical Pathology, Otago; Fellow, Royal College of Pathologists (Australasia); Cancer Society travelling grants, USA 1978, Australia 1984; Institute in Cytology for Pathologists, Johns Hopkins Hopsptial,

Baltimore, USA. *Appointments include:* House Surgeon 1967, Registrar, Assistant Lecturer in Pathology 1969-74, Senior Lecturer in Pathology/Consultant pathologist 1974-, Head, Diagnostic Cytology 1980-, Dunedin Hospital; Examiner, Anatomic Pathology, Royal Australasian College of Pathologists, 1983-84; Examinr & Moderator, Histology & Cytology, New Zealand Laboratory Technologist Board/Board member, 1985-. *Memberships:* Otago Medical School Research Society; Otago Medico-Legal Society; New Zealand Society of Pathologists; Cytology Society of New Zealand; International Academy of Pathology; Clinical Medical Staff Group, University of Otago (secretary, 5 years); New Zealand Society for Colposcopy & Cervical Pathology. *Publications include:* Author/co-author, over 25 research papers, various medical journals. *Honour:* Prize, preventive & social medicine, Royal College of General Practitioners, 1965. *Hobbies:* Photography; Growing orchids; Oil painting; Stamp collecting; Music. *Address:* Pathology Department, Otago University Medical school, PO Box 913, Dunedin, New Zealand.

CHANG, Ching-jer, b. 17 Oct. 1942, Hsinchu, Taiwan. m. Shu-fang, 25 Dec. 1978, Taipei, 1 son, 1 daughter. *Education:* BS, Chemistry, National Cheng Kung University, 1965; PhD, Organic Chemistry, Indiana University, USA, 1972. *Appointments:* Post-doctoral Associate, Bio-organic Chemistry, 1972-73, Assistant Professor, 1972-78, Associate Professor, 1978-84, Professor, 1984-, Medicineal Chemsitry, Purdue University, USA. *Memberships:* American Chemical Society; Academy of Pharmaceutical Science; American Association for Cancer Research; American Society for Pharmacognosy; Phytochemical Society of North America. *Publications:* Articles include: "Chemcial Modification of Nucleic Acids, Methylation of Calf Thymus DNA Investigated by Mass Spectrometry and Liquid Chromatography", Analysis of Nucleic Acids and Food Products", 'Food and Drug Administration', 1984. *Honours:* Lions Club Cancer Research Award, 1983. *Hobbies:* Gardening; Stamp Collection. *Address:* Dept. of Medicinal Chemistry, Purdue University, West Lafayette, IN 47907, USA.

CHANG, Kuang Hsiung, b. 20 Aug. 1941, Tokyo, Japan. Obstetrician and Gynaecologist in Private Practice. m. Fang-Mai Chen, 25 Feb. 1967, Taiwan, Republic of China, 2 daughters. *Education:* MD, Taipei Medical college, 1967. *Appointments:* Resident, Changhua Christian Hospital, 1968-71; Rotating Intern 1972-73, Resident in Surgery 1973-74, St Mary's Hospital, Waterbury, Connecticut, USA: Resident in Obstetrics-Gynaecology, Hahnemann Medical College and Hospital, Philadelphia, Pennsylvania, 1974-76; Private practice: Princeton, Indiana, 1976-79; Watsonville, California, 1979-80; Salinas, California, 1980-. *Memberships:* Fellow, American College of Obstetricians and Gynecologists; American Fertility Society; International Microsurgical Society. *Honour:* Diplomate, American Board of Obstetrics and Gynecology. *Hobbies:* Classical music; The outdoors. *Address:* 1115 Los Palos Drive, Salinas, CA 93901, USA.

CHANG, Kuo C, b. 13 Oct. 1943, Taiwan. Chief of Department of Allergy and Immunology. m. Helen S. Wang, 16 Sept. 1978, Portland, Oregon, USA, 1 daughter. *Education:* MD, National Taiwan University, College of Medicine, 1969. *Appointments:* Rotating Internship, Mercy Hospital and Medical Centre, Chicago, USA, 1971-72; Pediatric Residency, Cook County Hospital, Chicago, 1972-73; Paediatric Residency, University of Kansas Medical Centre, 1973-74; Private Practice and Staff Physician at Wesley Medical Centre, Wichita, Kansas, 1974-75; Fellowship in Allergy/Immunology, National Asthma Centre, Denver, Colorado, 12975-77; Chief, Department of Allergy and Immunology, Kaiser Permanent Medical

Centre, Portland, Oregon and Clinical Assistant Professor of Medicine, Oregon Health Science University -. *Memberships:* American Academy of Allergy nd Immunology; American Thoracic Society; Western Society of Allergy and Immunology; Oregon Society of Allergy and Immunology. *Publications:* Co-author: 'Impaired Response to hypoxia after bilateral carotid body rejection for treatment of asthma' in 'chest', 1978; Co-author: 'Linear Growth of Children with chronic Asthma: the effect of the disease and various forms of steroid therapy' in 'Clinical Allergy', 1982; Co-author: 'Diphenylmethane diisocyanote: Induced Asthma' in 'Clinical Allergy', 1984. *Hobbies:* Tennis; Backpacking; Microcomputers; Skiing. *Address:* 3414 North Kaiser Centre Drive, Portland, OR 97227, USA.

CHANG, Weining, b. 1 May 1945, Nanking, China. Professor of Psychology. *Education:* BA Law, National Taiwan University,1967; MA Psychology, 1971, PhD Psychology, 1973, University of Houston, USA. *Appointments:* Assistant Professor, Texas Southern University, 1973-78, Associate Professor of Psychology, 1979-. *Memberships:* American Psychological Association; International Association of Cross-cultural Psychology. *Publication:* "A Cross-cultural Study of Depressive Symptomatology" (in culture, Medicine & Psychiatry, 1985. *Hobbies:* Travel; Reading; Gardening; Writing. *Address:* Department of Psychology, Texas Southern University, Houston, TX 77004, USA.

CHANGEUX, Jean-Pierre, b. 6 Apr. 1936, Domont, France. Professor, College de France, Professor, Pasteur Institute. m. 1 child. *Education:* ENS, Paris, 1955-58; Faculty of Sciences, University of Paris; Certificates of Higher Studies: Botany and General Physiology, 1956, Zoology and Geology, 1957; DES Dip. Higher Studies, 1958; Graduate Teacher, Natural Sciences, 1958; State Doctorate Sciences,1964. *Appointments:* Entered Pasteur Institute, 1959; Assistant in Metabolic Chemistry, Faculty of Sciences, Paris, 1960; Assistant Visiting Professor, SUNY, Buffalo, NY, USA, 1965; Eleanor Roosevelt Research Fellow, International Union against Cancer, University of California, Berkeley, 1965; Dernham Fellow in Oncology, American Cancer Society, California Division, 1966; Assistant Visiting Profesosr, Neurology, Columbia University, 1967; Deputy Director, College de France, Paris (Chair Molecular Biology), 1967; Head, Laboratory of Molecular Neurobiolgoy, Pasteur Institute, Paris, 1972-; Professor, 1975-; Professor, College de France, 1975-. *Membershps:* Neurosciences Research Program, Massachussetts Institute of Technology and Rockefeller University, USA, Associate Foreign Member; European Molecular Biology Organization; European Neuroscience Association; American Association for Advancement of Science; French Association of Pharmacologists; American Society for Neurosciences. *Honours include:* Commander, French National Order of Merit for Scientific Research, 1976; Chevalier, French Legion of Honour for Scientific Research, 1980; Officer, Order of Arts and Letters, 1983; Several Honorary Lectureships and Prizes in USA, France and Canada. *Address:* Laboratoire de Neurobiologie Molecular Institute Pasteur, 75724 Paris Cedex 15, France.

CHANTLER, Cyril, b. 12 May 1939, Bury, England. Professor of Paediatric Nephrology. m. Shireen Saleh, 13 July 1963, 2 sons, 1 daughter. *Education:* BA, St Catherine's College, Cambridge, 1960; MB B Chir, Distinction in Physic, Guys Hospital, London, 1963; MA 1963, MD 1972, Cambridge; Member, Royal College of Physicians, London, 1967. *Appointments:* Residency training at various hospitals including: Guys Hospital, Royal Postgraduate Medical School and Hospital for Sick Children, Great Ormand Street, London, 1963-71;

Clinical Research Fellow, Medical Research Council, 1969-70; Medical Research Council Travelling Fellow, University of California, San Francisco, USA, 1971-72; Senior Lecturer and Consultant Paediatrician 1972, Professor of Paediatric Nephrology 1981, General Manager, Guys Hospital, London, England; Professor of Paediatric Nephrology, Evelina Children's Hospital, United Medical and Dental Schools of Guys and St Thomas Hospitals. *Memberships:* Member of Academic Board, British Paediatric Association; Past Member Registration Committee, European Dialysis and Transplant Association; Past Councillor, European Society for Paediatric Nephrology; Councillor, International Paediatric Nephrology Association. *Hobbies:* Squash; Reading; Opera. *Address:* Evelina Children's Hospital, Guys Hospital, London SE1 9RT, England.

CHAPMAN, Barry Lloyd, b. 6 June 1936, Tamworth, New South Wales, Australia. Staff Specialist in Cardiology. m. Dr Janice Margaret Bishop, 21 Jan. 1961, Sydney, New South Wales, 2 sons, 2 daughters. *Education;* MB BS, University of Sydney, 1960; Fellow, Royal Australasian College of Physicians, 1972. *Appointments:* Resident Medical Officer, 1960-62, Medical Registrar, 1963-66, Fellow in Medicine and Director of Coronary Care, 1967-70, Staff Physician, 1973-,. Royal Newcastle Hospital, Newcastle, New South Wales; Senior Registrar and Research Fellow, West Middlesex Hospital and Royal Postgraduate Medical school, Hammersmith Hosptial, London, England, 1971-73; Clinical Lecturer, Medicine, University of Newcastle, New South Wales, Australia, 1977-. *Memberships:* Cardiac Society of Asutralia and New Zealand; Fellow, Scientific Council, Internatioanl College of Angiology and Royal Society of Medicine; New York Academy of Sciences, USA. *Publications:* 'Effect of coronary care on myocardial infarct mortality', in 'British Heart Journal', 1979; author of numerous other papers on myocardial infarction, liver cirrhosis, peptic ulcers, coeliac disease, ploymyalgia rheumatica, medical audit and history of medicine. *Honours:* Efficiency Decoration, Australian Army, 1969. *Hobbies:* Statistics; Computers; Music; English literature; Writing poetry; Military History. *Address:* York Wing, Royal Newcastle Hospital, Newcastle, NSW 2300, Australia.

CHAPMAN, Charles Frederick, b. 15 Mar. 1929, Elmhurst, Illinois, USA. Co-ordinator, Editorial Office, LSU School of Medicine, New Orleans. m. Norma Kathleen Magaw, 20 June 1954, Oregon, Illinois, 3 daughters, 4 sons. *Education:* BS, Medical Journalism; PhB, Psychology. *Appointments:* Copy Editor, speicialty journals, American Medical Association, 1955; News Editor, 'JAMA', 1956-59, Chief Copy Editor, 'Jama', 1959-63, Special Projects Editor, Science Publications, 1963-73, Assistant Managing Editor, 1973-74, Managing Editor, 1974-75, Scientific Publications, American Medical Association. *Memberships:* American Medical Writers Association, President, Chicago Chapter, 1974-75; Academy of Political Science; Council of Biology Editors; Group on Public Affairs, Association of American Medical Colleges. *Publications:* "Writing for Communication in Science and Medicine", co-author, 1980; "Medical Dictionary for the Nonprofessional", 1984; "Risk Factors for Senility", Co-ordinating Editor, 1984; "Virology in Medicine", Co-ordinating Editor, 1986. *Honours:* President, Chicago Chapter, American Medical Writers Association, 1974; Nellie Westerman Prize, Honourable Mention with J. Rao, MD, American Federation for Clinical Research. *Hobbies:* Humour: Photography; Hydrogen as a Fuel; Psychological Study of Innovation. *Address:* 1400 Lowerline St., New Orleans, LA 70118, USA.

CHAPMAN, Christine M., b. 15 Oct. 1927, England. Director, Nursing Studies. *Education:* BSc. Honours, Sociology; MPhil, Sociology, Nursing. *Appointments:* Ward Sister; Nurse Tutor; Lecturer,

Management Studies. *Memberships:* Deputy Chairman, United Kingdom Central Council for Nursing Midwifery and Health Visiting; Deputy Chairman, Welsh National Board for Nursing, Midwifery and Health Visiting; Chairman, Board of Education, Royal College of Nursing; Chairman, Education & Training Committee, Royal College of Nursing; Moderator, Special Interest Session, ICN Congress, Mexico, 1973; Chairman, Council of Europe European Public Health Select Committed of Experts on Post Basic Training for Nurses, 1981-84; etc. *Publications:* Numerous articles in professional journals; (Books) "Medical Nursing", 1972, 9th edition 1977; "Sociology for Nurses", 1978, 2nd edition, 1982. *Honours:* OBE, 1984; SRN; SCM; RNT; FRCN. *Hobbies:* Embroidery; Gardening. *Address:* Dept. of Nursing Studies, University of Wales College of Medicine, Heath Park, Cardiff, Wales.

CHAPMAN, John Edmon, b. 5 July 1931, Springfield, Missouri, USA. Dean of Medicine; Professor of Pharmacology; Professor of Medical Administration and Chair, Vanderbilt University. m. Judy Jean Cox, 9 Mar. 1968, Nashville, Tennessee. *Education:* BSc, Education; BSc, Biology and Chemistry; MD; Certificate of Pharmacology, 1962. *Appointments:* assistant Professor; Associate Professor; Assistant Dean; Associate Dean; University of Kansas School of Medicine, 1960-67; Associate Dean, 1967; Acting Dean, 1971-72; Acting Vice-Chancellor, 1972-74; Dean of Medicine, 1975-; Vanderbilt University School of Medicine. *Memberships:* Association of American Medical Colleges; American Medical Assocition, Section on Medical Schools; American Scoiety of Pharmacology and Therapeutics; American College of Clinical Pharamcology, etc. *Publications:* Several. *Honours:* Recipient several honours and awards including Post-Doctoral Fellowship, 1962. *Address:* Vanderbilt University School of Medicine, 21st Avenue at Garland, Nashville, TN 37232, USA.

CHAPMAN, Loring, b. 4 Oct. 1929, Los Angeles, Californ ia, USA, University Professor, m. Toy Farrar, 14 June 1954, Lake Tahoe, California, 2 sons, 1 daughter. *Education:* PhD, University of Chicago, 1950. *Appointments:* Assistant Professor, Cornell University Medical College, 1955-61; Associate Professor, University of California, Los Angeles, 1961-65; Branch Chief, National Institutes of Health, 1966-67; Professor and Chair Behavioral Biology, 1967-80, Professor fo Psychiatry, 1980-, Professor of Physiology, Neurology, 1969-80, Uiversity of California, Davis; Director of Research, Fairview Hospital, 1965-66; Clinical Professor of Paediatrics, Georgetown University Medical school, 1966-67; Visiting Professor, University Sao Paulo, Brazil, 1959, 1977; Visiting Professor Anatomy, University College, London, England, 1969-70; Visiting Professor Exptl Pathology, University of Florence, Italy, 1979-80. *Memberships:* American Physiological Society; American Psychological Association; Society Neurosciences. *Publications:* "Pain and Suffering" 3 volumes, 1967; "Head and Brain" 3 volumes, 1971; "The Eye"(with E Dunlap), 1981. *Honours:* Wilson Prize, 1958; Public Health Service Career Award, 1962; Commonwealth Award, 1970; Fogarty Senior Fellow, 1979-80. *Hobbies:* Sailing; Music. *Address:* Department of Psychiatry, University of California, School of Medicine, Davis, CA 95616, USA.

CHAPMAN, Warren, Howe, b. 30 Oct. 1925, Chicago, Illinois, USA, Professor of Urology, University of Washington, m. Barbara Brueggeman, 16 Sep. 1950, Chicago, 3 sons, 2 daughters. *Education:* BS, Massachusetts Institute of Technology, 1946; MD, University of Chicago, 1952. *Appointments:* Internship, St Lukes Hospital, Chicago, 1952-53; Residency in Urology, 1953-56, Instructor in Urology, 1956-57, University of Chicago. *Memberships:* AMA; AUA; Western Section, AUA; American Association of Cancer Research; Society

University Urologists; Canadian Urological Association. *Publications:* Author of 3 books, 1967-79; Contributor of articles, 1956-85. *Hobby:* Sailig. *Address:* Department of Urology, RL-10, University of Washington, Seattle, WA 98195, USA.

CHAPNICK, Paul, b 21 Mar. 1938, Toronto, Canada. Oral & Maxillofacial Surgeon, Private Practice; Associate, Faculty of Dentistry, University of Toronto. m. Joyce Leslie Peiser, 27 June 1965, New York, USA, 2 sons, 1 daughter. *Education:* DDS, University of Toronto; Diploma, Oral Surgery, Graduate School of Medicine, Boston Unviersity, USA; Inern, Harlem Hospital New York, 1964; Senior Chief Resident, Doctors Hospital, Toronto, 1965; FRCD (C). *Appointments:* Chief, Oral Surgery, Mount Sinai Hospital, Toronto, 1972-81; Chief, Dentistry, Northwestern Hospital, Toronto 1970-80; Lecturer, School of Dental Hygiene, University of Toronto; Lecturer, George Brown College, Toronto. *Memberships:* Past President: North Toronto Dental Society & Ontario Society of Oral Surgeons; Past President Elect, Alpha Omega Dental Fraternity, Academy of Dentistry, Toronto; Ontario Society of Oral & Maxillofacial Surgery: Great Lakes Society of Oral & Maxillofacial Surgeons; Fellow, International Association of Oral Surgeons; Fellow, American Dental Society of Anesthesiology; many other professional organisations.*Publications:* Numerous articles in professional journals including: 'American Dental Association Journal of Oral Surgery'; 'Canadian Dental Association Journal'. *Honours:* Horace Wells Medal in Anaesthesia, University of Toronto, 1962; Fellowship, Oral Surgery, Royal College of Dentists, Canada, 1970; Diplomate, American Board of Oral & Maxillofacial Surgery, 1972; Fellowship, American Dental Society Anaesthesia, 1974. *Hobbies:* Art Collecting; Photography - Portraits; Jogging; Skiing; Sports; Travel; Lecturing. *Address:* 235 St Clair Ave West, Suite 102, Toronto M4V 1R4, Ontario, Canada.

CHARKATZ, Harry Marvin, b. 18 June 1940, Baltimore, Maryland, USA. Private Practice, General Psychiatry; Assistant Clinical Professor of Psychiatry. m. Susan J Busch, 14 June 1967, Chicago, Illinois, 2 sons, 1 daughter. *Education:* AA, George Washington University; BS, MD, Northwestern University Medical School; Psychiatry Residency, Northwestern University Medical School. *Appointments:* Instructor, Psychiatry, Northwestern University Medical School, currently, Private Practice in General Psychiatry; Assistant Clinical Professor of Psychiatry, University of Illinois. *Memberships:* Chicago and Illinois State Medical Societies; American Medical Association; Illinois Psychiatric Society; American Psychiatric Association. *Address:* 701 Lee Street, Suite 780, Des Plaines, IL 60016, USA.

CHARLES, Douglas G., b. 26 Jan. 1955, Brooklyn, New York, USA. Owner, Director Carillon Chiropractic Clinic, Houston. m. Lynda A. Mandy, 15 Dec. 1984, Houston. *Education:* BA, Psychology; DC; Graduate, Parker Chiropractic Research Foundation. *Memberships:* American, Texas Chiropractic Associations; ACA Councils of Roentgenology, Nutrition; Foundation for Chiropractic Education and Research; Texas Chiropractic College Alumni Association; Bay Area Chiropractic Society. *Honours:* Team Doctor, Delia Stewart Dance Company. *Hobbies:* Reading; Bicycling; Swimming; Camping. *Address:* 10001 Westheimer, Suite 2115, Houston, TX 77042, USA.

CHASE, Barbara Ann, b. 6 July, 1946, USA. Assistant Professor and Associate Dean. m. Russell K Kramp, 1 son, 2 daughters. *Education:* BA, Wellesley College, USA; MD, Tufts University School of Medicine. *Appointments:* Assistant Professor, Department of Medicine, and Department of Pediatrics, Associate Dean for students, Tufts University School of Medicine, Boston,

Massachussetts, USA. *Memberships:* Fellow, American Academy of Paediatrics; American Medical Association; Society for Medical Desicion Making; American Medical Womens' Association. *Publications:* Co-Author with S.G. Pauker 'Recurrent Endocarditis in a Patient with a Permanent Transvenous Pacemaker' in "Medical Decision Making", volume 2, No. 2, 1982; Co-Author 'How Many Blood cultures should be obtained in Suspected Bacterial Endocarditis? A Bayesian Approach' abstract in 'Clinical Research', 1982; Co-Author: 'Abdominal Pain, Atherosclerosis and Atrial Fibrillation' in "Medical Decision Making", volume 2, No. 3, 1982. *Hobby:* Travel. *Address:* Tufts University School of Medicine, 145 Harrison Avenue, Boston, MA 02111, USA.

CHASSAGNE, Daniel Jean Marie René, b. 9 July 1927, Trelissac, France. Head Radiation Dept.; Professor, Radiotherapy. m. Soulas Marie-Elizabeth, 11 June 1959, Hossegor, 3 sons, 1 daughter. *Education:* Interne Des, Hospitauk, 1952; MD, 1959; Board of Radiotherapy, 1957; Assistant, Hospitals of Paris, 1961; Residency, Memorial Hospital, Cornell University, USA, 1960. *Appointments:* Assistant, 1961, Chief of Service, 1970, Chief, Dept. of Radiation, 1983-, Institut Gustave-Roussy; Professor, Agrégé Faculty of Medicine, Paris, 1964; Professor, Sans Chaire, 1975; Professor, Radiotherapy, 1982; Co-ordinator, Oncology Teaching, 1985. *Memberships:* Societe Franc de Radiologie; Society Franc Gynaecologie; Societe Fr de Chirurgie Plastique; Bureau de L'E-S-T-R-O; Groupe European de Curietherapie; Editorial Board, Radiotherapy and Oncology; etc. *Publications:* "Precis De Curietherapie", 1964; "Brachytherapy", 1978; "Bracytherapy", 1985; "Risques De la Radiotherapie of Chimiotherapie", 1985. *Honours:* Premio Nazionale De Medicina, Naples, 1984. *Hobbies:* Gardening; Skiing. *Address:* Institut Gustave-Roussy, Villejuif, 94 805 Cedex, France.

CHATTERJEE, Purnendukumar, b. 30 May, 1912, Feni, India. Head of Hospital Medicine Department. m. Sova Banerjee, 30 June, 1944, Calcutta, India, 2 sons, 1 daughter. *Education:* MB, Calcutta University, India; FRCP, London, England; FCCP; FSMF (WB). *Appointments:* Visiting Physician, National Infirmary, Chest Department, Islamia Hospital, 1948-55; Chest Department, Calcutta National Medical College, 1949-55, Associate Professor, 1955-67, Professor of Medicine, 1967-72, Emeritus Professor, 1972-; Consultant to Hooghly District Tuberculosis Association Hospital and Chest Clinic, Serumpore, 1953-80; Extramural Lecturer in Medicine, Calcutta University College of Medicine, 1957-82; Head of Department of Medicine, B.B. Hospital, Behala, Calcutta, India -. *Memberships:* Association of Physicians of India; Cardiological Society of India; International Academy of Chest Physicians and Surgeons of the American College of Chest Physicians; Indian Medical Association; Calcutta Medical Club. *Publications:* "Sudden and Emergent Illness" (in Begalee language), 1979; "Diseases of Chest and Pulmonary Tuberculosis", 1982; "Diabetes Mellitus and its Treatment" (in Bengalee), under publication; 82 scientific articles in various professional journals; 7 presentations to professioanl conferences. *Honours:* Manash Memorial Lecture, IMA, Calcutta, 1963 and 1975; A.C. Ukil Oration, IMA, Bengal, 1974; Narendra Nath Memorial Oration, Calcutta Medical Club, 1982; Fellow of State Medical Faculty, West Bengal. *Address:* 59 Block D, New Alipore, Calcutta 700 053, India.

CHAVEZ, (Jr) Ignacio, b. 14 Nov. 1928, Mexico City, Mexico, Head of Teaching Division, Sub-director, Instituto Nacional de Cardiología 'Ignacio Chávez' de México. m. Ofelia de la Lama, 26 Nov. 1934, México City, 2 sons, 2 daughters. *Education:* MD. *Appointments:* Assistant Chief Resident, 1959-61, Chief Resident, 1961-65, Cardiologist in Clinical Services, 1959-73, Head of Teaching Division,

1965-73, Head of Clinical Service, 1973-, Sub-director, Teaching Division, 1983-, Instituto Nacional de Cardiología de México; Professor of Cardiology, National University of México, 1959-. *Memberships:* President, 1986-85, National Academy of Medicine; Secretary-Treasureer, 1972-76, Interamerican Society of Cardiology; Former President, Mexican Society of Cardiology; Member, Nominating Committee, International Society and Federation of Cardiology; Fellow, American College of Physicians; American College of Chest Physicians; American College of Cardiology. *Publications:* "Coma, Síncope, Shock", 1966, 1976; "Cardioneuzologia", 1973; "Cardiopatia isquémica por aterosclerosis Coronaria", 1979, 1982; "Hypertensión Arterial", 1985; Contributor of over 70 articles. *Honours:* Member of the Government of the National University of México. *Address:* Instituto Nacional de Cardiología 'Ignacio Chávez', Juan Badiano 1, Tlalpan, México 14080, DF México.

CHAVIN, Walter, b. 6 Dec. 1924, Professor. *Education:* BS, CCNY, 1946; MS, 1949, PhD, 1954, New York University. *Appointments:* Instructor, College of the City of New York, 1946-47; Researcher, Genetics lab., New York Aquarium, New York Zoological Society, 1947-49; Instructor, University of Arizona, Tucson, 1949-51; Research Specialist, American Museum Natural History, 1951-53; Professor, Wayne State University, Detroit, 1953-; Professor, Radiobiology, Wayne State University Medical School, 1975-80. *Memberships:* AAAS; American Association Cancer Research; American Physiological Society; American Society Cell Biology; American Society Zoology; Endocrine Society; Internatioanl Pigment Cell Society; Society Francaise d'Endocrinology; many other professional organisations. *Honours:* Fellow, American Association Advancement of Science, 1958; Senior Postdoctoral Fellow, NSF, 1960; Faculty Research Award,1968; Sigma Xi; US Coordinator for US-Japan International Meeting, 1970; WSU Faculty Alumni Service Award, 1975; Fellow, New York Academy of Sciences, 1976; Distinguished Graduate Faculty Award, 1979. *Hobbies:* Sailing; Scuba Diving; Photography; Computer Programming. *Address:* 368 Joliet Place, Detroit, MI 48207, USA.

CHEN, Fu-Min, b. 21 Apr. 1936, China. President Chung-Shan Hospital, Taipei. m. 15 Mar. 1964, Taipei, 1 son, 2 daughters. *Education:* MD, National Defence Medical Center, Taipei; Diploma, American Board of Obstetrics and Gynecology; FACOG; FACS: FICS. *Appointments:* Resident, Chief Resident and Fellow, Department of Obstetrics and Gynecology, Beth Israel Medical Center, New York, USA; Attending Obstetrician and Gynecologist, Chief, Department of Obstetrics and Gynecology, Tri-Service General Hospital Taipei, Taiwan; Physician in Charge, Maternity and Child Health Demonstration Project, Republic of China; Lecturer, Associate Professor, National Defence Medical Center, Taipei; Associate Professor, Youth and Children Welfare Department, University of the Chinese Culture; Superintendent, Chung-Shan Hospital, Taipei; currently President (and Director, Department of Obstetrics and Gynecology), Chung-Shan Hospital, Taipei. *Memberships:* China Medical Association; Association of Obstetrics and Gynecology of Republic of China; Surgical Association of Republic of China; American Fertility Society; International Federation of Gynecology and Obstetrics. Fellow: American College of Obstetricians and Gynecologists; American College of Surgeons; International College of Surgeons. *Publications:* Contributor, "The Challenge-The Effort", 1973; "Clinic Experience of Female Sterlization by One Finger Method", 1975; "Experience of Oxytocin Challenge Test in Monitoring High Rish Pregnancies", 1979; "Pregnancy Following Tubal Ligation", 1982. *Honours:* Honours Graduation, National Defence

Medical Center, 1962. *Hobbies:* Swimming; Bridge; Singing; Drawing; Reading. *Address:* 4-5 Lane 468, Tun-Hwa South Road, Taipei, Taiwan, Republic of China.

CHEN, Hsing, I. b. 28 July 1943, Tainan, Taiwan, Republic of China. Professor and Chairman, Department of Physiology and Biophysics. m. Julie S L Chang, 22 Feb. 1972, 3 daughters. *Education:* MD, National Defense Medical Center, Taipei, Taiwan, 1969; PHD, University of Mississippi School of Medicine, Mississippi, USA, 1976. *Appointments:* Assistant Investigator, Department of Medical Research, Veterans General Hospital, Republic of China, 1969-73; Visiting Assistant Professor, Department of Pharmacology, University of Texas Health Science Center, San Antonio, Texas, USA, 1975-76; Associate Professor 1976-80, Professor and Chairman, 1980-, Department of Physiology and Biophysics, National Defense Medical Center, Taipei, Taiwan, Republic of China. *Memberships:* Biomedical Engineering Society of Republic of China; Cardiology Society of Republic of China, Honorary Member and Editorial Board Member; Chinese Medical Association; Chinese Pharmacological Society; Chinese Physiological Society, Executive Committee and Editorial Board; Chinese Society of Aerospace Medicine; Formosan Medical Association: Neurological Society ofRepublic of China. *Publications:* "Cardiovascular Function", 1978; "The Great Stories Behind Medical Discoveries", 1976; "Brain Injury and the Cardiovascular System", 1977; contributor of 90 scientific papers, abstracts and reviews. *Honours:* 10 Outstanding Young Men Award, Republic of China, 1978: Award for Outstanding Publications in Military Medicine, 1980, 83; Academic Award, Ministry of National Education, 1984. *Hobbies:* Sports; Gardening; Reading. *Address:* Department of Physiology and Biophysics, National Defense Medical Center, PO Box 8244, Taipei, Taiwan, Republic of China.

CHEN, Ying C, b. 18 Nov. 1945, Taiwan. Chairman, Department of Obstetrics and Gynaecology, Palomar Memorial Hospital, Escondido, California, USA. m. Sue Lynn Chen, 20 June 1975, New York City, 1 son, 1 daughter. *Education:* MD, Taipei Medical College; Resident, in Medicine, Mackay Memorial Hospital, 1972-73; Resident in Obstetrics and Gynaecology, St. Joseph Hospital, Chicago, Illinois, 1974--78. *Appointments:* Attending Physician, Obstetrics and Gynaecology Department, St. Joseph Hospital, Chicago, 1978-79; Medical Staff, Obstetrics and Gynaecology Department, Palomar Memorial Hospital and Pomerado Hospital, California, 1978-; Chairman, Department of Obstetrics and Gynaecology, Palomar Memorial Hospital, Escondido, California, 1985-. *Memberships:* Fellow, American College of Obstetricians and Gynaecolgosits; American Medical Association; California Medical Association; San Diego County Medical Association; Diplomate, American Board of Obstetrics and Gynaecology. *Hobbies:* Tennis; Golf. *Address:* 735 E. Ohio Avenue, Suite 201, Escondido, Ca 92025, USA.

CHENG, Chia-chung, b. 5 May 1925, Tientsin, China. Professor of Pharmacology. m. Katherine Cheng, 30 May 1953, Texas, USA, 4 daughters. *Education:* BS, National University of Chekiang, China, 1948; MA 1951, PhD, Organic Chemistry, 1954, University of Texas, USA. *Appointments include:* Research Associate, New Mexico Highlands University 1954-57, Princeton University 1957-59; Head, Medicinal Chemistry Section, Midwest Research Institute, Kansas City, Missouri, 1959-78. *Memberships:* American Chemical Society; American Association for Cancer Research; Research Society of America; Sigma Xi. *Publications include:* Over 200 scientific publications in organic chemistry, medicinal chemistry, malaria research, cancer research. *Honours:* Science award, Council of Principal Sciences, Midwest Research Institute, 1973; Faculty Research Award, University of Kansas Medical Centre, 1983. *Hobby:* Photography. *Address:* Drug Development Laboratory, University of Kansas Medical Centre, Kansas City, KS 66103, USA.

CHENG, Leslie Yu-Lin, b. 27 May 1905, Soochow, China. Retired Professor. m. 3) Elissa Chin, 25 Oct. 1980, Taipei, Taiwan, 1 son and 5 daughters from previous marriages. *Education:* MD, Peking Union Medical College, 1928; Certification, American Board of Psychiatry and Neurology, Diplomat: General Psychiatry, 1957; General Neurology, 1959; Child Neurology, 1969. *Appointments:* Associate, Neurology and Psychiatry, Peking Union Medical College, 1933-36; Associate Professor, Neurology and Psychiatry, 1936-38, Professor and Chairman, 1938-46, National Central University Medical College; Professor, West China Union University, Cheloo University and Peking Union Medical College; Professor and Chairman, Lingnan University Medical College, 1946-47; Director, National Neuropsychiatric Institute, Ministry of Health, Nanking, 1947-49; Professor, National Defense Medical Center, National Taiwan University, 1949-50; Clinical Assistant Professor, University of Washington, Seattle, USA, 1958-59; Clinical Professor, Michigan State University, College of Human Medicine, 1972-73, 1975-78; Professor and Chairman, Undergraduate Psychiatry, Michigan State University, 1973-75; Visiting Professor, National Defense Medical Center, National Yang Ming Medical College, 1978-81. *Memberships Include;* Life Member, Chinese Medical Association; 1st President, Life Member, Chinese Mental Health Association; Life Fellow, American Psychiatric Association; Senior Fellow, American Academy of Neurolgy. *Publications:* In Chinese: "Neurology", 1948; "Clinical Neurology", 1983; "Dynamic Psychiatry", 1983; "Medical Aspect of Mental Retardation", forthcoming. *Hobby:* Music. *Address:* 9129 Bonny Brook, San Antonio, TX 78239, USA.

CHENG, Renato, b. 25 May 1946, Marikina, Philippines. Department Head, Lung Center of Philippines. m. Erlinda P Santos, 11 May 1976, Marikina, Philippines, 1 daugher. *Education:* Doctor of Medicine; Fellow, American College of Chest Physicians; Fellow, Philippines College of Chest Physicians. *Appointments:* Head, Cardiopulmonary Laboratory and Therapy, Quezon Institute Hospital; Head, Pulmonary Section, Delos Santos Medical Center; Head, Pulmonary Department, Waterous General Hospital; Head Department of Pulmonary Therapy and Medical Intensive Care Unit, Lung Center of the Philippines. *Memberships:* Philippine Academy of Family Physicians; Philippine Medical Association; Markina Valley Medical Association; International Academy of Chest Physicians and Surgeons. *Honour:* Fellow in Pulmonary Phsyiology and Critical Care Medicine, World Health Organisation, 1981-82. *Hobbies:* Painting; Reading. *Address:* Lung Center of the Philippines, Quezon Boulevard Extension, Diliman, Quezon City, Philippines.

CHERMOL, Brian Hamilton, b 24 June 1944, Pennsylvania, USA. m. Annie LaurieMahone, 8 Jan. 1983, San Antonio, Texas, 2 daughters. *Education: BA; MA; PhD; University of Missouri, 1972; University of South Carolina, 1977; Army Command and General Staff College, 1979. Appointments:* Psychologist, Veterans Administration; Company Commander, Medical Company, Kansas National Guard; Psychologist, US Army Reserve; Staff Psychologist, Walter Reed Army Medical Center; Chief, Department of Psychiatry, Army Aviation Medical Center; Chief, Behavioural Science Branch, Academy of Health Science; Deputy Chief, Medical Training Team, US Army in El Salvador; Commander, 142nd Medical BN (Panama).

Memberships: American Psychological Association; American Society of Clinical Hypnosis; Association for the Advancement of Psychology. *Publications:* "Behavioural Science Specialist Handbook", 1983; Author of 16 articles on battle fatigue, hypnosis, combat psychiatry and World War II psychiatry in professional and military journals: Author òf article in Spanish on psychological casualties. *Honoùrs:* Man of the Year, Columbus, Georgia, 1963; Phi Kappa Phi; Psi Chi. *Hobbies:* Sailing; Travel; Fishing; Jogging; Scuba diving. *Address:* Headquarters, 142nd Medical Battalion, Panama APO Miami 34004, USA.

CHERRY, James D., b. 10 June 1930, Summit, New Jersey, USA. Professor, Paediatrics; Chief, Paediatric Infactious Diseases. m. Jeanne Fischer, 3 sons, 1 daughter. *Education:* BS, Springfield College, 1953; MD, University of Vermont, 1957; MSc., Epidemiology, London School of Hygiene and Tropical Medicine, England, 1983; Internships, Residencies, various hospitals, 1957-60; Fellowship, Harvard Medical School and Thorndike Memorial Laboratory, Boston City Hospital, 1961-62. *Appointments:* Instructor, Paediatrics, University of Vermont College of Medicine, 1960-61; Assistant Professor, Paediatrics, Associate Attending Physician, Madison General Hospital, University of Wisconsin, 1963; Associate Professor, University of Wisconsin School of Medicine, 1966; Associate Professor, Paediatrics, 1967, Medical Staff, Cardinal Glennon, Memorial Hospital for Children, St Louis University Hospitals, 1967; Associate Professor, Microbiology, 1968, Professor, paediatrics, 1969, Vice-Chairman, Paediatrics, 1970, St Louis University School of Medicine; Professor, Paediatrics, 1973-, Acting Chairman, Paediatrics, 1977-79, University of California School of Medicine. *Memberships:* Member, numerous professional organisations. *Publications include:* Co Editor, "Textbook of Paediatric Infectious Diseases", 1981; Numerous book chapters in 'Textbook of Pediatric Infectious Diseases'; numerous articles in professional journals. *Honours:* John and Mary R. Markle Scholar in Academic Medicine, 1964; Alpha Omega Alpha, 1980; Fellowship, Milbank Memorial Fund, 1982-83; University of Vermont Distinguished Medical Alumnus, 1984. *Address:* Dept. of Paediatrics, Centre for Health Sciences, University of California at Los Angeles School of Medicine, Los Angeles, CA 90024, USA.

CHESS, Stephen John, b. 29 June 1914, West Virginia, USA. Chief Surgeon, Buenaventura Medical Clinic, Inc. m. Dorothy Anne Haasch, 21 Nov. 1940, Waukon, 3 sons, 2 daughters. *Education:* BS, MS, Neuroanatomy, Marquette University; MD, Medical College of Wisconsin; PhD, Surgery, University of Illinois; Fellowship, Surgery, Research & Educational Hospitals; Diplomate, American Board of Surgery; Diplomate, American Board Abdominal Surgery. *Appointments:* Assistant Chief Surgeon, Chicago, Milwaukee St. Paul & Pacific R.R. Wesley Memorial Hospital, Faculty, Northwestern University School of Medicine, 1948-49; Organized Buenaventura Medical Clinic, Inc., 1950; Staff Member, Ojai Valley Community Hospital; St John's Hospital, Oxnard; Chief of Staff, Ventura County Hospital, 1971; Chief of Staff, Community Memorial Hospital, 1973; Chief, Surgery, 1978; President, Ventura County Medical Society, 1975; President, Professional Standards Review Organisation; Medical Advisory Committee to So. California Hospital Association, 1975-; Board of Governors, California Medical Review Inc., 1985. *Publications:* Numerous articles in medical journals. *Honours:* Served in Medical Corps as Surgeon in Portable Surgical Hospital, Pacific Theatre of Operations, WW2, rank of Major; Awarded Bronze Star Medal, Okinawan Campaign. *Hobbies:* Gardening; Ranching. *Address:* 155 Lakewood Ave., Ventura, CA 93004, USA.

CHESTER, Charles John, b. 15 June 1953, Chicago,

Illinois, USA. Physician Administrator, Adult Services, De Paul Hospital. m. Sharon Carthew, 1 Oct. 1983, 1 son. *Education:* AB, cum laude, Harvard College, 1975; MD, Dartmouth Medical school, 1978; Psychiatric Residency, Tulane, 1978-82; Board Certified in Psychiatry, 1984. *Appointments:* Private Practice of General Psychiatry and Psychoanalysis, 1982-; Physician Administrator, Outpatient Services, De Paul Hospital. 1982-85; Medical Director, Jefferson Substance Abuse Clinic, 1983-; Clinical Assistant Professor, Tulane Medical School, 1984-. *Memberships:* American Medical Association; American Psychiatric Association; American Academy of Psychoanalysis; Louisiana Psychiatric Association; Tulane Psychoanalytic Medicine Society. *Honours:* Mead Johnson Fellowship, 1981; Laughlin Fellowship, 1981. *Hobbies:* Gourmet Dining; Volleyball. *Address:* 1040 Calhoun Street, New Orleans, LA 70118, USA.

CHEUNG, Mung Wa, b. 28 Sept. 1921, Hong Kong. Medical Practitioner. m. Chan Yuen Kau, 6 June 1948, New York, USA, 1 son, 2 daughters. *Education:* MB, BS, Hong Kong, 1946; Diploma of Paediatrics, New York University, USA, 1949; Licentiate of the American Board of Paediatrics, 1952. *Appointments:* Houseman, Kowloon Government Hospital, Hong Kong, 1946, Medical Officer, 1947; Intern, University of Southern California, Los Angeles, USA, 1948; Fellow in Paediatrics, New York University, 1949-51, Instructor, 1951-55; Medical Director, and Paediatrician, Kwong Wai Siu Free Hospital, Singapore, 1955-64. *Memberships:* Singapore Paediatric Society. *Publications include:* Articles in professional journals including: 'Minimal Requirement of Infants for Certain Amino Acids' in 'American Journal of Diseases of Children', (co-author), 1953; 'Observations on Amino Acid Metabolism in Kwashiorkor' in 'Journal of Tropical Paediatrics', (co-author), 1955; 'Phenylalanine Requirement of the Normal Infant' in 'Journal of Nutrition', (co-author), 1955; 'Observations on Amino Acid Metabolism in the Pluricarencial Syndrome' in 'Boletin Medico del Hosptial Infantil, Mexico', (co-author), 1956; 'Renal Concentration Mechanism in Sickle-Cell Anaemia' in 'Journal of Laboratory and Clinical Medicine', (co-author), 1957. *Honour:* Recipient of the Public Service Silver Star, Singapore Government, 1964. *Hobby:* Tennis. *Address:* 9 Bukit Tunggal Road, Singapore 1130.

CHIANG, Benjamin N, b. 8 July 1929, China. Professor and Chairman, Department of Medicine. m. Annie Y H Shia, 23 Aug. 1958, Taipei, 2 daughters. *Education:* MD; FRCP; FACC; FCCP. *Appointments:* Chief, Division of Cardiology, 1964-79, Chairman, Department of Medicine, 1980-, Veterans General Hospital, Taipei; Profesor of Medicine, National Defense Medical Center, Taipei, 1970-79; Professor and Chairman, Department of Medicine, National Yang-Ming Medical College, Taipei, 1980-. *Memberships:* Fellow: Royal College of Physicians, Glasgow, Scotland; American College of Cardiology; American College of Chest Physicians; Chinese Medical Association. *Publications:* Contributor over 110 original papers including works to: 'Annals of Internal Medicine'; 'Circulation'; 'Progress in Cardiology'; 'The Lancet'. *Honours:* One of 10 Most Outstanding Youths, Republic of China, 1966; 1 of 10 Most Outstanding Veterans, Republic of China, 1979. *Hobbies:* Music; Arts. *Address:* 128-9B Sec 4 Chung-Hsiao E Road, Taipei 10646, Taiwan, Republic of China.

CHIETI, Anna Maria, b. 13 May, 1954, Casamassima, Italy. Psychologist. *Education:* Degree in Clinical Psychology, Italy. *Appointment:* Psychologist, Hospital 'Miulli', Acquaviva, Italy. *Memberships:* On list of experts attached to Appeal Court in Bari; List of experts in Hypnotherapy and Autogenic training. *Publications:* Conference Papers: 'Profili di Personalita in Paxienti Emicranici', 1985; 'Profilo di

Personalita in Soggetti Affetti da Enicrania e da Cefalea a Grappolo'; 1985; 'Personality Profiles in Migraine Patients', 1985. *Hobbies:* Music; Theatre; Literature. *Address:* Via Vecchia S Michele 22, 70010 Casamassima, Bari, Italy.

CHIGAROS, Helen Mae Tuttle, b. 22 May 1944, Kankakee, Illinois, USA. Instructor, Kankakee Community College, Illinois; Staff Development Coordinator, Americana Healthcare Center. m. William Lee Chigaros, 3 Nov. 1973, Kankakee, 2 daughters. *Education:* Nursing Diploma (RN), Illinois Masonic School of Nursing, Chicago, 1965; Certificate, Institute of Physical and Rehabilitative Medicine, Peoria, Illinois, 1976; BS, Health, College of St. Francis, Joliet, Illinois, 1978. *Appointments:* Staff Nurse to Assistant Director of Nursing, Riverside Medical Center, Kankakee, 1965-69, 1970-74; Staff Nurse, Disneyland, Anaheim, California, 1969; Staff Nurse to Inservice Director, Fontainbleu Nursing Center, Kankakee, 1974-80. *Memberships:* Association of Rehabilitative Nurses. *Publication:* Author and Presenter of Seminar, Restorative Nursing: the Geriatric Client. *Honour:* One of first registered nurses to be Certified by Exam in Rehabilitation in the USA. *Hobbies:* Travel; Golf; Fishing; Crewel Embroidery. *Address:* 555 South May Avenue, Kankakee, IL 60901, USA.

CHIN, Edward Jin-Hung, b. 3 Sept. 1930, Hong Kong. Obstetrician; Gynecologist. m. Mary Pao-Ven Lo, 2 Jan. 1968, Hong Kong, 1 son, 1 daughter. *Education:* BSc; MD; CM; Fellow, American College of Obstetricians and Gynecologists; Diplomates of American Boards of Obstetricians and Gynecologists and of Abdominal Surgeons. *Appointments Include:* Rotating Intern, St Michael Hospital, University of Toronto, Canada, 1959-60. Resident: Medicine and Surgery, Queen Mary Hsopital, Hong Kong, 1961; Obstetrics and Gynecology, Kapiolani Hospital, Hawaii, 1961-62; Kaiser Hospital, Oakland, California, USA, 1962-64; Childrens Hospital, San Francisco, 1964-65; Surgery, East Toronto General Hospitals, Canada, 1965-66. Medical Officer, Tung Wah Group of Hospitals, Hon Kong, 1966-68; Physician in Charge, Emergency Department, Fairmont Hospital 1968-69; Active Medical Staff, Merritt-Peralta-Providence Hospitals, Oakland, California, USA, 1971-, Memorial Hospital, San Leandro, 1984-. *Memberships:* Medical Councils of Canada, Newfoundland and Hong Kong;College of Physicians and Surgeons, Ontario; Commonwealth List of Register, General Medical Council, England; Affiliate, Royal Society of Medicine; American Medical Association; California Medical Association; International College of Surgeons; American College of Obstetricians and Gynecologists; American Society of Abdominal Surgeons; Association of American Gynecological Laparoscopists; Physicians Opinion Network; Society for Continuing Medical Education. *Hobbies:* Swimming; Travel; Table tennis; Bowling; Fishing; Chess. *Address:* 2820 Summit Street, Suite 7, Oakland, CA 94609, USA

CHIPHANGWI, John David, b. 17 Dec. 1936, Mulanje, Malawi. Chief Specialist, Obstetrics and Gynaecology. m. Stella, 13 Aug. 1974, Blantyre, 2 sons. *Education:* MB ChB, Aberdeen University, Scotland, 1966; DObs, 1971, MMed, 1973, Makerere University; MRCOG, London, England, 1973. *Appointments:* Junior Medical Officer, 1966-67; District Medical Officer, Dedza, 1967-69; Acting Medical superintendent, Zomba. 1969-70; Post Graduate Training, Makerere University, Uganda and St Mary's Hospital, London, England, 1970-73; Specialist, Obstetrics and Gynaecology, 1973-75, Senior Specialist, 1975-79, Principal Specialist, 1979-83, Chief Specialist, 1983-, Queen Elizabeth Central Hospital, Blantyre. *Memberships:* Past Chairman, Medical Association of Malawi; Royal College of Obstetricians and Gynaecologists; Chairman, Health Sciences Research Committee,

Malawi; National Research Council of Malawi; Committee, African Organisation for Research and training in Cancer; Fellow, Association of surgeons of East Africa; University Council, University of Malawi. *Publications:* 'Obstetric Problems in a Developing Country' in 'Medical Quarterly', 1983; 'Female Genital TB' in 'Journal of Obstetrics and Gynaecology of East and Central Africa'; 'Cervical Carcinoma in Malawi', in 'Cancer', 1981; contribution to Transactions of Royal Society of Tropical Medicine and Hygiene, 1982. *Hobbies:* Sports and Sport administration (Chairman, Olympic and Commonwealth Games Associations of Malawi). *Address:* Queen Elizabeth Central Hospital, Box 95, Blantyre, Malawi.

CHIPPERFIELD, Barbara, b. 30 May 1936, Bradford, Yorkshire, England. University Lecturer in Biochemistry. m. John Robert Chipperfield, 14 Oct. 1961, Cambridge, 2 daughters. *Education:* BA Natural Sciences (Part II Biochemistry) 1958, MA 1962, PhD (Department of Radiotherapeutics) 1962, Newnham College, Cambridge. *Appointments:* Scientific Assistant to Regius Professor of Physic, University of Cambridge, 1961-65; Research Assistant in Department of Botany 1965-66, Demonstrator 1966-80, Lecturer 1980-, Department of Biochemistry, University of Hull; Part-time Course Tutor and Tutor-Counsellor 1971-, Assistant Staff Tutor 1976-81, The Open University. *Publications include:* Contributions to: 'Nature'; 'International Journal of Cancer'; 'Clinica Chimica Acta'; 'Lancet'; 'American Heart Journal'. *Honours:* State Scholarship, 1954; Open Scholarship, Newnham College, Cambridge, 1955. *Hobbies:* Gardening; Knitting. *Address:* 284 Cottingham Road, Hull HU6 8QA, England.

CHISHOLM, Geoffrey Duncan, b. 30 Sep. 1931, New Zealand. Professor, Surgery, University of Edinburgh; Consultant Urological Surgeon, Western General Hospital, Edinburgh, Scotland. m. Angela J. Holden, 9 June 1962, Radlett, 2 sons. *Education:* MB, ChB, 1955, ChM, 1965, St Andrews; FRCS Edinburgh, 1959; FRCS England, 1960. *Appointments:* Research Fellow, John Hopkins, Baltimore, USA, 1961-62; Senior Urological Registrar, 1962-67, Consultant Urologist, Surgeon, 1967-74, Hammersmith Hospital, London; Senior Lecturer, St Peter's Hospital & Institute of Urology, 1972-77; Senior Urological Surgeon, Hamersmith Hospital, London, 1974-77; Professor, Surgery, University of Edinburgh, 1977-. *Memberships:* Royal College of Surgeons of Edinburgh, Council 1984-89; British Prostate Group, Chairman, 1975-80; European Society of Urological Surgeons, Vice President, 1985-86. *Publications:* "Postgraduate Teaching in Urology", 1980; "Scientific Foundations of Urology II", 1982; Senior Editor, "Clinical Practice in Urology"; various articles in professional journals. *Honours:* Ravenal Lecture, Charleston, USA, 1980; Kee Lecturer, Sydney, 1983; Honeyman Gillespie Lecture, 1985; Francisco Diaz Medal, 1985; Ballanger Memorial Lecture, 1986, Pybus Lecture, 1986. *Hobbies:* Medical Writing; Oenology. *Address:* Dept. of Surgery/Urology, Medical School, Teviot Place, Edinburgh EH8 9AG, Scotland.

CHITWOOD, Walter Randolph, Junior, b. 16 Jan. 1946, Pulaski, Virginia, USA. Professor and Chief, Division of Cardiac Surgery, East Carolina University, School of Medicine. m. Tamara S Whitt, 27 July 1968, Wytheville, Virginia, 1 daughter, 1 son. *Education:* BS, Hampden-Sydney College, Virginia, 1968; MD, University of Virginia, Charlottesville, 1974. *Appointments:* Textile Chemist, E.I. DuPont de Nemours & Company Incorporated, Wilmington, Delaware, 1968-70; Biology Instructor, Hampden-Sydney College, Virginia, 1970-71; Surgical Resident, Duke University Medical Center, Durham, North Carolina, 1974-84. *Memberships:* American Heart Association; American Association for History of Medicine; American Medical Association; International Society for Heart Transplantation; Association for Academic Surgery; North Carolina Medical Society; Pitt County Medical Society; Sigma Xi. *Publications:* Author of numerous articles in professional journals; Book Reviews; Author and co-author of several books and textbook chapters including: Myasthenia Gravis: Basic Surgery: A Textbook for Medical Students, Editor D C Sabiston Jr., 1985. *Honours:* Aplha Omega Alpha. National Institutes of Health Cardiovascular Training Grant, 1976-78; North Carolina Heart Association Research Grant, 1977-78; John Horsley Research Prize, 1978. *Hobbies:* Photography; Antiquarian Book Collecting; Amateur Radio. *Address:* Division of Cardiac Surgery, East Carolina University, School of Medicine, Greenville, NC 27834, USA.

CHIU, John Francis Sung-Fun, b. 21 Aug. 1954, Hong Kong. Private Practice, Family Medicine. *Memberships:* College of Physicians & Surgeons, Alberta & British Columbia; Alberta Medical Association; College of Family Physicians of Canada. *Hobbies:* Skiing; Sailing; Windsurfing; Motor Racing. *Address:* 5706-19A Avenue, Edmonton, Alberta, Canada.

CHIU, Shiau-Yen, b. 21 Mar. 1937, HongChow, Republic of China, Professor, m. L C Fu, 14 June 1964, Minneapolis, Minnesota, USA. *Education:* MB, 1955-62; ECFMG, 1962; PhD, Graduate School, Department of Microbiology, School of Medicine, University of Minnesota, USA, 1966; MD. *Appointments:* Research Fellow, Caltech, Calif, USA; Lecturer, Associate Professor, Department Head, Departmentn of Bacteriology, College of Medicine, National Taiwan Unviersity, Republic of China. *Memberships:* Chinese Society of Immunology, Taipei; Formosan Medical Association; Chinese Society of Microbiology; Chinese Society of Agricultural Chemistry. *Publications:* "Immunology", 2nd Edition, 1978; "Manual of immunology", 1973; "Principle of Virology", 1975; "Clinical Virology", 1974; "Immune Response during Hyperimmunization I-XVIII", 1973-81. *Honours:* The Women of the Year, Republic of China, 1976; Appreciation Award, the Philippine Society for Microbiology and Infectious Diseases. *Hobbies:* Photographs; Videos. *Address:* Rm 743, 7th Floor, Building of Basic Medical Sciences, 1/Jen-Ai Road, Taipei 100, Republic of China.

CHIUTEN, Delia F., b. 24 Apr. 1943, Philippines. Assistant Internist; Assistant Professor of Medicine. *Education:* BS, University of San Carlos, Philippines, 1966; MD, University of the Philippines, 1971. *Appointments:* NCI, Oncology Consultant, Veterans Administration, Washington DC, USA, 1978; Faculty Associate, Instructor, Developmental Therapeutics, MS Anderson Hospital & Tumour Institute, University of Texas System Cancer Centre, 1979-80; Consultant, Officer of Health Resources Opportunity Programme, Public Health Service, HEW, 1981-82; Assistant Internist, of Texas System Cancer Centre, 1980-. *Memberships:* American Society of Clinical Oncology; American Association for Cancer Research; International Association for Study of Lung Cancer; American Federation for Cancer Research; American Association for the Advancement of Science; American Society for Internal Medicine; American Society for Microbiology; Texas Society for Internal Medicine. *Publicaitons:* Articles in professional journals; book chapters etc. *Hobbies:* Symphony; Ballet; Skiing; Tennis; Jogging. *Address:* 3414 Broadmead St., Houston, TX 77025, USA.

CHLUMECKY, Jiri, b. 4 July 1935, Brno, Czechoslovakia. Director, MSB Animal Centre. m. Vera Sommerova, 21 July 1962, Brno. *Education:* MSc Animal Science, University of Agriculture, Brno, 1959; PhD Animal Genetics, ibid, 1965. *Appointments:* Distric Agriculturalist, State Animal Breeding Station, Jevicko, Czechoslovakia;

Chairman, Department of Laboratory Animal Care, Staff Scientist, Institute of Biophysics, Czechoslovak Academy of Sciences, Brno; Assistant Professor, Department of Animal Genetics, University of Agricultural Brno; Postdoctoral Fellow, Department of Animal Science, University of Alberta, Canada; Research Assistant, Department of Food Science, University of Alberta; Associate Director, Laboratory Animal Breeding Centre, Acting Director, Director, Health Sciences Animal Centre, University of Alberta, Edmonton, Canada. *Memberships:* Canadian & American Assoiations for Laboratory Animal Science; Laboratory Animal Science Association of Great Britain; Committee for Preservation of Genetic Stocks of Laboratory Animals of International Committee on Laboratory Animal Science; Canadian Council on Animal Care, Assessment Panel Member. *Publcations:* 24 publications, mainly on new strain of hairless laboratory mouse, 1965-68; ''Effect of Cold Environments with Energy Exchange of Young Beef Cattle', 1970; 'Guide to the Care & Use of Experimental Animals' volume 2, chapters on laboratory mouse & rat, 1984. *Hobbies:* Riding; Swimming; Game-ranching; Travel. *Address:* MSB Animal Centre, University of Alberta, Edmonton, Alberta, T6G 2H7, Canada.

CHMIELEWSKI, Henryk Mikolaj, b. 10 Sept. 1934, Myszyniec, Poland. Head of Neurological Department, Military Medical Academy. m. Wanda Serafin, 27 June, 1956, 1 son, 1 daughter. *Education:* MD, 1966; Associate Professor, 1974; Professor, 1984. *Appointments:* Physician, 1957-1960; Assistant in Neurology Clinic, Warsaw, Poland, 1960-62; Head of Department of Neurology in Ladek Sanatorium, 1962-70; Senior Assistant, Lodz Neurolgoy Clinic, 1970-73, Head of Neurolgoy Clinic, 1974-present. *Memberships:* General Secretary of the Polish Association of Neurology in Warsaw; President of Regional Department of the Polish Association of Neurolgoy in Lodz; Polish Acadmey of Sciences, Neurochemistry and Pain-Pathophysiology. *Pubications:* 132 articles published in Polish medical periodicals and journals. *Honour:* 1st degree Award for article ''Vertigo Epidemica'', 1975. *Hobby:* Gun collecting. *Address:* Zgierska 142/19, Lodz, Poland.

CHO, Jae Yone, b. 26 Dec. 1936, Korea. Psychiatric Centre Clinical Director. m. Song Sik Chun, 18 Nov. 1964, Korea, 1 son, 2 daughters. *Education:* MD, Catholic Medical College, Seoul, Korea, 1962; Rotating Internship, Detroit MaComb Hospital Association, USA, 1966-67; Psychiatric Resident, Traverse City State Hospital, Michigan, USA, 1967-70. *Appointments:* Staff Psychiatrist, Traverse City State Hospital, Michigan, USA, 1970-75; Private practice in Psychiatry, 1976-; Consultant Psychiatrist, St Mary's Hospital, St Luke's Hospital, Saginaw, Michigan; Attending Psychiatrist, Saginaw General Hospital, Saginaw; currrently, Clinical Director, White Pine Psychiatric Center, Saginaw. *Memberships:* American Medical Association; American Psychiatric Association; American Social Psychiatric Association; Michigan Psychiatric Society; Michigan State and Saginaw County Medical Societies. *Hobbies:* Black belt marshal arts; Tennis; Swimming. *Address:* 5856 Bircherest, Saginaw, MI 48603, USA.

CHODAK, Gerald Walter, b. 13 Mar. 1947, New York, USA, Associate Professor of Surgery. *Education:* BA, University of Rochester, 1965-69; MA, 1969-71; MD, 1971-75, State University of New York, Buffalo, NY. *Appointments:* Assistant Resident, Surgery, Bufffalo General Hospital, 1975-76; Clinical Lecturer, Surgery, SUNY School of Medicine, Buffalo, NY, 1975-76; Assistant Resident, Surgery, UCLA Medical Centre, 1976-77; Clinical Lecturer, Surgery, UCLA School of Medicine, 1976-77; Assistant Resident, Surgery/Urology, Peter Bent Brigham Hospital Medical Centre, Boston, Mass, 1977-79; Research Associate, Surgery, 1978-79, Research Associate, Department of Surgery, 1981-82, Children's Hospital Medical Centre, Boston, Mass; Senior, Chief Resident in Urology, 1979-81, Research Associate, Section of Urology, 1981-82, University of Chicago; Assistant Professor, 1982-85, Associate Professor 1985, Urology, University of Chicago. *Memberships:* American Urological Association. *Publications:* Author of numerous articles including: 'Wound infections and systemic Antibiotic Prophylaxis in Gynaecologic Surgery: A Review', (with M E Plaut), 1978; 'Angiogenesis Assay of Benign and Malignant Mammalian Urothelium', (with I Summerhays, J Folkman), 1980; 'A Technique for Continuous Infusion into the Mouse Bladder', (with E N Guillery), 1984; 'Detection of Angiogenesis Activity in Malignant Bladder Tissue and Cells;, (with I Summerhays), 1984; 'Partial Characterization of a Cell Motility Factor from Human Urine', (with M Klagsbrun, Y W Shing), 1985; Author of reviews, abstracts and presentations to meetings. *Honours include:* NIH National Cancer Scientist Trainee Fellowship, 1969-73; 1971-73; 3rd Prize, Chicago Urological Society, 1980; 1st Prize, Amrican Urological Association, 1980; American Urological Association Scholar, 1981-83; University of Chicago Gould Foundation Faculty Scholar, 1983-84; Chicago Community Trust Award, 1983-84. *Address:* The University of Chicago, Box 403, 5841 Maryland Avenue, Chicago, IL 60637, USA.

CHODYNICKI, Stanislaw, b. 18 Apr. 1933, Terespol nBug, Poland. Professor of Otolaryngology. m. Bozena Cechmistro, 21 Oct. 1967, Bialystok, 2 sons, 1 daughter. *Education:* MD, Medical Academy, Bialystok. *Appointments:* Assistant 1954-60, Senior Assistant 1960-63, Lecturer 1963-69, Department of Histology & Embryology; Lecturer, 1963-69, Assistant Professor 1971-76, Head of Department 1977-, Professor 1984-, Department of Laryngology, Medical Academy. *Membership:* Polish Otolaryngological Society. *Publcations:* Various articles in field. *Hobbies:* Jogging; Photography. *Address:* ul. Parkowa 14 m 70, 15-224 Bialystok, Poland.

CHOJANCKI, Tadeusz Jan, b. 4 Jan. 1932, Lagiewniki, Poland. m. Jolanta Pacynko, 12 Feb. 1955, 1 daughter. *Education:* MD, 1955, PhD, 1961, Medical School, Warsaw; Docent, Polish Academy of Sciences, 1966; Assistant Professor, 1972, Professor, 1978, Polish Academy of Sciences. *Appointments:* Research Assistant, Medical School, Warsaw, 1955-58; Research Assistant, Docent, Professor, Institute of Biochemistry and Biophysics, Polish Academy of Sciences, 1958-85; Research Fellow, University of Birmingham, England, 1961, 1964, 1965; Professor, Institute of Mother and Child, 1971-80; Deputy Secretary, Professor, Division of Biological Sciences, 1982-86, Polish Academy of Sciences. *Publications:* Articles in professional journals. *Honours:* 5 Awards for Experimental Studies on Galactosaemia and Polyprenoid Lipids, Polish Biochemical Society, Polish Academy of Sciences, 1968, 1972, 1973, 1976, 1977. *Hobbies:* Botany; Skiing; Hunting. *Address:* Institute of Biochemistry & Biophysics, Polish Academy of Sciences, Rakowiecka 36, 02-532 Warsaw, Poland.

CHOLNOKY, Peter Johnm, b. 8 Sept. 1932, Pécs, Hungary. Professor of Paediatrics. m. Sophia László, 15 Aug. 1961, Pécs, Hungary, 3 daughters. *Education:* MD; PhD; Specialist in Paediatrics, Laboratory Medicine and Human Genetics. *Appointments:* University Department of Paediatrics, Pécs, Hungary, 1956-69; University Department of Paediatrics, Groningen, The Netherlands, 1964-65; Professor of Paediatrics, Teaching Hospital, Szombathely, Hungary. *Memberships:* European Society for Paediatric Nephrology; Société des Pédiatres de Langues Latines; Advisory Board of the National Institute of Child Health, Hungary; Presidium of Hungarian

Society of Paediatricians. *Publications:* 49 publications in the field of paediatrics. *Honours:* Excellent Physician Award of the Ministry of Health, Hungary, 1977; Bokay Memorial Medal, 1978; Hungarian Red Cross Gold Medal, 1980. *Hobbies:* Gardening; Swimming. *Address:* Markusovszky Hospital, Szombathely, POB 143, H-9701, Hungary.

CHONG, Beng Hock, b. 29 Oct. 1945, Ipoh, Malaysia. Consultant Haematologist. m. Saw Gaik Lim, 2 sons. *Education:* MBBs, University of Malaya, 1966-72; Member, Royal College of Physicians, UK, 1976; Fellow, Royal College of Pathologists of Australasia; Fellow, Royal Australian College of Physicians; PhD, University of Sydney, Australia, 1981-83. *Appointments:* Intern, Medical Registrar/Resident, University Hospital, Kuala Lumpur, Malaysia, 1972-76; Haematology Registrar, Southern General Hospital, Glasgow, Scotland, 1976-77; Paediatrics Haematology Registrar, Prince of Wales Hospital, Sydney, Australia, 1977-78; Haematology Registrar 1980-81, Consultant Haematologist 1985-, St George Hospital, Sydney; Research Fellow, Westmead Medical Centre, Sydney, 1981-83; Consultant Haematologist, Royal Melbourne Hospital, Melbourne, 1983-85. *Memberships:* Haematology Society of Australia; Australian Society of Medical Research. *Publications include:* 'Heparin-induced thrombocytopenia: Effects of heparin platelet antibody on platelets', (with CS Crace and MC Rosenberg), 1981; 'Heparin-induced thrombocytopenia: Association of thrombotic complication with a heparin-dependent IgG antibody which induced platelet aggregation, release and thromboxane synthesis', (with WR Pitney and PA Castaldi), 1982; 'Quinidine-induced thrombocytopenia and leukopenia: Demonstration and characterisation of distinct antiplatelet and antileukocyte antibodies', (with MV Berndt, J Kouts and PA Castaldi), 1983; 'Drug-induced thrombocytopenia: A study of the mechanisms of thrombocytopenia caused by heparin and quinidine', PhD thesis, 1985. *Honours:* Postgraduate Medical Research Scholarship, National Health and Medical Research Council of Australia. *Hobbies:* Painting; Sports; Tennis; Badminton. *Address:* 31 Atkinson Street, Arncliffe, New South Wales, Australia.

CHONG, Mary Druzillea, b. 8 Mar. 1930, Fairview, Oklahoma, USA. Director of Nursing. m. Nguk Choy Chong, 24 Aug. 1952, Tustin, California (divorced) 1968), 1 son, 1 daughter. *Education:* AA, El Camino Junior College, 1950; Graduate Nurse, Los Angeles General Hospital School of Nursing, 1983; PHN, BSN, California State University, Los Angeles. *Appointments:* Staff Nurse, Los Angeles County General Hospital, 1957-58; Staff Nurse, 1958-69, Head Nurse, 1969-72, Harbor General Hospital; Instructor, LVN Program, YWCA Job Corps, 1972-74; MICN Emergency Room, Victor Valley Hospital, 1974-79; Director of Nursing, San Vicente Hospital, 1980-82; Director of Nursing, Upjohn Healthcare Service, 1982-85; Director of Nursing, Bear Valley Community Hospital Home Health Agency, 1986-. *Memberships:* National Association Female Executives; American Association University Women; California State University at Los Angeles Alumni Association; Internatioanl Platform Association. *Address:* P.O. Box 697, Lucerne Valley, CA 92356, USA.

CHONG TONG MUN, b. 7 Nov. 1924, Singapore, Republic of Singapore. Medical Practitioner, General Practice; Clinical Teacher in General Practice. m. Tan Geok Cheng, 31 Dec. 1953, 2 sons, 3 daughters. *Education:* MB BS, University of Malaya in Singapore, 1957; MD, University of Singapore, 1970. *Appointments:* General Medical Practitioner, 1958-, specialising in hypnotherapy, psychotherapy, 1962-; Clinical Teacher in General Practice, University of Singapore and now National University of Singapore, 1974-; Research Committee, College of General Practitioners, Singapore, 1976-. *Memberships:* Fellow, Society for Clinical and Experimental Hypnosis; Honorary Fellow, American Society of Clinical Hypnosis; Singapore Medical Association; College of General Practitioners, Founding Member; Association of Private Medical Practitioners of Singapore; Founding Member, President, Singapore Society for Clinical Hypnosis; International Society of Hypnosis. *Publications:* 'Singapore Medical Journal'; 'Medical Journal of Malaya'; 'British Medical Journal'; 'Journal of Singapore Pediatric Society'; 'American Journal of Clinical Hypnosis'; 'British Journal of Medical Hypnosis'; 'British Journal of Clinical Hypnosis'; 'Journal of the Society of Private Practice'; 'Nursing Journal of Singapore'; various others,. "The Truth About Hypnosis", book, 1975. MD Thesis published, University of Singapore, 1970. *Hobbies:* Fishing; Photography. *Address:* 86 Frankel Avenue, Singapore 1545, Republic of Singapore.

CHOO, Teck Chuan, b. 9 Feb. 1932, Singapore. Senior Partner, Specialist Group, Dental practitioners. m. Margaret, 16 Apr. 1958, Singapore, 3 daughters. *Education:* BDS, Eastman Dental Hospital, University of London, UK; FDSRCS (Eng); FDSRC (Edin); D.Orth RCS (Eng); FICD; FADI. Specialities, Orthodontics, crown & bridgework. *Appointments:* Demonstrator, Assistant Lecturer, Lecturer in Orthodontics, currently part-time tutor, University of Singapore. *Memberships:* Singapore Dental Association; Federation Denataire Internationale. *Hobby:* Golf. *Address:* 0539 Tanglin Shopping Centre, Singapore 1024.

CHOPRA, Hari Dass, b. 14 June 1939, India. Senior Consultant Psychiatrist. m. Narinder Chopra, 13 Dec. 1964, India, 2 sons, 2 daughters. *Education:* DPM, 1966; MD, 1968; Fellow, Royal Australian and New Zealand College of Psychiatrists; Member, Royal College of Psychiatrists, London; MBBS, Punjab, India, 1962. *Appointments:* Medical Officer/Lecturer, Central Institute of Psychiatry, India, 1966-69; Psychiatrist, Consultant Psychiatrist, Lakeside Hospital, Autralia, 1969-72; 1974-76; Assistant Professor, Psychiatry, Postgraduate Institute of Medical Education & Research, Chandgarh, India, 1972-73; Consultant Psychiatrist, Senior Consultant Psychiatrist, Royal Park Hospital, Melbourne, Australia, 1982. *Memberships:* Corresponding Fellow, American Psychiatirc Association; Fellow, Indian Psychiatric Society. *Publications:* "A Socioeconomic Status and Manic Depressive Psychosis - A study based on Hospital Cases", 'Indian Journal of Psychiatry', 1970; "Family Psychiatric Morbidity, Parental Separation and Socioeconomic Status in Cases of Mania", 'British Journal of Psychiatry', 1975. *Honour:* Best DPM Postgraduate, 1966. *Hobbies:* Travel; Indoor Sports. *Address:* Footscray Psychiatric Hospital, 160 Gordon St., Footscray, Victoria 3011, Australia.

CHOPRA, Inder Jit, b. 15 Dec. 1939, India. Professor of Medicine. m. Usha, 15 Oct. 1966, New Delhi, 1 son, 2 daughters. *Education:* MBBS 1961, MD Internal Medicine 1965, All India Institute of Medical Sciences, New Delhi. *Appointments:* Intern and Resident in Medicine 1962-65, Registrar in Medicine 1966-69, All India Institute of Medical Sciences, New Delhi; Research Officer, Indian Council of Medical Research, 1966; Resident in Medicine, Queen's Medical Center, Honolulu, Hawaii, USA, 1967-68; Fellow in Endocrinology, Harbor-Univeristy of California at Los Angeles Medical Center, Torrance, Los Angeles, California, 1968-71; Assistant Professor 1968-71, Associate Professor 1974-78, Professor 1978-, School of Medicine, University of California at Los Angeles. *Memberships:* American Society for Clinical Investigation; Association of Amercian Physicians; Endocrine Society; American Thyroid Association; American Federation for Clinical Research; Western Asssociation of Physicians; Sigma Xi Fellow, American College of

Physicians. *Publications include:* "Triiodothyronines in Health and Disease"; "Endocrines and Liver", (co-edior); Over 170 research papers and reviews. *Honours:* Research Career Development Award, NIH, 1972; Van Meter Prize, American Thyroid Association, 1977; Ernst Oppenheimer Award, Endocrine Society of USA, 1980. *Address:* Department of Medicine, University of California at Los Angeles Center for the Health Sciences, Los Angeles, CA 90024, USA.

CHOUDHURY, Subhabrata Roy, b. 31 Aug. 1937, Howrah, India. University Professor. m. Madhuri Bose, 14 Apr. 1968, Calcutta, 1 son, 1 daughter. *Education:* MBBS, Calcutta; Fellow Royal College of Surgeons (Edinburgh); MSc, PhD, Manchester University. *Appointments:* Lecturer in Anatomy, Senior Lecturer in Anatomy, Manchester University; Visiting Associate Professor of Anatomy, Iowa University, USA; Professor of Anatomy, Chairman of Anatomy, Kuwait University. *Memberships:* Fellow, Royal College of Surgeons (Edinburgh); Anatomical Society of Great Britain and Ireland; American Anatomical Society; Society for Neuroscience; Japanese Teratological Society; Australian Biochemical Society. *Publications:* Over 25 major publications in international medical journals. *Honours:* Certificate of honours in Physiology, Pharamacology, Chemistry, Medicine, Obstetrics and Gynaecology; Teacher of the Year. *Hobbies:* Computer programming; Listening to Oriental Classical Music. *Address:* Department of Anatomy, Faculty of Medicine, Kuwait University, PO Box 24923 Safat, Kuwait, Arabia.

CHOW, Khuen Wai, b. 6 Dec. 1925, Medan, Indonesia. Director, Hospital Radiology Department. m. Jessie Wong, 8 Dec. 1956, Singapore, 1 son, 1 daughter. *Education:* MB, BS, Malaya, 1954; DMRD (RCP&S), London, England, 1959; MRCP, Glasgow, Scotland, 1962; AM, Singapore, 1962; FRCP, Glasgow, Scotland, 1972; Fellow of American College of Cardiology, 1973; Fellow of Royal College of Radiologists, 1976. *Appointments include:* Medical Officer, Ministry of Health, Singapore, 1955-59; Registrar, Singapore General Hospital, 1959-61, Senior Registrar, 1961-62, Consultant, 1962-68, Head Department of Diagnostic Radiology, 1968-84; Clinical Associate Professor, Radiology, National University of Singapore. *Memberships include:* Singapore Medical Council; Asian-Oceanic Society of Radiologist; President, 1979-83, Master 1982-83, 1983-84, Academy of Medicine, Singapore. Board of Postgraduate Medical Studies, National University of Singapore, 1981-84; Radiation Protection Advisory Committee; Medical Research Committee, Ministry of Health; Ethics Committee, Singapore Medical Association; Chairman of Scientific and other sub-committees of several Asian-Pacific Congresses on Cardiology, Gastroenterology, Endoscopy and Radiology. *Honour:* Public Administration Gold Medal, Singapore. *Hobbies:* Reading; Golf. *Address:* Department of Radiology, Mount Elizabeth Hospital, 3 Mount Elizabeth, Singapore 0922, Republic of Singapore.

CHOWDHURY, A.H.M. Towhidul Anowar, b. 11 Oct. 1937, Dhaka, Bangladesh. Professor, Obstetrics, Institute of Postgraduate Medicine, Dhaka. m. Farida Khatun, 26 June 1966, 3 daughters. *Education:* MB, BS, Dhaka University, 1960; FRCS, Royal College of Surgeons, Edinburgh, 1964; MRCOG, Royal College of Obstetricians & Gynaecologists, London, 1965; FCPS, Bangladesh College of Physicians and Surgeons, Dhaka, 1972; FRCOG, Royal College of Obstetricians & Gynaecologists, London, 1978. *Appointments:* Assistant Surgeons, Dhaka Medical College Hospital, & Mitford Hospital, Dhaka, 1961-66; Associate Professor, Obstetrics & Gynaecology, Sir Salimullah Medical College, Dhaka, and Chittagong Medical College, 1966-72; Professor, Chittagong Medical College, 1972;

Professor, Obstetrics & Gynaecology, Institute of Postgraduate Medicine and Research, Dhaka, 1972-. *Memberships:* Bangladesh Medical Association; Vice President, Obstetrical & Gynaecological Society, Bangladesh; Honorary Secretary, college of Physicians & Surgeons, Bangladesh; Medical Research Council, Banladesh; Ethical Review Committee, International Centre for Diarrhoel Diseases; Executive Committee Member, Fertility Research Programme. *Publications:* 15 articles in professional journals; "Special Supplement on Mortality and Morbidity due to Pregnancy & Childbirth"; "Manual for the Management of Infertility at Peripheral Hospitals in Bangladesh". *Honours:* Honours, Obstetrics & Gynaecology, MB., BS Examination; ATCO Gold Medal, MB, BS, Examination, Dhaka University. *Hobbies:* Reading; Travel. *Address:* 165/A Shantinagar, Dhaka 17, Bangladesh.

CHOWDHURY, A K M Nazimunddowla, b. 30 Sep. 1929, Professor, Doctor of Psychiatry. m. Mahbuba Chowdhury, 6 Sep. 1953, Dhaka, 2 sons, 2 daughters. *Education:* MB BS, Dhaka Medical College, Bangladesh, 1946-51; DPM, Institute of Psychiatry, University of London, England, 1957-60; Fellowship, Royal College of Psychiatrists, England, 1980. *Appointments:* Assistant Surgeon, Clincial Assistant, Clical Pathologist, Dhaka Medical College, 1952-57; Medical Superintendent, Mental Hospital, Pabna, 1960-71; Associate Professor 1971-74, Professor of Psychiatry 1974-, Institute of Postgraudate Medicine & Research, Dhaka; Director, P G Hospital, Dhaka, 1981-83. *Memberships:* Panel of Experts Committee on Mental Health, World Health Organisation; Vice-President, College of Physicians & Surgeons, Bangladesh; President, Bangladesh Association of Psychiatrists; Vice-President, Foundation of Mental Health, Bangladesh. *Publications:* Various articles on Mental Health in Bangladesh & East Pakistan. *Hobbies:* Reading; Travel; Indoor Games. *Address:* Institute of Postgraduate Medicine, & Research, Dhaka, Bangladesh.

CHOY, Daniel Shu Jen, b. 29 May 1926, China. Research Scientist, Investigative Cardiology Laboratory, St. Luke's-Roosevelt Hospital Center. 1 son, 1 daughter. *Education:* BA, Columbia College, USA, 1944; MD, Columbia University College of Physicians and Surgeons, 1949. *Appointments:* Intern, Meadowbrook Hospital; Resident, Goldwater Hospital; Resident, Columbia Presbyterian Medical Center; Research Scientist, Aeromedical Laboratory, USAF; Chief, Tumor Service, Fench Hospital; Chief, Tumor Clinic, City Hospital; Attending Physician, Lenox Hill Hospital; Associate Attending Physician, St. Luke's Hospital; Director. American Board of Laser Surgery. *Memberships:* FACP, 1964; Fellow, Explorers Club, 1970; New York Academy of Science; American College of Physicians; American Society of Clinical Oncology; American Society of Lasers for Surgery and Medicine. *Publications:* Contributor to professional journals; Chapters in books including: 'Lasers in Cardiovascular Disease' in "Recent Advances in Cardiovascular Surgery" (in press); Books include: "A New Local Treatment for Burns", US Armed Forces, 1953; Invited Papers; Reports. *Hobbies:* Yachting; Skiing; Scuba Diving; Soaring; Music; Photography; Travel; Exploration. *Address:* 170 E. 77 Street, New York, NY 10021, USA.

CRICHTON-BROWN, Sir Robert, KCMG 1980, KT 1972, CBE 1970, TD, b. 23 Aug. 1919, Melbourne, Australia. m. Norah Isabelle, 1941, 1 son, 1 daughter. *Education:* Sydney Grammar School. War Service, 1939-45, BEF; Major Royal Artillery and Gen. Staff, France, Iceland, India, Burma (despatches twice). *Appointments:* Executive Chairman: Rothmans International plc (1985-); Chairman: Edward Lumley Ltd (1983-); Security Life Assurances Ltd; Security & General Insurance Co. Ltd; NEI Pacific Ltd (1961-85); Rothmans of Pall Mall

(Australia) Ltd (1981-85); Commercial Banking Co. of Sydney Ltd (1981-85); Commercial & General Acceptance Ltd (1977-82); Westham Dredging Co. Pty. Ltd. (1975-85); Vice Chariman: National Australia Bank Ltd (1982-85); Custom Credit Corporation (1982-85) Director: Daily Mail & General Trust Ltd (UK) (1979-); Rothmans of Pall Mall (Australia) Ltd (1971-81); Commercial Banking Co. of Sydney Ltd. (1970-82); Royal Prince Alfred Hospital, 1970-84; Fed. Pres., Institute of Directors in Australia, 1967-80 (Chairman, NSW Branch, 1965-80; Hon. Life Member). *Memberships:* President, Medical Foundation, University of Sydney; Hon. Life Governor, Australian Postgraduate Federation in Medicine; Australian Nat. Chairman United World Colleges (Australia) Trust (1984-85); Federal Exec. and Federal Hon. Treasurer of The Liberal Party of Australia (1973-85); Advisory Board, Girl Guides Association of Australia, 1973-85; International Forum and Panel, Duke of Edinburgh's Award (Nat. Co-ordinator, Duke of Edinburgh's Award Scheme in Australia, 1979-84); National Councillor, Scout Association of Australia, 1980-85; Advisory Board, Salvation Army (1973-85); Committee Member: Royal Australian College of Physicians, 1973-85; Underwriting Member of Lloyd's, 1946-; Council of Imperial Society of Knights Bachelor (UK); Vice Chairman, Pacific Reg., Imperial Society of Knights Bachelor. *Honours:* Member, Australia's Winning Admiral's Cup Team (BALANDRA), UK, 1967, Winner, Sydney-Hobart Yacht Race (Pacha), 1970. *Address:* 15 Hill Street, London W1X 7FB, England.

CHRIST, Jacob, b. 10 Feb 1926, Switzerland. Psychiatrist. m. Jane Lippincott Smith, 6 Jan 1979, Atlanta, Georgia, USA, 2 sons 2 daughters from previous marriage. *Education:* MD, University of Amsterdam, Netherlands, 1952; MD, University of Zurich, Switzerland, 1952. *Appointments:* Assistant/-Associate Psychiatrist/Director of Outpatient Service, McLean Hospital, Belmont, Massachusetts, 1956-70; Assistant/Instructor/Clinical Associate, Harvard University Medical school, Boston; Associate Professor, Emory Medical School, Atlanta, Georgia, 1970-79; Psychiatrist-in-Chief, Outpatient Services, Baselland, Switzerland. *Memberships:* Graduate of American Boards of Neurology and Psychiatry, 1959; Swiss Speciality Certificate, 1980; Fellow, American Psychiatric Association; Fellow, American Group Psychotherapy Association; Boston and Atlanta Psychoanalytic Societies. *Publications:* 'Outpatient Treatment of Adolescents and their Families" chapter 23 in "American Handbook of Psychaitry" 2nd edition 1973 edited by Ariete S; "Contemporary Marriage; Structrue, Dynbamics and Therapy" co-editor with H Grunebaum, 1976. *Address:* Externe Psychiatrische Dienste Baselland, Goldbrunnenstrasse 14, 4410 Liestal, Switzerland.

CHRISTIAN, Melville, b. 13 May 1932, Madras, India. Chief, Schieffelin Leprosy Research and Training Centre. m. Thankamma Varughese, 5 Jan. 1967, Jamshedpur, 2 sons. *Education:* MBBS, Madras University; DTM & H, Calcutta University; Diploma in Epidemiology, Post-graduate Medical School, Prague. *Appointments:* Deputy Assistant Director General, Central Bureau of Health Intelligence, DGHS, Government of India, New Delhi, 1970-71; Medical Superintendent, Central Leprosy Teaching and Research Institute, Chingleput, 1972-76; Officer-in -Charge, Assessment of National Leprosy Control Programme, Indian Council of Medical Research, 1976-78; Chief, Branch of Epidemiology and Leprosy Control, Schieffelin Leprosy Research and Training Centre, Karagiri, North Arcot District, Tamil Nadu 1979-. *Memberships:* International Leprosy Association; Indian Association of Leprologists; Christian Medical Association of India. *Publications:* Associated as memebr with the 'WHO Study Group on Chemotherapy of Leprosy for Control Programmes',' WHO Technical Report Series,'1982;' WHO Study Group on Epidemiology

of Leprosy in Relation to Control' TRS 716, 1983. *Honours:* Councillor for Asia and the Far East, International Leprosy Association; Contributing Editor, International Journal of Leprosy; Member, THELEP Steering Committee, WHO HQ, Geneva, 1983-. *Hobbies:* Reading; Music; Gardening. *Address:* Schieffelin Leprosy Research and Training Centre, Karigiri-632 106, North Arcot District, Tamil Nadu, India.

CHRISTIANSEN, John, b. 17 Nov. 1934, Denmark. Chief Surgeon. m. Inge Brydensholt, 5 Sep. 1959, Tranekaer, 2 daughters. *Education:* MD, 1961, PhD, 1972, University of Copenhagen. *Appointments:* Surgical Resident of Copenhagen Hospitals; Senior Resident, Department of Surgery D, Glostrup Hospital, 1970-72; Senior Resident, Department of Surgery A, Bispedjerg Hospital, Copenhagen, 1972-76; Chief Surgeon, Deartment of Surgery D, Glostrup Hospital, University of Copenhagen, 1976-. *Memberships:* The American Society of Colon and Rectal Surgeons; Society of Surgery of the Alimentary ract; Collegium Internationale Chirurgiae Digestivae. *Publications:* "Postoperative Cardiac Risk" 1972; Papers on colo-rectal surgery and gastric physiology. *Address:* Bregentved Alle 24, 2820 Gentofte, Copenhagen, Denmark.

CHRISTOPHER, Michael Robert Anthony, b. 5 Oct. 1939, London, England. Lecturer in Oral Biology and Oral Surgery; Consultant Oral Surgeon; Specialist Private Practice. m. Brenda Amy, 9 Nov. 1973, Durban, Republic of South Africa, 4 sons, 1 daughter. *Education:* MDSc, Queensland, Australia, 1981; BDS, Rand, 1962; Fellow in Dental Surgery, Royal College of Surgeons, Edinburgh, Scotland, 1977, England, 1977. *Appointments* Registrar, Department of Restorative Dentistry, School of Dental Surgery, 1964, Lecturer, Department of Anatomy, 1976, Clinical Lecturer, Department of Oral Surgery, 1977, Royal Dental Hospital, London, England; Lecturer, Department of Oral Surgery, Dental School, University of Queensland, Australia, 1978-; Consultant Oral Surgeon, Tweed Heads Hospital, New South Wales, current; Specialist Private Practice, Gold Coast. *Memberhips:* Australian Dental Association; Asutralian and New Zealand Association of Oral and Maxillofacial Surgeons; British Association of Oral and Maxillofacial Surgeons; International Association of Oral andMaxillofacial Surgeons. *Publications:* Thesis: "Radionuclide Assessment of Healing of Mandibular Fractures", 1981. *Hobbies:* Photography; Tennis. *Address:* Suite 10, Evandale Medical Chambers, 45 Blundell Road, Surfers Paradise, Gold Coast, Queensland 4217, Australia.

CHROM, Vivian Hawawiah, b. 3 Jan. 1931, London, England. Family Physician. m. Eleanor Fitch, 1 July 1959, Toronto, Ontario, Canada, 1 son, 1 daughter. *Education:* BSc, McGill University, Canada, 1954, MD, University of Toronto, 1958; Certification, College of Family Practice of Canada (CCFP), 1973. *Appointments include:* Delegate, Council, Ontario Medical Association, 1970-; President, Medical staff, Scarborough General Hospital, 1974-75; Inspector, Medical Review Committee, College of Physicians & Surgeons of Ontario, 1974-77; Chief, Department of Family Practice, Scarborough General Hospital, 1977-83. *Memberships:* Ontario & Canadian Medical associations; College of Family Practice of Canada; Israel Medical association. *Hobbies:* Bridge; Golf; Music. *Address:* 2901 Lawrence Avenue East, no.201, Scarborough, Ontario, Canada M1P 2T4.

CHRUSCIEL, Tadeusz Leslaw, b. 30 Jan. 1926, Lwów, Poland. Professor, Chairman. m. Maria Sliz, 11 Apr. 1955, Zakopane, 2 sons, 1 daughter. *Education:* BM, 1950, MD, 1951, Candidate of Medical Science, 1956; Docent, 1958; Professor, 1964. *Appointments:* Research Assistant, Pharmacology, Medical School, KraKkw, 1948-55,

Senior Research Worker, 1952-56, Polish Academy of Sciences; Professor, Pharmacology, Silesian Medical School, Zabrze, 1956-68; Consultant, Clinical Pharmacology, Katowice, 1965-68; Rockefeller Fellow, Pharmacology, Oxford, England, 1959-60; Senior Medical Officer, WHO, Geneva, 1968-75; International Narcotics Control Board, Vienna, 1977-81; Deputy Director, Drug Research & Control Institute, Warsaw, 1975-85; Professor, Chairman, Clincial and Social Pharmacology, Postgraduate Medical School, Warsaw, 1985-. *Memberships:* Polish Medical Society; Polish Pharmacological Society; Royal Society of Medicine, Affiliate Member; Collegium Internationae Psychoneuropharmacologicum; International Society for Biochemical Pharmacology, Polish Section; Society for Prevention of Drug Abuse, Vice President; WHO Expert, Advisory Panel on Drug Dependence and Alcoholism, 1976-. *Publications:* Contributing Author: "Physiology of Animals", 1964, "Treatment of Iatrogenic Diseases", 1977, "Drug Dependence", 1978, "Dependence Liability of 'non-narcotic' Drugs", with H. Isbell, 1970; "Clinical Pharmacology", 1985; "Pharmacologic. a. Therapeutic Classification of Drugs", 1982; several articles on drug dependence, psycho pharmacology and clincal pharmacology in professional journals. *Honours:* Exemplary Health Service Medal, 1953; Silesian Health Service Silver Medal 1965; Warsaw Health Service Gold Medal, 1982; Polonia Restituta Cross, 1983; 40th Anniversary Medal, 1985; Awards for Research Accomplished, 1966, 1982. *Hobbies:* Travel; Philately; Books; Swimming. *Address:* Dzika 6 m. 284, PL-00 172 Warsaw, Poland.

CHU, Ann Maria, b. Hong Kong. Professor and Chairman. *Education:* I. Sc; MD. *Appointments:* Assistant Radiologist, Massachussetts General Hospital, Boston; Visting Radiologist, Gray Laboratory, Mount Vernon Hospital, England; Visiting Scientist TND, Radiobiological Institute, Netherlands; Director, Residency Training Program, Tufts-New England Medical Centre, Boston; Director, Clinical Radiotherpy, University of Louisville, Kentucky; Chairperson, Department of Radiation Oncology, Temple University Hospital, Philadelphia. *Memberships:* American Medical Association; American College of Radiology; American Society of Therapautic Radiologists; British Institute of Radiology; Radiation Research Society; American Association of Cancer Education; American Association for the Advancement of Science; American Association of Physicists in Medicine; Society of Chairman of Academic Radiology Departments; New York Academy of Sciences; several other organizations. *Publications:* Contributor of articles and papers to professional journals, etc, including: Co-author, 'Patterns of local regional recurrance and results in state I and II breast cancer treated by radiation foillowing limited surgery An update', 'American Journal of Clinical Oncology', 1984; Co-Author, 'Dyserminonoma of the ovary', 'Journal of Surgical oncology', 1984. *Hobbies:* Travel; Chamber Music; Art; Anthropology. *Address:* Radiation Oncology Department, Temple University Hospital, 3401 North Broad Street, Philadelphia, PA 19140, USA.

CHU, David Z.J., b. 4 Apr. 1948, China. Assistant Professor of Surgery. m. Bettina Brownstein, 1 daughter. *Education:* BS, Physics; MD, Medicine. *Appointments:* Intern, University of California, San Diego; Resident, Surgery, University of California, David; Fellow, Surgical Oncology, M.D.Anderson Hospital, University of Texas; Faculty associate, ibid; Assistant Proffessor in Surgery, University of Arkansas for Medical Sciences. Candidate for Academic Surgery. American College of Surgeons; Southwest Oncology Group; Association for Academic Surgery. *Honour:* Career development award, Clinical Oncology, American Cancer Society, 1985-88. *Hobbies:* Sierra Club; Soccer. *Address:* Department of Surgery, University of Arkansas for Medical Sciences, 4301 W.Markham Street, Slot 520, Little Rock, AR 72205, USA.

CHU, Dong S. Associate Professor of Medicine. m. 26 Nov 1964, 1 son, 2 daughters. *Education:* MD, 1960; MS, 1963; Diplomate, American Board of Physical Medicine and Rehabilitation, 1970. *Appointments:* Attending Physician, New York University Medical Center, USA; Associate Professor, School of Medicine, New York University. *Memberships:* American Medical Association; American Academy of Physical Medicine and Rehabilitation; New York State Medical Society. *Publications* include: "Peripheral Nerve Injuries"; Approximately 20 scientific publications. *Honours* inlcude: Many from American Medical Association. *Hobbies* include: Gardening; Swimming. *Address:* 400 East 34th Street, New York, NY 10016, USA.

CHUA, Philip (Felipe) S., Cardiac Surgeon, Head, 4 Man Open-Heart Team, b. 26 May 1936, Manila, Philippines. m. Farida Isip-Chua, MD 21 June 1959, Quezon City, 5 children. *Education:* AA, University of the Philippines, 1956; MD, Far Eastern University, Manila, 1961. *Appointments:* Intern, Ravenswood Hospital, Chicago, 1963; Resident General Surgery, Vascular Surgery, 1965-69, Thoracic-Cardiovascular Surgery, 1969-72, VA Hospital, Hines, Illinois; Pediatric CV Surgery Rotation, Childrens Memorial Hospital, Chicago, 1971; Denton A. Cooley fellow, Cardiovascular Surgery, Texas Heart Institute, Houston, 1972. *Memberships:* Fellow, American College of Chest Physicians, Royal Society of Medicine, International College of Surgeons, Philippine College of Surgeons, Indiana Thoracic Society, American College of Angiology, Charles B Puestow Surgical Society, Denton A. Cooley Cardiovascular Surgical Society, International Society of Heart Transplantation; Past President: Beta Sigma, Student PMA, Philippine Medical Association in Chicago, Charles B Puestow Surgical Society, Denton Cooley Cardiovascular Surgical Society, American Heart Association, Society of Philippine Surgeons in America Inc.; Member, American Medical Association; Indiana State Medical Association; Lake County Medical Society. *Hospital Positions:* Chief of Staff, President, St Mary Medical Centre, 1981-82; St Anthony Medical Centre, 1982-84; The Methodist Hospitals Inc., 1986-86; Board Trustee, Lake County Medical Society 1983- , FEU Medical Alumni Foundation, 1986- ; Founder Editor, The Medical Student, FEU; Editor, PMAC Bulletin; Editor, The Philippine Surgeon; Contributing Editor, The APPPA News; Founder, The Mended Hearts Club, Northwest Indiana, 1982; Founder, President, Chairman of the Board, Comprehensive Healthcare Utilization Alternative, inc., 1984; *Honours and Awards:* Most Outstanding Intern, FEUCSO, 1961; Philippine Delegate, IFMSA, Jerusalem, Israel, 1961; Grantee, Asia Foundation, 1961; Many other awards. *Address:* 1830 Mirmar Road, Munster, IN 46321, USA.

CHUJYO, Nobuyuki, b. 1 Nov. 1923, Tokyo, Japan. Professor and Chairman of University Department of Pharmacology. m. Yayoi Yamamoto, 10 Jan. 1952, 1 son, 1 daughter. *Education:* Bachelor of Veterinary Medicine, The Imperial University of Tokyo, 1946; PhD, The University of Tokyo, 1957. *Appointments:* Associate Professor, The University of Chiba School of Pharmaceutical Science, 1955-62; Fulbright Exhange Professor, University Medical Center, 1960-62; Professor and Chairman, Toho University School of Pharamceutical Science, 1962-. *Memberships:* The Japanese Pharmacological Society; The Japanese Society of Smooth Muscle Research; The Society for Research in Asiatic Music. *Publications:* "Pharmacology", 1960; "Modern Pharmacology", 1969; "Physiology and Pharmacology of Smooth Muscle", 1974; "Laboratory Technique in Pharmacology", 1981;

"Bioassay", 1983. *Hobbys:* Licensed teacher of Koto and Sangen, Japanese string instruments. *Address:* 2-6-14 Moto-Ohkubo, Narashino, Chiba, 275 Japan.

CHUNG, Jin-Tack, b. 12 June 1926, Jinju, Korea. Private Practice; Chief, Department of Thoracic Surgery. m. Jae-Sook Lee, 30 Jan. 1953, Seoul, 2 sons, 1 daughter. *Education:* MD, College of Medicine, Seoul National University, 1950. *Appointments:* Surgeon, Chief of Department of Thoracic Surgery, 36th Army Hospital, 1955-68; Private Practice, Chung's Surgical Clinic. *Memberships:* International Academy of Chest Physicians and Surgeons; Thoracic-Cardiovascular Surgical Society, Korea. *Publications:* "Thoracomediastinal plication", 1962; "Extraperiosteal plombage for pulmonary tuberculosis", 1968; "Resection of Pulmonary Tuberculosis", 1972. *Hobbies:* Tennis; Listening to classical music. *Address:* 49-5 Sanho-dong, Masan City, 610 Korea.

CHUNG, Tai-Ho, b. 2 Dec. 1932, Taegu, Korea. Professor, Biomedical Research Laboratory, Dept. of Biochemistry. m. Hyuk-Ja Kwon, 20 Apr. 1958, Taegu, 1 son, 1 daughter. *Education:* MD, 1958, MS, 1962, PhD, 1968, Kyungpook National University. *Appointments:* Research Fellow, Biochemistry, George Washington University School of Medicine, USA, 1966-67; Research Fellow, Internal Medicine, VA Hospital and Medical College of Virginia, USA, 1971-73; Professor, Biochemistry, 1977-; Visiting Professor, New York State University, Buffalo, USA, 1975-76; Visiting Professor, Rigs Hospital of Copenhagen University, 1979; Director, Biomedical Research Laboratory, Kyunpook National University. *Memberships:* Korean Biochemical Society, President, 1984; Korean Cancer Society; Korean Immunology Society; New York Academy of Science. *Publications:* "Gastric Cancer", 1984; "Immunology for Medical Students", 1985; "Cancer Immunotherapy with Tubercin-3", (article), 1983; "Gastric Cancer in Korea", (article), 1986. *Honour:* Award, 20 years service in Kyungpook National University, 1984. *Hobbies:* Collection of old Oriental Medical Books (Acupuncture). *Address:* 3-210, Dong-Suh Apartment, 1450 Dae-Shin-Dong, Taegu, Korea 630.

CHURCH, William Kimball, b. 13 Dec. 1926, Spokane, Washington, USA. Osteopathic Physician, Private Practice. m. Rosemary Elaine Heath, 9 Aug. 1947, Kitchener, 3 sons, 1 daughter. *Education:* BSc., Northwest Missouri State University; DO, Kirksville College. *Appointments:* President, Canadian Osteopathic Association; Secretary, Ontario Osteopathic Association. *Memberships:* American Osteopthic Association; Canadian Osteopathic Association; Ontario Osteopathic Associaiton; American Academy of Osteopathy; Cranial Academy of Osteopathy. *Publications:* Articles in health Magazine; 'Journal of the Ameriucan Osteopathic Association'; 'D.O. Magazine'. *Honours:* Co-Founder, Big Brothers of Orillia and District Service Award. *Hobbies:* Painting; Sailing; Skiing; Swimming; Wood Carving; Stained Glass. *Address:* 85 Neywash St., Orillia, Ontario, Canada L3V 1X4.

CHUSED, Judith Fingert, b. 20 Aug. 1941, St Louis, Missouri, USA. Vice-Chairman, Psychiatry, Children's Hospital, District of Columbia; Training and Supervising, Psychoanalyst, Private Practice. m. Thomas M. Chused, Appleton, 1 son, 1 daughter. *Education:* BA, Wellesley College, 1963; MD, Harvard Medical School, 1967; Washington Psychoanalytical Instutute. *Appointments:* Medical Intern, Cleveland Metropolitan General Hospital, 1967-68; Psychiatric Fellow, Children's Hospital, 1969-71; Psychiatric Resident, George Washington University Medical School, 1971-72; Associate Clinical Professor, Psychiatry, George Washington University School of Medicine, 1976-. *Memberships:*

Association for Child Psychoanalysis; American Psychoanalytic Association; International Psychoanalytic Association; Washington Psychoanalytic Society; Washington Psychiatric Society; American Psychiatric Association. *Publications:* "Neutrality and Use of Child Analysis as New Object", 1982; "Differential Diagnosis of a Functional Symptom", 1971 "Fathers as Mothers", "Idealization of the Analyst by the Young Adult", in press. *Honours:* Journal of American Psychoanalytic Association Prize, 1982; Sigma Xi, 1963. *Hobbies:* Art Collection; Opera; Music; Travel. *Address:* 1805 Randolph St., NW, Washington, District of Columbia 20011, USA.

CHVAPIL, Milos, b. 28 Sep. 1928, Klando, Czechoslovakia, Professor and Head, Section of Surgical Biology. m. Milena, 1953, Prague, Czechoslovakia, 1 son, 1 daughter. *Education:* MD, Charles University Medical School, 1952; PhD, Czechoslovak Academy of Sciences, 1956; DSc, Charles University Medical School, Pathological/Physiolgoy Department, 1965. *Appointments:* Scientist, Institute of Industrial Hygiene and Occupational Diseaes, Prague, 1952-56; Consulting Scientist, Ministry for Food Industry, Ministry of Light Industry, 1958-68; Head, Division of Occupational Diseases Institute of Industrial Hygiene and Occupational Diseases, Prague, 1959-68; Fellowship, D S Jackson, Department of Surgery, Oregon University Medical School; Portland, Oregon, USA, 1963; Associate Professor of Experimental Pathology, Charles University Medical School, Prague, Czechoslovakia, 1965; Scientific Fellowship, Max Planck Institute für Eiweiss und Lederforschung, Munich, Federal Republic of Germany, 196869; Visiting Professor of Medicine, School of Medicine, University of Miami, Florida, USA, 1969-70; Professor of Surgical Biology Section of Surgical Biology, 1970-, Head, Section of Surgical Biology, 1976-, Director of Research Laboratories, Surgical Biology, 1973-, Department of Surgery, University of Arizona Health Sciences Centre, Tucson, Arizona, USA. *Memberships:* American Society for Experimental Pathology; Society for Development Biology; Society for Experimental Biology and Medicine; American Association of University Professors. *Publications:* Author of numerous articles in professional journals. *Honours:* Invited Speaker, Nobel Symposium, Stockholm, Sweden, 1977; Winner Concorso Internationale por la Preventione de la Silicosi, Rome, Italy, 1969. *Hobbies:* Horse riding; Skiing. *Address:* Department of Surgery, Section of Surgical Biology, University of Arizona Health Sciences Centre, Tucson, AZ 85724, USA.

CICCONE, Joseph Richard, b. 21 Mar. 1943, New york, USA. Director; Associate Professor. m. Natalie A Caputo, 9 Dec. 1967, New York USA., 2 sons, 1 daughter. *Education:* AB, Columbia College, 1963; MD, University of Pittsburgh, School of Medicine, 1968. *Appointments:* Instructor in Psychiatry, 1971-72; Assistant Professor of Psychiatry, 1974-80, Associate Professor of Psychiatry, 1980-, University of Rochester School of Medicine and Dentistry. *Memberships:* American Psychiatric Assn.; American Academy of Psychiatry and Law; American Academy of Forensic Sciences; American Assn. for the Advancvement of Science; American Society for Law and Medicine; International Academy of Law and Mental Health; American College of Legal Medicine. *Publications:* Numerous contributions to professional journals including 'The Ethical Practice of Forensic Psychiatry: A View from the Trenches', 1984; (co-author); 'Privilege and Confidentiality: Psychiatry and Legal Considerations', 1984; 'Applied Clinical Ethics or Universal Principles', 1985, (with CD Clements); 'Law and Psychiatry: Rethinking the Relationship' in press, (with CD Clements); 'Important Forensic Issues in Psychiatric Education' in press. *Address:* University of Rochester School of Medicine and Dentistry, Department of Psychiatry, 300 Crittenden

Blvd., Rochester, NY 14642, USA.

CIMONETTI, Thomas, b 28 Nov. 1928, USA. Regional Director of Mental Health. *Education:* BA, St Michaels; MD, University of Maryland School of Medicine; Certification, American Board of Psychiatry and Neurology. *Appointments:* Instructor, Aquinas College, Nassau, Bahamas; Overseas Representative, Carribean, Bishops' Relief Fund, US Catholic Conference; Administrator, Metropolitan New York, Prudential Insurance Group Insurance Department; Associate Professor, part-time, Loyola College, Baltimore, Towson State University; Clinical Assistant Professor, University of Maryland School of Medicine; Private Practice, Psychiatry, and Organisation Development; Co-Founder, Human Resources Institute Inc., Maryland Psychological Assessment Centre. *Memberships:* American Psychiatric Association; American Medical Association; International Society of Clinical and Experimental Hypnosis; American Society of Clinical Hypnosis; Medical and Chirurgical Faculty of Maryland, Council & House of Delegates; Commission on Medical Discipline; Society for International Students; American Group Psychotherapy Association. *Honour:* Fellow, American Psychiatric Association, 1984. *Address:* Eastern Shore Hospital Centre, Shore Drive, Box 800, Cambridge, MD 21613, USA.

CINOTTI, Alfonse A, b. 1 Jan. 1923, Jersey City, New Jersey, USA. Chairman of Department of Ophthalmology. m. Kathleen D Higgins, 26 June 1948, 3 sons, 2 daughters. *Education:* BS, Fordham University, 1939-43; MD, State University of New York Downstate, 1943-46; Residency, New York Eye and Ear Infirmary, 1950-53. *Appointments:* Director Residency Training 1955-59, Director of Spect. Clinics 1956-58, Director of Glaucoma 1959-64, Consultant 1964-, New York Eye and Ear; Associate Professor 1963-72, Professor, Chairman, Department of Ophthalmology, Seton Hall College of Medicine and Dental College, CMDNJ (formerly Seton Hall CMD); Professor and Chairman, Department of Ophthalmology, New Jersey Medical College. *Memberships:* New Jersey Society to Prevent Blindness; National Society to Prevent Blindness; Medical Society of New Jersey; National Association for Crippled Children; New Jersey State Commission for the Blind. *Publications:* Contributor, "Glaucoma Update", 1979; Contributor, "Sports Medicine for the Athletic Female", 1980; Contributor, "Geriatric Handbook", 1984; "Handbook of Ophthalmic Emergencies", (editor), 1985. *Honours:* Service Medal, Newark Host-Lions Clubs, 1976; Honor Award, American Academy of Ophthalmology, 1978; Outstanding Citizen's Award, New Jersey Lions District 16A, 1981. *Hobbies:* Painting; Photography. *Address:* Eye Institute of New Jersey, 15 South 9th Street, Annex, Newark, NJ 07107, USA.

CLAGNAZ, Peter John, b. 27 Feb. 1951, New York, USA. Psychiatrist. m. Roban Miller, 2 Mar. 1979, Westbury, New York, 2 sons, 1 daughter. *Education:* BA, Hofstra University; MD, University of Rochester. *Appointments:* Chairman, Department of Psychiatry, Dean, Medical Centre. *Memberships:* American College of Physicians; American Psychiatric Association; American Medical Association; Physicians for Social Responsibility. *Publications:* Various articles in medical journals. *Honours:* Nassau County Medical Scoiety Award, 1973; Class of 1976 Prize, School of Medicine, Rochester University. *Hobby:* Reading. *Address* 2744 Florann Drive, Madison, WI 53711, USA.

CLARK, Duncan William, b. 31 Aug. 1919, New York City, USA. Professor Emeritus of Preventive Medicine, Downstate Medical Cenier of State University of New York, Brooklyn. m. (1) Carol Dooley, 30 Jan. 1943 (deceased); (2) Ida O'Grady, 10 June 1972, Brooklyn, New York, 2 sons, 1 daughter. *Education:* AB, Fordham University, 1932, MD, Long Island College of Medicine, 1936; Certified, American Speciality Boards in Internal Medicine, 1942 and Preventive Medicine, 1965. *Appointments:* Internship, Brooklyn Hospital, 1936-38; Residency, Internal Medicine, Kings County Hospital. 1938-40; Commonwealth Fund Fellow in Medicine, Yale University, USA, 1940-41; Private Practice, Internal Medicine, Brooklyn, 1941-43; Assistant and Associate Dean, 1943-48, Dean, 1948-50, Long Island College of Medicine; Visiting Professor of Social Medicine, University of Birmingham, England, 1961; Chairman and Professor, Environmental Medicine and Community Health, 1950-82; Professor of Preventive Medicine, Downstate Medical Center, 1978-82; Professor Emeritus, 1982-. *Memberships:* International Epidemiological Association; Harvey Society; New York Academy of Medicine, President, 1983, 84; Fellow, American College of Physicians; Fellow, American College of Preventive Medicine; Association of Teachers of Preventive Medicine, President, 1953-56; Alpha Omega Alpha. *Publications:* Text "Preventive and Community Medicine", Co-editor, 1981; Articles on medicine, public health and medical education. *Honours:* Alumni Medallion for Distinguished Service to American Medicine, (DMC), 1983. *Address:* 35 Prospect Park West, Brooklyn, NY 11215, USA.

CLARK, Gregory Dale, b. 14 Feb. 1951, Canton, Ohio, USA. Dentist. m. Andra Gail Wyant, 22 Dec. 1979, Gainesville, Georgia, 2 daughters. *Education:* BA, Chemistry, Emory University, 1973; DDS, Emory University School of Dentistry, 1978; Member, United States Dental Institute studying orthodontics, 1979-. *Appointments:* Dentist in private practice, Gainsville, Georgia, 1978 -; Part-time Seminar Instructor, Clark Chiro-Dental Associates. *Memberships:* American Orthodontic Society; International Association of Orthodontics; Atlanta Craniomandible Society; Georgia Dental Association; American Dental Association; Northen District Dental Society; Hall County Dental Society. *Hobbies:* Boating; Skiing; Computer programming; Scuba diving. *Address:* Rt 1 Box 436, Oakwood, GA 30566, USA.

CLARK, Harry Edgar, b. 12 Apr. 1925, Canton, New York, USA. Pharmacist owner of Clarke Pharmacy, Waverly, New York; Staff Pharmacist, Veterans Adminsitration Outpatient Clinic, Sayre, Pennsylvania. *Education:* BS, Pharmacy, Ithaca, New York, 1949-51; Partner-Pharmacist, Clarke Pharmacy, Waverly, New York, 1951-71; Owner-Senior Pharmacist, Clarke Pharmacy, Waverley, 1971-; Staff Pharmacist, Veterans Adminsitration Outpatient Clinic, Sayre, Pennsylvania, 1984-. *Memberships:* National Association Retail Druggists; American Pharmaceutical Association; New York State Pharmaceutical Society; Academy of General Practice. *Honours:* American Cancer Society Fellow, Strong Memorial Hsopital, Rochester, New York, 1980; American Cancer Society Award for Outstanding Service, 1985. *Hobby:* Photography. *Address:* 444 Clark Street, Waverly, NY 14892, USA.

CLARK, Robert A, b. 14 Jan. 1942, Oswego, New York, USA. Professor of Medicine. m. Patricia Ann Tangi, 26 June 1965, Binghamton, New York, 2 sons, 1 daughter. *Education:* AB, Syracuse University, New York, 1963; MD, Columbia University, New York, 1967; Intern in Medicine; University of Washington, Seattle, 1967-68; Resident in Medicine, Columbia University, New York, 1968-69; Postdoctoral Fellow, National Institute of Health, Bethesda, Maryland, 1969-72; Chief Resident in Medicine, University of Washington, Seattle, 1972-73. *Appointments:* Assistant Professor, Associate Professor of Medicine, Boston University of Washington, 1973-77; Associate Professor, Professor of Medicine, Boston University, Boston, Massachusetts, 1977-83; Professor of Medicine, University of Iowa, 1983-.

Memberships; American Society for Clinical Investigation; Association of American Physicians; American Federation for Clinical Research; European Society for Clinical Investigation; American Association; of Immunologists; American Society for Cell Biology. *Publications:* "The Neutrophil: Function & Clinical Disorders" (with S J Klebanoff), 1978; Some 75 scientific papers. *Honours:* Research Career Development Award, National Cancer Centre, 1975; Medical Investigator Award, Veterans Administration, 1985. *Hobbies:* Travel; Fishing; Hiking. *Address:* Department of Internal Medicine, University of Iowa, Iowa City, IA 52242, USA.

CLARK, Ronald George, b. 9 Aug. 1928, Aberdeen, Scotland. University Professor of Surgery and Dean of Faculty of Medicine and Dentistry, m. Tamar W Harvie, 12 Sep. 1960, Duntocher, 2 daughters. *Education:* MB ChB cum laude, University of Aberdeen; Fellow, Royal College of Surgeons, Edinburgh; Fellow, Royal College of Surgeons, England. *Appointments:* House Appointments, Royal Infirmary, Aberdeen, 1956-57; Registrar, Western Infirmary, Glasgow, 1958-60; Surgical Research Fellow, Harvard University, USA, 1960-61; Lecturer in Surgery, University of Glasgow, Scotland, 1961-65; Senior Lecturer in Surgery, University of Sheffield, England, 1966-72; Examiner: Universities of Aberdeen, Glasgow, Edinburgh, Liverpool, Newcastle, Leicester, London, Southampton, Malta, Ibadan and Jos; Royal College of Physicians and Surgeons, Glasgow; Royal College of Surgeons of Edinburgh; Currently Dean of Faculty of Medicine and Dentistry, Professor of Surgery, University of Sheffield; Honorary Consultant Surgeons, Northern General Hospital, Sheffield. *Memberships:* Chairman 1982-86, European Society of Parenteral and Enteral Nutrition; Council of Nutrition Society, 1982-85; General Medical Council, 1983-88; Association of Surgeons of Great Britian and Ireland; Surgical Research Society. *Publications:* Editorial board, 'Scottish Medical Journals', 1962-65; Editor-in-Chief, 'Clinical Nutrition', 1980-82; Publications on surgical topics and metabolic aspects of acute disease. *Hobby:* Golf. *Address:* 2 Chesterwood Drive, Sheffield, S10 5DH, England.

CLARK, Timothy John Hayes, b. 18 Oct. 1935, London, England. Consultant Physician and Hospital Dean. m. Elizabeth Ann Day, 6 May 1961, Peterborough, England, 2 sons, 2 daughters. *Education:* Guy's Hospital Medical School 1954-60, BSc, Hons, Physiology, 1958, MRCS LRCP, 1960; MB BS (Hons) London 1961; MRCP, London 1962; MD London 1967 FRCP London 1973. *Appointments:* Registrar, Hammersmith Hospital, 1964-66; Senior Lecturer, in Departments of Medicine and Physiology, Guy's Hospital Medical school, 1966-68; Consultant Physician, Guy's Hospital, 1968-70; Currently: Consultant Physician, Guy's and Brompton Hospitals, Professor of Throacic Medicine and Dean of Guy's hospital. *Memberships:* Medical Research Society; British thoracic Society; Association of Physicians of Great Britian and Ireland. *Publications:* "Topical Steroid Treatment for Asthma and Rhinitis" co-author, 1980; "Clinical Investigation of Respiratory Disease" 1981; "Asthma" 2 editions 1977 and 1983 co-author; "Steroids in Asthma" 1983; "Bronchodilator Therapy" 1984 co-author; "Practical Management of Asthma" co-author 1985. *Hobby:* Cricket. *Address:* Dean's Office, Guy's Hosital, London SE1 9RT, England.

CLARKE, Cyril Astle (Sir), b. 22 Aug. 1907, Leicester, England. Director, Research Unit; Honorary Nuffield Research Fellow. m. Frieda Margaret Mary Hart, 27 Dec. 1935, London, 3 sons. *Education:* Caius College, Cambridge University; Guys Hospital Medical School; MD; DSc. Fellow: Royal College of Physicians; Royal Society; Royal College of Obstetricians and Gynaecologists; Royal College of Pathology, Honorary. *Appointments Include:* House Physician, Guy's Hospital, London; Demonstrator in Physiology and Pathology, Clinical Assistant In Dermatology, Guy's Hospital; Life Insurance Practice, 1936-39; Medical Specialist, Acting Surgeon Lieutenant Commander, 1939-46; Medical Registrar, Queen Elizabeth's Hospital, Birmingham; Consultant Physician, United Liverpool Hospitals and Broadgreen Hospital, Liverpool, 1946-72; Reader, 1958-65, Professor, 1965-72, University of Liverpool; President, Royal College of Physicians, London, 1972-77; Director, Medical Services Study Group, Research Unit, Royal College of Physicians, 1977-. *Memberships Include:* Fellow: Royal Society; Institute of Biology; American College of Physicians; Royal Colleges of Physicians, Scotland, Canada and Ireland, Australia. Chairman, Council, British Heart Foundation. *Publications:* "Genetics for the Clinician", 2nd Edition, 1969; "Selected Topics in Medical Genetics", Editor; "Human Genetics and Medicine", 1970, 3rd edition, 1986; "Prevention of Rhesus Hoemolytic Disease", co-author, 1972; "Rhesus Haemolytic Disease", Editor, 1975. *Honours Include:* CBE, 1969; KBE, 1974; Honorary DSc, Edinburgh, 1971, Leicester, 1971, Birmingham, Liverpool, Sussex, 1974, Hull, 1977, Wales, 1978. London, 1980; Numerous medals and awards from learned societies. *Hobbies:* Small boat sailing; Breeding butterflies. *Address:* 43 Caldy Road, West Kirby, Wirral, Merseyside, L48 2HF, England.

CLARKE, Edwin Ralph Hunter, b. 12 Mar. 1914, Australia. Haematologist, Commonwealth Pathological Laboratory, Tamworth, Australia. m. Florence Sarah Penberthy, 18 Dec. 1943, Camberwell, Victoria, Australia, 2 sons. *Education:* BSc; BMed.; B.Surg; Diploma of Civil Engineering; Diploma of Tropical Medicine and Hygiene. *Appointments:* Medical Officer, Victoria Health Department, 1952; Medical Officer, Commonwealth Serum Laboratories, Victoria,1953-62; Medical Officer, Commonwealth Pathology Laboratory, Bendego, Victoria, 1963-66; Haematologist, Royal Newcastle Hospital, Newcastle, New South Wales, 1967-70; Haematologist, Commonwealth Pathology Laboratory, Bendego, 1971; Haematologist, Commonwealth Pathology Laboratory, New South Wales, 1972-. *Memberships:* Fellow, Royal College of Pathologists Australasia; Haematology Society of Australia; International Society of Haematology, Asian-Pacific Division; International Academy Pathology, Australasian Division. *Hobbies:* Reading History; Music; Gardening; Swimming; Trekking in Far Places. *Address:* 15 Myrene Avenue, Tamworth, New South Wales 2340, Australia.

CLARKE, Edwin Sisterson, b. 18 June 1919, Felling-on-Tyne, England, Honorary Curator, Sherrington Room, University Laboratory of Physiology, Oxford. *Education:* MB, BS, University of Durham, UK: MD, University of Chicago, USA: MD (Durham); FRCP. *Appointments include:* Lecturer in Neurology/Consultant Neurologist, Royal Postgraduate Medical School, London; Assistant Professor, History of Medicine, Johns Hopkins University, USA; Visiting Associate Professor, Yale University, USA; Director, Wellcome Institute for History of Medicine. *Memberships:* Fellow, Royal Society of Medicine; Member, Association of British Neurologists. *Publications include:* "The Human Brain & Spinal Cord", 1968; "Modern Methods in the History of Medicine", 1971; "Illustrated History of Brain Function", 1972; Translation, "History of Crystal Neurophysiology", M. Neuburger, 1981. *Hobby:* Topography, N.E. England. *Address:* University Laboratory of Physiology, Parks Road, Oxford, OX1 3PT, England.

CLAY, Barbara Ellen Maire, b. 27 Dec. 1936, Mitcham, Surrey, England. Consultant Radiologist;

Consultant in Administrative Charge of Department. m. Ronald Pearce, 24 Mar. 1962, Mitcham, Surrey, 2 sons. *Education:* Royal Free Hospital; MRCS; LRCP; 1961; FFR, 1973; FRCR. *Appointments:* House Physician and House Surgeon, St. Charles Hospital, Paddington; House Surgeon, Hull Maternity Hospital; SHO (Obstetrics and Gynaecology), Louth County Hospital, Lincs.; G.P. Trainee, Alford, Lincs; SHO, Registrar, Senior Registrar in Radiology, Central Middlesex Hospital; Senior Registrar, Institute of Urology, London; Approved Consultant, Radiologist, Princess Margaret Hospital, Swindon, Wilts., 1974-; Postgraduate Clinical Tutor, Swindon District, 1985. *Memberships:* Royal College of Radiologists: British Institute of Radiology; British Nuclear Medicine Society; Fellow, Royal Society of Medicine; British Medical Association; Member of Council of Radiology Section, Royal Society of Medicine. *Hobbies:* Tennis; Badminton; Needlework. *Address:* Princess Margaret Hospital, Swindon, Wiltshire, England.

CLAY, Trevor, b. 10 May 1936, Nuneaton, England. General Secretary, Royal College of Nursing, UK. *Education:* Brunel University; London Business School; RGN, 1957; RMN, 1960; M.Phil, 1976. *Appointments:* Staff Nurse, Charge Nurse, Guy's Hospital, London, 1960-65; Assistant Matron, Psychiatric Unit, Queen Elizabeth II Hospital, Welwyn Garden City, 1965-67; Assistant Regional Nursing Officer, North West Metropolitan Regional Hospital Board, London, 1967-69; Director of Nursing, Whittington Hospital, London, 1969-70; Chief Nursing Officer, North London Group Hospital Management Committee, 1970-74; Area Nursing Officer, Camden and Islington Area Health Authority, London, 1974-79; Duputy General Secretary, 1979-82, General Secretary, 1982-, Royal College of Nursing. *Memberships:* Royal College of Nursing, UK; Board of Directors, International Council of Nurses. *Publications:* "The Workings of the Nursing and Midwifery Advisory Committees in the National Health Service", 1974. *Honours:* Fellowship, Royal College of Nursing, 1985. *Hobbies:* Work; Good Friends; Mozart. *Address:* 20 Cavendish Square, London W1M 0AB, England.

CLAYFIELD, Ronald Lewis, b. 21 Sept. 1925, Melbourne, Australia. Private Practitioner, Medical Hypnosis. m. Alison Shepherd, 15 Dec. 1953, Millicent, South Australia, 2 sons, 1 daughter. *Education:* MB BS, Melbourne University, 1954; Member, Australian Society of Hypnosis. *Appointments:* Resident Medical Officer, Hamilton Base Hospital, Victoria, 1954-55. General Practitioner: Portland, Victoria, 1955-62; Adelaide, South Australia, 1962-76. Clinical Assistant, Exvale Hospital, Exminster, Devon, England, 1977-79; Medical Officer, Hillcrest Hospital, Adelaide, Australia, 1979-80; Acting Medical Officer in Charge, St Anthony's Alcohol and Drug Addict Treatment Board, Adelaide, 1980-82; Private Practice, Medical Hypnosis, Walkerville, South Australia, 1982-. *Memberships:* Australian Medical Association; Australian Society of Hypnosis; International Society of Hypnosis; American Society of Clinical Hypnosis. *Hobbies:* Wood carving; Oil painting; Lawn bowls. *Address:* 7 Redford Street, Vale Park, SA 5081, Australia.

CLAYTON, Alastair James, b. 17 Apr. 1933, Glasgow, Scotland. Director General, Laboratory Centre for Disease Control, Ottawa, Canada. *Education:* MB, ChB, St. Andrews University, Scotland, 1958; Diploma of Public Health. *Appointment:* Director of Preventive Medicine, Canadian Forces Medical Services. *Memberships:* Fellow, Royal College of Physicians and Surgeons of Canada; Fellow, The Faculty of Community Medicine, UK; Fellow, The American College of Preventive Medicine; Canadian Society for Tropical Medicine and International Health; Canadian Public Health Association; Canadian Hospital Infection Control Association. *Publications:* Contributor to professional journals, etc. *Honour:* Canadian Decoration, 1972. *Hobbies:* Philately; History. *Address:* Laboratory Centre for Disease Control, Tunney's Pasture, Ottawa, Ontario K1A DL2, Canada.

CLAYTON, Barbara Evelyn, b. 2 Sep. 1922, Liverpool, England. Professor of Chemical Pathology. m. Eilliam Klyne (deceased,) 22 Apr. 1949, 1 son, 1 daughter. *Education:* MB ChB, MD, PhD, University of Edinburgh, Scotland, Fellow, Royal College of Physicians; Fellow, Royal College of Physicians of Edinburgh. *Appointments:* Consultant in Chemical Pathology, The Hospitals for Sick Children, London, 1959-70; Professor of Chemical Pathology, Institute of Child health, University of London, Honorary Consultant in Chemical Pathology, The Hospitals for Sick Children, 1970-79; Professor of Chemical Pathology & Human Metobolism, University of Southampton, 1979-. *Memberships include:* British Paediatric Association; Biochemical Society; Past President, Association of Clinical Biochemists; Society for Endocrinology; Royal Commission on Environmetnal Pollution; President, Royal College of Pathologists; Commonwealth Scholarships Commission; General Medical Council; Standing Medical Advisory Committee (DHSS); Deputy Chairman, Committee on Toxicity of Chemicals in Food & Consumer Products & the Environment (DHSS); Past President, Board of Governors, The Hospitals for Sick Children, London. *Publications:* Numerous publications in the fields of trace elements paediatric biochemistry, environmental pollution. *Honours:* CBE, 1983; Freeland Barbour Fellowship for Medical Research, 1952; Jessis MacGregor Prize for Medical Research (Royal College of Physicians), 1985. *Hobbies:* Natural History; Rambling; Gardening. *Address:* Dean's Office, Level C, South Academic Block, Southampton General Hospital, Southampton, England.

CLEATON-JONES, Peter Eiddon, b. 5 Mar. 1941, Johannesburg, South Africa. Professor of Experimental Odontology; Director, Medical Research Council m. Marguerite Ginette France Thorpe, 11 Mar. 1967, Johannnesburg, South Africa, 1 son. *Education:* BDS, University of the Witwatersrand, Johannesburg, 1963; MB, BCh, 1967; PhD, 1975; DTMEH; DPH; DA, college of Medicine of South Africa, 1975. *Appointments:* Dental Officer, Johannesburg City Council, 1963; Technical Officer, Dental Research Unit, Wits. University, Johannesburg, 1963-67, Anatomy Tutor, 1964-67; Intern in Medicine and Surgery, Baragwanath Hospital, Johannesburg, 1968; Researcher, Director. Wits. University Dental Research Unit, Johannesburg, 1969-; Part time Casulty Officer, Johannesburg non-European Hospital, 1970-84; Part time Anaesthetist, Johannesburg Hospital, 1975-. *Memberships:* Dental Association of South Africa; Medical Association of South Africa; British Medical Association; International Association for Dental research. *Publications:* 175 in total, including 1 book, 4 book chapters, numerous articles in professioanl journals. *Honours:* Prizes in Conservative Dentistry, Children's Dentistry, Anaesthesia, Oral medicine, Prosthetic Dentistry, 1963; Prize for Clinical Pathology, 1964; Prize in Internal Medicine, 1966; Colgate Prize of IADR, 1969; many research grants. *Hobbies:* Model Engineering, live steam locomotives; Dinghy Sailing; Philately; Photography; Boy Scouts. *Address:* MRC/University of the Witwatersrand, Dental Research Institute, 1 Jan Smuts Avenue, Johannesburg 2001, Republic of South Africa.

CLEMENT, Michael Scott, b. 31 Mar. 1939, Logan, Utah, USA. Assistant Director, Arizona Dept. of Health Services. m. Roberta Edwards, 11 May 1979, Utah, 1 son, 2 daughters. *Education:* MD, University of Utah, 1963. *Appointments:* Captain, US Army Medical Corps, 1944-46; Post-Doctoral Research Fellow, Ped., College of Medicine, University of Utah, 1966-68;Pediatrician, Private Practice, Murray, Utah, 1968-72; Pediatrician, Thomas-Davis Clinic, Tucson, 1972-75, Private Practice, Sierra Vista, 1975-80; Director, Cochise County Health Dept., Bisbee, 1978-80. *Memberships:* Maricopa County Pediatric Society; American Academy of Pediatrics, Arizona Chapter; American Public Health Association; US-Mexico Border Health Association; Arizona Perinatal Society; American Association for the Advancement of Science. *Publications:* 'Proceedings of the Society of Experimental Biology & Medicine', 1968; 'Journal of Laboratory and Clinical Medicine'; "Capitation & Child Health Services", Discussion Paper Series, University of California, 1984. *Honours:* American Legion Constitution Award, 1953; American Legion School Award, 1954; Leaders of Tomorrow Scholarship, University of Arizona, 1956-57; Pershing Rifles National Achievement Award, 1956-59; Mosby Research Award, 1960; National Association of Counties Achievement Award, 1982. *Hobbies:* Hunting; Photography; History. *Address:* 1820 E. Gary, Mesa, AZ 85203, USA.

CLEMENT, Richard Thierry, b. 27 Jan 1950, France, Doctor of Medicine. m. Amanda Adey Langford, 1985, 1 son. *Education:* ECFMG, 1974; MD, Paris, France, 1976. *Appointments:* Manager, Caribbean Therapy Clinics, Anguilla, West Indies. *Memberships:* Florida Society of Clinical Hypnosis, USA; British Homoeopathic Society; Club Medecine et Informatique, France. *Hobby:* Water skiing. *Address:* Caribbean Therapy Clinics Ltd, PO Box 324, Anguilla, West Indies.

CLIFFORD, Donald, b. 7 June 1925, Burlington, Vermont, USA. Professor & Director. m. Virginia Beatty, 13 Aug. 1954, Duluth, Minnesota, 4 sons. *Education:* DVM, University of Montreal, Canada, 1950; MPH 1955, PhD 1959, University of Minnesota, USA. *Appointments include:* Instructor 1952, Assistant Professor 1959, Veterinary Surgery & Radiology, University of Minnesota; Medical Associate/Director, Veterinary Services Brookhaven National Laboraotry, Upton, New York, 1962; Associate Professor, University of Minnesota, 1964; Associate Professor/Director, Division of Laboratory Animal Medicine, Medical College of Ohio, 1971; Professor & Director, ibid, 1977-. *Memberships:* American Veterinary Medical Association; Diplomate, American College of Veterinary Surgeons, American College of Laboratory Animal Medicine; American Association for Accreditation of Laboratory Animal Care; American Society of Laboratory Animal Practitioners. *Publications include:* Chapter, 'The Esophagus' in "General Small Animal Surgery", ed. Gourley & Vasseur, 1975; 'Preanesthesia, Anesthesia, Analgesia & Euthanasia' in "Laboratory Animal Medicine", ed. Fox, Cohen & Loew, 1974; etc. *Honours:* Prize, Veterinary Surgery, University of Montreal; Biographical listings. *Hobbies:* Stamp collecting; History; Gun collecting. *Address:* Medical College of Ohio, CS 10008, Toledo, OH 43699, USA.

CLIFT, John Vinton, b. 14 Mar. 1926, Baltimore, Maryland, USA. Dept. of Emergency Medicine, Beebe Hospital. m. Georgia Obrecht, 27 Nov. 1980, Oatlands. *Education:* BS, Hampden-Sydney College, 1949; MD, magna cum laude, University of Maryland School of Medicine, 1953. *Appointments:* Intern, Surgical Resident, 1953-59; Private Practice, General Surgery, Baltimore, 1960-62, Washington DC, 1963-67, Vienna, Virginia, 1965-84; Emergency Medicine, Front Royal, Virginia, 1978-84; Chief, Surgery, Commonwealth Doctors Hospital, 1970-75; Chief of Staff, Commonwealth Doctors Hospital, Fairfax, 1975-76; Department of Emergency Medicine, Beebe Hospital, Lewes, 1984-; etc. *Memberships:* Fellow, American College of

Surgeons, American College of Abdominal Surgeons, American College of Emergency Physicians, American Society of Clinical Hypnosis; Johns Hopkins Medical and Surgical Association; Washington Academy of Surgery; Northern Virginia Academy of Surgery. *Publications:* Various, 1959-60. *Hobbies:* Arabian Horses; Woodwork; Flying; Skiing; Gardening. *Address:* R.D.§5, Box 171, Harbeson, DE 19951, USA.

CLIFTON-HADLEY, Christopher Breen, b. 16 Dec. 1948, Esher, Surrey, England. Clinic Director. m. Virgina Fiona Duck, 1 Mar. 1980, Richmond, Surrey, 1 daughter, 1 son. *Education:* Doctor of Chiropractic, 1972. *Appointments:* Private practice; Director, Hadley Chiropractic Clinic, Richmond, Surrey, 1980-. *Memberships:* British, American and International Chiropractic Associations: Acupuncture Society of America; Parker Chiropractic Research Foundation. *Honours:* Chiropractor of the Year, 1983, (sole achiever in UK); Outstanding Contribution Award, National Chiropractic Antitrust Committee, 1980. *Hobbies:* Windsurfing; Weightlifting; Snooker; Carpentry. *Address:* Hadley Chiropractic Clinic, 155-157 Kew Road, Richmond, Surrey, England.

CLINTON, Lawrence Paul, b. 27 Apr. 1945, Lubbock, Texas, USA. Private Practice; Assistant Clinical Professor. m. Bonnie Gail Orenstein, 22 June 1969, Columbus, Ohio, 2 sons, 2 daughters. *Education:* BA, Southern Connecticut State University, 1966; MS, Ohio State University, 1968; MD, Hahnemann University, Pennsylvania, 1972. *Appointments:* Rotating Internship, 1972-73, Resident, Department of Mental Health Sciences, 1973-76, Hahnemann University; Private Practice, Vineland, New Jersey, 1976-; Psychiatric Director, Goldman Clinic, James C Guiffre Medical Centre, Philadelphia, Pennsylvaniam, 1975-78. Psychiatric Consultant: Child Development Centre, Norristown, Pennsylvania, 1974-77; Superior Court of New Jersey, 1977-; Equity Services, Haddonfield, New Jersey; Vanguard Facility, Santa Monica, California. *Memberships:* Phi Lambda Kappa; American Psychiatric Association; Pennsylvania and New Jersey Psychiatric Societies; International Association for Group Psychotherapy; American Medical Association; New York Academy of Science. *Publications:* Contributions to: 'North American Radiological Society', 1970; 'International Journal of Addictions', 1981 and others. *Honours:* Departmental Honours: Chemistry, Southern Connecticut State University, 1966; Radiation Therapy and Nuclear Medicine, Hahnemann University, 1972. Leadership Award, American Security Council, 1983; Diplomate, National Board of Medical Examiners, 1973, American Board of Psychiatry, 1982. *Hobbies:* Books; Historical tours; Gardening; Art collecting; Reading; Travel; Enjoying good conversation. *Address:* 1207 Manoa Road, Philadelphia, PA 19151, USA.

CLODIUS, Leo John, b. 29 Apr. 1930, Osnabruck, Switzerland. Head, Division of Plastic Surgery. m. Maria Tobler, 22 Sep. 1965, Zurich. *Education:* MD; Foreign diplomate, American Society for Plastic and Reconstructive Surgery Privat docent for plastic surgery. *Appointments:* Resident, General Surgery, Boston City Hospitals, Boston and Mass Memorial, USA; Resident, 1960-63; Chief Resident, 1962-63, Plastic Reconstructive Surgery St Barnabas Medical Center, New Jersey; Head, Unit for Plastic and Reconstructive Surgery, University of Zurich, Switzerland, 1969-(Docent, 1982-). *Memberships:* Swiss Society for Plastic, Reconstructive and Esthetic Surgery; Zurich Society for Plastic, Hand and Maxillofacial Surgery; Zurich Medical Society; Swiss Medical Society; Corresponding member, Angiological Society, Brazil; International Lymphological Society; Swiss Hand Surgery Society; European Society for Ophthalmic Plastic and Reconstructive Surgery Oculplastic Fellowship Society of New York. *Publications:* "Lymphedema",

1977; "Progress in Lymphology", 1981; Author of over 140 articles on plastic surgery and reconstructive surgery to medical journals. *Honours:* Award for Best Science Presentation, Tucson, Arizona, 1974; Angiology International Award, Baden-Baden, Federal Republic of Germany, 1976; Scudo d'Oro Award, City of Sienna, Italy, 1979; Purkynje Medal, Brno University, Czechoslovakia, 1982; President, Swiss Society of Plastic and Reconstructive Surgery, 1974-76, International Lymphology Society, 1977-79. *Hobbies:* Winter and summer sports; Bonsai growing. *Address:* Unit for Plastic Surgery, University Hospital, CH-8091, Zurich, Switzerland.

CLONINGER, Claude Robert, b. 4 Apr. 1944, Beaumont, Texas, USA. Professor,Psychiatry & Genetics, Washington University Medical School. m. Sharon Lee Roga, 11 July 1969, St Louis, 2 sons. *Education:* BA, Honours, University of Texas, 1966; MD, Washington University, St Louis, 1970; Psychiatric Residency, Barnes & Renard Hospitals, 1970-73. *Appointments:* Instructor, 1973-74, Assistant Professor, 1974-78, Associate Professor, 1978-81, Psyhciatry, Associate Professor, Genetics, 1979-81, Professor, Psychiatry & Genetics, 1981-, Washington University Medical School; Director, Outpatient Psychiatry, Jewish Hospital of St Louis, 1976-; Visiting Professor, Genetics, University of Hawaii, Manoa, 1978-79. *Memberships:* Fellow, American Psychiatric Association; Fellow, Treasurer, American Psychopathological Assocation; American Society of Human Genetics; Behaviour Genetics Association; Psychiatric Research Society; Society of Biological Psychiatry; Research Society on Alcoholism. *Publications:* 105 articles including "The Multifactorial Model of Disease Transmission : III Familial Relationshp Between Sociopathy and Hysteria (Briquet's Syndrome)", 'British Journal Psychiatry'. 1975; "Genetic Diversity, Genome Organization and Investigation of the Etiology of Psychiatric Diseases", 'Psychiatric Developments', 1983. *Honours Include:* Phi Beta Kappa, 1966; National Institute of Mental Health Research Scientist Award, 1975-90; Milton Parker Lecturer, Ohio State University, 1983; Honorary Doctor of Medicine, Umea University, Sweden, 1983; Editor, 'Behaviour Genetics', 1980-83; Associate Editor, 'American Journal of Human Genetic', 1980-83; Associate Editor,' Genetic Epidemiology', 1983-; Associate Editor, 'Journal of Clinical Psychiatry', 1981-. *Hobbies:* Photography; Gardening; Reading; Travel. *Address:* Dept. of Psychiatry, Jewish Hospital of St Louis, 216 So. Kings Highway Blvd., P O Box 14109, St Louis, MO 63178, USA.

CLULEE, Carol Kipp, b. 11 Dec. 1943, Norman, Oklahoma, USA. Audiologist; Speech Pathologist. m. Nicholas H Clulee, PhD, 16 June 1973, Hyndman, Pennsylvania, 2 daughters. *Education:* BA, Speech Pathology/Audiology, Indiana University of Pennsylvania, 1965; MEd, Speech Pathology, The Pennsylvania State University, 1966; Postgraduate: The George Washington University; Frostburg State College. *Appointments:* Speech Pathologists: Medical College of Virginia, Richmond; McGuire Veterans Hospital, Richmond; Sacred Heart Hospital, Cumberland; Allegany County Public Schools, Cumberland; Speech Pathologist/Audiologist; Sacred Heart Hospital, Cumberland; Allegany Hearing and Speech Associates, Cumberland. *Memberships:* Maryland Speech-Language-Hearing Association; Pennsylvania Speech-Language-Hearing Association; American Speech-Language-Hearing Association. *Hobbies:* Harpsichordist; Church Choir Director. *Address:* Allegany Hearing and Speech Associates, 925 Bishop Walsh Road, Cumberland, MD 21502, USA.

CLUNIE, Gordon James Aitken, b. 29 Mar. 1932,

Suva, Fiji. Professor of Surgery. m. Jess A Crozier, 27 Dec. 1957, Edinburgh, 1 son, 2 daughters. *Education:* MB ChB, ChM, 1968, University of Edinburgh, Scotland; FRCS, Edinburgh, 1961, England, 1962; FRACS, 1969. *Appointments:* Lecturer, Surgical Science, University of Edinburgh, Scotland, 1963-67; Reader in Surgery, 1968-73, Professor of Surgery, 1974-78, University of Queensland, Australia; Professor of Surgery, University of Melbourne, 1978-. *Memberships:* Clinical Oncological Society of Australia; Transplantation Society; Transplantation Society of Australia and New Zealand; Surgical Research Society of Australasia; Australasian Society of Nephrology; Australian Society for Medical research. *Publications:* Co-Editor, "Integrated Management of Cancer", 1984. Author of numerous articles on transplantation immunology, organ transplantation and oncology. *Hobbies:* Music; Reading. *Address:* Department of Surgery, Royal Melbourne Hospital, Melbourne 3050, Australia.

COBO, E. Joseph, b. 26 Oct. 1928, Cuba. Internal Medicine, Private Practice. m. Carolina Cobo, 31 July 1952, Cuba, 1 son. *Education:* Graduate, Havana University Medical School, 1950; University of Miami Medical School, USA, Jackson Memorial Hospital, 1961; Florida State Medical Board, 1969. *Appointments:* Internal Medicine, Cardiology, Private Practice, Havana, 1950-61; (Staff Phsyician, Cardiorespiratory Diseases, W.T. Edwards Hospital, Florida, USA, 1965-66; Internships, St Mary's Hospital, West Palm Beach, 1965-66;) Resident, Broward General Medical Centre, 1966-69; Private Practice, 1969-. *Memberships:* American Society of Internal Medicine; Florida Society of Internal Medicine; American College of Chest Physicians; American Thoracic Society; American Geriatric Society; American College of Physicians and Surgeons; American Medical Association; World Medical Association. *Publications:* Numerous articles in professional magazines, Cuba & USA. *Honours:* Fellow, Royal Society of Health, England. *Hobbies:* Tennis; Fishing. *Address:* 809 East Broward Boulevard, Fort Lauderdale, FL 33301, USA.

COBOC, C Edgard, b. 27 Aug. 1932, Cali, Colombia. Professor Emeritus of Obstetrics and Gynecology. m. Bertha Helena Corey, 22 Feb. 1969, Cali, 1 son, 1daughter. *Education:* MD, National University of Colombia, 1959; Board of Obstetrics and Gynecology, University of the Valley, Cali, 1959; Fellow, National University of Uruguay, 1959-61; Fellow, Population Council, New York, USA, 1969. *Appointments:* Instructor, 1959, Assistant Professor and Founder and Chairman, Section of Reproductive Physiology, 1961, Associate Professor, 1965, Full Professor, 1969, Professor and Chairman Obstetrics and Gynecology, 1972, Professor Emeritus, 1984, University of the Valley, Cali. *Memberships Include:* Federation of Societies of Obstetricians and Gynecologists of Colombia; Latin-American Association for Investigation on Human Reproduction; American Federation of Clinical Research; American Association forAdvancement of Science; American Fertility Society. *Publications:* "Human Reproduction", 5 volumes, 1973, 75; "Lactogenic Hormones, Fetal Nutrition and Lactation", 1974; "Reproduction", 1979. Various papers contributed to professional journals. *Honours:* 25th Anniversary Award for Scientific Research, Medical School, Cali, 1979; Annual Award for Scientific Research, Public Welfare of the State, 1980; Medal Simon Bolivar, for outstanding contributions to Education, Science and Culture, Ministry of National Education, 1985. *Hobbies:* Music; Latin-American Literature. *Address:* Departamento de Obstetricia y Ginecologia, Facultad de Salud, Universidad del Valle, AA 2188 Cali, Colombia.

COBURN, Robert Lee, b. 12 June 1950, West

Columbia, Texas, USA. Chiropractor. m. Melba Ann Bruce, 27 June 1969, Old Ocean, 2 sons. *Education:* Graduate, Texas Chiropractic College, 1965; National Board of Chiropractic Examiners, 1975. *Appointments:* Private Practice, 1975-. *Memberships:* American Chiropractic Association; Texas Chiropractic Assocation; World Wide Christian Chiropractic Association; Gonstead Clinical Studies Society; School Board of Trustee, Sweeny Independent School District. *Honour:* Outstanding Young Men of America, 1980. *Hobbies:* Golf; Fishing. *Address:* 211 N. Colombia Drive, West Columbia, TX 77486, USA.

COCHRAN, Jerry L., b. 4 June 1940, Tacoma, Washington, USA. Private Practice. m. Karen E. Freeman, 2 Feb. 1969, Spokane. *Education:* DPM; BSc., Bacteriology; BSc., Basic Medical Sciences. *Appointment:* Private Practice. *Memberships:* Fellow, American College of Foot Surgeons; Diplomate, American Board of Podiatric Surgery; Associate, American Academy of Podiatric Sports Medicine; American College of Sports Medicine; American Podiatric Medical Association. *Hobbies:* Amateur Astronomy; Bicycling; Photography. *Address:* Suite 128 N. 5901 Lidgerwood, Spokane, WA 99207, USA.

COCKBURN, Forrester, b. 13 Oct. 1934, Edinburgh, Scotland. Samson Gemmell Professor of Child Health, University of Glasgow. m. Alison Fisher Grieve, 15 Jan. 1960, Edinburgh, 2 sons. *Education:* MB, ChB; MRCP (Edin); MRCP (Glasgow); FRCP (Glasgow) DCH. *Appointments include:* Huntingdon-Hartford Research Fellow, Paediatric Metabolic Disease, USA, 1965; Assistant Visiting Professor, Paediatrics, Puerto Rico, 1965; Nuffield Senior Research Fellow, Oxford, 1966; Wellcome Senior Research Fellow, Neonatal & Paediatric Research, 1971; Senior Lecturer, 1977; Samson Gemmell Professor, 1977-. *Memberships:* British Medical Association; British Paediatric Association; Society for the Study of Iborn Errors of Metabolism. *Publications include:* Textbook, "Neonatal Medicine", with C.M.Drillien,. 1974; "A Handbook for Children's Doctors", 1984; "Practical Paediatrics", 1986. *Hobbies:* Walking; Sailing. *Address:* University Department of Child Health, Royal Hospital for Sick Children, Yorkhill, Glasgow, G3 8SJ, Scotland.

COFFMAN, Ted, b. 13 June 1946, Salina, Kansas, USA. Director of Clinics, Chiropractic Associates P.C. Divorced, 1 son, 1 daughter. *Education:* BA, University of Kansas, 1968; BS, 1972, DC, 1972, Logan College, St Louis; Diplomate, National Board of Chiropractic Examiners; Board Certified, Acupuncture, Columbia Institute. *Appointments:* President, Chairman, Board, Chiropractic Associates Clinics. *Memberships:* American, International Chiropractic Associations; Professional Chiropractic Association of America; New Mexico Chiropractic Association. *Publications:* "The Chiropractic Epitome", 'Chiropractic Economics', 1985; "How to Be Up no matter What's Going Down", 1986. *Honours:* Post Graduate Extension Lecturer Parker Chiropractic Research Foundation, Logan College. *Hobbies:* Giant Slalem Ski Racer: Colorado Nastav Silver Medalist, 1983-84, 1984-85. *Address:* 1820 Juan Tabo NE, Albuquerque, NM 87112, USA.

COGNETTI, Goffredo, b. 16 May 1942, Pisa, Italy. Associate Professor, Developmental Physiology. m. Maria Gabriella Amari, 8 Oct. 1972, Pisa, 1 son. *Education:* Lauren, University of Modena, Italy, 1967. *Appointments:* Postdoctoral Fellow, MII, Cambridge, Massachusetts, USA, 1968-69; Assistente Supplente, 1969-72, Assistente Ordinario, 1972-75, Professore Incaricato, 1975-81, Professore Associatoo, 1981-, University of Palermo, Italy. *Memberships:* International Society of Developmental biologists; Society for Developmental Biology Inc; Societa Italiana di Biofisica e Biologia Molecolar; Associazione di biologia Cellulare e del Differenziamento; Unione Zoologica Italiana. *Publications:* Articles in professional journals including: 'Journal Molecular Biology'; 'Biochemistry', 1981. *Address:* Dipartmento di Biologia Cellulare e dello Sviluppo, Via Archirafi 20, I-90141 Palermo, Italy.

COHEN, Alec Michael, b. 23 Sep. 1945, London, England. Orthodontic Consultant. m. Susan Bennett, Finchley, London, 16 July 1970, 2 sons, 2 daughters. *Education:* BDS, PhD, London Hospital Medical College, University of London; Fellow, Dental Society; Doctor of Orthodontics, Royal College of Surgeons (England). *Appointments:* House Officer, London Hospital Dental Department; Orthodontic Course, Eastman Dental Hospital Senior House Officer, University College Hospital Dental Department; Registrar, London Hospital Dental Department; Senior Registrar, Eastman Dental Hospital; Lecturer, University College Dental School, London; Honorary Consultant, Senior Lecturer in Orthodontics, University College Dental School. *Memberships:* British Society of Study of Orthodontics, Curator, Council Member; British Society for Dental Research. *Publications:* Various articles in dental journals. *Honours:* Francis Farmer Scholarship, 1964; Gensersal Dental Council Scholarship, 1964-69. *Address:* 42 Bramley Road, London N14 4HR, London, England.

COHEN, Betty Joan Berg, b. 16 Nov. 1930, New York, USA. Senior Medical Writer/Manager, Medical Writing Group, Medical Research, Syntex Research. m. Albert Cohen, 28 Aug. 1952, New York, 1 son, 1 daughter. *Education:* BA, 1952, MA, 1953, Biology, Brooklyn College; PhD, Epidemiologic Science, University of Michigan, Ann Arbor, 1965; Postdoctoral NIH Fellow, Genetics, Stanford University Medical School, 1975. *Appointments:* Researcher, Biochemistry, Rockefeller Institute for Medical Research, 1952-56; Research Scientist, Biochemistry, Columbia University College of Physicians & Surgeons, New York, 1958-60; Doctoral NIH Trainee, University of Michigan, 1960-65; NIH Postdoctoral Fellow, Genetics, Stanford University Medical School, 1974-75; Medical Literature Research Scientist/Writer, Alza Corp, Palo Alto, 1977-81; Senior Medical Writer, International Clinical Studies, Syntex Research, Palo Alto, 1981-86; Manager, Medical Writing Group, Medical Research Syntex Research, Palo Alto, 1986-. *Memberships:* American Medical Writers Association; Society for Technical Communication; American Association for the Advancement of Science; New York Academy of Science. *Publications:* Co-Author, "Metabolic and Endocrine Effects of Medicated Intrauterine Devices", 'Endocrine Mechanisms in Fertility Regulation', 1983;"Review: Anemia and Menstrual Blood Loss", 'Obstetrics Gynecology Survey', 1980; "Growth Characteristics of influenza virus in primary calf kidney tissue culture", 'Autoradiographic Studies', 1965; Author, "Aspects of Influenza Virus Biosynthesis", 1965; Numerous articles in 'International Clinical Studies for Publication in Scientific Journals. *Honours:* Sigma Xi; Phi Beta Kappa; Magna cum Laude, Honours in Biology, 1952; Kappa Phi Scholarship in Biology, 1952; Kappa Delta Pi. *Hobbies:* Music; Swimming; Reading. *Address:* 745 Mayfield Avenue, Stanford, CA 94305, USA.

COHEN, Barry Victor, b. 1 Mar. 1952, Brooklyn, New York, USA. Private Practice. m. Janet Ellen Schanker, 5 Jan. 1975, Watermill Inn, 1 son, 1 daughter. *Education:* Associate in Science; BS, Science; Doctor of Chiropractic. *Memberships:* American Chiropractic Association; New York State Chiropractic Association; Council on Nutrition, Council on Roengenology, American Chiropractic Association; Foundation for Chiropractic Education & Research. *Honours:* Diplomate, National Board of

Chiropractic Examiners. *Hobbies:* Sailing; Dance. *Address:* 357 E. Main St., (25A), Centerport, NY 11721, USA.

COHEN, Harris Roger, b. 22 Aug. 1946, New York, New York, USA. Doctor of Chiropractic, Private Practitioner. m. Iris Rochelle Berg, 21 June 1970, Bellrose, Queens, New York, 1 son, 1 daughter. *Education:* BA, Hartwick College; MS, C W Post College; DC, New York Chiropractic College. *Appointments:* Teacher: Elwood Junior High School; Calhoun High School. Faculty Member, New York Chiropractic College. *Memberships:* American, New York State and Suffolk County Chiropractic Associations; Alumni Association of New York Chiropractic College; National Speakers Association. *Publications:* "Chromosone Mapping of I-Coli", 1967. *Honours:* Deans List, 1967, 78, 79; Certificates of Merit, 1979; Certificate, 1979; Silver Star Award, 1983. *Hobbies:* Body building; Jogging. *Address:* 19 Middle Country Road, Middle Island, NY 11953, USA.

COHEN, Harvey Jay, b. 21 Oct. 1940, Brooklyn, New York, USA. Professor of Medicine, Director of Duke Aging Center. m. Sandra Helen Levine, June 1964, Brooklyn, 1 son, 1 daughter. *Education:* BS, Brooklyn College, 1961; MD, Downstate Medical Center, State University of New York, 1965. *Appointments include:* Chief Medical Service 1976-82, Associate Chief Staff of Education 1982-84, Director of Geriatric Research, Education and Clinical Center 1984-, VA Medical Center, Durham, North Carolina; Professor of Medicine 1980-, Director of Center for Aging 1982-, Duke University, Durham. *Memberships:* Fellow, American Geriatrics Society; American Society of Clinical Oncology; American Association of Hematology; American Association of Cancer Research Alpha Omega Alpha; Fellow, American College of Physicians. *Publications include:* "Medical Immunology", (with M Thaler and R Klausner), 1977; 'An Approach to Monoclonal Gammopathies in the Elderly', (with J C Crawford), 1982; "Effect of Age on Response to Treatment and Survival in Multiple Myeloma', (with H R Silberman, W Forman, a Bartolucci and C Liu), 1983; 'Comparison with Two Long-Term Chemotherapy Regimens, With or Without Agents to Modify Skeletal Repair, In Multiple Myeloma', (with H R Silberman, K Tornyos and A Bartolucci), 1984; 'Aging and Neoplasia', (with J Crawford), 1984; 'Carbohydrate Metabolism in Transforming Lymphocytes from the Aged', (with T O Tollefsbol), 1985; 'The Essential Role of L-Glutamine in Lymphocyte Differentiation in Vitro', (with J C Crawford), 1985. *Honours include:* Physicians Recognition Award, American Medical Association, 1984-87. *Address:* Director, Center for the Study of Aging, Box 3003, Duke University Medical Center, Durham, NC 27710, USA.

COHEN, Ian Thomas, b. 4 Mar. 1942, Republic of South Africa. Associate Professor of Paediatric Surgery. m. Sharon Dianne, 8 Aug. 1971, Johannesburg, 2 sons. *Education:* BS, University of Natal, Durban, 1962; MB, BCh, University of Witwatersrand. Johannesburg, 1968. *Appointments:* Internship: Johannesburg General Hospital and University of Witwatersrand, 1969; Military Service, Lieutenant, S. African Defense Force, 1970; Surgical Residency, Johannesburg General Hospital and University of Witwatersrand, Registrar, Urology, 1971; Registrar, General Surgery, Hammersmith Hospital and Royal Postgraduate Medical School, London, England, 1972; Senior Registrar, Trauma and Orthopaedics, St. Peter's Hospital, Chertsey, Surrey, England, 1972-73; Senior Registrar, Surgery, Johannesburg General Hospital and University of Witwatersrand, 1973-74. *Memberships:* North American Society of Paediatric Gastroenterology; Association for Surgical Education; Society for Nutrition Education; Worcester County Paediatric Society; Medical Association of South Africa; South African Association of Paediatric Surgeons.

Publications: Papers presented to learned societies; Chapters in Books; Contributor to professional journals including: Co-author, 'Accessory Diagphragm in an Infant', 'Journal of Pediatric Surgery, 1981; Co-author, 'Nutritional Care of the Surgical Neonate' in 'Journal of the American Dietetic Association', 1983; Co-author, "Nutrition and the Pediatric Cancer Patient", American Dietetic Association, Audio-cassette series, 1985. *Honours:* Outstanding Medical Educator, University of Massachusetts Medical School, 1983, 84. *Address:* University of Massachusetts Medical Center, Department of Surgery, 55 Lake Avenue North, Worcester, MA 01605, USA.

COHEN, James R., b. 6 Oct. 1945, Norfolk, Virginia, USA. Director of Oncology, Good Samaritan Hosptial, San Jose, California. *Education:* BA 1967; MD 1971. *Appointments:* Medical intern, resident, New York Hospital, 1971-73; Staff internist, USAF Regional Hospital, Fort Worth, Texas, 1974-76; Oncolgoy-Haematology Fellow, 1976-78, Clinical Instructor 1978-85, Stanford University; Director, Oncolgoy, Good Samaritan Hospital, 1982-. *Memberships:* Fellow, American College of Physicians; American Society of Internal Medicine; Board 1982-84, American Cancer Society; New York Academy of Science; American Association for the Advancement of Science; Clinical Investigator, Northern California Oncology Group; Board president, Hospice & Valley, 1983-85; Liaison associate in Cancer, American College of Surgeons; etc. *Publications include:* Numerous contributions to professioanl journals. *Honour:* Alpha Omega Alpha, 1971. *Hobbies:* Racquetball; Travel; Jogging. *Address:* 2410 Samaritan Drive, San Jose, CA 95124, USA.

COHEN, John Simon Henry, b. 20 Apr. 1937, London, England. Senior Lecturer. m. Wanda, 18 July 1971, 2 sons, 1 daughter. *Education:* MB, BS, University of London, 1961; LRCP, MRCS, 1961; MRCGP, Royal College of General Practitioners, 1973; Dip.Soc., University of London, 1980; FRGS, 1983; MSc., 1984. *Appointments:* House Physician, Barnet General Hospital, 1961; House Surgeon, St George's Hospital, London, 1961-62; Senior House Officer, Royal Marsden Hospital, London, 1962-63; Medical Registrar, Harefield Hospital, 1964-66; Registrar, Clinical Pathology, Harefield Hospital, 1966-67; General Practitioner, London NW11, 1967-82; Assistant Physician, Manor House Hospital, London, 1967-75; Part-time Lecturer, General Practice, Royal Free Hospital School of Medicine, 1976-82; Lecturer, Health Education, London Business School, 1975-83; Senior Lecturer, General Practice, Middlesex Hospital Medical School, London. *Memberhips:* British Medical Association; BCGP; Israel Medical Association; Royal Society of Medicine; MDU. *Publications:* Articles in professional journals including: 'The Practitioner'; 'Journal of the Royal society of Medicine'; etc. *Honours:* Stanning Overseas Fellowship, 1976, Upjohn Travelling Fellowship, 1979, Royal College General Practitioners. *Hobbies:* Exploring; Travel; Reading; Stamp Collecting; Writing. *Address:* Academic Sub-Department of General Practice, Middlesex Hospital Medical School, London W1P 8PN, England.

COHEN, Jules, b. 26 Aug. 1931, Brooklyn, New York, USA. Senior Associate Dean for Medical Education, University of Rochester School of Medicine and Dentistry. m. Doris Eidlin, 25 Mar. 1956, Rochester, New York, 2 sons, 1 daughter. *Education:* AB (High Distinction), 1953; MD (Hons.), 1957, University of Rochester. *Appointments:* Intern in Medicine, Beth Israel Hospital, Boston, 1957-58; Resident, Fellow in Medicine, Strong Memorial Hospital, Rochester, 1958-60; Research Associate, National Institutes of Health, Bethesda, 1960-62; Research Associate, Royal Postgraduate Medical School, London,

England, 1962-63; Instructor, 1963-64, Senior Instructor, 1964-66, Assistant Professor, 1966-69, Associate Professor, 1969-73, Professor of Medicine, 1973-, University of Rochester School of Medicine and Dentistry; Chief, The Medical Service, Rochester General Hospital, 1976-82; Senior Associate Dean for Medical Education at Rochester, 1982-. *Memberships:* Fellow, American College of Physicians; Fellow, American Heart Association, Council on Clinical Cardiology; Fellow, American College of Cardiology; American Physiological Society; American Federation for Clinical Research; Sigma Xi. *Publications:* Contributor to professional journals including: Co-author: 'Hypertrophic obstructive cardiomyopathy', 1964; 'Determinants of thyroxine-induced cardiac hypertrophy in mice', 1966; Effects of energy availability on protein synthesis in isdated rat atria', 1969; 'Conserving effect of thyroid hormone on myocardial energy stores in vitro', 1973; Book chapters include: 'Cardiac manifestations of the neuromuscular disorders' in "Advances in Neurology" (R.C. Griggs & R.T. Moxley, Editors), 1977; Co-author, "Polycythemia" in 'Hematology for Practitioners' (M.A. Lichtman, Editor), 1978. *Honours:* DSPHS Research Grants, 1963-69, 1974-77; Research Career Development Award, MH, 1970-75; American Heart Association Grant, 1970-72; Gold Medal, University of Rochester Medical Alumni Association, 1985. *Hobbies:* Tennis; Gardening; Reading; Theatre. *Address:* Box 601, University of Rochester Medical Center, Rochester, NY 14642, USA.

COHEN, Kenneth David, b. 16 Mar. 1928, Philadelphia, USA. Psychiatrist; Psychoanalyst. m. Ann Fedorka, 13 Mar. 1955, Philadelphia, 3 sons. *Education:* BA, University of Pennsylvania, 1949; MD, University of Health Sciences, Chicago Medical School, 1953; Institute for the Philadelphia Association of Psychoanalyis, 1966. *Appointments:* Mental Hygiene Consultation Service, Ft. Geo. G. Meade, 1957-59; Senior Staff Psychiatrist, 1959-62, Clinical Director, 1973-80, Director, Professional Education, 1974-80, Philadelphia Psychiatric Centre; Chief, Psychiatric Consultation Service, VA Hospital, Philadelphia, 1970-72; Associate Chief, Psychiatry, Presbyterian, University of Pennsylvania Medical Centre, 1980-83; Director, Professional School, Institute of Philadelphia Association for Psychoanalysis, 1984-. *Memberships:* Member, numerous professional organisations. *Publications:* "Significance of Illness to the Patient", 1960; Numerous articles in professional journals including: 'Audio Digest'; 'Biological Psychiatry'; 'American Law Institute'; 'Journal of National Psychiatric Hospitals'; etc. *Honours:* Certificate of Commendation, US Army, 1971; Fellow, Pennsylvania Psychiatric Society, 1971; Fellow, American Psychiatric Association, 1974; Fellow, Royal Society of Health, 1978; Fellow, College of Physicians of Philadelphia; Philadelphia Psychiatric Centre Medical Staff Distinguished Service Award, 1981; Commendation, Board of Directors, Philadelphia Psychiatric Centre, 1983. *Hobbies:* Reading; Swimming; Cross Word Puzzles. *Address:* 37 East Princeton Road, Bala Cynwyd, PA 19004, USA.

COHEN, Mervyn David, b. 4 Aug. 1944, Johannesburg, South Africa (USA Immigrant Visa Held). Professor. *Education:* BSc (Hons.), Microbiology, 1966, MB ChB, 1968, University of Edinburgh; DCH, 1971, MRCP, 1971, FRCR, 1978 (England); MD, University of Edinburgh, 1978; Board Examination of American College of Radiology, 1982; Postgraduate Medical Training: Children's Hospital, Johannesburg, South Africa, Baragwanath Hospital, Johannesburg, Children's Hospital, Edinburgh, Scotland. *Appointments:* Chief Medical Officer, Turks and Caicos Islands, West Indies, 1972-74; Locum General Practitioner, Edinburgh, Scotland, 1975; Consultant in Medical & Scientific Section. *Publications:* Over 180 publications in scientific journals; "Control of Enzyme Activity", 1976, 2nd edition 1983, translated into Spanish, German, Italian, Russian & Malay. *Honours:* Colworth Medal, British Biochemical Society, 1978; Anniversary Prize, Federation of European Biochemical Societies, 1977; Elected Member, European Molecular Biology Organisation, 1982; Fellow, Royal Society of Edinburgh, 1984; Fellow, Royal Society, 1984. *Hobbies:* Golf; Chess; Natural History. *Address:* Inverbay, Invergowrie, Dundee, DD2 5DQ, Scotland.

COHEN, Sheldon Gilbert, b. 21 Sep. 1918, Pittston, Pennsylvania, USA. Director, Immunology, Allergic and Immunologic Diseases, National Institute of Allergy and Infectious Diseases. *Education:* BA, Ohio State University, 1940; MD, New York University, 1943; DSc (Hon). *Appointments:* Intern, Bellevue Hospital, New York; Medical Corps, US Army Air Force; Hospital Residencies, various hospitals; Research Fellow, University of Pittsburgh; Chief, Allergy, Mercy Hospital; Professor, Experimental Biology, Wilkes College; Consultant, Internal Medicine, Allergy and Research, VA Hospital, Wilkes-Barre; Chief, Allergy and Immunology, EAP, NIAID; Director, IAID Programme, NIAID. *Memberships include:* Fellow, American Academy of Allergy and Immunology; American College of Physicians; American College of Allergists; Association of American Physicians; American Association of Immunologists; many other professional organisations. *Publications:* Numerous articles in scientific journals. *Honours:* Distinguished Service Awards: American Academy of Allergy, 1971, Wyoming Seminary, 1978, Asthama and Allergy Foundation of America, 1981; Clemens von Pirquet Award, Georgetown University, 1981; DSc., Honorary, Wilkes College, 1976. *Hobbies:* Sailing; Fishing; Art; Medical History. *Address:* Building 31, Room 7A-52, National Institutes of Health, Bethesda, MD 20892, USA.

COHEN, Sidney Maximilian, b. 25 May 1919, Morristown, New Jersey, USA. Associate in Clinical Neurology. m. Lea Astor, 26 Feb. 1955, White Plains, 2 sons, 1 daughter. *Education:* BS, Columbia University, 1939; MD, Long Island College of Medicine, 1943; Dr.Med.Sc., Neurology, 1952. *Appointments:* Rotating Intern, Assistant Resident, Medicine, Cumberland Hospital, Brooklyn, New York, 1943-44; Chief Psychiatrist, US Disciplinary Barracks, North Camp Hood, Texas, 1945; Chief, Neuropsychiatric Section, 98th General Hospital, Munich, Germany, 1946; Psychiatric Consultant, Dachau War Crimes Board, 1946; Assistant Attending, Neurologist, Chief, POD, Neurology, Roosevelt Hospital, Neurological Institute (Vanderbilt Clinic), 1951; Lecturer, Dean's Office for Postgraduate Medical Education, P & S Columbia University, 1983. *Memberships:* Fellow, American Academy of Neurology; Association for Research in Nervous & Mental Diseases; AMA; American Association for Advancement of Science; New York Academy of Science; Royal Society of Health. *Publications:* "History of Neurological & Related Research at Neurological Institute", 'Neurological Institute of New York 1909-1974', 1975; "Localization of Cord Tumors by Electromyography", 1950; "Thalamic Loci of Afferent Activity Initiated by Afferent Impulses in Cat", 1954; etc. *Honours:* Scroll of Honour, United Jewish Appeal, 1971; Society of Sigma Xi, 1950; Citation, New York City Director of Selective Service System. *Hobbies:* Art Collector; Travel; Theatre; Ballet. *Address:* 1213 Park Avenue, New York, NY 10128, USA.

COHEN, Sydney, b. 18 Sep. 1921, Johannesburg, South Africa. Professor, Chemical Pathology, Guy's Hospital, London, England. m. June Bernice Adler, 29 June 1950, Johannesburg, 1 son, 1 daughter. *Education:* MB.ChB, 1944, MD, 1954, Witwatersrand University; PhD, London University, 1959.

Paediatrics, Western Memorial Hospital, Corner Brook, Newfoundland, Canada, 1975; Registrar in Diagnostic Radiology, Leeds Area Health Authority, England. 1975-76; Senior Registrar, Diagnostic Radiology, Yorkshire Region Health Authority, Leeds, 1976-79; Assistant Professor, Paediatric Radiology, 1980-82, Associate Professor, 1982-84, Professor, 1984-, James Whitcomb Riley Hospital for Children, Indiana University Medical Center, Indianapolis, Indiana, USA; Director of Paediatric Radiology, 1983-. *Memberships:* Royal College of Physicians, London; Royal College of Radiologists, London; British Medical Association; British Institute of Radiology; Society for Paediatric Radiology; Midwest Paediatric Radiology Group; Radiological Society of North America; American Medical Assocition; Marion County Medical Association; American Academy of Paediatrics; American College of Radiology; American Roentgen Ray Society; Society of Magnetic Resonance in Medicine. *Publications:* Contributor to professional journals; Abstracts and Letters; Books including: 'New Techniques and Concepts in the Evaluation of the Small Bowel in Children' in "Clinical Radiology of the Small Intestine", 1986; Scientific exhibits at National and International Meetings; Presentations. *Honours include:* Several Grants, Fellowships and Awards; Certificate of Merit awarded by American Roentgen Ray Society for scientific exhibit, 1982. *Address:* Department of Radiology, James Whitcomb Riley Hospital for Children, Radiology S-139, 702 Barnhill Drive, Indiana University Medical Center, Indianapolis, IN 46223, USA.

COHEN, Philip, b. 22 July 1945, London, England. Research Professor. m. Patricia Townsend Wade, 17 Feb. 1969, London, 1 son, 1 daughter. *Education:* BSc Biochemistry, 1966, PhD Biochemistry, 1969, University College, London. *Appointments:* Science Research council/NATO Postdoctoral Fellow, University of Washington, Seattle, USA, 1969-71; Lecturer in Biochemistry, 1971-78, Reader in Biochemistry, 1978-81; Professor of Enzymology, 1981-84, Royal Society Research Professor, 1984-, all University of Dundee. *Memberships:* British Biochemical Society; British Diabetic Association; *Appointments:* Emergency Medical Service, England,1944-46; House Physician, Postgraduate Medical School, London, 1947; Lecturer, Senior Lecturer, Physiology, Witwatersrand Medical school, 1948-53; Scientific Staff, Biophysics, National Institute for Medical Research, London, 1954-60; Director, MRC Metabolic Unit, Whittington Hospital, London, 1957-60; Reader, Immunology, St Mary's Hospital Medical School, London, 1960-65. *Memberships:* British Society for Immunology; Royal Society of Medicine; Zoological Society, London; Royal Society of Tropical Medicine & Hygiene. *Publications:* "Immunology of Parasitic Infections", Co-Editor, 2nd edition, 1982. *Honours:* Founder Fellow, Royal College Pathologists, 1964; CBE, 1978; FRS, 1978. *Hobbies:* Golf; Gardening; Travel. *Address:* 4 Frognal Rice, London WW3 6RD, England.

COID, Charles Routledge, b. 15 Apr. 1926, Whithorn. Head, Division of Comparative Medicine, m. Marjory M Keay, 2 Jan. 1952, Pittenweem, Fife, Scotland, 1 son, 1 daughter. *Education:* BSc, Royal (Dick) School of Veterinary Studies, University of Edinburgh, 1945-50; PhD, University of Reading, England, 1956; FRCVS; FRCPath; FIBiol. *Appointments:* Clinical Assistant, Royal (Dick) School of Veterinary Studies, University of Edinburgh, Scotland, 1950-51; Senior Scientific Officer, Agricultural Research Council, 1951-56; Scientist, Medical Research Council, 1956-61; Head, Veterinary Research Unit, Glaxo Laboratories, 1961-64; Director of Animal Studies, Royal College of Surgeons of England, 1964-67; currently, Head, Division of Comparative Medicine, Medical Research Council, Clinical Research Centre, Harrow, Middlesex. *Memberships:* Fellow: Royal College of Veterinary Surgeons; Royal College of Pathologists.

Publications: "Infections and Pregnancy", Editor, 1977; "The Multiplication of Three Different Isolates of Group B Streptococci in Pregnant Mice", 1981; "Campylobacters as Placental Pathogens", 1983. *Honours:* Elected: Award of Diploma of Fellowship of Royal College of Veterinary Surgeons, 1983. *Hobbies:* Gardening; Beekeeping. *Address:* Division of Comparative Medicine, Clinical Research Centre Watford Road, Harrow, Middlesex HA1 3UJ England.

COLE, Madison Brooks, Jr., b. 30 Aug. 1940, Worcester, Massachusetts, USA. Principal Investigator, Orthopaedic Research Chief, Electron Microscopy & Histology Laboratory. m. Ada Lynn Asbury, 9 Oct. 1967, Knoxville, Tennessee, 1 son. *Education:* BA, Colgate University, 1962; Graduate work, Brown University, 1962-64; PhD, University of Tennessee, 1969; Postdoctoral training, New York University, 1975. *Appointments include:* Assistant Professor, Biological Sciences, Oakland University, Rochester, Michigan, 1969-74; Assistant Professor, Orthopaedic Surgery, Loyola University Medical Centre, 1975-82; Research Physiologist/Principal Investigator in Orthopaedic Research/Chief, Electron Microscopy & Histology, Veterans Administration Hospital, Hines, Illinois, 1983-; Consultant, Structure Probe Inc., Westchester, Pennsylvania, 1983- *Memberships:* American Association for the Advancment of Science; American Association of Anatomists; American Society for Cell Biology; New York Academy of Science; Orthopaedic Research Society; Sigma Xi. *Publications include:* 40 articles & abstracts, 1964-. *Honours:* Sigma Xi, 1967; National Science Foundation Fellow, 1970. *Hobbies:* Stamp collecting (member, American Philatelic Society); Masonic bodies (past high priest, RAM); Boy Scouts of America (Eagle Scout, Scoutmaster, Wood Badge, Vigil Honour, OA). *Address:* Orthopaedic Research Laboratory, Research Service, Veterans Administration Hospital, Hines, IL 60141, USA.

COLE, Philip, b. 5 Oct. 1917, England. Associate Professor. m. Raya A Cole, 12 Jan. 1943, 2 sons. *Education:* MB, ChB 1951, MD 1954, Victoria University of Manchester, Manchester, England. *Appointments include:* Research Associate, The Gage Research Institute, Toronto, Ontario, Canada, 1975- ; Lecturer 1978-82, Assistant Professor 1982-83, Associate Professor 1983- , Department of Ear, Nose and Throat, University of Toronto, Toronto; Staff, University of Toronto, Department of Ear, Nose and Throat, Saint Michael's Hospital, Toronto; Lecturer 1979-83, Associate Professor 1983- , Department of Preventive Medicine and Biostatistics, University of Toronto; Staff, Department of Ear, Nose and Throat, The Hospital for Sick Children, Toronto, 1980- , Synnybrook Medical Centre, Toronto 1981- . *Memberships:* Fellow, Royal College of Physicians and Surgeons, Canada; Royal College of Physicans and Surgeons, England. *Publications include:* Contributions to over 50 abstracts, articles, reviews, and book chapters in scientific publications, including: 'Mechanisms of nasal obstruction in sleep' (with J S J Haight), 1984; 'Health status of residents in homes insulated with urea formaldehyde foam compared with controls' (co-author), 1984; 'The choana and nasal obstruction' (co-author), 1985. *Hobbies:* Sailing; Skiing. *Address:* 21 Dale Avenue, Apartment 803, Toronto, Ontario N4W 1K3, Canada.

COLE, Philip John, b. 8 Aug. 1918, Essex, England. Ophthalmic Optician. m. Ruby Kathleen Crosier, 15 Mar. 1960, Brentwood, Essex, 1 daughter. *Education:* Fellow, British College of Opticians; Fellow, British Ophthalmic Association (HD). *Appointments:* Founder President, British College of Ophthalmic Opticians, 1980-82; Chairman, Advisory Committee, Worshipful Company of Spectacle Makers, 1972-80. *Memberships:* Briitsh College of Ophthalmic Opticians; Council, Association of Optical Practitioners; Member of Court, Worshipful

Company of Spectacle Makers. *Honour:* Honorary DSc, University of Bradford, 1983. *Address:* 2 John Raven Court, Feering Hill, Kelvedon, Essex, CO5 9NB, England.

COLES, George William, b. 20 Nov. 1933, Ridgewood, New Jersey, USA. Professor of Pathology. m. Florence Parker, 13 Aug. 1955, Philadelphia, Pennsylvania, 3 sons, 1 daughter. *Education:* BA Chemistry, University of Pennsylvania, 1954; MD, University of Miami, Florida, 1958. *Appointments:* Instructror, Haematology & Internal Medicine, University of Miami, 1963-66; Assistant Professor of Clinical Pathology, 1966-70, Director, Outpatient Laboratory Operations, Clinical Laboratories, 1970-72, Associate Professor, 1970-73, Professor & Vice-Chairman, Department of Pathology, University of Alabama at Birmingham; Director, Division of Clinical Pathology, Professor & Medical Director, Clinical Laboratory Sciences, School of Public & Allied Health, Assistant Professor of Internal Medicine, Director, General Haematology & Chemistry Clinical Laboratories, all at University of Alabama at Birmingham; Consultant, VA Medical Centre, Birmingham, Alabama; Director, Clinical Laboratories, University of Alabama Hospitals. *Memberships:* Academic Clinical Laboratory Physicians & Scientists; American Medical Association; American Society of Clinical Pathologists; College of American Pathologists; National Committee for Clinical Laboratory Standards; American Pathology Foundation (Board of Trustees 1983-86). *Publications:* Various articles in medical journals of Patholgoy. *Address:* Department of Pathology, University of Alabama at Birmingham, Medical Centre, Birmingham, AL 35294, USA.

COLEMAN, Ralph Edward, b. 2 Jan. 1943, Indiana, USA. Professor of Radiology. m. Jeanne Fording, 30 Dec. 1967, Kansas City, Missouri, 1 son, 2 daughters. *Education:* BA, University of Evansville, Evansville, Indiana, 1965; MD, Washington University School of Medicine, St Louis, Missouri, 1968. *Appointments:* Instructor in Radiology 1974, Assistant Professor of Radiology 1975-76, Washington University, St Louis, Missouri; Assistant Professor of Radiology 1976-78, Associate Professor of Radiology 1978-79, University of Utah, Salt Lake City, Utah; Professor of Radiology, Duke University Medical Center, Durham, North Carolina, 1979-. *Memberships:* Society of Nuclear Medicine; Radiologic Society of North America; American College of Nuclear Physicians; American Roentgen Ray Society; American Heart Association; American Association for the Advancement of Science; Association of University Radiologists; American College of Radiology; American Medical Association; North Carolina State Medical College. *Publications:* 1 book, 32 book chapters and 130 general articles. *Address:* Box 3808, Department of Radiology, Duke University Medical Center, Durham, NC 27710, USA.

COLETT, Ilse Vivien, Assistant Clinical Professor of Psychiatry, University of California Medical School, San Francisco, Fresno Branch; Consultant Clinical Psychiatrist, Cant Val Regional Center and Local Hospital, Fresno, California, 1967-; President Colett Medical Corporation, Fresno, California, USA, 1969-. *Education:* Medicine: University of Wien Faculty of Medicine; MD, 1939; Postgraduate Training: PGYl, USPHS, New York City, 1943-45; Psychiatric Resident, Norwich St. Hospital, Connecticut, 1945-49; Psychiatric Training: Fresno County Department of Mental Health, 1951-60; Berkeley St. Mental Hygiene Clinic, 1954-55; Langley Porter Psychiatric Institute, San Francisco, 1946-69; PsAn Training, 1954-5. *Appointments:* Hospital Affiliate: VA Medical Center, Fresno; St. Agnes Hospital and Medical Center, Fresno; Ethics Commitee, Central California Psychiatric Association, 1980-81; Chairperson, Psyhciatric Department, Fresno City Hospital, 1966-70; Chairperson, Department of

Psychiatry, Valley Medical Center, 1972-75; Former Acting Director, Fresno St. Mental Hygiene Clinic, Fresno, 1958-60; Consultant PT, Fresno MHC & Bureau of Social Work, Fresno, 1965-67; Consultant, Fresno City Mental Health Department, 1967-77. *Memberships:* American Medical Association; Association World Social Psychiatry; Phys. Socl. Respon. *Publications:* Contributor of articles and papers to professionaljournals etc. *Address:* 126 N. Howard, Fresno, CA 93701, USA.

COLETTE, Claude Gaston Felix Elisée, b. 4 Feb. 1929, France. Professor of Clinical Gynaecology & Obstetrics. m. M J Dhoutaut, 12 Mar. 1960, Besançon, France, 2 sons, 3 daughters. *Education:* MD, 1956; Certification to teach Medicine (Gynaecology & Obstetrics), 1962; Licence Degree in Natural Sciences, 1964. *Appointments:* Hospital Obstetrician & Gynaecologist, 1957; Clinical Professor, 1969. *Memberships:* Vice-President, International Professional Union of Obstetricians & Gynaecologists; President, National Syndicate of French Obstetricians & Gynaecologists; Board Member, French National College of Obstetricians & Gynaecologists; Delegate, European National Union of Specialist Doctors; Vice-President, Academy of Besançon. *Publications:* "Echographie obstetricale", 1970; "Microcirculation uteroplacentaire", 1975; "Ideologies de la sexualité", 1980; "Activité motrice du foetus", 1984. *Hobbies:* History of Ideologies; Mountaineering. *Address:* La Mère et l'Enfant, C.H.U. de Besançon, 25030 Cedex, France.

COLLIER, Joseph Gavin, b. 22 Jan. 1942, Manchester, England. Senior Lecturer and Honorary Consultant in Clinical Pharmacology. m. Roham, Sep. 1968, France, 3 sons. *Education:* MB, B Chir; MA; MD; Fellow, Royal College of Physicians. *Appointments:* House Physician, Registrar/Lecturer, Senior Registrar/Lecturer, Consultant/Senior Lecturer, St Georges Hospital Medical School, London. *Memberships:* Briitsh Pharmacological Society; British Hypertension Society. *Publications:* Deputy Editor, 'Drug and Therapy Bulletin'; Articles about drug usage and drug policy in 'The Times', 'The Gardian' and 'Lancet'; 'Capasicin inhalation in man and the effects of disodium cromozlycate', 1984. *Hobby:* Writing. *Address:* Department of Pharmacology and Clinical Pharmacology, St Georges Hospital Medical School, London SW17, England.

COLLINS, Patrick Gerard, b. 17 Oct. 1923, Cork City, Ireland. Professor, Clinical Surgery, Chairman, Surgery, Royal College of Surgeons in Ireland. m. 1978. *Education:* MB, BCh., BAO, National University of Ireland, 1947; M.Ch.; FRCSI; FRCS; FACS. *Appointments:* Senior Surgical Registrar, Shefield Royal Infirmary, 1957-59; Visiting Consultant Surgeon, Charitable Infirmary, Dublin, 1959-, St Luke's Hospital, Dublin, 1962-. *Memberships:* President, Royal Academy of Medicine in Ireland; 1983-85; Past President, Pancreatic Society of Great Britain & Ireland, Past President, Irish Society of Gastroenterology. *Publications:* "An Atraumatic Surgical Approach for Transgastric Internal drainage of pseudo systs", 'Journal Irish College Physicians & Surgeons', 1985; Co-Author, 'Iatrogenic Biliary Stricture – presentation & Management", 'British Journal Surgery', 1984. *Honours:* Elected, Honorary Life Member, Warren Cole Society, Chicago, USA, 1983. *Hobbies:* Reading; Fresh Water Fishing. *Address:* The Charitable Infirmary, Jervis Street, Dublin I, Ireland.

COLLINS, William Patrick, b. 23 May 1939, England. Professor, Reproductive Biochemistry, Director, Diagnostics Research Unit. m. Patricia Olive Norris, 2 June 1962, Ilford, 1 son, 2 daughters. *Education:* BSc; PhD; DSc; FRSC; C,Chem. *Appointments:* Biochemist, 1965, Senior Biochemist, 1965-69, Principal Biochemist, 1969-72, Biochemical Endocrinology, & Institute of Obstetrics &

Gynaecology, University of London; Senior Lecturer, 1972-75, Reader, Biochemical Endocrinology, 1975-79, Professor, Reproductive Biochemistry, 1979-, Director, Diagnostics Research Unit, 1983-, Obstetrics and Gynaecology, King's College School of Medicine & Dentistry, London. *Memberships:* Association of University Teachers; Association of Clinical Biochemistry; Royal Society of Chemistry; British Andrology Society. *Publications:* 180 articles in professional journals and books; "Alternative Immunoassays", Editor. *Hobbies:* Gastronomy; Natural Philosophy. *Address:* Obstetrics & Gynaecology Dept., King's College School of Medicine & Dentistry, Denmark Hill, London SE5 8RX, England.

COLLIS, Julian, b. 31 May 1932, Johannesburg, South Africa. Private Practice as Specialist Prosthodontist; Examiner in Prosthetics at Universities of Pretoria and Witwatersrand. m. Maureen Ethel Young, 5 July 1960, Johannesburg, 1 son, 2 daughters. *Education:* BDS, University of Witwatersrand, 1954; Higher Dental Diploma, University of Witwatersrand, 1960; Registered as Specialist Prosthodontist with South African Medical and Dental Council, 1972; MSc (Dental) , University of Witwatersrand 1981; Fellow, International College of Dentists, 1985. *Appointments:* Private General Practice, 1955-69; practice confined to Removable Prosthodontics, 1969-; Honorary Visiting Assistant Dental Surgeon, Clinical Lecturer in Prosthetics and Cleft Palate Section of Orthodontic Department, School of Dentistry, University of Witwatersrand, 1960-71; Part-time Assistant Dental Surgeon, Lecturer, 1970-71; Part-time Senior Lecturer, Senior Clinician, 1972-79; Part-time Principal Specialist, Senior Lecturer, 1980-81; Department of Prosthetic Dentistry, University of Witwatersranhd; Examiner in Pre-Clinical Prosthetics, Oral and Dental Hospital, Pretoria, 1980-. *Memberships include:* Founder Member and Executive Member, Prosthodontic Society of South Africa. *Publications:* Contributor to 'Journal of the Dental Association of South Africa'. *Honours:* PROSSA Presidential Medal, 1978; S.Tvl. President's Medal, 1979; Research Development Fund Grants, 1978, 85; University Study Grants, 1978, 80. *Hobbies:* Reading: Music; Tennis; Gymnastics; Jogging; Appearances on radio & TV general knowledge quiz shows. *Address:* 3 Rosebank Medical and Dental Centre, 11 Sturdee Avenue, Rosebank, Johannesburg 2196, South Africa.

COLMAN, Bernard Harold, b. 17 Oct. 1924, Wolverhampton, England. University Lecturer; Consultant Surgeon. m. Ilse Meschenmoser, 17 July, 1957, Edinburgh, Scotland. *Education:* MB, ChB, FRCS, ChM, Edinburgh; MA, MSc, Oxford University, England. *Appointment:* Lecturer in Otolaryngology, Oxford University, England; Consultant Surgeon, Radcliffe Infirmary,-Oxford, England -. *Memberships:* Fellow, Royal Society of Medicine; Collegium Otolaryngologicum Amicitiae Sacrum, etc. *Publications:* Co-author "Diseases of Nose, Throat and Ear"; various papers, mainly relating to Otology. *Honours:* Hon. Member Spanish Otolaryngological Society, 1981; Hon. Member, Hungarian Otolaryngological Society, 1985. *Hobbies:* Sailing; Ski-ing; Hill-walking. *Address:* Department of Otolaryngology, Radcliffe Infirmary, Oxford OX2 6HE, England.

COLMAN, Wendy, b. 6 July 1950, New York, USA. Associate Professor; Director of Graduate Education, Temple University. *Education:* BS, Occupational Therapy, Tufts University, 1972; MA, Occupational Therapy, 1977, PhD, Occupational Therapy, 1984, New York University. *Appointments:* Extended Family Center, San Francisco, California, 1973-75; Roosevelt Hospital, New York City, 1975-77; Teaching and Curriculum Design, Undergraduate and Graduate Level, New York

University, 1977-80; Assistant Professor, Boston University, 1980-83; Associate Professor, Temple University, 1984-. *Memberships:* American Occupational Therapy Association; American Occupational Therapy Foundation; World Federation of Occupational Therapy; Pennsylvania Occupational Therapy Association; AOTA Mental Health Special Interest Section. *Publications:* Articles include: Occupational Therapy and Child Abuse, Organizational Relationships, in professional publications. *Honours:* First person to be awarded a PhD in Occupational Therapy, 1984: Grant Award, Psychosocial Research, Affective Responses to Activities, 1985. *Hobbies:* Sports: Music: Pleasure Reading: Raising Dogs. *Address:* Department of Occupational Therapy, Temple University College of Allied Health Professions, 3307 North Broad Street, Philadelphia, PA 19140, USA.

COLON, Vicente Franklin, b. 22 Nov. 1937, Ponce, Puerto Rico. Physician. m. Marjorie Ruth Kunkel, 4 Aug. 1961, Lincoln, Nebraska, 3 sons. *Education:* BA, Nebraska Wesleyan University, 1959; MD, University of Nebraska College of Medicine, 1963. *Appointments:* Partner, Zimmer and Colon, Friend, Nebraska, 1964-77; Associate Professor, 1977-83; Professor, Family Medicine, University of Cincinnati, 1983-. *Memberships:* Cincinnati Academy of Medicine; Ohio State Medical Association; American Medical Association; Southwestern Ohio Society of Family Physicians; Ohio Academy of Family Physicians; American Academy of Family Physicians. *Publications:* (book) "A Clinician's Guide to Diagnostic Cytology", (with CG Schumann), 1982; (articles) 'Toxic Effects of the Brown Spider Bite', 1967; 'Vaccinia Necrosum as a Clue to Lymphatic Lymphoma', 1968; (book chapters) 'Cardiovascular Medicine for Family Medicine: Principles and Practice', 1978, 1982. *Honours:* Governors Highway Safety Award, Nebraska, 1974; Nebraska Leadership Award for Community Improvement, 1976; Family Medicine Residency Teacher of the Year, 1983-84. *Hobbies:* Medical Politics; Issues in Law and Medicine; Reading; Golf. *Address:* 455 Flemridge Ct., Cincinnati, OH 45231, USA.

COLQUHOUN, Joseph, b. 25 Mar. 1926, Auchinlech, Scotland. Associate Radiologist, SLEH/TCH/THI, Houston, Texas, USA; Assistant Professor, Clinical, Baylor College of Medicine, Houston. m. Eileen Norris, 29 Mar. 1952, Habbaniya, Iraq, 1 son, 3 daughters. *Education:* MB BS, London; DMRD; FRCR. *Appointments:* Registrar, Radiology, Addenbrooke's Hospital, Cambridge, England; Assistant Radiologist, Ulleval Hospital, Oslo, Norway; Senior Fellow, Radiology, Children's Hospital, Cincinnati, Ohio, USA; Senior Registrar, Radiology, Addenbrooke's Hospital, Cambridge; Chief Radiologist, Bradford Hospitals, England; Associate Radiologist, University Hospitals, Cleveland, Ohio; Assistant Professor, Radiology, Western Reserve University, Cleveland, Ohio. *Memberships:* British Institute of Radiology; Fellow, Royal Faculty of Radiologists; American College of Radiology; American Roentgen Ray Society; Texas Medical Association; Texas and Houston Radiologic Societies. *Hobby:* Cattle Ranching. *Address:* 6621 Fennin Street, Houston TX 77030, USA.

COLSTON, Michael Joseph, b. 6 Oct. 1948, Birmingham, England. Laboratory Head. m. Kay Barrett, 4 Sep. 1971, Oxford, 2 sons. *Education:* BSc honours Microbiology, PhD Medical Microbiolgoy, London University. *Appointments:* Central Public Health Laboratories, Colindale, London, 1970-72; St George's Hospital Medical school, London, 1972-78 and 1981-82; SRI International, California, USA, 1978-80; Biomedical Research, SRI International, California, 1980-81; Head, Laboratory for Leprosy and Mycobacterial Research, National Institute for Medical Research, Mill Hill, London, England, 1982-. *Memberships:* American Society of Microbiology; British Society of Immunology. *Publications include:*

About 35 articles and abstracts including: 'The nude mice in studies of leprosy' (with K Kohsaka) in "The nude mouse in experimental and clinical research" volume 2 (editors: J Fogh and B C Giovanella), 1982; 'Lymphatic leukemia and retrieval of defective Friend virus in athymic nude rats' (with A H Fieldsteel and P J Dawson), 1982; 'Elevated macrophage activity in nude mice' (with A K Sharp), 1982 and 1984; 'Leprosy in the nude mouse' (co-author), 1982 and 1984; 'Transplantation of human malignant tumors to the athymic rat' (co-author), 1982; 'Mycobacterium leprae infection in nude mice: bacteriological and histological responses to primary infection and large inoculi' (co-author), 1983; 'Infection of the congenitally athymic rat with Mycobacterium leprae' (with P J Dawson and A H Fieldsteel), 1983; 'The regulation of macrophage activity in congentially athymic mice' (with A K Sharp), 1984; 'Possible idiotypic suppression of cell-medicated immunity in lepromatous leprosy' (co-author), 1984; Immunoregulation in leprosy', 1984. *Hobbies:* Sports; Sculpturing; Painting. *Address:* National Institute for Medical Research, The Ridgeway, Mill Hill, London NW7 1AA, England.

COLWELL, John Amory, b. 4 Nov. 1928, Boston, USA. Professor of Medicine. m. Jane Kuebler Colwell, 16 June 1954, 2 sons, 2 daughters. *Education:* AB, Princeton University, 1950; MD, 1954, MS, Medicine, 1957, PhD, Physiology, 1968, Northwestern University Medical School, Chicago; Internships, Residencies, various hospitals. *Appointments:* ADA NIH Trainee, Diabetes, Northwestern University medical Centre, 1960-62; Clinical Investigator, VA Research Hospital, Chicago, 1962-64; Instructor, medicine, 1960-62, Associate, 1962-65, Assistant Professor, 1965-69, Associate Professor, 1969-71, Professor, Medicine, Director, Endocrinology Metabolism Nutrition, 1971-, Medical University of South Carolina; Associate Chief of Staff, Research & Development, VA Medical Centre, Charleston, 1971-. *Memberships include:* American Association for the Advancement of Science; American College of Physicians; American Diabetes Association; American Federation for Clinical Research; Charleston County Medical Society; Endocrine Society; European Association for the Study of Diabetes; etc. *Publications:* Author, over 130 articles and books. *Honours:* John A. Colwell Award for Excellence in Diabetes Research, S.C. Affiliate, American Diabetes Association (1st Recipient), 1983; Ralph Colp Award, Mt. Sinai Journal of Medicine (co-recipient). *Hobbies:* Golf; Tennis. *Address:* Medical University of South Carolina, 171 Ashley Avenue, Charleston, SC 29425. USA.

COMARR, Avrom Estin, b. 15 July 1915, Chicago, Illinois, USA. Professor of Urology. m. Ruth Harriette, 1 daughter. *Education:* AB, University of Southern California, Los Angeles, 1937; MB 1940, MD 1941, Chicago Medical School, Chicago; Diplomate, American Board of Urology, 1953; Diplomate, American Board of Spinal Cord Injury, 1978. *Appointments:* Internship, Evangelical Deaconess Hospital, Cleveland, Ohio, 1940-41; Residency, Polyclinic Hospital, Cleveland, 1941-42; US Army Service & Military Hospitals, 1942-52, discharged as Major; Clinical Instructor in Urology, School of Medicine, University of California, 1953-55; Assistant Clinical Professor of Urology, 1955-58, Assistant Professor 1958-59, Associate Clinical Professor 1959-66, Clinical Professor 1966-82, Emeritus Clinical Professor of Urology, 1982- , Loma Linda University School of Medicine; Clinical Professor of Surgery (Neurological-Urology), 1966-81, Emeritus Professor, 1981-, University of Southern California School of Medicine. *Memberships include:* American Medical Association; American Association of General Practice; American Urological Association; American College of Surgeons; International College of Surgeons; Founder, Past President, American Paraplegia Society; International Medical Society of Paraplegia; World Medical Association; American Spinal Injury Association.   *Publications:* "Neurological-Urology-Physiology of Micturition: Its Neurological Disorders & Sequalae", 1971; "Sexual Rehabilitation of the Spinal Cord Injuired Patient" (forthcoming). Over 500 articles in medical journals; over 1900 papers & lectures. *Honours:* Numerous Honours and Awards. *Address:* 4235 Clubhouse Drive, Lakewood, CA 90712, USA.

COMERFORD, Francis Rory, b. 17 Nov. 1933, Dublin, Ireland. Lecturer in Experimental Medicine. m. Philomena O'Toole, 14 Jan. 1960, 1 son, 2 daughters. *Education:* MB, BCh, BAO, University College Faculty of Medicine, Galway, Ireland, 1957, MD, 1974. *Appointments:* Internship, Regional Hospital, Galway, Ireland, 1957-58; Junior Resident in Medicine, Lemuel Shattuck Hospital, Boston, USA, 1960-61; Fellow in Medicine, Rheumatology, Boston University Medical Centre, 1961-64; Resident in Medicine, Boston City Hospital, 1965-66; Staff Member, Arthritis Section, Boston University Medical Centre, 1966-68; Director of Rheumatology, Boston Veteran's Administration Hospital and Assistant Professor of Medicine, Boston University School of Medicine, 1969-74; Lecturer in Experimental Medicine, University College, Galway, Ireland, 1974-. *Memberships:* Royal Academy of Medicine in Ireland; Irish Association of Rheumatology and Rehabilitation; Irish Society for Electron Microscopy; Arthritis Foundation of Ireland. *Publications:* Co-author 'The Nephropathy of Systematic Lupus Erythematosus' in 'Medicine', 1967; Co-author 'The Evolution of the Glomerular Lesion in NZB Mice' in 'Lab. Invest.', 1967; 'A Review of Glomerular Ultra-structure in Systematic Lupus' in 'Irish Journal of Medical Science', 1977. *Hobby:* Reading. *Address:* Department of Experimental Medicine, University College, Galway, Ireland.

CONANT, Steven G., b. 8 July 1949, Elkhart, Indiana, USA. Psychiatrist. *Education:* MD, Indiana University School of Medicine, 1975; Psychiatry Residency, Illinois Medical Centre, 1978. *Appointments:* Assistant Professor, Psychiatry, Illinois Medical Centre, 1978-80; Consulting Psychiatrist to 4 County Mental Health Centers and to Kennedy Clinic; Psychiatrist, Metrohealth & Gallahue Mental Health Centre; Consultant, Hawky Army Hospital, Fort Benjamin Harrison. *Memberships:* American Psychiatric Association; Indiana Psychiatric Society; American Academy of Clinical Psychiatrists; Fellow, American Association of Social Psychiatry; MENSA. *Honour:* Diplomate, American Board of Psychiatry & Neurology. *Hobbies:* Paino; English/Contemporary Literature; Antiques; Collecting American/Indian Impressionist Art. *Address:* 4030 N. Pennsylvania, Indianapolis, IN 46205, USA.

CONDON, Henry Arthur, b. 8 June 1921, London, England. Consultant Anaesthetist, Royal National Throat, Nose & Ear Hospital, London. m. Margaret Elizabeth Morris, 2 June 1945, London, 1 son, 1 daughter (dec.). *Education:* DA, 1949; MRCS; LRCP; FFARCS, 1954. *Appointments:* Resident anaesthetist, Charing Cross Hospital, 1944-46; Captain, Royal Army Medical Corps, 1946-48; Senior registrar, Department of Anaesthesia, Postgraduate Medical School of London, 1949-51; Consultant Anaesthetist, Bromley Hospital, Kent 1951-78; Regional Thoracic Surgery Unit, Brook Hospital, London SE, 1951-78. *Memberships:* Fellow, Royal Society of Medicine; Fellow, Association of Anaesthetists; Member, British Medical Association. *Publications:* Various papers on aspects of anaesthesia, learned journals. *Hobbies:* Music; Travel. *Address:* 88 Southborough Road, Bromley, Kent. BR1 2EN, England.

CONDORELLI, Mario, b. 19 July 1932, Naples, Italy. Chief, 1st Clinical Medicine, 2nd School of Medicine, University of Naples. m. Paola Chiariello, 3 June 1963, 1 son, 2 daughters. *Education:* Medicine and Surgery Degrees, summa cum laude, 1956; University Teaching, Medical Pathology, 1961; University Teaching, General Clinical Medicine and Therapy, 1964. *Appointments:* Researcher, CNR, 1964; Assistant Professor, Medical Pathology, University of Rome, 1964-68; Chief, Medical Pathology, University of Messina, 1968-70; Chief, Medical Pathology, 1970-72, Chief Medical Pathology, 2nd School of Medicine, 1972-82, Chief, 1st Clinical Medicine, 2nd School of Medicine, 1982 -, University of Naples; Chief, School for Italian Board in Cardiovascular Diseases, 2nd School of Medicine, University of Naples. *Memberships:* Fellow: International College of Angiology; American Association for the Advancement of Science; European Association of Internal Medicine; Societa Argentina di Medicina Interna; Societa Nazionale di Scienze, Lettere end Arti di Napoli; Accademia Publiese della Scienze; Accademic medica di Roma; Accademia Peloritana dei Pericolanti; Governor, Italian Chapter, American College of Chest Physicians; Board of Directors; Societa Italiana di Cardiologia, Societa Italiana di Medicina Interna. *Publications:* Author, several boks on cardiology and internal medicine; author, more than 800 publications in National and International journals. *Honours:* Medal of Merit, Public Health; National Prize of Sciences, 1982; International Prize, Universun Giovanni XXIII, 1983; Senator, Italian Republic, Member, Health Committee, Senate of Italy. *Address:* Via Chiatamone 57, Naples, Italy.

CONELL, Lawrence J., b. 12 June 1950, Hartford, Connecticut, USA. Psychiatrist. m. Reneé K Ganczewski, 7 Oct 1978, New Hope, Pennsylvania, 1 son. *Education:* BA, Syracuse University, 1972; MA, Catholic University of America, 1974; MD, Eastern Virginia Medical School, 1977; Psyuchiatric Residency, Georgetown University Medical Center, completed 1981; Consultation/Liaison Fellowship, Georgetown Medical Center through Fairfax Hospital, completed 1983. *Appointments:* Clinical Instructor, 1982-84, Clinical Instructor, 1982-84, Clinical Assistant Professor, 1985, Department of Psychiatry, Georgetown University Medical Center; Medical Director, Psychiatric Services, Mary Washington Hospital, 1985- . *Memberships:* American Medical Association; American Psychiatric Association; Psychiatric Society of Virginia; American Psychosomatic Society. *Publications:* 'Withdrawal after substitution of a short-acting Benzodiazepine' JAMA 1983; 'Withdrawal symptoms after long-term treatment with therapeutic doses of Flurazepam: A case report', American Journal of Psychiatry, 1983. *Address:* 434 Bridgewater Street, Fredericksburg, VA 22401, USA.

CONINE, Tali, b. 9 Nov. 1933, Tehran, Iran. Professor of Physical Therapy/Director, School of Rehabilitation Medicine. m. Col Robert E Conine, 9 July 1959, 1 son. *Education:* BSc, Physical Therapy, 1955, MA, Administration, 1956, New York University; Doctor of Health Science, Indiana University, 1966. *Appointments:* Chief Adviser, Rehabilitation of Disabled, World Health Organisation, Japan, 1962-66; Chairman, Graduate Allied Health Sciences Department, Indiana University School of Medicine, 1968-79; Director of School of Rehabilitation Medicine and Professor of Physical Therapy, University of British Columbia, Vancouver, Canada. *Memberships:* American Society of Allied Health Professions; American Physical Therapy Association. *Publications:* Contributor of numerous articles to scientific journals in the field of Physical Therapy and Rehabilitation Medicine. *Honours:* Pi Lambda Theta; Honorary Member, Iranian Red Lion and Sun (Red Cross) 1959-78; Honorary Member, Egyptian

Physical Therapy Association, 1978-; Honorary member, Japan Junior Red Cross, 1965-; Distinguished Service Medal, Government of Japan; Meritorious Service Award, State of Indiana, Department of Public Instruction; Certificate of Outstanding Service, American Society of Allied Health Professions, Journal of Allied Health; 1978; Outstanding Service Award, Indiana Allied Health Association, 1979; Meritorious Service Citation, Governor of Indiana, 1979; Distinguished Service Award, Japan Physical Therapy Association, 1982; Fellow, American Society of Allied Health Professions, 1984 etc. *Address:* 3287 West 48th Avenue, Vancouver, B.C.,Canada V6N 3P7.

CONN, Hadley Lewis, b. 6 May 1921, Danville, Indiana, USA. Professor of Medicine. m. Betty Jean Aubertin, 27 Sep. 1946, Wabash, Indiana, 4 sons, 1 daughter. *Education:* BA 1942, MD 1944, Indiana University; Resident in Medicine, University of Pennsylvania, 1948-51; Research Felow, American Heart Association, 1951-53. *Appointments:* Assistant Scientist, Haven National Laboratory, 1953-55; Assistant Professor of Medicine 1956-60, Associate Professor of Medicine 1960-64, Professor of Medicine 1964-69, Director of Clinical Research Center 1970-71, University of Pennsylvania; Chief, Department of Medicine, Presbyterian-University of Pennsylvania Medical Center, 1964-69; Professor and Chairman of Department of Medicine 1972-82, Director of Cardiovascular Institute 1982-, UMDNJ-Rutgers. *Memberships:* American Physical Society; American Society for Clinical Investigation; Fellow, American College of Physicians; Fellow, Board of Trustees 1959-63, American College of Cardiology; Clinical Cardiology Fellow, Established Investigator 1954-59, American Clinical and Climatological Association; Association of University Cardiologists; Phi Beta Kappa; Alpha Omega Alpha; Chairman, ECFMG Test Committee,1974-; President, Philadlephia Heart Association, 1967; President, John Morgan Society, 1965; President, Leola Detweiler Research Foundation, 1974-85; Chairman 1961, American Federation for Clinical Research; NIH-GCRD Council, 1972-76. *Publications include:* 152 papers and books including: "The Myocardial Cell", (with SB Briller), 1966; "Cardiac and Vascular Disease", (with O Horwitz), 1971; "Platelets, Prostaglandins and Lipids", (with PT Kuo), 1980; "Health and Obesity", 1983. *Honour:* Honorary MS Science, University of Pennsylvania, 1972. *Address:* 253 Wendover Road, Princeton, NJ 08540, USA.

CONN, P Michael, b. 12 May 1949, Pennsylvania, USA, Professor and Chairman, Pharmacology, University of Iowa College of Medicine, 1984-. *Education:* BS, CEd, University of Michigan, 1971; MS, North Carolina State University, 1973; PhD, Baylor College of Medicine, 1976; Fellow, NIH, NICHD, 1978. *Appointments:* Assistant Professor of Pharmacology, 1978-82, Associate Professor of Pharmacology, 1982-84, Duke Medical Centre. *Memberships:* Endocrine Society; Society for the Study of Reproduction; American Society for Cell Biology; American Society for Pharmacology and Experimental Therapeutics. *Publications:* "Methods in Enzymology", 1983, 1986; "The Receptors"; "Cellular Regulation of Secretion", 1982; Contributor of over 100 scientific articles in professional journals. *Honours:* JJ Abel Award, American Society for Pharmacology and Experimental Therapeutics, 1985; Weitzman Award of the Endocrine Society, 1985. *Address:* Department of Pharmacology, University of Iowa College of Medicine, Iowa City, IA 52242, USA.

CONNOLLY, Kevin Joseph, b. 29 July 1937, Ashton-under-Lyne, Lancashire, England. Professor of Psychology. m. Mary Colette Loughran, 26 July 1963, Liverpool, 3 daughters. *Education:* BSc, University of Hull, 1961; PhD, Birkbeck College, University of London, 1969. *Appointments:*

Assistant Lecturer 1962-63, Lecturer 1963-65, Birkbeck College, University of London; Research Assistant MRC Project 1961-62, Lecturer 1965-69, Senior Lecturer 1969-71, Professor of Psychology 1971-, Head Department of Psychology 1972-80 and 1983-86, Dean Faculty of Pure Sciences, 1986-88, University of Sheffield. *Memberships:* President 1980-81, British Psychological Society; Society for Research in Child Development; Association for Child Psychology and Psychiatry; Experimental Psychology Society; Royal Institute of Philosophy; President Section J 1983-84, British Association for the Advancement of Science; Genetical Society. *Publications include:* ''Maturation and Development: Biological and Psychological Perspectives'', (edited with H F R Prechtl), 1981; 'The Assessment of Motor Performance in Children' in ''Malnutrition and Behaviour: Critical Assessment of Key Issues'', (editors J Brozek and B Schürch), 1984; 'Maternal Thyroid Hormone Levels in Pregnancy and the Subsequent Cognitive and Motor Performance of the Children', (with P O D Pharoah, R P Ekins and A G Harding), 1984; 'Poverty and Human Development in the Third World', 1985; 'Psychological Aspects of Infertility', (with R J Edelmann), 1986; 'Experimental Studies of the Preschool Environment: The Sheffield Project', (with P K Smith) in ''Advances in Early Education and Daycare Volume IV'', (editor S J Kilmer), 1985. *Honours:* Spearman Medallist 1970, Myers Lecturer 1985, British Psychological Society; Greenwood Lecturer, University of Exeter, 1985. *Hobbies:* Calligraphy; Music; Hill walking. *Address:* Department of Psychology, University of Sheffield, Sheffield S10 2TN, England.

CONNOR, James Michael, b. 18 June 1951, Grappenhall, Cheshire, England. Wellcome Trust Senior Lecturer and Honorary Consultant in Medical Genetics. m. Dr Rachael Alyson Clare Brooks, 6 Jan. 1979, Icklesham East Sussex. *Education:* BSc Honours, Class 1 in Anatomy, 1972, MB ChB, Honours, 1975, MD, 1981, University of Liverpool; Member, Royal College of Physicians, London. *Appointments:* General Professional Training in Medicine and Paediatrics, Liverpool and Johns Hopkins Hospital, Baltimore, Maryland, UsA, 1975-79; University Research Fellow in Department of Medicine, Liverpool, England, 1979-81; Instructor, Medical Genetics, John Hopkins Hospital, Baltimore, Maryland, USA, 1981-82; Consultant in Medical Genetics, Duncan Guthrie Institute of Medical Genetics, Glasgow, Scotland, 1982-84. *Memberships:* Clinical Genetics Society; European and American Societies of Human Genetics; Scottish Society of Physicians; Liverpool Medical Institution. *Publications:* Soft Tissue Ossification'', 1983; ''Essential Medical Genetics'', with M A Ferguson-Smith, 1984; ''Self Assessment in Medical Genetics'', with J R W Yates, 1985; Author of various original articles on aspects of medical genetics. *Honours:* Samuels Memorial Prize for Medical Research, University of Liverpool, 1981; Wellcome Trust Senior Lectureship, 1984. *Hobby:* Country pursuits. *Address:* Westbank Cottage, 84 Montgomery Street, Eaglesham, Strathclyde, Scotland.

CONRAD, Gladys Pearl Krause, b. 1 Aug. 1917, Wisconsin, USA. Self-employed; Staff Psychiatrist. m. David M. Conrad, 17 Apr. 1949, San Diego, California, 2 daughters. *Education:* BA, MA, MD; Rotating Intern,; Residency in Psychiatry. *Appointments:* Staff Psychiatrist, California Youth Authority, Metropolitan State Hospital, California; Psychiatrist, Student Services, California State University, Fullerton and Fullerton Junior College; Clinical Faculty, University of California Medical School and Medical Center, Irvine; Staff Psychiatrist, Orange County Health Care Agency, Mental Health, *Memberships:* American Psychiatric Association; Orange County Psychiatric Association; Orange County Medical Association. *Hobbies:* Music; Art;

Swimming; Exercise; Clothes designing; Baking bread. *Address:* 657 Camino de los Mares, Suite 243, San Clemente, CA 92672, USA.

CONRAD, Harold Theodore, b. 25 Jan. 1934, Milwaukee, Wisconsin, USA. Medical Director. m. Elaine Marie Blaine, 1 Sep. 1962, New Orleans, 4 sons, 1 daughter. *Education:* AB, 1954, SB, Anatomy, 1955, MD, 1958, University of Chicago; FAPA; FRSH. *Appointments:* Chief, Psychiatry, USPHS Hospital, New Orleans, 1962-68; Chief, National Institute of Mental Health Clinical Research Centre, Lexington, 1969-73; Consultant, Psychiatry, National Institute of Mental Health Regional Office, San Francisco, 1973-79; Director, Adolescent Programme, Alaska Psychiatric Institute, 1979-81; Director, Alaska Psychiatric Institute, 1981-85; Medical Director, Bayou Oaks Hospital, Houma, Louisiana. *Memberships:* American Medical Association; American Psychiatric Association, Fellow; Alaska Psychiatric Association, Secretary, 1981-83; President, 1983-85; American Academy of Medical Directors; American College of Physician Executives; Royal Society of Health, Fellow; Association of Military Surgeons of the United States. *Publications:* Numerous articles in professional journals including: ''Heroin and Marijuna'', 'Archivos de Investigacion Medica', 1974; ''Rehabilitation of the Narcotic Addict'', 'Archivos de Investigacion Medica', 1974; ''Psychiatric Treatment of Narcotic Addiction'', 'Handbuch der Experimentelln Pharmakologie', 1977; ''Orthomolecular Psychiatry'', A Report to the Alaska State Legislature, 1985. *Honours:* Alpha Omega Alpha, 1958; Commendation Medal, US Public Health Service, 1970; Omegi Psi Phi National Award for Studies in Drug Abuse, 1971; Resolution of Commendation, Guam Legislature, 1977. *Address:* Bayou Oaks Hospital, 855 Belanger, Houma, LA 70360, USA.

CONRAD, Marcel Edward, b. 15 Aug. 1928, New York, New York, USA. University Professor; Cancer Center Director. 3 sons, 2 daughters. *Education:* BS, 1949, MD cum laude, 1953, Georgetown University, Washington. *Appointments* Intern, 1953-54, Resident, Internal Medicine, 1955-58, Chief Resident, Department of Medicine, Assistant Chief, Haematology, 1958-60, 1961-65, Chief, 1965-74, Chief, Clinical Investigation Service, 1971-74, Consultant in Haematology to Surgeon General, 1965-74, Walter Reed General Hospital; various positions, Walter Reed Army Institute of Research; Clinical Assistant Professor, Medicine, 1964-74, Clinical Associate Professor, 1968-74, Georgeotwn University School of Medicine; Director, Division of Haematology and Oncology, 1974-82, Professor of Medicine, 1974-82, University of Alabama; Director, Director of Haematology and Oncology, Professor of Medicine, University of South Alabama, 1983-; Director, USA Cancer Center, 1985-. *Memberships include:* Association of American Physicians; American Society for Clinical Investigation; American Federation for Clinical Research; Southern Society for Clinical Research; American Physiological Society; American College of Physicians; International Society of Haematology. *Publications:* Consultant Editorial Reviewer for numerous professional journals including: 'Journal of Clinical Investigation'; 'Gastroenterology'; 'Blood'; 'Annals of Internal Medicine'; 'Science'; 'Lancet'; 'Nature'; 'American Journal of Medicine'. Author of 350 scientific publications in hematology, oncology and gastroenterology. *Honours include:* MD cum laude, 1953; Gold Medal, Georgeotwn University Medical School, 1953; Hoff Medal, Walter Reed Army Institute of Research, 1961; John Shaw Billings Award; Legion of Merit, 1971; Walter Reed Award, 1974. *Hobby:* Boating. *Address:* USA Cancer Center, Mobile, AL 36688, USA.

CONROY, James Francis, b. 20 Aug. 1931,

Providence, Rhode Island, USA. Professor. 2 daughters. *Education:* BS, University of Rhode Island, 1951-54; DO, Philadelphia College of Osteopathic Medicine, 1965; MSc., Medicine, Philadelphia College of Osteopathic Medicine, 1971. *Appointments:* Director, Clinics, Instructor, Medicine, Philadelphia College of Osteopathic Medicine, 1967-68; Assistant Professor, Medicine, 1972-75, Clinical Assistant Professor, Pharmacology, 1972-75, Associate Professor, 1975-79, Professor, 1979-, Medicine, Hahnemann University; Professor, Medicine, Philadelphia College of Osteopathic Medicine, 1973-. *Memberships:* American College of Osteopathic Internists; American College of Physicians; American Osteopathic Association; American Society of Clinical Oncology; American Association for CA Education; American Society of Haematology; etc. *Publications:* Articles in professional journals including: 'Journal of Medicine'; 'JAOA'; 'American Association of Cancer Research'; 'American Society of Clinical Oncology'; 'Osteopathic Annuals'; 'Leukemia Research'; etc. *Honours:* McCaughan Scholarship Award, 1962; Mosby Bood Award, 1965; B and A Flack Award, Medicine, 1965; Lambda Omicron Gamma Alumni Award, 1973; Bruner Award in Medicine, 1965; Student Council Teaching Award, PCOM, 1975; Distinguished Achievement Award, Survivors Club, PCOM, 1980; President, Survivors Club, PCOM. *Address:* Hahnemann University Hospital, 230 N. Broad St., Philadelphia, PA 19102, USA.

CONSIGLI, Richard A, b. 3 Feb. 1931, New York, USA. Distinguished Professor. m. Barbara J. Seel, 2 June 1960, 3 daughters. *Education:* BS, Brooklyn College, 1954; MA, 1956, PhD, 1960, Kansas University. *Appointments:* Instructor, University of Kansas, 1959-60; Postdoctoral Fellow, University of Pennsylvania, 1960-63; Assistant Professor, 1963-65, Associate Professor, 1965-69, Professor, 1969-, Kansas State University; Visiting Professor, University of Geneva, Switzerland, 1972-73; Senior Scientist, Kansas Unviersity Cancer Centre, 1975-; Distinguished Professor of Biology, Kansas State University, 1985-. *Memberships:* American Society for Microbiology; Aemrican Society for Virology; New York Academy of Sciences; American Association for Cancer Research; American Academy for Microbiology; Society for Experimental Biology & Medicine; American Association for Advancement of Science. *Publcations:* 120 articles in scientific journals. *Honours:* NIH Research Career Development Award, 1968-73; Distinguished Graduate Faculty Member Award, 1976; CASE Silver Medal Award, 1985; University of Pennsylvania Scholar in medical Science, 1959-60; Elected Member, American Academy of Microbiolgoy, 1977; Sigma Xi; Phi Sigma; Outstanding Educators of America Award, 1975. *Hobbies:* Athletic Events; Reading. *Address:* Kansas State University, Division of Biology, Manhattan, KS 66506, USA.

CONWELL, Timothy Daniel, b. 7 Jan. 1950, Denver, Colorado, USA. Chiropractic Physician. m. Lori Jean Fahrenbruck, 21 Apr. 1979, Ft. Collins, 2 daughters. *Education:* BSc, Ohio State University, 1972; Postgraduate Studies, Colorado State University, 1972-75; DC, Logan College of Chiropractic, 1981; Board Certified Clinical Thermographer, 1985. *Appointments:* Faculty, Instructor of Microbiology, Logan College of Chiropractic. *Memberships:* American, Colorado Chiropractic Associations; Jefferson County Chiropractic Society; International Thermographic Society; California Thermographic Society; ACA Councils on Roentgenologyu Orthopedics and Nutrition; ACA Council, Nutrition Foundation of Chiropractic Education and Research. *Honour:* Graduated Cum Laude, Logan College of Chiropractic, 1981; Fellow, California Thermographic Society. *Hobbies:* Backpacking; Skiing; Water Skiing; Softball. *Address:* 1555 South Kipling Parkway, Lakewood, CO 80226, USA.

COOK, Christine L, b. 8 Feb. 1946, Eugene, Oregon, USA. Associate Professor. m. Larry Norman Cook, MD, 17 June 1973, 1 son, 1 daughter. *Education:* BA, Oregon State University, 1967; MD, University of Louisville, 1971. *Appointments:* Instructor, Department of Obstetrics and Gynaecology, 1976-78; Assistant Professor, Department of Obstetrics and Gynaecology 1978-83; Fellow, Division of Rep. Endo. and Inf., Department of Obstetrics and Gynaecology, 1980-82; Associate Professor, Department of Obstetrics and Gynaecology, 1984-; University of Louisville. *Memberships:* Fellow, American College of Obstetricians and Gynacologists; Association of Professors of Obstetrics and Gynaecology; American Fertility Society; American Association of Gynaecologic Laparoscopists; American Medical Women's Association; Kentucy Medical Association. *Publications:* Contributor to professional journals; Chapters in books; Abstracts; Presentations including: (with Sally Chaney MD), "Hysterosalphingogram Follow-Up in Women with Bilateral Fallope Ring Application", American Association of Gynaecologic Laparoscopists, Tenth Annual Meeting, Nov. 1981. *Address:* Department of Obstetrics and Gynaecology, University of Louisville School of Medicine, 550 S. Jackson Street, Louisville, KY 40292, USA.

COOK, John Charles, b. 19 ApOr. 1951, Hahira, Georgia, USA. Preclinical Research Coordinator. *Education:* BA, Biology; Certificate, Hospital Corpsman, United States Navy; Certificate, Clinical Laboratory Administrator, US Navy; Graduate work, Communication, Rensselaer Polytechnic Institute, Troy, New York. *Appointments:* Research Biologist, Toxicology, Sterling Winthrop Research Institute, Rensselaer, New York; Research Biologist, Virology; Medical Writer, Ive's Laboratories, New York City; Senior Medical Writer, Ayerst Laboratories, New York City; Preclinical Research Coordinator, Boehringer Ingelheim Limited. *Memberships:* American Medical Writers Association; Drug Information Association; New York Academy of Sciences; Society of Toxicology; Society for Technical Communication; Health Science Communication Association. *Publication:* Listed and acknowledged as preparer of manuscripts. *Hobbies:* Snow skiing; Tennis; Swimming. *Address:* 90 East Ridge, PO Box 368, Ridgefield, CT 06877, USA.

COOK, Stuart Donald, b. 23 Oct. 1936, Boston, Massachusetts, USA. University Professor and Chairman. m. 3 children. *Education:* AB, Chemistry, Brandeis University, Waltham, Massachusetts, 1957; MS, Neuroanatomy, 1959, MD, 1962, University of Vermont. *Appointments include:* Assistant Professor, Department of Neurology, College of Physicians and Surgeons, Columbia University, New York, 1969-71; Professor of Medicine (Neurology) and Director of Division of Neurology, College of Medicine and Dentistry 1971-72, Professor and Chairman, Department of Neurosciences University of Medicine and Dentistry, 1972-, New Jersey Medical School, Newark, New Jersey; Visiting Scientist, Swiss Institute for Experimental Cancer Research, Lausanne, Switzerland, Jan. 1985 – July 1985. Hospital Appointments: Chief, Neurology Service, VA Medical Center, East Orange, New Jersey, 1971-; Attending Physician, University Hospital, Newark, New Jersey, 1971-; Consultant, Welkind Neurological Hospital, Chester, New Jersey; 1973-; Consultant, St Barnabas Medical Center, Livingston, New Jersey, 1973-; Consultant, St Michael's Hospital, Newark, New Jersey, 1973-; Consultant, Hackensack Hospital, Hackensack, New Jersey, 1975-. *Memberships:* Fellow, American Academy of Neurology; Associate Member, American Association of Neuropathologists; American Neurological Association; Association for Research in Nervous and Mental Disease; National Multiple Sclerosis Society, United States; New York

Academy of Sciences etc. *Publications:* Numerous articles in Medical Journals and Papers presented to Medical Conferences. *Honours:* Woodbury Prize in Medicine, University of Vermont, 1960; Carbee Prize in Obstetrics, University of Vermont, 1962; Lamb Foundation Prize, University of Vermont, 1962; S. Weir Mitchell Research Award, American Academy of Neurology, 1968. *Address:* Swiss Institute for Experimental Cancer Research, Lausanne, Switzerland.

COOMBES, Bevan Harvey, b. 26 Mar. 1930, Sydney, Australia, Specialist Pathologist, m. June Elyson Phelps, 27 Nov. 1956, Sydney, 2 sons, 2 daughters. *Education:* MB, BS, DCP, Sydney University; FRCPA. *Appointments:* Junior Medical Officer, 1956, Senior Medical Officer, 1957, Resident, Pathologist, 1958-62, Assistant Pathologist, 1962, Sydney Hospital; Fellow in Pathology, Memorial hospital, New York, USA, 1963-64; Visiting Pathologist, Hornsby Hospital, 1964-80; Examiner, Pathology, RCRA, 1974-80; Visiting Pathologist, Goldcoast Hospital, 1981-. *Memberships:* Australian Medical Association; Royal Australasian College of Pathologists. *Hobbies:* Tennis; Gardening; Travel. *Address:* PO Box 157, Southport, Australia, 4215.

COOMBS, Maurice Martin, b. 29 Jan. 1929, London, England. Head, Chemistry Laboratory, Imperial Cancer Research Fund. m. Anne E.M. Chaplin, 1957, London, 1 son, 2 daughters. *Education:* BSc., Chemistry, 1951, PhD, Organic Chemistry, 1954, University of London. *Appointments:* Research Assistant, Wellcome Laboratories of Tropical Medicine, 1945-51; Chemist, Radio Chemical Centre, 1954-55; Research Fellow: Zoology, King's College, 1955-57, Imperial College, 1957-59; Present Position, 1959-. *Memberships:* Chemical Society; Biochemical Society; British and American Associations of Cancer Research; UK Environmental Mutagen Society. *Publications:* "Potentially Carcinogenic Cyclopentaphenanthrenes", Parts 1-11, 'Journal of the Chemical Society', 1966-83; many papers in Cancer Research, Carcerogenesis, etc. *Hobbies:* Hill Walking; Music. *Address:* Chemistry Laboratory, Imperial Cancer Research Fund, Lincoln's Inn Fields, London WC2A 3PX, England.

COOPER, Arnold Michael, b. 9 Mar. 1923, Brooklyn, New York, USA. Professor. m. Madge Huntington, 2 sons, 1 daughter. *Education:* BA, Columbia University, 1943; MD, University of Utah Medical School, 1947; Medical Internship, Presbyterian Hospital, New York, 1948-50; Psychiatric Resident, Belevue Hospital, New York, 1950-53; Certificate in Psychoanalytic Medicine, Columbia University, 1956. *Appointments:* Chief Psychiatrist, Presbyterian Hospital, 1959-63; Attending Psychiatrist & Clinical Professor, Psychiatry, Columbia University, 1959-74; Attending Psychiatrist, Professor of Psychiatry, Cornell University Medical College, 1974-. *Memberships:* International Psychoanalytic Association, Vice President, 1985-86; American Psychiatric Association; American Psychoanalytic Association, President Elect, 1979-80, President, 1980-82; Association for Psychoanalytic Medicine, President, 1975-77. *Publications:* Articles in scientific journals including: 'Journal Clinical Investigation'; 'Psychoanalytic Quarterly'; 'American Journal of Psychiatry'; etc. *Honours:* John F. Kennedy Lecturer, University of Miami, Department of Psychiatry, 1984; Sandor Rado Lecturer, Columbia Psychoanalytic Centre, 1985. *Address:* 525 East 68 Street, New York, NY 10021, USA.

COOPER, Betsy Jane, b. 7 Sep. 1947, Jersey City, New Jersey, USA. Psychiatrist. *Education:* BA cum laude Psychology, University of Rochester, New York, 1969; MD, Meharry Medical College, Nashville, Tennessee, 1974; Diplomate, National Board of Medical Examiners, 1974; Diplomate, American Board of Psychiatry and Neurology, 1984.

Appointments Include: Supervisor, Medication Clinic, Woodburn Community Mental Health Center, Annandale, Virginia, 1982-83; Consultant, Family Counselling Center, Alexandria, Virginia, 1982-; Staff Psychiatrist, Program Administrator, O'Malley Division, Saint Elizabeth's Hospital, Washington, District of Columbia, 1982-; Psychiatirc Consultant, Camelot Hall Nursing Home, Arlington, Virginia, 1983-; Psychiatric Consultant, Geropsychiatry Clinic, Arlington County, Arlington, Virginia, 1985-. *Memberships:* American Medical Women's Association; American Psychiatric Association. *Hobbies:* Needlecraft; Travel; Dancing. *Address:* 5501 Seminary Road §2405, Falls Church, VA 22041, USA.

COOPER, Cary L, b. 28 Apr. 1940, California, USA. Professor of Organisational Psychology, University of Manchester, England. Remarried Rachel Davies, 28 Aug. 1984, 1 son, 3 daughters. *Education:* BSc; MBA, University of California, Los Angeles; MSc, Manchester University, England; PhD, Leeds University, England. *Appointment:* Lecturer in Psychology, Southampton University, England. *Memberships:* Fellow, British Psychological Society; Former Chairman, M.E.D. Division, US Academy of Management; Member, International Association of Applied Psychology; Occupational Psychiatry Section of World Psychiatric Association. *Publications:* "The Stress Check", 1981; "Psychosocial Stress of Cancer", 1983 and 30 more books; 175 scholarly articles in professional journals; Editor-in-Chief, 'Journal of Occupational Behaviour'. *Honours include:* Advisor (temporary) to World Health Organization; Myers Lecture Award of British Psychological Society. *Hobbies:* Swimming; 19th Century Russian Literature. *Address:* University of Manchester, Institute of Science and Technology, P.O. Box 88, Manchester M60 1QD, England.

COOPER, Douglas E, b. 21 May 1912, New Boston, Ohio, Consultant Chemist, m. Anita H Hansen, 26 Sept 1959, Detroit, Michigan, USA. *Education:* MS, University of Tennessee, 1940; PhD, Purdue University, 1943. *Appointments:* Chief Chemist, Bristol Laboratories, 1944; Research Associate, 1965, Medical Manufacturing Liaison, 1975, Ethyl Corporation; Consultant, Cooper Associates, 1977. *Memberships:* American Chemical Society; American Industrial Hygiene Society; Health Physics Society; Association of Consulting Chemists and Chemical Engineers. *Publications:* Author of 5 technical publications and 16 patents. *Hobby:* Photography. *Address:* 3065 Argonaut, Sunset Whitney Ranch, Rocklin, CA 95677, USA.

COOPER, Max Dale, b. 31 Aug. 1933, Hazlehurst, Mississippi, USA. Professor of Paediatrics and Microbiology. m. Rosalie Cooper, 6 Feb. 1960, 3 sons, 1 daughter. *Education:* MD, Tulane University Medical School, New Orleans, Louisiana. *Appointments Include:* Assistant Professor, Department of Pediatrics, University of Minnesota, Minneapolis, 1966-67; Professor, Department of Pediatrics 1967-, Department of Microbiology 1971-. Director of Research, Rehabilitation Research and Training Center 1968-70, Senior Scientist, Comprehensive Cancer Center 1971-. Multipurpose Arthritis Center 1979-. Cystic Fibrosis Research Center 1981-, Director, Cellular Immunobiology Unit, Tumor Institute 1976-, University of Alabama, Birmingham, Alabama; Visiting Scientist, Tumor Immunology Unit, Department of Zoology, University College London, England, 1973-74. *Memberships:* American Association of Immunologists; American Society for Experimental Pathology; American Society for Clinical Investigation; Society for Pediatric Research ; American Pediatric Society; President 1975, Southern Society for Pediatric Research. *Publications Include:* 170 primary contributions, including: 'Delineation of the thymic and bursal lymphoid systems in the chicken' (with R D A Petersen, R A Good), 1965; 'Agammaglobulinemia with B lymphocytes: A specific defect of plasma cell differentiation' (with A R Lawton, D E Brockman), 1971; 'Developmental defects of T and B cell lines in humans' (co-author), 1973; 'The development of the immune system' (with R A Lawton), 1974; 'Pre-B cells; Normal and abnormal development', 1981; 'Immunoglobulin heavy chain switching in pre-B leukemias' (co-author), 1983. *Honours:* Samuel J Meltzer Founder's Award, 1966; VAB Distinguished Faculty Lecturer, 1982. *Hobbies:* Sailing; Tennis. *Address:* University of Alabama at Birmingham, University Station-224, Tumor Institute, Birmingham, AL 35294, USA.

COPELAND, Edward Meadors III, b. 6 Oct. 1937, USA, Professor and Chairman, Department of Surgery, University of Florida College of Medicine, m. Martha Patterson 24 Apr. 1964, Washington DC, 1 son, 1 daughter. *Education:* AB, Duke University; MD, Cornell University Medical College; Surgical Residency, Hospital of the University of Pennsylvania; Surgical Oncology Fellowship, University of Texas MD Anderson Hospital and Tumour Institute. *Appointments:* Professor of Surgery, University of Texas Medical School at Houston; Professor of Surgery, University of Texas M D Anderson Hospital and Tumour Institute. *Memberships:* American Surgical Association; Southern Surgical Association; Society of University Surgeons; Association for Academic Surgery; American College of Surgeons; Society of Clincial Surgery; American Gastroenterological Association; Society for Surgery of Alimentary Tract; American Board of Surgery; Society Internationale de Chirurgie. *Publications:* 'The complex nature of small bowel control of gastric secretions', (with L D Miller and G P Smith), 1968; 'Axillary metastasis from an unknown primary site', (with C M McBride), 1973; 'Effect of intraVENOUS hyperalimantation on established delayed hypersensitivity in the cancer patient', (with B V McFadden jr and S J Dudrick), 1976; 'Nutritional aspects of cancer', (with S J Dudrick), 1976; 'Nutrition as an adjunct to cancer treatment in the adult', (with J M Daly and S J Dudrick), 1977; ''Surgical Oncology'', 1983. *Honours:* Bronze Star, 1970; Seake Harris Award, 1984; Edward R Woodward Professorship, 1985. *Hobbies:* Golf; Tennis; Fishing. *Address:* University of Florida, Department of Surgery, Box J-286, JHMHC, Gainesville, FL 32610, USA.

COPELAND, Larry James, b. 1 Dec. 1947, Brampton, Ontario, Canada. Associate Professor, Gynaecology; Associate Surgeon. *Education:* BSc., 1969; MD, 1973; Psotgraudate, 1973-77; Fellow, Gynaecologic Oncology, 1977-79. *Appointments:* Assistant Surgeon, Assistant Professor, Gynaecology, 1979-82, Associate Surgeon, Associate Professor, Gynaecology, 1982-, University of Texas System Cancer Centre, M.D. Anderson Hospital & Tumour Institute. *Memberships:* Society of Obstetricians & Gynaecologists of Canada; Felix Rutledge Society; Society of Canadian Gynaecologic Oncologists; Society of Gynaecologic Oncologists; American Radium Society; Society of Surgical Oncology; Houston Gynaecological & Obstetrical Society; Houston Surgical Society; Harris County Medical Society; Texas Medical Association; American Medical Association; FACOG; FACS; Fellow, Royal College of Surgeons, Canada. *Publications:* Articles in professional journals including: ''Cancer'', 1985; Books – ''Malignant Gynaecologic Tumors'', 'Clinical Pediatric Oncology', 3rd edition 1984; ''Second-Look Laparatomy in Ovarian Cancer Patients'', ''Clinical OB/GYN''. *Honours:* Bobby Bauer Memorial Hockey Scholarship, 1966; Horner Gold Medal, Graduation, 1973; Purdue Fredick Award, 1984. *Address:* Univeristy of Texas System Cancer Centre, MD Anderson Hospital & Tumour Institute, 6723 Bertner

Avenue, Houston, TX 77030, USA.

COPLAND, William Alexander, b. 12 July 1924, Aberdeen, Scotland. Consultant Radiologist. m. Elizabeth June Hunter, Dec. 1952, Gosforth, Northumberland, 3 daughters. *Education:* MB ChB, Aberdeen University, 1946; DMRD, Bristol Univeristy, 1952. *Appointments:* House Officer, Aberdeen Royal Infirmary; Registrar, Radiology, United Bristol Hosptials; Senior Registrar, Middlesex Hosptial, London; Consultant, Edinburgh Western and Northern General Hospitals; Clinical teaching Staff, Medical Radiology, University of Edinburgh; Consultant in Adminstrative Charge, Western Genral Hosptial, Edinburgh. *Memberships:* Royal College of Radiologist; Royal College of Surgeons of Edinburgh; British Institute of Radiology; British Medical Ultrasound Society; Scottish Radiologial Society. *Honour:* Queens Honorary Physician, 1973. *Hobbies:* Sailing; Golf. *Address:* Rowallan, 51 Barton Avenue, Edinburgh, Scotland.

COPLAND-GRIFFITHS, Michael Charles, b. 7 Nov. 1946, Newbury, Berkshire, England. President, British Chiropractic Association. m. Noelle Mary (Penny) Trehane Spencer, 6 Dec. 1980, Blandford Forum. *Education:* Anglo-European College of Chiropractic, 1973-77;Diplomate, Natinal Board of Chiropractic Examiners, USA, 1978. *Appointments:* Faculty Member, Anglo-European College of Chiropractic, 1977-81; Member, College Council, Anglo-European College of Chiropractic, 1978-80; Assistant Secretary, British Chiropractic Association, 1979-85; Advisory and Education Committees, Institute for Complementaryand Alternative Medicine, 1984-5. *Memberships:* British Chiropractic Association. *Honour:* Graduated, Best All Round Student, Anglo-European College of Chiropractic, 1977. *Hobbies:* Archaeology; Natural History; History; Post Medieval Pottery. *Address:* Trowle House, Wingfield, Trowbridge, Wiltshire BA14 9LE, England.d

CORALL, Ian Mitchell, b. 20 Sep. 1944, India. Consultant Anaesthetist, Honorary Senior Lecturer, King's College Hospital, London. m. Sara Wendy Howard, 28 Feb. 1970, 2 sons. *Education:* LRCP, MRCS, St Bartholomews Hospital, London; FFA, RCS (Eng), King's College Hospital, London. *Appointments:* House Surgeon, St Bartholomew's Hospital, 1969; House Physician, Bethnal Green Hospital, 1970; Senior House Officer: Brook Hospital, London, 1970-71; King's College Hospital, 1971; Registrar, King's College Hospital, 1971-73; Beckwith Smith Research Fellow, King's College Hospital, 1973-74; Senior Registrar, 1973-75, Consultant/Honorary Senior Lecturer, 1975-, King's College Hospital and Medical School, London. *Memberships:* Associate Member, European Academy of Anaesthesiology; Training Sub-Committee, Anaesthesia, South East Thames Regional Post Graduate Committee, 1981; Faculty Representative, Regional Health Authority Appointment Committees for Consultant Posts, 1984; Council of Section of Anaesthetics, Royal Society of Medicine, London. *Publications:* Numerous articles in professional journals; Audio-Visual Presentations; Review articles. *Address:* East Pelham, Manor Park, Chislehurst, Kent BR7 5QE, England.

CORDER, Michael Paul, b. 20 Jan. 1940, Zanesville, Ohio, USA. Chief, Division of Oncology/Haematology/Department of Medicine, Kern Medical Centre; Adjunct Professor of Medicine, Unviersity of California, Los Angeles (UCLA). 3 daughters. *Education:* BS, Capital University, 1963; MD, Ohio State University, 1965; Internship, Residency, San Francisco, 1966-69; Fellowship, National Cancer Insitute, Bethesda, Maryland, 1971; Diplomate, Internal Medicine, Medical Oncology,

American Board of Internal Medicien. *Appointments include:* Assistant, Chief, Haematology/Oncology Service 1971-75, Chief, Oncology Section 1972-75, Letterman Army Medical Centre, San Francisco; Assistant, Associate Professor of Medicine, Director of Oncology/Associate Professor of Preventive Medicine & Environmental Health, Univesity of Iowa, 1975-83; Kern Medical Centre, 1983-. *Memberships include:* Membership Committee, American Society of Clincial Oncology; American Associaton for Cancer Research; American Federation for Clincial Research; American Association for the Advancement of Science; American Society of Haematology; Fellow, American College of Physicians; Fellow, International Society of Heamatology; etc. *Publications include:* 'Phytohemaglutanin Induced Lymphocyte Transformation' in 'Blood', 1972; 'A Financial analysis of Hodgkin Lymphoma Staging' in 'American Journal of Public Health', 1981; 'A decision analysis methodology for consideration of morbidity factors in clinical decision-making' in 'American Journal of Oncology', 1984; 57 manuscripts in refereed journals; 7 textbook chapters; 77 abstracts & letters to editors. *Honours:* 'A' professional designation, US Army Surgeon General, 1980; Biographical listings; A.Blaine Brower travelling scholarship, ACP, 1981; Consultant, National Cancer Institute, 1978-. *Hobbies:* Tennis; Oriental carpets. *Address:* Department of Medicine, Kern Medical Centre, 1830 Flower Street, Bakersfield, CA 93305, USA.

CORDERY, Joy, b. 24 Feb. 1926, Stamford, England. Coordinator of Rehabilitation Services, New York Hospital. *Education:* Diplomate, Association of Occupational Therapists, 1947; Registered Occupational Therapist, American Occupational Therapy Association, 1954. *Appointments:* RAF Chessington, Surrey, UK, 1947-52; University of Michigan Medical Centre, USA, 1956-57; Detroit Memorial Hospital, Wayne State University, Michigan, USA, 1957-59; Henry Ford Hospital, Detroit, 1959-61; Consultant Occupational Therapist, Michigan Arthritis Foundation, Detroit, 1961-62; Director, Occupational Therapy, Hospital of Medical Research Centre, Brookhaven National Laboratory, New York, 1962-65; Senior Research Occuaptional Therapist, Institute of Rehabilitation Medicine, New York University Medical Centre, 1965-68; Research Associate, Rehabilitation Medicine, College of Physicians & Surgeons, Columbia University, 1968-72; Coordinator of Rehabilitation Services, The New York Hospital, 1972-. *Memberships:* Amrican Occupational Therapy Association; New York State Occupational Therapy Association; World Federation of Occupational Therapists; Arthritis Health Professions Association. *Publicaitons include:* Contributions to various professioal journals, conference presentations, mongraphs. *Honour:* Associated Medical Services Award, Arthritis Foundation, 1964. *Hobbies:* Sailing; Gardening. *Address:* 7 Castle Street, E.Patchogue, NY 11772, USA.

CORN, Milton, b. 17 Jan. 1928, Berlin. Dean of School of Medicine. m. Virginia Emma Lynn Gettys, 19 Dec, 1954, New Haven, Connecticut, 1 son, 2 daughters. *Education:* BS, MD, Yale University, Hartford, Connecticut. *Appointments:* Haematologist, 1960-63, Director of Medical Education, 1962-63, St Michael's Hospital, Newark, New Jersey; Chief of Haematology, 1963-73, Chief of Medicine 1970-73, George Washington University Medical Division, D C General Hsopital, Washing D C; Director of Blood Bank, 1973-78, Director of Emergency Department, 1973-78, Director, Emergency Medicine Residency Training Program, 1975-78, Director, Clerkship in Junior Medicine, 1978-, Vice Chairman, Department of Medicine, 1978-, Director, Thrombosis and Haemostasis Service, 1984-, Dean, School of Medicine, 1985,

Georgetwon University School of Medicine and Georgetown University Hsopital, Washington. *Memberships:* Diplomate, American Board of Internal Medicine; American Board of Haematology., *Publications:* Contributor of numerous articles in the field of Haematology to professional journals and magazines. *Honours:* Campbell Prize (Highest Academic Rank in Graduating Class) Yale University, School of Medicine, 1955; Golden Apple Award, George Washington University Student Medical Association, 1971; Laurence H. Kyle Award for Excellence in Housestaff Education, Georgetown University Medical Center, 1974; Golden Apple Award, Georgetown University Student Medical Association, 1979 and 1983; Kaiser-Permanente Teaching Award, 1983. *Address:* Georgetown University, School of Medicine, 3900 Reservoir Road N W, Washington, DC 20007, USA

CORNAGLIA-FERRARIS, Paolo, b. 19 Feb. 1952, Cagliari, Italy, Head, Scientific Secretariat, National Tumour Institute I.S.T. Genova, Italy, m. Benedetta Costa, 31 May 1982, Genoa, 1 son, 1 daughter. *Education:* MD; Haematology, 1979; Paediatrics, 1984. *Appointments:* Assistant Professor in clinical haematology, University of Genoa, 1976-79; G Gaslini Scientific Institute for Children, Head, Paediatric Oncology Research Laboratory, 1979-86; Visiting Assistant Professor and Research Scientist, University of South Florida Medical College, Tampa, Florida, USA, 1983-84. *Memberships:* New York Academy of Science; International Society of Immunopharmacology; International Society of Experimental Haematology; American Society of Paediatric Hematol-oncology. *Publications:* 'Pharmacology in Pediatric Oncology'. *Hobby:* Travel. *Address:* I.S.T National Cancer Institute, General Direction, Viale Benedetto XV, 16132 Genova, Italy.

CORNWELL, Gibbons Gray, b. 17 Jan. 1933, West Chester, Pennsylvania, USA. Professor of Medicine. m. 13 Sep. 1958, Syracuse, New York, 1 son, 2 daughters. *Education:* BS, Yale University, 1954; MD, University of Pennsylvania, 1963. *Appointments:* Medical Resident, University of Pennsylvania Hospital, 1963-64 and 1965-66; Hematology Research Fellow, University of Cambridge, Cambridge, England, 1964-65; Research fellow in Biochemistry 1968-70, Assistant Professor of Medicine 1971-74, Associate Dean for Student and Academic Affairs 1973-76, Associate Professor of Medicine 1974-80, Chairman of Section of Haematology and Oncology 1977-84, Programme Director of Clinical Research of Norris Cotton Cancer Center 1977, Professor of Medicine 1980-, Dartmouth Medical School, New Hampshire, USA; Visiting Research Professor, Institute of Immunology, Oslo, Norway, 1976-77. *Memberships:* Fellow, American College of Physicians; American Society of Haematology; American Federation of Clinical Research. *Publications:* 65 papers and 31 abstracts on amyloidosis, multiple myeloma and other haematologic disorders. *Hobbies:* Cycling; Stamps; Whales. *Address:* Department of Medicine, Dartmouth Hitchcock Medical Center, Hanover, NH 03756, USA.

CORTESE, Carl John, b. 20 Jan. 1942, Brooklyn, New York, USA. Doctor of Podiatric Medicine; Assistant Professor. widowed, 3 sons. *Education:* BS, Farileigh Dickinson University; Graduate, New York College of Podiatric Medicine; DPM. *Appointments include:* Resident, 1971, Staff Member, Hopedale Medical Complex; Podiatry Surgical Staff, John Warner Hospital; Assistant Professor, Department of Allied Health Professions, Illinois State University; Director, Sports Medicine and Running Clinic, Bloomington; Podiatric Doctor, Bloomington, Pontiaic, Normal and Clinton. *Memberships:* Fellow,

American College of Foot Surgeons; Diplomate, American Board of Podiatric Surgery; American Podiatry Association; Illinois Podiatry Society; Diplomate, National Board of Podiatry Examiners; Secretary, Illinois Podiatry Examing Committee, Illinois Department of Registration and Education; Sept. 1986 President, Illinois Podiatric Medical Association; American Podiatric Medical Association. *Publications:* "The Evaluation and Treatment of Basic Foot Deformities", contributor, 1974; "Complications in Foot Surgery", Co-Author, 1977. Contributor: 'APA Journal'; 'Journal of American College of Foot Surgery'. Presentor, 61st Annual Meeting, American Podiatry Association, Washington. Lecturer, Illinois State Society Annual Meeting, 1975. *Honour:* Man of the Year Award, 1969. *Address:* 1607 Visa Dr., Normal, IL 61761, USA.

COURTNEY, James McNiven, b. 25 Mar. 1940, Glasgow, Scotland. University Senior Lecturer. m. Ellen Miller Copeland, 26 June 1965, Glasgow, 2 sons, 1 daughter. *Education:* BSc Applied Chemistry, University of Glasgow, 1962; ARCST Applied Chemistry, Associate of the Royal College of Science and Technology, 1962; PhD Chemistry, University of Strathclyde, 1969; Dr sc nat Biochemistry, Wilhelm Pieck University, Rostock, German Democratic Republic, 1984. *Appointments:* Rubber Technologist, Maclellan Rubber Limited, Scotland, 1962-65; Rubber Technologist Uniroyal Limited, 1965-66; Lecturer 1969-81, Senior Lecturer 1981-85, Reader 1986-, Bioengineering Unit, University of Strathclyde: Visiting Professor, Clinic for Internal Medicine, Wilhelm Pieck University, Rostock, German Democratic Republic, 1978. *Memberships:* Fellow, Royal Society of Chemists; Fellow, Plastics and Rubber Institute; International Society for Artificial Organs. *Publications include:* Approximately 100 publications in the areas of membranes and sorbents for blood purification and in polymers in medicine and surgery. *Hobby:* Football spectator. *Address:* University of Strathclyde, Bioengineering Unit, 106 Rottenrow, Glasgow G4 0NW, Scotland.

CORVILAIN, Jacques, b. 11 Dec. 1923, Charleroi, Belgium. Professor of Internal Medicine. m. Christine Delvigne, Boston, 1 son, 2 daughters. *Education:* MD, Agrégé de L'Enseignement Supérieur. *Appointments:* Assistant, University Hospital St Pierre; Adjoint, University Hospital Brugmann; Chief, Department of Endocrinolog· Professor of Endocrinology, University Hospital Brugmann; Professor of Internal Medicine, Brussels University; Chief, Department of Medicine, University Hospital Brugmann. *Memberships:* Belgian Society of Internal Medicine; Belgian Society of Endocrinology; European Calcified Tissue Society; American Society of Bone & Mineral Research. *Publications:* Various articles in British Medical Journal, Journals of Physiology, Clinical Endocrinology, Clinical Investigation; The Lancet; Archives of Internal Medicine; New England Journal of Medicine. *Honours:* Member, Royal Academy of Belgium; Prix Assubel. *Hobbies:* Literture; Tennis. *Address:* 30 rue Marie Depage, 1180 Brussells, Belgium.

COSSACK, Zafrallah Taha, b. 20 Nov. 1948, Damascus. Associate Professor and Director of Human-Clinical Nutrition Programme, Odense University, Denmark. m. Johanna, 4 June 1980, Riverside, California, USA, 2 sons, 1 daughter. *Education:* BSc, Agricultural Sciences; MSc, Nutrition; PhD, Nutritional Sciences. *Appointments:* Research Assistant, Department of Animal Nutrition, University of Alexandria, Egypt, 1972-74; Nutritionist, Omar Kazak Company, Amman, Jordan, 1974-75; Research Technician, Department of Animal Nutrition, Iowa State University, Ames, USA, 1976; Research Assistant, Department of Nutrition and Food Sciences and Department of

Plant Science, University of Arizona, USA, 1978-80; Lecturer, Department of Chemistry, Schoolcraft College, Livonia, Michigan, US, 1980; Consultant, Diabetes and Endocrinology Center, Clinical Laboratory, Bloomfield Hills, Michigan; Research Associate in Clinical Nutrition, Wayne State University School of Medicine, Detroit; Co-ordinator of Clincial Research in Nutrition and Medicine, Wayne State University School of Medicine, Department of Medicine and The Veterans Administration Medical Center, Medical Research, Allen Park, and Detroit, Michigan; Senior Guest Investigator, Interuniversity Reactor Institute, Nuclear Biotechnique Division, Delft, The Netherlands, 1984. *Memberships:* British Society for Nutrition; American Association for Advancement of Science; American Institute of Nutrition; American Society of Animal Sciences; American Federation for Clinical Research; American College of Nutrition; Sigma Xi; Scientific Society; American Society for Nutritional Medicine; Netherlands Nutrition Society; International Society for Trace Elements Research in Human. *Publications:* Contibutor to professional journals; Chapters in Books; Presentations. *Honours:* OGEM International, The Netherlands, Scholarship recipient, 1976-77; MEPIER Scholarship recipient, 1978-79; Arizona Honorary Citizen Award, 1979. *Hobbies:* Swimming; Ping Pong; Soccer. *Address:* Odense University, Institute of Physiology and College of Medicine, Campusvej 55, DK-5230 Odense, M, Denmark.

COSTA, Alberto, b. 9 Sep. 1951, Biella, Italy. Surgical Oncologist. m. Fiamma Buranelli, 3 Dec. 1982, Milan, 1 son. *Education:* MD: Specialisation in Oncology, University of Genoa; Specialisation in Surgery, University of Milan. *Appointments:* Assistant, National Cancer Institute, Milan; Secretary General, European School of Oncology; Scientific Secretary, Special Project on Oncology, Italian National Research Council. *Memberships:* Italian Society of Cancerology; Italian Association of Medical Oncology; European Society of Surgical Oncology. *Publications:* Contributions to : 'International Advances in Surgical Oncology', 1984; "Clinics in Oncology", 1982; "Clinical Trials in Cancer Medicine", 1985. *Honours:* Special Award of Italian Edition of Scientific American, 1976. *Hobbies:* Music; Reading. *Address:* Istituto Nazionale Tumori, Via Venezian 1, 20133 Milan, Italv.

COSTA, Paul T, b. 16 Sep. 1942, Franklin, New Hampshire, USA. Psychologist/University Professor. m. Karol S Eagle, 5 June 1964, Dudley, Massachusetts, 1 son, 2 daughters. *Education:* AB, Psychology, Clark University; MA, Human Development, PhD, Human Development, University of Chicago. *Appointments:* Lecturer in Clinical Psychology, Harvard University, 1970-72; Associate Professor of Psychology, University of Massachusetts, Boston, 1972-78; Research Psychologist, VA Outpatient Clinic, 1974-77; Visiting Associate Professor, Duke University Medical Center, 1977-78; Assistant Professor of Behavioural Biology, Department of Psychology, The Johns Hopkins University School of Medicine, 1979-; Adjunct Associate Professor of Medical Psychology, Duke University Medical Center, 1984-; Chief, Stress and Coping Section, Gerontology Research Center, National Institute on Aging, Baltimore, Maryland. *Memberships:* Gerontological Society of America; American Psychological Association; Society of Behavioural Medicine; International Society for Study of Individual Differences; American Public Health Association. *Publications:* "Humanism in Personology: Allport, Masalov and Murray" 1972; "Emerging Lives, Enduring Dispositions: Personality in Adulthood" 1984; "Normal Human Aging: The Baltimore Longitudinal Study of Aging" 1984; 'Hypochondriasis, Neuroticism and Aging: When are Somatic Complaints Unfounded?' American Psychologist, 1985. *Honours:* Fellow, Gerontological

Society, 1977; Fellow, American Psychological Society, 1977; President, Adult Development Division 20, APA 1984-85. *Hobbies:* Jazz; Gardening; Jogging. *Address:* National Institute on Aging, Gerontologic Research Center, Francis Scott Key Medical Center, Baltimore, MD 21224, USA.

COSTA E SILVA. Jorge Alberto, b. 26 Mar. 1942, Rio de Janeiro, Brazil. Professor and Chairman, Department of Psychiatry. m. 9 Feb. 1970, Rio de Janeiro, 2 sons, 1 daughter. *Education:* MD, Medical School, 1966, Special sation in Psychiatry, 1967, State University of Rio de Janeiro; PhD, 1975. *Appointments:* Concelors, Ministry of Health, 1973; Chief of Psychiatric Service, University Hsopital, 1974; Editor in Chief, Informacao Psiquiatrica (Medical Journal), • 1976; Concelor Adviser, Universitary Hospital, 1975; Scientific Director, Sanatoriio Botagogo, 1978; Dean, Medical School, State University of Rio de Janeiro, 1983-; Chairman, Council, Medical School, 1984-. *Memberships:* National Academy of Medicine; Director, Assistant Secretary, World Psychiatric Assocation: Fellow, American Psychiatric Association; International Academy of Science; Pan American Medical Association; Director, World Association for Social Psychiatry. *Publications:* "A Doenca e o Doente Mental", 1979; "Benzodiazepines and Depression", 1979; contributor, 'Annales Medico-Psychologiques', 1979; "Urgences psychiatriques: Modalite d'assistance des cadres cliniques des cas d'urgence au Bresil", 1980. *Honours:* Medallion, Merito Clementiono Fraga, for service to Brazilian Community, Rio de Janeiro, 1974. *Hobbies:* Writing; Travelling; Classical music concerts; Operas; Organisation of International scientific meetings. *Address:* Rua Getulio das Neves 22, 22461 Lagoa, Rio de Janeiro, Brazil

COSTELLO, John Francis, b. 22 Sep. 1944, Dublin, Republic of Ireland. Consultant Physician. m. Christine White, 11 Nov. 1972, Westminster, 3 sons. *Education:* MB BCh, BAO, University College, Dublin, 1968; Member, 1972, Fellow 1983, Royal College of Physicians, *Appointments:* Pre-registration, Mater Hospital, Dublin; Senior House Officer, Royal Northern Hospital, Hammersmith Hospital, Brompton Hospital; Registrar, Brompton Hospital; Lecturer, University of Edinburgh, Scotland; Assistant Professor, University of California at San Francisco, USA; Consultant Physician, King's College Hospital; Director, Department of Thoracic Medicine, King's College School of Medicine & Dentistry, 1983-. *Memberships:* Thoracic Society; American Thoracic Society; Harveian Society; Medical Society of London. *Publications:* Author of chapters, reviews and scientific papers on respiratory medicine. *Hobbies:* Music; Travel; Running; Political Biographies. *Address:* Department of Thoracic Medicine, King's College School of Medicine & Dentistry, Denmark Hill, London SE5 8RX, England.

COSTELLO, Philip, b. 22 Apr. 1946, England. Director of Computed Tomography/Assistant Professor of Radiology. m. Sheila M Payne, 1 June 1970, Solihull, England, 2 daughters. *Education:* MB, BS, London University; FRCP(C) University of Toronto. *Appointments:* Westminster Medical School, 1969-70; Toronto General Hospital, 1970-75; New England Deaconess Hospital 1975-. *Memberships:* American College of Radiology; Royal College of Physicians of Canada; Society of Thoracic Radiology; Massachusetts Radiological Society; New England Roentgen Ray Society. *Publications:* 41 articles in medical journals and 2 book chapters. *Honours:* Calveley Prize 1968; Chadwick Prize, 1969. *Hobbies:* Antiques; Gardening. *Address:* Radiology Department, New England Deaconess Hospital, 185 Pilgrim Road, Boston, MA 02215, USA.

COTCHETT, John Craig, b. 21 Sep. 1948, New York,

USA. Obstetrician/Gynaecologist. *Education:* BA, University of California - Berkeley, 1970; MD, Northwestern University, Chicago, 1974. *Appointments:* Intern, Highland Hospital, Oakland, California, 1974-75; Assistant Director Emergency Department, Stanislaus Memorial Hospital, Modesto, California, 1975-78; Resident Physician, Kaiser Hospital, San Francisco, California, 1978-81; Private Practice of Obstetrics and Gynaecology, San Mateo, California, 1981-. *Memberships:* Fellow, American College of Obstetrics and Gynecology; California Medical Assocation; San Mateo County Medical Society; Peninsula Gynecologic Society. *Honours:* Chief Resident Physician, Kaiser Hospital, San Francisco, 1980; Board Certification, American College of Obstetrics and Gynecology, 1983. *Hobbies:* Tennis; Skiing; Golf. *Address:* 101 South San Mateo Drive, San Mateo, CA 94401, USA.

COUCH, James Russell, Jr., b. 25 Oct. 1939, Bryan, Texas, USA. Professor & Chief of Neurology, Southern Illinois University (SIU) Medical School. m. Pamela Durre, 14 Apr. 1964, Bryan, Texas, 2 sons. *Education:* BS, Texas A&M University, 1962; MD 1965, PhD 1966, Baylor University College of Medicine. *Appointments include:* Fellowship, National Institute of Mental Health Laboratory of Neuropharmacology, Washington DC, 1967-69; Residency, Neurology, Washington University Medical School, St. Louis, 1969-72; Assistant Professor 1972-76, Associate Professor 1976-79, Department of Neurology, University of Kansas Medical Centre. *Memberships:* American Academy of Neurology; American Neurological Association; Neurosciences Society; American Association for the Study of Headache (offices); etc. *Publications include:* Numerous research papers in professional journals, eg. 'Brain Research', 'Advances in Neurology', 'Consultant', 'Life Sciences', 'Headache', etc; Presentations to various seminars & conferences; Abstracts; Book chapters in "Manual of Medical Therapeutics", 1971; "Neuropeptides in Neural Transmission", 1980; "Cluster Headache"; "Controversies & Variants of Migrane", "The Handbook of Clinical Neurology", Volume 4, 1984. *Honours:* Phi Eta Sigma, 1958; Phi Kappa Phi, 1960; Alpha Omega Alpha, 1965; Sigma Xi, 1966; Fellow, American Academy of Neurology, American Neurological Academy; Assistant secretary/treasurer, American Academy of Neurology. *Address:* Department of Neurology, SIU Medical School, Springfield, IL 62708, USA.

COUTINHO, Roeland Arnold, b. 4 Apr. 1946, Laren, The Netherlands, Head, Department of Public Health, Municipal Health Service, Amsterdam, The Netherlands, m. Johanna Wiggelendam, 21 Mar. 1970, Roermond, 1 son, 1 daughter. *Education:* MD; PhD. *Memberships:* Dutch Society for Infectious diseases; Society for Epidemiologic Research; British Society for the Study of STD; Dutch Society for the Study of STD. *Publications:* Author of numerous publications on professioanl subjects. *Hobbies:* Soccer; Music; Reading. *Address:* Municipal Health Service, PO Box 20244, 100 HE Amsterdam, The Netherlands.

COURTICE, Frederick Colin, b. 26 Mar, 1911, Bundaberg, Queensland, Australia. Emeritus Professor; Visiting Professor. m. Joyce Mary Seaton, 19 Dec. 1937, London, 1 son, 3 daughters. *Education:* BSC, 1933, DSc, 1946, University of Sydney, Australia; PhD, 1935, MA, 1945, University of Oxford, England; MRCS, LRCP, 1937, London Hospital; Fellow: Royal Australasian College of Physicians; Royal Australasian College of Surgeons; Royal College of Pathologists of Australia; Australian Academy of Science. *Appointments Include:* Rhodes Scholar, 1933-35; Beit Fellowship for Medical Research, 1937-38; Nuffield Research Scholar, 1939-40; Senior Experimental Officer, Chemical Research Experimental Station, Poreton, 1940-45; Reader in Human Physiology, Oxford,

1945-48; Lecturer in Physiology, New College, Oxford, 1945-48; Director, Kanematsu Memorial Institute, Sydney Hospital Australia, 1948-58; Professor of Experimental Pathology, John Curtin School of Medical Research, Australian National University, 1958-73; Director, John Curtin School of Medical Research and Howard Florey Professor of Medical Research, 1973-76; Emeritus Professor, Australian National University, 1977-; Visiting Professor, University of New South Wales, 1980-. *Memberships Include:* Physiological Society; Australian Physiolgocal and Pharmacological Society; Australian Society of Experimental Pathology; Australian Cardiac Society; International Society of Lymphology. *Publications:* "Lymphatics, Lymph and Lymphoid Tissue", co-author, 1956; "Lymphatics, Lymph and the Lymphomyeloid Complex", co-author, 1970; Author of numerous book chapters and articles in professional journals. *Hobbies:* Gardening; Walking. *Address:* 3 Bonney Close, St Ives, NSW 2075, Australia.

COVEL, Mitchel Dale, b. 10 July 1917, Oakland, California, USA. University Associate Dean, Clinical Affairs. m. Susan Day Giles, 12 June 1971, Los Angeles, 1 son, 3 daughters. *Education:* BA, 1939, MD, 1942, University of California. *Appointments include:* Intern, 1942-43, Resident, Internal Medicine, 1946-49, Los Angeles County Hospital, California; Chief, Outpatient Service, 1949-52, Junior Attending Physician, 1949-5, Senior Attending Physician, 1955-60, Los Angeles County Hospital; Instructor in Medicine, 1949-51, Assistant Clinical Professor, 1951-57, Associate Clinical Professor, 1957-60, Loma linda University; Associate Clinical Professor, Medicine, 1957-60; Assistant Clinical Professor, 1960-65, Associate Clinical Professor, 1965-73, Clinical Professor, 1973-, Associate Dean, Clinical Affairs, 1979-, School of Medicine, University of California, Los Angeles. *Memberships include:* Fellow: American College of Physicians; American College of Cardiology; Council of Clinical Cardiology, American Heart Association; New York Academy of Sciences; Founding Fellow, Royal Society of Health. Founding Fellow, American Geriatric Society. Past President: Los Angeles County Heart Association; California Heart Association. *Publications:* Contributions to: 'California and Western Medicine'; 'Annals of Internal Medicine'. Contributor to various symposium and seminars. *Honours:* Distinguished Achievement Award, 1959, Distinguished Service Award, 1961, Heart of Gold Award, 1978, Honorary Member, Board of Directors, 1978, American Heart Association; The Aesculapians Service Award, 1983. *Hobbies:* Sports; Tennis; Music; Travel. *Address:* School of Madicine, University of California, Los Angeles, CA 90024, USA.

COWAN, John Scott, b. 30 Aug. 1943, Toronto, Canada. University Professor and Head of Department of Physiology. m. Jill G Greenweel, 8 Mar. 1985, Ottawa. *Education:* BSc, Hons, Maths and Physics, 1965, MSc, Physiology, 1967, PhD, Physiology, 1969, Toronto University; Post Doctoral Fellow of MRC, University Laval, Quebec, 1969-71. *Appointments:* Assistant Professor of Physiology, 1971-76, Associate Professor of Physiology, 1976-80, Professor and Head of Department of Physiology, 1980, University of Ottawa. *Memberships:* Canadian Physiological Society, Secretary 1978-81, President 1982-83, Canadian Federation of Biological Societies, President 1980-81, Member, Board of Directors, 1978-84; American Physiological Society. *Publications:* Contributor of numerous articles to medical journals. *Address:* University of Ottawa, School of Medicine, 451 Smyth Road, Ottawa, Canada K1H 8M5.

COWELL, John Walter Frederick, b. 16 Apr 1944, Ottawa, Canada. Vice-President, Occupational Health & Safety. m. Monika M Schulte, 20 Aug,

1966, Ottawa, Canada, 2 sons, 1 daughter. *Education:* MD, MSc, Hon BSc, Certified, Canadian College of Family Practice, Canadian Board of Occupational Medicine. *Appointments:* Medical Director, Toronto Tansit Commission, 1972-77; Medical Director, Springhurst Community Health Centre, 1972-77; Manager, Health Safety & Environment & Company Medical Director, Canadian General Electric, 1977-81; Vice-President, Occupational Health & Safety, NOVA, an Alberta Corporation, 1981-. *Memberships:* Occupational Medical Association of Canada; Canadian Board of Occupational Medicine; Permanent Commission & International Association on Occupation Health; American Occupational Medical Association; Canadian Medical Association. *Publications:* (with G Hetenyi Jr) 'The Effect of Pheoxybenzamine & Propranol and their Combination on the Restoration of Glucose Homeostasis after Insulin Induced Hypoglycemia' (in 'Archives Internationales de Pharmacodyname et de Thérapie) 1969; (with A Booth) 'Crowding & Health' (in Journal of Health & Social Behaviour 1976); 'Organisation & Management of Occupational Health & Safety Programs' (in Occupational Health in Ontario) 1985; Co-editor, Proceedings of 11th International Congress on Occupation Health in the Chemical Industry, 1983. *Honour:* President, Occupational Medical Association of Canada, 1984-. *Hobbies:* Music; Sport. *Address:* c/ NOVA Corporation, P O Box 2535 Station M, Calgary, T2P 2N6, Canada.

COWGILL, Roert, b. 27 Jan. 1944, New York, USA. Private Practice. m. Diane, 2 Mar. 1974, Atlanta, Georgia, 1 son, 4 daughters. *Education:* BA, English, 1965, MD, 1969, University of Virginia. *Appointments:* Fellow, Surgical Oncology, Memorial Hosptial for Cancer, New York, 1976-78; Senior Consultant, Surgery, King Faisal Spoecialist Hospital, Riyadh, Saudi Arabia, 1980-83; Private Practice, Surgical Oncology. *Memberships:* Fellow, American College for Surgeons; Society of Surgical Oncology; Amrican Society of Clinical Oncology; Medical Association of Georgia. *Publications:* Articles in professional journals including: 'American Journal Physiology'; 'Journal of Trauma'; 'Diseases of the Colon and Rectum'; 'Atlanta Medicine'; 'Journal of the Medical Association of Georgia'; 'Gastroenterology'; 'King Faisal Specialist Hospital Medical Journal'; etc. *Hobbies:* Tennis; Hiking. *Address:* 5669 Peachtree Dunwoody Road NE 2§345, Atlanta, GA 30342, USA.

COY, Lawrence Bernard, b. 28 Apr. 1934, Sydney, Australia. Area Medical Research Director. m. Elizabeth Hansen, 2 Apr. 1959, Sydney, 2 sons, 2 daughters. *Education:* MB BS, University of Sydney, 1958; Fellow, Royal Australasian College of Physicians. *Appointmetns:* Intern, Royal Prince Alfred Hospital, Sydney, 1958; Senior Resident, Lewisham Hospital, Sydney, 1959; Registrar, Internal Medicine, St Vincent's Hospital, Sydney, 1960-63; Private Practice, 1963-73; Consultant Physician, St Vincent's Hospital, 1964-66; Visitng Specialist, Eastern Suburbs Hospital, 1966-74; Prince of Wale's Hospital, Sydney, 1973-74, Mater Misericordiae Hospital, Sydney, 1968-85. *Memberships:* Australian & New Zealand Cardiac Society; Australian Thoracic Society; Australian Society of Clinical & Experimental Pharmacologists. *Hobbies:* Golf; Tennis. *Address:* 36 Benelong Crescent, Bellevue Hill, New South Wales 2023, Australia.

CRABBE, Jean, b. 12 Aug. 1927, Brussels, Belgium. Professor of Human Physiology & Internal Medicine. m. Marie de Guchteneere, 10 Aug. 1954, 3 sons, 2 daughters. *Education:* MD, 1951, Agrégé, 1962, Catholic University of Louvain. *Appointments:* Research Assistant, University Hospital of Geneva, Switzerland, 1954-55; Assistant in Medicine, 1955-58, Intern, 1958-59, P B Brigham Hospital, Boston, Massachusetts, USA; Clinical & Research

Fellow, Massachusetts General Hospital, Boston, 1959-60; Assistant, Department of Medicine, University Clinics St Raphael, Louvain, Belgium, 1961-62; Lecturer, 1966, Associate Professor, 1967, Professor of Human Physiology & Internal Medicine, Catholic University of Louvain Medical School, 1972-; Chairman, Department of Physiolgoy, 1972-75. *Memberships:* American Society for Clinical Research; American Endocrine Society; Société Belge de Médecine Interne, d'Endocrinologie, de Physiologie, de Gastroentérologie (honorary); European Society for Clinical Investigation; Association des Physiologistes; New York Academy of Sciences; American Assciation for the Advancement of Science; Sociètè Française d'Ednocrinologie; Editorial Boards of 'Journal of Steroid Biochemistry', 'Archives internationales de Physiologie et Biochimie', 'Physiological Reviews', 'Molecular & Cellular Endocrinology', 'Pflügers Archiv'. *Publications:* More than 280 papers & abstracts in medical journals. *Honours:* Prix des Alumni (Medical Sciences), Fondation Universitaire, Belgium, 1963; Various Visiting Professorships. *Address:* Faculté de Médicine – UCL 5530, Laboratorie d'Endocrinologie, Avenue Hippocrate 55, B-1200 Brussels, Belgium.

CRABBE, Michael James Cardwell, b. 28 May 1951, Aden. Senior Research Biochemist. *Education:* BSc, University of Hull, 1971; MSc, PhD, University of Manchester; FRSC, C Chem. *Appointments:* Demonstrator in Biochemistry, University of Manchester Institute of Science and Technology, 1971-72; Graduate Research Assistant , Fellow, Manchester University, 1972-77; Wellcome Trust Fellow, Nuffield Laboratory of Ophthalmology, 1977-79, Guy Newton Stipendiary Junior Research Fellow, Natural Sciences, Wolfson College, 1979-82, Lecturer in Biochemistry, New College and St Peter's College, Principal Investigator, Nuffield Laboratory of Ophthalmology, Oxford University, 1982-86; Senior Research Biochemist, Dyson Perrins Laboratory Oxford University. *Memberships:* Biochemical Society; Blair Bell Research Society; International Society for Eye Research; Association for Eye Research; Association for ,Research in Vision and Ophthalmology; International Society for Clinical Enzymology; EURAGE. *Publications:* "The Lens" in "The § Eye", 3rd edition, Co-Author, 1984; Author of numerous articles in biochemical journals and works on experimental eye research. Book contributions on enzymology, kinetics, diabetic complications and computing. *Honours:* Holroyd Prize, 1968; Research Fellow, Wolfson College; Award, Association for Eye Research, 1984. *Hobbies:* Music; Recording; Oenology; Astronomy. *Address:* Wolfson College, Oxford OX2 6UD, England.

CRADDOCK, David Robert, b. 16 Dec. 1936, Townsville, Australia. Director, Cardio-Thoracic Surgery. m. Diane Strachan, 22 May 1961, Brisbane, 1 son 1,daughter. *Education:* MB BS, Queensland, 1960; FRCS, Edinburgh, Scotland, 1964; FRCS, England, 1965; FRACS, 1968. *Appointments:* Resident, 1960-61, Surgical Registrar, !962-63, Royal Brisbane Hospital; Senior Surgical Registrar, Cardio Thoracic Surgical Unit, Royal Infirmary, Edinburgh, Scotland, 1964-67; Cardio-Thoracic Surgeon, 1968-72, Assistant Director, Cardio-Thoracic Unit, 1973-77, Royal Adelaide Hospital, Australia; currently, Director, Cardio-Thoracic Surgery, Royal Adelaide Hospital. *Memberships:* Cardiac Society of Australia and New Zealand; Thoracic Society of Australia. *Publications:* Numerous. *Hobbies:* Golf; Tennis. *Address:* 3 Trinity Street, College Park, Adelaide 5069, Australia.

CRAIG, Kenneth Denton, b. 21 Nov. 1937, Calgary, Canada. Professor, Psychology. m. Sydney Grace Smith, 10 Apr. 1971, Calgary, 2 son, 1 daughter. *Education:* BA, Sir George Williams University,

1958; MA, University of British Columbia, 1960; PhD, Purdue University, 1964; Fellow, medical Psychology, University of Oregon Medical School, USA. *Appointments:* Associate Professor, University of Calgary, 1969-71; Professor, University of British Columbia, 1963-. *Memberships:* Canadian Psychological Associaton, Fellow; American Psychological Association, Fellow; Academy of Behavioural Medicine Research. *Publications:* Numerous articles in professional journals, most recent "Facial Expression during Induced Pain", 'Journal of Personality and Social Psychology', 1985; "Developmental Changes in Infant Pain Expression During Immunization Injections", 'Social Sciences and Medicine', 1984; Chapter, "Emotional Aspects of Pain", in 'Textbook of Pain'; etc. *Honours:* President, Canadian Psychological Association, 1986-87; President, British Columbia Psychological Associations, 1977. *Hobbies:* Running; Skiing; Sailing. *Address:* Dept. of Psychology, University of British Columbia, Vancouver, BC, Canada V6T 1Y7.

CRANKSHAW, David pilkington, b. 28 Mar 1939, London, England. Senior Lecturer in Anaesthetics. m. Susan Mary Selkirk, 30 Apr. 1965, Ballarat, Australia, 1 son, 1 dauaghter. *Education:* MB BS, 1963, PhD, 1973, University of Melbourne, Australia; Fellow, Faculty of Anaesthetists, Royal Australasian College of Surgeons, 1969; Board of Medical Examiners, FLEX, California, USA, 1974; Australian Computer Society, 1980. *Appointments:* Assistant Professor of Anesthesia, Stanford University, 1971-73; Specialist Anaesthetist, 1974-75, Senior Medical Staff, 1984-. Royal Melbourne Hosiptal; Senior Lecturer in Anaesthetics, University of Melbourne, 1975-. *Memberships:* Examiner, Past Regional Committee Member, Faculty of Anaesthetists, Royal Australasian College of Surgeons; Australian Society of Anaesthetists; Australian Society for Clinical and Experimental Pharmacology; Australian Phys. and Pharmcol Society; International Anaesthesia Research Society; Australasian Anaesthesia Research Group, Past President. *Publication:* Contributions to: "Muscle Relaxants", 1975; 'Journal Pharm Pharmcol'; 'Neuropharmacology'; 'Anaesth. Intens. Care'; 'European Journal of Clinical Pharmacology'. *Hobbies:* Field hockey; Wave sailing. *Address:* University Department of Surgery, P O Royal Melbourne Hospital, Victoria 3050, Australia.

CRANWELL, Richard Wayne, b. 8 Nov. 1946, St Louis, Missouri, USA. Associate Professor of Chiropractic Technique. m. Denise Ann Minnigerode, 2 Oct. 1976, St Louis, 1 daughter. *Education:* BS Biochemistry, St Louis University, 1970; DC, Logan Chiropractic College, 1976; MS Nutrition, Bridgeport University, 1983; Diplomate, National Board of Chiropractic; Diplomate, Gonstead Chiropractic Technique. *Appointments:* Quality Control Technician, Animal Feed Department, Ralston Purina Company, St Louis, 1969-70; Medical Technologist, Clinical Chemistry Laboratory, Barnes Hospital St Louis, 1971-76; Chief Intern, Gonstead Chiropractic Clinic, Mt Horeb, Wisconsin, 1976-77; Private Practice, St Louis, Missouri, 1977-; Instructor in technique 1977-80, Clinic Director of Logan Chesterfield Clinic 1977-78, Clinic Director of the Hosea House Clinic 1978-82, Assistant Professor 1980-83, Student Clinic Director 1982-, Associate Professor 1983-, Logan College of Chiropractic, St Louis. *Memberships:* National Board of Chiropractic Examiners; American Chiropractic Association; International Chiropractic Association; Logan College of Chiropractic Alumni. *Publications:* 'Alzheimers Disease – Current Nutrition', 1979; 'Gonstead Case Management Notes'; 'Enhanced Absorption of Oral Vitamin B12 From a Resin Absorbate Administered to Normal Subjects'. *Address:* 6704 Parkwood Place, St Louis, M0 63116, USA.

CRAWFORD, George Patrick Mitchell, b. 12 Oct. 1946, Aberdeen, Scotland. Director, Haematology. m. Allison McLeane Irvine, 27 July 1967, 1 son, 1 daughter. *Education:* MB ChB, Honours, 1970, MD, Honours, 1975, University of Aberdeen; MRCP (UK), 1972; FRACP, 1981; FRCPA, 1982. *Appointments:* Resident House Officer: Medicine, 1970-71, Surgery, 1971, University of Aberdeen; Research Fellow, 1971-72, Junior Research Fellow subsequently Hon. Registrar, 1972-75, Lecturer, Medicine (Senior Registrar), 1975-76, University of Aberdeen; Senior Lecturer, Medicine & Haematology, University of London, Consultant Physician, Director, Haemophilia Centre, Hammersmith Hospital, 1976-77; Senior Lecturer, Medicine, University of Western Australia, Consultant Physician, Haematologist, Sir Charles Geirdner Hospital, Perth, 1977-82; Head, Haematology, Freemantle Hospital, Director, Haematology, Sir Charles Gairdner Hospital, 1982-. *Memberships:* Haematology Society of Australia; Australian Society of Blood Transfusion; Australian Medical Association. *Publications:* "Assays of inhibitors of the fibrinolytic enzyme system: functional and immunological", 'Progress in Chemical Fibrinoysis and Thrombolysis', Volume II, 1976; "Heparin and its Current Therapeutic Role", 'Recent Advances in Blood Coagulation', 1977; "Platelets and Fibrinolysis'', 'Haemostasis: Biochemistry, Physiology and Pathology'', 1977. *Hobby:* Sailing. *Address:* 18 Grenfell Way, Leeming, Western Australia 6155.

CRAWFORD, Priscilla Ruth, b. 13 Oct. 1941, Ferndale, Michigan, USA. *Education:* BA, Butler University, 1962; Fulbright Scholar, Goethe University, Frankfurt, Germany, 1963; PhD, 1970, MA, 1965, Ohio State University, Columbus. *Appointments:* Research Associate, Gary Income Maintenance Experiment, 1970-73; Programme and Research Development, 1973-77; Director, manpower, Indiana Department of Mental Health, 1978-; Clinical Assistant Professor, Indiana University School of Medicine, Department of Psychiatry; Associate Faculty, Women's Studies School of Liberal Arts, IUPUI. *Memberships:* American Sociological Association; Eastern, Midwest and North Central Sociological Societies; Ohio Academy of Science; American Association of University Professors; American Management Association; Board Member, Indiana Academy of the Social Sciences. *Publications:* Various articles in professional journals; papers read at National and International meetings. *Honours:* Various 1st Place Awards, Public Speaking & Debate Competitions; Twice Tau Kappa Alpha National Debating Champion; American Chemistry Society Award; Faculty Senior Scholar; Hub and Wheel Awards; Andrew Mellon Grant; Fulbright Scholar; Special University Fellow; Fellow, National Institute of Mental Health; Toured health and mental health facilities, People's Republic of China, as member of specially-organized tour sponsored by Governor's State University/NIMH representatives, December 1981-January 1982, many other honours and awards. *Address:* PO Box 30254, Indianapolis, IN 46230, USA.

CREASON, Nancy S., b. 7 Aug. 1938, Elkader, Iowa, USA. Assistant Dean, Regional Programme; Associate Professor, Medical/Surgical Nursing. *Education:* BSN, University of Iowa; MSN, Wayne State University; PhD, University of Michigan. *Appointments include:* Acting Director, Family Planing, Tiffin, Ohio, 1972-73; Assistant Professor, School of Nursing 1973-74, Chair, Fundamentals School of Nursing 1975-77, University of Michigan; Associate Professor, Associate Dean, Director of Baccalaureate Programme, College of Nursing, University of Utah, 1977-78; Associate Professor, College of Nursing, University of Illinois, 1978-. *Memberships:* American & Illinois Nurses Associations; ANA Council of Nurse Researchers; North American Nursing Diagnosis Association;

East Central Illinois Nursing Research Network; Nurses' Coalition for Action in Politics; etc. *Publications include:* Contributions to nursing journals, book chapters, conference proceedings. *Honours:* Sigma Theta Tau, 1959; Fellowship, University of Michigan, 1974-75; Danforth Associate, 1980; Grant, US DHSS-Public Health Service, 1981-86. *Hobbies:* Reading; Cross-country skiing; Walking; Swimming; Sqaure dancing. *Address:* 1820 Sadler Drive, Chapaign, II 61821, USA.

CREASY, Robert Kenwood, b. 13 Nov. 1934, San Francisco, California, USA. Professor, Chairman of Obstetrics, Gynaecology and Reproductive Sciences. m. Judith Davidson, 19 Oct. 1963, Oberlin, Ohio, 1 son, 1 daughter. *Education:* BA Zoology, Dartmouth College, Hanover, New Hampshire, 1957; MD, New York University College of Medicine, 1961; MA Physiology, University of California, San Francisco, 1971. *Appointments:* Clinical Instructor 1968-71, Assistant Professor 1971-73, Associate Professor 1973-78, Professor 1978-84, Department of Obstetrics and Gynaecology, Associate member of Cardiovascular Research Institute 1973-84, University of California, San Francisco; Obstetrician-Gynecologist 1968-84, Chief of Obstetrical Service 1971-81, Moffitt Hospital, University of California Medical Center; Professor and Chairman of Department of Obstetrics, Gynaecology and Reproductive Sciences, Chief of Obstetrical and Gynaecological Service of Hermann Hospital, University of Texas Health Science Center, Houston, Texas, 1984-. *Memberships include:* American College of Obstetricians and Gynaecologists; Perinatal Research Society; Royal Society of Medicine; Society for Gynaecological Research; American Academy of Pediatrics; Society of Perinatal Obstetrics; American Gynecological and Obstetrical Society. *Publications include:* "New Hope For Problem Pregnancies, Helping Babies Before They Are Born", (with D Hales), 1982; "Maternal-Fetal Medicine: Principles and Practice", (with R Resnick), 1984; Numerous abstracts and articles. *Address:* University of Texas Health Science Center-Houston, Department of Obstetrics, Gynaecology and Reproductive Sciences, 6431 Fannin – Rm 3286, Houston, TX 77030, USA.

CREEDY, Brian Edward, B. 19 Dec., 1942, Brisbane, Australia. Private Practitioner. m. Genevieve Dempsey, 19 Aug. 1967, Brisbane, 2 sons. *Education:* BDSc., Queensland, 1965; FRACDS, 1978. *Appointments:* Dental Superintendent, Cloncurry Base Hospital, 1966, Longreach Base Hospital, 1967-70; Dental Superintendent Dalby General Hospital, 1970; Private Dental Practice, Townsville, 1970-. *Memberships* Australian Dental Association; Australian Society of Prosthodontists; Asustralian Society of Endodontology; Australian Society of Peridontology; Australian Society of Implant Dentistry; Australian Society for the Advancement of Anaesthesia and Sedation in Dentistry. *Hobbies:* Photography; Hunting; Fishing; Horse Riding. *Address:* 340 Flinders St., Townsville, Queensland 4810, Australia.

CRIELAERS, Peter J A, b. 15 Jan. 1941, Nijmegen, The Netherlands. Association Vice President. m. Josephine A M Jurgens, 10 Dec. 1966, Nijmegen, 1 son, 2 daughters. *Education:* Tandartsdiploma, University of Utrecht, 1967; Diploma in Dental Public Health, Royal College of Surgeons, England, 1970; Diploma in Dental Health, University of Birmingham, 1972; MD, University of Utrecht, 1977. *Appointments:* Chairman, Department of Social and Preventive Dentistry, University of Amsterdam, 1970-78; Chairman, Dental Group Practice, Abcoude, 1973-78; Director, School Dental Service, 1978-; Board Member, 1979-81, Vice President, 1981-, Dutch Dental Association; Board Member, International Health Development Foundation, 1983-; Treasurer, Dutch Association for the Study of Social Dentistry, 1983-. *Memberships:* Dutch Dental

Association; Nederlands Tandheelkundig Genootschap; Supporting Member, Federation Dentaire Internationale; Consultant, Commission on Research and Epidemiology; Committee de Liaisson des Practiciens de l'Art Dentaire dans les Pays de la CEE; Fellow, International College of Dentists; Behavioural Scientists in Dental Research. *Publications:* 'Dental Knowledge, Dental Attitudes and Oral Health of Birmingham Dental Hospital Patients', 1972; 'Op weg naar mondigheid. A Social dental investigation into the etimology of oral diseases', 1977. *Honour:* Fellowship, World Health Organisation, USA, 1971. *Hobbies:* Travel ; Bridge; Music; Reading. *Address:* 23 Peppinghof, 1391 BB Abcoude, The Netherlands.

CRISTIANO, Domenico, b. 18 Sept 1940, Gasperona, Italy. Psychoanalyst. *Education:* Degree in Modern Languages, Bocconi University of Milan, 1972; Degree in Psychology, University of Pedove, 1984. *Appointments:* Teacher in State school; Psychoanalyst. *Memberships:* Accademia Tiberina, Roma; Liberea Post Universita delle Nuove Medicine, Milan; Centro Coperenico per la reicvece psicoenolitico sui gruppi, Milan. *Hobbies:* Travel; Tennis; Photography. *Address:* Via di Torrevecchia 73, Rome, Italy.

CRISWELL, Eleanor Camp, b. 12 May 1938, Norfolk, Virginia, USA. Professor of Psychology, Sonoma State University, California; Clinical Director, Biotherapeutics, Kentfield Medical Hospital. m. Thomas L. Hanna, 25 June 1974. *Education:* BA, Elementary Education, University of Kentucky, 1961; MA, Counselling and Guidance, University of Kentucky, 1962; EdD, Educational Psychology, University of Florida, 1968. *Appointments:* Jacksonville University, Florida, 1966; University of Florida, 1968; California State College, Fullerton, 1967; California State College, Hayward, 1969; College of the Holy Names, 1969-75; Humanistic Psychology Institute, Saybrook Institute, Founder-Director, 1970-77. *Memberships:* American Psychological Association; California State Psychological Association; Association for Humanistic Psychology, President, 1976-77; Aerospace Medical Association; Biofeedback Society of American; Biofeedback Society of California, Past Executive Director, 1979-84. *Publications:* Co-Editor, "Biofeedback and Family Practice Medicine", 1983; Patentee, Optokinetic perceptual learning device, US Patent; Research section twice yearly, 'Somatics' magazine-journal of bodily arts and sciences (international journal), also managing editor, 1976-. Other articles in various magazines, journals and books. Publisher, Freeperson Press. *Hobbies:* Computers; Guitar; Gardening; Writing; Travel. *Address:* Psychology Department, Sonoma State University, Rohnert Park, CA 94928, USA.

CROGHAN, Gary Alan, b. 2 Oct. 1954, Fort Wayne, Indiana, USA. Cancer Research Scientist; Director, Laboratory for Ovarian & Breast Cancer Antigens. m. Ivana Tallerico, 3 July 1982, Newburgh. *Education:* BA, Wabash College, 1973; PhD, State University of New York, Buffalo, 1983; Fellow, Cancer Immunology, Cancer Research Institute, 1984-86. *Appointments:* New York State Cancer Research Fellowship, Roswell Park Memorial Institute, 1978-82; Cancer Research Affiliate, 1982-83; Postdoctoral Fellow, 1983-84; Fellow, Cancer Immunology, Cancer Research Institute, 1984-86; Director, Laboratory for Ovarian & Breast Cancer Antigens, Diagnostic Immunology Research & Biochemistry, 1984-; Medical Student, State University of New York, Buffalo, 1986-. *Memberships include:* American Association for the Advancement of Science; New York Academy of Sciences; American society for Microbiology; International Society for Breast Cancer Research; Sigma Xi; American Public Health Association. *Publications:* 15 articles in professional journals; 5 abstracts for National Meetings in cancer research.

Honours: Fellowship, Cancer immunology, Cancer Research Institute, 1984-86; DAAD Summer Exchange Scholarship, 1981; New York State Cancer Fellowship, 1978-82; several grants, 1982-85. *Hobbies:* Community Outreach Programmes on Cancer Prevention & Detection; Oil Painting; Travel; Fishing. *Address:* 209 E. Winspear Ave., Buffalo, NY 14215, USA.

CROKER, James Meyrick, b. 17 May 1927, Mackay, Queensland, Australia. President, 24th Australian Dental Association Congress. m. Joan Catherine Morris, 22 Feb. 1952, Brisbane, 4 daughters. *Education:* BDSC, Queensland; FICD. *Appointments:* Chairman, numerous committees, Queensland Branch, Australian Dental Association; Executive Member, President, Queensland Branch, Australian Dental Association. *Memberships:* Federation Dentaire International; Consultant, Dental Health; International College of Dentists; Dental Circle Post Graduate Study Club; Delta Sigma delta; Executive Officer, Federal Australian Dental Association; Executive Member, President, Queensland Council of Professions, Australian Council of Professions; Life Member, Queensland Branch, Australian Dental Association, 1985-. *Honours:* Distinguished Service Award, Queensland Branch, Australian Dental Association; Paul Harris Fellowship, Rotary, 1981; Member German Division, Order of Australia (AM) (for services to the profession of Dentistry) 1986. *Hobbies:* Lawn Bowls; Stamp Collecting; Fishing. *Address:* 8 Bougainvillea Avenue, Indooroopilly, Brisbane, Queensland, Australia.

CROKER, Joseph McCall, b. 20 Sep. 1939, Glen Falls, New York, USA. Chiropractor. m. Angelita, 13 Jan, 1942, 2 sons, 2 daughters. *Education:* BS, Human Biology, University of Pittsburg, Pennsylvania; DC, Lincoln Chiropractic College, 1967; Diplomate, National Board of Chiropractic Examiners; Certified Hypnotherapist, American Council of Hypnotist Examiners; Graduate, Institute of Chiropractic Hypnosis; Certified in Practice of Hypnosis, Miami School of Medicine. *Appointments:* Private Practice, 1970-; Founder, Director, The Institute of Applied Hypnosis. *Memberships:* American Chiropractic Association; Secretary, Michigan State Chiropractic Association; Florida Chiropractic Association; Colorado Chiropractic Association; Parker Chiropractic Research Foundation; Association for the Advancement of Ethical Hypnosis; Charter Member, International Society of Professional Hypnotists; President, Board of Education, Reading Community School System. *Publications:* "The Psychodynamics of Weight Control"; several articles in various journals; several poems. *Hobbies:* Fishing; Lecturing. *Address:* 729 South Main Street, Reading, MI 49274, USA.

CROLL, Una Joan, b. 15 June 1928, Australia. Medical Director, Sydney Square Diagnostic Breast Clinic, Australia. m. Frank Croll, 2 Sep. 1955, 4 daughters. *Education:* MB BS, Sydney University, 1951; Educational Affiliate, Royal Australasian College of Radiologists. *Appointments:* Junior RMO, Orange Base Hospital, New South Wales, 1952; Resident in Pathology, Prince Henry Hospital, Sydney, 1954; Pathologist for Northern Territory, 1954-55; Teaching Fellow in Pathology, Sydney University, 1955; Assistant Medical Director, Medicheck Referral Centre, Sydney, 1975-; Medical Director, Sydney Square Diagnostic Breast Clinic, 1978-. *Memberships:* Educational Affiliate, Royal Australasian College of Radiologists; National Consensus Committee on Breast Cancer Screening; Clinical Oncological Society of Australia; Australian Society Ultrasound in Medicine; Australian Medical Association. *Hobbies:* Fly Fishing; Reading; Golf; Needlework. *Address:* Sydney Square Diagnostic Breast Clinic, St Andrew's House, Sydney Square, New South Wales, Australia 2000.

CROMBIE, Alexander Leaster, b. 7 Aug. 1935, Cork, Republic of Ireland. Professor of Ophthalmology. m. Margaret Ann Adamson, 26 Aug. 1961, Edinburgh, Scotland, 2 sons. *Education:* MB ChB, University of Edinburgh. *Appointments:* House Officer, Medicine, Peel Hospital, Galashiels, 1959-60; House Officer, Surgery, Western General Hospital, Edinburgh, 1960; Senior House Officer 1960-62, Registrar 1962-64, Senior Registrar 1964-67, Opthalmology, Royal Infirmary, Edinburgh; Consultant Opthalmolgoist, Royal Victoria Infirmary, Newcastle upon Tyne, 1967-76; Professor of Opthalmology, University of Newcastle upon Tyne, 1976-. *Memberships:* Fellow, Royal College of Surgeons of Edinburgh; Fellow, Royal Medical Society; British Medical Association; Opthalmological Society of the United Kingdom; Faculty of Opthalmologists; Royal Society of Medicine. *Publications:* 'Adrenergic Supersensitisation as a therapeutic tool in Glaucoma', 1974; Book chapters: 'The Eye in Thyroid Disease' (editor: Trevor-Roper), 1975; 'Adverse Drug Reactions and the Eye' (editor: Davies), 1975 and 1977; 'Medical Opthalmology' (editors: Foster and Horler), 1978. *Honours:* Strang-Steel Bursary, 1953; Alexander Pigott Werner Research Fellow, Medical Research Council, 1965-66. *Hobbies:* Walking; Golf; Music; Reading. *Address:* 19 Graham Park Road, Gosforth, Newcastle upon Tyne N3 4BH, England.

CRONIN, Dennis Patrick, b. 17 Oct. 1954, Iowa, USA. Director. m. 28 Mar. 1981, Greensboro, North Carolina, 1 son, 2 daughters. *Education:* BS, University of SD; DC, Logan College of Chiropractic, St Louis, MO. *Appointments:* President, IA Chiropractic Society, 1981; Board Member, American Cancer Society; President, American Pain Control and Research Consultants. *Memberships:* American Chiropractic Assn.; Pain control and Research Consultants; Acupuncture Society of America; Professional Physicians; Assn. *Hobbies:* Flying; Art; Music; Weight Training. *Address:* 4612 West Market Street, Greensboro, NC 27407, USA.

CRONIN, Francis J. b. 22 Feb. 1940, Elizabeth, New Jersey, USA. Hospital President and Chief Executive. married, two children. *Education:* AB, Georgetown University, Washington DC, USA, 1962; Graduate Study in Chemistry, Louisiana State University, Baton Rouge, 1962-63; MBA, George Washington University, Washington, 1965. *Appointments:* Administrative Assistant, St. Elizabeth Medical Centre, New Jersey, 1963-64; Administarative Resident, Perth Amboy General Hospital, 1965-66, Administrative Assistant to the Director, 1966-67; Assistant Administrator, Kessler Institute for Rehabilitation, New Jersey, 1967-69; Principal Assistant Administrator, St. Joseph Hospital, Stamford, 1969-75; President and Chief Executive Officer, Elliot Hospital, Manchester, New Hampshire, 1975-present. *Memberships include:* American College of Hospital Administrators; American Academy of Medical Administrators; American Public Health Association; New Hampshire Hospital Association; Blue Cross/Blue Shield of New Hampshire; International Hospital Federation; Royal Society of Health. *Publications:* "A Search Procedure for Full Time Physicians", 1979. Numerous presentations to hospital assemblies; various radio and television interviews. *Address:* 36 Holly Hill Drive, Amherst, NH 03131, USA.

CROXSON, Michael Sutherland, b. 30 Apr. 1942, New Plymouth, New Zealand. Endocrinologist. m. Margaret Christine Cunningham, 2 sons. *Education:* MBChB, Otago University Medical School, 1960-65; Member 1970, Fellow 1975, Roayl Australasian College of physicians. *Appointments:* Fogarty International Fellow 1974-76, Associate Professor of Clinical Research Centre, 1977, University of Southern California, USA; Endocrinologist, Auckland Hospital, Auckland, New Zealand, 1977-; Part-time Clinical Lecturer, Auckland University, 1977-. *Memberships:* American Thyroid Association; American Endocrine Society; New Zealand Endocrine Society; New Zealand Society for Study of Diabetes. *Publications:* 35 in medicine endocrinology, 1970-85; 3 reveiws, 1978-84; 9 abstracts in proceedings, 1973-83. *Honours:* University Natioal Schoalrship, 1959; Fulbright International Fellow, 1974-76. *Hobbies:* Sport; Golf; Tennis; Running; Home; Family. *Address:* 18 Montrose Terrace, Mairangi Bay, Auckland 10, New Zealand.

CRUESS, Richard Leigh, b. 17 Dec. 1929, London, Ontario, Canada. Dean, Medicine, McGill University. m. Sylvia Robinson, 30 May 1953, Cleveland, 2 sons. *Education;* AB, Princeton University, 1951; MD, Columbia University, 1955. *Appointments:* Orthopaedic Surgeon-in-Charge, 1968-71, Assistant Surgeon-in-Chief, 19790-81, Royal Victoria Hospital; Surgeon-in-Chief, Shriners Hospital for Crippled Children (Montral Unit), 1970-82; Professor, Surgery, Chairman, Orthopaedic Surgery, 1976-80, Dean, medicine, 1981-, McGill University. *Memberships:* Royal Society of Canada; Royal College of Physicians & Surgeons; American College of Surgeons; Canadian Orthopaedic Association; American Academy of Orthopaedic Surgeons; American Orthopaedic Association; etc. *Publications include:* Numerous articles in professional journals inlcuding 'Journal of bone and Joint Surgery'; 'Journal of Trauma'; 'Orthopaedic Review'; etc.; Abstracts. *Honours:* Fellow, Royal College of Physicians & Surgeons of Canada; American Academy of Orthopaedic Surgeons; American Orthopaedic Association; Fellow, Royal Society of Canada. *Hobbies:* Fishing; Skiing; Photography. *Address:* 526 Mount Pleasant, Montreal, Quebec, Canada H3Y 3H5.

CRUL, Jan F, b. 31 July 1922, Batavia, Indonesia. Professor and Chairman of University Department of Anesthesiology. m. Ella J Sluijter, 20 June 1950, 5 sons. *Education:* MD, Leiden University, Netherlands, 1939-47; Specialisation in Anesthesiology 1950-52, PhD Medicine (pharmacology) 1955, University of Groningen. *Appointments:* Senior Medical officer, Dutch Army, 1947-50; Anesthesiologist, Laurentius Hospital, Roermond, 1952-57; Reader in Anesthesiology 1957-69, Professor of Anesthesiology 1969-, University of Nijmegen; Visitng Professor of Anesthesiology, Hospital of the University, Pennsylvania, USA, 1964-65. *Memberships:* Member of the Board 1964-65, Secretary 1959-62, Dutch Society of Anesthetists; Chairman, Anesthetic Council, 1963-66; Chairman 1966-68, Dutch Society for the Advancment of Surgical sciences; Chairman of Reanimation Committee 1963-66, Royal Dutch Society Het Orange Kruis; Chairman of the Committee on Statutes and Bylaws, Member of Executive Commitee, Member of the Scientific and Educational Committee, World Federation of Societies of Anesthesiologists, 1968-; FFARCS; Association of Anesthetists of Great Britain and Ireland; Honorary member, Association of University Anesthetists, USA; Fellow, Faculty of Anesthesiology, Royal College of Surgeons, Great Britain; Dutch representative, Union Européne des Médecins Spécialistes; Chairman, Dutch Committee of Anesthesiology; Resuscitation Committee, Oranje Kruis; committee Disaster Medicine; Representative for University Hospital of Nijmegen, Committee for Disaster Medicine for the Netherlands; Honorary member, Society of Anesthesiologists of Indonesia, 1985. *Honour:* Officer (Knighthood), Order of the House of Orange, 1970. *Hobbies:* Field Hockey; Swimming; Walking. *Address:* Bijleveldsingel 60, 6524 AE Nijmegen, The Netherlands.

CRUSE, Julius M., b. 15 Feb. 1937, New Albany, Mississippi, USA. Pathologist. *Education:* BA, Chemistry & German, 1958, BS, Medicine, 1958, University of Mississippi; D.Mikrobiologie, Fulbright

Fellow, University of Graz, Austria, 1958-60; MD, 1964, Phd, Pathology, 1966, University of Tennessee medical Units, Memphis; USPHS Predoctoral Fellow, Pathology, 1964-67. *Appointments:* Professor, Pathology, 1974-, Director, Immunopathology, 1978-, Director, Graduate Studies Programme, Pathology, 1974-, various other offices, University of Mississippi Medical centre, Jackson; Adjunct Professor, Immunology, Mississippi College, 1977-. *Memberships:* Member, numerous professional organisations including: Fellow, American Academy of Microbiology, Royal Society of Health, Great Britain, American Association for the Advancement of Science; American Association of Pathologists and Bacteriologists American Society for Experimental Pathology; American Association of Pathologists; American Association of Immunologists; International Academy of Pathology; American Society of Clinical Pathologists; etc. *Publications:* Author, over 150 articles in profesional journals including 'Neurosurgery'; 'Diagnostic Immunology'; 'Conceptual Immunology'; 'Experimental and Molecular Pathology'; etc.; Editorial Appointments include: Editor in Chief, 'Survey of Immunologic Research', 1982-, 'Survey and Synthesis of Pathology Research', 1983-; Editor, 'Concepts in Immunopathology', 1984-; Editor, "The Year in Immunology", 1983, 1984-85; etc. *Honours:* Fulbright Fellowship, University of Graz, Austria, 1958-60; American Cancer Society Grantee, University of Tennessee Medical Units, 1964-66; Research Corporation, New York, Brown-Hazen Fund, 3 Grants for Cancer Research, 1968-70; AMA Physician's Recognition Award, 1969, 1979; Outstanding Educator of America, 1971, 1975; Founder, Member, Visiting Professorship (Michelson), Pathology Committee, University of Tennessee Medical Units; etc. *Address:* Dept. of Pathology, University Medical Centre, Jackson, MS 39216, USA.

CSABA, Béla, b. 17 Jan. 1931, Bucsa, Hungary. Professor, Immunology & Pathophysiology. m. (1) Ilona Ruder, 31 Mar. 1936, died 1979, 1 son, 1 daughter, (2) Katlain Czeli, 1982. *Education:* MD; CMSci.; D.Sc.; Professor, Immunology and Pathophysiology; Postgraduate Training, Immunology, Copenhagen, 1970. *Appointments:* Assistant, Pathophysiology, University Medical School, Debrecen, 1956-63; Adjunct, Docent, Pathophysiology, 1963-72, Professor, Pathophysiology, 1972-, Deputy Rector, Teaching Programmes, 1968-74, University Medical School, Debrecen; WHO Fellow, 1965, England; WHO Consultant, WHO Regional Centre for Europe, Copenhagen, Denmark, 1973. *Memberships include:* International Union of Physiological and Immunological Societies; European Allergology and Clinical Immunology; Hungarian Physiological Microbiological, Immunological and Clinical Immunological Societies; Hungarian Society for Medical Education; Founder, Executive Committee, Immunological and Medical Education Societies, Hungary. *Publications:* "Practical Works in Immunology", 1983; "Allergische Reaktionen vom Typ I. in Allergologie", 1980; Articles in Professional Journals. *Honours:* Honorary Member, Czechoslovak Medical Society; J.E. Purkine, 1976; Corresponding Honorary Member, Sociedad Cubana de Allergologia, 1975; Doctor of Merit, 1966; Golden Order of Labour, 1970; Pro Universitate of Debrecen, 1975; Eminent Pedagogue in Higher Education, 1975. *Hobby:* Listening to Music. *Address:* Vörös Hadsereg u. 34, Debrecen 4024, Hungary.

CSABA, Gyorgy, b. 31 May 1929, Törökszentmiklós, Hungary. Professor; Director. m. (1) Dr Clara Hegyi, 5 Dec. 1954, (2) Katalin Kallay, 5 Aug. 1970, 2 sons, 2 daughters. *Education:* MD 1953; PhD 1957; DSc 1969. *Appointments:* Assistant, 1953-59, 1st Assistant 1959-63, Assistant Professor, 1963-70, Assistant Professor, 1970-71, Histology and

Embryology, Professor, Director, Biology, 1971-, Semmelweis University of Medicine, Budapest. *Memberships:* Society of Hungarian Biologists, Member of the Presidium; European Teratology Society, European Tissue Culture Society; European Neuroscience Association; International Society of Phychoneureondocrinology, etc. *Publications:* 22 books (textbooks, monographs, etc); 450 scientific papers. *Honour:* Outstanding Teacher, 1983; Huzella Prize, 1984. *Hobbies:* To write Papers & Books on the Present and Future of Human Beings. *Address:* Dept. of Biolgoy, Semmelweiss University of Medicine, H-1445 Budapest POB 370, Hungary.

CSABA, Imre Ferenc, b. 2 Nov. 1926, Tolna, Hungary. Obstetrician and Gynaecologist. m. 2 Apr. 1953, 1 son, 1 daughter. *Education:* Diploma, Medical University, 1951. *Appointments:* Assistant Professor, 1973, Director of Institute, 1975, Professor, 1975. *Memberships:* Scientific Evaluating Committee of Sciences; Colleges of National Institute of Gynaecology and Obstetrics; Editorial Board of 'Journal Magyar Nöorvosok Lanpa'; Honorary Member Society of Gynaecologists of the Bulgarien. *Publications:* "Clinical and Morphological picture of Polycystic ovaries", 1965; "Child and Adolescent Gynaecological Medication", 1984; over 200 articles in scientific journals. *Honour:* Excellent Physician, 1968. *Address:* Department of Obstetrics and Gynaecology, Medical University, Édesanyák u.17, 7624 Pecs, Hungary.

CSERR, Robert, b. 29 May, 1936, Perth Amboy, New Jersey, USA. Psychiatrist. m. Helen Fitzgerald, 28 May, 1962, 1 daughter. *Education:* AB, magna cum laude, Harvard College, USA: MD, Harvard Medical School. *Appointments:* Co-ordinator, Alcohol Clinic, Massachusetts General Hospital; Assistant Superintendent, Medfield State Hospital, Superintendent, Medfield State Hospital; Area Programme Director, Medfield, Norwood area, 1971-74; Board of Directors, Flynn House Christian Fellowship Consultant, our Brother's Place; President, Medfield Foundation, 1974-; Director, Outlook, 1974-76; Medical Director, Charles River Hospital, 1976-80; Vice President for Clinical Affairs, Communtiry Care Systems Inc.–; Psychiatrist in Chief, Charles River Hospital-; Psychiatrist in Chief, Hahnemann Hospital-; Private Psychiatric practice-. *Membershisp:* Massachusetts Medical Society, Committee on Mental Health; American Psychiatric Association; Massachusetts Psychiatric Society; Member, Board of Overseers, Mount Desert Island Biological Laboratory. *Publications:* Contributed to "Final Report on the Massachussetts Mental Hospital Planning Project", 1973; 'Community Mental Health and the Mental Hospital' (whilst chairman, Task Force on Community Based Care of the Adult Mentally Ill), in 'American Journal of Psychiatry', 1973; Discussion of Torrey and Taylor 'Cheap Labour from Poor Nations'. *Honours:* Valedictorian, 1954; Four year full academic shcolarship, 1954-58; Four year scholarships, 1958-62; Boylston Medical Society of Harvard Medical School, 1961. *Address:* Green Acres, North Dighton, MA 02764, USA.

CSIKY, Miklós, b. 7 May 1931, Bucharest, Romania. Senior Consultant, Department of Surgery, m. Sipos Gaudi Julianna, 2 Mar. 1963, Marosvásárhely, 3 sons, 4 daughters. *Education:* Medical diploma, 1956; Candidate, Medical Sciences, 1971. *Appointments:* Assistant Professor, Department of Anatomy, 1958-66, Assistant Professor, Department of Surgery, 1967-76, University School of Medicine, Marosvásárhely, Romania; Senior Consultant, County Hospital Szombathely, Department of Surgery, Hungary, 1977-79; Senior Consultant, Department of Surgery, County Hospital of Salgotarjan, Hungary, 1980-. *Memberships:* Hungarian Surgical Society; Hungarian Oncological Society; ESSO. *Publications:* 'Erfahrungen mit den wegen kolon und rektum tumor durchgeführten erweiterten Operationen', 1985; 'Experiences with primary resection of tumors of the left colon and rectum causing ileus', 1983; 'Operations performed becasue of tuberculotic alterations of the intestines', 1983; 'Experimental and clinical applications of a new anastomotic apparatus in low anterior resection', 1983. *Honours:* Kivalo orvos, 1985. *Hobbies:* Gardening. *Address:* County Hospital Salgótarján, Department of Surgery, Vörőshadsereg Street 64, 3100 Salgótarján, Hungary.

CUCHILLO, Claudi M, b. 28 Jan. 1941, Barcelona, Spain, Professor of Biochemistry and Head of Department and Director of Institute of Fundamental Biology, m. Maria Lluisa Torrents, 27 Apr. 1966, Barcelona, 1 son, 2 daughters. *Education:* PharmM, 1964, PharmD, 1967, University of Barcelona; PhD, University of London, England, 1974. *Appointments:* Member, Department of Biochemistry, Member, Insitute of Fundamental Biology, 1969, Head of department, 1977-, Director of the Institute, 1981-, Autonomous University of Barcelona. *Memberships:* Societat Catalana de Biologia; Sociedad Español de Bioquimica; The Biochemical Society, England; American Association for the Advancement of Science The New York Academy of Sciences; Academia de Medicina de Catalunya i Belears; Sociedad Farmaceutica del Mediterraneo Latino. *Publications:* 'Bovine pancreatic ribonuclease: Substrate binding and mechanism of action', 1970; 'The Specificty of the interaction of bovine pancreatic rebonuclease A with natural and halogernated purine nucleotides', 1978; 'The reaction of bovien pancreatic ribonuclease A with 6-cholorpurine riboside 5-monophosphate', 1980; 'Preparation purification and group separation of mono and dinucleotides by combining charge-transfer and affinity chromatography', 1982; 'Evidence of the existance of a purine ligand induced conformational change in the active site of bovine pancreatic ribonuclease A Studies by proton nuclear magnetic resonance spectroscopy', 1982; 'Separation of RNA derivatives by high-performance anion-exchange liquid chromatography', 1985. *Honours:* Prize August Pi i Sunyer, Institut d'Estudis Catalans, 1979. *Hobbies:* Music; Photography; Mountaineering. *Address:* Department de Bioquimica, Facultat de Ciencies, Universitat Autonoma de Barcelona, Bellaterra, Spain.

CUESTA, Francisco, b. 21 July 1929, Santander, Spain. Lecturer on Pneumology. m. Mercedes Briceno, 18 Jan. 1964, San Cristobel, 1 son. *Education:* DMS, Madrid; Pulmonary Disease; Cardiovascular diseases. *Appointments:* Resident: National Sanatorium Pedrosa, Santander, Spain; Sanatoriums El Algodonal, Caracas, Venezuela; National Institute of Cardiology, Mexico. Head Physician, Antituberculosis San., San Cristobel, Venezuela; Doctor attached Pneumology, Venezuelan Institute Society Sec S C ; Lecturer of Pneumology, University of Los Andes School of Medicine. *Memberships:* Venezuelan Society of Tisiology and Pneumology; Venezuelan Society of Cardiology; Venezuelan Society of Internal Medicine; Fellow, American College of Chest Physicians; International Union on Tuberculosis; Board of Directors, Red Cross of Venezuela; Teaching staff, University of Los Andes and Catholic University Andres. *Publications:* "Radiological Synopsis of Thoracic Diseases", 1966; "Traumatic Hemothorax", 1974; "Pulmonary Paracoccidiodiomicosis", 1976; "Heart in the Aged", 1984; "Bronchial Asthma", 1985. *Honours:* Dr Domingo Semedei Prize, 1966; Dr Alfredo J Gonzalez Prize, 1975; Recognition, Catholic University Andres Bello, 1978. *Hobbies:* Piano; Photography; Radioficion. *Address:* Av Francisco Cardenas 23-113, Qta Casuca Pirineos, San Cristobel, Estado Tachira, Venezuela.

CUEVAS-SOSA, Andres Alejandro, b. 10 Nov. 1939, Mexico. Medical Doctor; MSc; Director, Centre for Research on Psychoanylis and Psychotherapy. m.

Ma. de Lourdes Ramos, 8 May 1971, Mexico City, 2 sons, 2 daughters. *Education:* MD, National Autonomous University of Mexico, 1964; MSc., University of Michigan, USA, 1967; Psychoanalyst, National Autonomous University of Mexico, 1974. *Appointments:* Member, Research Dept., Mexican Institute of Social Security, 1967-68; Professor, Medicine, National Autonomous University of Mexico, 1968-72; Chairman, Human Genetics, General Hospital of Mexico; Founder, Director, Centre for Research on Psychoanalysis and Psychotherapy, 1979-. *Memberships:* Academy for Scientific Investigation, 1970; New York Academy of Sciences; American Society of Clinical Hypnosis. *Publciations:* "Crossing-over and the centromere", 'Cytogentics', 1967; "Human Chrosomology : Random Segregation of Chormatids in deploid cells in-vitro", 'Nature', 1968; "Human Chrosomology : random association of acrocentrics", 'Genetica', 1970; "Dreams-myths", 'Naturaleza', 1980; (book) "Psychoanalysis and Cognitive Behaviourism", 1982. *Honours:* Guest Researcher, Institute of Arthritis and Metabolic Diseases of The National Institutes of Health at Bethesda, USA. *Hobby:* Nature Watcher. *Address:* Patricio Sanz 1449-B-101, Col. del Valle, Delegation Benito Juarez 03210, Mexico DF, Mexico.

CULBERTSON, Frances Mitchell, b. 31 Jan. 1921, Boston, USA. Professor, Psychology, University of Wisconsin; Clinical Psychologist. m. John Mathew Culbertson, 27 Aug. 1947, Ann Arbor, 1 son, 3 daughters. *Education:* BS, MS, PhD, Psychology, University of Michigan; Postdoctoral studies, University of Wisconsin, Madison. *Appointments:* Teaching Fellow, University of Michigan, 1948-50; Research Psychologist: Children's Hospital, Washington DC, 1957, C. Wisconsin Col. and Training School, 1958-59; Clinical Psychologist, Wisconsin Diagnostic Centre, 1962-65; Chief Clinical Psychologist, University of Wisconsin Medical School, 1965-66; School Psychgologist, Madison Board of Education, Wisconsin, 1967-68; Professor, University of Wisconsin, Whitewater, 1968-; Clinical Psychologist, Private Practice, 1983-. *Memberships include:* American Psychological Association; President, 1979, International Council of Psychologists Inc.; International association of Applied Psychology; etc. *Publications:* Numerous articles in professional journals. *Honours:* Member, New York Academy of Sciences, 1985; Invited Lecturer, University of Sorbonne, Paris, France, 1984; Vice President, Midwest, Psi Chi, APA, 1983-85; Psi Chi, 1981; Brazilian Clinical Psychologists, Honorary President, 1979. *Hobbies:* Cross Country Skiing; Photography of Wild Flowers; Bird Watching; Swimming. *Address:* Dept. of Psychology, University of Wisconsin, Whitewater, WI 53190, USA.

CUNEO, John A Jr. b. 5 May 1929, New York, USA. Executive Director. m. Gloria F. Britting, 28 June 1952, New York, 1 son, 1 daughter. *Education:* BSc.; MSc., Hospital Administration; FRSH. *Appointments:* Officer, USAF (MSC), 1951-53; Assistant Administrator, Mid Island Hospital, Bethpage, 1955-59; Administrator, Pelham Bay General Hospital, Bronx, 1959-74; Executive Director, Parkway Hospital, Forest Hills, 1974-. *Memberships:* American Hospital Association; American College of Hospital Administrators; Royal Society of Health; Hospital Administrators Discussion Group; New York State Public Health Association; New York Academy of Science; Association of Private Hospitals Inc., President. *Address:* 650 Meadow Court, Westbury, NY 11590, USA.

CUNLIFFE, William James,. Consultant Dermatologist. *Education:* BSc., Manchester; MD, Manchester; FRCP (London); MRCS England; LRCP, London. *Appointments:* Senior Registrar, Dermatology, Royal Victoria Infirmary, Newcastle;

Senior House Officer, Manchester Royal Infirmary; Lecturer, Pathology, University of Manchester; Consultant Physician, Skin Disease, United Leeds Hospitals. *Membership:* Secretary, European Society of Dermatology. *Publications:* Papers on Vasculiitis & Fibrinolytic Activity, Acne & Village & Auto-Immunity. *Address:* The General Infirmary at Leeds, Great George Street, Leeds LS1 3EX, England.

CUNNINGHAM, Mary A. VanDemark, b. 20 Mar. 1931, Kingston, New York, USA. Specialist, Rehabilitation, Royal Insurance Company. m. Thomas F. Cunningham II, 13 Oct. 1951, Stoneridge, New York, 2 sons, 1 daughter. *Education:* RN, Methodist Hospital School of Nursing, 1951; BS St Joseph's College, Brooklyn; Certified: Occupational Health Nurse, 1981, Health Care safety Professional, 1982, Rehabilitation Counsellor, 1982, Rehabilitation Nurse, 1983, Insurance Rehabilitation Specialist, 1984. *Appointments:* Occupational Health Nurse, Republic Aviation Corp., Farmingdale, 1954-64; Airborne Instrument Laboratories, Eaton Corp, Commack, 1965-69; Rehabilitation Nurse, Liberty Mutual Ins. Co., 1969-79. *Memberships:* Professional Rehab Association, Founder, 1981, President, 1981-84; RN Study Group, Vice President, 1970-74; American Association Occupational Health Nurses'; Alumnae Association, Methodist Hospital. *Publications:* "Acute Care of Spinal Cord Injury", 1974; "The Role of the Rehabilitation Insurance Nurse", 1976; "Low Back Pain — Differential Diagnosis and Treatment", 1980. *Honours:* Recipient, various honours and awards. *Hobbies:* Sailing; Antique Hunting; Community and Church Work. *Address:* Royal Insurance, 195 Froehlich Farm Blvd., Woodbury, NY 11797, USA.

CURNOW, David Henry, b. 4 June 1921, Bunbury, Western Australia. Emeritus Professor. m. Norma Somers, 18 Oct. 1952, Chiswick, England, 4 sons. *Education:* BSc., University of Western Australia, 1942; PhD, University of London, 1950. *Appointments:* Head, Biochemistry, Royal Perth Hospital, 1953-73; Head, Combined Clinical Biochemistry Service, Queen Elizabeth II Medical Centre, 1974-85; Head, Clinical Biochemistry, University of Western Australia, 1976-82; Emeritus Professor, Clinical Biochemistry, University of Western Australia. *Memberships:* Australian Association of Clinical Biochemists; Biochemical Society; Royal College of Pathologists of Australasia. *Publications:* 85 scientific publications; 1 monograph. *Honours:* Hackett Overseas Studentship, 1947; Honorary Fellow, Royal College of Pathologists of Australasia, 1970; Honorary Life Fellow, Australian Association of Clinical Biochemists, 1985. *Hobby:* Sailing. *Address:* C/o University of Western Australia, Nedlands 6009, Western Australia.

CURTEIS, Peter Gregan, b. 28 Sep. 1939, Sydney , Australia., Consultant Cardiologist. m. Marie Jeanette Weston, 22 May 1968, Newcastle, Australia, 1 son, 2 daughters. *Education:* MB BS, Sydney, 1964; MRACP, 1971; FRACP, 1976. *Appointments:* RMO: Mater Hospital, Newcastle, 1964-67; Repatriation Hospital, Concord, 1968-70. Cardiologist, Registrar, Repatriation Hsopital, Concord, 1971; VMO, Royal Newcastle Hospital, 1972-75, Mater Hospital, Newcastle, 1972-75; Visiting Cardiologist, Royal Newcastle Hospital, 1976-, Mater Hospital, 1976-; Clinical Lecturer, University of Newcastle, 1980-. *Memberships:* Australian Medical Association; Cardiac Society of Australia and New Zealand. *Hobbies:* Work; Food; Wine. *Address:* Suite 3.3, 133 King Street, Newcastle 2300, Australia.

CURTIS, Adam Sebastian Genevieve, b. 3 Jan. 1934, London, England. Professor, Cell Biology, Chairman, University of Glasgow, Scotland. m. Ann Park, 3 May 1958, 2 sons. *Education:* BA, Kings College, Cambridge, 1955; PhD, University of Edinburgh,

1957; MA (Cantab) 1958. *Appointments:* Honorary Research Assistant, Anatomy, University College, London, 1957-62; Lecturer, Zoology, University College, London, 1962-67; Professor, Cell Biology, Glasgow University, 1967-. *Memberships:* Fellow, Royal Society, Edinburgh; Fellow, Institute of Biology; Member, Chemical Society; American Society, Cell Biology; British Society Cell Biology; International Society Developmental Biology; etc. *Publications:* "The Cell Surface", 1967; "Cell Adhesion and Movement", 1980; "Cell Behaviour", 1982. *Hobbies:* Sports; Scuba Diving; Gardening. *Address:* Dept. of Cell Biology, University of Glasgow, Glasgow G12 8QQ, Scotland.

CURZON, Gerald, b. 29 Apr. 1928, Leeds, England. Professor, Neurochemistry, Institute of Neurology, University of London. m. Stella Schatzberg, 25 Apr. 1952, 2 daughters. *Education:* BSc., Chemistry, 1948, PhD, Biochemistry, 1951, Leeds; DSc., Biochemistry, London, 1968. *Appointments:* Research Assistant, Institute of Orthopaedics, London, 1951-53; Research Fellow, 1953-61, Senior Lecturer, Biochemistry, 1961-68, Reader, Biochemistry, 1968-76, Professor, Neurochemistry, 1976-, Institute of Neurology. *Memberships:* Biochemical Society; British Pharmacological Society; International Society for Neurochemistry; Collegium Internationale Neuropsychopharmacologium. *Publications:* In various scientific journals. *Address:* Institute of Neurology, Queen Square, London WC1N 3BG, England.

CUSHING, Marian Catherine, b. 17 May 1937, Montreal, Canada. Child Psychiatrist. *Education:* BA, 1960, MDCM 1964, McGill University; FRCP (C) 1974; Psychiatry Residency, Cincinnati, Ohio, USA, 1966-70. *Appointments:* Fellow, Community Child Psychiatry, 1970-72; Private Practice: Hamilton, Ohio, 1972-73, Scarborough, 1973-79, Toronto, Ontario, 1973-79; Staff Psychiatrist, Thistletown, Rexdale, 1979-80; Private Practice, London, Ontario, 1980-. *Memberships:* Canadian and American Psychiatric Associations; Association for Humanistic Psychology; Association for Transpersonal Psychology. *Hobbies:* Hiking; Outdoor Sports; Music; Films. *Address:* 765 Hellmuth Ave., London, Ontario, Canada N6A 3T6

CUTHBERT, Alan William, b. 7 May 1932, Peterborough, England. Shield Professor, Pharmacology, University of Cambridge. m. Harriet Jane Webster, 22 Apr. 1952, Abernethry, Scotland, 2 sons. *Education:* B.Pharm, London, 1953; BSc., St Andrews, 1956; PhD, London, 1962; MA, Cambridge, 1964; FRS, 1982. *Appointments:* Pharmacist, Leicester Royal Infirmary, 1952-53; Leiutenant, Royal Navy, 1956-59; Research Fellow, 1959-60, Assistant Lecturer, 1960-63, London University; Demonstrator, 1963-66, Lecturer, 1966-73, Reader, 1973-79, Cambridge University; Fellow, Jesus College, Cambridge, 1968-; Director, Medical Studies, Jesus College, 1974-79; Shield Professor, Pharmacology and Head, Pharmacology, Cambridge University, 1979-. *Memberships:* British Pharmacological Society; Physiological Society; Society for General Physiology, US; Fellow, Zoological Society. *Publications:* 150 articles in professional journals. *Honours:* Pereira Medal, Pharmacuetical Society, 1953; Sir James Irvine Medal, Chemistry, St Andrews, 1955. *Hobbies:* Painting; Sculpture & Screen Printing; Gardening; etc. *Address:* Dept. of Pharmacology, University of Cambridge, Hills Road, Cambridge CB2 2QD, England.

CUTHBERTSON, Robert Fred, b. 15 Dec. 1929, Phoenix, Arizona, USA. Family Physician. m. Shirley June Hermann, Phoenix, 1953, 1 son, 2 daughters. *Education:* Phoenix College, 1947-49; University of California at Berkeley, 1949-50; MD, University of Southern California School of Medicine, Los

Angeles, 1950-54; Internship, Los Angeles County General Hospital, 1954-55. *Appointments:* US Naval School of Aviation Medicine, 1955-56; LT, Naval Flight Surgeon, US Navy 1955-58, Kwajalein, Marshall Islands, 1956-57. *Memberships:* Diplomate, American Board of Family Physicians; Fellow, American Board of Family Practice; American Medical Association; American Academy of Family Physicians; Governor, District 549, Rotary International, 1985-86. *Hobbies:* Motorcycling; Four-wheeling; Photography; Flying; Soaring. *Address:* 4426, Eat Indian School Road, Phoenix, AR 85018, USA.

CUTHBERTSON, William Francis Jack, b. 30 Jan. 1916, Great Yarmouth, England. Consultant. m. Elona S Severs, 18 Apr. 1951, London, 1 son. *Education:* BSc Botany, Zoology and Chemistry 2nd class Honours, BSc Chemistry 1st class Honours, PhD Biochemistry, London University. *Appointments:* Lecturer – Senior Lecturer, Faculty of Medical Sciences, University College, London; Head of Biochemistry (research), Glaxo Laboratories; Senior Lecturer in Charge, Physiology and Biochemistry Department, University College, Ibadan, Nigeria; Director, Glaxo Group Research. *Memberships:* Nutrition Society; Physiology Society; Biochemical Society; Society of Chemical Industry; Atherosis Discussion Group; Fellow, Institute of Biology; Fellow, Royal Society of Chemistry; Fellow, Institute of Food Science and Technology; Association for Study of Obesity. *Publications:* Numerous. *Honour:* Order of the British Empire, 1976. *Hobbies:* Photography; Avoidance of exercise. *Address:* 4 Coppermill Lock, Harefield, Middlesex, UB9 6JA, England.

CUTLER, Leslie S, b. 20 Jan. 1943, New Brunswick, USA. Professor and Chairman, Department of Oral Diagnosis. m. Terry Grubman. 30 July 1966, 2 sons. *Education:* DDS, Washington University School of Dentistry, USA, 1968; PhD, Pathology, State University of New York at Buffalo, 1973; MS, Management, Hartford Graduate Centre, Hartford, Connecticut, 1983. *Appointments:* Assistant Professor, Department of Oral Biology, University of Connecticut School of Dentistry, USA, 1973-77; Associate Professor and Chairman, Department of Oral Diagnosis, 1977-81, Professor and Chairman, 1981-. *Memberships:* American Association for the Advancement of Science; International Association of Dental Research; Histochemical Society; American Society for Cell Biology; Society for Developmental Biology. *Publications:* Over 100 publications of chapters, articles and abstracts. *Address:* Department of Oral Diagnosis, University of Connecticut School of Dental Medicine, Farmington, CT 06032, USA.

CUZICK, Jack Martin, b. 11 Aug. 1948, USA. Head of Department of Mathematics, Statistics and Epidemiology. m. Jane Valerie Beanland, 5 Nov. 1971, California, 1 son. *Education:* BSc Mathematics and Physics with Distinction and Departmental Honours, Harvey Mudd College, 1966-70; MSc Mathematics, University of London, England, 1970-71; PhD Mathematics, Claremont Graduate School, USA, 1971-74. *Appointments:* Assistant Professor, Columbia University, 1975-78; IARC Research Fellow 1978-79, ICRF Research Fellow 1979-82, Oxford University, England; Head of Department of Mathematics, Statistics and Epidemiology, Imperial Cancer Research Fund, London, 1982-. *Memberships:* Institute of Mathematical Statistics; Royal Statistical Society. *Publications:* 'Radiation Induced Myelomatosis', 1981; 'Palmar Keratoses and Cancers of the Lung and Bladder', 1984; 'Multivariate Generalizations of the Proportional Hazards Model', 1985; 'Prognostic Value of B_2 Microglobulin in Myelomatosis', 1985. *Honour:* Henry S Mudd Memorial Scholarship Award, 1970-71. *Hobby:* Flute playing. *Address:* Department of Mathematics, Statistics and Epidemiology, Imperial Cancer Research Fund, PO Box 123, Lincoln's Inn Fields, London WC2A 3PX, England.

CVETKOVICK, Miodrag, b. 1923, Professor of Department of Biochemistry, Faculty of Medicine, Univerzitet u Beogradu. *Education:* MD, Biochemistry, Univerzitet u Beogradu. *Appointments:* Assistant, Lecturer, Associate Professor, department of Biochemistry (Biochemistry of proteins and nucleic acids; enzymology and toxicology of snake venoms), Univerzitet u Beogradu, 1953-77; Professor, Department of Biochemistry, Faculty of Medicine, Univerzitet u Beogradu, 1953-. *Memberships:* Savez Biohemijskih Drustava Jugoslavije (Yugoslavian Association of Biochemicatl Societies); Savez Drustava Fiziologa Jugoslavije (Yugoslav Association of Physiological Societies); Sociata Italiana di Anatomia (Italian Society of Anatomy). *Publications:* Approximately 70 research publications in medical journals (Biochemistry proteins and nucleic acids; enzymology and toxicology of snake venoms); Editorial Board of 'Medicinska enciklopedija', Larousse-Vuk Karadzic, Beograd, 1976 and 'Medicinski leksihon', Larousse-Vuk Karadzic, Beograd, 1983. *Hobbies:* Classical Music; History; Byzantine Art; Phylology; Ethnology. *Address:* Faculty of Medicine, Univerzitet u Beogradu, Dr. Subotica 8, 11000 Beograd, Yugoslavia.

CYWINSKI, Jozef, b. 13 Mar. 1936, Warsaw, Poland, Executive Vice-President, Medinet Incorporated, m. Hann Zawistowska, 27 Apr. 1957, Warsaw, Poland, 1 son. *Education:* MSc, 1960, DSc, 1967, Warsaw Institute of Technology. *Appointments:* Fellow in Physiology, University of Pennsylvania Medical School, USA, 1967-69; Associate Professor of Radiology and Bioengineering, University of Missouri, 1969-70; Principal Associate in Anesthesiology, Harvard Medical School, 1970-81; Chief, Medical Engineering Department, Massachusetts General Hospital, 1970-82; Lecturer, Massachusetts Institute of Technology, 1970-81; Vice-President, Bio-Medical Research Ltd, 1981-82; Executive Vice-President, Medinet Incorporated, 1982-86; President, Corsan Engineering Incorporated, 1973-. *Memberships:* American College of Cardiology; Institute of Electrical and Electronic Engineers; New York Academy of Science; Biomedical Engineering Society. *Publications:* 'The Essentials in Blood Pressure Monitoring'', 1980; Author of over 100 scientific articles for medical journals and engineering periodicals, 1965-85; Author of 5 chapters in medical books and textbooks; 10 Inventions and patents in field of Bioengineering. *Honours:* Fellow, American College of Cardiology, 1978; Senior Member, IEEE, 1969; Senior Member, BMES, 1976. *Hobbies:* Inventing new medical devices; Mountaineering; Windsurfing; Tennis; Classical music; Theatre. *Address:* 372 Fifth Avenue No 7E, New York, NY 10018, USA.

CZAPLICKI, Jeremi Julian, b. 3 July 1930, Lozy, Poland. Head, Chairman, Biology & Genetics. m. Dr. Stefania Swierczek, 26 Jan. 1963, Katowice, 2 daughters. *Education:* MD, 1958, Doc.Dr.Hab., 1970, Professor 1985, Silesian Academy of Medicine. *Appointments:* Junior Assistant, 1950, Assistant, 1954, Senior Assistant 1955, Adjunkt, 1958, Senior Lecturer, 1963, Head, Biology, 1972; Dean of Pharmacy Faculty, 1978-81, Vice-Rector 1982-87. *Memberships:* Polish Medical Association; Polish Occulist Association; World Transplantation Association. *Publications:* Series of papers on the effects of early foetal thymic extracts on the immunology and biological state of adult organisms; Major papers; 'Surgery', 1961, 1962; 'Experimentia', 1963; 'Nature', 1964; 'Folia biologica/Praha', 1964, 1968, 1977; 'Thymus', 1980, 1981, 1982, 1983, 1984, 1985. *Honours:* 3rd & 2nd Degree, Scientific Awards, Silesian Academy of Medicine, 1981, 1982, 1983, 1984. *Hobbies:* Music;

Poetry; Sight-seeing Tours; Travel; Swimming. *Address:* Brynowska Str. 53/6, 40-584 Katowice Poland.

CZAPLINSKI, Waclaw Bogdan, b. 18 July 1923, Sycyna, Poland. Parasitologist. m. Danuta Laganowska, 19 May 1945, Zamość, Poland, 2 sons. *Education:* PhD, 1956; Assistant Professor, 1962, Extraordinary Professor, 1968, Professor, 1983. *Appointments:* Assistant, Department of Zoology & Parasitology, 1947, Senior Assistant, 1950, Lecturer, 1954, University of Warsaw; Lecturer, Department of Parasitology, Polish Academy of Science, 1955; Head of the Department of Biology, Medical Academy, Warsaw, 1963-. *Memberships:* World Federation of Parasitologists, 1974-78, Vice-President, 1978-82, President, Chairman of Committee for Parasitological Terminology; Polish Academy of Sciences, Committee for Parasitology, Secretary 1962-72, President 1972-81, Member, 1981-; Polish Society for Parasitology, Member of Scientific Council of Medical Faculty, Veterinary Faculty, Institute of Parasitology, Institute of Biostructure. *Publications:* "Helminthiases of Poultry", 1955; "Hymenolepididae of Some Domestic & Wild Anseriformes in Poland", 1956; "Nematodes & Acanthocephalans of Anseriformes in Poland", 1962; "Human Nematodes" (in Principles of Human Parasitology), 1979; "Human Helminthology" ibid, 1983. *Honours:* Association of Veterinarians (for Studies & Handbook), 1950-55; Polish Academy of Sciences, Division of Biological Sciences for PhD dissertation, 1956; Honorary Membership of All Union Society for Helminthology, 1974; Ministry of Health (for Handbook), 1984. *Hobby:* Swimming. *Address:* Francuska 10 A/5, 03-906 Warszawa, Poland.

CZECZUGA, Bazyli, b. 30 Oct. 1930, Plutycze, Poland. Professor, Head, Biology. m. Ada Matusewicz, 15 July 1956, 1 daughter. *Education:* MSc., University of Minsk, 1956; Sci.Dr., Academy of Agriculture & Technology, Olsztyn 1960; Assistant Professor/Dozent, Academy of Agriculture & Technology, 1963; Extraordinary Professor, natural Science, 1972, Ordinary Professor, 1984, Medical Academy Bialystok. *Appointments:* Assistant, 1956-61, Assistant Professor, Head, Biology, 1962-71, Professor, head, General Biology, 1972-, Medical Academy, Bialystok, Poland. *Memberships include:* President, Polish Botanical Society, Polish Hydrobiological Society, Polish Parasitological Society, Polish Natural Society, Societas Scientarium Bialostocensis; New York Academy of Sciences; International Association of Limnology; numerous other professional organisations. *Publications:* Monograph: "Ecological-physiological aspects of Chironomidae/Diptera", 1962; "The Nature of North-East of Poland", 1973; "The Wigry Lake", 1970; 368 scientific works. *Honours:* Gold Order of Merit, 1976; Order Polonia Restituta, 1977; Order of Merit Teacher, 1978; Prize, Polish Academy of Science, 1975; 17 prizes, Health Ministry. *Hobbies:* Mushrooming; History of Nations. *Address:* ul. Szpitalna 35a, M50, 15-295 Bialystok, Poland.

CZENKAR, Béla, b. 4 Nov. 1930, Losonc, Hungary, Head of Surgical Department and Vascular Surgery, Hospital of County Heves, Eger, Hungary, 1977-, m. Judith Csányi, 22 July 1961, 1 son, 1 daughter. *Education:* MD, Semmelweis University, Budapest, 1954; Specialist in Pathology, 1957; Specialist in Surgery, 1961; Specialist in Vascular surgery, 1980. *Appointmetns:* Assistant, Pathological Institute of the Medical University, Debrecen, Hungary, 1954-58; Surgeon, County Hospital Heves, Eger, Hungary, 1958-77. *Memberships:* Member of Council, Vascular Surgery, Hungary; Surgical Society, Hungary. *Publications:* Contributor of over 35 articles in medical and scientific journals. *Honours:* Recipient of several awards. *Hobbies:* Hunting; Chess. *Address:* Megyei Kórház, Széchenyi u 27, H-3300 Eger, Hungary.

CZLONKOWSKA, Anna, b. 15 June 1943, Warsaw, Poland, Head of Cerebrovascular Diseases Clinic Psychoneurological Institute, Warsaw, m. Andrej Czlonkowski, 24 Oct. 1968, Warsaw, 2 sons. *Education:* Finished Medical School, 1966; MD, 1971; Habilitation, 1977; DSc. *Appointments:* Department of Genetics, Psychoneurological Institute, Warsaw, 1969-84, Head of Immunology Unit, 1973-, Docent, 1977-. *Memberships:* Polish Society for Neurology; Polish Society of Imunology; British Society of Immunology; Medical Advisory Board of International Federation of Multiple Sclerosis. *Publications:* "Clinical Neurology", (Co-editor, Co-author), 2nd edition, 1980, 3rd Edition in print; "Medical Genetics", (Co-author) 1984; "Immunological and Clincial Aspects of Multiple Sclerosis", (Co-author), 1984. *Address:* Psychoneurological Institute, Sobieskiego 1/9,. 01-957 Warsaw, Poland.

D

DABELSTEEN, Erik, b 19 Dec. 1941, Copenhagen, Denmark, Professor and Head of Department of Oral Diagnosis, *Education:* Dr odont. *Appointments:* Associate Professor, Department of Oral Pathology, Visting Professor, Department of Oral Pathology, University of Iowa, USA. Associate Professor, Department of Oral Diagnosis, Royal Dental College, Copenhagen, Denmark. *Memberships:* President, Experimental Pathology Group, IADR, 1985; Secretary, Danish Society of Pathology, 1976-. *Publications:* Author of numerous publication on professional and medical subjects. *Address:* Department of Oral Diagnosis, The Royal Dental College, Nørre Alle 20, DK-2200 Copenhagen N, Denmark.

DAENEN, Willem Joris Erik, b. 6 Feb. 1941, Leuven, Belgium. Professor; Medical Doctor. m. 30 July 1966, Stymans, 1 son, 1 daughter. *Education:*MD, University Leuven, Belgium, 1966: Qualified, Cardiovascular Surgeon, University Leuven, 1972; Training, Congenital Heart Surgery, Hospital for Sick Children, London, England, 1975-76. *Appointments:* Vascular Surgeon, Salvator Hospital, 1971-72; Consultant Cardiovascular Surgeon, University Hospital, Leuven, 1972; Lecturer, 1975, Associate Professor, Cardiac Surgery, 1985- , University Leuven. *Memberships:* Belgian Royal Society of Surgery; Nederlandse Vereniging voor Thoraxchirurgie; European Club of Heart Surgeons; Society of Angiology. *Publications:*Numerous articles in professional journals including: "The Senning Correction of Simple Transposition", 'Journal of Cardiovascular Surgery', 1985; Co-Author: "Pacing in Children", 'British Heart Journal', 1985: "Preliminary Results of 156 Ionescu-Shiley Biprosthetic Valvular Replacements with and without Anticoagulant Treatment", 'Journal of Cardiovascular Surgery', 1985; Editorial: "Right Ventricular Outflow Tract Enlayment - The Solution to Diminutive Pulmonary Arteries", 'International Journal of Cardiology', 1983; etc. *Hobbies:* Windsurfing; Volleyball. *Address:* University Hospital Gasthuisberg, Dept. Cardiovascular Surgery, B-3000 Leuven, Belgium.

DAHL, Ronald, b. 9 Aug. 1945, Aarhus, Denmark, Senior Registrar. m. Inge Blaabjerg, 18 Mar. 1967, Aarhus, 1 son, 2 daughters. *Education:* Cand med, Aarhus, 1973; PhD, Uppsla, 1978; MD.*Appointments:* General Practitioner, Pajala, Sweden. Registrar: Department of Respiratory medicine, Aarhus, Denmark; Department of Medicine, Department of Surgery, Nassjo, Sweden; Department of Lung Medicine, Aarhus, Denmark; Department of International Medicine, Aarhus; Research Fellow in Internal Medicine, Senior Registrar, Department of Respiratory Medicine, Aarhus, Denmark; Assistant Professor, University of Aarhus, 1980; Docent, Experimental Allergology, University of Uppsala, 1981. *Memberships:* Danish Society for Allergy and Immunology; Danish Society for Chest Diseases; Danish Society for Allergy; European Society for Pneumology; Swedish Lung Phys.; European Academy for Allergy and Clinical Immunology. *Publications:* "Blood eosinophil granulocyte and eosinophil cationic protein. Studies in patients with bronchial asthama", Thesis, 1978; "Importance of duration of treatment with inhaled budesoide on the immediate and late bronchial reaction", 1982; "Generation of heat-labile chemotaotic activity in blood after inhalation challenge", 1982; "The Gordon phenomenon induced by the eosinophil cationic protein and eosinophil protein X". *Address:*Department of Respiratory Diseases, Aarhus Kommunehospital, 8000 Aarhus C, Denmark.

DAHLENBURG, Geoffrey Wyatt, b. 31 May 1933, Victoria, Australia. Dean, Faculty of Medicine , University of Adelaide. m. Marcia Elizabeth Jones, 19 Dec. 1980, Adelaide; 1 son , 2 daughters by previous marriage. *Education:* MB BS, MD, University of Melbourne; Fellow, Royal Australasian College of Physicians. *Appointments:* Resident, Clinical Supervisor, Royal Children's Hospital, Melbourne; Research Fellow, Nuffield Neonatal Research Unit, Hammersmiith Hospital, London, England; Consultant Neonatal Paediatrician, Royal Womens Hospital, Melbourne; Reader in Neonatal Paediatrics, University of Adelaide; Dean, Faculty of Medicine, University of Aldelaide. *Memberships:* Australian College of Paediatrics; Australian Perinatal Society; Australian & New Zealand Society of Intensive Care. *Publications:* Numerous articles in medical journals on aspects of neonatal care. *Hobbies:* Farming; Horse-Racing. *Address:* The Medical School, University of Adelaide, Adelaide 5001, Australia.

DALE, David Chandler, b. 19 Sep, 1940, Knoxville, Tennessee, USA. Professor of Medicine and Dean, m. Rose Marie Wilson, 22 June 1963, Knoxville, Tennessee, 2 sons, 1 daughter. *Education:* BS Chemistry, Carson-Newman College, Jefferson City, Tennessee, 1962; MD, Harvard Medical School, Boston, Massachusetts, 1966. *Appointments include:* Clinical Associate 1968-70, Senior Staff Fellow 1970-71, Senior Investigator 1972-74, Laboratory of Clinical Investigation, National Institute of Allergy and Infectious Diseases, National Institute of Health, Bethesda, Maryland; Consultant in Infectious Diseases, National Naval Medical Center, Bethesda, Maryland, 1972-74; Associate Chairman, Department of Medicine 1976-82, Associate Dean, Clinical Affairs 1982-, Dean, School of Medicine 1982-, University of Washington School of Medicine, Seattle, Washington. *Memberships include:* American Society of Hematology; American Federation for Clinical Research; Infectious Diseases Society of America; American College of Physicians; American Society for Clinical Investigation; Association of American Physicians; American Medical Association. *Publications include:*Over 150 contributions, on leucocyte physiology, host defense mechanisms, and related topics. *Honours:* James Tolbert Shipley Award, Harvard University, 1966; AOA Visiting Professor, University of Pennsylvania, 1980. *Hobbies include:* Woodworking; Gardening; Backpacking; Sailing. *Address:* School of Medicine, Office of the Dean, SC-64, University of Washington, Seattle, WA 98195, USA.

DALGAARD, Jorgen Brems, b. 11 June 1918, Viborg, Denmark. Professor of Forensic]Consultant Pathologist. m. 1. Ena Bach, 3 daughters; 2. Anne Marie Jexner, 1 daughter. *Education:* MD, 1943, PhD, 1950, University of Copenhagen. *Appointments:* Intern Swedish hospitals, 1943-45; Assistant, Department of Anatomy, 1951-53, Senior Assistant, Department of Pathology, 1951-53, University of Aarhus Denmark; Assistant Professor, Pathology and Forensic Pathology, Gade Institute, University of Bergen, Norway, 1954-58; Visiting Professor, University of Rochester, Minnesota (Mayo Clinic) 1958; Consultant Pathologist, Danish Health Service, 1951-; Ord Professor of Forensic Medicine, 1959-, Dean, Faculty of Medicine, 1963-64, University of Aarhus, Denmark; Medical Examiner for Jutland, Ministry of Justice, Denmark, 1959-. *Memberships:* Danish Medical Association; Danish Association of Pathologists; Scandinavian Association of Forensic Pathologists; British Association of Forensic Medicine; Deutsche Gesellsch. Rechtsmed.; Danish and Scandinavian Association of Traffic Medicine (Board Member); International Association Accident and Traffic Medicine; American Association of Autom. Medicine. *Publications:* Exp invest on the cause of increase in serum phosphatase in obstructive jaundice (thesis 1950); Carbon monoxide deaths through suicide, accident or homicide, 1961; "Killed in a car" 1978; Bus accidents 1983; and numerous papers on the subjects of pathology, forensic medicine and traffic medicine. *Honours:* Danish Red Cross Memorial Medal, 1943; Knight of Dannebroge, 1970; Knight Ist class, 1984. *Hobby:* Orienteering. *Address:* Elmehojvej 32, DK 8270 Hojbjerg, Denmark.

DALLAPICCOLA, Bruno Pio, b. 7 May 1941, Bricherasio. Director, Chair, Genetics. m. Aldrovandi Maria Cristina, 21 Sep. 1968, Ferrara, 2 daughhters. *Education:* Professor, Human Genetics. *Appointment:* Assistant Professor, Clinical Medicine, University of Ferrara, Italy; Assistant Professor, Medical Genetics, 1st University of Rome; Director, Chair, Genetics , Public Health & Molecular Biology, IInd University of Rome. *Memberships:* European Society of Human Genetics; Associazione Italiana di Citogentica Medica, President; Italiana di Genetica Medica; Associazion Italiana di Biologia Cellulare e del Differenziamento. *Publications:* "I dermatologlifi dlla Mano", 1968; La Patologia Cromosomica", 1973; Nuove sindromi cromosomiche : patologia autosomica", 1978; Diagnosi Prenatale precoce", 1980; Citogentica Oncologica", 1982. *Address:* Cattedra di. Genetica, Dept. Sanita Pubblicae Biologia Cellulare, Via Orazio Raimondo II Universita, di Roma, 00173, Rome, Italy.

DALRYMPLE, Christopher Guy, b. 2 Sept. 1958, Beaumont, Texas, USA. Doctor of Chiropractic; Chiropractic Clinic Administrator. m. Angela Hackley, 15 Dec. 1979, Dallas, Texas, 1 son, 1 daughter. *Education:* DC, Texas Chiropractic College, 1982. *Appointments:* Intern, Texas Chiropractic College, 1981-82; Associate, Brassard Chiropractic Clinic, 1982-84; Administrator, Brenham Chiropractic Clinic, Texas, 1985-. *Memberships:* American, International and Texas Chiropractic Associations; Delta Sigma Chi; Diplomate, National Board of Chiropractic Examiners; American Chiropractic Association Council on Roentgenogogy; Foundation for Chiropractic Education and Research. *Hobbies:* Hunting; Running; Reading. *Address:* PO Box 2350, Brenham, TX 77833, USA.

DALY, Michael de Burgh, b. 7 May 1922, York, England. Distinguished Visitor, Department of Physiology, Royal Free Hospital School of Medicine. m. Beryl Esmé Nightingale, 4 Sep. 1948, London, 2 sons. *Education:* BA, MA, Physiology, Natural Science Tripos parts I and II, Cambridge University; MB, B Chir, St Bartholomew's Hospital, London; ScD, MD Cambridge University; FRCP. *Appointments:* House Physician, St Bartholomew's Hospital, 1947-48; Lecturer in Physiology, University College, London, 1948-54; Rockefeller Foundation Travelling Fellow in Medicine, 1952-53; Locke Research Fellow of the Royal Society, 1955-58; Chair of Physiology, St Bartholomew's Hospital Medical College, 1958-84; Distinguished Visitor, Department of Physiology, Royal Free Hospital School of Medicine. *Memberships:* Physiological Society; Society of Experimental Biology; Fellow, Royal Society of Medicine; Undersea Medical Society Incorporated; European Undersea Biomedical Society; Treasurer 1983-84, Governor 1975-, St Bartholomew's Hospital Medical College. *Publications:* Numerous publications on the physiology of the respiratory and cardiovascular system; Films, 'William Harvey and the Circulation of the Blood'. *Honours:* Gold Medal, British Medical Association, 1973; G L Brown Lecturer, Physiological Society, 1985-86. *Hobbies:* Model Engineering; Model yachting. *Address:* Department of Physiology, Royal Free Hospital School of Medicine, Rowland Hill Street, London NW3 2PF, England.

DAMSKER, Beca, b. 15 Jan. 1923, Romania. Associate Director and Assistant Professor of Clinical Microbiology. m. Mircea, 11 May 1944. *Education:* MD, Bucharest University, Romania, 1950; MSc, University of Montreal, Canada, 1969. *Appointments:* Intern, Resident and Fellow, Bucharest, Romania, 1950-59; Specialist Physician, Clinical Laboratory, Hospital of Extrapulmonary Tuberculosis, Bucharest, Romania, 1959-63; Research Physician, Hadassah Hebrew University, 1964-66; Director, Clinical Laboratory, Jerusalem, Israel, 1966-67; Clinical Laboratory Supervisor, Assistant Director, Mount Sinai Hospital, New York City, USA, 1969-80; Instructor, Assistant Professor, Mount Sinai Medical School, 1970-; Associate Director, Microbiology, Mount Sinai Hospital, 1980-. *Memberships:* American Medical Association; American Society for Microbiology. *Publications:* 23 publications, mainly Mycobacteriology, 1953-85. *Honours:* American Medical Association Physician's Recognition Award in continuing medical education, 1971, 1981, 1984. *Hobbies:* Member of the Metropolitan Museum, New York; Member of New York Film Society. *Address:* 11 Riverside Drive, New York, NY 10023, USA.

DANCUART, Frank, b. 21 Mar. 1950, Lima, Peru. Staff Radiotherapist. *Education:* MD, Cayetano Heredia University, Lima, 1975: Diploma, Medical Radiotherapy, University of Toronto, Canada, 1979, Board Certified, Therapeutic Radiology, American College of Radiology, 1982. *Appointments:* Intern, Sinai Hospital, Detroit, USA, 1975-76; Resident, Internal Medicine, Wayne State University Affiliated Hospital, USA, 1976-77; Resident, Radiation Oncology, Princess Margaret Hospital, Toronto, Canada, !977-80; Fellow, Radiotherapy, MD Anderson Hospital and Tumour Institute, Houston, USA, 1980-82; Staff Radiation Oncologist, LAC/University of Southern California Medical Centre, Los Angeles, 1982-83; Staff Radiotherapist, Instituto Nacional De Enfermedades Neoplasicas, Lima, 1984- . *Memberships:* America Society of Therapeutic Radiology and Oncology; American Society of Clinical Oncology; Radiological Society of North America; Canadian Association of Radiologists; Gilbert H Fletcher Society; University of Texas MD Anderson Associates. *Publications:* Articles in professional journals including 'Cancer'. *Hobbies:* Classical Music; Cinema; Theatre; World Travel; Biking; Swimming. *Address:* Instituto Nacional De Enfermedades Neoplasicas, Av. Alfonso Ugarte 825, Lima, Peru.

DANKS, David Miles, b. 4 June 1931, Melbourne, Australia. Professor of Paediatric Research; Institute Director. m. June McMullin, 21 Oct. 1957. Melbourne, 4 sons, 1 daughter. *Education:* MB BS 1954, MD 1957, Melbourne. *Appointments:* Various medical posts, Royal Melbourne Hospital, Royal Childrens Hospital, Melbourne and Hospital for Sick Children, London, England ; Research Fellow, Clinical Genetics Unit, Institute of Child Health, London; Research Fellow, Department of Medical Genetics, Johns Hopkins Hospital, Baltimore , USA; Paediatrician, Royal Childrens Hospital, Melbourne, Australia; Reader in Human genetics, Stevenson Professor of Paediatrics, Melbourne; Currently: Director, Murdoch Institute for Research into Birth Defects; Professor of Paediatric Research, Royal Childrens Hospital, Parkville, Melbourne. *Memberships:* Member 1958, Fellow 1970, Royal Australian College of Physicians; Australian College of Paediatrics; Human Genetics Society of Austrlasia; American Society for Human Genetics; Society for Study of Inborn Errors of Metabolism; Society for Metabolic Diseases. *Publication:* 220 original articles on medical genetics, inborn errors of metabolism, liver disease in infants and copper metabolism. *Honour:* Honoury Member, Swiss Peadiatric Society. *Hobbies:* Sailing; Music. *Adress:* Royal Childrens Hospital, Parkville, Melbourne 3052, Australia.

DANN, Oliver Townsend, b. 10 Aug. 1935, Mansfield, Ohio, USA. Clinical Professor, Psychiatry, University of Miami School of Medicine; Training & Supervising Analyst, Baltimore District of Columbia Institute for Psychoanalysis. m. Linda Marie Schweers, 15 July 1961, Milwaukee, 3 sons, 1 daughter. *Education:* AB, Columbia College, 1958; MD, Yale University School of Medicine, 1962; Psychiatric Residency, Fellowship, Yale New Haven Medical Centre, 1963-67; Western

New England Institute for Psychoanalysis, New Haven, 1967-74. *Appointments:* Private Practice, Adolescent & Adult Psychiatry & Psychoanalysis, 1968- ; Staff Psychiatrist, Yale University Health Services, 1968; Staff Psychiatrist, VA Hospital, West Haven, 1968-79; Instructor, 1967-68, Clinical Instructor, 1968-72, Assistant Clinical Professor, 1972-79, Psychiatry, Yale University School of Medicine; Attending Psychiatrist, Yale New Haven Hospital, 1972-76; Clinical Associate Professor, 1979-82, Clinical Professor, 1982- , Psychiatry, University of Miami School of Medicine; Teaching Analyst, Baltimore District of Columbia Institute for Psychoanalysis, 1980- . *Memberships:* American Psychiatric Association; American Psychoanalytic Association; many other professional organisations. *Publications:* Co-Author, "Cycloserine inhibition of gamma-aminobutyric-alpha-ketoglutaric transaminase", 'Biochemical Pharmacology', 1964; "Self Presentation: an outgrowth of the therapeutic community", 'Frontiers of Hospital Psychiatry', 1967; "Dynamics of psychedelic drug abuse", 'Archives General Psychiatry', 1967; Author, "A Case Study of Embarrassment", 'Journal American Psychoanalytic Association", 1977; etc. *Honours:* Phi beta Kappa; Fellowship, American Psychiatric Association, 1984. *Hobbies:* Sailing; Mountaineering. *Address:* 1900 Coral Way, Miami, FL 33145, USA.

DANON, Abraham, b. 2 Mar. 1939, Sofia, Bulgaria. Associate Professor and Director of Clinical Pharmacology Unit, m. Batya Arzi, 19 Nov. 1963, Haifa. 2 sons 1 daughter. *Education:* MD, Hebrew University, Hadassah Medical School, Jerusalem, 1965; PhD, Hebrew University, Jerusalem, 1971. *Appointments include:* Research Associate, Department of Applied Pharmacology, Hebrew University School of Pharmacy, Jerusalem. 1967-1970; Fellow, in Clinical Pharmacology, Department of Medicine, University of Pittsburgh, School of Medicine, Pittsburgh, Pennsyvania, USA, 1970-71 Research Associate, Division of Clinical Pharmacology, Vanderbilt University, School of Medicine, Nashville, Tennessee, USA, 1971-74; Associate Professor and Clinical Pharmacology Unit Director, Ben Gurion University and Soroka Medical Center, Beer Sheva, Israel. 1974- . *Memberships:* Israel Society of Physiology and Pharmacology; Israel Society of Endocrinology. *Publications include:* 'Plasma protein binding of imipramine: Effect of hyperlipoproteinemia' in "Clinical Pharmacology Therapy" 1979: with Z Chen: 'Antiulcer activity of hypertonic solutions in the rate possible role of prostaglandins' in "European Journal of Pharmacology", 1979; with G Assouline; 'Effects of asprin, indomethacin, flufenamic acid and paracetamol on prostaglandin output: output from rat stomach and renal papilla in vitro and ex vivo' in "Journal of Pharmacy and Pharmacology", 1983. *Honours:* Merck, Sharp and Dohme International Fellowship in Clinical Pharmacology, 1970-72; Charles E Smith Fellow in Psychobiology, 1974-75; Eugene Hecht-Professorship in Clinical Pharmacology. *Address:* Ben Gurion University of Negev, P.O.B. 653, 84105 Beer Sheva. Israel.

d'APICE, Anthony John Fredrick, b. 24 Apr. 1943, Sydney, Australia. Assistant Director. m. Christine Gearin, 21 Feb. 1970, Sydney, 1 son, 3 daughters. *Education:* MBBS, Sydney University, 1968; MRACP, 1971; FRACP, 1975; MD, Melbourne University, 1975; FRCPA, 1979. *Apointments:* RMO, 1968-69, Medical Registrar, 1970, Renal Registrar, 1971, St Vincent's Hospital, Sydney; Renal Registrar, 1972, Assistant Physician, 1973, Physician in Transplantation, 1974, Royal Melbourne Hospital; Research fellow, Renal Division, Peter Bent Brigham Hospital, Boston, USA, 1974-75; Physician, Nephrology, 1976-79, Assistant Director, Nephrology, 1980- , Royal Melbourne Hospital. *Memberships:* Royal Australasian College of Physicians; Royal College of Pathologists of Australasia; Transplantation Society; AmericanAssociation of Immunologist; Australian Socities for immunology; Nephrology, Medical Research. *Publications:* 100 articles and book chapters. *Address:* Department of Nephrology, Royal Melbourne Hospital, Victoria 3050, Australia.

DARBY, Francis, b. 24 Feb. 1920, London, England. Consultant in Occupational Medicine. m. Pamela Lisbeth Hill, 20 Dec. 1969, Aldridge, Staffordshire, 3 sons. *Education:* MB ChB (Sd), 1950; DIH, (Soc. Apoth. London), 1963; DMJ (Soc. Apoth. London), 1965; MRCGP, 1970. *Appointments:* Hospital Appointments, 1950-51; General Practice, 1951-64; Medical Civil Service, 1964-82; Medical Officer, 1964-70; Senior Medical Officer, 1970-74; PMO, 1974-78; Deputy Chief Medical Adviser, DHSS, 1978-80; Chief Medical Adviser, DHSS, 1980-82; Chief Medical Officer and Consultant Physician, Caymen Island, British West Indies, 1983-85. *Memberships:* British Medical Association; Society of Occupational Medicine; Fellow, Royal Society of Medicine; Liveryman, Worshipful Society of Apothecaries of London. *Publication:* Papers on prescribing medical administration and disablement. *Honours:* Mention in Dispatches, 1943; TD, 1964; Freeman, City of London, 1979; Queens Honourary Physician, 1980. *Hobbies:* Sailing; Literature. *Address:* Ruardean, Captains Row, Lymington, Hampshire SO4 9RP, England.

DARDANO, Guillermo Jose, b. 22 May 1925, Panama Canal Zone. Assistant Professor of Psychiatry; Chief Psychiatrist. m. Elisabeth Schimmel, 24 May 1958, San Salvador, El Salvador, 2 sons, 3 daughters. *Education:* MD, 1958, PhD, 1958, University of El Salvador; Residency in Psychiatry, Stanford University California, USA, 1958-62; Fellowship, Geriatric Psychiatry, University of South Florida, 1980 *Appointments:* Chief Ward Psychiatrist, El Salvador State Hospital, 1962-75; Director of Psychiatry, El Salvador Military Hospital, 1972-80; Assistant Professor of Psychiatry, University of South Florida; Chief Psychiatrist, Florida Mental Health Institute, Tampa, Florida, USA. *Memberships:* Royal College of Psychiatrists, England; American Psychiatric Association; American Association of Geriatric Psychiatrists. *Honours:* MD Summa Cum Laude; Chief Resident, Psychiatry, University of South Florida, 1981-; Award as Best Resident in Psychiatry, University of South Florida, 1981. *Hobby:* Reading. *Address:* 607 Warren Road, Lutz, FL 33549, USA.

DARROW, Robert Person, b. 14 Aug. 1922, Connecticut, USA. Surgeon. m. Susan Miller Ackerman, 27 Dec. 1948, New Haven, 2 sons, 2 daughters. *Education:* BA, Middlebury College, 1944; MD, Yale University School of Medicine, 1947. *Appointments:* Intern, 1947, Assistant Resident, 1948, Medicine, New Haven Hospital; Resident, Surgery, Hospital University of Pennsylvania, 1949-51; US Navy, 1951-53; Resident, Surgery, Hospital University of Pennsylvania, 1953-56; Surgeon, Rutland Regional Medical Centre, 1956- , Former Chief, Surgery, Former, Chief Staff. *Memberships:* American Board of Surgery; American College Surgeons, Executive Committee, Board of Governors, 1982-86; Rutland County Medical Society, past President; Vermont State Medical Society; American Medical Assoication; New England Surgical Society. *Publications:* articles in various journals. *Honours:* Board of Directors, Vermont Health Services; Board of Trustees, Vermont Division, American Cancer Society; Board of Directors: HH, Vermont Blue Cross & Blue Shield, Natiomnal Association Blue Shield Plans, Rutland Regional Medical Centre. *Hobbies:* Skiing; Fishing; Hunting; Hiking; Canoeing; Tennis. *Address:* C/o Green Mountain Surgeons, 98 Allen Street, Rutland, VT 05701, USA.

DAS, Gopal, b. 7 Mar. 1937, India. Professor of Medicine, Chief of Cardiology, University of North Dakota School of Medicine, Fargo, USA. m. Jean Tilley, 19 Aug. 1969, New Jersey. *Education:* MB, BS, MD, Prince of Wales Medical College, Patna

University, 1957-62; Intern, Patna Medical College Hospital, India, 1962-63; Intern, St John's Hospital, Cleveland, Ohio, USA, 1963-64; Resident, Internal Medicine, St. Vincent's Hospital, New York, 1964-67; Fellow in Cardiology, St. Barnabas Medical Center, Livingston, New Jersey, 1967-69; Clinical Research Fellow, St. Barnabas Medical Center, 1967-69. *Appointments include:* Director, Cardiovascular Research Laboratories, VA Hospital, Allen Park, Michigan, 1971-79; Associate Professor of Medicine, Wayne State University School of Medicine, Detroit, 1975-79; Assistant Professor of Medicine, 1971-75; Clinical Assistant Professor of Medicine, The Ohio State University School of Medicine, Columbus, 1969-71; Currently Professor of Medicine, Chief of Cardiology, University of North Dakota School of Medicine, Fargo. *Memberships:* American Heart Association; American Federation for Clinical Research; American Heart Association, North Dakota Affiliate. *Publications include:* 'Physiology of Thirst', 'Prince of Wales Medical College Bulletin', 1961; 'New Observations on the Effects of Atropine on Sino-atrial and Atrioventricular Nodes in Man', 'Journal of Cardiology, 1979, and contributions to medical journals. *Honours include:* Golden Apple Award, Outstanding Teacher, presented by sophomore class of University of North Dakota School of Medicine, Grand Forks, 1984. *Hobbies:* Music; Fishing. *Address:* 1919 Elm Street N, Fargo, ND 58102, USA.

DAS, Jadunath Prasad, b. 5 Aug. 1933, Khurda, India. Professor and Head of Department of Cardiology, SCB Medical College, Cuttack. m. Gayatri, 2 sons. *Education:* MB BS (Hons.), Utkal University; DTM & H, Edinburgh; MRCP, Edinburgh; FRCP; DM, Cardiology, Madras University. *Appointments:* Assistant Professor of Medicine, 1963-68, Associate Professor of Cardiology, 1968-70, Professor of Cardiology, 1970-, SCB Medical College, Cuttack; Chief of Cardiology, SCB Medical College Hospital, Cuttack, 1970- . *Memberships:* Fellow, Royal College of Physicians of Edinburgh, 1975; Fellow, American College of Cardiology Fellow, National Academy of Medical Sciences, India; Life Member: Association of Physicians of India, Carediological Society of India; Indian Society of Medical Ultrasound. *Publications:* Over 50 scientific publication in professional journals. *Hobbies:* Painting; Writing. *Address:* SCB Medical College, Cuttack 753007, India.

DATSHKOVSKY, Jacob, b. 9 July 1931, Mexico. Private Practice. 1 daughter. *Education:* BSc., Centro Universitario, Mexico, 1948; MD, UNAM, Mexico, 1957; Rotating Internship, Methodist Hospital, Dallas, USA, 1958; Psychiatric Residency, Fellowship, Austin State Hospital, Texas. *Appointments:* Chief, Neuropsychiatry,Ruben Lenero Hospital, 1961; Lecturer, Consultant, Psychiatry, Austin State Hospital, 1962-63; Professor, Psychiatric Nursing, American British Cowdray Hospital, 1963; Expert Psychiatrist, Attorney General's Office, District of Justice of Federal Territories, 1962-63; Psychiatric Consultant, mental Health of Austin, Travis County, 1964; Consultant, Southwest Education and Research Laboratory, Austin, 1969. *Memberships:* Founder Member, Instituto Mexicano de Psicodrama, 1976; ARS Medici; American Psychiatric Association; American British Cowdray Hospital; American Association for Marriage and Family Therapy; etc. *Honours:* Diplomas: National Medical School and Mexican Red Cross, 1956, Hospital Jesus Aleman Perez, 1956; Centrol Materno Infantil, 1956. *Hobbies:* Music; Piano; Composition; Reading. *Address:* Sierra Tarahumara 120, Lomas de Chapultepec, Mexico D.F., 11000, Mexico.

DAUBENSPECK, George Thomas, b. 7 Jan. 1944, Pennsylvania, USA. Private Practice. m. Marlene Faye Armentrout, 2 Apr. 1976, Las Vegas, 3 sons, 1 daughter.*Education:* DC, Lincoln Chiropractic College, 1965. *Memberships:* American Chiropractic Association; Ohio Academy of Chiropractic Physicians. *Address:*

2141 Park Road, Springfield, OH 45504, USA.

DAUDEL, Raymond, b. 2 Feb. 1920, Paris, France. Professor, University Pierre Et Marie Curie. m. Salzedo Pascaline, 28 June 1944, Paris, 2 sons. *Education:* DSc., University of Paris. *Appointments:* Assistant, 1945, Maitre De Conferences, 1957, Professor, 1962, Pierre et Marie Curie, Paris; Counsellor, Curie Institute, 1973. *Memberships:* Scientific Committee, Acta Oncologica, 1980; Council Member, Ramazzini College, 1983; Co-Responsible, Club of Chemical Carcinogenesis, 1976. *Publications:* "Chemical Carcinogenesis and Molecular Biology", with P. Daudel, 1966; "Mecanisme de la Formation Des Cellules Malignes", co-author, 1983. *Honours:* Doctor Honoris Causa, Uppsala, 1977; Leuven, 1978; Barcelona, 1984; President, European Academy, 1980. *Address:* 60 Rue Monsieur Le Prince, 75006, Paris, France.

DAVAJAN, Val, b. 19 Feb, 1934, Tehran, Iran. Medical Doctor, Professor of Obstetrics and Gynaecology. Divorced, 2 daughters. *Education:* BA, Stanford University, USA, 1956; MD, George Washington University School.of Medicine, 1960. *Appointments:* Assistant Professor Obstetrics/Gynaecology, University of California, Los Angeles, 1965-69; Assistant Professor Obstetrics/ Gynaecology 1969-71, Associate Professor 1971-78, Professor 1978- , University of Southern California Medical Center; Co-Director, Center for Gynecologic Endocrinology, Infertility, and Endoscopy, Hospital of the Good Samaritan, Los Angeles, 1977- , *Memberships include:* President 1975-76, Pacific Coast Fertility Society; Fellow; American College of Obstetricians and Gynecologists; Los Angeles Obstetrical and Gynecological Society; American Association of Obstetricians and Gynecologists, *Publications include:*'Postcoital Testing: The Cervical Factor as a Cause of Infertility'; 'Evaluation of the Infertile Couple', (with Dr Mishell); 'Secondary Amenorrhea (without galactorrhea or androgen excess)', (with O A Kletzky); 'Intrauterine Insemination with Washed Sperm to Treat Infertility', (with J M Vargyas, O A Kletzky, March et al), 1983; 'The Effect of Exercise on the Menstrual Cycle', 1985; 'Infertility: Causes, Evaluation and Treatment', (with R Israel), 1985. *Honours:* 3 Squibb Prize Papers, 1968, 1973 and 1976. *Hobby:* Tennis. *Address:* 1240 North Mission Road, Los Angeles, CA90033, USA.

DAVEY, Martin Geoffrey, b. 29 June 1936, Sydney, Australia. Assistant National Director of Canadian Red Cross Blood Transfusion Service. *Education:* MB BS, University of Sydney 1960; MA, University of Adelaide, 1965; Fellow, Royal College of Pathologists of Australasia, 1973; Fellow, Royal Australasian College of Physicians, 1978. *Appointments:* include: National Heart Foundation of Australia Research Fellow, Department of Medicine, University of Adelaide, 1961-64; National Heart Foundation of Australia Overseas Fellow, Theodor Kocher Institute, University of Berne, Switzerland, 1964-66; Wellcome Trust Research Fellow in Clinical Pathology, Radcliffe Infirmary, Oxford, England, 1966-67; Director, Western Australia Red Cross Blood Transfusion Service, 1967-80; Editor in Chief 1970-79, Corresponding Editor 1980-82, for Africa, Asia and Ausralasia, 'Vox Sanguinis'; Assistant National Director, Canadian Red Cross Blood Transfusion Service, 1981-; Associate Professor of Pathology, University of Toronto, 1982-. *Memberships:* American Association of Blood Banks; American Society of Hematology; Australian Society of Blood Transfusion; Canadian Haematology Society; Haematology Society of Australia; International Society of Blood Tranfusion; International Society of Thrombosis and Haemostasis; International Society of Haematology. *Publications include:* 'The behaviour of infused human platelets during the first twenty four hours after infusion', (with H Lander), 1964; 'The survival and destruction of human platelets', 1966; 'Biochemical aspects of platelets and hemostasis', (with EF Luscher), 1968; 'Release reactions of human platelets iduced by thrombin and other agents', (with EF Luscher), 1968; 'Prevention of rhesus immunization in Australia: the first seven years', 1975; 'The prevention of rhesusisoimmunization', 1979. *Hobbies:* Camping; Canoeing; Orienteering; Cross country skiing; Music. *Address:* 95 Wellesley Street East, Toronto, Ontario M4Y 1H6, Canda

DAVIDOFF, Michail Slavtchev, b. 18 July 1940, Sofia, Bulgaria, Professor, m. Angelina Nikolai Djelepova, 1 Nov 1970, Sofia, 1 son, 1 daughter. *Education:* MD, Hogher Medical Institute, Sofia, 1966; PhD, 1970, Dr S, 1977, Bulgarian Academy of Sciences; Professor. *Appointments:* Scientific Research, 1967-74, Assistant Professor, 1974-82, Professor, 1982, Bulgarian Academy Science, Regen Research Laboratory; Assistant, Department Anatomy, 1967-74, Assistant, Department Histology, 1971-74, Medical Academy; Assistant Professor, Medical Institute, Pleven, 1977-78; Professor, Department Anatomy, University of Würzburg, FRG, 1978-79, 1980-81. *Memberships:* Secretary, 1971, President, Histochem section, 1982, Society Bulgarian Anatomy, Histology, Embryology; Histochemische Ges (FRG), 1969; Anatomische Gesellschaft, 1972. *Publications:* 'Structure and Functions of Lysosomes', 1981; 'Lysosomen und lysosmale Enzyme im Zentralnervensystem der Ratte', 1974; 'Guinea Pig Placenta', 1977. *Hobbies:* Photography; Music; Sport. *Address:* Regeneration Research Laboratory, Bulgarian Academy of Sciences, Zdrave Str 2, 1431 Sofia, Bulgaria.

DAVIDSON, Eugene Abraham, b. 27 May 1930, New York, USA. Professor and Chairman of Biological Chemistry. m. Alice A Howell, 25 Jan. 1952, 2 sons, 2 daughters. *Education:* BS, University of California at Los Angeles, 1950; PhD, Columbia University, New York, 1955. *Appointments:* Resident Associate Biochemistry, University of Michigan, Ann Arbor, Michigan, 1955-58; Assistant Professor 1958-62, Associate Professor 1962-65, Professor 1965-67, Duke University, Durham, North Carolina; Professor and Chairman of Biological Chemistry, The M S Hershey Medical Center of The Pennsylvania State University, Hershey, Pennsylvania, 1967-. *Memberships:* American Association for Cancer Research; American Chemical Society; American Society for Biological Chemists; President 1982-83, Society for Complex Carbohydrates; Public Affairs Representative, Association of Medical School Departments of Biological Chemistry. *Publications include:* About 150 scientific publications and texts. *Honours:* Research Grants, National Institute of Health, Bethesda, Maryland, 1967-. *Hobbies:* Sailing; Bridge. *Address:* The M S Hershey Medical Center, Department of Biological Chemistry-B-506, PO Box 850, Hershey, PA 17033, USA.

DAVIDSON, Geoffrey Paul, b. 28 Jan. 1942, England. Head, Gastroenterology Unit. m. Marion Esther Flint, 14 Feb. 1969, Adelaide, 1 son, 1 daughter. *Education:* MB BS, 1967, MD, 1978, Adelaide, Australia; FRACP, 1976. *Appointments:* Resident Medical Officer, Royal Adelaide Hospital, 1968; Junior Resident Medical Officer, Adelaide childrens Hospital, 1969; Medical Registrar, Royal Adelaide Hospital, 1970; Medical Registrar, Royal Childrens Hospital, Victoria, 1971; Research Fellow, Gastroenterology Department, Royal Childrens Hospital, 1973; Division of Gastroenterology, Hospital for Sick Children, Toronto, Canada, 1975; Staff Gastroenterologist, 1978, Head, Gastroenterology Unit, 1981-, Adelaide Childrens Hospital, Australia. *Memberships:* Royal Australasian College of Physicians; American Gastroenterology Association; Australia College of Paediatrics; Gastroenterology Society of Australia; Paediatric Research Society of Australia; Australian Society for Infectious Diseases. *Publications:* Contributor to: "Principles of Paediatrics: Health Care of the Young", 1978;"Gas-

troenterology and Nutrition in Infancy", 1981. Author or co-author of some 55 papers in professional journals including: 'Medical Journal of Australia'; 'Lancet'; 'Journal of Clinical Pathology';'Gastroenterology'; 'Japanese Journal of Paediatrics'; 'Acta Paediatr. Scand'; 'Patient Management'; 'Annals of Clinical Biochemistry'; numerous others. *Honours:* Mead Johnson Prize of Paediatrics, 1967; Eli Lilly International Fellowship, 1975. *Hobbies:* Orienteering; Golf; Tennis; Australian history and stamps. *Address:* Gastroenterology Unit, Adelaide Childrens Hospital, North Adelaide, SA5006, Australia.

DAVIDSON, Roslyn Sirlin, b. 29 Nov. 1933, New York, USA. Administrative Director, Rehabilitation. m. Fred L. Davidson, 23 Oct. 1954, New York, 2 sons, 1 daughter. *Education:* Certificate in Physical Therapy, New York University, 1954; BS, New York University, 1954; MPA, C W Post University, Long Island University, Greenvale, New York, 1981. *Appointments:* Staff Physical Therapist, NCMC, East Meadow, New York, 1954-55; Private Physical Therapist, Great Neck, New York, 1955-56; Staff Physical Therapist, Mercy Hospital, Rockville Centre, New York, 1966-68; Chief Physical Therapist, Hempstead General Hospital, New York, 1968-81; Administrative Director, Rehabilitation, Hempstead General Hospital, 1981-; Private Practice, Physical Therapist, 1973-. *Memberships:* American Physical Therapy Association; Long Island Chief Physical Therapists Forum. *Publications:* "Rehabilitation Administration Procedures for Extended Care Facilities", 1973; Co-Editor: "Coping With Stroke", 1977; Co-Author: "Quality Assurance Manual", 1981. *Honours:* Certificate of Appreciation, APTA, 1983; Merit Award, APTA, 1981; Certificate of Appreciation, Heart Association, Annually 1972-79, 1981; Continuing Education Awards, numerous annually. *Hobbies:* Reading; Knitting; Swimming; Bowling. *Address:* Clearwater Drive, 100-21 Baker Court, Island Park, NY 11558, USA.

DAVIES, Gordon Robert Wyndham, b. 23 Mar. 1944, Sydney, Australia. Consultant Psychiatrist. m. Rosalind Anne Henderson, 4 Feb. 1978, Sydney, 2 sons, 1 daughter. *Education:* MB BS, University of Sydney, 1967; DPM,Royal Colleges of Physicians & Surgeons of London, 1972; Member, Royal College of Psychiatrists, 1973; Member, Australian Psychological Association, 1977. *Appointments:* Junior Resident Medical Officer, Royal North Shore Hospital, Sydney, 1967; Senior Resident Medical Officer, Canterbury District Memorial Hospital, 1968; General Practitioner and Psychiatric Medical Officer, The Wollongong Hospital, 1969-70; Psychiatric Medical Officer, Wollongong Clinic, Gladesville Hospital, 1970; Hon. Clinical Assistant in Neurology, The London Hospital, England, 1971; Registrar in Psychological Medicine, The Middlesex Hospital, England, 1971-73; Honorary Psychiatrist, The Wollongong Hospital, 1974-84. *Memberships:* South Eastern Medical Association, 1973-, (President, 1981-84); Association of Psychiatrists in Training, 1972-73; Australian Medical Association, 1967-, (Member New South Wales Branch Council, 1976-, Chairman, Hospitals Committee, 1978-79, Ethics Committee,1981-82, Organisation & Public Relations Committee, 1983-); Board Member, Hospital Contribution Fund, NSW, 1979-83 (Vice-President 1982-83); Board Member, Royal Flying Doctor Service (NSW Branch), 1985-; Aviation Medical Society of Australia & New Zealand, 1967-, (Committee 1974-81, Treasurer, 1981-). *Publications:* 'Data Processing in General Practice' (in Medical Journal of Australia), 1970; 'A Clinical Trial of the Effects of Cyclandelate' (ibid 1971); 'In-Flight Medical Facilities' (in Aviation Space & Environmental Medicine), 1982. *Hobby:* Aviation. *Address:* Suite 1, 1 Darling Street, Wollongong, NSW 2500, Australia.

DAVIES, Hugh de la Haye, b 25 Jan. 1929, Cardiff, Wales. Medico-legal Practitioner. m. Gillian May Blanshard, 2 Jan. 1958, Northampton, England, 3 sons, 2 daughters. *Education:* MA, University of Oxford; BM BCh, 1955; Diploma of Medicine

Jurisprudence (Clinical), 1965. *Appointments:* General Medical Practitioner, 1958-81; Police Surgeon, 1958-67, Principal Police Surgeon, 1967-, Northamptonshire Police; Medical Advisor, Avon Cosmetics (UK), 1965-; Clinical Assistant of Forensic Medicine, The London Hospital, 1965-; Honorary Lecturer, Forensic Medicine, University of Leicester, 1980-; Visiting Lecturer, Metropolitan Police Dective Training School, Hendon, 1979-. *Memberships:* Association of Police Surgeon of Great Britain, Honorary Secretary, 1975-; British Academy of Forensic Sciences. *Publication:* Various book chapters, papers on medico-legal subjects. *Hobbies:* Foxhunting; Beagling; Country Pursuits. *Address:* Creaton House, Creaton, Northampton, England.

DAVIES, John Edward, b. 11 Feb. 1921, Loughour, South Wales. Professor and Chairman, Department of Epidemiology and Public Health. m. 16 Sept. 1944. *Education:* MB BS, Middlesex Hospital; London University; Royal College of Physicians and Surgeons, England, LRCP; MRCS, 1944; MPH, Harvard School of Public Health, USA, 1961. *Appointments:* Currently, Professor and Chairman, Department of Epidemiology and Public Health, University of Miami School of Medicine. *Memberships:* American and Florida Public Health Associations; Dade County Medical Association; International Epidemiologic Association; Society for Teachers of Preventive Medicine; Florida Medical Association; Society for Occupational Health and Safety; American College of Preventive Medicine; American Medical Association; Royal College of Physicians; Fellow, American College of Epidemiology. *Honour:* Elected a member of the Royal College of Physicians, London, England, 1984. *Hobbies:* Golf; Deep sea fishing. *Address:* Department of Epidemiology and Public Health, University of Miami School of Medicine, 1550 N W 10th Avenue, Suite 100, Miami, FL 33136, USA.

DAVIES, John Wynford, b. 18 Mar. 1927, Swansea, Wales. Medical Administrator. m. Lorraine Cluett, 8 Feb. 1969, Ottawa, Canada. *Education:* MB BS, London Hospital Medical School, 1950; DPH, School of Hygiene, University of Toronto, 1956; MSc, Harvard University USA, 1966; Fellow, Faculty of Community Medicine, Royal College of Physicians, London, 1982. *Appointments:* Assistant Chief Medical Officer of Health, 1956-59, Chief Medical Officer of Health, 1959-62, Province of Newfoundland, Canada; Medical Consultant, 1962-66, Chief, Division of Epidemiology, 1967-71, Department of National Health and Welfare, Ottawa; Director, Bureau of Epidemiology, Laboratory Centre for Disease Control, Department of National Health and Welfare, Ottawa, 1971-; Adjunct Professor, Department of Epidemiology and Community Medicine, University of Ottawa. *Memberships* Canadian Medical Association, Canadian Public Health Association. *Publication:* Numerous articles in medical journals. *Honours:* Mountain Memorial Award, University of Toronto, 1956; Delta Omega Society, Harvard University, 1966. *Hobbise:* Carpentry; Gardening; Collecting Antiques. *Address:* 7 Oaks Wood Lane, Kanata, Ontario, K2K 2B3, Canada.

DAVIES, Norman Thomas, b. 2 May 1933, Southport, Lacashire, England. Registrar, General Dental Council. m Penelope Mary Agnew, 14 Feb. 1961, Great Kimble, Buckinghamshire, 1 son, 1 daughter. *Education:* Passed Technical Staff Course RMCS Shrivenham, 1966; Passed Staff College, Camberley, 1967; BA, Open University, 1979. *Appointments:* Commissioned Royal Artillery, 1954; Regimental and Staff appointments, Malaya, Germany and UK, 1954-64; Military Assistant to Chief of Staff HQ Northern Army Group, 1968-69; Commanded C Battery Royal Horse Artillery and Second in Command 3rd Regiment Royal Hores Artillery, 1970-72; GSOI (DS), Staff College, Camberley and Canadian Land Forces Command and Staff College, 1972-74; Commanded 4 Field Regiment Royal Artllery, 1975-77; Military Director of Studies, Royal Military College of Science, Shrivenham, 1977-80. *Honours:* MBE.1970; JP Hants., 1984. *Hobbies:* Golf: Gardening: Wine. *Address:* Lowfields Cottage, London Road, Hartley Wintney, Hampshire RG27 8HY, England.

DAVIES, Peter, b. 12 Feb. 1937, Blackwood, Gwent, Wales. Consultant Radiologist, Nottingham City Hospital, England. m. Jennifer Ann Rees, 1 June 1963, Pyle, South Glamorgan, 2 sons. *Education:* MB BS, Royal Free Hospital of Medicine, 1962; DMRD, 1962, FFR, 1971, FRCR, 1975, University of Bristol; DM, University of Nottingham, 1981. *Appointments:* House Surgeon, Hampstead General Hospital; House Physician, Dreadnought Seamens Hospital; House Surgeon, Birmingham Accident Hospital; SMO, Pathology, Miller General Hospital; SMO, Surgery, United Cardiff Hospitals; Registrar, Radiology, United Bristol Hospitals; Senior Registrar, Radiology, United Bristol and Bath Hospitals. *Memberships:* Royal Society of Medicine; Royal College of Radiologists; British Institute of Radiology; British Thoradic Society; Royal Society of Arts; British Medical Ultrasound Society, former Honorary Secretary, President-elect; Member of British delegation to European Association of Radiology and European Union of Medical Specialists. *Publication:* Contrbutor of articles and papers to professional journals in his field. *Hobbies:* Cooking; Computers; Linguistics. *Address:* X-Ray Department, City Hospital, Nottingham, England.

DAVIS, John Michael Gordon, b. 25 Mar. 1935, Horsham, Sussex, England. Head of Pathology Unit. m. Julia Ann Nicholls, 25 June 1960, Felstead, Essex, 2 daughters. *Education:* BA 1957, MA 1959, PhD 1961, Cambridge University. *Appointments:* Research Fellow 1961-68, Assistant Director of Research 1968-71, Cambridge University; Head of Pathology Branch, Institute of Occupational Medicine, Edinburgh, Scotland, 1971-. *Memberships:* British Association of Cancer Research; British Association of Lung Research; British Society of Inhalation Toxicology; British Occupational Hygiene Society. *Publications include:* Over 100 scientific publications. *Hobbies:* Opera; Aeronautics; Fly fishing; Golf. *Address:* Institute of Occupational Medicine, 8 Roxburgh Place, Edinburgh, Scotland.

DAVIS, Lawrence Ronald, b. 17 Oct. 1953, Florida, USA. Chiropractic Physician. m. Deborah Dean, 4 Apr. 1981, Minneapolis, 1 son, 1 daughter. *Education:* DC, Northwestern College of Chiropractic, 1977; Advanced Education, Orthopedics, Los Angeles College of Chiropractic, 1984. *Appointments:* Private Practice, 1977-. *Memberships:* American Chiropractic Association; American College of Chiropractic Orthopedics; ACA Council on Roentgenology; Council on Chiropractic Education; Foundation for Chiropractic Education and Research. *Honours:* Past President, 2 terms, Vice President, Secretary/Treasurer, Western Nevada Chiropractic Association. *Hobby:* Music. *Address:* 650 Greenbrae Dr., Sparks, NV 89431, USA.

DAVIS, Lowell Livingston, b. 14 Dec. 1922, Verbanna, Virginia, USA. Thoracic and Cardiovascular Surgeon. *Education:* BS, Morehouse College, 1949; MS, Atlanta University, Georgia, 1950; MD, Howard University, 1955; Internship, Jersey City Medical Centre, 1955-56; Residencies, various hospitals, 1956-1969; Fellowships, various Hospitals, and Medical Centres 1972-73, including: Hospital for Sick Children, London, England, 1977-78, Texas Heart Institute, 1983. *Appointments include:* Instructor: Meharry medical College, 1950-51, University of Illinois, College of Medicine, 1969; Clinical Instructor, Thoracic Surgery, 1981-83, Clinical Assistant Professor, Surgery, 1983-, University of Southern California Medical School; Private Practice, New York, 1964-65; Senior

Surgeon, Military Practice, United States Naval Hospital, New York, 1965-67, Staff Thoracic Surgeon, 1969-70, Chief, Thoracic & Cardiovascular Surgery, 1970-71; Private Practice, Thoracic and Cardiovascular Surgery, 1975-; various hospital appointments including: Active Staff, Thoracic & Cardiovascular Surgeon, Hospital of Good Samaritan, Los Angeles, California Lutheran Hospital Medical Centre, Los Angeles; etc. *Memberships include:* Fellow: American College of Angiology, International College of Angiology, International College of Surgeons, New York Academy of Medicine, American College Chest Physicians, American College of Surgeons, American College of Cardiology; Member, Society of Thoracic Surgeons; American Association for Thoracic Surgery; Founding Member, Albert Starr Cardiac Surgical Society, 1974; etc. *Publications include:* "Ingestion of Corrosive Agents", co-author, 'Chest', 1962; "Pneumogastrography in the Diagnosis of Perforated Gastro-Duodenal Ulcers", co-author, 'New York Journal of Medicine', 1973; "Pulmonary Mainline Granulomatosis – Talcosis Secondary to Intravenous Heroin Abuse with Characteristic X-ray Findings of Asbestosis", 'Journal of the National Medical Association', 1983. *Honours:* Recipient, numerous honours & awards including: American Campaign Medal, World War II; Occupational Medal, Asia, etc. *Address:* 1245 Wilshire Blvd., Suite II 414, Los Angeles, CA 90017, USA.

DAVIS, Richard Edward, b. 7 July 1924, London. Haematologist. m. Norma Mackinnon, 9 Nov 1960, Perth, 1 son. *Education:* Diploma in Haematology, London, 1952; Diploma in Microbiology, London, 1955; Fellow, Institute of Medical Laboratory Science, 1955; MSc, 1970, D Phil, 1974, University of Western Australia; Fellow, Australian Association of Clinical Biochemists, 1982. *Appointments:* Royal Army Medical Corps, 1943-47; Medical Scientist Royal Postgraduate Medical School; Medical Scientist, Anglo Iranian Oil Company; Colombo Plan project re-organising the pathology services of East Pakistan with Professor H E Shortt; Chief Technologist, Department of Haematology, Royal Perth Hospital; Haematologist, Royal Perth Hospital, Western Australia. *Memberships:* Fellow, Australian Association of Clinical Biochemists; Fellow, Royal Society of Health; Fellow, International Society of Haematology; Australian Society for Medical Research; Australian Society of Haematology. *Publications:* In "Advances in Clinical Chemistry" "Clinical Chemistry of Thiamin" volume 23, 1983, "Vitamin B6" volume 23, 1983, "Vitamin B12" volume 24, 1985, "Folate" volume 25 1986. More than 150 scientific papers. *Hobbies:* Furniture designing; Stamp collecting. *Address:* 4 Janet Street, Rossmoyne, Western Australia 6155.

DAWSON, Anthony George, b. 26 Sep. 1940, Huddersfield, England. Head, Department of Biochemistry. m. Andrea Mary Elsworth, 27 June 1970, Kirby Muxloe, Leicestershire, England, 1 son, 1 daughter. *Education:* BSc (Hons) Physiology 1962, PhD Physiology, 1966, University of Sheffield, England; Diploma in Tertiary Education, University of New England, 1986. *Appointments:* Research Fellow, Department of Biochemistry, University of Melbourne, 1966-68; Medical Research Council Research Fellow, Department of Physiology, University of Leicester England, 1969-70; Lecturer, Senior Lecturer, Department of Biochemistry, University of Sydney, Australia, 1970-80. Head; Department of Biochemistry, New South Wales Institute of Technology, 1980-. *Membership:* Australian Biochemistry Society. *Publications:* 43 publications mainly on antimetabolic actions of drugs & on the metabolism of alcohol. *Hobbies:* Cycling; Bushwalking; Home Computers. *Address:* School of Biological & Biomedical Sciences, New South Wales Institute of Technology, P.O. Box 123, Broadway, NSW 2007, Australia.

DAWSON, Peter, b. 17 May 1945, Sheffield,

England. Senior Lecturer, Honorary Consultant, Royal Postgraduate Medical School, & Hammersmith Hospital, London. m. Hilary Sturley, 20 July 1968, Amersham, 1 son, 1 daughter. *Education:* BSc., 1st Class Honours, Mathematics, Physics, PhD, Physics, London University; MMBS, Westminster Hospital Medical School, London; MRCP, FRCR, England. *Appointments:* Senior House Physician, Renal Medicine, Hammersmith Hospital, Medical Oncology, Royal Marsden Hospital, London; Registrar, Diagnostic Radiology, Guy's Hospital, London; Senior Registrar, Diagnostic Radiology, The Middlesex Hospital, London. *Memberships:* Institute of Physics; Royal College of Physicians; Fellow, Royal Collge of Radiologists. *Publications:* Many scientific papers in professional journals. *Honours:* Barclay Prize, British Institute of Radiology, 1984. *Hobbies:* Grand Opera; Great Singing (Other People's); Good Wine; Bad Snooker. *Address:* Beechers, 18 Green Lane, Chesham Bois, Amersham, Bucks HP6 5LQ, England.

DAY, Elizabeth Anne Dadley (Captain), b. 8 June 1957, Perth, Western Australia. Captain Dental Officer, Royal Australian Army Dental Corps, m. John Charles Stewart Bogle, 5 May 1984, 1 daughter. *Education:* Perth College, 1969-74; University of Western Australia, 1975-79; BDSc (WA). *Memberships:* RAADC. *Hobbies:* Classical music; Playing piano; Equestrian sports. *Address:* 39 Padbury Road, Darlington, Western Australia 6070.

DAY, John Howard Dadley, b. 24 Dec. 1955, Perth, Western Australia. Dental Surgeon, m. Leigh Ellen Abercromby, 1 Dec. 1984, Guildford, Western Australia. *Education:* BSc., BDSc., University of Western Australia. *Appointment:* Dental Surgeon, Perth Dental Hospital. *Membership:* Australian Dental Association. *Honour:* Cruickshank-Routley Memorial Prize, 1981, University of Western Australia. *Hobbies:* Photography; Philately. *Address:* 30 Constance Street, Darlington, WA 6070, Australia.

DAY, Michael Herbert, b. 8 Mar. 1927, London, England, Head of Division of Anatomy, United Medical and Dental Schools of Guy's and St Thomas's Hospitals, m. Jose'Ashton Hankins, 12 Apr. 1952, Accrington, England, 1 son. *Education:* MRCS, LRCP, 1954; MB BS, London, 1954; PhD, London, 1954; DSc, London, 1982. *Appointments:* Assistant Lecturer in Anatomy, Royal Free School of Medicine, 1957-62; Lecturer in Anatomy, 1962-64; Senior Lecturer in Anatomy, 1964-69, Reader in Physical Anthropology, 1969-72, Middlesex Hospital Medical School; Professor of Anatomy, 1972-, Sub-Dean, 1977-84, United Medical and Dental Schools of Guy's and St Thomas's Hospitals. *Memberships:* President, Section of Medical Education, !978-79, Fellow, The Royal Society of Medicine; President, 1979-83, Fellow, The Royal Anthropological Institute; Fellow, The Zoological Society of London; Fellow, The Linnean Society; Vice-President, 1980, Member, The Anatomical Society og Great Britain and Ireland; Member , The British Association of Clinical Anatomists; Member, The Society for the Study of Human Biology; Member, The British Medical Association; President, 1976-79, Member, The Primate Society of Great Britain; Member, The International Primatological Union; Member, The American Association of Physical Anthropology; Member, The Association of Vertebrate Palaentologists. *Publication:* Author of numerous publications including, 'A Case of bilateral median nerve compression with denervation of muscle in the hands'., 1960; 'The anatomy of the lumbo-sacral plexus of nerves with particular reference to the blood supply', 1962; 'The biood supply to the lumbar and sacral plexuses in the human foetus', 1964; Guide to Fossil Man', 1965, 4th edition, 1986; The Fossil History of Man', 1972, Revised edition, 1984; Human Evolution', (editor), 1973; 'Homosapiens', 1973; 'Vertebrate Locomotion',

1981; 'Keep Taking The Tablets', 1984; 'The Postcranial remains of Homoerectus from Africa, Asia and Possibly Europe'. *Hobbies:* Game Fishing; Watching cricket; Athletics and Rugby; Motor Cars. *Address:* Division of Anatomy, United Medical and Dental Schools of Guy's and St Thomas's Hospitals, St Thomas's Campus, Lambeth Palace Road, London SE1 7EH, England.

DAYEM, Mohamed Khairy Abdel, b. 5 Feb. 1937, Cairo, Egypt. Professor, Cardiology, University of Ain Shams, Cairo City. m. Dr Kouka Saad-El-Din Abdel Wahab, 17 Apr. 1964, London, England, 2 sons, 1 daughter. *Education:* MB; BCh., 1959; Dip.Med., 1961; PhD, London; FRCP (Edinburgh); MRCP (London). *Appointments:* Lecturer, 1966-72, Assistant Professor, 1972-78, Cardiology, University of Ain Shams; Cardiologist, Dar El Shefa Hospital, 1980-, Miss International Hospital, 1983-; Associate Editor, Ain Shams Medical Journal. *Memberships:* Fellow, Royal College of Physicians of Edinburgh; Fellow, American College of Cardiology; Fellow, American College of Chest Physicians; Fellow, New York Academy of Science; Council Member, Epidemiology, International Society and Federation of Cardiology; Egyptian Society of Cardiology. *Publications:* "Understanding Cardiology", 1975, 3rd edition 1981; "The Wellbeing of Your Heart", 1983; Co-Author, 5 other books in Arabic; over 40 scientific articles in medical journals. *Honours:* Elected Treasurer, Egyptian Society of Cardiology, 1974- ; Elected Chairman, Middle Eastern and North African Pacing Group, 1984-85. *Hobbies:* Swimming; Music. *Address:* 32 Babel Street, Dokki, Cairo, Egypt.

D'CRUZ, Manuel Joseph, b. 25 Dec. 1928, Nairobi, Kenya, Consultant Ear, Nose and Throat Surgeon. m. Dr Clara da Silva. 22 Jan. 1972, Nairobi. *Education:* MB BS, B J Medical College, Ahmedabad, India. *Appointment:* Consultant Ear, Nose and Throat Surgeon. *Memberships:* Licenciate Royal College of Physicians and Surgeons, Edinburgh; Licenciate, Royal Faculty of Physicians and Surgeons, Glasgow; Licenciate, Royal College of Physicians and Surgeons of England; Fellow, Royal College of Surgeons of England; Past President, Kenya Medical Association; Fellow, Association of Surgeons of Eastern Africa; Past President, Association of Professional Societies in East Africa. *Hobbies:* Gardening; Reading; Outdoor Living. *Address:* PO Box 43774, Nairobi, Kenya

DEAN, Joseph Geoffrey, b. 5 Dec. 1918, Wales. Director of Medical Research. m. 5 Feb. 1962, Port Elizabeth, Republic of South Africa, 3 sons, 2 daughters. *Education:* MB, ChB, 1942, MD 1951, Liverpool; FFCM, 1975; FFCMI. *Appointments:* Medical Officer, Royal Air Force, 1943-45; Medical Registrar, Liverpool Royal Infirmary, Liverpool, England, 1945-47; Internist, Port Elizabeth, Republic of South Africa, 1948-68; Director, Medico-Social Research Board of Ireland, Dublin, Republic of Ireland, 1968-85. *Memberships:* Fellow, Royal College of Physicians, London; Fellow, Royal College of Physicians, Dublin; Royal College of Physicians, South Africa; Irish Medical Organisation. *Publications include:* "The Porphyries - A Story of Inheritance and Environment", 1963, 2nd edition 1971; Many papers on multiple sclerosis, smoking and health, research topics of the Medico-Social Research Board. *Honour:* Mentioned in Despatches, World War II, 1945. *Hobbies:* Reading; Swimming; Tennis; Travel. *Address:* Medico-Social Research Board, 73 Lower Beggot Street, Dublin, Republic of Ireland.

DECKER, Ronald McNeill, b. 27 Apr. 1928, Australia. Proprietor, Centreway Pharmacy, Melbourne. m. Leslie Hayne, 14 Apr. 1982, Melbourne, 3 sons, 3 daughters. *Appointments:* Australian Delegate, International Diabetic Congresses, 1964, 1976, 1979; Vice President, International Diabetic Foundation, 1980- . *Memberships:* Pharmaceutical Society of Australia;

Australian Institute of Pharmacy Management; Australian Diabetes Society; Board of Management, International Diabetic Foundation, 1982; Chairman, Diabetes Foundation, Victoria, 1973-83; President, Diabetes Federation of Australia, 1977. *Honour:Anzac Award for work in Diabetes. Hobbies:* Golf; Tennis. *Address:* 1a Fenwick St., Kew 3101, Victoria, Australia.

DEBAKEY, Michael Ellis, b. 7 Sep. 1908, Lake Charles, Louisiana, USA. Chancellor, Distinguished Service Professor and Chairman, Department of Surgery, Baylor College of Medicine; Cardiovascular Surgeon. m. Katrin Fehlhaber, 4 sons, 1 daughter. *Education:* BS; MD; MS, Tulane University, New Orleans, Louisiana. *Appointments:* Instructor, Department of Surgery, 1937-40; Assistant Professor of Surgery, 1940-46; Associate Professor of Surgery, Tulane University, 1946-48; Professor and Chairman, Department of Surgery, 1948-; Vice-President for Medical Affairs, 1968-69; Chief Executive Officer, 1968-69; President, 1969-79, Chancellor Baylor College of Medicine. *Memberships include:* American Association for Thoracic Surgery, President, 1959; Honorary Fellow, Royal College of Surgeons; International Cardiovascular Society, President, 1959; British Medical Association; Royal Society of Medicine, London; Academy of Medical Sciences, USSR;Association of International Vascular Surgeons, President, 1983. *Publications:* Author of over 1100 articles in medical journals and textbooks and of several books including: A Surgeon's Diary of a Visit to China, 1974; The Living Heart, 1977; The Living Heart Diet, 1984; Editor, Journal of Vascular Surgery. *Honours:* Numerous Honours, Awards and Honorary Degrees from throughout the world including: Presidential Medal of Freedom with Distinction, Hektoen Gold Medal, American Medical Association, 1970; Merit Order, Egypt; Independence of Jordan Medal; American Surgical Association Distinguished Service Award. *Address:* Baylor College of Medicine, One Baylor Plaza, Houston, TX 77030, USA.

DEBOER, Gerrit, b, 14 May 1942, The Netherlands, Head of Biostatistics, Ontario Cancer Institute, Canada, m. Annette Renata, 12 May 1965, Strathroy, Ontario, 1 son, 2 daughters. *Education:* BSc, University of Western Ontario, 1965; MSc, 1967, PhD, 1070, University of Toronto Department of Medical Biophysics. *Appointments:* Assistant, Physics Department, 1965-69, Assistant Professor, Department of Medical Biophysics, 1973-, University of Toronto; Postdoctoral Fellow, Department of Radiological Sciences, The Johns Hopkins University, USA, 1970-73. *Memberships:* Member, Biophysical Society, Member, Society for Clinical Trials; Member, Canadian Organisation for Advancement of Computers in Health. *Publications:* Author of numerous publications including, 'Herpes Zoster in Patients with Carcinoma of the Lung', (with R Feld, W K Evans), 1982; 'Modulatory activity of chemotherapeutics agents on phagocytosis and intracellular bactericidal activity in Human polymorphonuclear and mononuclear phagocytes', (with W Pruzanski and S Saito), 1983; 'Use of an information system to Foster research', (with J E Till), 1983; 'Combined modality induction therapy without maintenance chemotherapy formsmall cell carcinoma of the lung', (with R Feld, W K Evans, I C Quirt, F A Shepherd, J L Yeoh, J F Pringle, D G Payne, J G Herman and D Chamberlain), 1984. *Honours:* Ontario Scholarship, 1961; The International Nickel Company Scholarship, 1961-65; The Raymond Compton Dearle Gold Medal for Honours Physics and Mathematics, 1965; Medical Research Council Studentships and Fellowships, 1965-1973. *Hobbies:* Camping; Music. *Address:* Ontario Cancer Insitute, 500 Sherborne Street, Toronto, Ontario, Canada M4X 1K9.

DE CLERCQ, Erik Desire Alice, b. 28 Mar. 1941, Dendermonde, Belgium. Professor, Microbiology & Biochemistry, Katholieke Universiteit, Leuven. m.

Godelieve De Nef, 31 Aug. 1968, 1 son. *Education:* MD, 1966; M.Med.Sc., 1967; PhD, 1972. *Appointments:* Research Assistant, national Fund for Scientific Research, Belgium, 1966-72; Docent, 1972-75, Professor, 1975-, Katholieke Universiteit Leuven. *Memberships include:* American Association for the Advancement of Science; American Association for Cancer Research; American Association of Immunologists; American Chemical Society; American Federation for Clinical Research; American Society for Microbiology; Belgian Society of Biochemsityr; Belgian Immunological Society; Dutch Scoiety for Microbiology; Biochemical Society, UK; etc. *Publications:* Over 400 articles in scientific journals; Editor, 'Antiviral Research'; Editor, 2 books in the NATO Advanced Study Institutes Series, 1979, 1984. *Honours:* Awards, Belgian Academy of Medicine, 1973, 1974; G. Zambon Benelux Award, 1979; Award, Belgian League Against Poliomyelitis, 1984. *Hobbies:* Sports. *Address:* Rega Institute for Medical Research Katholieke Universiteit Leuven, Minderbroedersstraat 10, B-3000 Leuven, Belgium.

DEELEY, Thomas James, b. 2 Aug. 1925, Dudley, Worcestershire, England. Director and Consultant in Administrative Charge, South Wales Radiotherapy and Oncology Service. m. Sarah Clement Jones, 18 July 1953, Dudley, 1 son, 1 daughter. *Education:* MB,ChB, University of Birmingham; FRCR, Royal Postgraduate Medical School, Hammersmith Hospital, London. *Appointments:* include: Registrar, Birmingham United Hospital; Assistant, Consultant Radiotherapist, Royal Postgraduate Medical School, Hammersmith Hospital. *Memberships:* Royal College of Radiologists; British Institute of Radiologists; Institute of Biologists; National Radiological Protection Board; International Society for the Study of Lung Cancer. *Publications:* include: Approximately 13 books on aspects of oncology, radiotherapy, statistics, cancer education; over 400 articles covering a wider range of subjects. *Honours:* Member, Order of the British Empire (OBE). 1985; Glyn Evans Medal, Royal College of Radiologists, 1982. *Hobies:* Antiques; Antique books. *Address:* South Wales Radiotherapy and Oncology Service, Velindre Hospital, Velindre Road, Whitchurch, Cardiff, CF4 7XL, Wales.

DEGA, Wiktor, b. 7 Dec. 1896, Poznan, Poland. Consultant on Rehabilitation, Professor, Orthopaedic Surgeon, Educator. m. Maria Zelewska, 28 Nov. 1928, 1 son, 1 daughter. *Education:* Doctor Medicinae Universae, 1924; Docent, 1933; Professor Extraordinary, 1946; Professor Ordinary, 1950. *Appointments:* Assistant Resident, Clinic of University of Poznan, 1924-30; Chief Assitant, Orthopaedic Institute, Poznan, 1930-38; Head of Orthopaedic Department, Municipal Hospital, Bydgoszcz, 1938-39; Head of Department of Children's Surgery, Karol and Maria Hospital, Warsaw, 1940-45; Director of Orthopaedic Surgery Clinical Medical Faculty, University and Academy of Medicine, Poznan, 1945-67; Professor Emeritus, 1967; Currently Head Consultant on Rehabilitation, Ministry of Health and Social Care. *Memberships:* include: Corresponding member, American Academy of Orthopaedic Surgeons; Foreign member, Academy of French Surgeons, Paris; International Society of Surgery; International College of Surgeons; Rehabilitation International; Polish Academy of Sciences; Several honorary memberships. *Publications:* 'Etiology and Pathogenesis of Congential Dislocation of the Hip', 1932; "Crippled Child", 1947 and 1951; "Orthopaedics and Rehabilitation", handbook, 1964, 3rd editon 1983; "Medical Rehabilitation", handbook 1983. *Honours:* Doctor honoris causa: Academy of Medicine Poznan 1969, Cracow 1974, Wroclaw 1973, Lodz 1977, Halle/Wittenberg 1977,Academy of Physical Education, Poznan 1979; Polish State Award, 1951, 1968 and 1973; Municipal National Council Award, Poznan, 1951; Albert Lasker Award, 1966; Alfred Jurzykowski Foundation Award, New York, 1973. *Address:* 28 Czerwca 1956 Nr 135, Institut for Orthopaedy and Rehabilitation, Poznan 61-545, Poland.

DE GRANDI, Pierre, b. 13 Sep. 1941, Vevey, Switzerland. Medical Doctor; FMH Specialist, Gynaecology and Obstetrics. m. Elisabeth Fissé, 1 Sep. 1967, La Sarraz, 1 son, 1 daughter. *Education:* MD,1966; ECFMG, 1967; MD, 1970; Specialist, OB/GYN, 1975; Private Docent, 1981; Professeur Ordinaire, 1982. *Appointments:* Hospital St Loup, 1967; Institute of Pathology, 1970; Institute of Pathology, Zurich, 1971; Surgical Clinic, Lausanne, 1972; Frauenklinik Basel, 1973-75; Department of Gynaecology & Obstetrics, Lausanne, 1976-81; Department of Gynaecology & Obstetrics, Lausanne-CHUV, 1982- . *Memberships:* Societe Suisse de Gynecologie; Société Suisse de Fertilité et Sterilité; European Society for Oncology; International Continence Society. *Publications:* "Eléments d'oncologie gynécologique", 'Cancer Information', 1980; "Incontinence Urinaire en gynecologie", 1980; "Les Operations cesariennes", 'Encyclopedia Obstetricale', 1985. *Hobbies: Music; Sailing. Address:* Dept. de Gynécologie-Obstétrique, Maternité, CHUV, CH-1011 Lausanne, Switzerland.

DE GROOT, Leslie Jacob, b. 20 Sep. 1928, Fort Edward, New York, USA. University Professor. m. Helen Searls, 31 Jan. 1955, Washington, District of Columbia, 1 son, 4 daughters. *Education:* BS, Union College, MD, Columbia University. *Appointments:* Assistant in Medicine, Howard Medical Centre; Associate Professor of Medicine, MIT, Cambridge; Professor of Medicine, University of Chicago. *Memberships:* Endo Society; American Thyroid Society; Association of American Physicians; etc. *Publications:* Around 200 published articles etc. *Address:* University of Chicago Medical Center, 5841 S Maryland, Chicago, IL 60637, USA.

DeJOHN, Charles Samuel, b. 26 Nov. 1940, Houston, Texas, USA. Psychiatrist. m. Tania, June 1976, Houston, 1 son, 2 daughters. *Education:* BS, University of St Thomas, 1962; MS, 1965, PhD, 1968, University of Houston; MD, University of Texas Medical Branch, 1976; Psychiatry Residency, Baylor College of Medicine, 1979. *Appointments:* Predoctoral and Postdoctoral Fellowships, University of Houston, 1965-68; Research Physicist, Shell Development Corporation, 1968-72; Medical Student, Instructor, Blood Bank Technician/Medical Historian, University of Texas Medical Branch, Galveston, 1972-76; Director, Substance Abuse Section, Texas Research Institute of Mental Sciences, 1979-82; Private Practice. *Memberships:* American Physical Society; American Medical Association; American Psychiatric Association; Harris County Medical Society; American Psychiatric Association; Houston Psychiatric Society; Harris County Biofeedback Society. *Honours:* Honour Roll, University of St Thomas; Sigma Pi Sigma; Phi Kappa Phi; Diplomate, National Medical Boards. *Address:* 7580 Fannin, Suite 315, Houston, TX 77054, USA.

DE JONG, Jan Willem, b. 13 Aug. 1942, The Hauge, The Netherlands. Associate Professor, Director Cardiochemistry Laboratory. m. 9 Oct. 1968, 2 daughters. *Education:* BSc Chemistry 1964, MSc Biochemistry 1966, Leyden University; PhD, Medical Faculty, Rotterdam, 1971. *Appointments:* Instructor, Assistant Professor, Department of Biochemistry, Medical Faculty, Rotterdam, 1966-74; Teacher, Rotterdam Advanced Analytical School, 1968-69; Member, Medical Faculty Board, Rotterdam, 1974-76; Member, Medical Faculty Executive Committee, Rotterdam, 1979-81; Consultant, Department of Anesthesiology, University of Texas Medical Center, Houston, Texas, USA, 1982-83; Associate Professor, Director, Cardiochemical Laboratory, Thorax Centre, Erasmus University, Rotterdam, The Netherlands. *Memberships:* American Heart Association; American Physiology Society; Dutch Biochemistry Society; International Union of Biochemistry; Dutch Society of

Cardiologists; European Society of Cardiology; European Society of Clinical Investigation; International Society for Heart Research. *Publications include:* 'Palmitate Activation: Aspects of Palmitate Metabolism' (theses), 1971; About 180 other publications. *Honours:* Fulbright Fellow, 1973; Established Investigator, Netherlands Heart Foundation, 1975-80; German Academic Exchange Fellow, 1981. *Hobbies:* Tennis; Ornithology (Inspector, Birds Protection Act, 1971-85); Photography. *Address:* Cardiochemistry Laboratory, Thorax Centre, Erasmus University Rotterdam, PO Box 1738, 3000 DR Rotterdam, The Netherlands.

DEKARIS, Dragan, b. 21 Jan. 1936, Zagreb, Yugoslavia. Professor of Immunology, Medical Faculty, University of Zagreb; Science Cousellor. m. Ivana Cornioni, 4 May 1963, Rijeka, 2 daughters. *Education:* Medical Faculty, University of Zagreb, 1960; PhD, 1964; Associate Professor, 1976; Professor, 1984. *Appointments: Assistant, Institute Rugjer Boskovic, 1960-65; Visiting Investigator, Institute Pasteur, Paris, France, 1966-68; Research Associate, Institute Rugjer Boskovic, 1968-71; Scientific Counsellor, Head, Department for Immunological Research and Teaching, Institute of Immunology, 1971-; Immunologist, Clinical Hospital, Dr M. Stojanovic, 1983-. Memberships:* Medical Academy of Croatia, 1974; Yugoslav Academy of Science and Arts, 1975; Societe Francaise d'Immunologie, 1967; Yugoslav Immunological Society, 1968; European Reticulo-Endothelial Society, 1974. *Publications:* Contributions to over 140 scientific journals; Co-author of several books; Author: Basic Allergology, 1983. *Honours:* Rugjer Boskovic Prize of Republic of Croatia, 1973; Pavao Culumovic Prize of Medical Academy of Croatia, 1974. *Adress:* Institute of Immunology, Rockerfellerova 2, 41000 Zagreb, Yugoslavia.

de KOEKKOEK, Lasurens Jan, b. 13 Feb. 1930, Amsterdam, The Netherlands, Doctor of Chiropractic. m. Sheila Whitaker, 4 May 1957, Ndola, Zambia, 2 sons, 1 daughter. *Education:* DC; ND; Diplomate, National Board of Chiropractic Examiners; Diploma, X-ray and Spinography. *Appointments:* Private General Practice. *Memberships:* European Chiropractic Union; Netherlands Chiropractic Association; Mississippi State Board of Chiropractic Examiners; Southern Naturopathic Physician Association; International Academy of Nutritional Consultants. *Hobbies:* Music; Rowing. *Address:* Staringlaan 40, 1215 BS Hilversum, The Netherlands.

DE LA CRUZ, Mariano Villaroman, b. 23 Aug. 1928, Philippines. Professor, Anatomy; College Secretary. *Education:* AA, 1949, DM, 1954, University of the Philippines; Diplomate, American Board of Colon and Rectal Surgery; Diplomate, Philippine Society of Anatomists. *Appointments:* Instructor, 1963, Assistant Professor, 1966, Associate Professor, 1971, Professor, 1974, Chairman, 1972-85, Clinical Associate Professor, Surgery, 1981, College Secretary, 1985, College of Medicine, University of the Philippines. *Memberships:* Associate Member, National Research Council of the Philippines; Fellow, Director, Philippine Society of Colon and Rectal Surgeons; Fellow: Philippine College of Surgeons, Philippine Society of Anatomists; President, Philipine Society of Anatomists; Sports Medicine Association of the Philippines. *Hobbies:* Bowling; Jogging. *Address:* College of Medicine, University of the Philippines, 547 Pedro Gil, Ermita, Manila, Philippines.

DEL CAMPO, Carlos, b. 13 Mar. 1949, Madrid, Spain. Cardiovascular and Thoracic surgeon, Halifax Infirmary, Canada. m. Pamela M. A. Nicholls, 19 June 1982, Windsor, Ontario, Canada. *Education:* Medical School: University of Mexico, 1967-71; ECFMG, 1972; MD (Hons.), University of Mexico City, 1973; Internship, Regina General Hospital, 1974; Hematology, Immunology Diploma, Hospital General Mexico, 1975; Residency in General Surgery: Strong Memorial Hospital, New York, 1975-77, Memorial University

of Newfoundland, 1977-79; FRCS(C). 1979; Residency Cardiovasc & Thorac Surgery, London Ontario, Canada, 1979-81; LMCC, 1981 FRCS(C) Cardiovascular and Thoracic Surgery, 1981. *Appointments:* Assistant Professor of Human Histology, University of Mexico, 1968-73; Assistant Professor, University of Mexico City, 1970-73; Attending Staff, Victoria General Hospital, Nova Scotia and Halifax Infirmary, Nova Scotia, 1982-86; Clinical Instructor in Surgery, Dalhousie University, 1984; Acting Director, Surgical Intensive Care Unit, Halifax Infirmary, 1985; Director, Non-Invasive Vascular Laboratory, Halifax Infirmary, 1985; Lecturer in Surgery, Dalhouise University, 1985. *Memberships:* Canadian Medical Association; Royal College of Physicians and Surgeons of Canada; Medical Society of Nova Scotia; Canadian Cardiovascular Society; Heart Transplantation Society; Provincial Medical Board of Nova Scotia; Surgical Section Medical Society of Nova Scotia; New York Academy of Sciences. *Publications:* Numerous abstracts and papers in professional journals. *Honours include:* First Award at National Congress of Surgeons, Mexico City for Experimental work, New Design of A-V Valve Replacement with Autologous Tissue, 1972. *Hobbies:* Soccer; Downhill Skiing; Tae-Kwan-Do; Painting; Chess. *Address:* Room 412, Gerard Hall, 5303 Morris Street, Halifax, Nova Scotia, Canada B3J 1B6.

DEL CAMPO, John Avelino, b. 7 Sep 1941, Dansville, New York, USA. Dentist. m. Jo Ellen Kaiser, 4 Oct 1975, Rochester, New York, USA, 1 son 1 daughter. *Education;* BSc, Niagara University, 1963; DDS, Fairleigh Dickinson School of Dentistry, 1967; Oral Surgery Intern, San Francisco General Hospital, 1969. *Appointments:* Allegany Co Representative to Eighth District Dental Society, 1976-77; Chairman, Department of Dentistry, 1977-84, Board of Directors, 1979-81, St James Mercy Hospital; Honorary Adjunct Professor, Alfred University School of Nursing, 1982-; Lecturer, SUNY at Alfred School of Allied Health, 1983-; Secretary, Vice President, President Elect, President (ADA Delegate) Eighth District Dental Society, 1980-83. *Memberships:* American Dental Association; Dental Society of State of New York; Eighth District Dental Society; Allegany County Dental Society; Steuben County Dental Society; Academy of general Dentistry; Pierre Fauchard Academy; Pankey Institute Alumni Association; American Society of Clinical Hypnosis. *Honours:* President, Science Club, Niagara University,1963; Navy Achievement Medal and Combat 'V' 1969; Fellow, Academy of General Dentistry, 1977. *Hobbies:* Jogging; Skiing; Gardening; Collecting small antique American arms. *Address:* 49 Hillcrest Drive, Alfred, NY 14802, USA.

DELEON, Patrick Henry, b 6 Jan. 1943, Waterbury, Connecticut, USA. United States Senate Staff, Executive Assistant for Senator Inouye. m. Jean Louise Murphy, 15 June 1968, Carolina. Rhode Island, 1 son, 1 daughter. *Education:* MS, PhS, Clinical Psychology, Purdue University, 1966-69; MPH, University of Hawaii, 1973; Columbus School of Law, Catholic University, 1980. *Appointments:* Training Office, Peace Corps, University of Hawaii, 1969-70; Staff Psychologist, State of Hawaii, 1070-73. *Memberships:* American Psychological Association; American Bar Association; Hawaii Public Health Association. *Publications:* Over 100 articles, book chapters, etc. *Honours: Distinguished Early Career Contributions to Psychology in the Public Interest Award, American Psychological Association, 1984; Harold M. Hildreth Award, Public Service Division of American Psychological Association, 1985. Hobby:* Writing. *Address:* c/o United States Senator D.K. Inouye, United States Senate, Washington, DC 20510, USA.

DELGADO, Jose M R, b. 8 Aug. 1915, Ronda, Spain. Director, Centre for Neurobiological Studies. m. Caroline Stoddard, 26 May 1956, New Haven, Connecticut, USA, 1 son, 1 daughter. *Education:* MD, 1940, DSc,1942, Universsity of Madrid.

Appointments: Associate Professor of Physiology, Medical School, University of Madrid, 1940-46; Investigator, Spanish National Research Council, 1946-49; Instructor, Assistant Professor, Associate Professor, Full Professor of Physiology, Yale Medical School, New Haven, Connecticut, USA, 1950-71; Professor of Physiology, Autonomous Medical School, Madrid, 1971-81; Director of Research, 'Ramom y Cajal' Centre, Madrid, 1974-85; Director, Centre for Neurobiological Studies, Madrid, 1985-. *Memberships:* American Physiological Society; American College of Neuropsychopharmacology; European Brain and Behaviour Society; Fellow, New York Academy of Science; Spanish Chapter Club of Rome. *Publication:* "Physical Control of the Mind: Towards a Psychocivilised Society", 1969, translated into 6 languages; Over 400 scientific articles and 4 scientific films. *Honours:* Ramon y Cajal Prize, 1952; Guggenheim Fellow, 1963; Gold Medal, American Psychiatric Society, 1971; Gold Medal, International Society of Biological Psychiatry, 1974; Rodriguez Pascual Prize, 1975. *Address:* Centro de Estudios Neurobiologicos, Caleruega 29, 28033 Madrid, Spain.

DEL GUERCIO, Louis R.M., b. 15 Jan. 1929, New York City, USA. Professor and Chairman, Department of Surgery. m. Paula de Vantibault, 18 May 1957, 4 sons, 4 daughters. *Education:* BS, cum laude, Fordham University, 1949; MD, Yale University, 1953. *Appointments:* 1953-54 Resident, St. Vincent's Hospital, New York City; 1954-58 Cleveland City Hospital, 1958-60, practice medicine specialising in thoracic surgery, 1960 - member faculty Albert Einstein College of Medicine, New York City 1960-71, Associate Professor 1966-70, Professor of Surgery 1970-71, Director, Clinical Research Center, 1967-71, Clinical Professor of Surgery, New Jersey College of Medicine, Newark, 1971-76, Professor of Surgery, New York Medical College, 1976 -, Chairman of Department of Surgery, Metropolitan Hospital Center, Westchester County Medical Center; 1976 - Consultant Surgeon at other Hospitals. *Memberships include:* American Board of Surgery; American Board of Thoracic Surgery, 1970-74; Member Surgical Study Section NIH; Member, Committee on Shock NRC National Academy of Sciences 1969-71; Founder Member, American Trauma Society; Founder Member, President 1976, Society for Critical Care Medicine; Chairman, Board of Directors, Daltex Medical Sciences,Inc. *Publications:* "Urology 1956 with BG Clarke"; "The Multilingual Manual for Medical History Taking", 1972; "Septic Shock in Man", 1971 with SG Hershey and R McConn; Contributor of Numerous articles to medical journals. *Honours:* Gold Award, American Academy of Pediatrics, 1973; Alumni Award in Medicine, Fordham University, 1974. *Address:* 14 Pryer Lane, Larchmont, NY 10538, USA.

DELMONT, Jean Pierre,B. 18– Jan. 1933, Bordeaux, France. Head of Department of Hepatogastroenterology. m. Morita Mauri, 5 Jan. 1955, Marseilles, 2 sons, 2 daughters. *Education:* MD, Marseilles, 1961; Professor of Internal Medicine, 1965. *Appointments:* Hospital Resident, 1957-61, Assistant in Radionuclear Medicine, 1962-65, Associate Professor of Chair of Clinical Gastroenterology, 1965-70, Marseilles; Professor of Gastroenterology, 1971-76, Professor of Internal Medicine, 1976-, Nice Medical School; Head, Department of Hepatogastroenterology, University Hospital, Nice, 1970-,*Memberships:* Various societies of gastroenterology; Permanent Secretary, Franco-Spanish Conference in Gastroenterology; European Association for Cancer Research; New York Academy of Sciences. *Publications:* "The Treatment of Small Bowel Diseases", 1972; "The Sphincter of Oddi.", 1977; "Milk Intolerances", 1983; "Cancer of the Exocrine Pancreas", 1985. *Honours:* Prize, Marseilles Medical School, 1952, 60; Prize, Academie Francaise de Medecine, 1966; Chevalier des Palmes Academiques,

1979. *Hobbies:* Arabic and Jewish middle age medicine; Pre-Columbian art; Mountain trekking; Honorary President, University Omnisport Club, as former rugby player. *Address:* Centre d'Hepato-Gastro-Entérologie, Hospital de Cimiez, 4 Avenue Reine Victoria, 06000 Nice, France.

DELLA PORTA, Giuseppe, b. 2 Apr. 1926, Milan, Italy. Professor of Experimental Oncology and Pathology. *Education:* MD. *Appointments:* Post Doctoral Fellow, Department of Morbid Anatomy, University of Milan; 1951-55; Research Associate, Division of Oncology, Chicago Medical School, Chicago, 1956-60; Head, Section of Experimental Carcinogenesis, 1961-70, Director Division of Experimental Oncology A, 1971 -, Instituto Nazionale Tumori, Milan. Vice Director General, Instituto Nazionale Tumori, Milan, Italy. *Memberships:* American Association of Cancer Research; American Association of Pathologists; European Association of Cancer Research; Patholigical Society of Great Britain and Ireland; Societa` Italiana di Cancerologial Gruppo di Cooperazione in Immuniologia; Socita` Italiana di Cancerologial di Immunologia. *Publications:* Author of over 100 papers on Various aspects of experimental oncology including studies on chemical carcinogenesis, viral leukemogenesis and immunology of experimental and human tumors. *Address* Istituto Nazionale Tumori, Via G Venezian 1, 20133 Milan, Italy.

DELOOZ, Herman H R B, b. 6 Aug. 1936, Hasselt, Belgium. Professor of Anaesthesiology and Critical Care Medicine. m. Gilberte Cornil, 11 July 1961, Heverlee, 3 daughters. *Education:* Standard Certificate, Educational Council for Foreign Medical Graduates, USA, 1961; MD, Catholic University of Leuven, Brlgium, 1962; Honorary Clinical Assistant, Department of Anaesthetics, Royal Postgraduate Medical School, Univeristy of London, England, 1967; PhD, Anaesthesiology, Catholic University of Leuven, 1971. *Appoinments:* General Practice, Herne, Belgium 1962-64; Resident, Department of Anaesthesiology, 1964-66, Deputy Director, 1966 Lecturur, 1969, Docent, 1971, Department of Anaesthesiology, Catholic University of Leuven; Director, Emergency Department and Emergency Medical Servies, University Hospital Sint-Rafael, Leuven, 1972; Professor of Anaesthesia, University of Antwerp, 1972-75; Visiting Professor, University of Limburg, Belgium, 1973-85; Professor of Anaesthesiology and Critical Care Medicine, Catholic University of Leuven, 1974-; Vice-President, National Committee for Advice on Problems on Emergency Medical Care, Ministry of Health, 1978, President 1980-82. *Memberships:* Titular Member, Belgian Society of Anaesthesia and Resuscitation, 1971; Society of Critical Care Medicine, USA, 1973; European Academy of Anaesthesiology, 1978; Founding Member, 1980, President, 1982-1983, Belgian Intensive Care Society; University Association for Emergency Medicine, USA, 1983; Council Member, Belgian Society of Anaesthesia and Resuscitation, 1985. *Publications:* Editorial Board, International Journal of Clinical Monitoring and Computing; More than 80 publications. *Address:* Korbeeklostraat 98, B-3000 Leuven, Belgium.

DEL TORTO, Ugo, b. 26 Aug. 1923, Naples, Italy. Chairman and Director of Orthopaedic Institute, Naples University. m. 4 Feb. 1948, Naples, 1 son, 1 daughter. *Education:* Graduated with honours, School of Medicine, Naples University, 1947; Medical Radiology and Physical Therapy, University of Naples, 1949; Orthopaedy and Traumatology, University of Bologna, 1951. *Appointments:* Intern, United Hospital, Naples, 1947-49; Voluntary Assistant, Chair of Surgery, Naples University, 1949-53; Voluntary Assistant, Chair of Orthopaedic Surgery, University of Rome, 1953-57;Regular Assistant, for National Concours, same Chair, 1957-59; First Assistant, 1959-62; Professor of Orthopaedy and

Traumatology, Medical School of University of Naples, 1962-64; Professor of Orthopaedy and Traumatology, Italian Universities, 1964-; Chairman and Director of Orthopaedic Institute of First Medical School of Naples University, 1964-; Visiting Professor, Medical School of California University in San Francisco, USA and Mount Sinai Medical School, New York. *Memberships:* Italian Society of Orthopaedy and Traumatology (Past President); Italian Society of Medical Gymnastics (Past President); Italian Association of Students of Medicine and Law of the Traffic, (President);Societa di Ortopedia a Traumatologia dell 'Italia Merionale ed Insulare (Past President); Fellow, International College of Surgeons and several other organizations. *Publications:* More than 200 papers. *Honours include:* Government Grant, 1951; In 1957 first of the pass list at National Concours for free Professorship. *Address:* Universita di Napoli, Orthopaedics and Traumatology Clinic, Andrea delle Dame 4, 80138 Naples, Italy.

DEMARTINI, John Fredric, b. 25 Nov. 1954, Houston, Texas, USA. Chiropractic, Clinic Director. m. Denise A Childs, 13 Nov. 1983, Houston, Texas, 1 son, 1 daughter. *Education:* AA, Wharton Junior College; BSD Biology and Chemistry, University of Houston; DC, Texas Chiropractic College. *Appointments:* Clinic Director, Chiropractic Family Center; Founder and Professor of Health Education and Awareness Lectures. *Memberships:* President, Cancer Prevention and Control Association; Council on Nutrition, Council on Roentgenology, American Chiropractic Association; International Academy of Neurovascular Disease; Parker Chiropractic Research Foundation; Chiropractic Association; American Association of Nutritional Counsultants; Metabolic Research Foundation; Texas Chiropractic College Alumni Association; The Society for Neurolinguistic Programming; Association for Childbirth at Home International; Alpha Epsilon Delta. *Publications:* "The Moderate Guidelines Towards Health", 1982; "The Illusional Basis For Man's Health and Disease", 1983; "Your Body Speaks Out About Your Nutrition", 1984; "Lessons for Life", 1985; 'Demartini's Sign (For referred pain identification)'. *Honours:* Salutatorian, 1982; Magna cum laude, 1982; Special Achievement Award in Clinical Practice, 1982. *Hobbies:* Jogging; Surfing; Yoga; Writing; Public Speaking. *Address:* 13155 Westheimer Suite 110, Wind Chimes Center, Austin, TX 78752, USA.

DEMEDTS, Maurits Germain Paul, b. 11 June 1941, Tielt, Belgium, Professor of Medicine. m. Tan Toan Leng, 4 Apr. 1964, Wemmel, 2 daughters. *Education:* Medical Doctor, University of Leuven; Geaggregeerde Van Het Hoger Onderwys; Baccalaureus in Thomistic Philosophy. *Appointments:* Resident, Department of Internal Medicine, University Hospitals, Leuven, 1967-70; Research Fellow, McGill University, Montreal, Canada, 1970-71; Assistant Head of Pulmonary Division 1972-, Professor of Medicine 1981-, Catholic University of Louvain, Belgium. *Memberships:* Associate Editor, 'Clinical Physiology', SEPCR; Secretary, Belgian Society of Pneumology; Fellow, American Thoracic Society; Governor, American College of Chest Physicians. *Publications:* 'Regional Gas Distribution and Single-Breath Washout Curves in Head-Down Position', (with I Clarysse, M Verhamme, M Marcq and M De Roo, 1983; 'Cobalt Lung in Diamond Polishers', (with B Gheysens, J Nagels, E Verbeken, J Lauweryns, A van den Eeckhout, D Lahaye and A Gyselen), 1984; 'The Inherited Association of Interstitial Lung Disease, Hypocalciuric Hypercalcemia, and Defective Granulocyte Function', (with J Auwerx, P Goddeeris, R Bouillon, R Gyselen and J Laumeryns), 1985. *Honours:* Specia Award, 1965; de Falloise Award, 1976; Boehringher Award for Pneumology, 1978. *Address:* University Hospital 'Gasthuisberg', Herestraat, Leuven B 3000, Belgium.

DEMIRJIAN, Arto, b. 11 Feb. 1931, Istanbul, Turkey.

Director, Human Growth Research Center; Professor of Anatomy, University of Montreal, Canada. m. Sonia Giragosyan, 13 Sep. 1959, Montreal, Quebec, 1 son, 1 daughter. *Education:* BA, College St. Michel, Istanbul, 1949; Diploma, Dental Surgery, University of Istanbul, 1953; DDS, University of Montreal, 1959; MSc.D, University of Toronto, 1961. *Appointments:* Assistant Professor of Anatomy, Department of Oral Biology, Faculty of Dentistry, University of Montreal, 1961-65; Associate Professor in charge of Gross Anatomy and Growth and Development, 1965-71; Director, Human Growth Research Center, 1966-; Professor of Anatomy, Faculty of Dentistry, 1971-, University of Montreal. *Memberships:* Canadian Dental Association; College of Dental Surgeons, Province of Quebec; International Association for Dental Research; American Association of Physical Anthropology; French Canadian Association for the Advancement of Sciences; International Association of Anthroplogist; International Society of Cranio-Fracial Biology. *Publications:* Contributor to professional journals including: Co-author, 'Sexual diferences in dental development and prediction of emergence', 'Journal of Dental Research', 59; Co-author, 'Inter-relationships between somatic, skeletal, dental and sexual maturity', 'American Journal of Orthodontics'; Chapters in Books; Presentations. *Honours:* First Prize of War Award from CDA, 1960; Scholarship from CDA, 1960; Scholarship from NRC, 1960; Scholarship from MRC, 1973; Scholarship from CFDA, 1973; Award from MRC, 1975. *Hobbies:* Camping; Photography. *Address:* 1545 Lucerne Road, Town of Mount Royal, Quebec H3R 2JI, Canada.

DEMNER, Sigfrido, b. 25 Aug. 1923, Viena. Hospital Chairman; Professor, Surgery. m. Peria Goldstein, 30 May 1953, 1 son, 1 daughter. *Education:* MD; FACS; FCCP;FICA; Internship, Samaritan Hospital, Bogota; Residency, Samaritan Hospital, Hospital Santa Clara, Bogota; Internship, Lebanon Hospital, New York; Residency, Vancouver General Hospital, Canada; etc. *Appointments:* Assistant Surgeon, Hospital Santa Clara, Bogota; Assistant Surgeon, Thoracic, Associate Surgeon, Gral., Associate Chairman, Surgery, Hospital Samaritana; Assistant Professor, Thoracic, General Surgery, Professor, Surgery, University Javeriana, Bogota. *Memberships:* American College of Surgeons; American College of Chest Physicians; International Society of Surgery; International Society of Angiology; Colombian Academy of Medicine; Interamerican Academy of Medicine; Jeruselem Academy of Medicine; New York Academy of Sciences; many other professional organisations. *Publications:* "Preliminary Study of Empiema"; "A Case of Hydatidic Cyst of the Lung"; "Efageal Carcinoma found in 10 Years at the Samaritan Hospital"; "Lung Cancer in 10 Years at the Samaritan Hospital"; "Trauma of the Chest"; "Endothoracic Goiter"; "Pleuro-pulmonar ambissis"; "Asbestosis" *Hobbies include:* Tennis. *Address:* Calle 95 No. 10-70, of 201, Bogota, Colombia, South America.

DENKER, Hans-Werner, b. 4 Jan. 1941, Erfurt, Germany. Professor. m. Ulrike Denker, 10 Sep. 1976, Aachen, 1 son, 1 daughter. *Education:* Dr.rer.nat (PhD), 1969, MD, 1970, University of Marburg; Licensed Physician, 1970; Habilitation, RWTH Aachen, 1976; Professor, RWTH Aachen 1978. *Appointments:* Wissenschaftlicher Assistent and Oberassistent, Max-Planck-Institut fur Immunbiologie, Freiburg, 1968-74; Obersassistent, Professor, Abteilung Anatomie of the Medical Faculty, Rheinisch-Westfalische Technishe Hochschule, Aachen, 1974-. *Memberships:* Gesellschaft fur Histochemie; Anatomische Gesellschaft; Society for the Study of Reproduction; Gesellschaft fur Entwicklungsbiologie; Society for the Study of Fertility; Cell Tissue and Organ Culture Study Group; Deutsche Ges f Zellbiologie. *Publications:* "Implantation: The Role of Proteinases, and Blockage of Implantation by

Proteinase Inhibitors'', 1977. *Address:* Nordhoffstr. 12, D-5100 Aachen, Federal Republic of Germany.

DENNERSTEIN, Graeme Joseph, b. 8 Aug. 1939, Melbourne, Australia. Obstetrican and Gynaecologist. m Grazia, 8 Mar. 1985, 2 sons fom previous marriage. *Education:* MB BS, Melbourne University; MRCOG, 1967; FRACOG, 1979; FROCOG, 1984. *Appointments:* RMO, Alfred Hospital, 1962; SRMO 1963, Surgical Registrar 1964, Royal Perth Hospital; RMO, 1965, Registrar 1966, Royal Women's Hospital, Melbourne, Currently; Obstetrician and Gynaecologist, Western General and Essendon and District Memorial Hospital and Consultant in Gynaecology to Director General of Air Forces Health services, Royal Australian Air Force. *Memberships:* Fellow, International Society for the study of Vulvar Disease; Committee Member, Aviation Medical Society of Australia and New Zealand; President, Essendon Hospital Clinical Society. *Publications:* 'Cytology of the Vulvar' in 'Journal of Obstetrics and Gynaecology British Commonwealth', 1968; 'Multiple Pregnancy and Cervical Incompetence' in "Australia and New Zealand Journals of Obstetrics and Gynaecology", 1971; Several papers on vaginitis 1970-85. *Hobbies:* Pilot Licence with Instrument Rating; Violoncello and Piano. *Address:* 998 Mt. Alexander Road, Essendon, Victoria 3040, Australia.

DEN OTTER, Willem, b. 8 Aug. 1938, Alphena/dRÿan, Netherlands. Professor of Experimental Pathology. m. Hetty Bruins, 30 Aug. 1963, 4 sons, 2 daughters. *Education:* PhD Biology, University of Utrecht, Netherlands; Post-doctoral study, Chester Beatty Research Institute, Sutton, Surrey, England. *Appointments:* Teacher, Infant school, Enschede, 1957-59; Teacher, Secondary School, Rotterdam, 1963-65; Teacher, Biology, Secondary School, Amersfoort, 1963-70; Research Scientist, Pathologisch Instituut, State University, Utrecht, 1965-80;; Professor of Experimental Pathology, ibid, 1980-. *Memberships:* European Association for Cancer Research; Dutch Pathological Society; Dutch Society for Immunology. *Publications:* Various articles in medical journals, especially in the field of cancer. *Honour:* Editor, 'Cancer Immunology Immunotherapy'; 'In Vivo'; 'Research Monographs in Immunology'; Advisor, National Insitute of Health, Netherlands; Advisor, Utrecht Academical Hospital. *Hobby:* Music. *Address:* Department of Experimental Pathology, Pathologisch Instituut, Pasteurstraat 2, Utrecht, The Netherlands.

DENNIS, Kenneth John, b. 9 Aug. 1929, Selkirk, Scotland. Professor of Human Reproduction ad Obstetrics. m. Elizabeth Mary McLearly, 19 July 1952, Edinburgh, 2 sons, 2 daughters. *Education:* MB; ChB; University of Edinburgh, 1947-52; Fellow, Royal college of Surgeons, Edinburgh, 1958; Member, Royal College of Obstetricians and Gynaecologists, 1961; Fellow, Royal College of Obstetricians and Gynaecologists. *Appointments:* Captain, Royal Army Medical Cors, 1953-56; Senior House Officer, Royal Infirmary, Edinburgh, 1956-57; Surgical Registrar, Stracathre Hospital, 1957-59; Registrar, Obstetrics and Gynaecology, Perth Royal Infirmary, 1959-60; Registrar, Obstetrics and Gynaecology, Aberdeen Maternity Hospital, 1960-61; Lecturer in Obstetrics and Gynaecology, Aberdeen University, 1961-63; MRC Fellow, Obstetrics Medical Research Unit, Aberdeen, 1963-65; Senior Lecturer, Obstetrics and Gynaecology, Aberdeen University, 1965-71. *Memberships:* British Medical Association; Blair-Bell Research Society; Society for the Study of Fertility; South-West Obstetrical and Gyaecological Society; Obstetric Computer Society. *Publications:* Contributor to professional journals; 'Proteinuria in Pregnancy' In recent progress in perinatal medicine. Postgraduate Symposium, Budapest, Hungary, 1983. *Hobbies:* Social History; Classical Music.

Address: 21 Westwood Road, Southampton S02 1DL, England.

DENNISS, Alan Robert, b. 30 Sept. 1952, Brisbane, Australia. Ralph Reader Fellow National Heart Foundation of Australia. *Education:* BSc Med, 1974, MB BS 1977, MSc, 1978, MD 1986, University of Sydney, Australia; Fellow, Royal Australasian College of Physicians, 1983. *Appointments:* Research Assistant, Department of Physiology & Biophysics, University of Alabama, Birmingham, USA, 1976; Resident Medical Officer, Royal Prince Alfred Hospital, Sydney, Australia, 1977-78; Medical Registrar, St Vincent's Hospital, Sydney, 1979; Cardiology Registrar, Westmead Hospital, Sydney, 1980-81; Cardiology Research Fellow, National Health & Medical Research Council, Westmead Hospital, Sydney, 1982-84; Ralph Reader Fellow, National Heart Foundation of Australia at St Thomas' Hospital, London, England, 1985, Harvard Medical School, Brigham Hospital, Boston, Mass, USA, 1986, Westmead Hospital, Sydney, 1987 *Memberships:* Australian Medical Association; Cardiac Society of Australia & New Zealand; International Society for Heart Research; Section on Epidemiology & Prevention, International Society & Federation of Cardiology. *Publications:* Some 20 publications, 65 abstracts, including publications in 'American Journal of Physiology' & 'American Journal of Cardiology'. *Honours:* Chapman Prize, University of Sydney, 1976; Ralph Reader Prize (Young Investigators Award), Cardiac Society of Australia & New Zealand, 1982. *Hobbies:* Classical Music; Violin, Singing; Farming. *Address: Cardiology Unit, Westmead Hospital, Westmead, NSW2145, Australia.*

DENTON, Derek Ashworth, b. 27 May 1924. Tasmania. Australia. Director and Research Professor of Experimental Physiology and Medicine. m. Catherine Margaret Mary Scott, 13 May 1953, 2 sons. *Education:* MB, BS, University of Melbourne, *Appointments:* Research Fellow 1949-60, Principal Research Fellow 1960, National Health and Medical Research Council of Australia; Director 1971-, Research Professor of Experimental Physiology and Medicine 1978-, Howard Florey Institute of Experimental Physiology and Medicine, University of Melbourne. *Memberships:* First Vice President, International Union of Physiological Sciences; Fellow, Royal Australian College of Physicians; American Endocrine Society; Physiological Society. *Publications:* "The Hunger For Salt", 1982; Contributed to over 200 articles; Reviews in Scientific Journals. *Honours:* Fellow, Australian Academy of Sciences; Foreign Medical Member, Royal Swedish Academy of Sciences. *Hobbies:* Music; Fly Fishing; Tennis; Wine. *Address:* 816 Orrong Road, Toorak, Victoria 3142, Australia.

DENNY, Suanne E., b. 27 Feb. 1947, Rochester, New York, USA. Haematology Supervisor; Assistant Laboratory Manager. *Education:* AAS, 1967, BS, 1969, Rochester Institute of Technology; ASCP, St Mary's Hospital School of Medical Technology, 1969; Continuing Education, University of Rochester, 1970-82. *Appointments:* St Mary's Hospital, 1968-70; Soldiers & Sailors Memorial Hospital, 1970-84; Animal Reference Laboratories, Houston, 1985-. *Memberships:* American Society for Medical Technology; American Society of Clinical Pathologists; National Cetifying Agency. *Honours:* MT(ASCP), 1969; S(ASCP), 1980. *Hobbies:* Photography; Animal Welfare. *Address:* 1011 South Kansas St., La Porte, TX 77571, USA.

DE PERGOLA, Elio, b. 21 July 1923, Acquaviva, Bari, Italy. Chief of Private Clinic of Medicine and Geriatrics; University Full Professor of Endocrinology and Internal Medicine. m. Castellaneta Giacomina, 2 Apr. 1949, Acquaviva, 2 sons. *Appointments:* Medical Assistant, Istituto di Patologia Medica, Bari University; Medical Assistant, Clinica Medica, Ferrara University; Chief of Internal Medicine Department, Acquaviva Hospital, 1954-61; Chief of Internal Medicine

Department, Bari "Di Venere" Hospital, 1962-83. *Memberships:* Life Member, New York Academy of Sciences; Societa Italiana di Medicina Interna; Societá Italiana di Endocrinologia; Societá Italiana di Geriatria; Societá Italiana di gastroenterologia. *Publications:* 'Il Metodo Psicodiagnostico di Rorschach" Astrolabio) 1952; "Le sindromi iperfunzionale del surrene (Pozzi) 1955; "L'impiego degli ormoni in terapia (Circito) 1969; "L'ordinamento sanitario italiano (JOB) 1985; Many articles on Endocrinology, Gastroenterology, Cardiology. *Hobbies:* Pictures; Television; Computers. *Address:* Via Principe Amedo 144, Bari, Italy.

DE RIVAS, Carmela, b. 25 Nov. 1920, Italy. Medical Director. m. Aureliano Rivas, MD, 30 Oct. 1948, Philadelphia, Pennsylvania, USA, 1 son, 3 daughters. *Education:* MD, Women's College of Pennsylvania, USA, 1946. *Appointments include:* Clinical Director, Morristown State Hospital, 1957-61, Assistant Superintendent, 1961-63, Superintendent, 1963-70; Psychiatrist, Penn Foundation, Sellersville, Pennsylvania, 1970-72; Psychiatric Consultant, Norristown State Hospital, 1970-79; Clinical Suprvisor and Consultant, Central Montgomery Mental Health/Mental Retardation Centre, Norristown, Pennsylvania, 1979-81, Consultant, 1981-; Acting Assistant Superintendent for Clinical Services, Norristown State Hospital, 1980-82, Clinical Director with Special Assignments, 1980-84, Medical Director, 1984-. *Memberships include:* Fellow, Pennsylvania Psychiatric Society; Fellow, American Psychiatric Association, member of nominating Committee, 1982; Member, House of Delegates, Pennsylvania Medical Society; Fellow, Philadelphia College of Physicians; New York Acadmey of Sciences; Continued Medical Education Committee, Montgomery County Medical Society; Board of Directors, Arthur P. Noyes Research Foundation Inc. *Honours:* Woman of the Year, Norristown Business and Professional Women's Club, 1966; National Amita Golden Lady Achievement Award, 1976; Woman of the Year Citation, Pennsylvania Federation Business and Professional Women's Clubs; Citation, Legion of Honour, The Chapel of Four Chaplains, 1979. *Hobbies:* Gardening; Crafts. *Address:* 700 Joseph Drive, Wayne, PA 19087, USA.

deRos-DAWSON, Rosemary Grace, b. 21 Feb. 1947, Belfast, Northern Ireland. President, Principal Owner, Regency Investigations Inc. *Education:* SRN, England; Private Investigator, New York, State, USA; RN, USA. *Appointments:* Staff Nurse, Royal Victoria Hospital, Belfast, 1968; Charge Nurse: United Hospital, Port Chester, New York, 1968-72; Memorial Hospital, Sloan Kettering Institute, New York, 1972-78; Director, medical Malpractise Defense & Investigative Unit, Compass Investigators, White Plains, 1978-85; President, Principal Owner, Chairman, Regency Investigations Inc., 1985-. *Memberships:* Royal College of Nurses; American Nursing Association; New York State Nursing Association; Albany Claims Association. *Publications:* Papers: "The Expert's Report and Medical Records – Making Them Work for You". *Hobbies:* Tennis; Reading; Handcrafts; Sailing; Travel; Writing. *Address:* 700 Scarsdale Avenue, PO Box 58-H, Scarsdale, NY 10583, USA.

DESAI, Jagdish, b. 25 Sep. 1947, India. Solo Practitioner/Anaesthetist. m. Rekha Desai, 6 June 1972, Maroli, India, 1 son, 1 daughter. *Education:* MB ChB Birmingham University, England; DA London. *Appointments:* House Officer, Surgery and Medicine, Walsgrave Hospital, Coventry; SHO, Obstetrics, Marston Green, Birmingham; SHO, Anaesthetics, George Eliot Hospital, Nuneaton; Active Staff, Kirkland Lake Hospital, Kirkland Lake, Ontario; Active Staff, Brantford General Hospital, Brantford, Ontario; Active Staff, St. Joseph's Hospital, Brantford, Ontario; Consulting Staff,

Willett Hospital, Paris. *Memberships:* Brant District Health Council; College of Family Practitioners, Ontario; College of Physicians and Surgeons, Ontario; Faculty of Anaesthetists, (Royal College) London UK. *Hobbies:* Reading; Travelling; Plate collection. *Address:* P O Box 252, 161 Dundas Street, Brantford, Ontario, Canada N3R 1S6.

DESAI, Vajendra J., b. 19 Nov 1947, Hyderabad, India. Psychiatrist. m. Vinutha, 25 Nov 1977, Chicago, 1 son, 1 daughter. *Education:* Medical Education, Institute of Medical Sciences, Osmania Medical College, 1964-70; General Psychiatry Residency Training, Warren State Hospital, Warren, Pennsylvania, 1972-74; Child Psychiatry Training at University of Illinois, Institute for Juvenile Research, Chicago, 1974-77; Diplomate of American Board of Psychiatry and Neurology. *Appointments:* Chairman, Division of Child Psychiatry, 1980-81, Chairman, Division of Adolescent Psychiatry, 1981, Cook County Hospital, Chicago, Illinois, Assistant Professor of Clinical Psychiatry, Abraham Lincoln School of Medicine, University of Illinois, Chicago, 1979-81; Chairman, Department of Psychiatry and Chief, Division of Child Psychiatry, Saint Vincents Health Centre, Erie, Pennsylvania; Diplomare, American Board of Child Psychiatry. *Memberships:* American Psychiatric Association; American Academy of Child Psychiatry; Pennsylvania Psychiatric Association; American Association of Psychiatrists from India. *Publication:* 'Failure to Thrive with No Organic Etiology - A Critical Review of the Literature' International Journal of Eating Disorders, 1983. *Hobbies:* Carpentry, Reading, Music. *Address:* Department of Psychiatry, Saint Vincents Health Centre, 232 West 22nd Street, Erie, PA16544, USA.

DE SCHRYVER, André Emmanuel, b. 24 Dec. 1926, Gent, Belgium. University Professor (Radiotherapy). m. Ann Fredholm, 9 June 1961, Stockholm, Sweden, 1 son, 1 daughter. *Education:* Medical Degree, Belgium, 1953, Diploma of Radiotherapy, 1961; Swedish Medical Licence, 1965; PhD, Karolinska Institute, Stockholm, Sweden, 1974, Docent in Radiotherapy, 1974. *Appointments:* Radiotherapist, Radiuhemmet, Stockholm, Sweden, 1963-75; Head of Radiotherapeutic Department, University Hospital, Gnent, Belgium, 1975-present. *Memberships:* Belgian Radiological Society; Belgian Society for Radiotherapy and Oncology; Swedish Radiological Society; British Institute of Radiology; American Society for Therapeutic Radiology and Oncology. *Publications include:* Articles on Radiotherapeutic and Oncologic subjects. *Address:* Department of Radiotherapy and Nuclear Medicine, University Hospital, De Pintelaan 185, B-9000 Gent, Belgium.

DESGREZ, Alex, b. 7 Sep. 1929, Lapleau, France, Head of Biophysics and Nuclear Medicine Department, m. Anita Kirgo, 1 Aug. 1955, 3 daughters. *Education:* MD; Agrege of medical physics; Professor. *Appointments:* Ingenieur, Atomic Energy Commission, 1960; Full Professor, Paris XI University; Head of Nuclear Medicine Service, Bicetre Hospital, 1974. *Memberships:* Societe Francaise de Biophysique et Medecine Nucleaire; European Society of Nuclear Medicine; Society of Nuclear Magnetic Resopance. *Publications:* "Abrege de Medecine Nucleaire", 1977; "Biophysique des Radiations", 1980; Contributor of numerous professional articles and papers. *Honours:* Medaille de la Jeunesse et des Sports. *Hobbies:* Yachting; Pistol shooting; Antiques. *Address:* 70 rue d'Auteuil, F75016 Paris, France.

DESIKAN, Kothapalle Vedanta, b. 1 Jan. 1927. Director. m. Kamala, 29 July 1957, 1 daughter. *Education:* MBBS, 1950; MD, pathology, 1966. *Appointments:* House Surgeon, K.R. Hospital, Mysore, 1950-51; Medical Officer, Gandhi Memorial Leprosy Foundation, Wardha, 1952-62;

Demonstrator, Lecturer, Pathology, Christian Medical College & Hospital, Vellore, 1962-67; Assistant Director, Central Leprosy Teaching & Research Institute, Chingleput, 1967-76; Director, Central JALMA Institute for Leprosy, Taj Ganj, Agra, 1976-. *Memberships:* Indian Association of Leprologists, Vice-President, 2 years, Secretary 4 years, Treasurer 2 years, Central Council member, 15 years, Currently President; International Leprosy Association, Councillor; Honorary Member, Instituto de Investigaciones, Argentina; Indian Association of Pathologists. *Publications:* Contributor, Chapters, Dharmendra's Text Book on Leprosy. *Honour:* JALMA Trust Fund Oration Award. *Hobby:* Social Work, especially for Leprosy Patients. *Address:* Central JALMA Institute for Leprosy, Taj Ganj, Agra 282001, India.

DESOMBRE, Eugene Robert, b. 6 May 1938, Sheboygan, Wisconsin, USA, Professor, Ben May Laboratory for Cancer Research, The University of Chicago, m. Nancy L Cox, 10 Sep. 1960, Mound, Minnesota, 1 son, 1 daughter. *Education:* SB, 1960, MS, 1961, PhD, 1963, The University of Chicago. *Appointments:* Instructor, Ben May Laboporatorry for Cancer Research, 1964, Assistant Professor, Ben May Laboratory for Cancer Research, 1967, Associate Professor, Ben May Laboratory for Cancer Research, 1974, Director, Biomedical Computation Facilities, 1980, University of Chicago. *Memberships:* American Association for Cancer Research; The Endocrine Society; International Association for Breast Cancer Research. *Publications:* Contibutor of over 114 articles and chapters on books including, 'Steroid receptors in breast cancer', 1984; 'Progestin modulation of estrogen-depentent marker protein synthesis in the endometrium', 1985. *Honours:* Research Cancer Developoment Award, NIH, 1971; Elected to Endocrine Society, 1970; Elected to American Association for Cancer Research, 1973. *Hobbies:* Piano; Running; Photography; Computer programming. *Address:* Ben May Laboratory for Cancer Research, University of Chicago, 5841 South Maryland, Chicago, IL 60637, USA

DES ROCHES, Bernard Paul, b. 5 Dec. 1939, Timmins, Ontario, Canada. Senior Editor, Director of Education, Ontario College of Pharmacists. m. Nellie Kroon, 22 Aug. 1964, Ottawa, 3 sons, 1 daughter. *Education:* BSc.Phm., Toronto; MS.Phm., Wisconsin; PHD, Wisconsin. *Memberships:* American Association of Colleges of Pharmacy; Royal Society of Health; Canadian Pharmaceutical Association; Canadian Conference on Continuing Education in Pharmacy; Ontario Pharmacists Association; Canadian Society of Hospital Pharmacists; Canadian Institute for History of Pharmacy. *Publications:* "Women in Pharmacy", 1973; "Women in Pharmacy - a 1984 Perspective", 1985. *Honours:* Rho Pi Phi, 1968; Guest Lecturer, New South Wales Centennial, 1976. *Hobbies:* Photography; Curling. *Address:* Ontario College of Pharmacists, 483 Huron Street, Toronto, Ontario M5R 2R4, Canada.

DETRE,Thomas, b. 17 May 1924, Budapest, Hungary. Distinguished Service Professor. m. Katherine Maria Drechsler, 15 Sep. 1956, Pittsburgh, USA, 2 sons. *Education:* Horthy Miklos University School of Medicine, Szeged, Pazmany Peter University, Budapest, 1945-47, Rome University School of Medicine, Italy, 1952. *Appointments:* Intern, Morrisania City Hospital, New York, USA, 1953-54; Resident, Psychiatry, Mt. Sinai Hospital, New York, 1954-55; Yale University Medical School, 1955-57; Chief Resident, Instructor, 1957-58. Instructor, 1958-59, Assistant Professor, 1959-62, Associate Professor, 1962-67, Professor, 1970-73, Psychiatry, Yale University School of Medicine; Director, Psychiatric Inpatient Services, 1960-68, Assistant Chief, Psychiatry, 1965-68, Psychiatrist in Chief, 1968-73, Yale-New Haven Hospital; Chairman, Psychiatry, 1973-82, Associate Senior Vice Chancellor, Health Sciences,

1982-85, Senior Vice President for Health Sciences, 1985-, University of Pittsburgh. *Memberships:* Academy of Behavioral Medicine Research; American College of Neuropsychopharmacology, Fellow; American Psychiatric Association, Fellow; Collegium Internationale Neuro-Psychopharmacologicum; Pan American Medical Association, Life Member; Society of Behavioral Medicine, Fellow; Many other professional organisations. *Publications include:* (Book) "Modern Psychiatric Treatment", co-author, 1971; Consulting Editorships: 'American Journal of Psychiatry'; 'Archives of General Psychiatry'; 'The Medical Letter'; 'Hospital and Community Psychiatry'; Editorial Boards: 'Addictive Behaviors'; 'Dialogues in Psychiatry'; 'Health Policy Quarterly'; Evaluation and Utilization'; 'International Journal of Partial Hospitalization'; numerous articles in professional journals. *Hobbies:*Travel; Photography. *Address:* 3811 O'Hara Street, Pittsburgh, PA 15213, USA.

DEUS FOMBELLIDA, Javier, b. 27Dec. 1950, Renteria (Guipuzcoa) Spain. Professor of Surgery. *Education:* Doctor in Medicine & Surgery; Specialist in General & Digestive Tract Surgery; Specialist in thoracic surgery. *Appointments:* University Surgery Service, University of Lausanne, Switzerland (under Prof F Saegesser); Surgery Service, Zaragoza University Hospital (under Prof R Lozano); Thoracic Surgery Service, Marie Lannelongue Surgical Centre, Paris, France (under Prof H Le Brigand); Experimental Surgery Service, University of Lausanne, Switzerland (under Prof V Mirckovitz); Titular Professor of Surgery, University of Zaragoza, Spain; Adjunct Professor, University Hospital, Zaragoza. *Memberships:* Spanish Association of Surgeons; Francophone Thoracic & Cardiovascular Surgery Society; French Association of Surgery; American College of Chest Physicians; International Society of Surgeons; European Society for Surgical Research. *Publications:* (editor) "Pathology of the Adrenal Glands", 1982; Some 31 learned articles in medical journals. *Hobbies:* Reading; Music; Cinema; Tennis; Swimming. *Address:* Hospital Clinico Universitario de Zaragoza, Servicio de Cirugia "A", Avda Gomez Laguna s./n., 50009 Zaragoza, Spain.

DEUTMAN, August Frans, b. 30 Sept 1939, Leiden, Netherlands, Professor of Ophthalmology. m. Elise Catharina Rueb, 10 Sept 1966, Velsen, 2 sons, 2 daughters. *Education:* MD, Leiden University; PhD, Erasmus University, Rotterdam. *Appointments:* Research Fellow, University of Chicago, 1971-72; Member of Staff, Rotterdam Eye Hospital, 1972-73; Professor of Ophthalmology, Nijmegen University, 1973-; Chairman, Institute of Ophthalmology, Nijmegen, The Netherlands, 1975-. *Memberships:* Secretary General, International Council and Federation of Ophthalmological Societies; Member of Dutch, French, German, Swiss Ophthalmological Societies; Jules Gonin Club; Hippocrates etc. *Publications:* "Hereditary Dystrophies of the Posterior Pole of the Eye" 1971; "New Developments in Ophthalmology" 1976; "Neurogenetics and Neuroophthalmology" 1978. *Honours:* Graig Lecturer (Belfast) 1978; Turine Lecture (Los Angeles) 1978; Elliot Lecture (Vancouver) 1984; Reiner Science Prize (Wuppertal) 1980; Franceschetti Lecture 1986 etc. *Hobbies:* Rotary club; Sport; Music. *Address:* Adrianaweg 14, 6523 MV - Nijmegen, The Netherlands.

DEUTSCH-KEMPNY, Erwin, b. 12 Apr. 1917, Klagenfurt, Austria. Head, First Department of Medicine. m. Alma Sitte, 18 Apr. 1958. *Education:* MD, University of Vienna, 1940. *Appointments:* Assistant: Internal Medicine, University of Vienna, 1940-41; Internal Department, KH Neunkirchen/Saar, 1941-45; Hospital, City of Neustadt, Pfalz, 1945; Hospital Frankenholz, Saar Knappschaft, 1945. Assistant Professor, 1945, Associate Professor, 1963, Professor, Head of Department, 1964-, Internal Medicine, University of Vienna. *Memberships include:* New York (USA) and Austrian Academies of Science; International Society of Haematology; German Academy of Natural Science; Fachbeirat d Osterr. Bundesinstitutes f Gesundheitswesen, 1973-77, 1981-83; Fulbright Commission in Austria, 1973-83. *Publications:* "Hemkorper-Hamophilie", 1950; "Blutgerinnungsfaktoren", 1955; "Blutgerinnung u Operation", 1973; Editor, 'Thormbosis et Diathesis Haemorrhagica', 1957-79; 'Wiener klinische Wochenschrift', 1964-; 'Haemostasologie', 1981-. *Honours:* Theodor Körner Award, 1957; Award for Natural Sciences, City of Vienna 1968; Bergmann Medal Bundesärztekamer, Federal Republic of Germany, 1972; Golden Medal, Stadt Klagenfurt, 1974; GroBes Silbernes Ehrenzeichen für Verdienste um die Republik Osterreich und Goldenes Ehrenzeichen Für Verdienste um das Land Wien, 1982. *Hobbies:* Classical music. *Address:* 1st Department of Medicine, University of Vienna, Lazarettgasse 14, A-1090 Vienna, Austria.

DeVORE, Dale Paul, b. 13 Mar. 1943, Phillipsburg, New Jersey, USA. Director of Product Development, Medchem Products Inc., Massachusetts. m. Sandra B. Grebowiec, 27 Dec. 1965, Belvidere, New Jersey, 1 son, 1 daughter. *Education:* BS 1966, MS 1971, PhD 1972, Rutgers University. *Appointments include:* Research scientist 1972-74, Staff scientist 1974-76, Principal scientist 1976-79, Battelle Memorial Institute, Columbus, Ohio; Research specialist, 3M, Riker Laboratories 1979-85; Director, Product Development, Medchem, 1985-. *Memberships:* American Rheumatism Association; International Association for Dental Research; Midwest Connective Tissue Association; Academy of Ophthalmology. *Publications include:* Contribution to professional journals: 'Effects of D-penicillanine on Lymphocyte Modulation of Collagnase Production', 1979; 'Collagnase Inhibitors Retarding Invasion of a Human Tumor in Nude Mice', 1980; 'Inhibitors of Connective Tissue Degradation and their Patential as Antiarthritics', 1982 'Comparison of Anti-inflammatory Compounds', 1985. *Honours:* Alpha Zeta, 1966; 3M Circle of Technical Excellence, 1983. *Hobbies:* Antiquarian books; Antique Medical Devices; Tennis; Golf; Crosscountry Skiing. *Address:* Medchem Products Inc., 232 West Cummings Park, Woburn, MA 01801, USA.

DEVOS, Paul G M J M, b. 19 Apr. 1943, Elsene, Belgium. Director of Nuclear Medicine. m. Jacqueline Van Driessche, 29 July 1968, Ronse, 1 son, 1 daughter. *Education* MD; Specialist in Internal Medicine, Nuclear Medicine. *Appointments:* Director, Department of Nuclear Medicine, Bonheiden; Assistant Head, Department of Nuclear Medicine, School of Medicine, University of Louvaine. *Memberships:* Belgian Society of Nuclear Medicine; European Nuclear Medicine Society. *Address:* Minderbroederstraat 25, B-3000 Leuven, Belgium.

DE VOS-CLOETENS, Christine Andrée Mathilde, b. 4 Apr. 1947, Brussels, Belgium. Head of Immunophar-macology. m. Louis De Vos, 17 Dec. 1969, Brussels, 1 son, 1 daughter. *Education:* Secondary School Teacher Diploma, distinction 1968, Doctor in Zoology, high distinction 1968, PhD Zoology, highest distinc-tion 1972, Free University of Brussels. *Appointments:* Fellowship 1968-73, Post-Doctoral Fellowship 1973-77, Fonds National de la Recherche Scientifique; Fellowship, European Molecular Biology Organisa-tion, 1969-71; Post-Doctoral Fellowship, IRSIA, 1977-79; Head of Immunopharmacology Department, UCB Pharmaceutical Section, 1979-. *Memberships:* Belgium Immunological Society; Société Française d'Immunologie; International Society of Immunopharmacology; Société Belge d'Allergologie et d'Immunologie Clinique; Société Belge de Biologie Cellulaire; European Academy of Allergology and Clinical Immunology. *Publications:* 'Pharmacology of a new orally active antiallergic: pyrido (1, 2, -a)

pyrimidine, UCB L140 (Chinoin 1045) in rats' (various authors), 1982; 'A simple and rapid method for the detection of Il2 presence in a physiological medium' (with W Libert), 1984. *Hobbies:* Downhill skiing; Water skiing; Cinema; Music;Reading. *Address:* 109 Dreve du Duc, B-1170 Brussels, Belgium.

DeVOSS, B Scot, b. 15 June 1952, Washington State, USA. Chiropractor, *Education:* DC; Diplomate, National Board of Chiropractic Examiners. *Appoint-ments:* United States Air Force, Medical; Material Management, Electronics; Doctor of Chiropractic. *Memberships:* American Chiropractic Association; California Chiropractic Association; Santa Clara County Chiropractic Association. *Honour:* National Dean's List, 1981-82. *Hobbies:* Back packing; Fishing; Boating; Skiing. *Address:* 451 Castro Street, Moun-tain View, CA 94041, USA.

DEWAN, Mantosh, b. 22 July 1951, Bombay, India. Associate Professor of Psychiatry; Director, Undergraduate Education, State University of New York Upstate Medical Center; Acting Chief of Psychiatry, VAMC, Syracuse, New York. m. Anita, 21 June 1975, Bombay, 1 son, 1 daughter. *Education:* MB BS, Bombay University, 1973; Internship, T N Medical College, Bombay University, 1974-75; Internship-Residency, State University of New York Upstate Medical Center, Syracuse, 1975-79. *Appointments:* Assistant Professor, Psychiatry, SUNY Upstate Medical Center, 1975-85; Staff Psychiatrist, VA Medical Center, Syracuse, 1975-85; Assistant Director, Undergraduate Education, SUNY Upstate Medical Center, 1982-85. *Memberships:* American Psychiatric Association; American Association of Psychiatrists from India. *Publications:* Contributor to professional journals; Presentations of Papers to professional associations. *Hobbies:* Cricket; Hockey; Football (European). *Address:* Department of Psychiatry, 650 E. Adams Street, Syracuse, NY 13210, USA.

DEWHURST, David John, b. 8 Jan. 1919, Australia. Managing Director, Bioengineering Systems Pty. Ltd. m. Hilda Marjorie Wilmot, Caulfield, 2 sons, 1 daugh-ter. *Education:* BA Honours, 1940, BSc, 1948, MSc, 1952, PhD, 1958, University of Melbourne; FIE Aust; MIBME (Aust). *Appointments:* Lieutenant, Australian Imperial Force, 1940-46; Lecturer, 1949-52, Senior Lecturer, 1953-59, Physiology, Reader, Biophysics, 1959-71, University of Melbourne; Reader, Biomedi-cal Engineering, Electrical Engineering, University of Melbourne, 1972-84. *Memberships:* Australian Physiological Society; Biomedical Engineering Soci-ety, USA, Charter Member; Biological Engineering Society, UK; Honorary Life Member, Past President, International Federation for Medical & Biological Engineering; Life Member, Past President, Institute of Biomed Engineering, Australia; Fellow, Institution of Engineers, Australia. *Publications:* "An Introduction to Biomedical Instrumentation", 1966, 2nd edition 1976; 30 papers on Physiological and Bioengineering topics, 1948-84. *Honour:* IEEE Centenary Medal, 1984. *Hobbies:* Bushwalking; Oil Painting; Carpentry. *Address:* 37 Culwell Avenue, Mitcham, Victoria 3132, Australia.

DEWHURST, William George, b. 21 Nov. 1926, Fros-terley, England, Professor, Chairman, Psychiatry; Co-Director, Neurochemical Research Unit. m. Mar-garet Dransfield, 17 Sep. 1960, Sussex, England, 1 son, 1 daughter. *Education:* BA, 1947, BM, B.Ch., 1950, MA, 1962, Oxford University; MRCP, 1955; Academic DPM, Distinction, 1961; FRCP (C), 1978; FAC.Psych., 1980; FAPA, 1980; FRCPsych, 1982. *Appointments:* House Physician, Surgeon, London Hospital, 1950-52; Captain, Royal Army medical Corps, 1952-54; JUNIOR Registrar/Registrar, London Hospital, 1954-56; Registrar, Senior Registrar, Mauds-ley Hospital, 1957-62; Lecturer, 1962-64, Senior Lec-turer, 1965-69, Institute of Psychiatry, London; Associate Professor, 1969-72, Professor, 1972-, Pro-fessor & Chairman, 1975-, Co-Director, Neurochemical Research, 1979-,Psychiatry, University of Alberta, Canada. *Memberships include:* Alberta College of Physicians and Surgeons; Alberta Medical Association; American Association for the Advancement of Science; American Association of Chairmen of Departments of Psychiatry; Association for Academic Psychiatry; British Medical Association; Canadian Medical Association; Canadian Psychiatric Association; New York Academy of Sciences; World Psychiatric Association; etc. *Publications:* Co-Editor, "Pharmacotherapy of Affective Disorders", 1985; Co-Editor, "Neurobiology of Trace Amines", 1984; Author, over 80 scientific publications in professional journals, 1958-. *Honours:* Recipient, numerous honours and awards including: Open Scholarship, King's College, Taunton, England, 1942; Open Exhibition, Natural Science, University College, Oxford, 1944; Senior County Scholarship, Somerset County, 1944; Elected, Foundation Member, Royal College of Psychiatrists, London, 1971; Elected Founding Vice President, Canadian College of Neuropsychopharmacology, 1980; President, Canadian College of Neuropsycho Pharmacology, 1982-84; President, Canadian Psychiatric Association, 1983-84. *Hobbies:* Music; Hockey; Football; Chess; Athletics. *Address:* Dept. of Psychiatry, 1-122 Clinical Sciences Building, University of Alberta, Edmonton, Alberta, Canada T6G 2G3.

DEXTER, James Riley, b. 22 Feb. 1948, Loma Linda, California, USA. Chief of Hospital Pulmonary Section. m. Kathryn Louise Hutchinson, 18 Dec. 1972, 1 son, 1 daughter. *Education:* BA, Modern Languages, 1971; MD, 1974. *Appointments include:* Assistant Chief, Pulmonary Section, 1980-82, Medical Director, Pulmonary Function Laboratory, 1980-82, Medical Director, Respiratory Care, 1980-, Jerry L Pettis Memorial Veterans Hospital, Loma Linda, California;Program Chairman, Medical Chest Conference, Loma Linda University, 1980-82; Medical Director, Sleep Laboratory, Jerry L Pettis Memorial Veterans Hospital, Loma Linda, 1981-83, Acting chief Pulmonary Section, 1982-83; ICU Committee, Redlands Community Hospital, 1982-83; California Thoracic Society, Respiratory Care Assembly Steering Committee, 1982-; Co-medical Director, School of Respiratory Care, Victor Valley College, 1982-; Medical Director, California Society of Respiratory Care, Southern Californa Chapter 1982-83; Medical Director, Pulmonary Rehabilitation, Jerry L Pettis Memorial Veterans Hospital, Loma Linda, Californa, 1983-. *Memberships:* American College of Chest Physicians, American College of Physicians; American Medical Association; American Medical Writers Association; American Thoracic Society; California Medical Association; California Thoracic Society; Critical Care Society; Inland Society of Internal Medicine; San Bernardino County Medical Society. *Publications:* Author and co-author of numerous articles in medical journals and chapters in edited medical books. *Honours:* American Thoracic Society Fellowship Award, 1978-79 and 1979-80. *Hobbies:* Snow skiing; Water skiing; Sailing; Horsemanship. *Address:* Loma Linda VA Hospital (111P), 11201 Benton Street, Loma Linda, CA 92357, USA.

DEXTER, Wayne Robbins, b. 4 Dec. 1944, American Fork, Utah USA. Psychologist; Health Care Administrator. m. Donna Lee Johnson, 20 Apr, 1964, 2 sons, 2 daughters. *Education:* BS, Brigham Young University, 1967; MS, 1968; PhD, University Otago, New Zealand, 1973. *Appointments include:* Instructor, Research Assistant, Brigham Young University, 1967-68; Instructor, Psychology, University of Alaska, 1969-70; Research Fellow, University Otago, New Zealand, 1971-73; Assistant Professor, Psychology, University of Alaska, 1973-74; Conultant, National Spinal Cord Injury Data Research Center, 1975-80; Psychologist, Southwest Regional System Spinal Cord Injury Treatment, 1974-80; Psychologist, Good Samaritan Hospital, 1974-81; Director, Department

Psychology, Institute Rehabilitation Medicine, Good Samaritan Medical Center, 1981-83; Vice-Chairman, Institute of Behavioral Medicine, Good Samaritan Medical Center, Phoenix, 1983-; Adjunct Associate Professor, Rehabilitation, University Arizona, 1982-. *Memberships Include:* American Psychology Association; American Congress of Rehabilitation Medicine; American Society Clinical Hypnosis; Psi Chi. *Publications:* Contributor of articles to journals in psychology and medicine. *Honours:* Road Safety Research Award, New Zealand Ministry of Transport; Grantes, National Council Licensed Trade, Wellington, New Zealand, *Hobbies:* Skiing; Climbing; Photography. *Address:* 4856 E. Cheryl Drive, Paradise Valley, AZ 85253, USA.

DHAWAN, Indar Kumar, b. 22 June, Simla, India. Professor of Surgery. m. Sushila, 10 Dec. 1961, Kanpur, 1 daughter. *Education:* MBBS; MS. *Appointments:* Assistant Professor, 1961-70, Associate Professor, 1970-79, AIIMS; Professor, Surgery, All India Institute of Medical Sciences, 1979- , Head, Department of Surgery, 1982-. *Memberships:* Association of Surgeons of India; Association of Plastic Surgeons of India, Ex-President; Indian Society of Oncology, Ex-President. *Honours:* Fellow, Academy of Medical Sciences. *Hobbies:* Photography; Travel. *Address:* Department of Surgery, All India Institute of Medical Sciences, New Delhi 110029, India.

DIAMOND, Jared M, b. 10 Sept. 1937, Boston, Massachusetts, USA. Professor of Physiology. m. Marie Cohen. *Education:* BA, Biochemical Sciences, Harvard, 1958; PhD, Physiology, Cambridge University, England, 1961. *Appointments:* Junior Fellow, Society of Fellows, Harvard University; Associate in Biophysics, Harvard Medical School; Associate Professor, currently Professor of Physiology, University of California Medical School, Los Angeles, California; Research Associate, Department of Ornithology, American Museum of Natural History. *Publications:* Co-Author of contributions to: 'Journal of General Physiology', 1967; 'American Journal of Physiology', 1983. Co-Author: "Community Ecology", 1985. *Honours:* Bure Award, National Geographic Society, 1979; Bowditch Lecturer, American Physiological Society, 1976; Distinguished Achievement Award, American Gastroenterological Association, 1975. *Address:* Department of Physiology, University of California Medical School, Los Angeles, CA 90024, USA.

DIAMAND, Salim, b. 17 Apr. 1914, Bolechow, Poland. Physician. m. Hildegard Lucht, 18 Oct. 1972, Toronto, Canada, 1 daughter. *Education:* MD Surgery, Naples, Italy, 1939-40; LMCC Canada, 1952; Specialist in Paediatrics, Italy. *Appointments:* Senior Medical Officer, UNRRA & IRO (Italy), 1947-50; Medical Officer, of Health, City of Naples, Italy; Senior Member, College of Family Medicine of Canada. *Memberships:* Academy of Medicine of Toronto; Medical Society; Staff Member (courtesy), Toronto General Hospital; Staff Member, Doctor's Hospital, Toronto; New York Academy of Sciences; Life Member, Canadian Tuberculosis Association. *Honour:* Life Member, College of Family Physicians of Canada, 1984. *Hobbies:* Writing; Reading; Debating; Travel. *Address:* 206 Rosemary Road, Toronto, Ontario, M5P 3E1, Canada.

DIANZANI, Mario Umberto, b. 13 June 1925, Grosseto, Italy. Professor of General Pathology. m. Nor Maria Assunta, 18 Aug. 1956, Genoa, Italy, 1 son, 3 daughters. *Education:* MB BS, 1948, Degree in Pharmacy, 1950, University of Siena; Honorary Doctorate, Brunel University, Uxbridge, England. *Appointments:* Assistant in General Pathology, University of Siena 1948-50, University of Genoa 1950-58; Professor of General Pathology, University of Cagliari, 1958-64, University of Siena 1964-65, University of Turin 1965-; Dean Faculty of Medicine, University of Turin, 1971-84, Rector Magnificus,

1984-. *Memberships:* Ordine di Medici, Turin. *Publications:* "Trattato di Patologia Generale", 1st edition 1970, 5th edition 1985. *Honours:* Feltrinelli Award, Academia dei Lincei, 1979. *Hobbies:* Archaeology; Numismatics. *Address:* Corso d'Azeglio 118, 10126 Turin, Italy.

DIAZ-INFANTE, Augosto Jr, b.10 Apr. 1942, San Luis Potosi, Mexico. Chief, Obstetrics & Gynaecology, Faculty of Medicine, Universidad Autonoma De S.L.P. m. Rosa Maria Villarreal, 20 Jan. 1966, San Luis Potosi, 3 daughters. *Education:* MD, Facultad de Medicina, University Autonoma De S.L.P., 1966; Speciality Biology of Reproduccion, Instituto Nacional de la Nutricion, Mexico City, 1967-68; Speciality Obstetrics & Gynaecology, Universidad Nacional Autonoma de Mexico, 1969-72;Fellow, University of Pennsylvania School of Medicine, USA 1972-73. *Appointments:* Professor, Obstetrics & Gynaecology, Faculty of Medicine, Universidad Autonoma De San Luis Potosi, 1973-; Private Practice. *Memberships* American College of Obstetricians and Gynaecologists; American Fertility Society; Academia De Investigacion en Biologia de la Reproducion; Sociedad Mexiacan de Nutricion y Endoecrinologia; Sociedad Potosina de Ginecologia Obstetricia; Soceidad Mexicana Para Estudio Fertilidad y Reproduccion. *Publications;* Author, numerous articles to professional journals including 'Journal Clinical Endocrinology', 1969;'Prostaglandins';'Fertility and Sterility'; 'Ginec. Obstet. Mexico'; etc. *Hobbies:* Tennis; Jogging. *Address:* Scop §300, San Luis Potosi, S.L.P, 78270 Mexico.

DIAZ-OLIVEROS, Jesus , b. 16 Sep. 1937, Guadalajara, Mexico. Consultant Pneumologist. m. Cecilia Vallarino Lavista, 19 June 1965, Mexico City, 2 sons, 4 daughters. *Education:* MD, Universidad Autonoma De Guadalajara, 1962. *Appointments:* Trainee, Hospital Sanatorio Regional Del Pacifico, 1958; Trainee. Hospitasl Infantil De La Luz, Guadalajara, 1958; Resident, Pneumology Unit, Hospital General De La Secretaria De Salubridad y Asistencia, Mexico, 1962-64; Head, Residents, Pneumology, Hospital General De La SSA; External Physician, 1965-67, Assistant Physician, 1967-75, Head, Experimental Surgery, 1967-71, Hospital General De La SSA; Mexico; Consultant, Instituto Nacional De Las Enfermedades De La Nutricion, 1965-; Associate Professor, Universidad Nacional Autonoma De Mexico, 1964-75; Associate Professor, Respiratory Disease Clinic, Escuela Superior De Medicina, Instituto Politecnico Nacional, 1969-81; various other positions related to the Pharmaceutical Industry, including Advisor-Consultant to Undersecretary of Educational Planning in issues related to the field of medicine, 1984-. *Publications:* Author numerous articles in professional journals including "Bronquitis Plastica Recidivante", 'Revista Medica Del Hospital General De Mexico', 1973; "Pharmacological Basses in Anti-Inflammatory Therapy"','Ciudad Obregon', Sonora, 1978. *Memberships:* Sociedad Mexicana De Neumologia y Cirugia De Torax; Sociedad Medica Del Hospital General De La SSA, Secretary, 1970-71; Asociacion De Medicos Del Instituto Nacional De Las Enfermedades De La Nutricion; American College of Chest Physicians; Sociedad Medica Del Hospital Mocel; National Council of Respiratory Diseases; etc. *Honour:* Distinguished Visitor of the City of Jalapa, Veracruz, Mexico, 1971. *Hobbies:* Tennis; Chess; Swimming; Classical Music. *Address:* Puente Metlac 158, C/o Puente Colorado, Mexico 20, D.F., Mexico.

DIBIA, Godwin Okechukwu, b. 3 May 1947, Lagos, Nigeria. Consultant-chest Physician. m. Matilda O Wenene, 19 Apr. 1975, Kampala, Uganda, 1 son, 4 daughters. *Education:* MB ChB. Makerere University, Uganda, 1976; General Hospital, Aba, Nigeria; DTCD, University of Wales, 1981; Fellow,

American College of chest Physicians, 1982. *Appointments:* Medical Officer, Department of Medicine, 1977-78, Head, Chest Unite, 1978-80, General Hospital, Aba, Nigeria; Consultant Physician, Nigerian Christian Hospital, Aba, 1981-83; Consultant chest physician and head, Ugonna Hospitals Limited and Chest Unit, Aba, 1983-. *Memberships:* Nigerian Medical Association; British Thoracic Society; American College of Chest Physicians; International Academy of Chest Physicians and Surgeons. *Publications.* "Pattern of Valvular Damage in Rheumatic Heart Disease", 1976; "Population Dynamics and Problems Faced", 1976. *Hobbies:* Reading; Tennis; Chess; Travelling. *Address:* Ugonna Hospitals Limited and Chest Unit, Box 3307, Aba, Nigeria.

DICK, Robert, b. 7 Nov. 1937, Sydney, New South Wales, Australia. Chairman of Radiology. m. Dr Ann Diana Fairclough, 22 July 1967, Sussex, England, 1 son, 3 daughters. *Education:* MB BS, Sydney University, Australia; Fellow, Royal Australian College of Radiologists, Royal College of Radiologists, UK; Foundation Courses, Open University, England, 1979. *Appointments:* Currently: Chairman of Radiology,Royal Free Hospital and School of Medicine, London, England. *Memberships:* British Institute of Radiologists Royal College of Radiologists; Royal Australian College of Radiology; British Medical Association. *Publications:* Book. "Imaging in Hepato-Biliary Disease", Blackwells Co-author, 1986; 'Interventional Radiology of the Portal System' in Annals of Radiologie', 1982. *Hobbies:* Opera; Cinema; Punting; Tennis. *Address: Milton Lodge, 5 Milton Close, Hampstead Garden Suburb, London N2, England.*

DICKERMAN, Joesph David, b. 9 Mar. 1938, New York, New York, USA. Professor of Pediatrics and Director of Pediatric Hematology and Oncology. m. Jennifer Sichel, 30 June 1962, Princeton, New Jersey, 2 sons, 1 daughter. *Education:* BA, Johns Hopkins University; MD, Cornell University Medical College. *Appointments:* Intern - Assistant Resident - Senior Resident, Childrens Medical Center, Universityy of Texas, Southwestern Medical School; Lieutanmant Commander, United States Naval Reserve, United States Naval Hospital, Newport, Rhode Island; Research Fellow in Pediatrics Hematology, Johns Hopkins University School of Medicine; Assistant Professor - Associate Professor - Professor of Pediatrics, University of Vermont School of Medicine. *Memberships:* American Society of Hematology; American Society of Clinical Oncology; Society for Pediatric Research; American Pediatric Society; New England Pediatric Society; New England Cancer Society; Sigma XI; American Medical Association; American Academy of Pediatrics; American Society of Pediatric Hematology/Oncology; American Board of Pediatrics; American Board of Pediatrics-Sub Board of Pediatric Hematology and Oncology. *Address:* University of Vermont School of Medicine, Department of Pediatrics, Given Medical Building, Burlington, VT 05401, USA.

DICKENSON, Thomas Coston, b. 13 Mar. 1927, USA. Physician. m. 3 sons, 2 daughters. *Education:* MD, Emory University Medical School; Intern, Crady Memorial Hospital; Resident in Medicine, Atlanta Veterans Administration Hospital; Cardiac Fellowship, Logue Fellowship, American Heart Association of Emory University. *Appointments:* Florida Hospital South, Orlando, Florida; Florida Hospital North, Altamonte Springs; Winter Park Memorial Hospital, Winter Park. *Memberships:* Fellow: American College of Chest Physicians; Council of Clinical Cardiology, American Heart Association; American College of Angiology. Past Governor, State of Florida, Chairman of Board of Trustees, 1978, Fellow, American College of Cardiology; American and Florida Medical

Associations; Orange County Medical Society. Board of Directors and Past President, Central Florida Heart Association; Past Board of Directors, Florida Heart Association; Phi Sigma; AOA Honor Medical Society; Diplomate, American Board of Internal Medicine. *Honour:* Certified, Subspeciality Boards of Cardiovascular Diseases, 1967. *Hobbies:* Golf; Tennis; Sailing. *Address:* 500 East Colonial Drive, Orlando, FL 32803, USA.

DICKSON MABON, Jesse, b. 1 Nov. 1925, Glasgow, Scotland. Visiting Physician, The Manor House Hospital. m. Elizabeth Sarah Zinn, 6 Jan. 1970, House of Commons, London, 1 son. *Education:* MB ChB; DHMSA; MFH; FIP: Fellow, Royal Society of Apothecaries; Diploma in the History of Medicine, Society of Apothecaries of London. *Honours:* Member of Her Majety's Privy Council; Silver Jubilee Honours List, 1977. *Address:* 2 Sandringham, Largs, Ayrshire, KA30 8BT, Scotland.

DIEZ, Jose, b. 11 Apr. 1950, Mexico City, Mexico. Chiropractor. m. Ana Maria De Diez, 13 June 1981, Mexico City, 2 daughters. *Education:* Doctor of Chiropratic; Certificate of Proficiency in X Ray; Diplomate of National Board of Chiropractic Examiners. *Appointments:* General Director, Diez International Chiropractic Center; Instructor in Pierce Stillwagon Chiropractor System. *Memberships:* Charter Member, We Care Chiropractic Clinics Association; International Chiropractors Association; Scientific Society of Chiropractic in Mexico; Representative of Palmer College of Chirocpractric as a Regional Director in Latin America. *Publication:* Contributor to major newspaper in Mexico City *Hobbies:* Swimming; Bowling; Tennis; *Address:* Indiana § 188 Col. Napoles, CP 03810, Mexico DF, Mexico.

DIGGORY, Harold James Peter, b. 8 Sep. 1932, England. Director, Caribbean Epidemiology Centre. m. Mona D. Jaggassar, 18 Aug. 1961, London, 1 son. *Education:* MB; ChB; DPH; DTM&H. *Appointments:* Casualty Officer, Royal Southern Hospital, Liverpool, 1957; House Officer, Liverpool Royal Children's Hospital, 1957-58; Medical Officer, Public Health, Trinidad and Tobago, 1958-61; County Medical Officer of Health, Nariva, Mayaro, Trinidad, 1962-63; Medical Officer of Health, City of Port of Spain, 1963-66; PAHO/WHO Country Representative, Barbados and the Western Caribbean, 1966-71; PAHO/WHO County Representative, Jamaica and the North Caribbean, 1971-75; Chief of Surveillance, 1975-83, Director, 1983-, Caribbean Epidemiology Centre, Port of Spain, Trinidad. *Memberships:* Fellow; Royal Society of Health, Royal Institute of Public Health and Hygiene, Royal Society of Tropical Medicine and Hygiene; International Epidemiology Association; Trindad and Tobago Medical Association. *Publications:* "Fatal Parathion Poisoning caused by Contamination of Flour", in 'International Commerce American Journal of Epidemiology', 1977; "The Caribbean Epidemiology Centre", 'Bulletin of PAHO', 1979. *Honours:* Meritorious Award, 1977, Service Award, 1981 and 1986 PAHO/WHO . *Hobbies:* Fishing; Automobile Engineering. *Address:* Caribbean Epidemiology Centre, PO Box 164, Federation Park, Port of Spain, Trinidad, West Indies.

DIJKMAN, Joop H, b. 11 Jan. 1933, Doetinchem, Netherlands. Head of Department of Pulmonology, University Hospital, Leiden, Netherlands. *Education:* University of Nijmegen Medical School, 1951-58; Department of Medicine, University Hospital, Nimegen, 1961-65, Registered Internist, 1965; Department of Pulmonology, University Hospital, Groningen, 1965-67; Brompton Hospital, London, England, 1967-68, Registered Pulmonologist, 1968. *Appointments:* Pulmonologist, University Hospital, Nijmegen, 1968; Associate Professor of Medicine, Nijmegen, 1972; Professor of Medicine, Leiden, 1976-. *Memberships:* Association of Dutch Chest

Physicians (President 1984-); Thoracic Surgery Association; American College of Chest Physicians; European Society of Pulmanologists; European Society on Pulmonology & Clinical Respiration; Algemene Ziektekundige Vereniging (NL). *Publications:* 'Allergic bronchial reactions to inhalation of enzymes of Bacillus subtilis' (American Review of Respiratory Diseases) 107, 1973; 'Epidemiology of alpha-l-antitrypsin deficiency in the Netherlands' (Human Genetics 53, 1980); 'Enzymes & Enzyme-inhibitors in the small airways' (European Journal of Respiratory diseases 63, 1982); Transbronchial lung biopsy by the thoracoscopic route in patients with diffuse interstitial pulmonary disease' (Chest 82, 1982). *Address:* Department of Pulmonology, University Hospital. Rijnsburgerweg 10, 2333 AA Leiden, Netherlands.

DI LEO, Francesco Biagio, b. 3 Feb. 1940, Lecce, Italy. Association President. *Education:* BA, Zoology; MD; Board Certified in Psychiatry and Neurology. *Appointments:* Staff Physician, Research Associate, Maryland Psychiatric Research Center, Baltimore, Maryland, USA, 1972-75; Medical Director, Narcotic Clinic, Friends Medical Science Research Center, 1973-75; currently, President, American Association of Physicians for the Advancement of Psychedelic Medicne. *Memberships:* American Psychiatric Society; Maryland Psychiatric Society; International Transpersonal Psychology Association. *Publications:* Articles contributed to: 'Journal of Altered States of Consciousness', 1975; 'Journal of Psychoactive Drugs', 1981; 'Journal of Religion and Psychical Research', 1984. *Honour:* Phi Beta Kappa, 1963. *Hobbies:* Photography; Music. *Address:* Menmosyne Institute, Professional Arts Building, 101 West Read Street, Suite 703, Baltimore, MD 21201, USA.

DILLING-OSTROWSKA, Ewa Wladyslawa, b. 11 Apr. 1934, Lvov, Poland. Neurologist. m. Lucjan Ostrowski, 9 Apr. 1958, Sopot, Poland, 1 son, 1 daughter. *Education:* Diploma of Physician, 1957, MD 1965, Habilitation 1974, Medical Academy in Gdansk; Specialisation in General Neurology, 1960, Child Neurology, 1964. *Appointments:* Assistant, 1957, Senior Assistant 1964, Assistant Professor 1970, Associate Professor 1977, Head of Department, 1977, Department of Development Neurology, Medical Academy in Gdansk. *Memberships:* Polish Neurological Society; Polish Medical Society; Polish Scientific Academy; Commission of Developmental Neurology; Commission of Speech Disorders; European Federation of Child Neurology Societies; International Child Neurology Association. *Publications:* Chapters in "Speech Disorders of Childhood", 1982; Chapters in "Child Neurology", 1985; More than 50 articles in medical journals on neurological problems in children. *Honours:* Founder Member of International Academy for Research in Learning Disabilities, Ann Arbor, USA, 1979. *Hobbies:* Classical Music, especially Opera; Playing the Piano. *Address:* 81-831 Sopot, ul. Swierczewskiego 16/2, Poland.

DIMARCO, Jack Peter, b. 24 Dec 1953, New York, USA, Medical Director, Our Lady of Lourdes Rehabilitation Centre, Camden, New Jersey, USA. *Education:* BS, St John's University, NY, 1975; MD, Washington University School of Medicine, St Louis, Mo, 1979. *Appointments:* Internship, the Bryn Mawr Hospital, Bryn Mawr, Pa, 1979-80; Residency, The Hospital of the University of Pennsylvania, Physical Medicine and Rehabilitation, 1980-83. *Memberships:* AMA; American Academy of Physical Medicine and Rehabilitation; American Congress of Physical Medicine and Rehabilitation. *Hobbies:* Playing piano; Ice skating. *Address:* Lourdes Rehabilitation Centre, 1600 Haddon Avenue, Camden, NJ 08103, USA.

DING, Guang-sheng, b. 23 July 1921, Beijing, China. Professor of Pharmacology; Editor-in-Chief. m. Chuan-qing Zhou, 3 Dec. 1951, Shanghai, 2 sons, 1 daughter. *Education:* MD, College of Medicine, 1944, MSc, Department of Biochemistry, 1947, Central University; PhD, Department of Pharmacology, University of Chicago, Illinois, USA, 1950. *Appointments:* Assistant Resident (Captain), Department of Medicine, Military Hospital, Chengdu, 1944-45; Assistant , Department of Biochemistry, Central University, 1945-47; Assistant Resident, Anesthesiology, 1947-48, Resident, 1948-49, Postdoctoral Fellow, 1949-51, Department of Surgery, University of Chicago, Illinois, USA; Associate Professor, Pharmacology, 1951-64, Professor, 1964-, Pharmacology, Institute of Materia Medica, Chinese Academy of Sciences; Editor in Chief, Acta Pharmacologica Sinica, 1980-, New Drugs and Clinical Remidies, 1982-, President Shanghai Association of Scientific Journal Editors, 1985. *Memberships:* American Society of Anesthesiologists; International Anesthesia Research society; Chinese Society of Physiological Sciences; Chinese Medical Association; Chinese Pharmaceutical Society; Gesellschaft fur Arzneipflanzenforschung. *Publications:* 'Development of Clinical pharmacology in the Peoples Republic of China' in 'International Journal of Clinical Pharmacology Ther Toxicol'', 1985; 'Chinese medicinal materials for cardiovascualr diseases' in "Advances in Chinese Medicinal Materials Research", 1985, 'European Journal of Pharmacology'; 'La Riforma Media'; 'Journal of Biomedical and Environmental Sciences'. *Honours:* Elected: Society of Sigma Xi, Chicago, Illinois, USA, 1949; New York Academy of Sciences, 1981. *Address:* Institute of Materia Medica, 319 Yue-yang Road, Shanghai 200031, China.

DINTENFASS, Leopold, b. 29 Apr. 1921, Tarnow, Poland. Clinical Haemorheologist, Director, Department of Heamorheology, Sydney, Australia. m. Irene Kurzer, 26 Sept. 1954, Sydney. *Education:* MSc 1958, PhD 1962, University of Mew South Wales, Australia; FRACI; MACPSM; FICA. *Appointments:* Senior Research Fellow, Department of Medicine, University of Sydney, 1961-76; Director, Haemorheology & Biorheology Department, Sydney Hospital, 1976-84, Rachel Forster Hospital , Sydney, 1984-86; Commonwealth Visiting Professor, University of Strathclyde, Scotland, 1970-71; Senior Research Fellow, Department of Medicine, Glasgow Royal Infirmary, Scotland, 1970-71; Honorary Associate, Department of Medicine. Hebrew University, Jerusalem, 1974; Director, Advanced Studies Institutes, NATO, 1982-83; Principal Investigator, NASA Space Program, 1977-86. Led First experiment in Biorhsology on the space shuttle 'Discovery' Flight STS SI-C, 1985. *Memberships:* New York Academy of Sciences; Royal Society of Medicine (aff) Royal **Australian** Chemical Institute; Cardiac Society of Australia & New Zealand; British Society of Rheology; International Society of Biorheology. *Monographs:* "Blood Microrheology, Viscosity Factors on Blood Flow, Ischaemia & Thrombosis", 1971; "Rheology of Blood in Diagnostic & Preventive Medicine" 1976; "Hyperviscosity in Hypertension", 1981; "Blood Viscosity in Heart Disease and Cancer", (editor) 1981, "Heart Perfusion, Energetics and Ischemia", 1983.. " Blood Viscosity, Hyperviscosity & Hyperviscosaemia", 1985; some 240 papers (author or co-author). *Honors:* Honorary Associate, Department of Medicine, University of Sydney. 1977-; Honorary Member, Australian Society of Rheology, 1985. *Hobbies:* Reading; Travel. *Address:* Department of Medicine, University of Sydney, NSW 2006. Australia.

DIRENZO, Alfred Michael, b. 3 Nov. 1934, Passaic, New Jersey, USA. General Surgeon. 3 sons, 1 daughter. *Education:* BS, University of Maryland, 1956; DO, Kirksville College of Osteopathic Medicine, 1960. *Appointments:* Attending General Surgeon, Beth Israel Hospital, Passaic; Passaic General Hospital, Kennedy Memorial Hospital, Saddle Brook, New Jersey. *Memberships:* Royal Society of Health; American Academy of Sports Medicine; Former Councilman, City of Lodi, New Jersey; Lodi Kwanis Club. *Hobbies:* Boating; Hunting; Fishing. *Address:* 167 Grove Street, Lodi NJ 07644, USA.

DIPLOCK, Anthony Tytherleigh, b. 24 July 1935, London, England. University Professor. m. Lynn Christine Richards, 1 Apr. 1980. Chichester, Sussex. *Education:* BSc Physiology and Chemistry, University of Bristol, 1954-56; PhD Biochemistry, Guy's Hospital Medical School, University of London, 1962-66; DSC, London, 1976. *Appointments:* Research Biochemist - Head of Biochemical Research, Vitamins Limited, Tadworth, Surrey, 1956-67; Reader in Biochemistry, Royal Free Hospital Medical School, University of London, 1967-77; Professor and Head, Department of Biochemistry, Guy's Hospital Medical School, now United Medical and Dental Schools, Guy's Hospital, London, 1977 -. *Memberships:* Bichemical Society; Nutrition Society; Founder Member, Society of Free Radical Research; Senate, University of London, 1981-; Chairman, Standing Sub-Committee, Medicine, Acedemic Council, University of London, 1984-; Dean Faculty of Medicine. University of London, 1986-. *Publications:* Approximately 120 papers on fat-soluble vitamins, free radicals, selemium etc including: Editor, "Fat Soluble Vitamins", 1985. *Hobbies:* Sailing; Gardenig; Renovating old houses. *Address:* Division of Biochemistry, The United Medical and Dental Schools, Guy's Hospital, London SE1 9BT, England.

DISAIA, Philip J, b. 14 Aug 1937, Providence, Rhode Island. Professor of Obstetrics and Gynaecology. *Education:* Brown University, Providence, Rhode Island, (Cum Laude) 1959; MD (Cum Laude) Tufts University School of Medicine, Boston, 1963 Intership 1963-64, Residency 1964-67 Yale University School of Medicine, New Haven Hospital; Senior Fellow of the National Institutes of Health, University of Texas, Anderson Hospital and Tumor Institute at Houston. *Appointments:* UC Irvine Membership Gynecologic Oncology Group, Chairman, Immunology Committee Principal Investigator, 1977-,Professor and Chairman of Obstetrics and Gynecology 1977-, Professor of Radiology, Division of Radiation Therapy, 1978-, Director, Cancer Center, 1979-, Director, Residency Program in Obstetrics and Gynecology, 1977, Director, Postresidency Fellowship Program in Gynecologic Oncology, Department of Obstetrics and Gynecology 1977-, University of California, Irvine, California College of Medicine. *Memberships Include:* Fellow American College of Surgeons; American Society of Clinical Oncologists; Western Association and Society of Gynecologic Oncologists; Society of Pelvic Surgeons; American Radium Society; California Medical Association; American Medical Association; Americam College, South Atlantic and American Associates of Obstetricians and Gynecologists; American Society of Obstetrics and Gynecology Pacific Coast Obstetrics and Gynecology Society; Society of Gynecologic Investigation. *Honours Include:* 1st Prize Annual Clinical Training Research Project Competition 1970, First Distinguished Alumnus Award, MD Anderson Hospital and Tumor Institute, University of Texas, Houston; 1st Prize,President's Award,American College of Obstetrics and Gynecology; Lauds and Laurels Professional Achievement Award, UCI Alumni Association, 1983; Hubert Houssels Award for outstanding contributions to educational program of Center for Health Education, Memorial Hospital Medical Center, Long Beach. 1983. *Publications:* Numerous contributions to medical journals in the field of Obstetrics and Gynecology. *Address:* Department of

Obstetrics and Gynecology, University of California Irvine Medical Center, 101 City Drive South, Orange, CA 92668, USA.

DISHOTSKY, Norman I, b. 12 May 1940, New York City, USA. Professor of Psychiatry/Director, Laboratory for study of Violence and Criminal Behavior. m. Genevieve Nancy Wright, 21 July 1967, San Francisco, California, 2 sons, 1 daughter. *Education:* Queens College, City University of New York, BS, 1962; MD, State University of New York, Syracuse, 1966; Interm (Rotating) Herrick Memorial Hospital, Berkley, California and Children's Hospital, Oakland, California, 1966-67; Resident in Psychiatry, Mendocino State Hospital, 1968-70; Resident in Psychiatry,Stanford University, 1971-72. *Appointments:* Clinical Teaching Assistant in Psychiatry, Stanford University School of Medicine, 1972-73; Clinical Instructor in Psychiatry, 1973-76, Clinical Assistant Professor of Psychiatry, 1976-82, Stanford University School of Medicine; Director. Laboratory for the study of Violence and Criminal Behavior, Palo Alto Veterans Administration Medical Center, 1979-, Clinical Associate Professor of Psychiatry and Behavioral Sciences, Stanford University School of Medicine, 1982-, Fellow, Stanford Center for the Study of Youth Development Stanford University 1984-. *Memberships:* Fellow American Psychiatric Association 1985-; American Association for the Advancement of Science; American Academy of Political and Social Science; American Academy of Psychiatry and the laws; American Criminal Justice Research Association; Forensic Mental Health Association of California; Federation of American Scientists; Union of Concerned Scientists; Physicians for Social Responsibility; American Association of College Professors for Peace in the middle East; Co-Founder, Palo Alto Writers Workshop. *Publications:* Extensive contributor to medical and other Scientific journals. *Hobbies:* Travel; Literature and the Arts; Athletics; Nature. *Address:* 828 Bryant Street, Palo Alto, CA 94301, USA.

DITTRICH, Adolf, b. 11 Aug. 1941, Rumburg, Germany. Clinical Psychologist; Researcher. m. Jane Plattner, 13 Aug. 1971 (divorced). *Education:* Diploma. University of Cologne, 1965;, 66; Dr. rer. nat. 1972; Privatdozent, University of Zurich, 1983. *Appointments:* Psychologist, Psychiatric Clinic, Burgholzli, Zurich, 1967-68; Resident Psychologist, 1970-; Resident Psychologist, F. Hoffmann-La Roche, Basle, 1968-70; Lecturer, University of Zurich, 1972-; Member, Scientific Committee Schweizerische Gesselschaft fur Forschung auf Wissenschaftlichen Grenzgebieten, 1980-. *Publications:* Author: "Astiologieunabhangige Strukturen veranderter Wachbewusstseins-zustande"; main author and project Manager, "International study of Altered States of consciousness"; Contributor of articles to professional journals. *Memberships:* Schweizerischer Verband des Personals Offentlicher Diensts; Chase Manhattan Bank grantee, Geneva, 1975; Schweizerischer Nat. fonds zur Forderung des wissenchaftlichen forschung grantee, 1979; Member, Deutsche Geselschaft fur Psychologie; Schweizerische Gesallschaft fur Psychologie und ihre Anwendungen; World Pasvchiatric Association.*Address:* Im Ahorn 14, Zollikerberg, Zurich CH8125, Switzerland.

DIXIT, Hemang, b. 11 June 1937, Kathmandu, Nepal. Reader in Child Health. m. Asha Upadhaya, 7 July 1962, Kathmandu, 2 sons, 2 daughters. *Education:* MBBS, University of London, England; LRCP; London; MRCS, England; DTM&H, England; DCH, England. *Appointments:* House Officer, Charing Cross Hospital, London, 1961-62; Paediatrician, Bir and Kanti Hospital, Kathmandu, Nepal, 1965-75; Reader in Child Health 1978 and 1983-85; Professor in Child Health 1986; Dean 1979-82, Institute of Medicine, Kathmandu. *Memberships:* Life Member: Nepal Medical Association; Nepal Paediatric Society; Nepal Pharmaceutical Association; Nepal Leprosy Relief Association. *Publications:* "Medicine in Nepal", 1974; "Medical Bibliography of Nepal", 1978 and 1982. *Hobbies:* Writing medical articles in lay press; Writing books of health related subjects; Writing novels. *Address:* GA 1-636 Dillibazar, Kathmandu 2, Post Box 2730, Nepal.

DIXON, Adrian Kendal, b. 5 Feb. 1948, Cambridge, England. University Lecturer in Radiology. m. Anne Lucas, 16 June 1979, London, 1 son, 1 daughter. *Education:* MA, Kings College, Cambridge; MB BCh, St Bartholomew's Hospital Medical College, London; Member of the Royal College of Physicians; DMRD; Fellow; Royal College of Radiologists. *Appointments:* House Officer posts, London and Nottingham; Registrar, Senior Registrar, Radiology, St Bartholomew's Hospital, London; EMI Scanning Research Fellow, St Bartholomew's Hospital Medical School, London; Currently University Lecturer, Department of Radiology, University of Cambridge, Cambridge. *Memberships:* British Insitute of Radiology; British Medical Association; Royal College of Radiologists; Royal College of Physicians. *Publications:* "Roads to Radiology", (co-author), 1982; "Body CT", 1983; Papers mainly on Computed tomography. *Hobbies:* Golf; Tennis. *Address:* University Department of Radiology, Addenbrooke's Hospital, Hills Road, Cambridge, CB2 2QQ, England.

DIXON, David, b. 20 May 1927, London, England. Consultant Orthodontist. m. Joyce Lilian Dixon, 6 Oct. 1956, 1 son, 3 daughters. *Education:* MDS, Edingburgh, 1956; FDSRCS Eng.; DDO, Glasgow. *Appointments:* Lecturer, Orthodontics, Edingburgh University, 1956-62; Chairman, BDA Hospital Group, Scotland, 1962; Council Member, British Society of Study of Orthodontics, 1963-66; President, Northern Counties Branch, BDA, 1973; Clinical Postgraduate Tutor, University of Newcastle, 1968-72; Consultant Orthodontist, General Hospital, Sunderland; Visiting Consultant, Orthodontics, PEI Canada, 1975; Visiting Professor, Dental Health, Adelaide, Australia, 1973; Visiting Lecturer, Indian University, 1976. *Memberships:* British Dental Association; British Society for Study of Orthodontics; British Association of Orthodontics; Royal Society of Medicine; Pacific Coast Society of Orthodontics, USA. *Publications:* "Abonormalities of the Teeth and Supporting Structure", in 'The Cause and Natural History of Cleft Palates', 1966; over 200 papers. *Honours:* First Chapman Research Prize, British Society for Study of Orthodontics, 1963. *Hobbies:* Stereophotography; Fishing; Travel. *Address:* Orthodontic Department, General Hospital, Sunderland, England.

DIXON, Kendal Cartwright, b. 16 Feb. 1911, Dublin, Eire. Fellow, King's College, Cambridge; Emeritus Professor. m. Annette Sybil Darley, 20 Dec. 1938, Co. Dublin, 1 son, 1 daughter. *Education:* BA, 1933, MA, PhD, 1937, MB.BChir, 1939, MD, 1956, Cambridge University; FRCpath. *Appointments:* Fellow, King's College, Cambridge, 1937-; Medical Officer, RMAC, 1940-45; Official Fellow, King's College, 1945-73; University Lecturer, Chemical Pathology, Cambridge, 1949-62; Director of Studies in Medicine, King's College, 1959-73; Reader. Cytopathology, Cambridge University, 1962-73; Visiting Professor, Pathology, Columbia University, New York, 1978; Professor, Cellular Pathology, Cambridge University, 1973-78; Professor Emeritus, Cellular Pathology, Cambridge University. *Memberships:* Founder, Fellow, Royal College of Pathologists. *Publications:* "Cellular Defects in disease", 1982; Book Chapters, articles in medical journals etc. *Address:* King's College, Cambridge CB3 0DX, England.

DJAJIC, Dragoljub, b. 28 Aug. 1925, Titovo Uzice,

Yugoslavia. Professor of Periodontology and Oral Diseases. m. Dr Ljubica, 31 Oct. 1953, Belgrade. *Education:* Graduated from Faculaty of Stomatology, Belgrade 1953; Assitant Professor, 1956; Docent 1961, Associate Professor 1967; Professor 1972. *Appointments:* Director, Clinic for Oral Diseases and Periodontology, Faculty of Stomatology, University of Belgrade. *Memberships:* Serbian Medical Association; Society of Stomatologists of Yugoslavia; Society for Oral and Dental Diseases and Periodontology of Yugoslavia. *Publications:* Co-author of the following textbooks and books: "Bolesti usta" (Oral Diseases) 1966 and six subsequent editions; "Parodontopatije" (Peridontal Disease) 1980; "Oboljenja mekih tkiva usne duplje" (Diseses of soft oral tissues) 1981; "Bolseti usta" (Oral Diseases 1985; "Lekarski priručnik" (Doctor's Handbook) 1981. 102 scientific and profesional papers in Yugoslavian and other magazines. *Honours:* Annual Award of Serbian Medical Association, 1983; Charter of Serbian Medical Association, 1985; Labour Order with Golden Wreath, 1983; October's Award of Belgrade for Research Work, 1981. *Address:* ulica Prote Mateje 69, 11000 Beograd, Yugoslavia.

DJORDJEVIC, Milan, b. 14 Aug. 1933, Smed. Palanka, Yugoslavia. Professor, Surgery; Cardiovascular Surgeon; Director, National Pacemaker Centre; Board Director, Institute of Surgery. m. Maria Jovanovic, 24 Nov. 1961, 1 son, 1 daughter. *Education:* MD, University of Belgrade, 1961; Board Licence General Surgeon, 1974; Cardiovascular Surgeon, 1974; Dr.Sci., 1975. *Appointments:* Practiced General Medicine, Foca, Bosnia, 1960-64; Specialization of General Surgery, 1964-69; Secretary, Surgery, Belgrade Medical Faculty; Head, Research, Cardiovascular Surgery, 1971-73, Assistant Professor, Surgery, 1969-77, University of Belgrade; Associate Professor, Surgery, 1977-82; Director, National Pacemaker Centre, 1981; Professor, Surgery, 1982; Board Director, Institute of Surgery, 1985. *Memberships:* Yugoslav Society of Surgery; Yugoslav Society of Cardiology; President, Yugoslav Working Group on Cardiac Pacing; American Society for Artificial Internal Organs; Michael DeBakey International Cardiovascular Society; Nucleous Europena Working Group on Cardiac Pacing; Duropena Cardiovascular Surgical Society. *Publications:* "Heart block and Pacemakers", 1971; Editor in Chief, "Proceeding Book - 1st Yugoslav Symposium on Cardiac Pacing", 1979; 150 articles in professional journals. *Honours:* October Award for the best published book, "Heart Block and Parcemakers", 1981. *Hobbies:* Tennis; Photography. *Address:* Cardiovascular Clinic, Pacemaker Centre, Medical Faculty, Belgrade, Yugoslavia.

DJUKANOVIC, Dragoslav, b. 9 Dec. 1935, Belgrade, Yugoslavia. Professor. m. Mara, 4 Mar. 1962, Belgrade, 2 daughters. *Education:* Diploma 1960, MS 1968, DDS 1974, Faculty of Stomatology, University of Belgrade. *Appointments:* Assistant to Professor 1963, Docent 1972, Associate Professor 1977, Full Professor of Periodontology and Oral Diseases 1980-, Vice-Dean 1978-80 and 1981-82, Faculty for Stomatology, University of Belgrade. *Memberships:* Society of Oral and Dental Disease and Periodontology of Yugoslavia; Member of Presidency, Chairman of Stomatological Section, Chairman of Section for Oral and Dental Diseases, Serbian Medical Association; Consultant in Scientific Program Committee, Member of Commission for Oral Research and Epidemiology, Federation Dentaire Internationale. *Publications:* "Atlas of Oral Diseases", 1979; "Parodontopatije", (periodontal Diseases), textbook, 1980; Contributor, "Medical Lexicon", 1981; "Bolesti Usta", (Oral Diseases), textbook, 1985; "Bolesti Usta" (Oral Diseases For Nurses), 1985 Contributor, "Mala Prosvetina Enciklopedija", 1986; 108 scientific and professional papers. *Honours:* Annual Award 1978,

Charter 1982, Serbian Medical Association; Labour Order with Golden Wreath, 1983. *Hobby:* Stamp Collecting. *Address:* ulica Dr Subotica 4, Faculty for Stomatology, Universtiy of Belgrade, Fah 506, 11000 Belgrade, Yugoslavia.

DJURIC, Dušan S, b.24 Apr. 1920, Kragujevac, Yugoslavia. Professor of Internal Medicine, Belgrade, Yugoslavia. m. 8. Feb. 1947, 2 sons, 1 daughter. *Education:* MD, 1950; Doctor of Medical Sciences, 1973 *Appointments:* Assistant Professor, 1954, Associate Professor, 1959, Professor of Internal Medicine School of Medicine, University of Belgrade, 1969-, Head of Clinic for Endocrinology, Diabetes & Metabolism, School of Medicine, Belgrade. *Membershipos:* European Thyroid Association; Serbian Medical Society; Yugoslavia Endocrine Association; L'Union Médicale Balkanique; International Endocrine Association. *Publications:* "Endocrinology", 1967; "Textbook of Internal Medicine", 4th edition 1985; (chapter on Endocrinology); "Clinical Physiology" (chapter on Endocrinology), 1982; "Diabetes Mellitus", 1980; "Functional Investigations of the Endocrine System", 1982; "Basic Clinical Neuroendocrinology", 1985 (all in serbo-croate); also 120 articles in the international journals. *Honours:* President, Yugoslav Endocrine Association, 1962; President most domestic & International meetings; Honorary Member, L'Union Medicale Balkanique. *Hobbies:* History; Chess. *Address:* Clinic for Endocrinology, Diabetes & Metabolism, School of Medicine, U1 Dr Subotic 13, Belgrade, Yugoslavia.

DOBBING, John, b. 14 Aug. 1922, Sheffield, England. Emeritus Professor of Child Growth and Development. *Education:* BSc 1st class honours, University of London, 1950; MB, BS, St Mary's Hospital, University of London, 1953; DSc, University of Manchester, 1982; Fellow, Royal College of Pathologists; Fellow, Royal College of Physicians. *Appointments:* House Physician, St Mary's Hospital, London; Obstetric House Surgeon, Perivale Maternity Hospital, London; Lecturer in Pathology and Gull Student, Guy's Hospital, London; Senior Lecturer in Physiology, The London Hospital, London; Senior Lecturer in Growth and Development and Honorary Consultant, Hospital for Sick Children and Institute of Child Health, London; Senior Lecturer in Child Health and Honorary Consultant, Manchester University and United Manchester Hospitals; Professor of Child Growth and Development, University of Manchester. *Memberships:* British Medical Association; Neonatal Society; British Paediatric Association; Nutrition Society; Manchester Medical Society. *Publications include:* "Applied Neurochemistry", 1968; "Scientific Foundations of Paediatrics", 1974, 2nd edition 1981; "Maternal Nutrition in Pregnancy", 1981; "Prevention of Spina Bifida", 1983; "Scientific Studies in Mental Retardation", 1984; "Maternal Nutrition and Lactational Infertility", 1985; "Early Human Development" (editor-in-chief); Over 150 articles in the scientific literature. *Hobbies:* France and the French; Travel; Editing. *Address:* Higher Cliff Farm, via Birch Vale, via Stockport, Cheshire SK12 5DL, England.

DOBRESCU, Dumitru, b. 12 Mar. 1927, Bucharest, Romania. University Professor. m. Vasilica Niculescu, 1 Mar. 1950, Bucharest, 1 son, 2 daughters. *Education:* MD; BSc., Pharmacy; Pharmacologist; Homoeopathic physician. *Appointments:* Assistant Pharmacology, Assistant Professor, Medical Faculty, Bucharest; Professor, Chief, Pharmacodynamics, Bucharest; Dean, Pharmacy, Bucharest; President, Commission of Medicament of Romania; Clinical Pharmacologist; Homoepathic Physician; Expert, WHO. *Memberships:* Vice President; Union of Medical Sciences Society of Romania, Society of Pharmacy of Romania. *Publications:* "Pharmacology", 1965;

"Practicum of Pharmacodynamics", 1967, "Phymacodynamics", 1970; "General Pharmacodynamics", 1972; 2nd edition 1977; "Interactions of Medicaments", 1977; "Pharmacotherapy", 1981. *Honours:* Emeritus Professor, 1980; Award, medicine, Academy of Romania, 1981. *Hobbies:* Music; Literature. *Address:* Strada Dr. Felix No.59, Bloc A1, Apartment 5, 78136 Bucharest, Romania.

DOBROW, Matthew Isle, b. 1 Mar. 1948, New York City, USA. Professor, Medicine; Honorary Consultant, Pediatrics. m. Grace Reynolds, 24 Oct. 1972, Maryland, 2 sons. *Education:* AB, Havard University, 1968; MD, 1972, PhD, 1974, Johns Hopkins University. *Appointments:* Intern, Resident, Pediatrics, Penn State, Hershey, 1974-76; Chief Resident, Pediatrics, Dartmouth Hitchcock Medical Center, 1976-77; Assistant Professor, Child Health, Dartmouth Medical School, 1977-79; Assistant Professor, Clinical, 1979-80, Associate Professor, Clinical, 1980-81, University of Roch School of Medicine; Professor, Medicine, Ross University School of Medicine, Portsmouth, Dominica, 1982-. *Memberships:* American Society of Clinical Hypnosis; International Society of Clinical Hypnosis; American Academy of Pediatrics; Society for Research in Child Development; Society for Behavioral Pediatrics. *Publications:* "Ziai -Bedside Pediatrics", "Ziai - Assess of the Newborn", Contributor to both books ; Editor, "Text of Pediatrics". *Hobbies:* Sailing; Gardening . *Address:* PO Box 235, Roseau, Comm. of Dominica. West Indies.

DOBRYSZYCKA, Wanda Maria, b. 26 Feb. 1921, Dabrowa, Gornicza, Poland. Pharmaceutical Biochemist. m. R Dobryszycki, 20 Apr. 1945, Poznań, Poland, 2 sons. *Education:* Master of Pharmacy, 1952, PhD 1960, Habilitation, 1965. *Appointments:* Assistant, Department of Organic Chemistry, Medical Academy, Poznań, 1952; Assistant, 1953-60, Adjunct, 1960-65, Department of Biochemistry, Medical Academy, Wroclaw; Scientific Stay, Laboratory of Biochemistry, University of Paris, France, 1962, Hektoen Institute for Medical Research, Chicago, USA, 1967-68; Vice-Director, Director, Bio-pharmaceutical Institute, 1969-81, Associate Professor, 1972, Professor of Pharmaceutical Science, 1978; Head of Department of Clinical Investigation, Director, Department of Pharmaceutical Biochemistry, Faculty of Pharmacy, Medical Academy, Wroclaw, Poland. *Memberships:* President, Silesian Branch, Polish Society of Laboratory Diagnostics; Member of Board, Polish Biochemical Society and Polish Pharamceutical Society; Past National Representative, International Federaiton of Clinical Chemistry; Former Vice-President, Clinical Biology Section, International Pharmaceutical Federation. *Publications:* Over 150 publications in scientific & medical journals, book chapters. *Honours:* Order of Polonian Restituta, 1973; Order of Merit in Teaching, 1981; Scientific Awards of FEBS, Ministry of Health, Polish Academy of Sciences, Ministry of Higher Education,. Sciences & Technics. *Hobbies:* Collecting Ceramics, Porcelain, Sculpture; Stamps with an avian motive; Travel; Cooking. *Address:* Swierczewskiego 1/9, 50048 Wroclaw, Poland.

DOERING, Jeffrey Louis, b. 26 May 1949, Chicago, Illinois, USA, Assistant Professor of Biology, Loyola University of Chicago, m. Marilyn K Large, 8 June 1974, Oak Park, Illinois, 2 daughters. *Education:* PhD, 1975, BA, General and Special Honours, 1971, University of Chicago. *Appointments:* Predoctoral Student and Teaching Assistant, Microbiology and Development Biology, University of Chicago, 1971-75; Postdoctoral Fellow, Carnegie Institution of Washington, Department of Embryology, 1975-77; Assistant Professor, Departments of Biological Sciences and Biochemistry, Molecular and Cell Biology, Northwestern University, 1978-83.

Memberships: American Society for Cell Biology; Sigma Xi; New York Academy of Sciences. *Publications:* 'Identification and genomic organization of human Trnalys genes', 1982; 'DNA methylation patterns in the 5s DNAs of Xenopus laevis', 1983; 'Evolution of chick type I procollagen genes', 1985. *Honours:* Phi Beta Kappa, 1971; National Science Foundation Graduate Fellow, 1971-74; National Institutes of Health and Postdoctoral Fellowship, 1975-77. *Hobbies:* Cycling; Gardening; Choral singing. *Address:* Department of Biology, Loyola University of Chicago, 6525 North Sheridan Road, Chicago, IL 60626, USA.

DOHERTY, Ralph Leonard, b. 16 Dec. 1927,. Pro-Vice Chancellor, Health Sciences, University of Queensland, Australia. m. Margaret Frankie Bevan, 13 Feb. 1953, Brisbane, 4 sons, 5 daughters. *Education:* MB, BS, 1950, MD, 1973, University of Queensland; MPH, Harvard School of Public Health, 1955-57. *Appointments:* Resident Medical Officer, Brisbane Hospital, 1951; Medical Superintendent, Alpha Hospital, 1952; Queensland Institute of Medical Research, 1953-77, Director 1966-77; Professor, Social & Preventive Medicine, 1977-78, Dean, Medicine, 1978-82, University of Queensland. *Memberships:* Australian Medical Association; Royal Australasian College of Physicians; Royal College of Pathologists of Autralia; Royal Society of Tropical Medicine & Hygiene, former Local Secretary; Australian Society for Microbiology, former President. *Publications:* Scientific papers on infectious disease research in Australia. *Honours:* Various Awards, Undergraduate Medical Course; Bancroft Orator, Australian Medical Association, Queensland Branch, 1977; Cilento Medal, Commonwealth Dept. of Health, 1982. *Hobbies:* Reading; Music. *Address:* University of Queensland Medical School, Herston Road, Herston, Queensland 4006, Australia.

DOLLERY, Colin Terence, b. 14 Mar. 1931, Lincoln, England. Professor of Clinical Pharmacology, Consultant Physician. m. Diana Myra Stedman, 1958, 1 son, 1 daughter. *Education:* BSc, Birmingham, 1953; MB, ChB honours, 1956. *Appointments:* House Officer, Queen Elizabeth Hospital, Birmingham, Hammersmith and Brompton Hospitals, London, 1956-58; Medical Registrar 1958-60; Senior Registrar and Tutor in Medicine 1960-62; Hammersmith Hospital, London; Consultant Physician 1962-; Lecturer in Medicine 1962-65, Professor of Clinical Pharmacology 1965-, Royal Postgraduate Medical School, London; Member, Medical Research Council, 1982-84; Member, University Grants Commission, 1984-. *Memberships:* Fellow, Royal College of Physicians; Medical Research Society; Research Defence Society; Physiological Society; Cardiac Society; British Pharmacological Society; Association of Physicians of Great Britain and Ireland; Fellow, Royal Society of Medicine; Past President, European Society for Clincial Investigation; Honorary member, Association of American Physicians. *Publications include:* "The Retinal Circulation" (co-author), 1971; 'The role of prostacyclin' (co-author) in "Atherosclerosis – Mechanisms and Approaches to Therapy", 1984; 'Drug treatment of heart failure' (with L Corr), 1985. *Honour:* Chevalier dans l'Ordre National du Merite, 1976. *Hobbies:* Travel; Amateur radio; Work. *Address:* 101 Corringham Road, London NW11 7DL, England.

DONAHUE, Hayden Hackney, b.4 Dec. 1912, El Reno, Oklahoma, USA. Director, Oklahoma Institute for Mental Health Education & Training. m. Patrcia Toothaker, 22 Feb. 1948 Almo, 3 daughters. *Education:* BS, 1939, MD, 1941, University of Kansas. *Appointments Include:* Flight Surgeon, 1942-43, Group Surgeon, 1943-44, USAAF; Assistant to chief Psychiatrist, 12th Air Force Mediterranean Area, 1943-44; Director, Professional Services, AAF Neuropsychiatric Center, 1944-45; Assistant Chief,

Hospital Operations, US Veterans Administration, Washington DC, 1946; Executive Officer, US Veterans Hospital, North Little Rock, 1946-49; Director, Education & Research, Arkansas State Hospital, 1949-51; Consultant, Psychiatry, Arkansas Health Department, 1949-51; Associate Proffeor of Psychiatry, University of Arkansas, 1949-50-60; Assistant Medical Director, Texas State Board for Hospitals & Special Schools, 1951-52; Lecturer Legal Medicine, University of Texas, 1951-, Director, Mental Health, Oklahoma, 1952-59; Director, Projects, Arkansas State Hospital, 1959-61; Superintendent, Central State Friffin Memorial Hospital, Norman, 1961-79; Assistant Director, 1966-70, Director, 1970-78, Mental health, State of Oklahoma; Clinical Professor of Psychiatry, University of Oklahoma School of Medicine, 1967-, Director, Oklahoma Institute for Mental Health Education & Training, 1979-. *Memberships:* Fellow; American Association for Advancement of Sciences, American College of Psychiatrists (president 1978), American Psychiatric Association (Treasurer & Board of Trustees 1969-73) Sciences, American Geriatric Society, American College of Psychiatric Administrators; Board of Trustees, Pan American Training Exchange in Psychiatry, 1961-63, American Association of Medical Superintendents of Mental Hospitals (Presdient 1974-75); Treasurer, Benjamin Rush Society 1980-84. *Publications:* 31 Professoinal articles in fields of psychiatry, institutional medicine, personnel management, professional education,hospital administration, forensic psychiatry. *Honours Include:* Community Service Award, Oklahoma Medical Association, 1979-, Distinguished Service Award, American Psychiatric Association, 1984-. *Address:* 1109 Westbooke Terrace, Norman, OK 73069, USA.

DONALD, Alastair Geoffrey, b. 24 Nov. 1926, Scotland. General Practitioner. m. Edna Patricia Ireland, 3 Apr. 1951, Edinburgh, 2 sons, 1 daughter. *Education:* MA, Cambridge University; MB, ChB, Edinburgh University. *Appointments:* Chairman of Council, Royal College of General Practitioners; Chairman, Joint Committee on Postgraduate Training for General Practice. *Memberships:* Royal College of General Practitioners; Royal College of Physicians of Edinburgh. *Honour:* OBE, 1982. *Hobbies:* Golf; Reading 'The Times'. *Address:* 30 Cramond Road North, Edinburgh, Scotland.

DONOGHUE, Brigid Veronica Cristina, b. 22 June 1952, Galway, Ireland. Consultant Paediatric Radiologist. *Appointments:* Pre-Reg., Surgical, Regional Hospital, Galway, Ireland, 1976-77; Pre-Reg., Medical, Nenagh, Co Tipperary, 1977; S.H.O. Medical, Tralee, Co. Kerry, 1977-78; Registrar in Diagnostic Radiology, 1978-81, Senior Registrar in Diagnostic Radiology, Manchester Area Health Authority, 1982-83; Clinical Fellow, Paediatric Radiology, Division of Special Procedures, 1984, Clinical Fellow, Paediatric Radiology, General Division, Hospital for Sick Children, Tornoto, Canada, 1983-84. *Memberships:* European Society Paediatric Radiology; Imaging Group of British Paediatric Assn.; British Institute of Radiology; Irish Radiological society; Irish Paediatric Assn. *Publications:* 'Transient Portal Venous Gas in Necrotizing Enterocolitus', 1982; 'Intraspinal Epidermoid Cysts' 1984; CT Appearances of Sacroiliac Joint Trauma in Children', 1985; 'CT Features of Reactive Periostitis in the Humerus: a Lesion Resembling Myositis', 1985. *Hobbies:* Music; Reading. *Address:* Radiology Department, The Children's Hospital, Temple Street, Dublin 1, Ireland.

DONOHUE, Stephen Thomas, b. 11 Jan. 1925, Minneapolis, USA. Executive Director, Royal Society of Medicine Foundation; President, The Stephen T. Donohue Co. *Education:* BA, Journalism, University of Minnesota. *Appointments:* Director, Public Relations, American College of Physicians; Assistant Director, Communications, Director, Media Relations, American Medical Association. *Memberships:* Past Treasurer, American Medical Writers Association; National Association of Science Writers. *Honour:* Honour Award, New York State Society of Internal Medicine. *Address:* 405 East 56th Street, New York, NY 10022, USA.

DOOMS-GOOSSENS, Anne, b. 20 Oct. 1950. Oudenaarde, Belgium. Doctor in Biomedical Sciences, Contact Dermatitis Unit, University Hospital, Leuven. m. Marc Dooms, 19 May 1973, Jette, 3 sons. *Education:* Pharmacist, Katholieke Universiteit Leuven; Certificat d'etudes superieures de Cosmeto-pharmacie, Université de Nantas, France; Doctor in de Biomedische Wetenschappen, Katholieke Universiteit, Leuven, Belgium. *Memberships:* Belgian Ministry of Health, Pharmacopoeial Commission, Commission on Cosmetics; European Environmental Contact Dermatitis Research Group; Groupe d'etude et de recherche en dermato-allergologie; Belgian Tri-Contact Dermatitis Group; Corresponding Member of the Swedish Society for Dermatologists. *Publications:* "Allergic Contact Dermatitis to Ingredients used in topically appled Pharmaceutical Products and Cosmetics", PhD thesis, Katholieke Universiteit Leuven, 1983; "Computers and Contact Dermatitis", Chapter in "Contact Dermatitis", Editor A A Fischer, 1985. *Honour:* Award of Belgian Society of Dermatology, 1980. *Address:* Bondgenotenlaan 155, 3000 Leuven, Belgium.

DOONGAJI, Dinshaw Rustom, b.25 Feb 1932, Bombay, India. University Professor. m. Kerman Jehangir Davar, 29 Mar. 1964, Bombay, 2 daughters. 3*Education:* MB, BS, 1955, MD, 1959, DPM, 1961, University of Bombay; MS University of Minnesota, USA, 1969, MRCPsy., 1973, FRCPsy, 1976, Royal College, England. *Appointments:* Private Practice, Consultant Physician, 1961-. Honorary Assistant Psychiatrist, Honorary Assistant Professor, K.E.M. Hospital & G.S. Medical College, 1961-67; Honorary Associate Psychiatrist, Nanavati Hospital, Bombay, 1961-73; Honary Associate Psychiatrist, Honorary Associate Professor, 1971-74, Honorary Psychiatrist, Honorary Professor-in-Charge, K.E.M. Hospital & G.S. Medical College; Honorary Psychiatrist in Charge, Gujarat Research Society, Child Guidance Clinic, Bombay, 1963-73; Honorary Consultant Psychiatrist, Bhatia General Hospital, 1973-, Petit Parsee General Hospital 1973-83, Tata Memorial Cancer Hospital, 1978-, Consultant Psychiatrist, Atomic Energy Establishment, Central Government Health Scheme, 1977-, Head Psychological Medicine, 1981-, Associate Clinical Pharmacology, 1981-, K.E.M. Hospital & G.S. Medical College. *Memberships Include:* Fellow: National Academy of Medical Sciences, Royal Society of Medicine, London, Royal College of Psychiatrists; Honorary Fellow, American College of Physicians; Foundation Member, Royal College of Psychiatrists; Indian Academy of Medical Science, Many other professional organisations. *Publications:* More than 73 articles in professional jourals including: "Some Problems in th Conduct of Psychotropic Drug Trials – A Review", 'Journal of Postgraduate Medicine', 1982; "Elevated Cerebrospinal fluid noradrenaline in Tardive dykineasia", 'British Journal of Psychiatry', 1984. *Honours Include:* Recipient, Sandoz National Award in Psychiatry, 1968, Co-Recipient, 1975; Marfatia Award, Psychiatry, 1977; Merck Gold Medal, 1977, 1979; many other honours and awards. *Hobbies:* Photography; Painting; Music. *Address:* 33/B Empire Estate, Cumballa Hill, Bombay 400 036, India.

DOROBIALA, James Francis, b, 19 May 1941, Rochester, New York, USA, Chiropractor. m. Ngoc Lan M, 31 Aug, 1974, 2 sons, 2 daughters. *Education:* BA, University of Tampa, 1965; B.Fgn. Trade, 1968, M.Intl.Mgmt., 1973. American Graduate School of International Management; DC, Los Angeles College of Chiropractic, 1978; Licence Dr. Chiropractic, California, Florida, New Mexico; Additional Studies,

University of Maryland; Munich, Ger. Institute de Estudios Iberoamericanos, Saltillo. Mexico, 1969; American University Alumno Association, Bangkok, Thailand, 1971; California Community Colleges Teaching Credentials. *Appointments Include:* Assistant Superintendent, Kelliher Construction Company 1960-64; US Army, SSGT, BNTNGNCO, Munich Germany, 1965-68; Educational Counsellor, University of Maryland, Munich, Germany, 1966-68; High School Teacher, Monroe County School System 1968-70; Operations Manager, International Division, Chase Manhattan Bank 1970-74; Holistic Chiropractor/Director, North Valley Chiropractic Clinic Granada Hills, California 1979-; Ext. Faculty, Los Angeles College of Chiropractic, *Membership:* California Sacro-Occipital Research Society, President 1977-79; Director, Education & Research American Academy of Holistic Chiropractic, 1984-86; American, New York, Chiropractic Associations; many other professional organisations. *Honours:* John A. Fischer Memorial Scholarship, James Parker Scholarship, 1978. *Hobbies:* Metaphysics; Taoist Martial Arts; Meditation. *Address:* 17038 Chatsworth Street, Granada Hills, CA 91344, USA.

DOSHI, Sharat B. b. 3 Feb. 1946, Kenya, East Africa. Dental Director. m. Kumud Shah, 8 Dec. 1972, London, England, 1 son, 1 daughter. *Education:* BDS, University of London, England, 1969; LDSRCS, Royal College of Surgeons, England, 1969; DDPH, University of Toronto, Canada, 1980; currently studying for MSc, Memorial University of Newfoundland. *Appointments:* Private Dental Practice, London, England, 1969-75; Community Dental Officer, Barnet, London, 1976-77; Public Health Dentist, Department of Health, Newfoundland, Canada, 1977-82, Dental Director, 1983-present. *Memberships:* Newfoundland Dental Association; Canadian Dental Association; Canadian Society of Public Health Dentists; Federation Dentaire Internationale; British Dental Association; American Association of Dental Schools; International Association for Dental Research. *Honour:* WHP Fellow, 1985. *Hobbies:* Travel; Tennis; Badminton; Table Tennis. *Address:* 14 Prince Charles Place, St. Johns, Newfoundland, Canada A1A 2N9.

DOS REMEDIOS, Cristobal Guillermo, b. 19 Dec, 1940, Kobe, Japan. Associate Professor, Anatomy; Director, Institute of Molecular Biophysics, m. Patricia Anne Harrison, 29 May 1965, Sydney, Australia, 4 sons. *Education:* BSc 1965,PhD 1969, University of Sydney, *Appointments Include:* Lecturer, University of Sydney; Fellow, American Heart Association, USA; Assistant Professor, University of California, Berkeley, USA; Senior Lecturer, Anatomy, Univeristy of New South Wales, University of Sydney; Director, Muscle Research Unit, University of Sydney. *Memberships;* Australian Biochemical Society, Physiological & Pharmacological Society, Society for Biophysics; Anatomical Society of Australia; Scientists Against Nuclear Arms. *Publications Include:* Contributions to 'Proceedings, National Academy of Science, USA', 1972; 'Nature', 1978; 'Cell Calcium', 1981; Book, "Actin in Muscle Nonmuscle Cells", 1983; 'Biochemistry International', 1983; 'Biochemistry & Biophysics', 1984. *Honours:* Louis N, Katz Prize, Basic Research, 1971; Matsumae International Foundation Fellow, 1984. *Hobbies:* Sailing; Skiing; Tennis. *Address:* Muscle Research Unit, Department of Anatomy, University of Sydney, Sydney 2006, Australia.

DOSS, Larry Lee, b. 24 Oct. 1947, Searcy, Arkansas, USA. Acting Director, Radiation Oncology; Associate Professor of Radiology. m. Kara Veronique Remington, 20 Oct. 1984, North Little Rock, Arkansas, 1 son. *Education:* BS, Biology, State College of Arkansas, 1969, MD, University of Arkansas Medical School, 1973. *Appointments:* Assistant Scientist, Cancer Research Center, Columbia, Missouri, 1977-81; Associate Director, Radiotherapy, 1977-79, Associate

Director, Radiobiology and Clinical Research, 1980-81, Ellis Fischel State Cancer Hospital, Columbia; Assistant Professor, Radiology, University of New Mexico Cancer Center, Albuquerque, 1981-84; Associate Professor, Radiology, 1984-; Medical Director, School of Radiation Therapy, 1984-; Acting Director, Radiation Oncology, University of New Mexico Cancer Center, Albuquerque, New Mexico, 1984-. *Memberships:* Fellow, American College of Physicians; Albuquerque and Bernalillo County Medical Association; Arkansas Medical Society; American Medical Association; American College of Radiology; American Society of Clinical Hypnosis; American Society of Therapeutic Radiologists; Society for Clinical Trials, *Publictions:* Author of numerous articles, abstracts, presentations, etc, *Hobbies:* Guitar; Swimming. *Address:* University of New Mexico Cancer Center, Radiation Oncology Division, 900 Camino de Salud N,E,, Albuquerque, NM 87131, USA.

DOSS, Sherif Doss Adly, b. Dec. 1952, Cairo, Egypt. Consultant Physician. m. Dr Shahira Loza, 1 Feb, 1981, Maadi, Cairo, 1 son, 2 daughters. *Education:* MB BCh, 1976; MSc, Internal Medicine, 1981; MD Candidate. *Appointments:* House Officer, Cairo University Hospitals, 1977-78; Resident Physician Department of Internal Medicine, 1978-81, Cairo University; Clinical Assistant, Hillingdon Hospital, Uxbridge, London, England, 1981; Consultant Physician, As Salam International Hospital, Cairo, Egypt, 1982-; Nile Badrawi Hospital, 1985. *Memberships:* American and Egyptian Heart Associations; American College of Chest Physicians; American College of Physicians; American College of Cardiology; American and Egyptian Medical Association; Fellow International College of Tropical Medicine. *Publications:* MSc and MD theses, 1981, 83, *Honours:* Student of the Year, Victory College, Maadi Cairo, 1970; Student of the Year, Faculty of Medicine, Cairo University, 1974. *Hobbies:* Travelling; Reading. *Address:* PO Box 50 Maadi 11431 Cairo, Egypt.

DOSSETOR, Roberts Simon, b. 20 Oct. 1942, England. Consultant Radiologist. m. Helen Kalantidou, 19 Oct. 1969, London, 1 son, 1 daughter. *Education:* BM; BCh.; BA (Oxon); DMRD; FRCR. *Appointments:* Registrar, Radiology, Senior Registrar, Radiology, Radcliffe Infirmary, Oxford. *Membership:* British Scoiety of Neuroradiologists. *Publications:* "A Simple New Formula for Relating Changes in Renal Length to Changes in Renal Volume", 'British Journal Radiology', 1976; "Computerised tomography lymphangiography and ultrasound in the diagnosis of lymph node enlargement - A Comparison", 'Total Body Computerised Tomography', 1979; "Diagnosis of a small acoustic Neuroma by metrizamide Computer Assisted Tomography", 'British Journal Radiology' 1979; "Some Medical Aspects of Holography", 'Proceedings XV International Congress, Radiology', Brussels, 1981; "Angiography assisted by a new Videostore System", 'British Journal Radiology', 1981. *Hobbies:* Reading; Music; Sailing. *Address:* 8 Orpen Road, Hove, East Sussex, England.

DOTT, Wolfgang, b. 23 Apr. 1949, Koblenz, Federal Republic of Germany. Professor and Head, Department of Hygiene. m. Elke Caspari, 26 Mar. 1970, Neuwied, 3 daughters. *Education:* Diploma in Microbiology, 1975, PhD, 1977, University of Bonn; Habil in environment hygiene, 1982. *Appointments:* Microbiologist, Institute of Mikrobiobiology, Bonn, 1975; Assistant, Edgar Thofern Hygiene Institute, Bonn, 1977; Assistant Professor, Hygiene Institute, Bonn, 1983; Head, Department of Hygiene, Technical University, Berlin, 1985-. *Memberships:* Dt. Ges fuer Hygiene and Mikrobiolgoie; American Society for Microbiolgoy; Vereinigung fuer allgem und Angewandte Mikrobiologie. *Publications:* Author of some 50 papers on enzymology and regulation of sulfurmetabolism in wine yeasts, hygiene related to water, waste water and hospitals, microbiology and ecology in professional publications including: 'Zbl. Bakt. Hyg', 'Archives of Microbiology'. *Address:* Fachgebiet Hygiene, Fachbereich 21 Umwelttechnik, Technische Unviersität Berlin, Amrumer Str 32, D-1000 Berlin 65, Federal Republic of Germany.

DOUCET, Jean-Paul-Marie-Gustave, b, 4 Mar, 1919, Paris, France. Professor of Parasitology. m. (1) Martine Geismar, 3 Mar, 1948, Tananarive, Madagascar, (deceased), (2) Andree Labuzan, 20 Sept. 1956, Abidjan, Ivory Coast, (divorced), 2 daughters. *Education:* B Ph 1937, MD 1947, BSc 1957, DSc 1965, Professor 1965, Paris, France. *Appointments:* Staff 1948-, Director of Research 1962, Office de la Recherche Scientifique et Technique d'Outre-Mer; Chief, Laboratory Entomological Institute, Institute Recherche Scientifique, Madagascar, 1948-51; Chief, Laboratory Medical Parasitology, Institute Recherche Tropical Abidjan, 1951-65; Maitre Conference Agrege Faculte Medicine, 1966; Chief, Laboratory Centre Hospitalier Abidjan, 1966-82; Director, Laboratory Analytical Medical Institute Technology, Abidjan, 1969-77; Associated Professor 1966-74, Professor 1974-82, University of Abidjan, Ivory Coast; Professor, Univerity of Nice, France, 1982-. *Memberships:* Societe Francaise Pathologie Exotique; Societe Francaise Microbiologie; Societe Francaise Parasitologie; Societe Francaise Mycologie Medicale; Honorary Member Societe Belge Medecine Tropicale; International Society of Human and Animal Mycology; Royal Society of Tropical Medicine and Hygiene; American Association for the Advancement of Science. *Publications:* "Les Anopheles de Madagascar", 1950; "Les Serpents de la Republique de Cote d'Ivoire", 1963; "HEtude anatomique, histologique et histochimique des Pentastomes", 1965; Various articles. *Honours:* Croix de Guerre, 1945; Chevalier de la Legion d'Honneur, 1974; Chevalier, 1967; Officer, 1974, des Palmes Academiques. *Hobbies:* Lions Club; Mensa; Fellow, Explorer's Club; National Geographical Society; Planetary Society. *Address:* 3 Boulevard de Parc Imperial, 06000 Nice, France.

DOUGLAS, Charles Primrose, b. 17 Feb. 1921, Ayr, Scotland. Professor of Obstetrics and Gynaecology. m. Angela Francis, 10 Apr., 1948, Edinburgh, Scotland, 3 sons, 1 daughter. *Education:* MA, Cambridge, England; MB, ChB, Edinburgh, Scotland; FRCOG: FACS: Hon.FACOG. *Appointments:* William Waldorf Astor Fellowship to USA, 1956; Research Fellow, Duke University of North Carolina, USA, 1956; Senior Lecturer/Consultant, University of the West Indies, Jamaica, 1958-65; Professor Obstetrics and Gynaecology, Royal Free Hospital School of Medicine, University of London, England, 1965-76; Professor of Obstetrics and Gynaecology, Cambridge Clinical School, Cambridge, England-. *Memberships:* Royal Society of Medicine; British Medical Association; International Society for the Study of Vulva Disease; American College of Surgeons; Royal College of Obstetricians and Gynaecologists. *Publications:* Co-author "Disease of the Vulva", 1968; Editor, "Mental Retardation: Prenatal Assessment", 1972; 'Vulva Dystrophies' chapter in "Progress in Obstetrics and Gyaecology". *Honour:* Honorary Fellowship, American College of Obstetrics and Gynaecology, 1983. *Hobbies:* Painting; Equestrian events. *Address:* Rosie Maternity Hospital, Robinson Way, Cambridge CB2 2SW, England.

DOUGLAS, James Iain, b. 5 Dec. 1950, Workington, England. Private Practice as Dentist. m. Beryl Dianne Thomas, 9 Feb. 1983, Adelaide, Australia. *Education:* BDS, Adelaide. *Memberships:* Australian Dental Association; L D Pankey Institute, Miami, Florida, USA. *Hobbies:* Flying and building aircraft; Snow skiing; Sailing. *Address:* 53 Charles Street, Narrandera, 2700, Australia.

DOUGLASS, John Michael, b. 13 Apr., 1939, Takoma Park, Maryland, USA. Nutrition Consultant; Consultant in Engineering (Biomedicine for Domestic Industry); Coordinator, Health Improvement Service; Lecturer in Eating Style, Lifestyle and Health Improvement. m. Sue Nan Peters, 15 May 1962, 2 daughters. *Education:* BA, Zoology, Columbia Union College, Takoma Park, Maryland; MD, University of Southern California, Los Angeles, *Appointments include:* Home Care Physician; Emergency Room and Ambulance Physician; Medical Consultant, Trauma Research Group; Instructor in Engineering Medicine Training; Assistant Science Advisor, Injury Control Program; Medical Specialties Consultant; Internal Medicine Consultant; Instructor in Internal Medicine; Senior Medical Investigator; Lecturer in Kinematics; Internist, Kaiser-Permanente Medical Center, Los Angeles, 1970-; Nutrition Consultant for Specialty and Mass Market Food Conpanies, US Government, Universitites, Attorneys, etc. 1967-; Coordinator, Health Improvement Service, Kaiser-Permanente Medical Center, Los Angeles, 1980-; Lecturer in Eating Style, Lifestyle and Health Improvement, University of Southern California School of Public Administration, 1978-. *Memberships include:* Phi Delta Epsilon; Fellow, American College of Physicians; American Medical Association; California Medical Association; American Society of Internal Medicine; American Association for Automotive Medicine. *Publications:* Books and Booklets; Contributor to professioanl journals; Presentations. *Honours include:* Salemi Collegium Scholarship Awards, 1961-63; Bronze Medal, Teaching Exhibit, 1969; AMA Physician's Recognition Award, 1969-; Letter of the Month, Medical Tribune, July 1981. *Hobbies:* Oriental Rugs; Camping. *Address:* Kaiser-Permanente Medical Center, 1526 N. Edgemont, Los Angeles, CA 90027, USA.

DOWLING, Robert Hermon, b. 29 Sep. 1934, Belfast, Northern Ireland. Professor of Gastroenterology, Honorary Consultant Physician. m. Evelyn Graig, 11 Sep. 1964, Magilligan, County Londonderry, 2 sons, 1 daughter. *Education:* MB, B Ch, BAO 1959, MD 1968, Campbell College of Belfast, Queens University, Belfast. *Appointments:* Junior Hospital appointments, Queens University and Royal Victoria Hospital, Belfast, 1959-63; Research Fellow, Honorary Registrar and Senior Registrar 1964-66, Lecturer in Medicine and Honorary Consultant Physician 1968-73, Royal Postgraduate Medical School, Hammersmith Hospital, London, England; Medical Research Council Travelling Fellow, Junior Faculty Member, Boston University, Boston, Massachusetts, USA, 1966-68; Senior Lecturer and Consultant Physician 1974-76, Professor of Gastroenterology and Honorary Consultant Physician 1976-, Guy's Hospital and Medical School, London (now United Medical and Dental Schools of Guy's and St Thomas' Hospitals). *Memberships:* Fellow, Royal College of Physicians; British Society for Gastroenterology; American Gastroenterological Association; European Society for Clinical Investigation; British Association for Study of the Liver; American Association for Study of the Liver; European Association for Study of the Liver; Honorary member, Gastroenterology Societies of Australia, Belgium, Hungary and Switzerland. *Publications:* 'Small bowel adaptation and its regulation' in "Basic Science in Gastroenterology. Structure of the Gut", 1982; Contribution to 'Clinics in Gastroenterology', 1982; 'Hormones and polyamines in intestinal and pancreatic adaptation' (co-author) in 'International Workshop on Drugs, Hormones, Integrity and Structure of the Small Bowel and Pancreas', 1985. *Hobbies:* Squash; Skiing; Trout fishing; Modern languages. *Address:* Gastroenterology Unit, 18th Floor, Guy's Tower, Guy's Hospital, London SE1 9RT, England.

DOWSETT, John, b. 22 Nov. 1935, Melbourne, Australia. Director, Teaching & Research Resources, Westmead Hospital. m. Suzanne Wendy, 26 Apr. 1962, Sydney, 3 sons, 1 daughter. *Education:* MB, BS, University of Sydney; FRACGP; MHPEd., University of New South Wales. *Appointments:* RMO, Royal North Shore Hospital, 1959-63; Clinical Superintendent, 1964-65; General Practice, St Ives, 1966-74; Clincial Assistant, Paediatrics, Royal North Shore Hospital, 1966-78; Associate Physician, Hornsby and District Hospital, 1964-74; Clincial Lecturer, General Practice, Dept of Community Medicine, 1977-78; Honorary Secretary, NSW Faculty, FACGP, 1973-76; State Director (NSW) RACGP Family Medicine Programme, 1974-78; Member, Professional Services Advisory Council, Health Commission of NSW, 1979-81; APMA Medical Representatives Advisory Council, 1984-85. *Memberships:* Fellow, Royal Australian College of General Practitioners; Australian and New Zealand Association for Medical Education; Australian Sports Medicine Federation; Councillor, Australian Council on Hospital Standards. *Publications:* Editorial Advisor, "Family Health and Medical Library", 1981; "The Intern or Pre registration year", 'Research and Development in Higher Education', 1984. *Hobbies:* Watching Sport; Gardening; Cine Photography. *Address:* Westmead Hospital, The Parramatta Hospitals, Westmead, NSW 2145, Australia.

DOYLE, J. Stephen, b. 22 Dec. 1929, Dublin, Republic of Ireland. Professor. m. Catherine Harrington, 22 June 1963, Dublin, 1 son, 2 daughters. *Education:* MD. BcH., BAO, University College, Dublin, 1955; DCH; DPH; FACCP; FRCPI. *Appointments:* Tutor, Medicine, St Vincents Hospital; Fellow, Medicine, Lahey Clinic, Boston, USA; Senior Registrar, Medicine, St Laurence's Hospital, Dublin; Research Fellow, Medical College of Virginia, USA; Professor Chairman, Department of Medicine, RCSI & Gastoenterologist, St Laurence's Hospital, Dublin. *Memberships:* Royal Society of Medicine; Royal Academy of Medicine of Ireland; Association of Physicians of Great Britain & Ireland; American Gastroenterology Association; American College of Chest Physicians. *Publications:* Numerous papers and articles in professional journals. *Honours:* Honorary fellow, Amini Academy of Medical Sciences, Bahrain. *Hobbies:* Horse Riding; Gardening. *Address:* Professorial Unit, RCSI, St Laurence's Hospital, Dublin 7, Republic of Ireland.

DOYLE, Patrick John, b. 17 Nov 1926, Moosejaw, Saskatchewan, Canada, Professor and Head, m. Irene Strilchuk, 21 May 1949, Edmonton, Canada, 3 sons, 3 daughters. *Education:* MD; FRCS(C) Otolaryngology; Diplomate, American Board of Otolaryngology. *Appointments:* Assistant Professor, 1965-67, Associate Professor of Otolaryngology, 1967-70, University of Oregon Medical School, USA; Clinical Instructor, 1963-65, 1971-72, Associate Professor, Head, 1972-77, Professor, Head, Otolaryngology, University of British Columbia, Canada; Chairman, Department of Surgery, St Paul's Hospital, 1978-80. *Memberships:* Fellow, The Triological Society; American Academy of Otolaryngology, Head and Neck Surgery; Canadian Otolaryngological Society; Fellow, American Laryngological, Rhinological and Otological Society; Fellow, American Academy of Facial Plastic and Reconstructive Surgery. *Publications:* Author of numerous professional publications including 'Surgical Treatment of Abductor Laryngeal Paralysis', 1964; 'Approach to Tumours of the Nose, Nasoharynx and Paranasal Sinuses', 1968; 'Clinical Research in Head and Neck Cancer', 1976; 'Vocal Cord Paralysis', 1976; 'Surgery for Tumours of the Deep Lobe of the Parotid Gland', 1982. *Honours:* American Medical Association Physicians Award, 1971; Certificate of Appreciation, American Academy of O&O, 1975; Fellow, American Laryngological Society, 1976; American Academy of

O&O Award of Merit, 1977. *Hobby:* Golf. *Address:* 1081 Burrard Street, Vancouver, British Columbia, Canada V6Z 1Y6.

DOYLE, Robert Alan, b. 12 June 1935, Chicago, USA. Psychiatrist. m. 10 May 1969, Palm Beach, 2 sons, 1 daughter. *Education:* BS, Michigan State University; Yale University Medical School; MD, Duke University. *Appointments:* Chief of Staff, Coral Ridge Psychiatric Hospital, Fort Lauderdale; Consultant, The Priory, Roehampton, London, England; Staff Psychiatrist, Broward General Hospital, Fort Lauderdale; Staff Psychiatrist, Community Hospital, Monterey Peninsula, Carmel, California. *Memberships:* American Psychiatric Association; American Medical Association; Florida Medical Association; Broward County medical Association. *Hobbies:* Gardening; Collecting Chinese Export Armorial China. *Address:* PO Box 223231, Carmel, CA 93922, USA.

DRÄGAN, Ioan, b. 26 Feb. 1930, Bucharest, Romania. Professor. m. Georgeta Dragan Popescu, 31 Oct. 1954, 1 daughter. *Education:* MD, 1953; Certificate, Sports Doctor, 1954; Specialization, Sports Medicine, Munich, 1965; D.MSc., 1972; Professor, Sports Medicine, 1977. *Appointments:* Sports Doctor, 1953; Urologist Neurologist, 1954; Specialist, Sports Medicine, 1958; Director, Sports Medicine Centre, Bucharest, 1966-; Professor, Sprots Medicine, Bucharest, 1977-. *Memberships:* Romanian Olympic Committee; FINA medical Committee; FIMS. *Publications:* "Sports Medicine", Editor, 1983; "Nuclear Medicine", Chapter, 1982; "Ultrasounds in Medicine", Editor, 1983; more than 200 articles. *Honours:* FINA Silver Fin, 1982; Order Sports Meritus, Bucharest, 1981. *Hobbies:* Sports; Music. *Address:* Sports Medicine Centre, Boul. Muncii 37-39, District 2, Bucharest, Romania.

DRAGANESCU, Nicolae, b. 22 May 1927, Bucharest, Romania. Head of Department in Institute of Virology. *Education:* MD, PhD Medical Sciences, Faculty of Medicine, University of Bucharest. *Appointments:* Assistant in Faculty of Medicine; Chair of Virology; Scientific Researcher, Currently Senior Scientific Researcher, Stefan S Nicolau Institute of Virology, Bucharest. *Membership:* Union of Medical Science Societies. *Publications:* "Human Viral Encephalitides", 1962; "Herpes", 1967; "Arboviruses", 1970; 'Slow Viral Encephalitides and Encephalopaties', 1974; 'Laboratory Diagnosis of Arboviruses', 1976; "Handbook of Neurology", (co-author), volume 1 1979, volume 3 1981. *Honours:* Katherine Hadot Prize, Laureate of the Academy of Medicine Paris, 1963; Dr V Babesa Prize, Laureate of the Romanian Academy, 1970. *Hobbies:* Music; Poetry; Gardening. *Address:* Cosmonautilor 33, Bucharest, cod 70141, Romania.

DRAGO, Joseph Rosario, b. 28 Oct. 1947, New Jersey, USA. Director, Division of Urology, Ohio State University Hospitals. m. Diane Lavacca, 17 June 1972, New York, 3 daughters. *Education:* BS; MD. *Appointments:* Instructor of Urology, Pennsylvania State University College of Medicine, 1976-77; Assistant Professor of Urology, Director of Urologic Oncology, Pennsylvania State University College of Medicine, Hershey, 1979-80; Associate Professor of Surgery, Director of Urologic Oncology, Pennsylvania State University College of Medicine, Hershey, 1980-85; Professor of Surgery, Director of Urologic Oncology, Pennsylvania State University College of Medicine, Hershey, 1985; Director, Division of Urology, The Ohio State University Hospitals, Columbus - present position. *Memberships include:* ACS Liaison Fellow Commission on Cancer, 1983; ACS Program Committee, American Society of Andrology; American Urologic Association (Mid-Atlantic Section); Association for Academic Surgery; Association for Surgical Education. *Publications:* Contributions to professional journals, etc. *Honours Include:* Thomas Reeves Award, University of Illinois 1975; Academic Coordinator, Breast and Prostate Cancer Seminar,

1985; External Referee, Journal of Anticancer Research. *Hobbies:* Swimming; Racquetball; Music; Reading. *Address:* Division of Urology, The Ohio State University Hospitals, 456 Clinic Drive, Room 4829, Columbus, OH 43210, USA.

DRASKOCI, Miroslav, b. 25 May 1921, Senjski Rudnik, Yugoslavia. Professor. m. Slobodanka Grozdanović, 25 Jan. 1969, Belgrade, 1 son. *Education:* MD; DSc.; WHO Fellow, National Institute for Medical Research, London, England, 1958-59. *Appointments:* Assistant, Pathological Physiology, Belgrade Medical Faculty, 1949-53; Assistant, Pharmacology, University of Belgrade, 1953-61; Assistant Professor, Chairman, Pharmacology, 1961-73, Associate Professor, Chairman, Pharmacology, 1973-78, Professor, Chairman, Pharmacology, 1978-, University of Belgrade. *Memberships:* Scientific Society of SR Srbija; Yugoslav Pharmacological Society. *Publications:* Articles in professional journals including: 'Journal of Physiology'; 'Nature'; Yugoslav Physiological Pharmacology Acta'; 'Experientia'; 'British Journal Pharmacology'; etc. *Address:* Faculty of Pharmacy, University of Belgrade, dr Subotica 8, 11000 Belgrade, Yugoslavia.

DREW, Jessie Whitmarsh, b. 14 May 1947, Long Branch, New Jersey, USA. Research Assistant, University of Rochester and Full-time Student, University of Rochester. *Education:* BSN, Alfred University, 1970; MS, Rehabilitation Nursing, Boston University, 1973; Certification as Family Nurse Practitioner; University of Southern Maine, 1979; Doctoral Student, PhD, University of Rochester. *Appointments:* Staff Nurse, Massachusetts General Hospital, 1970; Staff Nurse, Quinar City Hospital, 1971; Staff Nurse, Children's Hospital, Boston, 1972-73; Clinical Nurse Specialist in Rehabilitation Nursing: R C. Peace Hospital, 1973-74, Maine Medical Center, 1974-75; Instructor in Nursing, Mercy Hospital, 1975-76; Consultant in Rehabilitation Nursng (Private), 1976-81; Clincial Nurse Specialist, Family Nurse Practitioner, Maine Medical Center, 1979-82; Assistant Professor of Nursing, Alfred University, 1982-85; Research Assistant, University of Rochester, 1984-85. *Memberships:* Sigma Theta Tau; American Nurses Association; Association of Rehabilitation Nurses; New York State Nurses Association. *Publications:* 'Aphasia: What Every Nurse Should Know', 'Maine Nurse', 1974; 'Questions on Certification', 'ARN' 10, 1984; 'Certificaiton in Rehabilitation Nursing', 'ARN' II, 1985. *Honours:* Writing Award, ANA, 1974; Chairperson, ARN Certification Board, 1982-85; Predoctoral Fellowship, USD of HEW Division of Nursing, 1984-85; Certification of Appreciation, ARN, 1985. *Hobbies:* Sailing; Bicycling; Photography; Sewing. *Address:* Helen Wood Hall, University of Rochester Medical Center, 601 Elmwood Avenue, Rochester, NY 14642, USA.

DREWS, Robert Seymour, b. 25 Dec. 1900, Brooklyn, New York, USA. Private Practice of Psychiatry (Retired). m. Josephine Sandoef, 21 June 1925, Detroit, Michigan, 1 daughter. *Education:* MS, University of Michigan, 1935; MD, Wayne University, 1926; DPH, University of Michigan 1938; Postgraduate work: University of Michigan, Temple University, Columbia University, Johns Hopkins University; Continuing Medical Education: Providence Hospital, Southfield, Michigan; St, Joseph Hospital, Pontiac, Michigan, *Appointments:* Assistant Director, Department of Neurology, Children's Hospital, Detroit, Michigan, 1930; Assistant Director, Department of Neurology, Women's Hospital, Detroit, 1930; Instructor, Department of Neuropathology, Wayne University, 1930. *Memberships:* American Medical Association; Academy of Psychosomatic Medicine; American Psychiatric Association; American Association of the Advancement of Psychotherapy; American Society of Group Psychotherapy and psychodrama,

Publications: A History of the Public Health Movement of Detroit, Michigan 1700-1854, 1938; A History of the Sick Poor of Detroit 1700-1854; The Role of the Modern Executive in the Course of Emotional Contagion, 1954. *Honours:* Recipient of several honours and awards. *Hobbies:* Music; Travel; Lecturing on Mental Health. *Address:* 16300 West 9 Mile Road, Apt. 210, Southfield, MI 48075, USA.

DRIESSENS, Ferdinand Clemens Maria, b. 26 Feb. 1937, Venray, Netherlands. Scientist. m. M.G. Boltong, 20 May 1961, 3 daughters. *Education:* MSc., University of Utrecht, 1962; PhD, Technical University, Eindhoven, 1964. *Appointments:* Chemical Assistant DSM, Geleen, 1954-57; Teacher, Physics, Chemistry, Van der Putt Lyceum, Eindhoven, 1961-62; Scientist Coworker, Technical University, Eindhoven, 1962-66; Senior Scientist, Philips Research Labs, Eindhoven, 1966-67; Lecturer, Dental Materials Science, Catholic University, Nijmegen, 1967-70; Professor, Scientist, Technologist, Dental Materials, 1970-, Catholic University, Nijmegen; Guest Scientist: Max Planck Institut fur Physik.Chem., Gottingen, 1965, Nat.Bur. Standards, Gaithersburg, Maryland, USA, 1968-69. *Memberships:* Dutch Standardization Committee on Dentistry, Chairman; Board, Fundamental Health Research Organisation, Netherlands; International Association Dental Research; European Organisation for Caries Research; Academy of Dental Materials; etc. *Publications:* "Mineral Aspects of Dentistry", 1982; "Tooth Development and Caries", co-author, 1985; "Biominerals", co-author, in Press; 150 papers. *Hobbies:* Philosophical Anthropology; Stamp Collecting. *Address:* Dept. of Oral Biomaterials, Catholic University, PO Box 9101, 6500 HB Nijmegen, The Netherlands.

DRIJANSKI, Ruben, b. 21 Sep. 1944, Mexico. Consultant in Internal Medicine. m. Nora Brucilovsky, 16 Dec. 1967, Mexico, 2 daughters. *Education:* Dr. of Medicine, National University of Mexico, 1968. *Appointments:* Internship in Internal Medicine, Sinai Hospital of Baltimore, USA, 1969, Resident, 1970; Resident in Internal Medicine, Mayo Clinic Postgraduate School of Medicine, USA, 1971-72, Associate Consultant, 1973-74; Head, Medical Education, CFE Medical Services, Mexico, 1974-76; Chief of Residents Medical Education, ABC Hospital, Mexico, 1976-78, Head, Emergency Room, 1980-81; Chief Medical Consultant in Internal Medicine, Mexico Psychoanalytical Association, Consultant in Internal Medicine, ABC Hospital, Mexico, both from 1974 to present. *Memberships:* Fellow, Mayo Alumni Association; American Society of Internal Medicine; Medical Society of ABC Hospital, Mexico; Mexican Internal Medicine Association. *Publications:* 'Afibrinogenemia with Severe Head Trauma' in 'JAMA', 1972; 'Trombeombolia Pulmonar' in "Archives of the Institute of Cardiology of Mexico", volume 148, 1978. *Honour:* Intern of the Year Award, Sinai Hospital of Baltimore, USA, 1969. *Hobbies:* Fishing; Tennis; Cooking; Reading non fiction; Pen collecting. *Address:* Sierra Gorda 185-1, Mexico DF 11000, Mexico.

DRINKWATER, John Stuart, b. 20 Apr. 1951, Burnie, Tasmania. Chriopractor, Private Practice. *Education:* Dip.App.Sci., Human Biology; Dip.App.Sci., Chiropractic; B.App.Sci., Chiropractic; Dip.N.B.C.E. (USA). *Appointments:* Foundation President, Chiropractic Alumni Association, Phillip Institute of Technology, 1982; Secretary, Australian Council on Chiropractic Alumni Association of Phillip Institute of Technology; Australian Spinal Research Foundation; Australian Council on Chiropractic Education. *Honours:* Meritorious Service Awards, Chiropractic Students Association, 1985. *Hobbies:* Music; Wood Carving; Tennis. *Address:* 404 Main Road West, St. Albans, Victoria 3021, Australia.

DROZ, Bernard, b. 25 Mar. 1930, Paris, France. Professor of Histology and Embryology; Institute Director. m. Anne-Marie Barrois, 23 Mar. 1956, 1 son, 2 daughters. *Education:* MD Histology, Faculty of Medicine, Paris; PhD Anatomy, McGill University, Montreal, Canada; DSc Cell Biology, Faculty of Sciences, Paris, France. *Appointments:* Associate Professor of Histology and Embryology, Faculty of Medicine, Angers; Professor of Physiology, University Pierre et Marie Curie, Paris; Scientific Advisor, Atomic Energy Commission, Saclay; Professor and Director, Institute of Histology and Embryology, University of Lausanne, Switzerland. *Memberships:* European Molecular Biology Organisation; Swiss National Science Foundation; European Science Foundation. *Publication:* 'Techniques in radioautography', 1976; 'Role of axoplasmic transport' in "Perspective on Neuroscience", 1985. *Honour:* Doctor honoris causa, Catholic University of Louvain, Belgium, 1980. *Address:* Institut d'Histologie et Embryologie, Rue du Bugnon 9, Lausanne, Switzerland.

DRUCKER, Harvey, b. 1 Jan 1941, Chicago, Illinois, USA, Associate Laboratory Director, Biomedical and Environmental Research, Argonne National Laborarory, m. Betty Baldridge, 20 Aug. 1965, Hinsdale, Illinois, 2 daughters. *Education:* BS, 1963, PhD, 1967, University of Illinois; Fellow, Cardiovascular Research Institute, University of California Medical Cantre, San Francisco, 1967-69. *Appointments:* Manager, Biology department, 1979-83, Manager, Molecular Biology and Biophysics Section, 1972-79, Senior Research Investigator-Biochemistry, 1969-72, Battelle Pacific Northwest Laboratories. *Memberships:* American Chemcial Society; American Society for Microbiology; Sigma Xi; American Society of Biologic Chemists; AAAS. *Publications:* Contributor of numerous articles on scientific subjects in profesional journals. *Honours:* Fellowship, 1967-69; Fellow of the Cardiovascular Research Institute, University of California Medical Centre, San Francisco. *Hobbies:* Music; Reading; Bicycling. *Address:* Argonne National Laboratory, 9700 South Cass Avenue, Argonne, IL 60439, USA.

DRUKKER, Bruce H, b. 8 Sept. 1934, Passaic, New Jersey, USA. Professor and Chairperson, Department of Obstetrics and Gynaecology. m. Esther van Manen, 19 June 1956, Grand Rapids, Michigan, 2 sons, 1 daughter. *Education:* MD, Cornell University Medical College, 1959. *Appointments:* Senior Staff Physician, 1966-73, Chairman, Department of Gynaecology and Obstetrics, 1973-84, Henry Ford Hospital, Detroit, Michigan; Professor and Chairperson, Department of Obstetrics and Gynaecology, Michigan State University, East Lansing, Michigan, 1984-. *Memberships:* American College of Obstetricians and Gynaecologists; Society of Gynaecologic Oncologists; Central Association of Obstetrics and Gynaecology; Society for the Study of Breast Disease; Association of Professors of Gynecology and Obstetrics. *Publications:* Numerous papers contributed to professional journals including: 'Cont. Obstetrics and Gynaecology'; 'Archieves of Surgery'; 'American Journal of Obstetrics and Gynaecology'. *Address:* Department of Obstetrics and Gynaecology, B-316 Clinical Center Michigan State University, East Lansing, MI 48824-1315, USA.

DRURY, Michael, b. 5 Aug. 1926, Birmingham, England. Professor. m. Joan Williamson, 7 Oct. 1950, Winsford, 3 sons, 1 daughter. *Education:* MRCS (England); LRCP (London), 1949; MB ChB (Birmingham), 1949; MRCGP 1960; FRCGP 1970; PRCGP 1985. *Appointments:* Prescription Pricing Authority, 1982; Member, General Medical Council, 1983; President, Royal College of General Practitioners, 1985. *Memberships:* Member, BMA, Royal Society Medicine. *Publications:* "Treatment", 1985; "Introduction to General Practice", 1977;

"Medical Secretary's Handbook", 1986; 'Nurse Management of Hypertension Clinics with Computer', 1985. *Honour:* OBE, 1982. *Hobbies:* Gardening; Music; Walking; Bridge. *Address:* Rossall Cottage, Church Hill, Belbroughton, Near Stourbridge, West Midlands, England.

DSANE-SELBY, Kofi, b. 24 July 1931, Cape Coast, Ghana. General Practitioner. m. Rosamund Wamcell, 26 Sep. 1959, London, England, 1 son, 5 daughters. *Education:* MD, University of Geneva, Switzerland, 1960; St Raphael's Hospital, New Haven, connecticut, USA, 1960. *Appointments:* Medical Officer, Ministry of Health, Ghana; 1961-62; Medical Director in Charge, Bimpeh Hill Hospital, 1962-69, 1972-; Ghana Ambassador to France & Spain, 1969-72. *Memberships:* Ghana Medical Association, 1961-; President, 1980-82; GMA Delegate to World Medical Assembly, 1976-81; Treasurer, Confederation of African Medical Associations & Societies, 1982-. *Hobbies:* Golf; Reading. *Address:* Bimpeh Hill Hospital, P.O. Box 645, Kumasi, Ghana.

DUCAT-AMOS, Barbara Mary, b. 9 Feb. 1921, London, England. State Registered Nurse. *Education:* Higher School Certificate. *Appointments:* Sister, General Wards, Princess Mary's Royal Air Force Nursing Service, 1944-47; Midwifery Student and Maternity Nurse, St. Thomas' Hospital, 1947-48; General Nurse, South and South West Africa, 1948-52; Rejoined PMRAFNS 1952, served as General Ward Sister, Theatre Charge Sister, Nursing Officer, UK, Germany, Cyprus, Aden and Changi, Singapore, 1952-67; Matron, RAF Hospital, Nocton Hall, 1967; Senior Matron, RAF Hospital, Changi, 1968; Principal Matron (Group Officer), Ministry of Defence, 1970; Matron-in-Chief (Air Commandant) PHRAFNS, London, 1972; Matron-in-Chief PHRAFNS and Director, RAF Nursing Services, 1976-78; Nursing Sister (Officer), Cable and Wireless PLC, London, 1978-85; Chairman Girls Venture Corps 1982-. *Memberships:* Royal College of Nursing; RAF. *Honours:* Royal Red Cross First Class 1971; Companion of the Bath, 1974; Queen's Honorary Nursing Sister, 1972-78; Commander (Sister) St, John, 1975. *Hobbies:* Music; Theatre; Travel. *Address:* c/o Barclays Bank PLC, King Street, Branch, P.O. Box 27, Reading, Berkshire RG1 2HD, England.

DUDENHOEFER, Paul Anthony, b. 7 Sep. 1927, Milwaukee, Wisconsin, USA. Medical Director. m. Rosemary Longe, 16 June 1951, Ionia, Michigan, 2 sons, 2 daughters. *Education:* BS 1948, MD 1951, Marquette University, Milwaukee, Wisconsin. *Appointments:* Staff Physiatrist, Brooke Army Hospital, San Antonio, Texas, 1956-58; Chief, Physical Medicine and Rehabilitation, Veterans Administration Center, Wood, Wisconsin, 1958-60; Associate Director 1960-70, Director 1970-, Department of Physical Medicine and Rehabilitation, St Francis Hospital, Milwaukee, Wisconsin; Associate Clinical Professor, Physical Medicine and Rehabilitation, Medical College of Wisconsin, 1975-. *Memberships:* Fellow, American Academy of Physical Medicine and Rehabilitation; American Congress on Rehabilitation Medicine; Life member, National Rehabilitation Association; American Association of Electromyography and Electrodiagnosis; Past President, Wisconsin Society of Physical Medicine and Rehabilitation. *Honour:* Service Award, Marquette University, 1984. *Hobbies:* Swimming; Music. *Address:* St Francis Hospital, 3237 South 16th Street, Milwaukee, WI 53215, USA.

DUDKIEWICZ, Jan, b. 13 July 1931, Szczecno, Poland. Head of Chair, Clinic of Obstetrics and Gynaecology. m. 23 Oct. 1963, 1 son. *Education:* Diploma, Silesaian School of Medicine, 1959; 1st and 2nd degree specialisation; MD, 1964, Doctor habil, 1974, Silesian School of Medicine; Professor, 1982; FIAC. *Appointments:* Assistant, Human Anatomy Institute, 1955-64, Assistant, Senior

Assistant, Adjunct, 1st Clinic of Obstetrics and Gynaecology, 1959-64, Senior Lecturer, Obstetrics and Gynaecology, 1964-73, Associate Professor, Head of Gynaecological and Endocrinological Department, 1974-77, Director of Obstetric and Gynaecological Institute, 1977-82, Professor, Head of Chair, Clinic of Obstetrics and Gynaecology, 1982-, Silesian School of Medicine, Poland. *Memberships:* Fellow, International Academy of Cytology. Vice President: Polish Association of Clinical Cytology; Katovice Region, Polish Gynaecological Association. Polish Endocrinological Association. *Publications:* Co-Author or Author of over 140 papers contributed to professional publications including: 'American Journal of Obstetrics and Gynaecology'; 'Gynaecologia'; 'Acta Cytol'. *Honours:* Award of 1st degree, Polish Ministry of Health, 1974; Rectors Awards for Research and Teaching, Annually. *Hobby:* Ancient history of Greece and Rome. *Address:* P1 24 Stycznia 8/3, 41-800 Zabrze, Poland.

DUDLEY. Richard Gilbert Jr., b. 15 May 1946, Pennsylvania, USA, Psychiatrist. *Education:* BS, Wheaton College, 1968; MD, Temple University School of Medicine, 1972. *Appointments:* Deputy Commissioner, New York City Department of Mental Health, Mental Retardation and Alcoholism Services; Medical Director, Washington Heights, West Harlem Community Mental Health Centre; Assistant Director, Professional Services, Roche Laboratories; Private Practice; Assistant Professor, Psychiatry, New York Medical College; Adjunct Assistant Professor, Law, New York University School of Law. *Memberships:* American College of Psychiatrists; Black Psychiatrists of America; American Academy of Psychiatry and Law; American Society for Adolescent Psychiatry; American Psychiatric Association; National Medical Association. *Hobbies:* Swimming; Classical and Modern Dance. *Address:* 466 West 144 St, New York, NY 10031, USA.

DUDLEY, William N., b. 29 Sep. 1929, Detroit, Michigan USA. Director of Chiropractic m, Gloria, 12 Dec, 1959, Detroit, 2 daughters, 2 sons. *Education:* DC, 1952. *Appointments:* President, Jackson MI Area Chiropractic Association, Guest Lecturer, National College of Chiropractic; Postgraduate Lecturer, Life Chiropractic College; President, International Thermographic Society, 1983-84; Board Member; Interntional Thermographic Society; Board Member, NAIRTA; Board Member, American Board of Clinical Thermology. *Memberships:* Michigan Chiropractic Council; American Chiropractic Association; International Chiropractic Association; Diplomate, American Board of Clinical Thermology 1985. *Publications:* Numerous articles in professional journals including 'Michigan State Chiropractic Journal'; 'MSC Journal'; 'Science Review of Chiropractic; 'American Chiropractic Association Journal'. *Honours:* International Chiropractic Association for Thermographic Research, 1968; International Thermographic Society for Thermographic Research, 1986. *Hobbies:* Fishing; Hunting; Flyng. *Address:* 120 State Street, Howell, MI 48843, USA.

DUERDEN, Brian Ian, b. 21 June 1948, Nelson, Lancashire, England. Professor of Medical Microbiology, Honorary Consultant Microbiologist. m. Majorie Hudson, 5 Aug. 1972, Nelson. *Education:* BSc Medical Science honours Bacteriology 1970, MB Ch B 1972, Edinburgh University Medical School, Edinburgh, Scotland; MD, Edinburgh, 1979. *Appointments:* House Officer, City Hospital, Edinburgh, 1972-73; Lecturer, Department of Bacteriology, Edinburgh University, 1973-76; Lecturer 1976-79, Senior Lecturer 1979-83, Professor 1983-, Department of Medical Microbiology, Sheffield University, Sheffield, England; Honorary Consultant Microbiologist, Children's Hospital, Sheffield, 1979-. *Memberships:* Sureditor, Journal of Medical Microbiology; Standing Advisory Committee on Medical Microbiology 1982-85, Royal College of Pathologists; Committee 1982-86, Pathological Society of Great Britain and Ireland; Founder member of Steering Committee, Assistant Secretary 1984, Honorary Secretary 1985-, Association of Medical Microbiologists; British Association for Antimicrobial Chemotherapy; Hospital Infection Society; British Society for the Study of Infection; Committee 1984-, Anaerobe Discussion Group; Founder member, Steeering Committee 1984-, STD Discussion Group. *Publications inlcude:* "Short Textbook of Medical Microbiology" (with D C Turk, I A Porter and T M S Reid), 5th edition 1983; Chapters on Bacteroides and Anaerobe Infections in Topley and Wilson's "Principles of Bacteriology, Virology and Immunity"; Over 30 articles on isolation, identification and classification of bacteroides, genito-urinary infections, antibiotics – laboratory and clinical studies, 1974-85. *Honour:* C L Oakley Lecturer, Pathological Society of Great Britain and Ireland, 1980. *Hobbies:* Cricket; Travel; Gardening; Politics. *Address:* 17 Wollaton Road, Bradway, Sheffield S17 4LD, England.

DUERS, John Allen, b, 25 May 1938, Hudson Falls, New York, USA. Senior Psychiatrist; Chairman, Department of Psychiatry; Private Practice. m. Victoria Ann Brooks, 9 July 1963, Albany, 1 son, 1 daughter. *Eduction:* BA, Colgate University, New York, 1960; MD, Albany Medical College of Union University, New York, 1960; MD, Albany Medical College of Union University, New York, 1964. *Appointments:* Certified Board of Psychiatry and Neurology in Psychiatry, 1972; Chief Resident in Psyciatry, 1968, Upstate Medical Centre 1966-68, Clinical Professor of Psychiatry 1968, Upstate Medical Centre, Syracuse new York; Director of Neuropsychiatry Ward (Major), Fort Leonard Wood, Missouri, 1968-70; Associate Professor of Psychiatry, 1970-75, Associate Professor, Department of Medicine, 1972-70; Associate Professor of Psychiatry, 1970-75, Associate Professor Department of Medicine, 1972-75, Upstate Medical Centre Syracuse New York; Assistant Medical Director, Natchaug Hospital Incorporated, 1984-85; Senior Psychiatrist, Windham C M Hospital; Private Practice, Willimantic Connecticut. *Memberships include:* American Medical Society; American Association of General Hospital Psychiatrists; Windham County Medical Association; Nation member, Smithsonian Association; American Professional Practice Association. *Publications:* "The Chronic Patient and The Private Sector"; "Inovations in Partial Hospitalization"; various conference proceedings; various panel discussion documents. *Honours:* Honours in German and Psychiatry, 1964. *Hobbies:* Meterology; Minerology; Astronomy; Gardening; Jogging; Travel. *Address:* 196 Conantville Road Willimantic, CT 06226, USA.

DÜHMKE, Eckhart, b. 22 July 1942, Berlin, Germany. Professor & Chairman, Department of Radiotherapy, University of Göttingen. m. Eva Bagge, 31 Dec. 1970, Kiel, Federal Republic of Germany, 1 son, 3 daughters. *Education:* Studies at the Universities of Marburg/Lahn & Kiel; Staatsexamen (graduation), 1968, MD, 1969, University of Kiel; Specialist in Radiology, 1974; University Lecturer, University of Kiel (Habilitation), 1980; Specialist in Radiotherapy, 1980. *Appointments:* Resident Physician, 1970, Senior Radiologist, 1974, Department of Radiology, University of Kiel. *Memberships:* German Roentgen Society; American society for Therapeutic Radiology & Oncology. *Publications:* "Diseases of the thoracic Aorta", (Handbook of Medicinal Radiology) with Gremmel & Schelte-Brinkmann, 1974; "Medicinal Radiography with fast Neutrons", 1980; Several articles in the field of radiotherapy, malignant non-Hodgkin-lymphomas & the use of compensators in radiotherapy. *Honour:* Visiting Professor, Department of Radiation Oncology & Nuclear Medicine, Hahnemann University, Philadelphia, USA, 1984. *Address:* Department of Radiotherapy, Göttingen University Medical Centre, D-3400 Göttingen, Federal Republic of Germany.

DUIC, Marko David, b. 12 May 1958, Zagreb, Yugoslavia. Clinical Fellow, Women's College Hospital, Toronto, Canada. *Education:* MD; CCFP. *Memberships:* Ontario Medical Association; American Institute of Physicians; College of Family Physicians. *Honours:* 3rd Year Class award, 1981; Lauge Award, 1981; Graduating Class Award, 1982; Ciba Geigy Award, 1982; Dr. D.S. Hoare Award, 1982; University of Toronto Medical Society Honour Award, 1982. *Hobbies:* Music; Skiing; Hiking; Cookery. *Address:* Department of Family Medicine, Women's College Hospital, Burton Hall, 60 Grosveneor Street, Toronto, Ontario, Canada M5S 1B6.

DUMON, Jean-Francois Marie Jerome, b. 3 Dec. 1939, Marseilles, France. Doctor of Medicine. m. Theodora Lecourtois, 18 June, 1966, Marseilles, France, 1 son, 2 daughters. *Education:* MD, Marseilles Medical School, France; Chest Physician; Certified Public Hospital Doctor. *Memberships:* Fellow, American College of Chest Physicians. *Publication:* "YAG Laser Bronchoscopy", USA. *Hobbies:* Video; Painting; Windsurfing; Gardening. *Address:* Clos d'Albizzi, 13260 Cassis, France.

DUNBAR, Jacqueline M, b. 7 Jan. 1942, Michigan, USA. Director of Nursing, Professor. *Education:* RN Nursing, Presbyterian University Hospital, Pittsburgh, Pennsylvania, 1959-62; BS Nursing, Florida State University, 1966-68; MS Nursing, University of California, San Francisco, 1968-69; Post-MS Certificate in Nursing, Child Psychiatric & Family Therapy, 1969-70, University of California. *Appointments:* Staff Nurse, Western Psychiatric Institute & Clinic, 1962-63; Head Nurse, South Florida State Hospital, Hollywood, Florida, 1963-66; Night Charge (Intensive Care Paediatrics), Tallahassee Memorial Hospital, Florida, 1966-68; Lecturer in Nursing, University of California at San Francisco, 1968-72; Lecturer, Department of Nursing, San Jose State University, 1970-75; Assistant Professor, Deapartment of Family Medicine, University of Iowa, 1977-79; Clinical Assistant Professor, Department of Psychiatry, Stanford University, 1980-84; Assistant Professor, Department of Psychiatry, University of Pittsburgh, 1984-; Director of Nursing, Western Psychiatric Institute & Clinic, 1984-. *Memberships:* American Heart Association; Divison of Health Psychology, American Psychological Association; Associaiton for the Advancemnet of Behaviour Therapy; Society of Behavioural Medicine; Society for Clinical Trials; American Diabetes Association; American Nurses Association. *Publications:* Author & Co-Author of some 20 articles in professional journals. *Honours:* National Honour Society, 1958; Phi Kappa Phi, 1966; Sigma Theta Tau, 1978. *Hobbies:* Gourmet cooking; Reading. *Address:* Western Psychiatric Institute & Clinic, 3811 O'Hara Street E.501, Pittsburgh, PA 15213, USA.

DUNCAN, Archibald Sutherland, b. 17 July 1914, Darjeeling, India, Retired: Emeritus Professor of Medical Education, Edinburgh. m. Barbara Holliday, Penrith, Cumbria, 12 Apr. 1939. *Education:* Universities of Neuchatel and Heidelberg (short periods); University of Edinburgh; MB ChB, 1936; FRCSED, 1939; FRCOG, 1955 (M, 1941); FRCPED, 1969. *Appointments:* Junior Hospital appointments in Edinburgh and London; Surgical Specialist, RNVR; Lecturer in University and Part-time Consultant Obstetrician and Gynaecologist, Aberdeen, 1946-50; Senior Lecturer, University of Edinburgh and Obstetrician and Gynaecologist, Western General Hospital, Edinburgh, 1950-53; Professor of Obstetrics and Gynaecology, Welsh National School of Medicine, University of Wales, 1953-66; Consultant Obstetrician and Gynaecologist, United Cardiff Hospitals and Advisor in Obstetrics and Gynaecology to Welsh Hospital Board, 1953-66; Executive Dean of the Faculty of Medicine and Professor of Medical Education, University of Edinburgh, 1966-76. *Memberships:* Honorary Member, Alpha Omega, USA; British Medical Association; Edinburgh Obstetrical Society; James IV Association of Surgeons; Welsh Obstetrical and Gynaecological Society, Founder and Former President; Institute of Medical Ethics, Vice-President; Association for Study of Medical Education. *Publications:* "Of Medical Education" University of Edinburgh Inaugural Lecture, 1967; "Medical Education through the Eyes of James Young Simpson', Journal of Obstetrics and Gynaecology of British Commonwealth', 1972; Joint Editor, "Dictionary of Medical Ethics", 1981; "Hospital Medicine and Nursing in the 1980-s", Joint Editor, 1984. *Honours include:* DSC, 1941; Honorary MD Edinburgh, 1984; various other honours. *Hobbies:* Mountains; Photography; Home Computing. *Address:* 1 Walker Street, Edinburgh EH3 7JY, Scotland.

DUNCAN, David Frank, b. 26 June, 1947, Kansas City, USA. University Professor. Divorced, 1 son. *Education:* BA, Psychology, University of Missouri at Kansas City, USA, 1970; Dr.PH in Community Health, University of Texas Health Science Centre at Houston, 1976. *Appointments:* Caseworker and Project Director, Texas Research Institute of Mental Sciences, 1971-73; Chief Trainer, Inlet Crisis Counselling Centre, Houston, Texas, 1973-76; Acting Director, Reality Island Halfway House, Houston, 1974-75; Research Associate, Office of the Governore, Austin, Texas, 1975; Research Associate, Institute of Clinical Toxicology, Baylor College of Medincine, Houston, Texas, 1975-76; Associate Professor, State University of New York, 1976-78; Professor of Health Education and Co-ordinator of Community Health Programmes, Southern Illinois Univresity, Carbondale, Illinois, 1978-present. *Memberships:* American Public health Association; American College of Epidemiology; Society for Epidemiologic Research; Society for Controlled Trials; Group for Medical Education. *Publications:* "Drugs and the Whole Person", 1982; "Epidemiology: Bases for Disease Prevention and Health Promotion" (in press); 44 articles in scientific journals. *Honour:* Presidential Medal of Merit, 1984. *Hobby:* Book collecting. *Address:* Department of Health Education, Southern Illinois University, Carbondale, IL 62901, USA.

DUNCAN, Margaret Elizabeth, b. 9 Dec. 1937, Glasgow, Scotland, Consultant Obstetrician and Gynaecologist. *Education:* MB ChB, 1961, Faculty of Medicine, Edinburgh University; D Obst, FCOG, 1964; MRCOG, 1967; FRCS Ed, 1967; FICS, 1972; FRCOG, 1979; MD, Hons, Edinburgh, 1983; Cum Amplissimam Laudem with Gold Medal. *Appointments:* House Officer, 1961-64, Surgery, Royal Infirmary, Edinburgh; House Officer, Obstetrician, 1967-68, Edinburgh Medical Missionary Society Hospital, Nazareth; House Officer, Robroyston Hospital, Glasgow, Scotland; Senior House Officer, Falkirk and District Royal Infirmary, Scotland, 1964; Registrar, Obstetrics and Gynaecology, Elsie Inglis Memorial Hospital, Bruntsfield Hospital, Edinburgh 1964-67; Senior Registrar, Tutor, Leeds University, England, 1968-70; Assistant Professor, Haile Selassie I University, 1970-75; Consultant Obstetrician Gynaecologist, Princess Tsehai Memorial Hospital, St Pauls Hospital, Addis Ababa, Ethiopia, 1970-75; Consultant Gynaecologist, NAMRU-5, Addis Ababa, 1974-77; Consultant Gynaecologist, Fistula Hospital, Addis Ababa, 1975-78; Research Obstetrician, Medical Research Council Leprosy Project, Addis Ababa, 1975-78; Associate Professor, Acting Head of Department, Addis Ababa University, 1977-78; Research Obstetrician, MRC Leprosy Project, NIME, 1978-81; Part-time General Practitioner, Seham, Tyne and Wear, England, 1981; Consultant Obstetrician and Gynaecologist, MODA Hospital, Jeddah, Saudi Arabia, 1981; Attached to Department of Bacteriology, University of

Edinburgh, Scotland, 1978-83; Consultant Obstetrician and Gynaecologist, Al Qassimi Hospital, Sharjah, United Arab Emirates, 1983-86. *Memberships:* Medical Protection Society; International Leprosy Association; Royal Society of Tropical Medicine and Hygiene; Full registration with General Medical Council. *Publications include:* "Tropical Infections in Obstetrics", 1986; 'Perspectives in Leprosy' 1985; 'Leprosy in Young Children – past, present and future', 1985; 'Leprosy and Procreation – a historical review of social and clinical aspects', 1985. *Address:* 'Ahlaine', Cardrona, Peebles, Scotland.

DUNLOP, William, b. 18 Aug. 1944, Kilmarnock, Scotland, Professor of Obstetrics and Gynaecology University of Newcastle-upon-Tyne. m. Sylvia Louise Krauthamer 25 Mar. 1968, Glasgow. 1 son, 1 daughter. *Eduction:* MBChB, Glasgow 1967, MRCOG 1971, FRCS (Ed), 1971, PhD 1982, Newcastle-upon-Tyne, FRCOG, 1984. *Appointments:* Registrar, Obstetrics and Gynaecology Queen Mother's Hospital and Western Infirmary, Glasgow, 1971-74; Lecturer, Department of Obstetrics and Gynaecology, University of Nairobi, Kenya, 1972-73; Scientific Staff, Medical Research Council Reproduction and Growth Unit, Newcastle-Upon-Tyne, 1974-75 Senior Lecturer, Department of Obstetrics and Gynaecology, University of Newcastle-Upon-Tyne,1975-82; Visiting Associate Professor, Department of Obstetrics and Gynecology, Medical University of South Carolina, Charleston, South Carolina, USA, 1980. *Memberships:* British Medical Association; Royal College of Obstetricians and Gynaecologists; International Society for the Study of Hypertension in Pregnancy; Blair Bell Research Society; Gynaecological Visiting Society. *Publications include:* 'The Effect of Normal Pregnancy upon the Renal Handling ofUric Acid', British Journal of Obstetrics and Gynaecology, 1977; 'Renal Hemodynamics and Tubular Function in Normal Human Pregnancy', Kidney International, 1980; 'Serial Changes in Renal Haemodynamics During Normal Human Pregnancy', British Journal of Obstetrics and Gynaecology, 1981; 'Obstetrical Epidemiology', Editoris: S. L. Barron, A. M. Thomson, (contributor), 1983. *Hobbies:* Music, Literature, Drama, Films. *Address:* 30 Eslington Terrace, Jesmond, Newcastle-upon-Tyne, NE2 4RN, England.

DUNN, David Christy, b. 12 Feb. 1939, Colchester, England. Consultant Surgeon; Medical Director of Studies. m. Anne Collet, 2 May 1969, 2 sons, 3 daughters. *Education:* BA, 1960, MB, B.Chir., 1963, St John's College, Cambridge; St Bartholomew's Hospital Medical School, London; FRCS; Fellow, St John's College, Cambridge. *Appointments:* House Physician, Royal Portsmouth Hospital; House Surgeon, Surgical Registrar, St Bartholomew's Hospital, London; SHO, Accident Service, Luton & Dunstable Hospital; Anatomy Demonstrator, University of Cambridge; RSO, Brompton Hospital, London; Surgical Registrar, St Albans City Hospital; Assistant Director of Research, Surgery, University of Cambridge; Consultant General Surgeon, Addenbrooke's Hospital, Cambridge; Director Medical Studies, St John's College, Cambridge. *Memberships:* British Medical Association; Fellow, Royal College of Surgeons of England; European Society of Surgical Research; Moynihan Chirurgical Travelling Club. *Publications:* "Arterial Sling Tourniquet: A New Method of Clamping Vessels", 'British medical Journal', 1971; "A Trial of Highly Selective Vagotomy in the Treatment of Chronic Duodenal Ulcer", 'Surg. Gynae. & Obst.', 1980; "Rat and Rabbit Kidney Grafts", 'M. Chir Thesis', 1972; "Surgical Diagnosis and Management", 1985. *Hobbies:* Coach to Cambridge University Boat Race Crew, 1986; Member, Cambridge Flying Group; Exhibitor Addenbrooke's Hospital Art Exhibition. *Address:* Dept. of General Surgery, Unit E7, Addenbrooke's Hospital, Cambridge CB2 2QQ, England.

DUNN, Graham Douglas, b. 21 Feb. 1957, Capetown,

South Africa. Registrar, Department of Diagnostic Radiology, Hammersmith Hospital, London, England. m. Debra-Ann Roblin, 8 Dec. 1984, Queenstown, South Africa. *Education:* MB ChB (Honours), University of Cape Town, 1979; MRCP (UK), 1982; DCH (UK), 1983; DMRD, 1985. *Appointments:* Intern, General Medicine, Groote Schuur Hospital, Cape Town, 1980; Intern, General Surgery, Neurosurgery and Paediatric Surgery, Groote Schuur Hospital and Red Cross Chilren's Hospital, Cape Town, 1980; Locum Senior House Officer, Medicine, Hammersmith and Brompton Hospitals, London, England, 1981; Senior House Officer, Cardiology and General Medicine, Hammersmith Hospital, 1982; Senior House Officer, Neurology, Maudsley and Kings College Hospitals, London, 1983; Senior House Officer, Paediatrics, Hillingdon Hospital, London, 1983. *Address:* 2 Holwood Close, Rydens Road, Walton-on-Thames, Surrey KT12 3AE, England.

DUNSTER, Herbert John, b. 27 July 1922, Bexhill, Surrey, England. National Board Director. m. Rosemary Elizabeth Gallagher, 10 Dec. 1944, Preston, Lancashire, 1 son, 3 daughters. *Education:* BSc, London University; ARCS, Imperial College of Science and Technology. *Appointments:* Scientist, UK Atomic Energy Authority, 1946-71; Assistant Director, National Radiological Protection Board, 1971-76; Deputy Director General, Health and Safety Executive, 1976-82; currently, Director, National; Radiological Protection Board. *Membership:* Society for Radiological Protection. *Publications:* Author of over 100 articles and publications in technical journals. *Honours:* Companion, Order of the Bath (CB), 1979; Melchett Medal, 1981. *Hobbies:* Music; Photography. *Address:* 5 Shoe Lane, East Hagbourne, Oxon OX11 9LP, England.

DUPONT, Jules St Martin, b. 3 Oct. 1921, Houma, Louisiana, USA. Medical Director, Cardiology. m. Louise Munsun, 7 May 1949, Albania Plantation, 2 sons, 2 daughters. *Education:* MD, School of Medicine, Tulane University, 1945. *Appointments:* Interne, 1945-46, Resident in Medicine, 1946, Charity Hospital, New Orleans, Louisiana, USA; Interne, American Hospital, Paris, France, 1946-47; Fellow in Medicine, School of Medicine, Louisiana State University, New Orleans, 1948-49; Clinical Assistant Professor of Medicine, Trainee in Cardiology, 1949-50; Resident in Medicine, Charity Hospital, New Orleans, 1950-51; Medical Director, Cardiology, Terrebonne General Medical Centre. *Memberships:* American Society of Internal Medicine; American College of Chest Physicians; Fellow, Royal Society of Health, London, England; Fellow, American College of Angiology; Musser-Burch Society, Tulane University. *Honours:* National Institute of Health Trainee Scholarship, 1949-50. *Hobbies:* Reading; Cooking; Fishing. *Address:* Apt 1, Austin Drive, Houma, LA 70360, USA.

DURRANT, Keith Ronald, b. 8 Apr. 1935, England. Physician in Administrative Charge, Department of Radiotherapy and Oncology, Oxford; Clinical Lecturer, University of Oxford. m. 28 May 1960, 1 son, 2 daughters. *Education:* MB BS, University of London St. Bartholomews Hospital; MRCP; FRCR; DMRT. *Appointments:* House Officer, St. Bartholomew's Hospital, London; Registrar, Senior Registrar, Radcliffe Infirmary, Oxford; Resident, Institut Gustave Roussy, Paris, France. *Memberships:* Fellow, Royal Society of Medicine; Royal College Radiologists; British Oncological Association; British Institute of Radiology; EORTC Gynaecology Cancer Group. *Publications:* Papers and articles on radiotherapy and oncology in 'The Lancet', 'British Medical Journal', on carcinoma breast and bronchus. *Hobbies:* Fly Fishing; Hill-Walking; Sailing. *Address:* Old Rectory, St. Michaels Lane, Beabroke, Oxford OX5 1RT, England.

DUSTING, Gregory James, b. 27 Sep. 1949, Melbourne, Australia. Senior Lecturer. m. Helen K. L.

Wong, 8 July 1978, London, England, 1 son, 1 daughter. *Education:* BSc., Honours, 1971; PhD, University of Melbourne, *Appointments:* Research Scientist, Welcome Research laboratorities, Beckenham, Kent, England, 1976-78; Senior Research Fellow. University of Melbourne, 1978-85. *Memberships:* Australian Phsyiological and Pharmacological Society; Australian Society for Clinical and Esxperimental Pharmacologists; Australian Society for Medical Research; British Pharmacological Society; High Blood Pressure Research Council of Australia; International Society for Hypertension. *Publications include:* "Prostacyclin is the endogenous metabolite responsible for relaxation of coronary arteries induced by arachidonic acid", 'Prostaglandins', 1977; "Prostacyclin (PG12) release accompanying angiotensin conversion in rat mesenteric vasculature", 'European Journal of Pharmacology 1981; "Stimulation of prostacyclin release from the epicardium in anaesthetized dogs", 'British Journal of Pharmacology', 1981; "Prostacyclin: its biosynthesis actions, and clinical potential", 'Prostaglandins and the Cardiovascular System', Raven Press 1982; "Vascular prostacyclin and Goldblatt hypertensive rats", 'Journal of Hypertension', 1984. *Honours:* C & F DeMuth Young Investigator Award, 1981; R, T, Hall Prize, Cardiology, Cardiac Society of Australia and New Zealand, 1981; David Syme Research Prize. *Hobbies:* Bushwalking; Driving. *Address:* Dept. of Physiology, University of Melbourne, Parkville, Victoria 3052, Australia.

DUTHIE, Herbert Livingston, b. 9 Oct 1929, Glasgow, Scotland. Provost, University of Wales College of Medicine. m. Maureen McCann, 31 Mar 1959, Glasgow, Scotland, 3 sons 1 daughter. *Education:* MB ChB 1952; MD Hons 1962; ChM Hons 1959, University of Glasgow; FRCS Ed 1956; FRCS 1957. *Appointments:* Senior House Officer, Registrar and Lecturer in Surgery, Western Infirmary, Glasgow, 1956-59; Rockefeller Travelling Fellow, Mayo Clinic, Rochester, Minnesota, USA, 1959-60; Lecturer in Surgery, University of Glasgow, 1960-61; Senior Lecturer in Surgery, University of Leeds, 1961-63; Reader 1964; Professor of Surgery, University of Sheffield, 1964-79; Dean, Faculty of Medicine, 1976-78; Provost, University of Wales College of Medicine, 1979-. *Memberships:* General Medical Council; Association of Surgeons of Great Britain and Ireland; British Scoiety of Gastroenterology; Surgical Research Society. *Publications:* Articles on Gastroenterological and educational topics. *Address:*86 Dan-y-Bryn Avenue, Radyr, Cardiff CF4 8DQ, South Wales.

DUX, Kazimierz, b. 9 June 1915, Kiev, Russia. Professor of Medicine. m. Maria Brzezińska, 23 Jan. 1940, Warsaw, 2 sons. *Education:* Faculty of Medicine, University of Poznań, 1933-38; Diploma of Physician, Faculty of Medicine, University of Warsaw, 1940; MD, 1945; Habilitation, Associate Professor, 1948; Professor of General & Experimental Pathology, 1949. *Appointments:* Physician, Wolski Hospital, Warsaw, 1940-41; Physician, Miastków, near Warsaw, 1941-44; Assistant, Chair of Histology, University in Lublin, 1944-45; Assistant, Chair of Histology, University of Poznań, 1945-49; Professor of Experimental Pathology, Silesian Medical School, Zabrze, Head of Department of Tumour Biology, Institute of Oncology, Gliwice, 1949-55; Head of Department of Tumour Biology, Marie-Curie-Sklodowska Institute of Oncology, Warsaw, 1955-85. *Memberships:* Polish Oncological Society; European Association for Research into Cancer. *Publications:* Various articles in medical journals. *Honours:* Polish State Prize, 1951; Honorary Member, Polish Endocrinological Society, 1981. *Hobbies:* Fine Arts; Gardening. *Address:* Kanie, ul. Nadarzyńska 4, 05-805 Otrebusy, Poland.

DYBING, Erik, b. 3 June 1943, Oslo, Norway. Chief Medical Officer. m. Tone Borgenhov, 21 Aug. 1965,

Sandvika, 1 son, 1 daughter. *Education:* MD, University of Gottingen, Federal Republic of Germany, 1968; PhD, Pharmacology, University of Oslo, Norway, 1974. *Appointments:* Research Fellow, Institute of Pharmacology, University of Oslo, 1971-74; US Public Health International Fellow, National Institutes of Health, Bethesda, Maryland, USA, 1974-75; Deputy Head, 1974-81, Head, 1981-, Department of Toxicology, National Institute of Public Health, Oslo, Norway. *Memberships:* Norwegian Society of Pharmacology and Toxicology; Society of Toxicology; International Society for the Study of Xenobiotics. *Publications:* Author of over 100 scientific publications. *Honour:* Frank R, Blood Award, Society of Toxicology, 1984. *Hobbies:* Running; Sports administration. *Address:* Department of Toxicology, National Institute of Public Health, Geitmyraveien 75, 0462 Oslo 4, Norway.

DYCK, George, b. 25 July, 1937, Hague, Saskatchewan, Canada. Medical Director/University Professor. m. Edna Margaret Krueger, 27 June 1959, Gretna, Manitoba, Canada, 3 sons, 1 daughter. *Education:* B Chr Ed, Canadian Mennonite Bible College, 1959; MD, University of Manitoba, 1964; Diploma in Psychiatry, Menninger School of Psychiatry, 1968. *Appointments:* Prairie View Inc, Newton, Kansas, 1968-73; Chairman, Department of Psychiatry, 1973-80, Professor of Psychiatry 1973-, University of Kansas School of Medicine at Wichita; Medical Director, Prairie View Inc, *Memberships:* American Medical Association; American Psychiatric Association; Kansas Psychiatric Society. *Address:* Prairie View Inc, 1901 East First Street, Newton, KS 67114, USA.

DYER, Lois Edith, b. 18 Mar. 1925, Gosport, England. *Education:* MCSP. *Appointments:* Physiotherapist, Middlesex Hospital, London, 1945-47; Senior Physiotherapist, Coronation Non-European Hospital, Johannesburg, South Africa, 1948-51; Superintendent Physiotherapist, Johannesburg Group of Hospitals, 1951-56; Superintendent Physiotherapist, Westminster Hospital, London, 1958-61; Superintendent Physiotherapist, Royal National Orthopaedic Hospital, Stanmore, Middlesex, 1965-70; Physiotherapy Officer, Department of Health and Social Security, London, 1976-85. *Memberships:* Chartered Society of Physiotherapy, Honorary Life Vice-President; society for Research Rehabilitation. *Publications:* Numerous articles in journals in UK and abroad during last 30 years; "Care of the Orthopaedic Patient", 1977; Co-Editor, "Physiotherapy Practice', 1985. *Honour:* OBE, 1984. *Hobbies:* Music; Country Pursuits; Bridge; Food and Drink; Bird-watching; Animal Welfare; Conservation. *Address:* Garden Flat, 6 Belsize Grove, London NW3 4UN, England.

DYKEN, Mark Lewis, b. 26 Aug. 1928, Laramie, Wyoming, USA. University Professor, Chairman, Department of Neurology. m. Beverly All Dyken, 8 June 1951, Bloomington, Indiana, USA, 3 sons, 3 daughters. *Education:* BS, Anatomy and Physiology, Indiana University, 1985; MD, Indiana University Medical School, 1954; Internship, Indianapolis General Hospital 1954-55; Residency in Neurology, Indiana University Medical Center, 1955-58. *Appointments:* Clinical Director and Director of Research, New Castle State Hospital, New Castle, Indiana, 1958-61; Assistant Professor, 1961-64, Associate Professor, 1964-69, Professor, 1969-, Chairman, 1971-, Department of Neurology, Indiana University. *Memberships:* Chairman, Stroke Council, American Heart Association, 1984-86; President-elect, American Association of University Professors of Neurology, 1984-86; President 1986-88; Fellow, American Academy of Neurology; Member, American Neurological Association; County, State and National American Medical Association. *Publications:* In excess of 100 published papers on cerebral vascular disease, blood flow, epilepsy, electroencephalography, muscle disease etc. *Honours:* Selected Outstanding Teacher in Clinical Sciences by members of the

Medical Class of 1979, 1982 and 1986; Alpha Omega Alpha Medical Society, Faculty Member, Honorary, Indiana University Chapter, 1981. *Address:* Department of Neurology, 125 Emerson Hall, Indiana University School of Medicine, 545 Barnhill Drive, Indianapolis, IN 46223, USA.

DYKMAN, Roscfoe Arnold, b. 20 Mar. 1920, Pocatello, Idaho, USA, Professor and Head, Division of Behavioural Sciences, m. (1), 2 sons, 2 daughters, (2) Kathryn Donita Bowman, 10 May 1980, Fayetteville, Arkansas. *Education:* Diploma, Idaho State College, Pocatello, Idaho; BS, George Williams College, Chicago, Illinois; PhD, University of Chicago, Illinois. *Appointments:* Instructor, Illinois Institute of Technology, 1948-50; Postdoctoral Fellow, Johns Hopkins Medical School, 1950-52; Instructor, Johns Hopkins Hospital, 1952-55; Assistant Director of Studies, 1953-55; Professor and Director, Psychiatric Research Laboratory, University of Arkansas Medical Center, 1955-61, 1961-75; Professor and Director of Behavioural Science, University of Arkansas College of Medicine, 1975-. *Memberships:* American Association for Advancement of Science, 1950-; 2nd President Elect, 1985, Pavlovian Society of America, 1955-; Society of Psychophysiological Research, 1960-; Psychonomic Society, 1960-; American Psychological Association, 1950-; Sigma Xi, 1949-. *Publications:* Contributor of numerous articles to professional journals, 1950-. *Honours:* Research Award, University of Arkansas, 1961-72; Distinguished Scientist Award, Pavlovian Society of America, 1970; President-Elect, Pavlovian Society of America, 1986. *Hobbies:* Golf; Group workshops; Computers; Mathematics. *Address:* University of Arkansas for Medical Sciences, 4301 West Markham, MS-588, Little Rock, AR 72205, USA.

DYMECKI, Jerzy Marian, b. 27 Apr. 1926, Warszawa, Poland, Head of Department of Neuropathology, Psychoneurological Institute, Warszawa, 1968-, m. Janina Bem, 10 Feb. 1954, Gdynia, 1 daughter. *Education:* Diploma of Physician, Medical Academy, Gdansk, Poland, 1952; DMS, 1962, Docent of Neuropathology, 1968, Medical Academy, Warsaw; Professor of Medicine, State Council of Polish Republic, Warsaw, 1978. *Appointments:* Director of Province Dispensary of Mental Health, Gdansk, 1952-54; Senior Assistant, Neurological Clinic, Psychoneurolotgical Institute, Warsaw, 1954-62. *Memberships:* International Society of Neuropathology; Polish Association of Neuropathologists; Polish Neurological Society; Member of Commission of Neuropathology of Polish Academy of Sciences; Member, Editorial Board, 'Polish Neuropathology' and 'Polish Neurology and Neurosurgery'. *Publications:* "Neuropathology", (Editor, Co-author), 1981; 'Pathogenesis and pathomorphology of cerebral stroke', 1978; 'Pathogenesis and pathomorphology of subarachnoid haemorrhage', 1978; 'Effects of intracerebral transplantations of immature substantia nigra in rats with experimentally induced Parkinson's Disease', 1985. *Hobbies:* Travel; Mountain climbing. *Address:* Dobra Str 4 app 62, 00388 Warsaw, Poland.

DZBENSKI, Tadeusz Hubert, Lipiny. Head of Department. m. Regina Dabrowska, 20 June 1964, Gdańsk, 1 son, 2 daughters. *Education:* Physician, Medical Academy, Warsaw, 1962; DAPE, London School of Hygiene and Tropical Medicine, 1965; MD, Medical Academy, Gdansk, 1973; Doktor Habilitowany, National Institute of Hygiene, Warsaw, 1978. *Appointments:* Assistant, Institute of Marine Medicine, Gdansk, 1962-72; Assistant, Medical Academy, Gdansk, 1972-73; Adiunkt/Tutor, National Institute of Hygiene, Warsaw, 1974-80; Head, Department, National Institute of Hygiene, Warsaw, 1980-. *Membership:* Polish Society of Parasitology. *Publications:* Articles in Professional journals. *Hobby:* Sport. *Address:* Chocimska 24, 00 791 Warsaw, Poland.

E

EASTMAN, Alan Richard, b. 16 Oct. 1949, Surrey, England, Associate Professor, Eppley Institute for Research in Cancer, Omaha, Nebraska, USA, m. Teresa, 19 Feb. 1983, Hinesburg, Vermont, USA. *Education:* BTech, Brunel University, London, England, 1972; PhD, Chester Beatty Research Institute, University of London, 1975. *Appointments:* Research Associate, Medical College of Georgia, Augusta, Georgia, USA, 1976; Research Associate, 1976-78, Research Assistant Professor, 1978-83, department of Biochemistry, University of Vermont College of Medicine, Burlington, Vermont; Assistant Professor, Eppley Institute for Research in Cancer, University of Nebraska Medical Centre, Omaha, Nebraska, 1983-85. *Memberships:* American Association for Cancer Research; American Association of Biological Chemists. *Publications:* 'Molecular and Cellular Biology', (with R Ding, K Ghosh, E Bresnick), 1985; Contributor of over 30 papers in professional journals. *Honours:* Junior Faculty Research Award, American Cancer Society, 1980-85; Research Career Development Award, National Cancer Institute, 1983-88. *Hobby:* Soccer. *Address:* Eppley Institute for Research in Cancer, University of Nebraska Medical Centre, Omaha, NE 68105, USA.

EATON, James Eugene, b. 31 Mar. 1926, Torrington, Wyoming, USA. Chiropractor. m. Wilda Maxine Hinds, 16 Jan. 1946, Bernalillo, 4 daughters. *Education:* DC, Palmer College of Chiropractic, 1966, BSc., 1979, MSc., 1983, Clayton University, St Louis; FACACN; Diplomate, National Board of Chiropractic Examiners. *Appointment:* Chiropractic & Preventive Therapeutic Applied Nutritionist. *Memberships:* Kansas and American Chiropractic Associations; International Academy of Preventive Medicine; Midwest Academy of Preventive Medicine; International Academy of Clinical Acupuncture; World Wide Chiropractic Christian Association; The Gideons International; Kiwians, *Honours:* Palmer Chiropractic College Class President, 1965-66; Kansas Chiropractic Association, President 1972-73; Northwest Chiropractic Association, President 1982-84. *Hobbies:* Collecting Antique Sad Irons and Small Hand Tools. *Address:* 311 Williams, Great Bend, KS 67530, USA.

EBAUGH, Franklin G. Jnr, b. 25 Dec. 1921, Philadelphia Pennsylvania, USA. Professor of Medicine. 3 daughters. *Education:* AB, Magna Cum Laude Dartmouth College, 1944; MD, Cornell Medical College, 1946. *Appointments:* Internship in Medicine, 1946-47, Assistant Resident in Medicine, 1948, Resident in Haematology, 1949-50, New York Hospital; Research Associate, Evans Memorial Hospital, Boston, 1950-53; Surgeon, US Public Health Service, 1953-55; Associate Director of Laboratories, Hitchcock Clinic and Mary Hitchcock Memorial Hospital, 1955-64; Dean, Boston University School of Medicine, 64-69; Dean, University of Utah School of Medicine, 1969-71; Associate Dean of VA Affairs Stanford University School of Medicine, 1972- Chief of Staff Veterans Adminsitration Medical Center, Palo Atto, 1972-. *Memberships:* American Academy of Arts and Sciences; American Society of Clinical Investigation; American Society of Haematology; AOA Cornell Sigma Xi; Western Association of Physicians; American College of Physicians, *Publications:* Editor: "Management of Common Problems in Geriatric Medicine", 1981; In Press: "The Radioactive Sodium Chromate Method for Erythrocyte Survival" with J. F. Ross. 46 articles between 1946 and 1969 and 3 between 1977 and present. *Honours:* Army Achievement Medal for Meritorius Service 1980-82; The Army Commendation Medal, 1984. *Hobbies:* Skiing; Mountain climbing; Squash. *Address:* 3801 Miranda Avenue, Palo Alto, CA 94304, USA.

EDELMAN, Norman H, b. 21 May 1937, New York

City, USA. Professor and Associate Chairman, Medicine, Associate Dean for Research, University of Medicine and Dentistry of New Jersey, Rutgers Medical School. m. Ida Nadel, 21 June 1959, New York City, 1 son, 2 daughters. *Education:* AB, Brooklyn College; MD, New York University. *Appointments:* Resident, New York University Medical Center; Research Fellow NIH National Heart Institute; Visiting Fellow Columbia University; Research Associate, Michael Reese Medical Center; Assistant Professor, University of Pennsylvania. *Memberships:* Association of American Physicians; American Society of Clinical Investigation; American Physiological Society; American Thoracic Society; American College of Chest Physicians; American College of Medicine; Member, NIH Pulmonary Disease Advisory Committee; Member, NIH Study Section, *Publications:* Over 100 Scientific Papers; Editorial Boards: 'American Review of Respiratory Disease', 'Journal of Applied Physiology'. *Address:* Department of Medicine, UMDNJ-Rutgers Medical School, CN 19, New Brunswick, NJ 08901, USA.

EDELSTEN, Geoffrey Walter, b. 2 May 1943, Melbourne, Australia. Principal, The Edelsten Group. m. Leanne Margaret Nesbit, 29 July 1984, Sydney, Australia. *Education:* MB, BS, Melbourne University. *Appointments:* RMO, Royal Melbourne Hospital, 1967; Medical Superintendent, Aramac Hospital, Queensland, Australia 1968; Acting Medical Superintendent, Barcaldine Hospital, Queensland, Australia, 1968; Honorary Medical Officer, Walgett District Hospital, New South Wales, 1969-72; Honorary Medical Officer, Fairfield District Hospital, 1972; Honorary Medical Officer, Bankstown District Hospital, 1975; Honorary VMO, Liverpool District Hospital, New South Wales, 1972-. *Membership:* Australian Medical Association. *Hobbies:* Popular music; Flying. *Address:* 631 Old Northern Road, Dural, New South Wales 2158, Australia.

EDERER, Fred, b. 5 Mar. 1926, Vienna, Austria. Private Consultant, Epidemiologic Research. m. Hilda Tomar, 30 Mar. 1958, Washington District of Columbia, USA, 1 son, 2 daughters. *Education:* BS, College of the City of New York; MA, American University, Washington. *Appointments:* Research Biostatistician: National Cancer Institute, 1957-64, National Heart Institute, 1964-71; Head, Clinical Trials, 1971-75, Chief, Biometry & Epidemiology, 1975-84, Associate Director, 1984-85, Biometry & Epidemiology, National Eye Institute; Private Consultant. *Memberships:* Fellow: American College of Epidemiology, American Statistical Association; Society for Epidemiologic Research; Clinical Trials Society; Biometric Society. *Publications:* Articles in: 'Journal Chronic Diseases'; 'Biometrics'; 'Epidemiology', etc. *Honours:* Sustained High Quality Work Performance Award, Directors, National Institutes of Health, 1974; Superior Service Award, Dept. of Health Education & Welfare, 1975; David Rumbugh Scientific Award, Juvenile Diabetes Foundation, 1983. *Hobby:* Playing Chamber Music (Viola). *Address:* 5504 Lambeth Road, Bethesda, MD 20814, USA.

EDGERTON, Milton Thomas, b. 14 July, 1921, Atlanta, Georgia, USA. Plastic Surgeon. m. Patricia Jane Jones, 30 June, 1945, New York, USA, 2 sons. *Education:* BA, Emory University, USA, 1941; MD, Johns Hopkins University School of Medicine, 1944; Diplomat of the American Board of Surgery, 1951; Diplomat of the American Board of Plastic Surgery, 1951. *Appointments Include:* Assistant Resident in Surgery, Johns Hopkins University, 1949-51, Instructor in Plastic Surgery, 1951-53, Surgeon in Charge, Plastic Surgery, 1952-70, Assistant Professor of Plastic Surgery, 1951-53, Associate Professor, 1953-62, Professor, 1962-70; Plastic Surgeon in Chief, University of Virginia Medical Centre, 1970-present. *Memberships include:* Phi Beta Kappa, 1941; Eta Sigma Psi, 1941; American

Medical Association; American Association for the Advancement of Science; American Surgical Association; Fellow, American College of Surgeons; Pan American Medical Association; Society of Head and Neck Surgeons; American Psychosomatic Society; American Leprosy Missions Inc; Transplantation Society; Alpha Omega Alpha Honour Medical Society, 1985. *Publications:* Chapter: 'Emergency Care of Maxillofacial and Neck Injuries' in "The Management of Trauma", 1968; Chapter: 'Surgical Treatment of Male Transsexuals' in "Clinics in Plastic Surgery", 1974; "Vascular and Lymphatic Tumors in Infancy - Current Problems in Cancer", 1978; Chapter: 'Steroid Therapy of Hemangiomas' in 'QQ'. *Honours include:* Numerous visiting professorships. Recipient of many prizes and awards including Clinician of the Year Awards 1980 and 1981, American Association of Plastic Surgeons. *Hobbies:* Ski-ing; Tennis; Golf; Farming; Family related activities. *Address:* University of Virginia Medical Centre, Department of Plastic Surgery, Box 376, Charlottesville, VA 22908, USA.

EDMAN, K A Paul, b. 28 Nov. 1926, Mörlunda, Sweden. Professor of Pharmacology. m. Anna-Greta Björk, 24 June 1955, Karlskoga, 1 son, 1 daughter. *Education:* B Med 1949, MD 1955, PhD 1959, Uppsala. *Appointments:* Assistant Professor of Pharmacology, Uppsala, 1959-62; Honorary Research Associate in Physiology, University College, London, England, 1960-61; Associate Professor of Pharmacology, Umeå and Lund, Sweden, 1962-69; Research Professor in Physiology, University of California, Los Angeles, California, USA, 1968-69; Professor of Pharmacology, Lund, Sweden, 1969-. *Memberships:* Royal Physiographic Society, Lund; Scandinavian Physiological Society; Scandinavian Pharmacological Society; British Pharmacological Society; Associate Member, Physiological Society, Britain; Biophysical Soiciety, USA. *Publications:* Publications based on research work mainly in muscle physiology and pharmacology. *Hobbies:* Gardening; Fishing. *Address:* Department of Pharmacology; University of Lund, Sölvegatan 10, S 223 62 Lund, Sweden.

EDMONDS, Charles John, b. 17 Apr, 1929, London, England. Consultant Physician/Endocrinologist, Clinical Scientist, m. Gillian Mary Riggott, 13 Mar, 1965, Sevenoaks, Kent, 3 sons. *Education:* BSc 1st Class Honours Physiology, University College London, 1950; MB, BS, University College Hospital Medical School, 1953; Biophysics Laboratory, Harvard Medical School, USA, 1961-62; MD 1961, DSC 1982, University of London. *Appointments:* Flight Lieutenant RAF Institute of Aviation Medicine, Farnborough; Senior Clinical Assistant and Research Fellow Department of Therapeutics, Royal Infirmary, Sheffield; House Physician and Surgeon, Senior Registrar, Consultant Physician and Clinical Scientist in Department of Clinical Research, University College Hospital, London; Consultant Physician/Endocrinologist and Clinical Scientist, Medical Research Council, Northwick Park Hospital, Harrow, Middlesex. *Memberships:* British Medical Association; Royal Society of Medicine; Association of Physicians; Medical Research Society; Endocrine Society; Physiological Society, London. *Publications:* "The Large Intestine", (co-author), 1981; Many publications on Diuretics; Water and electrolyte pathophysiology; Intestinal, renal and endocrine physiology; Thyroid and adrenal disease. *Honours:* Bucknill Scholarship, University College Hospital, 1947; Sir William Dunn Scholarship, physiology, University of London, 1950; Rockefeller Travelling Fellowship, 1961; Fellow Royal College of Physicians (London) 1972. *Hobbies:* Walking; Cycling; Various sports. *Address:* 18 Beech Avenue, Radlett, Hertfordshire, WD7 7DE, England.

EDVINSSON, Lars Ingvar Herbert, b. 22 Sep. 1947, Malmö, Sweden, Consultant, M. Marie-Louise, 21 July 1979, Hultsjö, 1 son. *Education:* PhD 1975, MD 1979. *Appointments:* Research Fellow, 1971-76;

General Medicine, 1979-80; Resident, Clinical Pharmacology, 1980-86; Adjunct Professor of Pharmacology, SIU, Illinois, USA, 1982-86. *Memberships:* Swedish Physicians Association; International Neurochemical Society; British Pharmacological Society; Scandinavian Pharmacological Society; Scandinavian Physiology Society; International Society for Cerebral blood flow metabolism. *Publications:* Some 350 scientific papers 1970-85; Thesis 1975, Pharmacologcal Reviews 1976; 'Neurogenic Control of Brain Circulaion', 1977. *Honours:* Honorary Fellow Stroke Council; American Heart Association; Member, Editorial Boards 'Cephalalgia'; Journal of Cerebral blood-flow metabolism; Cerebral Aging Prevention. *Address:* Departments of Clinical Pharmacology and Internal Medicine, University Hospital, 221 85 Lund, Sweden.

EDWARDS, David Iwan, b. 14 Aug. 1940, Porthcawl, Wales. Reader and Head of Chemotherapy Research Unit. m. Jenifer Ann Brown, 1 Jan 1966, Gidea Park, Essex, England, 1 son, 1 daughter. *Education:* MIBiol Biochemistry, Barking College of Technology, 1968; PhD Microbiology, Queen Elizabeth College, University of London, 1971; Biochemistry Institute, University of Vienna, Vienna, Austria, 1975. *Appointments:* Technician, Research Laboratories, May and Baker Limited, Dagenham, Essex, England, 1961-66; Lecturer in Biochemistry, Paddington Technical College, London, 1966-71; Lecturer in Microbial Biochemistry 1971-72, Senior Lecturer in Microbiology 1972-79, Reader in Microbiology and Head of Chemotherapy Research Unit, 1979-, North East London Polytechnic, London. *Memberships:* Society for General Microbiology; Biochemical Society; British Society for Antimicrobial Chemotherapy; Association for Radiation Research; Society for Free Radical Research; Fellow, Royal Society of Chemistry. *Publications:* "Antimicrobial Drug Action", 1980; "Chemotherapeutic Strategy", 1983; 'Metronidazole' in "Antibiotics", Volume 6 (editor: F E Hahn), 1983; 'Mechanism of action of antitrichomonal drugs', 1984; Contribution to 'International Journal of Radiation Oncology, Biology and Physics', 1984. *Honour:* Royal Society Senior European Research Fellow, 1975. *Hobbies:* Wine; Viticulture; Cooking; Travel; Classical music; Writing; Golf. *Address:* Chemotherapy Research Unit, Department of Paramedical Sciences, North East London Polytechnic, Romford Road, London E15 4LZ, England.

EDWARDS, Hollis Alexander, b. 14 Nov. 1933, Tobago, West Indies. Director Toronto Family Therapy Institute; Director, Family Unit, Toronto East General Hospital, Canada. m. Gayle Catherine Farden, 3 Apr. 1965, Winnipeg, 2 sons. *Education:* MD (Man), 1964; FRCP (C); Dip. Psych. (Mcgill), 1969. *Appointments:* Chief Consultant, Psychiatry, Child & Family Section, Scarborough Community Mental Health; Director, Day Treatment Programme, Toronto East General Hospital; Director, In Patient Dept of Psychitry, Toronto East General Hospital. *Memberships:* Canadian and American Psychiatric Associations; Canadian Medical Association; Royal College of Physicians and Surgeons; American Family Therapy Association; Ontario Medical Association; Canadian Association for the Treatment and Study of the Family; etc. *Publication:* "A Model of Change in Family Systems", 'The Family', Volume 1, 1977. *Honours:* Founder, Toronto Family Therapy Institute, 1978. *Hobbies:* Music; Drama; Photography; Sports. *Address:* 1716 Bayview Avenue, Toronto, Ontario, Canada M4G 3C4.

EDWARDS, Larry D., b. 20 June 1937, Macomb, Illinois, USA. University Dean/Medical Director, Medical and Research Center. m. Ann L. Will, 31 Mar 1959, 1 son, 2 daughters. *Education:* MD, University of Illinois College of Medicine, Chicago, Illinois. *Appointments:* Assistant Professor, Department of

Medicine and Preventive Medicine, Assistant Scientist Department of Micro, Rush Medical College, Chicago; Associate Professor of Medicine, Professor of Medicine, Director, Division of Infectious Disease, Deputy Head, Department of Biomedical Sciences, Rockford School of Medicine, University of Illinios School of Public Health, Chicago, Illinois; Department Affiliate, University of Illiniois Department of Medicine, Abraham Lincoln School of Medicine, Chicago, Illinois; Director, Division of Infectious Diseases, Professor of Medicine, Chairman, Department of Internal Medicine, Associate Dean for Clinical Sciences, Dean, Oral Roberts University School of Medicine, Tulsa, Oklahoma. *Memberships:* American Society of Microbiology; American Federation for Clinical Research; Oklahoma Infectious Disease Society; Association of Professors of Medicine; Christian Medical Society. *Publications include:* 'Nongonococcal Urethritis: A survey of clinical and laboratory features' Sexually Transmitted Diseases 1980 with T. E. Root and P. J. Spengler; Adjunct Associate Professor in Epidemiology. University of Illinoi.'Office practice management of bronchitis and pneumonia due to Mycoplasma pneumoniae' Postgraduate Medicine Communications, 1981 with T. E. Kratzer and T. R. Vikander; 'Comparative Methods on 101 Intravenous Catheters. Routine, Semiquantitative and Blood Cultures' Arch Int Med, 1983, with M. Moyer and L. Farley; 'The Tri-plate as an Accurate Cost Effective Site Screening System for Neisseria gonorrhoeae' Journal of Clinical Microbiology, 1984 with T. Gartner. *Honours:* Smith, Kline and French Fellowship for study in Ethiopia, 1964; Letter of commendation for study on hospital infections, US Public Health Service Hospital, Staten Island, New York, 1968; Oral Roberts University School of Medicine Outstanding Faculty Member of Year, 1983. *Address:* Oral Roberts University School of Medicine, 8181 South Lewis, Tulsa, OK 74137, USA.

EDWARDS, Mary Frances, b. 13 Mar. 1947, McAlester, Oklahoma, USA. Director, Hawkeye Health & Rehabilitation Programmes. *Education:* BS, Oklahoma State University; MA, Northwestern University. *Appoointments:* Speech pathologist, Portsmouth Rehabilitation Centre, New Hampshire; Vista volunteer, Elkins, Arizona; Head Start Director, Winslow, Arizona; Speech/Language pathologist, St. Luke's Hospital, Cedar Rapids, Iowa; Rehabilitation Administration Assistant, St. Luke's Hospital. *Memberships:* American Speech & Hearing Association; Iowa Speech & Hearing Association. *Publication:* Book Chapter, 'Rehabilitative Home Care' (Continuity of Care: Advancing the Concept of Discharge Planning, 1985). *Honour:* Fellow, Iowa Speech-Language-Hearing Association, 1983. *Hobbies:* Bowling; Softball; Tennis. *Address:* 2025 D Street, Iowa City, IA 52240, USA.

EDWARDS, Robert George, b. 1 Jan. 1928, England. Deputy Director, Institute of Medical & Veterinary Science, Adelaide, Australia. m. Fay Madeline Gaffney, 18 Feb. 1956, Adelaide, 1 son, 3 daughters. *Education:* BSc, MSc, London, 1950, 1954 MB, BS, Adelaide, 1959; FRCPA 1963; FAACB, 1968; FRCPath 1977; FRACP, 1978. *Appointments:* Staff, Medical Research Counil Unit, Department of Human Anatomy, Oxford, 1953-55; Resident Medical Officer, Queen Elizabeth Hospital, 1960; Pathology Registrar, IMVS, 1961; Southwestern Medical School, University of Texas, Dallas, USA, 1963-64; Pathologist, IMVS, 1965; Head, Division of Clinical Chemistry 1967, Deputy Director 1977, Institute of Medical & Vetinary Science (IMVS). *Memberships:* President 1981-83, Royal College of Pathologists of Australia; Royal College of Pathologists, UK; Royal Australasian College of Physicians; Australian Association of Clinical Biochemists. *Publications:* Various papers on physiology, chemical pathology. *Hobby:* Sailing. *Address:* Institute of Medical & Veterinary Science, Frome Road, Adelaide, South Australia 5000.

EGAN, Robert Lee, b. 9 May 1920, Arkansas, USA. Professor of Radiology, Emory University School of Medicine. m. Mary Alice Vetterley, 28 Oct. 1950, 5 daughters. *Education:* MD; Intern US Naval Hospital, Virginia, 1950-51; Resident, Jefferson Hospital, Philadelphia, 1953-55; Fellow, M.D. Anderson Hospital, Houston, 1955-56; American Board of Radiology, 1956. *Appointments:* Assistant, Associate Professor, Radiology, University of Texas, 1956-62; Chief, Experimental Radiology, M.D. Anderson Hospital, 1962; Radiologist, Methodist Hospital, Indiana, 1962-64; Associate Professor 1964-68, Chief, Section of Mammography 1964-81, Professor of Radiology 1968-, Chief, Breast Imaging Centre 1981-83, Chief, Breast Research 1981-, Emory University. *Memberships:* American Roentgen Ray Society; Radiological Society of North America; Public Cancer Association of America; Pan-Pacific Surgical Society; American Cancer Society; New York Academy of Science; etc. *Publications include:* 14 medical books; Approximately 50 chapters in medical books; Over 200 refereed scientific articles; 560 lectures, papers, scientific exhibits. All on cancer, mostly cancer of breast. *Honours:* Lucy Wortham James Clinical Research Award, Society of Surgical Oncology, 1977; Distinguished Service Award, American Cancer Society, 1975; 3rd Annual Wendell G. Scott Memorial Lecture, 1975. *Hobbies:* Gardening; Water sports; Orchids; Bees. *Address:* Department of Radiology, Emory University School of Medicine, Woodruff Memorial Building, Atlanta, GA 30322, USA.

EGGERS, Hans J., b. 26 July 1927, Baumholder, Federal Republic of Germany. Professor of Virology. *Education:* ärztl. Vorprüfung, University of Köln, 1949; mediz. Staatsexamen, 1953, mediz. Doktorexamen, 1953, University of Heidelberg. *Appointments:* Karolinska Institutet, Stockholm, Virusinstitutionen (S Gard), 1954; Nervenklinik, University of Köln (W Scheid), 1955-57; Children's Hospital, University of Cincinnati, Ohio, (A B Sabin) 1957-59; The Rockefeller Institute, New York (F L Hossfall, I Tamm), 1959-64; Max-Planck-Institut für Virusforschung, Tübingen, 1965; Professor of Virology, Univeresität Giessen, 1966-72; Professor of Virology, Universität zu Köln, 1972-. *Memberships:* The Harvey Society; American Association of Immunologists; Society of Experimental Biology and Medicine; American Society of Microbiology; Deutsche Gesellschaft für Hygiene und Mikrobiologie; Paul Ehrlich Gesellschaft für Chemotherapie. *Publications:* 'Specific Inhibition of Replication of Animal Viruses' in 'Science' 1963; 'Antiviral Chemotherapy' in 'Ann Rev Pharmacol' 1966; 'Benzimidazoles: Selective Inhibitors of Picornavirus Repook of Experimental Pharmacology' 1982. *Honour:* Member, Deutsche Akademie der Naturforscher Leopoldina, 1982. *Hobbies:* Music; Literature. *Address:* Institut für Virologie der Universität zu Köln, Fürst-Pückler-Str 56, D-5000 Köln 41, Federal Republic of Germany.

EHRENSING, Rudolph Henry, b. 17 Nov, 1939, New Orleans, Louisiana,USA. Medical Director; Hospital Medical Staff President.m. Gayle F.Wurzlow, MD, 8 Apr 1967, 2 sons, 2 daughters. *Education:* BS, cum laude, University of Notre Dame, USA, 1961; MD, Cornell University Medical College, New York, 1965. *Appointments:* Director, Adolescent Inpatient Treatment Unit, DePaul Hospital New Orleans, 1972-73; Medical Staff, Department of Psychiatry, Houma Medical and Surgical Clinic, Houma, Los Angeles (part time), 1972-74; Associate Head, Department of Psychiatry, Oschner Clinic and Foundation Hospital, New Orleans, 1974-75; Vice President, Medical Staff, Oschner Foundation Hospital, New Orleans, 1983-85; Associate Medical Director Ochsner Clinic and Chairman, Department of Psychiatry, Oschner Clinic, President of Medical Staff, Oschner Foundation Hospital-. *Memberships Include:* Fellow, American Psychiatric Association; Fellow, American College of Psychiatrists; Fellow, Southern Psychiatric Association; American Medical

Association; American Psychosomatic Society; International Society of Psychoneuroendricrinology; American Board of Psychiatry and Neurology. *Publications Include:* 15 conference papers; numerous articles in medical journals; co-author book sections including: 'Clinical Effects of Hypothalmic-Pituitary Peptides Upon the Central Nervous System' in 'Clinical Neuropharmacology', 1978; 'Effects of MIF-I and TRH on the Brain' in 'Hormones and the Brain', 1980; 'MIF' in 'Encyclopedia of Neuroscience', 1984. *Hobbies:* Gardening; Fishing; Hunting. *Address:* 1514 Jefferson Highway, New Orleans, LA 70121, USA.

EHRLICH, George Edward, b. 18 July 1928, Vienna, Austria. Vice-President, Ciba-Geigy Pharmaceuticals; Adjunct Professor of Clinical Medicine, New York University. m. Gail Abrams, 30 Mar. 1968, Philadelphia, USA, 2 sons, 1 daughter. *Education:* AB, cum laude, Harvard University, 1948; MB, MD, Chicago Medical School, 1952. *Appointments:* Instructor in Medicine, Cornell University; 1959-64; Assistant- Associate Professor to Professor of Medicine and Rehabilitation Medicine, Temple University; Director, Arthritis Center and Rheumatology, Albert Einstein Medical Center and Moss Rehabilitation Hospital, 1964-80; Professor of Medicine and Director of Rheumatology, Hahnemann University, Philadelphia, 1980-83. *Memberships:* American College of Physicians; American Medical Association; academy of Rehabilitation Medicine; academy of Medicine; New York Academy of Sciences; Philadelphia College of Physicians; British Society of Rheumatology; 12 other medical societies. *Publications:* 'Total Management of the Arthritic Patient', 1973; 'Oculocutaneous Manifestations of Rheumatic Conditions', 1973; 'Prognosis', 1980; 'Rehabilitation Management of Rheumatic Conditions', 1980, 2nd Edition, 1986; 'Rheumatoid Arthritis', 1985; Books; More than 200 scientific articles; more than 50 chapters in books edited by others. *Honours:* Philip Hench award, 1971; Distinguished Alumnus Award, Chicago Medical School, 1969; numerous other citations and awards and named lectureships. *Hobbies:* Classical Music; Opera. *Address:* 38 Holly Drive, Loveladies, NJ 08008, USA.

EICHNER, Eduard, b. 11 Nov. 1905, Cleveland, Ohio, USA. Doctor of Medicine (Gynaecology, Endocrinology and Oncology). *Education:* AB, Western Reserve University, 1925; MD, School of Medicine, Western Reserve University, 1929; Intern, St. Alexis Hospital, School of Medicine, Western Reserve University, 1929; Intern, St. Alexis Hospital, Cleveland, 1929-30; Resident, Obstetrics, St, Ann Hospital, Cleveland, 1930-31; Proctor Training, Obstetrics and Gynaecology, 1932-36. *Appointments:* Consultant in Obstetrics and Gynaecology, Cleveland State Hospital, 1949; Associate, 1954; Director, Family Planning Clinic, Mt, Sinai Hospital, 1954-75; Associate, Clinical Professor, Obstetrics and Gynaecology, CWRU School of Medicine, 1973; Private Practice, General Medicine. 1931-37, Obstetrics and Gynaecology, 1938-72, Gynaecology Endocrinology and Oncology, 1973-; Emeritus Clinical Professor, Obstetrics and Gynaecology, 1983. *Memberships include:* American Medical Association; Central Association of Obstetricians & Gynaecologists; Diplomate, American Board of Obstetrics and Gynaecology; Fellow, American College of Surgeons; Founding Fellow, American College of Obstetricians and Gynaecologists; Fellow, American College of Surgeons; American Fertility Society; New York Academy of Science; Medical Alumni Association; Kappa NU; Phi Lambda Kappa Sigma Xi, etc, *Publications:* Contributor to professional journals, etc. *Honours include:* Awards for Original Investigation, American College of Obstetricians and Gynecologists, 1954, 63, Ohio Medical Association, 1955, 63, ACS 1955, Modern Medicine 1956; Gold Medal Award, Original Investiation, Ohio State Medical Association, Columbus, 1955; Julius E,

Goodman Award, Mt. Sinai Hospital, 1979. *Address:* Severance Medical Arts Building, Severance Circle, Cleveland Heights, OH 44118, USA.

EICHSTAEDT, Hermann Warner, b. 15 Feb. 1948. Alten-Buseck, West Germany. Professor of Cardiology; Senior Lecturer. m. Regina Actmann, 8 Oct. 1971, 1 son, 1 daughter. *Education:* MD; PhD; Studied Medicine at Universities of Mainz and Dusseldorf. *Appointments:* Participated in resarch projects in cardiac surgery at University Hospital of Dusseldorf, 1972-74; Resident in Cardiology, Cardiological Clinic, Bad Krozingen, 1975-77; Radiology in Freiburg; Special Training in Internal Medicine, University of Tuebingen, 1977-79; Researcher and Teacher, Cardiology Department, University Hospital, Berlin-Charlottenburg, 1979-; Lecturer, Internal Medicine, 1981-; Member of the Directory of the Department of Internal Medicine, 1981-; Attended almost all the major German and European congresses on nuclear cardiology and has visited American clinics for supplementary training in this field. *Memberships include:* Fellow, American College of Chest Physicians 1982. Publications: Authors of papers and contributions to journals and textbooks of over 200 articles, *Honour:* Elected, as an Active Member, to the New York Academy of Sciences. *Address:* Arzt f. Innere Medixin u. Kardiologie, Leibnizstrasse 58, 1000 Berlin 12, Federal German Republic.

EISDORFER, Carl, b. 20 June 1930, Bronx, New York, USA. Professor of Psychiatry & Neuroscience. *Education:* BA 1951, MA 1953, PhD 1959, New York University; MD, Duke University Schools of Medicine, Durham, North Carolina, 1964; Internship (Medicine), 1964-65, Psychiatric Training 1964-67, Duke University Medical Centre, Durham; Programme for Health Systems Management, 1981. *Appointments include:* Social Work Posts, New York City, 1952-54; US Army Clinical Psychology Specialist, 1954-56; Research Assistant 1956-68, Professor of Psychiatry 1968-72, Professor of Medical Psychology 1968-72, Duke University; Professor & Chairman, Department of Psychiatry & Behavioural Sciences, School; of Medicine, Adjunct Professor, Department of Psychology, University of Washington, Seattle, 1972-81; Professor, Departments of Psychiatry & Neuroscience, Albert Einstein College of Medicine, Bronx, New York, 1981-. *Memberships include:* Fellow, New York Academy of Medicine, 1981; American Psychological Association; Gerontological Society of America, President 1971-72; American Geriatric Society; American Psychiatric Association; American College of Psychiatrists; Member, American Psychopathological Association; Sogma Xi; American Psychosomatic Society; American Association for Geriatric Psychiatry; Various editorial responsibilities especially in field of aging. *Publications:* Author & Co-author of some 200 articles in field of Geriatric Psychiatry & other areas. *Honours:* Numerous awards, recognitions, certificates; Fellow, American Association for the Advancement of Science, 1977; Alpha Omega Alpha, 1978. *Address:* 111 East 210th Street, Bronx, NY 10467, USA.

EISENBERG, Bruce Elliot, b, 22 July 1955, Staten Island, New York, USA. Doctor of Chiropractic. *Education:* Bachelor of Science, Brooklyn College, City University of New York; Doctor of Chiropractic, New York Chiropractic College, 1979; Course for certificate in sports injuries, National college of Chiropractic, Lombard, Illinois, 1984. *Appointments:* Co-Director, Eisenberg Chiropractic Office; Co-Director, Raritan Valley Chiropractic Center; Panel of Examining Physicians, Strassberg Medical Services. *Memberships:* New York State Chiropractic Association, President, Staten Island, District; American Chiropractic Association; New Jersey Chiropractic Society; Foundation of Chiropractic Education and Research; New York Academy of Sciences; American Council on Mental

Health of American Chiropractic Association etc. *Publications:* Articles on Health and on Masonry in 'Staten Island Mason" 1983. *Honours Include:* Certificate of achievemnt in Science, National Science Teachers Association, 1966; Outstanding Young Men of America, 1977; National Honor Society in Psychology, 1977; Award of Achievement from Borough President, Staten Island, 1984; Certificate of Merit, Brotherhood Fund, Grand Lodge of Free and Accepted Mansons of New York, 1982. *Hobby:* Writing. *Address:* 941 Jewett Avenue, Staten Island, NY 10314, USA.

EISENBERG, Karen Sue Byer, b. 11 Mar. 1954, Brooklyn, New York, USA. Assistant Nursing Director, Pathology, Downstate Medical Centre, Brooklyn. m. Howard Eisenberg, 11 May 1974. *Education:* BS, Long Island University, 1976; MPS, Health care Administration, 1977; Numerous postgraduate courses & seminars. *Appointments include:* Utlisation Review Analyst, 1976, Nursing Supervisor 1976, Seagrit Health Related Facility, New York; Staff nurse 1978, Intensive care nurse 1978-79, Dowstate Medical Centre, New York; Assistant Nursing Director, Pathology/Clinical Researh Associate, Research Foundation of the State of New York, Dowstate Medical Centre, 1979-. *Memberships:* New York Academy of Sciences; Oncology Nursing Society; American Nurses Association; etc. *Publications include:* Contributions to various nursing & medical journals. *Address:* Downstate Medical Centre, 450 Clarkson Avenue, Box 25, Brooklyn, NY 11203, USA.

EITINGER, Leo Shua, b. 12 Dec. 1912, Lomnice. Professor Emeritus/Head of Board for Forensic Psychiatry in Norway. m. Elisabeth Lisl Kohn, 1 July 1946, Stockholm, Sweden. *Education:* MD, 1937, Doctor of Medical Science 1957. *Appointments:* Psychiatric Consultant to Norwegian Armed Forces; Intern, Assistant, Clinical Director, Medical Superintendent and Head of Department and University Institute of Psychiatry, University of Oslo. *Memberships:* Norwegian Medical Association; Norwegian Medical Society; Norwegian Psychiatric Association; Danish Psychiatric Association; Corresponding Member; American Psychiatric Association, Corresponding Fellow; German Psychiatric Association, Corresponding Member; Australian Society of Forensic Psychiatry, Honorary Member; Norwegian Academy of Sciences. *Publications:* Textbooks on Neuroses, Psychoses and Forensic Psychiatry, several editions 1961-85; "Psychiatric Investigation of Refugees in Norway" 1957; "Concentration Camp Survivors in Norway and Israel" 1964; "Mortality and Morbidity after Excessive Stress" 1971; Antisemitism in Our Time" 1985 and about 20 others. *Honours:* HM the King's Gold Medal, 1954; Commander of the Royal St. Olav's Order, 1978. *Address:* Ø.Ullern Terr. 67, N-0380 Oslo 3, Norway.

EKERT, Henry, b. 28 July 1936, Poland. Director, Department of Clinical Haematology and Oncology. m. Barbara Joan Terry, 28 Dec. 1958, Dandenong, Victoria, Australia, 1 son, 2 daughters. *Education:* Bachelor of Medicine and Surgery, 1960; MRACP, 1964; FRACP, 1972; FRCPA, 1973; MD, University of Melbourne, 1978. *Appointments include:* Haematology and Oncology Research Fellow, Children's Hospital of Los Angeles, California, USA, 1967-69; Lecturer in Paediatrics, University of London, Great Ormond Street Hospital for Sick Children, 1969-70; Clinical Haematologist and Senior Research Fellow, 1970-71, Deptuy Director of Haematology Clinic and Senior Research Fellow, Research Foundation, 1971-73, Director Haematology Clinic/Deputy Head Haematology Research Unit, 1973-74, Director, Department of Clinical Haematology and Oncolgoy, 1974-, Royal Children's Hospital, Melbourne, Australia; Sabbatical 6 months in research capacity at Oxford Haemophilia Centre, 1976; Sabbatical 6 months in research capacity at the Weizman Institute 1983. *Memberships:* Australian Paediatric Research Society; Australian Society for Medical Research; Australian College of Paediatrics; Haematology Society of Australia; International Society of Haematology; Member of the Senate of the international College of Paediatrics; International Society of thrombosis and Haemostasis; Clinical Oncology Society of Australia; World Federation of Haemophilia; The American Society of Pediatric Heamtology/Oncology; CCSG Corresponding Member. *Publications:* Clinical Paediatric Haematology and Oncology" 1982; 107 publications in scientific journals etc. *Honour:* Hellenic Distinction, 1983. *Hobbies:* Reading, particularly biographical history; Music appreciation; Tennis; Travel; Gardening. *Address:* Royal Children's Hospital, Flemington Road, Parkville; Victoria 3052, Australia.

EKPECHI, Onuora Louis Victor, b. 8 Dec. 1930, Nigeria. Professor of Medicine. m. Georgina Obiagelia Ekun-Melie, 2 Jan. 1960, Liverpool, England; 2 sons, 3 daughters. *Education:* PhD, 1964; MB, London, England; FRCP, 1972; FWACP, 1971; FMCP, 1972. *Appointments:* Associate Lecturer, University of Ibadan, 1965; Senior Lecturer, 1967, Reader 1972, Professor, 1973, Medicine, University of Nigeria; Research Fellow, Hammersmith Hospital, London, England, 1963; Visiting Professor, Medicine, Kings College, 1979; Senior Research Scientist, Massachusetts Institute of Technology, Cambridge, Massachusetts, USA, 1980; Regional Coordinator for Africa, International Council for the Control of Deficiency Diseases: currently, Professor of Medicine, College of Medicine, University of Nigeria. *Address:* Department of Medicine, College of Medicine, University of Nigeria, Enugu, Nigeria.

ELFENBEIN, Gerald Jay, b. 4 Mar. 1945, USA. Associate Professor of Medicine; Medical Director, Bone Marrow Transplant Unit. m. C. Dianne Strobel, 22 June 1968, Towson, Maryland, 1 son, 1 daughter. *Education:* AB, Harvard College, 1966; MD, Johns Hopkins University, 1970. *Appointments include:* Fellow in Oncology 1974-76, Assistant Professor, Oncology & Medicine, Johns Hopkins University, 1976-81; Investigator, Howard Hughes Medical Institute, 1976-80; Associate Professor, Medicine & Immunology/Medical Microbiolgoy, University of Florida, 1981-; Medical Director, Bone Marrow Transplant Unit, Shands Hospital, 1981-. *Memberships include:* American Federation for Clincial Research; American Association of Immunologists; American Society of Haematology; American Society of Clincial Oncolgoy; American Association for Cancer Research; International Society for Experimental Haematology; Transplantation Society; Southeastern Cancer Study Group; etc. *Publications include:* 56 journal articles; 90 abstracts; 16 book chapters. *Honours:* Phi Beta Kappa, 1966; Summa cum laude, 1966; Alpha Omega Alpha, 1970; Award, American Institute of Chemists, 1966; Mosby Scholarship Award, 1970. *Hobbies:* Volleyball; Jogging. *Address:* Box J-277, J. Hillis Miller Health Centre, University of Florida, Gainesville, FL 32610, USA.

ELIA, Mumtaz Hamid, b. 29 Dec. 1945, Iraq. Consultant. m. Caroline, 20 July 1977, Glasgow, Scotland. *Education:* MB Ch.B., Baghdad University, Iraq, 1969; DMRT (UK), 1977; FRCR, Radiotherapy and Oncolgy, (UK), 1978. *Appointments:* SHO, Institute of Radiology and Nuclear Medicine, Baghdad, Iraq; Clinical Assistant, Glasgow Institute of Radiotherapy & Oncology, Scotland; Clincial Assistant, Royal Marsden Hospital, London & Surrey, England; Registrar, Radiotherapy & Oncology, Royal Free Hospital, London; Senior Registrar, Radiotherapy & Oncology, Newcastle General Hospital; Consultant, Radiotherpay & Oncology; Director, North Scotland Cancer Registry, Raigmore Hospital, Inverness. *Memberships:* Fellow, Royal college of Radiologists, UK; American

Society of Radiology and Oncology. *Publications:* Contributor to: 'Atlas of Cancer Morbidity of Scotland'; 'Cancer Incidence in Five Continents'. *Hobbies:* Swimming; Photography. *Address:* Department of Radiotherapy & Oncology, Raigmore Hospital, Inverness, Scotland.

ELIAS, Richard A. b. 9 July 1930, West Virginia, USA. Boards of Trustees and Directors, Miami Heart Institute; Clinical Professor; Chief of Professional Services. m. 1)Joan Awad Elias, deceased, 2 sons, 1 daughter. 2) Susan H Wells, 14 May 1983, Oklhahoma City. *Education:* BA, West Virginia University, 1951; MD, Columbia University 1955. Fellowships: American College of Chest Physicians;American College of Angiology American College of Physicians; Pan American Medical Association; Diplomate member in Internal Medicine. *Appointments:* Intern, Columbia Division, Bellevue Hospital,1955-56; Military Duty, 1957-59; Fellow, Mayor Foundation for Medical Education and Research, 1959-61; Private Practice, 1962-, with hospital affiliations including Miami Heart Institute, Jackson Memorial Hospital and Veterans Administration Hospitals; Professor of Medicine, University of Miami Medical School, 1962-. *Memberships Include:* Board of Trustees and Director, Miami Heart Institute; Past President,Heart Association of the Greater Miami; Board of Directors, United Health Foundation. *Publications:* 'Anticoagulant Therapy in Ischemic Heart Disease', contributor, 1965; author or co-author of several papers contributed to professional journals including 'Journal of Clinical Investigation; 'US Armed Forces Medical Journal'; 'Clinical Research'. *Honours:* US Submarine Base Insignia, 1957-58; Award for Meritorious Service, American Heart Association, 1969; Silver Medallion, Miami Heart Institute, 1972; Meritorious Service, American College of Chest Physicians, 1970-71; Certificate for instruction, 1971-72; Certificate for instruction, 1971-72, Trustee, 1979, Grovernor, Medical School, 1979, University of Miami; Builders Silver Shovel Award, Miami Heart Institute. *Hobbies:* Running; Tennis; Golf. *Address:* 550 Brickell Avenue, Suite 610, Miami, FL 33131, USA.

ELKINS, Gary Ray, b. 5 Oct, 1952, Hot Springs, Arkansas, USA. Director, Stress Disorders Clinic. m. Dorothy J Elkins, 31 May 1975, Hot Springs. *Education:* BA, Henderson State University, 1975; MA, East Texas State University, 1976; PhD, Texas A & M University, 1980. *Appointments:* Chief Clinical Psychologist, Mental Health Service, Grand North Dakota School of Medicine, 1981-82; Programme, Director Management Programme, Scott & White Clinic, Texas, 1982-84; Director, Stress Disorders Clinic, Scott and White Clinic & Hospital; Assistant Professor, Psychiatry, Texas A & M University School of Medicine. *Memberships:* American Psychological Association; American Society of Clinical hypnosis; Society for Clinical and Experimental Hynosis; Academy of Psychosomatic Medicine. *Publications:* 24 publications including: 'Hemispheric Asymmetry as a Model for Hypnotic Phenomina: A Review and Analysis', 'American Journal of Clinical Hypnosis'. *Hobbies:* Golf; Camping. *Address:* Dept. of Psychiatry, Scott and White Clinic, Temple, TX 76501, USA.

ELKOWITZ, Edward B, b. 1 May 1934, USA. President, American College of Osteopathic Medicine. m. Pamelia, 22 Oct. 1980, New York, USA, 1 son, 1 daughter. *Education:* BS, Columbia University, USA, 1955; DO, Chicago College of Osteopathic Medicine, 1960; DMS, State University of New York;1979. *Appointments:* Chairman, Department of Geriatric Medicine, Interbord Hospital New York; Clinical Assistant Professor, Down State Medical Center; Preceptor, Department of Gerontology, New York University Medical Centre; Chairman, Department of Geriatric Medicine, NY Com., New York; Assistant Clinical

Professor, New York College of Osteopathic Medicine; Preceptor, Clinical Medicine, Texas College of Osteopathic Medicine; President, American College of Osteopathic Medicine. *Memberships:* American Osteopathic Assocaiton; New York state Osteopathic Association; American Geriatric Society; National Institute of Aging; Gerontological Society; American Osteopathic College of Geriatric Specialists. *Publications Include:* "Geriatric Medicine for the Primary care Practitioner", 1981; "The Family Physician and Care of the Dying Abed" in "the Life Threatened Elderly", 1984. *Honours;* Fellow, American Geriatric Society; Fellow, American Osteopathic College of Geriatric Medicine; Fellow, Internaitonal College of Physicians and Surgeons. *Hobbies:* Horticulture; Oil Painting; Model Building. *Address:* 1610 Ralph Avenue, Brooklyn, NY 11236, USA.

ELL, Peter Josef, b. 7 May 1944, Lisbon, Portugal. Director, Institute of Nuclear Medicine. m. Yvonne Yolantha Maya Brink, 19 Aug. 1980, 2 sons. *Education:* MD, Lisbon University, 1969; MSc, London University, England, 1972; Private Docent, University of Bern, Switzerland, 1981; Member, Royal College of Physicians, 1984; Fellow, Royal College of Radiology, 1984. *Appointments:* Currently, Director, Institute of Nuclear Medicine, Middlesex Hospital Medical School, London, England; Secretary, European Nuclear Medicine Society; Council Member; Society of Nuclear Medicine/Europe; British Institute of Radiology; British Nuclear Medicine Society. *Publications:* Co-Author: "Nuclear Medicine: An Introductory Text", 1981; "Atlas of Computerized Emission Tomography", 1980; "Radionuclide Section Scanning", 1982; "Radionuclide Ventricular Function Studies", 1982; "Gamma Camera Emission Tomography", 1984; "Diagnosis of Metabolic Bone Disease", 1985; author of over 130 scientific publications. *Honour:* Corresponding Member, Finnish Nuclear Medicine Society. *Hobbies:* Study of languages; The Arts. *Address:* Institute of Nuclear Medicine, Middlesex Hospital Medical School, Mortimer Street, London W1N 8AA, England.

ELLIOTT, Donald Wesley, b. 2 Feb. 1924, Canada. Family Physician; Clincial Assistant Professor. m. Mary Tutton, 2 July 1949, Hamilton, 2 sons, 1 daughter. *Education:* PhmB, University of Toronto, 1948; MD, University of Western Ontario, 1964; Certification in Family Medicine, College of Family Physicians of Canada, 1971. *Appointments:* Family Physician; Clinical Assistant Professor, Faculty of Medicine, University of Western Ontario. *Memberships:* College of Family Physicians of Canada; Canadian Medical Association; Ontario Medical Association. *Honour:* Serving Brother, Order of St John, 1981. *Hobbies:* Piper of Highland Bagpipes; Part-time farmer. *Address:* 335 Wharncliffe Road North, London, Ontario N6G 1E4, Canada.

ELLIS, Harold b. 13 Jan. 1926, London, England. Professor of Surgery m. Wendy Levine, 20 Apr. 1958, London, 1 son, 1 daughter. *Education:* BM, BCh, Oxford University, England, 1948, M.Ch, 1956, DM, 1962.*Appointments:* Resident Posts, Oxford, 1948-49; Captain, Royal Army Medical corps, 1950-51; Resident Surgical Posts in Oxford, Sheffield and London, 1952-60; Senior Lecturer, Westminster Hospital Medical School, 1960-62; Professor of Surgery -. *Memberships:* Vice President, Royal College of Surgeons; Consultant Surgeon to the Army; Member of Council, Royal Society ofMedicine. *Publications:* "Clinical Anatomy", 7th edition, 1983; "Maincot's Abdominal Operations", 1984; "Famous Operations", 1984; "Wound Healing for Surgeons", 1984, etc. *Honours:* Hallett Prize, Royal College of Surgeons, 1950.*Hobbies:* Medical History; Hiking. *Address:* Department of Surgery, Charing Cross and Westminster Medical School, Westminster Hospital, Page Street Wing, London SW1P 2AP, England.

ELLIS, Peter Stephen Joseph, b. 26 Oct. 1950, London, England. Consultant Pathologist. m. Catherine, 15 Sep. 1973, London, 2 son, 1 daughter. *Education:* MA, University of Cambridge, England, 1974; MB ChB London Hospital Medical College, 1974-75; Fellow, Royal College of Pathologists of Australasia, 1980. *Appointments:* House Physician, Southend General Hospital, 1974; House Surgeon, The London Hospital, 1975; Senior House Officer, Northwick Park Hospital, 1975-77; Registrar in Pathology, Princess Alexandra Hospital, Brisbane, Australia, 1977, 1979; Registrar in Pathology, Flinder Medical Centre, Adelaide, 1978; Pathologists, State Health Laboratory, Brisbane, 1980-81; Consultant Pathologist, Queensland Medical Laboratory. *Memberships:* Australian Medical Association, President, Sunshine Coast branch, 1984-85; Internatioanl Academy of Pathology; International Dermatopathology Society. *Publications:* Articles in field of pathology. *Honour:* Arthur Burrows Prize in Dermatology, London Hospital, 1974. *Hobbies:* Tennis; Cooking; Music. *Address:* PO Box 320, Nambour, Queensland 4560, Australia.

EL-MAHDI, Anas Morsi, b. 7 July 1935, Egypt, Professor and Chairman, Department of Radiation Oncology and Biophysics, Eastern Virginia Medical School, USA. m. Nancy Webb, 1 son, 1 daughter. **Education:** MB BCh, Cairo University, Egypt, 1959; ScD, Johns Hopkins University, USA, 1970. *Appointments:* Instructor, Cancer Institute, Cairo University, 1963-65; Instructor, Radiology, Johns Hopkins University School of Medicine, 1967-71; Assistant Professor, Johns Hopkins University School of Medicine, 1967-71; Associate Professor, Radiology, University of Virginia Hospital and Medical School, 1971-75; Professor, Radiology, University of Virginia Hospital and Medical School, 1975-76; Professor and Chairman, Department of Radiation Oncology and Biophysics, 1975-76; Professor and Chairman, Department of Radiation Oncology and Biophysics, 1975-; Consultant in Radiation Oncology; Co-Editor, Cancer Trends, 1979-; Active Staff Member, Virginia Beach General Hospital, 1984-. *Memberships include:* American Association for Advancement of Science; American Association for Cancer Research; American Association for Advancement of Science; American Association for Cancer Research; American Association of University Professors; American Medical Associations; New York Academy of Sciences; International Society for Preventive Oncology. *Publications:* Contributor to professional journals, etc. *Honours:* American Medical Association Physicians Recognition Awards, 1969, 78, 81, 84. *Hobbies:* Art; Pen and Ink Sketching. *Address:* Eastern Virginia Medical School, Department of Radiation Oncology and Biophysics 600 Gresham Drive, Norfolk, VA 23507, USA.

ELTON, Arnold, b. 14 Feb. 1920, London, England. Consultant Surgeon. m. Billie Pamela Briggs, 9 Nov. 1952, London, 1 son. *Education:* MB BS, Member, Royal College of Surgeons, Member, Royal College of Physicians, 1943; Fellow, RCS, 1946; MS, 1951, all University College and University College Hospital, London, England. *Appointments:* HS HP and Casualty Officer, University College Hospital; Registrar, Bolinbroke Hospital; Senior Registrar, Charing Cross Hospital; Member, Court of Examiners, Royal College of Surgeons, 1971-77; Examiner, FRCS, 1977-83; Surgical Tutor, Royal College of Surgeons, 1970-80. *Memberships:* Chairman, Conservative Medical Society; Fellow, Hunterian Society; Fellow, Royal Society of Medicine; Member, Thyroid Club; British Association of Surgical Oncology; Fellow, Association of Surgeons. *Publications:* Various medical articles in journals. *Honours:* Commander of the Order of the British Empire, 1982; Queen's Medal for Local Community Service, 1977; Gosse Research Scholarship, 1948. *Hobbies:* Cricket; Music. *Address:* 22 St Stephen's Close, Avenue Road, London, NW8, England.

EMAD, Jamal, b. 6 Aug. 1931, Shiraz. Psychiatrist;

Physician. m. Jean, 23 July 1982, Syracuse, 2 sons, 1 daughter. *Education:* MD, Tehran Medical School, 1957; Rotating Internship, Mercy Hospital, Hamilton, USA, 1958; Psychiatric Resident, Longview State Hospital, 1959. *Appointments:* Psychiatric Resident, Marcy Psychiatric Center, Marcy, 1960-62; Residency, Syracuse Psychiatric Centre and Albany Medical Centre, 1960-62; Senior Psychiatrist, 1963-64, Supervising Psychiatrist, 1967-73, Unit Chief, 1973-, Marcy Psychiatric Centre, Marcy, New York; Private Practice, 1965-; Affiliated, St. Lukes Hospital, Utica, New York; St. Elizabeth Hospital, Utica, New York; Rome City Hospital, Rome, New York. *Memberships:* American Pyschiatric Association; American Orthpsychiatric Associates; New York State Medical Society; Oneida County Medical Society, *Publications:* "Meckles Diverticulum Diseases and Treatment", 1957; various other articles. *Hobbies:* Hunting; Fishing; Poetry. *Address:* 1627 Genesee St., Utica, NY 13501, USA.

EMAMI-NOURI, Mohammed, b. 26 Apr. 1937, Kashmar, Iran. University Professor/Private Practitioner. m. Irmgard, 24 May 1966, Vienna, 3 daughters. *Education:* Theatre and Literature, Paris; MD, Vienna University, 1968; as Professor, University of Vienna, 1978; University Professor Ferdowssi, Mashad, Iran. *Appointments:* Head of Neurology Department, University of Vienna, 1975; Head, Department ENT Centre, University Ferdowssi Mashad, Iran, 1976. *Membership:* HNO-Gesselschaft, Vienna; Austrian HNO - Gessellschaft; German HNO and Chirurgie Gessellschaft. *Publications:* Contributor of numerous articles to medical and scientific journals. *Hobbies:* Gardening; Sports. *Address:* Hutteldorferstr 197/2, 1140 Vienna, Austria.

EMENER, William George, b. 10 June 1943, New York City, USA. Associate Dean; Professor. m. Rae Dorothy Torgensen, 26 June 1965, 1 son, 2 daughters. *Education:* BA, Trenton State College, 1965; MA, New York University of Georgia, 1971; Certified Rehabilitation Counsellor; Certified Psychologist. *Appointments:* Resident Assistnat, Trenton State College, 1965; Teacher, Secondary High school English, Northern Burlington County Regional High school, 1965-66; Substitute Teacher, Bordentown Twp. Schools, 1966-67; Internship, Vocational Guidance counsellor, E.R. Johnstone Training & Research Center, 1968-69; Assistant Professor, Murray state University, 1971-74; Psychologist, Private Practice, Murray, 1972-74; Assistant Professor, Florida State University, 1974-77, Associate Professor, 1977-78. *Memberships Include:* American Personnel and Guidance Association; Association for Counsellor Education & Supervision; National Rehabilitation Assocation; American Rehabilitation Counselling Association; etc. *Publications:* Co-Author: "Rehabilitation Administration & Supervision", 1981; "Selected Rehabilitation issues and their Impact on People", 1984; "Employee Assistance Programmes: A Multidisciplinary Approach", 1985; "Rehabilitation Counsellor Preparation and Development: Selected Critical issues", 1986; numerous articles Din professional journals, book chapters, etc. *Honours Include:* Gold Medal, Washington for Heroism, 1959; Citizenship Award, 1961; Recipient, various scholarships. *Hobbies:* Athletics; Reading. *Address:* 16404 Shagbark Place, Tampa, FL 33618, USA.

EMERSON, Peter Albert, b. 7 Feb 1923, London, England. Consultant Physician. m. Ceris Hood Price, Knightsbridge, London, 1 son 1 daughter. *Education:* MB, BCH, 1947, MA, 1948, Cambridge University; MRCP, London University; MD, Cambridge University; FRCP, London. *Appointments:* House Physician, St George's Hospital, 1947; S/Ldr, RAF Medical Branch, 1948-52; Medical Registrar, St George's Hospital, 1952-54; Senior Medical Registrar, Brompton Hospital, 1955-57; Assistant Professor of Medicine, State University of New York, 1958; Dean, Westminster Medical School, 1981-84; Consultant Physician, Westminster Hospital, London, currently; Civilian

Consultant Physician to the Royal Navy, currently; *Memberships:* British Thoracic Society; British Medical Association; Association of Physicians; American college of Physicians, Honorary Fellow; Royal College of Physicians, Vice President; Society of Medical Decision Making, USA. *Publications:* Editor: "Thoracic Medicine"1981; Chapters in various medical textbooks; Various papers on Thoracic Diseases and on Medical Decision Analysis. *Honours:* Bracenbury Prize, Medicine, St George's Hospital, 1946; Mitchell Lecturer, Royal College of Physicians, 1969; Procensor, Censor and Senior Censor, Royal College of Physicians, 1978-86. *Hobbies:* Tennis; Computer Medicine; Renovating old buildings. *Address:* 3, Halkin Street, Belgrave Square, London SW1X 7DJ, England.

EMERY, Alan Eglin Heathcote, b. 21 Aug. 1928, Manchester, England. Emeritus Professor of Human Genetics, Professorial Fellow, University of Edinburgh. m. Rosalind Skinner, 7 Sep. 1973, Edinburgh, 1 daughter. *Education:* BSc, Hons, MSc, DSc, MB, ChB, MD, Manchester University; PhD, Johns Hopkins University. *Appointments:* University Lecturer/Reader in Medical Genetics, Manchester University, 1964-68; Foundation Professor and Chairman, Department of Human Genetics, Edinburgh University, 1968-83, Consultant Physician. *Memberships:* Fellow, Royal Society, Edinburgh; Fellow of the Linnean Society; Fellow, Royal College of Physicians; Clinical Genetics Society, President Elect 1980-83; Genetical Society, Vice President 1984-. *Publications:* Books: "Elements of Medical Genetics" 6 editions 1983; "Principles and Practice of Medical Genetics" 1983; "Psychological Aspects of Genetic Counselling" 1984; "An Introduction to Recombinant DNA" 1984; "Methodology in Medical Genetics" 2 editions 1985. *Honours:* National Foundation International Award for Research into the Cause and Prevention of Genetic Disease, 1980; Wildred Card Medal 1985. *Hobbies:* Marine Biology; Painting; Writing poetry. *Address:* The Medical School, Teviot Place, Edinburgh WH8 9AG, Scotland.

EMERY, Paul Emile, b. 2 May 1922, Montreal, Canada, Medical Doctor. m. Olga V. Kennick, 27 July 1979, Concord, New Hampshire, USA. 3 sons, 2 daughters. *Education:* MD, University of Montreal, 1948. *Appointments include* Private Practice, Concord. New Hampshire. 1962-85; Consultant, Veteran's Administration Hospital, Manchester, 1962-64, 1982-85; Consultant, New Hampshire Division of Public Health Program on Alcoholism and Drug Abuse, 1962-71; Medical Director, Forensic Unit, New Hampshire Hospital, 1980-82; Medical Director, New Hampshire Forensic Center, Concord, 1982-85;Staff, Center for Stress Recovery, Brecksville, Ohio, 1985-. *Memberships include:* Fellow, American Psychiatric Association; American Society for Adolescent Psychiatry; American Acadamy of Law and Psychiatry: American Society of Law and Medicine; American College of Forensic Psychiatry. *Publications include:* 'Remarks on Narcissistic Identification', 1956; 'Adolescent Depression and Suicide', 1983; 'Language in Senile Dementia of the Alzheimer Type', 1983; 'Normal Aging and Linguistic Decrement', 1983. *Honours include:* Honoured for Services to the Profession, New Hampshire Psychiatric Society, 1984. **Hobbies:** Reading, Walking. Travelling. *Address:* Center for Stress Recovery, VA Medical Center, 1000 Brecksville Rd, Brecksville, OH 44141, USA.

EMMERSON, Bryan Thomas, b. 5 Sep. 1929, Townsville, Australia. Professor of Medicine. m. Elva Brett, 28 Apr. 1955, Brisbane, 2 sons. *Education:* MB BS, 1952; MD, 1962; PhD, 1973. *Appointments:* Senior Lecturer in Therapeutics 1960-62, Head, Department of Medicine 1985-, University of Queensland; Research Associate, Westminster Hospital, London, England, 1963; Reader in Medicine 1964-72, Professor of Medicine 1974-, University of Queensland, Princess Alexandra

Hospital; United States Public Health Service Postdoctoral Fellowship, University of Pennsylvania, 1967; Chairman of Medicine, Princess Alexandra Hospital, 1981-83. *Memberships include:* Member 1957, Fellow, 1967, Royal Australasian College of Physicians; Councillor, Queensland Institute of Medical Research; Director, Australian Kidney Foundation; Councillor, Queensland Consevatorium of Music; Numerous professional and scientific medical socities. *Publications:* Numerous publications in scientific medical literatu̇re and contributions to postgraduate textbooks in medicine, nephrology and rheumatology. *Honours:* Open Scholarship 1946, Weinholt Prize and Masonic Bursary 1950, University of Queensland; Parr Prize for research in rheumatic disease, 1966; Susman Prize for contribution to knowledge, Royal Australasian College of Physicians. *Hobbies:* Music; Swimming. *Address:* Department of Medicine, Princess Alexandra Hospital, Brisbane, Queensland 4102, Australia.

EMSLIE, Ronald Douglas, b. 9 Mar. 1915, London, England. Professor Emeritus. m. Dorothy Dennis, 18 Mar. 1951, Paris, Illinois, USA, 4 sons. *Education:* BDS, Guys Hospital Dental School, London, England; MSc, College of Dentistry, University of Illinois, USA; FDS, Royal College of Surgeons, England. *Appointments:* Surgeon Lieutenant (D)-Surgeon Lieutenant Commander (D), Royal Navy Voluntary Reserve; Half-time Assistant, Head, Reader, Professor, Department of Preventive Dentistry, Professor of Periodontology and Preventive Dentistry, Dean of Dental Studies, retired 1980, Guys Hospital Medical and Dental Schools; Research Fellow, University of Illinois, USA. *Memberships:* Fellow, British Dental Association; British Society of Periodontology; International Dental Federation; International Association for Dental Research; Fluoridation Society; Past member of Board of Faculty of Dental Surgery, Royal College of Surgeons; Past member of Odontological Section, RSM; Past member of Dental Education Advisory Council; Past member of Board of Studies in Dentistry, University of London. *Publications:* Various in dental literature; Scientific Assistant Editor, :British Dental Journal', 1951-61. *Honours:* Merit Award, International Dental Federation, 1979; Fellow, British Dental Association, 1975. *Hobbies:* Tennis; Sailing; Old Motor Cars. *Address:* Little Hale, Woodland Way, Kingswood, Tadworth, Surrey, KT20 6NW, England.

EMUCHAY, Dick Waobianyi, b. 5 Aug. 1919, Azumini, Imo State, Nigeria. Medical Director. m. 4 Aug. 1956, 5 sons, 3 daughters. *Education:* LFIBA; MB ChB, St Andrews, Scotland; Licentiate of the Royal College of Surgeons, Edinburgh; Licentiate of the Royal Faculty of Physicians and Surgeons, Glasgow; DTM & H, Liverpool, England. *Appointments:* House Physician 1950, House Surgeon 1951, Gynecological House Officer 1951-52, Medical Officer in charge of rural areas 1955-57, Medical Officer in charge of Maternity Hospital 1957-58, Medical Officer in charge of General Hospital 1958-59, Degema, Nigeria; Senior Medical Officer, General Hospital, Aba, 1959-61; Superintendent 1961-71, currently Medical Director, Cottage Hospital, Azumini. *Memberships:* Nigerian Medial Association; Fellow, Postgraduate Medical College of Nigeria. *Publications:* 'Tetanus of the New Born' in 'Eastern Nigeria Medical Bulletin', 1967. *Honour:* Member of the Federal Republic of Nigeria. *Hobbies:* Swimming; Playing chess. *Address:* Cottage Hospital, PO Box 10, Azumini, Via Aba, Imo State, Nigeria.

ENGESET, Jetmund, b. 22 July 1938, Vega, Norway. Consultant Surgeon. m. Ann Graeme Robertson, 3 June 1966, Aberdeen, 2 daughters. *Education:* University of Oslo, Norway; MB ChB, University of Aberdeen, Scotland; FRCSE; FRCSG; ChM. *Appointments:* House Officer, Aberdeen Royal

Infirmary, 1964-65; Research Fellow, Senior House Officer, Registrar in Surgery, Aberdeen Royal Infirmary & University of Aberdeen, 1965-70; Lecturer in Surgery, University of Aberdeen, 1970-74; Senior Surgical Registrar, Aberdeen Royal Infirmary, 1971-74; Senior Lecturer in Surgery, University of Aberdeen, 1974-, Consultant Surgeon, Aberdeen Royal Infirmary, 1974-; Surgeon to the Queen in Scotland, 1985-. *Memberhips:* British Medical Association; Surgical Research Society of Great Britain & Ireland; Briitsh Vascular Society; British Transplantation Society. *Publications:* Numerous publications on vascular, surgical & transplantation topics. *Hobbies:* Gardening; Squash; Skiing. *Address:* Pine Lodge, 315 North Deeside Road, Milltimber, Aberdeen, AB1 0DL, Scotland.

ENGLAND, Mary Jane, b. 22 Julv 1938, Boston, Massachusetts, USA. Assistant Dean and Director, Lucius N. Littauer Master in Public Administration Program, Harvard University, John F. Kennedy School of Government. 1 son, 2 daughters. *Education:* AB, Regis College, 1959; MD, Boston University School of Medicine, 1964; Internship, Framingham Union Hospital, Mass., 1964-65; Resident, Psychiatry; University Hospital, Boston, 1965-66; Mt. Zion Hospital, San Francisco, 1966-67; Resident, Child and Adolescent Psychiatry, Boston City Hospital, 1967-69. *Appointments:* Director, Child Psychiatry, St. Elizabeth's Hospital of Boston, 1969-72; Director, Clinical Psychiatry, Brighton-Allston Mental Health Clinic, 1972-74; Director, Planning and Manpower for Children's Services, Mass. Department of Mental Health, Boston, 1974-76; Associate Commissioner, Mass. Department of Mental Health, 1976-79; Commissioner, Mass. Department of Social Services, 1979-83; Consultant, 1983-; Associate Dean and Director, Lusius N. Littauer Master in Public Administration Program, Harvard University, John F. Kennedy School of Government, 1983-. *Memberships include:* American Academy of Child Psychiatry; American College of Mental Health Administration; American Medical Women's Association, President, 1986; American Orthopsychiatric Association; American Psychiatric Association; American Society for Public Administrators; Association for Psychiatric Treatment of Offenders; Boston Network for Women in Politics and Government; Massachusetts Psychiatric Society; New England Council of Child Psychiatry. *Honour:* Honorary Doctor of Sciences, Regis College, 1985; Honorary Doctor of Humane Letter, Massachusetts School of Professional Psychology. *Hobbies:* Reading; Travel. *Address:* 100 Goodenough Street, Brighton, MA 02135, USA.

ENGLISH, John Michael, b. 7 Sept 1934, Southampton, Hampshire, England, General Practitioner m. Wendy Frances Webb, 19 July 1958, Hatfield, Hertfordshire, 3 sons, 2 daughters. *Education:* MB, ChB, 1957; MRCGP, 1958; MF Hom, 1971; GP Trainer, 1978; FRCGP, 1981; Trained, Transpersonal Psychology. *Appointments:* House Physician, Paediatric Unit, Bristol, 1957-58; Senior House Officer, Burnley, Lancashire, 1959; National Service, Nigeria, 1959-62; Senior House Officer, Southampton, Hampshire, England, 1962; Medical Registrar, Salisbury General Hospital, 1962-64; Medical Registrar, Ealing General Hospital, 1964-66; General Practice, Principal in Hayes, 1966; Instructor, Touch for Health Foundation, 1981-. *Memberships:* Complaints Committee, District Health Authority; Regional Advisory Sub-committee in General Practice, North West Thames Region Medical Committee, Regional Health Authority. BMA; RCGPBM Acupuncture Society; British Association for Autogenic Training and Therapy; British Holistic Medicine and Association; British Association for Counselling; LMC, Hillingdon Health Authority; Regional General Practitioner Sub-Committee. *Publications:* 'How do we teach

Homeopathy', 1982; 'One week study of Homeopathy', 1971; 'Not milking the cow..', 1984. *Hobbies:* Piano; Keeping fit; Madrigal singing; Tai Chi. *Address:* 20 Grosvenor Avenue, Hayes, Middlesex UB4 8NL, England.

ENGLISH, Terence Alexander Hawthorne, b. 3 Oct. 1932, South Africa. Consultant Cardiothoracic Surgeon, Papworth Hospital. m. Ann Margaret Smartt Dicey, 23 Nov. 1963, Plettenberg Bay, South Africa, 2 sons. *Education:* BSc, Engineering, Witwatersrand University, 1954; MB, BS, London University, England, 1962; FRCS, England, 1967; FRCS, Edinburgh, 1967; MA, Cambridge University, 1977; FACC, 1985. *Appointments:* SHO, Thoracic Unit, 1963, Demonstrator in Anatomy, 1964, Guy's Hospital, London; Surgical Registrar, Bolingbroke Hospital, London, 1966; Surgical Registrar, Brompton Hospital, London, 1967; Senior Registrar, Brompton National Heart and London Chest Hospitals, 1968-72; Surgical Research Fellow, University of Alabama, Birmingham, USA, 1969; Consultant Cardiothoracic Surgeon, Papworth and Adenbrooke's Hospitals, 1973; Director, BHF Heart Transplant Research Unit, Papworth, 1980. *Memberships:* President, International Society for Heart Transplantation, 1984-86; President, Society of Perfusionists, 1985-86; British Medical Association; British Cardiac Society; Society of Thoracic and Cardiovascular Surgeons of Great Britain; The Transplantation Society; Member of Council, Royal College of Surgeons of England; Member, General Medical Council; Member, Council, British Heart Foundation; Fellow, American College of Cardiology. *Publications:* 'Cardiac transplantation' in "The Scientific Foundation of Cardiology", 1983; 'Surgery of the Thorax and the Heart' In "Short Practice of Surgery", 19th Edition, 1984; 'Transplantation of the Heart' in "Assisted Circulation", 2nd Edition, 1984. *Hobbies:* Reading; Walking; Tennis. *Address:* 19 Adams Road, Cambridge CB3 9AD, England.

EPSTEEN, Casper Morley, b. 6 May 1902, USA. m. Aline G. Grossman, 6 May 1922, Chicago, 1 son, 1 daughter. *Education:* BSc., Medicine, 1923, MD, 1925, University of Illinois; Intern, Michael Rees Hospital, Chicago; Postgraduate Studies, Maxillofacial and Plastic Surgery, University of Pennsylvania; DDS, Loyola University, 1930. *Appointments:* Instructor, Anatomy, 1923, Pathology, 1924, University of Illinois College of Medicine; Professor, Maxillofacial Surgery, Cook County Graduate School of Medicine, 1947-59; Clinical Professor, Surgery, Chicago Medical School-University of Health Sciences, 1962-; Senior Attending Surgeon, Michael Rees Hospital and Medical Centre, over 50 years; Attending Surgeon, Cook County Hospital of Chicago, 1947-59; Consulting Staff, various hospitals. *Memberships include:* President, 1962-63, Chicago Medical Society; President, 1963-64, American Society of Maxillofacial Surgeons; 2nd Vice President, 1964, 1st Vice President, 1965, Illinois State Medical Society; Founder, Organizer, South Side Medical Assembly, 1938; Chicago, Illinois State, American Medical Societies; American Burn Association; Royal Society of Medicine, England; Fellow, American College of Surgeons, International College of Surgeons; Illinois Society for Medical Research; Fellow, Educational and Scientific Foundation, Illinois State Medical Society; International Society, International Association of Maxillofacial Surgeons; Pan American Medical Association; etc. *Publications:* Numerous articles in professional journals; Co-Author, Chapter, "Stomatitis", 'Tice's Practice of Medicine', Volume 7. *Honours:* Special Achievement Awards including American Society of Maxillofacial Surgeons Distinguished Award 1966; Honorable Mention from American Society of Plastic and Reconstructive Surgeons; other numerous honours and awards include Special Achievement Award, American Society of Maxillofacial Surgeons, 1982; Guest of Honour,

International Congress of Maxillofacial Surgeons, Venice, Italy, 1971; Career Achievement Award, Professional Fraternity Association, 1984. *Hobby:* Photography. *Address:* 5750 Kenwood Avenue, Chicago, IL 60637, USA.

EPSTEIN, Alan Lee, b. 14 Aug. 1949, Brooklyn, New York, USA. Assistant Professor of Clinical Pathology. m. Lindsay Dianne Mount, 19 Dec. 1976, Los Altos, California, USA, 2 sons. *Education:* BA, Wesleyan University, Middletown, Connecticut, 1971; MD, Stanford University, California, 1978, PhD, 1979. *Appointments:* Post-Doctoral Fellow, Eleanor Roosevelt Institute for Cancer Research, 1978-80; Assistant Professor of Medicine, Medical Oncology Section, Northwestern University School of Medicine, Chicago, USA, 1980-84; Assistant Professor of Clinical Pathology, University of Southern California, Los Angeles, 1984-. *Memberships:* American Society of Haematology; American Society for Advancement of Science; American Society for Cell Biology; American Society for Cancer Research; American Society of Clinical Oncology; American Society of Microbiology; New York Academy of Sciences. *Publications include:* 28 articles in professional journals; 6 book chapters including :Functional and Cytogenetic Characterisation of Established Human Malignant Lymphoma Cell Lines' ''Human Lymphocyte Differentiation: Its Application to Cancer: INSERN Symposium'', vol. 8, 1978; 'Intracranial Heterotransplantation of Human Hematopoietic Tumours in the Nude Athmyic Mouse' in ''Thymusaplastic Nude Mice and Rats in Clinical Oncology'', 1981; 'Immunohistolgic Techniques: Their Impact in Tumour Diagnosis with Particular Reference to Lymphomas' in ''Lymphoproliferative Diseases: Pathogenesis, Diagnosis, Therapy'', 1985. *Honours include:* Junior Faculty Award, American Cancer Society, 1981-84; Searle Scholar, 1982-84; Co-recipient Benson-Yalow Award, 1984. *Hobbies:* Woodwork; Photography; Piano; Tennis. *Address:* Department of Pathology, USC Medical Centre, 2025 Zonal Avenue, Los Angeles, CA 90033, USA.

EPSTEIN, John Howard, b. 29 Dec. 1926, San Francisco, California, USA, Clinical Professor of Dermatology, University of California at San Francisco, m. Alice V Thompson, 16 Nov. 1953, San Francisco, 1 son, 2 daughters. *Education:* BA, University of California at Berkeley, 1949; MD, University of California at San Francisco, 1952; MS, University of Minnesota, 1956; Diplomate. American Board of Dermatology, 1957; Intern, Stanford, 1952-53; Residency. Mayo Clinic, 1953-56. *Appointments:* Chief of Dermatology, San Francisco General Hospital, 1959-69; Chief of Dermatology, Mt Zion Hospital and Medical Centre, 1971-81; Clinical Professor of Dermatology, University of California, San Francisco Medical Centre, 1972-; Chief Editor, Archives of Dermatology, 1973-78; Editorial Board, Western Journal of Medicine, 1979-; Assistant Editor, Journal of the American Academy of Dermatology, 1978-; Editorial Board, Photodermatology, 1983-; Editorial Board, Journal of the AMA, 1977-79; Editorial Board, Photochemistry and Photobiophysics, 1985-; Consultant to Letterman Army Medical Centre, San Diego, 1959-. *Memberships:* American Academy of Dermatology, 1956-; American Board of Dermatology, 1957-; AMA; American Dermatologic Association, 1964-; Society Investigative Dermatology, 1957; Fellow, American College of Physicians and Surgeons; American Federation for Clinical Research; International Society of Tropical Dermatology; American Association for Cancer Research; Pacific Dermatology Association. *Publications:* Contributor of over 189 scientific articles to professional journals. *Honour:* Silver Award, American Academy of Dermatology, Meeting, 1962; Gold Award for Investigation Merit, AAD, 1969; Essex Professor, Australia, 1977; Permanent Visiting Professor, Zagazig University,

Egypt, 1982; M B Sulzberger International Lecturer, 1985. *Hobbies:* Skiing; Tennis. *Address:* 450 Sutter Street, Suite 1306, San Francisco, CA 94108, USA.

EPSTEIN, Michael Anthony, b. 18 May 1921, London, England. Medical Scientist/Emeritus Professor. *Education:* Perry Exhibitioner, Trinity College, Cambridge, 1940; MRCS, LRCP, Middlesex Hospital Medical School, London, 1944; MA & MB, BChir, Cantab, 1949; MD,Cantab, 1951; PhD, London, 1952; DSc, London 1963; FRCPath, 1963. *Appointments:* House Surgeon, Middlesex (London) and Addenbrooke's (Cambridge) Hospitals, 1944; Lieutenant and Captain, Royal Army Medical Corps, 1945-47; Assistant Pathologist, Bland Sutton Institute, Middlesex Hospital Medical School, 1948-65, with leave as French Government Fellow, Institut Pasteur, Paris, 1952-53 and Visiting Investigator, Rockefeller Institute, New York, 1956; Reader in Experimental Pathology (University of London) at Middlesex Hospital Medical School and Honorary Consultant in Experimental Virology, The Middlesex Hospital, London, 1965-68; Professor of Pathology, 1968-85, Head of Department of Pathology and Honorary Consultant Pathologist, 1968-82, University of Bristol; Medical Scientist/Emeritus Professor, Nuffield Department of Clinical Medicine, University of Oxford, John Radcliffe Hospital, Headington, Oxford, 1985 -. *Memberships:* Pathology Society of Great Britain and Ireland; Society of Gen. Microbiology; Fellow, Royal Society of Medicine; Society of Experimental Biology; British Biophysics Society; British Society of Cell Biology; British Association for Cancer Research. *Publications:* Joint Founder Editor,'International Review of Experimental Pathology' vols 1-28, 1962-85; Joint Editor: ''Oncogenesis and Herpesviruses'' Parts 1 and 2, 1975; ''The Epstein-Barr Virus'' with B G Achong, 1979; ''The Epstein-Barr Virus: Recent Advances'' with B G Achong, 1985; More than 200 original publications in leading scientific journals. *Honours:* Paul Ehrlich & Ludwig Darmstaedter Prize and Medal, West Germany, 1973; Membre d'Honneur, Belgian Society for Cancer Research, 1979; Honorary Professor, Zhongshan Medical College, Guangzhou, People's Republic of China, 1981; Bristol-Myers Award for Distinguished Achievement in Cancer Research, New York, 1982; Commander of the British Empire, 1985. *Address:* Nuffield Department of Clinical Medicine, University of Oxford, John Radcliffe Hospital, Headington, Oxford OX3 9DU, England.

EPSTEIN, Sandra-Gail Schneiderman, b. 19 July 1939, Boston, Massachusetts, USA. Psychologist. m. 1963, 1 daughter. *Education:* AB, Boston University; MA, 6th year professional diploma, PhD, University of Connecticut. *Appointments:* School Psychological Examiner, Northeastern Connecticut; Staff Psychologist, Day Kimball Hospital Mental Health Clinic; School Psychologist, Northeastern Connecticut; Lecturer, Quinebaug Valley Community College; Lecturer, Psychology, Annhurst College; Founding Director, Together Inc., Woodstock; Consultant, School Psychology, Northeast Area Regional Education Service; Staff Psychologist, Thompson Medical Centre; Consultant, Regional Educational Assessment and Consultation Team, Capitol Region, Hartford; Consultant, Voluntown Public Schools; Consultant, The Bess and Paul Sigel Hebrew Academy of Greater Hartford; Private Practice, Woodstock and Farmington; Member, Psychiatry Dept., Day Kimball Hospital. *Memberships:* American Association for the Advancement of Science; American Psychological Association; American Society of Clinical Hypnosis; Connecticut Psychological Association; Connecticut Association of School Psychologists; International Society of Hypnosis; many other professional organisations. *Publications:* ''Diagnostic Decision making Among Children's Mental Health Professionals in Connecticut'', 1978; ''An Experimental Analysis of Decision Making of Mental Health Professionals, Convention proceedings, National Association of

School Psychologists", 1980. *Honours:* Dean's Recognition Award, Boston University, 1958; Boston University Hillel Award, 1959; Fellowship, University of Connecticut, 1968. *Hobbies:* Music; Reading. *Address:* Woodstock Hill, Route 169, Woodstock, CT 06281, USA.

EPSTEIN, Stanley Winston, b. 2 Dec. 1937, Sydney, Cape Breton, Nova Scotia, Canada, University Professor/Medical Consultant. m. Paula Rivka Gorman, 21 Mar 1965, Toronto, 3 sons, 1 daughter. *Education:* MD, Dalhousie University, 1962; Fellow: Royal College of Physicians of Canada, 1966, American College of Chest Physicians, 1972. *Appointments:* Honorary Research Assistant, Postgraduate Medical School, Hammersmith Hospital, London, 1967-68; Associate, 1968-71, Assistant Professor, 1971-, Department of Medicine, University of Toronto; Active Attending Staff, Chest Physician, Respiratory Division, Department of Medicine, Toronto, Western Hospital, 1968-; Active Attending Staff, Medical, Hillcrest Hospital, Toronto, 1971-; Consulting Staff, Special Privileges, Diaphragm Pacing and Post Polio Clinic, West Park Hospital, Toronto, 1975-; Director, Chest Clinic, Ambulatory Care Department, Toronto Western Hospital, 1982-. *Memberships:* Ontario and Canadian Medical Associations, Ontario; American and Canadian Thoracic Societies; American College of Chest Physicians; Canadian Society of Allergy and Clinical Immunology; American Academy of Allergy; Canadian Chapter of the Israel Medical Association; Defence Medical Association of Canada; International Association of Asthmology; Alpha Omega Alpha; Academy of Medicine, Toronto; Clinical Research Society of Toronto; Canadian Societyof Pulmonary and Cardiovascular Technologists; Brompton Hospital Association. *Publications:* Extensive contributor to numerous medical journals. *Honours include:* Dr. Henry A Beatty Scholarship, Faculty of Medicine, University of Tornto, 1967-68; Visiting Lecturer, Regional Chest Allergy Unit, McMaster University, Hamilton, Ontario, 1981; Member, Cecil Lehman Mayer Research Forum Committee, American College of Chest Physicians, 1982; Toronto Chairman, Leadership Gift Campaign, American College of Chest Pysicians, 1983; Sixth Owen Clarke Memorial Lecturer, University of Western Ontario, London, Ontario, 1983. *Hobbies:* Canadian and Inuit Art; Woodworking; Gardening. *Address:* Toronto Western Medical Building, 25 Leonard Avenue, Professional Suite No, 407, Toronto, Ontario, Canada M5T 282.

ERAJ, Yusuf Ali, b. 6 Mar, 1923, Nairobi, Kenya. Consultant Obstetrician and Gynaecologist. m. Vajiha, 24 Dec. 1953, Nairobi, 1 son, 2 daughters. *Education:* MB BS, Punjab University, 1947; DRCOG, 1953; Member and Fellow, Royal College of Obstetricians and Gynaecologists. *Appointments:* Consultant Obstetrician and Gynaecologist, His Highness the Aga Khan P. J. Hospital; Senior Obstetrician and Gynaecologist, Head, Department of Maternal and Child Health, Somalia Secretary General, Kenya National Academy for the Advancement of Arts and Sciences; Chairman, Kenya Medical Association. *Memberships:* National Council for Population and Development; National Council for Science and Technology; Consultant, International Federation of Institutes of Advanced Studies; Pugwash. *Publications:* 'Umplanned Pregnancy in Kenya' in 'The Journal of the American Medical Association', 1966; 'Trade Union -ism in Medicine in the Developing Countries', Paper presented at Kenya Medical Association meeting, 1967 and included in 'Kenya Digest', 1975. *Honours:* Fellow: Royal College of Obstetricians and Gynaecologists, 1982; East Africa Association of Surgeons. *Address:* Jubilee Insurance House, Wabera Street, PO Box 43789, Nairobi, Kenya.

ERFFMEYER, John Edward, b. 21 June 1952, San Diego, California, USA, Medical Physician. *Education:* BS 1974, MD Honours Program, 1976 Northwestern University. *Appointments:* Internship 1976-77, Residency 1977-79, Internal Medicine, Alton Ochsner Medical Foundation, New Orleans, Louisiana; Fellowship, Allegry and Clinical Immunology, University of Tennessee Center for the Health Sciences, Memphis, Tennessee, 1979-81. *Memberships:* American College of Physicians; American Academy of Allergy and Immunology; Joint Council of Allergy and Immunology; American Thoracic Society. *Publications include:* 'Adverse Reactions to Penicillin', 1981; 'Exercise-induced urticaria, angioedema, and anaphylactoid episodes' (co-author), 1981; "Treatment of Infective Endocarditis, Editor: A Bisno (contributor), 1981. Honours: First Place, Clemens Von Pirquet Award, American College of Allergists, 1981. Fellow, American College of Physicians, 1986. *Hobby:* Fishing. *Address:* 8210 Walnut Hill Lane, Suite 818, Dallas, TX 75231, USA.

ERICKSON, Kim L., b. 1 Oct. 1951, Ft. Atkinson. Wisconsin, USA. Oral and Maxillofacial Surgeon. m. Veronica Meriel Cottam, 18 Dec. 1982, Abergele, North Wales. *Education:* BA, Economics, Kalamazoo College, 1973; DDS, School of Dentistry, University of Michigan, 1977; Completed Training Programme, Oral and Maxillofacial Surgery, Mt. Sinai Medical Centre, New York, 1981. *Appointments:* Oral and Maxillofacial Surgery, Clwyd Health Authority, Glan Clwyd Hospital, British National Health Service, 1981; Visitor, Oral and Maxillofacial Surgery, John Peter Smith Hospital, Fort Worth, Texas, 1982; Oral and Maxillofacial Surgeon, Scarsdale, New York; Member, White Plains Hospital Medical Centre, Dept. Oral and Maxillofacial Surgery, Centre of Craniofacial Deformities, Montefiore Medical Centre, Albert Einstein Medical Centre, Bronx, New York, 1982-86; American Association of Oral and Maxillofacial Surgeons, American Dental Society of Anesthesiology; American Cleft Palate Association; American Dental Association; New York State Society of Oral and Maxillofacial Surgeons. *Publications:* Developer, Instrument, Erickson Model Platform and Model Block; Articles include: "Dental Considerations in Clinical Anesthesia", 'Anesthesiology Review', 1979; "Current Concepts in the Surgical Management of Patients with Myasthenia Gravia", 'Journal of Oral Surgery', 1981; "Fatal Brain Abscess following Periodontal Therapy: A Case Report", 'Mount Sinai Journal of Medicine', 1981; "The Model Platform and Model Block: A Device for making Accurate Presurgical Measurements", in preparation; "Model Surgery", Parts I and II, in preparation; Presenter, numerous Lectures. *Honours:* Recipient, various honours and awards. *Hobbies:* Alpine and Cross Country Skiing; Tennis; Astronomy; Photography. *Address:* Blodgett Memorial Hospital, 1900 Wealthy Street, Grand Rapids, MI 49506, USA.

ERIKSON, Uno Eurgen, b. 15 June 1930 Uppsala, Sweden. Professor, Chairman, Diagn. Radiology. m. Birgit Ryden, 1966, Copenhagen, 1 son, 2 daughters. *Education:* Swedish Med.Lic., 1953; Swedish State Board to Practice Medicine & Surgery, 1959; Swedish MD, 1965; Professor, Diagn. Radiology, University of Uppsala, 1982-. *Memberships:* Swedish Medical Association; Association of Senior Medical Offices of Teaching Hospitals; Swedish Society of Medical Radiology; Uppsala Medical Society. *Publications:* "Circulation in Traumatic Amputation Stumps: An angiogra phical investigation", 'Acta Radiologica Suppl.', 1965; "Polymeric contras media for roentgenologic examinaiton of gastrointestinal tract", 'Invest. Radiology', 1970; "Aspects on functional analysis in vasular radiology by analogous and digitized methods", 'Ann Radiol', 1985; etc. *Honours:* President, European Society of Cardiovascular Radiology. *Hobbies:* Mathematics; Chess; Sailing. *Address:* Konsumvägen 33A, S-752 45 Uppsala, Sweden.

ERIKSSON, Elof, b. 8 June 1943, Backe, Sweden. Associate Professor, Plastic Surgery; Director, Burn Centre. m. Gudrun Eriksson, 2 June 1974.

Education: MD, University of Gothenburg School of Medicine, 1969; PhD, University of Gothenburg, 1972. *Appointments:* Associate Professor, Plastic Surgery, University of Gothenburg, 1980-82; Associate Professor, Plastic Surgery, Southern Illinois University School of Medicine, USA, 1982-. *Memberships:* European Society for Microcirculation; American Society for Microcirculation; American Burn Association; Swedish Society for Plastic Surgery; Swedish Medical Society; Gothenburg Medical Society; many other professional organisations. *Publications:* Co-Author, "Growth and differentiation of blood vessels", 'Microcirculation', Volume 1, 1977; "Microcirculatory effects of pressure", 'Pressure Ulcers: Principles and Techniques of Management', 1980; "Microcirculatory Changes in the Acute Burn Wound", 'Proceedings of the Wound Healing Symposium', 1980; Co-Author, "Arrangement of the vascular bed in different types of skeletal muscles", 1984; Articles in numerous professionaljournals. *Honours:* Grand Prize, Senior Resident's Conference, Dallas, Texas, 1979; Best Research Paper, at 'Resident's Night', Chicago Plastic Surgery Society, 1976; Winner, Chicago Committee on Traumas, Trauma Paper Competion. *Hobbies:* Hunting; Sailing; Skiing; Swimming. *Address:* Southern Illinois University School of Medicine, 800 North Rutledge Street, Room D330, Springfield, IL 62702, USA.

ERIMOGLU, A. Cevdet, b. 23 July 1922, Divrigi, Turkey. Director, Basic Scia Dept. m. 16 Aug. 1947, 1 daughter. *Education:* MD, University of Istanbul, 1947. *Appointments:* Assistant, Anatomical Dept. , Medical Faculty, Istanbul, 1949; Assistant Professor, 1970, Professor, 1971-, Director, Basic Scia Dept. 1982-, Dentistry, University of Istanbul. *Publications:* "Insan Anatomisi", 1975; "Anatomi terimleri kilavuzu", 1982; "Anatomical Dictionary", 1982. *Address:* Faculty of Dentistry, Istanbul University, Capa, Istanbul, Turkey.

ERSEVIM, Ismail Hakki, b. 11 Oct. 1929, Istanbul, Turkey. Private Practitioner, Adult and Child Psychiatry; Senior Psychiatrist. divorced, 3 sons. *Education:* MD, Istanbul University School of Medicine, 1952; Board of Certification in Psychiatry and Neurology, 1955; Graduate, Istanbul Conservatory of Music, 1955. *Appointments:* Psychiatric Intern, Ottawa, Canada, 1957-58. Resident: Buffalo Univesity, USA, 1958; Medfield State Hospital, 1959;63. Child Psychiatrist Fellowship, Harvard, 1963-65; Staff Psychiatrist, Bradley Home, Rhode Island, 1966; Newport County Mental Health Director. Rhoce Island; 1967; Chief, Rhode Island Mental Hygiene Services, 1967-70; Assistant Chief, Veterans Administration Hospital, Rhode Island, 1970; Adjunct Professor, Psychology, Salve Regina College and University of Rhode Island, 1967-70; Staff Psychiatrist, Mystic Valley Mental Health Clinic, Lexington, Massachusetts, 1971; Director Eastern Middlesex Guidance Center, Melrose, 1971-73; Director, Narcotics Programme, Cambridge, Harvard University, 1976-77; Instructor, Boston University School of Medicine, Lynn Hospital, Lynn, 1978; currently, Private Practitioner and Senior Psychiatrist, New Hampshire Hospital, Concord, New Hampshire. *Memberships include:* Turkish Neuro-Psychiatric Association; American Psychiatric Association; American Medical Association; Royal Society for Promotion of Health, past member; Life Member, New England Council of Child Psychiatry; World Medical Association. *Publications:* Numerous translations from the Medical press featured in professional journals and books. *Honours:* No 8th Writer in Short stories, Turkey, 1955; Professional Member, The National Writers Club, USA. *Hobbies include:* Opera; Ballet; Travelling; Poetry and short story writing; Book and record collecting. *Address:* 55 North Acres Road, Manchester, NH 03104, USA.

ESGUERRA, Alfonso, b. 24 Mar. 1939, Colombia,

South America. Director General. m. Gloria Gonzalez, 29 June 1962, Bogota, 2 daughters. *Education:* BS, Universidad de los Andes, Bogota, 1960; MD, Yale University School of Medicine Connecticut, USA, 1964; Intern, Hospital, University of Pennsylvania 1964-65; Residency, Diagnostic Radiology, Yale New Haven Medical Center, 1965-68. *Appointments:* Instructor in Radiology, Yale University School of Medicine, New Haven, Connecticut, USA, 1968-69; Radiologist, clinica de Marley, Bogota, Columbia, 1969-79; Assistant Clinical Professor, Radiology, Yale University School of Medicine, USA, 1969-84; Director General, Fundacion Santa Fe de Bogota, Columbia, 1979-. *Memberships:* Interamerican and American Colleges of Radiology; American College of Chest Physicians, Fellow; American Thoracic Society; International Academy of Chest Physicians and Surgeons; New York Academy of Science. *Publications:* Co-Author of articles contributed to 'Journal of American Medical Association' and 'American Review Respiratory Diseases'. *Honour:* Wirt Winchester Fellow, Yale University School of Medicine, New Haven, Connecticut, USA, 1966-68. *Hobby:* Raising trout. *Address:* Fundacion Santa Fe de Bogota, Calle 119 9-33, Bogota, Columbia, South America.

ESPY, Rene Organ, b. 20 Dec. 1944, Flushing, Long Island, New York, USA. Doctor of Chiropractic. *Education:* BA, MA, Psychology and Religion; DC. *Appointments:* Worked with Women's Olympic Volleyball Team, 1976, 1984. *Memberships:* American Chiropractic Association; International College of Applied Kinesiology; Parker Chiropractic Research Foundation. *Publications:* "Candida Alibcans, The Misdiagnosed Friend", 'American Chiropractor', 1984. *Honours:* Special Achievement Award, Clinical Proficiency, Texas Chiropractic College, 1980. *Hobbies:* Writing; Skiing; Research. *Address:* 17125 SW Boones Ferry Rd., Lake Oswego Or 97034, USA.

ESQUIBEL, Edward V, b. 28 May 1928, Denver, USA. Staff Psychiatrist, Veteran's Administration. m. Lillian D, Robb, 11 Jan. 1961, County Seat, 2 sons, 4 daughters. *Education:* MD; Diplomate, American Board of Psychiatry & Neurology. *Appointments:* Director of Undergraduate Programme, Psychiatry, Chicago Medical School, 1965-66; 1st Chief, Forensic Services, State of Colorado, 1981; Chief, Outpatient Services, Psychiatry, Veteran Administration, Associate Clinical Professor, Psychiatry, Quillen-Dishner Medical College, Johnson City 1982-84. *Memberships:* American Medical Association; American Psychiatric Association; American Group Psychotherapy Association; American Association of Psychoanalytic Physicians. *Publications:* "PTSD in the VA: Limitations, Caveats, and Observations on War Neurosis", 'VA Practitioner', 1985; "The Rationale and Need for Privilege Monitoring: An Apologia for the Establishment of a Liaison Committee on Privileges: On the Clinical Care of Sociopathy" 'Treatise', 1981. *Honours:* Fellowships, APPA, AGPA; Plaque of Honour, Southern Psychiatric Institute, 1964; International Personnel Research Creativity Award, 1972. *Hobbies:* Movies; Collecting; Restortions of Bric-a-Brac, etc. *Address:* Va Outpatient Clinic, Port of Palm Beach Executive Plaza, 301 Broadway, Riviera Beach, FL 33404, USA.

ESSOMBA, René, b. 6 Apr. 1932, Mbalmayo, Cameroun. Professor of Surgery. m. Julienne Etoundi, 28 June 1959, 2 sons, 2 daughters. *Education:* MD. *Appointments:* Consultant Surgeon, 1960-69; Head, Department of Surgery, University of Yaounde, 1969-80; Surgeon, 1980-. *Memberships include:* Société Internationale de Chirurgie; College Internationale des Chirurgies; Fellow, West African College of Surgeons; Royal Society of Medicine, London; Academie de Chirurgie, France. *Publications include:* "Surgery in the Tropics"; About 100 publications in the international press. *Hobbies:* Jogging; Fishing. *Address:* PO Box 219, Yaounde, Cameroun.

EUBANKS, Jerry J., b. 21 Apr. 1953, Long Beach,

California, USA. Owner, Automobile Collision Cause Analysis. m. Cheryl M. Ramsey, 28 July 1978, San Diego, California, 2 daughters. *Education:* Technical Accident Investigation, Accident Reconstruction, Northwestern University; Certified Traffic Collision Investigator. *Appointments:* Police Officer, City of San Diego; Owner, Automobile Collision Cause Analysis. *Memberships:* International Association of Accident Reconstruction Specialists; Charter member and Cerification Board, Society of Accident Reconstrutionists; American Association for Automotive Medicine. *Hobby:* Computer Evaluation of Traffic Collisions. *Address:* 2768 Grandview Street, San Diego, CA 92110, USA.

EVANS, Alun Estyn, b. 27 Sept. 1944, Northern Ireland. Senior Lecturer, Consultant in Community Medicine, Director, Belfast MONICA Project. m. Kathleen Field, 14 Dec. 1973, Belfast, 1 son, 2 daughters. *Education:* MB, BCh (Hons) Queen's University, Belfast, 1968; Member, Royal College of Physicians, London, 1971; Diploma Society of Medicine, Edinburgh, Scotland, 1973; MFCM London, 1974; MD, Queen's University, Belfast, 1984. *Appointments:* House Officer, Royal Victoria Hospital, Belfast, 1968-69; Junior Tutor, Senior House Officer in Medicine, 1969-71; General Practitioner, British Columbia, Canada, 1971-72; Senior Registrar in Community Medicine, Queen's University, Belfast, 1973-85, Senior Lecturer, 1985-. *Memberships:* International Society & Federation of Cardiology; - Scientific Section of Epidemiology & Prevention; Society for Social Medicine; all-Ireland Society for Social Medicine (Committee Chairman); Irish Cardiac Society; American Heart Association Council on Epidemiology; European Society of Cardiology Working Group on Epidemiology & Prevention. *Publications:* Various articles on epidemiology and coronary care, 1974-85. *Address:* Department of Community Medicine, Institute of Clinical Science, Royal Victoria Hospital, Belfast, BT12, 6BJ, Northern Ireland.

EVANS, David Alan Price, b. 6 Mar. 1927, Birkenhead, England. Director of Medicine, Riyadh Armed Forces Hospital, Saudi Arabia. *Education:* BSc, University of Liverpool, England, 1948, MB, ChB, 1951, MSc, 1957, MD, 1959, PhD, 1965, DSc, 1981; MRCP, London, 1956, FRCP, 1968. *Appointments Include:* Registrar in General Internal Medicine, Stanley Hospital, Liverpool, England, 1956-58; Fellow, Department of Medicine, Johns Hopkins Hospital, Baltimore, USA, 1958-59; Registrar, David Lewis Northern Hospital, Baltimore, USA, 1959-60; Lecturer, University of Liverpool, 1960-62, Senior Lecturer, 1962-68, Professor, 1968-72, Professor and Chairman, Department of Medicine and Director, Nuffield Unit of Medical Studies, 1972-83; Director of Medicine, Riyadh Armed Forces Hospital, Saudi Arabia -. *Appointments:* British Medical Association; British Society for Gastroenterology; Genetical Society; Association of Physicians of Great Britian and Ireland; The John Hopkins University Alumni Association John Hopkins Meidical and Surgical Association. *Publications:* Articles in scientific literature; chapters in books on various topics in the field of medicine, particularly medical genetics. *Honours Include:* Kelly Meda, 1951; Owen T. Williams Prize, 1951; Roberts Prize, 1959; Samuels Prize, 1965; (all preceding from the University of Liverpool); Thornton R. Wilson award, Eastern Psychiatric Association, USA, 1964; Poulsson Lecturer and Medallist, University of Oslo, Norway, 1971; Sir Henry Dale Lecturer and Medallist, Johns Hopkins Hospital, USA, 1972; Watson Smith Lecturer, Royal College of Physicians of London, 1976. *Hobby:* Farming. *Address:* C123 Riyadh Armed Forces Hospital, PO Box 7897, Riyadh 11159, Kingdom of Saudi Arabia.

EVANS, Edward Frank, b. 30 Mar. 1936, Birmingham, England. Professor. m. Diana

Marguerite Price, 20 July 1963, Brighton,1 son, 1 daughter. *Educaiton:* BSc, PhD, MB, ChB, University of Birmingham. *Appointments:* House Physician, General Hospital, Birmingham, 1960; House Surgeon, Dudley Road Hospital , Birmingham, 1961; Research Fellow, University of Birmingham Neurocommunications Unit, 1961; Visiting Associate, National Institutes of Health, Bethesda, USA; 1965-67 Senior Research Fellow, Department of Communication and Neuroscience, 1967; Reader 1973, Professor of Auditory Physiology 1978, Head of Department, Department of Communicational and Neuroscience, University of Keele, 1982. *Memberships:* Physiological Society of UK; Acoustical Society of America;International Audiological Society; Institute of Acoustics; Collegium Oto-Rhino-Laryngologicum Amicitiae Sacrum; Royal College of Physicians of London; British Society of Audiology; Brain Research Association I.B.R.O. *Publications:* 'Classification of unit responses in the auditory cortex of the unanaesthetized and unrestrained cat', (with I C Whitfield), 1964; 'The frequencey response and other properites of single fibres in the guinea pig cochlear nerve', 1972; 'The sharpening of cochlear frequencey selectivity in the normal and abnormal cochlea', 1975; 'Psychophysics and physiology of Hearing' (with J P. Wilson) Eds., 1977; 'Hearing', Chapters 13-15, In 'The Senses'. *Honours:* Norman Gamble Prize in Otology, 1984; T.S.Littler Prize of British Society of Audiology, 1974; Elected, MRCP, 1985; FIOA 1982; Fellow, Acoustical Society of America, 1977; Collegium OtoRhinoLaryngologicum Amicitae Sacrum 1979. *Hobbies:* Church Work; Sailing; Music. *Address:* Department of Communmication and Neuroscience, University of Keele, Staffs., ST5 5BG, England.

EVANS, Jane Alison McLaren, b. 1 Aug. 1948, France Lynch, England. Associate Professor of Genetics. m. David Evans, 9 Aug. 1969, Mapledurham, England, 1 son, 1 daughter. *Education:* BSc Biological Sciences, University of Birmingham, England; PhD Genecology, University of Leicester, England; FCCMG, Canada. *Appointments:* Research Fellow, University of Manitoba, 1972-74; Consultant Biologist, Canadian Wildlife Service, Manitoba Museum of Man & Nature, City of Winnipeg, 1974-77; Research Associate, Health Sciences Centre, Winnipeg, 1975-77; National Health Research Fellow, University of Manitoba, 1977-79; Consultant, St Amant Centre for the Mentally Handicapped, Winnipeg, 1979-; Member, Medical (Scientific) Staff, Health Sciences Centre Winnipeg, 1980-; Consultant Geneticist, Manitoba Provincial Congenital Anomalies Registry, 1984-; Associate Professor, Department of Human Genetics, University of Manitoba. *Memberships:* Fellow, Canadian College of Medical Geneticists; American Society of Human Genetics. *Publications:* 'Tracheal agenesis and associated malformations' (co-author), American Journal of Medical Genetics, 1985; 'Cloacal exstrophy and related abdominal wall defects in Manitoba' (co-author), Clinical Genetics', 1985; 'Differences in hospital usage patterns of handicapped children and matched controls', Canadian Journal of Public Health, 1985; 'A Study of Institutionalized Mentally Retarded Children in Manitoba: overrepresentation by Canadian Indian Children (co-author), Journal of Mental Deficiency Research, 1985; 'A cytogenetic survey of 14,069 newborn infants IV Further follow-up on the children with sex chromosome anomalies' (co-author), Birth Defects, 1982; 'Numerical taxonomy in the study of birth defects', Advances in the Study of Birth Defects Volume V, 1982; 'Down's Syndrome and recent domographic trends in Manitoba', Journal of Medical Genetics, 1978. *Honour:* Open Entrance Scholarship, University of Birmingham, 1966-69; Rh Institute Award for Outstanding Research in the Health Sciences, 1985. *Hobbies:* Reading; Gardening; Golf. *Address:* Department of Human Genetics, University of Manitoba, 250-270 Bannatyne Avenue, Winnipeg, Manitoba, R3E 0W3, Canada.

EVANS, Kenneth Theodore, b. 4 May. 1925,

Llanidloes, Wales. Professor and Director of Radiology. m. Susanne Mary MacGregor, 6 Aug. 1953, 4 daughters. *Education:* MB; ChB; FRCP; FRCR; FFR(RCSI); DMRD. *Appointments:* Junior appointments in medicine 1946-56; Senior Registrar Radiology, Hammersmith Hospital, 1956-59; Consultant/Radiologist, United Bristol Hospitals, 1959-66; Visiting Lecturer, University of Ibadan, Nigeria, 1962-63; Professor of Radiology, University of Wales College of Medicine, 1966-; Director of Radiology, University Hospital of Wales, 1966-. *Memberships:* Association of Physicians of Great Britain and Ireland; British Society of Gastroenterology; Fellow, Royal College of Radiologists; British Institute of Radiologists; Fellow, Royal College of Physicians. *Publications:* Co-author: "Mammography, Thermography and Ultrasonography" 1973; "Forensic Radiology" 1981; "Clinical Radiology for Medical Students" 1982. *Hobby:* Golf. *Address:* The Meadows, Graig Road, Lisvane, Cardiff, South Wales.

EVANS, Louise, b. San Antonio, Texas, USA. Clinical Psychologist; Lecturer. m. Tom R Gambrell, 23 Feb. 1960, Fullerton. *Education:* BS, Northwestern University, 1949; MSc., 1952, PhD, 1955, Purdue University; Internship, Menninger Foundation, 1953; Post-Doctoral Fellow, Clinical Child Psychology, Menninger Clinic, 1956. *Appointments:* Teaching Assistant, Purdue University, 1950-51; Staff Psychologist, Kankakee State Hospital, 1954; Head, Staff Psychologist, Child Guidance Clinic, Kings County Hospital, Brooklyn, 1957-58; Clinical Research Consultant to Episcopal Diocese (City Mission), St Louis, Missouri, 1959; Director, Psychology Clinic, Barnes Hospital, Instructor, medical Psychology, Washington University School of Medicine, 1959; Private Practice, Clinical & Consulting Psychology, Fullerton, 1960-; Psychology Consultant, Fullerton Comunity Hospital, 1961-81; Staff Consultant, Martin Luther Hospital, Anaheim, California, 1963-70. *Memberships Include:* Internaitonal Council of Psychologists incorporated; Intercontinental Biographical Association, England; Royal Society of Health, England; American Association for Advancement of Science; American Orthopsychiatric Association; American Psychological Association; American Biographical Institute; World Wide Academy of Scholars, New Zealand; Diplomate, American Board of Professional Psychology; etc. *Honours:* Recipient, numerous honours and awards including: Statue of Victory, Personality of the Year Centro Studi E. Richerche Delle Nazioni, Italy, 1985. *Hobbies:* Antiques; Travel. *Address:* 905-907 W. Wilshire Ave., Fullerton, CA 92632, USA.

EVERETT, Melinda Jan Brown, b. 29 June 1946, Humboldt, Tennessee, USA. Public Relations Writer, Worcester Memorial Hospital, Massachusetts. m. Wayne Humphreys Everett, 15 Aug. 1970, Newbury, 2 sons. *Education:* AB, English, Sweet Briar College, 1968; Msc., Journalism, Boston University School of public Communications, 1970. *Appointments:* English and Journalism Instructor, Newburyport High School, 1968-69; Senior public Information Specialist, New York State Narcotic Addiction Control Commission, 1970-71; Public Relations Consultant, Laplante Associates, 1975-79; Associate Editor, Landmark Newspaper, Holden, 1979-83; Public Relations Writer, Worcester Memorial Hospital, 1983-. *Memberships:* Worcester County Public Relations Association; American Medical Writers' Association; Boston University Womens Club. *Publications:* Writer for 'Pacemaker'. *Honours:* Tau Phi; Outstanding Young Woman in Holden, 1978. *Hobbies:* Collecting Royal Doulton Toby Jugs; Reading; Movies; Theatre; Counted Cross Stitch Embroidery. *Address:* Lane's End, 44 Appletree Lane, Holden, MA 01520, USA.

EVRARD, Philippe, b. 1 Jan. 1942, Courcelles, Belgium. University Professor of Paediatric Neurology and Neuroanatomy. m. Ghislaine Evrard-Botteman, 1 son. *Education:* Physician, MD, Medical School, 1966, Neurologist and Paediatric Neurologist, 1970, University of Louvain Medical School, *Appointments:* Resident, University of Louvain Medical School, 1966. Research Fellow; Council of Europe and INSERM, University of Paris, France, 1970, 72. Postdoctoral Research Fellow: National Institutes of Health, USA; Harvard Medical School, massachusetts General Hospital, 1972 Associate Professor: Harvard Medical School, 1980; Massachusetts General Hospital, 1980; Professor, Paediatric Neurology and Neuroanatomy, University of Louvain Medical School, Brussels, Belgium, 1980-. *Memberships:* National and International Societies in Paediatric Neurology, Developmental Neuroscience and Paediatrics; President, Sociète Europeenne de neurologie Pediatrique. *Publications:* Author of various papers, books and book chapters in paediatric neurology and developmental neuroscience. *Honours:* French Literature, Amities Francaise, Belgium, 1959; SPECIA Award, 1966; International Postdoctoral Fellow, Research, National Institutes of Health, USA, 1972; Award for Sabbatical leave, Fonds National Belge de la Recherche Scientifique, 1980. *Address:* Service de Neurologie Pediatrique, Universite de Louvain Faculte de Medicine, Avenue Hippocrate 10, Boite 10/1303, B-1200 Brussels, Belgium.

EWER, Micheal S., b. 19 Sep. 1942, New York, USA. Associate Professor, Medicine. m. Jane Tobias, 14 July 1973, Norfolk, Connecticut, 2 sons, 1 daughter. *Education:* BA, Hunter College, 1964; MD, University of Basel, Switzerland, 1969; American Board of Internal Medicine, 1980; Diploma, Tropical Medicine, Swiss Tropical Institute, 1973. *Appointments:* Teaching Fellow, Brown University, 1974-75; Associate Internist & Assistant Professor, Medicine, 1983-84, Assistant Internist, Assistant Professor, Medicine, 1979-83, Associate Internist, Associate Professor, Medicine, 1984-, University of Texas System Cancer Centre, M.D. Anderson Hospital, & Tumour Institution, Houston, Texas. *Memberships:* American College of Emergency Physicians; American College of Physicians; Critical Care Society; American Heart Association. *Publications:* Articles in professional journals. *Honour:* Special Recognition Award, Norwalk Hospital, Connecticut, 1971. *Hobbies:* Flying; Music. Address: M.D. Anderson Hospital, Cardiopulmonary, Box 70, 6723 Bertner, Houston, TX 77030.

EWO, Sonia Udechuka, b. 22 Oct. 1925, Nigeria. Assistant Chief Matron, General Hospital, Lagos. m. Martin Ewo, 1955, London, England, 1 son, 1 daughter. *Education:* SNR; SCM; Fellow, West African College of Nursing; Dip.M.C.W.; Dip. H. Adm. (Nursing); CIFP. *Appointments:* Staff Nurse, 1952; Nursing Sister, 1960; Senior Nursing Sister, 1974; Matron 1978; Assistant Chief Matron, 1983. *Memberships:* Royal College of Nursing, England; Royal Institute of Public Health and Hygiene; Foundation Fellow, West African College of Nursing; National Association Nigerian Nurses and Midwives; Registered Senior Nurse Administrators; ICN. *Hobbies:* Counselling - Spiritual, Matrimonial and Social. *Address:* General Hospital, Lagos, Nigeria.

EYCKMANS, Luc A F, b. 23 Feb. 1930, Antwerp, Belgium. Professor of Infectious Diseases and Director of Institute for Tropical Medicine. m. Godelieve Cornelissen, 3 Sep. 1957, Houthalen, Belgium, 4 sons, 3 daughters. *Education:* MD, Medical School Leuven, Belgium, 1954; Specialisation in Internal Medicine, Leuven, 1961; Diploma in Tropical Medicine, Antwerp, 1957; Fellow in Infectious Diseases, Baylor University, Dallas, Texas, 1961-63; and Cornell University, New York, 1963-64; PhD, University of Leuven,. 1972. *Appointments:* Medecin des Hopitaux, Kisantu (former Belgian Congo) 1957-60; Assistant Professor of Medicine, University of Leuven, 1965-72; Professor of Medicine and President Medical Faculty, University of Antwerp, 1973-76; Director,

Institute of Tropical Medicine, Antwerp, 1976-; Visiting Professor of Infectious Diseases, Universities of Antwerp and Leuven. *Memberships:* The Royal Academy of Overseas Sciences; Belgian Society of Tropical Medicine, Secretary; Council of Directors of Tropical Medicine Institutes of Europe, Secretary; International Federation of Tropical Medicine, Secretary General; Royal Society of Tropical Medicine and Hygiene; Societe de Patholige Exotique etc. *Publications:* 96 scientific publications in profesional journals and chapters in edited books. *Honour:* Prix Jean Degroff, 1964. *Hobby:* Hiking. *Address:* Institute for Tropical Medicine, Nationalestraat 155, B2000 Antwerp, Belgium.

EYSKENS, Erik Joannes Maria, b. 20 July 1935, Leuven Belgium. Professor of Surgery; Chairman, Department of Surgery. m. Julie Ponet, 10 Oct. 1965, Tongeren, 2 sons, 1 daughter. *Education:* MD; Intern, Hospital of Paris, France; Research Fellow, Harvard University, USA; Specialist in Surgery; Doctor in Surgical Sciences. *Appointments:* Lecturer, Catholic University, Leuven, Belgium; Assistant Professor, Catholic University; currently, Professor of Surgery, University of Antwerp; Chairman, Department of Surgery, University Hospital, St Vincentius, Antwerp. *Memberships:* Admission Board for Surgery, Brussels; Foreign Associate, Academie de Chirurgie, Paris, France; Royal Society of Surgery, Belgium; Belgin Society of Gastroenterology; French Society of Surgery; International Society of Surgery. *Publications:* "Leerboek Chirurgie", 1983; "Codex Medicus", 1985; Author over 50 articles in national and international reviews. *Hobbies:* Walking; Swimming; Cycling. *Address:* Troyentenhoflaan 14, 2600 Antwerp-Berchem, Belgium.

F

FABB, Wesley Earl, b. 19 Mar. 1930, Ultima, Victoria, Australia. National Director, Family Medicine Programme, Royal Australian College of General Practitioners. Divorced, 2 sons, 1 daughter. *Education:* MB BS, University of Melbourne, 1955. *Appointments:* National Director of Education, Family Medicine Programme, Director of Examination Research and Development, Royal Australian College of General Practitioners; Honorary Senior Lecturer, Department of Community Medicine, Monash University, Melbourne; Assistant Physician, General, Review Clinics, Casualty Department, Alfred Hospital, Melbourne; Honorary Secretary, Treasurer, World Organization of National Colleges, Academics and Academic Organizations of General Practitioners, Family Physicians. *Memberships:* Fellow, Royal Australian College of General Practitioners; Honorary Fellow, Royal Australian College of General Practitioners; Honorary Fellow, College of General Practitioners, Singapore; Honorary Fellow, Faculty of General Practice, College of Medicine of South Africa; Honorary Member, College of Family Physicians of Canada. *Publications:* 'Focus on Learning in Family Practice', 1976; 'The Nature of General Family Practice, 1983; 'The Assessment of Clinical Competance in General Family Practice', 1983; 'Principles of Practice Management on Primary Care', 1985; Several other books and articles in professional journals; International and national presentations. *Honour:* Recipient of several honours. *Hobbies:* Reading; Photograpy; Music; Travel. *Address:* 59 Glen Park Road, North Eltham, Victoria 3095, Australia.

FABRICIUS, Jorgen C F Schack, b. 10 July 1920, Copenhagen, Denmark. Senior Physician/University Professor. m. Kristen Madsen, 12 Mar 1955, twin sons. *Education:* Graduated in medicine, 1947; Thesis 1959; Specialist in cardiology, 1967; Specialist in clinical physiology, 1967. *Appointments:* House Office, Copenhagen Country Hospital, 1947; Registrar, Medical Department, Aalborg General Hospital, 1948-52; Senior Registrar, Medical Department B, Rigshospitalet, Copenhagen, 1952-61; Senior Registrar, Clinical Chemistry, Blegdamshospital, Copenhagen, 1961-63; Senior Physician, Department of Clinical Physiology, Odense University Hospital, 1963-; Professor of Clinical Physiology, Odense University, 1970-. *Membeships:* Former Member, Danish Medical Research Council; Danish Society for Biomedical Engineering, Past President; Danish Society for Clinical Physiology, Past President; Publications: 'Isolated pulmonary stenosis' Thesis 1959; Papers on clinical physiology. *Honour:* Knight of the Dannebrog. *Hobby:* Numismatics. *Address:* Department of Clinical Physiology, Odense University Hospital, DK-5000 Odense C, Denmark.

FABRIS, Fabrizio, b. 24 Sep. 1935, Rome, Italy. Director of University Institute of Gerontology. m. Maria Grazia Batori, 15 Sep. 1962, Valmadonna, 3 sons. *Education:* MD; Specialisation in Gerontology and Geriatrics; Cardiology; L D Internal Medicine, Gerontology and Geriatrics. *Appointments:* Lecturer, Senior Lecturer, Faculty of Medicine, University of Turin; currnelty: Director, Institute of Gerontology, Faculty of Medicine, University of Turin. *Memberships:* President, Italian Study Group of Geriatric Therapy. *Publications:* "Atlas of Geriatrics" 1986; About 150 publications mostly in the field of Gerontology and Vascular disease. *Honour:* Fornaca Award, Turin 1970. *Address:* Institute of Gerontology of the University of Turin, Molinette Hospital, Corso Bramante 88, Turin, Italy.

FABRIZIO, Tuula Inja Jokinen, b. 13 May 1931, Helsinki, Finland. Physician. m. John A Fabrizio, 4 Aug, 1962, Portland, Maine, USA, 2 sons. *Education:* MD, University of Helsinki, 1957; DMS, University Central Hospital, Helsinki, 1958; Intern in USA, continuing study in orthopaedics, general surgery & traumatology. *Appointments:* Physician in Hospital Emergency departments at Bridgeport 1964, Norwalk 1966-69, Milford 1973-77, St Vincent's Medical Centre, Bridgeport 1977-79; presently Physician in practice of Occupational & Preventive Medicine, Norwalk, Connecticut. *Memberships:* American Board of Family Practice, 1971; Fellow, American College of Preventive Medicine, 1971; Charter Fellow, American Academy of Family Physicians, 1972; American Medical Association; Connecticut State Medical Society; American College of Emergency Physicians; American Public Health Association; American Association for Automobile Medicine; International College of Paediatrics; Acadmey of Political Science; American Medical Writers Association; American Association for the Advancement of Science; New York Academy of Science. *Publications:* Numerous scientific articles in 'Acta Chirugica Scandinavica'; 'Journal of the Finnish Medical Association', *Honours:* Bronze Medal Award of the Finnish Medical Association, 1980; Medal award, Finnish Medical Journal, 1982. *Hobby:* Traffic Safety. *Address:* 42 Stevens Street, Norwalk, CT 06850, USA.

FAERBER, Eric Norman, b. 22 Nov, 1942, Johannesburg, South Africa. Radiologist. m. Esme Emanuel, 18 Nov. 1975, Johannesburg, South Africa, 1 son, 1 daughter. *Education:* MB,BCh, University of Witwatersrand, Johannesburg, 1966; DMRD, London, England, 1972; Diplomate of American Board of Radiology, 1979. *Appointments:* Consultant Radiologist, Baragwanath Hospital, Johannesburg, 1974, Principal Consultant, 1976; Fellow, Neuroradiology, Tufts, New England Medical Centre, Boston, USA, 1976-78, Fellow, Paediatric Radiology, 1978-80; Attending Radiologist, St. Christopher's Hospital for Children, Philadelphia, 1980-present; Attending Radiologist, Medical College of Pennsylvania, 1980-present; Assistant Professor of Radiology, Temple University School of Medicine, Philadelphia, 1980-86, Associate Professor from 1986; clinical Associate Professor of Diagnostic Imaging, Medical College of Pennsylvania Medical School and Hospital, 1985-present. *Memberships:* British Institute of Radiology; American Roentgen Ray Society; American Society for Neuroradiology; Society for Paediatric Radiology. *Publications:* Chapter: 'Cerebral Trauma' in 'Central Nervous System: Approaches to Radiology Diagnosis', 1979; Monograph: 'Cranial Computed Tomography in Infants and Children', 1986; Articles: 'Computed Tomography of Spinal Fractures' in'Journal of Computer Assisted Tomography', 1979; 'Usual Manifestations of Neonatal Pharyngeal Perforation' in 'Clinical Radiiology', 1980; Co-author 'Computed Tomography of Neuroblastic Tumours' and 'The Role of Digital Subtraction angrography in Paediatric Cerebrovascular Occlusive Disease', 1984; *Honours:* Cluver Prize for Social and Preventive Medicine', 1964; Victor Vaughan Teaching award, 1983. *Hobbies:* Music; Reading; Philately; Motoring; Tennis *Address:* Department of Radiology, St. Christopher's Hospital for Children, 2600 N. Lawrence, Street Philadelphia, PA 19133, USA.

FAGRAEUS, Lennart, b. 30 Nov. 1938, Stockholm, Sweden. Professor of Anaesthesiology. m. Elisabet Ingeborg, 2 July 1965, Leksand, Sweden, 2 daughters. *Education:* MD, Medical School, PhD, Department of Physiology, Lecturer in Physiology, Faculty of Medicine, Karolinska Institutet, Stockholm, Sweden. *Appointments:* Surgeon Lieutenant Commander, 1963-70, Surgeon Commander, 1970-75, Medical Corps, Royal Swedish Navy Reserve; Visiting Assistant Professor, Department of Anaesthesiology, Duke University Medical Centre, Durham, North Carolina, USA, 1974-75; Member of Core Faculty F H Hall Laboratory for Environmental Physiology, Duke University Medical Centre, 1975-82; Assistant Professor, Department of Physiology, Faculty of Medicine, Karolinska Institutet, Stockholm, Sweden, 1975-; Assistant Professor, 1978-79, Associate Professor (Tenure), 1979-82, Department of Anaesthesiology, Duke University Medical Centre; Professor & Chairman, Department of Anaesthesiology, University of Oklahoma Health Sciences Centre, College of Medicine, Oklahoma City, 1983-. *Memberships:* American Medical Association; American Society of Anaesthesiologists; Association of University Anaesthetists; International Anaesthesia Research Society; Oklahoma State Medical Association; Sigma Xi; Society of Academic Anaesthesiology Chairmen; Society of Cardiovascular Anaesthesiologists; Society for Obstetric Anaesthesia & Perinatology; SwedishMedical Association. *Publications:* Over 130 articles, papers, abstracts & book chapters in medical & professional journals. *Hobbies:* Sailing; Tennis. *Address:* Department of Anaesthesiology, College of Medicine, Oklahoma University, Health Sciences Centre, P.O Box 53188, Oklahoma City, OK 73152, USA.

FAHEEM, Ahmed Daver, b. 7 Mar. 1948, Nizamabad, India. Clinical Associate Professor of Psychiatry. m. Najma, 4 June 1972, Hyderabad, India, 2 daughters. *Education:* MD; MRC Psychiatry, UK; DPM; UK: Certified by American Board of Psychiatry and Neurology, USA. *Appointments:* Senior House Officer, Walsgrove Hospital, Coventry, England, 1973-74; Registrar, Central Hospital, Warwick, 1974-76; Fellowship in Psychosomatic Medicine 1976-78, Assistant Professor 1978-82, University of Missouri, Columbia, Missouri, USA; Clinical Associate Professor, University of West Virginia, Morgantown, West Virginia, 1983-; Solo private practice in General and Adolescent Psychiatry, Beckley, 1982-. *Memberships:* American Psychiatric Association; American Society of Clinical Hypnosis; West Virginia State Medical Association; Raleigh County Medical Society, West Virginia. *Honours:* Elected Giant in Medicine, University of Missouri Medical School Graduating Class, 1981; Best Teacher Award, Residents in Psychiatry, University of Missouri, 1979, 1980 and 1981; Examiner, American Board of Psychiatry and Neurology, 1981. *Hobbies:* Theatre; Public Speaking; Jogging; Movies. *Address:* 113 Greenwood Drive, Beckley, WV 25801, USA.

FAHIMI, H Dariush, b. 7 May 1933, Tehran, Iran. University Professor of Antomy; Cell Biologist. 1 son, 1 daughter. *Education:* MD, University of Heidelberg, Federal Republic of Germany. *Appointments:* Associate Professor of Pathology, Harvard University Medical School, Boston, USA; Professor and Chairman, Department of Anatomy, University of Heidelberg, Federal Republic of Germany. *Memberships:* American Society of Cell Biology; Histochemical Society; American Association of Pathologists; Anatomische Gesellschaft. *Publications:* Over 100 scientific papers in speciality journals on Histochemistry and Cell biology. *Honour:* Research Career Development Award, National Institute of Health, USA, 1972-77. *Hobbies:* Skiing; Swimming; Tennis. *Address:* Department of Anatomy, University of Heidelberg, D 6900 Heidelberg, Federal Republic of Germany.

FAINE, Solomon, b. 17 Aug. 1926, Wellington, New Zealand. Professor of Microbiolgoy. m. Eva Rothschild, 17 May 1950, 1 son, 2 daughters. *Education:* B.Med.Sc., 1946, MB ChB, 1949, MD 1958, Otago University, New Zealand; D.Phil., University of Oxford, England, 1955. *Appointments:* Assistant Lecturer, Bacteriology, 1950-51, Lecturer, Microbiology, 1952-58, Otago University, New Zealand; On leave & Nuffield Dominions

Demonstrator, Sir William Dunn School of Pathology, University of Oxford, England, 1953-55; Senior Lecturer, 1959-63, Associate Professor, Clinical Bacteriology, 1963-68, University of Sydney, Australia; Professor of Microbiology, Chairman of Department, Monash University, Australia, 1968-. *Memberships:* Executive Board, Vice-Chairman 1974-78, Chairman 1978-82, Division of Bacteriology, International Union of Microbiological Societies; Chairman, Taxonomic Subcommittee Leptospira, International Committee Systematic Bacteriology, 1973-82, Chairman, Medical Microbiology Interdisciplinary Committee, 1982-86, International Union of Microbiological Societies; National Committee for Microbiology, Australian Academy of Sciences, 1981-83; Member, 1959-, President, 1969-70, Chairman, Standing Committee for Clinical Microbiology, 1984-, Australian Society for Microbiology; Foundation Member, Australasian Society for Infectious Diseases, 1976-; Fellow, American Academy of Microbiology, 1979-; Australian Society for Immunology, 1979-; Society for General Microbiology (UK), 1953-; UK Pathological Society, 1955-; American Society for Microbiology, 1965-. *Publications:* "Guidelines for the Control of Leptospirosis", WHO Geneva, 1982; Numerous publications in scientific journals. *Honours:* Peter Bancroft Prize for Research, Sydney University, 1965; Exchange Scholar, French Government, Institut Pasteur, Paris, 1971-72; Fulbright Award, 1978; Exchange Senior Fellowship, Federal German Government, 1979; Medallion for Distinguished Service, International Union of Microbiological Societies, 1982. *Hobbies:* Music; Photography. *Address:* Department of Microbiology, Monash University, Wellington Road, Clayton, Victoria 3168, Australia.

FAIREY, George Gage, b. 17 Sep. 1948, Detroit, Michigan, USA. Clinical Director, Psychiatrist in Charge, Islip Centre. m. Joanne Slocum Woodle, 13 May 1978, 1 son, 2 daughters. *Education:* BSc., 1971, MD, 1975, University of South Carolina; Residency, Psychiatry, New York Medical College, 1978. *Appointments:* Assistant Clinical Instructor, Metropolitan Hospital Centre, New York, 1978-81; Staff Psychiatrist, Craig House Hospital, Beacon, 1980-82; Clinical Director, Psychiatrist II, Islip Centre, 1982-. *Memberships:* American Psychiatric Association; American College Psychosomatic Obstetrics & Gynaecologists. *Honours:* Board of Directors, Mental Health Association of Suffolk County. *Hobbies:* Swimming; Sailing; Rock Music; Making Videos. *Address:* Islip Centre, 1747 Veteran's Highway, Central Islip, NY 11722, USA.

FAIRWEATHER, Denys Vivian Ivor, b. 25 Oct 1927, Forfar, Scotland, Professor, Director, Department of Obstetrics and Gynaecology, Vice-Provost (Medical), University College, London, m. Gwendolen Yvonne Hubbard, 21 Apr. 1955, Heckington, Lincs, England, 1 son, 2 daughters. *Education:* MB ChB, MD, University of St Andrews; DRCOG, MRGOG, FRCOG, Royal College of Obstetricians and Gynaecologists, London. *Appointments:* Royal Air Force Medical Branch, 1949-54; Registrar in Obstetrics and Gynaecology to Sir Duglad Baird, Aberdeen, Scotland, 1955-59; First Assistant. Senior Lecturer in Obstetrics and Gynaecology, University of Newcastle on Tyne, England, 1959-66; Professor and Director, Department of Obstetrics and Gynaecology, 1967-, Dean, Faculty of Clinical Sciences, 1982-84, Vice-Provost (Medical), 1984- University College, University College Hospital, London. *Memberships:* Royal Society of Medicine. *Publications:* 'Amniotic Fluid - Research and Clinical Application', (Editor, Co-author), 1978; 'Labour Ward Mannual'; (Editor, co-author); 'Nausea and Vomiting during Pregnancy', 1978; 'Obstetric management and follow up of the very low birth-weight infant', 1981; 'Obstetric outcome and problems of midtrimester fetal blood sampling for ante-natal diagnosis', 1981; 'How to deliver the under 1500 gram infant', (with A L Stewart), 1983; 'A randomized double-blind controlled trial of the value of stilboestrol therapy in pregnancy: long term follow-up of mothers and their offspring', (with M P Vessey, B Norman-Smith, J Buckley), 1983; 'The effect of amniocentesis and drainage of amniotic fluid on lung development in Macaca fascularis', (with A Hislop, R J Blackwell, S Howard), 1984; 'Screening in pregnancy for congenital abnormality', 1984. *Honours:* Fulbright Scholar, Western Reserve, Cleveland, USA, 1964; FAARM (Hon), 1969; Honorary Fellow, University College London, 1985. *Hobbies:* Gardening; Travel; Tennis. *Address:* Department of Obstetrics and Gynaecology, Faculty of Clinical Sciences, University College London, 88-96 Chenies Mews, London WC1E 6HX, England.

FALCONE, Alfonso Benjamin, b. 24 July 1923, Bryn Mawr, Pennsylvania, USA. Physician. m. Patricia J. Lalim, 22 Oct. 1955, 2 sons. *Education:* AB, with distinction in Chemistry, 1944, MD (Hons.), 1947, Temple University; PhD, Biochemistry, University of Minnesota, 1954; Diplomate, American Board Internal Medicine, subspeciality Board Endocrinology and Metobolism. *Appointments:* Intern, 1947-48, Resident, Internal Medicine, 1948-49, Philadelphia General Hospital; Teaching Fellow, Internal Medicine, University Hospitals, University of Minnesota, 1949-51; Assistant Clinical Professor, Medicine, 1956-59, Associate Clinical Professor, 1959-63, University of Wisconsin, Madison; Assistant Professor, Institute for Enzyme Research, 1963-66; Visiting Professor, 1966-67; Cons. practice Medicine specializing in endocrine and metobolic diseases, Fresno, California, 1968-; Member, Active Staff, Fresno Community Hospital, Chairman, Department Medicine, 1973; Member Active Staff, St. Agnes Hospital, Fresno; Member, Honorary Staff, Valley Medical Center, Fresno; Senior Corr., Ettore Majorana Center for Sciences, Culture, Erice, Italy. *Memberships:* California Academy of Medicine; NIH Postdoctoral Fellow, 1951-53; Fellow A.C.P; American Society Biological Chemists; Central Society Clinical Research; American Federation Clinical Research; American Chemical Society; American Medical Association; American Society Internal Medicine; American Association for Study Liver Disease; Sigma Xi; Phi Lambda Upsilon. *Publications:* Contributor of articles to professional journals. *Honours include:* NIH Research Grantee, 1958-68. *Address:* 2240 E. Illinois Avenue, Fresno, CA 93701, USA.

FALK, Katherine, b. 17 June 1944, New York, USA. Clinical Assistant Professor, Psychiatry, Columbia University College of Physicians and Surgeons; Private Practice, Psychiatry. *Education:* AB, Barndard College; MD, Mount Sinai School of Medicine; Diplomate: National Board of Medical Examiners, 1981, American Boards of Psychiatry & Neurology, 1977. *Appointments:* Intern, Assistant Resident, Medicine, St Lukes Hospital, New York City, 1970-72; Resident, Psychiatry, St Lukes Hospital, 1973-75; Instructor, Psychiatry, Cornell University Day Hospital, Cornell Medical College, 1976-77; Staff Psychiatrist, Student Health Psychiatric Services, Columbia Presbyterian Medical Centre, 1977-78; Clinical Instructor, Psychiatry, Columbia University, 1981-83; etc. *Memberships:* Fellow, American Psychiatric Association; American Medical Womens Association; Hastings Centre Institute of Society Ethics and Life Sciences. *Publications:* "A Comparison of the Syndrome Associated with a Partial Delition of the Short Arms of Chromosomes no, 4 and no, 5", 'The Mount Sinia Journal of Medicine', 1970; "Myoglobinunia with Reversible Acute Renal Failure", 'New York State Journal of Medicine', 1973. *Hobbies:* Sculpture; Painting; Collecting Art; Anti-nuclear War Activities; Skiing; Hiking. *Address:* 141 East 88th St., New York, NY 10128, USA.

FARLEY, H. Fred, b. 15 Feb. 1950, Pittsburgh, Pennsylvania, USA. Assistant Director of Nursing, University Hospitals of Cleveland, Ohio. m. Jonny D. Harger, 23 Dec. 1985, Pittsburgh, Pennsylvania, 3 daughters. *Education:* BA, Biology; BS, Nursing; MS, Nursing in Nursing Administration and Education. *Appointments:* Staff Nurse, Cardiac Intensive Care, Head Nurse, Hemodialysis, Assistant Director of Nursing, University Hospitals of Cleveland; Clinical Instructor, Frances Playne Bolton School of Nursing, Cleveland. *Memberships:* Greater Cleveland Nursing Association; Ohio Nurses Association; American Nurses Association; American Assembly for Men in Nursing; American Association of Nephrology Nurses. *Publications:* 'Altruism: A Complex Sociobiological Concept Applied to Renal Transplantation', 'AANNT Journal;', 1982; 'Assessment of Urinary System', "Medical/Surgical Nursing", 1985; 'Problems of the Heart and Major Blood Vessels', "Essentials of Medical/Surgical Nursing", 1985; 'Problems of Urinary System', "Medical/Surgical Nursing", 1985. *Honours:* Beta Beta Beta; Sigma Theta Tau; Cushing-Robb Award for Outstanding Scholarship, 1978, 81; Outstanding Services Award, Ohio Nurses Association, 1983; Service Award, Greater Cleveland Nurses Association, 1984; Award for Contribution to Paer Assistance, Ohio Nurses Association, 1984. *Hobbies:* Programming Home Computer with education programs for his three children; Writing; Reading Fiction. *Address:* University Hospitals of Cleveland, 2074 Abington Road, Cleveland, OH 44106, USA.

FARNSWORTH, Wells E., b. 7 Oct. 1921, Hartford, Connecticut, USA. Professor & Chairman, Biochemistry. m. Marjorie Anne Whyte, 15 Sep. 1945, Detroit, Michigan, 1 son, 1 daughter. *Education:* MA, PhD, University of Missouri. *Appointments include:* Biochemistry, 1962-80, Urology 1971-80; Clincal Assistant Professor, Medical Technology 1974-80, State University of New York, Buffalo. *Memberships:* American Society of Biology Chemistry; American Psychological Society; Endocrine Society; American Association for Cancer Research. *Publications include:* Contributions to various professional journals; Book chapters in "Some Aspects of the Aetiology & Biochemistry of Prostetic Cancer", 1970, "Scientific Foundations of Urology", 1976; 1983, "Benign Prostatic Hypertrophy", 1983; etc. *Address:* Chicago College of Osteopathic Medicine, Biochemistry Department, 5200 South Ellis Avenue, Chicago, IL 60629, USA.

FARQUHAR, Robin Hugh, b. 1 Dec. 1938, Victoria, British Columbia, Canada. President, Vice-Chancellor, University of Winnipeg. m. Frances Harriet Caswell, 6 July 1963, 3 daughters. *Education:* BA, Honours, MA, English, University of British Columbia; PhD, Educational Administration, University of Chicago, USA. *Appointments:* Teacher, Counsellor, Edward Milne Secondary School, Sooke, 1962-64; Staff Associate, Univeristy of Chicago, 1964-66; AssociateDirector, University Council for Educational Administration.Columbus, Ohio, 1966-69; Assistant Professor, Ohio State University, 1967-70; Deputy Director, University Council for Educational Administration, Columbus, Ohio State University, 1970-71; Department Chairman, Ontario Institute for Studies in Education, Toronto, 1971-73; Assistant Director, 1973-76; Professor, University of Toronto, 1974-76; Dean, Education, Professor, University of Saskatchewan, 1976-81; President, Vice-Chancellor, and Professor University of Winnipeg, 1981-. *Memberships Include:* President, Commonwealth Council for Educational Administration; Former President, Canadian Society for the Study of Education; Board Member: Intern-American Society for Educational Administration, Canadian Education Association. *Publications:* Author, 6 books and monographs, 60 book chapters and articles and 12 papers. *Honours:*

Fellow, Commonwealth Council for Educational Administration; Winner, $5,000 Edward L. Bernays Foundation Award, for proposal of comprehensive programme to futher understanding between the peoples of the United Kingdom and the USA, 1986. *Hobbies:* Golf; Swimming; Reading. *Address:* 49 OaK Street, Winnipeg, Manitoba, R3M 3P6, Canada.

FARRELL, Patricia Ann, b. 11 Mar. 1945, New York City, USA. Staff Clinical Psychologist I. *Education:* BA, Queen's College, City University of New York, 1976; MA, New York University, 1978; PhD Candidate, New York University, 1980-. *Appointments:* Associate Editor, Publishers Weekly Magazine, New York City, 1968-72; Editor, Best-Selling Magazine, New York City, 1972-73; Associate Editor, King Features Syndicate, New York City, 1973-78; Staff Psychologist, Intake Co-ordinator, Mid-Bergen CMHC, Paramus, New Jersey, 1978-84; Consultation and Education Specialist, Family Counselling Service, Ridgewood, New Jersey, 1984-; Adjunct Instructor, Psychology, Bergen Community College, New Jersey, 1978-; Clinical Psychology Internship, State of New Jersey Marlboro Psychiatric Hospital, 1984-85; Staff Clinical Psychologist I, Marlboro Hospital, 1985-. *Memberships:* Associate Member, American Psychological Association; Associate Member, New Jersey Psychological Association. *Publications:* Articles in various newspapers; also 'Writers' Digest'; 'Real World'; Book: "It's A Crazy Business". *Honours:* Good Citizen Award, 1958; National Honor Society, 1958; Social Science Award, 1976. *Hobbies:* Racquetball; Kite Design; Nautilus. *Address:* Station A Marlboro Psychiatric Hospital, Marlboro, NJ 07746, USA.

FARRELL, Robert Edmund, b. 10 July 1960, Providence, Rhode Island, USA, Instructor of Biology, The Catholic University of America, Washington DC. *Education:* MS, Catholic University of America, Washington, DC; BS, Providence College, Providence, Rhode Island. *Memberships:* New York Academy of Sciences; American Society for Cell Biology. *Publications:* 'Cell Proliferation and the expression of myc and ras oncogenes in normal and malignant fibroblasts', (with J J Greene and J R Wu), 1984. *Hobbies:* Water skiing; Travel. *Address:* Department of Biology, The Catholic University of America, Washington DC 20064, USA.

FARUGUI, Azhar M.A., b. 10 June 1948, Karachi, Pakistan. Consultant Cardiologist, National Institute of Cardiovascular Disease, Karachi. m. Shashida, Karachi, 2 sons. *Education:* MB BS; FRCP (C); Diplomate, American Board of Internal Medicine; Diplomate, American board of Cardiovascular Diseases. *Appointments:* Intern and Resident, Cardiology Fellow, Emory University School of Medicine, Atlanta, USA; Tutor, Royal Postgraduate Medical School, London, England; Director, Cardiac Cath. Laboratory and Assistant Professor, Emory University School of Medicne, Atlanta, USA. *Memberships:* American College of Cardiology; American Heart Associaiton; Royal College of Surgeons and Physicians of Canada; Pakistan Cardiac Society. *Publications:* 80 Scientific papers and two monographs; Editor, 'Pakistan Heart Journal'. *Honours:* Internationsl Fellow, Council on Clinical Cardiology of American Heart Association, 1985; Clinical Professor of Medicne, Age Khan Medical University, Karachi. *Hobbies:* Writing for lay press; Computers. *Address:* 116 Al Humra Society, Karachi, 8016, Pakistan.

KAULKNER, Kenneth Keith, b. 28 Apr. 1926, Barbourville, Kentucky, USA. Professor & Head, Department of Anatomical Sciences, University of Oklahoma College of Medicine. m. Jane Bullock 13 Aug. 1955, Oklahmoa City, 1 son, 2 daughters. *Education:* BSc, Lincoln Memorial University, 1949; MSc 1951, PhD 1955, University of Oklahoma. *Appointments:* Instructor, Lincoln Memorial University, 1949; Instructor, 1954, Assistant

Professor 1955, Associate Professor 1965, Professor 1970-, Vice Chairman 1970-75, Acting Chairman 1975-76, Interim Chairman 1981-82, Chairman 1982-, Uiversity of Oklahoma. *Memberships:* American Association for the Advancemnt of Science; Sigma Xi; American Association of Anatomists; Association of Anatomy Chairmen; Oklahoma State Anatomical Board. *Publications include:* "Case Studies in Anatomy", with E. Lachman, 3rd edition 1981; 'Surgical anatomy of the pubovesical (puboprostatic) ligament', co-author, 'Journal of Urology', 1973; 'The effects of scapular restriction an manual work space', with C.K. Rozier, 'Human Factors', 1975. *Hobbies:* Sports; Classical music; Current events. *Address:* 4420 Redbud Place, Edmond, OK 73013, USA.

FAUVE, Robert Marc, b. 19 Oct. 1930, Epernon, France. Professor, Pasteur Institute. m. Louise Hovhannessian, 6 Oct. 1953, 1 son, 1 daughter. *Education:* MSc., Faculty of Sciences, Paris, France, 1950, Md, Faculty of Medicine, 1957. *Appointments:* Research Associate, Rockefeller Institute, 1960-61; Assistant, Pasteur Institute, France, 1962-66, Chief of Laboratory, 1967-73, Professor, 1973-. *Memberships:* World Health Organisation – Export in Immunology, 1976, Member of Advisory Committee on Medical Research, 1976-80; National Committee of the National Scientific Research Centre, 1976-80; Editorial Board, Annales d'Immunologie, since 1976. *Publications:* Research on Immunophysiology and cancer; Medical film "Les Macrophages", 1972; Invention: Six French and foreign patents. *Honours:* Medical Doctor magna cum laude, 1957; Medical thesis Prize, 1958; French Medical Film Festival Award, 1971; Chevalier de la Legion d'Honneur, 1975. *Hobby:* Music. *Address:* Institut Pasteur, Unite d'Immunophysiologie cellulaire, 25 Rue du Dr Roux, 75724, Paris Cedex 15, France.

FAVARO, Mary Kaye (Asperheim), b. 30 Sep. 1934, Edgerton, Wisconsin USA. Physician; Author. m. B. Philip Favaro, 31 May 1969, Madison, Wisconsin, 1 son, 1 daughter. *Education:* BS, Pharmacy University of Wisconsin, 1956; MS, Pharmacy St, Louis College of Pharmacy 1965; MD, University of Wisconsin, 1969. *Appointments:* Instructor, Pharmacology, St. Louis University, 1959-64; Internship, Albany Medical College, NY, 1969-70; Residency, Albany Medical College, 1970-71; Residency, Medical University of South Carolina, 1972-73; Assistant Professor of Paediatrics, 1973-79; Private Practice, Family Practice and Pediatrics, Charleston, South Carolina, 1974-; Board Certified Pediatrics. *Memberships:* American Medical Association; South Carolina Medical Association; Charles County Medical Society; Hospital Staff, Roper Hospital, St. Francis and Baker Hospitals, Charleston, South Carolina. *Publications:* "Pharmacologic Basis of Patient Care", 5th Edition, 1985; "Pharmacology, An Introductory Text", 6th Edition, 1986. *Hobbies:* Piano; Gardening. *Address:* 1866 Capri Drive, Charleston, SC 29407, USA.

FAWCETT, Robert George, b. 12 Nov, 1946, Cleveland, Ohio, USA. Psychiatrist. m,. Letty Lee Ringman, 14 June 1975, 2 daughters. *Education:* BS, Michigan State University, 1968; MD, Wayne State University School of Medicine, 1975. *Appointments:* Partner, Chairman, Department of Psychiatry, Burns Clinic Medical Center, PC; Director, Mental Health Unit, Chairman, Department of Psychiatry, Northern Michigan Hospitals. *Memberships:* American Psychiatric Assn.; American Medical Assn; Michigan State Medical Society; Northern Michigan Medical Society. *Hobbies:* Cross Country Skiing; Fishing. *Address:* Burns Clinic Medical Center PC, 560 W Mitchell, Petoskey, MI 49770, USA.

FAZLI, Ahmet (Sir), b. 12 Apr. 1931, Afghanistan, Chief of Microbiology and Basic Medicine Departments and of Health Institute. m. Suphiye Acikel, 23 Oct. 1957, 1 son, 2 daughters. *Education:* BS, 1955;

MS, 1958; PhD, 1960; Associate Professor, 1969; Full Professor, 1981. *Appointments:* Lecturer and Staff member 1961-66, Staff member, Dean, Senate member, Member Academic Degrees Evaluation and University Development Committees 1970-79, Kabul University, Afghanistan; Chief Assistant Professor and Research Staff, Medical Faculty, Ankara University, Turkey, 1966-70; Staff member, Chief of Medical Science and Microbiology Department of Medical Faculty, Chief of Health Science Institute, Eriyes Univerisyt, Turkey. *Memberships:* Turkish Microbiology Association; Ankara Microbiology Society; Turkish Society for Parasitology; Culture Collection and Industrial Microbiology Assocition. *Publications:* "Immunology, Serology and Allergy"; "Microbiology of Food, Water and Sewage for Kabul University"; 64 articles in national and international journals related to public health. *Honours:* Afgan Educational Medal, 1974; Plaque for 25 years Service in professional field, 1984. *Hobbies:* Playing and talking with children; Students; Planting and care of flowers. *Address:* Erc, Univ. Tip Fakultesi, Mikrobiyoloji Anabilim Dali Kayseri, Turkey.

FEDORYK, Donald Joseph, b. 18 July 1953, USA. Chiropractic Physician, m. Linda Kruse, 26 Nov 1977. *Education:* BA, Rutgers College; Certified Chiropractic Sports Team Physician; Diplomate, National Board of Chiropractic Examiners; Phi Chi Omega Chiropractic Scholastic Honour Society; Doctorate of Chiropractic. *Memberships:* New Jersey Chiropractic Society; American Chiropractic Association; ACA Council on Sports Injuries. *Hobbies:* Triathlete; Porsch Club Membership. *Address:* 2035 Brooks Boulevard, S Somerville, NJ 08876, USA.

FEENEY, James, b. 7 Aug. 1936, St Helens, Lancashire, England. Centre Controller, MRC Biomedical NMR Centre, National Institute for Medical Research. m. Mary Margery Foster, 31 May 1960, St Helens, Lancashire, England, 2 sons, 2 daughters. *Education:* BSc, Chemistry, 1958, PhD, 1961, DSc, 1975, Liverpool University. *Appointments:* Lecturer in Chemistry, Liverpool University, 1960-64; Director, European Laboratories, Varian Associates, Walton-on-Thames/Zurich, 1964-69; Special Appointment, MRC, 1971; MRC, Molecular Pharmacology Unit, Cambridge 1969-72; National Insitute for Medical Research, Mill Hill, 1972-; Centre Controller, Biomedical NMR Centre, National Institute for Medical Research, 1980-; Visiting Professor, Chemistry Department, University of Essex, 1982-; Visiting Professor, Chemistry Department, University of Surrey, 1985-. *Memberships:* Royal Society of Chemistry; Biophysical Society. *Publications:* Co-author of two textbooks on 'High Resolution NMR Spectroscopy'; Editor of 18 volumes on 'Progress in MNR Spectroscopy'; Numerous scientific papers on MNR Spectroscopy as applied to Bicyhemistry and Molecular Pharmacology. *Honours:* Fellowship of Royal Society of Chemistry (FRSC); 1969; Medallist of Liverpool University Chemical Society, 1973. *Hobbies:* Squash; Conversation; Guitar. *Address:* Biomedical NMR Centre, National Institute for Medical Research, Mill Hill, London NW7 1AA. England.

FEFERMAN, Irving Jacob, b. 1 July 1947, Toronto, Canada. Director of Emergency Services. m. Margot Rentate Snow, 30 Dec, 1971, Toronto, 2 sons, 1 daughter. *Education:* MD; Certification in Emergency Medicine, Canadian College of Family Physicians. *Appointments:* Casualty Officer, Mount Sinai Hospital, Toronto, 1974-75; Consultant, Science International, Television series, 1980; Chairman, Community Hospitals Emergency Department Directors, 1984-; Vice Chairman, Medical Advisory Board, Department of Ambulance Services; currently, Director of Emergency Services, Scarborough General Hospital; Family Physician. *Memberships:* Royal College of Physicians and Surgeons; Canadian College of Family Physicians; American College of Emergency Physicians. *Publications:* 'Pica: A Review', in 'Modern Medicine of Canada'; 'Screening for Hypertension', in 'Canadian Family Physicians', 1973; 'Simple Methods for Administering Endotracheal Medication', 1980; 'Use of Surgical Glove When Repairing Finger Injuries', 1985. *Hobbies:* Jogging; Piano: Water skiing. *Address:* 2432 Eglinton Avenue East, Scarborough, Ontario, Canada M1K 2P8.

FEHER, Janos, b. 23 Nov. 1932, Kisbarat, Hungary. Director, Professor of Medicine. *Education:* MD, Semmelweis University of Medicine, Budapest, 1958; Specialist in Pathology, 1961; Specialist in Internal Medicine, 1965; PhD, 1975; Specialist in Gastroenterology, 1980-; DSc, 1981. *Appointments:* Resident, 1958; Assistant Professor, 1961; Research Fellow, Department of Pathology, University Dental School, Newcastle upon Tyne, England, 1970; Associated Professor 1979, Director and Professor of Medicine 1983, Department of Medicine, Semmelweis Medical University, Budapest, Hungary. *Memberships include:* General Secretary, Hungarian Arteriosclerosis Society; International Association for the Study of the Liver; International Arteriosclerosis Society; International Association for Oncodevelopment Biology and Medicine. *Publications:* 'Glycoprotein Metabolism in Experimetnal tissue Alterations and in Chronic Liver Diseases', PhD thesis, 1975; 'Autoimmunity Autoimmune Diseases' in "Allergology", 1979; 'Spirohetal Hepatitis' in "International Textbook of Medicine", 1981; 'Pathogenesis and Prognosis of Chronic Active Hepatitis', DSc thesis, 1981; 'Icterus. Diagnosis and Differential Diagnosis', 1986; 'Free Radicals in Medicine', 1985; More than 100 publications in journals, mostly in the field of liver disease. *Address:* Szentkiralyi u 46, Budapest, H 1088, Hungary.

FEHRENBACH, Alice Regina, b. 14 Nov 1910, Denver, Colorado, USA. Clinical Psychologist. m. (1) Frank Martin O'Sullivan, Colorado Springs, (deceased); (2) Carl Ernst Fehrenbach, Ogden, Utah (deceased). *Education:* AB, Barnard College, Columbia University, 1931; MA, 1944, PhD, 1955, University of Denver; Fellow, American Psychological Association, 1967; Diplomate, ABPP, 1970. *Appointments:* Teacher, Denver Public Schools, 1931-47; Psychologist, Denver Public Schools, 1948-68; Full Professor/Director of Counseling, 1968-76, Professor Emeritus, 1976-, Regis College; Private Practice, Psychology, 1948-; Ancillary Staff, Mount Airy Psychiatric Center, 1976-. *Memberships:* Past President, CPA; Board Member, Rocky Mountain Psychology Association; ABPP Intermountain Regional Board 1978-83. *Publications:* Many Journal articles some which have been abstracted by medical educational publications; Articles in feature sections of public press; Articles in alumnae publications. *Honours:* Distinguished Service Award, 1969, Past Presidents Award 1985, CPA; Social Action Award, Mental Health Association of Colorado, 1974; Distinguished Service Award, Rocky Mountain Psychology Association, 1982; Distinguished Service Award, Intermountain Regional Board, ABPP. *Hobbies:* Travel; Reading; Mountain Climbing. *Address:* 3232 St Josephine Street, Denver, Co 80210, USA.

FEICHTINGER, Wilfred, b. 19 Oct. 1950, Vienna. Associate Director, Institute of Reproductive Endocrinology and In Vitro Fertilization. *Education:* Medical Degree 1975; Specialization for Obstetrics and Gynaecology, 1983. *Appointments:* IInd Department of Obstetrics and Gynaecology, University of Vienna, 1977-82; Founder of In Vitro Fertilization Program 1979-; Institute of Reproductive Endocrinology and In Vitro Fertilization (with Dr P. Kemeter) 1983-. *Memberships:* American Fertility Society; Austrian Society of Obstetrics and Gynaecology; Austrian

Society of In Vitro Fertilization; Austrian Society of Parinatal Medicine; Austrian Society of Psychosomatics in Gynaecology and Obstetrics; Foreign Correspondent Member, Sociedad Espanola de Fertilidad; Middle European Society of Reproductive Medicine; European Society of Human Reproduction and Embryology. *Publications:* Numerous articles on in vitro fertilization; Book: "Recent Progress in Human In Vitro Fertilization", 1984. *Hobbies:* Travelling; Singing; Fishing; Sailing; Hunting; Skiing; Horseriding. *Addresds:* Trauttmansdorffgasse 3a, A-1130 Vienna, Austria.

FEINBERG, Joseph George, b. USA. Visiting Professor, St. Thomas's Hospital Medical School, London, England. m. London, 1 daughter. *Education:* BS, Brooklyn College; MS, DVM, Kansas State University. *Appointments:* Small Animal Practice; Veterinary Pharamceutical Chemist; Veterinary Inspector, Bureau of Animal Industry, Civilian Conservation Corps, U.S. Army; Director of Research, Beecham Research Laboaratories (Bwncard Division), Miles Laboratories (Dome Division); Director of Studies in Immunology, University of London (Chelsea College); Visiting Professor in Immunology, University of London (St. Thomas's Hospital Medical School). *Memberships:* American Association of Immunologists; American Academy of Allergy and Immunology; British Society for Allergy and Clinical Immunology; British Society for Immunology; European Academy of Allegology and Clinical Immunology; Royal Society of Medicine; Institute of Biology; Zoological Society of London; International Med. Club. *Publications:* 'Experimental Studies in Penicillin Allergy' in "Penicillin Allergy; Receent Advances", 1970; "Paper and Thin Layer Chromatography and Electrophoresis" with I. Smith, 1972; "The Chain of Immunology" with Mark Jackson, 1983. *Honour:* Citation from European Academy of Allergy for contributions to research in allergy and immunology. *Address:* Department of Immunology, Rayne Institute, St. Thomas's Hospital, London SE1 7EH, England.

FEINSILVER, David B, b. 11 Nov. 1939, Boston, Massachusetts, USA. Psychiatrist. m. Miriam Hoffman, 21 Apr. 1963, 1 son, 1 daughter. *Education:* AB, Brandeis University, 1961; MD, Tufts University Medical school, 1965; Internship, Mount Zion Hospital, 1965-66; Psychiatric Residency, Yale University, Connecticut Mental Health Centre & Yale Psychiatric Institute, 1966-69. *Appointmetns:* In Private Practice, 1969-; Staff Psychiatrist, Chestnut Lodge Hospital, 1971-. *Memberships:* Chestnut Lodge Research Committee; Washington Psychoanalytic Society Research Committee; Associate Member, American Psychoanalytic Association; American Psychiatric Association. *Publications:* Various articles in medical & psychiatric journals. *Hobbies:* Tennis; Skiing; Photography. *Address:* 2800 McKinley Place NW, Washington, DC 20015, USA.

FEINSILVER, Donald Lee, b. 24 July 1947, Brooklyn, New York, USA. Associate Professor, Psychiatry. *Education:* BA, Alfred University, 1968; MD, Autonomous University of Guadalajara, 1974. *Appointments:* Intern, Internal Medicine, Long Island College Hospital, Brooklyn, 1975-76; Resident, 1978-79, Chief Resident, 1979-, Psychiatry, State University of New York, Down State Medical Center; Assistant Professor, 1980-85, Associate Professor, 1985-, Psychitry, Medical College of Wisconsin, *Memberships:* American Psychiatric Association; American Medical Association; Academy of Psychosmatic Medicine; American Association for the Advancement of Science; American Academy of Psychiatry and the Law; American Society of Law and Medicine. *Publications:* Editor, "Crisis Psychiatry: Pros and Cons", 'Issue of Psychiatric Annals', 1982; Author, "Emergency Room Psychiatry: Role Conflicts, Future Directions", 'Current Psychiatric Theraies', volume 21, 1982;

"Psychiatric Diagnostic Procedures in the Emergency Department", 'Handbook of Psychiatric Diagnostic Procedures', 1982. *Address:* 8700 W. Wisconsin Avenue, Milwaukee, WI 53226, USA.

FEINSTEIN, Alvan Richard, b. 4 Dec. 1925, Philadelphia, Pennsylvania, USA. Professor of Medicine and Epidemilogy, Yale University School of Medicine, New Haven, Connecticut. *Education:* BS, 1947, MS, Mathematics, 1948, MD, 1952, University of Chicago. *Appointments:* Assistant Professor of Medicine, New York University, 1956-62; Medical Director, Irvington House, New York, 1956-62; At Yale and New Haven since 1962; Chief, Cooperative Studies Support Center, Veterans Administration Hospital, West Haven, Connecticut, 1967-74. *Memberships:* Association of American Physicians; American Board of Internal Medicine, Governing Member; American Society for Clinical Investigation; American Epidemilogical Society; Institute of Medicine. *Publications:* Books: "Clinical Judgement", 1967; "Clinical Biostatistics", 1977; "Clinical Epidemiology", 1985. *Honours:* Francis Gilman Blake Award, Yale University, 1969; Distinguished Service Award, University of Chicago, 1975; Ludwig Hailmeyer Society Gold Medal Award, 1981; Richard and Hinds Rosenthal Foundation Award, American College of Physicians, 1982; Charles V. Chaplin Medal Award, 1983. *Hobbies:* Guitar; Folk Songs. *Address:* Yale University School of Medicine, 333 Cedar Street, P.O. Box 3333, New Haven, CT 06510, USA

FELD, Harvey J, b. 16 Mar. 1949, St Petersburg, Florida, USA. Physician, Pathologist. m. Karen W Markman, 2 June 1973, 1 son. *Education:* BS Chemistry 1971, Masters Programme in Science Education 1971-73, University of Florida, Gainesville; MD, University of the East, Philippines, 1977; Clinical Clerkship, Long Island College Hospital, Brooklyn, New York, USA, 1977-78; Resident in Pathology, The Mount Sinai School of Medicine, New York, 1978-82; Fellow in Cytopathology, M D Anderson Hospital and Tumor Institute, Houston, Texas, 1982-83; Diplomate, American Board of Pathology, 1985. *Appointments:* Pathologist, Humans Hosp-Pasco, Dade City, Florida, 1983-; Pathologist, East Pasco Medical Center, Zephyrhills, Florida, 1983-. *Memberships:* Fellow, College of American Pathologists; Fellow, American Society of Clinical Pathologists; Associated Alumni of Mount Sinai Medical Center; Founding member, M D Anderson Associates. *Publications:* 'Spontaneous Perforation of Intestinal Duplications', 1982; 'Hypernephroma Metastatic to a Parathyroid Adenoma 18 years After Nephrectomy', 1982; (Both Mt Sinai Journal of Medicine. *Honour:* Ralph Colp Award of journalistic excellence, 'Mount Sinai Journal of Medicine', 1982-83. *Hobbies:* Rock collecting; Coin collecting. *Address:* 14714 Tall Tree Drive, Lutz, FL 33549, USA.

FELLOWS, Cheryl Wolf, b. 9 June 1950, Illinois, USA. Private Practice in Psychology. m. David B, Fellows, 23 Apr, 1982, Tampa, Florida, USA, 1 son. *Education:* AA Nursing; BA Social Sciences; MA Psychology; PhD Clinical Psychology. *Appointments:* Director, Children's Program, Parents' Training Program, Child Management Program, University of South Florida; Consultant, Mental Health Services of Pinellas County, Florida; Mental Health Counsellor, Horizon Hospital, Clearwater, Florida; Assistant Director, Family Violence Project, Pinellas County, Florida. *Memberships:* American Psychological Association; International Neuropsychology Society; Florida Psychological Association; Southeastern Psychological Association; American Society of Clinical Hypnosis; Florida Society of Clinical Hypnosis; Psychology & Law Division, American Psychological Association. *Publications:* 'Alcohol-related Advertisements in a College Newspaper', Journal of Addictions; 'Family Violence: Intervention Techniques for Therapists'. *Honours:* Graduate Fellowship, University of South Florida, 1979-81; Phi Kappa Phi Honor Society. *Hobby:* Jogging. *Address:* 655 Ulmerton Road Suite 1o-A, Largo FL 33541, USA.

FELLS, Peter, b. 6 Sep. 1935, Sheffield, England. Consultant Ophthalmologist. m. Christine Gurowich, 3 Sep. 1960, Worthing, England, 3 daughters. *Education:* MA, Cantab, Hons, MB, BChir, FRCS, DO. *Appointments:* House Physician and House Surgeon, University College Hospital, London 1960-61; Resident Surgical Officer, Bristol Eye Hospital, 1961-63; Resident Surgical Officer, 1963-66, Senior Lecturer, Professional Unit, 1968-71, Moorfields Eye Hospital; Honorary Consultant Ophthalmologist, Royal Postgraduate Medical school, Hammersmith Hospital, London 1968-74; Consultant Ophthalmologist, Moorfields Eye Hospital, 1971-. *Memberships:* Ophthalmological Society of U.K.; B.M.A.; Fellow, Royal Society of Medicine; Council Member, International Strabismological Association; Court of Examiners, Royal College of Surgeons; European Strabismological Association; Chairman, Britsh Orthoptic Council. *Publications:* Editor of "Transactions of International Strabismological Association" 1971 and 1976; Chapters and papers on strabismus surgery, dystyroid eye disease and orbital blow-out fractures. *Honours:* Hallett Prize, Royal College of Surgeons, 1961; Harkness Fellow of the Commonwealth Fund, 1966-67. *Hobbies:* Music, listening and playing clarinet and recorder; Cycling. *Address:* 20 East End Road, Finchley, London N3 3QT, England.

FENECH, Frederick Francis, b. 20 Feb. 1934, Malta. Professor and Chairman Department of Medicine. m. Marie Rose Galea, 1 Nov. 1957, Malta, 1 son, 1 daughter. *Education:* MD, University of Malta; FRCP, London; FRCP, Edinburgh; FRCP, Glasgow; FACP. *Appointments:* Consultant Physician and Lecturer in Medicine and Clinical Pharmacology, Royal University of Malta; Professor and Head of Department of Medicine, University of Malta; Dean, Malta Medical School; Foundation Professor and Chairman, Department of Medicine, University of Kuwait. *Memberships:* Association of Physicians of Great Britain and Ireland; British Medical Association; British Diabetic Association; Medical Association of Malta; European Association of Internal Medicine. *Publications include:* "Effect of intravenous Prehisolone in Asthmatics with adrenegic induced responsiveness" Lancet 1975; "Guidelines to Management of Common Medical Emergencies in Adults" 1985. *Hobbies:* Reading; Walking; Swimming; Historical Research. *Address:* Department of Medicine, PO Box 24923 Safat, Kuwait.

FENNER, Harold Allan Jr, b. 12 Apr. 1924, Nebraska, USA. Department Orthopaedic Surgery, Norte Vista Medical Centre, div, 2 sons, 1 daughter. *Education:* BS, 1947, MD, 1948, University of Nebraska; Orthopaedic Surgery, US Air Force, 1951-53; Surgery of Trauma, University of Texas, 1951-52. *Appointments:* American Medical Association Committee Medical Aspects of Automotive Safety; Consultant to Department of Transportation, National Accident Sampling Survey (NASS); US Department Transportation, National Motor Vehicle Advisory Committee, National Highway Safety Advisory Committee; Consultant Surgeon, General Committee on Emergency Health Care and Injury Control; Past President, American Association for Hand Surgery; American Association for Automotive Medicine; Fellow, American College of Sports Medicine; Fellow, International College of Surgeons (Orthopaedics). *Publications:* 'Types of Vehicle Injuries and Treatment' 1966; 'Rating the Degree of Tissue Damaged' 'Football Injuries and Helmet Design', 1964; 'Devlopment of Medicably Acceptable Injury Scale', 1969; 'Adoption of Racing Helmet Design for Head Protection in Football and Other Sports', 1970. *Honours:* Snell Memorial

Foundation Director, 1984; American Airpower Heritage Foundation, 1985. *Hobbies:* Relation of auto and aircraft injuries to interior design; Flying. *Address:* Norte VISTA Medical Centre, 2410 North Fowler, Hobbs, NM, 88240, USA.

FENTON, Elaine Reiman, b. 13 Apr. 1937, Cincinnati, Ohio, USA. Director, Manhattan Speech/Language/Voice Pathology Service. m. Bradford Donaldson Fenton, 23 May, 1964, 1 son. *Educaiton:* BA, Marymount College, New York City, USA, 1959; MA, Hunter College of CUNY, 1962; CCC, American Speech-Launage Hearing Association, 1966; PhD, New York University, 1971; New York State Licence, Speech-Language Pathology, 1976; Certificate in Speech Communication, MIT Post Doctoral Institute, 1979 and 1982; Professional Education Certificates, American Speech-Language Hearing Association, 1982 and 1985. *Appointments include:* Assistant Professor of Speech Pathology and member of graduate faculty, Douglass College of Rutgers University, New Brunswick, USA, 1971-76; Research Associate, Speech Production, Haskins Laboratories, New Haven, Connecticut, 1974-81; Research Associate, Neurology, New York Hospital, 1975-80; Director, Manhattan Speech/Language Voice Pathology Service, 1982-. *Memberships include:* New York Academy of Sciences; New York City Speech Hearing and Language˙ Association; Acoustical Society of America; American Speech-Language Association; American Association of Phonetic Sciences; Psycholinguistic Circle of New York, etc. *Publications include:* Co-author 'Parkinson's Disease: Acoustical Analysis of Phonation' in 'ASHA', 1975; Co-author 'Stroboscopic Invertigation of Larynges in Parkginson's Disease Patients' in :ASHA', 1976; Co-author 'Symptoms in Parkin's Disease' in 'Annals of Otology, Rhin. & Laryngocology', 1982. *Honours:* Awarded scholarships to undergradute college and for post-doctoral studies; Recipent funds for research studies. *Hobbies:* Poetry; Gardening; Civic Work. *Address:* 36 Sutton Place South, New York, NY 10022, USA.

FENTON, George Wallace, b. 30 July 1931, Londonderry, Northern Ireland. Professor, Psychiatry, University of Dundee. *Education:* Queen's University of Belfast Medical School, 1948-54; MB. BCh. BAO, 1954; DPM (England), 1957; MRCP (Edinburgh), 1960; MRCP (London), 1963; FRCP (Edinburgh), 1974; FRC Psych. 1976. *Appointments:* Lecturer, Academic Dept. of Psychiatry, Middlesex Hospital Medical School, University of London, 1964-66; Senior Lecturer, Institute of Psychiatry, University of London, 1967-75; Consultant Neurophysiologist, 1968-75, Consultant Psychiatrist, 1967-75, Maudsley Hospital; Professor, Mental Health, Queens University of Belfast, 1976-83. *Memberships:* Fellow, Royal College of Psychiatrists; Fellow, Royal Society of Medicine; EEG Society; Association of British Clinical Neurophysiologists; British Association of Behavioural Psychotherapists. *Publications:* "Research Interests: The Behavioural Aspects of Epilepsy, Clinical Neurophysiology and Neuropsychiatry"; Author, over 90 papers and joint author, 1 research monograph. *Address:* Dept. of Psychiatry, University of Dundee Medical School, Ninewells Hospital, Dundee DD1 9SY, Scotland.

FENTON, John Vincent, b. 24 Oct. 1945, New York, USA. Director, Rehabilitation, Brotman Medical Centre. m. Stella, 1 son, 2 daughters. *Education:* BS, Manhattan College, 1968; Phys. Therapy, Columbia University, 1969; MBA, Health Science Management, Century University, Beverly Hills, California, 1981; Certificate, Nursing Home Extended Care Facilities Administration, 1973; Lic. Phys. Therapist, California, New York, Michigan, New Jersey. *Appointments:* Recreational Assistant, Cardiac Hospital, St Frances Hospital, New York, 1962-64; Emergency Medical Technician, St.

Vincent's Hospital, New York City, 1964-69; Director, Cerebral Palsy Treatment Centre, Albany, 1964-69; Assistant Administrator, Director, Rehabilitation Services. Menorah Home and Hospital, Brooklyn, 1971-73; Executive Administrator, New York Medical College, Mental Retardation Institute, Valhalla and New York City, 1973-76; Administrator, Jewish Board of Guardians, New York City, 1977-78; Corp. Officer, Executive Director, Professional Services, Cons., Creative Escapes, Beverly Hills, 1980-; Director, Rehabilitation Services, Brotman Medical Centre, 1982-. *Memberships Include:* American Phys. Therapy Association; American Association Mental Deficiency; American Hospital Association; American College of Sports Medicine; American College Nursing Home Administrators; Association Administrators, Mental Health and Retardation Facilities. *Address:* Brotman Medical Centre, 3828 Delmas Terrace, Culver City, CA 90230, USA.

FERGUSON, Donald John, b. 19 Nov. 1916, Minneapolis, USA, Professor of Surgery, m. Lillian Elizabeth Mack, 26 June 1943, St Paul, Minnesota, 2 sons, 1 daughter. *Education:* BS, Yale University, 1939; MD, 1943, MS, 1951, PhD, 1952, University of Minnesota. *Appointments:* Instructor to Professor of Surgery University of Minnesota, 1952-60; Professor of Surgery, University of Chicago, 1960-. *Memberships:* American College of Surgeons; American Surgical Association; Society of University Surgeons; International Surgical Society; Holsted Society. *Publications:* 'Pulmonary arteriosclerosis', 1962; 'Magnetic meters', 1966; 'Surgical wounds', 1971; 'Staging laparotomy', 1973; 'Tumourilysin', 1980; 'Extended mastectomy', 1985. *Hobbies:* Music; Reading. *Address:* 5629 South Blackstone, Chicago, IL 60637, USA.

FERGUSON, James E, b. 25 Oct. 1951, Glendale, California, USA, Assistant Professor. m. Lynn Carpening, 21 June 1975, Asheville, North Carolina, 3 sons. *Education:* AB History, Marquette University, Milwaukee, Wisconsin, 1971-73; MD, Wake Forest University, Bowman Gray School of Medicine, 1973-77. *Appointments:* Attending staff, Medical Park and Forsyth Memorial Hospitals, Winston-Salem, 1981-82; Private Practice, Winston-Salem, 1981-82; Clinical Faculty, Department Obstetrics-/Gynecology, Bowman Gray School of Medicine, 1981-82; Associate medical staff, Santa Clara Valley Medical Center, San Jose, California, 1982-; Consultant, Mid-Coastal California Perinatal Outreach Program, 1982-; Attending staff, Stanford University Hospital, 1984-; Assistant Professor Section of Maternal-Fetal Medicine, Department of Gynecology and Obstetrics, Stanford University School of Medicine, 1984-. *Memberships include:* Phi Beta Kappa; Phi Alpha Theta; Junior Fellow, American College of Obstetricians and Gynecologists; Shufelt Society; Association of Professors of Gynecology and Obstetrics. *Publications include:* "Obstetric Anesthesia", (with G. A. Albright and D. K. Stevenson); Several contributions to learned journals. *Honours include:* Lange Award, C. Hampton-Mauzey Award, Bowman Gray School of Medicine, 1977; Mellon Foundation Fellow, Stanford University School of Medicine, 1984-85. *Hobbies:* Running; Music, *Address*; Section of Maternal-Fetal Medicine, Stanford University School of Medicine, Stanford, CA 94305, USA.

FERGUSON, Peter Edwin, b. 10 Feb. 1946, Iowa, USA. Psychiatrist; Medical Director. 1 daughter. *Education:* BS, Iowa State University, 1971; MD, University of Iowa College of Medicine; Psychiatric Residency, Wilford Hall USAF MC, San Antonio, 1974. *Appointments:* Chief Resident, Psychiatry, Wilford Hall USAF MC; Chief, In-Patient Service, USAF Hospital Elmendorf, Anchorage; Staff Psychiatrist, Alaska Psychiatric Institute; Psychiatrist, Anchorage Children's Centre; Consultant, USCG Clinic Kodiak; Associate Clinical Professor, University of Washing-

ton, Seattle, West Virginia University, Morgantown; Psychiatrist, Appalachian Mental Health Centre; Medical Director, Elkins, West Virginia. *Memberships:* American Psychiatric Association; Society of US Air Force Psychiatrists; American Association of Community Mental Health Center Psychiatrists. *Publication:* "What is a Psychiatrist? What is Mental Illness?", co-author, APA Task Force Report, 1975. *Honours:* National Merit Scholar, 1964-68; All Mid-America Rugby Select XV, 1970; Falk Fellow, American Psychiatric Association, 1972-75. *Hobbies:* Music; Log Cabin Building. *Address:* Appalachian Mental Health Centre, PO Box 1170, Elkins, WV 26241, USA.

FERGUSON-PELL, Martin William, b. 11 Sept. 1950, Luton, England. Chief of Rehabilitation Engineering Unit. m. 29 Dec 1973, Ledbury. *Education:* BSc, University of Strathclyde, Scotland, 1976-82; Chief, Rehabilitation Engineering Unit, Helen Hayes Hospital, West Haverstraw, New York, USA, 1982-present; Adjunct Associate Professor, Rensselaer Polytechnic Institute, New York; Associate Research Scientist, Columbia University, New York. *Memberships:* Institute of Physics; Hospital Physicists Association; Biological Engineering society; Rehabilitation Engineering Society of North America; American Society for Laser Medicine and Surgery. *Publications:* Articles:'Pressure Sore Prevention for the Wheel Chair bound Spinal Injury Patients', co-author, in 'Paraplegia', 1980; 'Design Criteria for the Measurement of Pressure at Body Support Interfaces', in 'Engineering in Medicine', 1980; Co-Editor 'Computing in Medicine', 1982; 'Establishing a Sore Prevention Service' in 'Chronic Ulcers of the Skin', 1984; Conference papers. *Hobby:* Photography. *Address:* Helen Hayes Hospital OERC, Route 9W, West Haverstraw, NY, 10993, USA.

FERDANDES, Carlos Manuelo Coelho, b. 21 Mar. 1945, Madeira. Acting Head Otorhinolaryngology, University of Natal, Durban; Private Practice. m. Carol-Anne Swimmer, 9 Sep. 1982, Durban, 2 sons, 1 daughter. *Education:* JMBMatriculation; Hoer Taalbond; MB; BCh; FCS (SA) Otol. *Appointments:* Head, Dept., Baragwanath Hospital, 1975-77; Professor , head, Otorhinolaryngology, University of Natal, Durban, South Africa, 1977-; Academic Head, Edendale Hospital, 1977-; Honorary Head, Speech Therapy, University of duraban, Westville, 1977-84. *Memberships:* South African Society of Otorhinolaryngology, Honorary Treasurer, 1982-85. *Publications;* Numerous articles in professional journals including: 'The Discharging Ear', 'South African Journal Continuing Medial Education', Volume 1, 1983; 'Paediatrics and Child Health - A Handbook for Health Practitioners in the Third World', 'Supplement to SA Prescriber'; 'Surgery for the Correction of Bilateral Choanal Atresia', 'Laryngoscope', 1985. *Hobby:* Tennis. *Address:* Chelmsford Medical Centre, Chelmsford Road, Durban 4001, South Africa.

FERMADEZ-POL, Blanca Dora, b. 5 Mar, 1932, Buenos Aires, Argentina. Psychiatrist; Chief, Continuing Treatment Programme, Department of Psychiatry. *Education:* MD, 1958. Diplomas: Questioned Documents Examiner, Buenos Aires, Argentina, 1961; Forensic Medicine, Buenos Aires, 1960; Psychiatry, Buenos Aires, 1964; American Board of Psychiatry and Neurology, USA, 1979. *Appointments:* General Practitioner Hospital Espanol, Buenos Aires, Argentina, 1959-62; Forensic Psychiatrist, Criminology Institute, Buenos Aires, 1963-65; Professor of Psychology, University of Moron, Buenos Aires, 1962-67; Assistant Professor of Psychiatry, New York Medical College, New York, USA, 1972-74; Clinical Attending Psychiatrist, Bellevue Psychiatric Hospital, New York, 1971-75; Major, Medical Corps, US Air Force, 1978-81; Chief Psychiatric Services, US Air Force Hospital, Yokota,

Japan, 1980, Homestead, Florida, USA, 1981; Assistant Clinical Professor of Psychiatry, Albert Einstein College of Medicine, Bronx, New York, 1982-; Chief Continuing Treatment Programme, Department of Psychiatry, Bronx-Lebanon Hospital Bronx, New York, currently. *Memberships:* American Psychiatric Association; Association of Military Surgeons of Us; The New York Academy of Sciences; American Medical Society on Alcoholism and Addictions; New York University-Bellevue Psychiatric Society. *Publications:* Contributions to: 'Journal of Psychiatric Society. *Publications:* Contributions to: 'Journal of Psychiatry', 1980; Alcoholism. Clinical and Experimental Research' 1985;'Journal of Studies on Alcohol', 1986. *Hobbies:* Painting; Sculpture; Travel. *Address:* PO Box 1644, Brooklyn, NY 11202, USA.

FERNANDES, Marcus Thomas, b. 18 June 1930. Calcutta, India. Professor Member, Medical Faculty; Consultant Surgeon. m. Patricia Horne, 27 Oct. 1962, Calcutta, 1 son. *Education includes:* Fellow: Royal College of Surgeons, Dublin, Republic of Ireland; College of Chest Physicians, USA; International College of Angiology, USA. FIAGP, India; FRIPH&H, UK; LM, Dublin; DCH; DIH; DPH; DTM&H, England; FPA Certificate, FPA London and Royal College of Obstetricians and Gynaecologists, London; Member, Honorable Society of Lincolns Inns, London; MFCM, Faculty of Community Medicine, Royal College of Physicians, London, England. *Appointments include:* Senior House Surgeon, Registrar to Professor of Surgery, NRS Medical College, Calcutta Islamia Hospital; Lecturer, Department of Anatomy, NRS Medical College; Assistant Professor, Surgery, Sammelani Medical College, West Bengal; Registrar, London Chest Hospital; Clinical Assistant, St Mary's Medical School, Guys Medical School, Kings College Hospital, London Hospital Medical College, St Georges Medical School, Queen Mary's Hospital for Children, United Sheffield Hospitals, Luton and Dunstable Hospital and Cardiff Hospital Part time Lecturer, Royal Instistute of Hygiene and Public Health, British Red Cross Society, St Johns Ambulance Association; Police Surgeon, Scotland; Joint Editor, Medical Year Book, London, 1972; currently, Professor, Medical Faculty, Indian Academy of General Practice and Consultant Surgeon. *Memberships:* Indian Medical Association; All India General Practitioners; Association of Physicians and India; Association of Surgeons of India; Indian Academy of Paediatrics; American College of Chest Physicians; International College of Angiology; Indian Medical Academy of Medical Specialities. *Publications:* "Management of Common Diseases", 1976; "Cardiac Arrest", 1962; 'Surgical Management of Tuberculosis', 1984; 'Surgical Management of Duodenal Ulcer', 1985. *Honours:* Order of St John, 1984. *Hobbies:* Writing; Golf; Tennis; Badminton. *Address:* 17/A Brabohrne Court, 1 Chandney Chowk Street, Calcutta 700013, India.

FERNANDEZ, Louis Agnelo Victor, b. 30 May 1944, Karachi, Pakistan. Associate Professor of Medicine. m. Virginia, 17 Nov. 1973, Halifax, Canada, 1 son, 1 daughter. *Education:* MBBS Medicine; Fellow, Internal Medicine and Hematology, Royal College of Physisians, Canada; ABIM, Internal Medicine and Hematology; FACP Internal Medicine and Hematology. *Appointments:* Assistant Professor of Medicine 1976-81, Associate Professor of Medicine 1981-, Dalhousie University, Nova Scotia, Canada. *Memberships:* Canadian Society of Clinical Investigation; Canadian Hematology Society; Medical Society of Nova Scotia; Nova Scotia Society of Internal Medicine; American Society of Hematology. *Publications:* 30 articles in referred journals. *Hobbies:* Tennis; Music. *Address:* Camp Hill Hospital, 1763 Robie Street, Halifax, Nova Scotia B3H 3G2, Canada.

FERNANDEZ, Osberto B., b. 11 Nov. 1931, Colon, Cuba. Psychiatrist. m. Mariblanca Fuentes, 27 Dec, 1959, Cuba, 1 son, 2 daughters. *Education:* MD, University of Havanna, Cuba and Salamanca, Spain;

ECFMG-Psychiatric Training, Univeristy of Louisville, Kentucky, Department of Psychiatry and Behavioral Sciences. *Appointments:* Director, Out Patient Clinic; Community Mental Health, Danville, Kentucky, Hillsborough County; Crisis Centre, Community Mental Health Center, Tampa; Private Practice. *Memberships:* American Psychiatry Association; Florida Psychiatric Association; American Medical Association; Cuban Medical Association in Exile, Cuban Civic Club; Defensa Civica Lubana; Tampa Psychiatry Society; Hillsborough County Medical Association. *Honours:* Commonwealth of Kentucky; Kentucky Colonel. *Hobbies:* Fishing; Photography; Music; Outdoor Activities. *Address:* 500 Vonderburg Drive, Suite 202, Brandon, FL 33511, USA.

FERREIRA, Armando Dos Santos, b. 18 Nov. 1920, Lisbon, Portugal, Resident of Portugal, Nationality Portuguese. Professor of Anatomy m. Adelina Dias, 17 Oct, 1954, Lisbon, 2 daughters. *Education:* Graduate, Faculty of Medicine, Lisbon University, 1947; Surgeon and Urologist, 1955; PhD, (Medicine and Surgery), 1956, Fellow, School of Medicine, 1963, Director, Anatomy Institute, 1964, Professor of Anatomy, 1967-86, Lisbon Medical University; Director of Anatomo-functional research center, Angiology, 1968-79. Dean of Faculty of Medicine, University of Lisbon, Nov. 1985. *Appointments:* Director, Anatomy Institute, Lisbon Medical Faculty, 1963; President,Angiology Department, 8th Internaitonal Anatomy Congress, Wiesbaden, 1965;President, juri for admission examinations to Lisbon Medical University, 1969-73; Member, Ministry of Education, National Council for Public Health, 1973; Co-Chairman, 10th Internaitonal Anatomy Congress, Tokyo, 1975; President, Portugese Anatomic Society, 1977; President, 3rd Luso-Brazilian Anatomy Congress, Funchal, 1979; Vice President, 5th European Anatomy Congress, Prague, 1979; Chairman 4th International Symposium on the Morphological Sciences, 1979; Member, International Committee, 11th International Anatomy Congress, Mexico, 1980; President, Urology Department, 9th International Anatomy Congress, Leningrad, 1970. *Memberships:* Luso-Hispano-American Anatomy Society; Association des Anatomistes; Paris Anatomic Society; Luso-Brazilian Society; Portuguese Anatomic Society; Lisbon Medical Sciences Society; Brazilian Anatomic College; Lisbon Geographic Society, Anthropology Department; Paris Anthropologic society. *Publications:* Approximately 200 works including: Lymphatic system of the stomach and their path ways of drainage; Angioarchitecture macrosopique des tumeurs malignes technique d'injection-corrosion ("La Semaiane des Hopitaux"); Surgical and Anatomic architecture of the human liver; Segmentation arterielle du rein ("Bulletin de l'Association des anatomistes"); Anaotmic Aspects of the Hepatic Hilum; Study of the Anatomic Radiology of the coronary arteries; Arterial Microcirculation of the Ovary, ("International Surgery"); Les grandes voies lymphatiques abdomino-thoraco-cervicales. *Address:* Av. do Brasil No 132, 7° Esq. 1700-Lisbon, Portugal.

FERRIS, Ernest John, b. 17 Nov. 1982, Adams, Massachusetts, USA, University Professor and Chairman of Radiology. m. Alice Manchester, 28 May 1960, 2 sons, 2 daughters. *Education:* MD, Tufts University School of Medicine, 1958. *Appointments:* Instructor 1964-66, Professor of Radiology 1970-77, Boston University School of Medicine; Assistant Professor, Boston University, 1966-67; Associate Director, Department of Radiology, Boston City Hospital, 1967; Clinical Instructor in Radiology, Harvard University, 1970-77; Professor and Chairman, Department of Radiology, University of Arkansas for Medical Sciences, Little Rock, Arkansas, 1977-. *Memberships include:* Fellow, American College of Radiology, Society of Nuclear Magnetic Resonance; American Roentgen Ray Society; Society of Magnetic Resonance Imaging; The Radiological Society of North America; Society of Thoracic Radiology; American College of Chest Physicians; Alpha Omega Alpha. *Publications include:* "Textbook of Venography", 1980 and 1983; "Urinary Tract and Adrenalglands", 1980; Pelvic and Abdominal Veins", contributing author, 1981. *Hobbies:* Tennis; Golf. *Address:* Department of Radiology, University of Arkansas for Medical Sciences, 4301 West Markham Street, Little Rock, AR 72205, USA.

FERSHT, Alan Roy, b. 21 Apr. 1943, London, England. Professor of Biological Chemistry. m. Marilyn Persell, 18 Aug. 1966, London, 1 son, 1 daughter. *Education:* MA, PhD, Gonville and Caius College, Cambridge. *Appointments:* Medical Research Council Laboratory of Molecular Biology, Cambridge, 1969-77; Currently: Wolfson Research Professor, The Royal Society; Professor of Biological Chemistry, Imperial College of Science and Technology, fLondon. *Memberships:* Fellow, Royal Society; Biochemical Society. *Publication:* 'Enzyme Structure and Mechanism', 2nd edition 1985. *Honour:* FEBS Anniversary Prize, 1980. *Hobbies:* Chess; Horology. *Address:* Department of Chemistry, Imperial College of Science and Technology, South Kensington, London SW7 2AY, England.

FETTNER, Ann Couper Giudici, b. 25 Feb. 1939, New York City, USA. Consultant, Advisor, Communications, 5 sons, 1 daughter. *Education:* MS Biology; BA Journalism. *Appointments:* Senior Advisor, Health Education, Ministry of Health, Kenya; Director of Education, International Eye Foundation, Nairobi, Kenya; Director of Education, National Arthritis Foundation, Atlanta, Georgia, USA; Advisor, Communications Consultant, Government of Jamaica. *Memberships:* Authors Guild; New York Academy of Science; American Association for the Advancement of Science; International Federation of Public Health; Association of African Physicians in North America; National Association of Science Writers; American Medical Writers Association. *Publicatins:* "AIDS: Evolution of an Epidemic", 1984; 'Potpourri', 1972-79, 1984. *Honours:* Cine film Awards, 1968, 1972, 1974; 1st Prize, Technical Communications, 1983; Rehabilitation Association Film Award, 1982; John Muir Medical Film Award, 1983; AIDS Book, 1st Prize American Medical Writers Association. *Hobbies:* Tropical Gardening; Raising Children. *Address:* 3927 Massachusetts Avenue NW, Washington, DC 20016, USA.

FEURESTEIN, Walter, b. 19 Mar. 1920, Vienna, Austria, Dermatologist/Assistant University Professor. m. Gertrud Reisetbauer, 17 Apr 1946, 3 sons, 2 daughters. *Education:* MD, University of Vienna, 1945. *Appointments:* Oberarzt, Department of Dermtology, Lainz-Hospital Vienna; Consultant Dermatologist, Hospital Modling NO; Chairman of Dermatologists, Chamber of Physicians, Vienna; Assistant Professor, University of Vienna. *Memberships:* Austrian Society of Dermatology; German Society of Dermatology; Austrian Society of Angiology; German Society of Phlebology; French Society of Phlebology; Society of Physicians of Vienna; International Society of Tropical Dermatology; International Society of Dermatologic Surgery. *Publications:* "Venenpraxis" 1969; More than 50 papers in the field of Dermatology and Phlebology published in books or journals in Austria, Germany, France and Switzerland. *Honours:* Member of Honor, Dermatological Society of Styria, 1980; Gold Medal for Merit of the Chamber of Physicians of Vienna, 1981; Scientific Award by the Mayor of Vienna, 1980 and 1983. *Hobbies:* Sailing; Tennis; Organ playing. *Address:* Lainzerstrasse 8, A-1130 Vienna, Austria.

FEYGE, Margaret Mary (Peg), b. 26 Sept. 1950, San Francisco, California, USA. Senior Occupational Therapist. m. Paul Allen Kvam, 10 Aug. 1979. *Education:* BSc, Occupational Therapy. *Appointments:*

Prevocational Evaluator, Hope Rehabilitation Services; Therapist, Ralph K. Davies Medical Center; currently, Senior Occupational Therapist, Washoe Medical Center, Reno, Nevada. *Memberships:* Associate Member, American Society of Hand Therapists; Past President, Nevada Occupational Therapy Association; World Federation of Occupational Therapists; American Occupational Therapy Foundation. *Hobbies:* Skiing; Dance, Ballet and jazz; Wind surfing; Stained glass. *Address:* Lake Tahoe, Box 3097, Incline Village, NV 89450, USA.

FIANDRA, Orestes Alfredo, b. 4 Aug. 1921, Montevideo, Uruguay, Cardiologist, m. Maria Elida de Leon, 15 June 1953, Montevideo, 2 sons, 1 daughter. *Education:* BSc, University of Uruguay, 1940; MD, Faculty of Medicine of Uruguay, 1953; Cardiologist, Escuela de Graduados, Faculty of Medicine, Uruguay; Associate Professor of Cardiology, 1962-74, Professor of Cardiology, 1975-85, Faculty of Medicine, Montevideo, Uruguay. *Appointments:* Cardiologist, Hospital Espanol, Montevideo; Cardiologist, CASMU, Montevideo; Director del departmento de Marcapasos del Instiuto Nacional de Cirugia Cardiaca, Montevideo, Urugauy. *Memberships:* Sociedad de Cardiologia del Uruguay; New York Academy of Sciences; Former President, Sociedad de Medicina de Montevideo; Former President, Procardias; Sociedad de Historia de la Medicina del Uruguay; Instituto Nacional de Cirugia Cardiaca Uruguay. *Publications:* "Aparto Respiratorio", (Co-author), 1966; "Electrocardiografia", 1972; "Marcapasos Cardiacos", 1971; "Marcapasos Cardiacos", (Co-author, 1985; Author of over 162 medical publications. *Honours:* Premio Sanguinetti, 1954; Premio 2 Congreso de Radiologia de Culture Latina, Espana, 1957; Premio President de la Sociedad Argentina de Urologia, Buenos Aires, 1957; Premio Balga del Congreso Latino de radiologia, Portugal-Lisboa; Premio Sociedad de Medicina de Montevideo, 1971-74; Premio Academia Nacional de Medicina, Montevideo, 1978-81; Implanted the second pacemaker in a human being in the world, 1960. *Hobbies:* Sailing; Boating. *Address:* Gral Paz 1367, Montevideo, Uruguay.

FICHTNER, Heinz-Joachim, b. 4 July 1927, Neisse, Germany. Director of Dental Health Service for Neuss District. *Education:* Specialist Recognition as Dentist for Public Health; Lecturer, Academy of Public Health, Düsseldorf. *Appointments:* Chairman, Federal Association of Dentists in Public Health Service, 1965-; Editor and Publisher of journal 'Zahnärztlicher Gesundheitsdienst'; Committee Member, German Committee for Youth Dental Care of the Federal Association of Doctors in Public Health Service; many other committee activities. *Publications:* Numerous articles on health politics, both specialist and also of Public Dental Health Service in the Federal Republic of Germany 1965-85. *Honours:* Gold Needle of Honour, German Dental Association, 1982; Order of Merit of Federal Republic of Germany with Band, 1977; Cross of Merit, 1st Class, 1984. *Hobbies:* Painting; Music. *Address:* Carossastrasse 1, D-4040 Neuss, Federal Republic of Germany.

FIELD, Stuart, b. 22 June 1944, Ashby de la Zouch, Leicester, England. Consultant Radiologist, Canterbury and Thanet Health Authority. m. Margaret Dawes, 20 July 1968, Watford, 2 daughters. *Education:* MA, MB, B.Chir, Gonville & Caius College, Cambridge University; Kings College Hospital Medical School. *Appointments:* House Physician, Medical Unit, House Surgeon, Surgical Unit, Kings College Hospital, 1969-70; Registrar, Senior Registrar, Diagnostic Radiology, Kings College Hospital, 1970-74; Clinical tutor, Kent Postgraude Medical Centre, 1978-82. *Memberships:* British Institute of Radiology; British Medical Association. *Publications:* Chapters on 'Plain Film Radiology of the Acute Abdomen' in: "Radiological Atlas of Gastro-Intestinal Disease", D.J. Nolan,

1983; "Clinics in Gastroenterology", Editor, J.W. Laws, 1984; "Textbook of Organ Imaging", Editors, R. Grainger and D.J. Allison, 1985; "Textbook of Radiology and Imaging" Editor, D Sutton, 1986; 'The Erect Abdominal Radiograph in the Acute Abdomen: Should its routine use be abandoned?', 'British Medical Journal', 1985. *Honours:* Exhibition, 1964, Scholarship, 1965, Gonville & Caius College, Cambridge; Tancred Studentship in Physics, Gonville & Caius College, 1965; Burney Yeo Scholarship, Kings College Hospital Medical School, 1966-69. *Hobbies:* Music (playing the Violin); Rugby Football; Athletics; Gardening. *Address:* Department of Diagnostic Radiology, Kent and Canterbury Hospital, Ethelbert Road, Canterbury, Kent CT1 3NG, England.

FIGGIS CLOSE, Rhondda Elaine, b. 27 July 1933, Sydney, New South Wales, Australia. President, Pharmaceutical Society of Australia, New South Wales Branch; Chief Pharmacist, The Nepean Hospital, Penrith, New South Wales, Australia. m. John Kenneth Close, 12 Nov. 1981, Sydney, New South Wales. *Education:* PhC; Diploma of Educational Studies (Health Education). *Appointments:* Pharmacist: St, John's Hospital, Lewisham, England; Vale of Leven, Dunbartonshire; Bromley Hospital, Kent; Dreadnought Seamen's Hospital, Greenwick; Chief Pharmacist: Thursday Island Hospital, Queensland, Australia; The Parramatta Hospital, New South Wales, Australia. *Memberships:* Pharmaceutical Society of Australia, New South Wales Branch, President; Society of Hospital Pharmacists of Australia, New South Wales Branch; Pharmacy Practice Foundation; Federation Internationale Pharmaceutique. *Publication:* Contributor and Member of Editorial Panel, Pharmacology and Drug Information for Nurses. *Hobbies:* Opera; Ballet; Music; Skiing; Travel. *Address:* 137 Lanhams Road, Winston Hills, New South Wales, Australia.

FIGUEIRA-FO, Antonio Simao dos Santos, b. 25 Sept 1946, Recife, Brazil. Associate Professor/Director of Breast Unit. m. Elisabeth Horcades dos Santos Figueira, 22 Nov 1973, Rio de Janeiro, 2 sons 2 daughters. *Education:* MD, Faculty of Medical Sciences, University of Recife, Brazil, 1971; Master of Science (MSC), Oxford University, 1977. *Appointments:* Resident in General Surgery, Ipanema Hospital, 1972-73; Junior Assistant, Professor, I Pitanguy's Clinic, 1974; SHO Nuffield Department of Surgery, 1974, Registrar Breast Unit, 1975-76, Radcliffe Infirmary, Oxford, England; Senior Registrar, Breast Unit, Guy's Hospital, London 1977; Assistant Professor, Department of Surgery, Medical School, Recife, 1978-82; Associate Professor, Department of Surgery, Medical School, Federal University Recife, Brazil, 1982-. *Memberships:* Fellow, Brazilian College of Surgeons; Fellow, Royal Society of Medicine; Fellow, International College of Surgeons; Fellow, Brazilian Society of Medicine. *Publications:* Books and articles about: breast cancer, the relationship between mammary dysplasia and cancer, breast reconstruction after mastectomy, plastic surgery of the breast and benign breast diseases. *Honour:* Honoured Professor by the Doctors graduated 1983 (Medical School, Federal University, Recife, Brazil. *Hobby:* Motor racing. *Address:* Rua Nicaragua, 99, Espinheiro, 50000 Recife, Brazil.

FINCKH, Ernest Sydney, b. 13 June 1924, Sydney, Australia. Director, Institute of Clincial Pathology and Medical Research and Clinical Professor of Pathology. m. Nancye Kathleen Llewelyn, 26 Mar. 1955, London, England, 3 sons. *Education:* MBBS, 1946, DCP, 1951, MD, 1964, Sydney University; MRCOA, 1956, MRACP, 1959, FRCPath, 1969, FRACP, 1969, FRCPA, 1971. *Appointments include:* Pathologist, Clinical Research Unit, Walter and Eliza Hall Institute, Melbourne, 1951-54; Visiting Research Scholar, Department of Morbid Anatomy, University College Hospital, London 1955-56; Senior Lecturer

in Pathology, 1956-62, Associate Professor in Experimental Pathology, 1962-69, University of Sydney; Guest Investigator, Rockefellor Institute, New York, 1964-65; Deputy Director, Institute of Clinial Pathology and Medical Research, Health Commission of New South Wales and Associate Professor of Pathology, University of Sydney, 1969-78; Director, Institute of Clincal Pathology and Medical Research, Westmead and Clinical Professor of Pathology, University of Sydney, 1978-. *Memberships:* Australian Medical Association; British Medical Association; Society of Pathologists, Great Britain and Ireland. *Publications:* 55 scientific papers on gastritis, hepatitis, cirrhosis, acute tubular necrosis, cellular migration, multiplication and differentiation, the cell biology of tumours and related conditions. *Honours:* Nuffield Dominion Travelliong Fellow (UK) 1955-56; Peter Bancroft Prize for Medical Research, University of Sydney, 1964; Senior Fulbright Scholar, 1964-65 (USA); President, Royal College of Pathologists of Australasia, 1979-81. *Hobby:* Yachting. *Address:* Westmead Hospital, Westmead, New South Wales 2145, Australia.

FINESCHI, Gianfranco, b. 17 Mar. 1923, Florence, Italy. Orthopaedic Clinic Director. m. Carla Pavignani, 3 daughters. *Appointments:* Assistant, Associate, Orthopaedic Clinic, University of Florence, Tuscany, Italy; currently Lecturer in Orthopaedics and Traumatology and Director of Orthopaedic Clinic, Catholic University of Rome, Italy. *Memberships:* Italian Society of Orthopaedic and Traumatological Surgery; International Society of Orthopaedic Surgery and Traumatology; Member of the editorial board of 'International Orthopaedics'. *Publications:* 'The posterior prolapse of the intervertebral disc' (Monography), 1954; 'Vascular and nervous lesions in traumas typical of modern life' (Monography), 1966; 'Pathology and treatment of cervical disc lesions (Monography), 1966. Editor of 'Archivio Putti' (Italian Review on Orthopaedic Surgery); Co-editor of the 'Italian Journal of Orthopaedics'; author of 110 original papers. *Honours:* Recipient of several honours and awards for medical science including Premio Nazionale delle Scienze, 1981; Targa Europa per la Sezione Scienze, 1983. *Hobbies:* Rose growing: owner of main private rose garden in Europe, with over 6,000 specimens. Music lover (symphonic and opera). *Address:* Via Oslavia 12, 00195, Rome, Italy.

FINKE, Joachim, b. 4 Feb. 1927, Leignitz. Medical Director ot Neurological Hospital, Burgerhospital, Stuttgart. m. Waltraut Hoffmann, 27 Sep. 1952, Halle/Saale, 3 daughters. *Education:* Diploma, Psychology, Halle/Saale, 1950; Doctorate, Halle/Saale, 1951; Habil, Tubingen, 1965; Associate Professor, Tubingen, 1972. *Appointments:* Intern, University of Halle/Saale, 1951-53; Resident: Charite Hospital, Berlin, 1953-58; Bethesda Hospital, Stuttgart, 1959; Research Assistant, University of Tubingen, 1960-65; Lecturer, University of Tubingen, 1965-72; Associate Professor, University of Tubingen, 1972-; Medical Director of Neurological Hospital, Burgerhospital, Stuttgart, 1970-. *Membership:* German Neurological Association. *Publications:* "Ophthalmodynamographie", 1966; "Die neurologische Untersuchung", 1968; "ODG Syumposium", 1974; "Neurol. Untersuchungskurs", 1975; "Schafstorungen" (co-author with W. Schute), 1970, 2nd Edition, 1979; "Neurologische Erkrankungen", 1981; "Neurologie fur die Praxis", 1985. *Hobbies:* Painting; Piano. *Address:* Tunzhofer Strasse 14-16, D-7000 Stuttgart 1, Federal Republic of Germany.

FINLEY, Wayne House, b. 7 Apr. 1927, USA. Professor of Paediatrics. m. Sara Crews, 6 July 1952, Lineville, Alabama, USA, 1 son, 1 daughter. *Education:* BS, Jacksonville State University, USA, 1948; MA, University of Alabama, 1950, MS, 1955, PhD, 1958; MD, University of Alabama School of Medicine, 1960. *Appointments:* Trainee, Medical

Genetics, University of Uppsala, Sweden, 1961-62; Assistant Professor of Paediatrics, University of Alabama at Birmingham, USA, 1962-66, Director, Laboratory of Medical Genetics, 1966-; Associate Professor of Paediatrics, 1966-70, Professor of Paediatrics, 1970-; Senior Scientist, Comprehensive Cancer Centre, University of Alabama, at Birmingham, 1970-., Professor of Public Health, 1977-., Adjunct Professor of Biology, 1980-., Senior Scientist, Cystic Fibrosis Research Centre, 1981-. *Memberships:* American Association for the Advancement of Science; American Society of Human Genetics; New York Academy of Science; Southern Medical Association; Medical Association of State Alabama; Jefferson County Medical Society. *Publications:* Co-author: "Birth Defects: Clinical and Ethical Considerations", 1983; 'Cytogenetic Perspectives' in "Perspectives of Progress in Mental Retardation", volume III, "Biomedical Aspects", 1984; many articles in professional journals. *Honours:* Sigma XI, 1963; American Medical Associations Physicians Recognition Award, 1971, 1975, 1981, ODK, 1976; Distinguished Medical Alumni Award, University of Alabama School of Medicine, 1978; Distinguished Faculty Lecturer, Medical Centre, 1983. *Hobby:* Reading. *Address:* 3412 Brookwood Road, Birmingham, AL 35223, USA.

FINN, William F. b. 23 July, 1915, New Jersey, USA. Retired Gynaecologist. m. Doris I. Henderson, 21 Sept. 1943, New York, USA, 2 sons, 1 daughter. *Education:* BA, Holy Cross College, USA, 1936; MD, Cornell Medical College, 1940; MA, New York University, 1985. *Current Appointments:* Consultant Gynaecologist, Mercy Hospital; Clinical Professor, Obstetrics and Gynaecology, Cornell Medical College; Honorary Obstetrician/Gynaecologist, North Shore University Hospital. *Memberships:* American College of Surgeons; American College of Obstetricians. *Publications:* "Women and Loss" (2 volumes), 1985; 45 articles on Gynaecology, Pathology and Biomedical ethics in various journals. *Honour:* Long Island Diocese Bishop's Distinguished Service Award. *Hobbies:* Biomedical Ethics; Travel; Wine Tasting; Gourmet Dining. *Address:* 3 Aspen Gate, Manhasset, NY, USA 11030.

FINNBERG, Elaine Agnes, b. 2 Mar. 1948, Brooklyn, New York, USA. Licensed Psychologist. m. Rodney L. Herndon, 1 Mar. 1981, San Francisco, California, 1 son. *Education:* BA, Psychology, Long Island University, Brooklyn, New York, 1969; MA Psychology, New School for Social Research, New York, 1973; PhD Clinical Psychology, California School of Professional Psychology, Berkeley California, 1981. *Appointments include:* Editor, Writer, Consultant, The Foundation of Thanatology, Columbia-Presbyterian Medical Center, New York, 1971-76; Director, Grief Psychology and Bereavement Counseling Programme, San Francisco College of Mortuary Science, 1977-81; Research Associate, Department of Epidemiology and International Health, School of Medicine, University of California, San Francisco, 1979-81; Medical Panel, California State Department of Rehabilitation, Salinas, 1983-; Director of Community Services, Suicide Prevention Center of Monterey, California, Carmel, 1984. *Memberships include:* American Psychological Association; American Medical Writers Association; The Foundation of Thanatology. *Publications:* 'Anticipating side effects of relaxation treatment', 1983; 'What's Your CQ (Counselling Quotation)?', 1983; 'Sudden Death: The Crisis for Funeral Directors and other Helping Professions', 1983. *Hobbies:* Travel; Art. *Address:* Natividad Medical Center, Neuropsychiatric Unit, 1330 Natividad Road, Salinas, CA 93905, USA.

FINZI, Aldo Fabrizio, b. 16 June 1931, Perugia, Italy. Professor of Dermatology. m. Maria Luisa Rigi-Luperti, 26 Apr. 1962, Florence, 2 sons. *Educaiton:* MD, PhD, University of Perugia.

Appointments: Professor of Investigative Dermatology, University of Ferrara Medical School; Chairman, 2nd Department of Dermatology, University of Milan Medical School. *Membership:* Vice-President, Italian Society of Dermatology. *Publications:* 112 scientific publications. *Hobbies:* Sailing; Skiing; Hunting. *Address:* 2nd Department of Dermatology, University of Milan, Via Pace 9, 20122 Milan, Italy.

FIREMAN, Philip, b. 28 Feb. 1932, Pittsburgh, Pennsylvania, USA. Professor of Paediatrics. m. Marcia Levick, 27 Nov. 1957, 4 sons, 1 daughter. *Education:* BS, University of Pittsburgh, 1953; MD, University of Chicago School of Medicine, 1957; Internship, Philadelphia General Hospital, 1957-58; Resident in Paediatrics, University of Pittsburgh, Children's Hospital of Pittsburgh, 1958-60; Clinical Fellow, 1960-62, Chief Paediatric Resident, 1961-62, National Institutes of Allergy & Infectious Diseases, Bethesda, Maryland; Fellow, Allergy & Immunology, Department of Paediatrics, Harvard University & Childrens Hospital, Boston, 1962-63. *Appointments:* Instucter, 1963-64, Assistant Professor, 1964-69, Associate Professor, 1969-76, Professor of Paediatrics, 1976-, University of Pittsburgh School of Medicine; Research Collaborator, Brookhaven National Laboratory, Upton, New York, 1964-70; Visiting Professor of Paediatric, University of Lausanne, School of Medicine, Switzerland, 1972-73; Visiting Scientist, Swiss Institute for Experimental Cancer Research, Lausanne, Switzerland, 1972-73; Director, Division of Allergy & Immunology (& training programme), Children's Hospital of Pittsburgh, 1968-. *Memberships:* Society for Paediatric Research; Fellow, American Academy of Paediatrics; Fellow, American Academy of Allergy; Fellow, American College of Allergy; American Thoracic Society; American Association of Immunologists; Federation of American Societies for Experimental Biology; Phi Beta Kappa. *Publications:* Author & Co-author of some 125 articles & papers in medical journals; Reviewer for 'Journal of Allergy & Clinical Immunology', 'Journal of Paediatrics', 'Paediatrics', 'Paediatric Research'. *Honours:* NIH Special Research Fellowship, 1962-64; Inter-state Postgraduate Medical Society Research Award, 1964; NIH Research Career Development Award, 1965-74. *Hobbies:* Skiing; Hiking. *Address:* Childrens Hospital of Pittsburgh, 125 Desoto Street, Pittsburgh, PA 15213, USA.

FIRESTONE, Ronald Lee, b. 12 Mar 1950, La Paz, Bolivia. Private Practice; Extension Faculty, Los Angeles College of Chiropractic; President, Vacation Samaritans Mission. m. Esther Violet Cepeda, 24 Dec. 1969, Los Angeles, 1 son, 1 daughter. *.Education:* AA, Pasadena City College; BA, Edison State College; MS, University of Bridgeport; DC, Los Angeles College of Chiropractic; MD; ABD PhD, Walden University. *Appointments:* Ordained Minister, Church of God, Anderson; Private Practice, 1972-; College Instructor; Clinical Director, Church of God Clinic, Bolivia, South America; Missionary Physician with Church of God, Anderson; Adjunct Professor, Biochemistry & Nutrition, Los Angeles College of Chiropractic. *Memberships:* American and California Chiropractic Associations; Christian Chiropractors Association; Bolivian College of Medicine. *Publications:* "You and the Uniterm", 'ACA Journal', 1970. *Honours:* ACA Research Fellow, 1962-72; student Body President Pasasena City College, *Hobbies:* Reading; Travel; Preaching; Teaching. *Address:* 57610 Crestview Drive, Yucca Valley, CA 92284, USA.

FIROZA BEGUM, Syeda, b. 1 Apr. 1930, Comilla, Bangladesh. Professor and Head, Department of Obstetrics and Gynecology. m. Professor M. A. Jalil, 1956, 1 son, 1 daughter. *Education:* MB BS, Dhaka; Member and Fellow, Royal College of Obstetrics and Gynecology. *Appointments:* Senior House Officer, Hammersmith Post Graduate Medical Institute; Associate Professor, currently Professor and Head,

Department of Obstetrics and Gynecology, Dhaka Medical College Hospital, Dhaka, Bangladesh, *Memberships:* Member and Fellow, Royal College of Obstetrics and Gynecologists, England. *Publications:* "The Surgical Treatment of Recurrent Late Abortion", 1969; "Maternity Care Services in Bangladesh", 1972; "Medical Problems in Obstetrics Practice", 1974. *Honours:* Award for outstanding activities in research, teaching and population control, Path Finder Fund, USA, 1983. *Hobbies:* Music; Story from the noble. *Address:* 19/E Green Road, Dhaka, Bangladesh.

FISHBURNE, John Ingram, b. 18 Aug. 1937, Charleston, South Carolina, USA. Professor of Obstetrics and Gynaecology. m. Jean Crawford, 10 June 1961, Savannah, Georgia, 2 sons, 1 daughter. *Education included:* AB, Princeton University, Princeton, New Jersey, 1959; MD, Medical University of South Carolina, Charleston, 1963; Diplomate, American Board of Obstetrics and Gynecology, 1972 and 1977; Diplomate, American Board of Anesthesiology, 1973. *Appointments include:* Instructor 1970-71, Assistant Professor 1971-74; Associate Professor 1974-75, Department of Obstetrics and Gynecology, University of North Carolina School of Medicine, Chapel Hill; Associate Professor of Anesthesiology 1975-83, Associate Professor 1975-78, Professor 1978-83, Obstetrics and Gynecology, Bowman Gray School of Medicine, Wake Forest University, Winston-Salem; Director of Maternal-Fetal Medicine, Department of Obstetrics and Gynecology, Forsyth Memorial Hospital, Winston-Salem, 1977-83; Adjuct Professor of Anesthesiology, Professor and Chairman of Obstetrics and Gynecology, Oklahoma University Health Sciences Center, Oklahoma City, Oklahoma, 1983-. *Memberships include:* American Society of Anesthesiologists; Society for Obstetrical Anesthesia and Perinatology; Fellow, American College of Anesthesiologists; Fellow, American College of Obstetricians and Gynecologists; Alpha Omega Alpha. *Publications include:* Chapters in books inclding: "Clinics in Perinatology", 1982; "Obstetric Anesthesia: The Complicated Patient"; "Managemnt of High-Risk Pregnancy", (editor JT Queenan), 1985; Numerous conbributions to journals. *Honours:* NIH Research Fellowship, Medical University of South Carolina, Charleston, 1961-62; American Cancer Society Clinical Fellowship, University of North Carolina, Chapel Hill, 1968-69; Public Health Service Clinical Fellowship, Case Western Reserve University Hospitals, Cleveland, Ohio, 1969. *Hobbies:* Tennis; Volleyball; Reading; Skiing. *Address:* Department of Obstetrics and Gynaecology, Post Office Box 26901, Oklahoma City, OK 73190, USA.

FISCHER, Daniel Edward, b. 22 Apr. 1945, New Haven, Connecticut, USA. Psychiatrist. m. Linda Lee Bradford, 12 June 1969, Houston, 2 daughters. *Education:* BA, Boston University, 1969; MD, Boston University School of Medicine, 1969; Residency, Psychiatry, Washington University School of Medicine, Barnes & Renard Hospital; JD, William & Mary Marshall Wythe School of Law, 1986. *Appointments:* Instructor, Psychiatry, Washington University School of Medicine, 1973; Chief, Mental Health Services, US Army Hospital, Seoul, Korea, 1974; Psychiatric Consultant, 8th US Army Republic of Korea, 1974; Staff Psychiatrist, Fitzimons Army Medical Center, Denver, Colorado, 1975; Instructor, Psychiatry, Eastern Virginia Medical School, 1976-; Private Practice, Hearst, Fischer & Schreiber Ltd., 1975-. *Memberships:* Royal College of Psychiatrists; American Medical Association; American Psychiatric Association; Virginia Medical Society; Academy of Psychosomatic Medicine; American Academy of Psychosomatic Medicine. *Publications:* Co-Author, "Frequency and Patterns of Drug Abuse in Psychiatric Patients", 'Diseases of the Nervous System', Volume 36, 1975. *Honours:* Army Commendation Medal, 1975; Physicians Recognition Award,

1976, 1981; Fellowship, American Academy of Psychosomatic Medicine, 1981. *Address:* Pembroke 5 Bldg., Suite 331, Virginia Beach, VA 23462, USA.

FISCHER, Josef, b. 7 May 1937, New York, USA. Professor of Surgery. m. Karen Down, 24 Oct. 1965, 1 son, 1 daughter. *Education:* BS, Yeshiva College, MD, Harvard Medical School, USA. *Appointments:* Teaching Fellow in Surgery, Fellow, American Cancer Society, Harvard Medical School, 1968-69; Instructor in Surgery, Harvard Medical School, 1970-72; Assistant in Surgery, Massachusetts General Hospital, 1970-73; Chief, Surgical Physiology Laboratory, Massachusetts General Hospital, 1970-78; Assistant Professor of Surgery, Harvard Medical School, 1972-75; Chief, Hyperalimentation Unit, Massachusetts General Hospital 1972-76; Assistant Surgeon, Massachusetts General Hospital, 1973-76; Associate Professor of Surgery, Havard Medical School, 1975-78; Associate Visiting Surgeon, Massachusetts General Hospital, 1976-78; Christian R. Holmes Professor, Chairman, Department of Surgery, University of Cincinnati, 1978-. *Memberships include:* Fellow, American College of Surgeons, 1973; American Federation for Clinical Research; American Gastroenterological Association; American Medical Association; American Physiological Society; American Society for Clinical Investigation; American Surgical Association; New York Academy of Sciences; Society of Univesity Surgeons; and others. *Publications:* Some 400 scientific articles in medical journals. *Honours:* McCurdy-Rinkel Award (Honorable Mention), 1971; Jame IV Surgical Fellow, 1974; Oscar Schuberth Lecture, Swedish College of Surgeons, 1979. *Address:* University of Cincinnati College of Medicine, Department of Surgery, 231 Bethesda Avenue, Cincinnati, OH 45267-0558, USA.

FISHMAN, Jacob Robert, b. 6 Aug. 1930 New York City, USA. Chairman, Board of Directors, Renaissance Health Group. m. Tamar Hendel, 1 June 1958, New York City, 2 sons, 2 daughters. *Education:* AB, Columbia College, New York, 1951; MD, Boston University School of Medicine, 1956; Intern, Department of Internal Medicine, Albert Einstein College of Medicine, Bronx Municipal Hospital Center, 1956-57; Resident, Department of Psychiatry, 1957-59; Resident in Psychiatry, National Institute of Mental Health, 1959-60. *Appointments include:* Research Psychiatrist, 1959-61; Surgeon, US Public Health Services, 1959-61; Attending Psychiatrist, Howard University Hospital, 1962-69; Director, Human Behaviour Undergraduate Teaching Program, 1961-69; Assistant and Associate Professor of Psychitry, 1961-69; Director, Juvenile Delinquency Training Center, 1963-68, Howard University College of Medicine; Director, Psychiatric Services, DC General Hospital, 1967-69; Board of Directors, Webster College, 1977-75; Medical Director, Dominion Psychiatric Center, 1977-78; Chairman, Psychiatry, Southern Maryland Hospital Center, 1978-80; President, Cumberland Mental Health Center Inc., 1980-84; Medical Director, Cumberland Psychiatric Hospital, 1982-84; President, Horizon Health Group, 1982-84; Chairman, Potomac Psychiatric Associates, 1980; Chairman, Renaissance Health Group, 1985-. *Memberships:* Member several professional organizations. *Publications:* Numerous papers and articles in medical journals. *Honours:* Phi Lambda Kappa Gold Medal, 1957; Distinguished Service Award, DC Public Health Association, 1968; Distinguished Lecturer, Northwestern University School of Medicine. *Address:* 5000 N Ocean Boulevard, Fort Lauderdale, FL 33308, USA.

FITCH, Frank W., b. 30 May 1929, Illinois, USA. University Professor. m. Shirley Dobbins, 23 Dec 1951, Nushnell, Illinois, 1 son, 1 daughter. *Education:* Monmouth College, Monmouth, Illinois, 1947-49; MD, 1953, SM, 1957, PhD, 1960, University of Chicago. *Appointments:* Instructor of Pathology, 1957-60, Assistant Professor of Pathology, 1960-63,

Associate Professor of Pathology 1963-67, University of Chicago; Visiting Scientist, Institute of Biochemistry, University of Lausanne, 1965-66; John Simon Guggenheim, Memorial Foundation Fellow, 1975; Visiting Professor, Swiss Institute for Experimental Cancer Research; Associate Dean for Medical and Graduate Education, 1976-78, Associate Dean for Academic Affairs, Dean for Academic Affairs, 1985-, University of Chicago. *Memberships:* American Association of Immunologists; American Association of Patholologists. *Publications:* "Isolation, Characterization and Utilization of T Lymphocyte Clones", 1982; Scientific reports in Journal of Immunology and Immunological Reviews. *Honours:* Alpha Omega Alpha 1952; Lederle Medical Faculty Award, 1958-61; John and Mary R, Markle Scholar in Academic Medicine, 1961-66. *Address:* Department of Pathology, The University of Chicago, 5841 Maryland Avenue, Chicago, IL 60637, USA.

FLAUTNER, Lajos, b. 13 Nov. 1938, Ujpest, Hungary. Associate Professor of Surgery, Vice-Director of National Institute of Surgery. m. Lilian Salamon, 29 July 1961, 1 son, 1 daughter. *Education:* MD, 1962; Specialization in General Surgery, 1966. *Appointments:* Medical Centre of National Institute of Physical Education, 1962; 1st Surgical Department, Semmelweis Medical University, 1970-. *Memberships:* Hungarian Society of Surgery; Hungarian Society of Gastroenterology; University Council; Collegium International Chirurgiae Digestive, European Pancreatic Club. *Publications:* "Komplikation Nach Duodenopankreatektomie bei Chronischer Pankreatitis Chirurg'', 1985; 'Pancreatogastrostomy: An Ideal Complement of Pancreatic Head Resection with Pylorus Preservation in the Treatment of Chronic Pancreatitis' in 'American Journal of Surgery, 1985. *Honours:* 1st Prize for best publication of the year, Hungarian Society of Gastroenternology; 1st Prize, MOTESZ, National Association of Medical Societies, 1985; Award for Distinguished Work, Ministry of Health, 1985. *Hobbies:* Fine Art; Tennis; Skiing. *Address:* 1st Surgical Department, Semmelweis Medical University, üllöi ut 78, Budapest 1082, Hungary.

FLECK, Adam, b. 19 Oct. 1932, Glasgow, Scotland. Professor of Chemical Pathology, Charing Cross and Westminster Medical School, University of London. m. Elizabeth MacLean, 12 July 1960, Glasgow, 1 son, 2 daughters. *Education:* BSc (Hons. 1); MB ChB; PhD, University of Glasgow. *Appointments:* Lecturer. Biochemistry, University of Glasgow; Senior Registrar, Victoria Infirmary, Glasgow; Consultant Biochemist, Glasgow Royal Infirmary; Senior Lecturer, Pathological Biochemistry, Honorary Consultant, Biochemist, Western Infirmary, Glasgow. *Memberships:* Association of Clinical Biochemists; Association of Clinical Pathologists; Royal Society of Medicine; Biochemical Society; Fellow, Royal Society of Edinburgh; Royal Society of Chemistry; Royal College of Pathologists; Royal College of Physicians and Surgeons, Glasgow. *Publications:* Contributor to: 'British Medical Bulletin'; 'Annals of Clinical Biochemistry'; 'The Place of Albumin' in "Care of the Postoperative Surgical Patient", J.A.R. Smith and J.Watkins, 1985. *Honour:* Vickers Award of Association of Clinical Biochemists, 1982. *Hobby:* Golf. *Address:* Department of Chemical Pathology, Charing Cross Hospital, Fulham Palace Road, London W 6 8RF, England.

FLECK, Mariann Bernics, b. 1922, San Francisco, California, USA. Health Scientist and Counsellor. m. Jack Fleck, 28 Mar. 1980, 3 sons. *Education:* BVE 1965, BA 1965, California State University, Long Beach; MA, California State University, Los Angeles, 1968; PhD, Laurence University, Santa Barbara; Postgraduate Studies; University of California at Los Angeles, 1960-75; Cerritos College, 1964; Whittier College, 1964; Calfornia State University, 1969;

Santa Ana School of Hypotherapy, Newport University, 1979; International University, Santa Monica. *Appointments:* Professor, Life Sciences Division, and Adminstrator, Fullerton College, 1960-75; Consultant, Dr Mariann Health Programs, Incorporated, 1965-; International Lecturer, 1973-85; Professor and Administrator, Health Sciences, Cypress College, 1975-80; Private Practitioner, Professional Services Associated Counselling, Santa Ana, 1975-80; Director, Owner, American Health Institute, La Mirada; Director, Owner, Hypnosis Center, La Mirada, 1975-80; Health Editorial, 'Awake and Alive', Boonville, Arkansas, 1981-85; 'Dr Mariann Health Program', KJON Radio Station, 1980-85; Guest Artist, Channel 5 and Chanel 24 Television. *Publications include:* Numerous articles. *Honorus include:* Scholarship, University of California at Los Angeles, 1966; Honorary Life Credential, Physical Education and Health Fitness, 1974; Professor Emeritus, North Orange County College District, California, 1980. *Address:* Route 1 Box 15A, Magazine, AR 72943, USA.

FLECKNOE-BROWN, Stephen Crisford, b. 26 Feb. 1960, Australia, Consultant Haematologist, m. Diane Elizabeth Dunkley, 14 Feb. 1974, Sydney, 2 sons *Education:* MB, BS, Monash University, 1973 FRACP; FRCPA. *Appointments:* Intern, Resident Registrar, Royal Prince Alfred Hospital, Sydney 1974-79; Research Fellow, Sydney University, 1980; Haematology-Oncology Fellow, University of California, Los Angeles, USA, 1980-82; Private Practice, Sydney, Australia, 1982-. *Memberships:* Australian Medical Association; Haematology Society of Australia; Clinical Oncology Society of Australia; President, Warringah District Medical Association. *Honours:* E and O Hewitt Medical Research Scholar, 1980. *Hobbies:* Cooking; Running; Family pursuits. *Address:* 14 Glenroy Avenue, Middle Cove, New South Wales 2068, Australia.

FLEISCHHAUER, Kurt Johann Maximilian, b. 14 Oct. 1929, Dusseldorf, Federal Republic of Germany. Professor and Head of University Department of Anatomy. m. Sabine Waller, 1965, Kiel, 1 son, 2 daughters. *Education:* Medical Studies, Universities of Freiburg im Breisgau, Kiel and Dusseldorf, 1949-54; Statsexamen, University of Freiberg im Breisgau, 1954; Dr med 1954, Dr med habil Anatomy 1960, University of Kiel. *Appointments:* Assistant, Medical Clinic, Dusseldorf and Munich, 1954-56; Assistant, Department of Anatomy, University of Kiel, 1956; British Council Scholar, 1956-58, Scientific Staff 1960-62, National Institute for Medical Research, Mill Hill, London, England; Head, Division of Neuroanatomy 1962-64, Full Professor of Anatomy 1964-68, University of Hamburg, Federal Republic of Germany; Full Professor of Anatomy and Head of Anatomical Institute, University of Bonn, 1968-. *Memberships:* Anatomische Gesellschaft; JERO; Associate member, Physiological Society; Fellow, Royal Society of Medicine. *Publications include:* Numerous papers in scientific journals; Managing Editor, 'Anatomical Embryology', 1978-; Editor, new edition of Benninghoff "Anatomy" volume 2, 1985. *Address:* Anatomisches Institut, Nüssallee 10, D-5300 Bonn, Federal Republic of Germany.

FLEMING, Patrick John, b. 6 June 1947, Massachussets, USA. Associate Professor. *Education:* BA, Kalamazoo College; PhD, University of Michigan, Ann Arbor. *Appointment:* Assistant Professor, Associate Professor, Biochemistry, Georgetown University. *Memberships:* American Society of Biological Chemistry; American Association for the Advancement of Science; New York Academy of Science. *Publications:* Articles in: 'Journal Biological Chemistry'. *Honours:* Established Investigatorship, American Heart Assocaition. *Hobbies:* Sailing; Flying. *Address:* Department of Biochemistry, Georgetown

University Medical Centre, Washington, DC 20007, USA.

FLEMING, Peter George, b. 8 Oct. 1932, Melbourne, Australia. Director of Educational Development. m. Wenda Cordingley, 31 Dec. 1955, Melbourne, 2 sons, 2 daughters. *Education includes:* BSc, BEd, Melbourne; PhD, Monash University. *Appointments:* Teacher of Mathematics and Science: Victorian Education Department, 1956-64; Tanzania, 1965-66; Victorian Education Department Australia, 1967. Lecturer, 1968-71, Senior Lecturer, 1972-75, Secondary Teachers College, Melbourne; Coordinator of Studies, Melbourne State College, 1976-79; Exchange Professor of Education, University of Oregon, USA, 1980; National Educator/Researcher, 1981-82, Director, 1982-, Family Medicine Programme, Melbourne, Australia. *Memberships:* South Pacific Association of Teacher Education; Higher Education Research and Development Society of Australia; Australian and New Zealand Association of Medical Educators. *Publicaitons:* "Matriculation Chemistry: A Programmed Reading Guide", 1969; 'An Integrated Programme of Vocational Training for General Practice', RACGP, 1985. Contributions to: 'Australian Family Physician'; 'Journal of Australia and New Zealand Association of Medical Educators'. *Hobbies:* Bushwalking; Travel; Jogging; Photography. *Address:* Family Medicine Programme, 4th Floor, 70 Jolimont Street, Jolimont, Melbourne 3002, Australia.

FLEMINGER, Rafael, b. 16 June 1932, Romania. Deputy Chief, Oncology. m. Ruth, 1 son, 2 daughters. *Education:* MD, National University of Colombia, 1959; Residency, Internal Medicine, Israel, 1967-72; Fellowship, Clinical Oncology, 1972-74, Radiation, 1978-80, USA. *Appointments:* Deputy Chief, Oncology Institute, Beilinson Medical Centre. *Memberships:* Israel Medical Association; Israel Society of Internal Medicine; Israel Society of Oncology; American Society of Clinical Oncology. *Honours:* Certified specialist: Internal Medicine, Oncology, Israel; Eligible Boards of Internal Medicine, Medical Radiology, USA. *Address:* 17 Snunit St., Hofit Y0295, Israel.

FLETCHER, David Jeffrey, b. 30 Sept. 1954, Doctor of Preventive Medicine. m. Glen Ellyn, 22 Mar 1978, Illinois, 2 daughters. *Education:* BA, University of Illinois, Champaign, Illinois, 1976; MD, Rush Medical College, Chicago, 1979; MPH, University of California, Berkley, 1982. *Appointments:* Kaiser-Permanente Hospital Staff, San Jose, California, 1982-86; Preventive Medicine Service, Ft Ord, California, 1982-830; Assistant Chief Preventive Medicine Service, Madigan Army Medical Center, Tacome, Washington, 1983-86; Private Preventive Medicine Practice, Tacoma, Washington, 1986-. *Memberships:* Fellow, American College of Preventive Medicine; American Public Health Association; Society for Prospective Medicine; Physicians for Social Responsibility; American Medical Association. *Publications:* 'Health Promotion for the Primary Care Practitioner' series in Postgraduate Medicine, 1985-86; 'Free Clinic Movement; Alive and Well' Lancet, 1982; 'Current Treatment Approaches for Gonorrhea', Military Medicine, 1984. **Honours:** David J, Fletcher Scholarship, Illinois Alcoholism and Drug Abuse Association, 1980; Smoking Prevention Award, American Cancer Society, 1983; UC Berkeley, student Weissman Award for outstanding research, 1983. *Hobbies:* Writing; Hiking; Music. *Address:* 5405 64th Avenue West, Tacoma, WA 98467, USA.

FLETCHER, James Pearse,b. 25 Oct. 1928, Bristol, England. Louis Cohen Professor and Head, Department of Dental Surgery Liverpool University. m. Judith Mary Abbott, 8 Sept. 1962, Caerleon, 1 son, 1 daughter. *Education:* BDS Honours, University of Bristol, 1951; LDS, 1952, FDS, 1956, Royal College of Surgeons of England. *Appointments:* House Surgeon, United Bristol

Hospitals, 1952; Assistant in Private and General Dental Practice, 1953,57; Dental Officer, Armed Forces, 1953-55; Dental Registrar, South West Regional Hospital Board, 1955-57; Senior Dental Registrar, United Bristol Hospitals, 1957; Lecturer in Parodontal Diseases, Liverpool University, 1957-58; Lecturer in Dental Surgery, 1959, in Dental Medicine, 1959-63, Consultant, Senior Lecturer, Dental Medicine, 1963-80, Dental Clinic Dean, 1972-75, 78, Chairman, Board of Dental Studies, 1975-78, Senate Member, 1971-75, 1979-80, Court Member, 1979-80, Bristol University; currently, Louis Cohen Professor, Head of Department of Dental Surgery, Liverpool University. *Memberships Include:* Fellow, Royal Society of Meidcine; British Dental Association; British Society of Periodontology; International Association for Dental Research; British Society for Oral pathology; British Society for Oral Medicine. *Publicaitons Include:* 'Human Disease for Dental Students', co-author, 1981; contributions to professional journals including, 'Journal of Dental Research', 'Oral Surgery' and 'Journal of Applied Bacteriology;. *Honours:* Chairman, Bristol, Bath and District Section, 1963-64, British Dental Association; Presidnet, 1981-82, Chairman, Teachers Section, 1976-77, Council Member, 3 terms, British Society of Periodontology; Council Member, 1982-85, British Society for Oral Medicine. *Hobbies:* Music; Watercolours; Photography. *Address:* Department of Dental Surgery, School of Dental Surgery, Pembroke Place, Liverpool L69 3BX, England.

FLETCHER, John Perry, b. 25 Sep. 1946, Perth, Australia. Senior Lecturer, Surgery University of Sydney and Westmead Hospital, 1978-. m. Beryl Duplex, 22 Jan. 1969, Perth, 2 sons. *Education:* MBBS, Univeristy of Western Australia, 1970; FRACS, 1975; FRCS, 1976. *Appointments:* Intern, Napier Hospital, New Zealand, 1970; Captian, RAAMC, 2nd Military Hospital, New South Wales, 1971-72; Surgical Registrar: Royal Prince Alfred Hospital Sydney, 1972-75, Stoke Manderville Hospital, England, 1975-77; Special fellow, Cleveland Clinic, Ohio, USA, 1975-78; Temporary Lecturer, University of Sydney and Royal Prince Alfred Hospital, Sydney, 1978. *Memberships:* Australian Medical Association; Australian Association of Surgeons; Pan-Pacific Surgical Association; International Society for Cardiovascular Surgery; Cleveland Clinic Surgical Society; John Loewenthal Club. *Publications:* 35 articles on Vascular Surgery and Surgical Nutrition in various professional journals. *Hobbies:* Family; Cricket; Football; Music. *Address:* Department of Surgery, Westmead Hospital, Westmead, NSW 2145, Australia.

FLERKO, Bela, b. 14 June 1924, Pécs, Hungary. Professor of Anatomy. m. Vera Bárdos MD, 23 July 1951, Pécs. *Education:* MD, University Medical School of Pécs, 1948. *Appointments:* Instructor, 1948-51, Assistant Professor, 1951-61, Associate Professor, 1961-64, Professor & Head of Deparmtent of Anatomy, University Medical School of Pécs, 1964-; Rector of the University Medical school 1979-85. *Memberships:* President, Hungarian Society of Endocrinology & Metabolism, 1973-81; Vice-President, International Society of Neuroendocrinolgoy, 1972-76; Executive Committee, International Brain Research Organisation, 1973-85, also Council Member, International Society of Endocrinology, 1973-81; Council Member, International Society for Research in Reproduction; President, Hungarian Society of Anatomists, Histologists & Embryologists, 1982-. *Publications:* Some 114 publications including book chapters in field of neural control of gonadotrophin secretion. *Honours:* Corresponding Member 1970, Member 1982, Hungarian Academy of Sciences; Honorary Member, Czechoslovakian Society of Endocrinology, 1977; Honorary Member, Society for Endocrinolgoy, German Democratic Republic, 1978,

Poland, 1985; Recipient, National Prize, 1978; Honorary Doctorate, Kuopio University, Finland, 1982. *Hobby:* Music. *Address:* József utca 7, H-7621 Pécs, Hungary.

FLIGHT, George Hubert. b. 15 Sep.1926, Broad Cove, Newfoundland. Professor; Associate Dean. m. Celeste Mylinda Sanderson, 28 Mar. 1951, 1 son, 2 daughters. *Education:* MD, CM, 1950; FRCS(C), 1958. *Appointments:* Specialty Practices, St John's, Newfoundland, 1958-62, Halifax, Nova Scotia, 1962-68; Professor, Chairman, Memorial University, Newfoundland, 1968-73; Associate Professor, Obstetrics & Gynaecology, Dalhousie University, 1973-74; Professor, Chairman, 1975-82, Obstetrics & Gynaecology, Associate Dean, 1982-, Acting Dean, 1985-86, Health Sciences, McMaster University. *Memberships:* Fellow: Society of Obstetricians & Gynaecologist of Canada, American College of Obstetricians & Gynaecologists, Royal College of Physicians & Surgeons, Canada; Niagara Society of Obstetricians & Gynaecologists; Canadian Fertility & Andrology Society; etc. *Publications:* Articles in professional journals including: 'Minnesota Medical Bulletin'; 'Journal American Medical Association'; 'Nova Scotia Medical Bulletin'; etc. *Hobby:* Golf. *Address:* Faculty of Health Sciences, McMaster University, 1200 Main Street West, Hamilton, Ontario L8N 3Z5, Canada.

FLOCH, Herve Alexandre, b. 3 Oct. 1908, Brest, France. Doctor of Medicine; Biologist. m. Lucie Henry, 1 Aug. 1932, Brest, France, 2 sons, 1 daughter. *Education:* Doctor of Medicine, Biological, Tropical and Pasteur medicine. *Appointments include:* Director, Gau da loupe Institute, 1968-71; Head, Anti-malarial services, Director of Blood Transfusion Centre; Honorary Director of Pasteur and Gau da loupe Institutes of French Guyana; Head of Laboratory, Paris Pasteur Insitute; Head of Biological Laboratory, Morlaix Hospital, 1974-79; Professor of Microbiology, Brest, 1978-85; Specialist in Parasite Sicknesses, World Organisation of Health. *Memberships:* Member of numerous medical and scientificasocieties, in France and internationally. *Publicaitons:* Over 900 articles in journals and reviews both in France and internationally. *Honours:* Officer of the Legion of Honour; Commander of the Order of Merit; Medal for the Epidemic Medicine; Laureat of National Academy of Medicine (seven prizes) and of the Academy of Sciences, 1974. *Address:* 45 Avenue Camille Desmoulins, 29200, Brest, France.

FLUHARTY, Arvan Lawrence, b. 10 June 1934, Haines, Oregon, USA. Professor. m. Clarie L Boyd, 24 June 1961, 2 sons, 1 daughter. *Education:* BS Chemistry, University of Washington, Seattle 1956; PhD Biochemistry, University of California at Berkeley, 1959. *Appointments:* Postdoctoral Research, Baltimore, Maryland, 1959-61; Assistant Professor of Biochemistry, 1962-66, Associate Professor 1966-68, Adjunct Associate Professor 1969-72, Adjunct Professor 1972-75, School of Medicne, University of Southern California at Los Angeles; Adjuct Professor 1975-79, Professor in Residence, 1979-, University of California at Los Angeles Research Group, Domona, California; Research Group Coordinator, ibid, 1980-. *Memberships include:* American Society for Biological Chemistry; Biochemical Society; American Society for Neurochemistry; American Association for the Advancement of Science; Sigma Xi; Phi Beta Kappa. *Publications:* Author & Co-author of some 160 papers & abstracts in field; various editorial responsiblities. *Honours:* Numerous awards & recognitions. *Hobbies:* Sport; Swimming; Senior Refferee (Soccer), 1977-84. *Address:* UCLA/MRRC Lanterman Development Centre Research Group, P.O. Box 100-R, Pomona, CA 91769, USA.

FLUKES, William Kenilworth, b. 8 Jan. 1943,

Sydney, Australia. Physician. m. Vicki, 15 Feb. 1985, Hobart. *Education:* BSc, Medicine, 1964, MB BS, 1967, University of Sydney; FRACP, 1974. *Appointments:* Resident Medical Officer, 1967-68, Medical Registrar, 1969-70, Royal Prince Alfred Hosptial, Sydney; Registrar in Respiratory Medicine, London Chest Hospital UK, 1971; Cardiology Registrar, The Brompton Hospital, UK, 1971-72; ICU Registrar, Royal Prince Alfred Hospital, Sydney, 1973; Staff Physician ICU, 1974-75, Physican in Charge/ICU/CCU Co-Director, 1975-, Royal Hobart Hospital, Hobart, Tasmania; Teacher in Clinical Medicine, Department of Medicine, University of Tasmania, 1975-; Medical Adviser, Ambulance Service of Tasmania, 1975-. *Memberships:* Fellow, The Royal Australasian College of Physicians; Cardiac Society of Australia and New Zealand; Australian and New Zealand Intensive Care Society; Western Pacific Association of Critical Care Medicine; Australian Society of Parenteral and Enteral Nutrition. *Honours:* BSc, Bichemistry Hons Class I 1964; MBBS, Hons Class II 1967. *Hobbies:* Squash; Golf; Diving; Canoeing; Sailing; Skiing; Trekking. *Address:* Royal Hobart Hospital, Liverpool Street, Hobart, Tasmania 7000, Australia.

FLYE, M. Wayne, b. 23 June 1942, Tarboro, North Carolina, USA. Professor of Surgery and Immunology; Director, Organ Transplantation & Immunobiology. m. Phyllis Webb, 2 sons. *Education:* BS, University of North Carolina, Chapel Hill, 1964; MD, University of North Carolina School of Medicine, 1967; MA, Immunology, PhD, Immunology, 1980, Duke University; MA (Hon), Yale University, 1985. *Appointments:* Guest Worker, Transplantation Biology, Immunology, National Cancer Institute, 1976-77; Staff Surgeon, Organ Transplant Unit, Walter Reed Army Medical Centre, 1976-78; Senior Investigator, Chief, Thoracic Surgical Services, NIH, Bethesda, 1977-79; Assistant Professor, Surgery & Microbiology, 1979-80, Chief, Vascular Surgery, 1979-83, Associate Professor, Surgery and Microbiology, 1980-83, University of Texas Medical Branch; Consultant, National cancer Institute, 1979-; Associate Professor, Surgery, 1983-84, Director, Organ Transplatation & Immunobiology, Washington University School of Medicine, St Louis, 1985-. *Memberships include:* Chi Psi; Alpha Omega Alpha; Sigma Xi; British Society of Immunology; Southern Medical Association; Transplatation Society; North Carolina, Durham-Orange County Medical Societies; Association for Academic Surgeons; American Society of Transplant Surgeons; Daryl Hart Surgical Society; American College of Cardiology, Fellow; American College of Surgeons, Fellow; Royal Society of Medicine; British transplantation Society; etc. *Publications:* Numerous articles in professional journals. *Honours:* American Field Service Exchange Student Scholarship to Germany, 1959; John Motley Morehead Scholarship, 1960-64, Alpha Omega Alpha, 1967, Award for Excellence, 1967, University of North Carolina; Mosby Book Scholarship Award, 1967; James W. McLaughlin Medal, 1982; etc. *Hobbies:* Sport; History. *Address:* Washington University School of Medicine, 4989 Barnes Hospital, Suite 5108 Queeny Tower, St Louis, MO 63110, USA.

FOGLIA, Virgilio Gerardo, b. 13 Nov 1905, Argentina. Medical Doctor m. Maria Angelica Vivanco de Foglia, 6 July 1950, 2 sons 1 daughter. *Education:* MD, Univeristy of Buenos Aires, 1928; Scholarship, McGill University, Montreal, Canada, 1937-38; Special Research Fellow, NIH, Bethesda, Maryland, USA, 1949-50; College de France, Paris, 1957. *Appointments:* Researcher, Facultad de Medicina, Buenos Aires, 1929-43; Researcher, Instituto de Bioloiga Medicina Experimental, Buenos Aires, 1944-45; Full Professor of Physiology, Facultad de Medicina, Buenos Aires, 1956-71; Director, Instituto de Biologiay Medicina Experimental, 1972-86; President, National

Academy of Medicine, Buenos Aires, 1986-88. *Memberships:* Societe d'Endocrinologie, Paris; Academia Medica di Roma, Italy; Intern, Diabetes Federation, London; Cherny's Foundation, Secretary, Buenos Aires; Berson's Foundaiton, USA; Hervert M Evans Memorial Committee, San Francisco, USA. *Publications:* About 500 original papers on Medicine. The majority on experimental research on: endocrinology, diabetes, metabolism, stress, lymph hearts, tumours etc. *Honours:* Honorary Doctorates: univ Mayor Real Pontificia, Sucre, Bolivia, 1962, Univ Complutense Madrid, Spain, 1975, Univ Nacional de Asuncion, Paraguay, 1979, Univ de la Republica, Uruguay, 1984; Prizes: Faculty de Ciencias Medicas, Thesis, Buenos Aires, 1931; Miguel Couto Acad Medic de Rio de Janeiro, Brazil, 1944; Bernardo A Houssay OEA Washington, USA, 1981; Hagedorn Latin American Association for Diabetes, Santiago, Chile, 1983. *Address:* Callao 1695- Piso 12, 1024 Buenos Aires, Argentina.

FOK, Po-Kai Frederick, b. 24 Oct. 1940, Hong Kong. Private Practice. m. Dr Angela Chan Yuen Yuen, 16 Oct. 1971, 2 daughters. *Education:* MB, BS, (HK) 1965; LRCP (London), MRCS (England), 1971; LMSSA (London), 1971; MRCP (UK) 1971; FCCP, 1975; FRCPE, 1983. *Address:* Room 610 Melbourne Plaza, 33 Queen's Road C, Hong Kong.

FÖLDES, István, b. 12 Dec. 1921, Budapest, Hungary; Director, Microbiological Research Group. m. Edit Beregi, 21 Dec. 1947, 1 son, 1 daughter. *Education:* MD, 1950; Can.Med.Sc., 1954; DMSc., 1966; Professor, 1972. *Appointments:* Assistant Professor, 1st Institute of Pathology, Semmelweis Medical School, 1950-51; Aspirant, National Institute of Hygiene, 1951-54; Head, Pathophysiology, National Insitute of Tuberculosis and Pneumology, 1954-57; Scientific Director, 1954-72; Director, Microbiolgical Research Group, Hungarian Academy of Sciences, 1972-. *Memberships:* Executive Committee, Hungarian Associations of Microbiology, Immunology, Oncology and Pneumology; Editorial Board, Acta Microbiol. Hung., and Pneumologia Hungarica, Interferon y Biotecnologia. *Publications:* 190 articles in International and Hungarian Medical Journals; "Allergy and Immunity in Tuberculosis", 'Immunological Aspects of Allergy and Allergic Disease', 1976; etc. *Honours:* Merited and Eminent Doctor of Hungary, 1961; Gold Medal of Labour, 1970; medal, Socialist Hungary, 1985; etc. *Hobby:* Bridge. *Address:* Pihenó ut 1, 1529 Budapest, Hungary.

FÖLDI, Michael, b. 10 Jan. 1920, Budapest, Hungary. Director, Clinic of Lymphology and its College. m. Ethel Börcösk, 27 Sep. 1970, 3 daughters. *Education:* University Medical School, Szeged, Hungary, 1938-44. *Appointments:* Director, 2nd Dept., of Internal Medicine, Szeged, Hungary, 1960-69. *Memberships:* Secretary General, International Society of Lymphology; etc. *Publications:* Co-Author, 'Lymphangiology', 1983, etc. *Honours:* Gold Medal, (Athenaeum Angiologicum Santorianum, 1979;) Gold Medal, Curatorium Internationale Angiologorum, Ratschow, 1983. *Hobbies:* Clasical Music & Literature. *Address:* Tullastr. 72, 7800 Freiburg, Federal Republic of Germany.

FONTANA, Paul Andre, b. 23 May 1954, Abbeville, Louisiana, USA. Manager of Physician's Occupational Therapy Service. m. Rose Kallok, 24 July 1981, 1 son, 1 daughter. *Education:* Louisiana State University, Baton Rouge, 1972-74; BS, Occupational Therapy, Louisiana State University Medical Center, New Orleans, 1976; Post. Bacc. Work, Augusta College, Georgia, 1977-79; MBA Program, Indiana University School of Business, Gary, Indiana, 1980-84. *Appointments:* Staff Therapist, Medical College of Georgia, Augusta,

1976-77; Staff Therapist, Veterans Administration, Augusta, 1977-79; Chief Therapist for Restorative Services Incorporated at St. Mary Medical Center, Gary and Hobart, Indiana, 1979-81; Occupational Therapy Supervisor for Restorative Services Incorporated, Hobart, Indiana, 1981-83; Manager of Occupational and Speech Therapy Divisions of Restorative Services Incorporated, Hobart, Indiana, 1983-. *Memberships:* American Occupational Therapy Association Member, Co-chair, 1987, AOTA Conference; Indiana Occupational Therapy Association; Illinois Occupational Therapy Association; Ohio Occupational Therapy Association; Kentucky Occupational Therapy Association. *Publications:* 'Private Practice Offers Professional Growth and Financial Returns', AOTA newspaper, Nov. 1984; Numerous articles published in Indiana Occupational Therapy Association Newsletter. *Honour:* Indiana Occupational Therapy Association Distinguished Service Award, 1985; President's Award RSI, 1984. *Hobbies:* Family; Church; Singing; Hiking; Hunting; Camping; Playing Guitar; Outdoor sports; Coaching Little League Football, Baseball and Basketball. *Address:* 1400 South Lake Park Avenue, Suite 400, Hobart, IN 46342, USA.

FOON, Kenneth A, b. 7 Mar. 1947, Detroit, Michigan, USA. m. Rebecca Garrett, 1 son, 2 daughters. *Education:* University of Michigan, 1964-66; BS 1968, MD with high distinction 1972, Wayne State University. *Appointments include:* Reserch Associate, National Eye Institute, 1973-75; Guest Worker 1973-75; Clinical Associate 1975-76, Laboratory of Microbiology and Immunology, National Institute of Dental Research, National Institutes of Health, Bethesda, Maryland; Junior Assistant Resident, Washington VA and Georgetown University Hospitals, Washington DC, 1976-77; Hematology-Oncology Fellowship 1977-80, Assistant Professor of Medicine 1980-81, University of California, Los Angeles, School of Medicine; Research Associate, VA Wadsworth Medical Center, Los Angeles, 1980-81; Head Monoclonal Antibody-Hybridoma Section 1981-82, Head Clinical Investigations Section 1982-85, Biological Therapeutics Branch, Biological Response Modifiers Program, Division of Cancer Treatment, National Cancer Institute-Frederick Cancer Research Facility, Frederick, Maryland; Associate Professorial Lecturer in Medicine, George Washington University School of Medicine and Health Sciences, 1984-85; Associate Director, Division of Hematology and Oncology and Associate Professor, Department of Medicine, University of Michigan, 1985-. *Memberships:* Fellow, American College of Physicians; Alpha Omega Alpha; American Society of Hematology; American Association for the Advancement of Sciences; American Society of Clinical Oncology; American Association for Cancer Research; American Federation for Clinical Research. *Publications include:* "Monoclonal Antibody Therapy of Human Cancer", (Edited with A. C. Morgan); Numerous papers. *Honours include:* Dr A, Ashley Rousuck Award in Internal Medicine, 1972; Gordon B. Myers Award in Internal Medicine, 1972. *Address:* Simpson Memorial Research Institute, 102 Observatory, Ann Arbor, MI 48109, USA.

FORBES, Iain, b. 23 Oct. 1942, Inverness, Scotland. Family Physician. m. Anna D'Agostino, 4 Mar. 1971, London, 2 sons, 1 daughter. *Education:* MB, Ch.B; LMCC. *Appointments:* House Physician, City Hospital, Aberdeen; House Surgeon, Childrens Hospital, Aberdeen; Senior House Physician, Queen Elizabeth Hospital for Children, London, England; Family Physician: Lethbridge, Alberta, Canada, Parksville, British Columbia, Victoria, British Columbia, Canada. *Memberships:* Canadian College of Family Physicians; Canadian Society of Aviation Medicine. *Hobbies:* Travel; Languages. *Address:* 211, 3749 Shelbourne Street, Victoria, BC, Canada V8P 5N4.

FORD, Larry Creed, b. 29 Sept. 1950, Provo, Utah,

USA. Associate Professor. *Education:* BS, Brigham Young University, Provo, Utah, 1971; Md, University of California Los Angeles School of Medicine, Los Angeles, California, 1975. *Appointments include:* Associate Professor, Department of Obstetrics and Gynecology, University of California Los Angeles School of Medicine, Los Angeles, California, 1980-; Director of Research, Center for Ovarian Cancer, University of California, Los Angeles School of Medicine, Los Angles, California, 1981-; Chairman, Medical Advisory Board, Chantal Pharmaceutical Corporation, Los Angeles, California, 1983-. *Memberships:* Founding Member, International Society for Infectious Diseases in Obstetrics and Gynecology; Fellow, Infectious Diseases Society for Obstetrics and Gynecology; American Society for Microbiology; New York Academy of Science; American Association for the Advancement of Science. *Publications include:* "Cost Effective Use of Antibiotics", 1983; "Antihormones and Hormonal Receptors in Fungi and Parasites", 1983; 'Estrogen and progesterone receptors in ovarian neoplasms', 1983; "New Antibiotics in OB-GYN", 1984; "Connective Tissue in Modulation with Ethasyn", 1986; Contributor to various Medical and Scientific Journals. *Hobbies:* Hunting; Shooting. *Address:* Department of Obstetrics and Gynecology, University of California, Los Angeles School of Medicine, Los Angeles, CA 90024, USA.

FORD, Ronald Stanley, b. Cheshire, England. Consultant Psychiatrist (part-time). m. Dr. Joan Mary Thomas, 25 July 1959, Risley, Derbyshire, 2 sons, 1 daughter. *Education:* MBChB, Liverpool University, 1958; MRCPscych., 1971; DPM, 1965; DPM, Manchester University, 1965. *Appointments:* Consultant Psychiatrist and Deputy Medical Superintendent, Cheadle Royal Hospital; Previously Neuropsychiatric Unit, Sefton General Hospital, Liverpool; Neurosurgical Unit, Walton Hospital, Liverpool. *Memberships:* Member, Chartered Society of Physiotherapy, 1947; British Medical Association; Fellow, Manchester Medical Society. *Hobbies:* Outdoor Activities; Travel; Egyptology; Comparative Religion; Music; Metaphysics. *Address:* "Green Hallow", 60 Carrwood Road, Wilmslow, Cheshire SK9 5DB, England.

FOREMAN, John Charles, b. 6 Feb 1949, Peterborough, England. Lecturer in Pharmacology. *Education:* BSc, Hons, Pharmacology, 1970, PhD, Pharmacology, 1973, University College London; MB,BS, University College Hospital Medical School, 1976. *Appointments:* House Physician 1977, House Surgeon, 1977, Peterborough District Hospital, England; Visiting Instructor of Medicine, Johns Hopkins University School of Medicine, Baltimore, USA, 1978-79; Lecturer in Pharmacology and Sub Dean and Tutor, Faculty of Medical Sciences, University College London. *Memberships:* Fellow Royal Society of Medicine; Physiological Society; British Pharmacological Society; American Society of Pharmacology and Experimental Biology; British Medical Association. *Publications:* 'Textbook of Immunopharmacology' with M M Dale, 1984; 'Pharmacological control of immediate hypersensitivity' in 'Annual Review of Pharmacology' 1981; 'Neurogenic inflammation' in 'Trends in pharmacological Science' with C C Jordan, 1984; 'Receptors for immunoglobulin E' in 'The Receptors' vol 1 with R Healicon, 1984. *Honour:* Faculty of Science Silver Medal, University College London, 1970. *Hobbies:* Music; Squash; Walking; Travel. *Address:* Department of Pharmacology, University College London, Gower Street, London WC1E 6BT, England.

FORGON, Mihaly, b. 22 June 1919, Debrecen, Hungary. Head, Traumatologic Clinic. m. 27 Apr. 1953, Debrecen, 1 daughter. *Education:* MD; DSc., Hungarian Academy of Sciences; Specialisation: General Surgeon, Trauma Surgeon, Orthopaedic Surgeon, Plastic Surgeon. *Appointments:* Lecturer,

General Surgery, University Medical School, Debrecen, 1943-49; Senior Lecturer, Orthopaedic Surgery, University Medical Schools, Debrecen, & Budapest, 1949-69; Professor, Traumatology, University Medical School, Pecs, 1969-. *Memberships:* Hungarian Traumatologic Society; Hungarian Orthopaedic Society; Hand. Surgery Section, Plastic Surgery Section, Hungarian Surgical Society; Yugoslavian Association of Traumatology; SICOT. *Publications:* 112 articles in Hungarian, German, English Journals. *Honours:* President, Hungarian Traumatological Society; Honorary Member, Yugoslavian Association of Traumatology; Kivalo Orvos, Hungarian Ministry of Health. *Hobby:* Painting. *Address:* Traumatological Clinic, University Medical School, 7643 Pécs, Hungary.

FORMBY, David John, b. 14 Mar. 1937, Birmingham, England. Consultant Paediatrician; Chairman, Federal Assembly, Australian Medical Association. m. Valerie Campbell, 4 Jan. 1961, Perth, 4 daughters. *Education:* MB BS (WA), 1959; DCH (London) 1965; FRCP (London), 1967; FRACP, 1978. *Appointments:* Registrar, St Andrews Hospital, London, 1955-56; RMO: Royal Perth Hospital, 1960, Princess Margaret Hospital for Children, 1961, King Edward Memorial Hospital for Women, 1962; General Practitioner, Albany, 1962-64; Registrar, Sheffield Childrens Hospital, 1966-67; Deputy Director, Princess Margaret Hospital, 1968-72; Consultant Paediatrician, Perth, WA, 1972-. *Memberships:* Australian Medical Association; Australian College of Paediatrics; Australian College of Physicians; Royal College of Physicians, London. *Publications:* Articles in professional journals including: 'Journal of Pathology'; 'Developmental medicine & Child Urology'; 'Australian Paediatric Journal';"Care & Management of Spinal Cord Injuries", 1981. *Honour:* Fellowship, Australian Medical Association, 1980. *Hobbies:* Golf; Reading. *Address:* Unit 3-4 25 Hamilton St., Subiaco, WA 6008, Australia.

FORMIGLI, Leonardo, b. 23 Mar. 1949, Cairo, Egypt. Manager, Reproductive Biology Laboratory. m. Graziella Badulli, 6 Oct. 1979, Milan, Italy. *Education:* Graduate in Medicine & Surgery, University of Pavia Medical School; Specialist in Obstetrics & Gynaecology, Pharmacology & Toxicology. *Appointments:* Head of Reproductive Medicine Unit, Milan, Italy. *Memberships:* American Association of Tissue Banks; Consultant for Fertility & Genetics Research, Chicago; Italian Association for Semen Cyrobanking. *Publications:* 'Semen Analysis & In Virtro Fertilization', 'Artificial Insemination by Donor Results in Relation to Husband's Semen' (in Archives of Andrology 1985). *Honour:* Head of first & only team in Italy to perform Embryo Donations of 'in vivo' fertilized human eggs. *Hobby:* Swimming. *Address:* Viale Umbria 44, 20 135, Milan, Italy.

FORRESTER, Dennis Hugh George, b. 21 Sept. 1951. Kingston, Jamaica. Family medical practitioner. m. Althea Roselle Taylor, 26 June, 1976, Toronto, Canada, 3 sons. *Education:* BSc, Chemical Engineering; Master of Applied Science; Biomedical Engineering; MD; Certification in the College of Family Physicians of Canada. *Appointments:* Chief Resident in Family Medicine, Toronto General Hospital; Active Staff, Mississauga General Hospital; currently active staff, Credit Valley Hospital, Staff Physician - Peel Regional Health Department, Family Practitioner, Ontario, Canada. *Memberships:* Toronto Academy of Medicine; College of Physicians and Surgeons of Ontario; College of Family Physicians of Canada. Ontario Medical Association. Christian Medical and Dental Society of Canada. Board of Directors, Family Services of Peel. *Publication:* 'Conditions for the Induced Adhesion of Hydrophobic Polymers to soft tissue' published in volume XX of "Trans American Society Artificial Internal Organs", 1974. *Honours:* The Jamaica Scholarship for Boys 1969; Univeristy of the West Indies Open Scholarship, 1969; Charles R Massey Prize, Most Outstanding Student in Engineering UWI, 1972; Alcan Overseas Postgraduate Scholarship, 1972; Doctor and Mrs. M. Pollock Award, 1975; Junior Fellowship, Massey College, University of Toronto, 1975; PSI Foundation Scholarship, 1984. *Hobbies:* Poetry and drama; Table tennis. *Address:* 6855 Meadowvale Towne Centre Circle, Suite 208, Mississauga, Ontario Canada L5N 2YI.

FORSSMAN, Sven Peter Magnus, b. 5 Feb. 1911, Lund, Sweden. Professor Emeritus, Consultant. m. (1) Mait Gudrun Bengtsson (deceased), 17 Sept. 1937, Dalby, Sweden, (2) Barbara Strandberg, 29 May 1973, Simris, Sweden; 3 sons, 3 daughters. *Education:* BSc Chemistry, 1930, MD, 1938, Resident Physician, Department of Internal Medicine, 1941-42, University of Lund. *Appointments:* Associate Professor of Pharmacology, University of Lund, 1941-44; Professor, Chief, Department of Ind. Hygiene, National Institute of Public Health, Stockholm, 1943-51; Associate Professor of Occupational Health, Karolinska Institute, Stockholm, 1951-73; Medical Advisor, Swedish Employers' Confederation, Stockholm, 1951-66; Consultant in periods to World Health Organisation, in Occupational Health, Geneva, Copenhagen, Alexandria, New Delhi, Manila, 1950-84; Chief, Occupational Health Section, WHO, Geneva, 1965-66; Director-General, National Institute of Occupational Health, Stockholm, 1966-72; WHO Cheif Technical Advisor, UNDPWHO Lodz, Poland, 1973-77; WHO Consultant ot Denmark, 1976-79; ILO Consultant to Argentina, 1979-80, United Kingdom, 1980-81. *Memberships:* American Association of Occupational Health; Swedish Medical Society; Swedish Associaton for Occupational Health Physician (past Vice-President); Honorary Member: American Medical Association; Ergonomic Society; Occupational Medicine Societies of Argentina, Finland, Hungary, Mexico, Poland, United Kingdom; Faculty of Occupational Medicine, Royal College of Physicians, Ireland; American Union of Occupational Medicine; International Commission on Occupational Medicine (President 1954-69). *Publications:* Some 500 publications on industrial toxicology, occupational health services, health of older workers, occupational health services in different countries. *Honours:* William P Yant Award, 1967; Lucas Lecture, 1985; Knight Commander of Northern Star, Sweden; Finnish Lion; Order of the United Arab Republic; Knight, Polish Order of Merit. *Hobbies:* History; Botany; Rotary Club (Swedish Member); Traveller's Club. *Address:* Blockhusringen 39 n.b. S-115 25 Stockholm, Sweden.

FORSTER, Arnold E, b. 21 Sep. 1934, Brooklyn, New York, USA. Doctor of Chiropractic, 1960; MS Biology, University of Bridgeport; Diplomat, National Board of Chiropractic Examiners. *Appointments:* Instructor, Physiology principles and practice, Columbia Institute of Chiropractic, 1960-65; Instructor, Masters Course in Nutrition, University of Bridgeport, 1980-1982; Visiting Professor, Department of Clinical Instruction, New York Chiropractic College. *Memberships:* Fellow, American College of Chiropractors; Fellow, International College of Chiropractors; Council on Nutrition, American Chiropractic Association; President Brooklyn District 1969, District Delegate 1971, 1979 and 1980, New York State Chiropractic Association; Chinese Acupuncture Institute; World Iridology Fellowship; Chairman 1980 and 1981, Chiropractic Knights of the Round Table; President, FACTS Unlimited. *Publications:* ''Iridology Explained''. *Honours:* Awarded Testimonial, Board of Trustees, Columbia Institute of Chiropractic, 1968; Citation for Distinguished Service, New York State Chiropractic Association, 1977 and 1978. *Address:* 448 Marlborough Road, Brooklyn, NY 11226, USA.

FORTAK, Waldemar Jan, b. 17 Nov. 1929, Lodz,

Poland. Chief, Histology & Embryology, Medical Academy, Lodz. m. Maria Anna Warezak, 6 Apr. 1958, Lodz, 1 son, 1 daughter. *Education:* B.Med., MD, D.Med.Sc., Docent, Professor, Medical Sciences, Medical Academy, Lodz, 1955-73; Diploma, Master of Internal Diseases, Medicine, Health & Social Welfare Dept., Lodz. *Appointments:* Scientific Worker, Medical Academy, Lodz, 1952-62; Medical Practitioner, Internal Diseases, Hospital of M. Pirogov, Consulting Unit of Internal Diseases, Consulting Unit of Heavy Industry, 1955-62, Dept. of Health & Social Welfare, Lodz. *Memberships:* European Academy of Allergology and Clinical Immunology; Interasma; Polish Anatomical Society; Polish Histochemical and Cytochemical Society; Polish Endocrinological Society; Polish Society of Allergology; Polish Society of Prevention of Allergic Diseases; Polish Society of Internists; Lodz Scientific Society. *Publications:* ''Histological and Histochemical Studies on the Sources and Pathways of Liver Regeneration in White Rats'', 1961; ''Histologic and Histochemical Studies on Experimental Asthma in Guinea Pigs'', 'Annals Polish Academy of Sciences', 1966; many other articles in professional journals. *Honours:* Gold Cross of Merit, 1968; Knight Cross of Polonia Restituta, 1973; Medal, Committee of National Education, 1985; Award of Polish Academy of Sciences, 1962; Award, Ministry of Health & Social Welfare, 1985. *Hobbies:* Car; Handy Man; Allotments. *Address:* Dept. of Histology & Embryology, Institute of Biomorphology, Medical Academy, Lodz, Poland, Narutowicza 60, Lodz 90-136, Poland.

FOULKES, Ernest C., b. 20 Aug. 1924, Karlsruhe, Germany. Professor of Environmental Health & Physiology. m. Valarie Hopton, 19 Jan. 1946, Sydney, Australia, 3 sons, 1 daughter. *Education:* BSc; MSc (Sydney); DPhil (Oxon). *Appointments:* Investigator, Australian National Health & Research Council; Associate, May Institute for Medical Research; Established Investigator, American Heart Association; Assistant Professor, Associate Professor, Professor, University of Cincinnati College of Medicine, USA. *Memberships:* American Physiological Society; American Society of Nephrology; Biophysical Society; American Society of Biological Chemistry; American Association for the Advancement of Science; Society for Experimental Biological Medicine; Society of Toxicology; American Association of University Professors. *Publications:* Over 100 papers in scholarly journals; Editor, ''Biological Role of Metallothionein'', Elsevier, 1982, ''Cadmium'', Springer, 1986. *Hobbies:* Canoeing; Cave exploration; Reading history. *Address:* Department of Environmental Health, University of Cincinnati College of Medicine, Cincinnati, OH 45267-0056, USA.

FOWLER, Godfrey Heath, b. 1 Oct. 1931, Wolverley, England. University Professorial Fellow; General Medical Practitioner. m. Sissel Vidnes, 15 Sep. 1962, Oslo, Norway, 2 sons. *Education:* MA, University College, Oxford, England; BM, BCh, University College Hospital, London; DCH; DRCOG. *Appointments:* Various Junior posts, University College Hospital, 1956-59; Currently: Professorial Fellow, Balliol College, Oxford; General Practitioner; Clinical Reader, Oxford University. *Memberships:* British Medical Association; Fellow, Royal College of General Practitioners. *Publications include:* ''Preventive Medicine in General Practice'' (co-author), 1983; ''Essentials of Preventive Medicine'' (co-author), 1984; Numerous papers on preventive medicine. *Hobbies:* Mountaineering; Sailing. *Address:* Orchard House, Squitchey Lane, Oxford OX2 7LD, England.

FOWLER, Michael William, b. 6 Apr. 1944, Birmingham, England. Professor; Institute Director. m. Judith M. Vaugh, 7 Sep. 1968, Harrow, 2 sons, 1 daughter. *Education:* BSc., Honours, Biochemistry, Chelsea College, University of London, 1966; PhD, Biochemistry, Fitzwilliam College, University of Cambridge, 1969; C.Biol.; F.I.Biol; Fellowship, Royal Society of Arts, 1986. *Appointments:* ICI Research Fellow, University of Leicester, 1969-71; Lecturer, 1971-77, Senior Lecturer, 1977-80, Professor, Institute Director, Institute of Biotechnology, 1981-, University of Sheffield. *Memberships:* Fellow, Institute of Biology; Society of Chemical Industry; Biochemical Society; Society of General Microbiology. *Publications:* Articles in professional journals. *Honour:* Fellowship, Institute of Biology, 1982. *Hobbies:* Sailing; Sheep Farming; Gardening. *Address:* Wolfson Institute of Biotechnology, The University, Sheffield S10 2TN, England.

FOX, Anthony Dunstan, b. 12 Feb. 1943, Wellington, Somerset, England. Medical Physician. m. Jennifer A Kilford, 20 May 1967, Drewsteignton, 1 son, 2 daughters. *Education:* BSc, MB, BS, Diploma Obstetrics and Gynaecology, Diploma Child Health, London University. *Appointments:* SMO, Paediatrics, Obstetrics, Gynaecology, Nottingham; SMO, Medicine, Registrar, Phychiatry, Chesterfield; Principal, General Practice, Medical Officer, Geriatrics, Keynsham, Bristol; Assistant, Bristol Homeopathic Hospital. *Memberships:* Member, British Medical Association Faculty of Homeopathy; Member, Royal College General Practitioners; British Society of Clinical Ecology; British Society of Nutritional Medicine. *Publications:* 'Role of Homeopathy in Clinical Ecology', 1985. *Honour:* 3rd prize, International Clinical Ecology Competition, 1983. *Address:* 54 Barton Court Avenue, Barton-on-Sea, New Milton, Hants. BH25 7HG, England.

FOX, Mervyn, b. 13 Aug. 1936, London, England. Developmental Paediatrician; Associate Professor of Paedriatrics. m. Dr Hannah Jacob, London, 1 son, 1 daughter. *Education:* MB BS,Middlesex Hospital Medical School, University of London; Fellow, Royal College of Physicians and Surgeons, Canada; DCH. *Appointments:* Lecturer in Paediatrics, MRC Group on Neonatal Physiology and Metabolism , London Hospital Medical College, University of London, England; Honorary Lecturer, Developmental Paediatrics, Wolfson Centre, Institute of ChildHealth, University of London; Principal Physician, Child Health, Camden Area Health Authority and Inner London Educational Authority, London; currently, Medical Director, Thames Valley Childrens Centre; Associate Professsor, Paediatrics, University of Western Ontario, Canada. *Memberships:* Royal Society of Medicine; Royal College of Physicians and Surgeons, Canada; British Paediatric Association; Canadian Paediatric Society; American Academy for Cerebral Palsy and Developmental Medicine; Association for Child Psychology and Psychiatry; Society for Behavioural Paediatrics; Council for Exceptional Children. *Publications:* "They Get This Training But They Don't Really Know How You Feel". 1975; contributor to "Practical Psychiatry", Volume 1, 1981; Proceedings of 1st Canadian Conference on Education and Development of the Deaf-Blind, 1983. *Hobbies:* Photography; Travel; Literature; Indian sub-continent; Opera. *Address:* Department of Paediatrics University of Western Ontario, Childrens Hospital of Western Ontario, 800 Commissioners Road, London, Ontario, Canada, N6A 4GS

FOX, Rick, b. 6 Apr, 1957, Toronto, Canada, Resident in Otorhinolaryngology. m. Anna Bakerspigel, 4 Nov. 1984, Toronto. *Education:* Undergraduate 1976-78, Medical School 1978-82, MD, University of Toronto; Internship, Mount Sinai Hospital, Toronto. 1982-83; Residency - Otorhinolaryngology, Dalhousie University, Halifax, Nova Scotia, 1983 -. *Memberships:* Canadian Society of Otolaryngology; American Academy of Otolaryngology - Head and Neck Surgery; American Academy of Otolaryngolic

Allergy. *Address:* Halifax Infirmary, 1335 Queen Street, Halifax, Nova Scotia, B3J 2H6, Canada.

FRANCHI, Giuseppe, b. 16 Nov. 1924, Siena, Italy. University Professor. m. 12 Dec. 1951, Siena, 1 son. *Education:* Laurea, Pharmacy, 1948; Libera Docenza, 1958; Libera Docenza, 1962. *Appointments:* 1st Assistant, Pharmaceutical Chemistry, 1950, Lecturer, Pharmaceutical Technology & Legislation, 1958, Professor, Pharmaceutical Technology and Legislation, 1975-, Director, Pharamceutical Chemistry, 1976-81, President, Faculty of Pharmacy, 1976-, University of Siena. *Memberships:* Societa Chemica Italiana; Societa Italiana di Scienze Farm.; Associazione Docenti e Ricercatori Italiani Tecnica e Legislazione Framaceutica, Vice President, 1979-81; President, 1982 Societe de Pharmacie de la Mediterranee Latine. Accademia dei Fisiocritici Siena, Councillor, 1978-80; Ordine dei Farmacisti di Siena, Councillor, 1957, President, 1970-76. *Publications:* 62 articles; 2 patents. *Honours:* Diploma di Prima Classe Benemeriti Scuola, Cultura e Arte. *Hobbies:* Numismatics; Philately. *Address:* Faculty of Pharmacy, Siena University, Banchi di Sotto, 55 53100 Siena, Italy.

FRANCIOSA, Joseph Anthony, b. 24 Apr. 1936, Easton, Pennsylvania, USA. Professor of Medicine. m. Barbara A Neilan, 3 Aug. 1973, Rockville, Maryland, 1 son. *Education:* BA Sociology, University of Pennsylvania, 1954-58; MD, Faculty of Medicine, University of Rome, Italy, 1958-63. *Appointments Include:* Instructor 1971-73, Assistant Professor 1973-74, Department of Medicine, Georgetown University Medical School, Washington DC; Assistant Professor 1974-77, Associate Professor 1977-79, Department of Medicine, University of Minnesota Medical School, Minneapolis; Associate Professor, Department of Medicine, University of Pennsylvania School of Medicine, Philadelphia, 1979-82; Professor of Medicine, University of Arkansas for Medical Sciences, Little Rock, 1982 - ; Director, Cardiovascular Division, University of Arkansas for Medical Sciences and VA Hospital, Little Rock 1982 -. *Memberships Include:* Fellow, American College of Physicians; Fellow, American College of Cardiology; Fellow, American College of Chest Physicians; American Heart Association. *Publications include:* 93 original articles; 125 abstracts; Lectures and reviews. *Honours:* Numerous grants. *Address:* Cardiovascular Division, Mail Slot 532, University of Arkansas for Medical Sciences, 4301 West Markham Street, Little Rock, AR 72205, USA.

FRANCIS, Robert Lloyd, b. 2 Nov. 1931, Los Angeles, California, USA. Internist & Cardiologist. m. Laverne Louise Francis, 30 June 1956, Los Angeles, 2 sons, 2 daughters. *Education:* BA, Pomona College, 1953; MD, University of Southern California, 1957; MSc, University of Minnesota, 1961. *Appointments:* Partner, Fullerton Internal Medicine Center, 1966-; Fullerton Community Hospital Director of Cardiology, 1966-; Associate Professor of Medicine, School of Medicine, University of Southern California, 1967-73; Sports Medicine Staff, 1975-; Director, Fullerton Cardiac Rehabilitation Center, 1972-84; Co-director, St Jude Hospital Rehabilitation Center, Outpatient Cardiac Rehabilitation Department, 1984-. *Memberships:* Fellow, American College of Physicians; Fellow, American College of Sports Physicians; Fellow, American College of Chest Physicians; Fellow, American College of Angiology; Associate Fellow, American College of Cardiology. *Publications:* 'A Clinical Pathological Study of Patients with and without Angina Pectoris Preceding Initial Myocardial Infarction', 1964; Chapter on 'The Treatment of Angina Pectoris' in "Current Therapy", 1965. *Hobbies:* Golf; Jogging; Travel. *Address:* 433 W Bastanchury Road, Fullerton, CA 92635, USA.

FRANCO-SAENZ, Roberto, b. 13 July 1937, Colombia, South America. Professor of Medicine. Kathleen Netzley, 7 Sept 1973, Toledo, Ohio, USA, 2 sons. *Education:* BSc (premed), Instituto Nacional Nicolas Esguerra, Bogotá, Colombia, 1955; MD, Universidad Nacional de Colombia, 1962. *Appointments:* Assistant Professor of Medicine, 1971-75, Associate Professor, 1975-79, Professor of Medicine, 1979-. Medical College of Ohio at Toledo; Acting Chief of Endocrinology & Metabolism, 1973-75, Chief of Endocrinology & Metabolism Section, 1981-. Medical College of Ohio at Toledo. *Memberships:* Fellow, American College of Physicians; Endocrine Society; American Federation for Clinical Research; Central Society for Clinical Research; AOA-Delta Chapter of Ohio. *Publications:* Over 90 articles ,papers and abstracts in medical & professional journals etc. *Honours:* Honour Diploma, 1962, Daniel Vega Award, 1962, Universidad Nacional de Colombia; Golden Apple Award, Medical College of Ohio, 1974, 1975, 1976, 1978; Alpha Omega Alpha; Sigma XI. *Hobbies:* Jogging; Soccer; Music. *Address:* 2457 Hempstead, Toledo, OH 43606, USA.

FRANKEL, Herman Morris, b. 30 Mar. 1938, Brooklyn, New York, USA. Director Portland Health Institute. m. Ruth Ellen Wallach, 16 June 1963, Brooklyn, New York, 2 daughters. *Education:* BA Magna cum laude with distinction in Psychology, Columbia College, 1958; MD, College of Physicians and Surgeons, Colombia University, 1962; Diplomate, American Board of Pediatrics, 1967. *Appointments:* Medical-Surgical Intern, Montefiore Hospital, New York, 1962-63; Resident in Pediatrics, New York Hospital - Cornell Medical Center, New York, 1963-65; Fellow in Language and Communication Disorders in Children 1965-67, Instructor in Pediatrics 1967-69, University of Oregon Medical School; Director, Prescriptive Education Program, Portland Public Schools, 1969-73; Pediatrician, Kaiser-Permanente Medical Care Program of Oregon, 1973-77; Clinical Instructor in Pediatrics, Oregon Health Sciences University, 1973-; Senior Investigator Kaiser-Permanente Health Services Research Center 1977-84; Adjunct Associate Professor of Health and Physical Education, Portland State University 1983-; Director, Portland Health Institute, Portland, Oregon, 1984-. *Memberships:* American College of Sports Medicine; American Society of Bariatric Physicians; American Society of Clinical Hypnosis; American Medical Joggers Association; Multnomah County Medical Society; Phi Beta Kappa. *Honours:* Award for Exemplary Community Health Promotion and Disease Prevention, State of Oregon, 1983; Award of Excellence for Community Health Promotion and Disease Prevention, US Secretary of Health and Human Services, 1984; Nobel Prize for Peace, (International Physicians for the Prevention of Nuclear Wars), 1985; Endurance exercise; Cooking; Juggling; Travelling. *Address:* Portland Health Institute, 5757 SW Macadam Avenue, Portland, OR 97201, USA.

FRANKL, William Stewart, b. 15 July 1928, USA. Professor of Medicine. m. Razelle Sherr, 19 June 1951, Philadelphia, USA, 2 sons. *Education:* BA, Temple University, USA, 1951, MD, 1955, MS 1961; Fellowship in Cardiovascular Medicine, University of Pennsylvania, 1962. *Appointments:* Instructor, Assistant Professor of Medicine, Associate Professor, Temple University Health Sciences Centre, USA, 1961-68; Chairman, Department of Medicine, Physician in Chief, Springfield, Hospital Medical Centre, Spingfield, USA, 1968-70; Professor of Medicine and Chief of Cardiology, Medical College of Pennysylvania, 1970-79; Professor of Medicine and Associate Chief, Division of Cardiology, Thomas Jefferson University and Medical College, 1978-84; Professor of Medicine, Co-Director, Lik offCardiovasclar Institute of Hahnemann University, 1984-. *Memberships*

Include: Fellow, American college of Physicians; American College of Cardiology; American College of Clinical Pharmacology; Council on Clinical Cardiology; Council on Atherosclerosis; Royal Society of Medicine; New York Acadmey of Sciences; American Federation on Clinical Research, etc. *Publications:* Co-author: "Cardiovascular Therapeutics in Clinical Practice", 1983; Co-author: "Valvular Heart Disease: Comprehensive Evaluation and Treatment", 1985; numerous conference papers and ariticles in professional journals. *Honours:* Golden Apple Award for Teaching, Temple University, 1967; Golden Apple Award for Teaching, Medical College of Pennysylvania, 1972; LindbackAward for Excellence in Teaching, Medical College of Pennysylvania, 1975; Fogarty International Fellowship, London University, 1978; Residents' Award for Excellence in Teaching, Thomas Jefferson University, 1982, etc. *Hobbies:* Baroque Music; Films; Photography. *Address:* Hahnemann University Hospital, 230 North Broad Street, Philadelphia, PA 19102, USA.

FRANKLIN, Alexander, b. 19 Dec. 1932, London, England. Industrial Medical Consultant. m. Cornelia De Valois, 18 Dec. 1982, Toronto, Canada, 1 son. *Education:* Harrow School; MB, BS, London, 1959; Diploma Physical Medicine (UK) 1964; ECFMG, Certificate, 1972; FLEX Lic. (USA), 1974; Diploma of Public Health, Toronto, 1974; Diploma of Industrial Health, Toronto, 1975. *Appointments:* Orthopaedic House Surgeon, Addenbrooke's Hospital, Cambridge, England; House Physician, Area Neurology Unit, Royal Surrey County Hospital, Guildfaord, England; Senior House Officer, Department of Rheumatology & Rehabilitation, West Middlesex Hospital, London; Registrar, West Middlesex Hospital, Whittington Hospital, St Stephen's Hospital, Westminster Teaching Group, University of London; St Luke's Geriatric Hospital & Centre for Spastic Children; Consultant to 5 hospitals in the Netherlands. Director of Treatment, Ontario Workers Compensation Board Hospital & Rehabilitation Centre, Downsview, Toronto, Chief Physician, Senior Citizens Programmes, Homes for the Aged, Ontario, Ministry of Community & Social Services, Canada. *Memberships:* British Association for Rheumatology and Rehabilitation; Biological Engineering Society; Royal Society of Medicine; Society of Apothecaries of London; Canada & Ontario Public Health Associations; American Industrial Hygienist & Occupational Medical Associations; Permanent Commission & International Association on Occupational Health; Canadian Association of Physical Medicine; Canadian Council of Occupational Medicine; British Medical Association; Canadian Medical Association. *Publications:* 'A New Reading Apparatus';, Annals of Physical Medicine, 1963; 'Vitamin C Deficiency in Physical Medicine Patients', Excerpta Medica, Paris, 1964; 'Seamless Shoes in Rheumatoid Arthritis', British Medical Journal, 1968; (co-author with A St J Dixon); 'Treatment of Writer's Cramp by postural re-education'. (EMG Congress, Brussels), 1971. *Honours:* Certificate of Merit 1978, Service Award 1983, Canadian Red Cross (Ontario Division). *Hobbies:* Languages (French, Italian, Russian); Rotary International; Writing. *Address:* 8 Appleton Avenue Suite 100, Toronto, Ontario, M6E 3A3, Canada.

FRANKUM, Wilbur Max, b. 14 Feb. 1950, Missouri, USA. Medical Doctor; Veterinarian. m.Debby Mackoy, 7 Mar. 1980, St Moritz, Switzerland. *Education:* BS, 1971, DVM, 1975, University of Missouri; MD, University of Kansas School of Medicine, 1981; Rotating Internship, St Luke's Hospital, 1982. *Appointments:* Parasitology Instructor, University of Missouri, 1974; Research Assistant, Dalton Research Centre, Columbia, 1975; Microbiologist, Public Health Service, Kansas City, 1976-77; Histology Instructor, St George's University, 1978-79; Emergency Veterinarian,

Animal Emergency Clinic, Kansas City, 1980-82; Veterinarian, Private Practice, Kansas City, 1980-82; Medical House Officer, St Luke's Hospital, Kansas City, 1981-82; Emergency Physician, Emergency Medicorp, Olathe, 1981-82; Consulting Physician, Alpha Therapeutic Corporation, Honolulu, 1982-; Attending Physician, Doctors on Call, Honolulu, 1982-. *Publications:* "Management of Myelomeningocele", 1981; "Evaluation of Spontaneous Variations in Canine Urine Electrolyte Excretion", 1976; "Adjective Check List Analysis of Personality Traits for Veterinarians", 'Journal of Veterinary Medical Education', 1975. *Honours:* Phi Kappa Phi; Phi Zeta; National Honours Society of Veterinary medicine; Outstnading Pathologist of the Year. Eagber Ebert Award for Excellence in Medicine and Surgery; Gamma Sigma Delta; Pi Omicron Sigma; Alpha Zeta; Dean's lists; Chancellor's Honors Committee; Beta Beta Beta. *Address:* Suite 1505, 1778 Ala Moana Blvd., Honolulu, HI 96815, USA

FRANTZ, Kurt Smith, b. 27 Jan. 1948, Enid, Oklahoma, USA. University Professor; Private Practitioner. m. Ivana Bohdal, 1 May, 1976, Montreal, Canada, 1 son, 2 daughters. *Education:* BA, Univeristy of Oklahoma, USA, 1970; MD, Washington University, St. Louis, Missouri, 1974. *Appointments:* Chief Resident, Family Pracitce, Montreal General Hospital, McGill UniversityCanada, 1976; Chief Resident, University of Oklahoma Health Science Centre, 1977; Assistant Clinical Professor, Department of Family Medicine, 1977; Chief, Department of Family Practice, Baptist Hospital Enid, Oklahoma, 1981-82, Cheif of staff, 1985. *Memberships:* American Medical Association; Oklahoma State Medical Association; American Academy of Family Practice; Garfield County Medical Association; American Academy of Family Practice; Garfield County Medical Association; Diplomate, American Board of Family Practice; Society of Teachers of Family Medicine. *Honours:* Phi Beta Kappa, 1974; Top Ten Senior Men, Univeristy of Oklahoma, 1974; Outstanding Resident, MCGill University Montreal General Hospital, 1976. *Hobbies:* Hunting; Fishing; Team Sports; Farmpond Ecology. *Address:* 615 East Oklahoma, Enid, OK, 73701, USA.

FRASER, Donald McRobie, b. 25 Oct, 1926, Ottawa, Canada. Clinical Assistant Professor, Orthopaedics, Strong Memorial Hospital, New York. m. Barbara Sampson 10 Oct. 1952, Toronto, 2 sons, 1 daughter. *Education:* MD;FCFP;CCFP; Fellow, Society of Orthopaedic Medicine, England. *Memberships:* Vice President, Society of Orthopaedic Medicine; Past President, North American Academy of Manipulative Medicine; American Medical Association; Canadian Medical Association; Ontario Medical Association; College of Family Physicians, Canada; British Association of Manipulative Medicine. *Publications:* 'Post Partum Backache - A Preventable Condition', 'The Family Physicians', 1977; "Observations of Whiplash Injuries in Private Practice", "Federation of International Manual Medicine", 1977. *Address:* 5147 Lewiston Road, Lewiston, NY 14092, USA.

FRASER, Gordon Martin, b. 24 Mar. 1929, Carlisle, England. Consultant Radiologist, Western General Hospital, Edinburgh. m. Susan Mary Stanton, 16 May 1970, Penn, Bucks., 1 son, 1 daughter. *Education:* MB; ChB; DMRD; MRCP(Ed); FRCR. *Appointments:* Senior Registrar in Radiodiagnosis, Cardiff Royal Infirmary; Consultant Radiologist, Falkirk and District Royal Infirmary; Consultant Radiologist, Leith Hospital, Edinburgh. *Memberships:* British Medical Association; British Institute of Radiology; British Society of Gastroenterology. *Publications:* The Double Contrast Enema in Ulcerative and Crohn's Colitis (with J M Findlay), Clinical Radiology, 1976; "Percutaneous Transhepatic Cholangiography with the Chiba Needle" (co-author), Clinical Radiology, 1978; The Double Contrast Barium Meal in Patients with Acute Upper Gastrointestinal Bleeding, Clinical Radiology, 1978; Contrast Radiology (with K C Simpkins) in Gastrointestinal Haemorrhage, 1981; The Double Contrast Barium Meal: A Correlation with Endoscopy (with P M Earnshaw), Clinical Radiology, 1983; The Small Bowel Barium Follow Through Enhanced with an Oral Effervescent Agent (with P G Preston), Clinical Radiology, 1983. *Hobbies:* Gardening; Fishing; Shooting; Skiing. *Address:* 17 Park Road, Edinburgh EH6 4LE, Scotland.

FRAZER, Gregory James, b. 28 Sep. 1952, Sacramento, California, USA. Director of Audiology. *Education:* BA, Speech Pathology and Audiology, California State University, Scaramento; MS, Audiology and Counselling Deaf/Hearing Impaired, University of Utah, Salt Lake City; PhD, Audiology, Wayne State University, Detroit, Michigan. *Appointments include:* Director of Audiology, Midwest Health Center, Dearborn, Michigan, 1981; Director of Audiology, Pulec Ear Clinic, Los Angeles, California, 1982; Director of Audiology, Auditory-Vestibular Center, Panorama City, California, 1982-; Director of Audiology, Olive View Medical Center, Van Nuys, California, 1984-. *Memberships include:* American Speech-Language-Hearing Association; California Speech-Language-Hearing Association; International Electric Response Audiometry Study Group; American Tinnitus Association; American Auditory Society. *Publications:* Contributor of articles to journals in the field of Audiology. *Honours:* California State Scholarship, 1970-71; Rehabilitation Services Grant 1974-76; Phi Kappa Phi Honor Society, 1976; Wayne State University Graduate Professional Scholarship 1979-80; Deans Honor List 1970-74. *Hobbies:* Snow skiing; Water skiing; Golf; Tennis; Backpacking; Jogging. *Address:* Auditory-Vestibular Center, 14427 Chase Street, Suite 103, Panorama City, CA 91402, USA.

FREE, Noel, b. 25 Dec. 1946, Washington, District of Columbia, USA. Director of Psychotherapy Training, University of Cincinnati, Department of Psychiatry. m. Jill Dolence 27 July 1985, Seattle, Washington. *Education:* AB, Chemistry, University of North Carolina, Chapel Hill; MD, University of North Carolina College of Medicine, Chapel Hill. *Appointments:* Medical Director, Outpatient Drug Dependency Treatment Unit, Cincinnati Veterans Adminsitration Hospital; Assistant Chief of Psychiatry, Cincinnati Veterans Administration Hosptial, Cincinnati. *Memberships:* American Psychiatry Association; Society for Psychotherapy Research; Association for the Advancement of Psychotherapy. *Publication:* 'Empathy and Outcome in a Brief Focal Dynamic Therapy', 'American Journal of Psychiatry', Aug. 1985. *Honours:* Columbus Award for Outstanding Physician Dedication; Hedgepeth Award. *Hobbies:* Skiing; Mountain Climbing; Music. *Address:* Central Psychiatric Clinic, University of Cincinnati, ML 539, Cincinnati, OH 45267-0539, USA.

FREELING, Paul, b. 5 Aug. 1928, London, England. Professor in General Practice and Primary Care, St George's Hospital. m. Shirley Valerie Stanley, 21 Oct. 1953, Hendon, England, 1 son, 1 daughter. *Education:* MB, BS, St Mary's Hospital Medical School. *Appointments:* Principal in General Practice; Senior Lecturer (part-time) in General Practice, King's College Hospital Medical School, London; Nuffield Tutor, Royal College of General Practitioners; Reader in General Practice, St George's Hospital Medical School, London. *Memberships:* Fellow, Royal College of General Practitioners. *Publications:* "In-service Training - A Study of the Nuffield Courses of the Royal College of General Practitioners", 1982; "The Future General Practitioner - Learning & Teaching (Jointly), 1972;

"Talking with Patients" (co-author), 1980; "The Doctor-Patient Relationship" (co-author), 3rd edition 1983; "Communication between Doctors" (co-author), 1984; "A Workbook for GP Trainees" (co-author), 1983. *Honours:* Order of the British Empire, 1981. *Hobbies:* Sailing; Chess; Bridge; Theatre; Music. *Address:* Department of General Practice, St George's Hospital Medical School, Cranmer Terrace, Tooting, London, SW17 0RE, England.

FREEMAN, Hugh Lionel, b. 4 Aug, 1929, Salford, England. Consultant Psychiatrist, Salford Health Authority; Editor, British Journal of Psychiatry; Honorary Lecturer, Universities of Manchester & Salford; consultant, WHO. m. Sally Joan Casket, 24 Mar. 1957, Manchester, 3 sons, 1 daughter. *Education:* MA, BM; BCh (Oxon); MSc.; DPM; FRC Psych. *Appointments:* House Surgeon, Neurosurgery, Manchester Royal Infirmary; House Physician, Withington Hospital, Manchester; Area Psychiatrist, Royal Army medical Corps; Registrar, BeBethelm Royal & Maudsley Hospitals, London; Senior Registrar, Littlemore Hospital, Oxford; Consultant Psychiatrist, Salford Royal Hospital. *Memberships:* Royal College of Psychiatrists, Chairman, Journal Committee, Member of Council, etc; Honorary Society of Clinical Psychiatirsts; Pembroke College, Oxford, Senior Common Room; Manchester Medical Society, Council Member, President, Section of Psychiatry, 1979; Collegium International Neuro-Psychopharcalogilum; European Association of Science Editors; many other professional organisations. *Publicaitons:* "Trends in the Mental Health Services", 1963; "Psychiatric Hospital Care", 1967; "New Aspects of the Mental Health Services", 1968; "Treatment of Mental Disorders in the Community", 1968; "Progress in Behaviour Therapy", 1969; "Progress in Mental Health", 1982; "Dangerousness", 1985; "Mental Health and the Environment", "Mental Health Services in Europe", "Schizophrenia New Pharmacological and Clinical Developments", 1986; "Planning Mental Health Services: The Way Ahead", (all edited); 22 Chapters in books; 59 papers in learned journals. *Honours:* Recipient, numerous honours and awards. *Address:* Hope Hospital, Salford M6 8HD, England.

FREEMAN, Jeremy Louis, b. 3 Mar. 1949, Hamilton, Ontario, Canada. Staff Otolaryngologist; Assistant Professor. m. Elayne Bonnie Naiman, 15 Dec. 1973, Toronto Canada, 2 daughters. *Education:* MD, University of Toronto Medical School, 1969. *Appointments Include:* Staff Otolaryngologist, Mount Sinai Hospital, Toronto, Ontario, 1980-; Toronto General Hospital, Toronto, 1982-; Sunnybrook Medical Centre, Toronto, 1983-; Consultant Otolaryngologist, Princess Margaret Hospital, Toronto, 1980-81; Toronto-Bayview Clinic, Toronto, 1981-; Workman's Compensation Board of Ontario, 1983; Assistant Professor of Otolaryngology, Faculty of Medicine, Univeristy of Toronto, 1980-. *Memberships Include:* American Academy of Facial Plastic and Reconstructive Surgery, 1983-; American Nasal and Facial surgery Institute, Vice President, 1979-; American Society for Head and Neck Surgery, 1980-; Ontario College of Physicians, 1978-; Ontario Medical Associaiton, 1978-. *Publications:* Several publicaitons in professional journals 'Late Post-Radiation Necrosis and Fibrosis of the Larynx' (with co-authors), 1984; 'The Clinical Significance of Radionuclide Bone and Gallium Scanning in Osteomyelittis of the Head and Neck' (co-authors). 1984; 'Hair Bearing Flaps in the Head and Neck Reconstructive Surgery' (co-author), 1984. *Honours Include:* ISSEI Scholarship in Medicine and Surgery; Gordon Richards Fellowship in Oncology; Mclauglin Travelling Fellowship. *Address:* Mount Sinai Hospital, 600 University Avenue, Suite 405, Toronto, Ontario M5G 1X5, Canada.

FREEMAN, Neill Verner, b. 19 Feb. 1930, Tabora, Tanzania. Consultant Paediatric and Neonatal Surgeon; Senior Lecturer in Paediatric Surgery. m. Pamela Amy MacGregor, 19 Jan. 1957, Johannesburg, Republic of South Africa, 3 daughters. *Education:* MB BCh, Witwatersrand University, 1954; Fellow, Royal College of Surgeons, Edinburgh, Scotland, 1959; Fellow, Royal College of Surgeons, England, 1964; 1st part MCh, Liverpool, 1964. *Appointments:* House Surgeon, Professorial Unit, General Hospital, Johannesburg, Republic of South Africa; Senior House Officer in Pediatric Surgery, Children's Hospital, Johannesburg; Senior House Officer in Orthopaedic Surgery, Princess Margaret Hospital, Edinburgh, Scotland; Senior House Officer in General Surgery, Redhill, Surrey, England; Medical Officer, Willamson Diamonds, Tanzania; Senior House Officer in Paediatric Surgery, Great Ormond Street Hospital, London, England; Registrar-Senior Registrar and Consultant, Alderley Children's Hospital, Liverpool; Consultant Paediatric Surgeon, Al Sabah Hospital, Kuwait; Currently Consultant Paediatric and Neonatal Surgeon and Senior Lecturer in Paediatric Surgery, Wessex Regional Centre for Paediatric Surgery, Southampton General Hospital, Southampton, England. *Memberships:* Council member, British Association of Paediatric Surgeons; Honorary Member, Polish Paediatric Surgeons; British Paediatric Gastroenterology Group; British Paediatric Association; Society for Research into Hydrocephalus and Spina Bifida. *Publications include:* 2 chapters in "Neonatal Surgery", 1969; 'Congenital Defects' in "Basic Clinical Surgery for Nurses and Medical Students", (McFarland), 1973 and 1980; 2 chapters in "Essential Surgical Practice", (editors A Cushieri, GR Giles and AR Moosa), 1982; Several articles in medical journals. *Hobbies:* Woodwork; Photography; Natural history. *Address:* 3 Blackwater House, Blackwater, Lyndhurst, Hampshire, SO43 7FJ, England.

FREITAG, Frederick Gerald, b. 12 Feb. 1952, Milwaukee, Wisconsin, USA. Staff Physician, Diamond Headache Clinic, Chicago. m., Lynn N. Stegner, 10 Sep. 1977, Milwaukee. *Education:* BSc, Biochemistry, University of Wisconsin, Madison, 1974; DO, Chicago College of Osteopathic Medicine, 1979. *Appointments:* Director, Twinsburg Family Clinic; Clinical Associate Professor, Ohio University College of Osteopathic Medicine; Visiting Lecturer, Department of Family Medicine, Chicago College of Osteopathic Medicine; Associate Staff, Louis A Weiss Memorial Hospital. *Memberships:* American Medical Association; American Osteopathic Association; American Association for the Study of Headache; American Association of Osteopathic Specialists (Headache); Illinois and Chicago Medical Societies; American Academy of Osteopathic Medicine; American College of General Practitioners in Osteopathic Medicine and Surgery; Illinois Association of Osteopathic Physicians and Surgeons; North American Academy of Manual Medicine. *Publications:* Author of numerous articles; Books: Contributor with others to: The Practising Physicians Approach to Headache (in press). *Hobbies:* German Oenologist; Goldfish raising and breeding; Home Carpentry. *Address:* c/o Diamond Headache Clinic, 5252 N. Western Avenue, Chicago, IL 60625, USA.

FREITAS E COSTA, Manuel Francisco, b. 27 Dec. 1928, Mocambique. Head of Department of Respiratory Diseases. m. Maria Amelia Pereira de Lima, 27 Jan 1960, Lisbon, 2 sons, 2 daughters. *Education:* Graduate in Medicine; MD; DSc; PhD. *Appointmetns:* Intern; President, Pneumology; Consultant, Pneumology; Assistant Professor; Full Professor; currently, Head, Department of Respiratory Diseases, Hospital Santa Maria. *Memberships:* Founder and President, Sociedade Protuguesa de Patologia Respiratoria; Founder, Societas Europaea Pneumologica; Governor for Portugal, International

College of Chest Physicians. *Publications:* "Broncoarteriografia Selectiva Apliccacao Clinica", 1971; "Biopsia Transtoracia nas Doencas Pulmonares Difusas", 1972; Author of 86 published articles in Portuguese, English, French, German, Italian and Dutch medical reviews. *Hobbies:* Cinema; Reading; Music; Squash. *Address:* Clinica de Doencas Pulmonares, Faculty of Medicine Lisbon, Av Prof egas Moniz, 1699 Lisboa, Portugal.

FRENCH, Charles Marcus, b. 13 June 1938, Dar Es Salaam, Tanganyika. Institute Director. *Education:* BA, 1959, BChir, 1962, MB, 1963, MA, 1963, MD, 1967, Cambridge University, England; DTM & H, Royal college of Physicians and Royal College of Surgeons, 1971; MRCGP, 1972. *Appointments:* Lecturer, Physiology, London Hospital Medical School, England, 1963-66; Royal Army Medical Corps, retired as Major, 1966-75; Research Officer in Charge, Research Unit, African Medical and Research Foundation, Kenya, 1976-83; Honorary Lecturer, Parasitology, Liverpool School of Tropical Medicine, England; currently, Director, Mumbiastros and Medicinal Pracitices Research Institute, Kenya. *Memberships:* Fellow; Royal society of Medicine; British and Kenyan Medical Associations; Life Member, Aero Club of East Africa. *Publications:* Co-author of papers contributed to 'Annals of Tropical Medicine and Parasitology' and 'East African Journal of Medicine'. *Honours:* Kenya Open Scholarship, 1955; Andrew Elliot Prize, London Hospital, England, 1962; De Chanmont Prize, 1967, Parks Medal, 1971, Katharine Webb Medal, 1971, Montetiore Medal, 1971, Leishaman Medal, 1st Order of Merit, 1971, Royal Army Medical Corps, London. *Hobbies:* Private pilot and aircraft operator; Life member, International Wine and Food Society; Classical music. *Address:* Mumbiastros, PO Box 11366, Nairobi, Kenya.

FRENKEL Eugene Phillip, b. 27 Aug. 1929, Detroit, Michigan, USA. Professor of Internal Medicine & Radiology. m. Rhoda Beth Smilay, 21 Dec. 1958, 1 son, 1 daughter. *Education:* Instructor in Medicine, Research Associate in Haematology-Oncology, University of Michigan, Simpson Memorial Institute, Ann Arbor VA Hospital, 1959-62; Assistant Professor, 1962, Associate Professor, 1966, Professor, 1969, Professor of Radiology & Internal Medicine, 1973, University of Texas Health Science Centre at Dallas (Southwestern Medical School); Chief, Section of Haematology-Oncology, Department of Internal Medicine, Univeristv of Texas, Dallas, 1962-. *Memberships:* Association of American Physicians; American Society for Clinical Investigation; American College of Physicians; American Society of Haematology; American Society of Clincial Oncology; American Society of Biological Chemists; American Association for Cancer Research; International Society of Haematology; American Federation for Clinical Research; International Association for the Study of Lung Cancer; and others. *Publications:* Over 170 publications in medical journals. *Honours:* Professorship of Clincial Oncology, American Cancer Society, 1973-78; Treasurer, American Society of Haematology, 1976-84; Associate Editor, Journal of Clinical Investigation, 1975-77; American Board of Internal Medicine, Board of Governors, 1980-85; Chairman, Membership Committee, American Society of Clinical Oncology, 1983-. *Address:* Division of Haematology-Oncology J5.126, Department of Internal Medicine, UTHSCD, 5323 Harry Hines Boulevard, Dallas, TX 75235-9030, USA.

FREUND, Deborah Anne, b. 9 June 1952, New York City, USA. University Professor. m. Thomas J Kneiser, 3 Jan 1981, New York City. *Education:* AB, Washington University; MA, MPH, PhD, The University of Michigan. *Appointments:* Program Officer, The Robert Wood Johnson Foundation; Economist, The National Center for Health Services Research; Assistant Professor, Associate Professor, The University of North Carolina. *Memberships:* The American Public Health Association; The American Economics Association. *Publications:* "Medicaid Reform: 4 studies of Case Management" 1984; 'Length of Stay: Differences between Voluntary and Proprietory Hospitals' Inquiry, 1985. *Honour:* Jay S. Drotman Award from the American Public Health Association, 1981. *Hobbies:* Tennis; Home design. *Address:* 263 Rosenau Building, The University of North Carolina, Chapel Hill, NC 27514, USA.

FREUND, Hans-Joachim, b. 17 Aug 1935, Neukirchen Moers, Germany, University Professor. m. Elsche Denecke. 8 Dec 1960, Hamburg, 3 sons. *Education:* MD, Universities of Hamburg and Freiburg, Federal Republic of Germany. *Appointments:* Assistant, Department of Physiology, 1962-64, Resident, Department of Neurology, 1964-68, Assistant, Department of Neurology, 1968-73, Professor Associate of Neurology, 1973-77, University of Freiburg. *Memberships:* German EEG Society, President 1983-84; German Neurological Association; German Physiological Association; Society of Neuroscience; American Neurological Association Corresponding Member. *Publications:* Various Contributions in journals and books. *Address:* Neurologische Universitatsklinik, Moorenstrasse, 5, D-4000 Dusseldorf, Federal Republic of Germany.

FREUND, Jerome Robert, b. 6 May 1940, Tilda, India. Director, The Counselling Center of the Florida Conference, United Methodist Church. m. Elisabeth Lee Patterson, 16 Sep. 1967, Norfolk, Virginia, USA. 1 son, 1 daughter. *Education:* BA, Westminister College, Fulton, Missouri, 1962; St. Mary's College, St. Andrews University, Scotland, 1963; M/Div, Union Theological Seminary, New York, 1968; Diploma, Ecole d'Administration, Brussels, Belgium, 1965; MS, 1970, PhD, 1972, University of Florida, Gainesville. *Appointments:* Counsellor, Brookwood Hall, E. Islip, New York; Associate Pastor, Dairsie and Flotta, Scotland; Missionary to Zaire and Malawi with Board of Global Min. UMC and Church World Service and Church of Central Africa, Presby; Youth Pastor, Elmhurst, New York; Mental Health Chaplain, Eastern State Hospital, Williamsburg, Virginia; Clinical Psychologist, Guidance Center, Daytona Beach; Clinical Psychologist, Comm. Mental Health Center, Eustis, Florida; Clinical Psychologist, Private Practice, Leesburg, Florida; Director, Florida Conference Counselling Center, Lakeland. *Memberships:* Zeta Tau Delta; Phi Kappa Phi; American Psychological Association; American Society for Clincial Hypnosis; Florida Conference United Church of Christ. *Honours include:* Fulbright Scholar, 1962-63. *Hobbies:* Flying (private pilot); Reading; Piano; Walking. *Address:* 714 Oakway Place, Glendale, MO 63122, USA.

FREUNDT, Eyvind Antonius, b. 1 Aug. 1919, Elsinore, Denmark. Professor of Medical Mircobiology. m. Jette Schultz, 26 July 1979, Fruering, 1 son. *Education:* Graduate in Medicine, University of Copenhagen, 1946; MD, 1959. *Appointments:* Scientific Assistant, later Chief Physician, Statens Serum Institute, Copenhagen, 1948-62; Head of Department & Lecturer in Veterinary Virology, Royal Veterinary & Agricultural College of Copenhagen, 1962-64; Professor of Medical Mircrobiolgoy (Virology), Univeristy of Aarhus, 1964-; Director, FAO/WHO Collaborating Centre for Animal Mvcoplasmas, University of Aarhus; Cuest Professor, Christian-Albrachts,-University, Kiel, Federal Republic of West Germany, 1981. *Memberships:* American Society of Microbiology; Society of General Microbiology;' ICSB Subcommittee on the Taxonomy of Mollicutes, (Chairman); World Federation of Culture Collections; International Organisation for Mycoplasmology, President, 1982-84. *Publications:* Numerous papers, especially on mycoplasmology, in international scientific journals, contributor to medical handbooks etc. *Honours:* Gold Medal for treatise on subject in Prehistoric archaeology, University of Copenhagen, 1946; Owesen Foundation Award 1966; Honorary Member, Indian Association of Medical Microbiologists, 1975; Kjærgaard Foundation award in science, 1983. *Hobbies:* Prehistoric Archaeology; Humanics. *Address:* Skovbrynet 13, DK-8660 Skanderborg, Denmark.

FRIBERG, Lars Torsten, b. 25 Feb. 1920, Malmö, Sweden. Professor of Environmental Hygiene. m. (1) Britt-Marie Friberg, 18 Aug. 1951, Stockholm, 3 sons; marriage dissolved, m. (2) Monika Lundin, 12 Apr. 1986. *Education:* MD, Karolinska Insitute, Stockholm, 1945; Doctor of Medical Sciences, 1950; Training in Internal Medicine, Occupational Medicine, Environmental Hygiene & Toxicology, 1945-56. *Appointments:* Professor, Chairman, Department of Environmental Hygiene, Karolinska Institute, 1957-; Visiting Professor, University of Cincinnati, USA; 1967; Director, WHO Collaborating Center of Environmental Health Effects, Karolinska Institute, 1976-; Division of Environmental Health, World Health Orgnaisation, Geneva, Switzerland, 1978; Director, National Institute of Environmental Medicine, Stockholm, 1980-. *Memberships:* WHO Advisory Board on Occupational Health; UN Joint Group of Experts on Scientific Aspects of Marine Pollution, 1981-; Chairman, Working Group on Potentially Harmful Substances; Board of International Commission on Occupational Health, 1975-81, Chairman, Scientific Committee on Toxicity of Metals, 1969-; Project Director, UNEP/WHO Global Biological Monitoring Programme, 1978-82; Member, Nobel Assembly, Karolinska Institute, 1957-85; Trustee, Nobel Foundation, 1984-85; Advisory Boards, Swedish Armed Forces, Board of Swedish Nuclear Power Inspectorate, 1981-86. *Publications:* Some 200 scientific papers, especialy on metal toxicology & Epidemiology; Contibuting Editor, various journals, especially in environmental reseach. *Honours:* Jubilee Prize, Swedish Society of Medical Sciences, 1955; William P Yant Award, American Industrial Hygiene Association, 1985; Honorary Member, New York Academy of Sciences, Corresponding Member, Purkinje Society, Finnish Industrial Medicine Society. *Hobbies:* Music (Cello, flute); Radio Amateur (SMO BTA). *Address:* Department of Environmental Hygiene, Karolinska Institute, S-104 01 Stockholm, Sweden.

FRIED, Marvin P., b. 10 June 1945, New York City, USA. Professor. *Education:* BS, City College of New York, 1965; MD, Tufts University School of Medicine, Boston, 1969. *Appointments:* Assistant & Fellow, Otolaryngology, Washington University School of Medicne, 1971-75; Fellow, National Institute of Neurological Disease & Stroke, 1971-75; Instructor, Otolaryngology, Eastern Virginia Medical School, 1975-77; Surgeon, Chief of Otolaryngology, US Public Health Service Hospital, Norfolk, 1975-77; Assistant Professor, 1977-79, Clinical Instructor, 1977-, Assistant Professor, 1979-83, Associate Professor, 1984-, Boston University School of Medicine. *Memberships include:* American Academy of Otalaryngology, Head & Neck Surgery Fellow; New England Otalaryngology Society; Massachusetts Medical Society; American Medical Association; Fellow, American College of Surgeons, Fellow; Royal Society of Medicine; New York Academy of Sciences; many other professional organisations. *Publications:* Articles in professional journals; Co-Author, "Manual of Otolaryngology", 1985; Co-author, "Complications of Laser Surgery of the Head & Neck", in press; "The Larynx", 1986. *Honours:* Phi Beta Kappa; New York City Council Jonas Salk Award for Study in the Field of Medicine, 1965; Anatomy Award, Tufts University School of Medicine, 1968; Recipient, 1st Place, Basic Research in Otalaryngology, American Academy of Ophthalmology and Otalaryngology, 1975; Boston University and Tufts Otalaryngology Teaching

Award, 1979; Edmund Prince Fowler Award for Basic Science Research, Triologic Society, 1984. *Address:* 140 Shaw Road, Brookline, MA 02167, USA.

FRIEDELL, Morris Theodore, b. 8 May 1913, Minneapolis, Minnesota, USA. President & Chairman of the Board, Jackson Park Hospital Foundation. m. Barbara Fishbein Friedell, 3 July 1937, 2 sons, 2 daughters. *Education:* BSc, 1936, MD, 1937, MS Surgery, 1940, University of Minnesota; Fellowship in Surgery, Mayo Foundation, 1937-41. *Appointments:* Attending Surgeon, Cook Country Hospital, Michael Reese & Mercy Hospitals; Chairman, Surgery, Jackson Park Hospital; President, Jackson Park Hospital; Chairman, Board of Directors, Hektoen Institute of Cook County Hospital. *Memberships:* International College of Surgeons; American Medical Association; American Board of Surgery; American College of Surgeons, Chicago Medical Society; Illionois State Medical Society; Alpha Omega Alpha; Sigma Xi; Chicago Surgical Society. *Publications:* Over 100 scientific & medical publications. *Honours:* Physicians Recognition Award, American Medical Association, 1984; Gold Medal Award, Phi Lambda Kappa, 1978; Letter of Service, US Navy (Submarines). *Hobbies:* Golf; Computers; Swimming; Reading. *Address:* 7531 Stony Island Avenue, Chicago, IL 60649 USA.

FRIEDLAENDER, Gary Elliott, b. 15 May 1945, Detroit, Michigan, USA. Professor & Chief, Orthopaedic Surgery, Yale University School of Medicine. m. Linda Beth Krohner, 16 Mar. 1969, Southfield, Michigan, 1 son, 1 daughter. *Education:* BS 1967, MD 1969, University of Michigan. *Appointments:* Director, US Navy Tissue Bank, 1974-76; Assistant Professor 1976-79, Associate Professor 1979-84, Professor & Chief or Orthopaedic Surgery 1984-, Yale University; Chief, Orthopaedic Surgery, Yale-New Haven Hospital, 1984-. *Memberships include:* American Academy of Orthopaedic Surgeons; American College of Surgeons; American Council on Transplantation; American Association of Tissue Banks; American Society of Transplant Surgeons; Transplantation Society; Society for Surgical Oncology; etc. *Publications:* Over 100 scientific articles, chapters, books & abstracts including: "Osteochondral Allografts: Biology, Banking & Clincial Applications", co-editor, 1983; "Tissue Banking for Transplatation", with K.W.Sell, 1976. *Honours:* Kappa Delta Award, outstanding research, 1982; President, American Council on Transplation, 1983-85; President, American Association of Tissue Banks, 1983-85; Presidential Guest Lecturer, British Orthopaedic Research Society, 1984; Honorary MA, Yale University, 1984. Consulting editor, research, 'Journal, Bone & Joint Surgery', 1981; Board, advising editors, 'Clinical Orthopaedic & Related Research', 1986-; Member, Orthopaedic & Musculoskeletal Study Section, National Institutes of Health, 1985-89. *Address:* Yale University School of Medicine, 333 Cedar Street, New Haven, CT 06510, USA.

FRIEDLANDER, Robert Lynn, b. 9 Nov. 1933, Detroit, Michigan, USA. Medical College President and Dean. m. Mary Louise Cloon, 27 Nov. 1960, 2 daughters. *Education:* BS Chemistry 1955, MD 1958, Wayne State University, Detroit, Michigan. *Appointments Include:* Resident 1962-63, Chief Resident 1964, Assistant Attending 1965, Dispensary 1969, Acting Chairman 1971-72, Department of Obstetrics and Gynecology, Albany Medical Center Hospital; Instructor 1964, Assistant Professor 1965, Associate Professor 1969, Acting Chairman 1971-72, Medical Coordinator Primary Care Preceptorship Training Program 1972-75, Assistant to Dean 1973, Assistant Dean 1974, Professor in Department of Obstetrics and Gynecology 1976, Associate Dean 1976, Executive Associate Dean 1978, Acting

President and Dean 1979, President and Dean 1980 -, Albany Medical College. *Memberships:* New York Academy of Medicine; Association of American Medical Colleges; American Medical Association; Medical Society of State of New York; American College of Obstetricians and Gynecologists; New York Academy of Sciences; Alpha Omega Alpha. *Publications Include:* 'Oral Medroxyprogesterone Acetate in the Management of Endometriosis', (with E S Henriques, V R Raman and D P Swartz), 1978; 'Long-Term Follow-Up of Endometriosis Treated with Danazol'; 'Endometriosis: A Case-Study Approach to Diagnosis and Treatment', (with R W Kistner as commentator), 1979; 'The Role of the Faculty', 1983. *Honours Include:* Lederle Laboratories Fellowship, 1955; NIH Research Fellowship, 1957; Certification, American Board of Obstetrics and Gynecology, 1967; Distinguished Alumnus of the Year, Wayne State University, 1980. *Hobby:* Photography. *Address:* 47 New Scotland Avenue, Albany,NY 12208, USA.

FRIEDMAN, Eli A, b. 9 Apr. 1933, USA. Professor of Medicine; Chief of Renal Division, Downstate Medical Center. m. Berrett-Lennard, 16 June 1957, Brooklyn, New York, 3 daughters. *Education:* BS; MD, Downstate Medical Center, 1957; DSc, Madras University, India, 1985. *Appointments:* Instructor in Medicine, Emory University, 1961-63; Assistant Professor of Medicine, 1963-67, Associate Professor of Medicine, 1968-71; Professor of Medicine, 1971-, Downstate Medical Center. *Memberships:* Transplantation Society; American College of Physicians; Association of American Physicians; American Society of Nephrology. *Publications:* Books: "Strategy in Renal Failure", 1978; "Dietetic Renal-Retinal Syndrome", 1980; "Diabetic Nephropathy", 1985; 250 Papers. *Honour:* Alumni Medallion, Downstate Medical Center, 1978. *Hobbies:* Photography; Exploration. *Address:* Box 52, Downstate Medical Center, 450 Clarkson Avenue, Brooklyn, NY 1203, USA.

FRIEDMAN, Herman, b. 22 Sept. 1931, Philadelphia, USA. Professor and Department Chairman. m. Ilona, 27 Dec, 1958, 1 son, 3 daughters. *Education:* AB, 1953. AM, 1955; PhD, 1957. *Appointments:* Instructor, Hahnemann Medical College, Philadelphia, USA, 1957-58; Chief, Allergy Research Laboratory, Pittsburg VA Hospital, 1958-59; Head, Department of Microbiology, Albert Einstein Medical Centre, Philadelphia, 1959-78; Professor and Chairman, Department of Medical Microbiology, University of South Florida, Tampa, Florida, 19 8-. *Memberships:* American Association of Immunology; Society of Experimental Biology and Medicine; American Society of Microbiology; American Academy of Allergy; American Acadmey of Microbiology, etc. *Publications:* Editor or author of 40 books; author or co-author of 450 articles. *Honours:* President Eastern Pennysylvania American Society of Microboiology, 1970-72; Outstanding Alumni Award, Hahnemann Medical College, 1971; President, Florida American Society of Microbiology, 1982-84. *Address:* University of South Florida College of Medicine, Box 10, 12901 North 30th Street, Tampa, FL 33612, USA.

FRIEDMAN, Marion, b. 15 Aug. 1918, Onley, Virginia, USA. Associate Chief of Medicine, North Charles General Hospital. m. Esther Lerner, 29 May 1941, Baltimore, Maryland, 1 son. *Education:* BS, University of Maryland College of Arts and Sciences, 1938; MD, University of Maryland School of Medicine, 1942; Rotating Internship, US Marine Hospital, Norfolk, 1942-43; Resident in Internal Medicine, US Marine Hospital, Baltimore, Maryland, 1946-49. *Appointments:* Assistant Health Officer, Montgomery County, Kansas; Health Officer, Cherokee County, Kansas; Assistant Health Commissioner, St. Louis County, Missouri; Assistant in Medicine, University of Maryland School of Medicine; President of Staff, North

Charles General Hospital; President, Maryland Academy of Family Physicians; Private Practice of Family Medicine and Internal Medicine, 1949-84. *Memberships:* Baltimore City Medical Society; Medical and Chirurgical Faculty of State of Maryland; American Medical Association; Maryland Academy of Family Physicians; Fellow (charter), American Academy of Family Physicians; Fellow, Pan-American Medical Association; American Physicians Fellowship Incorprorated for Medicine in Israel; Associate Member, World Medical Association; Maryland Heart Association; American Heart Association; American Thoracic Society; Maryland Thoracic Society, Phi Lambda Kappa; Phi Kappa Phi. *Publications:* Presentations; Papers; Scientific Exhibits; First in world to suggest use of cortisone use in treatment of subedeltoid bursitis. *Hobbies:* Gardening; Photography; Stamp and Coin collecting. *Address:* 7906 Terrapin Court, Baltimore, MD 21208, USA.

FRIEDRICH, Eduard Georg, b. 21 Oct. 1937, Chicago, Illinois, USA. Professor of Obstetrics and Gynaecology. *Education:* HAB 1963. LL D Honours 1982, Xavier University, Cincinnati, Ohio; MD,JOHNS Hopkins University, Baltimore, Maryland, 1963. *Appointments:* Pathology Instructor 1970, Obstetrics/Gynaecology Instructor 1970, Assistant Professor 1972, Associate Professor 1976, Medical College of Wisconsin, Milwaukee; Director Medical Research, Kimberley-Clark Corporation, 1976-79; Professor and Chairman, Department of Obstetrics/Gynaecology, University of Florida, 1979-. *Memberships:* Secretary-General 1970-79, President 1982, International Society for the Study of Vulvar Disease; Vice-President 1984, International College of Surgeons; Fellow, American Gynaecologist and Obstetricians Society; Fellow, American College of Obstetricians and Gynaecologists; Vice-president 1980, American Venereal Disease Association. *Publications:* "Vulvar Disease", 1983; "Poems", 1983; 'Serum levels of sex hormones in Vulvar Lichen Sclerosus', 1984; 'Foundations of the Arch'. 1984; 'Genetic Aspects of Lichen Sclerosus', 1984. *Honours:* Senior Class Award for Teaching Excellence, 1974; ACOG Film Award, Motion Picture of the Year, 1979; Outstanding Residency Program Director, ACOG Dist IV, 1983. *Hobbies:* Sailing; Shooting; Singing; Poetry. *Address:* Box J-294 JHMHC, Gainesville, FL 32610, USA

FRIEND, Gary Jay, b. 20 June 1951, New York City, USA. Podiatrist. m. Lois Wolff, 25 May 1975, Rochester, New York, USA. *Education:* BA, Biology, State University of New York at Buffalo, 1973; DPM, Pennsylvania College of Podiatric Medicine, 1977. *Memberships:* American Academy of Podiatric Sports Medicine; American Podiatric Medical Association. *Publications:* "Sequential Metatarsal Stress Fractures after Keller Arthroplaty with Implant" in "Journal of Foot Surgery" 1981; "Correction of elongated under lapping lesser toes by middle phalangectomy and skinplasty" in "Journal of Foot Surgery" 1984. *Hobby:* Photography. *Address:* 459 Lake Cook Road, Box 326, Deerfield, IL 60015, USA.

FRIESEN, James Donald, b. 4 Nov. 1935, Saskatchewan, Canada. University Professor and Chairman, Department of Medical Genetics. m. Lynn Arnason, 6 Sep. 1958, Saskatoon, 2 sons, 1 daughter. *Education:* BA 1956, MA 1958, Department of Physics, University of Saskatchewan; PhD, Department of Medical Biophysics, University of Toronto, 1962. *Appointments:* Assistant Professor 1965-67, Associate Professor 1967-69, Department of Physics, Kansas State University, Kansas, USA: Associate Professor, 1969-72, Professor 1972-81, Department of Biology, York University, Ontario, Canada; Professor and Chairman, Department of Medical Genetics, University of Toronto, Ontario, 1981-. *Memberships:* American Society of

Microbiology. *Publications:* 77 publications. *Address:* Department of Medical Genetics, Medical Sciences Building, University of Toronto, Toronto, Ontario M5S 1A8, Canada.

FRIGAS, Evangelos, b. 26 Sept. 1945, Greece, Consultant. m. Carole Bobroski, 6 Sept. 1974, Lond Island, New York, USA. *Education:* MD, Graduate University of Rome, 1971; FACP; FAAAI. *Appointments:* Consultant, Internal Medicine, Allergy/Immunology Mayo Clinic, 1980. *Memberships:* Fellow, American College of Physicians; American Academy of Allergy/Immunology; Member, American Medical Association. *Publications:* "Increased Levels of Eosinophil Major Basic Protein in Paitents with Asthma", (Co-author), 1981; 'Dosage Radioimmunologique de la Protein Basique du Granule Eosinophile Dans L'Expectoration. Un Appoint Diagnostique Dans L Asthme', (co-author), 1983; "Eosinophils in Bronchial Asthma", book Chapter, (co-author), forthcoming. *Honours:* MD, cum laude, 1971; FACP, 1983; FAAAI, 1983. *Address:* Mayo Clinic, 200 First Street SW, Rochester, MN 55905, USA.

FRIIS-HANSEN, Bent Julius, b. 2 Feb 1920, Copenhagen , Denmark. Paediatrician/University Professor. m. Bente Marianne Wessel, 20 Aug 1964, 2 sons. *Education:* MD, PhD, RaD. *Appointments:* Research Fellow, Harvard Medical school, Boston, USA, 1948-50; Physician in Chief, Department of Neonatology, University Hospital, Rigshospitalet, 1964; Visiting Professor, Babies Hospital, Columbia University, New York, 1968; Professor in Pediatrics and Neonatology, Departmewtn of Neonatology, University Hospital, Rigshospitalet, 1970 -. WHO Nutritionist and Head of Health and Nutrition Scheme, Zambia, 1958-59; Director of WHO Danish seminar on malnutrition in Kenya, 1969 and in Thailand 1971. Chairman, WHO International Paediatric Association Workshop, Buenos Aires, 1970-81; Co-founder and Associate Editor, Journal of Paediatric Research 1967-72; Member of Advisory Board of Acta Paediatrica Scandinavica. Member (ass.) Danish Board of Technical assistance to developing countries DANIDA 1964-81; Visiting Professor, Brown University, 1984. *Memberships:* European Society for Pediatric Research; Danish Pediatric Society; International Pediatric Association; Danish Society for Family Planning; The New York Academy of Sciences. *Publications:* Editor in Chief, "Scandinavian Textbook of Paediatrics" 7th edition, 1973 8th edition 1978 and 9th edition 1985; Co-editor: "Intensive Care in the Newborn" vol 1 1977, vol II 1979, Vol III 1981. "Physiologic Foundations of Perinatal Care" 1985; More than 100 scientific papers. *Honours:* Knight of the Order of Dannebrog, 1979; The Odd Fellow Orden, Denmark, Jubilee Prize for Research, 1969; Consul General Ernst Karlsen's Foundation Research Prize, 1974; NOVO Pharmaceutical Ltd Foundation, The Novo Prize, 1979; Honorary Scientific Adviser to Foundation Princesse Marie Christine, Belgium and to International Center for Child Studies, Bristol and to Pediatric Societies of Finland, Austria, and France Neonatal Society, England and Nordic Pediatric Association; Swedish Paediatric Association The Niels Rosen von Rosenstein Medal, 1984. *Hobbies:* Tennis; Sailing. *Address:* Department of Neonatology, University Hospital, Rigschospitalet, Blegdamsvej 9, DK-2100 Copenhagen, Denmark.

FRIMAN, L Göran G, b. 17 Feb. 1940, Säffle, Sweden. Head, Director, Infectious Diseases. m. G. Margareta Jonsson, 5 Jan. 1968, Uppsala, 1 son, 2 daughters. *Education:* MD, 1967, PhD, 1976, Uppsala University; Diploma, Tropical Medicine, Karolinska Institute, 1984. *Appointments:* Internship, Residency, Internal Medicine & Cardiology, Academic Hospital, Uppsala, 1967-70, Infectious Diseases and Clinical Physiology, 1970-76;

Consultant, Lecturer, Infectious Diseases, Academic Hospital, 1976-81; Research Fellow, 1978-79, US Army Medical Research Institute of Infectious Diseases, Fort Detrick, Frederick, Maryland, USA; Head, Director, Infectious Diseases, Academic Hospital, Uppsala, 1981-. *Memberships:* Swedish Medical Association; Infectious Diseases Society; American Federation for Clinical Research; Scandinavian Society for Antimicrobial Cheotherapy; Swedish Society for Tropical Medicine. *Publications:* Articles in professional journals including: 'Journal of Infectious Diseases'; 'Acta Med. Scand.'. *Hobbies:* Languages; History; Wines; Exercise. *Address:* Dept. of Infectious Diseases, Academic Hospital, S 751 85 Uppsala, Sweden.

FRINDEL, Emilia, b. 1925. *Education:* MD, University of Paris. *Appointments:* Director, 250 Cell Kinetics Research Unit, Institut National de la Sante et de la Recherche Medicale, 1960. *Memberships:* European Tissue Culture Society; International Society of Differentation; European Cell Biology; International Society for Experimental Haematology; Cell Kinetic Society; Radiation Research Society; European Stem Cell Club; American Association for Cancer Research. *Address:* 250 Cell Kinetics Research Unit, Institut National de la Sante et de la Recherche medicale, rue Camille Desmoulins, 94805 Villejuif, France.

FRISELL, Wilhelm Richard, b. 27 Apr. 1920, Two Harbors, Minnesota, USA. Chairman and Professor of Biochemistry. m. Margaret Jane Fleagle, 6 Mar. 1948, 2 sons. *Education:* BA summa cum laude, St Olaf College, 1942; MA 1943, PhD 1946, The Johns Hopkins University. *Appointments:* Research Associate, the Johns Hopkins University, 1946-47; Postdoctoral Fellow and Instructor in Physiological Chemistry, Johns Hopkins School of Medicine, 1947-51; John G Berquist Fellowship, American Scandinavian Foundation, Uppsala University, Sweden, 1949-50; Assistant Professor 1951-58, Associate Professor 1958-64, Professor 1964-69, University of Colorado School of Medicine; Professor and Chairman Department of Biochemistry 1969-76, Acting Dean of Graduate School of Biomedical Sciences 1971-73, College of Medicine and Dentistry of New Jersey,New Jersey Medical School; Professor and Chairman, Department of Biochemistry, Assistant Dean for Graduate Affairs, School of Medicine East Carolina University, 1976-. *Memberships:* American Scoiety of Biological Chemists; Fellow, American Association for the Advancement of Science; American Chemical Society; President Colorado chapter 1968-69, Sigma Xi; New York Academy of Sciences; Harvey Society; Society for Experimental Biology and Medicine; American Society of Microbiologists; Secretary 1980-83, Vice-President 1983-85, The Johns Hopkins Alumni Association of North Carolina; Secretary, Association of Medical School Biochemistry Departments, 1984-86; Phi Beta Kappa. *Publications:* "Acid-Base Chemistry in Medicine", 1968; "Human Biochemistry", 1982; 64 technical publications. *Honours Include:* Golden Apple Award, 1972; Centennial Award, University of Colorado School of Medicine, 1983. *Hobbies:* Oil Painting; Philately. *Address:* 209 Fairlane Road, Greenville, NC 27834, USA

FROM, Henri (Heinrich Karl), b. 18 Dec. 1947, Kümmersbruck, Oberpfalz, Federal Republic of Germany. Professor of Experimental Psychoanalysis. m. Amanda Lear, 1977. *Education:* in colleges with Professors, privately; qualifications in psychology, mental disorders, Psychoanalysis; social, art & law education. *Appointments:* Director of the Henri From Group International Co., 1970-85; Art Advisor, Babylon Gallery, Brussels, Belgium, 1978; Senator; Counsellor of Arts; General Secretary, Academy, Citta di Boretto; General Manager of Bank, Asfine & Creamberg; General

Manager of SOSJ; Instructor of the Supreme Court of Justice, Federal Republic of Germany. *Memberships:* World Association of Psychiatry; Acadmey of Sciences, Paris, France; German Acadmey for Psychoanalysis; Accademia Tiberina; Acadmey of Noble Sciences; LE Education Social, Paris; University Humanum del Vita. *Publications:* "Book of Art & Psychoanalysis" (2 volumes), 1978. *Honours:* Oscar de France, LUBP, Paris; Encouragement Public, Paris; LEES, Paris; Gold Medal, Silver Medal, Tiberina etc. *Hobby:* Cycle Racing, 1964-85. *Address:* Postfach 1431, D-8450 Amberg/Oberpfalz, Federal Republic of Germany.

FROMM, David, b. 21 Jan 1930, New York, USA. Professor and Chairman, m, Barbara Solter, 13 June 1961, 2 sons, 1 daughter. *Education:* MD, California; FACS. *Appointments:* Assistant professor of Surgery, 1973-78, Associate Professor of Surgery, 1977-78, Harvard Medical School; Professor and Chairman, Department of Surgery, State University of New York Health Science Centre, Syracuse, 1978-. *Memberships:* American Surgical Association; Society for Clinical Surgery; The Society of University Surgeons; American Gastro-intestinal Association. *Publications:* "Complications of Gastric Surgery", 1977; "Gastrointestinal Surgery", (author, editor), 1985; Contributor to numerous scientific journals. *Honours:* Grantee, NIH career development; NIH Research. *Hobbies:* Sailing; Skiing. *Address:* Department of Surgery, University Hospital, 750 E Adams Street, Syracuse, NY 13210, USA.

FROST, Dwight Maurice, b. 20 Aug. 1920, Fort Wayne, Indiana, USA. Medical Director, Immanuel Rehabilitation Centre, Immanuel Medical Centre, Omaha. m. Carol Lanham Frost, 15 Apr. 1967, Omaha, 2 sons, 3 daughters. *Education:* BS, Medicine; MD. *Appointments:* Founder, University Nebraska, Douglas County Rehabilitation Centre, Omaha, 1955; Chairman, PMR Department, Nebraska College of Medicine, 1955-68; Medical Director, Founder, Childrens Therapy Centre, Omaha, 1958-60; Director, Amputee Clinic, Nebraska College of Medicine, 1955-68; Medical Director, Immanuel Rehabilitation Centre, Omaha, 1968-. *Memberships:* Metro Omaha Sarpy Medical Society; Nebraska Medical Society; American Medical Association; American Congress of Rehabilitation Medicine; International Society PM & R; International Society of Inst. Fellows. *Honours:* Nebraska Physician of the Year, 1970; Distinguished Service Award, Immanuel Medical Centre, 1979. *Hobbies:* Travel; Fishing; Horticulture. *Address:* 4929 East Ridge Drive, Omaha, NE 68134, USA.

FRY, William James, b. 28 Mar. 1928, Ann Arbor, Michigan, USA. University Professor and Chairman. m. Martha Earl, 18 June, 1949, Detroit, Michigan, USA, 2 sons. *Education:* MD, University of Michigan Medical School, 1952. *Appointments include:* Associate Professor of Surgery, 1964-67, Chief, Red Surgical Service, 1964-67, University of Michigan Medical School; Head, Section of General Surgery, 1967-74, Professor of Surgery, 1967-76, University of Michigan; Senior Active Medical Staff, Parkland Memorial Hospital, Dallas, Texas, 1976-; Active Attending Staff, Children's Medical Center, Dallas, 1976-; Chief of Surgical Services, Parkland Memorial Hospital, Dallas, 1976-. *Memberships include:* American College of Surgeons; American Surgical Association; American Board of Surgery; Society for Vascular Surgery; International Society for Cardiovascular Surgery. *Publications:* Numerous chapters on various aspects of Surgery in learned medical textbooks. *Honours:* Lee Hudson-Robert Penn Professorship, University of Texas Southwestern Medical School, 1976-; Frederick A Coller Professorship, University of Michigan Medical School, 19740-76; Galens Shovel Honorary Medical Society, University of Michigan Medical School, 1970. *Hobby:* Golf. *Address:* Department of Surgery, University of Texas Health Science Center,

Southwestern Medical School, 5323 Harry Hines Boulevard, Dallas, TX 75235, USA.

FRYKLÖF, Lars-Einar, b. 23 Sept. 1929, Stockholm, Sweden. Managing Director, Swedish Pharmaceutical Society. m. (2) Maud Forsslund, 25 Apr. 1981, Stockholm, 1 son, 2 daughters; 2 step-sons. *Education:* MSc Pharmacy, 1954; PhD Pharmaceutics, 1957. *Appointments:* Lecturer in Pharmaceutics, Royal Pharmaceutical Institute, Stockholm, 1954-69; Research Scientist, Central Laboratory of the Pharmaceutical Society, Stockholm, 1956-59; Assistant Manager, 1959-63, Technical Manager, 1963-70, Pharmaceutical Society, Stockholm; President, ACO Läkemedel AB (ACO Pharmaceuticals Ltd), Stockholm, 1971-79; Managing Director, Swedish Pharmaceutical Society, Stockholm, 1979-. *Directorships:* National Bacteriological Laboratory, Stockholm, 1973-, Deputy Chairman, 1982-; Deputy Chairman, ACO Läkemedel AB, Stockholm; Swedish Pharmaceutical Press, 1979, Chairman, 1981-; Association of Swedish Cooperative Building Societies, 1965-, Deputy Chairman since 1971. *Publications:* Some 25 papers, especially on autoxidation of essential oils, mixing problems, sustained release preparations (inventor of the Durules principle) & rheology. *Address:* Swedish Pharmaceutical Society, P.O. Box 1136, S-111 81 Stockholm, Sweden.

FRYKLUND, Linda, b. 27 Feb. 1945, Sweden. Director of Research and Development, Peptide Hormones, KabiVitrum AB. m. (1) 19 June 1965, Pinner, England; (2) Mats Jernfält, 15 Jan. 1983, Sollentuna, Sweden, 1 son, 2 daughters. *Educatio* University of Bristol, England; University Uppsala, Sweden; BSc, Biochemistry, 1966; Phil.Li 1970; PhD, Biochemistry, 1973. *Appointments* Junior Lecturer, Department of Biochemsitry, University of Uppsala, 1966-73; Protein Chemist, KabiVitrum, R & D, Stockholm, Sweden, 1973-76; Docent in Biochemistry, 1975. *Memberships:* Swedish Biochemistry Society; Swedish Society of Endocrinology. *Publications:* Conference Proceedings; Contributor to professional journals including: Co-author: 'Serum Levels of Immunoreactive Somatomedin A in the Rat: Some developmental aspects', 'Endocrinology', 1980; Co-author: 'Somatomedins', 'Excerpta Med.', Volume 500, 1980; Co-author: "Somatomedin B: Mitogenic activity derived from contaminent epidermal growth factor", 'Science', 1981. *Hobbies:* Gardening; Music; Painting. *Address:* KabiVitrum AB, R & D Peptide Hormones, S-112 87 Stockholm, Sweden.

FUHRMANN, Walter Johann Georg, b. 12 Sept. 1924, Berlin, Germany Director, Institute of Human Genetics, Justus Liebig Universitat, Giessen. m. Annemarie Fuhrmann-Rieger, 30 Sep. 1958, Berlin, 1 son, 2 daughters. *Education:* Dr. Med., Freie Universitat, Berlin, 1951; Speciality Boards, Pediatrics, 1958; Venia Legendi in Pediatrics, 1961; Venia Legendi, Pediatrics & Human Genetics, Universitat Heildelberg, 1964. *Appointments:* Internship, Residnecy, Elizabeth, New Jersey, Boston, Massachusetts, USA, 1951-53; Assistant Physician, Universitatskinderklinik, Freie Universitat Berlin, 1954-62; Fellowship, Childrens Memorial Hospital, North Western University, Chicago, USA, 1963; Privatdozent, Institut fur Humangenetik der Universitat Heidelberg, 1964-67; Professor, Director, Institute of Human Genetics, University Giessen, 1967-. *Memberships:* Gesellschaft fur Anthropologie und Humangenetik; Deutsche Gesellschaft fur Kinderheilkunde; Gesellschaft fur Genetik; European Society of Human Genetics; Clinical Genetics Society. *Publications:* "Taschenbuch der allgemeinen und klinschen Humangenetik", 1965; "Genetische Familienberatung", co-author, 1968, 3rd edition, 1982 (also in English, Spanish, Japanese, Italian, Portuguese Polish); numerous artticles & book chapters. *Address:* Institute of

Human Genetics, Am Schlangenzahl 14, D 6300 Giessen, Germany.

FUJIMOTO, Takeo, b. 30 Mar 1936, Miyazaki, Japan. University Professor. m. Motoko Horio, 14 June 1963, Miyazaki, Japan, 3 sons. *Education:* MD, Kyoto Prefectural University of Medicine, 1960; PhD, Kyushu University School of Medicine, 1972. *Appointments:* Internship, Kyoto Citizen Hospital, Kyoto, Japan, 1960-61; Residency in Pediatrics, 1961-64, Fellow in Pediatrics, 1964-69, Kyushu University Hospital; Clinical Fellow in Pediatrics, University of Texas System Cancer Center, M D Anderson Hospital and Tumor Institute, 1969-71; Lecturer in Pediatrics, Aichi Medical University, 1979-. *Memberships:* Chairman, Children's Cancer and Leukemia Study Group of Japan; Councilor, Japan Society of Clinical Hematology; American Society of Clinical Oncology; Corresponding Member, American Association for Cancer Research; Councilor, Japan Hematological Society; councilor, Japanese Academy of Pediatrics, 1984-, Director, 1984-, Editorial Board, 1985-; Corresponding Member, Children's Cancer Study Group in USA. *Publications:* 'Childhood Cancer: Current Topics and Comprehensive Care' 1984; "Treatment of Childhood Acute Leukemia" in "Acta Hematology, Japan" 1980; etc. *Honours:* Research Awards for "Prognositc Factors and Treatment Regimes in Childhood Hematologic Malignacies" Japanese Foundation for Multidisciplinary Treatment of Cancer, 1982. Special Award for "Multicentral Co-operative Studies for Treatment in Childhood Cancer" Tokai Acadmey of Science, 1983. *Hobby:* Tennis. *Address:* 54-2 Shimodouchi, Inokoshi, Itaka-cho, Meito, Nagoya, Japan 465.

FUJINAGA, Kei, b. 8 July 1931, Fukuoka, Japan. Professor/Director, Cancer Research Institute. 1 son, 1 daughter. *Education:* MS, Biochemistry, PhD, Microbiology, Hokkaido University. *Appointments:* Instructor, Hokkaido University, School of Medicine, Sapporo; Senior Scientist, Institute for Molecular Virology, St Louis University Medical School, St Louis, Missouri, USA, 1964-68; Section Head, Aichi Cancer Research Institute, Nagayo, 1968-71; Professor, Director of Cancer Research Institute, Sapporo Medical College. *Memberships:* ASM; The Japanese Cancer Association; The Japanese Biochemical Society; The Molecular Biology Society of Japan; The Society of Japanese Virologist. *Publications:* 'Fundamental Technique in Virology' co-author, 1969; "Molecular Biology in Cancer" (in Japanese) 1976; 'Curr. Top. Microbiol. Immunol.' co-author, 1984. *Honour:* The Hokkaido Kagaku Gizyutsu Sho, 1983. *Hobbies:* Skiing; Golf. *Address:* 6-25, Asahigaoka 5 chöme, chuo-ku, Sapporo 060, Japan.

FUJITA, Michiya, b. 19 July 1933, Osaka, Japan. Professor of Biochemistry. m. Taeko, 1960, Tokyo, 2 sons, 1 daughter. *Education:* BM, University of Tokyo; DMSc, University of Tokyo Postgraduate School. *Appointment:* Associate Professor, Tokyo Medical and Dental University School of Medicine, 1972-78. *Memberships:* Japanese Society of Biochemistry; Japanese Society of Physiology; Japanese Society of Cell Biology; Japanese Society of Membrane Science; Japanese Society of Gastroenterology. *Publications:* "Bioassembly Lines: A General Mechanism for Maintaining the Specific Architecture of A Cell", 1982; "Asymmetric Distribution of Ouabain-Sensitive At Pase in Intestinal Mucosa", 1971. *Hobbies:* Water Colour Painting; Old Books. *Address:* Hamamatsu University School of Medicine, 3600 Handa-Cho, Hamamatsu 431-31, Japan.

FUKUSHIMA, Masanori, b. 30 Nov. 1948, Nagoya, Japan. Cancer Center Section Head. m. Masae Maehara, 29 May 1973, Nagoya, 1 son, 2 daughters. *Education:* MD, Nagoya University School of Medicine, 1973; PhD, Kyoto University, 1979.

Appointments: Resident, Nagoya Red Cross Hospital, 1973-74; Assistant Professor, Department of Biochemistry, Hamamatsu University School of Medicine, 1976-78; Visiting Assistant Professor, Department of Pharmacology, Baylor College of Medicine, Houston, Texas, USA 1980; Section Head, Department of Internal Medicine, Aichi Cancer Center. *Memberships:* Japanese Biochemical Society; Japanese Cancer Association; American Federation for Clinical Research; American Association for Cancer Research; American Society of Clinical Oncology. *Publications:* Contributor to various medical journals. *Honours:* Japanese Cancer Association Award, 1985; Editorial Board, Japanese Journal of Cancer Research, 1986. *Hobbies:* Playing with the children; Travelling. *Address:* Aichi Cancer Center, Tashiro-cho, Chikusa-ku, Nagoya 464, Japan.

FULTON, Woodrow Wilson, b. 1 Aug. 1917, Neshoba, Mississippi, USA. Director, Physical Therapy, StaHome Health Agency Incorporated. m. Ophia Fox Blanton, 19 Oct. 1942, Clinton, Mississippi, 1 daughter. *Education:* BA, Mississippi College, Clinton, 1942; MA, University of Alabama, Tuscaloosa, 1951; RPT, Tulane University and Charity Hospital, New Orleans, 1956; Prosthetics, New York University, 1957; Post-graduate Study, Millsaps, University Center, Jackson. *Appointments:* Associate Professor of Health and Physical Education and Athletic Coach, Mississippi College, Clinton, 1946-55; Technical Director and Chief Therapist University Medical Center Hospital, 1956-58; Executive Director, Alumni Relations and Assistant to President, Mississippi College, Clinton, 1958-61; Executive Director an Chief Therapist, Greenwood Leflore Hospital, Greenwood, 1962-81; Self-employed Physical Therapist, Contractual Quality Home Health Agency, 1981-83; Physical Therapist, StaHome Health Agency Incorporated, 1984-. *Memberships:* Retired Officers Association; Mississippi Gulf Coast Retired Officers Association; Charter Member, Republican Presidential Task Force, 1985; American Physical Therapy Association; Phi Delta Kappa. *Honours:* Nathan H Palmer Academic Award, 1956; Little All-American Football Sports Hall of Fame; Service Award, Greenwood Leflore Hospital, 1977; Community Affairs Award, First Baptist Church, Greenwood, 1977; Purple Heart, 1944. *Hobbies:* Reading; Fishing; Sports; Hunting. *Address:* 210 Walda Drive, Biloxi, MS 39531, USA.

FURLAN-HRABAR, Jana, b. 14 July 1931, Ljubljana, Yugoslavia. Consultant, Pneumonology, University Institute Golnik. m. Dr Bogo Hrabar, 30 Aug. 1958, divorced, 1 son, 1 daughter. *Education:* MD; DRSc.; Assistant Professor. *Appointments:* Chief, Pneumonology; Assistant, Internal Medicine, Assistant Professor, Internal Medicine, Medical Faculty Ljubljana. *Memberships:* President, Slovene Association for Allergology and Clinical Immunology; European Academy of Allergology and Clinical Immunology. *Publications:* "Living with Asthma", in press; 57 published articles. *Honours:* Award, Yugoslav Association for Allergology and Clinical Immunolgy, 1980; Award, Yugoslav Association for Pneumophtysiology, 1983. *Hobbies:* Painting; Skiing. *Address:* University Institute of Diseases of the Chest and TB, 64204, Golnik, Yugoslavia.

FURTADO, Tancredo A, b. 13 Apr. 1923, Brazil. Dean, Faculty of Medicine. m. Maria de Conceiçào Barbosa Mello, 12 Dec. 1950, Belo Horizonte, 1 son, 5 daughters. *Education:* MD, Federal University of Minas Gerais, Belo Horizonte. Fellow: Dermatology, University of Kansas, USA, 1947; University of Southern California, 1951-52; New York University, 1953. *Appointments include:* Assistant Professor, 1947, Associate Professor and Livre-Docente (equivalent to Doctor), 1955, Professor and Chairman of Dermatology, 1975-, Chief of

Dermatology Service, 1975-82, Coordinator of Post Graduation, 1977-80, Faculty of Medicine, Federal University of Minas Gerais; Professor and Chairman of Dermatology, 1963, Chief of Dermatology Service, 1963-74, Faculty of Medical Sciences of Minas Gerais; Visiting Professor, University of Illinois, USA and Armed Forces Institute of Pathology, Washington, 1959-61, University of Mexico, 1982. *Memberships include:* American Association of Dermatology; American Academy of Dermatology; National Societies of Dermatology of Brazil, France, Uruguay, Venezuela and Argentina; Bolivian Federation of Dermatology; Investigative Society of Dermatology; International Societies of Tropical Dermatology, Leprosy, Humans and Animal Micrology; Brazilian National Academy of Medicine. *Publications:* "Intensive Treatment of Syphilis", 1953; 'Late Yaws Mainifestations', thesis, 1955; 'Kerato-acanthoma and related conditions', thesis, 1962; "O Aleijadinho (The Little Cripple) and Medicine", 1970; "Themes on Medical Education", 1974; 'Abrikossoff's granular cell tumor', thesis, 1974. Contributor of numerous books chapters, 152 articles published in Brazil and 53 worldwide. *Honours:* Antonio Aleixo Award, Brazilian Society of Dermatology, 1953; National Prize of Monographs, 1961; Carlos Chagas Medal, 1981; Honour Medal of Inconfidence, 1983; Carlos Chagas Award, 1984. *Address:* Rua da Bahia 1032, Belo Horizonte 30,000, Brazil.

FUSTER, Valentin, b. 20 Jan. 1943, Barcelona, Spain, Chief, Division of Cardiology, Mount Sinai Medical Centre; Arthur M and Hilda A Master Professor of Medicine, m. Angela-Maria Guals, 3 Sep. 1968, Barcelona, Spain, 1 son, 1 daughter. *Education:* Baccaluarate, Colegio Jesuitas, Barcelona, 1954-61; MD, Barcelona University, Barcelona, 1961-67. *Appointments:* Assistant Professor of Medicine and Cardiovascular Diseases, 1974-77, Associate Professor of Medicine and Cardiovascular Diseases, 1978-81, Associate Professor of Paediatrics, 1980-, Professor of Medicine and Cardiovascular Diseases, 1981-82, Mayo Medical School, Rochester, Minnesota, USA; Authur M and Hilda A Master Professor of Medicine, Mount Sinai School of Medicine, New York, USA, 1982-. *Memberships:* Editorial Board, American Journal of Cardiology, 1982; Exectuive Committee, Council on Thrombosis, AHA, 1982; Editorial Board, Arteriosclerosis; Board of Directors, New York Cardiological Society. *Publications include:* 'Long term results of total correction for Tetralogy of Fallot', 1978; 'Biography of Professor V Carulla', (with J Fuster), 1978; 'Medical and Surgical long-term follow-up of ventricular septal defect with pulmonary vascular obstructive disease', (with A S Iskandrian), 1979; 'Pathogenesis of atherosclerosis and the role of risk factors', 1981; 'Miocardiopatias', 1981; 'Pathophysiology of atherosclerosis', 1982; 'Diseases of the Heart', 1982; Contributor of over 180 articles and 164 abstracts. *Honours:* D C Balfour Award for Outstanding Research Achievement, 1974; Miguel Servet 1st International Award for Cardiovascular Research, Madrid, Spain, 1976; Chosen among leading investigators in Cardiovascular disease, Press Meeting, AHA, 1979. *Address:* Mount Sinai Medical Centre, Division of Cardiology, 1 Gustave L Levy Place, New York, NY 10029, USA.

FYSH, Peter Norman, b. 1 Dec. 1942, Melbourne, Australia. Chiropractor. m. Maggie La Ragy, 31 Dec. 1983, Melbourne. *Education:* Bachelor of Applied Science (Chiropractic); Diploma in Applied Science (Human Biology); Diploma in Applied Science (Chiropractic). *Appointments:* Lecturer, School of Chiropractic, Phillip Institute, Melbourne; President, Chiropractic Alumni Association, Phillip Institute of Technology, Melbourne. *Memberships:* Australian Chiropractors Association; American Chiropractors Association; Council on Troentgenology of American Chiropractors Association. *Hobbies:* Computer Programming; Squash. *Address:* 226 Springvale Road, Glen Waverley, Victoria 3150, Australia.

G

GAAFAR, Yousef, b. 8 Nov. 1940, Egypt. Radiologist; Head, Radiology Dept., Bolak El Dakror General Hospital. m. Safaa Elsabbahy, 7 Oct. 1971, 1 son, 1 daughter. *Education:* MB; BCH; DMRE, Cairo University, 1969. *Appointments:* General Practitioner, 1964-66; Trainee, Radiology Registrar, 1966-69; Radiologist, Egyptian Hospitals, 1969-71; Radiologist, Libyian General Hospital, 1971-75; Saudian General Hospital, 1975-81; Chief Radiologist, Head, Radiology, Egyptian General Hospital, 1982-. *Memberships:* Egyptian Society of Radiology & Nuclear Medicine; British Institute of Radiology; Egyptian Society of Ultrasound. *Hobby:* Chess. *Address:* 12 Rashdan St., Dokkin, Cairo, Egypt.

GABOR-IONESCU Silvia, b. 4 Jan. 1925, Cluj, Romania. Scientific Researcher. m. Dr Nicolae Ionescu, 7 Jan. 1958, 1 son. *Education:* Physician, Institute of Medicine, Cluj-Romania, 1949; Doctor of Medicine, Institute of Medicine, Leningrad USSR, 1954. *Appointments:* Associate Professor, 1954-70, Head of Occupational Health Department, 1954-85, Head of Hygiene Department, 1970-73, Institute of Hygiene and Public Health, Cluj-Romania. *Memberships:* International Section for Research on Prevention of Occupational Risks (Paris) 1983; International Society for Trace Element Research in Humans, 1985. *Publications:* "Effect of silica on Lipid Peroxidation' 1974; 'Effect of Asbestos on Lipid Peroxidatin in the red cells' 1975; 'In vitro action of guartz on alveolar macrophage lipid peroxides' 1975; 'Cadmium-induced lipid peroxidaiton' 1978; 'Mechanisms of Toxicity and Hazard Evaluation' 1980; 'The in vitro Effects of Mineral Dusts' 1980; VI International Pneumoconiosis Conference Proceedings, 1984. *Hobbies:* Walking (preferably in the forest); Gymnastics; Orchestral music. *Address:* Racovita Street 38, 3400 Cluj-Napoca, Romania.

GABRIELSON, Ira Wilson, b. 27 Nov. 1922, New York, USA. Professor and Chair, Department of Community and Preventive Medicine, Medical College of Pennsylvania. m. Mary Oliver, 4 Sep. 1948, Williamsburg, Massachusetts, 2 sons, 2 daughters. *Education:* BA, Columbia College, New York, 1944; Columbia University Graduate Faculties (Zoology), 1944-45; MD, College of Physicians and Surgeons of Columbia University, 1949; MPH, The Johns Hopkins University School of Hygiene and Public Health, Baltimore, 1950; University of Michigan Center for Population, Planning, Summer 1965; Internship and Assistant Resident, Internal Medicine, Roosevelt Hospital, New York, 1949-51; Assistant Resident, Paediatrics, Yale New Haven Community Hospital, 1951-53. *Appointments:* Administrative Assistant, Office of the Vice-President, The Johns Hopkins Medical Institutions, 1953-54; Administrative Assistant and Assistant Director, The Johns Hopkins Hospital, 1954-57; Instructor, Public Health Administration and Paediatrics, Johns Hopkins, 1958-59; Director, Community Program for Retarded Children, New Haven, Connecticut, 1959-61; Assistant Attending Paediatrician, Yale-New Haven Community Hospital, 1959-68; Clinical Instructor, 1959-61, Assistant Professor of Public Health and Paediatrics, 1961-68, Executive Officer, Department of Epid. and Public Health, 1962-67, Yale School of Medicine; Clinical; Professor of Maternal and Child Health, University of California, Berkeley, 1968-71 Professor and Chairman, Department of Community and Preventive Medicine, Medical College of Pennsylvania, 1971-; Visiting Professor, University of Hawaii School of Public Health, 1977. *Memberships:* Fellow, American Public Health Association; Fellow, American Academy of Paediatrics; College of Physicians of Philadelphia;

American Association for the Advancement of Science; Sigma Xi; Delta Omega. *Publications:* Book Reviews; Presentations; Abstracts; Contributor to professional journals. *Honour:* Fellow, National Foundation, 1958-59. *Hobbies:* Photography; Mountain Hiking. *Address:* Department of Community and Preventive Medicine, Medical College of Pennsylvania, Philadelphia, PA 19129, USA.

GADA, Manilal Talakshi, b. 12 Jan. 1947, Kutch, India. Consultant Psychiatrist, Psychotherapist. m. Manjula, 24 May 1973, Bombay, 2 daughters. *Education:* MB, BS, University of Bombay; DPM, College of Physicians and Surgeons of Bombay; MD, Psychological Medicine, University of Bombay. *Appointments:* Research Assistant, Seth G.S. Medical College, & K.E.M. Hospital; Senior Research Fellow, Psychopharmacology in India, W.H.O. Collaborating Centre; Honorary Assistant Professor, Honorary Assistant Psychiatrist, L.T.M. Medical College and Hospitals; Head, Psychiatry, Rajawadi Municipal General Hospital, Bombay; Honorary Psychiatrist, Pragati Hospital; Panel Consultant, Air India. *Memberships:* Fellow, Indian Psychiatric Society; Corresponding Member, American Psychiatric Association; British Association of Social Psychiatrists; Executive Committee, Indian Psychiatric Society, West Zone Branch; Indian Medical Association, NEBS Branch; Honorary Treasurer, Kutchi Medicos; Association of Medical Consultants of Bombay. *Publications Include:* (Book Chapter) "Treatment of Mental Disorder in India", "Perspectives in Psychopharmacotherapy", 1979; (Papers) Co-Author, "Diabetes Mellitus - A Psycho-Somatic Study of 147 Cases", 'Journal of Post-graduate Medicine', 1975; "Treatment of Mental Disorders in India", 'Prog. Neuro Psychopharmacology', 1979; "Psychopharmacotherapy in India - I Antipsychotic Drugs", 'Psychopharmacology Bulletin', 1983; "Psychopharmacotherapy in India II Antidepressant Drugs", 'Psychoparmacology Bulletin', 1984; etc. *Honours:* Invited by Mental Health Division of WHO to attend meetings at Copenhagen, 1977, Bombay 1979, Geneva, 1982, 1983; Recipient, many other honours and awards. *Hobbies:* Cricket; Public Speaking. *Address:* 6 Laxmi Niwas, M.G. Road, Ghatkopar (W), Bombay 400 086, India.

GADD, Kenneth Gordon, b. 19 June 1922, Manchester, England. Head of Chemical Pathology, SAIMR. m. Barbara Collingwood Borradaile, 25 Nov. 1952, Edinburgh, Scotland, 2 sons. *Education:* MB ChB, Edinburgh University, 1946; DCP, London University, England, 1957. *Appointments:* House Physician, North Staffordshire Royal Infirmary, Stoke on Trent, 1946-47; Medical Officer, 1st Northern Rhodesia Redgiment, Lusaka, Northern Rhodesia, 1947-49; Pathologist, Northern Rhodesia Government, 1950-56; Director, Public Health Laboratory, Lusaka, 1957-63; Director, Public Health Laboratory, Salisbury, Rhodesia, 1963-78; Chairman of Board of Studies, Diploma Medical Technology, Honorary Lecturer, University of Rhodesia, 1963-78; Head of Chemical Pathology, Baragwanath SAIMR, Johannesburg, Republic of South Africa, 1978-. *Memberships:* Founder member, College of Pathologists; Fellow, Royal College of Pathologists; South African Association of Clinical Biochemists. *Publications:* 13 papers. *Honour:* Knight, Military and Hospitaller Order of St Lazarus of Jerusalem, 1972. *Hobby:* Communication Electronics. *Address:* SAIMR, Baragwanath, Box 1038, Johannesburg 2000, Republic of South Africa.

GADOMSKA, Helena, b. 25 May 1913, Tashkent. Medical Doctor; Professor, Oncology; Head, Polish Cancer Registry. m. Witold Gadomski, 26 Dec. 1937, Poznan, 3 sons, 1 daughter. *Education:* Medical University Graduate, Poznan; Doctorate, medicine, Warsaw; Specialisation, Gynaecology & Obstetrics II; Organisation of Health Protection II; Epidemiology & Medical statistics Diploma,

INSERM, Paris, 1965; Institute G. Roussy, 1967; University Libre Bruxelles, 1970. *Appointments:* Junior Researcher, University of Poznan, 1934-39; Research Worker, Transfiguation Hosptial, Warsaw, 1939-; Head, centre of Mother & Child's Health Protection, 1949-62; Deputy Direcotr, UNICEF Course, Social Paediatrics, 1959-62; Head, Epidemiology, Institute of Oncology, 1969-72; Deputy Director, Institute of Oncology, 1979-83; Head, Polish Cancer Registry, 1984-; Co-ordinator, Problem No. 7, Cancer Epidemiology, Council for Mutual Economic Assistance, 1975-; Programme Council for Health Education Films, 1985. *Memberships Include:* International Association of Medical Women; International Association of Cancer Registries; French Speaking Epidemiological Association; Accademia Tiberina; Polish Medical Society; Polish Oncological Society; Polish Gynaecological Society; Polish Pathological Society; etc. *Publications:* "Cancer Registry Report in Selected Areas of Poland 1965-1970", 1972; "Cancer in Poland" – City of Warsaw and Selected Rural Areas 1963-72", 1977; "Cancer Epidemiology in Poland 1952-82", 1985; 3 films on public health education. *Honours:* Golden Cross of Merit, 1966; 100 Years of Brussels Medal, 1978; Warsaw Uprising Cross, 1982; Polonia Restitute Officer's Cross, 1984. *Hobbies:* Ancient History; Travel. *Address;* Grochowska 221, Apt. 21, 04-077 Warsaw, Poland.

GAINOTTI, Guido, b. 12 Mar. 1939, Parma, Italy. Director of Service of Clincial Neuropsychology. m. Amann Merete, 3 Apr. 1971, Geneva, 1 son, 1 daughter. *Education:* Doctor of Medicine, Associate Professor of Neuropsychology. *Appointments:* Assistant Professor, Neurology, University of Perugia; Assistant Professor, Neurology, Catholic University of Rome; Associate Professor of Clinical Neuropsychology and Director of Service of Clinical Neuropsychology, Catholic University of Rome. *Memberships:* Secretary of Research Group on Aphasia of the World Federation of Neurology; Società Italiana di Neurologia. *Publications:* Books: "Neuropsicologia Clinica" co-author, 1977; "Struttura e Patologia del Linguaggio" editor, 1983; Chapter: 'Constructional Apraxia' in "Handbook of Clincial Neurology" vol 1 1985. *Address:* Clinica Neurologica, Policlinico A Gemelli Largo A Gemelli 8, 00168 Roma, Italy.

GAINSFORD, Ian Derek, b. 24 June 1930, Twickenham, England. Dean, Faculty of Clinical Dentistry, King's College, London. m Carmel Liebster, 13 June 1957, London, 1 son, 2 daughters. *Education:* BSS, London University; LDS, MGDS, FDS, Royal College of Surgeons, UK: DDS, Honours, Toronto University, Canada. *Appointments:* Lecturer, King's College Hospital Medical School 1956-57, London Hospital Medical College 1957-60; Senior Lecturer, London Hospital Medical College, 1960-70; Senior Lecturer/Consultant, King's College Medical School, 1970-; Vice-Dean, King's College Medical School Dental Faculty, 1973-77; Dean, Faculty of Clinical Dentistry, King's College London/Director, Clinical Dental Services, 1977-. *Memberships:* President 1982-83, American Dental Society of London; President 1982-83, American Dental Society of Europe; President 1973-74, British Society for Restorative Dentistry; Fellow, Council Member 1983, Royal Society of Medicine; Fellow, International College of Dentists. *Publication:* "Silver Amalgam in Clinical Practice", 1965. *Honours:* Honorary member, American Dental Association, 1983; Fellow, International College of Dentists; Fellow, King's College, London, 1984. *Hobby:* Theatre. *Address:* 31 York Terrace East, Regents Park, London NW1 4PT, England.

GALASKO, Charles Samuel Barnard, b. 29 June 1939, Johannesburg, South Africa. Professor, Orthopaedic Surgery. m. Carol Freyda Lapinsky, 29 Oct. 1967, Welkom, 1 son, 1 daughter. *Education:*

MB.BCH., 1st Class Honours, Witwatersrand, 1962; FRCS, Edinburgh, 1966; FRCS, England, 1966; M.Ch., Witwatersrand, 1970; MSc., (Honorary), Manchester, 1980. *Appointments:* House Surgeon, 1963, House Physician, 1963-64, Part-time Casualty Officer, 1964, Johannesburg General and Non-European Hospitals; Lecturer, Anatomy, 1964, Part-time Lecturer, Anatomy, 1965-66, University of Witwatersrand; General Practitioner Locum, 1964-65; Senior House Surgeon, 1965, Registrar, 1965-66, Orthopaedic Surgery, Johanesburg General Hospital; House Surgeon, 1966-67, Surgical Registrar, 1967-69, Hammersmith Hospital & Royal Postgradute Medical School, London, England; Lord Nuffield Scholar, Orthopaedic Surgery, Nuffield Orthopaedic Centre, Oxford, 1969; Registrar, Accident Service, Radcliffe Infirmary, Oxford, 1970; Senior Orthopaedic Registrar, Nuffield Orthopaedic Centre & Accident Service, Radcliffe Infirmary, 1970-73; Director, Orthopaedic Surgery, Hammersmith Hospital, Royal Postgraduate Medical School, 1973-76; Professor, Orthopaeic Surgery, University of Manchester, 1976-. *Memberships:* Numerous profesional organisations. *Publications:* "Radionuclide Scintigraphy in Orthopaedics", 1984; "Principles of Fracture Management", 1984; "Neurological Problems in Orthopaedics", in press; "Skeletal Metastasis", in press; numerous articles in proferssional journals. *Honours:* Recipient numerous honours, awards & scholarships. *Hobbies:* Sport; Theatre. *Address:* Dept. of Orthopaedic Surgery, Clinical Sciences Building, Hope Hospital, Eccles Old Road, Salford M6 8HD, England.

GALE, Alan William, b. 24 Nov. 1944, New South Wales, Australia. Chairman of Cardiothoracic Surgery. m. Helen Margaret Budge, 20 Nov 1968, Sydney, 2 sons. *Education:* MB BS, Honours, Fellow: Royal Australian College of Physicians, 1975; Royal Australian College of Surgeons, 1975; Royal College of Surgical iology, 1978; Australian Cardiac Society, 1984. FACC, 1979. *Appointments:* RMO/Registrar, 1969-72, Cardiac Registrar, 1973, General Surgecn, 1974, Royal Prince Alfred Hospital, Sydney; Anatomy Demonstrator, Sydney University, 1972; Paediatric Surgeon, RAHC, Sydney, 1975; Senior Registrar, Cardiothoracic, St Vincent's, Sydney, 1976; Fellow, Cardiovascular Surgery, University of Oregon, USA, 1977; Evarts A Graham Fellow, American Association for Thoracic Surgery, 1977-78; Cardiovascular Fellow, Mayo Clinic, Minnesota, 1979; Staff Specialist, St Vincents, Sydney, Australia, 1979-83; Visiting Cardiothoracic Surgeon, Royal North Shore Hospital, Sydney and Sydney Adventist Hospital, 1983-; currently, Chairman, Cardiothoracic Surgery, Royal North Shore Hospital. *Memberships:* Cardiac Society of Australia; Cardiac Society of New South Wales; Thorocotomy Society of Australia; Sydney Cardiac Surgical Society. *Address:* Suite 10, Garden Mews, 82-86 Pacific Highway, St Leonards, NSW 2086, Australia.

GALE, Ernest Frederick, b. 15 July 1914, Luton, Bedfordshire, England. Emeritus Professor of Chemical Microbiology. m. Eiry Mair Jones, 28 Aug 1937, Cardiff, 1 son. *Education:* BA, 1936, PhD, 1939, ScD, 1944, St. John's College, Cambridge. *Appointments:* Senior Student, Royal Commission Exhibition of 1851, 1939; Beit Memorial Fellow, 1941; Staff Medical Research Council, 1943; Reader in Chemical Microbiology, 1948-60, Director, Unit of Chemical Microbiology, 1948-62, Professor of Chemical Microbiology, 1960-81, Biochemistry Department, University of Cambridge. *Memberships:* Society for General Microbiology; Meetings Secretary, 1954-60, International Representative 1963-67, President 1967-69. *Publications:* Research publications in 'Biolchemical Journal', 'Journal for General Microbiology' 'Biochimica Biophysica Acta' etc. Reviews and books on Bacterial Metabolism: mode of action of antibiotics e.g. "The Molecular Basis of Antibiotic Action" with others, 1981. *Honours:* Fellow of the Royal Society 1953- (Leeuwenhoek Lecturer 1956); Fellow of St John's College, Cambridge, 1939-. *Hobbies:* Photography; Reading; Gardening. *Address:* 25 Luard Road, Cambridge, England.

GALIBERT, Francis, b. 25 May 1934, Asnieres, France. Scientist; Molecular Biologist. m. Francoise Mercier, 18 Apr. 1964, 2 daughters. *Education:* Graduated, Pharmaceutical Faculty, Paris; DSc., Science, Paris. *Appointments:* Head, Clinical Laboratory, Hospital Necuer Enfants Malades, 1959-61; Head, Experimental Hemaetology, 1982-, Head, Genetic Recombinant DNA, 1981-, C.N.R.S., 1962-. *Publications:* Articles in: 'Nature', 1965, 1966, 1973, 1979. *Honours:* Prix de Academie des Sciences, Henriette Regnier, 1972; Prix Rosen de Cancerologie, 1976; Silver Medal, CNRS, 1976. *Hobbies:* Sailing; Surfing; Wind Surfing; Classical Music. *Address:* 7 Av. Simon Hayem, Saint Gratien, France.

GALL, James, b. 21 Apr. 1924, Wishaw, Scotland, Deputy Chief Dental Officer, m. Margaret Law Cran, 20 Sept 1952, Aberdeen, Scotland, 1 son, 2 daughers. *Education:* LDS; RFPS (G). *Appointments:* General Dental Surgeon, Law Hospital, Lanarkshire, 1949-74; Visiting Dental Surgeon, Hartwood Hospital, Lanarkshire, 1950-74; Visiting Clinical Teacher, Glasgow Dental School and Hospital, 1966-74; Lecturer, Dental Surgery Assistant Course, Lanarkshire College, 1960-84; Professional Member, Scottish Dental Estimates Board, 1972-74; Chairman of Council, British Society of Medical and Dental Hypnosis, 1973-77; President, British Society of Medical and Dental Hypnosis, 1977-80; Visiting Dental Surgeon, Clinical Teacher, Glasgow Dental Hospital and School, 1964-74; Honorary Visiting Dental Surgeon, Glasgow Dental Hospital and School, 1974-. *Memberships:* British Dental Association; Royal Society of Medicine, London; British Society Medical and Dental Hypnosis; Life Member, Federation Dentaire Internationale; Life Fellow, Royal Zoological Society, Edinburgh; Royal Odontological Society, Edinburgh; Glasgow Odontological Society. *Publications:* 'The Difficult Dental Patient', 1982; 'Hypnosis in Dentistry', 1966. *Hobbies:* Gardening; Golf; Sailing; Bridge; Reading; Photography; Video Photography. *Address:* "The Bungalow", 21b Douglas Gardens, Uddington, Glasgow G71 7HB, Scotland.

GALLETTI, Pierre M, b. 11 June 1927, Monthey, Switzerland. Professor, Medical Science; Biomedical Researcher. m. Sonia Aidan, 31 Dec. 1959, Atlanta, USA, 1 son. *Education:* BA, St Maurice College, Switzerland, 1945; MD, University of Lausanne, 1951; PhD, University of Lausanne, 1954. *Appointments:* Resident in Internal Medicine, University Hospital, Zurich, 1954-57; Research Fellow, Institute for Medical Research, Cedars of Lebanon Hospital, Los Angeles, USA, 1957-58; Emory University, Atlanta, 1958-67; Eleanor Roosevelt Fellow, International Union Against Cancer, University of Palermo, Italy, 1964-65; Senior Guest Scientist, University of Nancy, France, 1978-79; Professor, Medical Science, 1967-, Vice President, Biology and Medicine, 1972-, Brown University. *Memberships:* American Society for Artificial Internal Organs, President, 1969-70; American College of Cardiology, Fellow; American Physiological Society; Institute of Electric and Electronic Engineers; American Association for the Advancement of Science; Biomedical Engineering Society; etc. *Publications:* Co-Author, "Heart-Lung Bypass: Principles and Techniques of Extracorporeal Circulation", 1962, 4th edition 1979; Numerous articles in professional journals. *Honours:* Honorary DSc., Roger Williams College, Rhode Island, 1979; Honorary Doctoral Degree, University of Nancy, 1982; Frank W. Hastings Lecture, Devices & Technology Branch, National

Heart, Lung & Blood Institute, 1979; John H. Gibbon Junior Award, American Society of Extra-Corporeal Technology Inc., Philadelphia, 1980; Plenary Lecture, World Biomaterials Congress, Vienna, Austria. *Hobbies:* History; Gardening. *Address:* Box G, Division of Biology and Medicine, Brown University, Providence, RI 02912, USA.

GALLI, Claudio, b. 10 May 1938, Bergamo, Italy. Professor of Experimental Pharmacology. m. Daniela Re Cecconi, 8 Oct. 1966, Milan, Italy, 1 son, 1 daughter. *Education:* MD, 1962; PhD Pharmacology, 1971. *Appointments:* Research Fellow. City of Hope Medical centre, Duarte, California, USA, 1962-65; Fellow, Mutiple Sclerosis Society, University of Milan, 1965-67; Assistant Professor of Pharamcology, Faculty of Medicine, University of Milan, 1967-70; Associate Professor, 1970-80, Professor of Experimental Pharmacology, Faculty of Pharmacy, University of Milan, 1980-. *Memberships:* International Society of Biochemical Pharmacology; International Societies of Neurochemsitry & Pharmacology. *Publications:* Various articles in medical journals; various co-editorships. *Hobbies:* Photography; Mountian Hiking. *Address:* Via Andrea del Sarto 21, 20129 Milan, Italy.

GALOFRE, Alberto, b. 10 Dec. 1937, Santiago, Chile. Associate Dean for Curriculum. m. Nancy Kay Evert, 23 June 1968, 3 daughters. *Education:* BSc, Catholic University, Santiago, 1959; MD, University of Chile, 1962; MEd, University of Illinois, Urbana, USA, 1974. *Appointments:* Instructor in Pediatrics, 1963-70, Assistant Professor of Pediatrics, 1970-73, Catholic University, Santiago; Assistant Professor, Pediatrics and Human Development, Michigan State University, East Lansing, 1974-78; Assistant Professor, Internal Medicine, 1978-79; Assistant Dean for Curriculum, 1979-84; Associate Professor, Internal Medicine, 1985-; Associate Dean for Curriculum, 1985-; St. Louis University, Missouri. *Memberships:* American College of Physicians; American Educational Research Association; National Council on Measurement in Education; American Association for the Advancement of Science; American Public Health Association; American Association for Higher Education. *Honours:* MD, summa cum laude; W K Kellogg in Pediatric and Developmental Biology, 1967-78; Public Health Service Fellowship in Medical Education, 1974-75; Grant, National Fund for Medical Education. *Hobbies:* Nature Photgraphy; Tennis; Jogging; Golf; Scuba. *Address:* 1402 S Grand Boulevard, St. Louis, MO 63104, USA.

GALTON, David Jeremy, b. 2 May 1937, London, England. Consultant Physician, St. Bartholomew's Hospital. m. Merle Gywynne James, 16 Apr. 1969, Boston, Massachusetts, USA, 1 son, 1 daughter. *Education:* BSc (1st class Hons.), 1957; MB BS (Hons), Medicine, 1960; MSc, Biochemistry, 1962; MD, Biochemistry, 1967; FRCP, London, 1976. *Appointments:* Postdoctoral Research Fellow, National Institutes of Health, Bethesda, Maryland, USA; Lecturer, Clinical Biochemistry, Hammersmith Hospital, London; Senior Lecturer, Medicine; Consultant Physician, St. Bartholomew's Hospital, London; Consultant Physician, Moorfields Eye Hospital. *Memberships:* Association of Physicians; Medical Research Society; Biochemical Society; British Diabetic Association. *Publications:* "The Human Adipose Cell: A Model for Errors in Metabolic Regulation", 1971; "Molecular Genetics of Metabolic Disease", 1985. *Hobbies:* Skiing; Tennis; Sailing; Music. *Address:* St. Bartholomew's Hospital, West Smithfield, London, EC1, England.

GALVIN, Mary Anne, b. 3 June 1954, Worcester, Massachusetts, USA, Consulting Psychologist, Private Practice; McBerg and Company, Boston. *Education:* EdD, University of Massachusetts, 1980; MEd, 1978; BS, Wheelock College, Boston, 1976; Diplomate, American Board of Professional

Psychology. *Appointments:* Instructor, Tufts University School of Medicine; Pscyhologist and Clincial Director, Department of Psychiatry, Tufts-New England Medical Centre, Boston; Assistant Professor in Psychology, University of New Hampshire; Psychologist Instructor, University of Massachusetts; Instructor, Mt Holyoke College. *Memberships:* American Psychological Association; National Register of Health Service Founders in Psychology; Massachusetts Psychological Association; International Council of Psychologists. *Publications:* Contributor of numerous articles in professional journals and chapters in books. *Honours:* Graduate Fellowship, Massachusetts Federation of Women's clubs, 1976; Visiting Fellowship, University of Stockholm Sweden, 1975; National Science Foundation Travel Grant, 1985. *Hobbies:* Swimming; Dance; Skiing; Tennis; Sailing; Piano; Literature; Creative writing. *Address:* 232 Newbury Street, Boston, MA 02116, USA.

GAMEL, John Worth, b. 21 Jan, 1944, Selma, Alabama, USA. Associate Professor of Opthalmology. *Education:* BA cum laude Mathematics; MD, Stanford Medical School. *Appointments:* Associate Professor, University of Louisville School of Medicine, Department of Opthalmology, Louisville, Kentucky, 1977-. *Memberships:* American Academy of Opthalmology; Kentucky Academy of Eye Physicians and Surgeons; Louisville Academy of Opthalmology; Association for Research in Vision and Opthalmology; American Association of Opthalmic Pathologists; Georgian Dvorak Theobald Society; Jefferson County Medical Society; Kentucky Medical Association; American Medical Association. *Publications:* 30 contributions to books and scientific journals, including: 'Computerized histopathologic assessment of malignant potential' (co-author: I W McLean), 3 articles 1982-84; 'Modern developments in histopathologic assessment of uveal melanomas' (co-author: I W McLean), 1984; 'Mucoepidermoid carcinoma of the conjunctiva' (co-authors: R A Eiferman, P Guibor), 1984. *Honours:* Harvard National Scholar; Fellowship, Opthalmic Pathology; Wesley Award, Outstanding Opthalmology Resident, 1974; Patrick O'Connor Award, Outstanding Teacher, 1979. *Hobbies:* A wide variety of interests. *Address:* University of Louisville School of Medicine, Department of Opthalmology, 301 East Muhammad Ali Boulevard, Louisville, KY 40202, USA.

GAMMEL, Charles Lee, b. 2 Aug. 1950, Corinth, Mississippi, USA. Executive Director. m. Sue Vandiver, 31 Aug. 1969, Corinth, 1 son, 2 daughters. *Education:* BA, Mississippi College, 1971; Washington University, 1973; PhD, University of Southern Mississippi, 1980. *Appointments:* Assistant Professor, Mississippi College. *Memberships:* Alexander Graham Bell Association; Council for Exceptional Children; American Speech and Hearing Association; Mississippi Speech and Hearing Association. *Publications:* Reading in the Preschool; The Effects of Vibrotactile Stimulation on the Speechreading Performance of Profoundly Deaf Children; The Auralingual Method: An Auditory Based Curriculum for Deaf Children; Hearing Aid Fitting and Training for Very Young Profoundly Deaf Children. *Hobby:* Camping. *Address:* Magnolia Speech School Incorporated, 733 Flag Chapel Road, Jackson, MS 39209, USA.

GANELLIN, Charon Robin, b. 25 Jan. 1934, London, England. Chemical Researcher. m. Tamara Greene, 27 Dec. 1956, 1 son, 1 daughter. *Education:* BSc 1955, PhD 1958, Queen Mary College, University of London; DSc, 1986; Fellow, Royal Society of Chemistry. *Appointmnts:* Research Chemist, Smith Kline & French Laboratories Ltd, 1958-59, 1961-62; Research Associate, Massachusetts Institute of Technology, USA, 1960-; Department Head in Medicinal Chemistry, Smtih Kline & French Laboratories Ltd, 1962-75; Honorary Lecturer, Department of Pharmacology, University College, London, 1975-; Director, Histamine Research, Smith Kline & French Labs Ltd, 1975-80; Honorary Professor of Medicinal Chemistry, University of Kent at Canterbury, 1979; Advisory Tutor, Department of Chemistry, Polytechnic of North London, 1979-83; Vice-President, Research, Smith Kline & French Labs Ltd, 1980-. *Memberships:* American Chemical Society; British Pharmacological Society; European Histamine Research Society; Royal Society of Chemistyr; Society of Chemical Industry; Society for Drug Research, Chairman, 1985-. *Publications:* "Pharmacology of Histamine Receptors", 1982; "Frontiers in Histamine Research", 1985; "Definition & Antagonism of Histamine H_2-Receptors (in 'Nature', 1972); 'Medicinal Chemistry & Dynamic Structure Activity Analysis' (in 'Journal of Medicinal Chemistry', 1981.) *Honours:* UK Chemical Society Medallion in Medicinal Chemistry, 1977; Prix Charles Mentzer from La Société de Chimie Thérapeutique (France), 1978; Division of Medicinal Chemistry Award, American Chemical Society, 1980; Elected Honorary member of the Sociedad Espanola de Quimica Terapeutica, 1982; Tilden Medal, Royal Society of Chemistry, 1982. *Hobbies:* Walking; Sailing; Music. *Address:* Smith Kline & French Research Ltd, The Frythe, Welwyn, Hertfordshire, England.

GARCIA-CALDERON, Pedro Antonio, b. 13 June 1945, Cartagena, Spain. Consultant in Immunology; Director, Inmunolab Center. m. Ma José Muriel Villoria, 29 July 1969, Cartagena, 1 son. *Education:* BMed, 1968, MMed, 1970, Salamanca University; PhD, Medicine, Autonoma University, Barcelona, 1972. *Appointments:* Resident Doctor, St Cruz and San Pablo Hospital, 1968-70; Assistant Lecturer, Autonoma University, Barcelona, 1970-72; Consultant, Immunological Unit, St Cruz and San Pablo Hospital, Barcelona, 1972-75; Lecturer, Immunology, Autonoma University, 1972-75; Consultant Immunologist, Spanish Social Security Service, 1976-; Director, Inmunolab, Immunology and Allergy Research Center, Barcelona, 1980-. *Memberships:* Spanish Immunology Society; Spanish Society of Allergy and Immunology; Spanish Society of Biopathology; Association of Medical Dominicana; Catalana Society of Allergy and Clinical Immunology; Catalana Society of Immunology; European Academy for Allergy and Clinical Immunology; European Committee for Clinical Laboratory Standards. *Publications:* "A New Rapid and More Sensitive Microcytotox Test", 1971; "Lymph. transform, test in fixed drug eruption", 1975; "Immune regulators in transfer factor", 1979; "An in vitro study of lymph. in pat. with atopia", 1983; "Cell mediated immun in perenn. allergic rhinitis", 1984; "Immune complexes in retinitis pigmentosa", 1984. *Honours:* Honorary Member, Dominican Academy of Medicine. *Hobbies:* Reading; Philosophy; Classical music; Cinema. *Address:* Inmunolab, Pau Claris 162 1°, 08037 Barcelona, Spain.

GARCIA-PUEYO, Felix Raul, b. 9 Aug. 1938, Iquites, Peru. Physician. m. 16 June 1963, 2 sons, 1 daughter. *Education:* MD, San Marcos University; Fellow, Internal Medicine, University of Miami. *Appointments:* Resident Physician, Huachocolpa's Hospital, 1964-68; Resident, Internal Medicine, Clinica Internation, 1969; Physician, Las Palmas Hospital, 1970; Chief Physician, Air Force Group Nine, Pisco, 1971-74; Assitant Physician, Central Aeronautics Hospital, 1975-; Head, Medical Division, Buenaventura Mining Co, 1975-; Fellow, Internal Medicine, University of Miami, 1983-84; Chief Physician, Clinica Vesalio, Lima, Peru, 1985-. *Memberships:* Daniel A Carrion Peruvian Society; New York Academy of Sciences; Aerospace Medical Association; Peruvian Society for Occupational Health. *Publication:* "Human Factors in Aircraft Accident" 1977. *Hobbies:* Pictures; Sculpture;

Chess. *Address:* Av Javier Prado Este 3250, San Broja, Lima, Peru.

GARCIA-WEBB, Peter, b. 12 Oct 1942, England. Clinical Biochemist. m. Janet I Mason, 23 Aug 1974, Melbourne, Australia, 2 sons, 2 daughters. *Education:* MBBS, Guy's Hospital, London University, 1965; Md, University of Western Australia, 1982. *Appointments:* Senior Lecturer/Specialist, University of Western Australia/Sir Charles Gairdner Hospital, 1976-85; Associate Professor/Specialist, University of Western Australia/Sir Charles Gairdner Hospital, 1985; Head, Department of Clinical Biochemistry, University of Western Australia, 1985-; Head, Combined Clinical Biochemistry Service, Queen Elizabeth II Medical Centre, 1986-. *Memberships:* Secretary, Asian and Pacific Federation of Clinical Biochemistry; Fellow, Royal College of Pathologists of Australasia; Fellow, Australian Association of Clinical Biochemists. *Publications:* 36 scientific publications. *Hobby:* Bridge. *Address:* c/o Department of Clinical Biochemistry, Queen Elizabeth II Medical Centre, Nedlands, Western Australia 6009.

GARDNER, David Godfrey, b. 24 Feb. 1936, Darlington, England. Professor & Chairman, Department of Pathology & Radiology, University of Texas Dental Branch, USA. m. Nancy C. Foggo, 4 June 1960, Toronto, Canada, 3 daughters. *Education:* DDS, University of Toronto, 1958; MSD, Oral Pathology, Indiana University, USA, 1965; Diplomate, American Board of Pathology, 1969. *Appointments:* Dental officer, Royal Canadian Dental Corps, 1958-63; Assistant Professor 1966, Profesor 1973, Chairman, Division of Oral Pathology, University of Western Ontario, Canada, 1966-84. *Memberships:* American Academy of Oral Pathology; Canadian Academy of Oral Pathology; International Academy of Oral Pathologists; American Association of Dental Schools. *Publications:* Total, 63 including: 'Epithelial Cysts of the Jaws' (Inter. Path. 1976), co-author; 'Treatment of Amelo Blastoma Based on Pathologic & Anatomic Principles' (Cancer, 1980), co-author; 'Plexiform Unicystic Ameloblastoma' (Cancer), 1984, co-author. *Honours:* Fellowships, National Research Council of Canada, 1963-65, Physician's Services Inc. 1973-74, Ontario Ministry of Health 1981-82, Canadian Academy of Oral Pathology 1972-73; President, American Academy of Oral Pathology, 1985-86. *Hobbies:* Canoeing; Woodwork; Watercolours. *Address:* Department of Pathology & Radiology, University of Texas HSC at Houston, Dental Branch, PO Box 20068, Houston, TX 77225, USA.

GARDNER, Richard Lavenham, b. 10 June 1943, Dorking, Surrey, England. Research Professor of Royal Society and Director of the Imperial Cancer Research Fund Developmental Biology Unit. m. Wendy Joy Cresswell, 14 Dec. 1968, Cobham, Surrey, England, 1 son. *Education:* BA, Hons, Physiology, 1966, MA, 1970, PhD, 1971, Cambridge University. *Appointments:* Research Assistant, Physiological Laboratory, Cambridge University, 1969-73; Lecturer in Development and Reproduction, Department of Zoology, University of Oxford, 1973-77; Student, Christ Church, Oxford, 1974-; Henry Dale Research Professor of the Royal Society, 1978-; Honorary Director of the Imperial Cancer Research Fund Developmental Biology Unit, 1985. *Memberships:* British Society for Developmental Biology; Society for the Study of Fertility; Fellow of the Institute of Biology; Fellow of the Royal Society. *Publications:* Gardner and Lyon (1971) Nature (London) 231; Gardner and Papaioannou (1975) The Early Development of Mammals; Gardner (1983) International Review of Experimental Pathology. *Honours:* Scientific Medal of the Zoological Society of London, 1977; Fellow of the Royal Society. *Hobbies:* Ornithology; Sailing;

Painting; Music. *Address:* ICRF Developmental Biology Unit, Department of Zoology, University of Oxford, South Parks Road, Oxford OX1 3PS.

GARDNER, Sandra Lee, b. 1 Dec. 1946, Louisville, Kentucky, USA, Director, Professional Outreach Consultation. *Education:* RN, Sts Mary and Elizabeth Hospital School of Nursing, 1964-67; BSN, Spalding College, 1973; MS, University of Colorado, Denver, 1975; Pediatric Nurse Practitioner, 1978. *Appointments:* Staff Nurse, Methodist Evangelical Hospital, KY, 1967-71; Charge Nurse, Newborn Intensive Care Unit Children's Hospital, Louisville, KY, 1971-73; Charge Nurse, Newborn Intensive Care Unit, Children's Hospital, Denver, 1973; Perinatal Outreach Education Coordinator, 1974-76; Assistant Professor, MCN Program, UCMSC, Denver, Col, 1976-79; Co-Founder, Director, Pediatric Services, Alternative Birth Center, Denver, 1978-79; Director, Profesional Outreach Consultation, 1980-; Authorised Lact-Aid representative, 1983-. *Memberships:* Kentucky Nurses Association, 1967-73; Colorado Nurses Association, 1973-; Colorado Perinatal Care Council, 1976-; Neonatal Nursing Education Foundation, 1982. *Publications:* 'Mothering – The Unconcsious Conflict between Nurse and new Mothers', 1978; 'Care of High Risk Neonate', 1980; 'Modular Study Guide to MCN Nursing', in 1983; "Handbook of Neonatal Intensive Care", (Co-author, Co-Editor); 1985; "Perinatal Grief and Loss", 1986; "Helping Families", 1986. *Honours:* Magna Cum Laude, 1973; National Honour Society of Secondary Schools, 1964; Gerald L Hencemann Memorial Award, 1978. *Hobbies:* Skiing; Reading; Sewing; Backpacking; Camping. *Address:* 12095 East Kentucky Avenue, Aurora, CO 80012, USA.

GARDNER-THORPE, Christopher, b. 22 Aug. 1941, Cosham, Hampshire, England. Consultant Neurologist. *Education:* MB, BS, London, England, 1964; MRCP, 1968; MD, London, 1973; FRCP, 1985. *Appointments:* House Surgeon, Peace Memorial Hospital, Watford, England, 1964; House Physician, Royal South Hampshire Hospital, 1964-65; Senior House Officer in Neurology, Southampton General Hospital, 1965-66; Medical Registrar, North Staffordshire Infirmary and City General Hospital, 1966-67; Registrar in Neurology, Southampton General Hospital, 1967-69; Neurological Registrar then Research Registrar, Leeds General Infirmary, 1969-71; Senior Registrar in Neurology, Newcastle General Hospital, 1971-74; Consultant Neurologist, South Western Regional Health Authority, 1974-; Honorary Consultant Neurologist, Wessex Regional Health Authority, 1981-; Honorary Tutor in Neurology, University of Exeter Postgraduate Medical School, 1983-. *Memberships:* Fellow, Royal Society of Medicine; British Epilepsy Association; Association of British Neurologists; Harveian Society; Society of Internal Medicine; Society of Authors and Medical Writers, etc. *Publications Include:* 47 articles and editorials in medical journals including: 'Some Synonyms of Antiepileptic Drugs', in 'Ibid', 1973; 'Anterior Interosseous Nerve Palsy: Spontaneous Recovery in two Patients' in 'Journal of Neurology, Neurosurgery and Psychiatry', 1974; 'Summing Up', in "Clinical Pharmacology of Antiepileptic Drugs", 1975; Introduction in "Antiepileptic Drug Monitoring", 1977; 'Spinal Cord Compression - a Neurological Emergency' in 'Modern Medicine', 1979; 'Self Help Approach in a Tank' in 'Current Practice', 1984; etc. *Address:* The Coach House, 1A College Road, Exeter, Devon EX1 1TE, England.

GARDOS, George, b. 8 July 1927, Budapest, Hungary. Deputy Director of the National Institute of Haematology and Blood Transfusion, NIHBT, Budapest. m. Agatha Rein, 14 July 1953, Budapest, 2 sons. *Education:* Diploma, Chemistry, 1950; PhD, 1958; D.Sc, 1969. *Appointments:* Lecturer, 1949-62; Senior Lecturer, 1962-64, Department of Medical

Chemistry, Medical University of Budapest; Head, Department of Cell Metabolism, National Institute of Haematology and Blood Transfusion, Budapest, 1964-; Deputy Director, NIHBT, Budapest, 1980-. *Memberships:* Hungarian Biochemical Society; Hungarian Biophysical Society; Hungarian Physiological Society; Hungarian Medical Nuclear Society; International Cell Research Organization, ICRO; European Cell Biology Organization, ECBO. *Publications:* 'Accumulation of K ions in human erythrocytes', 'Acta Physiol. Hung.' 6, 1954; 'The Function of Calcium in the Potassium Permeability of Human Erythrocytes', 'Biochim. Biophys'. Acta 30, 1958; 'Postassium Accumulation in Guinea Pig Brain Cortex Slices', 'Journal of Neurochemistry', 5, 1960; "The Function of Calcium in the Regulation of Ion Transport", Proc.Symp. Membrane Transport and Metabolism, Prague, 1961; "Mechanism of Ca-dependent K Transport in Human Red Cells", FEBS Proc. 35, 1975; General Editor, FEBS Proceedings, Volumes 31-37, 1975. *Address:* Daróczi u. 24, H-1113 Budapest, Hungary.

GARNER, Margaret Flora, b. 20 Feb. 1927, Sydney, Australia. Staff Specialist/Chief Serologist/Head and Chief Investigator, WHO Collaborating Centre for Venereal Diseases. *Education:* MBBS, Sydney University, 1950; MRCPath, England, 1965; FRCPA (Royal College of Pathologists of Australia) 1968; FRCPath, England, 1977. *Appointments:* Resident Medical Officer, Goulburn Base Hospital, New South Wales, Australia; Resident Anaesthetist and House Physician, Nelson Hospital, London; Pathology Registrar, Queen Mary's Hospital for East End, London; Medical Officer, Microbiological Laboratory, New South Wales Health Department, Australia; Senior Specialist Pathologist, then Staff Specialist and Chief Serologist, V.D. Reference Laboratory, Institute of Clinical Pathology and Medical Research, Westmead Hospital, Westmead, New South Wales, Australia; Also Head and Chief Investigator, WHO Collaborating Centre for Venereal Diseases and Treponematoses Reference and Research, Western Pacific Region. *Memberships:* Royal College of Pathologists of England; Royal College of Pathologists of Australia; Venereology Society of New South Wales; Australasian Society for Infectious Diseses. *Publications:* 56 publications in overseas and Australian medical and scientific journals. *Honours:* NHMRC Travelling Fellowship 1963; WHO Exchange of Research Workers Grant 1970. *Hobbies:* Gardening; Handicrafts. *Address:* Institute of Clinical Pathology and Medical Research, PO Box 60, Wentworthville 2145, Australia.

GARLICK, David George, b. 17 Jan 1933, Sydney, Australia. Senior Lecturer. 1 daughter. *Education:* BSc (Med) 1957; MBBS, 1959, Sydney University; PhD, Australian National University,1963. *Appointments:* Junior Resident Medical Officer, Parramatta Hospital, 1959; Commonwealth Research Scholar, Australian National University, 1960-62; Registrar in Pathology, Prince Henry Hospital, 1963; Lecturer in Pathology, University of New South Wales, 1964-65; ANU Travelling Fellow, Duke University, 1966-68; Research Fellow, Copenhagen University, 1968-69; Currently Senior Lecturer, University of New South Wales. *Memberships:* Australian Physiological and Pharmaocolgical Society; Anatomical Society of Australia and New Zealand; Ergonomics Society of Australia and New Zealand. *Publications:* Editor: "Progress in Microcirculation Research" 1981; "Proprioception, Posture and Emotion" editor, 1982; Editor: "Festschrift for F C Courtice" 1981; "Progress in Microcirculation Research II" co-editor with F C Courtice and M A Perry, 1984; "Frontiers in Physiological Research" co-editor with P I Korner, 1984. *Hobbies:* Aerobic exercise; Music; Reading. *Address:* School of Physiology and Pharmacology, University of New South Wales, Kensington, New South Wales 2033, Australia.

GARNER, Alec, b. 1 June 1932, Accrington, England.

Professor and Director of Pathology. m. Catherine Mary Watling, 25 June 1959, Seven Kings, Essex, 2 sons, 1 daughter. *Education:* MB ChB 1960, Md 1966, PhD 1972, University of Manchester Medical School. *Appointments:* House Physician and Surgeon, Crumpsall Hospital, Manchester, 1960-61; Resident Clinical Pathologist, Manchester Royal Infirmary, 1961-62; Assistant Lecturer in Pathology 1962-66, Lecturer 1966-67, University of Manchester; Senior Lecturer in Pathology 1967-70, Reader in Experimental Pathology 1970-78, Professor and Director of Pathology 1978-, Institute of Ophthalmology, London. *Memberships:* Royal College of Physicians; Royal College of Pathologists; Royal Society of Medicine; Pathological Society of Great Britain; Ophthalmological Society of the United Kingdom. *Publications:* "Immunopathology of the Eye", (co-author), 1976; "Pathobiology of Ocular Disease", (Co-editor and contributor),1 982. *Hobbies:* Reading; Snooker; Music. *Address:* Institute of Ophthalmology, 17/25 Cayton Street, London EC1V 9AT, England.

GARRETT, John Raymond, b. 28 Mar. 1928, Winchester, England. Professor and Head of Department of Oral Pathology. m. Daphne Anne Parr, 28 Apr. 1958, London, 1 son, 1 daughter. *Education:* BSc 1st class honours; MB BS honours Obstetrics and Gynaecology; LDSRCS; PhD, 1965. *Appointments:* Dental Health Service 1950, Nuffield Research Fellow, Morbid Anatomy 1961-64, Senior Lecturer, Oral Pathology 1964-68, Reader, Oral Pathology 1968-71, Professor and Head of Department of Oral Pathology 1971-, King's College Hospital, London; Captain, Royal Army Dental Corps, 1951-52. *Memberships:* Fellow, Royal College of Pathologists; Worshipful Society of Apothecaries; President 1980-82, Royal Microscopical Society; Royal Society of Medicine; Physiological Society; Pathological Society; International Association of Dental Research; Secretary 1984, Interntional Federation of Societies of Histochemistry and Cytochemistry. *Publications include:* Numerous articles including: 'Adventures with autonomic nerves: perspectives in salivary glandular innervations', 1982; 'myenteric plexus of hind-gut: developmental abnormalities in humans and experimental studies' in 'Development of the Autonomic Nervous System', 1981. *Honours:* Isaac Schour Award, International Association of Dental Research, 1979; Honorary MD, Lund University, Sweden, 1985. *Hobbies:* Rugby football; Medical History. *Address:* Department of Oral Pathology, The Rayne Institute, King's College School of Medicine and Dentistry, London SE5 9NU, England.

GARY, Nancy Elizabeth, b. 4 Mar. 1937, New York, USA. Professor of Medicine & Associate Dean, University of Medicine & Dentistry of New Jersey-Rutgers Medical School. *Education:* BS, Springfield College, 1958; MD, Medical College of Pannsylvania, 1962. *Appointments:* Clinical & research fellow, National Institutes of Health, Georgetown University Medical Centre, 1965-67; Chief, Nephrology, St. Vincent's Hospital, New York City, 1967-74; Instructor, Clincial Medicine, New York University School of Medicine, 1967-74; Assistant, Associate Professor of Medicine, University of Medicine & Dentistry of New Jersey-Rutgers Medical School, 1974-81. *Memberships:* Fellow, American College of Physicians; New Jersey, American & International Societies of Nephrology; American Medical Association; Harvey Society. *Publications include:* Over 65 contributions, various medical journals. *Honours:* Alpha Omega Alpha, 1984; UMDNJ-Rutgers Medical School teaching award, 1983. *Hobbies:* Travel; Art; Theatre. *Address:* UMDNJ-Rutgers Medical School, University Heights, Busch Campus, Piscataway, NJ 08854, USA.

GASTON, Lawrence Randolf, b. 19 Jan. 1954. Doctor

of Podiatric Medicine. *Education:* BA, University of Kansas, 1976; Doctor of Podiatric Medicine, Illinois College of Podiatric Medicne, 1982; First year podiatric surgical residencey program, Windom Area Hospital, 1983. *Memberships:* Associate, American College of Foot Surgeons; Member, American Podiatry Medical Association; Kansas Podiatry Medical Association. *Address:* 3301 Clinton Parkway Court, Lawrence, KS 66046, USA.

GASTON, Peter Francis, b. 13 June 1914, Budapest, Hungary. Supervising Psychiatrist. m. Sara Klein, 12 May 1944, Carei Mare, 1 son. *Education:* MD, Budapest Pazmany Peter University, 1938; Qualified Psychiatrist, 1962; Diploma, Speciality of Psychiatry, 1963. *Appointments:* Resident, Psychiatry, Kings Park, New York, USA, 1957-61; Supervising Psychiatrist, Mental Hygiene, Outpatients Clinic, New York, 1961-; Assistant Psychiatrist, Bellevue Hospital, New York, 1961-66; Instructor, Clinical Psychiatry, Columbia University, New York, 1973-77. *Memberships:* Life Member, New York County Medical Society; Life Member, American Psychiatric Association. *Honours:* Diploma, Psychiatry, 1963; Certificate of Appreciation for Efficient Patient Care, Manhattan St. Hospital, New York, 1973. *Hobbies:* Model Railroading; Music. *Address:* 55 East 87th St., New York, NY 10028, USA.

GATELL, Jose M., b. 14 Jan. 1951, Brafim, Physician/Associate Professor of Medicine. m. Rosa M Aused, 29 Sep. 1975, Barcelona, Spain. 1 son, 2 daughters. *Education:* MD, 1976; PhD, 1981; ECFMD Certificate 1976; Visa Qualifying Examination, 1977. *Appointments:* Residency in Medicine, 1976-80; Residency in Infectious Diseases 1981; Physician, Infectious Diseases Unit, 1982-; Assistant Professor of Medicine, 1976-78; Associate Professor of Medicine, 1978-. *Memberships:* Secretary, Catalan Association of Internal Medicine; New York Academy of Sciences; American Society of Microbiology; American Public Health Association. *Publications:* Co-author: "Farreras-Rozman Medicina Interna" 1982; "Aminoslycoside Toxicity Antimicrobial Acents Chemotherapy, 1982; Prophylaxis in Orthopedic Surgery and Bone Joint Surgery" 1984 etc and several articles about Infections in Drug Addicts. *Hobbies:* Skiing; Tennis. *Address:* Santapau 62, 08016 Barcelona, Spain.

GAUME, James Garnet, b. 14 Sep. 1915, Byron, Oklahoma, USA. Biomedical Consultant in Accident Litigation. m. Jean Hemstreet, 1 June 1940, Omaha, Nebraska, 1 son, 2 daughters. *Education:* BS, Chemistry, Kansas State University, Manhattan, Kansas; MD, Creighton University School of Medicine, Omaha, Nebraska. *Appointments include:* Director, Life Sciences, Northrop Space Laboratories, Hawthorne, California, 1962-64; Chief Aerospace Medicine, Douglas Aircraft Company, Santa Monica, California, 1964-66; Manager, Aviation Medicine and Safety Research, McDonnel Douglas Corporation, Long Beach, California, 1966-82; President, James G Gaume and Associates, Inc, Biomedical Consultant in Accident Litigation, 1982-. *Memberships include:* International Academy of Aviation and Space Medicine; International Society of Air Safety Investigators; Aerospace Medical Association; Airlines Medical Directors Association etc. *Publications:* Numerous articles in professional journals in the field of Aviation and Space Medicine and Safety. *Honours include:* Liljencrantz Award, Aerospace Medical Association, 1985; Fellow of Aerospace Medical Association, 1972 Associate Fellow, American Institute of Aeronautics and Astronautics. *Hobbies:* Camping; Swimming and diving; Music; Geneaology; Aviation buff. *Address:* James G Gaume and Associates, Inc, 2550 Via Tejon, Suite 3H, Palos Verdes Estates, CA 90274, USA.

GAUR, Shailendra Nath, b. 23 May 1952, Delhi, India. Lecturer in Chest Medicine. m. Meera Gaur, 30 June 1982, Delhi, 1 daughter. *Education:* MB BS 1973, MD 1977, MLN Medical College, University of Allahabad, Uttar Pradesh, India. *Appointments:* Intern 1974, House Officer Medicine 1975, Registrar TB and Chest Diseases 1976, Tutor 1977-78, SRN Hospital, MLN Medical College, Allahabad; Senior Resident, TB and Chest Diseases, Goa Medical College, Panaji, Goa, 1978-79; Medical Officer, TB Clinic, Gorakhpur, 1979-80; Lecturer in Chest Medicine, VP Chest Institute, University of Delhi, 1980 - . *Memberships:* Fellow, American College of Chest Physicians; Fellow, National College of Chest Physicians; Fellow, Indian College of Allergy and Applied Immunology; Life Member, Asthma and Bronchitis Foundation of India. *Publications:* 'Blastomycosis Dermatitidis in India', 1983; 'Amoebic pl. eff. - diagnosed by microscopy', 1984; 'Curschmann's spirals : A cytological finding in chronic bronchitis', 1984; 'A viral study in acute episodes of wheezy bronchitis in children', 1983; 'Etiol. significance of insects in allergy', 1985. *Hobbies:* Chess; Badminton; Table-Tennis. *Address:* Clinical Research Centre, VP Chest Institute, University of Delhi, Delhi 110007, India.

GAUSSET, Philippe Emmanuel Lucien, b. 21 May 1945, Lisbon, Portugal. Medical Director. m. Michele Paduart, 30 Sept. 1967, Brussels, Belgium, 1 son, 2 daughters. *Education:* MD, Free Unviersity fo Brussels, Belgium, 1969; Diploma Universitaire de Transfusion Sanguie, University of Paris, France, 1981. *Appointments:* Currently, Medical Director, Centre A Hustin Blood Bank, University Hospital Saint Pierre, Brussels, Belgium. *Memberships:* International and French Societies of Blood Transfusion; American Association of Blood Banks; European Society for Clinical Investigation; European Society for Clinical Immunology adn Allergology; Belgian Society for Allergology and Clincial Immunology; Berlgian Society of Immunology. *Publications:* 'In Vitro response of subpopulations of human lymphotytes - II DNA synthesis, induced by anti immunoglobulin antibodies' in 'Journal of Immunology', 1976. *Hobby:* Music. *Address:* Ave de la Fauconnerie 57, B-1170 Brussels, Belgium.

GAVIRIA, Moises, b. 28 Dec. 1943, Peru. Associate Professor of Psychiatry and Preventive Medicne. m. Eliana, 2 sons. *Education:* Premedical School, 1959-60, Medical School, 1961-66, MD, Universidad Nacional Major de San Marcos; Intern, Arzobispo Loayza Hosptial, Lima, 1966-67; Psychiatric Resident, Universidad Nacional Major de San Marcos, 1967-70, University of Connecticut, USA, 1971-74; Fellow, Community and Social Psychiatry, Illinois State Psychiatric Institute, Chicago, Illinois, USA, 1974-75. *Appointments include:* Clinical Instructor, 1966-69, Director of Undergraduate Education, Department of Psychiatry, 1969-70, Universidad Nacional de San Marcos, Lima; Assistant Professor, 1975-79, Associate Professor, Psychiatry and Preventive Medicine, Health Sciences Center, 1979-, Director, Affective Disorders Clinic, 1975-, Director, Social Psychiatry Research Unit, Department of Psychaitry, 1983-, Director, Simon Bolivar Research and Training Program, 1984-, University of Illinois, USA; Consultant, Pilsen Little Village Community Mental Health Center, 1975-, Psychiatric Inpatient Service, West Side Veterans Administration Hosptial, 1980-. *Memberships include:* Past Presidnet, American Society of Hispanic Psychiatrists; Illinois Psychiatric Society; American Psychiatric Association; Honorary Member, Peruvian Psychiatric Society; American Board of Psychiatry and Neurology Examiner. *Publications:* "Affective Disorders: Psychopathology and Treatment", co-editor, 1982; "Psychological Management in Affective Disorders: Psychopatholology and Treatment", 1982. Author of 46 papers contributed to refereed professional journals and about 24 papers presented at national and international confereneces. *Honours include:* Licensed, Illinois State, 1975, American Board of Psychiatry and Neurolgoy, 1977; Consultant, Peruvian National Institute of Mental Health. *Address:* 912 Southwood Street, Chicago, IL 60612, USA.

GEDDES, LaNelle Evelyn, b. 15 Sep. 1935, Houston, Texas, USA. Professor and Head of University School of Nursing. m. Leslie Alexander Geddes, 3 Aug. 1962, Houston, Texas. *Education:* BS Nursing, PhD Biophysical Sciences, University of Houston; Postdoctoral Fellowship in Cardiovascular Physiology, Baylor College of Medicine. *Appointments:* School Nurse, Houston Independent School District; Assistant Professor of Nursing, Texas Woman's University; Assistant Professor of Physiology, Baylor College of Medicine; Associate Professor of Medicine, Currently Professor and Head of School of Nursing, Purdue University, West Lafayette, Indiana. *Memberships:* American Nurses Association; National League for Nursing; American Association of Critical Care Nurses; Sigma Theta Tau; Phi Kappa Phi; Iota Sigma Phi. *Publications include:* 'The measurement of cardiac output by means of electrical impedance', 1971; 'Contrasting twitch and latency relaxation in skeletal muscle', 1972; 'Thoracic impedance changes following slaine injection into right and left ventricles', 1972; Other abstracts and book chapters, 1972-81. *Honours:* Predoctoral and Postdoctoral Fellowships, 1965-72; James G Dwyer Undergraduate Teaching Award, 1977; Amoco Foundation Outstanding Undergraduate Teaching Award, 1984. *Hobbies:* Travel; Culinary arts. *Address:* School of Nursing, Purdue University, West Lafayette, IN 47907, USA.

GEERTINGER, Preben Gert, b. 3 Feb. 1923, Copenhagen, Denmark. State Forensic Pathologist, Professor MD. m. Lilan Woldum, 22 Sep. 1966, 1 daughter. *Education:* Graduate Copenhagen University Medical School, 1956; MD Sc, University of Copenhagen, 1966. *Appointments:* Practice of Forensic Pathology 1959-; Director, Government Institute of Forensic Medicine, University of Umea and University of Gothernburg, Sweden, 1964-70; Professor of Forensic Medicine, University of Copenhagen, 1970-; Secretary, Danish Medico-Legal Board, 1970-. *Publications:* "Sudden Death in Infancy" 1968; Contributor of articles to medical journals. *Honours:* King Christian X's Foundation Award, 1962, 1964; Danish Heart Foundation Awards 1971, 1977. *Address:* Aurehøjvej 26 B, 2900 Hellerup, Denmark.

GEELHOED, Glenn William, b 19 Jan. 1942, Grand Rapids, Michigan, USA. Professor, Surgery, George Washington University Medical Centre. 2 sons. *Education:* AB, 1964, BS, 1965, Calvin College; MD, University of Michigan Medical School, 1968;' Internship, Residnecies, various hospitals, 1968-70. *Appointments:* Assistant, Surgery, Harvard Medical School, 1969-70; Clinical Associate, National Institue of Health, 1970-72; Senior Staff, National Cancer Institute, NIH, 1972-73; Associate, 1973-74, Instructor, 1974-75, Assistant Professor, 1975-76, Surgery, Associate Director, Clinical Scholar Programme, 1977-79, Associate Professor, 1976-84, Professor, 1985-, Surgery, George Washington University Medical College. *Memberships include:* Fellow, American College of Surgeons; Society of Univeristy Surgeons; Association for Academic Surgery; many other professional organisations. *Publications include:* "Problem Management in Endocrine Surgery", 1983; "Endocrine and Metabolic Responses to Illness & Injury", co-author, 1983; "Correlative Surgical Endocrinology", co-author, 1984; "Surgical Infection and Its Prevention", co-author; "Surgery of the Sdrenal Cortex"; "Perioperative Care of the Surgical Patient", 1985; numerous articles in professional journals. *Honours include:* Bausch & Lomb Science Medal, 1960; National Merit Scholarship, 1960;

Conrad Gobst Award, 1975; etc. *Hobbies include:* Natural History; Adventure Travel; Photography. *Address:* 2Dept. of Surgery, George Washington University Medical Centre, 2150 Pennsylvania Ave NW, Washington, DC 20037, USA.

GEFFNER, Donna Sue, b. New York City, USA. Speech Pathologist; Audiologist; Educator. *Education:* BA, magna cum laude, Brooklyn College, L'SA, 1967; MA, New York University, 1968; PhD (NDEA Fellow), 1970; Postgraduate Student, Advanced Institute Analytic Psychotherapy, 1973-75. *Appointments:* Assistant Professor, Lehman College, CUNY,. 1971-76; Professor, Department of Speech, Com. Sci. and Theatre, St. John's University, 1976-; Director, Speech and Hearing Centre, Chairperson, Department of Speech, Com. Sci. and Theatre, 1983-. *Memberships:* New York State Speech Language and Hearing Association President, 1978-80; American Speech-Language-Hearing Association, Legislative Councillor, 1978-87. *Publications:* Contributor of articles to professional journals and textbooks; Issue Editor "Journal Topics in Language Disorders", 1980; Editor and contributor to 'Monograph' Speech Language and Communication Skills of Deaf Children, 1980. *Honours:* New York Research Foundation grantee, 1972; New York State Educational Department grantee, 1976-78; President's Commission on Employment for the Handicapped; Developed Bachelors' and Masters' Degree Programme, St. John's University, New York, USA. *Address:* St. John's University, Jamaica, NY 11439, USA.

GEHA, Alexander Salim, b. 28 June 1936, Beirut, Lebanon, Professor of Cardiothoracic Surgery, Yale University. m. Diane Redalen, 25 Nov. 1967, Lanesboro, Minnesota, 3 daughters. *Education:* BS 1955, MD 1959, American University of Beirut; MS, University of Minnestoa Mayo Graduate School of Medicine, 1967. *Appointments:* Assistant Professor of Thoracic & Cardiovascular Surgery, University of Vermont, 1967-69; Assistant Professor of Surgery (tenure), 1969-73, Associate Professor of Surgery (tenure), 1973-75, Washington University School of Medicine; Associate Professor of Surgery (tenure), 1975-78, Professor of Surgery (tenure), 1978-, Yale University School of Medicine; Associate Chief, 1978-82, Chief, 1982-, Section of Cardiothoracic Surgery, Yale University School of Medicine. *Memberships include:* American Association for Throacic Surgery; American College of Cardiology; American College of Chest Physicians; American College of Surgeons; American Heart Association; American Medical Association; American Surgical Association; American Thoracic Society; Association for Academic Surgery; International Society for Heart Transplantation; Société Internationale de Chirurgie; Society of University Surgeons. *Publications:* Some 120 published papers as author & co-author in medical & surgical journals. *honours:* Alpha Omega Alpha, American University of Beirut Chapter, 1958; Sigma Xi, Mayo Foundation Chapter, 1968; MA Privatum, Yale University, 1978. *Address:* Department of Surgery, Yale University School of Medicine, 333 Cedar Street, PO Box 3333, New Haven, CT 06510, USA.

GEISELMAN, Paula J, b. 30 June 1944, Ohio, USA. Visiting Assistant Professor of Psychology. m. Dr. R Edward Geiselman, 20 Mar. 1976, Ohio. *Education:* AB Psychology with High Honour 1971, MS Experimental Psychology 1976, Ohio University; PhD Physiological Psychology, University of California, Los Angeles, 1983. *Appointments:* Instructor, Department of Psychology, Ohio University, 1974-76; Predoctoral Fellow (National Institute of Mental Health) 1977-81, Research Associate (National Institue of Neurological and Communicative Diseases and Strokes) intermittently 1978-81, Teaching Assistant 1981, Teaching Fellow 1982, Staff Research Associate (National Institute of

Drug Abuse) 1983, Currently Visiting Assistant Professor, Department of Psychology, University of California, Los Angeles. *Memberships include:* Society for Neuroscience; American Association for the Advancement of Science; American Psychological Association; North American Association for the Study of Obesity; Association of Academic Women; Association for the Advancement of Psychology; International Brain Research Organization/World Federation of Neuroscientists; Sigma Xi; Psi Chi. *Publications include:* 'Dietary Implications for the Control of Food Intake and Body Weight', 1984; 'Appetite, Hunger, and Obestity as a Function of Dietary Sugar Intake: Can These Effects be Mediated by Insulin-induced Hypoglycemia? A reply to Commentaries', 1985; 'Feeding Patterns Following Normal Ingestion and Intragastric Infusion of Glucose, Fructorse, and Galactose in the Rabbit'. *Honours include:* UCLA Medal, 1983; Graduate Woman of the Year Award, UCLA chapter, Association of Academic Women, 1983; Several grants. *Hobbies:* Opera; Ballet; Early music; Italian renaissance; Mesoamerica. *Address:* Department of Psychology, Franz Hall, 1405 Hilgard Avenue, UCLA, Los Angeles, CA 90024, USA.

GELDER, Michael Graham, b. 2 July 1929, Ilkley, Yorkshire, England, Professor of Psychiatry, University of Oxford; Fellow, Merton College, Oxford, m. Margaret Anderson, 21 July 1954, Edinburgh, Scotland, 1 son, 2 daughters. *Education:* Hasting Scholar, Theodore Williams Prize, 1949, 1st Class Honours Physiology, Queens College, Oxford University; Goldsmit Scholarship, University College Hospital; MA; MD; FRCP; FRCPsych. *Appointments:* House Physician, House Surgeon, Casulaty Medical Officer and Senior House Officer, Psychiatry, University College Hospital; Registrar, Senior Registrar, Maudsley Hospital; MRC Fellow in Clinical Research; Lecturer, Senior Lecturer, Institute of Psychiatry, London; Consultant Psychiatrist, Bethlem and Maudsley Hospitals. *Memberships:* Association of Physicians; British Association of Psychopharmacology; Society for Psychotherapy Research. *Publications:* "Oxford Textbook of Psychiatry", (Co-author), 1983; "Agoraphobia, Nature and Treatment", (Co-author), 1981; Contributor to "Oxford Textbook of Medicine", 2nd Edition, 1986 and "Oxford Companion to Medicine", 1986; Contributor of numerous articles in scientific journals. *Address:* University Department of Psychiatry, Warneford Hospital, Oxford OX3 7JX, England.

GENSTER, Helge Gotfred, b. 24 May 1932, Copenhagen, Denmark. Chief Surgeon. m. Hanne, 8 Feb. 1958, Haderslev, 3 daughters. *Education:* MD, University of Aarhus, 1958; Speciality Board, Surgery 1967, Urology 1972, Denmark. *Appointments:* Resident, Odense and Sønderborg Hospitals; Resident, V A Hospital, Madison, Wisconsin, USA, 1968; Resident 1969-75, Chief Urologist 1975-78, University Hospital, Aarhus, Denmark; Chief Surgeon, Sønderborg Hospital, 1978 -. *Memberships:* Danish Surgical Society; Scandinavian Urological Association; International Society of Urology; Royal Society of Medicine, London. *Publications:* Articles on surgical and urological topics. *Honour:* Prize winning essay, American Urological Association, 1968. *Hobby:* President, Rotary Club Sønderborg Syd, 1986. *Address:* Department of Surgery K, Sønderborg Hospital, DK 6400 Sønderborg, Denmark.

GENTLESK, Michael John, b. 23 May 1938, Haddon Heights, New Jersey, USA. m. Jurate Elizabeth Pauliukonis, 5 Oct. 1963, Holy Maternity Church, 4 sons, 3 daughters. *Education:* BS, 1960, MD, 1964, Georgetown University, Washington. *Appointments:* Director of Paediatrics and Patient Services, Childrens Heart Hospital, 1972-73; Chief, Department of Allergy and Immunology,

Paediatrics, Our Lady of Lourdes Medical Centre, 1982-; Currently, Associate Professor of Paediatrics, Thomas Jefferson University, Philadelphia, Pennsylvania, Clinical Associate Professor of Paediatrics, Rutgers University and Adjunct Clinical Assistant Professor of Paediatrics, Temple University, St Christophers Hospital. *Memberships:* Fellow: American Academy of Paediatrics; American College of Allergists; American Academy of Allergy and Clinical Immunology; American College of Chest Physicians; American Medical Association. *Publications:* Author or co-author of papers contributed to professional journals including: 'American Journal of Nursing'; 'Annals of Allergy and Immunology'; 'Cutis'; 'International Archives of Allergy and Clinical Immunology'; 'Journal of Pharmacy and Therapeutics'. *Honours:* Elected Delegate, New Jersey Medical Society to American Medical Association meetings, 1983-86. *Hobbies:* Fishing; Tennis; Golf; Stamp collecting; Antique car collecting. *Address:* 1942 East Marlton Pike, Route 70, Cherry Hill, NJ 08003, USA.

GEORGE, Charles Frederick, b. 3 Apr 1941, Birmingham, England. Professor of Clinical Pharmacology. *Education:* BSc, Anatomy, 1962, MB, ChB, 1965, University of Birmingham, MRCP, London, 1968; MD, Birmingham, 1974; FRCP, London, 1978. *Appointments:* Tutor in Medicine and Clinical Pharmacology, Royal Postgraduate Medical School, London; 1971-73; Senior Lecturer in Clinical Pharmacology, 1973-75, Professor of Clinical Pharmacology, 1975-, Deputy Dean, Faculty of Medicine, 1984, University of Southampton; Honorary Consultant Physician to Southampton and Southwest Hants Health Authority, 1975-. *Memberships:* Committee on the Review of Medicines; Administration of Radioactive Substances Advisory Committee; British Pharmacological Society Committee; Association of Physicians of Great Britain and Ireland. *Publications:* "Topics in Clinical Pharmacology" 1980; "Presystemic Drug Metabolism" with Shand D G and Renwick A G, 1982; 'Drug induced disorders of the Small Intestine' with G E Holdstock, in "Disorders of the Small Intestine" edited by Booth CC and Neale G, 1985. *Honour:* Merck Sharp and Dohme International Fellowship in Clinical Pharmacology, 1973 (not taken up). *Hobbies:* Windsurfing; Squash; Jogging; Music. *Address:* The University of Southampton, Medical and Biological Sciences Building, Bassett Crescent East, Southampton SO9 3TU, England.

GEORGE, Phyllis Ann, b. 18 Feb. 1925, Sedgley, Staffordshrie, England. Surgeon, Royal Free Hospital. *Education:* LRCP; MRCS; MBBS; FRCS Eng.; Royal Free Hospital School of Medicine. *Appointments:* House Surgeon, Casualty Surgeon, Royal Free Hospital; House Surgeon, Central Middlesex Hospital; SHO Surgeon, Gt. Ormond Street Hospital for Sick Children; Senior Surgeon Registrar, Royal Free Hospital; Resident Surgeon, Memorial Hospital, New York Spec.; Fellow, Surgeon, Sloan Kettering Institute, New York. *Memberships:* Member Council Royal College of Surgeons of England; Member, Court Examiners Final FRCS Royal College of Surgeons, England; Immediate Past-President, Section Surgery, Royal Society of Medicine; Association of Surgeons of Great Britian and Ireland. *Publications:* Chapters in books and articles on biliary tract surgery, panc. surgery, breast surgery, melanoma. *Honours:* Squibb Olin Travelling Fellowship New York, 1968; Marsden Travelling Fellowship to Australia and New Zealand, 1978. *Hobbies:* Cooking; Walking; Woodland Conservation. *Address:* Royal Free Hospital, Pond Street, London NW3 2QR, England.

GEORGIEVA-TANCHEVA, Kichka, b. 7 Aug. 1930, Haskovo, Bulgaria. Head of Department of Oral and Maxillofacial Surgery. m. Peter Tanchev, 16 July 1948, 1 son. *Education:* Doctor of Dental Surgery,

Professor, PhD. *Appointments:* Lectuer 1953-61, Assistant Professor 1961-72, Professor 1972-, Head of Department of Oral and Maxillofacial Surgery, 1977-, Dean, Faculty of Stomatology 1977-83, Vice President of the High Institute of Medicine, Sofia, 1983-. *Memberships:* President, Association Medicale Scientifique Republicaine de Stomatologie; Head of Editorial Staff of Bulgarian Dental Journal "Stomatology". *Publications:* Textbooks: "Oral and Maxillofacial Surgery" 1975, 1979; "Urgent Aid in Stomatology" 1981; "Propaedeutics of the Dental Surgery" 1982 and many others. *Honours:* Medal of People's Republic of Bulgaria (major honorary title of merit in science in Bulgaria. *Hobbies:* Poetry and Belles Letters. *Address:* Medical Academy, Faculty of Stomatology, 1 "G. Sofiski" Bld, Sofia 1431, Bulgaria.

GEORGOTAS, Anastasios, b. 28 Mar. 1946, Corfu, Greece. Professor of Psychiatry and Director of Depression Studies Programme, New York University; Medical Director, Clinical Research Center; Director, Biological Psychiatry and Psychopharmacology, NYU Bellevue Medical Center. *Education:* MD, Athens University Medical School; Intern, Boston University Medical Center, USA; Resident, Columbia University; Chief Resident, Massachusetts Mental Health Center, Harvard University; Teaching and Research Fellowships, Harvard University. *Appointments:* Assistant Professor, Psychiatry, New York University; Attending Psychiatrist, Bellevue and University Hospitals; Research Psychiatrist, Neuropsychopharmacology, New York University; Research Collaborator, Brookhaven National Laboratories; Consultant Psychiatrist, New York Veterans Administration Medical Center; Adjunct Associate Professor, Neuropsychiatry, Seoul National University, College of Medicine, Korea; Associate Professor of Psychiatry, Patras University, Greece; currently: Professor of Psychiatry and Director, Depression Studies Programme, New York University, USA; Medical Director, National Institute of Mental Health Clinical Research Center; Director, Biological Psychiatry-Psychopharmacology, Bellevue Medical Center. *Memberships:* New York Academy of Sciences; Harvard Medical Alumni Association; New York University Medical Alumni Association; American Psychiatric Association; Society of Biological Psychiatry; Collegium Internationale Neuro-Psychopharmacologicum. *Publications:* "Frontiers in Neuropsychiatric Research", 1983; "Depression and Mania A Comprehensive Textbook", 1986; Author over 20 book chapters, 1978- and 50 published articles, 1978-. *Honours Include:* MD Summa cum laude, Athens University, Greece, 1968; Physicians Recognition Award, American Medical Association, 1974-77, 1977-80; Grants, National Institute of Mental Health, 1978-86. *Address:* New York University Medical Center, Department of Psychiatry, 550 First Avenue, New York, NY 10016 USA.

GERASH, Helen, b. 9 Oct. 1930, Los Angeles, California, USA. Psychiatrist; Private Practitioner. 2 sons. *Education:* BA, Berkeley, 1952, Graduate School, 1953, University of California; MD, University of Colorado School of Medicine, 1961; Psychiatric Residency completed, University of Colorado School of Medicine, 1967. *Appointments:* Psychiatrist, Private Practice; Lecturer; Consultant to Mental Health, Religious, Humanist and Women's Issues organisations. *Memberships:* Denver Medical Society; American Psychiatric Association; American Medical Womens Association; Colorado Child and Adolescent Psychiatric Society; Physicians for Social Responsibility. *Honours:* BA with honours, University of California, Berkeley, 1952. *Hobbies:* Sociological and political reading and Activities; Travel; Hand crafts. *Address:* 4770 East Iliff Avenue, Suite 111, Denver, CO 80222, USA.

GERGELY, Mihály, b. 1 Mar. 1933, Kassa, Hungary.

Professor Surgery. m. Ildikó Adorján, 31 Mar. 1958, Diósgyör, Hungary, 4 sons, 1 daughter. *Education:* Graduation, Debrecen Medical University, 1958; Specialsit in Surgery (=FRCS), 1963; Candidate of Medical Science (+PhD), 1973; Honorary Docent, Szeged Medical University, 1978; Honorary Professor, Szeged Medical University, 1984. *Appointments:* Senior House Officer, 1958-63, Registrar, 1963-67, Postgraduate Research Fellow, 1967-70, 1st Surgical Clinic, Institute of Experimental Surgery, Szeged Medical University; Senior Registrar, 1970-75, Consultant of Surgery, 1975-; Senior House Officer to Mr G H Wooler, Thoracic Surgical Department, Killingbeck Hospital, Leeds, England, 1973-74. *Memberships:* Hungarian Society of Surgeons; Hungarian Society of Gastroenterology; Hungarian Society of Gerontology; Collegium Intern. Chirurgiæ Dig; European Society of Surgical Oncology. *Publications:* Book Chapters, some 70 articles in surgical journals. *Honour:* Award for Excellent Work, Ministry of Health, 1985. *Hobbies:* Riding; Driving; Gardening; Surgery. *Address:* 1st Department of Surgery, County Hospital, 5004 Szolnok POB 2, Hungary.

GERMAN, Albert A, b. 17 Mar. 1917. Tours France. Professor of Virology & Immunology. m. Charlotte Haeberlin, 29 June 1943, Paris France, 1 son, 3 daughters. *Education:* Internship in Paris Hospitals, 1938; Pharmacists Internship, Paris, 1944; State Doctor of Pharmacy, 1947; Certification to teach in Faculties of Pharmacy, 1952; State Doctor of Sciences, 1953. *Appointments:* Hospital Pharmacist, 1945; Hospital Biologist, 1972; Professor of Virology & Immunology, University of Paris-Sud, 1953-. *Memberships:* Vice-President, Council of the Order of Pharmacists, France; French Society of Immunology; Expert to European Pharmacopoeia; National Academy of Phamacy, France. *Publications:* "Précis de Microbiologie", 1959; 250 papers in Virology & Immunology & on Interferons and Immunodiagnostics of viral diseases. *Honours:* Chevalier, French National Order of Merit, 1972; Chevalier, French National Order of the Legion of Honour, 1980. *Hobbies:* Mountain Walking; Swimming. *Address:* 9 avenue des Etats-Unis, F-78000, Versailles, France.

GERHARDT, Uta, b. 11 June 1938, Zella-Mehlis. Director, Institute of Medical Sociology. m. Dr. Walter Gerhardt, 22 Oct 1960, Frankfurt, divorced 1969. *Education:* Diplomsoziologe, Dr. rer. soc. *Appointments:* Teaching Assistant: Free University of Berlin, University of Konstanz; Assistant Professor, University of Konstanz; Visiting Professor, University of Tubingen; Visiting Researcher, University of California (San Francisco, Berkeley); Lecturer, University of London. *Memberships:* German Sociological Association; German Society of Medical Sociology; European Society of Medical Sociology; German/British Society of Social Medicine; New York Academy of Sciences. *Publications:* "Hochschule in der Demokratie" co-author, 1965; "Rollenanalyse als Kritische Soziologie" 1971; "Stress and Stigma: Explanation and Evidence in the Sociology of Crime and Illness" with M E J Wadsworth, 1985; "Patienten Karrieren'", 1986. *Hobbies:* Opera; Hiking. *Address:* Friedrichstrasse 24, 6300 Giessen, Federal Republic of Germany.

GERTHARDT, John Joseph, b. 20 Apr. 1920, Nowy Sacz, Poland. Doctor; Assistant Professor. m. Margarethe (Greta) A.J. Tatscher, 21 June 1947, Graz, Austria, 1 son, 1 daughter. *Education:* Kaiser Wilhelm University Medical School Berlin, 1942; Karls University Medical School, Prague, 1944; MD, 1945, Karl Franzens University Medical School, Graz, Austria, 1948; Orthopaedisches Spital Wien, Certificate Orthopaedics, 1956; Certificate PM & R Veterans Administration Hospital, Portland, USA, 1971. *Appointments:* Surgical Assistant, County

Hospitals, Austria, until 1956; Staff Physician, Dixon State Hospital, USA, Family Practice, Prohetstown, 1959-66; Residency in Physical Medicine and Rehabilitation, Veterans Administrative Hospital, Portland Oregon, 1966-69; Research & Education Associate in PM & R, Veterans Administrative Hospital, Portland, Oregeon, 1969-71; Chief Physiatry Kaiser Permanente, 1971- ; Assistant Professor, Orthopedics and Rehabilitation, Oregon Health Sciences University, Voluntary Faculty; Attending Physician, VA Hospital, Portland, Oregon; Consultant, Rehabilitation, Shriners Hospital for Crippled Children, Portland. *Memberships:* American Association of Orthopaedic Medicine; American Rheumatism Society; American Medical Society of Vienna; American Medical Association; Oregon Medical Association; Clackamas County Medical Society; International Rehabilitation Medicine Association; many other professional organisations. *Publications:* Co-Author, "Immediate Postsurgical Prosthetics, Rehab. Aspects", 'American Journal Physical Medicine', 1970; "International SFTR Method of Recording Joint Motion & Position", 1976; "A Device to Control Ambulation Pressure", 'Prosthetic Research'; "Amputations", 1982; others. *Hobbies:* Photography; Painting; Sculpture; Music; Skiing; Travel. *Address:* Kaiser Sunnyside Medical Center, 10180 S.E. Sunnyside Road, Clackamas, OR 97015,USA.

GERLACH, Eckehart, b. 2 Apr.1927, Göttingen, Germany. Professor, Chairman, Head of Department. m. (1) Ingrid Bues, 18 Dec. 1954 (deceased 1977) (2) Christine Günther, 16 Oct. 1981; 1 son, 2 daughters. *Education:* MD, University of Heidelberg, 1954; Dr.med.habil, University of Freiburg, 1960. *Appointments:* Assistent, University of Heidelberg, 1954-56; Senior Rassistant, 1956-59, Lecturer, 1960-66; Professor of Physiology, Chairman & Head of Department, Technical University of Aachen,1 966-74; Professor of Physiology, Chairman & Head of Department, University of Munich, 1974-. *Memberships:* German Physiological Society; German Society for Heart & Circulation Research; German Society for Biological Chemistry; Society for Nephrology; New York Academy of Sciences; International Society for Heart Research (European Section). *Publications:* Numerous articles in professional journals; Editor of several proceedings of scientific conferences; Editorial Board, 'Journal of Molecular & Cellular Cardiology', 1970-77; 'Herz-Kreislauf', 1971-; Pfluegers Archiv Europ. Journal of Physiology 1972-; Basic Research in Cardiology, 1973-; Herz u. Gefäße, 1981-. *Honour:* Paul Morawitz award, German Society for Heart & circulation Research, 1980. *Address:* Department of Physiology, University of Munich, Pettenkoferstrasse 12, D-8000 München 2, Federal Republic of Germany.

GEROW, James Hadley, b. 16 Nov 1910, Hutchinson, Kansas, USA. Medical Practitioner. m. Freddy Deubel, 12 Nov 1965, Oregon City, 1 son. *Education:* BA, 1940, MD, 1942, University of Oregon. *Appointments:* US Naval Reserve Lieutenant JG, 1943-45; Lieutenant 1945-46. Assigned to Fleet Marine Force, 2nd Marine Division as combat surgeon in South Pacific. Inactive status 1946-55. Family Pratice, 2 man clinic, Oregon City, Oregon, 1946-56; Family Practice, solo, Oregon City, Oregon, 1956-82; Semi-retired, Volunteer work with migrants 1982 -. *Memberships:* Charter Fellow, American Academy of Family Practice; American Medical Association; Oregon Medical Association; Past President, Clackamas County Medical Society; Oregon Thoracic Society; American Academy of Hypnosis; Secretary-Treasurer, Portland Academy of Hypnosis; Past President, Physicians Association of Clackamas County; Board of Directors for Nursing and Health Services, Oregon Trail Chapter, American Red Cross. *Honour:* Recognition of 25 years of service, American Academy of Family

Physicians, 1982. *Hobbies:* Reading; Music; Theatre. *Address:* 20822 S W Johnson Road, West Linn, OR 97068, USA.

GERSCHMAN, Jack Allen, b. 3 June 1947, Germany, Dental Surgeon. m. Tania Manowicz, 19 Dec. 1976, Melbourne, 2 sons. *Educations:* BD Sc 1971, PhD 1983, Melbourne; LDS, Victoria, 1971: FIBA, 1984. *Appointments:* Co-ordinatior Oro-Facial Pain Clinic 1972 -, Clinical Assistant 1974-, Department of Dental Medicine and Surgery, Lecturer 1976 -, Research Associate in Department of Psychiatry 1976 -, Examiner and member of Board of Examiners in Faculty of Dental Science 1984 -, University of Melbourne, Honorary Dental Hospital 1974 -, Austin Hospital 1983 -, Melbourne; Postgraduate Lecturer, Australian Dental Association, 1977 -; Co-Director, The Melbourne Pain Management Clinic, 1979 -; Scientific Consultant, Journal of Australian Society for the Advancement of Anaesthesia and Sedation in Dentistry, 1983 -, ConsultingEditor, International Journal of Psychosamatics. *Memberships:* Board of Education and Censors, Australian Society of Hypnosis Ltd; Australian Dental Association; International Association of Dental Research; Federation Dentaire Internationale/International Association for the Study of Pain. *Publications Include:* "Diagnosis and Management of Oro-Facial" (in Press), Over 40 book chapters and scientific articles. *Honours:* Research Prize, Melbourne University, 1970; Nominee for BHP Pursuit of Excellence Award, 1984. *Hobbies:* Literature; Music. *Address:* 15 Snowdon Avenue, Caulfield, 3162 Melbourne, Australia.

GERSTEIN, Lawrence M., b. 13 Sept. 1947, Brooklyn, New York. Chiropractic Physician. m. Joy F E Gerstein, 27 Sept. 1975, Orlando, Florida. *Education:* BS, DC, CLT. *Appointments:* Associate Professor of Clinical Science, 1976; Director of Laboratories, 1977; Clinic Director, 1979; Secretary, Treasurer, Missouri Chiropractic Committee for Political Action, 1981. *Memberships:* American Chiropractic Assn.; Missouri State Chiropractic Assn.; Council of Chiropractic Orthopedics. *Publications:* 'Enchanced Absorption of Oral Vitamin B12 from a Resin Adsorbate', 1982; 'Kinisiology', 1976. *Honours:* Montgomery Award, Logan College, 1979; Certificate of Merit, Logan College, 1979; Honours Award, MO State Chiropractic Assn., 1980. *Hobbies:* Fishing; Hunting. *Address:* 819 West 5th Street, Washington, MO 63090, USA.

GERSTENBERGER, Dean L, b. 17 Oct. 1948, Lincoln, Nebraska, USA, Medical Director. m. Marta Martin, 6 Sep. 1975, Topeka, Kansas, 2 sons, 1 daughter. *Education:* BS, Baker University, 1970; MD, University of Kansas, 1974; Diplomate, American Board of Psychiatry and Neurology, 1980. *Appointments:* Staff Psychiatrist, Rochester State Hospital, Rochester, Minnesota, 1978; Surgeon, National Health Service Corp, 1978-80; Medical Director 1978-82 and 1985-, Staff Psychiatrist 1983-85, Coconino Community Guidance Center, Flagstaff, Arizona. *Memberships:* Coconino County Medical Society; Arizona Medical Society; American Society of Clinical Hypnosis. *Publication:* 'Patient-Partner Satisfaction in the Inflatable Penile Prosthesis', 1978. *Honour:* Commissioned Officer Award, National Health Service Corps, 1980. *Address:* 1355 North Beaver, Flagstaff, AZ 86001, USA.

GHAHERI, Manoutchehr, b. 12 Dec. 1923, Tehran, Iran. Head of Aeromedical Department of Iran Air. m. Maryam, 2 Apr. 1948, Tehran, 2 sons, 1 daughter. *Education:* MD; AMD; Specialist in Internal Diseases and Aerospace Medicine. *Appointments:* General Director, Ministry of Health, Iran, 1957; Aerospace Medical positions: Senior Aviation Medical Examiner, 1962; FAA Senior Aviation Medical Examiner, 1968; British Senior Aviation Medical Examiner, 1969; Head, Medical Services Division of

Iran Air, 1978-. *Memberships:* International Aerospace Medical Association, Associated Fellow, 1972, Fellow, 1974, Academician, 1974, Vice-President, 1975-76, Selector Academician, 1977; International Medical Civil Aviation Association; International Federation Aeronautics, Vice-President, 1977, 78, 79. *Publications:* "Medical Handbook for Pilots", 1967; "Guide for Sanitation in Aviation", 1968; "First Aid in Flight" 1970; "Aviation Medicine", 1975; Books translated: "Manual of Civil Aviation Medicine", 1975; "Guide for Aviation Medical Examiners", 1975; "International Health Regulations", 1975; "Medical Manual", 1977; '"Personal Licensing Annex One", 1979. *Hobbies:* High Jumping (three times Champion of Iran, 1941, 43, 44); Swimming; Volleyball. *Address:* 92 Aban Street, Tehran 15987, Iran.

GHALI, Anwar Youssef, b. 30 May 1944, Cairo, Egypt. Clinical Associate Professor,Psychiatry. m. Dr Violette S. Ghali, 23 May 1968, Cairo, 1 daughter. *Education:* MB., B.Ch., 1966, DPM, 1970, DM, 1971, Cairo University; Diplomate, American Board of Psychiatry & Neurology, 1979; Certified, Administrative Psychiatry, APA, 1984. *Appointments:* Rotating Internship, Cairo University Hospitals, 1966-67; Forensic Physician, Egyptian Forensic Medicine Dept., 1967-68; Resident, Psychiatry, Ahmed Maher Hospital, Cairo, 1969-71; Psychiatrist, Shoubra General Hospital, Cairo, 1971-72, Shihar Hospital, Taif, Saudi Arabia, 1972-73; Registrar, Psychiatry, 1973-74, Assistant Psychiatrist, 1974, Woodilee Hospital, Glasgow, Scotland; Resident, 1974-77, Instructor, 1977-78, Clinical Assistant Professor, 1978-79, Assistant Professor, 1979-83, Psychiatry, New Jersey Medical School, USA;. *Memberships:* Christian Medical Society; American medical Association; American Psychiatric Association; New Jersey Psychiatric Association; New Jersey Medical Society. *Publications:* "Masking of Tardive Dyskinesia with Four Times-A-Day Administration of Chlorpromazine" 'Diseases of the Nervous System', 1977; "Sleep Disorders Prevalence, Reported Prevalence and Continuing Medical Education", 'Sleep Research', 1981; "Sleep in a Small Space : Results of an Office Brief Psychophysiological Training and Evaluation", Sleep Research', 1981. *Honours:* Exceptional Merit Award, College of Medicine & Dentistry of New Jersey, 1981. *Hobbies:* Swimming; Stamp Collecting. *Address:* 22 Benvenue Avenue, West Orange, NJ 07052, USA.

GHARIB, Reza, b. 20 Apr. 1929, Iran. Professor of Paediatrics. m. Parvin Sadeghi, 6 Oct. 1962, 1 son, 2 daughters. *Education:* MD, Tehran University, Iran, 1954; MS, Mayo Clinic and University of Minnesota, USA; Diplomate, American Board of Paediatrics, 1960. *Appointments:* Dean, School of Medicine, Chief, Nemazee Hospital, Shiraz Medical Center, Chairman, Department of Paediatrics, School of Medicine, Shiraz University, Iran. *Memberships:* President, Shiraz Section, Paediatric Society. *Publications:* Paediatric Physical Diagnosis", 2nd editin, 1982, in Persian. Contributions to 'AJDC', 'Paranasal Sinuses in Cystic Fibrosis', 1964; 'Sweat Chloride Concentration', 1965; 'Acute Rheumatic Fever in Shiraz', 1969. In 'Clinical Paediatrics': 'Lithiasis in the Urinary Tract', 1970; 'ECG in Children and Severe Chronic Anemia', 1972. *Address:* Nemazee Hospital, Shiraz, Iran.

GHATAK, Satyendra Nath, b. 19 July 1926, Kanpur, Uttar Pradesh, India. Deputy Director and Head of Biochemistry of Central Drug Research Institute. m. Ruby Bose, 29 June 1955, Lucknow, 1 son. *Education:* ISc, 1944; BSc 1946, MSc 1948, PhD 1958, Agra University; Diploma in German Language, Lucknow University, 1954. *Appointments:* Research Assistant, CSIR, Delhi, 1948-50; Technical Assistant, Publications Directorate, CSIR, New Delhi, 1950-51; Scientific Assistant 1951-57, Junior Scientific Officer 1957-61,

Senior Scientific Officer 1961-73, Assistant Director 1973-83, Deputy Director 1983-, Central Drug Research Institute, Lucknow; Visiting Scientist, German Academy of Sciences, Institute of Medical Microbiology, Jena, German Democratic Republic, 1964-65; Visiting Scientist, DAAD-CSIR Exchange Programme, Berhard Nocht Institute, Hamburg, Federal Republic of Germany, 1980. *Memberships:* Elected Associate, Royal Institute of Chemistry, London; Indian Science Congress; Society of Biological Chemistry, India; Association of Microbiologists, India; Indian Society of Parasitologists. *Publications include:* 122 scientific papers including: 'Purification and characterization of FDP-aldolase from Setaria cervi', (with JK Saxena and AA Ansari), 1982; 'Effect of chloroquine treatment in vivo on the cyclic AMP level of erythrocytes from normal and plasmodium berghei: infected mastomys natalensis', (co-author), 1982; 'Skin sensitizing allergen in the adults of Ascaridia galli', (with SK Mishra and KC Saxona), 1983; 'Effect of levamisole on the level of biogenic amines of Nippostrongylus braziliensis', (co-author), 1983; 'Effect of anticonvulsants, centazolone and centpropazine on gamma amino butyric acid metabolism in mouse brain', (co-author), 1985; 2 review articles in journals. *Honour:* Silver Jubilee Award, St John's College, Agra, 1946. *Hobbies:* Colour photography; Cricket. *Address:* Discipline of Biochemistry, Central Drug Research Institute, Lucknow – 226001, India.

GHETTI, Bernardino, b. 28 Mar. 1941, Pisa, Italy. Professor of Pathology and Psychiatry. m. Caterina Genovese, 8 Oct. 1966, Pisa, 1 son, 1 daughter. *Education:* Diploma Maturita Classica, 1959; MD, 1966; Diploma of Specialization in Mental and Nervous Diseases, 1969; Research Fellow in Neuropathology, 1970-73; Resident in Pathology, 1973-75; Resident in Neuropathology, 1975-76; Baord Certification in Neuropathology, 1982. *Appointments:* Postdoctoral Fellow, University of Pisa, 1966-68; Postdoctoral Fellow, University of Pisa and Visiting Fellow, University of Naples, 1968-70; Research Fellow in Neuropathology, Albert Einstein College of Medicine, 1970-73; Clinical Fellow and Resident in Pathology, 1973-75, Clinical Fellow and Resident in Neuropathology, 1975-76, AECOM; Assistant Professor of Pathology, 1976-77, Assistant Professor of Pathology and Psychiatry, 1977-78, Assocate Professor of Pathology and Psychiatry, 1978-83; Professor of Pathology and Psychiatry,1983-, Indiana University Medical Center. *Memberships:* American Association of Neuropathologists; Society for Neurosciences; Association for Research in Nervous and Mental Diseases; American Society for Cell Biology; New York Academy of Science; Sigma Xi. *Publications:* 55 papers, most of them in international scientific journals. *Honour:* Silver Medal of University of Pisa for MD degree cum laude. *Address:* Indiana University Medical center, Department of Pathology (Division of Neuropathology), 635, Barnhill Drive, MS A138, Indianapolis, IN 46223, USA.

GHOSH, Hemendra Kumar, b. 25 June 1933, Singapore. Director of Hospital; Clinical Microbiology Department. m. Molly Ray, 21 Feb. 1968, Kuala Lumpur, Malaya, 1 son, 1 daughter. *Education:* MBBs, Calcutta University India, 1957; Diploma in Bacteriology, University of Manchester, England, 1962; PhD Bacteriology, University of Edinburgh, Scotland, 1965; Fellow, Royal College of Pathologsts of Australasia, 1970; Australian Society for Microbiology, 1977. *Appointments include:* Associate Professor of Bacteriology and Acting Head of Pathology Department, Kasturba Medical College, Manipal, India, 1966-67; Lecturer, and Bacteriologist, Faculty of Medicine, University of Malaya, Kuala Lumpur, 1967-71; Senior Lecturer in Clincial Bateriology, Faculty of Medicine, Sydney University, Australia, 1971-72; Senior Clinical Microbiologist, Institute of Medical and Veterinary

Sciences, Adelaide, South Australia, 1972-74; Director of Clincial Microbiolgoy Department, Royal Newcastle Hospital Group, Newcastle, New South Wales, 1974-. *Memberships include:* Life member, Indian Association for the Advancement of Medical Education; British Medical Association; American Society for Microbiology. *Publications include:* 'The pathogenesis of experimental cholera' (with R Cruikshank and AL Mia) in "IX International Congress for Microbiology (Moscow)", 1966; 'Immunological observations in experimental cholera', 1970; Contributor to cholera section, 'Torpical Diseases Bulletin', 1962-66; 'Mebendazole therapy of whipworm (Trichuris trichiura) infestations: a clinical trial', (with JN Pereira, S Concklin and S Rayan), 1979; 'Bordetella bronchicanis (bronchiseptica) infection in man: review and a case report', (with J Tranter), 1979; 'Halophilic vibrios from Human tissue infections', (with TE Bowen), 1979. *Honours:* FC Chatterji Scholarship for Histology 1955, Shanks Medal for Clinical Pathology 1956, Gold Medal for Pathology 1957, Calcutta University. *Hobbies:* Yoga; Photography. *Address:* Box 664J, Newcastle, NSW 2300, Australia.

GIACOBINO, Jean-Paul, b. 27 Mar. 1938, Marseille, France. Adjunct Professor of Biochemistry. *Education:* MD; Private Dozent, University of Geneva. *Appointments:* Assistant, Department of Medical Biochemistry, Department of Pathology, Geneva; Head of Department & Research, Department of Medical Biochemistry, Geneva; Visiting Scientist, Enzyme Institute, Madison, Wisconsin, USA, Deparmtent of Biochemistry Buffalo, New York, USA. *Memberships:* Union of Swiss Societies of Experimental Biology; International Conference on the Biochemistry of Lipids; New York Academy of Sciences. *Publications:* Various artices in biochemical journals. *Hobby:* Kitsch. *Address:* Department of Medical Blochemistry, University Medical Centre, 9 Avenue de Champel, 1211 Geneva 4, Switzerland.

GIANNOULOPOULOS, Dimitris, b. 28 Mar. 1946, Athens, Greece. Senior Flight Surgeon. Major, Hellenic Air Force. m. Bassiliki Stiliou, 22 June 1972, Agrinion, Greece, 2 sons. *Education:* MD, FS, Athens, Greece. Studies in Aerospace Medicine, Texas, USA. *Appointments:* Chief Surgeon, 1972-74; Chief Surgeon, General Hospital, 1974-78; Chief Flight Surgeon, 1978-84; Senior Magistrate General Hospital, 1984-85; GNA, General Hospital, Aviation Centre, School of Aviation Medicine, 1985-present. *Memberships:* Greek Society of Surgeons; Aerospace Medical Association, USA. *Hobby:* Tennis. *Address:* 37 Karathanou Street, Larissa, Greece 41222.

GIBSON, Ray Allen, b. 15 Jan. 1941, Kentucky, USA. Private Practice. m. Nancy S Bailey, 28 Nov. 1963, Knoxville, 1 daughter. *Education:* BS, Berea College; MD, University of Louisville. *Appointments:* Intern, 1968-69, Resident, Obstetrician Gynaecologist, 1969-72, Louisville Hospitals; Major, US Army, 1972-74; Howard Clinic, Glasgow, 1974-83; Private Practice, 1982-. *Memberships:* American College of Obstetricians & Gynaecologists; Diplomate, American Board of Obstetrics & Gynaecology; Kentucky Medical Association; Barren County Medical Society. *Publications:* Articles in 'American Journal Obstetrics & Gynaecology'; 'Obstetrics & Gynaecology'. *Hobbies:* Boating; Cooking; Horse Riding. *Address:* 120 State Ave., Glasgow, KY 42141, USA.

GIELDANOWSKI, Jerzy Zbigniew, b. 16 Mar. 1925, Krakow, Poland. Head, Experimental Medicine. m. Zofia Zamorska, 18 Dec. 1951, Wroclaw, 2 daughters. *Eucation:* Physician, 1951, MD, 1961, Docent, 1963, Medical Academy, Wroclaw. *Appointments:* Assistant, Pharmacology, Medical Academy, Wroclaw, 1951-63; Assistant Professor, 1964-69, Professor, 1970-, Head, Experimental Medicine, Institute of Immunology and Experimental Therapy, Polish Academy of Sciences, Wroclaw. *Memberships:* Polish Pharmacological Society; Polish Immunological Society; Polish Physiological Society; Committee, Immunology, Polish Academy of Science; Commitee, Expeirmental Therapy, Committee, Physiological Sciences, Polish Academy of Sciences. *Publications:* Co-author, "immunologia praktyczna", 1970; "Farmakometria", 1982; "immunosupresja", 1984; 'Immunologia', 1985; Editor, Board, 'Immuniligia Polska'. *Honours:* Corresponding Member, Polish Academy of Sciences, 1983; Prizes, Scientific Secretary, Polish Academy of Science, 1970; 1971, 1974, 1977, 1981; Polonai Retituta Order, 1977. *Hobbies:* Stamp Collecting; Travel. *Address:* ul. Wieczysta 87/6, 50-550 Wroclaw, Poland.

GIER, Ronald E, b. 8 Jan. 1935, Bloomington, Indiana, USA. Professor of Oral Diagnosis. m. Patricia J Smelden, 23 Dec. 1982, Overland Park, Kansas, 4 sons, 1 daughter. *Education:* BS, Kansas State University, 1956; DMD, Washington University, St Louis, Missouri, 1959; MSD, Indiana University, 1967. *Appointments:* US Navy Dental Corps, 1959-61; Private Practice (Dentistry), 1961-65; Graduate Education, Indiana University, 1965-67; Professor, Chairman, Department of Oral Diagnosis, University of Missouri, Kansas City, 1967-. *Memberships:* American Dental Association; American Academy of Oral Pathology; International Association for Dental Research; Organisation of Teachers of Oral Diagnsis; American Association of Dental Schools; American Academy of Forensic Sciences; International Transactional Analysis Association. *Publications:* Various publications in field. *Honours:* Omicron Kappa Upsilon, 1969; Student Award, American Academy of Dental Medicine, 1969; Student Award, American Society of Dentistry for Children, 1969. *Hobbies:* Yard Work; Fishing; Home Repairs. *Address:* 650 East 25th Street, Kansas City, MO 64108 - 2795, USA.

GIFFORD, George Edwin, b. 6 Dec. 1924, Minneapolis, Minnesota, USA. Professor of Immunology and Medical Microbiology; widower, 1 son, 1 daughter. *Education:* BS cum laude, 1949, MS, 1953, PhD, 1955, University of Minnesota; Fellow, American Academy of Microbiology. *Appointments:* Instructor, University of Minnesota, 1955-56; Assistant Professor, 1957-64, Associate Professor, 1964-68, Professor, 1968-, University of Florida. Visiting Professor; Hadassah Medical School, Jerusalem, Israel, 1984; Fraunhofer Institute, Hannover, Federal Republic of Germany, 1985. *Memberships:* American Association for Advancement of Science; American Society for Microbiology; American Society for Virology; Society for General Microbiology; American Academy for Microbiology; American Association of Immunologists; Sigma Xi; Tissue Culture Association; Union of Concerned Scientists; American Institute of Biological Sciences; Reticuloendothelial Society; New York Academy of Science. *Publications:* Chapters on Tumor Necrosis Factor in: "Lymphokines", Volume 2, 1981; "Biological Response Modifiers", 1985. Chapter on Antivirals in "Kirk-Othmer Encyclopedia of Chemical Technology", 1979; author of some 85 papers in various scientific publications. *Honours:* Fellow: American Academy for Microbiology, 1966; American Association for Advancement of Science, 1967. *Hobbies:* Reading; Travelling; Hiking; Swimming. *Address:* Department of Immunology and Medical Microbiology, University of Florida, College of Medicine, Box J-266, Gainesville, FL 32610, USA.

GIFFORD, Ray W., b. 13 Aug. 1923, Westerville, Ohio, USA. Physician. m. Frances Anne Moore, 13 Jan. 1973, Cleveland Heights, 1 son, 3 daughters.

Education: BS, Otterbein College, 1944; MD, Ohio State University, 1947; MS, University Minnesota, 1952. *Appointments:* Staff Consultant, Mayo Clinic, Rochester, 1953-61; Assistant Professor, Medicine, Mayo Foundation, 1956-61; Staff, Cleveland Clinic Foundation, 1961-; Chairman, Hypertension & Nephrology, 1967-85, Vice Chairman, Medicine, 1978-, Senior Physician, Hypertension & Nephrology, Cleveland Clinic Foundation, 1985-. *Memberships:* Board of Governors, Cleveland Clinic Foundation; Assistant Attending Physician US Congress, 1954-56. *Memberships:* AHA, Board of Directors, 1969-72; Fellow, American College Cardiology, Gov. for Ohio, 1970-73; American Society for Clinical Pharmacology & Ther., President 1976-77; Fellow, American Chest Physicinas, Chairman, Committee on Hypertension, 1970-72; etc. *Publications:* Over 380 scientific articles; Co-author, "Pheochromocytoma". *Honours:* Weinland Chemistry Prize, Otterbein College, 1942; Alumni Achievement Award, Ohio State University, 1962; Distinguished Science Achievement Award, Otterbein College, 1970; Oscar Hunter Award, American Society Clinical Pharmacology & Therapeutics, 1979; Simon Rodbard Lectureship, American College Chest Physicians, 1982. *Hobbies:* Fishing; Coin & Stamp Collecting. *Address:* Department of Hypertension and Nephrology, Cleveland Clinic Foundation, 9500 Euclid Avenue, Cleveland, OH 44106, USA.

GIFT, Thomas Edward, b. 14 June 1946, Washington, District of Columbia, USA. Executive Director, Mental Health Centre, Associate Professor. m. Joan, 21 May 1976, Webster, New York. *Education:* AB Biology, Princeton University, 1968; MD, University of Chicago/Pritzker School of Medicine, 1972. *Appointments:* Instructor 1976-77, Assistant Professor 1977-83, Associate Professor 1983-, University of Rochester; Executive Director, Western Monroe Mental Health Center. *Memberships:* American Psychopathological Association; County of Monroe Medical Society; State of New York Medical Society; Genesee Valley District branch, American Psychiatric Association; American Medical Association; American Psychiatric Association. *Publications:* 'How Diagnostic Concepts of Schizophrenia Differ', 1980; 'Schizophrenia: Affect and Outcome'; 'Established Chronicity of Psychotic Symptoms in First-admission Schizophrenic Patients', 1981; 'The Severity of Psychiatric Disorder: A Replication', 1985. *Hobbies:* Gardening; Piano; Automotive repair. *Address:* Western Monroe Mental Health Center, 2633 West Ridge Road, Rochester, NY 14626, USA.

GIL, Lionel, b. 4 Aug. 1939, Santiago, Chile. Chairman, Department of Biochemistry, University of Chile. m. Carmen Cubillos, 21 Jan. 1967, Santiago, 1 son, 2 daughters. *Education:* Chemical Pharmacist, University of Chile, 1963; PhD, Cornell University, USA, 1973. *Appointments:* Assistant Professor, Faculty of Medicine, University of Chile, 1964; Consultant Syracuse University Research Corporation, 1972; Scientific Adviser, Regional Graduate Training Programme in Biological Sciences PNUD/UNESCO RLA, 1979-83; Chairman, Department of Biochemistry, Faculty of Medicine, University of Chile, 1977-present (full Professor in 1982). *Memberships:* Chilean Biological Society; Chilean Biochemical Society; Pan American Biochemical Society; Latin American Nutritional Society. *Publications:* Co-Author of several learned articles in professional journals. *Honour:* President of the Chilean Biochemical Society, 1981-1982. *Address:* Los Trigales 323, Las Condes, Santiago, Chile.

GILBERT, Roberta M., b. 17 Sept. 1935, Psychiatrist. *Education:* MS, Wheaton College; USA; MD, State University of NY, Buffalo. *Appointments:* Laboratory Instructor, West Suburban Hospital School of Nursing, Oak Park, Illinois; Private Practice, Psychiatry, Buffalo, NY; Staff Psychiatrist, Ward Psychiatrist, Director, After Care Clinic, Georgia Regional Hospital, Augusta, Georgia; Staff Psychiatrist, Rainbow Hospital, Kansas City, Kansas; Private Practie, Psychaitry, Prairie Village, Kansas; Meriam, Kansas; Clinical Assistant Professor, Psychiatry, School of Medicine, University of Missouri, Kansas City; Assistance Clinical Professor, Psychiatry, School of Medicine, University of Kansas, Kansas City, Kansas. *Memberships:* American Psychiatric Association; American Medical Women's Association; Johnson County Medical Society; Kansas State Medical Society; Johnson County Mental Health Association; Chairman of Department of Psychiatry, Professional Advisory Board Schawnee Mission Medical Center; Member, Executive Committee, 1979, 1980. *Publications:* 'Treatment Techniques for Pedophiles and Exhibitionists in a Community Environment', (with I J Barrish, Gerald H Vandenberg, Roberta M Gilbert); 'Patient-Drug Monitoring: Laboratory Studies for Psychotropic Drugs', (with Martha Knight), 1977; 'Breast Carcinoma: Current Diagnosis and Treatment'. *Address:* 4121 West 83rd, Suite 150, Prairie Village, KS 66208, USA.

GIL-DEL-REAL, Maria Teresa, b. 5 Jan. 1941, Colombia, Assistant Analyst, New Jersey Department of Health, Epidemiology Division, Cancer Epidemiology Programe, 1985-, m. John R Romano, 10 Oct 1964, New York City, USA, 1 son, 1 daughter. *Education:* Associate in Business, Bogota Business College, Bogata, Colombia, 1959; BA, Summa Cum Laude, Rutgers University, New Jersey, USA, 1979; MPH, Colombia University New York, 1986. *Appointments:* Freelance translator and simultaneous interpreter, 1974-78; Bilingual Editor, Princeton International translations, Princeton, New Jersey, 1979-80; Program Assistant, The Robert Wood Johnson Foundation, Princeton, New Jersey, 1980-83; Consultant, Ministerio de Sanidad y Consumo, Madrid, Spain, 1984. *Memberships:* Research Associate of America; Biographical Institute Research Association; Alpha Sigma Lambda Honour Society. *Publications:* 'Potlatching and Face Maintenance Behaviour Among the Kwakiutl of British Columbia', 1980. *Honours:* BA degree Summa Cum Laude. *Hobbies:* Oil painting; Reading; Tennis; Swimming. *Address:* 76 Princeton Avenue, Rocky Hill, NJ 08553, USA.

GILL, Jane Roberts, b. 6 Dec 1923, Boston, Massachusetts, USA, Clinical Social Worker, The Headache Research Foundation, Faulkner Hospital, Boston, Massachusetts, div, 3 sons, 1 daughter. *Education:* MSSS, Boston University School of Social Work, 1956; BA, Wellesley College and Boston University, 1954; Diploma, the Putney School. *Appointments:* Psychiatric Social Worker, Obstetrical Service, Beth Israel Hospital, Boston; Psychiatric Social Worker, The South End Family Program; Psychiatric Social Worker, The Margaret Gifford School; Senior Clinical Social Worker Supervisor, The Faulkner Hospital;, Cardian Rehabilitation Program, Coordinator for Outpatient Psychiatry/Social Service Clinic and the Oncolgoy Clinic; LICSW-MA, Private Practice. *Memberships:* National Association of Social Workers; Academy of Certified Social Workers; NASW Register of Clinical Social Workers; Academy of Psychosomatic Medicine; Social Services Committee, American Heart Association; Member, Social Workers Oncology Group; International Headache Society. *Publications:* 'Myocardial infarction in two patients with unresolved feelings about early parental loss', 1986; Contributor of numerous papers to professional meetings and conferences. *Hobbies:* Concerts; Opera; Gardening; Walking; Travel; Reading. *Address:* The Faulkner Hospital, Centre Street at Allandale Road, Boston, MA 02130, USA.

GILL, Thomas J. III b. 2 July 1932, Malden,

Massachusetts, USA. Professor of Pathology; Department Chairman; Pathologist-in-Chief. m. Faith L Etoll, 8 July 1961, Albany, New York, 2 sons, 1 daughter. *Education:* BA Summa cum laude, 1953, MA, 1957, Md, 1957, Harvard; Assistant in Pathology, Peter Bent Brigham Hospital, Boston, Massachusetts, 1957-58; Intern, Medicine, New York Hospital, Cornell Medical Center, New York, 1958-59; Junior Fellow, Society of Fellows, Harvard University, 1959-62. *Appointments:* Associate in Pathology, 1962-65, Assistant Professor, Pathology, 1965-70, Harvard Medical School, Boston, Massachusetts; Associate in Pathology, Peter Bent Brigham Hospital, Boston, 1962-70; Associate Professor, Pathology, Harvard Medical School, Boston, 1970-71; Senior Associate in Pathology, Peter Bent Bringham Hospital, Boston, 1970-71; Professor of Pathology, Chairman, Department of Pathology, School of Medicine, University of Pittsburgh, Pennsylvania, 1971-; Pathologist-in-Chief, University Health center of Pittsburgh, 1971-. *Memberships:* Past Vice President, Transplantation Society; Secretary General, International Society for the Immunology of Reproduction; American Medical Association; American Association of Immunologists; Genetics Society of America. *Publications:* Author of over 280 publications in various scientific journals and books. *Honours:* Trustee, American Board of Pathology, 1981-; Smith Kline distinguished Lecturer, Hahnemann Medical College, 1984; Whipple Lecturer, University of Rochester, New York, 1984; Distinguished Scientist Award in Genetics, Southwest Foundation for Biomedical Research, San Antonio, Texas. *Hobbies:* Swimming; Tennis; History; Music. *Address:* Department of Pathology, School of Medicine, University of Pittsburgh, Pittsburgh, PA 15261, USA.

GILLE, Paul, b. 5 Dec. 1927, Commercy, France. Head of Department of Pediatric Surgery. m. Francoise Barrucand, 26 Dec. 1955, 2 sons, 3 daughters. *Education:* Professor. *Appointments:* Professor of Pediatric Surgery, University of Besancon. *Memberships:* International College of Surgeons; French Society of Pediatric Surgery; French Society of Orthopedic Surgery. *Address:* 1A Avenue Denfert Rochereau, 25000 Besançon, France.

GILLESPIE, Iain Erskine, b. 4 Sep. 1931, Glasgow, Scotland. Professor of Surgery. m. Muriel McIntyre, 5 Sep. 1957, Glasgow, 1 son, 1 daughter. *Education:* MB, ChB, 1953, MD, Honours, 1963, University of Glasgow; FRCS(Ed); FRCS(England); FRCS (Glasgow). *Appointments:* House Officer Posts, Glasgow, 1953-56; Royal Army Medical Corps, 1954-56; MRC Grantee, 1956-58; Lecturer, Surgery, University of Sheffield, 1958-66; USPHS Postdoctoral Fellow, Los Angeles, 1960-61; General Lecturer, Reader, Titular Professor, University of Glasgow, 1964-70; Professor, Surgery, 1970-, Dan, Medicine, 1983-86, University of Manchester; Member, UGC Medical Subcommittee, 1974-; Member, Hong Kong UPGC 1984-. *Memberships:* Surgical Research Society Great Britain & Ireland; British Society for Gastroenterology; Association of Surgeons of Great Britain & Ireland; Association of Professors of Surgery of Great Britain & Ireland; Manchester Medical Society; North of England Gasteoenterology Society; Honorary Member, several overseas Gastroenterological Societies. *Publications:* Numerous articles, chapters, reviews, etc. *Address:* 27 Athol Road, Bramhall, Cheshire SK7 2BR, England.

GILLIAM, Paul Edwin, b. 13 Oct. 1952, Washington, District of Columbia, USA. Staff Surgeon, Chief, Emergency Services, Wiesbaden Regional Medical Centre, Federal Republic of Germany. m. Marlene Mailman, 17 Oct. 1981, Johnstown, USA. *Education:* BSc., US Air Force Academy, 1974; MD, University of Maryland Medical School, 1978. *Appointments:*

Chief, Surgery, Incilik AB, Turkey. *Memberships:* Society of Air Force Clinical Surgeons; Aerospace Medical Association; Candidate, American College of Surgeons; American Academy of Family Physicians. *Hobbies:* Skiing; Water Skiing; Flying; Travel; Handball; Squash; Amateur Astronomy. *Address:* PSC §2, Box 677, APO, NY 09220, USA.

GILLIATT, Roger William, b. 30 July 1922, London, England. Professor, Clinical Neurology, University of London; Chairman, University Dept. of Clinical Neurology; Honorary Consultant Neurologist, National Hospital for Nervous Diseases, and Hammersmith Hospital, London. m. Mary Elizabeth Green, 1963, 1 son, 2 daughters. *Education:* BA, 1946, MA, 1949, BM, BCh, 1949, DM, 1955 (Oxon); MRCP, London, 1951; FRCP, London, 1961. *Appointments:* Research Assistant, Spinal Injuries Unit, Stoke Mandeville Hospital, & University Laboratory of Physiology, Oxford, 1946-47; Houser Physician, Medical Registrar, 1950-52, Senior Registrar, 1955, Middlesex Hospital, London; House Physician, Resident Medical Officer, National Hospital for Nervous Diseases, 1953-54; Assistant physician, Middlesex Hospital, and National Hospital for Nervous Diseases, 1955-61. *Address:* University Dept. of Clinical Neurology, Institute of Neurology, Queen Square, London SC1N 3BG, England.

GIRARD, Marc Paul Fernand, b. 24 June 1936, Lyon, France. Scientific Director Pasteur Vaccins. m. (1) Anik Globa, 5 July 1958, Paris, 3 sons, (2) Jacqueline London, 5 Jan. 1985, 1 daughter. *Education:* DVM, Alfort, 1960; DSc, Paris, 1967. *Appointments:* Assistant, Veterinary College, Alfort, 1960-62; Post-doctoral Fellow, Massachusetts Institute of Technology, Cambridge, Massachusetts, USA, Albert Einstein College of Medicine, New York, Salk Institute for Biological Research, La Jolla, California, 1963-66; Research Assistant, Pasteur Institute, Paris, France, 1967-69; Research Director, Cancer Institute, Villejuif, 1970-74; Professor of Virology, Paris University, 1974-84; Head, Laboratory of Molecular Virology, Pasteur Institute, 1980-; Scientific Director, Pasteur Vaccines, 1984-. *Memberships:* Société Francaise de Microbiologie; American Society for Microbiolgoy. *Publications:* "Virologie Moleculaire", (with Leon Mirth), 1980; More than 100 major scientific publications in professional reviews. *Hobbies:* Mountains; Skiing. *Address:* Department of Virology, Pasteur Institute, 28 Rue du Dr Roux, 75015 Paris, France.

GIRDWOOD, Ronald Haxton, b. 19 Mar. 1917 Arbroath, Scotland. Chairman, Scottish National Blood Transfusion Association. m. Mary Elizabeth Williams, SRN, 31 July 1945, Calcutta, 1 son, 1 daughter. *Education:* MB, ChB (Hons.), 1939; PhD, 1952; MD Gold Medal, 1954; University of Edinburgh; MRCPE, 1941, FRCPE, 1945; MRCP, London, 1944; FRCP, London, 1956; FRCPath, 1964; FRSE, 1978; FRCPI, 1984. *Appointments:* Officer, RAMC, 1942-46; Lecturer in Medicine, 1946-50; Reckefeller Research Fellow, University of Michigan, Ann Arbor, USA, 1948-49; Senior Lecturer, then Reader, Department of Medicine, 1951-62; Professor of Therapeutics and Clinical Pharmacology, 1962-82; Dean, Faculty of Medicine, 1975-79; University of Edinburgh; Consultant Physician, Royal Infirmary of Edinburgh, 1948-82; President, Royal College of Physicians, Edinburgh, 1982-85. *Memberships:* Association of Physicians of Great Britain and Ireland; British Society for Haematology, President, 1963-64; Medico-Pharmaceutical Forum, Chairman Scottish National Blood Transfusion Association, 1985-; South East of Scotland Blood Transfusion Association, Chairman, 1981-. *Publications:* Editor: "Blood Disorders due to Drugs and Other Agents", 1973; "Clinical Pharmacology", 1976, 79, 84; Co-Editor: "Malabsorption", 1969; "Textbook of Medical Treatment", 1971, 74, 78; About 300 papers in medical journals, particularly relating to haematology, clinical pharmacology and medical history. *Honours include:* CBE, 1984; Several Fellowships and Scholarships: Cullen Prize, Royal College of Physicioans of Edinburgh, 1970. *Hobbies:* Photography; Painting in Oils; Gardening. *Address:* 2 Hermitage Drive, Edinburgh EH10 6OO, Scotland.

GIROD, Christian Alphonse, b. 31 Aug. 1930, Bone, Algeria. Professor and Chief of Department of Histology-Embryology. m. Raymonde Vaille, 19 Dec. 1955, Algiers, 5 daughters. *Education:* MD, Agrégé de l'Université, 1961; Professor, 1967; Dean of Faculty of Medicine, Alexis Carrel, 1971-76; Associate Director of Faculty of Human Biology, 1976-79; Biologiste des Hopitaux, Lyons, 1967-. *Appointments:* Associate Professor, Algiers, 1961-62; Lyons, 1962-67; Professor, 1967-. *Memberships:* Société de Biologie, Algiers and Lyons; Association des Anatomistes de Langue Francaise; Société Francaise de Cytologie Clinique; Société Francaise d'Histochimie; Société Francaise de Microscopie Electronique; Société d'Endocrinologie; Société de Neuroendocrinologie; Société d'Histoire de la Médecine; American Society of Primatologists; New York Academy of Sciences. *Publications:* Leçons sur les Glandes Endocrines, 1968; Histochemistry of the Adenohypophysis, 1976; Biologie de la Reproduction, 1977; Introduction à l'étude des glandes endocrines, 1980; Immunocytochemistry of the vertebrate Adenohypophysis, 1983. *Honour:* Officier des Palmes Académiques, 1975. *Hobby:* Symphonic Music. *Address:* Laboratoire d'Histologie-Embryologie, Faculté de Médecine Alexis Carrel, rue Guillaume Paradin, F-69372 Lyon Cedex 08, France.

GIROUD, Jean-Paul, b. 6 Nov. 1936, Paris, France. Professor of Pharmacology; Hospital Department Head. *Education:* MD, Paris School of Medicine; PhD, University of London, England; DSc, Paris Fauclty of Sciences. *Appointments:* Assistant Professor of Pharmacology, School of Medicine, Paris, France, 1965-66; Senior Lecturer in Pharmacology, 1966-67; Professor of Pharmacology, School of Medicine, Tours, France, 1967-70; Professor of Pharmacology, UER Cochin Port-Royal, Paris, 1970-82; Head of Department of Pharmacology, Cochin Hospital, Paris, 1982-. *Memberships:* French Society of Therapeutics; French Society of Immunology; French Society of Pharmacology; Pathological Society of Great Britain and Ireland; British Society of Immunology; Royal Society of Medicine; Founder Member of the International Society of Immuno-Pharmacology; British Immunological Society. *Publications:* More then 200 publications in the field of pharmacology and experimental pathology (inflammation); Editor two-volume text book in Clinical Pharamcology and the three-volume text book in the field of inflammation. *Honours:* Laureate of School of Medicine, Paris, Thesis Prize, Silver Medal, 1965; Ministry of Youth and Sports Prize, 1968; National Academy of Medicine Jansen Prize, 1969; Academy of Sciences Parkin Prize, 1974; Academy of Medicine Award for Research in Rheumatology, 1976; Academy of Medicine Award, 1984. *Address:* Department of Pharmacology, Cochin Hospital, 27 Rue du Faubourg Saint-Jacques, 75674 Paris Cedex 14, France.

GISLASON, Thorsteinn, b. 26 July 1947, Reykjavik, Iceland. Staff Urologist, St Josefs Hospital, Iceland. m. Svienbjornsdottir Ingveldur, 19 Sep. 1971. *Education:* Md, Icelandic University; Internship, Residency, Surgery & Urology, St Louis University Hospitals, USA; American Board of Urology. *Memberships:* Icelandic Medical Association; Icelandic Surgical Society; Icelandic Urological Society; American Urological Association. *Publications:* "Epididysoritis in Prepubertal Boys", 'Journal Urology', 1978; "Hemhorragic Cystitis treated with Formalin Instillabide", 'Urology', 1979;

"Bilateral Renal Carcinoma – Aggresive Surgical Management', 'Journal of Urology', 1980; etc. *Hobbies:* Hunting; Fishing. *Address:* St Josefs Hospital, 1010 Reykjavik, Iceland.

GIULIANO, Robert Paul. b. 7 Mar. 1943, New York, USA. Pharmacist; Founder, Chairman, President, US Home Health Care Corporation & Subsidairies – Steri – Pharm, Inc. m. Maja Hreljanovic, 2 July 1966, New York, 2 sons. *Education:* MS, Pharmacy, Long Island University, 1970; BS, Pharmacy, Forham University, 1965. *Appointments:* Pharmacy Residnet, 1965-66, Staff Pharmacist, 1966-70, Columbia Presbyterian Medical Centre, New York; Director, Pharmacy, St Barnabas Hospital Medical Centre, New York, 1970-71; Director, Pharmaceutical Sciences, 1971-79, Administrator, Ambulatory Care, 1979-81, Misericordia Hospital Medical Center, New York; Founder, President, US Home Health Care Corporation, Scarsdale, New York, 1981-. *Memberships:* American Society Hospital Pharmacists; American Pharmaceutical Association; American Society of Parenteral & Enteral Nutrition; National Intravenous Therapy Association; New York State Council of Hospital Pharmacists; National Association of Emergency medical Technicians, Founding Member; etc. *Honours:* G.B. Lambert Awards Committee Recipient, 1975; Recognized for significant contributions to Health Care; Robert Wood Johnson Foundation, 1985 Home Health Care Consultant. *Hobbies:* Photography; Numismatics; Philatelics. *Address:* 157 Oakland Ave., Eastchester, NY 10707, USA.

GIUNIO, Nenad, b. 14 Dec. 1920, Split, Yugoslavia, Chief of Pulmonary Department. Divorced, 2 sons, 1 daughter. *Education:* Medical Faculty 1948, Specialization in Physiology 1951, Primarius 1966, D Sc 1977, Medical Faculty, University of Zagreb. *Appointments:* Chief of Diagnostic Department 1954, Vicedirector 1957, Institute for tbc and pulmonary disease, Golnik; Director of Hospital for tbc and pulmonary disease, Kasindo. *Memberships:* American Trudeau Society; International Union Against Tuberculosis; American College of Chest Physicians. *Publications:* 'Testing of twofold tubercle bacilit', 1955 'Chemotherapy of previously treated patients with pulmonary tuberculosis', 1964. *Honours:* Diploma of Honorary member, Medical Association of Bosna and Herc.; Diploma of medical Association of Croatia, 1977; Charter and Medal, Institute of Pulmonary Disease, Golnik, 1981. *Hobby:* Fishing. *Address:* B Santini 43, Split 58000, Croatia, Yugoslavia.

GJERMO, Per Edvard, b. 11 Sept 1933, Oslo, Norway. University Professor. *Education:* Dr. Odont. 1974; DDS, University of Oslo, 1956. *Appointments:* Assistant Professor in Periodontology, 1968-78; Asscoiate Professor in Periodontology, 1978-83; Professor in Community Dentistry, 1983-. *Memberships:* International Association for Dental Research; Federation Dentaire International; Scandinavian Society of Periodontology. *Publications:* 'Studies on the Effect and Mode of Action of Chlorhexidine in Dental Plaque Inhibition" University of Oslo, Theseis, 1974; More than 50 scientific articles, 30 Reviews, Symposia etc. *Address:* Institute of Community Dentistry, Dental Faculty, University of Oslo, P B 1052, Blindern, Oslo 3, Norway.

GLANCY, Ross James, b. 22 Mar. 1946, Brisbane, Queensland, Australia. Histopathologist. m. Fay Patricia Edgeworth, 12 Dec. 1970, Brisbane, 1 daughter. *Education:* MB, BS, University of Queensland, 1970; Fellow, Royal College of Pathologists of Australasia, 1980. *Appointments include:* Princess Alexandra Hospital, Brisbane, Ayr District Hospital, North Queensland, University of Queensland, Sir Charles Gairdner Hospital & Royal Perth Hospital, Western Australia, 1971-75; Pathology registrar, Fremantle Hospital, Western

Australia, 1975-76; Histopathology registrar, Sir Charles Gairdner Hospital, WA, 1977-79; Pathologist, State Health Laboratory Services, WA, 1980-82; Histopathologist, Fremantle Hospital, WA, 1983-. *Memberships:* Pathology Group Convocation representative, Australian Medical Association; Honorary treasurer, Australian Society of Cytology; International Academy of Pathology. *Publications include:* Contributions to journals 'Pathology', 'International Journal of Cancer', 'Medical Journal of Australia', etc. Hobbies: Antiques; Reading; Australian Rules Football. *Address:* 13 Ambergate Drive, Karrinyup. Western Australia 6018.

GLANTZ, Per-Olof Johan, b. 23 July 1936, Lund, Seden, Professor; Chairman and Dean, m. Margaretha Weman, 7 Oct 1961, 1 son, 2 daughters. *Education:* LDS, Royal Dental School, Malmö, Sweden, 1961; Odont Doctor, University of Lund, 1969; Specialist Diploma in Prosthetic Dentistry. *Appointments:* Dental Officer, Public Dental Health System, Växjö, 1961-62; Lecturer, Prosthetic dentistry, Dental School, Malmö, 1962-67; Senior Lecturer, 1967-73; Professor, Dental technology, dental School, Gothenburg, 1973-77; Visiting Professor, Dental School, University of California, San Francisco, USA, 1977-78; Professor, Prosthetic Dentistry, 1977-, Dean, 1984-, Dental School, Malmö, Sweden. *Memberships:* International Association for Dental Research; Royal Physiographic Society, Lund; Academy of Dental Materials; British Society for the Study of Prosthetic Dentistry; American Chemical Society. *Publications:* Author of over 100 publications. *Honours:* IADR-prosthodontic award; Science Award of the Swedish Dental Society; Miller Award; Forsberg Award; Elander Award. *Address:* Dental School, S-214 21 Malmö, Sweden.

GLASER, Susanna Dorothea, b. 2 Mar. 1944, Basel, Switzerland. Ergotherapist, Occupational Therapist. *Education:* School of Occupational Therapy, Zürich, Switzerland; Registry & Certification, American Occupation Therapy Association; Professional Licence, New York State; Bobath-Method/Therapist for Cerebral Palsy; Graduate , Institut de l'Alliance Francaise, Paris, France; Work Evaluator (McCarron-Dial System). *Appointments:* Chief Occupational Therapist, Centre pour IMC, Hôpital Orthopédique, Lausanne, Switzerland, 1966-69; Consultant OT, Eger Nursing Home, New York, 1970-71; Senior Therapist, Mt Sànai Hospital Rehabilitation Department, New York, 1970-71; Consultant OT to numerous Extended Care Facilities, New York City, 1973-76; Consultant OTR, Chief Hand Therapist, Plastic Surgery Specialists Inc, Norfolk, Virginia, 1976-81; Independent OT, Norfolk, Virginia, 1981-82; Private Practice, Director & Owner, Comprehensive Rehabilitation Services of Tidewater Inc, Virginia Beach, VA, 1982-. *Memberships:* Occupational Therapy Association, Tidewater District, 1976-; Virginia OT Association, 1976-; American OT Association, 1970-; American Society of Hand Therapists, Founding member, 1978-. *Publications:* 'Functional Analysis of the reversed scissors & its application in the treatment of the injured hand', 1980; 'Overview of Isokinetics & the role of Cybex II in Hand Therapy' (Co-author), 1983; 'Breaking the Gridlock as OT in Private Practice', 1985. *Honour:* Certificate of Recognition, Virginia Occupational Therapy Association, 1984. *Hobbies:* Sailing; Swimming; Karate; Skiing; Playing the piano and flute. *Address:* Comprehensive Rehabilitation Services of Tidewater Inc, 1024 Independence Blrd., Virginia Beach, VA 23455, USA.

GLASER, Wolfram, b. 27 Feb. 1944, Breslau, Germany. Psychiatrist. m. Emily Pitts Glaser, 5 May 1979, Birmingham, Alabama, 3 sons, 1 daughter. *Education:* BA, Birmingham Southern College 1967; MD, School of Medicine, University of Alabama, 1971. *Appointments:* Chief, Department of Psychiatry, US Army Hospital, Berlin, Germany,

1975-76; Consultant, University of Alabama Drug Abuse Program, 1976; Chairman, Department of Psychiatry, Lloyd Noland Hospital and Health Center, 1976 -; Clinical Instructor, Department of Psychiatry, UAB School of Medicine, Birmingham, Alabama, 1976 -. *Memberships:* American Psychiatric Association; American Medical Association. *Honours:* Alpha Omega Alpha; National Honor Medical Society, 1969. *Hobbies:* Reading; Horticulture; Sailing. *Address:* Lloyd Noland Hospital & Health Center, 701 Ridgeway Road, Fairfield, AL 35064, USA.

GLASS, Gary Michael, b. 7 Nov. 1948, New Jersey, USA. Assistant Medical Director, Philadelphia Psychiatric Center. m. Shelli Demchick, 1 son. *Education:* BA, University of Pennsylvania, 1970; MD, Universidad Autonoma de Guadalajara, 1974; Internship, Pediatrics, New Jersey College of Medicine; Residency, Psychiatry, University of Pennsylvania; Fellowship, Forensic Psychiatry, University of Pennsylvania. *Appointments:* Director, Out Patients Department, Philadelphia Psychiatric Center, 1979-81; Assistant Director, 1979-81, Acting Director, 1981, Residency Training, University of Pennsylvania; Associate Director, Center for Law and Psychiatry, University of Pennsylvania, 1980-84; Adjunct Professor, St. Joseph's University School of Criminal Justice; Acting Medical Director, Phila Psychiatric Center 1983-84; Associate Professor Temple University School of Medicine, Department of Psychiatry. *Memberships Include:* Fellow, Philadelphia College of Physicians; American Medical Association; American Psychiatric Association; American Academy of Psychiatry and The Law; Fellow, American Society of Law and Medicine; National Association of Private Psychiatric Hospitals; Pennsylvania Association of Probation, Parole and Corrections; New Jersey and Pennsylvania Councils on Compulsive Gambling; Board of Directors, Phila Center for Human Development. *Honours:* Honored alumnus of Universidad Autonoma de Guadalajara,1985; John D. Nowiche Award, 1979; Laughlin Award of National Psychiatric Endowment Fund, 1979. *Address:* c/o Philadelphia Psychiatric Center, Ford Road and Monument Avenue, Philadelphia, PA 19131, USA.

GLASSMAN, Armand Barry, b. 9 Sept. 1938, New Jersey, USA. University Professor; Chairman of Laboratory Medicine. m. Alberta C. Macri, 30 Aug, 1958, Maryland, USA, 3 sons. *Education:* BA, Rutgers Unviersity, USA, 1960; Ms, Magna cum Laude, Georgetown University, 1965. *Appointments:* Assistant Professor, University of Florida School of Medicine, USA, 1969-71; Associate Professor, Medical College of Georgia, 1971-76; Director of Clinical Laboratories, Medical University Hospital, 1976-; Associate Medical Director, 1982-present; Director of School of Applied Laboratory Sciences and Assistant Dean, College of Allied Health Sciences, 1984-present; Director of Clinical Laboratories, Charleston Memorial Hospital, 1984-present; Acting Chairman, Department of Basic and Clinical Immunology and Microbiology, Medical University of South Carolina, 1985-. *Memberships include:* American Medical Association; American College of Physicians; American College of Nuclear Medicine; International Association of Medical Specialists; International Society of Blood Transfusion; American Society of Tropical Medicine and Hygiene; American Geriatrics Society; American Society of Microbiology; International Academy of Pathology; American Association of Blood Banks; Georgia Heart Association, etc. *Publications include:* "Hemotherapy: The Use of Blood and Blood Products", 1979; "Introduction to Nuclear Medicine", 1979; "Essentials of Laboratory Medicine", 1982, etc; over 70 articles in professional journals; 26 book chapters. *Honours include:* Johnson Foundation Scholarship, 1961-64;

Physician's Recognition Award, American Medical Association, 1970-73, 1973-76; 1976-79; 1979-82; 1982-85; 1985-88; Distinguished Service Award, 1975, etc. *Hobbies:* Running; Tennis. *Address:* Laboratory Medicine, Medical University of South Carolina, 171 Ashley Avenue, Charleston, SC 29425, USA.

GLENN, Mel B, b. 15 Feb. 1949, Fort Worth, Texas, USA. Staff Psychiatrist and Assistant Professor of Rehabilitation, New England Medical Center Hospital and Tufts University School of Medicine; Director of Rehabilitation, Greenery Rehabilitation and Skilled Nursing Center, Boston, Massachusetts. m. Judith A. Ashway, 20 Aug. 1976, Great Neck, New York, 1 son, 1 daughter. *Education:* BA, Sarah Lawrence College, Bronxville, New York, 1972; MD, New York University School of Medicine, 1978. *Appointments:* Residency, Physical Medicine and Rehabilitation, New York University Medical Center, New York, 1978-81; Fellowship, Spinal Cord Inury Medicine, New York University Medical Center, New York, 1981-82. *Memberships:* American Academy of Physical Medicine and Rehabilitation; Massachusetts Medical Society; New England Society of Physical Medicine and Rehabilitation; Advisory Board, Massachusetts Chapter of the National Head Injury Association. *Publications:* Co-author, 'Serum Albumin as a Predictor of Course and Outcome on a Rehabilitation Service', 'Arch. Phys. Med. Rehab.', 1985; Co-author, 'Rehabilitation Following Severe Traumatic Brain Injury', 'Sem. Neurol.', 1985; Co-author, 'Anticonvulsant Prophylaxis of Post-traumatic Seizure, Head Trauma Rehabilitation! (in press); Co-author, 'The Care and Rehabilitation of the Patient in a Persistent Vegetative State. Head Trauma Rehabilitation' (in press). *Address:* Box 107, New England Medical Center Hospitals, 171 Harrison Avenue, Boston, MA 02111, USA.

GLICK, Ira David, b. 15 Dec 1935, Brooklyn, New York, USA. University Professor. m. Sep. 1982, New York City, 1 son 1 daughter. *Education:* BS, Dickinson College, Carlisle, Pennsylvania, 1957; MD, New York Medical College, 1961. *Appointments Include:* Chief Clinical Research Ward 1968-78 (except 1971-73); Director, Medical Student Education, Department of Psychiatry, 1976-78; Assistant Clinical Professor of Psychiatry and Obstetrics and Gynecology, 1968-72; Associate Clinical Professor of Psychiatry and of Obstetrics and Gynecology, 1972-76; Professor of Psychiatry in Residence, 1976-78; Langley Porter Neuropsychiatric Institute and Department of Psychiatry, School of Medicine, University of California, San Francisco; Professor of Psychiatry, 1978 -, Associate Medical Director for Inpatient Services, 1978 -, The Payne Whitney Clinic and The New York Hospital Cornell University Medical College, New York. *Memberships:* American Psychiatric Association; Society of Biological Psychiatry; American College of Neuropsychopharmacology; Association of Academic Psychiatry; The Hastings Center - Institute of Society Ethics and the Life Sciences; American Family Therapy Association; Group for the Advancement of Psychiatry; Association for Clinical Psychosocial Research. *Publications Include:* 'Psychiatric Hospital Treatment for the 1980s: A Controlled Study of Short versus Long Hospitalization' with WA Hargreaves, 1979; 'Practical Considerations (Discussions of "The effects of social class on parental values and practices" by Kohn ML and of "The development of children in mother-headed families" by Hetherington EM, Cox M, Cox R)" in The American Family: Dying or Developing edited by Reiss D and Hoffman H, 1979; "Marital and Family Therapy" 2nd edition 1980 with DR Kessler; "Family therapy and research: An annotated bibliography of articles, books, videotapes and films published 1950-1979" 2nd edition 1982, with D Weber, D Rubinstein and J

Patten. Numerous articles in scientific journals and magazines. *Honour:* Fellow, American College of Neuropsychopharmacology. *Hobbies:* Sport; Reading. *Address:* The New York Hospital, 525 East 68th Street, New York, NY 10021, USA.

GLICK, John Harrison, b. 9 May 1943, New York City, USA. Professor of Medicine and Director, University of Pennsylvania Cancer Center. m. Jane, 1968, 2 daughters. *Education:* MD, Columbia University College of Physicians; AB, Princeton University (Magna Cum Laude). *Appointments:* Intern in Medicine, Presbyterian Hospital, New York City, 1969-70; Assistant Resident in Medicine, Presbyterian Hospital, 1970-71; Clinical Associate, Medicine Branch, National Cancer Institute, Bethesda, 1971-73; Post Doctoral Fellow in Medical Oncology, Stanford University, 1973-74; Assistant Professor of Medicine, 1974-79; Associate Professor of Medicine, 1979-83; Professor of Medicine, 1983-, University of Pennsylvania. *Memberships:* Fellow, American College of Physicians; American Society of Clinical Oncology; American Association for Cancer Education; American Association for Cancer Research; American Radium Society; American Society of Hematology; American Federation of Clinical Research; Fellow, College of Physicians of Philadelphia; John Morgan Society, University of Pennsylvania; Phi Beta Kappa. *Publications:* Numerous original papers, abstracts, chapters and books. *Honours:* Ann B Young Assistant Professor of Cancer Research, 1974; American Cancer Society Junior Faculty Fellowship, 1975-78; American Cancer Society Faculty Research Award, 1982-86. *Address:* University of Pennsylvania Cancer Center, 7 Silverstein, 3400 Spruce Street, Philadelphia, PA 19104, USA.

GLINDMEYER, Henry William, b. 6 Apr. 1947, New Orleans, Louisiana, USA. Associate Professor, Medicine; Associate Professor, Engineering. m. Pamela Jean Hayes, 18 Apr. 1980, New Orleans, 1 son. *Education:* BS, Louisiana State University, New Orleans, 1970; MS, 1971, D.Engr., 1976, Tulane University. *Appointments:* Research Associate, 1972-74, Instructor, 1974-76, Assistant Professor, Medicine, 1976-81, Adjunct Associate Professor, Physiology, 1977-81, Engineering, 1977-81, Associate Professor, medicine, 1981-, Associate Professor, Engineering, 1981-, Tulane University School of Medicine. *Memberships:* Fellow, American College of Chest Physicians; American Thoracic Society; Sigma Xi; Mensa. *Publications:* More than 20 Scientific & Medical Articles; 8 Chapter in Books; more than 30 Abstracts & Invited Papers. *Honours:* FCCP, 1984; Editor, Critical Reviews, Medical Informatics, 1984-. *Hobbies:* Family; Travel; Computer. *Address:* 1700 Perdido St., New Orleans, LA 70112, USA.

GLORIEUX, Francis Henri Maurice, b. 7 June 1939, Brussels, Belgium. Professor of Human Genetics and Surgery. m. Jacqueline Serruys, 20 June 1964, Ghistelles, 1 son, 2 daughters. *Education:* MD, University of Louvain, 1963; Certificate in Pediatrics, Brussels, 1968; MSc Genetics, University of Montreal, Canada, 1969; PhD Human Genetics, McGill University, Montreal, 1972; Fellow, Canadian College of Medical Geneticists, 1982. *Appointments Include:* Assistant Professor of Pediatrics and Surgery 1972, Associate Professor of Surgery 1976, Associate Professor of Pediatrics and Human Genetics 1980, Professor of Human Genetics and Surgery 1981, McGill University; Director of Research and Head of the Genetics Unit, Montreal Shriners Hospital for Crippled Children, 1972 -. *Memberships:* Belgian Pediatric Society; Canadian Society for Clinical Investigation; Club de Recherches Cliniques du Quebec; Orthopaedic Research Society; American Society of Human Genetics; Society for Pediatric Research; American Society for Bone and Mineral Research; Bone Group Sigma; European Calcified Tissue Society.

Publications: 85 book chapters and articles. *Honours Include:* Knight of the Order of the Crown, Belgium, 1980; Knight of Malta, 1985. *Hobbies:* Tennis; Squash; Cross Country Skiing; Wine Collection. *Address:* Genetics Unit, Shriners Hospital, 1529 Cedar Avenue, Montreal, H3G IA6 Canada.

GLOVER, Stuart William, b. 9 Dec. 1928, Crewe, England. Professor, Head, Dept. of Genetics. m. Monique Lauryssens, 16 Feb. 1965, Richmond, 2 sons. *Education:* BA 1953, MA, 1955, PhD 1956, ScD 1972, Trinity College, University of Dublin, Ireland. *Appointments:* Research Assistant, Cold Spring Harbor, New York, USA, 1953-55; Research Fellow, Irish medical Research Council, 1955-56; Research Staff, Medical Research Council, London, 1956-68; Assistant Director, Medical Research council Unit, Edinburgh, 1968-72; Professor, Genetics, Newcastle University, 1972-. *Memberships:* Society for General Microbiology; Genetical Society; Biophysical Society; Institute of Biology. *Publications:* "Genetics as a Tool in Microbiology", 1981; "Genetic Studies with Bacteria", 1956. *Hobby:* Gardening. *Address:* Dept. of Genetics, University of Newcastle, Newcastle upon Tyne NE1 7RU, England.

GLOVER, Walter Ernest, b. 4 May 1932, Belfast, Ireland. Dean, Medicine. m. Lillian Mary Johnston, 8 Aug. 1956, Belfast, 1 son, 1 daughter. *Education:* MB BCh BAO, 1955, MD, 1960, DSc., 1983, Queen's University of Belfast. *Appointments:* Fellow, Royal Australasian College of Physicians; House Surgeon & Physician, Ards Hospital, 1955-56; Assistant Lecturer, 1956-58, Lecturer, Physiology, 1958-65, Queen's University, Belfast; Royal Society & Nuffield Foundation Bursary, University of Adelaide, 1965-66; Senior Lecturer, Queen's University, Consultant Physiologist, Northern Ireland Hospitals Authority, 1966-68; Professor, Head, Physiology & Pharmacolgoy, University of New South Wales, Australia, 1969-85; Consultant Physiologist: Prince Henry, Prince of Wales Hospital, 1972-; St Vincents Hospital, Sydney, 1974-; Dean, Faculty of Medicine, University of New South Wales, Sydney, 1985-. *Memberships:* Physiological Society; Medical Research Society; Australasian Society for Clinical & Experimental Pharmacology; Australian Physiological and Pharamcological Society. *Publications:* Papers on Control of Peripheral Circulation in Man, and Vascular Physiology & Pharmacology, in 'Journal of Physiology'; 'British Journal of Pharmacology'; 'Clinical Science'; etc. *Hobby:* Sailing. *Address:* 2 Coolong Road, Vaucluse, NSW 2030, Australia.

GODFREY, Malcolm Paul Weston, b. 11 Aug. 1926, London, England. Second Secretary, UK Medical Research Council. m. Barbara Goldstein, 4 Sep. 1955, London, 1 son, 2 daughters. *Education:* University of London; King's College; MB, BS (London); FRCP (London). *Appointments:* Various Hospitals, UK National Health Service, 1950-60; Fellow, Medicine, Assistant Physician, Johns Hopkins Hospital, USA, 1957-58; Medical Research Administrator, UK Medical Research Council, 1960-74; Dean, Royal Postgrauldate Medical School, University of London, 1974-83. *Memberships:* Various professional societies. *Publications:* Articles on cardiac and respiratory disorders, various professional journals. *Hobbies:* Theatre; Reading; Walking; Cross Country Skiing. *Address:* Medical Research Council, 20 Park Crescent, London W1N 4AL, England.

GODLEWSKI, Andrej, b. 31 Oct. 1944, Drohobytsh, Russia. Junior Associate Professor. m. 2 Aug. 1969, 1 daughter. *Education:* DMSc., 1976. *Appointments:* Assistant, General Biology and Parasitology, 1968-73, Assistant, Histology & Embryology, 1973-74, Senior Assistant, 1974-76, Junior Associate Professor, Histology & Embryology, 1977-, Academy of Medicine, Biologic and Morphological Institute, Poland; Visiting Scientist, Physiology, University of

Connecticut Health Centre, USA, 1982-83. *Memberships:* Polish Society of Histochemistry and Cytochemistry; Polish Anatomical Society; European Academy Allergology Clinical Immunology; Polish Society of Parasitology. *Publications:* Articles in professional journals. *Honours:* Fellowship Award, 1982. *Hobby:* Classic Symphonic Music. *Address:* Department Histology and Embryology, Academy of Medicine, 90-136 Lodz, 60 Poland.

GOERTTLER, Klaus Juergen, b. 24 Mar. 1925, Munich,. Federal Republic of Germany. Chairman; University Professor; Director. *Education:* Dr.med. Venia Legendi; Ordinarius of the University Comparative and Experimental Pathology. *Appointment:* Director, Institute of Experimental Pathology, German Cancer Research Centre. *Address:* Institute of Experimental and Comparative Pathology, University of Heidelberg, Im Neuenheimer Feld 220, D-6900 Heidelberg 1, Federal Republic of Germany.

GOLAB, Boguslaw Kazimierz, b. 4 Aug. 1929, Borszczów, Poland, Chairman, Department of Normal Anatomy and Director, Bio-Morphological Institute Medical Academy, Lodz, m. 12 Jan. 1956, 1 daughter. *Education:* MD, Dr Hab, Medical Faculty of Medical Academy, Lodz, 1953; Professor. *Appointments:* Department of Normal Anatomy Bio-Morphological Institute Medical Academy, Lodz, 1953-. *Memberships:* President, Polish Anatomical Society; Anatomischer Gesellschaft; International Society of Lymphology, 1973-76. *Publications:* "Anatomy of the Lymphatic System", 1974; "Anatomy and Physiology of Man", 1981; "Functional Anatomy of the Central Nervous System", 1984. *Honours:* Gold Cross of Merit, 1970. *Hobbies:* Literature; Tourism. *Address:* Narutowicza 75c-7, 90-132 Lodz, Poland.

GOLD, Phil, b. 17 Sep. 1936, Montreal, Quebec, Canada. Professor of Medicine. m. Evelyn Katz, 20 Aug. 1960, Montreal, 2 sons, 1 daughter. *Education:* BSc Honours Physiology 1957, MSc MD CM 1961, PhD Physiology 1965, McGill University, Montreal. *Appointments Include:* Lecturer - Associate Professor 1964-74, Professor of Medicine and Physiology 1973 -, Director Cancer Centre 1973-80, McGill University, Junior Assistant - Associate Physician 1967-73, Senior Physician 1973 -, Director of Division of Clinical Immunology and Allergy 1977-80, Director McGill University Medical Clinic, Physician in Chief of Department of Medicine 1980-, Senior Investigator of Research Institute, Montreal General Hospital; Consultant, Department of Internal Medicine, Douglas Hospital Centre, Montreal, 1981 -; Chairman, Department of Medicine, McGill University, 1985-. *Memberships Include:* Fellow : Royal College of Physicians and Surgeons of Canada; Royal Society of Canada; American College of Physicians. *Publications:* 111 papers and reviews in learned journals. *Honours Include:* Companion of the Order of Canada, 1985; Heath Memortial Award, 1980; The FNG Starr Award, The Canadian Medical Association, 1983. *Hobbies:* Photography; Music. *Address:* The Montreal General Hospital, 1650 Cedar Avenue, Room 648, Montreal, Quebec H3G IA4, Canada.

GOLD, Richard Horace, b. 20 Nov. 1935, New York City, USA. Professor. m. Gittelle Schneider, 27 June 1965, New York City, 1 son, 1 daughter. *Education:* BA, New York University, 1956; MD, University of Louisville, 1960. *Appointments:* Internship, Pennsylvania Hospital, 1961; Fellowship, University of California, San Francisco, 1967-68; Assistant Professor, Radiology, University of California, San Francisco, 1968-72; Assistant Professor, 1972-74, Associate Professor, 1974-78, Professor, 1978-, Radiological Sciences, University of California, Los Angeles. *Memberships:* Association of University Radiologists; Radiological Society of North

America; American College of Radiology; International Skeletal Society; American Roentgen Ray Society. *Publications:* Co-Author, "Roentgen Appearance of the Hand in Diffuse Disease", 1975; Co-Author: "Clinical Arthography", 1981, 2nd edition 1985, "Mammography, Thermography, and Ultrasound in Breast Cancer Detection", 1982; "Hand Held and Automated Breast Untrasound", 1985. *Honours:* Fellow, American College of Radiology, 1977; US Public Health Service Commissioner's Special Citation, 1981; Editorial Boards of Investigative Radiology, 1983-; Alpha Omega Alpha. *Hobbies:* Classical Music; Fine Arts; Theatre; Reading. *Address:* Department of Radiological Sciences, UCLA Medical Centre, Los Angeles, CA 90024, USA.

GOLDBERG, Abraham (Sir), b 7 Dec 1923, Edinburgh, Scotland. Regius Professor of the Practice of Medicine, Glasgow University. m. Clarice Cussin, 3 Sept 1957, 2 sons 1 daughter. *Education:* MB, ChB, 1946, MD(Gold Medal) 1956, University of Edinburgh; DSc, University of Glasgow, 1966. *Appointments:* Nuffield Research Fellow, Medicine, University College Hospital, London, 1952-54; Eli Lilly Travelling Fellow, University of Utah, USA, 1956; Lecturer, 1956-67, Titular Professor, 1967-70, Department of Medicine, University of Glasgow; Regius Professor, Department of Materia Medica, University of Glasgow, 1970-78. *Memberships:* Association of Physicians of Great Britain; Fellow of Royal Society (Edinburgh); Fellow of Royal Colleges of London, Edinburgh and Glasgow. *Publications:* "Diseases of Porphyrin Metabolism" co-author, 1962; "Recent Advances in Haematology" co-editor, 1972; "Clinics in Haematology" 'The Porphyrias' 1980. *Honours:* KB, 1983; Sydney Watson Smith Lectureship RCP (Edinburgh) 1964; Henry Cohen Lectureship, Hebrew University, Jerusalem, 1973; Watson Prize Lectureship RCP (Glasgow) 1959; Alexander Fleck Award, University of Glasgow, 1967. *Hobbies:* Medical history; Literature; Writing; Walking; Swimming. *Address:* University of Glasgow, Department of Medicine, Gardiner Institute, Western Infirmary, Glasgow G11 6NT, Scotland.

GOLDBERG, Richard Thayer, b. 9 Nov. 1935, Cambridge, Massachusetts, USA. Director of Research. m. Dorothy Lewis, 19 Oct. 1958, Brookline, 1 son, 1 daughter. *Education:* AM, 1956, MAT, 1957, Harvard University; Ed.M., 1958, Ed.D., 1966, Boston University. *Appointments:* Rehabilitation Research Fellow, Boston University, 1962; Research Associate, Medfield Foundation, 1964; Instructor, Rehabilitation Administration, Northeastern University, 1969-72; Instructor, Psychology, Boston State College, 1973-81; Adjunct Professor, Boston University, Sargent College, 1978-; Director, Research, Massachusetts Rehabilitation Commission, 1966-. *Memberships:* Fellow, American Psychological Assocation; American Congress of Rehabilitation Medicine. *Publications:* "The Making of Franklin D. Roosevelt: Triumph Over Disability", 1981; Articles in professional journals. *Honours:* Valedictorian, Cambridge Latin School, 1952; Fellow, Office of Vocational Rehabilitation, 1961-62. *Hobbies:* Piano; American History; Opera. *Address:* Massachusetts Rehabilitation Commission, 20 Park Plaza, Boston, MA 02116, USA.

GOLDEN, Robert Neal, b. 27 Aug. 1953, Philadelphia, USA. Assistant Professor, Psychiatry. m. Shannon C. Kenney, 27 May 1979, San Rafael, 1 son, 1 daughter. *Education:* BA, cum laude, Yale University, 1975; MD, Boston University School of Medicine, 1979; Intern, Psychiatry & medicine, 1979; Resident, 1980, Chief Resident, 1982, Psychiatry, University of North Carolina. *Appointments:* Clinical Associate, Laboratory of Clinical Science, National Institute of Mental Health, 1983; Assitant Professor, Psychiatry, University of North Carolina School of Medicine, 1985-. *Memberships:* American

Psychiatric Association; American Association for the Advancement of Science; Society of Biological Psychiatry; Physicians for Social Responsibility. *Publications:* Co-Author: "Buproprion: biochemical effects and clinical response', 'Arch.Gen.Psych.', in press; "Bupropion : role of metabolites in clinical outcome'', 'Arch.Gen.Psych.', in press; etc. *Honours:* Ginsburg Fellowship, group for the Advancement of Psychiatry, 1980; Laughlin Fellowship, American College of Psychiatrists, 1983. *Hobby:* Photography. *Address:* Dept. of Psychiatry, University of North Carolina School of Medicine, Chapel Hill, NC 27541, USA.

GOLDFINCH, Conway Peter, b. 11 Feb. 1937, South Australia. Medical Services Director, Qantas Airways. *Education:* MB, BS, Adelaide University, Australia, 1960; DPH, Sydney University, Australia, 1966; DIPAvMed, United Kingdom, 1977; FACOM, Australia, 1982. *Appointments:* Medical Officer and Senior Medical Officer, Royal Australian Air Force, 1958-66; Senior Medical Officer, Royal Australian Air Force Reserve, 1966-79; Medical Services Director, Qantas Airways Limited, 1982-; Designated Aviation Medical Examiner, Australia and Fiji -. *Memberships:* Australian Medical Association; Treasurer, New South Wales Branch, Australian and New Zealand Society of Occupational Medicine; Aerospace Medical Association; Aviation Medical Society of Australia and New Zealand; Medical Adviser, Guild of Air Pilots, Australia; Adviser to Surf Lifesaving Association of Australia. *Hobbies:* Car Restoration; Languages; Aviation. *Address:* Qantas Medical Centre, Box 489 GPO, Sydney 2001, New South Wales, Australia.

GOLDFINE, Peter E, b. 5 Aug. 1939, New York City, New York, USA. Director of Child Psychiatry Training. m. Christina Curle, 3 Aug. 1968, San Francisco, California, 3 daughters. *Education:* MD Medicine, State University of New York, Downstate Medical Center, New York City, 1963. *Appointments include:* Asistant Clincial Professor of Psychiatry, Tufts University Medical school, 1972-80; Director of Psychiatric Training and Research 1972-74, Assistant Director of Psychiatry 1975-, Director of Child Psychiatry Training 1979-, Maine Medical Centre, Portland; Psychiatric Consultant, The Spurwink School, Portland, 1973-; Site Surveyor, Liaison Committee on Continuing Medical Education, American Medical Association, 1978-; Assistant Clinical Professor of Psychiatry 1980-83, Associate Clinical Professor of Psychiatry 1983-, University of Vermont Medical School; Associate in Clincial Research, Foundation for Blood Research, Scarborough, Maine, 1982-; Curriculum Advisory Committee, Division of Occupationl Therapy, University of New England, Biddeford, Maine, 1983-; Consulting Editor, 'Journal of Child and Adolecent Psychotherapy', 1984-; Psychiatric Consultant, Autism Demonstration Project, Bureau of Mental Retardation, Maine, 1985-. *Memberships include:* Phi Beta Kappa; American Psychiatric Association; Fellow, American Academy of Child Psychiatry. *Publications include:* 'Firesetting, Enuresis, and Animal Cruelty', (with G A Heath and V A Haresty), 1984; 'Association of Fragile X Syndrome with Autism', (with P M McPherson, G A Heath, V A Hardesty, L J Beauregard and B Gordon), 1985; 'Alternatives to Psychiatric Hospitalization for Children', (with G A Heath, V A Hardesty, H J Berman, B Gordon and N Werks-Lind), 1985. *Honours include:* Fulbright Fellow, Tavistock Clinic and Institute, London, England, 1966-67. *Hobbies:* Hiking; Canoeing; Skiing. *Address:* Maine Medical Center, 22 Bramhall Street, Portland, ME 04102, USA.

GOLDING, Stephen John, b. 3 July 1949, Worcestershire, England. Lecturer in Radiology and Consultant in charge of Oxford Regional Computed Tomography Service. m. Lesley Margaret Phillips, 12 Aug 1972, Southwark, 2 daughters. *Education:*

MB, BS, London University, Guy's Hospital, 1972; LRCP, MRCS, 1972; DMRD, 1977; FRCR, 1980. *Appointments:* House Surgeon, Orpington Hospital, Kent; House Physician, Franborough Hospital, Kent; Senior House Officer, Department of Surgery, Guy's Hospital; Senior House Officer, Brook Hospital, London SE18; Registrar in Radiology, Senior Registrar in Radiology, Guy's Hospital; Senior Lecturer, Institute of Cancer Research, Sutton, Surrey; Lecturer in Radiology, University of Oxford and Consultant in charge of Oxford Regional Computed Tomography Service. *Memberships:* British Medical Association; British Institute of Radiology; Royal College of Radiologists; Association for the study of Medical Education. *Publications:* 'Diagnostic Puncture in Renal Cystic Dysplasia' with H M Saxton, C Chandler and G D Haycock in 'British Journal of Radiology' 1981; 'Recent Body Computed Tomography' in ''Recent Advances in Radiology'' edited by R E Steiner, 1983; 'The Role of CT-Guided Needle Biopsy in an Oncology Service' with J Husband 'Clinical Radiology' 1983; 'The Role of Computed Tomography in the management of Bronchial Carcinoma' in ''Bronchial Carcinoma'' edited by M Bates, 1984. *Hobbies:* Music; History. *Address:* Regional CT Unit, Churchill Hospital, Headington, Oxford, England.

GOLDMAN, Howard Hirsch. Associate Professor Director. *Education:* BA 1970, PhD, Brandeis University, Waltham, MA, USA, 1978; MD, Harvard Medical School, Boston, 1974; MPH, Harvard School of Public Health, Boston, 1974. *Appointments:* Trainee, Chief Resident (1975-76), Social Research and Psychiatry, Worcester Youth Guidance Center and Worcester State Hospital, 1974-78; Lecturer, American Studies Department, Brandeis University, 1977; Research Psychiatrist, US Public Health Service, National Institute of Mental Health, Divsion of Biometry and Epidemiology, Office of the Director; Co-ordinator of NIMH Services Evaluation activities; Designer, Project Officer, Chapter Co-ordinator, 1978-80; Assistant Professor in Residence, Director of Medical Student Education, Department of Psychiatry, School of Medicine, University of California, 1980-83. *Memberships include:* Northern California Psychiatric Society, 1980-; American Public Health Assoc,; 1979-; Group for the Advancement of Psychiatry, 1982-. *Publications:* Various publications including Editorials; Abstracts; Book Reviews; 32 articles; Guest Editor in Professional Journals; Chapters in Books; Government Reports; Attended numerous Scientific; Professional meetings and Workshops, all involving paper presentations and Lectures; Books and Monographs ''The Enduring Asylum: Cycles of Scoial Reform at Worcester State Hospital'', with JP Morrissey, LV Klerman), 1980; ''Assessing Community Support Programs'', (with RC Tessler), 1982. *Honours:* BA, Magna Cum Laude, Brandeis University, 1970; US Public Health Service Fellowship (Jerusalem), 1972; US Public Health Service, Commissioned Corps, Plaque, 1980; Kaiser Teaching Award, Honorable Mention, 1982; Outstanding Teacher Award, UCSF Graduating Class, 1982. *Address:* Department of Psychiatry, School of Medicine, University of California, San Francisco, CA 94143, USA.

GOLDMAN, John Michael, b. 30 Nov. 1938, London, England. Consultant Physician. *Education:* BM BCh, University of Oxford, 1963; DM,. 1981. *Memberships:* British Society of Hematology; International Society for Experiemtnal Hematology; American Society of Hematology. *Publications:* Books, chapters & papers on Leucocytes, leukaemia, lymphoma & bone marrow transplatation. *Honour:* Fellow, Royal College of Physicians, London, 1979. *Hobby:* Skiing. *Address:* MRC Leukaemia Unit, Royal Postgraduate Medical School, London W12 0HS, England.

GOLDMAN, Louis Milton, b. 15 Mar. 1929, Lowood, Queensland, Australia, State Director, RACGP Family Medicine Programme, m. Margaret, 15 Apr. 1952, Sydney, 1 son, 1 daughter. *Education:* MBBS, Sydney, 1952; FRACGP. *Appointments:* Visiting Medical Officer, Bulli and Wollongong District Hospitals, 1954-62; Clinical Assistant, Department of Medicine, St Vincent's Hospital, Sydney, 1964-77; Medical Educator, 1978-79, State Director, 1979-, RACGP Family Medicine Programme, New South Wales; Honorary Secretary, 1980-83, Honorary Treasurer, 1985-, Australian Medical Society on Alcohol and Drug Related Problems. *Publications:* ''Take Care of Yourself'', (Co-author), 1981; 'Integrated approach to Curriculum Planning', 1983; 'Role of Hospital Unit in Alcohol and Drug Related Problems', 1983; 'Education and Training for General/Family Practice', 1984. *Hobbies:* Theatre; Classcial music; Golf; Tennis; Lawn bowls; Painting water colours. *Address:* 2/366 Edgecliff Road, Woollahra, 2025 New South Wales, Australia.

GOLDSCHMIDT, Arnold M, b. 20 May 1928, New York City, USA, President, Federation of Chiropractic Licensing Boards, Member NY State Board for Chiropractic, Director, National Board of Chiropractic Examiners, m. Lucille Cohen, 25 Aug 1984, New York; 1 son, 2 daughters, by previous marriage. *Education:* DC, Chiropractic Institute of New York, 1950; FACC; FICC. *Appointments:* Secretary, New York State Chiropractic Association, 1969-75; Vice President, New York State Chiropractic Association, 1975-77; Director, New York State Chiropractic Association, 1977-84; Vice President, Federation of Chiropractic Licensing Boards, 1983-85. *Memberships:* New York State Chiropractic Association; American Chiropractic Association; Alumni Association National College of Chiropractic; Alumni Association New York Chiropractic College; Association for History of Chiropractic Inc. *Publications:* 'Survey of 203 Chiropractic Cases of Industrial Injuries', 1982. *Honours:* Distinguished Service Citations, NYSCA, 1969-84; Award of Excellence, NYS Chiropractic Association; Fellow, American College of Chiropractors, 1970; Fellow, International College of Chiropractors, 1981. *Hobbies:* Tennis; Swimming; Cycling. *Address:* 60 East 42nd Street, New York, NY 10165, USA.

GOLFIN, Robert Allen, b. 24 Mar. 1952, Brooklyn, USA. Doctor of Chiropractic. m. Cheryl Klein, 10 Aug. 1974, New York City, 1 son, 1 daughter. *Education:* BS, Biology, Brooklyn College; BS, Human Anatomy, DC, National College of Chiropractic. *Appointments:* Intern, Lombard Clinic, Illinois, 1977; Course Director, Alphalogic School, Bristol; Director, Golfin Chiropractic Centre, Bristol, 1980-. *Memberships:* Connecticut Chiropractic Association; American Chiropractic Association; American Chiropractic Association, Council of Nutrition; Parker Research Foundation. *Honours:* Diplomate, National Board of Chiropractic Examiners; Appearances on Local TV and Radio. *Hobby:* Cooking. *Address:* 1098 Farmington Avenue, Bristol, CT 06010, USA.

GOMEZ, Jaime G b. 3 Apr. 1932, Bucaramanga, Columbia. Professor & Chairman of Department of Neurosurgery. m. Lucy Gonzalez, 28 Oct. 1956, Bogota, Columbia, 4 sons, 1 daughter. *Education:* National University of Columbia, 1955, Resident Neurosurgeon, National University Hospital, Columbia, 1956; Fellow, Neuropathology, Columbia University, 1957; Resident Neurologist, New York, USA, 1959-60. *Appointments:* Assistant Professor of Neurosurgery, Javerian University, Bogota; Neurosurgeon, Children's Hospital, Bogota, 1961, Military Hospital, Bogota, 1962; Director, Founder, Neurological Insititute, 1966; Associate Professor of Neurosurgery, Javeriana University, 1978; Consultant, World Health Organisation, 1980; Adjunct Professor of Neurosurgery, University of

Florida, USA, 1981. *Memberships:* National Academy of Medicine, Columbia; Corresponding Member, American Academy of Neurosurgery; Honorary Member, Equatorial Society of Neurological Sciences, Corresponding Member, Peruvian Society of Neurosurgery; Honorary Member, Chilean Society of Laser; President, Ibero-American Society of Laser. *Publications:* Over 100 articles in journals 'Enfermeria Neurologica', Guia Neurologica', 'Principios de Cirugia Neurologica'. *Honours:* Honorary Citizen of Dallas, 1975, Texas, 1975; City of Bogota Decoration, 1976; Distinguished Services Medal, 1956. *Hobby:* Golf. Address: Neurological Institute of Columbia, Transv 4H No 42-00, Apartado Aereo 56666 Bogota. Columbia, South America.

GONZALES, Primo E, b. 9 June 1928, Balanga, Bataan, Philippines. President, International College of Dentists. *Education:* DDM, University of Philippines College of Dentistry, 1952; Postgraduate, Prosthodontics, College of Dentistry, New York University, USA, 1954-55; Intern, Dental Surgery & Anaesthesia, Morrisania City Hospital, New York City, 1955-56. *Appointments:* Private Dental Practice, 1952-54 and 1956-; Part-time Lecturer & Demonstrator, University of Philippines College of Dentistry, 1959-61. *Memberships include:* Philippine Dental Association, President 1971-72, 1975-76; President, International College of Dentists-at-Large, 1986; Vice-President, Asian-Pacific Dental Federation, 1974-77; Fellow, International College of Dentists; Fédération Dentaire Internationale. *Address:* Solid Mills Building, Dela Rosa Street, Legaspi Village, Makati, Metro Manila, Philippines.

GONZAGA, Florante P, b. 17 May 1934, Philippines. Assistant Professor of Obstetrics and Gynaecology. m. Evelyn Recto, 30 Dec. 1969, Manila, 1 son, 1 daughter. *Education:* MD, University of the Philippines, 1958; FACOG; FACS. *Appointments:* Resident in Obstetrics and Gynecology, Philippine General Hospital, Manila, 1958-62; Fellow in Obstetrics and Gynecology, College of Physcicians and Surgeons, Columbia University, New York, USA, 1963-65; Temporary Adviser, World Health Organisation (Session on Ovulatory Cycle), Geneva, Switzerland, 1966,; Currenlty, Assistant Professor, Obstetrics and Gynaecology, College of Medicine, University of the Philippines. *Memberships:* Fellow: American College of Obstetricians and Gynaecologists; American College of Surgeons; Philippine Obstetricians and Gynaecologists Society; Philippine College of Surgeons. *Publications:* Co-author of papers contributed to : 'American Journal of Obstetrics and Gynaecology', 1985. *Hobby:* Photography. *Address:* Department of Obstetrics and Gynaecology, College of Medicine, University of the Philippines,

GONZALEZ, Mario L, b. 4 Mar. 1929, Carolina, Puerto Rico. Medical Director, Chief Radiation Therapy. m. Patrito S Gonzalez, Santiago, Spain, 9 Jan. 1954. *Education:* BSc, University of Puerto Rico, 1948; MD, School of Medicine, University of Santiago, Spain, 1955. *Appointments:* Director, Department of Radio Therapy, Long Island College Hospital, Brooklyn, New York and Brooklyn-Cumberland Hospital; Radiotherapist, M D Anderson Hospital, Houston, Texas; Medical Director, Head, Radiation Therapy, Rio Grande Cancer Treatment Centre, Inc., McAllen, Texas. *Memberships:* American Medical Association; American College of Radiology; American Society of Therapeutic Radiation & Oncology; Radiological Society of North America; New York Academy of Science; American Endocurietherpay Society; Gilbert H Fletcher Society; Texas Medical Society; Hidalgo-Starr County Medical Society. *Hobbies:* Painting; Hunting; Fishing; Gardening. *Address:* 501 North Ware Road, McAllen, TX 78501, USA.

GONZALEZ-GARCIA, Pedro Jose, b. 25 Mar. 1951,

Puerto Rico. Chiropractic Physician. m. Dora Nilsa Santiago-Gonzalez, 24 Aug. 1979, San Juan, 1 son. *Education:* BA, University of Puerto Rico; DC, Palmer College of Chiropractic, USA; 5th Degree Black Belt, Chi-I-Do Gojo-Ryu. *Appointments:* Elementary and Pre-School Teacher; Karate Instructor; President, Dr. Pedro J. Gonzalez, PC, Chiropratic Officers. *Memberships:* American, International, Southern Maryland and National Chiropractic Associations. *Publications:* Developed pre-school curriculum, 1978-79; "Quien es Meher baba", 1977. *Honours:* Clinic Examination Scholarship, 1981-82; Extern Scholarship, 1982; Hans Nielsen Member Scholarship, 1981-82; Diplomate, National Boards of Chiropractic Examiners, 1982. *Hobbies:* Photography; Record Collector. *Address:* 5408 Beech Avenue, Bethesda, MD 20814,USA

GONZALEZ-GONZALEZ, Remigio, b. 11 Oct. 1929, Pontevedra, Spain. Professor, Psychiatry. m. New Orleans, 2 sons, 1 daughter. *Education:* BA, Cornell College, USA; MD, Tulane University Medical School; Psychoanalytic Training, Adult, Adolescent & Child, New Orleans Psychoanalytic Institute. *Appointments:* Clinical Director, Director, Adolescent Service, Southeast Hospital, Mandeville; Director, Mental Health Region III, St Tammany Mental Health Centre, Bogalousa Mental Health Centre, Hammond Mental Health Centre, New Orleans Mental Health Centre; President, DePaul Hospital Medical Staff; President, River Oaks Medical Staff; President, New Orleans Adolescent Society; President, Louisian Child Council; Chairman, Child and Adolescent Training, Psychoanalysis, New Orleans, Psychoanalytic Institute; Associate Professor, Psychiatry, Tulane University. *Appointments Include:* Orleans Medical Society; Louisiana State Medical Society; Louisiana Psychiatric Association; American Psychiatric Association; Louisiana Child Council, American Academy of Child Psychiatry; New Orleans Psychoanalytic Society; American Psychoanalytic Society; International Psychoanalytic Society; etc. *Publications:* "Fencanfamin vs. Placebo in Depressed Patients", 'Journal of New Drugs'. 1964; "Hemogram Abnormalities in Chronic Schizophrenics Used as Placebo Controls", 'Psychopharmacology Service Center Bulletin', 1965; etc. *Honours:* Fellow, Geriatrics Society; Fellow, American Society for Social Psychiatry; Fellow, American Psychiatric Association. *Hobbies:* Golf; Travel. *Address:* 1303 Amelia Street, New Orleans, LA 70115, USA.

GONZALEZ SANTANDER, Rafael, b. 17 Aug. 1932, Leon, Spain. Professor and Chairman of Department of Histology and Embriology. m. Gloria Martinez Cuadrado, 26 Feb. 1963, Madrid, 2 sons, 1 daughter. *Education:* Surgery and Medical Doctor, University of Madrid, 1961. *Appointments:* Scientific Assistant, Institute Cajal CSIC, 1965; Adjunct Professor of Histology, Madrid, 1968; Scientific Researcher, Instituto Cajal CSIC, 1971; Medical School Secretary, Barcelona, 1974; Professor of Histology, Barcelona, 1975; Professor of Histology, 1980, Medical School Vice-Dean, 1981, Alcala de Henares. *Memberships:* Sociedad Mexicana de Anatomia; Sociedad Espanola de Citologia; Sociedad Espanola de Microscopia Electronica; Sociedad Espanola de Histologia. *Publications:* "Manual de Microscopia Electronica", 1966; "Tecnicas de Microscopia Electronica en Biologia", Editor, 1969; "Introduction a la Citogenetica Humana",. Editor, 1976. *Honour:* Ramon y Cajal Award (Royal Medicine Academy), 1968. *Address:* Facultad de Medicina, Universidad de Alcala de Henares, Madrid, Spain.

GOODALL, Charles Murray Maarire, b. 10 Mar. 1935, New Zealand. Experimental Oncologist. *Education:* MB ChB, University of Otago, New Zealand, 1959, MD 1963. *Appointments:* Research Fellow, Cancer Research Unit, Otago Medical School Dunedin, New

Zealand, 1963; Research Associate, Institute for Medical Research, Chicago Medical School, USA, 1963-67; Director, National Cancer Research Laboratory, Cancer Society, New Zealand, 1967-74; Director, Cancer Research Unit, University of Otago, Dunedin, 1974-. *Memberships:* Life Member: New York Academy of Sciences; American Association for Cancer Research; Otago Medical Research Foundation; Charter Member: International Society for the Study of Xenobiotics; Member: Society of Toxicology; Foreign Member, International Society for Preventive Oncology; Australian Society of Experimental Pathology; Endocrinology Society; New Zealand Society of Pathology; American Association for the Advancement of Science; New Zealand Biochemcial Society; Founder & Chairman, Cancer Research Trust; Founder President, New Zealand Society of Oncology. *Publications:* (with G Griffiths) "Maori Dunedin", Maori poetry and other works. 108 Scientific publications. *Honours:* Honorary Citizen, Boys Town, Nebraska, USA, 1964; George S Christie Memorial Award, Melbourne, 1985. *Hobbies:* Music Composition; Poetry; Trustee for several Maori & Community organisations. *Address:* PO Box 5190, Dunedin, New Zealand.

GOODALL, William MacKenzie, b. 1 Dec. 1940, Winnipeg, Canada. Associate University Dean. m. Eleanor Thompson, 27 Dec. 1961, Winnipeg, 3 daughters. *Education:* BSc, University of Manitoba, Canada, 1961, MD, 1965. *Appointments:* Private Practice, 1966-80; Associate Dean, University of North Dakota School of Medicine, USA, 1980-. *Memberships:* American Medical Association; North Dakota Medical Association; American Academy of Family Medicine. *Publications:* 'Cystitis in Women : Current Diagnosis and Management Standards' in 'Consultant' Magazine, 1983. *Honours:* C.V. Mosby Book Award for Excellence in Physiology, University of Manitoba, 1965; Ayerst Pharmaceutical Award, University of Manitoba, 1965. *Hobbies:* Aviation; Bicycling; Sailing; Ski-ing. *Address:* 501 Columbia Road, Grand Forks, ND 58201, USA.

GOODEN, Charlene Adelia, b. 19 May 1947, Suffern, New York, USA. Staff Nurse. 2 sons. *Education:* AAS, Nursing, New York Community College. *Appointments:* Staff Nurse, New York Hospital, 1968; Charge Nurse, La Guardi Hospital, 1969-70; Assistant Head Nurse, NYSDACC, 1973-76; Charge Nurse, University of Maryland Hospital, 1977-78; Staff Nurse, Sinai Hospital, 1983-85. *Memberships:* American Nurses Association; NLN. *Hobbies:* Dancing; Sewing; Boy Scout Activities; Little League Activities. *Address:* 3524 Carriage Hill Circle, Randallstown, MD 21133, USA.

GOODMAN, Stanley Sidney, b. 24 Nov. 1929, Philadelphia, Pennsylvania, USA. Private Practice. m. Pearl C. Cohen, 28 June 1953, 1 son, 2 daughters. *Education:* BA, University of Louisville; MA, Columbia University; MD, State University of New York; Diplomate, American Board Internal Medicine. *Memberships:* Chief of Staff, Plantation Hospital, 1973-75; Associate Director, Cardio Pulminary Service, Plantation Hospital, 1971-; Senior Active Staff, Broward Heneral Hospital; Vice Chairman, Board of Trustees, plantation Hospital, 1982-. *Memberships:* American Medical Association; Broward County Medical Association, President 1980-81; American College Chest Physicians, fellow; American College Cardiology. *Publications:* "Indcopathic Mycocarditis", 'Journal Florida Medical Association', 1984. *Hobbies:* Stone Sculpture; Sailing. *Address:* 333 N.W. 70 Ave., Ft. Lauderdale, Fl 33317, USA.

GOODWIN, Charles Stewart, b. 11 Dec 1932, London, England. Head of Department of Microbiology. m. Jean Elizabeth Bruce, 14 Mar 1959, Brenchley, 2 sons 2 daughters. *Education:* BA, 1954, MA, 1957, MD, 1965, Clare College, Cambridge; MB,

BChir, 1954-57, St Bartholomews Hospital, London; Diploma in Bacteriology, London, 1966; Member, 1970, Fellow, 1982, Royal College of Pathologists; Fellow, Royal College of Pathologists of Australasia, 1977. *Appointments:* House Surgeon, St Bartholomews Hospital, London, 1958; House Surgeon in Plastic Surgery, East Grinstead Hospital, UK, 1959; Registrar Hand Research Unit, Christian Medical College, Vellore, India, 1960; Physician and Pathologist, Hong Kong Leprosarium, Hong Kong, 1961-64; Senior Microbiology Registrar, St Mary's Hospital, Portsmouth, UK, 1966-67; Physician, All Africa Leprosy and Rehabilitation Training Centre, 1967-69; Senior Bacteriologist, St Mary's Hospital, Portsmouth, UK, 1969-71; Consultant Microbiologist, Northwick Park Hospital, London, UK, 1971-76; Asociate Professor in Clinical Microbiology, University of Western Australia 1976-86; Head of Department of Microbiology, Royal Perth Hospital. *Memberships:* Fellow, Royal Society of Tropical Medicine and Hygiene; Austalasian Society of Infectious Diseases; Australian Society of Medical Research; British Association for the Study of Infectious Diseases; Pathological Society of Great Britain; British Society for Antimicrobial Chemotherapy. *Publications:* Editor: "Microbes and Infections of the Gut" 1984; "Microbial Disease" with Tyrrell, Phillips and Blowers, 1979; "Essentials of Leprosy for the Clinician" 1963; Also many papers on Campylobacter pyloridis, leprosy, cephalosporins and other microbiological subjects. *Honour:* First Glaxo Orator, 1973. *Hobbies:* Biblical Exegesis and Christian Evangelism; Anthropology; Photography; Book Writing; Tennis; Swimming. *Address:* 162, Barker Road, Subiaco, Perth, Western Australia 6008.

GOODWIN, Frederick King, b. 21 Apr. 1936,. Cincinnati, Ohio, USA. Director of Intramural Research, National Institute of Mental Health. m. Rosemary Powers, 19 Oct. 1963, 2 sons, 1 daughter. *Education:* BS, Georgetown University, 1958; Graduate Fellowship in Philosophy, St. Louis University, 1958-59; MD, St. Louis University School of Medicine, 1963; Fellow, Washington School of Psychiatry, 1969-71. *Appointments:* Mixed Internship in Medicine and Psychiatry, State University of New York, Syracuse, 1963-64; Resident in Psychiatry, University of North Carolina, Chapel Hill, 1964-65; Clinical Associate, Adult Psychiatry Branch, NIMH, 1965-67; Special Research Fellow, National Heart Institute, 1967-68; Private Practice of Psychiatry and Psychopharmacology (part-time), 1967-; Chief, Clinical Research Unit, Section on Psychiatry, 1968-73, Chief, Section on Psychiatry, Laboratory of Clinical Science 1973-77, Chief, Clinical Psychobiology, 1977-81, Director, Intramural Research Program, 1982-, NIMH. *Memberships:* American Philosophical Association; American Association for the Advancement of Science; American Psychosomatic Society; Washington Psychiatric Society;' Society of Biological Psychiatry; American College of Neuropsychopharmacology; American Academy of Psychoanalysis; National Academy of Sciences, Institute of Medicine; Society of Neuroscience; International Group for the Study of Affective Disorders; Psychiatric Research Society. *Publications:* "Lithium Clinical Considerations", 1982; "Biological Rhythms and Manic-Depressive Illness", 1983; "The Natural Course of Recurrent Affective Illness", 1984; 'Biological Rhythms in Psychiatry' Editor with T. Wehr, 1983; "The Biology of Depression, conceptual issues", 1984; "Manic-Depressive Illness" (in preparation for 1986) with K. Jamison. *Honours:* A.E. Bennett Award, 1970; Psychopharmacology Research Prize, APA, 1970; Hofheimer Prize for Research, APA, 1971; International Anna Monika Prize for Research in Depression, 1971; Taylor Manor Award, 1976; Edward Strecker Award, 1983; UNC Distinguished Alumni Award, 1984; Elected to Institute of

Medicine of National Academy of Sciences, 1985. *Hobbies:* Skiing; Carpentry. *Address:* 9000 Rockville Pike, Building 10, Room 4N-224, Bethesda, MD 20892, USA.

GOODWIN, John Forrest, b. 1 Dec 1918, Ealing, England. Emeritus Professor of Clinical Cardiology. m. Barbara Cameron Robertson, 30 Oct. 1943, London, 1 son, 1 daughter. *Education:* MRCS, LRCP, 1942, MB, BS, University of London, MD, MRCP, FRCP. *Appointments:* Casulty House Surgeon, 1942, Casulty Physician, 1943, Medical Registrar, 1944, St Mary's Hospital, London; Physician Anglo-Iranian Oil Company, 1944; Medical 1st Assistant, Royal Infirmary, Sheffield, 1946; Lecturer, Senior Lecturer, Professor, Royal Postgraduate Medical School, London, 1949-84; Second Vice President, Royal College of Physicians, 1979-80. *Memberships:* Fellow, Royal Society of Medicine; Fellow, Royal College of Physicians of London; BMA; Association of Physicians of Great Britain and Ireland; Past President, British Cardiac Society, 1972-76; Past President, International Society and Federation of Cardiology, 1978-82; Honorary Member, American Heart Association Council on Clinical Cardiology. Fellow, American College of Cardiology, 1966. *Publications include:* "Medical and Surgical Cardiology" 1969; "Progress in Cardiology" annually since 1972; "Heart Disease" 1985; Numerous papers and articles in the field of Cardiology. *Honours:* Honorary Fellow, American College of Physicians, 1985; Star of Pakistan, 1962; Commander of the Icelandic Falcon, 1965; Honorary Doctorate, University of Lisbon, 1984; Gifted Teacher Award, American College of Cardiology, 1984. *Hobbies:* History; Travel; Photography. *Address:* 2 Pine Grove, Lake Road, Wimbledon, London SW19 7HE, England.

GOODWIN, Trevor Walworth, b. 23 June 1916, Neston, England. Professor Emeritus. m. Kathleen Sarah Hill, 28 Dec. 1944, Old Ollerton, 3 daughters. *Education:* BSc., Honours, 1938, Diploma, Education, 1939, MSc, 1940, D.Sc, 1950, University of Liverpool. *Appointments:* Extramural Scientist, Ministry of Food, 1940-44; Lecturer, 1944-50, Senior Lecturer, 1950-59, Biochemistry, University of Liverpool; Professor, Biochemsitry and Agricultural Biochemistry, University College of Wales, 1959-66; Johnston Professor, Biochemistry, head of Dept., 1966-83, Dean, Science, 1971-74, University of Liverpool. *Memberships:* Royal Society; Biochemical Society; Phytochemical Society; Institute of Biology; Royal Society of Chemistry; Federation of European Biochemical Societies; American Society of Plant Physiologists. *Publications:* Over 350 articles in professional journals; "Chemistry and Biochemistry of Plant Pigments", 2 volumes, 2nd editon 1975; "Introduction to Plant Biochemistry", 2nd edition 1982; "The Biochemistry of Carotenoids", 2 volumes, 2nd edition, 1982-83. *Honours:* Fellow, Royal Society, 1968; CBE, 1975; Ciba Medallist, 1970; Roussel Prizewinner, 1981; Honorary Member, Biochemical Society, 1985. *Hobbies:* Gardening; Photography. *Address:* 'Monzar', Woodlands Close, Parkgate, Wirral, Cheshire L64 6RU, England.

GOONETILLEKE, Udugama Koralalage Don Albert, b. 4 Feb. 1936, Colombo, Sri Lanka. Senior Lecturer; Consultant, Forensic Medicine, Charing Cross & Westminster Medical School, London, England. m. Sumanaseele Wijesinghe, 10 Jan. 1958, Colombo, 1 son, 1 daughter. *Education:* MB,BS, Ceylon, 1961; MD, 1984; FRCPA 1976; MRCPath, 1980; DMJ, 1970. *Appointments:* Medial officer, Health Department, Ceylon; Postgraduate & honorary lecturer, Edinburgh University, Scotland, UK; Lecturer, Forensic Medicine, Leeds; Registrar, Pathology, National Health Service, London; Lecturer, Forensic Medicine, Charing Cross & Westminster Medical School. *Memberships:* Fellow, British Association of Forensic Medicine; British Academy of Forensic Science; Medicolegal Society; British Medical Association; Adviser, Amnesty International, National Council for Civil Liberties, 'Inquest'. *Publications include:* Contributions to 'Medicine, Science & Law', 'Forensic Science International', etc. *Honours:* Gold Medal, best student, medicine, 1954; C.H.Milburn Award, BMA, 1982; Fellowship, King Edward Fund, 1981. *Hobbies:* Photography (still, cine & video); Ballroom dancing. *Address:* Department of Forensic Medicine, Charing Cross Hospital, Fulham Palace Road, London, W6, England.

GOOTENBERG, Joseph Eric, b. 9 Aug. 1949, Boston, Massachusetts, USA. Assistant Professor. *Education:* MD, Albert Einstein College of Medicine, 1975; AB, Harvard College, 1971. *Appointments:* Resident, Paediatrics, Medical Centre, Children's Hospital, Boston, 1975-78; Fellow, Paediatric Oncology, National Cancer Institute, Bethesda, 1978-82; Cancer Expert, National Cancer Institute, 1982-83; Assistant Professor, Paediatrics, Georgetown University School for Medicine. *Memberships:* American Society of Haematology. *Publications:* Articles in: 'Journal Experimental Medicine'; 'Journal Immunology'. *Honour:* AOA, 1975. *Address:* Division of Pediatric Oncology, Lombardi Cancer Centre, 3800 Reservoir Road NW, Washington, DC 20007, USA.

GORDON, (George Andrew) Douglas, b. 20 Aug. 1909, Richmond, Surrey, England. University Visiting Fellow. m. Hildegard Muriel Middleton, 31 Mar. 1935, Inverness, Scotland, 1 son, 3 daughters. *Education:* MB CHB, University of Edinburgh, Scotland, 1931; Diploma in Medical Radiology, Cairo University, Egypt, 1943; Diploma in Medical Radio-Diagnosis, England, 1945. *Appointments:* Radiologist, Willesden General Hospital, 1947-74; Radiologist and Electrophysiologist, West End Hospital for Neurology and Neurosurgery, 1947-70; Ultrasonic Radiologist, Whittington Hospital, 1970-74; Radiologist, Moorfields Eye Hospital, 1953-74; Visiting Professor of Bio-Medical Engineering, City University, 1975-81; Currently Visiting Fellow, City University. *Memberships:* British Medical Association; British Institute of Radiology; Fellow, Royal Society of Medicine; Founder Member, Biological Engineering Society; Honorary Fellow, American Institute for Ultra-Sonics in Medicine; Panel Member, BSI for ECT Equipment. *Publications:* Editor and Contributor, "Ultrasound as a Diagnostic and Surgical Tool", 1964 Joint Editor and Contributor, "Ultrasonic Techniques in Biology and Medicine", 1965; Contributor, "Electroconvulsive Therapy: An Appraisal", 1981. *Honours:* Corresponding Fellow, Toronto Academy of Medicine, Canada; Senior Member, Institute of Electrical and Electronic Engineers, USA. *Hobbies:* Cine and Videotape; Opera. *Address:* Flat A2, The Court, St Mary's Place, Shrewsbury SY1 1DY, England.

GORDON, Gregory Jay, b. Apr. 1943, Lynn, Massachusetts, USA. Doctor of Chiropractic. m. Marie Vitullo Gordon, 14 Sep. 1979, Chicago. *Education:* Diplomate of Chiropractic, National College of Chiropractic 1974; MEd., Boston University, 1970; BSc., National College, 1972; B.Ed., University of Miami, 1966. *Appointments:* President, North Shore Chiropractic Society (Mass.) 1984; Past Massachusetts Chairman, National College Alumni Assoc. *Memberships:* American Chiropractic Association; Massachusetts Chiropractic Society; North Shore Chiropractic Society; Foundation for Chiropractic Education and Research; Council on Roentgenology of American Chiropractic Association., Academy for International Medical Studies. Past President, Salem, Mass. Kiwanis. *Honours:* Chiropractic of the Year, North Shore Chiropractic Society, 1984. *Hobbies:* Fishing; Golfing; Travel; Sailing. *Address:* 76 Federal Street, Salem, MA. 01970 USA.

GORDON, Milton, b. 17 Sep. 1911, USA. Civil Air Surgeon, State of Israel. m. Natalie Blume, 24 Dec. 1939, Philadelphia, Pennsylvania, 1 son, 2 daughters. *Education:* BA, University of Pennsylvania, Philadelphia; MA, Jefferson University, Philadelphia; Internal Medicine, University of Pennsylvania Graduate School of Medicine and Aviation Medicine Certificates. *Appointments:* Private Practice, Internal Medicine, Camden, New Jersey, USA, to 1974; Consultant in Aviation Medicine and Cardiology, Teaching Faculty University of Pennsylvania; Senior Aviation Medical Examiner for USA FAA; Hospital Chief of Medicine for 10 years; Consultant to 50 Insurance Companies in USA; Certified Aviation Instrument Flight Instructor, FAA. *Memberships:* New Jersey State Medical Society; International Academy of Aviation and Space Medicine; Airlines Medical Directors Association; Civil Aviation Medical Association; Marco (Medical Amateur Radio Council). *Publications:* Contributor to professional journals including: Co-author, "Heat Stress Exposures of Agricultural Spray Pilots", "Aviation Space Environ. Med", 1980; 'Review of Argyria and report of a case', 'New Jersey State Medical Journal', 1941; Bulletins; Reports. *Honours:* John A. Tamisiea Award from Aerospace Medical Society, 1984; AMA Physicians Recognition Award, Fellow Aerospace Medical Association. *Hobbies:* Amateur Radio; Flying; Instructor Fl. Inst. Free Balloon rating. *Address:* 14 Shai Agnon St., POB 4079, Jerusalem, Israel.

GORDON, Susan, b. 18 Oct. 1928, Hungary. Senior Haematologist. m. Peter Gordon, 2 Apr. 1954, Sydney, Australia, 2 daughters. *Education:* MB BS, DCP, University of Sydney, Australia; Fellow, Royal College of Physicians of Australia; Fellow, Royal Australasian College of Pathologists; Fellow, Royal College of Pathologists. *Appointments:* Director of Haematology, Sydney Hospital, 1963-83. *Memberships:* New York Academy of Sciences; Australian Medical Association; Haematology Society of Australia; International Haematology Society; International Society of Blood Transfusion; Transplatation Society of Australia. *Publications:* 15 Publications in various journals. *Hobbies:* Classical Music; Bridge. *Address:* Haematology Department, St George's Hospital, Kogarah 2217, Australia.'

GORELICK, Kenneth Paul, b. 16 Apr. 1942, Paterson, New Jersey, USA. Chief of Continuing Medical Education. *Education:* BA, Rutgers University, 1962; MD, Harvard Medical School, 1967; Residency, Massachusetts Mental Health Center, Harvard Medical School, 1968-71; Internship, Mount Zion Hosptial and Medical Center, San Francisco, 1967-68. *Appointments:* Unit Director Area D Community Mental Health Center 1971-72, Psychiatrist United States Public Health service 1971-73, Chief of Continuing Medical Education, St Elizabeth's Hospital, Washington, DC; Assistant Clinical Professor Psychiatry and Behavioural Sciences, George Washington University School of Medicine. *Memberships:* Fellow, American Psychiatric Association; Diplomate in Psychiatry, American Board of Psychiatry and Neurology; President 1983, Medical Society St Elizabeth's Hosptial; Phi Beta Kappa; American Medical Association; American Psychiatric Association; Executive Board, National Association for Poetry Therapy. *Publication:* 'Great Literature As A Teaching Tool In The Education Of Mental Health Professionals', 1978. *Honour:* Fulbright Award to France, 1962. *Hobbies:* Reading Literature; History; The Arts. *Address:* 2625 Woodley Pl NW, Washinton, DC 20008, USA.

GOTFRIED, Mark, b. 4 Sep. 1952, Chicago, Illinois, USA, Practicing Physician, m. 7 Nov. 1977, Chicago, Illinois, 4 sons. *Education:* BS, University of Michigan; MD, University of Illinois. *Appointments:* Instructor of Medicine, University of Chicago, 1980;

Clinical Instructor, University of Arizona, 1981. *Memberships:* Fellow, American College of Physicians; Diplomate, American Board of Internal Medicine; Diplomate, American Board of Pulmonary Disease; American Thoracic Society; American College of Chest Physicians. *Publications:* 'Chemoprophylaxis of Tuberculosis', (with J Bloom and M D Lebowitz), 1983; 'Diffuse epithelial pleural mesothelioma presenting as a solitary lung mass', (with S F Quan and R E Sobonya), 1983; 'Obstructive sleep apnea – pathogenesis and treatment', (with S F Quan), 1984. *Honours:* Recipient of several honours and awards. *Address:* 715 West Tuckey, Phoenix, AZ 85013, USA.

GOTLIEB-STEMATSKY, Tamar, b. Israel. Associate Professor of Virology and Head of Central Virology Laboratory. 1 daughter. *Education:* MSc, PhD, Hebrew University, Jerusalem, Irael. *Appointments:* Research Associate, The Children's Hospital, Philadelphia, Pennsylvania, USA; The Public Health Research Institute, City of New York, New York, USA; The Goustave-Roussy Institute Cancer Research, Villejuif, France; The National Institute for medical Research, Mill Hill, London, England; National Institute of Health, Bethesda, Maryland, USA; Visiting Professor, Center for Experimental Cell Biology, Mount Sinai Medical School, New York; Division of Infectious Diseases, Stanford Medical School; Division of Virology, Montefiore Medical center, New York; Currently Associate Preofessor of Virology and Head of Central Virology Laboratory, Ch Sheba Medical Center, Tel-Hashomer and Tel Aviv University; Sackler School of Medicine. *Memberships:* Israel Society for Mircobiology; Cell, Tissue and Organ Culture Study Group, International Union Against Cancer; European Group for Rapid Viral Diagnosis; The New York Academy of Sciences. *Publications include:* "Human Herpes in the field of reactivation and recombination of influenza viruses, human cancer, Epstein-Barr virus, Viruses in neurological and Psychotic diseases. *Address:* Central Virology Laboratory, Ch Sheba Medical Center, Tel-Hashomer and Tel-Aviv University, Sackler School of Medicine, Department of Human Microbiology, Ramat-Aviv, Israel.

GOTTLIEB, Abraham Arthur, b. 14 Dec. 1937, USA. University Professor and Chairman Department of Microbiology and Immunology. m. Marise Suss MD, 1958, 2 daughters. *Education:* AB, Columbia University, 1957; MD, New York University School of Medicine, 1961. *Appointments include:* Research Fellow in Chemistry, Tutor in Chemistry, Harvard University, Assistant in Medicine, Peter Bent Brigham Hospital, Boston, Massachusetts, 1965-67; Associate in Medicine, Tutor in Biochemical Sciences, Harvard University, Associate in Medicine, Peter Bent Brigham Hosptial, Boston, 1968; Assistant Professor of Medicine, Harvard Medical School, Jan-June 1969; Associate Professor of Microbiology, 1969-72, Professor of Microbiology, 1972-75, Institute of Microbiology, Rutgers University, New Brunswick, New Jersey; Professor and Chairman Department of Microbiology and Immunology, Tulane University School of Medicine, New Orleans, Louisiana – present position, also Professor of Medicine, Tulane University School of Medicine. *Memberships include:* American Association for the Advancement of Science; American Association for Cancer Research; American Association of Immunologists; American Chemical Society; American Society of Biological Chemists; American Society for Cell Biology; American Society for Clinical Investigation; American Society for Microbiology; New York Academy of Sciences. *Publications:* Numerous articles in medical journals, chapters in edited volumes and papers presented to medical conferences. *Honours include:* Alpha Omega Alpha first prize for highest scholartic standing over four year medical school course; Recipient of Frances

Stone Burns Award of American Cancer Society, Massachusetts Division 1968; Travelling Fellow, Royal Society of Medicine; Fellow, American College of Physicians; Fellow, American Academy of Microbiology. *Hobby:* Travel. *Address:* Department of Microbiology and Immunology, Tulane University School of Medicine, 1430 Tulane Avenue, New Orleans, LA 70112, USA.

GOTTLOB, Rainer Maximilian Ewald, b. 17 Dec. 1918, Vienna, Austria. Doctor of Medicine; Lecturer in Surgery; Professor of Surgery (retired); General Surgeon. m. Dr. Hedwig Knapp, 26 Mar. 1952, Vienna, 1 son, 1 daughter. *Education:* MD, Prague University, 1941; Specialsit in Surgery, 1956. *Appointments:* Vienna Policlinic, Department of Surgery (including Institute of Pathology, Vienna University, Manchester Royal Infirmary, England, Leeds General Infirmary and Brompton Hospital, London), 1945-51; Traumatology, Lorenz Bohler, 5 months, 1951; Chief Assistant, Kaiser Franz Josef Hospital, Vienna, Department of Surgery, 1951-58; Department of Vienna Health Insurance Company, 1959-60; Head, Department of Experimental Surgery, First Surgical Clinic, Vienna University 1962-84. *Memberships:* Fellow, International College of Surgeons, President, Austrian Section, 1965-77; Fellow, International College of Angiology; International Society Cardiovascular Surgery, Board Member, 1970-84; Austrian Society of Surgery; German Society of Surgery; International Surgical Society; Gesellschaft der Arzte, Vienna; Honorary Member, Austrian Society of Experimetnal Surgery, 1982. *Publications:* "Angiographie und Klinik", 1956; "The Venous Valve", 1986; 260 papers in national and international journals mainly dealing with Vascualr Surgery, Vascular Endothelia, Angiography, Thrombolysis, Surgical Adhesives, Thermography and Fat Embolism. *Honours:* Theodor Korner Prize, 1954, Hoechst Prize of Vienna Medical Faculty, 1965, 66, 67. *Hobbies:* Practical Philosophy (in preparation a book "Living for What, Survive How?"); Epistemology; Gardening; Filming. *Address:* Kirchengasse 28, A-1070 Vienna, Austria.

GOURLAY, Desmond Robert Hugh, b. 2 Nov. 1922, Thunder Bay, Canada. Professor of Pharmacology and Chairman. m. Marjorie Edith Curl, 6 Sep. 1946, Toronto, 5 sons. *Education:* BA, 1945, PhD, 1949, University of Toronto; Postdoctoral Fellow, University of Virginia, USA, 1949-51; Fellow, Humboldt Foundation, W. Germany, 1968-69. *Appointments:* Demonstrator in Zoology, University of Toronto, 1945-49; Research Associate, Pharmacology, 1949-51, Assistant Professor of Pharmacology, 1951-53, Associate Professor, 1953-62, Professor, 1963-73, University of Virginia; Chairman, Pharmacology, University of Virginia, 1961, 1967-68; Professor and Chairman, Pharmacology, Eastern Virginia Medical School, 1973-; Adjuct Instructor, School of Continueing Education, University of Virginia, 1970-; Adjuct Professor, Chemical Sciences, Old Dominion University, 1975-. *Memberships:* American Physiological Society; American Society for Pharmacology and Experimental Therapeutics; Pharmacology Society of Canada; Association for Medical School Pharmacology; Society for Experimental Biology and Medicine. *Publications:* Books: "Interaction of Drugs With Cells", 1971; "Problems in Pharmacology", 4th Edition, 1981; "Essential Knowledge Objectives in Medical Pharmacology", 1985; More than 50 learned articles. *Honours:* Research Award, Virginia Academy of Sciences, 1952; Fellow, Humboldt Foundation, W. Germany, 1968-69; Excellence in Teaching Award, University of Virginia, 1973. *Hobbies:* Skiing; Photography; Scuba Diving. *Address:* Eastern Virginia Medical School, P.O. Box 1980, Norfolk, VA 23501, USA.

GOVINDARAJAN, Mirudhubashini, b. 10 Feb. 1947, Coimbatore, India. Head, Obstetrics and Gynaecology, Sri Ramakrishna Hospital, Coimbatore. m. Dr Kavetti S. Govindarajan, 9 Feb. 1970, Coimbatore, 2 sons. *Education:* MBBS Madras; FRCS Canada. *Appointments:* Obstetrics & Gynaecology Dept., St Boniface General Hosptial, Concordia General Hospital, Winnipeg, Manitoba, Canada; Physician in Charge, Endocrinology Clinic, Infertility, Winnipeg, 1977-79; Head, Obstetrics and Gynecology, Sri Ramakrishna Hospital, Coimbatore, India, 1981-. *Memberships:* Indian Medical Association; Indian Society of Obstetrics & Gynaecology; Society of Obstetrician and Gynaecologyists of Canada; American College of Obstetricians and Gynaecologyists. *Honours:* Certificates of Merit, Anatomy, Ophthalmology; Gold Medallist, Medicine, 1970; Merit Certificate, Preventive Medicine, 1970; Professors Scholarship for best Resident, 1975, 1976; Best Intern of the Year, 1972-73. *Hobby:* Reading. *Address:* C/o Dr. Saradha, 21 Thiruvenkataswamy Road, R.S. Puram, Coimbatore 641 002, India.

GOYAL, Ravindra Kumar, b. 24 Nov 1949, Nasirabad, India. Assistant University Professor. m. Damyanti, 15 Dec 1973, India, 2 sons. *Education:* MB, BS, MD, FCCP. *Appointments:* Attending Physician, Brookdale Hosptial Medical Center, Brooklyn, New York, 1979-; Attending Physician, 1979-, Co-ordinator in Long Term Care Medicine, 1983-, Kingsbrook Jewish Medical Center, Brooklyn; New York; Assistant Clinical Professor, Downstate Medical Center, Brooklyn, New York, 1984-. *Membership:* Fellow, American College of Chest Physician. *Hobbies:* Horse riding; Photography. *Address:* 51 Larch Drive, Manhasset Hills, NY 11040, USA.

GRABOWSKI, Nancy Jean, b. 29 Aug. 1954, Chicago, Illinois, USA. Chief Flight Nurse. *Education:* BSN, University of Arizona, 1977; MBA, University of Pungent Sound, 1983. *Appointments:* Certified Emergency Paramedic, Phoenix, 1977-78; Advanced Cardiac Life Support Programme Coordinator, Emergency Room Nurse, Seattle, 1978-80; Cardiac Nurse, Seattle, 1980-82; Neonatal Intensive Care Nurse, Seattle, 1982-84; Instructor, Flight Nurse/Flight Nurse, USAF Reserves, Travis AFB, 1981-. *Memberships:* Aerospace Medical Association, Air Transport Medicine Committee, Air Ambulance Subcommittee; National Flight Nurses Association; Americans Heart Association; Advanced Cardiac Life Support Instructor. *Publications:* "Inflight Medical Emergencies", 1983; "Medical Assistance on Board Aircraft", 1984; "Flight Nurse Evaluation & Selection", 1985. *Hobby:* Helicopter Pilot. *Address:* 308 N.I. St., Tacoma, WA 98403, USA.

GRAHAM, Geoffrey Smyth, b. 27 Aug. 1932, England. Dental Surgeon; Psychotherapist. m. Patricia Carol Dixon, 2 Aug. 1958, Malta, 2 daughters. *Education:* BDS; Numerous Courses, Psychotherapy, Hypnosis, both as Student & Lecturer, Worldwide. *Appointments:* Captain, Royal Army Dental Corp, 1 year; Assistant, General Dental Practice 1 year; Principal, General Practice Dental Surgery, 1959-; Private Practice, Psychotherapy, 1970-; Fellow, British Society of Medical & Dental Hypnosis; Fellow, American Society of Clinical Hypnosis; Fellow, Singapore Society of Clinical Hypnosis; Founder Fellow, Hypnosis Section, Royal Society of Medicine. *Publications:* "How to Become The Parent You Never Had", "Into & Out of the Mouths of Babies and Sucklings" and "Oral Gratification as a Defence", (all in Press); 2 papers in ASCH Journal; 2 papers in British SMDH Journal. *Honour:* Accredited Fellow, BSMDH, 1984. *Hobby:* Competition Winning Gardener. *Address:* 6 Whickham Park, Whickham, Newcastle Upon Tyne NE16 4EH, England.

GRAHAM, John Richard, b. 8 Aug. 1944, Sydney, New South Wales, Australia. Visiting Physician. m.

Philippa Dion Myers, 30 Nov. 1974, Sydney, 3 daughters. *Education:* BSc Honours, 1966, MB BS, Honours, 1969, Sydney University; MRACP, 1972; FRACP, 1975. *Appointments:* Clinical Lecturer, University of Sydney, 1972-83; Senior Medical Registrar, Sydney Hospital, 1973; Visiting Registrar, Outram Road General Hospital, Singapore, 1974. Visiting Physician: St Luke's Hospital, 1973-; Balmain Hospital, 1974-78; Ryde District Hospital, 1974-79; Sydney Hospital, 1977-; Prince of Wales Hospital, 1983-. Councillor, Australian Medical Association, New South Wales branch, 1979-; Member, Drug Committee of Health Commission of New South Wales, 1980-; Clinical Tutor, University of New South Wales, 1984-. *Memberships:* Australian Medical Association; Gastroenterological Society of Australia; British Society of Gastroenterology. *Publications:* "Common Problems in the Treatment of Peptic Ulcers", 1983; 'Nervous dyspepsia and biliary reflux' in 'Medical Journal of Australia', 1979; 'Gastric pseudolymphoma developing from chronic gastric ulcer, Endoscopic diagnosis and the effect of cimetidine' in 'Dig. Dis. Sci', 1982; Author of some 21 other publications in field of gastroenterology. *Honours:* James and Margaret Claffy Prize in Ophthalmology, University of Sydney, 1967; Life Governor, Sydney Hospital, New South Wales. *Hobbies include:* Flying; Golf; Tennis; Polo; Breeding quarter horses and Santa Gertrudis cattle. *Address:* 183 Macquarie Street, Sydney, NSW 2000, Australia.

GRAHAM, Kenneth Robert, b. 5 June 1943, Philadelphia, Pennsylvania, USA. Professor Head, Psychology, Muhlenberg College. m. Michele Monroe, 10 Aug. 1968, Stanford, 2 sons. *Education:* BA, University of Pennsylvania, 1964; PhD, Stanford University, 1969. *Appointments:* Research Psychologist, Unit for Experimental Psychiatry, Institute of Pennsylvania Hospital, 19069-70; Assistant, Associate, Professor, Muhlenberg College, 1970-; Private Practice, part-time, 1979-. *Membership:* American Psychological Associaiton; American Society of Clinical Hypnosis; Society for Clinical and Experimental Hypnosis. *Publications:* "Psychological Reserch: Controlled Interpersonal Interaction", 1977; "Perceptual Processes and Hypnosis: Support for Cognitive State Theory based on Internality", 'Annals of the New York Academy of Sciences', 1977. *Honours:* Sigma Xi; Past President 1980, Division of Psychological Hypnosis, American Psychological Association. *Hobby:* Collecting Glass Paperweights. *Address:* Muhlenberg College, Allentown, PA 18104, USA.

GRAHAM, Neil, b. 25 Jan. 1952, Bournemouth, England. Senior Registrar, Diagnostic Radiology, St. Bartholomew's Hospital. m. Lindsey Carey, 25 Nov. 1975, Leeds. *Education:* MB,ChB, Leeds University, 1977; FRCR, London, 1985. *Appointments include:* House officer, Edgware General Hospital, Wembley Hospital; Senior house officer, East Ham Memorial Hospital, Middlesex Hospital; Registrar, Diagnostic Ultrasound, Middlesex Hospital; Senior House Officer, Medical Oncology, Hackney Hospital; SHO/Registrar, Royal Northern Hospital; Registrar, Diagnostic Radiology, Middlesex Hospital. *Memberships:* British Institute of Radiology; British Medical Ultrasound Society; Fellow, Royal Society of Medicine. *Publications include:* Articles & presentations, general diagnostic ultrasound, 1979-. *Honour:* Letheby-Tidy Prize, Medicine, Royal Northern Hospital, 1981. *Hobbies:* Walking; Running; Cycling; Squash; Reading general/science fiction; Wine & Food. *Address:* 103 The Avenue, Tottenham, London N17 6TE, England.

GRAHAM, Neil Bonnette, b. 23 May 1933, Liverpool, England. University Professor. m. Marjorie Royden, 16 July 1955, 1 son, 3 daughters. *Education:* Associate of the London college of Music (ACCM) 1950; BSc, Hons, 1953, PhD, 1956, Liverpool University. *Appointments:* Research Chemist, Research Scientist, Canadian Industries Ltd., MacMasterville PQ, Canada 1956-67; Assistant Group Head then Group Head, Polymer Chemistry, ICI, Runcorn, Cheshire; Young Professor of Chemical Technology, Strathclyde University, 1973-82; Research Professor, Chemical Technology, Strathclyde University, 1982-; Technical Director, Polysystems Ltd., 1982-. *Memberships:* Advisory Committee on Dental and Surgical Materials, 1979-; Society of Chemical Industry Committee for Colloid and Surface Chemistry, 1975-79; Vice Chairman, West of Scotland Division, Chemical Society, 1974; Fellow, Chemcial Institute of Canada, 1965-; Fellow, Plastics and Rubber Institute 1973-; Fellow, Royal Society of Chemistry, 1974-; Governor, Keil School 1978-; Member of Editorial Boards of "Biomaterials", "Biomedical Polymers" and "Journal for Controlled Release'. *Publications:* Author of many papers, chapters of books reviews etc. *Honours:* Leblanc Medal, Liverpool University, 1953; Potts Medal, Liverpool University, 1974; Miscellaneous Memorial Lecturers; Prize winner in "Enterprise Scotland Competition" 1980; Prize winner in "Academic Enterprise Competition" 1982. *Hobbies:* Music; Walking. *Address:* University of Strathclyde, Department of Pure and Applied Chemistry, Thomas Graham Building, 295 Cathedral Street, Glasgow G1 1XL, Scotland.

GRAHAM, Saxon, b. 14 Jan. 1922, Buffalo, New York, USA. Professor & Chairman, Department of Social & Preventive Medicine, State University of New York (SUNY). m. Caroline Morgan, 2 sons, 1 daughter. *Education:* AB, 1943; AM 1949; PhD, Sociology, 1951. *Appointments include:* Director 1956-60, Acting Chief 1958-59, Community Epidemiological Studies, Roswell Park Institute; Assistant Professor, Medical Sociology, 1956-66; Professorial Lecturer, Sociology, 1958-65, Professor 1966-, SUNY at Buffalo; Associate Cancer Research Scientist, Roswell Park Institute 1960-65, Principal Scientist 1965; Professor & Chairman, Department of Social & Preventive Medicine, SUNY at Buffalo, 1981-. *Memberships:* Board of Scientific Counsellors, National Cancer Institute Society for Epidemiologic Research; American Public Health Association; Advisory Committee, Study of Long-Term Effects of Plutonium, Los Anlamos Scientific Laboratory, New Mexico. *Publications:* Contributions to scientific journals including: 'Epidemiologic Reviews', 'Journal, National Cancer Institute', 'Reviews in Cancer Epidemiology', 'American Journal of Epidemiology', etc; Books including "Nutrition in the Young & the Elderly", 1983, "Applications of Social Science to Clinical Medicine & Health Policy", in press. *Honour:* President, Society for Epidemiologic Research. *Hobbies:* Skiing; Golf. *Address:* Department of Social & Preventive Medicine, SUNY at Buffalo, 2211 Main Street, Building A, Buffalo, NY 14224, USA.

GRAHAM, Thomas P., b. 1 Mar. 1937, USA. Professor of Paediatrics; Director, Paediatric Cardiology. m. Carol Ann Noggle, 17 June 1960, Miami, 1 son, 2 daughters. *Education:* AB, 1959, MD, 1963, Duke University. *Appointments:* Resident, Physician, Childrens Hospital, Boston, 1963-65; Research associate, National Heart Institute, 1965-67; Fellow, Paediatric Cardiology, 1967-69; Assistant Professor, 1969-71, Duke University; Associate Professor, 1971-76, Professor, 1976-, Director, 1971-, Paediatric Cardiology, Vanderbilt University. *Memberships:* American Heart Association, Chairman, Council CV Disease in Young, 1982-83; American College Cardiology, Chairman, Paediatric Cardiology Committee, 1979-86; American Academy Paediatrics; SE Paediatric Cardiology Society. *Publications:* Over 140 articles, and book chapters. *Honours:* Phi Beta Kappa, 1958; 1969. *Hobbies:* Tennis; Travel. *Address:* Paediatric Cardiology Division, Vanderbilt

University Medical Centre, Nashville, TN 37232, USA.

GRAHAME-SMITH, David Grahame, b, 10 May 1933, Leicester, England. Rhodes Professor of Clinical Pharmacology. m. Kathryn Frances Beetham, 25 May 1957, Leeds, 2 sons. *Education:* MB BS, PhD, St Mary's Hospital Medical School, University of London; MA, Oxford; FRCP. *Appointments:* House Physican, Paddington General Hospital, London, 1956; House Surgeon, Battle Hospital, Reading, Berkshire, 1956-57; Registrar and Senior Registrar in Medicine, St Mary's Hospital, Paddington, London, 1957-60; HAM Thompson Research Scholar and Saltwell Research Scholar, Royal College of Physician, London, 1961-65; Wellcome Trust Research Fellow, 1965-66; Medical Research Council Travelling Fellow, Department of Endocrinology, Vanderbilt University, Nashville, Tennessee, USA, 1966-67; Senior Lecturer and Reader in Clinical Pharmacology and Therapeutics, Honorary Consultant Physician, St Mary's Hospital, Paddington, London, England, 1967-71; Currenlty: Rhodes Professor of Clinical Pharmacology, University of Oxford; Honorary Director, Medical Research Council Clinical Pathology Unit; Honorary Consultant Physician, Oxfordshire Health Authority. *Memberships:* British Pharmacological Society; Biochemical Society; Medical Research Society; Association of Physicians of Great Britain and Ireland; International Society of Neurochemistry; British Association of Psychopharmacology; Collegium Internationale Neuropsychiatricum. *Publications:* "The Carcinoid Syndrome", 1972; "Drug Internactions", (editor) 1977; "Psychopharmcology I", (editor), 1983; "Oxford Textbook of Clinical Pharmacology and Drug Therapy", 1984; Papers on clinical pharmacology and neuropharmacology in scientific journals. *Honours:* Anna Monika 2nd Prize (jointly), 1977; Paul Martini Prize in Clinical Pharmacology, (jointly), 1980. *Hobbies:* Piano; Horseriding. *Address:* Romney, Lincombe Lane, Boar's Hill, Oxford OX1 5DY, England.

GRAINGER, Ronald Graham, b. 14 Oct. 1922, Leeds, England. Professor of Radiology, University of Sheffield; Consultant Radiologist. m. Ruth Jason, 16 Oct. 1960, London, 2 sons. *Education:* MB, ChB (Honours); MD; FRCP; FRCR; FACR (Honorary); FRACR (Honorary). *Appointments include:* Radiological registrar, Sheffield United Hosptials, Westminster Hospital, London; Radiological Senior registrar, St. Thomas' Hospital, London; Consultant Radiologist, London Chest Hospitals, Royal Hallamshire Hospital & Northern General Hospital, Sheffield. *Memberships:* Royal College of Radiologists; British Institute of Radiology; American College of Radiology; Australasian Royal College of Radiology; British Cardiac Society; British Medical Association. *Publications include:* "Diagnostic Radiology: An Anglo-American Text on Organ Imaging", Ed. with D.H.Allison, 3 volumes, 1986; "Cardiac Catheterization & Angiocardiograhy", with D.Verel, 3rd edition, 1977; Over 100 original radiological research papers. *Honours:* Sir James Wattie Travelling Professor to New Zealand, 1978; Mackenzie Davidson Lecturer, London, 1981; George Simon Lecturer, London, 1985. *Hobbies:* Work; Medicine; Bridge; Reading; Walking. *Address:* Little Orchard, 8 Clumber Road, Sheffield S10 3LE, England.

GRAMMATICOS, Philip Constantin, b. 24 Oct. 1933, Thessaloniki, Greece. Director, Nuclear Medicine, Ahepa University Hospital. m. Efi Melphu, 28 Apr. 1965, 2 sons, 3 daughters. *Education:* Specialised: Internal Medicine, 1963, Nuclear Medicine, 1973; Research fellow, Royal Postgraduate Medical School, London, England, 1967, 1973; Research Professor, Temple University Hospital, Philadelphia, USA, 1985. *Appointments:* Staff, University of AHEPA Hospital, 1961-; Assistant Professor, University of Thessaloniki, 1976; Acting Director,

1968-85, Director, 1985-, Nuclear Medicine, Ahepa University Hospital. *Memberships:* Royal Society of Medicine; American Nuclear Medicine Society; British Nuclear Medicine Society; Britsh Society of Radiology; Institute of Radiation Protection. *Publications:* "Practical Applications and Basic Principles in Nuclear Medicine", 1984; "Measurement of splenic red blood cell mass", co author, 'Year Book of Nuclear Medicine', 1970; "Quantitative estimation of red cell uptake in spleen", 1968; etc. *Hobbies:* Collecting Greek Stamps and Butterflies. *Address:* 51 Hermou Street, Thessaloniki 546 23, Greece.

GRANDJEAN, Philippe Adam, b. 1 Mar. 1950, Copenhagen, Denmark. Professor of Environmental Medicine. m. Elaine Catherine Pysz, 22 Dec. 1978, Connecticut, USA. *Education:* MB, University of Copenhagen, Denmark, 1974, Diploma in Basic Medical Research, 1975, MD, 1979. *Appointments:* Research Fellowships, University of Copenhagen, Denmark, 1974-78; Fulbright Senior Scholar and Visitng Fellow, Mount Sinai School of Medicine, New York, USA, 1978-80; Director, Department of Occupational Medicine, Danish National Institute of Occupational Health, 1980-82; Professor of Environmental Medicine, Chairman of Institute of Community Health, Odense University, Denmark, 1982-present. *Memberships:* Association of Clinical Scientists; Danish Medical Association; International Commission on Occupational Health; International Union of Pure and Applied Chemistry. *Publications:* 'Widening Perspectives of Lead Toxicity' (Thesis), 1979; 'Biological Effects of Organolead Compounds', CRC Press 1984; 'Toxic Oil Syndrome - Mass Food Poisoning in Spain' 'World Health Organization' 1984; 'Environment and Prevention' (in Danish), 1984. *Honours:* Prize Essay in Medicine, University of Copenhagen, 1972; Keynote Speaker, Odense University Anniversary, 1983; Gitlitz Memorial Lecture, Newport, Rhode Island, USA, 1985. *Hobbies:* Ornithology; Nature Conservation. *Address:* Department of Environmental Medicine, Odense University, J B Winslows Vej 19, DK-5000, Odense, Denmark.

GRANGE, John Michael, b. 4 Apr. 1943, Dereham, Norfolk, England. Reader in Clinical Microbiology. m. Helga Jenke, 4 June 1968, Hamburg, Federal Republic of Germany. *Education:* MB BS 1967, MD 1974, Middlesex Hospital Medical School; MSc Immunology with Distinction, Chelsea College, University of London, 1981. *Appointments:* House Physician, Mount Vernon Hospital, Northwood, Middlesex, 1967-69; Lecturer in Pathology, Middlesex Hospital Medical School, 1970-76; Currently Reader in Clinical Microbiology, University of London. *Memberships:* Royal Society of Medicine; International Union Against Tuberculosis; British Thoracic Society; Society for Applied Bacteriology; British Society for Immunology. *Publications:* "Mycobacterial Diseases", 1980; Numerous original articles, chapters and reviews on Mycobacteria and Mycobacterial diseases. *Hobbies:* Travel; Photography; Classical music; Winemaking; Philosophy of Religion. *Address:* Cardiothoracic Institute, Fulham Road, London SW3 6HP, England.

GRANT, Alan Archie, b. 17 Mar. 1930, Victoria, Australia. Professor of Restorative Dentistry, University of Manchester, England. m. Anne Marie Fisch, 28 Dec. 1961, Melbourne, Australia, 2 sons, 1 daughter. *Education:* BDSc 1952, MDSc 1956, DDSc 1960, University of Melbourne; FRACDS, Royal Australasian College of Dental Surgeons, 1967; MSc, University of Manchester, 1974. *Appointments include:* General dental practice, 1952-60; Research worker, part-time, 1956-59, Lecturer, prosthetic dentistry 1960-64, Senior lecturer 1964-70, University of Melbourne; Visiting Associate Professor, Dental Materials, Northwestern University, Chicago, USA, 1965-66; Professor, Restorative Dentistry 1970-, Dean, Dental School 1977-81, Pro-Vice-Chancellor 1983-86, University of

Manchester. *Memberships:* British Dental Association; British Association for Dental Research; British Society for the Study of Prosthetic Dentistry; European Prosthodontic Association; British Society for Restorative Dentistry. *Publications include:* "An Introduction to Removable Denture Prosthetics", co-author, 1983; Numerous publications, professional literature. *Hobbies:* Indoor & outdoor gardening. *Address:* University Dental Hospital, Higher Cambridge Street, Manchester M15 6FH, England.

GRÄSBECK, (Armas) Ralph Gustaf, b. 6 July 1930, Helsingfors, Finland, Chief Physician, Professor, m. Christina Strömberg, 11 Sept 1954, Helsingfors, 2 sons. *Education:* Med Lic, 1953; Dr med & Chir, PhD, 1956. *Appointments:* Research Fellow, Johns Hopkins University, Baltimore, Md, USA, 1954-55; Research Fellow, Department of Biochemistry, Karolinska Institute, Stockholm, Sweden, 1957; Assistant Instructor, Department of Medical Biochemistry, Helsinki University, Finland, 1958-59; Chief Physician, Laboratory Department, Maria Hospital, Helsinki, Finland, 1960-; Docent, Clinical Chemistry, Helsinki University, 1959-; Secretary General, Minerva Foundation for Medical Research, 1959; Chief, Minerva Foundation Institute for Medical Research, 1971-; Exchange Visiting Professor, University of Wisconsin, USA, 1969; Editor, Scandinavian Journal of Clinical and Laboratory Investigation, 1965-75, Haematology, 1975. *Memberships:* Finnish Medical Society; Finnish Society of Sciences and Letters; Finnish Society for Nuclear Medicine; Finnish Chemical Society; International Society of Haematology; American Chemical Society. *Publications:* "Reference Values in Laboratory Medicine", (Co-editor T Alström), 1981; "Festschrift in Honour of Bertel von Bonsdorff", (editor), 1964; Author of over 250 professional and scientific articles. *Honours:* Finnish Medical Society, Runeberg Prize, 1956; Rosenquist prize, 1963; Honorary Member, 1985; Finska kemistsamfundet, Alfthan Prize, 1962; Oslo University Anders Jahre Prize, 1966; Finnish Society of Nuclear Medicine Honorary Member, 1984; Charter Member, Johns Hopkins Society of Scholars, 1969; conferred title of Professor, 1982. *Hobbies:* Living in Baltic Islands; Modern art. *Address:* Minerva Institute, PO Box 819, SF-00101 Helsingfors, Finland.

GRAY, Gary Michael, b. 4 June 1933, Seattle, USA. Professor of Medicine. m. Mary Alice Lassila, Aug. 1957, Seattle, 5 sons. *Education:* BS, Seattle University, 1955; MD, University of Washington, 1959. *Appointments include:* Fellow in Gastroenterology, Boston University School of Medicine, 1962-64; Fellow in Biochemistry, Chicago Medical School, 1963; Gastroenterologist, 1964-65, Chief of Metabolic Studies, 1965-66, US Army Tropical Research Medical Laboratory, San Juan P.R.; Assistant Professor of Medicine, 1966-70, Associate Professor of Medicine, 1970-77, Head of Division of Gastroenterology, 1971-, Professor of Medicine, 1978-, Stanford University School of Medicine. *Memberships:* AFCR; ASCI; American Gastroenterologic Association; Association of American Physicians; American Chemcial Society; American Society of Biological Chemists, etc. *Publications:* 70 publications in the area of Biochemistry of Intestinal Digestion and Absorption; Gastroenterology Section of "Scientific American Medicine". *Honours:* Student Scholarship Award from American Institute of Chemical Engineers, 1952; BS Magna Cum Laude 1955; Recipient of Research Grants from NIH(USPHS). *Hobbies:* Tennis; Photography; Auto Restoration. *Address:* Division of Gastroenterology S-069, Stanford University School of Medicine, Stanford, CA 94305, USA.

GRAY, Laman A Jr., b. 28 May 1940, Louisville, Kentucky, USA. Professor of Surgery. m. Julie, 3 daughters. *Education:* BA Wesleyan University, Middletown, Connecticut, 1963; MD, Johns Hopkins University, Baltimore, Maryland, 1967. *Appointments:* Internship, 1967-68, Resident, General Surgery, 1968-72, Resident, Thoracic & Cardiovascular Surgery, 1972-74, University of Michigan; Assistant Professor of Surgery, 1974-78, Associate Professor of Surgery, 1978-84, Acting Chairman, Theatre of Cardiovascular Surgery, 1975-76, Director, 1976-, Professor of Surgery, Director, Division of Thoracic & Cardiovascular Surgery, 1984-, School of Medicine, University of Louisville, Kentucky. *Memberships:* American Association for Thoracic Surgery; American College of Cardiology; American College of Chest Physicians; American College of Surgeons; American Thoracic Society; Société Internationale de Chirurgie; Southern Thoracic Surgical Association; Southern Surgical Association; Society of Thoracic Surgeons. *Publications:* Various articles in medical journals, book chapters especially on Thoracic surgery. *Honours:* Award for outstanding work in organic Chemistry, American Chemical Society, 1963. *Address:* Department of Surgery, University of Louisville, Louisville, KY 40292, USA.

GRAY, Michael Ian Hart, b. 12 July 1940, England. Senior Medical Officer, Gulf Air Medical Service, Bahrain. m. Patricia Margaret Stewart, 22 July 1964, Dundee, Scotland, 1 son. *Education;* MB ChB, University of St Andrews, 1965; Diploma in Aviation Medicine, 1976; Member, Faculty of Occupational Medicine, 1981; Accreditation in Occupational Medicine, 1982; Member, Royal Aeronautical Society, 1984. *Appointments:* House Surgeon, Bexhill Hospital; House Phsycian, Lewis Hospital, Stornaway, Scotland; Regimental Medical Officer, 4th/7th Royal Dragoon Guards; Trainee, Specialist in Pathology, Queen Alexandra Military Hospital; Pathologist, Chemical Defence Establishment, Porton Down; Pathologist, Tidworth Military Hospital; Trainee, Specialist in Aviation Medicine, Army Air Corps Centre; Advisor in Aviation Medicine to Director, Army Air Corps; Consultant in Aviation Medicine, King Abdul Aziz Military Hospital & King Faisal Air Base, Occupational Medicine; B ritish Academy of Forensic Science. *Publication:* 'Long Term Toxicity of CR by Skin Application to Mice' (in DCE Technical Bulletin) 1974. *Hobbies:* Sailing; Shooting; Riding; Scuba Diving; Flying; Reading; Music. *Address:* Nut Tree Cottage, Lower Chicksgrove, Tisbury, Salisbury, Wiltshire, England.

GRAZIANI, Joseph, b. 11 July 1983, Florence, Italy. Chiropractor. m. 2 sons. *Education:* BA, 1969, MA, 1970, C.Phil., 1971, PhD, 1973, University of California, Los Angeles, USA; DC, 1980. *Appointments:* Professor, Middle Eastern History & Semitic Languages, University of Nevada, Las Vegas, 1974-77; Doctor of Chiropractic, Director, Graziani Chiropractic Inc., Glendale, 1981-. *Memberships:* Association Society for the Near East; Middle Eastern Studies Association; Internal Organisation of Near Eastern Studies in the USA and Canada; American Professors for Peace in the Middle East; Speculum of Medieval Society; Harvard; Americans for Middle East Understanding; Clark County Foreign Language Association; many other professional organisations. *Publications:* "Arabic Medicine During the Eleventh Century", 1980; Articles in professional journals including: "The Climax of Arabic Medicine During the Eleventh Century", 'Egyptian Journal of Genetics and Cytology', 1975; "The Contribution of Medieval Arabic Medicine to the Health Profession Today", 'Episteme', 1980. *Honours:* Pre-Med Scholarship, 1964-66; Order of the Golden Bruin, Honorary Society, 1972; Delta Sigma Honorary Scholastic Society, 1980. *Hobbies:* Soccer; Tennis; Piano. *Address:* 809 W. Dryden, Glendale, CA 91202, USA.

GREEN, Alan Gordon, b. 29 Feb. 1928, Liverpool, England. General Dental Practitioner; Chairman,

Representative Board, British Dental Association. m. Joyce Ley, 19 Apr. 1952, Deganwy, North Wales, 2 daughters. *Education:* LDS, University of Liverpool, England; RCS, England. *Appointments:* House Surgeon, Liverpool Dental Hospital, England, 1950-51; Royal Army Dental Corps, 1951-53; General Dental Practitioner, 1953-74; Chairman, Annual Conference of Local Dental Committees, 1968-69; Area Dental Officer, Cheshire Area Health Authority, 1974-83. *Memberships:* British Dental Association; Liverpool and District Odontological Society; Federation Dentaire Internationale. *Publications:* Articles in 'British Dental Journal': 'A Survey of the Dental Condition of 19 year old Youths', 1953, 'The General Practitioner - His Representation and Political Lines of Communication in England', 1974, 'The Representation of Dental Officers Working for Area Health Authorities', 1980; 'The General Dental Service - Future Responsibilities', 'Royal Society of Health' Journal, 1972. *Hobbies:* Sailing; Skiing. *Address:* Foxwist, Tirley. Lane, Utkinton, Tarporley, Cheshire CW6 0JZ, England.

GREEN, Amy, b. 5 May 1939, New York, New York, USA, Psychiatrist and Psychoanalyst. m. Jack M Clemente, 2 Dec. 1967, 1 son, 1 daughter. *Education:* BA Psychology, Bard College, New York; MD, Faculty of Medicine, McGill University, Montreal, Canada; Rotation Internship, University of Illinois, Chicago, Illinois, USA; Psychiatric Resident, Metropolitan Hospital, New Yourk City. *Appointments:* Acting Chief, Psychiatric Emergency Service, San Diego County Community Mental Health Services, 1968-70; Clinical Instructor Psychiatry, University of California at San Diego Medical College, 1970; Liaison Psychiatrist, Beth Isreal Medical Center, New York City, 1970-76; Clinical Instructor, Department of Psychiatry, Mount Sinai Medical School, 1972-77; Currently private pratice of Psychiatry and Psychoanalysis. *Memberships:* The Society of Medical Psychonalysts; The American Academy of Psychoanalysis; The American Psychiatric Association; The American Medical Women's Association. *Address:* 85 Park Street, Montclair, NJ 07042, USA.

GREEN, Larry A, b. 27 Mar. 1948, Ardmore, Oklahoma, USA. University Professor and Departmental Chairman. m. Margaret, 27 Mar. 1971, Houston, Texas, USA, 1 son, 1 daughter. *Education:* BA, Psychology, University of Oklahoma; MD, Baylor College of Medicine, USA. *Appointments:* Physician, National Health Service Corps, Van Buren, Arkansas, USA; Assistant, Associate Professor and Residency Director, Department of Family Medicine, University of Colorado; Director, Mercy Medical Centre, Family Medicine Residency, Denver, Colorado, Professor and Chairman, Department of Family Medicine. *Memberships:* American Academy of Family Physicians; North American Primary Care Research Group; Society of Teachers of Family Medicine; International Epidemiological Association; Ambulatory Sentinel Practice Network. *Publications:* Articles: 'A Family Medicine Information System', 1978, 'Differences in Morbidity Patterns Among Rural, Urban and Teaching Practices', 1979, 'The Ambulatory Sentinel Practice Network: Purposes, Methods and Policies', 1984, in 'JFP'. *Hobbies:* Re-modelling old homes; Skiing; Water Sports; Tennis. *Address:* University of Colorado School of Medicine, 4200 E Ninth Avenue, Denver, CO 80262, USA.

GREEN, Leland J, b. 11 Aug. 1929, Minneapolis, Minnesota, USA. Director of Allergy Department. m. Gretchen H Kerr, 26 Oct. 1974, Gwynedd, Pennsylvania. *Education:* BA 1951, BS 1953, MD 1955, University of Minnesota; Diplomate, American Board of Allergy and Immunology, 1974. *Appointments:* Instructor, Department of Internal Medicine, University of Minnesota, 1960-63;

Instructor, Department of Medicine, Graduate Hospital, University of Pennsylvania, 1964-66; Medical Consultant Staff, Institute for the Achievement of Human Potential, Philadelphia, Pennsylvania, 1966 -. *Memberships:* American Medical Association; American Academy of Allergy and Immunology; American Society Clinical Hypnosis; New York Academy of Sciences; American Association for Certified Allergists. *Publications:* 'Neurological Organization in Primitive People', 1968. *Hobbies:* Philately; Music; Photography; Sailing; Skiing; Travel; Anthropology. *Address:* Lansdale Medical Group, Lansdale, PA 19446, USA.

GREENBERG, Irwin Morton, b. 21 Sept. 1930. Medical Director. m. Bonita Boone, 28 Dec. 1974, 1 son, 1 daughter. *Education:* MD, New York University College of Medicine, 1955; DMSc, State University of New York Downstate Medical Centre, USA, 1968. *Appointments include:* Staff Psychiatrist, Hillside Hospital, Glen Oaks, New York, 1960-62; Senior Staff Psychiatrist, 1962-67; Assistant Clinical Professor of Psychiatry, State University of New York, Downstate Medical Centre, 1964-67; Chief of Service, Bronx State Hospital, 1967-68; Deputy Director, 1968-69; Assistant Clinical Professor of Psychiatry, Albert Einstein College of Medicine, 1967-72; Director, Creedmoor State Hospital, 1969-72; Director of Psychiatric Services, Waterbury Hospital, 1972-84; Medical Director, Jackson Brook Institute, South Portland, Maine, 1984-86. *Memberships include:* American Psychiatric Association, Fellow; American Psychological Association; New York Academy of Sciences; American Association for the Advancement of Science; Diplomate of the American Board of Neurology and Psychiatry, 1962; Association of Medical Sueprintendents of Mental Hospitals, 1969-72. *Publications include:* Numerous articles in professional journals including: 'Approaches to Psychiatric Consultations in a Hospital Setting' in 'Archives of General Psychiatry', 1960; 'Attitudes Toward Death in Schizophrenia' in 'Journal of the Hillside Hospital', 1964; conference papers, including 'Studies on Attitudes Toward Death' at GAP Symposium on Death, No. 11, 1965; book sections including 'Social Calvinism, Free Will, Etiology and Treatment' in "State Hospitals: Problems and Potentials", 1980. *Honours include:* Mathematics Medal, New York University College of Arts and Sciences, 1950; Administration Building named after Dr. Greenberg at Creedmoor State Hospital. *Hobbies:* Swimming; Sculpting; Gardening. *Address:* PO Box 350, Taunton, MA, 02780, USA.

GREENBERG, Stephen Robert, b. 5 May 1927, Omaha, Nebraska, USA. Associate Professor. m. Constance Milder, 4 June 1952, Omaha, 2 sons. *Education:* BS, Biology, 1951, MS, Anatomy, 1952, PhD, Pathology, 1954, St Louis University, Missouri. *Appointment:* Assistant, Pathology, Clarkson Hospital, Omaha, 1954-55; Assistant, 1955-57, Instructor, 1957-62, Assistant Professor, 1962-69, Associate Professor, 1969-, Pathology, Chicago Medical School. *Memberships include:* American Association of Advancement of Science, Fellow; Association of Clinical Scientists; New York Academy of Sciences; American Association of Nephrology; International Acadmey of Pathology; Fellow, Society of Clinical Scientists; American Society of Clinical Pathologists; American Association of Anatomists; Sigma Xi; Society of Toxicologic Pathologists; etc. *Publications:* Articles in numerous journals including: 'Lancet'; 'Urologia Internationalis'; 'Journal Audiovisial Methods in Medicine'; 'Proceedings Institute of Medicine Chicago'; etc. *Honours:* Meritorious Service Award, Scottish Rite Bodies of Chicago, 1978; Distinguished Service Award, Grand Royal Arch Chapter, State of Illinois, 1984. *Hobby:* Photography. *Address:* Dept. of Pathology, University of Health Sciences, Chicago

Medical School, 3333 Green Bay Road, North Chicago, IL 60064, USA.

GREENE, Alice Mary, b. 19 Sep. 1952, Dublin, Republic of Ireland. General Practice; Private Practice. *Education:* Trinity College Dublin, MB, BCh, BAO (1977); DCH, National University of Ireland; Dip Obst, Royal College of Physicians, Ireland; MRCGP, London; MF Hom, Faculty Homoeopathy, London. *Appointments:* Junior House Officer, Sir Patrick Duns Hospital, Dublin. Senior House Officer Medical, Medicine/Accidents and Emergency, St James Hospital, Dublin; Obstetrics and Gynecology, St James Hospital; Paediatrics, Our Lady's Hospital for Sick Children, Dublin. General Practice, Dublin; Medical Registrar, Royal London Homoeopathic Hospital, London, England; General Practice, Hampstead, London and Hayes, Middlesex. *Memberships:* Medical Defense Union; Faculty of Homoeopathy; Royal College of General Practitioners; British Holistic Medical Association; Scientific and Medical Network. *Hobbies:* Jogging; Woodcarving; Reading; Music; Homoeopathy; Acupuncture; Alternative/Holistic medicine. *Address:* 13 Glenloch Road, Hampstead, London NW3, England.

GREENE, Beverly Ann, b. 14 Aug. 1950, New Jersey, USA. Clinical Psychologist. *Education:* BA, Psychology, New York University, 1973; MA, 1977, PhD, 1983, Clinical Psychology, Gordon F. Derner Institute of Advanced Psychological Studies, Adelphi University. *Appointments:* Various appointments, 1970-74; Psychology Fellow, New York Medical College, 1974-76; Consultant, Psychology, Williamsburg Child Development Centre, Brooklyn 1976-78, 1979-80; Psychology Intern, VA Medical Centre, East Orange, 1978-79; Research Assistant, New Jersey College of Medicine and VA Hospital, 1979-80; Psychology Trainee, Brookdale Hospital, 1980; School Psychologist, New York City Board of Education Committee on the Handicapped, 1980-82; Staff Psychologist, Clinical Instructor, 1982-84, Senior Psychologist, 1984-, Kings County Hospital; Clinical Assistant Professor, State University of New York, 1985-. *Memberships include:* Association for Women in Psychology; American Orthopsychiatric Association; National Association of Black Psychologists; International Neuropsychological Society; American Psychological Association; etc. *Publications:* Articles in professional Journals including: 'Women and Therapy'; 'Psychotherapy'; etc. *Honours:* National Institute of Mental Health Fellow, 1976-77; Mental Retardation Institute Psychology Fellow, 1974-76; New York University, Martin Luther King Scholar, 1968-72; New Jersey State Scholar. *Hobbies:* Photography; Music. *Address:* 26 St John's Place, Brooklyn, NY 11217, USA.

GREENFIELD, Lazar John, b. 14 Dec. 1934, Texas, USA, Stuart McGuire Professor and Chairman, Department of Surgery, Medical College of Virginia, Virginia Commonwealth University, 1974-, m. Sharon Dee Bishkin, 29 Aug. 1956, Houston, Texas, 2 sons, 1 daughter. *Education:* MD, honours, Baylor University College of Medicine, 1958; Intern, Surgery, 1958-59, Assistant resident, Surgery, 1961-65, Resident, Surgery, 1965-66, The Johns Hopskins Hospital; Senior Assistant Surgeon, NIH, USPHS, 1959-61. *Appointments:* Assistant Professor, Surgery, 1966-68, Associate Professor, 1968-71 Professor, 1971-74, Department of Surgery, University of Oklahoma Medical Centre; Chief, Surgical Service, Veterans Administrative Hospital, Oklahoma City, Oklahoma. *Memberships:* Member of numerous profesional organisations. *Publications:* Contributor of over 200 chapters, monographs, Abstracts and articles in professional and medical journals and books. *Honours:* Deans Award for Contributions to The School of Medicine, 1981; MCV Distinguished Service to Medicine Award, 1981; Thomas R Franklin Scholar, 1954;

Merck Award, 1958; Markle Scholar in Academic Medicine, 1968-73. *Hobbies:* Tennis; Bonsai. *Address:* Department of Surgery, Medical College of Virginia, Virginia Commonwealth University, Box 645 – MCV Station, Richmond, VA 23298-0001, USA.

GREENFIELD, Peter Rex, b. 1 Dec. 1931, Sheffield, England. Chief Medical Adviser, Social Security, DHSS. m. Faith Stella Gigg, 24 Sept. 1954, 8 sons, 2 daughters. *Education:* BA, Pembroke College, Cambridge, England, 1954; MB, B.Chir. St. George's Hospital Medical School, London, 1957, DObst., RCOG, 1960, MA, 1985. *Appointments:* House Appointments, St. George's Hospital, London, and St. Mary's Hospital, Croydon, 1958-59; General Practitioner, Sussex, England, 1959-69; Medical Officer, Vinehall School, Robertsbridge, Sussex, 1964-69; Medical Officer, Battle Hospital, Battle, Sussex, 1964-69; Divisional Surgeon, St. John Ambulance Brigade, 1965-date; Appointments at Department of Health and Social Security, 1969-date? Member of Joint Formulary Committee, British National Formulary, 1978-82; Chairman of Informal Working Group on Effective Prescribing, 1981-82. *Memberships:* British Medical Association; British Geriatrics Society; Associate, Royal College of General Practitioners. *Publications include:* Contributions to medical journals on geriatric day care and the DHSS Regional Medical Service. *Hobbies:* Golf; Walking; Music; Swimming. *Address:* Lorne House, Robertsbridge, East Sussex, EN32 5DW, England.

GREENHALGH, Roger Malcolm, b. 6 Feb. 1941, Ilkeston, Derbyshire, England. Professor of Surgery. m. Karin Maria Gross, 30 July 1964, Vienna, Austria, 1 son, 1 daughter. *Education:* MA, MD, MChir, Cambridge; Fellow, Royal College of Surgeons, England. *Appointments:* House Surgeon, St Thomas Hospital, London; Casualty Senior House Officer, St Thomas' Hospital; Lecturer and Senior Registrar, Surgery, St Bartholomew's Hospital; Senior Lecturer in Surgery, currently Professor of Surgery, Charing Cross Hospital Medical School and Westminster Medical School, London. *Memberships:* British Medical Association; Royal Society of Medicine; MDU. *Publications:* "Progress in Stroke Research", I, 1978, 2, 1983; "Smoking and Arterial Disease", 1981; "Hormones in Vascular Disease", 1981; "Fenoro Distal Bypass", 1981; "Extra anatomic and Secondary Arterial Reconstruction", 1982; "Vascular Surgical Techniques", 1984; "Diagnostic Techniques and Investigative Procedures in Vascular Surgery", 1985. *Honours:* Moynihan Fellow, 1974, Moynihan Prize, Association of Surgeons; Hunterian Professor, Royal College of Surgeons, 1980. *Hobbies:* Tennis; Skiing; Music. *Address:* Department of Surgery, Charing Cross Hospital, London W6 8RF, England.

GREENLAND, Sander, b. 16 Jan. 1951, Chicago, Illinois, USA, Associate Professor of Epidemiology. *Education:* AB, 1972; MA, 1973; MS, 1976; Dr PH, 1978. *Appointmetns:* Statistician, University of California at Los Angeles, 1975-78; Assistant Professor of Biostatistics, Harvard University, 1979; Assistant Professor of Epidemiology, 1980-84, Associate Professor of Epidemiology, 1984-, University of California at Los Angeles, School of Public Health. *Memberships:* Society for Epidemiologic Research; Biometric Society; International Epidemiologic Association. *Publications:* Contributor of over 60 articles in professional journals and chapters in books. *Honours:* Phi Beta Kappa, 1972; Regents Fellow, Mathematics, 1973; Regents Fellow, Public Health, 1978. *Address:* Division of Epidemiology, University of California at Los Angeles School of Public Health, Los Angeles, CA 90024, USA.

GREENOUGH, Anne, b. 25 Aug. 1954, Newcastle, England. Senior Lecturer, Honorary Consultant, Paediatrician. m. Charles G Greenough, 6 Sep. 1975,

Saltburn. *Education:* MB BS, London, 1978; MA, Cambrigde University, 1979; DCH, 1980; Member, Royal College of Physicians – Pediatrics, 1981; MD, 1986. *Appointments:* Clinical Lecturer, Department of Pediatrics, University of Cambridge; Honorary senior registrar, Hospital for Sick Children, Great Ormond Street, London; Director of Studies and Fellow of Girton College, University of Cambridge; Currently Senior Lecturer and Paediatrician, Department of Child Health, King's College Hospital, London. *Memberships:* Neonatal Society; paediatric Reseach Society; Paediatric Respiratory Group; Association of Perinatal Paediatricians. *Honours:* Scholar, Girton, Cambridge, 1974; Buxton Browne Prize, Harveian Society, 1985; Bye-Fellow, Girton College, Cambridge, 1985. *Hobby:* Travelling. *Address:* 57 Stradella Road, Herne Hill, London, England.

GREENWALL, Ryno Maurice Harrison, b. 28 June 1935, Cape Town, South Africa. Federal Councillor Dental Association of South Africa. m. Yvonne, 20 Jan. 1975, Cape Town, 2 sons, 3 daughters. *Education:* BDS, Witwatersrand, 1956. *Appointments:* President, Cape Western Branch, BASA, 1975-76; Federal Councillor, DASA, 1973-. *Memberships:* Dental Association of South Africa; IADR; Alpha Omega. *Publications:* "Artists and Illustrators of the Anglo Boer War" (in progress); Regular contributor to: 'Africana Notes and News'; 'SAPRG Newsletter'; 'Quarterly Bulletin S.A. Library'. *Honours:* Scholar of the University, 1953, 54; Stephen Goldfoot Prize, Witwatersrand University, 1954. *Hobbies:* Africana Collecting and Research into Pictorial Aspects of the Anglo Boer War; Golf; Snooker. *Address:* P.O. 14 Observatory, Cape Town 7935, South Africa.

GREENWAY, Clive Victor, b. 6 Mar. 1937,. Gloucester, England. Professor and Head of University Department of Pharmacology. m. Anne E Lawson, 6 June 1969, Winnipeg, Manitoba, Canada, 1 son, 2 daughters. *Education:* MA, PhD, University of Cambridge, Cambridge, England, 1961. *Appointments:* Demonstrator in Pharmaoclogy, University of Cambridge, 1960-63; Lecturer in Physiology, University of Aberdeen, Aberdeen, Scotland, 1963-67; Assistant Professor in Physiology, University of Alberta, Canada, 1967-68; Associate Professor 1968-79, Professor 1979-, Head 1983-, Department of Pharmacology, University of Manitoba, Winnipeg. *Memberships:* American Society of Pharmacological Therapy; American Physiological Society; Canadian Physiology Society; Canadian Pharmacological Society; Canadian Association for Gastroenterology. *Publications include:* 25 abstracts and 61 papers including: 'Hepatic vascular bed', (with RD Stark), 1971; 'Mechanisms and quantitative assessment of drug effects on cardiac output using a new model of the circulation', 1981; 'The role of the splanchnic venous system in overall cardiovascular homeostasis', 1983; 'Physiology and pharmacology of blood vessels in the liver' in "Blood Vessels and Lymphatics in Organ Systems" (editors DI Abramson and PB Dobrin), 1984; 'The hepatic vascular bed' in "Handbook of Physiology" (editor JD Wood), in press; 'The venous system, cardiac preload and cardiac output', (with WW Lautt), 1986. *Hobbies:* Music; Philately; Photography; Gardening. *Address:* Department of Pharmacology, University of Manitoba, 770 Bannatyne Avenue, Winnipeg, R3E 0W3, Canada.

GRENIER, Bernard, b. 11 Aug. 1925, Onzain (41), France. Professor of Infectious Diseases in Children. m. Nicole Farinaux, 14 Sep. 1955, Paris, France, 2 sons, 3 daughters. *Education:* Titular Professor. *Memberships:* French Society of Paediatrics; French-speaking Society of Infectious Pathology. *Publications:* "Pédiatrie en Poche"; "Développement et naladies de l'enfant". *Honour:* Officer, French Order of Academic Palms, 1985

Hobbies: Cycling tourism; Sailing. *Address:* 34 rue de Loches, F-37000 Tours, France.

GREWAL, Ripdaman Singh, b. 3 Dec. 1922, Narangwal, India. Member of Pharma Research Board, Ciby-Geigy Ltd., Basel, Switzerland. m. 27 May 1956, Simla, 1 son, 2 daughters. *Education:* BSc; MB BS; D.Phil, University of Oxford, England. *Appointments:* House Physician, Medicine, V H Medical College, Amritsar, India; Registrar in Medicine, Medical College, Dibrugarh; Reader in Pharmacology, Medical College Nagpur; Professor of Pharmacology, Medical College, Nagpur; Research Fellow, National Research Council of Canada; Deputy Director, Director, Ciba-Geigy Research Centre, Bombay, India; Member of Pharma Research Board, Ciba-Geigy Ltd., Basel, Switzerland. *Memberships:* British Pharamacological Society; Indian Pharmacological Society, President 1979; Association of Physiologists & Pharmacologists of India; Past Member: Canadian Pharmacological Society, New York Academy of Sciences. *Publications:* Over 120 publications in various international scientific journals. *Honours:* Fellow, Indian Academy of Sciences, 1975; Fellow, Maharashtra Academy of Sciences, 1977; Professor, UK Seth Oration, Hockey Blue, University of Oxford, 1980; Temporary Adviser, WHO, 1980, Member, Scientific & Technical Review. WHO, 1983. *Hobbies:* Tennis; Golf; Reading. *Address:* Unterer Rheinweg 44, 40457 Basel, Switzerland.

GRIBBLE, Michael de Gruchy, b. 4 May 1923, Oxford, England, Private Practice-Pathology, m. (1) Patricia Mary Watkins, (2) Judith Ann Crouch, 5 sons, 1 daughter. *Education:* MA, 1st class honours; BSc; DM, Oxford; FRCPA; FRC Path. *Appointments:* House Physician, House Surgeon, Senior House Physician, The London Hospital; Staff Member, FAR Institute of Aviation Medicine, Farnborough, Hants; Registrar, St Mary Abbots Group Laboratory, London; Senior Registrar, Maryfield Hospital, Dundee, Scotland. *Memberships:* Association of Clinical Pathologists; Haematology Society of Australia; International Society of Haematology; Australian Medical Association. *Hobbies:* Reading; Local History; Painting. *Address:* 45 Statenborough Street, Leabrook, South Australia 5068.

GRIEVE, Andrew Robert, b. 23 May 1939, Stirling, Scotland. Professor of Conservative Dentistry. m. Frances M Ritchie, 26 Sept 1963, Forfar, 2 daughters. *Education:* BDS, University of St. Andrews; DDS, University of Birmingham; Fellowship in Dental Surgery, Royal College of Surgeons, Edinburgh. *Appointments:* Junior hospital appointments, 1961-63; Lecturer in Conservative Dentistry, University of St Andrews, 1963-65; Lecturer, 1965-75, Senior Lecturer, 1975-80, University of Birmingham; Professor of Conservative Dentistry, University of Dundee, Consultant in Restorative Dentistry, Tayside Health Board, 1980-. *Memberships:* Dental Council, Royal College of Surgeons of Edinburgh; British Dental Association; Council Member, British Society for Restorative Dentistry; Council Member, Royal Odonto-Chirurgical Society of Scotland. *Publications:* Many publications on aspects of research related to Conservative Dentistry. *Hobby:* Hill walking. *Address:* Department of Conservative Dentistry, Dental School, The University, Dundee DD1 4HN, Scotland.

GRIEVE, Robert James, b. 28 July 1951, Rugby, England. Consultant Radiotherapist. m. Catherine Maria Christine Jackson, 21 Aug. 1976, Birmingham, England, 2 sons, 1 daughter. *Education:* MB ChB 1974; MRCP 1976; FRCR 1983. *Appointments:* House Physician, Selly Oak Hospital, Birmingham, 1974; House Surgeon, Queen Elizabeth Hospital, Birmingham, 1975; Senior Health Officer, Selly Oak Hospital Birmingham, 1975-76; Senior Health

Officer, Dudley Road Hospital, Birmingham, 1976; Research Registrar/CRC Fellow, Prof. Unit, Queen Elizabeth Hospital, Birmingham, 1976-79; Registrar, 1979-81, Senior Registrar, 1981-83, Christie Hospital Manchester. *Memberships:* British Institute of Radiology; British Association of Cancer Research; British Stomach Cancer Group. *Publications:* Numerous papers on cancer research. *Hobbies:* Cricket; Golf; Squash. *Address:* Ashfield House, Brooke Road, Kenilworth CV8 2BD. England.

GRIFFIN, Anthony William, b. 12 Nov. 1938, Sydney Australia. Radiologist. m. Helen Ruth Wheen, 2ʒ May 1966, Sydney, 3 sons, 1 daughter. *Education.* MBBS,University of Sydney, 1966; Fellow, Roya College of Surgeons, Edinburgh, Scotland, 1969 Fellow, Royal Australian College of Radiologists 1974. *Appointments:* Resident Medical Officer 1966-67, Registrar, 1968, St George's Hospital Sydney; Surgical Registrar, Essex County Hospital Colchester, England, 1970-71; Radiology Registrar, Royal Canberra Hospital, Australia, 1972-73; Staff Specialist Radiology, Royal Prince Alfred Hospital, Sydney, 1974-75; Visiting Radiologist to Royal Canberra Hospital, Woden Valley Hospital, Calvary Hospital, 1976-. *Memberships:* Australian Medical Association, Councillor, Capital Territory Group; Australian Association of Surgeons. *Hobbies:* Shooting; Farming; Football; Travel. *Address:* Corinna Chambers, Corinna Street, Phillip, Australian Capital Territory 2606, Australia.

GRIFFIN, John Parry, b. 21 May 1938. Director, Association of the British Pharmaceutical Industry. m. Margaret Cooper, 1962, 1 son 2 daughters. *Education:* BSC, 1959, PhD, 1961, MB BS, 1964, London Hospital Medical College, England; LRCP, MRCS, 1964, MRCP, 1980, MRCPath, 1982. *Appointments:* House Physician, London Hospital Medical Unit and House Surgeon, London Hospital Accident and Orthopaedic Department, 1964-65; Lecturer in Physiology, King's College, London, 1965-67; Head of Clinical Research, Riker Laboratories, 1967-71; SMO Medicines Division 1971-76; PMO; Medicines Division and Medical Assessor, Committee on Safety of Medicines, 1976-77; SPMO and Professional Head of Medicines Division, DHSS, 1977-84; Director, The Association of the British Pharmaceutical Industry. *Memberships:* Joint Formulary Committee for British National Formulary, 1978-84; UK, Representative, EEC Committee on Proprietary Medicinal Products, Chairman, Committee on Proprietary Medicinal Products Working Party on Safety Requirements, 1977-84; FRSM. *Publications:* Co-author, "Iatrogenic Diseases" 1972 3rd edition 1986; Co-author, "Manual of Adverse Drug Interactions" 1975, 3rd edition 1984; Co-author, "Drug Induced Emergencies" 1980; Numerous articles in scientific and medical journals mainly on aspects of neurophysiology and clinical pharmacology and toxicology. *Honours:* Lethby and Buxton Prizes, London Hospital Medical College, 1958; George Riddoch Prize in Neurology, 1962. *Hobbies:* Gardening; Local history. *Address:* 20 Mornington, Digswell, Herts AL6 0AJ, England.

GRIFFIN, Thomas W, b. 16 Feb. 1945, USA. Professor. m. Vicki Griffin, 8 Aug. 1971, 1 daughter. *Education:* BS, 1966; MD, 1970; Certification in Therapeutic Radiology, 1976. *Appointments:* Professor, University of Washington, Chairman, Department of Radiation Oncology, Director, University Cancer Center, Vice-Chairman, Radiation Therapy Oncology Group, University of Washington. *Memberships:* American College of Radiology; American Society of Therapeutic Radiology & Oncology; American Radium Society; Radiation Therapy Oncology Group. *Publications:* Over 100 published scientific articles. *Hobbies:* Mountain Climbing; Skiing. *Address:* University of Washington, Seattle, WA 98195, USA.

GRIFFIN DOUGALL, Beverly, b. Delhi, Louisiana,

USA. Professor and Director, Department of Virology. *Education:* MA; PhD, ScD, Cambridge University, England. *Appointments include:* Head, Nucleic Acid Chemistry Laboratory, Imperial Cancer Research Fund, London, England; Professor and Director, Department of Virology, Royal Postgraduate Medical School, London. *Memberships:* New York Academy of Sciences; Society for General Microbiology; Biochemical Society. *Publications:* Contributor to most learned journals of molecular biology and virology including: 'Nature'; 'EMBOJ'; 'Proceedings of National Academy of Sciences'; 'British Medical Journal of Virology'. *Hobbies:* Skiing; Music; Gardening. *Address:* Department of Virology, Royal Postgraduate Medical School, Lodnon W12, England.

GRIFFITHS, Peter Denham, b. 16 June 1927, Southampton, England. Professor of Biochemical Medicine. m. Joy Burgess, 9 Apr. 1949, Southampton, 3 sons, 1 daughter. *Education:* Guy's Hospital Medical school, London; BSc Physiology 1st class honours; MB BS; Licentiate, Royal College of Physicians; Member, Royal College of Surgeons; MD, London; Fellow, Royal College of Pathologists. *Appointments:* House Officer, Junior Lecturer, Registrar in Clinical Pathology, Guy's Hospital, London; Senior House Officer, New Cross General Hospital, London; Senior Registrar in Clinical Pathology, Guy's and Lewisham Hospitals; Consultant Pathologist, Harlow Group of Hospitals; Senior Lecturer in Chemcial Pathology, Honorary Consultant, University of St Andrews, Scotland; Professor of Biochemical Medicine 1968-, Vice Principal 1979-85, Dean of Faculty of Medicine and Dentistry 1985-, University of Dundee; Honorary Consultant, Tayside Health Board. *Memberships:* British Medical Association; Biochemical Society; Association of Clincial Pathologists; Association of Clincial Biochemists. *Publications include:* 'Serum Levels of ATP: Creatine Phosphokinase. The Normal Range and Effect of Muscular Activity', 1965; 'Multiple On-line Data Collection and Processing for RIA Using a Micro-computer System', 1980; Editorial Board, Joint Editor in Chief 1978-85, 'Clinica Chimica Acta'. *Honour:* Kone Award, Association of Clinical Biochemists, 1985. *Hobbies:* Music; Theatre; Domestic activities. *Address:* Charlemont, 52 Albany Road, Broughty Ferry, Dundee DD5 1NW, Scotland.

GRILLIOT, James Richard, b. 6 June 1954, St, Mary's, Ohio, USA. Chairman, Department of Radiology. m. Christine Ann Marie Diller, 15 Apr. 1978, Coldwater, Ohio, 2 sons. *Education:* BSc, Education – Biology; B App Sc, Human Anatomy; Doctor of Chiropractic; Diplomate, American Chiropractic Board of Roentgenology; Fellow, Chiroptractic Council on Radiology, Canada. *Appointments:* Research Assistant, Psychology Department, Bowling Green State University; Assistant Clinic Director, Montgomery Chiropractic Clinic; Radiologist, Canadian Memorial Chiropractic College; Radiology Department Chairman, Canadian Memorial Chiropractic College. *Membersisp:* American Chiropractic Association; Canadian Chiropractic Association; Ontario Chiropractic Association; American College of Chiropractic Roentgenologists; American Council of Chiropractic Radiology; Ohio State Chiropractic Society. *Publications:* Numerous original papers prepared for major seminars and scientific journals. *Hobbies:* Fishing; Camping; Backpacking; Hiking; Softball; Gardening; Music; Scuba Diving; Good Conversation. *Adddress:* 1900 Bayview Avenue, Toronto, Ontario, Canada M4G 3E6.

GRIM, Charles, b. 15 Aug. 1950, York, Pennsylvania, USA. Chiropractor. *Education:* BA, Temple University, 1972; DC, Palmer College of Chiropractics, 1982. *Appointments:* Chiropractor. *Memberships:* American Chiropractic Association;

American College of Chiropractic Orthopedics; Council on Chiropractic Orthopedics of ACA; American Chiropractic Association Council on Roentgenology; Pennsylvania Chiropractic Society; International Chiropractic Association. *Honours:* Honor Extern, Clinical Exam Center and Clinic, Palmer College, 1982. *Hobbies:* Running; Motorcycles; Reading; Physical activities. *Address:* 1409 MacDade Boulevard, Folsom, PA 19033, USA.

GRINER, Paul F, b. 1 Jan. 1933, Philadelphia, Pennsylvania, USA. General Director, Strong Memorial Hospital; Medical Center Director, University of Rochester Medical Center. 1 son, 1 daughter. *Education:* BA, Harvard College; MD, University of Rochester School of Medicine and Dentistry, Rochester. *Appointments:* Director of Medical Education, Rochester General Hospital, NY, 1965-67; Associate Chairman for Clinical Services, Department of Medicine, 1969-84; Head, General Medicine Unit, Department of Medicine, 1976-84; Acting Chairman, 1977-79; Associate Vice-President for Hospital Affairs, 1984-85; University of Rochester, School of Medicine and Dentistry; General Director, Strong Memorial Hospital of University of Rochester, 1984-; Director of Medical Center, University of Rochester Medical Center, Rochester, NY, 1985-. *Memberships:* American Clinical and Climatological Association; Alpha Omega Alpha; Sigma Xi; Association of American Medical Colleges; Fellow, American College of Physicians; American Society of Hematology; American Federation for Clinical Research; Clinical Chemistry Data Communications Group; Soiciety for Research and Education in Primary Care Internal Medicine; Society for Medical Decision Making. *Publications:* Contributor of professional journals; Co-editor, "Clinical Diagnosis and the Laboratory: Logical Strategies for Common Medical Problems" (in press). *Honours:* MD with Honor, 1959; Doran Stephens Prize, 1959; Alpha Omega Alplha, 1959; USAF Commendation Medal, 1964; University Mentor Award, University of Rochester, 1982. *Address:* 601 Elmwood Avenue, Box 612, Rochester, NY 14642, USA.

GRISHAM, Joe Wheeler, b. 5 Dec. 1931, Tennessee, USA. Professor and Chair, Department of Pathology. m. Evelyn Malone, 2 July 1985, Gordonsville, Tennessee. *Education:* BA, 1953, MD, 1957, Vanderbilt University. *Appointments:* Instructor, 1960-61, Assistant Professor, 1961-67, Associate Professor, Pathology, 1967-69, Professor of Pathology and Anatomy, 1969-73, Washington University, St Louis, Missouri; Assistant and Associate Pathologist, Barnes and Allied Hospitals, St Louis, 1960-73; Professor and Chair, Pathology, University of North Carolina, Chapel Hill, North Carolina, 1973-; Chief of Pathology, North Carolina Memorial Hospital, Chapel Hill, 1983-. *Memberships:* American Medical Association; American Association for Cancer Research; American Association of Pathologists; American Association for the Study of Liver Diseases; American Association for the Advancemnt of Science; American Society for Cell Biology Tissue Culture Association; International Academy of Pathology; Cell Kinetics Society. *Publications:* Author of over 100 articles in major biological research journals. *Honours:* President and Board Chairman, Federation of American Societies of Experimental Biology, 1984-85; Past President, American Association of Pathologists. *Address:* Department of Pathology, University of North Carolina, 305 Brinkhous-Bullitt Building 228-H, Chapel Hill, NC 27514, USA.

GRIX, Roy George Charles, b. 21 Jan 1928, London, England. Consultant Health Physicist. m. Patricia Margaret Hayden, 27 July 1957, Bromley, Kent, 1 son. *Education:* Teaching Diploma, Goldsmiths College, University of London; BSc honours, Birkbeck College, University of London; C Chem.

Appointments: Principal Lecturer, Nuclear Sciences, Suffolk College, 1963-84; Secretary, British Radiological Protection Association, 1978-81; Chairman, Association of University Radiation Protection Officer, 1980-83; Registrar, Institute of Radiation Protection, 1984-. *Memberships:* Association of University Radiation Protection Officers; Institute of Radiation Officers; Institute of Radiation Protection; Royal Society of Chemistry. *Publications:* Script Writer, Training Modules in Radiation Protection (video), 1981-84; "The Radman Guide to the Ionising Radiations Regulations", Co-author, 1985. *Hobby:* Badminton. *Address:* 14 Quintons Corner, East Bergholt, Colchester CO7 6RD, England.

GROAT, Ronald Douglas, b. 4 Mar. 1951, Minneapolis, Minnesota, USA. Psychiatrist. m. Jennifer L Groat, 23 Aug. 1975, 2 sons, 1 daughter. *Education:* BA, 1973, MD, 1976, University of Minnesota; Internship Rotating General, Hennepin County Medical Center, 1977; Resident in Psychiatry, 1980, Fellowship in Consultation Psychiatry, University of Minnesota Hospitals. *Appointments:* Medical Director, Psychiatric Service, St Marys Hospital, Minneapolis, Minnesota, 1982-84; Medical Director, Family Renewal Center, Fairview Southdale Hospitals, 1980-, Adult Psychiatry Programs, Fairview Hospitals, 1984-, Chemical Dependency Services, Fairview Southdale Hospitals, 1985-; Clinical Assistant Professor, Psychiatry, Deaprtment of Psychiatry, University of Minnesota Hospitals, 1980-. *Memberships:* American Psychiatric Association; American Medical Association. *Publications:* Contriubotor to: 'Journal of Nervous and Mental Diseases'; 'Journal of Clinical Psychopharmacology'. *Honours:* Fellowship in Consultation Psychiatry, 1980. *Hobbies:* Golf; Fishing; Music. *Address:* Suite 818, 606 24th Avenue South, Minneapolis, MN 55454, USA.

GROCHMAL, Stanislas, b. 13 Apr. 1911, Jureczkowa, Poland. Retired Professor, Medical Academy; Consultant, Neurolgical Rehabilitation. m. 11 Nov. 1939, 1 son, 1 daughter. *Education:* Diploma, Physician, Medical Faculty, University of Poznan, 1935; MD, University Poznan; Specialist, Neurology, 1953; Specialist, Rehabilitation Medicine, 1959; Associate Professor, Cracow, 1962; Professor, 1968. *Appointments:* Assistant Lecturer, Physiology, University Poznan, 1936, Army Medical Service, 1937-39; Regional Physician, Chief, Epidemic Hospital Tuchow, 1939-45; Assistant Lecturer, Clinical Hospital, Cracow, 1946-50; Assistant Lectuer, Neurolgoy, Medical Academy, 1951-62; Head, Medical Rehabilitation, Higher School of Physical Education, 1965-72; Rector, Higher School, Physical Education, Cracow, 1965-68; Head, Rehabilitation Department, Institute of Neurology, Cracow, 1972-82. *Memberships:* World Federation of Neruological Research; Royal Society of Medicine; International Cerebral Palsy Society; International Rehabilitation Medicine Association; Pavlovian Society of America; Commission, Rehabilitation, Polish Academy of Sciences; etc. *Publications:* "The Physiological Bases of Motor Rehabilitation", 1966; "Theory and Methodology of Relaxation-concentration Exercises", Editor, Co-author, 1979; "The Rehabilitation in Diseases of Nervous System", Editor and Co-Author, 1980; "The Bases of Motor Rehabilitaiton", co-author, 1981; "The Medical Rehabilitation", co-author, 1983. *Honours:* Cross of Merit with Swords, 1964; Cross of Underground Movement 1964; Cross of the Order Virtuti Militari, 1968; Cross and the Order Polonia Restituta, 1971. *Hobbies:* Poetry; Travel. *Address:* Institute of Neurology, Medical Academy, ul Botaniczna3, 31-503 Krakow, Poland.

GRÖNROOS, Matti, b. 20 Jan. 1931, Turku, Finland. Professor of Obstetrics & Gynaecology. m. Leena, 27 Oct. 1956, 3 sons, 1 daughter. *Education:* MD, 1965; Docent, Assistant Professor, Professor,

Obstetrics & Gynaecology, University of Helsinki. *Appointments:* Coordinating Physician for mass screening for cervical & breast cancer in Turku district; Consultant, Assistant Physician, Chief Physician, Obstetrics & Gynaecology;' Consultant Physician in Hormonal Cytology, Department of Pathology, University of Turku; Chief Physician, Outpatient Clinic of Finnish Cancer Association; Chief Physician (Gynaecological oncology), University Central Hospital, Turku. *Memberships:* Secretary-General, Scandinavian Association of Obstetricians & Gynaecologists, 1970-76, 1977-83; and others. *Publications:* Various publications in field of gynaecological oncology. *Honours:* Silver Medal for Merit, Ministry of Education, 1978; Medal for Recognition of Merit, Finish Ice-Hockey Association, 1979-1982; Silver Medal, Finnish Sports & Gymnastics Association; Professor honoris causa. *Hobbies:* Sports Medicine; Turku Archipelago; Finnish Red Cross; Work for Cancer Prevention; Blood Donor. *Address:* Department of Obstetrics & Gynaecology, University of Turku, Turku 52, Finland.

GROOPMAN, Jacob Elliot, b. 3 Aug. 1948, New York, New York, USA. Associate Director, Maimonides Medical Center Pulmonary Disease Division and Medical/Pulmonary Intensive Care Units. *Education:* BS, Magna cum laude, City College, City University of New York; MD Cum laude, Downstate Medical Center, Brooklyn, State University of New York. *Appointments:* Acting Associate Director of Medical Education, 1980-81, Acting Associate Director of Medicine, 1981-81, Assistant Director of Pulmonary Division, 1981-85, Assistant Director of Medical and Pulmonary Intensive Care Units, 1981-85, Associate Director, Pulmonary Disease Division and Medical/Pulmonary Intensive Care Units, 1985-, Maimonides Medical Centre, Brooklyn, New York. *Memberships:* Fellow: American College of Chest Physicians; American College of Physicians. Member: American Medical Association; American Thoracic Society; New York Academy of Science; American Association for the Advancement of Science; American Mensa Limited; Phi Beta Kappa. *Honours:* Research Prize Award for best clinical research paper, Maimonides Medical Centre, 1981; Alan Teitler Memorial Award for Excellence in Medicine, 1976. *Address:* 21-50 33rd Road, Long Island City, Queens, NY 11106, USA.

GRUBER, Walther S, b. 23 Nov 1941, Vienna, Austria, Assistant Professor, Department of Obstetrics and Gynaecology, University of Vienna, m. Ilse Schwarz, 16 June 1967, 2 sons, 1 daughter. *Education:* MD, University of Vienna; Universitätsdozent. *Appointmetns:* Fellow, Department of Obstetrics and Gynaecology, University of North Carolina Medical School, NC, USA, 1975-76. *Memberships:* Austrian Society for Obstetrics and Gynaecology; Austrian Society for Senology; Österreichische Gasellschaft für Perinatale Medizin. *Publications:* Author of 80 article published in Scintific Journals. *Hobbies:* Gardening; Music; Skiing; Windsurfing. *Address:* Bastiengasse 117, 1180 Vienna, Austria.

GRUMBACH, Melvin Malcolm, b. 21 Dec 1925, New York, USA. Chairman, University Department of Paediatrics. m. Madeleine F Butt, 3 sons. *Education:* MD, Columbia University, 1948. *Appointments:* Instructor in Pediatrics, Columbia University, College of Physicians and Surgeons, New York, 1955-56; Associate in Pediatrics, 1956-57, Assistant Professor of Pediatrics, 1957-61, Associate Professor of Pediatrics, 1961-66, Columbia University College of Physicians and Surgeons; Professor of Pediatrics, 1966-, Chairman, Department of Pediatrics, 1966-, Edward B Shaw Professor of Pediatrics, 1983-, University of California San Francisco. *Memberships include:* American Pediatric Society; Fellow, American Academy of Pediatrics; Society for Pediatric Research; Fellow, American Association for the Advancement of Science; American Society

for Clinical Investigation; Association of American Phsyicians; Ednocrine Society; Association of Medical School Pediatric Department Chairman, and many more. *Publications:* Contributor of numerous chapters to edited scientific textbooks and articles to medical journals. *Honours:* Career Scientists Award, The Health Research Council of the City of New York, 1961-66; Joseph Mather Smith Prize, Columbia University, 1962; Silver Medal, Bicentennial, Columbia University College of Physicians and Surgeons, for Distinguished Achievement, 1967; Borden Award for Research in Pediatrics, American Academy of Pediatrics, 1971; The Robert H Williams Distinguished Leadership Award, The Endocrine Society; Member, Institute of Medicine, National Academy of Sciences, 1983. *Address:* Department of Paediatrics, University of California San Francisco, San Francisco, CA 94143, USA.

GRUNDY, Paul Henry, b. 12 July, 1951, Providence, Rhode Island, USA. Department of State Regional Medical Officer. m. Kim Hyewon, 29 Dec. 1979, Seoul, Korea, 2 sons. *Education:* BA, Southern Californian College, USA, 1974; MD, MPH, University of California, 1978. *Appointments:* Chief of Hospital Services, USAF, Osan, Korea, 1979-80, Director of Occupational and Preventive Medicine, Chief of Flight Medicine, 1980-81; Physician in Residence, Johns Hopkins University, Baltimore, Maryland, 1981-82; Staff Preventive Medicine Officer, USAF, Texas, 1983-85; currently Regional Medical Officer, Department of State, US Embassy, Sanna, Yemen. *Memberships include:* Internatioanl Health Society; American Medical Association; American College of Preventive Medicine (Fellow); American Aerospace Association; Occupational Medical Scoiety; Delta Omega Honorary Medical Society; Zigma Zi Honorary Scientific Society. *Publications:* Conference papers and presentations to: School of Aerospace Medicine; Congress on Tropical Medicine; Congress of Electron Microscopy; Radiation Meeting, from 1974-83; various articles in professional journals, including 'Supply of Cuban Medical Personnel in Third World Countries' in 'The American Journal of Public Health', 1980. *Honours include:* Ex Luna Scientista Outstanding Contribution in Lunar Research, National Seronautics Space Administration, 1973; Regents Scholar, University of California, 1974; Meritorious Service Award for outstanding service in Korea, Defence Department, 1981; Delta Omega, Johns Hopkins University, Baltimore, 1982; Southern California College Alumnus of the year, 1983; Joint Meritorious Service Award for outstanding service in Saudi Arabia, 1985. *Hobbies:* Travel; Reading. *Address:* Department of State, SANAA, Washington DC 20520, USA.

GRUNHAUS, Leon, b. 11 Sep. 1948, Maracaibo, Venezuela. Assistant Professor, Director. m. Leora Zuriel, 7 Aug. 1979, Jerusalem, Israel, 1 son, 1 daughter. *Education:* MD, Graduate School, Universidad del Zulia, Maracaibo, Venezuela. *Appointments:* Instructor 1975, Lecturer 1978-79, Hebrew University, Jerusalem, Israel; Instructor 1977, Physician in Charge, Psychiatry Inpatient Service 1980, Hadassah Medical Centre, Jerusalem; Assistant Professor of Psychiatry, University of Michigan Medical School, 1983-; Director, Clinical Studies Unit, University of Michigan Psychiatric Hospitals, 1983-. *Memberships:* Honorary Member, Chilean Psychiatric Society; Israel Medical Association; Israel Psychiatric Association; Michigan Psychiatric Association; American Psychiatric Association; American Association for the Advancement of Science; Society of Biological Psychiatry. *Publications:* about 20 articles, including: 'Serial Monitoring of anitdepressant response to electroconvulsive therapy with sleep-EEG recording and dexamethasone suppression tests', 1985; 'Depression and panic in patients with borderline personality disorder', 1985;

'Simultaneous panic and depressive disorder', 2 articles 1985. *Honours:* Outstanding Medical Student Award, Universidad del Zulia, 1966; Faculty prize, Hebrew University, 1976. *Address:* Department of Psychiatry, University of Michigan Hospitals, 1405 East Ann Street, Ann Arbor, MI 48109, USA.

GUADALAJARA MACIAS, Joel, b. 10 Oct. 1930, Ags, Mexico. Director of General Hospital. m. Elsie Garza, 26 Aug. 1966, Monterrey, 1 son, 2 daughters. *Education:* MD, University of Nuevo Leon, Monterrey; Studied surgery, University of Tennessee Research Center and Hospital, Knoxville, Tennessee, USA; studied thoracic Surgery, Hahnemann Medical College and Hospital, Philadelphia, Pennsylvania, USA. *Appointments:* Attending Physician and Thoracic Surgeon, Acting Chief of Service of Thoracic Surgery, Chief Clinical Department, Director of Medical Clinic, currently, Director of General Hospital, Mexican Institute of Social Security, Monterrey. *Memberships:* Mexican Society of Pneumology and Thoracic Surgery; American College of Chest Physicians; Society of Thoracic Surgeons, USA; International Academy of Chest Physicians and Surgeons. *Publications:* Contributions to: 'Neumol. Cir. Torax Mexico', 'Diseases of the Chest'; 'International Surgery'; 'Gazeta Medica Mexico'. *Honours:* Mexican Board of Pulmonary Diseases, 1973; Mexican Board of Surgery, 1978. *Hobbies:* Music; Literature; History; Travel. *Address:* Via Triumphalis no 117, Colonia del Valle, Nuevo Leon 66200, Mexico.

GUAY, Michel, b. 11 July 1938, Quebec, Canada. ENT Specialist. m. Claudette Robitaille, 6 Oct. 1962, Lauzon, 3 sons. *Education:* MD; CSPQ; FRCS(C). *Appointments:* ENT Specialist, 1968; Chief, ENT Service, Hotel-Dien de Levis. *Memberships:* Canadian Oto Laryngological Society; Association of ENT, Quebec; Royal College of England; American Medical Association. *Hobbies:* Sports; Manual Works. *Address:* 15 Ave. Begin, Levis, Quebec, Canada G6V 4B6.

GUAY, Raymond M, b. 26 Nov. 1928, Lauzon, Canada. Otolaryngologist. m. Gaetane Boily, 21 June 1954, Lévis, 2 sons, 2 daughters. *Education:* MD, Laval University; CSPQ Otolaryngology; FRCS (C) Otolaryngology. *Appointments:* Chief of Otolaryngology, Hotel Dieu De Lévis Hospital, 1968-82. *Memberships:* Canadian Medical Association: Association Des Médecins de Langue Française du Canada; Royal Society of Medecine; American Academy of Otolaryngology. *Publication:* 'Meniere's Disease', 1970. *Honour:* President, Collaboration Santé Internationale. *Hobbies:* Golf; Skiing. *Address:* 15 Begin Avenue, Lévis, Quebec, G6V 4B6 Canada.

GUEDON, Jacques Joseph Marie, b. 28 Jan. 1927, France. Medical Research Director. m. Pierrette Gaillard, 4 Jan. 1954, Chantilly, 5 daughters. *Education:* MD, 1959. *Appointments:* Director, Research Unit on Clinical Pharmacology of Hypertension, National Institute for Health and Medical Research; Chief, Department of Nephrology and Hypertension, CMC Foch, Suresnes. *Memberships:* International Society of Nephrology; International Society of Hypertension; European Society for Clinical Investigation. *Publications:* about 100 papers in scientific journals. *Honour:* Chevalier de l'Ordre National du Merite. *Hobbies:* Tennis; Medieval History. *Address:* 9 Parc de Bearn, 92210 Saint Cloud, France.

GUELL, Ricardo, b. 22 Apr. 1935, Cuba. Research Professor of Paediatric Endocrinology. m. Today, 24 Feb. 1961, Esperanza, 2 daughters. *Education:* MD, University of Havana, 1960; Paediatric Endocrinologist, Havana, 1965. *Appointments:* Vice-Director, 1966-67, Head of Paediatric Department, 1966-76, National Institute of Endocrinolgoy, Havana; Vice-President, Instituto de la Infancia, Cuba, 1976-80; Research Professor of Paediatric Endocrinology, National Institute of Endocrinology, Havana, 1980-. *Memberships:* International Study Group of Diabetes in Children & Adolescents; Associacion Latino Americana de Diabetes; Federación Ibero-Americana de Diabetes; Sociedad Cubana de Endocrinología Pediátrica; Sociedad Cubana de Endocrinología; Sociedad Cubana de Diabetes; Sociedad Cubana de Pediatría. *Publications:* "Diabetes Mellitus". 1971; "Temmas de Endocrinología Infantil" (editor), 1974; Various articles in medical journals. *Hobby:* Camping. *Address:* Departimento Endocrinología Pediátrica, Instituto Nacional Endocrinología, Hospital Infantil Pedro Borrás, Havana 4, Cuba.

GUENTHER, Donna Marie, b. 20 Oct. 1938, Meadville, Pennsylvania, USA. Group Practice, Allergist. m. Malcolm Paul Scott, 15 July 1972, Wilmington, Delaware, 1 son. *Education:* BS, Allegheny College, 1960; MD, Temple University, 1967. *Appointmetns:* Internship 1967-68, Residency 1968-69, Chief Resident in Pediatrics, St Christopher's Hospital for Children, Philadelphia, 1969-70; Fellow, Pediatric Allergy and Immunology, Thomas Jefferson University, Philadelphia, 1970--71; Fellow, Immunology, University of Minnesota, Minneapolis, 1971-72; Fellow, Allergy and Immunogloy, 1972-73, Assistant Clinical Professor, Pediatrics and Immunology, University of California, San Francisco, 1977-; Chief of Allergy Divison, Children's Hospital Medical Center, Oakland, CA, 19730; Assistant Clinical Professor, Pediatrics – Allergy, University of California, San Diego, 1976-; Physician Kaiser Permanente Medical Group, S. San Francisco, California, 1985-. *Memberships:* Fellow, American Academy of Pediatrics; Amei na Academy of Allergy; American College of Allergists; Western Society for Pediatric Research; California Society of Allergy and Clinical Immunology; Western Society of Allergy and Immunology. *Publications incldue:* Author of several scientific papers inclduing 'Thymosin Effect in Patients with DiGeorge Syndrome', (co-author), 1978; 'Ataxia Telangiectasia with Burkitt's Lymphoma' (co-authro), 1978; 'Wiskott-Aldrich Syndrome and Systemic Necrotizing Vasculitis', (co-author), 1978. *Hobbies:* Running; Tennis; Writing; Photography. *Address:* 161 Alpine Terrace, Oakland, CA 94618, USA.

GUHL, Felipe, b. 14 July 1949, Bogatá, Colombia. Microbiologist, Parasitologist. m. Maria Teresa Samudio, 4 Aug. 1972, 2 sons, 1 daughter. *Education:* Degrees in Biology, Microbiology, 1973, MSc Parasitology, 1975, University of the Andes, Bogatá Colombia. *Appointments:* (medical): Instructor 1970-71, Lecturer 1972-77, General Biology Course; Instructor, basic Parasitology Course, 1973-74, Lecturer, postgraduate course, 1975, serology of tropical parasitic diseases; Lecturer, advanced immunology course, 1976; Lecturer, advanced serology course, 1978; Lecturer on training course for diagnostics & epidemiology of parasitic diseases, also General Biology & Biogeography, 1979-84, all University of the Andes, Bogotá; (administrative): General Coordinator, Department of Biological Sciences, 1976-77; Head of Microbiology (Parasitology Laboratories, 1977; Vice-Dean, Faculties of Arts & Sciences, 1981-82; Director, Department of Biological Sciences, Director, Microbiology & Parasitology Laboratories, 1982-. *Memberships:* 25 national congresses, 11 national symposia, 4 international congresses, 3 international symposia; President, Colombian Association of Biological Sciences, 1979-80, 1980-81; Colombian Representative on Continental Study Group on the Serology of Chagas Diseases, 1980; UNDP/World Bank/WHO Special Programme for Research & Training in tropical diseases, Sao Paulo, Brazil; ABAMA (Society of Microbiologists); Brazilian Society of Microbiology; Colombian Biology Society; Colombian Society for the

Advancement of Science; Latin American Society of Electronmicroscopy; Colombian Society for Clinical Pathology; Latin American Society of Parasitology & Tropical Medicine; Advisor to the Museum of Natural History, Bogotá; Executive Secretary, International Committee on Chagas Disease. *Publications:* Some 50 books and articles in professional journals etc. *Hobbies:* Tennis; Swimming; Climbing Mountains. *Address:* Laboratorio Microbiologia & Parasitologia, Unviersidad de Los Andes, Apartado Aereo 4976, Bogotá, Colombia.

GUIMARAES, Murilo José de Barros, b. 12 June 1952, Recife, Brazil. Assistant Professor; Chest Physician. m. Ana Christina Queiroz Monteiro, 26 Jan. 1973, Recife, 1 son, 1 daughter. *Education:* MD, Federal University of Pernambuco, 1976; Resident, Institute of Diseases of the Chest of Recife, 1977-78; Visiting Fellow, Cardiothoracic Institute, Brompton Hospital, England, 1979-80; MSc., Federal University of Pernambuco, 1983. *Appointments:* Physician, ICU, Hospital of IPSEP, Recife, 1977; Honorary Registrar, Pulmonary Medicine, Brompton Hospital, England, 1979-80; Assistant Professor, Faculty of Medical Sciences, University of Pernambuco; Chest Physician, Hospital of Public Servants of Pernambuco; Chest Physician, Portuguese Hospital, Recife. *Publications:* "Small Cell Bronchogenic Carcinoma : Present Concepts, Diagnostic Means and Prognosis", Thesis, 1982; "Lung Biopsy with Chiba Needle", 'Rev. Bras. Cirurgia', 1979; "Anomalies of Aortic Arches", 'Rev. Bras. Cirurgia', 1979; "Importance of Bronchofiberoscopy in the Staging of Lung Cancer", 'Jornal de Pneumologia', 1982; "CT Scannings of Thorax and Abdomen in the Staging of Lung Cancer", 'Jornal de Pneumologia', 1984; many other articles in professional journals. *Hobbies:* Stamp Collecting; Coin Collecting; Collecting Stamps of Bottled Beverages. *Address:* Av. Agamenon Magalhaes, 4261, Apto 801, Derby, Recife, 50.000, PE Brazil.

GULI, Edmondo Piero Gioggio, b. 17 July, 1929, Genoa, Italy. Chief of Hospital Division of Laboratory Medicine. m. Catherine Lindsay Yuncken, 24 May 1969, Melbourne, 2 daughters. *Education:* MD, Genoa, 1953, Diploma, Oncology, Pavia, 1956; Docente in Anatomical Pathology, Italy, 1961; MRCPath, 1970; FRCPA, 1971; FRCPath, 1982. *Appointments:* Lecturer, University of Pavia, Italy, 1953-54; Lecturer and Senior Lecturer in Pathology, University of Milan, 1955-62; NATO Scholar in Human Gentics, University of Birmingham, UK, 1962-63; Associate Professor, Acting Professor, and Chairman of Pathology, University of Siena, Italy, 1963-69; Associate Professor of Pathology and Immunology, Monash University, Melbourne, Australia, 1969-75; Director of Laboratory Medicine and Honorary Associate Professor, Queen Victoria Medical Centre, Melbourne, Australia, 1976-83; Chief, Division of Laboratory Medicine, The Royal Southern Memorial Hospital, Melbourne, Australia, 1983-. *Memberships:* Council Member and Member of Medical and Scientific Committee, Anti-Cancer Council of Victoria; Royal College of Pathologists, UK; Royal College of Pathologists of Australasia; Australian and New Zealand Society for Neuropathology; Human Genetic Society of Australasia; Australian Association of Neurolgoists; International Academy of Pathology; Australian Society of Pathology and Experimental Medicine. *Publications include:* "Anti-tumour Immunoreactivity in Colonic Carcinoma: A Guide to Early Recognition of Recurrence" in Australian and New Zealand Journal of Medicine, 1974; "Trisomy of Chromosome 18" in Handbook of Clinical Neurology Vol 42, 1981. *Honours:* Prize, University of Genoa, 1953; Golf Medal for Sciences, Society of Arts, Sciences and Letters, French Republic, 1961; NATO Scholarship in Human Genetics, 1962; Yearly Prizes for Scientific Work, Universities of Milan and Siena, 1962-67. *Hobbies:* Mechanics; Symbolic

Logic; Propositional Calculus. *Address:* 49 Talbot Road, Mount Waverley, Victoria 3149, Australia.

GUNN, John Charles, b. 6 June 1937, England, Professor of Forensic Psychiatry. *Education:* MBChB, Birmingham University Medical School; Acad DPM, Md, FRCPsych, Institute of Psychiatry; MD, Birmingham. *Appointments:* House Officer, Queen Elizabeth Hospital, Birmingham; Registrar, Maudsley Hospital; Research Worker, Senior Lecturer, Institute of Psychiatry; Director, Special Hospitals Research Unit. *Memberships:* Fellow of the Royal college of Psychiatrists; Member, British Medical Association; Fellow of the Royal Society of Medicine. *Publications:* "Violence in Human Society", 1973; "Epileptics in Prison", 1977; "Psychiatric Aspects of Imprisonment", 1978; 'The Relationship between Mental Disorder and Crime', 1977; 'Forensic Psychiatry as a Subspecialty', 1982; 'An Evaluation of Grendon Prison', 1982. *Honours:* Bronze Medal, RMPA, 1970. *Hobbies:* Walking; Photography; Opera; Theatre; Cinema. *Address:* Institute of Psychiatry, De Crespigny Park, Denmark Hill, London SE5 8AF, England.

GUPTA, Om Prakash, b. 5 July 1931, Gurgaon, India. Professor of Otolaryngology. m. Dr Saroj Gupta, 14 May 1960, New Delhi, 2 sons. *Education:* BSc, Agra University 1950; MBBS, Lucknow University, 1955; DO, Aligarh Muslim University, 1957; MS(ENT), Lucknow University, 1960. *Appointments:* Resident Surgical Officer/Registrar (ENT) 1959-60, Lecturer in ENT, Mar 1960-Sept 1960, Lucknow University; Reader in ENT, Medical College, Pondicherry, 1960-62; Reader in Otolaryngology, 1962-70, Professor of Otolaryngology 1970-, Banaras Hindu University. *Memberships:* Association of Otolarngologists of India; Fellow, International College of Surgeons; Indian Association for Advancement of Medical Education; Indian Society of Oncology; Faculty of Medicine and Academic Council, Banaras Hindu University. *Publications:* 99 papers in Indian and foreign journals. *Honours include:* Fellowship under sponsorship of US Agency for International Development for higher training in Otological Surgery in USA, 1965-66; Certificate for completing training in Otological Surgery, from Department of Health Education and Welfare, USA, 1966; Certificate of Achievement for successfully completing pariticpation in tecnical co-operation program under US Agency of International Development, 1966; Certificate of Participation in Seminar on Communication by Michigan Stat University, 1966; Mafatlal Gagalbhai Guest Lecturer Award, 1977, Laxmichand Bhagaji Guest Lecturer Award, 1978, L H Hirandani Guest Lecturer Award, 1980, Fransukhlal Hafatlal Guest Lecturer Award, 1983 all presented by the Association of Otolaryngologists of India. *Hobbies:* Photography; Badminton; Tennis. *Address:* Professor of Otolaryngology, 2-Medical Enclave, Banaras Hindu University, Varanasi-221 005, India.

GURFEIN, Hadassah Neiman, b. Brooklyn, New York, USA. Clinical Psychologist m. Elisa Gurfein, 31 July 1966, 3 sons. *Education:* BA, Barnard College, 1960; MA, CCNY, 1962; PhD, Fordham University, 1977. *Appointments:* Psychologist, Hadassah Hospital, Jerusalem, 1962-63; Psychologist, Clinical Fellow, Brooklyn College, 1963-64; Consultant Psychologist, L I Cons Center, 1963-64; School Psychologist, Lynbrook, New York also Fairfield, Connecticut, 1964-67; School Psychologist, Chairman, Child Study Team Dumont Public Schools New York, 1977-; Independent Practice, Psychotherapy, New York City, 1977; Part time Faculty Member, Department of Psychology, Fairleigh Dickinson University, 1977-78; Consultant Psychologist, Tourett Ticand Movement Disorder Clinic, Mount Sinai Hospital, New York City, 1981-; Clinical Instructor of Psychiatry, Mount Sinai School of Medicine, New York City, 1982-; Member Task Force, Mental Health Federation, Jewish

Philanthropies, 1981-. *Memberships:* American Psychological Association; Society of Clinical and Experimental Hypnosis; New York State Psychological Association; New Jersey Psychological Association; New Jersey Association of School Psychologists. *Honours:* Psi Chi; Phi Delta Kappa (Dissertation Award 1976). *Address:* 156, Sherwood Place, Englewood, NJ 07631, USA.

GUTHRIE, Anne, b. 3 Mar. 1941, Ayr, Scotland. Consultant Psychiatrist. m. dissolved, 1 son, 2 daughters. *Education:* MB ChB, DPM; MRC Psychiatry Member, Royal College of Psychiatrists. *Appointments:* House Physician, General Medicine, Stobhill General Hospital, Glasgow, Scotland, 1966-67; House Surgeon, General Surgery & Casualty, West Cumberland Hospital, Whitehaven, England, 1967; Post-registration House Physician in Neurology, Prof. J A Simpson Institute of Neurological Sciences, Glasgow, 1967-68; Registrar in Psychiatry, Gartnavel Royal Hospital, Glasgow 1968, Royal Dundee Liff & Maryfield Hospitals, 1968-70, (part-time) Sunnyside Royal Hospital, Montrose, 1972-75; Senior Registrar in Psychiatry, Dundee Psychiatric Services, 1975-78; Consultant Psychiatrist, Murray Royal & Murthly Hospitals, Scotland, 1978-81; Consultant Psychiatrist, Stratheden Hospital, Cupar, Fife, Scotland, 1981-83; Consultant Psychiatrist, Medical Director, St Brendan's Hospital, Bermuda, 1983-. *Memberships:* British Medical Association; Society for Study of Addiction to Alcohol & Other Drugs. *Publications:* Various articles in scientific & medical journals in Great Britian & USA. *Honours:* William Cullen Medal, Psychological Medicine, McKail Prize, Scare Prize, University of Glasgow Medical School, 1965; Scottish Hospitals Endowment Research Trust Grant 1975-78 for study of Early Cerebral Impairment in Alcoholism; World Health Organisation Fellow, 1977. *Hobbies:* Field Hockey; Road-running. *Address:* St Brendan's Hospital, Bermuda.

GUTIERREZ, Albert SJ, b. 28 Jan. 1920, Barcelona, Spain. Specialist Physician in Internal Medicine; Priest in the Society of Jesus. *Education:* Licentiate in Philosophy, Natural Sciences, Theology; MD. *Appointments:* Assistant, II University Clinic; Deputy Head Physician, Herz-Jesu Hospital; Head of Dialysis Unit, Vienna District Hospital Outpatients' Department; Internal Specialist, Outpatients' Department; Pastor of the Spanish-Speaking Community in Vienna. *Memberships:* Society of Jesus; Vienna Chamber of Physician. *Honours:* Commander, Order of Civil Merit, Spain. *Hobbies:* Music; Walking. *Address:* Rennweg 31, A-1030 Vienna, Austria.

GUTIERREZ-HERMOSILLO, Luis Elias, b. 12 Feb. 1942, Stockton, California, USA. Obstetrician and Gynaecologist. m. Martha G Suarez-Navarro, 12 July 1975, Guadalajara, Mexico, 1 son, 2 daughters. *Education:* BS, University of Santa Clara, USA; MD, University of Guadalajara, Mexico; PhD in Gynaecology, University of Guadalajara. *Appointments:* Chairman, Obstetrics and Gynaecology Department, Mexican-American Hospital, Guadalajara, Mexico; President, Obstetrics and Gynaecology Society of Guadalajara. *Memberships:* Fellow, American College of Obstetrics and Gynaecology; Fellow, American College of Surgeons; American Fertility Society; Latin American Group of Urogynecology and Vaginal Surgery. *Hobbies:* Gardening; Tennis. *Address:* Morelos 2122-B, 44680 Guadalajara, Jalisco, Mexico.

GUTTERIDGE, Bruce Heath, b. 10 Sep. 1928, Queensland, Australia. Senior Partner, Queensland Medical Laboratory. m. Elizabeth Mary Hodgkinson, 3 Dec. 1960, Brisbane, 1 son, 2 daughters. *Education:* MBBS, University of Queensland, 1951; DCP, University of London, 1956; FRCPA; FAACB; MIAC; FCAP; FIAC; FASMF. *Appointments:* Resident, Royal Brisbane Hospital, 1953; Registrar, Pathology, Royal Brisbane Hospital, 1955; Registrar, Chemical Pathology, 1956-57, Haematology, 1957-58, Royal Post Graduate Medical School of London; Senior Partner, Queensland medical Laboratory, 1959-; Senior Visiting Pathologist, Royal Brisbane Hospital, 1959-; Advisor, Pathology, Northern Command and Military Hospital, 1959-; Pathologist, 1 Australian Field Hospital, Vietnam, 1969; Director, Australian Sports Medicine Federation, Queensland Branch, 1983. *Memberships include:* Australian Medical Association; Association of Clinical Pathologists; Royal Collge of Pathologists of Australasia; American Society Clinical Pathologists; College American Pathologists; International Academy of Cytology; Australian Society of Cytology; etc. *Publications:* Numerous articles in professional journals including 'Therapeutic Nova'; 'British Medical Journal'; 'Medical Journal of Australia'; 'Annals of General Practice'; 'Australian Family Physician'; Australia, New Zealand, Journal of Medicine; etc. *Hobbies:* Skiing; Golf; Contract Bridge; Fine Art. *Address:* C/o Queensland Medical Laboratory, PO Box 410, West End, 4101 Brisbane, Queensland, Australia.

GUTTLER, Richard B., b. 19 June 1942, Chicago, Illinois, USA. Associate Clinical Professor of Medicine, University of Southern California School of Medicine. m. Delaney Ann, 1 June 1985, Malibu, 1 son, 2 daughters. *Education:* MD, University of Illinois, 1967. *Appointments include:* Director, Santa Monica Thyroid Diagnostic Centre, 1974-; Endocrine consultant, USC Rancho Los Amigos Hospital, 1969-84; National Institutes of Health Fellow, Thyroid, USC (Dr. J.T. Nicoloff), 1972-74; Resident/intern, LAC/USC Medical Centre, 1968-72. *Memberships include:* Fellow, American College of Physicians; American Federation for Clincial Research; American Thyroid Association; Affiliated member, Royal Society of Medicine, London, UK; American Boards, Internal Medicine, Endocrine; etc. *Publications include:* Contributions to various professional journals; Major research interests, pathogenesis of sporadic goiter & toxic nodular goiter, newer methods to evaluate the thyroid nodule, mechanism of action of throid hormones, pathogenesis of Graves' disease. *Honours:* Alpha Omega Alpha, 1966; NIH Fellowship Grant, 1972-74; Royal Society Travelling Fellowship, UK, 1974; Visiting Professor, Medical School, Papua New Guinea, 1980; Visitng Lecturer, Nairobi, Kenya, 1978. *Hobbies:* Long distance walking; Reading novels; World travel. *Address:* 1260 15th Street, Suite 1105, Santa Monica, CA 90404, USA.

GYDIKOV, Alexander, b. 7 Apr. 1929, Vidin, Bulgaria. Professor of Physiology. m. Vera Dimitrova Gydikova, 23 Jan. 1955, 2 daughters. *Education:* PhD 1961, MD 1966. *Appointments:* Bulgarian Academy of Sciences: Scientific Collaborator, 1957, Senior Scientific Collaborator 1962, Professor of Physiology, 1927, Deputy Director, Centre of Biology, 1976, Director, Central Laboraotry of Biophysics, 1982. *Membership:* IUPS Commission on Motor Control, 1973-79. *Publications:* "Cybernetics & Cortical Control of Movements", 1964; "Microstructure of the Voluntary Movements in Man", 1969; "The Theoretical Basis of Electromyogarphy", 1975; "Motor Control", 1973 (editor). *Honour:* Dimitrov Award for Science, 1976. *Address:* Central Laboratory of Biophysics, Acad G Bontchev Str b1 21, Sofia 1113, Bulgaria.

GYE, Richard Spencer Butler, Professor, Dean, Medicine, University of Sydney, Australia. *Education:* MA, D.Phil, Oxon; MB, BS, BSc (Med); FRCS; FRACS. *Appointments:* Sub-Lieutenant, RANR, 1945-47; RMO, Registrar, Roy Prince Alfred Hospital, 1955-60; Temporary Lecturer, Surgery, University of Sydney, 1960-61; Nuffield Dominion Travelling Fellowship, Oxford, 1961; Graduate Assistant and Senior Registrar, Neurological

Surgery, Oxford, 1962-64; Senior Lecturer, Associate Professor, Surgery, University of Syndey; Honorary Neurosurgeon, Roy Prince Alfred Hospital; Visiting Medical Officer, Concord Repal Hospital; Head, Neurological Surgery, Radcliffe Infirmary, Oxford, 1971-74; Honorary Consultant Surgeon, various Hospitals. *Memberships:* Board of Directors, Royal Alexandra Hospital for Children, Parramatta Hospitals and United Dental Hospital, New South Wales State Cancer Cl.; Sydney Committee, Ludwig Institute of Cancer; Research Director, Sir Robert Menzies Memorial Trust; Deputy Chairman, National Foundation; Chairman, Scientific Advisory Committee, Spinal Research Foundation; etc. *Address:* 14 Stanhope Road, Killara, NSW 2071, Australia.

GYHRA, Alberto Raul, b. 5 Jan, 1942, Concepción, Chile. Professor. m. Maria Imschenetzky, 8 Apr. 1967, Nacimiento, Chile, 1 son. *Appointments:* Instructor in Physiopathology, 1966-69; Instructor in Surgery, 1969-73; Auxilliary Professor in Surgery, 1973-75; Professor of Surgery, 1976-, Head of Cardiothoracic Team Hospital G Grant B, Concepción Chile, Director, Post-graduate Program, Faculty of Medicine, University of Concepción. *Memberships:* Medical Society of Concepción; Chilean Society of Thorax; Chilean Surgical Society; Chilean Society of Cardiology & Cardiovascular Surgery; American College of Surgeons; American College of Chest Physicians; Chilean Pediatrics Society; International Bronchoesophagical Society; Medical Society of Nuble. *Publications:* Various articles in scientific journals. *Honours:* Paul Hawley Guest International, American College of Surgeons, 1979; Virginio Gomez Award, Medical Society of Concepción, 1967. *Hobby:* Golf. *Address:* Martin Garcia Onez de Loyola 21, Lomas de San Andrés, Concepción, Chile.

GYORKOS, Theresa Walburga, b. 9 Apr. 1953, Canada. Faculty Lecturer, Department of Epidemiology and Biostatistics. *Educations:* PhD, Department of Epidemiology and Biostatistics, McGill University, 1985. *Appointments* Information Scientist, Institute of Parasitology, McGill University, 1976-82; Faculty Lecturer, Department of Epidemiology and Paiostatistics, 1985-. *Memberships:* Canadian Society for Tropical Medicine and International Health (Board of Directors), 1984-85; Chairman, Scientific Programme Committee, 1984-85; Chairman, Research Committee, 1985-86); Canadian Public Health Association; Canadian Society of Zoologists. *Publications:* A Comparative Study to Determine the Effects of Screening for Intestinal Parasites in newly-arrived Southeast Asian Refugees, PhD thesis, 1985; "Estimation of Parasite Prevalence based on Submissions to Provincial Laboratories, Canadian Journal of Public Health, 1983. *Honours:* IODE War Memorial Scholarship, 1980-82; PhD Fellowship, National Health and Welfare, 1981-84. *Address:* Department of Epidemiology and Biostatistics, McGill University, Purvis Hall, 1020 Pine Avenue West, Montreal, Quebec, Canada, H3A 1A2.

H

HAAB, Otto P., b. 19 Apr 1932, Zurich, Switzerland. Specialist in Internal Medicine and Haematology. m. Ingeborg K Peyer, 23 May 1959, Zuerich, 1 son, 2 daughters. *Education:* MD, University of Zuerich, Switzerland, 1959. *Appointments:* Intern, Resident, University of Salt Lake City, Utah, USA, 1963; Resident, University of Zuerich, Switzerland, 1969; Currently: Private Practice in Internal Medicine, Specialist in Haematology and Oncology, Zuercih, Switzerland. *Memberships:* American Society of Clinical Oncology; Swiss Society of Haematology; Swiss Society of Onclogy; International Society of Haematology. *Address:* Talstrasse 65, 8001 Zurich, Switzerland.

HAANEN, Clemens, b. 28 Dec. 1924, Amsterdam, The Netherlands. Professor, Haematology. m. Magda Rosier, 10 Jan. 1953. *Education:* MD, Medical School, PhD, University of Amsterdam. *Appointments:* Head, Out-patient Dept., 1961, Lecturer, 1967, Assistant Professor, 1969, Professor, Haematology, University of Nijmegen. *Memberships:* Councillor, International Society of Hematology, 1973-77; President, Netherland Society of Haematology, 1974-78; Councillor, Societé de médecin Interne Cancérologique, 1976-78; Netherlands Council for Health Research; Scientific Council, Institute of Radiation Pathology of the University of Leyden, 1978-83; Netherlands Cancer Institute, Amsterdam,1977-; Chariman, Leukemias and Hematosarcomas Cooperative Group, 1979-82; Member, Chairman, Advisory Committees, National Council for Health; Elected Member, Royal Netherlands Academy of Arts & Sciences, 1981; Invited, Vistiting Professor, haematology, M.S McLeod Fellowship Foundation, University of Adelaide, Australia, 1984. *Address:* 87 St Annastraat, NL 6524 EJ Nijmegen, The Netherlands.

HABER, Richard William, b. 22 Jan. 1933, Krakow, Poland. Consultant Physician. m. Edna Hochdorf, 12 Aug. 1982, Sydney, Australia, 2 sons, 1 daughter. *Education:* MB; BS:FRACP. *Appointments Include:* JRMO, Royal North Shore Hospital, Sydney, 1957; SRMO, Alfred Hospital, Melbourne, 1958; Registrar in Neurosurgery 1950, Fellow in Thoracic Medicine 1960, Royal Prince Alfred Hospital; Medical Registrar, Prince Henry Hospital, 1961-62; Honorary Physician, Fairfield District Hospital, 1962-66; Senior Visiting Specialist Physician, 1963-69; Clinical Teacher in Medicine, University of New South Wales, 1966-81; Consultant Physician in Private Practice; Visiting Physician, Prince Henry and Auburn District Hospitals. *Memberships:* Royal Australasian College of Physicians; Cardiac Society of Australia and New Zealand; Australian Medical Association; Fellowship of Jewish Doctors. *Publications:* 'Carcinoma of Lung - Results of Treatment', (with Dr Rowan Nicks), 1961; 'A review of 995 Cases of Primary Carcinoma of Lung', 1964; 'Pulmonary Hydatid Disease', (with Dr A F Grant), 1961. *Honours:* 2nd class honours on graduation, University of Sydney, 1957; Sir Harold Dew Prize, Sydney University, 1966; Recipient of Public Exhibition, University of Sydney. *Hobbies:* Tennis; Skiing; Travelling. *Address:* 183 Macquarie Street, Sydney, New South Wales 2000, Australia.

HACKETT, Mary-Jo, b. 12 Oct. 1940, New Jersey, USA. Founder and Working President of Rehab Consulting Service. m. Joseph E Hackett, 20 Jan. 1968, New Jersey, USA. *Education:* Registered Nurse, St. Mary's Hospital, Orange, New Jersey, USA, 1961, BA, Health Education and Nursing, City State College, 1965; Certification of Insurance Rehabilitation Specialist, 1985. *Appointments:* Head Nurse, Orthopaedic/Medical, Memorial General Hospital, 1961-65; Rehabilitation Nurse Consultant,

Liberty Mutual Insurance Company, 1965-75; Rehabilitation Specialist/Working President, Rehabi Consulting Service, 1975-present. *Memberships:* Association of Rehabilitation Nurses; National Rehabilitation Association; Rehabilitation Insurance Nurses Group; National Head Injury Foundation. *Honours:* 10 years of repetitive assignments from 40 major insurance companies. *Hobby:* Speciality areas of work. *Address:* Rehab Consulting Service, 40 Eisenhower Drive, Paramus, NJ 07652, USA.

HADDEN, Ronald Charles Munday, b. 26 Aug. 1917, Batavia, Java, Dutch East Indies. Private Consultant Radiotherapist. m. *Education:* MRCS; LRCP; DMR(Eng); ADMR(Lond); St. Thomas' Hospital Medical School, University of London. *Appointments include:* Consultant Radiotherapist, Torbay Hospital, Torquay, North Devon Infirmary, Barnstaple, Royal Devon & Exeter Hospital, Exeter; Director, School of Radiography, Exeter, retired 1982; Adviser, Radiation Hazards Committee, University of Exeter, current; Medical officer, Medical Advisory Service, Department Ionising Radiations (Area), current; Consultant Radiotherapist, Launceston General Hospital & Royal Hobart Hospital, Tasmania, Australia, 1984. *Memberships:* Faculty of Radiologists; Life member, British Institute of Radiology; BIR 'Larynx fractionation trials'. *Publications include:* 'Radiotherapy' in Butterworth's "Encyclopaedia of General Practice", In preparation, "Treatment of breast cancer by local excision/radiotherpay", "Cancer of the larynx". *Honour:* Anatomy prize, St. Thomas's Hospital, 1935. *Hobbies:* Philately; Oenology. *Address:* Hylton House, 10 Barnfield Hill, Exeter, Devon, England.

HAERLE, Franz, b. 17 July 1937, Berlin, Federal Republic of Germany, Head of Department, Oral and Maxillofacial Surgery, m. 4 Jan 1964, Bremen, 2 sons, 1 daughter. *Education:* Medical Diploma, 1962; MD, 1963; Med dent Diploma, 1964; Oral and Maxillofacial Surgery, 1969; Habilitation, 1971; Dr Med Dent, 1972; Plastic Surgeon, 1976; Professor, 1978. *Appointments:* Assistnat, Oral and Maxillofacial University Hospital, Freiburg, FRG, 1966-70; 2 Oberarzt, 1971-75, 1 Oberarzt, 1976-79, Head of Department, 1980-, Oral and Maxillofacial Surgery, University Hospital, Kiel, FRG. *Memberships:* Arbeitsgemeinschaft für Kieferchirurgie; Deutsche Ges für ZMK-Heilkunde; Deutsche Ges für MKG-Chir; Deutsche Ges für Plast u wie-derherstellungs-Chir; European Association Maxillofacial Surgery; International Association Oral and Maxillofacial Surgery. *Publications:* 'Die Zeitwahl der Osteoplastik bei LKG-Spalten', 1974; 'Le traitement chirurgical des fractures du cadre periobitaire', 1978; 'Surgical Correction in dentofacial Deformities', 1980; 'A Review of mandibular ridge Augmentation procedures: Proceedings Consensus Conference: The Relation Role of Vestibuloplasty and Ridge Augmentation in the management of the Atrophic mandible', 1984. *Honours:* Wassmund Preis, 1971. *Hobbies:* Skiing; Surfing; Fishing; Sailing. *Address:* Reventlouallee 5, D-2300 Kiel, Federal Republic of Germany.

HAGEN, Paul Beo, b. 15 Feb. 1920, Sydney, Australia. Professor of Pharmacology. m. Jean Himms, 29 Sep. 1956, Abingdon, England, 2 daughters. *Education:* MB, BS, University of Sydney, Australia, 1939-45. *Appointments:* Intern, Balmam Hospital, 1945-46; Resident Medical Officer, Lidcombe Hospital, 1946-48; Lecturer in Physiology 1948-50, Senior Lecturer 1950-51, Postgraduate Supervisor in Physiology 1949-51, University of Sydney; Senior Lecturer in Physiology, University of Queensland, 1951-52; Research Fellow in Pharmacology, Oxford University, England, 1952-54; Assistant Professor of Pharmacology, Yale University, USA, 1954-56; Assistnat Professor of

Pharmacology 1956-59, Director of NIH postgraduate training programme in pharmacology 1957-59, Harvard University; Professor and Chairman, Biochemistry Department, University of Manitoba Canada, 1959-64; Professor and Chairman, Biochemistry Department, Queen's University, Ontario, 1964-67; Director, National Research Council of Canada, 1967-68; Dean of Graduate Studies 1968-83, Professor and Interim Chairman, Pharmacology Department 1983-86, University of Ottawa. *Memberships:* Physiology Society, Great Britain; British Pharmacological Society; American Society of Pharmacology; Chairman of Biochemistry section 1963-64, Chemical Institute of Canada; American Association for the Advancement of Science; Ontario Medical Association. *Publications include:* 'Storage and release of catecholamines', 1959; 'The adrenal medulla and biosynthesis of pressor amines', 1956; 'Storage and release of amines in the chromaffin cell', 1960; 'Biosynthesis of indolealkylamines', 1965. *Honours:* C J Martin Felowship, Oxford, 1952; Fulbright Fellowship, 1954; Lederle Faculty Award, Yale, 1956; Fellowship, Chemical Institute of Canada, 1961; Jubilee Medal, 1977. *Hobbies:* Mountain hiking; Gardening. *Address:* Department of Pharmacology, University of Ottawa Medical School, Ottawa, Ontario K1H 8M5, Canada.

HAFFNER, Jon. b. 2 Mar 1940, Oslo, Norway. Consultant, Surgical Gastroenterology. m. Kokko, 1965, 1 son 2 daughters. *Memberships:* President, Norwegian Surgical Society; National Secretary, Nordic (Scandinavian) Surgical Society; National Representative, Internaitonal Federation of Surgical Colleges; IFS; CICD; ESSR. *Publications:* 'The Exitatory Adrenergic Response in Gastric Smooth Muscle' Oslo, 1973 (Thesis); 'Kirurgisk gastroenterologi' Oslo, 1985; Articles mainly on Surgical Gastroenterology 1967-85. *Address:* Department of Surgery, Ullevaal Hospital, (Oslo University), 0407 Oslo 4, Norway.

HAGES, Richard Joseph, b. 5 Nov. 1954, Bay City, Michigan, USA. Chiropractic Clinic Director. m. Cheryl Ann Wahlen, 20 Nov. 1981, New Orleans, Louisiana, 1 daughter. *Education:* DC, Palmer College of Chiropractic, 1975; Postgraduate, University of New Orleans, 1975-78; Postgraduate, National College of Chiropractic, 1978-81; Diplomate, National Board of Chiropractic Examiners. *Appointments:* Staff Doctor, Causeway Clinic, Metairie, Louisiana, 1975-77; Baker Clinic, Barton Rouge, 1977-78; Chiropractic Consultant, Louisiana Insurance and Legal Professions, 1978-83; Training Director, City of Kenner Civil Defence, 1983; Owner, Clinic Director, David Drive Chiropractic Clinic, Metairie, 1978-. *Memberships:* Council on Sports Injuries, American Chiropractic Association; Sacroocccipital Society Internation; Parker Chiropractic Research Society; Board of Directors 1983-84, Chiropractic Association of Louisiana; Motion Palpation Institute; Palmer College Alumni Association. *Honours:* Clinical Excellence Award, Palmer College, 1975; Appreciation Awards, Chiropractic Association of Louisiana, 1978 and 1984. *Address:* 2614 David Drive, Metairie, LA 70003, USA.

HAGLER, Henry James, b. 23 July 1941, Columbia, South Carolina, USA. Scientific Administrator. m. Jean Smith, 25 July 1964, 1 son 1 daughter. *Education:* BS, Biology, Wake Forest University, 1963; PhD, Physiology, Bowman Gray School of Medicine, Wake Forest University, 1969; Postdoctoral Trainee Mental Health Research Institute, University of Michigan, 1969-71. *Appointments:* Research Associate, Department of Psychiatry, Yale Univeristy 1971-74; Assistant Professor, 1974-80, Associate Professor and Director of Graduate Studies, 1980-82, Department of Pharmacology, Emory University; Section Head, CNS Pharmacology, G D Searle and Co., Skokie,

Illinois, 1982-. *Memberships:* Society for Neuroscience (President, Atlanta Chapter 1980-81); Society for Pharmacology and Experimental Therapeutics; American Association for the Advancement of Science. *Publications:* 'Serotonin Receptors in the Brain' in 'Fred.Proc.' 1977; with G K Aghajanian; 'Morphine and methionine-enkephalin differential effects' in 'J Pharmacol Exp Therap' 1980 with D A Hosford; 'Putative nociceptive neurotransmitters' in 'Life Sciences' 1981 with D D Spring. *Honour:* Magistral Lecturer Headace 80: Neurological Congress in Florence, Italy. *Hobbies:* Carpentry; Acrylic painting; Computers. *Address:* Section Head, CNS Pharmacology, 4901 Searle Parkway, Skokie, IL 60077, USA.

HAHN, Werner, b. 7 Mar. 1912, Trier, Germany. Director, Heinrich-Hammer Institute for Postgraduate Education, Kiel. m. G. Martini, 24 Oct. 1942, Berlin, 1 son, 2 daughters. *Education:* Dr.med; Dr.med.dent; Professor. *Appointments:* Surgical Department of Dental School; Berlin, 1936-40; Munster, 1952-62; Kiel, 1962-80 *Memberships:* I.A. of Oral Surgeons; I.A. of Cytology; Fed. Dent. Int. core and SPE Member; German Association for Dental Mouth and Jaw Disease; Member, Golden Needle, 1982. *Honour:* Gold Medal, Bologna, 1954; German Society of Medical Law. *Hobby:* Segeln. *Address:* Danziger Str. 10, 2300 Kiel 17, Democratic Republic of Germany.

HAIDER, Zulfiqar, b. 24 May 1930, Lahore, Pakistan. Physician and Director of Research Unit. m. Yasmin Zahra, 11 Nov. 1968, Lahore, 1 son. *Education:* MB BS, Punjab University, King Edward Medical College, Lahore, 1953; DTM&H, London School of Tropical Medicine, London, England, 1959; Member 1963, Fellow 1976, Royal College of Physicians, Edinburgh, Scotland. *Appointments include:* Medical Officer, Mayo Hospital, Lahore, Pakistan, 1955-58; Registrar, Seacroft Hospital, Leeds, England, 1961-63; Registrar, Halifax General Hospital, 1964-65; Physician 1965-66, Honorary Physician 1967-69, Pakistan Medical Research Council Medical Research Centre, Ganga Ram Hospital, Lahore, Pakistan; Fellow in Clinical Haematology, Department of Medicine, General Hospital, Ottawa, Canada, 1966-67; Resident in Neurology, University Hospital, Baltimore, USA, 1969-70; Head Physician in Charge, Pakistan Medical Research Council Clinical Research Unit, Ganga Ram Hospital and Fatimah Jinnah Medical College, Lahore, Pakistan, 1970-. *Memberships:* British Medical Association; Pakistan Medical Association; Fellow, Royal College of Physicians of Edinburgh; New York Academy of Sciences. *Publications include:* Nearly 60 research publications on Diabetes, Hypertension, Lipids and Liver disorders including: "Risk factors for Coronary Heart Disease in Pakistan", (co-author); "Diabetes Mellitus in Pakistan: A Seven Year Study in Retrospect", 1982; "Hypertension: A Study in lahore", 1984. *Hobbies:* Reading history and biography; Gardening; Agriculture; Tennis. *Address:* PMRC Clinical Research Unit, F J Medical College, Lahore, Pakistan.

HAJNAL, John, b. 26 Nov. 1924, Darmstadt, Federal Republic of Germany. Professor of Statistics. m. Nina Lande, 10 Sep. 1950, New York, USA, 1 son, 3 daughters. *Education:* Ma, University of Oxford, England, 1941-44. *Appointments:* Research Assistant, Royal Commission on Population, London, 1944-48; Statistician, United Nations, New York, USA, 1948-51; Office of Population Research, Princeton, New Jersey, 1951-53; Lecturer in Medical Statistics, University of Manchester, England, 1953-57; Lecturer in Demography 1957, Reader in Demography, Reader in Statistics, Currently Professor of Statistics, London School of Economics, London. *Memberships:* Royal Statistical Society; International Statistical Institute; International Union for the Scientific Study of

Population. *Publications:* 'A Method for Testing Analgesics in Rheumatoid Arthritis Using a Sequential Procedure', (with J SHarp and A J Popert), 1959; 'Artificial Insemination and the Frequency of Incestuous Marriages', 1961; 'Concepts of Random Mating and the Frequency of Consanguineous Marriages', 1963. *Honour:* Fellow of the British Academy, 1966. *Address:* London School of Economics, Houghton Street, London WC2A 2AE, England.

HAKANSSON, John Doren, b. 27 May 1947, Arvika, Sweden, Clinical Instructor, Department of Operative Dentisry, Karolinska Institute, Stockholm, 1980-; Private Practitioner, Kungsgatan, 1980-. *Education:* LDS, Karolinska Institute, Stockholm. *Appointments:* Practising Dentist, Public Health Service, Visby, Sweden, 1972-75; 1979-80; Instructor, Department of Operative Dentistry, University of Alabama, Birmingham, Alabama, USA, 1976-78. *Memberships:* Member, Swedish Dental Association and Lokal, Stockholm. *Address:* Kungsgarten 72, 11122 Stockholm, Sweden.

HALDEMAN, Scott, b. 23 June 1943, Canada. Consulting Neurologist. m. Joan Surridge, 27 Nov. 1965, Pretoria, South Africa, 2 sons. *Education:* DC, Palmer College of Chiropractic, 1964; BSc., 1968, MSc., 1970, University of Pretoria; PhD, 1973, MD, 1976, University of British Columbia; FCCS; FRCP(C). Private Practice, Chiropractic, 1964-77; Lecturer, Canadian Memorial Chiropractic College, 1970; Internship Medicine, 1976-77; Resident, Neurology, 1977-80; Assistant Adjunct Professor, Neurology, University of California, Irvine, 1980-81; Attending Physician, Lond Beach VA Medical Centre, 1980-81; Private Practice, Neurology, 1981-. *Memberships Include:* American Academy of Neurology; Orange County medical Society; California & American Medical Associations; International Society for the Study of the Lumbar Spine; American Back Society; North American Spine Association; North American Academy of Manipulative Medicine; American Chiropractic Association; International Chiropractic Association; etc. *Publications Include:* Editorial Board, 'Manual medicine', 1984-; Editorial Board, Australian Chiropractic Association, 1983; Advisory Council, various societies; Articles in numerous scientific journals including: 'American Chiropractic Association Journal'; 'Journal Canadian Chiropractic Association'; 'South African Medical Journal'; 'Brain Research'; 'Journal Neurochemistry'; 'Urology'; 'Gastroenterology'; etc. *Honours Include:* Pi Tau Delta; various prizes from Universities; Chiropractor of the Year, South African Chiropractors Association, 1968; Palmer College Alumni Award, 1968; South African Medical Research Council Overseas Study Bursary, 1972; Research Fellowship, Foundation for Chiropractic Education & Research, 1975; Honorary DSc., Western States Chiropractic College, 1981. *Address:* 1125 East 17th St., Suite W127, Santa Ana, CA 92701, USA.

HALE, Jacqueline Dee, b. 14 Jan. 1944, Battle Creek, Michigan, USA. Captain, US Air Force Nursing Corps. *Education:* Nursing diploma, Borgess School of Nursing, 1965; BSN, Marquette University, 1968; MS, University of Michigan, 1976. *Appointments:* Staff Nurse, Hospital Supervisor, Neurosurgical Clinical Specialist, Medical-Surgical Clinical Specialist, Leila Hospital, Battle Creek, 1965-80; Assistant Education Coordinator, Wright-Patterson Air Force Base, 1980-81; Charge Nurse, ibid, 1981-82; Flight Nurse/Flight Nurse Instructor, 1982-84, Clark Air Force Base, Philippines; Education Coordinator, Chanute Air Force Base, Illinois, 1984-85; Intermediate Supervisor, School of Health Care Science, Sheppard Air Force Base, Texas, 1985-. *Memberships:* Texas Nurses Association; Continuing Education Council,

American Nurses Association; Air Force Association; Aerospace Medical Association. *Honours:* Honour graduate, Flight Nurse, 1981; Commendation medals, 1982, 1983. *Hobbies:* Hot air ballooning; Horseback riding; Snow skiing. *Address:* 1710 Pearlie Drive, Wichita Falls, TX 76306-2212, USA.

HALIKIS, Spyros Emanuel, b. 29 Aug. 1925, Greece. Dental Surgeon. m. Maria Kailis, 4 Dec. 1949, Perth, Western Australia, 1 son, 2 daughters. *Education:* BDSc; Fellow, International College of Dentists. *Appointments Include;* Assistant Superintendent, Perth Dental Hospital, 1959-62; Member, Dental Board of Western Australia, 1972-75; Faculty of Dental Science, University of Western Australia, 1972-75; Board of Regents, International College of Dentists, Australasian Section; Executive Cocuncil, Asian Pacific Dental Federation; Consultant, Federation Dentaire International: Dental Surgeon in private general practice. *Memberships:* Australian Dental Association; International College of Dentists; International Association of Dental Research; Federation Dentaire International; Pierre Fauohard Academy; Greek-Australian Professional and Businessman's Association of Western Australia. *Publications Include:* 'The variation of eruption of permanent teeth and loss of deciduous teeth in Western Australia', parts I-IV, 1961-62; 'A study of dental caries in a group of Western Australian children', parts I-IV, 1962-65. *Honours:* Member of the Order of Australia, 1983; Honorary Life Member, Australian Dental Association Western Australian Branch, 1983. *Hobbies:* Stamp Collecting; Reading; Music. *Address:* 6 Hale Street, North Beach, Western Australia 6020, Australia

HALIKOWSKI, Boguslaw Kazimierz, b. 1 Mar. 1914, Brody. Director, Paediatric Institute. m. Jadwiga Guz, 23 Oct. 1942, Tarnopol, 5 daughters. *Education:* MD, John Casimir University, Lwow. *Appointments:* County Hospital, Przemysl; Children's Dept., Tuberculosis, Institute of Tuberculosis, Warsaw; Paediatric Dept., Medical academy, Gdansk; Paediatric Department, Medical Academy, Krakow; Institute of Paediatrics, Pomeranian Medical Academy, Szczecin; Child Health Centre, Warsaw; Paediatric Dept., University Rene Descartes V, Paris, France; Director, Paediatric Institute, Pomeranian Medical Academy, Szczecin, Poland. *Memberships:* European Society of Paediatric Research; International Association of Child Neurology; European Society of Social Paediatrics; International College of Paediatrics; Committee of Neurological Sciences of the Polish Academy of Sciences, Committee of Metablism. *Publications:* 106 scientific papers and clinical reports; 39 book chapters, learned articles; 1 monographic book, "Pneumonia in Children", 1968. *Honours:* Award, West German J. Korczak Society, 1979. *Hobbies:* Climbing; Music; History of Science. *Address:* Zawadzkiego 59/4, 71-246 Szczecin, Poland.

HALL, Eric John, b. 5 July 1933, England, Professor of Radiology, Columbia University, New York, USA. m. Bernice Williams, 27 July 1957, England, 1 son. *Education:* BSc, University College, London, 1953; DPhil, Oriel College, Oxford, 1962; MA Honoris causa, 1966, Dsc 1977. *Appointments include:* Fulbright Exchange Scholar, Visiting Assistant Professor of Radiological Physics, University of Colorado, USA, 1962-63; Principal Physicist, Churchill Hoispital Oxford, UK, 1963-68; Professor of Radiology, Columbia University, 1968-; Radiation Biologist, Radiology Service, Presbyterian Hospital, New York, 1983-; Director, Radiological Research Laboratory, 1984-. *Memberships:* British Institute of Radiology; Radiation Research Society; Association for Radiation Research; Hospital Physicists Association; Radiological Society of North America; American Society for Therapeutic Radiology & Oncology. *Publications Include:* "Radiobiology for the Radiologist", 1973, 1978; "Radiation & Life",

1976, 1985. *Honours:* Roentgen Award, British Institute of Radiology, 1976; Barclay Medal, ibid, 1983; Marie Curie Gold Medal, Health Physics Society, 1983; Memorial Lecturer, numerous societies, 1975-; Honorary Memberships, fellowship; Special Keynote Speaker, ASTRO, 1985. *Address:* Columbia University, College of Physicians & Surgeons, 630 West 168th Street, New York, NY 10032, USA.

HALL, Neil Rex, b. 12 Jan. 1933, Parramatta, New South Wales, Australia. Private Restorative Dental Practice. m. Judith Ann Holmes, 2 June 1956, Parramatta, 2 sons, 1 daughter. *Education:* BDS, University of Sydney; Created a Dental Colour Atlas, enabling tooth colour to be estimated and reproduced accurately. *Appointments:* General Dental Practice, Tumut, 1955, London 1957-62, Wahroonga, 1963-77; Private Restorative Dental Practice; Research Affiliate, Operative Dentistry, University of Sydney. *Memberships:* Australian Dental Association; International Society of Ceramics; Colour Society of Australia; Inaugural President, Dental Aesthetics and Ceramics Society. *Hobbies:* Art; Golf; Represented University of Sydney at Cricket and Rugby. *Address:* 229 Macquarie Street, Sydney 2000, Australia.

HALL, Roger Kingsley, b. 18 Aug. 1934, Australia. Chief Dental Surgeon, Royal Children's Hospital, Melbourne. m. Veronica Kertesz, 13 Sep. 1973, Melbourne, 3 sons, 2 daughters. *Education:* BDSc., 1956, MDSc., 1962, University of Melbourne; FRACDS. *Appointments:* House Officer, Royal Dental Hospital, Melbourne, 1956-57; Clinical Demonstrator, Dental faculty, University of Melbourne, 1958; Registrar, Eastman Dental Hospital, London, 1959-60; Chief Dental Surgeon, Royal Children's Hospital, 1960-; Lecturer, Senior Clinical Demonstrator, Conservative Dentistry and Dental Medicine & Surgery, and Paediatrics, University of Melbourne, 1971-. *Memberships:* International Association of Dentistry for Children, President, 1985-87; International Association of Dentistry for the Handicapped; International Association of Oral Surgeons; International Association for Dental Research; International Association Dento-Maxillofacial Radiology. *Publications:* 24 publications, 4 book chapters including "Ten Year Survey of Traumatic Injuries to Face & Jaws in Children". 1985; "Dental Management of the Chronically Ill Child", 1979; "Temporomandibular Joint Injuries in Children", 1974; "Injuries of Face & Jaws of Children", 1972. *Honours:* Ernest Joske Memorial Prize, 1956;. *Hobbies:* Photography; Gardening; Golf; Wine and Food; Ballet; Music; Film; Many Sports. *Address:* Dept. of Dentistry, Royal Children's Hospital, Flemington Road, Parkville, Victoria 3052, Australia.

HALLIDAY, William Ross, b. 9 May 1924, USA. Medical Director, Middle Tennessee Back Care Centre. m. Eleanore Hartvedt, 2 July 1951, Seattle, 1 son, 2 daughters. *Education:* BA, Swarthmore College; MD, George Washington University; FCCP; FACM. *Appointments:* Private Practice, Thoracic Surgery, 1957-65; Medical Consultant, Chief Medical Consultant, Medical Director, Washington State Department of Labour and Industries, Seattle and Olympia, Washington, 1965-76; Medical Director, Washington State Division of Vocational Medicine and Rehabilitation Medicine, Northwest Occupational Health Clinic, Seattle, 1983-84; Medical Director, Northwest Vocational Rehabilitation Group, Seattle, 1984; Medical Director, Middle Tennessee Back Care Centre, 1984-. *Memberships:* American Academy of Algology; American College of Chest Physicians; American College of Legal Medicine; American Congress of Rehabilitation Medicine; American Federation for Clinical Research ; American Medical Association; Charter Member, American Pain Society; International Association for the Study of Pain,

Founding Member; King County Medical Society; National Rehabilitation Association; Society of Thoracic Surgeons, Founding Member; Washington State Medical Association. *Publications:* "Rehabilitation of Injured Workmen with Psychosocial Handicaps", Chapter 17, 'Compensation in Psychiatric Disability and Rehabilitation', 1971; various articles, 1954-. *Honours:* Essay Prize, American College of Chest Physicians, 1953. *Hobbies:* Outdoor and Spelean Activities. *Address:* 209 Ward Circle, Brentwood, TN 37203, USA.

HALPERN, Daniel, b. 28 May 1917, New York, USA. Adjunct Professor, Rehabilitation Medicine, University of Wisconsin. m. Marylyn R. Johnson, 13 Dec. 1943, Chicago, 2 sons, 1 daughter. *Education:* BA, New York Univeristy, 1936; MD, Chicago Medical School, 1944; Fellow, Rehabilitation medicine, New York Medical College, Bird S. Coler Hospital, New York, 1961. *Memberships:* American Academy for Cerebral Palsy; American Academy of Paediatrics; American Acadmey of Physical Medicine and Rehabilitation; American Congress of Rehabilitation Medicine; American Association for Advancement of Science; American Association of University Professors. *Publications:* Numerous articles in professional journals including: 'Archives of Physical Medicine and Rehabilitation'; 'Minnesota Medicine'; 'Pathophysiology and Management'; Book Chapters include: 'Physical Therapy of Pulmonary Obstructive Disease', in'New Perspective in Chronic Respiratory Diseases in Children and Adolescents', 1970; 'Rehabilitaiton of Children with Brain Damage', in'Krusen's Handbook of Physical Medicine and Rehabilitation', 1982; etc. *Hobby:* Sailing. *Address:* Dept. of Rehabilitation Medicine, University of Wisconsin Clinical Science Centre, 600 Highland Ave., E3 352, Madison, WI 53792, USA.

HALPERT, Bernard, b. 26 May 1920, Brooklyn, New York, USA. Laboratory Director. m. Nancy Sager, 16 Aug. 1946, New York, 1 son, 3 daughters. *Education:* BA, Brooklyn College, 1940, BS, ibid, 1941; VMT, Army Medical School, 1942; Biotechnology, Carnegie Institute of Technology, 1943; MA, Hofstra University, 1954. *Appointments:* Chief Chemist, Puritan Dairies; Supervisor, Gardner Industries; Executive Director, Hempstead General Hospital; Direcotr, Williamsburg Laboratories; Director, Biometric Affiliated Research Laboratories; Executive Director, Biologic Consultants. *Memberships:* American Association of Consulting Chemists & Chemical Engineers; American Association for the Advancement of Science; American Institute of Chemists; American Public Health Association; Institute for Sanitation Management; New York Academy of Science; New England Association of Food & Drug Officials; Association of American Food & Drug Officials. *Honours:* New York Diabetes Association fellowship, 1949; Nassau Civic Club Award, 1962. *Hobby:* Swimming. *Address:* 76 Elm Street, New Canaan, CT 06840, USA.

HALPORN, Roberta, b. 9 Sept 1929, USA. Director, Center for Thanatology Research and Education. 1 daughter. *Education:* BA, MA, New York University. *Appointments:* Licensed Teacher, New York City Board of Education; Assistant Sales Manager, MacMillan Publishing Corporation; Assistant Sales Manager, Riverside Press; Sales Manager, Health Sciences Publishing Corporation; Currently: Founder/Director, Center for Thanatology, Adjunct Professor, Brooklyn College, Publishing Representative, Foundation for Thanatology. *Memberships Include:* Society for Scholarly Publishing; American Library Association; National Hospice Organisation; Children's Hospice Internation; Foundation of Thanatology; Association for Gravestone Studies Medcial Library Association; Forum for Death Education. *Publications:* 'The Thanatology Library' Monograph, 1977; 'The

Thanatology Librarian' Annoteted Book Newsletter, 1978; 'Lessons from the Dead' 1980; 'Bridges, For the Woman Alone' Newsletter, 1982; 'How to Create a Small Thantology Library and Make it Grow' 1984; Compiler and editor: 'Children and Dying' Sarah Sheets Cook et al, 1970; 'The Hospice Concept' Joan Kron et al, 1977; Editor: 'Thanatologic Aspects of Aging' M Tallmer et al, 1980; 'So You Want to See a Psychiatrist' Dr Bruce Danto, 1980; 'How to Run A Hospice Volunteer Training Program' 1980. Contributor of articles in the field of Thanatology. *Honour:* Past President, Publishers Library Promotion Group. *Hobby:* Gravestone Rubbing. *Address:* 391 Atlantic Avenue, Brooklyn, NY 11217, USA.

HALTTUNEN, Erkki Antero, b. 19 Mar. 1935, Kitee, Finland. Thoracic and Vascular Surgeon. m. Maire, 18 Aug. 1956, Finland, 1 son, 2 daughters. *Education:* MD; PhD. *Appointments:* Assistant Surgeon, 1963-69; Senior Surgeon, 1969-72; Senior Thoracic and Cardiovascular Surgeon, 1972-. *Memberships:* The Scandinavian Association for Thoracic and Cardiovascular Surgery; International College for Chest Physicians and Surgeons. *Publications:* 'New surgical correction of central airway collapse in an asthmatic patient', 1981; 'Surgical treatment of benign endobronchial tumors', 1982. *Hobbies:* Sport; Theatre. *Address:* Helsinki University Central Hospital, Haartmannink 4, 00290 Helsinki 29, Finland.

HAM, John Mackenzie, b. 20 May 1933, Manchester, England. Associate Professor of Surgery, Gastrointestinal Surgeon. Divorced, 2 sons, 1 daughter. *Education:* Honours graduate in medicine 1956, MD 1969, University of Sydney, Australia; FRACS, 1961; FACS, 1978. *Appointments Include:* Senior Surgical Registrar, Royal Prince Alfred Hospital, Sydney; Registrar and Lecturer, The Middlesex Hospital, London, England; Senior Lecturer in Surgery, University of New South Wales; President, Surgical Research Society of Australasia; Chairman of Board in General Surgery, Deputy Chairman of Court of Examiners, Council Member 1981 -, Royal Australasian College of Surgeons. *Memberships Include:* Surgical Research Society of Australasia; Gastroenterological Society of Australia; Pan-Pacific Surgical Association; Societe Internationale de Chirurgie; Asian-Pacific Association for the Study of the Liver; International Biliary Association. *Publications:* "Symptom Analysis and Physical Diagnosis", (with A E Davis and T D Bolin), 1985; Book chapters and articles. *Honours Include:* Clinical Fellowship in Cancer, New South Wales State Cancer Council, 1963; Glissan Prize, Royal Australasian College of Surgeons, 1969. *Hobbies:* Sailing; Windsurfing; Books. *Address:* Department of Surgery, Prince of Wales Hospital, Randwick, Sydney 2031, Australia.

HAMADA, Shigeyuki. b. 25 June 1942, Japan. Director of Department of Dental Research. m. 1973, 1 son, 1 daughter. *Education:* DDS General Dentistry, Osaka University Dental School, Osaka, 1967; PhD Microbiology, Osaka University, 1971. *Appointments:* Instructor, Oral Microbiology, Osaka University, 1971-77; Postdoctoral Fellow, Northwestern University Medical School, Chicago, Illinois, USA, 1974-76; Assistant Professor, Osaka University Dental School, 1977-80; Visiting Investigator, Northwestern University and University of Colorado School of Dentistry, Denver, Colorado, USA, 1978-79; Visiting Professor, University of Alabama, Birmingham, 1980-85; Director, Department of Dental Research, The National Institute of Health, Tokyo, Japan, 1980-. *Memberships:* Japanese Society for Bacteriology; Japanese Association for Oral Biology; International Association for Dental Research; American Society for Microbiology; American Association for Immunologists. *Publications:* 'Advances in Basic Cariology and Peridontology' in Japanese, Volumes 1-3, 1982 and 1985; 150 scientific papers, mostly in English. *Address:* Department of Dental Research, The National Institute of Health, 2-10-35 Kamiosaki, Shinagawa-ku, Tokyo 141, Japan.

HAMARD, Henry-Georges, b. 18 Feb. 1933, Le Havre, France. Professor, Head, University Eye Clinic, University Paris V, and Cochin Hospital. m. Monique Imbert, 2 Feb. 1960, Paris, 1 son, 2 daughters. *Appointments:* Non-Resident Medical Student, Paris Hospitals; Ophtalmogist; head of Service. *Membership:* General Secretary, French Ophthalmic Society. *Publications:* "Echographie oculaire", 1974; "Oeil et cortisone", 1975; "Ischemie aigue de la tete du nerf optique", 1977; "Neuropathies optiques", in press. *Hobbies:* History; Antiques. *Address:* 1, rue de Chazelles, 75017, Paris, France.

HAMBACHER, William O, b. 13 May 1925, Bloomfield, New Jersey, USA. Professor of Psychology; Consultant in Psychology. m. 30 June 1950, Bloomfield, 2 sons, 2 daughters. *Education:* PhD, University of Pennsylvania. *Appointments:* Head, Department of Psychology, Juniata College; Senior Staff Psychologist, East Moline State Hospital; Head, Department of Psychology, Augustana College; Manager, Staff Psychologist, HRB-Singer Project Director, Naval Medical Research Institute; Consulting and Private Practice; Professor of Psychology, California University of Pennsylvania. *Memberships:* American Psychological Association; Eastern Psychological Association; Pennsylvania Psychological Association; American Society of Clinical Hypnosis; Psychologists in Private Practice; American Association for the Advancement of Science; Society of Sigma Xi. *Publications:* "Self Concept of Psychiatric and Normal Subjects Revealed by the Way Test", 1962; "Effects of Daily Physical Exercise on the Psychiatric State of Institutionalized Geriatric Mental Patients", 1974; "A Note on the Use of Anticoagulant Therapy in Chronic Brain Syndrome", 1973; "Treatment Approaches with Psychiatric Elderly", 1977; "Psychological Assessment of Geriatric Patients: A Review", 1977. *Hobbies:* Gardening; Jogging. *Address:* P.O. Box 601 Edward Street, California, PA 15419, USA.

HAMBLEN, David Lawrence, b. 31 Aug. 1934, London, England. Professor of Orthopaedic Surgery. m. Gillian, 16 Nov. 1968, 1 son, 2 daughters. *Education:* MB BS, The London Hospital, University of London, 1952-57. *Appointments:* Orthopaedic Registrar, Lecturer, The London Hospital, 1963-66; Teaching Fellow in Orthopaedics, Harvard Medical School Massachusetts General Hospital, 1966-67; Lecturer in Orthopaedics, Nuffield Orthopaedic Centre, Oxford, 1967-68; Senior Lecturer in Orthopaedics, Honorary Consultant, University of Edinburgh, 1968-72; Professor of Orthopaedics Surgery, University of Glasgow, 1972-; Visiting Professor, University of Strathclyde. *Memberships:* Fellow, British Orthopaetdic Association; Chief Scientist Committee, Scottish Home & Health department, 1983-87; Chairman of Committee, Research on Equipment for Disabled, SHHD, 1983-87; Systems Board, Medical Research Council, London, 1983-87. *Publications:* Book chapters on total hip replacement & surgical physiology; numerous papers in orthopaedic journals. *Honours:* Senior Fulbright Exchange Scholarship to Boston, Massachusetts, 1966; British Orthopaedic Association; ABC Travelling Fellowship (to America, Canada, New Zealand & Australia), 1970. *Hobby:* Golf. *Address:* University Department of Orthopaedics, Western Infirmary, Glasgow G11 6NT, Scotland.

HAMBURG, David A., b. 1 Oct 1925, Evansville, Indiana, USA. Psychiatrist/President, Carnegie Corporation of New York. m. Beatrix A Hamburg MD, 26 May 1951, Chicago, Illinois, USA, 1 son, 1 daughter. *Education:* MD, Indiana University, 1947; Diplomate in Psychiatry, American Board of Psychiatry and Neurology, 1953. *Appointments include:* Chief Adult Psychiatry Branch, National Institute of Mental Health, Bethesda, Maryland, 1958-61; Professor and Chairman, Department of Psychiatry, Stanford University Medical School 1961-72; Reed-Hodgson Professor of Human Biology, 1972-76; Sherman Fairchild Distinguished Scholar, California Institute of Technology 1974-75; President, Institute of Medicine (National Academy of Sciences) Washington 1975-80; Director, Division of Health Policy Research and Education, Harvard University, Cambridge, Massachusetts, 1980-82; John D McArthur Professor of Health Policy and Management John F Kennedy School of Government, 1980-82; President, Carnegie Corporation of New York, 1983-. *Memberships:* American association for the Advancement of Sciences, President 1984-85, Chairman of the Board 1985-86; Advisory Committee on Medical research of World Health Organization; Board of Directors, Rockefeller University, Mt Sinai Hospital, New York. *Honours:* Recipient of numerous awards including: President's Medal Michael Reese Medical Center, 1974; American college of Physicians Award, 1977; MIT Bicentennial Medal 1977; Member, American Psychiatric association (Vestermark award 197). *Publications:* Contributor of numerous articles in medical journals and many chapters to edited medical textbooks. *Address:* Carnegie Corporation of New York, 437 Madison Avenue, New York, NY 10022, USA.

HAMERTON, John L., b. 23 Sep. 1929, Brighton, England. Profesor, head, Human Genetics. m. Irene, 13 Sep. 1967, 1 son, 3 duaghters. *Education:* BSc., Zoology, Honours II-I, 1951, DSc., Human Genetics, 1968, London University. *Appointments:* Scientific Staff, Medical Research Council, Radiobiological Research Unit, 1951-56; Senior Scientific Officer, HM Scientific Civil Service, British Museum (Natural History), Zoology, Mammal Section, 1956-59; Scientific Staff, British Empire Cancer Campaign, Zoology Dept., King's College, University of London, 1959-60; Lecturer, Head, Cytogenetics, Paediatric Research Unit, Guy's Hospital Medical School, University of London, 1960-62; Senior Lecturer, Head, Cytogenetics, Guy's Hospital, 1962-69; Associate Professor, Head, Genetics, Director, Gentics, Children's Hospital, Winnipeg, Canaca, 1969-72; Visiting Professor, Genetics, Hebrew University, Jerusalem, 1974; Head, Genetics, 1972-79, Associate Dean, Graduate Studies & Research, 1977-81, Professor, 1972-, Professor, Head, Human Genetics, 1984-, University of Manitoba. *Memberships include:* American Society of Human Gentics, President, 1975; Genetics Society of Canada, President, 1975; Linnean Society, Fellow; Canadian Society for Clinical Investigation; New York Academy of Sciences, Fellow, Royal Society of Medicine; etc. *Publications:* 3 Books: "Chromosomes in Medicine"; "Human Cytogetetics", Volume I; "Human Cytogenetics", Volume II. *Honours:* Robert Roessler de Villiers Award, Leukemia Society of America, 1956; Huxley Memorial Medal, Imperial college of Science an Technology, 1985; Research professor, Medical Council of Canada, 1981. *Address:* Dept. of Human Genetics, Faculty of Medicine, University of Manitoba, 250-770 Bannatyne Avenue, Winnipeg, Manitoba, Canada R3E 0WE.

HAMILTON, William Hall, b. 2 Mar., 1943, Visalia, California, USA. Professor; Psychologist. m. Terri A. Snell, 3 Aug. 1974, Visalia, California, 1 daughter. *Education:* BA, Psychology, San Jose State University, California, USA, 1965, MA, 1967; PhD, Clinical Psychology, California School of Professional Psychology, 1978. *Appointments;* Rehabilitation Counsellor, San Jose, California, 1966; Child Therapist, San Jose, 1967-68; Instructor, Psychology and Counsellor, Mount San Jacinto College, California, 1968-69; Private practice, Visalia, California, 1972-80; Clinical Psychologist and Director, Centre for Counselling and Psychotherpay, Visalia, California, 1980-85; Adjunct Faculty, Marital and Family Therapy Programme, School of Education, University of San Francisco, 1984-85; Professor and Head of Psychology Department, College of Sequoias, Visalia, California-; Adjunct Faculty, Department of Health Sciences, California State Univeristy, 1984; Private Practice in Clinical and Health Psychology, Visalia, California-. *Memberships:* American Psychological Association; American Association for Marital and Family Therapy; American Association for Sex Educators, Counsellors and Therapists; American Society of Clinical Hypnosis; Institute for the Advancement of Health. *Honour:* Teacher of the Year, College of the Sequoias, 1979. *Hobbies:* Jogging; Ski-ing; Water Ski-ing; Reading. *Address:* Department of Psychology, College of the Sequoias, Visalia, CA, 93277, USA.

HAMMER, Guy Saint Clair II, b. 3 Oct. 1943, West Virginia, USA. Associate Director, VA Rehabilitation R & D Evaluation Unit, 1985-. m. Jean Heather Wier, 29 Dec. 1976, Arlington, 2 sons, 1 daughter. *Education:* BSEE; EIT; CSE; FWAS; FRSH. *Appointments:* President, Instant Rain Inc., 1964-66; Nuclear Weapons Electronics Specialist, US Army, 1966-69; Research Staff, University of Maryland, 1970-73; Consulting Clinical Engineer, VA Hospital, 1973-78; Manager, Technical Development, Association for the Advancement of Medical Instrumentation, 1974-78; Director, Biomedical Engineering, Washingotn Hospital Centre, 1978-80; Consulting Clinical Engineer, Bechtel/Saudi Arabia Royal Commision, 1981-84; Consulting Clinical Engineer, Private Practice, 1976-; etc. *Memberships:* American Association for the Advancementof Science; american Society for Testing and Materials; Association for the Advancementof Medical Innstrumentation; Engineering in Medicine & Biology Society; many other professional organisations. *Publications:* Associate Editor, Engineering in Medicne & Biology Society Newsletter, 1980-81; Standards Editor, Clinical Engineering, 1977-78; Technical Editor, Medical Instrumentation, 1975-80;Staff Contributor, Standards Engineering, 1975-79; author, "SaudiMed: Medical Market Prospects & Agents in Saudi Arabia", 1985; "Technology Awareness: Electrical Safety, the Clinical Environment and Standards", 1983; etc. *Honours:* Phi Kappa Phi; Eta kappa Nu; Outstanding Achievement Award, 1974; Tau Beta Pi, 1973; Fellow, Royal Society for Health, 1983; Senior Member, SES; Senior Member, IEEE; Fellow, Washington Academy of Sciences, 1979; National Capital Award, 1979; President, Washington Society of engineers, 1979. *Hobbies:* Technological Art; Microcomputer Applications and Communications; Scuba Diving; Coaching T-Ball and Soccer; Hiking in Swiss Alps. *Address:* 8902 Ewing Drive, Bethesda, MD 20817, USA.

HAMMERLE, Ronald L. b. 20 Dec. 1942, Louisville, USA. President, Health Resources Ltd. and First Care Inc. *Education: DMn, MTh,* University of Chicago, 1969; AB, Hanover College ,Hanover, Indiana, USA. *Appointments;* Presidnet, Health Resources Limited and FirstCare Inc. *Memberships:* American Marketing Association; Greater Kansas City Medical Managers Association; American Hospital Association; Faculty, University of Missouri School of Medicine, Kansas City. *Publications:* "Is there a Conglomorate in Your Future" in 'Medical Economics', 1982; 'Are You Managing a Future National Medical Practice?' in 'Medical Group Management', 1983; 'What do you Do when your Largest Medical Group says "We're Selling?" in "Health Care Strategic Management", 1984. 'What Medical Managers can Learn from Henry Bloch' in 'Medical Group Management', 1985. *Address:* C/o

Health Resources Limited, River Road Professional Building, PO Box 14188, Kansas City, MO, 64152, USA.

HAMMOND, Donna Louise, b. 28 Oct 1953, Buffalo, New York, USA. Research Scientist. m. Herbert K Proudfit, 1 May 1983. *Education:* BS, Biochemical Pharmacology, State University of New York at Buffalo, 1975; PhD, Pharmaocology, University of Illinois Medical Center, Chicago, 1980. *Appointments:* Postdoctoral Fellow, Mayo Clinic, Rochester, Minnesota, 1980-82; Research Investigator, 1982-83, Research Scientist 1983-, G D Searle and Co., Skokie, Illinois. *Memberships:* American Association for the Advancement of Science; International Association for the Study of Pain; Society for Neuroscience; Women in Neuroscience. *Publications:* 'Neural circuitry mediating transmission of nociceptive information' in "Pharmacology and Therapeutics" 1981 (with T L Yaksh); 'Pharmacology of central pain modulating networks' in Vol 9 "Advances in Pain Research and Therapy" edited by H L Fields, R Dubner and F Cervero, 1985. *Honour:* National Research Service Award 1981-82. *Hobbies:* Equestrian events; Downhill Skiing. *Address:* G D Searle and Co., Research and Development Division, 4901 Searle Parkway, Skokie, IL, USA.

HAMMOND, G Denman, b. 5 Feb. 1923, Atlanta, Georgia, USA. Professor of Paediatrics, University of Southern California School of Medicine; Associate Vice-President, Health Affairs; Chairman, children's Cancer Study Group. m. Florence Williams, 30 Mar. 1946, Washington, DC, 3 sons, 1 daughter. *Education:* BA, University of North Carolina Chapel Hill, 1944; University of North Carolina School of Medicine, 1944-46; MD, University of Pennsylvania School of Medicine, 1948; US Naval School of Aviation Medicine, Pensacola, Florida, 1952; US Naval Flight Surgeon. *Appointments:* Instructor and Assistant Professor of paediatrics, University of California School of Medicine, San Francisco, 1954-57; Associate, children's Hospital of Los Angeles, 1957; Assistant Professor, Associate and Full Professor; Director, Kenneth Norris Junior Cancer Research Institute, 1978-81; Founding Director, USC Comprehensive Cancer Center, 1971-81; Associate Dean, School of Medicine, 1981-85; Childrens Cancer Study Group Chairman, 1968-; Associate Vice-President, Health Affairs, 1985-. *Memberships:* American Academy of Paediatrics; American Society of Clinical Oncology; American Society of Hematology; American Association of Cancer Research; International Society of Hematology; International Society of Paediatric Oncology; American Paediatric Society; Society of Surgical Oncology. *Publications:* Contributor to professional journals; Chapters in books; Books. *Honours:* Distinguished Alumnus Award, University of North Carolina, 1974; Admiral Chambliss Award, Navy League, 1979; Lucy Wortham James Award of Society of Surgical Oncology, 1984. *Hobbies:* Classic Car Restoration: Photography; Travel; Skiing. *Address:* University of Southern California, Health Affairs, 2025 Zonal Avenue, Keith §506, Los Angeles, CA 90033, USA.

HAMMOND, Michael Graham, b. 25 Aug. 1940, Durban, Republic of South Africa. Head of Transplantation Unit. m. Corrine, 1 Jan. 1965, Durban, 1 son, 4 daughters. *Education:* BSc, University of South Africa; PhD, University of Natal. *Appointments:* Currently Head of Transplatation Unit, The Natal Institute of Immunology, Durban. *Memberships:* The Transplantation Society; Founder member, South African Transplantation Society; Founder member, South African Immunological Society. *Publications include:* 18 contributions to series "Histocompatability Testing", 1972-84; 'HLA and Cancer of the Esophagus', in "Cancer of the Esophagus", 1982; 31 publications in refereed journals; 'Associations

Between HLA Antignes and Nephrotic Syndrome in African and Indian Children in South Africa', (with M Adhikari and H M Coovadia), 1985; 'Male Transmission of the Gene For Isolated Gonadtropin Releasing Hormone Deficiency', (with R J Norman, K Reddi, A Richards and S M Joubert), 1985. *Hobbies:* Gardening; Golf. *Address:* Natal Institute of Immunolgoy, PO Box 2356, 4000 Durban, Republic of South Africa.

HAMPTON, G Robert, b. 31 Mar. 1949, Ohio, USA. Clinical Assistant Professor. m. Janis Steinbaugh, 9 Jan. 1972, Canton, Ohio. *Education:* BS, Ashland College, Ohio, USA; MD, Case Western Reserve University School of Medicine, Cleverland, Ohio. *Appointments:* Assistant Professor, Albany Medical College, Albany, New York; Clinical Assistant Professor, SUNY Upstate Medcial Centre, Syracuse, New York-. *Memberships:* Fellow, American Academy of Ophtalmology; New York State Ophthalmological Society; Vitreous Society; Aerospace Medical Society; Flying Physicians Society; Eastern New York EENT Society. *Publications:* 'Visual Prognosis of Disciform Degeneration in Myophia Ophthalmology', 1983; 'Results of Argon Green Laser for Disciform Macular Degeneration' in "Graffes Archives of Ophthalmology"; 'Gaze Evoked Blindness' in "Annals of Ophthalmology". *Honours:* Wiggers Travel Fellowship, Albany Medical College, 1980; HEED Ophthalmic Foundation Fellow, 1981. *Hobbies:* Flying; Diving; Sailing; Skiing; Photography; Computing. *Address:* Retina-Vitreous Surgeons of Central New York, PC, 3107 East Genessee Street, Syracuse, NY 13224, USA.

HANAN, Christopher Mark, b.27 Oct. 1940, Dunedin, New Zealand. Specialist, Oro-Maxillio Facial Surgeon, Royal Darwin Hospital. m. Annie Hung Yip, 15 Dec. 1979, Darwin, 1 son. *Education:*BDS, University of Otago, 1964; Primary FDS Course, Royal College of Surgeons, England, 1967; Orthodontic Course, Eastman Dental Hospital, 1968-69; Dorth RES (Eng) 1969; FDSRCS(Ed); FDSRCS(Eng), 1972. *Appointments:* Resident, Dental Surgeon, Christchurch Hospital, New Zealanad, 1965-66; Registrar, Oral Surgery, Royal Free Hospital, Oxford, 1969-71; Senior Registrar, Oral Surgery, Aberdeen Royal Infirmary, Scotland, 1972-76; Senior Registrar, Oral Surgery, Mount Vernon Centre for Plastic & Oral Surgery, London, 1977-78. *Memberships:* British Association of Oral & Maxillofacial Surgeons; European Orthodontic Society; Australian & New Zealand Association of Oral & Maxillofacial Surgeons; New Zealand Dental Assocation; Australian Dental Association. *Hobbies:* Music; Boating; Fishing; Camping; Travel; Chinese Language & Cuisine. *Address:* Oro-Maxillofacial Unit, Royal Darwin Hospital, P O Box 41326 Casuarina, NT 5792, Australia. London, 1967-68, Registrar, Oral Surgery. Radcliffe Infirmary & Churchill Hospital.

HAND, Roger Peter, b. 25 Sep. 1938, New York, USA. Chairman of Internal Medicine and Professor of Medicine. m. Linda Schwartz, 1 Jan. 1986, Chicago, 1 son, 1 daughter. *Education:* BS, University College; MD, New York University School of Medicine. *Appointments:* Assistant-Associate Professsor, Department of Medicine and Microbiology 1973-78; Assistant-Associate Physician, McGill University Clinic, Royal Victoria Hospital, 1973-78; Professor of Department of Medicine 1978-84, Director 1980-84, McGill Cancer Centre; Currently Chairman of Internal Medicine, Illinois Masonic Medical Center; Currently Professor of Medicine, University of Illinois, Chicago. *Memberships:* American Society for Clinical Investigation; American Society of Biological Chemists; American Association for Cancer Research; American Society for Clinical Oncology; Cancer and Acute Leukemia Group B. *Publications:* Many articles in referred scientific journals.

Honours: International cancer Research Technology Transfer Receipt and visiting Professor, University of Bern, 1977; Visiting Scientist, National Institute of Health, 1983. *Hobbies:* United States Army Researve; Parachuting; Tennis; Fitness. *Address:* 836 W Wellington, Chicago, IL 60657, USA.

HANDS, Brian William, b. 10 July 1943, Toronto, Canada, Ear Nose and Throat Specialist. m. Cynthia Faire Goldstein, 23 Dec. 1967, Toronto, 2 sons. *Education:* MD, University of Toronto Medical School, 1968; Fellow, Royal College of Surgeons of Canada, 1973; *Appointments:* Clinical Demonstrator, University of Toronto, 1975-78; Active Staff, Central Hospital, Toronto, 1978-85; External Consultant, Ministry of Health, Province of Ontario, 1982; Consultant to the Canadian Opera Company for ear, nose and throat conditions. *Memberships:* Academy of Medicine, Toronto; Medico-legal Society of Upper Canada; Ontario Medical Association; Canadian Medical Association; Canadian Otolaryngological Society. *Publications:* 'Cancer of Larynx', audio-visual, 1970; 'Industrial Hearing Program', 1978; 'Hearing Conservation Program', 1979; 'Hearing in the Senior Population', 1981; 'Noise and Pollution', 1985. *Hobbies:* Sailing; Tennis; Gardening; Skiing; Bird-Watching. *Address:* 200 St Clair Avenue West, Suite 406, Toronto, Ontario M4V IRI, Canada.

HANDSCHUMACHER, Robert E, b. 16 Oct 1927, Abington, Pennsylvania, USA, Professor, Department of Pharmacology, yale University School of Medicine, 1964-, 2 sons. *Education:* BS, Drexel Institute, 1949; MS, 1951, PhD, 1953, University of Wisconsin. *Appointments:* Postdoctoral Fellow, Lister Institute of Preventive Medicine, 1953-54; Postdoctoral Fellow, Department of Pharmacology, 1955-56, Assistant Professor, 1956-60, Associate Professor, 1960-64, Professor, 1964-, Director, division of biological Sciences, 1969-72, Chairman, Department of Pharmacology, 1974-77, Yale University School of Medicine, New Haven, Connecticut. *Memberships:* Associate Editor of numerous Editorial boards, 1965-; Holder of numerous positions on professional committees and councils; American Association for the Advancement of Science Fellow; American Scoiety of Biological Chemists; American Society of Pharmacology and Experimental Therpautics; American Association for cancer research; American Chemical Society. *Publications:* Contributor of numerous articles and abstracts in professional and scientific journals. *Honours:* National foundation Postdoctoral Fellow, 1953-54; Squibb Postdoctoral Fellow, 1955-56; Scholar in Cancer research, 1957-62; Eleanor Roosevelt International Fellowship, UICC; American Cancer Society Research Professor, 1964-74; Lamson Memorial Lecturer, Vanderbilt University, 1973; Member, Connecticut Academy of Science and Engineering, 1976-; American Cancer Society Professor, 1977-; Schuler Haddow Visiting Fellow, Chester Beatty Cancer Research Institute, England, 1977-78; Fellow, American Association for the Advancement of Science, 1982-; Philips Memorial Lecturer. Memorial-Sloan Kettering, 1985. *Hobbies:* Sailing. *Address:* Yale University School of Medicine, New Haven, CT 06526, USA.

HANDWERGER, Stuart, b. 19 Dec. 1938, Baltimore, Maryland, USA. Professor of Paediatrics. m. Roberta Ann Blaker, 21 June 1964, Silver Spring, Maryland, 1 son, 1 daughter. *Education:* BA, Johns Hopkins University, 1960; MD, University of Maryland, 1964. *Appointments:* Intern, Paediatrics, Bronx Municipal Hospital Center, New York, 1964-65; Resident, Paediatrics, Mount Sinai Hospital, 1965-66; Clinical Associate, Paediatric Metabolism Branch, National Institutes of Health, Maryland, 1966-68; Fellowship in Endocrinology, Harvard Medical School, 1968-69; Beth Israel Hospital, 1969-71; Assistant Professor,

Paediatrics, 1971-76, Chief, Paediatric Endocrine Division, 1971-, Assistant Professor, Physiology, 1975-, Associate Professor, Paediatrics, 1976-81, Professor, Paediatrics, 1981-, Duke University Medical Center, Durham, North Carolina; Visiting Scientist, Guggenheim fellow, Departemnt of Hormone Research, Weizmann Institute of Science, Rehovot, Israel, 1978-79.*Memberships:* Alpha Omega Alpha; American Society of Clinical Investigation; American Federation for Clinical Research; Endocrine Society; Lawson Wilkins Paediatric Endocrine Society; Society for Paediatric Research; American Association for the Advancement of Science. *Publications:* Contributions to: Nature', 1971; 'Science', 1978. *Honours:* Phi Beta Kappa, 1955; Alpha Omega Alpha, 1963; Mosby Book Award, 1964; Research Career Development Award, 1975-80. *Hobbies:* Photography; Jogging. *Address:* Duke University Medical Center, Box 3080, Durham, NC 27710, USA.

HANEDOES, Peter, b. 11 Nov 1938, Amsterdam. Dentist. m. Rita Gouka, 10 Apr., 1965, 3 daughters. *Education:* Dentist, FICD. *Appointment:* Dentist - Chief Negotiator to the Government. *Memberships:* FICD; FIDI; Nederlandse Vereniging van Tandartsen; President, Dutch Dental Association. *Honour:* Member of the List of Honours of TSV "John Tomes". *Hobby:* Golf. *Address:* Rijksstraatweg 90, 7391 MV Twello, The Netherlands.

HANKOFF, Leon D, b. 17 June 1927, Maryland, USA. Director/Chairman, Department of Psychiatry, 4 daughters. *Appointments:* Programme Planning Consultant, New York City Department of Mental Health and Mental Retardation Services, 1969; Director/Chairman, Department of Psychiatry, Misericordia Hospital Medical Center, 1970-78; Chief, Consultation and Liaison Unit, University Hospital, Stony Brook, New York, 1980. *Memberships:* Fellow, American Psychiatric Association; American Public Health Association; Association for Psychiatric Treatment of Offenders; Sigma Xi; American Association for the Advancement of Science. *Publications:* "Emergency Psychiatric Treatment: A Handbook of Secondary Prevention", 1968; "Jewish Ethno-Psychiatry: A Manual for Inservice and House Staff Education", (senior author), 1977; "Suicide: Theory and Clinical Practice", (senior editor), 1979. *Honour:* Recipient of Revere Annual Award for paper 'A Reference Study of Ataraxics: A Two-Week Double Blind Outpatient Evaluation', 1962. *Hobbies:* Handball; Gardening; Writing. *Address:* Elizabeth General Medical Center, 925 East Jersey Street, Elizabeth, NJ 07201, USA.

HANNA, Saddik Mishriki, b. 4 Dec. 1929, Cairo, Eygpt. Professor. m. Aida Riad Istefanos, 25 Jan. 1960, Cairo, 3 sons. *Education:* DTM&H, Cairo, 1968; DMSc., Cairo, 1970; MD, Cairo, 1973; CES Immuno Paris, 1975; CES Bacteria & Virology Paris, 1977; CES Allergology & Immunology Paris, 1979; DERBH Biology Humaine, 1979. *Appointments:* Rural Health Services, 1957-60; Director, Rural Health Units, 1961-67; Director, Rural Health Units, 1961-67; Chief, Parisitology, Institute Research Tropical Medicine, Cairo, 1968-73; Scholarship in France: Allergology, Immunology, biology, 1974-79; Chief, Allergology and Immunology, Institute of Research for Tropical Medicine, Cairo, 1980-. *Memberships:* French Society of Allergy & Clinical Immunology; French Society of Parasitology; European Academy of Allergy and Clinical Immunology; British Society of Allergy and Clinical Immunology. *Publications:* Many articles in Parasitology, Allergology and Serology; "Les Allergies de la Paeu"; "Mecanism of Histamine Liberation, La Methode Elisa Appliquee a la Toxoplasmose Humaine Pathology", 'Biology'. *Hobbies:* Tennis; Volley Ball; Swimming. *Address:* 77 Gameat El Dewal El Arabia Street, Cairo, Egypt.

HANNUKSELA, Matti, b. 20 Sep. 1938, Laihia, Finland. Professor of Dermatology. m. Aila Tuhkanen, 22 June 1963, 1 son, 2 daughters. *Education:* MD. *Appointments:* Resident 1966-69, Head of the Allergy Department 1971-76, department of Dermatology, University of Helskini; Resident, Department of Medicine, Aurora Hospital, Helsinki, 1969-71; Currently Professor of Dermatology and Chairman of Department of Dermatology, University of Oulu. *Memberships:* Finnish Dermatological Society; European Academy of Allergology and clinical Immunology; Secretary, International Contact Dermatitis Research Group. *Publications:* "Erythema Nodosum", 1971; "Allergia", 1985. *Hobbies:* Gardening; Cross country skiing. *Address:* Department of Dermatology, University of Oulu, SF 90220 Oulo, Finland.

HANSEN, Daniels DuBose, b. 30 Mar. 1931, Denver, Colorado, USA. Chief of Medicine. m. Joanne Dixon, 23 Oct. 1958, Denver, 1 son, 1 daughter. *Education:* BA cum Laude, Princeton University, 1952; MD, University of California School of Medicine, Los Angeles, 1956; Internship and Residency, University of California, Los Angeles, 1957-59; Fellowship in Cardiology, University of Colorado, 1959-60; Fellowship in Psychosomatic Medicine, Menninger Foundation, Topeka, Kansas. *Appointments:* Clinical Assistant Professor, Medicine and Psychiatry, University of California Medical School, Los Angeles, 1963-78; Director of Professional Services, US Air Force Hospital, Columbus Air Force Base, 1960-62; Chief of Cardiology, 1970-76, Chief of Staff, 1973-75, Marina Mercy Hospital; Chief of Cardiology, Boise Veterans Administration Hospital, 1977-79; Medical Chief, Hemet Hospital, California, 1979-. *Memberships:* American College of Physicians; American College of Cardiology; American College of Chest Physicians; Pan American College of Physicians and Surgeons. *Publications:* Consultant, "The Patient Who Wants a Heart Attack"; 'Psychiatric Aspects of Medical Emergencies' in 'International Quarterly Journal of Psychiatry'. Editor of 2 books and 3 articles. Papers presented at conferences. *Honours:* National Scholar, Princeton University, 1948; Rockefeller Fellowship, Woods Hole, Massachusetts, 1953; National Institutes of Health Fellowship, Henninger Foundation, 1963. *Hobbies:* Flying; Fishing; Swimming; Tennis. *Address:* 26811 Sol Court, Hemet, CA 82344, USA.

HANSEN, James Edward, b. 4 Sep. 1926, Wisconsin, USA. Professor of Medicine. m. Beverly Kapke, 5 June 1948, Milwaukee, Wisconsin, 1 son, 3 daughters. *Education:* MD, Johns Hopkins University School of Medicine, 1945-49. *Appointments Include:* Chief, Physiology Division, US Army Medical Research and Nutrition Laboratory, Denver, 1962-65; Commander and Director, US Army Research Institute of Environmental Medicine, Natick, Massachusetts, 1965-71; Lecturer, Johns Hopkins School of Public Health, 1965-71; Chief, Clinical Investigation Service, Tripler Army Medical Center, Honolulu, 1971-75; Clinical Professor Physiology, University of Hawaii School of Medicine, 1971-75; Associate Professor of Medicine 1976-78, Professor of Medicine 1978-, University of California at Los Angeles; Director Clinical Respiratory Physiology Laboratory, Harbor-UCLA Medical Center, 1976-. *Memberships Include:* Fellow: American College of Physicians; American College of Chest Physicians. *Publications Include:* co-author: 'Predicted values for clinical exercise testing;, 1984; 'Principles of exercise testing and interpretation', 1986. *Honours Include:* Award for Medical Research, Association of Military Surgeons, 1971 and 1975; Legion of Merit, US Army. *Hobbies:* Tennis; Gardening; Piano. *Address:* Division of Respiratory Physiology and Medicine, Department of Medicine, Harbor-UCLA Medical Center, Torrance, CA 90509, USA.

HANSEN, Phyllis Jean, b. 30 Dec. 1943, Ohio, USA. Chief Nurse, 10th Aeromedical Staging Flight, United States Air Force, Nurse Corps. m. Richard James Hansen, 11 Mar. 1980, Scott Air Force Base, Illinois, 1 son. *Education:* California Hospital Nursing Diploma; BSN, Nursing, Public Health Nurse Certificate, Mt. St. Marys College; Masters of Nursing, University of California, Los Angeles. *Appointments:* Staff Nurse: Obstetrics, General Surgery and Recovery Room, Intensive Care and Coronary Care Unit, Emergency Room and General Therapy Clinic; Charge Nurse: Pediatric and General Therapy Clinic; Co-ordinator: General Surgery and Orthopedics, Coronary Observation Unit and Oncology Unit; Flight Nurse; Flight Nurse Instructor; Senior Flight Clinical Co-ordinator; Community Health Nurse and Nurse Consultant to PACAF/SG; Chief Nurse and Nurse Consultant to AF/SG on Aeromedical Staging. *Memberships:* American Heart Association; American Nurses Association; Aerospace Medical Association; Associate Fellow, Flight Nurse; American Public Health Association; Association of Military Surgeons of the United States. *Publications:* Air Transport of the Man Who Needs Everything in Aviation Space and Environmental Medicine, 1980; A Look at Quality Assurance Through the Audit Process in Aviation Space and Environmental Medicine, 1980; A New Approach for Quality Assurance in Aviation Space and Environmental Medicine, 1981. *Honours:* Medical Flight Nurse of the Year, 4th Air Force Reserve, 1977; Humanitarian Service Medal, 1975 Operation New Life, Viet Nam. *Hobbies:* Flying; Sightseeing; Shopping. *Address:* 6204 Sally Ford Court, Fairfax Station, VA 22039-9998, USA.

HANSMAN, David John, b. 10 Jan. 1930, Sydney, New South Wales, Australia. Director, Microbiology department, Adelaide Children's Hospital. m. Miriam Veronica Mattock, 15 Mar. 1957, London, England, 1 son, 1 daughter. *Education:* MB, BS, University of Sydney, 1953; DCP, London, 1957; DTM&H, England, 1958; MRCPath, 1963; FRCPath 1975; MCAP 1964; FRCPA 1971; MASM, 1976. *Appointments include:* Senior Bacteriologist, Institute of Clinical Pathology & Medical research, Sydney, 1959-65; Bacteriologist/Clinical Pathologist, Women's Hospital, Crown Street, Sydney, 1966-70. *Memberhsips:* Australian Medical Association; Australian Society for Microbiology; British Medical Association; Royal Society of Medicine; Royal Society of Tropical Medical & Hygiene. *Publications include:* Contributions to 'New England Journal of Medicine', USA; 'Lancet', UK; 'Journal of Hygiene', UK. *Hobbies:* Birdwatching; Gardening; Photography. *Address:* Microbiology Department, Adelaide Children's Hospital, North Adelaide 5006, South Australia.

HANSON, David Gordon, b. 16 Nov. 1943, USA. Associate Professor of Surgery; Vice Chief, Division of Head & Neck Surgery, University of California Los Angeles (UCLA) School of Medicine. m. Terri Dangerfield. *Education:* BS, Wheaton College, Illinois; MS, University of Washington; MS, University of Minnesota. *Appointments:* Staff scientist, executive secretary, Communticative Disorders Study Section, NINCDS, NIH/Senior surgeon US Public Health Service, Communicative Disorders Programme, NINCDS, NIH, 1975-78; Assistant Professor of Surgery, UCLA School of Medicine, 1975-83; Chief, Section of Head & Neck Surgery, VA Medical Centre, West Los Angeles, 1982-. *Memberships:* American Broncho-Esophagological Association; American College of Surgeons; American Medical Association; American Academy of Otolaryngology/Head & Neck Surgery; American Society for Head & Neck Surgery; Association for Research in Otalaryngology; etc. *Publications include:* Invited articles, book chapters, research papers in refereed journals, etc. *Honours:* US PHS

Medal of Commendation, 1975; Head & Neck Surgery honour award, American Academy of Otolaryngology, 1985. *Hobbies:* Sailing; Skiing. *Address:* Division of Head & Neck Surgery, UCLA School of Medicine, Los Angeles, CA 90024, USA.

HANSON, Lars A, b. 10 Aug. 1934, Naverstad, Sweden. Professor of Clinical Immunology. m. Monika Tunback-Hanson, 15 Aug. 1958, Paris, France, 1 son, 1 daughter. *Education:* MD; PhD. *Appointments:* Research Associate, Department of Bacteriology University of Göteborg, Sweden; Research Association, Rockefeller Institute, New York, USA; Assistant Professor, Department of Paediatrics, Karolinska Institute, Stockholm, Sweden; Assistant Professor, Department of Paediatrics, Associate Professor, Department of Immunology, Professor & Physician-in-chief, Department of Clinical Immunology, University of Göteborg, Sweden. *Memberships:* Collegium Internationale Allergologium; Academy of Science, Cordoba, Argentina; American College of Nutrition; European Society of Paediatric Research; European Society for Clinical Research; European Group for Immunodeficiency; European Society for Paediatric Haematology & Immunology; and others. *Publications:* Over 350 scientific articles, 8 books on Immunology. *Honours:* Various awards & Visiting Professorships in USA, Norway, Australia. *Hobbies:* Sailing; Skating; Skiing; Sailskating; Music; Literature. *Address:* Vastergatan 2, S-411 23 Göteborg, Sweden.

HANZLIK, Janusz – Andrzej, b. 15 Feb 1933, Sokal, Poland. Chairman, University Medical Department. m. Maria Langwinska, 26 Aug. 1958, 1 son, 1 daughter. *Education:* MD, 1964, Professor of Medicine 1978. *Appointments:* Assistant Professor, Department of Physiology, 1957-58, Assistant Professor, Department of Medicine, 1959-70, Associate Professor, Department of Medicine, 1971-78, Professor of Medicine, 1978-, University Medical School, Lublin, Poland. *Memberships:* Polish Society of Internal Medicine, First Vice President, 1973-; Polish Society of Cardiology; Lublin's Scientific Society. *Publications:* 'Atherosclerosis' in "Internal Medicine" edited by Wojtczak, PZWL, Warsaw, 1983; "Isolation of Proteoglycans from Human Aorta Artery" 1978; Apolipoprotein Gene Polymorphism and Susceptibility to Non Insulin-Dep. Diabetes Mell American Journal of Human Genetics, 1985. *Honour:* Award of the Polish Society of Internal Medicine, 1964. *Hobbies:* Music; Electronics. *Address:* ul. Grottgera 7/8, Lublin, Poland.

HARBERT, John Charles, b. 21 Mar. 1937, McMinnville, Oregon, USA. Professor of Medicine and Radiology, Division of Nuclear Medicine, Georgetown University Hospital. *Education:* MD, Northwestern University Medical School; Professor of Medicine and Radiology. *Appointments:* Staff Physician, 1966-68, Chief, Diagnostic Nuclear Medicine Section, 1968-69, Clinical Center, National Institutes of Health, Bethesda, Maryland; Director, Division of Nuclear Medicine, Georgetown University Hospital, Washington, DC, 1969-83; Assistant Professor of Medicine and Radiology, 1969; Associate Professor, 1973; Professor, 1979. *Membership:* Society of Nuclear Medicine. *Publications:* Co-Editor, "Symposium on Cisternography and Hydrocephalus", 1972; Co-author, "Textbook of Nuclear Medicine: Basic Science", 1978; Co-author, "Textbook of Nuclear Medicine: Clinical Applications", 1979; Contributor to "CRC Handbook Series in Clinical Laboratory Sciences. Section A Nuclear Medicine I", 1977; 'Radioisotope Cisternography' in "Mosby's Manual of Nuclear Medicine Procedure", 1981; Co-author, 'Reported adverse reactions to lung scanning procedures' in "Handbook Series in Clinical Laboratory Science" Section A: "Nuclear Medicine" Volume II, 1982; 'Efficacy of bone and liver scanning in malignant diseases; facts and opinions' in "Nuclear Medicine Annual 1982", 1982; Co-author, 'Cardiovascular Nuclear Medicine' in "Essentials of Clinical Cardiology", 1983; "Efficacy of liver scanning in malignant disease", Semin. Nuclear Medicine, 1984; Co-author, "Textbook of Nuclear Medicine: Volume I Basic Sciences", 1985; Co-author, "Textbook of Nuclear Medicine. Volume II. Clinical Applications", 1985. *Hobbies:* Sailing; Tennis. *Address:* Division of Nuclear Medicine, Georgetown University Hospital, 3800 Reservoir Road, NW, Washington, DC 20007, USA.

HARBISON, Paula Kay, b. 27 Apr, 1955, California, USA, Physician of Podiatric Medicine and Surgery. m. James F Cook, 10 Sep. 1983, California. *Education:* BS Biological Sciences; BS Medical Sciences; DPM Podiatric Medicine. *Appointments:* Resident in Podiatric Medicine and surgery, Detroit, Michigan, 1983; Solo practitioner in Podiatric Medicine and Surgery, Escondido, California, 1983-. *Memberships:* Associate, American College of Foot Surgeons; American, California, and San Diego Podiatry Association; American Association of Women Podiatrists. *Publications:* 'Vasolressin and Oxytocin Levels in Swiss Webster Mice', 1977. *Honour:* Graduation with Honours in Research, University of California, Irvine, 1977. *Hobbies:* Writing; Public speaking; Informational Seminars; Skiing; Mountaineering. *Address:* 910 E Ohio Street, Suite 203, Escondido, CA 92025, USA.

HARCOURT, John Kenneth, b. 27 June 1931, Melbourne, Victoria, Australia. Reader in Restorative Dentistry. *Education:* BDSc 1953, MDSc 1956, DDSc 1968, Melbourne University; Fellow, Royal Australasian College of Dental Surgeons, 1965. *Appointments:* Staff Dentist, Dental Hospital of Melbourne, 1954; Senior Demonstrator and Tutor in Dental Prosthetics 1954-57, Lecturer 1957-63, Australian College of Dentistry; Honorary Senior Clinical Assistant 1963-82, Consultant 1983-, Royal Dental Hospital of Melbourne; Visiting Associate Professor, Department of Biological Materials, 1967-69 and Visiting Professor, Departments of Biological Materials and Removable Prosthodontics, Northwestern University Dental School, Chicago, Illinois, USA, 1979-80; Senior Lecturer in Dental Prosthetics 1964-73, Reader in Department of Dental Prosthetics 1974-82, Assistant Dean in Faculty of Dental Science 1976, Deputy Dean 1977-79, Reader in Department of Restorative Dentistry 1983-, University of Melbourne. *Memberships include:* Australian Dental Association; International Association for Dental Research; Australian Prosthodontic Society; Federation Dentaire Internationale; Pierre Fauchard Academy; The Royal Australasian College of Dental Surgeons, International College of Dentists. *Publications include:* "Materials Science in Dentistry", (with E H Greener and E P Lautenschlager), 1972; "Dental Assistant's Manual", co-editor with AA Grant of 2nd edition 1977, Editor 3rd edition 1979; Numerous articles and papers; Acting Editor, Australasian Dental Journal, 1985-. *Hobbies:* Photography; Computing; Tennis. *Address:* School of Dental Science, 711 Elizabeth Street, Melbourne, Victoria 3000, Australia.

HARDARSON, Thordur, b. 14 Mar. 1940, Reykjavik, Iceland. Professor. m. Sólrún B Jensdóttir, 4 Feb. 1962, 2 sons, 1 daughter. *Education:* Canad. Med et Chir., 1967, University of Iceland Medical School; PhD, University of London, 1974. *Appointments:* Research Cardiologist, University Hospital, San Diego, California, 1975-76; Consultant Cardiologist, University Hospital, Reykjavik, Iceland, 1976; Chief of Medicine, Reykjavik City Hospital, 1977-82; Professor & Chief of Medicine, University Hospital, Reykjavik, Iceland, 1982-. *Memberships:* British Cardiac Society; American College of Cardiology; American Heart Association (Member, International

Council in Clinical Cardiology); Icelandic Medical Association; Icelandic Cardiological Society. *Publications:* Numerous articles on Medicine & Cardiology, in: 'The Lancet'; 'British Heart Journal'; 'Circulation'; 'American Journal of Cardiology'; 'American Heart Journal'; 'American Journal of Medical Science'; 'Thorax'; 'Acta Medica Scandinavica'; and others. *Hobbies:* Chess; Music; History. *Address:* 10 Helluland, 108 Reykjavik, Iceland.

HARDCASTLE, Jack Donald, b. 3 Apr. 1933, Yorkshire, England. Professor & Head, Department of Surgery, University Hospital, Nottingham. m. Rosemary Hay-Shunker, 18 Dec. 1965, 1 son, 1 daughter. *Education:* BA, MB, BChir, MA, Cambridge University; MRCP, London; FRCS, England; MChir, distinction, Cambridge; FRCP, London. *Appointments include:* The London Hospital, 1958-60, 1962-65, Junior appointments; Senior Registrar, Surgery, Metropolitan & London Hospitals, 1965-68; Senior Registrar, St. Mark's Hospital, London, 1968; Senior Lecturer, Surgery, London Hospital, 1968-70. *Memberships:* President 1982-83, Section of Surgery, Royal Society of Medicine; Surgical Research Society; British Society of Gastroenterology; International Surgical Group; Moynihan Chirurgical Club. *Publications include:* "Isolated Organ Perfusion", with H.D. Ritchie, 1973; Over 100 contributions to scientific journals. *Honours:* State scholarship. 1951; Albert Hopkinson Prize 1952, Senior Scholarship 1954, Windsor Postgraduate Scholarship 1960, Emmanuel College, Cambridge; Open Scholarship 1955, James Anderson Prize 1955, T.A.M. Ross Prize 1955, 1956, London Hospital; Sir Arthur Sims Commonwealth Travelling Professor, touring Canada, South Africa, Zimbabwe, 1985. *Address:* 'Wild Briars', Goverton, Bleasby, Nottingham, England.

HARDIN, Alice I (Randall), b. 4 Oct. 1936, Preble, New York, USA. Director of Rehabilitation Services, Pan American Hospital, Miami, Florida. m. Robert B. Hardin, 26 Nov. 1969, Homestead, Florida, 6 sons, 3 daughters. *Education:* AA (Hons), Miami-Dade Community College; AS in P.T. Technology with Honours, Miami-Dade Community College; BS, Physical Therapy, Florida International University. *Appointments:* Director, Hialeah Pain Control Center; Staff P.T., Cedars of Lebanon, Miami, Florida; Staff PTA, Hialeah Hospital, Hialeah, Florida. *Memberships:* Phi Theta Kappa; Dade's Employ the Handicapped Committee; Florida Rehabilitation Association (Secretary, 1984-85); Advisory Board, Miami-Dade Community College PTA Program; Advisory Council, Florida Association of Rehabilitation Facilities; American and Florida Phyther. Association; Founder of First and Only Spanish Stroke Club in State of Florida for Stroke Patients and Families. *Honours:* Class Vice-President, Junior Year at Florida International University, 1977-78; Class President as Senior, 1978-79. Several High School honours. *Hobbies:* Camping; Hiking; Canoeing; Swimming; Horseback Riding; Crocheting. *Address:* 27000 S.W. 142 Avenue, Naranja, FL 33032, USA.

HARDING, Graham Frederick Anthony, b. 19 Mar. 1937, Birmingham, England. Professor of Clinical Neurophysiology; Hon. Consultant, Birmingham Central District Health Authority. m. Margaret, 6 Mar. 1961, Sutton Coldfield, England, 2 daughters. *Education:* BSc. Hons., University College, London, England; 1961, PhD, University of Birmingham, 1968. *Appointments:* Research Assistant, Applied Psychology, Aston University, England, 1961-62, Research Fellow, 1962-64, 1964-69, Professor of Clinical Neurophysiology, 1973-, Head of Department of Vision Sciences, 1981-; Honorary Consultant Neuropsychologist, Birmingham Area Health Authority, 1973-. *Memberships:* British Psychological Society; 1961; The EEG Society;

ISCEV. *Publications:* "Advances in Ophthlmology", 1974; "Photosensitive Epilepsy", 1975; "Visual Evoked Potentials in Man: New Developments", 1977; ''International Handbook of Electroencephalography'', 1977; "Evoked Potentials", 1980; "Clinical Applications of Evoked Potentials in Neurology", 1982. *Hobby:* Railway enthusiast. *Address:* Department of Vision Sciences, Aston University, Duke Street, Gosta Green, Birmingham B4 7ET, England.

HARDINGHAM, Michael, b. 16 Oct 1939, Birmingham, England, Consultant Ear, Nose and Throat Surgeon, m. 25 Sep. 1982, Gloucester, 1 son. *Education:* LRCP, MRCS, 1963, MB, BS, 1963, St Mary's Hospital Medical School, University of London; FRCS, Edinburgh, 1971; FRCS, London, 1973. *Appointments:* Senior House Officer, Royal Hospital for Sick Children, Edinburgh, Scotland, 1967; Regsitrar, Paediatric Surgery, Childrens Hospital, Gothenburg, Sweden, 1969; Senior Registrar, Otorhinolaryngology, St Mary's Hospital and Royal Marsden Hospital, London, England, 1971; Consultant Ear Nose and Throat Surgeon, Cheltenham General Hospital and Gloucester Royal Hospital, 1974. *Memberships:* Royal Society of Medicine; Association of Head and Neck Oncologists of Great Britain; National Association of Laryngectomy Society of Head and Neck Surgeons, USA. *Publications:* 'Management Recurrent Oral Malignant Disease', 1979; 'Reconstruction of Facial Defects', 1982; 'Cancer of Floor of Mouth – Clinical Oncology', 1977. *Hobbies:* Skiing; Sailing; Chairman, Board of Directors, Gloucester Arts. *Address:* 19 College Green, Gloucester GL1 2LR, England.

HARDJONO, Iskak Sastroredjo, b. 6 Oct. 1938, Semarang, Jawa, Indonesia. Head of Biochemistry Laboratory, University Diponegoro, Faculty of Medicine. m. Mrs. Siswanti, 1 Sep. 1966, Semarang, 3 sons, 1 daughter. *Education:* MD, Diponegoro University, Faculty of Medicine; PhD, Kyushu University School of Medicine, Fukuoka, Japan. *Appointments:* Assistant, Biochemistry Department, 1966; Junior Lecturer, 1974; Senior Lecturer, 1979; Head, Biochemistry Department, 1977-; Diponegoro University Faculty of Medicine. *Membership:* Perhimpunan Biokimie Indonesia. *Publications:* "2, 3-DPG and its correlation to hematocrit value (Observation on Indonesian people)", M.K.I. 11-12, 1976; 'Transport of phosphoenolpyruvate through the Erythrocyte Membrane', 'Biochem. Journal', 1978; "Effect of Osmolarity and Echinocytogenic Drugs on the Transport of phosphoenolpyruvate through the Red Cell Membranes", "Cell Structure and Function", 1980. *Hobbies:* Music; Swimming. *Address:* Biochemistry Laboratory, Diponegoro University Faculty of Medicine, jl.dr. Sutomo 18, Semarang 50231, Indonesia.

HARDMAN, Joel Griffeth, b. 7 Nov. 1933, Colbert, Georgia, USA. Professor of Pharmacology. m. Georgette Johnson, 16 July, 1955, Athens, USA, 1 son, 3 daughters. Education: BS, University of Georgia, USA, 1954, MS, 1959; PhD, Emory University, 1964. *Appointments:* Instructor of Pharmacy, University of Georgia, 1957-60; Instructor of Physiology, Vanderbilt University, 1964-67, Assistant Professor, 1967-70, Associate Professor 1970-72, Professor, 1972-75, Professor of Pharmacology and Department Chairman, 1975-. *Memberships:* American Society for Pharmacology and Experimental Therapeutics; American Society of Biological Chemists; American Association for the Advancement of Science; Basic Science Council of the American Heart Association. *Publications Include:* 82 articles in professional journals including: 'Calcium Induced Release from Platelet Membranes of Fatty Acids that Modulate Soluble Guanylate Cyclase' (co-author), in'Journal of Pharm. Exp. Terhap.', 1983; 'Cycling Nucleotides and Regulation of Vascular Smooth Muscle' in

'Cardiovascular Pharmacology', 1984; 'Differences in the Association of Calmodulin with Cyclic Phosphodiesterase in Relaxed and Contracted Arterial Strips', (co-author), in 'Biochemistry', 1985; 46 abstracts including 'Is Calmodulin-Sensitive Phosphodiesterase Activity Regulated by Changes in CA Levels in Intact Cells?' in 'Advances in Cyclic Nucleotide Research', (co-author), 1984; Numerous conference presentations. *Honours:* Franqui Foreign Visiting Professor, Free University of Brussels, 1974; H.B. Van Dyke Award, Columbia University, 1981. *Hobbies:* Reading; Music; Gardening. *Address:* Rt 1, Box 152, Primm Springs, TN, 38476, USA.

HARDY, Leslie Karen, b. 8 Mar. 1947, Sudbury, Ontario, Canada. Director and Associate Professor, School of Nursing, University of Lethbridge. divorced. *Education:* RN, Royal Victoria Hospital School of Nursing, Montreal, 1968; BN, McGill University, 1977; MScNed, PhD, University of Edinburgh, 1977, 83. *Appointments:* Instructor, School of Nursing, University of British Columbia, Vancouver, 1978-80; Associate Professor, School of Nursing, University of Lethbridge, Alberta, 1983-. *Memberships:* Alberta Association of Registered Nurses; Canadian Nurses Foundation; Canadian Health Education Society; International Council for Women's Health Issues. *Publications:* Contributor to professional journals including: "The Emergence of Nursing Leaders: A case of in spite of, not because of', 'Nursing Times', 12 Jan. 1983; co-author with J. Hughes, 'Learning Manipulation', 'Nurse Education Today', 1984; With L. Coutts, 1986, "Teaching for Health"; Presentations; Proceedings; Video Course on nursing elective "Women and Health", Jan. 1985; Book Reviewer for 'Nursing Times'; Participated in making video about communication skills with University of British Columbia Biomedical Communications Department, 1979. *Honours:* Overseas Research Student (ORS) Award, 1980; Commonwealth Scholar, 1981-83. *Hobbies:* Writing; Travelling. *Address:* School of Nursing, University of Lethbridge, 4401 University Drive, Lethbridge, Alberta T1K 3M4, Canada.

HARE, David Linley, b. 4 Sep. 1947, Melbourne, Australia. Medical Director; Assistant Cardiologist; Clinical Tutor. m. Jillian L Gleadow, 10 June 1974, Melbourne, 3 sons, 1 daughter. *Education:* MB BS 1972, DPM 1978, University of Melbourne; Fellow, Royal Australasian College of Physicians; Fellow, Royal Australian and New Zealand College of Psychiatrists. *Appointments:* Medical Registrar 1975, Psychiatry Registrar 1976-77, Senior Psychiatry Registrar 1978, Fellow in Cardiology 1980, Assistant Physician in Cardiology and General Medicine 1981-85, Currently Assistant Cardiologist, Austin Hospital, Melbourne; Medical Registrar, Guy's Hospital, London, England, 1979; Cardiologist 1981-84, Currently Medical Director, National Heart Foundation, Victoria Division, Australia; Currently clinical Tutor in Medicine, University of Melbourne. *Memberships:* Fellow, Royal Australasian College of Physicians; Fellow, The Australian and New Zealand College of Psychiatrists; Cardiac Society of Australia and New Zealand; Australian Medical Association; British Medical Association; Scientific Council on Rehabilitation, International Society of Cardiology. *Publications:* Research articles. *Address:* 11 View Street, Canterbury, Victoria 3126, Australia.

HARGARTEN, Stephen William, b. 5 Jan. 1949, Milwaukee, Wisconsin, USA. Medical Doctor; Emergency Staff Physician. 1 daughter. *Education:* BA, University of Wisconsin, 1971; MD, Medical College of Wisconsin, 1975; MPH, Johns Hopkins School of Public Health, 1984. *Appointments:* Staff Physician: St Marys Hospital, Milwaukee, Wisconsin, 1977; St Lukes Hospital, Milwaukee, 1985-. Assistant Clinical Professor, Department of Surgery, Emergency of Surgery, Emergency Medicine Section, Medical College of Wisconsin,

Milwaukee, 1985-. *Memberships:* American College of Emergency Physicians; American Medical Association; American Public Health Association. *Publications:* 'Facilaties in the Peace Corps', in 'Journal of American Medical Association', co-author, 1985. *Hobbies:* Squash; Cross Country; Skiing; Golf; Canoeing. *Address:* 1216 East Vienna Avenue, Milwaukee, WI 53212, USA.

HARIK, Sami I, b. 27 July 1941, Beirut, Lebanon. Professor of Neurology & Pharmacology. m. Wafa Bashir, 2 June 1968, 3 daughters. *Education:* BS, School of Arts & Sciences, MD, School of Medicine, American University of Beirut, Lebanon. *Appointments:* Assistant Neurologist, American University Medical Centre, 1973-76; Assistant Professor of Neurology, University of Miami School of Medicine, 1976-78; Attending Neurologist, Jackson Memorial Hospital, VA Medical Centre, 1976-91; Associate Professor of Neurology, 1978-81,Associate Professor of Pharmacology, 1979-81, University of Miami School of Medicine; Professor of Neurology, 1981-, Professor of Pharmacology, 1982-,Associate Neurologist, 1981-. Case Western Reserve School of Medicine. *Memberships:* American Academy of Neurology, 1969-81; Fellow, 1981-; Society for Neuroscience, 1971-; The Johns Hopkins Medical & Surgical Association, 1974-; Sigma Xi; Internaitonal Brain Research Organisaiton, 1975-; American Neurological Association, 1980-; Winter Conference on Brain Research, 1980-; International Society for Cerebral Blood Flow & Metabolism, 1981-. *Publications:* Over 70 articles & book chapters in medical publications. *Address:* Department of Neurology, University Hospitals of Cleveland, Cleveland, OH 44106, USA.

HARING, Gene Frances, b. 4 July 1940, San Francisco, California, USA. Psychiatrist. *Education:* BS, Jamestown College, North Dakota, 1961; MD 1965, Internship in Internal Medicine and Neurology 1965-66, Medical College of Pennsylvania, Philadelphia, 1965; Residency, Adult Psychiatry, Eastern Pennsylvania Psychiatirc Institute, Philadelphia, 1966-69; Certification, American Board of Psychiatry and Neurology, 1972. *Appointments:* Director of Structured Services 1969-77, Medical Director 1977-79, Luzerne-Wyoming Counties Mental Health Center, Wilkes-Barre, Pennsylvania; Chief of Psychiatry and Director of In-patient Psychiatric Services, Wilkes-Barre General Hospital and Luzerne-Wyoming Counties Mental Health Center, Wilkes-Barre, 1972-77; Private Practice, Adult Psychiatry, Kingston, 1979-. *Memberships:* American Psychiatric Association; American Group Psychotherapy Association; American Medical Women's Association; International Association of Social Psychiatry; Secretary-Treasurer, Northeastern Pennsylvania Psychiatric Association; International Society for the Study of Multiple Personality; Pennsylvania Psychiatric Association; American Association of Social Psychiatry. *Publications:* 'Embezzlement and Multiple Personality', 1982. *Honour:* Outstanding Professional in Human Services, The American Academy of Human Services, 1974-75. *Hobbies:* Music; Opera; Travel; Reading; Gardening. *Address:* 841 Wyoming Avenue, Kingston, PA 18704, USA.

HARNDEN, David Gilbert, b. 22 June 1932, London, England. Director of Paterson Laboratories and University Professor of Experimental Oncology. m. Thora Margaret Seatter, 9 July 1955, 3 sons. *Education:* BSc, 1954, PhD, 1957, University of Edinburgh; Royal College of Pathologists, Member 1970, Fellow 1982. *Appointments:* Assistant Lecturer, University of Edinburgh, 1956-57; Scientific Member of Medical Research Council, Radiobiology Unit, Harwell, 1957-59; Scientific Member of Medical Research Council, Clinical and

Population Cytogenetics Unit, Edinburgh, 1959-69; Research Fellow in Oncology, University of Wisconsin, 1963-64; Professor and Head of Department of Cancer Studies, University of Birmingham, 1969-83; Director of Paterson Laboratories and Professor of Experimetnal Oncology, University of Manchester, 1983-. *Memberships:* Fellow of Institute of Biology; Honorary Fellow and (currently) President, Association of Clincial Cytogenetecists; Member and (currently) Chairman, British Association for Cancer Research; Genetical Society; British Society for Cell Biology; Clinical Genetics Society. *Publications:* Many publicaitons in professional journals and books. *Honour:* Fellow of Royal Society of Edinburgh, 1982. *Hobbies:* Sketching; Gardening. *Address:* 'Tanglewood' Ladybrook Road, Bramhall, Stockport, Cheshire SK7 3NE, England.

HARNOIS, Gaston P, b. 6 Aug. 1933, Trois-Rivieres, Quebec, Canada. Douglas Hospital Centre, Director General. m. Renee Fortin, 10 Aug. 1957, Shawinigan, 2 sons, 1 daughter. *Education:* MD, University of Ottawa, 1959; Postgraduate, Wayne State University, Michigan, USA, 1964; Certificate in Hospital Administration, University of Montreal, Canada, 1970; Certificate in Community and Social Psychiatry, Columbia University, New York, USA, 1975; *Appointments:* Medical Superintendent, Hospital Pierre-Janet, Hull, Quebec, 1964-71; President, Conference of Hospital Psychiatrists, Quebec, 1973-76; Secretary, Chairman of Scientific Committee, Co-Chairman, Programme Committee, World Federation for Mental Health, 1975-84; President, Comité de la santé mentale du Quebec, 1980-; Consultant, Mental Health Division, World Health Organisation, Geneva, Switzerland, 1984-, Health and Welfare Canada; Associate Professor, Department of Psychiatry, McGill University, 1981-; Director General, Douglas Hospital Centre and Montreal World Health Organisation Collaborating Centre. *Memberships:* Canadian and American Psychiatric Associations; Canadian Mental Health Association; International Hospital Federation; World Psychiatric Association; World Federation for Mental Health; American Orthopsychiatric Association. *Publications:* "International Trends in the Delivery of Mental Health Services for Adults", 1978: contributor toProceedings of the VII World Congress of Psychiatry, Vienna, Austria, 1983; chapter in "Cultures in Collison", 1975. *Honours:* Fellow: Royal College of Physicians and Surgeons, Canada; American Psychiatric Association. Prix Vigor for outstanding contribution to field of hospital administration, 1984. *Hobbies:* Music; Theatre. *Address:* Douglas Hospital Center, 6875 LaSalle Boulevard, Verdun, Quebec, Canada H4H 1R3

HARPER, Clive G., b. 21 Apr. 1943, Sydney, Australia. Professor, Neuropathology. m. Jann Pullman, 4 Dec. 1965, Sydney, 2 sons, 1 daughter. *Education:* MB BS, Sydney; FRCPA. *Appointments:* Resident Medical Officer, Royal North Shore Hopspital, Sydney; Lecturer, Neuropathology, Glasgow University, Scotland; Medicin Assistant, Hopital Cantonal de Lausanne, Switzerland; Neuropathologist, Royal Perth Hospital; Postgraduate Fellow, Neuropathology, University of Pennsylvania, USA; Neuropathologist, Royal Perth Hospital; Professor, Neuropathology, University of Sydney. *Memberships:* British Neuropatholgoy Society; Australian Association of Neurologists; Australian & New Zealand Society of Neuropathologists; American Association of Neuropathologists; Australian neuroscience Society. *Publications:* Articles in professional journals. *Address:* Department of Pathology, University of Sydney, NSW 2006, Australia.

HARRINGTON, Douglas Stephen, b. 9 Jan. 1953, Butte, Montana, USA. Physician/University Fellow. m. Beth Anne Boardman, 27 Dec. 1982, Denver, Colorado, USA. *Education:* BA, Molecular, Cellular and Devleopmental Biology, 1975; MD, University of Colorado Medical Center, 1978. *Appointments:* House Surgeon, North Canterbury Hospital Board, Christchurch, New Zealand, 1978-79; Surgery Resident, University of Arizona Health Sciences Center, 1979-81; Pathology Resident, 1981-84, Instructor in Surgery, 1985, University of Colorado Health Sciences Center; Attending Physician, Littleton Clinic, Swedish Hospital, St Joseph's Hospital, Aurora Humana, all in Denver Colorado, 1985; Fellow, Hemato-Pathology, University of Nebraska, Health Sciences Center, 1985-86. *Memberships:* FCAP; ASCP; AMA; DMS; CMS; Aero MA; Phi Beta Kappa; AED; PSA. *Publications:* US Patent 4, 113, 467, 1978; "Characterization of the Pulmonary Esterases" JCR 1976; "Malignant Lymphoma in XLP Males" IAP 1986; "Immunopeenotype Characterization of B-Cell Malignant Lymphomas" 1985. *Honours:* Alfred Packer Award for Outstanding Achievement in Surgery, 1978; UCHSC Student Research Fellowship, 1976; Boetcher Health Professions Grant and Scholarship 1975-76; Alpha Epsilon Delta 1973; Phi Beta Kappa, 1975; CPCC Academic Excellence Award, 1977. *Hobbies:* Photography; Skiing; Guitar. *Address:* 11305 Evans Street §2, Omaha, NE 68164, USA.

HARRIS, Edmund Leslie, b. 11 Apr. 1928, Benoni, South Africa. Deputy Chief Medical Officer, DHSS. m. Robina S. Potter, 6 Aug. 1959, London, England. *Education:* MB BCh, University of the Witwatersrand, 1952; MRCP, 1959, FRCP, 1975, London; MRCP, 1959, FRCP, 1971, Edinburgh; HFCM, 1978; FFCM, 1980. *Appointments:* House Officer, Baragwanath Hospital & General Hospital, Johannesburg, 1953; General Practice, Benoni, South Africa, 1954; Medical Registrar, Tropical Medicine, Queen Marys Hospital, Roehampton, England, 1956; Medical Registrar, Royal Surrey County Hospital, Guildford, 1958; Senior Medical Registrar, General Hospital, Birmingham, 1959; Medical Director, Pharmaceutical Industry, 1962; Senior Medical Officer, 1969, Principal Medical Officer, 1972, Senior Principal Medical Officer, Head of Medicines, 1974, Deputy Chief Medical Officer, 1977-, DHSS; National Biological Board, 1975-77; Member, Public Health Laboratory Service Board, 1977-; Member, Central Blood Products Laboratory Authority, 1982-85. *Memberships:* Royal Society of Medicine; British Pharmacological Society. *Publications:* Various on: Clincial Trials, Adverse Drug Reactions, Drug Regulation. *Honour:* CB, 1981. *Hobbies:* Walking; Gardening; Photography. *Address:* Dept. of Health & Social Security, Alexander Fleming House, Elephant & Castle, London SE1 6BY, England.

HARRIS, James C, b. 6 Nov. 1940, Birmingham, Alabama, USA. Associate Professor. m. Catherine DeAngelis, 26 May 1979, Ossining, New York. *Education:* BS cum laude, University of Maryland, 1962; MD, George Washington University School of Medicine, Washington DC, 1966. *Appointments Include:* Director, Pediatric Neuropsychology, John F Kennedy Institute, Baltimore, 1976-; Director Child Psychiatry 1978-82, Director Psychiatric Education 1982-, Associate Professor, Psychiatry, Pediatrics 1982-, Johns Hopkins University. *Memberships Include:* American Psychiatric Association; American Association of Mental Deficiency; American Academy of Child Psychiatry. *Publications Include:* 'Neuroleptic Serum Levels in Mentally Retarded Boys Taking Thioridazine', (with L E Tune, M Kurtz and J T Coyle), 1982; 'Disappearance of a Urinary Antigonadotrophin Following HCG Administration in Prader Willi Syndrome', (with K Knigge), 1982; 'The Biological Basis for Self Injury in the Mentally Retarded', (with M F Cataldo), 1982;

'Comparison of Behavioural and Learning Disabled Children in Special Schools', (with S King, J Reifler and L Rosenburg) 1984; 'Hyperlexia in Infantile Autism', (with D Whitehouse and A O'Quinn), 1984; 'Sleep Disordered Breathing and Circadian Disturbances of REM Sleep in Prader Willi Syndrome', 1985. *Honours Include:* Pollen Award, 1965. *Hobby:* Swimming. *Address:* CMSC 337, Johns Hopkins Hospital, Baltimore, MD 21205, USA

HARRIS, Jules Eli, b. 12 Oct. 1934, Toronto, Ontario, Canada. Director, Medical Oncology. m. Josephine, 2 sons, 4 daughters. *Education:* MD, University of Toronto, 1959; Fellow, Royal College of Physicians & Surgeons of Canada, 1965; Fellow, American College of Physicians, 1967. *Appointments include:* Assistant Professor, Associate Professor, Professor of Medicine, University of Ottawa, Canada, 1969-78; Samuel G. Taylor III Professor of Medicine, Rush Medical College/Director, Section of Medical Oncology, Rush-Presbyterian-St. Luke's Medical Centre, Chicago, 1978-; Professor of Immunology, Rush Medical College, 1978-. *Memberships include:* Reticuloendothelial Society; Central Society for Clinical Research; American Association for Cancer Education; American Association for the Advancement of Science; American Federation for Clinical Research; Sigma Xi; etc. *Publications:* Author/co-author, numerous contributions to medical journals; Abstracts & letters; Series editor, Medical & Paediatric Oncology Adult Tumour Board. Books: "Immunology of Malignant Disease", with J.G.Sinkovics, 1970, 1975; Proceedings, 5th Leukocyte Culture Conference", editor, 1970; "Problems in Clincial Immunology", editor, volume 56, 1972; "Pathophysiology of Malignant Disease", editor with A.H. Rossof, in press; "Hormone Manipulation in the Therapy of Human Malignant Disease" in "Reviews on Endocrine-Related Cancer", ed. with S.G. Taylor, 1980. *Honours include:* Scholarship, awards, University of Toronto, 1953-59; Alpha Omega Alpha, 1958; Ernest Freyman Fellowship, 1962-63; Archibald Hutchinson Fellowship, 1966; Memorial Lecturer, Toronto 1974, Prince Edward Island 1973, Chicago 1977, 1983; Royal College of Physicians & Surgeons of Canada Lecturer, University of Ottawa, 1983; Visiting Professor, American Cancer Society (California division), 1984; etc. *Address:* Rush-Presbyterian-St. Luke's Medical Centre, Section of Medical Oncology, 1725 West Harrison Street, Suite 830, Chicago, IL 60612, USA.

HARRIS, Keith Wallington Hills, b. 15 July 1920, Grenfell, New South Wales, Australia. Consultant, Tuberculosis; Senior Chest Physician. m. Barbara Rosalind Birt, 29 Dec. 1948, Tambellup, 2 sons, 1 daughter. *Eduction:* MB., BS, Sydney; DPH, Sydney; FRACMA, Australia; FCCP, America. *Appointments:* RMO, Royal Perth Hospital, 1950-51; Senior Medical Officer, 1952, Assistant TB Physician, 1953-58, Public Health, Western Australia; Deputy Director, Tuberculosis, Dept. of Public Health, New South Wales, 1958-60; Lt. Col. CO7, 13 Fd. AMB., 1956-58, CO, 1 Fd.Amb, 1958-61; COL. CO, 1 Gen. Hospital, 1962-66; Director, Tuberculosis, Public Health & Commission, New South Wales, 1960-80;Director, Community Health & Antituberculosis Association, 1960-, Vice President, 1983-; Member, National Tuberculosis Advisory Council, 1960-80; Honorary Secretary, Ausrtralian TB & Chest Association, 1972; Secretary General, Eastern Region Internaitonal Union Against TB, 1974-76, 1984-; Director, St John Ambulance Association, 1975-, Deputy Chairman, 1983-85, Chairman, 1985-. *Memberships:* Thoracic Society of Australia; Australasian Society of Infectious Diseases; ANZSERCH; Australian College of Medical Administrators. *Honours:* Efficiency Decoration, 1962; Serving Brother, Order of St John of Jerusalem, 1982. *Hobbies:* Photography; Motoring; Fishing; Music. *Address:* Wandeen Road, Clareville 2107, NSW, Australia.

HARRIS, Malcolm, b. 8 Nov. 1934, Leeds, England. Professor; Consultant; Head, Oral & Maxillofacial Surgery. m. Naomi Cohen, 10 Jan. 1964, London, 1 son, 2 daughters. *Education:* MD; FDS; RCS; FFD; RCSI. *Appointments:* Formerly Consultant, Oral & Maxillofacial Surgeon, King's College Hospital, London; Currently Professor, Head, Oral & Maxillofacial Surgery, Eastman Dental Hospital and University College Hospital. *Memberships:* Bone & Tooth Society; British Association of Oral Surgeons; Alpha Omega; Association of Head and Neck Surgeons of Great Britain; International Association of Oral and Maxillofacial Surgeons; Patey Society; British Dental Association; Anglo-Israeli Medical Association; Royal Society of Medicine; International Association for Dental Research. *Publications:* "Psychogenic Facial Pain"; "Connective Tissue Destruction"; a variety of surgical topics. *Hobbies:* Music; Painting. *Address:* Eastman Dental Hospital, 256 Gray's Inn Road, London WC1 8LD, England.

HARRIS, Patrick Donald, b. 30 March 1940, Nebraska City, Neb, USA, University Chairman and Professor, m. Doris Jean, 18 July 1959, 2 sons, 1 daughter. *Education:* BS Hons, 1962, MS Hons, 1963, University of Missouri; PhD, Northwestern University, 1967; Postdoctoral Fellow in Physiology, Indiana University, 1967-68. *Appointments:* Assistant Professor, 1968-71, Associate Professor, 1971-74, Invesitgator, Dalton Research Centre/Associate Professor, 1974-77, Investigator, Dalton Research Centre, Professor of Physiology, 1977-80, Associate Director, Dalton Research Centre/Professor, 1980-81, University of Missouri; Visitng Associate, Biomed Engr, Division Engineering and Applied Science, California Institute of Technology, 1977-78; Professor, Chairman, Department Physiology and Biophysics, University of Louisville School of Medicine, Kentucky, 1981-. *Memberships:* President-elect, President, Past-President, 1985-88, National Executive Committee, 1982-86, National Committee Membership, 1979-83, National Committee Chairman, Landis Award, 1975-76, Nominations, 1974-75, National Committee Finance, 1970-74, Microcirculatory Society, 1965-; Fellow, Cardiovascular Section, 1982, APS-FASEB Programme Advisory Committee, 1982-84, APS Programme Executive Committee, 1984-87, American Physiological Society, 1970-; Institute of Electrical and Electronic Engineers, 1961-; Council on Basic Science, Council on Circulation; Council on High Blood Pressure Research, 1978-; American Heart association; Shock Society, 1981-. *Publications include:* 'Effects of tissue acidosis on skeletal muscle microcirculatory responses to hemorrhagic shock in unanesthetized rats', (with H M Cryer, H Kaebnick, L M Flint), 1985; 'Progressive microvascular alterations with the development of renovascular hypertension', (with I G Joshua, D L Weigman, F N Miller), 1984; 'Distributions of intra-vascualr pressure in skeletal muscle of one-kidney, one-clip, two-kidney, one-clip and Deoxycorticosterone-salt hypertensive rats', (with G A Meininger, I G Joshua), 1984. *Honours:* Recipient of numerous honours and awards. *Address:* Department of Physiology and Biophysics, School of Medicine 1115A HSC, University of Louisville, Louisville, KY 40292, USA.

HARRIS, Phillip John, b. 18 May 1945, Sydney, Australia. Director, Clinical Cardiology. m. Margaret Joan Fenton, 10 Dec.1970, Sydney, 1 son, 2 daughters. *Education:* BSc. Medicine, Honours, 1967, MB BS Honours I, 1973, University of Sydney; D.Phil., University of Oxford,1970. *Appointments:* Resident Medical Officer, 1973-74, Cardiology registrar, 1975-77, Royal Prince Alfred Hospital, Sydney; Cardiology Fellow, Duke University, USA, 1977-79; Staff Specialist, Cardiology, Royal Prince Alfred hospital, 1979-84; Director, Clinical Cardiology, Royal Prince Alfred Hospital.

Memberships: Fellow: American College of Cardiology, Royal Australasian College of Physicians, Clinical Cardiology Council, American Heart Association; Cardiac Society of Australia and New Zealand, Secretary, 1983-85. *Publications:* Numerous articles in professional journals including: 'American Journal Cardiology'; 'Journal Physiology'; 'Paraplegia'; etc. *Honours:* Rhodes Scholar, 1967. *Hobby:* Sailing. *Address:* Dept. of Cardiology, Royal Prince Alfred, Missenden Road, Camperdown, NSW 2050, Australia.

HARRIS, Trevor John, b. 19 Jan 1931, Warwick, Queensland, Australia. Plastic Surgeon. m. Dorothy Lowther, 4 May 1956, Brisbane, 2 sons, 4 daughters. *Education:* MB,BS,Queensland University; Fellow, Royal College of Surgeons, Glasgow, 1964; Fellow, Royal Australasian College of Surgeons, 1967. *Appointments:* Registrar, Glasgow and West of Scotland Regional Plastic Surgery service, 1964-65; Honorary Plastic Surgeon, Mater Misericordiae Hospital, Brisbane, 1967-72; Specialist Plastic Surgeon, Departemnt of Veterans' Affairs Hospital Greenslopes, 1967-74; Plastic Surgeon, Royal Brisbane Hospital, 1967-; Senior Surgeon to Head and Neck Clinic, Queensland Radium Institute, 1969-; Senior Platic Surgeon and Head of Department of Plastic Surgery, Royal Brisbane Hospital, 1971-. *Memberships:* Associate Member, British Association of Plastic Surgeons; Foreign Corresponding Member, Society of Head and Neck Surgeons, USA; President, Australian Society of Plastic Surgeons, 1983-85; Chairman, Division of Plastic and Reconstructive Surgery, 1983-85, Royal Australian College of Surgeons; Chairman, Head and Neck Section, Clinical Oncological Society of Australia, 1981-86; Board Member, RACS Board of Plastic and Reconstructive Surgery, 1983-. *Publications:* 'Intra-Oral Carcinoma' with AJJ Emmettin 'Operative Plastic and Reconstructive Surgery' edited by Barron and Saad, 1980; Sections in 'Malignant Skin Tumours' edited by Emmett and O'Rourke, 1982; 'Morbidity of Radical Neck Dissection' in Journal of Otolaryngological Society of Australia, 1980; 'Melanoma of the Head and Neck in Queensland' with DM Hinckley in 'Head and Neck Surgery' 1983. *Honour:* Foundation Lecturer, RACS (Queensland) 1984. *Address:* Morris Towers, 149, Wickham Terrace, Brisbane, Queensland 4000, Australia.

HARRISON, Donald Dean, b. 11 May 1946, Port Angeles, Washington, USA. Doctor of Chiropractic. m. Sanghak Oh, 1 Jan, 1986, Reno. Nevada, 2 sons, 1 daughter. *Education:* BS Mathematics, University of Washington; MS Mathematics, University of Texas at El Paso; Additional Year's Study, Washington State University; Secondary Teaching Certificate, Western Washington State College; DC, Western States Chiropractic College; International Chiropractors Research Programme (with Prof Chung Ha Suh), University of Colorado. *Appointments:* Instructor, Washington State University; Instructor, Peninsula Community College; Instructor, Mount Hood Community College; Instructor & President, Harrison Chiropractic Seminars Inc; Post graduate Faculty, Life Chiropractic Colleges, Georgia & California; Assistant Professor of Biomechanics, Northern California College of Chiropractic. *Membership:* International Chiropractic Association. *Publications:* "Chiropractic Biophysics", volume 1 1980, volume 2 1982 (College Text); "X-Ray Workbook for Chiropractic Biophy"; 1980; Original corrective procedures taught in his textbooks, by applying mechanics to the spine, human posture. *Hobbies:* 3-Dimensional computer-aided analysis of spine; Fishing; Hunting. *Address:* Evanston Chiropractic Centre, 170 Yellow Creek Road Suite D, Evanston, WY 82930, USA.

HARRISON, Glenn Richard, b. 19 Dec. 1947, Port Angeles, Washington, USA. Doctor of Chiropractic, Private Practice. m. Irene D Duval, 15 July 1967, Port Angeles, 1 son, 1 daughter. *Education:* AA, Peninsula Junior College; BA, University of Washington; DC Western States Chiropractic College; Distinguished Fellow, International Chiropractors Association, 1983; Fellow, Society of Public Health Educations. *Appointments:* Private Practitioner; Continuing Education Faculty, Life Chiropractic College and Palmer College, Pasadena College of Chiropractics. *Memberships:* Secretary, Wyoming State Board of Chiropractic Examiners; State Representatvie, International Chiropractors Associations; Board Member, Wyoming Chiropractic Society (Past President); American Public Health Association; Association for the History of Chiropractic; Past President, Lander Kiwanis Club; Chamber of Commerce; Elks; Shrine; Master Mason, Blue Lodge. *Publications:* 'The Physics of Spinal Correction', Co-author, volume II, 1982; 'History of Scientific Chiropractic and Spinal Correction', presented at Upper Cervical Conference, Wyoming, 1984and published in 'Chiropractic Economics'. *Honours:* Distinguished Fellow, International Chiropractic Association, 1983; Fellow, Society of Public Health Educators, 1984; Meritorious Service Award, President of International Chiropractors Association, 1984. *Hobbies:* Fishing; Hunting. *Address:* 550 Main Street, Suite 1, Lander, WY 82520, USA.

HARRISON, Saul I., b. 4 Nov, 1925, New York, NY, USA. Professor; Director. *Education:* MD,University of Michigan, 1948. *Appointments:* Instructor, Psychiatry, Temple University Hospital and School of Medicine. Philadelphia, 1954-56; Assistant Professor 1956-61, Associate Professor 1961-66, Professor 1966-84, Professor Emeritus, University of Michigan School of Medicine, Ann Arbor, Michigan Medical center, Ann Arbor; Professor and Director of Child and Adolescent Psychiatry. Harbor UCLA Medical Center, Torance, California, 1984-. Director of Child and Adolescent Psychiatry Education, University of Michigan Medical Center, Ann Arbor; *Memberships:* FAPA; FACP;FACCP;FAOA; GAP; American Psa. Assn. *Publications Include:* "A Guide to Psychotherapy", (with D J Varek), 1966; "Childhood Psychopathology", (co-editor with J F McDermott), 1972; "Psychiatric Treatment of the Child", (co-editor with J F McDermott), 1977; "Therapeutic Interventions"; (editor), Volume III of Noshpitz's Basic Handbook of Child Psychiatry, 1979; "New Directions in Childhood Psychopathology, Volume I: Developmental Considerations", (with J F McDermott Jr), 1980; "New Directions in Childhood Psychopathology, Volume II: Deviations in Development", (editor with J F McDermott),1982; Author of 80 Chapters in books and artricles; Abstracts; Reviews; Panel Discussions. *Honour:* Commonwealth fund Fellowship, 1966. *Address:* Harbor-UCLA Medical Center, 1000 West Carson Street, Torrance, CA 90509, USA.

HART, George Babe, b. 29 January 1930, Lamesa, Texas, USA. Director, Baromedical Department. m. Sara McVey Hart, 20 Dec. 1953, Galveston, Texas, 3 sons, 2 daughters. *Education:* BA Biology, 1952; MD, 1956. *Appointments:* Chief of Surgery, Naval Hospitals, Guantanamo Bay, Cuba 1965-67, Naval Regional Medical Centre, Lond Beach, California, 1967-75; Director, Hyperbaric Oxygen Research, 1968-75, Director, Surgical Education, 19698-75, Naval Regional Medical Center, Long Beach; Assistant Clinical Professor of Surgery, University of California at Irvine, 1970-; Chief of Surgery, Director of clinical Services, Naval Regional Medical Center, Corpus Christi, Texas, 1975-77; Visiting Professor of Thoracic Surgery, University of Texas, 1975-77; Staff Surgeon, Director, Baromedical Unit, Shrine Burn Institute, Galveston, Texas, 1975-77; Director,

Baromedical Department, Memorial Medical Centre, Long Beach, 1975-. *Memberships:* American Medical Association; Diplomate, American Board of Surgery; Diplomate, Board of Thoracic Surgery; Fellow, Society of Thoracic Surgeons; Fellow, American College of Surgeons; Fellow, American College of Chest Physicians; International Society for Burns; American Burn Association; International Congress on Hyperbaric Medicine; Fellow, Royal Society of Medicine (GB); and others. *Publications:* Various articles on emergency medicine in medical journals. *Honours;* Navy Commendation Medal, 1977; Physicians Recognition Award, 1977, 1981, 1984. *Hobbies:* Golf; Sailing; Medical & Recreational Photography. *Address:* 2888 Long Beach Boulevard, Suite 240, Long Beach, CA 90806, USA.

HART, Francis Dudley, b. 4 Oct. 1909, Glossop, Derbyshire, England. Consulting Physician. m. Mary Josephine Tully, 18 Dec. 1944, Barletta, Italy, 1 son, 2 daughters. *Education:* Bachelor of Medicine, Bachelor of Surgery, Edinburgh, Scotland, 1933; MD, Edinburgh, 1939; Member, Royal College of Physicians, 1937, Fellow, 1949, London, England. *Appointments:* Medical Registrar, Royal Northern Hospital, 1935-37; Medical Registrar, Westminster Hospital, 1939; Medical Specialist, Officer Commanding Medical Division, RAMC, 1942-46; Consultant Physician, Westminster Hospital, 1946-74, Chelsea Hospital for Women, 1950-74, St Stephen's Hospital, 1960-74, Hospital of St John & St Elizabeth, 1960-74; Honorary Civilian Consultant in Medicine to the Army, 1972-74. *Memberships:* Fellow, Royal College of Physicians; Fellow, Royal Society of Medicine; Honorary Members, British Society for Rheumatology; Medical Society of London; Honorary Member, Ligue Français Contre le Rheum; Rheumatism Associations of America, Italy & Australia. *Publications:* Editor, 3 editions of "French's Index of Differential Diagnosis", 1973, 1979, 1985; "Practical Problems in Rheumatology", 1983; Editor, 2 editions "Drug Treatment of the Rheumatic Diseases", 1978, 1982; (with E C Huskisson) "Joint Disease" (3 editions), 1973, 1975, 1978. *Honour:* Mentioned in Despatches, 1945. *Hobbies:* Music; Travel. *Address:* 24 Harmont House, 20 Harley Street, London, W1N 1AN, England.

HART, John Lewis, b. 8 Sep. 1942, Kansas City, Missouri, USA. Director, Physical Medicine & Rehabilitation. m. Sandra K , 1 daughter. *Education:* BA, University of Missouri; DO, Kansas City College of Osteopathic Medicine. *Appointments include:* General practice, Fredericktown, Missouri, 4 years; Madison Memorial Hospital, 1970-74; Assioate Professor, PM&R, University of Missouri, Columbia, 1977; Director, Physical Medicine & Rehabilitation, Charles E. Still Osteopathic Hospital, Jefferson City, Missouri, 1978-. *Memberships:* President, Fellow, Board Certified, American Osteopathic College of Rehabilitation Medicine; Board Certified, American College of Physical Medicine & Rehabilitation; American Association of Electrodiagnosis & Electromyography; National, State, Local Osteopathic Societies; International Society for the Study of Pain; American Society for the Study of Pain. *Publications include:* 'Herniated Disc, How to Treat Without Surgery', (Modern Medicine, 1984); 'The Secret Disorders of Stroke Patients' (Cooperation, 1984); 'Non-Operative Treatment of Herniated Disc', 1985. Various presentations, professional conferences. *Honour:* Osteopathic Physician of the Year Award, 1984. *Hobby:* Sailing. *Address:* Route 3, Box 464, Holts Summit, MO 65043, USA.

HARTER, Alan Campbell, b. 13 Mar. 1925, Canton, Ohio, USA. Executive Director, Fairview Health Systems Inc., Great Barrington, Massachusetts. m. Barbara Elliott Weeks, 21 Mar. 1981. 2 sons, 1 daughter. *Education:* AB, Williams College, Massachusetts, 1949; MD, State University of New York, Buffalo, 1955; Internship/residency, Dartmouth Medical School, Hanover, New Hampshire, 1955-59; MPH, Harvard University, 1966; Diploma, US Air Force School of Aerospace Medicine, 1965; Diploma, US Navy School of Deep Sea Divers, 1967. *Appointments include:* Chief, Launch Site Medical Operations, NASA, Kennedy Space Centre, Florida, 1966-70; Chief, Medical Services, NASA, ibid, 1970-72; Adjunct Professor, Aerospace Medicine, Florida Institute of Technology, 1970-72; Division Medical Director, General Electric Company, Erie, Pennsylvania, 1972-84; Medical Director, Occupational Health, Control Data Corporation, Rockville, Maryland, 1984-85; Executive Director, Fairview Health Systems Inc., 1985-. *Memberships:* Fellow, American College of Preventive Medicine, American Occupational Medical Association; Member, American Academy of Occupational Medicine, Aerospace Medical Association, Massachusetts Medical Society. *Honour:* Presidential Medal of Freedom, US Government, 1972,. *Hobbies:* Flying; Skiing. *Address:* PO Box 1129, Stockbridge, MA 01262, USA.

HARTMAN, Boyd Kent, b. 21 Oct. 1939, Wichita, Kansas, USA. Professor. m. Ann Quatrevaley, 20 Aug. 1960, Haddonfield, New Jersey, 1 son, 1 daughter. *Education:* AB, 1962, MD, 1966, University of Kansas. *Appointments:* Associate Professor, 1974-78, Psychiatry, Associate Professor, 1975-82, Professor, 1982-, Neurobiology, Professsor, Psychiatry, 1978-, Washington University School of Medicine, St Louis. *Memberships:* American Psychiatric Association; American Psychopathological Association Inc; American Society for Neurochemistry; American Society of Biological Chemists; American Society Pharmacology & Experimental Therapeutics; St Louis Medical Society; Society for Neuroscience; Eastern Missouri Psychiatric Society; International Society Neurochemistry; Psychiatric research Society. *Publications:* Articles in scientific journals including: 'Science'; 'American Journal Pathology'; 'Biochemistry'; 'Pharmacologist'; 'Brain Research'; etc. *Honours:* Sheard-Stanford Award, 1966; A.E. Bennett Award, 1971; Falck Fellow, 1971-72; Research Scientist Development Award, 1972; Phi Lamda Upsilon; Phi Beta Kappa; Alpha Omega Alpha. *Hobbies:* Skiing; Camping. *Address:* Washington University School of Medicine, Department of Psychiatry, 4940 Audubon Avenue, St Louis, MO 63110, USA.

HARTMAN, Charles Richard, b. 1 Oct. 1937, Kansas City, Missouri, USA. Professor of Medicine. 1 son, 2 daughters. *Education:* AB, University of Kansas, 1962; MD, University of Kansas Medical School, 1966. *Appointments:* Internship, Wesley Medical Center, 1966-67; Chief of Endocrinology 1972-83, Consultant 1983-, Veterans Administration Hospital; Resident in Internal Medicine 1967-69, Endocrinology Fellowship 1969-70 and 1972-73, Assistant Professor of Medicine 1973-78, Associate Professor 1978-82-, Director of Emergency Services 1977-83, Vice-Chancellor for Clinical Affairs 1979-83, Chief of Staff 1979-, University of Kansas Medical Society; Wyandotte County Medical Society; Fellow, American College of Physicians; American Federation for Clinical Research; The Endocrine Society. *Publications:* 'Evidence for the Biosynthesis of PTH-like Peptides by a Human Squamous Cell Carcinoma', (with R R MacGregor, L L H Chu, C S Anast, D V Cohn and J W Hamilton), 1977; 'Hypertensive Crisis resulting From Avocados and an MAO Inhibitor', (with J A Generali, L C Hogan, M McFarlane and s Schwab), 1981; "Correlation of Hemoglobin A C and Nurve Conduction Studies in Diabetic Patients', (with P A Singer, B W Festoff, A N Reeder, L Spencer and K Hassanein), 1981. *Address:* 8921 Horton, Overland Park, KS 66207, USA.

HARTMAN, Nancy Lee, b. 29 July 1951, Philipsburg, Pennsylvania, USA. Physician. *Education:* BA, Biology, Lycoming College, 1972; MS, Medical Biology, Long Island University, 1977; MD, American University of Carribbean, 1981. *Appointments:* Various Hospitals, 1971-78; Laboratory Supervisor, CLI Labs Inc., Westbury, 1981-82; Medical Internship Program, Interfaith Medcial Centre, Brooklyn, 1983-84; EMSI, Dallas, Texas, 1984-85; Medical Centre, Brooklyn, 1984-85; Medical Consultant, Malpracitc Law Firm, Shapiro, Baines & Saasto, Mineola, 1985-. *Memberships:* International Platform Association; New York Academy of Science; American Society of Clinical Pathologists; American Society for Microbiology. *Publication:* "The Hand Pocketbook of Infectious Agents and Their Treatments". *Awards:* Recipient, Allied Health professions Traineeship Grant, 1975-77. *Hobbies:* Jogging; Scuba Diving; Travel; Skiing; Flying; Tennis; Free Lance Modelling. *Address:* PO Box 98, Roslyn, NY 11576, USA.

HARTOCOLLIS, Peter, b. 29 Nov. 1922, Greece. Professor of Psychiatry. m. Pitsa (Calliope) Palli, 8 Apr. 1953, Greece, 1 son, 2 daughters. *Education:* AB, Clark University, Worcester, Massachussetts, USA, USA; MD, Lausanne Medical School, Switzerland; Certificate American Board of Psychiatry and Neurology; Certificate, Topeka Institute for Psychoanalysis. *Appointments:* Hospital SectionChief, The Menninger Foundation, Topeka, Kansas, USA; Director of Hospital Research, Hospital Director; Training and Supervising Analyst, Topeka Institue for Psychoanalysis; *Memberships:* Hellenic Psychoanalytic Association; American Psychoanalytic Association; International Psychoanalytic Association; American Psychiatric Association. *Publications:* Editor "Borderline Personality Disorders", 1977; "Time and Timelessness", 1984; "Introduction to Psychiatry" (in Greek), 1986; over 50 scientific articles. *Honours:* Spencer Foundation Fellow in Advanced Studies, 1976-79; Visiting Professor, New York Hospital Cornell Medical Centre, 1978; Visiting Professor, Langley Porter Institute, University of California at San Francisco, 1978. *Hobbies:* Chess; Literature. *Address:* Psychiatry Department, University of Patras Medical School, PO Box 1045, 261 10 Patras, Greece.

HARVALD, Bent Jergen, b. 11 Feb. 1924, Copenhagen, Denmark. Professor. m. Ulla Agnethe Neilson, 5 Apr. 1952, 2 sons, 1 daughter. *Education:* MD, 1947; PhD, 1954; Professor, 1969. *Appointments:* Lecturer, Clinical Genetics, University of Copenhagen, 1961-69; Chief Physician, Internal Medicine, C, Bispebjerg Hospital, Cophenagen, 1961-69; Chief Physician, Queen Ingrid Hospital, Godthab, Greenland, 1965-66; Professor, Chief Physician, Dept. B, Odense University Hospital, 1981, 1969-81, Professor, Chief Physician, Dept. C., 1981-, Odense University Hospital. *Memberhips:* Danish Medical Research Council, 1968-76; Danish Registration Committee for Genetic Engineering; Nordic Council for Arctic Medical Research; Danish Medical Association; Danish Association of Internal Medicine; Danish Association of Clinical Pharmacology; International Society for Twin Studies; International Society of Hypertension. *Publications:* "Heredity in Epilepsy" 1954; "Circumpolar Health", 1981; Papers in professional journals etc. *Honours:* The Odd fellow Prize, 1971; The Carlsen Prize, 1976; The Gaardon Prize, 1984; Knight of Dannebrog 1st Degree, 1983. *Hobby:* Studies of Arctic Nature. *Address:* Langelinie 163, DK 5230 Odense M, Denmark.

HARVARD-DAVIS, Robert, b. 14 June 1924, Cardiff, Wales. Professor, General Practice. m. Valerie Smart, 5 Aug. 1953, Radyr, 1 son, 1 daughter. *Education:* Marlborough College; MA, DM, BM, Bch, Queen's College, Oxford; Guy's Hospital, London;

FRCGP. *Appointments:* Principal, General Practice, Cardiff, 1950-68; Senior Lecturer, 1968-75, Reader, 1975-79, Professor, 1979-, General Practice, University of Wales College of Medicine. *Memberships:* Past Member, Central Health Services Council; Standing Medical Advisory Committee, Medicines Commission; Committee on Child Health Services; Chairman, Committee, Organisation of Group Practice. *Publications:* "General Practice for Students of Medicine", 1975; "Parathyroid Insufficiency", 1961; "The Organisation of Group Practice, HMSO", 1971; "The Potential in each Primary Care Consultation", 1979. *Hobbies:* Cricket; Golf; Fishing; Travel. *Address:* Little Acre, Corntown, Mid Glamorgan CF35 5BB, Wales.

HARVEY, Michael William, b. 25 Sept, 1950, Schenectady, New York, USA. Managing Editor; Program Director. *Education:* MLS/MA, Columbia University Schools of Library Services and Journalism, New York, 1973; BA, Columbia University, New York; MA, in progress, City University of New York. *Appointments:* Medical Research Editor, MEDCOM, Inc., New York, NY., 1974-76; Editor, "Diabetes Outlook", Science and Medicine Publishing Company, New York, NY, 1976-78; Senior Writer and Editor, Emergency Medicine Magazine, New York, NY, 1978-80; Managing Editor, Transitions In Medicine, VICOM Association, San Fransisco, CA, 1980-82; Senior Editor for all VICOM Medical Publications. *Memberships:* American Medical Writers Association; Naitonal Audobon Society. *Honours:* Pfizer Award for Outstanding Medical Journalism, 1977; Best in the West Award for Transitions, 1981. *Hobbies:* Short Story Writing; Musicology Composition; Tennis; Travel; Swimming; Interior Design. *Address:* 1570 10th Avenue, San Francisco, CA 94122, USA.

HARVIN, James Shand, b. 19 Dec. 1929, Sumter, South Carolina, USA. Associate Professor and Head of Plastic and Maxillofacial Surgery. m. Abbie Leah Bradham, 1 Sep. 1951, Sumter, 2 sons, 2 daughters. *Education:* AB, Duke University, 1951; MD, Medical University of South Carolina, 1953. *Appointments include:* Assistant Chief 1961-62, Chief 1962-63, Plastic Surgery, Wright-Patterson Air Force Base Hospital, Dayton, Ohio; Assistant Chief 1963-64, Chief 1964-67, Plastic Surgery, Wilford Hall United States Air Force Base, San Antonio, Texas; Associate Professor, Head of Plastic and Maxillofacial Surgery, Medical University of South Carolina, Charleston, 1967-. *Memberships include:* South Carolina Surgical Society; Fellow, American College of Surgeons; American Society of Plastic and Reconstructive Surgeons; Military Association of Platic Surgeons; Society of Air Force Clinical Surgeons; Society of Head and Neck Surgeons; Southeastern Society of Plastic and Reconstructive Surgeons; American Medical Association; South Carolina Medical Association; Pi Kappa Alpha. *Publications include:* "Plastic and Reconstructive Surgery", (with James Barret Brown), 1961; 'Homotransplantation of a cadaver neoplasm and renal homograft', (co-author), 1965; 'The role of the orthodontist on the cleft palate team in a military hospital', (co-author), 1966; 'Team approach cure of cleft lip and palate', (with H Gruber), 1966. *Hobbies:* Horseback riding; Boating. *Address:* 171 Ashley Avenue, Charleston, SC 29425, USA.

HARWOOD-NASH, Derek Clive, b. 11 Feb. 1936, Bulawayo, Southern Rhodesia (Zimbabwe). Radiologist-in-Chief and Professor of Radiology m. Barbara Jordan, 9 Mar. 1963, Ontario, Canada, 3 daughters. *Education:* MB ChB, University of Cape

Town, Republic of South Africa; LMCC, Canada; DMR, University of Toronto; Fellow, Royal College of Physicians and Surgeons of Canada. *Appointments:* Paediatric Neuroradiologist, 1968, Radiologist in Chief, 1978-, Hospital for Sick Children, Toronto, Ontario Canada; Professor of Radiology, University of Toronto. *Memberships:* Radiological Society of North America; Canadian Association of Radiology; American Association of Neurological Surgeons. President: Society of Paediatric Radiology; American Society of Neuroradiology. *Publications:* "Neuroradiology in Infants and Children", 1976; "CT and Myelography of the Spine and Cord", 1982; "Anomalies of the Central Nervous System", 1985; author of 157 scientific articles and book chapters. *Honours;* Sir Alfred Beit Scholar, 1961-63; Honorary Member, Swedish Society of Medical Radiology and Medalist; 37 Visiting Professorships, Worldwide. *Hobbies:* Cross country skiing; Classical music and opera; Rare wines and Gourmet food. *Address:* c/o Hospital for Sick Children, 555 University Avenue, Toronto, Ontario, Canada M5G 1 XB.

HASAN, Mohammad Khalid, b. 16 Dec. 1942, India. Psychiatrist in Private Practice; Staff Psychiatrist. m. Surayia, 1 son, 2 daughters. *Education:* BSc, MB, BS, MD, Allahabad University; Diploma of Psychological Medicine, Conjoint Board of England; Fellow, Royal College of Psychiatry. *Appointments Include:* Senior House Officer, Internal Medicine, Bromsgrove General Hospital, England, 1969-70; Training in Adult Psychiatry, 1971-74; Psychiatry Senior Registrar and Honorary Lecturer, Medical School, University of Birmingham, 1974-75; Staff Psychiatrist, Cherry Hospital, North Carolina, USA, 1975, Beckley Appalachian Regional Hospital and FMRS Mental Health Center, 1975-77; Chief, Division of Psychiatry, Beckley Appalachian Regional Hospital, 1977-; Assistant Clinical Professor, Marshall University; Clinical Associate Professor, West Virginia University; currently, Private Practice, Raleigh Psychiatry Services Incorporated. *Memberships Include;* American and Canadian Psychiatric Associations; Raleigh County Medical Society; Royal College of Psychiatrists, UK; Biofeedback Society of America; American Geriatric Society; West Virginia State Health Planning and Development Agency. *Publications:* Numerous including: "Overseas Doctors in Psychiatry", 1975; "Psychogenic-Fever - An Entity or Non-Entity", 1979; "Depression and Thyrotoxicosis", 1981; "Establishing Lithium Clinics in Office Practice", 1982; "Diagnosis and Treatment of Alzheimer's Disease"; "Monoamine Oxidase Inhibitors: Clinical Profile of Responders", 1983. *Honours:* Certified: American Board of Psychiatry and Neurology, 1980; Royal College of Physicians and Surgeons, Canada, 1977; Royal College of Physicians, London, England, 1971. *Hobbies:* Tennis; Racquetball. *Address:* Raleigh Psychiatric Services Incorporated, 24 Mallard Court, PO Box 1025, Beckley, WV 25802-1025, USA.

HASAN, Mushtaq, b. 7 Apr. 1919, Jehlum, Punjab, Pakistan. Professor. m. Zubaida Malik, 17 Apr. 1955, Rawalpindi, Pakistan 1 son, 1 daughter. *Education:* MD, Punjab; Fellow, Royal College of Physicians, Edinburgh, Scotland; FCPS Pakistan; Europahjelpen Fellow in Tuberculosis, Norway. *Appointments:* House Physician, Mayo Hospital, Lahore, 1942-43; Assistant Demonstrator, Department of Pathology, King Edward Medical College, Lahore, 1943-48; Lecturer in Medicine, 1948-53, Assistant Professor of Medicine, 1953-56, Dow Medical College, Karachi; professor of Medicine, Nishtar Medical College, Multan, 1956-60; Professor of Medicine, Liaquat Medical College, Hyderabad, 1960-61; Professor of Medicine, F.J. Medical College, Lahore, 1961-63; Professor of Medicine, Dow Medical College, Karachi, 1963-79; Professor & Head of Department of Medicine, karachi University, 1966-79.

Memberships: Pakistan Medical Association; British Medical Association; Founder Fellow, Pakistan Cardiac Society; Fellow, Royal Society of Tropical Medicine & Hygeine, London; Fellow, American College of Chest Physicians; Fellow, International College of Angiology; Member, Rotary Club of Karachi. *Publications:* Various articles in medical and scientific journals. *Address:* 54 Khayaban-1-Hafiz, Defence Housing Authority, Phase V, Karachi-46, Pakistan.

HASHMI, Farrukh Siyar, b. 12 Sep. 1927, Guyrat, Pakistan. Consultant Psychiatrist. m. Shahnaz, 1972, 1 son, 2 daughters. *Education:* MB, BS, MRCPsych; DPM; FRCPsych, King Edward Medical College, Punjab University, Lahore. *Appointments:* Senior House Officer, Brook General Hospital, Woolwich, 1955-56; Senior House Officer, Snowdon Road Hospital, Bristol, 1956; Assistant MOH, Co. Berwicks, 1957; Registrar, Uffculme Clinic and All Saints Hospital, Birmingham, 1960-063; Research Fellow, Department of Psychiatry, Birmingham University, 1963-66; Senior Registrar, Uffculme Clinic and All Saints Hospital, Birmingham, 1966-69; Chairman of Psychiatric Division, West Birmingham Health District, 1977-83. *Memberships:* Commission for Racial Equality; West Midlands Regional Health Authority; Central District Authority, Birmingham; UK Committee, World Federation for Mental Health and many others. *Publications:* "Pakistan Family in Britian" 1965; "Mores, Migration and Mental Illness" 1966; "Psychology of Racial Prejudice" 1966; "Community Psychiatric Problems Among Birmingham Immigrants" 1968; "In a Strange Land" 1970; "Measuring Psychological Distrubance in Asian Immigrants to Britain" 1970. *Honour:* OBE, 1974. *Hobbies:* Writing; Reading; Music. *Address:* 5 Woodbourne Road, Edgbaston, Birmingham B15 3QJ, England.

HASLAM, Colleen, b. 19 Apr. 1952, Clovis, New Mexico, USA. Registered Nurse, Department Head, Medical/Surgical & Oncology Unit. *Education:* BS Nursing, University of Utah; Master of Organizational Behaviour, Brigham Yound University. *Appointments:* Staff Registered Nurse, LDS Hospital, 1974-75; Health Mission, Taipei, Taiwan, 1975-77; Head Nurse, Department Head, LDS Hospital, 1977-78; Management Intern, IBM, 1980; Assistant Director of Nursing, Idaho Falls Consolidated Hospital, 1981-82; Department Head, Cottonwood Hospital, 1982-. *Memberships:* National Oncology Nursing Society; Utah Air National Guard; Association of Air National Guard Nurses; Educational Sub-committee, American Cancer Society; Association of Military Surgeons of the US. *Publications:* 'Chemotherapy' Certification Programme, 1984. *Hobbies:* Sports; Music; Poetry. *Address:* 1958 South 400 East, Bountiful, 84010, USA.

HASLER, John Clendinnen, b. 21 Feb. 1937, London, England. General Practitioner; Clinical Lecturer. m. Lindsay Willans, 28 Apr. 1962, 4 sons. *Education:* MB, BS, 1960, MD, 1982, Middlesex Hospital Medical School, University of London; FRCGP; DA; DCH. *Appointments:* House Surgeon, Surgical Studies, Middlesex Hospital, 1961; House Physician, Mount Vernon Hospital, 1961; Casualty Surgical Officer, Middlesex Hospital, 1962; Senior House Officer, Anaesthetics, Salisbury Hospitals, 1962; Nuffield Practitioner, British Posgraduate Medical Federation, Wessex Region, 1963; Clinical Assistant Anaesthetist, Reading Hospitals, 1966; General Practitioner, Sonning Common Health Centre; Regional Postgraduate Adviser, Clinical Lecturer, General Practice, University of Oxford. *Memberships:* Council Member, Chairman, Royal College of General Practitioners; Reading Pathological Society; Non-Residential Visiting Fellow, Green College, University of Oxford. *Publications:* Numerous articles on Health Team, GP

Education, etc.; Joint Editor: "Doctor Patient Communcation", 1983; "Continuing Care: chronic Disease", 1984; "Primary Health Care 2000", in press. *Honours:* OBE, 1984. *Hobbies:* Gardening; Walking; Photography. *Address:* Crossways Kingwood, Henley on Thames, Oxon RG9 5LR England.

HASSI, Jaakko Juhani, b. 13 Sept. 1943, Raahe, Finland. Director. m. Tyne Kivihalme, 30 Jan. 1976, 3 sons, 1 daughter. *Education:* MD; Docent. *Appointments:* Director, Merikoski Rehabilitation Centre, 1969-71; Assistant, Institute of Occupational Health, 1972-73; Director, Oulu Regional Institute of Occupational Health; 1973-. *Memberships:* International Commission on Occupational Health; Laakariseura Duodecim; Suomen Teollisuuslaaketieteen yhdistys. *Publications:* "The Brown Adipose tissue in man", "Acta Universitatis Ouluensis", 1977; 'Arrangement of municipal occupational health services for small workplaces', co-author, "Scandinavian Journal Work Environmental Health", 1979; etc. *Hobby:* Hiking. *Address:* Oulu Regional Institute of Occupational Health, PO Box 451, SF 90101 Oulu, Finland.

HASTINGS, Garth Winton, b. 24 Mar. 1932, Portsmouth, Hampshire, England. Head of Biomedical Engineering Unit. m. Theresa Helen Dunford, 12 Apr. 1958, Chingford, Essex, 2 sons, 2 daughters. *Education:* BSc 1953, PhD Polymer Chemistry, 1956, DSc 1980, University of Birmingham. *Appointments:* Senior Scientific Officer, Ministry of Aviation, 1956-61; Senior Lecturer, Polymer Science, University of New South Wales, Sydney, Australia, 1961-72; Principal Lecturer, Biomedical Engineering, North Staffordshire Polytechnic, 1972-83; Visiting Professor, Technische Hogeschool Twente, Enschede, Netherlands, 1968-69; Visiting Professor, University of Karlsruhe, Federal Republic of Germany, 1984; Head, Biomedical Engineering Unit, North Staffordshire Polytechnic & Health Authority. *Memberships:* Fellow, Royal Society of Chemistry; Fellow, Plastics & Rubber Institute; President, Biological Engineering Society, 1982-84; British Orthopaedic Association (Companion Fellow). *Publications:* "Plastics Materials in Surgery" (with B Bloch), 2nd edition 1972; "Structure Property Relationships in Biomaterials" (editor with P Ducheyne of a series), 1984; Over 70 publications in learned journals; Editor of "Biomaterials". *Hobbies:* Poetry & Play-writing; Music; Photography; Gardening. *Address:* Biomedical Engineering Unit, c/o Medical Institute, Hartshill, Stoke-on-Trent, ST4 7NY, England.

HATCHER, James Donald, b. 22 June 1923, St Thomas, Ontario, Canada. Dean, Faculty of Medicine, Dalhousie University. m. Helen Edith Roberts, 14 June 1946, 2 daughters. *Education:* MD, University of Western Ontario, 1946; PhD, University of Western Ontario, 1951; LL.D Honorary, Queen's University, 1985; FRCP (C), 1977. *Appointments:* Instructor, medicine, Boston University School of Medicine, USA, 1950-52; Assistant Professor, 1952-55, Associate Professor, 1955-59, Professor, Chairman, Physiology, 1959-62, Professor, Head, 1962-76, Physiology, Associate Dean, Medicine, 1968-71, Queens University; Sabbatical Leave, University of California, 1971-72; Professor, Physiology, Dean, Medicine, 1976-85; Advisor Research and Technology Transfer, 1985-. Dalhousie University. *Memberships Include:* Canadian Medical Association; Nova Scotia Medical Society; Halifax Medical Society; Canadian Federation of Biological Societies; Canadian Physiological Society; etc. *Publications:* "Physiology of Human Survial", co-author, 1965; "International Symposium on the Cardiovascular and Respiratory Effects of Hypoxia", co-author, 1965; 41 papers in professional journals. *Honours:*

Recipient, various honours & awards including: Markle Scholar, medical Science, Queen's University, 1952-57; Nuffield Travelling Fellowship, England, 1956; Ontario Heart Foundation, 1975-72; Queen's Jubilee Medal, 1977. *Hobbies:* Painting; Gardening; Music;Reading. *Address: 24 Rockwood, Halifax, Nova Scotia B3N 1X5, Canada.*

HATFIELD, Kenneth Daniel, b. 20 Aug. 1924, Sydney, New South Wales, Australia. Radiologist. m. Harriet Astrid Bech, 30 Mar. 1979, Sydney. *Education:* MB BS, Sydney University, 1946; DMRD England, 1951; FRACR, 1956; FIR Hon, 1979. *Appointments:* Consultant Radiologist, Royal Australian Air Force, 1955-79; Radiologist, St Vincents Hospital, Sydney, 1960-83, Coffs Harbour and District Hospital, currently; Honorary Secretary, New South Wales Branch, 1960-75, Chairman, 1975-77, Council Member, 1977-79, Royal Australasian College of Radiologists. *Memberships:* Australian Medical Association; British Medical Association; British Institute of Radiology. *Publications:* Contributions to 'Australian Radiology' of papers: 'The Combined Barium Meal and Gall Bladder Examination', 1962; 'The Preauricular Sulcuss', 1966; 'Normal Pressure Hydrocephalus', 1979; 'The Displaced Pineal, Case Report', 1985. 'Barium Sulfate for Abdominal CT' in Journal CAT', 1980. *Hobbies:* Golf; Skiing; Travel; Reading; Farming. *Address:* Box 337, PO Coffs Harbour 2450, Australia.

HATTORI, Takao, b. 9 June 1926, Shanghai, China. Professor of Surgery. m. Kyoko Ide, 21 June 1956, Tokyo, Japan, 2 sons. *Education:* MD; Intern and Postgraduate surgical training, PhD, Tokyo University, 1956. *Appointments:* Professor of Surgery, Research Institute for Nuclear Medicine, and Biology Hiroshima University, Japan, 1948-; Research Assistant, Department of Surgery, Research Institute for Infectious Diseases, Tokyo University, 1958-62; Chief Surgeon, National Cancer Center Hospital, Tokyo, 1962-66; Associate Professor of Surgery, Kyushu University, 1966-73. *Memberships:* Japan Surgical Society; Japanese Association for Thoracic Surgery; Japanese Society for Clinical Surgery; Japanese Society of Gastroenterological Surgery; Japanese Cancer Association; Japan Society for Cancer Therapy; International College of Surgeons; Japanese Society for Chemotherapy. *Publications:* 'Postoperative chemotherapy with futrafal and mitomycin C and chemoimmunotherapy for gastric cancer' i 'Oncoglogy', 1983; 'Experimental Studies of operative stress on tumor growth in rats', in 'Basic Mechanism and Clinical Treatment of Tumour Metastasis', 1985. *Hobbies:* Music; Reading; Travelling. *Address:* 4-7-302 Teppo-cho Naka-ku, Hiroshima 730, Japan.

HAUSMAN, William, b. 25 July, 1925, New York City, USA. Professor of Psychiatry. m. Lillian Margaret Fuerst, 12 June, 1947, St.Louis, USA, 3 sons, 1 daughter. *Education:* MD, Washington University Medical School, St. Louis, USA, 1947; FACP. *Appointments:* US Army - including Chief Behavioural Science Research Branch, Office of the Surgeon General and Deputy Director, Division of Neuropsychiatry, Walter Reed Army Institute of Research, 1949-60; Associate Professor of Psychiatry, Johns Hopkins University, 1966-69; Professor and Head, Department of Psychiatry, University of Minnesota, 1969-80. *Memberships:* Fellow, American College of Psychiatry; American Psychaitric Association; International Association for Social Psychiatry; Diplomate, American Board of Psychiatry and Neurology, 1953. *Publications:* 25 published papers inlcuding: 'Applications of the Military Medical Models of Civilian Psychiatry' in 'Journal of Psychiatric Research', 1971; 'The Re-organisation of a University Department of Psychiatry: A Blueprint for Change' in 'Task and Organisation', 1976; 'National Culture vs. Professional Culture: a comparative study of psychiatric educators in two countries' in 'Culture Medicine and Psychiatry', 1983. *Honour:* Legion of Merit, US Army, 1969. *Hobbies:* Sailing; Skiing; Photography. *Address:* Box 393 Mayo Building, 420 Delaware Street South East, Minneapolis, MN 55455, USA.

HAUSMANOVA-PETRUSEWICZ, Irena, b. 27 Dec. 1918, Warsaw, Poland. Professor of Neurology. m. Kazimier Petrusewicz, 26 July 1956, Warsaw, 1 daughter. *Education:* MD 1941, PhD 1949, Doctor of Medical Science (veniam legendi), 1951. *Appointments:* Assistant 1948-51, Assistant Professor 1951-53, Associate Professor 1954-58, Professor & Head of Department of Neurology, Medical School, Warsaw, 1959-. *Memberships:* Past President, Polish Neurological Society; Deputy President, Neurological Committee, President, Commission of Muscular Diseases, Polish Academy of Sciences; Deputy President, Neuromuscular Research Group, World Federation of Neurology; Corresponding Member, American, French, Italian, Bulgarian, East German, West German Neurological Societies; and others. *Publications:* "Muscle Diseases", 2nd edition 1977; "Sponal Muscular Atrophy", 1978; "Clinical electromyography", 1980; "Therapy of Neurological Diseases", 1983; 250 scientific papers. *Honours:* Awards for Research in Neuromuscular diseases from Polish Ministry of Health, 1967, 1979, Polish Academy of Sciences 1973, 1975, 1978, 1981, 1983; Hans Beregr Medal, 1973; Ducherine-Erb Award, Federal Republic of Germany, 1985. *Hobbies:* History; Theatre. *Address:* 2 Brodzins Kiego, 01557 Warsaw, Poland.

HAWKINS, Richard Bruce, b. 8 Nov. 1941, New Jersey, USA. Arthroscopic Orthopaedic Surgeon. m. Anne Louise Lovgren, 25 June 1966, Swarthmore, Pennsylvania, USA, 2 sons. *Education:* AB cum laude, Harvard University, Cambridge, ,Massachusetts, 1963; MD, University of Pennsylvania, 1969. *Appointments:* Arthritis Research Fellow, Robert Brigham Hospital, Boston, 1970-71; Orthopaedic Resident, Peter Bert Brigham & Massachusetts General Hospitals, 1972-74: Chief Resident, Orthopaedics, Peter Bert Brigham Hospital, Boston, 1975; Senior Orthopaedic Surgeon, Burbank Hospital, Fitchburg, Massachusetts, 1975-; Arthroscopic Orthopaedic Surgeon, Burbank Hospital, Fitchburg, Mass., 1981-. *Memberships:* Fellow, American Academy of Orthopaedic Surgeons; Fellow, Arthroscopic Association of North America; International Arthroscopic Association. *Publications:* "Techniques in Orthopaedics" (Arthroscopic Surgery Update), edited John T S McGinty, 1985; Chap 15, 'Arthroscopic Reconstruction for Chronic Lateral Ankle Instability'. *Honour:* CARE-Medico 1981 for Volunteer service in Bangladesh (teaching Orthopaedics Residents). *Hobbies:* Cycling; The Triathlon. *Address:* 1480 John Fitch Highway, Fitchburg, MA 01420, USA.

HAWSON, Geoffrey Arthur Thomas, b. 30 Dec. 1945, Ipswich, Queensland, Australia. Director of Haematology & Oncology. m. Laraine Robin Skinner, 30 Dec. 1967, Toowoomba, 1 son, 1 daughter. *Education:* MB, BS, University of Queensland, 1969; Fellow, Royal Australasian College of Physicians (FRACP), 1976; Fellow, Royal College of Pathologists of Australia (FRCPA), 1980. *Appointments include:* Haematologist, Sullivan & Nicolaides Laboratory, 1976; Medical Registrar 1977-78, Haematology Registrar 1979, Locum Haematologist Oncologist 1980, Princess Alexandra Hospital; Visiting Haematologist/Oncologist 1981, Director 1982-, Prince Charles Hospital. *Memberships:* Haematology Society of Australia; Australasian Society of Blood Transfusion; Clinical Oncologial Society of Australasia (COSA); Medical Oncology Group, COSA. *Publications include:* Contributions to: 'Medical Journal of Australia',

'Medical & Paediatric Oncology', 'Australia & New Zealand Journal of Medicine'. *Hobbies:* Charismatic renewal; Reading; Photography; Tropical fish. *Address:* The Prince Charles Hospital, Rode Road, Chermside, Brisbane, Queensland 4032, Australia.

HAY, David Russell, b. 8 Dec. 1927, Chirstchurch, New Zealand.Cardiologist; Medical Director, National Heart Foundation of New Zealand. m. Jocelyn Valerie Bell, 22 Feb. 1958, 2 daughters. *Education:* MD (NZ), 1960; FRCP (London), 1971; FRACP, 1965. *Appointments:* Physician, North Canterbury Hospital Board, 1959-64; Head, Cardiology, 1969-78, Chairman, Medical Services, 1978-84, Canterbury Hospital Board; Clinical Lecturer, 1973-80, Clinical Reader, 1980-, University of Otago; Foundation Councillor, National Heart Foundation of New Zealand, 1968-; WHO Expert Advisory Panel on Smoking and Health, 1977-; New Zealand Government Advisory Committee on Smoking and Health, 1974; New Zealand Government Advisory Committee in the Prevention of Cardiovascular Diseases, 1985-. *Memberships:* Cardiac Society ANZ, Past Chairman, NZ Region and Councillor, 1977-82; Past President, Canterbury Division, British Medical Association, 1972; Past Councillor, Censor, 1974-75; Royal Australasian College of Physicians; Chairman, Christchurch Hospitals Medical Staff Association, 1983-85. *Publications:* 74 papers in scientific journals; Editor, "Coronary Heart Disease, Prevention and Control in 1983", 1983; Editor, "Technical Report Series, National Heart Foundation of New Zealand", 1975-. *Honour:* CBE, 1981. *Hobbies:* Golf; Tennis. *Address:* 20 Greers Road, Christchurch, New Zealand.

HYMAN, Max. b. 19 Dec. 1908, Winnipeg, Canada. 1 son, 1 daughter. *Education:* BSc, 1929, MD, University of Manitoba, Winnipeg, Canada, 1935. *Appointments:* Senior Assistant Physician, Springfield State Hospital, Maryland, 1937; Assistant, Department of Psychiatry, Johns Hopkins School of Medicine, 1937-38; Resident in Neurology, Columbia University College of Physicians and Surgeons, NY, 1939; Fellowship Institute of Living, Hartford, Conn., 1940-41; President, Director, Psychiatric Hospitals - Compton Foundation Hospital, Compton, CA., 1955-80; Westerly Hospital, Los Angeles, 1964-65; Westwood Hospital, Los Angeles, 1970; Vista Hill Psychiatric Foundation, 1968-75. *Memberships:* Emeritus, Mount Sinai Hospital, LA, CA; Fellow, American Psychiatric Association; American Psychoanalytic Association; American Medical Association on Alcoholism; Former Professor of Psychiatry, UCLA School of Medicine, 1970. *Publications:* "Alcoholism Mechanism and Management"; 40 papers on Psychoanalysis, Psychiatry, Drugs and Alcoholism. *Honour:* Clinical Prize of International J. Psychoanalys. *Hobbies:* Tennis; Travel. *Address:* 1423 San Lorenzo Road, Palm Springs, CA 92264, USA.

HÄYRY, Pekka Juha, b. 13 Dec. 1939, Finland. Professor of Transplantation Surgery & Immunology. *Education:* MD 1965, DSc Experimental Pathology 1966, University of Helsinki. *Appointments:* Post-doctoral Fellow, Wistar Institute of Anatomy & Biology, University of Pennsylvania, USA, 1967-70; Resident, Department of Surgery, 1970-74; Lecturer in Immunology, 1970-79, University of Helsinki; Lecturer in Surgery & Transplantation Surgery, University of Oulu, 1974-80; Visiting Professor, University of Paris, Hospital Necker, France, 1974; Duke University & University of North Carolina USA, 1977, University of Adelaide, Adelaide, S Australia; Associate Chief in Surgery, University of Helsinki Central Hospital, 1973-79; Professor of Transplantation Surgery & Immunology, University of Helsinki, 1980-. *Memberships:* Transplantation Society; Board

Member, Scandinavian Society for Immunology; International Society of Heart Transplantation; American Association for Immunology; American Society of Transplant Surgeons. *Publications:* Some 250 articles, reviews & book chapters in professional publications. *Hobbies:* Agriculture; Forestry. *Address:* Transplantation Laboratory, University of Helsinki, Haartmaninkatu 3, SF-00290 Helskinki 29, Finland.

HAYS, David S, b. 31 July 1920, Boston, Massaachusetts, USA. Psychiatric Consultant. m. Norma Lear (deceased), 13 Aug. 1944, New Haven, Connecticut, 2 sons, 2 daughters. *Education:* BS cum laude 1941, MD 1944, Tufts University. *Appointments:* Consultant, Childrens Village, Dobbs Ferry, New York, Leake and Watts Childrens Home, Yonkers, New York, Briarcliff College, Briarcliff, New York, Childrens Clinic, Rockland State Hospital Satellite, Newburgh, New York, Board of Cooperative Educational Services, Westchester County, 1952-81; Director, Tappan Zee Mental Health Center, Tarrytown, 1953-57; Chief Psychiatrist, Sing Sing Prison, Department of Mental Hygiene, New York State, 1953-61; Medical Director, Cooperative Consultation Services, White Plains, New York, 1954-81; Chief, Division of Psychiatry, Phelps Memorial Hospital, Tarrytown, New York, 1960-69; Psychiatric Consultant, New York State Division of Parole, Executive Department, 1964-69; Chairman, Group Therapy Services, Bureau of Child Guidance, Board of Education of City of New York, 1970-74; Psychiatric Consultant, St Agatha's Group Home, Pound Ridge, New York 1981-, Office of Mental Hygiene New York State, Bedford Hills Correction Facility, Bedford Hills, New York. *Memberships:* Fellow, American Psychiatric Association; Fellow, American Group Psychotherapy Association; Associate, American Academy of Neurology; American Society of Adolescent Psychiatry. *Publications Include:* 'The Aged Offender: A Review of the Literature and Two Current Stadies from the New York State Division of Parole', 1969; 'Intentional Groups with a Specific Problem Orientation Focus' in "TheIntensive Group Experience" (with Y Danieli), 1976; 'The Teaching of Psychiatry in the Correctional Setting: A New Dimension in the Medical School Curriculum', 1985. *Hobbies:* Flying; Sailing; Photography; Dog Breeding. *Address:* 163 Limekiln Road, Ridgefield, CT 06877, USA.

HAYS, Howard L, b. 14 Feb. 1931, Council Bluffs, Iowa, USA. Chief Operating Officer. m. Beverly Baptist Bonical, 11 Oct. 1980, Omaha, Nebraska, 3 sons, 1 daughter. *Education:* BSc, University of Nebraska at Omaha, 1957; Master of Hospital Administration, Washington University, St Louis, Missouri, 1959. *Appointments:* Administrative Resident, 1958-59, Administrative Assistant 1959-60, Iowa Methodist Hospital, Des Moines, Iowa; Assistant Administrator, 1960-62, Dallas County Hospital District (Parkland Memorial Hospital), Dallas, Texas; Assistant Administrator, University of Utah Hospital, Salt Lake City, Utah, 1962-65; Assistant Administrator, Presbyterian Hospital of Dallas, Texas, 1965-69; Associate Administrator 1969-84, Chief Operating Officer 1984-, Bishop Clarkson Memorial Hospital, Omaha, Nebraska. *Memberships:* American College of Healthcare Executives; Nebraska Hospital Association; Association of University Programmes in Health Administration. *Honours:* Fellow, American College of Healthcare Executives, 1970; Elected Council of Regents, 1983-; President, Omaha Hospital Association 1978-79, Nebraska Hospital Association, 1980-81. *Hobbies:* Golf; Racquetball; Music; Spectator Sports. *Address:* 12911 Lafayette Avenue, Omaha, NE 68154, USA.

HAZELL, Jonathan Walter Peter, b. 28 Mar, 1942, England. Neuro-Otologist m. Dr Rena Graham , 2 sons, 2 daughters. *Education:* Natural Science Tripos, Emmanuel College, Cambridge University, 1960-63; MB, 1966; BChir, 1967; Clinical Studies, Middlesex Hospital Medical School, London, 1963-66. *Appointments Include:* House Physician, 1966-67, House Surgeon, 1967, Middlesex Hospital; Surgical Registrar, Otolaryngology, 1972-74, Honorary Lecturer, 1974-76, Honorary Senior Lecturer, 1976-77. University College Hospital; Honorary Consultant Neuro-Otologist, University College Hospital, 1977-; Consultant Neuro-Otologist, Royal National Institute for the Deaf,London, 1977-; Senior Lecturer, University College, London University, 1977-; Honorary Consultant, Audiological Medicine, Royal National Throat, Nose and Ear Hospital, London, 1977-. *Memberships:* Fellow: Royal Society of Medicine. International Electric Response Audiometry Study Group; Council Member, British Society of Audiology; British Association of Audiological Physicians; International Association of Physicians in Audiology; Council, International Tinnitus Study Group. *Publications:* Author or co-author of some 30 papers contributed to professional publications including: "Disesases of the Ear, Nose and Throat", 4th edition, 1979; "Fotal and Neonatal Physiological Measurements", 1981; "Advanced Medicine", 1982; "British Journal of Audiology"; 'Archives of Diseases of Childhood'; 'Modern Medicine'; "Journal of Laryngology". 'Medical International'. *Honours:* Windsor Scholarship for Post graduate study of anatomy, University of Cambridge, 1967. *Hobbies:* Music; Computing; Skiing; Water sports. *Address:* Royal National Institute for the Deaf, 105 Gower Street, London WC1E 6AH, England.

HEALY, Thomas Edward John b. 11 Dec. 1935, Doncaster, England. Professor of Anaesthesia. m. Lesley Edwina Sheppard, 3 Nov. 1966, Westminster, 1 son, 2 daughters. *Education:* BSc; MSc, University of Manchester; MD, Guy's Hospital; University of London FFARCS; DA. *Appointments:* Reader in Anaesthesia, University of Nottingham. *Memberships:* Association of Anaesthesia of Great Britain and Ireland; Academician, European Academy of Anaesthesiologists; Worshipful Society of Apothecaries of London. *Publications:* "Aids to Anaesthesia", Book 1 - Basic Science, Book 2 - Clinical Practice, (co-author), 1984; "Publications Pharmacology and Clinical Pharmacology Related to Anaesthesia". *Address:* University Department of Anaesthesia, University Hospital of South Manchester, Manchester, M20 8LR, England.

HEARD, Frederick Stanley, b. 30 Oct. 1930, London, England, General Practitioner, m. Stella McLoughlin, 28 Jan. 1961, Westhead, Lancashire, 2 daughters. *Education:* MB, ChB, University of Liverpool, 1959; D Obst FCOG; Certificant, College of Family Practice Canada (CCFP); LMCC. *Appointments:* House physician, House surgeon, Liverpool Royal Infirmary; House Officer, Mill Road Maternity Hospital; General Practice, Formby, Lancashire, 1961-66; General Practice, Victoria, British Columbia, Canada, 1966-. *Memberships:* BMA; CMA (BCMA); American Geriatrics Society; New York Academy of sciences. *Hobbies:* Squash; Polo. *Address:* No 205, 2020 Richmond Avenue, Victoria, British Columbia, Canada V8R 6R5.

HEARON, Kevin G, b, 4 Oct 1950, Everett, Washington, USA, Doctor of Chiropractic. *Education:* DC; FIACA; FASA. *Appointments:* Present Post Graduate Faculty Member, Western States Chiropractic College, Portland, Ore, Life Chiropractic College, Marietta, Ga, Life Chiropractic College, San Loranzo, Calif, Los Angeles College of Chiropractic, Whittier, Calif; Teacher, Sports Medicine; Team Teacher, Parker Chiropractic

Research Foundiaton. *Memberships:* President, North Olympic Chiropractors Association, 1984, 1985. *Publications:* "What you should know about Extrmity Adjusting", 1981. *Hobbies;* Soccer; Rugby; Cycling; Golf; Arm/Wrist Wrestling. *Address:* P O Box 1824, 461 W Washington, Sequim, WA 98382, USA.

HEATH, Douglas Ross, b. 5 Mar. 1942, Cedar Rapids, Iowa, USA. Editor; Associated Chiropractors. m. Kathryn Elizabeth Whalen, 25 Feb. 1985, Cedar Rapids, 2 sons, 2 daughters. *Education:* sBS, Upper Iowa University, 1964; MA, University of Northern Colorado, 1974; DC, Palmer College of Chiropractic, 1982. *Appointments:* Cedar Rapids Community School District Teacher, 1964-79; President, Heath Diagnostic Equipment, 1979-; Union Carpenter Local §308, 1968-; Chiropractic Physician, 1982-. *Memberships:* AAHPER; NEA; AFT; Phi Delta Kappa; American College of Sports Medicine; Student, American Chiropractic Association; Christian Chiropractic Association; Illinois Chiropractic Association; National Board of Chiropractic Examiners, Diplomate, 1981. *Honours:* Palmer Clinic Intern Programme, Gold Coat, 1981; Student, American Chiropractic Association, 3 Time National Delegate, 1979-81. *Hobbies:* Bicycle Riding; Canoeing; Hiking. *Address:* 1800 Memorial Dr. SE, Cedar Rapids, IA 52403, USA.

HECHT, Jeffrey S., b. 29 Dec. 1952, Lansing, Michigan, USA. Co-Director, Brain Injury Programme, Rehabilitation Institute of New Orleans, Herbert Hospital; Physiatrist, Southern Baptist Hospital. m. Shelley A. Hecht, 1 son, 1 daughter. *Education:* BA, 1975, MD, 1979, University of Michigan; Internship, Residency, Baylor College of Medicine, Houston, 1979-82. *Appointment:* Patricia Neal Rehabilitation Centre, Knoxville. *Memberships:* American Medical Association; Louisiana State Medical Society; Orleans Parish Medical Society; American Academy of Physical Medicine and Rehabilitation; American Association of Electromyography and Electrodiangosis; American Society for Evoked Potentials; Louisiana Physical Medicine and Rehabilitation Society, Secretary; Southern Society of Physical medicine & Rehabilitation; etc. *Publications:* Articles in professional journals including: 'Archives of Physical medicine and Rehabilitation'; etc. *Honours:* Branstom Prize, 1970; Angell Scholar, 1971; Cardiovascular Research Training Programme, 1974-75; English Honours Programme, magna cum laude, 1975; Certified: American Board of Physical medicine and Rehabilitation, 1983, American Association of Electromyography and Electrodiagnosis, 1984. *Hobbies:* Juggling (IJA Member); Mandolin; Philately; Fly-fishing. *Address:* 4708 Taft Park, Metairie, LA 70002, USA.

HEGDE, Belle Monappa, b. 18 Aug. 1938, Pangal, India. Professor of Medicine, K. M. C. Mangalore; Visiting Professor, Cardiology, Middlesex Hospital Medical School, London, England. m. Malathi Hegde, 5 May 1960, Udupi, 1 son, 2 daughters. *Education:* MBBS, Madras University, 1960; MD, Lucknow University, 1964; MRCP, England, 1970; FRCP, London, 1981; FRCP, Glasgow, 1985; FACC, 1985. *Appointments:* Lecturer, medicine, Kasturbamed College, India; Reader, Associate Professor; Registrar, Cardiology, Middlesex Hospital, London; Clinical Assistant, Cardiology, Heart Hospital, London. *Memberships:* Indian medical Association; Association of Physicians of India; Cardiological Society of India; International Society of Hypertension. *Publicaitons:* Many articles on Hypertension; various articles in professional journals including: 'British Journal of Vascula Disesase'; 'British Heart Journal'; etc. *Honours:* Gold Medal in MBBS; Prize, Medicine; Commonwealth Fellowship in Cardiology; Chest & Heart Foundation UK Fellowships. *Hobbies:*

Reading; Lecturing; Swimming. *Address:* Ganesh, Lower Bendur, Mangalore 575002, India.

HEGSTRAND, Linda Kozel, b. 14 Feb 1947, Rockford, Illinois, USA. Associate Scientist in Psychiatry. m. Lee Hegstrand, 19 May 1973, 1 son. *Education:* BA, Chemistry, Magna Cum Laude, Hope College; PhD, Physiological Chemistry, MD, University of Wisconsin, Madison. *Appointments:* Postdoctoral Fellow in Pharmacology, Yale University, New Haven, Connecticut; Instructor in Pharmacology, University of Colorado, Denver; Assistant Scientist in Psychiatry, Associate Scientist in Psychiatry, University of Wisconsin, Madison. *Memberships:* Sigma Xi; Society for Neuroscience; American Women in Science; American Medical Women's Association. *Publications:* Contributor of numerous articles to professional journals including: 'Evidence of Involvement of Protein Kinase in the Activation of Adenosine' J Biol Chem, 1975; 'Histamine-Sensitive Adenylate Cyclase in Mammalian Brain' Nature, 1976; 'Simultaneous Determination of Beta-1 and Beta-2 Adrenergic Receptors' Mol Pharmacol 1979. *Honours:* Woodrow Wilson Fellowship 1969; American Institute of Chemists' Award, 1969; Motar Board 1969; Multiple Sclerosis Fellowship 1973; Colorado Heart Association Grant, 1978; National Institute of Mental Health Grant, 1982. *Hobbies:* Competitive tennis, volleyball and softball; Bicycle touring; Canoe camping; Skiing. *Address:* 765 Waisman Center, Neurochemistry Section, Madison WI 53705, USA.

HEESE, Hans De Villiers, b. 15 July 1928, Bloemfontein, South Africa. Professor. m. Margaret Ann Lawrence, 1 son, 1 daughter. *Education:* BSc., University of Stellenbosch, 1948; MB, ChB, 1953, MD, 1959, University of Cape Town; DCH, Royal College of Physicians & Surgeons, London, England, 1955; MRCP, Royal College of Physicians, Edinburgh, 1957; FRCP, Royal College of Physicians, Edinburgh, 1970. *Appointments:* Research Fellow, Child Health, University of Bristol, England, 1957-58; Senior Registrar, Paediatrician, Senior Paediatrician, 1959-67, Professor, Head, Paediatrics & Child Health, 1970-86, University of Cape Town and Red Cross War Memorial Children's Hospital; Professor, Paediatrics, University of the Witwatersrand, 1968-70. *Memberships:* South African paediatric Association; Medical Association of South Africa; British Medical Association; Fellow, Royal Society of Medicine; Life Member, London House Fellowship. *Publications:* Co-author, 13 book chapters; Author, co-author over 90 articles in refereed medical journals. *Hobbies:* Hiking; Fishing; Gardening. *Address:* Department of Paediatrics & Child Health, Institute of Child Health, Red Cross War Memorial Children's Hospital, Rondebosch, 7700, Republic of South Africa.

HEFFRON, Warren Allen, b. 7 Nov. 1936, St Louis, Missouri, USA. Professor. m. Rosalee Bowdish Heffron, 10 June 1961, Columbia, 1 son, 3 daughters. *Education:* Ab, Chemistry, University of Missouri, 1958; MD, University of Missouri School of Medicine, 1962. *Appointments:* Medical Officer, USPHS Quarantine Station, Staten Island, 1963-64; General Medical Officer, USPHS Indian Hospital, Fort Defiance, 1964-66; Physician, Hospital Castaner, Puerto Rico, 1966-68; Resident, Internal Medicine, 1968-71, Assistant Professor, Family, Community and Emergency Medicine, 1971-76, Director, Family Medicine Residency Programme, 1971-82, Associate Professor, Assistant Chairman, 1976-82, Acting Chairman, 1979-80, Chief, Medical Staff, University of New Mexico Hospital, 1980-81, Professor, Chairman, Family Community and Emergency Medicine, 1982-, University of New Mexico, Albuquerque. *Memberships:* American Academy of Family Physicians; American Medical Association; Society of Teachers of Family Medicine; New Mexico Academy of Family Physicians; Bernalillo

County Academy of Family Physicians. *Publications:* Numerous articles in professional journals including: 'Annals of Internal Medicine'; 'American Journal of Medical Sciences'; 'Yearbook of Medicine'; 'Rocky Mountain Medical Journal'; 'Missouri Medicine'; 'Paediatrics'; 'American Family Physician'; 'Journal of Family Practice'; 'Drug Therapy'; 'Resident and Staff Physician'; 'British Journal of Clinical Pharmacology'; 'Family Practice Research Journal'; etc. *Honours:* Robbins Award for Community Serivce, New Mexico Society, 1981; American Medical Association Physician Recognition Award, 1977, 1980, 1983. *Hobbies:* Travel; Skiing; Backpacking. *Address:* Dept. of Family, Community and Emergency Medicine, University of New Mexico School of Medicine, Albuquerque, NM 87131, USA.

HEIN, David William, b. 17 Aug. 1955, USA. Associate and Adjunct Assistant Professor of Pharmacology. m. Karla, 4 Mar, 1978, Madison, Wisconsin, 1 son. *Education:* BS Chemistry, University of Wisconsin, Eau Claire; PhD Pharmacology, University of Michigan. *Appointments:* Instructor, Huron Valley Lutheran High School, Westland, Michigan; Assistant Professor, Acting Chairman, Currently Associate Professor and Chairman of Pharmacology, Morehouse School of Medicine, Atlanta, Georgia; Adjunct Assistant Professor, Emory University School of Medicine. *Memberships:* American Chemical Society; American Association of Medical School Pharmacology. *Publications include:* Co-author: 'A unique pharmacogenetic expression of the N-acetylation polymorphism in the inbred hamster', 1982; 'Identification of homozygous rapid and slow acetylators of drugs and environmental carcinogens among established inbred rabbit strains', 1982; 'Relationship between N-acetylator phenotype and susceptibility towards hydrazine-induced lethal central nervous system toxicity in the rabbit', 1984; 'Inheritance of liver N-acetyltransferase activity in the rapid and slow acetylator inbred hamster', 1985; 'N-acetylation pharmacogenetics', 1985; 'Biochemical investigation of the basis for the genetic N-acetylation polymorphism in the inbred hamster', 1985. *Honours:* Outstanding Senior Award, 1977; Teacher of the Year Award, 1983; Teaching Awards, 1984 and 1985; Dean's Award for Faculty Achievement, 1985. *Address:* Department of Pharmacology, Morehouse Schol of Medicine, 720 Westview Drive, Atlanta, GA 30310, USA.

HEIN, Werner Wilfried Victor, b. 20 Dec. 1933, Hof/Barn, Germany. Dentist. m. Ruth Reimer, 28 July 1958, 1 son, 1 daughter. *Education:* Dr. med. dent., University of Munich. *Appointments:* Assistant Dentist, Switzerland and Federal Republic of Germany, 1957-63. *Memberships:* Executive Committee, Bavarian Dental Organizations, Munich, Regensburg; Executive Committee, Bavarian Dental Oral Health Organization; Chairman, Committee of Oral Health Education, Bavarian Dental Organization. *Publications:* "Oral Hygiene - Prevention of Caries and Peridontal Disease", 'Quintessence', 1980; "Standortbestimmung der Zahnheilkunde der 80er Jahre", 'Quintessence', 1982; "Arbeitsgemeinschaft : Gesundes Kauorgan", 'Weltgesundheitstag Gesundheit fur unsere Kinder', 1984. *Honours:* Certificate of Appreciation, Japanese Dental Association, 1983; Ehrennadel of the German Dental Association, 1981; Certificate, meritorious service, Institute of Myofunctional Therapy, Miami, USA, 1981. *Hobbies:* Golf; Skiing; Classical Music; European Classical Literature. *Address:* Posteig 1, D-8470 Nabburg, Federal Republic of Germany.

HEINS, Marilyn, b. 7 Sept. 1930, Boston, Massachusetts, USA. Vice-Dean, College of Medicine, University of Arizona. m. Milton P Lipson, 9 Sept. 1958, 1 son, 1 daughter. *Education:* AB, Radcliffe College, 1951; MD, College of Physicians & Surgeons, 1955; Internship, Paediatrics, New York Hospital; Residence, Paediatrics. *Appointments:* Assistant & Associate Physician, Department of Paediatrics, Assistant to Chief of Department, Detroit Receiving Hospital, 1960-64; Director, Department of Paediatrics, Detroit General Hospital, 1965-71; Assistant Professor of Paediatrics, Wayne State University School of Medicine, 1966-70; Associate Dean for Student Affairs, Wayne State University, 1970-79; Associate Dean for Academic Affairs, University of Arizona, 1979-83; Vice Dean, College of Medicine, 1983-; Associate Professor, 1978-85; Professor of Paediatrics, 1985-, University of Arizona. *Memberships Include:* Diplomate American Board of Paediatrics; Fellow, American of Paediatrics; American Medical Association; American Public Health Association; Ambulatory Paediatric Association; Fellow, American Orthopsychiatric Association; Member, National Board of Medical Examiners for the American Hospital Association, 1983-. *Publications:* 55 articles & book chapters in field of paediatrics & child abuse. *Honours:* Wayne State University Alumni Faculty Service Award, 1972, Recognition Award, 1977. *Hobbies:* Travel; Literature. *Address:* 1501 North Cambell Avenue, AHSC, Tucson, AZ 85724, USA.

HEINZER, François Charles, b. 29 Mar. 1942, Vevey. Private Practice. m. Rose-Marie Schmutz, 16 Dec. 1967, Lausanne, 3 sons. *Education:* MD, University of Lausanne; Mayo Graduate School, Rochester, Minnesota, USA; Hammersmith Postgraduate School, London, England; FMH, Internal Medicine, Pneumology. *Appointments:* Chef de Clinique, Chest Diseases, University Hospital, Lausanne; Director, School of Physiotherapy, Lausanne; Consultant, Chest Diseases, University of Lausanne; Private Practice. *Memberships:* Board Member, Swiss Society of Pneumology, Swiss Association against Tuberculosis and Respiratory Diseases; American College of Chest Physicians, Swiss Representative to European Council; American Thoracic Society; Founding Member, Societas European Pneumologica. *Publications:* "Posterior oblique romography at an angle of 55° in Chest Roent Genology", 'American Journal Roentgenology', 1974; "La pneumonie peribulleuse Schweiz med Wschr 104", 1974; "Le diagnostic precoce du syndrome pulmonaire obstructif", 'Praxis'. 1973; etc. *Hobbies:* Skiing; Sailing; Mountain Climbing; Photography; Cinema. *Address:* Boulevard de Grancy 7, Lausanne, CH 1006, Switzerland.

HEISER, Jon Franklin, b. 27 July 1939, Lakewood, Ohio, USA. Director of Clinical Psychopharmacology Service; m. Nanette Denise, 26 June 1983, Norwalk, California, 2 daughters (1 from previous marriage). *Education:* BA, Hons, Williams College, Williamstown, Massachusetts, 1961; MD, Case-Western Reserve University, Cleveland, Ohio, 1965. *Appointments:* Intern, University of Illinois Research and Education Hospitals, Chicago, Illinois, 1965-66; Resident, Stanford Medical Center, Palo Alto, California, 1966-69; Psychiatrist, US Naval Hospital, Oakland, California, 1969-71; Associate Clinical Professor, University of California Irvine Medical Center, Orange, California, 1971-78; Associate Professor, University of Texas Medical Branch, Galveston, Texas, 1978-80; Staff Psychiatrist, 1980-, Chief, Clinical Psychopharmacology Service, 1982-, Metropolitan State Hospital, Norwalk, California; Medical Director, Mental Health Services, Presbyterian Inter-Community Hospital, Whittier, California, 1984. *Memberships:* Diplomate in Psychiatry, American

Board of Psychiatry and Neurology, 1972; Collegium Internationale Neuro-Psychopharmacologicum; American Association for Artificial Intelligence; Special Interest Group in Artificial Intelligence; American Psychiatric Association; Southern California Psychiatric Society. *Publications:* 'Reversal of Anticholinergic Drug-Induced Delirium and Coma with Physostigmine' with J C Gillin in American Journal of Psychiatry, 1971; 'Can Psychiatrists Distinguish a Computer Simulation of Paranoia from the Real Thing?' with K M Colby, W S Faught and R C Parkison, in Journal of Psychiatric Research, 1979. *Honours:* Bendict Prize in Mathematics, Williams College, 1959; Merck Award to Outstanding Premedical Student, 1960; Gargoyle Senior Honor Society, 1960; Canby Athletic Scholarship Prize, 1961. *Hobbies:* Roller skating; Reading; Cinema. *Address:* 11400 Norwalk Boulevard, Norwalk, CA 90650, USA.

HEISTRACHER, Peter, b. 19 Apr. 1931, Bad Hofgastein, Austria. University Professor. m. Elisabeth Oberhammer, 22 July 1961, Salzburg, 3 daughters. *Education:* MD, University of Innsbruck Medical School, 1956. *Appointments:* Research Assistant, Institute of Pharmacology, University of Vienna, Austria; Research Fellow and Research Associate, Department of Physiology, Yale University School of Medicine, New Haven, Connecticut, USA; Associate Professor, Institute of Pharmacology, University of Vienna; Professor and Head, Institute of Pharmacodynamics and Toxicology, University of Vienna. *Memberships:* Austrian Physiological Society; Austrian Biochemical Society; German Pharamcological Society; American Association for the Advancement of Science; New York Academy of Science; Editor: Naunyn-Schmiedeberg's Arch Pharmacol. *Publications:* 'The relation of membrane changes to contraction in twitch muscle fibres' Journal of Physiology, London 1969 (with C C Hunt); 'Mechanism of action of antifibrillatory drugs' Naunyn-Schmiedebergs Arch. Pharmak. 1971. *Hobby:* Beekeeping. *Address:* Institut für Pharmakodynamik und Toxikologie der Universität Wien, Währinger Strasse 17, A-1090 Vienna, Austria.

HELLER, Abraham, b. 17 Mar. 1917, Claremont, New Hampshire, USA. University Professor and Vice Chairman of Psychiatry. m. Lora S Levy, 16 June, 1957, Waltham, Massachusetts, USA, 1 son. *Education:* BA, Brandeis University, USA, 1953; MD, Boston University, USA, 1958; Diplomate, American Board of Medical Examiners, 1958; Certified in Psychiatry, American Boardof Neurology and Psychiatry, 1966. *Appointments include:* Director, Psychiatric Internship, Residency Training, Denver General Hospital, Colorado, 1969; Director, Community Mental Health Centre, Denver General Hospital, 1970-72, Associate Director, Division of Psychiatric Services, 1971-73; Clinical Associate Professor of Psychiatry, Brown University, Rhode Island, USA, 1973-77; Director, Newport County Communitty Mental Health Centre, Newport, Rhode Island, 1973-77; Professor, Departments of Psychiatry and Community Medicine, School of Medicine, Wright State University, Dayton, Ohio, 1977-, Vice Chair, 1980-. *Memberships Include:* American Public Health Association; American Academy of Psychiatry and the Law; American Psychiatric Association; American Orthophysichiatric Association. *Publications Include:* Numerous contributions to professional journals; book sections including: 'Hamlet's Parents: The Dynamic Formulation of a Tragedy' in "American Imago", 1960 (co-author); 'Exgension of Wyatt to Ohio Forensic Patients' in "Wyatt v. Stickney, Retrospect and Prospect", 1981. *Hobbies:* Music; Theatre; Literature; Hiking. *Address:* Department of Psychiatry, Wright State School of Medicine, Box 927, Dayton, OH 45401, USA.

HELLER, Paul, b. 8 Aug. 1914, Czechoslovakia. Senior Medical Investigator; Veterans Administration; Professor of Medicine, University of Illinois College of Medicine. m. Alice H. Florsheim, 3 Aug. 1946, New York City, USA, 1 son, 1 daughter. *Education:* MD, Chales University Medical School, Prague, 1938. *Appointments:* Clinical Instructor in Medicine, George Washington University Medical School, Washington, DC, 1948-51; Associate in Medicine, University of Nebraska School of Medicine, Omaha,. 1952-54; Assistant Chief, Medical Service, Veternas Administration Hospital, Omaha, 1952-54; Assistant Professor, 1954, Associate Professor, 1960; Professor of Medicine, 1963, University of Illinois College of medicine; Hemaologist and Attending Physician, Veterans Adminsitration and University of Illinois Hospitals, 1954-66; Chief, Medical Service, Veterans Administration Hospital and Attending Physician, University of Illinois, 1966-69; Senior Medical Investigator, Veterans Administration, 1969-; Attending Physician and Hematologist, University of Illinois Hospital, 1969-. *Memberships:* Association of American Physicians; American College of Physicians; American and International Society of Hematology; Central Society for Medical Research; American Federation of Clinical Research; Association of American Immunologists; American Society of Human Gentics. *Publications:* Author of 158 publications including: 'Hemoglobinopathic Dysfunction of the Red Cell', American Journal of Medicine', 1966; ''Refactory Anaemias', 'Disease-a-Month', Apr. 1967; 'Sickle Cell Disorders and Their Clinical Implications', ''Surgery Annual'', 1974; Annual reviews of progress in hematology. ''Yearbook of Medicine'', 1969-76. *Honours include:* Middleton Award for Medical Research, 1975; Esther Langer Award for Cancer Research, 1980; Distinguished Faculty Award, University of Illinois, 1981. *Hobbies:* Literature; Music; History of Medicine; European History of 19th Century. *Address:* Veterans Administration Westside Medical Center, P.O. Box 8195, Chicago, IL 60680, USA.

HELLGREN, Lars Gustav Inge, b. 26 Dec. 1930, Tranås, Sweden, Professor, Dermato-venereology. m. Marianne Nilsson, 30 Nov. 1959, Dörarp, 4 sons. *Education:* Med.Lic., 1956; MD, 1966; Ass. Professor, 1967. *Appointments:* Assistant Professor, Sahlgrenska Hospital, University of Sweden; Professor, Head, Dermato-venerology, University of Trondheim, Norway; Professor, Head, Dermo-venerology, University of Umeå, Sweden. *Memberships:* Swedish, Danish, Finnish, Norwegian Societies of Dermatologists; Nidaros Dermatology Society; Svenska läk.förbundet. *Publications:* "An Epidemiological Survey of Skin Disease", 1967, "Psoriasis", 1967, "Tattooing", 1967; 180 articles on dermato-venereology, 1959-85. *Address:* Dept. of Dermatolgoy, University of Umeå, 901 87 Umeå, Sweden.

HELLING, Dennis Keith, b. 3 Aug. 1948, St louis, Missouri, USA. Associate Professor and Head of University Division of Clinical/Hospital Pharmacy. *Education:* BS, St Louis College of Pharmacy, St Louis, Missouri, 1971; Pharm D, University of Cincinnati College of Pharmacy, Cincinnati, Ohio, 1973; Residency, Cincinnati General Hospital, 1973; Fellow, American College of Clinical Pharmacy, 1985. *Appointments:* Assistant Professor 1973-77, Associate Professor and Head 1978-, Division of Clinical/Hospital Pharmacy, College of Pharmacy, University of Iowa, Iowa City. *Memberships:* American College of Clinical Pharmacy; American Society of Hospital Pharmacists; Chairman of Section on Clinical Practice 1985, American Pharmaceutical Association; Chair-elect of section of Teachers of Clinical Instruction 1985, American Association of Colleges of Pharmacy. *Publications:* Contributions to: 'Drug Intelligence Clinical Pharmacy', 1982 and 1984; 'Journal of Family Practice', 1982 and 1984; 'American Journal of

Hospital Pharmacy', 1983; 'Journal of clinical Hospital Pharmacy', 1985. *Honours:* Award for Achievement for Sustained Contributions to the Literature of Hospital Pharmacy, 1985. *Address:* Division of Clincal/Hospital Pharmacy, College of Pharmacy, University of Iowa, Iowa City, IA 52242, USA.

HELLMAN, Bo Olof Alexander, b. 30 June 1930, Mariestad, Sweden. Professor of Medical Cell Biology. m. Birgit Inga Margareta Nilsson, 14 Oct. 1961, Linköoing, 3 sons, 1 daughter. *Education:* MD 1952, ML 1958, MD 1959, University of Uppsla. *Appointments:* Assistant Professor, Histology, University of Uppsala, 1960-62; Researcher, Experimental Diabetes, Swedish Medical Research Council, 1963-64; Associate Professor, Karolinska Institute, Stockholm, 1964-66; Professor, Histology, University of Umea, 1966-76; Professor, Medical Cell Biology, University of Uppsala, 1976-. *Memberships:* Vice President 1970-73, European Association for the Study of Diabetes; American Diabetes Association; Board 1971-76, Swedish Medical Research Council. *Publications include:* "Structure & Metabolism of the Pancreatic Islets", co-editor, 1964, 1970; Numerous publications, experimental diabetes. *Honours:* Minkowski Award, European Association for the Study of Diabetes, 1969; Eriksson Prize, Royal Swedish Academy of Science, 1983. *Address:* Hösträngvägen 22, S-75247, Uppsala, Sweden.

HELLMAN, Ronald, b. 2 Jan. 1948, Baltimore, USA. Psychiatrist. *Education:* MD, State University of New York, Downstate Medical Centre, 1975, MS, School of Graduate Studies, 1975; *Appointments:* Psychiatric Residency, State University of New York, Stony Brook, USA, 1978; Research Fellow, Human Sexuality, 1979; Private Practice-; Staff Psychiatrist, South Beach Psychiatric Centre-. *Memberships:* American Medical Association; American Psychiatric Association; American Veneral Disease Association; New York Physicians for Human Rights. *Publications:* 'Growth in Hypothalamic Neurons; in 'Psychoneuroendocr', 'Neuroendocrine Response to Estrogen' in 'Science', 1984. *Address:* 129 Barrow Street, New York, NY 10014, USA.

HELMAN, Judith Gail, b. 5 Mar. 1952, Lynn, Massachusetts, USA. Occupational Therapist. *Education:* BSc, Sargent College of Allied Health Professions, Boston University, 1973. *Appointments:* Occupational Therapist: Hogan Regional Center, Hathorne, Massachusetts, 1974-76; Robert B Brigham Hospital, Boston, 1976-80; Brigham and Womens Hospital, Bosotn, 1980-82; New England Baptist Hospital, Boston, 1982-. *Memberships:* American and Massachusetts Occupational Therapy Association; Allied Health Professional Section, Arthritis Foundation; American Society of Hand Therapists. *Publications;* 'Orthopaedics Upper Exteremity Orthopaedics', Co-Author of Chapter 3 in 'Adult Rehabilitation: A Team Approach for Therapists', 1982. *Hobbies:* Aerobic dancing; Duplicate bridge. *Address:* 105 Larch Road, Cambridge, MA 02138, USA.

HELMCHEN, Hanfried, b. 12 June 1933, Berlin, Federal Republic of Germany. Professor, Psychiatry. *Education:* Studied Medicine, Universities of Berlin & Heidelberg, 1950-55; Research Fellow, Max Planck Institute for Medical Research, Heidelberg, 1954-58; Resident, Neurology, Heidelberg, 1956-58; MD, 1956; Resident, Psychiatry, Berlin, 1959-63. *Appointments:* Senior Consultant, Berlin, 1964-70; Lecturer, Psychiatry, Neurology, 1967; Head, Psychiatry, Free University, Berlin, 1971, Professor, 1972-. *Memberhsips:* President, Deutsche Gesellschaft fur Psychiatrie und Nervenheikunde, 1979-80; President, Abeitsgemeinschaft fur Neuropsychopharmakologie und Pharmakopsychiatrie, 1978-79; President, deutsche

Sektion der Internationalen Liga gegen Epilepsie, 1973-75. *Publications:* "Bedingungskonstellationen paranoid-helluzinatorischer Syndrome", 1968; "Entwicklungstendezen biologischer Psychiatrie", 1975; "Psychiatrische Therapieforschung. Ethische u. Juristische Probleme", 1978; "Fernsehen in der psychiatrie", 1978; "Psychotherapie in der Psychiuatrie", 1982; "Depression, Melancholie, Manie", 1982. *Address:* Eschenallee 3, D 1000 Berlin 19, Federal Republic of Germany.

HELMREICH, Ernst J.M., b. 1 July 1922, Munich, Germany. University Professor and Chairman. m. Rosemarie Hartmann, 31 May 1949, Munich, 2 daughters. *Education:* MD 1949; Elementary and advanced graduate training in chemistry, Department of Organis Chemistry, Munich Institute of Technology, 1948-51. *Appointments include:* Visiting Fellow, National Academy of Sciences, USA, Department of Biological Chemistry, 1954-56, Assistant Professor in Biochemistry in Medicine, 1956-60, Assistant Professor for Biological Chemistry, Department of Biological Chemistry, 1960-61, Washington University, St Louis, USA; Associate Professor, 1961, Full Professor and Chairman, Department of Physiological Chemistry, 1968-, University of Wurzburg, Federal Republic of Germany. *Memberships include:* German Chemical Society; Society for Biological Chemists (President 1973-75); American Chemical Society; American Society for Biological Chemists; Editor of several journals. Advisor of NSF, DFG, Max Planck Society, A v Humbolt Foundation a.o. *Publications:* About 160 publications in international biochemical journals. *Hobby:* Mountaineering. *Address:* Werner-von-Siemens-Str 83, D-8700 Wurzburg, Federal Republic of Germany.

HELMS, Sandra Ann, b. 27 Apr. 1945, San Antonio, Texas, USA. Medical Editor. m. 1) Harvey M Fleming, 1 Jan 1964, San Antonio, 1 son. 2) William Radford Helms, 22 Mar. 1980, San Antonio, 1 stepson, 1 stepdaughter. *Education:* American Medical Writers Programme. *Appointments:* Medical Transcriptionist, 1964-73, Medical Secretary, 1974, Managing Editor, BAMC Progress Notes and Medical Editor, Department of Medicine, 1975-79, Senior Education Technician, Graduate Medical Education, Office of the Commander, 1979-80; Medical Transcriptionist, 1981-83, Medical Editor, Department of Medicine, 1983-, Brooke Army Medical Center, Fort Sam Houston, Texas. *Memberships:* Council of Biology Editors; American Medical Writers Association; American Association for Medical Transcription. *Publications:* Editor of various medical literature. *Honours:* Multiple sustained superior performance awards and outstanding performance appraisals, during Civil Service career. *Hobbies:* Genealogical research; Reading Ayn Rand novels; Walks. *Address:* Route 1 Box 252, Hampshire, TN 38461-9998, USA.

HELZER, Paul Laurence, b. 21 Mar. 1952, California, USA. Director. m Beverley A Hoover, 2 daughters. *Education:* Pre-Medical training, Mount San Antonio College, Pomona; Professional Training, Palmer College of Chiropractic; Graduate Training, Cleveland College of Chiropractic, 1975; PhD, Newport University, 1982. *Appointments:* Director, Helzer Chiropractic Offices, Bellflower, California. *Memberships:* Extension Faculty: Wesley Medical Technical College, Bellflower; Los Angeles College of Chiropractic. California and American Chiropractic Associations; American Psychological Association. *Publications:* Writer of Health Column, 'Bellflower Hearald American'; contributor to 'American Chiropractic Magazine', 'American Chiropractic Journal', 'Journal of the Parker chiropractic Research Foundation'. *Honours:* X-Ray Supervisorand Operator Permit; Licensed to practice, Iowa, Arizona and California; Diplomate, National Board of Chiropractic Examiners;

Journalist Service, Parker Chiropractic Research Foundation, 1982; Selected as delegate of 2nd cultural exchange programme of Chiropractors invited to travel to China to teach chiropractics, 1983. *Hobbies:* Fishing; Scuba diving; Travelling. *Address:* 9461 Flower Street, Bellflower, CA 90706, USA.

HEMINGWAY, Anne Patricia, b. 1 Mar. 1951, Essex, England. Senior Lecturer; Honorary Consultant. *Education:* BSc.; MRCS; LRCP; MB.BS; MRCP; DMRD; FRCR. *Appointments:* House Surgeon, Guy's Hospital, 1975; House Physician, Greenwich District Hospital, 1975-76; Junior Registrar, Cardiology, Guy's Hospital, 1976; Senior House Officer, General Medicine, St Olaves Hospital, 1976-77; Registrar, Respiratory Medicine, Brook Hospital, 1977-78; Registrar, Diagnostic Radiology, Hammersmith Hospital, 1979-83; Senior Lecturer, Royal Postgraduate Medical School. *Memberships:* Royal College of Physicians; British Institute of Radiology; Royal College of Radiologists; British Medical Association; European College of Angiography. *Publications:* "Gastrointestinal Angiography" in 'Nolan D. Ed. An Atlas of Gastrontestinal Disease", 1983; "Venography" in "Diagnostic Imaging", 1985. *Honour:* Duke of Edinburgh's Gold Award, 1972. *Hobbies:* Music; Cookery; Royal Icing & Australian Cake Decorating. *Address:* Dept. of Radiology, RPMS, Hammersmith Hospital, Du Cane Road, London W12 0HS, England.

HAMPFLING, Linda Lee, b. 28 July 1947, Indianapolis, Indiana, USA. Medical Auditor & Chart Reviewer, Med-Charge Analysis Inc. *Education:* Diploma, Indiana Methodist Hospital School of Nursing, 1968; Studies, DePauw University 1968; Joliet Junior College 1969; Currently working for BSPA, Health Care Administration, St. Joseph's College, North Windham, Maine. *Appointments include:* Nurisng positions, Indiana, Illinois, New York, Texas, 1968-76; Unit Manager, Operating Rooms, Hermann Hospital, Houston, Texas, 1976-78; Unit Manager/Purchasing Coordinator, Operating Rooms, ibid, 1979-83; Medical auditor & Chart Reviewer, Med-Charge Analysis Inc., 1984-. *Memberships:* Association of Operating Rooms Nurses; American Nurses Association; Greater Houston Chapter, AORN; Texas Nurses Association; National Leauge for Nursing. *Honours:* Scholarship, Future Nurses of America, 1965; National Merit Scholar, 1965. *Hobbies:* Avid reader; Swimming; Arts & Crafts. *Address:* 12419 Landsdowne Drive, Houston, TX 77035, USA.

HENDERSON, Alexander Scott, b. 7 Dec. 1935, Aberdeen, Scotland. Research Unit Director. m. Priscilla Helen Gill, 24 Feb. 1963, Sydney, Australia, 2 sons, 3 daughters. *Education:* MD, University of Aberdeen, Scotland. *Appointments:* House Physician, Aberdeen Royal Infirmary; Registrar, Ross Clinic, Aberdeen; Senior Registrar, Prince Henry Hospital, Sydney, Australia; Scientific Staff, Medical Research Council Unit for Epidemiological Studies in Psychiatry, University of Edinburgh, Scotland; Foundation Professor of Psychiatry, University of Tasmania, Australia; Director, National Health and Medical Research Council Social Psychiatry Research Unit, The Australian National University, Canberra. *Memberships:* Fellow, Royal Australasian College of Physicians; Fellow, Royal College of Psychiatrists; Fellow, Royal Australian and New Zealand College of Physicians; Royal College of Physicians; Fellow, Academy of Social Sciences in Australia. *Publications:* "Neurosis and the Social Environment" (with D G Byren and P Duncan-Jones), 1981; 'The epidemiology of Alzheimer's disease', 1986. *Honour:* Director, World Health Organisation Collaborating Centre in the Epidemiology of Mental Disorders, 1983. *Hobbies:* Hill Walking; Ornithology; Fly-fishing. *Address:* National Health and Medical Research Council Social Psychiatry Research Unit, The Australian National University, Canberra 2601, Australia.

HENDERSON, David Lorne, b. 9 Jan. 1947, Canada. Staff Officer, Hyperbaric Medicine; Head, School of Operational Medicine. m. Donna Ann Daye, 25 Mar. 1972, Halfax, Nova Scotia, 1 son, 1 daughter. *Education:* BSc 1968, MD 1973, Dalhousie University; MPH, University of Texas, USA, 1982. *Appointments include:* Regimental medical officer, 3rd Royal Canadian Horse Artillery, 1973-75; Company Commander, 1st Field Ambulance, Calgary, Alberta, 1975-77; Operational Support/Diving Medical Officer, Victoria, British Columbia, 1977-81; Fellow, American College of Preventive Medicine/MPH, San Antonio, Texas, USA, 1981-82; Defence & Civil Institute of Environmental Medicine, Toronto, 1982-. *Memberships:* Undersea Medical Society; Occupational Medical Association of Canada; Canadian Medical Association; Canadian College of Family Physicians. *Publications include:* Contributions to medical & aviation journals. *Honours:* Canadian decoration, 1981; Schering postgraduate study award, 1974. *Hobbies:* Scuba diving; Skiing; Coin collecting; Jogging. *Address:* 1133 Sheppard Avenue West, Downsview, Toronto, Ontario, Canada M3M 3B9.

HENDERSON, Derek, b. 9 Apr. 1935, London, England. Consultant Oral and Maxillo-Facial Surgeon. m. Jennifer Jill Anderson, 1961, 1 son, 1 daughter. *Education:* BDS (Hons.), MB BS (Hons.), 1963, London University; FDSRCS (Eng.), 1960; LDS, 1956; MRCS, LRCP, 1963; Dental and Medical Training, Kings College Hospital, London, 1952-56, 1959-63. *Appointments:* House Surgeon appointments, Kings College Hospital and Royal Dental Hospital, 1956-59; Kings College Hospital; Lecturer in Dental Materials, 1958-65; ENT House Officer and Casualty Officer, 1964; Registrar in Oral Surgery, Queen Mary's Hospital, Roehampton and Westminster Hospital, 1965; Senior Registrar in Oral Surgery, United Cardiff Hospitals, 1965-67; Consultant Oral Surgeon to Eastern Region Hospital Board, Scotland and Dundee Dental Hospital, 1967-69, Hon. Senior Lecturer, University of Dundee; Consultant in-charge-of Maxillo-facial Service to Glasgow and West of Scotland, based on Canniesburn Plastic and Oral Surgical Unit, Glasgow, 1969-75, Hon. Clinical Teacher, Glasgow Unitersity; Hon. Civilian Consultant, Queen Elizabeth Military Hospital, Woolwich (formerly Queen Alexandra Military Hospital, Millbank), 1976-81. *Memberships:* Royal College of Surgeons (Eng.) Council, 1984-, Board of Faculty of Dental surgery, Vice-Dean, 1985; Central Committee for Hospital Dental Services, 1978, Member, Exectuive Committee, 1980-;' Central Committee for University Dental Teachers and Research Workers, 1978-81; Negotiating Sub-committee, CCHMS, 1980-; European Association for Maxillo-Facial Surgery; British Medical Association; BDA; Craniofacial Society, Council Member, 1973-77; Oral Surgery Club Great Britain, Fellow; BAOS, Council, Member, 1977-80; International Association of Oral Surgeons; Hon. Member, American Association of Oral Surgeons in Europe; Hon. Associate Life Member, Society of Maxillo-Facial and Oral Surgeons of SA; Hon. President, Institute of Maxillo-Facial Technology, 1977-78. *Publications:* A Colour Atlas and Textbook of Orthogmathic Surgery, 1985; Contributions on general oral surgery to 'British Joruanl of Oral Surgery' and 'British Dental Journal' and expecially on surgery of facial and jaw deformity to 'British Journal of Oral Surgery' and 'British Journal of Plastic Surgery'. *Honours:* Recipient of numerous honours and awards as Dental Student and Medical Student; Hunterian Professor, Royal College of Surgeons of England, 1975-76. *Hobby:* Fly fishing. *Address:* Mallington, Headley Road, Leatherhead, Surrey KT22 8PU, England.

HENDERSON, (Donald) James, b. 7 Aug. 1940, Sudbury, Ontario, Canada. Elected to Ontario Legislature, 1985; Associate Professor, Medicine,

University of Toronto. m. Karen Andrea Santolini, 2 Sep. 1977, Toronto, 3 sons. *Education:* MD, 1964; MPH, Johns Hopkins University, USA, 1966; FRCP(C); DABPN; FAPA. *Appointments:* Director, Out-Patient & Community Services, Lakeshore Psychiatric Hospital, Toronto; Director, Psychiatric Services, Royal Victoria Hospital, Barrie, 1976-83; Psychiatrist in Chief, University Health Service, University of Toronto. *Memberships:* Ontario Psychiatric and Ontario medcial Associations; Canadian Medcial Association; Canadian Psychiatric Association; American Psychiatric Association; Alpha Omega; Alpha Honour Medical Society. *Honours:* Gold Medallist, University of Toronto Diploma Programme, Psychiatry, 1970; Elected to Alpha Omega, 1962; Elected Fellow, American Psychiatric Association, 1983; Elected, Ontario Legislature, 1985; *Hobbies:* Skiing; Sailing; Jogging; Canoeing. *Address:* 14 Fieldstone Road, Etobicoke, Ontario M9C 2J6, Canada.

HENDERSON, James Stuart, b. 26 May 1928, Dundee, Scotland. Professor. m. Ursula Offenbacher, 16 Mar. 1956, Durham, USA, 2 sons. *Education:* MB, ChB, St Andrew's University, Scotland, 1951; Cours de Perfectionment en Pratique Obstetricale, University of Paris. *Appointments:* Rotating Internship, Muhlenberg Hospital, New Jersey, 1951-52; Royal Army Medical Corps, Korea, 1952-54; Instructor, Pathology, Duke University, USA, 1955-57; Research Associate to Peyton Rous, Rockefeller Institute, New Yrok, 1957-61; Assistant Professor, Rockefeller University, 1961-70; Professor, University of Manitoba, Canada, 1970-. *Memberships:* British Medical Association; Pathological Society of Great Britain and Ireland; Fellow, Royal Society of Medicine; American Association for Advancement of Science; Sigma Xi; Ameircan Association of Pathologists; American Association for Cancer Research; New York Academy of Sciences; etc. *Publications:* "View from the Centre of a World", 'A Notable Career in Finding Out', 1971; articles in professional journals. *Hobby:* Theatre. *Address:* Department of Pathology, Faculty of Medicine, University of Manitoba, 770 Bannatyne Avenue, Winnipeg, Canada R3E OW3.

HENDERSON, Maureen McGrath, b. 11 May 1926, Tynemouth, England. Head, Cancer Prevention Programme, Fred Hutchinson Cancer Research Centre; Professor of Medicine & Epidemiology, University of Washington, USA. *Education:* MB, BS, 1949; DPH 1956, University of Durham School of Medicine, UK. *Appointments:* Clinical epidemiologist, Medical Research Council Group of Research on Atmospheric Pollution, St. Bartholomew's Hospital, London, UK, 1958-60; Professor of Social & Preventive Medicine 1968-75, Chairman of Department 1971-75, University of Maryland Medical school; Associate Vice President, Health Sciences, 1975-81, Professor of Medicine & Epidemiology 1981-, University of Washington. *Memberships:* President 1970-72, Association of Teachers of Preventive Medicine; American Epidemiological Society; Exective Officer 1971-76, International Epidemiological Association; Chairman 1969-70, Society for Epidemiologic Research; Council 1981-84, Institute of Medicine; Royal Society of Medicine. *Publications include:* "Epidemiology as a Fundamental Science: Its Use in Health Service Planning, Administration & Evaluation", with K.L.White, 1976; Numerous contributions to scientific journals. *Honours:* John & Mary R. Markle Scholar in Academic Medicine, 1963-68; Luke-Armstrong Scholarship, Epidemiology, University ofDurham, 1956-57. *Hobbies:* Golf; Sailing. *Address:* Fred Hutchinson Cancer Research Centre, 1124 Columbia Street, Seattle, WA 98104, USA.

HENDERSON-SMART, David John, b. 30 June 1944, Johannesburg, South Africa. Director, Newborn Intensive Care. m. Cheryl Mary Alderson, 6 Dec. 1968, Sydney, 3 daughters. *Education:* MB BS, University of Sydney, 1969; MRACP, 1973; FRACP, 1978; PhD, Physiology, University of Sydney, 1978. *Appointments:* Junior Resident Medical Officer, Sydney Hospital, 1969; Resident Medical Officer, Waikato Hospital, New Zealand, 1970; Registrar in Paediatrics, Royal Alexandra Hospital for Children, 1971-74; Post Doctoral Research Fellow, Nuffield Institute for Medical Research, Oxford, 1978-79. *Memberships:* Australian College of Paediatrics; Royal Australasian College of Physicians; Australian Physiological and Pharmacological Society; Paediatric Research Society of Australia (President 1985-86); Australian Perinatal Society (current Secretary). *Publications:* "Regulation of Breathing During Sleep in Newborn Babies and Animals", PhD Thesis, 1978. Contributor of papers and articles to professional journals, etc. *.Honours:* Bushells Travelling Fellowship, Royal Australasian College of Physicians, 1978. *Hobbies:* Sailing; Golf. *Address:* Perinatal Medicine, Royal Pripce Alfred Hospital, Missenden Road, Camperdown, Sydney, New South Wales, 2050, Australia.

HENDLER, Nelson Howard, b. 15 Aug. 1944, New York City, USA. Clinical Director, Mensana Clinic. m. Lee Meyerhoff, 20 Oct. 1974, Owings Mills, 2 sons, 2 daughters. *Education:* BA, Princeton University, 1966; MD, 1972, MS, 1974, University of Maryland; Residency in Psychiatry, Johns Hopkins Hospital, 1972-75. *Appointments:* Assistant Professor, Psychiatry, Assistant Professor, Neurosurgery, Johns Hopkins School of Medicine. *Memberships:* American Medical Association; American Psychiatric Association; International Society for Study of Pain. *Publications:* "Diagnosis and Non-Surgical Management of Chronic Pain", 1981; "Diagnosis and Treatment of Chronic Pain", 1982; "Coping with Chronic Pain", 1979. *Honours:* Board Citation, Psychiatry, American Board of Psychiatry and Neurology; Honourable Mention, William Meninger Award; Falk Fellow, American Psychiatric Association. *Hobbies:* Hunting; Skeet Shooting; Fishing. *Address:* Mensana Clinic, 1718 Greenspring Valley Rd., Stevenson, MD 21153, USA.

HENDLEY, Edith Dipasquale, b. 5 Sept 1927, New York, USA. University Professor. m. Daniel Dees Hendley, 21 Apr 1952, New York, 1 son 2 daughters. *Education:* AB, Hunter College of City of New York, 1948; MSC, Ohio State University, Columbus, Ohio, 1950; PhD, University of Ilinois Professional Schools, Chicago, 1954. *Appointments:* Instructor, University of Chicago Department of Physiology, 1954-56; Assistant Lecturer in Physiology, University of Sheffield, England, 1955-57; Instructor, Ophthalmology Department, 1963-66, Research Associate, Pharmacology and Experimental Therapeutics 1966-72, Johns Hopkins University; Senior Investigator, Environmental Neurobiology, Friends Medical Science Research Center, 1972-73; Professor, Department of Physiology and Biophysics, University of Vermont College of Medicine, 1973-. *Memberships:* American Physiological Society; Society for Neuroscience; American Society of Pharmacology and Experimental Therapeutics; Sigma X1; AAAS; Association for Women in Science. *Publications:* Author of 35 original articles in journals and 5 chapters in books. *Honours:* Phi Beta Kappa; University Scholarship Ohio State University; Grantee of National Institute of Health, American Heart Association, The Sugar Association. *Hobbies:* Books; Music; Theatre. *Address:* Department of Physiology and Biophysics, University of Vermont College of Medicine, Burlington, VT 05405, USA.

HENDRY, William Forbes, b. 15 June 1938, Birmingham, England. Consultant Genitourinary Surgeon. *Education:* MB ChB, 1961, ChM 1971, University of Glasgow. *Memberships:* British Association of Urological Surgeons; British

Andrology Society. *Publications:* "Recent Advances in Urology" (editor); "Textbook of Genitourinary Surgery" (co-editor). *Adress:* 149 Harley Street, London W1, England.

HENISEY, Otis Edward, b. 21 Dec. 1934, Houston, Texas, USA. Dentist, Behavioural and Nutritional Therapist. m. Charmaine LeFleur, 1 June 1962, Houston, 2 sons, 1 daughter. *Education:* DDS, University of Texas, 1961; Diplomate, International Board of Psychohygienics, 1969; PhD, National Christian University of Missouri, 1974; Certificate (Myotronics) in Craineomandibular Orthopedics, 1978; Mastership, Fellowship, Academy of GeneralDentistry. *Appointments Include:* Private practice of dentistry, 1964-83; Chief of Dental Services, Harris County Health Department, 1976-78; Administration and Management, Otis E Henisey DDS Inc, 1983-. *Memberships Include:* American Dental Association; Academy of General Dentistry; Academy of Psychosomatic Medicine; International Academy of Preventive Medicine; International College of Applied Nutrition; Pierre Fauchard Academy; American· Society of Clinical Hypnosis; American Society of Dentistry for Children. *Publications:* Editor, 'Journal of Psychophysical Sciences and Hypnosis', 1965-72; "Psychosomatics and Hypnosis in Dentistry", 1967; "Stress Management and the Brain Computer", 1978; "Dentists Action Guide to Success", 1978: 'Positive Power Plateaus", 1984. *Honours Include:* FAGD, 1969; MAGD, 1974; FAPM, 1975; FICAN, 1976. *Hobbies:* Painting; Writing poetry; Singing; Swimming. *Address:* 17926 Bamwood, Houston, TX 77090, USA.

HENK, John Michael, b. 14 Mar. 1935, Newcastle-under-Lyme, England. Consultant in Radiotherapy and Oncology, Royal Marsden Hospital, London. m. Ailsa Marie Craig, 14 July 1962, Kensington, 2 daughters. *Education:* MA (Cantab); MB; B.Chir; FRCR: Emmanuel College, Cambridge; St. Georges Hospital Medical School. *Appointments:* House Physician, Casualty Officer, St. Georges Hospital, London; Resident Medical Officer, Atkinson Morleys Hospital; House Physician, Radiotherapy Registrar, Royal Marsden Hospital; Consultant Radiotherapist, United Cardiff Hospitals and Welsh Hospital Board. *Memberships:* British Medical Association; British Institute of Radiology; Royal Society of Medicine. *Publications:* Co-author, "Tumours of the Oral Cavity", 1985; Publications on radiotherapy, head and neck cancer, hyperbaric oxygen, in various medical journals. *Honours:* Open exhibition to Emmanuel College, Cambridge, 1952; Brackenburgh Prize in Medicine, St. Georges Hospital Medical School, 1956. *Hobbies:* Lawn Tennis; Member of Society of Lawn Tennis Referees. *Address:* 76 The Crescent, Belmont, Surrey, England.

HENKEN, Bernard Samuel, b. 30 May 1919, Everett, Massachusetts, USA. Psychologist; Clinical Counselor, Medford Pediatric Associates; Editor, Clinical Counseling Bulletin. m. Charlotte, 30 Dec. 1953, Boston, Massachusetts, 2 daughters. *Education:* Boston College, 1938-41; BSc, Harvard University, 1947; MSc, Psychology, Purdue University Graduate School, 1950; Graduate work: Boston University Graduate School, 1950-51; Harvard Graduate School of Education, 1951-53; DSc, Psychology, Calvin Coolidge College of Liberal Arts, 1955. *Appointments Include:* Staff Psychologist, Carney Hospital, Boston, 1950-52; Speech Pathologist, Massachusetts General Hospital, 11951-52; Chief of Speech Department, Staff Psychologist, Audiology Center, Lynn, 1951-55; Clinical Counselor, Alfano Medical Institute, 1956-70; Chief of Psychology and Clinical Counseling Services, Brusch Medical Center, Cambridge 1956-76, 1978-79; Professor of Psychology, Director of Department, Calvin Coolidge College of Liberal Arts, 1958-69; Psychologist and Clinical Counselor, Medford Pediatric Association, 1974-; Speech Pathologist, Everett Public Schools, 1955-68; School Psychologist, 1968-85; Lecturer in Psychology, Massachusetts Department of Education University Extension Services at Harvard University, 1960-68; Psychologist, Wakefield Education Center, 1963-82; Psychologist and Clinical Counselor, North Shore Children's Hospital, 1966-74. *Memberships:* National Association of School Psychologists; Fellow, National Academy of Counselors and Family Therapists; American Psychological Association; Diplomate, American Association of Clinical Counselors; Society of Pediatric Psychology; Massachusetts Speech and Hearing Association; American Association for Counseling and Development; Massachusetts Teachers Association; American Rehabilitation Counselors Association. *Publications:* Contributor to professional journals, etc. *Honours Include:* Leadership Plaque from Massachusetts School Psychologists Association, 1974. *Address:* 118 Waverly Avenue, Melrose, MA 02176, USA.

HENLEY, Edgar (Ed) Floyd, b. 11 Feb. 1940, Corpus Christi, Texas, USA. Pharmacist/Consultant Pharmacist. m. Sylvia Nesbit Atwell, 26 Dec, 1981, Smackover, Arizona, 1 son. *Education:* BS Pharmacy; PhD Behavioural Science. *Appointments:* Intern, Murray-Hart Drug Company, Pine Bluff, Arkansas; President, Bruce Drugs Inc, Smackover; Pharmacy Consultant, AMI Corporation, Smackover. *Memberships:* Arkansas Pharmacists Association; Arkansas Academy of Consultant Pharmacists; National Association of Retail Druggists; Fellow, American Society of Consultant Pharmacists; Chairman, University of Arkansas for Medical Sciences Alumni Advisory Council, 1986; Curriculum Committee, UAMS College of (1986) Pharmacy; Educational Affairs Council, American Society of Consultant Pharmacists, 1986. *Honours:* Community Service Award, Arkansas Pharmacists Association, 1974; Bowl of Hygeia Award, A H Robins, 1974. *Hobbies:* Psy-Ops studies; Politics; Firearms. *Address:* 1101 Cedar, Smackover, AR 71762, USA.

HENNON, David Kent, b. 20 Oct 1933, Midland, Indiana, USA. Professor of Pedodontics. m. Clarice Faye Graves, 16 June 1957, Bloomington, Indiana, 2 sons. *Education:* AB, 1957, DDS, School of Dentistry, 1960, MSD, School of Dentistry Graduate School, 1975 Certificate (Orthodontics), School of Dentistry Graduate School, 1983, Inidana University. *Appointments;* Lecturer in Nutrition, 1960-62, Assistant Professor of Preventive Dentistry, 1962-71, Associate Professor of Preventive Dentistry, 1971-74, Associate Professor of pedodontics, 1974-76, Acting Director, Graduate Pedodontic Clinic, 1976-82, professor of Pediatric Dentistry, 1979-, Indiana University, School of Dentistry; House Staff, Riley Hospital for Children, Indiana University Medical Center, Indianapolis, Indiana. *Memberships Include:* Fellow, American Academy of Pediatric Dentistry, Diplomate, American Board of Pediatric Dentistry; American Dental Association; American Society of Clinical Hypnosis; American Society of Dentistry for Children, and many more. *Publications:* Contributor of numerous articles to scientific journals and presenter of many papers in the field of Dentistry. *Honour:* Omicron Kappa Upsilon, Honorary Dental Fraternity. *Hobbies;* Fishing; Piano. *Address:* 1121 West Michigan Street, Indianapolis, IN 46202, USA.

HENRY, Jack Hopkins, b. 20 Apr. 1937, Lubbock, Texas, USA. Orthopaedic Surgeon. m. Jane Underwood Henry, 19 June 1965, Lubbock, 2 sons. *Education:* BA, Texas Technical University, 1960; MD, University of Texas Medical Branch, Galveston, 1964; Internship, Hospital of the University of Pennsylvania, 1965-66; Fellow, Hip Surgery,

Columbia Presbyterian Medical Centre, 1971-72; Sports Medicine, 1971; Carl Berg Travelling Fellowship, 1972. *Appointments include:* Assistant Clinical Professor, Adjunct Assistant Professor, Anatomy, University of Texas Health Science Centre, San Antonio; Consultant, Hip Service, Audie Murphy Veterans Hospital, San Antonio, Bexar County Hospital, San Antonio; Orthopaedic Consultant, Athletic Medicine, Southwest Texas State University, San Marcos; Texas Lutheran College; Team Physician & Orthopaedic Surgeon, San Antonio Spurs Basketball Team, San Atnonio Gymnastics School; Orthopaedic Consultant, Brook Army Medical Centre, Fort Sam Houston, San Antonio Dodgers Professional Baseball Club; Adjunct Assistant Professor, University of Texas Health Science; Staff Appointments, various hopitals. *Memberships include:* Texas Medical Association; American Academy of Orthopaedic Surgeons, Fellow; American College of Surgeons, Fellow; American Orthopaedic Society for Sports Medicine; Texas Medical Association; Texas Society of Sports Medicine; etc. *Publications:* Numerous articles in professional journals. *Honours:* Phi Gamma Delta; Outstanding Medical Student Award, University of Texas Medical School, 1963; Nu Sigma Nu, Vice President, 1964. *Hobbies:* Hunting; Golf. *Address:* 8042 Wurzbach, Suite 540, San Antonio, TX 78229, USA.

HENRY, Jean Yves, b. 11 May 1947, Paris, France. Doctor. m. 1 son, 1 daughter. *Education:* Graduated, Homeopathology, 1976, Acupunture, 1979, Immunology, 1981. *Appointment:* Teacher, Ecole Europeenne de Medecine Naturelle, 1983-. *Memberships:* Scientific Adviser, CEIA. *Publications:* 'Fichier D'Homeopathie', 1983; articles in professional journals. *Hobby:* Yachting. *Address:* Le pre curieux, 74500 Evian Les Bains, France.

HENSHAW, Nta Elijah, b. 5 Nov. 1928, Calabar, Nigeria. Chief Professor of Restorative Dentistry, University of Lagos. m. 1957, Lagos, 6 sons, 2 daughters. *Education:* Fellow of Dental Surgery; Royal College of Physicians & Surgeons; Doctor of Dental Science; FMCDS; FWACS. *Appointments:* House Officer, 1957-58, Lecturer, 1968, Senior Lecturer, 1971, Associate Professor, 1974, Dean, School of Dental Sciences, 1974, Professor, 1976; Deputy Provost, 1976, Acting Provost, 1978-79, College of Medicine, University of Lagos; Hon. Commissioner for Health 1979, for Finance, 1981-82, Cross River State Government. *Memberships:* Secretary-General, Nigerian Medical Association, 1968-72; Member & Registrar, Nigerian Medical Council, 1974-78; Secretary, National Postgraduate Medical College, 1975-79; President, National Dental Association, Nigeria, 1976; Chairman, Calabar Education Foundation; President, Federation of African Dental Associations, 1985-87. *Publications;* 20 Scientific articles in international dental journals. *Honours:* Chief Gbabimo of Odwa, 1968; Chief Bajito of Lagos State, 1969; Chief Ada-Idagha Ke Iboku Calabar, 1975; Chief Obong Mboko, Ekpe Lodge, Calabar, 1983. *Hobbies:* Music; Soccer; Tennis. *Address:* 28 Ekpo Edem Street, off New Airport Road, Arartigha, Calabar, Nigeria, West Africa.

HERAK, Janko, b. 5 Feb. 1937, Brasljevica. Professor. m. 1 Apr. 1961, Zagreb, 2 daughters. *Education:* BSc., 1960, MSc., 1964, Physics, Phd, Biophysics, 1967, University of Zagreb. *Appointments:* Assistant, Rudjer Boskovic Institute, Zagreb, 1960-64; Research Associate, Duke University, Durham, USA, 1964-66; Scientist 1966-73, Head, Physics, 1975-76, Rudjer Boskovic Institute, Zagreb; Visiting Professor, University of British Columbia, Canada, 1973-74; Professor,

Pharmacy & Biochemistry, University of Zagreb, 1976-. *Memberships:* Council Member, European Physical Society, 1974-76; President, Yugoslav Biophysical Society, 1982-84. *Publications:* Articles in professional journals; Co-Author, "Magnetic Resonance in Chemistry and Biology", 1975; "Supramollcular Structure and Function", 1983. *Address:* Department of Pharmacy and Biochemistry, University of Zagreb, Zagreb, Yugoslavia.

HERCZEG, Béla, b. 16 Sep. 1933, Kunszentmárton, Hungary. Head of Surgery Department. m. Ilona Kovalszky, 10 June 1972, 1 son, 1 daughter. *Education:* Candidate of Medical Sciences. *Appointments:* Assistant Surgeon, County Hospital, Baja, 1958-65; Adjunct, Chief of Section, Department of 1st Clinic of Surgery, Semmelweis University, 1965-73; Head of Department of Surgery, Róbert Károly Hospital, Budapest, 1973-. *Memberships:* Hungarian Society of Surgery; Hungarian Society of Gastroenterology. *Publications:* Various articles in surgical journals & proceedings. *Hobbies:* Serious Music; Fine Arts; Painting. *Address:* Istenhegyi u.39/c, 1125 Budapest, Hungary.

HERING, Egbert Raymond, b. 8 Apr. 1945, Windhoek, Namibia. Senior Lecturer, University of Cape Town; Medical Specialist, Scientist (Medical Physics), Groote Schuur Hospital. m. Linda May, 31 Dec. 1981, Cape Town, 1 son, 1 daughter. *Education:* BSc (Hons), 1968; MSc, 1971; PhD, 1973, University of Cape Town. *Appointments:* Medical Physicist Groote Schuur Hospital and University of Cape Town, 1971; Principal Medical Physicist, 1974; Chief Medical Physicist, 1981; Medical Specialist Scientist, 1984-. *Memberships:* Institute of Physics, London; Institute of Biology, London; Institute of Radiation Protection, London; British Institute of Radiology; South African Association of Physicists in Medicine and Biology; South African Association of Nuclear Medicine. *Publications:* Observations on the Combined Effect of Ultrasound and X-Rays on the Growth of the Roots of Zea Mays, Physics in Medicine and Biology (co-author); A Comparison of the Biological Effect of 125I and 192I Gamma Rays on the Roots of Vicia faba using a Specially Designed Applicator, British Journal of Radiology; The evaluation of an RBE for Iodine-125 Relative to Iridium-192 from a Human Erythematous Skin Reaction Using a New Approach to Skin Scoring, British Journal of Radiology (co-author). *Hobby:* Philately. *Address:* Department of Medical Physics, Groote Schuur Hospital, Observatory, Cape Town 7925, South Africa.

HERLINGER, Hans, b. 19 Apr. 1915, Graz, Austria Professor of Radiology. m. Betty Nield, 19 Dec. 1950, London, England, 2 sons. *Education:* MD: DCH: DTM & H: DMRD, FRCR. *Appointments:* Medical Officer, Colonial Service, British Guiana, 1948; Specialist in Radiology, British Guiana, 1956; Consultant Radiologist, St. James' Hospital, Leeds, England, 1961; Senior Clinical Lecturer, University of Leeds, Head of Department of Radiology, 1964; Professor of Radiology, University of Pennysylvania, Philadelphia, USA. 1979. *Memberships:* Radiological Society of North America; American Society of Gastroenterology; Society of Gastrointestinal Radiologists; Royal College of Radiologists; Royal Society of Medicine. *Publications:* 'Clinical Radiology of the Liver' (2 volumes), 1984; 'Jejunal fold seperation in adult Celiac disease', in 'Radiology', 1986; 'Non specific involvement of Bowel adjoining Crohn's disease' in 'Radiology', 1986. *Honour:* 'A' Merit Award, UK, 1978. *Hobbies:* Golf; Swimming; Walking; Music; Bridge; Travelling. *Address:* 1118 North Woodbine Avenue, Penn Valley, PA 19072, USA.

HERMAN, Judith Lewis, b. 31 Mar. 1942, New York,

USA. Assistant Clinical Professor of Psychiatry. m. Jerry Berndt, 8 May 1978, Cambridge, Massachusetts, 1 daughter. *Education:* BA, Radcliffe College, Cambridge, Massachusetts, 1964; MD, Harvard Medical School, Boston, 1968; Residency and Fellowship, Community Psychiatry, Boston University Medcial Center, 1970-75. *Appointments:* Psychaitric Director, Founding Member, Women's Mental Health Collective Incorporated, Somerville, Massachusetts, 1973-; Assistant Clinical Professor, Psychaitry, Harvard Medical School, Boston, 1981-. *Memberships:* General Member, Committee on Women, 1982-84, Chairperson, Committee on Women, 1984-85, Member, Committee on Abuse 'Misuse of Psychiatry, 1985-, American Psychaitric Association. *Publications:* 'Father-Daughter Incest', 1981. *Honours:* Phi Beta Kappa, 1963; C Wright Mills Award, 1981; Guggenheim Fellowship, 1984; Mary Ingraham Bunting Institute Fellowship, 1984. *Address:* 61 Roseland Street, Somerville, MA 02143, USA.

HERMAN, Lawrence, b. 22 May 1924, New York City, USA. Professor & Chairman, Department of Anatomy, New York Medical College, Valhalla, New York. m. Janice Mae Helmer, 21 Jan. 1960, 2 sons. *Education:* AB, New York University, 1947; MA, Columbia University, 1948; PhD, University of Chicago, 1956. *Appointments include:* Instructor, biology, various colleges, 1948-55; Teaching assistant, University of Chicago, 1955-56; Research Associate, Cornell University Medical school, 1956-57; Assistant, Associate Professor, 1957-68, Professor, Pathology, 1968-76, State University of New York. *Memberships include:* Electron Microscope Society of America; American Society for Cell Biology; Sigma Xi; American Society of Zoologists; American Association of Pathologists; American association for the Advancement of Science; etc. *Publications:* Over 30 research papers in professional journals, conference proceedings, etc. *Honours:* US Public Health Service Special Fellow, Department of Biochemistry, University of Cambridge, UK, 1968-69; Fulbright Fellow, Biophysics, Indian Institute of Medical Sciences, New Delhi, 1975-76; Fogarty Scholar, Clinical Chemistry, Cambridge University/Addenbrookes Hospital, Cambridge, UK, 1978. *Address:* Department of Anatomy, New York Medical College, Valhalla, NY 10595, USA.

HERMAN, Zbigniew Stanislaw, b. 17 Dec. 1935, Tluste, Poland. Professor of Pharmacology. m. Anna Dyaczynska, 29 Apr. 1972, Katowice. *Education:* MD 1959, PhD 1970, Professor Extraordinarius 1978, Medical Faculty, Silesian School of Medicine, Katowice. *Appointments:* Assistant, 1959-65, Senior Lecturer, 1966-69, Head of Department of Pharmacology, 1970-, Silesian School of Medicine, Katowice. *Memberships:* Polish Pharmacological Society; Polish Physiological Society; Polish Biochemical Society; Society of Polish Internists; New York Academy of Sciences; European Society of Biochemical Pharmacology. *Publications:* 181 publications in journals in the field of Psychopharmacology & Clinical Pharmacology; "Pharmacology of Circulation" (co-editor 1983); "Clinical Pharmacology" (co-editor 1985). *Honours:* First Award of Polish Pharmacological Society, 1970; Awards of Polish Ministry of Health, 1975, 1980; Riker Fellowship, 1966. *Hobby:* Music. *Address:* Ordona 14/59, 40-164 Katawice, Poland.

HERMANN, Robert E, b. 28 Jan. 1929, Highland, Illinois, USA, Chairman, Department of General Surgery, Cleveland Clinic Foundation, Cleveland, Ohio, m. Barbara Bower, dec, 23 Aug 1952, 3 sons. *Education:* AB, cum laude, Harvard University, 1950; MD, Washington University, 1954. *Appointments:* Intern and Resident in surgery, University Hospitals of Cleveland, 1954-61; Cirle, Bunts and Lower Fellow in surgery, Western Reserve University, 1961-62; Instrucotr-Assistant Clinical Professor, Associate Clinical Professor in Surgery, 1961-78, Clincial Professor of Surgery, 1978, Case Western Reserve University. *Memberships:* Certified by American Board of Surgery; Fellow, American college of Surgeons; Central Surgical Association; Society for Surgery of Alimentary Tract; Society of Surgical Oncology; American Surgical Association; International Society of Surgery; Collegium Internationale Chirurgiae Digestivae; James IV Associaiton of Surgeons. *Publications:* Contributor of over 169 medical articles including, 'Basic Factors in the Pathogenesis of Pancreatitis', 1963; 'Clinical aspects of pancreatitis', 1964; 'Operative Cholangiography', 1966; 'Transabdominal repair of esophageal histus hernia anterior to the esophagus', 1968; 'T-Tube catheter drainage of the duodenal stump', 1973; 'Shunt operations for portal hypertension', 1975; 'Obstructing duodenal ulcer', 1976; 'Surgery of the pancreas', 1978; 'Patient selection and classes of risk', 1980; 'Carcinoma of the pancreas', 1981; 'The training of surgeons', 1983; 'Bile duct cysts', 1985. *Honours:* Honorary member, Minnesota Surgical Society; Southern Illinois Medical Association, British Columbia Surgical Society, Ecquadorian Surgical Scoiety, Colombia Surgical Society and Surgical Research Society of South Africa. *Hobbies:* Tennis; Sailing; Music; Travel. *Address:* Department of Surgery, Cleveland Clinic Foundation, 9500 Euclid Avenue, Cleveland, Ohio 44106, USA.

HERMUS, Rudolf J J, b. 10 June 1941, Kludert, Netherlands, Managing Director, m. Bernardina A M van Mook, 2 Nov 1966, Wamel, 1 daughter. *Education:* BSc, MSc, Dairy Science and technology; PhD Argicultural Sciences, 1975; Prof Dr Ir. *Appointments:* Research Assistant, 1968-72, Lecturer, 1972-75, Senior Lecturer, Human Nutrition, 1976-79, Argicultural University, Wageningen; Temporary Director, Netherlands Heart Foundation; 1975-76; Head Department Nutrition, 1979-83, Director, 1984-, TNO-Institute CIVO-Toxi-cology and Nutrition, Zeist; Extra-ordinary Professor Human Nutrition, State University Limburg, Mastricht, Faculty Medicine and Health Sciences, 1981-. *Memberships:* National Nutrition Counci; Committees of National Health Council; Group of European Nutritionists; Netherlands Association for Nutrition and Food Technology; Deutsche Gesellschaft für Ernährung; British Nutrition Society. *Publications:* "Experimental Atherosclerosis in Rabbits", 1975; 'Blood and Arterial Wall in Arherogenesis andArterial Thrombosis', 1975; "Atheroscerosis and the Child", 1977; "Alcohol, Health and Society", 1983. *Honours:* Golden Heart of the Netherlands Heart Foundation: *Hobby:* Gardening. *Address:* CIVO-TNO, P O Box 360, 3700 AJ Zeist, Netherlands.

HERNANDEZ-SERRANO, Ruben, b. 12 Oct. 1944, Caracas, Venezuela. Deputy Secretary General, Medical Federation of Venezuela. m. Oris Perez-Benavides, 18 Dec, 1970, Caracas, 2 sons, 1 daughter. *Education:* MD, Central University of Venezuela; Postgraduate course, Psychiatry, Vargas Hospital; Postgraduate course, Psychiatry, University of London Maudsley; Postgraduate Course, Criminology, Central University, Venezuela. *Appointments:* Intern, University Hospital of Caracas; Resident Vargas Hospital of Caracas; Director, Hospital El Junquito, Caracas; Clinical Assistant; Maudsley Hospital, London; Deputy Director, Vargas Hospital, Caracas; Forensic Psychiatrists, Medico-Legal Institute, Caracas; Director of Mental Health, Ministry of Health, Venezuela; Director, Sex Education and Therapy Unit, Venezuela; Assistant Professor, Forensic Psychiatry, Central University; Psychiatrist, Child Guidance Clinic, Caracas. *Memberships:* Membership Advisor, World Psychiatric

Association; General Secretary/Vice President, College of Physicians Miranda; Doctrine Secretary, Medical Federation of Venezuela; Associate' Secretary, World Association of Sexology; Board Member, International Council Prison Medical Services, Forensic Psychiatry Section, World Psychiatric Association. *Publications:* "Manual Practico para Dosificaciones y Use Psicofarmacos" 1982; International Symposia Sexuality: Female 1978, Child 1979, Male 1980, Handicapped 1981, Culture-Anthropology 1982, Law-Violence 1983, Infidelity 1984. 150 Video-cassettes of Forensic Psychiatry Cases, 1974-85. *Honours:* Dr Obdulio Alvarez Prize, College of Physicians, Miranda, 1976; Dr Patrocinio Penuela Prize, Medical Federation Venezuela, 1983; President El Dorado Country Club, 1985-87. *Hobbies:* Tennis; Jogging; Opera. *Address:* Apartado 17302 El Conde, Caracas, 1015-A, Venezuela.

HERNANDEZ-YAGO, José, b. 1 Oct. 1942, Torrente, Valencia, Spain. Chairman, Department of Electron Microscopy. m. Pilar Andreu, 12 Oct. 1967, Torrente, Valencia, 2 sons, 2 daughters. *Education:* Agronomy Engineer, Polytechnic University of Valencia, 1965, PhD 1973. *Appointments:* Assistant Professor of Biochemistry, Polytechnic University of Valencia, 1967-74; Chairman, Electron Microscopy Department, Institute for Cell Research, Valencia, 1974-; Research Associate Professor, University of Kansas, USA, 1980-; Professor of Biochemistry, Polytechnic University of Valencia, 1984-. *Memberships:* American Society for Cell Biology; Royal Microscopical Society (United Kingdom); French, Spanish Societies of Electron Microscopy. *Publications:* Various articles & papers in medical journals. *Honours:* Secretary to Governing Board, Institute for Cell Research, Valencia, 1978-; Scientific Vice-Director, ibid, 1978-. *Hobby:* Music (Completed studies of flute 1959 & violin 1960, Conservatory of Valencia. *Address:* Avenida P Valenciano 64-10a, Torrente (Valencia), Spain.

HERRALD, Gordon Alexander, b. 18 Oct. 1945, Sacramento, California, USA. Private Practitioner, Obstetrics and Gynecology. m. Anne Rutherford, 25 July 1971, Oxnard, California, 2 sons. *Education:* BA, 1969, MD, 1974, University of Colorado; Diplomate, National Board of Medical Examiners and American College of Obstetrics and Gynecology. *Memberships:* Fellow, American College of Obstetrics and Gynecology; California Medical Association; Santa Barbara County Medical Society; Tri-Counties Obstetrics and Gynecological Society. *Hobbies:* Snow skiing; Ocean sailing; Scuba diving. *Address:* 219 Nogales Avenue, Suite A, Santa Barbara, CA 93105, USA.

HERRERA-HERNANDEZ, Manuel, b. 18 Feb. 1932, Las Palmas, Islas Canarias, Spain. Paediatrician; Allergy Specialist. m. Maria Dolores Artiles, 28 July 1960, Telde, Islas Canarias, 3 sons, 3 daughters. *Education:* Lic.med., 1957; MD cum laude, 1963; Paediatrics & puericulture specialist, 1963; Adjunct Professor, Paediatrics, Cadiz University, 1957-59; Peurinculture Medicus, State, 1974; Allergy specialist, 1982. *Appointments include:* Director & Professor, Puericulture School, Las Palmas, 1978-; Public Health Paediatrician, 1960-85; School Medical Inspector, 1970-76. *Memberships:* President 1983-, Sociedad Canaria de Pediatria; Asociacion Espanola de Pediatria; Sociedad Espanola de Alergia; International Association of Asthmology; European Academy of Allergology & Clinical Immunology. *Publications include:* Articles in professional journals: 'Pepsinogeno plasmatico y urinario (uropepsina) en neurologia', 1965; 'Skin test & igE specific in asthma', 1978; 'Food Allergy in Childhood', 1982; 'Shock anafilactico', 1984; etc. *Honours:* Honorary Member, Asociacion Espanola de Pediatria, Spain, 1984, Sociedad Canaria de Pediatria, Spain, 1978; Academician, Royal Medical Academy of Canarias, 1975. *Hobbies:* Tennis; Golf; Reading (biographies). *Address:* Avenida Primero de Mayo, 33-1B, 35002 Las Palmas, Gran Canaria, Spain.

HERRMANN, Hans W., b. 21 Aug 1914, Berlin, Germany. Emeritus Professor. m. Elisabeth Muller, 24 July 1954, Bonn, 2 daughters. *Education:* Dental State Board ex. 1937; Dr. med dent, 1942; Habilitation 1963; Professor, 1968. *Appointments:* 1st Assistant, Department of Oral Surgery, 1947-55; Head of Department of Proth. Dentistry, 1955-71; Head, Department of Dental Materials and Roentg. 1971-79. *Memberships:* FDI Member CDP, Incogudet, DGZMK, DIN NA Dent, Convenor WG Metals, Convenor WG Terminology, DGZPW, ISO TC 106. *Publications:* Over 100 publications in dental books and magazines. *Honours:* Needle of Honour of the German Dental Profession, 1977; Hon. M. Turkish Dental Society of Prosth. and Implant, 1982; Honorary Member, DGZPW, 1982. *Hobbies:* Photography; Hiking; Fishing. *Address:* Am Hhnchen 13, 5300 Boon 3, Federal Republic of Germany.

HERSHEY, David William, b. 15 Aug. 1940, Ann Arbor, Michigan, USA. Private Practice, Psychiatry and Psychoanalysis. 2 sons. *Education:* BA, Yale University, 1962; MD, University of Michigan, 1966; Graduate, Baltimore District of Columbia Institute for Psychoanalysis, 1977. *Appointments:* Chief, Behavioral Sciences Branch 3320th Retraining Group, Lowry AF Base, Denver, 1971-73; Staff Psychiatrist, Chestnut Lodge, Rockville, Maryland, 1973-77, 1980-81; Clinical Assistant Professor of Psychiatry, Georgetown University, 1977-81; Clinical Assistant Professor of Psychiatry, University of Texas Health Science Center, Dallas, 1981-; Teaching Psychoanalyst, New Orleans Psychoanalytic Institute, 1982-. *Memberships:* International Psychoanalytical Association; American Psychoanalytical Association; Baltimore DC Society for Psychoanalysts; New Orleans Psychoanalytic Society; American Medical Association; American Psychiatric Association. *Publications:* Contributor to professional journals. *Honour:* Lewis B Hill Award for best paper by a psychoanalytic candidate, Baltimore, DC, Institute for Psychoanalysis, 1976. *Hobbies:* Writing; Literature; Mountaineering; Swimming. *Address:* 8226 Douglas, Suite 432, Dallas, TX 75225, USA.

HERSHMAN, A Gloria, b. 9 May. 1931, Newark, New Jersey, USA. Director and President, Hand Rehabilitation Center, Management Development Services. m. Paul Hershman, deceased, 2 daughters. *Education:* BS, Milwaukee-downer College, 1952; Graduate School, 1968, Post Graduate Medical School, 1971, New York University; MA candiate, Seton Hall University. *Appointments Include:* Consultant OTR: Evergreens Nursing Home, 1961-66; Multiple Sclerosis Treatment Center, Chester, New Jersey, 1964-68; Clinical Instructor, Rehabilitation, Columbia University, 1975-79; Member, Advisory Council for Occupational Therapy Curriculum, 1975-, Adjunct Faculty, 1979- Kean College; President, Owner, Management Consulting Firm, Management Development Services, Scotch Plains, New Jersey, 1976-; Management Consultant, Performance Improvement Programes, Allied Health, tennessee, 1978-; President, Owner, hand Rehabilitation Center, 1982-. *Memberships:* American Occupational Therapy Association; American Society of Hand Therapists; American Association for Hand Surgery; National Association of Rehabilitation Professionals; New Jersey Occupational Therapy Association. *Publications:* 'Journal of the American Occupational Therapy Association'; 'American Society for Plastic Surgeons Journal'; various other papers contributed to professional journals, Special task forces and position papers and numerous professional presentations. *Honours Include:*

Registrations, American Occupational Therapy Association, 1953, American society of Hand Therapists (Founding Member), 1978; Elected to Roster of Fellows, American Occupational Therapy Association, 1981. *Hobbies:* Boating; Fishing; Bicycling; Tennis; Reading; Attending fine arts, music and theatre. *Address:* 2216 Coles Avenue, Scotch Plains, NJ 07076, USA.

HERSZKOWICZ, Akiva Iehuda, b. 6 Aug. 1933, Buenos Aires, Argentina. Cardiologist. m. Sara Schitter, 14 May 1960, 1 son, 1 daughter. *Education:* MD, 1959, Industrial Medical Doctor, 1961, University of Buenos Aires; ECFMG (USA) 1972. *Appointmetns:* Assistant Physician, Cardiology Division, JA Fernandez Hospital, Buenos Aires, 1960-77; Internal Doctor at Clinica Albertal, Buenos Aires, Medical Doctor, National Institute of Social Services for the Retired and Pensioned, Cardiologist at the Policlinico Gral. San Martin, Saavedra, Cardiologist at the Italian association, Belgrano, Buenos Aires. *Memberships:* Argentine Society of Cardiology; Argentina Association of Atherosclerosis; Argentine Society of Angiology; Argentine Society of Flebolinfology. *Publications:* 'Evaluation of Y-Aminobutiric acid with Vitamin B6 in primary arterial hypertension' ''Chemical Abstracts'' 1965; 'Hydrochlorate of Pargiline in the treatment of Arterial Hypertension' ''La Semana Medica'' 1964; 'Our experince in the treatment of the Arterosclerosis disease with clofibrate-taurina' Acts of the 3rd Interamerican Congress of Arterosclerosis, 1968 etc. *Honours:* ECFMG (USA) 1972; Cardiologist, Ministry of Social Assistance and Public Health, R Argentina 1965. *Hobbies:* Chess; Swimming; Music; Philately. *Address:* Congreso 1737, 2°A. Buenos Aires, 1428, R Argentina.

HERTZ, Alan B., b. 7 June 1946, Bronx, New York, USA. Medical Director, Family Service Institute; Clinical Assistant Professor. *Education:* MD; Fellowship, Psychosomatic Medicine, State University of New York. *Appointments:* Assistant Instructor, Medicine, State University of New York; Instructor, Clinical Assistant Professor, Psychiatry, State University of New York, Downstate. *Memberships:* American Psychiatric Association; Brooklyn Psychiatric Society, Secretary, Treasurer. *Address:* c/o Family Service Institute, 142 Joralemon St., Brooklyn, NY 11201, USA.

HERTZ, Dan (George), b. 15 July 1923, Miskolc, Hungary, Director of Psychiatry Clinic. m. Judith Schoenberger, 6 July 1954, Jerusalem,Israel, 1 son, 1 daughter. *Education:* MD, Hebrew University Medical School; Psychoanalytic Institute, Boston, Massachusetts, USA; Psychoanalytic Institute, Jerusalem, Israel; Post-graduate speciality training in psychiatry, Hadassah University Hospital, Israel. *Appointments:* Assistant and Research Fellow in Psychiatry, Harvard Medical School, Boston, Massachusetts, USA; Director, Mental Health Center, Liberia; Past Chairman, Psychiatric Faculty, Professor of Psychiatry, Hebrew University-Hadassah Medical School, Israel; Director of Psychiatric Consultation Service, currently Director of Psychiatric Clinic, Hadassah University Hospital. *Memberships:* Past Vice-President, International College of Psychosomatic Medicine; International Psychoanalytic Association; Past Secretary-General, Israel Psychiatric Association; Past President, Israel Psychoanalytic Society; Corresponding Fellow, American Psychiatric Association; Fellow, Royal Society of Medicine; Active member, New York Academy of Sciences; American Psychosomatic Society. *Publications include:* 'The Stress of Migration: Adjustment Reactions of Migrants and Their Families' in ''Strangers in the World'', 1980; 'Unwanted Pregnancy' chapter in ''Handbook of Psychosomatic Obstetrics and Gynecology'', 1983; ''Psychosomatik der Frau'', 3rd edition, 1985;

'Homesickness and Psychosomatic Illness' in ''Psychotherapy and Psychosomatic Medicine'', 1985. *Honours:* Grand Commander Star of Africa, 1965; Gustav Bychowski Prize, 1979; Silver Medal, International College of Psychosomatic Medicine, 1979. *Hobbies:* Swimming; Gardening; Watchmaking. *Address:* 30 Tchernikovsky Street, Jerusalem, 92585 Israel.

HERZ, Marvin I, b. 24 Dec 1927, New York City, USA, Professor, Chairman of Psychiatry. m. Beatrice Leslie Mittelman, 13 Sept 1952, NY, NY, USA, 1 son, 2 daughters. *Education:* BA, University of Michigan, 1949; MS, Yale University, 1951; MD, Chicago Medical School, 1955; Internship, University of Illinois, Research and Educational Hospital, 1955-56; Residency, Michael Reese Hospital, Chicago, Ill, 1956-59; Certificate in Psychoanalysis, Columbia University, 1968. *Appointments:* Teaching and Research Assistant, Department of Psychology , Yale University, 1949-51; Director, Inpatient Service, Division of Psychiatry, Montefiore Hospital, New York, 1961-63; Director, Westchester Day Hospital, Albert Einstein Medical School, NY; Instructor to Assistant Professor of Psychiatry, Albert Einstein College of Medicine, NY, 1963-65; Ward Administrator to Director, Washington Heights Community Service New York State Psychiatric Institute, NY; Assistant Attending Psychiatrist, Presbyterian Hospital, NY; Associate in Psychiatry, College of Physicians and Surgeons, Columbia University, NY, 1965-77; Medical Director, Director of Research in Delivery of Mental Health Services, Georgia Mental Health Institute, Atlanta, Ga; Professor of Psychiatry, Emory University, Atlanta, Ga, 1977-78. *Memberships:* Diplomate, American Board of Psychiatry and Neurology in Psychiatry; National Board of Medical Examiners; Fellow, American Psychiatric Association; American College of Psychiatrists; American Academy of Psychoanalysis; American College of Psychoanalysts; American College of Mental Health Administration. *Publications include:* 'Partial Hospitalization, Brief Hospitalization and Aftercare', 1980; 'Course, Relapse and Prevention of Relapse', 1984. *Honours:* Alpha Omega Alpha; Consultant, Psychiatry Education Branch, NIMH, 1978-; NIMH Special Rev Comm, 1981-; *Hobbies:* Tennis; Hiking; Sailing. *Address:* Department of Psychiatry, School of Medicine, SUNY at Buffalo, 462 Grider Street, Buffalo, NY 14215, USA.

HERZBERG, Bernard, b. 11 Oct. 1948, Munich, Germany. Assistant Director, Non-Invasive Cardiac Laboratory, Mount Sinai Medical Centre, Miami Beach, USA. m. Marion, 4 Jan. 1975, Great Neck, New York, 2 sons. *Education:* BA, University College of California, Los Angeles, 1970; MD, New Jersey Medical School, 1977; FACC, 1984. *Appointments:* Medical Resident, New Jersey Medical School Affiliated Hospitals, 1977-79; Chief Medical Resident, Newark Beth Israel Medical Centre & New Jersey Medical Affiliated Hospitals, 1979-80; Cardiology Fellowship, Mount Sinai, 1980-82; Associate Attending Cardiologist, Mount Sinai Medical Centre, & Philip Samet Cardiology Associates, Miami Beach, 1982-. *Memberships:* Fellow,American College of Cardiology; American College of Physicians; American College of Chest Physicians; American Society of Internal Medicine; American Medical Association; American Heart Association. *Honours:* Fellowship, American College of Cardiology, 1984; Diplomate: American Board of Internal Medicine, 1980; American Board of Cardiovascular Diseases, 1983. *Hobbies:* Swimming; Jogging. *Address:* 4300 Alton Road, Miami Beach, FL 33160, USA.

HES, Joseph Philip, b. 5 May, 1925, Culemborg, Holland. Director of Psychiatric Services. m. Hindle Sarah Swartenberg, 6 Mar. 1955, Rehoboth, Israel, 2 sons, 1 daughter. *Education:* MD, Utrecht, Holland, 1954; Specialist of Psychiatry, 1961. *Appointments:* Staff Psychiatrist, Talbieh Hospital Jerusalem, Israel,

1959; Director, Psychiatric Outpatient Clinic, Jerusalem; Director, Municipal Psychiatric Services, Tel Aviv-; Associate Professor, Tel Aviv University-. *Memberships:* Israel Medical Association; Israel Psychiatric Association; Israel Association for Medical Psychotherapy; National Representative, International Association for Suicide Prevention. *Publications:* About 70 articles in scientific journals. *Honour:* Meir Prize for Medical Science, 1967. *Hobbies:* Music; Playing the Clarinet; Swimming; Travel. *Address:* 15 Eli Cohenstr. Ramath Hasharon 47239, Israel.

HESS, Leslie Alan, b. 20 July 1953, Manhattan, New York, USA. Clinical Instructor, Pharmacy and Podiatry; Private Practitioner. m. Jeanne Lindley, 8 Feb. 1981, Turnersville, New Jersey, 1 son. *Education:* BS, Brooklyn College of Pharmacy, 1975; DPM, Penn College of Podiatric Medicine, 1979; Resident, Surgery, 1979-80. *Appointments:* Clinical Instructor: Philadelphia College of Pharmacy and Science, 1980, 81-83; Penn College of Podiatric Medicine, 1981-. Staff Podiatrist: J F K Hospital; Elmer Hospital; Burlington County Hospital. *Memberships:* American Pharmaceutical Association; American Podiatric Medical Association; Board of Trustees, New Jersey Podiatric Medical Society. *Publications:* 'Physiological Changes in the foot during Pregnancy' in 'Journal of Podiatric Medical Association', 1985. *Honours:* Peripheral Vascular Disease Award, 1979; Board of Trustees, New Jersey Podiatric Medical Society, 1984,85. *Hobbies:* Numismatics; Sports. *Address;* Ganttown Professional Plaza, RD 3 Box 429 Ganttown Road, Sewell, NJ 08080, USA.

HESSEL, Louwrens Willem, b. 11 Apr. 1931, The Hague, Holland. Duputy Director, Gaubius Institute for Cardiovascular Research. m. Jacoba van der Kooij, 12 Aug. 1955, 1 son, 3 daughters. *Education:* MSc., Technical University, Delft, Holland; PhD., University of Leiden, Netherlands. *Appointments:* Scientific Investigator, Royal Shell Laboratory, Amsterdam, Holland; Senior Lecturer, Murray College, Sialkot, Pakistan; Deputy Director, Gaubius Institute TNO for Cardiovascular Research-. *Memberships:* Royal Chemical Society; European Atherosclerosis Group; International Atherosclerosis Society. *Publications:* First-author 'Phosphatidic acids and derivatives' 1954; First-author 'The crystal structure of anhydrous manganic acetate', 1969; Editor, 'Liproprotein metabolism and endocrine regulation', with HMJ Kraus, 1979; Author, 'Advances in clinical fibrinolysis', with C Kluft, 1986. *Address:* 9 Plantsoen, 2311 KE, Leiden, Netherlands.

HESSION, Reginald William, b. 16 June 1929, Sydney, Australia. Dentist in Private Practice. m. Pamela Ann, 2 July 1955, London, 1 son, 2 daughters. *Education:* Bachelor of Dental Surgery, 1953, Master of Dental Surgery, 1960, Doctor of Dental Science, 1977, Sydney University. *Appointments include:* Dental Registrar, Royal North Shore Hospital, 1956; Private Practice Sydney, 1957-; Part-time Senior Tutor in Dentistry, University of Sydney, 1959-72; Course Controller, Lecturer and Examiner in Prosthetic Dentistry for the Dental Board of New South Wales, 1961-63; Lecture and Examiner in Restorative Dentistry, Dental Assistants Training Course, 1962-65; Course Designer and Lecturer in Endodontics for the Post Graduate Committee in Dental Science, University of Sydney, 1965-; Senior Visiting Consultant, United Dental Hospital of Sydney, 1983-; Member of Faculty of Dentistry, University of Sydney, 1984-. *Memberships include:* Endodontic Society of New South Wales, President 1965-66; Australian Society of Endodontology; The American Association of Endodontists; Royal Australasian College of Dental Surgeons (Honrorary Secretary 1984-, serving on

various Committees); Fellow, International College of Dentists; Honorary Member, New Zealand Dental Association; Associate, Dental Health Education and Research Foundation, University of Sydney. Pierre Fauchard Society; Australian Dental Association, President 1980-82, Honorary Life Member; New South Wales Branch of Australian Dental Association, President 1971, and various others. *Publications:* Contributor of numerous articles to dental journals and chapters to edited textbooks. *Honour:* AM (Member of the General Division of the Order of Australia). *Hobbies:* Music; Sailing; Skiing; Antiques. *Address:* 53 Telegraph Road, Pymble 2073, New South Wales, Australia.

HETTINGER, Matthew Kevin, b. 31 Dec. 1955, Sturgis, Michigan, USA. Graduate Student. *Education:* BA, Biology, Albion College; MA, Biology, Western Michigan University. *Appointments:* Analytical Chemist, Lear Stegler Inc., Mendon, Michigan, 1978-79; teaching Assistant, Biology, Western Michigan University, 1979-81; Pre-doctoral Research Fellow, Physiology, Biophysics, Health Sciences Centre, University of Illinois, Chicago, 1982-85. *Memberships:* National Coalition for Science and Technology; Society for Neuroscience; American Association for the Advancement of Science. *Publications:* "Intranigral Muscimol Suppresses Ethanol Withdrawal Seizures", 'Brain Research', 1984; "Effects of Physostigmine on Septo-Hippocampal Averaged Evoked Potentials", 'Brain Research', 1984. *Honours:* Predoctoral Alcohol and Drug Abuse Training Fellowship, NIAAA, 1982-85; Beta Beta Beta. *Hobbies:* Computers; Electronics; Swimming; Basketball; Singing; Piano. *Address:* Dept. of Physiology and Biophysics, University of Illinois at Chicago, Health Sciences Centre, Chicago, IL 60680, USA.

HETZEL, Basil Stuart, b. 13 June 1922, London, England. Chief CSIRO Division of Human Nutrition. m. (1) Helen Eyles, 3 Dec. 1946, Adelaide (deceased 1980) (2) Anne Gilmour Fisher, 1 Oct. 1983, Melbourne; 3 sons, 2 daughters. *Education:* MB BS 1944, MD 1949, University of Adelaide; Member, Royal Australasian College of Physicians 1949, Fellow, 1958; Member, Royal College of Physicians 1962, Fellow, 1972; FFCM 1980, FTS 1981. *Appointments:* Resident Medical Officer, Clinical Pathology Registrar, Medical Registrar, Royal Adelaide Hospital, Australia, 1945-49; Clinical Research Officer, Institute of Medical & Veterinary Science, Adelaide, 1949-51; Fulbright Research Fellow, Cornell-New York Hospital, USA, 1951-54; Research Fellow, Department of Chemical Pathology, St Thomas' Hospital Medical School, London,. 1954-55; Michell Research Scholar/Reader in Medicine, University of Adelaide, 1954-58; Honorary Physician, Queen Elizabeth Hospital, Adelaide, 1958-63; Michell Professor of Medicine, 1964-68; Visiting Commonwealth Professor, University of Glasgow, Scotland, 1972-73; Professor of Social & Preventive Medicine, Monash University, Melbourne, 1968-75; Chief, CSIRO Division of Human Nutrition, Adelaide, 1975; Chief, CSIRO, 1975-85; Executive Director, International Council for Control of Iodine Deficiency Disorders, 1986-. *Memberships:* International epidemiological Association, Deputy Chairman 1977-81; Australasian Society for Epidemiology & Research in Community Health; Endocrine Society of Australia, President, 1964-66; Nutrition Committee, NH & MRC; Australian Nutrition Foundation, Chairman 1979-84; Chairman, Scientific Advisory Committee, Menzies Foundation; Corresponding Member, American & Latin-American Thyroid Associations. *Publications:* Numerous publications in field. *Honours:* Susman Prize for Medical Research, 1984; Mallinckrodt Prize Lecturer, 9th International Thyroid Congress, Sao Paulo, 1985. *Hobbies:* Music; Landscape Painting. *Address:* 139 Kermode Street, North Adelaide, South Australia 5006, Australia.

HEWITT, Doris Woodruff, b. 22 Feb 1941, Turner County, Georgia, USA, Marriage and Family Therapist, Director of Therapy, Cross Keys Counselling Centre, m. Clifford S Hewitt Jr, 11 Aug 1963, Sycamore, Georgia, 1 son, 1 daughter. *Education:* MS, Family Relations, PhD, Marriage and Family Therapy, Florida State University, Tallahassee, Fla; Approved Supervisor of marriage and family therapy. *Appointments:* College Counsellor, Assistant Professor of Psychology, St Andrews College, Laurinburg, NC; Associate State Director, Family Planning, Georgia Bureau of Planning, Atlanta, Georgia; Currently Adjunct Professor of Psychology, Georgia State University, Atlanta, Ga. *Memberships:* American Association of Marriage and Family Therapists (AAMFT); State Vice President, GAMFT; American Psychological Association (APA); American Society of Clinical Hypnosis (ASCH). *Publications:* Author of numerous articles in Christian publications on school age pregnancy. *Hobbies:* Reading; Biblical and pre-historic archaeology; Gardening. *Address:* 2014 Winmar Lane, Conley, GA 30027, USA.

HEWITT J C, b. 19 May 1933, Orangeburg, South Carolina, USA. Director of Nuclear Medicine. m. 15 July 1955, Orangeburg, South Carolina, 1 son, 1 daughter. *Education:* BS, Presbyterian College; MD, Medical University of South Carolina. *Appointments:* Assistant Radiologist, Medical University of South Carolina, 1962-63; Physician Director, Schools of Nuclear Medicine and X-Ray Technology, Hillsborough Community College, 1967-77; Co-Director, 1968-70, Director, Radiology Residency Program, 1968-70, Tampa General Hospital; Associate Clinical Professor of Radiology, University of South Florida School of Medicine, 1975-77; Director of Nuclear Medicine, Grand Strand General Hospital, Myrtle Beach, South Carolina, 1977-. *Memberships:* AMA; ACR (Fellow); RSNA; SNM; American Society of Clinical Hypnosis; ACNM. *Publications:* Approximately 53 Papers and publications. *Honour:* Fellow, American College of Radiology, 1984. *Hobbies:* Fishing; Tennis. *Address:* Radiology Department, Grand Strand General Hospital, Myrtle Beach, SC 29577, USA.

HICKEY, Andrew J, b. 9 Feb. 1949, Galway, Ireland. Consultant Cardiologist. m. Dr Camille Schodel, 18 Dec. 1976, Brisbane, Australia, 1 son, 1 daughter. *Education:* MB ChB, BAO, University College, Dublin, Republic of Ireland, 1972; MRCP, UK, 1974; FRACP, Australia, 1979; MD, University of New South Wales, 1985. *Appointments:* Intern, Lourdes Hospital, Dogheda, Ireland, 1972-73; SHO, Hull Royal Infirmary, Yorkshire, England, 1973-75; Medical Registrar, Mater Hospital, Brisbane, Australia, 1975-76. Cardiology Registrar: Canberra Hospital, 1976-77; Research, St George Hospital, Sydney, 1977-78; Prince Henry Hospital, Sydney, 1978-80; Research, Prince Henry Hospital, 1980-85. Consultant Cardiologist, Royal Newcastle Hospital, 1985-. *Memberships:* Royal College of Physicians, Engalnd; Royal Australasian College of Physicians; Member, Cardiac Society of Australia and New Zealand. *Publications:* Author or co-author of over 29 papers contributed to professional publications including: 'Australia and New Zealand Journal of Medicine'; 'Lancet'; 'Medical Journal of Australia'; 'British Heart Journal'; 'Thrombosis Research'; 'Circulation'; 'American Heart Journal'; 'Biochemistry Journal'; 'Journal of American College of Cardiology'. Presenter of 9 papers at international meetings. Ralph Reader Prize Presentation, Cardiac Society of Australia and New Zealand, 1985; R T Hall Prize, for papers published on mitral valve prolapse syndrome, 1985. *Hobbies:* Tennis; Bush walking. *Address:* 76 Watkins Street, Merewether, Newcastle, Australia.

HIDAYATALLA,Abdalla, b. 6 Oct. 1933, Omdurman. Professor, Radiotherapy & Oncology. m. Wadida Hassan Ali, 27 Jan, 1966, Omdurman, 3 sons, 2 daughters. *Education:* MBBS; DMRT. *Appointments:* House Officer, Khartoum Hospital; Medical Officer, Rumbeck Hospital, Bahr El Guzal Province; Medical Registrar: The Middlesex Hospital, London, England, University College Hospital, London; Consultant, Radiotherapy, Radiation & Isotope Centre, Khartoum; Clinical Assistant, Royal Marsden Hospital, Surrey, England; Professor, Radiotherapy & Oncology, University of Khartoum. *Memberships:* British Institute of Radiology; Royal College of Radiologists; Sudanese Doctors Union; Sudanese Association of Radiologists. *Publications:* Articles in various professional journals including: 'Sudan Medical Journal'; 'British Journal of Cancer'; 'European Journal of Cancer & Clinical Oncology'. *Honours:* Vice Chairman, Technical Committee, Review Conference of Non-Proliferation Treaty, Geneva, 1975; Rapporteur, UN Scientific Committee on Effects of Atomic Radiation, Vienna, 1983-86. *Hobbies:* Music; Tennis. *Address:* PO Box 677, Khartoum,Sudan.

HIDEG, Janos, b. 25 Jan. 1933, Kalazno, Hungary. General Major, Hungarian People's Army. m. Zsuzsanna Kulcsar, 18 Aug. 1962. *Education:* Semmelweis Medical Academy, 1959; Flight Surgeon, 1970; Holder, Candidate's Degree in Medicine, 1984. *Appointments:* Flight Surgeon, 1959; First Assistant, Pressure Chamber, Hungarian Aeromedical Research Institute, 1960; Head Surgeon, Physiological Dept., 1964-67, Commandant, 1969-70, Hungarian Aeromedical Research Institute; Chief, Flight Surgeons, 1970-83; Head, Hungarian People's Army Medical Corp, 1984-. *Memberships:* Intercosmos Council, Hungarian Academy of Sciences; Hungarian Gastroenterologic Society; Governing Body, Hungarian Physiological Society; President, Gravitational Physiology Section, 28th International Congress of Physiological Sciences; Vice President, Medico-Biological Special Committee, Intercosmos Council, Hungarian Academy of Sciences; International Astronautical Federation Bioastronautic Committee; Aerospace Medical Association; Presidencey, Hungarian Aviation Association; Corresponding Member, International Astronautic Academy; etc. *Publications:* Author, numerous articles in professional journals; "Advances in Physiological Sciences", 'Proceedings of the 28th International Congress of Physiological Sciences', Budapest, 1980, Editor; "Modern Method and Instrument for Measuring Psychic Performance", '34th Congress of the International Astronautical Federation', 1983; etc. *Honours:* Merited Doctor of the Hungarian People's Republic, 1972; Golden Order of Labour, 1980. *Hobby:* Tennis. *Address:* Ajtosi Durer Sor 25/A, Budapest 1146, Hungary.

HIERHOLZER, Klaus Hermann, b. 8 June 1929, Konstanz, Germany. Professor of Clinical Physiology. m. Christel Mauthe, 6 Oct. 1958, Opladen, Federal Republic of Germany, 2 sons, 2 daughters. *Education:* MD, University of Freiburg, Federal Republic of Germany, 1954; Research Fellow, Department of Physiology, Cornell University, USA, 1957-60. *Appointments:* Fellow, Department of Pharmacology, University of Freiburg; Assistant, Department of Medicine, University of Frankfurt, Federal Republic of Germany; Private Docent, Chairman, Professor, Department of Physiology, Free University of Berlin, Germany. *Memberships:* International Society of Nephrology (Member of Council); German Physiological Society, President 1979, 1984; Senator, Deutsche Forshungsgemeinschaft, 1985-. *Publications:* "Textbook of Endocrinology", 1977; "Distal Na-Transport" (editor Seldin & Giebisch), 1985; "Renal Physiology & Pathophysiology", 1960-85; 'Renal Physiology' American Journal of Physiology, 1957-60. *Honours:* Schoeller-Junkmann Prize, 1967; Member, Academy Leopoldina, Halle,

German Democratic Republic, 1982. *Hobbies:* Collecting Art, Books; Chamber Music; Gardening. *Address:* Thielallee 26, D-1000 Berlin 33, Germany.

HIGENBOTTAM, Timothy William, b. 12 Mar. 1947, England. Consultant Physician. m. Patricia Mary Sidebotham, 21 Aug. 1971, Bramhall, 2 sons. *Education:* BSc., Biochemistry, Honours; MD; MBBS; MRCP. *Appointments:* House Officer, House Surgeon, Guy's Hospital, 1971; Senior House Officer; Greenwich District Hospital, 1972, Brook General Hospital, 1972, London Chest Hospital, 1973, National Hospital for Nervous Diseases, 1974; Resident Medical Officer, University College Hospital, 1974; Medical Registrar, Guy's Hospital, 1974-75; Research Assistant, Thoracic Medicine, Guy's Hospital, 1975-77; Senior Medical Registrar, Guy's Hospital and Brook General Hospital, 1977-80; Assistant Clinical Tutor, Guy's hospital Medical school, 1980-81. *Memberships:* British Thoracic Society; Medical Research Society; British Society for Allergy and Clinical Immunology; British Society for Lung Research; European Society of Clinical Respiratory Physiology; Breathing Club, Honorary Secretary; etc. *Publications:* Articles in professional journals including: 'Journal of Epidemiology and Community Health'; 'World Smoking and Health'; 'Journal of Applied Physiology'; 'British Medical Journal'; 'Clinical Respiratory Physiology'. *Hobbies:* Reading; Jogging; Oil Painting; Computer Programming. *Address:* The Respiratory Function Laboratory, Papworth Hospital, Papworth Everard, Cambridge CB3 8RE, England.

HIGGINS, Peter Matthew, b. 18 June 1923, London, England. Professor of General Practice. m. Jean Margaret Lindsay Currie, 27 Sep. 1952, London. 3 sons, 1 daughter. *Education:* MB BS, University College Hospital, London; Fellow, Royal College of Physicians; Fellow, Royal College of General Practitioners. *Appointments:* House Physician, Professorial Unit, University College Hospital, London, 1947; Royal Army Medical Corps, 1948-50; Resident Medical Officer 1950-52, Assistant Medical Registrar 1953, University College Hospital; General Practice, Rugeley, Staffordshire, England, 1954-66; Castle Vale, Birmingham, 1966-68; Senior Lecturer, Guy's Hospital Medical School, 1968-74; Professor of General Practice, Guy's Hospital Medical School, 1974-; Chairman, Division of General Practice, United Medical Schools of Guy's & St Thomas'; Vice-Chairman: South East Thames Regional Health Authority, 1976-; Governors of Linacre Centre for Study of Medical Ethics; Regional Adviser in general Practice. South East Thames. *Memberships:* Fellow, Royal Society of Medicine; Britsh Medical Association. *Publications:* Various articles in medical journals; Chapter in "Mental Health & the Environment" (edited H Freeman), 1985. *Honour:* Wander Lecturer, Royal Society of Medicine, 1983. *Hobbies:* Squash; Tennis; Swimming; Literature; Music. *Address:* United Medical Schools of Guys & St Thomas', Guys Hospital, London SE1 9RT, England.

HIGGINS, Robert W., b. 9 Nov, 1934, Uniontown, Washington, USA. Chief of Staff, Naval Hospital, Bremerton, Washington. m. Barbara J. Wright, 19 Aug. 1956, Walla-Walla, Washington, 2 sons, 1 daughter. *Education:* BS 1957, MD, University of Washington, 1965. *Appointments:* Medical Officer, USS Tutuila, US Navy, 1966-68; Private Medical Practice, Wenatchee, Washington, 1968-72; Chairman, Department of Family Medicine, Naval Hospital, Charleston, SC, 1972-78; Assistant Clinical Professor, Medical University of SC, 1972-78; Chairman Department of Family Medicine, Naval Hospital, Camp Pendleton CA, 1978-80; Bremerton, WA, 1980-; Chief of Staff, Naval Hospital, Bremerton, WA, 1983-; Associate Clinical Professor, University of Washington School of Medicine, 1980-; Consultant in Family Medicine, to the Surgeon General, US Navy, 1973-85; Faculty Core

Content Review in Family Medicine, 1975-. *Memberships:* American Medical Association, Director, 1980-83, Chairman of Board 1982-83, President Elect, 1983-84, President, 1984-85, American Academy of Family Physicians; Uniformed Services Academy of Family Physicians; Uniformed Services Academy of FP; National Medical Veterans Association; Association of Military Surgeons of the US; Society of Medical Consultants to the Armed Forces; US Naval Institute. *Publications:* (chapter) 'Behavioural Disorders of children and adolescents', 3rd edition, 1982; 'Stimulation of sodium reabsorption in the invitro dog kidney by diphenylhydantoin', 1962. *Honours:* Secretary, Navy Commendation Medal, 1967; Navy Commendation Medal, 1978. *Hobbies:* Sailing; Jogging; Birdwatching; Fly Fishing; Stamp Collecting; Cornet. *Address:* 1995 Kaster Court NE, Bremerton, WA 98310, USA.

HILES, Richard A, b. 31 Aug. 1943. Vice President and Technical Director. m. Karen S Lietzell, 22 July 1966, East Lansing, Michigan, USA. *Education:* BS Chemistry, Clemson University, 1965; PhD Biochemistry, Michigan State University, 1970. *Appointments:* Research Assistant, University of Minnesota, 1970-71; Staff in Research, Procter and Gamble Company, 1971-78; Toxicologist, President and Technical Director, Springborn Institute for Bioresearch, Spencerville, Ohio, 1978-; Adjunct Professor of Pharmacy, Ohio Northern University, 1979-. *Memberships:* Society of Toxicology; Cosmetic Chemists Society. *Publications:* 34 articles and reports, including; 'A method for determining the maximum tolerated dose for in vivo cytogenetic analysis' (with E O Thompson), 1981; 'Inorganic tin: chemistry, disposition and role in nuclear medicine diagnostic skeletal imaging agents' (various co-authors), 1981; 'Subchronic toxicity of N, N-Dimethylaniline (DMA) to F344 rats and B6C3F1 mice' (with K Abdo, M Wolf; sponsor: P V Thadani); 'Lethality study in CD2F1 mice and toxicity studies in Fischer 344 rats and Beagle dogs of Benzisoquinolinedione' (various co-authors), 1985; Two-year carcinogenicity bioassay reports in preparation, National Toxicology Program, National Institute of Environmental Health Sciences. *Hobbies:* Agriculture, Scuba Diving; Tennis. *Address:* Springborn Institute for Bioresearch, Incorporated, 553 North Broadway, Spencerville, OH 45887, USA.

HILL, Christopher Rowland, b. 26 July 1929, Carshalton, England. Professor of Physics as Applied to Medicine, University of London. m. Patricia Susan Gale Maguire, 16 Sep. 1953, Woking, 2 sons, 2 daughters. *Education:* BA, Physics, University of Oxford, 1951; PhD, Biophysics, 1960, DSc, 1976, University of London. *Appointments:* Trainee, Electrical Research Association, 1947-48; 2nd Lieutenant, REME (National service), 1951-53; Development Engineer, Canadian General Electric Company, 1953-57; Staff Scientist, Institute of Cancer Research, 1960-63; Visitng Reader (part-time), University of Surrey, 1967-76. *Memberships:* Fellow, Institute of Physics; Institution of Electrical Engineers; Royal Institution of Great Britain; British Institute of Radiology; Honorary Member, American Institute of Ultrasound in Medicine; British Medical Ultrasound Society, Past President. *Publications:* "Ultrasound in Tumour Diagnosis", 1978; "Investigative Ultrasonography", 1980;' "Medical Ultrasound Images: Formation, Recording, Display and Perception", 1981; "Acoustical Imaging", Volume 12, 1982; Approximately 80 scientific papers. *Honours:* Co-prizewinner of International Ultrasound in Medicine and Biology Prize, 1982, 83; Barclay Prizewinner, British Institute of Radiology, 1983. *Hobby:* Enjoying the World at large. *Address:* Physics Department, Institute of Cancer Research, Royal Marsden Hospital, Sutton, Surrey, England.

HILL, James Howard, b. 10 June 1947, Howell, Michigan, USA. Assistant Professor; Otalaryngologist. 3 sons, 2 daughters. *Education:* MSc., University of Michigan, 1979; MD, University of Michigan Medical School, 1974. *Appointments:* Chief, Otolaryngology, Landstuhl Army Regional Medical Centre, Federal Republic of Germany, 1981-82; Assistant Professor, Otolaryngology, University of Illinois, Chicago; Chief, Otalryngology, Chicago Illinois West Side VA Medical Centre. *Memberships:* Chicago Laryngological and Otologic Society; Midwest Bio-Laser Institute; American Academy of Facial Plastic and Reconstructive Surgery; American Academy of Otolaryngology; American College of Surgeons; Walter P. Work Society; Skin Cancer Foundation; Society of University Otolaryngologists – Head and Neck Surgeons. *Publications:* Articles in, 'Laryngoscope', 'American Journal Pathology', 'American Journal Otolaryngology'; Editor, (with others), "Otolaryngology-Head and Neck Surgery", 1986. *Honours:* US Army Commendation Medal for Meritorious Service, 1982; Appointment to Task force on New Materials for Continuing Medical Education, American Academy of Otolaryngology, 1983-; Appointment, Board of Directors, Midwest Bio-Laser Institute, 1985-. *Hobbies:* Downhill Skiing; Contract Bridge. *Address:* University of Illinois, Eye and Ear Infirmary, Suite 2.42, 1855, West Taylor Street, Chicago, IL 60612, USA.

HILL, Lawrence T, b. 15 Jan. 1947, Washington, District of Columbia, USA. Director, Radioation Oncology, Washington County Hospital Association. m. Greta Dixon 4 Sep. 1982, Georgetown University, Washington, District of Columbia. *Education:* BS, Natural Science, Muhlenberg College, Allentown; MD, Howard University of Medicine. *Appointments:* Associate Director, Radiation Medicine, Georgetown University Medical Center; Director, Radiation Oncology, Washington County Hospital. *Memberships:* Medical Society of District of Columbia; American College of Radiology; ASTRO; ASCO. *Honours:* Frederick Drew Award, 1972; Certificate Award, US Virgin Islands, 1975; Physicians Recognition Award, American Medical Association, 1983. *Address:* 251 E. Antietam Street, Hagerstown, Md 21740, USA.

HILL, Ralph Kelly, b. 31 Oct. 1952, Houston, Texas, USA. Family Physician, Associate Medical Director, Consultant. m. Ellen Albright Smith, 12 Nov. 1977, St Paul's, Houston, 1 son, 1 daughter. *Education:* BA, Rice University, 1973; MD, Baylor College of Medicine, 1976. *Appointments Include:* ER Physician 1978 and 1982-83, Director 1979, Memorial Southwest Hospital; Flight Surgeon, US Air Force, 1979-82; ER Physician, Rapides Hospital, 1980-82; ER Physician, Leesville Hospital, 1981; Private practice of family medicine, 1983 -; Preventive Medicine, The Houstonian Preventive Medical Clinic, 1985 -. *Memberships Include:* American Medical Association; MENSA; American Academy of Family Practice; American College of Emergency Physicians; Society of Teachers of Family Medicine; American Association of Professional Hypnotists; American College of Medicine; American Society of Clinical Hypnosis. *Publications Include:* 'Cold Calamities', 1984; Editor, Martial Arts Newsletter, 1983 -; 'Is our treatment worse than the disease?", 1985; 'Review of Frostbite', 1985; "Ninja Knifefighting", martial arts book, 1985. *Honours Include:* Physicians Recognition Award, 1980 and 1983; Fellowship, American College of Medicine; Black Belt of the Year, 1984. *Hobbies Include:* Martial Arts; Weightlifting; Writing; Tennis; Running. *Address:* 909 Frostwood, Suite 333, Houston, TX 77024, USA.

HILLEMAND, Bernard Jean Pierre Hippolyte, b. 22 Aug. 1923, Paris, France. Titulary Professor; Medical Doctor. m. 31 Jan. 1959, Paris. *Education:* Professor, University of Rouen. *Appointments:* Externe, Paris Hospitals, 1946; Interne, Paris Hospitals, 1950; Faculte de Medecine de Paris, 1955; Chief, Medical Clinic, Faculty of Medicine, Paris, 1956; Maitre de Conférence Agrégé, 1966; UER of Medicine, & Pharmacy of Rouen; Chief of Service, Public Hospitals, Rouen, 1969; Professor, Without Chair, Rouen, 1971; Professor, a titre personnel, Therapeutics, UER of Medicine and Pharmacy of Rouen, 1974-; Expert auprès du Haut Comité d'Etude et d'Information sur l'Alcoolisme (Services du Premier Ministre). *Memberships:* French national Society Gastroenterology; French National Society Proctology; French National Society Allergy; French Society Hepatology; French Society Alcoholy; Spanish Society of Digestive pathology; Correspondant National de l'Académie Nationale de Médecine; etc. *Publications:* 241 articles in professional journals; Monographies; Chapters in Books; 17 Communications or reports at Congress. *Honour:* Officer of Academic Palms, 1983. *Hobby:* Sailing. *Address:* 52 Rue Grand Pont, 7600 Rouen, France.

HILLMAN, Harold, b. 16 Aug. 1930, London, England. Reader, Physiology; Director, Unity Laboratory. m. Elizabeth Holland, 16 Oct. 1974, London, 2 sons, 2 daughters. *Education:* MB, BS; BSc.; MRCS; LRCP; PhD. *Appointments:* Honorary Lecturer, Biochemistry, University of London; Research fellow, Honorary Docent, University of Goteborg, Institute of Neurobiology; Biochemist, Lecturer, Applied Neurobiology, Institute of Neurology, London; Reader, Physiology, Director, Unity Laboratory, University of Surrey. *Memberships;* British Medical Association; Physiological Society; Biochemcial Society; International Society for Neurochemistry; Brain Research Association; Society of Experimental Biology. *Publications:* "Certainty and Uncertainty in Biochemical Techniques", 1972; "Living Cell – A Re-examination of its Fine Structure", co-author, 1980; "Cellular structure of Mammalian Nervous System", 1986; 120 papers in professional journals. *Honour:* Medal, Free University of Brussels, 1974. *Hobbies:* Writing Short Stories; Microscopy. *Address:* Unity Laboratory of Applied Neurobiology, University of Surrey, Guildford, Surrey GU2 5XM, England.

HILLMAN, Sandra Mary, b. 12 May 1947, Wtby, Connecticut, USA. College Dept. Chairperson. m. Henry Matthew Hillman, 22 Nov. 1970, Hartford. *Education:* BSc., University of Connecticut, 1969; MSc., Boston University, 1976; PhD, Boston College School of Education, 1983. *Appointments:* Public Health Nurse, Waterbury, 1969-75; Independent Clinician, Boston, 1975-83; Instructor, Public Health, University of Lowell, 1976-77; Instructor, Community Health, Northeastern University, 1977-78; Assistant Professor, Boston College, 1978-83; Consultant, 1984-; Clinical Field Nurse, Home Health Care, San Francisco Visiting Nurse Association, 1984-; Course Coordinator, Instructor, Community Health Nursing, 1984-86, Chairperson, Social and Organizational Health Systems, 1985-86, Samuel Merritt College of Nursing, Oakland; Assistant Professor, Community and Mental Health Department, University of California, San Francisco, 1986-. *Memberships:* American Educational Research Association; National Association of Female Executives; National Association of Women Deans and Counsellors; National League for Nurses; Society for Research in Nursing Education. *Publications:* Numerous articles in professional journals; Guest Lecturer; Workshop Coordinator. *Honours:* Unico Scholarship Award for Undergraduate Education, 1965; National Fellowship for Graduate Education, 1975; Sigma Theta Tau, 1978. *Address:* 942 Via Casitas, Greenbrae, CA 94904, USA.

HILSON, George Richard Forsyth, b. 19 June 1919, United Kingdom. Emeritus Professor/Research

Fellow. m. (1) Margaret McGroch, 13 Nov 1943, Wigtownshire, Scotland, 2 daughters, (2) Patricia Joan Eaton, 17 June 1976, Sutton, Surrey, England, 1 son. *Education:* MB, BS, King's College, Strand and St George's Hospital Medical School, London, 1938-43; MD Pathology (London) 1960. *Appointments:* Lecturer, Senior Lecturer, Reader in Bacteriology, St George's Hospital Medical School, 1947-69; Honorary Consultant in Bacteriology, St George's Hospital London SW1 and London SW17, 1955-84; Professor of Bacteriology, University of London, 1969-84; Emeritus Professorand Research Fellow, St George's Hospital Medical School, London, 1984-. *Memberships:* British Medical Association; Fellow, Royal College of Pathologists; Pathological Society. *Publications:* Publications in animicrobial chemotherapy; tuberculosis; leprosy. *Honours:* Fulbright Fellowship to Communicable Disease Center, Atalanta, Georgia, USA, 1964-65; Research Grants form U S P H S, M R C, W H O, etc 1957-84. *Hobbies:* Tennis; Sailing; Bridge; Computing. *Address:* 37 Wilderness Road, Earley, Reading, Berks. RG6 2RU, England,

HINCKLE, Thomas Wendell, b. 22 Mar. 1929, Brunswick, Maryland, USA. Professor, Mississippi State University; Private Practice, Psychotherapy. m. Susie May Armstrong Hartley, 6 July 1956, Biloxi, 2 sons, 1 daughter. *Education:* BS, MS, Psychology, University of Southern Mississippi; Ed.D., Counselling and Educational Psychology, Mississippi State University; Certified Rehabilitation Counsellor, Commission on Rehabilitation Counsellor Certification. *Appointments:* Psychologist, US Veterans Administration; Medical Clinic Director, Wiggins Clinic Ltd., Mississippi; Counsellor, Mississippi Employment Service. *Memberships:* American Psychological Association; American Association of Professional Hypnotherapists; American Society of Clinical Hypnosis; Academy of Psychologists in Marital Sex and Family Therpay. *Publications:* "Understanding Stress", 'Mississippi Business Review', 1985; 29 publications and professional presentations, 1973-85. *Hobby:* Magic. *Address:* Rt. 4, Box 183, Starkville, MS 39759, USA.

HINCKLEY, Elmer D., b. 11 Jan. 1903, Margaretville, New York, USA. Professor Emeritus. m. 1 Jan. 1927. *Education:* AB, University of Florida, 1924; PhD, University of Chicago, 1929. *Appointments:* Statistician, Merrill Palmer School, Detroit, 1925-26; Assistant Professor to Professor, 1926-63, Head of Dept., 1930-57, Psychology, University of Florida; Director, Bureau of Vocational Guidance and mental Hygiene, 1931-50, Director, Florida Merit System, 1940-46, University of Florida; Consultant: Florida Parole Commission, Veterans Administration. *Memberships include:* American Psychological Association, Fellow; American Association for Advancement of Science, Fellow; Psychometric Society; National Vocational Guidance Association, Professional Member; Florida Psychological Association, President 1948-49; Florida Academy of Sciences; Florida Educational Association; Sigma Xi; Phi Beta Kappa; Phi Kappa Phi. *Publications:* "Scale for Measuring Attitude Toward the Negro", 1930; Articles in Professional journals; "Brainard Occupational preference Inventory", Reviewed in Fourth Mental Measurements Yearbook, 1953; "Vocational Interest Blank for Men", Revised, Reviewed in Fourth Mental Measurements Yearbook, 1953. *Address:* Box 12007, University Station, Gainesville, FL 32604, USA.

HIND, Joseph Edward Jr., b. 2 Apr. 1923, Chicago, Illinois, USA. University Professor and Chairman of Department of Neurophysiology. m. Ruth A Lueders, 12 Sep. 1947, Oshkosh, Wisconsin, USA, 2 sons, 1 daughter. *Education:* BSEE, Communications Engineering, Illinois Institute of Technology, Chicago, 1944; PhD, Physiological Psychology, University of Chicago, 1952. *Appointments:* Assistant Manufacturing Engineer, Western Electric Co., Chicago, 1944-45; Radar Engineer, US Naval Research Laboratory, Washington DC, 1945-46; Research Assistant , University of Chicago, Division of Otolaryngology, 1946-53; Research Associate, Central Institute for the Deaf, St Louis, Missouri, 1953-54; University of Wisconsin, Madison, 1954-, Professor of Neurophysiology 1964-, Director, Laboratory Computer Facility, 1965-68, Chairman, Department of Neurophysiology 1973-. *Memberships:* American Physiological Society; Accoustical Society of America; Accoustical Society of Japan; Society of Neuroscience; International Brain Research Organization; Association for Research in Otolaryngology; American Association for the Advancement of Science. *Publications:* Author and co-author of articles on: 'microelectrode studies at several levels of the auditory nervous system, including the eighth nerve, cochlear nucleus, inferior colliculus and cerebral cortex' and 'application of digital computers to neurophysiological research'. *Honours:* Fellow, Accoustical Society of America, 1967; Sigma Xi; Tau Beta Pi; Eta Kappa Nu. *Hobbies:* Bicycling; Hiking. *Address:* Department of Neurophysiology, University of Wisconsin Medical School, 1300 University Avenue, Madison, WI 53706, USA.

HINDIEH, Farid George, b. 1 Mar. 1942, Alappo, Syria. Doctor of Medicine. m. Nadia Salameh, 2 July 1966, Harissa, Lebanon, 2 sons, 1 daughter. *Education:* Docteur en Medicine (French State Diploma), 1966; Certificate of the Educational Council for Foreign Medical Graduates, USA, 1973. *Appointments:* Resident Physician, Hospital Des Enfants Malades, Beirut, Lebanon, 1966-71; S.H.O.' Casualty, Haroldwood Hospital, England, 1971; Physician, Internal Medicine, Lebanese Hospital, Jeddah, Saudi Arabia, 1972-74; Senior Medical Officer, Lockheed Aircraft International, Jeddah, Saudi Arabia, 1974-80; General Practitioner (Private), Sharjah, United Arab Emirates, 1980-. *Memberships:* Aerospace Medical Association, USA; Senior Medical Examiner for F.A.A., USA. *Hobbies:* Reading; Listening to Music. *Address:* 2300-51 Ogilvie Road, Gloucester, Ottawa, Ontario KIJ 7X8, Canada.

HINDLEY, Colin Boothman, b. 4 July 1923, Bolton, England. Professor. *Education:* MB. ChB, University of Manchester, 1946; BSc., Psychology, University College, London, 1949. *Appointments:* House Physician, Hope Hospital, Salford, 1946-47; Research Psychologists, 1949-66, Senior Lecturer, 1966-72, Professor, Child Development, 1972-84, Emeritus Professor, 1984-, Institute of Education, University of London. *Memberships:* British medical Association; Fellow, British Psychological Society; Founding Committee Member, Chairman, 1967-68, Association for Child Psychology and Psychiatry; International Society for the Study of Behavioral Development; Association de Psychologie Scientifique de Langue Francaise. *Publications:* Editor, 'Journal of Child Psychology and Psychiatry'', 1959-69; Co-editor, Contributor, 'Development in Adolescence: Psychological, Social and Biological Aspects', 1983; 33 papers in learned journals and books. *Honour:* Fellow, British Psychological Society. *Hobbies:* Gardening; Walking; Swimming; Literature; Philosophy. *Address:* Dept of Child Development and Educational Psychology; University of London, Institute of Education, 20 Bedford Way, London WC1, England.

HINTON, John Mark, b. 5 Mar. 1926, London, England. Research Fellow; Honorary Consultant. m. Moira Patricia Watkins, 15 Aug. 1950, 1 son, 1 daughter. *Education:* MD; FRCP; FRCPsych; DPM. *Appointments:* House Officer, King's College Hospital, 1949-50; RAMC Sierra Leone, 1950-52;

SHO, Medical Registrar, King's College Hospital, 1953-55; Assistant House Physician, National Hospital for Nervous Diseases, 1955; SHO, Registrar, Senior Registrar, Maudley Hospital, 1955-61; Senior Lecturer, Hon, Consultant, Middlesex Hospital, 1961-66; Professor, Psychiatry, Middlesex Hospital Medical School, 1966-83; Research Fellow, Hon Consultant, St Christopher's Hospitce, London. *Memberships:* Royal Society of Medicine. *Publications:* Articles in professional journals. *Honours:* Emeritus Professor, Psychiatry, University of London, 1983. *Hobbies:* Ornithology; Gardening. *Address:* 99 Auckland Road, London SE19 2DT, England.

HIRAKAWA, Kimiyoshi, b. 18 Aug. 1934, Fukuyama City, Japan. Professor & Chief of Neurosurgery, Kyoto Prefectural University of Medicine. m. Atsuko Nakatsuka, 30 May 1968, 2 daughters. *Education:* MD, University of Tokyo, 1959; DMSc, ibid, 1970. *Appointments include:* Assistant of Neurosurgery 1963-69, Chief Assistant 1966-69, Assistant Professor 1969-72, Associate Professor 1972-78, University of Tokyo. *Memberships:* Japan Neurosurgical Society; Japanese Congress of Neurological Surgeons. *Publications include;* 'Mechanical Study on the traumatic optic nerve injury' (Neurol.Med.Chir., Tokyo, 1971); 'Effect of human leukocyte interferon on malignant brain tumor' (Cancer, 1983); 'Proton MNR study on brain oedema' (Recent Progress in the Study & Therapy of Brain Edema, ed. Go & Baethman, 1984). *Hobby:* Photography. *Address:* Kyoto Prefectural University of Medicine, Department of Neurosurgery, Kawaramachi-Hirokoji, Kamigyo-ku, Kyoto 602, Japan.

HIRAYAMA, Chisato, b. 6 Nov. 1923, Kagoshima, Japan. Chairman, 2nd Dept., of Medicine, Tottori University School of Medicine, Yonago. m. Kimiko Ueno, 4 May 1954, 1 son, 1 daughter. *Education:* MD, 1947, PhD, 1956, Kyushu University, Fukuoka. *Appointments:* Assistant Professor, 1953-62, Associate Professor, 1966-76, Kyushu University; Professor, Tottori University, 1977-; Director, Tottori University Hospital, 1984-. *Memberships:* Japan Society Hepatology, Director, 1980-, President 1984-85; Fellow, Japan Society Gastroenterology, Japan Society Hematology; International Association for Study of Liver Desease. *Publications:* "Diseases of the Liver", 1977; "Pathophysiology of Liver Function", 1984; Editor: "Plasma Proteins", 1979, "Treatment of Hepatology Disease", 1980, "Pathobiology of Hepatic Fibrosis", 1985. *Honours:* Japan Society of Electrophoresis, 1968. *Hobbies:* Reading; Travel. *Address:* 343 Nagae, Yonago 683, Japan.

HIROSE, Sadao, b. 1 Mar. 1918, Osaka, Japan. Emeritus Professor, Nippon Medical School; Honorary Superintendent, Tama Chuo Hospital. m. Katsuyo, 27 Mar. 1955, Tokyo. *Education:* MD, University of Tokyo, 1941; Degree, DMSc., Neuropsychiatry University of Tokyo, 1955. *Appointments:* Medical Officer, 1946-54, Chief, Psychiatry, 1954-59, Matsuzawa Mental Hospital; Consultant Psychiatrist Neuropsychiatry, University of Tokyo, 1957-59; Professor, Director, Neuropsychiatry, 1960-83, Postgraduate Dean, 1975-83, Nippon Medical School; Emeritus Professor, Nippon Medical School, 1983; Honorary Superintendent, Tama Chuo Hospital, Tokyo; Consultant Psychiatrist, Tama Hospital, Tokyo. *Memberships:* World Psychiatric Association; American Psychiatric Association, Corresponding Fellow; World Association for Social Psychiatry, Fellow; International Psychiatric Association for the Advancement of Electrotherapy, Charter Member; International Society of Psychiatric Surgery, Founding Member; International Society for Criminology; etc. *Publications:* "Lobotomy : Indications & Results", Japanese, 1951; "The Case Selection of Mental Disorder for Orbito-ventromedical Undercutting", 'Psychosurgery', 1972; "Depression and Homicide", 'Medical Journal', 1979; "Long Term Follow-up of Psychosurgical Operations in Epilepsy with Explosive Behaviour and Episodic Confusional States in Atypical Psychoses", 'Limbic Epilepsy & The Dyscontrol Syndrome', 1980; etc. *Hobbies:* Travelling Abroad; Photography; Theatre. *Address:* 1-10-20 Honkomagome, Bunkyo-ku, Tokyo 113, Japan.

HIROSE, Teruo Terry, b. 20 Jan. 1926, Tokyo, Japan. Cardiovascular, Thoracic & General Surgeon. m. Tomiko Kodama, 1 June 1976, New York City, USA, 1 son. *Education:* BS, Tokyo College, 1944; MD, 1948, PhD, 1958, Chiba University; Clinical Professor, Surgery, New York Medical College, 1974. *Appointments:* Intern, Chiba University Hospital, 1948-49; Resident, Surgery, 1949-52, Resident, Surgery, 1954, American Hospital, Chicago; Resident Thoracic Surgery, Hahnemann Medical College, Philadelphia, 1955-56, New York Medical College, 1961-62; Practice Medicine, Surgery, Chiba, Japan, 1952-53; Chief, Surgery, Tsushimi Hospital, Hagi, Japan, 1958-59; Assistant Professor, Surgery, Chiba University, 1959; Research Fellow, Advanced Cardiovascular Surgery, Hahnemann Hospital, 1959; Teaching Fellow, Surgery, New York Medical College, 1959-60; Instructor, 1961-62; Practice, Surgery, New York City, 1965- , New Jersey 1975-; Director, Cardiovascular Lab, St Barnabas Hospital, New York City, 1965-82; Senior Attending Surgeon, 1965-82; Chief Vascular Surgery Union Hospital, New York City, 1966-67; Attending Surgeon, Flower Fifth Avenue Hospital, 1973-79; Jewish Hospital & Medical Center, New York, 1976-80; St Vincent's Hospital, 1976-; Maimonides Hospital, 1976-78; Passaic General Hospital, New Jersey, 1977-; Westchester County Hospital, 1977-78; Yonkers Professional Hospital, 1978-80; Westchester Square Hospital, 1978-; Pelham Bay General Hospital, 1979-; St Joseph's Hospital, 1980-; Yonkers General Hospital, 1980-. *Memberships:* Member numerous professional organisations including: Diplomate, American Board Surgery; American Board Thoracic Surgery; Fellow, American College Chest Physicians; American College Cardiology; International College Surgeons; American Association Thoracic Surgery; etc. *Publications:* Approximate 200 articles in field of cardiovascular surgery and general surgery in American and Japanese Medical Journals. *Honours:* Hektoen Bronze Medal, 1965, Gold Medal, 1971, American Medical Association. *Hobbies:* Fishing; Swimming; Golf; Skiing; Painting; Writing. *Address:* 5830 Tyndall Avenue, Bronx, NY 10471, USA.

HIROTA, Yukinori, b. 29 Jan, 1930, Hiemji, Japan. Head, Microbial Genetics, National Institute of Genetics. m. Aiko Hirota, 2 Dec. 1961, Osaka, 1 son, 2 daughters. *Education:* MSc., DSc., 1958, Graduate School, University of Osaka. *Appointments:* Research Assistant, University of Wisconsin, USA, 1958; Research Associate, Stanford Univeristy, 1959; Assistant Lecturer, Univeristy of Osaka, School of Science, 1961-70; Maitre de Recherche, Institut Pasteur, Paris, 1967-70; Dirige du Unite, 1970-73; Head, National Institute of Genetics, Japan, 1973-. *Memberships:* Japanese Society of Genetics; Japanese Society of Molecualr Biology. *Publications:* 110 articles in professional journals. *Honours:* Prize, Japanese Society on Genetics, 1965. *Address:* National Institute of Genetics, 1,111 Yata, Mishima, Shizuoka-ken, Japan 411.

HIRSCH, Lawrence L. b. 20 Aug. 1922, Chicago, USA. Professor; Departmental Chairman, Chicago Medical School. *Education:* BS, University of Illinois, 1943, MD, 1950. *Appointments:* Private Practice of

Family Medicine, 1951-70; Medical Director of Ambulatory Care, Illinois Masonic Medical Centre, 1970-72, Director, Family Practice Residency, 1972-75; Professor and Chairman, Department of Family Physicians (Fellow); American Geriatric Society (Fellow); American Association for the Advancement of Science (Fellow); Association of Departments of Family Medicine, (Treasurer); Charter Diplomate, twice recertified American Board of Family Practice; Society of Teachers of Family Medicine. *Publications:* Numerous book reviews and articles in professional journals including 'Journal of the American Medical Association', 'Family Medicine', etc. *Honours:* Past National President, Illinois Academy of Family Physicians; Member of Medical Examining Board, State of Illinois; Speaker, House of Delegates, Illinois State Medical Society. *Hobbies:* Chess; Backpacking; Comparative Religion and Mythology. *Address:* 3333 Green Bay Road, North Chicago, IL 60064-3095, USA.

HIRSCH, Michelle Linda, b. 12 June 1947, USA. Assistant Clinical Professor of Psychiatry, Columbia University. m. Patricio Paez, MD, 24 July 1979, New York City, 1 son, 1 daughter. *Education:* BSc, City College of New York; MD, Upstate Medical School, Syracuse, New York. *Appointments include:* Instructor, Psychiatry, College of Physicians & Surgeons, Columbia University, 1980-. *Memberships:* American Psychiatric Association; American Academy of Child Psychiatry. *Publications include:* Co-author, 'The Assessment of Affective Disorders in Children & adolescents by Semistructured Interview'. *Honour:* Phi Beta Kappa, 1968. *Hobbies:* Music; Dance. *Address:* 3333 Henry Hudson Parkway, Riverdale, NY 10463, USA.

HIRSCHOWITZ, Basil Isaac, b. 29 May 1925, Bethal, South Africa. Professor of Medicine; Professor, Physiology & Biophysics. m. Barbara Louise Burns, 6 July 1958, Ann Arbor, USA, 2 sons, 2 daughters. *Education:* BSc., BCh.;MD (Witwatersrand); FRCP; FACP; FRCP; (Edinburgh). *Appointments include;* Instructor, Physiology, University of Witwatersrand, 1944-45; Intern, Resident, Johannesburg General Hospital, 1947-49; Clinical Assistant, Research Associate, Central Middlesex Hospital, London, 1951; Medical Registrar, Central Middlesex Hospital, 1952-53; Instructor, Research Associate, Gastroenterology, 1953-55, Assistant Professor, Medicine, 1955-57, University of Michigan, USA; Assistant Professor, Medicine, Temple University,1957-59; Associate Professor, Medicine, 1959-64, Director, Gastroenterology, 1959-, Assistant Chairman, medicine, 1963-64, Professor, Medicine, 1964-, Associate Professor, Physiology & Biophysics, 1964-71, Professor, 1971-, University of Alabama, Birmingham, USA. *Memberships include:* South African, British Medical Associations; Medical Research Society of Great Britain; American Federation for Clinical Research; New York Acadmey of Science; American Physiological Society; Alabama Academy of Science; etc. *Publications Include:* Over 260 articles published; 200 Abstracts; numours presentation; 4 teaching films; 2 tapes; Reviewer; etc. *Honours Include:* Sigma Xi; Alpha Omega Alpha; Fellow, American Associationfor the Advancement of Science, 1963; Fellow, Royal College of Physicians (Edinburgh), 1966; McArthur Lecture, University of Edinburgh, Scotland, 1966; Fellow, American College of Physicians, 1967; Distinguished Professor Lecture, Univeristy of Cincinnati, 1973; Jerome Levy Lecture, Univeristy of Arkansas, 1974; Fellow, Royal College of Physicians, London, 1975; Stuart Distinguished Lecture, Pan American Gastroenterology Congress, 1981; Distinguished Visiting Professor, Royal Free School of Medicine, London, England, 1983; etc. *Hobbies:* Philately; Photography. *Address:* Dept. of Medicine, University of Alabama, University Station, Birmingham, AL 35294, USA.

HIRTZLER, Raoul, b. 3 July 1923, Karlovac. Professor. m. Muk Ljerka, 3 May 1969, Poreč. *Education:* MD, University of Zagreb Medical School, 1946; Specialist Examination, Pathology, Sarajevo, 1951; DMSc., University of Zagreb, 1977. *Appointments:* Assistant, 1946, Junior Lecturer, 1956, Senior Lecturer, 1958, Reader, 1963, Professor, 1970, Pathology, Medical School, Zagreb; Chairman, Council of Management, 1967-68, Chairman, Chair of Pathology, 1976-79, Head, Pathology, 1979-85, Zagreb Medical School; Consultant Pathologist, Hospital of Infectious Diseases, Zagreb, 1955-85. *Memberships:* Medical Association of Croatia, Chairman, Pathology Section, 1966-74; Medical Academy of Croatia; Association of Yugoslav Pathologists, Vice President 1970-74; Affiliate, Royal Society of Medicine. *Publications:* Papers on Pathology; Editor, 'Proceedings of the First Congress of Yugoslav Pathologists', 1970; Editor, 'Pathologic Basis of Disease', Croation Translation of L.S. Robbins Book. *Honours:* Yugoslav Order of Work with Golden Wreath, 1968; Yugoslav Order of Merits for the People with Silver Rays, 1974. *Address:* Department of Pathology, Medical School, PO B 936, Zagreb 1001, Yugoslavia.

HO, John Hung-Chiu, b. 6 July 1916, Hong Kong. Chairman Medical and Health Department, Institute of Radiology and Oncology, Hong Kong. m. Florence Tin-yau Kwok, 24 Oct. 1940, Tientsin, the People's Republic of China, 1 son, 2 daughters. *Education:* MRCP; FRCP; DMRD; DMRT; FRCR(D); FRCR(T). *Appointments:* Resident House Physician to Professor of Medicine, University of Hong Kong, 1940; Chinese Army Medical Corps, 1941-45; Medical Officer in Charge, Lai Chi Kok Infectious Disease Hospital, Hong Kong, 1945-46; Junior Assistant Radiologist, Hammersmith Hospital, London, England, 1947-49; Radiologist, Queen Mary Hospital, Hong Kong, 1949-50; Chairman, Medical and Health Department, Institute of Radiology and Oncology, Hong Kong, 1950-85; Honorary Clinical Professor in Radiation Oncology, University of Hong Kong, 1950-. *Memberships Include:* Chairman, Hong Kong Anti-Cancer Society; President, Hong Kong Society of Radiation Therapy and Oncology; International Commission on Radiological Education; British Medical Association; Hong Kong Medical Assocation; Fellow, Royal College of Physicians, London; Royal College of Radiologists; Royal Society of Medicine; International College of Surgeons. *Publications Include:* 'Salted Fish and Nasopharyngeal Carcinoma', (with D P Huang), 1983; 'Is Passive Smoking an Added Risk Factor for Lung Cancer in Chinese Women?', (with L C Koo and D Saw), 1984; 'Nasopharynx', 1984; 'An Analysis of Some Risk Factors For Lung Cancer in Hong Kong', (with L C Koo and N Lee), 1985; 'Prognosis and Histology in Stage 1 Nasopharyngeal Carcinoma(NPC)', (with D Saw, M Fong, C L Chan, C H Tse and W H Lau), 1985. *Honours:* OBE, 1966; Cavaliere of the Order 'Al Merito della Repubblica Italiana', 1982; CBE, 1985. *Hobbies:* Reading Chinese History; Chinese Ceramics; Swimming; Hiking. *Address:* 11Briar Avenue, 1st Floor, Hong Kong.

HO, Yau-Cheung, b. July 1924, Hong Kong. Physician. m. Dr Jane S P Lee, 8 Nov 1952, Hong Kong, 1 son, 1 daughter. *Education:* MD, Lingnan University, Canton, China, 1950. *Appointments:* Intern and Surgery Resident, Dr Sun Yet Sui Hospital, Canton, 1950-52; Medical Officer of Hong Kong Government, Tung Wah Hospital, Hong Kong, 1952-54; Intern, St Luke's Hospital, Denver, Colorado, USA, 1954-55; Resident, New Mount Saini Hospital, Toronto, Ontario, Canada, 1955-66; Resident, Doctors Hospital, Toronto, 1956-57; Private Practice in Toronto, 1958-. *Memberships:* Ontario College of Physicians and Surgeons; Fellow, American Geriatric Society; Fellow, The Royal Society of Health etc. *Honours:* Heavyweight Boxing

Champion of China, 1948. *Hobbies:* Badminton; Tennis; Swimming. *Address:* 21 Lynedock Crescent, Don Mills, Ontario, Canada M3A 2A7..

HOAK, John Charles, b. 12 Dec. 1928, Progress, Pennysylvania, USA. Professor and Chairman, University Department of Medicine. m. Dorothy Witmer, 21 Dec. 1952, Harrisburg, Pennsylvania, 1 son, 2 daughters. *Education:* BS, Lebanon Valley College, USA, 1951; MD, Hahnemann Medical College, 1955; *Appointments;* Instructor in Medicine, University of Iowa, USA, 1961-62; Visiting Research Staff, Oxford University, England, 1962-63; Assistant Professor of Medicine, University of Iowa, 1963-67, Associate Professor, 1967-70, Professor, 1970-84, Director, Division of Haematology-Oncology, 1972-84; Professor and Chairman, Department of Medicine, University of Vermont, 1984-present. *Memberships Include:* Phi Alpha Epsilon; Alpha Omega Alpha; American Medical Association; American College of Physicians; Sigma XI; American Physiological Society; Association of American Physicians; Association of Professors of Medicine; American Society of Haematology; International Society on Haematology; American Heart Association; American Federation for Clinical Research. *Publications Include:* Over 100 articles in professional journals; Chapter in "Synopsis of Surgery", 1972; "Thrombosis: Animal and Clinical Models", 1978; contributions to other publications including "Textbook of Hemostasis and Thrombosis", 1980; "The Regulation of Coagulation", 1980. *Honours Include:* Special Mention, Annual Cochems Competition, 1966-69; American Men of Science, 1973. *Hobbies:* Golf; Travel; Gardening. *Address:* Department of Medicine, University of Vermont College of Medicine, Fletcher House, Room 311, Medical Centre Hospital of Vermont, Burlington, 05405, USA.

HOAKEN, Paul Clement Spencer, b. 18 Dec. 1930, Toronto, Ontario, Canada. Professor of Psychiatry. m. Ellen Brooke Moore, 4 Nov. 1961, Greensboro, North Carolina, USA, 2 sons, 2 daughters. *Education:* BA, 1953, MD, 1957, University of Toronto, Canada. *Appointments:* Attending Psychiatrist, North Carolina Memorial Hospital, Chapel Hill, North Carolina, USA, 1962-63; Assistant Director, Female Service, Kingston Psychiatric Hospital, Kingston, Ontario, Canada, 1963-64; Lecturer, 1964, Professor, 1983-, Faculty of Medicine, Queens University, Kingston, Ontario. *Memberships:* Canadian and Ontario Medical Associations; Canadian, Ontario and American Psychiatric Associations; American Association for the Advancement of Science; Society for Health and Human Values. *Publications;* 'Psychopathology in Klinefelter's Syndrome', in Psychosomatic Medicine', 1964; 'Paranoid Depressive Relationships' in 'Canadian Psychiatric Association Journal', 1973; 'Jealousy as a sympton of Psychiatric Disorder', in 'Australian and New Zealand Journal of Psychiatry', 1976; 'Genetic Factors in Obsessive-Compulsive Neurosis', in 'Canadian Journal of Psychiatry', 1980. *Honours:* President, Ontario Psychiatric Association, 1980. *Hobbies:* Creative writing; Music; Tennis; Running. *Address:* 1050 Johnson Street, Kingston, Ontario, Canada.

HOBACK, Florence Kunst, b. 26 Oct. 1922, Grafton, West Virginia, USA. Psychiatrist. m. John Holland Hoback, 27 October, 1945, Baltimore, 1 son, 1 daughter. *Education:* MD, University of Maryland; Intern, St Mary's Hospital, Huntington; Resident Medicine, St Mary's Hospital; Resident, Psychiatry, Medical College, Virginia, 1961-65. *Appointments:* VA Hospital, 1954-60; Resident, 1961-65; Private Practice, Psychiatry, 1965-. *Memberships:* American Medical Association; American Psychiatric Association; Southern Medical Association; West Virginia Medical Association; Cabell County Medical

Association. *Publications:* "Psychiatry in West Virginia", 1968, 3rd edition 1976, Editor; several articles in professional journals. *Honours:* Police Commission, Huntington, 1976-78; President, West Virginia Branch, APA, 1976-77; Residency Review Board, Psychiatry & neurology, 1980-82. *Hobbies:* Sewing; Gardening. *Address:* 2658 3rd Avenue, Huntington, WV 25702, USA.

HOBBS, Alan Dean, b. 18 May 1946, Jacksonville, Illinois, USA. Doctor of Chiropractic. m. Evelyn Directo Taluba, 14 June 1970, Lemon Grove, 2 sons, 1 daughter. *Education:* BSc., Illinois College, 1969; Doctor of Chiropractic, Palmer College of Chiropractic, Davenport, 1982. *Appointments:* Staff Microbiologist, Kelco Co., San Diego, 1969-79; Doctor of Chiropractic, Hobbs Clinic of Chiropractic. *Memberships:* International Chiropractic Association; American Chiropractic Association; Colorado State Chiropractic Society. *Honours:* Diplomate, National Board of Chiropractic Examiners, 1982; John Connolly Award, Palmer College, 1982; Centurian, Palmer College, 1981, 1982; Certificate of Merit, Palmer College, 1982. *Address:* Hobbs Clinic of Chiropractic, 1135 N. Lincoln Avenue, §1 F2, Loveland, CO 80537, USA.

HOBKIRK, John Andrew, b. 17 Dec. 1944, Newcastle-upon-Tyne, England. Professor of Prosthetic Dentistry, University of London; Head of Department of Prosthetic Dentistry, Institute of Dental Surgery and Eastman Dental Hospital. m. Kathryn Lauderdale, 15 Aug. 1970, Alnwick, 2 sons. *Education:* BDS (Hons.), Dunelm, 1967; FDS RCS (Eng.), 1970; FDS RCS (Ed.), 1970; PhD, University of Newcastle, 1975. *Appointments:* House Officer, Newcastle-upon-Tyne, 1967-68; Resident Senior House Officer, Regional Oral Surgery and Maxillo-Facial Unit, Withington Hospital, Manchester, 1968-69; Registrar, Newcastle-upon-Tyne Dental Hospital, 1969-70; Lecturer, Prosthodontics, University of Newcastle-upon-Tyne, 1970-75; Visiting Lecturer, University of Gothenberg, Sweden, 1974; Senior Lecturer, Department of Prosthetic Dentistry with Honorary Consultant status, Institute of Dental Surgery, Eastman Dental Hospital, London, 1976-79. *Memberships:* British Dental Association; British Society for the Study of Prosthetic Dentistry; European Prosthodontic Association; International Association for Dental Research; Biological Engineering Society. *Publications:* Scientific papers; textbooks as author or contributor, including: Co-author, "The Influence of the Gingival Tissues of Prostheses Incorporating Gingival Relief Area', 'Journal of Dentistry', 7; 'Progress in Implant Research', 'International Dental Journal', 33; "A Clinical Atlas of Complete Dentures"; Consultant Editor, "Clinical Materials". *Honour:* Reckitt Prize, British Society for the Study of Prosthetic Dentistry, 1975. *Hobbies:* Music; Hillwalking; Woodworking. *Address:* Institute of Dental Surgery, Eastman Dental Hospital, 256 Gray's Inn Road, London, WC1X 8LD, England.

HOBO, Sumiya, b. 1 Jan. 1937, Tokyo, Japan. Professor, Tohoku Dental University; Director, International Dental Academy; Visiting Professor, University of California, USA. m. Toshiko Kiuchi, 17 Aug. 1961, 2 sons, 1 daughter. *Education:* DDS, Nihon University, 1961; MSD, Indiana University, 1964; PhD, Tokyo Dental College, 1983. *Appointments:* Graduate Assistant, Fixed and Removable Partial Prosthodontics, Indiana University, 1962-63; Instructor, Fixed and Removable Partial Prosthodontics, 1963-65, Assistant Professor, Head, Dental Ceramics, 1969-70, Indiana University, School of Dentistry, USA; Assistant Professor, Fixed Prosthodontics, University of California, USA, 1970-72. *Memberships:* American Academy of Crown and Bridge Prosthodontics; American Academy of Esthetic Dentistry; International Academy of

Gnathology; International College of Dentists; International Association for Dental Research; Japan Academy of Gnathology. *Publications:* "Cast Gold Preparation", 1974; "Encyclopedia of Occlusion", 1978; "Fundamentals of Fixed Prosthodontics", 2nd edition, 1981; "Dental Ceramics", 1983; "Restoration of the Partially Dentate Mouth", 1984. *Honours:* Merito Integracao Nacional, Government of Brazil, 1983; Beverly B. McCollum Award, International Academy of Gnathology, 1983; National Invention Prize, Japan Institute of Invention and Innovation, 1984. *Hobby:* Golf. *Address:* 2-9-2, Motoazabu, Minato-ku, Tokyo 106, Japan.

HOBSON, Douglas Paul, b. 22 July 1952, Louisville, Kentucky, USA. Director of Residency Training. m. Vicki Lyn Hoofnel, 18 Dec. 1976, Louisville, Kentucky, 1 son. *Education:* MD, University of Louisville, 1978; MA, Baylor University, 1983; Psychiatry Residency, Yale University School of Medicine; Psychosomatic Fellow, Massachusetts General Hospital. *Appointments:* Assistant Professor of Psychiatry and Director of Residency Training, Department of Psychiatry and Health Behavior, Medical College of Georgia, 1983-. *Memberships:* American Medical Association; American Psychiatric Association; Academy of Psychosomatic Medicine. *Honour:* Order of Kentucky Colonels, 1977. *Hobbies:* Antiquarian Books; Classical Music; Tropical Fish. *Address:* Department of Psychiatry and Health Behaviour, Medical College of Georgia, 1515 Pope Avenue, Augusta, GA 30912, USA.

HOBSON, John Allan, b. 3 June, 1933, Hartford, Connecticut, USA. University Professor; Laboratory Director; m. Joan, 23 June, 1956. Providence, Rhode Island, USA, 2 sons, 1 daughter. *Education:* AB, Wesleyan University, USA, 1955; MD, Harvard Medical School, 1959. *Appointments:* Director, Laboratory of Neurophysiology, Massachussetts Mental Health Centre, USA, 1967-; Assistant Professor of Psychiatry,Harvard Medical School, 1969-74, Associate Professor of 1974-78, Professor, 1978-. *Memberships:* Board of Scientific Counsellors, NIMH, Chairman from 1982; Boston Museum of Science; Association of the Psycho-physiological Study of Sleep; Society for Neuroscience. *Publications Include:* 64 articles in professional journals; 112 abstracts; 16 reviews; 18 book chapters including 'Cellular Neurophysiology and Sleep Research' in 'The Sleeping Brain', 1972; 'The Cellular Basis of Sleep Cycle Control' in "Advances in Sleep Research", 1974; 'How does the Cortex Know What to Do? in "Dynamic Aspects of Neocortical Function", in press. Co-author: "Neuronal Activity in Sleep", 1971; "The Recticular Fromation Revisited: Specifying Function for a Non Specific System", 1980 (co-author), etc. *Honours;* Sigma XI, 1959; Benjamin Rush Gold Medal for Best Scientific Exhibit, American Psychiatric Association, 1978. *Hobbies:* Painting; Photography; Design; Farming. *Address:* Laboratory of Neurophysiology, Harvard Medical School/MMHC, 74 Fenwood Road, Boston MA 02115, USA.

HOCKETT, Steven Leon, b. 22 Aug. 1952, Springfield, Ohio, USA. Doctor of Chiropractic. m. Deborah K Reeder, 2 Sep. 1972, New Carlisle, Ohio, 1 son, 1 daughter. *Education:* Associate degree, Medical Laboratory Technology; BSc Human Biology; Doctor of Chiropractic. *Appointments:* Medical Technologist, registered with American Society of Clinical Pathologists and Department of Health Education and Welfare; Teaching Fellowship in Microbiology, National College of Chiropractic. *Memberships:* Diplomate, American Board of Chiropractic; Ohio State Chiropractic Association; American Chiropractic Assocation. *Address:* 23 East Blagrove Street, Richwood, OH 43344, USA.

HODGE, Warren Wise, b. 29 Apr. 1934, Martinsville, Virginia, USA. Director, Medical Services, Naval Hospital, Pensacola. m. Irene Ann Vasil, 29 June 1961, Corpus Christi, Texas, 1 son, 1 daughter. *Education:* BSc., 1955, MD, 1958, University of Louisville; MPH, Harvard School of Public Health, 1964. *Appointments:* Naval Flight Surgeon, Resident, Aerospace Medicine, US Navy; Senior Medical Officer, USS Shangri-La CV38; Assistant Director, Training, Naval Aerospace Medical Institute, Pensacola; Senior Medical Officer, USS Independence CV62; Director, Professional Services, Navy Clinic, Brunswick; Director, Clinical Services, Naval Hospital, Cherry Point; Regional Health Care Coordinator, NRMC Oakland. *Memberships:* Fellow: American college of Preventive Medicine, Aerospace Medical Association; Association of Military Surgeons of US; Society of Naval Flight Surgeons. *Honours:* Meritorious Service Medal and Star for Second Award; Navy Commendation Medal. *Hobbies include:* Sports – Certified USSF Soccer Referree; Music; Art. *Address:* 120 Nandina Road, Gulf Breeze, FL 32561, USA.

HODGES, T(erence) Mark, b. 18 June 1933, Sheffield, England. Librarian. m. Judith Leanore Rosenbloom, 5 Aug. 1963, New York, USA, 1 son, 1 daughter. *Education:* Associate of the Library Association. *Appointments:* City Libraries, Sheffield, England; Hamilton College Library Clinton, New York, USA: Swarthmore College Library, Swarthmore, Pennsylvania, USA; Brooklyn Public Library, USA; Countway Library of Medicine, Harvard University, Boston, Massachusetts, USA; Calhoun Medical Library, Emory University, Atlanta, Georgia, USA; Currently Director, Medical Center Library, Vanderbilt University, Nashville, Tennessee, USA. *Memberships:* American Association of Universiyy Professors; Association of Academic Health Sciences Library Directors; Library Association; Medical Library Association. *Address:* Medical Center Library, Vanderbilt University, Nashville, TN 37232, USA.

HODGKIN, Alan Lloyd, b. 5 Feb 1914, Banbury, England. Emeritus Professor of Biophysics. m. Marion de Kay Rous, 1944, New York, USA, 1 son, 3 daughters. *Education:* MA, ScD, University of Cambridge. *Appointments:* Fellow of Trinity College, Cambridge, 1936-; University Demonstrator in Physiology, Cambridge, 1939-45; Scientific Officer in Radar for Air Ministry, 1939-45; Lecturer then Assistant Director of Research, Department of Physiology, University of Cambridge, 1945-52; Royal Society Foulerton Research Professor of Physiology, 1952-69; John Humphrey Plummer Professor of Biophysics, University of Cambridge, 1970-81; Master of Trinity College, Cambridge, 1978-84. *Memberships:* Physiological Society; Marine Biological Society, President 1966-67; Fellow, Royal Society, 1948-; President 1970-75; etc. *Publications:* "Conduction of the Nervous Impulse" 1964; "Chance and Design in the Pursuit of Nature"; Papers in Journal of Physiology and others on Nerve, muscle, vision 1937-85. *Honours:* Nobel Prize for Medicine and Physiology, 1963 with A F Huxley and J C Eccles; KBE; OM; Royal Medal 1958 and Copley Medal 1965 of Royal Society; Baly Medal, Royal College of Physicians. *Hobbies:* Gardening; Ornithology. *Address:* Physiological Laboratory, Downing Street, Cambridge CB2 3EG.

HODGKIN, John Elliott, b. 22 Aug. 1939, Portland, Oregon, USA. Clinical Professor of Medicine; Medical Director, Center for Health Promotion and Rehabilitation. m. Dorothy Jean Walker, 6 Sept. 1980, Glendale, California, 2 sons, 3 daughters. *Education:* BS, Walla Walla College, 1960; MD, Loma Linda University, School of Medicine 1964; Internal Medicine Residnecy, Loma Linda Medcial Center, 1965-66, 1968-70; Pulmonary Fellowship, Mayo Clinic, 1970-72; *Appointments Include:* Chief,

Pulmonary Section: Loma Linda University School of Medicine, 1974-80; Pettis Memorial Veterans Administration Hospital, Loma Linda, 1977-82. Medical Director: Respiratory Care Department, Loma Linda University Medical Center, 1974-81; Respiratory Care and Pulmonary Rehabilitation Center, St Helena Hospital, st Helen, 1983-; Clinical Professor of Medicine, University of California School of Medicine, Davis, 1983-. *Memberships Include:* Fellow: American College of Physicians; American College of Chest Physicians. American Thoracic Society; American Medical Association; sigma Xi; National Association of Medical Directors for Respiratory Care. *Publications:* Editor: "Chronic Obstructive Pulmonary Disease: Current Concepts Regarding Diagnosis and Treatment", 1979; "Pulmonary Rehabilitation: Guidelines to Success", 1984. Co-Editor: "Respiratory Care: A Guide to Clinical Practice", 1984. Author or co-author of some 119 papers in professional journals inlcuding: "Respiratory Therapy"; 'West Journal of Medicine'; 'American Journal of Surgery'; 'Critical Care Medicine'; 'Practical Cardiology'. *Honours Include:* Hoffman-La Roche Award, 1962; Avalon Scholarship Award, 1962; Avalon Scholarship Award, 1963; Presidents Award, 1964, Comstock Award, 1968, Loma Linda University; Fellowship Award, American Thoracic Society, 1972. *Hobbies:* Tennis; Softball; Trumpet. *Address:* St Helena Hospital and Health Center, Deer Park, CA 94576, USA.

HODKINSON, Henry Malcolm, b. 28 Apr. 1931, Cheshire, England. Barlow Professor of Geriatric Medicine. Divorced, 4 daughters,. *Education:* MA DM, Brasenose College, Oxford University; Middlesex Hospital Medical School; Fellow, Royal College of Physicians. *Appointments:* Junior posts, Middlesex, Central Middlesex, St Stephens and Whittington Hospitals, London, 1956-62; Consultant Geriatrician, North Middlesex and St Anne's General Hospitals, London, 1962-70; Consultant Geriatrician, Member of MRC Scientific Staff, Northwick Park Hospital and Clinical Research Centre, Harrow, Middlesex, 1970-78; Senior Lecturer, Geriatric Medicine, 1978-79, Professor of Geriatric Medicine, 1979-84, Royal Postgraduate Medical School, Hammersmith Hospital, London; currently, Barlow Professor of Geriatric Medicine, University College, London. *Memberships:* British Medical Association; British Geriatrics Society; British Society for Research in Aging; Medical Research Society; Governor, British Foundation for Age Research. *Publications:* "An Outline of Geriatrics", 1975, 81, various translations; "Common Symptoms of Disease in the Elderly", 1976, 80, Turkish edition, 1983; "Biochemical Diagnosis in the Elderly", 1977; "Clinical Biochemistry of the Elderly", Editor, 1984. *Hobbies:* British glass and ceramics. *Address:* 8 Chiswick Square, Burlington Lane, Chiswick, London W4 2QG, England.

HODNETT, Ellen Donnelly, b. 13 July, 1948, New Jersey, USA. Assistant Professor, Faculty of Nursing. m. Michael James Hodnett, 5 July, 1969, New Jersey, USA, 1 son, 1 daughter. *Education:* BSN, Georgetown University, Washington DC, USA, 1969; MScN, University of Toronto, Canada, 1980, PhD, 1983. *Appointments:* Unit Administrator, Labour and Delivery, North York General Hospital, Willowdale, Ontario, Canada, 1970-75; Lecturer, University of Toronto Faculty of Nursing, Toronto, Canada, 1975-83; Assistant Professor-. *Memberships:* College of Nurses of Ontario; Nurses Association of the American College of Obstetricans and Gynecologists; Registered Nurses Association of Ontario. *Publications:* 'Mothers' Perceptions of their Labour Experiences' in 'Matt. Ch. Nurs. J.' 1980, (with P.Butani); 'Patient Control During Labour: Effects of Two Types of Foetal Monitors' in 'J.O.G.N Nurs.' 1982; 'Comparisons Between Home and Hospital Birth Choosers in Metropolitan Toronto' - proceedings, 10th National Nursing Res.

Conference, Toronto, 1985. *Honours:* Canadian Nurses Foundation Fellowship, 1979-80; Ontario Ministry of Health Fellowships, 1979-80, 1981-83. *Hobbies:* Reading; Travel. *Address:* University of Toronto, Faculty of Nursing, 50 St. George St Toronto, Ontario, Canada, M5S 1A1.

HOEMAN, Shirley A. Pollock, b. 15 Oct. 1942, USA. Director, Research, Education and Professional Studies; Assistant Professor, Columbia University (College Physicians and Surgeons). *Education:* BS, University of Missouri, Columbia, 1964; PNA Certificate; MPH, University of Minnesota, Minneapolis, 1974; MA, 1982, PhD, 1984, Rutgers, The State University, New Brunswick, New Jersey. *Appointments:* Director of Nursing, Sister Kenny Rehabilitation Institute, Minnesota; Supervisor, Infant and Child Health Programs, State of Minnesota; Assistant Professor, University of Minnesota; Assistant Professor and Grant Management Team, Kellogg Grant for Total Systems Curriculum Design Project, Creighton University; Assistant Professor, Rutgers, New Brunswick; Consultant, Private Practice; Director, Home Health Agency, New Brunswick; Assistant Professor, Columbia University, College of Physicians and Surgeons; Director, Research, Education and Professional Standards, Kessler Institute for Rehabilitation Incorporated. *Memberships:* American Public Health Association; American Anthropological Association; Medical Anthropology Society; Sigma Theta Tau. *Honours:* St. Charles Clinic Award, 1960-64; National Science Foundation Scholarship, 1960-64; USPHS Titale ll Traineeship, 1972-74. *Hobbies:* Herb Gardening; Cross Country Skiing. *Address:* 6 Camp Washington Road, Long Valley, NJ 07853, USA.

HOFFBRAND, Allan Victor, b. 14 Oct. 1935, Bradford, England. Professor of Haematology. m. Irene Jill Mellows, 3 Nov. 1963, London, 2 sons, 1 daughter. *Education:* The Queens College, Oxford, Oxford University, 1953-57; London Hospital, 1957-60; MA,DM,BCh, 1960; FRCP; FRCPath; FRCP(Edin). *Appointments:* House Appointments and Registrar, London Hospital, 1960-62; Diploma in Clinical Pathology, Research Fellow and Registrar in Haematology, Royal Postgraduate Medical School, 1962-66; Lecturer in Haematology, St Bartholomew's Hospital, 1966-67; Research Fellow, New England Medical Center, Boston, Massachusetts, USA, 1967-68; Lecturer in Haematology, Royal Postgraduate MedicalSchool, England, 1968-74; currently, Professor of Haematology, Royal Free Hospital and School of Medicine, London. *Memberships:* British and American Societies of Haematology. Fellow: Royal College of Physicians; Edinburgh Royal College of Pathologists. *Publications:* Editor: "Clinics in Haematology", 1976; "Recent Advances in Haematology", 3rd and 4th editions, 1982, 85. Joint Editor: "Tutorial in Postgraduate Medicine", 1972; "Postgraduate Haematology", 1980; "Recent Advances in Haematology", 1977, "Clinics in Haematology," 1986; Joint Author: "Essential Haematology", 1980, 84. *Honours:* Lewis Smith Travelling Scholarship, London Hospital, 1962; MRC Travelling Scholarship, 1966; Various Guest Lectureships internationally including 3 Memorial Lectures. *Hobbies:* Squash; Chess; Bridge; Antiques. *Address:* 57 Camden Square, London NW1 9XE, England.

HOFFMAN, Leon, b. 6 Dec 1941, Dominican Republic, Psychiatrist and Psychoanalyst. m. Anne J Golomb, 18 June 1967, New York, USA, 2 daughters. *Education:* AB, Columbia College, 1963; MS, State University New York, Buffalo, 1967; Graduate, New York Psychoanalyst Institute, 1979; Qualified Child Psychoanalyst, 1983. *Appointments:* Psychiatrist in charge, Child Psychiatry Unit, Mt Sinai Medical Centre, NY, 1978-84; Assistant Clinical

Professor, Mt Sinai School of Medicine, NY, 1978-85; Clinical Assistant Professor, Cornell Medical Centre, 1985-. *Memberships:* American Psychoanalytic Association; New York Psychoanalytic Institute and Society; International Psychoanalytic Association; Association for Child Psychoanalysis; American Psychiatric Association; American Academy Child Psychaitry. *Publications:* "Evaluation and Care of Severly Disturbed Children", 1982; "Painter Model Theme in Picasso", 1984; "Play Group Psychotherapy", 1979. *Honour:* M Ralph Kaufman Chief Resident, 1974. *Hobbies:* Reading; Sport. *Address:* 167 East 67, New York, NY 10021, USA.

HOFFRICHTER, Manfred, b. 14 Oct. 1919, Königsberg, Germany. International Aviation Medical Examiner; Chief, Fliegerärztliche Untersuchungsstelle Kronberg. m. Rose-Marie Kuales, 21 May 1982, Kronberg, 1 son. *Education:* MD, University of Prague; University of Berlin; Medical Academy of Danzig; University of Prague; GP 1951; Licence of Flight Surgeon by Government Darmstadt, 1951; Aviation Medical Examiner, Federal Aviation Administration, 1964-; Flight Surgeon by Contract of German Lufthansa Airline, 1969; Chief Aviation Medical Examiner in 6242, 1972-; General Practice, Sports Medicine; Lt.Col (Reserve), German Air Force. *Memberships:* Aerospace Medical Association; Federal Aviation Administration; Deutsche Gesellschaft fur Wehremedizin und Wehrpharmazie e.V; Deutsche Gesellschaft fur Luft-und Raumfahrtmedizin. *Publications:* What About the German Research in Space Medicine? in Astronautik, 1967; Special article by request of Wissenschaftliche Gesellschaft fur Luftfahrt on international regulations of airman medical examinations, 1961; Lecture on "Actual Problems of Aviation Medicine" at Sanchenberg Museum, Frankfurt-am-Main, 1967. *Honours:* Ambassador at Large of Oklahoma City, USA, 1967; Corresponding Member of Harmann-Oberth Gesellschaft, 1972; Appreciation of Aerospace Medical Association for more than 25 years service and membership. *Hobbies:* Long Distance Skiing; Painting; Life in the Alps and Lake Constance. *Address:* Goethestrasse 15, 6242 Kronberg-Taunus, Federal German Republic.

HOGAN, Bartholomew Toner, b. 17 Oct. 1934, Honolulu, Hawaii, USA. Head, Naval Hospital Psychiatry Department. m. Judith Fields, 10 Jan, 1976, Chevy Chase, Maryland, 2 sons, 1 daughter. *Education:* BA History, University of Virginia, 1952-56; MD, Johns Hopkins Medical School, 1956-60. *Appointments:* Chief of Neuropsychiatry, US Naval Hospital, Charleston, South Carolina, 1964-66; Staff Psychiatrist, Bethesda Naval Hospital, Bethesda, Maryland, 1966-68; Director of Neuropsychiatry, Knud Hansen Memorial Hospital, Charlotte Amalie, Saint Thomas, Virgin Islands, 1971-72; Private Practice, Psychiatric Institute, Washington DC, 1968-70 and 1972-73; Private Practice, Montgomery Village Professional Center, Gaithersburg, Maryland, 1978-80; Director of Residency Training 1980-84, Head, 1984-, Psychiatry Department, Naval Hospital, Bethesda. *Memberships:* Committee on Preventive Psychiatry 1966-69; Hofheimer prize review Board 1969-71; American Psychiatric Association; Washington Psychiatric Association; Johns Hopkins Medical and Surgical Association; Association of Military Surgeons of the United States; Phi Beta Kappa. *Publications Include:* 'The Action of Optical Antipodes on Acctylcholinestease Inhibition', (with Friers, Whitcomb and French), 1958. *Hobbies:* Gardening; Woodworking. *Address:* Naval Hospital, Naval Medical Command, NCR, Department of Psychiatry, Bethesda, MD 20814, USA.

HOGAN, Joseph Thomas, b. 25 Nov. 1943, Cooperstown, New York, USA. Podiatrist. m. Kathleen M. Sullivan, 22 July 1978, 3 sons, 2 daughters. *Education:* BA, University of Notre Dame; DPN, Illinois College of Podiatric Medicine. *Appointments:* Residency, St Mary Hospital, Philadelphia, 1975, 1976; Clinical Instructor, Upstate Medical Centre, Syracuse, 1981; Surgical Staff, Lourdes Memorial Hospital, Binghamton General Hospital, Witson Memorial Hospital; Founder, Diabetic Foot Clinic, Wilson Memorial Hospital, 1982; *Memberships:* American Public Health Association; Board of Directors, New York State, American Diabetes Association; Board of Directors, Diabetic Association of Southern Tier, 1983; American Podiatric Medical Association; New York State Podiatry Society; New York Academy of Sciences; Pennsylvania Podiatric Medical Association, (Faculty Hershey Surgical Seminar, 1985). *Honours:* Fellow, American College of Foot Surgeons, 1984; Diplomate, American Board of Podiatric Surgery; Fellow, American Association of Hospital Podiatrists; President, Notre Dame Club of Triple Cities. *Address:* 41 Oak Str., Binghamton, NY 13905, USA.

HOH, Joseph Foon Yoong, b. 12 Dec. 1936, Kuala Lumpur. Reader in Physiology. m. Helen Lising, 18 Nov. 1966, Hong Kong, 2 sons. *Education:* BSc(Med), 1961, MB. BS, 1964, Sydney University, Australia; PhD, Australian National University, 1969. *Appointments:* Junior Residential Medical Officer, Prince Henry and Prince of Wales Hospitals, New South Wales, 1964; Lecturer, Phsyiology, University of Malaya, 1965; Medical Research Scholar, Australian National University, 1966-69; Research Associate, University of Illinois, Chicago, 1969-71; Lecturer, 1971-72, Senior Lecturer, 1973-80, Sydney University; Reader, Physiology, University of Sydney. *Memberships:* Australian Physiological & Pharacological Society; Australian Biochemical Society; International Heart Research Society, Australian Section; Australian and New Zealand Society for Cell Biology. *Publications:* Co-Author: "Myosin isoforms in normal & dystrophic muscles", 'Muscle Gene Expression'; "Ventricular isomyosins and tonic regulation of cardiac contractility", 'Advances in Myocardiology'. *Honours:* Medical Research Scholar, Australian National University, 1966-69; An Experimental proposal to investigate the effects of zero-gravity on skeletal isomyosins was accepted by NASA as a flight experiment in the Spacelab Life Sciences programme, 1979. *Hobby:* Personal Computers. *Address:* Dept. of Physiology, University of Sydney, NSW 2006, Australia.

HOLBROOK, L Bruce, b. 26 July 1950, Charleston, West Virginia, USA. Clinical Director. *Education:* BA, Marshall University; BSc, Palmer College; Doctor of Chiropractic, Palmer College of Chiropractic. *Appointments:* Team Physican, USA Karate Team, 1981-83; Member, National AAU Karate Sports Medicine Committee, Co-Chairman, 1981-83; Tournament Physician, World Karate Championships, Taipei, Taiwan, 1982, various national and International Karate Tournaments, 1981-84; President, Physicians Federation on Martial Arts, 1981-85; Member, International Council Arts Education, 1982-85; Physical Fitness Committee, AAU, 1982-85; Member of National AAU Sports Medicine Committees for Jujitsu and Kung-Fu, USA, 1984-85; Tournament Physician, World Jujitsu Championships, Trinidad, 1985; Team Physician, USA Jujitsu Team 1984-85; Tournament Physician, World Jujitsu Championships, Ontario, Canada, 1984; Member, National AAU Sports Medicine Committee; currently, Clinical Director, Holbrook Clinic, West Virginia. *Memberships:* National Association for Sport and Physical Education; American Alliance for Health, Physical Education, Recreation and Dance; Association for the Advancement of Health Educaiton; Amateur Athletic Union fofthe USA. *Publications:* "Training Manual for Weight Lifting" for USA Karate Team, 1983; series of articles written for American Karate Association on sports medicine and athletic care.

Honours: Outstanding Young Men of America, 1982; Distinguished West Virginian Award, 1982; Association Chairmans Award, Amateur Athletic Union, 1982; West Virginia Ambassador of Goodwill, 1982; Congressional Certificate of Achievement and Award by US Congress, 1983. *Hobbies:* Dog training; Karate; Reading; Music. *Address:* PO Box 617, St Albans, WV 25177, USA.

HOLESH, Shura Alexandra, b. 4 Feb. 1922. Consultant Radiologist, Kingston and Cromwell Hospitals. *Previous Appointment:* Senior Registrar, Radiology Department, Westminster Hospital, London, England. *Memberships;* Royal College of Radiologists; British Medical Ultrasound Society; British Institute of Radiology; Royal Society of Medicine; British Medical Association; European Society of Paediatric Radiology. *Publications:* 'Diagnosis of Tumours of the Glomus Jugulare', 1955; 'Unusual X-Ray Appearances in Hodgkins' Disease', 1955; 'Transposition of the Great Vessels with Absence of the Aortic Arch', 1957; 'Selective Angiography of the right Heart', 1958; 'Dissecting Aneurism of the Aorta', 1958; 'The Mediastinum' in 'British Authors', 1962 and 1973; 'Cystitis Emphysematosa', 1969. *Hobbies:* Music; Ballet; Travel; Skiing. *Address:* 31 Princes Court, Brompton Road, London SW3 1ES, England.

HOLLAN, Susan R, b. 26 Oct. 1920, Budapest, Hungary. Professor of Haematology. m. Prof György Révész, 1944, 1 son, 1 daughter. *Education:* MD 1947, Candidate of Medicine, 1956, University Medical School, Budapest; DSc, University Medical School, Hungarian Academy of Science, 1971. *Appointments:* Research Fellow, 1st Department of Medicine, University Medical School, Budapest, 1950-54; Scientific Adviser, Institute for Experimental Medicine, Budapest, 1954-; Director, National Institute of Haematology Blood Transfusion, Budapest, 1959-85; Professor of Haematology, Postgraduate Medical School, Budapest, 1970-; Director-General, National Institute of Haematology and Blood Transfusion, Budapest, 1985. *Memberships:* Hungarian Academy of Sciences, 1973-; Member of Praesidium, Hungarian Academy of Sciences, 1976-84; Honorary Member, Purkinje Society /CS/; Turkish, German, Soviet, Polish & Romanian Societies of Haematology; Honorary President, Hungarian Society of Genetics; Corresponding Member, Collège de France, Société de Biologie. *Publications:* "Basic Problems of Transfusion", 1965; "Haemaoglobins & Haemoglobinopathies", 1972; "Hungarian Medical Encyclopaedia" (editor), 1967-72; Advances in Physiological Science Volume 6: Genetics, Structure, Function of Blood Cells" (editor), 1982; Editor-in-Chief, 'Haematologie' (quarterly), 1967-; Editor, 'recent Advances in Haematology, Immunology, Blood Transfuction', 1983; Numerous professional papers. *Honours:* Hungarian Academic Award, 1970; Hungarian National Prize, 1974. *Address:* H.1502 Budapest, Pf 44, Hungary.

HOLLAND, Ian Mackay, b. 30 June 1948, Embsay, North Yorkshire, England. Consultant Neuroradiologist, University Hospital, Nottingham. m. Angela Mary Naylor, 4 Sep. 1971, Ashton-under-Lyne, 3 sons. *Education:* Manchester University; Mb.ChB, 1972; DMRD, 1977; FRCR, 1979; Certificate Specialist Training GMC, 1983. *Appointments:* HO, Medicine, HO Professional Surgical Unit, Manchester Royal Infirmary; SHO, Obstrrics and Gynaecology, St. Mary's Hospital, Manchester; SHO, Medical Oncology, Royal Marsden Hospital, Sutton, Surrey; Registrar Radiology, Sheffield, A.H.A (T); Senior Registrar, Radiology/Neuroradiology, Hammersmith Hospital, National Hospital, Queen Square,`Hospital for Sick Children, Great Ormond Street; Senior Registrar, Neuroradiology, National Hospital Queen Square; Consultant Neuroradiologist, Yorkshie Regional Health Authority. *Memberships:* Britsh Society of Neuroradiologists; European Society of Neuroradiologists; French Society of Neuroradiology; British Institute of Radiology; British Medical Association; Royal Colelge of Radiologists; British Institute of Radiology; Royal Society of Medicine. *Publications:* Contributor to professional journals including: 'Computed Tomography in Alexander's Disease', 'Neuroradiology', 1980; 'Multiple Sclerosis Plaque Mimicking Tumour on CT', 'British Medical Journal', 285. *Honours:* Bradford City Scholarship to Bradford Grammar School, 1959; Reginald G. Reid Memorial Fellowship, 1983. *Hobbies:* Photography; Music. *Address:* 21 Marlborough Road, Woodthorpe, Nottingham NG5 4FG, England.

HOLLANDER, Ellen Catherine Collins, b. 6 Mar. 1946, Cambridge, Massachusetts, USA. Assistant Director, Personnel, Southwest Texas Methodist Hospital. *Education:* BA, Boston College, 1967; MA, Incarnate Word College, 1976. *Appointments:* Teaching Supervisor, Massachusetts General Hospital, 1963-67; Teacher, Guidance Counsellor, St Peter Claver Academy, 1967-69; Supervisor, Radiology, Genesse Hospital, 1970-77; Instructor, Health Careers, St Philip's College, 1971-73; Teaching Training Consultant, 1975-76, Instructor, Management, 1983-, San Antonio College; Adjunct Faculty, Southwest Texas State University, 1976-. *Memberships:* American Hospital Association; American Society for Healthcare Education & Training; Texas Hospital Association; Texas Society for Hospital Educators. *Publications:* "Identifying Healthcare Training Needs", 1984; Articles in professional journals. *Honours:* Outstanding Service Award, Texas Society for Hospital Educators, 1981; Distinguished Service Award, American Society for Healthcare Education & Training, 1982; Outstanding Young Women of America, 1982.*Hobbies:* Needlepoint; Poetry; Reading. *Address:* 6123 Walking Gait Drive, San Antonio, TX 78240, USA.

HOLLENDER, Lars Gösta, b. 22 Oct. 1933, Weinge, Sweden. Professor & Head, Oral Radiology, University of Göteborg, Sweden. 2 sons, 2 daughters. *Education:* DDS, 1958; Odont.Dr., 1964; Professor, 1968; Specialist, Oral Radiology, 1982; Diplomate, American Board of Oral & Maxillofacial Radiology, 1982. *Appointments:* Assistant, Associate Professor, School of Dentistry, Malmö, Sweden, 1958-68; Professor & Head, Oral Radiolgoy, University of Göteborg, Sweden, 1969-; Visiting Professor, Oral Radiology, University of California, Los Angeles, USA, 1980-82; University of Washington, Seattle, 1984-. *Memberships:* American Board of Oral & Maxillofacial Radiology; Swedish Dental Association; International Association of Dento-Maxillofacial Radiology; Swedish Association of Medical Radiology; Swedish Association of Oral Radiology. *Publications include:* Approximately 70/80 papers, aspects of oral radiology, 1960-85; Thesis, "Determining the interior orientation at radiography", 1964. *Honours:* Research prizes, South Swedish Dental Society 1964, Swedish Dental Society 1965; Elander Research Prize, 1976. *Hobbies:* Skiing; Golf; Literature; Music. *Address:* 7504 39th NE, Seattle, WA 98115, USA.

HOLLER, Joseph, b. 15 Dec. 1932, Witt, Illinois, USA. Consulting Psychologist. *Education:* BS, MA, Clinical Psychology, MA, Counseling Psychology, Ball State University, Muncie, Indiana; PhD, Clinical Psychology, Purdue University, Indiana. *Appointments include:* Senior Partner, Joseph Holler and Associates, 1946-; President, Landscape Associates Inc, 1965-; Psychologist, Muncie Psychiatric Clinic, 1972-74; Assistant Registrar, Ball State University, 1973-74; Psychologist, Purdue University, 1974; Psychologist, Human Resources Center, 1976-77; Consulting Psychologist, Artist-in-Residence and Visiting Scholar, Purdue

University, 1977-. *Memberships:* International Society of Consulting Arborists; American Personnel and Guidance Association; American Orthopsychiatric Association; American Psychological Association; American Association for Marriage and Family Therapy, Clinical Member. *Publications:* 100 features on Psychology broadcast on National Public Radio (1980) Poetry and Special Features 1975-85; "Guidelines for Living" in press. *Honours:* Registrar's Roll of Honour, 1972; Dean's List 1972, BS Magna cum laude 1972, Ball State University. *Hobbies:* Crossword Puzzles; Hiking; Landscape design; Reading. *Address:* 207 Ann Street, Paris, IL 61944-1218, USA.

HOLLIDAY, Robin, b. 6 Nov. 1932, Palestine. Head of Division of Genetics, National Institute for Medical Research. m. Diana Collet Parsons, 12 July, 1957, London, 1 son, 3 daughters. *Education:* BA, 1955, PhD, 1959, Cambridge University. *Appointments:* Scientific Staff, John Innes Institute, Bayfordbury, Hertford, 1958-65; Scientific Staff, 1965-, Head of Division of Genetics, 1970-, National Institute for Medical Research, Mill Hill, London. *Memberships:* Fellow of Royal Society; 1976; Genetical Society. *Publications:* "The Science of Human Progress" 1981; About 150 articles on Genetic Recombination and Repair, Cell Ageing, Gene Expression and Cancer. *Hobbies:* Sculpture; Travel. *Address:* National Institute for Medical Research, Mill Hill, London NW7 1AA, England.

HOLMDAHL, (Svante) Martin Hison. b. 10 June 1923, Gothenburg, Sweden. Professor of Anaesthesiology, President, University of Uppsala. m. (Karin) Barbro Jehander, 24 Mar. 1949, 3 sons, 1 daughter. *Education:* MD 1950, PhD Medicine 1956, University of Uppsala. *Appointments:* Assistant Surgical Clinic, 1950-55, Assistant Professor of Physiology, 1956, University of Uppsala; Assistant Lecturer, Department of Anaesthesiology, Post-graduate Medical School, London, England, 1956-57; Head of Department of Anaesthesiology, University of Uppsala, 1957-80; Visiting Professor, Columbia University, New York, 1960-61; Professor of Anaesthesiology, 1965-, President, 1978-, University of Uppsala. *Memberships:* Fellow, Royal College of Surgeons, London, 1971; Honorary Member, American Society of University Anaesthesiologists, 1970, Swedish and German Societies of Anaesthesiologists, Faculty of Anaesthetists, Royal College of Surgeons. *Publications:* Various publications in field of anaesthesiology. *Honour:* Honorary Doctor of Science, University of Miami, USA, 1972. *Hobbies:* Tennis; Sailing. *Address:* Döbelnsgatan 26 A, S-752 37 Uppsala, Sweden.

HOLT, John Michael, b. 8 Mar. 1935, England. Consultant Physician, John Radcliffe Hospital, Oxford. m. Sheila Margaret Morton, 1 son, 3 daughters. *Education:* MB ChB, 1959, MD (high commendation), 1964, University of St. Andrews; MSc, Queens University, Ontario, Canada, 1965; MRCP (London), 1965; FRCP (London), 1964. *Appointments:* Registrar, Lecturer, Nuffield Department of Medicine, Radcliffe Infirmary, Oxford, 1964-68; Medical Tutor, University of Oxford, 1968-73; Director of Clinical Studies, University of Oxford, 1972-76. *Memberships:* Association of Physicians; British Society Haematology. *Hobby:* Sailing. *Address:* John Radcliffe Hospital, Oxford, England.

HOMBO, Zen-ichiro, b. 8 Aug. 1922, Tokyo, Japan. Professor, Chairman. m. Nishida Sachiko, 30 May 1948, Tokyo, 2 sons, 1 daughter. *Education:* MD, 1947, DMSc., 1955, Tohoku University School of Medicine. *Appointments:* Instructor, Radiology, Tohoku University School of Medicine, 1950-54; Assistant Professor, 1954-67, Professsor, Chairman, 1967-, Radiology, Nagasaki University School of

Medicine; Member, Medical X-ray Technicians Examination Committee, 1963-64; Member, Radiological Board Examination Committee, 1970-73; Councillor, Nagasaki University, 1983-85. *Memberships:* Japan Radiological Society, Councillor; Japanese Society of Nuclear Medicine, Councillor; Japan Angiological Society, Councillor; Japanese Society of Gastroenterological Mass Survey, Councillor; Japanese Society for Cancer Therapy; Japan Circulation Society; Japan Society of Chest Disease; Japan Lung Cancer Society; American College of Chest Physicians. *Publications:* "Period required for disappearance of iodized oil after bronchography", 1956; "Cineangiocardiography by means of a grid controlled X-ray tube", 1960; "Evaluation of angiocardiography as a method of diagnostic imaging", 1980; "Digital Radiography", 1983; "DSA of Coronary Artery", 1983. *Honours:* Award, Special Lecture, 37th Annual Meeting of Japan Radiological Society, 1978. *Hobbies:* Music; Art; Short Wave Listening; Swimming; Motoring; Kendo. *Address:* Dept. of Radiology, Nagasaki University School of Medicine, 7-1 Sakamoto-Machi, Nagasaki 852, Japan.

HONDERICK, Edwina Barnett, b. 15 Aug. 1946, Lyon County, Kansas, USA. Director, Physical Therapy, Maryvale Samaritan Hospital. *Education:* BS, Physical Therapy, University of Kansas, 1968. *Appointments:* Staff Therapist, University of Kansas Medical Centre, Kansas City, 1968-69; Administrative Co-ordinator, Chief PT, Rehabilitation Centre, Hadley Regional Medical Centre, 1969-75; Chief, PT, Osteopathic Hospital of Wichita, 1975-77; Chief PT,Patient Services Co-ordinator, Mid-America Rehabilitation Inc., Warrensburg, Missouri, 1977-82; Director, Physical Therapy, Maryvale Samaritan Hospital, 1982-. *Memberships:* American Physical Therapy Association; PT Directors, Phoenix, 1982-. *Hobbies:* Camping; Hiking. *Address:* Maryvale Samaritan Hospital, 5102 N. Campbell Ave., Phoenix, AZ 85031, USA.

HÖNIGSMANN, Herbert, b. 26 Mar. 1943, Vienna. Professor; Vice Chairman. m. Alexandra Billeg, 5 June 1971, Vienna, 1 son, 1 daughter. *Education:* MD 1968. *Appointments:* Resident in Dermatology, Department of Dermatology I, Associate Professor, 1981, Full Professor and Vice-Chairman, Department of Dermatology I., University of Vienna, 1983; Member of Staff, Division of Experimental Dermatology, Lecturer, Dermatology, Associate Professor, University of Innsbruck, 1977. *Memberships:* European Society for Dermatol. Res.; Society for Invest. Derm.; American Academy of Dermatology; American Society for Photobiology; Association Internationale de Photobiologie; International Pigment Cell Society; Austrian Society for Dermatology; German Society for Dermatology. *Publications:* 135 publications, including 32 book chapters; Editor, Current Problems in Dermatology'. *Honours:* Hoechst-Preis, 1982; Max-von-Ritter-Award, 1976, 1978; Award of the State of Tyrol, 1979; Corresp. Member Swedish Derm. Society, 1985. *Hobbies:* Skiing; Mountain Hiking. *Address:* Department of Dermatology I., University of Vienna, Alserstrasse 4, A-1090 Vienna, Austria.

HÖÖK, Robert Olof (Olle), b. 30 Oct. 1918, Skinnskatteberg, Sweden. Professor Emeritus. m. Kerstin Lundevall, 31 Jan. 1943, 2 sons, 2 daughters. *Education:* Medical Licentiate, Karolinska Institute, 1944; MD, 1958. *Appointments:* Assistant Chief Physician, 1957-63, Assistant Professor, 1959-66, Neurology, Karolinska Institute; Head, Neurological Rehabilitaiton, Karolinska Hospital, 1963-66; Professor, Chairman, Institute of Rehaiblitaiton Medicine, University of Goteborg, 1966-83. *Memberships Include:* Executive Committee, International Rehabilitation Medicine Association,

1974-78; Chairman, Research Group in Neurological Rehabilitation within World Federation of Neurology; Chief Editor, Scandinavian Journal of Rehabilitation Medicine, 1968-; Medical Science Council, National Board of Health, 1967-84; Advisory Council, World Federation Fund, 1977-; Medical Science Council, Medical Board of the Armed Forces; Past Chairman, Swedish Neurological Society, Swedish Society of Rehabilitation & Physical Medicine and Restorative Neurology; National Swedish Social Insurance Court, 1962-64; etc. *Address:* Lindgatan 10, S-753 28 Uppsala, Sweden.

HOOPES, John Michael, b. 6 Feb 1947, Canton, Ohio, USA. Associate Professor of Family Medicine and Clinical Pharmacy. m. Janet L Ward, 6 Nov. 1971, Kenton, Ohio, 1 son, 2 daughters. *Education:* BSc, Pharmacy, Ohio Northern University, Ada, Ohio, 1970; Doctor of Pharmacy, Duquesne University, Minerva, Ohio; Resident in Hospital Pharmacy, Yale-New Haven Hospital, New Haven, Connecticut. *Memberships:* American Society of Hospital Pharmacists; Society of Teachers of Family Medicine; American Association of Colleges of Pharmacy. *Publications:* 'Constipation and Diarrhoea' (with A E Gunnett) in Clinical Pharmacology and Therapeutics in Nursing, 1985; 'Patient assessment and consultation' (with W Klein-Schwartz) in Handbook of Non-Prescription Drugs, 7th Edition, 1982; (Sequelae and management of urinary infection in patients requiring chronic catheterization' (with J W Warren, H L Muncie, E J Bergquist) in Journal of Urology, 1981; 'Ineffectiveness of cephalexin in treatment of cephalexin-resident bacteriuria in patients with chronic indwelling urethral catheters' (with J W Warren, H L Muncie, and W C Anthony) in Journal of Urology, 1983. *Hobbies:* Music; Running; Painting. *Address:* 807 Hollywood Boulevard, Crownsville, MD 21032, USA.

HOOVER, John E, b. 24 July 1929, Ohio, USA. Consultant in Biomedical Communications. m. Marcia Lavanish Crawford, 15 May 1971, Kettering, Ohio, 1 daughter. *Education:* BSc Pharmacy, Ohio State University, 1952. *Appointments:* Consultant, Biomedical Communications, 1954-; Community/Hospital Pharmacist, 1954-58; Managing Editor, Mack Publishing Co., 1958-75; Manager of Special Services, Mack Printing Co., 1960-66; Director of Communications, Philadelphia College of Pharmacy & Science, 1966-68; Director of Administration, 1975-78; Consultant to the President, Delmont Laboratories Inc., 1979-. *Memberships:* American Pharmaceutical Association; American Medical Writers Association; Council of Biology Editors; Drug Information Association; American Institute for the History of Pharmacy. *Publications:* "Remington's Pharmaceutical Sciences" (12th-15th, 17th editions); "Dispensing of Medication" (formerly Husa's Pharmaceutical Dispensing), 5th, 6th, 8th editions; "American Journal of Pharmacy" (volumes 138-present); "Mosby's Medical & Nursing Dictionary"; "Tile & Till". *Hobbies:* Aviation; Basketball; Swimming. *Address:* 363 Riverview Road, Swarthmore, PA 19081, USA.

HOPKINS, John Bryan, b. 10 July, 1945, Sacramento, California. Associate Professor; Director of Behavioural Medicine. m. Sharon Dellinger, 11 June, 1983, Newburne, Tennessee, USA, 1 daughter. *Education:* AB, University of California, Davis, USA, 1970, MA, 1972; PhD, George Peabody College, Vanderbilt University, USA, 1976. *Appointments:* Senior Clinical Psychologist, Naval Hospital, Beaufort, South Carolina, 1977-80; Senior Clinical Psychologist, Branch Clinic, US Marine Corps Air Station, Beaufort, South Carolina, 1978-80; Lecturer in Psychology, University of South Carolina, 1978-80;

Assistant Professor of Psychology, University of Alabama,Huntsville, 1980-82; Assistant Professor of Family Medicine, 1982-85; Associate Professor of Family Medicine and Director of Behavioural Medicine for Family Medicine Programmes-. *Memberships:* Society of Teachers of Family Medicine; American Psychological Association; Society for Research in Child Development; Alabama Psychological Association; Alabama Licenced Psychologists Association; South Carolina Psychological Association. *Publications:* "The Effect of Early and Extended Neonatal Contact on Mother-Infant Interaction", 1976; With S.E Hopkins 'Hyperemesis Gravidarum: A Biophysmosocial Treatment Plan' in 'The Journal of the Alabama Academy of Science', 1985. *Hobbies:* Jogging; Tennis; Golf. *Address:* University of Alabama in Huntsville, School of Primary Medical Care, 201 Governors Drive, Huntsville, AL 35801, USA.

HOPPE, Roy Walter, b. 30 Nov. 1954, Squamish, British Columbia, Canada. Chiropractic Physician. m. Cynthia Ellen Schultz, 28 June 1980, Glen Ellyn, 1 son.*Education:* AA, San Jacino College; BSc., DC, National College of Chiropractic; Diplomate, National Board of Chiropractic Examiners. *Appointments:* Intern, NCC Clinic, Illinois; Associate, Winchester Chiropractic Clinic, Indiana; Director, Willowbrook and Huntwick Chiropractic Clinics. *Memberships:* American, Texas Chiropractic Associations; Indiana Society of Chiropractic Physicians; American Public Health Association; ACA Council on Sports Injuries; Alumni of the National College of Chiropractic; XPE, (Chi-Rho-Sigma) - International Professional Fraternity. *Honours:* Commendation for Inflight Emergency, Delta Airlines, 1981. *Hobbies:* Marksmanship; Hiking; Photography; Naturalism. *Address:* 13713 Farm Road 149, Houston, TX 77086, USA.

HOPPS, John Alexander, b. 21 May 1919, Winnipeg, Canada. Secretary General International Union for Physical Engineering Sciences in Medicine. m. Eleanor Isabel Smith, 1 May, 1943, Winnipeg, Canada, 2 sons, 1 daughter. *Education:* BSc, EE, University of Manitoba, Canada, 1941, Honorary DSc, 1976. *Appointments:* President, Canadian Medical and Biological Engineering Society, 1965-69; President, International Federation for Medical and Biological Engineering, 1971-73, Secretary-General , 1976-85; Principal Research Officer and Head of Medical Engineering, National Research Council of Canada (retired 1979). *Memberships:* Fellow, Canadian Medical and Biological Engineering Society; Honorary Life Member, International Federation for Medical and Biological Engineering. *Publications:* Scientific Journal papers. *Honours:* Award of Merit, Canadian Standards Association, 1981; A.G.L. McNaughton Award, IEEE, 1985; Distinguished Scientist Award, North American Society of Pacing and Electrophysiology, 1985. *Hobbies:* Woodwork; Writing. Address: IUPESM Secretariat, Building M-50, Room 302, National Research Council of Canada. Ottawa, K1A OR8, Canada.

HORECKER, Bernard Leonard, b. 31 Oct. 1914, Chicago, Illinois, USA. University Dean. m. Frances Goldstein, 12 July 1936, 3 daughters. *Education:* BS, 1936, PhD, 1936, University of Chicago. *Appointments:* Biochemist, USPHS, NIH, Bethesda, Maryland, 1941-59; Chief, Laboratory of Biochemistry and Metabolism, National Institute for Arthritis and Metabolic Disease, 1956-59; Professional Lecturer, Enzyme Chemistry, George Washington University, 1950-57; Professor of Microbiology/Chairman of Department, New York University College of Medicine, 1959-63; Professor of Molecular Biology/Chairman of Department, 1963-72, Albert Einstein College of Medicine; Member, Roche Institute of Molecular Biology,

Nutley, New Jersey, 1972-84; Adjunct Professor, Cornell University Medical College, 1972-84; Professor of Biochemistry/Dean of Graduate School of Medical Sciences, Cornell University Medical College, 1984-. Visiting Professor to Universities in US, South America, Japan and Europe. *Memberships:* American Chemical Society; Biochemistry Society (England); Honorary Member: Swiss Biochemistry Society; Spanish Biochemistry Society; Japanese Biochemistry Scoiety; Hellenic Biochemistry and Biophysics Society; Indian National Science Academy; Brazilian Academy of Sciences. American Society of Biological Chemists; National Academy of Sciences; American Academy of Arts and Sciences; PanAm Association of Biochemistry Societies. *Publications:* 365 publications. *Honours:* Paul Lewis Laboratories Award in Enzyme Chemistry, 1952; Superior Accomplishment Award, Federal Security Agency, 1952; Rockefeller Public Service Award, 1957; Hillebrand Prize, American Chemistry Society, 1954; Award in Biological Sciences, Washington Academy of Science, 1954; Fulbright Travel Award, 1963; Commonwealth Fund Fellow, 1967; Merck Award, ASBC; Fellow AAAS (American) Association for the Advancement of Sciences; Phi Beta Kappa; Sigma Xi. *Hobbies:* Gardening; Bird Watching; Music. *Address:* Cornell University Graduate School of Medical Sciences, 1300 York Avenue, New York, NY 10021, USA.

HORDER, John Plaistowe, b. 9 Dec 1919, Ealing, London. Visiting Professor. m. Elizabeth June Wilson, 20 June 1940, 2 sons, 2 daughters. *Education:* MA, BM, B Ch, Oxford; FRCP (London) FRCP (Edinburgh); FRCGP; FRC Psych. *Appointments:* General Practitioner, London 1951-81; Consultant, Expert Committee, WHO, Geneva, 1960-; WHO Fellow 1964 and 1983; Consultant Adviser, DHSS, 1977-83; Secretary, Leeuwenhorst European Working Group, 1974-82; Visiting Fellow, King Edward's Hospital Fund for London, 1983-85; Visiting Professor, Royal Free Hospital Medical School, 1983-. *Memberships:* Fellow, Royal College of Physicians, London; Fellow, Royal College of Physicians, Edinburgh; Fellow, Royal College of General Practitioners; Fellow, Royal College of Psychiatrists; British Medical Association, etc. *Publications:* Editor and part author: "The Future General Practitioner – Learning and Teaching". Numerous papers on General Practice. *Honours:* OBE 1972; CBE 1981; Honorary Member, Canadian College of Family Practitioners, 1982; Honorary Fellow, Royal Society of Medicine, London, 1983; Honorary MD, Free University of Amsterdam, 1985. *Hobbies:* Playing piano and organ; Painting water-colours; Cutting grass. *Address:* 98 Regent's Park Road, London NW1, England.

HORGAN, John Anthony, b. 17 Dec. 1930, Melbourne, Australia. General Practitioner; Treasurer, Australian Medical Association, Victorian Branch. m. Sandra E.Neil, 3 sons, 3 daughters, 2 step-sons, 1 step daughter. *Education:* MBBS, Melbourne. *Appointments:* Resident Medical Officer, St Vincents Hospital, Melbourne, 1956, Royal Childrens Hospital, Melbourne, 1957, Queens Memorial Infectious Diseases Hospital, Fairfield, 1957; General Practice, Solo, 1957-61, in Partnership, 1961-. *Memberships:* BMA, Victorian Branch, Australian Medical Association, 1978-84, Branch Council, Victorian branch, 1982-, Treasurer, 1984-; Medical Service Committee of Enquiry of Victoria, 1983-; Local Medical Officers Advisory Committee of Veteran Affairs Dept.; Surgeon of Moonee Valley Racing Club, 1972-79; Royal Australian College of General Practitioners. *Hobbies:* Reading; Tennis; Music; Opera; Australian Rules Football. *Address:* Lot 8 Metary Road, Eltham, Victoria, Australia 3095.

HORNBEIN, Thomas Frederic, b. 6 Nov. 1930, St Louis, Missouri, USA. Anesthesiologist; Professor and Chairman of University Department of Anesthesiology. m. Kathryn Mikesell, 21 Dec. 1971, Seattle, Washington, 1 son, 5 daughters. *Education:* BA Geology, University of Colorado, 1948-52; MD, Washington University School of Medicine, 1952-56. *Appointments:* Instructor in Anesthesiology, Washington University, St Louis, 1960-61; Assistant Professor 1963-67, Associate Professor 1067-70, Professor 1970-, Chairman 1978-, Department of Anesthesiology, University of Washington School of Medicine, Seattle, Washington. *Memberships:* American Psychological Society; American Society of Anesthesiologists; Treasurer 1969-72, President 1974-75, Association of University Anesthetists; Society of Academic Anesthesia Chairmen; Alpha Omega Alpha. *Publications:* "Everest The West Ridge", 1965; "Regulation of Breathing", (editor), 1981. *Honours:* Hubbard Medal; George Nolin Award, University of Colorado, Denver, 1970; Alumni Centennial Symp Award, University of Colorado, 1975; Distinguished Teaching Award, University of Washington, 1982. *Hobby:* Mountain climbing. *Address:* Department of Anesthesiolgoy RN-10, University of Washington School of Medicine, Seattle, WA 98195, USA.

HOROWITZ, Harvey A. b. 2 Aug. 1942, Philadelphia, Pennsylvania, USA. Director, Adolescent Coordinate Programme, Assistant Director, Adolescent Services. m. Claudia Fondersmith, 7 Oct. 1979, Villanova, 2 daughters. *Education:* BA, Susquehanna University, 1960-64; MD, Temple University, 1964-68. *Appointments:* Chief Resident in Adolescent Psychiatry 1974-74, Associate Director 1974-77, Associate Attending Psychiatrist 1974-80, Director 1977-79, Adolscent Treatment Unit. *Memberships:* President, Philadelphia Society for Adolescent Psychiatry; Fellow, American Society for Adolescent Psychiatry; American Psychiatric Association; Pennsylvania Psychiatric Society; Philadelphia Psychiatric Society. *Publications:* 'Impromptu Group: Beyond Crisis Intervention', (with L H Crabtree), 1974; 'The Use of Lithium in the Treatment of the drug Induced Psychotic Reaction', 1975; 'Lithium and the Treatment of Adolescent Manic Depressive Illness', 1977; 'Mind Influencing Drugs and Adolescents', 1978; 'Psychiatric Casualties of Minimal Brain Dysfunction in Adolescence', 1982; 'Minimal Brain Dysfunction in Adolescents and Young Adult Psychiatric Inpatients', (with L H Crabtree and B Gever), 1983. *Honours:* Mathey Award, 1972 and 1974; Excellence in Teaching Award, Institute of Penna Hospital, 1983. *Hobbies:* Folk Music; Reading; Art; Sports. *Address:* 111 N 49th Street, Philadelphia, PA 19139, USA.

HORROCKS, Elisabeth Ninette, b. 21 Feb 1944, Stoke-on-Trent, Staffs, England. Hospital Consultant. m. Anthony Michael Horrocks, 15 June 1974, Harrow, England. *Education:* BChD, University of Leeds Dental School, 1968; D Orth RCS, Institute of Dental Surgery, University of London, 1973; FDSRCS (England) 1972. *Appointments;* House Officer, Leeds Dental Hospital; Senior House Officer, United Bristol Hospitals; Registrar, United Bristol Hospitals and Frnchay Hosptial; Junior Clinical Assistant Orthodontic Registrar senior Registrar, Eastman Dental Hospital. *Memberships:* Honorary Secretary, British Society for the Study of Orthodontics; British Association of Orthodontists; European Orthodontic Society; Consultant Orthodontists Group; Asociation of University Teachers of Orthodontics; UK Begg Study Group. *Publications:* "Proprioceptive Innervation of the Toungue" with A K Adatia, in jouranl of Anatomy, 1971; "Bilateral Inferior Alveolar and Lingual Nerve Block" with A K Adatia, in British Dental Journal, 1972. *Honours:* Percy Leigh Medal, 1965; Award of American Society of Dentistry for Children, 1968, etc. *Hobbies:* Squash; Tennis; Cycling; Travel. *Address:* Orthodontic Department, Eastman Dental Hospital, 256 Grays Inn Road, London WC1X 8LD, England.

HORSNELL, Arthur Maxwell, b. 6 July 1912, Brentwood, Essex, England. Emeritus Professor of Dental Health. m. Agatha Frances Mary Hatt, 28 Mar 1940, Hampstead, England, 4 daughters. *Education:* Fellow in Dental Surgery, Royal College of Surgeons, (England) Hon Caus, 1950; Fellow, Royal Australasian College of Dental Surgeons (Founding Fellow) 1965; Fellow, International College of Dentists, 1973. *Appointments:* Dental House Surgeon, Registrar Posts, London Hospital, 1935-40; Medical Officer, RAF, 1940-46; Director, Conservative Dentistry, London Hospital Medical College, 1949-58; Professor of Dental Science 1959-71; Professor of Dental Health, 1971-77, Dean, Faculty of Dentistry, 1959-63, and 1971-75, Professor Emeritus, 1978-, University of Adelaide. *Memberships:* British Dental Association; Australian Dental Association; Federation Dentaire Internationale; Australian Society of Dentistry for Children; International Association of Dentistry for Children; Honorary Life Member, International Association for Dental Research. *Publications:* Various papers on Restorative Dentistry; Children's Dentistry and Dental Education; *Honour:* Officer of the Order of Australia for Service to Dentistry, 1984. *Hobbies:* Gardening; Golf; Woodwork; Editor, Newsletter of Australian Society of Dentistry for Children. *Address:* 28 Lockwood Road, Erindale, South Australia 5066

HORST, Antoni, b. 4 June 1915, Zakrzewo, Poland. Professor of Pathophysiology & Human Genetics. m. Maria Halina Horst, deceased 1969, 3 daughters. *Education:* Graduated 1942, MD 1945, PhD 1947, Faculty of Medicine, University of Poznań. *Appointments:* Assistant Professor, Department of Microbiology, 1942-44, Associate Professor, Department of Internal Medicine, 1944-46, University of Warsaw; Associate Professor, Department of Internal Medicine, University of Poznań, 1946-50; Professor of General Pathology, Medical Faculty, Medical Academy of Poznan, 1950; Professor of Human Gentics, Medical Faculty, 1963; Director, Institute of Human Genetics, Polish Academy of Sciences, 1974. *Memberships:* Polish Academy of Sciences, 1969-;' Head, Poznań Section, Polish Genetic Society; Head, Psthophysiological Section, Polish Physiological Society; Polish Biochemical Society; President, Committee of Cell Pathophysiology, Medical Section of Polish Academy of Sciences; Member of Scientific Councils: Institute of Immunology & Experimental Therapy (Wroclaw), Centre of Experimental & Clinical Medicine (Warsaw), Institute of Biogenic Amines (Lodz – President of the Council). *Publications:* "Pathological Physiology – A Textbook for Students" (8 editions to 1982); "Molecular Pathology" monograph (2 editions to 1970); "Molecular bases of pathogenesis of Diseases" monograph, 1979; "Human Ecology", 1976; Series of Papers on gene regulation in eukaryotes, especially rôle of non-histone chromatin proteins in immunocopetent cells during immunization with various antigens (1980-81). *Address:* ul. Podhalańska 14, 60-615 Poznań, Poland.

HORYD, Wanda Irena, b. 29 Jan. 1923, Warsaw, Poland. Associate Professor. *Education:* MB, Warsaw University, 1948; Cand Sc Med, Medical Institute, Moscow, USSR, 1953; MD Habilit., Medical Academy, Warsaw, Poland, 1973. *Appointments:* Lecturer in Department of Psychiatry 1947-48, Lecturer in Department of Neurology 1949-53, Warsaw University; Senior Lecturer, Department of Neurology, Medical Academy, Gdansk, 1953-59; Senior Lecturer, Department of Neurology, Psychiatric Hospital and in Psychoneurological

Institute, Pruszkow and Warsaw, 1959-75; Assistant Professor, EEG Department, Psychoneurological Institute, Warsaw, 1976-. *Memberships:* Polish Society of Neurology; Polish Society of EEG and Clinical Neurophysiology. *Publications Include:* 60 publications in the field of Electroencephalography and Neurology. *Honours:* Korean PDR Order of National Banner, 1955; Cross of Warsaw Insurrection and Polish Golden Cross of Merit, 1983. *Hobby:* Classical Music. *Address:* Psychoneurological Institute, Department of EEG/EMG, A1. Sobieskiego 1/9, 02-957 Warsaw, Poland.

HOSAKA, Yasuhiro, b. 8 Jan. 1931, Kyoto, Japan. Professor. m. Tomoko Hosaka, 2 Nov. 1958, 2 sons, 1 daughter. *Education:* MD, Nagoya University School of Medicine, 1955; Dr. Med. Sci., Osaka University Graduate Course of Medicine, 1960. *Appointments:* Research associate, 1960, Associate Professor, 1974, Research Institute for Microbial Diseases, Osaka Univeristy; Associate Scientist, Wistar Institute of Anatomy and Biology, 1974-76. *Memberships:* Society of Japanese Virolotgists; Japanese Society of Electron Microscopy; Japanese Society for Immunology; American Society of Microbiology. *Publications:* "Virology", Volume 29, 1966, Volume 29, 1972; "Handbook of Viruses", in Japanese, 1972; "Virus Infection and the Cell Surface", "Cell Surface Review", Volume 2, 1977; "Cell Membranes and Viral Envelopes",. 1980; "Illustration by Electron Micros.", "Virology", 1979. *Honours:* Dr Seto Memorial Prize, Japanese Society of Electron Microscopy, 1967. *Hobbies:* Tennis; Travel; Music. *Address:* Research Institute for Microbial Diseases, Osaka University, Suita, Osaka 565, Japan.

HOSKINS, Trevor William, b. 24 Feb. 1931, London, England. Medical Officer. m. Janet Crewdson Lloyd, 1 May 1965, Riverhead, Kent, 3 sons. *Education:* MA, MB, BChir, Emmanuel College, University of Cambridge; DCH; D Obst Royal College of Obstetricians and Gynaecologists, Guy's Hospital Medical School, London. *Appointments:* House Physician, Resident Obstetrician, Guy's Hospital, London; Physiologist, Army Operational Research Group; Senior House Physician, Kent and Sussex Hospital; General Practitioner and Clinical Assistant, Sevenoaks, Kent; Senior Medical Officer, British Petroleum Exploration Company (Libya) Limited; Medical Officer, Christ's Hospital, Horsham, West Sussex, England. *Memberships:* Royal College of Surgeons; Licenciate, Royal College of Physicians; Past President, Medical Officers of Schools Association; Royal Society of Medicine; British Medical Association. *Publications include:* Editor, "Handbook of School Health", 1984; 13 articles including: 'Collaboration between psychiatrist and doctor in a boys' boarding school', 1979; 'Rugby injuries to the cervical spine in English schoolboys', 1979; 'Assessment of inactivated influenza A vaccine after three outbreaks of influenza A at Christ's Hospital' (co-author), 1979; 'Investigation of an outbreak of adenovirus type 3 infection in a boys' boarding school' (co-author), 1984. *Hobbies:* Music; Theatre; Travel. *Address:* Hollowcroft, Christ's Hospital, Horsham, West Sussex, RH13 7LE, England.

HOSODA, Yutaka, b. 25 May 1926, Tokyo, Japan, 1 son, 1 daughter. *Education:* MD; Dr.Med.Sc; Post Graduate Course, Rome University, Carlo Forlanini Institute; Guest, Edinburgh University, Scotland, Uppsala University. *Appointments:* Assistant, Chiba University School of Medicine; Chief, Occupational Health, JNR Central Health Institute. *Memberships:* Fellow: Japanese Society of Tuberculosis; Japanese Society of Chest Disease; Japanese Society of Transportation Medicine; Member, Japanese Society of Radiology; Honorary Fellow, American

College of Radiology. *Publications:* "Sarcoidosis", Editor, 1979; "Industrial Health", Co-Author, 1985; "Diseases of the Pleura", co-author, 1983. *Hobbies:* Music; Travel. *Address:* Higashinakano 1-41-4, Nakano, Tokyo 151, Japan.

HOUCHENS, James Reid, b. 3 June 1943, Bloomington, Illinois, USA. Private Practice. m. Susan K. Ryan, 20 Feb. 1971, Mexico, Missouri, 1 son, 2 daughters. *Education:* DC, 1965; Postgraduate, X-Ray Research, 1968. *Appointments:* Private Practice, Chiropractic. *Memberships:* American Chiropractic Association; Acadmey of Missouri Chiropractors, Board Member, 1982-86; Pettis County Chiropractic Association, Presidnet, 1982; Pi Kappa Chi. *Honours:* University of Missouri Leadership Honour Roll, 1975. *Hobbies:* Hunting; Fishing; Photography. *Address:* 805 West Eleventh, Sedalia, MO 65301, USA.

HOUGHTON, William Charles Stanley, b. 13 June 1942, Brisbane, Australia. Medical Director. m. Elizabeth Joy Houghton, 12 Mar. 1968, Sydney, 2 sons, 1 daughter. *Education:* MBBS, Sydney University, 1967; FFARACS, 1971. *Appointments:* Resident Medical Officer, 1967-68, Anaesthetic Registrar, Repatriation General Hospital, Concord, 1969-71; Anaesthetic Registrar, Royal Alexandra Hospital for Children, Camperdown, Royal Prince Alfred Hospital, 1972; Director, Anaesthetics and Intensive Care, Albur Base Hospital, 1973-84; Medical Director, Abbott Australasia, 1984-; Visiting Anaethetist Royal South Sydney Hosptial, 1984-. *Memberships:* Australian Society of Anaesthetists; Australian and New Zealand Intensive Care Society; Australian Society of Parenteral and Enteral. Nutrition; Association for Medical Directors of the Australian Pharmaceutical Industry; Association of Regulatory and Clinical Scientists; The Australian Society of Clinical and Experimental Pharmacologists; The Australian Society for Infectious Diseases.*Address:* PO Box 101, Cronulla, NSW Australia 2230.

HOUSE, Stanley Gartenhaus, b. 15 Feb. 1920, New York City, USA. Editor in Chief, The Physicians' Geriatrics Digest. m. Lillian Nathan, 11 Apr. 1943, Washington DC, 3 sons, 1 daughter. *Education:* MBA, Loyola College, Baltimore, Maryland, 1980. *Appointments Include:* Member, Editorial Department, Washington Post, 1941-42; Editor in Chief, Labour Relations Institute, New York City, 1943-48; Chairman and President, Stanley G House and Associates Incorporated, Washington DC, 1952-84; Public Relations Consultant, Group Health Association of Washington DC, 1958-78; President, Healthcare Interaction Consultants Incorporated, Rockville MD, 1981-85; Editor in Chief, The Physicians' Geriatrics Digest, 1983-85. *Memberships:* American Medical Writers Association; President 1962, National Capital Chapter, Public Relations Society of America; Charter Member Health Care Academy, American Marketing Association. *Publications:* "Democratic Processes for Modern Health Agencies", (co-author), 1978. *Address:* 9912 Carter Rd, Bethesda, MD 20817, USA.

HOUSSEMAYNE DUBOULAY, Edward Philip George, b. 28 Jan. 1922, Alexandria, Egypt. Emeritus Professor, neurodradiology; Radiologist, Institute of Zoology; Director, Radiological Research Trust. m. (2) Pamela Mary Verity, 23 Feb. 1968, Marylebone, 6sons, 2 daughters. *Education:* MB,BS,DMRD,FRCR, FRCP. *Appointments:* House Officer, Charing Cross Hospital, Derby City Hosptial; Medical Officer, RAF & Army Emergency, Reserve; Senior Registrar, St Bartholowmess Hospital & St George's Hosptial; Consultant Radiologist, National Hosptial for Nervous Diseases, St Bartholomews Hospital; Radiologist, Institute of Zoology, Zoological Society of London; Head, Radiology, National Hosptial for Nervous Diseases. *Memberships:* Honorary Member, British Institute of Radiolgy; Swedish Society of Neuroradiology; German Society of Neuroradiology; Honorary Fellow, American College of Radiology; Fellow, Royal Society Medicine; Royal College of Physicians; Royal College of Radiology; President, European Society of Neuroradiolgy; British Society Neuroradiolgy;etc. *Publications:* Numerous articles on neuroradiolgy & related subjects. *Honour:* CBE, 1985. *Hobby:* Gardening. *Address:* Old Manor House, Brington, Huntingdon, Cambs PE18 OPX, England.

HOUSTON, Ian Briercliffe, b. 11 Sep. 1932, Blackpool, Lancashire, England. Professor of Child Health. m. Pamela Beryl Rushton, 12 May 1956, Machester, 1 son, 2 daughters. *Education:* MB ChB Honours 1955, MD 1963, University of Manchester; DCH. *Appointments:* House Physician in Medicine 1955-56, Resident Clinical Pathologist 1956-57, Senior House Officer, University Department of Medicine 1957-59, Manchester Royal Infirmary; House Surgeon in Paediatric Surgery 1956, Medical Registrar in Paediatrics 1959-62, Royal Manchester Children's Hospital; Senior Registrar in Paediatrics, Royal Manchester Children's Hospital and St Mary's Hospital, Manchester, 1962-63; Lecturer in Child Health 1963-69, Senior Lecturer in Child Health 1969-74, Honorary Consultant Paediatrician 1969-, Professor of Child Health 1974-, University of Manchester; Nuffield Research Fellowship, Paediatric Renal Unit, Albert Einstein College of Medicine, New York, USA, 1965-67. *Memberships:* Fellow, Royal College of Physicians; European Society for Paediatric Nephrology; Renal Association; British Paediatric Association; Manchester Medical Society; Manchester Paediatric Club; International College of Paediatrics; British Association of Paediatric Nephrologists; European Dialysis and Transplant Association; International Society of Nephrology; International Paediatric Nephrology Association. *Publications:* 'Pus cell and bacterial counts in diagnosis of urinary tract infections in childhood', 1963; 'Fanconi syndrome with renal salt wasting and metabolic alkalosis', 1968; 'Growth and Development of the Kidneys', (book chapter), 1974. *Hobbies:* Squash; History; Archaeology. *Address:* University Department of Child Health, Royal Manchester Children's Hospital, Pandlebury, Manchester M27 1HA, England.

HOUSTON, John Boag, b. 5 Dec. 1936, Toronto, Canada. Private Practice: Speciality of Dental Prosthetics. m. 17 June 1960, 1 daughter. *Education:* DDS, Toronto, 1961; MS, University of Iowa, USA, 1968, DABP, 1970; FACP, FRSP, FRSH, MRCD, Canada. FAIDS; FICP. *Appointments:* Assistant Professor, UCLA, School of Dentistry, USA, 1969-75; Associate Professor, University of Colorado School of Dentistry, 1975-76; Professor and Director of Clinics, University of Toronto Faculty of Dentistry, Canada, 1976-79. *Memberships:* International and American and Canadian Association for Dental Research; American College of Prosthodontists; Canadian and Ontario Prosthodontic Associations; Canadian and Ontario Dental Associations. *Publications:* 13 articles 1968-79. *Honours:* Sigma PSI National Research Fraternity, 1974; Omicron Upsilon Honour Dental Fraternity, 1976; Fellow, Association of International Dental Studies. *Address:* 700 Bay Street, Toronto, Ontario, Canada, M5G126.

HOUSTON, Robin William, b. 25 Nov. 1944, Toowoomab, Australia. Consultant, Oral and Maxillo Facial Surgery. m. Carol Gibson, 18 Aug. 1973, Great Harwood, 1 son, 2 daughters. *Education:* BDSc, University of Queensland, Australia 1967; FDSRCS, England, 1973; MB BCh, Welsh School of Medicine, 1976; FRCS, Edinburgh, 1981. *Appointments:* Registrar, The London Hosptial, 1971-73; Medical and Surgical Resident, 1976-77, Senior Medical and

Surgical Resident, Toowoomba General Hospital, 1977-79; Registrar, General Surgery, Peterborough District Hospital, 1979-80; Maxillo Facial Surgery, Cannies Burgh Hosptial, Glasgow, 1980-82; Consultant, Maxillo Facial Surgeon, St Vincent's Hospital and St Andres's, Toowoomba, 1982-. *Memberships:* Member, British Association of Oral and Maxillo Facial Surgeons; Australian Dental Association; Australian Medical Association; Australian and New Zealand Association of Oral and Maxillo Facial Surgeons; Fellow, Royal College of Surgeons of Edinburgh; Dental Surgery RCS of England. *Hobbies:* Tennis; Classical and Jazz Music; Squash; Swimming. *Address:* 165A Russell Street, Toowoomba, Queensland 4350, Australia.

HOVI, Urpo Tapani, b. 28 Apr. 1942, Sauvo, Finland. Head of Enterovirus Laboratory, Department of Virology. m. Liisa Mirjami Nikkilä MD, 29 May 1965, Kerava, Finland, 2 sons, 1 daughter. *Education:* MD, University of Helsinki, 1972. *Appointments:* Research and Teaching Assistant, Department of Virology, University of Helsinki, 1968-73; Visiting Scientist, Division of Cell Pathology, MRC Clinical Research Centre, Harrow, Middlesex, 1974-75; Research Fellow, Department of Virology, University of Helsinki, 1975-80; Head, Medical Department of 'Suomen Astra Oy' Espoo, 1980-81; Acting Associate Professor/Professor, Department of Virology, University of Helsinki, 1982-83. Head of Enterovirus Laboratory, Department of Virology, National Public Health Institute, Helsinki, 1983-. *Memberships:* Finnish Medical Association; Finnish Medical Society 'Duodecim'; Finnish Foundation for Research on Viral Diseases, Secretary: Societas Biochemica, Biophysica et Microbiologica Fenniae, Council Member; Scandinavian society for Antimicrobial Chemotherapy (Council Member); Society for General Microbiology (UK); American Society for Microbiology. *Publications:* Original research reports and review articles on rubella virus (1969-72), control mechanisms of cell proliferation in fibroblast and lymphocyte cultures (1973-79), physiology and pathology of monocytes antiviral chemotherapy (1980-), poliovirus and poliomyelitis (1985-). *Hobbies:* Woodwork; Weeding; Walking. *Address:* Department of Virology, National Public Health Institute, Mannerheimintie 166, SF-00280, Helsinki, Finland.

HOWARD, Edward Richard, b. 2 Nov. 1936, London, England. Consultant General & Paediatric Surgeon, Kings College Hospital, London. m. Ann Harriet Cullis, 19 Nov. 1960, Coleford, Gloucestershire, 2 daughters. *Education:* MRCS, LRCP, 1960; MB, BS, London, 1960; FRCS, London, 1965; MS, London, 1970. *Appointments include:* Senior surgical registrar, Kings College Hospital, 1970-72; Chief resident, paediatric surgery, University of South Carolina, USA, 1972-73; Consultant Surgeon, Kings College, 1974-. *Memberships:* Royal Society of Medicine; British Society of Gastroenterology; Harveian Society; British Association of Paediatric Surgeons; Association of Surgeons of Great Britain. *Publications include:* Contributions to Books: "Rob's Operative Surgerey", ed. Prof. Dudley, 1978; "Liver & Biliary Disease", 2nd edition, Ed. Wright et.al., 1985; "Somatic & Nerve-Muscle Interactions", 1983; "Maingot's Abdominal Operations", 8th edition; "Neonatal Gasterenterology", 1984. Numerous research articles, professional journals. *Honours include:* Jocelyn Almond Prize, research, children's diseases, 1968; Charlton-Briscoe research prize, 1971; Senior Fulbright-Hays scholarship, USA, 1972-73; Gold Medal, surgical research, Southeastern Surgical Congress, USA, 1973; British Council travel grant, India & Japan, 1981; Hunterian Professor, Royal College of Surgeons (Hirschsprung's Disease), 1970; Hunterian Professorship, RCS, (Biliary Atresia), 1983. *Hobbies:* Choral singing; Pianoforte; Contemporary music; Oenology; Medical history. *Address:* 'Silverton', 34 Thorpewood Avenue, Sydenham, London SE26 4BX, England.

HOWARD, Peter, b. 15 Dec. 1925, Aldershot, Hants. Commandant, RAF, Institute of Aviation Medicine/Dean of Air Force Medicine. m. Norma Lockhart Flectcher, 24 June 1950, Lambeth, London, 1 son, 1 daughter. *Education:* MB, BS, PhD. *Appointments:* Research Registrar, St. Thomas' Hospital, 1950-51; Director of Research, 1971-85, Commandant, 1975-, RAF Institute of Aviation Medicine; Dean of Air Force Medicine, 1985-. *Memberships:* International Academy of Astronautics; Worshipful Society of Apothecaries; Aerospace Medical Association; Royal Society of Medicine; International Academy of aviation and Space Medicine. *Publications:* Contributions to: "The Theory and Practice of Public Health" ed. W Hobson, 1971, "A Textbook of Aviation Physiology" ed. J A Gillies, 1965; "Emergencies in Medical Practice" ed C Allen Birch, 1967. *Honours:* OBE, 1957; QHP 1983. *Hobbies:* Trout fishing; Music. *Address:* 135 Aldershot Road, Church Crookham, Hampshire, England.

HOWAT, Henry Taylor, b. 16 May 1911, Pittenweem, Fife, Scotland. Emeritus Professor. m. Rosaline Green, 29 June 1940, Manchester, 2 sons, 1 daughter. *Education:* MB ChB, St Andrews, 1933; MRCP, London, 1934; FRCP, London, 1948; MD, St Andrews, Honours & University Medal, 1960; MRCP, Edinburgh, 1961; FRCP Edinburgh, 1965. *Appointments:* House Surgeon, House Physician, Dundee Royal Infirmary, 1933-34; Junior RMO, City of Dundee Sanatorium, 1934; Resident Physician, Edinburgh City Fever Hospital, 1935; Resident Clinical Pathologist, Manchester Royal Infirmary, 1935-36; Resident Medical Officer, MRI, 1938-40; Chief Assistant to A Medical Unit MRI, served in RAMC, 1940-46, Lieutenant Colonel; Physician, Ancoats Hospital, Manchester, Physician, Manchester Royal Infirmary, 1946-62; Physician in Charge, University Department of Gastroenterology, 1948-76; Private Practice, Consulting Physician, Manchester, 1972-76; Assistant Lecturer, 1946-48, Lecturer, 1946-48, Reader, Medicine, Professor, Gastroenterology, 1969-72, University of Manchester. *Memberships:* British Society of Gastroenterology, President 1968-69; European Pancreatic Club, President, 1965; President, 1978-79, Pancreatic Society of Great Britain & Ireland; etc. *Publications:* Articles in numerous journals; Co-author, "The Exocrine Pancreas", 1949. *Honours:* CBE (Civil), 1971; MSc., Manchester, 1975; Honorary MD, Louvain, 1945; Medalist J.E. Parkine Czechoslovak Medical Society, 1968; Manchester Man of the Year, 1975. *Hobby:* Golf. *Address:* 3 Brookdale Rise, Hilton Road, Bramhall, Sky 3AG, England.

HOWE, Geoffrey Richard, b. 2 Dec. 1942, England. Deputy Director, Epidemiology Unit; University Professor. *Education:* BSc Honours Chemistry, University College, London, 1965; PhD Theoretical Chemistry, University of Liecester, 1969. *Appointments:* Research Chemist, Imperial Chemical Industries, Cheshire, 1965-66; Research Fellow, Department of Chemistry, Brock University, St Catherine's Ontario, Canada, 1969-71; Research Analyst, Kalium Chemicals, Regina, Saskatchewan, 1971-72; Biostatistician 1972-75, Senior Biostatistician 1975-85, Deputy Director 1985-, Acting Director 1985, National Cancer Institute of Canada Epidemiology Unit, Toronto, Ontario; Associate Professor 1976-82, Professor 1982-, Department of Preventive Medicine and Biostatistics, University of Toronto, Ontairo; Visiting Professor, Oxford University, England, 1983. *Membeships:* Society for Epidemiologic Research; Biometric Society; American Statistical Assocation; New York Academy of Sciences. *Publications:* 71 articles including: 'Age at first pregnancy and risk of colo-rectal cancer; a case-control study' (with K J P

Craig and A B Miller), 1985; 'Effects of age, cigarette smoking and other factors on fertility: findings in a large prospective study' (co-author), 1985; 'Methodological Issues in Cohort Studies: Point Estimators of the Rate Radio', 1986; 'Selection of women at high risk of breast cancer for initial screening' (with M T Schechter and A B Miller), 1986. *Honours:* Eleanor Roosevelt International Cancer Fellowship, 1983; Visiting Fellowship, Wolfson College, Oxford University, England, 1983. *Hobby:* Music. *Address:* National Cancer Institute of Canada Epidemiology Unit, McMurrich Building, 3rd Floor, 12 Queen's Park Crescent West, University of Toronto, Toronto, Ontario M5S 1A8, Canada.

HOWELL, John Bernard Lloyd, b. 1 Aug. 1926, Swansea, Wales. Professor of Medicine. m. Heather Joan Rolfe, 12 July 1952, London, 2 sons, 1 daughter. *Education:* BSc; MB; PhD; FRCP; FACP (Hon); Middlesex Hospital Medical School; University of London. *Appointments:* House Physicina, Middlesex & Brompton Hospitals; Lecturer, Physiological Medicine, Middlesex Hospital; Eli Lilly Travelling Fellow, Johns Hopkins Hospital, USA; Lecturer, Pharmacological Medicine, Middlesex Hospital; Senior Lecturer, Medicine, Manchester Royal Infirmary, and Honorary Consultant Physician; Consultant Physician, Manchester Royal Infirmary. *Memberships:* Physiological Society; Medical Research Society; Association of Physicians; British Thoracic Society. *Publications:* Articles in professional journals including: 'Lancet'; 'British Medical Journal'; 'Journal of Physiology'; 'Clinical Science' etc. *Honours:* Goulstonion Lecturer RCP, 1966. *Hobbies:* Wine; DIY. *Address:* Southampton General Hospital, Tremona Road, Southampton, England.

HOWELL, Stephen Barnard, b. 29 Sep. 1944, Shirley, Massachusetts, USA. Associate Professor of Medicine. m. 7 Sep. 1968, Cambridge, Massachusetts, 2 sons. *Education:* AB, Biology, University of Chicago, 1966; MD, Immunology, magna cum laude, Harvard Medical School, 1970; Diplomate in Internal Medicine; Diplomate in Oncology. *Appointments:* Medical Intern, 1970-71, Medical Resident, 1971-72, Massachusetts General Hospital, Boston; Research Associate, National Cancer Institute, 1972-74; Medical Resident, University of California Hospital, San Francisco, 1974-75; Fellow in Oncology, Sidney Farber Cancer Institute, Boston, 1975-77; Assistant Professor of Medicine, University of California, San Diego, 1977-81; Director, Laboratory of Pharmacology, University of California, San Diego, Cancer Center, 1978-; Associate Professor of Medicine, University of California, San Diego, 1981-. *Memberships:* Biochemical Modulation Advisory Group, Division of Cancer Treatment, NCI; Ad hoc Advisory Group to Diagnosis Program, NCI; ASCO Scholarship Awards Committee; Cancer Research Coordinating Committee; Program Committee, American Society for Clinical Oncology; Phi Beta Kappa; Alpha Omega Alpha. *Honours:* Highest General Academic Honors, Special Honors in Biolgoy, 1966; Fogarty Senior International Fellowship Award, 1984. *Hobbies:* Sailing; Skiing. *Address:* University of California, San Diego, Department of Medicine, T-012, La Jolla, CA 92093, USA.

HOWELLS, John Gwilym, b. 24 June, 1918, Wales. Private Medical Practitioner. m. Ola Margaret, 12 Dec. 1943, 3 sons, 1 daughter. *Education:* MD; LRCP; MRCS; FRCPsych; DPM; AKC; Attended Chairing Cross Medical School, University of London; Institute of Psychiatry, University of London. *Appointments:* Founder and Director Institute of Family Psychiatry, Ipswich, England (affiliated to University of Cambridge), 1949-83; Private Practice -. *Memberships:* British Medical Association; Fellow, Royal Society of Medicine; Fellow, Royal College of Psychiatrists. *Publications:* Editor and author of 27 books and 150 scientific papers; "Family Psychiatry", 1963; "Principles of Family Psychiatry", 1975; "World History of Psychiatry", 1974; "Intergral Clinical Investigation", 1982. *Honours:* Founder Fellow, Royal College of Psychiatrists, 1972; Distinguished Fellow, American Psychiatric Association. *Hobbies:* Growing clematis; Opera; Travel; Walking; Ruminating. *Address:* Hill House, Higham, Colchester, England.

HOYT-BATES, Sharon Jean, b. 21 Feb. 1946, Federicton, Canada. Nursing Quality Assurance Co-Ordinator. m. Richard L. Bates, 1 July 1978, Ogden, Utah, USA. *Education:* Diploma, Barnes Hospital School of Nursing, 1967; BSN, University of Utah, USA, 1978; MPA, Golden Gate University, 1985. *Appointments:* Staff Nurse, Surgical Ward, 1967-68; (Military Career) Staff Nurse, Pulmonary Disease Services, Intensive Care Unit, and 1st Aeromedical Staging Flight, 1968-70; Flight Nurse, 56 Aeromedical Evacuation Squadrom and 10th Aeromedical Evacuation Squadrom, 1970-72; Nurse Advisor, 3502 USAF Recruiting Group, 1972-75; Staff Nurse, General/Medical Surgical Unit, and Staff Nurse/Assistant Charge Nurse, Medical/Surgical Unit, 1975-76; Charge Nurse Multiservice Nursing Unit, 1978-84; Supervisor, Outpatient Services, 1984-85; Quality Assurance Coordinator, Assistant Chief Nurse, 1985-. *Memberships:* Sigma Theta Tau; Phi Kappa Phi; Aerospace Medical Association; Air Force Association; Business and Professional Women, USA. *Honours:* USAF: Meritorious Service Medal, 1984, Commendation medal with 2 Oak Leaf Clusters, 1975, 1976, 1978; Viet Nam Service Medal, 1970; Honour Graduate BSN and MPA Programmes. *Hobbies:* Downhill Skiing; Volksmarching ; Tennis; Music. *Address:* 13409 Shawnee Road, Apple Valley, CA 92308, USA.

HREBIEN, Leonid, b. 12 April, 1949, Regensburg, Germany. Research Physiologist; Biomedical Engineer. m. Linda A. Macaw, 22 July 1978, Philadelphia, USA, 1 daughter. *Education:* BA, Electrical Engineering; MS, PhD, Biomedical Engineering. *Appointments include:* Assistant Professor, Adjunct Associate Professor, Drexel University, Philadelphia, Pennsylvania, USA. *Memberships:* Associate Fellow, Aerospace Medical Association; Chapter Chairman, Philadelphia, Institute of Electrical & Electronics Engineers; New York Academy of Sciences. *Publications include:* Research papers, professional journals: 'An In-Vitro Study of Cardiac Pacemaker Optimization by Pulse Shape Modification', 1976; 'Anti-G Suit Inflation Effects on G-Protection', 1985. *Honours:* Eta Kappa Nu, 1972; Tau Beta Pi, 1972; Sigma Xi, 1975. *Address:* Naval Air Development Centre, Code 60B1, Warminister, PA 18974, USA.

HRILJAC, Michael James, b. 31 Oct. 1950, Illinois, USA. Doctor of Podiatric Medicine. m. Patricia A Turek, 31 July 1977, St. Neoards. *Education:* BS; BA; DPM. *Appointments:* Surgical Staff, Chicago Center Hospital; Surgical Staff, Chicago Speciality Hospital; Surgical Staff, Jackson Park Hospital; Surgical Staff, Mercy Health Care and Surgical Center; Surgical Staff, Oak Park Hospital. *Memberships:* American Podiatric Medical Association; Illinois Podiatric Medical Association; American College of Foot Surgeons, Associate Member. *Honour:* Diplomat, American Board of Podiatric Examiners. *Hobbies:* Woodworking; Photography; Antiques; Shooting. *Address:* 3124 Wesley, Berwyn, IL 60402, USA.

HSIEH, Hsien-Chen, b. 10 May 1924, Taiwan, Republic of China. President of Kaohsiung Medical College; Director of Graduate Institute of Medicine, Kaohsiung Medical College. m. Hsieh Cheng Kuei-Wu, 9 Oct. 1949, Taiwan, 5 sons. *Education:* MD, National Taiwan University College of Medicine; DTM & H, University of London, England;

D.Med.Sc., Kagoshima University, Japan. *Appointments:* Technical Expert of Taiwan, Provincial Malaria Research Institute, 1949-57; Visiting Professor, Brigham Young University, USA, 1960; Medical Consultant, World Health Organization, 1961; Principal Investigator of Hookworm Project of American Foundation for Tropical Medicine, 1964-69; Member of WHO Expert Advisory Panel for Parasitic Disease, 1964-74; Professor, Dean of Studies, Kaohsiung Medical College. *Memberships:* Royal Society of Tropcial Medicine and Hygiene; Amrican Society of Parasitologists; American Society of Tropical Medicine and Hygiene; The Chinese Society of Microbiology. *Publications:* "Combining MTFC and Stoll Dilution Egg Counting for Species Analysis of Hookworm in Men", 1971; "Distribution of Necator americanus and Ancylostoma duodenale in Liberia", 1972; "Epidemiologic Studies of Eosinophilic Meningitis in Southern Taiwan, 1975. *Honour:* President's Prize for Successful Military Malaria Control, 1957. *Hobbies:* Reading; Fishing. *Address:* Kaohsiung Medical College, 100 Shih-Chuan 1st Road, Kaohsiung City, Taiwan, Republic of China.

HSIEH, Yuan-Ching, b. 25 Aug. 1926, Kian-Si, China. Consultant Physician. m. Shih-Lan Sun, 26 June 1959, Taipei, Taiwan, Republic of China, 1 son, 2daughters. *Education:* BM, National Defence Medical Center, Taipei, Taiwan, Republic of China, 1953; Postdoctoral Research Fellow, Department of Medicine, Indiana University Medical Center, Indianapolis, Indiana, USA, 1966-68. *Appointments Include:* Intern, Assistant Resident, Chief Resident, Visiting Physician, Department of Medicine, First Army General Hospital, Taipei, Taiwan, 1952-67; Attending Physician and Section Chief, Chest Section, Department of Medicine, Chairman of Department of Medicine, Deputy Director and Director of Professional Department, Triservice General Hospital, Taipei, Taiwan; Assistant, Instructor, Associate Professor, Professor and Chairman of Medicine, Department of Medicine, National Defense Medical Center, Taipei, 1956-83; Commissioner, Examination Committee for Medical Personnel of Examination Yuan, Republic of China, 1980-83. *Memberships Include:* Fellow, American College of Chest Physicians; American Thoracic Society; Chinese Medical Association; The World Association for Bronchology; International Academy of Chest Physicians and Surgeons, Thoracic Society, Republic of China. *Publications Include:* 'Pulmonary diffusing capacity response to inverted posture', 1973; 'A new method for measurement of Respiratory resistance', (co-author), 1983. *Honours Include:* Outstanding Service Achievement, Surgeon General, Chinese Army. *Hobbies:* Tennis; Photography; Travel; Chinese Food; Cooking. *Address:* 37-114 4th Section, Jen-Ai Road, Taipei, Taiwan 10649, Republic of China.

HSU, Chung Yi, b. 14 Oct. 1944, Taipei, Taiwan, Republic of China. Associate Professor of Neurology. m. Amy Yang, 27 Dec. 1974, Charlottesville, Virginia, USA, 1 son, 2 daughters. *Education:* MD, National Taiwan University School of Medicine, Taipei, Taiwan, Republic of China, 1970; PhD Pharmacology, University of Virginia School of Medicine, Charlottesville, Virginia, USA, 1975. *Appointments Include:* Fellow, Clinical Pharmacology, 1977-80, Assistant Professor, Department of Neurology, 1981-84, Director of Anticonvulsant Laboratory and Coordinator of Clinical Research, 1982-, Department of Neurology, Medical University of South Carolina, Charleston, South Carolina; Attending Neurologist, Medical University Hospital, Charleston, 1981-; Consultant, Charleston Veteran Administration Medical Center, Charleston, 1981-. *Memberships Include:* Fellow, American Heart Association; American Academy of Neurology; American Society for Neurological Investigation; Society for Neuroscience; New York

Academy of Science. *Publications:* 50 Research Articles in Scientific and Medical Journals. *Honours Include:* National Institute of Health TIDA, Award, 1983. *Hobbies:* Literature, History, Table Tennis, Basketball, Photography, Computers. *Address:* Department of Neurology, Medical University of South Carolina, Charleston, SC 29425, USA.

HSU, Jing, b. 18 Dec. 1937, Harbin, China. Associate Professor, John A. Burns School of Medicine; Chief of Psychiatry, St. Francis Hospital. m. Wen-Shing Tseng, 1 son, 2 daughters. *Education:* MD, School of Medicine, National Taiwan University, Taipei, 1961. *Appointments:* Associate Professor, Department of Psychiatry, Taipei Medical School, 1969-70; Fellow of Open Grants, East-West Center, and Research Fellow, Culture and Mental Health Program, Social Science Research Institute, University of Hawaii, 1971-72; Assistant Clinical Professor, Department of Psychiatry, University of Hawaii School of Medicine, 1972-73; Assistant Professor, Department of Human Development, University of Hawaii, 1973-74; Assistant Professor, 1976-80, Associate Professor, 1980-, Department of Psychiatry, University of Hawaii School of Medicine; Chief, Department of Psuchiatry, St. Francis Hospital, Honolulu, Hawaii, 1981-. *Memberships:* American Family Therapy Associt3ion; National Council of Family Relations; American Psychiatric Association; Hawaii Psychiatric Society; Life Member, Chinese National Association of Neurology and Psychoalogy. *Publications:* 11 articles in various journals; 10 chapters in books; 4 books. *Honours:* American Association of University Women Fellow and Fulbright Fellow, 1966-68; East-West Center Fellow, Culture and Mental Health Program, 1971-72; "Excellence in Teaching" in Psychiatry, John A. Burns School of Medicine, 1983. *Address:* University of Hawaii School of Medicine, 2230 Liliha Street Honolulu, HI 96817, USA.

HSU, John Tseng-tung, b. 15 Sep. 1932, Shanghai, China. Associate Professor of Radiology. m. Philomena Tang, 22 Apr. 1961, Pittsburgh, Pennsylvania, USA, 1 son. *Education:* MD, National Defence Medical Center, Taiwan, Republic of China; Diplomate, American Board of Radiology; Fello in Radiation Oncology, Memorial Cancer Center, New York, New York, USA. *Appointments:* Instructor of Radiology, Boston University Medical Center, Boston, Massachusetts: Instructor of Radiology, Albert Einstein College of Medicine, New York; Assistant Professor of Radiology, New York Medical College, New York; Associate Attending Radiologist, Saint Luke's-Roosevelt Hospital Center, New York; Associate Clinical Professor of Radiology, Columbia University, New York. *Memberships Include:* American Medical Association; Fellow, American College of Chest Physicians; Radiological Society of North America; New York Roentgen Society; Founding Member, Society of Thoracic Radiology. *Publications Include:* 'Radiological Assessment of Bronchopleural Fistula with Empyema' (with G M Bennett, E Wolff), 1972; 'Limited Form of Wegener's Granulomatosis', 1976; 'Adult Respiratory Distress Sydnrome' (co-author), 1977; 'Lung Absess Complicating Transbronchial Biopsy of a Mass Lesion' (with C R Barrett), 1981. *Hobbies:* Swimming, Music. *Address:* 2 Cindy Lane, Irvington, New York, New York 10533, USA.

HUANG, Alice S, b. 22 Mar. 1939, Nanchang, Kiangsi, China. m. David Baltimore, 8 Oct 1968, Cambridge, Massachusetts, USA, 1 daughter. *Education:* MA, Wellesley College, Wellesley, Massachusetts, USA, 1957-59; BA, Johns Hopkins University School of Medicine, Baltimore, 1961; MA, Johns Hopkins University, Department of Microbiology, 1963; PhD, Johns Hopkins University Department of Microbiology, 1966. *Appointments include:* Professor of Microbiology in Health Sciences and Technology, Harvard-Massachusetts

Institute of Tehcnology Program, 1979-; Professor of Microbiology and Molecular Genetics, Harvard Medical School, 1979-; Director, Laboratories of Infectious Diseases, Children's Hospital, Boston, Massachusetts, 1979-; Visiting Associate Professor of Virology, Rockefeller University, New York, 1975-76; Wellcome Visiting Professorship in the basic Medical Sciences, University of Mississippi, 1980. *Memberships:* Sigma Xi; American Society for Microbiology; American Association for the Advancement of Science; American Society of Biological Chemists; Fellow, Infectious Diseases Society of America; American Society for Virology; American Academy of Microbiology; Member of Numerous advisory boards and committees. *Publications:* Contributor of over 83 articles in professional and scientific journals. *Honours include:* Opportunity Fellow, The John Hay Whitney Foundation, New York, 1960-61; American Society for Microbiology Foundation Lecturer, 1975-76; Eli Lilly Award in Microbiology and Immunology, 1977; Alumnae Citation Award, National Cathedral School, Washington DC, 1978; MA, Honorary, Harvard University, 1980; The Sixth Hattie Alexander Memorial lecturer, Columbia University, 1981; DSC, Honorary, Wheaton College, 1982; Lee Kuan Yew Distinguished Visitor, National University of Singapore, 1985. *Address:* 26 Reservoir Street, Cambridge, MA 02138, USA.

HUANG, Liang, b. 8 Apr. 1920, Shanghai, People's Republic of China. Professor of Medicinal Chemistry. m. Dr C H Liu, 22 June 1949, Ithaca, New York, USA, 1 daughter. *Education:* BS Chemistry, St John's University, Shanghai, China, 1942, PhD Organic Chemistry, Cornell University, USA, 1949. *Appointments:* Post-doctoral Fellow, Bryn Mawr college, 1949-50, Cornell University 1950-52, Wayne University 1952-54, Iowa State University 1954-56, all USA; Associate Professor 1957-64, Professor, 1964-, Chairman of Department of Medicinal Chemistry, 1961-83, Institute of Materia Medica, Chinese Academy of Medical Sciences, Peking. *Memberships:* Committee of Directors, Chinese Chemical Socity, 1978-; Chinese Cancer Society i978-85; Chinese Pharmaceutical Society; Editorial board, Chinese Medical Encycolopaedia. *Publications:* Research papers in the fields of anticancer & antivirus agents, contraceptives, natural products. *Honours:* Phi Kappa Phi, 1948; Sigma Xi, 1949; Fellow, Academis Sinica. *Hobby:* Bridge. *Address:* Institute of Materia Medica, Chinese Academy of Medical Sciences, Beijing, Republic of China.

HUANG, Ting Fei, b. 23 Dec. 1920, Taipei, Taiwan. Professor of Physiology. m. Shu Chin Kuo, 21 Jan. 1945, 2 sons, 1 daughter. *Education:* MB, College of Medicine, Taihoku University, 1942; MD, Nagoya University, 1952; Downstate Medical Center, State University of New York, 1957-58; Columbia University 1966-67. *Appointments:* Instructor of Physiology, National Taiwan University, 1951-56; Associate Professor 1956-60, Professor 1960- *Memberships:* Formosan Medical Association; Chinese Physiological Society. *Publications:* "Experimental arrhythmias" "Chemoreceptor and diving bradycardia". *Honours:* Academic Award for Medicine, Ministry of Education, ROC, 1976. *Hobbies:* Classical music; Swimming. *Address:* Department of Physiology, College of Medicine, National Taiwan University, 1 Jen Ai Road, 1st Section, Taipei, Taiwan; Republic of China.

HUANG, Zhi-Qiang, b. 1 Jan 1922, Guangdong PR China. Professor of Surgery. m. Jean Yu, 1 May 1950, Chungqing, China, 2 sons. *Education:* MD. *Appointments:* Lecturer, 1950-53, Associate Professor of Surgery, 1953-63, Professor of Surgery and Head of Department of General and Hepato-biliary Surgery 1963-, Military Postgraduate Medical College, Chinese PLA General Hospital, The 3rd military Medical College; Vice Director of the Southern West Hospital, Chungqing, China, 1980-.

Memberships: International Society of Surgery; Chinese Medical Association. *Publications:* "Operative Surgery" (in Chinese) 1975; "Biliary Surgery" (in Chinese) 1976; "Surgery of the Liver" (in Chinese) 1982; "Treatment of Trauma" co-author, 1982. *Honour:* National Academic Award, 1978. *Hobbies:* Swimming; Photography. *Address:* Department of Surgery, Chinese PLA General Hospital, 28 Fuxin Road, Beijing, Republic of China.

HUAPAYA,Luis Victor Manuel, b. 13 May, 1926, Lima, Peru. Psychiatrist. m. Reine Roy, 31 Oct. 1964, Montreal, Canada, 1 son, 1 daughter. *Education:* MD, Lima, Peru, 1955; Diploma Course in Psychiatry, McGill University, Montreal, Canada, 1959-63, Diploma in Psychiatry, 1964; *Appointments:* Staff Psychaitrist, Hospital des-Laurentides l'Annonciation, Quebec, Canada, 1964-71; Staff Psychiatrist, Community Psychiatric Centre, Douglas Hosptial, Verdun, Quebec, Canada, 1971-75; Staff Phychiatrist, St. Mary's Hosptial, Montreal, Canada, 1971-84; Assistant Professor, Department of Psychiatry, McGill University, Montreal, 1977-84; Staff Psychiatrist, Adult Outpatient Psychiatric Clinic, Ottawa General Hosptial-; Psychiatric Consultant, Division of Neurology, Ottawa General Hospital 1984-. *Memberships:* Peruvian Psychiatrict Association; Canadian Psychiatric Association; Quebec Psychiatric Association, 1970-84; American Psychiatric Association Fellow; Royal College of Physicians of Canada; (Fellow) New York Academy of Sciences; American Association for the Advancement of Science; Peruvian American Medical Society. *Publications:* 'Psychogenesis and Somatogenesis of Common Symptoms' in 'Canadian Medical Association Journal, 1975; 'Seven Cases of Somnambulism Induced by Drugs' in 'American Journal of Psychiatry', 1979; 'Depression Associated with Hypertension: A Review', in 'Psychiataric Jouranl of Ottawa', 1980 (Co-author); 'Trastornos de los Estados Profondes des Sveno Precipitados per los Medicamentos' in 'Rev. Neuro-Psiquiatria', Peru. *Address:* Ottawa General Hospital, Department of Psychiatry, 501 Smyth Road, Ottawa, Ontario, KIH 8L6, Canada.

HUBBS, Roy Sears, b. 12 Dec. 1895, Dawson Minnesota, USA. Consultant, Psychiatry Neurology. m. Clara Margreet Eidamp, 19 June 1927, Gary, Dakota, 2 sons, 1 daughter. *Education:* BS, 1927, BM, 1929; DM, 1930. *Appointments;* Associate Physician, Physician, Senior Physician, Vet. Admin. Hospitals, 1930-42; Senior Medical Officer, C.O., Army Field Hospital, SW Pacific Area, 1942-46; Chief, Out Patient Service, Assistant Chief, Professional Services, Vet. Admin. Hospital Services, Palo Alto, California; Teacher, Clinical Psychiatry, University of California Medical School, 1949-54; Stanford University Medical School, 1954-62; Voluntary Professional Work, Consultant in Psychiatry and Neurology, Private Practice; Emirutus Clinical Faculty, Stanford. *Memberships:* Fellow, American Psychiatric Assoc.; American College of Physicians. *Publications:* 'Early Diagnosis of Neurosyphilis', 1932; 'Myocardial Disease', 1938; 'The Sheltered Workshop in Psychiatric Rehabilitation', 1958; 'The Sheltered Workshop in Psychiatric Rehabilitation', 1964; co-author of 4 other papers. *Honours:* Fellow, American College Physicians, 1954; American Psychiatric Assoc., 1956; Commendation and bronze plaque, founder of shelterd workshop, psychiatric patients, 1973; Certificate of Service Award, 1976. *Hobbies:* Ham Radio; Golfing. *Address:* 1303 Waverley Street, Palo Alto, CA 94301, USA.

HUBERMAN, Eliezer, b. 8 Feb. 1939, Lukow, Poland. Director; Professor. m. Lily Ginsburg, 11 May 1967, Tel Aviv, Israel, 2 sons. *Education:* MSc, Tel-Aviv University, 1964; PhD, The Weizmann Institute of Sciences, Rehovot, Israel, 1969. *Appointments:*

Visiting Associate, Etiology Branch, 1968, Visiting Scientist, Etiology Branch, National Cancer Institute, 1971; Postdoctorate, Department of Oncology, University of Wisconsin, 1969-71; Scientist, Department of Genetics, 1971-73, Senior Scientist and Associate Professor, Department of Genetics, Weizmann Institute of science, 1973-77; Group Leader, Biology Division, Oak Ridge National Laboratory, 1976-81; Director and Senior Scientist, Division of Biological and Medical Research Argonne National Laboratory, 1981-; Professor of University of Chicago, 1982-. *Memberships:* American Association for Cancer Research; Radiation Research Society. *Publications include:* Over 100 papers including 'Recombinant gamma-interferon and lipopolysaccharide enhance 1,25-dihydroxy-vitamin D3 induced cell differentiation in human promyelocytic leukemia (HL-60) cells', 1985; (co-author); 'An interlaboratory comparison of transformation in Syrian hamster embryo cells using model and coded chemicals' in press 1985 (co-author)' 'The Role of Chemicals and Radiation in the Etiology of Cancer', 1985; 'Specific protein phosphorlylation in human promyelocytic HL-60 leukemia cells susceptible or residant to induction of cell differentiation by phorbol 12-myristate 13-acetate', 1985. *Address:* Division of Biological and Medical Research, Argonne National Laboratory, 9700 South Cass Avenue, Argonne, IL 60439, USA.

HUDAK, Christine Angela, b. 13 Dec. 1950, Cleveland, Ohio, USA. Health Care Analyst; Information Specialist. *Education:* BSN, Nursing, Case Western Reserve University, 1974; M.Ed., Post Secondary Education, Cleveland State University, 1980; Post-master's Work, Computer Applications/Education, Cleveland State University, 1980-. *Appointments:* Public Health Nurse, 1974-75; Clinical Preceptor, Physician's Assistant Programme, Cuyahoga Community College, 1975-77; Staff Development Instructor, Cleveland Metropolitan General Hospital, 1978-85; Health Care Analyst, Information Specialist, Cleveland Metropolitan General Hospital, 1985-. *Memberships:* Centre for Professional Ethics; Educational Computer Consortium of Ohio; Association for Development of Computer Based Educational Systems; American Association of Artificial Intelligence. *Publications:* "Parts of a Sympton", self-instructional unit, 1976. *Honours:* Phi Delta Kappa; Pi Lambda Theta; Sigma Theta Tau; etc. *Hobbies:* Aerobics; Playing Keyboard & Cello; Cross Country Skiing; Recreational Computing. *Address:* 18421 Chagrin Road, Shaker Hts, OH 44122, USA.

HUDES, Marc Jay, b. 19 Feb. 1948, New York, USA. Podiatrist. m. Judith M Sims, 30 Aug. 1970, Whitestone, New York, 2 sons, 1 daughter. *Education:* BS, Biology, Fairleigh Dickenson University, Teaneck, New Jersey, 1968; Doctor of Podiatric Medicine, New York College of Podiatric Medicine, 1972. *Appointments:* Chief of Podiatry Department, Community General Hospital of Sullivan County, 1973-; Clinical Instructor, New York College of Podiatric Medicine, 1977-; President Mid Hudson Division, Podiatry Society of the State of New York, 1979-81. *Memberships:* Fellow, American Association of Hospital Podiatrists; Fellow, American Academy of Ambulatory Foot Surgeons; Associate American College of Foot Surgeons. *Hobby:* Past President, Monticello Rotary Club. *Address:* 237 Broadway, Monticello, NY 12701, USA.

HUDGENS, Richard Watts, b. 10 Jan. 1931, Greenville, South Carolina, USA. Physician; Professor of Clinical Psychiatry. m. Shirley Ann, 2 sons, 2 daughters. *Education:* BA, Princeton University, USA, 1952; MD, Washington University, 1956. *Appointments:* Professional ranks - Clinical Professorship from 1963-74, Wahsington University School of Medicine, 1967-73; Physician, Professor of Clinical Psychiatry-. *Memberships:* Fellow, American Psychiatric Association; American Medical Association; Alpha Omega Alpha Honour Society. *Publications:* 26 scientific articles; Book "Psychiatric Disorders in Adolescents", 1974. *Honour:* Alpha Omega Alpha Honour Society, Washington University School of Medicine; Magna cum Laude, Princeton University, 1952. *Hobby:* Historical studies. *Address:* 777 South New Ballas Road, St. Louis, MO 63141, USA.

HUDGSON, Peter, b. 3 Feb. 1936. Consultant Neurologist; Senior Lecturer in Neurology; Clinical Director, Muscular Dystrophy Research Laboratories. m. Margaret Jean Stevenson, 23 Sept. 1967, Newcastle upon Tyne, England, 3 daughters. *Education:* MB; BS; University of Melbourne Medical School, Australia; Royal Melbourne Hospital Clinical School; FRCP; FACP. *Appointments:* Resident Medical Officer, Senior Medical Registrar, Prince Henry's Hospital, Melbourne, Australia, 1959-64; Senior House Officer, Registrar, Honorary Senior Registrar and Research Associate in Neurology, 1964-667; 1st Assistant in Neurology, University of Newcastle upon Tyne, England, 1967-68; Visiting Professor of Medicine (Neurology), Duke University Medical Centre, Durham, North Carolina, USA, 1980-81; currently, Consultant Neurologist and Senior Lecturer in Neurology, Clinical Director, Muscular Dystrophy Research Laboratories, Newcastle General Hospital, England. *Memberships include:* New York Academy of sciences, USA; Association of Physicians of Great Britain and Ireland; Association of British Neurologists; Fellow, Royal Society of Medicine; American Association for Advancement of Science. *Publications:* "Syringomyelia", 1973; chapter in "Handbook of Clinical Neurology", 1980. Contributions ot' 'Brian" "Journal of the Neurological Sciences". *Honours:* Senior Fulbright Scholar, 1980-81. *Hobbies:* Squash; Golf; Gardening; Listening to Classical music; Reading. *Address:* Regional Neurological Centre, Newcastle General Hospital, Westgate Road, Newcastle Upon Tyne NE4 6BE, England.

HUDOLIN, Vladimir, b. 2 Apr 1922, Ogulin, Head of University Department of Neurology, Psychiatry and Alcoholism. m. Visnja, 30 Apr 1952, Zagreb. *Education:* MD, Faculty of Medicine, Zagreb University, 1948; Specialist in Neurology and Psychiatry, 1951, Dr. Sci. 1961, Zagreb University. *Appointments:* Deputy Head 1953-59, Head, 1959-, Department of Neurology and Psychiatry, Dr M Stojanovic Hospital, Zagreb; University Professor and Chair of Neurology, Psychiatry and Social Psychology, Faculty of Dentistry, Zagreb University, 1961-. *Memberships:* Past President and Honorary President, World Association of Social Psychiatry; President and Founding Member, Mediterranean Sociopsychiatric Association; Polish Psychiatric Association; Member of Expert Committee for Alcoholism and Drug Dependency of WHO; Association of Alcohologists of Yugoslavia; President, International Commission for the Prevention of Alcoholism; Czechoslovakian Psychiatric Association; American Psychiatric Association; International council on Alcohol and Addictions; International Commission for the Prevention of Alcoholism; *Publications:* More than 500 papers and 60 books and handbooks including: "Working Ability of Alcoholics and Drug Addicts - A Handbook for General Practitioners" 1978; "Dependencies" 1977; "Psychiatry" 1981; "Alcoholism in the Youth" 1981; "The Truth About Drugs" 1982; "Clubs of Treated Alcoholics"; "Alcoholism - What is Alcoholism?" 8th edition 1979; Editor; "Social Psychiatry" 1984. *Honours:* Award ofthe Association for Medical Education and Research in Substance Abuse, (AMERSA), 1982; Gold Medal of the Red Cross; Wagnsson's Medal of the I O G T, 1982. *Hobbies:* Botany; Gardening.

Address: University Department for Neurology, Psychiatry, Alcoholism and Other Dependencies, Dr M Stojanovic University Hospital, Vinogradska 29, 41000 Zagreb, Yugoslavia.

HUDSON, Arthur James, b. 3 Aug. 1924, Toronto, Ontario, Canada. Professor, Medicine, Neurology. m. Jean Margaret Glanville, 22 Dec. 1956, South Wales, 2 sons, 1 daughter. *Education:* MD; BSc; FRCP(C). *Appointments:* Faculty of Medicine, University of Western Ontario; Department of Medicine, Instructor 1958, Assistant Professor, 1967, Associate Professor, 1969, Professor, 1974-; Department of Clinical Neurological Sciences, Associate Professor, 1969, Professor, 1974-, Biochemistry, Honorary Lecturer, 1964-; Director, Neurochemistry Laboratory, University Hospital University of Western Ontario, 1974-; Senate, University of Western Ontario, 1980-82; Senate Committee, University Planning and Committee on Budget and Finance, University of Western Ontario, 1982-85; News Editor, Canadian Journal of Neurological Sciences, 1982-84; Founder, Amyotrophic Lateral Sclerosis Society of Canada, (ALSSOC), 1976; Chairman, Scientific Advisory Committee, ALSSOC; Co-Founder, Rossiter Research Conference. *Memberships Include:* Canadian Neurological Society, Secretary/Treasurer, 1969-73, Vice President 1974, President, 1975; Royal College of Physicians & Surgeons of Canada, Neurology Committee, 1972-73; Society for Neuroscience, USA, Programme Committee, 1975-77; Canadian Congress of Neurological Sciences, President, 1975; etc. *Publications:* Author, 100 publications; Contributor to number of books including "Basic Research in Myology"; 'Exerpta Medical Foundation', 1974; "The Diagnosis and Treatment of Amyotrophic Lateral Sclerosis", 1979; etc. *Honours:* Recipient, J H Richardson Fellow, University of Toronto, 1951-52; Muscular Dystrophy Association of Canada Research Award, 1960-74; Medical Research Council of Canada Research Award, 1976-83; Cdn. Diabetic Research Award, 1982-84; Ontario Mental Health Foundation Research Award, 1984-86. *Hobby:* Writing Poetry. *Address:* Dept. Clinical Neurological Sciences, University Hospital, 339 Windermere Road, London, Ontario, N6A 5A5, Canada.

HUDSON, Eric Hamilton, b. 11 July 1902, Littleborough, Lancashire, England. Retired. m. (1) Jessie Marian Mackenzie, 10 July 1940, Elstree, died 1968, 2 sons, 1 daughter, (2) Nora Joan Pitman, 16 Apr. 1972. *Education:* Radley College; Emmanuel College, Cambridge; Guy's Hosptial, London; MRCS London, 1927; NAMB. Bch., Cantab, 1931; MRCP, 1935; FRCP, 1941. *Appointments:* Medical Registrar: London Chest Hospital, Charring Cross Hospital, 1934; Consultant Physician: London Chest Hospital, 1935, West London Hospital, 1936, Papworth Village & Settlement, 1946, King Edward VII Hospital, Midhurst, 1947, Manor House Hospital, 1950, Brompton Hospital, 1960; Senior Medical Officer, Prudential Assurance Co., 1965. *Memberships:* Senior Member, Association of Physicians, Thoracic Society, Hunterian Society; Past President, West London Medico Churugical Society. *Publications:* Section: "Diagnosis & Medical Treatment Respiratory Tuberculosis", 'Heafs Symposium of Tuberculosis'; Section, 'Pulmonary Tuberculosis', 'Diseases of the Chest', 'Perry & Holmes Sellors,. *Hobbies:* Hobbies: Fishing; Gardening. *Address:* The Shieling, Highclere, Nr. Newbury, Berkshire, England.

HUDSON, James Irvin, b. 5 Jan. 1928, Nashville, Tennessees USA. Associate Dean; Professor, Epidemiology and Preventive Medicine. m. Judith Anne Quinn, 30 Oct. 1976, 1 son, 2 daughters. *Education:* BA, Cornell University USA, 1948; MD, Johns Hopkins University School of Medicine, 1952. *Appointments:* Director, Comprehensive Child Care Programme and Associate Professor of Paediatrics, Johns Hopkins University Medical School, 1966-71; Director, Programme Planning and Evaluation, Project Hope, Washington DC,. 1971-73; Director, Department of Health Services, Association of American Medical Colleges, Washington DC, 1973-80; Assistant to Director, CBO, National Organisation for Quality Assurance in Hospitals, Utrecht, The Netherlands, 1980-82; Associate, Johns Hopkins Centre Hospital, Finance and Managemetn-; Associate Dean, Administration, University of Maryland School of Medicine-. *Memberships:* American Academy of Paediatrics; American Public Health Association; Medical and Chirurigal Faculty of State of Maryland; Association for Health Services Research; American Health Planning Association. *Publications:* Co-author "Principles of Quality Assurance and Cost Containmetn in Health Care: A Guide to Medical Students, Residents", 1982;'The Changing Character of Quality Assurance Activities in Acute Care Hospitals' in "Effective Health Care", 1983; "Measuring Costs and Benefits of Quality Assurance" pp 164-166, 1983. *Address:* Office of the Dean, University of Maryland School of Medicine, 655 Ø Balto Street, Baltimore, MD, USA 21201.

HUDSON, Leslie, b. 24 Oct. 1946, England. Professor and Chairman of Immunology. m. Katharine Elaine Buxton, 31 Aug. 1968, Littleover, Derbyshire, 1 son, 1 daughter. *Education:* BSc, 1st Class Honours, Imperial College of Science and Technology, University of London, 1968; ·PhD, Middlesex. Hospital Medical School, 1975; Associate, Royal College of Science. *Appointments:* SRC Studentship, Imperial Ccollege, London University, 1969-70; MRC Research Assistant, Department of Immunology, Middlesex Hospital Medical School, 1970-73; Research Member, Basel Institute for Immunology, Switzerland, 1974-75; Senior Scientist, Wellcome Research Laboratories, England, 1975-77; Special Lecturer, Immunology, Imperial College, 1975-77; Senior Lecturer, Immunology, 1977-82, Reader, Immunology, 1982-85, Professor and Chairman, Immunology, 1985-, St George's Hospital Medical School, London. *Memberships:* British Society for Immunology; British Society for Parasitology; Fellow, Royal Societyfor Tropical Medicine and Hygiene; Antibody Club. *Publications:* "Practical Immunology", 3rd edition, 1986; "The Biology of Trypanosomes", 1985; 'A monoclonal antibody defining antigenic determinants on subpopulations of neurons and Trypanosoma cruzi parasites' in 'Nature', 1982. *Honours:* Forbes Medal and Prize, Imperial College of Science and Technology, London University, 1968. *Hobbies:* Reading; Fencing; Painting; Old houses. *Address:* Department of Immunology, St George's Hospital Medical School, Cranmer Terrace, London SW17 0RE, England.

HUGHES, Austin, b. 28 Mar. 1940, Whiston, Lancashire, England. Director, National Vision Research Institute of Australia, Professor, University of Melbourne. m. Gurli M A Nielsen, 30th Oct. 1962, 2 sons. *Education:* BA 1963, MA 1968, Pembroke College, Oxford University; DIC, Imperial College, London University, 1966; PhD 1968, DSc, 1982, Edinburgh University, Scotland. *Appointments:* Assistant Lecturer, Edinburgh University Medical School, 1964-68; Demonstrator in Physiology,. Oxford University, 1968-72; Extraodinary Lecturer, New College, Oxford, 1969; Postdoctoral Fellow, 1972-74, Senior Research Fellow, 1974-83, John Curtin School for Medical Research, Australian National University, Canberra, Australia. *Memberships:* Physiological Society (UK); Australian Physiological & Pharmacological Society; Australian Neuroscience Society; Association for Research into Vision & Ophthalmology; Fellow, American Academy of Optometry. *Publications:*

Numrous papers on visual optics, neuroanatomy & neurophysiology in professional journals, Contributor to Springer Handbook of Sensory Physiology. *Honours:* Medical Research Council Postgraduate Scholarship, 1963; Ellis Prize in Physiology, Edinburgh University, 1966. *Hobbies:* Books; Personal Computers. *Address:* National Vision Research Institute of Australia, 386 Cardigan Street, Carlton, Victoria 3053, Australia.

HUGHES, Leslie Ernest, b. 12 Aug. 1932, Parramatta, Australia. m. Marian Castle, 19 Dec. 1955, Parramatta, 2 sons, 2 daughters. *Education:* MB BS, University of Sydney, 1955; FRACS 1959; FRCS, England, 1959; DS, Queensland, 1975. *Appointments:* Surgical Trainee, Sydney Australia, 1955-59; Surgical Registrar, Derby & London, England, 1959-61; British Empire Cancer Campaign Research Fellow, King's College Hospital, London, 1962-63; Reader, Surgery, University of Queensland, Australia, 1964-71; Eleanor Roosevelt International Scholar, Roswell Park Memorial Institute, Buffalo, New York, USA, 1969-70; Professor, Surgery, University of Wales, College of Medicine, 1971-. *Memberships:* Fellow: Royal Australasian College of Surgeons, Royal College of Surgeons of England, Royal Society of Medicine; James IV Association of Surgeons; British Medical Association; British Society of Gastroenterology; British Association of Surgical Oncology; Surgical Reseach Society. *Publications:* Papers on Surgical Immunology, surgical oncology etc. *Honours:* Visiting Professor to Universities of Queensland, Allahabad, Sydney, Witwater rand, Cairo, Melbourne, Lund, Albany New York. *Hobby:* Music. *Address:* Dept. of Surgery, University of Wales College of Medicine, Heath Park, Cardiff CF4 4XN, Wales.

HUGHES, Michael Clement, b. 12 Feb. 1937, Merrill, Wisonsin, USA. Director, Hughes Mental Health Center. divorced, 1 son. *Education:* BS, University of Notre Dame, 1959; MD, University of Wisconsin, 1962; Intern in Medicine, Columbia University, 1962-63; Resident in Psychiatry, University of Wisconsin, 1963-65; Resident, Child Psychiatry, Harvard Medical School, 1965-67. *Appointments:* Harvard Medical School and Children's Hospital Medical Center, 1965-75; Director, Inpatient Consultantion Service, 1972-74; Director, Child and Adolescent Psychiatry, University of Miami School of Medicine, 1975-77; Clinical Professor of Psychiatry, University of Miami School of Medicine, 1985-; Director, Hughes Mental Health Center, 1985-. *Memberships:* Fellow, American Psychiatric Association, President, S Florida Chapter, 1985; American Society for Adolescent Psychiatry; American Academy of Child Psychiatry; Society of Professors of child Psychiatry, Emeritus; Alpha Omega Alpha. *Publications:* 'Recurrent Abdominal Pain and Childhood Depression', 'American Journal of Orthopsychiatry', 1984; ''Hyperactivity and the Attention Deficit Disorder', 'American Family Physician', 1983; 'Chronically Ill Children in Groups', 'American Journal of Orthopsychiatry'. *Honour:* Casuso Essay Award, Florida Psychoanalytic Society, 1982. *Hobbies:* Tennis; Boating; Theater; Reading. *Addres:* Hughes Mental Health Center, 5900 W 73 Street, Suite 301, South Miami, FL 33143, USA.

HUGHES, Patrick Lawrence, b. 11 Mar, 1955, Kansas City, Missouri, USA. Staff Psychiatrist, Medical Director, Inpatient Clinic, Psychiatry, Scott & White Clinic; Assistant Professor, Psychology, Texas A & M Medical School. m. Jane Elizabeth Nelson, 15 Aug. 1981, Rochester, 1 daughter. *Education:* BA, Liaberal Arts, Kansas University, Lawrence; MD, Kansas University Medical Centre. *Appointment:* Psychiatric Residencey Training, Mayo Clinic, Rochester, 1980-84. *Memberships:* American Psychiatric Association; American Medical Association; American Federation of Clinical Reserarch; Anorexia Nervosa and Associated

Disorders Association; Texas Medical Society. *Publications:* Articles in professional Journals including 'Journal of the American Medical Association'. *Honours:* Kansas University Owl Society, 1974;Outstandiang Senior Resident, Mayo ClinicPsychiatric Residency Training Programme, 1983-84. *Hobbies:* Golf; Fishing; Water Skiing; Railing; Tennis; Fiction. *Address:* Dept. of Psychiatry and Psychology, Scott & White Clinic, Temple, TX 76508, USA.

HUGHES-PARRY, Robert, b. 3 Nov, 1895, Caernarfon, Wales. Retired. m. 12 Apr. 1924, Wanstead, 2 sons, 2 daughters. *Education:* University College of Wales; Middlesex Hospital Medical School, London; Lyall Scholar, Gold Medallist, Brodenip Scholar; MD; FRCP; DPH; Honorary Physician to H.M. King George VI, H.M. Queen Elizabeth. *Appointments:* CMO, CSO, Middlesex Hospital; Chief Officer, medical Services, Bristol City Council, 1930-56; Visiting Professor, Yale University, USA, 1956; Consultant in Public Health to WHO, 1960. *Memberships:* Royal College of Physicians, London; Honorary APHA, USA, 40 years. *Publications:* Several on Cancer & Health Centres; ''Under the Cherry Tree'', 1969; ''Within Lifes Span'', 1970. *Honours:* KHP to the late King George VI; QHP, to H.M. Queen Elizabeth II. *Hobbies:* Formely Golf & Gardening. *Address:* 7 Gwaen Canal, Cricweth, Wales.

HUGHES, Sean Patrick Francis, b. 2 Dec. 1941, Farnham, England. Professor of Orthopaedic Surgery, University of Edinburgh. m. Felicity Mary Anderson, 1 son, 2 daughters. *Education:* MS; FRCS (Edinburgh); FRCS Ed.Orth.; FRCSI. *Appointments:* Senior Registrar, Orthopaedics, Middlesex Hospital and Royal National Orthopaedic Hospital; Research Fellow, Mayo Clinic, USA; Director of Orthopaedic Unit, Royal Postgraduate Medical School, London. *Memberships:* Member of Council, Royal College of Surgeons of Edinburgh; Research Committees: Action Research, British Orthopaedic Research Society. *Publications:* Co-editor: ''The Basis and Practice of Orthopaedics'', 1980; Editor; ''The Basis and Practice of Traumatology'', 1983; Author: ''Blood Flow: Thoery and Practice'' in ''Transport of Small Molecules Across Capillaries in Bone'', 1980; Papers in infection in bone, eternal fixation of fractures, bone blood flow and mineral transport in bone. *Hobbies:* Golf; Sailing; Lying in Sun. *Address:* 9 Corrennie Gardens, Edinburgh, Scotland.

HUGHS, Clifford Frederick, b. 1 Sept. 1945, Sydney, New South Wales, Australia. Visiting Medical Officer in Cardiothoracic Surgery. m. Elizabeth Ann Renn, 23 Aug. 1969, Sydney, 1 son, 2 daughters. *Education:* MB BS, University of New South Wales, 1969; FRACS, 1974; Post Doctoral Fellow, Johns Hopkins Hospital, Baltimore, Maryland, USA, 1978-79; FACS, 1985; FCCP, 1985; FACC, 1986; JP. *Appointments:* Junior Resident Medical Officer, 1969, Senior Resident Medical Officer, 1970, Surgical Registrar, 1972-73, Senior Surgical Registrar, Professional Registrar in Surgery, 1974-75, Royal North Shore Hospital, Sydney; Lecturer, Anatomy, University of Sydney, 1971; Senior Surgical Registrar, Cardiothoracic Surgery, Royal Prince Alfred Hospital, Sydney, 1976; Senior Surgical Registrar, Greenlane Hospital, Auckland New Zealand, 1976-78; Post Doctoral Fellow, Cardiac Surgery, Johns Hopkins Hospital, Baltimore, Maryland, USA, 1978-79; currently, Visiting Medical Officer in Cardiothoracic Surgery, Prince Alfred Hospital, Sydney, Australia. *Memberships Include:* Fellow: Royal Australasian College of Surgeons; American College of Surgeons. Australian Medical Association; Affiliate, Royal Society of Medicine American College of Chest Physicians; Australian Associations of Surgeons; Cardiac Society of Australian and New Zealand, American College of Cardiology, Life Member: Royal Blinc Society; Red Cross Society of New South Wales. *Publications:*

Papers contriubuted to: 'Radiology', 1977; 'Annals of Thoracic Surgery', 1981; 'Cardiovascular Research', 1983; 'Thorax, 1986; 'Australia and New Zealand Journal of Surgery' 1986; 'Journal of Thoracic & Cardiovascular Surgery', 1986. *Address:* 100 Carillon Avenue, Newtown, NSW 2024, Australia.

HUGHS, Owen Peter, b. 10 July 1942, Durban. Medical Practitioner; Family Physician. m. Karin Paul, 10 May 1969, Sudbury, Canada, 1 son, 3 daughters. *Education:* MD; MBA: B.MED.Sc.: B.Sc. (Eng.). *Appointments:* Professional Engineer, 1968-81; Assistant Professor, Community Medicine & Business Administration, University (Memorial) of Newfoundland, 1977; Preceptor, Family Medicine, University of Ottawa, 1979-. *Memberships:* LMCC; CCFP. *Publications:* "Economics of Home Care", co-author, 'International Journal of Health Services', 1976. *Hobbies:* Tennis; Squash. *Address:* 551 Cambridge Street S., Ottawa, Ontario K1S 4J4, Canada.

HUHTIKANGAS, Aarre Erkki, b. 8 May 1938, Helsinki, Finland. Professor of Pharmaceutical Chemistry. m. Leena Riitta Suontaa, 30 May 1963, Helsinki, 1 son, 3 duaghers. *Education:* MS Pharmacy, 1967; Pharm Lic, 1972; Dr Pharm, 1976. *Appointments:* Assistant in Pharmacognosy, Associate Professor of Pharmacognosy, University of Helsinki; Associate Professor of Pharmaceutical Chemistry, Professor of Pharmaceutical Chemistry, Dean of the Department of Pharmacy, University of Kuopio. *Publications:* Publications in the fields of natural products, analytical pharmaceutical chemistry, pharmaceutical chemistry and biochemistry. *Hobbies:* Private aviation; Music; Literature. *Address:* Lakkapolku, 6B, 70280 Kuopio, Finland.

HUIZAR, Sanchez Pompilio, b. 16 Aug. 1938, El Sauz Tostado, Colotlan, Jal. Mexico. m. Celerina Noemi Sanchez Argaez; M.D. 27 Sept. 1969, Mexico, D.F. 3 sons. *Education:* MD 1963, MS 1969, PhD, CIEA of Instituto Politenico Nacional of Mexico, 1973. *Appointments:* Associate Professor 1967-72, Full Professor 1967-72, Full Professor 1985, Escuela Superior de Medicina IPN, Head of Graduate Studies, Department Interdisciplinary Health Sciences Center, Instituto Politecnico National de Mexico, 1976; Visiting Associate Researcher, University of Pennsylvania, USA 1972-73; UNC Physiol. Department, Chapel Hill NC, 1973-75; Full Professor, Committee Head, Elaboration of the curriculum, Biomedical Engineering Master's Degree, DCBI, UAH-I, 1978-80, Co-Director, Division de Ciencias Biologicas y de la Salud, 1981-83, Head, Master's Program, Animal Reproductive Biology, DCBS, 1983-84, Temporary Director, DCBS, University Autonoma Metropolitana at Iztapalapa, Mexico D.F, 1984. *Memberships:* Regular Member, Sociedad Mexicana de Ciencias Fisiologicas, 1971; Society for Neurosciences 1974; Sociedad Mexicana de Ingenieria Biomedica, 1978. *Publications:* Scientific and Original papers in: Ciencia, Mexico; Acta Fisiologica Latino-Americana; Acta Politencinca, Mexico; J.Physiology, London; Internal Documents. *Honours:* Fellowships, Ministry ofEducation for MS Studies, 1965-69, Doctoral Studies, 1969-83; Fellowship, Grass Foundation, 1972,*Hobbies;* Tennis; Electronics; Automechanics. *Address:* Km 6 ½Carretera Panormaica al Ajusco, Cruz del Farol, Ejidos de San Andres Totoltepec Tlalpan, Mexico D.F., Mexico.

HUKUHARA, Takehiko, b. 16 Oct. 1930, Niigata, Japan. Director, Department of Pharmacology. m. Yoko Hukuhara, 6 July 1959, Tokyo, 1 son, 1 daughter. *Education:* MD, Faculty of Medicine, 1950-54, Internship, 1954-55, DMSc, Graduate School of Medical Sciences, 1955-58, University of Tokyo. *Appointments:* Research Associate, 1958-66, Associate Professor, 1966-75, Department of Pharmacology, Faculty of Medicine, Tokyo University, Japan; Visiting Research Fellow, University of Goettingen, 1960-62; Visiting Scientist, Mental Health Research Institute, University of Michigan, USA, 1967-68; Professor, Director, Department of Pharmacology II, Jikei University School of Medicine, Tokyo, Japan, 1975-; Visiting Professor, Ruhr University, Bochum, Germany, 1976. *Memberships:* Japanese Pharmacological Society; Physiological Society of Japan; Japan Society of Neurovegetative Research; Japan Society of Electroencephalography and Electromyography.*Publications:* "Central Rhythmic and Regulation", 1973; "Central Interaction between Respiratory and Cardiovascular Control Systems of Breathing and Circulation", 1983; "Mechanisms of Blood Pressure Waves", 1984. *Hobbies:* Classical Music appreciation. *Address:* Department of Pharmacology II, Jikei University Medical School, 3-25-8 Nishishinbashi, Minato-ku, Tokyo 105, Japan.

HULL, Christopher James, b. 1 Mar. 1938, Bath, Somerset, England. Professor of Anaesthesia. m. Joan Mary, 31 Dec. 1961, Darlington, Co. Durham, 3 sons, 1 daughter. *Education:* MB BS, London, 1961; Member, Royal College of Surgeons, London; Licentiate, Royal College of Physicians, 1961; DA, 1963; Fellow, Faculty of Anaesthetists, Royal College of Surgeons, 1966. *Appointments:* House Appointments, Medicine & Surgery, 1961, Senior House Officer in Anaesthetics, 1962, Registrar in Anaesthetics, 1963, Cumberland Infirmary, Carlisle. Registrar in Anaesthetics, Royal Victoria Infirmary, Newcastle-upon-Tyne, 1964; Senior Research Assistant, 1966, First Assistant, 1967, Senior Lecturer, 1970, Professor, Department of Anaesthesia, University of Newcastle-upon-Tyne. *Memberships:* Academician, European Academy of Anaesthesiology; Past President, North of England Society of Anaesthetists; President, Society of Anaesthetic Laboratory Technicians; Member, Board of Faculty of Anaesthetists, Royal college of Surgeons; Association of Anaesthetists of Great Britain & Ireland; Scottish Society of Anaesthetists; Anaesthetic research Society; Newcastle-upon-Tyne & Northern Counties Medical Society. *Publications:* "Principles of Clinical Measurement" 2nd edition, 1980; Various articles in medical journals in field; Honorary Editor, 'Clinical Physics & Physiological Measurement'; Honorary Associate Editor, 'British Journal of Anaesthesia'. *Honours:* 13th Nuffield Prize, Royal College of Surgeons, 1964; 1st Pinkerton Lecture, Association of Anaesthetists, 1983; Thomas Vicary Lecture, Royal College of Surgeons, 1985. *Hobbies:* Sailing; Jogging. *Address:* Department of Anaesthesia, Royal Victoria Infirmary, Newcastle-upon-Tyne, NE 4LP, England.

HULME, Russell LeRoy, b. 14 Oct. 1926. Associate Clinical Professor of Obstetrics and Gynecology. m. Joy Haws, 6 June 1949, 2 sons, 6 daughters. *Education:* BA, University of Utah, 1950; MD, University of Utah Medical School. 1952. *Appointments:* Clinical Instructor, Clinical Assistant Professor, Clinical Associate Professor, Stanford University Medical School. *Memberships:* Fellow, American College of Obstetricians and Gynecologists; Fellow, American College of Surgeons; San Francisco Gynecologists Society; Peninsula Gynecologists Society; Shofelt Obstetrics-Gynecology Society of Santa Clara Valley; Phi Beta Kappa; Phi Kappa Alpha; Alpha Omega Alpha. *Honours:* Photography; Movie making; Skiing; Boating; Water-skiing. *Address:* 15000 Los Gatos Boulevard §200, Los Gatos, CA 95030, USA.

HULT, Frederick E, b. 21 Mar. 1954, Kankakee, Illinois, USA. Chiropractic Physician. m. Karen Hilger, 19 Apr. 1980, Western Springs, Illinois. *Education:* BS Biology, University of Illinois, Champaign, Illinois, 1976; DC, National College of

Chiropractic, Lombard, Illinois, 1980. *Appointments:* Instructor, Department of Anatomy 1976-80, 1982-, Department of Clinical Practice 1979-80, National College of Chiropractic, Lombard, Illinois; Associate Practice, Champaign, Illinois, 1980-82; Private Practice, McHenry, Illinois, 1982- . *Memberships:* American Chiropractic Association; Illinois, and Northern Illinois Chiropractic Societies. *Honours:* Administrative Council Outstanding Senior Award, Infraternity Council Anatomy Exellence Award, National College of Chiropractic; Diplomate, National Board of Chiropractic Examiners. *Hobbies:* Tennis; Golf. *Address:* 803 North Front Street, McHenry, IL 60050, USA.

HUMPHREYS, Gerald Stanley, b. 5 Feb. 1932, Nottingham, England. Cardiologist in Private Practice and Miami Heart Institute, Florida, USA. Divorced, 2 sons, 3 daughters. *Education:* MBBS, Charing Cross Hospital, London, University, 1955; FRCP (Edinburgh); MRCP. *Appointments:* House Surgeon, Harrow Hospital, 1955; House Physician, Charing Cross Hospital, 1955-56; Medical Officer, RAF, 1956-58; Medical Registrar, San Fernando, 1958-61; Medical Registrar, Bromley Group Hospitals, 1961-64; Medical Registrar, Cardiac Surgical Department, Leeds University, 1964-65 Consultant Physician, Kingston, Jamaica, 1965-75; Consultant Physician, University of West Indies, Kingston, 1968-75; Director, Intensive Care Unit, Brandon, Manitoba, Canada, 1975-77; Visiting Cardiologist, S.S. Hope (Project Hope), Jamaica, 1971. *Memberships:* Fellow, American College of Cardiology; Fellow, American College of Chest Physicians; Fellow, American College of Angiology; Member British Cardiac Society. *Publications:* Contributor to: Oral Pathology, West Indies Medical Journal, Gerontology Clinics, Manedsskrift for Praktisk Laegegering, British Medical Journal and General Practitioner. *Honour:* Governor's Clinical Gold Medal, Charing Cross Hospital, 1955. *Hobbies:* Skiing; Scuba; Golf. *Address:* 1065 Kane Concourse, Bay Harbour Island, Miami, FL 33154, USA.

HUMPHREYS, Gwynfor Owen, b. 3 Apr 1946, Llandudno, Wales, Director of Research Development, m. Linda Ann Foster, 28 Dec 1970, Plymouth, Devon, England, 2 sons. *Education:* BSc, 1965-68, PhD, 1968-71, University College London. *Appointments:* Scientist, Enteric Reference Laboratory, Central Public Health Laboratory, Colindale, England, 1971-75; Lecturer, Microbiology Department, University of Liverpool, 1975-81. *Memberships:* Society for General Microbiology, 1971-; American Society for Microbiology, 1974-. *Publications:* Author of over 50 professional papers on scientific subjects. *Honours:* Medal and Prize, Faculty of Science, University College London, 1968; Jack Drummond Prize, University College of London, 1967. *Hobbies:* Music; Playing violin; Squash; Golf. *Address:* Apcel Ltd, 545 Ipswich Road, Slough, Berkshire SL1 4EQ, England.

HUMPHRIES, John O'Neal, b. 22 Oct, 1931, Columbia, South Carolina, USA. Physician Educator. m. Mary Cregan, 13 Mar. 1954, Baltimore, Maryland, USA, 2 sons, 1 daughter. *Education:* MD. Johns Hopkins University, Baltimore, MD, USA, 1956; BS, Duke University, Durham, NC, USA, 1952. *Appointments:* Instructor 1964, Assistant Professor, Associate Professor, Robert Levy Professor of Cardiology, Professor, Johns Hopkins University School of Medicine; Professor, Chairman, 1979, O. B. Mayer Sr., Jr. Prof. of Medicine, 1980, Dean, School of Medicine, University of South Carolina, 1983. *Memberships:* American Federation for Clinical Research; American Clinical And Climitalolgical Association; American Heart Association; American College of Cardiology. *Publications:* Editor, (with D.G.Julian), "Cardiology Volume 2, Preventive Cardiology", 1983; 'Myocardial Infarction in Sickle Cell Anmemia', (with

O'N. Barrett, D.E. Saunders, D.E. McFarland), 1984. *Honours:* Alpha Omega Alpha, 1966; Sir William Osler Award, University of Miami, 1979; Boron Visiting Professor of Medicine, UCLA, 1980. *Hobby:* Golf. *Address:* School of Medicine, University of South Carolina, Columbia, SC 29208, USA.

HUMPHRIES, Laurie Lee, b. 26 Apr. 1944, Atlanta, Georgia, USA. Assistant Professor of Psychiatry. m. Dr. Asa Alan Humphries, 22 July, 1972, Decatur, Georgia, 1 daughter. *Education:* BA, Emory College, Georgia, 1966; MD, Emory University School of Medicine, Atlanta, Georgia, 1963. *Appointments:* Assistant Professor, Emory University School of Medicine, Atlanta, Georgia, USA, 1978-81; Assistant Professor, Department of Psychiatry, University of Kentucky College of Medicine, Lexington, Kentucky, 1981-. *Memberships:* American Psychiatric Association; American Academy of Child Psychiatry; American Medical Women's Association; Sleep Reserach Society. *Publications:* 'Daily Patterns of Scrotonin Uptake in Platelets from Psychiatric Patients and Control Volunteers' i 'Biological Psychiatry', 1985; 'Sequential Quantitative EEG Analysis in Acute Lymphatic Leukaemia of Children' in 'Clinical EEG', 1985. *Honours:* Child Mental Health Faculty Development Award, National Institute of Mental Health, 1983-84; Kappa Kappa Gamma Fraternity Alumnae Achievement Award, 1986. *Hobbies:* Tennis; Cooking. *Address:* Department of Psychiatry, University of Kentucky, College of Medicine, Lexington, KY, 40536 USA.

HUNCHAK, John Franklin, b. 24 Aug, 1945, Winnipeg, Manitoba, Canada. m. Dianne Lynn Fletcher, 6 Aug. 1971, Winnipeg, Manitoba, Canada. 1 son, 2 daughters. *Education:* BSc.; MD. *Appointments:* Active Staff, Oshawa General Hospital. *Memberships:* Canadian and Ontario Medical Associations; Ontario Society of Clinical Hypnosis; American Society of Clinical Hypnosis. *Publications:* 'Hypnotic Induction by Entopic Phenomena', 1980; 'Calm, Cool and Collected', 1985. *Address:* R.R, 1, Pickering, Ontario, Canada LIV 2 P8.

HUNG, Tao, b. 10 Oct. 1931, Shandong, Peoples Republic of China. Professor, Institute of Virology, China National Centre for Preventive Medicine. m. Chang Jiayu, 24 May 1955, Tsinan, 2 daughters. *Education:* MD, Shandong Medical College, 1949-55; Diploma, Candidate, medical sciences (PhD), Institute of Virology, Academy of Sciences, Bucharest, 1955-61. *Appointments:* Chief, Morphopathology, 1960-69, Head, Virus Morphology, 1971-78, Associate Professor, Head, Virus Morphology, 1978-84, Professor, Head, Virus Morphology and Viral Diarrhoea, Institute of Virology, China National Centre for Preventive Medicine; Physician, Vice Director, Germu Hospital, Tsinghai, 1969-71; Visiting Professor, Univeisyt of Chicago, Pennsylvania State Univeristy, 1981; Vice Director, Institute of Geriatrics, Beijing Hospital, 1984- . *Memberships:* Vice President, Chinese Society for Medical Virology; President, EM Division, China Society for Medical Imaging Technology; Chinese Society for Microbiology; Electron Microscopic Society of America; Steering Committee, CDD WHO. *Publications:* "Ultrastructure & Electron Microscopy in Biomedicine", 1980; "Atlas of Biomedical Electron Microscopy", 1978; "Progress & Perspectives in Virology", 1981; "Viral Diarrhoea", 1984; Numerous scientific articles published in: 'Lancet'; 'Archives of Virology'; Chinese Journals; etc. *Honours:* Achievement Award, National Science Congress, 1978; Achievement Award, 1st National Congress of Medical Sciences, 1978; Achievement Awards, Academy of Medical Sciences, 1979, 1980, 1983; 1st Class Awards for research on HFRS & ADRV, 1984, 1985. *Hobby:* Oil Painting. *Address:* Institute of Virology, China National Centre for Preventive

Medicine, 100 Ying Xing Jie, Xuan Wu Qu, Beijing 100052 Peoples Republic of China.

HUNNINGHAKE, Gary William,. b. 10 July 1946, Seneca, Kansas, USA. Professor of Medicine. m. 1968, 3 children. *Education:* BS, summa cum laude, St. Benedict's College, 1968; MD, Kansas University, 1972. Diplomate, American Boards, Internal Medicine, Allergy & Immunology, Pulmonary Disease. *Appointments include:* Clinical Associate 1974-76, Medical Officer 1976-77, Laboratory of Clinical Investigation, National Institute of allergy & Infectious Diseases, National Institutes of Health (NIH), Bethesda, Maryland; Senior Investigator, Pulmonary Branch, National Heart, Lung & Blood Institute, NIH, Bethesda, 1977-81; Consultant, Pulmonary Diseases, ibid, 1977-81; Associate Professor 1981-84, Professor of Medicine, 1984-, University of Iowa College of medicine; Director, Pulmonary Disease Division, University of Iowa Medical Centre/VA Hospital, Iowa City, 1981-. *Memberships include:* Alpha Omega ALpha; American Federation for Clinical Research; American College of Physicians; American Association of Immunologists; Central & American Societies for Clinical Research; etc. *Publications:* Numerous contributions to professional journals, abstracts, conference proceedings, book chapters, etc. Areas of research interest: Lung Immunology & Host Defences; lung infections, interstital lung diseases, chronic obstructive lung disease, asthma, oxidant lung injury. *Honours:* G.Milton Shy Award, Neurology paper; L.L. Marcell Award, outstanding medical student, 1971 & 1972; Award, outstanding medical intern,. 1973. *Address:* Department of Internal Medicine, University of Iowa College of Medicine, Iowa City, IA 52242, USA.

HUNT, Vere David Urquhart, b. 20 May 1939, Woking England. Director of Cardiology. m. Julie Essington King, 24 Nov. 1964, Melbourne, 3 sons, 1 daughter. *Education:* MBBS, 1962, MD, 1966, University of Melbourne; MRACP, FRACP, Royal Australasian College of Physicians; FACC, American College of Cardiology; DDU, Society of Medical Ultrasound. *Appointments include:* Medical Registrar, 1966, Cardiology Registrar, 1967, Royal Melbourne Hospital; Visiting Lecturer in Medicine, University of Hong Kong, 1967; Cardiology Research Fellow, Royal Melbourne Hospital, 1968; Instructor in Medicine, University of Alabama, 1969 and 1970; Honorary Physician to Outpatients, 1971-74, Assistant Director of Cardiac Laboratory, 1977-77, Assistant Director of Cardiology, 1977-80, Director of Cardiology, 1980-, Royal Melbourne Hospital; Senior Associate, Department of Medicine, University of Melbourne, 1971-, Consultant Cardiologist, Royal Women's Hospital Melbourne, 1978-. *Memberships:* Australian Medical Assocation; American College of Caridology; Royal Australasian College of Physicians; Cardiac Society of Australia and New Zealand; British Cardiac Society. *Publications:* Numerous contributions to medical journals and to edited volumes. *Hobbies:* Swimming; Tennis. *Address:* Department of Cardiology, Royal Melbourne Hospital, Melbourne 3050, Australia.

HUNT, Wayne Philip, b. 4 Feb. 1947, Baltimore, Maryland, USA. Psychologist. m. Janice Lee Staples, 1 daughter. *Education:* BS, Mars Hill College, 1969; MS, The Johns Hopkins University, 1974; EdD, The George Washington University, 1982. *Appointments include:* Mental Health Counselor, Health and Welfare Council of Central Maryland, 1975-78; Co-ordinator of Counseling Services, Counseling and Consultation Services, 1978-80; Consulting Psychologist, Chestnut Hill Development, Center, 1982-84, Board of Directors 1983-84; Psychologist, St Francis School, for Special Education 1978-83; Clinical Psychologist, State of Delaware Youth Diagnostic Center, 1983-84; Chief Psychologist, Maryland Reception-Diagnostic and Classification Center, 1984-. *Memberships:* American Psychological Association; National Association of School Psychologists; Maryland Psychological Association; Maryland School Psychologists Association; The Johns Hopkins Club. *Publications:* 'The Effects of Learning the American Indian Gestural Code on the IQs of Mildly, Moderately and Severely Retarded Students' 1982 (Dissertation). *Address:* 708 Dunkirk Road, Baltimore, MD 21212, USA.

HUNTER, Harlen C. b. 23 Sept. 1940, Esterville, Iowa, USA. Orthopaedic Surgeon, Sports Medicine. m. Joan Wilson, 30 June, 1962, Hudson, Iowa, USA, 1 son, 1 daughter. *Education:* BA, Drake University, Des Moines, Iowa; DO, College of Osteopathic Medicine and Surgery, Des Moines. *Appointments:* Normandy Orhtopaedic Inc. 1972-79; Iowa Orthopaedic Sports Medicine Clinic, 1982-83; St. Louis Orthopaedic Sports Medicine Clinic, 1979-present. *Memberships:* American Osteopathic Association; American College of Osteopathic Surgeons; American Osteopathic Acadmey of Orthopaedics; MissouriAssociation of Osteopathic Physicians and Surgeons; American College of Sports Medicine. American Osteopathic College of Sports Medicine (Founder Member); American Orthopaedic Society for Sports Medicine; American Medical Association; St. Louis Metropolitan Medical Society; Missouri Medical Association. *Publications include:* Many articles in Osteopathic annuals and journals. *Honours:* Clinic Speaker Award, Iowa High School Baseball Coaches Association; Honorary Member of Alpha Episilon Delta Pre-Medical Society, Drake University; Men of Achievement, volume Xi, 1984. *Hobby:* Professional Racing Photographer for Daytona, Talladega, Darlington and Indy. *Address:* 1230 Walnut Hill Farm, Chesterfield, MO 63017, USA.

HUNTER, John Angus Alexander, b. 16 June 1939, Edinburgh, Scotland. Professor of Dermatology. m. Ruth Mary Farrow, 26 Oct. 1968, Spalding, Lincolnshire, England, 1 son, 2 daughters. *Education:* BA, University of Cambridge, 1960; MB ChB 1963, Member, Royal College of Physicians of Edinburgh, 1967, MD (Gold Medal), 1977, Fellow, RCPEd, 1978, Edinburgh. *Appointments:* Research Fellow, Institute of Dermatology, London, 1967; Registrar, Department of Dermatology, Royal Infirmary, Edinburgh, 1968-70; Exchange Reseach Fellow, Department of Dermatology, University of Minnesota, 1968; Lecturer, Department of Dermatology, University of Edinburgh, 1970-74; Consultant, Dermatology, Lothian Health Board, 1974-80; Grant Professor of Dermatology, University of Edinburgh, 1980-. *Memberships:* Executive Committee, Investigative Group of British Association of Dermatologists, 1977-79; Secretary, Scottish Dermatological Society, 1980-82; Specialist Advisory Committee (Dermatology), Joint Committee on Higher Medical Training, 1983; Member, Scottish Committee for Hospital Medical Services, 1983. *Publication:* "Common Diseases of the Skin" (Co-editor). *Honours:* Gold Medal MD, Edinburgh, 1977; Dowling Orator, London, 1982. *Hobbies:* Music; Gardening; Tropical Fish; Golf. *Address:* Leewood, Rosslyn Castle, Roslin, Midlothian, EH25 9PZ, Scotland.

HUNTER, Kenneth Crawford, b. 3 Aug. 1947, Coleraine, Northern Ireland. Family Practitioner. m. Gea Faber, 16 Dec. 1982, Vancouver, Canada, 1 daughter. *Education:* MB, BCh, BAO, Queen's University Belfast Northern Ireland, 1972; LMCC, 1980. *Appointments:* Family Practice, Prince George, British Columbia, 1977-79, Hanna, Alberta, 1979-81, Delta, Vancouver, British Columbia, 1981 -. *Memberships:* Canadian Medical Association; British Columbia Medical Association; Canadian Medical Protective Association; Delta Hospital Medical Society. *Hobbies:* Sailing; Skiing; Golf; Fishing; Badminton; Swimming. *Address:* 409

English Bluff Road, Delta, South Vancouver, British Columbia V4M 2M9, Canada.

HUNTER, Marlene Elva, b. 30 Nov, 1931, Toronto, Canada. Family Physician. m. Redner Jones, 2 sons, 3 daughters. *Education:* BA; MD; CFPC (C). *Appointments:* Medical Officer PCEA Hospital, Tumutumu, Kenya, 1967-71; Chief of Department of General Practice, Lions Gate Hosptial, North Vancouver BC, 1975-79 Member, Joint Conference Advisory Committee, BCMA/CFPC (B.C.Div.), 1979-; Member at Large, Board of Provincial Chapter of College of Family Physicians, Canada, 1982-83; Secretary 1983-85, President Elect 1985-86; Teachinng Faculty, Canada Society Clinical Hypnosis, (B.C.) 1976-; President Canadian Society of Clinical Hypnosis, (B.C.) 1982-83; 3rd Vice President, American Society Clinical Hypnosis, 1984-85, 1985-86; Chairman, Federation of Canadian Societies of Clinical Hypnosis, 1984-85. *Memberships:* Certificant, College of Family Physicians of Canada; British Columbia Medical Assoc.; Canadian Society Clinical Hypnosis; American Society Clinical Hypnosis; International Society Hypnosis; Swedish Society Clinical and Experimental Hypnosis. *Publications:* ''Psych Yourself In: Hypnosis and Health'', 1984. *Hobbies:* Stained Glass; Quilt-Making. *Address:* 1411 Bellevue Avenue, West Vancouver, BC, Canada V7T 1C3.

HUSBAND, Janet Elizabeth, b. 1 Apr. 1940, Chinnor, Oxon, England. Consultant Radiologist, Department of Diagnostic Radiology, Royal Marsden Hospital, Sutton, Surrey. m. Dr. Peter Husband, 20 July 1963, Princes Risborough, 3 sons. *Education:* MRCS LRCP, 1964; MB BS, London, 1964; DCH, England, 1966; DObst.RCOG, 1967; MRCP, London, 1969; DMRD, 1974; FRCR, 1976. *Appointments:* Registrar, Diagnostic Radiology, Queen Mary's Hospital, London, 1974-75; Registrar, Diagnostic Radiology, Kings College Hospital, London, 1975-76; Clinical Scientist (Senior Registrar), EMI Whole Body Scanner Unit, Northwick Park Hospital, Harrow, 1976-77; Research Fellow, CRC CT Scanning Unit, Royal Marsden Hospital and Honorary Senior Lecturer, Institute of Cancer Research, Surrey, 1977-80; Consultant Radiologist, BUPA Medical Centre, London, 1977-81; Consultant Radiologist, Royal Marsden Hospital and Honorary Senior Lecturer, Institute of Cancer Research, Sutton, 1980-; Director, CT Scanning Unit, BUPA Medical Centre, London 1981; Director, Cancer Research Campaign CT Scanning Unit, Royal Marsden Hospital, Sutton (now Cancer Research Campaign Radiology Research Group), 1982-. *Memberships:* American Society of Computed Body Tomography; European College of Body CT; American Society of Thoracic Radiology; British Institute of Radiology; Fellow, Royal College of Radiologists. *Publications:* Computed Tomography of the Body: A Radiological and Clinical Approach (co-author), 1981. Contributor to professional journals. *Honour:* Couch Award, Royal College of Radiologists, 1976. *Address:* 7 Malbrook Road, Putney, London SW 15 6UH, England

HUTCHINSON, Jeffrey Stuart, b. 8 Apr. 1944, Melbourne, Australia. Senior Lecturer.m. Svetlana Cvetic, 5 Feb. 1972, Melbourne, 1 son, 1 daughter. *Education:* BSc, Monash University, 1969; MSc, 1971, PhD, 1974, Melbourne University. *Appointments:* Alexander von Humboldt Fellow, University of Heidelberg, 1973-75; Senior Research Officer, Baker Medical Research Institute, 1975-77; Senior Reserach Officer, 1978-81, Research Fellow, 1982, University of Melbourne Department of Medicine, Austin Hospital; Senior Lecturer, Department of Pharmacology, Faculty of Medicine, National University of Singapore, 1983-. *Memberships:* International Society of Hypertension; High Blood Pressure Research Council of Australian; Endocrine Society of Australia; Australian Neuroscience Society; Australasian Society of Nephrology; Australian Neuroscience; Singapore Biochemical Society. *Publications:* Book contributions include: 'Central Nervous Control of Nat Balance'; ''Central Actions of Angiotensin and Related Hormones'', 1977. Papers contributed to professional journals including: 'Australasian Annals of Medicine'; 'Journal of Endocrinology'; 'Annals of New York Academy of Sciences'; 'Acta Medica Academiae Scientarium Hungarici'; 'Clinical Science and Molecular Medicine'; 'The Medical Journal of Australia'; 'Hypertension'; 'Clinical and Experimental Pharmacology and Physiolgy'; 'Clinical and Experimental Pharmacology and Physiology'; 'Clinical Science'; 'Experimental Brain Research'; 'American Journal of Cardiology'; 'Life Sciences'; 'British Journal of Pharmacology'. Co-Author of Pharmacoalogy'. Co-Author of over 70 abstracts. *Hobbies:* Reading; Photography; Chess; Sailing; Judo. *Address:* 33 Prince Charles Street, Clayton, Victoria, 3168, Australia.

HUTCHISON, William McPhee, b. 2 July 1924, Glasgow, Scotland. Professor of Parasitology. m. Isabella Duncan McLaughland, 15 Mar. 1963, Glasgow, 2 sons. *Education:* BSc, 1952; PhD, 1959; DSc, 1971. *Appointments:* Assistant Lecturer, 1952; Lecturer, 1954; Senior Lecturer, 1969; Professor, 1971. *Memberships:* Fellow, Institute of Biology; Chartered Biologist; Fellow, Royal Society of Tropical Medicine anad Hygiene; Fellow, Linnean Society; Fellow, Royal Society Edinburgh; Royal Philosophical Society; American Society Parasitologists; Society of Protozoologists; British Society of Parasitologists. *Publications:* 80 papers in major scientific and medical journals mostly on Toxoplasmosis. *Honours:* Robert Koch Medal and Prize. *Hobbies:* Do-it-Yourself; Gardening; Collecting scientific specimens. *Address:* Department of Bioscience and Biotechnology, George Street, Glasgow, G1 1XW. Scotland

HUTT, Michael Stewart Rees, b. 1 Oct. 1922, England. Professor Emeritus. m. Elizabeth N Jones, 4 May 1946, Hinchley Wood, Surrey, England, 1 son, 3 daughters. *Education:* MB, BS, 1945, Member, Royal College of Physicians 1946, MD, 1949, Fellow, Royal College of Physicians 1967, Fellow, Royal College of Pathologists, 1967, all London. *Appointments:* Senior Lecturer in Clinical Pathology, St Thomas' Hospital Medical School, London, 1957-62; Professor of Pathology, Makerere University of East Africa, Kampala, Uganda, 1962-70; Professor of Geographical Pathology, St Thomas' Hospital Medical School, London, 1970-83, Emeritus Professor, 1983-, University of London. *Memberships:* Royal Society of Tropical Medicine & Hygiene; Royal Society of Medicine; International Academy of Pathology; Pathological Society of Great Britain. *Publications:* 180 papers and chapters published; Joint Editor, ''Medicine in a Tropical Environment'',1972; Joint Editor, ''Cardiovascular Disease in the Tropics'', 1974. *Honours:* Maud Abbott Lecturer, International Academy of Pathology, 1977; Honorary Fellow, East African Association of Surgeons, 1969. *Address:* Gwernvale Cottage, Brecon Road, Crickhowell, Powys, NP8 1SE, Wales.

HUTTUNEN, Jussi K, b. 27 Aug. 1941, Helsinki, Finland. Director, National Public Health Institute of Finland. m. Raili Seppälä, 6 Apr. 1963. *Education:* MD, Dr of Medical Science, 1966 University of Helsinki. *Appointments:* Research Assistant, Department of Medical Chemistry, University of Helsinki, 1963-69; Research Fellow, University of California at San Diego, USA, 1969-70; Assistant Physician, Assistant Physician-in-chief, Third Department of Medicine, University of Helsinki, 1971-75; Associate Professor of Medicine,

Department of Medicine, 1975-78; Director, Professor, National Public Health Institute of Finland, 1978-. *Memberships:* Secretary & Treasurer, Scandinavian Society for Atherosclerosis Research, 1977-79; Vice-President, European Society for Clinical Investigation, 1979; President, Finnish Society for Internal Medicine, 1981-83. *Publications:* 150 publications on medical biochemistry, metabolism, internal medicine, nutrition, public health. *Honour:* Jacob Poulsen Award, 1985. *Address:* National Public Health Institute, Mannerheimintie 166, 00280 Helsinki, Finland.

HUUSKONEN, Matti Sakari, b 20 Dec 1945, Sonkajarvi, Finland. Chief Medical Officer. m. Pirkko-Liisa Anneli Nyman, 1 May 1969, Helsinki, Finland, 1 son, 3 daughters. *Education:* BM 1967, MD 1969, Doctor Degree 1979. University of Helsinki; MSc Physiology 1980, School of Public Health Harvard University; *Appointments:* Plant Physician, Nokia Company Limited, 1972-73; Occupational Health Physician, Lauttasaari Reseach Centre, 1973-74; Associate Physician 1974-77, Consultant in Occupational Medicine 1978-83, Institute of Occupational Health, Helsinki; Acting Chief Physician of the Health Centre Department of the Medical Council of Finland, 1977; Medical Director, Finnish Farmers Meat Marketing Association, Helsinki, 1981-; Chief Medical Officer, Uusimaa Regional Institute of Occupational Health, Helsinki, 1983-. *Memberships Include:* Finnish Medical Association, Finnish Occupational Health Association; New York Academy of Sciences; American College of Chest Physicians; International Commission on Occupational Health; Occupational Medical Association. *Publications Include:* Various articles on occupational lung diseases, espeically of asbestosis and silicosis, of wollastonite, and of lung diseases in tobacco workers, 1976-; Articles on muscle tendon disorders of the upper extremeties in repetitive work, 1983-. *Hobbies:* Sport; Nature. *Address:* Kotitontuntie 17 D, 02200 Espoo, Finland.

HUXLEY, Hugh Esmor, b. 25 Feb. 1924, Birkenhead, England. Research Scientist; Joint Head, Structural Studies Division/Deputy Director, MRC Laboratory of Molecular Biology. m. Frances Fripp, 12 Feb. 1966, Concord, Massachusetts, USA, 1 daughter, 3 step-children. *Education:* BA, 1st Class Honours 1948, MA 1950, PhD (ScD) 1964), Christ's College, Cambridge University. *Appointments include:* Postdoctoral Fellow, Commonwealth Fund, Biology Department, Massachusetts Institute of Technology, USA, 1952-54; Scientific Staff, medical Research Council (MRC), 1954-, including External MRC Staff & Research Associate, University College, London, 1956-62. *Memberships include:* Council, Royal Society, 1973-75, 1984-85; President's Advisory Board, Rosenstiel Basic Medical Sciences Centre, Brandeis University, USA, 1971-77; Scientific Advisory Council, European Molecular Biology Laboratory, 1975-; Instrumentation Policy Planning Committee, ibid, 1981; etc. *Publications include:* Articles in scientific journals, on molecular structure & function of biological systems, especially muscle. *Honours include:* Member, Order of British Empire

(MBE), military, 1948; Fellow, Royal Society, 1960; Feldberg Prize, experimental medical research, 1963; Hardy Prize, Biological research, 1965; Louisa Gross Horwitz Prize, 1971; Feltrinelli International Prize, Medicine, 1975; Royal Medal, Royal Society of London, 1977; E.B. Wilson Award, American Society for Cell Biology, 1983; Numerous honorary degrees, memberships of overseas societies. *Hobbies:* Skiing; Sailing. *Address:* MRC Laboratory of Molecular Biology, Hills Road, Cambridge CB2 2QH, England.

HYLES, Rudolph Samson Patrick, b. 15 Mar 1945, Trinidad. Family Physician. m. Dianne Clare Prevatt, 5 July 1969, Port-of-Spain, Trinidad, 1 son 2 daughters. *Education:* MD, Dalhousie University, Halifax, Nova Scotia. *Appointments:* Family Physician (Private Practice) 1972-; Active Staff 1972-, Chairman, Education Committee, 1976-78, Member, Medical Staff Executive, 1981-83, President of Medical Staff, 1983, Member, Board of Governors, Chairman, Credentials Committee 1982-83, Oakville Trafalgar Memorial Hospital. *Memberships:* Canadian Medical Association; Ontario Medical Association; College of Family Physicians of Canada. *Address:* 1758 Wedmore Way, Mississauga, Ontario, Canada L5J 2J9.

HYMAN, Edward Sidney, b. 22 Jan. 1925, New Orleans, Louisiana, USA. Private Practice of Medicine; Independent Research. m. Jean Simons, 29 Sep. 1956, 1 son, 3 daughters. *Education:* BS, Louisiana State University, 1944; MD, The Johns Hopkins Medical School, 1946. *Appointments:* Intern, Barnes Hospital, St. Louis, 1946-47; Sterling Fellow in Medicine, Stanford Medical School, 1949-50; Assistant Resident in Medicine, Stanford Hospital, 1950-51; Assistant Resident in Medicine, Peter Bent Bringham Hospital, Boston, 1951-53; Teaching Fellow in Medicine, Harvard Medical School, 1952-53; Director, Kidney Unit, Charity Hospital, New Orleans, 1953-55; Investigator, Touro Research Institute, New Orleans, 1959-; Senior Active Staff, Internal Medicine, Touro Infirmary; Chief of Staff, Sara Mayo Hospital, New Orleans; Consultant, Water Quality (Sewerage and Water Board) City of New Orleans, 1978. *Memberships:* Fellow, American College of Physicians; American Federation for Clinical Research; American Society for Artificial Internal Organs; Biophysical Society, Membrane Subgroup, Chairman, Local Arrangements, 1971, 77, 81, 87; American Physiological Society, Renal Subgroup; American Society for Microbiology; AAAS. *Publications:* Contributor of articles and papers to professional journals including: 'Acquired Iron-Deficiency Anaemia Due to Impaired Iron Transport', 'The Lancet', Jan. 1983; 'Acquired Iron-Deficinecy Anaemia caused by an Antibody Against the Transferrin Receptor', NEJM', July 1984. *Honours include:* Research Advisory Committee, Cancer Association of New Orleans, 1976-; Research Advisory Committee, Louisiana State Board of Regents, 1983-. *Address:* 3525 Prytania Street, Suite 220, New Orleans, LA 70115, USA.

I

IADAROLA, Vincent, b. 20 July 1957, Framingham, Massachusetts, USA. Assistant Director of Area Chiropractic Centre. m. Rosemary Ann Morris, 7 Aug. 1983, Milford, Massachusetts. *Education:* Medical Technology, Northeastern University, 1975-77; Doctor of Chiropractic cum laude, Palmer College of Chiropractic. *Appointments:* Associate Doctor, Milford Area Chiropractic Center, 1982-83; Chiropractor, Egg Harbor City Chiropractic Center, 1983; Assistant Director, Area Chiropractic Center, Schaumberg, Illinois. *Memberships:* American Chiropractic Association; Palmer College of Chiropractic Alumni Association; Council on Roentgeology to American Chiropractic Association; Mass Chiro Association; New Jersey Chiro Association. *Honours:* Northeastern University Milford Community Scholarship, 1975; National Powerlifting Referee Certified, 1981. *Hobbies:* Weightlifting; Swimming. *Address:* 2250 Hassell Road, Hoffman Estates, IL 60195, USA.

IBE, Ibe Onuka. b. 23 Sep. 1945, Nigeria, West Africa. University Professor. m. Afocha Ngozi, 30 Mar. 1975, Nigeria, 1 son, 3 daughters. *Education:* Diploma Electrical Engineering, Yaba College of Technology, Lagos, Nigeria, 1963; MB, BS, University of Ibadan, Nigeria, 1973; Diploma, American Board of Psychiatry and Neurology. *Appointments:* Residency in Psychiatry, University of Missouri, USA, 1977-80, Instructor in Psychiatry, 1980-82, Assistant Professor of Psychiatry, 1982-present, Assistant Director, Consultation Liaison Psychiatry, 1983-present. *Memberships:* American Medical Association; American Psychiatric Association; Eastern Missouri Psychiatric Society; Psychosomatic Society of America. *Publication:* contributions to the 'American Journal of Psychiatry' include: 'Schizophrenia to Manic Depression: Mutation of Mis-diagnosis', June, 1980 (with J.L. Barton); 'Diagnosing Schizophrenia with DSM III', September, 1981 (with J.L. Barton); contributions to the 'Journal of the American Medical Association: 'Differentiations of Delirium from Dementia', 1983; 'Causes of Impotence', 1983. *Hobbies:* Lawn Tennis; Dancing. *Address:* Department of Psychiatry, St. Louis University, 1221 South Grand, St. Louis, MO 63104, USA.

IBRAHIM, Saad Ahmed, b. 10 Oct. 1931, Khartoum, Sudan. Professor of Medical Biochemistry. m. Douria Musa, 3 July 1958, Khartoum, 3 sons, 2 daughters. *Education:* DSKM, Khartoum; PhD, Guy's Hospital Medical School, London, England; MRCP, London. *Appointments:* Head, Biochemistry Department, 1966; Director, Board for Postgraduate Medical Studies, 1976; Dean, Faculty of Medicine, 1977. *Memberships:* Biochemical Society, England; International Society of Toxinology, Geneva; Royal College of Physicians. *Publications:* 'Haemoglobinopathies'; 'Red-Cell Anomalies'; 'Inborn Errors of Metabolism'; 'Toxicology of Scorpion and Snake Venoms'. *Hobbies:* Fishing; Hunting; Classical Music; Ballet. *Address:* Department of Biochemistry, Faculty of Medicine, PO Box 102, Khartoum, Sudan.

IDICULLA, Anne A, b. 30 Jan. 1944, India. Director, Amputee Service/Assistant University Professor. widowed, 2 sons, 1 daughter. *Education:* MBBS, 1967, MD, Internal Medicine, 1972, Punjab University, India; Diplomat of American Boards of Physical Medicine and Rehabilitation, 1979. *Appointments:* Lecturer, Department of Internal Medicine, Christian Medical College, Ludhiana, Punjab, India; 1971-72; Assistant Clinical Professor, Temple University, Philadelphia, USA, 1978-; Attending Physiatrist Moss Rehabilitation Hospital, Philadelphia, 1978-. *Memberships:* American Medical Association; Academic Physiatrist Association of America; American Women's Medical Association; American Academy of Physical Medicine and Rehabilitation; American Congress of Physical Medicine and Rehabilitation. *Publication:* "Psychology for Living" 1985. *Address:* Moss Rehabilitation Hospital, 12th and Tabor Road, Philadelphia, PA 19161, USA.

IDZOREK, Scott, b. 11 Mar. 1944, Iowa, USA. Psychiatrist. m. Nancy Henkel, 7 June 1969, Dallas, Texas, 1 son, 1 daughter. *Education:* BA, University of Dallas, Texas, 1965; MD, University of Texas Medical School, 1969; Diplomate, National Board of Medical Examiners; Diplomate, American Board of Psychiatry and Neurology in Psychiatry. *Appointments:* Internship, Maricopa County General Hospital; General Medical Officer, US Air Force, 1970-72; Psychiatry Residency, University of Texas Health Science Centre, San Antonio, Texas, 1972-75; Staff Psychiatrist, Arizona Health Plan, 1975-80; Private Practice in Psychiatry, 1980-. *Memberships:* American Psychiatric Association. *Publications:* 'A Functional Classification of Hypochrondriasis with Specific Recommendations for Treatment', 1975; 'Antiparkinsonian Agents and Fluphenazine Decanoate', 1976; 'A Practical Approach to Hypochrondriasis', 1977; 'The Evolution of Psychiatric Services in a Health Maintenance Organization', (with T E Bittker), 1978. *Hobbies:* Jogging; Tennis. *Address:* 7125 East Lincoln Drive, Suite 206, Scottsdale, AZ 85253, USA.

IFFY, Leslie, b. 17 May 1925, Budapest, Hungary. Professor, Obstetrics & Gynaecology; Director, Maternal-Fetal Medicine. m. Maureen B. Deeney, 8 Dec. 1962, London. *Education:* MD, Budapest; LRCP & S, Edinburgh; LRFPS Glasgow; Fellow, American College of Obstetricians & Gynaecologists; Fellow, Royal College of Surgeons, Canada; Diplomate: American College of Obstetricians & Gynaecologists, Royal College of Surgeons of Canada, American College of Obstetricians & Gynaecologists. *Appointments:* Assistant Professor, Obstetrics & Gynaecology, Temple University School of Medicine; Associate Professor, Obstetrics & Gynaecology, University of Illinois School of Medicine, Chicago; Director, Obstetrics & Gynaecology, Episcopal Hospital, Philadelphia. *Memberships:* Central Association of Obstetricians & Gynaecologists; Royal College of Medicine, London; Chicago Gynaecological Society; American College of Legal Medicine, etc. *Publications:* "Perinatology Case Studies, Garden City, New York", co-author, 1978; "Principles and Practice of Obstetrics & Perinatology", co-author, 1981; "Operative Perinatology", co-author, 1984; etc. *Honours:* Dr. Robert Jardine Research Prize, Glasgow, 1962. *Hobbies:* Chess; Travel; Music. *Address:* Room F247, University Hospital, 100 Bergen Street, Newark, NJ 07103, USA.

IGHODARO, Irene Elisabeth Beatrice, b. 16 May 1916, Freetown, Sierra Leone. Private Medical practitioner; Consultant, WHO Consultant, Maternity & Child Health. m. Samuel Osarogie Ighodaro, 25 Jan. 1947, Newcastle upon Tyne, England, 3 sons, 1 daughter. *Education:* MBBS, Durham, 1944; Fellow, Medical Council in General Practice, Nigeria. *Appointments:* House Surgeon, Royal Victoria Infirmary, 1944-45; General Practice, Newcastle-on-Tyne, 1945-46; House Surgeon, Royal Sussex Hospital, Brighton, 1946; Private Practice, East Croydon, 1948; Private Practice, Benin City, Nigeria, 1950-52, Ibadan, Nigeria, 1952-68; Benin City, Nigeria, 1968-; First Chairman, Management Board, University of Benin, Teaching Hospital, 1971-75. *Memberships:* British Medical Association; Trustee, Nigerian Medical Association; Medical Womens Association of Nigeria; etc. *Publications:* "Baby's First Year", 1966; "Earth the Village of Our Times", series of 6 lectures on Nigerian National Broadcasting, 1976; various other lectures & articles in professional journals. *Honours:* MBE, 1958. *Hobbies:* Reading; Writing; Gardening; Music; People in General. *Address:* PO Box 499, Osama, 33 Boundary Road, G.R.A., Benin City, Bendel State, Nigeria.

IGNACIO, Lourdes Ladrido, b. 5 Nov. 1939, The Philippines. Professor in Psychiatry. m. Antonio B Ignacio, 7 Juen 1964, Iloilo, Philippines (deceased), 2 sons, 2 daughters. *Education:* MD, University of the Philippines. *Appointments:* Staff Consultant Psychiatrist Manila Electric Company; Medical Center, Manila; Chairman, Department of Psychiatry, College of Medicine, University of the Philippines; Chief Investigator, WHO Collaborative Study, Strategies for Mental Health Care. Founding President, Philippine Psychiatric Association; Former and Vice-President, Philippine Mental Health Association and World Federation for Mental Health; Member, American Psychiatric Association; Royal Australian and New Zealand College of Psychiatry. *Publications:* Co-Editor: "Today's Priorities in Mental Health", 1982; Co-author: "Knowledge and Attitudes of Primary Health Care Personnel on Mental Health Problems", 'American Journal of Public Health', 1983; Co-author: 'Research Screening Instruments as Tools in Training Primary Health Worker for Mental Health", Tropical and Geog. Medicine, 1983. *Hobby:* Swimming. *Address:* Department of Psychiatry, College of Medicine, University of the Philippines, 547 P.Gil Street, Manila, Philippines.

IHLENFELD, Charles L., b. 31 July 1937, Wheeling, West Virginia, USA. Assistant Professor of Clinical Psychiatry. *Education:* AB, Princeton University, Princeton, New Jersey, 1959; MD, New York University, 1963. *Appointments:* Clinical Instructor, Psychiatry, Columbia University College of Physicians and Surgeons, New York City, 1979-; Assistant Professor, Clinical Psychiatry, SUNY-Stony Brook, Stony Brook, New York, 1984-. *Memberships:* American Psychiatric Association; Harry Benjamin International Gender Dysphoria Association, Inc. *Publications:* 'Thoughts on the Treatment of Transsexuals' in 'Journal of Contemporary Psychotherapy' 1973. *Address:* 222 Manor Place, Greenport, NY 11944, USA.

IKEJIANI, Okechukwu, b. 19 Dec. 1922, Nigeria. Pathologist-in-Chief and Director of Laboratories. m. Patricia Duncan Remi, 4 sons, 6 daughters. *Education:* BSc, University of New Brunswick, Canada; MSc, University of Chicago, Illinois, USA: MD, Unviersity of Toronto, Canada; DSc, Lincoln University, Pennsylvania, USA. Fellow: Royal College of Pathology; West African College of Physicians; FMCPath; RM(CCM). *Appointments:* Demonstrator, Department of Pathology, University of Ibadan, Nigeria; Director, National Clinic, Nigeria; Pathologist and Director of Laboratories, Railway Medical Centre, Nigeria; Pro-Chancellor and Chairman of Council, University of Ibadan; Medical Director, Pfizer Products, Nigeria; currently, Pathologist in-Chief, Director of Laboratories, Gace Bay Community and General Hospitals, Nova Scotia, Canada. *Memberships:* New York Academy of sciences; British and Canadian Medical Associations; Canadian Association of Medical Microbiologists; Canadian College of Microbiologists; Canadian Association of Pathologists. *Publications:* "Nigerian Education", 1964; "Nklemdilim", 1975; contributor to journals including 'Journal of Parasitology', 'West African Medical Journal', 'Nova Scotia Medical Bulletin' and 'West African Journal Boil. Medicine'. *Honours:* CON, Commander of the Order of the Niger, Nigeria. *Hobby:* Writing. *Address:* Department of Laboratory Medicine and Pathology, Glace Bay General Hospital, Glace Bay, Nova Scotia, Canada.

IKIC, Drago, b. 2 July 1917, Foĉa, Yugoslavia. Institute Director. m. Smiuljka (deceased), 10 May 1948, Zagreb, Yugoslavia, 1 daughter. *Education:* Diploma, Medical Faculty, Hygiene and Social Medicine, Bacteriology, Virology, Parasitology and Immunology; ScD Immunology. *Appointments:* Director, Institute for Control and Research of Vaccines, Serovaccinal Institute, Institute of Immunology, Institute for Research and Standardization of Immunological Substances of the Yugoslavian Academy of Science and Arts, Zagreb, Yugoslavia. *Memberships include:* Full Member, Yugoslav Academy of Sciences and Arts; Foreign Member, Academy of Medical Sciences of the USSR; Various appointments, World Health Organisation; British Royal Society of Medicine; New York Academy of Sciences; All-union Scientific Society of Microbiologists and Epidemiologist. *Publications include:* 'The safety of human diploid cell strains for man', 1968; "Attenuation of characterization of Edmonston-Zagreb measles virus',. 1972; 'Application of human leucocyte interferon in patients with urinary bladder papillomatosis, breast cancer and melanoma', 1981; As Editor: "Clinical Use of Interferon", 1975; "Stability and Effectiveness of Measles, Poliomyelitis, and Pertussis Vaccines", 1976. *Honours:* Ruder Boskovic Prize, 1972; Life Achievement Prize, 1980. **Address:** Institute for Research and Standardization of Immunologic Substances, Demetrova 18/II, 41000 Zagreb, Yugoslavia.

ILBERY, Peter Leslie Thomas, b. 20 Mar. 1923, Perth, Australia. Consultant. m. Marianne Boyer, 8 May 1951, Sydney, 2 sons, 2 daughters. *Education:* MB., BS, 1952, MD, 1960, University of Sydney; Diploma, Medical Radiology (Therapy), Royal College of Physicians & Surgeons. *Appointments:* Honorary Radiotherapist, Royal Prince Alfred Hospital, Sydney, 1963-74; Honorary Chemotherapist, The Women's Hospital, Sydney, 1964-74; Associate Professor, Radiobiology, University of Sydney, 1970-74; Medical Director, Cancer Institute, Melbourne, 1975-78; Assistant Director General, Health, Canberra, 1979-. *Memberships:* Australian Medical Association; Fellow, Royal Australasian College of Radiologists; Fellow, Royal Australasian College of Phgysicians; European Oncological Society. *Publications:* 100 scientific articles on tumour biology. *Honours:* Cancer Council Award to MRC Radiobiological Research Unit, Harwell, 1956; Rockefeller Award to Middlesex Hospital, London, 1961; Phillips Award to ABC Hiroshima, 1969. *Hobbies:* Sailing; Farming. *Address:* 93 Hawkesbury Crescent, Farrer, ACT 2607, Australia.

ILIAS, Wilfried Karl, b. 10 Mar. 1947, Güssing. Attending Anaesthesiologist, University of Vienna, Austria, m. Egger Isolde Amalie, 20 July 1974, Bolzano, 2 sons. *Education:* MD. *Appointments:* Residency, Attending Anaesthesiologist, University of Vienna; Visiting Professor, Texas Technical University, El Paso, USA. *Memberships:* Austrian Society of Anaesthesiology; Austrian Society for Artificial Organs; Biomaterials and Medical Replacement Devices; Interdisciplinary Centre of Research & Development in the field of Intensive Care Medicine; American Society of Anaesthesiologists; American Society of Regional Anesthesia; American Physiological Scoiety. *Publications:* 56 articles, 1977-. *Hobbies:* Skiing; Ice Hockey; Swimming; Climbing; Music. *Address:* 1 Lammgasse 1/12a, A1080 Vienna, Austria.

ILIOPOULOS, John, b. 7 July 1944, Greece. Assistant Professor of Surgery. *Education:* MD; Board Certified in General Surgery; Fellow in Vascular Surgery, University of Kansas, USA. *Appointments:* Attending Surgeon, Veterans Administration Medical Center, Kansas City, Missouri, 1981-;

Attending Surgeon, University of Kansas Medical Center, Kansas City, Kansas, 1982-. *Memberships:* American Medical Association; American Association for Academic Surgery; Southwestern Surgical Society; Kansas City Surgical Society; American Society for Laser in Medicine and Surgery; American College of Surgeons; Sigma Chi. *Publications include:* As co-author: 'Trnasmesocolic amentoplasty: A technique for abdominal aortic graft coverage', 1983; 'Aortoiliac reconstruction combined with nonvascular operations', 1983; 'Renal microembolization syndrome' (RMS): A cause for renal dysfunction after abdominal aortic reconstruction', 1983; 'Trends in reconstruction for atherosclerotic renal vascular disease', 1984; 'Incidence of recurrent stenosis following carotid endarterectormy determined by digitalized subtraction angiography', 1984; 'Subtotal parathyroidectomy for secondary hyperparathyroidism', 1984; 'The effect of biliary decompression on morbidity and mortality in pancreatoduodenectomy', 1984. *Hobbies:* Bicycling; Swimming; Photography. *Address:* University of Kansas Medical Center, 39th Street and Rainbow Boulevard, Kansas City, KS 66103, USA.

ILLMAN, Arnold M., b. 1 Jan. 1934, Boston, Massachusetts, USA. Orthopaedic Surgeon. m. Lois Illman, 2 daughters. *Education:* AB, Harvard College, Cambridge, Mass., 1955; MD, Boston University School of Medicine, 1960. *Appointments:* Attending Staff, Brunswick General Hospital, Amityville, NY; Active Staff, Mid Island Hospital, Bethpage, NY; Courtesy Staff, Central General Hospital, Plainview, NY; Attending Staff, South Oaks Hospital, Amityville, NY; Attending Teaching Staff, Paediatric Orthopedic Division, Nassau County Medical Center, East Meadow, NY; Associate Professor Orthopedic Surgery, Stony Brook Medical School. *Memberships:* Fellowship, American College of Surgeons; International College of Surgeons; American Academy of Orthopedic Surgeons; American Academy of Compensation Medicine; American Medical Association; NY State Society of Orthopedic Surgeons; Founding Member, International Arthroscopic Society; North American Arthroscopic Society' Nassau County Medical Society; Nassau Surgical Society; World Medical Assoc.; Eastern Orthopedic Assoc.; American College of Sports Medicine; Member, National Strength and Conditioning Assoc. *Publications:* (Articles) 'Equipment/Sports Med.', 1983; 'Common Shoulder Injuries', 1983; 'Sports Medicine', 1983. *Hobbies:* Scuba Diving; Tennis; Photography. *Address:* 4180 Sunrise Highway, Massapequa, NY 11758, USA.

ILLSLEY, Raymond, b. 6 July 1919, Derbyshire, England. Professorial Fellow; Project Leader. m. Jean Mary Harrison, 5 June 1948, Oxford, 2 sons, 1 daughter. *Education:* BA, University of Oxford, 1947; PhD, 1956, University of Aberdeen; DSc. *Appointments:* Director, MRC, Medical Sociology Unit, Aberdeen, 1964-83; Professor of Sociology, 1964-73, Professor of Medical Sociology, University of Aberdeen, 1973-83. *Memberships:* European Society of Medical Sociologists; Society for Social Medicine. *Publications:* "Professional or Public Health", 1980; "Low Birth Weight", (with R.G. Mitchell), 1984; "Individual Choice and Enabling Structures", (with R. Taylor), 1985. *Honours:* Commander of British Empire, 1980; DSc., Honoris Causa, University of Hull, 1984. *Hobby:* Rough Husbandry. *Address:* School of Humanties and Social Sciences, University of Bath, Claverton Down, Bath BA2 7AY, England.

IMBESI, Antonio, b. 1 Apr. 1912, Scilla, Italy. Director, Pharmaco-Biological Dept., Dean, Pharmacy, University of Messina. m. Maria Giuliano, 14 Sep. 1946. *Education:* Diploma in Farmacia, 1932; Laurea Chimica, 1933; Laurea Farmacia, 1937; Laurea Medicina e Chirurgia, 1942. *Appointments:* Assistant, Chemistry, 1932, Lecturer, Pharmacology, 1935, Professor, Pharmacognosy, 1960, Professor, Pharmacology & Pharmacognosy, 1963, Director, Institute Pharmacology & Pharmacognosy, 1963, Director, Specialisation School of Pharmacognosy, 1963, Dean, Pharmacy, 1968-, Director, Pharmaco-Biological dept., 1981-82;, University of Messina. *Memberships:* Italian Society Pharmacognosy, President; Pharmaceutical Society Latin mediterraneo, President; National Academy of Sciences of the XL, Rome; Italian Association Pharmacy biologists; Medical Academy, Rome; American Society Pharmacognosy; Greek Pharmaceutical Society; New York Academy of Sciences. *Publications:* "Index Plantarum quae in omnium populorum pharmacopoeis sunt adhuc receptae", 1964; 150 scientific articles in professional journals. *Honours:* Gold Medal, Ministry of Education, 1972; Canals Medal, services to the Pharmaceutical Society Latin Mediterraneo. *Hobbies:* Research on History & Legends of Messina's Straits (Scilla and Cariddi). *Address:* Pharmaco-Biological Dept., University of Messina, Villaggio Annunziata, 98010 Messina, Italy.

IMBODEN, John Baskerville, b. 17 Sep. 1925, USA. Associate Professor, Psychiatry, Johns Hopkins University, USA; Psychiatrist-in-Chief, Sinai Hospital, Baltimore. m. Anne Grimes, 21 June 1969, 1 son, 1 daughter. *Education:* MD, Johns Hopkins University. *Memberships:* American Psychoanalytic Association; American Psychiatric Association. *Publications:* "Practical Psychiatry in Medicine", co-author, 1978; Section Editor, "Psychiatry in Principles & Practice of Medicine", 1984. *Honour:* Sigma Xi. *Address:* 111 West Lake Ave., Baltimore, MD 21210, USA.

IMSANDE, Marcus Edward, b. 8 July 1954, Dearborn, Michigan, USA. Doctor of Chiropractic. m. Patricia Ann Fragner, 5 May 1984, 1 daughter. *Education:* Certificate in Disability & Impairment Evaluation; Certified & Registered as Disability Evaluation Physician; Certified, Master of Personnel Management & Motivation; Certification in Roetgenology, Practical Clinical Laboratory Diagnosis, Physiotherapy. *Appointment:* Successful private practice leading to the establishment of Health Care Centre in Dearborn, Michigan. *Memberships:* American Chiropractic Association; Michigan State Chiropractic Association; National Association of Disability Evaluation Physicians; Council on Roentgenology; Chamber of Commerce. *Publications:* 'Amyotropic Lateral Sclerois: A Professioanl thesis to patient diagnosis, treatment 5 management'; 'Common Neurological Manifestations'. *Hobbies:* Competitive Athletics; Reading; Travel. *Address:* 2119 Monroe, Dearborn, MI 48124, USA.

INDRISO, Andrew Charles, b. 20 Sep. 1952, Philadelphia, Pennsylvania, USA. Chiropractic Physician. m. Frances Lafferty, 26 July 1981, 1 son, 2 daughters. *Education:* Pre-medical Studies, Camden County Community College, Blackwood, New Jersey, 1970-72; Medical Laboratory Technologist, Our Lady of Lourdes Hospital, Camden, 12972; Cardiac Catheterization Surgery Assistant, Thomas Jefferson Hospital, Philadelphia, Pennsylvania, 1973; DC, Pennsylvania Chiropractic College, 1980; Certificate of Honours, 1978; Diplomate, Pennsylvania State Board of Chiropractic Examiners, 19980. Various Post-Graduate study courses. *Appointment:* Chiropractic Physician, Philadelphia. *Memberships:* American and International Chiropractic Academic Standards Association; Parker Chiropractic Research Foundation; Foundation for Chiropractic Education and Research; Greater Philadelphia Chamber of

Commerce; Philadelphia Jaycees; Charter Contributor National Cystic Fibrosis Foundation; Peoples Medical Society; Student Referral Counsellor, Pennsylvania Chiropractic College. *Honours:* Award for Roetgenology Internship, 1980; Award for Clinic Internship, 1980; Honour Award, Pennsylvania Chiropractic College, 1980; President, Pennsylvania Chiropractic College of Alumni Association. *Hobbies:* Baseball; Golf; Travel; Basketball; Spending time with family. *Address:* 1426 Spruce Street, Philadelphia, PA 19102, USA.

INGALL, Michael Alexander, b. 8 July 1940, Boston, Massachusetts, USA. Psychiatrist. m. Carol Krepon, 18 June 1961, Boston, 1 son, 1 daughter. *Education:* BA, Harvard College, 1961; MD, Chicago Medical School, 1966; Internship, University Hospital, Boston, 1966-67; Psychiatric Residency, Boston University Medical Center, 1967-68, 1970-72; Fellowship, Child Psychiatry, ibid, 1971-72. *Appointments:* Medical Director, Providence Mental Health Centre, Rhode Island, 1972-84; Clinical Associate Professor of Psychiatry, Brown University Medical School, 1980-; Chief, Department of Psychiatry, Rhode Island Group Health Association, Warwick, Rhode Island, 1984-. *Memberships:* Fellow, American Psychiatric Association; American Group Psychotherapy Association; Rhode Island Medical Society; Physicians for Social Responsibility. *Publications:* Several publications in medical literature. *Honours:* Alpha Omega Alpha, 1966; Roche Award, 1966; Alumni Association Award, 1966. *Address:* 150 Upton Avenue, Providence, RI 02906, USA.

INGLE, Ronald Ferguson, b. 8 May 1927, Tsingtao, China. Lecturer, Medical University of Southern Africa. m. Pauline Marshall, 13 Feb. 1960, All Saints. *Education:* MA; MB,BChir (Cantab), 1952. *Appointments:* Medical officer, RAF Butterworth, Malaya, 1953-55; Surgical officer, RAF Hospital, Ely, UK, 1955-57; Medical Officer, All Saints Mission Hospital, Transkei, South Africa, 1958-60, Medical Superintendent, ibid, 1960-76; Chief Medical Officer, Primary Health Care, Department of Health, Republic of Transkei, 1977-80; Director, Medical Services, ibid, 1980-81; Head, Professional Services, ibid, 1981-82. *Memberships:* Transkei & Ciskei Research Society; SA National Council for Health Education, 1977-82; British Medical Association; South African Medical Association; Transkei & Ciskei Association of Mission Hospitals, 1964-76; Consultative Committee, SA Medical Missions, 1970-76. *Publications:* 'Modern doctors, old-fashioned tubverculosis & the community', 1980, 'Childhood mortality rates, infant feeding & use of health services in rural Transkei', 1984, both in 'South African Medical Journal'. *Honour:* Noristan Prize, best contribution by general practitioner, Southern African medical journal, 1980. *Hobbies:* Reading; Music; Wildlife; Travel. *Address:* 678 Punctata Street, Pretoria North, Republic of South Africa 0182.

INMAN, Frank Pope, b. 2 Aug. 1937, Amlet, North Carolina, USA. Professor and Chairman of Biochemistry. m. Barbara Jean Bullock, 30 Aug. 1959, North Carolina, 1 son, 1 daughter. *Education:* AB, University of North Carolina 1959, PhD, 1964; Post Doctoral Fellow, University of Illinois, 1964-66; MA, Harvard Medical School, 1976. *Appointments:* Assistant Professor of Microbiology and Biochemistry, University of Georgia, USA, 1966-70, Associate Professor, 1970-75, Professor, 1975-77; Professor and Chairman, Department of Biochemistry, Quillen-Dishner College of Medicine, East Tennessee State University, 1977-; Division of Clinical Nutrition, 1985-. *Memberships:* American Association of Immunologists; American Society of Biological Chemists; American Society of Microbiology; American Chemical Society; Association of Medical School Departments of Biochemistry; New York Academy of Sciences. *Publications include:* Over 50 articles, book chapters and abstracts; co-editor of 6 books including "Contemporary Topics in Immunochemistry", volume 1, 1972; "Contemporary Topics in Molecular Immunology," volumes 4, 7, 8, 9, and 10, 1975-85. *Honours include:* John M. Morehead Scholarship, University of North Carolina, 1955-59; M.G. Michael Award for Research, University of Georgia, 1969; AAI Travel Award for Second International Congress in Immunology, England, 1974; American Cancer Society Scholar, 1976; Personalities of America, 1979 and 1983; Personalities of the South, 1983. *Hobbies:* Photography; Landscape Design; Architecture. *Address:* Department of Biochemistry, Quillen-Disher College of Medicine, East Tennessee University, Johnson City, TN 37614, USA.

INMAN, William Howard Wallace, b. 1 Aug. 1929, Surrey, England. Research Unit Director. m. June Halfpenny, 21 July 1962, Macclesfield, 3 daughters. *Education;* MA, MB, B Chir, University of Cambridge; FRCP; FFCM. *Appointments:* Various Clinical posts at Addenbrooke's Hosptial, Cambridge; Medical Advisor, Pharmaceuticals Division, Imperial Chemical Industries Limited, -1964; Principal Medical Officer, Committee on Safety of Drugs -1971. Medicines-1980; Director, Drug Surveillance Research Unit, Southampton, 1980-; Professor, Pharmaco-Epidemiology, University of Southampton, 1985. *Memberships include:* British Medical Association. *Publications include:* Editor, 'Monitoring for Drug Safety'; Over 100 papers on Drug Epidemiology, Adverse Reactions to Drugs, Safety of Oral Contraceptives, and related topics. *Honours:* First Chair in Pharmaco-Epidemiology in World, 1985. *Hobbies:* Fly-fishing, Gardening. *Address:* Southcroft House, Botley, Hampshire S03 2BX, England.

INNIS, Michael Derrick, b. 8 July 1919, Delhi, India. Consultant Haematologist, Repatriation General Hospital, Brisbane, Australia. m. Elizabeth Osborne, 28 Jan. 1944, 2 sons, 1 daughter. *Education:* MBBS (Madras); DTM & H (Liverpool); FRC Path; FRCPA. *Appointments:* Indian Army medical Corps; Registrar, Pathology, Royal Infirmary, Doncaster, England; Assistant Pathologist, Adelaide Childrens Hospital, Australia; Consultant Haematologist, Princess Alexandra Hospital, Brisbane; Consultant Haematologist, Repatriation General Hospital. *Memberships:* Royal Society of Medicine. *Publications:* "Oncogenesis and Poliomyelitis Vaccine", 'Nature', 1968; "Heredity and Oncogensis in Childhood", 1971, "Hereditary Theory of Childhood Oncogenesis", 1972, 'Oncology'. *Honours:* Blacklock Golf Medal, University of Madras, 1942. *Hobbies:* Sailing; Short Story Writing; Acupuncture. *Address:* 11 Trudgian Street, Sunnybank 4109, Brisbane, Australia.

INNS, Harry Douglas Ellis, b. 4 June 1922, Ontario, Canada. Doctor of Optometry, Private Practice & Industry Consultant. 1 son, 1 daughter. *Education:* University of Toronto, 1946-48; Graduate, Optometry, Ontario College Optometry, 1950; D.Optometry, 1958. *Memberships include:* Canadian Association of Optometrists; Ontario Association of Optometrists; Canadian Society of Safety Engineering; Canadian Public Health Association; American Society of Contact Lens Specialists; American Optometric Association; American Association for the Advancement of Science; Better Vision Institute, USA; National Eye Research Foundation; etc. *Publications:* Articles in 'Canadian Journal of Optometry'; 'Contacto'; 'Contact Lens Forum'; 'American Academy of Optometry'; 'Societe D'Optometrie, D'Europe Journal'; 'International Contact Lens Clinic'; 'Optical Index', 1985; etc.; Lectures include: International Society of Contact Lens Specialists Congress, England 1980, Israel, 1981; Heart of American Contact Lens

Congress, Kansas City; etc. Inventor, Inns Extension Disc to extend the range of the Keratometer. *Honours:* Education Programme Award, 1976, Contact Lens Programme Award, 1978, Contact Lens Programme Award 1978; International Lecture Award, 1979; Appreciation Award, 1980; Distinguished Service Award, 1981, Ontario Association of Optometrists; Recipient, numerous other honours and awards. *Hobby:* Captain 78th Fraser Highlanders. *Address:* 36 King George Road, Brantford, Ontario N3R 5K1, Canada.

INSALL, John Nevil, b. 19 June 1930, Bournemouth, England. Professor of Orthopaedic Surgery. m. Mary Insall, 1 son, 1 daughter. *Education:* Sherborne School, 1943-48; BA, MB, BCh, University of Cambridge, England, 1950-53; MD, London Hospital Medical School, 1953-56; London Royal College of Physicians; Member, Royal College of Surgeons, 1956; Diplomate, American Board of Orthopaedic Surgery, 1968; House Surgeon, St Bartholomew's Hospital, Rochester, Kent, 1957; House Physician, 1957, Casualty Officer, 1958, Royal Free Hospital, London; Junior Assistant Resident, General Surgery, 1958-59, Assistant Resident, Orthopaedic Surgery, 1959-60, Royal Victoria Hospital, Montreal, Canada, Resident, Orthopaedics, Shriners Hospital for Crippled Children, Montreal, Canada, 1960-61. *Appointments:* Fellow, Orthopaedics, Hospital for Special Surgery, New York, 1961-62; Senior House Officer, Royal National Orthopaedic Hospital, London, England. 1962-63; Registrar, Orthopaedics, Bristol Royal Infirmary, Winford Orthopaedic Hospital, Bristol, England, 1963-64; Attending Orhtopaedic Surgeon, Chief, Knee Service, Hospital for Special Surgery & New York Hospital, 1965-; Professor of Orthopaedic Surgery, Cornell University Medical College, New York. *Memberships:* American Orthopaedic Association; American Academy of Orthopaedic Surgeons; International Society of the Knee; SICOT; New York Academy of Medicine; President, The Knee Society; Honorary Member, Virginia Orthopaedic Society; Corresponding Member, Argentine Orthopaedic Association; Colombian Society of Orthopaedic Surgery. *Publications:* "Surgery of the Knee", 1984; Over 100 articles in orthopaedic journals, mainly on knee surgery. *Hobbies:* Art; Golf. *Address:* 535 East 70th Street, New York, NY 10021, USA.

INTAGLIETTA, Marcos, b. 10 Aug. 1935, Buenos Aires. Professor. *Education:* BS, University of California at Berkeley, 1957; MA 1958, PhD 1964, California Institute of Technology; Research Fellow, Los Angeles County Heart Association, 1964-66. *Appointments:* Assistant Professor 1966-71, Associate Professor 1971-76, Professor 1976-. *Memberships:* Microcirculatory Society; American Physiological Society; Bioengineering Society; International Institute for Microcirculation. *Honours:* Hoffman La Roche Fellow, 1974; Swedish Medical Council Award, 1976; Humboldt Award, 1983; Abbott Distinguished Lecturer, 1985; Honorary Professor, Chinese Academy of Medical Sciences, Beijing, China, 1984. *Address:* University of California at San Diego M-005, La Jolla, CA 92093, USA.

IONESCU-STOIAN, Stefan Petre, b. 14 Jan. 1909, Petresti, Romania. Emeritus Professor. m. Micaela Ghitescu, 18 Apr, 1966, Bucharest, 1 son. *Education:* B.Pharm, PhD, Bucharest. *Appointments:* Assistant Lecturer, Faculty of Pharmacy, Bucharest, 1937-48; Lecturer, Faculty of Pharmacy, Cluj, 1948-56; Professor, Faculty of Pharmacy, Bucharest, 1956-76; Director, State Institute for Drug Control & Pharmaceutical Research, 1956-76; President, Romanian Pharmacopoeia Committee, 1958-76; President, Drug Commission, 1960-73; WHO Expert, from 1969-; President, National Commission for Drugs & Drug Monitoring, 1973-76. *Memberships:* Academy of Medical Sciences, Romania; Illinois

State Academy of Science; Corresponding Member, Academy of Pharmacy, Paris, France; Royal Academy of Pharmacy, Spain; President, Pharmaceutical Society of Romania. *Publications:* More than 140 works in various Romanian & foreign journals. *Honours:* Honorary Member, Polish Pharmaceutical Society, 1971; Romanian Orders, Military Merit 3rd Class, 1954, 1st Class 1959; Sanitary Merit 2nd Class, 1963; Scientific Merit 3rd Class 1966, 2nd Class 1971. *Hobby:* Trout Fishing in Mountain Rivers. *Address:* Str. Cobalcescu 50, R-70768 Bucharest, Romania.

IPPOLITO, Ferdinando, b. 3 Dec. 1919, Rome, Italy. Director, Dermatologic Institute of St. Gallicano, Rome. m. Spezzano Giulia, 24 Aug. 1940, 1 son. *Education:* MD; Dermatologist. *Appointment:* Professor of Allergic and Occupational Dermatology, Dermatologic Clinic, University of Rome Medical School. *Memberships:* Secretary, Italian Society of Dermatology and Venereology; Member Correspondant de la Société Francaise de Dermatologie. *Publications:* Several articles especially in the fields of occupational skin disease and thermagraphy in dermatology. *Hobbies:* Swimming; Hunting. *Address:* Istituto Dermatologico S. Gallicano, Via S. Gallicano 25/A, 00153 Rome, Italy.

IRANI, Katie D., b. 18 Aug. 1933, Bombay, India. Assistant Professor, Physical Medicine & Rehabilitation, Baylor College of Medicine, USA. m. Dinshaw K. Irani, 15 Oct. 1961, Bombay, India, 1 son, 1 daughter. *Education:* MB.BS, University of Bombay, 1957. *Appointments:* Chief, Physical Medicine and Rehabilitation, Ben Taub General Hospital, Houston, Texas, 1974-; Director, Inpatient Rehabilitation Service, Physical Medicine and Rehabilitation, Methodist Hospital, Houston, USA, 1980-81; Private General Medicine, Bombay, 1963-66, 1967-69; Assistant Medical Officer, Public Health, Bombay Municipal Corporation, 1958-62. *Memberships include:* American Academy of Physical Medicine & Rehabilitation; American Medical Association; Texas, Hariss County Medcial Associations; Houston Physical Medicine and Rehabilitation Society; American Association of Academic Psychiatrists; etc. *Honours:* American Medical Association Physician's Recognition Award, 1982. *Hobbies:* Social Work; Swimming. *Address:* Ben Taub General Hospital, Physical Medicine and Rehabilitation, 1502 Taub Loop, Houston, TX 77030, USA.

IRONSIDE, Wallace, b. 31 July 1917, People's Republic of China. Emeritus Professor, Consultant in Psychomatic Medicine. m. Vera June Ironside, 8 Jan 1942, Aberdeen, Scotland, 2 daughters. *Education;* MD, ChB, MD, Aberdeen University; DPM (RCP, RCS). *Appointments:* Registrar, Aberdeen Royal Infirmary, Chrichton Royal Institution; Senior Lecturer, Leeds University, England, University of Otago, New Zealand; Assistant Professor, University of Rochester, New YORK, USA; Foundation Professor of Psychological Medicine, University of Otago, New Zealand, Monash University, Australia. *Memberships:* Australian Medical Association; Fellow, American Psychiatric Association; American Psychosomatic Society; Foundation Fellow, Royal College of Psychiatrists; Foundation Fellow, President 1972-73, Royal Australian and New Zealand College of Psychiatrists; Fellow, Royal Australian and New Zealand College of Psychiatrists; President 1975-80, Victorian Association of Psychotherapists. *Publications:* 50 articles in various psychiatric and medical journals. *Honour:* Mentioned in despatches, Major, Royal Army Medical Corps, 1943. *Address:* 93 Leopold Street, South Yarra, Victoria 3141, Australia.

IRVINE, Allan Turner, b. 20 Oct. 1953, Surrey, England. Senior Registrar in Diagnostic Radiology. *Education:* MB, BS, University College Hospital Medical School, 1972-77; Member, Royal College of Physicians, 1980; DMRD, Royal College of Radiologists 1985; Fellow, Royal College of Radiologists. *Appointments:* House Physician, St Pancras Hospital, London, 1977-78; House Surgeon, George Eliot Hospital, Nuneaton, England, 1978; Medical Resident, 1978-79, Neurology Resident, 1979-80, Victoria General Hospital, Dalhousie University, Halifax, Nova Scotia, Canada; Medical Registrar, Wycombe General Hospital, High Wycombe, Buckinghamshire, England, 1980-81; Senior House Officer, National Hospital for Nervous Diseases, London, 1981-82; Registrar, 1982-84, Senior Registrar, 1984-, Diagnostic Radiology, St Mary's Hospital, London. *Memberships:* British Medical Association; Collegiate Member, Royal College of Physicians (London); Fellow, Royal College of Radiologists. *Publications:* (with A Coral) "Multiple Choice Tutor: Radiological Anatomy, Physics & Techniques", 1985; 'Treatment of Fisher's Variant of Guillain Barre syndrome by exhange transfusion' (with J Tibbles) in 'Canadian Journal of Neurological Science', 1981. *Hobbies:* Tennis; Squash; Collecting old medical instruments; Croquet. *Address:* 283 Waldegrave Road, Strawberry Hill, Twickenham, Middlesex, TW1 4SU, England.

IRVINE, Donald Hamilton, b. 2 June 1935, Newcastle upon Tyne, England. Principal in General Practice; University Regional Adviser in General Practice, 2 sons, 1 daughter. *Education:* MB BS Dunelm; MD, Newcastle;' FRCGP; D Obst RCOG. *Appointments:* House Physician, Royal Victoria Infirmary, Newcastle, 1958-60; Senior House Officer in Obstetrics, Queen Elizabeth Hospital, Gateshead, 1960; Currently: Principal in General Practice, Ashington; Regional Adviser in General Practice, University of Newcastle upon Tyne. *Membershisp:* Fellow, Royal College of General Practitioners; Fellow, British Medical Associaiton; General Medical Council; ASME, *Publications:* 'BMA Planning Unit Survey of General Practice', (co-author), 1967; "The Future General Practitioner; Learning and Teaching", (co-author), 1972; 'The Quiet Revolution', 1975; 'Quality of Care in General Practice: Education Development and Evaluative Research in Northern Region', (co-author). *Honour:* OBE, 1979. *Hobbies:* Bird watching; Motor cars; Photography. *Address:* 'Redesdale', Wansbeck Road, Ashington,. Northumberland, England.

IRWIN, Michael Henry Knox, b. 5 June 1931, London, England. Medical Director, United Nations, UN Development Programme, UNICEF. m. Frederica Todd Harlow, 9 Apr. 1983, New York, 3 daughters by previous marriage. *Education:* MB, BS, St Bartholomew's Hospital, London University, 1955; MPH, Columbia University, New York, 1960. *Appointments:* UN Medical Service, New York, 1957-61; Deputy Resident Represenative, UN Development Programme, Pakistan, 1961-63; UN Medical Service, New York, 1963-73; UN Medical Director, 1969-73; Director of Personnel, UN Development Programme, New York, 1973-76; UNICEF Representative in Bangladesh, 1977-80; Senior Adviser, UNICEF, New York, 1980-82; Medical Director of UN, 1982-. *Memberships:* Fellow, Royal Society of Medicine, 1982-; Consultant, American Association of Blood Banks, 1984-; Member, Board of Governers, American Acadmey of Compensation Medicine, 1984-. *Publications:* "Check-Ups: Safeguarding Your Health", 1962; "Overweight: A Problem for Millions", 1964; "Travelling without Tears", 1966; "What do we know about Allergies?", 1972; "Aspirin: Current Knowledge About an Old Medication", 1983; "Can We Survive Nuclear War?", 1984; "The Cocaine Epidemic", 9185. *Honour:* Officer Cross, International Federation of Blood Donor Organisations, 1984. *Hobbies:* Travel; Cycling; Writing. *Address:* United Nations, New York, NY 10017, USA.

ISA, Nessim Naguib, b. 22 June 1935, Egypt. Obstetrician and Gynaecologist. m. Laraine Walsh, 1 Dec. 1962, Blackburn, England, 2 sons, 1 daughter. *Education:* MB, B Ch, Cairo University, Egypt, 1959; Diploma in Obstetrics and Gynaecology, Ain-Shams University, Cairo, 1964; RACS, QRCS, McGill University, Royal Victoria Hospital, Montreal, Canada, 1970. *Appointments:* Assistant Professor, Medical Faculty, Dalhousie University, Halifax, Nova Scotia, Canada; Obstetrician and Gynaecologist, Regional Hospital and 'St Joseph's Hospital, Saint John, New Brunswick; Director: Division of Gynaecological Oncology, Colposcopy Clinic, Saint John Regional Hospital, Saint John, New Brunswick. *Memberships Include:* Canadian Medical Association; Royal College of Surgeons of Canada; Fellow, American college of Obstetricians and Gynaecologists; President, Atalantic Society of Obstetricians and Gynaecologists; American Society for Laser Medicine and Surgery. *Publications:* 'Correlations of Abnormal Pap Smear with Histological Diagnosis', 1977; 'Use of Antibiotics in Gynaecology', 1978; 'Management of Vulvar, Vaginal and Cervical Condylomata Acuminta', 1979; 'Diagnosis and Management of Premature Labour', 1979; 'Collposcopy and Cryosurgery', 1983; 'Management of Abnormal Pap Smear, Treatment of Premalignant Disease of the Cervix', 1983; 'Problems and Managment of Menopause', 1986. *Hobbies:* Photographay; Gardening; Fishing; Reading; Travelling. *Address:* 45 Park Lawn Court, Saint John, NB B2K 2B7, Canada.

ISAACSON, Keith Geoffrey, b. 25 Oct. 1935, Woolwich, London, England. Consultant Orthodontist. m. J R Townsend, 26 Mar. 1966, London, 1 son, 1 daughter. *Education:* Postgraduate Orthodontic Training, Royal Dental Hospital; DOrth RCS, England; Postgraduate Oral Surgery Training, The London Hospital; FDS RCS, England. *Appointments:* Senior House Officer, Hospital for Sick Children, Great Ormond Street, London; Registrar in Oral Surgery, The London Dental Hospital; Registrar in Orthodontics-Senior Registrar, Royal Dental Hospital; Currently Consultant Orthodontist, Oxford Regional Health Authority; Adviser to Faculty of Dental Surgery 1981-, Examiner 1983-, Member of Orthodontic Standards Working Party 1983-, Royal College of Surgeons. *Memberships:* British Dental Association; Council member, British Society for the Study of Orthodontics, 1982-; British Association of Oral and Maxillo Facial Surgeons; American Association of Orthodontists. *Publications:* "An Introduction to Fixed Appliances", 3rd edition 1984; "Orthodontic Treatment With Removable Appliances", 2nd edition 1980; 'Overbit and facial height', 1970; 'Construction of Harvold', 1983; 'Orthodontic techniques' in "General Dental Practice", 2nd edition 1985; 'The modified harvold activator', 1984. *Address:* Royal Berkshire Hospital, London Road, Reading, Berkshire, England.

ISHIZAKA, Kimishige, b. 3 Dec. 1925, Tokyo, Japan. University Professor. m. Teruko Matsuura, 4 Dec. 1949, Tokyo, 1 son. *Educaiton:* MD, University of Tokyo School of Medicine; PhD Immunology, University of Tokyo. *Appointments include:* Research Member, National Institues of Health, Tokyo, 1950-53; Chief, Department of Serology, Division of Immunoserology, Tokyo, 1953-62; Research fellow in Immunochemistry, California Institute of Technology, California, USA, 1957-59; Chief, Department of Immunology, Children's Asthma Research Institute and Hospital, Denver, Colorado, 1962-70; Assistant Professor 1962-65,

Associate Professor 1965-70; University of Colorado Medical School, Denver; Wellcome Visiting Professorship in Basic Medical Sciences, 1977-78; Research fellow in Immunology 1959, School of Hygiene and Public Health, Professor of Biology in Faculty of Arts and Science 1970-, O'Neill Professor of Medicine and Microbiology 1970-81, O'Neill Professor of Immunology and Medicine 1981-, Director of Subdepartment of Immunology 1981-, School of Medicine, John Hopkins University, Baltimore, Maryland. *Memberships:* American Association of Immunologists; American Academy of Allergy; American Association for the Advancement of Science; Society for Experimental Biology and Medicine; Japanese Society of Allergy; Société Française d'allergie; American Society for Experimental Pathology; Collegium Internationale Allegologicum; Fellow, American Academy of Arts and Sciences; Foreign Associate, National Academy of Sciences. *Publications include:* Nearly 300 papers and chapters in books; "Biological role of Immunoglobulin E System", (co-editor and contributor), 1972I; Editor or co-editor of several journals including: 'Clinical Immunology and Immunopathology', 'Immunopharmacolgoy', 'Journal of Clincial Immunology'. *Honours include:* Passano Foundation Award, USA, 1972; Emperor's Award, Japan, 1974; American College of Physicians Award for Achievement in Medical Sciences, 1985. *Address:* 4 North Good Samaritan Hospital, 5601 Loch Raven Boulevard, Baltimore, MD 21239, USA.

ISLAM, Nurul, b. 1 Apr. 1928, Chittagong. Director, Professor, Medicine, IPGMR; Chairman, Bangladesh Medical Research Council. m. Anwara Islam, 26 Dec. 1962, Chittagong, 1 son, 2 daughters. *Education:* MB.Call; TDD Wales; FCPS.Pk; FRCP.Ed.; FRCP. London; FCCP, USA. *Appointments:* Lecturer, medicine, Dhaka Medical School; Physician-in-Charge, TB Ward, Mitford Hospital; Associate Professor, medicine, Dhaka Medical College; Professor, Medicine, Chittagong Medical College; Nuffield Fellow, Royal Free Hospital; Joint Director, Professor of Medicine, Institute of Postgraduate Medicine & Research, Dhaka; Director, Professor, medicine, Institute of Postgraduate Medicine & Research, Dhaka, Physician to the Founding Father of Bangladesh, Sheikh Miyibar Rahman. *Memberships:* President, Bangladesh Association for Advancement of Medical Sciences; Chairman, Standing Recognition Committee, Bangladesh Medical & Dental Council; Chairman, Faculty of Medical Sciences, Bangladesh College of Physicians & Surgeons; Vice Chairman, Academic Council, Birdem; Councillor, Bangladesh Academy of Sciences; Diabetic Association of Bangladesh; etc. *Publications:* Over 90 scientific papers indexed in 'Index Medicus'; Author, 9 books including: "A Simplified Tuberculosis Control Programme for East Pakistan", 1983; "Tropical Eosinophilia", 1964; "Symposium on Medicine", 1969; "Essentials of Medical Treatment", 1974; "Shyastha Shambande Kichu Khata", 1978; "History of IPGMR", 1978; "Medical Diagnosis and Treatment", 1978, 2nd edtion 1980 53rd edition 1986; "Prescriptions", 1984, second edition, 1985; Essential Drugs in Village Practice, 1986. *Honours:* President's gold medal, Pakistan TB Association, 1963; Sitara-E-Imtiaz (SI) Highest National Academic Distinction, 1970; Gold Medal, Meritorius Services, Chittagong Association, Dhaka, 1979, Academy of Sciences Gold Medal, 1982. *Hobbies:* Travel Abroad; Reading; Writing. *Address:* Gulmeher, 63 Central Road, Dhanmondi R.A. Dhaka 5, Bangladesh.

ISMADI, Muryanto, b. 10 Oct. 1927, Yogyakarta, Indonesia. Professor of Medical Biochemistry. m. Siti Dawiesah M.D., 1 Dec. 1955, Yogyakarta, Indonesia, 2 sons, 2 daughters. *Education:* MD, 1958, PhD, 1976, Gadjah Mada University, Yogyakarta, Indonesia. *Appointments:* Instructor in Biochemistry, 1952-55, Assistant in Biochemistry, 1956-60; Lecturer in Biochemistry, 1961-66; Associate Professor in Biochemistry, 1967-76; Professor of Biochemistry, 1977-, Gadjah Mada University, Yogyakarta, Indonesia. *Memberships:* The Indonesian Association of Physicians; The Indonesian Biochemistry Association; The Federation of Asian and Oceanian Biochemists. *Publications:* "The Effect that Sonchus Arvensis Linn leaves on the dissolution of Urinary Stones" bulletin 1967; "A Study of Calculogenesis with special reference to the Biochemical Properties of Urine" dissertation, 1976. *Honour:* Satyalancana Karya Satya tingkat II 1980. *Hobbies:* Music; Sport. *Address:* Faculty of Graduate Studies, Universitas Gadjah Mada, Yogyakarta, Indonesia.

ISMAIL, Rusdi, b. 21 July 1939, Western Sumatra, Indonesia. Head, Pediatrics, School of Medicine. m. Samsinar, 11 Sep. 1965, Simabur, Indonesia, 1 son, 2 daughters. *Education:* MD, School of Medicine, 1965, Pediatrician, 1969, School of Medicine, University of Indonesia; Dioploma, WHO/Unicef Course, Senior Teachers of Child Health, Institute of Child Health, University of London, England, 1977. *Appointments:* Assistant Lecturer, Child Health, University of Indonesia, 1964-69; Director, Jayapura General Hospital, Irian Jaya, 1969-71; Senior Lecturer, Child Health, 1972-, Head, Pediatrics, Palembang General Hosptial, 1980-, School of Medicine, Sriwijaya Unvierisyt. *Memberships:* Indonesian Pediatric Association; International College of Pediatrics. *Hobbies:* Tennis; Bridge. *Address:* Kompleks R.S.U. No. 22, J1. Madang, Palembang, Indonesia.

ITO, Ryuta, b. 4 Mar. 1922, Hiroshima, Japan. Professor of Pharmacology. m. Ryuriko, 17 Mar. 1957, 1 son, 1 daughter. *Education:* MD, Doctor of Medical Sciences, Faculty of Medicine, University of Tokyo; Research Fellow, Department of Pharmacology, Cornell University Medical College, USA. *Appointments:* Instructor, University of Tokyo, Japan; Fellow, Iatrochemical Institute of Pharmacological Foundation; Research Fellow, Cornell University; Associate Professor, Department of Pharmacology, School of Medicine, Toho University, Tokyo, Japan. *Memberships:* Japanese Pharmacological Society; Japanese Society of Allergology; International College of Paediatricians; World Medical Association. *Publications:* "Introduction to Experimental Sciences", 1961; "Some Aspects of Pharmacodynamics", 1974; "Developmental Pharmacology", 1978; "Clinical Pharmacology and Therapeutics", 1980; "Japan Medical Terminology";", 1975; "Animal Models for New Drug Detection", 1985. *Honours:* Music Concours, Japan, 1950 and 1957; Riker International Fellowship, Pharmacology section, International Union of Physiological Sciences, 1961; Niwa Prize, Japanese Centre of Scientific Information, 1969; 19th, 24th Festival of Arts, Japan. *Hobbies:* Composition of music; Conducting. *Address:* Department of Pharmacology, Toho University School of Medicine, Omori Nishi 5-21-16, Ota-ku, Tokyo 143, Japan.

ITTI, Roland, b. 31 Oct. 1940, Mulhouse, France. Professor, Biophysics. m. Heitz Eliane, 7 Aug. 1964, Illzach, 2 sons, 1 daughter. *Education:* PhD, University of Strasbourg, 1966; MD, University of Tours, 1978. *Appointments:* Professor Biophysics, University of Tours; Chief, Nuclear Medicine & Ultrasounds, University Hospital, Tours. *Memberships:* Fench and European Societies of Nuclear Medicine; Society of Nuclear Medicine, USA; Society of Magnetic Resonance in Medicine, USA. *Publications:* "Les explorations cardiovasculaires", 1980; "Gamma-Cardio 82", 1982; 150 articles in professional journals. *Address:* Chateau De Noire, 37500 Chinon, France.

ITTKIN, Paul, b. 28 Sept. 1908, Montreal, Canada. Senior Attending Staff Consultant. m. Edith Charlap Nobleman, 28 Oct. 1967, Montreal, Canada, 2 sons. *Education:* BSC; Md; CM; Diploma AB of O; Certification FRCS (C); CPS., Quebec, Canada; Fellow, AAO – Hns. AAFPRS: ACS. *Appointments:* Rotating Internship, Reddy Memorial Hospital, 1933-34, Resident, 1934-35; General Practice, 1935-46; Attending Staff St. Joseph & Lutheran Hospital, North Dakota, USA: Basic Science in OTL University of Illinois, USA, 1946-47; Senior Resident, 1948-49, Clinical Assistant OTL R.M.H. 1952-54; Junior Assistant, OTL, J.G.H.; 1954-55; Assistant, TOL, 1R.M.H., 1955-58; Clinical Assistant, OTL, J.G.J. 1958-62, Assistant, OTL, 1962-67, Associate, OTL, 1967-71, Chief, OTI, 1971-73, Attending Staff, 1973-85, Senior Attending Staff, 1985-. *Memberships:* AAO: HNS: ACS: AAFPRS: COS - HNS: AOPQ; CMA; AMA; QMA; MCA; ND; SMS; ISMS. *Publications:* 'Penicillen and Syphilis of the Ear' in 'EENT', 1951; 'Studies of Syphilis of the Ear ad Penicillne' in 'A.J. of M.S.', 1953; 'Foreign Body Embedded in Retropharyngeal Space' in 'A of ORL' 1961. *Honours:* Med. - Chi Soc - Sec of OTL (Pres 1969-71); Sec. Treas., 1957-65, Vice Pres. 1965-69. *Hobbies:* Music; Golf. *Address:* Ellendale Medical Building, Suite 535, 5845 Cote des Neiges Road, Montreal, Quebec, Canada H3S 1Z4.

IWA, Takashi, b. 7 Dec. 1925, Nagano, Japan. Professor; Chairman. m. Kazue Kabayashi, 17 May 1952, 1 son, 1 daughter. *Education:* MD; PhD, Surgery. *Appointments:* Assistant Professor, Thoracic & Cardiovascular Surgery, Sapporo Medical College; Instructor, Surgery, University of Illinois College of Medicine, USA; Associate Professor, Professor, Chairman, Surgery (1), Kanazawa University School of Medicine. *Memberships:* American College of Surgeons; Society of Thoracic Surgeons; American College of Chest Physicians; International Cardiovascular Society; International Association for Lung Cancer; International Society for Artificial Organs; International College of Surgeons; Societe Internationale de Chirurgie; Pan-Pacific Surgical Association; Association of Thoracic and Cardiovascular Surgeons of Asia. *Publications:* 650 medical articles. *Address:* Dept. of srugery (1), Kanazawa University School for Medicine, Takara-machi 13-1, Kanazawa, Japan 920.

IWARSON, Sten Axel, b. 28 Apr. 1940, Sweden. Professor of Infectious Diseases, University of Gothenburg. m. Birgitta Rennerfelt, 1969, 2 sons, 2 daughters. *Education:* MD; PhD. *Appointment:* Currently, Director, Department of Infectious Diseases, Ostra Hospital, Gothenburg. *Memberships:* Swedish Medical Association; European Association Study of the Liver, etc. *Publications:* About 200 scientific papers in the medical field (infectious dieseases) and one major textbook. *Hobbies:* Sailing; Chairman of Swedish Triss-jolle Association. *Address:* Department of Infectious Diseases, Östra Hospital, S-41685 Gothenburg, Sweden.

IVERSEN, Leslie Lars, b. 31 Oct. 1937. Executive Director, Merck, Sharp & Dohme Neuroscience Research Centre, Harlow, Essex, England. m. Susan Diana Kibble, 1 son, 2 daughters (1 deceased). *Education;* BA, Biochemistry, PhD, Pahrmacology, Trinity College, Cambridge; Harkness Fellow, USA; Fellow, Trinity College, Cambridge. *Appointments:* With Dr J. Axelrod, National Institute of Mental Health, and Dr. E. Kravitz, Dept. of Neurobiology, Harvard Medical School, 1964-66; Locke Research fellow, Royal Society, Dept. of Pharmacology, University of Cambridge, 1967-71; Director, MRC Neurochemical Pharmacology Unit, Cambridge, 1971-82. *Memberships:* Associate, Neurosciences Research Programme; Fellow, Royal Society. *Publications:* "The Uptake and Storage of Noradrenaline in Sympathetic Nerves", 1967; "Behavioural Pharmacology", with S.D. Iversen, 1975, 2nd Edition 1981; numerous scientific articles in professional journals. *Hobbies:* Reading; Gardening. *Address:* Merck, Sharp & Dohme Neuroscience Research Centre, Terlings Park, Eastwick Road, Near Harlow, Essex CM20 2QR, England.

IYER, Prema Venkatraman, b. 17 May 1942, Bombay, India. Senior Specialist Pathologist, Tissue Pathology, IMVS; Clinical Lecturer, Pathology, University of Adelaide, Australia. m. Dr V.S. Iyer, 22 Oct. 1965, Bombay, 1 son, 1 daughter. *Education:* MBBS; FRCPA. *Memberships:* International Society of Gynaecological Pathologists; Australian Dematopathology Society; Australian Society for Colposcopy & Cervical Pathology; Royal Australian College of Ophthalmologists, Associate Member, Fellow of the Royal College of Pahtologists of Australasia; International Academy of Pathology. *Address:* Division of Tissue Pathology, Institute of Medical & Veterinary Science, Adelaide, South Australia 5000.

IZOR, Glenn Edward, b. 4 Sep. 1949, Dayton, Ohio, USA. Chiropractic Physician. m. Teresa Elaine Gilmore McNelly, 28 July 1974, Centerville, Ohio, 1 son, 1 daughter. *Education:* BS, MEd, Miami University, Oxford, Ohio: DC, Palmer College of Chiropractic, Davenport, Iowa. *Appointments:* Private practice. *Memberships:* Central Ohio Chiropractic Association (Member board of directors and past Secretary Treasurer); Ohio State Chiropractic Assocaiton (Member Board of Directors, Workers' Compensation Chairman and past Publci Relations Director); American Chiropractic Assoc.; Foundation for Chiropractic Education and Research; Palmer Colllege of Chiropractic Alumni Association. *Honours:* Leadership Award, Ohio State Chiropractic Assoc., 1983; President's Award, Ohio State Chiropractic Assoc., 1984; Forum Award, Excellence in professional Series Writing on Diet and Nutrition, 1983. *Hobbies:* Golf; Reading; Family. *Address:* Izor Chiropractic Center, 5945 Sawmill Road, Dublin, OH 43017, USA.

J

JABLONSKI, Leon Wawrzyniec, 22 Jan. 1931, Ploskie, Poland. Professor of Epidemiology. m. Miroskawa Wysocka, 5 July 1954, Lublin, 1 daughter. *Education:* Diploma of Physician, 1955, Specialisation in Internal Diseases, 1958, in Medical microbiology, 1961, in Medical epidemiology, 1974, Medical Academy of Lublin. *Appointments:* Assistant, Department of Medical Microbiology, 1955, MD Adjunct, 1962, Assistant Professor, 1967, Associate Professor, 1976, Head, Department of Epidemiology, 1978-, Dean, Faculty of Medicine, 1975-78, currently Professor, Medical Academy of Lublin. *Memberships:* Polish Society of Microbiology; Polish Society of Epidemiology and Physicians of Infectious Diseases; Polish Society of Social Medicine; various-other memberships. *Publications:* "Medical Virology", 1969, 4th edition, 1979; "Review of Medical Microbiology", 1971, 4th edition, 1986; "Clinical Virology", 1974; "Epidemiology", 1980, 3rd edition, 1985; author of some 200 professional papers. *Honours:* Cavalier's Cross, 1974, Officers Cross, 1980, Polonia Restituta; Deserving Teachaer of Polish Republic, 1983; numerous other awards. *Hobbies:* Collecting old arms; Hunting; Gardening. *Address:* Leonarda 11-55, 20-625 Lublin, Poland.

JACKS, Brian Paul, b. 23 May 1943, Canada. Associate Clinical Professor of Psychiatry. m. Brooke Ann Foland, 14 Nov. 1976, Los Angeles, USA. 1 daughter. *Education:* MD, University of Toronto, Canada, 1967; Residency, University of Southern California, 1968-72; Certified American Board of Psychiatry and Neurology, 1974; Certified American Board of Psychiatry and Neurology, Child/Adolescent, 1976. *Appointments:* Assistant Director, Child/Adolescent Psychiatric Outpatient Services, LAC/USC Medical Center, 1972-76; Ward Chief, Long-Term Intensive Adolescent Inpatient Services and Director of Residency Training for Child/Adolescent Psychiatry, 1976-79; Associate Clinical Professor of Psychiatry, University of Southern California; Full-time private practice, 1979 -; Delegate to Regional Councils of American Academy of Child Psychiatry as representative from Southern California, 1979-81; Independent Medical Examiner, State of California Department of Industrial Relations, 1981 -. *Memberships:* Past President, Southern California Society for Child Psychiatry; Past President, Southern California Society for Adolescent Psychiatry; Chairman, Child/Adolescent Psychiatry Committee, Southern California Psychiatric Society; American Psychiatric Association. *Publications:* "Overactivity in Children" Continuing Education for the Family Physician, 1974; 'Psychopathology in Children' and 'Psychopathology in Adolescence' (with S Russak) both in "Basic Psychopathology: A Programmed Text" edited by C W Johnson et al, 1975. *Honour:* Fellow, American Academy of Child Psychiatry, 1979. *Hobbies:* Travel; Art; Chess. *Address:* 435 North Bedford Drive, Penthouse West, Beverly Hills, CA 90210, USA.

JACKSON, Andrew H Junior, b. 18 Apr. 1948, LaFayette, Indiana, USA. Private Practice as Chiropractor. m. Barbara Ellen VanGeem 18 Nov. 1978, Ellisville, Missouri, 1 daughter. *Education:* Associate of Applied Science; DC, National College of Chiropractic, Lombard, Illinois, 1973; Diplomate, American Chiropractic Board of Roentgenology, 1979. *Appointments:* Resident in Roentgenology, National College of Chiropractic; Instructor in Radiology, National College of Chiropractic; Head, Department of Radiology, Logan College of Chiropractic, Chesterfield, Missouri; Private Practice with radiological consultation service, Illinois, 1979-. *Memberships:* Amercian and Southwestern Illinois Chriropractic Associations; Illinois Chiropractic Society; Council on Roentgenology and College of Roentgenology, American Chiropractic Association. *Honour:* Life Member, Delta Sigma Chi. *Hobbies:* Photography; Camping; Hiking. *Address:* 700 Carlyle Avenue, Belleville, IL 62221, USA.

JACKSON, Barry Trevor, b. 7 July 1936, London, England. Surgeon to H.M. Royal Household; Consultant Surgeon, St. Thomas' Hospital, London; Consultant Surgeon, King Edward VII Hospital for Officers, London. m. Sheila May Wood, 25 Apr. 1962, Bollington, 2 sons, 1 daughter. *Education:* King's College, London; Westminster Medical School, London; MB, BS, 1963; FRCS (Eng.), 1967; MS (London), 1972. *Appointments:* Junior Surgical Posts: St. James' Hospital, Baltham; St. Peter's Hospital, Chertsey; St. Helier Hospital, Carshalton; St. Thomas' Hospital, London. *Membershiprs:* Association of Surgeons of Great Britain and Ireland; Royal Society of Medicine; British Society of Gastroenterology; British Medical Association; British Society of Surgical Oncology; Osler Club of London. *Publications:* Numerous articles and chapters in books on surgery and surgery of the gastrointestinal tract. *Honour:* Arris and Gale Lecturer, Royal College of Surgeons of England, 1973. *Hobbies:* Reading; Book Collecting; Opera; Medical History. *Address:* St. Thomas' Hospital, London SE1 7EH, England.

JACKSON, Bernard Richard, b. 19 Apr. 1918, Atlantic City, USA. Chairman, Department of Surgery. m. 1 Oct. 1949, Cleveland, Ohio, 1 son, 1 daughter. *Education:* Wake Forest University, North Carolina, 1936-39; MD, Temple University Medical School, Philadelphia, 1943; Internship, US Naval Hospital, Philadelphia, 1943; Special Surgical Course, US Naval Hospital, Pa, 1944-45; Residency, Philadelphia General Hospital (General Surgery), 1945-46; Fellowships (General Surgery), Cleveland Clinic Foundation, 1946-47; College of Medical Evangelists, Loma Linda University, Los Angeles, California, 1954-56. *Appointments:* Private Practice, Colon & Rectal Surgery, Raleigh, North Carolina, 1947-54, Los Angeles, 1956-; Attending staff, California Hospital Medical centre, 1954-57, 1975-, Chairman, Department of Surgery, 1976-80, Chairman, Colon & Rectal Oncology, Director of Clinical Service, Southern California Cancer Centre, 1975-; Attending Staff, St Vincent Hospital Medical Centre, 1956-, Chairman, Department of Colon & Rectal Surgery, 1962-, Chairman, Tumour Board, 1972-76, Chairman, Surgical Section, 1985-, Chairman, Department of Surgery, 1986-. *Memberships include:* American Medical Association; American Society of Colon & Rectal Surgeons; Pan American Medical Society; American Radium Society; Society of Surgical Oncology (James Ewing Society); Royal Society of Medicine, England; American Endocurietherapy Society. *Publications:* Various articles in surgical journals in field. *Honorus:* Various invitations for lectures, especially in area of cancer treatment. *Address:* Medical Square Ste 3, 2206 West 3rd Street, Los Angeles, CA 90057, USA.

JACKSON, David Huntsman, b. 17 July 1937, Tuscaloosa, Alabama, USA. Physician (Cardiologist). m. Sara Elizabeth Wyatt, 12 June 1960, 2 daughters. *Education:* BS, Biology, University of Alabama, 1959; MD, Medical College of Alabama, 1963; Intern University Hospital and Hillman Clinic, Birmingham, 1963-64; Residency, Harvard Medical Services, Boston City Hospital and Thorndike Memorial Laboratory, 1967-69. *Appointments:* Instructor in Medicine, 1970-71, Assistant Professor of Medicine, 1971-74, University of Alabama School of Medicine; Staff, University of Alabama Hospitals and Clinics, 1971-74; Staff, Bessemer Carraway Hospital, 1974-76, 1983-; Staff, Brookwood Hospital, Birmingham, 1974-; Staff, South Highlands Hospital, Birmingham, 1976-; Chief of Cardiology, 1981-84, Vice-Chairman, Department of Medicine, 1984-,

Brookwood Hospital; Staff, Shelby Medical Center, Alabaster, 1984-. *Memberships include:* American Federation for Clinical Research; Alabama Heart Association, Elected to Board, 1975; American Heart Association; Fellow, Council on Clinical Cardiology, American Heart Association; Diplomate, National Board of Medical Examiners; Fellow; American College of Physicians; American College of Chest Physicians; American College of Cardiology. *Publications:* Contributor to professional journals; Invited Book Reviews; Abstracts; Presentations; Monographs; Books, etc. *Honour:* Board Certified by American Board of Internal Medicine and Cardiovascular Section of American Board of Internal Medicine. *Address:* 2022 Brookwood Medical Center Drive, Suite 510, Birmingham, AL 35209, USA.

JACKSON, Douglas, b. 5 Mar. 1918, Oldham, Lancashire, England. Emeritus Professor, University of Leeds. m. Majorie Kenyon, 15 Apr. 1944, Bury, 1 son, 2 daughters. *Education:* MDS, DDS, University of Manchester; FDS, Royal College of Surgeons. *Appointments:* Lecturer, University of Manchester, 1947-49; Lecturer, Senior Lecturer, University of Leeds, 1951-64; Chair in Children's and Preventive Dentistry, 1964-81; Honorary Consultant Dental Surgeon, 1962-81. *Memberships:* British Dental Association; British Paedodontic Association; British Association Study of Community Dentistry. *Publications:* 90 published papers on dental epidemiology and fluoridation. *Honour:* Chairman, British Fluoridation Society, 1981-. *Hobbies:* Writing; Gardening. *Address:* 5 Croft Park, Menston, Near Ilkley, West Yorkshire L529 6NA, England.

JACKSON, Edgar Basil, b. 19 June, 1932, Ireland. Medical Director. m. Elizabeth Cathcart, 1 daughter. *Education:* MB, Queen's University, Belfast, Ireland; DPM, University of Dublin, Ireland; MD, State University of New York, USA; PhD, ThD, California Graduate School of Theology; DSc, Hanyang University, South Korea; MRCP, London, England; LRCS, LRCP, Edinburgh, Scotland. *Appointments include:* Medical Director, Psychiatric Clinic, Buffalo, New York, 1963-64; Instructor in Psychiatry, Marquette School of Medicine, Milwaukee, Wisconsin, USA, 1964-69, Associate Professor, 1969-71; Associate Clinical Professor of Psychiatry, Medical College of Wisconsin (formerly Marquette School of Medicine), 1971-; Professor of Psychiatry, University of Wisconsin, 1974-; Chief of Psychiatry, Wood VA Hospital, Wisconsin-; Director of Graduate Psychiatric Education, Marquette University Medical School. *Memberships:* American Psychiatric Association; British Medical Association; American Medical Association; American Child Psychiatry Academy; American Psychosomatic Academy and many others. *Publications:* Numerous lectures, presentations, seminars, papers and columns including "All Your Anxiety"; "Why Do Kids Take Drugs?"; "Faith with Assurance", etc. Books: "Memory Loss in ECT; The Effect of Unilateral Electro-Convulsive Therapy on Verbal and Visual-Spatial Memory", 1981; "New Voices in American Poetry", 1979 and 1980. *Honours include:* Musgrave Pathology Prize, Queen's University, Belfast, 1956; Allen-Bradley Research Grants, 1967 and 1968; Citizen of the Year Award, Milwaukee, 1982, and many others. *Hobbies:* Flying; Sky Diving; Biblical Languages. *Address:* 2130 North Mayfair Road, Milwaukee, WI 53226, USA.

JACKSON, Richard Howell, b. 6 Aug. 1925, Havana, Cuba. Chief of Allergy Service; Associate Professor of Medicine; Senior Partner, Allergy Clinic. m. Bobbette Burke, 17 Mar. 1951, Lincoln, Nebraska, USA, 1 daughter. *Education:* BA, Institute of Higher Education, Havana, Cuba, 1942; MD, Havana Medical School, 1949. *Appointments:* Chief Resident, Internal Medicine Training, Baylor University Medical School, Houston, Texas, USA,

1951-53; Associate Professor, Baylor Medical School, 1954-; Chief of Medical Service, Fort Crowder US Army Hospital, Missouri, 1955-57; Chief of Allergy Clinic, Hermann Hospital, 1972-; Chairman, Pharmacy and Therapeutic Committee, Park Plaza Hospital, 1975-; currently, Associate Professor of Medicine, Univeristy of Texas Medical School and Senior Partner, Houston Allergy Clinic. *Memberships:* Fellow: American Academy of Allergy and Immunology; American College of a Allergists; American Association for Clinical Immunology and Allergy; American Association of Certified Allergists; Member of the House of Delegates of the Texas Medical Associations. *Publications:* Author of papers contributed to: 'Diseases of the Chest'; 'Industrial Medicine and Surgery'; 'Annals of Allergy'; 'Texas State Journal of Medicine'; 'Medical Record and Annals'; 'Journal of the Kansas Medical Society'. *Honours:* President: American Association for Clinical Immunology and Allergy, 1972-73; Houston Allergy Society, 1983-84. The National Registrar of Prominent American and International Notables. *Hobbies:* Music; Woodworking; Boating; Watersports. *Address:* Houston Allergy Clinic, 444 Park Plaza Professional Building, 1213 Hermann Drive, Houston, TX 77004, USA.

JACKSON, Ruth, b. 13 Dec. 1902, Greene County, Iowa, USA. Orthopaedic Surgeon. *Education:* BA, University of Texas, 1924; MD, Baylor University College of Medicine, Dallas, Texas, 1928; General Internship, Memorial Hospital, Worcester, Massachusetts, 1928-29; Internship in Orthopaedic Surgery, University Hospitals, University of Iowa, 1929-30; Resident Orthopaedic Surgeon, Memorial Hospital, Worcester, 1930-31; Resident Orthopaedic Surgeon, Texas Scottish Rite Hospital for Crippled Children, Dallas; Assistant. Carrell-Driver-Girard Clinic, Dallas, 1931-32. *Appointments:* Orthopaedic Surgery Practice, Dallas, 1932-; Chief, Orthopaedic Surgery, Parkland Memorial Hospital, Dallas, 1936-41; Clinical Instructor in Orthopaedic Surgery, Baylor University College of Medicine, Dallas, 1936-43; Presently Honorary Consulting Orthopaedic Surgeon, Baylor Medical Center, Parkland Memorial Hospital, Dallas; Assistant Clinical Professor of Orthopaedic Surgery, Southwestern Medical School, University of Texas. *Memberships Include:* American Medical Association; Texas Orthopaedic Association; Texas Rheumatism Association; Fellow, American College of Surgeons; Fellow, International College of Surgeons; American Academy of Orthopaedic Surgeons; American Association for Automotive Medicine; National Association of Disability Examiner. *Publications:* Some 30 papers, numerous lectures delivered. *Hobbies:* Fishing; Hunting; Raising Livestock (Registered Paint Horses & Cattle); Grapefruit & Oranges in Southern Texes. *Address:* 3629 Fairmount, Dallas, TX 75219, USA.

JACOB, Ruthard Josef, b. 23 Aug. 1925, Tauberbischofsheim, West-Germany. Professor. m. Paula Jacob, 29 Dec. 1956, 2 sons, 1 daughter. *Education:* MD, University of Heidelberg, 1953; Habilitation, University of Wurzburg, 1966. *Appointments:* Clinical Work, 1952-59; Certified Internist, 1967; Assistant Professor, Institute of Physiology, University of Wurzburg, 1959-68; Residential Work, Department of Physiology, University of Virginia, Charlottesville, 1969; Head of Sub-division, Cardiac Circulation Research, Department of Physiology, 1970, Head of Chair II, Institute of Physiology, 1971, Dean of the Faculty, Theoretical Medicine, Universisty Tubingen, 1976-77. *Memberships:* German Society for Heart and Circulation Research; European Section, International Society for Heart Reserach; German Physiological Society; American Physiological Society. *Publications:* "Handbook of Internal Disease, Volume I"; "Handbook of Hypertension". *Honour:* Fraenkel Prize, 1967. *Hobby:* Classical

Music. *Address:* Institute of Physiology II, University of Tübingen, Gmelinstrasse 5, D-7400 Tübingen, Federal Republic of Germany.

JACOBS, Conrad Raymond, b. 6 Sep. 1935, Newark, New Jersey, USA. Psychiatrist. m. Beverly Jacobs, 1 July 1977, Hallandale, Florida, 1 son, 2 daughters. *Education:* AB, Cornell University; MD, Medical College, NY. *Appointments:* Captain, Medical Corps, Chief Inpatient Service, Martin Army Hospital, Columbus, CA; Staff Psychiatrist, South Florida Staff Hospital. *Memberships:* AMA; Florida Medical Assoc.; American Psychiatric Assoc.; American Association for Geriatric Psychiatry. *Honours:* Alpha Epsilon Delta, 1956; Alpha Omega Alpha, 1960. *Hobbies:* Bass Fishing; Opera. *Address:* 4420 Sheridan Street, Hollywood, FL 33021, USA.

JACOBS, Douglas George, b. 25 Aug. 1945, New York, USA. Professor of Psychiatry. m. Mary Winik, 13 Apr. 1969, New York, 2 daughters. *Education:* AB, Trinity College, 1967; MD, School of Medicine, University of Pennsylvania, 1971. *Appointments:* Director, Psychiatric Emergency Services, 1975-83; Director, Continuing Education Division, 1977-85; The Cambridge Hospital; Medical Director, Metropolitan State Hospital, 1983-84; President, Professional Psychaitric Associates & Consultants; Assistant Professor of Psychiatry, Harvard Medical School. *Memberships:* Massachusetts Psychiatric Society; Examiner, American Board of Psychiatry & Neurology. *Publications:* Various articles on care and psychopharmacological management of emergency psychiatric patients. *Honour:* Founder of Continuing Education Division, Department of Psychiatry, The Cambridge Hospital. *Hobby:* Tennis. *Address:* 31 White Oak Road, Waban, MA 02168, USA.

JACOBS, Edwin Max, b. 8 Sep. 1925, San Francisco, California, USA. Associate Executive Officer. *Education:* BA, Reed College, 1950; MD, Cornell University Medical College, 1954; Intern, Resident, Fellow, Bellevue Hospital, and Memorial Sloan-Kettering, New York, 1954-60. *Appointments:* Associate Clinical professor, Medical & Radiation Science, Head, Clinical Cancer Research, University of California, San Francisco, 1960-76; Deputy Branch Chief, Clinical Investigations, National Cancer Institute, Bethesda, 1976-85; Associate Executive Officer, Northern California Oncology Group, 1985-. *Memberships:* American Medical Association; American Society Clinical Oncology; American Association Cancer Research; American Society Haematology; Society Surgical Oncology; New York Academy of Sciences; American Association for Advancement of Science; Fellow, American College of Physicians. *Publications:* Co-author, "Testicular Cancer: The Role of Adjevant Chemotherapy", 1980. *Honours:* Squibb Olin Fellowship, 1965; Visiting Physician, Royal Marsden Hospital, London, England, 1970; Special Achievement Award, National Institute of Health, Bethesda, and USA, 1983. *Hobby:* Music. *Address:* 1860 16th Ave., San Francisco, CA 94122, USA.

JACOBS, Hayman Dudley, b. 12 Apr. 1924, South Africa. Consultant Physician Cardiologist. m. Beatrice Jacobs, 12 Dec. 1948, Johannesburg, 1 son, 2 daughters. *Education:* MB, CH B 1948, MD 1953, University of Witwatersrand; MRCP 1953, FRCP 1973, Edinburgh; FRACP, Sydney, 1980. *Appointments:* Intern Professorial Unit, Johannesburg General Hospital, 1949-50; Medical Registrar 1950-52, Lecturer in Medicine 1954-56, University of Witwatersrand; Clinical Assistant, Department of Cardiology, Royal Infirmary, Edinburgh, Scotland, 1953; Assistant Registrar, National Heart Hospital Institute of Cardiology, London, England, 1953-54; Consultant Physician, Pnewmoconiosis Bureau, Johannesburg, South Africa, 1956-64; Physician in Charge, Discoverers'

Hospital, Florida, 1957-79. *Memberships:* Royal Society of Medicine of England; Australian Medical Association; Australian Society of Experimental and Clinical Pharmacologists; Cardiac Society of Australasia and New Zealand; Medical Directors Association of the Pharmaceutical Industry of Australia. *Publications:* 'Cardiac Aneurysm', 1953; :Techniques of Drug Evaluation', 1972; 'Hyperuricaemia as a risk factor in coronary heart disease: Purine metabolism in man', 1977. *Honours:* Medical Graduates Association Prize in Medicine, University of Witwatersrand, 1948; Nuffield Dominion Travelling Fellowship in Medicine, 1953. *Hobby:* Model Railroads. *Address:* 2/6 Longworth Avenue, Point Piper, 2027 New South Wales, Asutralia.

JACOBS, Leo I, b. 8 Mar. 1935, Biest, Belgium. Senior Attending Psychiatrist, Forest Hospital, Des Plaines, Illinois, USA. m. 12 July 1964, 2 daughters. *Education:* BSc, 1956; MD, 1960, Catholic University of Louvain, Belgium; Residency in Psychiatry, Illinois State Psychiatric Institute, Chicago, 1961-63; Board Certified by American Board of Psychiatry and Neurology, 1967. *Appointment:* Assistant Clinical Professor of Psychiatry, Chicago Medical School. *Memberships:* Fellow, American Psychiatric Association; Illinois Psychiatric Society. *Address:* 555 Wilson Lane, Des Plaines, IL 60016, USA.

JACOBS, Paul A., b. 25 July 1930, New York, USA. Orthopaedic Surgeon. m. Elizabeth J. Hottenstein, 30 May 1957, New York City, 4 duaghters. *Education:* BA, Syracuse University; MD, State University of New York, Downstate Medical Centre. *Appointments:* President, Milwaukee Orthopaedic Society, 1975-77; Team Physician, Milwaukee Brewer Baseball Team, 1975-; Governing Staff, Milwaukee Children's Hospital, 1977-79; President, Association of Professional Baseball Physicians; 1979-80; Associate Chief, Surgery, Mount Sinai Medical Centre, 1983-85. *Memberships:* American Academy of Orthopaedic Surgeons; Clinical Orthopaedic Society; American Orthopaedic Society for Sports Medicine; Musculoskeletal Tumor Society; Paediatric Oncology Group. *Publications:* Articles in numerous professional journals including: 'American Journal of Surgery'; 'Wisconsin Medical Journal'; 'Clinical Orthopaedics'; etc. *Address:* 1218 W. Kilbourn Avenue, Milwaukee, WI 53233, USA.

JACOBS, Roland William, b. 1 Nov. 1952, New York City, USA. Medical Director. *Education:* MD, Psychiatrist, Rutgers Medical School, UMDNJ, 1979; BA, Rutgers University, Newark, 1975. *Memberships:* AMA; APA; Society for Neuroscience; Honorary Member, British Brain Research Assoc.; European Brain and Behaviour Society. *Publications:* 'Alzheimer's dementia and reduced nicotinamide adenine dinuclcotide' (NADH) - diaphorase activity in senile plaques and the basal forebrain', 1985; 'Plague-like lesions in the basal forebrain in Alzheimer's disease', 1985; 'Histopathology of the basal forebrain and its targets in Alzheimer's disease', 1985; 'Pathology of the basal forebrain in Alzheimer's disease and other dementias', in 'Biological Substrates of Alzheimer's diseases', 1986. *Honours:* Phi Beta Kappa 1975; Bessie Dolgan Award for Outstanding Premedical Achievement, 1975. *Hobbies:* Skiing; Photography; Tennis. *Address:* 1127 Rosario Drive, Topanga, CA 90290, USA.

JACOBSEN, Ole Victor, b. 8 Feb. 1951, Farsund, Norway. General Practitioner. m. Tora Berg Jacobsen, 29 Dec. 1979, Valle, Norway, 2 sons, 1 daughter. *Education:* MD, University of Oslo, 1976. *Appointments:* District Physician, Ibestad, 1978; Neurology & Internal Medicine Practice, Oslo & Farsund, 1979-. *Memberships:* General Practitioner Dnlf, 1984-; Seaman's Doctor, 1983-. *Hobby:* Rotary International. *Address:* Kirkegt 6, 4550 Farsund,

Norway.

JACOBSON, Gary, b. 14 Sep. 1948, Brooklyn, New York, USA. Doctor of Chiropractic. m. Marsha Anhold, 14 Aug. 1983, Fort Lauderdale, Florida, USA. *Education:* BA, Brooklyn College, New York, 1971; DC, Life Chiropractic College, 1980; Diplomate, National Board of Chiropractic Examiners, 1979. *Appointments:* Instructor, Tathology & Clinic Proficieny, Life Chiropractic College, 1979-80; Guest Lecturer, Nutrition & Health, Miami area, 1981-. *Memberships:* American Chiropractic Association; Florida Chiropractic Association; American Chiropractic Association Council on Roentgenology; Life Chiropractic Alumni Association; Pi Tau Delta International Chiropractic Honor Society. *Publications:* Author of Syndicated Secience-fact articles entitled 'Beginnings', 1971-73; Computer medical software for GSR Systems Ins. 1985. *Honours:* Nocturne Magazine Short Story Award, 1971; Pi Tau Delta Award for Scholastic Excellence, 1980. *Hobbies:* Short story writing; Electronics; Computer programming. *Address:* 14737 W Dixie Hyway, Miami, FL 33181, USA.

JACOBSON, Gerald Frederick, b. 30 May 1922, Berlin, Germany. Executive Director, Didi Hirsch Community Mental Health Centre. 1 son, 2 daughters. *Education:* AB, University of California, Berkely, 1942; MD, Medicine, University of Southern California, 1951; Intern, Resident, various hospitals, 1950-54. *Appointments:* Executive Director, Didi Hirsch Community Mental Health Centre, Los Angeles Psychiatric Service, 1959; Asociate Clinical Professor, Psychiatry, University of Southern California, 1974; Associate Clinical Professor, Psychiatry, University of Southern California, 1974-; Attending Staff, Psychiatry, St John's Hospital and Health Centre, Santa Monica, 1979. *Memberships:* American Psychoanalytic Association; Southern California Psychiatric Society; Fellow, American Psychiatric Association; American Medical Association; etc. *Publications:* Numerous articles in professional journals; "The Multiple Crises of Marital Separation and Divorce", 1983. *Honours:* Phi Beta Kappa; Alpha Omega Alpha; Mental Health Award for Service to the Mentally Ill & Retarded. *Hobby:* Research. *Address:* 4760 South Sepulveda Boulevard, Culver City, CA 90230, USA.

JACOBSON, Jean Hjelte, b. 6 Feb. 1924, Honolulu, Hawaii. Mobile Unit Physical Therapist. m. Carl T. Jacobson, Senior, 2 July 1976, Coos Bay, Oregon, USA, 3 sons, 1 daughter (all by previous marriage). *Education:* BS, University of California Los Angeles; Certificate in Physical Therapy, University of Southern California. *Appointments:* Staff Physical Therapist, Indiana University Medical Center, Indianapolis; Chief Physical Therapist, Sacred Heart General Hospital, Eugene, Oregon; Staff Physical Therapist, Memorial Hospital, Salem, Oregon; Physical Therapist with Drs. Holm and Embick, Salem; Chief of Physical Therapy and Occupational Therapy, Sunshine School, Fresno, California; Mobile Physical Therapist, California Elks Organization, Fresno County, California; Part-time Physical Therapist with Carl Edd, R.P.T., North Bend, Oregon; Mobile Physical Therapist for Easter Seal Society of Oregon for Coos, Curry and Douglas Counties. *Memberships:* American Physical Therapy Association; Member, Geriatric Section of APTA; Oregon Physical Therapy Association; Licensed in Oregon and California States as R.P.T. *Hobbies:* Sports: Swimming; Horseback Riding; Walking, etc; Gardening. *Address:* 1441 N 14th Cooes Bay, OR 97429, USA.

JACOBSON, Steven A, b. 29 Oct. 1952, Brooklyn, New York, USA. Private Practitioner in Chiropractics. *Education:* BA, Florida Atlantic University; DC, Life Chiropractic College; Diplomate, National Board of Chiropractic Examiners. *Appointments:* Faculty Member, Clinic Proficiency, Technique and Pathology Laboratory, Life Chiropractic College, 1979-80; Guest CPR Lecturer, American Red Cross, Greater Miami Area, Florida, 1983-; Private Practitioner, Miami. *Memberships:* American and Florida Chiropractic Associations; Council on Physical Therapy, American Chiropractic Association; Phi Tau Delta; Past Board of Directors, Life College Alumni Association. *Honours:* Award for Scholastic Excellence, Pi Tau Delta, 1980; Student Council Award for Outstanding Service, Alumni Award for Outstanding Service, Life College. *Hobbies:* Computers; Water Skiing; Music. *Address:* 14737 West Dixie Highway, Miami, FL 33181, USA.

JACOBUS, Dwight Aubrey, b. 12 Aug. 1947, Paterson, New Jersey, USA. Chairman, Department of Orthopaedic Surgery. m. Diane Elaine Ribe, 26 May 1968, Succasunna, 2 sons, 1 daughter. *Education:* BA, Taylor University; DO, Kansas City College of Osteopathic Medicine. *Appointments:* Clinical Instructor, Orthopaedic Surgery, Ohio University; Secretary, Department of Surgery, Childrens Medical Center, Dayton, Ohio; President, Dayton District Academy of Osteopathic Medicine; currently, Chairman, Department of Orthopaedic Surgery, Grandview Hospital, Dayton. *Memberships:* American and Ohio Orthopaedic Associations; Dayton District Academy of Osteopathic Medicine; Dayton Surgical Society; Dayton Orthopaedic Society; American Osteopathic Academy of Orthopaedics; American College of Osteopathic Specialists; National Osteopathic Foundation; Academic Achievement Society. *Publications:* "Natural History of Talises Equinovqrus Deformity", 1977; 'Subtalor Extra-articular Arthrodesis in the Treatment of Progressive Calcaneal valgus deformity', 1978; 'Supracondylor Fractures of the Humerous in children-Operative Treatment', 1982; 'Subtalor dislocations without associated fractures' in 'Journal of American Osteopathic Association'; 1982. *Honours:* Academic Achievement Society; Phi Sigma Gamma. *Hobbies:* Karate; Snowmobiling; Golf; Swimming; Model ship building. *Address:* 4959 Ashwyck Place, Kettering, OH 45429, USA.

JACYSZYN, Kazimierz, b. 23 Apr. 1925, Sambor. Professor. m. 1 July 1948, 2 daughters. *Education:* University of Poznan, 1951; ScD, University of Wroclaw, 1964; PhD, Academy of Medicine, Wroclaw, 1970; Associate Professor, Academy of Medicine, 1978. *Appointments:* V Director, Epidem. Station, Ostrow Wlkp., 1952-55; Assistant, Nephrological Clinica, 1956-69, Assistant Professor, 1970-78, Associate Professor, 1978-, Toxicology, V-Director, Institute of Environment Investigation, 1975-81, Academy of Medicine, Wroclaw. *Memberships:* Polish Academy of Sciences, Committee of Human Ecology; Societe des Sciences de Wroclaw; Polish Society of Toxicology, President, Low Silesia Section; Polish Association of Biochemistry; European Society of Human Ecology. *Publications:* "Aminotranspherases in Urine", 1968; "Isoenzymes of gamma-Glutamyltrans-peptidase, Leucly Arylamidase and Lactac Dehydrogenase in Urine", 1972; Articles in professional journals. *Honour:* 1st Prize, Ministry of Health, 1966. *Hobbies:* Numismatics; Skiing. *Address:* Skibowa Str. 105, 50 322 Wroclaw, Poland.

JADHAV, Narayanarao Ambajeerao, b. 10 Aug. 1931, Davangere, Karnataka State, India. Consulting Physician. m. Dr. Kantha, 7 Sep. 1961, Mysore City, 2 sons. *Education:* MBBS, Mysore University, 1953; MRCP, 1959, FRCP, 1977 Edinburgh University, FNCCP, Delhi; FCCP, USA: FICA, USA: MNAS, New York. *Appointments:* Lecturer in Medicine, Government Medical College, University Medical College, 1955-57; Assistant Professor in Medicine, 1961-62, Reader in Medicine and Associate Professor of Medicine, 1962-72, Professor and Head of Department of Medicine, 1972 -, Government Medical College, Mysore City; Medical

Superintendent, K R Hospital, Mysore City, 1974-76; Honorary Lecturer in Neurology and Consulting Physician, All India Institute of Speech and Hearing, Mysore City, 1972-. *Memberships:* Indian Medical Association; Life Member, Association of Physicians of India; Life Member, the Cardiological Society of India; Life Member, Association of Chest Physicians of India. *Publications:* 'Studies on Oxyfedrine in Cardiac Patients' presented at Madras Symposium, 1977; About 80 Research dissertations for postgraduate medical students for MD since 1962. *Hobbies:* Music; Gardening; Philosphy. *Address:* 65 Lakshmamba Sadan, 3rd Cross, M H Road, J L Puram, Mysore-370 012, Karnataka State, India.

JAEGER, Sharon A., b. 9 Feb. 1952, Adrian, Michigan, USA. *Education:* DC, National College of Chiropractic, 1976; BS, 1975. *Appointments:* Chairman, Department, Cleveland College of Chiropractic, 1980-81. *Memberships:* American Chiropractic Assoc.; San Fernando Valley Chiro. Assoc.; Council on Roentgenology; American College of Chiropractic Roentgenologists: Delta Tau Alpha Honorary Fraternity; Honorary Member, Sigma Chi Psi Fraternity; Glendale Chapter, American Business Women's Assoc.; Former Member, Joint Commission of Education for the Chiro. Radiological Technologists. *Publications:* (Roentgen Briefs): 'Giant Cell Tumor Case Study'; 'The Many Faces of the Osteochondroma'; 'Hereditary Multiple Exostosis'; 'Aneurysmal Bone Cyst'; Short Articles for Family Physician Magazine; 'Fibrous Dysplasia', article for ACA journal, 1978; "Positioning Manual", 1980; (article) 'Stop, Look and Listen'; (Textbook), "Radiographic Postioning and Normal Anatomy and Variants", pending. *Honours:* Illinois Delegate, Outstanding Young Women in America; Outstanding Woman Graduate (NCC); Joseph Janse Outstanding Senior Award, (NCC); Outstanding New D. C. in San Fernando Valley; Woman of Year, American Business Women's Assoc. *Hobbies:* Home Decoration; Sewing. *Address:* P.O. Box 7134, Canoga Park, CA 91304, USA.

JAEN, Ruben J, b. 11 Feb. 1926, Caracas, Venezuela. Professor Cardiovascular Surgery. m. Helena Urrutia P, 8 Dec. 1949, Caracas, 2 sons, 1 daughter. *Education:* MD, Central University of Venezuela; Fellow, Cardiovascular Surgery, Baylor University, Houston, Texas, USA. *Appointments:* Chief Surgeon, Hospital Vargas, Caracas, Venezuela; Assistant Surgeon, Military Hospital, Caracas, Assistant Surgeon, Venezuelan Red Cross Hospital; Chief Cardiovascular Surgery, Ministry of Health, Venezuela; Professor and Chairman, Cardiovascular Surgery, Central University of Venezuela. *Memberships:* Miembro Honorario de las Sociedades Cardiovasculares de Brasil, Perú, Chile, Uruguay Cuba; Sociedad Venezolna de Cirugiá Cardiovascular; President Latin American chapter, Vice-President, International Society for Cardiovascular Surgery; Fellow, American College of Surgeons; Fellow, American College of Cardiology; Fellow, American Association of Thoracic Surgeons; Fellow, American College of Chest Physicians. *Publications Include:* 'Atlas de Patologia Vascular', 1964; Surgery of aneurysms of the aorta'; 'Complications of open heart surgery'; 'Aneurysms of thoracic aorta'; About 120 published papers. *Honours:* Orden Rafael Urdaneta, 1958; Orden Andres Bello, 1973; Orden Francisco de Miranda, 1975; Award Rene Fontaine, 1984. *Hobby:* Big game fishing. *Address:* Centro Medico de Caracas, San Bernardino, Caracas, Venezuela.

JAFFE, Daniel Solomon, b. 11 May 1914, New York, New York, USA. Clinical Professor. m. Caroline Raifman, 14 May 1941, Washington District of Columbia, 2 sons, 1 daughter. *Education:* BA, New York University; 1935; MD, George Washington University, 1938. *Appointments:* Interne, Queens General Hospital, New York, 1938-40; Fellow,

Neuropathology, George Washington University, Washington DC, 1940-41; Resident in Neurology, Gallinger Municipal Hospital, Washington DC, 1941-42; Resident in Psychiatry, St Elizabeths Hospital, Washington DC, 1942; Neuro Psychiatrist, Valley Forge Hospital, (Army), 1943-44; Major, Medical Corps, US Army Division Neuropsychiatrist, 97th Infantry Division, 1944-46; Private Practice, Neuro-Psychiatry and Psychoanalysis, Washington DC, 1947-. *Memberships:* DC Medical Society; American Medical Association; Washington Psychaitric Society; American Psychiatric Association; Washington Psychoanalytic Society; American Psychoanalytic Association; International Psychoanalytic Assoc. *Publications:* 'The Masculine Envy of Women's Procreative Function', 1968; 'The Mechanism of Projection', 1968; 'Forgetting and Remembering', 1970; 'The Role of Ego Modification and the Task of Structural Change in the Analysis of a case of Hysteria', 1971; 'Aggression: Instinct, Drive Behaviour', 1982; 'Some Relations Between the Negative Oedipus Complex and Aggression in the Male, 1983; 'On Words and Music: A Personal Commentary', 1983; 'Empathy, Counteridentification, Countertransference', 1986; etc. *Honours:* Clinical Essay Prize, British Psycho-analytic Society, 1970; Vicennial Medal, Georgetown University, 1966. *Honours:* Photography; Gardening; Hiking; Swimming. *Address:* 3741 Huntington Street, NW, Washington, DC 20015, USA.

JAFFE, Kenneth Marc, b. 8 Apr. 1948, New York, USA. Director, Department of Rehabilitation Medicine, Children's Orthopaedic Hospital, Seattle, Washington; Assistant Professor, Department of Rehabilitation Medicine and Paediatrics, University of Washington School of Medicine. m. Ada Shen, 27 Oct. 1973, 1 son. *Education:* BA, Tufts University, 1970; MD, Harvard Medical School, 1975; Master of Rehabilitation Medicine, University of Washington, 1982. *Appointment:* Associate Director, Department of Rehabilitation Medicine, Children's Orthopaedic Hospital, 1982-83. *Memberships:* American Academy of P.M. & R; American Congress of P.M. & R; American Academy of C.P. and Developmental Medicine; American Association of Electromyography and Electrodiagnosis; Association of Academic Psychiatrists. *Publications:* Author of numerous publications. *Address:* Children's Orthopaedic Hospital, Box C-5371, Seattle, WA 98105, USA.

JAFFE, Yoram, b. 17 Dec. 1944, Tel-Aviv, Israel. Professor of Psychology. m. Sharon, 1968, 1 son, 1 daughter. *Education:* PhD, University of California at Los Angeles, USA, 1974. *Appointments:* Department of Psychology, University of Tel-Aviv, Israel, 1974-79; Department of Psychology, Ben-Ilam University, Israel, 1979-81; Department of Psychology, UCLA, USA, 1981-83; Department of Psychology, University of Southern California, 1984-present. *Memberships:* American Psychological Association; Israel Psychological Association. *Publication:* Co-Editor, "Perspectives on Behaviour Therapy in the Eighties", 1983. *Honour:* Phi Beta Kappa, 1968. *Hobby:* Art Collection. *Address:* Department of Psychology, SGM Building, University of Southern California, University Park, Los Angeles, CA, 10089, USA.

JAGGARAO, Nattama S V, b. 19 Feb. 1946, Viskhapatnam, AP, India. Consultant Cardiologist. m. N Lakshmi, 30 July 1979, Madras, India, 1 daughter. *Education:* BSc, MBBS, Andhra University, India; DTM&H, University of Liverpool, England. *Appointments Include:* Resident Intern, Mount Sinai Medical Center, Milwalkee, USA, 1973-74; Good Samaritan Hospital, Cincinatti, USA, 1974-75; University Hospital, Saskatoon, Canada, 1975-76; Registrar, Hammersmith Hospital, London, England; British Heart Foundation Overseas Fellow, Roayl Sussex County Hospital, Brighton, England,

1980-81; Cardiologist, Visakhapatnam, India; Consultant Cardiologist, King Fahad Hospital, Al Baha, Saudia Arabia. *Memberships:* Royal College of Physicians; Fellow, American College of Chest Physicians; Fellow, International College of Angiology. *Publications Include:* 'Amiodorone increases digoxin concentration', 1981' 'Use of automatedexternal defibrillation- Pacemaker by ambulance staff', 1982; 'Defibrillation at a football staduim. An experiment with Brighton and Hove Albion', 1982; 'Effects of Amiodaroneon thyroid function', 1982. *Hobby:* Radio amateur. *Address:* 31-32-81 Daba Gardens, Visakhapatnam 530020 AP, India.

JAGODZINSKI, Zbigniew Adam, b. 24 Dec 1929, Lodz, Poland. Head of Neurotraumatologic Department, Medical Academy, Lodz. Widower. 1 daughter. *Education:* MD, 1966, PhD, 1976, Diploma of Postgraduate School of Neurosurgery, 1965. *Appointments:* Assistant, Human Physiology Department Medical Academy, Lodz, 1953-58; Adjunct and Assistant Professor in Neurosurgical Department, Medical Academy, Lodz, 1958-83; Neurosurgical Consultant, Hospital in Lask, 1966-; Head of Neurotraumatological Department, Medical Academy, 1983-. *Memberships:* Polish Neurosurgical Society; European Association of Neurosurgical Society; World Federation of Neurosurgical Societies. *Publications include:* "Neurogenic pulmonary edema, cerebral blood flow and energy metabolism in acceleration head injury" Neurol. Neurochir. Pol. 1975; "Application of laser in neurosurgery" with G F Lombard, Neurol. Neurochir. Pol. 1983. *Hobbies:* Tourism; Chess; Bridge. *Address:* Neurotraumatologic Department of Medical Academy, Maria Sklodowska-Curie's Hospital, ul. Parzeczewska 35, 95-100 Zgierz, Poland.

JAHNSEN, Tore, b. 27 Jan 1954, Ski, Norway. Researcher. *Education:* MD, Faculty of Medicine, University of Oslo, 1982; PhD, University of Oslo, 1983. *Appointments:* Internship in Surgery, Jan-July 1983, Internship in medicine, July-Dec, 1983-84, Nordland Sentralsykehus, Bod, Norway; Researcher (Oslo University) Institute of Pathology, Rikshospitalel, Oslo 1, Norway, 1983-; Research Associate, Department of Cell Biology, Baylor College of Medicine, Houston, Texas, USA, 1984-86. *Memberships:* Norwegian Endocrine Society; Norwegian Medical Association; Norwegian Society for Biochemistry; The Nordic Association for Andrology; The Endocrine Society. *Publications:* "Regulation of gonadotropin responsive adenylyl cyclases in ratetestes" Doctoral thesis, 1983. Contributor of chapters to textbooks, numerous articles in scientific journals, published abstracts and book reviews. *Honours:* Fulbright Fellowship, 1984. *Hobbies:* Tennis; Soccer. *Address:* Institute of Pathology, Rikshospitalet, Oslo 1, Norway.

JAIN, Mahasukhlal Kapurchand, b. 28 Sep. 1940. Patan, India. Honorary Associate Professor of Paediatrics. m. Maya H. Vora, 18 May 1968, Bombay, 1 son, 2 daughters. *Education:* MBBS, MD Paediatrics; DCH (London); DCH (Bombay). *Appointments:* Lady Tata Research Fellow, 1967-69; Resident Senior Medical Officer, Park Hospital, 1969-70; AlderHay Children's Hospital, England, 1970; Resident Registrar in Paediatrics, Essex County Hospital, 1970-72; Honorary Assistant Professor of Paediatrics, Seth G.S. Medical College and K.E.M. Hospital, 1972-82; Recongnized Post-graduate Teacher for MD (Ped.), of University of Bombay, 1976-. *Memberships:* Indian Academy of Pediatrics; Indian Medical Association; Nutrition Society of India; Consultants Association of India; Indian Society of Gastro-enterology; National Neonatology Forum; Staff Society and Research Society, K.E.M. Hospital, Bombay. *Publications:* Malabsorption - physiological concept, Golden Jubilee Commemoration Volume, 1978; Evaluation of Clinical Criteria in the Management of Acute

Diarrhea in Infants and Children, Indian Pediatrics, 1983; Pancreatic Enzymes in Malnouriushed Children. Proceeding of Diarrhea and Malnutriton in Children of Commeonwealth, 1984. *Honour:* Mrs I.C. Zaveri Gold Medal for standing first in D.C.H. (Bombay) Examination, 1966. *Hobbies:* Reading; Photography. *Address:* 34 S.V. Road, Suvarna Deep Building, Santacruz (W), Bombay 400 054, India.

JAIN, Rajiv, b. 23 Aug. 1949, Ambala, India. Chief, Haematology - Oncology. m. Kavita, 14 Dec. 1976, Ambala, India, 1 son, 1 daughter. *Education:* MB, BS, MP, Shah Medical College, Jamnagar, Gujarat, India, 1972; Diplomate, American Board of Internal Medicine, 1978; Diplomate in Internal Medicine, subspeciality haematology, 1980; Diplomate in Medical Oncology, 1983. *Appointments:* Chief, Haematology - Oncology Section, VA Medical Centre, Salem, Virginia, USA; 1979-; Assistant Professor of Medicine, University of Virginia School of Medicine, 1979-85; Associate Professor, 1985-. *Memberships:* Fellow, American College of Physicians; Virginia Society of Haematology – Oncology. *Publications:* Various articles in medical journals. *Honours:* Sahu Jain Trust Merit Scholarship, 1966-70. *Hobbies:* Tennis; Camping. *Address:* VA Medical Centre, Salem, VA 24153, USA.

JAIN, Shukan R, b. 14 Sep. 1929, India, Senior Consultant in Cardiology, Choithram Hospital and Research Centre, Indore. m. Sumati, 8 Dec, 1948, Deoli Pabuji, Rajasthan, 4 sons. *Education:* LMP (MP), 1951; MBBS, 1954; MD, 1957, Agra Univeristy. *Appointments:* Senior House Physician, K.E.H. Medical School, Indore, 1954-55; Casualty Medical Officer, M.Y. Hospital, Indore, 1955-58; Lecturer in Cardiology, 1958-65, Reader in Medicine, 1965-73; M.G.M. Medical College and M.Y. group of hospitals, Indore; Professor of Medicine, various medical colleges of M.P., 1973-81; After voluntary retirement in 1981 Senior Consultant in Cardiology, Choithram Hospital and Research Centre, 1981-. *Memberships:* Indian Medical Association; M.P Cancer Society; Life Member, Association of Physicians of India; Life Member, Cardiology Society of India; Fellow, College of Chest Physicians; Fellow, International College of Angiology. *Publications:* Contributor of research papers to professional journals including: 'Acta Cardiologica'; 'Indian Heart Journal'; 'Clinical Trials Journal', etc. *Honour:* Justice Renade Medal for Standing Highest in Surgery in L.M.P. Examination, 1951. *Hobbies:* Gardening; Lions Club of Indore. *Address:* 28/1 South Tukoganj, Indore 452 001, India.

JAIN, Sukhbir Prasad, b.23 May 1917, Bombay, India. Consultant Surgeon. m. Shakuntala Mithal, 21 July 1942, New Delhi, India, 2 sons, 1 daughter. *Education:* MB, BS, Lucknow University, India,1940, MD, 1942; LRCS, Edinburgh, 1949, FRCS, 1950; FACS, 1963. *Appointments:* House Physician, 1940-41; Lecturer, Pathology, 1941-42; Assistant Surgeon, 1942-46; Resident Surgeon, Medical College Hospital, Agra, India, 1946-47; Reader in Pathology, SN Medical College, Agra University, 1947-48; Orthopaedic Officer and Surgical Registrar, England, 1950; Professor and Head, Anatomy Department, SN Medical College, Agra University, India, 1950-58; Medical and Surgical Specialist and Civil Surgeon, 1958-60; Professor and Head of Surgery, Maulana Azad Medical College and Irwin Hospital, Delhi University, India, 1960-66; Surgeon to Government of Somalia under Indian Aid Mission, 1966-70; Professor of Surgery, Chief Surgeon, and Hospital Director, Public Health College, Haile SellassieUniversity, Ethiopia, 1970-76; Surgeon, Haile Sellassie Hospital, Addis Ababa, Ethiopia, 1976-77, Professor of Anatomy, 1977-78; Consultant Surgeon, Professor and Head, Department of Anatomy and Sub-Dean Medical Faculty, Jos University Hospital, Nigeria, East

Africa,-. *Memberships:* Anatomical Society of India; Association of Surgeons of India; Indian Medical Association; British Medical Association; Indian Association of Medical Education; British Association of Clinical Anatomists. *Publications:* 42 research papers; Review of operative findings in 325 cases of oesophagogastro-intestinal obstruction in Ethiopia, 1976; Pattern of Neoplastic Disease in Ethiopia, 1976, etc. *Honours:* Distinction in Anatomy, Obstetrics and Gynaecology, MBBS; 11 medals and 7 certificates; WHO Fellowship 1964. *Hobby:* Travel. *Address:* Jos University Teaching Hospital, PMB 2084, Jos, Nigeria.

JAKAB, Tivadar, b. 16 Feb. 1925, Debrete, Hungary. Professor in Anaesthesia. 1 son, 1 daughter. *Education:* MD, Medical University of Budapest; PhD, D Sc, Hungarian Academy of Science. *Appoinments:* Senior House Officer – Registrar 1951-72, Assistant Professor 1972-79, 2nd Surgical Department of Budapest; Professor and Director, Department of Anaesthesia, Postgraduate Medical School, National Institute of Anaesthesiology, Budapest, 1979-. *Memberships:* General Board, WFSA; Founding Member, European Academy of Anaesthesia; Board Member, Hungarian Academy of Science; Honorary President 1984, Hungarian Society of Anaesthesia and Intensive Care. *Publications:* "General Anaesthesia", 1972; 'Intensive Care' in 'Medicina', 1975-77; "A Practice of General Anaesthesia", 1978; "Pain Relief", 1982. *Address:* Anaesthesiology and Intensive Therapy, Orvostovábbképzö Intézet, H 1389 Budapest Pf 112, Hungary.

JAKOB, Andreas Franz, b. 25 Oct 1935, Samaden. Head of Research group, University Biochemical Department. m. Rosemarie Haas, 7 July 1960, Geneva, 1 son, 3 daughters. *Education:* MD, University of Zurich. *Appointments:* Internship in Internal Medicine; Research fellowships; Resident, Internal Medicine, University of Zurich; currently Head of Research Group, Biochemistry Department, University of Basel, Switzerland. *Memberships:* Swiss Society for Biochemistry, Secretary, 1985; German Biochemical Society; European Association for the Study of Diabetes. *Publications:* Biochim. Biophys. Acta 404, 57-66, 1975; European Journal of Biochemistry 106, 233-240, 1980; Molecular Aspects of Medicine, Vol 4, 369-455, 1982. *Address:* Department of Biochemistry, University of Basel, Vesalianum, Vesalgasse 1, CH-4051 Basel, Switzerland.

JALALI, Behnaz, b. 26 Jan. 1944, Iran. Associate Professor, Psychiatry. m. Mehrdad Jalali, 28 Sep. 1968. *Education:* MD, Tehran University School of Medicine, 1968; Residency, Psychiatry, University of Maryland Hospitals, USA. *Appointments:* Assistant Professor, Psychiatry, Rutgers University School of Medicine, 1973-76; Assistant Professor, 1976-81, Associate Professor, 19081-85, Psychiatry, Yale University; Associate Professor, Psychiatry, University of California, Los Angeles, 1985-. *Memberships:* American Psychiatric Association; American Orthopsychiatric Association; American Family Therapy Association; Word Federation for Mental Health; American Association for Social Psychiatry. *Publications:* Numerous articles in professional journals. *Hobbies:* Photography; Painting. *Address:* University of California, at Los Angeles, VA Medical Centre, Brentwood Psychiatry Service, 11301 Wilshire Blvd., Los Angeles, CA 90043, USA.

JALBERT, Michel Raymond, b. 29 Mar., 1956, Montreal, Canada. Doctor of Chiropractic. *Education:* DEC in Human Sciences, Rosemont College, Montreal, Canada; currently attending post-graduate studies in industrial chiropractic and chiropractic Sport Sciences. *Appointment:* engaged in private practice of Chiropractic since graduation. *Memberships:* Fédération Professionelle Chior-Québec; Canadian College of Chiropractic Sports Sciences; American College of Sports Medicine; American Chiropractic Association; Canadian Chiropractic Association; Association des Chiropracticiens du Québec; Ordre des Chiropracticiens du Québec. *Publications:* "Talking About Your Health", (French edition), to be published spring, 1986; articles: "What is Chiropractic"; 'How to Choose a Chiropractor;' 'What to Expect from Chiropractic Care'; 'Good Health Habits', etc. *Honour:* Graduation "cum laude", Palmer College of Chiropractic, Iowa, USA, 1979. *Hobbies:* Ski-ing; Racquetball; Golf; Windsurfing; Yoga; Running; Scuba Diving; Swimming; Reading. *Address:* CP 248, 167 Laurier Boulevarde, Laurier-Station, Quebec, Canada, GOS-INO.

JALIL, Muhammad Abdul, b. 4 Feb. 1928, India. Director, X-Ray Centre, Sharq, Kuwait. m. Ann Owens, 8 Apr. 1961, London, England, 2 daughters. *Education:* MBBS, DTM & H, DMRD, London. *Appointments:* Senior Registrar, Radiology, Derbyshire Royal Infirmary, Derby, 1961-63; Consultant Radiologist, Southwell Hospital, Ahmadi, K.O.C., Kuwait, 1963-64; Director, X-Ray Centre, Sharq, Kuwait, 1964-; Consultant Radiologist, American Mission Hospital, Kuwiat, 1964-67; Overseas Radiologist, American Mission Hospital, Kuwait, 1964-67; Overseas Radiologist, The Middlexsex Hospital, London, 1972-73. *Memberships:* Royal College of Radiologists, London; British Insitute of Radiology, London; British Medical Association. *Publications:* "Rosetta Stone Booklet" of British Museum translated into Urdu, 1964. *Hobbies:* Painting; Photography; Languages; Charity; Walking; Gardening. *Address:* Hilali Street, Sharq, Kuwait.

JAMAL. Sinnamohideen, b. 1 Jan. 1934, India. Professor of Plastic Surgery. m. Rahima, 10 June 1965, India, 3 sons. *Education:* MBBS, Madurai Medical College, Madras University, 1960; FRCS, Edinburgh and Glasgow General Surgery, 1964; Certificate, American Board of Plastic Surgery, 1967. *Appointments:* Assistant Professor of Plastic Surgery, Madurai Medical College, 1968; Assistant Professor of Plastic Surgery, Thanjavur Medical College, 1970; Reader of Plastic Surgery and Head of Department of Plastic Surgery, 1977, Professor of Plastic Surgery, 1978, Professor of Plastic Surgery and Chief, Clinical Filarial Research Unit, 1981, Thanjavur Medical College; Professor of Plastic Surgery, Madras Medical College, 1985. *Memberships:* Association of Surgeons in India; Association of Plastic Surgeons of India; Indian Medical Association; International Society of Lymphology. *Publications:* Numerous articles in medical journals, chapters in edited volumes etc, concerning the surgical management of filarial elephantiasis. *Hobbies:* Photography; Lionistic and Masonic activities. *Address:* Professor of Plastic, Madras Medical College, Madras, India 600 003.

JAMES, David Geraint, b. 2 Jan. 1922, Treherbert. Dean and Consultant Physican, Royal Northern Hospital, Holloway Road, London, England. m. Professor Dame Sheila Sherlock, 2 daughters. *Education:* MA; MD; FRCP; LL.D; Jesus College, University of Cambridge, 1939-41; Middlesex Hospital Medical School, University of London, 1941-44. *Appointments:* House Physician and Casualty Officer, Middlesex Hospital, 1944-45; Medical Registrar, Royal Postgraduate Medical School, 1948-50; College of Physicians and Surgeons, Columbia University, New York, USA, 1950-51; Senior Medical Registrar and Leverhulme Research Fellow, Middlesex Hospital, 1951-59; Lecturer in Medicine, Royal Postgraduate Medical School, 1964-73. *Memberships:* Past President, Harvey Society of London, Medical Society of London and Osler Club; Member of Council, Royal College of Physicians; Member of Council,

Hunterian Society. *Publications:* "Diagnosis and Treatment of Infections", 1957; "Sarcoidosis", 1970; "Circulation of the Blood", 1978; "A Colour Atlas of Respiratory Diseases", 1984; "Sarcoidosis and Other Granulomatous Disorders", 1985. *Honours:* Comyns Berkeley Fellow, Middlesex Hospital Medical School, 1950-51; Research Fellow, Columbia University, New York City; Ethel Reilly Scholarship, Middlesex Hospital Medical School, 1955; Leverhulme Scholar, Middlesex Hospital Medical School, 1955-57; First Prize, Scientific Exhibition, British Medical Association Congress, Newcastle-upon-Tyne, 1957; Chesterfield Medallist, Institute of Dermatology, University of London, 1957; First Prize, Barraquer Institute of Ophthalmology, Barcelona, 1958; Honorary Doctor of Laws, University of Wales, 1982; Carlo Forlaninin Gold Medal, Italian Thoracic Society, 1983; White-Robed Member of the Gorsedd, 1984. *Hobbies:* History of Medicine; International Welshness; Rugby Football. *Address:* 149 Harley Street, London W1 1HG, England.

JAMES, John Anthony, b. 2 Apr. 1913, South Africa. Neurosurgeon (retired). m. Millicent Ward, 8 Mar. 1941, Perth, Western Australia, 3 sons, 1 daughter. *Education:* FRACS, Melbourne, 1947;' MB, BS, Melboune University, 1938. *Appointments:* Neurosurgical Registrar, Alfred Hospital, Melbourne, 1944-47; Assistant Neurosurgeon, Dunedin Hospital, Otago, 1948-51; Senior Lecturer in Neurosurgery, Dunedin, 1951-64; Director, Neurosurgical Unit, Visiting Neurosurgeon, 1965-67, Wellington Hospital. *Memberships:* New Zealand Commitee of RACS; Neurosurgical Society of Australasia; New Zealand Neurological Society; Asian and Australasian Society. *Honour:* CMG, 1973. *Hobbies:* Fishing; Golf; Sailing; Painting; Gardening. *Address:* 136 Vipond Road, Whangaparada, North Auckland, New Zealand.

JAMIESON, John L., b. 21 Aug. 1943, Vancouver, Canada. Associate Professor; Chairman, Department of Psychology. m. Trudy Jamieson, 18 Aug. 1967, Lakehead University, Vancouver, 1 son, 1 daughter. *Education:* BA, MA, PhD, University of British Columbia. *Memberships:* Canadian Psychological Association; American Psychological Association; Society of Behavioral Medicine Society for Psychophysiological Research. *Publications:* "Type A behaviour and heart rate recovery from a psychosocial stressor", Journal of Human Stress, 1983; "Aerobic Power and tonic heart rate responses to psychosocial stressors", Personality and Social Psychology Bulletin, 1979. *Address:* Department of Psychology, Lakehead University, Thunder Bay, Ontario, Canada P7B 5E1.

JAMISON, James Starrett, b. 4 Jan. 1948, Roanoke, Virginia, USA. Psychologist m. Ruth Miller Craddock, 9 Nov. 1974, Roanoke, Virginia, USA. *Education:* BA, Roanoke College, Salem, Virginia, USA, 1971; MA, Radford University, Radford, Virginia, 1976. *Appointments:* Staff, Emergency Services of Mental Health Services, Roanoke Valley, Roanoke, Virginia, 1975-80; School Psycologist, Franklin County Public Schools, Rockymount, Virginia, 1980-86. *Memberships:* American Psychological Assoc,; Virginia Psychological Assoc; National Education Assoc; Virginia Education Assoc; Franklin County Education Assoc; Kappa Delta Pi; American Association for the Advancement of Science; Roanoke Valley Regional Association of School Psychologists. *Publications:* 'The Ames Distortion Room: An Experimental Test of the Concept of Environment Transaction as the Theoretical Basis for this Perceptual Phenomenon in Pre-School Aged Children', 1976 (unpublished); Paper read at Virginia Academy ofScience Annual Meeting, 'A Test of the concept of environmental transation in pre school children using The Amnes Distortion Room, 1978. *Honour:* Member, Kappa Delta Pi. *Hobby:* Travel. *Address:* 2388 Carlton Road

SW, Roanoke, VA 24015, USA.

JAMISON, Rex L., b. 8 July 1933. Professor; Acting Chairman; Acting Physician-in-Chief. m. Dorothy Tufts Lockwood, 3 Mar. 1962, Cambridge, Masschusetts, 2 sons. *Education:* AB, 1955, University of Iowa; BA, 1957, MA, 1961; Oxford University, England; MD, Harvard Medical School, Boston, 1960. *Appointments:* Intern, Medicine , Massachusetts General Hospital; Assistant Resident, Medicine, Boston; Senior Assistant Resident, Medicine, New York; Clincial Associate, Laboratory of Kidney & Electrolyte., NIH; Assistant Professor, Medicine, Washington School of Medicine; Associate Professor, Medicine, Chief, Division of Nephrology, Professor, Medicine and Physiology, Stanford University. *Memberships include:* AHA Council on Kidney in Cardiovascular Disease; American Physiological Society; American Society for Clincial Investigation; American Society of Nephrology; Association of American Physicians; Association of Professors of Medicine; Association of American Rhodes Scholars; California Academy of Medicine; etc. *Publications:* Co-author, "Urinary Concentrating Mechanism: Stucture and function", 1982; "Transplantation in the 1980's : Recent Advances", Editor, 1984; articles in professional journals. *Honours:* Phi Beta Kappa: John Briggs Award, 1951; Rhodes Scholar, 1955; Markle Scholar, 1968; USPHS Research Career Development Award, 1968; Honorary Member, Peruvian Society of Nephrology, 1980; Fellow, Guggenheim Foundation, 1977. *Hobbies:* Music; Tennis. *Address:* Stanford University School of Medicine, Stanford University Medical Centre, Rm. S102, Stanford, CA 94305, USA.

JANKOWSKI, Janet Marie, b. 5 Nov. 1949, Worcester, Massachusetts, USA. Speech and Language Pathologist. m. John Paul Chmielowiec, Stamford, Greenwich, Connecticut, 1 son. *Education:* BA, French, Anna Maria College, Paxton, Massachusetts, 1971; MS, Speech, Emerson College, Boston, Massachusetts, 1974. *Appointments:* Volunteer Speech Pathologist, Mercy Center, Worcester, Massachusetts, 1974; French Teacher, St. Mary's High School, Worcester, Massachusetts, 1974; Speech and Language Pathologist, Stamford Public Schools, Stamford, Connecticut, 1974-. *Memberships:* American Speech and Hearing Association (Certificate in Clinical Competence in Speech); Alpha Mu Gamma, National Foreign Language Honor Society. *Hobbies:* Reading; Travel. *Address:* 34 Huntington Court, Bethel, CT 06801-1436, USA.

JANSKY, Jeannette Louis Jefferson, b. 27 Nov. 1927, Urbana, Illinois, USA. Educational Director. m. Curtis M. Jansky (divorced) 14 Aug. 1949, Urbana, Illinois, 1 son. *Education:* BS, University of Illinois, USA; MS, College of the City of New York; PhD, Columbia University. *Appointments:* Speech Therapist, Blythedale Convalescent Home, Valhalla, New York, 1950-51; Clinician, Language Disorders Clinic, Columbia Presbyterian Medical Centre, 1951-57 and 1965-72; Associate, Private Practice, Katrina de Hirsch, 1951-79; Director, Language Disorder Clinic, 1972-74; Private Practice, Diagnosis/Treatment of Language and Learning Disabilities, Educational Director, de-Hirsch-Robinson Reading Clinic-. *Memberships:* American Psychological Association; American Orthopsychiatric Association; International Reading Association; Editorial Board, Orton Dyslexia Society. *Publication:* "Predicting Reading Failure",. 1966, with de Hirsch and Langford; "Preventing Reading Failure", 1972, with de Hirsch; Chapter 'A Critical Review' in "Dyslexia, An Appraisal of Current Knowledge", 1978; "A Clinician in the Classroom", Part 1, 1981, Part II, 1982; Chapter 'Developmental Reading Disorders' in "Comprehensive Textbook of Psychiatry", volume II, 1982; Chapter 'Developmental Reading Disorders' in

"Comprehensive Textbook of Psychiatry", volume III, 1980, volume IV, 1985. *Honours:* Sigma Xi, 1970; Orton Society Inc. New York State Branch, Honours for Year 1977. *Hobbies:* Reading; Photography; Cycling; Walking; Bridge. *Address:* 120 East 89th Street, New York City, NY 10128, USA.

JANSSEN, Carl Wilhelm, b. 10 Sep. 1929, Bjugn in Fosen, Norway. Assistant Professor, Surgery. (Gastroenterology).m. (1) Anne Fougner, 14 Mar. 1956, deceased, 2 sons, 1 daughter; (2) Eldrid Munck, 22 Dec. 1984. *Education:* MD. *Appointments:* Registrar: Rikshospitalet, Oslo, 1960-61, Pathology Dept., Haukeland Hospital, Bergen, 1961-64, Surgery Dept., Haukeland Hospital, 1965-69; Assistant Professor, Haukeland Hospital, 1970-. *Memberships:* Norwegian and Nordic Surgical Associations; Scandinavian Association of Thoracic and Cardiovascular Surgery. *Publications:* Numeorus in professional journals. *Hobbies:* Mountaineering; Hiking; Skiing. *Address:* Surg. dept., N-5016 Haukeland Sykehus, Norway.

JANUS, Cynthia, b. 10 May 1946, New York, New York, USA. Associate Professor of Clinical Radiology. m. Sam Janus, 31 July 1977, Ferndale, New York, 1 son, 1 daughter. *Education:* BA, New York University, New York, 1967; MD Jefferson Medical College, Philadelphia, Pennsylvania, 1971. *Appointments:* Attending Staff, Radiology, Roosevelt Hospital, 1975-78; Associate Professor of Clinical Radiology, Mount Sinai Hospital and School of Medicine, New York City, New York. *Memberships:* Radiologic Society of North America; American College of Radiology; New York Roentgen Society; American College of Medical Imaging; American Medical Association. *Publications:* 'Diagnosis of Popliteal Cyst: Double Contrast Arthography and Sonography', 1981; 'Percutaneous Localizaion of Non-Palpable Breast Lesions', 1983; 'Radio-Pathological Correlation of Occult Tumor of the Breast', 1984. *Honour:* Founder and President of the New York Chapter of the American Association of Women in Radiology. *Hobbies:* Writing, Dance, Piano. *Adress:* 983 Park Avenue, New York, NY 10028, USA.

JARMAN, Bernard Alvin, b. 15 May 1948, Newfoundland, Canada. Psychotherapist. Divorced, 1 son. *Education:* BA Pre-Medical Studies, Rollins College, Winter Park, Florida, USA; MA Counseling Psychology, Chapman College, Orange, California; PhD Counsiling Psychology, Arizona State University, Tempe, Arizona. *Appointments:* Psychologist Assistant to Chief Psychologist, Naval Regional Medical Center, San Diego, California, 1974-75; Psychotherapist, Muscle Shoals Mental Health Center, Florence, Alabama, 1975-77; Doctoral Intern in Counseling Psychology 1977-79, Staff Psychotherapist 1977-, Center for Behavioral Health, Mesa Lutheran Hospital, Mesa, Arizona. *Memberships:* American Psychological Association: Arizona Counselors' Association; Phi Lambda Theta. *Honours:* Rollins College Achievement Award Scholarship, 1966; A S Sullivan Award Scholarship, 1968; Arizona State Universtiy Tuition Scholarship, 1977. *Hobbies:* Tennis, Soccer, Reading, Theatre. *Address:* 3030 South Alma School Road, §31, Mesa, AZ 85202, USA.

JAROSZ, Marek Mieczyslaw, b. 14 Jan. 1928, Warsaw, Poland. Professor of Psychiatry. m. Anastazja Len, 2 sons. *Education:* MA, Psychology, University of Lodz, 1952; MD, Lodz Medical School, 1961. *Appointments:* Assistant 1954-59, Senior Assistant, 1960-64, Adjunct 1965-67, Docent, 1968-75, Professor of Psychiatry 1976-, Dept of Psychiatry Lodz school of Medicine; Head of Department of Medical Psychology, Lodz Medical School 1977-83. *Memberships:* Polish Psychiatric Association; Polish Psychological Association; International Association of Applied Psychology;

International College of Psychosomatic Medicine; Member of Editorial Board of "Psychiatria Polska" (Journal of Polish Psychiatry). *Publications:* Books (all in Polish) "Medi la Psychology" 1971, 1973, 1978, 1983; "Psychology and Psychopathology of Everyday Life", 1975, 1976; "The Psychiatrist and his Patient" 1982; Co-editor: "Bases of Psychiatry" 1976, 1978, 1980, 1983; Articles in medical journals. *Hobbies:* Painting; Drawing; Numismatics. *Address:* ul Kolinskiego 27/24, Os. Zagajnikowa, 91-849 Lodz, Poland.

JARROLD, Ashleigh Edward, b. 1 Apr. 1952, Sydney, Australia. Dental Surgeon. *Education:* HSC, Waverley College 1969; BDS, Sydney University, 1975. *Appointments:* Private Practice. *Memberships:* Australian Dental Association; Federation Dentaire Internationale; Australian Society for the Advancement of Anaesthesia and Sedation in Dentistry. *Hobbies:* Numismatism,Tennis. *Address:* 62 Watt Street, Newcastle, 2300, Australia.

JARROTT, Bevyn, b. 5 Apr. 1943, Brisbane, Australia. Clinical Pharmacologist. m. Margaret Kaye Trembath, 30 June 1973, Heyfield, Victoria, Australia, 2 daughters. *Education:* Bachelor of Phanmacy, University of Queensland, Australia, 1965; PhD, University of Cambridge, England, 1969. *Appointments:* Lecturer, Department of Physiology, Monash University, Australia, 1970-74; Senior Lecturer, Clinical Pharmacology & Therapeutics Unit, University of Melbourne, 1974-84; Reader, 1984-. *Memberships:* Australasian Society of Clinical & Experimental Pharmacologists (Assistant Treasurer 1980-82, Treasurer 1983-85); Australianm Phsyiological & Pharmacological Society, International Society of Hypertension; Australian Neuoscience Society. *Publications:* 'Clonidine & Related Compounds' (in "Handbook of Hypertension"), 1984; "Cellular Aspects of Catecholaminergic neurons' (in "Handbook of Physiology"), 1977. *Hobbies:* Standardbred Horseracing; Microcomputers; Oenology; Genealogy. *Address:* Clinical Pharmacology & Therapeutics Unit, Department of Medicine, University of Melbourne, Austin Hospital, Heidelberg, Victoria 3084, Australia.

JASINSKI, Wladyslaw Kazimierz, b. 22 Jan 1916, Warszawa, Poland, Professor and Head, Department of Nuclear Medicine, Institute of Cardiology, Warsaw, m. Janina Groyecka, 3 May 1941, Warsaw, 1 son, 1 daughter. *Education:* MD, Jagiellonian University, Cracow, 1946; DSc, University of Wroclaw, 1954. *Appointments:* Institute of Oncology/Radium Institute, Warsaw, 1937-41; Institute of Oncology, Warsaw; Cancer Control Adviser, WHO, 1973-75; Professor and Head, Nuclear Medicine, Postgraduate Medical School, Warsaw, 1976-85; Professor and Head, Department of Nuclear medicine, Insitute of Cardiology, Warsaw, 1986-. *Memberships:* Polish Academy of Sciences; Polish Society of Nuclear Medicine; European Society of Nuclear Medicine; Society of Nuclear Medicine, USA. *Publications:* 'Physical Bases of Radiotherapy of Cancer', 1950; 'Clinical Use of Radioactive Isotopes', 1965; 'Quantitative Liver Scintigraphy in Oncology', 1970; 'Clinical Scintigraphy', 1971; 'The Use of Radioactive Ca-47', 1966; 'Cancer Control Programming', 1979; 'Nuclear Cardiology', 1983. *Hobbies:* Photography; Computer Science; Skiing. *Address:* Institute of Cardiology, Department of Nuclear Medicine, Alpejaka 42, PL-04-628 Warsaw, Poland.

JASMIN, Claude, b., 12 Dec. 1938, Reims, France, Professor, Medical Faculty Paris XI, Head of Department of Haematology and Biology of Tumours, m. Evelyn Drylewicz, 5 Dec. 1965, 1 son, 1 daughter. *Education:* Baccalaureat, 1955; Medical Study, Medical Faculty, Paris, 1957-65; MSc, University of Paris, 1963-64; Professor of Oncology, Faculty of Medicine of Paris, 1974. *Appointments:*

Externe, 1959-61, Interne, 1962-67, Hopitaux de Paris; Fellow, Wistar Institute, Philadelpia, USA, 1962-63; Chef de Clinique, 1967-74, Professor of Oncology 1974, Faculty of Medicine, Paris; Acting Head of Department, 1974-82, Head of Department of Haematology and Biology of Tumours, Hopital Paul Brousse, Villejuif. *Memberships:* National Scientific Commission No 2, National Institute for Health and Medical Research; Scientific Commission, Associaiton pour le Recherche sur le Cancer; National committee for evaluation and prospective medical and biological engineering; National Expert in clinical Pharmacology; Past Member, EORTC Council, European Organization. *Publications:* Author of numerous publicitions on medical and scientific subjects; Contributor of numerous articles to medical and scientific journals. *Honours:* Recipient of Isaac Wistar Lecture, Philadelphia, USA, 1983. *Hobbies:* Guitar; Singing; Table tennis; Arts. *Address:* Service d'hématologie, Hôpital Paul Brousse, 14 Avenue Paul Vaillant Counturier, 94804 Villejuif Cédex, France.

JAYASINGHE, Asoka Wimalananda, b. 7 Apr 1945, Kandy, Sri Lanka, Medical Director, Advanced Mental Health Services of Los Angeles, Norwalk, California, USA. *Education:* MD, Diplomate American Board of Psychiatry and Neurology. *Appointments:* Private Practice, Psychiatry, 1977; Assistant Clinical Professor of Psychiatry, University of California, Los Angeles School of Medicine. *Memberships:* Member, American Psychiatric Association; Southern California Psychiatric Society; Fellow, American Association for Social Psychiatry. *Address:* 606 Paramount Blvd., Long Beach, CA 90805, USA.

JAYES, Percy Harris, b. 26 June 1915, Bromley, Kent, England. Consultant Plastic Surgeon. m. Aileen Mary McLaughlin, 26 Aug. 1964, 1 son, 1 daughter, 2 sons 1 daughter by previous marriage. *Education: MB: BS: FRCS England. Appointments:* Consultant Plastic Surgeon: Queen Victoria Hospital, East Grinstead, Sussex, 1948-73, St. Bartholomew's Hospital, London, 1950-73, King Edward VII's Hospital for Officers, London, 1965-85, Royal Air Force (Civil Consultant), 1961-82. *Memberships:* British association of Plastic Surgeons; British Association of Aesthetic Platic Surgeons. *Publications:* "Plastic Repair After Seperation of Cranipagus Twins", 'British Medical Journal', 1964. *Honour:* McIndoe Medal, Royal College of Surgeons, 1964. *Address:* 149 Harley Street, London W1N 2DE, England.

JEANNET, Michel, b. 22 Apr. 1932, Geneva, Switzerland. Transplantation Immunologist. m. Marie-Claire, 1 Mar. 1979, Geneva, 1 son, 1 daughter. *Education:* Medical Degree, 1956, Md 1960, University of Geneva Medical School; Private-Docent, 1972, Chargé de Cours, 1974, Faculty of Medicine of Geneva. *Appointments:* Internship, Department of Surgery, 1957, Department of Medicine, 1957-60, University of Geneva Medical School; Internship, Department of Haematology, Hôpital St-Louis, Paris, France, 1960-61; Research Fellow, Central Laboratory of the Swiss Red Cross Blood Transfusion Service, Bern, 1961-63; Internship, Department of Medicine, University of Geneva Medical School, 1963-65; Clinical Reserch Fellow, Department of Surgery & Medicine, Harvard Medical School, Boston, Massachusetts, USA, 1966-68; Head Transplantation Immunology Unit & National Reference Laboratory for Histocompatibility, Hôpital Cantonal Universitaire, Geneva, Switzerland. *Memberships:* Swiss Society of Haematology; Swiss Society of Allergology & Immunology; French Society of Haematology; French Society of Transplantation; British Society for Immunology, International Society for Experimental Haematology; International Transplantation Society. *Publications:* 'The Main

istocompatibility System in Man' (in "Transplantation, Handbuch der allgemeinen Patholgie"), 1977; "HLA-DR in immune-mediated disease' (in "Human class II Histocompatibility Antigens: Theoretical & Practical Aspects, Clinical Relevance"), 1986-. *Hobbies:* Tennis; Sailing; Skiing; Windsurfing. *Address:* Transplantation Immunology Unit, Division of Immunology & Allergology, Hopital Cantonal Universitaire, 1211 Geneva 4, Switzerland.

JEANRENAUD, Bernard, b. 16 Mar. 1930, La Chaux-de-Fonds. Professor and Head of Laboratories of Metabolic Research. m. Francoise Rohner, 19 May 1979, 3 sons. *Education:* Faculte des Sciences and Premier propedeutique, 1949-50; Ecole de Medecine, Deuxiene propedeutique, 1950-55; MD degree, 1955. *Appointments:* Internship, Mount Auburn Hospital, Cambridge, USA; Assistant in Medicine and Research Fellow, Harvard University, USA; Guest Investigator and Assistant Physician, Rockefeller University, USA; Research Fellow, New York; Assistant in Medicine, Instructor, Geneva; Doctorate in Medicine, Geneva; Assistant Dean, Faculty of Medicine, Geneva; Privat Docent, Faculty of Medicine, Geneva; Associate Professor and Head; Full Professor of Medical Research, Geneva; Head of Laboratories of Metabolic Research. *Memberships:* European Association for the Study of Diabetes; American Diabetes Association; Biochemical Society; European Neuroscience Association; New York Academy of Sciences; Federation of European Nutrition Societies; International Diabetes Federation; Union des Societes Suisses de Biologie Experimentale; American Physiological Society; Endocrine Society, USA. *Publications:* More then 200 articles in field of experimental endocrinology (diabetes) and metabolism. *Honours:* Minkowski Award, 1970; John Kellion Medal, Australia, 1983; Fellowship of Japanese Society for the Promotion of Science, 1983. *Address:* Laboratoires de Recherches Metaboliques, University of Geneva Medical School, 64 av. de la Roseraie, 1211 Geneva 4, Switzerland.

JEANTY, Maxence, b. 7 May 1940, Haiti. Psychiatrist. married, 2 sons, 1 daughter. *Education:* Diplomate, American Board of Psychiatry & Neurology, 1982; Diplomate, American National Board of Psychiatry, Inc, 1982. *Memberships:* American Medical Association; American Psychiatric Association; Academy of Psychosomatic Medicine; International College of Physicians & Surgeons; American College of International Pysicians; American Association for Geriatric Psychiatry; American Orthopsychiatric Association, Inc; Southern Medical Association; New York Academy of Sciences. *Address:* 18739-2 Innsbrook, Northville, MI 48167, USA.

JEFFERSON, James W, b. 14 Aug 1937, USA, Professor of Psychiatry, Director, Centre for Affective Disorders, Co Director, Lithium Information Centre, m. Susan M Cole, 25 Jun 1965, New York, New York, USA, 1 son, 2 daughters. *Education:* BS, Bucknell University, 1958; MD, University of Wisconsin, 1964. *Appointments:* Internship, St Lukes Hospital, NY, 1964-65; Residency, Internal Medicine, 1965-67, Residnecy, Psychiatry, 1971-74, Assistant Professor, Psychiatry, 1974-78, Associate Professor, Psychiatry, 1978-81, Professor of Psychiatry, 1981-, University of Wisconsin; Fellowship, Cardiology, University Chicago, 1967-68. *Memberships:* American Psychiatric Association; Collegium International Neuropsychopharmacologium (CINP); American Psychopathological Association. *Publications;* "Primer of Lithium Therapy", 1977; "Neuropsychiatric Features of Medical Disorders", 1981; "Treatment of Mental Disorders", 1982; "Lithium and Manic Depression: A Guide", 1982; "Lithium Encyclopedia for Clinical Practice", 1983; "Depression and its Treatment: Help for the Nations

- 1 Menal Problem'', 1984; ''Anxiety and its Treatment: Help is Available'', 1986; 'A Review of the Cardiovascular effects and toxicity of tricycle antidepressants', 1975. *Hobbies:* Running; Lithium artifact collecting. *Address:* Department of Psychiatry, University of Wisconsin Clinical Centre, 600 Highland Avenue, Madison, W1 53792, USA.

JELJASZEWICZ, Janusz, b. 8 Aug. 1930, Wilno, Poland. Head of Laboratory of Bacterial Metabolites, National Institute of Hygiene, Warsaw; President, Scientific Advisory Council to Minister of Health and Social Welfare; Adviser for Science to Minister. divorced, 1 daughter. *Education:* MD; PhD, University Medical School, Poznan. *Appointments:* Research Associate, Department of Microbiology, University of Poznan Medical School, 1952-60; Research Associate, Department of Microbiology, University of Warsaw Medical School, 1960-65; Assistant Professor, National Institute of Hygiene, Warsaw, 1963-73; Professor of Microbiology and Head, Department of Bacteriology, 1973-79; President, Scientific Advisory Council to Minister of Health and Social Welfare, 1979-; Adviser for Science to Minister, 1981-. *Memberships:* Polish Society for Microbiology; Polish Medical Association; American Society for the Microbiology; Infectious Diseases Society of America; American Association for the Advancement of Sciences; British Society for Antimicrobial Chemotherapy; Paul Ehrlich Gessellschaft fur Chemotherpie; Deutsche Gesellschaft fur Hygiene and Mikrobiologie, etc. *Publications:* Over 350 publicaitons in leading International scientific journals; 30 books including: ''Staphylococci and Staphylococcal Infections'', 1966, 71, 76, 81, 85; ''Medical Microbiology'', 5 volumes, 1980-85; ''Bacterial Toxins and Cell Membranes'', 1978; ''Bacteria and Cancer'', 1981; ''Chemotherapy and Immunity'', 1985. *Honour:* State Prize for Scientific Achievements, 1976. *Hobbies:* Collection of old books and maps, old silver; Studies on Human Motivation. *Address:* 28A Okrezna, 02-916 Warsaw, Poland.

JELLINS, Jack, b. 5 Nov. 1938, Vienna, Austria, Head Ultrasonic Imaging, Ultrasonics Institute. m. Maureen Varga, 5 Sep. 1981, Sydney, Australia, 2 sons, 1 daughter. *Education:* B Sc 1960, BE 1961, University of Sydney. *Appointments:* Consultant in Ultrasound, Royal Prince Alfred Hospital, Camperdown, Sydney, 1974; Consultant in Clinical Ultrasonics, Royal North Shore Hospital, St leonards, Syney, 1978; Currently Head, Ultrasonic Imaging, Ultrasonics Institute. *Memberships:* Australian Society of Ultrasound in Medicine; Australian College of Physical Scientists in Medicine; American Institute of Ultrasound in Medicine. *Publications:* 'Ultrasonic Grey Scale Visualisation of Breast Disease', (with G Kossoff, T S Reeve and B H Barraclough), 1975; 'Proceeding of the Third International Congress on the Ultrasonic Examination of the Breast', (edited with T Kobayashi), 1983. *Honour:* Honorary Fellow, American Institute of Ultrasound in Medicine, 1985. *Hobbies:* Literature; Music; Photography. *Address:* P O Box 479, Double Bay, NSW 2028, Australia.

JENDEN, Donald James, b. 1 Sep. 1926, Horsham, Sussex, England. Professor of Biomathematics. m. Jean Ickeringill, 18 Nov. 1950, 1 son, 2 daughters. *Education:* BSc Physiology, King's College, University of London, England, 1947; MB BS with Distinction in Pathology, Pharmacology & Therapeutics, Medicine, Surgery & Gynaecology & Obstetrics, Westminster Medical School, University of London, 1950. *Appointments:* Demonstrator in Pharmacology, St Bartholomew's Hospital Medical School & King's College, University of London, 1948-49; Lecturer in Pharmacology, University of California Medical centre, San Francisco, 1950-51; Assistant Professor 1952-56, Associate Professor of Pharmacology 1956-60, Acting Chairman,

Department of Pharmacology, 1956-57, University of California Medical centre, Los Angeles; NSF Senior Postdoctoral Fellow, Honorary Research Associate, Department of Biophysics, University College, London, 1961-62; Member, Brain Research Institute, Professor & Chairman, Department of Pharmacology, Professor of Biomathematics, University of California at Los Angeles, 1962-. *Memberships include:* American Association for the Advancement of Science; Fellow, American College of Neuropsychopharmacology; American Physiological Society; American Society for Mass Spectrometry; American Society for Medical School Pharmacology; American Society of Neurochemistry; American Society for Pharmacology & Experimental Therapeutics; New York Academy of Science; Physiological Society (London); Society for Neuroscience. *Publications:* Author & Co-author of some 330 articles & papers. *Honours:* University Gold Medal, London, 1950; Honorary Doctorate, University of Uppsala, Sweden, 1980; Fulbright Short-term Senior Scholar Award, Australia, 1983; Wellcome Visiting Professor, University of Alabama,. 1984. *Address:* Department of Pharmacology, School of Medicine CHS, University of California, Los Angeles, CA 90024, USA.

JENDRISAK, Edward Anthony, b. 20 Nov 1946, Akron, Ohio, USA, Vice President, Lake Erie Institute of Rehabilitation, m. Ann Wilkie, 11 June 1977, Cincinnati, Ohio. *Education:* BSc; MA; LPT; NHA. *Appointments:* Director, Rehabilitation Unit, F. Edward Herbert Hospital New Orleans, LA; Assistant Administrator, Rehabilitation Institute of Oklahoma, Oklahoma City, Okla; Associate Administrator, Rehabilitation Hospital for Special Services York, Pa. *Memberships:* Association of Medical Rehabilitation Directors and Coordinators; American College of Hospital Administrators; American Congress of Rehabilitation Medicine; American Acadmey of Medical Administrators. *Address:* LEIR, 137 West Second Street, Erie, PA 16507, USA.

JENKINS, David Malvern, b. 22 Dec. 1936, South Wales. Professor of Obstetrics and Gynaecology. m. 29 July 1963, 1 son, 4 daughters. *Education:* MB ChB BAO 1960, MD 1973, Queen's University, Belfast, Northern Ireland; Member 1966, Fellow 1977, Royal College of Obstetricians and Gynaecologists, London, England. *Appointments:* Senior Lecturer, Department of Obstetrics and Gynaecology, Leeds University, 1973-78; Professor of Obstetrics and Gynaecology, University College, Cork, Republic of Ireland, 1978-. *Memberships:* Gynaecological Club of Great Britain and Ireland; Royal Academy of Medicine of Ireland; Institute of Obstetrics and Gynaecology; Royal College of Physicians of Ireland. *Publications:* Chapters on Immunology of Reproduction in ''Clinical Immunology'' (editor C W Parker), 1980, and in ''Immunology of Human Reproduction'' (editors Scott and Jones); 'Breech in Clinics' in 'Obstetrics and Gynaecology', 1980; ''Undergraduate Guide to Gynaecology'', in press. *Honours:* Edgar Research Fellow, Royal College of Obstetricians and Gynaecologists, 1978; Birthright Research Award, 1984. *Hobbies:* Oil painting; Game fishing. *Address:* c/o Department of Obstetrics and Gynaecology, Erinville Hospital, Western Rd, University College Cork, Cork, Republic of Ireland.

JENKINS, ElRay, b. 12 Nov. 1938, Logan, Utah, USA. Commander US Army; Consultant. m. Uta Elke Dzierzon, 18 Dec. 1964, Salt Lake City, Utah, USA, 1 son, 5 daughters. *Education:* BS 1964, MS, University of Utah, 1965; MD, University of MO, 1969; MPH, Harvard School of Public Health, 1979. *Appointments:* Flight Surgeon, 32d Air Defense Command, Sembach, Germany, Sembach, Germany, 1970-75; Chief, Professional Services, Flight Surgeon, Aviation Medicine Consultant, Imperial Army Aviation of Iran, 1975-78; Chief

Education and Training, 1980-82, Commander, US Army Aeromedical Center, 1983-, Director, Army Aeromedical Activity, Fort Rucker, AL, 1982-83; Consultant, Aerospace Medicine, to US Army Surgeon General, 1984-. *Memberships:* Aerospace Medical Assn.; Asn of US Army; Assn. of Military Surgeons of US; Society of US Army Flight Surgeons; Space Medicine Branch. *Publications:* Contributor to Aerospace Medicine, 1985. *Hobbies:* Fishing; Computers; Skiing. *Address:* Commander, US Army Aeromedical Center, Fort Rucker, AL 36362, USA.

JENKINS, Peter Anthony, b. 10 Sep. 1936, Cardiff, Wales. Director, Mycobacterium Reference Unit. *Education:* BSc., Wales. PhD, London. *Appointments:* Research Officer, Clinical Immunology Research Group, Medical Research Council; Senior Scientific Officer, Principal Scientific Officer, Tuberculosis Reference Unit (Public Health Laboratory Service). *Memberships:* British Thoracic Society; IUAT; Association Clinical Pathologists. *Publications:* Over 73 publications. *Honours:* Recipient, various honours. *Hobbies:* Walking; Drinking; Music; Squash. *Address:* PHLS Mycobacterium Reference Unit, University Hospital of Wales, Heath Park, Cardiff, South Glamorgan CF4 4XW, Wales.

JENKNER, Fritz Lothar, b. 7 Dec. 1923, Vienna, Austria. Head, Neurosurgery Clinic and Pain Clinic of Ambulatorium Süd, Vienna. m. Uta Friedl, 8 June 1957, Klagenfurt, 1 son, 1 daughter. *Education:* Dr. Univ. Med, University of Vienna, 1949; Univ. Doz, University Graz, 1962; Univ. Doz, 1972; Univ. Prof., 1978, University of Vienna. *Appointments:* Fulbright Fellow to University of Cincinnati School of Medicine, Department of Neurosurgery, 1950-51; Research Assistant, University of Washington, Department of Neurosurgery, 1951-52; First Resident, Dozent, University of Graz, Department of Surgery and Division of Neurosurgery, 1953-67; Visiting Professor, Georgetown University, USA, 1964; Head, Neurosurgery Clinic and Pain Clinic of Ambulatorium, Süd, Vienna, 1976-; Pain Consultant to L. Boltzmann Institute for Clinical Oncology, Vienna City Hospital, Lainz, 1974-80; Visiting Professor, University of Manitoba, Canada, 1983. *Memberships:* German Neurosurgical Association; Association for Study of Pain for Austria, Germany and Switzerland; Member of Jury for Award "Project Pain"; Medicine-Meteorological Association of Austria, Scientific Advisory Board. *Publications include:* "Cervical Syndrome", 1983; "Rheoencepholography", 1962, 1986; over 130 papers in professional journals. *Honour:* Theodor Korner Award, 1961. *Hobbies:* Sports (Skiing, Tennis, Surfing, Biking, etc.); Gardening. *Address:* Fichtnergasse 22, A-1130 Vienna, Austria.

JENNINGS, Garry Lawrence, b. 29 Dec. 1946, Melbourne, Victoria, Australia. Deputy Director, Clinical Research Unit. m. Janis Rouvray, 3 sons. *Education:* MB BS, Monash University; MD; Member Royal College of Physicians (UK); Fellow, Royal Australasian College of Physicians. *Appointments:* Resident Medical Officer, Alfred Hospital, 1970-72; General Medical Registrar, Cardiology registrar & Lecturer in Cardiology, St Mary's Hosptial, London, England, 1972-75; Staff Physician, Clinical Research Unit, Alfred Hospital; Joint Head, Human Hypertension & Vascular Laboratory, Baker Medical Research Institute. *Memberships:* International Society of Hypertension; Cardiac Society of Australasia; Australian Society of Clinical & Experimental Pharmacology. *Publications:* Various articles in medical journals. *Honour:* Young Investigators Award, Cardiac Society of Australia, 1980. *Hobbies:* Thoroughbred Horse Racing; Breeding. *Address:* Clinical Research Unit, Baker Medical Research Institute, Alfred Hospital, Commercial Road, Prahran, Victoria 3181, Australia.

JENNINGS, Roger Dennis, b. 29 July 1933, Los Angeles, California, USA. Professor and Department Head. m. Jean Louise Cottrell, 9 Aug. 1957, San Francisco, 1 son, 1 daughter. *Education:* AA, City College of San Francisco; BA, University of California, Berkeley; MA, San Jose State College, San Jose, California; PhD, University of Colorado, Boulder. *Appointments:* NIMH Postdoctoral Trainee, University of California Medical Center, San Francisco; Postdoctoral Psychology Assistant, Veterans Administration Hospital, Palo Alto, California; Research Associate, Oceanic Institute, Waimanalo, Oahu, Hawaii; Research Associate, Portland State University, Oregon; Associate Professor, Portland State University. *Memberships:* New York Academy of Sciences; Animal Behavior Society; Undersea Medical Society. *Publications:* Co-author, 'Rat Operant Responding: An indicator of Nitrogen Narcosis', 'Aviation, Space and Environmental Medicine', 1977; Co-author, 'Behavioral Observations and the Pedestrian Accident', 'Journals of Safety Research', 1977. *Hobbies:* Scuba Diving; Sailing. *Address:* Psychology Department, Portland State University, P.O. Box 751, Portland, OR 97207, USA.

JENSEN, Ditlev Frimann Nergaard, b. 27 Nov. 1942, Oslo, Norway. Senior Resident House Physician. m. Aase Fystro Jensen, 27 Dec. 1966, 2 sons. *Education:* MD, University of Oslo, 1969, awarded Dr Med 1981, Consultant in Neurology, 1984. *Appointments:* Junior Resident, Neurology, Ulleval Hospital, Oslo; Junior Resident, Psychiatry, Ulleval Hospital, Oslo, Senior Resident, Neurology, National Hospital, Oslo. *Memberships:* Norwegian Medical Association; Norwegian Neurological Association; Norwegian Association of Clinical Neurophysiology; International Continence Society; International Medical Society of Paraplegia. *Publications:* Articles concerning neurogenic bladder dysfunction in various medical journals including: 'Scandinavian Journal of Urology'; Acta Neurol. Scandinavia'; etc. *Hobbies:* Gardening; Summerhouse; Stamps. *Address:* The National Hospital, Dept. of Neurology, 0027 Oslo 1, Norway.

JEPSEN, Carl Henry, b. 27 Aug. 1940, Tacoma, Washington, USA. Co-Founder, The Health Centre for Medical, Dental and Psychological Services. divorced, 2 sons. *Education:* DDS, University of Washington, Seattle, USA, 1965; PhD, Human Behaviour, US International University, 1983. *Appointments include:* Dental Hygienists Liaison Officer, San Diego County Dental Society; California, USA, 1967; Facilitator, Human Dimensions in Dentistry Seminar, 1973-76; Senior Training Co-ordinator, Lifespring, 1977-78; Co-Founder, The Health Centre for Medical, Dental and Psychological Services, 1982; Founder, Institute for Behavioral Research in Health Care, 1983. *Memberships include:* Fellow, American Academy of General Dentistry; American Dental Association; Delta Sigma Delta; American Academy of Operative Dentistry; American Society for Preventive Dentistry; Lambda Chi Alpha; Pi Omicron Sigma. *Publications:* 'Anatomy of a Study Club' in 'AAGFO Journal', 1973; Chapter 'Dentistry' in "Logotherapy in Action", 1973; "Developmental and Implementation of a Model Training Programme in Family Dentistry", as task force member and consultant, University of Southern California, 1976-78; 'Relationship Between Dental Team and Dental Patient Inclusion, Control and Affection Behaviours and Dental Patient Compliance', USIU, 1983; Numerous conference presentations, essays, seminars. *Honours:* Turnipseed Outstanding Active 20-30 Member, 1967; Deputy Sheriff of San Diego County, 1973; Community Services Headliner, San Diego Press Club, 1974. *Hobbies:* Gardening; Snow Ski-ing; Tennis; Private Pilot. *Address:* 4632 Van Dyke Avenue, San Diego, CA 92116, USA.

JEPSON, Joanne Hope, b. 22 Mar. 1931, Fort

Wayne, Indiana, USA. Associate Professor of Clinical Radiology and Neurosurgery. *Education:* BA, University of California, Berkeley, USA, 1953, MA, 1956; MD, CM, McGill University, Montreal, Canada, 1959. *Appointments:* Fellow, Special Fellow, Haematology, McGill University, Canada, 1963-66; Assistant Professor, 1966-70; Associate Professor of Medicine, Pharmacology, Chariman Haematology/Oncology, Medical College of Pennsylvania, Philadelphia, USA, 1970-72; Professor of Medicine, 1972-77; AMCA Society Fellow, University of California, San Francisco, 1977-79, Associate Professor, Clinical Radiology, 1979-82; Associate Professor, Clinical Radiology/Neurosurgery, 1982-; Senior Radiotherapist, University of Southern California, Southern California Cancer Centre-; Kenneth Norris Jr Cancer and Research Hospital. Los Angeles, California-. *Memberships:* American College of Physicians; American College of Radiology; American Society of Clinical Oncology; American Society of Haematology; American Society of Therapeutic Radiology and Oncology; California Radiology Society; California Radiation Therapy Association; Los Angeles Radiology Society; Los Angeles Radiation Therapy Society; Executive Board, American Cancer Society, Los Angeles. *Publications:* "Haematological Problems in Cardiologic Practice", 1977; 'Haematologic Problems in Pregnancy', 1979; Over 60 research papers. *Honours:* McGill University Scholar, 1957-59; Alpha Omega Alpha, 1958. *Hobbies:* Painting; Sculpting; Sports; Travel. *Address:* Southern California Cancer Centre, University of Southern California, 1414 South Hope Street, Los Angeles, CA 90015, USA.

JEREB, Berta, b. 25 May 1925, Dravograd, Yugoslavia, Radiation Oncologist. m. Marjan Jereb, 26 Sep. 1961, Stockholm, Sweden, 1 son, 1 daughter. *Education:* MD, Medical School, University of Ljubljana, 1950; DMedSc, 1973, Docent, 1973, Karolinska Institute, Stockholm, Sweden. *Appointments:* Assistant Professor, Oncological Institute, Ljubljana, Yugoslavia, 1957-61; Radiation Oncologist, Radiumhemmet, Stockholm, Sweden, 1963-73; Radiation Oncolgoist, Memorial Sloan-Kettering Cancer Centre, New York, USA, 1973-75, 1977-83. *Membership:* President, 1976-80, International Society of Paediatric Oncology; Swedish Radiological Society; American Society for Therapeutic Radiology and Oncology. *Publications:* 'Carcinoma of the Thyroid in Children', 1972; "Ergonostic Aspects of Nephroblastoma", 1973; 'Anaplastic Giant-cell Carcinoma of the thyroid', 1975; 'Intrapleural Interferon in Breast Cancer', 1976; 'Ophthalmic Radiotherapy', 1983; 'Radiation for Medulloblastoma', 1984. *Address:* Kardeljeva 12, Ljubljana, Yugoslavia.

JEROME, John Anthony, b. 8 Apr. 1947, Detroit, Michigan, USA. Psychologist. m. Jaye L Hamilton, 17 Mar. 1978, Lansing, Michigan, USA, 1 son, 1 daughter. *Education:* BS Psychology, MS Rehabilitation Counselling, PhD Psychology, Michigan State Universtiy. *Appointments:* Staff, Orthopaedic Department, Ingam Medical Center, Lansing, Michigan; Adjunct Research Staff, Department of Human Medicine, Michigan State Universtiy; Clinical Assistant Professor, Department of Surgery, Michigan State University. *Memberships:* American Psychological Association; Michigan Psychological Association; Charter Member, Biofeedback Reasearch Society; Charter Member, American Association of Biofeedback Clinicians; Charter Member, American Pain Society; International Associetion for the Study of Pain. *Publications:* 'Chronic Back Pain Syndrome: An Analysis of Current Therapies' (in Michigan Osteopathic Journal), 1978; 'Back Clinic: Design, Results, Analysis', 1975. *Honours:* Distinguished Service Award, Arthritis Foundation, 1977; Fellowship & Educational Stipends, Department of Health Education & Welfare, 1981, 1982. *Hobbies:* Family; Hunting; Fishing. *Address:* East Lansing Orthopaedic Association, 4528 S Hagadon Road, East Lansing, MI 48823, USA.

JESTE, Dilip V, b. 23 Dec. 1944, Pimpalgaon, India, Chief of Unit on Movement Disorders and Dementia; Associate Clinical Professor of Neurology and Psychiatry. m. Sonali D Jeste, MD, 5 Dec. 1971, Poona, 2 daughters. *Education:* MB, BS, University of Poona, 1966; DPM, College of Physicians and Surgeons, Bombay, 1970; MD Psychiatry, University of Bombay, 1970; Certified, American Board of Psychiatry and Neurology, 1979,. *Appointments:* Honorary Assistant Professor in Psychiatry, KEM Hospital and Seth GS Medical College, Bombay, 1971-74; Staff Psychiatrist, Adult Psychiarty Branch NIMH, Saint Elizabeths Hospital, Washington DC, USA, 1977-82; Clinical Associate Professor of Psychiatry, Uniformed Services University of Health Sciences, Walter Reed Army Medical Center, National Naval Medical Center, Bethesda, Maryland, 1981-84. *Memberships Include:* American College of Neuropsychopharmacology; American Psychiatric Association; Society of Biological Psychiatry; American Academy of Neurology; Society for Neuroscience; Indian Psychiatric Society. *Publications:* "Understanding and Treating Tardive Syskinesia", (with R J Wyatt), 1982; "Neuropsychiatric Movement Disorder", (editor with R J Wyatt), 1984; " Neuropsychiatric Dementias: Current Perspectives", editor. *Honours:* Sandoz Award, Indian Psychiatric Society, 1973; A E Bennett Neuropsychiatric Research Award in Clinical Sceinces, Society of Biological Psychiatry, 1981. *Hobbies:* Tennis; Cricket; Music. *Address:* Neuropsychiatry Branch, National Institute of Mental Health, Saint Elizabeths Hospital, WAW Building, Washingon, DC 20032, USA.

JETMALANI,, Narain Bodaram, b. 24 Feb 1916, Shikarpur, Pakistan, Clinical Professor, Psychiatry, Adjunct Professor Psychoanalysis, Oregon Health Sciences, USA. m. Sheila, 3 Apr 1955, Bombay, India, 2 sons, 1 daughter. *Education:* MRCS; LRCP; DPM (England); MD (USA); Associate Member, British Institute of Psychoanalysis. *Appointments:* House Officer, Dulwich Hospital, London, England; Registrar, Senior Registrar, Netherne Hospital, Surrey, England; Senior Hospital Medical Officer, Claybury Hosptial, Essex; Joint Director, BM Institute Child Therapy, Ahmedabad, Inida; Director, Residency Training and Medical Education, Oregon State Hospital, Salem, USA; Private Practice, Psychiatric Association; Indian Psychiatric Association; Oregon Psychiatric Association; British Society of Psychoanalysis. *Hobbies:* Tennis; Camping; Hiking. *Address:* 2697 12th Place S E, Salem, OR 97302, USA.

JEVNE, Ronna Fay, b. 24 Nov. 1948, Alberta, Canada. Psychologist, Clinical Professor. m. Allen Eng, 1 Aug. 1981, 3 sons, 2 daughter. *Education:* BEd English, Sociology/Psychology, University of Alberta, 1970; MA Educational Foundations, 1974, PhD Counselling Psychology, 1978, University of Calgary. *Appointments:* Teacher, Calgary Schools, 1970-72; Graduate Teaching Assistant, University of Calgary, 1972; Student Counsellor, Calgary Board of Education, 1972-76; Consultant, Counsellor, 1976- (in private practice); Senior Psychologist, Cross Cancer Institute, Edmonton, 1978-; Associate Clinical Professor, University of Alberta, Work in Health Psychology and Psychosocial Oncology. *Memberships:* ATA Guidance Council; Psychologists Association of Alberta; Special Interest Group on Counselling PAA; Canadian Guidance & Counselling Association; Psychologists for Peace; Canadian Mental Health Association; Canadian Society of Clinical Hypnosis; American Society of Clinical Hypnosis; Sons of Norway. *Publications:* Various articles in professional journals on counselling & stress management;

several manuals. *Honours:* Some 15 grants & Fellowships for research 1966-84. *Hobbies:* Photography; Cooking. *Address:* 3103-104 Street, Edmonton, Alberta, T6J 3B2, Canada.

JEYASINGHAM, Kumarasingham, b. 5 Aug. 1933, Manipay, Ceylon. Consultant Thoracic Surgeon. m. Veronica Mary Kershaw, 9 Sept. 1965, Preston, England, 2 sons, 2 daughters. *Education:* MBBS, University of Ceylon, 1957; ChM; Liverpool, 1965; Higher Certificate Training in Thoracic Surgery, 1975. *Appointments:* Registrar, Cardiothoracic Surgery, Liverpool Regional Cardiothoracic Centre, England, 1962-65; Senior Lecturer in Surgery, University of Ceylon, Colombo, Ceylon, 1965-67; Senior Registrar, Cardiothoracic Surgery, South Western Regional Hospital Board, England, 1968-75; Research Fellow, Cardiac Surgery, University of Aarhus, Denmark, 1969-70; currently Consultant Thoracic Surgeon, Frenchay Hospital, Bristol, England. *Memberships:* Fellow, Royal Colleges of Surgeons; 1962 British Thoracic Society; British Society of Gastroenterology; European Society of Surgical Oncology; Society of Thoracic and Cardiovascular Surgeons of Great Britain and Ireland; British Oesophageal Group; Cosham Medical Society; Bristol Medico Chirurgical Society; West Country Society, etc. *Publications Include:* Chapter: 'Diaphragm', in 'Operative Surgery and Management', 1981; Chapter: 'Carcinoma of the Oesophagus and Stomach' in 'Operative Surgery and Management', second edition (in press, 1986); Contributions to professional journals including 'British Journal of Surgery', 'Thorax', 'Surgery', 'Surgical Gynaecology and Obstetrics'. *Honours:* Honorary Member Societa Medica Chirugica of Bologna, Italy, 1978; Visiting Lecturer, University of Athens, Greece, 1983; Visiting Professor, University of Indianapolis, USA, 1984; Elected to Panel of Examiners for the Fellowhsip in Cardiothoracic Surgery, Royal College of Surgeons, Edinburgh, 1984. *Hobbies:* Philately; Travel. *Address:* Prospect House, 3 Prospect Close, Winterbourne Down, Avon BS17 1BN, England.

JHEE, Heun-Taik, b. 16 May 1923, Seoul, Korea. Professor of Dentistry. m. Geum-Ja Lee, 14 Nov. 1952, Pusan, Korea, 1 son, 3 daughters. *Education:* DDS, College of Dentistry, Seaul National Universtiy, Graduate and Postgraduate of Dentistry, University of Michigan, Michigan, USA; Dr Med Sc, Graduate School of Medicine, Yonsei University, Seoul, Korea. *Appointments:* Assistant, Instructor, Assistant Professor, Associate Professor, Professor, Medical and Dental College, Yonsei University, Seoul, 1947-70; President, Korean Academy of Dental Materials 1968-70, Korean Academy of Prosthodontics 1972-74, Seaul Dental Association 1976-78, Korean Dental Association 1978-82; Vice President, Asian Pacific Dental Federation, 1979-85; Regent, International Federation of Dentists Korea; Advisor, Korean Dental Association; Visiting Professor, College of Dentistry, Yonsei University, Seoul. *Memberships:* Korean Dental Association; Asian Pacific Dental Federation; Federation Dentaire Internationale; Fellow, Intereational College of Dentist. *Publications:* 'A Study of Salivary Glands of Rats Injected with Aatinomycin D'. *Honours:* Medal, Kugmin Pojang 1972, Kugmin Hunjang Mokryunjang 1983. *Address:* Woo-Sung Apartment 7-406, San 90-I Secochodong Kangnam-ku, Seoul, Korea.

JOCHHEIM, Kurt-Alphons, b. 20 Jan. 1921, Hamburg, Federal Republic of Germany. Head, Rehabilitation Center. m. Eleonore, 26 Sept. 1948, Hamburg, 1 son, 2 daughters. *Education:* Final Examination in Medicine, 1946; MD; Lecturing License for Neurology and Psychiatry, 1958. *Appointments:* Intern, Neurological Department, Hamburg, 1946; Assistant, Department of Neurology and Psychiatry, University of Cologne, 1950; Assistant Professor, University Hospital, Cologne, 1964; Chairman, Rehabilitation Center,

1966-. Head of Institute for Rehabilitation and sport for the Disabled, 1964. *Memberships:* President, German Society for Rehabilitation for the Disabled; Council Member, Rehabilitation International (Past President). *Publications:* Grundlagen der Rehbilitation, 1958; Lumbaler Bandscheibenschaden, 1961 zus mit Loew u Rutt, Neurologie u. Psychiatrie fur Krankenschwestern und Krankenpfleger zus mit Arns u. Remschmidt, 5 Aufl. 1983; Das Neurologische Gutachten zus mit Rauschalbach 1984; Author over 250 articles in books and professional journals. *Honour:* Reichsbund Prize, 1978; Poppelreuther Medal, 1978; Bundesverdienstkreuz, 1984; Honorary Member, Dutch Society for Rehaiblitation Medicine, 1980; Columbian Society for Physicial Medicine and Rehaiblitation, Honorary Member, 1973. *Hobbies:* Riding; Sailing; Art collecting. *Address:* Sperberweg 10, Erftstadt, Federal Republic of Germany.

JOFFE, Barry Issac, b. 24 Oct. 1939, Johannesburg, South Africa. Associate Professor, Medicine, Senior Physician, Witwatersrand Medical School. m. Rebecca Berkowitz, 29 Nov. 1964, Johannesburg, 3 sons, 1 daughter. *Education:* MB Bch., Witwatersrand University Medical School, 1962; MRCP, London, 1966; FRCP, 1982; DSC. (Med), Witwatersrand, 1975. *Appointments:* House Physician, Baragwanath Hosptial, 1963-64; Postgraduate Student, Queen Square & Hammersmith Hospital, London, England, 1965-66; Physician and Senior Physician, Johannesburg Hospitals Teaching Complex, University of Witwatersrand, 1970-. *Memberships:* Society for Endocrinology, Metabolism & Diabetes of Southern Africa; Endocrine Society; Medical Graduates Association, Witwatersrand University. *Publications:* Articles in professional journals including: "Insulin Reserve in Patients with Chronic Pancreatitis", 'Lancet 2', 1968. *Honours:* Associate Professor, medicine, University of Witwatersrand, 1981. *Hobbies:* Swimming; Chess; Gardening. Address: Dept. of Medicine, University of Witwatersrand, Medical School, York Road, Parktown, Johannesburg 2193, South Africa.

JOHAL, Malkit Kaur, b. 18 Mar. 1948, Kenya, Family Physician; Clinical Instructor, University of Toronto; Staff, Toronto Western Hospital. m. Hardev Singh Johal, 25 July 1973, Chandigarh, India, 1 son, 1 daughter. *Education:* MBBS; CCFP. *Appointments:* Family physican. *Memberships:* College of Physicians and Surgeons of Ontario; College of Family Physicians of Canada; Ontario Medical Association. *Honours:* Silver Medal, Punjab University; President of India's Medal, Top Female Student of Punjab University, 1970-71. *Hobbies:* Reading; Knitting; Baking. *Address:* 5 Jill Crescent, Islington, Ontario, Canada M9B 6B2.

JOHANSSON, Barbro Birgitta, b. 23 Dec. 1933, Falkenberg, Sweden. Professor and Chairman, Department of Neurology. *Education:* MD, 1959, PhD, 1974, University of Goteborg; DTM & H, London School of Hygiene and Tropical Medicine, England, 1964. *Appointments:* Associate Professor, Department of Neurology, University of Goteborg; Consultant in Occupational Neurology, Department of Occupational Health, Goteborg University; Visiting Scientist, National Institutes of Health Bethesda Maryland, USA, 1967-68; currently, Professor and Chairman, Department of Neurology, University of Lund, Sweden. *Memberships:* International Society of Microcirculation; International Society of Hypertension; Stroke Council, American Heart Association; Research Committee, World Federation of Neurology; International Society for Cerebral Circulation; European Neuroscience Association; Royal Society of Medicine Committee for Medical Disasters, Swedish Defence Department. *Publications:* Author of about 200 medical articles in International Journals 10-15 book chapters. *Hobbies:* Music;

Underwater archaeology; Ethnographic art; Anthropology; International literature; Languages. *Address:* Department of Neurology, University of Lund, University Hospital, S-221 85 Lund, Sweden.

JOHANSSON, Börje E G, b. 29 July 1930, Afors, Sweden. Director of Preclinical Cardiovascular Research. m. Gun, 16 Mar. 1957, Göteborg, Sweden, 1 son, 1 daughter. *Education:* MD 1959, PhD 1962. *Appointments:* Assistant Professor, Department of Physiology, University of Göteborg, 1962-69; Professor of Physiology, University of Lund, 1970-80; Director of Preclinical Cardiovascular Research, AB Hässle, Mölndal, 1980-; Adjunct Professor of Physiolgoy, University of Lund, 1984. *Memberships:* Scandinavian, American Physiological Societies; Editorial Board, 'Journals of Cardiovascular Pharmacology'. *Publications:* More than 100 papers & reviews in professional journals. *Hobbies:* Hiking; Canoeing; Chess. *Address:* Hässle Research Laboratories, S-431 83 Mölndal, Sweden.

JOHNS, Richard Bell, b. 10 Aug. 1929, Sutton, Surrey, England. Professor. m. Pamela Marie Thurgood, 3 Apr. 1954, London, 2 sons, 3 daughters. *Education:* LDS RCS (Eng), 1955, PhD (London), 1974, Guy's Hospital Dental School. *Appointments:* Lecturer, 1969-74, Senior Lecturer, 1974-79, Reader, Sub-Dean, Dental Studies, 1976-79, Guy's Hospital Dental School; Professor, Restorative Dentistry, Dean, Dental Studies, Charles Clifford Dental Hospital, Sheffield. *Memberships:* British Endodontic Society, Honorary Member; British Society for Restorative Dentistry; International Association for Dental Research; Society for Biomaterials, USA; Royal Society of Medicine; European Society for Biomaterials; Biological Engineering Society. *Publications:* "A Study of the Response of Tissue to Endodontic and Endosseous Implants in Macaca irus Monkeys", 1974; Joint Editor in Chief Companion to Dental Studies, Blackwells; Articles in professional journals. *Hobbies:* Thinking; Silversmithing. *Address:* Dept. of Restorative Dentistry, School of Clinical Dentistry, Charles Clifford Dental Hospital, Wellesley Road, Sheffield S10 2SZ, England.

JOHNSON, Brian, b. 22 Jan. 1952, New York, USA. Clinical Instructor. Divorced, 1 son, 1 daughter. *Education:* BS, Columbia University, USA, MD, New York Medical College. *Appointments:* Staff Psychiatrist in charge of Psychiatric Service for Alcoholics, Metropolitan State Hospital, Waltham, Massachussetts, 1981-83; Clinical Instructor in Psychiatry, Harvard Medical School, 1981-83; Psychoparmacology Consultant, Cambridge Family and Children's Service, 1983-; Medical Director, Alcoholism Intervention Centre, Somerville, Massachussetts, 1983-; Clinical Instructor in Medicine, Harvard Medical School; Advanced Candidate, Boston Psychoanalytic Institute-. *Memberships:* Massachussetts Psychiatric Society, 1981; American Psychiatric Association, 1982; American Medical Society on Alcoholism, 1982; MPS Committee on Alcholism, 1982. (all current). *Address:* 10 Jacques Street, Somerville, MA 02145, USA.

JOHNSON, Dale G, b. 27 Sep. 1930, Salt Lake City, Utah, USA. Professor of Surgery and of Pediatrics; Chairman of Medical Centre Department of Surgery. m. Beverly Clark, 22 Dec. 1952, 2 sons, 2 daughters. *Education:* BS 1953, MD 1956, University of Utah; Internship and Residency in Surgery, Massachusetts, 1956-61; Residency in Pediatric Surgery, Children's Hospital of Philadelphia, 1964-65; Certified, American Board of Surgery, 1962; Certificate of Special Competance in Pediatric Surgery, 1975; Recertified in the Speciality of Pediatric Surgery, 1983. *Appointments:* Investigator in Experimental Surgery, Walter Reed Army Institute of Research, 1961-63; Research Associate in Surgery 1963-64, Assistant Professor of Pediatric Surgery

1966-71, University of Pennsylvania; Associate Professor of Surgery and Pediatrics 1971-76, Professor of Surgery 1976-, Professor of Pediatrics 1977-, Head of Pediatric Surgery Division 1971-, University of Utah College of Medicine; Chairman of Department of Surgery, Primary Children's Medical Center, Salt Lake City, 1971-. *Memberships:* American Academy of Pediatrics; American College of Surgeons; American Pediatric Surgical Association; American Society for Laser Medicine and Surgery; American Surgical Association; British Association of Pediatric Surgeons; Lilliputian Surgical Society; Pacific Association of Pediatric Surgeons; Societe Internationale De Chirurgie; Society of University Surgeons; Phi Beta Kappa; Alpha Omega Alpha; Society of Sigma Xi. *Publications include:* 'Treatment of Wilms' tumor in children', 1980; 'Ambulatory pediatric surgery' (with ME Matlak), in "Ambulatory Surgery and the Basics of Emergency Surgical Care", (editor Mark W Wolcott), 1981; 'Gastroesophageal reflux and respiratory disease: The place of the surgeon', (co-author), 1984; 'Current thinking on the role of surgery in gastroesophageal reflux', 1985. *Hobbies:* Classical music; History; Skiing; Gardening; Microcomputer applications. *Address:* Primary Children's Medical Center, 320 Twelfth Avenue, Salt Lake City, UT 84103, USA.

JOHNSON, Douglas William, b. 6 June 1954, West Point, New York, USA. Director, Radiation Oncology Section, David Grant USAF Medical Centre. m. Susan Mary Friedman, 23 July 1977, Centreville, Virginia, 1 daughter. *Education:* BSc, Virginia Polytechnic Institute, 1976; MD, Medical College of Virginia, 1979; Intern, Internal Medicine, Wilford Hall US Air Force Medical centre, 1980; Resident, Therapeutic Radiology, Stanford University Medical Centre, 1983. *Appointments:* Clinical Instructor, Department of Radiology (Radiation Therapy), Stanford University Medical Centre, 1983-; Director, Radiation Oncology, David Grant USAF Medical Centre, Travis Air Force Base, California, 1983-. *Memberships:* American Medical Association; American Society of Therapeutic Radiology & Oncology; American Society of Clinical Oncology; American College of Radiology; American Endocurie Therapy Society; California Radiology Society; Northern California Radation Therapy Association; Society of Air Force Physicians. *Publications:* Contributions to various medical journals, presentations to professional seminars & conferences, technical innovations: Outline, procedure for transposing CT-scan determined tumour volumes to set-up films, now integral part of pre-treatment, prostate cancer, Stanford University Medical Centre (with M.A. Bagshaw, MD); Design, adjustable breast bridge for use in interstitial implants of the breast, now routine use at Stanford. *Honours:* Alpha Omega Alpha, 1979; US Air Force Award, 1983. *Hobbies:* Tennis; Swimming; Flying (private pilot). *Address:* Radiation Oncology Section, SGHRT, David Grant USAF Medical Centre, Travis AFB, CA 94535-5300, USA.

JOHNSON, Glenn Michael, b. 28 Dec. 1948, Arizona, USA. Associate Psychologist. m. Mary-Louise V Copeland, 21 May 1978, Jackson, New Jersey, USA. *Education:* BA, Hunter College, City University of New York, 1979; MA, Clinical Psychology, University of Kansas, 1983; PhD, University of Kansas, 1986. *Appointments:* Counsellor/Therapist, Renaissance West Inc, 1983-84; Assistant Field Co-ordinator for Rehabilitation Psychology, Department of Psychology, University of Kansas Medical Center, 1984-85; Director of Residential Treatment Services, Renaissance West Ins, 1984-85; Associate Psychologist, 1985-86. *Memberships:* American Psychological Association (SA); Therapeutic Communications Cooperative; American Society of Clinical Hypnosis (SA); Institute for the Advancement of Health; American Association for the Study of Mental Imagery. *Publications:* Articles in professional journals. Honour: Summa Cum

Laude, Hunter College, 1979. *Hobbies:* Photography & Collage; Swimming; Computer Programming & Games; Creative Writing; Travel. *Address:* Norfolk Regional Center, Norfolk, NE 68701, USA.

JOHNSON, Marilyn b. 7 May 1925, Houston, Texas, USA. Private Practitioner, Obstetrics & Gynaecology. *Education:* BA, The Rice Institute, Houston, Texas, 1945; MD, Baylor University College of Medicine, 1950; Fellow, American College of Obstetrics & Gynaecology, 1963; Rotating Intern, New England Hospital for Women & Children, Tufts Teaching Hospitals, Boston, Massachausetts, 1950; Resident in Obstetrics & Gynaecology, Methodist Hosptial, Houston, 1951-53; Resident in Gynaecology, M D Anderson Tumour Institute, Houston, 1954; Fellow in Gynaecological Pathology, Free Hospital for Women, Brookline, Massachusetts, 1952, The Harvard Medical School. *Appointments Include:* Clinical Instructor, Obstetrics & Gynaecology, Baylor University College of Medicine, 1954-81, University of Texas Postgraduate School of Medicine, 1954-81; Gynaecologist, Depelchin Faith Home, Houston, 1954-80; Active Staff Member, various Texas Hospitals, 1954-81; Gynaecologist, Rice University, Houston, 1960-80. *Memberships Include:* American Medical Association; American Medical Womens' Association; American Infertility Society; Alpha Epsilon Iota; Medical Director, Birthright Organisation, Houston, 1973-81; Member, Board of Directors, Right ot Life Organisation, Houston, 1973-81; and others. *Hobbies:* Writing Poetry & Short Stories; Piano. *Address:* 204 West Schubert Street, Fredericksburg, TX 78624, USA.

JOHNSON, Michael L, b. 17 May 1941, Louisville, Kentucky, USA. Staff Psychiatrist. m. 1 son, 3 daughters. *Education:* BA, Earlham College; MD, Indiana University; Intern, Marion County General Hospital Indiana; Residency in Psychiatry, Barnes Renard Hospitals. *Appointemnts:* Staff Psychiatrist, Naval Hospital, Portsmouth, Virginia; Staff Psychiatrist, South Central CMHC, Bloomington, Indiana; Private Practice in Psychiatry, Bloomington; Consulting Psychiatry, Indiana Univeristy Student Health Services; Medical Director, Mental Health Unit, Milford Whitinsville Regional Hospital; Psychiatrist-in-Chief, Massachusetts Osteopathic Hospital and Medical Center; Staff Psychiatrist, Harvard community Health Plan-Cambridge Center; Clinical Instructor in Psychiatry, Harvard Medical School. *Memberships:* American Psychiatric Association; Boston Society Psychiatry and Neurology; Massachusetts Psychiatric Society; American Board Psychiatry and Neurology, 1976; Nityananda Institute (Cambridge). *Address:* 1611 Cambridge Street, Cambridge, MA 02238.

JOHNSON, Peter Roy, b. 3 Nov. 1942, Evanston, Illinois, USA. Programme Director, Meadowlands Health Care Centre. m. Joanne Bollinger, 31 Aug. 1963, 1 son, 1 daughter. *Education:* BS, Northern Illinois University, 1964; MS 1966, PhD 1971, University of Pittsburgh; Graudate study, Ohio State University, 1979-80. *Appointments include:* Experimental therapist, Home for Crippled Children 1966-67, University of Pittsburgh 1968-69; Lecturer, Duquesne University, 1968-; Assistant Professor, ibid, 1970-71; Assistant Director, Communications Department, Children's Hospital, 1971-73; Hearing/Speech Pathology & Audiology, Allegheny General Hospital. 1973-85. *Memberships:* American Speech, Language & Hearing Association; Pennsylvania Speech & Hearing Association; Adjunct professorial staff, Allegheny General Hospital. *Publications include:* 'The use of parent-child interaction patterns in therapy for young stutterers', co-author, 1972. *Honours:* Kappa Delta Pi; Sigma Alpha Eta; United Cerebral Palsy Scholarship. *Hobby:* Sailing. *Address:* 121 Wetzel Road, Glenshaw, PA 15116, USA.

JOHNSON, Suzanne Hall, b. 25 Oct. 1946, New Jersey, USA. Director. m. Steven H Johnson. *Education:* BS, Duke University; MN, UCLA; RN. *Appointments:* Edirot, 'Dimensions of Critical Care Nursing', Director, Hall Johnson Communications Inc', Faculty, Stanford University, Palo Alto, CA. *Memberships:* American Association of Critical Care Nurses; American Nurses' Association; Sigma Theta Tau; NAACOG. *Publications:* "High Risk Parenting", 2nd edition, 1986; "Marketing Continuing Education in a Recession, Journal of Continuing Education in Nursing", 1985. *Honour:* Distinguished Alumni, Duke University, 1982. *Address:* 9737 West Ohio Avenue, Lakewood, CO 80226, USA.

JOHNSON, William Michael, b. 20 Nov. 1940, Olean, New York, USA. Chief, Pulmonary Disease. m. Marlene Brill, 26 June 1965, Williamsville, New York, 1 son, 3 daughters. *Education:* AB, 1963, MD, 1968, Stanford University; MPH, 1970, MIH, 1971, Harvard University. *Appointments:* Intern Medicine, Buffalo Hospitals, State University of New York, 1968-69; Acting Deputy Director, Division of Field Studies and Clinical Investigations, National Institute for Occupational Safety and Health, Cincinnati, Ohio, 1971-73; Resident in Internal Medicine, 1973-75, Fellow in Pulmonary Disease, 1975-77, University of Arizona; Assistant Professor, Environmental Health, Adjunct Assistant Professor of Medicine, University of Washington, Seattle, 1977-80; Pulmonary Disease Physician, 1980-, Chief, Pulmonary Disease Service, 1983-. Eisenhower Army Medical Center, Fort Gordon, Georgia. *Memberships:* Fellow, American College of Chest Physicians; American Thoracic Society; Society for Occupational and Environmental Health; American Industrial Hygiene Association; New York Academy of Sciences. Diplomate: American Board of Internal Medicine; American Board of Preventive Medicine. *Publications:* Author of numerous articles on pulmonary disease and occupational cancer. *Address:* 2948 Foxhall Circle, Augusta, GA 30907, USA.

JOHNSON-LAIRD, Philip Nicholas, b. 12 Oct. 1936, Leeds, England. Assistant Director of Applied Psychiatry Unit. m. Maureen Mary Sullivan, 1 Aug. 1959, London, 1 son, 1 daughter. *Education:* BA Honours Psychology 1964, PhD Psychology 1967, University College, London. *Appointments:* Assistant Lecturer in Psychology 1966-67, Lecturer 1967-73, University College, London; Reader in Experimental Psychology 1973-78, Professor of Experimental Psychology 1978-82, Sussex University; Assistant Director, Medical Research Council Applied Psychiatry Unit, Cambridge, 1982-. *Memberships:* British Psychological Society; Linguistics Association; Experimental Psychology Society. *Publications including:* 5 books including: "Psychology of Reasoning", (with P C Watson), 1972; "Language and Perception", (with G A Miller), 1976; "Thinking", (edited with P C Watson), 1977; "Mental Models", 1983; 75 papers in psychgological, linguistic and scientific journals. *Honours:* Rosa Moriston Medal, University College, London, 1964; Spearman Medal, British Psychological Society, 1974; Honorary Doctorate, Gothenburg, Sweden, 1983; Presidents Award, British Psychological Society, 1985. *Hobbies:* Modern Jazz; Cinema; Theatre. *Address:* MRC Applied Psychology Unit, 15 Chaucer Road, Cambridge CB2 2EF, England.

JOHNSTON, Ivan David Alexander, b. 4 Oct 1929, Belfast, Northern Ireland. University Professor and Head of Department of Surgery. m. 3 Sep. 1958, Belfast, 2 sons. *Education:* MB BCh BAO, Hons, 1953 MCh, 1958 Commendation, Queen's University, Belfast; FRCS, Royal College of Surgeons, 1958.

Appointments: Senior Tutor in Surgery, Queen's University Belfast, 1955-58 and 1960-63; Research Assistant, Mayo Clinic, Rochester, Minnesota, 1958-59; Lecturer and Consultant Surgeon, Royal Postgraduate Medical School, London, 1963-66; Professor and Head of Department of Surgery, University of Newcastle-upon-Tyne. *Memberships:* Fellow of the Association of Surgeons of Great Britain and Ireland; Member of the Surgical Research Society; Fellow of the Royal Society of Medicine (past members of Council of Section of Oncology); Member, International Society of Surgery. *Publications:* "Advances in Clinical Nutrition" 1982; "Endocrine Surgery" 1983; "Design and Utilization of Operating Theatres" 1984; "Scientific Foundations Surgery" third edition. *Honours:* Hunterian Professor, Royal College of Surgeons of England, 1964; Schubert Medal, Swedish Medical Society, 1974; Honorary Fellow, American Surgical Association, 1980; Honorary Fellow, American College of Surgeons, 1984. *Hobbies:* Gardening; Photography. *Address:* 36, Woodside, Darras Hall, Ponteland, Northumberland NE20 9JA, England.

JOHNSTON, Janis Clark, b. 5 Jan. 1947, South Bend, Indiana, USA. Psychologist. m. Mark Johnston, 14 June 1969, Oak Brook, Illinois, 1 son, 1 daughter. *Education:* BA, Manchester College; EDD, Boston University. *Appointments:* Lexington Public Schools, Lexington, MA, 1972-78; Harvard University Pre-school project, 1973-74; Boston University Graduate School of Education, 1974-75; Hahnemann Medical College and Hospital of Philadelphia, PA., 1978-81; Acorn (Employee Assitance Program), Philadelphia, 1979-81; Oak Park and River Forest High School on Campus Behaviour Disorders Program, Oak Park, 1981-86. *Memberships:* American Psychological Assoc.,National Assoc. School Psychologists; Illinois School Psychologists Association. *Publications:* "School Consultation" with the "Classroom Family'", 1981; 'Burn Out Prevention Training for School Administrators', 1981; 'Psychologist as Negotiator in System Contracts with Adolescents', 1983; 'Balancing an Educational Mobile through Problem Solving Conferences', 1983; 'The on Campus Program: A Systemic/Behavioral Approach to Behavior Disorders in High School', 1983; 'Drama and Interpersonal Problem Solving: A Dynamic Interplay for Adolescent Groups', 1986. *Honours:* NDEA Title IV Fellowship, 1969; Outstanding Young Women of America, 1974; School Psychology Practitioner of the Year, Region 1, 11., 1984. *Hobbies:* Gardening; Embroidery; Sewing; Cooking; Reading; Tennis; Aerobic Dance. *Address:* 539 North Ridgeland Avenue, Oak Park, IL 60302, USA.

JOHNSTON, Oliver Budge, b. 9 Jan. 1930, Blackfoot, Idaho, USA. Chairman, Orthopaedic Department, Cottonwood Hospital. m. Nina Leishman, 16 Mar. 1956, Salt Lake City, 5 sons, 1 daughter. *Education:* BS; MD; American Board of Orthopedic Surgery. *Appointments:* Chief, Surgery, 1971, Chairman, Quality Care Committee, 1973, President, Medical Staff, 1974-75, Chief, Orthopaedics, 1978-79, Chairman, Orthopedics, 1985- , Cottonwood Hospital, Salt Lake City. *Memberships:* International Arthroscopy Association; Arthroscopy Association of North America; American Academy of Orthopedic Surgeons; American Medical Association. *Hobbies:* Skiing; Water Skiing; Motor Cycling; Backpacking. *Address:* 1927 E 5600 So., Salt Lake City, UT 84117, USA.

JOKLIK, Wolfgang Karl, b. 16 Nov. 1926, Vienna, Austria. Chairman of Department of Microbiology and Immunology. m. (1) Judith Vivien Nicholas, 9 Apr. 1955, Canberra, Australia, (died 1975), 1 son, 1 daughter, (2) Patricia Hunter Downey, 23 Apr. 1977, Durham, North Carolina, USA. *Education:* BSc 1947, MSc 1948, Sydney University, Australia, DPhil, Oxford University, England, 1952. *Appointments:*

Research Fellow, Department of Cytophysiology, University of Copenhagen, Denmark, 1953; Research Fellow 1953-56, Fellow in Department of Microbiology 1956-62, Australian National University, Canberra, Australia; USPHS Postdoctoral Fellow, Laboratory of Cell Biology, NIAID, NIH, Bethesda, Maryland, USA, 1959-60; Associate Professor 1962-65, Sienfried Ullman Professor of Cell Biology 1965-68, Albert Einstein College of Medicine, New York; Professor and Chairman, Department of Microbiology and Immunology, Duke University Medical Center, Durham, North Carolina, 1968. *Memberships:* American Society for Virology; American Society for Microbiology; American Society for Biological Chemists. *Publications:* Contributor and Senior Editor, 'Zinsser Microbiology' 15th-18th editions, 1972-84; Contributor and Senior Editor, 'Principles of Animal Virology', 1980 and 1984; Contributor and Senior Editor, 'The Reoviridae', 1983. *Honours:* James B Duke Professor of Microbiology and Immunology, 1972; Elected to National Academy of Sciences and to its Institute of Medicine, 1981. *Hobbies:* Golf; Tennis; Walking. *Address:* Department of Microbiology and Immunology, P O Box 3020, Duke University Medical Center, Durham, NC 27710, USA.

JOLIVET, Jacques, b. 7 Aug. 1953, Montreal, Canada. Research Associate; Physician. m. Paule L'Anglais, 15 June 1975, Montreal, 1 son. *Education:* MD, University of Montreal, 1976. *Appointments:* Cancer Expert, National Cancer Institute, Bethesda, Maryland, USA, 1981-83; Reseach Associate, Institut du Cancer de Montreal, Canada, 1983-. *Memberships:* Royal College of Physicians of Canada; American Association for Cancer Research; American Society of Clinical Oncology. *Publications:* 'Pharmacology & Clincial Use of Methotnexate' in 'New England Journal of Medicine', 1983; 'A Methotnexate Resistant Human Breast Cancer Cell Line' in 'Journal of Biological Chemistry', 1984. *Hobbies:* Classical music; Wine; Sport. *Address:* Institut du Cancer de Montreal, 1560 Sherbrooke Street East, Montreal, Canada H2L 4M1.

JOLLES, Christopher J, b. 17 May 1951, USA. Director of Gynecologic Oncology. m. Robin Ann, 15 May 1971, California, 1 daughter. *Education:* BA, University of California; MD, Yale University School of Medicine; Fellowship in Gynecologic Oncology, MD Anderson Hospital, University of Texas Systems Cancer Center. *Appointments:* Director of Gynecologic Oncology, University of Utah Medical Center, Salt Lake City, Utah. *Memberships:* Western Association of Gynecologic Oncologists; Candidate, Society of Gynecologic Oncologists; Salt Lake Surgical Society; Utah State Obstetrical and Gynecological Society; Felix Rutlege Society; Sigma Xi; Academic Senate; Fellow, American College of Surgeons, American College of Obstetricians and Gynecologists. *Publications:* 'Second Look Surgery for Ovarian Cancer'; 'Progesterone Production in Adenocarcinoma of the Colon', 1985; 'Complications of Extended Field Radiotherpay', 1986. *Hobbies:* Skiing; Backpacking. *Address:* Director of Gynecologic Oncology, University of Utah Medical Center, Salt Lake City, UT 84132, USA.

JOLLEY, Janina M, b. 26 Aug. 1956, San Pedro, California, USA. Assistant Professor of Psychology. m. Mark L Mitchell, 2 Aug. 1980, Leavenworth, Indiana. *Education:* BA Human Studies, California State University at Dominguez Hills, California; MA 1980, PhD Developmental Psychology 1982, Clarion University of Pennsylvania, Pennsylvania. *Appointments:* Director, The Ohio State Unitversity Poll, 1978-80; Adjunct Professor, Franklin University, Columbus, Ohio, 1981; Assistant Professor, Mansfield University of Pennsylvania, 1982-83; Assistant Professor of Psychology, Clarion University of Pennsylvania, 1983- : Consulting Editor, The Journal of Genetic Psychology, Genetic Psychology Monographs. *Memberships:* American Psychological Association; Gerontological Society of America; Northeastern Gerontological Society. *Publications:* 'How to wirte psychology papers; A survival guide for students in psychology and related fields', 1984; 'The relationship between self structure, adaptability, and age', 1984; "A process of discovery" (in press). *Hobbies:* Physical fitness, Photography, Computer programming. *Address:* Department of Psychology, Clarion University of Pennsylvania, Clarion, PA 16214, USA.

JOLLY, Hugh, b. 5 May 1918, Douglas, Isle of Man. Honorary Consultant Paediatrician. m. Geraldine Howard, 2 sons, 1 daughter. *Education:* BA Honours 1939, MB BChir, 1943, MA 1943, DCH 1949, MD 1951, Sidney Sussex College, Cambridge University, England. *Appointments include:* Casualty Officer, West London Hospital, 1943; House Physician 1943; Medical Assistant 1947-48, The Lonodn Hospital; House Physican 1948-49, House Surgeon 1949, Assistant Medical Registrar 1949-50, Senior Medical Registrar and Pathologist 1950-51, THe Hospital for Sick Children, London; Registrar, Gastroenteritis Flying Squad, 1949-50; Resident, The Children's Hospital, Cincinnati, Ohio, USA, 1951; Consultant Paediatrician, Plymouth Clinical Area, Devon, England, 1951-60; Professor of Paediatrics, University College Ibadan, Nigeria, 1961-62; Visiting Professor of Child Health, Ghana Medical School, Ghana, 1967-69; Consultant Paediatrician 1960-83, Physician in Charge, Department of Paediatrics 1965-83, Head, Academic Department of Paediatrics 1971-83, Honorary Consultant Paediatrician 1983-, Charing Cross Hospital, London. *Memberships include:* Fellow, Royal Society of Medicine; Neonatal Society; Vice President, Family Planning Association; Advisory Board, Parents' Centres, Australia; Patron, Down's Children's Association. *Publications:* "Sexual Precocity", 1955; "Diseases of Children", 1964, 5th edition 1985; "Book of Child Care", 1975, 4th edition 1985; "Commonsense About Babies and Children", 1973 and 1983; "More Commonsense About Babies and Children", 1978; "The First Five Years", 1985; "The Grandparents' Handbook", 1985; Numerous articles; 4 chapters in books. *Honours:* Raymond Horton-Smith Prize, Cambridge University, 1951; Medical Journalists' Association Award, 1978; Bronze Medal, British Medical Association Film Competition, 1978; The Meering Award, National Association of Nursery Matrons, 1980. *Address:* The Garden House, Warren Park, Kingston Hill, Surrey KT2 7HX, England.

JONECKO, Antoni Franciszek, b. 11 Feb. 1931, Odment, Upper Silesia. Associate Professor of Surgery; Medical Academy, Cracow; Chief of Clinical Department of General Surgery, Rzeszow. m. Urszula Maria Kubica, Dr Sc Med, 3 Oct. 1964, Krapkowice, 2 daughters. *Education:* Physician Diploma, Faculty of Medicine, Silesian Academy of Medicine, 1957; Dr.Sc.Med, 1962; Dr.Habil.Sc.Med. (Surgery), 1978; Docent Dr.Hail.Sc.Med.(Surgery), 1980. *Appointments:* Instructor, Assistant and Senior Assistant Lecturer, Silesian Medical Acaemy, 1956-68; Senior Scientific Assistant, Maria-Sklodwska-Curie Institute of Onology, Gliwice, 1963-69; Vice-Chief/Head, Miner's Hospital, Department of Surgery, Zabrze, 1969-73; Chief/Head, Department of General Surgery and Voivodship Expert of Surgery, Voivodship Hospital Plock, 1973-79; Associate Professor of Surgery, Medical Academy, Cracow, 1979; Head, Clinical Department of Surgery at Rzeszow of this Academy to date; Voivodship-Expert of Surgery, Rzeszow, 1979-. *Membership:* Chairman, Rzeszow Department of Polish Association of Surgeons. *Publications:* 157 scientific articles, 1957-85; 1 mongraph, 1975. *Honour:* Dozenten-Stipendium of Alexander-von-Humboldt-Stiftung (Bad Godesberg), 1966. *Hobbies:* Manual Labour; Sports; History of Medicine. *Address:* Medical Nicolaus Copernicus Academy, ulica Sw.Anny 12, Cracow (PL-31-008 Krakow), Poland.

JONES, Beverly Ann, b. 14 July 1927, Brooklyn, New York, USA. Assistant Administrator, Nursing. m. Kenneth L. Jones, 5 Sep., 1953, Bayshore, New York, 2 sons. *Education:* BS, Nursing; Numerous seminars, courses, workshops on an ongoing basis. *Appointments include:* Associate Director, Nursing, Anne Arundel General Hospital, Anapolis, Maryland, 1966-70; Assistant Adiminstrator, Nursing, Alexandria Hospital, Virginia, 1972-73; Assistant Administrator, Nursing, Longmont United Hospital, Colorado, 1977-. *Memberships:* Colorado Society for Nurse Executives, Board Member, 1978-82, 1984-86, President, 1980-81; American Organization of Nurse executives; etc. *Publications:* "Nursing Management", 1981; "Focus", printed testimony given to National Commission on Nursing Hearing, Denver, Colorado. *Honours:* Nominee, Programme of Recognition of Excellence, Nursing Service Adminsitration of the American Organisation of Nurse Executives, People to People, US Nurse Leaders, 1980. *Hobbies:* Music; Travel; Entertaining; Theatre; Reading. *Address:* 8902 Quail Road, Longmont, Co 80501, USA.

JONES, Christopher Ernest, b. 4 Nov. 1952, Clinton, Indiana, USA. Chief, Toxicology Section, USAF School of Aerospace Medicine. *Education:* BS, Biology, University of Houston, Texas, 1973; PhD, Pharmacology, Baylor College of Medicine, Houston, 1979. *Appointments:* Postdoctoral Fellow, Northwestern University Medical School, Chicago, 1979-81; Chief, Clinical Pathology Laboratory, 1982-85, Chief, Toxicology Section, 1985-, USAF School of Aerospace medicine, Brooks AFB, Texas. *Memberships:* American Association for the Advancement of Science; American Chemcial Society; Society of Armed Forces Medical Laboratory Scientists; Aerospace Medicine Association and its Space Medicine Branch; Southwestern Association of Toxicologists. *Publications:* Co-author, 'Sequence-Specific DNA-Protein Internaction: The Lac Repressor', 'Journal Theoretical Biology', 1977; Co-author, 'Site of Phosphorylation in Nucleolar Protein B23' in 'Biochim et biophys. Acta', 1980; Co-author, 'Phosphodipeptide Analysis of Nonhistone Nuclear Proteins' in 'International Journal Peptide and Protein Research', 1980. *Honours:* National Merit Scholarship, 1970-73; University of Houston Outstanding Male Freshman, 1971 and Top Five Student, 1972; Achieveemnt Rewards for College Scientists, 1972; Air Force Commendation Medal, 1985. *Hobbies:* Flying; Stamp Collecting. *Address:* 7730 Clear Ridge, San Antonio, TX 78239-4010, USA.

JONES, Clyde William, b. 29 Sept. 1929, Barbados, West Indies. Anaesthesiologist. m. Norma Anita Smith, 14 Sept. 1963, San Diego, California, USA, 3 sons. *Education:* BS, City College of New York; MD, Howard University College of Medicine, Washington DC; Residency in Anaesthesiology, Naval Regional Medical Centre, San Diego, California, 1963-66. *Appointments:* Chairman, Department of Anaesthesiology, Naval Regional Medical Centre, San Diego, 1973-79; Chief of Anaethesiology, USA Naval Hospital, Guam, 1969-71; Clinical Associate Professor of Anaesthesiology, University of California, San Diego, 1979; Chief, Department of Anaesthesiology, Kaiser Permanente Medical Centre, San Diego. *Memberships:* American Society of Anaesthesiologists; California Society of Anaesthesiologists; International Anaesthesia Research Society; American Society of Clinical Hypnosis. 'The Use of Hypnosis in Anaesthesiology' in 'Journal of National Medical Association', 1975; (co-author) 'Hypnosis for Monitoring Intra-operative Spinal Cord Function, Anaesthesia & Analgaesia', 1976; (co-author) 'Ventilatory & Cardiovascuar Effects during spontaneous Ventilation in Man' in 'Anaestheisa & Analgaesia', 1978. *Honours:* Meritourious Service Medal, Certificate of Merit, US Navy. *Hobbies:* Hypnosis; Coin-collecting;

Harmonica-playing; Jogging. *Address:* 5201 Countryside Drive, San Diego, CA 92115, USA.

JONES, David Gareth, b. 28 Aug. 1940, Cardiff, Wales. Professor of Anatomy. m. Beryl Watson, Newcastle-upon-Tyne, England, 30 July 1966, 2 daughters. 2 sons. *Education:* BSc, Hons, University college, London, 1961; MBBS, University College Hospital Medical School, 1965; DSc, University of Western Australia, 1976. *Appointments:* Lecturer in Anatomy, University College, London, 1965-70; Senior Lecturer in Anatomy, 1970-76, Associate Professor of Anatomy, 1977-83, University of Western Australia; Professor of Anatomy and Chairman of Department, University of Otago, New Zealand, 1983-. *Memberships:* American Scientific Affiliation; Anatomical Society of Great Britain; Anatomical Society of Australia and New Zealand; Australian Neuroscience Society; Institute of Biology; Hastings Center; New York Academy of Sciences; Sigma Xi. *Publications:* "Brave New People" 1984/85; "Current Topics in Reseach on Synapses" editor Vols 1-3, 1984/86; "Our Fragile Brains" 1981; "Neurons and Synapses" 1981; "Synapses and Synaptosomes" 1975. *Honours:* W E Adams Travelling Fellowship of Anatomical Society of Australia and New Zealand, 1975; Fellow of American Scientific Affiliation, 1985. *Hobbies:* Reading; Walking; Listeing to music. *Address:* Department of Anatomy, University of Otago, P O Box 913, Dunedin, New Zealand.

JONES, Franklin Del, b. 22 Sep. 1935, Hereford, Texas, USA. Associate Director for Combat Stress. m. June Kim Jones, 30 Nov. 1957, Hereford, 3 sons, 1 daughter. *Education:* MD, University of Texas Southwestern Medical School, Waco, 1961; Certified, American Board of Psychiatry and Neurology, 1969. *Appointments Include:* Director, Research Ward 108 1968-74, Assistant - Chief of Psychiatry Department 1969-74, Director Psychiatric Education and Chief of Forensic Psychiatry Service 1974-78, Walter Reed Army Medical Center, Washington DC; Psychiatry and Neurology Consultant, Army Surgeon General, 1978-81; Chief, Combat Psychiatry Branch, Associate Director for Combat Stress, Neuropsychiatry Division, Walter Reed Army Insitute of Research, 1981 -; Clinical Professor, Georgetown University Medical School, Washington DC, 1975 -; Clinical Professor, Uniformed Services University of Health Sciences, 1976 -. *Memberships:* Fellow, American Psychiatric Association; Secretary, Former President, military section, World Psychiatric Association; Clinical Fellow, Behavior Therapy and Research Society; Society of Medical Consultants to the Armed Forces; Association of Military Surgeons of the United States; Alpha Epsilon Delta. *Publications:* 'Medical and Psychiatric Treatment Policy and Practice in Vietnam', (with A W Johnson), 1975; 'Contingency Management of Hospital-diagnosed (BI) Soldiers', (co-author), 1977; "War and Its Aftermath", (editor with D Adelaja), 1983. *Honour:* Awarded Army Surgeon General's 'A' Professional Designation, 1978. *Hobbies:* Crabbing and Clamming; History of Military Psychiatry. *Address:* 6508 Tall Tree Terrace, Rockville, MD 20852, USA.

JONES, Ivor Hugh, b. 24 May 1930, Yorkshire, England. 1st Assistant, Department of Psychiatry, University of Melbourne, Australia; Federal Chairman, Forensic Section, Royal Australia & New Zealand College of Psychiatrists. m. Eileen Margaret Cooper, 22 Feb. 1958, 2 daughters. *Education:* MB,BS, University of London, 1954; MRCP, Royal College of Physicians, Edinburgh, 1960; DPM 1962, MD 1967, London; MRCPsych (foundation member), UK, 1971; FRANZCP, Australia, 1976; FRCP, Edinburgh, 1978; FRCPSych, UK, 1979. *Appointments include:* Research Fellow, Psychiatry, Oxford, UK, 1962-65; 2nd Assistant 1965-67, Sometime Acting Head 1967-, Examiner, 1967-, Department of Psychiatry, University of Melbourne;

Assistant Physician, St. Vincent's Hospital, Melbourne, 1965-67; Examiner in Psychiatry, Final MB, BS, University of Melbourne, 1967-; Sometime Examiner, Australian & New Zealand College of Psychiatry, 1967-. *Memberships:* Fellow, College of Psychiatrists, UK: Fellow, College of Psychiatrists, Australia & New Zealand; Honorary Fellow, Indian Psychiatric Association; Associate Member, Institute of Aboriginal Studies; Australasian Academy of Forensic Sciences. *Publications include:* Textbook, "Essentials of Forensic Psychiatry", in press; Articles in 'Perspectives in Biology & Medicine', 'Society of Science & Medicine'; Extensive publications in: Ethnological aspects of psychiatry, forensic psychiatry, schizophrenia, aboriginal studies. *Honours:* John F. Williams Prize, Australian & New Zealand College of Psychiatrists, 1968; Honorary Fellow, Indian Psychiatric Association, 1979. *Hobbies:* Sailing; Bushwalking; Foreign travel. *Address:* University Department of Psychiatry, St. Vincent's Hospital, Fitzroy, Australia 3065.

JONES, Ronald Coy, b. 24 Aug. 1932, Harrison, Arkansas, USA. Professor, Surgery, University of Texas Health Science Centre. m. Jane, 1 son, 2 daughters. *Education:* MD, University of Tennessee School of Medicine, 1957. *Appointments:* Instructor, 1965, Assistant Professor, 1965-69, Associate Professor, 1969-73, Professor, Acting Chairman, 1974-76, Professor, 1974-, Surgery, University of Texas Health Science Centre, Dallas. *Memberships:* Dallas County medical Society; Dallas Society of General Surgeons; American Cancer Society; Texas Medical Association; Texas Surgical Society; American College of Surgeons; American Medical Association; American Surgical Association; Southwestern Surgical Congress; etc. *Publications:* Numerous articles in professional journals including: 'Review of Surgery'; 'Arch. Surg.'; 'Cancer'; 'Police'; 'Journal of Oral Surgery'; 'Current Therapy'; 'Principles of Surgery'; 'American Journal Surgery'; etc., several book Chapters & Abstracts; Film, "Post-surgical nosocomial infections", 1976. *Address:* Dept. of Surgery, University of Texas Health Science Centre at Dallas, 5323 Harry Hines Boulevard, Dallas, TX 75235, USA.

JONG, Paul T V M de, b. 12 Sep. 1942, Heerlen, Netherlands. Chairman of Opthalmology. *Education:* MD, State University, Utrecht, 1969; PhD, University of Amsterdam, 1973. *Appointments:* Resident, Ophthalmology, 1971-75, Staff Member, Department of Opthalmology, 1975-82, University of Amsterda; Chairman, Opthalmology, Erasmus University, Rotterdam, 1982-. *Memberships:* Dutch, Belgian, German and United Kingdom Opthalmological Societies; ARVO Member. *Publications:* PhD thesis and numerous articles to professional publications. *Address:* Eye Hospital, Schiedannse Vest 180, 3011 BH Rotterdam, The Netherlands.

JONSSON, Arni, b. 30 Sept. 1952, Akureyri, Iceland. Dental Surgeon & General Medical Practitioner. m. 27 Dec. 1975, Reykjavik, Iceland, 1 son, 1 daughter. *Education:* Cand. med. et chir., University of Iceland, Reykjavik, 1978; Cand. Odontology, Oslo University, Norway, 1985; Licended for medicine & dentistry in Iceland & Norway, 1981-85, Intern, Medical, Patholgical & Surgical Departemnts, University Hospital, Reykjavik, 1978-79. *Appointments:* General Practitioner & Public Health Officer, Blonduos, Iceland, 1979-80; Resident, Paediatric Clinic, University Hospital, Reykjavik, 1980-81; Senior Resident, University Ophtalmic Clinic, Landakot Hospital, Reykjavik, 1981; Senior Resident, City Hospital Psychiatric Department, Reykjavik, 1981-82; General Practitioner, Kristiansund, Norway, 1982; General Medical Practitioner, Oslo & Sanderfjord, Norway, 1982-85; Dental Surgeon, General Medical Practitioner, Public Health Officer, Selfoss, Iceland, 1985-. *Memberships:* Icelandic Medical Association; Icelandic Dental Association; Norwegian Medical

Association; New York Academy of Sciences, USA. *Honour:* Educational Commision for Foreign Medical Graduates, 1981 (USA). *Hobbies:* Politics & Economics; Outdoor Living; Literature; Music. *Address:* Grashaga 18, IS-800 Selfoss, Iceland.

JONSSON, Bengt, b.2 Sept. 1937, Göteborg, Sweden. Professor of Work Physiology. *Education:* MD, 1965, PhD, Anatomy, 1970, University of Göteborg. *Appointments:* Assistant Professor of Anatomy, Göteborg, 1965-71; Assistant Professor of Anatomy, Umea, 1972-73; Professor (Laborator) of Work Physiology, Umea, Swedish National Board of Occupational Safety & Health, 1974. *Memberships:* Founder of for many years Secretary-General of International Society of Electrophsiological Kinesiology (ISEK); International Society of Biochanics,(ISB), formely Secretary-General. *Publications:* Some 100 articles in the areas of electromyographic kinesiology, biomechanics, ergonomic & muscle physiology. *Hobbies:* Mountains Walking; Camping; Nature; Skiing; formerly Flying. *Address:* Work Physiology Unit, National Board of Occupational Safety & Health, Box 6104, S-900 06 Umea, Sweden.

JONSSON, Carl-Evert, b. 15 Apr. 1936, Umea, Sweden. Assistant Head, Consultant, Department of Plastic Surgery, Karolinska Hospital, Stockholm. m. Kerstin, 22 June 1960, Uppsala, 1 son, 2 daughters. *Education:* MD, PhD, University of Uppsala; Assistant Professor, Experimental Surgery, University of Uppsala; Plastic Surgery, Karloinska Institute, Stockholm. *Appointment:* Registrar, University Hospital, Uppsala. *Memberships:* Tord Skoog Society of Plastic Surgeons; Swedish and Scandinavian Association of Plastic Surgery; Swedish Association Aesthetic Plastic Surgery. *Publications:* Prostaglandins in Burn Injury, 1972 (Thesis); Articles on experimental skin flaps, burn pathophysiology, Neuropeptides in skin, aesthetic surgery; Burn Injury (monograph in Swedish), 1985. *Hobbies:* Painting; Skiing; Tennis. *Address:* Department of Plastic Surgery, Karolinska Hospital, Stockholm S 104 01, Sweden.

JORDAN, Harold Willoughby, b. 24 May 1937, Newnan, Georgia, USA. Professor and Chairman of Psychiatry. m. Geraldine Crawford, 2 sons, 2 daughters. *Education:* BS, Biology, Morehouse College, 1958; MD, Meharry Medical College, 1962. *Appointments include:* Psychiatric Consultant, Florence Crittendon Home, July – Dec 1967; Psychiatric Consultant, Intensive Treatment Center, State Division of Vocational Rehabilitation, 1967-71; Psychiatric Consultant, Fisk University Student Counselling Center, 1969-71; Assistant Commissioner for Psychiatric Services, Tennessee Department of Mental Health and Mental Retardation, 1971-75; Commissioner, Tennessee Department of Mental Health and Mental Retardation, 1975-79; Professor and Chairman, Department of Psychiatry, Meharry Medical College, 1979-; Psychiatric Consultant, Tennessee State University, 1984-. *Memberships include:* National Association for the Advancement of Colored People; American Psychiatric Association; American Association of University Professors; Tennessee Medical Association; Tennessee Association of Mental Health Centers, President 1968-69. *Publications:* Numerous articles in medical journals and chapters in edited volumes. Co-author: "DSM IV: Diagnostic Criteria for the Self-Mutilation Syndrome", "Consultation Liaison Psychiatry: A Study of Referrals", "An Outline of Psychopharmacology". *Honours include:* Plaque for "Outstanding Contribution in the Efforts to Eliminate Institutional Racism" Minority Research Divsion, TN Dept. of Mental Health and Mental Retardation, 1979; Plaque for "Outstanding Achievements as Commissioner of the TN Department of Mental Health Mental Retardation" Harriet Cohn Mental Health Center, 1979; Plaque for "Leadership and Support" as Commissioner of the

TN Dept of Mental Health, Mental Retardation, 1971-79, Lakeshore Mental Health Institute. *Address:* School of Medicine, Vanderbilt University, Nashville, TN 37203, USA.

JORDAN, Jerry Dugger, b. 8 Oct 1930, Alexandria, Louisiana, USA. Diagnostic Cardiologist. m. Frances Brewer Jordan, 3 sons, 2 daughters. *Education:* MD, Louisiana State University, 1955; Internship, Confederate Member, Medical center, Shreveport, Louisiana, 1955-56; Residency: Confederate Member, Medical Center Pediatrics, 1956-57, Texas Children's Hospital, Houston, Pediatrics, 1959-60; Fellowship, Texas Children's Hospital, Pediatric Cardiology, 1960-62. *Appointments:* Pediatric Cardiologist, Ochsner Clinic and Foundation, New Orleans, 1962-67; Director, Division of Research, Alton Ochsner Medical Foundation, 1964-67; Clinical Instructor, Pediatrics, Louisiana State University, New Orleans, 1962-67; Consultant in Pediatric Cardiology, Crippled Child Program, New Orleans 1962-67; Director, Cardiovascular Laboratory, Mobile General Hospital and Co-Director, Department of Pediatrics, 1967-73; Currently Diagnostic Cardiologist/Pediatric and Adult. *Memberships:* Medical Society of Mobile County; Fellow, American Academy of Pediatrics; Fellow, American College of Cardiology; American Heart Association; Medical Association of the State of Alabama. *Address:* One Houston Street, Mobile, AL 36606, USA.

JORDAN, William Reynier Van Evera, b.4 Aug. 1928, Missouri, USA. Psychotherapist, Instructor. *Education:* MA, University of Northern Colorado, 1979; BS, Cum Laude, 1956; AA, University of Florida. *Appointments:* Instructor, Psychotherapist, Colorado Springs College of Business, Colorado Springs Colorado, 1979-80; Co-ordinator, Psychotherapist, 1980-81, Psychotherapist St Petersburg Free Medical Clinic, St Petersburg, FL., 1981-83; Psychoatherapist Affiliated Counselling Services, Phoenix, Arizona, 1983-84; Program Co-ordinator, Psychotherpist, Youth and Family connection, St Petersburg, FL., 1984; Case-Worker, Counselor, Suncoast Epilepsy Association, St Petersburg, FL., 1984-85; Psychotherapist (Volunteer), Bay Pines Veterans Administration Medical Center, 1985. *Memberships:* Clinical Member, International Acadmey of Professional Counseling and Psychotherapy; American Psychological Association; International Council of Sex Education and Parenthood; Silver Circle of Alpha Tau Omega; Sigma Delta Chi; President's Club of the Epilepsy Foundation of America; Retired Officers Association. *Publications:* Books of Poetry, "In the Darkness and the Shadows", 1975; "More Than Friends", 1978; "Heart Lightning", 1984; "Peppermint Trees", being completed; Foreign Policy, "No Eternal Enemies", being completed; numerous articles on psychological warfare, 1966-70; articles on intelligence and South Asia for military publications. *Honours:* Numerous citations and awards including, Legion of Merit with Oak Leaf Cluster; Meritorious Service Medal; Joint Services Commendation Medal; Army Commendation Medal. *Hobbies:* Photography; Writing Prose and Poetry; Volunteer work. *Address:* 5311 Burlington Ave North, St Petersburg, FL 33710, USA.

JORGENSON, Scott P., Chiropractic Doctor/University Professor. *Education:* Certified Electronics Technician, 1976; Associate of Arts Degree, 1976; BS, Biology, 1980; Doctor of Chiropractic, 1981; Diplomate, National Board of Chiropractic Examiners, 1981; Licensed Chiropractic Doctor, California, 1981; Licensed Chiropractic Physician, Minnesota, 1981; Certified in Rationg Physical Impairment, 1983; Diplomate, American Board of Chiropractic Orthopedists, 1985. *Appointments:* Internship, Goodfellow Chiropractic Clinic, El Monte, California, 1980-81; Preceptorship, Halburian Chiropractic Group, Glendora, California, 1981; Private Practice, Minnesota,

1981 -; Assistant Professor, Departments of Chiropractic and Clinics, Northwestern College of Chiropractic, Bloomington, Minnesota, 1981 -; Member, Postgraduate Faculty, Northwestern College of Chiropractic, Bloomington, Minnesota, 1983 -. *Memberships:* Fellow, Academy of Chiropractic Orthopedists; American College of Chiroparactic Orthopedists, Minnesota Chiropractic Orthopediuc Society; American Chiropractic Association; Council on Chiropractic Orthopedics; Council on Chiropractic Roentgenology; Alumni Association, Los Angeles College of Chiropractic etc. *Publications:* "A Review of Electrical Stimulation Techniques, Graduate Student Orthopedic Research and Clinical Obsevations: Collected Works" 1983; Presenter of numerous lectures and seminars in the field of Chiropratic. *Address:* 1627 Madison Street N E, Minneapolis MN 55413, USA.

JOSEPH, Douglas, b. 21 Jan 1925, Sydney, Australia, Nuffield Professor of Anaesthetics, Head of Department of Anaesthetics. *Education:* MB, BS, University of Sydney, 1947; DA (RCP&S), 1952; FFARCS, 1956; FFARACS, 1956. *Appointments:* Resident Medical Officer, Anaesthetic Registrar, Royal North Shore Hospital, Sydney, 1947-50; Anaesthetic Registrar, Royal Victoria Infirmary, Newcastle upon Tyne, England, 1952; Senior Registrar, Royal Infirmary, Edinburgh, Scotland, 1953-54; Director, Department of Anaesthetics and Resuscitation, Sydney Hospital, Australia, 1956-61; Christiana Hartley Research Fellow, Department of Anaesthetics, University of Liverpool, England, 1962; Nuffield Professor of Anaesthetics, University of Sydney, 1963-; Honorary Anaesthetist, Royal Prince Alfred Hospital, Sydney, Australia, 1963-. *Memberships:* Member, Board of Faculty Anaesthetists, Royal Australasian College of Surgeons, 1972-84; Dean, Faculty of Anaesthetics, RACS, 1980-82; Education Officer, 1974-78, Member, Court of Examiners, 1966-78, RACS; Member, Editorial Board, 'Anaesthesia and Intensive Care', 1972-84; Australian Society of Anaesthetists, 1951-. *Publications:* 'Awareness during Anaesthesia', 1984; 'The Attainment of National Standards', 1984. *Honours:* Gilbert Brown Award, Australian Society of Anaesthetists, 1970; Elected to Court of Honour, Royal Australasian College of Surgeons, 1984. *Hobbies:* Music; Art; Swimming; Ice skating. *Address:* 13 Bellevue Road, Bellevue Hill, New South Wales 2023, Australia.

JOSEPH, Steven Michael, b. 2 Apr. 1942, Chicago, Illinois, USA. Private Practice of Psychiatry. m. Corey L Hansen, 17 Dec. 1977, Albany, California, 4 sons. *Education:* California Institute of Techonology, 1959-61; Hebrew University, 1961-62; BA, Physics, University of California, Berkeley, 1964; MD, Stanford University School of Medicine, 1972; Internship and Residency: Kaiser Hospital, San Francisco, San Francisco Community Mental Health Services, 1972-76. *Appointments:* Emergency Psychiatrist (part-time), San Francisco General Hospital, 1975-81; Staff Psychiatrist, Berkeley (California) Mental Health Services, 1978-82; Visiting Lecturer, Health and Medical Sciences Program, University of California, Berkeley, 1976-83; Lecturer Center for Psychological Studies, Berkeley, 1983-. *Memberships:* The Psychotherapy Institute, Berkeley; East Bay Psychiatric Association, Berkeley. *Publications:* Contributor to 'The Psychaotherapy Institute Journal'; 'San Francisco Jung Institute Library Journal'. *Honours:* Analytic Candidate, C G Jung Institute, San Francisco, 1982-; President, The Psychotherapy Institute,Berkeley, 1981-83. *Hobby:* Study, practice and teaching of Kabbalistic Psychology. *Address:* 1235 Marin Avenue, Suite B, Albany, CA 94706.

JOSEPHSON, Mark Eric, b. 27 Jan. 1943, New York, New York, USA, Professor of Medicine, Chief of Cardiology Section. m. Joan E. Eisenberg, 27 Aug. 1967, Peekskill, New York, 2 daughters. *Education:* BS Cum Laude, Trinity College, Hartford, Connecticut, 1961-65; MD, Columbia University College of Physicians and Surgeons, 1965-69; Intern in Medicine 1969-70, Resident in Medicine 1970-71, Mount Sinai Hospital, New York; Research Associate in Electrophysiology, USPHS, 1971-73; Fellow in Cardiology, University of Pennsyulvania, Philadelphia, 1973-74. *Appointments:* Research Associate in Cardiology 1974-75, Assistant Professor of Medicine 1975-79, Associate Professor 1979-81, Robinette Foundation Associate Professor 1982-84, Robinette Foundation Professor of Medicine (Cardiovascular Diseases) 1984 -, University of Pennsylvania. *Memberships:* Fellow, American College of Cardiology; Fellow, American College of Physicians; Fellow, American Heart Association Council on Clinical Cardiology; American Federation for Clinical Research; American Heart Association; American Society for Clinical Investigation; Association of American Physicians; Phi Beta Kappa; Alpha Omega Alpha. *Publications:* "Clinical Cardiac Electrophysiology : Techniques and Interpretations", (with S F Seides), 1979; "Ventricular Tachycardia: Mechanisms and Management", editor, 1982; "Tachycardias: Mechanisms, Diagnosis and Treatment", (edited with H J J Wellens), 1984. *Honours:* Honorary MA, University of Pennsylvania, 1982; Medal for Excellence, Columbia University, 1982; Century IV Physician of the Year, Philadelphia Medical Society, 1982. *Address:* Section of Cardiology, Hospital of the University of Pennsylvania, 3400 Spruce Street, Philadelphia, PA 19104, USA.

JOSHI, Durga Datt, b. 10 May 1940, Nepal. Acting Chief Epidemiologist, Epidemiology and Statistics Division, Department of Health. m. K.D. Joshi, 15 May 1958, 1 son, 2 daughters. *Education:* B.V.Sc. and A.H., India; MPVM, USA; FISCD (NICD), India; Fellow, UNEP/USSR Zoonoses Management; Fellow, FAO/WHO Zoonoses and Foodborne Disease, Berlin West. *Appointments:* Chief, Zoonotic Disease Control Section, Department of Health Services; Chief, Rabies Control Project, Department of Health Services; Secretary, Nepal Medical Research Committee, Ministry of Health, HMG Nepal. *Membership:* Life Member: Indian Society of Malaria and other Communicable Disease, NICD, New Delhi; Nepal Pharmaceutical Association; Nepal Veterinary Association; Honorary Member, Nepal Medical Association. *Publications:* "Surveillance of Echinococdosis/Hydatidosis in Animals and Human of Kathmandu", 1984; "Epidemiological Surveillance Report on Japnaese Encephalitis in 1985"; "National Health Services Research Inventories; Nepal", 1984. *Honour:* Gorkha Dankhin Bahu Awarded by His Majesty King Birendra of Nepal, 1984. *Hobbies:* Swimming; Badminton. *Address:* Chief, Zoonotic Disease Control Section, Department of Health Services, 1885 Kathamndu, Nepal.

JOSHI, Preetinder Singh, b. 17 Nov. 1947, Rajpura (Pb), India. Project Director. m. Parveen Joshi, 7 Jan. 1977, Patiala, 2 daughters. *Education:* MBBS, Medical College, Amritsar Punjab University, Chandigarh, 1969; MD, Maulana Azad Medical College, Delhi University, Delhi, 1974; MRCP (UK), Royal College of Physicians, UK, 1978. *Appointments Include:* Medical Superintendant, Consultant Cardiologist, Consultant Physician, 1978-80, Consultant Cardiologist, Consultant Physician, Kidarnath Charitable Clinic and Laboratories, New Delhi, 1980-81; Medical Advisor, 1980-81, Medical Director, Chief Division of Cardiology and Internal Medicine, Escorts Medical Centre, Faridabad; Director, Research Activity for Escorts Hearth Institute and Research Centre, New Delhi; Advisor, Escorts Heart Institute and Research Centre, New Delhi; Project Director, Birla Centre for Medical Research, New Delhi, 1984-. *Memberships Include:* Fellow, International College of Angiology; American College of Chest Physicians; Associate Fellow, American College of Cardiology; Member,

International Society for Heart Research. *Publications Include:* Contributor to various journals; Author of several papers on heart disease. *Honours Include:* Stood First, punjab University Final Professional Examination, 1969; Best Graduate, Medical College, Amritsar, Session 1965-69. *Hobbies:* Classical Music; Indian Meditation Techniques. *Address:* A-314, Defence Colony, New Delhi - 110024, India.

JOSHI, Usha Madhusudan, b. 24 Aug. 1934, Varanasi, India. Research Director. m. Dr Madhusudan R Joshi, 7 Dec. 1957, Bombay, 1 son, 2 daughters. *Education:* MSc, PhD. *Appointments:* Senior Research Officer; Assistant Director, Deputy Director Institute for Research in Reproduction, Bombay, India. *Memberships:* Life Member: Endocrine Society of India; Association of Clinical Biochemists of India; Member, Nutrition Society of India; Association for the Study of Fertility & Sterility. *Publications:* Various papers & articles in medical journals. *Honour:* Smt Chandaben Patel VASVIK Award for Industrial Research, 1981. *Hobbies:* Reading; Travel; Classical Indian Music. *Address:* Institute for Research in Reproduction, Jehangir Merwanji Street, Parel, Bombay 400 012, India.

JOSKE, Richard Alexander, b. 6 Oct. 1925, Melbourne, Australia. Professor of Medicine. m. Enid Jocelyn Prudence Apperly, 5 Mar. 1952, Melbourne, 4 sons. *Education:* MB BS (Melbourne); PhD (W. Australia); FRCP; FRACP. *Appointments:* Resident Medical Officer, Royal Melbourne Hospital, 1949-50; Drug Houses of Australia Fellow, Clinical Research Unit, Royal Melbourne Hospital & Walter & Eliza Hall Institute, 1951; Associate Assistant, Walter & Eliza Hall Institute, 1953-55; Nuffield Dominion Fellow, Medicine, University College Hospital Medical School, London, England, 1955-56; Commonwealth Fund (Harkness) Fellow, Medicine, Massachusetts General Hospital & Harvard Medical School, USA, 1956-57; Adolph Basser Fellow, Medicine, 1957-62, Reader, Experimental Medicine, 1962-68, Professor, Medicine, 1968-, Dean, Medicine, 1978-80, 1982-, University of Western Australia. *Memberships:* Past President, WA Branch, Australian Medical Association; British Medical Association; Gastroenterological Society of Australia, Councillor, Past President; Immunology Society of Australia; etc. *Publications:* Over 100 papers in professional journals; "Changing Disease Patterns and Human Behaviour", Co-Editor, 1980. *Honour:* David Grant Prize, University of Melbourne, 1952. *Hobbies:* Gardening; Philately. *Address:* University Department of Medicine, Queen Elizabeth II Medical Centre, Nedlands, WA 6009, Australia.

JOSLIN, Charles Albert Frederick, b. 2 Apr. 1928, Braintree, Essex, England. Professor and Head of Department of Radiotherapy, University of Leeds. m. Elizabeth Ann Gibson, 3 Mar. 1956, London, 2 sons, 1 daughter. *Education:* MB BS, London, 1958; Chartered Engineer, 1958; DMRT, 1962; FFR, 1966; FRCR, 1975. *Appointments:* Senior Registrar, Charing Cross Hospital, London; Senior Registrar, Royal Postgraduate Hospital, Hammersmith; Consultant Radiotherapist, University Hospital of Wales, 1967-74; Clinical Teacher, Welsh National School of Medicine, 1967-74; Professor of Radiotherapy and Head of Department of Radiotherpay, University of Leeds, Cookridge Hospital, Leeds, 1974-. *Memberships:* Fellow, Royal College of Radiologists; Member, British Institute of Radiology. *Publications:* "The Long Term Effects of Combined Teletherapy and High Dose Rate Intracav. Treatment", 1985, Proceedings of 3rd International Selectron Users Meeting, 1984, Innsbruck, Editor R.F. Mould; "Radiobiology of Ionising Radiation Therapy in Gynaecological Malignancy. Scientific Basic of Obs. and Gynae", Editor R.R. Macdonald, 3rd edition, 1985. *Honour:* Roentgen Prize of British Institute of Radiology, 1977. *Address:* University of

Leeds Department of Radiotherapy, Tunbridge Building, Cookridge Hospital, Leeds LS16 6QB, England.

JOZEFOWICZ, Wlodzimierz, b. 15 Apr. 1932, Lódź, Poland. Professor of Prosthetic Dentistry. m. Grazyna Masierek, 25 June 1955, 2 daughters. *Education:* Dentist 1955, Physician 1966, Medical Academy of Lodz. *Appointments:* Assistant-Adjunct- Docent- Professor of Department of Prosthetic Dentistry 1955-, Vice-Dean of Medical Faculty 1981-, Medical Academy of Lodz; Director, Institute of Stomatology, Lodz, 1971-78; Professor, Department of Prosthetic Dentistry, University of Garyounis, Benghasi, Libya. *Memberships:* President, Polish Dental Association; Consultant, Federation Dentaire Internationale; European Prosthodontic Association; British Society for the Study of Prosthetic Dentistry. *Publications:* 'The Influence of Wearing Dentures on Residual Ridges', 1970; 'Cushioning Properties of the Tissues Forming the Basel Seat of Dentures', 1972; 'Pressure Yielding of the Maxillary Periosteum', 1972; 'Posterior Palatal Seal and its Role in Denture Retention', 1984. *Honour:* Award of the Scientific Council, Polish Ministry of Health and Welfare, 1970. *Hobbies:* Tourism; Chess. *Address:* 52 Nowa Str m 29, 90 – 030 Lódź, Poland.

JUDD, Ali Bradford, b. 9 Sep. 1929, Detroit, Michigan, USA. Private Practitioner. m. Eleanore Margueritte Gridley, 24 Feb. 1962. *Education:* AB Honours, Cornell University, 1950; MD, Harvard Medical School, 1954; Diplomate Psychiatry 1962, Child Psychiatry 1966, American Board of Psychiatry and Neurology. *Appointments:* Teaching Fellow, Harvard Medical School, 1957-61; Director of Training, Children's Psychiatric Center, New Jersey, 1961-67; Assistant Clinical Professor 1967-69, Research Neurobiologist 1974-, Cornell University Medical School, New York; Professor of Social Psychology, Newark State College, New Jersey, 1969-74; Private Medical Practice. *Memberships:* Telluride Association; Alpha Epsilon Delta; American Acadmey of Child Psychiatry; American Psychiatric Association; New Jersey Medical Society; American Orthopsychiatric Association; Society for Neuroscience; American Association for the Advancement of Science. *Publications:* 'One Aspect of Mind' (with Milton Greenblatt) in "Theories of the Mind" (editor: J Scher), 1962; 'Sex Education for Young Americans' 1966. *Honours Include:* New Jersey Broadcaster's Award, 1966. *Hobbies:* Wine making; Bee keeping; Farming; Writing. *Address:* 837 Broad Street, Shrewsbury, NJ 07701, USA.

JUDSON, Martyn, b. 10 Aug. 1948, Manchester, England. General Practitioner. *Education:* MB, ChB; D.Obst., RCOG; MRCGP; CCFP. *Appointments include:* House officer, Manchester Royal Infirmary, 1971-72; Senior house officer, St. Mary's Hospital, Manchester 1972-73, Park Hospital, Daveyhulme 1973-74. *Membership:* London Academy of Medicine. *Honours:* Canadian Master's Rowing Champion, 1983-, 1984, 1985. *Recreation:* Rowing *Address:* 1225 Wonderland Road North, London Ontario, Canada.

JUE, Ronald Wong, b. 9 Aug 1938, San Francisco, California, USA. Licenced Clinical Psychologist m. Naomi Iwashita, 18 Dec 1966, San Jose, California, 2 daughters. *Education:* PhD, 1976; MA 1973; BA, 1962. *Appointments:* Co-ordinator, Day Treatment Programme, 1975-77, Director of Special Programmes, 1977-81, Child Guidance Centre, Fullerton, Calif; Clinical Assistant Professor of Psychology, Fuller Theological Semindry, Pasadena, Calif, 1978-81; Instructor, University of California, Irvine, 1981-84; Private Practice, Fullerton and Newport Beach, Calif, 1981-. *Memberships:* American Psychological Association; American Society of Clinical Hypnosis; Asian American

Psychological Association; Association for Transpersonal Psychology; International Council of Psychologists; Orange County Society of Clinical Hypnosis; World Federation of Mental Health; Board Member, Institute for Health Facilitation, 1981-82; Board Member, Institute for Intergrative Therapy, 1981-82; Vice President, 1983-84, Presdient, 1984-86, Association for Transpersonal Psychology; Chairman of the Board, 1984-85, Kendall Foundation. *Publications:* Contributor to numerous lectures, seminars and workshops on profesional and scientific subjects. *Honours:* President, Association for Transpersonal Psychology, 1984-86; Fulbright Teaching Fellow to Indonesia, 1970-71. *Hobbies;* Collecting World Folk art; Primitive Art; Rare Flora; Photography. *Address:* P O Box 5805, Fullerton, CA 92635, USA.

JULIAN, Wayne Edmond, b. 2 Feb. 1951, New Orleans, Louisiana, USA. Medical Director, Methodist Psychiatric Pavilion, New Orleans, Louisiana; Assistant Clinical Professor of Psychiatric, Tulane Medical School, New Orleans. m. Anne Packer, 22 Apr. 1978, 1 daughter. *Education:* BS (cum laude with hons.), Tulane University, 1973; MD, Tulane University Medical School, 1977; Internship and Psychiatric Residency, Yale University School of Medicine, 1981. *Appointments:* Staff Psychiatrist, JoEllen Smith, F. Edward Hebert and Meadowcrest Hospital, 1981-84; Director, Psychiatric consultation/liaison services for Westbank Center for Psychotherapy, 1981-84; Director, Adult In-Patient Psychiatric Services, JoEllen Smith Psychiatric Hospital, 1981-84; Medical Director, Methodist Psychiatric Pavillion, 1985-; Consulting Psychiatrist, Willow Wood Nursing Home, 1985-. *Memberships:* American Psychiatric Association; American Association of Geriatric Psychiatry; Delta Phi Alpha; Alpha Epsilon Delta; Beta Beta Beta. *Publications:* "The Presence of 5-Hydroxtrayptamine in the Eyestalks and Brain of the Fiddler Crab Uca Pugilator, Its Quantitative Modification by Pharmacological Agents, and Possible Role as a Neurotransmitter in Controlling the Release of Red Pigment – Dispersing Hormone", 1974; Milton Finger and Wayne Julian, Department of Biology, Tulane University, New Orleans, 'Louisiana Journal of Comparative and General Pharmacology' Volume 5, 1974. *Honour:* Diplomat, American Board of Psychiatry and Neurology. *Hobbies:* Music; Sports. *Address:* 5430 Durham Drive, New Orleans, LA 70118, USA.

JULIUS, Demetrios Aristides, b. 12 Apr. 1945, Athens, Greece. Chief, Psychiatry Service; Associate Professor. m. Janice Weil, 16 Apr. 1977, Boston, Massachusetts, USA, 1 son. *Education:* Honors in chemistry and French, Western Reserve Academy; AB Magna cum Laude, Harvard College; Fellow, National Hospital, Queen Square; MD, Chief Resident, University of Cincinnati. *Appointments:* Research and Aministrative Psychiatrist, National Institute on Drug Abuse, Rockville, Maryland, USA, 1974-79; Private Practice, Psychiatry, Bethesda, Maryland and Tehran, Iran, 1975-79; Medical Director, Social Development Center, Tehran, 1977-79; Chief, Psychiatry Service, Veterans Administration Medical Center, Richmond, Virginia, USA, 1979-; Associate Professor, Medical College of Virginia. *Memberships:* Cum Laude Society; American Psychiatric Association; Virginia Psychiatric Society; International Society of Political Psychology; National Association of Veterans Administration Chief of Psychiatry. *Publications:* "The Old and the New: The Changing Values of Modern Greece", 1967; "Narcotic Antagonists: Naltrexone Progress Report", with P F Renault", 1976; "Psychodynamics of Drug Dependence", With J D Blaine, 1977; "Psychiatry and Foreign Affairs", with V D Volkan; contributions to 'American Journal of Psychiatry'. *Honors:* Magna cum Laude and Dunster House Shield, Harvard College, 1967; Book Prize for Out-standing Research, University of Cincinnati, 1970;

Vice Chairman, Committee on Psychiarty and Foreign Affairs, American Psychiatric Association, 1983-85. *Hobbies:* Music; Surrealist art; Athletics; International travel. *Address:* Psychiatry Service (116a), Veterans Administration Medical Center, 1201 Broad Rock Boulevard, Richmond, VA 23249, USA.

JUMA, Mahdi Buxali, b. 16 June 1931, Basrah, Iraq. Medical Director. m. Avelina M Cabahug, 18 Dec. 1967, Saskatoon, Canada, 2 sons, 2 daughters. *Education:* MBBS, 1955; MSc Basic Sciences with distinction, university of Karachi, Pakistan, 1963. *Appointments:* House Officer in Ophtalmology, Civil Hospital, Karachi, 1955-56; Instructor in Anatomy, Dow Medical College, Karachi, 1957-65; Research Assistant in Anatomy, Medical School, Saskatoon, Saskatchewan, Canada,1966-70; Rotating Internship, City Hospital, Saskatoon, 71970-71; Resident in Physical Medicine and Rehabilitation, University Hosptial, Saskatoon, 1971-75; Staff Physician in Geriatrics and Rehabilitation 1975-, Medical Director 1977-, Souris Valley Regional Care Center, Weyburn, Saskatchewan. *Memberships:* College of Physicians and Surgeons of Saskatchewan; Canadian Association of Gerontology; Saskatchewan Gerontological Association; Full Gospel Businesmen's Fellowship International. *Publications:* "Falls in Elderly", 1982; "Hepatitis-B Carriers in an Extended Care Facility", 1983; "Ascorbic Acid as Unique Salt Substitute", 1984; "Subcutaneous Fluid Drip in Geriatric Care", 1985. *Hobbies:* Books; Stamp collecting; Travel;' Research; Theology. *Address:* 729 Windsor Street, Weyburn, Saskatchewan S4H OX3, Canada.

JUMBE, James Joseph, b. 12 Feb. 1946, Chipata, Zambia. Commandant, Maina Soko Military Hospital. m. Lydia Phasha, 11 Mar. 1972, Lusaka, 1 son, 3 daughters. *Education:* BSc, Human Biology, 1970; MB, CHB, University of Zambia, 1973; Dip.Ave.Med., Bangalore University, India, 1977; Certificate of Aviation Medicine, Farnborough, England. *Appointments:* Junior Registrar, Department of Obstetrics and Gynaecology, 1975-76; Station Medical Officer, ZAF Mbala, 1977-81; Director of Medical Services, Zambia Airforce HQ, 1981-85; Commanding Officer, Maina Soko Military Hospital, 1985-, Commandant Maina Soko Military Hospital. *Memberships:* Aero-Medical Society of India; Aerospace Medical Association, USA. *Publications:* Zambia Medical Journal, 1969; Vibration and Visual Acuity (Postgraduate thesis), 1977. *Honours:* First Dirctor of Medical Service in Zambia Air Force, 1981-85; Appointed First Commanding Officer of Maina Soko Military Hospital (only military hospital in Zambia), 1985-. *Hobbies:* Lawn Tennis; Football; Music; Reading; Watching Wrestling. *Address* Maina Soko Military Hospital, P.O. Box 320091, Woodlands, Lusaka, Zambia.

JUNG, Lynnette Clair, b. 7 Aug. 1940, Billings, Montana, USA. Chairman, Department of Social Work. *Education:* BA, Sociology, College of St Catherine and St Paul, Minnesota, 1961; MSW, University of Utah, Salt Lake City, Utah, 1965. *Appointments include:* Psychiatric Social Worker, US Air Force, 1974-; Assignments at Andrews AFB, Maryland, 1974-79, Lowry AFB, Colorado, 1979-82 (Director of Human Development Program at Lowry AFB 1981-82); Chief, Mental Health Clinic, Osan AB, Korea 1982-83; Chief, Mental Health Clinic, Clark AB, Philippines, 1983-85; Chief, Social Services, MHC, Randolph AFB, Texas 1985; Chairman, Department of Social Work, Wilford Hall USAF Medical Center, 1985-. *Memberships:* National Association of Social Workers; Academy of Certified Social Workers; American Orthopsychiatric Association, Fellow; American Group Psychotherapy Association; American Association of Sex Educators, Counselors and Therapists; Society of AF Social Workers; Business and Professional Women; Women Officers Association. *Publucations:* 'Diagnostic Divorrce: Co-Therapist Impotence' in "Journal of Group Studies" 1977; Sexual Counseling for Penile Implant

Candidates in a Military Setting' in "AF Social Worker's Newsletter" 1982. *Honours:* Pi Gamma Mu, Social Science Honorary, 1961; USAF Commendation Medal 1980; USAF Meritorious Service Medal 1982 and 1983. *Hobbies:* Travel; Reading; Skiing. *Address:* 9003 Peuplier, San Anatonio, TX 78250, USA.

JUNQUEIRA, Luiz Carlos Uchoa, b. 5 Aug. 1920, Brazil. Professor. m. Luiza M Salles, 10 May 1957, Sao Paulo, 2 sons, 1 daughter. *Education:* MD. *Appointments:* Research Associate, University of Chicago, 1949; Assistant Professor, Associate Professor, Professor in field of cell bioogy & anatomy. *Memberships:* American Association of Anatomists; American Society of Cell Biology. *Publications:* Some 120 publications in indexed periodicals on cell biology & histology; 6 books, also translated. *Honour:* Honorary Research Associate, Harvard University, 1968. *Hobbies:* Gardening; Sailing; Skindiving. *Address:* Rua Rio Janeiro 316 apt 402, 01240 Sao Paulo, Brazil.

JURI, Hugo Oscar, b. 2 Oct. 1948, Argentina. Adjunct Professor of Biophysics, National University of Cordoba Medical School. m. Carmen B,b. 23 Dec. 1972, Cordoba, 2 sons.*Education:* MD, 1971, PhD, 1984, National University of Cordoba; Internship, Union Hospital, Fall River, Massachusetts, USA, 1973; Resident in Surgery (Chief Resident), Sisters Hosptial, Buffalo, NY 1974-77. *Appointments:* Fellow, Head and Neck Surgery, University of Buffalo, 1978; Chief of Surgery, Bella Vista Hospital, Los Angeles, 1978; Chief of Staff, Bella Vista Hospital, 1979; Chief of Surgery, Beverly Hills Hospital, Los Angeles, 1979; Chief, Department of Laser Surgery, Beverly Hills 1979. *Memberships:* Fellow: Interamerican College of Physicians and Surgeons: American Society of Laser Medicine and Surgery; Argentine Society; Argentine Society of Laser Medicine and Surgery; International Society of Laser Medicine and Surgery. *Publications:* "Co2 Laser in Decubitus Ulcer", 1984; Contributor to: "Hiperparatiroidismo L Vista", 1984. Articles in professional journals. *Honour:* Invited by President of Argentina to participate in the visit to West Germany, Sep. 1985. *Hobby:* Old Books Collections. *Address:* Virrey del Pino 2149 Cerro, Cordoba, Argentina 5009.

JURIN, Mislav, b. 29 Apr. 1939, Šibenik, Chief of Scientific Unit, Department of Experimental Biology and Medicine. m. Durdica Matkun, 11 Sep. 1976, Zagreb, 1 son, 1 daughter. *Education:* MD, MSc, DSc, University of Zagreb. *Appointments:* Research Assistant, Ruder Boskovic Institute, Zagreb, 1964-69; Project Investigator, MD Anderson Hospital and Tumor Institute, Houston, USA, 1969-72; Research Associate 1972-78, Research Adviser 1978-, Ruder Boskovic Institute, Zagreb; Teacher of Immunology at Medical Faculty University of Zagreb 1972-75 and of Experimental Oncology at University of Zagreb 1974-. *Memberships:* Yugoslav Immunological Society, Secretary General; Yugoslav Physiological Society; Croatian Medical Association; European Association for Cancer Research; MD Anderson Associates (Founding Member). *Publications:* Four chapters in "Fundamentals of Modern Oncology" Part 1 1977 and Part 2 1982; Chapter in "Textbook of Pathophysiology" to be published in 1986; both in Croatian. *Honours:* First Prize in Annual Clinical Training Research Project Competition at University

of Texas, Houston, 1972; Annual Prize of City of Zagreb, 1978. *Hobbies:* Photography; Travel. *Address:* Department of Experimental Biology and Medicine, Ruder Boxković Institute, Zagreb, Yugoslavia.

JUST, Gemma Rivoli, b. 29 Nov. 1921, New York, New York, USA. Vice President. m. Victor Just, 29 Nov. 1955, New York, New York. *Education:* BA, Hunter College, City of NY, 1943. *Appointments:* Medical Copywriter, William Douglas McAdams Inc., 1954-56; Copy Supervisor, Medical, Senior Copywriter, Print, Doherty, Clifford, Steers and Shenfield Inc., NY, 1956-58; Copy Group Head, Print and TV, Senior Copywriter, Print and TV, McCann-Erickson Inc., NY, 1958-62; Copy Supervisor, Print and TV, Morse International Inc., NY, 1962-67; VP Copy Director, 1967, VP Creative Services, 1969, Deltakos Division of j. Walter Thompson, NY,1967-75; VP Copy, Sudler and Hennessey Inc., NY, 1975-. *Memberships:* American Medical Writers Association, Executive Committee, is1974; Pharmaceutical Advertising Council. *Publications:* 'In Patients at risk of Coronary Heart Disease (CHD): Landmark Studies and Reports Have Significant Impact on the treatment of Dyslipidemias', 1984; 'Advances in Djyslipidemia Therapy: A Three-part Report. 1. The New View of Lipid Disorders: 2. The Need for HDL Determinations; 3.New Findings on HDL' 1982; 'Dyslipidemia and the Role fo Serum lipids and Serum Lipoproteins in Atherogenesis: A Clinical Update', 1981; 'Drug-Induced Changes in Plasma Lipoproteins Can inhibit Progress of Coronary Artery Lesions; Highlights of NHLBI Coronary Intervention Study', 1984. *Honours:* Andy Award of Merit, Tylox, 1982; Y and R Award of Excellence, 1981; Spectrum Award, 1980; Felix Mari-Ibanez Award, 1979; Aesculapius Award, 1979; Copywrite's Certificate of Distinction, 1979. *Hobbies:* Asian Travel; Photgraphy; Writing; Poetry; Mountain Trail Climbing. *Address:* 55 East 38th Street, Apt 160-5D, New York, NY 10016, USA.

JUSTICE, Blair, b. 2 July 1927, Dallas, Texas, USA. Professor of Psychology. m. Rita Norwood, 26 July 1972, Houston, Texas, 1 son, 2 daughters, (by previous marriage). *Education:* BA, University of Texas at Austin; MS, Columbia University; PhD, Rice University. *Appointments Include:* Medical Writer, New York News, 1955-56; Science and Medical Editor 1964-70, Houston Post; Professor, University of Texas Health Science Center, School of Public Health, Houston, 1969-; Faculty, Psychiatry Residency Program, Texas Research Institute of Mental Sciences, 1970- ; Faculty Associate, Center for Health Promotion, Research and Development, University of Texas Health Science Center, Houston, 1982-. *Memberships:* American Psychological Association; Society of Behavior Medicine; American Public Health Association; National Association of Science Writers. *Publications Include:* "The Abusing Family", 1976; "The Broken Taboo", 1979; "Who Gets Sick: Thinking and Health", (in press); 'Factors mediating child abuse as a response to stress', 1984; 'Needs assessments', 1985. *Honours:* Chairman, Mental Health Section, Governing Council, American Public Health Association; President, Houston Psycholgical Society. *Hobbies:* Marathorn running, Wine Collecting. *Address:* University of Texas School of Public Health, 1600 Herman Pressler Drive, Texas Medical Center, Houston, TX 77030, USA.

K

KAAK, Hans Otto, b. 27 Mar. 1938, Chicago, Illinois, USA. Professor Psychiatry. m. Kay DeYoung, 15 Jan. 1966, Sebowing, Michigan, 1 son, 2 daughters. *Education:* BS, Western Michigan University, 1959; MD, University of Michigan, 1964; Rotating Internship, Bronson Methodist Hospital, 1964-65; Family Practice Residency, Wesley Medical Centre, 1967-68; Psychiatric Residence, University of Michigan, 1968-70; Fellowship, Child Psychiatry, University of Michigan, 1970-72. *Appointments:* Assistant Professor 1972, Assistant Professor, Psychiatry & Paediatrics, 1976, Associate Professor, Psychiatry & Paediatrics, 1982, Director, Division of Child Psychiatry, 1982, University of Kentucky. *Memberships:* American Psychiatric Association; American Paediatric Association; Kentucky Academy of Child Psychiatry. *Publication:* "Child Abuse & Neglect Case Studies" (with A Fosson), 1976. *Hobbies:* Sailing; Music; Literature. *Address:* Department of Psychiatry, University of Kentucky Medical Centre, 800 Rose Street, Lexington, KY 40536, USA.

KÁDÁR, Anna, b. 15 Aug. 1935, Budapest, Hungary. Professor, Pathology. m. Dr Gábor Krakovits, 2 Oct. 1958. *Education:* MD, medical University, 1959; Specialisation in Pathology and Pathohistology, 1962; Candidate Medical Sciences, 1971; DMSc., 1980. *Appointments:* Assistant Professor, 1959, Adjunct Professor, 1971, Associate Professor, 1974, Professor, 1982-, 2nd Dept. of Pathology, Semmelweis Medical University. *Membership:* Secretary General, 1972-81, Vice President, Hungarian Society of Pathologists; Secretary General, Hungarian Division, International Academy of Pathology; Committee Member, European Artery Club; etc. *Publications:* "The Elastic Fiber", 'Ext.Path.Suppl', 1979; Monograph: "New Concepts in Elastic Tissue Disorders", 'Front. Matrix Biol.', Volume 8, 1980; 105 Publications; 164 presentations. *Honours:* Jendrassik Memorial Medal, 1981; Award, Higher Education, 1985. *Hobbies:* Tennis; Gardening. *Address:* 2nd Dept. of Pathology, Central Electron Microscope Laboratory, Semmelweis Medical University, Ulloi ut 93, 1091 Budapest, Hungary.

KAGAN, Benjamin M., b. 18 July 1913, Washington, Pennsylvania, USA. Senior Consultant. m. Katherine Hamburger, 2 June 1940, Baltimore, 2 sons. *Education:* AB; MD; FAAP; FACP; FIDA. *Appointments:* Instructor, Medical college of Virginia, Columbia Medical School; Associate Professor, University of Illinois; Associate Professor to Professor, Northwestern Medical School, Chicago; Clinical Professor to Professor & Vice Chairman, University of California, Los Angeles; Director, Chairman, Paediatrics, Michael Reese Hospital, Chicago, 1946-55, Cedars-Sinai Medical Centre, Los Angeles, 1955-84; Director, Cystic Fibrosis Centre, 1955-; Senior Consultant, Paediatrics, Cedars-Senai Medical Centre, 1984-. *Memberships Include:* Diplomate: American Board of Paediatrics, 1942, American Board of Nutrition, 1967; Official Oral Examiner, American board of Paediatrics, 1955-85; Chairman, Written Examination Committee, American Board of Paediatrics, 1960-85; Cystic Fibrosis Foundation; ASPS; Association Paediatric Ambulatory Service; LAPS; SPR; Southern Paediatric Society; Western Society for Paediatric Research; ASM; APHA; Los Angeles Academy of Medicine; Western association of Physicians; Western Society for Cllinical Research; etc. *Publications:* Articles in: 'Excerpta Medica'; 'Journal of Paediatric Opthalmology'; 'California Medicine'; 'Journal of Paediatric Surgery'; 'Audio Digest, Paediatrics'; 'Paediatric News'; etc. *Honours:* Distinguished Service Award, Army, 1945; Honorary Alumnus, of the Year Award, Cedars-Sinai Alumnus Association, 1977; Citation of the American Academy of Paediatrics for Outstanding Service Rendered as a Member of the Committee on Drugs, 1978. *Hobbies:* Fishing; Swimming; Playing Piano. *Address:* Cedars-Senai Medical Centre, 8700 Beverly Blvd., Los Angeles, CA 90048, USA.

KAHANOVITZ, Neil, b. 1 July 1949, Baltimore, Maryland, USA. Chief of Back Service, Hospital for Joint Diseases. m. Melanie, New York City, 1 daughter. *Education:* BS, Randolph-Macon College, 1970; MD, University of Maryland School of Medicine, 1975; Internship, General Surgery, 1975-76; Residency, Orthopaedic Surgery, 1976-80; Fellowship, Scoliosis Service, 1980-81. *Appointments:* Senior Clinical Association in Surgery, Cornell University Medical College, 1980-81; Junior Attending, Scoliosis Service, Hospital for Special Surgery, NYC, 1980-81; Surgeon, Orthopaedics, New York Hospital, 1980-81; Orthopaedic Fellow, Bone Tumor Service, Sloan-Kettering Cancer Center, NYC, 1980-81; Assistant Professor, Louisiana State University, 1981-82; Co-Director, Spine Unit, Children's Hospital, New Orleans, 1981-82; Co-Director, Acute Spinal Cord Injury Center, Hotel Dieu Hospital, New Orleans, 1981-82; Chief, Back Service, Hospital for Joint Diseases, Orthopaedic Institute, NYC, 1982-; Assistant Professor, Mt. Sinai School of Medicine, NYC, 1982-; Director, Outpatient Clilnics, Hospital for Joint Diseases, 1983-. *Memberships:* International Society for the Study of Lumbar Spine; American Academy of Orthopaedic Surgeons; Orthopaedic Research Society; North American Lumbar Spine Society. *Publications:* Co-author, Chapter 'Scoliosis' in "The Child with Disabling Illness", Editors Downey and Low, 1981; Abstracts; Contributor to professional journals; Presentations (local and national). *Honours:* USPHS Research Grant and March of Dimes Birth Foundation. 1980; Orthopaedic Research and Education Foundation Grant, 1981. *Address:* 10 West 86th Street §5A, New York, NY 10024, USA.

KAHN, Alvin, b. 21 Jan. 1928, Paterson, New Jersey, USA. Clinical Instructor, Psychiatry, Harvard Medical School. m. Betty North, Cambridge, 2 sons, 1 daughter. *Education:* BA, 1949, Harvard College; MD, Harvard Medical School, 1953. *Appointments:* Consultant: Cambridge Court Clinic, Cambridge Guidance Centre, Massachusetts Rehabilitation Commission. *Memberships:* American Psychiatric Association; Massachusetts Medical Society; New England Council of Child Psychiatry. *Publications:* "Love and Hate on the Tennis Court", co-author, 1977; "Psychotherapy with the Suicidal Patient", 1982; "Emergency Psychiatry", Chapter 5, "The Therapeutic Stance", 1984. *Honour:* Phi Beta Kappa, 1949. *Hobbies:* Tennis; Skiing; Piano; Camping; Lyricist. *Address:* 130 Brattle St., Cambridge, MA 02138, USA.

KAHN, Arlene Judy Miller, b. 16 Dec. 1940, Chicago, Illinois, USA. University Professor. m. Dr Roy M. Kahn, 1968, Reno, Nevada, 1 daughter. *Education:* AB, RN, MSN, University of Illinois, USA; EdD, University of San Francisco. *Appointments:* Head Nurse, Psychiatric Unit, Grant Hospital, Chicago, USA; Supervising Nurse, Illinois Psychiatric Institute; Lecturer/Assistant Professor, San Francisco State University; Consultant (NIMH Grant), Napa State Hospital, California; Associate/Full Professor, Psychiatric Nursing, California State University at Hayward, California. *Memberships:* California Nursing Association; Fellow, American Academy of Psychiatric Nurse Specialists; United Professors of California. *Publications:* 'The College Student as Untrained Mental Health Worker' in 'American Journal of Orthopsychiatry Newsletter', 1964; 'Relationship Between Nurses' Opinions about Mental Illness and Experience' in 'Nursing Research', 1976;

'Modifications in Nursing Students' Attitudes' in 'Nursing Research', 1980. *Honours:* Sigma Theta Tau, 1968; Research Grant Award, California State University, 1980. *Hobby:* Cooking. *Address:* School of Science, Department of Nursing, California State University, Hayward, CA 94442, USA.

KAHN, Faith-Hope Green, b. 25 Apr. 1921, New York, USA. Professional Registered Nurse; Author; Editor; Lecturer; Researcher; Administrator; Notary. m. Dr Edward Kahn, 29 May 1942, Highland Falls, 3 daughters. *Education:* RN, Beth Israel Medical Centre, 1942; preceptorships, and Higher Professional and Educational Qualifications, New York University; ITT Educational Services Special Courses and Continued Education. *Appointments:* 1st Scrub, Operating Room, Beth Israel Hospital, 1942; Supervisor, OR, Hunts Point General Hospital, 1942; New York Military-Civilian, Phoenixville General Hospital, Pennsylvania; Research, Gynaecology Reconstructive Procedures, Sydenham, Park East, West 1945-64; American Red Cross Disaster Field Hospital, Queens, 1950; Co-ordinator, 1st Scrub, Gyn Surgical Team with Dr Edward Kahn, 1945-84; Visiting Instructor, Upjohn and Rehabilitation, 1977-78. *Memberships:* American Academy of Ambulatory Nursing Administration; American College of Obstetrics and Gynaecology; National Association of Physician Nurses. *Publications:* Co-Author, Editor, "Traction Hysterography - An Improved Technique for the Diagnosis of Uterine Lesions", 1955; Patent Holder, Kahn Surgicap for Operating Room and Allied Fields; various other articles in professional journals. *Honours:* Citation, American Red Cross, 1951; Patriot USA Commenorative Gall, 1976-77; Bronze Medal, American Security Council Education Foundation, 1978; etc. *Hobbies:* Composing; Fencing; Riding; American Heritage; Music; etc. *Address:* 213-16-85th Avenue, Hollis Hills, NY 11427, USA.

KAHN, Stephen Mitchell, b. 25 Dec. 1936, Brooklyn, New York, USA. Clinical Psychologist, Assistant Professor. m. Ann Louise Grommesh, 3 Dec. 1977, Portland, Oregon, 2 daughters. *Education:* BBA, City College, New York, 1965; MA, University of Texas, 1968; PhD, University of Portland, 1974. *Appointments:* Research Associate, Human Resources Research Office; Research Psychologist, Raytheon Corporation; Psychologist, Oregon Corrections Department; Assistant Professor, University of Portland. *Memberships:* Oregon Psychological Association; American Society of Clinical Hypnosis; American Association of University Professors. *Honours:* Psi Chi, (Honorary Psychology Society), 1967; Elected President, S.V.O.I. Incorporated, 1984. *Hobbies:* Astronomy; Computer Programming; Writing Non-fiction Books. *Address:* 6130 SW Alfred Street, Portland, Oregon 97219, USA.

KAHRS, Trygve, b. 23 Nov 1942, Norway. Staff and Consultant Radiologist, Vest-Agder Sentral Hospital, Kristiansand. m. Johanna Anna Wilhelmina Wagenaar, 30 June 1973, Sittard, Netherlands, 1 son, 2 daughters. *Education:* MD, University of Groningen, Netherlands; Consultant, Medical Radiology, Oslo, Norway. *Appointments:* Assistant Radiologist, Lillehammar Sentral Hospital; Assistant Radiologist, Ulleval Hospital, Oslo; Consultant Radiologist, Norwegian Radium Hospital, Oslo; Consultant Radiologist, Ulleval Hospital, Oslo; Consultant Radiologist, Buskarud Sentral Hospital, Drammen; Currently: Staff and Consultant Radiologist, Vest-Agder Sentral Hospital, Kristiansand. *Memberships:* Norwegian Association of Doctors; Association of Medical Radiology. *Hobbies:* Travelling; Books; Winter Sports. *Address:* Bj0rnbakken 20, 4600 Kristiansand, Norway.

KAICK, Gerhard Heinrich Van, b. 21 Apr. 1935, Karlsruhe. Head, Diagnosis and Therapy in Oncology. m. Erika van Kaick, 19 Oct. 1963, 1 son, 1 daughter. *Education:* MD, 1962. *Appointments:* Postgraduate Fellow, Institute of Nuclear Medicine, German Cancer Research Centre, 1972-77; Head, Diagnosis and Therapy in Oncology, German Cancer Research Centre, Heidelberg. *Memberships:* Deutshe Rontgengesellschaft; Deutsche gesellschaft fur Ultraschall in der Medizin. *Publication:* Abdominal angiography", 1972; "Total Body Computerized Tomography", 1978; "The German Thorotrast Study", 1984. *Hobbies:* History; Philosophy; Theology; Hiking. *Address:* Deutsches Krebsforschungszentrum Heidelberg, Im Neuenheimer Feld 280, D-6900 Heidelberg 1, Federal Republic of Germany.

KAIMAL, P. K., b. 7 May 1939, Kerala, India. Consultant Cardiologist. m. 21 Aug, 1971, India, 1 son. *Education:* MD. *Appointments:* Assistant Director, National Exercise and Heart Disease Project; Assistant Professor of Medicine, Case Western Reserve University, Cleveland, Ohio, USA; Assistant Professor of Medicine, Chief of Cardiology, Director of Heart Station, University Medical Center, Lafayette, Louisiana. *Memberships:* Fellow, American College of Physicians; Fellow, Royal College of Physicians, Canada; Fellow, American College of Cardiology; Fellow, American College of Chest Physicians; Fellow, Council of Clinical Cardiology, American Heart Association; Louisiana State Medical Society; Rapides Parish Medical Society. *Publications include:* 'Echocardiographic Evaluation of Acquired Valvular Disease of the Heart' (with S. S. Hirschfield), 1979; 'Psychologic vs Exercise Stress. Comparison of Hemodynamic, Metabolic, and EEG Responses', 1980; 'Characteristics of National Class Race Walkers' (with B. A. Franklin, T. W. Moir and H. K. Hellerstein), 1981; 'Computed Tomography for Diagnosis of Pericardial Cyst', 1981; 'Cardiac Dysfunction in Trichinosis' (with B. E. Beyt), 1982; 'Transient Electrocardiographic Q Waves in Spontaneous Pneumothorax', 1983. *Address:* 201 4th Street, Box 30144, Alexandria, LA 71301, USA.

KAKKAR, Vijay Vir, b. 22 Mar. 1937, Sialkot. Professor, Surgical Science, University of London; Honorary Consultant Surgeon, King's College Hospital; Director, Thrombosis Research Unit, King's College School of Medicine, London. m. Dr Sauitri Karnani, 3 Apr. 1962, Chesterfield, 2 sons. *Education:* MBBS, Ghandi Medical College, Uikram University, 1960; Fellow, Royal College of Surgeons, 1964; Fellow, Royal College of Surgeons of Edinburgh, 1964. *Appointments:* Senior House Officer, Registrar, various institutions, 1961-64; Lecturer, Surgery, University of Oxford, England, 1964-65; Research Fellow, Honorary Senior Registrar, Surgery, 1965-68, Senior Registrar, Surgery, 1968-69; King's College Hospital, London; Lecturer, Surgery, 1969-71, Senior Lecturer, Honorary Consultant Surgeon, 1971-76, King's College Hospital Medical School, London. *Memberships:* President, British Society on Thrombosis and Haemotiasis; International on Thrombosis and Haemostasis; Honorary Fellow, Academy of Medicine, Singapore; Honorary Member, Association of Surgeons of India; Surgical Research Society; etc. *Publications:* "Vascular Diseases", 1969; "Thromoembolism : Diagnosis and Therapy", 1971; "Heparin; Chemistry & Clinical Usage", 1976; "Chromgenic Peptide Substrates", 1978; "Atheroma and Thrombosis", 1984; "Stimulus Response Coupling in Platlets", 1985; 300 articles in journals on Thrombosis and Vascular Diseases. *Honours:* Hunterian Professor, Royal College of Surgeons, 1969; David Patey Prize, Surgical Research Society, 1979; Gunnar Baver Memorial Lecture, 1971; Finnlayson memorial Lecture, 1975; Wrigth-Schulte Lecture, 1977; Cross Memorial Lecture, 1977; Freyer Lecture, 1981. *Hobbies:* Skiing; Tennis; Cricket. *Address:* Thrombosis Research Unit, King's College School of Medicine and Dentistry, Denmark Hill, London SE5 8RX, England.

KAKULAS, Byron Arthur, b. 29 Mar. 1932, Perth, Western Australia. Professor of Neuropathology; Medical Director, Neuromuscular Foundation and Institute of Western Australia. m. Valerie Anne Patsoyannis, 5 Feb. 1961, 1 son, 2 daughters. *Education:* MB BS, St. Mark's College University of Adelaide, 1956; MD, University of Western Australia, 1964; FRACP, 1971; FRCPA, 1975; FRCPath, 1975. *Appointments:* Resident and Registrar, Royal Perth Hospital, 1957-69; Resident and Fellow, Harvard Medical School, USA, 1953-65; Honorary Neuropathologist, Princess Margaret Hospital, 1965-; Reader in Pathology, University of Western Australia, 1967-71; Head, Departmnt of Pathology, Royal Perth Hospital, 1967-; Professor of Neuropathology, University of Western Australia, 1971-; Neuropathologist, Sir Charles Gairdner Hospital, 1972-; Dean of Medicine, University of Western Australia, 1976-78; Medical Director, Muscular dystrophy Research Association, 1967-; Medical Director, Neuromuscular Foundation, 1974-; and Neuromuscular Research Institute, 1982-. *Memberships:* Vice-President, IInd, IIIrd, IVth, International Congress on Muscle Diseases, 1971, 74, 78; Vice-President, Vth International Congress on Neuromuscular Diseases, 1982; World Federation of Neurology, 1967-; Australian Association of Neurologists, Councillor, 1972-75; Australian Brain Foundation, President, 1980-85; Western Australia Division of ANZAAS, Chairman, 1981-83; International Spinal Research Trust, 1983-; President, Australian and New Zealand Society for Neuropathology, 1985-. *Publications:* 4 books: "Basic Research in Myology"; "Clinical Studies in Myology", Excerpta Medica, 1973 (Editor); "Man Marsupials and Muscle", 1982; "Diseases of Muscle, Pathlgoical Foundations of Clinical Myology" 4th edition, 1985 (co-author); Over 200 scientific papers on neuro and myopathological topics. *Honours:* Honorary Member, Rotary Club of West Perth, 1967-; Officer of the Order of Australia, 1975; Didaktora (Honoris Causa), University of Athens. *Hobby:* Water Sports. *Address:* 59 Dampier Avenue, City Beach 6019, Perth, Western Australia.

KALE, Oladele Olusiji, b. 19 Nov. 1938, Ijebu-Ode, Nigeria. Professor and Head of Department of Preventive and Social Medicine. m. Dr. Aderonke Oderinde, 31 May 1969, London, 5 sons. *Education:* BA, 1961, MB, BCh, BAO, 1963; Trinity College, Dublin; DTM & H, Liverpool University, 1966; DPH, Bristol University, 1971; DMCPH, Nigeria, 1971; FWACP, 1971. *Appointments include:* Registrar, Tropical Diseases Hospital, St Pancras, London, 1967; Registrar, New Corss Hospital (Annex of Guy's Hosptial, London) 1969; Senior Registrar, University College Hospital, Ibadan, 1971-73; Lecturer/Consultant, 1973-76, Senior Lecturer/Consultant, 1976-78, Reader/Consultant, 1978-82, Professor and Head of Department of Preventive and Social Medicine, Director Ibarapa Community Health Programme, 1983-, University of Ibadan. *Memberships:* Nigerian Medical Association; Association of Community Physicians of Nigeria; Nigerian Medical Postgraduate Medical College; West African College of Physicians. *Publications:* 'Clinico-epidemiological profile of guinea-worm in the Ibadan district of Nigeria' American Journal of Tropical Medicine and Hygiene, 1977; 'A simplified technique for counting Onchocerca volvulus microfilariae in skin snips' Bulletin of WHO, 1978; 'Fall in incidence of guineaworm infection in Western Nigeria after periodic treatment of infected persons' Bulletin WHO 1982. *Honours:* Fellow of the Nigerian Postgraduate Medical College; Fellow of the West African College of Physicians. *Hobbies:* Reading; Writing; Scrabble; Darts. *Address:* Department of Preventive and Social Medicine, University of Ibadan, Ibadan, Nigeria.

KALIBAT, Francis P, b. 15 Nov 1941, New York, USA. Director, Institute for Integrative Therapy. m. Linda Watten, 21 June 1980, Washington, 2 daughters. *Education:* AB, Columbia University, 1963; MD, Albany Medical College, 1967. *Appointments:* Medical Intern, Hospital for the Good Samaritan, Los Angeles, California, 1967-68; Resident in Psychiatry, Los Angeles County, University of Southern California Medical Center, 1968-71; Staff Psychiatrist, National Institute of Mental Health, 1971-74; Senior Psychiatric Consultant, The Crossing Place, 1977-; Director, Institute for Integrative Therapy, Washington. *Memberships:* American Psychiatric Association; Washington Psychiatric Society; Diplomate, American Board of Psychiatry and Neurology (Psychiatry). *Publications:* "Crossing Place: A Residential Model for Crisis Intervention Hospital and Community Psychiatry" with M Kreske-Wolfe, S Matthews and L Mosher, 1984. *Honour:* Clinical Assistant Professor of Psychiatry, Georgetown University School of Medicine, 1983. *Hobbies:* Piano; Gardening; Skiing. *Address:* 3842 Macomb Street NW, Washington, DC 20016, USA.

KÄLLÉN, A J Bengt, b. 1 June 1929, Kristianstad, Sweden, Professor in Embryology. m. Ingegerd Mörck, 14 June 1951, 3 sons, 1 daughter. *Education:* PhD, 1952; MD, 1958. *Appointments:* Associate Professor Embryology, 1952-65, Full professor of Embryology, 1965-, University of Lund, Sweden; Research Fellow, University College, London, England, 1953; Rockefeller Fellow, Washington University, St Louis, Mo, USA, 1953-54. *Publications:* Author of scientific articles in embryology, teratology and immunobiology. *Address:* Galjevångsvägen 26, S-22365 Lund, Sweden.

KALLIOKOSKI, Pentti Juhani, b. 2 Aug. 1947, Helsinki, Finland. Professor of Environmental Health. m. Maija Leena Kouvinen, 19 June 1970, 2 sons, 1 daughter. *Education:* MSc, 1970, Lic. Sc. 1976, Technical University of Helsinki; PhD, Public Health, University of Minnesota, 1979. *Appointments:* Occupational Hygienist, Institute of Occupational Health, Helsinki, 1971-77; Assistant, School of Public Health, University of Minnesota, 1978; Senior Researcher, Institute of Occupational Health, 1978-79; Professor, 1979-, Dean 1984-, University of Kuopio, Finland. *Memberships:* International Commission on Occupational Health; The Finnish Association on Toxicology; The Finnish Industrial Hygiene Association. *Publications:* Over 100 publications in the field of occupational and environmental health. *Hobbies:* Outdor life; Skiing. *Address:* University of Kuopio, PO Box 6, 70211 Kuopio, Finland.

KALLISTRATOS, George, b. 21 May 1927, Cairo, Egypt. University Professor. m. Ursula Kahlert, 1 daughter. *Education:* University of Athens, Greece; Faculty of Science, Cairo University, Egypt; 2 Doctor degrees, Faculty of Medicine, Hamburg University, Federal Republic of Germany. *Appointments:* Institute of Physiological Chemistry 1955-56, Laboratory of Clinical Chemistry and Biological Institute 1956-57, Hamburg University; Department of Radiobiochemistry and Nutrition Physiology, Max-Planck Institute Mariensee, 1958-62; Max-Planck Institute Hamburg-Volksdorf, 1962-64; Department of Experimental Urology, Max-Planck Society, Grosshansdorf, 1965-70; Research Institute for Experimental Biology and Medicine, Borstel, 1971-77; Professor of Experimental Physiology 1978-, Dean 1978-79, Faculty of Medicine, Vice Rector, 1979-80, Rector 1980-81, Pro-Rector 1981-82, President Hydrobiological Research Center 1981-, University of Ioannina, Greece. *Memberships:* 1st President, Society for the Agricultural Development of Ipiros region; Ex- Board of Directors, European Mariculture Society; Max-Planck Society for the Advancement of Science; New York Academy of Science; German Society for Clinical Chemistry; American Association for the Advancement of Science; European

Association for Cancer Research; German Society for Science and Medicine; Union Medicale Balkanique; European Inland Fisheries Advisory Committee; Hellenic Society for Preventive Medicine; German Society for Solar Energy. *Publications include:* 160 scientific publications, 3 monographs and 2 articles including: 'Litholytic Agents, Preventive and Curative Drugs for Nephrolithiasis', 1973; 'Instrumental Kidney Stone Chemolysis', in German, 1973; 'Endogenous and Exogenous Inhibitors of PAH Carcinogenesis', 1980. *Address:* Department of Experimental Physiology Faculty of Medicine, The University of Ioannina, 45332 Ioannina, Greece.

KALLMAN, Harold, b. 6 June 1929, New York City, New York, USA. Physician; Profesor of Family Medicine. *Education:* Mini-Residency in Occupational Medicine, CMDNJ-Rutgers; Cardiology Fellow, National Institute of Health; Residency in Internal Medicine, Kings County Hospital, Brooklyn, New York. *Appointments:* Private practice, Edison Medical Group, 1959-81; Clinical Assistant Professor 1975-81, Half-time Faculty 1978-81, Clinical Associate Professor 1980-81, College of Medicine and Dentistry; Assistant Director, Family Practice Residency Program, J F Kennedy Medical Center, 1975-81; Professor and Director, Geriatric Division, Department of Family Medicine, East Carolina University, 1982-. *Memberships:* Gerontological Society of America; Fellow, American Geriatric Society; Society of Teachers in Family Medicine; American Academy of Family Physicians; North Carolina and Pitt County Medical Society; New Jersey Academy of Family Physicians Council on Graduate Medical Education. *Publications include:* 'Pericardiectomy for massive pericardial effusion', 1959; 'A health knowledge questionnaire survey of senior citizens', (with MR Stuart and Harris S Goldstein), 1982; 'Constipation in the elderly', 1983; 'Acute brain failure' in "Family Medicine Research Monograph" (editors D Revicki, H May and J Daugherty), 1983; 'Depression in the elderly' in "Desyrel (Tradodone HCl) A Compendium of Three Years of Clinical Use (Monography)", 1984; "Principles and Practices in Family Medicine" (with Ira Morganstern), (editor Robert B Taylor), 1982; 'Accidental Hypothermia', 1986. *Hobbies:* Tennis; Swimming. *Address:* Director of Geriatric Division, East Carolina University School of Medicine, PO Box 1846, Greenville, NC 27835-1846, USA.

KALOUSEK, Dagmar Karla, b. 8 Aug. 1943, Czechoslovakia. Associate Professor, Pathology, University of British Columbia. m. Joseph Kalousek, 27 Jan. 1964, Plzen, 2 daughters. *Education:* MD, Palachy University, Czechoslovakia, 1966; Fellowship, Royal College of Physicians and Surgeons of Canada, 1973; Fellowship, Canadian College of Medical Genetics, 1980. *Appointments:* Director of Cytogenetic Laboratory, Montreal Children's Hospital, Montreal, 1974-77; Program Head, Cytogenetics and Embryofetopathology, B.C. Children's Hospital, Vancouver, 1977-; Senior Scientific Staff, Terry Fox Laboratory for Haematology/Oncology Research, Career Control Agency of British Columbia, Vancouver, 1981- *Memberships:* American Society of Human Genetics; Society of Paediatric Pathology; Genetics Society of Canada; International Academy of Pathology; The Genetical Society of Great Britain. *Publications:* Co-author, "Chromosomal mosaicism confined to the placenta in human conceptions', 'Science', 1983; Co-author, "Embryonic and fetal pathology of abortion" in 'Surgical Pathology of the Human Placenta", 1984; 'Confined chorionic tissue mosaicism in human gestations' in "First Trimester Fetal Diagnosis", 1985; Co-author, 'The Pathology of abortion, the embryo and previable fetus' in "Textbook of Perinatal Pathology" (in press). *Address:* Cytogenetic Laboratory, British Columbia Children's Hospital 4480 Oak Street, Vancouver, British Columbia, Canada.

KALYANKAR, Govind D, b. 2 June 1925, Kolhapur, Maharashtra, India. Chairman, Department of Biochemistry, M/S. Ramaiah Medical College, Bangalore, India. m. Vijaya, 11 May 1955, Belgaum, 2 sons, 1 duaghter. *Education:* MSc; PhD (Biochemistry). *Appointments:* Post-Doctoral Fellow, University of California, Berkely, 1955-58; Research Associate, Tufts University Medical School, Boston, 1958-62; Chairman, Department of Biochemistry and Bio-Physics, St. John's Medical College, Nangalore, 1963-85; Vice-Dean, St. John's Medical College, Nangalore, 1980-85. *Memberships:* Life Member, Association of Clinical Biochemists of India, President-elect; Society of Biological Chemists, India; Association of Physiologists and Pharmacologists of India. *Publications:* 105 Articles in scientific journals; Article in "Methods of Enzymology", Volume 17, 1973; Editorial Committee, 'Journal of the Association of Physiologists and Pharmacologists of India'. *Hobby:* Reading. *Address:* M.S. Ramaiah Medical College, Gokula, Bangalore 560 054, India.

KAMATH, C Ramadas, b. 29 Mar. 1936, Udupi, India. Otolaryngologist. m. Savithri R Kamath, 16 Dec. 1965, Udupi, 1 son, 1 daughter. *Education:* MB, BS, Stanley Medical College, Madras, India, 1953-57; Rotating Internship, Ibid, 1958-59; Demonstrator in Anatomy, Christian Medical College, Vellore, India, 1959-61, Resident in Surgery & Medicine, 1961-62; Resident, Otolaryngology, King George Medical College Hospital, Lucknow University, India, 1962-65; Diploma in Laryngotology, Master of Surgery (Ear, Nose & Throat); Diploma, American Board of Otolaryngology (Head & Neck Surgery). *Appointments:* Assistant Professor, 1965-70, Associate Professor, 1970-72, Otolaryngology, Kasturba Medical College & Hospital, Manipal, India; Clinical Fellow in Otolaryngology, Tufts New England Medical Centre, Boston, Massachusetts, USA; 1971-72; Resident, General Surgery, Stamford Hospital, Connecticut, 1972-73; Resident in Otolaryngology, Rhode Island Hospital, Providence, RI, 1973-76; Chief, ENT Section, VA Medical Centre, Martinsburg, West Virginia, 1976-; Assistant Professor of ENT, Johns Hopkins Medical School, Baltimore, Maryland, 1982-. *Memberships:* Fellow, American Academy of Otolaryngology & Head & Neck Surgery, 1977; Fellow, American College of Surgeons, 1979; Fellow, American Society of Head & Neck Surgery, 1981; Rotary International, Martinsburg, West Virginia, 1984. *Publicaitons:* Various articles in medical journals in field of ENT surgery. *Honour:* CIBA Fellowship from India for Study at University of Basel, Switzerland, 1969-70. *Hobbies:* History; Medical History; Philately; Numismatics; Ancient India & USA. *Address:* VA Medical Centre, Martinsburg, WV 25401, USA.

KAMBOJ, Ved Parkash, b. 1 Apr. 1937, Jullundur City, India. Deputy Director. m. Dr Mridula Kamboj, 24 Jan. 1971, Pilkhuwa, 2 daughters. *Education:* BSc., Honours, 1959; MSc., Honours, 1960, PhD, 1965, DSc., 1970, Punjab University, India; Advanced Training in Reproductive Biology, Contraceptive Technology, West Germany, 1975. *Appointments:* Scientist B, 1965-70, Scientist C, 1970-78, Scientist E, 1978-82, Deputy Director, 1982-, Central Drug Research Institute, Lucknow, India. *Memberships:* WHO Steering Committee on Vaginal and Cervical Devices for Fertility Regulation, 1977-80; ICMR Task Forces, Postcoital Contraception, 1980-, Plants for Fertility Regulation, 1984-; Society for Study of Reproduction, USA; Life Member, Endocrine Society of India, Punjab University Zoological Society, UP Association for the Advancement of Science, Punjab University Alumni Association. *Publications:* 135 orignianl research papers and review articles; 4 book chapters; Co-inventor, 19 Patents. *Hobbies:* Reading; Table Tennis; Badminton. *Address:* Division of Endocrinology, Central Drug Research Institute, Chattar Manzil Palace, PO Box 173, Lucknow 226001, India.

KAMDAR, Hasmukh Harilal, b. 3 Feb 1931, Dumana, India. Consultant, General and Cardio-Thoracic Surgeon. m. Nirmala Malde, 15 Aug 1957, Bombay, 1 son, 1 daughters. *Education:* MS General Surgery, Bombay University, 1959; FRCS, Edinburgh, 1960; FRCS, England, 1961; FACS, ACS, USA, 1975. *Appointments include:* Honorary Assistant Surgeon, Byl Nair Hospital, Bombay, 1963-64; Honorary Lecturer in Surgery, T N Medical College, 1963-64; Consultant, Cardio-Thoracic Surgeon, Kenyette National Teaching Hospital, University of Nairobi, 1970-75 and 1981-; Consultant Surgeon, M P Shah Hospital, Nairobi; Consultant Cardio-Thoracic Surgeon, Aga Khan Hospital, Nairobi. *Memberships:* Council member, Past Chairman and Past Secretary, Kenya Medical Association; Fellow, Council member, Association of Surgeons of East Africa; BMA; Assistant Secretary, Kenya Cardiac Society. *Publications include:* 17 papers and other publications including: 'Repair of Oro-antral Fistula by Complete palatal Flap (25 cases)', 1962; 'Surgical Disorders of Diaphragm', 1972; 'Continuing Education in Medical Profession', 1980. *Honours:* Balkrishna Sudamji Prize of University of Bombay, 1955. *Hobbies:* Service Clubs; Lions. *Address:* P Box 44266, Nairobi, Kenya.

KAMHOLZ, Stephen Leonard, b. 16 Oct, 1947, New York, USA. Associate Professor of Medicine. m. Rosemary V Potucek, 6 May 1978, New York, 1 son, 2 daughters. *Education:* BA, New York University, 1968; MD, New York Medical College, 1972. *Appointments include:* Instructor in Medicine 1977-78, Assistant 1978-83, Associate 1983-, Professor of Medicine, Albert-Einstein Medical College, New York; Assistant 1977-79. Adjunct 1979-84, Associate 1984-, Attending Physician, Montefiore Medical Center, Bronx, New York. *Memberships include:* Fellow, American College of Physicians; Fellow, American College of Chest Physicians; American Thoracic Society; American Federation for Clinical Research; New York Society for Thoracic Surgery. *Publications include:* 13 abstracts; 7 chapters in books; 33 articles including: 'Lung Transplants, Part 1: Advances in immunosuppression and surgical techniques', with F J Veith, C M Montefusco and F P Mollenkopf, 1984; 'Lung Transplants, Part II: Postsurgical Considerations', with F J Veith, C M Montefusco and F P Mollenkopf, 1984; 'Maintenance Protocol for Potential Organ Donors in Multiple Organ Procurement', with C M Montefusco, F P Mollenkopf, J Goldsmith and F J Veith, 1984. *Honour:* Linn J Boyd Award in Internal Medicine, New York Medical College, 1972. *Address:* Division of Pulmonary Medicine, Montefiore Medical Center, 111 East 210 Street, Bronx, NY 10467, USA.

KAMOUN, Pierre-Prosper, b. 2 July, 1936, Algeria. Professor of Biochemistry. m. Annie Vuyet, 30 Mar 1963, Paris, France, 1 son, 2 daughters. *Education:* MSc; MD. *Appointments:* Professor-Assistant, Biochemistry, 1965-68; Chief of Laboratory in Clinical Nephrology, 1969-74; Professor of Biochemistry, Head of Clinical Chemistry Laboratory, Université René Descartes, Paris. *Memberships:* The Biochemical Society, London; French Society of Clinical Biology; The New York Academy of Sciences; American Association for Clinical Chemistry. *Publications:* "Appareils et méthodes en Biochimie", 1974, 2nd edition, 1977; "Aide mémoire de Biochimie", 1976, 2nd edition, 1979; "Guide des examens de laboratoire", 1977, 2nd edition, 1981; "Guia de examenes de laboratorio", 1981, 2nd edition, 1986; "Guida agli esami di laboratorio, 1983. Numerous articles on amino acids and serotonin in inborn errors of metabolism and Down's Syndrome, published in scientific journals and publications. *Honour:* Laureat, Academie des Sciences, Paris, 1984. *Hobbies:* Bridge; Gardening. *Address:* H0pital Necker-Enfants Malades, 75743 Paris Cedex 15, France.

KAMPER-JORGENSEN, Finn, b. 25 Mar, 1944, Copenhagen, Denmark. Director. m. Lise Koch, 11 July 1970, 1 son, 1 daughter. *Education:* MD, University of Copenhagen, 1970; ECFMG 1970; PhD, 1975. *Appointments:* Hospital Physician, Bispebjerg Hospital, Copenhagen, 1970; Various Research Fellowships, Institute for Social Medicine, University of Copenhagen, 1971-77; Deputy Director, Danish National Social Research Institute, 1978; Deputy Director, National Board of Health, Primary Health Services, 1980-81; Director, Danish Institute for Clinical Epidemiology, 1981-. *Memberships:* Danish Medical Association; Danish Society for Community Medicine; International Epidemiological Association. *Publications:* Societal Costs of Road Traffic Accidents in Denmark", 1967-69; "Health Economics with a Social-Medical Perspective", Publication 2, 1974; "Prevention and Health", with G Almind, 1985. *Honour:* Schering Prize, 1976. *Address:* The Danish Institute for Clinical Epidemiology, 25 Svanemøllevej, DK 2100 Copenhagen Ø, Denmark.

KAMPIK, Anselm, b. 24 Apr 1949, Dillingen, Federal Republic of Germany. Professor of Ophthalmology. m. Ursula Kapfer, 1972, 1 son, 2 daughters. *Education:* MD, University of Munich Medical School, 1975; Residency, University Eye Hospital, Munich (training in Ophthalmology), 1975-79; PhD Ophthalmology, 1981. *Appointments:* Fellow in Ophthalmology (Eye Pathology), Wilmer Eye Institute, Johns Hopkins Hospital, Baltimore, Maryland, USA, 1979-80; Senior Assistant, 1980-85, Professor of Ophthalmology, 1985-, University Eye Hospital, Munich. *Memberships:* German Ophthalmological Society; East African Ophthalmological Society. *Publications:* 153 publications on clinical research in Ophthalmology & eye Pathology (especially vitreous & corneal pathology); "Epiretinale aund vitreale Membranen", 1981. *Hobbies:* Sports; Music. *Address:* Augenklinik der Universität München, MathildenStrasse, D-8000 Münich, Federal Republic of Germany.

KAMPS, Joseph M, b. 29 Oct. 1931, Bandung. Deputy Director, KLM Medical Department. m. Alessie C.J.M., 2 Mar. 1973, Heemstede, 2 son, 3 daughters. *Education:* MD, University of Amsterdam; Occupational Medicine, University of Leyden. *Appointments:* Royal Dutch Navy, 1958-60; General Practitioner, 1960-68; Occupational Medicine, 1968-. *Memberships:* National Association of Occupational Medicine (Netherlands); Society of Occupational Medicine (UK); Aerospace Medical Association, USA; International Association for Physicians in Overseas Services (UK); Netherlands Association for Aerospace Medicine. *Publication:* Co-author of section 'Occupational Medicine' in "Codex Medicus", 8th Edition. *Hobbies:* History of Art; Tennis. *Address:* Medical Department KLM, POB 3700 Schiphol Airport 1117Z1, Netherlands.

KANAAR, Adrian Charles, b. 19 Feb. 1911, England. Consultant Psychiatrist, Private Practice. m. Mary S. Forster, 23 Dec. 1937, (dec'd 1984), Sunderland, England, 1 son. *Education:* MRCS; LRCP; MB., BS, London, 1936; FRCS, Edinburgh, 1937; MRCP, London, 1939; MD, London, 1939; FRCS, Canada, 1949; FRCP, 1974; NYS License, 1959; Diplomate, American Board of Physical Medicine and Rehabilitation, 1963. *Appointments inlcude:* Served to Captain, Royal Army medical Corps, 1939-46; Assistant Surgeon, Birmingham Accident Hospital & Rehabilitation Centre, England, 1947-48; Private Practice, Orthopedic Surgery, Hamilton, Ontario, Canada, 1950-54; Assistant Professor, Phys. Med. & Rehab., University of Buffalo Medical School, New York, USA 1959-64; Attending Staff, St Francis Hospital, Poughkeepsie, 1964, and Vassar Brothers Hospital, 1967; Consultant Staff, VA Hospital, Castle Point, 1965, Director, Hand Clinic, 1973; Consultant, Wassaic Dev. Centre, New York, 1967; Fishkill Correc. Facility, Beacon, 1967; Greenhaven Correc. Facility, 1980. *Memberships include:* Fellow, Royal Society Medicine; Fellow American Academy Physical Medicine and Rehabilitation; North

American Academy Manipulative Medicine, Programme Chairman, 1965-66; AMA; Medical Society, State of New York; etc. *Publications include:* "Neurofibromatosis: Report on 3 Cases", St Bartholomew's Hospital, Medical Journal, 1934; "Some Important Psychiatric Complications of Injury", Ontario Medical Review, 1952; Monograph published by Saskatchewan council for Crippled Children, 1958; "Sports; Performance or Spectacle?", Chpt. in 'Is It Moral to Modify Man', 1973; "Long Distance Swimming", Chapter in 'Games Doctors Play', 1973. *Hobbies:* Marathon Swimming; Research on Hypothermia; Vice President, American Med Swimming Association; etc. *Address:* 12 Forbus Street, Poughkeepsie, NY 12601, USA.

KANAKANEDALA, Raghavaiah, b. 21 June 1927, India. Staff Psychiatrist, Veterans Administration Hospital; Associate Clinical Professor, UCI. m. Jhancy Laxmi, 11 June 1948; India, 2 sons, 1 daughter. *Education:* MB BS, Andhra India, 1953; DCH, 1958; MD, Paediatrics, 1963; Diplomate, American Board of Paediatrics, 1976; Diplomate, American Board of P M & R, 1977. *Appointments:* Paediatrician, Guntur General Hospital, A.P. India; Professor, Paediatrics, G.M.C., A.P. India, 1972; Assistant Professor in P.M. & R, Rush Medical College, USA; Attending Physician, Schwab Rehabilitation Hospital, Chicago, 1975-81. *Memberships:* Fellow, American Academy of P.M. & R; Active Member, American Association of Electromyography and Electrodiagnosis; Association of VA Physicians. *Publications:* Abstracts; 'Case Report of Cruveilhier Baumgarten Syndrome in a two year old child', 'Indian Pediatrics', 1966; 'Cibital Tunnel Syndrome; letters to the editor', 'Journal of American Medical Association', Sep. 1979; Book Review, "Practical Electromyography", Edited by Ernest W Johnson, 1980; "Posterior Introsseous Nerve Syndrome Caused by an Intermuscular Lipoma", Co-author of paper presented at 46th Annual Assembly of American Academy of Physical Medicine and Rehabilitation, Oct. 1984 in Boston, Massachusetts. Published in 'Archives of Physical Medicine and Rehabilitation Vol. 66, 1985. *Hobbies:* Gardening; Playing Tennis. *Address:* Veterans Administration Medical Center, RMS. 117 5901 E. 7th Street, Long Beach, CA 90822, USA.

KANAZIR, Dušan, b. 28 June 1921, Mošorin, Yugoslavia. President of Serbian Academy of Sciences and Arts; University Professor. m. Mersiha, 6 Jan. 1945, Paris, France, 1 daughter. *Education:* MD, Medical Faculty, Belgrade, Yugoslavia, 1949; Specialization in radiobiology, Institute of Radium, Paris, France, 1951-53; Specialization in molecular biology, Centre of Molecular Biology, Brussels, Belgium, 1953-55; PhD Physiology, Université Libre, Brussels, 1955. *Appointments:* Head, Laboratory of Molecular Biology and Endocrinology, Institute Boris Kidric, Vinca, Yugoslavia, 1956; Assistant Professor 1957-62, Associate Professor 1963-69, Full Professor 1970-, Faculty of Sciences, Belgrade; Academicina 1970-, President 1981-, Serbian Academy of Sciences, Belgrade. *Memberships include:* European Society of Radiobiology; European Society of Mutagenesis; Biochemical Society of Europe; Biochemical Society of Belgium. *Publications:* "Progress in Nucleic Acid Research and Molecular Biology", 1969; 'The Stucture and regulatory functions of cortisol receptor', 1979; "Harmonaly Active Peptides", 1982; "Cell Function and Differentiation", 1982. *Honours:* Red Flag, Yugoslavia, 1961; Golden Star Order of Merit for Nation, Yugoslavia, 1965; Brotherhood and Unity with a Golden Wreath, Yugoslavia, 1976. *Address:* Serbian Academy of Sciences and Arts, 35 Knez-Mihailova, 11000 Belgrade, Yugoslavia.

KANEFIELD, Marvin, b. 18 Nov. 1935, Philadelphia, Pennsylvania, USA. Senior Staff Psychiatrist. m. Isabelle Kanefield, 1 son, 2 daughters. *Education:* AB, Central High School, Philadelphia, PA, 1953; BS, Villanova University, Villanova, Pennsylvania, 1957; DO, Philadelphia College of Osteopathic Medicine, 1961. *Appointments include:* Private Practice, Psychiatry, Philadelphia, 1973-; Chief, Psychiatric Consultation Service, John F. Kennedy Memorial Hospital, Philadelphia, 1976; Consultant in Psychiatry, Jeanes Hospital, Philadelphia, 1981-; Rolling Hill Hospital, Elkins Park, Pennsylvania, 1977; Lawndale Community Hospital, Philadelphia, 1985-; American Oncologic Hospital, Philadelphia, 1985-; Immaculate Mary Nursing Home, Philadelphia, 1978-; Protestant Home, Philadelphia, 1981-; Clinical Assistant Professor, Hahnemann University Hospital, Philadelphia, 1973-; Lecture, Medical/Surgical, Weekly Staff Conference, John F Kennedy Memorial Hospital, Philadelphia, 1974-. *Memberships include:* American Psychiatric Assn., 1971-, General Member 1972-, Elected Fellow 1980; Pennsylvania Psychiatric Society, 1972-, Councillor, 1985-86; Philadelphia Psychiatric Society, 1971-, President 1984-85; United Health Services of Philadelphia, Member, Board of Director, 1970-73. *Publications:* "DST as a Predictor of Relapse Following Treatment with ECT" (co-author), in press; Contributor to numerous lectures. *Address:* Roosevelt Boulevard and Adams Avenue, Philadelphia, PA 19124, USA.

KANFER, Julian N, b. 23 May 1930, New York City, New York, USA. Professor and Head of University Department of Biochemistry. 1 son, 1 daughter. *Education:* MS 1958, PhD 1961, George Washington University, Washington DC. *Appointments:* Chemist, National Heart Institute, Bethesda, Maryland, 1955-60; Research Fellow and Postdoctoral Fellow, National Science Foundation and National Institutes of Health, Harvard Medical School, Boston, 1961-62; Research Biochemist, National Institute of Neurological Disease and Blindness, Bethesda, 1962-68; Director of Biochemical Research, Eunice Kennedy Shriver Center, Waltham, 1969-75; Professor and Head, Department of Biochemistry, University of Manitoba, Winnipeg, Manitoba, Canada, 1975-. *Memberships:* American Society of Biological Chemistry; American Neurochemistry Society; International Neurochemistry Society; American Chemical Society; Sigma Xi; American Association for the Advancement of Science; Society of Complex Carbohydrates; National Correspondent, Federation of American Societies for Experimental Biology; Canadian Federation of Biological Societies, Board of Directors, M S Society of Canada; Canadian Biochemical Society; Assiociation of Medical School Departments of Biochemistry; Scientific Review Committee, HSC Research Foundation. *Publications:* 2 books. *Address:* Department of Biochemistry, University of Manitoba, 770 Bannatyne Avenue, Winnipeg, Manitoba R3E OW3, Canada.

KANG, C. Yong, b. 28 Nov 1940, Hadong, Korea. Professor and Chairman. m. Myung-Ja, 17 Dec 1966, Hamilton, Canada, 1 son, 2 daughters. *Education:* PhD, McMaster University, 1971; Postdoctoral training, McArdle Laboratories, University of Wisconsin, USA, 1971-74. *Appointments:* Assistant Professor, Department of Microbiology, University of Texas South-western Medical School, 1974-78; Associate Professor, Department of Microbiology, University of Texas Southwestern Medical School, 1978-82; Professor and Chairman, Department of Microbiology and Immunology, University of Ottawa, 1982-. *Memberships:* American Society for Virology; American Society for Microbiology; American Association for the Advancement of Science; Canadian Society of Microbiologists; Genetic Society of Canada. *Publications:* Viral Interference, Rhabdoviruses, Volume II, 1980. Contributions to: Journal of Virology; Proceedings of National Academy of Science. *Hobbies:* Golf; Music. *Address:* Department of Microbiology and Immunology, University of Ottawa School of Medicine, Ottawa, Ontario, Canada K1H 8M5.

KANNO, Yoshinobu, b. 28 June 1930, Tokyo. Professor and Chairman, Department of Physiology. m. Fumiko Harada, 29 Nov 1959, 2 sons. *Education:* MD, Niigata University School of Medicine, 1955; D Med Sci, Postgraduate School of Niigata University, 1960. *Appointments:* Associate, Tokyo Medical and Dental University, 1960-62; Research Associate, Colubia University, 1962-64; Instructor, Tokyo Medical and Dental University, 1964-66; currently: Professor and Chairman of Department of Physiology, Hiroshima University School of Dentistry. *Memberships:* Physiological Society of Japan, Councilor; Sigma Xi; Harvey Society of New York; International Association of Dental research; New York Academy of Sciences. *Publications:* "New Textbook of Physiology" co-author, 1979; Contributor: "Bioelectrochemistry" 1980; Contributor: "Dentistry in Japan 1982-83" 1984; "Dentistry in Japan 1983-84" 1985; Minireview in Japan Journal of Physiology, 1985. *Honours:* Invitation to participate in Symposium on Neurophysiology of Japan-US Scientific Co-operation Program, March 1964; 16 other seminars and symposia. *Hobbies:* Photography; Horticulture. *Address:* 17-34-101 Nishikasumi-cho. Minami-Ku, Hiroshima City 734, Japan.

KANTOCH, Miroslaw Henryk, b. 13 Jan. 1928, Poland. Head of Virology Department. m. Zofia-Wanda Rudzka, 27 Mar. 1952, Wroclaw, Poland, 2 sons. *Education:* Physician 1952; Doctor of Medical Sciences, 1956; Habilitated Doctor of Medical Science, 1961. *Appointments:* Assistant, Microbiology Department, Medical School, Wroclaw, 1950-55; Chief of Virology and Electronmicroscopy Laboratory, Institute of Immunology and Experimental Therapy, Polish Academy of Science, Wroclaw, 1956-61 and 1963-64; Rockefeller Foundation Fellow, Johns Hopkins University, Baltimore, USA, 1961-62; Head of Virology Department, National Institute of Hygiene, Warsaw, Poland, 1965-. *Memberships:* Member of Science Councils of: National Institute of Hygiene, Warsaw, Institute of Immunology and Experimental Therapy, Wroclaw, Ministry of Health and Social Welfare; International Editorial Board of Acta Virologica, Bratislava; Vice President of Microbiology Committee, Corresponding Member, Polish Academy of Sciences. *Publications:* 'Markers and Vaccines' in "Advances in Virus Research" 1978; 'Cell-mediated immune reactions in measles' Acta Virol. 1980; 'RIA in SSPE', Acta Virol. 1982; "Medical Virology" textbook in Polish, 1982, 1984. *Honours:* Scientific Prize of Polish Academy of Science, 1975; National Scientific Prize, 1978; Scientific Prize of Ministry of Health and Social Welfare, 1982, 1983. *Hobbies:* Historical literature; Growing fruit trees. *Address:* Chocimska-street 24, 00-791 Warsaw, Poland.

KAPLAN, Alex Hillier, b. 25 Sept 1912, England, Clinical Professor of Psychiatry, m. Ada Marie Liebson, 7 June 1936, St Louis, Missouri, USA, 2 sons, 1 daughter. *Education:* BSc, College of the City of New York, USA, 1932; MD, St Louis University School of Medicine, 1936; Graduate, Chicago Psychoanalytic Institute, 1956. *Appointments:* Psychiatrist in chief, Jewish Hospital of St Louis, 1959-66; Medical Director, St Louis Psychoanalytic Institute, 1965-72; Acting Director, Community Child Guidance Clinic, 1955-58, Lecturer in Social Psychiatry, School of Social Work, 1951-57, Clinical Professor of Psychiatry, 1977-, Washington University, St Louis, Miss. *Memberships:* President, 1958-59, Eastern Missouri Psychiatric Association; President, 1966-68, 1982-84, St Louis Psychaonalytic Association; President, 1978-79, Treasurer, 1971-77, American Psychoanalytic Association; Vice

President, 1985-86, American College of Psychoanalysis; Fellow, American Psychiatric Association. *Publications:* 'The Dying Psychotherapist', 1985; 'From Discovery to Validation', 1981; 'Psychosomatic Infertility in the male and female', 1972; 'Joint parent-Adolescent interviews in Psychotherapy', 1956; Author of Over 30 articles. *Hobbies:* Tennis; Photography. *Address:* 4524 Forest Park Avenue, St Louis, MO 63108, USA.

KAPLAN, Debra Lee, b. 17 Aug. 1951, Buffalo, New York, USA. Director, Clinical Psychology Internship, Beth Israel Medical Center, New York; Assistant Professor, Mt. Sinai School of Medicine, New York. m. Dr. Adrian Sandheimer, 13 Sep. 1981, 1 son. *Education:* BA, State University of New York at Binghamton, 1972; PhD, University of Pennsylvania, 1977. *Appointments:* Clinical Psychology Intern, Upstate Medical Center, Syracuse, New York, 1976-77; Postdoctoral Fellow, University of Rochester, School of Medicine and Dentistry, 1977-79; Instructor in Psychiatry, Obstetrics and Gynaecology, Duke University Medical Center, 1979-80; Supervising Psychologist, Beth Israel Medical Center; Instructor, Mt. Sinai School of Medicne, New York, 1980-83. *Memberships:* Phi Beta Kappa; American Psychological Association; Society for Sex Therapy and Research. *Publications:* 'Eating Style of Obese and non-obese Males', 'Psychosomatic Medicine', 1980; Co-author, 'Human Sexuality' in "Critical Issues in Psychiatry", 1981; Co-author, 'The Urethral Syndrome – Sexual Components', "Sexuality and Disability", 1983; Co-author, 'Evaluation of the first 70 patients in the center for male sexual dysfunction', 'Journal of Urology', 1984. *Honour:* Summa cum laude, 1972. *Hobbies:* Classical Music; Mysteries. *Address:* 320 West End Avenue, New York, NY 10023, USA.

KAPLAN, Gerson H, b. 16 Feb 1930, Chicago, Illinois, USA, Private Practitioner, Psychiatry, m, Ruth T Kaplan, 8 May 1957, Chicago, Illinois, 3 sons, 1 daughter. *Education:* BA, Stanford University, 1951; MD, Northwestern University Medical School, 1955. *Appointments:* Associate, Assistant Director, Northwestern University Medical School; Staff Psychiatrist, Psychiatric Institute of Circuit Court, Cook County; Clinical Assistant Professor of Psychiatry, University of Chicago, Ill. *Memberships:* American Psychiatric Association; Central Neurophychiatric Society; American Medical Association. *Publications:* 'Progress in Neurology and Psychiatry', 1957, 1958; 'Liasion Psychiatry in a Veterans Administration Hospital', 1962. *Hobby:* Travel. *Address:* 111 North Wabash, Suite 1119, Chicago, IL 60602, USA.

KAPLAN, Paul Elias, b. 26 Oct. 1940, New York City, USA. University Professor. m. Candia S Post, 18 June 1966, Guarden City, New York, USA, 1 son, 2 daughters. *Education:* BA, cum laude, Amherst College; MD, University of California, Los Angeles. *Appointments include:* Fellow in Rehabilitation Medicine, NIH and Resident in Rehabilitation Medicine, USC Medical Center, 1971-72; Resident in Rehabilitation Medicine, USC Medical Center, 1972-73; Private practice in Rehabilitation Medicine, Beverly Hills, California, 1973-74; Staff Attending Physician/Director of Clinical Stroke Program, Rehabilitation Institute of Chicago, 1974-. *Memberships:* Illinois Society of Physical Medicine and Rehabilitation, Past President; Association of Academic Physiatrists, President Elect; Fellow, American Academy of Physical Medical and Rehabilitation; Fellow, American College of Physicians; American Association EMG/EDX. *Publications:* "Physical Medicine and Rehabilitation" 1977, 1980; "Practice of Rehabilitation Medicine" 1982; "Practice of Physical Medicine" 1984; "Stroke Rehabilitation" 1985; "Yearbook of Rehabilitation" 1986. *Honours:* Residency Award, American Academy of Physical Medicine and Rehabilitation, 1973; Honorary Board

Member, EMG Clinical Neurophysiol; American Medical Association Continuing Education Awards 1969-. *Hobbies:* Swimming; Ice Skating; Reading; Music; Playing Clarinet; Stamp Collecting; Art. *Address:* Rehabilitation Institute of Chicago, 345 E Superior Street Rm 883, Chicago, Il 60611, USA.

KAPLAN, Philip Bernard, b. 9 Oct. 1931, Bridgeport, Connecticut, USA. Physician. m. Celine Benoliel, 11 Jan 1961, Cherry Point, North Carolina, 1 son, 1 daughter. *Education:* BA, 1953, MD, 1957, University of Vermont. *Appointments:* Battalion and Regimental Surgeon, Flight Surgeon, US Navy, 1958-62; Acting and Assistant Regimental Flight Surgeon, FAA, 1962-66; Private Practice, 1966-, 2 years as Chief, Department of Family Practice, Human Hospital, Huntington Beach, California. *Memberships:* OCMA; CMA; AMA; AAFP; Aerospace Medical Association. *Publications:* 'Relationship of Character and Behaviour Disorders to Aircraft Accidents' in "Aerospace Medical Journal" 1966. *Honours:* Fellow, American Academy of Family Practitioners; Diplomate, American Board of Family Practitioners. *Hobbies:* Tennis; Music. *Address:* 17822 Beach Boulevard §243, Huntington Beach, CA 92647, USA.

KAPLAN, Steven Paul, b., 5 Mar. 1954, Chicago, Illinois, USA, Rehabilitation Psychologist, St. Elizabeth Hospital, Wisconsin, USA. m. Marci Lee Paul, 15 Sept 1979, Madison, Wis, 2 sons. *Edcuation:* BS, University of Illinois, 1975; MS, 1979, PhD, 1981, University of Wisconsin. *Appointments:* Director of Rehabilitation, St. Vincent Hospital, Green Bay, Wisconsin, 1964-85; Counsellor, Division of Vocational Rehabiliation, Madison, Wis, 1979; Assistant Professor, Rehabilitation Counselling University of North Carolina, Chapel Hill, NC, 1981-84. *Memberships:* American Psychological Association; National Rehabilitation Association; National Rehabilitation Counselling Association; Association of Medical Rehabilitation Directors and Coordinators. *Publications:* 'Psychological and Social Factors in Obesity', 1979; 'Professional Attitudes towards the obese', 1982; 'Rehabilitation Perspectives on Obesity', 1983. *Honours:* Academic Achievement, Association of Medical Rehabilitation Directors and Coordinators, 1985. *Hobbies:* Softball; Jogging; Reading; Family. *Address:* 321 W Briar Lane, Green Bay, WI 54301, USA.

KAPPENBERG, Richard Paul, b. 5 Feb 1944, Jamaica, New York, USA. Chief Psychologist; Programme Director. m. Judith Nakashima, 27 Nov 1970, Honolulu, Hawaii, 1 son, 1 daughter. *Education:* BA, 1965, MA, 1966, Fairfield University; PhD, University of Hawaii, 1973; varied additional training in neuropsychology, pain management and hypnosis. *Appointments include:* Various internships, Hawaii, 1969-72; Assistant Professor, Department of Human Development, 1973-79, Chairman, 1980-, Adjunct Clinical Professor of Psychology, 1984-, University of Hawaii; Private practice, Psychology, 1974-; Peer Reviewer, Office of Civilian Health and Medical Plan for Uniformed Service, 1978-; Consultant, St Timothy's Preschool, 1978-; Clinical Consultant, Division of Vocational Rehabilitation, State of Hawaii, 1975-; Chief Psychologist, Rehabilitation Hospital of Pacific, Hawaii, 1981-86; Clinical Director, Head Injury Programme, Rehabilitation Hospital, Honolulu, 1984-86. *Memberships:* American Psychological Association; American Association for Advancement of Science. *Publications:* Contributions to professional journals including: 'The Rehab Journal'; various internal reports. Contributor to: "Encyclopedia of Psychology", 1984; "Peer Counselling Manual", 1978; "HOME Program Instructors Manual"; "Family Life Center Manual". Various conference participations. *Honours include:* Licensed Psychologist, State of Hawaii; Certified Mental Health Care Provider; Diplomate, American Academy of Behavioural Medicine; Numerous invited conference contributions; Numerous com-

mittee chairmanships. *Hobbies:* Jogging; Skin diving. *Address:* 99-1661 C Aiea Heights Drive, Aiea, HI 96701, USA.

KAPSTAD, Leif Olav, b. 10 Dec 1946, Bygstad, Norway. Surgeon. m. Judith, 14 Aug 1971. Surgeon. *Education:* MD, 1973; General Surgeon, 1985. *Appointments:* Intern, 1974-75; General Practitioner, 1975-81; Rendend, 1981-85; Consultant, 1985. *Memberships:* Sociatas Phlibologica Scandinavica. *Publications:* "Muscle Lift for Tennis Elbow", 1981; "Splenic Cysts", 1983; "Ulcus Venosum Cruris", 1983; "Short-bowel Syndrom", 1984; "Congenital Liver Cysts", 1985. *Hobbies:* Sports; Mountaineering. *Address:* Hospital SSSF, Surgical Department, 6800 Forde, Norway.

KARAM, Daoud B, b. 4 Aug. 1934, Lebanon, Director, Rehabilitation Medicine, Coler Memorial Hospital, New York Medical College, USA, m. Barbara, 8 Oct 1966, 2 daughters. *Education:* MD, St Joseph University, Beirut, Lebanon, 1962. *Appointments:* Long Island Jewish Medical Centre, Queens Hospital Centre Affiliation, 1970-79. *Memberships:* AMA; American Congress Rehab Medicine; American Academy PM & R. *Publications:* 'Tendon Reflex Latencies in upper extremity archives of PM & R', 1977. *Honours:* Assistant Professor, Stony Brook University, 1973-1979; Assistant Professor, New York Medical College, 1980-. *Address:* 12 Tower Court, Syosset, NY 11791, USA.

KARCZEWSKI, Witold Andrzej, b. 30 Aug. 1930, Lwow, Poland. Head of Neurophysiology. m. Elzbieta Wegrzyn, 1 Mar. 1962, 1 son. *Education:* MD, 1954; Dr.Med.Sc. 1961; PhD, 1965; DSc., 1971; Professor, 1979. *Appointments:* Research Assistant, 1954-56, Senior Research Assistant, 1956-59, Assistant Lecturer, 1959-65, Lecturer (Docent) 1965-71, Reader, 1971-79, Professor, 1979-, Neurophysiology, Head 1964-, Scientific Director, 1968-85, Polish Academy of Sciences Medical Research Centre. *Memberships:* Polish and British Physiology Societies; Association Medicorum J.E. Purkyne, Honorary Member; IBRO; Society European Physiology Clinical; Warsaw Scientific Society; Committee, Biocybernetics and Bioengineering, PAS. *Publications:* About 70 papers on respiratory reflexes, central control of breathing, etc. *Honours:* Scientific Award, Medical Dept., Polish Academy of Science, 1967; Scientific Awards, Scientific Secretary of the PAS, 1973, 1979, 1983; State Prize in Medicine, 1984. *Hobbies:* History; Sailing; Do It Yourself. *Address:* Dept. of Neurophysiology, PAS Medical Research Centre, Dwokowa 3, 00 784 Warsaw, Poland.

KARIITHI, Mary Wanjiku, b. 27 July 1948, Kenya. Senior Medical Laboratory Technologist, Haematology, Kenyatta N Hospital. 1 son, 1 daughter. *Education:* Certificate, Coagulation Techniques and Quality Control; Intermediate Diploma, Medical Laboratory Technology, East Africa; Final Diploma, Haematology, Blood Transfusion, East Africa; Certificate in Quality Control, Haematology. *Appointments:* Medical Laboratory Technologist III, 1971-75; Medical Laboratory Technologist III, in charge of Coagulation Section, Haematology, 1975-78; Medical Laboratory Technologist I, in charge of Haematology Department, 1978-82; Senior Medical Laboratory Technologist, in charge of Haematology Department, Kenyatta National Hospital, 1982-. *Memberships:* Association of Kenya Medical Laboratory Scientific Officers, Secretary to Executive Committee. *Publications:* "Haemorrhagic Disorders as seen in Kenyatta National Hospital", co-author, 'Tropical Doctor Journal', 1979; "External Quality Control in Blood Coagulation at the Kenyatta National Hospital", co-author, 'East African Medical Journal', 1984; "Investigations of Haemorrhagic Disorders at the Kenyatta National Hospital", 'Medicom', 1980. *Hobbies:* Reading; Gardening;

Cinema. *Address:* c/o National Public Health Laboratory Services, PO Box 20750, Nairobi, Kenya.

KÄRJÄ, Juhani, b. 25 Dec. 1934, Kalajoki, Finland. Professor of Otorhinolaryngology; Department Head. m. Magda Leena Niemi, 28 July 1961, 1 son, 1 daughter. *Education:* Candidate in Medicine, 1958; MD, 1960; Specialist in Otorhinolaryngology, 1966; Doctor of Medical Sciences, 1968., *Appointments:* Assistant Demonstrator, 1965-72, Assistant Chief Surgeon, 1974-74, Acting Associate Professor, 1974-75, Department of Otohinolaryngology, University of Kuopio, Finalnd; Professor, 1975-, Head, Department of Otorhinolaryngology, 1975-, Medical Director, Central Hospital, 1981-84, University of Kuopio. *Memberships:* Finnish Otolaryngological Society; Internal Society of Audiology; European Working Group in Paediatric Otorhinolaryngology; Collegium Oto-Rhino Laryngologicum Amicitiae Sacrum; New York Academy of Sciences, USA. *Publications:* "Perstimulatory suprathershold audiotry adaptation", 1960; Salmivalli - Jauhiainen - Karja - Raivio, "Kuulontutkimus ja kuntoutus" Finnish textbook; Editor of Finnish textbook, 1981. *Address:* University of Kuopio, Box 6, SF-70211 Kuopio, Finland.

KARLEN, John Richard, b . 4 Mar. 1942, Ohio, USA. Professor of Obstetrics and Gynaecology. m. Helen Bilello, 2 Sept. 1967, New Jersey, USA, 2 sons, 1 daughter. *Education:* BA, Alfred University, USA, 1965; MD, Northwestern University, 1969. *Appointment:* Professor of Obstetrics and Gynaecology, Northeastern Universities College of Medicine, USA,-. *Memberships:* Summit County Medical Society; Ohio State Medical Association; American Medical Association; American College of Obstetricians and Gynaecologists; Society of Gynaecologic Oncologists. *Publications:* Co-author: 'Carcinoma of the endometrium co-existing with pregnancy' in 'Obstetrics and Gynaecology', 1972; co-author: 'Renal scleroderma and Pregnancy' in 'Obstetrics and Gynaecology', 1974; co-author 'The mulitdisciplinary team approach to exenteration of the pelvis' in 'Surgical Gynaecology and Obstetrics', 1983; co-author 'Infected intrauterine Pregnancy presenting as septic shock' in 'Annals of Emergency Medicine', 1983; co-author 'Psychological implications of prenatal diethylstilbesterol exposure in females' submitted 1985. *Hobbies:* Running; Skiing; Golf. *Address:* 75 Arch Street, Suite 042, Akron OH 44304, USA.

KARMADJI, Ignatius, b. 19 June 1932, Pati, Indonesia. Flight Surgeon (retired). m. Yvonne Ratih Ekasari, 7 May 1959, Pati, Indonesia, 1 son, 2 daughters. *Education:* Aerospace Medicine, US Air Force, Brooks Air Force Base, Texas. *Appointments:* Air Force Medical Officer, 1963-73; Chief, Bureau of Education & Training, Armed Forces Population & Family Planning Unit, 1973-85; Project Officer, Population Education, Indonesian Armed Forces, National Family Planning Coordinating Board & United Nations Fund for Population Activities, 1979-85. *Memberships:* Indonesian Medical Association; Indonesian Population & Environmental Education Association; Aerospace Medical Association. *Publications:* "Population Education for Armed Forces Officers" (textbook), 1980; "Population Problems in Indonesia" (book, flipchart, slides, video), 1981-84. *Hobbies:* Photography; Books. *Address:* Komplek AURI Jatiwaringin, Jalan Wirajasa 2, Blok M-2, Jakarta 13620, Indonesia.

KAROLY, Paul, b. 18 Oct 1944, New York City, USA. Professor of Psychology and Director of Clinical Training. m. Linda S Ruehlman, 1 son from previous marriage. *Education:* BA, City College of City University of New York, 1966; PhD, University of Rochester, New York, 1971. *Appointments:* Assistant Professor, 1970-75, Associate Professor, 1975-80, Professor, 1980-82, Department of Psychology, University of Cincinnati, Cincinnati, Ohio; Professor of Psychology, and Director of Clinical Training, Department of Psychology, Arizona State University, Tempe, Arizona. *Membership:* American Psychological Association. *Publications:* Editor: "Child Health Psychology: Concepts and Issues" 1982; "Self Management and Behaviour Change" 1982; "Measurement Strategies in Health Psychology" 1985. *Hobbies:* Music; Reading; Hiking. *Address:* Department of Psychology, Arizona State University, Tempe, AZ 85287, USA.

KARPMAN, Harold L, b. 23 Aug. 1927, USA. Associate Clinical Professor of Medicine University of California Los Angeles School of Medicine. m. Molinda, 9 Aug. 1985, Versailles, France, 1 son, 1 daughter. *Education:* BA, University of California, Berkeley, 1950; MD, University of California Medical School, San Francisco, 1954; Post-graduate Training: Wyley Winsor Research Foundation, Los Angeles; Los Angeles County General Hospital; Beth Israel Hospital, Boston, Massachusetts; Diplomate, American Board of Internal Medicine, 1964. *Appointments:* Instructor of Medicine, Department of Medicine, Harvard Medical School, 1955-57; Clinical Instructor of Medicine, 1958-64; Assistant Clinical Professor of Medicine, 1964-72; Associate Clinical Professor of Medicine, 1971-72; University of Southern California School of Medicine, Los Angeles; Associate Clinical Professor of Medicine, University of California at Los Angeles School of Medicine, 1972-; General Partner, Camden Medical Building, Los Angeles, 1970-; Director, Noninvasive Vascular Laboratory, Brotman Medical Center, Culver City, California, 1976-. *Memberships:* Fellow: American College of Physicians; Ameican College of Cardiology; American College of Chest Physicians; International Cardiovascular Society; American College of Angiology; International College of Angiology; American Academy of Thermology; Alpha Omega Alpha, etc. *Publications:* Contributor to professional journals; Exhibits; Presentations. *Honours:* San Bruno Community House Award, 1953; Merk Award, 1953. *Hobbies:* Reading; Writing (books and articles). *Address:* 414 North Camden Drive, Beverley Hills, CA 90210, USA.

KARPOWICZ, Alexander Paul, Jr, b. 11 Oct 1942, Trenton, New Jersey, USA. Doctor of Chiropractic. m. Christine A Buchalski, 13 Mar 1982, Scranton, Pennsylvania, 1 son, 4 daughters. *Education:* Trenton Junior College, 1962; Doctor of Chiropractic, Logan Chiropractic College, 1965; Diplomate of International College of Applied Kinesiology, 1980. *Appointments:* Teaching for Diplomate, International College of Applied Kinesiology. *Memberships:* American Chiropractic Association; Pennsylvania Chiropractic Society. *Publications:* 'Urinalysis-Help for the Tough Cases', Success Express Magazine, 1984; 'Mirror, Mirror - On the Wall', American Chiropractor Magazine, 1984. *Honours:* Award of Merit, Pennsylvania Chiropractic Society, 1980; Certificate of Nutritional Counselling, Nutritional Academy, 1980; Logan College of Chiropractic Ambassador Club, 1969-70. *Hobbies:* Fishing; Hunting; Reading; Gardening. *Address:* Karpowicz Chiropractic Center, 1201 Wheeler Avenue, Dunmore, PA 18510, USA.

KARUSH, Aaron, b. 27 Nov 1912, New York, New York, USA. Professor. m. 24 June 1934, Boston, Mass., 2 sons. *Education:* BS, College of City of NY, 1931; MD, Boston University School of Medicine, 1935. *Appointments:* Research Assistant, 1947-49, Instructor, 1949-53, Associate, 1953-55, Assistant Clinical Professor, 1955-57, Associate Clinical Professor, 1964-75, Professor Clinical Psychiatry (Ret), Department of Psychiatry, Columbia University College of Physicians and Surgeons, 1975-78; Director, 1971-76, Training and Supervising Psychoanalyst, Columbia Psychoanalytic Center for Training and Research, 1948-; Attending Psychiatrist, Presbyterian Hospital, Columbia Presbyterian Medical Center, 1964-78. *Memberships:* Member 1948, Fellow 1967, American Psychiatric Assoc.; American Psychoanalytic Assoc. 1949; Association for Psychoanalytic Medicine, NY, 1978-; President, Association for Psychoanalytic Medicine, 1963-65; American Association for the Advancement of Science. *Publications:* 'Ulcerative Colitis Psychoanalyses of Two Cases', (with G E Daniels), 1953; 'A Methodological Study of Freudian Theory', (with Kardiner, A, Ovesey L,), 1959; 'Psychotherapy in Chronic Ulcerative Colitis', (with G E Daniels, J O'Connor, C A Flood, B Saunders), 1977; 'Working Through', 1967. *Honours:* Sandor Rado Lecturer, Tulane University, New Orleans, 1973; Rado Lecturer, Columbia Psychoanalytic Center, NY, 1981; Professor Emeritus, Clinical Psychiatry, Columbia University, 1978. *Hobby:* Writing. *Address:* 16 Devonshire Road, New Rochelle, NY 10804, USA.

KARZON, David Theodore, b. 8 July 1920, New York, USA. Professor and Chairman University Department of Pediatrics. m. Allaire Urban, 18 May 1950, Elizabeth, New Jersey, USA, 1 son, 1 daughter. *Education:* Yale University, New Haven, Connecticut, 1936-37; BS, MS, Ohio State University, Columbus, Ohio, 1937-41; MD, Johns Hopkins University School of Medicine, Baltimore, Maryland, 1941-44. *Appointments include:* Director, Virology Laboratory, State University of New York at Buffalo, 1954-68; Assistant Professor, Associate Professor, Professor of Virology, Department of Bacteriology and Immunology, State University of New York at Buffalo, 1954-68; Acting Chairman of Pediatrics, SUNY at Buffalo, 1964-65; James C Overall Professor and Chairman of Pediatrics, Vanderbilt University School of Medicine, Nashville, 1968-. *Memberships:* American Academy of Pediatrics; American Board of Pediatrics; Society for Pediatric Research; Southern Society for Pediatrics Research; American Pediatric Society; Ambulatory Pediatric Association; Association of Medical School Pediatric Department Chairmen; Infectious Diseases Society of America; Pediatric Infectious Diseases Society. *Publications:* 139 publications including: 'Considerations of Safety, Efficacy and Potential Applications of Vaccinia Vectors for Immunophrophylaxis: An Alternative Approach to Control of Human Diseases for which Vaccines are Available' in "Vaccinia Viruses as Vectors for Vaccine Antigens" edited by Gerald Quinnan, 1985; "The Cytotoxis T-Cell Response to Respiratory Syncytial Virus in Mice" in Journal of Virology, in Press co-author. *Honours:* US Public Health Service Research Fellowship, 1948-50; Lowell M Palmer Senior Fellowship, 1952-54; Markle Scholar in Medical Science, 1956-61; Research Career Award, National Institutes of Health, US Public Health Service, 1962-68; Alpha Omega Alpha 1975. *Address:* Department of Pediatrics, Vanderbilt University, School of Medicine, Nashville, TN 37232, USA.

KASHANI, Javad H., b. 30 Aug. 1937, Meshed. Professor, Psychiatry, Paediatrics & Internal Medicine, University of Missouri, Columbia; Director, Children's Services, Mid-Missiouri Mental Health Centre. m. Soraya, 23 Mar. 1962, 1 son, 1 daughter. *Education:* MD; FRCP (C). *Appointments:* Assistant Professor, Psychiatry, 1978-82; Associate Professor, Psychiatry, 1982-85; Director, Children's Inpatient Unit, Mid-Missouri Mental Health Centre. *Memberships:* American Psychiatric Association;' American Academy of Child Psychiatry; Fellow, Royal College of Physicians & Surgeons of Canada. *Publications:* Numerous articles in professional journals including: 'Archives of General Psychiatry'; 'American Journal of Psychiatry'; 'American Academy of Child Psychiatry'; 'Canadian Journal of Psychiatry'; 'British Journal of Psychiatry'. *Honours:* State of Missouri Commission on Mental Health Award, 1981; Fellow, American Academy of Child Psychiatry. *Hobby:* Oil Painting. *Address:* Dept. of Psychiatry, University of Missouri, 3 Hospital Drive, Columbia, MO 65201, USA.

KASTENBAUER, Joseph Rudolf, b. 6 July 1945, Schwabisch-Hall, Germany. Dentist; Doctor. m. Maritta, 6 May 1970, 2 sons, 1 daughter. *Education:* University of Munich; University of Erlangen-Nuremberg; MD; Dr.Med.Dent. *Memberships:* DGZMK (German Professional Dental Medicine Association; APW. *Publication:* ''Computer und neue Medien in der Zahnheilkunde'', 1983. *Honour:* Member, Rotary International. *Hobbies:* Skiing; Tennis; Golf. *Address:* Arzt, Zahnarzt, Bahnhofstrasse 14, 8262 Altötting, Democratic Germnan Republic.

KASTIN, Abba J, b. 24 Dec 1934, Cleveland, Ohio, USA. Physician/Endocrinologist/Research Scientist. *Education:* AB, Harvard College, 1956; MD, Harvard Medical School, 1960. *Appointments include:* Clinical Investigator, VA Hospital New Orleans, 1965-68; Chief, Endocrinology Section, VA Medical Center, New Orleans, 1968-; Associate. Graduate Faculty, University of New Orleans, 1976-; Professor, Deapartment of Medicine, Tulane University School of Medicine, New Orleans, 1974-. *Memberships:* Honorary Member: La Societe de Dermo-Chimie, 1966; Chilean Society of Endocrinology, 1970; Philippine Society of Endocrinology and Metabolism, 1976; Peruvian OB/GYN Society 1980; Peruvian Endocrine Society, 1980; Polsih Endocrine Society, 1980; Hungarian Endocrine Society, 1985; Also regular member of numerous other societies and associations; Editor-in-Chief of Peptides. *Publications:* 2Contributor of over 450 articles to professional journals. *Honours:* Tyler Fertility Award, 1975; listed among 100 most cited scientists in the world, 1978-; Copernicus Medal of Medical Faculty of Krakow, Poland, 1979; Honorary Doctorate, University, Peru, 1980; Middleton Award, 1982; Introductory "Honorary" scientific lecture, XVth International Congress of the International Society of Psychoneuroendocrinology, Vienna, 1984; Honorary Doctorate, University of New Orleans, 1984. *Hobbies:* Competitive swimming; Viola Playing; Foreign Travel. *Address:* VA Medical Center and Tulane University School of Medicine, 1601 Perdido Street, New Orleans, LA 70146, USA.

KATHOL, Roger Gerald, b. 15 Jan 1948, Wichita, Kansas, USA. Assistant Professor, Psychiatry and Internal Medicine. m. Mary Holman, 18 Nov 1972, Kansas City, USA, 2 sons, 1 daughter. *Education:* BA, University of Kansas, Lawrence; MD, University of Kansas Medical Centre; FACP. *Appointments:* Registrar, Fellow, Endocrinology, University of Otago Clinical School, Wellington, New Zealand, 1980; Fellow Associate in Internal Medicine and Psychiatry, 1980, Assistant Professor of Psychiatry and Internal Medicine, 1982-, University of Iowa, Iowa City, USA. *Memberships:* AMA; Iowa Psychiatric Association; Iowa Medical Society; American College of Physicians; Johnson County Medical Society; American Psychiatric Association; American Academy of Psychosomatic Medicine; Society Behavioral Medicine; American Academy Clinical Psychiatry; American Association Advancement of Science; Endocrine Society; Society of Biological Psychiatry; American Federation for Clinical Research. *Publications:* 'Functional Visual Loss', 1983; 'Provocative Endocrine Testing', 1984; 'Persistent Elevation of Urinary Free Cortisol', 1985; 'Corticosteroid Changes in Affective Disorders', 1985; 'Urinary Free Cortisol Levels and Dexamethasone Suppression Testing in Organic Affective Disorder', 1985. *Honours:* Fellowship Appointment, American College of Physicians, 1985. *Hobbies:* Running; Golf; Woodwork. *Address:* 1-301A Psychiatric Hospital, The University of Iowa, Iowa City, IA 52240, USA.

KATO, Ryuichi, b. 23 Feb. 1930, Hokkaido, Japan.

Professor of Pharmacology. m. Nagako Okabe, 27 May 1961, Tokyo, 1 son, 1 daughter. *Education:* MD, School of Medicine, Keio University, 1954; Doctor in Medical Science, Keio University, 1961; PhD, University of Milan, Italy, 1961, Internship, School of Medicine, Keio University, 1954-55. *Appointments:* Assistant, Department of Neuropsychiatry, School of Medicine, Keio University, 1955-57; Research Associate, Department of Pharmacology, School of Medicine, University of Milan, Italy, 1957-62; Visiting Associate, Laboratory of Chemical Pharmacology, NIH, USA, 1962-64; Head, Section of Biochemical Pharmcology, Department of Pharmacology, National Institute of Hygienic Sciences, Tokyo, Japan, 1964-70; Director, Biological Research Department, Central Research Laboratory, Fujisawa Pharmaceutical Co Ltd, Osaka, Japan, 1970-77; Chairman, Professor of Pharmacology, Department of Pharmacology, School of Medicine, Keio University, Japan, 1977-. *Memberships:* President, International Society for the Study of Xenobiotics, 1986-; Vice-Chairman, Section of Drug Metabolism, International Union of Pharmacologists, 1984-; Board of Trustees, Japanese Pharmacology Society, 1975-; Board of Trustees, Japan Toxicology Society, 1972-. *Publications:* 'Drug Metabolisms & drug effects', 1968; 'Microsomes, Drug Oxidation & Drug Toxicity', 1982; 'Sex-related differences in drug metabolism', 1974; 'Characteristics & differences in the hepatic mixed function oxidases of different species', 1974. *Honours:* Kitajima's Keio Medicine Award, 1966; Princess Takamatsu Cancer Research Award, 1983. *Hobbies:* Tennis; Igo. *Address:* 1-5-4-24 Osone-cho, Kouhoku-ku, 222 Yokohama, Japan.

KATO, Shiro, b. 4 Nov 1925, Dalian, China. Professor. m. 27 May 1951, Osaka, 2 daughters. *Education:* MD, 1950, PhD, 1956, Osaka University Medical School. *Appointments:* Associate Professor, 1956-64, Professor, 1964-, Director, 1980-84, Research Institute for Microbial Diseases, Osaka University. *Memberships:* Past President Society of Japanese Virologists; Japanese Cancer Association; Japan Society of Medical History. *Publications:* 'Marek's disease virus' in 'Advances in Virus Research', 1985. *Honours:* Prize of Princess Takamatsu, 1980; Cancer Research Fund. *Hobby:* Bird watching. *Address:* Fujishirodai 4-23-7, Suita, Osaka, Japan 565.

KATOCH, Vishwa Mohan, b. 18 Feb 1953, Hamirpur, India. Head, Microbiology, Central Jalma Institute for Leprosy, Agra, India. m. Dr Kiran Katoch, 17 Feb 1978, Jaipur, 1 daughter. *Education:* MBBS, HP, Medical College, Simla, India, 1974; MD, All India Medical Institute, New Delhi, 1978; Post Doctoral Fellow, TB Research Laboratory, VA Medical Centre, Long Beach, California, USA, 1981; British Council Exchange Visitor at NIMR, London, England, 1984-85. *Appointments:* Talent Search Scheme Fellow, 1976-78; Junior Resident, Obstetrics Gynaecology and Medicine, Safdarjang Hospital, New Delhi, 1976; Junior Resident, Microbiology, Allms, New Delhi, 1977-78; Research Officer, Head, Microbiology, Central Jalma Institute for Leprosy, Agra 1979-82; Senior Research Officer, Head, Microbiology, Central Jalma Institute for Leprosy, Agra, 1983-. *Memberships:* Indian Association of Medical Microbiologists; Indian Association of Leprologists; Indian Medical Association; Indian Science Congress; International Working Group on Mycobacterial taxonomy. *Publications:* Author, 33 publications in Indian, European and American Medical Journals, subjects include drug trials to drug resistance, mycobacterial taxonomy, metabolism and genetics of mycobacteria. *Honours:* 2nd Position, MBBS & Gold Medal in Obstetrics and Gynaecology; Selected for Research Service of ICMR by National Competition. *Hobbies:* Travel; Studying Social & Political Aspects of different Societies within India and Abroad. *Address:* Jajoli, PO Jalari, Distt. Hamir-

pur (HP), India.

KATOPODIS, Nonda, b. 13 Jan 1924, Greece. Chief Research and Development Director. m. Georgia Yola Tsagridis, 9 Nov 1952, Athens, Greece, 2 sons. *Education:* M.S. Organic Chemistry; PhD, Biochemistry. *Appointments:* Cancer Research, University of Athens, Greece, 1952-55; Cancer Research, Montreal Cancer Institute, Canada, 1956-60; New England Institute for Medical Research, Ridgefield, Connecticut, USA, 1965-70; Sloan Kettering Institute Memorial Hospital, New York, 1971-83; Medical Research, Dianon Systems Inc, 1983-. *Memberships:* Hellenic Anti-Cancer Society; American Chemical Society; American Association for Clinical Chemistry; International Society for Oncodevelopmental Biology and Medicine. *Publications:* Contributor of chapters to edited medical volumes and articles to scientific journals. Presenter of many papers to medical conferences. *Hobbies:* Chorus singing; Sailing; Fishing; Photography. *Address:* 80 Woodway Road, Stamford, CT 06907, USA.

KATZ, Eli, b. 15 Sep. 1912, USSR. Honorary Head of Department of Otolaryngology. m. Grace Gertrude Genesove, 19 Mar. 1942, Toronto, Canada, 2 sons, 3 daughters. *Education:* MDCM; FRCS(C). *Appointments:* Otolaryngologist 1952-60, Chairman of Department of Oytolaryngology 1960-79; Honorary Head of Department, Queen Elizabeth Hospital, Montreal. *Memberships:* American Academy of Otolaryngology and HNS; American Academy of Facial Plastic and Reconstructive Surgery; Canadian Otolaryngological Association; Canadian Medical Association; Quebec Association of Otolaryngologists and HNS. *Publication:* 'Intranasal Steroid Injection', 1985. *Hobbies:* Reading; Music; Astronomy; Hiking. *Address:* 5025 Sherbrooke West, Montreal, Quebec H4A 1S9, Canada.

KATZ, Elias, b. 22 Sept. 1912, New York, USA. Director, Institute of Art and Disabilities. m. Florence Ludins, 7 Dec. 1937, East Chester, New York, 1 son. *Education:* BA, 1932; MS (CCNY), 1933; PhD, Columbia University, USA, 1942; Diploma for Training in Community Psychiatry, Berkeley, California. *Appointments:* Chief Psychologist, US Navy, Berkeley, California, 1948-51; Chief Psychologist, CP Programme, UC Medical Centre, San Francisco, 1953-70; Lecturer, Department of Psychiatry, UC Medical Centre, 1970-; Founder and Co-Director, Creative Growth, Oakland, California, 1974-82; Founder and Co-Director, Institute of Art and Disabilities, 1982-. *Memberships:* Fellow, American Psychological Association; Fellow, American Association on Mental Deficiency; Society for Research in Child Development. *Publications:* "Retarded Adult in the Community", 1968, 3 reprints; "Retarded Adult at Home", 1970, 2 reprints; "Mental Health Services for Mentally Retarded", 1972; Creative Art of Developmentally Disabled", 1977; "Art and Disabilities", 1983. *Honours:* President, California Conference of Workshops for Handicapped, 1963-65; Special Consultant, President's Committe on Mental Retardation, 1970. *Address:* 2839 Ashby Avenue, Berkeley, CA 94705, USA.

KATZ, Hilton Collin, b. 7 July 1950, South Africa. Dental Surgeon. m. Maryann Shapiro, 1 September 1974, Johannesburg, 2 sons, 1 daughter. *Education:* BDS; MSc, Dentistry. *Memberships:* Australian Dental Association; Federation Dentaire International; Dental Association of South Africa; Australian Society of Endodontics; Australian Society of Periodontics. *Publications:* "A Critical Evaluation of Epithelial Dysplasia in Oral Muscosal Lesions using the Smith-Pindburg Method of Standardization", 'Journal of Oral Pathology', 1984. *Hobby:* Tennis. *Address:* 1c Hanover Road, Vermont South 3133, Melbourne, Australia.

KATZ, Jonathan David, b. 17 May 1945, Evanston, Illinois, USA. Physician. m. Evelyn Lee Singer, 28 June 1970, Pittsburgh, 1 son, 1 daughter. *Education:* BS, Zoology, Honors, 1967, MD, 1971, University of Michigan. *Appointments:* General Internal Medicine, Dean Clinic, Madison, Wisconsin, 1976-78; Physician, General Internal Medicine, Oxboro Clinic, Bloomington, 1978-. *Memberships:* American College of Physicians; American Medical Association; Minnesota Medical Association; American Society of Clinical Hypnosis; Minnesota Society of Clinical Hypnosis. *Hobbies:* Guitar; Tennis. *Address:* 9820 Lyndale Ave South, Bloomington, MN 55420, USA.

KATZ, J. Lawrence, b. 18 Dec. 1927, Brooklyn, New York, USA. Professor of Biophysics & Biomedical Engineering, Rensselaer Polytechnic Institute. m. Gertrude Seidman, 17 June 1950, Brooklyn, 1 son, 2 daughters. *Education:* BS 1950, MS 1951, PhD 1957, Physics, Polytechnic Institute of Brooklyn. *Appointments include:* Assistant, Associate, & Professor of Physics, 1956-72, Professor of Biophysics & Biomedical Engineering 1972-, Director, Biomedical Engineering Centre 1974-, Rensselaer Polytechnic Institute; Visiting Professor, University of Miami, USA 1969-70, University of London, UK 1985-86, Paris, France 1986; etc. *Memberships include:* Society for biomaterials; Biomedical Engineering Society; International Association for Dental Research; American Scoiety for Bone & Mineral Research; Fellow, American Physical Society; American Crystallographic Association; European Society of Biomaterials, etc. *Publications include:* Contribution to "Structure-Property Relationships of Biomaterials", ed. Hastings & Ducheyne, 1986; "Electromechanical Effects in Bone" in "Handbook of Bioengineering", ed. Shalak & Chen, 1986; Contributions to "Proceedings of 1st China-Japan-USA Conference on Biomechanics" 1985, "Encyclopaedia of Material Science" 1986, etc. *Honours include:* Fellowships, National science Foundation, John S. Guggenheim Foundation, Naitonal Institutes of Health; 3rd Annual Clemson Award, 1975; Elected President, Society for Biomaterials 1978-79, Biomedical Engineering Society 1983-84; Sigma Xi 1951, Sigma Pi Sigma 1958; Fellow, American Physical Society, 1972. Co-holder, 1 US Patent, 1976. *Hobbies:* Folk & Madrigal singing; World travel; Stamp collecting; Civic theatre; Swimming. *Address:* Department of Biomedical Engineering, Rensselaer Polytechnic Institute, Troy, NY 12180, USA.

KATZ, Morton Lawrence, b. 12 Mar 1946, Dallas, Texas, USA. Licensed Clinical Psychologist. m. Lu Ann Stella, 1 July 1984, Houston, Texas. *Education:* BA, Psychology, University of Houston, 1969; MA, General Psychology, California State University, Fresno, 1972; PhD, Clinical Psychology, California School of Professional Psychology, 1975. *Appointments:* Adjunct Faculty Member, Baylor College of Medicine, Houston; Consulting Psychologist, Alief Independent School District, Houston; Consulting Psychologist, Spring Branch Independent School District, Houston; Consulting Psychologist, 7 private schools, Houston area. *Memberships:* American Psychological Association; Texas Psychological Association; Houston Psychological Association; Association for the Advancement of Psychology. *Honours:* Recipient, various honours and awards. *Address:* 6671 Southwest Freeway, Suite 501, Houston, TX 77074, USA.

KATZ, Philip Arthur, b. 17 Oct. 1942, Newark, New Jersey, USA. Associate Vice President, Technology & Information Management. m. Leslie Ruth Levin Katz, 26 Aug. 1978, Englishtown, 2 sons, 2 daughters. *Education:* BS, Rensselaer Polytechnic Institute; PhD, University of Minnesota. *Appointments:* Research Associate, Argonne National Laboratory, 1966-70, University of Tel Aviv, Israel, 1970-72, Austrian Academy, Vienna, Austria,

1972-73; Director, Biomedical Engineer, Beth Israel Medical Center, Newark, 1973-77; Director, Biomedical Instrumentation, 1977-85, Associate Vice President, 1985-, Assistant Professor, Surgery, 1981-, Assistant Professor, Radiology, 1981-, Thomas Jefferson University; Adujnct Associate Professor, Drexel University, 1980-. *Memberships:* Clinical Engineering Societies of Pennsylvania and New Jersey, Board of Directors; Senior Member, Institute Electrical & Electronic Engineers; Editorial Consultant, Biosciences Information Service; Sigma Xi. *Honours:* Professional Recognition, Clinical Engineering Society of Pennsylania; Certification, Healthcare Safety Professioanl Certificate Board. *Hobbies:* Tennis; Golf. *Address:* Thomas Jefferson University, 1020 Walnut Street, 626 Scott Building, Philadelphia, PA 19107, USA.

KATZ, Rennee S, b. 13 Aug. 1959. Private Practitioner of Psychotherapy; Medical Social Worker. *Education:* BA, University of Washington, USA, 1980; MSW, University of California, Berkeley, 1982; PhD candidate, California School of Professional; Psychology. *Appointments:* Medical Social Worker, Merritt Peralta Medical Center, California' Clinical Consultant, American Cancer Society Consultant Instructor, Social Work Consultants Incorporated; Private Practitioner, Psychotherapy, Oakland, California; Medical Social Worker, Home Health and Counselling, California. *Memberships:* National Association of Social Workers; Bay Area Social Work Oncology Group; American Psychological Association; Alameda County Service and Rehabilitation Steering Committee, American Cancer Society. *Publications:* Editor, 'American Cancer Society Can Support Training Manual'. *Honours:* Scholastic Achievement Awards, University of Washington, 1978-80; Phi Beta Kappa, 1980; Summa cum laude, 1980; Leadership Award, American Cancer Society, 1985. *Hobbies:* Dancing; Running; Singing; Hiking; Gourmet cooking; Fine arts. *Address:* Hawthorne and Webster Streets, Oakland, CA 94609, USA.

KAUFMAN, Irving, b. 16 Sept. 1917, Orange, New Jersey, USA. Consultant Psychiatrist; Instructor in Psychiatry. remarried, 3 sons, 1 daughter. *Education includes:* BA, New York University, 1939; MD, George Washington University, 1943; Intern, Newark City Hospital, 1944; Resident, Pathology, Sibley Memorial Hospital, 1944-46, Psychiatry, Taunton State Hospital, 1946-48; Certified, American Board of Psychiatry and Neurology. *Appointments include:* Staff Psychiatrist, 1950 to Chief Research Psychiatrist, 1959, Judge Baker Guidance Center, Boston, Massachusetts; Clinical Director, 1959-60, Staff, Adult Unit, 1959-79, Staff, Supervison, Teaching and Research, 1959-, Metropolitan State Hospital; Consulting Staff, McLean Hospital, Belmont, 1979-; Consultant to various social agencies including Massachusetts Society for Prevention of Cruelty to Children. Teaching Positions include: Tufts University School of Medicine, 1952-62; Assistant In Psychiatry, 1954-56, Instructor, 1956-59, 1965-, Retired Harvard University School of Medicine; Simmons College, 1951-53, 1966-67; Faculty, Smith College School for Social Work, 1951-; Boston University, 1964-79. *Memberships include:* Fellow: American Medical Association; Academy of Psychosomatic Medicine; American Geriatric Society. Life Fellow: American Psychiatric Association; American Orthopsychiatric Association; American and International psychoantglic Associations; Various life memberships. *Publications:* "Character Disorders in Parents of Delinquents", co-author, 1959; Editor of 3 books, contributor of 11 book chapters, 29 papers in professioanl journals, 7 book reviews and a monograph. *Honours:* Numerous offices held in national and international professional associations. *Hobbies:* Cello; Chamber music; Folk and Square dancing; Karate, Black belt. *Address:* 40 Williston Road, Auburndale, MA 02166, USA.

KAUFFMAN, Nancy Allen, b. 14 Aug. 1936, Pennsylvania, USA. Occupational Therapist. m. Richard Genso Kauffman, 14 June 1958, Havertown, 1 son, 1 daughter. *Education:* BS, Occupational Therapy, University of Pennsylvania, 1958; Ed.M., Special Education, Temple University, 1979. *Appointments:* Occupational Therapist, Programme Director, Melmark Home, Berwyn, 1966-68; Research Assistant, Kruzen Research Centre & Devereux Foundation, Berwyn & Philadelphia, 1971-74; Perceptual Motor Specialist, School District of Philadelphia, 1973-81; Occupational Therapist, Crozer Chester Medical Centre, 1981-83; Private Practice. *Memberships:* American Occupational Therapy Association; Pennsylvania Occupational Therapy Association, Committee Chairmanships, 1979, 1980, 1981, 1985; Sensory Integration International. *Publications:* Book Chapter, in "Willaard and Spackman's Occupational Therapy", 1979, 1983; Co-author, book chapter, in "neurological Rehabilitation", 1985; Co-author, Research Paper, "Vestibular Activities For Learning Disabled Children", 1986. *Hobbies:* Violinist in Symphony Orchestra; Gourmet Cooking; Travel; Sailing. *Address:* 4016 Foxhill Lane, Newtown Square, PA 19073, USA.

KAUFMAN, S Harvard, b. 16 Dec 1913, Milwaukee, Wisconsin, USA. Clinical Professor. m. Leone M Van Gelder (dec), 29 Apr 1934, Madison, Wisconsin, 1 son, 1 daughter. *Education:* BS 1934, MD 1936, University of Wisconsin; Commonwealth Fellow, Forensic Psychiatry, University of Pennsylvania, 1941; Child Psychiatry Fellow, Philadelphia Child Guidance Clinic, 1942. *Appointments include:* Psychiatrist to Juvenile Court, Allegheny County, Pennsylvania, 1942-45; Psychiatry Instructor, University of Pittsburgh School of Medicine, 1944 and 1945; Chief Psychiatrist and Director, Seattle Guidance Clinic, State Department of Health, Washington, 1945-49; Lecturer in Psychiatry, University of Washington School of Social Work, 1947; Assistant Professor Psychiatry 1948-55, currently Clinical Professor Psychiatry, University of Washington School of Medicine. *Memberships:* Life Fellow, Former President Seattle chapter, American Psychiatric Association; Life Fellow, American Orthopsychiatric Association; Charter Fellow, American Academy of Child Psychiatry; King County Medical Society; Washington State Medical Association; North Pacific Society of Neurology and Psychiatry; Past President, Washington State Council of Child Psychiatry; Chairman Domestic Law Committee, American Academy of Psychiatry and Law; Sigma Xi. *Publications include:* 'New Approach to Undergraduate Teaching of Psychiatric Problems of Children', (with H S Ripley), 1953; 'How Psychiatry Serves the Juvenile Court', 1964; "Kinetic Family Drawings (K-F-D), An Introduction to Understanding Children Through Kinetic Drawings", (with R C Burns), 1970; "Actions, Styles and Symbols in Kinetic Family Drawings (K-F-D) An Interpretative Marvel", (with R C Burns), 1972. *Hobbies:* Owning thoroughbred racehorses; Fishing; Tennis. *Address:* 710-10 Avenue East, Seattle, WA 98102, USA.

KAY, Stanley Robert, b. 7 June 1946, New York, USA. Clinical Psychologist. m. Theresa Maria De Monte, 27 June 1970, Pleasantville, New York, USA, 2 daughters. *Education:* BA, New York University, 1968; MA, Fairleigh Dickinson University, 1970; PhD, State University of New York, 1980. *Appointments:* Psychometrist and Psychological Researcher, Klein Institute for Aptitude Testing, New York City, 1970; Clinical Psychologist and Research Scientist, Bronx Psychiatric Centre, New York, 1970-; Private Practice in Psychotherapy and Psychodiagnosis, Mahopac, New York, 1975-; Green Chimneys Children's Services, Brewster, New York, 1980-81; Clinical Psychologist and Research Scientist, Albert Einstein College of Medicine, New York, 1980-. *Memberships:* American Psychological Association; Eastern Psychological Association;

New York Psychologists in Public Service; American Biographical Institute (Hon Member); Behavioural and Brain Sciences (Associate); American Society of Distinguished Citizens (Hon Member). *Publications:* "Conceptual Disorder in Schizophrenia", 1980; "The Cognitive Diagnostic Battery: Evaluation of Intellectual Disorders", 1982; Editorial consultant for 7 professional journals in psychiatry and psychology, including 'Archives of General Psychiatry'; Over 70 articles in professional publications; 30 conference papers; 6 psychological tests; several clinical scales, book chapters and monographs. *Honours:* Hon Member, New York University Coat of Arms Society, 1968; Certificates for Distinguished Contribution to Psychology, 1981, and Outstanding Scientific Achievement, 1982 from American Biographical Institute; Selected for the Statue of Victory World Culture Prize for Letters, Arts and Sciences by the National Research and Study Centre, Italy, 1985. *Address:* Kirkwood Road, RFD 2 Mahopac, NY 10541, USA.

KAY, Won Chuel, b. 1 Jan. 1924, Sunchon, Korea. Director & Vice President, Civil Aeromedical Centre, Korean Air. m. Sukin Choi, 2 May 1952, Pusan, 1 son, 2 daughters. *Education:* MD, SUMC, Seoul, 1945; Diplomas, PCAM 1954, ACAM, 1960, USAF SAM; Certified, Korean Board of General Surgery, 1957; Certified, Korean Board Preventive Medicine, 1963; DMSc., Yonsei University, Korea, 1964; SM, Hygiene, Harvard University, USA, 1966. *Appointments:* Assistant, Surgery, Severance Hospital, 1945-48; Flight Surgeon, ROKAF, 1949-61; National Consultant to C/S ROKAF, 1964-; Visiting Professor, YUMC, Aerospace Physiology, 1964-; FAA Senior AME, 1966-; Medical Director, Korean Airlines, 1968-76; Director, Vice President, Medical Services 1976-83, Civil Aeromedical Centre, Korean Air, 1984-; Aeromedical Consultant, CAB, Ministry of Transportation, Korea, 1977-. *Memberships:* KMA; KMSA; KSGS; KSPM; KIHA; KSHE; ASMA; AMDA; IAASM; Past President, KMSA; Past Vice President, KMSA; ASMA; KIHA; IAASM; Fellow, Aerospace Medicine. *Publications:* "Antropometry of the ROKAF Pilots", 1961; "Physiological Effects of Rapid Decompression in the Rabbit", 1964; etc. *Honorus:* Military Merit Choongmu (3), 19050, ı1951, 1953; Bronze Star Medal, USA, 1950; Military Service Merit (2), 1957, 1964; Legion of Merit, USA, 1965; others. *Hobby:* Music Appreciation. *Address:* ÀDa-406 Garden Mansion 4-cha Apt., 445 Banpo-Dong, Kangnan-ku, Seoul, Korea.

KAYE, Robert Allen Charles, b. 5 June 1941, New Jersey, USA. Clinical Psychiatrist, Hypnotist. 2 sons. *Education:* BA, Zoology, Drew University; MD, Cornell University Medical School. *Appointments:* Staff Psychiatrist, Clinical Psychobiology, National Institute of Health, Bethesda, 1968-70; Psychiatric Resident, Yale University Medical School, 1970-73; Staff Psychiatrist, Chope Community Hospital, San Mateo, 1973-75. *Memberships:* American Society of Clinical Hypnosis; American Psychiatric Association; San Mateo County Medical Society. *Publications:* "The Role of the Liaison Psychiatrist in a Hemodialysis Programme", co-author, 'Journal of Psychiatry in Medicine', 1973. *Hobbies:* Nature Photography; Horticulture and Landscaping; Model Railroading; 19th Century Landscape Painting. *Address:* 101 South San Mateo Drive, Suite 208, San Mateo, CA 94401, USA.

KAYED, Khalil S, b. 26 Dec. 1933, Cairo, Egypt. Head, Clinical Neurophysiological Section. m. Line Sonnichsen, 20 Dec. 1969, Oslo, Norway, 2 daughters. *Education:* MD; Neurology and Psychiatry DPM, Cario, 1965; Clinical Neurophysiology, Oslo, Norway, 1968. *Appointments:* Laboratory of Clinical Neurophysiology, Air Force Hospital, Cairo, Egypt, 1960-64; Head, Laboratory of Clinical Neurophysiology, Maadi Hospital, Cairo, 1965-67.

Consultant: Ernest Conseil Hospital, Tunis, 1969-70; Sentralsykehuset i Tromso, Norway, 1974-77; Rikshopitalet, Oslo, 1974-77. Head, Clinical Neurophysiology Section, Akershus Central Hospital, Nordbyhagen, 1977-. *Memberships:* Norwegian Society of Clinical Neurophysiology; Norwegian Society of Neurology; Sleep Research Society; European Sleep Research Society; Scandinavian Sleep Research Society. *Publications:* Author of articles on clinical neurophysiology, neurology, sleep disorders and technical methods for sleep recording. *Hobbies:* Reading; Fishing. *Address:* Lysehagan 4, 0383 Oslo 3, Norway.

KEANE, Diarmuid Liam, b. 19 May 1963, Tipperary, Eire. Consultant Opthalmic Optician. *Education:* Diploma, Ophthalmic Optician, Dublin Institute of Technology. *Appointments:* Assistant Ophthalmic Optician, Sweeney's Opticians, Sligo, Eire. *Memberships:* Fellow, Association of Ophthalmic Opticians, Eire. *Hobbies:* Extensive sporting interests including rugby, squash, all of Ireland's National sporting activities. *Address:* 13 Main Street, Tipperary Town, Republic of Ireland.

KEANE, Ronald, b. 28 Dec 1923, Ebbw Vale, Wales. Consulting Physician. m. Celia Prince, 15 Sep 1954, Barry. *Education:* MRCS; LRCP; DC. *Appointments:* Consultant, Charterhouse Rheumatism Clinic, Weir Hospital; Tutor, Anglo European College of Chiropractic. *Memberships:* Bournemouth Medical Society; Honorary Secretary, Chiropractic Medical Association. *Publications:* "Manipulation of Cervical Spine", 1965. *Hobby:* Sailing. *Address:* 51 Canford Cliffs Road, Poole, Dorset, England.

KEANE, Terence Martin, b. 18 Feb. 1952, New York City, USA. Chief, Psychology Service, Boston, Massachusetts. *Education:* BA, University of Rochester, 1973; MA 1976, PhD, State University of New York, Binghamton, 1978. *Appointments:* Director, Behavioral Consultation Program, 1978-81, Chief, Psychology Service, VAMC-Jackson, MS, 1981-85; Instructor, Associate Professor, University of Mississippi Medical Center, 1978-85. *Memberships:* American Psychological Association; Assoc. for Advancement of Behavior Therapy; Southeastern Psychological Association; American Assoc. for Advancement of Science. *Publications include:* 'The empirical development of an MMPI - subscale for the assessment of combat-related PTSD', (co-author), 1984; 'Social support in Vietnam veterans with PTSD: A comparative analysis, (co-author), 1985. *Honours:* University of Rochester Student Life Award, 1973; Professional Research Award, MS Psychological Assoc., 1979. *Hobbies:* Running; Tennis; Racketball; Dining and Cooking. *Address:* Psychology Service (116b), Boston VA Medical Center, 150 S Huntingdon Avenue, Boston, MA 02130, USA.

KEATING, Thomas Patrick, b. 5 Jan 1949, Cleveland, Ohio, USA. Administrative Director for Materials Management, MUSC Medical Center, Charleston, South Carolina. m. Carolyn E Kraft, 4 Sep 1976, Fort Bragg, North Carolina, 1 son, 1 daughter. *Education:* BBA, Cleveland State University, Ohio, 1971; MBA, University of Toledo, Ohio, 1973; Certified Professional in Health Care Materials Management, 1985; Certified Purchasing Manager, 1983. *Appointments:* Hospital Supply and Services Officer, Womack Army Hospital, Fort Bragg, North Carolina, 1973-77; Assistant Director for Facilities Operations University of Kansas College of Health Sciences and Hospital, Kansas City, Kansas, 1977-80; Director, Management Services, Charleston County PRT, South Carolina, 1980-84; Administrative Director for Materials Management, Medical University of South Carolina Medical Center, Charleston, 1984-. *Memberships:* South Carolina Hospital Association; American College of Health Care Executives in Nominee Status; Health Care Materials Management Society; Toastmasters International. *Publica-*

tions: Author of numerous articles in professional journals, etc. *Honours:* US Army Commendation Medal (3rd OLC), 1982; 1982 NRPA Proposal Competition, 1982. *Hobbies:* Home Landscaping; Volunteer Work. *Address:* MUSC Medical Center, 171 Ashley Avenue, Charleston, SC 29425, USA.

KEATS, Theodore E, b. 26 June 1924, New Brunswick, New Jersey, USA. Professor, Chairman, Radiology, University of Virginia School of Medicine. *Education:* BS, Rutgers University, 1945; MD, University of Pennsylvania School of Medicine, 1947. *Appointments:* Internship, University of Pennsylvania Hospital, 1947-48; Residency, University of Michigan Hospital, 1948-51; Military Service - Army, ASTP 1943-46, Captain, Medical Corps, Army, 1951-53; Instructor, Radiology, 1953-54, Assistant Professor, 1954-56, Radiology, University of California School of Medicine; Associate Professor, 1956-59, Professor, 1959-63, Radiology, University of Missouri School of Medicine; Consultant, Ellis Fischel State Cancer Hospital, 1962-63; Visiting Professor, Karolinska Institute, Sweden, 1963-64; Professor, Chairman, Radiology, University of Virginia School of Medicine, 1963-. *Memberships:* American Board of Radiology; American College of Radiology; American Medical Association; American Roentgen Ray Society; Association of American Medical Colleges; Association of University Radiologists; many other professional organisations. *Publications:* Author numerous articles in professional journals including: "Missouri Medicine'; 'American Heart Journal'; 'American Journal Roentgenology'; 'Radiology'; 'The Military Surgeon'; 'Medical Times'; 'Virginia Medical Monthly'; 'Pediatrics'; (Books) "An Atlas of Roentgenographic Measurement", co-author, 1959; "An Atlas of Roentgenographic Measurement", 2nd Edition 1967, 5th Edition 1985; "An Atlas of Normal Roentgen Variants that may Simulate Disease", 1973, 3rd Edition 1984; "An Atlas of Normal Developmental Roentgen Anatomy", co-author, 1977; "Pediatric Disease (Second Series Syllabus)", 1982; "Emergency Radiology", Editor, 1983; "Lytic Lesions in Bone: Difficult Diagnoses", co-author, 1985; etc. *Honours:* Recipient, numerous awards and honours including: Phi Beta Kappa; Alpha Omega Alpha; Sigma Xi; Fellow, American College of Radiology; Trustee, American Board of Radiology; Guest Speaker, Asian Oceanian Congress of Radiology, 1979, 1983; Honorary Member, Australasian College of Radiologists, 1980; Editor in Chief, 'Skeletal Radiology', 1985; etc. *Address:* Dept. of Radiology, Box 170, University of VA Medical Centre, Charlottesville, VA 22908, USA.

KEE, Poo-kong, b. 12 Feb 1947, Malaysia. Senior Research Fellow. m. 15 May 1976, Singapore. *Education:* PhD, BA (Hons). *Appointments:* Counsellor, Department of Social Welfare, Kuala Lumpur, Malaysia; Research Fellow, Regional Institute of Higher Education and Development, Singapore; International Relations Officer, Singapore Airlines Ltd, Singapore; Research Scholar, Australian National University, Australia; Research fellow, East-West Population Institute, Honolulu, USA; Senior Research Fellow, Australian Institute of Multicultural Affairs, Australia. *Memberships:* American Psychological Association; Population Association of America; International Union for the Scientific Study of Populations; International Association for Cross-Cultural Psychology; Population Association of Australia. *Publications:* "Motivations for childbearing among Malaysians" in 'Journals of Biosocial Science' 1982; "Perceptions of methods of contraception: a semantic differential study" in 'Journal of Biosocial Science', 1981 "Sons or daughters? cross-cultural comparisons of the sex preferences of parents in Australia and Malaysia" in 'Population and Environment' 1981. *Honours:* Anna Florence Booth Prize for Thesis in Social Psychology, University of Adalaide, 1972; Australian Psychological Society Prize for Honours Psychology, 1972. *Address:* 16 Ruby Street, Balwyn, Victoria, Australia 3103.

KEELE, Reba L, b. 28 Oct. 1941, Emery, Utah, USA, Vice-President, Health Care Innovations. *Education:* PhD, Purdue University, 1974; MS, 1966, BS, 1963, Brigham Young University; AS, College of Eastern Utah, 1961; W K Kellogg Fellow. *Appointments:* Associate Director, Director, Honours Programme, 1974-78, Associate Professor, Organizational Behaviour, 1979-, Brigham Young University; Visiting Professor, Purdue University, 1978-79; Director, Centre for Women's Health, Cottonwood Hospital Medical Centre, 1984-85. *Memberships:* Academy of Management Health Care Division; Western Academy of Management; American Management Association. *Publications;* "Let's Talk: Adults and Children Sharing Feelings", 1977; Contributor of over 30 articles at professional conferences and in journals. *Honours:* W K Kellogg Fellow, Group VI, 1985; Honours Professor of the Year, Brigham Young University, 1983; Maeser Distinguished Teaching Award, Alumni Association, 1983; Women of Achievement, Utah Federation of BPW, 1985. *Hobbies:* Reading; Horses. *Address:* Suite 750, 5 Triad Centre, Salt Lake City, UT 84180, USA.

KEELER, Eileen C, b. 7 Apr. 1934, Chicago, Illinois, USA. Clinical Nursing Specialist. *Education:* BSN, St. Xavier College, Chicago; MSN, Catholic University of America, Washington, DC; Certification in Rehabilitation Nursing, 1984. *Appointments:* Instructor, St. Xavier College, Chicago, 1967-69; Clinical Nursing Specialist, Loyola University Medical Center, Maywood, Illinois, 1969-74; Clinical Nursing Specialist, Marianjoy Rehabilitation Center, 1974-. *Memberships:* Association of Rehabilitation Nurses; American Congress of Rehabilitation Medicine; International Association for the Study of Pain. *Publications:* Co-author: 'Chronic Pain and The Questionable Use of the Minnesota Multiphasic Personality Inventory', 'Archives of PMR', Aug. 1981. *Hobbies:* Cross-country Skiing; Swimming. *Address:* Marianjoy Rehabilitation Center, PO Box 795/26 W 171 Roosevelt Road, Wheaton, IL 60189-0795, USA.

KEELIN, Peter W, b. 11 Aug 1945, New York, New York, USA. Clinical Psychologist. 1 son. *Education:* BS, MS, State University of New York, Plattsburgh, 1963-69; PhD, Florida State University, Tallahassee. *Appointments:* Director of Counselling Services and Assistant Professor of Counsellor Education, Developmental Research School, Florida State University, 1971-74; Assistant Professor Counsellor Education, Oakland University, Rochester, Michigan, 1974-77; Private practice Clinical Psychologist, Clinical Resources Inc, Clarkston, Michigan, 1974-85; Assistant to Superintendent of Schools, Warren Consolidated Schools, Warren, Michigan, 1977-81. *Membership:* America Psychological Association. *Hobbies:* Vacationing; Sports. *Address:* 5885 Ortonville Road, Clarkston, MI 48016, USA.

KEELING, Marita Jane, b. 11 Aug. 1952, Rhodesia. Clinical Instructor. m. Michael S. Sinensky, PhD, 5 Oct. 1974, Newton, Massachusetts, USA, 1 son, 1 daughter. *Education:* AB, magna cum laude, Harvard University, USA, 1975; MD, University of Colorado Health Sciences Centre, 1980. *Appointment:* Clinical Instructor, University of Colorado Health Sciences Centre, USA-. *Memberships:* American Medical Association; American Medical Women's Association; American Psychiatric Association; American Psychoanalytic Association. *Honours:* Phi Beta Kappa, 1974; Alpha Omega Alpha, 1979. *Hobbies:* Gardening; Ballroom Dancing. *Address:* 4900 Cherry Creek South Drive, Denver, CO 80222, USA.

KEENEY, Virginia T, b. 23 Mar 1920, Albany, New York, USA. Child Psychiatrist; Director, Division of Humanities and Medicine. m. Arthur H Keeney, 27 Dec 1942, Albany, 2 sons, 1 daughter. *Education:* BS, College of William and Mary, 1942; MD, University of Louisville, School of Medicine, 1954. *Appointments:* Physicians Assistant, Provincial Leper Colony, Pusan, Korea, 1946-48; Intern, Kentucky Baptist Hospital, Louisville, Kentucky, USA, 1954-56; NINDB Trainee, Ophthalmology, University of Louisville, 1956-59; Staff Physician, American Red Cross Blood Center, Louisville, 1959-62; Assistant Professor, Ophthalmology, Temple University Medical School, 1967-73; Associate Professor, Community Health, 1974-, Director, Programme in Humanities and Medicine, 1974-, Resident in Psychiatry, 1975-81, Fellow in Child Psychiatry, 1981-84, Assistant Professor, Department of Psychiatry, 1984-, University of Louisville Medical School. *Memberships:* Jefferson County Medical Society; Kentucky and American Medical Associations; American Psychiatric Association; American Academy of Child Psychiatry; Society for Health and Human Values. *Publications:* "Dyslexia: Diagnosis and Management of Reading Disorders", Co-Editor, 1968; Chapters contributed to "Pediatric Ophthalmology", 1975 and "Geriatric Ophthalmology", 1985. *Honours:* Laughlin Award, National Psychiatric Endowment Fund, 1984; Citizens Laureate, Louisville, 1964; Woman of the Year Award, Business and Professional Women, Louisville, Kentucky, 1964. *Hobbies:* Tennis; Swimming; Sailing; History; Art appreciation. *Address:* University of Louisville, Louisville KY 40292, USA.

KEGLAR, Shelvy Haywood, b. 13 Dec 1947, Charleston, Mississippi, USA. Clincial Psychologist. m. Robbia Steward, 7 Mar 1970, Forrest City, Arkansas, USA, 3 sons, 2 daughters. *Education:* BA, Sociology, 1970, MA, Rehabilitation Psychology, 1974, Arkansas State University; PhD, Psychology, Indiana University, 1979. *Appointments:* Porogram Director, Hamilton Center, Terre Haute, Indiana; Mental Health Consultant, Atterbury Job Corps Center; Clinical Psychology Specialist, Ft Sam Houston, Texas; President, Mid-American Consulting Inc. *Memberships:* American Psychological Association; Association of Black Psychologists; National Rehabilitation Association Society for Personality Assessment; National Head Start Association; Society for Training and Development; Society for Experimental and Clinical Hypnosis. *Publications:* "Life-Style Analysis in Individual Appraisal" Monograph, 1977; "Depression in Alcoholics" in 'Health and Research World' 1979; "Alcoholics in Primary Care Facilities" in 'Alcohol, Health and Research World' 1979. *Honours:* Standing Senior Award, Akkansas State, 1970; Post Commendation Award, Ft Sam Houston, Texas, 1973; Miniority Fellow in Psychology, American Psycholigcal Association, 1976; Indiana Association of Black Psychologists Award, 1984; US Jaycess Outstanding Young Man of America, 1984. *Hobbies:* Music; Sport; Racing. *Address:* 9208 Fordham Street, Indianapolis, IN 46268, USA.

KELEMEN, Endre, Jr., b. 31 Oct. 1927, Budapest, Hungary. Chief Surgeon, County Hospital, Szekszard. m. 1979, 1 son. *Education:* MD; Spcialist, General Surgery, Vascular Surgery. *Appointments include;* Assistant Surgeon, Kaposvar County Hospital 1951-55, University Medical School, Budapest Surgical Clinic 1955-62; Chief Surgeon, Szekszard County Hospital, 1962-. *Memberships:* Hungarian Society of Surgeons; Hungarian Society of Vascular Surgeons; Colleges of State Institutes for Surgery, Oncology, General Medicine. *Publications include:* Books: "Physical Diagnosis of Acute Abdominal Diseases & Injuries", 1964, English & Hungarian editions; "Surgery of Renovascular Hypertension", 1984. Over 50 articles, various medical periodicals. *Honours:* Academy Prize, 1966; 'Creative Award of County Tolna', 1982; Honorary title, Pecs University Medical School. *Hobbies;* Music, especially jazz, plays vibes in 'Szekszard Jazz Quartet', amateur ensemble of doctors. *Address:* Megyei Kórház, H-7100 Szekszárd, Hungary.

KELEMEN, József, b. 23 Oct. 1931, Baltavár, Hungary. Assistant Professor of Paediatrics. m. Balogh Ibolya, 25 Sep. 1965, Budapest, 2 daughters. *Education:* PhD; Diploma of Medical Sciences. *Appointments:* Assistant, 1957-76; Assistant Professor, 1976-, Medical University. *Memberships:* European Academy of Allergology and Clincial Immunology; Interasma; European Pediatric Respiratory Society. *Publications:* Articles include: 'Physical activity of asthmatic patients', 1983; 'The natural course of complaints in asthmatic children', 1980; 'Asthma bronchiale in sport', 1980; 'Natural course of serious childhood asthma', 1981; 'Change of symptoms of asthmatic children upon one-year ketotifen treatment', 1983. *Hobbies:* Gardening; Travel. *Address:* Törökveasz u.2, Budapest, Hungary 1022.

KELEMEN, Zoltan Alexander, b. 20 June 1941, Hungary. Consulting Psychologist. m. Elizabeth, 20 Dec 1962, Sydney, Australia, 1 son. *Education:* BA, Macquarie University, Australia; PhD, International College of Post-Graduate Studies, USA; Diploma in Clinical Hypnosis, New South Wales School of Hypnotic Sciences, Australia; Diplomate, Medical Psychology, International Academy of Medicine and Psychology; Certificate of Registration, Victorian Psychological Council. *Appointments include:* Supervising Consultant Psychologist for Forensic Hypnosis, New South Wales Police Department, 1978; Principal and Programme Co-ordinator, New South Wales School of Hypnotic Sciences, 1979-; Founding Editor and Editor-in-Chief, 'The Australian Journal of Clinical Hypnotherapy and Hypnosis', 1980-; Clinical Associate Professor, Post Graduate Institute of Medical Forensic Psychotherapy, California, USA, 1981; Federal President, The Australian Society of Clinical Hypnosis, 1982-; Clinical Supervisor, Australian Society of Clinical Hypnotherapists, 1985-. *Memberships:* Fellow, Australian Society of Clinical Hypnotherapists; Fellow and Diplomate, International Academy of Medicine and Psychology; Australian College of Private Clinical Psychologists; Australian Association of Psychologists; New South Wales Counsellors Association; American Society of Group Psychotherapy and Psychodrama; International Psychosomatics Institute; International Academy of Ecclectic Psychotherapists; Australian Behaviour Modification Society; Australian and New Zealand Association of Psychiatry, Psychology and Law. *Publications:* Contributions to professional journals including 'Australian Journal of Clinical Hypnosis'; 'The Australian Behaviour Therapist'; 'Journal of Hollistic Medicine'; 'Australian Journal of Clinical Hypnotherapy and Hypnosis'. *Hobbies:* Reading; Music; Fishing; Painting. *Address:* Suite 2, 3 Trelawney Street, Eastwood, New South Wales 2122, Australia.

KELETI, Tamás, b. 13 May 1927, Budapest. Director, Institute of Enzymology. m. Márta Katona, 11 Sep. 1948, Debrecen, 1 son, 1 daughter. *Education:* Diploma, Chemistry, 1948; University Dr., Chemistry, 1950; PhD, Biology, 1957; DSC., Enzymology, 1965; Professor, Enzyme Kinetics, 1974; Corresponding Member, Hungarian Academy of Science, 1976. *Appointments:* Assistant, University Medical School Debrecen, 1948-50; Researcher, 1950-60, Senior Researcher, 1960-72, Institute of Biochemistry, Hungarian Academy of Sciences, Budapest; Deputy Director, Director, Institute Enzymology, Biological Research Centre, Hungarian Academy of Science, 1972-. *Memberships:* Chairman, Hungarian National Committee, IUB; Hungarian National Committee, ICSU; Hungarian Biochemical Society. *Publications:* "Basic Enzyme Kinetics", 1986; Articles in professional journals. *Honours:* Academic Prize First Degree, 1961. *Hobbies:* Music; Books; Photography; Travel. *Address:* Institute of Enzymology, Biological Research Centre, Hunagarian Academy of Sciences, H-1502 Pf. 7, Budapest, Hungary.

KELLER, Reed T., b. 26 May 1938, Aberdeen, South Dakota. Professor; Chairman. m. Mary Ann Keller, 14 June 1959, Bismarck, North Dakota, 3 daughters. *Education:* BA, summa cum laude, BS, summa cum laude, University of North Dakota, Grand Forks, North Dakota; MD, cum laude, Harvard Medical School, Boston, Massachusetts. *Appointments:* Instructor in Medicine, 1970-71; Senior Instructor in Medicine, 1971-72; Assistant Professor of Medicine, 1972-73, Case Western Reserve University School of Medicine, Cleveland, Ohio. *Memberships:* Fellow, American College of Gastroenterology, 1972-; American College of Physicians, 1975-; Assoc. of Professors of Medicine, 1973-; Member, American Gastrointestinal Assoc., 1973-; American Medical Assoc., 1973-; North Dakota Medical Assoc., 1973-. *Publications:* "Hereditary Pancreatitis: Evaluation of a Possible Kindred and a Review of Recent Literature", (with K. Naylor), 1982; "Zinc Metabolism in Gluten Enteropathy", (with W K Canfield), 1981. *Honours:* Representative to Board of Governor's, Mid-West region, American College of Gastroenterology, 1983-; National Board of Medical Examiners, 1984-. *Address:* Department of Internal Medicine, University of North Dakota, School of Medicine, Grand Forks, ND 58201, USA.

KELLEY, D.C., William Ronald, b. 24 Aug. 1948, Baltimore, Maryland, USA. Doctor of Chiropractic. m. Joane L. Kelley, 13 Feb. 1982, Knoxville, Tennessee, 1 daughter. *Education:* DC, Logan College of Chiropractic, St Louis, MO; BA, University of Virginia, Charlottesville, VA. *Memberships:* American Chiropractic Assoc.; International College of Applied Kinesiology (Athletic Advisory Board); Secretary, Tennessee Chiropractic Assoc., 1985; Various offices, Tennessee Valley Chiropractic Assoc; Council of Roentoenology of ACA. *Honours:* First D.C., US Olympic Training Center, 1984; First D.C., Medical Staff, National Sports Festival, 1985. *Hobbies:* Sports; Tennis; Golf; Reading; Jogging; Guitar; Piano Playing. *Address:* 6910 Kingston Pike, Knoxville, TN 37919, USA.

KELLEY, Robert Otis, b. 30 Apr. 1944, Santa Monica, California, USA. Professor. m. Judy Kathryn Varley, 22 Aug. 1965, Albuquerque, 2 daughters. *Education:* BS, Abilene Christian University, 1965; MA, 1966, PhD, 1969, University of California. *Appointments:* Assistant to Professor, University of New Mexico, 1969-. *Memberships:* American Society for Cell Biology; Society for Developmental Biology; International Society for Developmental Biology; American Association of Anatomists; Electron Microscopy Society of America. *Publications:* Articles in professional journals; "Limb Development and Regeneration", Volume II, co-editor, 1983; Book chapters etc. *Honours:* Research Career Development Award, NIH 1972-77; Kaiser Foundation Award for Teaching in Basic Science, 1976. *Hobbies:* Sailing; Skiing; Montaineering; Soaring; Travel. *Address:* Dept. of Antomy, University of New Mexico, School of Medicine, North Campus, Albuquerque, NM 87131, USA.

KELLY, John Franklin, b. 22 Sept. 1931, USA. Private Practitioner. *Education:* MD, University of Texas; Psychiatric Training, University of Colorado; Psychoanalytic Training, Denver Institute for Psychoanalysis. *Appointments:* Director, Psychiatric Inpatient Services, University of Colorado Health Sciences Center; Faulty Member, Denver Institute for Psychoanalysis. *Memberships:* American Psychiatric Association; American Psychoanalytic Association. *Publications:* Book review, Hidden Selves by M Masud Khan, in 'International Journal of PSA', 1985. *Honour:* Fellow, American Psychiatric Association, 1978. *Hobby:* Music. *Address:* 650 South Cherry Street, Suite 1400, Denver, CO 80222, USA.

KELLY, Jonathan Richard, b. 19 Jan. 1949,

Middlebury, Vermont, USA. Assistant Professor of Psychiatry m. Katherine Butler, 5 July 1974, Rochester, 1 son, 2 daughters. *Education:* BS, Biology, St John Fisher College, 1971; MD, Upstate Medical Centre, 1975; Internship, 1975-76, Psychiatry Residency, 1976-79, Strong Memorial Hospital; Forensic Psychiatry Fellowship, Rush-Presbyterian St Luke's Medical Centre, Chicago, 1979-80. *Appointments:* Clinical Instructor, Strong Memorial Hospital, 1975-79; Assistant Clinical Professor, Psychiatry, Rush-Presbyterian-St Luke's Medical Centre, 1979-. *Memberships:* American Acadmey of Forensic Sciences; American Association for the Advancement of Science. *Publication:* "Current Psychiatric Therapies", volume 21, 1982. *Honours:* Board Certified, Psychiatry & Neurology, 1981, Forensic Psychiatry, 1983. *Address:* 1720 W. Polk St., Chicago, IL 60612, USA.

KELLY, Michael A, b. 27 Feb. 1936, London, England. Consultant Surgeon Otolaryngology, Greater Niagara General Hospital. *Education:* MB, ChB, Glasgow; FRCS (Glasgow); FRCS (Canada); FACS; FICS. *Appointment:* Consultant Surgeon, Otolaryngology Grimsby and Louth Hospitals, Lincolnshire, 1965-66. *Memberships:* Scottish Otolaryngological Society; Ontario and Canadian Medical Associations. *Address:* § 103, 6150 Valley Way, Niagara Falls, Ontario, Canada.

KELLY, Michael John Anderson, b. 13 Jan 1931, England. Consultant Obstetrician-Gynaecologist. m. Barbara Anne Ralston, 7 July 1962, Huntsville, Canada, 1 son, 2 daughters. *Education:* MA, Oxford University, England; BM; B Ch; MRCOG, 1961; FRCSC, 1963; FACOG, 1964; FRCOG, 1981. *Appointments:* HS Urology, Middlesex Hospital, England, 1956; Intern, St Johns General Hospital, 1956-57; Surgical Resident, Newell H Chattanooga, Tennessee, USA, 1957-58; Assistant Resident 1958-59, Chief Resident 1959-60, Obstetrics-Gynaecology, Royal Victoria Hospital, Montreal, Canada; Captain, RCAMC I CBMU Iserlohn, Federal Republic of Germany, 1960-61; Whitehorse Military Hospital, Yukon, 1961-62; Teaching Fellow, University Hospital, Edmonton, Alberta, 1962-63; Consultant Obstetrician-Gynaecologist, Sault (Sainte) Marie, Ontario, 1963-. *Memberships:* BMA; CMA; SOGC; RCOG; RCPSC; ACOG. *Publications:* 'A New Preparation for the Suppression of Lactation', 1960; 'Management of the Perimenopausal syndrome' Obstetrics and Gynaecology', 1961; 'Virilizin Ovarian Tumours', 1961. *Hobbies:* Nordic Skiing; Boating; Travel; Mountaineering. *Address:* 1015 Queen Street East, Sault Sainte Marie, P6A 2C2, Ontario, Canada.

KELVIN, Frederick Maxwell, b. 9 May 1943, Leeds, England. Staff Radiologist. m. Anne Getty, 20 May 1979, 1 son, 1 daughter. *Education:* MB BS, University of London, 1966; MRCP (UK) 1969; FRCR 1972; MACR, 1976. *Appointments:* Registrar in Radiology, Kings College Hospital, London, 1968-70; Senior Registrar in Radiology, Southampton University Hospitals, Southampton, 1971-73; Senior Registrar in Radiology, Westminster Hospital, London, 1973-75; Assistant Professor 1975-80, Associate Professor 1980-85, Department of Radiology, Duke University Medical Center, Durham, North Carolina, USA; Staff Radiologist, Methodist Hospital of Indiana, Indianapolis, Indiana, USA, 1985-. *Memberships:* Royal College of Radiologists, Fellow; American College of Radiology; Society of Gastrointestinal Radiologists; Radiological Socity of North America; American Roentgen Ray Society. *Publications:* 'The Double Contrast Barium Enema in Crohns Disease and Elcerative Colitis' Am J Roentgen. 1978; 'The Lymphoid Follicular Pattern of the Colon in Adults' Am J Roentgen. 1979; 'Colorectal carcinoma missed on Double Contrast Barium Enema Study: A Problem in Perception' Am J Roentgen. 1981. 'The

Pelvis after Surgery for Rectal Carcinoma: Serial CT Observations with Emphasis on Non-beoplastic Features' Am J Roentgen, 1983 and other articles related to gastrointestinal radiology. *Hobbies:* Golf; Tennis; Listening to classical music. *Address:* Department of Radiology, Methodist Hospital of Indiana, 1604 N Capitol Avenue, Indianapolis, IN 46202, USA.

KELWALA, Surendra, b. 13 Dec 1951, Jabalpur, India. Assistant Chief of Service, Psychiatry, VA Medical Centre, Allen Park, Michigan, USA; Director, Residency Training. *Education:* MBBS; MD; Clinical Fellow, Harvard Medical School, 1978-80; Research Fellow, Wayne State University, Detroit, 1981-83. *Appointments:* Assistant Professor, Wayne State University, Detroit, 1983-. *Memberships:* Council Member, Michigan Association of Neuropsychiatrists; American Psychiatric Association. *Publications:* Co-Author, "Lithium Induced Accentuation of Extrapyramidal Symptoms in Alzheimer's Dementia", 'Journal Clinical Psychiatry', 1984; "History of Antidepressants: Successes and Failures", 'Journal of Clinical Psychiatry', 1983. *Honours:* Paul Harrison Prize, Neurology, Christian Medical College, Vellore, India, 1972; All India Science Talent Search Award, 1968. *Hobby:* Studying the Evolution of Monetary Systems. *Address:* VA Medical Centre, Dept. of Psychiatry (116A), Allen Park, MI 48101, USA.

KEMENY, Mary Margaret, b. 7 May 1946, Elizabeth, New Jersey, USA. Senior Surgeon, General & Oncologic Surgery, City of Hope National Medical Centre, California. *Education:* BS, Radcliffe College, 1968; MD, Columbia University, 1972; Internship, Residency, New York, Colorado, 1972-79. *Appointments include:* Fellowship, Tumour Oncology, Memorial Sloan-Kettering Cancer Centre, 1975-76; Research Fellowship. Thoracic Surgery, ibid, 1976-77; Clinical Associate, Surgical Branch, National Cancer Institute, National Institutes of Health, Bethesda, Maryland, 1979-81. *Membership:* Society of Surgical Oncology. *Publications include:* Numerous contributions to medical journals, abstracts, presentations. *Honours include:* Member, Study Goup, Women's Education, with Dr. Greta Bibring, Radcliffe College, 1965-68; Class Marshall, ibid, 1968; Cum Laude, Biology, Harvard University, 1968; Founder, Organisation of Female Medical Students, College of Physicians & Surgeons, 1969; Award, scholastic achievement, American Medical Women's Association, 1972. *Address:* City of Hope National Medical Centre, G&O Surgery, 1500 East Duarte Road, Duarte, CA 91010, USA.

KEMMANN, Ekkehard, b. 22 Apr. 1942, Germany. Associate Professor, Department of Obstetrics & Gynaecology. m. Amelia Gonzalez, 30 Mar. 1974, 2 daughters. *Education:* ABOG Certification, 1976; ABOG Subspeciality Certification, Reproductive/Infertility, 1978; Abitur, Gymnasium Avenue, Wuppertal, 1961; MD, University of Düsseldorf, 1967. *Appointments include:* Resident, Obstetrics & Gynaecology, Kings County Hospital, Brooklyn, New York, USA, 1970-74; Fellow, Reproductive Endocrinology, State University of New York, Brooklyn, 1974-76; Assistant Professor, Department of Obstetrics & Gynaecology, UMDNJ-Rutgers Medical School, 1976-80. *Memberships:* American College of Obstetrics & Gynaecology; American Fertility Society; Christian Medical Society; Endocrine Society; Charter member, Society of Reproductive Endocrinology; etc. *Publications include:* Co-author/co-editor, numerous research papers, abstracts, book chapters. *Honours:* Junior Fellow award, District II Meeting, ACOG, 1974; Merit Award, UMDNJ-Rutgers Medical School, 1985. *Hobby:* Skiing. *Address:* Department of Obstetrics & Gynaecology, UMDNJ-Rutgers Medical School, Academic Health Science Centre, CN 19, New Brunswick, NJ 08903, USA.

KEMP, Katherine Virdin, b. 4 Feb 1923, Baltimore, Maryland, USA. Clinical Assistant Professor of Psychiatry; Psychiatric Private Practice. m. Willis David Witter, 12 Oct 1946, Relay, Maryland, 3 sons, 1 daughter. *Education:* AB Biology, College of Notre Dame, Baltimore, 1943; MD, University of Maryland School of Medicine, Baltimore, 1948. *Appointments include:* Lecturer 1954-59, College of Notre Dame of Maryland, Chief Department of Rehabilitation Medicine 1970-72, Lutheran Hospital of Maryland; Instructor 1967-69, Assistant Professor 1969-72, Department of Rehabilitation Medicine, University of Maryland Medical School, Clinical Assistant Professor, Institute of Psychiatry and Human Behavior 1975-, University of Maryland School of Medicine; Chief Prosthetic Clinic 1967-72, Chief Outpatient Clinic, Department of Rehabilitation Medicine, 1967-70, University of Maryland Hospital; Disability Determination Services, State of Maryland Department of Education, 1968-, Physical Medicine and Rehabilitation Psychiatry, 1975-; Private Practice, Psychiatry and Rehabilitation Medicine, 1975-. *Memberships include:* American Medical Association; American Congress of Rehabilitation Medicine; American Psychiatric Association. *Publications include:* 'Distribution of Peripheral Neuropathies in Diabetic Amputees', 1971; 'Lithium in the Treatment of a Manic Patient with Multiple Sclerosis: A Case Report', 1977; 'Hospitalization of Personality Disorders', 1981. *Hobbies:* Gardening; Travel; Music. *Address:* 517 Old Orchard Road, Baltimore, MD 21229, USA.

KEMPER, Han C.G., b. 20 Mar., 1941, Amsterdam, The Netherlands. Professor, Health & Activity. *Education:* Teacher, Physical Education, Amsterdam; PhD, Physical Education, Brussels. *Appointments:* Teacher, Secondary School, Amsterdam; Lecturer, Academy of Physical Education, Tilburg; Assistant Professor, Psychophysiology, Health Sciences, University of Amsterdam; Professor, Health & Activitiy, University of Amsterdam, Interfaculty of Physical Education, Free University, Amsterdam. *Memberships:* Physiological Society; Growth Society; American Academy of Physical Education; Editorial Board, International Journal of Sports Medicine. *Publications:* "Growth Health and Fitness of Teenagers - Longitudinal Research in International Perspective", Medicine an Sport Science", Karger, Basel volume 20, 1985; "Children and Exercise XI", co-author, 'Sport Sciences' Human Kinetics campaign, volume 15, 1985. *Honours:* Sport Medicine, 1974. *Address:* Academic Medical Centre, Medical Faculty Working Group of Exercise Physiology & Health, Meibergdreef 15, 1105 AZ Amsterdam 20, The Netherlands.

KENDELL, Robert Evan, b. 28 Mar. 1935, Rotherham, Yorkshire, England. Professor of Psychiatry, University of Edinburgh. m. Ann Whitfield, 2 Dec. 1961, Lindfield, Sussex, 2 sons, 2 daughters. *Education:* BA, 1956; MA, 1959, University of Cambridge; King's College Hospital Medical School, 1956-59; MB. BChir., Cantab, 1959; MD, 1967; FRCP, London, 1974; FRCP, Edinburgh, 1977; FRCPsych., 1979. *Appointments:* Visiting Professor, University of Vermont, USA, 1969-70; Reader in Psychiatry, The Institute of Psychiatry, London, 1970-74. *Memberships:* Fellow: Royal Colleges of Physicians of London, Edinburgh and Royal College of Psychiatrists; Medical Research Council, 1984-88; World Health Organization's Expert Advisory Panel on Mental Health. *Publications:* "The Classification of Depressive Illnesses", 1968; "Psychiatric Diagnosis in New York and London", 1972; "The Role of Diagnosis in Psychiatry", 1975; Editor, "Companion to Psychiatric Studies", 1983. *Honour:* Gaskell Gold Medal of the Royal College of Psychiatrists, 1967. *Hobbies:* Over-eating; Walking up hills. *Address:* University Department of Psychiatry, Royal Edinburgh Hospital, Edinburgh EN10 5HF, Scotland.

KENNEDY, Carol Sue (Hawse), b. 2 Dec 1949, Petersburg, West Virginia, USA. Assistant Head Nurse, Emergency Center. *Education:* Diploma Nursing, 1970; Flight Nurse Training, 1972; Intensive Coronary Course, 1978; BSc, Nursing, 1978; Critical Care Practitioner, 1980; Candidate Masters Business Administration, 1982; Advanced Cardiac Life Support Nursing Service Management, 1984; Battlefield Nursing, 1985. *Appointments:* US Air Force Nurse Corps, 1971-76; Paramedic/Emt Instructor, 1977-78; Pediatric Clinic Supervisor, 1975; Head Nurse, Medical Surgery, 1976; Acting Head Nurse, Emergency Service, 1981; US Air Force Reserves Nurse Corps, 1982-; Immunization Clinic OIC, 1982-84; Chief Nurse, 901 TAC Clinic, 1983-84; Chief Nurse, 302 TAC Hospital, 1984-85; Mobility QIC, 1982-84; Emergency Services, OIC, 1982-; Memorial Hospital EMT Instructor, 1982; Assistant Head Nurse, Emergency Services, 1985; National Certified Emergency Nurse, 1984-. *Memberships:* National League of Nursing; National and Colorado Emergency Nurses Associations; Emergency Nurses Association, Front Range 1978, President, 1980; Aerospace Medical Association, Flight Nurse Division; Reserve Officers Association, Vice-President, 1985. *Honours:* US Air Force Outstanding Unit Citation, 1972-73; Outstanding Young Women of America, 1983; Nomination, Junior Officer of Year, 1983; Nomination, Nurse of the Year, 1983; Senior Nurse Badge, 1984. *Hobbies:* Skiing; Hiking; Reading. *Address:* 5110 Wagon Master Drive, Colorado Springs, CO 80917, USA.

KENNEDY, Charles Aidan Redmond, b. 26 Sept 1931, Shropshire, England, Private Practitioner, restorative dental surgery. *Education:* BDS, University of Birmingham, 1955; LDS RCS (England), 1978; DDS, Dalhousie, Canada, 1966; MSc, University of London, Periodontology, 1982; DRD RCS (Edinburgh), 1983. *Appointments:* House Surgeon, General Hospital, Birmingham, 1956; Senior House Officer, Wordsley Hospital Maxillofacial Unit, 1956; Dental Officer, Royal Air Force, 1956-58; Research Assistant, University of Manitoba, Canada, 1969; Clinical Assistant, 1978, Associate Specialist, 1983, Guy's Hospital, London, England. *Memberships:* Fellow, Royal Society of Medicine; Member, American Dental Society of London; Member, American Dental Society of Europe; Life Member, Federation Dentaire Internationale. Member, Anglo Ameican Medical Society; Member, British Society of Periodontology; Member, European Dental Society; Member, British Dental Association; Member, British Endodontic Scoiety; Carlton Club; RAF Club; RAC Club; Institute of Directors. *Publications:* 'Cephalometric Analysis of an Eskimo community, Igloolik, NWT, Canada', 1966; 'Osteoporosis in relation to periodontal disease', 1982. *Address:* 2 Harley Street, London W1N 1AA, England.

KENNEDY, Gary John, b. 1 Nov. 1948, USA. Psychiatrist. m. Jenny, 1 Sept. 1969, Dallas, Texas, USA. *Education:* BA, Biology, University of Texas, 1970; MD, University of Texas Medical School at San Antonio, 1975. *Appointments:* Fellow, Liaison-Psychosomatic Psychiatry, Montefiore Medical Center, Bronx, New York, 1979-81; Instructor in Psychiatry, Albert Einstein College of Medicine, New York, 1979-84; Assistant Attending Physician, Montefiore Medical Centre, Moses Division, New York, 1979-85; Psychobiology Research Fellow, National Research Service Award, Montefiore Medical Centre, Bronx, New York, 1980-82; Research Fellow, Division of Aging and Geriatric Psychiatry, Albert Einstein College of Medicine, 1982-84; Assistant Professor if Psychiatry, Albert Einstein College of Medicine,-. *Memberships:* American Psychiatric Association; American Psychosomatic Association; Society for Liaison Psychiatry; Gerontologic Society of America; North American Society for Pacing and Electrophysiology, affiliate; Faculty for continuing Medical Education, New York Academy of Medicine. *Publications:*

Co-author: 'Phases of change in the patient with Alzheimers Diseaes: A Conceptual Dimension for defining Health care Management' in 'Journal of the American Geriatrics Society'; 'Depression and Dementia in Patients at Risk for Sudden Death' in 'Psychosomatic Medicine', (co-author), 1985. *Honours:* US WHO Organisation Travel study fellowship, 1983; New Investigator Research Award, National Institutes of Health, 1984. *Address:* Department of Psychiatry, Montefiore Medical Centre, Moses Division, 111 East 210 Street, Bronx, NY 10467, USA.

KENDREW, (Sir) John (Cowdery), b. 24 Mar. 1917, Oxford, England. President of St. John's College, Oxford. *Education:* Scholar of Trinity College, Cambridge, 1936-39; BA, 1939; MA, 1942, PhD, 1949; ScD, 1962. *Appointments:* Deputy Chairman, Medical Research Council Laboratory of Molecular Biology, Cambridge, 1946-74; Fellow of Peterhouse, Cambridge, 1947-75; Reader, Davy Faraday Laboratory, Royal Institution, London, 1954-68; Director-General, European Molecular Biology Laboraotry, Heidelberg, 1975-82; President, St. John's College, Oxford, 1981-. *Memberships:* Fellow, Royal Society, 1960; Honorary or Foreign Member: American Society of Biological Chemists; American Academy of Arts and Sciences; Leopoldina Academy; Institute of Biology; Max-Planck Gesellschaft; Weizmann Institute; National Academy of Sciences, USA; Heidelberg Academy of Sciences; Bulgarian Academy of Sciences; Royal Irish Academy; British Biophysical Society. *Publications:* "The Thread of Life", 1964; publications in scientific journals. *Honours:* Honorary Fellow, Peterhouse and Trinity College, Cambridge; Honorary Professor, Heidelberg; Nobel prize in Chemistry, 1962; CBE, 1963; Knight Bachelor, 1974; Honorary: ScD, Keele, Reading; D.Sc, Exeter, Buckingham; Honorary Doctor, Pecs, Hungary. *Address:* St. John's College, Oxford OX1 3JP, England.

KENT, Gordon Arnold, b. 11 Nov 1950, Chicago, Illinois, USA. Dental Director; General Dentist; Implantologist. m. Nomi, 29 Jan 1972, Brockton, Massachusetts, 1 son, 2 daughters. *Education:* BA, Washington University, 1972; DMD, Tufts University, 1979. *Appointments:* General Dentist; Implantologist; Dental Director, Smile Centers. *Memberships:* American Dental Association; New York State Dental Association; 8th District Dental Association; Academy of General Dentistry; American College of Oral Implantology; American Academy of Dental Group Practice; American Academy of Orthodontists; American Association of Functional Orthodontics; American Orthodontic Society; International Congress of Oral Implantologists; Alpha Omega; American Academy of Orthodontics for the General Practitioner. *Hobbies:* Racquetball; Fishing. *Address:* Smile Center, 4427 Union Road, Cheektowaga, NY 14225, USA.

KENT, Herbert, b. 13 Mar. 1914, New York, USA. Clinical Professor, Preventive Medicine & Public Health, University of California Irvine College of Medicine; Chief, RMS, VA Medical Centre, Long Beach. m. Kathleen P, 1 June 1946, 1 son, 1 daughter. *Education:* MD, LRCPS, Royal College of Physicians & Surgeons, UK, 1938-43; Internship, Residency, New York, USA, 1944-48; Fellowship, Institute PM&R, Bellevue Medical Centre, New York, 1948-49. *Appointments include:* University of Oklahoma, various appointments, 1958-73; Associate Clinical Professor in PM&R, Department of Physical Medicine & Rehabilitation, California College of Medicine, University of California, Irvine, 1973-82; Vice Chairman, Department of Physical Medicine & Rehabilitation, ibid, 1982-. *Memberships include:* American & British Medical Associations; American Academy of Physical Medicine & Rehabilitation; American Congress of Rehabilitation Medicine; American College of Chest Physicians;

Association of Academic Physiatrists; American Association for Electromyography & Electrodiagnosis. *Publications include:* 23 total; Books, "Physical Medicine & Rehabilitation", 1952; "Orthotics Etcetera", 2nd edition 1980; "Disability Measurement", in press. *Hobbies:* Amateur radio; Computer science; Chess; Fencing. *Address:* Rehabilitation Medicine Service (117), V.A.Medical Centre, 5901 East 7th Street, Long Beach, CA 90822, USA.

KENZORA, John E, b. 10 Sep 1940, Toronto, Canada. Professor and Head of Division of Orthopaedic Surgery. m. Adrienne, 2 daughters. *Education:* MD, University of Toronto, 1965. *Appointments:* Instructor in Orthopaedic Surgery, Harvard Medical School, 1972-78; Associate Professor 1978-84, Professor of Surgery 1984-, University of Maryland. *Memberships:* Fellow, American Association of Orthopaedic Surgeons; Orthopaedic Research Society; Hip Society; Foot and Ankle Society; Maryland Orthopaedix Society; Alpha Omega Alpha. *Honours:* Kappa Delta Award, 1978; Nicholas Andry Award, 1978. *Address:* University of Maryland Hospital, Division of Orthopaedic Surgery NGW58, 22 S Greene Street, Baltimore, MD 21201, USA.

KEON, Wilbert Joseph, b. 17 May 1935, Sheenboro, Quebec, Canada. Professor. m. Barbara Anne Jennings, 2 July 1960, Sheenboro, 2 sons, 1 daughter. *Education:* MSc., Experimental Surgery, McGill University, 1963; MD, University of Ottawa, 1961. *Appointments:* Surgeon-in-Chief, Ottawa Civic Hospital, 1977-83; Associate Professor, Surgery, 1969-76, Professor, Chairman, Surgery, University of Ontario; Director General, University of Ottawa Heart Institute. *Memberships include:* Ontario & Canadian Medical Associations; Fellow, Royal College of Physicians and Surgeons of Canada; Academy of Medicine, Ottawa; Canadian cardiovascular Society; American Heart Association; fellow, American College of Surgeons; Affiliate, Royal College of Medicine, London; International Cardiovascular Society; American Association for Thoracic Surgery; Fellow, American College of Cardiology; Founding Member, Canadian Association of General Surgeons; many other professional organisations. *Publications include:* Co-Author, "Causes of Death in Aorto-Coronary Bypass Surgery – Experience with 1600 Patients", 1977; "Developments in the Surgical Management of Coronary Artery Disease", 1977; "Indications and Results of Reoperation", 1979; Co-Author, "The Location of the Indifferent Electrode in Unipolar Pacemaker Sensing", 1979; "Urgent Surgical Therapy for Unstable Angina", 1981; "Aortocornoary Bypass Surgery in Asymptomatic Patients with Coronary Artery disease", 1984; numerous other books, book chapters, articles etc. *Honours include:* Peter Ballantine Ewing Gold Medal, Surgery, 1961; McLaughlin fellowship, 1968; Ontario Heart Foundation Senior Fellowship, 1970-76; Alpha Omega Alpha Honorary Member, 1972; Man of the Year, Ottawa Knockers Club, 1973;' University of Ottawa Staff Research Award, 1975; Outstanding Alumnus Award, Carleton University, 1977; Queen Elizabeth II Silver Jubilee Medal, 1978; James IV Surgical Association Travelling Fellowship, 1979; Officer, Order of Canada, 1985; Paul Harris Fellow, Rotary International, 1985; Knight of Malter, Saint John of Jerusalem, 1985; etc. *Hobbies:* Skiing; Gardening; Fishing. *Address:* Dept. of Surgery, Ottawa Civic Hospital, 1053 Calring Ave., CPC 1st Floor, Ottawa, Ontario K1Y 4E9, Canada.

KEPRON, Donald, b. 25 Oct. 1922, Winnipeg, Manitoba, Canada, Director, Division of Prosthodontics, Department of Clinical Dentistry, McGill University, Montreal, 1977-. m. Joan, 5 sons. *Education:* BSc, University of Manitoba, 1947; DDS, McGill University, 1954; MSc, University of Michigan, USA, 1956; Examiner in Prosthodontics for the Royal College of Dentists of Canada; FRCD (C). *Appointments:* Lecturer, St Paul's College, Winnipeg, Manitoba, Canada, 1948-49; Assistant Physical Director, University of Manitoba, 1949-50; Assistant Professor, Department of Prosthodontics, 1956-59, Assistant Professor, Department of Occlusion, Graduate Prosthodontics, 1973-74, Associate Professor, Department of Occlusion, Graduate Prosthodontics, 1975-77, McGill Univeristy, Montreal; Consulting Prosthodontist, Sherbrooke General Hospital, Sherbrooke, Quebec, 1964-80; Associate Clinical Dentist, St Mary's Hospital, 1964-80; Dentist, Montreal General Hospital, 1973-78. *Publications:* 'Experiences with Modern Occlusal Concepts', 1971; "Role of Restorative Materials in Maintaining Occlusion', 1978; 'Variation of Condyle Position Relative to Centric Mandibular Recordings', 1979. *Address:* McGill University, Faculty of Dentistry, 740 Dr Penfield Avenue, Rm 425, Montreal, Quebec, Canada H3A 1A4.

KERBESHIAN, Jacob, b. 21 Jan 1944, Psychiatrist, Grand Forks Clinic, North Dakota, USA, m. Lynn Anderson 4 Feb 1966, 1 son, 3 daughters. *Education:* AB, Harvard College, 1966; MD, University of Rochester, 1970; Internship, Cleveland Metropolitan General Hospital, 1970-71. *Appointments:* Resident in Psychiatry, 1971-73, Resident in Child Psychiatry, 1973-75, University of Rochester; Medical Officer, USAF, 1975-77. *Memberships:* American Medical Association; American Psychiatric Association; American Academy of Child Psychiatry. *Honours:* Diplomate, American Board Psychiatry and Neurology, Psychiatry, 1976, Child Psychiatry, 1977. *Address:* 1000 S Columbia Road, Grand Frorks, ND 58201, USA.

KEREBEL, Bertrand Felix Jean Joseph, b. 30 Dec. 1931, Goulven, France. University Professor. m. Lise-Marie Praloran, 4 July 1977, Dirinon, France, 1 son, 2 daughters from first marriage. *Education:* Doctorat Universite Paris (Sorbonne) Biology; PhD, Dental Sciences. *Appointments:* Professor, Dental School, Nantes; Dean of Dental School, Nantes 1969-72, Chairman of Department of Peridontology, 1974-, Director of Research Unit 225 of the National Institute of Health and Medical Research, 1978-. *Memberships:* Academie Nationale de Chirurgie Dentaire; International Association for Dental Research. *Publications:* 220 publications in international scientific reviews. *Honour:* Officier de l'ordre des Palmes Academiques. *Hobbies:* Painting; Photography. *Address:* Faculté de Chirurgie Dentaire, INSERM U 225 Nantes, Place A Ricordeau 44042, Nantes, France.

KEREZSI, David Robert, b. 18 Jan 1944, New Bruns- wick, New Jersey, USA. Doctor of Chiropractic. m. Dona Lynn, 1 July 1967, 1 son, 1 daughter. *Educa- tion:* BA, University of Miami, 1967; BS, DC, Lincoln College, 1971. *Appointment:* Director, Kerezsi Chiropractic Center. *Memberships:* American Chiropractic Association; New Jersey Chiropractic Society; American Academy of Nutritional Consul- tants; American College of Chiropractic Orthopaed- ists; Council Member, Council on Roentgenology, American Chiropractic Association. *Honour:* Out- standing American Award, 1976; F Lorne Wheaton Award for Outstanding Clinician, 1971. *Hobbies:* Sailing; Swimming. *Address:* 7 Cedarwood Drive, Toms River, NJ 08753, USA.

KERMAN, Herbert D., b. 24 July 1917, Chicago, Illinois, USA. Director, Regional Oncology Centre, Halifax Hospital Medical Centre, Daytona Beach, Florida. m. Ruth Rice, 8 Jan. 1943, Durham, North Carolina, 4 sons. *Education:* AB, Duke University; MD, Duke University School of Medicine. *Appointments:* Assistant/Associate Professor of Radiology, University of Louisville, 1949-56; Director, Department of Radiology 1956-80, Director,

Division of Radiation Therapy 1980-, Director, Regional Oncology Centre 1984-, Halifax Hospital Medical Centre. Various other appointments. *Memberships include:* Fellow, American College of Radiology; American & Southern Medical Associations; American Association for the Advancement of Science; American Roentgen Ray Society; Radiological Society of North America; American Radium Society; Radiation Research Society; Florida Radiological Society; etc. *Publications include:* Numerous contributions, professional journals & conferences. *Honours:* Mosby Student Award in Cardiology, Duke Medical School, 1942; Alpha Omega Alpha; Volusia County Medical Society 'Physican of the Year'; Annual Florida Division distinguished service award, American Cancer Society; etc. *Hobbies:* Sailing; Reading. *Address:* Regional Oncology Centre, Halifax Hospital Medical Centre, PO Box 1990, Daytona Beach, Fl 32015, USA.

KERR, David Nicol Sharp, b. 27 Dec. 1927, London, England. Dean, Royal Postgraduate Medical school. m. Mary Eleanor Jones, 2 July 1960, Llanrhyddlad, 2 sons, 1 daughter. *Education:* MB, ChB (Hons), Edinburgh), 1951; MS, Wisconsin, USA, 1953; FRCP (Edinburgh), 1966; FRCP (London), 1967. *Appointments:* HP/HS Intern, Royal Infirmary, Edinburgh, 1951-52; Exchange Fellow, University of Wisconsin, 1952-53; Surgeon Lieutenant, RNVR, 1953-55; Assistant Lecturer, University of Edinburgh, 1956-57; Registrar, Hammersmith Hospital, 1957-59; Lecturer, Senior Lecturer, University of Durham, 1959-63; Senior Lecturer, University of Newcastle-upon-Tyne, 1963-68; Personal Professor of Medicine, 1968-70; Professor of Medicine (established Chair), Head of Department, 1970-83. *Memberships:* MRC Physiological Systems Board; Association of Physicians Great Britian and Ireland; Medical Research Society; International Society of Nephrology; European Renal Association; Royal Society Medicine; Renal Association. *Publications:* Author of books, chapters and papers on Renal Disease. *Honours:* Fulbright Scholar, 1952; Volhard Medal (Renal Medicine in Germany), Goulstonian Lecturer, 1968; Lumleian Lecturer, 1983, of RCP (L). *Hobbies:* Fell Walking; Jogging. *Address:* Royal Postgraudate Medical School, Du Cane Road, Shephards Bush, London W12 0HS, England.

KERR, Melville Greig, b. 2 Dec. 1929, Edinburgh, Scotland. Director of Division of International Development. m. Agnes Bain, 12 May 1956, Edinburgh, Scotland, 1 son, 1 daughter. *Education:* BSc, Mb, BCh; Fellow, Royal College of Surgeons; Fellow, Royal College of Obstetrics & Gynaecology. *Appointments:* Professor of Obstetrics & Gynaecology, McMaster University, Hamilton, Ontario, Canada; Professor of Obstetrics & Gynaecology, University of Edinburgh, Scotland; Professor, Head of Obstetrics & Gynaecology, University of Calgary, Alberta, Canada. *Memberships:* Royal College of Obstetrics & Gynaecology, London; Royal College of Surgeons of Edinburgh; Royal College of Physicians & Surgeons of Canada. *Hobbies:* Music; Literature. *Address:* University of Calgary, 2500 University Drive NW, Calgary, Alberta, T2N 1N4, Canada.

KERR, Peter James, b. 10 July, 1941, Glasgow, Scotland. Psychiatrist. m. Marion Ann O'Donnell, 11 July, 1965, Glasgow, Scotland, 2 sons, 2 daughters. *Education:* MB, CHB, University of Glasgow; CCFP, FRCP, MIAP, University of Ottawa, Canada. Diploma of American Board of Psychiatry and Neurology. *Appointments:* Family Practitioner; Lecturer in Psychiatry and General Pracitce, University of Ottawa. *Memberships:* Canadian Medical Association; Ontario Medical Association; Ottawa Psychoanalytic Association; International Psychoanalytic Association; Medicolegal Society of Ottawa; Academy of Medicine, Ottawa. *Hobbies:*

Piano; Philately; Calligraphy. *Address:* 436 Gilmour Street, Suite 101, Ottawa, Ontario K2P OR8, Canada.

KERSTEN, Walter Heinrich, b. 6 July 1926, Obersuhl, Federal Republic of Germany. University Professor and Head of Department of Biochemistry. m. Helga Kersten, 20 Apr. 1955. *Education:* Dr Med, University of Marburg; Dr med habil, University of Münster; Professor Ordinarius, University of Erlangen-Nürnberg. *Appointments:* Assistant Clinical Chemistry, Mannheim; Head of the Laboratory Landesbad, Aachen; Dozent, Institute Physiological Chemistry, University of Münster; Professor, McArdle Institute, Madison, Wisconsin, USA, 1964-65; Currently Professor and Head, Department of Biochemistry, University Erlangen-Nürnberg. *Memberships:* Deutsche Gesellschaft f Biol Chemie; Paul-Ehrlich-Society; Geselischaft Deutscher Naturforscher u Ärzte; AAA. *Publications:* "Inhibitors of Nucleic Acid Synthesis"; Editor, "Progress in Molecular and Subcellular Biology". *Address:* Fahrstr 17, D 8520 Erlangen, Federal Republic of Germany.

KESHISHIAN, John M, b. 15 Aug. 1923, Corfu, Greece. University Professor. *Education:* MD, George Washington University School of Medicine, 1950. *Appointments include:* Instructor in Surgery, 1955-56, Attending in Surgery, 1956-63, Associate in Surgery, 1964-65, George Washington University School of Medicine and Hospital; Assistant Clinical Professor of Surgery, George Washington University Medical Center, 1965-72; Consultant, US Air Force, Andrews Air Force Base, Washington DC, 1960-73; Consultant, Glenn Dale Hospital, Glenn Dale, Maryland, 1966-72; Attending in Surgery, District of Columbia General Hospital, 1958-68; Clinical Professor of Surgery, Uniformed Services University of the Health Sciences, Bethesda, Maryland, 1978; Clinical Professor of Surgery, George Washington University Medical Center, 1983-; Chief, Division of Vascular Surgery, The Washington Hospital Center; Consultant, Walter Reed Army Medical Center, Washington DC, 1973-; Consultant, Department of State, Washington DC; Consultant, Johnson and Johnson, New Brunswick, New Jersey, 1974-; Consultant, Ethicon Inc, Somerville, New Jersey; Consultant, Ely Lilly, Indianapolis, Indiana; Medical Director, Pan African Airlines (Nigeria) Ltd; Member, Air Transport Medicine Committee, Aerospace Medical Association, 1976-; Councillor, Southern Association for Vascular Surgery, 1978. *Memberships include:* Fellow, American College of Surgeons, 1959; Fellow, American College of Chest Physicians, 1963; Fellow, Southeastern Surgical Congress, 1964; American Medical Association; Society for Thoracic Surgeons; Society for Vascular Surgery; International Cardiovascular Society. *Publications:* Novel: "Autopsy for a Cosmonaut" with J Hay, 1969; Numerous articles published in medical journals and papers presented to medical conferences. Articles and photographs of archaological projects published in National Geographic Magazine and other journals. *Honours:* Hektoen Bronze Medal for "Clinical Experiences with the Modified Arteral Graft" (Bovine origin) in Man" AMA San Francisco 1972; Award of Merit Pan American World Airways, 1975 for services on board Pan American Clipper at altitude; Citation from National Geographic Society 1969 re medical evacuation of Geographic Employee from overseas hospital. *Address:* 3 Washington Circle, 23rd Street At Pennsylvania Avenue NW, Washington DC 20037, USA.

KESTEN, Mark M, b. 8 Feb 1938, Poland. Psychiatrist; Neurologist. m. 6 Sept 1979, New York City, 1 son. *Education:* MD, Hebrew University, Jerusalem, 1965. *Appointments:* Private Practice in Psychiatry, Neurology and Electroencephalograhpy; Assistant Clinical Professor, Mount Sinai School of Medicine, New York; Assistant Attending; Mount Sinai Hospital, New York; Attending, Gracie Square Hospital, New York; Attending, The Cabrini Medical Center, New York Associate Adjunct Physicians, Department of Medicine, New York Eye and Ear Infirmary; Attending, Medical Arts Center Hospital, New York; Assistant Attending, Joint Diseases North General Hospital, New York. *Memberships:* Medical Society of the State and County of New York; American Medical Society; American Psychiatric Association; American Electroencepholographic Society, American Academy of Psychoanalysis; Biofeedback Society of America. *Publications:* Contributor of articles to medical journals, author of chapters in edited medical publications and of scientific papers. *Hobbies:* Reading; Swimming; Exercise; Fine art; Music; Theatre. *Address:* 823 Park Avenue, New York, NY 10021, USA.

KESTENBERG, Jeffrey Meir, b. 16 Dec 1957, Melbourne, Victoria, Australia. Private Practice Dental Surgeon. m. Ruth Mitelman, 26 June 1983, Melbourne. *Education:* BDSc, MDSc, Melbourne; LDS, Victoria; FRACDS. *Appointments:* Honorary Clinical Assistant, 1981-84, Clinical Tutor, Advanced Dental Technician Training Course, 1982-83, Senior Registrar in Restorative Dentistry, 1983, Royal Dental Hospital of Melbourne; Senior Clinical Demonstrator, Faculty of Dental Science, University of Melbourne, 1981-84. *Memberships:* Australian Dental Association; Australian Prosthodontic Society; American Cleft Palate Association; Federation Dentaire Internationale; Cleft Palate and Lip Society. *Publications:* 'Speech Assessment in Dentistry', in 'Australian Dental Journal', 1983. *Hobbies:* Squash; Philately; Cooking. *Address:* 20 Collins Street, Melbourne, Victoria 3000, Australia.

KESWANI, Manohar Hariram, b. 8 Apr. 1931, Rohri (Sind). Consultant Plastic Surgeon. m. Lila Jotwani, 25 Dec. 1958, Bombay, 1 son, 2 daughters. *Education:* MS, University of Bombay; Training, Plastic Surgery, CMC Hospital, Vellore, 1958-59. *Appointments:* Lecturer, Surgery, CMC Hospital, Vellore, 1958-59; Honorary Assistant Urofessor, Surgery, 1960-63, Honorary Assistant Professor, Plastic Surgery, 1963-75, J.J. Hospital; Honorary Plastic Surgeon, Jaslok Hospital, 1974-82, Bhatia Hospital, 1978-83; Consultant Plastic Surgeon, Head of Burns, Bai Jerbai Wadia Hospital for Children. *Memberships:* Association of Surgeons of India; Association of Plastic Surgeons of India; Burns Association of India; International Society for Burn Injuries. *Publications:* "Haemorrhoidectomy – A Modified Technique", 'Indian Journal of Surgery', 1967; "Prevention of Burns – An Attempt to Educate the Mases", (Research in Burns', 1970; "The Treatment of Burns – First Aid and Transport", 1977; "A Decade in the Field of Burn Prevention", 1978, "The Boiled Potato Peel as a Burn Wound Dressing", 1985, 'Burn'. *Honour:* Peet Memorial Award, 1973. *Hobbies:* Photography; Writing Poetry. *Address:* Nirmal Kunj, 70 East Sion, Sion, Bombay 400 022, India.

KESZTHELYI, Lajos, b. 15 Feb. 1927, Kaposvár, Hungary, Director, Institute of Biophysics, Szeged, m. Sára Lándori, 23 Aug. 1951, Budapest. *Education:* Diploma of mathematics and physics, Roland Eotvos University, Budapest, 1950; Candidate of physics, 1955, Doctor of physics, 1962, Hungarian Academy of Sciences. *Appointments:* Scientific co-worker, Central Research Institute of Physics, Budapest, 1954-63; Head of Department for Nuclear Physics, Central Research Institute of Physics, 1954-57; Director of the Institute of Biophysics, Szeged, 1975-. *Memberships:* Member, International Society for the Study of Origin of Life; Member International Cell Research Organisation; Corresponding Member, of the Hungarian Academy of Sciences. *Publications;* "Scintillation Counters", 1962; 'The asymmetry of biomolecules and weak interaction', 1977; 'Electric signals associated with the photocycle of bacteriorhodopsin', 1980; 'Intramolecular charge shifts during the photoreation cycle of bacteriorhodopsin', 1984. *Honours:* Medal of the Roland Eotvos Physical Society, 1980; Gold Order of Work, Hungarian People's Republic, 1985. *Hobby:* Cooking. *Address:* Institute of Biophysics, Biological Research Centre, Szeged, 62 Oddesszai, H-6701 Hungary.

KETTLEWELL, Neil M., b. 27 May 1938, Evanston, Illinois, USA. Professor. *Education:* BS, Kent State University, Kent State, Ohio, 1962; MA 1966, PhD, University of Michigan, Ann Arbor, Michigan, 1969. *Appointments:* Departmental Tutor 1961-62, Teaching Assistant, Kent State, 1961-62; Research Assistant, Mental Health Research Institute, 1963-65; Assistant in Research, Inter University Consortium for Political Research of the Institute for Social Research, 1965-68; Teaching Fellow, Psychology, University of Michigan, 1964-67; Research Assistant, Psychology, 1966-68; Instructor, 1968-69, Assistant Professor, 1969-74, Associate Professor, University of Montana, 1974-. *Memberships:* Society for Neuroscience; British Brain Research Organization; New York Academy of Sciences. *Publications include:* 'The effects of an interpolated ITI stimulus on classical conditioning of the nictitating membrane response of the rabbit', (with M. Niel, James D. Papsdorf), 1967; 'Effects of attenuating cutaneous afferent activity on a pre-established nictitating membrane reponse in rabbits', (with D.C. Woolston, L.H.Berger), 1972; 'Extinction in rabbits under different levels of cutaneous afferent activity', (with L.H. Berger, J. Pezzino), 1973; 'The effect of cutaneous afferent activity on instrumental learning in rabbits', (with L.H. Berger), 1974; Various papers presented at meetings; participation on panels or symposia. *Honours include:* Psi Chi; Pi Mu Epsilon; Phi Eta Sigma. *Address:* 172 Fairway Drive, Missoula, MT 59803, USA.

KÉTYI, Iván Thomas, b. 16 July 1926, Pécs, Hungary. Microbiologist. m. Adele Vertényi, 30 Aug. 1952. *Education:* MD; Specialist in Medical Laboratory Investigation & Microbiology. *Appointments:* Lecturer 1952, Senior Lecturer 1954, Assistant Professor 1957, Associate Professor 1965, Professor, 1974, University Medical School, Pécs. *Memberships:* Association of Hungarian Microbiologists; Editorial Board, 'Acta Microbiologicæ Hungariae'; and others. *Publications:* "Medical Microbiology" (textbook), Edition I 1978, Edition II 1983; "Microbiological Genetics", 1981; Over 100 papers. *Hobby:* Dogs. *Address:* Institute of Microbiology, University Medical School, H-7643 Pécs, Szigeti Str. 12, Hungary.

KEUR, Johannes Jacobus, b. 13 Dec 1935, The Hague, Netherlands. Head of Radiology Department, Royal Dental Hospital, Melbourne. m. Jacoba Doornekamp, 17 Dec 1960, De Bilt, Netherlands, 2 sons. *Education:* Bachelor Dental Science, 1959; Doctor Dental Science, University of Utrecht, 1973; Licensed Dental Surgeon, Netherlands, 1960. *Appointments:* Lecturer Prosthetic Dentistry, 1960-67, Senior Lecturer Prosthetic Dentistry, 1967-76, Senior Lecturer, Oral Radiology, University of Utrecht, 1976-79. *Memberships:* Australian Dental Assoc.; International Assoc. of Dento-Maxillo-Facial Radiology; Associate Member, Royal Australasian College of Radiologists. *Publications:* 'Forminstability of certain thermoplastic materials used in Dentistry', £973; 'A rare earth screen-film system for dental panoramic radiography', 1983; Publication pending: 'Dental panoramic radiography with intra-oral X-ray tubes'; 'Radiographic localization techniques'; 'The Clinical significance of the elongated styloid process and the ossified related ligaments', 1986. *Hobbies:* Photography; Bushwalking. *Address:* 265 The Boulevard, East Ivanhoe, Victoria 3079, Australia.

KEY, Jack Dayton, b. 24 Feb. 1934, Enid, Oklahoma, USA. Librarian. m. Virgie Richardson, 12 Aug. 1956, Coggon, Iowa, 2 sons, 1 daughter. *Education:* BA, Phillips University, 1958; MA, University of New Mexico, 1960; MS, University of Illinois, 1962. *Appointments:* Assistant Librarian 1958-59, Medical Librarian 1965-70, Lovelace Foundation for Medical Education and Research, 1958-59; Staff Supervisor, Graduate Library, University of Illinois, 1960-62; Pharmacy Librarian, University of Iowa, 1962-64; Librarian, Mayo Clinic, 1970-; Instructor in History of Medicine 1973-, Assistant Professor of Biomedical Communications 1973-81, Associate Professor Biomedical Communications 1981-, Mayo Medical School, Rochester, Minnesota. *Memberships include:* American Library Association; American Medical Writers Association; Medical Library Association; American Osler Society. *Publications include:* Over 235 publications including: "Library Automation; The Orient and South Pacific", (editor), 1975; "Automated Activities in Health Sciences Libraries", 1975-78; "The Origin of the Vaccine Inoculation by Edward Jenner", (with CG Roland), 1977; "Classics and Other Selected Readings in Medical Librarianship", (edited with TE Keys), 1980; "Medical Vanities", (with RJ Mann), 1982; "William A Hammond, MD (1828-1900); The Publications of An American Neurologist", (with BE Blustein), 1983; "Classics in Cardiology", (with JA Callaghan and TE Keys), 1983; "Medical Casebook of Doctor Arthur Conan Doyle – From Practitioner to Sherlock Holmes and Beyond", (with AE Rodin), 1984. *Honours include:* University of New Mexico Fellow, 1958-59; Special Author's Award, 'Minnesota Medicine', 1980; Knight of the Icelandic Order of the Falcon, President of Iceland, 1980. *Address:* 624 N E 23rd Street, Rochester, MN 55904, USA.

KHAJAVI, Farrokh, b. 26 Jan. 1940, Iran. Private Medical Practitioner. m. Teli, 28 Oct. 1979, Paris, France, 1 son. *Education:* MD, University of Tehran, Iran. *Appointments:* Internship, Illinois Masonic Medical Centre, Chicago, USA; Residency in Psychiatry, Illinois State Psychiatric Institute; Unit Director, Health Corporation, Iran; Lecturer, Harvard Medical School, Boston, Massachussetts; Consultant, Boston School Department; Consultant, Commonwealth of Massachussetts Department of Youth Service; Consultant, Boston Model City Programme; Director, Tri City Mental Health Centre, Malden, Massachussetts; Chairman, Department of Psychiatry, Whidden Memorial Hsopital, Everett, Massachussetts. *Memberships:* Fellow, American College of Physicians; Fellow, American Psychiatric Association; Fellow, Royal Society of Health, London; Fellow, Massachussetts Medical Society; Fellow, Massachussetts Psychiatric Society; New York Academy of Scineces. *Publications include:* 2 editorials on Nursing Homes nad Predicaments of the elderly in 'Ettelaat', Tehran, Iran, 1970; Contributions to professional journals including 'Journal of American Medical Association'; 'British Journal of Educational Psychology'; 'American Journal of Community Psychology'; 'Journal of Clinical Psychology'; 'Some Correlates of Contemplated Suicide' in 'Psychological Report', 1977; 'Some Personality Correlates of Self Rated Academic Success' in 'Perpetual Motor Skills', 1978; Book chapter: 'Managing the Dynamics of Change and Stability' (co-author) in "Annual Handbook for Group Facilitators", 1975. *Honour:* Scholarship, Harvard Medical School, 1970. *Hobbies:* Swimming; Reading; Writing Music. *Address:* 5 Woodland Road, Stoneham, MA 02180, USA.

KHAMBATTA, Roeinton Burjor, b. 30 Sep 1924, Karachi. Visiting Physician, Royal Masonic Hospital, London; Consultant Cardiologist, Private Practice. m. Rhodabé F Patel, 19 January 1959, Karachi, 2 daughters. *Education:* MBBS, University of Bombay; FRCP London; FRCP Edinburgh; FCPS Pakistan; FACC; DTM & H, England. *Appointments:* Associate Physician, Cardiology, Dow Medical College, Karachi; Visiting Professor, Cardiology, F J Medical College, Lahore; Consultant Physician, West Pakistan Government Hospital, Karachi; Consultant Cardiologist, Parsi General Hospital, Karachi; Consultant Physician, Cardiologist, Lady Dufferin Lying-in-Hospital, Karachi; Academic Registrar, Secretary, Pakistan College of Physicians & Surgeons, Karachi. *Memberships:* British Medical Association; Royal Society of Medicine; Royal Society of Tropical Medicine & Hygiene; Hunterian Society; Medical Society of London; Society of Apothecaries. *Publications:* "Q-T interval in Myocardial Infarction", 'British Medical Journal', 1953; "I.V. Protoveratrine on Digital Pulse Volume", 'Circulation', 1955; "Natural History of Chronic Amoebiasis", 'Journal Pakistan Medical Association", 1957; "Whither Medical Education", Editor, Report of Conference of College of Physicians & Surgeons, Pakistan, 1974. *Honours:* Honorary Physician to President of Pakistan, 1973-77; Vice President, Pakistan Medical Association, 1961-63. *Hobbies:* Freemasonry; Horse Racing; Reading; Watching Cricket. *Address:* 35 Astell Street, London SW3 3RT, England.

KHAN, Ashfaq Alam, b. 19 June 1929, Mombasa, Kenya. Regional Adviser, World Health Organisation. m. Drakhshanda Jabeen, 10 Mar. 1957, Lahore, Pakistan, 2 sons, 1 daughter. *Education:* BSc; MB BS; Fellow, Royal College of Physicians; DCH; CPH; Doctor, Tropical Medical & Hygiene. *Appointments:* Head, Department of Paediatrics & Child Health, Kenyatta National Hospital, Nairobi, Kenya; Professor, Head, Department of Paediatrics & Child Health, University of Zambia, Lusaka; Regional Adviser, World Health Organisation, Maternal & Child Health, Family Health, Alexandria, Egypt. *Publications:* "Diseases of Children in Sub-tropics & Tropics" (3rd edition); Various papers in medical journals. *Hobbies:* Table-tennis; Tennis; Golf. *Address:* WHO Eastern Mediterranean Regional Office, Box 1517, Alexandria, Egypt.

KHAN, Fahim Ahmad, b. 5 Feb. 1921, Jullundar, India. Private Consultancy. m. Umeeda Niaz Rasul, 23 Oct. 1948, Lahore, 1 son, 2 daughters. *Education:* MBBS, DPH with distinction, University of Punjab; Fellowship in Community Medicine, College of Physicians and Surgeons, Pakistan. *Appointments:* Officer Commanding, Military Hospitals and Field Units; Senior staff appointments in the medical field; Director of Medical Services, Pakistan Air Force; Director-General Medical Services and Surgeon General Armed Forces Medical Services; National World Health Organization Representatives and Programme Coordinator in Pakistan. *Memberships:* President, Public Health Association of Pakistan; Fellow, Royal Society of Health, London. *Honours:* Hilal-i-Imtiaz, Military; Sitara-i-Basalat. *Hobbies:* Photography; Sight-seeing; Indoor games. *Address:* No 22 Ataul Haq Road, Westridge – I, Rawalpindi Cantonment, Pakistan.

KHAN, M Ibrahim, b. 5 Dec. 1943, Shahpur, Swat, Pakistan. Private Practitioner in Orthopaedic and Hand Surgery. m. Paula, 25 Dec. 1976, Henderson, Kentucky, USA, 1 son, 1 daughter. *Education:* MB BS, Lahore, Pakistan; Diplomate, American Board of Orthopaedic Surgery. *Memberships:* Fellow: Kleinert Hand Society; American Academy of Orthopaedic Surgeons. Charter Member, Mid American Orthopaedic Association; New York Academy of Science; Kentucky Orthopaedic Society; Pakistani Physicians Association. *Publications:* 'Carpal Tunnel Syndrome Associated with Aberrant Muscle', in 'Surigcal Rounds', 1983; 'Journal of Hand Surgery', Letters to the editor. *Address:* 10 Third Street, Suite 370, Henderson, KY 42420, USA.

KHAN, Muhammad Iqbal, b. 4 Apr. 1943, Kamalia. Medical Director, Woodside Hospital, Youngstown, Ohio, USA. m. Surriaya Begum, 30 Oct. 1969, Multan, Pakistan, 3 sons, 1 daughter. *Education:* MB, BS, University of Punjab, 1968; Educational Commission for Foreign Medical Graduates, 1973; Federal Licencing Examination, 1976; Diplomate, American Board of Psychiatry, 1979. *Appointments:* Medical Officer, Government of Punjab, Pakistan, 1968-73; Senior House Officer, Psychaitry, Oakwood Hospital, Maidstone, Kent, England, 1973-74; Registrar, Psychiatry, Powick Hospital, Worchester, England, 1974; Resident, Psychiatry, Fallsview Psychiatric Hospital, Cuyahoga Falls, Ohio, USA, 1974-77; Assistant Medical Director, Woodside Hospital, Youngstown, Ohio. *Membership:* American Psychiatric Association. *Honours:* First Professional MBBS New Scheme; First in College, Final Professional MBBS; Letter of Appreciation of Services from Dean, Northeast Ohio-Universities College of Medicine, 1983; Certificate of Exceptional Service from Governor of State of Ohio, 1982. *Hobbies:* Bridge (Master, American Contract Bridge Leauge); Golf. *Address:* 6188 Westington Drive, Canfield, OH 44406, USA.

KHANTZIAN, Edward John, b. 26 May 1935, Haverhill, Massachusetts, USA. Psychiatrist; Psychoanalyst; Educator. m. Carol Ann DeAndrus, 17 May 1959, Lawrence, Massachusetts. *Education:* AB, Boston University, 1958; MD, Albany Medical School, 1963; Internship, Rhode Island Hospital Providence 1963-64; Residency in Psychiatry, Massachusetts Mental Health Center, Boston, 1964-67; Diplomate, American Board of Psychiatry and Neurology, 1970; Boston Psychoanalytic Institute, 1967-73. *Appointments:* Chief, Psychiatric Consult. Service, 1967-71; Associate Director, 1976-80; Special Assistant to Director, 1980-82; Director, Departmental Liaison, 1982-85; Principle Psychiatrist for Addictive Disorders, 1985-; Cambridge Hospital Department of Psychiatry; Director, Drug Treatment Program, 1970-76; Associate Director, Clinical Services, 1976-80; Cambridge-Somerville Mental Health Center; Associate Professor of Psychiatry, Harvard Medical School, The Cambridge Hospital, 1978-. *Memberships:* American Psychiatric Association, Consultant, Committee on Drug Abuse; Massachusetts Medical Society, Chairman, Committee on Drugs and Therapeutics; Massachusetts Psychiatric Society, Chairman, Committee on Alcoholism. *Publications:* Contributor to professioanl journals; Book Chapters and Agency Publications. *Honours:* Felix and Helene Deutsch Prize, the Boston Psychoanalytic Society and Institute, 1973; Collegium of Distinguished Alumni (one of first 100 chosen during the Centennial Celebration), Boston University CLA, 1974. *Hobbies:* Tennis; Writing; Reading; Spectator Sports. *Address:* 160 Summer Street, Haverhill, MA 01830, USA.

KHAYAT, Azeez Victor, b. 13 Aug 1927, New York, USA. Physician, Psychiatrist. m. Waltraud Minna Ahlswede, 15 July 1965, Washington DC, USA, 1 son, 2 daughters. *Education:* BBA; Licentiae, Apothecaries' Hall of Ireland; B.Ch, BAO, MD, National University of Ireland, Dublin, Republic of Ireland. *Appointments:* Chief of Psychiatry, US Naval Hospitals, Portsmouth, New Hampshire, USA, 1962, Saigon, Vietnam, 1963-64; Chief of Service, St Elizabeth's Hospital, Washington DC, 1965-71; Private Practice, 1971-. *Memberships:* American Medical Association; American Psychiatric Association; Association of Military Surgeons of US; Medical Society of the District of Columbia; Montgomery County Medical Society; Medical & Chirurgical Society of Maryland; Washington Psychiatric Society; Medical Society of St Elizabeth's Hospital, Washington DC. *Publication:* 'Recognising Post-traumatic Stress disorder in the Vietnam Veteran' (in Journal of St Elizabeth's Hospital), 1965. *Honour:* Purple Heart, Vietnam, 1964. *Hobbies:* Cycling; Swimming; Hiking; Ballroom Dancing. *Address:* 5454 Wisconsin Avenue Suite 1435, Chevy Chase, MD 20815, USA.

KHOGALI, Mustafa Mohamed Hassan, b. 3 July 1936, Sudan. Professor and Chairman. m. Majda F.E. Abdalla, 13 July 1975, Omdurman, 2 sons, 2 daughters. *Education:* MB BS; MD; FFOM; MFCM; DTPH; DTCD. *Appointments:* Lecturer, Faculty of Medicine, 1964-69, Head, Department of Community Medicine, Faculty of Medicine, 1970, Khartoum; Senior Research Fellow (Senior Clinical Lecturer), London School of Hygiene and Tropical Medicine, University of London, England, 1975-80; Associate Professor, Faculty of Medicine, 1980, Acting Chairman, Department of Community Medicine, 1982, Professor and Chairman, Department of Community Medicine, 1984-, Kuwait University. *Memberships:* WHO Expert Committee on Vegetable Dust Diseases; Consultant to Ministry of Health, Saudi Arabia on Heat Illnesses; Scientific Committee of Permanent Commission, OHDC; Member, IEA; Member, Ed. Board of IJE; Ed. Board of Health Policy and Planning Journal. *Publications:* Contributor to books, professional journals including: 'Health Problems of Migrant Workers', 'Medicine Digest', 1984; Co-author, "Disseminated Intravascular Coagulapathy in Heat Stroke', 'British Journal of Haematology' (in press); Books include: Co-author, "Heat Stroke and Opiods" (in press). *Address:* Faculty of Medicine, Kuwait University, P.O. Box 24923, Safat, Kuwait.

KHOURI, Philippe John, b. 5 Oct 1947, France. Director, Residency Training; Associate Professor. m. Randa Rousse, 22 May 1972, 2 sons. *Education:* BSc, Biology; MD. *Appointments:* Research Associate, Laboratory of Psychology and Psychopathology, National Institutes of Health, Bethesda, Maryland, USA; Assistant Professor, Department of Psychiatry, Georgetown University, Washington, District of Columbia; Assistant Professor, Division of Psychiatry, American University of Beirut, Lebanon; Associate Professor, Department of Psychiatry, University of Tennessee Center for Health Sciences, Memphis, Tennessee, USA. *Memberships:* Sigma Xi Scientific Research Society; American Psychiatric Association; American Association for the Advancement of Science; Society for Biological Psychiatry; American Psychopathological Association; New York Academy of Sciences. *Publications:* Co-author of article in 'British Journal of Psychiatry', 1980; Book chapter in "Contemporary Issues in Psychopathology", 1985. *Honours:* Sandoz Award, 1974-75; Teacher of the Year Award, Department of Psychiatry, University of Tennessee Center for Health Sciences, 1984-85. *Hobbies:* Tennis; Classical music; History. *Address:* 66 North Pauline Street, Suite 633, Memphis, TN 38105, USA.

KIDD, James Douglas, b. 28 Apr. 1933, Sydney, New South Wales, Australia. Private General Practitioner. m. Margaret Joan Casey, 23 Mar. 1957, Mosman, New South Wales, 2 sons, 2 daughters. *Education:* MB BS, Sydney, 1957. *Appointments:* Resident: Royal North Shore Hospital, 1957; Royal Hobart Hospital, 1958-59. Medical Officer, Repatriation General Hospital, Concord, 1960-63; General Practitioner, Penrith, 1964-; HMO and VMO, Associate Surgeon, Nepean Hospital, 1964-. *Memberships:* Royal Asutralian College of General Practice; Foundation Member, WONCA; Member of Section of General Practice of NSW Branch of Past Chairman and Secretary, Australian Medical Association; New South Wales Branch Council member, Australian Medical Association; Vice President, NAGPA. *Hobbies:* Photography; Golf. *Address:* Brechindene, 125 River Road, Emu Plains 2750, Australia.

KIDD, Nancy van Tries, b. 6 May 1933, Huntington, Pennsylvania, USA. Psychologist. m. J. Thomas Kidd, 23 May 1970, 2 sons, 1 daughter. *Education:* BS, Journalism, Pennsylvania State University, USA, 1955; MEd. Temple University, 1969; DEd. Counseling Psychology, Pennsylvania State University, 1977. *Appointments:* Associate Professor, Psychology and Counseling, Community College of Rhode Island, 1973-81; Adjunct Faculty, Providence College, Glendale College, University of Richmond, Virginia; Child, Adult and Family Psychological Services, State College, Virginia; Psychologist, Counseling and Psychological Services, Richmond, Virginia; Psychologist, Divorce and Family Mediator, Psychological and Counseling Resources, Inc. *Memberships:* Board of Trustees, Pennsylvania State University; Phi Delta Kapp; Pi Lambda theta; American Psychological Association; Virginia Psychological Association; Virginia Counseling Psychological Association; Academy of Family Mediators. *Publication:* "Journal of College Student Personnel", 1970. *Hobbies:* The Arts; Travel. *Address:* 122 Stuart Avenue, Richmond, VA 23220, USA.

KIELER, Jøorgen von Fuhren, b. 23 Aug. 1919, Horsens, Denmark. Director of Research. m. Eva Fausbøll Mosbech, MD, 1 July 1947, Jersie, 2 sons, 1 daughter. *Education:* MD, 1947; D.Sc. 1954. *Appointments:* Clinical positions in Odense, Dianalund and Arhus, Denmark, 1947-52; Research Fellow, Memorial Center for Cancer and Allied Diseases, New York, USA, 1952-53; Lady Tata Senior Research fellow, Fibiger Laboratory, Copenhagen, 1953-54; Visiting Scientist, Carlsberg Laboratory, Copenhagen, 1954-55; Division Head, 1954-65, Director, 1965, Fibiger Laboratory, Copenhagen; Director of Research, Danish Cancer Society, 1980-. *Memberships:* Foreign Member, Polish Academy of Science; Danish Medical Society; The Danish Medical Association; The Danish Association for Cancer Research; The Danish Society for Pathology; The Scandinavian Society for Immunology; The Scandinavian Society for Cell Research; The Scandinavian Society for Mutagen Research; British Association for Cancer Research; American Society for Cell Biology and Medicine; European Association for Cancer Research; European Tissue Culture Society. *Publications:* Co-author, "Famine Disease in German Concentration Camps", 1952; "The History of a Resistance Group", 1982; Articles in international journals of cell metabolism, immunology and cancer. *Honours:* Awards: Petrargia, 1958; William Neilsen, 1963; Alfred Benzon, 1963; Marie Manson, 1968; Samuel Friedman's Rescue Award, 1984; Medals: Ebbe Munck, 1980; Copernicus (awarded by Polish Academy of Science), 1982; Knight of Dannebrog, 1980. *Hobbies:* Gardening; History; Art; Tennis. *Address:* Rungstedvej 107, 2960 Rungsted Kyst, Denmark.

KIELHOFNER, Gary Wayne, b. 15 Feb 1949, Missouri, USA, Associate Professor, Sargent College of Allied Health Professions, Boston University, m. Nancy Ann Croatt, 9 July 1977, Los Angeles, 1 son, 1 daughter. *Education:* DPH, University of California, Los Angeles; MA, University of Southern California; BA, St Louis University. *Appointments:* Co-ordinator of Training in Occupational Therapy, University Affiliated Facility, University of California at Los Angeles Neuropsychiatric Institute; Assistant Professor and Director of Graduate Studies, Virginia Commonwealth University. *Memberships:* American Occupational Therapy Associations; American Public Health Association; Massachusetts Occupational Therapy Association. *Publications:* "A Model of Human Occupation: Theory and Application", (Editor), 1985; "Psychosorial Occupational Therapy", (with Roann Barris and Janet Hawkins Watts), 1983; "Health Through Occupation: Theory and Practice in Occupational Therapy", (Editor), 1983. *Honours:* Academy of Research, Charter Member, American Occupational Therapy Foundation, 1984; Fellow of the American

Occupational Therapy Association, 1983; Outstanding Achievement Award, American Public Health Association, 1981. *Hobbies:* Designing and building furniture; Jogging; Travel. *Address:* 72 Newtonville Avenue, Newton, MA 02158, USA.

KIESZKIEWICZ, Teresa Pajszczyk, b. 15 Feb. 1930, Lodz, Poland. Head of Department of Pathological Pregnancy and Vice-Director of Institute of Gynaecology and Obstetrics. m. 11 Sep. 1958. *Education:* Doctor 1953, MD 1964, Medical Academy of Lodz; Dr habil med, 1973; Specialist in Obstetrics, Gynaecology, Perinatology. *Appointments:* Assistant 1953-64, Lecturer 1964-73, Assistant Professor 1973, Head of Department of Pathological Pregnancy, Currently Vice-Director, Institute of Gynaecology and Obstetrics, Medical Academy of Lodz. *Memberships:* Polish Gynaecological Society; Polish Medical Society; Polish Endocrinological Society. *Publications:* 'Biosynthese des Oestrogenes dans les Placentas Humains Perfuses in Vitro', 1969; 'Prevention de la Prematurite', 1970; 'Estrogens and Progesterone Biogenesis in Human Full-Term Placenta', 1970; 'Grossesse chez le Femme Porteuses des Prostheses Valvulaire', 1976; 'Pregnancy and Labour in Women With Rheumatic and Congenital Heart Disease', 1979; 'Pregnancy in Women with Valcular Prostheses', 1985. *Hobbies:* Tourism; Books; Cooking. *Address:* ul Uniwersytecka 8/10 m 4, 90-137 Lodz, Poland.

KILGORE, Thomas Blake, b. 4 Dec. 1943, Lynn, Massachussetts, USA. Professor of Oral Surgery; Assistant Dean. m. Susan Riker, 27 Dec. 1964, Sidney, New York, 2 daughters. *Education:* AB, University of Rochester, USA, 1965; DMD (Hons.), University of Pennsylvania School of Dental Medicine, 1969. *Appointments:* Internship, Massachussetts General Hospital, Department of Oral Surgery, 1969-70, Residency, 1970-73; Visiting Oral Surgeon: Sturdy Memorial Hospital, Massachussetts, 1971-72; Beverly Hospital, Massachussetts, 1973-77; University Hosptial, Massachussetts, 1973-; Associate Visiting Oral Surgeon, Hunt Memorial Hospital, Massachussetts, 1973-78; Active Staff, Boston City Hospital, 1973; Active Staff Kennedy Memorial Hospital, Massachussetts, 1978-. *Memberships include:* American Dental Association; Massachussetts Dental Society; Hon. Member, American Academy of Oral Medicine; Hon. Member, American Society of Dental Anaesthesiology; Omicron Kappa Upsilon; American Association of Dental Schools; Fellow, American Scoiety of Oral Surgery; Metropolitan Boston District Dental Society; Massachussetts Chapter of the Committee to Combat Huntingdon's Disease. *Publications include:* Contributions to professioanl journals including 'Auditory Canal Haemarrhage with Contralateral Condylar Fracture' in 'Journal of the Canadian Dental Association', 1976; Book chapters: 'Management of Dentoalveolar and Soft Tissue Trauma' in "Harvard School of Dental Medicine Oral Surgery Handbook"; 'Oral Surgery and Hospital Dentistry Protocol' in "Textbook of Paediatric Dentistry", 1980. *Honour:* Nominee for Metcalf Award, 1981. *Hobbies:* Sailing; Cycling; Philately. *Address:* BU School of Graduate Dentistry, 100 East Newton St, G407 Boston, MA 02118, USA.

KILLER, Douglas Victor, b. 14 Apr. 1943, Brisbane, Australia, Medical Superintendent, The Wesley Hospital, Brisbane. m. Laurell Jorgensen, 29 Jan 1966, Brisbane, 1 son, 2 daughters. *Education:* MBBS, University of Queensland, 1967; MRACP, 1975; FRACP, 1978; LMUSA, 1961; FACM, 1968; FTCL, London, 1974. *Appointments:* Resident Medical Officer, 1968-69, Medical Registrar, 1971-72, Gastroenterology Registrar, 1973-74, Princess Alexandra Hospital, Brisbane; Medical Registrar, Toowoomba General Hospital, Queensland, 1970; Medical Educator, RACGP Family Medicine

Programme, Brisbane, 1975-76; Fellow in Medical Education, McMaster University, Hamilton, Ontario, Canada, 1977-78; Part-Time Tutor, Department of Community Medicine, University of Sydney, Australia, 1980; Medical Educator, RACGP Family Medicine Programme, Sydney, 1979-85. *Memberships:* Royal Australian College of General Practitioners; Australian and New Zealand Association for Medical Education. *Publications:* 'Urinary Tract Infection in Primary Care', (with K Scherer, J G Ekins), 1977; "Take Care of Yourself", (with L M Goldman, W O Ogborne, J M Raine), 1981; 'Self Audit in General Practice', 1983; 'Practical Aspects of Learning Contracts', 1983; 'Learning by Contract in Family Medicine Training', 1984; 'Audit in General Practice; The Australian Experience', 1984. *Hobbies:* Musical performance; Tennis; Squash; Painting. *Address:* 4 McLaren Street, Fig Tree Pocket, Queensland, 4069, Australia.

KILPATRICK, George Stewart, b. 26 June 1925, Edinburgh, Scotland. Dean of Clinical Studies and Professor of Tuberculosis and Chest Diseases. m. Joan Askew, 11 May 1954, Penryn, Cornwall. *Education:* MD; FRCP; FRCP(Ed). *Appointments:* Various posts in the Edinburgh teaching hospitals; Brompton Hospital, London; MRC Pneumoconiosis Unit, Cardiff; Welsh National School of Medicine 1963-, now known as the University of Wales College of Medicine. *Memberships:* Member of Medical Advisory Committee of CVC's and P's; Member of numerous committees in the medical college; Chairman of Council of ASME; Association of Medical Deans in Europe; Chairman of Conference of Provincial Deans of Medical Schools of UK; Member of Council of British Thoracic Society. *Publications Several publications in relation to General Medicine, Respiratory Medicine and the teaching of medicine. Honour:* OBE, 1986. *Hobbies:* Walking; Reading. *Address:* Dean of Clinical Studies, University of Wales College of Medicine, Heath Park, Cardiff CF4 4XN, S Wales.

KIM, Damian Byungsuk, b. 15 Mar. 1934, South Korea, Chief, Psychiatric Ambulatory Care Services, Clinical Assistant Professor, SUNY, Downstate Medical Centre. m. Yung-Sook Lee, 15 May 1965, Rochester, New York, USA, 2 sons, 1 daughter. *Education:* MD, Medical College, Seoul National University, Seoul, Korea, 1959; Certified Psychoanalyst, American Institute for Psychoanalysis, 1980. *Appointments:* Staff Psychiatrist, 1969, Chief, Alcoholism Treatment Programme, 1978, Coney Island Hospital, USA. *Memberships:* American Psychiatric Association; American Society of Clinical Hypnosis. *Hobbies:* Golf; Hiking. *Address:* 2132 Victory Boulevard, Staten Island, NY 10314, USA.

KIM, Doohie, b. 17 Sep, 1935, Republic of Korea. Professor. m. Euryeong Gun, 24 March 1959, Kyungnam Province, 2 sons, 1 daughter. *Education:* BA, MD, School of Medicine, Kyungpook National University; MA, Medicine, PhD, Medicine, Post-graduate School, Kyungpook National University. *Appointments:* Teaching Assistant, Instructor, Assistant and Associate Professor, Preventive Medicine, Leader, Industrial Health and Welfare Division, Institute of Industrial Development, Director, Medical Library, Vice Dean, Student Affairs, Chairman, Preventive Medicine, Chairman, Preventive Medicine, Graduate School, Director, Faculty of Medicine, Chairman, Environmental Health, School of Public Health, Kyungpook National University; Major, Preventive Medicine, Republic of Korea Army; Director, Kyungpook Branch, Korean Industrial Health Association. *Memberships:* Committee, Korea Preventive Medicine Association; Departmental Head, Academy, Korea Preventive Medicine Association; Advisory Committee, Social Welfare, Kyungpook; Korean Public Health Association. *Publications:* "Environmental Sanitation", 1975; "Concept of Public Health", 1978; "Practice of School Health",

1979; "Preventive Medicine and Public Health", 1978, all in Korean; 74 articles in professional journals, 1961-. *Honours:* Letters of Commendation: from Prime Minister, 1963; C-in-C of Korean Forces in Vietnam, 1967; Minister of Health and Social Affairs, 1985. *Hobby:* Fishing. *Address:* NA-101 Rombard Apt, 1-3 Sooseong 2-Ga, Sooseong-Gu, Taegu, Korea.

KIM, Ho Yon, b. 26 Oct 1926, Wonsan, Korea. Staff Physician, Psychiatrist. m. Myung Ja Kim, 28 May 1944, Wonsan, Korea, 2 sons, 2 daughters. *Education:* Graduation, Medical College, Seoul National University, Seoul, Korea, 1952; MD 1952. *Appointments:* Staff Psychiatrist, VA Hospital Marion, Indian, USA, 1980-; Crafts-Farrow State Hospital, Colombia, South Carolina, 1978-80; Psychiatry Residency, Marlboro Psychiatric Hospital, Marlboro, NJ, 1977-78; St Louis State Hospital, St Louis, MI, 1974-76; Internship, Augustana Hospital, Chicago, 1973-74; Government Medical Officer, Guyana, South America, 1967-70; Staff Physician/General Practitioner, 1952-67. *Memberships:* American Psychiatric Assoc; American Medical Assoc. *Hobby:* Travel. *Address:* V A Hospital, Quarter 33-B, Marion, IN 46953, USA.

KIM, Jay S., b. 2 Oct. 1935, Taegu, Korea. Professor of Clinical Pathology. m. Hak P Pai, 12 May 1962, 2 sons, 3 daughters. *Education:* MD, Doctor of Medical Sciences, Kyungpook National University School of Medicine & Graduate School. *Appointments:* Assistant 1966, Instructor, Assistnat Professor, Associate Professor, Professor & Director, Department of Clinical Pathology. *Memberships:* Korean Society of Clinical Pathology; Korean Society of Clinical Pathology & Quality Control; Korean Society of Medical Associations; Korean Society of Cancer; World Association of Societies of Pathology. *Publications:* "Textbook of General Clinical Pathology", 2nd edition 1985; "Medical Microbiology", 1979; About 100 various papers in medical journals. *Honour:* 1st Prize, Seoul Medical News. *Hobbies:* Music; Collecting & growing oriental orchids. *Address:* 3-181 Daesin, 1st-Dong Joong-Goo, Taegu City, Korea.

KIM, Myunghee, b. 8 Nov. 1932, Korea. Psychiatrist, Teaching Staff. m. Peter Reimann, 29 June 1962, New York City, USA. 2 daughters. *Education:* MD, Medical School of Seoul National University, Korea. *Appointments:* Psychiatrist Staff, Roosevelt Hospital, NY; Staff Child Psychiatrist, Child Guidance and Family Service, Maplewood, Oranges and Milbun, NJ; Teaching Staff Psychiatrist, Bergen Pine Hospital, NJ. *Memberships:* American Psychoanalytic Assoc.; International Psychoanalytic Assoc.; American Psychiatric Assoc. *Publications:* 'Clinical Psychoanalytic Experience in America', Psychiatry Bulletin, Seoul National University, Korea. *Hobbies:* Oriental and Primitive Art Collection; Travel. *Address:* 272 Short Hills Avenue, Springfield, NJ 07081, USA.

KIM, Yong-Kook Augustine, b. 15 Aug 1939, Korea. Chief, Department of Psychiatry, Warminster General Hospital. m. Theresa Kwang-Oak, 5 Apr 1967, Korea, 4 daughters. *Education:* MD, School of Medicine, Seoul National University, Korea, 1964; Certified by American Board of Psychiatry & Neurology, 1981. *Appointments:* Director, Development Disability Unit, Albert Einstein Community Mental Health Center, Philadelphia, Pennsylvania; Director, Older Adult Unit, Horsham Clinic, Ambler, Pennsylvania; Director, ADAPT (substance abuse programme), Eugenia Hospital; Clinical Director, Chief of Department of Psychiatry, Warminster General Hospital, Warminster, Pennsylvania. *Memberships:* American Medical Association; Southern Medical Association; Philadelphia Medical Association; American Psychiatric Association; Pennsylvania Psychiatric Association; Philadelphia Psychiatric Association. *Honour:* Legion of Honour,

Chapel of Four Chaplains, 1982. *Hobbies:* Golf; Classical Music. *Address:* Suite 212, Warminster Medical Office Center, 205 Newtown Road, Warminster, PA 18974, USA.

KIMBER, Pamela Mary, b. 29 Nov 1934, Marlow, Bucks. Superintendent Radiographer. *Education:* Diploma of the college of Radiographers; Higher Diploma of the College of Radiographers; Fellowship of the College of Radiograpehrs. *Appointments:* 2Radiographer, Radcliffe Infirmary; Radiographer, Mayo Memorial Hospital, Mineapolis, Minnesota; Senior Neuro Radiographer, Radcliffe Infirmary; Superintendent Radiographer, Wessex Neurological Centre. *Membership:* College of Radiographers. *Publication:* "Radiography of the Head" 1983. *Honour:* Fellowship of College of Radiographers, 1968. *Hobbies:* Soroptimist International; Classical music. *Address:* Flat L, Windsor Court, Winn Road, Southampton SO2 1EL, England.

KIMBERLEY, A Gurney, b. 14 Feb 1905, Northfield, Vermont, USA. Retired. m. Marjorie A Smith, 14 Feb 1943, Portland, Oregon, 4 sons, 3 daughters. *Education:* BSc, 1926, MD, 1930, Oregon University; DMS, Columbia University Medical School, 1937; Anna C Kane Fellowship, New York Dispendary and Hospital, 1934-37. *Appointments:* Private practice, Portland, Oregon, 1937-; Founding Partner, Orthopaedic Consultants P C; Senior Surgeon, US Public Health Service and Consultant, Selective Service, Oregon (World War II); Consultant, Veterans Hospital, US Public Health Service and Crippled Childrens Programme; Emeritus Professor of Orthopaedics, University of Oregon Medical School; Visiting Professor, Autonomous University, Gualalajara, Mexico. *Memberships:* Charter Member and 1st President, Portland Orthopaedic Club. Past President: North Pacific Orthopaedic Society; Oregon Chapter, Western Orthopaedic Society; Northwestern Medical Association; Staff of the Good Samaritan Hospital, Portland. *Publications:* Associate Editor, 'Western Journal of Surgery', 20 years. *Honours:* Board Certified, Diplomate in Orthopaedics, 1938; Outstanding American under 35 years, National Junior Chamber of Commerce, 1938. Life Member: Academy of Orthopaedic Surgery; American Medical Association; Pan American Medical Society; Pan Pacific Surgical Society; various others. *Hobbies:* Skiing, served as President, American Society of Skiing Doctors; Mountain climbing; Hiking; Gardening. *Address:* 01837 South West Greenwood Road, Portland, OR 97219, USA.

KIMURA, Masayasu, b. 19 May 1930, Tokyo, Japan. Professor of Chemical Pharmacology. m. Ikuko Kimura, May 1970, 2 sons. *Education:* PhD Pharmacology, University of Tokyo. *Appointments:* Professor, Chemical Pharmacology, University of Toyama, 1958-79. *Memberships:* Councillor, Japanese Pharmacological Society, 1963-; Councillor 1972-73 and 1980-81, Pharmaceutical Society of Japan; Director, Medical and Pharmaceutical Society for Wakan-Yaku, 1984-. *Publications:* "Chemical Pharmacology" in Japanese, 1975; "Developmental Pharmacology" in Japanese, 1979; "Pharmacology of Medicinal Herbs in East Asia" in Japanese, 1982. *Honours:* Stimulus Award of Pharmaceutical Society of Japan, 1966; Abbott Prize, 1972; Culture Prize of Toyama Press, 1973; Invention Prize, Invention Association Toyama branch, 1973; Workshop Organiser, International Congress of Pharmacology, 1981. *Hobby:* Game of Go. *Address:* Department of Chemical Pharmacology, Faculty of Pharmaceutical Sciences, Toyama Medical and Pharmaceutical University, 2630 Sugitani, Toyama 930-01, Japan.

KINALSKI, Ryszard Jerzy, b. 27 Feb. 1929, Lwów, Poland. Chairman of Department of Rehabilitation; Consultant in Rehabilitation. m. Teresa Ida, 30 July, 1955, Bialystok, Poland, 2 sons, 1 daughter. *Education:* Master of Physical Education, University

College of Physical Education, 1950; MD, Medical Academy, 1955; PhD, 1969. *Appointments:* Assistant, Neurology Department, 1956-63; Chairman, Medical Rehabilitation Department, 1963-present; Provincial Consultant in Rehabilitation, 1965-present; Deputy Specialist in Rehabilitation Medicine in Mongolia, 1977; Appointed by World Health Organisation as Consultant in Rehabilitation Medicine for Mongolia, 1979; Assistant Professor, Medical Academy, Bialystok, 1983. *Memberships:* Polish Medical Society; Polish Neurological Society; Polish Society for Rehabilitation of the Disabled; Polish Society for EEG and Clinical Neuro-Physiology; International Rehabilitation Medicine Association. *Publications include:* Contributions to professional journals. *Honours:* Silver Cross of Merit, 1970; Gold Mark of Polish Society for Rehabilitation of the Disabled, 1971; Medal of National Education, 1976. *Hobbies:* Skiing; Travel; Tinkering. *Address:* ul.B Chrobrego 6 Z m.42, 15-057 Bialystok, Poland.

KINDT, Thomas James, b. 18 May 1939, Cincinnati, USA. Chief, Laboratory of Immunogenetics, NIAID, NIH, m. 4 Sep. 1964, Urbana, Illinois, 1 son, 1 daughter. *Education:* PhD Biochemistry, BA cum Laude Chemistry, University of Illinosi, Thomas More College. *Appointments:* Postdocotral Fellow, 1967, Assistant Research Scientist, 1969, Department Immunology, City Hope National Medical Center, California; Postdoctoral Fellow, Laboratory Bacteriology and Immunology, 1970, Assistant Professor, Laboratory Immunology and Immunochemistry, 1971, Associate Professor, Laboratory Immunology and Immunochemistry, 1973, Acting Head, Laboratory Immunology and Immunochemistry, 1975, Rockefeller University; Adjg Associate Professor, Department of Medicine, Cornell University Medical School, 1971; Visiting Scientist, Laboratory Analytical Immunochemistry, Institut Pasteur, Paris, France; Chief, Laboratory Immunogenetics, NIAID, NIH, 1977-; Adjunct Professor, Department of Microbiology and Paediatrics, Georgetown University School of Medicine and Dentistry, Washington DC, 1981-. *Memberships:* American Association of Immunologists; American Heart Association; Harvey Society; Sigma Xi; American Society of Biological Chemists; Member of 7 editorial and review boards. *Publications:* "The Antibody Enigma", (with DD CApra), 1984; Contributor of 145 articles in scientific research and medical journals. *Honours:* NIAID Award and Bonus for High Quality Work Performance, 1981, 1982, 1983, 1984, 1985; Professional Achievement Award, Thomas More College, 1975; Professional Achivement Award, 1970-75; Established Investigator, American Heart Association; Postdoctoral Fellow, NIH, 1967-70; Predoctoral Fellow, NIH, 1964, 1967; Undergraduate Fellow, National Science Foundation, 1962-63. *Hobbies:* Gardening; Photography; Hiking. *Address:* Laboratory of Immunogenetics, NIAID, NIH, Building 5, Room B1-04, Bethesda, MD, 20892, USA.

KING, Barbara J.F., b. 28 June 1941, Missouri. Coronary Intensive Care Nurse. m. C B King Jr., 4 Sep. 1972, Weatherford, Texas, USA, 2 sons. *Education:* Diploma of Nursing with BSN in progress. *Appointments include:* Assistant Head Nurse, Pediatric Unit, John Peter Smith Hospital, Fort Worth, Texas, 1978-79; Head Nurse, Bridgeport Hospital and Clinic, Bridgeport, Texas, 1979-81; Relief Head Nurse, Bowie Memorial Hospital, Bowie, Texas, 1979-81; Instructor of Vocational Nurses, Coke County Junior College, Gainesville, Texas, 1981-83; Nurse on Coronary and Intensive Care Unit, Decatur Community Hospital, Decatur, Texas, 1983-. *Memberships:* ABI; ANA; IPA; AAAPF. *Honour:* ABI Medal of Honor, 1986. *Hobbies:* Music; Fishing; Reading; Dancing. *Address:* Rt 1 Box 198, Alvord, TX 76225, USA.

KING, Frederick Alexander, b.10 Mar. 1925, Glen Rock, New Jersey, USA. Director, Yerkes Regional Primate Research Centre. m. dissolved, 1 son, 1 daughter. *Education:* AB, Psychology & Biological Sciences, Stanford University; AM, PhD, Physiological Psychology, Johns Hopkins University. *Appointments:* Instructor, Department of Psychology, Johns Hopkins University, 1954-56; Instructor, 1956-57, Assistant Professor, 1957-59, Department of Psychiatry, College of Medicine, Lecturer, Department of Psychology, Ohio State University; Assistant Research Professor, Division of Neurosurgery, College of Medicine, University of Florida, 1959-68; Assistant Professor, 1959-63, Associate Professor, 1963-68, Department of Psychology, University of Florida; Director, Centre for Neurobiological Sciences, 1965-78, Research Professor, Division of Neurosurgery, 1968-69, Professor, Department of Psychology, 1968-78, Professor & Chairman, Department of Anatomical Sciences, 1969-70, Professor & Chairman, Department of Neuroscience, 1970-78, University of Florida College of Medicine; Research Neurophysiologist, VA Hospital, Gainesville, Florida, 1968-72; Director, Yerkes Regional Primate Research Centre of Emory University, Professor of Anatomy, Associate Dean, Emory University School of Medicine, Adjunct Professor of Psychology, 1978-; Adjunct Professor of Psychology, Georgia Institue of Technology, 1984-. *Memberships:* Society for Neuroscience; International Neuropsychology Society; American Association of Anatomists; American Physiological Society; American Psychological Association; Fellow, American Association for the Advancement of Science; Sigma Xi; New York Acadmey of Sciences; American Association of Unviersity Professors; and others. *Publications:* Numerous papers, articles, lectures, book chapters etc. *Honours:* John Carrol Fulton Scholar, Johns Hopkins University, 1953-55; Predoctoral Research Fellow, National Institute of Health, ibid, 1955-56; Special Fellow, NIH, University of Pisa, Itlay, 1961-62. *Hobbies:* Tennis; Motorcycling; Rain Forest Exploration. *Address:* Yerkes Regional Primate Research Centre, Emory University Atlanta, GA 30322, USA.

KING, Harold, b. 8 Dec. 1922, Bedford, Indiana, USA. Director. m. Betty Jane Fink, 30 Aug. 1952, Bloomington, 2 sons. *Education:* Indiana University, 1940-43; MS, Yale University School of Medicine, 1946. *Appointments:* Instructor, Surgery, 1955-58, Assistant Professor, 1958, Associate Professor, 1961, Professor, 1964, Surgery, Director, Thoracic and Cardiovascular Surgery, Indiana University Medical Centre. *Memberships:* American Medical Association; American College of Surgeons; American Association for Thoracic Surgery; Society for Vascular Surgery; Chest Club; Central Surgical Association; International Cardiovascular Society; Society of University Surgeons; International Society of Surgery; American Surgical Association; Society of Thoracic Surgeons; American College of Cardiology; American College of Chest Physicians; Midwestern Vascular Surgical Society. *Publications:* "Splenic Studies I, Susceptibility to Infection after Splenectomy Performed in Infancy", co-author, 'Annals of Surgery', 1952. *Hobby:* Golf. *Address:* 545 Barnhill Drive, Emerson Hall 212, Indianapolis, IN 46223, USA.

KING, Michalene Ann, b. 28 Sep. 1951, Wheeling, WVa USA, Faculty Member, Ohio Valley Hospital School of Nursing. m. George Thomas King, 26 Oct 1974, Steubenville, Ohio, 1 daughter. *Education:* Nursing Diploma, Ohio Valley Hospital School of Nursing, Steubenville; BSN, West Liberty State College, WVa; MSEd, University of Dayton, Dayton, Ohio; Student, Master of Science degree in Nursing, West Virginia University, Morgantown, WVa. *Appointments:* Staff nurse, Ohio Valley Hospital, Steubenville, Ohio, 1972-82; Faculty Member, Ohio Valley Hospital School of Nursing, 1982-. *Memberships:* American Nurses Association; Ohio

Nurses Association. *Honours:* Women's Advisory Award, Ohio Valley Hospital School of Nursing, 1972. *Hobbies:* Needlecrafts; Community Volunteer; Parent Nurturing Programme. *Address:* 142 Susan Drive, Wintersville, OH 43952, USA.

KING, Richard Ewart, b. 6 May, 1921, Chicago, Illinois, USA. Director of Orthopaedic Education. m. Lorraine Klingler, 28 Mar. 1945, New Orleans, Louisiana, USA, 1 son, 1 daughter. *Education:* BS, MD, University of Illinois, USA. *Appointments:* Associate Professor, Orthopaedic Surgery, Tulane University, New Orleans; Clinical Professor, Orthopaedic Surgery, Emory University, Atlanta, Georgia; Director, Orthopaedic Residency Education, Georgia Baptist Medical Centre, Atlanta, Georgia-. *Memberships:* Georgia Orthopaedic Society; Southern Orthopaedic Association; American Academy of Orthopaedic Surgeons; American Orthopaedic Association; SICOT: Russell A Hibbs Society. *Publications:* Chapters and co-editor "Fractures in Children"; Chapter 'Proximal Femoral Focal Deficiency' in "Surgery of the Hip Joint"; Chapter "Current Practice in Orthopaedic Surgery"; Chapter 'The Hip', Proceedings of Hip Society, 11th Open Scientific Meeting; Chapter, Section 1 "Paediatric Orthopaedics Postgraduate Textbook of Clinical Orthopaedics"; Articles in 'Journal of Bone and Joint Surgery, 1954, 1973, 1982. *Honour:* Good Samaritan Award, Variety Club, Atlanta, Georgia, 1965. *Hobbies:* Photography; Stamp and book collecting; Hunting; Fishing. *Address:* 340 Boulevard NE, Atlanta, GA 30312, USA.

KINGSTON, Josephine Mary, b. 20 May 1943, Pontefract. Senior Medical Officer, RAF Odiham. m. Roger Michael Kinston, 5 Nov. 1966, 1 son, 2 daughters. *Education:* MB, BS; LRCP; MRCS; Dip.Ave.Med. *Appointments include:* Berkshire County Medical Officer of Health; General practitioner, Windsor, Berkshire; FAR Medical Officer, Brize Norton; RAF Senior Medical Officer, High Wycombe. Farnborough Institute of Aviation Medicine; Senior Medical Officer/Flight Medical Officer, RAF Odiham, Hampshire. *Memberships:* British Medical Association; Aerospace Medical Association. *Hobbies:* Flying; Swimming. *Address:* 118 Belgrave Road, London SW1, England.

KINNAMON, Kenneth E, b. 28 May, 1934, Deniston, Texas, USA. Associate Dean for Operations. m. Arlene Edwards, 30 May, 1981, Silver Springs, Maryland, USA, 3 sons. *Education:* BSc., Oklahoma State University, USA, 1956; Doctor of Veterinary Medicine, Texas A & M University, 1959; MSc., University of Rochester, USA, 1961; PhD, University of Tenessee, 1971. *Appointments include:* Walter Reed Army Institute of Research, 1971-75; Director, Multidiscipline Laboratories, 1975-76, Associate Professor of Physiology, 1975-79, Uniformed Services University of the Health Sciences, Betheseda, Maryland, Acting Assistant Dean for Instructional and Research Support, 1976-77, Director, Envirnomental Health and Occupational Safety, 1976-77, Director, Grants Management, 1976-78, Assistant Dean, Instructional and Research Support, 1977-80, Professor of Physiology, 1979-. *Memberships:* American Physiological Society; American Public Health Association; American Veterinary Medical Association; Society of Sigma Xi; American Society of Tropical Medicine and Hygiene; American Association for the Advancement of Science; Health Physics Society, etc. *Publications:* Contributor to "Microautoradiography", in "Selected Histochemical and Histopathological Methods", 1966; 'Stratetic Employment of Food' in 'Ethics in Science and Medicine', 1980; Numerous articles in professional journals, abstracts, reports and conference papers. *Honours:* Consultant, National Cancer Institute; Armed Forces Radiobiology Research Institute; US Army Surgeon General.

Hobbies: Former professional baseball player, Kansas City organisation; Church activities. *Address:* Uniformed Services University of the Health Sciences, 4301 Jones Bridge Road, Betheseda, MD 20814, USA.

KINO, Isamu, b. 18 July 1932, Tokyo, Japan. Professor of Pathology. m. Shizuko Hara, 10 Nov 1963, Tokyo, 1 son, 2 daughters. *Education:* MD 1957, Doctor of Medical Science 1965, Faculty of Medicine, University of Tokyo. *Appointments:* Assistant in Department of Pathology 1965, Associate Professor of Pathology 1973, Faculty of Medicine, University of Tokyo, Professor of Pathology, School of Medicine, Hamamatsu University, 1974-. *Memberships:* International Academy of Pathology; Japanese Pathological Association; Japanese Cancer Association. *Publications:* "Histopathology of the Gastrountestinal Tract - Biopsy Interpretation", 1980; "Textbook of Pathology; Gastrointesinal Pathology and Gynaecological Pathology", 1980. *Hobbies:* Golf; Mountaineering. *Address:* 3600 Handa-Cho, Hamamatsu 431-31, c/o School of Medicine, Hamamatsu University, Japan.

KIRBY, Norman George, b. 19 Dec. 1926, England. Consutlant Casualty Surgeon, Guy's Hospital, London. m. Cynthia Bradley, 1 Oct. 1949, Birmingham, 1 son, 1 daughter. *Education:* MB ChB; MRCS; LRCP; 1949; FRCS England; FRCS Edinburgh; FICS. *Appointments:* Surgical Registrar, Birmingham Accident Hospital; Surgical Registrar, Postgraduate Medical school, London; Consultant Surgeon, Britisah Military Hospitals, Cyprus, Aldershot, London, Germany; Consulting Surgeon to the Army; Honorary Surgeon to H.M. The Queen. *Memberships:* Fellow, Casualty Surgeons Association; British Orthopaedic Association; Association of Surgeons of Great Britain and Ireland; Medical Society of London. *Publications:* Field Surgery Pocket Book, 1981; "Biallieres Handbook of First Aid, 1985; "New Health Encyclopaedia", Volume 2, "Anatomy Physiology", 1985. *Honours:* Officer of Order of British Empire, 1971; Officer of Order of St. John, 1977. *Hobbies:* Motoring; Travel; Reading. *Address:* Accident and Emergency Department, Guy's Hospital, London Bridge, London SE1 9RT, England.

KIRCHNER, John Albert, b. 27 Mar. 1915, Waynesboro, Pennsylvasnia, USA. Professor Emeritus, Otolaryngology, Yale University. m. Aline Legault, 11 Nov. 1947, Baltimore, Maryland, 3 sons, 2 daughters. *Education:* MD, University of Virginia, 1940; Honorary MS, Yale University, 1952; Commonwealth Fund Fellow, Physiology, Royal College of Surgeons, London, UK, 1963-64. *Appointments include:* Captain, US Army, 1942-46; Resident, Otolaryngology, Johns Hopkins, 1946-50; Private Practice, Cincinnati, Ohio, 1950-51; Assistant Professor, Associate Professor, Professor, Otolaryngology, 1951-85, Professor Emeritus 1985-, Yale University. *Memberships:* President 1965-66, New England Otolaryngological Society; President 1977-78, American Society of Head & Neck Surgery; Vice President 1978-79, American Academy of Otolaryngology; President 1979-80, American Laryngological Association; President 1981-82, American Layrngological, Rhinological & Otolaryngological Society; Collegium Orlas. *Publications include:* Over 125 scientific papers, presentations, etc. 1985, 'Landmarks in Laryngology', 'Laryngeal Perichondritis & Abcess', 'Treatment of Laryngeal Cancer' (in book, "Head & Neck Cancer"). *Honours:* Bronze Star Medal, 1946; Mosher Award, ALROS, 1958; Casselberry Award, ALA, 1966; Newcomb Award, ALA, 1969; Semon Medal, University of London, 1981; DeRoaldes Medal, ALA, 1985. *Hobby:* Vegetable gardening. *Address:* PO Box 3333/333 Cedar Street, New Haven, CT 06510, USA.

KIRCHNER, Peter Thomas, b. 2 July 1939. Hungary.

Professor of Radiology. m. Mary Coleman, 1965, Sussex, England, 1 son, 2 daughters. *Education:* BA Physics, Yale University; 1956-60; MD, Columbia University, 1960-64; Internship 1964-65, Residency Medicine 1966-69, Chief Resident, Medicine, 1969-70, National Naval Medical Centre, Bethesda, Maryland; Fellow, Nuclear Medicine, Johns Hopkins Medical Institution, 197-72. *Appointments:* Attending Physician, Internal Medicine, National Naval Medical Centre, Bethesda, 1973-77; Assistant Professor of Radiology, George Washington University, Washington DC, 1973-77; Chief, Nuclear Medicine Division, 1972-77, Director, Nuclear Medicine Residency Programme, 1974-77, National Naval Medical Centre, Bethesda; Associate Professor of Radiology, 1977-81, Associate Director, Nuclear Medicine, 1978-81, University of Chicago; Director, Division of Nuclear Medicine, 1981-, Associate Professor of Radiology, 1981-83, Professor of Radiolgoy, 1983-, Univeristyof Iowa. *Memberships:* Society of Nuclear Mediciine; American Medical Association; American College of Physicians (Fellow 1983); American College of Nuclear Physicians (Fellow 1983); American College of Radiolgoy; Radiological Society of North America; American Heart Association; American Clinical Research. *Publications:* Over 50 scientific publications, numerous abstracts, one book. *Honours:* Fellowships in ACP and ACNPP Accrediation Council for Graduate Medical Education. *Hobby:* Tennis. *Address:* Department of Radiology, University of Iowa, Iowa City, IA 52242, USA.

KIRKMAN, Hadley, b. 14 Mar. 1901, Richmond, Indiana, USA. Professor of Anatomy, Emeritus, Active, Stanford University. m. Gladys Tracy, 5 Apr. 1942, Chicago, 1 daughter. *Education:* AB, University of Iowa, 1925, MS, University of Chicago, 1929, PhD, Columbia University, 1937. *Appointments include:* Instructor, Anatomy, New York Medical College 1929-32, Columbia University 1934-36, Stanford University 1936-38; Assistant Professor 1938-43, Associate Professor 1043-49, Professor of Anatomy 1949-65, Stanford University; Professor of Anatomy, Active Emeritus, 1965-. *Memberships:* Fellow, New York Academy of Science; Fellow, American Assocation for the Advancement of Science; Fellow, Royal Society of Medicine, UK; American Association of Anatomists; American Association for Cancer Research; Histochemical Society, 1952-72; American Association of University Professors; Physicians for Social Responsiblity; Sigma Xi. *Publications include;* Over 100 research articles in profeessional journals, on histology, embryology, Pathology, teratology, hormonal carcinogenisis, 1930-85. *Honours:* Senior Fellow, National Science Foundation, 1957-58; Special Fellow, US Public Health Service, 1958-59; Fellow, New York Academy of Science, 1949; Fellow, AAAS, 1945-; Member, Section of Fellowships, Committee on Growth, Fellowship Advisory Council, Division of Medical Sciences, National Research Council, 1952-54; Teaching awards, 1964, 1965, 1973. *Recreation:* Reading. *Address:* Division of Human Anatomy, Department of Surgery, Stanford University School of Medicine, Stanford, CT 94305, USA.

KIRSCHNER, Henryk Wladyslaw, b. 27 June 1929, Lvov. Director, Medical School. m. Joanna Belniak, 20 Oct. 1956, Warsaw, 1 son. *Education:* Diploma of Physician, 1954; Specialist in Epidemiology, 1955; MD, 1959; Doctor Habilitatis in Physiology, 1971; Professor, 1980. *Appointments:* Assistant, Hygiene Dept., 1954-57, Senior Assistant, Assistant Professor, Applied Physiology 1958-72, Director, Institute of Social Medicine, 1973-, Medical School, Warsaw. *Memberships:* Polish Academy of Sciences, Committee of Ergonomics Society; Polish Society of Hygiene. *Publications:* 100 papers in professional journals; Author, "Analysis of Work", 1963; "Ergonomics in Practice", 1967; "Physiology

of Physical Activity", co-author, 1970; "Work and Nutrition", 1979. *Honours:* Council of State, 1977, 1982; Polish Society of Hygiene, 1975, 1978; Minister of Health, 1973, 1984; Trade Unions, 1963. *Hobbies:* Theatre; Hiking. *Address:* ul Oczki 3, 02 007 Warsaw, Poland.

KIRSCHNER, Paul A, b. 30 Dec. 1917, New York, New York, USA. Clinical Professor of Surgery. m. Charlotte Gordon, 2 Oct, 1945, New York City, 1 son, 2 daughters. *Education:* BS magna cum laude, New York University, 1937; MD, Columbia University College of Physicians and Surgeons, 1941. *Appointments:* Assistant in Surgery 1949-53, Instructor 1953-57, Associate 1957-63, Columbia Univeristy; Clinical Assistant Surgeon 1949-53, Assistant Attending Surgeon 1953-63, Associate Attending Surgeon of Thoracic Surgery 1962-71, Attending Surgeon for Thoracic Surgery 1971-, Mount Sinai Hospital, New York; Adjunct Thoracic Surgeon, Montefiore Hospital, Bronx, New York, 1949-54; Chest and General 1949-53, Associate Visiting Surgeon Chest 1953-63, Believe Hospital, New York; Attending Thoracic Surgeon 1951-63, Senior Consultant in Thoracic Surgery 1963-, Veterans Hospital, Bronx, New York; Clinical Assistant Professor of Surgery, Albert-Einsten College of Medicine, 1963-68; Associate Visiting Surgeon, Bronx Municipal Medical Center, 1963-68; Associate Clinical Professor of Surgery 1966-71, Clinical Professor of Surgery 1971-, Mount Sinai School of Medicine; Chief, General Thoracic Surgery Section, Mount Sinai Medical Center, 1979-. *Memberships:* Fellow, American College of Surgeons;American Association for Thoracic Surgery; American College of Chest Physicians; American Thoracic Surgery; Society of Thoracic Surgeons; American Medical Association; International Association for the Study of Lung Cancer; Phi Beta Kappa; Alpha Omega Alpha. *Publications:* 'Hemodynamics of Mitral and Aortic Valve Disease', (with A Gordon and H Moscovitz), 1961; 62 articles; 125 papers presented at meetings. *Honours:* Wm Perry Watson Prize in Pediatrics, Surgery Prize, Columbia University College of Physicians and Surgeons. *Hobbies:* Photography; Atheltics; Music. *Address:* 2 East 92 Street, New York, NY 10128, USA.

KISFALUDY, Lajos, b. 30 Aug 1924, Saj0g0m0r, Hungary. Head, Research Department of Chemical Works of G Richter. m. Maria Makovits, 9 Apr, 1949, Budapest, 1 son, 1 daughter. *Education:* Diploma, Chemical engineering, Technical University of Budapest, 1948; Doctor of University, 1963; Candidate of Science, 1963; DSc, 1975; Corresponding Member, Hungarian Academy of Sciences, 1982. *Appointments:* Assistant Professor, Technical University of Budapest, 1948-56; currently, Head, Research Department of Chemical Works of Gedeon Richter. *Memberships:* Correspondening Member, Hungarian Academy of Sciences; Past President, Organic and Medical Chemistry section, Hungarian Chemical Society; Member of numerous scientific committees; Board Member, Technical University, Budapest. *Publications:* Author of over 150 publications including book chapters and holder of 70 patents. *Honour:* State Prize, 1st degree, 1970. *Hobbies:* His work; Sports. *Address:* PO Box 27, H-1475 Budapest 1o, Hungary.

KISIDA, Elek, b. 22 July 1936, Viszlo, Hungary. Docent. m. Magdolna Kadi, 28 July 1952, 3 daughters. *Education:* Medical Diploma, 1961; General Surgery 1967, Thoracic Surgery, Specialization exam, 1970; Candidacy in Medical Sciences, 1976. *Appointments:* Assistant, Institute of Micro-biology, Hungarian Acadmey of Sciences, 1961; Resident, 2nd Department of Surgery, The "Semmelweis", University of Medicine, 1963; Specilized Surgeon, 1967; Assistant Professor of Surgery, 1977; Docent, 1984. *Meberships:*

Hungarian Society of Surgeons; Hungarian Society of Gastroenterology. *Publications:* "Einfluss de Omentektomie auf die Erythrophagocytose Langenbeck's Arch", 1965; "Primer Retroperitonealis Tumorok", 1968; "Experimentelle Untersuchungennüber die Leberschadigende Wirkung des Halothans", 1969; "Toxicity of Peritoneal fluids form dogs with occulded SMA", 1974; "Experimental Retroperitoneal Infection", 1985. *Hobbies:* Educating Children; Photography; Collecting Old Maps; Sculpture; Greek Orthodox Liturgy; Skiing; Mountain Climbing. *Address:* Budapest, XIII, Budakeszi ut 46/a, 1121, Hungary.

KISSEL, Charles Gregory, b. 8 June 1951, Lackawana, NY. Chief, Section of Podiatry. m. Carol Ann Cook, 29 July 1977, St Bernadette's, 2 sons. *Education:* DPM, Ohio College of Podiatric Medicine, 1978; BS, State University of New York at Buffalo, Cume Laude, 1973. *Appointments:* Director, Residency Training, Hutzel Hospital, Detroit, MI; Chairman, Scientific Committee, MI Podiatric Medical Assoc.; Podiatric Consultant, Macomb Oakland Regional Center; Group Health Plan of Michigan; Clinical Instructor, University Health Center, Wayne State, Detroit Receiving Hospital; Clinical Investigator, Sutter Biomedical Products. *Memberships:* Diplomat, American Board of Podiatric Surgery; Fellow, American College of Foot Surgeons; Member, Michigan Podiatric Medical Association; American Podiatric Medical Association. *Publications:* 'Syndactylism and its Surgical Repair', 1981; 'Implants of the First MPJ', 1983; 'Calcaneal Osteotomies', 1984; 'Allogenic Bone Grafts', 1984. *Honour:* Pi Delta National Honor Society, 1977. *Hobbies:* Water Skiing; Skating; Photography. *Address:* 3600 East Twelve Mile Road, Warren, MI 48092, USA.

KISZONAS, Richard A. b. 15 May 1931, USA. Radiologist. *Education:* BS, Ursinos College, USA; DD, MSc (Rad), Philadelphia College of Osteopathic Medicine. *Appointments:* Associate Radiologist, Tri County Hosptial, 1963-77; Asociate Radiologist, Metropolitan Hospital, 1977-81; Radiologist, Southeastern Medical Centre, 1981-present; Clinical Assistant Professor, Radiology, Southeastern College of Osteopathic Medicine, 1983; Clinical Associate Professor, Radiology, University of Miami Medical School, 1983. *Memberships:* American Osteopathic Association; American Osteopathic College of Radiology; British Institute of Radiology. *Publications:* 'Use of Chest Radiograph Screening in Hospital Admissions' in 'ADA Journal', 1963; 'Use of Zero Radiography inoother than Mammography', in 'Medical Imaging', 1976. *Honours:* Fellow, AOCR, 1979; Trenery Lecturer, AOCR, 1981. *Hobby:* Music. *Address:* 1000 Quayside Terrace, 1512 Miami, FL 33138, USA.

KIT, Saul, b. 25 Nov. 1920, Passaic, New Jersey, USA. Professor & Head, Division of Biochemical Virology, Baylor College of Medicine, Houston, Texas. m. Dorothy Anken, 28 Sep. 1945, Miami, Florida, 2 sons, 1 daughter. *Education:* BA, Highest Honours, 1948, PhD, Biochemistry 1951, University of California, Berkeley. *Appointments include:* Postdoctoral Fellow, National Federation for Infantile Paralysis & National Cancer Institute, University of Chicago, 1951-52; Research Biochemist to Biochemist & Chief, Section of Nucleoprotein Metabolism, University of Texas M.D. Anderson Hospital & Tumour Institute, 1953-62; Assistant Professor, Associate Professor, Professor, Baylor College of Medicine, 1956-. *Memberships:* American Society of Biological Chemists; American Association for Cancer Research; American Society for Cell Biology; American Society for Microbiology; Corresponding member, Argentine Society of Virology; American Society for Virology. *Publications include:* Over 200 research papers, various professional journals. *Honours:* Abraham Rosenberg Predoctoral Fellow, University of California, 1949-50; Polio Foundation & National Cancer Institute Postdoctoral Fellow, University of

Chicago, 1952; Research Career Award, US Public Health Service, 1963-; Numerous research grants, USPHS, American Cancer Society, Leukaemia Society, National Science Foundation. *Hobbies:* Theatre; Music; Sports; Books; Politics. *Address:* Division of Biochemical Virology, Baylor College of Medicine, One Baylor Plaza, Houston, TX 77030, USA.

KITAMOTO, Osamu, b. 17 Sep 1911, Japan. Emeritus Professor. m. Jasuko Joshida, 7 June 1939, 2 sons, 1 daughter. *Education:* MD, University of Tokyo Medical School, 1935; DMSc, University of Tokyo, 1940; Research, Pasteur Institute, Paris, France, 1950-51. *Appointments:* Associate Professor of Medicine, 1948, Professor of Medicine, 1951-72, University of Tokyo, Japan; Professor of Medicine, 1972-81, Dean, Faculty of Medicine, 1974-81, Vice President, 1978-81, Kyorin University; Emeritus Professor, University of Tokyo and Kyorin University. *Memberships:* Honorary Member, International Organisation for Micoplasmology; Regent for Japan, International Academy of Chest Physicians and Surgeons of American College of Chest Physicians; President, Societe Franco-Japonaise de Medecine; Honorary Member, Japanese Society of Internal Medicine, Chest Diseases, Tuberculosis Infectious Diseases and others. *Publications:* "Diseases of the Chest", 1968; "Textbook of Internal Medicine", 1956; "Pulmonary Tuberculosis", 1972; "Atlas of Differential Diagnosis of Lung Cancer", 1968; contributor, "Klinische Pharmacologie and Pharmocotherapie", 1971. *Honours:* Chevalier de l'Order National de la Legion d'Honneur, France, 1974; Second Order of Merit, Japan, 1984. *Hobbies:* Painting; Golf. *Address:* 5-18-1 Honkomagome, Bunkyoku, Tokyo 113, Japan.

KITCHEN, Alice Dean, b. 12 Sept. 1927, Kansas City, Kansas, USA. Assistant Dean of Student Affairs; Assistant Professor of Psychiatry; Director, Consultant Liaison Psychiatry. *Education:* BS, Zoology, Wheaton College, Illinois, USA; MD, Univeristy of Kansas School of Medicine, 1955. *Appointments:* Rotating Internship, St. Lukes's Hospital, Kansas City, USA; General Practice Residency, Sacramento County Hospital, California, 1956-57; Staff Physician, Mission Hospital, West Pakistan, 1957-63; Medical Director, 1964-67; Psychiatric Residency, University of Rochester, New York, USA, 1967-70; Instructor in Psychaitry, Univeristy of Missouri, 1970-72, Assistant Professor, 1972-74, Director, Residency Training Programme, 1972-74, Director Psychiatric Nurses' Programme, 1972-74; Assistant Professor of Psychiatry, st. Louis University School of Medicine, 1974-; Chief CL Division, Department of Psychiatry, JCVA Hospital, St.Louis, 1974-79; Director CL Psychiatry, St Louis University Medical Centre, 1979-, Assistant Dean for Students, 1981-. *Memberships:* Eastern Missouri Psychiatric Society; American Medical Association, etc. *Publications:* Medical School Course Syllabi, 1979-84; Videocassettes: 'Slow Death', 1978, 'An Adolescent Copes with Cancer' 1979, 'A Family Copes with Malignant Uncertainty', 1979, 'The Mourning Process', 1979 (HECSA Award of Merit, 1980); articles in scientific journals. *Honours:* Alpha Omega Alpha, 1955; Certification, American Board of Psychiatry and Neurology, 1973; Fellow, American Psychiatric Association, 1976, etc. *Hobbies:* Swimming; Snorkeling; Scuba Diving. *Address:* 1402 South Grand Avenue, St. Louis, MO 63104, USA.

KITTLE, C Frederick, b. 24 Oct. 1921, Athens, Ohio, USA. Professor of Surgery; Director of Section of Thoracic Surgery; Director, Cancer Centre. m. 1) Jeane Groenier, 1945, 2 sons, 2 daughters. 2) Ann C Bates, May 1971. *Education:* BA, Ohio University; MD, University of Chicago, Illinois; KS, University of Kansas; LLD, Ohio University. *Appointments:* Associate Professor of Surgery, University of Kansas Medical School; Professor of Surgery,

University of Chicago,Illinois; Currently, Professor of Surgery, and Director, Rush Cancer Center, Rush Presbyterian St Luke's Medical Center. *Memberships:* American Association of Thoracic Surgery; American College of Surgeons; American Surgical Association; International Cardiovascualar Society; International Society of Surgery; Society of Clinical Surgery; Society of Surgical Oncology; Society of Thoracic Surgery; Society of University Surgeons; American Association for History of Medicine. *Publications:* Author of numerous articles on general Surgery, cardiar and thoracic surgery. *Honours:* Markle Scholar, 1953-58; Phi Beta Kappa; Alpha Omega Alpha. *Hobbies:* Arthur Conan Doyle; Back-packing. *Address:* 1725 West Harrison, Chicago, IL 60612, USA.

KJERSEM, Jens Anders, b. 8 May 1945, Aalesund, Norway. Leader of own Chiropractic Clinic. m. Judith, 2 Mar. 1974, Sykkylven, 2 sons, 1 daughter. *Education:* DC, Palmer College of Chiropractic, 1969. *Appointments:* Editor, Norwegian Chirorpractic Association's Journal, 1973-75; Treasurer, Norwegian Chiropractic Association, 1981-86. *Memberships:* Norwegian Chiropractic Association; European Chiropractic Union; American Chiropractic Association; International Chiropractic Association. *Publications:* "Kiroprakrikk for pasienten" (booklet), 1971; Speaker at European Chiropractic Union's Convention, 1985; Speaker at Swedish post-graduate seminar on 'Computer Technology and Systems relating to Chiropractic Clinics', 1983. Inventor and designer of the "Tilt" chair (orthopedic chair), for correct active sitting position. *Hobbies:* Marathon Runner (Ran the London Marathon in May 1983 and raised more than N.Kr.7000 for Anglo-European Chiropractic College in Bournmouth, England; former Wrestler (Greco-Roman Style). *Address:* Einarvikgt 1, 6000 Aalesund, Norway.

KLEBER, Herbert David, b. 19 June 1934, Pittsburgh, Pennsylvania, USA. Professor of Psychiatry; Director, Substance Abuse Treatment Unit. m. Joan Fox, 9 Sept. 1956, Philadelphia, 1 son, 2 daughters. *Education:* BA cum laude with high distinction, Dartmouth College, 1956; MD, Jefferson Medical College, 1960; Lederle Research Fellowship, 1959-60; Rotating Intern, Health Care Hosptials of University of Pittsburgh, 1960-61; Psychiatric Residency, Yale University School of Medicine, 1961-64. *Appointments:* Assistant Chief, Hill-West Haven Division, 1966-67, Outpatient and Admissions Coordinator, 1967-68, Director and Founder, Drug Dependence Unit, 1968-, Connecticut Mental Health Center; Assistant Professor, 1966-70, Associate Professor, 1970-75, Professor, 1970-75, Professor, 1975-, Psychiatry, Medical School, Yale University. *Memberships:* Fellow, American Psychiatric Association; American College of Neuropsychopharmacology; Executive Committee, Committee on Problems of Drug Dependence Incorporated. *Publications:* Author or Co-author of over 120 publications contributed to professional journals including: 'Journal of Clinical Psychiatry'; 'Archives of General Psychiatry'. *Honours:* Gold Award, 1975, Foundation Fund Prize for Research in Psychiatry, 1981, American Psychiatric Association; Lapides Foundation Fund Meritorious Service Award, 1979; Board of Scientific Counsellors of the Addiction Research Center, 1982-84. *Hobby:* Swimming. *Address:* 34 Park Street, New Haven, CT 06519, USA.

KLEINBERG, Israel, b. 1 May 1930, Toronto, Canada. Professor and Chairman, Department of Oral Biology and Pathology. m. Constance Louise Sfreddo, 19 Sep 1955, Dryden, Ontario, 3 sons, 1 daughter. *Education:* DDS, University of Toronto, 1952; PhD, University of Durham, England, 1958; Fellow, Royal College of Dentists, Canada, 1969. *Appointments:* Assistant Professor, 1958-59, Associate Professor, 1959-61, Associate Professor, Oral Biology, Head,

Biochemistry, Faculty of Dentistry, 1961-65, Professor of Oral Biology, Head of Oral Biology and Biochemistry, 1965-73, University of Manitoba; Professor and Chairman, Department of Oral Biology and Pathology, School of Dental Medicine, State University of New York, Stony Brook, New York, USA, 1973-. *Memberships:* International and American Associations for Dental Research; American Society of Microbiology; Royal College of Dentists of Canada. *Publications:* "Saliva and Dental Caries", with S A Ellison and I D Mandel, 1979; Author of numerous original scientific papers contributed to professional journals and books including: 'British Dental Journal'; 'Journal of Dental Research'; 'Archives of Oral Biology'; 'Journal of Periodontal Research'; 'International Dental Journal'; 'Israel Journal of Chemistry'; 'Caries Research'; 'Calcified Tissue Research'; and numerous others. *Honours:* Canada Centennial Medal, Government of Canada, 1967; Fellow, Dental Science, Royal College of Dentists of Canada, 1969; Honorary DSc, University of Manitoba, 1983. *Hobby:* Gardening. *Address:* Department of Oral Biology and Pathology, School of Dental Medicine, Health Sciences Center, State University of New York, Stony Brook, NY 11794, USA.

KLEINER, Charlotte Antoinette, b. 12 Feb 1922, Germany. Consultation-Liaison Psychiatrist and Psychoanalyst. m. Wolfgang O Grube, 4 Sep 1949, North Bergen, New Jersey, USA, 1 son, 3 daughters. *Education:* BA, Washington Square College, New York University; MD, New York University College of Medicine, 1945. *Appointments:* Internship, Pathology Residency, Newark City Hospital, New Jersey; Internal Medicine Residency, New York Infirmary for Women; Intensive post-graduate OB Training, Margaret Hague Hospital, Jersey City; General practice of Medicine; School Physician; Psychiatric residency and Psychoanalytic training; Inpatient ward attending, Inpatient Ward Chief, Metropolitan Hospital. *Memberships:* Society for Consultation-Liaison Psychiatry; Burgen County, New Jersey Medical Society; New Jersey branch, American Psychiatric Association; American Academy of Psychoanalysis; Academy of Medical Psychoanalysts; AOA of New York University. *Hobbies:* Music; Playing piano; Boating - active in US Coast Guard Auxiliary; Gardening; Cooking; Reading. *Address:* 350 Summit Avenue, Leonia, NJ 07605, USA.

KLEPPE, Geir, b. 7 Dec. 1950, Oslo, Norway. Registrar in Plastic Surgery, Haukeland sykehus, Bargen. m. Mariana Burmester, 11 Nov. 1978, Quinta do Malpique, Santarem, Portugal, 1 son, 2 daughters. *Education:* MD, Faculty of Medicine, Oporto, 1970-77; Additional course foreign medical students, Oslo, 1977. *Appointments:* Training in Surgery and Medicine, Vestfold Sentralsykehus, 1978-79; Supervised training in general practice, Sand Suldal – 1980; Registrar in Surgery, Ulleval sykehus, 1980-83; Interrupted as ship surgeon on board Royal Viking Sea in 1981; Registrar in Plastic Surgery, Telemark Sentralsykehus Skien, 1983; Registrar, General Surgery, 1984; Registrar in Plastic Surgery, Haukeland sykehus, Department of Plastic and Reconstructive Surgery, 1984-. *Memberships:* Portuguese Medical Association Ordem dos Medicos de Portugal; Norwegian Medical Association Den Norske Legeforening; Norwegian Plastic Surgery Society; International Society for Burns Injuries. *Hobbies:* Jogging; English Classic Cars. *Address:* Forstander-smuget 8, 5000 Bergen, Norway.

KILMAN, Gilbert Wallace, b. 14 Dec 1929, Brooklyn, New York, USA, m. Nancy Berezin, 15 Feb 1981, Nassau, Bahamas, 2 sons, 2 daughters. *Education:* MD, Harvard Medical School, Boston, Mass, 1953; BA, University of Cincinnati, Ohio, 1949; Internship, University California Medical School, San Francisco, Calif, 1953-54. *Appointments:* Chief, Psychiatry and

Neurology, United States Naval Hospital, Bainbridge, MD, 1955-67; Consultant, Windward School, NJ, 1957-59; Founder and Medical Director, The Centre for Preventive Psychiatry, NY, 1965-79; Consultant, Children's Television Workshop, NY, 1976; Consultant, Centre for Preventive Psychiatry, NY, 1979; Founder, Editor-in-chief, Journal of Preventive Psychiatry, 1981-; Lecturer, 1983-, Associate Clinical Professor, Columbia Division of Child Psychiatry, NY; Director, Foster Care Unit, Columbia Univeristy College of Physicians and Surgeons, 1984-. *Memberships:* American Acadmey of Psychiatry and the Law; American Psychoanalytic Association; Fellow, American Acadmey of Child Psychiatry; Fellow, American Psychiatric Association; Westchester Psychoanalytic Association; Association for Child Psychoanalysis; Foundation of Thanatology; Westchester Medical Society; Westchester Psychiatric Society; Social Issues Committee, American Psychoanaltic Association, 1976-83; Prevention Committee American Academy of Child Psychiatry, 1983-; Committee for Establishing a Training Programme, Westchester Psychoanalytic Society, 1978-82; Executive Committee, 1965-78, Planning Committee, 1970-79, The Centre for Preventive Psychiatry. *Publications:* Author of numerous articles and papers; 'Children and the Death of a President', (with Martha Wofstein, editor), 1965; 'Psychological Emergencies of Childhood', 1968; 'The Open FamilySeries', (with Sarsah Bonnett Stein, Consultant Editor), 1974; 'Responsible Parenthood: The Child's Psyche Through The Six Year Pregnancy', 1980; 'The Journal of Preventive Psychiatry', Vol I, 1983, Vol II, 1983-84; 'Preventive Mental Health Services for Children Entering Foster Family Care', (with M Harris Schaeffer, M Friedman), 1984. *Address:* 555 Westchester Avenue, Rye Brook, NY 10573, USA.

KLIMEK, Rudolf, b. 12 Dec 1932, Krakow, Poland. Professor of Obstetrics and Gynaecology. m. Ewa Kownacka-Klimek, 21 Apr 1961, Krakow, Poland, 1 son. *Education:* Physician-Diploma with Distinction, 1955, MD 1961, PhD Obstetrics & Gynaecology, 1964, Extraordinary Professor of Medicine, 1972, Ordinary Professor of Medicine 1980, Copernicus University Medical School. *Appointments:* Assistant, Senior Assistant, Department of Biochemistry, 1952-57, Senior Assistant, Department of Obstetrics & Gynaecology, 1957-64, Head, Central Endocrine Laboratories, 1965-69, Assistant Professor, Associate Professor, 1967-69, Head of Endocrinology Department, 1969-, Chairman, Director of Obstetrics & Gynaecology Department, 1969-, all Copernicus University Medical School, Krakow. *Memberships:* Scientific Board, International Federation of Obstetrics & Gynaecologists; Scientific Board, Polish Health Ministry; New York Academy of Sciences; American Association for the Advancement of Science; American Fertility Society; International Society for Biochemical Pharmacology; Society of Magnetic Resonance in Medicine; All-Union & Hungarian Gynaecological Society; Polish Society for Biochemistry, Gynaecology & Endocrinology. *Publications:* "Oxytocin and its analogues", 1964; "Clinical Neuroendocrinology", 1972; "Clinical Sexology", 1974, 1978; "High-risk Pregnancy", 1978, 1984; "Gynaecology", 1977, 1982; "Cancer: Cause, Predisposing factors & Host-defence", 1985; "Infertility-cured or not", 1977, 1981, 1985; Over 250 articles in professional & medical journals. *Honours:* Medal for Exemplary Services, 1969; Individual 1st Grade Awards, Polish Health Ministry, 1972, 1976, 1977; Bachelor's Cross of the Order of Polonia Restituta, 1975; Gold Medal of Krakow City, 1978. *Hobbies:* Polish Highlanders Folklore; Tourism. *Address:* Sebastiana 10/3, 31-049 Krakow, Poland.

KLINE, Howard Jay, b. 5 Nov 1932, White Plains, New York, USA. Clinical Professor of Medicine, 2 sons. *Education:* MD; NIH Fellowship in Cardiology; FACP; FACC. *Appointments:* Assistant Professor of

Medicine, Research Assistant in Cardiology 1962-67, Mount Sinai Hospital and Medical Centre; Chief of Cardiology, Valley Forge General Hospital, Lt Colonel US Army Medical Corps, 1967. *Memberships:* Fellow, American College of Cardiology; Fellow, American College of Physicians; Fellow, Council on Clinical Cardiology, American Heart Association; Fellow, American College of Chest Physicians. *Publications:* 'Mechanical Increase of Vascular Resistence in Experimental Myocardial Infarction with Shock', 1966; 'Thermodynamic metabolic effects of Hypervaric Rejection', 1970; Numerous articles in Cardiology journals. *Honours:* Gold Medal, Nihon University School of Medicine, Tokyo, Japan, 1984; Visiting Professor. *Hobbies:* Reading; Painting; Running; Skiing; Backpacking. *Address:* 2100 Webster Street, Suite 518, San Francisco, CA 94115, USA.

KLINE, John Andrew, b. 2 Jan 1930, Lancaster, Pennsylvania, USA. Chairman, Department of Pathology, Grim-Smith Hospital, Kirksville, Missouri. m. (1) Gloria Ziliak, 13 June 1955, Philadelphia; (2) Jane Ann Moore, 27 July 1974, Kirksville, Missouri, 2 sons, 1 daughter. *Education:* BS, Franklin and Marshall College, Pennsylvania; DO, Philadelphia College of Osteopathy; Residency in Pathology, Osteopathic Hospital of Maine, Portland; Flint Osteopathic Hospital, Michigan ; Certified American Osteopathic Board of Pathology (Anatomic Pathology and Laboratory Medicine). *Appointments:* Assistant Professor of Pathology, Chicago College of Osteopathic Medicine; Chairman, Department of Pathology, Waterville Osteopathic Hospital, Maine; Chairman, Department of Pathology, Grand Rapids Osteopathic Hospital, Michigan; Professor and Chairman, Department of Pathology, Kirksville College of Osteopathic Medicine; Several Public positions including: Member, Missouri Mental Health Commission, 1982-. *Memberships:* US-Canadian Division of International Academy of Pathology; Member of Board of Members, American Registry of Pathology (Armed Forces Institute of Pathology, Bethesda, Maryland); American Osteopathic Association; Missouri Association of Osteopathic Physicians and Surgeons; Northeast Missouri Association of Osteopathic Physician and Surgeons; American Osteopathic College of Pathologists (Past President). *Publications:* Contributor to various professional journals. *Honours:* Citizen of the Year, Kent County Association for Retarded Citizens, 1972; Citizen of the Year, Michigan Council for Exceptional Children, 1972. *Hobbies:* Creating Trees from semi-precious Gems; Woodcarving; Canoeing. *Address:* 3 Woodland Lane, Kirksville, MO 63501, USA.

KLINE, Michael James, b. 18 Feb 1949, USA, President, College of Natural Therapies, Chiropractor and Naturopathic physician, m. Kathleen Elizabeth Murphy, 14 Dec 1974, Kansas City, Missouri, USA, 1 son. *Education:* Geneva College, 1967-69; Lincoln College of Chiropractics, 1969-70; Canadian Memorial Chiropractic College, 1970-72; Palmer Chiropractic College, 1972; DC, Cleveland Chiropractic College, 1972-74; ND, Institute of Drugless Therapies. *Appointments:* Associate Doctor, Fore Clinic, Lenexa, Kansas; Director, Overland Park Clinic; Associate Doctor, The Havana Clinic, Denver, Colorado; Director, Back Pain Relief Centre, Kansas City, Miss. *Memberships:* Board of Directors, National Board of Massage Examiners; Missouri State Chiropractic Association District II; Guild of Drugless Practitioners. *Publications:* 'Referred Visceral Pain - A Clinical Diagnostic Aid', 1983; 'The Essentials of Massage', 1985. *Honours:* Diplomate, National Board of Chiropractic Examiners, 1974; Certificate of Registration, Canadian Chiropractc Examining Board, 1974; Licences, Missouri, Hawaii, Colorado, Kansas. *Hobbies:* Martial Arts; Chess; Swimming; Reading. *Address:* Suite No 113 Doctors Building East, 751 East 63rd Street, Kansas City, MO, 64110, USA.

KLING, Suzanne K., b. 11 Sep. 1918, Budapest, Hungary. Private Practice; Assistant Clinical Professor. m. William Kling, 28 June 1940, New York, USA, 2 sons, 1 daughter. *Education:* BA, Smith College, Northampton, USA, 1940; MD, George Washington University, 1943; Graduate, British Institute of Psychoanalysis, London, England, 1953; Certification, Psychoanalysis, American Psychoanalytic Association. *Appointments:* Private Practice; Assistant Clinical Professor, Psychiatry, Georgetown University School of Medicine. *Memberships:* American Psychoanalytic Association; British Psychoanalytic Society; Baltimore District of Columbia Society for Psychoanalysis; American Psychiatric Association; American Medical Association; Medical Society of District of Columbia; American Medical Womens' Association; Washington Psychiatric Society. *Hobbies:* Swimming; Reading; Theatre; Films; Dance; Cookery. *Address:* 1616-18th St. N.W., Washington, DC 20009, USA.

KLINNER, Werner Wenzel Franz Bruno, b. 28 Nov 1923, Neudorf, Federal Republic of Germany. University Professor of Cardiac Surgery. *Education:* Study of Medicine, University Breslau and Marburg, 1942-49; MD, 1949; Doctor's Degree, 1950. *Appointments:* Cardiac Surgery staff 1958, Assistant Professor of Surgery 1961, Associate Professor of Surgery 1967, Head of Department of Cardiac Surgery 1971, University of Munich. *Memberships:* German Society of Surgeons; German Society of Thoracic and Cardiovascular Surgeons; Pan Pacific Surgical Association; Fellow, American College of Surgeons; Corresponding member, Peruvian Society of Cardiology; Society of Thoracic Surgeons; American Heart Association Council on Cardiovascular Surgery; Honorary memberships: Polish Society of Surgeons; Austrian Society of Surgeons; Medical Society of Thessaloniki. *Publications include:* 189 publications mostly concerning cardiac surgery including: "Tetralogy of Fallot", 1969 and 1982; "Textbook of Surgery", editor, 1978. *Honours:* Silver Medal pro meritis, University of Graz, Austria, 1962; Bayerischer Verdienstorden, 1981; Honorary Doctor of Medicine, University of Wroclaw, Poland, 1983. *Hobby:* Fishing. *Address:* Herzchirurgische Klinik, Klinikum Grossadern, MarchioniniStrasse 15, D 8000 Munich 70, Federal Republic of Germany.

KLOPPER, Ralph Maurice, b. 6 Sept. 1935, Kansas City, Missouri, USA. Psychiatrist. m. Ruth Friedman, 2 sons. *Education:* BA, 1957, MD, 1961, University of Missouri. *Appointments:* Staff Psychiatrist, Keesler Air Force Base, Biloxi, Mississippi, US Air Force, 1965-67; Unit Chief, Georgia Mental Health Institute, 1967-72; Clinical Assistant Professor, Psychiatry, Department of Psychiatry, 1967-, Instructor, Psychoanalysis, School of Psychoanalytic Medicine, 1974-, Emory University, Atlanta; Consultant, Atlanta Regional Hospital, 1971-72; Lecturer, Atlanta Psychoanalytic Society, 1974-; Examiner, Psychiatry, American Board of Psychiatry, 1980. *Memberships:* Medical Associations of Georgia and Atlanta; Atlanta Psychoanalytic Society; American Psychoanalytic Association. *Hobbies:* Jogging; Golf. *Address:* 456 East Paces Ferry Road North East, Atlanta, GA 30305, USA.

KLOTZ, Marvin David, b. 24 Nov. 1935, Toronto, Canada. Paedodontist. m. Susan Alberta, 30 Aug. 1968, Toronto, 2 sons, 1 daughter. *Education:* DDS, University of Toronto, 1960; MS, Northwestern University, 1964; FRCD(C), Toronto, 1967; FICD, 1984. *Appointments:* President, Ontario Society of Paedodontists, 1967; Board of Governors, Ontario Dental Association, 1968-74; Chairman, ODA Public Relations Committe, 1970-72; Chairman, ODA Communications Committee 1973-75; Editor, ODA, 1978-81; Editorial Committee, Canadian Dental Association, 1980-86; Editor, Canadian Society of Dentistry for Children; Editor, Ontario Society for Preventive Dentistry; Editor, DATA, Faculty of Dentistry, University of Toronto. *Memberships:* Ontario Dental Association; Canadian Dental Association; Alpha Omega; Pierre Fouchard; American Academy of Pediatric Dentistry;' Canadian Academy of Pediatric Dentistry. *Publications:* "Corticosteroids in experimental pulp injection", thesis, Northwestern University, Chicago, 1964; Contributor of articles to professional journals. *Honours:* FICD, 1984; Pierre Fouchard, 1984. *Hobbies:* Skiing; Cycling; Tennis; Sailing; Golf; Music; Hi-Fi; Writing Humour Columns. *Address:* Suite 403, 4800 Leslie Street, Willowdale, Ontario, Canada MLJ 3KG.

KLÖTZER, Walter T, b. 13 Feb 1932, Neuss, Germany. University Professor/Head of Prosthodontic Department. m. Sibyulle Klotzer-Vierhub, 1967, 1 son. *Education:* Zahnarzt, 1955, Doctor of Dental Medicine, 1959, Physician, 1965, Doctor of Medicine, 1968, Habilitation in Dental Medicine, 1972, University of Tubingen; Professor 1973, Professor apl, 1975, Full Professor, Chairman and Head Prosthetic Department, 1976, University of Marburg. *Appointments:* Department for Prosthetics and Dental Materials, Munchen, 1955-67; Department for Crown and Bridges and Dental Materials, Zürich, Switzerland, 1967-69; School of Dental Medicine, Biomaterials, General Dentistry, Hartford, Connecticut, USA, 1969-70; Department of Prosthetic Dentistry and Dental Materials and Department of Restorative Dentistry and Biomaterials, Tübingen, Germany, 1970-76; Full Professor and Head of Prosthodontic Department, University of Marburg 1976-. *Memberships include:* German Prosthodontic Association; German Dental Association; American Dental Association; International Association for Dental Restoration; European Prosthodontic Association; Federation of Dentistry International; Chicago Dental Society. *Publications:* Around 50 printed papers and textbook chapters; also around 100 papers presented in Austria, Australia, Bahamas, Belgium, Brazil, England, Finland, France, Germany, Hong Kong, Mexico, Netherlands, Switzerland, Turkey and USA. *Address:* Klinik und Poliklinik fur Zahn -, Mung- und Kieferkrankheiten der Universität Marburg, Georg-Voight-Strasse 3, D-3550 Marburg 1, Federal Republic of Germany.

KLUG, Margarita Cochran, b. 20 Jan. 1941, New York City, USA. Consultant, Psychiatric Occupational Therapy. m. Donald Klug, 27 Apr. 1974, Cambridge, Massachusetts, 2 daughters. *Education:* BS, Occupational Therapy, Tufts University, 1963. *Appointments:* Staff Occupational Therapist, 1963-68, Director, Psychiatric Occupational Therapy, 1968-74, Massachusetts Mental Health Center, Boston; Director, Psychiatric Occupational and Recreational Therapy Department, St. Lukes Hospital, New York City, 1974-77; Consultant, Psychiatric Occupational Therapy, St. Lukes/Roosevelt Hospital, New York City, 1978-85; New York State Regional Research Liaison for The American Occupational Therapy Foundation, 1985-. *Memberships:* American Occupational Therapy Association, Fellow; New York State Occupational Therapy Association. *Hobbies:* Photography; Tennis; Stenciling. *Address:* Bushnell Road, Chatham, NY 12037, USA.

KLYMAN, Cassandra M, b. 1 Jan 1938, New York City, New York, USA, Private practitioner, Assistant Clinical Professor, Psychiatry, Wayne State University. m. Calvin Klyman, 26 June 1960, New York, USA, 2 sons. *Education:* Graduate, Michigan Psychoanalytic Institute, 1977; MD; FAPA. *Appointments:* Chair, Female Sexuality Study Group, 1977-80, Chair, Cont Ed Committe, 1980-86, chair, Legislative Committee, 1983-86, Michigan Psychoanalytic Society. *Memberships;* American Psychoanlytic Society; American Psychiatric Association; AMA; Michigan Psychoanalytic Society; Michigan Psychiatric Society. *Publication:*

'An Operatic Accompaniment to an Analysis;', 1980; 'Communtiy Parental Surrogates Role for Adolescent Devleopment', 1985. *Honours:* Outstanding Teacher, Sinai Hospital, 1975; Fellow, American Psych Association 12979; Service to Michigan Psychiatry, Michigan Psychiatric Society, 1985. *Hobbies:* Tennis; Travel; Art. *Address:* 3060 Chickering Lane, Bloomfield Hills, MI Y8013, USA.

KNAPP, Raymond Walter, b. 19 Apr 1948, Sterling, Illinois, USA. Chiropractic Physician. m. Raye Fletcher Knapp, 8 Sep 1973, Monmouth, Illinois, 1 son. *Education:* AA, Sauk Valley College; BS, Northern Illinois University; Doctor of Chiropractic, Palmer College of Chiropractic. *Appointments:* Chairman, Education Committee, Chiropractic Association of Oklahoma; Chairman, March of Dimes. *Memberships:* Educational Chairman, Executive Council member, Fellowship of Chiropractic Physicians; International Academy of Neurovascular disease; Council on Chiropractic Orthopedics; American Chiropractic Association. *Publication:* "Diagnosis and the Medical Examiner", 1982. *Honours:* Honorary member, Belle Starr Gang, 1981; Century member, Boy Scouts of America, 1983-84; Clinic Excellence, 1983, 1984 and 1985. *Hobbies:* Bike Riding; Horse back riding; Flying; Fishing; Riflery; Weight Lifting. *Address:* 201 West Main, Wilburton, OK 74578, USA.

KNIGHT, Andrew David Eric, b. 22 Sep. 1930, New Zealand, Director/Proproetor, Kings Park Medical Laboratory, m. Vivi Sepp, 22 Jan. 1964, Christchurch, New Zealand, 3 daughters. *Education:* MB, ChB, University of New Zealand, 1961; FRCPA, Sydney, Australia, 1966. *Appointments:* Waikato Hospital, 1962-63; Christchurch Hospital, 1964; Alfred Hospital, Melbourne, Australia, 1965-66. *Hobbies:* Computer science; Pistol shooting. *Address:* AMA House, 8 Kings Park Road, West Perth, Western Australia 6005.

KNIGHT, Bernard Henry, b. 3 May 1931 Cardiff, Wales, Professor. .m. Jean Gwenllian Ogborne, 11 June 1955, Swansea, 1 son. *Education:* MB.BCh, Wales, 1954; MD, Wales, 1966; MRCPath, 1964; FRCPath, 1976; DMJ Path, 1966; MRCP, 1984; Barrister, Gray's Inn, 1967. *Appointments:* House Surgeon, Cardiff Royal Infirmary; House Physician, Swansea General Hospital; SHO, Pathology, United Cardiff Hospitals; Captain, RAMC, Junior Specialist in Pathology, Malaya; Lecturer, Forensic Medicine, London Hospital, Welsh National School of Medicine; Senior Lecturer; Reader, Professor, Forensic Pathology, University of Wales College of Medicine; Professor, Forensic Pathology, Home Office Pathologist. *Memberships:* BMA; British Association Forensic Medicine; International Academy of Legal & Social Medicine, Vice President; Forensic Science Society; Finnish Forensic Medicine Society; International Study Group in Sudden Natural Death; Crime Writers Association. *Publications:* "Legal Aspects of Medical Practice", 3rd edition 1982; "Coroners Autopsy", 1983; "Pocket Atlas of Forensic Medicine", 1985; "Sudden Infant Death", 1983; "Postmortem Technicians Handbook", 1984; "Laywers Handbook of Forensic Medicine", 1983; etc.; 150 articles. *Honours:* 1984 Oddfellows Literary Prize for Book on Cot Death; University of Helsinki Medal for Forensic Medicine, 1978. *Hobbies:* Writing Crime & Historical Novels, Biography, Radio and TV Drama and Documentaries. *Address:* Institute of Pathology, Royal Infirmary, Cardiff CF 2 1SZ, Wales.

KNIGHT, Geoffrey MacDonald, b. 5 May 1946, Sydney, Australia. Dental Practitioner. m. Sinikka Virtanen, 11 Jan 1975, Tampere, Finland, 3 sons. *Memberships:* Australian Dental Association; Australian Society of Periodontology; British Society of Periodontology. *Publications:* "The Effects of Hormonal Contraceptives on the Human Periodontium Journal of Periodontal Research", co-author; "The use of adhesive materials in the conservative restoration of selected posterior teeth", 'Australian Dental Journal', 1984. *Hobbies:* Sailing; Skiing; Running. *Address:* 20 Carpenter Street, Middle Brighton, Victoria 3186, Australia.

KNIGHT, Irving A., b. 3 Jan. 1922, Chicago, Illinois, USA. Medical Doctor. m. Helen, 26 Jan. 1947, Chicago, 2 daughters. *Education:* BS, MD, University of Illinois. *Appointments include:* Assistant Professor of Surgery, University of California. *Memberships:* American Board of Surgery; American College of Surgeons; American Society of Clinical Oncology. *Publications include:* 'Evidence for & Against Wide Local Excision for Breast Cancer' (Contemporary Surgery, 1973); 'Partial Mastectomy for Breast Carcinoma: A Personal Approach' (California Cancer Journal, 1980); 'Letter of Information for Breast Cancer Patients' (Breast, 1983). *Hobbies:* Tennis; Golf. *Address:* 433 No Camden Drive 1177, Beverly Hills, CA 90210, USA.

KNIGHT, James Allen, b. 20 Oct. 1918, St. George, South Carolina, USA. Professor of Psychiatry, Louisiana State University School of Medicine in New Orleans. *Education:* AB, Woodford College, South Carolina, 1941; BD, Duke University Divinity School, 1944; MD, Vanderbilt University School of Medicine, 1952; MPH, Tulane University School of Medicine, 1962; various other Univerisities. *Appointments incldue:* Assistant in Psychiatry, Tulane University School of Medicine, 1955-57; Instructor, 1957-58; Assistant Professor Psychiatry, 1958-61; Assistant Dean, 1960-61; Baylor University College of Medicine; Associate Professor of Psychiatry and Preventive Medicine, 1961-63; Director, Section on Community Psychiatry, 1961-63; Tulane University; Director, Program in Psychiatry and Religion, Union Therological Seminary, New York, 1963-64; Professor of Psychiatry, Tulane University, 1964-74; Dean and Professor of Psychiatry, Texas A & M University, 1974-77; Professor of Psychiatry, Louisiana State University, New Orleans, 1977-. *Memberships:* Member several professional and honorary societies including; American Academy of Psychoanalysis; American Osler Society, Blue Key; Delta Omega; Phi Beta Kappa. *Publications:* Contributor to professioanl journals; Chapters in Books; Books include: "A Psychiatrist Looks at Religion and Health", 1964; "For Love of Money", 1968; "Conscience and Guilt", 1969; "Medical Student: Doctor in the Making", 1973, revised edition, 1981; "Doctor-to-be: Coping with the Trials and Triumphs of Medical School", 1981. *Honours:* Most Outstanding Clinical Professor Award, Louisiana State University School of Medicine, Graduating Class 1979; The John P. McGovern Award Lecture in the Medical Humanities, UTMB, Galverston, Texas, 1983. *Address:* 7450 Pearl Street, New Orleans, LA 70118, USA.

KNIGHT, John James, b. 10 Sep. 1920, London, England, Honorary Consulting Physicist, Royal National Throat, Nose & Ear Hospital. m. Julie Doris Smith, 2 Feb. 1952, Ealing, 1 daughter. *Education:* BSc., Honours, ARCS, Imperial College, London, 1941; Postgraduate Research, Ultrasonics, 1946-49; ibid; PhD, Physics (Auditory Hazards), Kings College Hospital Medical School, London, 1962. *Appointments include:* Commission, Royal Air Force, 1941-46; Physicist, Deafness Aid Clinic, Royal National TN&E Hospital, 1949-53; Member, Scientific staff, M.R.C Wernher Research Unit on Deafness, King's College Hospital Medical School, 1953-64; Physicist, Institute of Laryngology & Otology, University of London, 1964-85; Honorary Consulting Physicist, Royal National TN&E Hospital, 1974-. *Memberships:* Fellow, Institute of Physics; Fellow, Institute of Acoustics; Hospital Physicists Association; Founder member, British Society of Audiology. DHSS Advisory Committees on

Audiology, 1970-82; Hearing Aid Council, 1975-81; BSI & IEC Committees on Acoustics, Noise, Medical Ultrasonics, current. *Publications include:* Over 100 papers & textbook chapters, acoustics, noise, hearing loss, hearing aids, diagnostic procedures in audiology. *Honour:* Member, Order of British Empire (OBE), 1984. *Hobbies:* Dogs; Horticulture; Photography. *Address:* Royal National Throat, Nose & Ear Hospital, 330 Gray's Inn Road, London WC1X 8DA, England.

KNISELY, William Hagerman, b. 3 Feb. 1922, Houghton, Michigan, USA. Professor of Anatomical Sciences; Executive Associate Dean, College of Medicine; Associate Dean, Graduate College. m. Marguerite Marie Labasse, 18 Jan. 1947, Orange, New Jersey, 3 sons, 2 daughters. *Education:* PhD; MS; BS; PhB; Litt D; LHD. *Appointments include:* Teaching Assistant, Anatomy, Medical College, South Carolina, 1951-54; Instructor, 1954-56, Assistant Professor, 1957, Associate Professor, Anatomy, Assistant Professor, Medicine, 1958-59, Duke University; Vice Chancellor, Health Affairs, Texas University System, 1970-75; President, 1975-82, Distinguished University Professor, 1982, Medical University, South Carolina; Professor, Anatomical Sciences, 1982-, Executive Associate Dean, College of Medicine, 1982-, Associate Dean, Graduate College Health Sciences Center, 1982-, Acting Dean, 1983, University of Oklahoma. *Memberships include:* Fellow, Royal Microscropical Society, England; American Association of Anatomists; Microcirculatory Society; Human Biology Society, Oxford, England; Sigma Xi, USA; American Association for History of Medicine. *Publications:* Co-Author: Report to the Coordinating Board, Texas College and University System, 1974; contribution to 'American Heart Journal', 1957. *Honours:* Sesquicentennial Distinguished Alumnis Award, Medical University, South Carolina, 1974; Honorary Member, Dallas Southern Clinical Society, 1972; Honorary Member, American Dietetic Association, 1976, Alpha Omega Alpha, 1978; Established W H Knieely Award for top student in Anatomy, University of Kentucky, 1981. *Hobbies:* Reading; Polishing stones. *Address:* 12413 Arrowhead Terrace, Oklahoma City, OK 73120, USA.

KNOBLOCH, Ferdinand Jiri, b. 15 Aug. 1916, Prague, Czechoslovakia. University Professor. m. (1) Zuzana Hartman, deceased, Auchwitz Concentration Camp, 1944; m. (2) Dr. Jirina Skorkovska, 5 Sept. 1947, Prague, Czechoslovakia, 2 daughters. *Education:* MD, Charles University, Prague, 1945, Med.Sc.C. 1957; Fellow, American Academy of Psychoanalysis, 1968; FRCP, Canada, 1970. *Appointments:* Teaching Fellow, Department of Psychiatry, Charles University, Prague, 1949-61; Assistant Professor, 1961-65; Associate Professor, 1965-70; Visiting Professor, University of Illinois, USA, 1968-69; Columbia University, New York, USA, 1969; Albert Einstein Medical College, 1969-70; Assosciate Professor, University of British Columbia, Canada, 1970-71, Professor, 1971-. *Memberships:* World Psychiatric Association; Psychotherapeutic Section Vice Chairman; Canadian Psychiatric Association; American Psychiatric Association, Fellow; American Group Psychotherapeutic Association, Fellow; American Academy of Psychoanalysis, Fellow; Canadian Society for Integrated Psychotherapy and Psychoanalysis, President. *Publications:* Contribution to the 'Technique of Family Psychotherapy', 1954 (in Czech); 'On the theory of a Therapeutic Community for Neurotics' in 'International Journal of Group Psychotherapy', USA, 1960; "Forensic Psychiatry", Orbis, Prague, 1957/65 (in Czech); "Integrated Psychotherapy", New York, 1979, Translated into German 1983, Japanese, 1984. *Honours:* Prize of the Czech Medical Association for the book "Forensic Psychiatry; Hon. Director of Psychodrama, Moreno Institut, USA, 1969. *Hobbies:* Music; Windsurfing.

Address: 4137 W 12 Vancouver, British Columbia, Canada V6R 2P5.

KNOLLE, Peter, b. 5 July 1931, Gadderbaum, Germany. International Consulting President, Cappamed Incorporated, New York, USA; Institute for Medical Research, Lausanne, Switzerland. m. Gisela Bartelt, 20 Dec. 1962, Berlin, 1 son. *Education:* Chemistry, Microbiology, Medicine, University of Mainz, West Berlin, Germany; Purdue University, Lafayette, Indiana, USA; MS; PhD. *Appointments:* Post-doctoral studies, Purdue University, USA, Indiana University, USA: Assistant, Senioir Assistant, Max Planck Institute for Comp. Heredit Biology and Pathology, West Berlin; Research Associate, New York University School of Medicine, USA; Assistant Professor of Microbiology, New York University School of Medicine; Visiting Professor of Molecular Biology, Northwesternb University, Illinois, USA; Head, Chemotherapy Research, Hoffman La Roche, Basel, Switzerland; Medical Director, Head of research and Development, Scientific Coordinator, Mundipharma, Frankfurt/Limburg, German; Hote: Swiss Institute for Experimental Cancer Research, Lausanne, Switzerland. *Memberships include:* American Association for the Advancemnt of Science; American Society Microbiology; Dt.Ges Hygiene; Drug Information Association; European Academy Allergology; International Society for Burn Injuries. *Publications:* Numerous journal contributions (more than 60), editorials, commentaries since 1960; Editor of and contributor to several books. *Hobbies:* Music (cello, organ); Central American Archaeology. *Address:* Institute for Medical Research, Chemin du Pâqueret 24A, CH-1025 Saint Sulpice pr. Lausanne, Switzerland.

KNOWLING, Russell J, b. 17 Nov 1938, Auckland, New Zealand. Private practice - specialising in spine and nerve rehabilitation. m. Jane Murray, 27 June 1970, Ottawa, Ontario, Canada, 1 son. *Education:* TTC, Auckland Teacher's College, New Zealand, 1960-61; BA Sociology, York University, Toronto, Canada, 1973; DC, Palmer College of Chiropractic, Davenport, Iowa, 1978; Postgraduate studies, National College of Chiropractic. *Appointments:* School Teacher, Auckland, New Zeland, 1962-63; School Teacher, London, England, 1964-65; School Teacher, Saskatchewan, Canada, 1965-66; Librarian, Toronto Board of Education, Toronto, Canada, 1966-68; House Master, The Crescent School, Toronto, Canada, 1968-73; School Teacher, Kitchener, Ontario, 1973-75; Private practice, Belleville, Illinois, USA, 1978-79; Private practice, Wauchula, Florida, 1979-. *Memberships:* American Chiropractic Association; Florida Chiropractic Association; ACA Council on Roentgenology; ACA Council on Physiological Therapeutics; Foundation for the Advancement of Chiropractic Education; FCA Council on Orthopedics; Southwest Florida Chiropractic Society. *Honours:* Honorary Kentucky Colonel, 1964; Deacon, First Presbyterian Church. *Hobbies:* Travel; Patron, Asolo State Theatre, Sarasota; Music. *Address:* 4950 Hall Road, Orlando, FL 32817, USA.

KNUPFER, Genevieve Louise, b. 19 Mar. 1914, Düsseldorf, FRG, Consultant, Alcohol Research Group, Berkeley, California, USA, Private Practitioner, Psychiatry. m. Edward Thommen, 14 Feb 1952, New York, USA, 1 daughter. *Education:* BA, Wellesley College, Mass, USA, 1935; Licence, en Sciences Sociales, University Libre de Bruxelles, Belgium, 1936; Ma, 1938, PhD, 1946, Columbia University, NY, USA: MD, University of Rochester School of Medicine and Dentistry, Rochester, NY, 1951. *Appointments:* Intern, Bellevue Hospital, NY, 1951-52; Resident in Psychiatry, 1953-55, Staff Psychiatrist, 1971-74, V A Hospital, Menlo Park, Calif; Consultant, San Mateo County Mental Health Service, 1970-71; Medical Director, Methadone Clinic, Central Medical Centre, Santa Clara County,

1975-78; Staff Psychiatrist, Geriatric Services, Mission District, San Francisco Department of Mental Health, 1979-84; Private Practitioner, Psychiatry, Redwood City/Menlo Park, Calif, 1956-; Consultant in research, Alcohol Research Group, Medical Research Institute, Berkeley, 1979-. *Memberships:* American Psychiatric Association. *Publications include:* 'Portrait of the Underdog', 1947; 'Age, Sex and Social Class as Factors in Amount of Drinking in a Metropolitan Community', (with Robin Room), 1964; 'The Mental Health of the Unmarried', (with Walter Clark, Robin Room), 1966; 'Problems Associated with Drunkenness in Women: some research issues', 1982; 'The Risks of Drunkenness, or, Ebrietas Resurrecta: a comparison of frequent intoxication indices and of population sub-groups as to problem risks', 1984. *Hobbies:* Camping; Crossword puzzles; Swimming. *Address:* 188 Elliott Drive, Menlo Park, CA 94025, USA.

KOBAYASHI, Akio, b. 2 Jan. 1927, Japan. m. Apr. 1956, 1 son, 3 daughters. *Education:* MD; DMSC. *Appointments:* Chief, 1st Division, National Institute of Health of Japan, Parasitology Dept., 1954-70; Profesosr, Jikei University School of Medicine, 1972-. *Memberships:* President, Japanese Society of Parasitology, 1978-79; Japanese Society of Tropical Medicine; Japaneses Society of Allergology. *Publicaitons:* Contributor, "Human Ecology and Infectious Diseases", 1983; Editor, 1967-83, Chief Editor, 1984-, 'Japanese Journal of Parasitology'. *Honour:* Katsurada Prize, 1981. *Address:* 2-3-11 Sakura, Setagaya-ku, Tokyo 156, Japan.

KOBLENZER, Caroline Scott, b. 26 Sep 1929, Bolton, England. Assistant Clinical Professor of Dermatology and Dermatology-in-Psychiatry. m. Peter Johann Koblenzer, 12 May 1951, Bolton, 2 sons, 1 daughter. *Education:* 2nd MB, 1947-49, MB BS, Honours, 1949-53, Royal Free Hospital School of Medicine, University of London; Certified, American Board of Dermatology, 1968, Board of Professional Standards. American Psychoanalytic Association, 1982. *Appointments:* House Officer, Royal Free Hospital, London, 1953; Lady Medical Officer, Civil Hospital, Anglo-Egyptian Sudan, 1953-55; Consultant Physician, Civil Hospitals of Kudat and Tawau, British North Borneo, 1955-57; Rotating Intern, West Jersey Hospital, USA, 1962-63; Resident, 1964-66, Chief Resident, 1966, Dermatology Skin and Cancer Hospital, Temple University, Philadelphia, Pennsylvania; Clinical Instructor, Dermatology, Medical College of Pennsylvania, 1967-69, Skin and Cancer Hospital, Temple University, 1967-73; Assistant Clinical Professor, Dermatology, Skin and Cancer Hospital, Philadelphia, 1973-79; currently, Assistant Clinical Professor, University of Pennsylvania; Associate Faculty, Institute of Philadelphia Association for Psychoanalysis. *Memberships include:* Fellow: American Academy of Dermatology; College of Physicians of Philadelphia; Dermatology Foundation; American Medical Association; American Psychoanalytical Association; British Medical Association; International Society of Dermatology. *Publications:* Contributor of papers in: "Clinical Dermatology", 1985; "Practical Management of the Dermatologic Patient"; 'Archives of Dermatology', 1983, 85. *Hobbies:* Literature; Music; Movies; Theatre. *Address:* 1812 DeLancey Place, Philadelphia, PA 19103, USA.

KOCHENOUR, Neil Kraybill, b. 30 Apr. 1941, Lancaster, Pennsylvania, USA, Director of Division of Maternal-Foetal Medicine, UUMC, m. Edie Osborne, 22 June 1963, 1 son, 1 daughter. *Education:* BME, Graduate Assistant, Department of Psychiatry, MD, Cornell University, Ithaca, New York; Internship, Residency, University of Colorado, Denver; ABOG Certified, 1975; ACOG, Maternal-Foetal Medicine Boards, 1981. *Appointments:* Obstetrics and Gynaecology, US Army, Fort Knox, Kentucky, 1973-75; Instructor, 1975-77, Assistant Professor, department of Obstetrics and Gynaecology, 1977-78, University of Louisville; Assistant Professor, 1978-82, Associate Professor, 1982-, Department of Obstetrics and Gynaecology, Chief, Maternal-Foetal Medicine, 1978-, Adjunct Assistant Professor, Department of Paediatrics, 1980-, University of Utah. *Memberships:* ACOG; Board of Directors, 1981-, NPOA; President Elect, 1970, President, 1980-82, UPA; UOG Society; American Association of Professors of Obstetrics and Gynaecology; USMS; CAOG; SLL County Medical Society; Fellow, ACOG, 1976. *Publications:* Author of Articles in Profesional and Medical journals. *Honours:* Phi Eta Sigma, Cornell University, 1960; Pi Tau Sigma, Cornell University, 1964; Alpha Omega Alpha, Cornell University Medical college, 1969; The Gustav Seelingmannn Prize for Efficiency in Obstetrics and Gynaecology, Cornell University Medical College, 1969; Galloway Fellowship in Gyecologic Oncology, Memorial Hospital for Cancer and Allied Diseases, 1971. *Address:* Department of Obstetrics and Gynaecology, University of Utah School of Medicine, 50 North Medical Drive, Salt Lake City, UT, 84132, USA.

KOCSIS, James Howard, b. 20 June 1942, Torrington, Connecticut, USA. Associate Professor, Clinical Psychiatry, Cornell University Medical School. m. Randy Lehrer, 11 May 1984, New York, 1 son, 1 daughter. *Education:* BA, Amherst College, 1964; MD, Cornell University Medical College, 1968. *Appointments:* Assistant Professor, Psychiatry, 1977-83; Lt. LCDR, US Navy, 1970-71, Resident, Psychiatry, 1969-70, 1972-75; Instructor, Psychiatry, 1975-76. *Membership:* American Psychiatric Association. *Publications:* "Lithium in Acute Treatment of Mania", 'Handbook of Lithium Therapy', 1980; numerous articles in professional journals; 3 book chapters. *Hobby:* Tennis. *Address:* Payne Whitney Clinic, 525 East 68th Street, New York, NY 10021, USA.

KOECH, Davy Kiprotich, b. 21 Aug 1951, Kenya. Principal Research Officer. *Education:* BSc, University of Nairobi, Kenya, 1974; MS, Duquesne University, Pittsburgh, USA, 1977; PhD, University of Nairobi, 1980. *Appointments:* Research Assistant (Immunologist), Wellcome Trust Research Laboratories, Nairobi, 1974; Parasitologist/Immunologist, Ministry of Health, Kenya, 1975-80; Fulbright-Hays Scholar, Duquesne University, Pittsburgh, Departments of Medicine & Biological Chemistry, Harvard University Medical School, Boston, USA, 1976-78; Honorary Lecturer, University of Nairobi Medical School, 1981-; Senior Immunologist, Ministry of Health, Kenya, 1981-83; Head, Division of Vector-borne Diseases, Kenya, 1981-84; Director, Clinical Research Centre, 1982-84; Principal Research Officer Director, Biomedical Sciences, Research Centre, Kenya Medical Research Institute, Nairobi, Kenya. *Memberships:* East African Society of Parasitologists; British Society for Immunology; British Transplantation Society; Institute of Biology; Institute of Professional Managers. *Publications include:* "Macrophages, Lymphocytes and their Interactions in Visceral Leishmaniasis", PhD Thesis; "The Case for Clinical Immunology Laboratories in Developing Countries", 'East African Medical Journal', 1984; Co-authored numerous articles on Medical Research; Contributor of reviews, monographs, articles to professional journals and conferences. *Honours:* Presidential Award (State Investiture) of the Decoration of the 'Silver Star of Kenya', 1984; Chartered Biologist, 1984. *Address:* Kenya Medical Research Institute, PO Box 54840, Nairobi, Kenya.

KOFFMAN, David Michael, b. 30 July 1946, Erie, Pennsylvania, USA. Doctor of Chiropractic. m. Francine Herold, 2 sons. *Education:* Pre-medical Studies, Gannon College, Erie, 1962-64; BA Psychology, University of Youngstown, Ohio, 1967; Doctoral Studies, Clinical Psychology, Columbia University, New York, 1967-68; Ordination, Cantor,

Jewish Theological Seminary of America, New York, 1970; Doctor of Chiropractic, Columbia Institute of Chiropractic, New York, 1974. *Appointments:* President, David M Koffman PC, 1974-; President, Conical Corp, 1979-; President, Slipped Disc Recording Co, 1978-; Seminar Coordinator for Licence Renewal, Massachusetts Chiropractic Society, 1980-. *Memberships:* American Chiropractic Association, Councils on Neurology & Orthopaedics; Massachusetss Chiropractic Society; Foundation for Chiropractic Education & Research; Board Vice-Chairman, International Systemic Health Organisation, 1981; Vice-President, 1980-81, International Craniopathic Society; Board Chairman, Sacro Occipital Research Society International, 1981-85; Freemason, 1977; Cantor, Congregational Sons of Zion, 1975-; Director, Congregational B'nai Israel, 1977-78; Career Counsellor, Columbia Institute of Chiropractic, 1975-. *Honours:* Honorary Member, Jewish Liturgical Music Society of America, 1970-; Foundation for Chiropractic Education & Research Service Award; International Systemic Health Organisation, Founders Award; Outstanding Young Men of America, 1984. *Address:* Hampshire Chiropractic Centre, 293 Elm Street, Northampton, MA 01060, USA.

KOKOT, Franciszek, b. 24 Nov. 1929, Olesno, Silesia, Poland. Professor of Medicine. m. Malgorzata Kokot, 26 Dec. 1955, Rokitnica, 4 sons. *Education:* MD 1957, Docent 1962, Extraordinary Professor 1969, Ordinary Professor 1982, Silesian School of Medicine, Katowice. *Appointments:* Senior Assistant, Department of Pharmacology, 1953-57, Senior Assistant, 1957-62, Assistant Professor 1962-69, Extraordinanry Professor 1969-74, Head of Nephrological Clinic, 1974-, all Silesian School of Medicine Department of Internal Medicine. *Memberships:* Polish Academy of Sciences; New York Academy of Sciences; International Society of Nephrology; European Dialysis & Transplantation Society; Polish Society of Nephrology; Polish Society of Internal Medicine. *Publications:* 3500 scientific publications, more than 50 chapters in 20 medical textbooks. *Honours:* Purkyni Medal, University of Prague, Czechoslovakia; J Sniadecki Award, Polish Academy of Sciences, 1976. *Hobbies:* Bee-keeping. *Address:* Armii Czerwonej 8/162, 40-004 Katowice, Poland.

KOKOWSKI, Palma A, b. 15 Aug 1947, Beaver Fall, Pennsylvania, USA. Medical and Rehabilitation Specialist. m. Clifford, 2 Oct 1971, Emsworth, Pennsylvania, 1 daughter. *Education:* RN Diploma; CIRS. *Appointments:* Staff Nurse, South Side Hospital; Charge Nurse, Greater Pittsburgh Guild for the Blind; Field Nurse, Field Supervisor, Rehabilitation Nurse; Rehabilitation Coordinator, Upjohn Health Care Services; Medical and Rehabilitation Specialist, Champion Claim Service Incorporated. *Memberships:* Pennsylvania Association of Rehabilitation Nurses, National and Local; Pennsylvania Claims Association. *Hobbies:* Camping; Crocheting; Swimming, Other crafts. *Address:* Champion Claim Service Incorporated, Suite 205, 109 Dewalt Avenue, Pittsburgh, PA 15227, USA.

KOLB, David Allen, b. 14 May 1946, El Paso, Texas, USA; Director and Head Physician. m. Barbara Paul Carey, 3 May 1980, Austin, Texas, 1 son. *Education:* Associate in Applied Science, Odessa College, 1967; BA, University of Texas, 1971; Doctor of Chiropractic, Palmer College of Chiropractic, 1979; Certified, Acupuncturist, National College of Chiropractic, Illinois, 1983; Electroacupuncture and Homeopathic Physician, Occidental Institute of Chinese Studies, 1981, 83. *Appointments:* Computer Operator; Computer Programmer, 4 years; Director and Head Physician, Professional Healthcare Services Incorporated, Austin, Texas. *Memberships:* America, Texas and Colorado Chiropractic Associations; Travis County Chiropractic Society; International Founda-

tion for Homeopathy; Occidental Institute Research Foundation. *Publications:* Contribution of work by 1st research group published in 'Todays Health', 1972, combined work by 1st and 2nd research groups published in Maharishi International University on the comparison of reaction times after meditation to resting with eyes closed for 20 minutes, 1975. *Honours:* Graduate Magna cum laude, Pi Tau Delta, Palmer College of Chiropractic, 1979; Various awards for sport, high school and college, 1960-71; Music Scholarship, College, 1967-71. *Hobbies:* Jogging; Hiking; Swimming; Exercising; Camping; Research seminars; Good science fiction; Meditation. *Address:* Professional Healthcare Services Incorporated, 1004 West 31st Street, Austin, TX 78705, USA.

KOLBAS, Eugene Dean, b. 6 Feb. 1928, Yugoslavia. Chief of Obstetrics/Gynaecology Department, CIGNA, Region III, Los Angeles, California, USA. m. Deanna Neimar, 30 Jan, 1961, Diest, Belgium, 1 son, 2 daughters. *Education:* State College, Vukovar, Yugoslavia, 8 years; Medical School, Zagreb, 5 years; Internship, County Hospital, Vinkovci, 1 year; Residency in OB/GYN, University Hosptial, Jezero, Sarajevo, 3 years; USA Internship, Wheeling Hosptial, West Virginia; USA Residency OB/GYN, Altcona Hospital, Pennsylvania, 3 years; MD, USA Board of Certified Specialist in Obstetrics, Gynaecology and Infertility. *Appointments:* Staff OB/GYN Doctor, St. Joseph Hospital, Diest, Belgium 1960-61; Chief, OB/GYN Department M. Lousteau Hospital, Oujda, Morocco, and State Hospital, Marrakesh, Morocco, 1961-63; House Doctor, Jean Talon Hosptial, Montreal, Canada, 1963-65; Practicing OB/GYN at Ross Clinic, Merrilville, Indiana, USA, 1968-70; Practice OB/GYN, Los Angeles area, California, 1970-. *Memberships:* American Medical Association; California Medical Association; Los Angeles County Medical Association; Los Angeles OB/GYN Society; California OB/GYN Association; Los Angeles OB/GYN Society; California OB GYN Association; Fellow, American College of OB/GYN; Member, World Medical Association. *Honours:* American Medical Association Recognition Awards, 1977, 83; California Medical Association Certification for continuing medical education, 1977, 83; Advanced Sex Counseling and Therapy Certificates, University of San Francisco, 1977, 81. *Hobbies:* World Travel; Photography; Hunting; Swimming; Growing Flowers, Roses, exotic fruit trees and plants. *Address:* 3559 Ballina Canyon Road, Encino, CA 91436, USA.

KOLFF, Willem Johan, b. 14 Feb. 1911, The Netherlands. Professor of Surgery. m. Janke, 4 sons, 1 daughter. *Education:* MD, University of Leiden Medical School, Netherlands, 1938; PhD, University of Groningen, Netherlands, 1946. *Appointments:* Assistant, Pathology, Anatomy, University of Leiden, 1934-36; Assistant, Medical Department, University of Groningen, 1936-41; Head, Medical Department, Municipal Hospital, Kampen, Holland, 1941-50; Private Dozent, University of Leiden Medical School, Netherlands, 1950-51; Staff of Research Division, Cleveland Clinic Foundation, USA, 1950-63; Assistant Professor, later Professor of Clinical Investigation, Education Foundation of the Cleveland Clinic Foundation, 1950-67; Staff of Surgical Division, Cleveland Clinic Foundation, 1958-67; Scientific Director, Artificial Organs Programme, 1958-67; Professor of Surgery, Head, Division of Artificial Organs, Department of Surgery, School of Medicine, Research Professor of Engineering & Bioengineering, College of Engineering, Director, Institute for Biomedical Engineering, University of Utah; Distinguished Professor of Medicine & Surgery, University of Utah, Professor of Internal Medicine, 1981-; Adjunct Professor, Department of Surgery, Temple University, Philadelphia, 1985-. *Memberships include:* American Association for the Advancemnt of Science; American Association of University Professors; American Medical Association; American Physiological Society; American Society of Nephrology; New York Academy of Sciences; Royal Society for The Encouragement of the Arts, London, England; Sigma Xi; International Society for Heart Transplantation, 1982. *Publications:* More than 600 publications, especially in renal and artificial organ surgery, book chapters, various editorial responsiblities. *Honours;* Numerous awards & recognistions. *Hobbies:* Mountaineering; Bird-watching; Carving. *Address:* Division of Artificial Organs, 535 Dumke Building, University of Utah, Salt Lake City, UT 84112, USA.

KONDRASKE, George Vincent, b. 13 Oct. 1956, USA. Associate Professor of Electrical & Biomedical Engineering, University of Texas, Arlington. m. Linda King, 2 daughters. *Education:* BS, University of Rochester, 1978; MS, University of Texas, 1980. *Appointments:* Supervisor, Biomedical Instrumentation & Computer Laboratory, 1979-82, Director, Centre for Advanced Rehabilitation Engineering (NIHR grant)/Principal Investigator, various nationaly funded/private funded research projects, medical instrumentation, 1982-, University of Texas, Arlington. *Memberships:* Board, Centre for Computer Assistance to the Disabled; Trustee, Visiting Committee, University of Rochester; Chairman, IEEE Engineering in Medicine & Biology Society. *Publications include:* Book chapter, 'Neurophysiologic Measurements' (Biomedical Instrumentation, 1985); Journal articles, 'Disk Synchronization to increase continuous data acquisition rate', 'A microprocessor-based system for adaptable calibration & linearization of hall effect position sensors', 1985. *Honours:* Research award, Sigma Xi, 1983; Student award, biomedical engineering, UTA, 1979, 1980, 1982; Outstanding Engineer, Class of 1978, University of Rochester. *Hobbies:* Amateur radio; Piano; Cookery. *Address:* Department of Electrical Engineering, PO Box 19016, University of Texas, Arlington, TX 76019, USA.

KÖNIG, Klaus G, b. 22 Sep. 1931, Nürnberg, Germany. Professor of Preventive & Community Dentistry. *Education:* MD Dentistry, University of Würzburg, Federal Republic of Germany, 1954; PhD, University of Zürich, Switzerland, 1962. *Appointments:* Staff Member, Private Practice of Dentistry, 1954-56; Dental School, 1956-66, Associate Professor, 1966-68, 1969-, University of Zürich; Professor, Head of Department, Institute of Preventive & Community Dentistry, University of Nijmegen, Netherlands. *Memberships:* International Association for Dental Research; European Organisation for Caries Research; Corresponding Member, German Society for Oral, Dental & Jaw Medicine; Association for Dental Education in Europe. *Publications:* "Der Nürberger Stadtarzt Georg Palma 1543-91", 1961; "Karies und Karies-prophylaxe" 2nd edition 1974; "Karies und Parodontitisprophylaxe", 3rd edition, 1982; 200 scientific articles on research in dental caries, 1957-85. *Honours:* Honorary Member, Gesellschaft für Kinderstomatologie, German Demoncratic Republic 1978; Honorary Member, Royal Belgian Dental Society, 1984. *Hobby:* Mediaeval Medical History. *Address:* Faculty of Medicine & Dentistry, University of Nijmegen, P.O. Box 9101, NL-6500 HB Nijmegen, Netherlands.

KONOPINSKI, Virgil James, b. 11 July 1935, Ohio, USA. Director of Industrial Hygiene and Radiological Health. m. Joan Mary Wielinski, 27 June 1964, Toledo, Ohio, 1 son, 2 daughters. *Education:* BS, University of Toledo, 1956; MS, Pratt Institute, New York, 1960; MBA, Bowling Green State University, Bowling Green, Ohio, 1971; Registered Professional Engineer; Certified Industrial Hygienist; Certified Safety Professional. *Appointments include:* Industrial Hygienist and Contract Engineer, WB Waste Control, Tulsa, Oklahoma, 1973-75; Director, Divi-

sion of Industrial Hygiene and Radiological Health, Indiana State Board of Health, Indianapolis, Indiana, USA, 1975-. *Memberships:* American Industrial Hygiene Association; American Conference of Governmental Industrial Hygienists; American Society of Safety Engineers; US Naval Institute; Member, AIHA Finance Committee; ASSE, Indiana Section. *Publications include:* Contributions to various journals including 'Archives of Environmental Health'; 'American Industrial Hygiene Association Journal'; 'Golf Course Management'; presentations to various American and international symposiums. *Hobbies:* Fishing; Gardening; Model Building; Golf; Reading. *Address:* 60 Irongate Drive, Zionsville, IN 46077, USA.

KONOPKA, Lech-Jerzy, b. 3 Feb. 1938, Wilno, Poland. Head of Medical Department and of Isotope laboratory. m. 21 July 1960, 2 daughters. *Education:* Medical Academy, Warsaw, 1955-62; 1968; Associate Professor, 1976; Professor of Medicine, 1985. *Appointments:* Staff 1963-, Currently Head of Department of Internal Medicine and of Isotope Laboratory, Institute of Haematology, Warsaw. *Memberships:* International Society of Haematology and Transfusiology; Internationalle Gesellschaft für Chemo-Immunotherapie. *Publications:* 150 papers, 6 books and 15 chapters in books. *Hobbies:* Sport; Music. *Address:* Bonifacego 79 m 42, Warsaw, Poland.

KONRAD, Klaus, b. 22 Aug. 1942, Vienna, Austria. Professor of Dermatology. m. Edda, 15 May, 1971, Insbruck, Austria, 2 sons, 1 daughter. *Education:* Matura, 1960; MD, 1966; University Docent, 1978, Professor, 1984. *Appointments:* Professor of Dermatology, University of Vienna. *Memberships:* European Society for Dermatological Research; International Pigment Cel Society; German Dermatological Society; International Society of Dermatopathology. *Publications:* "Das Melanin Pigmentsystem der Haut", 1977. *Hobbies:* Skiing; Surfing; Mountain Climbing. *Address:* Hofzeile 21/1/3, A-1190 Vienna, Austria.

KOPER-DULAJ, Nance Lillian Irene, b. Chicago, Ill, USA. Columnist; Model; Artist. 2 sons, 1 daughter. *Education:* AA, Bogan College, 1962; Proficiency exams, Polish and Spanish Languages, Roosevelt University, 1970; BA, St Xavier College, 1970, 1982; Business Law and Commerce, Northwestern University School of Commerce, Chicago Teachers College; Diploma, School of Furniture Retailing; John Marshal Law School, 1981; Graduate, John Robert Powers Finishing and Modelling School, 1984; MBA Candidate, St Xavier College, 1984. *Appointments:* Teacher, Oak Law High School, Ill; Elementary Education, Remedial and Junior High, Queen of Martyrs School, Evergreen Park, Ill; Assistant Secretary to Financial Vice-President, Lyons Container International, 1970-73; Executive Secretary to Vice President and Patent Counsel, Velsicol Chemical Corporation, 1973-77; Evening Reservations Manager, The Drake Hotel, 1973-75; Administrative Assistant, Thomas Havey and Company, CPA's, 1977-80; Evening Reservations Manager, Ritz-Carlton Hotel, 1976-79; Paralegal/Secretary, Maher and Newman Ltd., 1980; Evening Reservation Manager, Rephael Hotel, 1980; Administative Assistant to Assistant Commissioner of Mental Health, Chicago Department of Health, 1980-82; Evening Reservation Manager, Park-Hyatt Hotel, 1981; Administrative Assistant to Commissioner of Health, Bureau of Laboratories, 1982-. *Publications:* "Legacy", 1970; "Ode to St Xavier", 1970; 'Ethnic Recipes', 1983; Has appeared in numerous stage shows and musicals. *Memberships:* American-European Student Union; City of Chicago "Executive Development Class Alumni Association"; Chicago Council on Foreign Relations; Chicago Historical Society; Chicago Plan Commission; Coalition of Polish American women; Contact/Chicago Teleministries, 1985; Galena

Chamber of Commerce; National/Illinois/Chicago Legal Secretaries Association; National Association of Female Executives. *Honours:* Outstanding Achivements Award for News Specials, 21st Chicago Emmy Awards Dinner, 1979; Continuing Legal Education Recognition Award, NALs, 1983. *Address:* 7235 South Avers Avenue, Chicago, IL 60629, USA.

KOPILOFF, George, b. 20 Jan. 1934, Argentina. Chief, Day Hospital, K Jerry L Pettis Memorial, Veterans Administration Hospital, Loma Linda, California. m. Nelly Caceres, 19 Apr. 1963, 1 son, 1 daughter. *Education:* MD; Diplomate, American Board of Psychiatry and Neurology. *Appointments:* Attending Psychiatrist, Riverside General Hosptial and Hemet Valley Hosptial. *Memberships:* American Psychiatric Association, Former Veterans Administration Physicians. *Honour:* Board Certified in Internal Medicine, Uruguay, South America. *Hobbies:* History; Geography; Politics. *Address:* 25110 Tulip Avenue, Loma Linda, CA 92354, USA.

KOPP, Claire B., b. 7 Aug. 1931, New York, USA. Adjunct Professor, Psychology, University of California, Los Angeles. m. Eugene Howard, 31 Aug. 1950, 2 sons, 1 daughter. *Education:* BS, New York University, 1951; MS, University of Southern California, 1961; PhD, Claremont Graduate School, 1970. *Appointments:* Rancho Los Amigos Hospital, 1955-57; School for Cerebral Palsied Children, Los Angeles, 1961-63; Los Angeles Children's Hospital, 1963-64; University of California, Los Angeles, 1970-. *Memberships:* American Association for the Advancement of Science; American & Western Psychology Associations. *Publications include:* 4 books, over 30 articles, over ten book chapters. *Hobbies:* Flying (private pilot); Sports. *Address:* 483 West Avenue 46, Los Angeles, CA 90065, USA.

KOPP, Sigvard Frans Otto, b. 4 Oct. 1947, Gothenburg, Sweden. Professor of Stomatogmathic Fhysiology, School of Dentistry, University of Lund, Sweden. m. Birgit, 5 May 1979, Gotheburg, 1 son, 1 daughter. *Education:* DDS; Odont.Dr. *Appointment:* Associate Professor, School of Dentistry, University of Gothenburg, Sweden. *Memberships:* International Association for the Study of Pain; Scandinavian Association for the Study of Pain; International Association of Dental Research; Society of Oral Physiology, former Store Kro Club. *Publications:* 'Topographical distribution of sulphated glycosaminoglycans in human temporomandibular joint disks', in 'Journal of Oral Pathology', 1976; 'Temporormandibular joint osteoarthrosis. A histochemical and clinical study', Thesis, University of Gothenburg, Sweden, 1977; 'Clinical microscopical and biochemical investigation of synovial fluid from temporomandibular joints', 'Scandinavian Journal of Dental Research', 1983. *Hobbies:* Sailing; Tennis. *Address:* Department of Stomatognathic Physiology, School of Dentistry, Carl Gustavs v 34, S-214 21 Malmö, Sweden.

KOPP, Torsten Pen-Ingvar, b. 16 May 1949, Boras, Sweden. Chiropractor.m. Beate Busch, 27 Dec. 1977; Oslo, Norway, 2 chilren. *Education:* DC, Anglo-European College of Chiropractic, Bournemouth, 1976. *Appointments:* Chiropractor, Simcoe Clinic, Southampton, 1976-77; Private Practice, Stockholm, 1977-82; Private Practice, Boras Sweden, 1980-; Private Practice, Alingsas, Sweden, 1982-. *Memberships:* Swedish Chiropractic Society; European Chiropractors' Union; American Chiropractic Association; Associated member, British Chiropractors'Association; Anglo-European College of Chiropractic Alumni Association. *Publications:* 'A comparative Study of Gonstead X-Ray Analysis and Movement Palpation of the Sacrolliac Joint', 1976. *Hobbies:* Literature; Art; History of Culture; Astronomy; Photography; Cars. *Address:* Österlånggatan 65, S-502 32 Borås,

Sweden.

KOPTA, Joseph Antony, b. 9 May, 1936, Boston, Massachussetts, USA. Professor and Head, Department of Orthopaedic Surgery. *Education:* BS, University of Oklahoma, USA, 1958, MD, 1962; M.Ed. University of Illinois, 1970. *Appointments:* Reserach Associate, Office of Research Medical Education, University of Illinois, Chicago USA, 1969-70; Fellowship in Medical Education, University of Illinois, 1969-70; Assistant Porfessor or Orthopaedic Surgery Washington University, St. Louis, Missouri, 1970-74, Assistant Professor of Preventive Medicine, 1972-74; Director, Irene Walter Johnson Institute of Rehabilitaiton, St. Louis, Missouri, 1972-73; Professor and Head, Department of Orthopaedic Surgery and Rehabilitation, Oklahoma University, Oklahoma City, 1974-. *Memberships:* American Acadmey of Orthopaedic Surgeons; Association of Bone and Joint Surgeons; American College of Surgeons; Orthopaedic Research Society; American Orthopaedic Association; Rocky Mountain Traumatologic Sociey. *Honours:* Alpha Omega Alpha, 1962; Vernon P. Thompson Award, Western Orthopaedic Association, 1967. *Address:* PO Box 26901, 920 Stanton L. Young Boulevard, Oklahoma City, OK 73190, USA.

KORCZAK, Director, b. 10 Mar. 1948, Weissenstadt, Federal Republic of Germany. Proprietor and Managing Director, Research Group. *Education:* Dr re pol, Diplom-Vilkswirt, University of Cologne. *Appointments:* Group Head, Psychological Research, Marplan, Offenbach, Federal Republic of Germany, 1973-74; Assistant Professor, Sociology, Research Institute of Sociology, University of Cologne, 1975-76; Head, Department for Qualitative Research, Reemtsma Company, Hamburg, 1978-79; Director, Research, in Field of Drug and Alcohol Abuse, and International Health Research, Infratest, Munich, 1980-84; Consultant, European Economic Community, 1985-; Proprietor and Managing Director, GP Research Group, 1985-. *Memberships:* Deutsche Gesell. fur Medizinsoziologie; Committee of Family Research; International Sociological Association; Berufsverband der Markt-und Sozial forscher. *Publications:* "Neue Formen des Zusammenlebens", 1978; "Ruckkehr in die Gemeinschaft", 1981; "Die betiaubte Gesellschaft", 1986; "Psychiatrie und offentliche meinung", 1983. *Hobbies:* Writing; Water sports. *Address:* GP Forschungsgruppe, Asamstr 7, D-8000 München 90, Federal Republic of Germany.

KÖRLOF, Bengt Nils Helge, b. 23 Feb. 1926, Haparanda, Sweden. Head, Department of Plastic and Reconstuctive Surgery, Karolinska Hospital, Stockholm, Sweden. m. Ulla Styrman, 21 July 1950, 1 son, 1 daughter. *Education:* Medical degrees at University of Uppsala, Sweden; Dissertation, 1956; Associate Professor of Plastic Surgery. *Appointments:* University Hospital, Uppsala; Gallivare County Hospital; University Hospital, Uppsala; Karolinska Hospital, Stockholm. *Memberships:* Member to some ten national and international associations. *Publications:* "Infection of Burns", 1956; 110 other publications. *Hobbies:* Travel; Lake Fishing. *Address:* Furusangsvägen 28, 16128 Bromma, Stockholm, Sweden.

KORMAN, Hanahh Cherie, b. 4 Feb. 1952, Kalamazoo, Michigan, USA. Administrator, alternative Rehabilitation Nursing Services Inc. *Education:* BA; Certificate, Rehabilitation Registered Nurse (CRRN). *Appointment:* Pioneer in founding professionally owned rehabilitation nursing services corporation providing home health care/case management, as well as legal consulting. *Memberships:* Association of Rehabilitation Nurses; Washington State Nurses Association; Washington Thoracic Society. *Hobbies:* Travel, US & international; Singing; Jewellery making. *Address:*

10201 65th Avenue South, Seattle, WA 98118, USA.

KORNBLUTH, Ralph Ross, b. 18 Apr. 1938, Montreal, Canada. Private Psychiatric Practice. m. Anita Dubow Kornbluth, 2 Apr. 1966, Montreal, 2 sons, 1 daughter. *Education:* BSc., 1962, MDCM, 1964, McGill University; Rotating Internship, Jewish General Hospital, Montreal, 1964-65; Residency Training Programme,Psychosomatic and Psychiatric Institute, Michael Reese Hospital & Medical Centre, Chicago, USA, 1965-68. *Appointments:* Consultant, Douglas Hospital, Verdun, Canada, 1965; Consultant, Illinois State Hospital System, 1968; Officer, Medical Corps, United States Navy, LCDR, 1968-70; Staff Psychiatrist, Portsmouth Psychiatric Centre, Virginia, USA, 1970-71. *Memberships:* American Psychiatric Association; American Physicians Fellowship; Medical Society of Virginia; Fairfax County Medical Society; Washington Psychiatric Society; American Group Psychotherapy Association; Washington Seminar in Family and Group Psychotherapy; etc. *Publications:* "A Study of Coping Behavior Exhibited in a Training Program for the Home Treatment of Hemophilia", 'Illinois Psychiatric Society Journal', 1968. *Honours:* Physicians Recognition Award, American Medical Association, 1969-72, 1979-82; Resident Award, Psychosomatic and Psychiatric Institute, 1968; Resident Award, Illinois Psychiatric Society, 1969. *Hobbies Include:* Breeding Tropical Fish; Swimming; Sports; Reading. *Address:* 8303 Arlington Blvd., Suite 297, Fairfax, VA 22031, USA.

KORTTILA, Kari, b. 11 Jan. 1948, Turku, Finland. Associate Professor of Anaesthesiology. m. Ritva Tiirikka, 28 Mar. 1970, 1 son, 1 daughter. *Education:* MD, University of Helsinki, 1972; Doctoral Thesis, Helsinki, 1975. *Appointments:* Research Assistant, 1973-76, Lecturer in Anaesthesia, 1977-78, Department of Anaesthesia & Pharmacology, University of Helsinki; Resident & Lecturer in Anaesthesia, Helsinki University Central Hospital, 1978-79; Visiting Assistant Professor & Staff, Department of Anaesthesia, University of Iowa Hospitals & Clinics, Iowa City, USA, 1979-81; Associate Professor of Clinical Anaesthesiology, University of Helsinki, 1983-; Head of Department of Anaesthesia at Departments I & II of Obstetrics & Gynaecology, Helsinki University Central Hospital, 1984-. *Memberships:* Finnish, Scandinavian, American Societies of Anaesthesiologists; Association of Anaesthetists of Great Britain & Ireland; European Academy of Anaesthesiology; International Anaesthesia Research Society. *Publications:* Over 100 articles, reviews & book chapters on anaesthesiology & Clinical pharmacology. *Hobbies:* Golf; Tennis; Slalom. *Address:* Department of Anaesthesia at Departments I & II of Obstetrics & Gynaecology, SF-00290 Helsinki, Finland.

KOSASIH, Andre, b. 28 June 1939, Jakarta, Indonesia. Head, Fixed Prosthodontics; Chairman, Indonesian Prosthodontics Society, Jakarta. m. Arsianti Winardi, 15 Oct 1961, Bandung, 2 sons. *Education:* drg; Continuing Education, Technical Prosthodontics, Ivoclar, Liechtenstein, Vita, Federal Republic of Germany, Unitek, USA. *Appointments:* Head, Dental Technology, Trisakti University, Faculty of Dentistry, 1968-79; Clinical Instructor, Crown & Bridge, Trisakti University, 1979-85; Head, Dental Materials, Trisakti University, 1968-. *Memberships:* International Dental Federation; Indonesian Dental Association; Indonesian Prosthodontic Society; Treasurer, Jakarta Branch, Indonesian Prosthodontic Society, 1978-83; Chairman, Trisakti Alumnee of Dental Surgeons, 1980-85. *Hobbies:* Tennis; Knowledge Exchange in Dental Prosthetic and Dental Materials Science. *Address:* jL Patrakumala 1, Jakarta 11430, Indonesia.

KOSBAB, F (rederic) Paul (Gustav), b. 29 Mar. 1922, Berlin, Federal Republic of Germany. Professor of Psychiatry and Behavioral Sciences. m. Marianne E Bodmann, 2 May 1951, Goettingen. *Education:* MD, Friedrich Wilhelms Universitaet, Berlin, 1945; Certified in Internal Medicine, Federal Republic of Germany Speciality Board; Diplomate, American Board of Psychiatry and Neurology Inc. *Appointments Include:* Private practice in internal medicine, Kaiserslautern, 1951-55; Unit Medical Director, Oregon State Hosptial, Salem, Oregon, USA, 1962-63; Assistant Progessor 1964-66; Associate Professor, 1966-69, Profesor 1969-73, Acting Chairman 1969-70, Associate Chairman 1970-73, Department of Psychiatry, Medical College of Virginia; Medical Director, East Plains Mental Health Centre, Nassau County New York, 1974-76; Professor of Psychiatry, Eastern Virginia Medical School, 1977-; Chief, Psychiatry Service, Veterans Administration Medical Center, Hampton, Virginia, 1977-82; Professor and Chairman, Department of Psychiatry and Behavioral Sciences, Oral Roberts University School of Medicine, 1982-; Chief, Department of Behavioral Medicine and Psychiatry, City of Faith Medical and Research Center, Tulsa, Oklahoma, 1982-. *Memberships Include:* American Medical Association; Fellow, American Psychiatric Association; Fellow, Royal Society of Medicine, London, England; Honorary Fellow, Arbeitsgemeinschaft F Katathymes Bilderleben, Federal Republic of Germany; Oklahoma State Medical Society. *Publications Include:* "Neurologie Fuer Studierende", 1948; 'Camptocormia - A Rare Case in the Female', 1961; 'A Buddy System for Hospitalized Geriatric Patients', 1962; 'Psychoanalysis and Modern Concepts in Psychotherapy', 1967; 'The Physician, The Nurse, and the Dying Patient', 1968; 'Suicide Prevention in Physicians', 1972; 'Imagery Techniques in Psychiatry', 1974. *Honour:* Virginia Commonwealth University Service Award, 1972. *Hobbies:* Boating; Amateur Radio. *Address:* Oral Roberts University School of Medicine, Medical Research Center, 8181 South Lewis Avenue, Tulsa, OK 74137, USA.

KOSCIELAK, Jerzy, b. 6 Sep. 1930, Lodz, Poland. Professor of Biochemistry. 1 daughter. *Education:* MB 1953, MD 1960, DSc/Dozent 1966, Medical Academy, Warsaw; Associate 1973, Full Professor 1982. *Appointments:* Junior Assistant, Department of Physiological Chemistry, Dental Academy, Warsaw, 1950-51; Staff 1951-, Head 1969-, Biochemistry Department, Scientific Secretary, Institute of Hematology, Warsaw; Research Fellow, Harvard Medical College, Boston, Massachusetts, USA, 1964-65. *Memberships:* Correspondent, Polish Academy of Science; International Society of Blood Transfusion; International Society of Hematology; Polish Biochemical Society; Polish Hematological Society. *Publications:* About 140 papers mainly on chemistry, biosynthesis and immunological properties of glycosphingolipids including: 'Enzymatic Sythesis of Neolactotetraosylceramide by the N-acetyllactosamine Synthase of Human serum', (with J Zielenski), 1982; 'Lactosylsphingosine-reactive Antibody and CEA in Patients With Coloractal Cancer', (with W Józwiak), 1982. *Honours:* Scientific Awards of the 6th Medical Division, Polish Academy of Science, 1965 and 1970; Special Scientific Award of the President, Polish Academy of Science and the Minister of Science, Higher Education and Technology, 2nd Congress of Polish Science, 1973; Sniadecki Award, 6th Division of Polish academy of Science, 1977; Parnas Award, Polish Biochemical Society, 1977; State Scientific Award, 1980. *Address:* Institute of Hematology, ul Chocimska 5, 00-957 Warsaw, Poland.

KOSTIAL ŠIMONOVIĆ, Krista, b. 19 Dec. 1923, Osijek, Yugoslavia. Head of Department of Mineral Metabolism. m. Ivan Šimonović, 18 July 1953, Zagreb, 1 son. *Education:* MD 1949, PhD 1955, Medical Faculty, Professorship in Faculty of Natural Sciences 1965, University of Zagreb; World Health Organisation Postgraduate Fellowship, University

College, London, England, 1952-53; IAEA, Medical Research Council Radiobiology Research Unit, Harwell, 1960-61. *Appointments:* Honorary Research Assistant, University College, London, 1952-53; Research Assistant 1950-58, Scientific Consultant/Full Professor 1964-, Head of Department of Mineral Metabolism 1964-, Deputy Director at various times 1970-, Institute for Medical Research and Occupational Health, Zagreb, Yugoslavia. *Memberships:* Physiological Society, England; American Nuclear Society; International Association of Human Biologists; Biochemical Pharmacology; Yugoslav Physiological Society; World Health Organisation Consultant. *Publications:* About 120 scientific papers in international journals. *Honours:* Decorated with State Awards for Scientific Achievements, 1965 and 1983. Rudjer Boskovic Republican Scientifc Award, 1969. *Hobbies:* Gardening; Tennis. *Address:* Amruševa 19, 41000 Zagreb, Yugoslavia.

KOSTIC, Hranimir, b. 5 Feb. 1930, Pirot, Yugoslavia. Director of Institute for Tuberculoses and Chest Diseases of Medical Faculty in Nis. m. 15 Apr. 1963, a daughter. *Education:* Specialisation of Chest Diseases; Subspecialisation of Chest Oncology Diseases; Dr.Med.Sci. *Appointments:* Chief of Chest Diseases Department in Hospital, Prokuplje; Deputy Director of Chest Diseases Clinic in Nis. *Memberships:* Chest Diseases Community, Yugoslavia; Presidnecy of Serbian Union Against Cancer; American College of Chest Physicians; International Union Against Tuberculosis. *Publications:* "Microbiology", 1964; "Rentgenologic Diagnositc of Chest Diseases", Institute of Tuberculoses and Chest Diseases, Nis, 1976; "Regional Particularities of Chest Malignity in the Region of Nis", Institute of Tuberculoses and Chest Diseases, 1982; Numerous professional books and articles in this field. *Honours:* State Ward for Special Merits against Tubercluoses; Two Award of Town Nis for Special Merits against Tubercluoses. *Hobby:* History. *Address:* Hajduk Veljkova 35/10, 18000 Nis, Yugoslavia.

KOTOULAS, Othon B, b. 18 July 1932, Athens, Greece. Professor and Chairman of the Department of Anatomy, Histology and Embryology, Medical School, University of Ioannina. m. Angeliki Sideris, MD, 22 Jan. 1961, Athens, 2 sons. *Education:* MD, National University of Athens, 1957; PhD, Pathology, McGill University, Montreal, Canada. 1970. *Appointments:* Resident, Internal Medicine, National University of Athens, 1960-63; Postdoctoral Research Trainee, Washignton University Barnes Hospitals, St. Louis, Missouri, USA, 1963-65; Resident and Graduate Student in Pathology, Barnes Hospitals, 1965-67; Clinical Fellow and Graduate Student in Pathology, Royal Victoria Hospital, McGill University, Canada, 1968-69; Senior Resident and Graduate Student in Pathology, Montreal General Hospital, 1970; Resident in Electron Microscopy and Pathologist, Alexandra Hospital, Athens, 1970-73; Lecturer, Department of Histology, National University of Athens, 1973-75; Pathologist in Veterans Hospital, Athens, 1974-75; Associate Professor, Medical School, National University of Athens, 1975-77; Professor and Chairman, Department Anatomy, Histology and Embryology, Medical School, University of Ioannina, 1977- Dean of Medical School, University of Ioannina, 1979-80; Consultant in Pathology, General Military Hospital of Athens, 1984-; Pathologist, Committee for Biomedical Research of National Health System, Greece, 1984-; Member of Board of Hellenic Public Universities Center for accridation of titles from foreign institutions, 1984-. *Memberships:* Hellenic Society of Pathology; Society for Medical Studies, Greece, Editorial Director, 1975-77; New York Academy of Sciences; Association des Anatomistes, France; Hellenic Biochemical and Biophysical Society Greece. *Publications:* Contributor to professional journals.

Hobbies: Reading; Chess. *Address:* Department of Anatomy, Histology and Embryology, Medical School, University of Ioannina 45332, Greece.

KOTTEGODA, Sri Ramachandra, b. 12 Nov. 1919, Sri Lanka. Research Professor. m. Damayanthi Rambukpota, 12 May 1950, Colombo, 2 sons, 2 daughters. *Education:* BSc., London, 1942; MBBS, Ceylon, 1947; D.Phil, Oxford, 1954; FFARCS (Eng), Conferred, 1974. *Appointments:* Medical officer, Dept. of Health, Ceylon, 1947-49; Lecturer, Senior Lecturer, 1949-68, Professor, Head, 1968-82, Pharmacology, Dean, Medicine, 1970-82, University of Ceylon (Sri Lanka); Research Professor, Obstetrics & Gynaecology, National University of Singapore. *Memberships:* British Pharmacological Society; Physiological Society, London; President, Sri Lanka Association for the Advancement of Science, 1979; President, Sri Lanka Academy of Science, 1981-82. *Publications:* Articles in professional journals including: 'Journal Physiology'; 'Australian New Zealand Journal of Obstetrics & Gynaecology'; Contributor to: "Smooth Muscle", 1970; "Advances in Prosteglandin & Throboxane Research", 1980; "Neuronal and Extraneuronal Events in Autonomic Pharmacology", 1985. *Honours:* Rockefeller Research Fellow, Pharmacology, Harvard Medical School, 1958; Commonwealth Medical Fellow, University of Oxford, 1967; Hon. FFARS, Royal College of Surgeons, England, 1975; WHO Visiting Scientist, 1979; Visiting Professor, National University of Singapore; Professor Emeritus, University of Colombo, Sri Lanka, 1983; Hon. DSc, University of Colombo, 1985. *Hobbies:* Photography; Cricket; Gardening. *Address* 19 Welikadawatte Rajagiriya, Sri Lanka.

KOWALEWSKI, Jan Kazimierz, b. 30 Mar. 1921, Chelm, Poland. Professor. m. Jadwiga Grabowska, 31 Dec. 1948, Lublin, 1 son, 1 daughter. *Education:* Graduated, Medicine, Medical School, Lublin, 1950; Specialist, Internal Diseses, Haematology & Rheumatology. *Appointments:* Emergency Service, Lublin, 1949-50; Assistant, 1950-67, Associate Professor, 1968, Head, 2nd Dept. of Medicine, 1969-70, Head, Haematology, 1971-, Medical school, Lublin. *Memberships:* International Society of Haematology; Scientific Councils of the Institutes of Haematology, Warsaw, Rheumatology, Warsaw, Balneoclimatology, Poznan; Vice President, Polish Society of Haematology & Blood Transfusion. *Publications:* "Morphology and Cytochemistry of Inflammatory Exudate Cells in Leukaemic Patients ", 1967; "Cytochemical Criteria of Differential Diagnosis of Acute Leukaemias", 1974; "Nonrandom Chromosome Rearrangements in human myeloid leukaemia", 1977; "Platelet Function in Diabetics", 1981. *Honours:* Scientific Award, Polish Minister of Health, 1975, 1979. *Hobbies:* Touring; Camping. *Address:* Department of Haematology, ul. Jaczewskiego 8, 20-950 Lublin, Poland.

KOUNS, Alan Terry, b. 31 Dec. 1941, Long Beach, California. Medical Writer. *Education:* MA Comunications, University of Pennsylvania. *Appointments:* News paper Reporter, 1961-; work as documentary writer-producer, media fund-raiser, magazine journalist, freelance writer; Public Relations Writer, University of Southern California, 1965; Health Sciences Writer, 1970-72; Associate Producer of Medical TV News, funded by Corporation for Public Broadcasting, 1973; Consultant & Writer for Health Care Multimedia, D'Antoni & Associates, 1974; Training ex Corporation, 1980-81; Correspondent for US Information Agency, 1975-81; 1982-; Lecturer in Communication Arts, California State Polytechnic University, Pomona, 1981; Writer-Pulicist, City of Hope National Medical Centre, 1981-82. *Memberships:* American Film Institute; American Medical Writers' Association; Centre for the Study of Early Man; International Documentary Association; L S B Leakey Foundation; National Association of Science Writers. *Publications:* Book Chapter on water supplies & hygiene, "Third World Development" 1985 edition; "Organ Procurement Bills in Congress" in "Dialysis & Transplantation", 1984; "The Inner Journey of Anais Nin" in "Dreamworks" 1981; "Vermont's Junior Rescue Squad" in 'Emergency Medical Services'. 1984. *Honours:* Ford Motor Co Journalism Scholarship, 1958; University of Pennsylvania Communications Scholarship, 1966. *Hobbies:* University Alumni activities. *Address:* 9936 Ramona Street apt 21, Bellflower, CA 90706, USA.

KOUVALAINEN, Kauko Einari, b. 15 July 1930, Iisalmi, Finland. Professor of Pediatrics. m. Marita Kilander, 19 May 1956, 1 son, 1 daughter. *Education:* MD, 1958, MScD 1963. *Appointments:* Resident, Children's Hospital of Helsinki, 1959-63; Assistant Professor of Pediatrics, University of Helsinki, 1964-67; Associate Professor of Pediatrics, University of Turku, 1967-72; Professor of Pediatrics, 1972-, Vice Dean, Medical Faculty, 1975-78, Dean of the Medical Faculty, University of Oulu, 1972-. *Memberships:* Finnish Pediatric Association (President); European Society for Pediatric Research; European Society for Pediatric Hematology and Immunology; European Group for Immunodeficiencies; Member, Advisory Boards, Acta Paediatrica Scandinavica, Annals of Clinical Research, Zeitschrift für Kinderchirurgie. *Publications:* Some 250 publications on pediatrics, pediatric immunology and pharmacology; "Drug Therapy in Children" (in Finnish), 1968-82 (3 editions); "Pediatrics for Parents" (in Finnish), 1982. *Honours:* Corresponding Member, Austrian Pediatric Association, 1975; Honorary Member, Turkish National Society of Pediatrics, 1984. *Hobby:* Nature. *Address:* Department of Pediatrics, University of Oulu, SF-90220, Oulu, Finland.

KOVACHY, Edward Miklos, Jr, b. 3 Dec 1946, Cleveland, Ohio, Private Practitioner: Psychiatry, Medication, Management Consulting. m. Susan Light, 21 June 1981, La Honda, California. *Education:* BA, Magna cum Laude, 1968, JD 1972, MBA, Harvard University, 1972; MD, Case Western Reserve University, 1977. *Appointments:* Intern, Resident in Psychiatry, 1977-81, Chief Resident in Psychiatry, Stanford University Medical Center, 1980-81. *Memberships:* American Psychiatric Assoc.; Northern California Psychiatric Society; Assoc. of Family and Conciliation Courts; North American Society for the Psychology of Sport and Physical Activity; San Francisco Academy of Hypnosis. *Publications:* Columnist, The Peninsula Times Tribune (Palo Alto), California, 1983-85. *Honours:* Diplomate, National Board of Medical Examiners, 1978; Licensed Physician and Surgeon, State of California, 1978-; Falk Fellowship, American Psychiatric Assoc, 1978-80. *Hobbies:* Athletics; Musical Comedy; Personal and Social Activism. *Address:* 1187 University Drive, Menlo Park, CA 94025, USA.

KRAFT, David Peterson, b. 23 Mar, 1942, Waterbury, Connecticut, USA. Director, University Health Services. m. Stephanie Barlett, 11 June, 1966, Wheaton, Illinois, USA, 1 son, 1 daughter. *Education:* AB, Wheaton College, Illinois, 1964; MD, Northwestern University Medical School, Illinois, 1968. *Appointemnts:* Internship, University of Vermont Medical Centre, Burlington, USA; General Psychiatry Residency, University of Rochester, New York, Medical Centre, 1969-72; Surgeon US Public Health Service, assigned as Prinicpal Mental Health Officer, Job Corps Health Office, Washington DC, 1972-74; Staff Psychiatrist, University of Massachussetts Health Service, Amherst, Massachussetts, 1974-76, Assistant Director, Mental Health Division, 1976-78, Director, 1978-83, Executive Director, 1984-. *Memberships:* Fellow, American Psychiatric Association; Member,

American College Health Association. *Publications:* Co-author: 'Suicide by Persons with and Without Psychiatric Contacts' in "Archives of General Psychiatry", vol. 33, 1976; 'A comprehensive prevention program for college students' in "Prevention of Alcohol Abuse: Current Issues and Future Directions", 1984. *Honour:* Certified in General Psychiatry, American Board of Psychiatry and Neurolgy, 1975. *Hobbies:* Swimming; Household Repairs. *Address:* University Health Services, University of Massachussetts, Amherst, MA 01003, USA.

KRAFT, Garry G, b. 6 Oct 1945, San Francisco, CA, USA. Doctor of Chiropractic; Partner. *Education:* BS; DC, Los Angeles College of Chiropractic, Glendale, California. *Appointments:* Automobile Parts Manager, Heuberger Volkswagen, Colorado Springs, Colorado, 1972-75; Veterans Counselor, Veterans Outreach Program, Colorado Springs, 1976-77; Teaching and Laboratory Assistant, Los Angeles College of Chiropractic, Glendale, California, 1981; Associate Preceptorship, Hobson Clinic, Glendora, California, 1982-83; Chiropractor, Citrus Health Center, Azusa, California, 1983-84; Owners Anacapa Health Care Center, Port Hueneme, California 1984-. *Memberships:* American Chiropractic Association; California Chirpractice Association; Foundation for Chiropractic Education and Research; American Public Health Association; ACA Council on sports injuries and Physical Fitness; Sigma Chi Psi, Alumni Division; Los Angeles College of Chiropractic Alumni Association. *Publications:* Oral Presentations, 'Giardiasis as a factor in Malabsorption Syndrome', 1972; 'Some effects of the circadian rhythm of rats and mice', 1972; 'Case Presentation: Twisting injury to the low back complicated by right inguinal hernia', 1983. *Honours:* Colorado Scholar's Award, University of Colorado, 1977; Nomination to "Who's Who in American Colleges and Universities, 1981; Outstanding Senior Award, Los Angeles College of Chiropractic, California, 1981. *Hobbies:* Sailing; Restoration of old Porsches; Auto Racing; Reading. *Address:* PO Box 43, Port Hueneme, CA 93041, USA.

KRAMER, Barnett Sheldon, b. 29 July 1948, Baltimore, Maryland, USA. Associate Professor of Medicine. m. Ruth Solomon, 25 June 1972, Baltimore, 1 son. *Education:* MD, University of Maryland, 1973. *Appointments include:* Clinical Associate, National Cancer Institute, USA, 1975-78; Associate Professor of Medicine/Associate Division Chief, Medical Oncology, University of Florida College of Medicine, 1983-. *Memberships:* American Society of Clinical Oncology; American Association for Cancer Research. *Publications include:* Author/co-author, numerous papers in refereed journals, book chapters, etc. *Honour:* Alpha Omega Alpha, 1972. *Hobbies:* Photography; Tennis. *Address:* J.H. Miller Health Centre, Box J-277, Gainesville, FL 32610, USA.

KRAMER, Charles H, b. 31 May 1922, Oak Park, Illinois, USA, Professor of Psychiatry and Behavioral Sciences, Northwestern University Medical School, m. Jeannette Ross, 15 Sept 1945, Urbana, Illinois, 5 sons, 1 daughter. *Education:* BS, 1944, MD, 1945, University of Illinois; Diplomate, American Board of Psychiatry and Neurology, General, 1960, Child Psychiatry, 1961; Graduate, Institute for Psychoanalysis, Chicago, Ill, 1967. *Appointments:* General practice, Medicine and Surgery, 1947-51; Captain, US Air Force, 1951-53; Staff Psychiatrist, Elgin State Hospital, 1953-54; Fellow, Faculty, Institute for Juvenile Research, 1955-70; Founder, President, Family Institute of Chicago, 1968-; Founder, Director, Centre for Family Studies, 1975-; Attending Psychiatrist, Northwestern Memorial Hospital, 1975-; Founder, President, Plum Grove Nursing Home, 1953-83; Founder, President, Kramer Foundation, 1961-. *Memberships:* Chicago Psychoanalytic Society; Illinois Council of Child

Psychiatry; Illinois Psychiatric Society; American Psychiatric Association; American Family Therapy Association; American Association for Marital and Family Therapy. *Publications:* "Psychoanalytically-oriented Family Therapy", 1968; "The Relationships between Child and Family Psychopathology", 1968; "Beginning Phase of Family Treatment", 1968; "Basic Principles of Long-Term Patient Care", 1976; "Becoming a Family Therapist", 1980. *Honours:* Sigma Xi, 1945; Better Life Award, 1970; Book of the Year, American Nursing Association, 1976. *Hobby:* Sailing. *Address:* 417 No Kenilworth, Oak Park, IL 60302, USA.

KRAMER, Herbert J, b. 24 Dec. 1939, Bad Kreuznach, Federal Republic of Germany. Profesor of Medicine. m. Hella Schirra, 13 Dec. 1963, Homburg/Saar, 2 sons. *Education:* University of Munich; University of Paris, France; MD 1963, Habilitation 1972, University of Saarland, Federal Republic of Germany; Associate 1976, Professor of Medicine 1980. *Appointments:* Resident 1965, Assistant Professor 1972, Department of Medicine, University of Saarland, Homburg/Saar; Resident, Department of Medicine, University of California, Los Angles, USA, 1968; Assistant Professor of Medicine 1973, Assoicate Professor 1976, Professor 1980, Department of Medicine, University of Bonn, Bonn. *Memberships:* German Association of Internal Medicine; German Association of Endocrinology; German Association of Nephrology; International Society of Hypertension; European Dialysis and Transplant Association; Euroepan Society Clinical Investigation; International Society Nephrology; American Society Nephrology; American Federation Clinical Research; New York Acadmey of Sciences; Aemrican Israeli Nephrology Association. *Publications:* "Natriuretic Hormone", 1978; Articles on hormonal regulation of body fluid and electrlytes. *Honorus:* Claude Bernard-Prize, University of Saarland, 1972; Theodor Frerichs-Prize, German Association of Internal Medicine, 1973. *Hobbies:* Music; Tennis. *Address:* Medical University Poliklinik, Wilhelmstrasse 35-37, 5300 Bonn 1, Federal Republic of Germany.

KRAMER, Richard Alan, b. 12 Jan 1949, Monticello, New York, USA. Clinical Social Worker/Consultant. m. Dora Gutman, 2 Sep 1979, Denver, Colorado, 1 daughter. *Education:* AA, Miami Dade Junior College, Miami, Florida, 1969; BSc Social Work, Florida International University, Miami, 1974; MSW, University of Denver Graduate School of Social Work, Colorado, 1977. *Appointments:* Counselor, Highland Park General Hospital/Human Resource Institute, 1974; Youth Counselor, Runaway Intervention Program/Dade County Department of Youth and Family Development, 1975; Family Counselor and Chief Evaluation Specialist; Regional Youth Services, 1977; Director of Counseling Services, Columbine Center Safe-House for Battered Women, Volunteers of America, 1978; Project Supervisor, New Emotional Adjustment Treatment Program, Southeast Metropolitan Board of Cooperative Services, 1979-82; Family Consultant-Training Supervisor, Cenikor Foundation Inc, 1983-85; Consultant and Associate Counselor, Joseph Osoro Consultant Associates, 1984-85; Private practice Therapist-Consultant, 1984-. *Memberships:* Colorado Addictions Counselors Certified Counselor/Supervisor Level III; Licensed Clinical Social Worker Level II, State of Colorado; National Association of Social Workers; Academy of Certified Social Workers; National Register of Clinical Social Workers. *Hobbies include:* Photography; Baseball. *Address:* 7150 E Hampden Avenue Suite 307, Denver, CO 80224, USA.

KRAMP, Ronald Arthur, b. 13 July 1938, Antwerp, Belgium. Professor of Physiology and Pathophysiology. m. Cécile Claus, 15 May 1968, Tournai, Belgium, 2 sons, 1 daughter. *Education:* Md, University of Louvain, 1964, Specialist in Internal Medicine, 1970, PhD, 1976. *Appointments:* Clincial Fellow in Internal Medicine, University of Louvain, 1964-67; Post Doctoral Fellow, University of North Carolina, USA, 1967-69, Career Investigator, Fellow American Heart Association, 1969-1970; Established Investigator, Foundation for National Scientific Research, University of Louvain, 1971-75; Director Merck Sharp & Dohme Research Laboratories, Brussels, 1975-79; Professor, and Chair of Physiology, Faculty of Medicine, University of Mons, 1979-present. *Memberships:* Euoprean Society for Clinical Investigation; American Society for the Advancement of Sciences; Société Belge des Maladies Internes; International Society of Nephrology; Fellow of the Royal Society of Medicine, London; New York Academy of Scicences; Société Belge de Physiologie et de Pharmacologie Fondamentales et Cliniques; Societé des Sciences, des Arts et des Lettres du Hainaut; Club de la Fondation Universitaire. *Hobbies:* Field Hockey; Tennis; Music; Painting; Books. *Address:* Service de Physiologie, Faculte de Medecine, Universite de l'Etat a Mons, 7000 Mons, Belgium.

KRANTZ, Sanford Burton, b. 6 Feb. 1934, Chicago, Illinois, USA. Staff Physician, Nashville Veterans Adminstration Medical Center; Professor of Medicine, Vanderbilt University School of Medicine; Director of Hematology, Vanderbilt and Veterans Administration Medical Center. m. Sandra Rae Goldstein, 28 Dec. 1958, Chicago, Illinois, 2 sons, 2 daughters. *Education:* AB; MD. *Appointments:* Intern in Medicine, 1959-60, Assistant Resident in Medicine, 1960-62, USPHS Postdoctoral Fellow, 1962-63, University of Chicago Hospitals, Chicago; Research Associate and USPHS Postdoctoral Fellow, Department of Medicine, University of Chicago, 1963-64; NATO Postdoctoral Fellow, University of Glasgow, Scotland, 1964-65; Assistant Professor, Medicine, University of Chicago Hospital and Argonne Cancer Research Hospital, 1965-68; Staff Associate, 1968-69, Assistant Chief, 1969-70, Hematology service NIH, Bethesda; Associate Professor of Medicine, Vanderbilt University School of Medicine, Nashville, 1970-75; Chief, Hematology Section, 1970-, Coordinator, Heamtology Training Program, 1970-, Veterans Administration Medical Center, Nashville; Director, Hematology Section, 1974-, Professor of Medicine, 1975-, Vanderbilt University School of Medicine; Visiting Professor, University of Chicago, Department of Biochemistry, 1983-84. *Memberships:* Sigma Xi; Felow, American College of Physicians; American Federation for Clinical Research; American Association for Advancement of Science; Aemrican Society of Hematology; Central Society for Clinical Research; Southern Society for Clinical Investigation, Councillor, 1982-84, President, 1985; American Society for Experimental Pathology; American Society for Clinical Investigation; New York Academy of Sciences; American College of Physicians; Society for Experimental Biology and Medicine. *Publications include:* Contributor to professional journals; Proceedings; "Erythropoietin and the Regulation of Erythropoiesis", University of Chicago Press. *Honours:* Leukemia Society Scholar, 1965-68; Distinguished Service Award, Medical Alumni Association of University of Chicago, 1979. *Hobby:* Hiking. *Address:* Hematology Division, Vanderbilt University School of Medicine, 21st Avenue South at Garland Avenue, Nashville, TN 37232, USA.

KRANZLER, Elliot Mark, b. 29 June 1951, New York, USA. Psychiatrist. m. Adinah Schnall, 10 Aug. 1975, 1 son, 1 daughter. *Education:* BA, Johns Hopkins University, 1973; MD, Albert Einstein College of Medicine, 1978. *Appointments:* Internship, New York Hospital, Cornell University Medical College, 1978; Residency in Psychiatry, New York Hospital-Payne Whitney Clinic, Cornell University Medical College, 1979-82; Fellowship in Child Psychiatry, Columbia-Presbyterian Medical Center, 1982-84;

Fellowship in Clinical Research in Child Psychiatry, Columbia University College of Physicians and Surgeons, 1984-86; Private practice. *Memberships:* American Psychiatric Association; American Medical Association; American Academy of Child Psychiatry. *Honour:* Edward Sachar Award for Clinical Excellence in Child Psychiatry, New York State Psychiatric Institute, 1984. *Address:* 451 West End Avenue, New York, NY 10024, USA.

KRASNER, David Steven, b. 8 Nov. 1951, New York, USA. Doctor of Chiropractic. m. April Rosublatt, 17 Dec. 1978, Flushing, New York, 1 son. *Education:* Hofstra University, Hempstead, New York; BS, DC, National College of Chiropractic, USA. *Appointments:* Private Practice, Glendale, New York, 1975-80; Private Practice, Oklahoma City, Oklahoma, 1981-82; Clinic Director, Brooks Clinic, Oklahoma City, 1982-83; Private Practice, Staten Island, New York, 1983-. *Memberships:* Affiliated at various times to: American Chiropractic Association; Chiropractic Association of Oklahoma. *Honours:* Diplomate, National board of Chiropractic Examiners. *Hobbies:* Guitar Playing; Camping; Restoring old cars. *Address:* 3131 Hycao Boulevard, Staten Island, NY 10306, USA.

KREB, Roberta Alexia Revling, b. 19 Jan. 1953, Tampa, Florida, USA. Director of Speech and Language Pathology Services Clinic. m. Gary Sherwood Kreb, 8 June 1977, Minneapolis, Minnesota, 1 daughter. *Education:* BA, Communication Disorders, University of Minnesota, 1974; MD, Speech-Language Pathology, St Cloud State University, 1976. *Appointments:* Clinic Director, Kreb Speech and Language Pathology Services, Inc. *Memberships:* Chairperson, Minnesota Speech-Language-Hearing Association; Publicity Chairperson, MSHA Spring Convention, 1985; Chairperson on Licensure, 1985-86, MSHA of Minnesota; American Speech-Language-Hearing Association. *Address:* 4001 Stinson Boulevard, Suite 312, Minneapolis, MN 55421, USA.

KREMBERG, Marvin Roy, b. 19 Mar. 1951, New York, USA. Chief Psychiatrist, Inwood Mental Health Clinic of Catholic Charities, New York. *Education:* BA, Brooklyn College, 1972; MD, Columbia College of Physicians & Surgeons, 1976; Fellowship, St Luke's Hospital, New York, 1978-80; Residencies, various hopsitals. *Appointments include:* Assistant Attending, Psychiatry, St Luke's Hospital, 1980-; Instructor, Clinical Psychiatry, Columbia College of Physicians and Surgeons, 1981-; Medical Director, Gestalt Association of New York, 1982-85; Acting Director, Psychiatry, Jewish Memorial Hospital; Attending, Psychiatry, St Vincent's Hospital, 1983-. *Memberships:* American Psychiatric Association; American Academy of Child Psychiatry; New York Council on Child Psychiatry; American Academy for Adolescent Psychiatry; etc., *Publications:* Articles in numerous professional journals. *Honours:* APA Physicians Recognition Award, Psychiatry, 1980; AMA Physicians Recognition Award, Psychiatry, 1980. *Hobbies:* Painting & Drawing; Art History; Oriental Antiquities; Marine Life; Swimming; Horticulture. *Address:* 315 West 57th Street, New York, NY 10019, USA.

KRENZ, Eric W, b. 31 Mar 1946, Stockton, California, USA. Adjunct Assistant Professor. m. Vickie Eddington, 21 June 1975, Lynwood Fourquare, 1 son, 1 daughter. *Education:* BA, California State University, Los Angeles; MA, California Family Studies Center, Azusa Pacific University, Azusa, California; PhD, University of Utah. *Appointments:* Teaching Assistant 1979-82, Adjunct Associate Instructor 1982-83, Adjunct Assistant Professor 1983-, University of Utah; Sports Psychology Consultant for several collegiate athletic teams, 1981-. *Memberships:* American Psychological Association; American Alliance on Health, Physical Education, Recreation and Dance; North American Society for the Psychology of Sport and Physical Activity; Western Psychological Association; Rocky Mountain Psychological Association; Utah Society for Clinical Hypnosis; Utah Association for Health, Physical Education, Recreation and Dance; Associate member, Sigma Xi. *Publications:* 'Research and Utilization of Hypnosis in Sports', (with B Jencks), 1980; 'How To Relax', (with J Curtis and D Dieterich, 1981;) 'Effects of Hypnosis on State Anxiety and Stress in Male and Female Intercollegiate Athletes', (with R Gordin and S W Edwards), 1982; 'Modified Autogenic Training (MAT) for Athletes', (with J Jencks), 1982; 'Stress Management for the Special Athlete', (with T Madden), 1983; 'Modified Autogenic Training', 1983; 'Gaining Control: Making Stress an Asset with Modified Autogenic Training, 1983; 'Hypnosis in Sports', (with B Jencks), 1983; 'Improving Competitive Performance: Hypnotic Suggestions and Modified Autogenic Training in Sports', 1984; 'Hypnosis vs Autogenic Training: A Comparison', 1985; 'The Effect of Modified Autogenic Training on Stress in Athletic Performance', (with K P Henschen). *Hobbies:* Golf; Walking. *Address:* PO Box 8181, Salt Lake City, UT 84108, USA.

KRIEDMAN, Warren Steven, b. 6 July 1948, New York, USA. Physician (private practice). *Education:* BA, New York University, 1970; MD, University of Pennsylvania, 1974; Rotating Internship, Hahnemann Medical College, 1975; Residency in Psychiatry & Neurology, Institute of the Pennsylvania Hospital, Philadelphia, 1978. *Appointments:* Attending Psychiatrist, Montgomery County Emergency Service, 1978-83; Consultant Psychiatrist, Lower Merion Counselling Service, 1978-81; Psychiatric Practice, Medical Towers, Philadelphia, Pennsylvania, 1978-83; Attending Physician, Overlook Hospital, Summit, New Jersey, 1983-; also Newark Beth Israel Medical Center, 1983-; Private Practice, Millburn, 1983-. *Memberships:* American Psychiatric Association; American Medical Association; Fellow, American Orthopsychiatric Association; New Jersey Medical Society; Federation of State Board Medical Examiners; New Jersey Psychiatric Association; Essex County Medical Society; Fellow, Masters & Johnson Institute; Physicians Advisory Panel, Medical World News. *Honours:* Phi Beta Kappa, 1970; Founders Day Award, New York University, 1970; Diplomate, National Board of Medical Examiners, 1975; Certificate of Achievement, US Department of Justice, 1980; American Medical Association Physicians Award, 1985. *Address:* 90 Millburn Avenue, Millburn, NJ 07041, USA.

KRIKLER, Dennis Michael, b. 10 Dec. 1928, Cape Town, South Africa. Consultant Cardiologist and Senior Lecturer, Royal Postgraduate Medical School and Hammersmith University of London. m. Liese Winterstein, 3 July 1955, Cape Town, 1 son, 1 daughter. *Education:* MD; FRCP; FACC. *Appointments:* House Physician and Surgeon, Professorial Departments, Groote Schuur Hospital, Cape Town, 1952; Registrar and Tutor, Department of Pathology, University of Cape Town, 1953; Medical Registrar, Groote Schuur Hospital, 1954-55; Fellow in Medicine, Lahey Clinic, Boston, Massachusetts, USA, 1956-57; Senior Medical Registrar, Groote Schuur Hospital, 1957-58; Consultant Physician, Salisbury area hospitals, Rhodesia, 1958-66; Clinical Assistant, Medical Unit, Westminster Hospital, 1966-68; Consultant Physician, The Prince of Wale's General Hospital and St. Ann's General Hospital, London, England, 1967-73; Clinical Tutor, North London Postgraduate Medical Centre, 1969-73. *Memberships include:* British Cardiac Society, Treasurer, 1976-81, Ex-Officio Councillor, 1981-; Honorary Fellow, Council on Clinical Cardiology, American Heart Association; Fellow, American College of Cardiology; Fellow, Royal Society of Medicine (former Member of Council of Clinical Section); Honorary Corresponding Member, Societé Francaise de Cardiologie; various other

associations; Editor, 'British Heart Journal', 1981-
Member, Editorial Committee, 'Cardiovascular
Research', 1975-; Member, various scientific
councils. *Honours:* C.J. Adams Memorial Travelling
Fellow, 1956; Sir William Osler Award, University of
Miami, USA, 1981; International Lecturer, 57th
Scientific Sessions, American Heart Association,
1984; Paul Dudley White Citatiion for International
Achievement, American Heart Association, 1984.
Hobbies: Photography; Reading; Current History.
Address: 81 Harley Street, London W1N 1DE,
England.

KRISHNAN, Nanguneri Ramanujam, b. 18 Sept.
1928, Tinnevelly. Senior Consutlant, m. Padma
Krishnan, 2 June 1954, Madurai. *Education:* MBBS,
Andhra University, 1951; MD, Pune University, 1964.
Appointments: Graded Specialist, Classified
Specialist, Senior Advisor, Consultant in Medicine,
Armed Forces Medical Services, India, 1953-;
Reader, Associate Professor, Professor of Medicine,
Armed Forces Medical College, Pune. *Memberships:*
Association of Physicians of India; Cardiological
Society of India; Indian Society of
Electrocardiology; American College of Chest
Physicans; Indian Society for Clincial Pharmacology
and Therapeutics. *Publications:* Chapters on Effects
of Heat, Cold and Aviation Medicine, in textbook of
"Medicine", 1985; approximately 30 papers in
Indian journals. *Hobbies:* Photography; Music.
Address: Office of DGAFMS, Ministry of Defence, M
Block, New Delhi 110001, India.

KRISS, Joseph Pinkus, b. 15 May 1919,
Pennsylvania, USA. Professor of Radiology and
Medicine; Chief, Division of Nuclear Medicine,
Stanford University School of Medicine. m. Regina
Tarlow, 15 June 1948, Portland, Oregon, 3 sons.
Education: BA (summa cum laude), Pennsylvania
State University, 1939; MD (cum laude), Yale
University, 1943. *Appointments:* Intern in Medicine,
1943-44, Assistant Resident in Medicine, 1944,
Associate Resident in Metabolism, 1944-45,
Resident in Medicine, 1945, New Haven Hospital;
Instructor in Medicine, Yale University School of
Medicine, 1944-45; Research Fellow in Metabolism,
Washington University School of Medicine, 1946-48;
Research Associate in Endocrinology and
Metabolism, Michael Reese Hospital, 1948; Clinical
Instructor in Medicine, 1948-50, Assistnat Clinical
Professor of Medicine, 1951-56, Associate Professor
of Medicine and Radiology, 1957-62, Stanford
University School of Medicine. *Memberships:*
Association of American Physicians; Western
Association of Physicians; Western Society for
Clinical Research; American Thyroid Association;
American Heart Association, Council of
Cardiovascular Radiology; American Association for
Advancement of Science; Scottish Society for
Experimental Medicine. *Publications:* Contributor of
over 150 articles and papers to professional
journals; Presentations, etc., including:
'Pathogenesis and treatment of Graves'
ophthalmopathy' in 'Thyroid Today', Mar-Apr. 1984;
Co-author, "Limitations of Creatinine as a Filtration
Marker in Glomerulopathic Patients", submitted to
'Kidney International', Apr. 1985. *Honours:* Henry J.
Kaiser Award, Stanford University School of
Medicine, 1975; Distinguished Alumnus Award,
Pennsylvania State University, 1978; Alumni Fellow
Pennsylvania State University, 1979; Western
Regional Society of Nuclear Medicine Award, 1978.
Hobbies: Sculpture and Painting; Martial Arts;
Bicycling; Golf. *Address:* Division of Nuclear
Medicine, Department of Radiology, Stanford
University School of Medicine, Stanford, CA 94305,
USA.

KRISTENSEN, Henning Gjelstrup, b. 27 Oct. 1939,
Aarhus, Denmark. Professor of Pharmacy, Rector.
m. Agne Kjaervig, 23 Apr. 1966, 2 sons. *Education:*
Graduated in Pharmacy, 1963; Licentiatus
Pharmacia, (=PhD), 1969; Doctor Pharmaciæ, 1981.
Appointments: Pharmaceutical Assistant, School of

Pharmacy, 1969; Research Fellowship, 1970-73;
Senior Lecturer, School of Pharamcy, 1973;
Professor of Pharmacy, 1978, Rector, Royal Danish
School of Pharmacy, 1981-. *Memberships:* Danish
Pharmaceutical Society, Chairman 1978-84; Danish
Pharmacophœia Council, Chairman; European
Pharmacopœia Commission; Nordic Medicine
Council Sub-Committee of Drug Standardisation;
Chairman, Board of Postgraduate Education.
Publications: Several textbooks on Pharmaceutics &
Pharmaceutical technology; Some 50 scientific
publications in area of drug manufacture & control.
Hobby: Sailing. *Address:* Royal Danish School of
Pharmacy, 2 Universitetsparken, DK-2100
Copenhagen Ø, Denmark.

KRISTOFFERSEN, Alf Oskar, b. 4 Aug 1945, Harstad,
Norway. Chief Medical Officer. m. Kari Johanne
Stenby, 21 Oct 1967, Oslo, 1 son, 2 daughters. *Edu-
cation:* Medical Graduate, 1970, Diploma of Tropical
Medicine, 1970, Basel, Switzerland; Specialist in
Gynaecology and Obstetrics, 1984; Specialist in
General Medicine, 1985. *Appointments:* Medical
Officer of Health, Karlsoy, Norway, 1973-74; Regis-
trar, Department of Surgery, Harstad Hospital,
1974-75; General Practitioner, Harstad, 1975-80;
Registrar, Gynaecology and Obstetrics, Region Hos-
pital, Tromsoe, 1980-84; currently, Chief Medical
Officer, 6 Division, Norway. *Membership:* Nor-
wegian Medical Association. *Hobby:* Fishing.
Address: Hålogalandsgt 27, 9400 Harstad, Norway.

KRIZ, Svetanir, b. 12 Feb. 1933, Prague, Czechos-
lovakia. Staff Physician, Huronia Regional Centre,
Orillia, Ontario, Canada. m. Olga Moravkova, MD, 7
Sep 1957, Plzen, 2 sons. *Education:* Medical Faculty
of Charles University, Prague, 1958; MD; CCFP;
LMCC; ECFMG. *Appointments:* General Practice,
Czechoslovakia, 1958-68; Current position, 1969-72;
Postgraduate Training in Family Medicine, Sunnyb-
rook Hospital, Toronto, Canada, 1972-74; Current
position, 1974-. *Memberships:* Canadian Medical
Association; Ontario Medical Association; Orillia
Medical Society; American Epilepsy Society; The
College of Physicians and Surgeons of Ontario; The
College of Family Physicians of Canada, Ontario
Chapter. *Honour:* PSI Foundation Postgraduate
Award, 1981, 1982. *Hobbies:* Jogging; Swimming;
Downhill and Cross-country Skiing; Travel; Classical
Music; Science Fiction. *Address:* Huronia Regional
Centre, PO Box 1000, Orillia, Ontario, Canada L3V
6L2.

KROEGER, Hans, b. 11 Feb. 1928, Hamburg. Chief,
Biochemistry Dept. m. Inge Janssen, 31 Aug. 1959,
Leer, 1 daughter. *Education:* Prof.Dr.rer.nat.; MD.
Appointments: Research Assistant, Biochemisches
Institut, Universitat Freiburg i. Breisgau, 1957-59;
Post Doctoral Fellow, Biochemistry, New York
University, McArdle Memorial Institute, Wisconsin,
USA, 1960-61; Assistant Professor, 1962-69,
Biochemisches Institut, Universitat Freiburg i.
Breisgau, 1962-69. *Memberships:* Various scientific
societies. *Publications:* in various journals. *Address:*
Robert Koch Institut, Nordufer 20, D-1000 Berlin 65,
Federal Republic of Germany.

KROKAN, Hans Einar, b. 18 Feb. 1945, Folldal,
Norway, Manager, Research Centre. m. Ruth, 19
Sept. 1980, Tromsø, Norway, 3 sons, 2 daughters.
Education: MD, Oslo University, Norway, 1970; PhD,
(Biochemistry), University of Tromsø, Norway, 1977.
Appointments: Intern, Medical and surgical,
1970-71; Intern, General Practice, 1971-72; Military
Service, 1972; Research Fellow, University of
Tromsø, 1972-77; Post-doctorate, Harvard Medical
School, USA, 1977-79; Associate Professor,
Biochemistry, University of Tromsø, 1979-83;
Visiting scientist, NCI, NIH, Laboratory for Human
Carcinogenisis, 1983-84; Manager, Norsk Hydro
Research Centre, section for biotechnology,
Norway, 1985l. *Memberships:* Norweigan Medical
Association; Norweigan Biochemical Society,
President from January, 1986. *Publications:*

Approximately 50 scientific articles in international biochemical and carcinogenetic journals on DNA replication, DNA repair, carcinogenetics, and photobiology. *Honours:* Fogarty International Fellowship, 1977-79; Eleanor Roosevelt Fellowship, 1983-89. *Hobbies:* Music; Playing the Cello. *Address:* Norsk Hydro, Research Centre Porsgrunn, Section for Biotechnology, N-3901 Porsgrunn, Norway.

KROLL, Phillip Dorian, b. 25 Apr. 1941, Detroit, Michigan, USA, Chief, Alcohol Rehabilitation Unit, m. Syma Kantor, 1 Sept 1980, Ann Arbor, Michigan, 2 daughters. *Education:* MD, University of Michigan School of Medicine, Ann Arbor, Michigan; BA, Brandeis University, Waltham, Mass. *Appointments:* Assistant Chief, Psychiatry Service, 1973-84, Chief, Alcohol Rehabilitation Unit, 1975-, Ann Arbor VA Medical Centre, Mich; Instructor, Department of Psychiatry, 1973-79, Assistant Professor in Psychiatry, 1979-, University of Michigan Medical School, Ann Arbor, Mich. *Memberships:* American Psychiatric Association; Michigan Psychiatric Association. *Publications:* 'Cerebral Cortical Atrophy in Alcoholic Men', 1981; 'The Schizotyal Personality on an Alcohol Treatment Unit', 1983; 'The Dexamethosone Suppression Test in Patients with Alcoholism', 1983; 'The Behaviour of Adult Alcoholic Men Abused as Children', 1985. *Honours:* Phi Beta Kappa, 1962. *Hobbies:* Running; Sailing. *Address:* 2547 Bunker Hill Drive, Ann Arbor, MI 48105, USA.

KROLL, Una Margaret Patricia, b. 15 Dec. 1925, London, England. Senior Clinical Medical Officer, Hastings Health Authority. m. Rev. Leopold Kroll, 1 June 1957, Birmingham, 1 son, 3 daughters. *Education:* MB.B.Chir.; MRCGP; Deaconess, Church of England, 1970. *Appointments:* Missionary Doctor, Liberia/Namibia, 1956-61; Principal, National Health Service, Family Doctor, Orpington & Wimbledon areas, 1961-81; Community Health Service, Hastings, 1981-. *Membership:* Royal College of General Practitioners. *Publications:* "Cervical Cytology", 'British Medical Journal', 1971; "Sexual Counselling", 1983, 4 other books, many articles. *Hobbies:* Ecclesiastical Politics; Staying Alive. *Address:* Datcha, Clinton Way, Fairlight Cove, East Sussex, England.

KROUSKOP, Thomas Alan, b. 11 July, 1945, Washington DC, USA. Head, Rehabilitation Engineering Program. m. Arlene Swatsworth, 20 Jan. 1968, Pittsburgh, Pennsylvania, 2 sons, 1 daughter. *Education:* BS, Civil Engineering; MS, Civil Engineering and Biotechnology; PhD, Civil Engineering and Biotechnology. *Appointments:* Project Director, Biodynamic Tolerances Project, Department of Highway Traffic Safety Administration, 1971-72; Assistant Professor of Bioengineering, Texas A & M University 1971-74; Adjunct Assistant Professor, Bioengineering, 1972-79, Associate Professor Bioengineering, 1974-79, Tenured in 1977, Texas A & M University; Assistant Professor, 1979-82, Associate Professor, 1982-, Tenured in 1982, Department of Rehabilitation and Physical Medicine, Baylor College of Medicine. *Memberships:* American Society for Testing and Materials; National Society of Professional Engineers; American Congress of Rehabilitation Medicine; Rehabilitation Engineering Society of North America; Patent Committee, Baylor College of Medicine. *Publications:* 'Predicting the Loaded Shape of an Amputee's Residual Limb' published in the proceedings for the 8th Annual Conference of the Rahabilitation Engineering Society of North America Meeting, Memphis, Tennessee, June 1985, with B Goode, D Dougherty and E Hemmen. *Honours:* American Society for Testing and Materials Student Research Award, 1967; NIH Trainee-Civil Engineer, Carnegie-Mellon University 1967-70; Sigma XI. *Hobbies:* Camping; Scouting; Coin collecting. *Address:* TIRR-REC, 1333

Moursund Avenue, Houston, TX 77030, USA.

KRUEGER, Alan Lee, b. 31 July 1941, Brooklyn, New York, USA. Medical Director. m. Susan M Krueger, 11 Feb. 1977, 4 sons. *Education:* BA, Baker University, Baldwin, Kansas, 1963; MD, University of Kansas, 1967. *Appointments include:* Medical Member, Pacific Air Force Command, Drug Education Team, 1970-71; Assistant Professor, Psychiatry, University of Kansas Medical Center, 1974-78; Visiting Fellow, Psychiatry, Menninger Shcool of Psychiatry, 1976-78; Clinical Associate Professor, Psychiatry, Bowman Gray School of Medicine, Wake Forest University, 1978-; Member Psychiatric Active Medical Staff, 1978-, Medical Director, Appalachian Hall, Asheville, NC, 1981-. *Memberships include:* American Medical Assn.; American Psychiatric Assn.; Buncombe County Medical Society; North Carolina Medical Society; North Carolina Psychiatric Assn.; American Psychosomatic Society. *Publications include:* 'Confidentiality and Third Parties' (co-author), APA Task Force Report, 1975; 'Four Audits From One: The Result of Medical Audit Subcommittee Review' (co-author); (Book reviews) "Neurology for Psychiatrist", 1980; "Classic Contributions in the Addictions", 1981; "Substance Abuse: Clinical Problems and Perspectives", 1981; "Drug Abuse: A Guide for the Primary Care Physician", 1981; "Your Guide to Mental Help", 1983. *Honours include:* Chief Resident, Department of Psychiatry, University of Kansas Medical Center, 1973-74; Board of Directors, NC Peer Review Foundation, Executive Committee, 1985-88; APA Fellowship, 1985. *Hobbies:* Golf; Fishing. *Address:* Appalachian Hall, PO Box 5534, Asheville, NC 28813, USA.

KRUGLIK, Meyer, b. 3 Nov. 1914, New York City, USA. Consultant Psychiatrist. m. Gertrude Barbara Ginsburg, 4 Feb. 1938, Chicago, USA, 3 sons, 1 daughter. *Education:* BS, University of Illinois, USA, 1936, MD, 1939. *Appointments:* Intern, University Hospital, 1938-39; Cook County Hospital, 1939-41; Physician in Chief, Zuni Hospital, 1941-42; Psychiatric Training, Veteran Administration, 1942-47; Captain, US Army Medical Corps, 1944-46; Private Practice of Psychiatry, 1947-; University of Health Sciences, Psychiatric Faculty, 1948-58; Post Graduate Training, Illinois Neuropsychiatric Institute, 1948; Psychiatric Consultant to Illinois Department of Corrections,-. *Memberships:* American Psychiatric Association, Life Member; Illinois Psychiatric Society, Life Member; Emeritus Member of: Chicago Medical Society, Illinois Medical Society and American Medical Association. *Hobby:* International Travel. *Address:* 6 North Michigan Avenue, Chicago, IL 60602, USA.

KRUS, Stefan, b. 20 June 1926, Warsaw, Poland. Pathologist. m. Anna Elzbieta Korczak, 30 Apr. 1959, 2 sons, 2 daughters. *Education:* Medical Faculty, Medical Academy, Warsaw, 1951. *Appointments:* Assistant, Senior Assistant, Associate Professor, 1965, Professor, 1975, Chief, 1970-, Pathological Anatomy, Medical Academy, Warsaw. *Membership:* Polish Society of Pathologists, President, 1979-83. *Publications:* "Pathomorphology of Liver", 1973; "Pathomorphology of Kidneys", 1973; "Pathomorphology of Heart", Editor, 1979; "Pathological Anatomy", Textbook, Editor, 1972, 1980; Principles of Patho Morphology", Co-Editor, 1984. *Honours:* Honroary Member, Warsaw Medical Society, 1984; Meritorious Teacher of Polish People's Republic, 1984. *Hobbies:* Teaching Pathology; Classical Music; Poetry; Publishing Humanistic Essays; Travel; Wine. *Address:* Grochowska 325-7, 01-823 Warsaw, Poland.

KRZEMINSKA-PAKUA, Maria, b. 28 Aug. 1938, Zieleniec, Poland. Head, Department of Internal Medicine and Cardiology. m. Jan Pakua, 18 Jan. 1966. *Education:* Diploma, Medical Faculty, Medical Academy, Lodz, 1963; MD, 1969; Degree of

Assistant Professors, 1975; Degree of Professor, 1984. *Appointments:* Studied, Medical Faculty, 1957-63, Assistant, 2nd Department, 1963-72, Assistant-Adjunct, Institute of Cardiology, 1973-77, Head, Department of Internal Medicine and Cardiology, 1978-, Medical Academy, Lodz, Poland. *Memberships:* Polish Society of Cardiology; Polish Society of Internal Mediicne; International Society of Non-Invasive Cardiology; European Society of Cardiology. *Publications:* 'Angiographic and Polycardiographic Study of Patients with Left Ventricular Aneurysm' in 'Excerpta Medica', 1979; 'Left Parasternal Impulse in Mitral Valve Disease-Recent Advances in Noninvasive Cardiology', Brussels, 1981; 'Nieinwazyjna diagnostyka chorob ukladu krazenia - PZWL Warsawa', 1982; 'Late complications due to replacement valves protheses' in 'European Heart Journal', 1984; 'Surgical treatment of infective endocarditis', 1985. *Honours:* Several awards, Polish Health Minister. *Hobbies:* Literature; Travelling. *Address:* ul. Mxynarska 14/18m. 22, 91-823 Lodz, Poland.

KUCH, Klaus, b. 2 May 1941, Federal Republic of Germany. m. Wendy Parkinson, 19 Dec 1983. *Education:* MD, Doctorate dissertation cum laude in Pathology, University of Heidelberg; FRCP(C); Diplomate, American Board Psychiatry and Neurology; ECFMG (USA); LMCC (Canada). *Appointments:* 3 years Psychiatric residency training, University of Florida, USA; 1 year Psychiatric residency training, Assistant Professor 1980, University of Toronto, Canada; Staff Psychiatrist, St Michael's Hospital, 1972-; Currently Part-time Staff Psychiatrist, Toronto General Hospital. *Memberships:* Ontario Medical Association; Ontario Psychiatric Association; Canadian Psychiatric Association; Fellow, Royal College of Physicians and Surgeons of Canada; American Psychiatric Association; Peer review group, Canadian Research Foundation. *Publications include:* 'Helle Zellen in the Pancreas of the Horse', 1968; Contributor to "Psychotherapy Handbook", 1980; Several papers on anxiety posttraumatic stress disorder. *Honour:* Anclone Manor Award, Department of Psychiatry, Gainesville, Florida, 1971. *Hobbies:* Windsurfing; Skiing; Tennis; Fishing. *Address:* 10 Roxborough Street West, Toronto M5R 1T8, Canada.

KUCZYŃSKI, Leonard Ignacy, b. 15 Nov. 1913, Sejny, Poland, Professor Emeritus, m. Irena Bokun, 6 Oct. 1945, Osnabrück, 1 son. *Education:* Ing chem, Tehncial University of Lowow; Dr tech scis, Technical University of Wroclaw, 1949; Prof extraordinary, 1954, Profesosr ordinary, 1966, Academy of Medicine, Wroclaw. *Appointments:* Dean, Faculty of Pharmacy, 1956-58, 1960-62, Prorector, 1962-68, Rector, 1968-72, Director, Inst Chem and Techn of Drugs, 1966-81, Academy of Medicine, Wroclaw. *Memberships:* Polish chemical Scoiety; Polish Pharmacy Society. *Publications:* "Technologie of Drugs", 1954, 1971; "Synthesis of pryidine derivatives with expected therapeutic activity, Part I-II', 1961; Author of over 60 learned articles and books. *Honours:* Decorated Officers and Commandory Cross of Polonia Resitituta, 1965, 1971; Doctor honoris causa of Medical Academy of Lodz. *Hobbies:* Photography; Tourism. *Address:* Technology of Drugs Department, Faculty of Pharmacy, Akademia Medyczna we Wroclawiu, pl Nakiera 1, 50-140 Wroclaw, Poland.

KUENH, John Lampert, b. 8 Nov. 1930, Toledo, Ohio, USA. Professor of Psychiatry. m. Jane Oker Kleinmann, 27 Dec. 1952, Cincinnatti, Ohio, USA, 2 daughters. *Education:* AB, Ohio Wesleyan University, USA, 1952; MD, Ohio State University, 1957. *Appointments:* University Psychiatrist, Indiana University, 1964-66; Resident Psychiatrist, Peace Corps Training Centre, Hawaii, 1966; Director, Counselling and Mental Health Services, Louisiana State University, 1966-75; Medical Director, Mental Health Centre, Canton, Ohio, 1975-79; Programme

Director for Psychiatry, Canton Campus, Ohio, 1979-82; Professor of Psychiatry, Northeastern Ohio Universities Colleges of Medicine, 1982-. *Memberships:* Fellow, American Psychiatric Association, etc. *Publications:* 17 published contributions to profesional journals including 'Encounter at Leyden: Gustav Mahler consults Freud' in 'Psychoanalytic Review', 1966; 'Some Issues in Understanding and Counselling the Compulsive Student Drug User and His Family' in 'Bulletin of the Menninger Clinic', 1970, re-published in book 'The Behavioural Effects of Drugs', 1972; 'A Pilot Programme of Mental Health Education for Faculty' in 'American Journal of College Health', 1974; 'No Balm in Gilead? Mental Health Beliefs in a Time of National Renewal' in 'Current Concepts in Psychiatry', 1978; 'The Physician and the Community Mental Health Centre Revisited' currently being reviewed by 'Behavioural Medicine'. *Honour:* Omicron Delta Kappa, 1970. *Hobbies:* Clasical Music; History; Sailing. *Address:* c/o Portage Path Mental Health Centre, 3405 Broadway, Akron, OH USA 44308.

KUETTNER, Klaus Eduard, b. 25 June 1933, Bunzlau, FRG, University Chairman and Professor, m. Yolanda Adler, 25 Aug. 1975. *Education:* BS, Minden, FRG, 1956; MS, University of Freilburg, 1958; PhD, University of Berne, Switzerland, 1961. *Appointments:* Research Associate, Presbyterian St Lukes Hospital, Chicago, Ill, USA, 1964-66; Instructor, Department of Biology, University of Illinois College of Medicine, 1964-65; Assistant Professor, 1971-72, Associate Professor, 1972-77, Professor, Biochemistry and Orthopaedics, 1972-77, Chairman, Department of Biochemistry, 1980, Rush Presbyterian St Lukes Medical Centre, Chicago. *Memberships:* American Chemical Society; Orthopaedic Research Scoiety; American Society for Biol Chemistry; International Association for Den Res; American Society for Cell Biochemistry; Sigma Xi; Gesellschaft für Biologische Chemie; New York Academy of Science; American Association for the Advancemnet of Science; American Rheumatism Association. *Publications:* 'Basic Concepts of the Resistance of Cartilage Tumour Invasion', (with B U Pauli), 1984; "Articular Cartilage Biochemistry", (Co-Editor), 1986. *Honours:* Kappa Delta Award, 1978; Chairman, Gordon Res Conference on Chem Phjysiology and Structure of Bones and Teeth, 1978; Chairman, Gordon Res Conference on Proteoglycans, 1984. *Address:* Rush Presbyterian St Luke's Medical Centre, Department of Biochemistry, Chicago, IL 60612, USA.

KUHN, Endre Ferenc, b. 19 Feb. 1928, Kispest, Hungary. Professor; Director. m. Agota Gergely, 22 sept. 1951, Budapest, 1 son. *Education:* MD C, sci Diploma of Radiology; Diploma of Clinical Oncology. *Appointments:* Staff Radiologist, Budapest, Uzsoki Hospital, 1952-61; Lecturer of Radiology, 1962-72, Professor, Director, Department of Radiology, University Medical School, Pesc, Hungary, 1973-. *Memberships:* Council of Institute of Radiology; Council of Institute of Oncology; Vice Chairman, Committee of Radiology of Ministry of Health and Hungarian Acadmey of Sciences; EACR. *Publications:* 91 publications, radiological diagnosis and radiotherapyof malignat tumours; 'Radic herapy' in Encyclopaedia of Physicians, 1977; 'Radiologic Evaluation of Malignant Lymphomas', forthcoming 1986. *Honour:* Honour of Education, 1976. *Hobbies:* Music; Literature. *Address:* Department of Radiology. University Medical School, H-7643 Pécs, If juság u. 31. Hungary.

KUHN, Irvin Nelson, b. 18 Aug. 1928, Manitoba, Canada. Associate Chief of Staff of Education ACOS (E). m. Doreen M. Elvedahl, 3 July 1956, Los Angeles, California, USA, 1 son, 2 daughters. *Education:* BA, Chemistry, 1950; MD 1955, Loma Linda University, California. *Appointments:* Consultant & staff, North York Branson Hospital,

Willowdale, Ontario, Canada, 1960-61; Consultant & staff in medicine, Chief of Medicine Service, Bangkok Adventist Hospital, Thailand, 1961-64; Consultant & staff, haematology & oncology, Loma Linda University Medical Centre, California, 1965-. *Memberships:* Ontario & Candian Medical Associations, 1960-62; Thailand Medical Association, 1962-64; San Bernardino, California & American Medical Associations, 1966-; Fellow, Royal College of Physicians (Canada), 1973; Member & Fellow, American College of Physicians, 1967-. *Publications include:* Teaching materials, journal articles for San Bernardino County Medical Society, book chapters, theses, abstracts. *Honour:* Alpha Omega Alpha, 1975. *Hobbies:* Jade carving; Hiking; Skiing. *Address:* 36333 Panorama Drive, Yucaipa, CA 92399, USA.

KÜHN, Klaus, b. 1 May 1927, Breslau. Director. m. Barbara Bleimund, 1 son, 2 daughters. *Education:* BSc., MSc., Chemistry, University of Munich; PhD, Biochemistry, Max Planck Institute. *Appointments:* Fellow, Deutsche Forschungsgemeinschaft, Institute of Technology, Darmstadt, 1956-58; Assistant Professor, Institute Organic Chemistry, 1958-60; Associate Professor, Chemistry, University of Heidelberg, 1960-66; Director, Connective Tissue Research, Max Planck Institute, 1966-; Executive Director, MPI, Martinsried, 1977-80; Scholar in Residence, Fogarty International Centre, NIH, Bethesda, USA, 1981-82. *Memberships:* Gesellschaft fur Biologishe Chemie; Gesellschaft Deutscher Chemie; American Society for Biological Chemists; Editorial Board, Biological Chemistry Hoppe Seyler; etc. *Publications:* Over 200 articles in professional journals; "New Trends in Basement Membrane Research", Editor, 1982; "Rheumatology", Volume 8; etc. *Honours:* Prize, Verein f. Gerberei, Chemie u. Technik, 1960; Richard Zsigmondy Stipendium of the Kolloid Gesellschaft, 1961; Fogarty International Scholarship, 1981. *Address:* Max Planc Institut für Biochemie, D 8033 Martinsried b., Münich, Federal Republic of Germany.

KUHNLEY, Edward John, b. 14 Aug. 1951, Spangler, Pennsylvania, USA. Director, Child & Adolescent Services. m. Carol Bowie, 22 June 1974, Charlottesville, 2 daughters. *Education:* BS, Old Dominion University, 1972; MD, University of Virginia, 1976; Residency, Psychiatry, Eastern Virginia Medical School, 1979; Fellowship, Child Psychiatry, Yale University, 1981. *Appointments:* Director Child & Adolescent Services, Meadows PsychiatricCenter, Centre Hall, Pennsylvania. *Memberships:* American Psychiatric Association; American Medical Association; American Acadmey of Child Psychiatry; American Society of Adolescent Psychiatry. *Publications:* Articles in professional journals including: 'Psychiatric Opinions'; etc. *Hobbies:* Basketball; Hunting. *Address:* Meadows Psychiatric Centre, RD-1, Box 259, Centre Hall, PA 16828, USA.

KULCZYCKI, Jerzy Witold, b. 21 May 1928, Lwow, Poland. Head, Neurological Department, Psychoneurological Institute, Warsaw. m. Hanna Binder, 31 Dec. 1951, Skierniewice, 2 sons. *Education:* Graduate, Pommeranian Medical Academy, Szczecin, 1954; Md 1962; Dr.habil. 1972, Professor, 1982. *Appointments include:* Assistant, Docent, Neurological Department, Pommeranian Medical Academy, 1955-76. *Memberships:* World Federation of Neurology; Polskie Towarzystwo Neurologiczne (Polish Neurological Society); Stowarzyszenie Neuropatologow Polskich (Association of Polish Neuropathologists,. *Publications include:* "Types & Morphologic Analysis of Primary & Secondary Haemorrhages into the Brain Stem", 1964; "Zur Morphologie der Entwicklungsstörungen der Grosshirnrinde beim Menschen", 1967; "Correlation of Vascular Changes & Morphology of Lacunae in the So-called Lacunar Cerebral State", 1972. *Hobby:* Photography. *Address:* Puszczyka 3/92, 02-777 Warsaw, Poland.

KULIN, Howard Eric, b. 2 May 1937, Worcester, Massachusetts, USA, Associate Professor of Pediatrics m. Hanne Hoirup, 2 Jan 1965, 3 sons. *Education:* MD, Cornell University College of Medicine; 1963, BA, Harvard University, USA, 1969. *Appointments:* Internship, and Junior Residency, Children's Hospital Medical Centre, Boston, Mass, 1963-. Clinical Associate, Endocrinology Branch, National Cancer Institute, 1965-67, Senior Investigator, Reproduction Research Branch, National Institute of Child Health and Human Development, 1970-72, National Institutes of Health, Bethesda, Md; Senior Lecturer, Pediatrics Unit, St Marys Hospital Medical School, London, England, 1967-68; Pediatric Endocrinology Fellowhsip, University of California Medical Centre, San Francisco, Calif, USA, 1968-70; Associate Professor, Pediatrics Chief, Division of Pediatric Endocrinology, The Milton S Hersey Medical Centre, Pennsylvania State University College of Medicine, 1972-; Visiting Professor of Pediatrics, University of Nairobi School of Medicine, Nairobi, Kenya, 1979-80. *Memberships:* Society for Pediatric Research, 1970; The Endocrine Society, 1970; Society for the Study of Reproduction, 1970' Fellow, The American Academy of Pediatrics, 1973; American Federation for Clinical Research, 1974; The Lawson Wilkins Pediatric Endocrine Society, 1975; American Society of Andrology, 1977; Chilean Society of Endocrinology and Metabolism, 1982; The Amercian Pediatric Society, 1985. *Publications:* Author of over 70 professional and scientific articles. *Address:* R D No 5, Box 696A, Elizabethtown, PA 17022, USA.

KULKA, Fred, b. 31 Jan. 1925, Sahy, Hungary, Professor and Head of Surgical Department of Postgraduate Medical School, Budapest, m. Ester, 3 Apr. 1956, 1 son, 1 daughter. *Education:* MD; Professor of Surgery; Specialist in surgery, thoracic surgery and pulmonology. *Appointments:* Head. Thoracic Surgical Department, University of Szeged. *Memberships:* American Thoracic Surgical Society; Society of Thoracic Surgeons, Great Britain; International College of Chest Physicians; International College of Surgeons. *Publications:* Author of 167 publications and 4 chapters in books. *Honours:* Recipient of numerous awards from the Hungarian Government. *Hobbies:* Surgery; Theatre. *Address:* 1 Surgical Clinic of Postgraduate Medical School, Pf 112, Budapest 1389, Hungary.

KULSHRESTHA, Om Prakash, b. 23 Dec. 1931, Jodhpur, India. Professor of Ophthalmology. m. Jyoti Bala Deva, 14 June 1955, 1 son, 2 daughters. *Education:* MB, BS with Honours in Physiology; MS (Ophthalmology); Sawai Man Singh Medical College, Jaipur, 1958; Fellowship for advanced training in Oculo-plastic Surgery, Universities of Toronto & Montreal, Canada, 1965-66. *Appointments:* Lecturer in Ophthalmology, 1958-59, 1962-65, Reader & Head of Ophtalmology, 1965-68, RNT Medical College, Udaipur; Professor & Head, Udaipur, 1968-71; Professor of Ophtalmology, Sawai Man Singh Medical College, Jaipur, 1971-, Professor & Head of Ophtalmology, 1976-; Advisor in Ophtalmology to Government of Rajasthan. *Memberships:* All India Ophtalmological Society; Indian Medical Association; Indian Academy of Medicine. *Publications:* Various articles in field of ophtalmology, several papers on surgery of Galucoma by Trabeculectomy & CCT. *Honours:* Guest of Honour, Gold Medal, Bihar State Ophtalmic Society, 1982; Fellow, National Academy of Medicine (India) (highest honour for medical profession in India), 1985; Chairman of many scientific sessions, All-India Ophtalmic Society Congress. *Hobbies:* English Fiction; Bridge. *Address:* 20 Uniara Garden, Moti Dungri Road, Jaipur 302004, India.

KUNZ, Robert Joseph, b. 7 Jan 1953, Chicago, Illinois, USA. Chiropractic. m. Donna Sommerer, 16 Nov 1974, 1 son, 2 daughters. *Education:* BS Anatomy, 1975; DC, Certificate in X-ray, Acupuncture, Physiotherapy and Laboratory Diagnosis, National College of Chiropractic, 1977; Diplomate, National Board of Chiropractic Examiners, 1977; Graduate, Parker Chiropractic Research Foundation, 1978; Electrocardiograph Technical Certificate, Burdick Corporation, 1978; Activator Proficiency Rated, 1985. *Appointments:* Lecturer and Laboratory Instructor, Gross-Viceral Neuroanatomy, National College of Chiropractic, Lombard, Illinois, 1975-76; Assistant Chiropractic, Research Anatomy Department, 1976-77; Staff, Joseph Janse Research Center, 1983-84. *Memberships:* American Chiropractic Association; Illinois Chiropractic Society; Chicago Chiropractic Society. *Publications:* "Biomechanics of the Fixated Atlas"; "Effects of Manipulation and Adhesions in the Intervertebral Foramina; Contributor, Journal of Manipulative and Physiological Therapeutics. *Hobbies:* Model Trains; Reading; Church Activities; Sports; Enjoying children and spouse. *Address:* 4731 Willow Springs Road, LaGrange, IL 60525, USA.

KUO, Paul C, b. 22 May 1947, Beijing, China. Associate Professor. m. Leslie Anne Will, 14 Aug. 1982, Columbus, USA, 1 daughter. *Education:* BA, Carleston College; AM, Anatomy, Harvard University; DMA, Harvard University School of Dentistry; MD, Harvard University Medical School. *Appointments:* Teaching Fellow, Anatomy, Harvard Medical School, Biology, Harvard College; Assistant Professor, Oral and Maxillofacial Surgery, Assistant Professor, Surgery, Priteker School of Medicine, Consultant, Oral & Maxillofacial Surgery & Sports Dentistry, Sports Medicine Centre, Consultant, Clinical Neurophysiology Laboratory and Sleep Disorder Centre, University of Chicago; Professor, Chairman, Oral and Maxillofacial Surgery, Loyola University; Chief, Oral Maxillofacial Surgery, Loyola University of Chicago Stritch School of Medicine. *Memberships:* Fellow, American Association of Oral and Maxillofacial Surgeons; Charter Member, Society of Educators in Oral and Maxillofacial Surgery; Oral and Maxillofacial Research Group, International Association for Dental Research; American Cleft Palate Association. *Publications:* Articles in professional journals including: 'Journal American Academy Dental Radiology'; 'Oral Surgery'; etc. *Honours:* Sigma Xi, Associate Member, Carleton Chapter, 1970; Andelot Fellow, Medical Sciences, Harvard, 1971; John Parker Fellow, Medical Sciences, Harvard, 1972; Jeffrey Wyman Fellow, Anatomy, Harvard, 1973. *Hobbies:* Travel; Photography. *Address;* Loyola University Medical Centre, 2160 S. First Ave., Maywood, IL 60153, USA.

KUO, Sow-Hsong, b. 17 Dec. 1940, Taiwan. Associate Professor; Consultant. m. Chuen-Mei Hsu, 9 Mar. 1970, Taipei, 2 sons. *Education:* MB. *Appointments:* Resident, Chief Resident, Internal Medicine; Lecturer Department of Clinical Pathology; Consultant Chest Physician, Internal Medicine, National Taiwan University Hospital. *Memberships:* Fellow, Internal College of Chest Physicians and Surgeons; Member, International Academy of Cytology. *Publications:* 'Primary lung cancer in Taiwan', 1976; 'Fine Needleaspiration cytology in the diagnosis of cervical lymphadenopathy', 1979; 'Cytophotometric measurements of nuclear DNA content of bronchogenic carcinomas', 1985. *Hobbies:* Table Tennis; Music. *Address:* 10 Lane 185,Sec, 2 Ching-Shan South Road, Taipei, Taiwan, 10604, Republic of China.

KUPFERBERG, Cyril William, b. 1 Nov. 1927, Chicago, Illinois, USA. Assistant Senior Vice President, Medical Center; Associate Dean, College of Medicine. m. Louis Grusin, 19 June 1949, Chicago, 4 sons. *Education:* BS, 1949, MS, 1950, University of Illinois. *Appointments Include:* Research Chemist, Ethicon Incorporated, 1952-57; Assistant Director for Administration, 1961-69,

Executive Assistant, Department of Medicine, Business Administrator, 1969-76, University of Chicago, Pritzker School of Medicine, Illinois; Assistant Dean, Clinical Services, 1976-77, Associate Dean, Administration, 1977-79, University of Illinois, Abraham Lincoln Medical School; Assistant Dean, Management and Finance, 1979-81, Associate Dean, 1981-83, Assistant Senior Vice President, Medical Centre, Associate Dean, 1983-, University of Cincinnati College of Medicine. Former Consultant to various organisations. *Memberships Include:* Past Member of various committees, Past Committee Chairman, Past Vice Chairman and Secretary-Treasurer, Midwest Great Plains Region, Association of American Medical Colleges; Several past professional memberships; Member of numerous civic groups. *Honours:* Omega Beta Phi; various biographical entries. *Hobbies:* Fishing; Photography; Camping; Carptentry. *Address:* University of Cincinnati Collegeof Medicine, Medical Center Administrative Services, Eden and Bethesda Avenues, 151 Health Professions Building ML 553, Cincinnati, OH 45267, USA.

KURER, Peter Frank, b. 22 Apr. 1931, Austria, Dental Surgeon. m. Heather Gillian Goldstone, 11 Sept. 1955, Manchester, England. 1 son, 3 daughters. *Education:* LDS, University of Dunelm, 1955; MGDSRCS, Royal College of Surgeons, 1980. *Appointments:* Dental Officer, Royal Air Force, 1955-57; Dental Surgeon, Family Group Practice. *Memberships Include:* Member, International Association for Dental Research; British Dental Assoc.; British Endodontic Society; British Society for Restorative Dentistry; Alpha Omega Chapter of Dentists. *Publications:* Presentation of Scientific Papers in various countries; 'A Graphic Illustration of the Kurer Anchor System', (with Jean Perry, 1967; 'Trenica para applicacao do attachment Kurer', 1979; 'The Fin LockSystemfd', 1979; 'Questions and Answers on Post Crown Restorations'; 'Das Kurer System, Das Zahnarztliche Mitteilungsblatt fur den Prakiker', 1981; 'Il Sistema Kurer Press Stud', 1981; (books) 'The Kurer Anchor System - An approach to the Restoration and re-use of Endodontically Treated Teeth', 1984; 'The Kurer Anchor System', German and Japanese translation, 1985. *Honours Include:* President, British Society for Restorative Dentistry, 1983-84; President, Newcastle Dental Graduates' Association, 1985-86; Fellow, International College of Dentists. *Hobbies:* Music; Photography. *Address:* 39 Deansgate, Manchester M3 2AD, England.

KURITZ, Harold Michael, b. 31 Mar. 1942, Boston, Massachusetts, USA, Podiatric Physician, Surgeon. m. Roslyn Susan Seltzer, 3 Aug. 1969, Brookline, Massachusetts, 1 son, 1 daughter. *Education:* BA, Boston University, 1965; MSc, Northeastern University, 1968; DPM, California College of Posiatric Medicine, 1973. *Appointments:* Assistant Director, Residency Training, 1975-77, Director Residency Training, Hayward Vesper Hospital, 1977-80; Secretary Treasurer, 1979-80, President, Alameda-Contra Costa Podiatric Medical Association, 1980-81; Chief, Department of Podiatry Veteran's Administration Hospital, Livermore, 1982-; Chief Podiatric Surgery, Valley Memorial Hospital, Livermore, 1983-. *Memberships:* American Podiatry Medical Assoc.; California Podiatric Medical Assoc.; American Academy of Podiatric Laser Surgery; American Academy of Podiatric Micro Surgey; American College of Foot Surgeons; Alumni Assoc., California College of Podiatric Medicine. *Publications:* 'Locus of the Action of serum and the Role of Lysozmye in the Serum Bactericidal Reaction', 1968; 'Locus of the Lethal Event in the Bactericidal Reaction', 1968; 'Tarsal Tunnel Syndrome', 1975; 'Congenital Claw Food Deformity, A Case Report', 1977; 'Anterior Entrapment Syndromes' 1977; 'Post Traumatic Ossification in the Flexor Hallucis Longus Tendon Sheath: A Case Presentation', 1977. *Honours:* Pi Delta National

Podiatric Honour Society, 1973; Fellowship, American College of Foot Surgeons, 1977; Diplomate, American Board of Podiatric Surgery, 1975. *Hobbies:* Computer Technology; Landscaping; Remodelling; Jogging. *Address:* 155 Haven Hill Court, Danville, CA 94526, USA.

KURIYAMA, Kinya, b. 11 July 1932, Kyoto, Japan. Professor and Chairman, Department of Pharmacology. m. 10 Dec 1959, Kyoto, Japan, 2 sons. *Education:* MD, 1957, PhD, 1963, Kyoto Prefectural University of Medicine. *Appointments include:* Associate Resident Scientist, 1964-66, Head, Section of Neuropharmacology, 1966-69, City of Hope Medical Centre; Associate Professor, Loma Linda University School of Medicine, 1966-69; Director of Neuropharmacology, Department of Psychiatry, State University of New York, Downstate Medical Center, 1969-71; Professor and Chairman, Department of Pharmacology, 1971-, Director of Research 1979-83, Kyoto Prefectural University of Medicine. *Memberships:* Board of Directors, Japanese Society of Pharmacology; Board of Directors, Japanese Society of Neurochemistry; Council, International Society of Neurochemistry; Council, International Society of Developmental Neurosciences; Board of Directors, International Society of Biomedical Research on Alcoholism; President, Japanese Society of Studies of Alcohol; Board of Directors, Japanese Neurochemical Society. *Publications:* "Pharmacology of Brain" 1978; "Biochemical Pharmacology" 1982; "Sulfur Amino Acids Biochemical and Clinical Aspects" 1982; "Clinical Pharmacology and Therapeutics" 1982; "Pharmacology of Brain and Nerve" 1985; "Function and Structure of Synapses" 1979; "Therapeutics for Neuropsychiatric Disorders" 1984. *Honour:* Achievement Award from Japanese Medical Society, 1980. *Hobbies:* Travel; Tennis. *Address:* 69-1 Iwagakakiuchi-Cho, Kamikamo, Kita-Ku, Kyoto 603, Japan.

KURJAK, Asim, b. 13 Sep. 1949, Banja Luka, Yugoslavia, Professor and Chairman, Department of Obstetrics and Gynaecology, University of Zagreb, m. Biserka Funduk, 10 July 1972, Zagreb, 2 sons. *Education:* MD, 1967; PhD, 1977; Professor of Obstetrics and Gynaecology, 1981. *Appointments:* Director of Health Centre, Kotor Varos, 1967; Assistant Professor of Obstetrics and Gynaecology, University of Zagreb, 1969; Professor of Obstetrics and Gynaecology, 1980; Head, Ultrasonic Institute, Zagreb, 1981; Head, Department of Obstetrics and Gynaecology. 1985. *Memberships:* Honorary Member of Societies for Obstetrics and Gynaecology in Italy, Poland and Chile; Honorary Member, Ultrasonic Societies of Australia, Indonesia and Egypt; Vice-President, European Federation of Ultrasound in medicine and Biology. *Publications:* Contributor of numerous articles to professional journals. *Honours:* National Prize for Young Scientist, 1971; Gold OSIM, Italian prize for scientific work, 1980; National Prize for scientific work 'Rudjer Boskovic', 1985. *Hobbies:* Classical music; Literature; Swimming; Skiing. *Address:* Ljubinkovac stube 1, 41000 Zagreb, Yugoslavia.

KURKJIAN, Henry Joseph, b. 28 June 1920, Basra. Thoracic Surgeon; Public Health Administrator. m. Jacqueline. *Education:* Certified General and Thoracic Surgeon; Executive Public Administrator; BA; MD; FRCS(C); FACS; FACP; FACEP; MPA. *Appointments:* Thoracic Surgeon, Santa Calisini and Queen Elizabeth Hospitals, Montreal, Canada; In Charge of Thoracic Surgery, Lakeshore General Hospital, Montreal, Canada; Staff Thoracic Surgeon, St Vincent Medical Center, Los Angeles, USA; Chief, Medical Administrative Studies, Olive View Medical Center, Los Angeles. *Memberships:* American College of Surgeons; American College of Chest Physicians; Royal College of Surgeons; Royal Society of Medicine; American College of Emergency Medicine. *Hobbies:* Photography; Real Estate.

Address: PO Box 4069, North Hollywood, CA 91607, USA.

KURNICK, Nathaniel Bertrand, b. 8 Nov. 1917, New York, USA. Director, Bixby Oncology Laboratory. m. Dorothy Manheimer, 4 Oct. 1940, 2 sons, 1 daughter (deseased). *Education:* BA, Harvard College, 1936; MD, Harvard Medical School, 1940; Certified, National Board of Medical Examiners 1942, American Board of Internal Medicine 1951, Medical Oncology 1973, Harmatology 1974; Research Fellow, Harvard University, 1940-41, Rockefeller Institute 1947-48, Karolinska Institute, Stockholm, Sweden, 1948-49. *Appointments:* Intern, Mount Sinai Hospital, New York, 1941-42; Medical Officer, US Army, Pacific Area, 1942-46; Resident in Medicine, Mount Sinai Hospital, 1946; Fellow, American Cancer Society, Rockefeller Institute for Medical Research, 1947-48; Assistant Professor of Medicine, Tulane University School of Medicine, 1949-54; Associate Clinical Professor of Medicine, University of California at Los Angeles, 1954-65; Associate Professor of Medicine in Residence, University of California at Irving, 1965-68; Associate Research Internist, University of California, 1959-67; Clinical Professor of Medicine, University of California at Irving, 1968-; Chairman, Director of Haematology-Oncology Laboratory, Long Beach Community Hospital, 1981-. *Memberships include:* Histochemical Society; Society for Experiemtnal Biology & Medicine; International Societies for Biological Chemistry, for Cell Biology; American Medical Association; Sigma Xi; Fellow, American college of Physicians; International Society of Haematology; Radiation Research Society. *Publications:* Research articles on Bone Marrow storage & repopulation, radiation effects, Chemo-sensitivity assay of Cancer, Nucleic acid biochemistry & Histochemistry, stain technology. *Hobbies:* Sailing; Skiing. *Address:* 1760 Termino Avenue, G20, Long Beach, CA 90804, USA.

KURUP, Viswanath P, b. 20 Jan 1936, India. Associate Professor, Medicine. m. Indira, 2 Nov 1962, Kerala, 2 sons, 1 daughter. *Education:* BS, Fergusson College, Poona, 1957; MS, Botany, University of Poona, 1959; PhD, Medical Mycology, V P Chest Institute, University of Delhi, 1967. *Appointments:* Mycologist, Medical College, Trivandrum, 1967-68; Research Associate, Ohio State University, USA, 1969-70; Microbiologist, St Anthony Hospital, Columbus, 1970-73; Assistant Professor, Pathology, Medical College, Wisconsin, 1973-77; Microbiologist, Research Service VA Medical Centre, Milwaukee, 1973-; Associate Professor, Medicine, Medical College, Wisconsin, 1977-. *Memberships:* International Society of Human & Animal Mycology; Mycological Society of America; American Society for Microbiologists; Academy of Allergy & Clinical Immunology; Medical Mycological Society of Americas; International Society of Aerobiology. *Publications include:* Co-Author, "Hypersensitivity Pneumonitis", 'Mould Allergy", 1984; "Thermophilic actinmoyetes: their role in HP", 'Biological, Biochemical & Biomedical Aspects of Actinomycetes', 1984; "Serological diagnosis of hypersensitivity pneumonits", 'Microbiology', 1985; over 80 other publications in professional journals. *Honours:* Elected Fellow, American Academy of Microbiology, 1985; Chaired HP Session, ASM Meeting, St Louis, 1984; Fulbright Fellow, University of Kuopio, Finland, 1984; Visiting Professor, Ponce School of Medicine, Puerto Rico, 1981-83. *Address:* Allergy-Immunology Section, Medical College of Wisconsin, Research Service, 151, Clement J Zablocki VA Medical Centre, 5000 W National Avenue, Milwaukee, WI 53295, USA.

KUTINA, Kenneth Lee, b. 10 Sept. 1936, Cleveland, Ohio, USA. Senior Associate Dean, University Medical School. m. Judith Jones, 27 Nov. 1958, Massilon, Ohio, USA, 1 son, 1 daughter. *Education:* PhD, Management; MBA, Economics and Statistics; MS, Industrial Engineering and Statistics; BS,

Mechanical Enginering. *Appointments:* Engineer, Standard Oil of Ohio; Instructor, Department of Statistics, Western Researve University, Ohio, USA, Lecturer, Deaprtment of Statistics; Senior Engineer, Stadard Oil Co. of Ohio, Senior Analyst, Management Science Staff; Planning Officer, University Plans and Programmes, Case Western Reserve University, Director of Operations, Planning and Analysis, School of Medicine, Assistant Dean for Planning and Administration, Associate Dean, Assistant Professor of Community Health-; Assistant Professor, School of Management-. *Memberships:* The Society for Computer Simulation; Institute of Management Sciences; Association for Institutional Research; Society for College and University Planning; Association of American Medical Colleges, Planning Co-ordinators and Business Officers Sections. *Publications include:* Numerous conference papers and monographs; Chapter 'Program Planning and Faculty Activity Analysis' in "A Flexible Design for Health Professions Education", 1976; co-author 'Faculty Vitality Given Retrenchment - a Policy Analysis' paper presented at the 20th Annual Forum of Association for Institutional Research, and published in "Research in Higher Education", 1981. *Honours:* Sigma Xi; Tau Beta Phi; Theta Tau; Phi Kappa Alpha; Blue Key; Cornell Graduate Fellowship, 1959; Beta Gamma Sigma, 1967. *Hobbies:* Sailing; Ski-ing; Photography; Tennis. *Address:* School of Medicine, Case Western Reserve University, 2119 Abington Road, Cleveland, OH 44106, USA.

KUUSK, Sven, b. 24 July 1941, Tartu. Nursing Home Proprietor. m. Geraldine Margaret Rowett, 4 Feb. 1967, Marryatville, 1 son, 1 daughter. *Education:* BDS; MDS; RFD; FRACDS; BDS (Hons.). *Appointments:* House Surgeon Professional Unit, RAH; Teaching Dental Registrar, QEH; Part time Tutor, University of Adelaide; Orthodontist, Private Practice, 1973-. *Memberships:* Australian Society for Orthodontists; Royal Australian College Dental Surgeons; United Services Institution; Military Historical Society of Australia; Commanding Officer, Adelaide University Regiment. *Publications:* "Deciduous Crown Morhology in Australian Aborigines". *Honours:* Reserve Forces Decoration, 1984; National Medal, 1977. *Hobby:* Collecting Militaria. *Address:* 163 North Ice, Adelaide 5000, South Australia.

KWAAN, Hau C, b. 30 Sep 1931, Hong Kong. Professor of Medicine. m. Louise P L Kwaan, 1958, 1 son, 1 daughter. *Education:* MB BS, 1952; MD, 1958; Member, Royal College of Physicians (Edinburgh), 1958. *Appointments:* Lecturer in Medicine, University of Hong Kong, 1959-61; Senior Investigator, James F Mitchell Foundation, Washington DC, USA, 1962-65; Clinical Assistant Professor of Medicine, Georgetown University School of Medicine, 1964-65; Associate Professor 1966-71. Professor of Medicine 1972-, Northwestern University School of Medicine, Chicago, Illinois; Chief, Haematology/Oncology Section, VA Lakeside Medical Centre, Chicago, 1966-; Attending Physician, Northwestern Memorial Hospital, Chicago, 1972-. *Memberships:* Fellow, Royal College of Physicians (Edinburgh); Fellow, American College of Physicians; American Society for Clinical Investigation; American Physiological Scoiety; American Socity of Haematology; American Society of Clinical Oncology; Central Society of Clinical Research; International Society on Thrombosis & Haemostasis; American Medical Association;

Council Member on Thrombosis, American Heart Association; Alpha Omega Alpha. *Publications:* More than 175 articles, book chapters & papers in field. *Honours:* China Medical Board of New York Research Fellowship, 1958; Elwood Sharp Award for Contribution to the field of blood Coagulation, Wayne State University, Detroit, 1972; Distinguished Service Award, Department of Medicine, Northwestern University Medical School, 1978; Senior Fulbright Travel Scholarship, 1974. *Hobbies:* Underwater photography; Painting. *Address:* 347 Jeffery Lane, Northfield, IL 60093, USA.

KWAPISZEWSKI, Wincenty, b. 9 Nov 1927, Kamieniec Lit. Poland. University Professor. m. 29 Nov 1955, 1 daughter. *Education:* Graduated, Pharmaceutical Faculty, University of Poznan, 1952; Doctor of Pharmacy, 1962, Doctor Habil, 1974, Medical Academy of Warsaw. *Appointments:* Assistant, Pharmaceutical Chemistry Department, Medical Academy of Poznan, 1952-54; Adjunct, 1955-58, Associate Professor and Head, 1969-83, Professor and Head, 1983-84, Pharmaceutical Chemistry Department, Medical Academy of Warsaw; Vice-Dean, Pharmaceutical Chemistry and Drug Analysis Department, Medical Academy of Lodz. *Memberships:* President, Organising Committee, 36th FJP Congress, Warsaw, 1974-76; President, Polsih Pharmaceutical Society, 1977-; Vice-President, Federation of Polish Medical Societies, 1978-; Member FKP Council, 1977-; Member, Board of Polsih Scientific Societies at Polish Academy of Sciences, 1978-; Member, Scientific Board of Ministry of Health and Social Welfare, 1978-; Member, Scientific Board of Ministry of Chemical Industry, 1984-; Member, Editorial Committee, Polish Pharmacy 'Acta Poloniae Pharmaceutica''. *Publications:* "Chemical Quantitative Analysis of Drugs" 1975; "Chemistry of Drugs" co-author, 1978; More than 130 scientific papers and review articles. *Honours:* Honorary Member, Pharmaceutical Society of Czechoslovak Republic, 1981; Honorary Member, Pharamceutical Society of Soviet Union, 1980. *Hobbies:* Synthetic history of world and culture; Music; Tourism. *Address:* Department of Pharmaceutical Chemistry and Drug Analysis, Muszynskiego Str Nr 1, 90-145 Lodz, Poland.

KYNASTON, Bruce, b. 27 Apr. 1931, Brisbane, Australia. Deputy Director, Queensland Radium Institute. m. Gwynneth Anne Harris, 17 Nov. 1956, Brisbane, Australia, 1 son, 1 daughter. *Education:* MB, BS, University of Queensland, Australia, 1954; Diploma, Royal Australasian College of Radiologists, 1958; Fellowship, Royal College of Radiologist, England, 1963; Fellowship, Royal Australian College of Medical Administrators, 1984. *Appointments:* Resident Medical Officer, Brisbane General Hospital, Australia, 1955; Medical Officer, Queensland Radium Institute, 1956-58, Radiation Oncologist, 1958-77, Assistant Director, 1977-83, Deputy Director, 1983-present. *Memberships:* Australian Medical Association; Royal Asutralian College of Radiologists; British Institute of Radiology; Clinical Oncological Society of Australia; Royal Australian College of Medical Administrators; Royal Australian Institute of Public Administrators; National Health and Medical Research Council, 1976-84; Australian Ionizing Radiation Advisory Council, 1983-present. *Honour:* Fellowship, Australian Medical Association, 1985. *Hobbies:* Gardening; Creative Embroidery; Wood Carving. *Address:* 30 Janie Street, Aspley, Queensland 4034, Australia.

L

LAAGE, Thomas Allen, b. 22 Apr. 1951, USA. Assistant Psychiatrist; Instructor. m. Carmen L Jaquier, 5 June 1976, Norwalk, Conn. *Education:* AB, Harvard College, 1973; MD, A Einstein College of Medicine, 1976. *Appointments:* Internship and Residency, Internal Medicine, Peter Bent Brigham Hospital, Boston, MA, 1976-79; Residency in Psychiatry, McLean Hospital, Belmont, MA, 1979-82. *Memberships:* American Psychiatric Assoc.; MA Medical Society; MA Psychiatric Society. *Publications:* 'Urine Culture After Treatment of Incomplicated Cystitis in Women' (with Winschoff, Wilmer, Gull, Barnett), 1981, Southern Medical Journal. *Honours:* Phi Beta Kappa, 1972; Alpha Omega Alpha, 1976. *Hobbies:* Philosophy; Golf. *Address:* 32 Kensington Road, Arlington, MA 02174, USA.

LABAR, Boris, b. 9 Apr. 1947, Zadar, Yugoslavia. Head, Division of Haematology. m. Zeljka Dujmic MD, 24 July 1971, Zadar, 2 sons. *Education:* Medical Faculty, University of Zagreb, 1970; Postgraduate Course in Clinical Laboratory Correlations, 1972-75; Board Examination in Internag Medicine, 1976; Master of Science, 1979; Doctor of Medical Sciences, Medical Faculty, Zagreb, 1982. *Appointments:* Assistant of Internal Medicine, Medical Faculty, University of Zagreb, 1978-84; Head, Bone Marrow Transplantation Unit, Division of Haematology, Department of Medicine, Clinical Hospital Centre, University of Zagreb, 1982-85; Associate Professor of Internal Medicine, Medical Faculty, University of Zagreb, 1984-; Head, Division of Haematology, Department of Medicine, Clinical Hospital Centre, University of Zagreb, 1985-. *Memberships:* Croatian Society of Haematology; Yugoslav Society of Haematology; European Bone Marrow Transplant Group; International Bone Marrow Transplant Registry. *Publications:* "Bone Marrow Transplantation" 1985; "Principles of Haematology and Transfusiology" 1986. *Hobbies:* Waterpolo; Basketball. *Address:* Hegedusiceva 6, 41000 Zagreb, Yugoslavia.

LABARRE, Jean-François René, b. 1 June 1936, Nancy, France. Chemical Engineer. m. Dr M-C Malick-Parlange, 26 July 1958, Toulouse, France, 3 sons, 2 daughters. *Education:* ENSCT Chemical Engineer, 1958; Doctor of Science 1963. *Appointments:* Research Probationer, CNRS, 1958; Research Attaché, CNRS, 1959; In charge of Research project, CNRS, 1963; Master of Research, CNRS, 1965; Director of Research, CNRS, 1974; Director of 'Structure et Vie' Laboratory, Paul Sabatier University, Toulouse. *Publications:* 350 papers in 40 French & other international journals (mostly in English). *Honours:* Silver Medal of CNRS, 1972; Pierre Sue Award, French Chemical Society, 1975; Paul Pascal Award of French Academy of Sciences, 1975; Silver Medal, Soviet Lomonosov Institute, 1976; Toulousain of the Year, 1981. *Hobbies:* Classical Music; Gospels; Spirituals; Good wines; humour. *Address:* 30 rue des Géraniums 31400 Toulouse, France.

LABORDE, James Monroe, b. 27 Mar. 1947, New Orleans, LA, USA, Orthopaedic Surgeon, Touro Infirmary, Clinical Assistant Professor, Tulane University. m. 5 July 1969, 3 sons, 1 daughter. *Education:* BSc, 1969, MD, 1973, Tulane University; MSc, Case Western Reserve University, 1976. *Appointments:* Assistant Professor of Orthopaedics, Vanderbilt University; Chief of Orthopaedics, Veterans Administration Hospital, Nashville, Tenn. *Memberships:* Nashville Academy of Medicine; Davidson County Medical Society; Nashville Orthopaedic Society; Vanderbilt Orthopaedic Society; Orthopaedic Research Society; Orleans Parish Medical Society; Greater New Orleans Orthopaedic Society; Louisiana Orthopaedic Association; Tulane Caldwell Society; American Occupational Medical Association; American Academy for Cerebral Palsy and Development Medicine; American Academy of Orthopaedic Surgeons;

Catholic Physician's Guild of New Orleans. *Publications:* 'Inertial Properties of a Segmented Cadaver Trunk: Their Implications in Acceleration Injuries', 1971; 'Arthritis in Hemachromatosis-A Case Report', 1977; 'Experimental Comparison of Internal Fixation of Fractures of the Dorsolumbar Spine', 1980; 'Comparison of Fixation of Spine Fractures', 1980; 'Cadaver Studies in Spinal Stability', 1980; 'A Method of Analyzing the Three- Dimensional Stiffness Properties of the Intact Human Spine', 1981; 'Workman's Compensation, Litigation and Lumbosciatic Syndrome'. *Honours:* Tau Beta Pi; Omicron Delta Kappa; Alpha Epsilon Delta; Pi Mu Epsilon; AMA Physicians Recognition Award, 1980. *Hobbies:* Tennis; Jogging. *Address:* 3525 Prytania Street, No 402, New Orleans, LA 70115, USA.

LABRECQUE, Jean-Marie, b. 3 May 1930, Beaumont, Quebec, Canada. University Professor. m. Danielle Duchesne, 9 June 1984, Trois Rivieres, Quebec, 2 sons from previous marriage. *Education:* BA, University of Ottawa, Canada, 1954; BSc, 1956, BEd, 1957, MA, (Psychology), 1962. *Appointments:* Clinical Psychologist, Ontario Hospital, Kingston, Ontario, 1958-62; Clinical Psychologist, Director of Psychological Services, Institut Psycho-Social, Trois Rivieres, 1962-69; Professor, University of Quebec at Trois Rivieres, 1969-85. *Memberships:* La Corporation des Psychologues de la Province de Quebec; Ontario Board of Examiners in Psychology; American Psychological Association; National Council on Family Relations. *Publications:* "La Famille: Quatre Priorités", 1977; 'Premier Mandat: Une Prospective a court terme du gouvernement Péquiste' in 'Les Editions de l'Aurore'; editorial of volume I "Systemes Humains", 1985. *Hobbies:* Skiing; Swimming; Hunting. *Address:* Department de Psychologie, Université du Quebec a Trois Rivieres, CP500 Trois Rivieres, Quebec Province, Canada G9A 5H7.

LABUSCHAGNE, Izak, b. 2 Feb 1928, Zastron, Republic of South Africa. Ear, Nose and Throat Specialist. m. Margaret Antoinette Eglington, 23 May 1973, Johannesburg, 5 sons, 1 daughter. *Education:* MB, ChB, Pretoria University; Fellow, Royal College of Surgeons, Edinburgh, Scotland. *Appointments:* Lieutenant Colonel, South African Defence Force; Founder Member, International Rugby Board Medical Sub-Committee; Executive Member, South African Rugby Board Medical Sub-Committee. *Memberships:* Civil Aviation Medical Association; Federation Internationale Medicine de Sport; International Aerospace Medical Association; British Sport Medical Association; Royal College of Medicine; World Boxing Association Medical Sub-Committee. *Publications:* Contributions to: 'World Boxing Association Bulletin Medical Review', 1983-84; The South African Texbook of Sports Medicine"; 'South African Medical Journal of Medicine'. *Honours:* Honorary Fellow, South African Aeronautical Society, 1985. *Hobbies:* Boxing and rugby administration. *Address:* 83 Central Avenue, Houghton, Johannesburg 2196, Republic of South Africa.

LACERENZA, Andrew, b. 13 Mar. 1956, Sicily. Doctor of Chiropractic. m. Frances P D'Amico, 12 Apr. 1980, 1 son, 1 daughter. *Education:* AA, Nassau Community College; BA, Bloomfield College, New Jersey; DC, New York Chiropractic College. *Appointments:* Member of Faculty, New York Chiropractic College; Associate Clinic Director, Outpatient Facility, New York Chiropractic College; Member, President's Task Force for Student Affairs, ibid. *Memberships:* New York State Chiropractic Association; American Chiropractic Association; National Academy of Research Biochemists; Society for Non-Inovosive Vascular Testing; Member of the Board, Suffolk County Chiropractic Association. *Publication:* "A Manual for the Chiropractic Assistant", 1985. *Honours:* Dean's List, 1978, 1979, President's Club, 1979, Distinguished Service, 1979, New York Chiropractic College. *Hobbies:* Music; Sports; Consultant to JAFCO Video Production. *Address:* 199 N Wellwood Avenue, Lindenhurst, NY 11757, USA.

LACHMANN, Peter Julius, b. 23 Dec. 1931, Berlin. Sheila Joan Smith Professor for Tumour Immunology. m. Sylvia Stephenson, 7 July 1962, Haywards Heath, 2 sons, 1 daughter. *Education:* BA, Trinity College Cambridge; MD B Chir, University College Hospital, London; PhD, ScD, Cambridge University; FRCP; FRCPath. *Appointments:* Visiting Investigator, Assistant Physician, Rockefeller Institute, New York, USA, 1960-61; Arthritis and Rheumatism Council Fellow, University of Cambridge, 1962-64; Assistant Director, Research, Pathology, University of Cambridge, 1964-71; Professor, Immunology, RPMS, London, 1971-75; Sheila Joan Smith Professor of Tumour Immunology, University of Cambridge & Honorary Director, MRC MITI Unit. *Memberships:* British Society of Immunology; American Association of Immunology; Fellow, Royal Society of Medicine; Series Editor, 'Progress in Allergy'; Council Member, Board, 'British Journal Experimental Pathology', member, Editorial Boards, 'Immunology'; 'European Journal Immunology'; 'Sandinavian Journal Immunology'; 'Medical Microbiology and Immunology'; 'Springer Sem in Immunopathology'; 'Immunological Communications'; etc. *Publications:* Articles in numerous professional journals including: 'Immunology'; 'Experimental Cell Research'; 'Immunochemistry'; 'Lancet'; 'Journal of Immunology'; 'Nature'; 'British Medical Bulletin'; etc. *Honours:* FRS, 1982. *Hobby:* Beekeeping. *Address:* Mechanisms in Tumour Immunity Unit, MRC Centre, Hills Road, Cambridge, England.

LACOURSIERE, Roy Barnaby, b. 9 Aug 1937, Windsor, Canada. Psychiatrist. m. (2) Joanna Robinson, 27 Sep 1982, Topeka, 1 son, 3 daughters. *Education:* BA, University of Windsor, Windsor, 1962; MD, McGill University, Montreal, 1966; FAPA; FACP; FRCP. *Appointments:* Director Community Service Office and Research and Foundation Departments, Menninger Foundation, Topeka, 1971-75; Psychiatrist and group coordinator, Topeka State Hospital, Topeka, 1972-75; Consultant 1974-75, Chief of Chemical Problem Treatment Unit, Veterans Administration Hospital, Topeka; Visiting Professor, Washburn Law School; Faculty, Menninger School of Psychiatry. *Memberships include:* American Psychiatric Association; Canadian Psychiatric Association; American Public Health Association; American Academy of Psychiatry and Law; American Medical Society Alcoholism; Sigma Xi; Research Society in Alcoholism. *Publications include:* 'Traumatic Neurosis in the etiology of alcoholism: Vietnam Combat and other trauma', 1980; "The Life Cycle of Groups: Group Development Stage Theory", 1980. *Honours:* Governor General's Medal, University of Windsor, 1966; Gold Medal in Obstetrics, McGill University, 1966; Distinguished Writing Award, Menninger School of Psychiatry, 1970. *Hobbies:* Classical Music; Legal Psychiatry; Reading. *Address:* Veterans Administration Hospital, Topeka, KS 66622, USA.

LADENSON, Jack Herman, b. 8 Apr. 1942, Philadelphia, Pennsylvania, USA. Clinical Chemist. m. Ruth E. Carroll, 23 June 1968, Washington, District of Columbia, 1 son, 1 daughter. *Education:* BS, Pennsylvania State University, 1964; PhD, Analytical Chemistry, University of Maryland, 1971; Postdoctoral Fellow in Clinical Chemistry, Hartford Hospital, 1979-82. *Appointments:* Assistant Professor of Pathology and Medicine, 1972-79; Associate Professor of Pathology and Clinical Chemsitry in Medicine, 1979-84; Professor of Pathology and Clinical Chemsitry in Medicine, 1984-, Washington University School of Medicine, St. Louis, Missouri; Assistant Director of Clinical Chemistry, Division of Laboratory Medicine, Barnes Hospital, St. Louis, Missouri, 1972-76; Co-Director of Clinical Chemistry, 1976-79; Director of Clinical Chemistry, 1980-, Head, Section of Clinical Chemistry and Clinical Computing, 1980-, Division of Laboraotry Medicine, Washington University School of Medicine, St. Louis. *Memberships:* American Association for Clinical Chemistry, Board of Directors, 1981-83, 1985-87; President, 1986; Academy of Clinical Laboratory Physicians and Scientists, Executive Council, 1984-; American Board of Clinical Chemistry, Board of Directors, 1975-85; Commission of Accreditation in Clinical Chemsitry, Vice-President, 1981-85. *Publications:* Over 70 articles and book chapters; Editorial Boards of: 'Clinical Chemistry', 'Critical Reviews in Clinical Laboratory Sciences', 'Clinical Chemistry Outlook'. *Honour:* NSF Pre-doctoral Fellowship, 1966-70. *Hobbies:* Handball; Cycling; Skiing. *Address:* Washington University School of Medicine, Division of Laboratory Medicine, Box 8118, St. Louis, MO 63110, USA.

LADWIG, Harold Allen, b. 11 May 1922, Manilla, Iowa, USA. Practicing Neurologist, City of Wilson, North Carolina; Electroencephalographer, Wilson Memorial Hospital. m. Marjorie Lois Foster, 26 June 1946, Sioux City, Iowa, 1 son, 1 daughter. *Education:* MD, University of Iowa College of Medicine, 1947; BA, University of Iowa, 1952. *Appointments:* Instructor, Department of Neurology, University of Minnesota; Associate Professor of Neurology, Creighton University School of Medicine and Nebraska College of Medicine; Associate Director, Rehabilitation Center, Creighton Memorial, St Joseph's Hospital; Associate Director, Children's Therapy Center, Omaha, Nebraska; President, Omaha Neurological Clinic; Director of Electroencephalographic Laboratory, Creighton Memorial St Joseph Hospital, Children's Hospital and Archbishop Bergen Mercy Hospital, Omaha, Nebraska; President, Omaha Neurological Clinic Incorporated, 1972-83. *Memberships:* North Carolina State Medical Association; North Carolina Neurological Society; Fellow, American Academy of Neurology; Fellow, American College of Physicians; Fellow, American Electroenceph; Member, American Medical Association; The American Congress of Rehabilitation Medicine; Associate Member, American Society of Electromyography and Electrodiagnosis; Society of Neuro-Imaging; Diplomat, National Boards; Beta Beta Beta; Phi Beta Phi; Phi Beta Kappa. *Publications:* Multiple publications of topics pertaining to Neurology in National and State Journals, 'Rehabilitation of the Hemiplegic Patient', 'Current Therapy', 1966. *Honours:* Recipient of several honours. *Hobbies:* Gardening; Antiqueing. *Address:* 1600 Canal Drive, Wilson, NC 27893, USA.

LAEMMEL, Klaus, b. 20 July, 1931, Switzerland. Director, Department of Psychiatry, Lucerne Cantonal Hospital. *Education:* Doctorate in Medicine, Zurich, Switzerland, 1956; Licence to practice Medicine in New York, USA, 1960; Diplomate, American Board of Psychiatry; Certified Psychiatrist in Switzerland. *Appointments:* Director, St. Agatha Home, Nauet, New York, 1963-76; Consultant Psychiatrist, Metropolitan Hospital, New York, USA, Grasslands Hospital, Walhalla, New York, 1963-76; Assistant Clinical Professor of Psychiatry, New York Medical College, 1964-76; Director of Psychiatry, Lucerne General Hospital-; Private Psychiatric Practice, Lucerne, Switzerland-. *Memberships:* Fellow, American Psychiatric Association; Swiss Medical and Psychiatric Association. *Publications:* 'Sex and the Arts' in "The Sexual Experience", 1976; Numerous papers in medical journals. *Hobbies:* Painting; Mountaineering. *Address:* Psychiatrische Klinik, Kantosspital Lucerne, 6004 Lucerne, Switzerland.

LAHAM, Michel Nicolas, b. 7 Sep. 1946, Jacksonville, Florida, USA. Medical Doctor. m. Hala Laham, 24 Nov. 1976, Gainesville, FLA, 1 son, 1 daughter. *Education:* MD, 1971, BA, University of Florida, 1967. *Appointments:* Assistant Chief of Allergy, 1976-78, Chief of Immunology, Brooke Army Medical Center, 1978-82; Staff, Department of Medicine, Metropolitan

General Hospital, San Antonio, 1982; Baptist Medical Center, San Antonio, 1983; Santa Rosa Medical Center, San Antonio, 1982; Associate Clinical Professor, Department of Pediatric, University of Texas Health Science Center at San Antonio, 1982. *Memberships:* American College of Physicians; American College of Allergists; American Academy of Allergy and Immunology; American Association of Certified Allergists; Joint Council of Allergy and Immunology. *Publications include:* 'Increased Induction of Immunoglobulin Secreting Cells in the Presence of Drugs that Induce Lupus Erythematosus', (with D G Burleson), 1981; 'Frequency of Clinical Isolation and Winter Prevalence of Different Aspergillus Species at a Large Southwestern Army Medical Center', (with J L Carpenter, B Jeffery), 1982; "Modulation of Lymphocyte Proliferative Responses to Mitogens and Antigens by Complement Components C1, C4 and C2', (with R S Panush, J C Caldwell), 1982. *Honours:* Phi Alpha Theta, 1966; BA, Cum Laude, 1967; Fellow, American College of Physicians, 1982; American College of Allergists, 1983. *Hobbies:* Sailing; Music. *Address:* 1303 McCullough, Suite 161, San Antonio, TX 78212, USA.

LAHTINEN, Aira Liisa, b. 2 Mar. 1941, Helsinki, Finland. Assistant Editor, Dental Journal. m. Pekka Lahtinen, 23 Aug. 1963, 2 daughters. *Education:* Licentiate in Dentistry, 1966; Specialist in Clinical Dentistry, 1978. *Appointments:* Lecturer, School for Dental Assistants and Hygienists, 1975-; currently, Assistant Editor, Finnish Dental Journal. *Memberships:* Finnish Dental Association; Finnish Dental Society; FDI; Scandinavian Society of Peridontology; Scandinavian Division, International Association for Dental Research. *Publications:* Author of 30 articles on oral health promotion in Finnish journals for dentists and other health professionals, Health Education material, booklets, contributions to encyclopedias, articles for public in magazines and newspapers, 1972-. *Address:* Finnish Dental Association, Akavatalo, Rautatieläisenkatu 6, 00520, Helsinki, Finland.

LAIDLAW, Thomas Angus, b. 21 Dec. 1916, Saint John, New Brunswick, Canada. Medical Adviser. m. Dorothy Isabel Higgins, Dec. 1983, 1 son, 1 daughter. *Education:* McGill Diploma Course, Surgery; BA, Mt Allison; MDCM, Dalhousie University; FRCS (C); FACS. *Appointments:* General Surgery Practice, Charlottetown, Prince Edward Island, 1950-82; Chief of Staff, Prince Edward Island Hospital, Canada, 1951-82; Visiting Surgeon, Thoracic, Provincial Sanitorium, 1950-80; Medical Adviser, DVA, Government of Canada. *Memberships:* President, 1959, Prince Edward Island Medical Society; SR Member, Canadian Medical Society; Royal College P&S Canada. *Hobby:* Summer cottage. *Address:* 48 Summer Street, Charlottetown, Prince Edward Island, Canada C1A 2R1.

LAJAM, Fouad Elias A, b. 4 Nov 1937, Israel. Assistant Professor. m. Joanne Termine, 27 November 1965, New York City, New York, USA, 1 son, 2 daughters. *Education:* MD, University of Santo Domingo; Diplomate, American Board of Surgery, American Board of Thoracic Surgery. *Appointments:* Instructor, Surgery 1968-69, Cardio-Thoracic Surgery 1971-72, Associate in Surgery 1972-75, Assistant Professor, Cardio-Thoracic Surgery 1975-, Mount Sinai School of Medicine, New York, New York; Attending 1972-75, Chief 1975-, Cardio-Thoracic Surgery, Mount Sinai Hospital Services, City Hospital Center at Elmhurst, Elmhurst, New York; Clinical Assistant, Surgery 1972-75, Assistant Attending, Cardio-Thoracic Surgery 1975-, Mount Sinai Medical Center, New York, New York, Section Chief, Cardio-Thoracic Surgery, Bronx Veteran's Administration Hospital, Mount Sinai Hospital Services, Bronx, New York, 1973-. *Memberships:* Fellow, American College of Surgeons; Fellow, American College of Cardiology; Fellow, American College of Chest Physicians; Society of Thoracic Surgeons; New York Society of Chest Physicians. *Publications include:* 16 papers and articles

including: 'One State Surgery for Bilateral Bullous Emphysema via Median Sternotomy: Report of Three Cases', (with Lee Mannoon, Douglas L Prisco and Herbert W Berger), 1983. *Address:* 105 East 73 Street, New York, NY 10021, USA.

LAKE, C Raymond, b. 6 July 1943, Nashville, Tennessee, USA. Professor of Psychiatry and Pharmacology. m. Susan Frances de la Houssaye, 12 Aug 1967, New Orleans, Louisiana, 2 daughters. *Education:* BS Zoology, MS Biology, Tulane University, Louisiana; PhD Physiology and Pharmacology, Duke University Graduate School, Durham, North Carolina; MD, Duke University Medical School, Durham. *Appointments:* Research Associate 1974-75, Clinical Associate 1975-77, Staff Psychiatrist in Section on Experimental Therapeutics 1977-79, Laboratory of Clinical Science, Institute of Mental Health, NIH, Bethesda, Maryland; Clinical Assistant Professor, Department of Psychiatry, Georgetown Medical Center, Washington DC, 1974-79; Associate Professor Psychiatry/Pharmacology 1979-80, Professor of Psychiatry and Associate Professor of Pharmacology 1980-81, Professor of Psychiatry and Pharmacology 1981-, Uniformed Services University of Health Sciences, Bethesda, Maryland; Consultant, NHLBI, Behavioural Medicine branch, 1985-. *Memberships:* Grants Merit Review Committee, USUHS, 1979-82; Protection of Human Subjects Committee, Navy Hospital, Bethesda, 1982-; NIDA Review for Acquired Immune Deficiency Syndrome Grants, 1983; NHLBI Study Section for RFA on Behavioural Stress, Neuroactive Peptides and Cardiovascular Disease, 1985. *Publications:* "Norepinephrine", (edited with M G Ziegler), 1984; 'Psychiatric Clinics of North America', (editor) in "Clinical Psychopharmacology", volumes I and II, 1984; "The Catecholamines in Psychiatric and Neurologic Disorders", (edited with M G Ziegler), 1985. *Honour:* Physicians Recognition Award, American Medical Association of Continuing Medical Education, 1982-85. *Hobby:* Tennis. *Address:* B-3049, USUHS F Edward Hebert School of Medicine, 4301 Jones Bridge Road, Bethesda, MD 20814-4799, USA.

LAL, Satish Kumar, b. 24 Jan. 1942, Chhapra, Bihar, India. Orthopaedic Surgeon; Assistant Clinical Professor. m. Sushma Sharan, 25 Apr. 1970, New Delhi, 2 sons, 1 daughter. *Education:* MBBS, 1963, MS, 1968, All India Institute of Medical Sciences, New Delhi; Diplomate, American Board of Orthopaedic Surgery, USA, 1982; FICS; FACS. *Appointments:* Registrar, Department of Rehabilitation and Artificial Limbs, All India Institute of Medical Sciences, New Delhi, India, 1969-70; Lecturer, Department of Orthopaedic Surgery, Goa Medical College, Panajim, Goa, 1970-73; Assistant Professor, Department of Orthopaedic Surgery, Post-Graduate Institute of Medical Education and Research, India, 1973-76; Staff Orthopaedist, Kaiser Permanente Medical Center, Fontana, California, USA, 1980-; Instructor, 1980-84, Assistant Clinical Professor, Orthopaedic Surgery, Loma Linda University School of Medicine, Loma Linda, 1984-. *Memberships:* California Orthopaedic Association; American Academy of Orthopaedic Surgery; American College of Spinal Surgeons; California Medical Society. Fellow: International College of Surgeons; American College of Surgeons. *Publications:* Author of over 23 papers contributed to professional journals: 'Indian Journal of Orthopaedics'; 'The Clinician'; 'Indian Journal of Surgery'; 'Surgical Journal of Delhi'; 'Indian Medical Gazette'; 'Indian Journal of Pediatrics'; 'Abstract of Virology'; 'Archives of Medical Science'; 'Indian Journal of Medical Science'; 'Bulletin of PGI'; 'Journal of Trauma'; 'Contemporary Orthopaedics'. *Hobbies:* Photography; Tennis. *Address:* 9655 Almond Street, Alta Loma, CA 91701, USA.

LALA, Peeyush Kanti, b. 1 Nov. 1934, Chittagong. Professor and Chairman, Department of Anatomy, University of Western Ontario, London, Ontario, Canada. m. Arati, 7 July 1962, 2 sons. *Education:* MB BS, 1957; MD, 1962; PhD, Medical Biophysics, 1961, Calcutta

University. *Appointments:* Demonstrator, Pathology, Calcutta University, 1958-62; Resident Research Associate, Argonne National Laboratory, 1963-64; Research Biologist, Biophysicist, Laboratory of Radiobiology, University of California, San Francisco, 1964-66; Research Associate, Chalk River Nuclear Laboratory, Ontario, 1967-68; Assistant Professor of Anatomy, Associate Professor, Professor, McGill University, Montreal, 1968-83; Visiting Professor, Walter and Eliza Hall Institute of Medical Research, University of Melbourne, Australia, 1977-78; Professor and Chairman, Department of Anatomy, University of Western Ontario, 1983-. *Memberships include:* International Society of Experimental Hematology; International Society of Immunology of Reproduction; American Association of Cancer Research; Canadian Association of Anatomy and many other Societies. *Publications:* Contributor to many professional journals; Chapters in books; Presentations. *Honours:* T Ahmed Medal in Ophthalmology, Calcutta University, 1957; Fulbright Travel Scholarship, 1962; University of Melbourne Scholarship, 1977. *Hobbies:* Photography; Painting; Music. *Address:* Department of Anatomy, University of Western Ontario, London, Ontario, Canada N6A 5C1.

LAM, Albert Hoi-King, b. 12 May 1945, China. Senior Radiologist, Children's Hospital, Sydney, Australia. m. Catherine Kit-Fong Wong, 29 June 1972, Hong Kong, 1 son. *Education:* MB; BS; DRACR; FRACR; DDU. *Appointments:* Clinical Fellow, Paediatric Radiology, Los Angeles Hospital for Children, USA. *Memberships:* Royal Australasian College of Radiologists; Senior Member, American Institute of Ultrasound; Australian Society for Ultrasound in Medicine; Australian College of Paediatrics; Society of Paediatric Radiology, USA; Australian Society of Paediatric Imaging. *Publications:* Articles in professional journals including: 'Journal of Ultrasound in Medicine'; 'AJNR'; 'Journal of Clinical Ultrasound'; 'Paediatric Radiology'; 'Australasian Radiology'; several Abstracts including "Ultrasound of Hepatic Haemangioma in Neonates", 1985, "Sonography of Intracranial Bacterial Infections', 1985, both Proceedings of 4th WFUMB Scientific Meeting. *Hobby:* Travel. *Address:* Radiology Dept., Royal Alexandra Hospital for Children, Camperdown, NSW 2050, Australia.

LAMB, Joseph Fairweather, b. 18 July 1928, Brechin, Scotland. Chandos Professor. m. Olivia Jane Horne, 10 Sep. 1955, Edinburgh, 3 sons, 1 daughter. *Education:* MB, CHB, BSc, PhD, Edinburgh University; FRCP (E); FRS (E). *Appointments:* Resident in Surgery, Dumfries and Galloway Royal Infirmary, Resident in Medicine, Eastern General Hospital, Edinburgh, 1955-56; Lecturer in Physiology, Royal (Dick) School of Veterinary Studies, Edinburgh, 1958-61; Lecturer, Senior Lecturer, Physiology, Institute of Physiology, Glasgow University, 1961-69; Chandos Professor of Physiology, St Andrews University, 1969-; Honorary Senior Secretary of the Physiological Society, 1982-85. *Memberships:* Physiological Society; Pharmacological Society; Biochemical Society. *Publications include:* 'Genetic control of sodium pump density Developmental and physiological correlates of Cardiac Muscle' (co-author-, 1975; 'Occurence of passive furosimide-sensitive transmembrane potassium transport in cultured cells', (co-author), 1981; 'Internalization of Ouabain and Replacement of Sodium Pumps in the Plasma Membranes of HeLa Cells following block with Cardiac Glycosides' (co-author), 1982; 'Essentials of Physiology', 2nd edition, 1984; (co-author); 'The turnover of sodium pumps in human cultured cells and its significance for the action of cardiac glycosides', (co-author), 1985. *Honours:* DUX, Breckin High School, 1947; FRCP (E) 1984; FRS (E) 1984. *Hobbies:* Sailing; Boat Building. *Address:* Kenbrae, Millbank, Cupar KY15 5DP, Scotland.

LAMBA, Jogindar Singh Surg, Commodore, b. 20 July 1925, Poona, India. Consultant. m. Bala Thapar, 1 Mar.

1950, Karnal, 2 sons, 1 daughter. *Education:* MBBS, Bombay University; Dip. Anaesthesiology, Delhi; MD, Poona; MAMS, India; PhD; FCAM; DcCM, India; FCCP, USA. *Appointments:* House Surgeon, 1948-49; Regimental Medical Officer, 1949-52; Instructor, Army Medical Corps, 1953-57; Anaesthesiologist, 1957-67; Advisor Anaesthesiology, Surgeon Commander, Post Graduate Teacher, 1968-76; Senior Advisor, Surgeon Captain, Post Graduate Teacher and Examiner DA and MD, 1976-80; Consultant Anaesthesiology, Commandant Indian Naval Hospital Ship, Asvini and Institute of Naval Medicine, Bombay, 1981-83. *Memberships:* Indian Society of Anaesthetists; International College of Chest Physicians and Surgeons; National Academy of Medical Sciences; Indian Medical Association. *Publications:* 'Progress in cardio vascular diseases', 1979; 'Ketamine Hydrochloride anaesthesia in dental chair'; 'Management of Hypo volaemic shock afloat'; 'Epidural Morphine for Pain Relief'; 'Role of acupuncture and hypnosis in management of pain'; 'Parentral Hyperalimentation'. *Honour:* Distinguished Service Order, AVSM, 1983. *Hobbies:* Golf; Riding; Divinity. *Address:* Guru Kirpa, 1519 Sector - 33 'D', Chandigarh - 160 031, India.

LAMBERG, Bror Axel, b. 1 Mar. 1923, Helsinki, Finland, Professor of Endocrinology, University of Helsinki, m. Carin Anita Emilia Olin, 21 Dec. 1947, Helsinki, 1 daughter. *Education:* Lic med, 1949, Dr med and chir, 1953, University of Helsinki. *Appointments:* Assistant Physician, 1952-55, Assistant Professor, 1959-62, Assistant Head Physician, 1962-65, Associate Professor of Medicine, 1965-70, Professor of Endocrinology, 1971-, University of Helsinki; Assistant Physician, Ma ia Hospital, Helsinki, 1955-59; Director, Minerva Foundation Institute for Medical research, Helsinki, 1959-71. *Memberships:* Chairman, 1979-, Signe and Ane Gyllenberg Foundation; Chairman, 1984-, Minerva Foundation, Helsinki; Chairman, 1984-, Nordic Insulin Foundation, Copenhagen; European Thyroid Association; American Thyroid Association; Finnish Society for Endocrinology; Finnish Society for Nuclear Medicine; Finnish Society for Internal Medicine; Finnish Medical Society; Duodecim; European Nuclear Medicine Society; Society of Nuclear Medicine of Europe. *Publications:* 'Radioactive phosphorus as indicator in a chick assay of thyrotrophin', 1953; "The Thyroid and Its Diseases", 1968, 1969; "Clinical Endocrinology", (Editor), 1978, 2nd Edition, 1984; "The 25 Years History of the Finnish Society of Nuclear Medicine", 1985; Contributor of over 300 articles on professional and medical subjects. *Honours:* Liberty Cross 4, 1944; Commander, Swedish Nordstjernan Order, 1977; Commander, Finnish Lions Order, 1983; Honorary Member, Swedish Society of Endocrinology, 1972; Honorary Member, Swedish Society of Medicine, 1983; Honorary Member, Danish Society of Nuclear Medicine, 1982, Finnish Society of Endocrinology, 1979, Finnish Society of Nuclear Medicine, 1981 and Polish Society Endocrinology, 1985; Matti AraPAA Award, 1979; J W Runeberg Award and Medal, 1985. *Hobbies:* Music; Architecture; Rome. *Address:* N Mossavägen 17, SF-02700 Grankulla, Finland.

LAMBERT, Kenneth Lawrence, b. 28 Sep 1938, Missouri, USA. Orthopaedic Surgeon. m. Sandra Louise Palmer, 6 Aug 1965, Columbia, 1 daughter. *Education:* BS, Mathematics; MD; Fellowship, Association for Study of Internal Fixation; Certification, American Board of Orthopaedic Surgery. *Appointments:* Contributing Editor, 'Advances in Orthopaedic Surgery'; Instructor, ASIF; Physician, US Ski Team. *Memberships:* American Academy for Orthopaedic Surgeons; American Orthopaedic Society of Sports Medicine; American Academy of Science; Western Orthopaedic Association. *Publications:* "The Weight-bearing Function of the fibula", 'Journal of Bone & Joint Surgery', 1971; "Vascularized patellar tendon graft with rigid internal fixation...", 'Clinical

Orthopaedics', 1983; "The Syndrome of the Torn Anterior Cruciate Ligament", 'Advances in Orthopaedic Surgery', 1984; "Surgical Technique of Rupture of Anterior Cruciate Ligament", "The Crucial Ligaments", in press; "Frostbite: The Role of the Orthopaedic Surgeon", 'Advances in Orthopaedic Surgery', in press; etc. *Hobby:* Astronomy. *Address:* 557 E Broadway, PO Box 2770, Jackson, WY 83001, USA.

LAMBO, Thomas Adeoye, b. 29 Mar 1923, Abeokuta, Nigeria. Deputy Director-General, World Health Organisation. m. Dinah Violet Adams, 3 sons. *Education:* MB, ChB, Medical School, Birmingham University, England, 1948; DPM 1953, MD 1954, London University Institute of Psychiatry, 1952-54. *Appointments include:* Medical Officer in Charge, General Hospital, Gusau, 1951-52; Medical Officer, Special Grade, 1953-56; Consultant Psychiatrist, University College Hospital, Ibadan and Associate Lecturer, University of Ibadan, 1956-63; Specialist 1957-60, Senior Specialist 1960-63; Western Region Ministry of Health, Neuropsychiatric Centre; Professor and Head of Department of Psychiatry, Neurology and Neurosurgery 1963-71, Dean of Medical School 1966-68, Vice-Chancellor 1968-71, University of Ibadan; Assistant Director General 1971-73, Deputy Director-General 1973-, World Health Organisation. *Memberships include:* International Advisory Panel, International Hospital Federation; International Epidemiological Association; Advisory Scientific Panel, Centre for Advanced Study in the Development Sciences; Executive Committee, World Federation for Mental Health; Nigeria Medical Council; Scientific Council of the World Future Studies Federation; President 1979-81, World Society for Ekistics; Advisory Board, Earthscan; Co-Chairman, International Society for the Study of Human Development; Vice-President, World Association of Social Psychiatry; Member, Pontifical Academy of Sciences, 1974. *Publications include:* "Psychiatric Disorders Among The Yorubas", 1963; Over 150 articles. *Honours include:* OBE, 1962; Haile Selassie African Research Award, 1970; Nigerian National Order of Merit, 1979, Commander of the Order of Niger, 1979; 13 honorary degrees. *Hobby:* Collecting old medical books. *Address:* World Health Organisation, 1211 Geneva 27, Switzerland.

LAMBRIGHT, Robert Lamar, b. 28 Nov. 1926, Louisville, Kentucky, USA. Psychiatrist. m. Virginia Lee Carmitchel, 20 Aug. 1975, St. Joseph, Missouri, USA, 2 sons, 1 daughter. *Education:* BS University of Mississippi, USA, 1947; MD, Vanderbilt Medical School, 1950. *Appointments:* Internship in Surgery, Vanderbilt Medical School Hospital, 1951; Resident in Surgery, Vicksburg Hospital, Mississippi, 1954-55; Assistant in Surgery, St Tammany Parish Hospital, Louisiana, 1955-56; Resident in Psychiatry, University of Missouri Medical School, 1966-69; Physician, Baptist Hospital, Kediri, Java, Indonesia, 1958-65; Private Practice of Psychiatry, 1969-80; Flight Surgeon, US Air Force, 1980-82; Staff Psychiatrist, USAF Regional Medical Centre, Wiesbaden, West Germany, 1982-85; Staff Psychiatrist, US Army 97th General Hospital, APO NY 09757, Frankfurt, West Germany. *Memberships:* American Psychiatric Association; American Medical Association. *Hobbies:* Reading; Travel; Photography. *Address:* Palmengartenstrasse 4, 6000 Frankfurt 1, Federal Republic of Germany.

LAMMERANT, Jacques André, b. 28 Jan. 1925, Brussels, Belgium. Professor of Medicine. m. Evelyne Guillemare, 23 June 1962, Antwerp, 3 sons, 1 daughter. *Education:* MD 1942-49, PhD 1955-57, University of Louvain Medical School; Internal Medicine, University of Louvain, 1949-51 and 1952-55; Harvard Medical School, Boston, Massachusetts, USA and Columbia University College of Physicians and Surgeons, New York, 1951-52. *Appointments:* Professor of Medicine, Université Lovanium Medical School, Léopoldville – now Kinshasa, Belgian Congo, 1957-60; Established investigator of the Fonds National de la Recherche

Scientifique, Belgium, 1961-62; Professor of Medicine, Head of Department of Physiology, FNDP-Facultés Universitaires Notre Dame de la Paix Medical School, Namur, 1962-. *Memberships:* Société Belge d'Endocrinologie; Société Belge de Cardiologie; Société Belge de Médecine Interne; Société Belge de Physiologie et de Pharmacologie; Association des Physiologistes; International Society for Heart Research; European Society of Cardiology. *Publications include:* Numerous papers including: 'A Moderate Increase of Ketonemia Inhibits the Rise of Cardiac Free Fatty Acid Uptake and Oxygen Demand Induced by Norepinephrine', (with T Huynh-Thu and J Kolanowski), 1984; 'The Prolonged Stimulatory Effect of ACTH on 11 Beta-hydroxylation and its Contribution to the Steroidogenic Potency of Adrenocortical Cells', (with F Lambert and J Kolanowski), 1984; 'Arginine D(-)-3-hydroxybutyrate Reduces Free Fatty Acid Uptake and Acidosis in the Acutely Ischemic Myocardium', (with T Huynh-Thu and J Kolanowski), 1984. *Honours:* Résisant Armé Groupement AS, 1944; Officier de l'Ordre de Léopold, 1966; Commandeur de l'Ordre de la Couronne, 1976; Fellow of the Scientific Council of the International College of Angiology, 1983. *Address:* F N D P School of Medicine, Department of Physiology, Rue de Bruxelles 61, B 5000 Namur, Belgium.

LaMONICA, Michael Steven, b. 19 Apr. 1955, New York, USA. Chiropractic Physician. m. Carmela, 13 Aug. 1978, Queens, New York, 2 sons. *Education:* BSc, Manhattan College, 1977; DC, New York Chiropractic College, 1980. *Appointments:* Private Practice, Chiropractic Office, Bronx, New York, 1981-84; established, LaMonica Chiropractic Centre, Stamford, Connecticut, 1982-; Chiropractic Physician, Stamford Marathon, 1986. *Memberships:* Past President, Student Association, Connecticut Chiropractic Association (Examining Committee for State Licensure); American Chiropractic Association; Council on Roentgenology, Diagnosis and Orthopedics (District Representative for Public Relations Committee). *Publications:* Contributor, "The Temporomandibular Joint Syndrome", 'The Digest of Chiropractic Economics', 1984. *Honours:* Epsilon Sigma Pi, 1977; Inducted to Presidents Club, New York Chiropractic College, 1979; Diplomate, National Board of Chiropractic Examiners. *Hobbies:* Reading; Sports. *Address:* 427 Strawberry Hill Avenue, Stamford, CT 06902, USA.

LAMPE, Istvan, b. 27 Sep. 1932, Jászberény, Hungary. Doctor; Professor; Head of Department, Sub-Rector, Medical University of Debrecen. m. Pap Agnes, 14 Sep. 1957, 2 sons, 1 daughter. *Education:* Candidate in Medical Studies, Medical University, *Memberships:* Society of Hungarian Otorhinolaryngologists; Leading Member, Audiological Section, Editorial Board, Hungarian National Scientific Review on Otorhinolaryngology; President, National College of Otorhinolaryngological Institute; President, Tiszantul Section, National Otorhinolaryngologists; Secretary General, Hungarian Otorhinolaryngology Society. *Publications:* Candidate's Dissertation, "The Importance of the Parameters of the Acoustical Stimuls in the Producing of vein-response in audiogen peripheral vein-response", 1971; "Great Report: Intracranialis otorhinolaryngological complications", ENT Society, 1969; "The Characteristics and the Useful Possibilities of the Produced Potentials in the Brain Stem", 1982. *Honours:* Doctor of Merit, 1966; Eminent Doctor, 1971; Order of Labour, 1973; Silver Degree, 1976; Eminent Worker of Education, 1976; DOTE "Pro Universitatae", 1977; Order of Labour-Golden Degree, 1979. *Hobby:* Stamp Collecting. *Address:* Debreceni Orvostudományi Egyetem Fül-Orr-Gégeklinika, Nagyerdei krt 98, Debrecen 4012, Hungary.

LAMPRECHT, Friedhelm, b. 17 July 1941, Wittichenau. Medical Director of Psychosomatic Clinic Schomberg and Professor, Free University, Berlin. m. Annette Marie Roth, 4 June 1965, 3 daughters. *Education:* Study of Medicine and Psychology at Universities of Heidelberg, Vienna, Freiburg and Goettingen; MD, University of Goettingen, 1966; Doctoral thesis, University of Freiburg, 1968; Habilitation, Experimental Neurology, 1975; Psychosomatics and Psychotherapy, 1982; Psychoanalysis, Yale Department of Psychiatry, 1974; Institute of Psychotherapy, Berlin, 1976-82. *Appointments:* Medical Assistant, Country Hospital, Eberbach, 1966-68; Research Associate, Heidelberg, 1969-71; Visiting Associate, NIMH, Bethesda, USA, 1971-73; Psychiatric Resident, Yale University, 1973-74; Department of Neurology and Clinical Neurophysiology, Berlin, 1975-79; Department of Psychosomatic Medicine, Free University of Berlin, 1979-82; Medical Director, Psychosomatic Clinic Schoemberg; Professor, Department of Psychosomatic Medicine and Psychotherapy, Free University of Berlin, 1983-. *Memberships:* Member several professional organizations including Corresponding Member, American Psychiatric Association. *Publications:* Contributor to professional journals, etc; Presentations. *Hobbies:* Music; Farming. *Address:* Psychosomatische Klinik Schömberg, Dr Schroeder-Weg 12, D-7542, Schömberg, Federal Republic of Germany.

LAMVIK, Jon Ofstad, b. 21 May 1929, Tingvoll, Norway. Professor of Medicine (Haematology and Clincial Immunology), The Medical Faculty, University of Trondheim. m. Signe Valebjorg, 5 Apr. 1958, 1 son, 1 daughter. *Education:* BMed, 1955: Ph.D, 1969. *Appointments:* Lecturer in Pathology, The Gade Institute, University of Bergen, 1963-70; Reader in Medicine, 1970-73, Professor of Medicine, 1973-76, The Norwegian Institute of Technology, University of Trondheim; Dean, Faculty of Medicine, University of Trondheim, 1974-78. *Memberships:* The Royal Norwegian Society of Science and Letters; The Norwegian Academy of Technical Sciences; The Norwegian Cancer Society. *Publications:* "Antibody Synthesis in Rabbit Blood Lymphocyte Cultures", 1969; Approximately 60 publications related to haematology, cellular biology and immunology. *Hobbies:* Winter Sports; Mountain Climbing. *Address:* Trondheim University Hospital, Department of Medicine, N-7000 Trondheim, Norway.

LANDRY, Edmund Carl, b. 15 Jan. 1952, Houma, Louisiana, USA. Orthopaedic Surgeon. m. Kit Lozes, 20 May 1977, New Orleans, Louisiana, 1 son, 3 daughters. *Education:* Tulane University, 1970-73; MD, Louisiana State University School of Medicine, 1973-77. *Appointments:* Orthopaedic Resident, Tripler Army Medical Center, 1977-81; Staff Orthopaedic Surgeon, Reynolds Army Community Hospital, Fort Sill, Oklahoma, 1981-84; Assistant Clinical Professor of Orthopaedic Surgery, Tulane University School of Medicine, 1984-. *Memberships:* Diplomate, American Board of Orthopaedic Surgery; Fellow, American Academy of Orthopaedic Surgeons. *Hobbies:* Swimming; Photography. *Address:* 3525 Prytania Street Suite 501, New Orleans, LA 70115, USA.

LANDRY, Mark Edward, b. 24 May 1950, Washington District of Columbia, USA. Director, Podiatric Education, Clinical Assistant Professor, University of Health Sciences, University of Missouri; Private Practice. m. Mary Ann Kotey, 7 Sep. 1974, Independence, 2 sons, 1 daughter. *Education:* MS, Biomechanics/Kinesiology, University of Kansas; DPM, Ohio College of Podiatric Medicine; Diplomate, National Board of Podiatry Examiners; Diplomate, American Board of Podiatric Surgery; Fellow, American College of Foot Surgeons; Fellow, American Academy of Podiatric Sports Medicine. *Appointments:* Lieutenant, Emergency Care Instruction, Ocean City Beach Patrol, Maryland, 1971-73; Podiatric Surgeon, US Air Force, 1974-77; Private Practice, Kansas City, 1977-; Chairman, Podiatry, Dept. of Surgery, University Hospital, Kansas City, 1980-. *Memberships:* American Board of Podiatric Surgery; American College of Foot Surgeons; American Academy of Podiatric Sports Medicine; American Medical Joggers Association; American Association of Military Surgeons, 1974-77; Honorary Fellow, Podiatry Association of Great Britain. *Publications:* "The Inversion Sprain in the Athlete", 'Journal American Podiatry Association', 1976; "Anatomical Variance in Runner's Knee", Thesis, 1981; "Evolution of the Human Foot", 'American Podiatry Association', 1982; "Biomechanical Principles in Running Injuries", 1985; "Analysis of 100 Knees in High School Runners", 1985; 'Journal American Podiatry Association'. *Honours:* Mayor's Award, Ocean City, Maryland, 1972; Footprints Literary Award, 1975, President's Award, 1974, 1975, Ohio College of Podiatric Medicine. *Hobbies:* Swimming; Surfing; History; Architecture. *Address:* 8120 W 99th Street, Overland Park, KS 66212, USA.

LANE. Frederick M, b. 27 May 1928, USA. Associate Clinical Professor of Psychiatry. m. Carol Harmon, 2 Apr. 1978, New York, 1 son, 3 daughters. *Education:* AB, Cornell University, 1949; MD, Yale University School of Medicine; Certificate in Psychoanalysis, Columbia University Center for Psychoanalytic Training and Research. *Appointments:* Instructor in Psychiatry, Albert Einstein College of Medicine, 1960-62; Instructor in Psychiatry, 1967-71, Assistant Professor, 1972-84, Associate Clinical Professor, 1984-, Columbia University; Training and Supervising Analyst, Columbia University Center for Psychoanalytic Training and Research, 1972-. *Memberships:* American Medical Association; American Psychiatric Association, Fellow; American Psychoanalytic Association; International Psychoanalytical Association. *Publications:* Editor: "The Psychology of Men: New Psychoanalytic Perspectives" 1985; Chapter on 'Definition of Terms' in "Transference and Counter Transference" edited by Helen Meyers. *Honours:* Phi Beta Kappa, 1948; Alpha Omega Alpha, 1953. *Address:* 125 East 87th Street, New York, NY 10128, USA.

LANE, Joseph Michael, b. 27 Oct. 1939, New York City, USA. Orthopaedic Surgeon. m. Barbara Greenhouse, 23 June 1963, 2 daughters. *Education:* AB, Chemistry, Columbia University, 1961; MD, Harvard University, 1965. *Appointments include:* Attending Chief, Met Bone Disease Unit, Hospital for Special Surgery, 1976-; Chief, Orthopaedic Surgery Division, Memorial Sloan-Kettering Cancer Center, 1977-; Associate Member, Sloan Kettering Institute for Cancer Research, 1977-84; Associate Professor, Orthopaedic Surgery, Cornell University Medical College, 1978-84; Professor of Surgery, 1984-. *Memberships:* American Academy of Orthopaedic Surgeons; American College of Surgeons; Orthopaedic Research Society; American Rheumatism Association; American Federation for Clinical Research; American Geriatrics Society; American Medical Association; Medical Society of State of New York; Musculoskeletal Tumor Society; American Society of Bone and Mineral Research; Orthopaedic Forum; Society of Surgical Oncology; American Orthopaedic Association. *Publications:* 157 papers in professional publications. *Honours include:* NIH Career Research Development Award, 1977-82; Butz Frame Development Award, University of Pennsylvania, 1973-76; Resident Guest, AOA, 1973; Carl Berg Travelling Fellowship, OREF, 1973. *Hobbies:* Gardening; Golf; Tennis. *Address:* The Hospital for Special Surgery, 535 East 70th Street, New York, NY 10021, USA.

LANGBAKK, Bodil Nelly, b. 2 Feb 1951, Spitzbergen, Norway. Scientific Assistant. m. Jens Høstmark, 2 August 1974, Paris, France, 1 son. *Education:* Candidatus Medicinae. *Appointments:* Assistant Physician, Department of Gynaecology and Obstetrics, Department of Psychiatry, Haukeland Sukelius. *Memberships:* Norwegian Medical Association; Norwegian Biochemical Association. *Publications:* 'Identification and partial purification of human lactoperoxidase', 1984; 'Purification and partial characterization of human lactoperoxidase', in press. *Hobbies:* Music, Art collecting. *Address:* Wergelandsåsen 7, 5032 Minde, Norway.

LANGDELL, John Irving, b. 19 Apr. 1922, Chino, California, USA. Associate Clinical Professor of Psychiatry. m. Patricia L Waterman, 9 June 1942, Los Angeles, 2 sons. *Education:* MD, Stanford University; Residency, Neurology, Psychiatry and Child Psychiatry, University of California, San Francisco; Diplomate, American Board of Psychiatry and Child Psychiatry. *Appointments:* Director, Division of Mental Hygiene, San Francisco Department of Public Health, 1954-56; Psychiatric Consultant, US Army, Sonoma State Hospital; Child Psychiatry Consultant, Joint Commission on Hospital Accreditation. *Memberships:* American Psychiatric Association; American Society of Clinical Hypnosis; International Hypnosis Society. *Publications:* Author of 24 scientific articles and book chapters on childhood schizophrenia, phenylketonoria, sex education for children and family therapy. *Hobbies:* Camping; Scuba diving; Development of new breed of guinea pig. *Address:* 1756 14th Avenue, San Francisco, CA 94122, USA.

LANGFJÆRAN, Snorre, b. 19 Aug. 1956, Oslo Norway. General Practitioner. m. Anne Mette Østby, 7 July 1979, Gjøvik, 1 daughter. *Education:* MD. *Appointment:* Turnus Candidate, Lovisenberg Hospital, Oslo. *Membership:* KMMA. *Hobbies:* Music; Sailing; Family. *Address:* Ånnerudskogen 70, 1370, Asker, Norway.

LANGE, Dieter Ernst, b. 10 July 1933, Emden, Federal Republic of Germany. Chairman and Director, University Department of Periodontology and Periodontics. m. Dr. Margarita R Richter, 1958, 2 sons, 1 daughter. *Education:* Dr. med. dent. *Appointments include:* Senior Lecturer, 1966-69, docent in oral medicine and periodontology, University of Kiel 1969, docent dept cardiology and periodontology, University of Zurich, Switzerland, 1970-71; Professor of Periodontology and Oral Medicine, University of Kiel, 1973; Professor Director Department of Periodontology University Dental Hospital, Munster, Germany, 1974; Director and Chairman, Department of Periodontology, University School of Dental Medicine, Munster, Germany, 1974-. *Memberships:* Fellow, International College of Dentists; Pierre Fauchard Academy; Mem Deutsche Gesellschaft fur angewandte Zytologie; Deutsche Gesellschaft fur Parodontologie; Deutsche Gesellschaft for Histochemie; International Association for Dental Research; Periodontal Research Group; Member of Joint Research Group FDI/WHO. *Publications:* "Zellphysiologie und Funktion des menschlichen Gingivaepithals" 1972; "Parodontologie in der taglichen Praxis" 1984; around 180 publications in medical and dental journals. *Honours:* Rene Jaccard Award, Int. ARPR Berlin 1966; Miller Award, German Society of Dentistry, 1969; ARPA Award, German Society of Periodontology, Wurzburg, 1969. *Hobby:* Sea-sailing. *Address:* Department of Periodontology and Periodontics, University School of Dental Medicine, University of Münster, Waldeyerstr 30, D-4400 Münster, Federal Republic of Germany.

LANGEBAEK, Jørgen Aaris, b. 27 Sep 1929, Copenhagen, Denmark. Head of Department. m. Helle Schackinger, 24 Nov 1952, 2 sons, 1 daughter. *Education:* DDS, 1954. *Appointments:* Clinical Instructor, 1955-63, Assistant Professor, 1963-68, Associate Professor, 1968-79, Royal Dental College; Director, School for Public Health Dental Assistants, Kampala, Uganda, 1972; Secretary, Committee Continuing Education, 1959-63; Head of Department, Danish Dental Association, 1979-; Private Practice, 1955-. *Memberships:* Danish Dental Association; various Dental Societies. *Publications:* About 30 articles in professional journals. *Honours:* Honorary Prize, Periodontal Society, Denmark, 1972. *Address:* Arnevangen 24, DK 2840 Holte, Denmark.

LANGELAND, Tor, b. 27 Apr. 1949, Oslo, Norway. Medical Doctor. m. Kritin Petersen, 18 June 1976, 2 sons. *Education:* MD, University of Oslo, 1984. *Appointments:* Assistant Doctor, 1977-78, 1983-, Dermatology, Lecturer, Medicine, 1979-83; Rikshospitalet. *Memberships:* Norwegian Society of Dermatology; Norwegian Society of Allegology and Immunopathology. *Publications:* Numerous articles in professional journals. *Hobbies:* Sailing; Skiing. *Address:* Department of Dermatology, University Hospital, Oslo 1, Norway.

LANGMOEN, Iver Arne, b. 7 Apr. 1952, Hof in Solør, Norway. Clinical Neurosurgeon. m. Bente Sund, 1977, 2 sons, 1 daughter. *Education:* MD; PhD. *Appointments:* Research Fellow, Institute of Neurophysiology, Oslo University, 1977-81; Resident in Neurosurgery, Ullevaal University Hospital, Oslo, 1981-85; Clinical Neurosurgeon, University of Oslo National Hospital, Oslo, 1985-. *Memberships:* Various Physiological, Neurobiological and Neurosurgical Societies. *Publications:* 'On the Mechanism of Synaptic Transmission in Hippocampal Pyramidal Cells', 1981; 40 other publications on the transmission of electrical impulses in the cerebral cortex, epilepsy and the effect of general anaesthetics on the brain. *Honour:* Ragnar Forsberg Prize, 1982. *Hobbies:* Basic brain research; Skiing; Mountaineering, former Glacier guide; Outdoor life. *Address:* Granasen 65B, 1347 Hosle (Oslo), Norway.

LANGS, Robert, b. 30 June 1928, Brooklyn, New York, USA. Programme Director, Lenox Hill Hospital, New York, USA. *Education:* MD, Chicago Medical School, 1953. *Memberships:* International Psychoanalytic Association; American Psychoanalytic Association; American Psychiatric Association. *Publications:* "The Listening Process", 1978; "The Psycho-Therapeutic Conspiracy", 1982; "Psychotherapy: A Basic Text", 1982; "Unconscious Communications in Everyday Life", 1983; "Workbooks for Psychotherapists, Vols I, II, III", 1985; "Madness and Cure", 1985. *Address:* 30 East 60th Street, New York, NY 10022, USA.

LANGSLEY, Donald G, b. 5 Oct. 1925, Topeka, Kansas, USA. Professor of Psychiatry. m. Pauline Royal, 9 Sep. 1955, Lincoln, Nebraska, 3 daughters. *Education:* AB, State University of New York, 1949; MD, University of Rochester, New York, 1953. *Appointments include:* Associate Professor Psychiatry, University of Colorado School of Medicine, 1961-68; Professor and Chairman, Department of Psychiatry, University of California, Davis School of Medicine, 1968-76; Professor and Chairman, Department of Psychiatry, University of Cincinnati School of Medicine, Ohio, 1976-81; Professor of Psychiatry, Northwestern University Medical School, 1981-; Executive Vice-President, American Board of Medical Specialties. *Memberships include:* President 1980-81, American Psychiatric Association; American College of Psychiatrists; American Medical Association; American Psychoanalytic Association; Signum Laudis; Sigma Xi. *Publications:* "The Treatment of Families in Crisis", 1968; "Mental Health Education in the New Medical Schools", 1973; "A Manual of Psychiatric Peer Review", 1976; "Handbook of Community Mental Health", 1981; "Evaluating The Skills of Medical Specialists", 1983; "Legal Aspects of Certification and Accreditation", 1983. *Honours include:* Hofheimer Award for Psychiatric Research, 1971; Sacramento Mental Health Award, 1973; Harold Miles Award, 1977. *Address:* One American Plaza 805, Evanston, IL 60201, USA.

LAPIERRE, Yvon Denis, b. 19 Oct. 1936, Bonnyville, Alberta, Canada. Professor, Psychiatry and Pharmacology; Director of Research. m. Nicole Beauregard, 3 sons. *Education:* BA 1957, MD 1961, University of Ottawa; MSc, Faculty of Medicine, University of Montreal, 1970; FRCP (C) Psychiatry, 1972. *Appointments:* Lecturer, Psychiatry and Pharmacology, 1970-73; Scientific Director, Pierre Janet Hospital, 1970-76; Assistant Professor 1973-76,

Associate Professor 1976-81, Professor 1981-, Psychiatry and Pharmacology, University of Ottawa; Associate Staff and Director of Psychopharmacology Unit, Ottawa General Hospital, 1975-79; Director, Adult Out-Patient, Inpatient Unit and Speciality Clinics and Laboratories, Royal Ottawa Hospital, 1979-. *Memberships:* Fellow, American Psychiatric Association; Canadian Psychiatric Association; Society of Biological Psychiatry; Collegium International Psychopharmacology; Canadian College of Neuropsychopharmacology; Canadian Society for Clinical Pharmacology; American Society for Clinical Pharmacology and Therapy; Society for Clinical Trials. *Publications:* 'Psychophysiological Correlates of Sodium Lactate', (with V J Knott and R Gray), 1984; 'Pharmacological Approaches to Mania', (with J Telner), 1985. *Honours:* Tait-Mackenzie Medal, Academy of Medicine, Ottawa, 1980. *Address:* 1145 Carling Avenue, Ottawa, Ontario K1Z 7K4, Canada.

LAPIS, Károly, b. 14 Apr. 1926, Turkeve, Hungary. Physician. m. Ibolya Keresztes, 30 Apr. 1955, Budapest, 1 son. *Education:* MD, Eotvos Lorand University Medical Faculty; PhD, DSc, National Scientific Qualification Board, Budapest. *Appointments:* Research Assistant, Budapest Medical University, 1950-51. Scientific Research Worker: Debrecen Medical University Institute of Pathology, 1951-54; Oncopathology Research Institute, Budapest, 1954-63. Professor, Chairman, Postgraduate Medical School, Budapest, 1963-68; Professor, Director, 1st Institute of Pathology and Experimental Cancer Research, Semmelweis Medical University, Budapest, 1968-; Deputy Rector, in charge for scientific affairs, Semmelweis Medical University, 1985-. *Memberships include:* President, Liver Section, Hungarian Society of Gastroenterology 14th International Cancer Congress of UICC; Member, European Association for Cancer Research; Leading Member, Hungarian Society of Pathologists and Hungarian Society of Oncologists; Board of Presidency, Hungarian Cancer Society; European Society of Pathology; French Electronmicroscopic Society; Hungarian Section, Institute of Academy of Pathology; Metastasis Research Society Corresponding Member, American Association for Cancer Research. *Publications:* Co-Author: "Lymphknotengeschwulste", 1966; "Liver Carcinogenesi", 1979; "Tumour Progression and Markers", 1982; "Mediastinal Tumours and Pseudotumours", 1984; "Regulation and Control of Cell Profliferation", 1984. Author of chapter contributed to "Electron Microscopy in Human Medicine", 1979. *Honours:* Golden Degree, Order of Labour, 1978; Klompecher Medal, Hungarian Cancer Society. *Hobby:* Gardening. *Address:* 1st Institute of Pathology and Experimental Cancer Research, Semmelweis Medical University, Olloi 26, H-1085 Budapest, Hungary.

LAPUCK, Robert A, b. 17 Jan. 1952, Boston Massachusetts, USA. Chiropractic Physician. m. 23 May 1983, Copley Plaza Hotel. *Education:* BA, University of Massachusetts; MSc, Long Island University; BS, DC, National College of Chiropractic; Certification in Acupuncture. *Appointments:* Fellowship, National College of Chiropractic; Teacher, Currey College (Microbiology and Anatomy). *Memberships:* Council on Roentgenology, American Chiropractic Association; American Public Health Association; Massachusetts Chiropractic Association; Public Health Advisory Board, Sharon, Massachusetts. *Publications:* 'Plasma Line - Argon Plasma Determination of Lead'. *Honours:* Included in biographical works. *Hobbies:* Skiing; Fishing; Music; Gardening. *Address:* 3 Cheshire Road, Sharon, MA 02067, USA.

LARAMORE, George Ernest, b. 5 Nov. 1943, USA, Professor; Physician, div, 2 sons. *Education:* BS, Purdue University, 1965; MS, PhD, University of Illinois, 1966, 1969; MD, University of Miami, 1976. *Appointments:* Research Associate, University of Illinois, 1969-70; Research Physicist, Sandia Laboratories, 1970-74; Assistant Professor, 1979-82,

Associate Professor, 1982-85, Professor, 1985-, University of Washington. *Memberships:* American Physical Society; American Vacuum Society; American Society of Therapeutic Radiology and Oncology; American College of Radiology. *Publications:* Contributor of over 100 articles on professional and scientific subjects. *Honours:* NSF Postdoctoral Fellow, 1965-69, 1969-70; American Cancer Society Fellow, 1977. *Hobbies:* Swimming; Mountain climbing; Camping. *Address:* Department of Radiation Oncology, University of Washington Hospital RC-08, Seattle, WA 98195, USA.

LARI, Manuochehr M, b. 12 May 1935, Mashhad, Iran. Professor of Medicine. m. Shahin Maghami, 20 Dec. 1971, Mashhad, Iran, 1 son, 3 daughters. *Education:* MD, 1965; Fellowship in Hematology, 1972. *Appointments:* Residency 1967-71, Assistant Professor 1972-78, Associate Professor 1978-83, Professor of Medicine 1983-. *Memberships:* New York Academy of Sciences; Royal College of Medicine, England; Fellow, American College of Chest Physicians; Fellow, American College of Medicine. *Publications:* 'Hepatic Amebiasis', 1970; 'Meningoencephalucele', 1972; 'An unusual Case of spontaneous pneumocephalus', 1973; 'Myeloma in Young Male', 1974; 'Glioma', 1974; 'Methotrexate', 1975; 'Hypercalcemia', 1975; 'Allergic Aspergilosis', 1976; 'Cytogenetic Changes in CML during plastic transformation', 1977; 'Renal transplantation', 1977; 'Parotid gland swelling', 1977; 'A case of SLE complicated by peritonitis. A Case of lupus peritonitis', 1977; 'An epidemiological approach to the study of echinococcosis in the northeastern region of Iran', 1983; 'Primary tumours and cysts of the mediastinum in eastern Iran', 1984. *Hobby:* Swimming. *Address:* 31 Pyrnia Avenue, Mashhad, Iran.

LARKIN, Charles Byrne, b. 6 June 1924, Madison, Wisconsin, USA. Associate Professor of Psychiatry. m. Irene L Schneider, 30 Aug. 1947, Madison, Wisconsin, 3 sons, 4 daughters. *Education:* BS Medical Science 1947, MD 1949, University of Wisconsin, Madison; Certificate, American Board of Psychiatry and Neurology, 1974. *Appointments:* Private practice, Madison, Wisconsin, 1950-61; Chief of Acute Medicine, Patton Hospital, Patton, 1961-66; Director Behavioural Science, San Bernardino General Medical Center, 1975-78; Adjunct Associate Professor of Psychiatry, University of California, Los Angeles, 1975-78; Associate Professor of Psychiatry, University of Nevada, Reno, 1982-85; Assistant Professor 1973-78, Associate Professor of Psychiatry 1974-82 and 1985-, Loma Linda University, California. *Memberships:* Fellow, American Psychiatric Association; American Academy of Neurology; American College of Physicians; American Medical Association; Blue Key; Sigma Alpha Epsilon; Nu Sigma Nu. *Publication:* 'Alaxia Teleangrectasia - Case Report', 1970. *Hobbies:* Sports; Travel; Reading. *Address:* VA Medical Center, 11201 Benton Street, Loma Linda, CA 92357, USA.

LARMI, Teuvo Kaarlo Ilmari, b. 4 July 1924, Turku, Finland. Chairman, 2nd Department of Surgery, Helsinki University Central Hospital. m. Margit Petri, 22 Apr. 1950, Helsinki, 3 sons. *Education:* Licentiate of Medicine, 1949; MD, 1954; Specialist, Surgical Diseases, 1957, Thoracic and Cardiovascular Surgery, 1960, Gastroenterological Surgery, 1980. *Appointments:* Assistant Surgeon, 2nd Surgical Dept., 1955-58, 3rd Surgical Dept., 1958-60, Temporary Assistant Chief Surgeon, 4th Surgical Dept., 1963, Helsinki General Hospital; Assistant Surgeon, Maria Hospital, 1960-63; Ward Surgeon, Aurora Hospital, 1963-64; Department Head Surgeon, Tampere Centre Hospital, 1964; Professor, Surgery, 1965-85, University of Oulu; Chief Surgeon, Oulu University Centre Hospital, 1965-85. *Memberships:* Federation of Oulu University Central Hospital Executive Board, 1971-76, 1981, Alternate Member, Executive Board, 1977-81, Central Council Member, 1972-77, Executive Board of the Hospital, 1972-85; etc. *Publications:* 280 articles in professional journals. *Honours:* Titulaire Member, Societe International de Chirurgie, 1966-; Societe Europeerme de Chirurgie Cardiovasculaire; European Society for Surgical Research 13th Congress, elected Member, Honorary Committee. Many other honours & awards. *Address:* Mäntytie 10 A 6, SF 00250 Helsinki 29, Finland.

LAROCCA, Felix E F, b. 27 May 1936, Santiago, Dominican Republic (US Citizen). Medical Director, BASH Treatment and Research Center for Eating and Mood Disorders. m. 3 children. *Education:* MD, University of Santo Domingo Medical School, 1959; Internships: J M Cabral-Báez Hospital, Santiago, 1959; Suburban Hospital Association, Bethesda, USA, 1959-60; District of Columbia General Hospital, 1961; Residencies: The Seton Psychiatric Institute, Baltimore, 1961-62; Washington University Medical School, St Louis, 1964-67; Further training at The Institute of Psychoanalysis, Chicago, 1970-74. *Appointments include:* Faculty Member, Postgraduate Education Training Program, St Louis University Department of Psychiatry, 1972-; President and Founder of BASH (Bulimia Alorexia Self-Help) Incorporated, 1981-, Medical Director, Treatment and Research Center, 1982-; Editor, BASH Newsletter, 1981-. *Memberships:* Member and Officer several professional and civic organizations. *Publications include:* "Adolescent and Preadolescent Management for The Family Practitioner" (pamphlet), 1979; "The Psychiatric Clinics of North America", Vol 5, 1984; "An Inpatient Model for the Treatment of Eating Disorders", Psychiatric Clinics of North America, Vol 5, 1984; "Anorexia, Bulimia and Eating Disorders". Treatment: A Precis" (in preparation); Presentations; Lectures on cassettes. *Honours include:* Award of Merit, The Education Council of 100, The College of Education of Southern Illinois University, Carbondale, 1983. *Address:* BASH Treatment and Research Center for Eating and Mood Disorders, Deaconess Hospital, 6150 Oakland Avenue, St Louis, MO 63139, USA.

LAROS, Gerald S, b. 19 July 1930, Los Angeles, California, USA. Professor and Chairman, Orthopaedic Surgery. m. Marilyn Wald, 1 son, 2 daughters. *Education:* BS, 1952; MD, 1955; Northwestern University, Chicago; Internship, Philadelphia General Hospital, 1955-56; Residency, VA Hospital, Hines, Illinois and Chriners Hospital for Crippled Children, Honolulu, Hawaii. *Appointments:* Assistant Professor of Orthopaedic, Surgery-Trauma Service, University of Iowa, 1970-71; Associate Professor of Orthopaedics, University of Arkansas, 1971-73; Professor of Surgery, 1973-84; Chairman, Section of Orthopaedics, 1973-83; The University of Chicago; Professor and Chairman, Orthopaedic Surgery Department, Texas Tech University Health Sciences Center, 1984-. *Memberships:* American Board of Orthopaedic Surgery; Texas Medical Association; American Academy of Orthopaedic Surgeons; Orthopaedic Forum; American Orthopaedic Association; International Society of Orthopaedic Surgery and Traumatology; Continental Orthopaedic Society; American College of Surgeons; Western Orhtopaedic Association; Association of Orthopaedic Chairmen; Association of Bone and Joint Surgeons; American Medical Association; Illinois Orthopaedic Society. *Publications:* 33 original publications; 16 abstracts. *Honours include:* Resident Paper Award, Western Orthopaedic Association, 1960; Scholl Faculty Fellow, 1975-81; Alpha Omega Alpha; President-elect, American Board of Orthopaedic Surgery, 1985. *Address:* Texas Tech University Health Sciences Center, Department of Orthopaedic Surgery, Lubbock, TX 79430, USA.

LARSEN, Jenniece Beryl, b. 9 August 1942, Bassano, Alberta, Canada. Professor and Director, School of Nursing, University of Manitoba. Divorced, 1 son, 1 daughter. *Education:* Diploma in Psychiatric Nursing, Alberta Hospitals, Edmonton; BScN, M.Ed, PhD, University of Alberta, Edmonton. *Appointments:* Nursing Instructor, School of Nursing, Edmonton General Hospital; Instructor, Department of Nursing, Grant MacEwan Community College, Edmonton; Chairperson, Allied Health Department, Grant MacEwan Community College, Assistant Professor, Associate Professor, Faculty of Nursing, University of Alberta, Edmonton; Professor and Director, School of Nursing, University of Manitoba, Winnipeg. *Memberships:* The Canadian Research Institute for Advancement of Women; Canadian Association of University Schools of Nursing; Canadian Nurses Association; Academic Women's Association; University of Alberta; Alberta Status of Women Action Committee; Alberta Association of Registered Nurses; Edmonton Women's Network; International Congress of Nurses; Canadian Nurses Foundation. *Publications:* Articles and papers in professional journals; Numerous presentations. *Honours:* Dissertation of the Year Award, Canadian Society for the Study of Higher Education, 1984; Undergraduate Teaching Award, Faculty of Nursing, University of Alberta, etc. *Hobbies:* Aerobic Exercise; Hiking; Gourmet Cooking; Canadian History. *Address:* Room 218 Bison Building, School of Nursing, University of Manitoba, Winnipeg, Manitoba R3T 2N2, Canada.

LATARJET, Raymond, b. 17 Oct. 1911, Lyon, France, Honorary Director, Intitut Curie, m. Jacqueline Bernard, 4 May 1940, Lyon, 2 sons, 1 daughter. *Education:* MD; Doctor of Physics; Doctor of Medicine. *Appointments:* Head, Department of Radiation Biology, 1948-81, Director, Biological Section, 1954-77, Honorary Director, 1977-, Intitut Curie, Paris, France. *Memberships:* French Academy of Sciences, 1972-. *Publications:* "Laponie", 1943; "D'abord Vivre", 1982; Author of 184 original papers on professional and medical subjects, 1933-. *Honours:* Commandeur, French Legion of Honour; French Sport Golden Medal; Finsen Medal. *Hobbies:* Skiing; Climbing; Golf; Literature. *Address:* Intitut Curie, 26 rue d'Ulm, 75005 Paris, France.

LATIOLAIS, Minnie Fitzgerald, b. 26 Dec. 1921, Vivian, Louisiana, USA. Supervisor, Supplies Processing & Distribution. m. Joseph Clifton Latiolais, 19 July 1947, Lafayette, Louisiana, 1 son, 5 daughters. *Education:* Diploma, School of Nursing, Tours Infirmary, New Orleans. *Appointments:* Assistant Night Supervisor, Tours Infirmary; Surgical Nurse, Orthopaedic Department, Ochsner Clinic, New Orleans; Assistant Director of Nurses, Ochsner Foundation Hospital, New Orleans; Supervisor of Obstetrics & Nursery, Recovery Room, Operating rooms, Sanatorium, Lafayette, Louisiana; Supervisor, Operating rooms, Lafayette General Hospital; Administrative Assistant, Supervisor, Operating rooms, Abbeville General Hospital; GE General Manager & Surgical Nurse, J Robert Rivet & Associates, Lafayette, LA; Director of Nurses, Acadin St Landrey Hospital, Church Point, LA; Associate Hospital Consultant, B J Landry & Associates, Lafayette; Supervisor, Supplies Processing & Distribution, University Medical Centre, Lafayette. *Memberships:* American Nurses Association; Louisiana State Nurses Association; Lafayette District Nurses Association. *Hobbies:* Newedlework; Reading; Voluntary Service. *Address:* 1121 South Washington, Lafayette, LA 70501, USA.

LATNER, Albert Louis, b. 5 Dec. 1912, London, England. Emeritus Professor of Clinical Biochemistry. m. Gertrude Franklin, 3 Sep. 1936, Liverpool. *Education:* ARGS (1st Hons.), 1931, BSc (1st Hons.), 1932; M.Sc, 1933, DIC, 1934, Imperial College of Science; MB ChB, 1939, MD, 1948, D.Sc, 1958, University of Liverpool. *Appointments:* Assistant Lecturer, Physiology, University of Liverpool, 1933-36, 1939-41; Royal Army Medical Corps, 1941-46; Senior Registrar, Chemical Pathology, British Post-Graduate Medical School, 1946-47; Lecturer in Chemical Pathology, University of Durham, 1947-55; Consultant, Royal Victoria Infirmary, 1947-78; Reader in Medical Biochemistry, University of Durham, 1955-61; PRofessor of Clinical Biochemistry, University of Newcastle-upon-Tyne, 1961-78; Director, Cancer Research Unit, University of Newcastle-upon-Tyne, 1967-78. *Memberships:* British Medical Association; Royal Society of Medicine; Association of Clinical Biochemists, President, 1961, 62; Physiological Society; Biochemical Society; Pathological Society; Association of Clinical Pathologists; Royal Society of Chemists; Honorary Fellow, American National Academy of Clinical Biochemsitry, 1977; Honorary Member, Association of Clinical Biochemists, 1984. *Publications:* Co-author, "Isoenzymes in Biology and Medicine", 1968; Co-Editor, "Advances in Clinical Chemistry", 1970-83; Author, "Cantarow and Trumper Clinical Biochemistry, 7th Edition, 1975; Numerous Chapters in Medical and Scientific Books; Several hundred research publications. *Honour:* Wellcome Prize, Clinical Biochemistry, 1976. *Hobbies:* Photography; Art; Gardening. *Address:* Ravenstones, 50 Rectory Road, Gosforth, Newcastle-upon-Tyne NE3 1XP, England.

LATTA, David George, b. 7 Aug. 1935, Toledo, Ohio, USA. Orthopaedic Surgeon. m. Joan Margaret Hanson, 19 June 1957, Burbank, California, USA, 1 son, 2 daughters. *Education:* BA, La Sierra College, Riverside, California; MD, Loma Linda University, Loma Linda, California; Cert. American Board of Orthopaedic Surgery; Diplomate, National Board of Medical Examiners. *Appointments:* Internship, Los Angeles County General Hospital, 1963-64, Resident Orthopaedic Surgeon, 1964-66; Chief of Orthopaedic Surgery, US Army Hospital, Augsberg, Germany, 1966-69; Resident Orthopaedic Surgeon, USC Medical Centre, 1969-70; Fellowship, Spinal Cord Injuries, Rancho Los Amigos Hospital, Downey, California, 1970; Private Practice -. *Memberships:* American Medical Association; California Medical Association; Fellow, American Academy Orthopaedic Surgeons; Fellow, American College of Surgeons; American Orthopaedic Society for Sports Medicine; Western Orthopaedic Association; Team Physician, US Ski Team; Chief Medical Officer, Summer Olympics, Los Angeles, 1984. *Hobbies:* Skiing; Sailing; Tennis. *Address:* 231 West Pueblo Street, Santa Barbara, CA 93105, USA.

LATTA, Loren Lee, b. 10 Jan. 1944, Michigan, USA. Director of Research, & Associate Professor, University of Miami School of Medicine. m. Joan Sue Tallman, 4 Nov. 1966, Chicago, 2 sons, 1 daughter. *Education:* BS, Mechanical Engineering, Michigan State University, 1966; MS, Biomedical Engineering, 1978, PhD, Mechanical Engineering, 1979, University of Miami. *Appointments:* Goss Division, MGD Corporation, Chicago, 1966-67; Purchasing Agent, Chief Engineer, Pope Brace Co, Kankakee, Illinois, 1967-69; Senior Research Engineer, Dow Chemical, Rocky Flats Division, 1969-71; Pope Brace Division, Parke-Davis & Co, Kankakee, 1971-72; University of Miami School of Medicine, Dept. of Orthopaedics & Rehabilitation, 1972-. *Memberships:* American Academy of Orthopaedic Surgeons; Societe Internationale de Recherche Orthopedique de Traumatologie; Rehabilitation Engineering Society of North America; Orthopaedic Research Society; etc. *Publications:* Co-Author, "Closed Functional Management of Fractures", 1981; "Principles of Fracture Healing", 'AAOS: Inst.Co.Lect.', 1984; "The Rationale of Functional Bracing Fractures", 'Clinical Orthopaedics', 1980. *Honours:* Kappa Delta Award for Orthopaedic Research, 1976; Honors College, Cum Laude, and 6 Honorary Fraternities, Michigan State University, 1963-66. *Hobbies:* Photography; Tennis; Softball; Running; Railroading. *Address:* Dept. of Orthopaedics & Rehabilitation, D-27, University of Miami School of Medicine, PO Box 016960, Miami, FL 33101, USA.

LATTIMER, Agnes Dolores, b. 13 May 1928, Tennes-

see, USA. Director, Fantus Health Center, Widow, 1 son. *Education:* BA, Fisk University, 1949; MD, The Chicago Medical School, 1954. *Appointments:* Pediatrics Residency 1956-57, Chief Resident Pediatrics 1957-58, Associate Attending 1959-66, Attending 1968-72, Director Ambulatory Pediatrics 1965-71, Michael Reese Hospital, Chicago; Research Fellow, Chicago Board of Health Heart Disease program, 1958-61; Attending 1961-66, Chairman of Department of Pediatrics 1964-65, Mary Thompson Hospital, Chicago; Rotating Internship 1954-55, Pediatrics Residency 1955-56, Director Ambulatory Pediatrics 1971-84, Director of Fantus Health Center 1984-, Cook County Hospital, Chicago. *Memberships:* Diplomate, National Board of Medical Examiners; Ambulatory Pediatric Association; President Illinois chapter, American Academy of Pediatrics; American Institute of Hypnosis; American Association for the Advancement of Science; Chicago Pediatric Society; Fellow, International College of Applied Nutrition; American Public Health Association; Institute of Medicine of Chicago. *Publications:* 'Syllabus on Behavioral Pediatrics', 1981; "Triage Training Manual for Clerks", 1982; 'Teaching Behavioral Pediatrics - A Truly Multidisciplinary Approach', 1983; 'A Study of Penicillamine Treatment of Lead Poisoning'. *Honours:* Professor of the Year Award, Phillip and Elsie Sang Award for Excellence in Teaching, Chicago Medical School, 1968; Distinguished Alumnus Award, Chicago Medical School Alumnus Association, 1971; Pediatrician of the Year, American Academy of Pediatrics, 1985. *Hobbies:* Duplicate Bridge; Bowling; Chess; Flying Airplanes; Tennis. *Address:* Cook County Hospital, 1825 W Harrison Street, Chicago, IL 60612, USA.

LAU, Henry Po Kun, b. 25 Feb. 1945, Kunming, China. Pathologist. Private Practice. m. Barbara Ruth Lawson, 12 June 1981, Townsville, Australia, 3 sons, 3 daughters. *Education:* MB, BS (Monash); FRCPA. *Appointments:* Junior Medical Officer, Western General Hospital, Burnie, Tasmania, 1971; Senior Medical Officer, 1972, Registrar, Pathology, 1973-78, St George Hospital, Kogarah, New South Wales; Registrar, Pathology, Private Practice, Burwood, 1979; Registrar, Biochemistry, REPAT. General Hospital, Concord, 1980; Specialist, Pathology, Australian Dept. of Health, Townsville, 1981-82; Pathologist, Private Practice, Consultant Pathologists, Townsville Pty Ltd, 1982-. *Memberships:* College of Pathologists, Australia; Royal Society, New South Wales; Pathological Society of Great Britain & Ireland. *Publication:* "Pitfalls in Hand Spectroscopy", 'Journal of Royal Society of New South Wales', 1980. *Hobbies:* Scuba Diving; Underwater Photography; Aquaculturist; Marine Biology. *Address:* 6 Suttor St, Mysterton, Townsville, Queensland 4812, Australia.

LAU, Henry Yee-Chee, b. 12 Feb. 1936, Amoy, China. Active staff member, Izaak Walton Killam Hospital for Children, Halifax, Nova Scotia, Canada; Assistant Professor of Surgery, Dalhousie University Medical school. m. Dr. Asian Wu Lau, 22 Dec. 1958, 1 son, 2 daughters. *Education:* MD; FRCS (C); FAAP. *Appointments include:* Internship, residency, Halifax hospitals; Resident, Genral Surgery, Victoria General Hospital, Halifax; Clinical Fellow, Paediatric Surgery & Cardiovascular Surgery, Izaak Walton Killam Hospital. *Memberships:* Canadian & Nova Scotia Medical Associations; Halifax Medical Association; President, Children's International Medical Service; Fellow, Royal College of Physicians & Surgeons of Canada; Fellow, American Academy of Paediatrics; Canadian Association of Paediatric Surgeons. *Address:* 5897 Inglis Street, Halifax, Nova Scotia, Canada B3H 1K7.

LAU, Kam-Yung, b. 7 October 1951, Hong Kong. Assistant Professor of Medicine, Pulmonary Division, Department of Medicine, Texas Tech University School of Medicine, El Paso, USA. m. Sylvia Ho, 30 June 1979, Hong Kong. *Education:* MD, National Defense Medical College, Taipei, Taiwan, 1973; Diplomate,

American Board of Pediatrics, 1980; Diplomate, American Board of Internal Medicine, 1984. *Appointments:* Intern in Pediatrics, 1974-75, Resident in Pediatrics, 1975-76, Misericordia Hospital, New York City; Memorial University of Newfoundland School of Medicine, St Johns, 1976-77; Resident in Internal Medicine, Texas Tech, University School of Medicine, El Paso, 1980-82; Fellow in Pulmonary Medicine, University of California Los Angeles, San Fernando Valley Program, Los Angeles, 1983-85. *Memberships:* American Medical Association; American College of Chest Physicians; American Thoracic Society; Texas Medical Association. *Publications:* "Kaposi's Sarcoma of the Tracheobronchial Tree Chest" (in press); 'Young's Syndrome: An Association Between Male Sterility and Bronchietasis', 'The Western Journal of Medicine', (in press). *Honour:* "Outstanding Overseas Student Award, The Overseas Affairs Commission, Government of Republic of China, 1973. *Hobbies:* Table Tennis; Chinese Kung Fu; Travel. *Address:* Department of Medicine, Texas Tech University School of Medicine, 4800 Alberta Avenue, El Paso, TX 79905, USA.

LAUDANSKI, Tadeusz Marian, b. 8 Sep. 1941, Vilnius. Associate Professor. m. Joanna Ciesielska, 4 June 1969, Lodz, 1 daughter. *Education:* MD, 1965; PhD, 1973; Doctor Habilitatus, 1980. *Appointments:* Internship, Surgery, Internal Diseases, Paediatrics and Gynaecology, 1965-67; Postgraduate Training, Gynaecology, Assistant, Medical Academy, Lodz, 1967-74; Assistant Professor, 1974, Head, Perinatology, Medical Academy, Lodz. *Membership:* Polish Gynaecological Society. *Publications:* Articles in professional journals. *Honorus:* Award, Rector, Medical Academy of Lodz for Scientific and Didactic Activity, 1978, 1980, 1982. *Hobbies:* Looking for the Truth; Contact with Nature. *Address:* Stafana Street 6/6, Lodz 91463, Poland.

LAURENT, Christian Etienne, b. 27 Dec. 1943, Paris, France. Doctor of Chiropractic. m. Landau Rhea Rautio, 16 Oct. 1971, Elmhurst, Illinois, USA, 1 son, 2 daughters. *Education:* DC, National College of Chiropractic, Lombard, Illinois, USA, 1971; National Board of Chiropractic Examinares (USA), 1969. *Appointments:* Lecturer, Institut Français du Chiropractic (on the biomechanical & clinical principles of Chiropractic). *Memberships:* French Chiropractic Association; European Chiropractic Union; American Chiropractic Association; National College of Chiropractic Alumni Association; International President, Cabinet, National College of Chiropractic; Member, ACA Diagnosis & Internal Disorders. *Publications:* "Differential Diagnosis of Cervical Syndromes" (to be published 1986). *Hobbies:* Painting illustrations; Hiking; Lions Club. *Address:* 10 Rue St Laurent, 77400 Lagny S/M, France.

LAURITANO, Albert A, b. 8 Feb. 1953, Brooklyn, New York, USA. Director, Clinical Research Department, Squibb-Novo Incorporated, Princeton, New Jersey. m. Barbara M Tanneberger, 26 July 1975, Fair Lawn, New Jersey, 2 daughters. *Education:* BS, Biology, Fairleigh-Dickinson University, New Jersey, 1975; MS, Pharmacology, Rutgers University, New Jersey, 1977. *Appointments:* Clinical Research Associate positions at Lederle Laboratories-USA and ICI Americas, USA; Director, Medical Research at BCD Products, New York; Assistant Vice-President, Pharmaceutical Division at Baurs-Krey Associates, New York. *Memberships:* American Diabetes Association; Optimist International; Trustee, Associates of Clinical Pharmacology; Phi Zeta Kappa; Phi Omega Epsilon. *Publications:* Various research papers on Type II Diabetes and Insulin Immunogenicity submitted to national/international diabetes meetings; 'New Drug Therapies and Psychometric Evaluation; American Diabetes Association meeting, 1985. *Hobbies:* Cooking; Wines; Participating in various sports. *Address:* Squibb-Novo Incorporated, 120 Alexander Street, Princeton, NJ 08450, USA.

LAVADOS, Jaime, b. 13 Feb. 1937, Talca, Chile. Prof-

essor of Neurology. m. Laura Germain, 1960, 4 sons, 1 daughter. *Education:* MD, University of Chile, 1960; Graduate Bachelor in Philosophy, 1960; Certified Neurologist, University of Chile, 1964; PhD, LOndon, England, 1973. *Appointments:* Member, General Council, University of Chile on behalf of the President of the Republic of Chile, 1966-70; Director, National Council of Scientific and Technological Research, 1967-70; Secretary, Faculty of Medicine, Orient. Secc. University of Chile, 1973-76, Director Office for Scientific Development, 1973-76, Professor in Charge of Neurology Course, School of Medicine, 1974-; President, Promocion Universitaria, 1975-. *Memberships:* Chilean Medical Association; Chilean Society of Neurology; Chilean Society for Advancement of Sciences; World University Service, Executive Secretary for Chile, 1964; Interamerican Society for Neuropsychology. *Publications:* 'La Investigacion y la Ensenanza de Ciencias Neurologicas' in 'Rev. Phronesis', Madrid, 1977; 'Organisation of Scientific and Technological Development in Latin America' in "Integration of Science and Technology with Development", 1979; 'Notas sobre Actividad Cientifica Biomedica y Salud en Chile' in "Desarrollo Social y Salud en Chile", 1980; editor "La Educacion Medica en Chile", 1985; 46 articles in national and international medical journals, etc. *Honours:* Medal for Distinguished Service, University of Laval, Canada, 1965; Medal Marquez de Rio Brancho, Brazil, 1966; Medal from the National Council for Research and Development, Israel, 1970. *Hobbies:* Literature; Tennis. *Address:* Jacques Cazotte 5666, Santiago, Chile.

LAVIGNE, Marilyn E, b. 3 Mar. 1933, Detroit, Michigan, USA. Chiropractic Physician. *Education:* RN, Indiana Methodist Hospital School of Nursing, 1955; BA, Taylor University, Indiana, 1956; Public Health Nursing Certification, University of Michigan, 1958; MA, Education, University of Michigan, 1963; Advanced Graduate work in Adult Education and Gerontology, University of Michigan, 1977; Certification in Aging, 1977; DC, Cleveland Chiropractic College, Kansas City, Missouri, 1981. *Appointments include:* Hospital Staff Nurse; Public Health Nurse; School Nurse and School Health Consultant; Visiting Lecturer in Health Education, 1969-70, Assistant Professor of Health Education, 1970-78, Eastern Michigan University; Chiropractic Physician and Director, Calabash Family Chiropractic Center, North Carolina, 1981-84; Private Practice, 1981-84; Chiropractic Physician and Director of Chiropractic Center, Longboat Key, Florida, 1984-85. *Memberships:* American Chiropractic Association; North Carolina Chiropractic Association; Florida Chiropractic Association; Chamber of Commerce, Longboat Key. *Publications:* Contributor to professional publications; Presentations. *Hobbies:* Sailing; Painting; Racquetball. *Address:* Suite 2, North Key Plaza, 5610 Gulf of Mexico Drive, Longboat Key, FL 33548, USA.

LAVIN, Justin Paul, b. 4 Aug. 1947, Haverhill, Massachusetts, USA. Chief of Division of Obstetrics. m. Louis J Miller, 18 Aug. 1974, Philadelphia, Pennsylvania, 3 sons. *Education includes:* BS Biology 1969, MD 1975, University of Pennsylvania; Fellow in Maternal Fetal Medicine, University of Cincinnati Medical Center, Ohio, 1979-81. *Appointments include:* Assistant Instructor in Obstetrics and Gynaecology, University of Pennsylvania School of Medicine, Philadelphia, 1977-79; Assistant Professor 1981-83, Associate Professor 1983-, Obstetrics and Gynecology, Northeastern Ohio Universities College of Medicine, Rootstown, Ohio; Head of Maternal-Fetal Medicne Service 1981-, Chief of Divsion of Obstetrics 1982-, Akron City Hospital, Akron; Co-Director, Akron Regional Perinatal Center, 1981-. *Memberships include:* Fellow, American College of Obstetricians and Gynecologists; Society of Perinatal Obstricians; American Institute of Ultrasound Medicine; Blockley Obstetrical Society; Ohio State Medical Society. *Publications include:* "Obstetrics for the House Officer", (with W F Rayburn), 1984; 5 chapters in books; 30 abstracts an articles. *Honours:* Sandoz Award, University of Pennsylvania School of Medicine, 1975; Obstetrical Bowl, Philadelphia Obstetrical Society, 1979; Teaching Awards 1982 and 1984, Best Consultant 1984, Akron City Hospital. *Hobbies:* Skiing; Tennis. *Address:* Perinatal Center, Akron City Hosptial, 525 E Market Street, Akron, OH 44309, USA.

LAVIN, Louise Miller, b. 20 May 1947, Altoona, Pennsylvania, USA. Mental Health Nurse Specialist, Private Practice. m. Justin P Lavin, Junior, 18 Aug. 1984, Philadelphia, Pennsylvania, 3 sons. *Education:* BSN (with distinction), University of Rochester; MSN, University of Pennsylvania; Doctoral Program in Psychiatry, Medical College of Pennsylvania (6 doctoral credits). *Appointments:* Nurse, thalidomide children, Orthopadische Klinik, University of Heidelberg, Germany; Clinical Nurse Specialist, Mental Health, Medical College of Pennsylvania; Faculty Member, Family Nurse Clinician Program (part-time), University of Pennsylvania; Faculty Member, Graduate Division, Psychiatric Nursing, University of Cincinnati College of Nursing and Health; Mental Health Nurse Specialist and Counselor, Private Practice, Akron, Ohio. *Memberships:* American Nurses Association; Ohio Nurses Association; Charter Member, Advanced Practitioners in Psychiatric Mental Health Nursing; Childbirth Education Specialist, New York; Pi Lambda Theta; Sigma Theta Tau. *Publication:* Abstract: "Group Process: A Model for Health Care Intervention with Individuals Experiencing the Chronic Disease of Diabetes Mellitus", Archives of Physical Medicine and Rehabilitation, November 1978. *Hobbies:* Tennis; Skiing; Water Sports; Camping; Music. *Address:* 1958 Garland Avenue, Akron, OH 44313, USA.

LAWLESS, Patrick E, b. 23 Aug. 1955, Erie, Pennsylvania, USA. Chiropractor, Private Practice. *Education:* BA, Washington and Jefferson College, 1977; DC, Palmer College of Chiropractic, 1982. *Appointments:* Chemist, Witco Chemical Company, 1977-80; Instructor in Technique, Palmer College of Chiropractic, 1982-. *Memberships:* Illinois Prairie States Chiropractic Association, Treasurer, 1983-; American Chiropractic Association; International Chiropractic Association; Florida Chiropractic Association. *Hobbies:* Golf; Racquetball. *Address:* 1831 W 7 Street, Davenport, IA 52802, USA.

LAWRENCE, Leonard Eugene, b. 27 June 1937, Indianapolis, Indiana, USA. Professor of Psychiatry, Pediatrics and Family Practice. m. Barbara A, 3 Mar. 1962, Indianapolis, 2 sons, 1 daughter. *Education:* BA Anatomy and Physiology 1959, MD School of Medicine 1962, Indiana University. *Appointments include:* Child Psychiatrist 1969-72, Chief 1970-72, Child Psychiatry Service, Wilford Hall USAF Medical Center, Lackland Air Force Base, Texas; Psychiatric Consultant, Ella Austin Community Center, San Antonio, Texas, 1969-73; Clinical Assistant Professor 1970-72, Associate Dean for Student Affairs 1983-, Professor of Departments of Psychiatry, Pediatrics and Family Practice, University of Texas Health Science Center, San Antonio; Consulting Staff 1972-, Clinical Director San Antonio Children's Center, 1972-77, Associate Medical Director 1977-81, San Antonio Children's Center, San Antonio. *Memberships include:* Alpha Epsilon Delta; Fellow, American Academy of Child Psychiatry; American Medical Association; Fellow, American Psychiatric Association; American Society for Adolescent Psychiatry; Kappa Alpha Psi; National Association for Medical Minority Educators Inc; National Medical Association. *Publications:* 'On The Role of the Black Mental Health Professional', 1972; 'An Educational Strategy for Teaching Psychosocial Pediatrics', (with William Weston), 1975; 'Black Child Care', 1976; 'The Black Child', (with Jeanne Spurlock), 1979; 'Mental Health Treatment for Minors', 1979; 'Stress and The Black Medical Family', 1983. *Honours include:* Outstanding Professor, University of Texas Medical School at San Antonio, 1981, 1982 and 1984. *Hobbies:* Music; Poetry; Baseball. *Address:* Universi-

ty of Texas Mental Health Science Center at San Antonio, 7703 Floyd Curl Drive, San Antonio, TX 78284, USA.

LAWSON, Gordon Edwin, b. 17 Mar. 1950, Toronto, Canada. Professor. m. Susan A Gillis, 23 Feb. 1985, Unionville, Ontario. *Education:* DC, Canadian Memorial Chiropractic College, Toronto; DHN, London School of Hygiene and Tropical Medicine, University of London, London, England; DABCN. *Appointments:* Nutritional Consultant, Food Policy and Planning Division, Food and Agricultural Organization of the United Nations, 1977-78; Lecturer, Human Nutrition 1978-80, Assistant Professor 1980-, Canadian Memorial Chiropractic College; Lecturer, Faculty Science, York University, Toronto, Canada, 1980-82; Editor, Nutritional Perspective Journal, 1980-; Secretary, Treasurer, College of Chiropractic Sports Science, 1984-. *Memberships:* Canadian Chiropractic Association; Council on Nutrition, Council on Sports Injuries and Rehabilitation, American Chiropractic Association; Canadian Council on Chiropractic Sports Sciences; Ontario Chiropractic Association; Osler Society. *Publications:* 'Role of Nutrition in Chiropractic Education and Practice', 1981; 'Rational Approach to the Management of Peptic Ulcer Disease', 1983; 'Rational Approacj to Nutrient Supplementation', 1984. *Hobbies:* Running; Ice Hockey; Rowing; Freemason. *Address:* 22 Bartley Drive, Toronto, Ontario M4A 1B8, Canada.

LAWSON, John Alexander Reid, b. 30 Aug. 1920, Dundee, Scotland. General Practitioner, President, RCGP. m. Pat Kirk, 19 July 1944, St Andrews, Scotland, 2 sons, 2 daughters. *Education:* MB ChB, University of St Andrews, 1943; Member, 1953, Fellow, 1969, Royal College of General Practitioners; Member, College of Family Physicians of Canada, 1984. *Appointments:* House Surgeon, 1943, House Physician, 1944, Royal Infirmary, Dundee; Major, Royal Army Medical Corps, 1944-47; Surgical Registrar, Royal Infirmary, Dundee, 1947-48; Principal, in General Practice, 1948-; Regional Adviser in General Practice, Tayside Region, 1971-82. *Memberships:* Member of Council, 1962-82, Chairman of Council, 1973-76, President, 1982-85, Royal College of General Practitioners; Chairman, Joint Committee, Post-graduate training for General Practice, 1976-78; Chairman of Council, World Organisation of National Colleges & Academies of General Practice, 1980-; British Medical Association. *Honour:* Order of the British Empire, 1979. *Hobbies:* Fishing; Golf; Gardening. *Address:* The Ridges, 458 Perth Road, Dundee DD2 1NG, Scotland.

LAWSON, William Bradford, b. 27 Nov. 1945, Richmond, Virginia, USA. Research Director, Metropolitan State Hospital; Assistant Professor, University of California, Irvine. m. Rosemary Jackson, 6 Aug. 1983, Chicago, Illinois. *Education:* BS, Howard University; MA, University of Virginia; PhD, University of New Hampshire; MD, University of Chicago Pritzker School of Medicine, 1978. *Appointments:* Assistant Professor, Department of Psychology, University of Illinois, Champaign-Urbana, 1971-74; Internship and Residency, Stanford University Medical Center, 1978-82; Staff Psychiatrist and Clinical Research Fellow, Adult Psychiatry Branch, Intramural Research Program, National Institute of Mental Health, St Elizabeth's Hospital, Washington, DC, 1981-84; Research Director, Metropolitan State Hospital, Norwalk, California, 1984-; Assistant Professor in Residence, Department of Psychiatry and Human Behavior, University of California, Irvine, 1984-. *Memberships:* American Association for the Advancement of Science; American Medical Association; American Psychiatric Association; Association of Black Psychologists; Black Psychiatrists of America; Black Psychiatrists of California; California and National Medical Associations; Society for Neuroscience; Southern California Psychiatric Association; Psi Chi. *Publications:* Contributor to professional journals; Abstracts and Presentations. *Honours include:* Medical Student Research Fellowship, Chicago Diabetic Association, 1974; Kazi Award for Service to Student National Medical Association, 1976; Alcohol, Drug Abuse and Mental Health Administration Service Award for police training in cross cultural issues, 1983; Appreciation and recognition, Norwalk Chapter, Alliance for the Mentally Ill, 1984. *Hobbies:* Judo; Science Fiction. *Address:* Metropolitan State Hospital, 11400 S Norwalk Boulevard, Norwalk, CA 90650, USA.

LAWWILL, Theodore, b. 16 Oct. 1937, Chattanooga, USA. Professor, Chairman, Ophthalmology, University of Kansas Medical Centre. m. Charlene Lascody, 25 May 1963, Chicago, 1 son, 1 daughter. *Education:* BA, 1958, MD, 1961, Vanderbilt University; Internship, University of Iowa Hospitals, 1962; Resident, Ophthalmology, University of Illinois Research & Education Hospitals. *Appointments:* Research Associate, NIH Fellow, University of Iowa, 1965; Research Ophthalmologist, Walter Reed Army Institute of Research, 1966-68; Assistant Professor, 1968-70, Associate Professor, 1970-78, Professor, 1978-80, Ophthalmology, University of Louisville School of Medicine; Professor, Chairman, University of Kansas Medical Centre, 1980-. *Memberships:* Fellow, American Academy of Ophthalmology; Association for Research in Vision and Ophthalmology; International Society for Clinical Electrophysiology of Vision; International Strabismological Society; Optical Society of America; Fellow, American College of Surgeons. *Publications:* Numerous articles in scientific journals including: 'American Journal Ophthalmology'; 'Investigative Ophthalmology'; 'Japanese Journal of Opthalmology'; 'Ophthalmology'; etc. *Honours:* Opthalmology Programmes Representative, American College of Surgeons Advisory Council, 1983-; Secretary, Vice President, Board of Directors, International Society for Clinical Electrophysiology of Vision. *Hobbies:* Tennis; Ham Radio; Aeroplane Pilot. *Address:* Dept. Ophthalmology, University of Kansas Medical Centre, 39th & Rainbow Boulevard, Kansas City, KS 66103, USA.

LAYMAN, William Arthur, b. 8 Feb. 1929, West New York, New Jersey, USA. Professor of Psychiatry. m. Barbara M LaBelle, 27 Feb. 1983, 1 son. *Education:* BS, St Peter's College, 1948-51; MD, Georgetown University Medical School, 1951-55. *Appointments:* Instructor of Psychiatry 1959-61, Assistant Professor 1961-65, Seton Hall College; Associate Professor of Psychiatry 1965-74, Executive Officer 1966-69, Clinical Professor 1974-77, Department Chairman Educational Services 1976-, Professor of Psychiatry 1977-, Professor and Acting Chairman 1983-, UMDNJ-New Jersey Medical School. *Memberships:* New Jersey Medical Society; Bergen County Medical Society; Fellow, American Psychiatric Association; American Association for University Professors. *Publications include:* 'University Affiliation For Medical Schools', 1966; 'Pseudo Incest', 1972; 'The Effects of Long Term Psychotherapy on Patients' Self-Perception', (with S Vora, E Mann and A Danesino), 1977; 20 others. *Honours:* Golden Apple Award, Student American Medical Association, UNDNJ-New Jersey Medical School, 1974; Excellence in Teaching Award, Foundation of UMDNJ-New Jersey Medical School, 1980-81. *Address:* 208 Anderson Street, Hackensack, NJ 07601, USA.

LAZARUS, Leslie, b. 11 Dec. 1929, Sydney, Australia. Director, Garvan Institute of Medical Research. m. Phillipa Heavey, 6 Aug. 1955, Sydney, 1 son, 2 daughters. *Education:* MB, BS, University of Sydney, 1953; FRACP; FRCPA; FAACB. *Appointments:* Staff Endocrinologist, St Vincent's Hospital, Sydney, 1962-68; Honorary Consultant Endocrinologist, Royal Alexandra Hospital for Children, Sydney, 1972-; Chairman, Human Pituitary Advisory Committee, Commonwealth Department of Health, 1976; Director,

Endocrine Diagnostic Services, St Vincent's Hospital, Sydney, 1977-; Associate Professor of Medicine, University of New South Wales, Sydney, 1984-. *Memberships:* Fellow, Australian Association of Clinical Biochemists; Fellow, Royal Australasian College of Physicians; Fellow, Royal College of Pathologists of Australasia; The Endocrine Society, USA; Endocrine Society of Australia; Australian Society for Medical Research. *Publications:* 'Growth Hormone' in "A Guide to the Diagnosis of Endocrine Disorders", Editors R A Donald, Marcell Dekker, 1984; 'Suspension of the Australian Human Pituitary Hormone Programme', 'Medical Journal of Australia', 1985; 173 other publications in endocrine and biochemical journals, 1957-. *Honour:* Honorary Life Member, Endocrine Society of Australia, 1983. *Hobby:* Reading. *Address:* Garvan Institute of Medical Research, St Vincent's Hospital, Sydney 2010, Australia.

LEACH, Robert Ellis, b. 25 Nov. 1931, Sandford, Maine, USA. Professor, Chairman, Orthopaedic Surgery, Boston University Medical School. m. 20 Aug. 1955, 3 sons, 3 daughters. *Education:* BA, Princeton University, 1953; MD, Columbia University, 1957. *Appointments:* Lieutenant Commander, US Navy, 1962-64; Staff Orthopaedic Surgeon, Lahey Clinic, 1964-67; Chairman, Orthopaedics, 1967-70; Professor, Chairman, Orthopaedics, Boston University Medical School, 1970-; Chairman, Board of Trustees, American Journal of Sports Medicine, 1979-; Associate Editor, 'Clinical Orthopedics and Related Research', 1969-; Deputy Editor, 'Clinical Orthopedics', 1982-84. *Memberships:* American Academy of Orthopaed Surgeons; International Society for Surgery of the Knee; Continental Orthopaedic Society; American Society for Sports Medicine; American Orthopaedic Society. *Publications:* "Controversies in Orthopedics", co-Author, 1982; "Tibia and the Ankle, Evarts' Surgery of the Musculoskeletal System", 1983; Editor, "Tibial Fractures". *Honours:* American British Canadian Travelling Fellowship, 1970; President, American Orthopaedic Society for Sports Medicine, 1983, 1984; Head Physician, US Olympic Teams, Los Angeles Games, 1984; Chairman, US Olympic Committee Council for Sports Medicine, 1985; American Board of Orthopaedic Surgery, 1985. *Hobbies:* Tennis; Skiing; Print Collecting. *Address:* 720 Harrison Ave, Suite 808, Boston, MA 02118, USA.

LEAL, Nancy Jeanne, b. 1 Apr. 1944, Windsor, Ontario, Canada. Private Family Practitioner. *Education:* BA, Honours, 1966; MD, 1970; CCFP, 1974. *Appointments:* Private Practice, 1971-73; Resident, Family Medicine, 1974; Lecturer, Faculty of Medicine, Department of Family Medicine, McMaster University, 1975; Private Practice, 1976-; Acting Staff Victoria General Hospital and Associate Staff, Royal Jubilee Hospital. *Memberships:* British Columbia College of Physicians and Surgeons; British Columbia Medical Association; Victoria Medical Society; College of Family Physicians of Canada. *Hobbies:* Golf; Gardening; Handwork. *Address:* 105-2020 Richmond Road, Victoria, British Columbia, Canada V8R 6R5.

LEARY, Bernard Deryck John, b. 14 Apr. 1927, London, England. General Practitioner. m. Margaret Ann Rooney, 7 Nov. 1952, London, 2 sons. *Education:* MBBS, St Bartholomews Hospital, 1944-49; DTM & H, Royal Army Medical College, 1958-59; MFHom, Royal London Homoeopathic Hospital, 1981; PSC, Staff College, Camberley, 1960. *Appointments:* HS, West Herts Hospital, 1950; RMO, Beckenham Maternity Hospital, 1950-51; General Duties MO, RAMC, 1951; MO & DC, Military Wing, RAF Hospital, Rinteln, 1952-53; OC, 11 Field Dressing Station, 1953-56; SMO (Army) Mauritius, 1956-58; Instructor, RAMC Field Training Center, 1961; DADG Ministry of Defence AMD 1, 1962-64; DDMS HQ Farelf. Retired as Lieutenant-Colonel, 1964-67; General Practice, Chesterfield, Derbyshire, 1967-. *Memberships:* Member of Council, Faculty of Homoeopathy; Member, British Medical Acupuncture Society; Associate, British Association Manipulative Medicine; Member, British

Society of Medical and Dental Hypnosis; Member, British Medical Association. *Publications:* Contributor to 'British Homoeopathic Journal'. *Hobbies:* Books; History; Raising Seeds; Watching TV. *Address:* Windycroft, Brimington, Chesterfield, Derbyshire S43 1AX, England.

LEBEGUE, Breck Jon, b. 23 July 1951, Brigham City, Utah, USA. Psychiatrist. m. 1 child. *Education:* AB 1972, MD School of Medicine 1975, Indiana University; Psychiatry Residency, University of Utah Affiliated Hospitals, 1975-78; Fellowship, Psychiatry and Law, University of Southern California School of Medicine, Institute of Psychiatry, Law and Behavioral Science, 1978-79. *Appointments include:* Flight Surgeon, US Air Force, Chief Aerospace Medicine Section, Utah Air National Guard, 1977-; Forensic Psychiatric Consultant, Sex Offender Unit, Patton State Hospital, Patton, 1979; Consultant Psychiatrist, Salt Lake County Jail, 1979-80; Medical Director, Adult Residential Treatment Unit, Salt Lake Mental Health, 1979-80; Forensic Psychiatric Consultant 1979-80, Medical Director Forensic Unit 1980-81, Acting Clinical Director 1980-81, Utah State Hospital, Assistant Clinical Professor, Director Forensic Psychiatry Services, Department of Psychiatry, University of Utah, 1979-; Adjunct Assistant Professor, Department of Clinical Psychology, Brigham Young University, 1979-; Medical Director and Chairman, Division of Psychiatry, Holy Cross Hospital, Salt Lake City, 1981-83; Consultant Forensic Psychiatrist, Forensic Psychiatric Service, Mental Health Division, Melbourne, Victoria, Australia, 1983-84. *Memberships:* Secretary 1981-83, Utah Psychiatric Association; American Academy of Psychiatry and Law; American Psychiatric Association; Salt Lake County Medical Society. *Publications:* 'Forensic Psychiatry: Application of the Principles', in "Lawyers Medical Encyclopedia, 1981; 'Incompetence to Receive Treatment: A Necessary Condition For Civil Commitment', 1981; 'Paraphilias in Pornography: Deviations Inherent in Title', 1984. *Hobbies:* Skiing; Flying; Gardening; Piano. *Address:* University of Utah, Department of Psychiatry, 50 North Medical Drive, Salt Lake City, UT 84132, USA.

LEBENTHAL, Emanuel, b. 12 Apr. 1936, Jerusalem. Professor of Pediatrics. m. Hannah Leichtung, 2 sons, 3 daughters. *Education:* MD, Hebrew University. Jerusalem, Israel. *Appointments:* Assistant in Medicine, 1972-74; Associate in Medicine, 1974-76, Children's Hospital, Boston; Associate Professor, St University of New York at Buffalo, 1976-80; Chief, Gastroenterology, Children's Hospital at Buffalo, 1976-; Professor of Pediatrics, St University of New York at Buffalo, 1980-; Director, International Institute for Infant Nutrition and Gastro-Intestinal Disease, 1984-. *Memberships:* Editorial Board, American Journal of Gastroenterology, 1979-; Study Section and Site Visit, NIH, 1980-; Recruitment Committee, St University of New York at Buffalo, 1982-. *Publications:* "Digestive Diseases in Children" Editor, 1978; "Gastroenterology and Nutrition in Infancy" Editor, 1981; "Chronic Diarrhea in Children" Editor, 1984; Contributor to Journal of Pediatric Gastroenterology and Nutrition. *Honours:* The International Prize of Modern Nutrition, 1984 presented by the International Dairy Federation, Locarno, Switzerland. *Address:* International Institute for Infant Nutrition and Gastrointestinal Diease, Children's Hospital, 219 Bryant Street, Buffalo, NY 14222, USA.

LEBLANC, Caroline Anne, b. 11 Dec. 1947, Worcester, Massachusetts, USA. Captain, US Army Nursing Corps. m. Jon R Hager, 24 May 1969, Worcester, Massachusetts, 2 sons. *Education:* BSN, Boston College, Massachusetts, USA, 1969; MS, University of Maryland, Baltimore, USA, 1977. *Appointments:* Public Health Nurse, Washington DC, 1969; Psychiatric Nurse, Okinawa, 1970; Occupational Health Nurse, Boston, Massachusetts, 1971-72; Senior Assistant Nurse Officer, US Public Health Service, Occupational Health Nurse Consultant, DHEW, 1972-74; Assistant Professor of Nursing, Bloomsberg State College,

Pennsylvania, 1978-81; Captain, US Army Nursing Corps, Head Nurse/Psychotherapist, Family Practice Clinic, Walson Army Hospital, Fort Dix, New Jersey. *Memberships:* American Nurses Association; American Orthopsychiatric Association; American Rural Health Association; Council on Psychiatric and Mental Health Nursing. *Publications:* 'The Role of the Occupational Health Nurse in the Health Promotion of the Worker' in 'Occupational Health', 1974; 'Perspective on Rural Nursing' - paper presented at the Fourth National Conference on Family Systems Theory and Nursing, Washington DC, 1984. *Honours:* Sigma Theta Tau - National Nursing Honour Society; The Honour Society of Phi Kappa Phi; Fellow and Research Scholarship Recipient, Mental Health Nursing, University of Maryland. *Hobbies:* Gardening; Hiking; Needlework; Reading. *Address:* 723 Crestbrook Avenue, Cherry Hill, NJ 08003, USA.

LEBLIQUE, Leopold Benjamin, b. 21 June 1926, Newcastle-upon-Tyne, England. Chief Physician. m. Carol Carey, 7 Sep. 1974. *Education:* BSc Physics, University of Durham, England, 1947; MD, University of Vienna, Austria and Innsbruck, Austria, 1973; American Board of Family Practice, 1978. *Appointments:* Private Practice, New Mexico, USA, 1975-81; Medical Director, Geriatrics Section, Family Practice Department, University of Louisville, Kentucky; Chief Physician for Geriatrics, Veterans Administration Medical Center, Lake City, Florida. *Memberships:* Fellow, American Geriatrics Society; Fellow, American Academy of Family Physicians; National Association of Veterans Administration Physicians; Columbia County Medical Society. *Hobbies:* Landscape painting, Aquatic sports, Photography. *Address:* Veterans Administration Medical Center, Lake City, FL 32055, USA.

LEBOVITZ, Phil Stanley, b. 11 Nov. 1940, Memphis, Tennessee, USA, Private Practitioner, Psychiatry and Psychoanalysis. m. Donna Rudnick, 20 June 1964, Manchester, New Hampshire, USA, 1 son, 1 daughter. *Education:* AB, Columbia University; MD, Baylor School of Medicine; Diplomate for Psychiatry, American Board of Psychiatry and Neurology. *Appointments:* Internship in Medicine; Residency in Psychiatry; Lieutenant Commander, US Navy; Staff Member in Psychiatry, Student Health Service; Lecturer in Psychiatry, Department of Psychiatry, Medical School, Northwestern University; Clinical Assistant Professor of Psychiatry, University of Health Sciences/The Chicago Medical School; Candidate, Chicago Institute for Psychoanalysis. *Memberships:* American Psychiatric Association; American Psychoanalytic Association; American Society for Adolescent Psychiatry. *Publications:* 'Feminine Behaviour in Boys: Affects of its outcome', 1971. *Hobbies:* Bicycling; Photography; Golf. *Address:* 111 North Wabash, Chicago, IL 60602, USA.

LECHNER, Enrique, b. 24 July 1943, Mexico. m. Michele Edelkind, 5 Mar. 1972, Monticello, New York, USA, 2 daughters. *Education:* MD, Universidad Nacional Autonoma de Mexico. *Appointments:* Head, Child and Adolescent Psychiatric Department, 20 de Noviembre Hospital, Mexico; Professor, Child Psychiatry, Universidad Nacional Autonoma de Mexico; Professor, Child Psychiatry, Pediatric Residents, Hospital Infantil Privado; Professor, Child Psychiatry, University UNITEC. *Memberships:* Sociedad Mexicana de Neurologia Psiquiatica; Founding Member, Asociacion Mexicana de Psiquiaticia Infantil; American Psychiatric Association; American Society of Clinical Hypnosis. *Publications:* 'Effemininate Behaviour in Boys', 1974; 'Infantile Psychosis - Classification and Clinical Features', 1975; 'Problems in the Pre-School Child', 1976; 'Preadolescence Puberty', 1976. *Hobbies:* Photography; Numismatics. *Address:* Paseo de las Palmas 745-404, Mexico 10, D F, Mexico.

LECKMAN, James Frederick, b. 3 Dec. 1947, Alburquerque, New Mexico, USA. Associate

Professor of Psychiatry and Paediatrics, Child Study Center, Yale University. m. Hannah Hone, 27 Dec. 1971, Redlands, California, 1 son, 1 daughter. *Education:* BA, The College of Wooster, Ohio, 1969; Md, University of New Mexico, Albuquerque, 1973. *Appointments:* Clinical Associate, National Institutes of Mental Health, Bethesda, Maryland, 1974-76; Postdoctoral Fellow, 1976-80, Assistant Professor, 1980-83, Associate Program Director, Children's Clinical Research Center, 1981-, Coordinator Research, Child Study Center, 1984-, Yale University. *Memberships:* American Association for the Advancement of Science; American Psychiatric Association; American Academy of Child Psychiatry. *Publications:* Over 100 papers and articles including: 'Family genetic studies and the identification of valid diagnostic categories in adult and child psychiatry' in 'British Journal of Psychiatry' (co-author), in press. *Honours:* Phi Beta Kappa, 1969; Alpha Omega Alpha, 1973; Sigma Xi, 1980; Editorial Board, 'Journal of American Academy of Child Psychiatry'; NIMH Research Review Committee. *Hobbies:* Hiking; Swimming; Badminton. *Address:* Room I-269 SHM, Child Study Center, Yale University School of Medicine, P.O. Box 3333, New Haven, CT 06510, USA.

LeCOMPTE, Dory (Dorothy Joan) Bookhamer, b. 2 Oct. 1938, Philadelphia, Pennsylvania, USA. Podiatric Physician and Surgeon. m. Professor Gare LeCompte, 28 Jan. 1961, Philadelphia, 1 son, 2 daughters. *Education:* BS, Temple University; DPM, Ohio College of Podiatric Medicine; studies, Pennsylvania State University, Albright College and American University. *Appointments:* Teacher, Public schools, Virginia, Pennsylvania, Massachusetts and Connecticut, 1961-68; Visiting Professor, University of Damascus, Syria, 1962-63; Resident, Podiatric Surgery, 1979-80; Private Practice of Podiatric Surgery, 1981-; Chairman, Board of Directors, International Institute of Continuing Medical Education, 1984-. *Memberships:* The New York Academy of Sciences, 1985; International College of Podiatric Laser Surgery; American Podiatric Medical Association; American Association of Women Podiatrists; Board of Trustees and Chairman of Credential (Diplomate) Examination, International College of Podiatric Laser Surgery. *Publications:* "Behavioural Factors in Podiatric Surgery", 1986. *Honours:* Diplomate, International College of Podiatric Laser Surgery, 1983; Fellow, New York Academy of Science, 1984, American Society of Podiatric Medicine, 1984, Academy of Ambulatory Foot Surgery, 1982. *Hobby:* Skiing. *Address:* 21206B 72nd Avenue West, Edmonds, WA 98020, USA.

LeCOMPTE, Gare, b. 15 Sep. 1937, Chicago, Illinois, USA. Executive Director, International Institute of Continuing Medical Education. m. Dr Dory Bookhamer LeCompte, 28 Jan. 1961, 1 son, 2 daughters. *Education:* BA, University of Washington; MA, American University; PhD, Social Sciences, School of International Service, American University; PhD, Behavioral Sciences, Case Western Reserve University. *Appointments:* Centre for Research on Social Systems, 1960-62; Visiting Professor, University of Damascus, Syria, 1962-63; Co-ordinator, R & D Creative Design Projects, General Dynamics, 1964-67; Adjunct Professor, University of Hartford, 1967-71; Director, Social/Behavioral Science Research, State of Connecticut Research Commission, 1968-71; Director, Research, New York-Pennsylvania Health Management Corporation, 1971-73; Dean, Professor, Behavioral Medicine, Ohio College of Podiatric Medicine, 1973-80; Executive Director, Academy of Ambulatory Foot Surgery, 1980-85; Private Practice, 1980-84; Executive Director, International Institute of Continuing Medical Education, 1985-. *Memberships:* Numerous professional organisations. *Publications:* 90 articles in professional journals. *Honours:* Stickel Research Medal, American Podiatric Medical Association, 1982; Strong Foundation Fellowships, 1965, 1975-78; Visiting Lecturer, Academy of Traditional Chinese Medicine, Beijing, 1984. *Hobby:* Skiing.

Address: 21206 72nd Avenue West, Edmonds, WA 98020, USA.

LEDER, Stefan, b. 12 Nov. 1919, Warsaw, Poland, Head of Department of Neurotic Disorders. m. Pola Landau, 1970, Warsaw, Poland. *Education:* MD, 1943; Spec Intern Med II, 1952; Spec Psychiatrist, 1957; Spec Psych II, 1961; Doc sc med, 1965; Doct sc med habil, 1972; Professor Extraordinary, 1979. *Appointments:* Army Physician, 1943-46; Hospital Assistant, Intern Department, 1947-53; Department of Psychiatry, 1953-58, Psychoneurological Institute, Warsaw, 1958-; Head of Department of Neurotic Disorders. *Memberships:* Polish Medical Association; Polish Psychiatric Association; Member, Board of Int Fed of Medical Psychotherapy. *Publications:* "Psychoterapia grupowa", (Editor), 1983; Author of chapters in books and numerous articles on medical subjects. *Honours:* Polish Orders, 1948, 1969, 1980. *Hobbies:* Classical music; Chess; Tourism. *Address:* Instytut Psychoneurologiczny, Al Sobiestkiego 1/9, 02-572 Warsaw, Poland.

LEE, Choon Huat, b. 17 Jan. 1946, Singapore. Consultant Physician; Hematologist. m. Vivien Wei Sih, 30 Jan. 1971, Adelaide, Australia, 2 sons, 1 daughter. *Education:* MB BS Honours, Adelaide University Medical School, Australia; Postgraduate, Prince Henry and Prince of Wales Hospitals, Sydney; FRACP; FRCPA. *Appointments include:* Medical Registrar, Clinical Fellow, Prince Henry and Prince of Wales Hospitals, New South Wales, Australia, 1975-79; Staff Specialist, Westmead Hospital, 1979-80; currently, Consultant Physician and Hematologist, Westmead and Nepean Hospitals, New South Wales. *Memberships:* Fellow: Royal Australasian College of Physicians; Royal College of Pathologists of Australia; Hematology Society of Australia; Clinical Oncology Society of Australia; Associate Member, Cardiac Society of Australia and New Zealand; Australian Medical Association. *Publications:* Contributions to: 'Australian and New Zealand Medical Journal'; 'Journal of Medical Genetics'; 'Cancer'; 'Clinical Experimental Immunology'; 'American Journal of Clinical Pathology'; Blood. *Honours:* Singapore's Presidents Scholarship and Colombo Plan Scholarship, for top student in biological science, 1966; Everard Scholarship, Adelaide University, Australia, 1971; Baikie Memorial Medal, 1981; Young Investigator, Hematology Society of Australia. *Hobbies:* Tennis; Fishing; Table Tennis; Computers. *Address:* 13 Tamboy Avenue, Carlingford, NSW 2118, Australia.

LEE, Don Seung, b. 4 Dec. 1940, YangYang, Korea. Professor of Anaesthesiology. m. Sung Hee Song, 27 July 1970, 2 sons, 2 daughters. *Education:* MD, FACA, Catholic Medical College, Seoul, Korea. *Appointments:* Assistant Professor of Anaesthesiology, 1974-81, George Washington University, Washington DC, USA, Associate Professor, 1981-present. *Memberships:* American Medical Association; IARS; SNANSC; American Society of Anaesthesiology; American Association for the Advancement of Science. *Publications:* 'Effects of PEEP on air embolisms and ICP during neurosurgical procedures in the sitting position' in 'Intercranial Pressure V', 1983; 'Neurogenic pulmonary edema associated with ruptured spinal cord AVM' in 'Neurosurgery', 1983; 'Migration of tips of central venous catheters in the seated patients' in 'Anaesthesia Analgesia', 1984; Low incidence of shivering with chronic propandol therapy. In 'Lancet', 1986; Malignant Hyperthermia: A Possible New Variant. In 'Cana. Anaes. Soc. Journ.', 1985. *Hobbies:* Hiking; Travel; Reading; Game of BADOOK. *Address:* 7628 Georgetown Pike, McLean, VA 22102, USA.

LEE, Francis H, b. 11 Nov. 1948, China, Associate Medical Director, Du Pont Pharmaceuticals, m. Sheila W Cheng, 10 Jan. 1974, Eugene, Oregon, USA, 1 daughter. *Education:* University of London Overseas General Education Cetificate, 1967; BA,

University of Oregon, 1971; PhD, State University of New York at Buffalo, 1975. *Appointments:* Graduate Research Fellow, State University of New York; Senior research Scientist, Sterling Winthrop; Research Group Leader/Senior Research Scientist, Bristol-Myers; Assistant Director, Bristol-Myers; Associate Director, Clinical Pharmacology, Associate Medical Director, Infectious Disease and Oncology, Du Pont Company. *Memberships:* American Society Clinical Pharmacology and Therapeutics; American Association for Cancer Research; American Society of Clinical Oncology. *Publications:* 'New platinum complexes in clinical trials', 1983; 'Bleomycin disposition in children with cancer', 1983; 'Phase II evaluation of mitomycin C in children with refractory solid tumor using the single high intermittent dose schedule', 1981. *Honours:* National Science Foundation, 1968. *Hobbies:* Chinese calligraphy. *Address:* 3333 Coachman Road, Surrey Park, Wilmington, DE 19803, USA.

LEE, Michael S W, b. 8 Feb. 1943, Hong Kong. Clinical Director, Psychiatric Day Hospital; Private Practitioner. m. Kay S Y, 17 Dec. 1967, Hong Kong, 1 son, 1 daughter. *Education:* MB, BS, Hong Kong, 1968; Fellow, Royal College of Physicians, Canada, 1973. *Appointments include:* Chief, Inpatients, Department of Psychiatry, Queensway-Carleton General Hospital, Ottawa, Canada; Chief, Clinical Services, Department of Psychiatry, Calgary General Hospital, Calgary, Alberta; Director of Clerkship in Psychiatry, Associate Professor, Department of Psychiatry, Faculty of Medicine, University of Calgary, 1980-83; currentlym Private Practice and Clinical Director, Psychiatric Day Hospital, Calgary General Hospital. *Memberships:* Canadian and American Psychiatric Associations. *Publications:* Author of several articles on psychopharmacology and alcoholism; Numerous lectures; currently working on textbook on psychiatric teaching. *Hobbies:* Skiing; Hiking. *Address:* Calgary General Hospital, Calgary, Alberta, Canada.

LEE, Roger B (Colonel), b. 10 Mar. 1941, Oakland, California, USA, Chief, Gynaecologic Oncology, Madigan Army Medical Centre, m. Sylvia Kwong, 26 June 1966, 1 son, 1 daughter. *Education:* BS, Stanford University, 1962; MD, Hahnemann University, 1968. *Appointments:* Clinical Associate Professor, University of Washington, 1980-86; Adjunct Assistant Professor, University of Oregon, 1980-86; Fellowship, Gynaecologic Oncology, Walter Reed Army Medical Centre, Washington DC, 1978-82. *Memberships:* Dioplomat, American Board of Obstetrics and Gynaecology, 1974; Diplomat ABOG Division of Gynaecologic Oncology, 1982; Fellow, American College of Obstetrics and Gynaecology; Fellow, Society of Gynaecologic Oncology; Founding Fellow, Gynaecologic Urolic Society. *Publications:* 'Outpatient sterilization under local anaesthesia', 1980; 'Cervical Carcinoma in pregnancy', 1981; 'Scalenenode biopsy in cervical carcinoma', 1981; 'Bladder dysfunction following radical hysterectomy', 1981; 'Malignant melanoma of the vagina', 1984. *Honours:* "A" Professional Designator, department of Army, 1985; Order of Military Medical Merit, 1985; Certificate of Achievement, 1985; Army Achievement Award, 1985; Best Scientific Exhibit 'Presacral Neurectomy', 1985. *Hobby:* Computers. *Address:* Department Ob-Gyn, Madigan Army Medical Centre, Tacoma, WA 98431-5097, USA.

LEE, Tze-Yuen, b. 21 Sep. 1949, China. Consultant Dermatologist. m. Vivian Lee, 4 Sep. 1978, 1 son, 1 daughter. *Education:* MB BS, Hong Kong; Member, Royal College of Physicians, London, England; Dip Perm, London. *Appointments:* Medical Officer, Registrar in General Medicine, United Christian Hospital, Hong Kong; Post-graduate Student, St John's Hospital for Skin Diseases, Institute of Dermatology; Sessional Consultant, Caritas Medical Centre; Honorary Consultant, Dermatologist, Baptist Hospital, Hong Kong; Honorary Dermatologist, United Christian Hospital, Hong Kong. *Memberships:* Secretary, Hong Kong Association of Dermatology. *Address:* No 23A Soares Avenue, Homantin, Kowloon, Hong Kong.

LEEDS, Sanford E, b. 14 Nov. 1909, San Francisco, USA. Director Experimental Surgery Laboratory. m. Syra Florence Nahman, 9 April 1941, Carson City, Nevada, USA, 1 son. *Education:* MD, University of California, 1936; Research Associate in Experimental Surgery, 1936-38, Vanderbilt University Medical School, Nashville, Tennessee; Resident in Surgery San Francisco General Hospital and University of California Hospital, 1938-41, certified by American Board of Surgery, 1942; Certified by American Board of Thoracic Surgery, 1952. *Appointments:* Research Associate Vanderbilt University Medical School, Nashville, Tennessee, Laboratory of Dr Alfred Blalock, 1936-38; Assistant Resident and Resident in Surgery, San Francisco General Hospital and University of California Hospital, 1938-41; US Army active service, 1941-46; Assistant Clinical Professor of Surgery, University of California Medical School, 1952-85; Director, Experimental Surgery Laboratory, Mount Zion Hospital, 1969-present. *Memberships include:* Fellow, American Medical Association; Fellow, American College of Surgeons. American Federation for Clinical Research; American Thoracic Surgical Association; American Heart Association. American Association for the Advancement of Science; Phi Beta Kappa; Alpha Omega Alpha; Sigma Xi. *Publications include:* Numerous papers presented to medical conferences; many contributions to journals and publications including: 'The American Journal of Physiology'; 'Israel Journal of Medical Science'; 'American Journal of Pathology' etc. *Honours:* Phi Beta Kappa, Sigma Xi, 1931; Alpha Omega Alpha, 1935; Awarded research grants from National Institutes of Health 34 consecutive years. *Hobbies:* History of Medicine; Collecting medical artifacts; collecting medical books; Civil War Round Table. *Address:* 3440 Washington Street, San Francisco, CA 94118, USA.

LEESON, Charles Roland, b. 26 Jan. 1926, Halifax, Yorkshire, England. Professor, Anatomy, University of Illinois, USA. m. Marjorie Martindale, 24 Apr. 1954, Windermere, Cumbria, 2 sons, 3 daughters. *Education:* BA, St Catharine's College, Cambridge University, 1947; MB, B Chir, King's College Hospital, London, 1950; MA, 1951, MD, 1959, PhD, 1971, Cambridge University. *Appointments:* Lecturer, Anatomy, University College of South Wales, 1955-58; Associate Professor, Anatomy, Dalhousie University, Nova Scotia, 1958-61, Queen's University, Kingston, Canada, 1962-63, University of Iowa, USA, 1963-66; Professor, Chairman, Anatomy, University of Missouri, 1966-78; Professor, Anatomy, University of Illinois, Urbana, 1978-. *Memberships:* Anatomical Society of Gt Britain; American Association of Anatomists; British Association of Clinical Anatomists. *Publications:* Co-Author, "Histology", 5th edition 1985; "Human Structure", 1972; "Atlas of Histology", 2nd edition 1985. *Honours:* Outstanding Instructor, University of Iowa, 1965; Golden Apple Award, University of Missouri, 1973. *Hobbies:* Photography; Climbing; Sailing. *Address:* 2503 Melrose Drive, Champaign, IL 61820, USA.

LEGGETT, James Francois, b. 17 June 1945, Tacoma, Washington, USA. Private Practitioner. *Education:* BA, University of Puget Sound, 1967; MS, University of Southern California, 1973; JD, University of Washington, 1975; US Air Force Squadron Officers' School, 1969; US Air Force Command and Staff College, 1979. *Appointments:* Commission Regular Air Force, Graduated from Pilot Training, 1968, 1967; Squadron Pilot, 1968-71; Chief, F-105 Wing Standardization and Evaluation and Tactics, Korat AFB, Thailand, 1971-72; Instructor, Nellis AFB, Nevada, 1972-73; Admissions-Liaison Officer, US Air Force Academy, 1973-; Private Practitioner, 1976-. *Memberships:* Aerospace Medical Associations; Phi Alpha Delta; Pi Gamma Mu; Red River Rats Fighter Pilot Association; Air Force Association; Past President, Pacific Northwest Region, Society of Air Safety Investigators; National Platform Association; SAFE; VFW Post 91;

Human Factors Society. *Publications:* "History of Mount Rainier National Park", 1975; 'An Objective Standard of Safety', 'Forum', 1972; 'Man vs Machine', Institute of Aerospace Safety and Management, USC, 1979 and several other articles. *Honours:* Distinguished Flying Cross with Four Oak Leaf Clusters, Air Medal with Fourteen Oak Leaf Clusters, 1972; Director, Boys' and Girls' Clubs, 1981-85; Trustee, Elks Lodge 174, 1979-82; City Urban Finance Committee, 1978-81. *Hobbies:* Fly Fishing; Flying; Gardening; Weight Lifting. *Address:* 1131 North 26th, Tacoma, WA 98403, USA.

LEGHA, Sewa Singh, b. 17 Dec. 1946, Punjab, India. Associate Professor of Medicine. m. Kuldip Gill, 12 Oct. 1975, Washington, District of Columbia, USA, 1 son, 2 daughters. *Education:* Pre-Med Diploma, Punjab University, DAV College, Chandigarh, Punjab, India, 1964-65; MBBS, Punjab University, Christian Medical College, Ludhiana, Punjab, 1965-70; FACP. *Appointments:* Assistant, Clinical Institute, Medical College of Wisconsin, Milwaukee, Wisconsin, USA, 1972-74; Special Assistant, Cancer Therapy Evaluation Program, Bethesda, Maryland, 1974-76; Faculty Associate 1977-78, Assistant Professor Medicine and Assistant Internist 1978-80, Associate Professor of Medicine and Associate Internist in Department of Developmental Therapeutics 1980-83, Department of Chemotherapy Research 1983-85, Department of Medical Oncology, 1985-. UTMD Anderson Hospital and Tumor Institute, Houston, Texas. *Memberships:* American Federation Clinical Research; American Association of Cancer Research; American Society of Clinical Oncology; American Medical Association; American Society Cancer Chemotherapy; American Society Internal Medicine; Harris County Medical Society; Texas Medical Association; American Association For Advancement of Science; European Association of Cancer; Indian Society Clinical Oncology; International Society Chemotherapy; International Medical Science Academy. *Publications include:* 83 articles; Chapters in books including: 'New Drugs in the Treatment of Cancer', 1984; In Press: 'Doxorubicin Administration by Continuous Venous Infusion'; 'Clinical Trials of Infusion Chemotherapy in Breast Cancer'. *Honours:* Fellow, American College of Physicians, 1977; Junior Faculty Clinical Fellowship, American Cancer Society, 1978-81. *Hobby:* Reading. *Address:* M D Anderson Hospital and Tumor Institute, Department of Medical Oncology, Box 77, 6723 Bertner, Houston, TX 77030, USA.

LEHMAN, Ralph Arnold Walter, b. 21 July 1937, Hamburg, Federal Republic of Germany. Professor of Surgery/Chairman of Division of Neurosurgery. m. Judith Ann Ryan, 26 Nov. 1966, Sausalito, California, USA. 1 son, 2 daughters. *Education:* AB, Harvard College; MD, Harvard Medical School. *Appointments:* Instructor, Assistant Professor, Washington University School of Medicine; Assistant, Associate Professor, University of Colorado Medical Center; Professor, College of Medicine, Pennsylvania State University, Chairman, Division of Neurosurgery, M S Hershey Medical Center. *Memberships:* Congress of Neurological Surgeons; American Association of Neurological Surgeons; Society of Neurological Surgeons; American Medical Association; American College of Surgeons. *Publications:* 'Degeneration and Regeneration in Peripheral Nerve' in 'Brain' 1967; 'Motor Co-ordination and Hand Preference' in 'Brain' 1968; 'Mirror-image Shape Discrimination' in 'Brain' 1973. *Address:* Division of Neurosurgery, M S Hershey Medical Center, Hershey, PA 17033, USA.

LEHMAN James A, b. 17 Aug. 1936, USA. Associate Professor of Plastic Surgery. m. Jacqueline K Campbell, 10 Sep. 1965, Ashtabula, Ohio, 2 sons, 2 daughters. *Education:* Princeton University; MD , Jefferson Medical College, 1961; Plastic Surgery, University of Pittsburgh, Pennsylvania, and Canniesburn Hospital, Glasgow, Scotland. *Appointments:* Director, Plastic Surgery Residency, Akron City Hospital, Akron, Ohio, USA; Chief, Division of Plastic Surgery,

Associate Professor of Plastic Surgery, Northeastern Ohio Universities College of Medicine. *Memberships:* American Society of Plastic and Reconstructive Surgeons; American Association of Plastic Surgeons; American Cleft Palate Association; Plastic Surgery Research Council; The Society of Head and Neck Surgeons; American Society of Maxillofacial Surgeons. *Publications:* "A Parents Guide, Cleft Lip and Palate and other Craniofacial Problems", "Secondary Repair, Bilateral Cleft Lip Deformities", 'Cleft Lip and Palate' in "Fundamentals of Plastic and Reconstructive Surgery". *Honours:* First Prize 1965, Second Prize 1966, Cleveland Surgical Society; First Prize, Ohio State Surgical Society, 1966. *Hobbies:* Tennis; Skiing; Soccer. *Address:* 300 Locust Street, Akron, OH 44302, USA.

LEHMAN, John Walter, b. 22 Oct. 1932, Pittsburgh, Pennsylvania, USA. Private Practitioner. m. Mary Lu Hamilton, 22 June 1958, 1 son, 2 daughters. *Education:* BSc; MSc; MD. *Appointments:* Orthopaedic Surgical Staff, Medical Center of Beaver County; Elwood City Hospital; Aliquippa Hospital. Courtesy Staff, Shriners Hospital, Philadelphia Unit. *Memberships:* American and Pennsylvania Medical Associations; AAOS; ACOS; AAMD; Medical Center Beaver County; Beaver County Medical Society; Beaver Valley Chamber of Commerce; Eastern Orthopaedic Society; Interstate Orthopaedic Society. *Honours:* Past President; Beaver County Medical Society; Medical Staff Beaver County Medical Center; Ellwood City Hospital. *Hobby:* Equestrian. *Address:* 1415 Sixth Avenue, Beaver Falls, PA 15010, USA.

LEHMANN, Egil Henrik, b. 20 Sep. 1936, Oslo, Norway. Physician. m. Torunn Moksheim, 25 June 1960, Avaldsnes, Karmoy, Norway, 1 son, 1 daughter. *Education:* Candidate of Medicine, Bergen, 1963; Licentis Practicandi 1965. *Appointments:* Teacher of Anatomy, Bergen, 1966; Research Grant and Amanuensis, Bergen, 1969; Senior Amanuensis, Tromso, 1973; Head of Medical Statistics and Data Processing/Consultant Medical Statistician, Bergen, 1982-83; Currently; Physician, General Practice, Haugesund, Teacher of History of Medicine, Tromso. *Memberships:* The Norwegian College of General Practitioners; The Norwegian Medical Association; The European Society for Mycobacteriology. *Publications:* About 20 titles on Laboratory studies of tuberculosis, medical statistics and data processing, epidemiology and cardiovascular disease. About 200 newspaper articles. *Hobbies:* Humanitarian work: Emmaus Movement; Import firm: Casa de Importacion Lehmann. *Address:* Breidablikgt 197, N-5500 Haugesund, Norway.

LEHMANN, Heinz Edgar, b. 17 July 1911, Berlin, DRG, Professor Emeritus. m. Annette Joyal, 28 July 1940, 1 son. *Education:* University of Freiburg, 1929, 1930-31; University of Marburg, 1929-30; University of Vienna, 1931-32; MD, University of Berlin, 1932-35; OC; FRSC. *Appointments:* Clinical Director, 1947-66, Director of Research, 1966-76, Douglas Hospital, Montreal, Canada; Professor of Psychiatry, 1965-81, Chairman, Department of Psychiatry, 1970-74, Emeritus Professor of Psychiatry, 1981-, McGill University, Montreal, Canada. *Memberships:* President, 1965-66, Life Member, American College of Neuropsychopharmacology; President, 1970-76, Fellow, International College Neuropsychopharmacology; Life Member, American Psychiatric Association; Fellow, Canadian College of Neuropsychopharmacology. *Publications:* "Handbook of Psychiatric Treatment in Medical Practice", (Co-author), 1962; "Pharmacotherapy of Tension and Anxiety", 1970; "Experimental Approaches to Psychiatric Diagnosis", 1971; Author of over 200 professional publications. *Honours:* Albert Lasker Award, Lasker Foundation, 1957; Order of Canada, Government of Canada, 1976; The Royal Society of Canada, 1970. *Hobbies:* Gemology; Astronomy; Magic; Skiing; Scuba diving. *Address:* Department of Psychiatry, McGill University, 1033 Pine Avenue West, Montreal, Quebec, Canada H3A 1A1.

LEHMKUHL, L Don, b. 2 Jan. 1930, Lodgepole, Nebraska, USA, Coordinator, Head Injury Programme, The Institute for Rehabilitation and Research; Clinical Neurophysiologist, m. Carol Dill, 3 Oct 1953, Belvidere, Nebraska, 3 daughters. *Education:* BS, University of Nebraska; MS, PhD, Certificate in Physical Therapy, University of Iowa. *Appointments:* Instructor, Physiology, University of Iowa, 1959-60; Assistant Professor, 1960-68, Associate Professor, 1968-70, Physical Therapy, Case Western Reserve University; Assistant Director, department Allied Health, American Medical Association, 1970-76; Assistant Professor, Rehabilitation and Physiology, Baylor College of Medicine, 1976-; Associate Director for Research, 1976-, Clinical Neurophysiologist, 1982-, Coordinator, Head Injury Programme, 1984-, The Institute for Rehabilitation and Research, Houston, Texas. *Memberships:* Sigma Xi; American Physical Therapy Association; American Physiological Society; American Association for the Advancement of Science; Society for Neuroscience. *Publications include:* 'Evoked spinal, brain stem and cerebral potentials', 1981; 'Measurement of maximal blood flow following a standardized fatiguing exercise for evaluation of the functional capacity of the peripheral circulation', (with C J Imig), 1961; 'Electrical activity of cultured heart cells', (with N Sperelakis), 1967; 'Electrophysiological characteristics of lumbosacral evoked potentials in patients with established spinal cord injury', (with M R Dimitrijevic and F Renouf), 1984; 'Evoked spinal brain stem and crebral potentials', 1981; 'Motor control in man after partial or complete spinal cord injury', (with M R Dimitrijevic, J Faganel and A M Sherwood), 1983; "Brunnstrom's Clinical Kinesiology", (with L K Smith), 1983. *Honours include:* Award for Excellence in Teaching, Case Western Research University, 1969; Certificate for Appreciation, Joint Review Committee for Respiratory Therapy Education, 1976; Certificate of Appreciation, Accreditation Committee of the American Occupational Therapy Association, 1976; Geneva R Johnson Lecture Award, 1985; Lucy Blair Service Award, 1983. *Address:* Department of Clinical Neurophysiology, The Institute for Rehabilitation and Research, 1333 Moursund, Houston, TX 77030, USA.

LEHRE, Knut Peder Daehlin, b. 10 Aug 1924, Nordstrand, Norway, Head, Psyk avd, Buskerud Sentralsykehus, Drammen, Norway, m. Kirsten Irene, 26 Oct 1968, 2 sons, 1 daughter. *Education:* MD, 1951; Psychiatryst, 1961; Neurologist, 1961. *Memberships:* Norsk Psykiatrisk Forening; Norsk Nevrologisk Forening; Norsk Selskap for biologisk Psykiatri; Skandinavisk Migreneselskap. *Publications:* 'Corticosteroidpsykose med Kristusforestilling hos kvinne', 1963; 'Erfaringer med Tegretol i neuropsykiatrien', 1967. *Hobbies:* Outdoor activities; Literature. *Address:* Trollstien 37, 3000 Drammen, Norway.

LEIBOW, David B, b. 28 June 1950, Hamilton, Canada. Assistant Professor of Psychiatry. m. Sandra Aaronson, 1 Jan. 1982, New York, 1 daughter. *Education:* BSc, Hons, Queen's University, Kingston, Ontario; MD, McMaster University, Hamilton, Ontario; Diplomate, American Board of Psychiatry and Neurology; FRCPC (Psychiatry). *Appointments:* Assistant Clinical Professor of Psychiatry, Columbia University College of Physicians and Surgeons, New York; Assistant Attending Psychiatrist, Columbia Presbyterian Medical Center, New York; Attending Psychiatrist, Gracie Square Hospital, New York. *Memberships:* American Psychiatric Association; American Association for the Advancement of Science; Ontario Medical Association; New York Academy of Science. *Honour:* Laughlin Fellowship, 1979. *Hobbies:* Swimming; Tennis; Architecture.

Address: 86, Avenue Road, Toronto, Ontario, Canada M5R 2H2.

LEIBOWITZ, Alan Irwin, b. 22 Apr. 1946, New York, USA. Associate Professor of Medicine; Associate Dean for Student Affairs. m. Lucille A Weber, 9 Jan. 1971, New York. *Education:* BA, Brooklyn College, City University of New York, 1966; MD, School of Medicine, State University of New York, Buffalo, 1970. *Appointments:* Assistant Professor, Medicine, State University of New York, School of Medicine, Buffalo, New York, 1976-79; Assistant Professor, Medicine, 1979-84, Associate Professor, 1984-, Assistant Dean, Student Affairs, 1982-84, Associate Dean, 1984-, College of Medicine, University of South Florida. *Memberships:* Fellow, American College of Physicians; American Association for the Study of Liver Diseases; American Gastroenterology Society; American Society for Gastro-Intestinal Endoscopy; American Federation for Clinical Research. *Publications:* Author or Co-Author of contributions to various books including: "Digestive Diseases in Children", 1978; "The Reticuloendothelial System and the Pathogenesis of Liver Disease", 1980; "Interferon: Properties and Clinical Uses", 1980; "Critical Care Gastroenterology", 1982; "The Doctors Guide to You and Your Colon", 1982; "Second International Workshop on Interferons". Author or co-author of 12 papers contributed to professional journals including: 'Biomedicine'; 'Annals of Internal Medicine'; 'Journal of the American Medical Association'; 'American Journal of Medicine'; 'Clinical Chemistry'; 'Cancer Letters'; 'British Journal of Haematology'. *Hobbies:* Sculling; Jogging; Amateur radio. *Address:* University of South Florida College of Medicine, 12901 North 30th Street, MDC Box 4, Tampa, FL 33612, USA.

LEIGH, Hoyle, b. 25 Mar. 1942, Korea, Professor of Psychiatry, Yale School of Medicine, USA. m. Vincenta M Masciandaro, 16 Sep. 1967, White Plains, New York, USA, 1 son. *Education:* MD, Yonsei University School of Medicine; MA (Hon), Yale University; FACP; FAPA; FICPM. *Appointments:* Rotating Intern, Long Island College Hospital, Brooklyn, NY, 1965-66; Resident in Psychiatry University of Kansas Medical Centre, Kansas, 1966-67; Resident in Psychiatry, Montefiore Hospital and Medical Centre, Bronx, NY, 1967-79; Fellow in Research and Psychosomatic Medicine, Albert Einstein College of Medicine, Montefiore Hospital, NY, 1969-71; Assistant Professor of Psychiatry, 1971-76, Associate Professor of Psychiatry, 1976-81, Professor of Psychiatry, 1981-, Director, Psychiatric Consultant-Liason and Ambulatory Services, 1979-, Yale University School of Medicine; Assistant Chief of Psychiatry, Yale New Haven Hospital, 1976-. *Memberships:* Fellow, American Psychiatric Association; Fellow, American College of Physicians; American Psychosomatic Society; Fellow, International College of Psychosomatic Medicine; NY Academy of Sciences; International Society for Clinical and Experimental Hypnosis; New Haven Medical Association. *Publications:* "The Patient: Biological, Psychological and Social Dimensions of Medical Practice", (with M D & M F Reiser, M D Plenum), 1980; "Psychiatry in the Practice of Medicine", (editor), 1983; "The Patient: Biological, Psychological, Social Dimensions of Medical Practice", 2nd edition, 1985; Author of 100 other publications. *Honours:* Diplomate, American Board of Psychiatry and Neurology, 1971. *Hobbies:* Reading; Music; Skiing. *Address:* Department of Psychiatry, Yale University School of Medicine, 333 Cedar Street, New Haven CT 06510, USA.

LELIEVER, William Charles, b. 9 July 1946, Toronto, Canada. Assistant Professor of Otolaryngology. m. Elizabeth S. Gunnis, 14 Feb. 1970, Ottawa, Canada, 3 sons, 1 daughter. *Education:* BSc, Waterloo Lutheran University; MSc, Anatomy, Queen's University, 1970, MD, 1974. *Appointments:* Fellow in Otoneurology, Sunnybrook Medical Centre, 1979; Assistant Professor of Otolaryngology, University of Texas Medical Branch, Galveston, Texas, USA; Director of Vestibular Laboratories, Ear Institute of Indiana, USA, Clinical

Associate Professor of Otolaryngology, Indiana University. *Memberships:* American Neurotology Society; Royal College of Physicians and Surgeons of Canada; American College of Surgeons; American Medical Association; American Academy of Facial Plastic and Reconstructive Surgeons. *Publications include:* Author and co-author of 16 articles in professional journals including 'Laryngoscope'; 'Archives of Otolaryngology'; 'Otolaryngology Head & Neck Surgery'; 8 book reviews including: "Disorders of the Facial Nerve Anatomy' Diagnosis and Management", 1982; "Temporal Bone Dissection Manual", 1983; "The Vestibular System: Fundamental and Clinical Observations", 1984; Book chapter in press: 'Head, Ears, Nose, Mouth, Throat and Neck' in "Introduction to Clinical Medicine". Numerous abstracts.*Honours:* Queen's University Research Scholarship, 1971; Queen's University Medical Book Award, 1972. *Hobbies:* Music; Sailing. *Address:* Ear Institute of Indiana, 8003 Clearvista Parkway, Indianapolis, IN 46256, USA.

LEMKAU, Paul Victor, b. 1 July 1909, Springfield, Illinois, USA. Professor Emeritus of Mental Hygiene. m. Ruth Claire Roehm, 22 Nov. 1934, Berea, Ohio, 1 son, 4 daughters. *Education:* BSc, Baldwin-Wallace College, Berea, Ohio, 1931; MD, Johns Hopkins University, 1935; Resident in Psychiatry, Henry Phipps Psychiatric Institute, Johns Hopkins Hospital, 1936-39. *Appointments:* Research Assistant through to Associate Professor, 1939-60, Chairman and Professor Department of Mental Hygiene, 1961-75, Professor Emeritus, 1975-, School of Hygiene and Public Health, Johns Hopkins University; Lieutenant to Lieutenant Colonel, Medical Corps, Chief of Professional Services, 150th General Hospital, US Army; Director, New York City Community Health Board, 1955-57; Consultant, temporary services, World Health Organisation, Yugoslavia, Japan, Venezuela, India and Suriman. *Memberships:* Numerous including: American Psychiatric Association, Life Fellow; Fellow, American Public Health Association. *Publications:* "Mental Hygiene in Public Health", 1949, 55; "Basic Issues in Psychiatry", 1957; "Epidemiology of Psychoses in Yugoslavia", 1984. *Honours:* Honorary DSc, Baldwin-Wallace College, 1954; Honorary DrPH, Dickinson College, 1958; Rema Laponrse Medal, Epidemiology of Mental Illnesses, American Public Health Association, 1975. *Hobbies:* Blacksmithing; Music.*Address:* Box 178, Lusby, MD 20657, USA.

LENFANT, Claude, b. 12 Oct. 1928, Paris, France. Institute Director. *Education:* BS, University of Rennes, France; MD, University of Paris. *Appointments:* Assistant Professor of Physiology, University of Lille, France, 1959-60; Clinical Instructor, Medicine, Physiology and Biophysics, 1961-65, Clinical Assistant Professor, 1966-67, Associate Professor, 1968-71, Professor, 1971-72, University of Washington, Seattle, Washington, USA; Acting Associate Director, Collaborative R&D Programme, 1970-72, Associate Director for Lung Programmes, 1970-72, Director, Division of Lung Disease, 1972-80, currently Director, National Heart, Lung and Blood Institute, Bethesda, Maryland; Associate Director, Int Res. 1981-82, Director, Fogarty Int. Res. 1981-82, National Institutes of Health. *Memberships include:* Association of American Physicians; American Society for Clinical Investigation; American Physiology Society; American Society for Clinical Research; International Federation for Medical Electronics; Society for Experimental Medicine and Biology; Undersea Medical Society; New York Academy of Sciences; Institute of Medicine, National Academy of Sciences; Honorary Fellow, Council on Clinical Cardiology, American Heart Association.*Publications:* Author of over 155 published articles and books. *Honours:* Thesis Prize, 1956; Commendation, Tohoku Medical Society, Japan, 1973; Superior Service Honour Award, DHEW, 1974; Regent's Professor, University of California, 1978; Testimonial Dinner, American Thoracic Society, 1979; Honorary Fellow, American College of Chest Physicians, 1979, Council on Clinical Cardiology, American Heart Association, 1984. Honorary Professor: National Yang-Ming Medical College, Taiwan, 1980; Universidad Peruana Cayetano Heredia, Peru, 1980. Various others. *Address:* National Heart, Lung and Blood Institute, Bethesda, MD 20892, USA.

LENIS, Armando, b. 20 Dec. 1942. Otologist Professor Texas A&M University College of Medicine, USA. m. Barbara Ann Winters, 13 Sep. 1972, Richmond, Virginia, USA, 1 son, 2 daughters. *Education:* Doctor of Medicine and Surgery, Universidad del Valle, Cali, Columbia; Residency, Otolaryngology, Medical College of Virginia, Richmond, Virginia; Residency, General Surgery, The Stamford Hospital, Stamford, Connecticut.*Appointments:* Senior Clinical Instructor, Case Western Reserve University, Cleveland, Ohio; Regional Chief Otolaryngology Services, Kaiser Medical Center, Cleveland, Ohio; Visiting Otologist, Cleveland Metropolitan Hospital, Cleveland, Ohio. *Memberships:* Fellow, American College of Surgeons; Fellow, American Academy of Otolaryngology, (Head and Neck Surgery); Fellow, American Auditory Society; Fellow, Pan Am Association of Otolaryngology. *Hobby:* Golf. *Address:* 2401 South 31st Street, Scott and White Clinic, Temple, TX 76508, USA.

LENKO, Jan., b. 18 June 1917, Lwow, Poland. Chief, Department of Urology. m. Antonina Mozer, 25 Oct. 1939. *Education:* Diploma of Physician, 1941; Doctors Degree, 1951; Assistant Professor, 1955, Associate Professor, 1960, Full Professor, 1967, Medicine. *Appointments:* States Hospitals, Lwow, 1941-44, Cracow, 1945-52; Chief of Urological Department, 1952-77; Director, Institute of Surgery, 1974-77; Pro-Rector, Army Medical Academy, Lodz, 1958-66; Urologist in Chief, Medical Service, Polish Army, 1956-77; currently, Chief, Department of Urology, Medical Academy, Krakow, Poland. 2Memberships: Past President: Polish Urological Society; Polish Section, International Society of Urology. Polish Surgical Association; Honorary Member, Polish Urological Society; Czechoslovak Urological Society. *Publications:* Author or Co-Author: "Emergency Urology", 1958, 66; "Urology for Students", 1970, 3rd edition, 1982; "Urolithiasis", 1976; "Gynecology", 1982; over 300 papers in professional Polish and foreign journals. Editor-in-Chief: "Builetyn WAM" (Bulletin of Army Medical Academy); 'Urologia Polska (Polish Urology), 1982-. *Honours:* Scientific Prize 11 degree, Minister of National Defence, 1977, City of Lodz, 1967; Officers and Commandory Cross of Order, Polonia Restituta, 1963, 74; Golden Cross of Merit, 1958; Medal, Committee of National Education, 1975; Golden Honorary Badge, Polish Red Cross, 1975. *Hobbies:* Philately; Bibliophylism; Hiking. *Address:* Sarego 17/7, 31-047 Cracow, Poland.

LENNOX, Stuart Craig, b. 25 May 1932, Aberdeen. Scotland. Consultant Cardio Thoracic Surgeon, Senior Lecturer. m. Brenda Giles, 6 July 1957, 3 sons, 1 daughter. *Education:* MB, BS, London Hospital Medical College, 1956.*Appointments:* Senior Registrar, London Hospital; Brompton Hospital; Honorary Consultant, St Mary's Hospital, W2; Honorary Senior Lecturer, St Mary's Hospital Medical School; Consultant Cardio Thoracic Surgeon, Brompton Hospital; Surgeon, Senior Lecturer, Cardio Thoracic Institute. *Memberships:* Member, British Cardiac Society; British Thoracic Society; Society of Thoracic Surgeons, GB and Ireland; American Association for Thoracic Surgery; European Cardiovascular Society; Fellow American College of Chest Physicians. *Publications:* Various Publications on Congenital and Acquired Heart Surgery and Lung Surgery. *Honours:* Evarts Graham Travelling Fellow; American Association for Thoracic Surgery, 1964. *Hobby:* Sport. *Address:* Marlowe House, 103 Dulwich Village, London SE21, England.

LENOX, Robert Howard, b. 4 Mar. 1943, Boston, Massachusetts, USA. Professor of Psychiatry. m. Barbara Susan Selig, 25 May 1968, 2 daughters. *Education:* BS, Massachusetts Institute of Technology, 1960-64;

MD, University of Vermont College of Medicine, 1964-68; Internship, University of Kentucky Medical Center, 1968-69; Psychiatric Residency, University of California, Los Angeles, 1969-70; Psychiatric Residency, Walter Reed General Hospital, 1970-72. *Appointments:* Research Psychiatrist 1972-75, Assistant Chief Neuroendocrinology, 1975-76, WRAIR; Assistant Chief Neurochemistry and Neuroendocrinology, WRAIR, 1976-77; Associate Professor of Psychiatry 1977-84, Director Neuroscience Research Unit 1977-, Director Psychopharmacology Consulting Clinic 1981-, Professor of Psychiatry 1984-, University of Vermont College of Medicine; Attenting in Psychiatry, Medical Center Hospital of Vermont, 1977-. *Memberships:* American Society for Neurochemistry; Alpha Omega Alpha; Diplomate, National Board of Medical Examiners; Diplomate, American Board of Psychiatry and Neurology; American Psychiatric Association; Vermont Psychiatric Association; American Association for Advancement of Science; Society for Neuroscience; New York Academy of Science; Sigma Xi; International Society for Neurochemistry. *Publications:* 50 articles in scientific journals; Contributor to "Handbook of Neurochemistry" Volume II, (edited by A Lajtha), 1982. *Honours:* Scholarship Award, Massachusetts Institute of Technology, 1961; Massachusetts Medical Scholarship Award, 1965; Pfizer Scholarship Award, 1966; Fellow, American Psychiatric Association, 1986. *Address:* Neuroscience Research Unit, Department of Psychiatry, University of Vermont College of Medicine, Burlington, VT 05405, USA

LENZI, Gian Luigi, b. 24 Oct. 1943, Siena, Italy. Full Professor, Neurosciences. div., 2 daughters. *Education:* Graduate, University of Pisa Medical School, 1967; Fellow, Institute of Physiology, ibid, 1970; Neurological postgraduate school, University of Rome, 1970-72. *Appointments include:* Assistant, Institute of Neurology, University of Siena, 1973-76; NATO Fellow, MRC Cyclotron Unit, Hammersmith Hospital, UK, 1976; Associated Professor, Institute of Neurology, University of Siena, 1977; Associate Professor, University of Rome, 1978-80; Senior Lecturer, Neurology, Royal Postgraduate Medical school, Hammersmith Hospital, University of London, UK/Coordinator of ECAT-Brain studies, MRC Cyclotron Unit, Hammersmith Hospital, 1979-80; Assoicate Professor, Neuropathology, University of Rome/Consultant neurologist, Department of Nuclear Medicine, S. Raffaele Hospital, University of Milan/External consultant neurologist, MRC Cyclotron Unit, Hammersmith Hospital, London, 1981-84; Full Professor, Neurosciences, 1985-. *Memberships include:* Societa Italiana di Neurologia; European Society for Clinical Investigation; Societa Italiana per l'Arteriosclerosi; Lega Italiana contro il Morbo di Parkinson; International Society for Cerebral Blood Flow & Metabolism; etc. *Publications include:* book chapters, research papers in professional journals, etc: Fields of research, neurophysiology, experimental CBF, 1967-75; Cerebral metabolism & blood flow in man, cerebrovascular diseases, emission tomography, 1976-. *Honours:* Premio Luigi Butturini, 1971; Premio de operosita scientifica della Universita di Siena per l'Anno Accademico 1973-74, 1976; Premio di operosita scientifica della Universita di Siena per l'Anno Accademico 1974-75, 1977; Premio della Associazione per lo Sviluppo dello Ricerca Neurologica, Milano, 1981. *Hobby:* Vine growing. *Address:* Department of Neurosciences, III Neurologic Clinic, V.le dell'Universita 30, 00185 Rome, Italy.

LENZNER, Abraham Samuel, b. 22 Feb. 1915, Buffalo, New York. Psychiatrist, Adjunct Professor, Dartmouth Medical School. m. Jean Farber Schwartz, 14 Sep. 1944, Queens Village, New York, 2 daughters. *Education:* BA 1937, MA, University of Michigan, 1938; MD, University of Buffalo, 1941. *Appointments:* Consultation Liaison Psychiatrist, Mount Sinai Hospital, NY, 1948-53; Director, Psychiatric Outpatient Services,

Hillside Hospital, NY, 1953-55; Associate Chairman, Director, Psychiatric Training, Department of Psychiatry, Nassau County Medical Center, 1965-67; Chief, Liaison Psychiatric Services, North Shore University Hospital, Manhattan, NY, 1953-72; Joint Committee, American Hospital Association and American Psychiatric Association, (Chairman 1966-67); Program Director, Psychiatric Education for Non-Psychiatric Physicians, Nassau (NY) Academy of Medicine, 1960-69; Chairman, Department of Psychiatry, Morristown Memorial Hospital, Morristown, NJ, 1975-78. *Memberships include:* Life Fellow, American Psychiatric Assoc; Fellow, American Geriatric Society; American Psychosomatic Society; American Academy of Psychiatry and the Law; American Medical Assoc; Vermont State Medical Society. *Publications:* 'Attitudes and Prognosis of Naval Psychiatric Dischargees', (with A Blau), 1946; 'Psychiatric Services in General Hospitals', 1961; 'Psychiatric Vignettes from a Coronary Care Unit', (with A L Aronson), 1972; 'Psychiatry of Aging' (Chapter), 1973. *Honours include:* CW Post Center of Long Island University, 1971; Distinguished Physician's Award, North Short (Cornell) University Hospital, Manhasset, NY, 1975. *Hobbies:* Gardening; Golf; Tennis; Cabinetry. *Address:* RR 1 Box 215, Bragg Hill Road, Norwich, VT 05055, USA.

LEON, Robert Leonard, b. 18 Jan. 1925, Denver, Colorado, USA. Professor; Chairman. m. Willena Lee Leon, 14 Sep. 1947, 2 sons, 2 daughters. *Education:* MD, University of Colorado School of Medicine, Denver, 1948. *Appointments:* Assistant Director, Acting Director, Child Psychiatry, Greater Kansas City Mental Health Foundation, Kansas City, MO, 1953-54; Chief, Mental Health Services, US Public Health Service, Region VI, 1954-57; Assistant Professor, Associate Professor, Professor, Psychiatry, Chief of Psychiatrics Clinics, The University of Texas Health Science Center at Dallas, 1957-67; Professor, Chairman, Department of Psychiatry, The University of Texas Health Science Center at San Antonio, 1967-; Chief of Psychiatry, Medical Center Hospital, San Antonio, 1967-. *Memberships:* Fellow, American Academy of Child Psychiatry; American Assn. of Chairmen of Departments of Psychiatry; Life Fellow, American Ortho-psychiatric Assn, Fellow, American Psychiatric Assn; American College of Psychiatrists; American Ass. for Advancement of Science; American Assn. for Social Psychiatry; American Medical Assn; Society for Study of Psychiatry and Culture. *Publications:* "Psychiatric Interviewing: A Primer", 1982; 'The Generation Gap-adult and child psychiatry', 1978. *Hobbies:* Photography; Sailing. *Address:* Department of Psychiatry, The University of Texas Health Science Center at San Antonio, 7703 Floyd Curl Drive, San Antonio, TX 78284, USA.

LEONG, John Chi-Yan, b. 10 July 1942, Hong Kong. Professor of Orthopaedic Surgery, Dean, Faculty of Medicine. m. Annie Hsu On-Pok, Jan. 1969, 2 sons. *Education:* MB BS (Hong Kong), 1965; Fellow, Royal College of Surgeons, Edinburgh 1969, England 1970; Fellow, Royal Australasian College of Surgeons, 1985. *Appointments:* Honorary Consultant Orthopaedic Surgeon, United Christiaq Hospital, Kowloon, Hong Kong, 1976-; Honorary Medical Superintendent, Duchess of Kent Children's Hospital, Hong Kong, 1981-; Consultant Orthopaedic Surgeon, ibid, 1982-; Honorary Consultant in Orthopaedic Surgery to the Army in Hong Kong, 1982-; Honorary Consultant Orthopaedic Surgeon, Medical & Health Services, Hong Kong Government, 1982; Professor & Head of Department, Orthopaedic Surgery, University of Hong Kong, 1981-; Dean, Faculty of Medicine, University of Hong Kong, 1985-. *Memberships:* British Orthopaedic Association; Fellow, Western Pacific Orthopaedic Association; Société Internationale de Chirurgie et de Traumatologie; Fellow, American Academy of Neurological & Orthopaedic Surgeons; and others. *Publications:* Some 60 articles in medical & orthopaedic journals. *Honours:* Numerous Visiting

Professorships, Invited Speaker in various countries. *Hobbies:* Tennis; Down-hill Skiing; Cycling; Golf. *Address:* Department of Orthopaedic Surgery, University of Hong Kong, Hong Kong.

LEON-GONZALEZ, Carlos, b. 14 June 1938, S/C Tenerife, Spain. Chief, Thoracic Surgery Unit; Associate Professor. m. Carmen Rodriguez, 1 June 1965, Barcelona, 2 sons, 1 daughter. *Education:* MD, 1963; FCCP. *Appointments:* Adjunto, Jefe Seccion, Thoracic Surgery, Hospital Valle Hebron. *Memberships:* American College of Chest Physicians; International Society for Diseases of the Oesophagus; European Club of Thoracic Surgery; Sociedad Espanola de Cirugia; Sociedad Espanola de Patalogic Resquiratorid. *Publications:* "Transplate pulmoner experimental", 1970; "Manometric Control of Pulmonary Pressure in Various Stages of Lung Re-implantation", 1970; "Early and Late Effects of Pulmonary Denervation in the Dog", 1973; "Carcinoide Bronquinal", 1974, 1985; "Mesotelioma Plural", 1976; "One Stage Surgical Treatment of Cardiac and Pulmonary Echinococcosis", 1981. *Hobbies:* Photography; Theatre; Gardening; Dance; Music. *Address:* Thoracic Surgery Unit, Hospital Santa Cruz of San Pablo, Avda. S. Antonio Maria Claret, 167, 08025 Barcelona, Spain.

LEOPOLD, Irving Henry, b. 19 Apr. 1915, Philadelphia, Pennsylvania, USA. Physician; Medical Educator. m. Eunice Robinson, 24 June 1937, 1 son, 1 daughter. *Education:* Student, Pennsylvania State University, 1934; MD, University of Pennsylvania, 1938; DSc, 1943. *Appointments include:* Director, Research, Wills Eye Hospital, 1949-64; Attending Surgeon, 1952-64; Medical Director, 1961-64; Consultant Surgeon, 1965-; Chairman, Department Ophthalmology, Mount Sinai School of Medicine, 1965-85; Professor, Chairman Department Ophthalmology, University of California, Irvine, 1975-85; Professor Emeritus, 1985-; Consultant Ophthalmologist various hospitals; Lecturer, Universities and Colleges in USA and Canada; Consultant, Chemical Warfare Service, US Army, 1948-52, 1981-; Surgeon General, OSPHS, 1953-; Chairman, Ophthalmology Panel US Pharmacopeia, 1960-70, Member, Revision Panel, 1970-. *Memberships include:* Association Research Ophthalmology; National Society Prevention Blindness; American Association for Advancement of Science; American Diabetes Association; American Medical Association; New York Academy of Science; Sigma Xi; Alpha Omega Alpha; Newport Beach Tennis Club; Big Canyon Country Club; Century Club, New York City. *Publications:* Contributor to professional journals, etc; Editor-in-Chief, 'Survey of Ophthalmology', 1958-62; Consultant Editor, 1962-; Editorial Board: 'American Journal of Diabetes', 1956-73; 'Investigative Ophthalmology', 1961-74, 'American Journal Ophthalmology', 1965- *Honours include:* Zentmayer Award, 1945, 49; Honor Award, American Academy Ophthalmology, 1955; Edward Lorenzo Holmes Citation and Award, 1957; Friedenwald Medal, Association Research Ophthalmology, 1960. *Address:* 1484 Galaxy Drive, Newport Beach, CA 92660, USA.

LEÖVEY, András, b. 20 Nov. 1926, Nyiregyháza, Hungary. Professor and Chief of I. Medical Department, University Medical School of Debrecen; Rector of University Medical School of Debrecen. m. Nandine Wolafka, 10 Nov. 1951, 1 son, 1 duaghter. *Education:* MD, 1951; PhD, 1968; Academic Doctor of Medical Sciences, 1982; PhD. *Appointments:* Resident II, 1951, Assistant Professor, 1968, Associate Professor, 1972, Head of Department, 1974, Vice-Rector, 1974-80, Rector, 1985-, University Medical School of Debrecen. *Memberships:* European Academy of Allergology and Clinical Immunology; American Thyroid Association; Hungarian Society of Allergology and Clinical Immunology; Hungarian Society of Endocrinology and Metabolism. *Publications:* 115 articles and 12 book chapters on Clinical Immunology and Endocrinology (Thyroid Diseases and Thyroid Immunology). *Honours:* 1st degree of Universitatpreis, Rostock, 1979; Medal of Pro Universitate Emlekerem, Debrecen, 1976. *Hobbies:* Hunting; Fishing; Tennis. *Address:* Szabó István alt. tér. 8 sz, 4032 Debrecen, Hungary.

LEPAGE, Denis Jean-Baptiste, b. 24 June 1947, Sherbrooke, Québec, Canada. Associate Professor and Chairman, Department of Psychiatry, University of Sherbrooke; Chief, Department of Psychiatry, Centre hospitalier universitaire de Sherbrooke. m. Michèle Héon, 25 Aug. 1979, Sherbrooke, 1 son, 2 daughters. *Education:* BA, 1966; MD, LCMC, 1971; CSPQ, 1975; FRCP (C), 1975. *Appointments:* Chief Resident, Chedoke Child and Family Center, McMaster University, Hamilton, Ontario, 1974-75; Assistant Professor, 1975-80, Program Director, Department of Psychiatry, 1979-83, University of Sherbrooke. *Memberships:* Quebec Psychiatric Association; Canadian Psychiatric Association; American Psychiatric Association; The Royal College of Physicians and Surgeons of Canada. *Publications:* 'Electroconvulsive Therapy' in "L'union médicale du Canada", No. 9 Sep, 1980; 'Electroconvulsive Therapy' in "Précis pratique de psychiatris" (co-author), 1981. *Address:* Centre hospitalier universitaire de Sherbrooke, Sherbrooke, Québec, Canada JIH 5N4.

LESSER, Leonard Irving, b. 18 Feb. 1916, Georgia, USA. Consulting Psychiatrist, New Orleans Adolescent Hospital. m. May Hyman, 9 Nov. 1947, New Orleans, Louisiana, 2 sons, 2 daughters. *Education:* University of Alabama; MD, Tulane University of Louisiana; Resident in Pediatrics, Emory University, Atlanta, GA, 1941-45; Residency in Psychiatry/Child Psychiatry, Johns Hopkins University Hospital, 1955-56; FAAP; FAACP; FAPA. *Appointments:* Director, Dade County Child Guidance Clinic, Fla; Director, Los Angeles Child Guidance Clinic; Co-Director, Out Patient Childrens Clinic, Los Angeles/University Southern California Medical Centre; Director, Orange County Child Guidance Clinic, Calif. *Memberships:* American Medical Association; American Academy of Pediatrics; American Psychiatric Association; American Academy of Child Psychiatry. *Publications:* 'Pulmonary Manifestations of Kerosene Intoxication', 1943; 'Early Infantile Autism', (with Leo Kanner), 1958; 'Anorexia Nervosa in Children', (with Ashenden, Debuskey, Eisenberg), 1960; 'The Children's Psychopharmacology Clinic; It's Role within a Total Program for Children's Psychiatric Services', 1970; 'Hyperkinesis in Children - An Operational Approach to Management', 1970; 'Physiological Studies of the Hyperkinetic child: 1', (with Satterfield, Cantwell, Podosin), 1972; 'EEG Aspects in the Treatment of Minimal Brain Dysfunction', (with Satterfield, Saul, Cantwell), 1972; 'CNS Arousal in Hyperactive Children', (with Satterfield, Saul Cantwell, Podosin), 1972; 'Response to Stimulant Drug Treatment in Hyperactive Children: Prediction with EEG and Neurological Findings', (with Satterfield, Cantwell, Saul, Podosin), 1972; 'Family Psychodynamics Chapter 11', (with Stewart), 1973. *Honours:* Alpha Omega Alpha; Diplomate, American Board Pediatrics; Diplomate, American Board Psychiatry and Neurology, General Psychiatry; Diplomate, American Board Psychiatry and Neurology, Child Psychiatry; Examiner, Child and General Psychiatry, American Board Psychiatry and Neurology. *Hobbies:* Photography; Music; Horticulture. *Address:* 4909 St Charles Avenue, New Orleans, LA 70115, USA.

LESSER-KATZ, Miriam, b. 29 Aug. 1942, Israel. Child Psychotherapist. m. Adrian Katz, 31 Mar. 1965, 1 son, 1 daughter. *Education:* MA, University of Chicago, Illinois, USA, 1977; BGS, Roosevelt University, Chicago, Illinois, 1976. *Appointments:* Head Nurse, Beilinson Medical Centre, University of Tel-Aviv, Israel, 1962-65; Operating Room Nurse, Yale University Medical Center, New Haven, Conn, USA, 1965-67; Surgical Nurse, 1968-75, Research Assistant, 1976-80, Child Psychotherapist, 1980-, Department of Child Psychiatry, University of Chicago, Chicago, ILL, USA.

Memberships: American Psychological Assoc; American Assoc. for Counseling Psychologist; Assoc. of Mental Health Private Practitioners. *Publications:* 'Some Effects of Maternal Drug Addiction on the Neonate', 1982; 'Elective Mutism in the Pre-school: Two Kinds of Strangers Reactions', 1986. *Honours:* The Franklin Honor Society, 1975. *Hobbies:* Music; Art; Squash. *Address:* 1125 E 53rd Street, Chicago, IL 60615, USA.

LETTON, A. Hamblin, b,. 23 May 1916, Tampa, Florida, USA. Private Practitioner, General Surgery & Oncology. m. Roberta Rogers, 7 Oct. 1938, 1 son, 1 daughter. *Education:* MD, Emory University School of Medicine, 1941. *Appointments:* Consulting surgeon, Sheffield Cancer Clinic, 1954-; Active attending surgeon, 1955-, Director, Breast Screening Project 1973-, Chairman, Executive Committee, Cancer Division 1976-, Georgia Baptist Medical Centre; Assistant Clinical Professor of Surgery, Medical College of Georgia, 1984-. *Memberships:* Fellow, American College of Surgeons; Fellow, Southeastern Surgical Congress; Honorary life member, board member, American Cancer Society; Southern Surgical Association; American Society of Nuclear Medicine; Tinian Medical Society; Various local & state medical associations; etc. *Publications include:* "Hernia", film, Ethicon, 1985; Contributions to 'Cancer', "American Surgeon", volume 4; etc. Chairman, editorial board, 'Oncology Times'; Editorial board member, 'International Advances in Surgical Oncology'. *Honours:* Distinguished service awards, Southeastern Surgical Congress, 1982, American Cancer Society 1980; President, American Cancer Society, 1972. *Hobbies:* Playing organ; Boating. *Address:* 315 Boulevard, Suite 500, Atlanta, GA 30312, USA.

LEUNG, Alexander Kwok-Chu, b. 1 Oct. 1948, Hong Kong. Clinical Assistant Professor in Paediatrics. *Education:* MB BS, Hong Kong; FLEX; LMCC; DCH, London; DCH, Ireland; DABP; MRCP, UK; MRCP, Ireland; FRCP, Canada; FAAP. *Appointments:* Lecturer, University of Hong Kong, 1974; Paediatric Resident, University of Calgary, Canada, 1975-77; Lecturer, Child Health, University of Queensland, Australia, 1977; Paediatric Endocrine Fellow, University of Calgary, Canada, 1977-79; Paediatric Consultant, Alberta Childrens Hospital and Foothills Hospital, Alberta, 1980-. *Memberships:* Royal Colleges of Physicians, Ireland and UK; Fellow, Royal College of Physicians of Canada, American Academy of Paediatrics, Royal Society of Medicine, Royal Society of Health, Canadian Paediatric Society; New York Academy of Sciences. *Publications:* Author of some 120 publications including: 'Spontaneous recovery from serum IgA deficiency' and 'Congenital hemihypertrophy and maternal systemic lupus erythematosis' in 'Proceedings of the Royal College of Physicians of Edinburgh', 1985; 'Dominantly inherited syndrome of microcephaly and congenital lymphedema' in 'Clinical Genetics', 1985. *Honours:* Physician Recognition Award, 1985. *Hobbies:* Collecting stamps and gold coins. *Address:* 330 Market Mall Professional Building, 4935 40 Avenue North West, Calgary, Alberta, Canada T3A 2N1.

LEVENSON, Alan Ira, b. 25 July 1935, Boston, Massachusetts, USA. Professor and Head of Psychiatry Department. m. Myra B Katzen, 12 June 1960, West Hartford, 1 son, 1 daughter. *Education:* AB, Harvard College 1957; MD, Harvard Medical School, 1957; MPH, Harvard School of Public Health, 1965; Residency in Psychiatry, Massachusetts Mental Health Center, Boston, 1962-65. *Appointments:* Staff Psychiatrist 1965-66, Assistant Chief Mental Health Facilities Branch 1966; Director Division of Mental Health Service Programs 1967-69, National Institute of Mental Health; Professor and Head, Department of Psychiatry, University of Arizona College of Medicine; President and Chief Executive Officer, Palo Verde Hospital and Palo Verde Mental Health Services.

Memberships: Fellow, President 1986-87, American College of Psychiatrists; Fellow, President 1982-83, American College of Mental Health Administration; Fellow, American Psychiatric Association; Fellow, American Association for Social Psychiatry; Group for Advancement of Psychiatry. *Address:* Department of Psychiatry, Arizona Health Sciences Center, Tucson, AZ 85724, USA.

LEVI, Salvator, b. 1 Aug. 1934, Brussels, Belgium. Gynaecologist. m. Catherine Cuykens, 13 June 1964, Brussels, 1 son, 1 daughter. *Education:* Doctor of Medicine, Surgery and Midwifery; Graduate in Gynaecology and Obstetrics. *Appointments:* Full-time Voluntary Assistant; Full-time Assistant; Full-time First Assistant; Full-time Titular Associate; Head of Clinic. *Memberships:* Royal Belgian Society of Gynaecology and Obstetrics; Belgian Society of Ultrasound Diagnostics; Yugoslav Society of Ultrasonography (Honorary Member); American Institute of Ultrasound in Medcine; Belgian Study Group on Mental Handicap; European Anthropological Association; Group of French Speaking Gynaecologists in Belgium; Italian Society of Perinatal Medicine (Honorary Member); French Society for Applications of Ultrasound in Medicine and Biology. *Publications:* "Le Diagnostic par les Ultrasons en Gynecologie et en Obstetrique", 1972; Co-author: 'Present and Future of Diagnostic Ultrasound', Kooyker Scientific, Rotterdam, 1976; Co-author: "Real-time Ultrasound in Perinatal Medicine", 1979; Co-author: "Les Grossesses a Haut Risque", 1980; "Ultrasound and Cancer", 1982; Hundreds of articles in different scientific journals. *Honours:* Chevalier, Order of Leopold III, Belgium, 1980; Honorary Assistant, St Mary's Hospital, 1962; Senior Research Scientist, Indianapolis, 1976. *Hobby:* Tennis. *Address:* Hospital Universitaire Brugmann, Service Gynecologie-Obstetrique, Place A Van Gehuchten 4, 1020 Brussels, Belgium.

LEVICK, Richard Keith, b. 23 June 1930, Exeter, Devon, England. Consultant Radiologist. m. Beti Roberta Price, 20 June 1959, Bridgend, Glamorgan, Wales, 3 daughters. *Education:* MB, BCh, Welsh National School of Medicine, 1949-54. *Appointments:* House Physician & Surgeon, United Cardiff Hospitals, 1954-55; Medical Officer, RAMC, 1955-57; Training Posts in Medicine & Radiology, Cardiff & Sheffield, 1957-64. *Memberships:* Royal College of Radiologists (Council 1980-83); Royal College of Physicians, Fellow 1976; Royal Society of Medicine; British Paediatric Association. *Publications:* Various articles on paediatric radiology. *Honours:* Order of St John (Officer), 1972; Territorial Decoration, 1970. *Hobbies:* Walking; Music; Vintage Cars. *Address:* 'Avalon', Hill Lane, Hathersage, via Sheffield, S30 1AY, England.

LEVICK, Stephen E, b. 9 Apr. 1951, Coral Gables, Florida, USA. Psychiatrist. *Education:* BA, Psychology and Philosophy, magna cum laude, Western Reserve College, 1973; MD, Case Western Reserve University School of Medicine, Cleveland, Ohio, 1977. *Appointments:* Resident in Psychiatry, Yale University School of Medicine, 1977-81 (1st year, medical internship, Norwalk Hospital); Fellow, Yale Psychiatric Institute, 1981-82; Post-doctoral research trainee, New York University Medical Center and Staff Psychiatrist, Bellevue Hospital, 1982-84; Staff Psychiatrist, Veterans Administration, Medical Center, West Haven and Assistant Professor, Department of Psychiatry, Yale University School of Medicine, 1984-. *Memberships:* American Psychiatric Association; American Medical Association; American Association for the Advancement of Science. *Publications:* 'With onions and tears: A multidimentsional analysis of a counter-ritual' in "Family Process" 1981 (co-author); 'Paradoxes of always-never land' in "Group and Family Therapy 1983 - An Overview" edited by L R Wolberg and M L Aronson, 1983; 'The role of the idealizing tranference in the treatment of psychotic patients' in Journal of Nervous and Mental Diseases, 1985. (with A V Tepp). *Honours:* Phi Beta Kappa, 1973. *Hobbies:* Swimming; Snorkeling; Visual arts; Hiking. *Address:* V A Medical Center 116A1, West Haven, CT

06516, USA.

LITTLE, William Lynn, b. 17 July 1947, Philadelphia, Pennsylvania, USA. Fleet Liaison Officer, Aviation Life Support Equipment. m. Sharlene Warbrick, b. 20 Aug. 1966, Langhorne, Pennsylvania, 3 sons, 1 daughter. *Education:* BS, Biology-Chemistry, Delaware Valley College of Science and Agriculture; MS, Systems and Safety Management, University of Southern California. *Appointments:* Aviation Physiology Training Units; Aircraft Accident Investigator; Aeromedical Safety Officer; Fleet Liaison Officer. *Memberships:* Aerospace Medicine; Aerospace Physiologist Society; SAFE. *Publications:* Contributor of several papers to Navy Journal and SAFE Association Journal. *Honours:* Aerospace Physiologist, 1983; Wiley Post Award, 1984; Operational Physiology-Aerospace Medical Association; Navy Commendation Medal 1980-83; Small Arms and Rifle Expert Marksman. *Hobbies:* Music; Woodworking; Sports. *Address:* 43 Sweetgum Road, Levittown, PA 19056, USA.

LEVINE, Aaron Martin, b. 5 Mar. 1947, Bronx, New York, USA, Physiatrist. m. Susan Labell, 4 September 1983. *Education:* BS; MD. *Appointments:* Assistant Professor, Baylor College of Medicine. *Memberships:* American Medical Association; Southern Medical Association; Texas Medical Association; American Association Electromyography and Electrodiagnosis; American Society Evoked Potentials; American Clinical Academy Physical Medicine; Association Academic Physiatrists; American Congress Rehabilitation Medicine. *Publications:* 'Management of Multiple Sclerosis', 1985; 'External Fixation in Quadriplegia', 1984; 'Elderly Amputee', 1984; 'Spinal Orthuses', 1984. *Hobbies:* Cinema; Theatre. *Address:* 6419 Coachwood, Houston, TX 77035, USA.

LEVINE, Edwin Rayner, b. 7 Nov. 1903, New York City, New York, USA. Consultant Physician; Professor. m. Ruth Freudenheim, 28 January 1932, New York, 1 son, 1 daughter. *Education:* BS, New York University, 1926; MD, Cornell University, 1930; Intern, Bellevue Hospital, 1930-31; Resident and Chief Resident, Chest Service, Metropolitan Hospital, 1931-34. *Appointments include:* Instructor in Medicine, New York Medical College, 1938-43; Medical Director, Edgewater Hospital, Chicago, Illinois, 1949-80, Edgewater School of Inhalation, 1955-73, Malcolm X College, Chicago, 1968-73, Central Young Mens Christian Association College, 1970-78. Attending Physician: Edgewater Hospital; Ravenswood Hospital Medical Center. Consultant, Department of Hospitals, New York City; Associate Professor, Chicago Medical School; Visiting Lecturer, Lovelace Foundation, New Mexico; Adjunct Professor, Antioch College, Ohio. Medical Director: School of Respiratory Therapy, Medical Careers Institute; Career Academy, Chicago; Center for Respiratory Therapy, Chicago. *Memberships include:* Fellow: American Medical Association; American College of Chest Physicians; American Association for Advancement of Science; National Association of Medical Directors of Respiratory Therapy. Chicago and Illinois Medical Societies; Association for Advancement of Medical Instrumentation; Association for Computing Machinery; American Academy of Geriatrics. *Publications:* "Effective Inhalation Therapy", "Dyspnea"; author of numerous articles in scientific journals; columnist 'Respiratory Therapy Magazine'; Member of 10 editorial boards; author of 21 chapters in medical textbooks and 25 scientific exhibits. Numerous International lectures. *Honours include:* Award, Central Young Mens Christian Association College, 1983; Senior Citizens Hall of Fame, Chicago, 1980; Certificate of Appreciation, Chicago Lung Association, 1975, American Medical Association, 1975. *Address:* 6033 North Sheridan Road, Chicago, IL 60660, USA.

LEVINE, Raphael, b. 10 May 1940, Allentown, Pennsylvania, USA. Associate Clinical Professor of Orthopaedic Surgery. m. Letha Sharon Schwartz, 14 Feb. 1965, Philadelphia, 2 sons, 3 daughters. *Education:* BA, Brandeis University, 1961; MD, Jefferson Medical College, 1965. *Appointments:* Orthopaedic Residency, Columbia Presbyterian Medical Centre; Chief, Childrens Surgical Services, Helen Hayes Hospital, New York, 1973-85; Acting Director, Orthopaedic Surgery, 1980-84; Associate Clinical Professor, Orthopaedic Surgery, Columbia Presbyterian Medical Centre, 1982-85; Associate Orthopaedic Surgeon, Passack Valley Hospital, Westwood, New Jersey; Associate Clinical Professor, Orthopaedic Surgery, College of Physicians and Surgeons, Columbia Presbyterian Medical Centre, New York. *Memberships:* American Academy of Orthopaedic Surgeons; American Academy for Cerebral Palsy. *Publication:* Chapter in "The Child with Disabling Illness", 1982. *Honour:* AOA Honour Medical Society. *Hobby:* Tennis. *Address:* 354 Old Hook Road, Westwood, NJ 07675, USA.

LEVINSON, Bernard, b. 5 May 1926, Johannesburg, Republic of South Africa. Consultant Psychiatrist. m. Sheila, 21 Jan. 1981, Johannesburg. *Education:* MB ChB, DPM (Rand). *Memberships:* Fellow, American Society of Clinical Hypnosis; Founder Chairman, South African Medical Arts Society; Founder Chairman, South African Institute of Human Sexuality. *Publications:* "From Breakfast to Madness" (poetry); "Learning to Love" (sex education); "Waiting on the Edge" (Art therapy). *Hobby:* Sculpting. *Address:* 20 Walter Street, Fellside 2192, Johannesburg, Republic of South Africa.

LEVITSKY, David Randolph, b. 12 July 1951, New York, New York, USA. Doctor of Podiatric Medicine and Surgery. *Education:* BA, Queen's College of the City of NY; Doctor of Podiatric Medicine, 1976. *Appointments:* Director, Residency Training Program, Detroit Central Hospital, Detroit, Michigan, 1980-84; Member, Surgical Research Program; Department of Health and Human Resources; Public Health Service-Food and Drug Administration; Pediatric Subtalar Arthroereisis Implant; Member, Credentials Committee and Residency Training Committee, Dearborn Medical Centre, Dearborn, Michigan. *Memberships:* Former Member, Students Division, APA; Diplomat, American Board of Podiatric Surgery; Associate, American College of Foot Surgery; Member, American Podiatry Assoc; Michigan State Podiatry Assoc; Southeast Michigan State Podiatry Assoc; American College of Sports Medicine. *Publications:* 'Percutaneous Osteoclasp Fixation of Akin Osteotomy', 1981; 'Rigid Compression Screw Fixation of 1st Proximal Phalanx Osteotomy for Hallux Abducto Valgus', 1982. *Honour:* Pi Delta. *Hobbies:* Skiing, Water and Snow; String Musical Instruments; Collector of Antique String Instruments; Sailing; Gymnastics; Weight Lifting; Solo Free Climbing; Kayak/Canoeing; Ornithology; Entomology. *Address:* 31228 Five Mile Road, Livonia, MI 48154, USA.

LEVITT, Harvey Lawrence, b. 12 Mar. 1931, Montreal, Quebec, Canada. Dental Specialty Practice (Orthodontics); Assistant Professor, Faculty of Dentistry, McGill University; Clinical Assistant Professor of Orthodontics and Periodontics, University of Pennsylvania, USA. m. Margaret Lucie Felberg, 1 Sep. 1958, Montreal, 2 sons, 2 daughters. *Education:* BSc (cum laude), 1953, DDS, 1955, McGill University; Certificate in Orthodontics, University of Montreal, 1956; FRCD (C); FICD; FAIDS. *Memberships:* Alpha Omega Dental Fraternity, President, Montreal Alumni Chapter, 1965-66, International Regent, 1974-75; Mount Royal Dental Society, President, 1966-67; Quebec Association of Orthodontists, President, 1971; Canadian Association of Orthodontists; American Association of Orthodontists; Northeastern Society of Orthodontists; Canadian Dental Association; Royal College of Dentists of Canada; International College of Dentists: Academy of International Dental Studies. *Contributor to:* 'Journal of Clinical Orthodontics'; Major contributor to "Altas od Adult Orthodontics", Marks and Corn (Textbook in progress). *Honours:* Man of the Year, Dental Division of State of Israel

Bonds, 1983; Honorary Member, Montreal Alumni Chapter, Alpha Omega Dental Fraternity. *Hobby:* Music. Former member of several amateur orchestras including Montreal Musica Viva and Hampstead Chamber Orchestra; First violinist of string quartet. *Address:* 5757 Decelles Avenue, Suite 3, Montreal, Quebec, Canada H3S 2C3.

LEVITT, Michael Norman, b. 15 Sep. 1933, Montreal, Quebec, Canada. Clinical Assistant Professor. (Divorced), 2 sons, 1 daughter. *Education:* BA 1958, MD, CM 1958, McGill University, Montreal. *Appointments:* Associate Otolaryngologist, Royal Victoria Hospital, Montreal, 1964-; Associate otolaryngologist, Montreal General Hospital, 1978-; Assistant Professor, Department of Otolaryngology, McGill University; Practising Otolaryngology Head and Neck Surgery, Chairman, Tumor Board, Co-Chairman, Cancer Committee, Cedars Sinai Medical Center, Los Angeles, California; Member, The Attending Staff; Clinical Assistant Professor, University of South California. *Memberships include:* Nu Sigma Nu; Canadian Medical Association; Canadian Otolaryngological Society; American Medical Association; Canadian Medical Association; Royal College of Physicians and Surgeons of Canada; Canadian Otolaryngological Society. *Publications include:* 'The Cricopharyngeus Muscle, An Electromyographic Study in the dog', (with H H Dedo and J H Ogura), 1965; 'Supraglottic Subtotal Laryngectomy', 1966; 'Hydatid Disease of the Parotid Gland', (with D H Greig), 1967; 'Ranula. A Case Report', 1968; 'Facial Paralysis and Muscle Agenesis in the Newborn', (with H E McHugh, K H Sowden and A Sheridan), 1969; 'Spontaneous Cerebrospinal Fluid Rhinorrhea', (with G Bertrand), 1969. *Honours:* American Cancer Society Award for Fellowship Study at Washington University, Barnes Hospital Center, St Louis, Missouri. *Hobbies:* Tennis; Golf. *Address:* 435 North Bedford Drive, Beverly Hills, CA 90210, USA.

LEVY, Jean Paul, b. 8 June 1934, Paris, France. Head of Department, Professor. m. Donnatienne Senot, 11 Oct. 1954, Rheims, 2 sons, 2 daughters. *Education:* MD; Professor of Medicine. *Appointments:* Professor of Medicine, Research Director, Hôpital Cochin, Paris. *Publications:* Over 250 papers etc. *Address:* Hôpital Cochin, 27 rue du faubourg St Jacques, 75014 Paris, France.

LEVY, Laurence Fraser, b. 16 Nov. 1921, London, England. Professor, Surgery, University of Zimbabwe. m. Lorraine Moyle Woest, 24 Dec. 1966, Harare, 2 sons. *Education:* MSc, New York University, 1954; MBBS, London, 1949; MRCSLRCP, 1945; FRCS England, 1956; FRCS (ED) (SN), 1982; FACS,1 962. *Appointments:* House Physician, Worthing Hospital, 1945-46; Assistant Resident Medical Officer, Royal National Hospital for Diseases of Chest, Isle of Wight, 1946; RAFVR, Medical Branch, 1946-49; Demonstrator, Anatomy, University of Toronto, 1949-50; Senior Intern, Surgery, Queen Mary Veteran's Hospital, Montreal, 1950-51; Assistant Resident, Surgery & Neurosurgery, New York University Post graduate Hospital, USA, 1951-53; Assistant Fellow, Neuropathology, Montreal Neural Institute, 1953-54; Senior Resident, Neurosurgery, Bellevue Hospital, 1954-55; Research Fellow, Neurosurgery, London Hospital, England, 1955-56; Consultant, Neurosurgery, Salisbury Group of Hospitals, Zimbabwe, Consultant, Neurosurgery, Governments of Zambia & Malawi, 1956-72. *Memberships include:* Congress of Neurosurgeons; British Medical Association; Zimbabwe Medical Association; etc. *Publications:* Various articles in professional journals; Chapter in book. *Honours:* Montreal Medico/Chirurgical Society Interns Research Prize, 1951. *Hobbies:* Chess; Equitation. *Address:* Uchani Ard-Na-Lea Close, Chisipite, Harare, Zimbabwe.

LEVY, Roy Denton Keith, b. 2 Apr. 1919, Kingston, Jamaica. Clinical Associate Professor, Family Medicine, McMaster University Medical Centre, Hamilton, Ontario, Canada. m. Marjorie Hepburn, 21 Nov. 1945, Reading, UK, 2 sons. *Education:* MA, BM, BCh (Oxon): MRCP (London), 1949; CCFP(Canada), 1976. *Appointments include:* Medical officer, 5th Battalion Dorsetshire Regiment, 1943-45; Major, Royal Army Medical Corps, Control Commission, Germany, 1945; Senior Medical Registrar, Radcliffe Infirmary, Oxford, UK, 1948; Consultant physician, Kingston, Jamaica, 1948-74; Associate Professor, McMaster University, 1974-83 (retired 1983); Clinical Associate Professor, ibid, 1983-. *Memberships:* British Medical association; Royal College of Physicians, UK; Jamaica Medical Association; Canadian & Ontario Medical Associations; College of Family Physicians, Canada; Hamilton Academy of Medicine;' Medico-Legal Society of Hamilton. *Honours:* Mentioned in Despatches, 1946; Knight of Grace, Order of St. John (K.St.J.), 1972. *Hobbies:* Cycling; Skiing. *Address:* 177 Parkview Drive, Hamilton, Ontario, Canada L8S 3Y4.

LEW, Dong-Joon, b. 2 Oct. 1937, Seoul, Korea. Professor of Preventive Medicine. m. Kwang-Soon Kim, 16 Sep. 1967, Seoul, 4 daughters. *Education:* Pre-Medical course, Yonsei University College of Science, 1961; MD, Yonsei University College of Medicine, 1965; Physicians License, Republic of Korea, 1965; MPH, 1967, PhD, 1977, Seoul National University; Certified, Korean Board of Preventive Medicine, 1969, Board of Tuberculosis, 1975; Fellow, American College of Chest Physicians, 1976. *Appointments:* Post-Graduate Residency training, 1965-69; Navy Physicians, Korean Navy, 1969-72; Director, HooSaing Clinic, 1972-75; Instructor, 1975-85, Assistant Professor, Associate Professor, Professor, currently, School of Medicine, Kyung Hee University, Seoul; Visiting Professor, School of Community Medicine and Public Health, University of Washington, USA, 1982-84. Fellow, American College of Chest Physicians; Korean Medical Association. Life Member: Korean Society of Internal Medicine; Korean Society of Preventive Medicine; Korean Academy of Tuberculosis; Korean Society of Gastroenterology. Korean Society of Circulation; Korean Academy of Family Medicine. *Publications:* "Home Clinic", 1975; "Preventive Medicine", 1976; "Management of Chronic Diseases", 1979; "The Famour Doctors - named 333 Physicians", 1981; "The Health Encyclopedia for Middle Aged", 1982; "Diabetes Mellitus", 1982. *Honours:* Fellow, American College of Chest Physicians, 1976; Executive Trustee, Korean Association of Chronic Diseases Control, 1982. *Hobbies:* Movie appreciation; Sight-seeing tours. *Address:* 507-609 Gocheung Apt, Jamsil 5 Dong, GangDongKu, Seoul 134, Korea.

LEWANDOWSKA, Janina, b. 18 May 1921, Krzeszowice, Poland. Professor of Paediatrics. Widow. *Education:* MD, Medical Academy, Krakow, 1951; Speciality Board in Paediatrics, 1957, 1960 and 1977; Habilitated Doctor of Medicine 1969, Associate Professor of Paediatrics 1975, Professor of Paediatrics 1982, Medical Academy, Wroclaw. *Appointments:* Director, Outpatient Allegology Clinic, Wroclaw, 1960-; Consultant, Karpacz Spa Respiratory Disease Center, Karpacz, 1969-; Director of Research Centre, Childrens Allergology Hospital, Szczawno Spa, 1969-; Committee of Speciality Boards in Allergology, Programme Committee of Speciality Board in Paediatrics, Medical Centre, Warsaw, 1973-; Professor of Paediatrics, First Departemnt of Paediatrics, Academy of Medicine Hospital, Wroclaw, 1982-. *Memberships:* Polish Society of Paediatrics; Polish Medical Association; Polish Society of Allergology; International Society of Asthmology; European Academy of Allergology and Clinical Immunology; Society of Allergology and Clinical Immunology of the Socialistic States. *Publications include:* 88 papers including: 'Bacteriological diagnostics of the otitis media in newborn', 1957; 'Singnificance of the allergological tests and their association with the function of adrenal glands', 1969; 'The effect of the experimental anaphylactic shock on glycosamien and polysacharide in serum and mucopolysacharides in the lung and the adrenals and liver of the Guinea Pig', 1971; 'Relationship between skin tests and behaviour of the ventilatory & idices after provocative inhalation tests in children with bronchial asthma', 1974; 'Immunoglobulines in asthmatic children during balneological treatment in Szczawno Spa', 1982. *Honours:* Gold Cross of Recognition, 1975; Chevaliery Cross of Polish Republic, 1985. *Hobby:* Travelling. *Address:* Ul Lukasiewicza 16 mn 1, 50-371 Wroclaw, Poland.

LEWICKY, Roman T, b. 1 Jan. 1942, Ukraine. Orthopaedic Surgeon. m. Puka Gizinski, 26 June 1965, Cleveland, Ohio, USA, 2 sons. *Education:* BS, Holy Cross College, 1964; MD, Northwestern University Medical School, 1968; Orthopaedic Surgeon, Northwestern University Medical Center, 1975. *Appointment:* Medical Officer, US Navy, 1969-71. *Memberships:* American Academy of Orthopaedic Surgeons; American College of Surgeons; American Board of Orthopaedic Surgeons; American Medical Association; American Orthopaedic Society for Sports Medicine; Western Orthopaedic Association. *Publication:* Article: 'Arthroscopy of the Knee', 'American Journal of Sports Medicine', Vol 10 No 1. *Honour:* Arizona Sports Medicine Physician of the Year Award, 1983. *Hobbies:* Windsurfing; Skiing; Hiking; Fishing. *Address:* 1355 N Beaver Street, Flagstaff, AZ 86001, USA.

LEWIN, Walter, b. 25 Aug. 1930, Hamburg, FRG. Private Practitioner, Psychiatry. m. Grace Bogart, 9 June 1956, Kansas City, Missouri, USA, 3 sons, 1 daughter. *Education:* BA, University of Kansas; MD, University Kansas Medical Centre, Kansas City, Residency in Psychiatry, Menninger School of Psychiatry, Topeka, Kansas, 1959-62. *Appointments:* Director, Outpatient Department, Prairie View Hospital, Newton, Kansas, 1962-67; Medical Director, Johnson County Mental Health Center, 1967-69; Private Practice, Psychiatry, Shawnee Mission, Kansas, 1969-. *Memberships:* Kansas Medical Society; Johnson County Medical Society; Kansas Psychiatric Association; American Psychiatric Association; American Orthopsychiatry Association. *Honours:* Chairman, Department of Psychiatry, Shawnee Mission Hospital, 1973-75, 1985-86; President, Medical Staff, Shawnee Mission Medical Centre, 1977. *Hobbies:* Literature; Music; Swimming; Travel. *Address:* 8901 West 74th Street, Shawnee Mission, KS 66209, USA.

LEWIS, Brian Joel, b. 24 Apr. 1943, Houston, Texas, USA. Clinical Professor of Medicine. m. Simone Kent, 17 Aug. 1976, San Francisco, 2 daughters. *Education:* BA, Rice University; MD, Harvard Medical School. *Appointments:* Director, Oncology Unit, San Jose Hospital, 1974-76; Special assistant for clinical affairs, Division of Cancer Treatment, National Cancer Institute, Bethesda, Maryland, 1976-78; Senior investigator, Medicine, ibid, 1978-80; Co-director, Faculty Group Practice, Cancer Research Institute, University of California, San Francisco, 1980-. *Memberships:* American Society of Clinical Oncology; Amrican Association for Cancer Research. *Honours:* Phi Beta Kappa, 1965; Alpha Omega Alpha, 1969. *Address:* Room A502, 400 Parnassus Avenue, University of California, San Francisco, CA 94143, USA.

LEWIS, David, b. 18 Oct. 1939, Ogmore Vale, England. Medical Director, Ansett Airlines of Australia. m. Anne Jennifer Hooton, 6 Feb. 1964, Worksop, Nottinghamshire, England, 3 sons. *Education:* MB ChB, Bristol University, England, 1963; DObstRCOG, London, 1965; DAVMed, London, 1976. *Appointments:* HO, Swansea General Hospital, 1963; HO, Southmead Hospital, Bristol, 1964; SHO, Obstetrics and Paediatrics, Morriston Hospital, Swansea, 1964; Short Service Commission Royal Air Force, 1965-68; Principal, NHS General Practice, Ogmore Vale, 1968-71; Permanent Commission, Royal Air Force, 1971-77; Chief,

Medical Standards, Aviation Medicine Branch, Department of Aviation, Australia, 1977-81; Medical Director, Ansett Airlines of Australia, 1981-. *Memberships:* Founder Fellow, Australian College of Occupational Medicine, 1983; Vice-President, Aviation Medical Society of Australia and New Zealand; Member, Aerospace Association; Australian Medical Association; Australia and New Zealand Society of Occupational Medicine. *Hobbies:* Rugby; Photography; Aviation. *Address:* Medical Centre, Ansett Airlines, 501 Swanston Street, Melbourne, Australia 3000.

LEWIS, David Henry, b. 17 Oct. 1946, London, England, Consultant Orthodontist, University Dental Hospital of Manchester; Private Orthodontic practice, m. Helen M Goodman, 20 June 1971, Manchester, 1 son, 3 daughters. *Education:* BDS, London Hospital Dental School, 1968; FDS RCS, England; Dip Orth RCS, England. *Appointments:* Resident House Officer in Oral Surgery, London Hospital; General Practice; Resident Senior House Officer, St Batholemews Hospital, London; Clinical Trainee, Registrar in Orthodontics, Eastman Dental Hospital, London; Senior Registrar in Orthodontics, Royal Dental Hospital, London, St Georges, Tooting, Kingston Hospital and Guildford. *Memberships:* Royal College of Surgeons; British Dental Association; British Society for the Study of Orthodontics; British Association of Orthodontists; Consultant Orthodontist Group; Association of University Teachers of Orthodontics; Aemrican Association of Orthodontists. *Publications:* 'Dilaceration – A Surgical/Orthodontic solution', 1984; 'Internal Resorption complications orthodontic tooth movement', 1984, (with J Brady); 'Improved cranio maxillary fixation using orthodontic appliances', (with J Ferguson, M E Foster), 1985; 'Instanding lateral incisor in the adult: A new method for its management'. *Hobbies:* Computers; Windsurfing. *Address:* Orthodontic Department, University Dental Hospital of Manchester, Higher Cambridge Street, Manchester M15 6FH, England.

LEWIS, Dorothy Otnow, b. 23 July 1937, New York, USA. Professor of Psychiatry, New York University Medical Centre, Clinical Professor of Psychiatry, Yale University Child Study Centre. m. Melvin Lewis, 30 May 1963, 1 son, 1 daughter. *Education:* Radcliffe College, 1959; Yale University School of Medicine, 1963; MD; FACP. *Appointments:* Clinical Instructor, Psychiatry, 1970-71, Assistant Clinical Professor of Psychiatry, 1971-75, Associate Clinical Professor of Psychiatry, 1975-79; Clinical Professor of Psychiatry, 1979-, Child Study Centre, Yale University; Research Professor of Psychiatry, New York University School of Med icine, 1979-81; Associate Director, Child and Adolescent Psychiatry, New York University Medical Centre, 1979-. *Memberships:* Connecticut Council of Child Psychiatrists, 1962-; Connecticut State Medical Society, 1970-; New Haven County Medical Association, 1970-; Fellow, The American Psychiatric Association; American Academy of Child Psychiatry, 1972-; Connecticut Psychiatric Society; Associate Fellow, Silliman College, Yale University. *Publications:* "Delinquency and Psychopathology", (with D A Balla), 1976; "Vulnerabilities to Delinquency", (Editor), 1981; 'Violent juvenile deliquents: psychiatric, neurological, psychological and abose factors', (co-author). *Honours:* Book Prize, Yale Medical School, 1963; Sigma Xi, 1972; Blanche F Ittleson Award, American Psychiatric Association, 1982. *Address:* 10 St Ronan Terrace, New Haven, CT 06511, USA.

LEWIS, Gerald Richard John, b. 22 Nov. 1941, Jaipore, India. Consultant Cardiologist. m. Beryl Monica Moodey, 4 Feb. 1967, Wellington, 3 daughters. *Education:* MBChB, Otago, 1967; MRACP, 1971; MRCP (UK), 1973; FRACP, 1975; MD, Otago, 1976. *Appointments:* House Physician, Christchurch Hospital, 1968-69; Medical Registrar, Christchurch, 1970-72; Cardiology Registrar;

Research Fellow, Clinical Pharmacology, Royal Postgraduate Medical school, London, 1974; National Heart Foundation's Cardiac Research Fellow, St Thomas' Hospital, London, England, 1975-76; Consultant Cardiologist, Princess Margaret Hospital, Christchurch, 1977-83; Consultant Cardiologist, Napier Hospital, New Zealand. *Memberships:* Fellow, Royal Australasian College of Physicians; Royal College of Physicans, UK; Cardiac Society of Australaia and New Zealand. *Publications:* "Changes in Myocardial Function Following Cardiac Surgery", 1976; Articles in various journals including: 'European Journal of Cardiology"; 'British Journal of Pharmacology'; 'New Zealand Medical Journal'; 'Australia & New Zealand Medical Journal'; etc. *Hobbies:* Cricket; Tennis; Sailing; Computing; Classical Music; Tramping; Camping; Fishing. *Address:* 7 Balquhidder Road, Napier, New Zealand.

LEWIS, Melvin, b. 18 May 1926, London, England. Professor of Pediatrics and Psychiatry. m. Dorothy, 30 May 1963, New York City, USA, 1 son, 1 daughter. *Education:* MB, BS, London, England; MA (Hon), Yale University, USA; FRC Psych. DCH. *Appointments:* Instructor, Assistant Professor, Associate Professor, Professor. *Memberships:* American Academy of Child Psychiatry; American Psychiatric Association; American Psychoanalytic Association; Association for Child Psychoanalysis; American Pediatric Society; Royal College of Psychiatrists. *Publication:* "Clinical Aspects of Child Development", 2nd edition, 1982. *Honour:* Editor, 'Journal of the American Academy of Child Psychiatry', 1975-. *Hobby:* Piano. *Address:* 333 Cedar Street, New Haven, CT 06510, USA.

LEWIS, Michael, b. 10 Jan. 1937, New York City, USA. Profesosor. m. Rhoda Rosenzweig, 18 Aug. 1962, 1 son, 1 daughter. *Education:* PhD, University of Pennsylvania, 1962. *Appointments:* Director, Infant Laboratory, Educational Testing Service, 1971-78; Director, Institute for the Study of Exceptional Children, Eductional Testing Service, Princeton, 1977-82; Professor, Paediatrics & Psychiatry, University of Medicine and Dentistry, New Jersey Rutgers Medical School, 1982-; Chief, Division of Child Development, Paediatrics, UMDNJ-RMS, Piscataway, 1983-. *Memberships:* Eastern Psychological Association; American Psychological Association; Society for Research in Child Development; New York Academy of Science; American Association for the Advancement of Science; International Association for Infant Mental Health. *Publications:* Co-Author, "Children's Emotions and Moods: Developmental Theory and Measurement", 1983; "Origins of Intelligence: Infancy and Early Childhood", 1983; "Beyond the Dyad", 1984. *Honours:* Fellow: New York Academy of Sciences, American Psychological Association, Japan Society for the Promotion of Sciences, 1984. *Address:* 921 Linwood Circle, Princeton, NJ 08540, USA.

LEWIS, Michael Ray, b. 24 Feb. 1956, Colorado Springs, Colorado, USA. Visiting Scientist, Space Biomedical Research Institute, Johnson Space Center. m. Karen Diane Komarek, 21 May 1977, Boulder, Colorado, 1 son. *Education:* BA, University of Colorado, Boulder, 1978; PhD, University of Texas Medical Branch, Galveston, 1986 *Appointment:* Research Associate, Neuropharmacology, UTMB, Galveston, 1984-86. *Memberships:* Society for Neuroscience; Aerospace Medical Association. *Publications:* An Electrophysiological Investigation of the Rate Medial Vestibular Nucleus, In Vitro, in Contemporary Sensory Neurobiology, 1985; Afferent Vestibular Transmission in Rate is Mediated by Putative G, Excitatory Amino Acid Receptor, 1985. *Hobbies:* Computer Programming; Christian Apologetics; Military Modelling; Softball; Fencing. *Address:* 7096 N Holiday Drive, Galveston, TX 77550, USA.

LEWIS, Peter Robert Frederick, b. 26 June 1948, En-

gland. Pathologist. Grafton & Coffs Harbour, with Dr Sullivan and Nicolaides and Partners. m. Virginia Elizabeth Saunders, 16 May 1970, Salisbury, South Australia, 1 son, 1 daughter. *Education:* MBBS; FRCPA. *Appointments:* Resident Medical Officer, Royal Adelaide Hospital, 1972, Hastings Memorial Hospital, New Zealand, 1973; Pathology Registrar, Auckland Hospital, 1974-77; IMVS, Adelaide, 1978; Specialist Pathologist, IMVS, 1979-80; Private Practice, 1980-; Visiting Pathologist, Grafton Base Hospital, 1982-. *Memberships:* Australian Medical Association; Royal College Pathologists Australia; South Pacific Underwater Medical Association; International Academy Pathology. *Publications:* "Skin Diving Fatalities in New Zealand", 'New Zealand Medical Journal', 1979. *Hobbies:* Skin Diving (CMAS Instructor); Karate; Horse Riding. *Address:* 25 Prince Street, Grafton 2460, New South Wales, Australia.

LEWIS, Philip Christie, b. 19 July 1942, Lincoln, Nebraska, USA. Private Practitioner. m. Rosa Elisa Dragone, 17 Sep. 1965, Cordoba, Argentina, 3 daughters. *Education:* MD; Colonel, Medical Corps, US Army Reserve. *Appointments:* Chief, Community Mental Health Activity, Fort Clayton, Canal Zone, Panama, 1975-79. *Memberships:* American Psychiatric Association, 1975-; Circulo Medico de Cordoba, 1982. *Honours:* Honorary Member, Asociacion Medica Panamericana (Capitulo Ecuatoriano), 1979; Diplomate, American Board of Psychiatry and Neurology, 1979. *Hobby:* Jogging. *Address:* Dorrego 1234, Barrio General Paz, 5000 Cordoba, Argentina.

LEWIS, Randall Jeffrey, b. 26 Jan. 1946, Boston, Massachusetts, USA. Associate Clinical Professor Orthopaedic Surgery. m. Patricia Gimbel, 1 Sep. 1968, Hamden, Connecticut, 1 daughter. *Education:* AB Summa cum laude, Yale University, 1965; MD cum laude, Harvard Medical School, 1969; Certified National Board of Medical Examiners, 1970; Certified, American Board of Orthopaedic Surgery, 1977. *Appointments:* Intern 1969-70, Resident 1970-71, Beth Israel Hospital, Boston; Clinical Associate, Surgery branch, National Cancer Institute, 1971-73; Resident, Orthopaedic Surgery, Hospital for Special Surgery, 1973-76; Assistant Professor 1976-79, Associate Professor 1978-81, Associate Clinical Professor 1981-, Orthopaedic Surgery, George Washington University. *Memberships include:* American Academy of Orthopaedic Surgeons; American Medical Association; District of Columbia Medical Society; American Rheumatism Association; Washington Orthopaedic Society. *Publications include:* 'Detection of Deep Vein Thrombosis with Doppler Ultrasound Techniques in Patients Undergoing Total Knee Replacement', (with J A Bradford, J M Giordano and C M Edwards), 1982; 'Closed Rodding of Pathologic Fractures with Supplement Cement', (with J Kunec), 1984; 'Osteoarthritis', 1982; "Emergency Orthopaedic Radiology", (with R J Neviaser, L S Eisenfeld and S W Wiesel), 1985. *Address:* 1915 Eye Street NW, Washington, DC 20006, USA.

LEWIS, Ronald Gordon, b. 9 Dec. 1928, Sydney, Australia. Consultant Physician and Cardiologist; Clinical Lecturer in Medicine, University of Sydney. m. Joan Elmer Barr, 21 July 1955, Melbourne, 3 sons, 2 daughters. *Education:* MB BS (second class honours), University of Sydney, 1951; MRACP, 1955; MRCB (London), 1956; FRACP, 1967; FRCP (London), 1976. *Appointments:* Junior RMO, Royal Prince Alfred Hospital, 1951; Senior, RMO, Royal Hobart Hospital, 1952-53; Senior House Officer, University Department of Medicine, Manchester Royal Infirmary, England, 1956; Clinical Assistant in Medicine; Honorary Assistant Physician; Honorary Physician; Visiting Medical Officer, Sydney Hospital, 1954-83; Visiting Physician - The Bankstown Hospital, 1957-; Honorary Consultant Physician, now Emeritus, Auburn District Hospital, 1962-; Honorary Consulting Physician, Sydney Hospital, 1983-; Associate Cardiologist, Royal Prince Alfred Hospital, 1983-. *Memberships:* Cardiac Society of Australia and New Zealand; Life Governor, Sydney Hospital. *Publications to:* 'Medical Journal of Australia'; 'Journal of Cardiovascular Pharmacology'; 'Bulletins of Post Graduate Committee in Medicine, University of Sydney'; 'Clinical Experimental Immunology'. *Hobbies:* Photography; Opera; Tennis; Travel. *Address:* 210A Burwood Road, Burwood, New South Wales 2134, Australia.

LEWY, John E, b. 22 Apr. 1935, Chicago, Illinois, USA. Reily Professor, Chairman, Department of Paediatrics. *Education:* BA, University of Michigan, 1956; MD, Tulane University School of Medicine, New Orleans, 1960. *Appointments include:* Associate in Pediatrics, 1967-68; Assistant Professof of Pediatrics, 1968-69, Chicago Medical School; Director, Section of Pediatric Nephrology, Michael Reese Medical Center, Chicago, 1967-70; Assistant Professor of Pediatrics, 1970-71, Associate Professor of Pediatrics, 1971-75, Professor of Pediatrics, 1975-78, Director, Division of Pediatric Nephrology, 1970-78, Cornell University Medical College; Professor and Chairman, Department of Pediatrics, Tulane University School of Medicine, New Orleans, Louisiana, 1978-. *Memberships include:* American Academy of Pediatrics; Society for Pediatric Research; American Pediatric Society; Association of Medical School Pediatric Department Chairmen (Executive Committee 1981-84); American Board of Pediatrics, Sub-Board of Pediatric Nephrology, 1980-85; American Society for Pediatric Nephrology, Secretary-Treasurer 1974-80, President 1980-81; International Pediatric Nephrology Association, Assistant Secretary General 1974-78; American Society of Nephrology; International Society of Nephrology and many more. *Publications:* Author of numerous published abstracts and articles to scientific journals. *Honours:* Intern of the Year Award, Michael Reese Hospital Medical Center, Chicago, 1961; Louisiana Pediatric Society Award, 1960; Alpha Omega Alpha, Tulane University School of Medicine, New Orleans, 1960. *Address:* Tulane Medical School, Department of Paediatrics, 1430 Tulane Avenue, New Orleans, LA 70112, USA.

LEY, Robert Edgar Yves, b. 26 Sep. 1940, Brussels, Belgium. Head, Plastic Surgery, St Pierre University Hospital, and Erasmus Academy Hospital. m. Janine Limpens, 17 July 1965, Brussels, 2 daughters. *Education:* MD, University of Brussels, 1965; Graduated, General Surgery, 1971, Plastic Surgery, 1980. *Appointments:* Resident, General Surgery, 1965-74, Adjoint, Plastic Surgery, 1976-82, Head, Plastic Surgery, 1983-. Saint Pierre University Hospital; Resident, Plastic Surgery, MacGill University, Montreal, Canada, 1974-76; Head, Plastic Surgery, Erasmus Academic Hospital, 1983-. *Memberships:* Titulary Member: Belgian Society of Surgery, Belgian Society of Plastic Surgery; President, Belgian Association for Burn Injuries; Associate Secretary General, International Society for Burn Injuries. *Publications:* 27 articles in European and American Medical Journals; Author, 52 Lectures in European, American & Asian Medical Meetings. *Honour:* Fleurice Mercier Award, 1964. *Hobbies:* Antique African, Pre-Columbian and Asian Art. *Address:* 3 Avenue des Hesperides, 1180 Brussels, Belgium.

LEYDEN, Michael John, b. 2 July 1946, Melbourne, Australia. Oncologist, St Andrew's Hospital. m. Prudence Alsop, 15 Dec. 1970, Melbourne, 2 sons, 1 daughter. *Education:* MBBS, 1970; FRACP; FRCPA. *Appointments:* Junior Resident Medical Officer, 1971, Senior Resident Medical Officer, 1972, St Vincent's Hospital, Melbourne; Medical Registrar, Canberra Hospital, 1973-75; Medical Registrar, Woden Valley Hospital, 1976; Haematology Registrar, 1977, Haematology Pathology Registrar, 1978, St George Hospital, Sydney; Haematology Registrar, Prince Alfred Hospital, 1979; Assistant Oncologist, 1980-85; Royal Melbourne Hospital; Private Practice, 1985-. *Memberships:* Australian Medical Association; Clinical Oncology Society of Australia; Haematology Society of Australia; Australian Transplantation Society. *Publ-*

ications: Articles in professional journals including: 'Pathology'; 'Cancer'; 'Medical Journal of Australia'; 'Lancet'. *Honours:* Ern Linton Research Award; Cancer Council of Victoria, 1984-86. *Hobbies:* Sailing; Skiing. *Address:* Suite 9, 12 St Andrew's Place, East Melbourne 3002, Australia.

LEYTON, Robert Edward Geoffrey, b. 9 May 1944, Oxford, England, Private practitioner, medicine; President, Canadian Holistic Medical Association. m. Jocelyne, 19 June 1965, London, Ontario, Canada, 1 son, 1 daughter. *Education:* BSc, Honours, MD, Western University; CCFP, Queen's University. *Appointments include:* Committee on Psychosomatic Medicine, Ontario Medical Association; Founding member, President 1983-86, Canadian Holistic Medical Association; Editor, 'Hologram', Newsletter, ibid. *Memberships also include:* College of Family Physicians. *Hobbies:* Skiing; Running; Theatre & Drama; Music; Art. *Address:* 13 ½ Lower Union Street, Kingston, Ontario, Canada K7Z 2N3.

LI, Hui-Feng, b. 12 Jan. 1935, Szechuan, China. Associate Professor and Dean of Research Institute. m. 8 Dec. 1956, 1 son, 1 daughter. *Education:* Graduate, West China University of Medical Sciences, 1956. *Appointments:* Assistant, Department of Oral Medicine, West China University of Medical Sciences, 1956-60; Assistant, Department of Oral Medicine, Hubei Medical College, China, 1960-63, Lecturer, 1963-78. Associate Professor, 1978-present. *Memberships:* Chairman, Hubei Branch, Society of Stomatology; IADR; ADEE; ICD. *Publications:* "Oral Syndromes", 1978; One of the Editors "Textbook of Oral Medicine", 1981; Articles: 'Lichen planus of Oral Mucosa' in 'Chinese Journal of Stomatology', 1980; 'Cigarette smoking and leukoplakia' in 'National Medical Journal of China', 1981; 'A Preliminary study of Sister Chromatid Exchanges and Chromosomal Abberation in Lymphocytes of Patients with Leukoplakia and Oral Carcinoma', in 'Chinese Journal of Stomatology', 1985, etc. *Hobbies:* Music; Sport. *Address:* Hospital for Stomatology, Wuhan, Hubei, People's Republic of China.

LIBERMAN, Robert Paul, b. 16 Aug. 1937, Newark, New Jersey, USA. Professor. m. Janet Brown, 16 Feb. 1973, Thousand Oaks, California, 2 sons, 3 daughters. *Education:* AB, Summa cum laude, Dartmouth College, 1959; MS, University of California School of Medicine, San Francisco, 1961; MD, Johns Hopkins University School of Medicine, 1963. *Appointments include:* Chief Rehabilitation Medicine Service, Brentwood, VA Medical Center, Los Angeles; Director, UCLA Mental Health Clinical Research Center for Schizophrenia and Psychiatric Rehabilitation, 1977-; Director, Clinical Research Unit at Camarillo State Hospital, 1970-; Research Psychiatrist, NIMH, 1968-70. *Memberships include:* Assn. for Advancement of Behaviour Therapy; American Psychiatric Assn; Assn for Clinical Psychosocial Research. Publications include: Numerous articles in professional journals 'Multiple family therapy for schizophrenics: A behavioral approach', (co-author), 1984; 'Social skills training for relapsing schizophrenics: An experimental analysis' (co-author), 1984; 'Behavioral analysis and therapy for aggressive psychiatric and developmentally disabled patients' (co-author), 1984; 'Behavioral family therapy with deliquent and substance abusing adolescents' (co-author), 1984. *Honours include:* Silvano Arieti Award, Academy of Psychoanalysis, 1986; Certificate of Appreciation, National Alliance for the Mentally Ill, 1985; Distinguished Service Award, California Alliance for the Mentally Ill, 1982; Numerous research grants from federal government. *Hobbies:* Tennis; Violin; Jogging; Cooking; Swimming. *Address:* Research Centers (691/B117) West Los Angeles VA Medical Center, Wilshire and Sawtelle Blvds, Los Angeles, CA 90073, USA.

LIBRACH, Samuel, b. 3 May 1927, Toronto, Canada. Hospital Department Chief. m. Evelyn Spector, 1 June

1952. Toronto, 3 sons, 1 daughter. *Education:* BA Honours Physiology and Biochemistry 1948, MD 1952, University of Toronto. *Appointments:* Chief, Department of Obstetrics and Gynaecology, Doctors Hospital, Toronto, 1972-. *Memberships:* Fellow, American College of Obstetrics and Gynaecology; Fellow, Royal College of Surgeons, Canada; Society of Obstetrics and Gynaecology of Canada; Toronto Society of Obstetrics and Gynaecology; American Association of Gynaecolgic Labaioseopists; Canadian Society of Sterility and Infertility. *Publications:* The Librach Uterine Elevator and Manipulator (invention). *Hobby:* Sailing. *Address:* 25 Brunswick Avenue, Suite 302, Toronto M5S 2L9, Canada.

LICHTMAN, Marshall A, b. 23 June 1934, New York, USA. Professor, Medicine, Radiation Biology & Biophysics. m. Alice Jo Maisel, 23 June 1957, 3 daughters. *Education:* AB, Cornell University, 1955; MD, University Buffalo School of Medicine, 1960; Resident, Internal Medicine, 1960-63, Chief Resident, 1965-66, Strong Memorial Hospital, University of Rochester Medical Centre. *Appointments:* Post Doctoral Research Fellow, Medicine, 1966-68; Assistant Professor, 1968-71, Associate Professor, 1971-74, Professor, 1974-, Chief, Hematology, 1975, Associate Dean, 1979, Senior Associate Dean, 1980, Academic Affairs & Research, University of Rochester School of Medicine and Dentistry. *Memberships include:* American Society for Clinical Investigation; Association of American Physicians; Fellow, American College of Physicians; American Society of Hematology; etc. *Publications:* 170 scientific articles, Chapters, etc; "Hematology for Practitioners", 1978; "Hematology and Oncology", 1980; "White Cell Mechanics: Clinical & Basic Sciences Aspects", 1984, co-editor. *Honour:* Scholar, Leukemia Society of America, 1969-74. *Address:* Box 610 University of Rochester Medical Centre, 601 Elmwood Avenue, Rochester, NY 14642, USA.

LIE, Terje, b. 30 Dec 1952, Sandefjord, Norway, Chief Medical Officer, The Medical Office for Seamen, Oslo, Norway. *Education:* MD, University of Oslo, 1979. *Appointments:* General Practitioner, Oslo; Assistant Doctor, Psychiatric Department, Lovisenberg Hospital, Oslo. *Memberships:* Board Member, The Norwegian Neutical Medicine Association, 1984-; Member, Norwegian Medical Association, 1979-. *Hobbies:* Music; Playing bass guitar; Dogs. *Address:* A Överlandsv 138, 0764 Oslo 7, Norway.

LIEBMAN, Mayer Crockin, b. 20 Aug. 1934, Norfolk, Virginia, USA. Psychiatrist, Psychoanalyist. m. Jane B. Olenstein, 14 June 1964, New York City, New York, USA, 2 sons. *Education:* BA, Johns Hopkins University, Baltimore, Maryland, 1952-56; MD, New York University, 1957-62; Internship, Kings County Hospital, Brooklyn, New York, 1962-63; Residency in Psychiatry, Bellevue Psychiatric Hospital, New York, 1963-66. *Appointments:* Chief Resident, Psychiatry, 1965-66; Surgeon, US Public Health Service, 1966-68; Staff Psychiatrist, Sheppard-Enoch Pratt Hospital, Baltimore, Maryland, 1968-71; Director, Community Mental Health Service, Sheppard-Enoch Pratt Hospital, 1971-75; Director, Adult Admission Office, Sheppard-Enoch Pratt Hospital, 1975-81. *Memberships:* AMA; American Psychiatric Association; American Psychoanalytic Association. *Publications:* Author of various book-reviews and chapters in books. *Honours:* Fellow, American Psychiatric Association, 1975; Certified APA, Psychiatric and Neurology, 1969; Certified APA, Mental Health Administration, 1979; Assistant Clinical Professor of Psychiatry, University of Maryland; Assistant Adjunct Professor, Expression Arts, Gouche College; Supervisor, Sheppard-Enoch Pratt Hospital. *Hobbies:* Community Service; Classical music. *Address:* 6229 N Charles Street, Baltimore, MD 21212, USA.

LIECHTY, Mary Waltner, b. 8 Sep. 1941, Philadelphia, Pennsylvania, USA. Psychotherapist, private practice. 1 son, 1 daughter. *Education:* MSW, Western Michigan University, 1973. *Appointments include:* Director, Samaritan Counselling Centre, Mishawaka, Indiana; Associate Professor, St. Mary's College, Notre Dame, IN; Assistant Director of Education, Oaklawn Centre, Elkhart, IN; Psychiatric Social Worker, ibid. *Membership:* National Association of Social Workers. *Honours:* Western Michigan University Fellow, 1972-73; Phi Delta Society, Bluffton College, Ohio, 1963. *Hobbies:* Swimming; Reading. *Address:* 171 C Avenue, Coronado, CA 92118, USA.

LIEBOWITZ, Genese, b. 10 Nov. 1937, New York, USA. Psychotherapist. Divorced, 1 son, 2 daughters. *Education:* BA, Brandeis University, 1959; MA, Social Work, University of Chicago, USA, 1961; 4 year certificate, Bioenergetic Analyst, 1975; ACSW. *Appointments:* Social Caseworker, Family Service Bureau, United Charities of Chicago, 1961-66; Family Therapist, Private Practice, 1971-73; Bioenergetic Therapist and Workshop Leader, 1973-present; Training Therapist, Northern California Bioenergetic Society, 1982-present. *Memberships:* Association for Humanistic Psychology; National Association of Social Workers; Northern California Bioenergetic Society. *Publication:* "Wilhelm Reich and the Sexuality of Women", (manuscript in preparation). *Honour:* One of the keynote speakers at the major Esalen Conference on the work of Wilhelm Reich, 1973. *Hobbies:* Gardening; Hiking; Beachcombing. *Address:* 251 Mariw Avenue, Mill Valley, CA 94941, USA.

LIEM, Han, b. 28 Mar. 1929, Pekalongan, Indonesia. Staff Psychiatrist, US Veterans Administration. m. Frieda G, 16 Oct. 1960, Bandung, Indonesia, 3 daughters. *Education:* MD, University of Indonesia, Jakarta, 1956; Board Certified in Psychiatry, American Board of Psychiatry, 1975. *Appointments:* Plant Physician, Garuda Indonesian Airways, Jakarta, 1956-66; General Practitioner in Jakarta, 1956-66; Assistenz-artz, St Franziskus Hospital, Bonn, West Germany, 1966-67; Private Practice in General Psychiatry, Levittown, Pennsylvania, USA, 1971-75. *Memberships:* American Psychiatric Association; Association of Medical Surgeons of the United States. *Hobbies:* Jazz; Piano; Gardening; Home Computers. *Address:* 712 Fitzwatertown Road, North Hills, PA 19038, USA.

LIEPMAN, Michael Roger, b. 25 Oct. 1946, St Louis, Missouri, USA. Assistant Professor of Psychiatry and Human Behaviour; Clinical Coordinator. m. Marcia Kurlan, 5 Apr. 1968, Ann Arbor, Michigan, 2 sons, 1 daughter. *Education:* BSc, 1968, MD, 1973, University of Michigan; Board Eligibility in Psychiatry, Neuropsychiatric Institute, 1977; Department of Human Genetics, 1971, School of Public Health, 1978, University of Michigan. *Appointments:* Intern, St Joseph Mercy Hospital, Ann Arbor, Michigan, 1973-74; Resident, University of Michigan Hospitals, 1974-77; Instructor, Psychiatry, Career Teacher in Alcohol and Drug Abuse, 1977-80, Assistant Professor of Psychiatry and Family Practice, 1981-82, University of Michigan; Assistant Professor of Psychiatry and Human Behaviour, Brown University, Providence, Rhode Island, 1982-; Chief, Alcohol Dependence Treatment Programme, 1982-84, Clinical Coordinator, 1984-, Veterans Administration Medical Centre, Providence. *Memberships:* Charter Member, Association of Medical Educators and Researchers on Substance Abuse, Academy of Psychosomatic Medicine; Research Society on Alcoholism; American Medical Society on Alcoholism and Other Drug Dependencies; American Society of Clinical Hypnosis; American Psychiatric Association; American Medical Association; American Orthopsychiatric Association; Sigma Xi Research Society. *Publications:* Co-Author: "Family Medicine Curriculum: Guide to Substance Abuse", 1984; "Family Practice and Preventive Medicine: Health Promotion in Primary Care", 1983. *Honours:* Sigma Xi; Phi Beta Kappa; Summa cum Laude, 1968; Cum Laude, 1973; National Foundation of Birth Defects Research Award, 1972. *Hobby:* Sailing. *Address:* 116A6 Veterans Administration Medical Center, Davis Park, Providence, RI 02908, USA.

LIESKOVSKY, Vladimir, b. 7 Apr. 1926, Hungary. Consultant, Forensic Injury Mechanics and Vision at Low Light-Levels. m. Silan Hung, 29 Nov. 1971, San Jose, California, USA, 3 daughters. *Education:* BS, Military Science and Physics and Mathematics; MS, Engineering Mechanics; MSc, Aeronautics Engineering, Postgraduate Medical School Coursework, Clinical Clerkship, Stanford University. *Appointments:* IBM Corporation; Stanford Research Institute; Spectra Physics Corporation; Visiting Scholar, Stanford University; Guest Lecturer, Biomechanics, Stanford School of Engineering; Lecturer in Clinical Biomechanics, PM&R Department, SCVMC, Stanford Medical School; currently, Consultant, Forensic Injury Mechanics and Vision at Low Light-Levels. *Memberships:* American College of Sport Medicine; American Academy of Forensic Science; Illuminating Engineering Society; Registered Professional Engineer. *Publications:* "Optical Interferometry", 1963; "Free Surface Fluid Flow", with C Ablow, 1968; "Biomechanics of Low-Back Pain", 1981; "Evaluation of Visibility", 1982; "Visual Observations", 1984; "Visual Observations, in Forensic Science International", 1985. *Hobby:* Travel. *Address:* 655 Manzanita Way, Woodside, CA 94062, USA.

LIGHT, Terry, b. 22 June 1947, Chicago, Illinois, USA. Associate Professor of Orthopaedic Surgery, Loyola University of Chicago. m. Hollis Smith, 4 June 1978, Cotuit, Massachusetts, 1 daughter. *Education:* BA, Yale University; MA, Chicago Medical School. *Appointments:* Instructor, Assistant Professor, Surgery, Yale University School of Medicine; Assistant Professor, Orthopaedic Surgery, Loyola University School of Medicine. *Memberships:* Twenty-first Century Orthopaedic Association; American Society for Surgery of the Hand; American College of Surgeons; Association of Bone and Joint Surgeons; American Academy of Orthopaedic Surgery. *Publications:* 'Kinesiology of the Upper Limb', Chapter for AAOS; "Atlas for Orthotics", 2nd Edition, 1985; 'Plate Fixation of Long Bones' Chapter for "Operative Surgery", 1985; 'Regional Osseous Flow Determination in Neonatal, Immature and Mature Canines", "Bone Circulation", 1984. *Honours:* Nicolas Andry Award, 1982; Carl Heinze Award, 1977. *Hobbies:* Historic Preservation, Frank Lloyd Wright Foundation; Philately. *Address:* Loyola University School of Medicine, Department of Orthopaedics, 2160 South First Avenue, Maywood, IL 60153, USA.

LIGHTFOOTE, William Edward, b. 6 Oct. 1942, Tuskegee, Alabama, USA. Private Practice of Neurology. m. Marilyn Frances Madry, 23 Oct. 1971, Jacksonville, Florida, 1 daughter. *Education:* Tuskegee Institute, 1959-60; AB, Grinnell College, Iowa, 1963; MD, Howard University College of Medicine, 1967; Internship and Residency: Cleveland Clinic Hospital, Veterans Administration Hospital, Washington, DC, George Washington University Medical 1967-75. *Appointments:* Major US Air Force Medical Corps, 1969-71; Commander, US Public Health Service, 1975-79; Medical Officer, Stroke Models Laboratory, National Institute of Neurological and Communicative Disorders and Stroke, 1975-76; Medical Officer, Experimental Therapeutics Branch, National Institute of Neurological and Communicative Disorders and Stroke, 1976-77; Group Leader of Neurologic and Analgesic Drugs, Food and Drug Administration, 1977-79, Medical Officer, 1979-80; Private Practice of Neurology, Washington, DC, 1979-; Private Practice of Neurology, Fort Washington, Maryland, 1984-. *Memberships:* American Academy of Neurology; American Academy of Emergency Physicians; Commissioned Officers Association of the US Public Health Service; Alpha Omega Alpha and numerous other professional organizations. *Publications:* Contributor to professional journals; Abstracts; Presentations. *Address:* 1328 Southern Avenue SE, Washington, DC 20032, USA.

LIM, Yean Leng, b. 19 Jan. 1948, Singapore. Associate Director; Consultant Physician; Honorary Lecturer. m. Wen Joy Lim, 20 Oct. 1973, Melbourne, Australia, 1 son. *Education includes:* Diploma in Fine Art, Nanyang Academy of Fine Art, Singapore, 1962; BMedSc Honours, 1970, MB BS, 1972, PhD, 1977, Monash University, Australia. FRACP; FACC; Academy of Medicine, Singapore, 1982. *Appointments include:* Junior Resident Medical Officer, Alfred Hospital, Melbourne, Australia, 1973; Clinical Tutor, Department of Medicine, Monash University, 1975-76; Senior Resident Medical Officer and Registrar, Alfred Hospital, 1977-78; Research Fellow, National Heart Foundation, Australia, 1979-80; Clinical and Research Fellow, Massachusetts General Hospital, USA, 1981-82; Visiting Cardiologist and Assistant Physician, 1982-83, Consultant Physician, Alfred Hospital, Melbourne, Australia; Associate Director, Department of Cardiology, Epworth Hospital; Honorary Lecturer, Department of Medicine, Monash University. *Memberships include:* Australian and New Zealand Cardiac Society; American Federation of Clinical Research; Education Sub-Committee, National Heart Foundation of Australia; Committee Member, Chinese Medical Society. *Publications:* "Revision Notes in Clinical Medicine", 1981. Author or co-author of 20 papers contributed to professional journals including: 'Journal of American College Cardiology'; 'American Heart Journal'; 'Patient Management'; 'Australia and New Zealand Journal of Medicine'. *Honours include:* Research Fellowship, 1979-80, Overseas Research Fellowship, 1981-82, National Heart Foundation of Australia; Gordon-Taylor Scholarship, Melbourne University, 1981; Bushell Fellowship, Royal Australasian College of Physicians, 1981. *Hobbies:* Chinese painting; Church choir conducting and singing; Photography; Piano playing; Table tennis. *Address:* Department of Cardiology, Epworth Hospital, 62 Erin Street, Richmond, Vic 3121, Australia.

LIMA, Bruno, b. 16 Mar. 1951, Porto Alegre, Brazil. Assistant Professor, Psychiatry, Johns Hopkins University. m. Maria H Lima, 18 Apr. 1973, Porto Alegre, Brazil, 1 son, 1 daughter. *Education:* MD, Porto Alegre Medical School, Brazil, 1974; MPH, Johns Hopkins School of Hygiene and Public Health, Baltimore, USA, 1979. *Appointments:* Assistant Professor, Psychiatry, Pontifical Catholic University School of Medicine, 1980-82; Public Health Officer, Mental Hygiene Administration, Rio Grande Do Jul State Health Secretariat, 1980-82; Member, Research Team, Vila Sao Jose Do Murialdo, WHO Collaborating Centre, Porto Alegre, 1980-82; Consultant, Pan American Health Organisation. *Memberships:* Maryland Psychiatric Society; American and Brazilian Psychiatric Associations; American Psychosomatic Society. *Publications:* Articles in professional journals including: 'Excepta Medica'; General Hospital Psychiatry, Bulletin of the Pan American Health Organization. *Honours:* Elected for Delta Omega, 1979. *Hobbies:* Tennis; Reading. *Address:* Dept. of Psychiatry, Johns Hopkins Hospital, 600 N. Wolfe Street, Baltimore, MD 21205, USA.

LIMPAPHAYOM, Manit, b. 2 Feb. 1938, Thailand. Professor of Orthopedic Surgery. m. Kobchitt Mangalabruk, 26 May 1967, Washington DC, USA, 2 sons. *Education:* MD (Hon); Diploma, American Board of Orthopedic Surgery. *Appointments:* Instructor in Orthopedic Surgery, 1971-73; Assistant Professor, 1973-76; Associate Professor, 1976-79; Professor of Orthopedic Surgery, 1979-. *Memberships:* American Academy of Orthopedic Surgeons; American College of Surgeons; Society of International Research in Orthopedics and Traumatology. *Publications:* "Bones and Joints" 1974; "Fractures and Dislocations" 1975; "Pediatric Orthopedics" 1979 etc. *Honour:* Anandhamahidol Foundation Grantee. *Hobbies:* Gardening; Tennis. *Address:* 567 Nakornchaisri Road, Bangkok, 10300, Thailand.

LIN, Chin-Tarng, b. 11 Dec. 1938, Taiwan, Republic of China. Assistant Professor. m. Emily Wu Lin, 4 June

1983, Houston, Texas, USA, 1 daughter. *Education:* DDS, College of Medicine, National Taiwan University, 1963; PhD, University of Texas Medical Branch, Galveston, Texas, USA, 1975. *Appointments:* Dental Officer, Military Service, 1963-64; Resident Doctor, Teaching Assistant, Department of Pathology, 1964-69, Instructor, 1969-75, Associate Professor, 1975-78, National Taiwan University; Research Associate, 1978-81, Research Instructor, 1981-83, Department of Cell Biology, Baylor University College of Medicine, Houston, Texas, USA; Assistant Professor, Department of Physiology, Pennsylvania State University, Hershey, Pennsylvania, 1983-. *Memberships:* American Society for Cell Biology; Society for Neuroscience; American Association for the Advancement of Science; Histochemical Society. *Publications:* Author or co-author of contributions to professional publications including: 'Journal of Histochemistry and Cytochemistry'; 'Brain Res.'; "Methods in Enzynology". *Honours:* 2nd place Research Award, National Student Research Forum, USA, 1975. *Hobbies:* Music; Classics. *Address:* Department of Physiology, Milton S Hershey Medical Center, Penn State University, Hershey, PA 17033, USA.

LIN, Jain I, b. 18 Mar. 1938, Taiwan, Republic of China. Pathologist. m. Elizabeth Lin, 24 June 1968, Ping Tung, Taiwqn, 2 daughters. *Education:* MD, Kachsiung Medical College, Kachsiung, Taiwan. *Appointments:* Staff Pathologist, United States Public Health Service Hospital, Staten Island, New York, USA, 1973-77, Veterans Administration Medical Center, Dayton, Ohio 1977-. *Memberships:* Fellow, American College of Pathologists; Fellow, American Society of Clinical Pathologists; American Association of Blood Banks; American Association of Medical History; American Medical Writers Association. *Publications:* 'Rudolf Virchow - the Creator of Cellular pathology', 1982; 'Rudolf Virchow's pathological report on Frederick III's cancer', 1984; "The Death of a Kaiser", 1985. *Hobbies:* Reading; Music. *Address:* 100 Terrace Villa Drive, Centerville, OH 45459, USA.

LIN, Kuo-sin, b. 21 Nov. 1927, Taiwan, Republic of China. Professor of Clinical Pathology and Paediatrics; Director of National Taiwan University Hospital. m. Shiu-Huei Chen, 14 Apr. 1957, 2 sons, 1 daughter. *Education:* MD, National Taiwan University; DMSc, Fuksuhima Medical University, Japan. *Appointments:* Professor and Chairman, Department of Clinical Pathology, College of Medicine, National Taiwan University; School of Medical Technology, National Taiwan University, 1978-84; Director, National Taiwan University Hospital, 1984, 1985-. *Memberships:* International Society of Hematology; Formosan Medical Association;' Hematology Society of the Republic of China; Paediatric Society of the Republic of China; Cancer Society of the Republic of China. *Publications:* Articles regarding Thalassemias and others. *Hobbies:* Tennis; Swimming; Music. *Address:* 1 Chang-Te Street, Taipei, Taiwan, Republic of China.

LIN, Po-Jung, (also known as Bor-Long Lin), b. 9 Jan. 1949, Taiwan, Republic of China. Clinic Chairman. m. Chen Po-Ching, 18 Dec. 1974, Taiwan, 1 son, 2 daughters. *Education:* MD, Graduate, CSMC, Taichung City, Taiwan. *Appointments:* Army Surgeon, 1972-73; Resident in Ophthalmology, 1974-77, V S of Ophthalmology, 1978-81, CSMCH; Surgeon, General Surgery, VS, Surgical Department, Nan-Tou Public Hospital, 1975-79; Head, Shang-Lin Clinic, 1982-. *Publications:* 'The Trachoma Ex Report of the Factory Workers near Chung-Shin Village' in 'Tomus (volume 19)', Transations of the Ophthalmological Association of Republic of China, 1980. *Honours:* Specialist in General Surgery in China, 1980; Specialist of Ophthalmology in China, 1980. *Hobbies:* Personal computer; Astronomy, having own observatory. *Address:* 117 2nd sec. Chang-Nan Road, Changhua City 50061, Taiwan, Republic of China.

LINDE, Shirley, b. 22 Mar. 1929, Cincinnati, Ohio,

USA. Medical Author; Publisher. 2 sons. *Education:* BS, Zoology, University of Cincinnati; MS, Physiology, University of Michigan Medical School; Graduate courses in journalism, television, publishing: New York University, University of Cincinati, Northwestern University; PhD, Nutrition, International College of Health Sciences, London. *Appointments:* Publisher and Editor, "Feeling Better", The Wholistic Health Newsletter; President, Pavilion Publishing Company; President, Med-Assist Incorporated; Medical Consultant, HLA Advertising Agency; Director, At Home Diagnostics; Associate Editor: 'Together', Methodist Publishing House; Chief, Information Services, Northwestern University Medical School; Copy Editor, Year Book Publishers; Assistant Editor, 'Journal of International College of Surgeons; Research Fellow, University of Michigan Medical school; Research Assistant, University of Cincinnati Medical School; Research Chemist, Andrew Jergens Company; Director, Lake Lotowana Writers Conference; Chicago Bureau Chief, Medical News, Medical Tribune, Tele-Med; Owner, Hilltop Restaurant, Treasure Cay, Bahamas. *Memberships:* National Association of Science Writers, National Executive Committee; American Medical Writers Association, Treasurer, Florida Chapter, National Secretary, Vice-President; American Association for the Advancement of Science; Florida Writers Association. *Publications include:* Newsletters; Contributor to magazines including: 'Readers Digest', 'This Week', 'Good Housekeeping', 'Better Homes and Gardens', 'Family Circle'; Various newspapers; radio stations; films; Books include: Editor, Emergency Family First Aid Guide", 1971; "Sickle Cell", 1972; "The Complete Allergy Guide", (co-author); "The Joy of Sleep", 1981; "The Whole Health Catalogue", 1980; "How to Beat a Bad Back", 1981; "Lifegain" (co-author), 1981; "201 Medical Tests You Can Do At Home", 1983; "US Directory to Wholistic Medicine and Alternate Health Care", 1985; "Dr. Lindner's California Countdown Diet" (in press). *Honours include:* American Medical Writers Association Outstanding Service Award; Brandeis University Communications Award. *Address:* 152 1st Avenue N, Tierra Verde, FL 33715, USA.

LINDENTHAL, Jacob Jay, b. 21 July 1941, Roanoke, Virginia, USA. Professor and Chief of Behavioural Sciences. m. Lorelle Naomi Michelson, 16 Sep. 1984, Bloomfield, Connecticut, USA. *Education:* BA, BHL, Yeshiva University, 1963, MA, 1967, PhD, 1973; MA, Yale University, 1966, PhD, 1967; Dr.PH, Columbia University, 1978. *Appointments:* Research Staff Sociologist, Department of Sociology, Yale University, 1967-71; Field Director, New Haven Pilot Population Survey, 1967-71; Assistant Professor, Department of Sociology, Newark College of Arts and Sciences, Rutgers University, 1971-73, Associate of the Graduate Faculty, 1973-76; Associate Professor, Department of Sociology, Newark College of Arts and Sciences Rutgers University, 1973-76; Visiting Associate Professor of the Sociology of Judaism, Bernard Revel Graduate School, Yeshiva University, 1973-76, Acting Chairman, Department of Sociology, 1973-78; Visiting Associate Professor, College of Medicine and Dentistry, New Jersey Medical School, 1973-77; Chief of Behavioural Sciences, Department of Psychiatry and Mental Health Science, 1978-; Professor of Psychiatry, 1982-. *Memberships:* American Association for Social Psychiatry (Fellow); New Jersey Academy of Medicine (Fellow); New York Academy of Medicine (Associate Fellow); New York Academy of Science (Fellow); Royal Society of Health (Fellow); Sigma Xi; Society for Epidemiological Research. *Honour:* Adjunct University Professor of Sociology; Yeshiva University, 1985. *Address:* Department of Psychiatry and Mental Health Science, New Jersey Medical School, 100 Bergen Street, Newark, NJ 07103, USA.

LINDLEY, Barry Drew, b. 25 Jan. 1939, Orleans, Indiana, USA. Associate Dean for Medical Education. m. Elizabeth Price, 24 Apr. 1982,

Cleveland Heights, Ohio, 2 sons, 1 daughter. *Education:* BA Chemistry, De Pauw University, Greencastle, Indiana, 1960; PhD Physiology, Western Reserve University, Cleveland, Ohio, 1964; Postdoctoral Fellow, Nobel Institute for Neurophysiology, Karolinska Institutet, Stockholm, Sweden. *Appointments:* Assistant Professor of Physiology, Western Reserve University, Cleveland, Ohio, USA, 1965-68; Assoicate Professor of Physiology 1968-84, Professor of Physiology 1984-, Associate Dean for Medical Education, Case Western Reserve University, Cleveland; Visiting Scientist, ARC Unit, Department of Zoology, University of Cambridge, Cambridge, England, 1972; Visitng Scientist, Duke University Marien Laboratory, USA, 1973. *Memberships:* American Physiological Society; Biophysical Society; Society of General Physiologists; American Association for the Advancement of Science; Phi Beta Kappa. *Publications:* Numerous contributions to scientific journals, 1964-. *Honours:* Sears National Merit Scholar, 1956-60; Lederle Medical Faculty Award, 1967-70; USPHS Research Career Development Award, 1971-76; Dreyfus Scholar, De Pauw University, 1983. *Hobbies:* Painting; Hiking; Poetry. *Address:* Office of Medical Education, Case Western Reserve University, Cleveland, OH 44106, USA.

LINEHAN, Brian Joseph, b. 16 July 1938, New Zealand. Chemical pathologist, Hamilton Medical Laboratory & Waikato Hospital. m. Annette Louise McCracken, 19 Feb. 1983, Whakatane, 1 son. *Education:* MB, ChB, University of New Zealand; Diploma, Obstetrics, University of Auckland; Fellow, Royal College of Pathologists of Australasia. *Appointments include:* Resident medical officer, pathology registrar, Auckland Hospital Board; Resident pathologist, Sydney Hospital, Australia. *Memberships:* Past president, New Zealand Society of Pathologists; Divisional president, New Zealand Medical Association; Australian Association, New Zeland Association, Clincial Biochemists; Association of Clinical Biochemists. *Publications include:* Contributions to 'Annals of Internal Medicine', 'British Journal of Haematology', 'New Zealand Medical Journal', 'American Journal of Tropical Medicine & Hygiene', etc; "Control of Cholera", report, South Pacific Commission sponsored regional workshop, Cholera & Epidemic Diseases of the Pacific, 1978; etc. *Honour:* E D, 1976. *Hobbies:* Scuba diving; Boating. *Address:* Hamilton Medical Laboratory, PO Box 52, Hamilton, New Zealand.

LINGARD, Jennifer Mary, b. Brisbane, Queensland, Australia. Senior Lecturer, Department of Biological Sciences, Cumberland College of Health Sciences. m. Philip Stocks Lingard, 1970, Brisbane. *Education:* BSc, Queensland, 1969; BSc (Hons), Queensland, 1970; PhD, Sydney, 1976. *Appointments:* Fractional Tutor, University of Queensland, 1969; Tutor, 1970, 75, Senior Tutor, 1976-79, University of Sydney; Senior Research Officer, National Health and Medical Research Council, at University of Sydney, 1980-82; Lecturer, 1983, Senior Lecturer, 1984-, Cumberland College of Health Sciences. *Memberships:* Australian Physiological and Pharmacological Society; Associate/Assistant Editor, 'Journal of Australian Physiological and Pharmacological Society', 1977-82; Member of Council, 1977-82. *Publications:* Co-Editor, "Secretion: Mechanisms and Control", 1984; Contributor of articles to professional journals. *Hobbies:* Music; Walking. *Address:* Department of Biological Sciences, Cumberland College of Health Sciences, PO Box 170, Lidcombe, New South Wales, Australia.

LINK, Deborah Shaw, b. 19 Apr. 1933, Boston, Massachusetts, USA. Psychoanalyst; Psychiatrist. 3 daughters. *Education:* BA, Smith College, Northampton, Massachusetts, USA, 1955; MA, Yale University, USA, 1956; MD, Albert Einstein College of Medicine, New York, 1971; Diplomate, American Board of Psychiatry and Neurology, 1976; Graduate of New York Psychoanalytic Institute, 1984; Certification in Adult Analysis, American Psychoanalytic Association, 1985. *Appointments:* Researcher, Newsweek Magazine; Assistant to Dean, Sarah Lawrence College, Bronxville, New York; Resident, Psychiatry, Albert Einstein-Bronx Municipal Hospital, 1971-74; Private Practice in Psychoanalysis and Psychiatry. *Memberships:* American Psychoanalytic Association; International Psychoanalytical Association; New York Psychoanalytic Society; American Psychiatric Association. *Honour:* Phi Kappa, 1955. *Hobbies:* Gardening; Photography. *Address:* 97 Marvin Ridge Road, New Canaan, CT 06840, USA.

LINNER, Ernst Axel Erik, b. 26 Feb. 1916, Stockholm, Sweden. m. Margrith Ida Luchsinger, 10 May 1952, 1 son, 1 daughter. *Education:* MD, Uppsala, 1946. *Appointments:* Assistant Professor, Ophthalmology, University of Uppsala, 1953; Associate Professor 1959, Professor, 1974-81, Ophthalmology, University of Gothenburg; Professor, Ophthalmology, University of Umea, 1967; Research Fellow, Bern, Zurich, Switzerland, 1949-50; Johns Hopkins University, USA, 1953-55; Visiting Consultant, National Eye Institute, Bethesda, USA, 1978; Grantee, National Eye Institute, 1979-82; Consultant, WHO, South East Asia, 1982. *Memberships:* European Council of Ophthalmology; Executive Committee, European Glaucoma Society; International Glaucoma Committee; Board, International Society for Eye Research. *Publications:* More than 100 articles in ophthalmology. *Address:* Lilla Danska vagen 6, S-412 74 Göteborg, Sweden.

LINTON, Alan Henry, b. 29 Jan. 1925, Bristol, England. University Professor and Head of Department of Microbiology. m. Muriel Hilda Speare, 3 Apr. 1948, Bristol, 1 son, 1 daughter (deceased). *Education:* BSc, MSc, PhD, DSc, University of Bristol. *Appointments:* Biochemist, Glaxo Laboratories, 1945-46; Bacteriologist Preventive Medicine Department, University of Bristol, 1946-49; Lecturer in Veterinary Bacteriology, Senior Lecturer, Reader, Professor of Bacteriology, and Head of Department of Microbiology, Bristol University. *Memberships:* Society for General Microbiology; Society for Applied Bacteriology; Fellow, Royal College of Pathologists. *Publications:* "Microorganisms – function, form and environment"; "Microbes, Man and Animal"; 82 articles published in scientific journals. *Hobbies:* Lay preacher; Photography. *Address:* Department of Microbiology, University of Bristol, Bristol BS8 1TD, England.

LIPIN, Theodore, b. 5 Dec. 1920, Germany, Medical Unit Chief. *Education:* MD, Harvard College and Harvard Medical School, USA, 1944; Specialist Accreditations: Neurology (USA), Psychiatry (USA and Sweden), Psychoanalysis (USA and Sweden). *Appointments:* Unit Chief, Fitzsimons General Hospital, Denver, Colorado; Consultant, Neurological Institute, New York, New York, and Staten Island Hospital, Staten Island, New York; Associate Clinical Professor, Downstate Medical Center, Brooklyn, New York, and New York University, New York, New York; Faculty, New York and Swedish Psychoanalytic Institutes; Unit Chief, St Goran's Hospital, Karolinska Medical School, Stockholm, Sweden. *Memberships:* Fellow, American Psychiatric Association; American Psychoanalytic Association; Swedish Psychoanalytic Association; Association for Research in Nervous and Mental Disease. *Publications:* 'Metastases of Uterine Carcinoma to Central Nervous System', 1948; 'Psychic Functioning in Patients with Undiagnosed Somatic Symptoms', 1955; 'The Repetition Compulsion and 'Maturational' Drive-Representatives', 1963; 'Sensory Irruptions and Mental Organization', 1969; "Compendium of Rulings of Board of Professional Standards, American Psychoanalytic Association", 1959-63. *Address:* Frödingsvägen 14, S-112 56 Stockholm, Sweden.

LIPPMAN, Glenn, b. 30 Jan. 1953, Washington, District of Columbia, USA. Director of Inpatient

Psychiatry, Good Samaritan Hospital. m. Gayle Ann Breneman, 22 Nov. 1980, Phoenix, Arizona, 1 daughter. *Education:* BS, 1974, MD, 1979, University of Arizona. *Appointments:* Microscopy Technician, 1973-74, Lab. Prep, 1973-74, Research Technician, 1974, University of Arizona; Research Associate, Clinical Nutrition, University of New Mexico, 1974-75; Resident PG-1, Department of Obstetrics and Gynaecology, University of Arizona, 1979-80; Resident PG-2, 3, 4, 1980-83, Chief Resident, 1981-82, Department of Psychiatry, Maricopa Medical Center; Staff Psychiatrist, Arizona Health Plan, Phoenix, 1982-83; Psychiatrist, Private Practice, 1983-85; Director of Inpatient Psychiatry, Good Samaritan Hospital, 1985. *Memberships:* American Medical Association; Maricopa Medical Society; American Psychiatric Association; Arizona Psychiatric Association; Phoenix Psychiatric Council; Arizona Society for Adolescent Psychiatry; Western Student Medical Research Committee of the American Medical Association. *Publications:* Co-author: "Nutritional Status of Infants and Children", 1977; Co-author, "Asialoprotein Uptake by Liver Cells", 1979; Co-author, "Nutrition, Infection and Immunity", 1980; "Nutrition", 1980. *Honours:* Graduation with High Distinction from University of Arizona, 1974; Roy Killinsworth Award for Excellence in Psychiatry, University of Arizona, 1979; Kirmsey Award for Excellence in OB/GYN, 1979. *Hobbies:* Ship Model Building; Travel. *Address:* 4626 E Shea Boulevard C-140, Phoenix, AZ 85028, USA.

LIPSCHITZ, Alan, b. 28 Aug. 1951, New York, USA. Director, Anxiety Clinic, Metropolitan Hospital, New York, Assistant Professor, New York Medical College. *Education:* BA, Columbia College, New York, 1973; MD, University of Miami, School of Medicine, Florida, 1977. *Memberships:* American Psychiatric Association. *Publications:* 'Diagnosis and Classification of Anxiety Disorders', 1985. *Address:* 1235 Park Avenue, New York, NY 10128, USA.

LIPSHUTZ, Daniel Minor, b. 24 Jan. 1906, New York, USA. Retired Psychiatrist. m. Eva Klein, MD, 24 Nov. 1934, Paris, France. *Education:* BA, Cornell University, New York, USA; MSc, University of California, Berkeley, California; MD, University of Paris, France; Certificate in Post Graduate Study in Psychoanalysis, New York Fifth Avenue Hospital, New York City. *Appointments:* Instructor in Neuroanatomy, University of California; Chief of Clinical Laboratory, US Marine Hospital, Cleveland, Ohio; Clinical Assistant, Mount Sinai Hospital, New York City; Chief of Out Patient Department of Psychiatry, Lebanon Hospital, Bronx, New York. *Memberships:* American Psychiatric Association; American Academy of Psychoanalysis; Society of the County of New York Medicine; New York State Society of Medicine; Society for the Advancement of Psychiatry. *Publications:* "The Standardization of the Hemolytic Index", 1930; 'La Mort par l'Insuffisance aigue des glandes surrenales'; 'Les Voies Atteintes chez les Jeunes Rats Manquant Vitamine E'; 'Some Observations upon Specificity in Psychosomatic Medicine'. *Hobbies:* Sailing; Swimming; Skiing; Horse Riding; Fishing. *Address:* 2621 Palisade Avenue, Riverdale, NY 10463, USA.

LIPSIE, Gregory Scott, b. 9 Feb. 1947, Pittsburgh, Pennsylvania, USA. Chiropractor. m. Rebecca A Wahl, 19 July 1974, Somerset, Pennsylvania. *Education:* BS 1975, DC 1977, Logan College of Chiropractic, Chesterfield, Missouri; Graduate, Dale Carnegie Course, 1981. *Appointments:* Intern, Logan College Out Patient Clinic, Chesterfield, Missouri; Private practice, Ciropractic, Somerset, Pennsylvania, 1977-. *Memberships:* American Chiropractic Association; Pennsylvania Chiropractic Association; Florida Chiropractic Association; Association for Research and Enlightment; International Chiropractic Association; Logan College Chiropractic Club. *Honours:* Academic High Honours 1973. High Honours 1973, California State College; Dale Carnegie Awards of Achievement.

Hobbies: Golf; Fishing; Hunting; Flying. *Address:* RD No 2, Box 238A, Somerset, PA 15501, USA.

LIPSKI, John Gabriel, b. 7 July 1914, Krakow, Poland. Chief In-patients Service, Mental Health Center. m. Eleanor Respondek, 29 July 1944, Edinburgh, Scotland, 1 son, 4 daughters. *Education:* BS, Wayne University, Detroit, Michigan, USA; MB, ChB, University of Edinburgh, Scotland, 1946; MD, Wayne University, Detroit, 1956; Fellow, Royal Society of Health, London, England; Captain, Royal Army Medical Corps. *Appointments:* Intern, Henry Ford Hospital, Detroit, 1952-53; Family Practice, Rogers City, Michigan, 1953-65; Psychiatric Residency, Traverse City, Michigan, 1965-68; Chief, Department of Psychiatry, Burns Clinic Medical Center, Petoskey, Michigan, 1967-79; Chief In-patient Service, Shiawassee County Mental Health Center, Owosso, Michigan, USA, 1979-. *Memberships:* American Medical Association, Life Member, 1956; American Psychiatric Association; Canadian Psychiatric Association, Life Member, 1970. *Publications:* 'Epidemic of Hepatitis in Midwestern Rural Community', American Public Health Journal, 1958; "A Structural Approach to Group Therapy in Psychiatric Residency Programme", 1959. *Honours:* Croix de Guerre (2), France, 1940; Polish Cross for Gallantry, Scotland (3), 1943; Recipient, American Medical Association Award for Continuing Education. *Hobbies:* Swimming; Golf; Skiing. *Address:* Shiawassee County Mental Health Center, 826 West King Street, PO Box 479, Owosso, MI 48867, USA.

LIPTAK, Jozsef Janos, b. 2 Sep. 1941, Budapest, Hungary. Pharmaceutical Inspector. m. Eva Csekey, 4 Feb. 1971, Budapest. *Education:* Degrees, Pharmacy, Budapest, 1965; Chemical Engineering, Budapest, 1969; Doctor of Pharmacy, Budapest, 1973. *Appointments:* Research Analyst, Drug Research Institute, Budapest, 1965-74; Lecturer, Pharmacognosy Institute of Medical University, Budapest, 1972-77; Pharmaceutical Inspector, National Institute of Pharmacy, Budapest, 1977-; Expert, Quality assurance, Programme UNDP, Nicaragua, 1984-85. *Membershisp:* Secretary, Hungarian Pharmaceutical Society; Editorial Board, 'Gyogyszereszet'; Technical Editor, 'Acta Pharmaceutica Hungarica'. *Publications:* Scientific papers, various journals; parts of professional books. *Hobbies:* Basketball; Tourist Guide. *Address:* PO Box 450, H-1372 Budapest, Hungary.

LIPTON, Allan, b. 29 Dec. 1938, New York City, USA. Professor of Medicine. m. Nancy E Whitcomb, 8 May 1965, Saratoga, New York, 2 sons, 1 daughter. *Education:* AB. Almherst College, 1959; MD, New York University School of Medicine, 1963. *Appointments:* Assistant Professor of Medicine, 1971-74, Associate Professor of Medicine, 1974-79, Professor of Medicine, 1979-, M S Hershey Medical Centre, Hershey, Pennsylvania. *Memberships:* American Society of Clinical Oncology; American Association of Cancer Research; American Society of Haematology. *Publications:* Contributor of over 90 professional articles in medical journals; Author of over 97 abstracts and 18 contributions to books. *Honours:* Phi Beta Kappa, 1959. *Hobbies:* Running; Tennis; Swimming. *Address:* Division of Oncology, M S Hershey Medical Centre, Hershey, PA 17033, USA.

LIPTZIN, Benjamin, b. 17 Sep. 1945, New York, USA. Director of Geriatric Psychiatry. m. Sharon Leslie Rothstein, 10 June 1968, New York, 1 son, 2 daughters. *Education:* BA, Yale University, 1966; MD, University of Rochester, 1971. *Appointments:* Resident in Psychiatry, University of Virginia Hospital, Charlottesville, Virginia, 1971-74; Medical Officer and Chief, Program Analysis and Evaluation Branch, National Institute of Mental Health, Rockville, Maryland, 1974-78; Director of Geriatric Psychiatry, McLean Hospital, Belmont, Massachusetts, 1978-. *Memberships:* American Psychiatric Association; Gerontological Society of America; American Association for Geriatric Psychiatry. *Publications:* 'Clinical perspectives on sexuality in older patients' in 'Journal of Geriatric Psychiatry' 1984; 'Treatment of mania' in "Clinical Geriatric Psychopharmacology" edited by C Salzman, 1984; 'Drug treatment of dementia in the elderly' with J O Cole, in "Handbook of Studies on Psychiatry and Old Age" edited by G Burrows and D Kay, 1984. *Honours:* PHS Commendation Medal, 1978; Fellow, American Psychiatric Association, 1983; Geriatric Mental Health Academic Award, National Institute of Mental Health, 1983. *Hobbies:* Tennis; Skiing. *Address:* McLean Hospital, 115 Mill Street, Belmont, MA 02178, USA.

LISTWAN, Ignacy Andrew, b. 9 May 1910, Cracow, Poland. Consultant Psychiatrist. m. (1) Elvira Halpern, 16 July 1935 (2) Jikita Coby, 23 Nov. 1985, 1 daughter. *Education:* MD, Croacow, 1934; MD Postgraduate Degree in Neurology and Psychiatry, Cracow, 1937; MB BS, Sydney, 1955. *Appointments:* Lecturer, Neurology and Psychiatry, University of Cracow, 1937-39; Member, Mental Health Tribunal, New South Wales, 1959-80; Medical Officer, Callan Park Mental Hospital, 1952; Hon Clinical Assistant, Psychiatry, Royal North Shore Teaching Hospital, Sydney University, 1957-58; Hon Clinical Assistant, Psychiatry, Sydney Hospital, 1953-60; Hon Consultant Psychiatrist, Canberra Community Hospital, 1955-62; Hon Consultant Psychiatrist; Canterbury District Memorial Hospital, Sutherland Shire Hospital, Parramatta District Hospital, Eric Hilliard Psychiatric Centre, Marriage Guidance Council of New South Wales; Consultant Psychiatrist to Department of Social Security, 1984-. *Memberships:* Fellow. Australian and New Zealand College of Psychiatrists; Fellow, Royal Australian and New Zealand College of Psychiatrists. *Publications:* Co-author, "Relax", 1970; Contributions to professional journals including: 'Psychodrama', 'Medical Journal of Australia', 1955; 'Psychological Aspects of Car Accidents', 'Medical Journal of Australia', 1958; Presentations include: "Relaxation Methods in Psychotherapy" read at 10th International Congress of Psychotherapy, Paris, July 1976. *Hobbies:* Tennis; Skiing. *Address:* 193 Macquarie Street, Sydney 2000, Australia.

LITHWICK, Norton Hertz, b. 29 June 1936, Ottawa, Ontario, Canada. Orthopaedic Surgeon. m. Nina Garbe, 8 Mar. 1980, Toronto, 1 son, 1 daughter. *Education:* BSc, McGill University, Montreal, Quebec, 1957; Ottawa University, Ottawa, Ontario; Rotating Internship, 1961-62, Junior Surgical Resident 1962-63, Montreal General Hospital. *Appointments include:* Research Fellow 1963-64, Resident-Senior Orthopaedic Resident 1964-66, Children's Hospital Medical Centre, Boston, Massachusetts, USA; Orthopaedic Resident, Massachusetts General Hospital, 1965-66; Senior Orthopaedic Resident, Robert Breck Brigham Hospital, Boston, 1967; Senior-Chief Orthopaedic Resident, Peter Bent Brigham Hospital, 1967; Chief Orthopaedic Resident, West Roxbury Veterans' Affairs Hospital, West Roxbury, Massachusetts, 1967-68; Teaching Fellow, Harvard University, 1967-68; Clinical and Research Fellow, Toronto East General and Orthopaedic Hospital, and Toronto General Hospital Department of Orthopaedics, Toronto, Canada, 1968-69; Fellowship, Royal College of Surgeons, Canada, 1969; Orthopaedic private practice, Weston, Ontario, 1970-; Lecturer, Canadian Back Institute, 1978-; Staff, St John's Convalescent Hospital, 1980-. *Memberships:* Fellow, American Academy of Orthopaedic Surgeons; College of Physicians and Surgeons of Ontario; Council Member 1981-83, Co-Chair of Symposium on The Whiplash Injury 1983, Medico-Legal Society; Canadian and Ontario Medical Associations; Academy of Medicine, Toronto; Canadian Orthopaedic Association; Canadian Civil Liberties Association. *Publications:* 'Micro-analysis of Bone By The Laser Microprobe', (with M K Healy and L Cohen), 1964; 'Methemoglobin Formation Following Intravenous Regional Anesthesia Produced With Prilocaine', (assisted Dr William Harris), 1968; 'Referring The Injured Plaintiff For An Orthopaedic Consultation',

1978. *Hobbies:* Tennis; Table Tennis. *Address:* 1436 Royal York Road 205, Weston, Ontario M9P 3A9, Canada.

LITTLE, John Miles, b. 28 Dec. 1933, Sydney, Australia. University Professor of Surgery. m. Penelope Ann Vincent, 29 July 1978, Sydney, Australia, 1 son, 3 daughters. *Education:* MB, BS, University of Sydney, 1959; University of Glasgow, 1966; MD; MS; FRACS. *Appointments:* Medical Officer, Registrar, Royal Prince Alfred Hospital, 1959-64; Research Fellow, University of Glasgow, 1966; Surgeon, Royal Prince Alfred Hospital, 1967-68; Senior Lecturer, Surgery, University of Sydney, 1967-71, Associate Professor, 1971-78; Professor and Chairman, Westmead Hospital, University of Sydney, 1978-present. *Memberships:* Fellow, Royal Australasian College of Surgeons; Member Société Internationale de Chururgie; Collegium Internationale Chirurgae Digestivae; International Biliary Association; Pan Pacific Surgical Association; Association of Surgeons of South East Asia. *Publications:* "The Management of Liver Injuries", 1971; "Major Amputations for Vascular Disease", 1975; Articles and book chapters, in surgical literature on vascular disease and gastroenterology. *Honours:* Nuffield Dominion Fellow, 1966; Glissan Memorial Prize, 1967; Windsor Lecturer, 1979; G Bong Oration, 1984; Coupland Oration, 1985. *Hobbies:* Bird Watching; Photography; Writing; Poetry. *Address:* Department of Surgery, Westmead Hospital, Westmead, New South Wales, 2145, Australia.

LITTLEFIELD, Michael Drew, b. 26 Feb. 1946, Maine, USA. Doctor of Chiropractic. m. Shiela, 2 May 1978, Davenport, Iowa, USA, 1 son. *Education:* BA, Temple University, Philadelphia, Pennsylvania, USA; DC, Palmer College of Chiropractic, Davenport, Indiana. *Appointment:* Clinical Teaching Resident in Diagnosis, Radiology, Technique and Clinical Procedure at Palmer College of Chiropractic, Davenport, Iowa. *Memberships:* American Chiropractic Association; Maine Chiropractic Association; Greater Portland Chiropractic Society. *Honour:* Clinte Masters' Red Shield for Distinguished Service to Humanity, 1984. *Hobbies:* Jogging; Music; Hiking; Raising Akita dogs. *Address:* 1 Downing Road, Kennebunk, ME 04043, USA.

LITVAK, Ronald, b. 11 Aug. 1938, Cleveland, Ohio, USA. Private Practitioner, Psychiatry. m. Betty Ann Resnick, 14 Aug. 1960, Cleveland, Ohio, 1 son, 2 daughters. *Education:* BA, 1960; MD, 1964; MS, 1968; Clinical Associate Professor, Psychiatry, Ohio State University College of Medicine; President, Medical Staff, Harding Hospital, 1980; Treasurer, NSPCO; American Board of Forensic Psychiatry. *Appointments:* Consultant, Veterans Administration Hospital, Ohio; Consultant, Forensic Psychiatry, Department Mental Health and Retardation, Ohio; Director, Outpatient Services, Harding Hospital; Consultant, US Department of State; Consultant, US Department Labour; Consultant, Office of City Attorney, Columbus, Ohio; Consultant, Office Attorney General, Ohio; Consultant, Commission on Grievances and Discipline, Ohio Supreme Court; Consultant, Industrial Commission of Ohio; Consultant, Worthington Police Department, State University Police Department, Columbus Police Department; Acting and Assistant Chief, Department Mental Hygiene Consultation Service; US Walson Army Hospital, Department Psychiatry and Neurology; Consultant, State Medical Board of Ohio; Consultant, Various county courts and private attorneys. *Memberships include:* Diplomate, American Board of Psychiatry and Neurology; Diplomate, American Board of Forensic Psychiatry; American Psychiatric Association; Ohio Psychiatric Association; American Academy of Psychiatry and Law. *Publications include:* 'Agranulocytosis, Leukopenia and Psychotropic Drugs', 1971; 'Dermatological Side Effects with Psychotropics', 1972. *Honours:* Chief Resident in Psychiatry, OSU Hospitals, Department Psychiatry, 1967-68; Certificate of Achievement with Citation, Commanding General, Fort Dix, NJ; Letters of Commendation, US Army; Fellow, American Psychiatric Association. *Hobbies:* Jogging; Hunting; Reading; Backpacking; Photography; Weight Lifting. *Address:* 1170 Old Henderson Road, Suite 201, Columbus, OH 43220, USA.

LITWIN, Stephen David, b. 30 Apr. 1934, New York, New York, USA. Scientific Director. m. Zelda Chemrinow, 24 Dec. 1961, Minneapolis, Minnesota, 1 son, 2 daughters. *Education:* BA, Brooklyn College, New York, 1956; MD, New York University, New York, 1959. *Appointments:* Medical Resident 1959-62, Medical Fellow 1962-64, Montefiore Medical Center, New York; Guest Investigator, Assistant Professor, Rockefeller University, New York, 1964-67; Assistant Professor of Human Genetics 1969-71, Associate Professor 1971-79, Professor 1979-82, Cornell Medical College, New York; Scientific Director, Guthrie Foundation for Medical Research, Sayre, Pennsylvania, 1982-. *Memberships:* American Association of Immunologists; American Society of Clinical Investigation; Phi Beta Kappa. *Publications include:* "Clinical Evaluation of Immune Function in Man", (editor), 1976; "Genetic Determinants of Pulmonary Disease", (editor), 1978; Over 80 original scientific papers. *Honours:* Competitive grants, National Institutes of Health, American Cancer Society; Career Development Award, United States Public Health Service. *Hobbies:* Reading; Sailing. *Address:* Guthrie Foundation for Medical Research, Sayre, PA 18840, USA.

LIU, Xiehe, b. 21 May 1928, Hunan, China. Chairman, Psychiatry, West China Medical University; Chief Librarian, West China Medical University. m. Jichun Kang, 17 Nov. 1956, Chengdu, 1 daughter. *Education:* Xiangya Medical College, 1947-49; Hunan Medical College, 1951-55; Institute of Psychiatry, University of London, England, 1980. *Appointments:* Assistant Psychiatrist, 1955-64; Attending Psychiatrist, 1964-78; Lecturer, Psychiatry, Associate Director, Psychiatric Research Unit, 1978-80; Associate Professor, Psychiatry, 1980-. *Memberships:* Board of Directors, Chinese Society of Psychology, Chinese Mental Health Association; Chairman, Neurology & Psychiatry, Chinese Society of Genetics; Chairman, Neurology & Psychiatry, Chengdu Branch, Chinese Medical Society. *Publications:* "A Textbook of Psychiatry", Co-author, 1964; "Mental Health Work in Sichuan", 'British Journal of Psychiatry', 1980; Board of Editors, 'The Chinese Medical Encyclopaedia', 1982; various other articles in professional journals. *Honours:* Model Worker, Sichuan Province, 1985. *Hobbies:* Chess; Reading Novels. *Address:* Dept. of Psychiatry, West China Medical University, Chengdu, Sichuan, China.

LJUNGBERG, Otto L, b. 11 June 1937, Svenljunga, Sweden, Associate Professor of Pathology. m. Judit Miklos, 12 May 1967, Lund, 3 daughters. *Education:* MD 1968, PhD 1972, University of Lund. *Appointments:* Associate Professor, Department of Pathology, General Hospital, Malmo. *Membership:* Thyroid Group, Swedish Medical Research Council. *Publications include:* 'On medullary carcinoma of the thyroid', 1972; "Atlas of Breast Pathology" (with F Linell), 1984; about 120 articles on endocrine pathology and related topics. *Hobbies:* Painting; Gardening. *Address:* Department of Pathology, University of Lund, General Hospital, S-21401, Malmo, Sweden.

LLANOS-BEJARANO, Guillermo, b. 18 Nov. 1933, Cali, Colombia, South America. Epidemiologist. m. Margarita, 16 May 1958, Cali, Colombia, 2 sons. *Education:* AB, San Luis College, Cali, Colombia, 1950; MD, University of Valle, Cali, 1960; MPH, Johns Hopkins University, Baltimore, USA, 1961. *Appointments:* Assistant Professor, Preventive Medicine, University of Valle, Cali, Colombia, 1962-68; Associate Professor and Chairman Department of Preventive Medicine, National University, Bogota, 1968-73; Professor and Chairman, Department of Social Medicine, University of Valle, Cali, 1973-80; Consul-

tant in Epidemiology, Pan American Health Organisation (PAHO/WHO) Lima, Peru, 1985-date. *Memberships:* Colombian Medical Association; International Epidemiology Association; American Public Health Association (Fellow); Society for Epidemiologic Research; American Statistical Association. *Publications include:* Lectures in Biostatics, University of Bogota, 1971, Readings in Epidemiology, 1972; Approximately 50 papers in Colombian and international journals. *Honour:* Professor Emeritus, University of Valle, Cali, Colombia, 1985. *Hobbies:* Soccer; Photography. *Address:* WHO/PAHO, Casilla 2117, Lima, Peru.

LLOYD, Joseph Davies Anthony, b. 29 Oct 1927, Anderson, Indiana, USA. Staff Psychiatrist. m. Norma Jean Bradbury, 2 Aug 1980, Tacoma, Washington, 2 sons, 1 daughter by previous marriage. *Education:* AB, Anatomy & Physiology, Indiana University, 1954; MD, Indiana University, of Medicine, 1958; Internship, Milwaukee County General Hospital, Wauwatosa, Wisconsin, 1958-59; Residency in General Psychiatry, Letterman Army Medical Center, San Francisco, California, 1962-65. *Appointments:* Chief, Department of Psychiatry & Neurology, Madigan Army Medical Center, 1965-67; Assistant Chief, Psychiatry & Neurology Consultants Branch, Office of the Army Surgeon General, 1967-68; Commander, 9th Medical Battalion, RVN, 1968-69; Chief, Graduate Medical Education Branch, Office of the Army Surgeon General, 1969-71; Assistant Chief, Director of Residency Training, Letterman Army Medical Center, 1971-75; Deputy Commander, US Army Medical Department Activity, Fort Polk, 1975-76; Commander, USA MEDDAC, Fort Polk, 1976-77; Chief, Department of Psychiatry, Chief, Community Mental Center, Madigan Army Medical Center, 1977-79; Staff Psychiatrist, Western State Hospital, 1979-. *Memberships:* American Medical Association; American Psychiatric Association; Association of Military Surgeons of the US; World Health Organization; World Federation for Mental Health. *Honours:* Fellow, American Psychiatric Association, 1975; Diplomate, American Board of Psychiatry & Neurology, 1969; Diplomate, Commission on Certification in Administrative Psychiatry, American Psychiatric Association, 1978. *Address:* 705 North 5th Street, Tacoma, WA 98403, USA.

LLOYD, Stephen Gareth, b. 23 Sep 1953, Hereford, England. Principal, Cardiff Chiropractic Clinic. m. Juliet Ann Denman, 3 Sep 1977, Broadwater, Worthing, England, 1 daughter. *Education:* BSc Upper 2nd class honours Biological Sciences, Portsmouth Polytechnic; DC, Anglo European College of Chiropractic, Bournemouth. *Membership:* British Chiropractic Association. *Publications:* 'Study of Backpain in Nurses', thesis, researched 1978-79, printed (with Alan Breen) 1985. *Hobbies:* Sport; Do-it-Yourself. *Address:* 154 Penylan Road, Cardiff, South Glamorgan CF2 5RE, Wales.

LOAVENBRUCK, Angela, b. 21 Nov. 1943, New Jersey, USA. Director, Loavenbruck Associates. m. Grant P. Loavenbruck, 21 Aug. 1965, Scranton, Pennsylvania, 2 sons, 1 daughter. *Education:* BA, State University of New York, Buffalo, 1965; MA, Speech Pathology, 1968, Doctorate, Audiology, 1973, Columbia University. *Appointments:* Speech pathologist, Helen Hayes Hospital, 1965-67; Coordinator, Speech & Hearing Department, Rockland County Centre for Physically Handicapped, 1968-70; Assistant Professor, Catholic University, 1972-73; Associate Professor, Columbia University, 1973-80; Director, Loavenbruck Associates, 1980-. *Memberships:* American Speech & Hearing Association; New York State Speech & Hearing Association. *Publications:* "Hearing Aid Dispensing for Audiologists: A Guide to Clinical Practice", 1980. *Honour:* Fellow, American Speech & Hearing Association, 1985. *Hobbies:* Cooking; Sailing. *Address:* 500 New Hempstead Road, New York City, NY 10956, USA.

LoBUGLIO, Albert F, b. 1 Feb. 1938, Buffalo, New

York, USA. Professor of Medicine. m. Rita Ann Decker, 19 May 1962, Buffalo, New York, 1 son, 4 daughters. *Education:* MD, Georgetown University Medical School, Washington DC, 1962; Medical Internship 1962-63, Medical Assistant Residency 1963-65, Presbyterian University Hospital, Pittsburgh, Pennsylvania; Research Fellow, Thorndike Memorial Laboraotry, Boston City Hospital, also Harvard Medical School, 1965-67; Clinical Fellow II & IV (Harvard), Boston City Hospital, 1965-67. *Appointments:* Instructor in Medicine, State University of New York at Buffalo School of Medicine, 1967; Assistant Professor of Medicine, 1968-69; Director of Blood Bank & Haematology, Erie County Laboratory, E J Myer Memorial Hospital, Buffalo, 1967-69; Associate Professor of Medicine, 1969-73, Professor of Medicine, 1973-78, Ohio State University College of Medicine, Division of Haematology & Oncology; Deputy Director, Comprehensive Cancer Centre, Ohio State University, 1973-78; Director, Division of Haematology & Oncology, Director of Simpson Memorial Research Institute, University of Michigan Medical Centre, Ann Arbor, Michigan, 1978-83; Professor of Medicine, Director, Comprehensive Cancer Centre, Director, Divsion of Haematology-Oncology, Departemnt of Medicine, University of Birmingham at Alabama, 1983-. *Memberships include:* American Society for Clinical Investigation; American Federation for Clinical Research; American Society of Haematology; American Association of Immunologists; American Society of Clinical Oncology; American Association for Cancer Research; New York Academy of Sciences; American Association for the Advancement of Science; Fellow, International Society of Harmatology. *Publications:* More than 250 papers & abstracts. *Honours:* American Cancer Society Professorship of Clinical Oncology, 1973-78; Alpha Omega Alpha; Member of Executive Committee, Dean's Office, University of Michigan Medical School. *Hobby:* Golf. *Address:* Comprehensive Cancer Centre, University of Alabama at Birmingham, University Station, Birmingham, AL 35294, USA.

LOCHBAUM, Kenneth Lewis, b. 23 Aug. 1944, Pittsburgh, Pennsylvania, USA. President of Rehabilitation Speciality Corporations. m. 1 son, 1 daughter. *Education:* BS, Penn State University; Certified Physical Therapy, New York University. *Appointments:* Chief Physical Therapist, Visiting Nurse Association of Erie County, Pennsylvania; Staff Physical Therapist, Hamot Medical Center, Erie. President: Lochbaum Rehabilitation Specialists; Rehabilitation at Home Services. *Memberships:* American Physical Therapy Association; Pennsylvania Physical Therapy Association; National Athletic Trainers Association. *Hobbies:* Boating; Fishing; Hunting; Travel. *Address:* 3049 Glenwood Park Avenue, Erie, PA 16508, USA.

LOCKETT, Harold James, b. 17 July 1924, Wilmington, Delaware, USA. Assistant Director. m. Betty Jean Griffin (dec), 11 June 1950, Indianapolis, Indiana, 1 daughter. *Education:* AB, Indiana University, 1948; MD, Meharry Medical College, 1952. *Appointments:* Staff Psychiatrist, Hawthorn Center. *Memberships:* American Academy of Child Psychiatry; American Psychiatric Assn; American Orthopsychiatric Assn; National Medical Assn; Black Psychiatrists of America; Society for Clinical and Experimental Hypnosis; International Society of Hypnosis. *Publications:* 'Tranquilizing Drugs in the Treatment of Emotionally Disturbed Children: Inpatients in a Residential Treatment Center' (with Shaw), 1963; 'Amitriptyline in Childhood Depression' (with Lucas and Grimm), 1965; 'The Day Treatment Center - A Proposal for a Community-based Intensive Treatment Facility for Emotionally Disturbed Minority Group Children and Families', 1972; "A Passive Aggressive Selective Mute', (with Morse), 1974. *Hobbies:* Tennis; Skiing. *Address:* 319 Brookside

Drive, Ann Arbor, MI 48105, USA.

LODZINSKI, Kazimierz, b. 28 Aug. 1922, Radziejow, Poland. Professor. m. Stanislawa Jozwik, 16 Jan. 1944, Warsaw, 3 sons. *Education:* Graduate, University of Warsaw, 1947; MD, 1951; Dr.Habil.Ass.Prof., 1966; Professor/nadzwyczajny, 1975; Professor/zwyczajny, 1985. *Appointments:* Dept. of Anatomy, Paediatric Surgery, University of Warsaw; Military Hospital; Institute of Mother and Child, Warsaw, 1953-. *Memberships:* Polish Association of Paediatric Surgeons, President, 1970-77, General Secretary, 1980-; British Association of Paediatric Surgeons; International Continence Society. *Publications:* "Ventriculoatriostomy in the Treatment of Hydrocephalus in Children with Congenital Encephalocele and Myelomeningocele", 1966; "Surgical Treatment of Myelomeningocele", 1973; "History of Paediatric Surgery in Poland", 1975; "Gastritis Necorticans in Children", 1981. *Honours:* Honorary Member, Polish Association of Paediatric Surgeons, 1980; Honorary Award, J.E. Purkyne Czechoslovakia Society of Physicians, 1983. *Hobbies:* Travel; Veterans Home Army Society. *Address:* Institute of Mother and Child, Department of Paediatric Surgery, ul. Kasprzaka 17a, Warsaw 01-211, Poland.

LOEBENBERG, Ralph, b. 12 June 1938, New York, USA. Consultant Obstetrician and Gynaecologist. m. Carol Lee Cohen, 2 July 1963, New York City, 1 son, 2 daughters. *Education:* BSc, cum laude, College of the City of New York; MD, Dalhousie University. *Appointments:* Consultant Staff, Halifax Infirmary, Victoria General Hospital, Grace Maternity Hospital, Camp Hill Hospital, Nova Scotia Rehabilitation Centre. *Memberships:* Fellow, Royal College of Physicians and Surgeons; Fellow, American College of Obstetrics and Gynaecology; Fellow, Society of Obstetricians and Gynaecologists of Canada; American Medical Association; Nova Scotia Medical Society. *Hobbies:* Professional Volunteer, Nova Scotia and Canadian Figure Skating Society; Baron de Hirsch Hebrew Benevolent Society, Honorary Council President. *Address:* 5991 Spring Garden Road, §255, Halifax, Nova Scotia, B3H 1Y6, Canada.

LOEDIN, Augustinus Alexander, b. 12 Jan. 1930, Tanjung, Pinang. Head, National Institute of Health Research & Development. Divorced, 2 sons, 3 daughters. *Education:* MD, University of Amsterdam, Netherlands; Surgeon, National Board, Airlangga University, Surabaya, Indonesia; PhD, Airlangga University. *Appointments:* Vice-Rector, Airlangga University; Chairman, Committee for Research Development, Directorate General Higher Education, Ministry of Education and Culture: Chairman, South East Asia Advisory Committee, Medical Research, WHO; Professor, Surgery, Airlangga University; Vice Chairman, National Research Council. *Memberships:* Indonesian Medical Association; Indonesian College of Surgeons. *Publication:* Over 60 Scientific publications. *Hobbies:* Photography. *Address:* Jalan Taman Wijayakusuma ID 16, Cilandak, Jakarta, Indonesia.

LOES, Michael William, b. 1 May 1950, Detroit, Michigan, USA. Private Practice; Consultant, University of Arizona. m. Lauren Francis Eidem, 14 July 1979, Tucson, 2 daughters. *Education:* BA, Linguistics, University of California, 1972; MD, University of Minnesota, 1978; Internal Medicine Residency, University of Arizona. *Appointments:* Private Practice; University of Arizona Health Service Consultant. *Memberships:* Pima County Medical Society; Arizona State Medical Society; American Society of Clinical Hypnosis; International Society of Clinical Hypnosis; International Society of Physicians Against Nuclear War. *Publications:* Co-Author, "The Kinetics of Red Blood Cell Electrolytes Alterations following Digoxin Administration", 'Journal of

Developmental Pharmacology', 1980; "The Impaired Resident", co-author, 'Arizona Medicine', 1982; etc. *Honours:* Recipient, American Pharmaceutical Fellowship, 1976-77; 2 Masonic Oncology Research Fellowships, 1975-76, 1976; Minnesota Medical Foundation Student Achievement Award, 1978; Delegate, National American Medical Student Association National Conventions, 1974, 1975; President, Tucson Housestaff Association, 1979, Treasurer, 1980. *Hobbies:* Athletics; Travel. *Address:* 5200 East Grant, Tucson, AZ 85712, USA.

LOFBERG, Maureen Stella, b. 6 June 1933, New York, USA. Occupational Epidemiology Nurse Coordinator. m. Robert Tor Lofberg, 23 Nov. 1974, San Antonio, Texas, USA. *Education:* Diploma, Nursing, 1954; BS, Biological Science, 1957; BA, Chemistry, 1963; Diploma, Flight Nursing, 1971; Diploma, Squadron Officers School, 1972; Diploma, Air Command and Staff College, 1979. *Appointments:* Staff Nurse, Hotel Dieu Hospital, El Paso, Texas, 1954; Staff/Float Nurse, Providence Memorial Hospital, El Paso, Texas, 1954-63; Staff Nurse/Charge Nurse, William Beaumont Army General Hospital, 1963-68; Staff Nurse/Nurse Epidemiologist for Medical Center, Wilford Hall, USAF Medical Center, Lackland AFB, Texas, 1968-72; Wing Flight Nurse (Metabolic Laboratory) School of Aerospace Medicine, Brooks AFB, Texas, 1972-75; Assistant Charge Nurse/Charge Nurse, 11th USAF Hospital, Utapao, Thailand, 1975-76; Administrative Assistant to Director of Nursing Services/Nurse Epidemiologist for Medical Center, Malcolm Grow USAF Medical Center, Andrews AFB, Maryland, 1976-79; Administrative Nurse (Human Engineering) Aerospace Medical Research Laboratory, Wright Patterson AFB, Ohio, 1979-82; Chief, Nursing Services, USAF Hospital George, George AFB, California, 1982-85; Nurse Co-ordinator (Occupational Epidemiology), School of Aerospace Medicine, Brooks AFB, Texas, 1985-. *Memberships:* American Nurses Association; Aerospace Medical Association; Association for Infection Control Practitioners; New York Academy of Science; American Chemical Society; Human Factors Society; Society for the Advancement of Science; American Association of University Professors; American Cancer Society; American Heart Association. *Publications:* "Epidemic Neuromyasthenia" Graybill et al, 'JAMA' 1972; "Dietary Prejudice" Aviation, Space and Environmental Medicine, 1971; "Anthropometric and Mass Distributing Characteristics of the Adult Female', 1983. *Honours:* W prefix 9756, Nurse Epidemiologist, Consultant USAF Surgeon General, 1978-; Meritorious Service Medal with one oak leaf cluster, 1980-82. *Hobbies:* Sewing: Cooking; Designing and decorating. *Address:* 4810 Chesterfield Avenue, El Paso, TX 79903, USA.

LOGAN, Jerome Anthony, b. 3 Dec 1929, Dayton, Ohio, USA. Medical Director, Dartmouth Hospital, Dayton, Ohio. m. Marilyn J Logan, 21 July 1979, Dayton. *Education:* BS, University of Dayton, Ohio, 1951; MD, School of Medicine, St Louis University, St Louis, Missouri, 1955; Diplomate, American Board of Psychiatry & Neurology, 1983. *Appointments:* Internship, St Elizabeth Hospital, Dayton, 1955-56; Medical Corps, US Navy, 1956-68; Private Practice, 1968-. *Memberships:* American Psychiatric Association; American Medical Association; American Group Psychotherapy Association; American Academy of Clinical Psychiatrists; American Society of Clinical Hypnosis; World Medical Association; American Geriatric Society. *Honour:* Fellow, American Psychiatric Association, 1984. *Hobbies:* Classical Guitar; Myth as Medical Meta History; Wines; Gourmet Cooking; Showing Bullmastiffs; Fishing; Boating. *Address:* 1038 Salem Avenue, Dayton, OH 45406, USA.

LOGAN, Kayleen Ann, b. 18 Jan. 1954, Rock Springs, Wyoming, USA. University Professor. *Education:* BS in Nursing, University of Utah, Salt Lake City, USA, 1976; MS in Psychiatric Mental Health Nursing, University of Colorado Health Science Centre, Denver, USA, 1984. *Appointments:* Staff Nurse, University of Utah Medical Centre, Salt Lake City, USA, 1976; Charge Nurse, Holy Cross Hospital, Salt Lake City, 1977-78; Charge Nurse, Public Health Nursing Services, Sweetwater County, Wyoming, 1978-80; Nursing Director, Miners' Clinic, Memorial Hospital of Sweetwater County, 1980-82; Assistant Professor, University of Wyoming off Campus Programme, Rock Springs, Wyoming, 1984-. *Memberships:* American Nurses Association; District 6 Nurses Association. *Honours:* Honours at Entrance Scholarship, 1972; March of Dimes Scholarship, 1972; Graduated Cum Laude, 1976; WICH Exchange Student, 1982. *Hobbies:* Outdoor activities; Skiing; Fishing; Camping; Three-wheeling; Photography; Cooking; Crafts. *Address:* 1116 McCabe, Rock Springs, WY 82901, USA.

LOMAX, James Welton, b. 7 Dec. 1944, San Antonio, Texas, USA. Director of Psychiatric Residency. m. Nancy Robinson, 3 Sep. 1966, Bellaine, Texas, 3 daughters. *Education:* BA, Rice University, 1967; MD, Baylor College of Medicine, 1971; Candidate, Houston-Galveston Psychoanalytic Institute, 1983-. *Appointments:* Assistant Coordinator, 1977-79, Coordinator, 1979-81, Director, 1981-, General Psychiatry Residency Programme, Director, Psychiatry Clinic, 1982-84, Baylor College of Medicine. *Memberships:* American College of Psychiatrists, 1982-; American Psychoanalytic Association, 1984-; American Association of Directors of Psychiatry Residency Training Programmes, 1977-; American Psychiatric Association, 1975-. *Publications:* "Psychotherapy of Psychophysiological Disorders" (in Phenomenology & Treatment of Psychological Disorders) co-edited with Williams, 1980; Various articles on stress & suicide in professional journals. *Honours:* Phi Beta Kappa, 1967; Delta Phi Alpha 1966; Alpha Omega Alpha 1971; Laughlin Fellow, 1975; Falk Fellow, 1975; Eugen Kahn Award, 1977. *Hobbies:* Tennis; Racquetball; Fishing; Yardwork. *Address:* Department of Psychiatry, Baylor College of Medicine, One Baylor Plaza, Houston, TX 77030, USA.

LONDON, Nathaniel Jacob, b. 16 Jan. 1927, Baltimore, Maryland, USA. Psychiatrist. m. Edythe Block, Nov. 1957, Baltimore, Maryland, USA, 3 sons, 1 daughter. *Education:* BA, The Johns Hopkins University; MD, University of Maryland. *Appointments:* President, Western New England Institute for Psychoanalysis; President, Connecticut Psychiatric Society; Director, Psychoanalytic Foundation of Minnesota; Faculty and Training Analyst, Chicago Psychoanalysis Institute; Clinical Professor of Psychiatry University of Minnesota. *Memberships:* International Psychoanalytic Association; American Psychoanalytic Association; American Psychiatric Association; Minnesota Medical Association. *Publications:* 'An Essay on Psychoanalytic Theory: Two Theories of Schizophrenia' Parts 1 and 11 International Journal of Psychoanalysis, 1973; 'The Play Element of Regression in the Psychoanalytic Process' in Psychoanalytic Inquiry, 1981; 'An Appraisal of Self Psychology' in International Journal of Psychoanalysis, 1985. *Hobbies:* Music; Canoeing; Bicycling. *Address:* 1837 Medical Arts Building, Minneapolis, MN 55402, USA.

LONDON, Ray William, b. 29 May 1943, Burley, Idaho, USA. Clinical, Consulting and Medical Psychologist. *Education:* AS 1965, BS 1967, Weber State College; Master of Social Work 1973, PhD 1976, University of Southern California. *Appointments include:* Consultant to public schools, Hospitals, businesses, nationally and internationally, 1973-; Clinical Consulting Psychologist, Orange Police Department, 1976-80; Private Practice Consultation and Assessment, Santa Ana, California, 1974-; President, Board of Governors, Human Factor Programs, 1976-; Faculty and Lecturer, University of California Irvine-California College of Medicine, University of Southern California, University of California Los Angeles, University of Redlands, California State Colleges; Consulting Psychologist, St Joseph's Hospital, Orange, 1979-. *Memberships include:* President and Fellow, International Academy of Medicine and Psychology; Board of Directors, American Board of Psychological Hypnosis; Elected Fellow, Board of Directors, Royal Society of Health; Board of Directors, Society for Clinical Social Work. *Publications include:* Books, chapters, papers, abstracts, films, television series; Editor, International Bulletin of Medicine and Psychology. *Honours:* Milton H Erickson Scholar Laureate; Certificate of Special Congressional Recognition for Psychosocial and Mental Health Consultation, US House of Representatives; Fellow, Institute for Social Scientists on Neurobiology and Mental Illness, 1978. *Hobbies include:* Writing; Reading; Riding. *Address:* 1125 East 17th Street, Suite E 211, Santa Ana, CA 92701, USA.

LONG, Carolyn J, b. 17 Nov. 1944, Mineral Wells, Texas, USA. Psychotherapist. m. Burton Paris, Feb. 1984, 2 sons. *Education:* MA 1973, MS 1976, PhD 1981, East Texas State University; National Certified Counsellor. *Appointments:* Counsellor, Richland College, Dallas, Texas, 1982-83; Psychotherapist in Private Practice, 1983-. *Memberships:* Life Member, American Association of Sex Educators, Counselors and Therapists; American Association for Counseling and Dvlp; Texas Association for Counseling and Dvlp; American Association for Marriage and Family Therapists; American Society of Clinical Hypnosis; American Association of Professional Hypnotherapists; North Dallas Chamber of Commerce; Metroplex Women's Association. *Honour:* Citation of Appreciation of Leadership, American Business Women's Association, 1983. *Hobbies:* Swimming; Golf; Pistol shooting; Snow skiing. *Address:* 8111 L B J Freeway, Suite 565, Dallas, TX 75251, USA.

LONGO, Michael William, b. 13 Sep 1945, Greenwich, Connecticut, USA. Chiropractic Physician. m. Arlene Griffen, 4 September 1972, Greenwich, 1 son. *Education:* BSc, Biology, Marquette University, 1968; BSc, 1977, DC, 1977, National College of Chiropractic. *Appointments:* Teacher, Biology and Mathematics, Dreketi Inter-Racial Secondary School, Drekati, Fiji, 1969 (Acting Principal, 1970); Health Teacher, Warwick High School, New York, USA, 1971-73; currently, Chiropractic Physician. *Memberships:* American Chiropractic Association; Hawaii County Chiropractic Society; International Academy of Nutritional Consultants. *Honours:* Vice President, 1981, President, 1982, Hawaii County Chiropractic Society. *Hobbies:* Piano; Hawaiian outrigger canoe paddling; Skiing; Hiking; Surfing; Diving. *Address:* 1474 Wailuku Drive, Hilo, HI 96720, USA.

LONIE, David Alistair, b. 15 Sep. 1936, England. Director of Training, Child Psychiatry; Private Practice. m. Isla Frew, 20 Nov. 1958, Dunedin, New Zealand, 1 son, 2 daughters. *Education:* MB, ChB (Otago); DPM (Sydney); FRANZCP; MRCPsych. *Appointments:* Resident Medical Officer, Gisborne, New Zealand, 1959-61; Medical Officer, Kingseat Hospital, 1962-63; NSW Psychiatric Hospitals, 1963-65; Psychiatrist, Glafewille Hospital, 1966-71; Fellow, Child Psychiatry, 1971-73; Consultant, Child Psychiatry, Ryde, 1973-. *Memberships:* FRANZCP; MRCPsych; Member, Past President, NSW Institute of Psychiatry; Board Member, New South Wales Institute of Psychiatry. *Hobby:* Sailing. *Address:* 16 Alfred St., Woolwich, NSW, Australia.

LONIEWSKI, Edward Anthony, b. 13 Jan 1932, New Jersey, USA. Orthopaedic Surgeon. m. Mary Joanne Rohrig, 18 July 1959, Detroit, Michigan, 3 sons, 2 daughters. *Education:* St Peter's College, 1953; DO, Kansas City College of Osteopathy and Surgery, 1957; Fellow, American College of Osteopathic Surgeons; Fellow, American Osteopathic Academy of Orthopaedics, 1978. *Appointments:* Chairman, Department of Orthopaedic Surgery, Botsford General Hospital. *Memberships include:* American

Osteopathic Association; Michigan Association of Osteopathic Physicians and Surgeons; American College of Osteopathic Surgeons; American Osteopathic Acacemy of Orthopaedics; Michigan Osteopathic Academy of Orthopaedic Surgeons; American Osteopathic Academy of Applied Osteopathy; American Osteopathic Academy of Sports Medicine; International Arthroscopic Association; North American Arthroscopic Association. *Publications:* 'Congenital Dislocation of the Hips', 1962; 'Athlete Knee Injuries", 1976; 'Arthroscopy of the Knee - a needed adjunct to the management of meniscal disease', 1979; 'External fixation for the difficult fracture', 1983; 'The ace colles fixator in the treatment of comminuted fracture of the distal radius', 1983; 'Treatment of infected nonunion with bone deficit', 1983. *Honours:* Knotty Cane Award, American Osteopathic Academy of Orthopaedics, 1979; Walter Patenge Medal of Public Service, Michigan State University College of Osteopathic Medicine, 1980; Distinguished Service Award, Michigan Association of Osteopathic Physicians and Surgeons, 1981. *Hobbies:* Golf; Skiing; Sailing; Tennis. *Address:* 28080 Grand River, Suite 308, Farmington Hills, MI 48024, USA.

LOOK HONG, William Andrew, b. 22 Mar 1942, Kingston, Jamaica, West Indies. Deputy Chief of Psychiatry. m. Jeanne Veronica Lyn, 5 August 1973, Kingston, Jamaica, 2 daughters. *Education:* BSc, McGill University, Montreal, Quebec, Canada; MB BS, University of the West Indies, Jamaica; FRCP (C), University of Toronto, Canada; Diplomate, American Board Psychiatry and Neurology; Diplomate, International Academy Professional Counselling and Psychotherapy. *Appointments:* Medical Officer, Kingston Public Hospital, Victoria Jubilee Hospital, Children's Hospital, Kingston, Jamaica; Family Physician, Spanish Town, Jamaica; Resident in Psychiatry, University of Toronto, Ontario, Canada; Deputy Chief of Psychiatry and Unit Director, Out-patients Services, General and Marine Hospital, Owen Sound, Ontario. *Memberships:* American Psychiatric Association; Canadian Medical Association; Ontario Medical Association; Canadian Psychiatric Association; American Academy of Clinical Psychiatrists; International Academy of Professional Counselling and Psychotherapy; American Association of Geriatric Psychiatry; Academy of Psychosomatic Medicine; Royal College of Physicians and Surgeons of Canada; College of Physicians and Surgeons of Ontario. *Honours:* Aaron Matalon Prize in Psychiatry, 1972. *Hobbies:* Photography; Art Collecting; Pistol Shooting; Swimming. *Address:* General and Marine Hospital, Owen Sound, Ontario, N4K 5H3, Canada.

LOOMER, Richard Leslie, b. 3 Oct. 1938, Minnesota, USA. Orthopaedic Surgeon. m. Diane Kolander, 21 Dec. 1963, Minnesota, USA, 1 son. *Education:* BA, Gustavus Adolphus College, St. Peter, Minnesota, USA, 1960; MD, University of Minnesota, 1965. *Appointments:* Internship, Philadelphia General Hospital, Pennsylvania, USA, 1965-66; Residency, Vancouver General Hospital, Canada, 3 years and University of Western Ontario, London, Ontario, Canada, 1 year; Medical Officer, USAF; Public Health Officer, Portland, Oregon, USA; Consultant Orthopaedic Surgeon to: Royal Columbian Hospital, New Westminster, British Columbia; St Mary's Hospital, New Westminster, British Columbia; University of British Columbia Sports Medicine Clinic, Vancouver, British Columbia, Canada; Assistant Clinic Professor, University of British Columbia Department of Orthopaedics. *Memberships:* Fellow, Royal College of Surgeons of Canada; Fellow, American Academy of Orthopaedic Surgeons; Canadian Orthopaedic Association. *Publications:* Author and co-author of several contributions to professional journals and publications including 'Non-Union in Fractures of the Humeral Shaft' in 'Injury', 1976; 'Elbow Injuries in Athletes' in 'C.J.A.S.S.' 1982; 'The Anterior Cruciate Dilemma' in 'C.J.A.S.S.' 1982; Book chapter 'The Arthogram Tomogram and the Diagnosis of Glenohumeral Instability' in "Surgery of the Shoulder"; 'Ankles in Aging Athletes' News Letter, Canadian Academy of Sports Medicine. *Hobbies:* Skiing; Mountaineering; Hiking. *Address:* 7061 Cypress Street, Vancouver, British Columbia, Canada U6P 5M2.

LOOMIS, Earl Alfred, b. 21 May 1921, Minneapolis, Minnesota, USA. Professor of Psychiatry. m. (1) Victoria Marie Malkerson, 1944 (2) Lucile Rebekka Meyer 1962 (3) Anita Muriel Peabody, 22 Mar. 1969, New York City; 4 daughters. *Education:* BA 1942, BS 1943, MD 1946, University of Minnesota; Internship, Internal Medicine & Paediatrics, Boston University Hospital, Massachusetts, 1945-46; Residencies, Psychiatry & Child Psychiatry, Western Psychiatric Institute & Clinic, Pittsburgh, 1946-48, Hospital of the University of Pennsylvania & Institute of the Penn. Hospital, Philadelphia, PA, 1948-49. *Appointments include:* Associate Professor of Child Psychiatry, School of Medicine, University of Pittsburgh, 1952-56; Chief, Division of Child Psychiatry, St Luke's Hospital, New York, 1956-62; Researcher in Residence, Institut J-J Rousseau, University of Geneva, Switzerland, 1962-63; Attending Psychiatrist, St Luke's Hospital, New York City, 1963-73; Attending Psychiatrist, Eastern Long Island Hospital, Greenport, 1973-81; Professor of Psychiatry, 1981-82, also Head, section of Child Adolescent & Family Psychiatry, Department of Psychiatry, Medical college of Georgia, Augusta, GA, 1982-. *Memberships include:* American Medical Association; Fellow, American Psychiatric Association; American Association for the Advancement of Science; American Psychosomatic Society; International Psychoanalytic Association; Fellow, American College of Physicians; Fellow, American Orthopsychiatric Association; American Academy of Child Psychiatry; and others. *Publications:* Chapter on 'Paul Tillich & the Psychoanalytic Tradition' in "The Intellectual Legacy of Paul Tillich", 1968; "The Self in Pilgrimage", 1960; 'The Significance of Religious Development', 1961; 'The Role of the Minister in Mental Health', 1949. *Honours:* Certificates of Commendation, American Psychiatric Association, 1962, Georgia School of Alcohol & Drug Studies, 1985; John Phillips Fellow, Exeter Academy, Amherst, Massachusetts, 1968; Blueberry Treatment Centre, 1981. *Hobbies:* Travel; Sailing. *Address:* Department of Psychiatry & Health Behaviour, Medical College of Georgia, 1515 Pope Avenue, Augusta, GA 30912-7300, USA.

LOPACIUK, Stanislaw Kazimierz, b. 4 Jan. 1935, Podbielskie Ogrodniki, Poland. Head, Clinical Biochemistry, Institute of Haematology, Warsaw. m. Halina Zywicka, 3 Sep. 1961, 1 daughter. *Education:* MB, Warsaw Medical School; PhD; Professor, Medicine. *Appointments:* Research Associate, 1958-61, Senior Research Associate, 1962-67, Internal Medicine, Head, Haematology & Clinical Biochemistry, 1968-, Institute of Haematology, Warsaw; Consultant, haematologist, Ministry of Public Health, Kuwait, 1980-82. *Memberships:* Chairman, Subcommittee, Haemostasis and Microcirculation, Committee on Clinical Pathophysiology, Polish Academy of Sciences; Vice President, Polish Haemophilia Committee; Council Member, Polish Society of Haematology and Blood Transfusion; International Society on Thrombosis and Haemostasis; International Society of Haematology. *Publications:* Over 120 original papers in Polish & International Medical Journals; Author, Chapters, 7 Medical Books. *Hobbies:* Gardening; Theatre. *Address:* Institute of Haematology, Chocimska 5, 00-957, Warsaw, Poland.

LOPATA, Alexander, b. 5 Apr. 1937, Warsaw. Reader, Dept. of Obstetrics and Gynaecology, University of Melbourne. m. Rena Sparber, 8 Aug. 1964, Melbourne, Australia, 1 son, 2 daughters. *Education:* MB, BS, 1961, PhD, University of Melbourne, 1971.

Appointments: Resident Medical Officer, Austin Hospital, Melbourne, 1962; Teaching and Research Fellow, Department of Pathology, University of Sydney, 1963; Surgical Registrar, Royal Children's Hospital, Melbourne, 1964; Lecturer, Department of Physiology, 1965-71, Senior Lecturer, Department of Obstetrics and Gynaec, University of Melbourne, 1980-85; Senior Lecturer Department of Obstetrics and Gynaec, Monash University, 1971-80. *Memberships:* Australian Society for Reproductive Biology; Fertility Society of Australia; Endocrine Society of Australia; Australian Physiological and Pharmacological Society; UCLA Chapter, Sigma Xi Society. *Publications:* 'Pregnancy Following intrauterine implantation of an embryo obtained by in vitro fertilization of a preovulatory egg', (with W I H Johnston, I J Hoult and A L Speirs), 1980; 'Successes and failures in human in vitro fertilization', 1980; 'Concepts in Human in vitro fertilization and embryo transfer', 1983. *Honours:* Fullbright-Hayes Fellowship for Senior Scholars, 1974; Lalor Foundation Fellowship, 1974. *Hobbies:* Old Books, Wine Collecting; Squash; Tennis. *Address:* 488 Barkers Road, Hawthorn 3122, Victoria, Australia.

LOPEZ, Arnaldo Victor, b. 19 May 1936, Havana, Cuba, Orthopaedic Surgeon. m. Emma de Albear, 25 Nov 1962, 1 son, 2 daughters. *Education:* MD, Havana University, 1962; MD, Universidad de Madrid, Spain, 1970; Certified, American Board of Orthopaedic Surgeons, 1977. *Appointments:* Orthopaedic Surgeon, Colon Hospital, Cuba, Pinar del Rio Hospital, Camagüey Hospital; Resident, Orthopaedic Surgery, Mount Sinai Hospital, Miami Beach, Florida, USA, 1971-75; Orthopaedic Surgeon in Private Practice, 1975-. *Memberships:* American Medical Association; Florida Medical Association; District of Columbia Medical Association; Fellow, American College of Surgeons; Fellow, American Association of Orthopaedic Surgeons; Fellow, International College of Surgeons; Affiliate, Royal Society of Medicine, London. *Hobbies:* Boating; Fishing. *Address:* 1545, South West First Street, Miami, FL 33135, USA.

LOPEZ-VELEZ, Eliud, b. 4 June 1938, Adjuntas, Puerto Rico. Professor & Director, Department of Pathology. m. Yvonne Dávila, 19 May 1962, 4 daughters. *Education:* National Boards of Medical Examination, 1966; American Board of Pathology, Anatomical & Clinical Pathology, 1969. *Appointments:* Head of Pathology Deaprtment, Caguas Subregional Hospital, Instructor, School of Medicine Pathology Department, University of Puerto Rico, 1969-72; Associate Pathologist, San Juan City Hosptial, Assistant Professor, School of Medicine Pathology Department, University of Puerto Rico, 1972-73; Associate Pathologist, San Rafael Hospital, Caguas, PR, 1969-; Medical Director, Blood Programme, American Red Cross, PR, 1973-74; Director, Pathology Service, I Gonzalez Martinez Oncological Hospital, 1974-78; Chairman, Department of Pathology, University of Puerto Rico School of Medicine & Affiliated Hospitals, 1978-; Director, Institute of Forensic Sciences, School of Medicine, University of Puerto Rico, 1983-85. *Memberships:* Puerto Rico Medical Association; Member, Chamber of Deputies, 1975-76. *Publications:* Various articles in medical journals in field. *Honour:* Alpha Omega Alpha, 1962. *Hobbies:* School Parent-Teachers' Activities; Director, Scientific Committee, PR Medical Association. *Address:* University of Puerto Rico, Medical Sciences Campus, GPO Box 5067, San Juan PR 00936, USA.

LORBER, Curt Gerhard, b. 28 May 1931, Saarbrücken, Federal Republic of Germany. Head, Department of Maxillo-Facial Surgery. m. Dr Edeltraud Hüthwohl, 20 March 1967, Kassel, 1 son, 2 daughters. *Education:* MD, 1958, DMD, 1960, University of Heidelberg; Habilitation on Maxillo-Facial Surgery, Cologne, 1970. *Appointments:* Senior Surgeon, Clinic for Maxillo-Facial Diseases, Associate Professor, University of

Cologne; Professor, 1976-, currently Head, Department of Maxillo-Facial Surgery, Justus-Liebig University, Giessen. *Memberships:* Leader, Working Group on History of Dentistry, International Dental Federation. *Publications:* Various on problems of maxillo-facial surgery, dental surgery and history of stomatology. *Address:* Zum Westergrund 49, D-633 Westzlar 21, Federal Republic of Germany.

LORENZI, Nancy M. Associate Senior Vice-President for University of Cincinnati Medical Center; Director, Medical Center Information and Communications Unit. *Education:* AB, Psychology and Sociology, Youngstown State University, 1966; MS, Library Science, Case Western Reserve, 1968; MA, Sociology, University of Louisville, 1975; PhD, Organizational Behaviour, University of Cincinnati, 1980. *Appointments:* Chief Medical Librarian, St Elizabeth Hospital, Youngstown, Ohio, 1963-67; Head, Information Services, University of Louisville Medical Library, 1968-69; Director, Regional Library Extension Program, University of Louisville, 1970-71; Acting Director, Medical Center Personnel, 1980-81; Medical Center Public Affairs-News Bureau, 1983-; Special Assistant to Senior Vice-President, University of Cincinnati; Director, Medical Center, 1976-83; Director, Medical Center Libraries, University of Cincinnati, 1972-83. *Memberships:* Medical Library Association, President, 1981-82; President-elect; National Committee regarding US in International Information policy, 1982-83; Medical Library Association Board of Directors, 1981-84; Chair, National Committee to plan for National Library of Medicine in 2005, 1985-86. *Publications:* Contributor to: 'Enterprise: The Journal of the University of Cincinnati College of Business Administration'; 'Bulletin of the Medical Library Association'. *Honours:* Scholarship to Case Western Reserve from US Public Health Service; Rittenhouse Award, Medical Library Association, 1968. *Address:* University of Cincinnati Medical Center, 231 Bethesda Avenue, Cincinnati, OH 45267-0574, USA.

LOSCHEN, Earl Lee, b. 10 Jan. 1944, Minden, Nebraska, USA. Associate Professor of Psychiatry. m. Marilyn Reinhardt, 15 June 1974, St Louis, Missouri, 2 daughters. *Education:* BS, Midland Lutheran College, 1966; MD, University of Nebraska, College of Medicine, 1970. *Appointments:* Assistant Professor, Psychiatry, University of Nebraska, College of Medicine, 1973-74; Assistant Professor, 1974-80, Associate Professor, 1980-, Psychiatry, Southern Illinois University School of Medicine, Springfield, Illinois. *Memberships:* American Psychiatric Association; American Medical Association; American Public Health Association; National Association for Rural Mental Health; American Association of Directors of Psychiatric Residency Training; American Orthopsychiatric Association; Association for Academic Psychiatry. *Publications:* Contributions to: "Innovations in Clinical Practice", volume 3, 1984; 'International Journal of Mental Health', 1983; 'Journal of Medical Education', 1985. *Honours:* Blue Key National Honorary Fraternity, 1966; Alpha Omega Alpha, 1970. *Hobbies:* Gardening; Photography; Antiques. *Address:* Southern Illinois University School of Medicine, PO Box 3926, Springfield, IL 62708, USA.

LOSOS, Joseph Zbigniew, b. 12 Dec 1943, India. Director, Bureau of Infection Control. m. Joanne Cameron Carr, 24 July 1975, Toronto, Canada, 2 sons, 1 daughter. *Education:* MD, DECH, University of Toronto; Fellow, Royal College of Physicians and Surgeons of Canada, American College of Preventive Medicine. *Appointments:* Medical Officer, Uganda; Clinical Teacher, University of Toronto, Canada; Project Officer, International Development Research Center, Canada; Consultant Epidemiologist, World Health Organisation, Zambia; Associate Director, Health Sciences, International Development Research Centre, Canada; Director, Bureau of Infection Control, Centre for Diseases Control, National Health and Welfare,

Canada. *Memberships:* President Elect, Canadian Society for Tropical Medicine and International Health; Board of Directors, Canadian Public Health Association; Canadian Hospital Infection Control Association. *Publications:* Numerous articles on travel medicine, parasitic diseases and epidemiology of nosocomial infections. *Honour:* Losos Award dedicated, for best report of elective education programme funded in Canada annually, Canadian Society for Tropical Medicine and International Health. *Hobbies:* Sports; Sketching; Classical music. *Address:* 175 Rothwell Drive, Ottawa, Ontario, Canada K1J 7G7.

LOSOWSKY, Monty Seymour, b. 1 Aug. 1931, London, England. Professor of Medicine. m. Barbara Malkin, 15 Aug. 1971, 1 son, 1 daughter. *Education:* MA ChB, MD. *Appointments:* Fellow in Medicine, Harvard Medical School, Boston, Massachusetts, USA, 1961-62; Lecturer in Medicine 1962-64, Senior Lecturer in Medicine 1964-66, Reader in Medicine 1966-69, University Department of Medicine, Leeds General Infirmary, Leeds, England; Professor of Medicine, University of Leeds, St James's University Hospital, Leeds, 1969-. *Memberships:* Fellow, Royal College of Physicians; Council, British Society of Gastroenterology; Nutrition Society; Association of Physicians of Great Britain and Ireland; British Association for the Study of the Liver; British Society for Immunology; British Society for Haematology. *Publications include:* "Malabsorption in Clinical Practice" (with B E Walker and J Kelleher), 1974; "The gut and systemic disease" (editor) in the series "Clinics in Gastroenterology", 1983; "Advanced Medicine" (co-editor with R P Bolton), 1983; "The Liver and Biliary System" (with P W Brunt and A E Read), 1984; "Clinical Nutrition in Gastroenterology" (co-editor with R V Heatley and J Kelleher), 1986; "Gut Defences in Clinical Practice" (co-editor with R V Heatley), 1986; "The Gastrointestinal Tract" (with A E Read and P N Brunt), 1986; Over 200 articles in the field of medicine, especially gastrointestinal, hepatic and nutritional disorders. *Address:* Department of Medicine, St James's University Hospital, Leeds LS9 7TF, England.

LOUDON, John Duncan Ott, b. 22 Aug. 1924, Edinburgh, Scotland. Consultant Obstetrician & Gynaecologist, Eastern General Hospital, Edinburgh. m. Nancy Beaton Mann, 10 Sep. 1953, Avoch, Ross-shire, 2 sons. *Education:* MB,ChB 1947, FRCS 1954, Edinburgh University; MRCOG 1956, FRCOG 1973. *Appointments:* Medical Officer, RAF, 1948-50; Surgical registrar, Royal Northern Infirmary, Inverness, 1953-54; Registrar/Senior registrar, Simpson Maternity Pavilion & Royal Infirmary of Edinburgh, 1955-60; External examiner, Universities of Leeds, Newcastle-upon-Tyne, Glasgow, Aberdeen, Dundee, Royal College of Surgeons of Ireland, Welsh National School of Medicine; Examiner, Royal Australian College of Gynaecologists, University of Khartoum; Adviser, Family Planning, Government of Malta, 1980, 1981; Vice President, Royal College of Obstetricians, 1981-84. *Memberships:* Edinburgh Obstetrical Society; British Fertility Society. *Publications:* Articles in obstetric journals. *Hobbies:* Gardening; Golf; Food & wine. *Address:* 94 Inverleith Place, Edinburgh EH3 5PA, Scotland.

LOUIS, Dean Sherwood, b. 17 May 1936, Dayton, Ohio, USA. Professor. Divorced, 2 sons, 2 daughters. *Education:* BS, University of NH, 1958; MD, University of VT, 1962. *Appointments:* Instructor, Assistant Professor, Associate Professor, Professor, Orthopaedic Surgery, University of Michigan. *Memberships:* American Society for Surgery of the Hand; International Federation of Societies for Surgery of the Hand; American Academy of Orthopaedic Surgeons; Robert E Carroll Hand Club. *Publications:* Numerous publications in scientific journals including, 'Recall injury from vinblastine: a case report', (with F. Hankin, R. Natale, T. Green, J. Blum), 1985; 'Long term follow-up of lipofibroma of the median nerve', (F. Hankin, T. Greene, H. Dick), 1985; 'Long term follow up of non-vascularized fibular autografts for distal radial reconstruction', (with R Noellert), 1985; 'Fluoroscopic and arthrographic evaluation of carpal instability', (with E Braunstein, T. Greene, F. Hankin), 1985. *Honours:* Upjohn Award, Outstanding Senior Resident, University of MI, 1970; Sr. Anne Kane Fellowship, Columbia Presbyterian Medical Center, 1970. *Hobbies:* Camping; Fishing; Snow Skiing. *Address:* University of Michigan Hospitals, 2912 Taubman Center 1500 E, Hospital Drive, Ann Arbor, MI 48109-0328, USA.

LOURENCO, Ruy Valentim, b. 25 Mar. 1929, Lisbon, Portugal, Naturalised USA, 1966. Physician; Educator. m. Susan Jane Loewenthal, 18 Jan. 1960, 1 son, 1 daughter. *Education:* Intern, Lisbon City Hospital, 1951-53; Resident, Internal Medicine, 1953-55. *Appointments:* Instructor, University of Lisbon, 1955-59; Fellow, Medicine, Columbia University, New York City, 1959-63; Assistant Professor, 1963-66, Associate Professor, 1966-67, New Jersey College of Medicine; Private Practice, 1967-; Attending Physician, Direct Respiratory Physiology Laboratory, Jersey City Medical Centre, 1963-67; Associate Professor, Medicine, Physiology, University of Illinois, Chicago, 1967-69, Professor, 1969-, Chairman, Medicine, 1977-, Foley Professor of Medicine, 1978-; Director, Respiratory Research Laboratory, Hektoen Institute, Chicago, 1967-71; Director, Pulmonary Medicine, Cook County Hospital, Chicago, 1969-70; Attending Physician, University of Illinois Medical Centre, 1967-, Director Pulmonary Section & Labs, 1970-77, Physician in Chief, 1977-, President Medical Staff, 1980-81; Consultant, Task Force on Research in Respiratory Diseases, NIH, 1972. *Memberships include:* Fellow, AAAS, ACP, American College Chest Physicians; American Federation Clinical Research; American Heart Association; American Physiological Society; American Society Clinical Investigation; American Thoracic Society, Chairman Scientific Assembly, 1974-75; American Lung Association, Committee on Smoking and Health, 1981-83; International academy of Chest Physicians and Surgeons; Chest Physicians, Chairman, Nominating Committee, 1984-; Association American Physicians; Association Professors of Medicine; many other professional organisations. *Publications:* Editorial Board, 'Journal Laboratory & Clinical Medicine', 1973-77, 1985-; American Review of Respiratory Diseases', 1985-; Contributor, numerous articles to professional journals. *Address:* 840 S. Wood St., Chicago, Il 60612, USA.

LOURIE, Reginald Spencer, b. 10 Sep. 1908, Brooklyn, New York, USA. Expert Consultant, Department Material and Child Health, National Institute of Mental Health. m. Lucille Radin, 26 Feb. 1931, Brooklyn, 3 sons. *Education:* BS, Cornell University, 1930; MD, Downstate Medical Center, State University of New York, 1936; Med Sc D, College of Physicians and Surgeons, Columbia University, 1942; Baltimore Psychoanalytic Institute, 1957; Residency Training: Pediatrics, 1936-38; Psychiatry, 1938-40; Child Psychiatry, 1940-43. *Appointments:* Research Associate, College of P & S, Columbia University, 1940-43; Pediatric-Psychiatry Liaison, University of Rochester, 1946-48; US Navy, 1943-45; Director, Department of Psychiatry, Children's Hospital, National Medical Center, 1948-75; Professor of Child Health and Development and Psychiatry and Behavioral Science, 1948-75; Emeritus, 1975; Senior Research Scientist, National Institute of Mental Health, 1975-85; Medical Director, Regional Center for Infants and Children, Rockville, Maryland, 1985-. *Memberships include:* American Academy of Child Psychiatry; American Psychiatric Association; American Psychoanalytic Association; American Medical Association, etc. *Publications:* 150 articles and chapters in books; Co-Editor: "Year Book of

Psychiatry and Allied Mental Health", 1965-; "Early Child Care, New Dimensions", 1965. *Honours include:* Commander of Order of the Phoenix, Greece; Dickenson Medal for Distinguished Contributions to American Medicine; McGavin Award for Prevention of Children's Disorders. *Hobbies:* Gardening; Fishing; Sailing. *Address:* 4305 Thornapple Street, Chevy Chase, MD 20815, USA.

LOUSBERG, Sister Mary Clarice, b. 21 Aug. 1929, Fleming, Colorado, USA. President, DePaul Hospital. *Education:* RN, St Joseph Hospital School of Nursing, Denver, 1952; BS, Nursing Education, St Mary College, Leavenworth, 1969; MPA, Health Care Administration, University of Southern California, 1971. *Appointments:* Nursing Supervisor, 1954-59, Supervisor, Obstetrics, 1959-63, St John's Hospital, Helena, Montana; Operating Room Supervisor, Providence Hospital, Kansas City, 1963-66; Director, Nursing Service, 1966-68, President, 1979-, DePaul Hospital; Administrator, St James Community Hospital, Butte, 1972-79. *Memberships:* American College of Healthcare Executives, Fellow; American Hospital Association, Nursing Council Member; Catholic Hospital Association; St Joseph Hospital, Board of Directors; Wyoming Hospital Association, Board Chairman; DePaul Hospital, Board of Directors, Secretary, Treasurer. *Publications:* "Top Planning Issues of 1984", 'Trustee Magazine', 1984; "DePaul Hospital responds to Disaster", 'Catholic Health World', 1985. *Honours:* American Business Women's Association, Boss of the Year, Cheyenne; Selected by American College of Hospital Administrators for People to People Goodwill Mission to Finland, Soviet Union and China, 1984. *Hobbies:* Knitting; Walking. *Address:* 2600 East 18th, Cheyenne, WY 82001, USA.

LOUVARIS, Kimon M, b. 15 May 1915, Athens, Greece. Psychotherapist and Counsellor. m. 7 June 1946, 3 sons, 1 daughter. *Education:* LLB, Lasalle University, Illinois, USA; MD, United America Medicine College; PhD, Clinical Psychotherapy, Thomas Edison College, New York; Licensed Steam and Diesel Engineer, Delehanty Institute; Licensed Psychotherapist, American Board of Examiners in Psychotherapy, Palm Beach Psychotherapy Training Center Incorporated, Florida. *Appointments:* Steam and Diesel Engineer, United States Merchant Marines during World War II, 1940-45; Executive Director, Panhellenic Society, Inventors of Greece in USA; Chairman, Greek American Counsellor, Center of Greece in USA, Merrick, New York; Director, Naturopathic Society of New York, New York Incorporated; Licensed Clinical Psychotherapist, New York, New York; Reverend Doctor, Episcopalian Ordination, Ministry of Charity, New York. *Memberships:* Olders Organisations of Greece; The Athens Inventors of Greece; Veterans of (FWY) USA and Greek Navy. *Publications:* Scientific letters, 1943; "External and Internal Engines", 1953; Educational books on the human brain and chemistry and erroneous zones. *Honours:* Victory Medal, World War II; Distinguished Service, Battle of the Atlantic; 6 honours and awards from the Washington Administration, Washington, District of Columbia. *Hobbies:* Boxing; Soccer; Horsemanship; Water Polo; Athletics. *Address:* 2053 Narwood Avenue, Merrick, NY 11566, USA.

LOVE, Jack Wayne, b. 20 Sep. 1930, Belleville, Illinois, USA. Associate Clinical Professor, Surgery. m. Elizabeth Jeanne Vogt, 19 Nov. 1960, 4 sons, 2 daughters. *Education:* D. Phil (Oxford); MD (Yale). *Appointments:* Instructor, Physiology, Yale Medical School, 1958-59; Associate Professor, Surgery, Johns Hopkins University, 1967-70; Associate Clinical Professor, Surgery, University of California, Los Angeles, 1974-; Various Hospital Staff Appointments including: Consulting Thoracic Surgeon, Good Samaritan Hospital & Mt. Wilson State Hospital, 1969-70; Santa Barbara Cottage Hospital, Goleta Valley Community Hospital, St Francis Hospital, Santa Barbara General Hospital, 1970-. *Memberships include:* Alpha Omega Alpha; Sigma Xi; Fellow:

American College of Surgeons, American College of Cardiology, American College of Chest Physicians; American Association for Thoracic Surgery; Society of Thoracic Surgeons; Society for Vascular Surgery; International Cardiovascular Surgery; many other professional organisations. *Publications:* Editorial Board; 'Journal of the American Medical Association', 1974-77; Co-Editor, 'Proceedings of the Santa Barbara Medical Foundation Clinic', 1983-; Numerous articles in professional journals; Editor, "Cardiac Surgery in Patients with Chronic Renal Disease", 1982; US Patent for a Blood Oxygenator, 1964; US Patent, for a Tricuspid Prosthetic Heart Valve, 1984. *Honours:* Recipient, various honours and awards. *Address:* Santa Barbara Medical Foundation Clinic, Santa Barbara, CA 93102, USA.

LOVRIC, Albert, b. 14 June 1926, Belgrade. Director. m. 13 Sep. 1958, Newcastle, 1 son, 4 daughters. *Education:* MB, BS, University Sydney, 1956; Diploma Clinical Pathology, University of Sydney; Fellow, Royal Australasian College of Physicians; Royal College of Pathologists; Royal Australasian College of Pathologists. *Appointments:* Registrar in Pathology, Haematologist, Senior Haematologist, Consultant Haematologist, Royal Alexandra Hospital for Children, Sydney; Visiting Haematologist, Concord Repatriation Hospital, Sydney. *Memberships:* Australian Society of Blood Transfusion; Australian Society of Haematology; International Society of Haematology. *Publications:* 72 Scientific Papers; articles in books, etc. *Hobby:* Fishing. *Address:* NSW Red Cross Blood Transfusion Service, 153 Clarence Street, Sydney, NSW 2000, Australia.

LOW, Morton David, b. 25 Mar. 1935, Alberta, Canada. Coordinator of Health Sciences; Professor of Medicine. m. Barbara Joan McLeod, 25 Aug. 1984, Penticton, British Columbia, 1 son, 3 daughters. *Education:* MD, CM 1960, MSc Medicine 1962, Queen's University, Kingston; PhD with honour, Baylor University College of Medicine, Houston, Texas, USA, 1966. *Appointments:* Teaching and Research Fellow in Anatomy, Queen's University, Kingston, Canada, 1961-62; Teaching and Research Fellow 1963-65, Instructor 1965-66, Assistant Professor 1966-68, Physiology, Baylor College of Medicine, Houston, Texas, USA; Assistant in Neurophysiology, The Methodist Hospital, Houston, Texas, 1966-68; Associate Professor of Medicine 1968-78, Professor of Medicine 1978-, University of British Columbia, Canada; Director, Department of Diagnostic Neurophysiology, Vancouver General Hospital, 1968-; Director, Vancouver General Hospital Research Institute, 1981-85. *Memberships:* Secretary 1981-85, International Federation of Societies for Electroencephalography and Clinical Neurophysiology; President 1972-74, Canadian Society of Clinical Neurophysiology; Council 1977-80, Canadian Society for Clinical Investigation; Fellow, American EEG Society; Sigma Xi. *Publications:* Numerous articles in professional journals; Several book chapters on topics in cerebral neurophysiology, particularly in the field of cognitive neuroscience. *Honours:* A E McRae Award in Social Engineering 1958, President of Alma Mater Society 1958-59, Tricolor Award 1959, Queen's University; Senior Medical Scientist-Research Professorship, Canada-France Exchange, 1978-79. *Hobbies:* Certified sailing instructor – keelboats; Photography; Volunteer ski patrol; Youth soccer coach; Western horseman; Private pilot. *Address:* Office of the Co-ordinator of Health Sciences, Suite 400, 2194 Health Sciences Mall, Vancouver, British Columbia V6T 1Z6, Canada.

LOW, Teong, b. 29 May 1946, Malaysia. Private practice - Orthodontics. m. Jackie Low, 28 June 1973, Kuala Lumpur, 1 son, 1 daughter. *Education:* BDS Honours, Singapore University; M S Children's Dentistry, London University; Diploma in Orthodontics, Royal College of Surgeons, London; AM, Malaysia;

FADI. *Appointments:* Tutor, University of Singapore, 1971-72; Lecturer, University of Malaya, 1972-79. *Memberships:* Malaysian Dental Association; British Society for Study of Orthodontics; International Association Dentistry for Children; Academy of Medicine, Malaysia; Fellow, Academy of Dentistry International. *Publications:* 'The bonding of a polymeric fissure sealant to topical fluoride treated teeth', 1975; 'Caries prevalence in different racial groups of school children in West Malaysia', 1975; 'The influence of topical fluoride in the invitro adhesion of fissure sealants', 1977. *Hobbies:* Golf; Swimming; Rotary Club. *Address:* 31 Jalan SS 21/3, Petaling Jaya, Selangor, Malaysia.

LOWE, Robert Wylie, b. 28 Oct. 1937, Morehead, Kentucky, USA. Orthopaedic Surgeon. m. Sara Herr Lowe, 23 Aug. 1963, 2 sons, 2 daughters. *Education:* BS, 1959, MD, 1964. Surgical Internship, Vanderbilt University Hospital, 1964-65; Orthopedic Surgery Residency, 1966-69; National Board of Medical Examiners, 1965. *Appointments:* Orthopedic Consultant: Former Orthopedic Consultant, St Claire Medical Center, Morehead, Kentucky; Huntington State Hospital and Veterans Administration Hospital, Huntington, West Virginia; Active Hospital Staff: St Mary's Hospital, Huntington, Cabell Huntington Hospital, Huntington. *Memberships:* West Virginia State Medical Society; Cabell County Medical Society; American Medical Association; Southern Medical Association; American Academy of Orthopedic Surgeons; American Academy of Cerebral Palsy; American College for Sports Medicine; Tri-State Orthopedic Society; American Orthopedic Society for Sports Medicine. *Publications:* 'Hematogenous Osteomyelitis' in 'Southern Medical Journal' 1970; 'Standing Roentgenograms in Spondylolisthesis' - 'Clinical Orthopedics' Volume 117, 1976; 'The Low Back School in Community Hospitals' 'Orthopedic Transactions' Volume II, 1981. *Honours:* First Annual Richmond Cerebral Palsy Award, 1970; Outstanding Alumnus Award, Morehead State University, 1973; Chairman, Orthopedic Section West Virginia State Medical 1973-74; President, Cabell County Medical Society, 1982-83. *Address:* 2828 First Avenue, Suite 400, PO Box 3127, Huntington, WV 25702, USA.

LOWE, Thomas George, b. 20 Feb 1937, Minneapolis, Minesota, USA. Associate Clinical Professor of Orthopaedic Surgery. m. Sally Ann Jones, 27 Dec 1963, Minneapolis, 2 sons, 1 daughter. *Education:* BA, Carleton College, Minnesota, 1959; MD, Northwestern University, Chicago, Illinois, 1963. *Appointments:* Intern, Hennepin County General Hospital, 1963-64; Battalion Surgeon, US Army Medical Corps, Federal Republic of Germany, 1964-66; Resident, Orthopaedic Surgery, Veterans Administration, University of Minnesota Hospitals, USA, 1966-70; Numerous hospital affiliations, Denver and Wheatridge, Colorado; Currently, Clinical Associate Professor of Orthopaedic Surgery, University of Colorado Medical School. *Memberships:* American Medical Association; Western Orthopaedic Association; American Academy of Orthopaedic Surgery; Russel Hibbs Society; Fellow, Scoliosis Research Society; Diplomat; American Board of Orthopaedic Surgery; Colorado State Board of Examiners. *Publications:* Author or co-author of articles contributed to: 'Journal of Bone and Joint Surgery'; 'Pediatric Newsletter'; 'Scoliosis Research Society Annual Meeting Programme'. *Honours:* Board of Councillors, American Academy of Orthosurgery, 1982-; Chairman, Morbidity and Mortality Committee, Scoliosis Research Society, 1985-; Russell Hibbs Award, 1984. *Hobbies:* Skiing; Tennis; Scuba diving. *Address:* 8370 West 38th Avenue, Denver, CO 80033, USA.

LOWENTHAL, Armand, b. 7 Sep. 1919, The Hague, The Netherlands. m. Suzanne Jokisch, deceased, 1 son. *Education:* MD, neurologist; Higher Aggregation, Brussels University. *Appointments include:* Consultant Neurologist, Medico-Surgical Institute, Charleroi; Consultant Neurologist, F.O.B. Polyclinic, Antwerp; Neurologist, Internal Medicine,

Stuivenberg General Hospital, Antwerp; Lecturer, Brussels University; Professor, Neurology, Universitaire Instelling Antwerpen; Professor, Neurochemistry, Universitaire Instelling Antwerpen; Scientific Coordinator, Born-Bunge Foundation; Adjunct Secretary Treasurer General, World Federation of Neurology; Secretary General, Research Groups, World Federation of Neurology; President, Commission of Neuro-psychiatry; Consultant Neurologist, Medico-legal Dept. City of Antwerp; Head, Neurology, Middelheim General Hospital, Antwerp; etc. *Memberships include:* Belgian Society for Neurology; Belgian Society for Psychiatry; Belgian Society for Oto Neuro Ophthalomlogy; French Society for Neurology; Fellow, Royal Society of Medicine, London; New York Academy of Sciences; French Society of Physiology; Peruvian Society for Neuro Psychiatry; Founding Member, European Society of Neurochemistry; Chairman, Belgian Research Group on Parkinsons Disease, 1975; many other professional organisations. *Publications:* Articles in professional journals including: 'Journal of Neurochemistry'; 'The Lancet'; 'Journal of Neurochemistry. *Honours:* Chevalier, Order of Leopold II, 1966; Chevalier, Order of the Crown, 1976; Commander, Order of the Crown, 1979. *Address:* University of Antwerp (UIA), Born Bunge Foundation, Universiteitsplein 1, B 2610 Antwerp-Wilrijk, Belgium.

LOWINGER, Paul, b. 14 Nov. 1923, Chicago, Illinois, USA; Private Practitioner, Psychiatry; Consultant; Medical Director. m. 1948, 3 children. *Education:* MD, 1949, MS, 1953, State University of Iowa; Intern, US Marine Hospital, 1949-50; Residencies in Psychiatry, State University of Iowa, 1950-53. *Appointments include:* Visiting Lectures: Traverse City State Hospital, Michigan, 1960-70; Pontiac State Hospital, 1960-70; Northville State Hospital, 1960-70. Psychiatric Consultant: US Public Health Service Hospital and Clinic, Detroit, 1958-74; Organiser and Chief, Senior Attending Physician, 1958-70, Consultant, 1970-74, Detroit Memorial Hospital; Associate Staff, San Francisco General Hospital, 1974-; Active Staff, Highland General Hospital, California, 1976; Active Attending Staff, Presbyterian Hospital of Pacific Medical Center, 1975-; Attending Staff, Herrick Hospital, 1979-; Mount Zion Hospital, 1982-; Medical Director, Occupational Stress Clinic, Institute for Labor and Mental Health, 1982-. Consultant to numerous Community organisations including: Family Service Agency, 1983-; Pacific Evaluation Group, 1984-. Private Practitioner, Psychiatry, Detroit, Michigan and San Francisco, California, 1957-; Clinical Professor, University of California, 1974-; Faculty, American College of Traditional Chinese Medicine, 1981-. *Memberships:* Numerous including: Fellow, American Psychiatry Association; American Orthopschiatric Association, American Association for Advancement of Science. *Publications:* Author of 65 scientific papers including 12 chapters in books and 75 health policy publications. Co-Author, "The Minds of the Chinese People". Member of various editorial boards. *Honours:* Recipient of numerous grants. *Address:* 77 Belgrave Avenue, San Francisco, CA 94117, USA.

LOWRY, Thomas Power, b. 24 Nov. 1932, Sacramento, California, USA. Leading Physician, Psychiatrist. m. Anthea Snyder, 26 Nov. 1967, Tijuana, Chihuahua, Mexico, 1 son. *Education:* AB 1954, MD 1957, Stanford University, USA. *Appointments:* Chief of Inpatient Psychiatry, Ross Hospital, Ross, California; Medical Director, New Mexico State Hospital; Assistant Clinical Professor of Psychiatry, University of California at San Francisco, San Francisco, California; Leading Physician, Napa State Hospital. *Membership:* Fellow, American Psychiatric Association. *Publications:* "Hyperventilation and Hysteria", 1967; "Camping Therapy", 1973; "The Clitoris", 1976; "The Classic Clitoris", 1978; "Isobutyl Nitrite", 1979. *Honour:* Survivor's Medal, Dipsea Race, 1985. *Hobbies:* Scuba diving; Genealogy. *Address:* PO Box 1744, Ross, CA 94957, USA.

LOWY, Frederick H, b. 1 Jan. 1933, Austria. Dean, Faculty of Medicine, University of Toronto. m. (1) Anne L. Cloudsley, 18 June 1965, Cincinnati, USA, 3 sons, (2) Mary K. O'Neil, 1 June 1975, Toronto, 1 daughter. *Education:* BA, 1955, MD, CM, 1959, McGill University, Montreal; American Board of Psychiatry and Neurology, 1967; Certificate, Royal College of Physicians & Surgeons of Canada, 1965. *Appointments:* Lecturer, Assistant Professor, Psychiatry McGill University; Staff Psychiatrist, Royal Victoria Hospital, Montreal; Associate Professor, Professor, Psychiatry, University of Ottawa, Chief, Psychiatry, Ottawa Civic Hospital; Professor, Chairman, Psychiatry, University of Toronto, Director, Clarke Institute of Psychiatry, Toronto; Dean, Faculty of Medicine University of Toronto. *Memberships:* Canadian Medical and Psychiatric Associations; American Psychiatric Association; American Psychosomatic Society; American Association for Advancement of Science; International Psycho-Analytical Society. *Publications:* Co-Author, "A Method of Psychiatry", 1980; Numerous articles in professional journals. *Honours:* Alpha Omega Alpha, 1958; Elected Fellow, American College of Psychiatrists and American College of Psychoanalysts, 1978. *Hobbies:* Reading; Music; Sports. *Address:* Medical Sciences Building, University of Toronto, Toronto, Ontario, Canada M5S 1A1.

LØYNING, Yngve, b. 6 Feb 1929, Oslo, Norway. Director, The National Centre for Epilepsy. m. Alvhild Seglem, 18 Dec 1954, Oslo, 4 sons. *Education:* MD, Oslo University, 1954; PhD, Australian National University, Canberra, Australia, 1966; Specialist, Neurology 1969, Clinical Neurophysiology 1972. *Appointments:* Intern, Departments for Internal Medicine and Lung Diseases, Oslo and Bergen, Norway, 1955-60; Part-time Commander, Submarine and Diving Medical Officer, The Norwegian Navy, 1957-62; Research Fellow, Institute for Neurophysiology, Oslo, 1960-62; Research Fellow, Australian National University, Canberra, 1962-65; Reader, Institute for Physiology, Oslo University, 1966; Intern, Departments for Neurology, Psychiatry and Clinical Neurophysiology, Oslo University Hospital, 1966-70; Resident, Laboratory for Clinical Neurophysiology 1971-74, Director 1974-, The National Centre for Epilepsy, Consultant; Department of Neurology, The National Hospital, Oslo University, 1974-85. *Memberships:* National Societies for Physiology, Clinical Neurophysiology, Neurology and Epilepsy. *Publications:* Articles on cold acclimatisation, neurophysiology of the hippocampus, effects of barbiturates and hypoxia on synaptic transmission, physical fitness, hyperbaric oxygenation, decompression in diving, myasthenia, treatment of epilepsy, EEG in epilepsy, 1958-73. *Address:* The National Centre for Epilepsy, 1301 Sandvika, Norway.

LUBIN, Bernard, b. 15 Oct. 1923, USA. University Professor. m. Alice Wiesbord, 5 Aug. 1957, Bellefontaine, Pennsylvania. *Education:* BA, Psychology, 1952, MA, Psychology, 1953, George Washington University; PhD, Psychology, Pennsylvania State University, 1958. *Appointments include:* Professor of Medicine and Director of Psychology, Greater Kansas City Mental Health Foundation, Kansas City, 1967-74; Professor of Psychology and Medicine and Director of Clinical Psychology Program, Department of Psychology, University of Houston, Houston, Texas, 1974-76; Professor of Psychology and Medicine and Chairman, Department of Psychology, University of Missouri at Kansas City, Kansas City, 1976-83. *Memberships:* Fellow, American Psychological Association; Fellow, American Group Psychotherapy Association; Fellow, American Association for the Advancement of Science. *Publications:* More than 164 publications including 6 books. *Honours:* N T Veatch Award for

Distinguished Research and Creative Activity, 1981; UKC Trustees Research Fellowship, 1984; Faculty Community Service Fellowship, 1985. *Hobbies:* Music; Reading; Drama. *Address:* 5319 Holmes Street, Kansas City, MO 64110, USA.

LUCCI, Joseph Anthony, Junior, b. 21 Aug. 1921, Italy. Academic Chief of Obstetrics and Gynaecology, St Joseph Hospital; Clinical Professor of Obstetrics and Gynaecology, University of Texas Medical School at Houston. m. Joan Evelyn Smith, 7 Mar. 1957, Houston, 2 sons, 3 daughters. *Education:* BS, St Peter's College, Jersey City, 1943; MD, Marquette University School of Medicine (now Medical College of Wisconsin), 1946. *Appointments:* Assistant Gynaecologist, 1953-57, Associate Gynaecologist, 1957-68, University of Texas M D Anderson Hospital and Tumor Institute; Consultant in Gynaecology-Obstertrics, 1968-; Clinical Associate Professor, University of Texas Medical Branch, Galveston, 1968-; Clinical Associate Professor, University of Texas Medical School at Houston, 1970-72; Clinical Professor of Obstetrics and Gynaecology, University Medical School at Houston, 1973-. *Memberships:* Herman Johnson Obstetrics-Gynaecology Society; Houston Academy of Medicine; Texas Medical Association; Harris County Medical Society; Houston Gynaecology-Obstetrics Society; Houston Surgical Society. *Publications include:* "Why a New Women's Hospital", 'St Joseph Hospital Medical Surgery Journal', December 1977; 'Carcinoma in Situ of the Cervix: Review of 326 Cases', December 1979; 'Prune Belly Syndrome: Report of Two Cases', 'The Medical Journal of St Joseph Hospital', December 1979. *Address:* Medical Education Department, 1919 LaBranch, Houston, TX 77002, USA.

LUDAN, Arturo, b. 20 May 1938, Philippines. Chairman, Department of Paediatrics. m. Maria Victoria Chanco, 1 June 1963, Manila, Philippines, 1 son, 2 daughters. *Education:* MD. *Appointments:* Assistant Clinical Instructor, Albert Einstein College of Medicine, 1966-67; Instructor, 1968-70, Assistant Professor, 1978-80, Clinical Assistant Professor, 1980-, University of the Philippines College of Medicine; Professorial Lecturer, University of the East College of Medicine, 1973-85; currently, Chairman, Department of Paediatrics, Cardinal Santos Memorial Hospital. *Memberships:* Editor-in-Chief, past Board of Trustees member, Philippine Pediatric Society. *Publications:* "A Digest of Pediatric Literature on Diarrheas", 1974; Contributor of chapters to "Textbook of Pediatrics", 1st and 2nd editions, 1976, 82, "Handbook of Rehydration", 1979 and "Manual for Physicians", 1985. *Honours:* Outstanding Young Men of the Philippines Awardee in Medicine, TOYM, 1977. *Address:* Department of Pediatrics, Cardinal Santos Memorial Hospital, Wilson Street, Greenhills, San Juan, Metro Manila, Philippines.

LUDBROOK, John, b. 30 Aug. 1929, New Zealand. Research Institute Director. m. Judith Ann Whitworth, 24 Aug. 1981, Melbourne, Australia, 1 daughter (1 son, 2 daughters by previous marriage). *Education:* MD, ChM, DSc, BMed.Sc., University of Otago, New Zealand; FRCS; FRACS. *Appointments:* Professor of Surgery, University of New South Wales, Australia, 1964-69; Professor of Surgery, University of Adelaide, 1969-80; Associate Director, Baker Medical Research Institute, Australia, 1980-. *Memberships:* Fellow, Member of Court of Honour, Royal Australasian College of Surgeons. *Publications:* "Aspects of Venous Functions in the Lower Limbs", 1966; "Guide to House Surgeons in the Surgical Unit", 8th edition, 1985; Scientific articles on cardiovascular physiology and disease. *Honour:* Professor Emeritus, University of Adelaide, 1981. *Hobbies:* Cooking; Italian. *Address:* Baker Medical Research Institute, PO Box 348, Prahran 3181, Victoria, Australia.

LUECKEN, Peter Grant, b. 18 Jan. 1950, Brooklyn, New York, USA. Doctor of Chiropractic. m. Roxanne Sammis, 20 Sep. 1975. *Education:* BA, Hofstra University, 1972; DC, New York Chiropractic College, 1975; Diplomate, National Board of Chiropractic Examiners; Fellow, American Chiropractic College. *Appointments:* Director of Program Development and Alumni Affairs, New York Chiropractic College, 1975-78; Associate, Rockaway Chiropractic Clinic, 1976-78; Director, Fairfield Chiropractic Office, 1978-. *Memberships:* Kentuckiana Children's Center, Member, Advisory Board; New York Chiropractic College Alumni Association, Board of Directors; Fairfield Chamber of Commerce, Vice-President, Director; Parker Chiropractic Research Foundation; American Chiropractic Association; Connecticut Chiropractic Association; International and Connecticut Arabian Horse Association; Pyramid Society. *Publications:* Article: 'Chiropractic and Sports Medicine' in 'Work Out Magazine'; Lecture tapes: "Attitudes of Health and Success". *Honours:* Kentucky Colonel, Commonwealth of Kentucky, 1976; Distinguished Service Citation, New York Chiropractic College, 1977; VIP Award, Fairfield Chamber of Commerce, 1981. *Hobbies:* Breeding Eygptian Arabian Horses; Opera. *Address:* 527 Tunxis Hill Road, Fairfield, CT 06430, USA.

LUGER, Anton F H, b. 20 Sep. 1918, Vienna, Austria. Head, Ludwig Boltzmann Institute for Dermato-Venereological Serodiagnosis. m. Margith Widy, 28 Dec. 1947, 2 sons. *Education:* A O University Professor, University of Vienna; Dr. Med. *Appointments:* Head, Department of Dermatology, Krankenhaus der stadt Nien-Lainz, 1963-85; Head, Ludwig Boltzmann Institute for Dermatovenereological Serodiagnosis, 1965-; President, International Union Against The Venereal Diseases and the Treponematoses, 1983-. *Memberships:* Executive Committee: International Society for Std. Research; Austrian Dermatological Society; Austrian Society for Tropical Medicine. *Publications:* Author of 253 papers; Books: "Antibiotic Treatment of Venereal Diseases", 1968; "Cytostatica in der Dermatologie", 1977; "Genitale Kontaktinfektienen", 1983; "Treponemal Infections", 1982; "Dermatologische Onkologie", 1983; "Infektionen mit Chlamydia Trachonatis", 1985. *Honours include:* Goldenes Ehrenzeichen Stadt Wien, 1979; Schaudinn Plakette Derm. Ges. GDR, 1981; Hofrat, 1983; Cidesco Preis, 1983. *Hobbies:* Classical Music; Archaeology. *Address:* Florianigasse 58, A-1080 Vienna, Austria.

LUGER, Thomas A, b. 6 Oct. 1950, Vienna, Austria. University Professor. m. Beatrice M Engel, 21 Nov. 1981, 1 son, 1 daughter. *Education:* MD, University of Vienna, Austria, 1975; Post Doctoral training, National Institute of Dental Research, Bethesda, USA, 1980-82. *Appointments:* Resident, Department of Internal Medicine, Vienna, Austria, 1975-76; Resident Assistant, Institute for Cancer Research, University of Vienna, 1976; Resident, Department of Plastic Surgery, 1976; Resident, Department of Urology, Vienna, 1977; Resident, Department Derm. II, University of Vienna, 1977-82; Staff Member, 1982-, Assistant Professor, 1984-. *Memberships:* Austrian Society of Allergy and Immunology; European Society of Derm. Research; Austrian Society of Dermatology; American Federation for Clinical Research; Society of Dermatological Research; American Association of Immunology; German Society of Dermatology; Society of Invest. Dermatology. *Publications include:* Author and co-author of numerous articles in professional journals; including 'HPLC Separation of Distinct Epidermal Cell Derived Cytokines' in "Journal of Chromatography", 1985; 'Characterization of the Immune Defect in Patients with Haemophilia' in 'Journal of Clinical Investigation', 1985; 'Human Epidermal cells synthesize HLA-DR alloantigens in vitro upon stimulation with y-Interferon' in 'Journal of Investigative Dermatology', 1985, etc. *Honours:* Visiting Fellowship, Max Kade Foundation, New York, USA; Denk Award, 1978; Hebra Award, 1982; Aesca Award, 1984. *Hob-

bies: Classical Music; Tennis; Skiing. *Address:* A-1080 Vienna, Florianigasse 58, Austria.

LUI, Sammy Sek-Chiu, b. 6 Feb 1950, Macau. Doctor of Chiropractic. *Education:* Doctor of Chiropractic, Palmer College of Chiropractic, Davenport, Iowa, USA. *Memberships:* Member, American Chiropractic Association; Canadian Chiropractic Association; Australian Chiropractic Association; Hong Kong Chiropractors' Association; Council on Roentenology of ACA. *Hobbies:* Tennis; Travel; Swimming. *Address:* Room 1205, 12/FL, Hanglung Centre, 2-20 Paterson Street, Causeway Bay, Hong Kong.

LUISADA, Aldo A, b. 26 June 1901, Florence, Italy. Distinguished Professor. m. Anna Passigli, 12 Apr 1931, Bologna, 1 son.*Education:* MD, Medical School, Royal University, Florence, 1924. *Appointments:* Instructor, Medicine, Royal University Medical School, Padua, 1927-30; Assistant Professor, Associate Professor, Medicine, Royal University of Naples, 1930-35; Professor, Chairman, Medicine, University of Sassari, and then Ferrara, Italy, 1935-38; Instructor, Physiology and Pharmacology, Tufts College of Medicine, Boston, USA, 1943-49; Associate Professor to Full Professor, Medicine, Chairman, Medicine, Mount Sinai Hospital, Chairman, Cardiovascular Research, Chicago Medical School, 1949-71; Chairman, Cardiology, Oak Forest Hospital, 1971-83; Distinguished Professor, Physiology and Medicine, Chicago Medical School, 1972-. *Memberships:* Fellow: American Medical Association; American College of Physicians; American Association for the Advancement of Science; American Heart Association, Council of Clinical Cardiology; American College of Cardiology, Trustee; American College of Angiology, Charter Member; American College of Chest Physicians; American Physiological Society; Institute of Medicine of Chicago; Sigma Xi; Alpha Omega Alpha, Charter Member; Member, numerous other professional organisations. *Publications:* "Cardiologia", 1938; "Heart", 1949, 2nd Edition 1954; "The Heart Beat", 1953; "Differential Diagnosis of Cardiovascular Diseases", co-author, 1965; "A Primer of Cardiac Examination", 1968; Author, numerous Monographs, Chapters of Books, and over 420 Scientific Publications.*Honours:* Recipient, numerous honours and awards including: Morris Parker Award for Research, 1953; Gold Medal for exhibit at AMA Meeting, 1954; Honorary Citizen, City of Agropoli, Italy, 1971; Senior Citizen, Chicago Hall of Fame, 1971; Grand Marshal, Commencement, Chicago Medical School, 1979-85; Honorary Staff Member, St Mary of Nazareth Hospital, Chicago, 1977; Distinguished Member, Honorary Staff, Michael Reese Hospital, 1985. *Address:* 5000 South Cornell Avenue, Chicago, IL 60615, USA.

LUKASEWYCZ, Omelan Alexander, b. 28 Sep. 1942, Mostyska, Poland. Assistant Dean for Curriculum Affairs; Associate Professor, Medical Microbiology and Immunology. m. Marta de Sas Tatomyr, 25 May 1968, Philadelphia, Pennsylvania, USA, 1 son, 1 daughter. *Education:* BA, Biology, St Joseph's College, Philadelphia, 1964; MSc, Physiology, Villanova University, 1968; PhD, Microbiology, Physiology and Genetics, Bryn Mawr College, 1972; Postdoctoral Scholar, Immunology, University of Michigan School of Medicine, 1972-75; College Management Program, Carnegie-Mellon University, Summer 1983. *Appointments:* Substitute High School Teacher, 1965-68; Trainee, National Institute of Infectious Diseases, Bryn Mawr College, 1968-70; Research Scientist Assistant, University of Texas, 1970-72; Research Associate/Postdoctoral Scholar, University of Michigan School of Medicine, 1972-75; Lecturer, University of Michigan, 1973-75; Assistant Professor, Medical Microbiology and Immunology, University of Minnesota, 1975-78; Assistant Dean for Curricular Affairs, School of Medicine, 1977-; Associate Professor, Department of Medical Microbiology and Immunology, 1978-. *Memberships:* American Association for the Advancement of Science; American Association for Immunologists; American

Association for Laboratory Animal Science; American Chemical Society; American Society for Microbiology; Federation of American Societies for Experimental Biology; Sigma Xi; Society of Teachers of Family Medicine. *Publications:* Contributor to professional journals; Presentations; Proceedings. *Honours include:* Academic Scholarship to St Joseph's College, 1960-64; Minnesota Medical Foundation Teacher of Year, 1977 and 1982; Honorable Mention for Basic Science Teacher of the Year, 1976, 79, 80, 81 and 83; Bush Foundation Summer Fellowship, 1983. *Hobbies:* Jogging; Downhill and Cross-country Skiing; Marathon Running. *Address:* School of Medicine, University of Minnesota, Duluth, MN 55812, USA.

LUNDBERG, Dag Bror Anders, b. 10 Feb. 1940, Arvika, Sweden. Professor and Chairman, Department of Anaesthesiology. m. Marie Hedberg, 11 Jan. 1975, 1 son, 2 daughters. *Education:* MD, Medical School, 1967, PhD, Pharmacology, 1970, Uppsala University. *Appointments:* Various teaching positions, Department of Pharmacology, University of Uppsala, 1964-70; Resident, Associate Professor, University of Goteborg, 1970-81; Visiting Professor, Department of Anesthesiology, University of North Carolina, Chapel Hill, North Carolina, USA, 1977-78; Professor and Chairman, Department of Anesthesiology, University Hospital, Lund, Sweden, currently. *Memberships:* Swedish and Scandinavian Societies of Anesthesiologists; European Academy of Anesthesiology; International and European Shock Societies; Swedish Society of Pharmacologists. *Publications:* Author of over 100 publications including books and papers on pharmacology, physiology and anesthesiology. *Honour:* Whasser Medal, Uppsala University, Sweden, 1970. *Hobbies:* Jogging; Tennis; Sailing. *Address:* Department of Anaesthesiology, University Hospital, S-22185 Lund, Sweden.

LUNDBERG, Per Olov Magnus, b. 12 Apr. 1931, Vänersborg, Sweden. Professor & Head, Department of Neurology, University Hospital, Uppsala. m. Kerstie, 4 Dec. 1960, Copenhagen, Denmark, 2 daughters. *Education:* MD, 1957; D.Med.sci. 1960, Uppsala University. *Appointments include:* Professor & Head Physician, Department of Neurology, University Hospital, Uppsala, 1974-; Medical Director, ibid, 1978-83; Scientific adviser, National Board of Health & Welfare, 1975-. *Memberships:* Secretary 1963-72, Uppsala Medical Society; Chairman 1968-70, Swedish Neurological Society; Founding member, President, Scandinavian Migraine Society; Member, International Society of Psychoneuroendocrinology, International Academy of Sex Research. *Publications:* Thesis, "Corticohypothalamic connections in the rabbit", 1960; "Updating in Headache", with V.Pfaffenrath & O.Sjaastad, 1985; Numerous publications in neuroanatomy, clinical neurology, neuroendocrinology, sexology. *Honour:* Member, Uppsala County Council, 1974-85. *Hobby:* Ornithology. *Address:* Tallbacksvägen 19, S-752 45 Uppsala, Sweden.

LUNDIN, Andrew Peter, b. 4 Jan. 1944, Kansas City, Missouri, USA. Associate Professor of Medicine, Downstate Medical Centre, Brooklyn. m. Maureen Fitzgerald, 14 Sep. 1974, Glens Falls, New York. *Education:* AB, Stanford University, 1968; MD, Downstate Medical Centre, 1972; Residency, King's County Hospital, Brooklyn, 1972-74; Fellowship, Nephrology & Transplant Immunology, Peter Bent Brigham Hospital, Boston, 1974-76. *Appointments include:* Chief, Haemodialysis, Brooklyn VA Hospital, 1977-80; Director, Ambulatory Haemodialysis, Downstate Medical Centre, 1980-. *Memberships:* American & New York Societies of Nephrology; American Society of Artificial Internal Organs; International Society of Nephrology; American Society of Transplant Physicians; Association for the Advancement of Medical Instrumentation, Council on Transplantation.

Publications include: Various papers, contributions to medical journals, eg, 'Chronic Renal Failure in Current Therapy', 1983, 1984. *Honours:* Summa cum laude, Downstate, 1972; Frank L. Babbott Alumni Award, distinguished service, 1982. *Hobbies:* Reading history; Travel; Gardening. *Address:* Downstate Medical Centre, Box 52, 450 Clarkson Avenue, Brooklyn, NY 11203, USA.

LUNN, John Neville, b. 29 Sep. 1933, Uxbridge, Middlesex, England, Editor of Anaesthesia; Reader in Anaesthetics, University of Wales College of Medicine; Honorary Consultant Anaesatist, South Glamorgan Health District, m. Anne Elizabeth Nicholson, 5 Jan 1963, Barningham, 2 sons. *Education:* MB, Westminster Hospital Medical School; BS, University of London, 1956; MRCS, LRCP, 1956; DA (RCS), 1958; FFARCS, 1962; MD, 1968. *Appointments:* Research Fellowships at the University of Pittsburgh, USA, the Welsh National School of Medicine, Cardiff, Wales and the University of Newcastle upon Tyne, England. *Memberships:* Association of Anaesthetists of Great Britain and Ireland; Royal Society of Medicine; British Medical Association. *Publications:* "Lecture Notes in Anaesthetics", 1972, 1982, 1986; 'Mortality associated with anaesthesia', (with W W Mushin), 1979; "Quality of Care in Anaesthetic Practice", 1984. *Hobbies:* Gardening; Bird watching; Classical music. *Address:* Department of Anaesthetics, University of Wales College of Medicine, Heath Park, Cardiff CF4 4XN, Wales.

LUNTZ, Maurice Harold, b. 27 July 1930, Republic of South Africa. Clinical Professor, Director of Ophthalmology. m. Angela June R Myerson, 22 June 1956, Johannesburg, 2 sons, 1 daughter. *Education:* MB, BCh, University of Cape Town, 1952; MD, University of Witwatersrand, Johannesburg, 1957; Diplomate, American Board of Ophthalmology, 1978; DOMS. *Appointments:* Lecturer in Ophthalmology, University of Oxford, Oxford, England, 1957-64; Professor and Chairman of Ophthalmology, University of Witwatersrand, Johannesburg, Republic of South Africa, 1964-78; Clinical Professor and Director of Ophthalmology, Mount Sinai School of Medicine, Beth Israel Medical Center, New York, New York, USA, 1978-. *Memberships include:* Fellow, Royal College of Surgeons, England; Fellow, American College of Surgeons; Ophthalmological Society, South Africa; Ophthalmological Society, United Kindgom; Oxford Ophthalmological Society; American Academy of Ophthalmology; International Microsurgery Study Group; International Council of Ophthalmology; Academia Ophthalmologica Internationalis. *Publications:* 5 books, 1972-85; 120 articles in scientific journals, 1957-85; 10 teaching movies. *Honours:* Officer, Order of Saint John of Jerusalem, 1977; Conrad Behrens Prize. *Hobbies:* Tennis; Map collecting. *Address:* 121 East 60th Street, New York, NY 10022, USA.

LUZZATTO, Lucio, b. 28 Sep. 1936, Genova. Professor of Haematology. m. Paolo Caboara, 9 Sep. 1963, 1 son, 1 daughter. *Education:* Maturita classica, Liceo Doria, Genova, 1953; MD, University of Genova, 1959; Special degree in Haematology, Pavia, 1962; Libera docenza, Biochemistry, Italian Ministry of Education, 1965. *Appointments:* Assistant, Biochemistry, Biophysics, University of Genova, 1960-62; Research Fellow, Haematology, Columbia, University, USA, 1963-64; Lecturer then Professor, Department of Haematology, University of Ibadan, 1964-74; Director, International Institute of Genetics and Biophysics, CNR, Naples, 1974-81; Professor of Haematology, Royal Post Graduate Medical School, London, 1981-. *Memberships:* Fellow, Royal College of Physicians; Fellow, Royal College of Pathologists; International Society of Haematology; British Society of Haematology; Honorary Member of the Nigerian and Italian Societies of Haematology. *Publications:* Editor: "Haematology in Tropical Areas" 1981; Editor: "Molecular Biology of Parasites" 1983; About 130 papers in scientific journals. *Honours:* Livierato Prize, University of Genoa, 1957; Pasetto Prize, University of Genoa, 1958; 1st Nazionale Assistenza Infortuni sul Lavoro Prize 1960; Carlo Erba Fellow 1961; Ministero della Publica Istruzione Fellow, 1962; Fulbright Senior Fellow, 1967; Henry M Stratton Lecture. XV Int. Congress of Haematology, 1974; Pius XI Medal 1976; Sanremo Int. Prize for Human Genetics, 1982. *Address:* Department of Haematology, Royal Postgraduate Medical School, Ducane Road, London W12 0HS, England.

M

MAANY, Iraj, b. 21 May 1941, Tehran, Iran. Assistant Professor. m. Iran, 18 June 1971, Tehran, 1 son, 1 daughter. *Education:* MD; Post-doctoral Fellowships in Psychopharmacology and in Behaviour Therapy. *Appointments:* Internship, 1969-70; Psychiatric Residency, 1970-73; Post-doctoral Fellowship, 1973-74; Assistant Professor, MCP, 1974-76; Assistant Professor, University of Pennsylvania, 1976-. *Memberships:* American Psychiatric Association; Chester County Neuro-Psychiatric Society. *Publications:* 'Treatment of Depression, Briquet's Syndrome', (co-author), 1981; 'Syndrome of Tardivo Dyskinesia', 1977; 'A Study of Growth Hormone Release in Depression Neuropsychobiology', (co-author), 1979. *Honour:* Veterans Appreciation Award, 1985. *Hobbies:* Horseback-riding; Hunting; Swimming. *Address:* PVAMC7E, University and Woodland Avenues, Philadelphia, PA 19104, USA.

MACARTNEY, Fergus James, b. 7 Dec. 1940, Uganda. Professor of Paediatric Cardiology. m. Jacqueline Grace Hooper, 28 Dec. 1963, Guildford, Surrey, England, 3 daughters. *Education:* BA, Cambridge University 1963; MD, B Chir, Cambridge University/St Thomas' Hospital; MRCP 1968, FRCP 1977, MA 1984. *Appointments:* House Physician, Medical Unit, St Thomas's Hospital; House Surgeon, West Norwich Hospital; SHO in Cardiology, Kilbingbeck Hospital, Leeds; Registrar in Cardiology, Brompton Hospital, London; Fellow in Paediatric Cardiology, Mayo Clinic, USA; Consultant in Paediatric Cardiology, General Infirmary and Killingbeck Hospital, Vandervell/British Heart Foundation, Leeds; Professor of Paediatric Cardiology, Institute of Child Health, London; Honorary Consultant, Hospital for Sick Children, Great Ormond Street, London. *Memberships:* Fellow, Royal College of Physicians; Fellow, American College of Cardiology; Scientific Secretary, Association of European Paediatric Cardiologists; British Cardiac Society; British Paediatric Association. *Publications:* "Paediatric Cardiology" vol 5, 1983; "Paediatric Cardiology" 1986. Author of over 80 invited chapters and over 120 original articles. *Honours:* Frodsham Scholarship, Queens' College, Cambridge; 1959; Foundation Scholarship, 1962; Melsome Memorial Prize, 1963; Open Scholarship, St Thomas's Hospital, 1963; Beaney, Pinniger, Seymour Graves Toller Prizes, St Thomas's Hospital, 1966. *Hobbies:* Photography; Nature study; Gardening; Carpentry; Car Maintenance; Singing; Preaching; Composing songs. *Address:* The Hospital for Sick Children, Great Ormond Street, London WC1N 3JH, England.

McBRIDE, Herbert, b. 29 Dec. 1938, Elizabeth, New Jersey, USA. m. Nancy O'Neill, 1 Feb. 1964, Elizabeth, New Jersey, USA, 2 sons, 3 daughters. *Education:* BA, Rutgers University, New Brunswick, USA, 1960; MD, Georgetown University School of Medicine, Washington, DC, 1978. *Appointments:* Assistant Clinical Professor, Psychiatry, Rutgers Medical School, New Jersey, 1982-; Medical Director, New Beginnings, 1982-; Diplomat in Psychiatry of American Board of Psychiatry and Neurology, 1984; Chairman, Impaired Physicians Committee, New Jersey Medical Society, 1985; Clinical Director, Dover Institute of Psychiatry. *Memberships:* American Psychiatric Association; American Medical Association; American Medical Society on Alcoholism and other Drug Dependencies. *Publications:* 'Glucoproteins in Brain Tumours' in 'Neurology' volume 15, 1965; 'Differential Alcoholics according to MBD, Family History and Drinking Patterns' in 'Archives of American Psychiatry', 1977. *Honour:* Alpha Omega Alpha Hon Medical Society. *Hobbies:* Sports. *Address:* No 4 Tunesbrook Drive, Toms River, NJ 08753, USA.

McCANN, Barbara Sue, b. 17 June 1957, Mount Vernon, Ohio, USA. Postdoctoral Fellow, Clinical Research Training. *Education:* BA Honours Psychology, University of Michigan, 1979; MS 1982, PhD 1984, Psychology, Rutgers University, New Jersey. *Appointments:* Research Assistant Alcohol Behavior Research Laboratory 1979-80; Visiting Lecturer 1983, Rutgers University, New Jersey; Biofeedback Therapist, John F Kennedy Medical Center, Edison, 1980-82; Editor's Assistant, Consulting Editor, Behavioral Medicine Abstracts. *Memberships:* American Psychological Association; Society for Psychophysiological Research; Society of Behavioral Medicine; Behavioral Medicine Special Interest Group, Association for Advancement of Behavior Therapy. *Publications include:* 'Hemispheric Asymmetrics and Early Infantile Autism', 1981; 'Effects of Meditation and Progressive Relaxation on Self-reported and Behavioral Symptoms of Stress', (with R L Woolfolk, P M Lehrer and A J Rooney), 1982; 'Progressive Relaxation and Meditation: A Study of Psychophysiological and Therapeutic Differences Between Two Techniques', (with P M Lehrer, R L Woolfolk, A J Rooney and P Carrington), 1983. *Honour:* Martha Muenzer Memorial Award for Outstanding Work in Psychology, University of Michigan, 1978. *Hobbies:* Horseback Riding; Backpacking. *Address:* University of Pittsburgh, Western Psychiatric Institute and Clinic, 3811 O'Hara Street, Pittsburgh, PA 15213, USA.

McCARL, Deborah Louise, b. 11 June 1949, Cleveland, Ohio, USA. Obstetrician; Gynaecologist, Central Minnesota Group Health Plan. m. Phillip Charles Jennings, 6 Sep. 1969, St Paul, Minnesota, 1 daughter. *Education:* BA, University of Minnesota; MD, University of Minnesota Medical School. *Memberships:* American College of Obstetrics and Gynaecology; American Medical Womens Association; Physicians for Social Responsibility. *Honour:* CIBA Award, 1977. *Hobby:* Gardening. *Address:* 709 N River Rd, St Cloud, MN 56301, USA.

McCARTHY, Joseph, b. 28 June 1949, Jersey City, New Jersey, USA. Assistant Professor of Orthopaedic Surgery, Tufts New England Medical Centre, Boston, Massachusetts, m. Kathleen 16 June 1973, 1 son. *Education:* AB, University of Notre Dame, Indiana, 1967-71; MD, Georgetown University Medical School; Internship in Internal Medicine, Georgetown University, 1975-76; Assistant Resident General Surgery, 1976-77, Orthopaedic Surgery, 1977-80, Tufts Medical Centre, Boston, Massachusetts. *Appointments:* Reconstructive Joint Surgery Fellowship, Massachusetts General Hospital, Boston 1980-81; Assistant Professor, Tufts University Department of Orthopaedic Surgery, 1981-; Assistant Orthopaedist, New England Medical Centre, Boston, 1981-. *Memberships:* American Board of Orthopaedic Surgery, 1983; Fellow, American Academy of Orthopaedic Surgeons, 1985. *Publications:* 'Bony Ingrowth Fixation of the Acetabular Component in Canine Hip Joint Arthroplasty', 1983; 'Loosening of the Femoral Components of Total Hip Replacement after Plugging the Femoral Canaal', 1982; 'Total Hip Replacement in Patients under 30 years of age: A 5 year follow-up', 1981. *Address:* 96 Robbins Road, Watertown, MA 02172. USA

MACCARTY, William Carpenter, b. 7 June 1945, Hanover, New Hampshire, USA. Orthopaedic and hand surgeon. m. Jorise, 21 May 1983, South Boston, Virginia. *Education:* AB, Dartmouth College, 1967; MB, Dartmouth Medical School, 1969; MD, Harvard Medical School, 1971; Fellow, AAOS. *Appointments:* Chief of Orthopaedic and hand surgery, 121 EVAC Hospital, US Army, Seoul, Korea, 1976-78; Active Staff, Halifax-South Boston Community Hospital, South Boston, Virginia, 1978-. *Memberships:* Fellow, American Academy of Orthopaedic Surgeons; Virginia Orthopaedic Society; Southern Orthopaedic Society; Mayo Hand Club; 38th Parallel Medical Society. *Hobbies:* Hunting; Fishing; Archery; Farming. *Address:* 2202 A Beechmont, South Boston, VA 24592, USA.

McCARY, Roger Glynn, b. 2 Dec. 1942, Freeport, Texas, USA. Psychiatrist. m. Marsha Dingle McCary, 12 June 1965, Freeport, Texas, 2 daughters. *Education:* BA, University of Texas at Austin, 1964; MD, University of Texas Medical Branch, Galveston, 1968. *Appointments:* Internship Medicine, Los Angeles County, University of Southern California Medical Centre, 1968-69; Resident in Psychiatry, 1969-72, University of Texas Medical Branch, Galveston; Chief Mental Health, USAF Hospital, Kirtland, Albuquerque, New Mexico, 1972-74; Unit Clinical Director, Acute Care Centre, Shoal Creek Hospital, 1982-83; Medical Director, Shoal Creek Hospital, 1983-; Private Practice. *Memberships:* Fellow, American Psychiatric Association; Texas Psychiatric Society; Austin Psychiatric Society; Travis County Medical Society; Texas Medical Association; American Medical Association; Titus Harris Psychiatric Society; Central Neuropsychiatric Association. *Honour:* Fellowship, American Psychiatric Association, 1984. *Hobbies:* Jogging; Sailing. *Address:* 301 Medical Park Tower, Austin, TX 78705, USA.

McCAWLEY, Austin, b. 17 Jan. 1925, Greenock, Scotland. Director of Psychiatry, St Francis Hospital, Hartford, Connecticut, USA. m. Gloria Klein, 15 Feb. 1958, Douglaston, New York, 1 son, 1 daughter. *Education:* MB; ChB; DPM; DRCOG; FAPA; FACP. *Appointments:* Senior Clinical Director, Institute of Living, Hartford, Connecticut, 1963-66; Medical Director, Westchester Branch of St Vincent's Hospital, Harrison, New York, 1966-72; Professor of Psychiatry, University of Connecticut Medical School, 1983-. *Memberships:* Fellow, American Psychiatric Association; Charter Fellow, American College of Psychiatrists. *Publications:* 'Physician Burn Out', 1983; 'A Double Blind Evaluation of Nomifernsine and Imipramine in Depressed Outpatients' , 1979. *Hobbies:* Music; Golf. *Address:* Department of Psychiatry, St Francis Hospital, 114 Woodland Street, Hartford, CT 06105, USA.

McCLELLAN, Roger Orville, b. 5 Jan. 1937, Tracy, Minnesota, USA. Director and President, Research Institutes. m. Kathleen Mary Dunagan, 23 June 1962, Tenino, Washington, 1 son, 2 daughters. *Education:* DVM, Highest honours, Washington State University, 1960; Master of Management, University of New Mexico, 1980. *Appointments include:* Junior to Senior Scientist, Biology Laboratory, Hanford Laboratories, General Electric Company, Richland, Washington, 1957-64; Scientist, Medical Research Branch, Division of Biology and Medicine, US Atomic Energy Commission, Washington, 1965-66; Assistant Director of Research and Director, Fission Product Inhalation Programme, 1966-73, Vice President and Director of Research, 1973-76, President and Director, Inhalation Toxicology Research Institute, 1976-, Lovelace Biomedical and Environmental Research Institute, Albuquerque, New Mexico; Adjunct Professor, University of Arkansas Medical School, 1970-; Clinical Associate, University of New Mexico Medical School, 1971-; Adjunct Professor, College of Veterinary Medicine, Washington State University, 1980-. *Memberships include:* American Board of Toxicology, American Board of Veterinary Toxicology; Chairman, Committee on Toxicology, National Research Council; Executive Committee, US Environmental Protection Agency Science Advisory Board; National Council on Radiation Protection; Society of Toxicology; American Association for Aerosol Research; Society for Risk Analysis; Health Physics Society; Radiation Research Society. Fellow: American Association for Advancement of Science; American Academy of Veterinary and Comparative Toxicology. *Publications:* Author or co-author over 200 articles in major journals. *Honours:* Elda E Anderson Award, Health Physics Society, 1974; Herbert E Stokinger Award, American Conference of Governmental Industrial Hygienists, 1985. *Hobbies:* Travel; Gardening; Camping; Architecture. *Address:* Inhalation Toxicology Research Institute, Lovelace Biomedical and Environmental Research Institute, PO Box 5890, Albuquerque, NM 87185, USA.

McCLELLAND, Shearwood Jr, b. 1 Aug. 1947, Gary, Indiana, USA. Assistant Professor, Clinical Orthopaedic Surgery , Columbia University College of Physicians & Surgeons. m. Yvonne S Thornton, MD, 8 June 1974, New York, New York, 1 son, 1 daughter. *Education:* AB, Princeton University, 1969; MD, Columbia University, 1974; Diplomate, American Board of Orthopaedic Surgeons, 1981. *Appointments include:* Fellow, Total Joint Surgery, Ohio State University, 1982; Acting Chief, Orthopaedic Surgery, Harlem Hospital Centre, New York, 1983-84; Attending Surgeon, Department of Orthopaedic Surgery, Harlem Hospital Centre, 1984-. *Memberships:* Fellow: American College of Surgeons, International College of Surgeons, American Academy of Orthopaedic Surgeons, New York Academy of Medicine; Sigma Xi; Association of Military Surgeons, USA. *Publications include:* Contributions to 'Journal of Trauma', 'Orthopaedic Review', etc. *Honours:* Honour graduate, Princeton University, 1969; Elected full memberships, Sigma Xi, 1983. *Hobbies:* Reading; Photography; Basketball; Baseball. *Address:* Department of Orthopaedic Surgery, Harlem Hospital Centre, KP-9101, 506 Lenox Avenue, New York, NY 10037, USA.

McCOMBS, Rollin Koenig, b. 17 Aug. 1919, Denver, Colorado, USA. Radiotherapist, Long Beach Community Hospital. m. 20 Sep. 1952, Long Beach, 3 sons, 2 daughters. *Education:* BA, Chemistry, 1941, MA, Physics, 1944, University of Colorado; MD, Stanford University, 1954. *Appointments:* Instructor, Physics, University of Colorado, 1942-48; Intern, Surgery, Stanford University Hospitals, 1953-54; Research Fellow, Associate Physician, Donner Laboratory of Medical Physics, University of California, 1954-57; Resident, Staff, Long Beach Veterans Administration Hospital, 1957-67; Radiotherapist, Long Beach Community Hospital, 1967-; Associate Clinical Professor, Radiology, 1983-, University of Southern California School of Medicine. *Memberships:* American Medical Association; British Institute of Radiology; American College of Radiology; American College of Nuclear Medicine; Society of Nuclear Medicine; American Society of Therapeutic Radiology & Oncology; American Association of Physical Medicine. *Publications:* "Experimental Observations of the Effects on Heart Action of an Electronic Pacemaker and Defibrillator", 'Surgical Forum', 1952; "Proton Irradiation of the Pituitary and its Metabolic Effects", 'Radiology', 1957; "Über die Verwendung radioaktiver Isotope in der Hamatologie", 'Handbuch der gesamten Hamatologie', 1960. *Honours:* Phi Beta Kappa, 1942; Sigma Xi, 1946; Memorial Fund Lecturer, America 1956; etc. *Hobbies:* Model Railroading; Guns & Target Shooting. *Address:* Dept of Radiation Oncology, Long Beach Community Hospital, 1720 Termino Avenue, Long Beach, CA 90804, USA.

McCORMACK, Judith Gail, b. 4 Oct. 1939, Chicago, Illinois, USA. Company Vice-President. m. Robert George McCormack, 17 Sep. 1960, Westchester. *Education:* BS, Roosevelt University; Medical Technology, Mount Sinai Hospital; MT (ASCP) I, Medical Technology and Immunology Certification, ASCP. *Appointments:* Serology Supervisor, Mount Sinai Hospital, Chicago, Illinois; Serology Supervisor, Memorial Hospital of DuPage County, Elmhurst; Immunovirology Supervisor, Lutheran General Hospital, Park Ridge; Immunology Supervisor, Elmhurst Memorial Hospital, Elmhurst; Currently Vice-President, Bion Enterprises Limited, Park Ridge. *Memberships:* American Society of Clinical Pathology; American Society of Microbiology, South Central Association for Clinical Microbiology. *Publication:* 'The place of Epstein-Barr virus testing in a clinical laboratory' in 'Laboratory Medicine', 1977. *Address:* 5 Oak Brook Club Drive, Oak Brook, IL 60521, USA.

McCORMICK, Donald Bruce, b. 15 July 1932, Front Royal, Virginia, USA. Executive Associate Dean for Science; Chairman of Biochemistry; Fuller E Callaway Professor, Emory University School of Medicine, 1985-. m. Norma Jean Dunn, 6 June 1955, St Louis, Missouri, 2 sons, 1 daughter. *Education:* AB, 1953, PhD, 1958, Vanderbilt University, Nashville, Tennessee; Postdoctoral Fellow, University of California, Berkeley, 1958-60. *Appointments:* Assistant Professor, 1960-63, Associate Professor, 1963-69, Professor, 1969-79, Graduate School of Nutrition and Section of Biochemistry, Cornell University, Ithaca, New York; Visiting Lecturer, University of Illinois, Urbana, Illinois, 1963; Visiting Professor, Universities of Basel, Switzerland and Wagenigen, The Netherlands, 1966-67. *Memberships:* American Association for the Advancement of Science; American Chemical Society; American Institute Biological Science; American Institute of Chemistry; American Institute of Nutrition; American Society Biological Chairman; American Society Microbiology; American Society of Photobiology; Biophysics Society; New York Academy of Science; Sigma Xi; Society of Experimental Biological Medicine. *Publications:* "Vitamins and Coenzymes", (Editor and author), 1970-71; 1979-80; 1986; "Vitamins and Hormones", (Editor and author), 1984-; Contributor of over 300 articles in professional journals; Editorial board member of several journals. *Honours:* 1st Prize of TN Academy of Science, 1947; Bausch and Lomb Award, 1947; Westinghouse Science Scholarship, 1950; NIH predoctoral Fellowship, 1957; NIH Postdoctoral Fellowship, 1958; Guggenheim Fellowship, 1966; Mead Johnson Award, 1970; Osborne and Mendel Award, 1978; Kiberty Hyde Bailey Professor, 1978; Wellcome Visiting Professor, University of Florida, 1986. *Hobbies:* Nature study; Gardening; Travel. *Address:* 2245 Deer Ridge Drive, Stone Mountain, GA 30087, USA.

McCORMICK, James Stevenson, b. 9 May 1926, Dublin, Republic of Ireland, Professor of Community Health, Trinity College, University of Dublin. m. Elizabeth Ann Dimond, 11 Sep. 1954, Fleet, Hampshire, England, 3 sons, 1 daughter. *Education:* MA; MB BCh, Cambridge; MRCPI; FRCPI; MRCGP; FRCGP; MFCM; FFCM. *Appointments:* House Physician, St Mary's Hospital, London, England; Captain, Royal Army Medical Corps; House Surgeon, Royal Sussex County Hospital; General Practice, Leicestershire, England and County Wicklow, Republic of Ireland; Professor of Social and Preventive Medicine; Professor of Community Health; Dean of the School of Physics. *Memberships:* Vice-Chairman of Council, Royal College of General Practitioners; General Medical Council; Medical Council of Ireland; Chairman, National Health Council; President, Irish College of General Practitioners. *Publications:* "The Doctor: Father Figure and Plumber", 1978; "Living Together"; "Holy Dread"; "Science and Medicine". *Honours:* James Mackenzie Lecturer, RCGP, 1974; Albert Wander Lecturer, RSM, 1975; Foundation Council Award, RCGP, 1985. *Address:* The Barn, Windgates, Bray, County Wicklow, Republic of Ireland.

McCORMICK, Kenneth James, b. 11 Sep. 1937, Toledo, Ohio, USA. Research Associate Professor, Otolaryngology. m. Nancy L Kellett, 15 June 1963, New Ulm, Minnesota, 1 son, 2 daughters. *Education:* BS, University of Toledo, Ohio, 1959; MS 1962, PhD 1965, University of Michigan, Ann Arbor, Michigan. *Appointments:* Instructor to Associate Professor, Baylor College of Medicine, Houston, Texas, 1965-75; Associate Laboratory Director, St Joseph's Hospital Laboratory for Cancer Research, Houston, 1975-80; Adjunct Associate Professor, Baylor College of Medicine, Houston, 1975-85; Research Scientist, Co-Director, Head & Neck Oncologic Therapy Laboratory, University of Iowa, 1980-84. *Memberships:* American Association for the Advancement of Science; American Association for Cancer Research; American Association of Immunologists; American Society for Microbiology; New York Academy of Sciences; Tissue Culture Association. *Publications:* 'Oncogenic Viruses & the nude mouse, The Nude

Mouse in Experimental & Clinical Research', 1982; 'Immunologic methods of diagnostic & prognostic value in tumour bearers', Advances in Immunology & Cancer Therapy, 1985; 'The Murine Subrenal Capsule (SRC) assay in head & neck cancer' Head & Neck Cancer, 1985. *Honours:* H H Rackham Fellow, 1959; USPHS Fellow in the Pathogenesis of Infectious Disease, 1960-63; F G Novy Fellow, 1964. *Hobbies:* Music; Reading. *Address:* Otolaryngology - Head & Neck Surgery, University of Chicago Medical Centre, 5841, S Maryland Ave, Box 412, Chicago, IL 60637, USA.

McCONCHIE, Ian Haig, b. 4 Mar. 1917, Melbourne, Australia. Consultant Thoracic Surgeon. m. Marjory Sutcliffe, 23 May 1942, 2 sons, 2 daughters. *Education:* MB, BS, 1941; MS, 1947; FRACS, 1948; MD, 1983; FCCP, 1983; Fellow, Queen's College, Melbourne University, 1970. *Appointments:* Honorary Thoracic Surgeon: Royal Melbourne Hospital, Royal Women's Hospital, Western General Hospital, 1966-77; Honorary Thoracic Surgeon, Preson Community Hospital, 1960-66; Visiting Thoracic Surgeon, Repatriation Hospital, 1948-82; Team Leader, Dept. Territorial, Thoracic Surgery Team, Papua, New Guinea, 1957, 1964; Chairman, Victorian State Committee: Thoracic Society of Australia, 1970, Royal Australian College of Surgeons, 1975-76; Chairman, Honorary Medical Staff, Royal Melbourne Hospital, 1976-77; Captain, Royal Australian Army Medical Corps, 1942-46. *Memberships:* Royal Australian College of Surgeons; Australian Association of Surgeons; Australian Medical Association; Cardiac Society of Australia and New Zealand; Thoracic Society of Australia, Life Member. *Publications:* Numerous articles on Thoracic Surgery, 1948-82. *Honour:* AM, 1984. *Hobbies:* Golf; Gardening; Reading. *Address:* 18 Edward St., Kew 3101, Victoria, Australia.

McCRAY, Glen M, b. 24 May 1920, Kansas, USA. Medical Director. m. Maurine Mong, 17 July 1945, Kansas City, Kansas, 1 son, 2 daughters. *Education:* AB, Kansas University, Lawrence, Kansas, 1947; MD, Kansas University School of Medicine, Kansas City, Kansas, 1950; Diplomate American Board of Psychiatry and Neurology 1982, American Board of Child Psychiatry 1983. *Appointments:* Private Practice in Medicine, 1951-62; Instructor, Department of Psychiatry 1965-66, Assistant Clinical Professor of Psychiatry 1966-75, University of Kansas School of Medicine, Kansas City; Assistant Professor, Paediatrics and Psychiatry, University of Missouri School of Medicine, Columbia, Missouri 1966-71, University of Missouri, Kansas City School of Medicine 1971-78; Associate Professor, Paediatrics and Psychiatry, University of Missouri School of Medicine, Kansas City, 1978-84; Medical Director, Marion Center, Saint John's Health Center, Springfield, Missouri, 1984-. *Memberships:* American Medical Association; American Psychiatric Association; American Academy of Child Psychiatry; Fellow, American Orthopsychiatry Association. *Publications:* 'Excessive Masturbation in Childhood', 1978; 'Sleep Apnea Syndrome, Diagnosis of Upper Airway Obstruction by Fluroscopy', 1978. *Hobbies:* Trout fishing; Gardening; Music; Reading. *Address:* Marian Center, Saint John's Regional Health Center, Springfield, MD 65804, USA.

MacCULLOCH, William Thomson, b. 6 Nov. 1929, Coatbridge, Scotland. Professor of Prosthetic Dentistry, University College, Cork of National University of Ireland. *Education:* BDS, University of Glasgow, 1953; PhD, University of Birmingham, 1961; MSc, University of Manchester, 1968; National University of Ireland, 1969-; FFD, Royal College of Surgeons, 1972. *Appointments:* House Surgeon, Glasgow Dental Hospital, 1953-54; Public Dental Officer, County of Stirling, Scotland, 1954-58; Research Fellow, University of Birmingham, 1958-61; Lecturer, Prosthetic Dentistry, University of Manchester, 1961-69; Professor of Prosthetic Dentistry, University College Cork of

National University of Ireland, 1969-; Consultant. *Memberships:* Fellow, Royal College of Surgeons; British Dental Association; Feda. Dentaire International; International Association Dental Research; British Standards Institute; British Society for the Study of Prosthetic Dentistry; European Prosthodontic Society; Institute of Metals; The Engineering Council. *Publications:* Contributed articles on dentistry metallurgy and ceramics to various journals. *Honours:* Dean Webster Prize of University of Glasgow, 1953; External Examiner: University of Birmingham Dental School, 1980-83, University of Manchester Dental School, 1981-84. *Hobbies:* Music; The Arts. *Address:* University Dental School and Hospital, Wilton, Cork, Republic of Ireland.

McCUNNEY, Robert J, b. 4 July 1948, Pennsylvania, USA. Medical Director. *Education:* BS, Drexel University, 1971; MS, University of Minnesota, 1972; MD, Thomas Jefferson University Medical School, 1976; MPH, Harvard School of Public Health, 1981. *Appointments:* Emergency Room Physician, Choate Memorial Hospital, Woburn, Sancta Maria Hospital, Cambridge, Massachusetts, 1979-80; Medical Director, Occupational Health Services, Sturdy Memorial Hospital, Attleboro, Massachusetts, 1981-83; Medical Director, Goddard Occupational Health Services, Stoughton, Massachusetts, 1982-; Corporate Medical Director, Cabot Corporation, Boston, Massachusetts, 1983-. *Memberships:* American Medical Association; American College of Physicians; American Public Health Association; New England Occupational Medical Association; American Occupational Medical Association; American Medical Association. *Publications include:* 'Does Work at Waste Water Treatment Plants Pose a Risk to Health?'; 'Video Display Terminals: What are the Health Risks?', 1984; 'The Role of Fitness in Preventing Heart Disease', 1985; Editor, "Health and Safety Manual of the Jewelry Industry", 1982. *Honours include:* Fellowship, American College of Preventive Medicine, 1983; Fellowship, American Occupational Medical Association, 1985. *Hobbies:* Skiing; Writing; Tennis; Squash. *Address:* Cabot Corporation, 125 High Street, Boston, MA 02110, USA.

McDANIEL, Ellen Garb, b. 21 Dec. 1941, Cleveland, Ohio, USA. Associate Professor of Psychiatry; Associate Dean of Admissions. m. John P McDaniel, 1 son, 1 daughter. *Education:* Carnegie-Mellon University, 1959-62; MD, University of Michigan School of Medicine, 1962-66; Residency, Ohio State University, 1967-68; Residency, University of Maryland, 1968-70. *Appointments:* Director of Brief Therapy Clinic, Director of Adult Ambulatory Care Division, Director Junior Year Clerkship, Associate Dean of Admissions, Associate Professor of Psychiatry Department of Psychiatry, University of Maryland School of Medicine, Private practice, 1970-. *Memberships:* American Psychiatric Association; American Medical Association; Maryland Psychiatric Society; Phi Kappa Phi; Medical-Chirurgical Faculty. *Publications:* "Psychiatric Foundations of Medicine" volume I-IV, (edited with E V Balis and L Eurmser), 1975; Book chapters include: 'Personality Disorders in Private Practice', in "Personality Disorders" (editor J Lion), 1981; 'Mid-Life Problems in Women' in "Clinical Medicine" (editor John A Spittel Jr), 1981; 'Psychodynamic Aspects of Violence' (with G Balis and S Strahan) in "Handbook of Violence and Prevention" (edited by J Field, E Ostrom and L Hertzberg); Articles in journals, book reviews. Honour: Fellowship, American Psychiatric Association, 1978. *Address:* 655 W Baltimore Street, Room 14-015, Baltimore, MD 21201, USA.

McDEVITT, Denis Gordon, b. 17 Nov. 1937, Belfast, Northern Ireland. University Professor of Clinical Pharmacology. m. Anne McKee, 20 July 1967, Belfast, 2 sons, 1 daughter. *Education:* MB BCh and BAO 1962, MD 1968, DSc 1978, Queen's University, Belfast; Fellow, Royal College of Physicians, Ireland,

1977; Fellow Royal College of Physicians, London, 1978. *Appointments:* Assistant Professor of Medicine, Christian Medical College, Ludhiana, Punjab, India, 1968-71; Senior Lecturer in Therapeutics 1971-76, Reader in Clinical Pharmacology 1976-78, Professor of Clinical Pharmacology 1978-83, Queen's University, Belfast, Northern Ireland; Merck International Fellow in Clinical Pharmacology, Vanderbilt University, Nashville, USA, 1974-75; Professor of Clinical Pharmacology, University of Dundee, Scotland, 1984-. *Memberships:* Chairman Clinical Section, British Pharmacological Society, 1985-; Association of Physicians of Great Britain and Ireland; British Thoracic Society; American Society of Clinical Pharmacology. *Publications:* Several articles on cardiovascular and respiratory clinical pharmacology in medical scientific journals. *Honours:* Merck International Fellowship in Clinical Pharmacology, Merck Foundation, 1974; Smith, Kline and French prize in Clinical Pharmacology, 1975; Graves Lecturer, 1977. *Hobbies:* Golf; Classical music. *Address:* Department of Pharmacology and Clinical Pharmacology, Ninewells Hospital and Medical School, Dundee DD1 9SY, Scotland.

MacDONALD, Alister Gordon, b. 25 Jan. 1940, London, England. Reader in Physiology. m. Jennifer Matthews 16 Sep. 1961, 1 son, 2 daughters. *Education:* BSc, Bristol University, England; PhD, Bristol and East Anglia Universities. *Appointments:* Senior Research Associate, University of East Anglian, England, 1964-69; Visiting Research Worker, Woods Hole Oceanographic Institution, USA, 1967; Lecturer in Physiology, University of Aberdeen, Scotland, 1969; Visiting Associate Professor, University of North Carolina, USA, 1973; Senior Lecturer, University of Aberdeen, Scotland, 1974, Reader in Physiology, 1984-. *Memberships:* Physiological Society; European Undersea Biomedical Society; Society for Experimental Biology; British Society for Cell Biology; High Pressure Technology Association. *Publications:* "Physiological Aspects of Deep Sea Biology: Monography of Physiological Society", 1975; 'Hydrostatic Pressure Physiology' in "The Physiology and Medicine of Diving", 1982; 'The effects of Pressure on the Molecular Structure and Physiological Functions of Cell Membranes' in 'Phil Trans. R. Soc. Lond. B.' 1984. *Hobbies:* Hill Walking; Badminton; Football; Music. *Address:* Physiology Department, Marischal College, Aberdeen University, Aberdeen AB9 1AS, Scotland.

MacDONALD, Allan Sullivan, b. 9 Apr. 1939, Antigonish, Nova Scotia. Associate Professor of Surgery; Attending Surgeon. m. Lorna Morrison, 3 July 1965, 1 son, 2 daughters. *Education:* St Francis Xavier University, Antigonish, Nova Scotia, 1956-58; MD, Dalhousie University, Faculty of Medicine, 1963; FRCS (Canada). *Appointments:* Rotating Internship, Halifax and St John's, Newfoundland, 1962-63; Resident in Surgery, Victoria General Hospital, Halifax, Nova Scotia, 1963-67; JD Tory Foundation Scholar and Research Fellow, Harvard Medical School, Boston, USA, 1967-69; Assistant Professor of Surgery, Dalhousie University, Halifax, 1969-71; Centennial Fellow, Medical Research Council of Canada and Fellow, University of Cambridge, England, 1971-72; Assistant Professor, Surgery, Dalhousie University; Attending Surgeon, Victoria General Hospital, 1972-80; Associate Professor of Surgery, 1980-, Director, Surgical Research, 1982-84, Dalhousie University, Halifax. *Memberships:* Nova Scotia Medical Society, President, Surgical Section, 1979-80; Canadian Transplantation Society, President; Canadian Oncology Society, President, 1984-85; National Cancer Institute; Medical Research Council; Royal College of Physicians and Surgeons; Canadian Association of General Surgeons, Founding Committee; Canadian Multi-Centre Transplant Study Group, President, 1982-83; Kidney Foundation of Canada. *Publications:* Books: Chapter B, "Present Status of BCG in Cancer Immunotherapy", 1976; "Regional Renal Failure Guidelines", 1980; "Vital Organ Transplants'', 1985; Over 100 publications. *Honours:* Medical Staff Prize, IWK, 1962; Medical Senior Intern, VG Hospital, 1962; IWK Scholarship, 1967; JD Tory Foundation Scholarship, 1967; Centennial Fellow, MRC, 1971; Fellowship, Royal College of Physicians and Surgeons, Canada, 1967. *Hobbies:* Squash; Sailing. *Address:* Room 4134, Ambulatory Care Centre, 5820 University Avenue, Halifax, Nova Scotia, Canada, B3H 1V0.

MACDONALD, Colin Bruce, b. 13 Mar. 1927, Chest Specialist. m. Margaret MacDonald, 22 Nov. 1958, Hobart, 2 sons. *Education:* MB, BS (Honours II), Sydney, 1950; FRCP Edin., 1969; MRCP, 1960; FRACP, 1978; MRACP, 1975; FCCP, 1965. *Appointments:* RMO, Royal Prince Alfred Hospital, Sydney, 1950; Launceston General Hospital, Tasmania, 1951; Austin Hospital, Melbourne, 1952-53; Gresswell Sanatorium Mont Park, Victoria, 1954-55; Repat. General Hospital Hobart, 1956-59; Registrar, Respirator Diseases, University of Edinburgh, 1960; Registrar, Cardiology, London Chest Hospital, 1961-62; Clinical Assistant, Cardiologist, Royal Hobart Hospital, 1963-65; A/Cardiology, 1966-67; Cardiologist, Royal Hobart Hospital, 1968; Thoracic Physician, Royal Hobart Hospital, 1964-85; Chest Physician, Tasmania Department of Health Services and Visiting Chest Specialist, Repat. Dept., Tasmania, 1964-65. *Memberships:* American Medical Association; National Heart Foundation, Tasmania, 1967; Honorary Secretary, Tasmania Board Thoracic Society, Australia; Chairman, Medical Advisory Committee, Asthma Foundation of Tasmania, 1972-84; Cardiac Society of Australia and New Zealand. *Publications:* "Upper Lobe Fibrosis Associated with Ankylosing Spondylitis", 'British Journal Diseases of the Chest', 1965; 'Heart Sounds and Murmurs in pregnancy', 'American Heart Journal', 1966. *Hobby:* Photography. *Address:* 335 Davey Street, South Hobart, Tasmania 7000, Australia.

McDONALD, Edward Lawson, b. 8 Feb. 1918, England. Consultant Cardiologist, National Heart Hospital, London. Divorced, 1 son. *Education:* MA, MD, Cambridge University; Fellow: Royal College of Physicians of London; American College of Cardiology. *Appointments:* Aisstant to Professor of Medicine, Middlesex Hospital, London; Rockefeller Travelling Fellow, Peter Bent Brigham Hospital; Research Fellow in Medicine, Harvard University; Assistant Director, Institute of Cardiology and Honorary Physician, National Heart Hospital, London; Consultant Cardiologist, The London Hospital. *Memberships:* British Cardiac Society; Association of Physicians of Great Britain and Ireland; International Fellow, Council on Clinical Cardiology, American Heart Association; Fellow, American College of Cardiology; Corresponding Member of various Societies of Cardiology internationally. *Publications:* Medical and Surgical Cardiology, 1969; Editor: Very Early Recognition of Coronary Heart Disease, 1978; Numerous contributions to learned journals. *Honour:* Member, Most Honourable Order of the Crown of Johore, 1980. *Hobbies:* Art; Mountain Walking; Skiing. *Address:* 9 Upper Wimpole Street, London W1M 7TD, England.

MACDONALD, Ian, b. 22 Dec. 1921, London, England. Head, Department of Physiology, Guy's Campus, UMDS, London, 2 sons 1 daughter. *Education:* MD; MB; BS; PhD; DSc; Fl.Biol, University of London. *Appointments:* Lecturer in Physiology, 1948-62; Reader in Physiology, 1962-67; Professor of Applied Physiology, 1967-. *Memberships:* Nutrition Society, President, 1980-83; Physiological Society; Medical Research Society; American Society of Clinical Nutrition; Chairman, British Nutrition Foundation, 1985-; Member, UK Food Advisory Committee. *Publications:* Several publications relating to Dietary Carbohydrate Metabolism in Man. *Honour:* International Award for Modern Nutrition, 1973. *Hobbies:* Walking; DIY. *Address:* Physiology Department, Guy's Hospital, London SE1, England.

MacDONALD, John Junior, b. 15 Oct. 1941, El Paso, Texas, USA. Mental Health Clinician, San Bernardino County Department of Mental Health, California. m. JoAnne Jessop, 2 July 1966, Mesa, Arizona, 4 sons, 3 daughters. *Education:* BA, Brigham Young University, 1967; MSW University of Utah, 1969. *Appointments:* Psychiatric Social Worker, Patton State Hospital, 1969-72; Senior Psychiatric Social Worker, San Bernardino County Public Health Department, 1972-75; Mental Health Clinician III, 1975-79, Mental Health Clinician IV, 1979-; San Bernardino County Department of Mental Health. *Memberships:* National Association of Social Workers; Academy of Certified Social Workers; Licensed Clinical Social Worker, California; North American Society of Adlerian Psychology; California Adlerian Society. *Publication:* "Disability types of self concept: A Study of the Relationship between Disability types and Self concept", Masters Thesis. *Honour:* National Institute of Mental Health Stipend, 1968, 69. *Hobbies:* Scoutmaster, Boy Scouts of America; Softball; Chess; Little League Baseball Coach and Manager; Soccer Coach, American Youth Soccer Organization; Board Member of Civitan Little League. *Address:* 5924 Newcomb Street, San Bernardino, CA 92404, USA.

MacDONALD, R. Neil, b. 6 Jan. 1935, Calgary, Alberta, Canada. Director, Cross Cancer Institute. m. Mary Jane, 30 June 1962, Montreal, 3 sons, 1 daughter. *Education:* BA, University of Toronto, 1955; McGill University, 1955-59; Intern, Resident, Royal Victoria Hospital, 1959-62; Sloan Kettering Institute, Fellow, Cancer Chemotherapy, 1962-63; Fellow, Haematology, Royal Victoria Hospital, 1963-65; Fellow, Internal Medicine, Royal College of Physicians of Canada, 1965; Certificate, Haematology, Quebec College of Physicians. *Appointments:* Demonstrator, 1965-66, Lecturer, 1966-67, Associate Dean, 1967-70, Assistant Professor, 1967-71, Professor, 1980-81, McGill University; Associate Director, Director, Oncology Day Centre, Royal Victoria Hospital, 1967-71; Executive Director, Provincial Cancer Hospitals Board, 1971-75; Professor, Medicine, 1971-80, Director, Oncology, 1976-80, Acting Director, Haematology, 1982-84, Professor, Medicine, 1981, Director, Oncology, 1981, Honorary Professor, Geriatric Medicine, 1981, University of Alberta; Director, Cross Cancer Institute, 1975-80, Director, 1981, Active Staff; Associate Director, McGill Palliative Care Centre, 1980-81; etc. *Memberships:* Royal College of Physicians & Surgeons of Canada; American College of Physicians; American College of Clinical Oncology, Chairman, Finance Committee, 1976-79, Secretary Treasurer, 1979-82; Alberta Medical Association, Chairman Public Relations Committee, 1978, 1981-; Edmonton Academy of Medicine, President, 1977; Alpha Omega Alpha; American Association for the Advancement of Science; Canadian Oncology Society, President, 1977; Canadian Haematology Society, etc. *Publications:* Articles in professional journals. *Honours:* Recipient, various academic awards; Queen's Jubilee Medal, 1977; Alberta Achievement Award, 1980; National Cancer Institute, Blair Award, 1980. *Hobbies:* Skiing; Squash; Amateur Historian. *Address:* Cross Cancer Institute, 11560 University Avenue, Edmonton, Alberta T6G 1Z2, Canada.

McDOUGALL, John, b. 22 May 1930, Cambuslang, Scotland. Head, Department of Microbiology, NSW Institute of Technology, Sydney, Australia. m. Margaret Green, 23 Mar. 1957, Leicester, England, 1 son, 2 daughters. *Education:* BSc, 1st class honours, Strathclyde, 1955; PhD, Nottingham, 1958; FRSC, London; FAIFST. *Appointments:* Research Officer, Distillers Ltd; Scientific Services Manager, General Foods Ltd; Reader in Microbiology, Massey University, New Zealand. *Memberships:* Fellow, Royal Society of Chemistry; Fellow, Australian Institute of Food Science and Technology. *Publications:* "Microbial Toxins", 1970; "New Problems of Food Safety Hazards of Salmonellae", 1968; 'Microbial Aspects of

Environmental Health', 1967; 'Sanitation Audit of Plant', 1969. *Honours:* International Microbiology Essay Prize, 1960. *Hobbies:* Wood sculpture; Boat building; Sailing. *Address:* Microbiology Department, New South Wales Institute of Technology, School of Biomedical Sciences, PO Box 123, Broadway, Sydney, NSW 2007, Australia.

McDOWELL, Charles Lindsay, b. 20 July 1933, Belmont, North Carolina, USA. Orthopaedic Surgeon. m. Virginia Carter Donnan, 17 Aug. 1957, Roanoke, Virginia, 3 sons. *Education:* BS, Wake Forest University, Winston-Salem, North Carolina, 1955; MD, Jefferson Medical College, Philadelphia, Pennsylvania, 1959; Internship, Residency in Orthopaedics, Jefferson Medical College Hospital, Philadelphia; Paediatric Orthopaedics, State Hospital for Crippled Children, Elizabeth Town. *Appointments include:* Chief of Upper Extremity Service 1966-80, Chief of Division of Orthopaedics 1968-70, Richmond Veterans Administration Hospital, Richmond, Virginia; Chief of Upper Extremity Service 1967-77, Currently Clinical Professor, Orthopaedic and Plastic Surgery (Hand), Medical College of Virginia. *Memberships include:* American Academy of Orthopaedic Surgeons; American Society for Surgery of the Hand; Secretary-Treasurer 1974-77, Virginia State Orthopaedic Society; Virginia Medical Society; President 1973-74, Jefferson Orthopaedic Society; R E Carroll Hand Club; American Medical Association; Fellow, American College of Surgeons; Past President of Richmond branch, Arthritis Foundation. *Publications include:* 'Rhabdomyosarcoma, embryonal cell type, of the hand', (with J Cardea), 1974, 'Malignant histiocytoma in hand (case report)', (with Bill Henceroth), 1977; Chapter in "Pressure Ulcers - Principles and Techniques of Management" by Dr Mark Constantian, 1980; Chapter in "Operative Hand Surgery" by Dr David Green, 1981. *Honours:* Annie C Kane Fellowship in Hand Surgery, Columbia Presbyterian Medical Center, DePalma Orthopaedic Prize, 1959. *Hobbies:* Sailing; Windsurfing. *Address:* 2911-2915 Grove Avenue, Richmond, VA 23221, USA.

MacFADYEN, Bruce Vischer Jr, b. 4 Nov. 1942, Philadelphia, Pennsylvania, USA. Associate Professor, Department of Surgery. m. Rosemary, 18 June 1965, 1 son, 3 daughters. *Education:* BS, Wheaton College; MD, Hahnemann Medical College and Hospital. *Appointments:* Assistant Instructor in Surgery, The University of Pennsylvania School of Medicine, 1969-72; Chief Resident in General Surgery, The University of Texas Medical School, Hermann Hospital, MD, Anderson Hospital and Tumor Institute, 1972-74; Instructor in Surgery, 1973-74, Assistant Professor of Surgery, 1974-77; Associate Professor of Surgery, 1977-, The University of Texas Medical School. *Memberships:* American College of Surgeons; American Medical Society; American Society for Parenteral and Enteral Nutrition; Collegium Internationale Chirurgiae Digestivae; International Society for Parenteral Nutrition; Society of Surgical Oncology; Society for Surgery of the Alimentary Tract. *Hobbies:* Tennis; Camping; Ham Radio. *Address:* 6431 Fannin 4164, Houston, TX 77030, USA.

McFADZEAN, James Anderson, b. 21 Sep. 1925, Troon, Scotland. Director of Research. m. 3 July 1950, Barrhead, Scotland, 1 son, 2 daughters. *Education:* MB ChB, 1948; MD, 1954; Fl Biol 1965; MRCP (Glasgow) 1980; FRCP (Glasgow) 1982; FRSE, 1985. *Appointments:* Professorial House Physician, 1948-49, Professorial House Surgeon, 1949, Glasgow Royal Infirmary; Colonial Medical Research Student, NIMR London, 1949-51; Medical Research Council, The Gambia, West Africa, 1951-55; Member Scientific Staff, National Institute for Medical Research, London, 1956-60; Head of Division of Experimental Chemotherapy, Chemotherapeutic Research Manager, Pharmaceutical Research Manager, Pharmaceutical Research and Development Manager, Director of Pharmaceutical Research and Develop-

ment, May and Baker Ltd, 1960-. *Memberships:* Fellow, Royal College of Physicians (Glasgow); Fellow, Institute of Biology; Fellow, Royal Society of Edinburgh. *Publications:* Numerous publications and chapters in textbooks, particularly on chemotherapy and topical medicine, 1951-. *Hobbies:* Painting; Golf; Reading; Fishing. *Address:* May and Baker Ltd, Rainham Road South, Dagenham, Essex RM10 7XS, England.

McFARLAND, James Joseph, b. 25 Sep. 1942, New Jersey, USA. Cardiovascular/Thoracic/General Surgeon. *Education:* BS, Upsala College, New Jersey, 1964; MS, Seton Hall University, New Jersey, 1966; MD, University of Bologna, Italy, 1976. *Appointments:* Rotating Internship, University of Bologna, Italy, 1976; Residency, General Surgery, New York Medical College, New York City, USA, 1976-78; Residency, General Surgery, Bridgeport Hospital, Connecticut, 1978-81; Residency, Thoracic and Cardiovascular Surgery, Tulane University, New Orleans, Louisiana, 1982-84; Residency, Thoracic and Cardiovascular Surgery, Wayne State University, Detroit, Michigan, 1984-85; Postgraduate Cardiac Transplantation Course, Stanford University, Stanford, California, 1985; Fellowship, Cardiovascular and Thoracic Surgery, St Thomas Hospital, Nashville, Tennessee, 1985-86. *Memberships:* American Association for the Advancement of Science; American Association for the History of Medicine; American Board of Surgery; American College of Chest Physicians; American College of Surgeons; American Federation for Clinical Research; American Medical Association; American Trauma Society; International Society for Heart Transplantation; Society of Critical Care Medicine; Association for the Advancement of Medical Instrumentation; National Association of Residents and Interns; New Jersey Academy of Science; New York Academy of Science; Surgical Society of New York Medical College. *Publications:* 'Nutritional Assessment in the Traumatized Patient', 1979; 'Penetration of Clindamycin into Decubitus Ulcers', 1978; 'Persistent Left Superior Vena Cava', 1976; 'Interaction of Pox Viruses with Ehrlich's Ascites Carcinoma', 1966. *Honours:* Gifted Child, Entered College at 15; Graduated top 20 per cent of Medical School, 1976; First Prize, Resident Paper Competition in Trauma, American College of Surgeons, 1979; Top 6 per cent Thoracic Surgery Examination in the USA, 1981. *Hobbies:* Jogging; Hiking; Camping; Tennis; Swimming; Painting; Music. *Address:* 3919 Westmont Avenue, Nashville, TN 37215, USA.

McFARLANE, Ronald Knox, b. 2 Feb. 1920, Dunedin, New Zealand. Consultant Diagnostic Radiologist. m. Mary Byars, 8 Sep. 1956, Waikaka, New Zealand, 1 son, 2 daughters. *Education:* MB, ChB, New Zealand; DMRD, Edinburgh, Scotland; Fellow, Royal Australasian College of Radiologists. *Appointments:* Radiological Registrar, Kew Hospital, Invercargill, New Zealand; Radiological Registrar, Western General Hospital, Edinburgh, Scotland; Junior and Senior Visiting Diagnostic Radiologist, Kew Hospital, Invercargill, New Zealand; Honorary Consultant Radiologist, Southland Hospital Board, Invercargill, New Zealand. *Memberships:* British Institute of Radiology; Royal College of Radiologists. *Hobbies:* Book Collecting; Photography. *Address:* 81A Don Street, Invercargill, New Zealand.

MACFARLANE, Thomas Wallace, b. 12 Dec. 1942, Glasgow, Scotland. Reader in Oral Medicine and Pathology/Consultant in Oral Microbiology. m. Agnes McEwan Fyfe, 1 Apr. 1971, Glasgow, 1 son. *Education:* BDS, 1966; Membership, Royal College of Pathologists in Oral Microbiology, 1973, Fellowship 1985; Doctor of Dental Surgery, Glasgow University, 1976. *Appointments:* Assistant Lecturer, Dental Histology and Pathology, 1966-69; Lecturer, Oral Medicine and Pathology, 1969-77; Senior Lecturer, Oral Medicine and Pathology, 1977-84 (Consultant in Oral Microbiology); Reader in Oral Medicine and Pathology/{

Consultant in Oral Microbiology, 1984-. *Memberships:* Royal College of Pathologists; Royal College of Physicians and Surgeons; Association of Clinical Pathologists; Pathological Society of Great Britain; British Society for Dental Research; British Dental Association; Society for General Microbiology; International Association for Dental Research. *Publication:* 'Oral Manifestations of Systemic Infection' in "Oral Manifestations of Systemic Diease" edited by Jones and Mason, 1980; "The role of dietary carbohydrates in the pathogenesis of oral candidosis" 1985; "Infectivity of Hepatitis B surface antigen positive patients", 1981 etc. *Hobbies:* Music, especially playing the clarinet; Reading English and Scottish literature. *Address:* Oral Microbiology Unit, Dental Hospital and School, 378 Sauchiehall Street, Glasgow G2 3JZ, Scotland.

McFARLANE OF LLANDAFF, Jean Kennedy (Baroness), b. 1 Apr. 1926, Cardiff, Wales. University Professor of Nursing. *Education:* BSc, Sociology, Bedford College, University of London, England; MA, Birkbeck College, University of London. *Appointments:* Staff Nurse, St Bartholomews Hospital, London, 1950-51; Health Visitor, Cardiff, Wales, 1954-59; Tutor 1960-62, Education Officer 1962-66, Research Organiser 1966-69, Director of Education 1969-71, Royal College of Nursing, London; Senior Lecturer 1971-74, Professor and Head of Department of Nursing 1974-, University of Manchester. *Memberships:* Fellow, Royal College of Nursing; Chairman 1971-74, Standing Conference on Health Visiting Training Schools; Chairman 1980-83, English National Board for Nursing Midwifery and Health Visiting; UK Central Council for Nursing Midwifery and Health Visiting, 1980-83. *Publications:* "Proper Study of the Nurse", 1970; "The Practice of Nursing Using the Nursing Process", (with G Castledine), 1982. *Honours:* Life Barony of the United Kingdom, 1979; MSc, Manchester, 1979; DSc, Ulster, 1981; DEd, CNAA, 1983; Fellow, Royal College of Nursing - Australia. *Address:* Department of Nursing, University of Manchester, Oxford Road, Manchester M13 9PT, England.

McGEE, James O'Donnell, b. 27 July 1939, Scotland. Professor, Morbid Anatomy. m. Anne McCarron Lee, 27 Aug. 1961, Glasgow, 1 son, 2 daughters. *Education:* MB ChB, 1962, PhD, 1964, MD, Honours, 1973, Glasgow University; MA, Oxford University, 1975; FRC Path, 1986. *Appointments:* Senior House Officer, Registrar, Research Fellow, Lecturer in Pathology, Glasgow University, 1963-69; MRC Travelling Fellow, Roche Institute of Molecular Biology, 1969-70; Visiting Scientist, Roche Institute of Molecular Biology, USA, 1970-71; Lecturer, Senior Lecturer and Honorary Consultant, Pathology, Glasgow University, 1972-75. *Memberships:* Pathological Society of Great Britain; British Society of Gastroenterology; International Academy of Pathology; Association of Clinical Pathology. *Publications:* Biopsy Pathology of Liver, 1980; Articles on Liver Disease, Collagen Metabolism, Oncogenes in human neoplasia. *Honours:* Bellahouston Medal, Glasgow University, 1972; Fellow, Linacre College, Oxford, 1975; Kettle Memorial Lecture, Royal College of Pathologists, London, 1980; Annual Guest Lecture, Royal Academy of Medicine, Ireland, 1985. *Hobby:* Talking With His Family. *Address:* University of Oxford, Nuffield Dept of Pathology, John Radcliffe Hospital, Headington, Oxford OX3 9DU, England.

McGEER, Edith G, b. 18 Nov. 1923, New York City, USA. University Professor. m. Patrick L McGeer, 15 Apr. 1954, Wilmington, Delaware, 2 sons, 1 daughter. *Education:* BA, Swarthmore College, Pennsylvania, 1944; PhD, University of Virginia, 1946. *Appointments include:* Research Associate, 1954-74, Associate Professor, 1974-78, Associate Professor and Acting Head, 1976-78, Professor, 1979-, Head and Professor, 1983-, Division of Neurological Science, University of British Columbia. *Memberships:* Canadian Biochemical Society; Fellow, Canadian College of Neuropsychopharmacology; International Brain Research Organization; International Society of

Neurochemistry; Society of Neuroscience etc. *Publications:* "The Molecular Neurobiology of the Mammalian Brain" co-author 1978; "Kainic Acid as a Tool in Neurobiology" co-editor 1978; "Glutamine, Glutamate and GABA" co-editor, 1973. 232 papers and chapters of which 225 are in the field of neuroscience. *Honours:* Sebring Scholarship 1941-42; Swarthmore Open Scholarship 1941-44; DuPont Fellow 1945-46; Sigma Xi; Phi Beta Kappa; Citation, Delaware Section, American Chemical Society, 1958. *Address:* 4727 West 2nd Avenue, Vancouver BC, canada V6T 1C1.

McGEHEE, Frank Owen, b. 8 Oct. 1911, USA. Private Practice. m. Joyce Lacy, 1 Jan. 1938, Shreveport, 1 son, 1 daughter. *Education:* MD, Tulane University; MS, University of Tennessee. *Appointments:* Associate Professor, Orthopedic Surgery, Baylor Medical School. *Memberships:* Harris County Medical Society; Texas State and American Medical Associations; American College of Surgeons; Southern Medical Association; Central, Houston, and Clinical Orthopaedic Societies; Texas Orthopaedic Association; Willis C. Campbell Clinic Club; Diplomate, American Board of Orthopaedic Surgery; American Academy of Orthopaedic Surgeons; Charter Member, Houston Surgical Society. *Publication:* McGehee Elbow Prosthesis", 1958. *Hobbies:* Golf; Photography. *Address:* 5220 Travis, Houston, TX 77002, USA.

MacGILLIVRAY, Barron Bruce, b. 21 Aug. 1927, Durban, South Africa. Consultant Physician; University Dean and Vice Chancellor. m. Ruth Marjorie Valentine, 7 Jan. 1955, Manchester, England, 2 sons, 1 daughter. *Education:* BSc, University of Witwatersrand, Johannesburg, South Africa, 1949; MRCS, England, 1955; LRCP, London, 1955; MRCP, London, 1959; MB, BS, London, 1962; FRCP, London, 1973. *Appointments include:* Registrar, National Hospital, Queen Square, London, 1960-61, Registrar (Neurology), 1961-62, Senior Registrar, 1962-64; Physician, Royal Free Hospital, 1964-; Consultant, Clinical Neurophysiologist, National Hospital, Queen Square, London, 1970-. *Memberships:* British Association of Neurology; Brain Research Association; Royal Society of Medicine; British Computer Society; Royal Institution; Association for the Study of Medical Education; EEG Society; Harveian Society. *Publications include:* Numerous articles in medical and scientific journals, including: 'Biochemical and Electrophysiological Studies in Cerebral Oedema', in 'Brain', 1965 (Co-author); 'The Diagnosis of Cerebral Death' in 'Pro Eu Dial Transpl Assoc' 1973; 'The Application of Automated Analysis to the Diagnosis of Epilepsy in EEG Informatics' (Book chapter), 1977; 'Brain Death and the EEG' in 'Lancet', 1981, (co-author); Various conference papers. *Hobbies:* Photography; Sculpture; Flying light aircraft. *Address:* Royal Free Hospital School of Medicine, Rowland Hill Street, London NW3 2PF, England.

McGINTY, John, b. 19 Nov. 1930, Boston, Massachusetts, USA. Professor. *Education:* AB, Harvard College, 1952; MD, Tufts University School of Medicine, 1956; Teaching Fellow, Harvard Medical School; Residency: Yale New Haven Community Hospital, 1956-57, Childrens Hospital Medical Centre, Boston, 1959-61, Massachusetts General Hospital, 1960, Peter Bent Brigham Hospital, Boston, 1961. *Appointments:* Chief, Orthopaedics, Newton-Wellesley Hospital, 1966-84; Associate Orthopaedic Surgeon, Peter Bent Brigham Hospital, 1966-84; Courtesy Staff, Childrens Hospital Medical Centre, 1966-84; Consultant Orthopaedic Surgeon, New England Medical Centre, 1974-84; Chief, Orthopaedic Service, VA Hospital, West Roxbury, 1966-74; Consultant Orthopaedic Surgeon, Fort Devens Army Hospital, 1967-84; Associate Staff, Orthopaedic Surgery, Hahnemann Hospital, Brighton, 1977-84; Professor, Chairman, Orthopaedic Surgery, Medical University Hospital, Charleston; Charleston County Memorial Hospital; VA Hospital, Charleston. *Memberships:* American Academy of Orthopaedic

Surgeons; American College of Surgeons; New England Orthopaedic Society; American Medical Association; many other professional organizations. *Publications:* Numerous papers and articles in professional journals. *Address:* Medical University of South Carolina, Orthopaedic Surgery Dept, 171 Ashley Ave, Charleston, SC 29425, USA.

McGIRR, Edward McCombie, b. 15 June 1916, Hamilton, Scotland. Emeritus University Professor. m. Diane Curzon Woods, 16 Apr. 1949, Birmingham, England, 1 son, 3 daughters. *Education:* BSc 1937, MB, ChB with honours, 1940, University of Glasgow; MD with honours and Bellahouston Medal, 1960; FRCP, London, Edinburgh, Glasgow; FACP (Honorary); FFCM; FRSE. *Appointments:* Various appointments in University of Glasgow including Professor of Medicine (Muirhead Chair) and Physician i/c wards, Glasgow Royal Infirmary, 1961-78; Dean of Faculty of Medicine, 1974-81, Professor of Administrative Medicine and Administrative Dean, 1978-81; Chairman of Scottish Council for Postgraduate Medical Education, 1979-85; Chairman, Scottish Health Service Planning Council, 1978-84; Honorary Physician to the Army in Scotland, 1975-71; Chairman, Scottish Council for Opportunities for Play Experience, 1985. *Memberships:* Association of Physicians of Great Britain and Ireland; Scottish Society of Physicians; Scottish Society for Experimental Medicine; Medical Research Society; Royal Medico-Chirurgical Society of Glasgow; Council Member, Royal Society of Edinburgh, 1982-85; British Nuclear Medicine Society; Corresponding Member, American Thyroid Association. *Publications:* Numerous publications in medical and scientific press on topics in thyroid disease, nuclear medicine, medical education and on the NHS. *Honours:* CBE 1978; Orator of Herveian Society of Edinburgh, President 1979. *Hobbies:* Detective fiction; Curling; Antiques. *Address:* Anchorage House, Bothwell, Glasgow, G71 8NF, Scotland.

McGLASHAN, Thomas Hamel, b. 20 Oct. 1941, Rochester, New York, USA. Hospital Director of Research. m. Patricia Gwiazdowski, 29 Aug. 1964, Meriden, Connecticut, 2 daughters. *Education:* BA Chemistry, Yale University, 1963; University of Pennsylvania School of Medicine, 1967; Specialty training in psychiatry, Harvard University, 1968-71; Psychoanalytic Training, Washington Psychoanalytic Institute, 1973-81. *Appointments:* Programme Head, Psychopharmacological Research, NIMH, 1971-73; Chief, Clinical Research Unit, NIH, 1973-75; Staff Psychiatrist 1975-77, Director of Adult Studies 1977-81, Director of Research 1981-, Chestnut Lodge Hospital. *Memberships:* Fellow, American Psychiatric Association; Washington Psychiatric Society; Washington Psychoanalytic Society; Extended Associate Member, American Psychoanalytic Association; International Psychoanalytic Association; Society for Psychotherapy Research; Association for Clinical Psychosocial Research. *Publications:* 'The Goals of Psychoanalysis and Psychoanalytic Psychotherapy', 1982; 'Intensive Individual Psychotherapy of Schizophrenia', 1983; The Chestnut Lodge Follow-up Study I:' 'Follow-up Methodology and Study Sample', II; 'Long-Term Outcome of Schizophrenia and the Affective Disorders', 1984; 'The Borderline: Current Empirical Research', editor, 1985. *Honour:* Gary Morris Research Award, Washington Psychoanalytic Society, 1980. *Hobby:* Skiing. *Address:* 3777 Oliver Street NW, Washington, DC 20015, USA.

McGOUGH, William Edward, b. 12 Nov. 1928, Union City, New Jersey, USA. Professor; Chief, Psychiatric Services, UMDNJ-Rutgers Medical School, Middlesex General University Hospital. *Education:* BS, St Peter's College, 1950; MD, Duke University School of Medicine, 1956; Psychiatric Residency, Yale University School of Medicine, 1957-60; Graduate Studies, Anthropology, Yale University Graduate School, and University of North Carolina, Chapel Hill, 1958-64. *Appointments:* Instructor, Psuchiatry, University of

Rochester School of Medicine, 1960, Duke University School of Medicine, 1961-63; Assistant Professor, Duke University School of Medicine, 1963-64; Assistant Professor, Founding Faculty Member, 1964-66, Associate Professor, 1966-72, Rutgers University School of Medicine; Professor, UMDNJ-Rutgers Medical School, 1972-, Associate Dean, 1972-76; Chief, Psychiatric Services, UMDNJ-Ritgers Medical School Middlesex General University Hospital, 1979-. *Memberships:* New Jersey Psychiatric Association; American Psychiatric Association; American Psychosomatic Society. *Publications:* "Importance of Empathic Communication in Anthropological Research", 'International Journal of Social Psychiatry', 1964; "Patterns of Fat Mobilization in Field Independent and Field Dependent Subjects", co-author, 'Psychosomatic Medicine', 1964; Chapter in Clinical Medicine for 'the Occupational Physician', Street and Mental Illness; 27 other publications. *Honours:* Fellow, American Psychiatric Association, 1973; Overseer, School of Veterinary Medicine, University of Pennsylvania, 1982-. *Hobbies:* Breeder & Judge, Pure Bred Dogs (International); Officer, Board Member, Monmouth County Kennel Club, President 1975-. *Address:* Department of Psychiatry, UMDNJ-Rutgers Medical School; Middlesex General-University Hospital, 180 Somerset Street, New Brunswick, NJ 08901, USA.

McGOWAN, David Alexander, b. 18 June 1939, Portadown, County Armagh, Northern Ireland, Professor of Oral Surgery, Consultant Oral Surgeon. m. Margaret Vera Macauley, 21 June 1968, County Down, Northern Ireland, 1 son, 2 daughters. *Education:* BDS, 1961, MDS, 1970, Dental School, Queens University, Belfast; PhD, London; FDSRCS, England; FFDRCS, Ireland; FDSRCPS, Glasgow. *Appointments:* Oral Surgery Training, Belfast and Aberdeen, 1961-67; Lecturer in Dental Surgery, Queen's University, Belfast, 1968; Lecturer, Senior Lecturer, Deputy Head of Oral and Maxillofacial Surgery, London Hospital Medical College, 1968-77; Professor of Oral Surgery, University of Glasgow, Scotland; Consultant Oral Surgeon, Greater Glasgow Health Board. *Memberships:* Postgraduate Adviser in Dentistry, University of Glasgow; Chairman, Dental Committee, Scottish Council for Postgraduate Medical Education; Vice-chairman, Conference of UK Postgraduate Dental Deans/Advisers; Secretary, Dental Council, Royal College of Physicians and Surgeons of Glasgow; Former Council Member, British Association of Oral and Maxillofacial Surgeons. *Publications:* 'Dental treatment of patients with valvular heart disease', (co-author), 1968; 'The antibotic prophylaxis of infective endocarditis', (co-author), 1982; 'Prophylaxis of experimental endocarditis in rabbits using one or two doses of amoxycillin', 1983. *Hobbies:* Sailing; Music. *Address:* Department of Oral Surgery, Glasgow Dental Hospital and School, 378 Sauchiehall Street, Glasgow G2 3JZ, Scotland.

MacGOWAN, William, b. 12 Jan. 1925, Dublin, Republic of Ireland. Professor Emeritus. m. Joan Craven, 19 May 1956, Newcastle-upon-Tyne, England, 3 sons, 1 daughter. *Education:* Fellow, Royal College of Surgeons of Ireland, 1951; Licentiate, Royal College of Physicians (Ireland); Licentiate, Royal College of Surgeons (Ireland); Fellow, American College of Surgeons, 1960. *Appointments:* Chairman, Department of Surgery, Professor of Surgery, Royal College of Surgeons of Ireland, St Laurence's Hospital, Dublin; Registrar, Royal College of Surgeons of Ireland; Professor Emeritus. *Memberships include:* Royal Society of Medicine; British Medical Association; Association of Surgeons of Great Britain & Ireland. *Hobbies:* Tennis; Boating. *Address:* Royal College of Surgeons of Ireland, St Stephen's Green, Dublin 2, Republic of Ireland.

McGREGOR, Ian Alexander, b. 26 Aug. 1922, Scotland. Professorial Fellow, Liverpool University. m. Nancy Joan Small, 30 Jan. 1954, Mapledurham, Oxon, England, 1 son, 1 daughter. *Education:*

Rutherglen Academy; Study of Medicine in Glasgow, 1940-45; LRCP Ed; LRCS Ed; LRFPS Glasgow, 1945; DTM & H, 1949; MRCP London, 1958; FRCP (London), 1967; FRS, 1983; Hon LLD, Aberdeen, 1983; Hon DSc, Glasgow, 1984; Hon FRCP & S, Glasgow, 1984. *Appointments:* Military Service, RAMC, 1946-48; Scientific Staff, Medical Research Council, 1949-84; Member, Human Nutrition Research Unit, 1948-53; Member, MRC Laboratories, The Gambia, 1953-80; Director, Laboratories, 1953-73, 1978-80; Head, Laboratory of Tropical Community Studies, National Institute for Medical Research, Mill Hill, London, 1974-77; Member, MRC External Staff, 1981-84; Professorial Fellow, Liverpool University at Liverpool School of Tropical Medicine, 1981-. *Memberships:* Fellow, Royal Society of Medicine; Fellow and Past-President, Royal Society of Tropical Medicine and Hygiene; Honorary Member, American Society of Tropical Medicine and Hygiene; Fellow, Royal College of Physicians; Fellow, The Royal Society. *Publications:* Approximately 150 scientific papers on Tropical Medicine, Tropical Immunology, Malariology and Child Health. *Honours:* Mentioned in Despatches, 1949; OBE, 1959; Chalmers Medal, Royal Society of Tropical Medicine and Hygiene, 1963; CBE, 1969; Stewart Prize in Epidemiology, British Medical Association, 1971; Darling Medal, World Health Organization, 1974; Knight Bachelor, 1981; Laveran Medal, Society de Pathologie Exotique de Paris, 1983. *Hobbies:* Gardening; Ornithology; Fishing. *Address:* The Glebe House, Greenlooms, Hargrave, Chester CH3 7RX, England.

MacHEMER, Christine Anna, b. 24 May 1933, Düsseldorf, Federal Republic of Germany, Assistant Clinical Professor of Psychiatry. m. Robert Machemer, 30 July 1961, Düsseldorf, 1 daughter. *Education:* Abitur, Luisenschule, Düsseldorf, 1953; Medical Diploma, 1959, Doctoral Thesis, 1959, Freiburg; Internship, Germany, 1960-61; Residency in Psychiatry, Miami, Florida, USA, 1968-72. *Appointments:* Clinical Instructor in Psychiatry, University of Miami School of Medicine, USA; Private Practitioner, Psychiatry, Miami, Florida, 1978; Clinical Assistant, Professor of Psychiatry, Duke University Medical Center, Durham, USA, 1978-. *Memberships:* American Psychiatric Association; North Carolina Psychiatric Association; Southern Medical Association; Durham-Orange County Medical Association. *Hobbies:* Hiking; Skiing; Gardening; Travelling. *Address:* Box 3125, Duke University Medical Center, Durham, NC 27710, USA.

MACHOVICH, Raymund, b. 3 Nov. 1936, Budapest, Hungary. m. Ildiko Machovich, 25 June 1968, Budapest. *Education:* MD, Semmelweis University Medical School, 1961; PhD, 1972; DSc, 1978. *Apppointments:* Staff, Internal Medicine, Municipal Hospital, Szolnok, 1961-63; Assistant Professor, Biochemistry, Semmelweis University, 1963-73; Invited Scientist, Cancer Research Institute, New England Deaconess Hospital, Boston, USA, 1970-71; Faculty Member, Medicine, Postgraduate Medical School, Budapest, 1973-80; Visiting Associate Professor, Pathology, McMaster University, Hamilton, Canada, 1978-79; Visiting Professor, Centre National de Transfusion Sanguine, Paris, France, 1982-83; Scientific Advisor, 2nd Institute of Biochemistry, Semmelweis University Medical School, 1980-. *Memberships:* International Society on Thrombosis and Haemostatis; Federation of European Biochemical Societies. *Publications:* "The Thrombin", Volumes I-II, 1984; "Blood Vessel Wall and Thrombosis", Volumes I-II, in preparation; Author of 50 articles in professional journals including 'Biochemical Journal'; 'Biochimica et Biophysica Acta; 'Blood'; 'Thrombosis Research'; etc. *Honours:* Recipient, Canadian Heart Foundation Award, 1978; Editor, Journal 'Thrombosis Research', 1981-85; 'Excerpta Medica', 1985. *Hobbies:* Classical Music; Fiction; Tennis. *Address:* Semmelweis University Medical School, 2nd Institute of Biochemistry, Puskin 9, H-1444 Budapest, POB 262, Hungary.

MACIEIRA-COELHO, Alvaro, b. 26 May 1932, Portugal.

Research Director, French National Institute of Health. m. Ana Maria Vieira da Cruz, 4 Aug. 1962, Lisbon, Portugal, 3 sons, 1 daughter. *Education:* MD, University of Lisbon, Portugal, DSc, University of Uppsala, Sweden. *Appointments:* Intern, University Hospital, Lisbon, Portugal; Research Associate, Wistar Institute, University of Pennsylvania, Philadelphia, USA; Research Associate, Pathology Department, University of Uppsala, Sweden; Head, Department of Cell Pathology, Institute of Cancerology and Immunogenetics, Villejuif, France; Research Director, French National Institute of Health. *Memberships:* New York Academy of Sciences; American Association for Cancer Research; American Society for Experimental Biology and Medicine; American Society for Cell Biology; European Association for Cancer Research. *Publications:* Contributor of numerous articles to medical journals. *Hobby:* Sailing. *Address:* 12, rue Claude Debussy, 78370 Plaisir, France.

McILWAIN, William Anthony, b. 29 May 1949, Waynesboro, Mississippi, USA. Orthopaedic Surgeon. m. Dian Wymer, 12 June 1971, Oak Ridge, 2 sons, 1 daughter. *Education:* BSc, University of Tennessee; MD, University of Tennessee College of Medicine; Rotating Intern, Brook Army Medical Centre, Fort Sam Houston; Orthopaedic Resident, Brook Army Medical Centre; Paediatric Orthopaedic Resident, Shriners' Crippled Children's Hospital, Shreveport Unit. *Appointments:* Assistant Chief, Orthopaedic Surgery, Landstuhl Regional Medical Centre, Second General Hospital, West Germany; Assistant Chief, Spinal Trauma Centre, Armed Forces Unit, Europe, Landstuhl; Chairman, Surgery, Bristol Memorial Hospital, Tennessee. *Memberships:* Fellow: American College of Surgeons, American Academy of Orthopaedic Surgeons; Diplomate, American Board of Orthopaedic Surgeons; Arthroscopy Association of North America; International Arthroscopy Association; Society of Military Orthopaedic Surgeons. *Publications:* "Mechanics and Clinical Applications of the Bipolar Hemiarthroplasty"; "A Retrospective Review of 225 Cases of Legg-Perthes' Disease Treated Non-surgically'. *Hobbies:* Skiing; Photography. *Address:* 28 Midway Street, Bristol, TN 37620, USA.

McINNES, Roderick R, b. 12 Oct. 1944, Halifax, Nova Scotia. Assistant Professor. 1 son, 2 daughters. *Education:* BSc, Honours, Biology, 1965, MD, Distinction, 1970, Dalhousie University; Fellowship, Paediatrics, Royal College of Physicians and Surgeons, Canada, 1977; PhD Biology, McGill University, 1978; Fellowship, Biochemical Genetics, Canadian College of Medical Genetics, 1982. *Appointments:* Visiting Assistant Professor, Paediatrics, Bayler College of Medicine, Houston, USA, 1984-85; Assistant Professor, Paediatrics, Medical Genetics, University of Toronto. *Memberships:* Canadian College of Medical Geneticists; Canadian Society for Clinical Investigation; American Association for the Advancement of Science; American Society of Human Genetics; American Society for Clinical Research; Society for Inherited Metabolic Disorders. *Publications:* Articles in scientific journals. *Honours:* CV Mosby Co Book Prize, 1968, Lang Book Prize, 1968, University Scholarship, 1968, MRC Summer Resident Fellowship, 1969, Andrew James Cowie, MD, Memorial Medal for Obstetrics, 1969; Dalhousie University Faculty of Medicine Research Prize, 1969, Fellow, Cystic Fibrosis Foundation of Canada, 1971-74, Fellow, MRC, 1974-76, Queen Elizabeth II Scientist, 1980-85, Dalhousie University Medical School. *Address:* Department of Genetics, Hospital for Sick Children, 555 University Avenue, Toronto, Ontario, Canada M5G 1X8.

MacKAY, Judith Mary Longstaff, b. 18 July 1943, England. Expert Advisor on Smoking and Health. m. John Fleming MacKay, 8 July 1967, Edinburgh, Scotland, 2 sons. *Education:* MBChB, Edinburgh University Medical School, 1966; MRCP, UK; FRCPE. *Appointments:* House Physician, City Hospital, Edinburgh, Scotland,

1966-67; House Surgeon, Royal Hospital for Sick Children, Edinburgh, 1967; Civilian Medical Practitioner, Her Majesty's Forces, Hong Kong, 1968-69; Research Assistant, Child Development Centre, Department of Paediatrics, 1971-73; Medical Registrar, Department of Medicine, University of Hong Kong, 1973-76; Deputy Head, Department of Medicine, United Christian Hospital, 1977-84. *Memberships:* British Medical Assoc.; Hong Kong Medical Assoc.; Hong Kong Chinese Medical Assoc.; Hong Kong Cardiological Society; Obstetrics and Gynaecological Society of Hong Kong; Hong Kong Anti-Cancer Society. *Publications:* 'Medicine in Hong Kong', 1981; 'Government Anti-Smoking Publicity Campaign', 1983; 'The Menopause in Chinese Women', 1984; 'Wife Battering in Hong Kong', 1985; 'Politics and Preventive Health', 1985. Honours: Hong Kong Woman of the Year, 1979; Zonta Award for Services to the Abused, 1984. *Hobbies:* Golf; Tennis; Swimming; Windsurfing; Walking; Environment; Corruption Prevention; Health Education. *Address:* Riftswood, 9th Milestone, 147 Clearwater Bay Road, Sai Kung, Kowloon, Hong Kong.

McKEEN, John (Jock) Herbert Ross, b. 19 Oct. 1946, Own Sound, Canada. President, PD Seminars Ltd, Gabriola Island, BC, Canada. *Education:* MD, University of Western Ontario, 1970; Lic Ac College of Chinese Acupuncture, Oxford, England, 1974; Internship, Royal Columbian Hospital, New Westminster, British Columbia, 1970-71. *Appointments:* Demonstrator, Department of Anatomy, University of Western Ontario, 1965-66; Medical Research, Department of Pharmacology, University of Western Ontario, 1967; Emergency Physician, Royal Columbian Hospital, New Westminster, BC, 1971-74; Private Practice, Vancouver, BC, 1973-75; Director, Resident Fellow Programme, Cold Mountain Institute, 1975-80; Faculty, Antioch College, Vancouver, 1974-80; Board of Directors, Cortes Centre for Human Development, 1980-; President, PD Seminars, 1982-; Senate, Academy of Science for Traditional Chinese Medicine, Victoria, BC, 1984-. *Memberships:* Canadian Medical Association; BC Medical Association; Association for Humanistic Psychology; College of Family Physicians of Canada; Traditional Acupuncture Foundation; Alpha Omega Alpha Honour Medical Society; Canadian Holistic Medical Association. *Publications:* 'The Transpersonal Experience Through Body Approaches' in 'Transpersonal Psychotherapy' (with B R Wong), 1980; 'Long-term Pherapeutic Effects of a 3-month Intensive Growth Group' in 'Journal of Clinical Psychiatry', 1981 (co-author); 'Adolescence & Drug Abuse' in 'Journal of the Royal College of General Practitioners, 1971. *Honours:* Medical Research Council of Canada Research Grant, 1967; R A Kinch Award for Community Medicine, 1970; Ontario & Queen Elizabeth Scholarships, 1964. *Hobbies:* Writing; Philosophy. *Address:* Davis Road, Gabriola Island, British Columbia, Canada V0R 1X0.

MACKELL, Thomas Edward, b. 7 July 1945, Philadelphia, Pennsylvania, USA. Orthopaedic Surgeon. m. Mary Ann Umstead, 4 Dec. 1982, Dublin, Pennsylvania, 1 daughter. *Education:* BS, Georgetown University, Washington, District of Columbia; MD, Jefferson Medical College, Philadelphia, Pennsylvania; Certified, American Board of Orthopaedic Surgery. *Appointments:* Intern 1972-73, Surgival Resident 1973-74, Hartford Hospital, Hartford, Connecticut; Resident 1974-78, Chief Resident 1978, Orthopaedic Surgery, Thomas Jefferson University Hospital, Philadelphia, Pennsylvania; Private Practice, Doylestown, Pennsylvania, 1978-; Consultant, Orthopaedic Surgery, Pleasant Manor Home for Children, Point Pleasant, Pennsylvania; Active Staff, Doylestown Hospital; Captain, Senior Pilot, Medical Officer, 907th Squadron, Civil Air Patrol, Valley Forge Wing. *Memberships:* Fellow, American Academy of Orthopaedic Surgeons; American Medical Association; Pennsylvania Medical Association; Pennsylvania Orthopaedic Society; Board of Directors, Bucks County Emergency Health Council; Professional Advisory Council, Bucks County Chapter, March of

Dimes. *Hobbies:* Private pilot; Skiing. *Address:* 800 West State Street, Doylestown, PA 18901, USA.

McKENNEY, Joel Ray, b. 21 Feb. 1934, Ponca City, Oklahoma, USA. Director of Community Mental Health Center. m. Louise McClure, 28 July 1956, Lawrence, Kansas, 2 sons, 3 daughters. *Education:* BS 1956, MS 1958, University of Kansas, Lawrence; PhD, University of Washington, Seattle, 1964; MD 1975, Residency in Psychiatry 1977, Medical College of Georgia, Augusta. *Appointments:* Research Scientist, General Electric, Richland, Washington, 1958-65; Research Scientist, Batelle-Northwest, Richland, 1965-67; Assistant Professor, Department of Physiology, Medical College of Georgia, 1967-74; Psychiatrist in private practice, 1978-85; Director, Carl Albert Community Mental Health Center, McAlester, Oklahoma, 1985-. *Memberships:* Radiation Research Society; American Medical Association; Pittsburg County Medical Society; Oklahoma Medical Association; American Psychiatric Association; Oklahoma Psychiatric Association. *Publications:* 'Early Uptake and Dosimetry of Zn65 in Sheep' (with R O McLellan and L K Bustad), 1962; 'Electrolyte Transport and Voltage Measure in a Preparation of the Irradiated Rat Ileum', 1968; 'Electrolyte Transport and Voltage Measure With Rat Intestine in Vitro', (with M F Sullivan), 1969; 'Radiation Research', (with R L Lieb and T F McDonald), 1977. *Honours:* Radiobiology Health Physics Fellowship, 1957-58; Biophysics Fellowship, 1962-64; Research Grant, Atomic Energy Commission, 1969-72; Chief of Psychiatry, University Hospital, August, Georgia, 1984. *Hobby:* Computer Science. *Address:* 703 Flamingo Road, McAlester, OK 74501, USA.

MacKENZIE, David James Masterton, b. 23 July 1905, New Zealand. m. Patricia Eleanor Margaret Bailey, 21 July 1934, Thaba Bosigo, Lesotho, 2 daughters. *Education:* MB ChB, 1929, DPH, 1948, University of Edinburgh, Medical School; FRCPE, 1959, Royal College of Physicians of Edinburgh. *Appointments include:* Medical Officer, Bechuanaland Protectorate (Botswana), 1934-43; DDMS, 1944-46, DMS, 1946-49, Bechuanaland Protectorate; DMS, Nyasaland (Malawi) Ex Officio Member of Nyasaland Legislative Council, 1949-55; DMS, Northern Nigeria, 1955-57; Director Medical and Health Services, Hong Kong, Ex Officio Member of Legislative Council, 1958-64; Visiting Scientist in the US Public Health Service at the Communicable Disease Center, Atlanta, Georgia, 1965-69; Honorary Research Associate, Department of Bacteriology (later Department of Medical Microbiology) University of Cape Town Medical School, 1970-84; Short term consultant assignments for the British Government and the World Health Organization, 1962-75. *Memberships:* Chairman of Hong Kong Medical and Dental and Nursing Councils and of Pharmacy and Midwives Boards, 1958-63; Permanent Representative of the UK on the Directing Council of the Pakistan/Seato Cholera Research Laboratory, Dacca, 1962-66. *Publications:* Articles on Cholera 1965, 1967, 1971; Articles on Subacute Sclerosing Pan Encephalitis (SSPE) 1972. *Honours:* MBE, 1944; OBE, 1947; Coronation Medal 1953; CMG, 1957. *Hobbies:* Fly Fishing; Golf. *Address:* 8 Avondrust Avenue, Bergvliet, 7945, Republic of South Africa.

MACKENZIE, Donald William Ross, b. 10 Apr. 1929, Edinburgh, Scotland. Director of PHLS Mycological Reference Laboratory. m. Joyce Suttie McCullam, 3 Oct. 1959, Cowdenbeath, 2 sons, 1 daughter. *Education:* BSc 1st class honours 1953, PhD 1958, University of Edinburgh. *Appointments:* Senior Lecturer in Medical Microbiology, Queens University of Belfast, Northern Ireland, 1960-67; Associate Professor of Microbiology, Cornell University Medical College, New York, USA, 1967-72; Professor of Medical Mycology, University of London, England, 1978-85; Currently Director, PHLS Mycological Reference Laboratory, Central Public Health Laboratory, London. *Memberships:* International Society for Human and Animal Mycology; British Society for Mycopathology; Association of Clinical Microbiologists; Association of Medical Microbiologists. *Publications:* 106 publications in medical mycology. *Hobby:* Golf. *Address:* Mycological Reference Laboratory, Central Public Health Laboratory, 61 Colindale Avenue, London NW9 5HT, England.

McKENZIE, Ian Farquhar Campbell, b. 22 July 1937, Melbourne, Australia. Director, Cancer and Transplantation Research Centre. *Education:* MB, BS, University of Melbourne, Australia, 1961; MD, MRACP, 1965; PhD, FRACP, 1970; FRCPA, 1976. *Appointments:* Resident Medical Officer, Royal Melbourne Hospital, Australia, 1962-69, Third Assistant, Department of Medicine, 1966-69; Research Fellow, Massachusetts General Hospital, Harvard Medical School, USA, 1969-73; Assistant Immunologist, Massachusetts General Hospital, 1973-74, Reader in Medicine, 1977, Personal Chair in Medicine, 1980; Director, Research Centre for Cancer and Transplantation, University of Melbourne, Australia, 1982-. *Memberships:* Australian Society for Immunology; American Association of Immunologists; International Transplantation Society; Clinical Oncology Society of Australia. *Publications:* 350 scientific publications. *Honour:* Susman Prize in Medicine, 1979. *Hobbies:* Sailing; Diving; Surfing. *Address:* Department of Pathology, The University of Melbourne, Parkville, Victoria 3052, Australia.

MACKENZIE, Thomas Brooke, b. 20 May 1944, Tampa, Florida, USA. Associate Professor of Psychiatry and Medicine. m. Jane Bell, 1 son, 1 daughter. *Education:* BA, Harvard College, 1966; MD, Harvard Medical School, USA, 1970. *Appointments:* Internship, University of California at San Francisco, 1970-71; Residency, Dartmouth Medical School, Adult Psychiatry, 1973-76; Instructor of Clinical Psychiatry, 1975-77; Assistant Professor of Psychiatry and Medicine, University of Minnesota Medical School, 1977-81. Associate Professor, 1981-. *Memberships:* American Psychiatric Association; Minnesota Psychiatric Society; Minnesota Medical Association; Hennepin County Medical Society; American Psychosomatic Society; Association of Directors of Medical Student Education in Psychiatry. *Publications include:* Author and co-author of 39 articles on psychiatric medicine in professor journals; numerous conference papers and presentations; Author and co-author of 8 book chapters including: "Psychiatric Diagnoses' in "Loosening the Grip", a handbook for Alcohol Counsellors, 1978; 'Credibility: the Problem of Psychiatry's Return to Medicine' in "Psychiatry in Crisis', 1982; 'Psychiatric Illness' in "Understanding Alcohol", 1982; 'Obsessive-Compulsive Neurosis' in "Medical Basis of Psychiatry", in press; Book Review: "Schizophrenia: The Epigenetic Puzzle", 1983. *Honours:* Alpha Omega Alpha, 1970; Best Journal Paper Award, Academy of Psychosomatic Medicine, 1981-82. *Address:* Mayo Box 393, 420 Delaware Street SE, Minneapolis, MN 55455, USA.

McKEOWN, Patrick Michael, b. 23 Nov. 1947, USA. Instructor in Psychology, Coordinator in Hospital Pharmacy Technology. *Education:* BS, Purdue University; MS, San Francisco State University, California, Certificates in Communications and Human Systems, Mental Research Institute, Palo Alto, California, 1970 and 1972; National Drug Abuse Training Program, 1971; Certificate in Social Services, University of California, 1975; Various Certificates of Training, State of California, Department of Health and Department of Mental Health. *Appointments:* Line Officer, United States Coast Guard; Management Service Ernst and Ernst, San Francisco, California; Social Control and Offender Habilitation, Alameda County, State of California; College Instructor of Psychology, Child Abuse, and Cooperative Work Experience Education; College Instructor, Work Experience Coordinator in Hospital Pharmacy Technology. *Memberships:* Academy of Criminal Justice

Sciences; American Academy of Forensic Sciences. *Publication:* 'A Study of the Short Form of the Luscher Color Test and Personality, Behavior and Social Characteristics of Adolescents', 1975. *Honours:* Various commendations; Superior Court and Head of Agency; Testimonial Loyalty Certificate, Purdue University, 1984. *Address:* San Ramon, CA 94583, USA.

MacKIE, Rona McLeod, b. 22 May 1940, Scotland. Professor of Dermatology. m. Euan Wallace MacKie, 18 Sep. 1963, Glasgow, 1 son, 1 daughter. *Education:* MB BCh, 1963, MD with commendation, 1970, Glasgow University. *Appointments include:* Currently, Professor of Dermatology, University of Glasgow, Scotland. *Memberships:* British Association of Dermatology. *Publications:* "Clinical Dermatology", 1981; "Eczema and Dermatitis", 1983; "Immuno Dermatology", 1982; "Malignant Melanoma", 1984. Editor, 'British Journal of Dermatology'. *Hobbies:* Skiing; Travel; Archaeology; Opera. *Address:* 7 Horseshoe Road, Beasden, Glasgow G61 2ST, Scotland.

McKINLEY, Laurence Mercer, b. 9 Sep. 1948, Dublin, Ireland. Consultant Orthopaedist. m. Mary Beth Proctor, 7 Oct. 1978, Glendale, California, USA. *Education:* University of Dublin, Trinity College; BA, 1970; MA, 1973; MB BCh BAO (Hons), 1972; MD, 1978. *Appointments:* Lecturer in Orthopaedics, University of Louisville, 1976; Lecturer in Orthopaedics, University of Southern California, 1977; Assistant Professor of Orthopaedics, University of Arkansas for Medical Science, 1978; Assistant Professor of Surgery, Michigan State University, 1979-81. *Memberships:* Diplomat, American Board of Orthopaedic Surgery; American Academy of Orthopaedic Surgeons; American Association for Hand Surgery; American Orthopaedic Society for Sports Medicine; Orthopaedic Research Society; International Medical Society of Paraplegia; American Congress of Rehabilitation Medicine; American Spinal Injury Association; American Paraplegic Society; American Academy of Neurological and Orthopaedic Surgery; California Medical Association; San Diego County Medical Society; MENSA. *Publications:* Contributor to professional journals, etc; Presentations; Exhibits. *Hobbies:* Sailing; Boat Building. *Address:* Pacific Spine Centre, 355 E Grand Avenue, Escondido, CA 92025, USA.

McKINNON, Bert, b. 20 July 1947, Kearny, New Jersey, USA. Orthopaedic Surgeon. m. Cynthia Anne Fish, 21 Aug. 1971, Red Bank, New Jersey, 3 sons. *Education:* BA, University of Pennsylvania, 1969; MMSc, Rutgers University, 1971; MD, University of Colorado, 1973. *Appointments:* Staff Surgeon, Naval Regional Medical Center, San Diego; Private Practice, Orthopaedic Surgeon. *Memberships:* Fellow, American Academy of Orthopaedic Surgeons; Arizona Medical Association; Coconino County Medical Society. *Publications:* "Congenital Dysplasia of the Hip: The Lax (Subluxatable) Newborn Hip" with M Bosse and W Browning in 'Journal of Pediatric Orthopaedics' 1984; "Pitfalls in the Use of the Pavlik Harness for Treatment of Congenital Dysplasia Subluxation and Dislocation of the Hip" with S Mubarek, S Garfin, R Vance, D Sutherland, in Journal of Bone and Joint Surgery, 1981. *Honours:* Colorado Tuberculosis Association Award, 1972; Norman T Kirk Award, 1979. *Hobbies:* Fishing; Boating. *Address:* 1350 North Rim Drive, Flagstaff, AZ 86001, USA.

MacKINNON, Sterling Alexander, b. 5 Dec. 1915, San Francisco, USA. Physician; Psychiatrist. m. Jane Nash, 11 May 1960, Philadelphia, 2 sons, 1 daughter. *Education:* BA, 1940, MD, Temple University, 1943. *Appointments:* Private Practice, Psychology, Norristown, PA, 1950-59; State Hospital, Psychology, 1960-1985. *Memberships:* Member, APA, 1947-85; Fellow, Royal Society of Health, 1970-1985. *Hobby:* Dogs. *Address:* 111 Fordham Circle, Pueblo, CO 81005, USA.

MACKLIN, Dennis James Senior, Chiropractic Osteopath. m. Carla Strober, 2 sons. *Education:* BSc,

Biology, USA; DC, USA; DO, UK. *Appointments:* Private Practice, Chiropractic Osteopath, Terni, Italy; Faculty Member, Palmer College of Chiropractic, USA, 3 years; Visiting Faculty Member, International College of Osteopathy and Alternative Therapeutics, London, England. *Memberships:* Past Chairman, Hygiene Committee, American Board of Chiropractic Examiners; Chairman, Italian Board of Chiropractic Examiners; Board of Governors, Anglo-European College of Chiropractic; Founding Member and Officeholder, Secretary, Society of Independent Chiropractors, Italy (Editor of Newsletter); International Academy of Psychobiophysics; American Chiropractic Association; Italian Chiropractic Association: Society of Independent Chiropractors, Italy. *Publications:* "The Human Spine: Gross Considerations", 1971; "Physiotherapy as Adjunct to Manipulative Therapy in Osteoarticular Disfunction", 1979; "Case Studies of Laser Application in Osteoarticular Disfunctions", 1981. *Honours:* World Progress Award in field of medicine, Italy, 1981. *Hobbies:* Photography; Music. *Address:* Viale dello Stadio 63, 05100 Terni, Italy.

MACKLIN, Martin, b. 27 Aug. 1934, Raleigh, North Carolina, USA. Administrative Director of Psychiatry. m. Anne Warren, Maryland, 25 May 1979, Honolulu, 3 daughters. *Education:* B Mechanical Engineering, Cornell University, USA, 1957, M. Industrial Engineering, 1958; PhD, Case Western Reserve University, 1967, MD, 1977. *Appointments:* Assistant Professor, Biomedical Engineering, Case Western Reserve University, Cleveland, Ohio, USA, 1967-72; Established Investigator, American Heart Association, 1969-74; Visiting Research Fellow, University of Sussex, England, 1970; Associate Professor, Biomedical Engineering, Case Western University, Cleveland, Ohio, 1972-81; Psychiatric Consultant, Mental Health Centre, 1979-81; Director of Professional Services, Horizon Centre Hospital, Warrensville Township, Ohio, 1981-83; Administrative Director, Psychiatry, Ashtabula County Medical Centre-; Assistant Professor, Psychiatry, Case Western Reserve University, Ohio. *Memberships:* American Psychiatric Association; Society of General Physiologists; Cleveland Psychiatric Association; Cleveland Academy of Medicine; American Medical Society on Alcoholism. *Publications include:* Numerous conference papers, letters, articles in professional journals including: 'Changes in the Conduction of the Fetal Electrocardiagram to the Maternal Abdominal Surface during Gestation', co-author, in 'American Journal of Obstetrics and Gynaecology', 1977; 'Cimetidine-Impramine Interaction: A Case Report', co-author in 'American Journal of Psychiatry', 1983; Chapter 20 'Alcoholism' in "Clinical Psychiatry", 1985. *Honours:* Established Investigator, American Heart Association, 1969-74; Laughlin Fellow, 1980. *Hobby:* Cabinet Making. *Address:* 2420 Lake Avenue, Ashtabula, OH 44004, USA.

McKNEW, Donald Harrison, b. 17 July 1933, Washington, District of Columbia, USA. Research Psychiatrist. m. Gretchen McKnew, 27 Nov. 1976, 1 son, 1 daughter. *Education:* BA, Yale University, New Haven, CT, 1955; MD, Johns Hopkins Medical School, Baltimore, MD, 1961. *Appointments include:* Research Associate, Department of Psychiatry Depression Study Group, Children's Hospital of DC and Hillcrest Children's Center, Washington, DC, 1968-73; Clinical Professor, Child Health and Development and of Psychiatry and Behavioral Sciences, George Washington University School of Medicine, Washington, DC, 1968-; Guest Worker, National Institute of Mental Health, Biological Psychiatry Branch, Bethesda, Maryland, 1973-77; Research Psychiatrist, Unit on Childhood Mental Illness, Biological Psychiatry Branch, 1977-82, Research Psychiatrist, Laboratory of Developmental Psychology, National Institute of Mental Health, Bethesda, Maryland, 1982-; Senior Attending Physician, Children's Hospital, Washington DC, 1976-. *Memberships:* American Psychiatric Assn; Washington Psychiatric Society;

American Psychopathological Assn (Honorary); American Academy of Child Psychiatry. *Publications include:* Author of numerous scientific papers including 'Treatment issues in childhood depression', (with L Cytryn), 1985; "Basic Handbook on Child Psychiatry", (with L Cytryn), in press. *Honours:* Alpha Omega Alpha, 1961; Fellow, American Psychiatric Assn, 1975; APA Blanche F Ittleson Prize for Research in Child Psychiatry, 1981. *Hobbies:* Tennis; Jogging. *Address:* 1127 Crest Lane, McLean, VA 22101, USA.

McKNIGHT, William Kuhn, b. 15 Feb. 1911, Beaver Falls, Pennsylvania, USA. Assistant Professor of Psychiatry. m. Elizabeth Frances Schum, 17 Mar. 1938, Grove City, Pennsylvania. *Education includes:* BS, 1934, MD, 1935, Medical School, University of Pittsburgh; Intern, Medical Center, University of Pittsburgh, 1935-36; Resident, New York Hospital, 1938-40; Fellow, Child Psychiatry, 1940-41. *Appointments include:* Chief, Psychiatric Service, General Hospital, US Army, 1944-45, Lieutenant Colonel, US Army Reserve, 1946-53; Assistant Superintendent, Clinical Director and Director, Friends Hospital, Philadelphia, 1946-53; Physician in Charge, New York Hospital, QPD West Division, Cornell Medical Center, 1957-69; Consultant, Psychiatry, Veterans Administration Hospital, Montrose, New York, 1967-73; Acting Director, Greater Bpt Comm Mental Health Center, 1975-; Instructor, 1957, Assistant Professor, Psychiatry, 1965, Emeritus, 1973-, Cornell Medical College. *Memberships include:* Honorary Member, New York Psychiatric Society; American Medical Association; Diplomate, American Board of Psychiatry; Fellow, American Psychiatric Association; Past President, Association of Community Clinic Psychiatrists and Psychiatric Society of Westchester County; Fellow, American Orthopsychiatric Association. *Publications:* Author or co-author of numerous professional publications including: 'Psychosomatic Medicine'; 'Journal of Nervous and Mental Disease'; 'New York State Journal of Medicine'; 'Westchester Medical Bulletin'; 'American Journal of Psychiatry'. Various contributions to international conferences. *Honours:* Activities Key, University of Pittsburgh; Honorary Secretary, New York Psychiatric Society; Diplomate, American Board of Psychiatry and Neurology; Commonwealth Fund Fellow, 1940-41; Numerous committee Chairmanships and Memberships. *Hobbies:* Painting; Music; History; Tennis; Swimming. *Address:* 704 Norfolk Court, Rio Rancho, NM 87124, USA.

MACLAREN, Noel Keith, b. 28 July 1939, New Zealand. Professor of Clinical Pathology. 2 daughters. *Education:* MB Ch B; FRACP; DC; Fellow in Endocrinology/Metabolism, Johns Hopkins and University of Maryland School of Medicine, USA, 1972-75. *Appointments:* Assistant Professor Pediatrics 1973-75, Associate Professor Pediatrics 1975-78, University of Maryland School of Medicine, Baltimore; Professor of Pathology/Pediatrics, Chairman of Department of Pathology, University of Florida College of Medicine, 1978-. *Memberships:* American Diabetes Association; Lawson Wilkins Society for Pediatric Endocrinologists; American Society Pediatrics; Society for Pediatric Research; American College Pathologists; American Society Clinical Pathologies. *Publications:* 'Adrenal Autoimmunity and Autoimmune Polyglandular Syndromes' (with R Blizzard), in "The Autoimmune Diseases", 1985; Many articles in learned journals. *Honour:* University of Florida Clinical Research Faculty Award, 1984. *Hobbies:* Golf; Chess; Bridge. *Address:* Department of Pathology, University of Florida College of Medicine, Box J-275, J Hillis Miller Health Center, Gainesville, FL 32610, USA.

McLEAN, David Ian, b. 8 June 1947, Canada. Assistant Professor of Medicine. m. Siu-Li Yong, 1 daughter. *Education:* BSc, MD, University of Manitoba, Canada, 1971; Fellow, Royal College of Physicians of Canada, Dermatology, 1976; Diplomate, American Board of Dermatology, 1977. *Appointments:* Research Fellow, Harvard University, 1976-77; Assistant Professor, Department of Medicine, University of British Columbia, 1977-; Chairman, Skin Tumour Group, Cancer Control Agency of British Columbia, 1977-. *Memberships:* Society for Investigative Dermatology; International Pigment Cell Society; Fellow, Canadian Dermatological Association; Fellow, American Academy of Dermatology. *Publications:* Numerous publications in medical journals. *Honours:* McEachern Award, Canadian Cancer Society, 1976; Research Scholar Award, British Columbia Health Care Research Foundation, 1979, 1980, 1981. *Address:* 855 West 10th Avenue, Vancouver, British Columbia, V5Z 1L7, Canada.

MacLEOD, Alastair William, b. 26 Aug. 1916, Canada. m. Ann Isobel Black, 18 Sep. 1954, Montreal. *Education:* BSc, Pure Science, 1938, MB, ChB, 1941, University of Glasgow, Scotland; Diploma, Public Health, University of Glasgow; Certificate, Tropical Medicine, University of Edinburgh, Scotland, 1943; Postgraduate Diploma, Psychological Medicine, University of London, England, 1944; Royal College of Physicians of London; Graduate, Institute of Psychoanalysis, London, 1951. *Appointments include:* Resident Clinical Clerk, Woodilee Mental Hospital, Corporation of Glasgow, 1938-42; Medical Officer, Bexley Hospital, London County Council, 1942-44; Clinical Assistant, Guy's Hospital, London, 1944-50; Resident House Physician, 1944-45, 1st Medical Officer, 1945, Assistant Medical Director, 1945-50, Acting Medical Director, 1945-47, Senior Registrar, 1949-50, Guy's Hospital, London; Senior Registrar, Cassel Hospital for Function Nervous Disorders, Richmond, 1950-51; Assistant Director, 1951-60, Associate Director, 1960-66, Medical Director, 1966-69, Executive Director, 1969-81, Mental Hygiene Institute Inc, Montreal, Canada; Lecturer, 1951-53, Assistant Professor, 1953-59, Associate Professor, 1959-64, 1964-72, Professor, 1972-81, 1981, McGill University, Canada. *Memberships include:* Royal Society of Tropical Medicine & Hygiene, Fellow; Fellow, Royal Society of Medicine; Associate Member, British Psychoanalytical Society; Associate Member, Institute of Psychoanalysis; Life Fellow, American Psychiatric Association; Life Member, Canadian Psychiatric Association; Canadian Psychiatric Association; Canadian Psychoanalytic Society; American Psychoanalytic Association; Fellow, American Association for the Advancement of Science; Royal College of Psychiatrists; Founding Committee, RM Bucke Memorial Society. *Publications:* Chapter, Co-author, "Basic Concepts", 'Recent Developments in Psychosomatic Medicine', 1954; Author, "Recidivism, A Deficiency Disease", 1965. *Hobbies:* Reading; Walking. *Address:* 3674 Peel Street, Montreal, Quebec H3A 1W9, Canada.

McMILLAN, Donald Edgar, b. 23 Sep. 1937, Butler, Pennsylvania, USA. Professor. m. Marjorie Ann Leavitt, 4 Feb. 1961, Philadelphia, 1 son, 1 daughter. *Education:* BS, Grove City College; MS, PhD, University of Pittsburgh. *Appointments:* Post-doctoral Fellow, Harvard Medical School, 1965-67; Instructor, 1968, Assistant Professor, 1968-69, Downstate Medical School, University of New York; Assistant Professor, 1969-72, Associate Professor, 1972-76, Professor, 1976-78, University of North Carolina School of Medicine; Professor, Chairman, University Arkansas for Medical Sciences, 1978-, Pharmacology, 1985-, University of Arkansas; Visiting Lecturer, Universidad Central, Caracas, 1974. *Memberships:* American Association Advancement of Science; Behavioral Pharmacological Society, President, 1982-84; American Society Pharmacology; Experimental Therapeutic Society; Sigma Xi; Neurobehavioral Toxicology Society. *Publications:* "Central Nervous System Pharmacology", 1979; over 150 papers on drug abuse, behavioral pharmacology etc. *Honours include:* Recipient, various honours and awards. *Hobbies:* Tennis; Antique Restoration. *Address:* Department Pharmacology & Interdisciplinary Toxicology, College of Medicine, University Arkansas for Medical Sciences, Little Rock, AK 72206, USA.

McMILLAN, Mae Frances, b. 12 May 1936, Austin, Texas, USA. *Education:* BA, BS, Summa cum Laude, Wiley College, Marshall, TX; MD, Honors, Meharry Medical College, Nashville, TN; FAPA. *Appointments:* Assistant Director, 1968-72, Director, Child Study Clinic, Division of Child Psychiatry, 1972-74, Director, Early Childhood Therapy Course and Clinic, TX Research Institute of Mental Sciences, 1974-; Part-time Private Practice, Child Psychiatry, Speciality pre-schooler, 1966-. *Memberships:* Harris County Medical Society; TX Medical Assn.; National Medical Assn.; American Society of Adolescent Psychiatry; Houston Society of Adolescent Psychiatry; TX Society of Child Psychiatry; American Psychiatric Assn.; TX Psychiatric Society; Black Psychiatrists of America. *Publications:* 'A Racial Minority: Black Americans and Mental Health Care' (with E A Kendrick, C A Pinderhughes), 1983; 'Child Psychiatry; Treatment and Research' (with S Henao), 1977; 'Children: Their Names are Today', 1979; 'Von Glierke's Disease in Siblings: A Case Study of Three Siblings and Review of the Literature',)with I A Kraft, and J L Wheeler), 1966. *Honours include:* Alpha Kappa Mo National Honour Society, 1953; Outstanding Young Women of America, 1971; Two Thousand Women of Distinction, 1972-82; Certificate, World's Who's Who of Women, 1973. *Hobbies:* Reading; Travel; Long Distance Walking; Piano Music; The Arts. *Address:* 4114 Cornell Street, Houston, TX 77022, USA.

McMINN, Alexander, b. 12 Dec. 1932, Liverpool, England. Executive Director, International Association of Medical Laboratory Technologists. m. Kathleen Frances Rannard, 18 Aug. 1956, Liverpool, 2 daughters. *Education:* Fellowship, Institute of Medical Laboratory Sciences, 1957; Member, Institute of Biologists, 1963; PhD, 1984. *Appointments:* Principal lecturer in Medical Science 1964-68, Head of Department of Medical Sciences 1968-72, Director of External Relations 1972-84, Liverpool Polytechnic; Consultant in Education, World Health Organisation, 1972-; Executive Director, International Association of Medical Laboratory Technologists, 1980-; Chief Executive, Health Manpower Services Ltd, Liverpool, 1982-; Honorary Senior Lecturer in International Community Health, Liverpool School of Tropical Medicine, 1985-. *Memberships:* Fellow, Institute of Medicine Laboratory Sciences; Institute of Biology; Fellow, Royal Society of Medicine. *Publications:* "Training of Medical Laboratory Technicians: A Handbook for Tutors", 1975; "Designing and Teaching Competency Based Curricula for Health Laboratory Workers", in press. *Honours:* Medal of the Council of Europe for Services to International Education, 1982. *Hobbies:* Water Sports; Playing the Organ; Cooking. *Address:* Health Manpower Services Limited, Mast House, Derby Road, Merseyside L20 1EA, England.

McMURRAY, Donald A, b. 4 Apr. 1945, Philadelphia, Pennsylvania, USA. Executive Director, Human Services Center Inc. m. Meredith Fogg, 7 July 1977, Ascutney, Vermont, 1 son, 1 daughter. *Education:* BS Political Science, Rollins College, 1968; MA Psychology, University of South Florida, 1972; PhD Psychology, University of Pittsburgh, 1975; Post doctorate hypnotherapy, American Society of Clinical Hypnosis, 1978; Post doctorate Family Therapy, Family Therapy Institute, 1981. *Appointments:* Program Chair, Chairman, Psychology Department, Keene, New Hampshire; Association Dean of Administration/Finance, Antioch University, Columbia, Maryland; Executive Director, Community Counselling Centre Inc, Cumberland, Maryland; Executive Director, Human Services Center Inc, New Castle, Pennsylvania; Psychologist in private practice, 1975-; Association Professor, Antioch University and Frostburgh State College. *Memberships:* Board of Directors, Pennsylvania Association of Community MH/MR Providers; American Psychological Association; American Society of Clinical Hypnosis; International Society of Clinical Hypnosis; Pittsburgh Psychoanalytic Center Inc; Western Pennsylvania

Group Psychotherapy Association. *Publication:* 'An Appraisal of a Doctoral Program in Counselor Education Based Upon a Value Analysis Method Derived From Harold D Lasswell's Policy Sciences Approach', dissertation, 1975. *Hobbies:* Skiing; Water Sports; Tennis; Basketball. *Address:* 301 Haney Building, PO Box 144, New Castle, PA 16103, USA.

McNAB JONES, Robin Francis, b. 22 Oct. 1922, Bristol, England. Consulting Surgeon and University Dean. m. Mary Garrett, 23 July 1950, Orpington, Kent, England, 1 son, 3 daughters. *Education:* St Bartholomew's Hospital Medical College, MBBS (London) 1945, FRCS (England) 1952. *Appointments:* House Surgeon, St Bartholomew's Hospital, 1946-47; MO, RAF 1947-50; Demonstrator of Anatomy, St Bartholomew's Hospital, 1950-52; Registrar, Royal National Throat Hospital, 1952-54; Senior Registrar, St Bartholomew's Hospital, ENT Department, 1954-59; Lecturer on Otolaryng, University of Manchester, 1959-61; Consultant Surgeon, Royal National Throat Hospital, 1962-83; Dean, Institute of Laryngology and Otology, University of London, 1971-76; Surgeon, ENT Department, St Bartholomew's Hospital, 1961-. *Memberships:* Royal Society of Medicine, President of Section of Laryngology 1982; British Association of Otolaryngologists, Member of Council 1978-; Royal College of Surgeons, England, Member Court of Examiners 1972-78, Member of Council 1983-. *Publications:* Chapters 'Examination of Nose' and 'Diseases of Nasal Passages' in "Price's Textbook of Medicine" 12th Edition 1978; Chapters on 'Anatomy and Physiology of Mouth, Pharynx and Oesophagus', 'Hyperpharyngeal Diverticulum and Oesoph Conditions' in Scott-Brown's "Diseases of ENT" 4th edition 1979; Chapters on 'Lavage of the Sinuses', Caldwell-Luc and Allied Operations' in Rob and Smith's "Operative Surgery" 4th edition 1982. *Hobbies:* Tennis; Golf; Skiing; Fishing. *Address:* 108 Harley Street, London W1N 1AF, England.

McNAMARA, Dan Goodrich, b. 19 Oct. 1922, Waco, Texas, USA. Professor of Paediatrics; Chief, Section of Cardiology, Baylor College of Medicine and Texas Children's Hospital. m. Ann Randolph Wier, 4 Jan. 1949, Houston, Texas, 2 sons, 3 daughters. *Education:* BS; MD; Internship, Jersey City Medical Center, 1946-47; Pediatric Residency: Hermann Hospital, Houston, 1949-50, St Louis Children's Hospital, 1950-51; Fellowship, Pediatric Cardiology, The Johns Hopkins Hospital, Baltimore, Maryland, 1951-53. *Appointments:* Instructor in Pediatrics, The Johns Hopkins University School of Medicine, 1951-53; Assistant Professor of Pediatrics, Baylor University College of Medicine, 1954-65; Associate Professor of Pediatrics, 1965-69, Professor of Pediatrics, 1969-, Baylor College of Medicine. *Memberships:* Diplomate, American Board of Pediatrics; Fellow, American College of Cardiology, President, 1981-82; Member, American Pediatric Society; Association of European Pediatric Cardiologists, Corresponding Member; Cardiology Society of Australia and New Zealand, Corresponding Member. *Publications include:* "Twenty-five Years of Progress in the Medical Treatment of Pediatric and Congenital Heart Disease", 'JACC', 1983; 'The Blalock-Taussig Operation and Subsequent Progress in Surgical Treatment of Cardiovascular Disease', 'Journal of American Medical Association', 1984. *Honours:* Distinguished Alumnus Award, Baylor University Alumni Association, 1981; Distinguished Faculty Award, Baylor Medical Alumni Association, 1980; "Al Merito", Republic of Ecuador, 1961. *Hobby:* Sailing. *Address:* 6621 Fannin Street, Houston, TX 77030, USA.

McNAMARA, Gregor, b. 5 Jan. 1954, Lowell, Massachusetts, USA. Podiatrist. m. Debra McNamara, 4 Apr. 1974, 1 daughter. *Education:* DPM, Ohio College of Podiatric Medicine, Cleveland, Ohio; MS, Public Health, Tufts University, Medford, MA; BS, Chemistry, Merrimack College, N Andover, MA. *Appointments:* Resident, Podiatric Medicine and Surgery,

Lutheran Hospital, Baltimore MD; Fellow, American Heart Association, Cleveland, OH; Instructor, Public Health, Ohio College of Podiatric Medicine; Clinical Staff, Veterans Administration, Bedford, MA. *Memberships:* Associate American College of Foot Surgeons; American Podiatric Medical Assoc.; American Public Health Assoc.; American Board of Podiatric Surgery. *Publications:* 'Local Sympathectomy of the Foot, A Quantitative Analysis', (with J M Louis, A Weinstein), 1980; 'Aneurysmal Bone Cyst of a Metatarsal: A Case Report and Review of the Literature', (with F Beheshti), 1982; 'Pseudomonas Osteomyelitis: A Case Report and Clinical Perspectives', (with R I Shor), 1982; 'Diabetic Neuro-Osteoarthropathy: A Case Report', (with R I Shor),'Diabetic Neuro-Osteoarthropathy: A Case Report', (with R I Shor), 1983; (abstracts) 'Characteristics of 1000 New Admissions to the Cleveland Foot Clinic', 1982; 'Effect of Cimetidine on dl-propranolol Disposition in the Isolated Rat Hepatocytes', (with Y Kwong), 1982. *Honours:* Pi Delta National Podiatric Honorary Society, 1980; Sigma Xi; Research Fellowship, The National Council on Air and Stream Improvement, 1976; Outstanding Young Man of America, 1979; USAF Armed Forces Health Professions Scholarship, 1978. *Hobbies:* Boating; Tennis. *Address:* 817 Merrimack Street, Lowell, MA 01854, USA.

MacNEILL, Alastair Duncan, b. 21 Apr. 1922, Dunoon, Argyll, Scotland. General Practitioner. m. Janet Kelso Campbell, 21 Apr. 1951, Glasgow, 1 son, 1 daughter. *Appointments:* House Surgeon, House Physician, Royal Alexandra Infirmary, Paisley; General Practice and SHMO Glasgow Homoropathic Hospital. *Memberships:* Fellow, Faculty of Homoropathy; Royal Medico-Chirurgical Society of Glasgow. *Hobby:* Golf. *Address:* 9 Victoria Park Gardens South, Glasgow G11 7BY, Scotland.

McNEILL, John Hugh, b. 5 Dec. 1938, Chicago, Illinois, USA. University Professor of Pharmacology and Toxicology. m. Sharon Louise Keneffly, 27 July 1963, Edmonton, Canada, 2 daughters. *Education:* BSc 1960, MSc 1962, Pharmacy, University of Alberta; PhD Pharmacology, University of Michigan, USA, 1967. *Appointments:* Instructor/Assistant Professor, Michigan State University, 1966-71; Associate Professor 1971-74, Chairman of Division of Pharmacy 1972-81, Professor of Pharmacology and Toxicology, 1974-, Medical Research Council Research Professor 1981-82, Associate Dean 1982-84, Dean 1985-, Faculty of Pharmaceutical Sciences, University of British Columbia, Vancouver, Canada. *Memberships:* Pharmaceutical Society of Canada; American Society of Pharmacology and Experimental Therapeutics; Western Pharmacology Society; International Society of Heart Research; American Association for the Advancement of Science; New York Academy of Sciences; Canadian Cardiovascular Society; American Pharmacological Association; British Columbia College. *Publications:* 181 papers on cardiovascular pharmacology; 25 review articles and book chapters. *Honours:* Upjohn Award, 1983; McNeill Award, 1983; Jacob Biely Prize, 1985. *Hobbies:* Travel; Reading history. *Address:* Faculty of Pharmaceutical Sciences, University of British Columbia, Vancouver, British Columbia, V6T 1W5, Canada.

McPHIE, John Milroy, b. 9 Jan. 1919, South Australia, Australia. Consultant Cardiologist. m. Joan Mahood, 30 March 1946, Adelaide, 4 daughters. *Education:* MB BS, 1942, MD, 1957. Adelaide; Member, 1948, Fellow, 1960, Royal Australian College of Physicians. *Appointments:* Resident Medical Officer, Royal Adelaide Hospital, 1942; Service with RAAMCS, 1942-46; Registrar, Hammersmith Hospital, London, England, 1953; Senior Cardiologist, Head, Clinical Cardiac Unit, Royal Adelaide Hospital, 1959-84; Consultant Cariologist, Veterands Administration, South Australia, 1953-75. *Memberships:* Australian Medical Association; Life Member and Past President, Cardiac Socoety of Australia and New Zealand. Fellow, Royal

Australasian College of Physicians; American College of Cardiology. *Publications:* Author or Co-Author of numerous articles contributed to professional publications including: 'Australasian Annals of Medicine'; 'Medical Journal of Australia'; 'American Heart Journal'; 'Australian and New Zealand Journal of Medicine'; 'The Lancet'; 'Circulation'. *Hobbies:* Golf; Tennis; Fishing. *Address:* 327 South Terrace, Adelaide, SA5000, Australia.

MacQUARRIE, Ronald Anthony, b. 30 Jan. 1943, Oakland, California, USA. Professor of Basic Life Sciences. m. Mary Lucinda Tupac, 2 Jan. 1983. 2 sons, 1 daughter. *Education:* BS, University of California; PhD, University of Oregon. *Appointments:* Assistant Professor 1973-79, Associate Professor 1972-83, University of Missouri, Kansas City; Chairman, Department of Chemistry 1982-83, Professor 1983-, ibid; Interim Dean, School of Basic Life Sciences, 1985-86. *Memberships:* American Association for the Advancement of Science; American Chemical Society; American Society of Biological Chemists; Sigma Xi. *Publications include:* 'Partial purification & properties of Acyl-CoA Hydrolase & Lysophosphatidyl Choline Acyltransferase from heart muscle microsomes' (Federal Proceedings, 1985), co-author. *Honours:* Postdoctoral Fellowship, National Institutes of Health, 1970-72; National Science Foundation research grants, 1975-80, 1985-88; NIH research grant, 1975-78. *Hobbies:* Running; Racket sports. *Address:* School of Basic Life Sciences, University of Missouri-KC, Kansas City, MO 64110, USA.

McROY, Ruth G Murdock, b. 6 Oct. 1947, Vicksburg, Mississippi, USA. Assistant Professor of Social Work. m. Myron L McRoy, 5 June 1968 (divorced), 2 daughters. *Education:* BA Sociology 1968, MSW 1970, University of Kansas; PhD, University of Texas, Austin, 1981. *Appointments:* Marriage and Family Counselor, Family Consultation Service, 1970-71; Adoptions Counselor, Kansas Children's Service League, 1971-72; Project Co-ordinator, Black Adoption Program and Services, Kansas City, 1972-73; Assistant Professor, University of Kansas School of Social Welfare, 1973-77; Assistant Professor, Prairie View A and M University, Prairie View, Texas, 1977-78; Technical Assistant Specialist, Region VI Adoption Resource Center, Austin, 1979-81; Assistant Professor of Social Work, University of Texas, Austin, 1981-. *Memberships:* National Association of Social Workers; Southwestern Social Science Association; Western Social Science Association; Council on Social Work Education. *Publications:* "Transracial and Inracial Adoptees: The Adolescent Years", 1983; "Alcohol Use and Abuse Among Blacks", 1985; "Alcohol Use and Abuse Among Mexican-Americans", 1985; "Cross-Cultural Field Supervision", 1985. *Honours:* Danforth Fellow, 1978; Graduate Fellow, Outstanding Dissertation Award, University of Texas, 1981; Lora Lee Penderson Teaching Excellence Award, 1984; Ruby Lee Presta Centennial Fellow, 1985; Phi Kappa Phi Scholar Award, 1986. *Hobbies:* Jogging; Travelling. *Address:* University of Texas School of Social Work, 2609 University Avenue, Austin, TX 78712, USA.

McSHERRY, James Andrew, b. 20 May 1942, Comrie, Scotland. Director, Student Health Service; Associate Professor, Family Medicine, Queen's University, Kingston, Canada. m. Helen Margaret Weetch, 3 Feb. 1968, Glasgow, 2 sons, 1 daughter. *Education:* MB, ChB, Glasgow, 1965; MRCGP, 1972; FRCGP, 1982; CCFP (C), 1976; FCFP (C), 1985; FAAFP, 1982; FRSH, 1980; FAGS, 1976; DObstRCOG, 1967. *Appointments include:* General Medical Practitioner, Glasgow, Scotland/Sarnia, Ontario, Canada; Attending Staff, Sarnia General Hospital/St Joseph's Hospital, Sarnia; Chief, Department of General Practice, St Joseph's Hospital, Sarnia; Attending Staff, Hotel Dieu Hospital, Kingston, Canada; Associate Staff, Kingston General Hospital. Former major, RAMC (V). *Memberships:* Various medical associations. *Publications include:* Numerous scientific articles, items of medical wit & wisdom. *Honour:* Territorial Army

Decoration, 1973. *Hobbies:* Scottish country dancing; Social bridge; Family activities. *Address:* Student Health Service, Queen's University, Kingston, Canada K7L 3N6.

MacSWEEN, Joseph Michael, b. 1 Mar. 1933, Antigonish, Nova Scotia, Canada. Professor of Medicine, Dalhousie University. m. Mary Walsh, 19 Oct. 1957, Halifax, 2 sons, 2 daughters. *Education:* BSc, St Francis Xavier University, 1952; MD, 1957, MSc, 1969, Dalhousie University; FRCP (Canada)), 1971. *Appointments:* General Practice, Halifax, 1957-66; Resident, Internal Medicine, Victoria General Hospital, Halifax, 1966-68; Research Fellow, Department of Medicine, Dalhousie University, 1968-69; Fellow, Clinical Immunology, Montreal General Hospital, 1969-70; MRC Fellow, Walter and Eliza Hall Institute, Melbourne, Australia, 1971-72. *Memberships:* Canadian Medical Association; Nova Scotia Medical Society; Royal College of Physicians, Canada; Canadian Society for Immunology; Canadian Society for Clinical Investigation; American Society for Transplant Physicians. *Publications:* Contributor to professional journals; Chapters in Books; Presentations. *Honours:* Lilly International Fellowship, 1966; Medical Research Council Fellowship, 1971. *Hobbies:* Swimming; Canoeing; Skiing. *Address:* Camp Hill Hospital, 1763 Robie Street, Halifax, Nova Scotia, Canada B3H 3G2.

McVICKER, Rowland Alexander Melville, b. 25 June 1916, Edinburgh, Scotland. Consultant Orthopaedic Surgeon. m. Mavis Dierdre Corry, 4 Apr. 1950, Comber, County Down, Northern Ireland, 2 sons, 1 daughter. *Education:* MB, Belfast, Northern Ireland. *Appointments:* Royal Army Medical Corps, 1940-46; Orthopaedic Registrar, Lewisham Hospital, London, England; Senior Orthopaedic Registrar, Manfield Orthopaedic Hospital, Northampton; Honorary Consultant, Coast Province General Hospital, Mombasa, Kenya, CMS Mission Hospital, Kaloleni, 1954-69; Honorary Consultant Orthopaedic Surgeon, APDK, Polio Clinic, Mombasa, 1965-. *Memberships:* British Orthopaedic Association; Kenya Medical Association; British Ornithological Union. *Honours:* Member of the British Empire, 1977. *Hobby:* Ornithology. *Address:* PO Box 90664, Mombasa, Kenya.

MADDOX, Yvonne Tarlton, b. 19 July 1936, Paducah, Texas, USA. Health Administrator. m. George F Allman, 2 Nov. 1974. *Education:* BA, Business Administration. *Appointments:* President and Founder, World Health Information Services Inc, New York City, 1970-83; Vice President, Health Education Technologies Division, Barton Barton Durstine and Osborn Inc, New York City, 1984-. *Memberships:* Pharmaceutical Advertising Council; American Women of Radio and Television (Past Director); Association of Independent Clinical Publications (Executive Secretary); Madison Square Garden Boys Club. *Hobbies:* Painting; Restoring Old Houses; Golf; Tennis. *Address:* Health Education Technologies Division, 488, Madison Avenue, New York, NY 10022, USA.

MADDREY, Willis Crocker, b. 29 Mar. 1939, Roanoke Rapids, North Carolina, USA. Magee Professor of Medicine and Chairman of the Department. m. Ann Marie Matt, 18 Apr. 1981, Baltimore, 3 sons. *Education:* BS, Wake Forest University, 1960; MD, Johns Hopkins University, 1964. *Appointments:* Internship, 1964-65, Assistant Resident, 1965-66, Osler Medical Service, Johns Hopkins Hospita; US Public Health Service, Office of International Research, Calcutta, India, 1966-68; Assistant Resident, 1968-69, Chief Resident 1969-70, Osler Medical Service, Johns Hopkins; Fellow, Liver Disease, Yale University School of Medicine, 1970-71; Assistant Professor of Medicine, 1971-75; Assistant Dean, Postdoctoral Programs and Faculty Development, 1975-79; Associate Director and Associate Physician in Chief, 1979-82; Professor of Medicine, Johns Hopkins University School of Medicine, 1980-82; Magee Professor of Medicine and

Chairman of Department, Jefferson Medical College, 1982-. *Memberships include:* Alpha Omega Alpha; American Society for Clinical Investigation; Fellow and Regent, American College of Physicians; American Association for the Study of Liver Disease, President, 1981; American Board of Internal Medicine, Subspecial Board on Gastroenterology. *Publications:* Books include: "Liver", 1984 (co-author); Contributor to professional journals, etc. *Honours:* Henry Strong Denison Scholar in the Medical Sciences, 1963-64; George Stuart Outstanding Teacher Award, Johns Hopkins, 1970; Distinguished Achievement Award Lecturer, American College of Nutrition, 1984. *Hobbies:* Golf; Travel. *Address:* 775 Mill Creek Road, Gladwyne, PA 19035, USA.

MADEN, William Leroy, b. 19 Oct. 1931, Georgia, USA. Associate Professor, m. Patricia E Raulerson, 16 July 1966, 2 sons, 1 daughter. *Education:* BA Biology, Emory University, Atlanta, Georgia; MD Medicine, University of Tennessee, Memphis, Tennessee; Certificate Psychoanalysis, Columbia University, New York, 1970. *Appointments:* Instructor in Psychiatry, Emory University 1961-62, Columbia University 1962-63; Director, State Intensive Care Unit, Grady Hospital, Georgia, 1961-62; Senior Staff Psychiatrist, Treatment Center, New York, 1963-68; Clinical Assistant in Psychiatry, Mount Sinai Medical School, 1969-77; Assistant Attending Psychiatrist, New York Hospital, 1977-79; Associate Professor of Psychiatry, 1979-, Chairman Admissions Committee 1980-82, Quillen-Dishner College of Medicine, ETSU, Johnson City, Tennessee; Staff Psychiatrist, Chief of Inpatient Unit, Veterans Administration Medical Center, Tennessee, 1979-. *Memberships:* Secretary, Program Chairman, Section of Neurology, Neurosurgery, and Psychiatry, Southern Medical Association; President, Upper East Tennessee Chapter of American Psychiatric Association; Tennessee Medical Society. *Publications:* 'Major Psychiatric Disorders' (with D G Doane) in "Family Practice" (editor: R E Rakel) 3rd edition 1983. *Hobbies:* Outdoor activities; White water boating. *Address:* Department of Psychiatry, Quillen-Dishner College of Medicine, PO Box 19, 501A ETSU, Johnson City, TN 37614-0002, USA.

MADIGAN, Michael Hoseph, b. 22 Mar. 1946, Wichita, Kansas, USA. Psychiatrist. m. Dixie Tucker, 23 Dec. 1969, New Orleans, USA, 1 son, 1 daughter. *Education:* BA, Southern Methodist University, 1968; MS, Clinical Psychology, North Texas State University, 1971; PhD, Psychology, Tulane University, 1976; MD, Louisiana State University, 1979; Psychiatry Specialisation, Timberlawn Psychiatric Hospital, 1984. *Appointments:* Sports Reporter for the 'Dallas Morning News', 1968; Graduate Assistant to Research Psychologist, Tulane University, 1971-74; Chief Psychiatric Resident, Timberlawn Psychiatric Hospital, 1983-84; Staff Psychiatrist. *Memberships:* Dallas County Medical Society; North Texas Psychiatric Society; Texas Medical Association; American Medical Association; American Psychiatric Association; Member of the Board of Trustees of the American Psychiatric Association, 1984. *Publication:* Co-author chapter in "The Broadscope of Ego Function Assessment", 1984. *Honours:* Falk Fellow, American Psychiatric Association, 1982-84; President of Falk Fellows, 1984; Member of the American Psychiatric Assoc iation's Board of Trustees, 1984. *Hobbies:* Basketball; Tennis; Cycling; Writing Poetry. *Address:* 4701 Samuell Boulevard F Dallas, TX 75228, USA.

MADORSKY, Julie G, b. 17 June 1945, Hungary. Medical Director. m. Arthur Madhorsky, 17 Sep. 1978, 3 sons, 2 daughters. *Education:* MD, 1969; Diplomate, National Board of Medical Examiners, 1969; Diplomate, American Board of Physical Medicine and Rehabilitation, 1975. *Appointments:* Assistant Professor of Rehabilitation Medicine, Temple University Hospital, Philadelphia, Pennsylvania, USA, 1973-74. *Memberships include:* Examiner 1981-, Quality Assurance and Health Care Financing Subcommittee 1982-, American Board of Physical Medicine and Rehabilitation; Diagnostic and Therapeutic Technology Assessment Reference Panel 1982-, American Medical Association; American Academy of Physical Medicine and Rehabilitation; American Association of Sex Educators, Counselors and Therapists; American Congress of Rehabilitation Medicine; American Medical Women's Association; American Society for Clinical Evoked Potentials; American Spinal Injury Association. *Publications include:* 'The role of Benzodiazepines in the management of neurological and muscular disorders', 1983; Editor, Epitomes of Progress, Physical Medicine and Rehabilitation, 'Western Journal of Medicine', 1984-; 'Wheelchair sports medicine', (with K A Curtis), 1984; 'Psychosocial aspects of death and dying in Duchenne Muscular Dystrophy', (with L M Radford and E M Neumann), 1984; 'Staged treatment of spasticity', 1984; 'Sexuality and disability', 1984; 'Wheelchair mountaineering', (with D P Kiley), 1984. *Address:* 255 E Bonita Avenue, Pomona, CA 91767, USA.

MAEDA, Hiroshi, b. 22 Dec. 1938, Hyogo-Ken, Japan. Professor and Chairman. m. Norico Soma, 1 Oct. 1968, Sendai, Japan, 2 sons. *Education:* BS, Tohoku University, Sendai, Japan, 1962; MS, University of California, USA, 1964; PhD, Tohoku University, 1968, MD, 1972. *Appointments:* Research Associate, Dana Farber Cancer Centre, Children's Hospital Medical Centre, Harvard University Medical School, USA, 1968-71; Associate Professor, Kumamoto University Medical School, Japan, 1972-80, Professor and Chairman, 1980-. *Memberships:* Japanese Biochemical Society; Japanese Cancer Association; Japan Society for Cancer Treatment; Japanese Society for Bacteriologists; American Chemical Society; American Society of Microbiologists; American Association for Cancer Research; Society of Sigma Xi; NY Academy of Sciences; Soc Exp Biol Med; Japan Society of Cell Biology. *Publications:* "Chemical Modification of Proteins" (in Japanese), 1982; "Physiology and Biochemistry of Diseases" (in Japanese), 1985; "Enhancement of Vascular Permeability upon Serratial Infection: Activation of Hageman Factor", 1985; Developed a new concept in cancer chemotherapy and a prototype macromolecular drug, Smancs; Articles in professional journals. *Honours:* Fulbright Award, 1962-64; Incett Award, 1980; Award for Multidisciplinary Treatment of Cancer, 1983; Princess Takamatsu Award for Cancer Research, 1985; Research Award from Sapporo Life Science Foundation, 1985. *Hobbies:* Photography; Travel; Swimming. *Address:* Hotakubo Honmachi 631-3, Kumamoto, Japan 862.

MAEKAWA, Nobuo, b. 30 Jan. 1921, Hokkaido, Japan. Professor of Medicine/Hospital Director. m. Chieko Tachikawa, 3 Nov. 1946, Ashiya, 1 son, 1 daughter. *Education:* MD, Faculty of Medicine, Kyoto University, 1944. *Appointments:* Associate Professor, 1956-70, Professor of Medicine, Chest Disease Research Institute, Kyoto University, 1970-. *Memberships:* International Union Against Tuberculosis; American College of Chest Physicians; International Association for the Study of Lung Cancer. *Publications:* "Pulmonary Manifestations of Systemic Diseases" 1976; "Respiratory Diseases", 1983. *Honour:* Emeritus Professor of Kyoto University, 1984. *Hobbies:* Travel; Photography. *Address:* 2-21, Matsunouchi-cho, Ashiya, Hyogo Pref, 659, Japan.

MAEKAWA, Tadashi, b. 29 Oct. 1924, Kyoto, Japan. University President. m. Masayo Fujikado, 28 Nov. 1953, Nagoya, 2 daughters. *Education:* Graduate, Faculty of Medicine, 1948, MD, DMS, 1957, Tokyo University. *Appointments:* Intern, Hospital, 1948-49, Research Fellow, 3rd Department of Internal Medicine, 1950-52, Research Associate, 1952-54, Tokyo University; Assistant Professor, 2nd Department of Internal Medicine, Gunma University School of Medicine, 1954-61; Research Fellow, City of Hope National Medical Center, USA, 1956-57; Associate Professor, 2nd Department of Internal Medicine, 1961-73, Chairman and Professor, 3rd Department of

Internal Medicine, 1973-86, Dean, School of Medicine, 1982-85; President, Gunma University, 1985. *Memberships:* International and Japanese Societies of Hematology; International and Japanese Societies of Thrombosis and Haemostasis; International and Japanese Societies of Internal Medicine. *Publications:* "Atlas of Hematology", 1972; "Textbook of Physical Diagnosis", 1983; "Disseminated Intravascular Coagulation, Its Diagnosis and Treatment", 1984. *Address:* 32-11 Shimoishikura-cho, Maebashishi, Japan 371.

MAFFEI, Lamberto, b. 21 Mar. 1936, Grosseto, Italy. Professor. m. Maria Grazia Fucci, 25 Nov. 1963, Pisa, 1 son, 1 daughter. *Education:* MD. *Appointment:* Assistant Professor, Professor, Director, Institute of Neurophysiology, Pisa. *Publications:* 150 articles in professional journals. *Honour:* Feltrinelli Award, 1979. *Hobbies:* Swimming; History; Sport. *Address:* Ist of Neurophysiology, Via S Zeno 51, Pisa, Italy.

MAGHAZAJI, Haider Ismail Ibrahim, b. 17 Dec. 1939, Baghdad, Iraq. Professor of Psychiatry, Medical College, Baghdad University. m. Sawsan Adel Al-Jadda, 2 Oct. 1960, Baghdad, 2 sons, 4 daughters. *Education:* MB; ChB; FRANZCP; DPM; Honours Graduate, Medical College, Baghdad University, 1964; Institute of Psychiatry and The National Hospital, London, England, 1968-70; Diploma in Psychological Medicine, London, 1970. *Appointments:* Clinical Assistant (Unpaid), St Olave's Hospital, London, 1968; S.HO and Registrar, Bexley Hospital, Dartford, Kent, England, 1969-70; Consultant Psychiatrist, Shammaiyah Mental Hospital, Baghdad, Iraq, 1970-71; Lecturer and Assistant Professor, Medical College, Baghdad University, 1971-84; Member of The Advisory Panel on Mental Health, WHO, 1982-. *Memberships:* Founding Member, The Iraqi Society of Psychiatrists and Neurologists; Affiliate of The Royal College of Psychiatrists, UK; Corresponding Member, The American Psychiatric Association; Australian and New Zealand College of Psychiatrists, Fellow, 1983. *Publications:* Some 30 published articles on psychiatry, neurology and mental health in professional journals, etc. *Honour:* Outstanding Member of The Teaching Staff from The Medical College, 1984. *Hobbies:* Presenting TV Programme for the last five years dealing with aspects of psychiatry of interest to the public; Also on Radio; Taking Movie Films. *Address:* Al-Magrib, Aadamiah, Dist 304, St 16, No 36, Baghdad, Iraq.

MAGNANI, Bruno, b. 13 Apr. 1926, Parma. Director, Institute Cardiovascular Diseases. m. 26 Oct. 1959, Ilaria, 1 son, 3 daughters. *Education:* MD, University of Parma. *Appointments:* Assistant, Institute of Pharmacology, University of Parma, 1950-53; Assistant, Medical Pathology, 1953-69, Professor, Internal Medicine, 1969-76, Professor, Cardiology, 1976-, Director, Postgraduate School of Cardiology, 1976-, University of Bologna. *Memberships:* Accademia delle Scienze dello Studio di Bologna; Italian Society of Cardiology; Italian Society of Internal Medicine; International Society of Hypertension; Union Therapeutique Internationale. *Publications:* "Le Cardiomiopatie ipertrofiche", 1974; "Beta-Blocking Agents in the Management of Hypertension and Angine Pectoris", 1974; "Potassium: the Heart and Hypertension", 1982; "Miocardiopatie", "Enciclopedia Medica Italiana', 1982; Cardiologia, Utet Ed 1985, 2 vol. 1986. *Address:* Institute of Cardiovascular Diseases, University of Bologna, Via Massarenti 9, 40138 Bologna, Italy.

MAGNETTI, Sandra Marie, b. 30 Apr. 1948, San Francisco, California, USA. Research Project Coordinator. *Education:* DrPH, University of Texas School of Public Health, 1983; MS, 1972, BA, University of California, Davis and Berkeley, 1970, Post graduate certificate. *Appointments:* Health Planning Intern, Golden Empire Health Planning Council, Sacramento, Calif, 1971-72; Health Programme Developer, Fazendas Aquiqui, Agro Industria, Ltda,

Belem, Para, Brazil, 1972-74; Founder, Director, Amazonian rural family planning clinics; Health Planner, Para State Health Department, Belem, Brazil, 1975-76; Founder, Coordinator, Student internship information, Ctr School Public Health, University of Texas, Houston, TX, USA, 1978-79; Senior Research Associate, Texas Research Institute, Houston, 1982-85; Research Project Coordinator, University of Pittsburgh, Western Psychiatric Institute and Clinic, Department of Behavioral Medicine, 1985-. *Memberships:* American Public Health Association; The Society of Behavioral Medicine. *Publications:* 'The Chronically Mentally Ill: A Survey of Professional Attitudes', 1985; 'The First National Health and Nutritional Examination Survey; Relationships Between Dietary and Biochemical Measures of Nutritional Status', 1981; "Psychological Development of the Child from Birth to 12 yrs - A Manual for Health in the State of Para Brazil", 1976. *Honours:* US Public Health Service Traineeship, 1976, 1977, 1978, 1979, 1981; Full Scholarship, Brazilian Chap of Planned Parenthood International. *Hobbies:* Jogging; Aerobics; Biking; Racquet ball. *Address:* University of Pittsburgh, Western Psychiatric Institute and Clinic, 3811 O'Hara Street, Pittsburgh, PA 15213, USA.

MAGNUS, Ian Allingham, b. 27 Oct. 1920, England. Professor Emeritus. m. Frances Bott, 10 Feb. 1945, St Ives Cornwall, 2 sons, 3 daughters. *Education:* BA, MA, MD, Cambridge University; MRCP; FRCP. *Appointments:* DADMS, Cyprus, 1947; Registrar and Research Fellow, Guy's Hospital Medical School, London, England, 1950-55; Lecturer, Senior Lecturer, Reader, Institute of Dermatology, London; Professor of Photobiology, University of London, 1974. *Publications:* "Dermatological Photobiology", 1976. *Honours:* Parks-Weber Prize, Royal College of Physicians, London, 1974; Purkinje Medal, Prague, Czechoslovakia, 1976. *Hobbies:* Music, especially opera; Victorian English culture; Travelling, particularly in India. *Address:* Department of Photobiology, Institute of Dermatology, Homerton Grove, London E9 6BX, England.

MAGNUSSEN, Finn, b. 11 July 1925, Bodo, Norway. Clinical Director, Adolescent Clinic, State Center for Child and Adolescent Psychiatry. m. Jorunn M, 7 Feb. 1959, 3 sons. *Education:* Cand Med, Oslo, 1952. *Appointments:* Residency, Psychiatric Training, Duke University Hospital, North Carolina, USA; Junior Staff, Gaustad Mental Hospital, Oslo, Norway; Junior Staff, Vestfold sentralsh psyk avd-Tonsberg, Norway; Clinical Director, Adolescent Clinic, State Center for Child and Adolescent Psychiatry. *Memberships:* Norwegian Medical Association; Norwegian Psych Association, Past President; International Federation Medical Psychotherapy, President; International Society for Adolescent Psychiatry, Council Member. *Publications:* Some 40 publications in fields of psychosomatic medicine, psychotherapy and adolescent psychiatry; Book: "Becoming Adult", 1983. *Address:* Bjornveien 127, Oslo 3, Norway.

MAHALIK, Stephen Louis, b. 29 May 1949, Joliet, Illinois, USA. Chiropractor. m. Patricia Anne Murphy, 13 Sep. 1975, Plainfield, Illinois, 4 sons, 1 daughter. *Education:* BS, Northern Illinois University; DC, National College of Chiropractic. *Appointments:* Medical Practice. *Memberships:* Illinois Chiropractic Society; Northern Illinois Chiropractic Society; Council on Roentgenology, Nutrition, American Chiropractic Association. *Hobby:* Arabian Horse Breeder. *Address:* 515 South State Street, Lockport, IL 60441, USA.

MAHER-LOUGHNAN, Gilbert Patrick, b. 19 Jan. 1917, Stoke-on-Trent, England. Consultant Physician. m. Helen Paterson, 14 Jan. 1943, London, 1 son. *Education:* BA Physiology, BM, BCh, MA, DM, Oxford University, Oxford. *Appointments:* House Physician 1942, Resident Medical Officer 1943, London Chest Hospital, London; Assistant Medical Officer, Senior

Registrar, Harefield Hospital, Middlesex, 1945-50; Consultant Physician, Colindale Hospital, London, 1950-78; Private Consultant, Wimpole Street, London, 1978-; Honorary Consultant Physician, Brompton Hospital, Colindale Hospital, London. *Memberships:* Honorary Member, British Thoracic Society; Fellow, Vice President, Royal Society of Medicine; Fellow, Vice President, British Society of Medical and Dental Hypnosis; Honorary Fellow, American Society of Hypnosis; International Society of Hypnosis. *Publications include:* 'An Investigation into Relapse of Pulmonary Tuberculosis, Artificial Pneumothorax', 1950; 'Plasma Cortisol Monitoring and Use of ACTH in Asthma'; 'Hypnosis, Clinical Applications in Medicine', 1960; 'Hypnosis for Asthma - A Controlled Trial', 1968; "Hypnosis and Autohypnosis in Treating Psychosomatic Illness" (chapter), 1976. *Honours:* National Health Service Merit Award, 1962, 1970. *Hobbies:* Golf; Bridge. *Address:* 7 Wimpole Street, London W1, England.

MAHESH, Virendra Bushnan, b. 25 Apr. 1932, Khanki, Punjab, India. m. Sushila Aggarwal, 29 June 1955, 1 son, 1 daughter. *Education:* BSc, Honours, Patna University, India, 1951; MSc, Chemistry, 1953, PhD, Organic Chemistry, 1955, Delhi University; D.Phil, Biological Sciences, Oxford University, England, 1958. *Appointments:* Travelling Fellow, Welcome Foundation, Basel, Switzerland, 1958; James Hudson Brown Memorial Fellow, Yale University, USA, 1959; Assistant Research Professor, 1959-63, Associate Research Professor, 1963-66, Professor, 1966-70, Regents Professor, 1970-, Endocrinology Medical College of Georgia, USA; Director, Center for Population Studies, 1971-, Chairman, Endocrinology, 1972-, Robert B Greenblatt Professor, Endocrinology, Medical College of Georgia, 1979-. *Memberships include:* American Association for Laboratory Animal Science; American Association for University Professors; American Fertility Society; American Physiological Society; Biochemical Society, England; Chemical Society; Endocrine Society; Sigma Xi; International Society for Neuroendocrinology; New York Academy of Sciences; Society of Biological Chemists. *Publications:* Editor: "The Menopausal Syndrome", 1974; "The Pituitary - A Current Review", 1977; "Functional Correlates of Hormone Receptors in Reproduction", 1981; "Recent Advances in Fertility Research, Part A & B", 1982; "Hirsutism and Virilism", 1983; "Unwanted Hair - Its Cause and Treatment", 1985; Author, numerous articles in professional journals; Editorial Boards: 'Journal of Clinical Endocrinology and Metabolism', 1976-81; 'Steroids', 1963-; Referee for Papers; etc. *Honours include:* Rubin Award, American Society for the Study of Sterility, 1963; Billings Silver Medal, 1965; Best Teacher Award, School of Medicine Class of 1972; Outstanding Faculty Award, School of Graduate Studies, 1981. *Address:* 2911 Sussex Road, Augusta, GA 30909, USA.

MAHLER, Dan, b. 22 Mar. 1933, Israel. Professor for Plastic Surgery. m. Sophia, 20 Aug. 1959, Israel, 2 sons, 2 daughters. *Education:* MD, Faculty of Medicine, Hebrew University, Jerusalem. *Appointments:* Chief, Surgical Division, Soroka University Hospital, 1982-84; President, Israel Association of Plastic Surgeons, 1977-79; Professor for Plastic Surgery, Ben Gurion University; Head of Department of Plastic Surgery and Burns, Soroka University Hospital, Be'er Sheva, Israel. *Memberships:* Israel Association of Plastic Surgeons; British Association of Plastic Surgeons; International Society of Burns; International Association of Plastic Surgeons. *Publications include:* 'The Retropectoral Route for Breast Augmentation' Aest Plastic Surgery, 1982; co-author; 'A Measuring Scale for Objective Evaluation of Nasal Shape' Aesth. Plastic Surgery, 1983; co-author; 'Pressure Garments for Hypertrophic Scars' Israeli Journals of Medical Science, 1984; co-author; 'Dermodress: A New Temporary Skin Substitute for Extensive Deep Burn Coverage' Plastic and Reconstructive Surgery, 1985, co-author; 'Burns caused by bromine

and some of its compounds' Burns, 1985, co-author and many others. *Address:* 39 Ha'mitnadev Str, Tel-Aviv, 69-690, Israel.

MAHLER, David Carl, b. 19 Apr. 1951, Brooklyn, New York, USA. Oral and Maxillofacial Surgeon. m. Linda Susan Altman, 11 Aug. 1974, Queens, New York, 2 sons. *Education:* BS magna cum laude, 1973; DDS, 1976; Fellow, American Board of Oral and Maxillofacial Surgery, 1985. *Appointments:* General Practice Residency in Dentistry, General Leonard Wood Army Hospital, Fort Leonard Wood, Missouri, 1976-77; Captain, United States Army Dental Corps, 1976-79; Clinic Chief, Dental Corps 2, Fort Harrison, Indiana, 1977-78; Resident, Oral and Maxillofacial Surgery, Massachusetts General Hospital - Harvard University 1979-82, Brigham and Women's Hospital, Boston, Massachusetts 1982; Clinical Fellow, Oral and Maxillofacial Surgery, Harvard University, 1981-82; Assistant Resident, Plastic Surgery, Children's Hospital Medical Center, Boston, 1982; Private Practice. *Memberships:* Phi Beta Kappa; American Dental Association; Fellow, American Association of Oral and Maxillofacial Surgery; Fellow, International Association Oral and Maxillofacial Surgery; Harvard Dental Alumni Association; International Brotherhood of Magicians. *Honours:* Certificate of Achievement, United States Army, 1978, 1979. *Hobbies:* Sports, Camping, Chess, Auto repair, Magic. *Address:* 27 Oak Street, Binghamton, NY 13905, USA.

MAHLER, Halfdan T, b. 21 Apr. 1923, Vivild, Denmark. Director-General, World Health Organization. m. Ebba Fischer-Simonsen, 2 sons. *Education:* MD, University of Copenhagen, 1948; Postgraduate Degree in Public Health. *Appointments:* Planning Officer, Mass Tuberculosis Campaign, Ecuador, 1950-51; Senior Officer attached to National Tuberculosis Campaign in India, 1951-61, Chief of Tuberculosis Unit and Secretary to Expert Advisory Panel on Tuberculosis, 1962-69, Director of Project Systems Analysis 1969, Assistant Director-General 1970-73, Director-General 1973-, World Health Organization, Geneva, Switzerland. *Memberships include:* Associate, Belgian Society of Tropical Medicine; Fellow, Royal College of Physicians, London; Honorary Fellow: Faculty of Community Medicine of the Royal Colleges of Physicians of the United Kingdom; Indian Society for Malaria and other Communicable Diseases; Royal Society of Medicine; London School of Hygiene and Tropical Medicine; College of Physicians and Surgeons, Dacca, Bangladesh; Several honorary memberships including: Société Médicale de Geneve; Union Internationale Contre la Tuberculose; Société Française d'Hygiène, de Médecine Sociale et de Génie Sanitaire. *Publications:* In the fields of: Epidemiology and control of tuberculosis; Priorities in the health sector; Application of systems analysis to health care problems. *Honours include:* Jana Evangelisty Purkyne Medal, Prague, 1974; Comenius University Gold Medal, Bratislava, 1974; Carlo Forlanini Gold Medal, Federazione Italiana Contro la Tubercolosi e le Malattie Polmonari Sociali, Rome, 1975; Grand Officer de l'Ordre National du Bénin, 1975; Grand Officier de l'Ordre National Voltaïque, Upper Volta, 1978; Ernst Carlsens Foundation Prize, Copenhagen, 1980; Georg Barfred-Pederson Prize, Copenhagen, 1982; Grand Officier de l'Ordre du Mérite de la République du Sénégal, 1982; Commandeur de l'Ordre National du Mali, 1982; Commander First Class of White Rose Order of Finland, 1983; Hagedorn Medal and Prize, Denmark, 1986; 11 honorary degrees. *Address:* World Health Organization, 1211 Geneva 27, Switzerland.

MAIER, Thomas, b. 7 Dec. 1934, Vienna, Austria. Chief of Psychiatry. m. Patricia McMartin, 11 Aug., 1957, 1 son, 1 daughter. *Education:* AB, University of Rochester, USA, 1956; MD, University of Virginia, 1961. *Appointments:* Internship, Genessee Hospital, Rochester, New York, 1961-62; Residency, Boston University Hospitals, 1962-65; Chief of Psychiatry,

249th General Hospital, US Army, Japan, 1965-67; Assistant in Psychiatry, Boston University Hospital, 1967-70; Chief, Psychiatric Liaison Service, 1970-71; Assistant Clinical Professor of Psychiatry, Boston University Medical School, 1971-. *Memberships:* Massachussetts Psychiatric Society; American Psychiatric Association; American Association of General Hospital Psychiatrists; Boston Society for Geriatric Psychiatry. *Address:* 29 Bloomfield Street, Lexington, MA, 02173, USA.

MAJ, Jerzy Michal Jozef, b. 14 July 1922, Brześć, Poland. Director of Institute of Pharmacology, Polish Academy of Sciences. m. Maria Tabeau, 31 Jan. 1950, 2 sons. *Education:* MSc Pharm, Jagiellonian University, Cracow, 1949; PhD, 1951, PhD habil, 1962, Medical Academy, Cracow. *Appointments:* Assistant - adiunkt Department Pharmacodyn, Medical Academy, Cracow, 1950-64; Associate Professor and Head, Department Pharmacology, Medical Academy, Lublin, 1964-67; Associate Professor, Professor, Institute of Pharmacology, Polish Academy of Sciences, Cracow, 1967-; Director, 1977-. *Memberships:* Corresponding Member, Polish Academy of Sciences; Polish Pharmacological Society; Hon Member, Hungarian Pharmacological Society; Corresponding Member, Pharmacological Society of Federal Republic of Germany. *Publications:* About 230 publications in scientific journals, including: "Current Developments in Psychopharmacology", 1976; Co-author, Revs Physiol Biochem Pharmac Volume 100, 1984. *Honours:* Issekutz Order of Hungarian Pharmaceutical Society, 1979; Buchheim Plaque of Pharmacological Society of German Democratic Republic, 1979; Polonia Restituta Officer Cross, 1980; Anna Monica Award, 3rd Class, 1981. *Hobby:* Sport. *Address:* Nad Sudolem 24/10, Pl 31-228 Cracow, Poland.

MAJERUS, Thomas Charles, b. 6 Aug. 1946, Red Wing, Minnesota, USA, Doctor of Pharmacy. m. (divorced), 1 son, 1 daughter. *Education:* BSc Pharmacy, 1969; Doctor of Pharmacy, 1976. *Appointments:* Clinical Pharmacist, Head of Clinical Pharmacology, MIEMSS, Baltimore, Maryland; Clinical Assistant Professor of Clinical Pharmacy, UMAB, School of Pharmacy, Baltimore, Maryland; Branch Manager, Home Medical Support Services, Columbia, Maryland. *Memberships:* American College of Clinical Pharmacy; Baltimore Critical Care Medicine Society; American Trauma Society; Shock Society; MSHP; SCCM; ASHP; ASPEN; NITA. *Publications include:* 'Nutritional Suport of the Critically Ill Patient' in "The Shock Trauma/Critical Care Manual", 1982; "Practice of Critical Care Pharmacy", 1985; 'Current Problems in Nutritional Support of the Critically Ill Patient' in "Critical Problems in Trauma Care II, Medical Management", 1986; 62 articles, book chapters, and monographs. *Honours:* Teacher of the Year, University of Maryland School of Pharmacy, 1977; Outstanding Young Men of America, 1980; United States Army Achievement Medal, 1985. *Hobbies:* Woodworking; Photography; Reading; Cooking; Maryland Army National Guard. *Address:* 2910 B Goodwood Road, Baltimore, MD 21214, USA.

MAJKOWSKI, Jerzy, b. 17 Feb. 1928, Bogate. Chief, Clinical and Experimental Neurology, Warsaw; Chief, Clinical & Experimental Neurophysiology, New York, USA. m. Barbara Cendrowska, 17 Feb. 1955, Warsaw, 2 daughters. *Education:* Physician Diploma, MD, Medical Academy, Warsaw, 1952; Specialist, Neurology, 1st degree, 2nd degree, 1957; dr med, 1958; dr.hab.med, 1964; Docent, 1968; Professor, 1975. *Appointments:* Fellowship, 1952-53, Assistant Professor, 1954-55, Senior Assistant, 1956-59, Neurology, Medical Academy, Warsaw; Research Scientist, Montreal Neurological Institute, Canada, 1959-60; Adjunct, 1960-67, Docent, 1968-74, Professor, Head, Neurology, 1975-82, Dean, Second Medical Faculty, 1976-78, Medical Academy, Warsaw; Research Scientist, New York Medical College,

California Institute of Technology, USA, 1964-66; Editor in Chief, 'Medycyna-Dydaktyka-Wychowanie", 1967-79; Visiting Professor, New York University, 1978-80, 1981-83, 1984-86. *Memberships:* Polish Neurological Society; Polish Society for Electroenceph and Clinical Neurophysiology; Polish Chapter, International League Against Epilepsy; International Brain Research Organization; German Electrodiagnostic Society; American Epilepsy Association; Neurological Committee of Polish Academy of Sciences. *Publications:* "Clinical Electromyography", 1960; "Atlas of Electroencephalography", 1975; "Posttraumatic Epilepsy and Pharmacological Prophylaxis", 1977; "Clinical Electroencephalography", 1979, Editor; "Epilepsy: A Clinical and Experimental Research", Editor, 1980; "Epilepsy: Diagnosis - Treatment-Prophylaxis", 1986; 170 articles in professional journals. *Honours:* Cross of the Brave, 1944; Medal for Victory, 1945; Medal for Warsaw, 1975; Gold Order of Merit, 1976; Gold Award, Special Contribution to Warsaw, 1976; Polonia Restituta Cross of Cavalier, 1979; Award, Polish Neurolical Society; 7 awards, Ministry of Health and Welfare; Award, Polish Academy of Sciences. *Hobbies:* Old Maps Collection; Gardening; World War II History. *Address:* Al Niepodleglosci 214 m4, 00-608 Warsaw, Poland.

MAKII, Michael, M, b. 7 May 1948, Hawaii, USA. Associate Professor of Gynaecology and Gynaecologic Oncology. m. Christine J Berlin, 24 Mar. 1979, Chicago, Illinois, 2 sons, 1 daughter. *Education:* BS, University of Oregon; MD, University of Hawaii. *Appointments:* Fellow, Pelvic Surgery, Union Memorial, Baltimore, Maryland, 1979-80; Fellow 1980-82, Assistant Professor 1982-83, Gynaecologic Oncology, University of Chicago, Chicago, Illinois; Assistant Professor, Director, Gynaecologic Oncology, Texas Technical University, Amarillo, Texas, 1983-86. *Memberships:* Canadiate Member, American College of Surgeons; Candidate Member, Society of Gynaecologic Oncologists; Fellow, American College of Obstetricians and Gynaecologists. *Honour:* Galloway Fellowship, 1977. *Hobbies:* Photography; Alpine skiing; Swimming. *Address:* 1835 W Harrison Street M-4022, Chicago, IL 60612, USA.

MALAWSKI, Stefan Kazimierz, b. 26 Dec. 1920, Rakow, Poland. Head of Orthopaedic Clinic. m. Natalia Przyborowska, 3 Apr. 1949, Warsaw, 3 daughters. *Education:* Diploma of Physician, University of Lublin, 1946; MD, Medical Academy of Warsaw, 1952. *Appointments include:* Director of Hospital for Bone and Joint Tuberculosis in Otwock, 1968-73; Head of Orthopaedic Department of Teaching Hospital, Medical Centre for Postgraduate Education, Otwock, 1974-80; Head of Orthopaedic Clinic, Medical Centre for Postgraduate Education, 1981-85. *Memberships:* Polish Society of Orthopaedic Surgery and Traumatology, Vice-President 1980-82, President 1983-86; International Society of Orthopaedic Surgery and Traumatology; World Federation of Spine Surgery and Spondyliatry, Vice Chairman of National Committee. *Publications:* Anterior decompression of the spinal cord in tuberculosis paralysis" 1955; "Traumatic injuries of the cervical spine" 1956; "Surgical treatment of spine tumors" 1964; "Liofilised grafts bone sterilised with gamma rays" 1968; "Tuberculosis of Bone and Joint" 1976; "Treatment of the pyogenic spine infection" 1977; "Stenosis of the lumbaer canal" 1979. *Honours:* Award of Faculty of Medicine, Polish Academy of Science, 1961; Award of Polish Council for Peaceful Application of Atomic Energy" 1966; Award of Scientific Council of Ministry of Health, 1975. *Hobbies:* History; Skiing. *Address:* ul Pesztenska 10B, 03-925 Warszawa, Poland.

MALAMUD, Nathan, b. 28 Jan. 1903, USSR, Professor Emeritus in Neuropathology. m. Rita K Malamud, 5 Sep. 1930, New York, USA, 1 son, 1 daughter. *Education:* MD. *Appointments:* Instructor, Assistant Professor, Associate Professor, Professor, in

Neuropathology, University of California, San Francisco School of Medicine, San Francisco, California. **Memberships:** Vice President 1959, American Association of Neuropathologists; American Psychiatric Association; American Academy of Neurology; World Federation of Neurology. *Publications:* Atlas of Neuropathology'', 1957, 2nd edition 1974; 18 chapters in books, 1937-80; 73 articles in journals, 1937-80. *Honours:* Outstanding Civilian Service Award, United States Army, 1966 and 1985; Medal, University of California, 1981; Meritorious Contribution to Neuropathology, American Association of Neuropathologists, 1985. *Address:* University of California, San Francisco School of Medicine, Department of Pathology, San Francisco, CA 94143, USA.

MALEC, Kathleen, b. 14 Mar. 1935, Cleveland, Ohio, USA. Health and Education Consultant. m. George N Malec, 28 May 1960, Cleveland, Ohio, 1 son 5 daughters. *Education:* Bachelor of Science in Nursing; Dr of Arts in Education. *Appointments:* Staff Nurse, Cleveland Clinic, Cleveland, Ohio; Public Health Nurse, Cleveland; Associate Professor, Lakeland Community College, Mentor, Ohio; Co-ordinator of Education, Richmond Heights General Hospital, Richmond Heights, Ohio; Director, Department of Education, Womans General Hospital, Cleveland; Consultant, Health and Education for Hospitals, Patient Education and Industry. *Memberships:* National League for Nursing; American Society for Healthcare Education and Training; Women Business Owners of the Western Reserve; Cleveland Area League for Nurses; Past President, Professional Instruction Developers Association for North-Eastern Ohio. *Publications:* Development of an Upper Division Level of Nursing Program: 2 + 2 Program; 1980; Over 25 Multiple Video Tapes for all areas of Nursing. *Honour:* Fellowship, Joint offering of Ohio Board of Residents and Lakeland Community College, 1976. *Hobbies:* Family; Reading. *Address:* 37442 Park Avenue, Willoughby, OH 44094, USA.

MALEK, Mehrdad, b. 25 Sep., 1945, Teheran, Iran. Director, Washington Orthopaedic & Knee Clinic, USA. m. 24 Oct. 1968, Feri Hamidi, 2 sons. *Education:* MD, National University of Iran, 1972; Orthopaedic Residency Program, Hamot Medical Centre, Erie, Pennsylvania, USA, 1975-78; Reconstructive Knee Surgery & Sports Medicine Fellowship, University of Cincinnati, 1978. *Appointments:* Clinical Instructor, Fellow, University of Cincinnati Sports Medicine Institute, 1978-79; Clinical Assistant Professor of Orthopaedic Surgery, Howard University, Washington DC, 1980-. *Memberships:* Fellow: American College of Surgeons, International College of Surgeons, American Academy of Orthopaedic .Surgeons; American College of Sports Medicine; Arthroscopy Association of North America; International Arthroscopy Association; American Society of Biomechanics; International Knee Society; Southern Orthopaedic Society; Southern Medical Association; Washington Orthopaedic Society. *Publications:* Some 16 articles in medical & professional journals, including 'Clinical Orthopaedics', 'Orthopaedics Today', 'Orthopaedics Review'. *Honours:* Dean's List, National University of Iran, 1969; Appreciation Award for Anatomy Instruction, Duke University Medical Centre, 1976; AMA's Physician Recognition Awards, 1978, 1980, 1983; Order of Merit Cum Laude, Orthopaedic Research & Education Foundation, 1982, 1984. *Hobbies:* Travel; Tennis; Photography. *Address:* 4600 King Street Suite 5N, Alexandria, VA 22302, USA.

MALEK-AHMADI, Parviz, b. 26 May 1943, Iran. Associate Professor. m. Marjorie A Smith, 15 Oct. 1978, Columbia, Missouri, USA, 2 sons. *Education:* MD, University of Tehran, Iran. *Appointments:* Assistant Professor of Psychiatry, School of Medicine, University of Missouri, Missouri, USA; Associate Professor of Psychiatry, University of Texas Medical Branch, Texas. *Memberships:* Sigma Xi; Fellow, Royal College of Physicians and Surgeons of Canada; American Psychiatric Association; Canadian Psychiatric Association; Royal Society of Medicine; American Society of Clinical Hypnosis. *Publications:* 'Biochemical correlates of schizophrenia', (with F E Fried), 1976; 'Psychopharmacology of morphinomimetic peptides in relation to schizophrenia', 1978. *Honours:* Department of Psychiatry, University of Missouri, Award for Teaching Excellence, 1978. *Hobby:* Camping. *Address:* Texas Tech University Health Sciences Center School of Medicine, Department of Psychiatry, Lubbock, TX 79430, USA.

MALER, Roger, b. 12 Mar. 1937, Brooklyn, New York, USA. President/Chief Executive Officer. m. Pamela Driscole, New Jersey, 2 sons, 3 daughters. *Education:* BA, Brooklyn College, 1959; Postgraduate, New York City Community College, 1961-62; Certified Business Communicator, 1979. *Appointments:* President/Chief Executive Officer, Maler, Miller and Brown, 1972; President/Chief Executive Officer, Dimedco, 1979; Currently: President/Chief Executive Officer, Roger Maler Inc. *Memberships:* Vice President, Board of Education, 1973-78; Mayor-Elect, 1979-84; Founder and President-Elect, Lakeland Mayors Association, 1980-84; Board of Directors, New Jersey Conference of Mayors, 1982-84; Business Professional Advertising Association; Pharmaceutical Advertising Association; Medical Writers' Association; Biomedical Marketing Association; Business Publications Audit; etc. *Publications:* Publisher: Scientific Review 1980-, Laboratory Perspectives, 1982-, Advances in Orthopaedics, 1984-, Inside Tract, 1983, Radio- immunoassay Review, 1979; published limited edition Micrographia Nova and Anatomica. *Honours:* Neographics Silver Award, 1983; Neographics Silver Award, 1984; Lakeland Mayors Association, 1984 etc. *Hobbies:* Tennis, Reading, Painting. *Address:* PO Box 435, Mount Arlington, NJ 07856, USA.

MALETZKY, Barry Michael, b. 25 May 1941, Schenectady, New York, USA. Director, Sexual Abuse Clinic; Professor, Clinical Psychiatry, Oregon Health Sciences University. m. Marjorie Ellen Tokat, 25 June 1969, Schenectady, 2 daughters. *Education:* BA, 1963; MD, 1967, Columbia University, New York City. *Appointments:* Internship, Psychiatry, Albany Medical Centre, 1967-68; Resident, Psychiatry, University of Oregon Medical School, 1968-71; Major, Medical Corps, US Army, Chief Neuropsychiatry, Fort Rucker, Alabama, 1971-73. *Memberships include:* American Psychiatric Association; Oregon Psychiatric Association; American & Oregon Medical Associations; International Psychiatric Association for the Advancement of Electrotherapy; Oregon Neuropsychiatric Society; etc. *Publications:* 37 articles in professional journals; numerous papers presented. *Honours:* Army Commendation Medal for Meritorious Service, 1973; Multnomah County Medical Society Distinguished Physician Award, 1979. *Hobby:* Mountain Climbing. *Address:* 8332 SE 13th Ave, Portland, OR 97202, USA.

MALIK, Muhammad Aslam, b. 27 Jan. 1929, Sialkot, Pakistan. Chief of Radiology, PNS Shifa (Naval Hospital). m. Ghulam Fatima, October 1946, 1 son, 3 daughters. *Education:* MB BS; MCPS (Pakistan). *Appointments:* Radiologist, Military Hospitals Sialkot and Lahore; Chief of Radiology, Military Hospitals Rawalpindi and Lahore; Chief of Radiology, Naval Hospital, Karachi (PNS Shifa). *Memberships:* British Institute of Radiology; International College of Surgeons; Radiological Society of Pakistan. *Publications:* 'Bezoars', 'AFM Journal', 1969; 'Fellots Tetrology', Case Report, 'AFM Journal', 1970; 'DMC Case Report', 'The Doctor', 1982; NMR review articles, 'AFM Journal', 1985. *Honour:* Sitara-i-Imtiaz. *Hobby:* Reading. *Address:* PNS Shifa, Karachi, Pakistan.

MALIN, Howard Gerald, b. 2 Dec. 1941, Providence,

Rhode Island, USA. Podiatrist; Journalist; Educator; National & International Lecturer. *Education:* AB, Biology, University of Rhode Island, 1964; Certificate, Cytotechnology, Our Lady of Fatima Hospital-Institute of Pathology, North Providence, 1965; Certificate D'Etudes Franciases, Universite de Poitiers, Touraine, France, 1965; SH, Universite de Tours, France, 1967; MA, Brigham Young University, USA, 1969; BSc, 1969, DPM, 1972, California College of Podiatric Medicine; MSc, Pepperdine University, 1978; various other certificates etc. *Appointments:* Private Practice, Podiatric Medicine & Surgery, Brooklyn, New York, 1974-77; Hospital Staff, Prospect Hospital, Bronx, New York, 1974-77; Chief Podiatry Service, David Grant USAF Medical Centre, Travis Air Force Base, 1974-77; Instructor, Advanced Cardiac Life Support, 1978-85, Hospital Staff, Podiatrist, 1977-80, David Grant USAF Medical Centre; Editorial Board: 'Archives of Podiatric Medicine and Foot Surgery', 1978-81, David Grant USAF Medical Centre, 1979-80; Chief Podiatric Medicine, VA Medical Centre, Martinsburg, 1980-; Hospital Staff, VA Medical Centre, Martinsburg, 1980-; Reserve Staff Podiatrist, Malcolm Grow USAF Medical Center, Andrews Air Force Base, 1980-. *Memberships include:* American Podiatry Student Association; American Public Health Association; American Podiatric Medical Association; New York Academy of Science; Academy of Podiatric Medicine; etc. *Publications include:* "An English Translation of Marc-Antoine Muret's Play Entitled 'Julius Caesar'," 1969; "The History of the Neuro-Myo-Vascular Glomus and of the Glomus Tumor: A Review of the Literature", 'Archives of Podiatric Medicine and Surgery', volume III; etc. *Honours:* Recipient numerous honours and awards. *Hobbies:* Legitimate Theatre; Oil Painting; Clarinet; Classics; etc. *Address:* c/oVA Medical Centre, Podiatric Section, Martinsburg, WV 25401, USA.

MALKA, Jeffrey, b. 10 Sep. 1940, Sudan. Orthopaedic Surgeon. m. Susan Gelfand, Philadelphia, USA, 4 daughters. *Education:* MD; Diplomate, American Board of Orthopaedic Surgeons; FACS; FAAOS. *Memberships:* American College of Surgeons; American Academy of Orthopaedic Surgeons; Fairfax County Medical Society; Virginia Medical Society. *Publications:* Numerous articles. *Hobbies:* Tennis; Gardening. *Address:* 6845 Elm Street, McLean, VA 22101, USA.

MALKINSON, Alvin Maynard, b. 5 Jan. 1941, Buffalo, New York, USA. Associate Professor. m. Lynn Ellen Reynolds, 26 Dec. 1967, White Plains, 1 son, 1 daughter. *Education:* BA, University of Buffalo, 1962; PhD, Biology, Johns Hopkins University, 1968; Postdoctoral Studies: University of Leicester, England, 1971-72, Yale University, 1972-74. *Appointments:* Lecturer, Co-Chairman, Veterinary Biochemistry, University of Nairobi, Kenya, 1969-71; Assistant Professor, University of Minnesota, 1974-78; Assistant Professor, Pharmacy, University of Colorado, 1978-83. *Memberships:* American Association for Cancer Research; American Society for Pharmacology and Experimental Therapeutics; Rho Chi; Environmental Mutagen Society; Society of Toxicology. *Publications:* "Hormone Action", 1975; articles in: 'Journal of National Cancer Institute'; 'Cancer Research'; etc. *Honours:* White House Summer Fellow, 1964; Principal Investigator on: NIH Special Postdoctoral Fellowship, 1972-74, National Foundation 1975-78, NIGMS, 1976-78, NIEHS, 1980-, NIC, 1982-. *Hobbies:* Reading: Films; Tennis; Table Tennis; Hiking; Music. *Address:* School of Pharmacy, University of Colorado, Boulder, CO 80309, USA.

MALLICK, Asrar Ahmad, b. 3 Jan. 1933, Patna, India. Director/Professor. m. J.N. Mallick, 17 June 1957, Patna, 3 sons, 1 daughter. *Education:* MB; BS; DTD; PhD; FNCCP; FCCP (USA); FAMS. *Appointments:* Resident Junior House-Staff, Resident Senior House-Staff, Honorary Clinical Assistant, Medical Officer, Epidemiologist, Director, T.B.D. and T.C., patna; T.B. Officer, T.B.Clinic, Buxar; Professor, T.B. and Chest Diseases, Patna University; Director, T.B. Control Programme, Bihar. *Memberships:* Life Member, Indian Medical Assoc; Life Member, Tuberculosis Assoc. of India; Founder Member, Indian Society of Chest; Member, International Union Against Tuberculosis; General Secretary, Bihar TB Assoc; Vice President, Bihar State Health Services Assoc. *Publications:* 'Study of Tuberculin reaction in the contacts and the General Population', 1964; 'Hospital and Home - in the Treatment of Pulmonary Tuberculosis', 1967; 'Isorin Therapy in Tuberculosis', 1975; 'Short Course Chemotherapy', 1982-83; 'Tuberculosis Control in India with Particular Reference to Bihar', 1984. *Hobbies:* Gardening; Book Reading. *Address:* 158, Chhajoobagh, Patna-800001, Bihar, India.

MALLORY, Thomas Howard, b. 10 Jan. 1939, Columbus, Ohio, USA. Clinical Instructor, Orthopaedic Surgery, Ohio State University. m. Kelly Lynn Smith, 31 Dec. 1964, Columbus, 3 sons. *Education:* AB, Miami University, Oxford, Ohio; MD, Ohio State University, Columbus; MA (Fellowship, Hip Surgery), Harvard Medical School, Boston, Massachusetts. *Appointments:* Teaching Fellow, Harvard Medical School/Tufts University, Boston, 1970. *Memberships:* American Academy of Orthopaedic Surgeons; American College of Surgeons; American Medical Association; Association of Bone and Joint Surgeons; Sir John Charnley Society; Ohio State Medical Society; Columbus Orthopaedic Society; The Hip Society; The Knee Society; Columbus Surgical Society; Ohio Orthopaedic Society; American Rheumatism Society; Mid-American Orthopaedic Society. *Publications:* Contributor of numerous papers and articles to professional journals, etc; Presentations. *Honour:* Diplomate, American Board of Orthopaedic Surgery. *Hobbies:* Polo; Jogging; Riding. *Address:* 720 East Broad Street, Columbus, OH 43215, USA.

MALMBORG, Anna-Stina, b. 20 Apr. 1929, Stockholm, Sweden. Clinical Head, Microbiology. m. Gunnar Höglund, 27 June 1960, Stockholm. *Education:* MD, PhD, Karolinska Institute, 1974. *Appointments:* Research Assistant, Karolinska Institute, 1953-59; Staff Physician, Karolinska Hospital, 1960-72; Associate Professor, Karolinska Institute, 1974-; Clinical Head, Clinical Microbiology, Huddinge Hospital, Karolinska Institute, 1976-. *Memberships:* Swedish Medical Association; Swedish Society of Medicine; American Society of Microbiology. *Publications:* 100 articles in professional journals. *Hobby:* President, Friends of the Museum of Modern Art, Stockholm. *Address:* Norr Mälarstrand 54, 112-20 Stockholm, Sweden.

MALONE, Charles Bruce III, b. 4 Feb. 1943, Nashville, Tennessee, USA. Associate, Austin Bone and Joint Clinic. *Education:* AB, Harvard University, USA, 1965; MD, Duke University School of Medicine, 1969. *Appointments:* Surgical Internship, Surgical Residency and Orthopaedic Specialty Residency, University Hospitals of Cleveland, Ohio, USA, 1969-75; Major, Medical Corps, US Air Force, 1975-77; Associate, Austin Bone and Joint Clinic, Austin, Texas, 1977-. *Memberships:* American Academy of Orthopaedic Surgeons; American Board of Orthopaedic Surgery; American Medical Association; Texas Medical Association. *Publication:* 'Mechanical Properties of Bone' in 'Clinical Orthopaedics', 1977. *Address:* 1011 East 32nd Street, Austin, TX 78705, USA.

MALPIEDE, Ronald Joseph, b. 6 Sep. 1947, Denver, Colorado, USA. Chiropractic - Orthopaedic Practitioner. m. Evelyn Rimbey, 3 Dec. 1971, 2 daughters. *Education:* AB, 1972; DC, Cleveland Chiropractic College of Kansas City, 1976. *Appointments:* Private Practice, 1976-. *Memberships:* American Chiropractic Association; Board of Directors, Colorado Chiropractic Association; American College of Chiropractic Orthopaedists; American College of Sports Medicine. *Publications:* "Chiropractic Podiatric Biomechanical

Interraltionships (pelvic- podiatric Biomechanical Interraltionships)", 1978. *Honours:* Outstanding Student Award, Cleveland Chiropractic College of Kansas City, 1973; Distinguished Service Award, Colorado Chiropractic Association, 1978; Board of Directors Award, Colorado Chiropractic Society, 1984. *Hobbies:* Golf; Travel. *Address:* 7400 West 14th Avenue, Lakewood, CO 80225, USA.

MAMEGHAN, Hedy, b. 25 May 1943, Tehran, Iran. Staff Radiation Oncologist. m. Jill Cutler, 9 Oct. 1976, 1 son, 1 daughter. *Education:* MA, BM, BCh, Oxford University, 1970; DMRT, 1974, FRCR, 1976; London; FRACR, Sydney, 1978. *Appointments:* Registrar in Radiotherapy, Charing Cross Hospital, London, 1972-74; Registrar in Radiotherapy, Royal Marsden Hospital, London and Surrey, 1974-77; Staff Radiation Oncologist, Prince of Wales Hospital, Randwick, New South Wales, Australia. *Memberships:* Royal College of Radiologists, (England); Royal Australasian College of Radiologists; American Society for Therapeutic Radiology and Oncology; European Society for Therapeutic Radiology and Oncology; Urological Society of Australia. *Publications:* "Bone Marrow Transplantation for Acute Leukaemia in Childhood" 1982; "Misonidazole and Radiotherapy in the Palliative Treatment of Lung Cancer" 1983; Radiation Hepatitis Following Moving Strip Radiotherapy" 1983; "Tumor Control with 1251 Seeds in Childhood Pelvic Yolk Sac Tumour" 1985; "Bone Marrow Transplantation for Malignant Histiocytosis in Childhood" 1985. *Hobbies:* Chamber Music (violin and viola); Tennis. *Address:* Institute of Oncology and Radiotherapy, Prince of Wales Hospital, Randwick 2031, New South Wales, Australia.

MANASSE, Gabriel Otto, b. 10 Feb. 1942, Durham, North Carolina, USA. Chief, Psychiatry Service. m. Patricia C. Arthur, 11 Dec. 1971, San Franscisco, USA, 1 son, 1 daughter (1 daughter by previous marriage). *Education:* BA, University of Michigan, Ann Arbor, Michigan, USA, 1964; MD, Temple University School of Medicine, 1969. *Appointments:* GMO in Psychiatry, US Public Health Service Hospital, San Francisco, 1970-72; Staff Psychiatrist, Brentwood VA Medical Centre, Los Angeles, 1975-79; Assistant Clinical Professor of Psychiatry, UCLA, 1976-79; Veterans Administration Administrative Scholar, Washington, DC Fellowship Programme, 1979-81; Chief, Psychiatry Service, VA Medical Centre, Tucson, Arizona, 1981-; Adjunct Associate Professor, Psychiatry, University of Arizona, 1984-. *Memberships:* American Psychiatric Association; Arizona Psychiatric Association, Treasurer 1985-6, co-Chairman Legislative Committee, 1984-; Tucson Psychiatric Society, Secretary-treasurer, 1984-85, President 1985-86, Delegate to State Executive Committee 1984-85; Arizona Medical Association; Pima County Medical Society; National Association of VA Chiefs of Psychiatry; Physicians for Social Responsibility. *Publications:* 'Patient Government: History, Structure and Ethics' in 'American Journal of Social Psychiatry', 1981; 'Patients' Participation in Facility Management at a VA Psychiatric Hospital' in 'Hospital and Community Psychiatry', 1981; etc. *Honours:* Leadership VA, 1978; Selected as VA Administrative Scholar (two year fellowship type programme), 1979-81. *Address:* Veterans Administration Medical Center, Tucson, AZ 85723, USA.

MANCALL, Elliott Lee, b. 31 July 1927, Hartford, Connecticut, USA. Professor of Neurology. m. Jacqueline Mancall, 27 Dec. 1953, Philadelphia, Pennsylvania, USA, 2 sons. *Education:* BS, Trinity College, 1948; MD, University of Pennsylvania Medical School, 1952; Intern, Hartford Hospital, 1952-53; Assistant Resident, Surgery, Hartford Hospital, 1953-54; Clinical Clerk (Fulbright Scholar), Queen Square, 1954-55; Assistant Resident, Neurological Institute, New York, 1955-56; Resident, Neuropathology, Massachusetts General Hospital, 1956-57. *Appointments:* Teaching Fellow, Neuropathology, Harvard Medical School, 1956-57; Assistant Professor of Neurology, Jefferson

Medical College, 1958-64; Associate Professor of Neurology, Jefferson Medical College, 1964-65; Professor of Neurology, 1965-76, Professor & Chairman of Neurology, 1976-, Hahnemann University, Philadelphia; Director, American Board of Psychiatry & Neurology, Inc. *Memberships:* Fellow, American Academy of Neurology; Member: American Neurological Association; American Association of Neuropathologists; American Association of University Professor os Neurology; American Medical Association; Society for Neuroscience. *Publications:* "Essentials of the Neurological Examination", 2nd edition, 1981; "Clinical Neurology", 6th edition (with Alpers), 1971; Various articles in medical journals in field. *Honours:* Oliver Memorial Prize in Ophthalmology, University of Pennsylvania, 1952; Medal from Columbia University for excellence in Neurological teaching, 1968; Christian R & Mary F Lindback Award for distinguished teaching, 1969; Plaques for excellence in teaching, 1976, 1980, Hahnemann University. *Hobbies:* Antiques; Skiing; Tennis; Art; Reading. *Address:* Department of Neurology, Hahnemann University, Broad & Vine, Philadelphia, PA 19102, USA.

MANDEL, Benjamin, b. 13 May 1944, Mexico City, Mexico. Dentist; Dental Consultant. m. Olga Mandel, 27 Dec. 1970, San Diego, 2 sons. *Education:* BS, Chemistry, University of California, Berkeley, 1966; MS, Chemistry, Polytechnic Institute, Mexico, 1969; Postgraduate, Biochemistry Advanced Studies, University of Wisconsin, 1970-71; DDS, New York University, 1975. *Appointments:* Research Associate, University of Wisconsin, 1970-72; General Practice Resident, VA Hospital, Martinez, 1975-76; Private Practice Dentistry, Santa Clara, 1976-; Consultant, Misson Convalescent Home, 1976-77; Founder, Chairman, Santa Clara County Perodontology Study Club; Lecturer on TMJ Disorders and relationships to headache, back and neck pain, (Hawaii), and Internationally, 1982. *Memberships:* Elected Member, California Dental Board of Examiners; Santa Clara Dental Society; Western Society of Peridontol; Santa Clara County, Orthopedic Study Club; American Society of Clinical Hypnosis; American Dental Association; California Dental Association; Hispanic American Dental Association; American Academy of Periodontology; Alpha Omega; etc. *Publications:* Author, "Dentistry for the 21st Century" 1977. *Honour:* Recipient, Appreciation Award, Mexican Centre for Research and Oral Rehabilitation, 1984. *Address:* 74 Harold Avenue, San Jose, CA 95117, USA.

MANDELL, Harvey N, b. 27 Sep. 1924, Norwich, Connecticut, USA. Medical Director/Associate Clinical Professor of Medicine. m. Marjorie, 22 Sep. 1951, Massachusetts, 3 sons. *Education:* BA, Dartmouth College, Hanover, New Hampshire; MD, Columbia University, New York. *Appointments:* Private Practice of Internal Medicine, Norwich, Connecticut (22 years); Medical Director, The William W Backus Hospital; Associate Clinical Professor of Medicine, Yale University School of Medicine. *Memberships:* Fellow, American College of Physicians; Connecticut Society of Internal Medicine; American Society of Internal Medicine; Connecticut Representative to New England Organization of Hospital Medical Staffs; Member, Connecticut Medical Examining Board. *Publications:* "Abdominal Angina" 'NEJM' 1957; "Cellists' Chest", 'NEJM', 1962; "Lactose Intolerance" 'Med Times' 1978; "Gases and Lytes Without Anguish" 'Postgrad Med' 1981; Editor: "Laboratory Medicine in Clinical Practice" John Wright, 1983; "The peer reviewed physician" in "The Physician - A Professional Under Stress" edited by J P Callan, 1983. *Honour:* Diplomate, American Board of Internal Medicine, 1958. *Hobbies:* Travel; Music; Chess; Writing. *Address:* The William W Backus Hospital, 326 Washington Street, Norwich CT 06360, USA.

MANDL, Herbert, b. 27 Apr. 1942, Vienna, Austria. University Professor. m. Gerda Pilz, Vienna, 3 daughters. *Education:* MD, University of Vienna, Medical

Faculty, 1968. *Appointments:* University Assistant, 2nd Surgical University Clinic, Vienna, 1968-72; University Assistant, 1973-75, Oberarzt, 1975-82, Assistant Professor, 1982-, Department of Plastic Surgery, 2nd Surgical University Clinic, Vienna. *Memberships:* Austrian Society for Plastic Surgery; Austrian Society for Surgery; Austrian Society for Experimental Surgery; Austrian Society for Senology; International Society for Microsurgery; German-speaking Group for Handsurgery; German-speaking Group for Microsurgery. *Publications:* 75 articles mainly on subjects in the field of Plastic Surgery e.g. Replantation Surgery; Lymph Vessel Surgery. *Honours:* Kardinal-Innitzer-Förderungspreis für Medizine, 1980; Förderungspreis der Ersten Österr. Spar-Casse, 1980; Theodor-Billroth-Preis, 1981. *Address:* Waehringerstrasse 2-4, A-1090 Vienna, Austria.

MANDOKI, Miguel, b. 4 Sep. 1950, Mexico. Director, Division of Child Psychiatry. *Education:* MD, Universidad Nacional Autonoma de Mexico; University of Toronto, Canada; Child Psychiatry, Albert Einstein College of Medicine. *Appointments:* Director, Childrens Day Treatment Unit, Bronx Children's Psychiatry Centre, USA; Albert Einstein College of Medicine, Bronx, New York; Staff Psychiatrist, St John's Episcopal Hospital, Catholic Charities Outreach Team; Clinical Instructor in Psychiatry, Albert Einstein College of Medicine. *Memberships:* American Psychiatric Association; American Academy of Child Psychiatry. *Address:* University Hospital of Jacksonville, 655 West Eight Street, Jacksonville, FL 32209, USA.

MANELL, Per, b. 10 Nov. 1948, Stjarnsund, Sweden. Pharmacist; Chief Pharmaceutical Officer. *Education:* Pharmacist; MSc; Computer Technology. *Appointments:* Teacher, Department of Social Pharmacy, Senior Administrative Officer, Faculty of Pharmacy, Uppsala University; currently, Chief Pharmaceutical Officer, Department of Drugs, National Board of Health and Welfare, Uppsala. *Memberships:* Board Member: Swedish Pharmaceutical Association; Swedish Academy of Pharmaceutical Sciences. Advisor, World Health Organisation. *Publications:* "Impact of Computer Technology on Drug Information", 1983; "Computing and Drugs", in Swedish, 1984; "The Drug Legislation'. in Swedish. 1985. *Hobby:* Swedish Tramwat Society. *Address:* Department of Drugs, National Board of Health and Welfare, Box 607, 5-571 25 Uppsala, Sweden.

MANGO, Enrico S, b. 29 June 1951, USA. Private Practice, Commack. m. Jean Ann Bagwell, 29 Dec. 1973, Queens, 3 sons, 3 daughters. *Education:* BS, Biology, Manhattan College, 1972; MD, Creighton University, 1976; LI, Jewish Hospital, New York, 1977; Residency, Orthopaedic Surgery, State University of New York, Stoney Brook, 1977-81; Certification, American Board Orthopaedic Surgeons, 1983. *Appointments:* Assistant Clinical Professor, Orthopaedic Surgery, State University of New York, Stony Brook; Founder, Editor in Chief, 'Orthopaedic Index', 'Orthobase'. *Memberships:* American College of Sports Medicine; American Medical Association; Fellow, American Academy of Orthopaedic Surgeons. *Publications:* "Isolated Traumatic Posterior Radial Head Dislocation: Case Reports and Anatomic Study", 'Orthopaedic Transactions', 1980; "Current Orthopaedic Practice", Co-Editor, 1986. *Honour:* Certificate, meritorious Achievement, State University of New York, Orthopaedic Dept., 1977. *Hobbies:* Jogging; Fishing; Hunting. *Address:* 160 Commack Road, Commack, NY 11725, USA.

MANIATIS, George, b. 25 Dec. 1934, Athens, Greece. Professor and Director, Biology Laboratory, University of Patras Medical School. m. Alice Kallinikos, 16 Nov. 1961, Athens, Greece, 2 sons, 1 daughter. *Education:* MD, University of Athens Medical School, 1959, Dr Med Sci, 1963; PhD, Biochemistry, Massachusetts Institute of Technology, 1969. *Appointments:* Research Fellow, Tufts University, USA,

1962-64; MIT Research Associate, 1965-71; Assistant Professor, Department of Human Genetics, Columbia University College of Physicians and Surgeons, 1971-77, Senior Research Associate, 1977-78; Rector, University of Patras, Greece, 1981-82; Visiting Professor, Massachusetts Institute of Technology, 1984. *Memberships:* American Society of Haematology; American Society for Cell Biology; American Federation for Clinical Research; Hellenic Society of Eugenics and Human Genetics, President; Hellenic Society of Biological Sciences; Hellenic Society for the Study of Medical Education. *Publications:* Numerous articles in scientific journals. *Honour:* J T Hirschl Career Scientist Award, 1973-78. *Address:* Laboratory of Biology, School of Health Sciences, University of Patras, GR-261, 10 Patras, Greece.

MANN, David W, b. 22 Feb. 1950, Riverside, California, USA. Medical Director. m. Livia Minica, 28 Jan. 1984, Cambridge, Massachusetts, USA, 1 daughter. *Education:* BA, sumna cum laude, University of Texas, 1975; Fulbright Scholar, Cybernetics and Theoretical Biology, Sussex University, England, 1975-76; Doctor of Medicine, University of Texas Southwestern Medical School, 1980. *Appointments:* Resident in Psychiatry, Massachusetts Mental Health Centre, 1980-83; Fellow in Psychiatry, Harvard Medical School, Boston, 1980-83; Staff Psychiatrist, MMHC, 1984-85; Instructor in Psychiatry, Harvard Medical School, 1984-; Medical Director, Cambridge-Somerville Units, USA, 1985. *Memberships:* Phi Beta Kappa; Phi Kappa Phi; Society for the Interdisciplinary Study of the Mind; American Psychiatric Association; Massachusetts Psychiatric Association; New Psychiatry Seminar. *Publications:* "This Proposition is False", 1977; "Crowding", 1981; "Reunion and War Within", 1982; "Six Months in the Psychotherapy of 2 Young Paranoid Schizophrenics", 1983; "The Question of Medical Psychotherapy", 1984. *Honours:* Phi Beta Kappa 1975; Phi Kappa Phi 1975; Fulbright Scholar to Great Britain 1975. *Hobbies:* Building furniture and automobiles; Gardening; Writing; Reading literature and philosophy. *Address:* 89 Magazine Street, Cambridge, MA 02139, USA.

MANNAIONI, Pier Francesco, b. 27 June 1932, Florence, Italy. Professor, Toxicology. m. Mariarosa Camerino 18 Mar. 1962, Florence, 2 sons, 2 daughters. *Education:* Diploma, Classic Lyceum, Florence; MD, University of Florence; Postdoctoral Fellow, Visiting Professor, Yale University, USA; Lecturer, Pharmacology; Lecturer, Toxicology. *Appointments:* Assistant Professor, Pharmacology, 1962; Associate Professor, 1967, Professor, 1975-, Toxicology, Florence University School of Medicine. *Memberships:* IUPHAR; European Society of Toxicology; European Histamine Research Society; Collegium Internationale Allergologicum. *Publications:* Articles in: 'British Journal Pharmacology', 1960; 'European Journal Pharmacology', 1968; Piccin Editor, 'Clinical Pharmacology of Drug Dependence', 1980; etc. *Honours:* Scientific Production Award, University of Florence, 1959-60, 1966-67, 1967-68. *Hobbies:* Skiing; Tennis; Opera. *Address:* Department of Preclinical and Clinical Pharmacology, Florence University, School of Medicine, Viale Morgagni 65, 50134, Florence, Italy.

MANNERVIK, Bengt, b. 19 Aug. 1943, Stockholm, Sweden. Senior Lecturer in Biochemistry. *Education:* PhD, 1969, Fil Lic, 1967, Fil Kand, 1964, University of Stockholm. *Appointments:* Secretary, Swedish Biochemical Society, 1976-82; Chairman of the Nordic Committee of Biochemistry, 1979-80; Senior Lecturer in Biochemistry, Department of Biochemistry, University of Stockholm, 1970-. *Memberships:* The Swedish Biochemical Society; The Biochemical Society (UK); Secretary, Swedish National Committee of Biochemistry, Royal Swedish Academy of Sciences. *Publications:* 'The Isoenzymes of Glutathione Transferase' in "Advances in Enzymology" vol 57, 1985. *Honours:* Senior Fulbright Scholar, 1981-82;

Sweden-America Foundation Award, 1981; Thanks to Scandinavia Award, 1982. *Address:* Department of Biochemistry, Arrhenius Laboratory, University of Stockholm, Stockholm S-10691, Sweden.

MANNINGER Jenó, b. 30 Oct. 1918, Rácbolypuszta, Hungary. Professor and Chairman of National Institute of Traumatology. m. Dr Elizabeth Turoczy, 16 Dec. 1949, Budapest, 2 sons, 1 daughter. *Education:* MD, 1942, Pecs; Specialist in Pathology 1949; Specialist in Surgery 1951; Specialist in Traumatology 1959; Candidate of Medical Sciences 1965, Budapest; Doctor of Medical Sciences 1980. *Appointments include:* Assistant to Professor as Traumasurgeon and Handsurgeon, 1950-56, Chief of Department for Injury of Extremities and Deputy Director of Institute, 1956-72, Professor and Chairman, 1978-, National Institute of Traumatology, Budapest; Professor of Traumatology for Postgraduate School of Medicine, Budapest, 1978-. *Memberships include:* Co-Chairman, Hungarian Society of Traumatologists; President, Hungarian Section, Hungarian Hand Surgeons; Executive Committee Member, Austrian Society of Traumatologists; Council Member, International Federation of Society for Surgery of the Hand; Emeritus Member, International Society of Orthopedy and Traumatology; Honorary Member, Society of Surgeons of DDR. *Publications:* 'Surgery of the Hand' in Littmann: "Chirurgische Operationslehre" 1977; Postgraduate Textbook for Traumatology, 3 editions 1976, 1978, 1984; "Die Phlebographie des Schenkelkopfes" 1979. 13C published papers. *Honours:* Honoured Physician of the Hungarian People's Republic, 1964; Golden Order of Labour, 1975. *Hobbies:* Gardening; Carpentry. *Address:* National Institute of Traumatology, Mezó Imre út 17, H-1081 Budapest VIII, Hungary.

MANOLIDIS, Leonidas, b. 26 Oct. 1924, Granitsa, Greece. Professor of ORL. m. Panagiota Delantoni, July 1964, 2 sons, 1 daughter. *Education:* MD, Athens University, 1952; ENT Degree, University of Thessaloniki, 1954; PhD, University of Frieburg, 1963. *Appointments:* Assistant: Athens University, 1953; University of Thessaloniki, 1954. Assistant Professor, 1960, Associate Professor, 1964, Professor, 1973, Head, 1974, ENT Clinic, University of Thessaloniki; currently, Head, ORL, AHEPA Hospital, Aristotelian University of Thessaloniki. *Memberships:* Founder: ORL Society of North Greece; Panhellenic ORL Society. President, Otoneuro-ophtalmologican and Neurosurgical Society; International Audiological Society; French ORL Society; Politzer Society, Acoological Society of Italy, American Academy of Facial Plastic and Reconstructive Surgery. *Publications:* Author of 3 books and over 150 papers of experimental nature in Greek and foreign medical journals. *Honours:* Honoured Member, Hungarian ORL Society and ORL Society of Austria; German ORL Society, Sercer Society, Member, British Royal ORL Society; Collegium, ORL, IFOS. *Address:* Department of ORL, AHEPA Hospital, Aristotelian University of Thessaloniki, Thessaloniki, 54006, Greece.

MANOLOV, Stephan, b. 11 June 1925, Sofia, Bulgaria. Director of Regeneration Research Laboratory. m. Maria Gueorguieva, 19 July 1959, Sofia, 1 daughter. *Education:* MD 1952, PhD 1965, Medical Faculty, Sofia; Dr es Sc, Bulgarian Academy of Sciences, Sofia, 1975. *Appointments:* Assistant 1953-64, Assistant Professor 1964-70, Professor 1970, Director 1982, Regeneration Research Laboratory, Bulgarian Academy of Sciences, Sofia. *Memberships:* International Society for Developmental Neuroscience; Bulgarian Society of Anatomy; Société Française de Microscocopie Électronique; Anatomische Gesellschaft; European Cell Biology Association. *Publications:* 'Histochemistry of Cholinesterases in the Nervous Tissue', 1976; 'Morphology of Neuromuscular Synapses', 1976; 'Ultrastructuyre of the Synapses in the C N S', 1979; 'Structure and Cytochemistry of the Chemical Synapses', 1982. *Honours:* Member of the Jury for International Prize

for Medical Sciences Saint Vincent, 7th and 8th Edition. *Hobbies:* Music; Tourism. *Address:* Regeneration Research Laboratory, Bulgarian Academy of Sciences, 1431 Sofia, Bulgaria.

MANOUKIAN, John Jack, b. 3 Feb. 1951, Alexandria, Egypt. Assistant Professor. m. Sossi Boghossian, 31 Aug. 1985. *Education:* Pre Med Natural Science 1970, Medical Education 1975, Alexandria University, Egypt; MBChB Diploma; Post Medical Education, Otolaryngology Speciality, McGill University, Montreal, Canada, 1984; Royal College of Physicians and Surgeons of Canada; Certified Diplomate, American Board of Otolaryngology; Corporation Professionelle des Medecins du Quebec Otolaryngology. *Appointments:* Clinical Pediatric Otolaryngology Fellowship, Cincinnati Children's Hospital Medical Center, University of Cincinnati, Ohio, 1985. *Memberships:* Canadian Society of Otolaryngology, Head and Neck Surgery; American Academy of Otolaryngology, Head and Neck Surgery; American Academy of Facial Plastic and Reconstructive Surgery; American Academy of Otolaryngic Allergy; Quebec Medical Association; The Royal College of Physicians and Surgeons of Canada; Quebec Association of Oto-Rhoni-Laryngology and Mexillo-Facial Surgery. *Publication:* 'Undifferentiated (Anaplastic) Carcinoma with Lymphoid Stroma of the Parotid Gland', 1984. *Honours include:* Premedical Medical Education Scholarship, Alexandria University and Gulbenkian Foundation, Lisbon, Portugal. *Hobbies:* Tennis; Travelling. *Address:* Montreal Children's Hospital, 2300 Tupper Street, Montreal, PQ H3H 1P3, Canada.

MANSCHRECK, Theo C, b. 21 June 1945, USA. Associate Professor; Clinical Director; Director. m. Janis L Gogan, 21 Jan. 1978, Cambridge, Massachusetts, 1 son, 1 daughter. *Education:* BA, Philosophy, Carleton College; MPH, Behavioural Sciences and Epidemiology, Harvard University; MD, Medicine, Cornell University. *Appointments:* Chief, Acute Psychiatry Service, 1975-76, Fellow, Psychosomatic and Liaison Psychiatry, 1976-77, Director, Investigative Psychiatry Training and Education Program, Massachusetts General Hospital, 1977-82; Director, Laboratory for Clinical and Experimental Psychopathology, 1977-; Chief, Adult Inpatient Services, Erich Lindemann Mental Health Center, Boston, 1980-84. *Memberships:* American Association for the Advancement of Science; American Psychiatric Assoc; Associate, The Behavioural and Brain Sciences; American Academy of Clinical Psychiatrists; Society of Biological Psychiatry. *Publications:* 'Schizophrenic Disorders', 1981; 'Disturbed Voluntary motor activity in schizophrenic disorder', (with B A Maher, M Rucklos, D Vereen), 1982; 'Neurological features and psychopathology in schizophrenic disorders', (with D Ames), 1984; 'The atypical psychoses, 1979; 'The paranoid syndrome', (with M Petri), 1978; Editor in Chief, Psychiatric Medicine Update: Massachusetts General Hospital Reviews for Physicians, 1979, 1981, 1984. *Honours:* Milton Fund Award, 1977; Rand Fund Award, (with Brendan Maher), 1980; Fulbridge Award, 1985-86. *Hobbies:* Computers; Gardening. *Address:* Department of Psychiatry, Lindemann 521, Massachusetts General Hospital, Boston, MA 02114, USA.

MANSFIELD, Morgan, b. 16 July 1920, Dublin, Ireland. Surgeon, Assistant Clinical Professor, m. Clare Waskerman, 18 Oct. 1952, New York, 3 sons, 2 daughters. *Education:* MB, BCh, BAO, National University of Ireland, 1946; Diplomate, American Board of Surgery; Diplomate, Board of Abdominal Surgery; Fellow, American College of Surgeons; Fellow, International College of Surgeons; Fellow, College of Chest Physicians. *Appointments:* Chief Surgeon, Chief of Staff, Atlantic Coastline Railroad, Waycross, Georgia, USA, 1953-55; Chief of Surgery, Assistant Chief Thoracic Surgeon, 3810 US Air Force Hospital, Montgomery, Alabama, 1955-57; Chief of Surgery, Memorial of Queens, NY, 1957-60; Director of Surgery, Interfaith Hospital, Queens, NY, 1965-67; Chairman, Department of Surgery, East Nassau Medical Group, Long Island, NY, 1968-84; Assistant Professor, Anatomy, Stonybrook Medical School, 1972-82; Professor, Assistant Clinical, SUNY Stonybrook Medical School, L I, NY, 1982-. *Memberships:* American Medical Association; NY State Medical Society; Suffolk County Medical Society LINY; American College Chest Physicians; NY State Chapter, College Chest Physicians; Fellow, American College of Surgeons; International College of Surgeons; American Society of Abdominal Surgeons. *Honours:* Richard Tobin Prize, St Vincents Hospital, Dublin, Ireland, 1942; McArdle Prize in Surgery, St Vincents Hospital, Dublin, Ireland, 1945. *Hobbies:* Sailing; Reading. *Address:* 35 Harbor Circle, Centerport, NY 11721, USA.

MANSFORD, Keith Robert Leonard, b. 12 Jan. 1932, Great Yarmouth, England. Chairman, Beecham Pharmaceuticals Research Division. m. Brenda Lazell, 29 Mar. 1958, 3 sons, 1 daughter.*Appointments:* Head of Toxicology and Drug Metabolism, Beecham Research Laboratories, 1954-64; Senior Research Fellow, Metabolic Reactions Research Unit, MRC, Imperial College, 1964-69; Director, Research Projects, 1969-84, Research Director, 1982-84, Beecham Pharmaceuticals Research Division; Group Board, Beecham Group plc, 1984-. *Memberships:* Royal Society of Chemistry; Society for Drug Research; Institute of Biology; Research and Development Society. *Publications:* 50 articles in scientific journals on synthetic organic chemistry, isolation of antibiotics, metabolism and absorption studies, cardiac metabolism, insulin and diabetes. *Hobbies:* Photography; Music; Tennis. *Address:* Beecham Pharmaceuticals Research Division, Brockham Park, Betchworth, Surrey RH3 7AJ, England.

MANSKY, Peter Alan, b. 2 Jan. 1943, Utica, New York, USA. Psychopharmacologist and Psychotherapist. m. Susan Ellen Malark, 27 Dec. 1984, 1 son, 1 daughter. *Education:* AB, Cornell University School of Arts and Sciences, Ithaca, New York, 1964; MD, State University of New York at Buffalo Medical School, New York, 1968; Diplomate, American Board of Psychiatry and Neurology 1978, National Board of Medical Examiners.*Appointments include:* Clinical Fellow in Psychiatry, Harvard University, Boston, 1972-75; Chief Resident Psychopharmacology Clinic, Massachusetts General Hospital, Boston, 1974-75; Director of Residency Education, Assistant Professor, Associate Unit Chief of Veterans Administration Hospital, University of Kentucky Medical Centre, 1975-78; Private Practice, 1975-; Associate Professor 1978-83, Clinical Associate Professor 1983-, Department of Psychiatry, Albany Medical College of Union University; Director Psychopharmacology Unit, Capital District Psychiatric Center, Albany, New York, 1978-84; Executive Editorial Board of the Psychiatric Quarterly, 1982-. *Memberships include:* American Psychiatric Association; American Association of Directors of Psychiatry Residency Training. *Publications include:* 26 articles on psychiatry and related topics in medical books and journals, including: 'Opiates: Human Psychopharmacology' in "The Handbook of Psychopharmacology" (editors: L Iverson, S Iverson and S Snyder), 1978. *Honours:* Scribe and Participant: MIT Neurosciences Program Work Session on Molecular Basis of Opiate Action; Cornell National Scholarship; American Medical Association Physicians Recognition Award, 1976; Discussant: Patient Conference, Massachusetts General Hospital, Department of Psychiatry 50th Anniversary Celebration, 1984. *Hobbies:* Skiing; Creative Writing, Swimming, Computer programming. *Address:* Executive Park East, Albany, NY 12203, USA.

MANSOUR, Salah, b. 14 Nov. 1942, Lebanon. Otolaryngologist. m. Ruth Williamson 17 June 1972, 3 sons. *Education:* MD, St Joseph University, Beirut, Lebanon, 1970; Licencié, Medical Council of Canada, Montreal, 1972; Certificate, Specialist in Otolaryngology, 1975. *Appointments:* Chief Resident, University of Montreal, Canada, 1975; Otolaryngologist, Honoré Mercier Hospital, St Hyacinthe, Quebec, Canada,

1976; Staff Otolaryngologist, Dar El Soha Hospital, Beirut, Lebanon, 1980. *Memberships:* Fellow, Royal College of Surgeons of Canada, 1975; American Academy of Otolaryngology, 1977; Fellow, American College of Surgeons, 1978; Canadian Society of Otolaryngology & Maxill-Facial Surgery; Quebec Society of Otolaryngology & Maxillo-Facial Surgery; Royal Society of Medicine, London, England. *Publications:* 'Manifestations Cochléo-vestibulaires du trou déchiré postérieur', Canadian Journal of Otolaryngology, 1975; 'Cylindrome de la tête et du cou', Révue de l'Union Médical du Canada, 1976; 'Hémangiome de la Mandibule', Canadian Journal of Otolaryngology, 1978; 'Triglycerid and sudden Hearing Loss', Arab Journal of Medicine, 1983; 'Neck Metastasis and Laryngeal & Orotharyngeal Cancer', Arab Journal of Medicine, 1984. *Honours:* Lauréat, French Faculty of Medicine, Beirut, St Hoseph's University, 1968; 1st Prize, Medical-surgical Society of Montreal, 1974, 1975; Best Resident of the Year Award, Montreal University, 1975; Award of Charities Foundation, Notre Dame Hospital, Montreal, 1975. *Hobbies:* Poetry; Literature. *Address:* Chatila Building Verdun Street, Beirut, Lebanon.

MANZ, Friedrich, b. 22 July 1941, Backnang, Federal Republic of Germany. Vice-Director for the Institute for Child Nutrition. m. Irmgard Manz, 26 Aug. 1966, 1 son, 1 daughter. *Education:* Dr med, 1968; Privat dozent, 1980; Professor, 1983. *Appointments:* University Children's Hospital, Bonn, 1970; University Children's Hospital, Heidelberg, 1971-83; Institute for Child Nutrition, 1983-. *Memberships:* European Society for Pediatric Research; European Society for Pediatric Nephrology; Society for the Study of Inborn Errors of Metabolism; Deutsche Gesellschaft für Kinderheilkunde; Deutsche Gesellschaft für Ernährung. *Publication:* 'Hereditäre Tubulopathien' (with K Schärer) in "Klinische Nephrologie" volume II (H Losse and E Renner), 1982. *Honour:* Milupa-Preis, Herbert-Quandt-Stiftung, 1983. *Address:* Forschungsinstitut für Kinderernährung, Heinstück 11, D 4600 Dortmund 50, Federal Republic of Germany.

MANZOOR-I-KHUDA, Abu Raihan Mahiuddin Mohammad, b. 1 Oct. 1933, Calcutta, India. Director, Drug Research & Development Institute, Bangladesh Council of Scientific and Industrial Research Laboratories. m. Khaleda Fancy Khanum, 19 July 1957, London, England, 1 son, 3 daughters. *Education:* BSc, (Honours) Applied Chemistry, 1953, MSc, Organo-Applied Chemistry, 1954, Dhaka University; DIC, Organic Chemistry, Imperial College of Science & Technology, London, 1958; PhD, Organic Chemistry, University of London, 1958. *Appointments:* Senior Research Officer, Principal Scientific Officer, Head of Research Division, CSIR, 1959-67; Director (Technology), Jute Research Institute, 1967-77; Director (-Planning), Bangladesh Council of Scientific & Industrial Research, Dhaka, 1977-78; Senator, University of Dhaka, 1974-77, University of Chittagong, 1983-; Member, National Council of Scientific & Technology, 1977-81; Director, BCSIR Laboratories, Chittagong, 1978-. *Memberships:* Fellow, Chemical Society, 1956; Life Member, Vice-President (1974-78), Bangladesh Association for Scientists & Scientific Profession; Life Member, Bangladesh Chemical Society; Member, Bangladesh Association for the Advancement of Science; Member, Vice-President (1978-84), Alumni Association for West German Universities. *Publications:* Over 100 research & review papers, patents, monographs, on Pharmacognostic & chemical studies; more than 10 monographs & articles on religion & science. *Honours:* Royal Exhibition of 1851 Fellow, London, 1955-57; Fellow, National Research Council of Canada, 1958-59; Fellow, Nuffield Foundation, UK, 1964-65; Senior Fellow, Alexander von Humboldt Stiftung, Federal Republic of Germany, 1971-73, 1978. *Hobbies:* Travel; Coin collecting; Photography. *Address:* B/2/1 Humayun Road, Dhaka-7, Bangladesh.

MAOZ, Beyamin, b. 31 Oct. 1929, Kassel, Germany.

Professor of Psychiatry, Ben Gurion University; Head of Department of Psychiatry, Soroka Medical Center. m. Elly Erna Orakker, 1 May 1957, 3 daughters. *Education:* MD; PhD, Social Psychiatry. *Appointments:* General Practitioner; Head of Outpatients Department, Psychiatric, GEHA Hospital. *Memberships:* International College of Psychosomatic Medicine; International Society of Clinical and Psychosomatic Hypnosis; International Society of the Menopause. *Publication:* Co-author, "A Time to Reap", 1981. *Hobby:* Music. *Address:* B Yiftah Hagiladi Str, Beer Sheva, Israel, 84234.

MAPLESON, William Wellesley, b. 2 Aug. 1926, London, England. Professor of Physics of Anaesthesia. m. Gwladys Doreen Wood, 10 July 1954, Cardiff, Wales, 1 son, 1 daughter. *Education:* BSc, 1947; PhD, 1953; DSc, 1973; Dunelm. *Appointments:* Lecturer, 1952-65; Senior Lecturer, 1965-69; Reader, 1969-73; Professor, 1973-; University of Wales College of Medicine (formerly called Welsh National School of Medicine).*Memberships:* Fellow, Institute of Physics; Fellow, Royal Society of Medicine; Member, Anaesthetics Research Society; Hospital Physicists Association; Biological Engineering Society. *Publications:* Contributor to professional journals including: "The Elimination of Rebreathing in Various Semi-closed Anaesthetic Systems', 'British Journal of Anaesthesia', 1954; 'Circulation time Models of the Uptake of Inhaled Anaesthetics and Data for Quantifying them', 'British Journal of Anaesthesia', 1973; Books include: Co-author, "Automatic Ventilation of the Lungs", 3rd edition, 1980. *Honours include:* Faculty Medal of the Faculty of Anaesthetists of the Royal College of Surgeons of England for services to anaesthesia, 1981; Honorary Member of the Sociedade Brazileira de Anestesiolgia, 1983.*Hobbies:* Theatre; Walking; Botany. *Address:* Department of Anaesthetics, University of Wales College of Medicine, Cardiff CF4 4XW, Wales.

MARAGOUDAKIS, Michael, b. 4 Aug. 1932, Crete. University Professor of Pharmacology. m. Jane Boyagis, 17 July 1968, Philadelphia, Pennsylvania, USA. 1 son, 1 daughter. *Education:* PhD, Oregon State University, USA. *Appointments:* Manager, Research Department, Ciba Geigy Pharmaceutical Company; Visiting Professor of Medicine, Albert Einstein College of Medicine; President, National Drug Industry, Greece; Currently Professor of Pharmacology, University of Patros Medical School. *Memberships:* American Society for Pharmacology and Experimental Therapeutics; American Society for Biological Chemists. *Publications:* Many articles in the field of biochemistry and pharmacology. *Honours:* NIH Fellowship; Greek State Scholarship Foundation. *Hobby:* Sailing. *Address:* Iroon Polytechnion 42, Patras, Greece.

MARCER, Guido Ruggero, b. 5 July 1947, Udine, Italy. Assistant Professor. *Education:* MD, Padva, 1973; Occupational Health and Safety; Allergy and Clinical Immunology. *Appointment:* Research Assistant, University of Padua. *Memberships:* European Academy of Allergology and Clinical Immunology; Societa Italiana di Medicina Del Gavoro Ediciene. *Publications:* Over 100 articles in Italian & International Journals. *Hobbies:* Chess; Cookery; Swimming. *Address:* Istituto Di Medicina Del Lavoro, Via Facciolati 71, 35100 Padova, Italy.

MARCH, Charles Michael, b. 26 July 1941, New York, New York, USA. Associate Professor of Obstetrics and Gynaecology. m. Antonia Delia Garcia, 7 Nov. 1976, La Canada, California, 1 son, 1 daughter. *Education includes:* BS, St Peters College, New Jersey, 1962; MD, State University of New York, 1966; Intern, St Vincents Hospital, New York, 1966-67; Resident, State University of New York, 1969-73; Fellow, Section of Reproductive Biology, University of Southern California, 1973-75. *Appointments include:* Assistant Instructor, Department of Obstetrics and Gynaecology, State University of New York, Downstate Medical Center, Brooklyn, New York, 1970-73; Instructor,

1973-75, Assistant Professor, 1975-79, Associate Professor, 1980-, Department of Obstetrics and Gynaecology, Chief Section of Gynaecology, University of Southern California School of Medicine, Los Angeles, California; various hospital appointments; Former Consultant to Los Angeles and United Nations Family Planning. *Memberships:* Fellow, American College of Obstetricians and Gynaecologists; American Fertility Society; Pacific Coast Fertility Society; Endocrine Society; Society for Gynaecologic Investigation; Fellow, Los Angeles Obstetrical and Gynaecological Society; Chilean Society of Obstetrics and Gynaecology. *Publications:* Author or Co-author of 41 papers in reviewed journals and 18 non-peer review journals, 4 other publications, 33 book chapters and 22 abstracts. *Honours include:* In-Training Award, 1974, Wyeth Award, 1978, Pacific Coast Fertility Society; Squibb Award, Pacific Coast Fertility Society Mtg, 1980; Codman Award for Best Scientific Film, American Fertility Society, 1984; Lester T Hibbard Outstanding Teacher Award, University of Southern California, 1984. *Hobbies:* Photography; Stamp collecting; Gourmet cooking. *Address:* 1240 North Mission Road, Los Angeles, CA 90033, USA.

MARCHALONIS, John Jacob, b. 22 July 1940, Scranton, Pennsylvania, USA. Professor and Chairman, Department of Biochemistry, Medical University of South Carolina. m. Sally Ann Sevy, 5 May 1978, Frederick, Maryland, 3 daughters. *Education:* AB, Lafayette College, Eastern Pennsylvania, 1962; PhD, Biochemistry, The Rockefeller University, New York, 1967; Postdoctoral Training, the Walter and Eliza Hall Institute of Medical Research, Melbourne, Australia. *Appointments:* Graduate Fellow, The Rockefeller University, New York, 1962-67; Postdoctoral Fellow, American Cancer Society, The Walter and Eliza Hall Institute of Medical Research, Melbourne, 1967-69; Assistant Professor, Medical Sciences, Brown University, Rhode Island, 1969-70; Head, Laboratory of Molecular Immunology, Walter and Eliza Hall Institute of Medical Research, 1970-76; Adjunct Professor, Department of Pathology, University of Pennsylvania School of Medicine, Philadelphia, 1977-83; Head, Cell Biology and Biochemistry Section NCI Cancer Biology Program, Frederick Cancer Research Center, 1977-79; Professor and Chairman, Department of Biochemistry, Medical University of South Carolina, Charleston, 1980-. *Memberships:* Phi Beta Kappa; American Association of Immunologists; American Society of Biological Chemists; American Society of Zoologists; American Association for the Advancement of Science. *Publications:* Editor, "Comparative Immunology", 1976; "Immunity in Evolution", 1977; Editor, "The Lymphocyte: Structure and Function", 1977; Co-editor, "Self/Non-Self Discrimination", "Contemporary Topics in Immunobiology" Volume 9, 1980; Co-editor, "Antibody as a Tool", 1972. *Honours:* Summa cum laude, 1962; High honours in Biology, 1962; Honors in Philosophy, 1962; Fellow of the Neuro Sciences Research Program, 1969; Frank R Lillie Fellow of the Marine Biological Laboratory, 1973. *Hobbies:* Tennis; Running; Reading. *Address:* 986 Casseque Province, Mt Pleasant, SC 29464, USA.

MARCUS, Douglas Alan, b. 6 Mar. 1947, Somerville, New Jersey, USA. Psychiatrist. m. Judith Ann Feinstein, 25 June 1970, New York City, 1 son, 1 daughter. *Education:* MD, Northwestern University Medical School, 1973; AB, Cornell University, 1969. *Appointments:* Director, Inpatient Services, Division of Child and Adolescent Psychiatry, Co-ordinator, Clinical Clerkships, 3rd Year, Department of Psychiatry, SUNY, Downstate, Brooklyn, NY. *Memberships:* American Society for Adolescent Psychiatry; American Psychiatric Association; American Orthopsychiatric Association; Nassau County Psychiatric Association; NY Council of Child Psychiatry.*Hobbies:* Tennis; Gardening; Skiing; Writing; Music. *Address:* 34 Elm Street, Great Neek, NY 11201, USA.

MARCUS, Eric Robert, b. 16 Feb. 1944, New York, New

York, USA. Director, Undergraduate Psychiatric Education. *Education:* BA, Columbia University, 1965; MD, University of Wisconsin, 1969; Intern, New York University, Bellevue, 1970; Psychiatric Resident, New York State Psychiatric Institute, Columbia Presbyterian Medical Center, 1975. *Appointments:* Co-Director, 1975-83, Director, 1984, Neuropsychiatric Diagnostic Unit, Columbia Presbyterian Medical Center; Director, Undergraduate Psychiatric Education, 1981-, Associate Clinical Professor of Psychiatry, 1981, Associate Clinical Professor of Social Medicine, 1981-, Columbia University. *Membership:* Fellow, American Psychiatric Association. *Publications:* 'Use of the acute hospital unit in the early phase longterm treatment of borderline psychotic patients', in 'Psychiatric Clinics of North America'; 'Psychoanalysis and Medical Student training in Advances in Consultation and Liaison', 1983. *Honours:* Fellow, American Psychiatric Association, 1985; Commencement Speaker, 1982, Most Distinguished Teacher, 1979, College of Physicians and Surgeons, Columbia University. *Address:* 722 West 168th Street, Box 125, New York, NY 10032, USA.

MAREK, Frederick Martin, b. 12 July 1910, Vienna, Austria. Associate Orthopaedic Surgeon. m. 17 Dec. 1970, New York, USA, 1 son, 1 daughter. *Education:* MD, University of Vienna Medical School, Vienna, Austria. *Appointments:* Attending Orthopedic Surgeon, Lincoln Hospital, USA; Attending Orthopedic Surgeon, Bronx-Lebanon Hospital; Associate Orthopedic Surgeon, Mount Sinai Hospital; Attending Orthopedic Surgeon, Doctors Hospital, New York. *Memberships:* American College of Surgeons; American Academy of Orthopedic Surgeons; New York Academy of Medicine; Fracture Association; Eastern Orthopedic Association. *Publications:* Numerous. *Hobbies:* Music; Art; Bridge. *Address:* 159 East 69th Street, New York, NY 10021, USA.

MAREK, Zdzislaw, b. 19 Nov. 1924, Bystra, Poland. Head, Institute of Forensic Medicine, Cracow. m. 30 Dec. 1954, 1 son, 1 daughter. *Education:* MD, 1962; Assistant Professor, 1967; Professor, 1976. *Appointments:* Assistant, Institute of Pathology, 1950-52; Pathologist, County Hospital, 1952-56; Assistant, 1957-, Head, 1972-, Institute of Forensic Medicine, Medical Academy, Cracow; Cardiologist and Internal Medicine Practitioner, 1952-65. *Memberships:* International Academy of Forensic and Social Medicine; Polish Society of Forensic Medicine and Criminology. *Publications:* Editor in Chief, "Archiv of Forensic Medicine and Criminology"; "Forensic Medicine Textbook for Students", co-author, 1972, 4th edition, 1983; articles in professional journals. *Honours:* Awards, Minister of Health for Scientific Results, Serology, 1967, Education, 1972, Publishing, 1976. *Hobbies:* Music; Garden. *Address:* ul Urzednicza 56/7, 30-040 Krakow, Poland.

MARGULIES, Alfred Salsbury, b. 9 Mar. 1948, Virginia, USA. Psychiatrist. m. Bonnie Hoffman, 16 June 1974, 2 daughters. *Education:* BA, University of Virginia, 1970; MD, Harvard Medical School, 1974; Residency, Massachusetts Mental Health Center, Harvard, 1974-77; Candidate, Psychoanalytic Institute of New England, East; First Elvin Semrad Teaching Fellowship, Massachusetts Mental Health Center, Harvard, 1979-80. *Appointments:* Teaching Consultant in Psychiatry, Hospital Improvement Program, Institute of Mental Health, Rhode Island, 1977-78; Teaching Consultant in Psychiatry, 1978-80, Co-Director of Psychiatric Education, 1980-81, Department of Mental Health, Region V, Massachusetts; Attending Psychiatrist, 1981-83, Chief Psychiatrist, 1983-85, Director, 1985-, Psychiatric Out Patient Fepartment, The Cambridge Hospital, Cambridge, Massachusetts; Director, Medical Student Education in Psychiatry, The Cambridge Hospital, Cambridge, Massachusetts. *Memberships:* Massachusetts Psychiatric Society; American Psychiatric Society; American Psychoanalytic Association; Affilitate Member; Associate of Directors od Medal Student Education in Psychiatry. *Publications:* 'The Initial Encounter: What to do First?' (with L Havens) American Journal of Psychiatry, 1981; 'Toward Empathy: The Uses of Wonder' American Journal of Psychiatry, 1984; 'On Listening to a Dream: The Sensory Dimensions' Psychiatry, 1985. *Honours:* University of Virginia: Echols Scholar, 1966-70, Du Pont Scholar, 1966-70, John Kenneth Crispell Scholar, 1969, Phi Beta Kappa, Junior Fellow, Society of Fellows, 1969-70, Raven Society, Dean's Prize for Academic Excellence in the College, 1970; Harvard (Medical): The Harvard National Scholarship, 1970-74. *Address:* The Cambridge Hospital, Department of Psychiatry, 1493 Cambridge Street, Cambridge, MA 02139, USA.

MARGULIS, Lynn, b. 5 Mar. 1938, Chicago, Illinois, USA. Professor of Biology. m. (1) Carl Sagan, June 1957, (2) T N Margulis, Jan. 1967, div, 3 sons, 1 daughter. *Education:* AB, University of Chicago, 1957; MS, University of Wisconsin, 1960; PhD, University of California at Berkeley, 1965. *Appointments:* Research Associate, Brandeis University, 1963-64; Lecturer, Brandeis Biology Department, 1962-65; Consultant, Staff Member, Elementary Science Study, Educational Services Incorporated, 1963-67, Biology Co-ordinator, Brandeis Peace Corps, 1965-66; Adjunct Assistant Professor, 1966-67, Assistant Professor, 1967-71, Associate Professor, 1971-77, Professor, 1977-, Boston University Biology Department; Visiting Professor, Scripps Institute of Oceanography, 1980; Visiting Professor, Cal Tech, 1980; Faculty, 1980, 1982, 1984, Co-Director, 1982, 1984, NASA Planatary Biological and Microbial Ecology Summer Course. *Memberships:* Elected Member, National Academy of Sciences, 1983; Space Science Board/NASA, 1977-81; NASA Advisory Council, 1982-; Commonwealth Book Fund Committee, 1982-; Society for Evolutionary Protistology; International Society for the Study of the Origin of Life; Marine Biology Laboratory. *Publications:* "The Origin of Eukaryotic Cells", 1970; "Symbiosis in Cell Evolution", 1981; "Five Kingdoms: An Illustrated Guide to the Phyla of Life on Earth", (with K V Schwartz), 1982; "Origins of Sex", 1986. *Honours:* Elected Member, National Academy of Sciences, 1983; Sherman Fairchild Distinguished Scholar, Cal Tech, 1976-77; Guggenheim Fellow, 1979; NASA Public Service Award, 1981; George Lamb Award, Outstanding US Botanist, 1971; Fellow to AAAS, 1975. *Address:* Boston University, Biology Department, 2 Cummington Street, Boston, MA 02215, USA.

MARIBONA, Ricardo P, b. 22 June 1935, Varadero, Cuba. Chief, Psychiatry Department. m. 29 Oct. 1960, Havana, 3 sons. *Education:* BS, National Institute of Higher Education, Cuba; MD, University of Valladolid, Spain. *Appointments:* Private Practitioner, 1973-; Psychiatry Resident, Dallas, Texas, USA, 1969-73; currently, Chief of Psychiatry Department, St Anthony's Hospital, Florida. *Memberships:* American, Pinellas County and Florida Psychiatric Associations; Florida Medical Association; Pinellas County Medical Society. *Hobbies:* Boating; Tennis; Fishing; Golf. *Address:* 5500 Central Avenue, Suite A, St Petersburg, FL 33707, USA.

MARINI ARAÚJO ABREU, Mario Manuel, b. 26 Sep. 1930, Coimbra, Portugal. Professor of Anatomy. m. Rosa Maria Fonseca Araújo Abreu, 1 May 1957, Coimbra, 2 sons, 3 daughters. *Education:* MD, Universidade de Coimbra; PhD, Universidade de Lourenço Marques, Mozambigue; Specialist in leprosy, tropical diseases, pediatrics and sanitary doctor. *Appointments:* Medical Doctor, Hansen disease, Hospital Rovisco Pais; Lecturer, Instituto de Medicina Tropical, Lisbon, Portugal; Lecturer in Anatomy, Professor in Anatomy, Universidade de Lourenço Marques, Mozambique; Professor of Anatomy, Instituto de Ciências Biomédicas Abel Salazar, Universidade de Porto, Porto, Portugal. *Memberships:* Anatomical Society of Southern Africa; Sociedade Anatómica

Portuguesa; Sociedade Brasilieira de Anatomia; Association des Anatomistes, Paris; Pan-American Association for Anatomy; Portuguese Society of Electron Microscopy. *Publications:* 'Vascularizaçao Arterial do Córtex Cerebeloso do Quirópteros', 1980; 'Hypoplastic Right Ventricle, Rare Malformation of the Heart', 1982. *Hobbies:* Pilately; Hunting. *Address:* Rua António Cândido, 66 - 4200 Porto, Portugal.

MARKMAN, Ronald Abraham, b. 29 Aug. 1936, Tel Aviv, Israel. Forensic Psychiatrist. m. Nitza Artsiel, 3 June 1962, 2 sons, 1 daughter. *Education:* BA, University of California at Los Angeles, 1957, MD, 1960; JD, University of West Los Angeles, 1979. *Appointments:* Assistant Clinical Professor, Psychiatry, UCLA, 1966-67; Assistant Professor, Psychiatry, University of Southern California, 1967-82, Associate Clinical Professor, 1982-; Medical Director, Airport Marina Counselling, 1969-; Private Practice of Forensic Psychiatry–. *Memberships:* American Academy of Psychiatry and Law; American Psychiatric Society; Southern California Psychiatric Society; Alpha Omega Alpha; Phi Beta Kappa. *Publications:* 'Juvenile Delinquincy in Israel' in 'American Journal of Psychiatry', 1966; 'Kleine-Levin Syndrome - Report of a Case' in 'American Journal of Psychiatry', 1967. *Honours:* Phi Beta Kappa, 1957; Alpha Omega Alpha, 1960. *Hobbies:* Skiing; Tennis; Cycling; Travel. *Address:* PO Box 6063, Beverly Hills, CA, USA 90212.

MARKOE, Arnold Michael, b. 15 Apr. 1942, New York, USA. Associate Professor of Radiation Oncology. m. Tana Kates, 3 Sep. 1967, Roslyn, New York, 1 daughter. *Education:* BA, Adelphi University, New York, 1963; MSc, University of Rochester, New York, 1966; ScD, University of Pittsburgh, Pennsylvania, 1972; MD, Hahnemann Medical College, Philadelphia, 1977. *Appointments:* Visiting Research Associate, Brookhaven National Laboratories, 1963-66; Research Associate, Radiology, Albert Einstein College of Medicine, 1966-69; USPHS Post-doctoral Fellow, Allegheny General Hospital, 1972-73; SR Instructor of Radiation Oncology, Hahnemann Hospital, 1976-81; Assistant Professor of Radiation Oncology, Hahnemann Hospital, 1981-85; Associate Professor, 1985-; Consulting Radiation Oncologist: St Agnes Medical Center, Philadelphia, 1984-; West Jersey Hospital System, 1983-; Delaware Valley Medical Center, 1986-. *Memberships:* American College of Radiology; American Society Therapeutic Radiology-Oncology; Keystone AREA Society of Radiation Oncology; Pennsylvania Medical Society; Philadelphia County Medical Society; Associate Member, Radiation Research Society; Alpha Omega Alpha; Beta, Beta Beta. *Publications:* Contributor to books and professional journals; Book Review Editor, 'American Journal of Clinical Oncology', 1982-. *Honours:* Radiation Research Society Travel Award, 1972; Nuclear Medicine Society Research Award, 1977; Upjohn Award for Research, 1977; Jane Stuart Prize in Radiation Oncology, 1977; Lindback Award for Outstanding Teaching, 1983. *Address:* Department of Radiation Oncology, Hahnemann Hospital MS200, Broad and Vine Streets, Philadelphia, PA 19102, USA.

MARKOFF, Richard Allan, b. 28 Feb. 1929, New York City, USA. Associate Professor, John A Burns School of Medicine; Clinical Director, Hawaii State Hospital. m. Sally, 31 Oct. 1961, New York, USA, 1 daughter. *Education:* AB, Washington Square College of Arts and Sciences of New York University, 1951; MA, Education, School of Education, New York University, 1954, MD, School of Medicine, 1959. *Appointments:* Resident in Psychiatry, Bellevue Hospital, New York, 1960-63, Psychiatrist, 1963-69; Psychiatrist, University Hospital, NYU Medical Centre, 1964-69; Unit Chief Psychiatrist, Clinical Director, Hawaii State Hospital, 1969-72; Clinical Assistant Professor of Psychiatry, Associate Clinical Professor, University of Hawaii School of Medicine, 1970-72, Assistant Professor of Psychiatry, 1972-74, Associate Professor, 1974-. *Memberships:* American Psychiatric Association; New York County Medical

Society; Hawaii Psychiatric Society; Royal Society of Health; New York Academy of Sciences; Member, American Pain Society; Fellow, American Psychiatric Association. *Publications:* 17 articles in various medical journals, 1973-; 3 book chapters in textbooks, 1977-81. *Honours:* Alpha Omega Alpha Medical Honour Society, 1958; Teaching Awards, Medical School, 1982, 1985; Residency Teaching Award, 1984. *Hobbies:* Bagpiping; Jogging. *Address:* UH School of Medicine, 2230 Liliha Street, Honolulu, HI 96817, USA.

MARKS, Charles, b. 28 Jan. 1922, Ukraine. Professor of Surgery; Senior Surgeon. m. Joyce Wernick, 11 Dec. 1949, Salisbury, Rhodesia (now Harare, Zimbabwe), 4 sons. *Education:* MB ChB, University of Cape Town, South Africa; MD, MS, Wisconsin, USA; PhD, Tulane University; FRCP, Edinburgh; FRCS, England; FRCCP; FACC. *Appointments:* Consultant Surgeon, Salisbury General Hospital, Rhodesia, 1953-63; Associate Professor, Surgery, Marquette University Medical School, USA, 1963-67; Attending Surgeon, Milwaukee General Hospital and Veterans Administration Hospital, 1963-67; Associate Clinical Professor, Surgery, Case West Reserve Medical School, Cleveland, Ohio; Director of Department of Surgery, Mount Sinai Hospital; Attending Surgeon, University Hospital and Veterans Administration Hospital, Cleveland, 1967-71; Professor of Surgery, Louisiana State University Medical School, New Orleans, Louisiana, 1971-; Senior Surgeon, Charity Hospital and Veterans Administration Hospital, New Orleans, 1971-. *Memberships include:* British and American Medical Associations; Royal Society of Medicine; Royal (England) and American Colleges of Surgeons; Societe Internationale de Chirug; American College of Cardiology; American College of Chest Physicians; American Association of Anatomists. *Publications:* "Atlas of Techniques in Surgery", 1965; "Applied Surgical Anatomy", 1972; "The Portal Venus System", 1973; "A Surgeon's World", 1973; "Carcinoid Tumors", 1979; "The Zimbabwe Story: A Sequence of Events", 1981. *Honours:* Hunterian Professor, Royal College of Surgeons, England, 1956; Clinical Teacher of the Year, Aesculapian Honour Society, Louisiana State University Medical School, 1972, 74, 79; President, New Orleans Surgical Society, 1981. *Hobbies:* Travel; Tennis; Writing. *Address:* 1680 State Street, New Orleans, LA 70118, USA.

MARKS, Gerald Samuel, b. 13 Feb. 1930, Cape Town, Republic of South Africa. Professor and Head of Department of Pharmacology and Toxicology, Queen's University, Kingston, Ontario, Canada. m. Marion Zoe Tobias, 6 June 1955, Cape Town, Republic of South Africa, 1 son, 1 daughter. *Education:* BSc, 1950, MSc, 1951, University of Cape Town; DPhil, Oxford, England, 1954. *Appointments:* Research Chemist, South African Institute for Medical Research, Johannesburg, Republic of South Africa; Post-doctoral Fellow, Pure Chemistry Division, NRC, Ottawa, Canada; Research Assistant, Instructor, Botany Department, University of Chicago, USA; Lecturer, British Empire Cancer Campaign Research Fellow, Department of Chemical Pathology, St Mary's Hospital, Medical School, London, England; Assistant, Associate and Full Professor, Department of Pharmacology, University of Alberta, Edmonton, Alberta, Canada; Visiting Professor, School of Pharmacy, University of California, San Francisco, USA. *Memberships:* Chemical Society, London; Canadian Pharmacological Society; American Society of Pharmacology and Experimental Therapeutics; New York Academy of Sciences; Canadian Toxicology Society. *Publications:* "Heme and Chlorophyll, Chemical, Biochemical and Medical Aspects", 1969; 'The effect of chemical on hepatic haem biosynthesis in chick embryo liver cells and the 17-day-old chick embryo. Differences between species in the response to porphyrin-inducing chemicals', Chapter 7 in 'Handbook of Experimental Pharmacology', 1978. *Honours:* Aesculapian Society Lectureship Award, Queens University, 1973; MRC Visiting Professor, Department of Pharmacy, Dalhousie University, 1974; Visiting Professor, Department of Pharmacy, University of Alberta, 1976. *Hobbies:* Tennis; Squash; Swimming. *Address:* Department of Pharmacology and Toxicology, Queen's University, Kingston, Ontario, Canada K7L 3N6.

MARKS, Isaac, b. 16 Feb. 1935, Cape Town, South Africa. m. 31 Mar. 1957, Cape Town, 1 son, 1 daughter. *Education:* MD: FRCPsych. *Appointment:* Professor, Experimental Psychopathology, Institute of Psychiatry, London, England-. *Publications:* "Patterns of Meaning in Psychiatric Patients", 1965; "Care and Cure of Neuroses", 1981; "Fears, Phobias and Rituals", 1986; 7 other books; 190 articles in scientific journals. *Honours:* Starkey Medal and Prize, Royal Society for the Promotion of Mental Health, 1969; Salmon Lecturer and Medallist, New York Society of Medicine, 1978; Fellow, Centre for Advanced Study in Behavioural Sciences, Stanford University, California, USA, 1981-82. *Hobbies:* Theatre; Hiking; Gardening. *Address:* Institute of Psychiatry, Maudsley Hospital, London SE5 8AF, England.

MARKS, Ronald, b. 25 Mar. 1935, London, England. Professor of Dermatology. m. Hilary Venmore, Nov. 1978, Cardiff, 2 daughters. *Education:* Guy's Hospital Medical School, London, 1953-58; BSc (Hons), Physiology, London, 1956; MBBS (Hons), London, 1959; DTM&H, England, 1961; MRCP, London, 1964; FRCP, London, 1977; MRCPath, 1980; FRCPath, 1985. *Appointments include:* Specialist in Dermatology; Registrar in Dermatology; Senior Lecturer, Institute of Dermatology, London and Honorary Consultant at St John's Hospital for Diseases of Skin, London, 1971; Consultant Dermatologist, St John's Hospital, 1972; Senior Lecturer in Dermatology, University of Wales College of Medicine, Cardiff, 1973; Honorary Consultant to University Hospital of Wales, 1973; Reader in Dermatology, 1977; Professor of Dermatology, University of Wales College of Medicine, Cardiff, 1980-. *Memberships:* Fellow, Royal Society of Medicine; Fellow, Royal College of Physicians; Fellow, Royal College of Pathologists; Member, British Association of Dermatologists; Society of Cosmetic Chemists; European Society for Dermatological Research, President, 1978-79; American Academy of Dermatology; International Society of Dermatopathology; Chairman, Society for Bioengineering and the Skin. *Publications:* "Common Facial Dermatoses", 1976; "Mechanisms of Action of Topical Corticosteroid", 1976; "Dermatology: Postgraduate Tutorials" (Co-editor and contributor), 1977; "Psoriasis", 1981; "Practical Problems in Dermatology", 1983; "Acne", 1984; Contributor to professional journals. *Hobbies:* Visual Art of the 19th and 20th Centuries; Squash. *Address:* Department of Medicine, University of Wales College of Medicine, Heath Park, Cardiff, CF4 4XN, Wales.

MARKS, Vincent, b. 10 June 1930, London, England. University Professor of Clinical Biochemistry. m. Averil Rosalie Sherrard, 27 Feb. 1957, London, 1 son, 1 daughter. *Education:* MA, BM, BCh, DM, University of Oxford, 1948-52; St Thomas Hospital Medical School, University of London, 1948-52. *Appointments:* Resident, St Georges Hospital, London; Registrar and Lecturer in Chemical Pathology, Senior Lecturer in Chemical Pathology, Institute of Neurology, London; Medical Research Council Research Fellow, Kings College Hospital, London; Currently Consultant Chemical Pathologist, Guildford, Surrey; Currently Professor of Clinical Biochemistry, University of Surrey. *Memberships:* Medical Research Society; American Diabetes Association; Association of Clinical Biochemists; Nutrition Society; Association of Clinical Pathologists; American Association of Clinical Chemists; Former President, Biomedical section, British Association for the Advancement of Science, 1975. *Publications:* "Hypoglycaemia", (co-author), 1964 and 1981; "Scientific Foundations of Clinical Biochemistry", (co-author), volume 1, 1978, volume 2, 1983; "Therapeutic Drug Monitoring",

(co-author), 1981; "Clinical Biochemistry Nearer the Patient", (co-author), 1985. *Honours:* Roman Lecturer, Australian Association of Clinical Biochemists, 1982; Wellcome Award, Association of Clinical Biochemists, 1985. *Hobbies:* Talking; Relaxing. *Address:* Department of Biochemistry, University of Surrey, Guildford, GU2 5XH, England.

MARKS-BROWN, Shirley F., b. 22 Oct. 1946, Prairie View, Texas, USA. Clinical Assistant Professor, Psychiatry, 1 son. *Education:* BA, Spelman College; MD, Harvard Medical School; MPH, Harvard School of Public Health. *Appointments:* Assistant Professor, Psychiatry, Clinical Assistant Professor, Psychiatry, Baylor College of Medicine; TV Personality, Medical Staff, 'Good Morning Houston', KTRK, Houston. *Memberships:* American Psychiatric Association; National Medical Association; American Orthopsychiatric Association; Harris County Medical Association; Texas Medical Association. *Honours:* Merrill Scholar, 1967-68; Houston's Most Influential Women's Award. *Hobbies:* Swimming; Sewing. *Address:* 2646 South Loop West, Suite 150, Houston, TX 77054, USA.

MARRIE, Thomas James, b. 13 Nov. 1944, Newfoundland, Canada. Associate Professor, Director of Infectious Diseases Programme. m. Kathleen Dingman Hebb, 16 Aug., 1969, Chester, Nova Scotia, 1 son, 3 daughters. *Education:* MD Cum Laude, Dalhousie University, 1970; FRCP(C) General Internal Medicine, 1977; Diplomate, American College of Physicians - Infectious Diseases, 1979; Certificate Special Competance - Infectious Disease, 1983. *Appointments:* Assistant Professor 1978, Associate Professor 1980-, Dalhousie University. *Memberships:* RCPS Canada; American College of Physicians; American Society for Microbiology. *Publications include:* 79 contributions to learned journals, 1977-85. *Hobby:* Sailing. *Address:* 6077 Cherry Street, Halifax, Nova Scotia B3H 2K4, Canada.

MARRS, Richard P, b. 6 Dec. 1947, Kerrville, Texas, USA. Associate Professor, Department of Obstetrics and Gynaecology. m. 1 child. *Education includes:* BA, 1970, MD, Medical Branch, 1974, Resident, 1974-76, Chief Resident, 1976-77, University of Texas; Fellowship in Reproductive Endocrinology, University of Southern California, 1977-79. *Appointments include:* Clinical Instructor, Onstetrics and Gynaecology, 1977-79, Assistant Professor, Endocrinology, Associate Professor, 1982-, Los Angeles County-University of Southern California School of Medicine; Assistant Clinical Professor, University of Texas Medical Branch, 1979-82. *Memberships:* American College of Obstetricians and Gynaecologists, Fellow; American Fertility Society; American Medical Association; Pacific Coast Fertility Society; Society for Gynaecologic Investigation; Endocrine Society; Society for Study of Reproduction. *Publications:* Author or Co-author of numerous contributions to peer review journals, non-peer review journals, books, and abstracts. *Honours include:* Schreiner Institute Scholarship, 1966-68; Jeanne Kempner Fellowship Award, 1978-79; Squibb Prize Paper Award, Pacific Coast Fertility Society, 1979; Scientific Exhibit Award, American College of Obstetricians and Gynaecologists, 1980; Senior Residents Award for Excellence in Teaching, 1980; Memorial Foundation Award, 49th Annual Meeting, Pacific Coast Obstetrical and Gynaecological Society, 1982. *Hobby:* Tennis. *Address:* 1240 North Mission Road, Los Angeles, CA 90033, USA.

MARSH, Anthony William, b. 24 Sep. 1955, Hoboken, New Jersey, USA. Director. *Education:* Doctor of Chiropractic, New York Chiropractic College. *Memberships:* American Chiropractic Association; ACA Council on Neurology; ACA Council on Roentgenology; Member, Chiropractic Council on Education; Federation of Chiropractic Education and Research; Candidate Elect, NY Academy of Sciences. *Publications:* 'Spinal Dysraphism', Journal of the ACA; 'Healthwise', Syndicated Column. *Honours:* Academic Excellence, NYCC, 1976; Diplomate, National Board of Chiropractic Examiners, 1980; Outstanding Young Men of America, 1980; Chiropractic Council on Education, 1984. *Hobbies:* Aerobics; Computers; Music; Chess.*Address:* Tower West, Suite B, 6050 Boulevard East, West New York, NJ 07093, USA.

MARSH, Ella Jean, b. 16 Dec. 1941, Chicago, Illinois, USA. Associate DME, Orlando General Hospital; Chairman, Department of Pediatric, Orlando General Hospital; Associate Clinical Professor, West Virginia College of Osteopathic Medicine and South-Eastern College of Osteopathic Medicine. *Education:* BA, St Mary of the Woods College, 1963; DO, Chicago College of Osteopathic Medicine; Fellow, American College of Osteopathic Pediatrics.*Appointments:* Assistant Professor of Pediatrics, Chicago College of Osteopathic Medicine; Associate Professor. *Memberships:* Vice-President, College of Osteopathic Pediatricians; AOA; American Medical Association; FOMA; Central Florida Pediatric Society; Orelando Chamber of Commerce; Active Staff, various Florida Hospitals. *Publications:* Contributor to professional journals. *Honours:* Donald Buckner Moore Scholarship, 1971; Pediatric Department Senior Student Award, 1971; Diplomate of American Board of Pediatricians, 1978; Diploma of the Osteopathic National Awards, 1972; Fellow, American College of Osteopathic Pediatricians, 1986. *Hobbies:* Water Sports; Antiques. *Address:* 7824 Lake Underhill, Suite D, Orlando, FL 32822, USA.

MARSH, Joanne Marilyn, b. 1 Feb. 1941, Drumheller, Alberta, Canada. Assistant Professor/Assistant Physician/Consultant. *Education:* BSc, 1962, MD, 1966, University of Alberta; FRCP (C) Internal Medicine, 1972. *Appointments:* Teaching Fellow in Rheumatology, University of Alberta, 1971; Research Fellow, Mathilda and Terrance Kennedy Institute of Rheumatology, London, England, 1972-74; Honorary Registrar, Charing Cross Group of Hospitals London, England, 1972-74; Currently: Assistant Professor, Dalhousie University, Halifax, Nova Scotia, Canada; Assistant Physician, Victoria General Hospital, Halifax, Nova Scotia, Canada; Consultant, Nova Scotia Rehabilitation Centre, Halifax, Nova Scotia, Canada. *Memberships:* Fellow, Royal College of Physicians of Canada; Fellow, Royal Society of Medicine (England); Tissue Culture Association (USA); British Society of Immunology; British Society of Rheumatology; Canadian Rheumatism Association; Arthritis and Rheumatism Association; Canadian Society for Clinical Investigation; Nova Scotia Society of Internal Medicine; Canadian Medical Association. *Publications:* Contributor of articles to medical and scientific journals. *Honours:* Canadian Arthritis and Rheumatism Research Fellowship, 1972-74; Canadian Arthritis and Rheumatism Society Associateship, 1974-81. *Hobbies:* Painting; Gardening; Music. *Address:* Room 4193 ACC, Victoria General Hospital, Halifax, Nova Scotia, Canada B3H 2Y9.

MARSHALL, Charles Edivard, b. 13 July 1912, Cowell, South Australia. Professor of Pathology (retired). m. Thelma B Simmonds, 31 Jan. 1941, 1 daughter. *Education:* Diploma in Clinical Pathology, University of London, England; Diploma in Pathology, Royal College of Physicians & Surgeons; Fellow, Royal College of Pathologists (England); Fellow, Royal College of Pathologists (Australasia); Diplomate, American Board of Pathology. *Appointments:* Resident Physician, Royal South Sydney Hospital, 1940; Captain, RAAMC, 1941-46; Resident in Pathology, Sydney Hospital, 1946-49; Assistant Morbid Anatomist, Hospital for Sick Children London, 1951; Assistant Bacteriologist, Sydney Hospital, 1953; Assistant Morbid Anatomist, Sydney Hospital, 1954-55; Teaching Fellow in Pathology, University of Sydney, 1953-55; Associate Professor of Pathology, Dalhousie University, Canada, 1955-57; Director of Laboratories, Group Health Medical Centre, Seattle, Washington,

USA, 1957-77; Clinical Assistant Professor of Pathology, University of Washington, 1958-77. *Memberships:* Australian Medical Association; British Medical Association; College of American Pathologists. *Publications:* Various articles in medical journals, especially in field of carcinoma of the cervix. *Honours:* BMA Prize-winning Essay on 'Infective Hepatitis & its Sequalae', 1958. *Hobbies:* Playing Clarinet in amateur Seattle Symphony Orchestra; Painting. *Address:* 1100 University Street Apt 8K, Seattle, WA 98101, USA.

MARSHALL, John, b. 16 Apr. 1922, Bolton, Lancashire, England. Professor of Clinical Neurology. m. Margaret Eileen Hughes, 9 Oct. 1946, Bolton, 2 sons, 3 daughters. *Education:* MB, ChB, 1946, MD, 1951, DPM, 1952, DSc, 1981, University of Manchester; Fellow, Royal College of Physicians (Edinburgh), 1957; Fellow, Royal College of Physicians (London), 1966. *Appointments:* Senior Registrar, Manchester Royal Infirmary, 1947-49; Lieutenant-Colonel, Royal Army Medical Corps, 1949-51; Senior Lecturer in Neurology, University of Edinburgh, 1954-56; Reader in Clinical Neurology, University of London, 1956-71; Professor of Clinical Neurology, 1971-, Dean, Institute of Neurology, University of London. *Memberships:* Association of British Neurologists; Association of Physicians of Great Britain & Ireland; Royal Society of Medicine; Honorary Member, Italian, Swiss & Portuguese Societies of Neurologists.*Publications:* "The Management of Cerebrovascular Disease", 3rd edition, 1976; "The Infertile Period: Principles & Practice", revised 1969.*Honours:* Honorary Fellow, Stroke Council of the American Heart Association, 1980; Auenbrugger Medal, University of Graz, Austria, 1983. *Hobbies:* Gardening; Walking. *Address:* 203 Robin Hood Way, London SW20, England.

MARSHALL, William Hext, b. 10 Apr. 1933, London, England. Professor of Immunology. m. Ingeborg C L Ristow, 16 Sep. 1961, Hildesheim, 2 sons, 1 daughter. *Education:* B Arts, 1954, MB BChir, 1957, MD, 1965, Cambridge University, England; MRCP, Royal College of Physicians, 1961; PhD, Melbourne University, Australia, 1966; FRCP, 1981. *Appointments:* Junior Lecturer, The London Hospital Medical College, 1961-63; Assistant Physician, 1963-68, Research Fellow, 1963-68, Walter and Eliza Hall Institute, Australia; Research Associate, New York University Medical Centre, 1967-68; Associate Professor of Immunology, 1968-70, Professor of Immunology, 1970-; Memorial University of Newfoundland. *Memberships:* Member, Canadian, Australian and US Societies for Immunologists; Transplantation Society; Genetical Society. *Publications:* Over 74 scientific papers on cellular immunology, clinical immunology and immunogenetics. *Hobbies:* Cinema; Theatre; Gardening; Outdoor Sports. *Address:* Immunology Laboratories, Faculty of Medicine, Memorial University of Newfoundland, St John's, Newfoundland A1B 3V6.

MARSTON, Jeffery Adrian Priestley, b. 15 Dec. 1927, London, England. Consultant Surgeon and Director of Vascular Unit. m. Sylvie Colin, 17 July 1952, 2 sons, 1 daughter. *Education:* MA, DM, MCh, University of Oxford, 1945-48, St Thomas's Hospital Medical School, 1948-52, Harvard Medical School, 1960-62. *Appointments:* Senior Surgical Registrar, St Thomas's Hospital, 1960-64; Instructor in Surgery, Harvard Medical School, Boston, USA, 1960-62; Senior Lecturer in Surgery, University of London, 1965-; Consultant Surgeon, The Middlesex Hospital, London, 1965-; Consultant Surgeon, The Royal Northern Hospital, 1970-85; Consultant Surgeon, University College Hospital, London, 1985-. *Memberships:* President, Section of Surgery, Royal Society of Medicine, 1978; President, Vascular Surgical Society of Great Britain and Ireland, 1985-86; President, Association of Surgeons of Great Britain and Ireland, 1985-86; Council Member, Royal College of Surgeons of England, 1985; Medical Society of London; British Society of Gastroenterology; British Medical Association. *Publications:* "Intestinal Ischaemia" 1977; "Contemporary Operative Surgery" 1979; "Reconstruction of the Visceral Arteries" 1984 etc. *Honour:* Kinmouth Memorial Lecturer, Royal College of Surgeons of England, 1985. *Hobbies:* Literature; Languages; Travel; Music. *Address:* 82 Harley Street, London W1N 1AE, England.

MARTIN, Donald William, b. 13 Aug. 1921, Columbus, Ohio, USA. Psychiatric Consultant. m. Clara Jane Jones, 23 June 1951, Tyrone, Pennsylvania, 1 son, 1 daughter. *Education:* BA, MD, Ohio State University; Certified in Psychiatry, American Board of Psychiatry and Neurology; Psychiatric Resident, Kings Park and Central Islip State Hospitals, New York. *Appointments:* Staff Psychiatrist, Central Islip State Hospital, New York and Summit County Receiving Hospital, Cuyahoga Falls, Ohio, 1951-59; Superintendent, Summit County Receiving Hospital (now Falls View Mental Health Center), Ohio, 1959-63; Director, Clinton Valley Center, Pontiac, Michigan, 1963-79;; Associate Clinical Professor of Psychiatry, Michigan State University, East Lansing, 1968-79; currently, Psychiatry Consultant. *Memberships:* American Psychiatric Association; American Medical Association; American Association of Psychiatric Administrators; Michigan Psychiatric Society; Michigan State Medical Society; Oakland County Medical Society, Michigan. *Honours:* Life Member, Phi Beta Kappa, 1942; Fellow, American Psychiatric Association, 1955 (Life Fellow, 1984). *Hobbies:* Reading; Writing; Bridge; Music; Theatre; Travel. *Address:* 1267 Southfield Road, Birmingham, MI 48009, USA.

MARTIN, Jean-Jacques, b. 16 Dec. 1935, Brussels, Belgium. Professor of Neurology. m. Liliane Sneesens, 8 Aug. 1959, Brussels. *Education:* MD 1959, Agrege de l'Enseignement Supérieur 1971, Free University of Brussels. Trainee in Neurology, 1959-63; Visiting Fellow, Columbia University, New York, USA, 1961-62; Research Fellow, Belgian Foundation for Scientific Research, 1964-72; Research Fellow 1973, Head of Laboratory of Neuropathology 1963-, Born Bunge Foundation. *Memberships:* Belgian, French and Italian Societies of Neurology; Belgian, French, German and Italian Societies of Neuropathology; International Brain Research Organization. *Publications:* 'Thalamic Pathology of Multiple System Atrophies', thesis, 1971; More than 200 papers on clinical neuropathology. *Honour:* Armand Kleefeld Award, 1959. *Hobby:* Shooting. *Address:* University of Antwerp, Department of Medicine, Building T Room 5.18, Universiteits Plein 1, B 2610 Wilrijk, Antwerp, Belgium.

MARTIN, Marion Veronica, b. 12 Dec. 1938, Panama. Chairman, Department of Microbiology; Consultant in Bacteriology. m. Professor Ruben Martin 30 June 1966, Panama, 2 sons. *Education:* MSc, Hygiene, Tulane University, 1969; BSc, 1960, MD, 1964, University of Panama. *Appointments:* Intern, Santo Tomas Hospital, Panama, 1964-65; Assistant, 1965-67, 1970-71, Auxiliary Professor, 1971-74, Associate Professor, 1974-77, Professor, 1978-, Chairman, 1982-, Department of Microbiology, School of Medicine, University of Panama; Consultant in Bacteriology, Social Security Hospital, Panama, 1971-. *Memberships:* National Medical Association, Panama; American Society for Microbiology; Medical Mycological Society of the Americas; Panamerican Association for Microbiology and Parasitology; International Society for Human and Animal Mycology; Association for Practitioners in Infection Control. *Publications:* 'Nosocomial Infections in Social Security Hospital', 1978; 'Yeasts as Contaminants in Hemodialysis Machines', 1980; 'Group B Streptococcus Colonization of Mothers and Neonates', 1983; 'Spectrum of Paracoccidioidomycosis in Panama', 1984; 'Reactivity of Panamanian Population to 3 Fungal Antigens', 1985; 'First Isolation of P Brasiliensis in Panama', 1985. *Honours:* Research Fellow, World Health Organisation and Panamanian Health Organisation, to Tulane University, 1968-69. *Hobbies:* Piano and organ

playing; Reading. *Address:* Department of Microbiology, University of Panama, School of Medicine, Estafeta Universitaria, Panama, Republic of Panama.

MARTIN, Renée Halo, b. 8 June 1948, Sweden. Associate Professor of Pediatrics. m. Kenneth D MacLean, 18 Aug. 1979, Vancouver, British Columbia, Canada, 2 sons. *Education:* PhD, University of British Columbia. *Appointments:* Instructor, Co-ordinator, Science Department, Fraser Valley College, Abbotsford, British Columbia, 1975-78; Assistant Professor of Pediatrics 1978-81, Associate Professor of Pediatrics 1981-, Division of Medical Genetics, University of Calgary, Alberta. *Memberships:* Fellow, Canadian College of Medical Genetics; American Fertility Society; American Society of Human Genetics; Genetics Society of Canada; Canadian Fertility and Andrology Society. *Publications include:* 62 articles, including: 'Analysis of human sperm chromosome complements from a male heterozygous for a reciprocal translocation t(11;22) (q23;q11)', 1984; 'A comparison of chromosomal abnormalities in hamster egg and human sperm pronuclei', 1984; 'Recognition of the Y chromosome in human spermatozoa' in "The cytogenetics of the Y chromosome" (editor: A A Sandberg), 1984; 'Chromosomal abnormalities in human sperm' in "Aneuploidy: Etiology and Mechanisms" (editors: V Vaughan-Dellarco, P Voytek and A Hollaender"), 1985. *Hobbies:* Skiing, Hiking, Swimming, Aerobic Dance, Pottery, Cooking, Snorkling, Travel. *Address:* Medical Genetics Clinic, Alberta Children's Hospital, 1820 Richmond Road, SW, Calgary, Alberta T2T 5C7, Canada.

MARTIN, Ronald Lawrence, b. 15 June 1945, Cleveland, Ohio, USA. Professor of Psychiatry. m. Kathryn, 2 Aug. 1980, 2 sons. *Education:* BA, Northwestern University College of Arts and Sciences, 1967; MD, Northwestern University Medical School, 1971; Intern, Denver General Hospital, 1971-72; Resident in Psychiatry, University of Southern California Medical Center, 1972-74; Resident in Psychiatry, Barnes Hospital and Washington University School of Medicine, 1974-75. *Appointments:* Instructor in Psychiatry, 1975-77, Assistant Professor, 1977-80, Washington University School of Medicine; Associate Professor, 1980-85, Professor 1985-, University of Kansas School of Medicine. *Memberships:* American Psychiatric Association; Society of Biological Psychiatry; American Association of Directors of Psychiatric Residency Training Programs; American Academy of Clinical Psychiatrists; American Medical Association; American Psychopathological Association. *Publications:* "Excess Mortality in 500 Psychiatric Out Patients: I and II"; 'Arch Gen Psych' 1985; "Frequency and differential diagnosis of depressive syndromes in schizophrenia" 'Journal of Clinical Psychiatry' 1985 and 30 others. *Honours:* Nu Garde Honorary Service Organization and Departmental Honors in Biology, Northwestern University; Pi Kappa Epsilon Honorary Service Fraternit, Northwestern University Medical School; Physician's Medical Association; American Medical Association.. *Hobbies:* Running; Skiing; Tennis. *Address:* University of Kansas Medical Center, Department of Psychiatry, 39th and Rainbow Boulevard, Kansas City, KS 66103, USA.

MARTIN, Thomas Allen III, b. 28 May 1947, Easton, Pennsylvania, USA. Child Psychiatrist. m. Margaret Marie Billowits, 27 Dec. 1969, Scarsdale, New York, 3 sons. *Education:* BS, Biology, St Joseph's University, Philadelphia, 1969; MD, University of Texas Medical School at San Antonio, Texas; Internship, 1978-79, Psychiatric residency 1979-82, Wilford Hall, USAF Medical Center. Appointments: Chief, Inpatient Psychiatry Service, Department of Mental Health, Wilford Hall, USAF Medical Center, Lackland AFB, San Antonio, Texas, 1982-84; Child and Adolescent Psychiatry Fellowship, Ohio State University, Columbus, Ohio, 1984-86. *Memberships:* American Medical Association; American Psychiatric Association; Society of USAF Psychiatrists; Alpha Omega Alpha, National Honor Medical Society. *Publications:* "Psychiatric

House Staff Guide", WHMC, 1982-83 and 1983-84 for Inpatient Psychiatry. *Honours:* Distinguished Military Graduate, ROTC with regular commission; Full sponsorship USAF for medical school and commendation medal; "Amicus Psychologia" WHMC Department of Psychology Staff and Residents, 1982-83; Department of Air Force Suggestion Award; The Neuropsychiatric Society of Central Ohio First Annual Psychiatric Residents Research Award, 1985. *Hobbies:* Reading; Numismatism; Philately; Collecting leather-bound books, Wedgewood porcelain, Music. *Address:* 1989 Samdda, Worthington, OH 43085, USA.

MARTINEZ, Humberto L, b. 20 Jan. 1944, Puerto Rico. Executive Director. m. Rita M Cobian, 6 June 1970, Puerto Rico, 1 son, 2 daughters. *Education:* BS 1965, MD 1970, University of Puerto Rico, Rio Pedras; Straight Psychiatric Internship, University, Hospital, San Juan, Puerto Rico, 1971; Psychiatric Residency, Albert Einstein College of Medicine, Bronx, New York, 1974; 1 year post graduate studies, School of Public Health, Columbia University, Manhattan, New York, 1974. *Appointments include:* Chief, Mental Health Clinic, United States Air Force Regional Hospital, Shaw Air Force Base, South Carolina, USA, 1974-76; Director, Partial Hospitalization Service, Lincoln Community Mental Health Center, Bronx, New York, 1976-77; Unit Director, Consultant Psychiatrist, Albert Einstein College of Medicine, Substance Abuse Service, Methadone Maintenance Treatment Program, Bronx, New York, 1977-79; Director, Lincoln Community Mental Health Center, Misericordia Hospital Medical Center, Bronx, New York, 1979-81; Executive Director, South Bronx Mental Health Council Incorporated, Community Mental Health Center, Bronx, New York, 1981-. *Memberships:* Phi Chi Medical Fraternity; American Public Health Association; American Psychiatric Association; American Society of Hispanic Psychiatrists; Fellow, Interamerican College of Physicians and Surgeons; American Medical Association; American Association for the Advancement of Science. *Publications:* 'A Socio-epidemiological Analysis on an Urban Ghetto Day Hospital Program' (with P Ruiz), 1980; 'Inner City Day Hospital Programs: An Ethnics Perspective' (with P Ruiz), 1980; 'Consumer Input in the Evaluation of Drug Addiction Services' (co-author), 1981. *Honours include:* Scholarship Award, School of Medicine, University of Puerto Rico, 1965; Meritorious Plaque, Lincoln Community Mental Health Center Advisory Board, 1979. *Hobbies:* Stamp collecting, Reading. *Address:* 781 East 142nd Street, Bronx, NY 10454, USA.

MARTINEZ DE ALVA, Hector, b. 5 Oct. 1913, Mexico DF. Pneumology Consultant. m. Maria Enriqueta Córdoba, 15 Oct. 1950, Tijuana BC, Mexico. 2 sons, 2 daughters. *Education:* Medicine Doctor and Surgeon, National University of Mexico, Distrito Federal, 1938; Postgraduate Courses: Dermatology - General Hospital, Mexico DF; Cardiology - National Institute of Cardiology, Mexico DF; Tuberculosis - Sanatorio Tuberculosos de Huipulco; Syphilis - General Hospital, Mexico DF. *Appointments include:* Chief of Pneumology Service, Sindicate of Electricians, Mexico DF; Almacenes Nacionales de Deposito. Physician. Mexico DF; Sub-Director of Mexican Institute of Social Security, Tijuana BC; Consultant of US Public Health Service, San Diego, California; Pneumology Consultant of Civil Hospital of Tijuana, Tijuana BC; Pneumology Consultant of Institute Social Service for Workers to the Service of the State, Tijuana, Baja California, Mexico. *Memberships:* Sociedad de Cirugia, Founder Member and President, Tijuana BC, Mexico; College of Physicians, Tijuana BC, Mexico; Fellow and Fellow Emeritus, American College of Chest Physicians, USA; Academic and Academic Emeritus, Mexican Acacemy of Surgery; American Academy of Tuberculosis Physicians; INTERASMA; American Trudeau Society; International Union Against Tuberculosis. *Publications:* '27 cases of Bronchial Asthma treated with resection of the carotid body' 1966; "Complications of Extrapleural Pneumothorax" 1944; "Plom-

naje with Lucite Spheres as a Substitute of the Thoracoplasty" 1961; "The Allergic States and Surgery" 1958; "Diabetes and Surgery" 1985; etc. *Hobbies:* Photography; Travel. *Address:* Avenida Cinco de Mayo 809, Tijuana, Baja California, Mexico 22000.

MARTINEZ-RIOS, Marco A, b. 31 Aug. 1937, Mexico City. Cardiologist, National Institute of Cardiology, Mexico. m. Beatriz Gomez, 13 July 1963, Mexico City, 2 sons, 1 daughter. *Education:* MD; FACC; FACP; FGCP. *Memberships:* Mexican Academy of Medicine; Mexican Academy of Surgery; Mexican Society of Cardiology; Fellow, American College of Cardiology, Physicians, Chest Physicians. *Publications:* "Arteriografia Coronaria", 1977; 92 papers in coronary artery disease in 'American Journal of Cardiology'; etc. *Honour:* Magna Cum Laude, Medical School, University of Mexico. *Hobbies:* Tennis; Scuba Diving. *Address:* Instituto Nacional de Cardiologia de Mexico, Juan Badiano I, Tlalpan, DF Mexico, Mexico.

MARTINI, Carlos Jose Maria, b. 4 Aug. 1938, Argentina. Association Vice President. m. Luisa Maria Nieto, 5 July 1963, Argentina, 1 son, 2 daughters. *Education:* MD, DPH, 1962, University of Buenos Aires; MPH, Yale University, USA, 1969; MSc, London University, England, 1972; MFCM, Royal College of Physicians, England, 1974. *Appointments:* Director, University Health Services, University of Buenos Aires, Argentina, 1963-65; Health Plan Manager, Center for Medical Education and Clinical Research, 1965-67; Lecturer, Latin American Center for Medical Administration, 1969-72; Senior Research Fellow, Nottingham University, England, 1972-75; Senior Lecturer, Department of Community Health Nottingham University, 1975-78; Consultant, Department of Health and Social Services, England, 1975-78; Professor of Community Health and Family Medicine, University of Colorado, School of Medicine, USA, 1978-85; Chairman, Department of Preventive Medicine and Biometrics, University of Colorado, 1982; Vice President, Medical Education, Americal Medical Association, 1985-. *Memberships:* Argentine and American Public Health Associations; UK Society for Social Medicine; American College of Preventive Medicine; International Epidemiological Association. *Publications:* "Participation in Health", with J McEwen, 1982. Contributor to: 'British Journal of Social and Preventive Medicine', 1976; 'International Journal of Epidemiology', 1976; 'International Journal of Health Services', 1977; 'British Medical Journal', 1978. *Honours:* Pan American Health Organisation, 1967-69; Millbank Memorial Fund, 1971-72; British Council, 1971-72; Fellow, Faculty of Community Medicine, 1984. *Hobbies:* Reading; Music; Woodworking. *Address:* 929 Valley Road, Glencoe, IL 60022, USA.

MARTINI, Luciano, b. 14 May 1927, Milan, Italy. Professor, Endocrinology. m. Elisabetta Nava, 11 Feb. 1957, Milan, 2 sons. *Education:* MD, 1950. *Appointments:* Professor, Pharmacology, Chairman, Pharmacology, University of Perugia, 1968-70; Professor, Pharmacology, Chairman, University of Pavia, 1970-72; Professor, Endocrinology, Chairman, Endocrinology, University of Milan, 1972-. *Membership:* National Board of Physicians. *Publications:* "Frontiers in Neuroendocrinology", Volumes 1-9, 1969-86; "Comprehensive Endocrinology", Volumes 1-13, 1978-85; "Clinical Neuroendocrinology", Volumes 1-2, 1978, 1982. *Honours:* Junkman-Schoeller Prize, 1968; Gold Medal, Italian Ministry of Education, 1978; Commandatore, The Ordine al Merito della Repubblica Italliana, 1979. *Hobby:* Music. *Address:* Istituto di Endocrinologia, Via Balzaretti 9, Milan, Italy.

MARUSIC, Matko, b. 4 Nov. 1946, Split, Yugoslavia. Professor of Physiology and Immunology, m. Ana, 15 Sep. 1984, 2 sons. *Education:* MD, 1970, PhD, 1975, School of Medicine, Zagreb; MSC, University of Zagreb, 1976; Postdoctoral Fellow, Oak Ridge National Laboratory, Oak Ridge, Tenn, USA, 1976-78.

Appointments: Assistant Teacher, 1971; Associate Professor, 1979, Professor, 1986, Department of Physiology, University of Zagreb Faculty of Medicine, Zagreb, Yugoslavia. *Memberships:* Secretary, 1974-76, 1978-79, President, 1979-83, Croatian Association of Physiologists; Croatian Immunological Society; The Transplantation Society; The New York Academy of Sciences. *Publications:* "Immunological Recognition", 1981; "1000 Multiple-Choice Test Questions", (Editor), 1984; 'Involvement of Mhc loci in immune responses that are not Ir-gene-controlled', (Co-author), 1982. *Honours:* Dean's Award for Distinguished Students, University of Zagreb, 1969; Jure Banovic's Award for Best Graduates, 1970. *Hobbies:* Writing children's stories; Football. *Address:* Vinogradska 101, 41000 Zagreb, Yugoslavia.

MARUTA, Toshihiko, b. 13 June 1946, Japan. Consultant, Associate Professor, Psychiatry, Mayo Clinic, 1 son, 1 daughter. *Education:* MD, Keio University School of Medicine, Tokyo; Master's Degree, University of Minnesota, USA. *Appointments:* Consultant, Psychiatry, Mayo Clinic, Rochester, USA; Director, Pain Management Centre, St Marys Hospital-Mayo Clinic; Assistant Professor, Psychiatry, Mayo Medical School. *Memberships:* International Association for the Study of Pain; American Association for the Advancement of Science; American Psychiatric Association; Sigma Xi; President, Midwest Pain Society; American Academy of Algology; American Pain Society. *Publications:* Over 78 articles in professional journals, most recent include: "Psychiatric Consultation", 'Psychosomatic Q & A', 1984; "On Team Approach", 'Psychosomatic Q & A', 1984; Co-author, "Neuroleptic Levels in Serum: Clinical Usefulness in Schizophrenic Patients", 'Clinical Research', 1984. *Address:* 200 SW 1 Street, Rochester, MN 55905, USA.

MARUYAMA, Shoji, b. 2 Jan. 1928, Nagaoka City, Japan. Associate University Professor. m. Sachiko, 5 May 1949, Niigata City, Japan. *Education:* Faculty of Liberal Arts (Sci), Niigata University, 1945-48; LLB, Faculty of Law, Nihon University, 1960-63; Dr Med Sci, (PhD) Niigata University, 1969. *Appointments:* Associate, Department of Pharmacology, Niigata University School of Medicine, 1951-71; Associate, Department of Neurophysiology, Brain Res Inst, Niigata University, 1971-74; Associate Professor, Department of Pharmacology, Yamagata University Medical School, 1974-76; Associate Professor, Department of Neurophysiology, Brain Res Inst, Niigata University, 1976-; Lecturer as additional post - Nihon Dental College, Niigata Womens College, Faculty of Education, Niigata University, 1971-. *Memberships:* Japanese Pharmacological Society, Councilor; Physiological Society of Japan, Councilor; Medical Electronics and Biological Engineering Society of Japan. *Publications:* Contributor: "Electrophysiology and Ultrastructure of Heart" 1967; Contributor: "Eubiotics" 1981; 'The presence and nature of inhibition in small slices of the dorsal LGN of rat and cat incubated in vitro' 1979; 'Involvement of S 35 protein, a cerebellar protein, in modulation of P cell activity of rat cerebellum' 1985. *Hobbies:* Painting; Photography; Go-play; Spectator sports. *Address:* Hakusanura 2-179, Niigata City 951, Japan.

MARYON DAVIS, Alan Roger, b. 21 Jan. 1943, London, England. Chief Medical Officer, Health Education Council, London, England. m. Anne Davies, 14 Mar. 1981, 2 daughters. *Education:* MA, MB, BChir, St John's College, Cambridge, England; MRCS, LRCP, St Thomas's Hospital Medical School, London; MSc Social Medicine, London School of Hygiene and Tropical Medicine; MRCP; FFCM. *Appointments:* House Physician, St Mary's Hospital, Portsmouth, England; House Surgeon, St Thomas's Hospital, London; Senior House Officer, Neurology and Rheumatology, St Thomas's Hospital, London; Registrar, General Medicine, Watford General Hospital; Registrar, Rheumatology, St Thomas's Hospital, London; Senior Registrar, Rheumatology, Middlesex

Hospital, London; Research Assistant, Paediatric Research Unit, Guy's Hospital, London; Medical Officer, Health Education Council, Chief Medical Officer-. *Memberships:* Royal College of Physicians; Faculty. of Community Medicine; British Medical Association; Medical Journalists' Association. *Publications:* "Family Health and Fitness", 1981; Numerous articles on health education for lay and professional readers. *Hobbies:* Eating; Drinking; Singing. *Address:* 33 Lillieshall Road, London SW4 0LN, England.

MASALIN, Kai Erik, b. 28 Jan. 1946, Lappeenranta, Finland. Assistant Executive Director, Finnish Dental Association. m. Arja Laatio, 1970, 1 son, 1 daughter. *Education:* DDS, 1971; MPH, 1981. *Appointments:* Study Secretary, Dentistry, Faculty of Medicine, University of Helsinki, 1969-71; Board Member, Dental Students Society, 1966-70, Vice President, 1969, Secretary, 1970; Member of Representatives, Students Union, University of Helsinki, 1968-69; Editor, Finnish Dental Journal, 1971-; Assistant Executive Director, Finnish Dental Association, 1972-; Secretary-Treasurer, Finnish National Committee, FDI, 1976-; Secretary of Advisory Council, National Board of Health for Specialization in Dentistry, 1980-84. *Memberships:* Finnish Dental Association; Finnish Dental Society; Society of Swedish-Speaking Dentists; Fellow, Academy of Dentistry International. *Publications:* 'Effects of a National Dental Health Campaign in Finland' Acta Odontol Scand 1984 with H Murtomaa; 'Dental Health Practices Among Finnish Adults' Community Dental Health, 1984 with H Murtomaa and P Laine; 'Public Image of Dentists and Dental Visits in Finland' Community Dent Oral Epideiol 1982 with H Murtomaa. *Honours:* The Sword of Honour of the Finnish Reserve Officer Association, 1965; The Badge of Merit of the Dental Students' Society, 1971; The Silver Medal of the Finnish Dental Association, 1977; The Golden Medal of the Finnish Dental Association, 1985. *Hobbies:* Aviation; Philately. *Address:* Jollaksentie 30, 00850 Helsinki, Finland.

MASERI, Attilio, b. 12 Nov. 1935, Italy. University Professor of Cardiovascular Medicine. m. Countess Garncesca Maseri Florio di Santo Stefano, 30 July 1960, 1 son. *Education:* MD, Padua University Medical School; Special bds in Cardiology, 1963 and in Nuclear Medicine 1965; FRCP. *Appointments:* Research Fellow: University of Pisa, 1960-65, Columbia University, New York, 1965-66, Johns Hopkins University, Baltimore, 1966-67; Assistant Professor, University of Pisa, 1967-70; Professor of Internal Medicine, 1970, Professor of Cardiovascular Pathophysiology, 1972-79, Professor of Medicine (Locum) 1972-79; Currently: Sir John McMichael Professor of Cardiovascular Medicine, Director of Cardiology, Royal Postgraduate Medical School, University of London. *Memberships:* Fellow, Royal College of Physicians (FRCP); Fellow, American College of Cardiology (FACC); Life Member, The Johns Hopkins Society of Scholars. *Publications:* "Myocardial Blood Flow in Man" 1972; "Primary and Secondary Angina" 1977; "Perspectives on Coronary Care" 1979; Articles in major international cardiological and medical journals. *Honour:* Chevalier d'honneur

MASHHOUR, Yehia A S, b. 23 Mar. 1939, Cairo, United Arab Republic. Consultant Cardio-Pulmonary Surgeon. m. Helen M Fraser, 18 Aug. 1978, Cairo, 2 sons, 2 daughters. *Education:* MB BCh 2nd Honours 1961, DGS Excellent 1964, Ein-shams University, Cairo. *Appointments include:* Registrar, Thoracic Surgery, Ministry of Public Health, Cairo 1963, Ein-shams University Hospital, Cairo 1963-65; Assistant Surgeon, Embala Cardiac Surgery Centre, Cairo, 1965-66; Senior House Officer, The Royal Infirmary, Bradford, England, 1966-67; Locum Registrar, Thoracic Surgery, Papworth Hospital, Cambridge 1967, The General Infirmary, Leeds 1967-69; Registrar, Thoracic Surgery, Cardiothoracic Surgeon, Catharina Hospital, Eindhoven, The Netherlands, 1979-. *Memberships:* Fellow, Royal College of Surgeons; Fellow, American College of Chest Physicians; Dutch Thoracic Surgical Society; Dutch Cardiology Society; Dutch Surgical Society; American Academy of Chest Physicians and Surgeons. *Publications:* 12 articles, including: 'Reconstructed heterograft aortic valves for human use; preparation and surgical implantation for mitral, aortic and tricuspid replacement' (with M I Ionescu and G H Wooler), 1968; 'A new atrial lead with bipolar configuration for temporary pacing after open heart surgery. A comparison with a series of gardlock electrodes' (co-author), 1981. *Hobbies:* Golf, Table Tennis, Swimming. *Address:* Catharina Ziekenhuis, Eindhoven, The Netherlands.

MASLINSKI, Czeslaw, b. 19 May 1921, Samara, Poland. Director, Biogenic Amines. m. (1) Halina Dmitrijuk, 12 July 1940, 2 sons, (2) Wieslawa A Fogel, 2 Aug. 1980. *Education:* MD, 1951, PhD, 1956, Pathophysiology, University School of Medicine. *Appointments:* Lecturer, 1949-50, Associate Professor, 1959-64, Professor, Head, 1964-70, Pathophysiology, University School of Medicine, Lodz; Deputy Chief, Institute of Aviation Medicine, Warsaw, 1951-54; Head, Pathophysiology, Pathomorfol Centre, Warsaw, 1954-59; Professor, Director, Biogenic Amines, Polish Academy of Sciences, 1970-. *Memberships:* Polish Academy of Sciences: Committees of Basic Sciences, Physiological Sciences; European Histamine Research Society; Polish Biochemical Society; Polish Physiological Society; etc. *Publications:* "Histamine", 1974; "Histamine and its Metabolism in Mammals: Part I Chemistry and Formation of Histamine, Part II, Catabolism of Histamine and Histamine Liberation", 1975; "Agents and Actions" 1975; 180 articles. *Honours:* Winner, Scientific Prizes, Secretary of Polish Academy of Sciences, 5 times; Minister of Health and Welfare, 2 times; 3 military, 4 civil decorations. *Hobbies:* Fishing; Music. *Address:* Piekna 41/43-19, 93 558 Lodz, Poland.

MASLOWSKI, Andrew Henry, b. 11 Sep. 1949, England. Cardiologist. *Education:* MB ChB, Bristol University Medical School, 1973; FRACP, 1984. *Appointments:* National Heart Foundation Cardiology Research Fellow, Christchurch, New Zealand, 1981-82; Cardiology Senior Registrar, Greenlane Hospital, Auckland, 1983-84; Consultant Cardiologist, Director of Coronary Care Unit, Middlemore Hospital, Auckland, 1984-. *Memberships:* Fellow, Royal Australasian College of Physicians; Associate Member, New Zealand Cardiac Society. *Publications:* 'Haemodynamic and Hormonal Responses to Captopril in Resistant Heart Failure', 'Lancet', 1981; "Haemodynamic Histopathological and Hormonal Features of Alcoholic Cardiac Beriberi", 'Quarterly Journal of Medicine', 1981; "Mechanisms in Renovascular Hypertension in Man", 'Hypertension', 1983; "Blood Pressure Response to Sodium Manipulation", 'Lancet', 1984. *Hobbies:* Chess; Skiing; Scuba Diving; Windsurfing. *Address:* Department of Cardiology, Middlemore Hospital, Auckland, New Zealand.

MASON, David Kean, b. 5 Nov. 1928, Scotland. Dean of Dental Education and Professor of Oral Medicine. m. Judith Anne Armstrong, 3 June 1967, Belfast, Ireland, 2 sons, 1 daughter. *Education:* LDS, 1951, BDS, 1952, University of St Andrews; FDS RCS, Edinburgh, 1957; MB ChB University of Glasgow, 1962; FDS FDS RCPS, Glasgow; MD (with commendation) University of Glasgow, 1967; MRCPath, 1967; FRCS (Glasgow) 1973; FRCPath, 1976. *Appointments:* House Surgeon in Oral Surgery, 1951, House Surgeon in Prosthetics and Orthodontics, 1952; Dundee Dental Hospital; Dental Officer, RAF Uxbridge, Halton and Cosford, 1952-54; Registrar, Oral Surgery, Dundee Dental Hospital and Dundee Infirmary, 1954-56; Locum Assistant Tutor, Department of Conservation, 1957-58, Dental Surgeon, 1958-63, Senior Registrar, Dental Surgery, 1964, Consultant Dental Surgeon and Honorary Lecturer in Preventive Dentistry, 1964-65, Senior Lecturer, Den-

tal Surgery and Pathology, 1965-67, Glasgow Dental Hospital; currently Dean of Dental Education and Professor of Oral Medicine, Glasgow Dental Hospital and School. *Memberships include:* Chairman, National Dental Consultative Committee 1976-80 and 1983-; Chairman, Dental Committee, University Grants Committee, 1983-; Joint MRC/Health Departments/SERC Dental Committee, 1984-. *Publications:* "Salivary Glands in Health and Disease" with D K Chisholm, 1975; "Introduction to Oral Medicine" with Chisholm, Ferguson and Jones, 1978; Preface in "Dental Care of the Handicapped" 1984; Scottish Home and Health Department, HMSO; Report on DEAC Conference on Teachers "Total Patient Care by Undergraduates" 1984 with C J Smith in British Dental Journal. *Honours:* Charles Tomes Lecturer, Royal College of Surgeons of England, 1975; John Tomes Prize, Royal College of Surgeons, 1979; Evelyn Sprawson Lecturer, London Hospital Medical College, 1984. *Hobbies:* Golf; Tennis; Gardening; Country Life. *Address:* Glasgow Dental Hospital and School, 378 Sauchiehall Street, Glasgow G2 3JZ, Scotland.

MASON, Dean Towle, b. 20 Sep. 1932, Berkeley, California, USA. Physician; Cardiologist; Physician-in-Chief. m. Maureen O'Brien, 22 June 1957, 2 daughters. *Education:* BA, Chemistry, 1954, MD, 1958, Duke University. *Appointments include:* Intern, Resident in Medicine, Johns Hopkins Hospital, 1958-61; Clinical Associate Cardiology branch, Senior Assistant Surgeon, 1961-63; Assistant Section Director, Attending Physician, Senior Investigator, Cardiology, 1963-68, USPHS National Heart Institute National Institutes of Health; Professor, Medicine and Physiology, Chief, Cardiovascular Medicine, University of California Medical School, 1968-83; Physician-in-Chief, Western Heart Institute, St Mary's Medical Center, San Francisco, 1983-. *Memberships include:* Fellow and Past President, American College of Cardiology; American Heart Association; American College of Chest Physicians; Royal Society of Medicine; Phi Beta Kappa. *Publications:* "Cardiovascular Management", 1974; "Congestive Heart Failure", 1976; "Advances in Heart Disease", volume 1, 1977; volume 3, 1980; "Cardiovascular Emergencies", 1978; "Clinical Methods in Study of Cholestrol Metabolism", 1979; "Principles of Noninvasive Cardiac Imaging", 1980; "Clinical Nuclear Cardiology", 1981; "Myocardial Revascularization", 1981; "Love Your Heart", 1982; "Cardiology", 1981, 82, 83, 84, 85; Author of numerous articles. Editor: 'Clinical Cardiology Journal'; Editor in Chief, 'American Heart Journal'. Member of numerous editorial board of scientific journals. *Honours include:* Faculty Research Award, University of California, 1978; Symbol of Excellence, Texas Heart Institute, 1979; Distinguished Alumnus Award, Duke University Medical School, 1979. *Address:* Western Heart Institute, St Mary's Medical Center, 450 Stanyan Street, San Francisco, CA 94117, USA.

MASON, Edward Allen, b. 18 Mar. 1919, Elmira, New York, USA. Associate Clinical Professor of Psychiatry; Director, Documentaries for Learning. m. Jean Ann Kaltwasser, 2 Sep. 1944, St Louis, Missouri, 1 son, 2 daughters. *Education:* BA, 1941, MD, 1944, Medical School, Washington University. *Appointments:* Paediatric Intern, New Haven Hospital, 1944-45; Psychiatric Resident, McLean Hospital, 1945-46; Fellow, Psychiatry, Massachusetts General Hospital and Putnam Center Childrens Hospital. Judge Bake Instructor, Boston University School of Social Work, 1951-53; Assistant Professor of Mental Health, Harvard School of Public Health, 1957-64. Currently: Director, Documentaries for Learning; Associate Clinical Professor, Psychiatry, Harvard Medical School. *Memberships:* American Psychiatric Association; American Orthopsychiatric Association; New England Council of Child Psychiatry; Educational Film Library Association. *Publications:* 'The Hospitalised Child' in 'New England Journal of Medicine', 1965. Video & Films: "Boys in Conflict", 1969; "Gee, Officer Krupke", 1975; "Forming an Alliance", 1981; "Breaking the Silence: The Generation After the Holocaust", 1984. *Honours:* Blue Ribbon, American Film Festival, 1970; Silver Hugo, Chicago International Film Festival, 1975; Blue Ribbon, 1976; 1st Muir Medical Film Institute, 1978; Bronze Awards, International Film and Television Festival, 1981, 82; Golden Eagle, CINE, 1984 and others. *Hobbies:* Photography; Painting. *Address:* 74 Fenwood Road, Boston, MA 02115, USA.

MASON, Scott Aiken, b. 23 May 1951, Boston, Massachusetts, USA. President, National Health Advisors. *Education:* BS, Duke University; MPA, Pennsylvania State University; DPA, George Washington University. *Appointments:* Health Systems Analyst, Health Systems Development Project; Consultant, Booz Allen and Hamilton; Staff Specialist, American Hospital Association; Corporate Director, Samaritan Health Service; currently, President, National Health Advisors, McLean, Virginia. *Memberships:* Society for Hospital Planning and Marketing; American Health Planning Association; Fellow, American College of Hospital Administrators; Member, American Association of Healthcare Consultants. *Publications:* Editor, "Multihospital Arrangements: Public Policy Implications", 1979. Contributor to: "Ambulatory Care and Regionalization in Multi-Institutional Health Systems", 1982; "Hospital Guide Survival Guide: Strategies for the '80s"; numerous professional journals including: 'Public Health Reports'; 'Public Health Reviews'; 'Journal of Hospital Financial Management'; 'Journal of Ambulatory Care Management'; 'Hospital and Health Services Administration'. Numerous speeches and guest lectureships. *Hobbies:* Basketball; Water skiing. *Address:* National Health Advisors, 6849 Old Dominion Drive, Suite 310, McLean, VA 22101, USA.

MASORO, Edward. Joseph. b. 28 Dec. 1924, Oakland, California, USA. Professor and Chairman, Department of Physiology, University of Texas Health Science Centre. m. Barbara Muir Weikel, 25 June 1947, St Helena, California, USA. *Education:* AB, Physiology, PhD, University of California, Berkeley, USA. *Appointments:* Assistant Professor, Department of Physiology, Queen's University, Kingston, Ontario, Canada, 1950-52; Assistant Professor, Department of Physiology, Tufts University School of Medicine, Boston, USA, 1952-55, Associate Professor, 1955-62; Research Associate Professor, Department of Physiology and Biophysics, University of Washington, Seattle, USA, 1962-64, Research Professor, 1964; Professor and Chairman, Department of Physiology and Biophysics, Medical College of Pennsylvania, Philadelphia, USA, 1964-73; Professor and Chairman, Department of Physiology, University of Texas Health Science Centre at San Antonio. *Memberships:* American Association for the Advancement of Science; American Association of University Professors; American Physiological Society; Society of Experimental Biology and Medicine; Canadian Biochemical Association; American Chemical Society; New York Academy of Sciences, etc. *Publications:* "Acid Base Regulations - Its Physiology, Pathology and the Interpretation of Blood Gas Analysis", 1977; 'Extending the Mammalian Life Span' in "Aging 2000: Our Health Care Destiny", 1985; 'State of Knowledge on Action of Food Restriction and Aging' in "Molecular Biology of Aging", 1985; contributions to professional journals. *Honours:* Sigma Xi; Christian R & Mary F Lindback Distinguished Teaching Award, 1967; SAMA Golden Apple Awards, 1966 and 1971. *Hobby:* Gardening. *Address:* Department of Physiology, University of Texas Health Science Centre, 7703 Floyd Curl Drive, San Antonio, TX 78284-7756, USA.

MASRI, As'ad Muhuyidin, b. 20 Apr. 1936, Nablus, Jordan. Psychiatrist, Medical Director. m. Linda Scott, Dec. 1961, 2 sons, 2 daughters. *Education:* BS, University of Cincinnati, USA, 1958; MD, University of Virginia, 1962. *Appointments:* Chairman of Medical Section 1966-, Vice Chief 1981, Chief of Staff 1982-83, Petersburg General Hospital; Medical Director 1973-82, President of Medical Staff 1973-80, Petersb-

urg Psychiatric Institute; Medical Director, Poplar Springs Hospital, 1982-; Clinical Director, Adult Unit, Poplar Springs, 1982-; Clinical Associate Professor of Psychiatry, University of Virginia Medical School, 1977-; Clinical Assistant Professor of Psychiatry, Medical College of Virginia, 1976-. *Memberships:* American Medical Association; Diplomate, American Board of Psychiatry; American Medical Political Action Committee; American Psychiatric Association; Cofounder member, University of Virginia Medical Society; Virginia Neuropsychiatric Society. *Publications:* "Treatment of Anger and Impulsivity in a Brain Damaged Patient, A Case Study Applying Stress Innoculation in Clinical Neurophychology", (with Frank T Lira, and W F Carne), 1983. *Honour:* Fellow, American Psychiatric Association. *Hobbies:* Surf Fishing; Reading. *Address:* 511 South Sycamore Street, Petersburg, VA 23803, USA.

MASSERMAN, Richard Lee, b. 26 June 1937, New York, USA. Orthopaedic Surgeon. m. Patricia Masserman, 23 Dec. 1962, Los Angeles, 1 son, 2 daughters. *Education:* BA, 1959, MA, UCLA, 1961; MD, UCI, 1965; FACS; FICS. *Memberships:* Fellow, American Academy of Orthopedic Surgeons; American College of Surgeons; International College of Surgeons; Diplomate, American Board of Orthopedic Surgery; Western Orthopedic Association. *Publications:* 'Congenital Pseudarthrosis of the Tibia Clinical Orthopedics and Research', 1974. *Address:* 16550 Ventura Blvd, Encino, CA 91436, USA.

MASTERS, David M, b. 4 Feb. 1924, Philadelphia, Pennsylvania, USA. Professor and Chairman, Department of Psychiatry. m. Rosalie Perelman, 15 Sep. 1965, 1 son. *Education:* BA, University of Pennsylvania; DO, Philadelphia College of Osteopathic Medicine; Intern, Massachusetts Osteopathic Hospital; Fellowship in Psychiatry, Philadelphia Mental Health Clinic. *Appointments include:* Unit Chief, Haverford State Hospital; Private Practitioner in Psychiatry; currently, Professor and Chairman, Department of Psychiatry, Southeastern College of Osteopathic Medicine, Florida. *Memberships:* American Psychiatric Association; American College of Neuropsychiatrists; American Osteopathic Association; Florida Osteopathic Medical Association. *Publications:* 'Psychodynamic Psychophysiological and Psychosocial aspects of Aging' in 'Bulletin of the American College of Neuropsychiatrists', 1973. *Hobbies:* Music; Travel. *Address:* 16666 North East 19th Avenue, North Miami Beach, FL, USA.

MASTRANGELO, Michael Joseph, b. 3 Oct. 1938, Phoenixville, USA. Professor, Medicine; Director, Medical Oncology, Jefferson Medical College. m. Ann Sunday, 30 May 1964, Bridgeport, 2 sons, 1 daughter. *Education:* MD, Johns Hopkins University School of Medicine, 1964; Intern, 1964-65, Medical Resident, 1967-69, Oncology Fellow, 1969-70, Chief Medical Resident, 1970-71, Jefferson Medical College Hospital. *Appointments:* Research Physician, Fox Chase Cencer Centre, 1972-84. *Memberships:* American Association Cancer Research; American Society for Clinical Oncology; American College of Physicians; American College Clinical Pharmacology. *Publications:* Author, numerous articles in professional journals. *Hobby:* Woodwork. *Address:* Jefferson Medical College, 1025 Walnut St, Philadelphia, PA 19107, USA.

MASUCCI, Elmo Francis, b. 19 Aug. 1920, Scranton, Pennsylvania, USA. Assistant Chief, Neurology Service; Professor of Neurology. m. Adrienne E Aldisert, 24 Aug. 1957, Pittsburgh, 1 son, 2 daughters. *Education:* BS, University of Scranton, 1942; MD, Hahnemann Medical College, 1945, Neurology Resident: Veterans Hospital, Pittsburgh, 1956, 57; Georgetown University Hospital, 1958. *Appointments:* Staff Psychiatrist, 1948-56, Resident in Neurology, 1956-57, Senior Resident, 1958, Veterans Administration, Scranton; Assistant Chief, Psychiatry and Neurology, 1959-63, Neurology Service, 1963-, Veterans Administration, Hospital, Washington; Instructor, 1958-69, Assistant

Professor, 1969, Associate Professor, 1982, Professor, 1985-, Neurology, Georgetown Medical School and University Hospital, Washington. *Memberships:* District of Columbia Medical Society (Section of Neurology and Neurosurgery Past Secretary and Chairman); Clinical Associate Member, American Academy of Neurology; Fellow, Council on Cerebrovascular Disease; New York Academy of Sciences; Various past professional memberships. *Publications:* Author or Co-Author of some 24 papers in professional journals: 'Annals' DC; 'Brain'; 'Acta Neurol LatinoAmer'; 'Diseases of the Nervous System'; 'Neurology'; 'Journal of the Neurological Sciences'; 'Annals of Neurology'; 'Annal of Ophthalmology'; 'Clinical Nuclear Medicine'; 'Archives of Neurology' and others. Contributor of chapters to editions of "Current Diagnosis". *Honours:* Vicennial Medal, Georgetown University, 1978; Service Award, Veterans Administration Medical Center, Washington, 1984. *Hobbies:* Sports, Bowling and golf; Reading; Music. *Address:* 3406 Glenmoor Drive, Chevy Chase, MD 20815, USA.

MASUREIK, Conrad Joffre, b. 22 Oct. 1944, Pretoria, South Africa. Private Practice; Part-time Consultant, Department Maxillo Facial & Oral Surgery, University of Pretoria. m. Jean Seccombe, 19 Jan. 1974, Pretoria, 1 son, 2 daughters. *Education:* BChD, LDS, 1971, MChD, 1977, University of Pretoria. *Appointments:* Private Practice, London, 1970-73; Registrar MFOS, Pretoria, 1973-77; Private Practice, Pretoria, 1977-; Consultant (Part-time), University of Pretoria. *Memberships:* Northern Transvaal Branch, Dental Association of South Africa, Executive Committee, 1978-83, Treasurer, 1984, Secretary, 1985; South African Society of Maxillo Facial and Oral Surgery, President, 1985. *Publications:* "Preliminary Clinical Evaluation of the Effects of Small Electrical Currents on Healing of Jaw Fractures", 'Clinical Orthopedics and Related Research', 1977; "Treatment of Maxillory Deficiency - a Le Fort I Down Sliding Technique", 'Journal of Oral and Maxillo Facial Surgery, 1985', 1985; etc. *Honours:* Henry St John Randal Medal, DASA. *Hobbies:* Fishing; Golf. *Address:* 616 Medforum, 412 Schoeman Street, Pretoria 002, South Africa.

MATERU, Adela Michael, b. 18 Feb. 1949, Moshi. Chief of Surgical Services. *Education:* MD (Dar); MMed Surgery (Dar); First Lady Surgeon, Tanzania and East Africa. *Appointments:* District Medical Officer, Arusha Region; Chief, Surgical Services, Arusha Region. *Memberships:* Medical Association of Tanzania; Association of Surgeons of East Africa. *Publications:* "Pancreatic Pseudoaysts in Children", 'Proceedings of the ASEA', 1981; "The Management of Urethral Strictures at Muhimbila Medical Centre", 'Proceedings of the ASEA', 1980. *Honours:* Scholarship, IPPF, University of Lagos, Nigeria, 1974; Scholarship from CMC New York for study tour on primary health care, India, 1982. *Hobbies:* Gardening; Housekeeping; Singing; Swimming. *Address:* PC Box 3092, Arusha, Tanzania.

MATHIS, James L, b. 30 Jan. 1925, Tennessee, USA. Professor and Chairman, East Carolina Medical School Department of Psychiatry. m. Anna K Weber, 2 June 1948, St Louis, Missouri, USA, 2 sons, 3 daughters. *Education:* MD, St Louis Medical School, Missouri, 1949. *Appointments:* Intern, Fitzsimons General Hospital, Denver, USA, 1949-50; GP Residency, Elk City, Oklahoma, 1950-55; Psychiatric Residency, University of Oklahoma, 1960-63; General Practice, Dayton, Tennessee, 1955-60; Assistant Professor of Psychiatry, University of Oklahoma Medical Centre, 1963-68; Associate Professor, Rutgers University Medical School, 1968-70; Professor and Chairman of Psychiatry, Medical College of Virginia, 1970-76; Professor and Chairman of Psychiatry, East Carolina University Medical School, 1976-. *Memberships:* American Psychiatric Association; University of Carolina Psychiatric Association, President, 1985-86; American Medical Association; Alpha Omega Alpha; American College of Psychiatrists. *Publications:* "Basic Psychiatry: A Primer of Concepts and Terminology, 1968, 1972; "Sexual Devia-

tions", 1972; "Psychiatric Medicine - A Handbook", 1984; 13 book chapters; 63 articles. *Honours:* Alpha Omega Alpha, 1948; Fellow, American Psychiatric Association; Fellow, American College of Psychiatrists. *Hobbies:* Gardening; Reading; Fishing. *Address:* Department of Psychiatric Medicine, East Carolina University Medical School, Greenville, NC 27834, USA.

MATKOVICS, Bela, b. 12 July 1927, Csongrád. Assistant Professor, University of Szeged, Hungary. m. M Áron, 15 May 1951, Szeged, Hungary, 3 daughters. *Education:* MD, University Medical School of Szeged, 1951; Medical Clinical Chemical Specialist, 1956; PhD, Natural Science Faculty, University of Szeged, 1966, Candidate of Chemical Sciences, 1966. *Appointments:* Practicant, 1950; Younger Assistant, 1951-55; Elder Assistant, 1955-67; Assistant Professor-. *Membersgips:* American Chemical Society; Chemical Society, London; International Society for Clinical Enzymology; Gesellschaft fur Biol Chemie; Hungarian Chemical Society; Society for Free Radical Research; Society of Hungarian Biochemists. *Publications:* 'The Radicals of molecular oxygen and enzymatic cell defence against some of them', Acta Univ Londziensis, Seria II, pp 103-145, 1977; Co-author "Biological and clinical aspects of superoxide and superoxide dismutase", pp 367-380, 1980. *Honours:* K Than Memorial Award, Hungarian Chemical Society, 1975; Medal for Excellent Work, Ministry of Education, 1983; Award for Service to the Community and Science, Lodz, Poland, 1985. *Hobbies:* Swimming; Tennis. *Address:* PO Box 539 Szeged 1, H-6701, Hungary.

MATSEN, Frederick A III, b. 5 Feb. 1944, Austin, Texas, USA. Professor. m. Anne Lovell, 24 Dec. 1966, Austin, Texas, 1 son, 2 daughters. *Education:* BA, University of Texas, 1964; MD, Baylor University College of Medicine, Houston, Texas, 1968. *Appointments:* Orthopaedic Residency, University of Washington, Seattle, 1974, Acting Instructor, 1974, Director, Medical Students Orthopaedic Education, 1975-78, Assistant Professor, Orthopaedics, 1975-79, Director, Orthopaedic Residency Programme, 1978-81, Associate Professor, Orthopaedics, 1979-82, Professor, Orthopaedics, 1982-; Chairman, Orthopaedics, 1986; Affiliate Professor, Nursing, University of Alaska, 1982-. *Memberships:* American Academy of Orthopaedic Surgeons; Association of Bone and Joint Surgeons; American Shoulder and Elbow Surgeons, Founder Member; Orthopaedic Research Society; American Medical Association; Western Orthopaedic Association; Washington State Medical Society. *Publications include:* 43 articles in professional journals; 24 conference papers; 2 book reviews: "Fractures and Joint Injuries", 1977; "Traumatic Dislocation of the Hip", 1980; 10 book chapters including: 'Biomechanics of the Shoulder' in "Basic Biomechanic of the Skeletal System", 1980; co-author chapter 'The Continuous Infusion Technique in the Assessment of Clinical Compartment Syndromes' in "Tissue Fluid Pressure and Composition", 1981; 'Glenohumeral Instability' in "Surgery of Musculoskeletal System", 1983, etc. *Honours:* Fellowship Award, International Society of Orthopaedic Surgery and Traumatology, Kyoto, Japan, 1978; Nicholas Andry Award, Canada, 1979; ABC Travelling Fellowship, American Orthopaedic Association, 1983. *Hobbies:* Participation in Triathlons; Hiking; Swimming. *Address:* Department of Orthopaedics, University of Washington, Seattle, WA 98195, USA.

MATSUBARA, Yoshito, b. 11 Dec. 1939, Kagoshima, Japan. Chief of Hospital Chest Diseases Centre. m. Yoshie Misawa, 10 Jan. 1974, Essen, West Germany, 1 son, 2 daughters. *Education:* MD, Medical School Kyoto University, Japan. *Appointments:* Medical Staff, Surgical Department, Chest Diseases Research Institute, Kyoto University; Medical Staff, Respiratory Division, Fukui Red Cross Hospital; Medical Staff, Respiratory Division, Kyoto-Katsura Hospital; Medical Staff, Ruhrlandklinik, West Germant. *Memberships:* American College of Chestr Physicians; World

Association for Bronchology; Japanese Cancer Association; Japan Surgical Society; Japanese Association for Thoracic Surgery; Japan Society of Chest Diseases; Japan Society for Cancer Therapy; Japan Lung Cancer Society; Japan Society for Clinical Surgery; Japan Society for Bronchology. *Publications:* "Illustrated Thoracic Surgery" 1980; 'Tumor spezifische Antikorper in der regionalen Lymphknoten von Patienten mit Bronchial-Karzinom' Prax Klin Pneumol, 1980; 'Prosthetic Reconstruction of the Airway' Japanese Journal of Bronchoesophagology Society, 1985; "Tennessee Antigen in Tumor Marker" 1985. *Hobbies:* Travel; Swimming; Bowling; Go Game; Japanese chess. *Address:* 4-8-15 Nishisakaidani-cho, Oharano, Nishikyo-ku, Kyoto, 610-11, Japan.

MATTHEIEM, Wolrad H, b. 16 Apr. 1928, Mayen, Federal Republic of Germany. Chief of Breast and Pelvic Surgical Clinic, Professor of Surgical Oncology, University of Brussels, Belgium. *Memberships:* Society Royale Belge de Chirurgie; Association Francaise du Cancer; European Organisation for Research and Treatment of Cancer; European Society of Surgical Oncology. *Address:* Institut Jules Bordet, 125 Boulevard de Waterloo, 1000 Brussels, Belgium.

MATTHES, Karl John Ludwig Max, b. 16 Dec. 1931, Leipzig, Germany. Professor of Internal Medicine, University of Giessen. m. (1) Doris Stemper, 3 Apr. 1965 (deceased 1978), Munster; (2) Bettina Kemkee, 4 Apr. 1981, Giessen, 1 son, 2 daughters. *Education:* Abitur, 1949; Staatsexamen, Dr. Med, 1954; Habilitation, Priv Doz, 1966; Prof Dr. Med, 1971. *Appointments:* Medical University Klinik, Heidelberg, 1954-56, 1960; Max-Planck Institut Biochemie, Munchen, 1956-59; Department of Physiology, University of California, Berkeley, USA, 1959-60, 1962; Medical University, Kliniken Munster, 1960-67; Professor of Internal Medicine, Medical University Kliniken Giessen, 1967-. *Memberships:* Deutsche Gesellschaft fur Innere Medizin; Deutsche Diabetes-Gesellschaft; European Association for the Study of Diabetes; German Association for the Study of the Liver, etc. *Publications:* "Biochem Untersuchungen Pathologie Leberstoffwechsel", 1969; Co-author: "Untersuchungsmethoden und Funktionsprufungen Innere Medizin", 1975; 83; Co-Editor, "High Density Lipoproteins", 1981; "Vitamin K, Metabolism and Vitamin K Dependent Proteins", Editor J W Suttie, 1979. *Hobbies:* Travel; Photography; Languages (English, Spanish, French). *Address:* Klinikstr 36, D-6300 Giessen, Federal Republic of Germany.

MATTHEWS, David Morling, b. 15 Dec. 1926, High Wycombe, England. Retired Professor. m. 20 Oct. 1960, Hornsey. *Education:* MB BS, University College and Hospital; PhD; MD; DSc; Fellow, Royal College of Physicians; Fellow, Royal College of Pathologists. *Appointments:* House Surgeon, University College Hospital; House Physician, Hackney Hospital; Assistant Lecturer, University of Sheffield, 1950-55; Lecturer in Physiology, University of Birmingham, 1956-58; Lecturer in Chemical Pathology, Royal Free Hospital, 1958-62; Senior Lecturer, Chemical Pathology, National Hospital, 1962-65; Reader in Chemical Pathology, Westminster Medical School, 1965-70; Professor of Experimental Chemical Pathology, Westminster Medical School, 1970-85. *Memberships:* Physiological Society; Biochemical Society; Association of Clinical Biochemists; Zoological Society of London; Royal Society of Medicine. *Publications:* "Peptide Transport in Protein Nutrition", Co-editor, 1975; "Cobalamin Absorption", 1975; "Cobalamin Metabolism and its Clinical Aspects", with Dr J C Linnel, 1984. *Honours:* Fellowes Gold Medal in Senior Clinical Medicine, 1948. *Hobbies:* Reading; Walking. *Address:* 7 Firs Avenue, Muswell Hill, London N10, England.

MATTINGLY, David, b. 1 Mar. 1922, London, England. Professor of Postgraduate Medical Studies; Medical School Director; Consultant Physician. m. Rosemary Joyce Willing, 10 Nov. 1956, Exeter, Devon, England, 1 son, 2 daughters. *Education:* MB, BS, St Thomas' Hospital Medical School, London, England; FRCP, London. *Appointments:* House Physician, St Thomas' Hospital, London, England; Resident Medical Officer, Royal Devon and Exeter Hospital, England; Registrar, Department of Metabolic Diseases, St Thomas's Hospital, London; Senior Medical Registrar, Hammersmith Hospital, London. *Memberships:* Fellow, Royal College of Physicians; Association of Physicians of Great Britain and Ireland; Medical Research Society; British Medical Association. *Publications:* 'Simple fluorimetric method for estimation of free 11-hydroxycorticoids in human plasma' in 'Journal of Clinical Pathology', 1962; 'Bedside Diagnosis", 12 edition, 1985. *Hobbies:* Amateur Radio; Conjuring. *Address:* 1 Moorview Close, Exeter, Devon EX4 6EZ, England.

MATTINGLY, Stephen, b. 1 Mar. 1922, Hampstead, England. Emeritus Consultant Physician, Middlesex Hospital, London. m. Brenda Mary Pike, 23 Nov. 1945, Finchley, 1 son. *Education:* TD, MB, BS (London), FRCP (London), DPhysMed, University College Hospital, London. *Appointments:* Consultant Physician/Medical Director, Garston Manor Rehabilitation Centre, 1956-82; Consultant Physician/Deputy Director, Department of Rheumatology, Middlesex Hospital, 1958-81. Regional Medical Consultant (part-time), Department of Employment, London & Southeast, 1960-74; Honorary Consultant, Rheumatology & Rehabilitation, Army, 1976-81; Member, Attendance Allowance Board, Department of Health & Social Security, 1978-83. *Memberships:* Life Member, British Society for Rheumatology; Senior Companion Fellow, British Orthopaedic Association. *Publications include:* Editor, "Rehabilitation Today", 1977, 1981; Chapters in "Textbook of the Rheumatic Diseases", ed W S C Copeman, 4th ed 1969, "Fractures & Joint Injuries", R Watson-Jones, 6th ed 1964. *Honour:* Territorial Decoration (TD), 1964. *Hobbies:* Gardening; Local History. *Address:* Highfield House, Little Brington, Northamptonshire, NN7 4HN, England.

MATTOCKS, Kyrle Maitland, b. 14 Apr. 1924, Maitland, New South Wales, Australia. Senior Chemical Pathologist. m. Pamela Fay Reynolds, 25 Sep. 1954, Kogarah, New South Wales, Australia, 2 daughters. *Education:* MB, BS (Hons II), 1947, DCP, Sydney, 1958; FRCPath, 1967; FAACB, 1968; FRCPA, 1971. *Appointments:* RMO, 1947-50, Resident in Pathology, 1950-52, Sydney Hospital; Lecturer in Biochemistry, University of Sydney, 1952-55; Chemical Pathologist, Royal Prince Alfred Hospital, 1955-68; Chemical Pathologist, The St George Hospital, Kogarah, 1968-; Board of Censors RCPA, 1968-74; Honorary Consultant Biochemist, The Sutherland Hospital, 1972-. *Memberships:* Fellow, Royal College of Pathologists of Australasia; Fellow, Royal College of Pathologists (London); Fellow, Australian Association of Clinical Biochemists; Australian Biochemical Society; Australian Medical Association. *Hobbies:* Gardening; Aboriginal artifacts. *Address:* Biochemistry Department, The St George Hospital, Kogarah, New South Wales 2217, Australia.

MATTON, Guido Emile Charles, b. 24 May 1930, Etterbeek, Belgium. Professor of Plastic and Maxillofacial Surgery. m. Dr Maria van Leuven, 14 June 1958, Mechelen. *Education:* MD, State University of Gent, Belgium, 1955; Diplomate, American Board of Plastic Surgery, 1961. *Appointments:* Instructor in Plastic Surgery, Duke University, Durham, North Carolina, USA; Professor of Plastic and Maxillofacial Surgery, University Hospital, Gent, Belgium. *Memberships:* American Society of Plastic and Reconstructive Surgery; American Cleft Palate Association; American College of Surgeons; Society of Head and Neck Surgeons; British Association of Plastic Surgeons; Netherlands Society of Plastic Surgeons (Hon Member); Society of French Chir Plast; Belgian Society of Plastic Surgeons (Past President); Belgian Hand Group (Past

President). *Publications:* 73 articles on plastic surgery in Plastic Surgical Journals and books. *Honour:* Perrin Galpin Fellow of the Belgian American Education Foundation, 1957 and 1958. *Address:* Kliniek voor Plastische Heelkunde, Akademisch Ziekenhuis, De Pintelaan 185, B-9000 Gent/Belgium.

MATTSON, Roger Albert, b. 12 May 1938, Ishpeming, Michigan, USA. Psychiatrist. m. Karen A Filby, 6 June 1964, Duluth, Michigan, 1 son, 3 daughters. *Education:* BA, Northern Michigan University, 1959; MD, University of Michigan, 1963; Aerospace Medicine Flight Surgeon, 1964; Psychiatry Resident, Mayo Clinic, 1967-69; Psychiatry Resident, University of Minnesota, 1969-70. *Appointments:* Internship, St Mary's Hospital, Duluth, 1963-64; Flight Surgeon, USAF, 1964-67; Lt Col USAFR, 1967-; Private Practice of Psychiatry, Hospital and Veterans Administration Consultant, 1970-. *Memberships:* St Louis County, Minnesota State and American Medical Societies; American Psychiatric Society; Aerospace Medical Association. *Publication:* 'Vietnamese Refugee Care Psychiatric Observations' Minnesota Medicine, 1978. *Honours:* Air Force Commendation Medal, 1976; Suomi College Award of Distinction, 1982. *Hobbies:* Travel; Gardening; Business. *Address:* 1015 Medical Arts Building, Duluth, MN 55802, USA.

MATUHASI, Tokyo, b. 3 May 1922, Japan. Director, Dept. of Applied Immunology, National Institute of Health, Tokyo, 1979-. m. Rina, 11 February 1947. *Education:* MD, School of Medicine, University of Tokyo; PhD; Post Graduate School of Medicine, University of Tokyo. *Appointments:* Professor, Allergology, Institute of Medical Science, University of Tokyo, 1968-83. *Memberships:* Japanese Societies of Immunology, Allergology, Clinical Pathology, Bacteriology, Blood Transfusion, etc. *Publications:* (In Japanese) ''Immunoglobulin'', 1968; ''Immunoserology'', 1975; ''Blood Bank Technology'', 1974. *Honour:* Honorary Professor, University of Tokyo, 1983. *Hobbies:* Fishing; Travel. *Address:* Institute of Medical Science, University of Tokyo, 4-6-1 Shirokanedai, Minato-ku, Tokyo, 108 Japan.

MATYCHOWIAK, Francis Anthony, b. 20 May 1926, Pinckneyville, Illinois, USA. m. Sally Kayser, 28 Oct. 1950, Riverside, Illinois. *Education:* BA, Miami University, Oxford, Ohio, 1947; BS, 1947, MD, University of Illinois, 1950. *Appointments:* General Practice, Knightstown, Indiana, 1951-52; Private Practice Psychiatry, 1956-; Consultant, California Correctional Institution, Tehachapi, 1958-; Consultant, Superior Court, Kern County, 1956-; Clinical Professor, School of Nursing, School of Arts and Sciences, California State College, Bakersfield, 1976-. *Memberships:* American Psychiatric Assoc, 1955-; American Psychiatric Assoc, Fellow, 1982; Kern County Medical Society, 1956-; California Medical Assoc, 1956-; American Medical Assoc, 1956 American Academy of Clinical Psychiatrists, 1978-American College of Forensic Psychiatry, 1980-. *Address:* 1901 Truxtun Avenue, Bakersfield, CA 93301 USA.

MAUMUS, Craig W, b. 1 Sep. 1946, New Orleans Louisiana, USA. Private Practice Psychiatry; Consultant to East Jefferson Mental Health Clinic; Clinical Assistant Professor of Psychiatry, Tulane Medical Center. m. Priscilla Guderian, 20 Jan. 1973, New Orleans, 1 son. *Education:* BS, Tulane University; MD, Tulane School of Medicine; Internship, Sunnybrook Hospital, University of Toronto, Canada; Psychiatry Residency, Veterans Administration Hospital, Tulane School of Medicine, New Orleans. *Appointments:* Private Practice, office and hospital, Adult Psychiatry, 1976-; Consultant: East Jefferson Mental Health Clinic, 1976-, St Mary's Domincan College, New Orleans, 1983-84; Active Staff: Touro Infirmary, 1976-, Coliseum Medical Center, 1976-81; Courtesy Staff, Coliseum Medical Center, 1981-; President of Medical Staff, Coliseum Medical Center, 1981; State Secretary, Louisiana Psychiatric Association, 1981-85. *Memberships:* New Orleans Area Psychiatric Association; Louisiana Psychiatric Association; American Psychiatric Association; Orleans Parish Medical Society; Louisiana Medical Society; American Medical Association; Southern Medical Association. *Honours:* Diplomate, American Board of Neurology and Psychology, 1981; AMA Physicians Recognition Award, 1976, 79, 82, 85; APA CME Certificate, 1979, 82, 85. *Hobbies:* Sailing; Photography; Model Railroading. *Address:* 1325 Amelia Street, New Orleans, LA 70115, USA.

MAUTNER, Henry George, b. 30 Mar. 1925, Prague, Czechoslovakia. Professor. m. 21 Nov. 1967, Munich, 1 son, 2 daughters. *Education:* BS, Chemistry, University of California, Los Angeles, 1943; MS, Organic Chemistry, University of Southern California, 1949; PhD, Medical Chemistry, University of California, 1955; Honorary MS, Yale University, 1967. *Appointments include:* Yale University School of Medicine, 1955-70; Professor, Head of Section, Medical Chemistry, 1967-70, ibid; Professor, Biochemistry 1970-, Chairman of Departments Biochemistry & Pharmacology, 1970-85, Tufts University School of Medicine; Visiting Fellow, Organic Chemistry, Uppsala University, Sweden, 1962; Visiting Professor, Max-Planck Institute, Munich, Germany 1967-68, University of Basel, Switzerland 1985. *Memberships:* American Chemical Society; American Society of Biological Chemists; Biophysical Society; American Society of Pharmacology & Experimental Therapy, Marine Biology Laboratory, Woods Hole, Massachusetts. *Publications include:* Over 120 articles, reviews, book chapters. *Honours:* Member, Study Section, Medical Chemistry, National Institutes of Health, 1968-79, Chairman 1971-72; Member, Neurobiology Panel, National Science Foundation, 1977-80; Editorial board, 'Journal of Medical Chemistry', 1968-70, 1976-81. *Hobbies:* Photography; Sailing; History. *Address:* 183 Ward Street, Newton Centre, MA 02159, USA.

MAXMEN, Jerrold S, b. 27 June 1942, Detroit, Michigan, USA. Associate Professor of Clinical Psychiatry. m. Mary Berman, 18 Dec. 1966. *Education:* BA, MD, Wayne State University, Detroit Michigan; Japanese studies, Sophia University, Tokyo, Japan. *Appointments:* Intern, Mount Zion Hospital, San Francisco, California, USA, 1967-68; Psychiatric Resident, Yale University, New Haven, Connecticut, 1968-71. Assistant Professor of Psychiatry: Dartmouth College, Hanover, New Hampshire, 1971-74; Albert Einstein College, Bronx, New York, 1974-77. Associate Clinical Professor of Clinical Psychiatry, 1977-, Director, Medical Student Psychiatric Training, 1977-80, Columbia University. *Membership:* American Psychiatric Association. *Publications:* "Rational Hospital Psychiatry", Co-author, 1974; "The Post-Physician Era: Medicine in the 21st Century", 1976; "A Good Night's Sleep", 1981; "The New Psychiatry", 1985; "Essential Psychopathology", 1986. *Honours:* Distinguished Psychiatrist Lectureship, American Psychiatric Association; Fellow, National Fund for Medical Education. *Hobbies:* Reading; Ice hockey. *Address:* 30 Fifth Avenue 6E, New York, NY 10011, USA.

MAXWELL, Ian David, b. 7 Mar. 1915, Vancouver, British Columbia, Canada. Consultant in Pathology, Halifax Infirmary. m. Rachel Anne Bompas, 27 July 1940, Broughton, Hampshire, England, 4 sons, 1 daughter. *Education:* BSc, University of Bristol, England, 1936; MS, ChB, University of Edinburgh, 1942; GMC (Gt Britain and Ireland), 1942; Provincial License (Med), Nova Scotia, 1943; LMCC (Canada), 1947; Cert Path RCP&S Canada, 1952; FRCP (C), 1965. *Appointments:* Director of Laboratory, Royal Columbian Hospital, 1953-58; Associate Professor, Pathology, Dalhousie University, 1958-63; Associate Director, Laboratory, Halifax Infirmary, 1963-84; Consultant in Pathology, Halifax Infirmary and Hants. Community Hospital, 1983-. *Memberships:* Canadian Medical Association; RMS; CAP; American Society Clinical Pathology; CSCC; NSSCC. *Publications:* Contributor to professional journals including: 'Medical Expenses in Cases Involving Litigation', 'Nova Scotia Medical Bulletin, 1967; 'Therapeutic Abortion and Sterilization', 'Nova Scotia Medical Bulletin', 1967; 'Responsibility for the Acts of Another', 4 Parts, 'Nova Scotia Medical Bulletin', 1968; 'Prothrombin Estimations', Canadian Medical Association Journal, 1968; 'Preparation Indium Colloids' (co-author), 'Journal Applied Radio Isotopes', 1969; 'Recent Advances in Laboratory Investigations', 'Nova Scotia Medical Bulletin', 1969; 'Sickle Cell Survey in Halifax County' (co-author), Nova Scotia Medical Bulletin', 1974. *Hobbies:* Woodcraft; Sailing. *Address:* Tancook Island, Nova Scotia, Canada.

MAY, Genevieve Stewart, b. 14 Aug., 1909, Pakistan. Consultant Psychiatrist. m. Philip R A May, 11 Nov. 1959, Malibu, California, USA. *Education:* BS; MD; Psychoanalytic Training, Los Angeles Psychoanalytic Institute. *Appointments:* Psychiatric Resident, Norristown, Pennsylvania State Hospital - St Elizabeth Hospital, Washington DC - Pennsylvania Hospital, Philadelphia; Staff Psychiatrist, Vet Admin Hospital, Sepulveda, California - Vet Admin Mental Hygiene Clinic, Los Angeles, California; Consultant, Camarillo State Hospital, California Research. *Memberships:* American Psychiatric Association; American Medical Association; Southern California Psychiatric Society; Los Angeles Psychoanalytical Society and Institute. *Hobbies:* Gardening; Cooking; Embroidery; Travel. *Address:* 28820 Cliffside Drive, Malibu, CA 90265, USA.

MAY, Kazimierz Leon, b. 31 July 1932, Warsaw, Poland. Adjunct/Assistant Professor. m. Halina Szucka, 10 Apr. 1965, Warsaw, 1 son, 1 daughter. *Education:* Doctor of Medicine, Warsaw Medical School, 1955; Specialist in internal disease, lower degree 1959, higher degree 1963; Specialist in Allergology, 1975; Doctor of Medical Sciences, 1968. *Appointments:* House Officer and Senior House Officer, Internal Departments, Municipal Hospitals, Warsaw, 1955-65; House Officer, Sully Hospital, Cardiff, Wales, 1961; Research Worker, Pulmonological Department, University Hospital Groningen, Netherlands, 1966-67; Registrar, Institute of Internal Diseases, 1967-70; Research Worker, Allergological Department, University Hospital Pamplona, Spain, 1975; Consultant Internist-regional, 1977-80; Adjunct Research Worker, TB and Chest Diseases Research Institute, Warsaw, Poland, 1971-. *Memberships:* Founder of Allergological Section, Polish Medical Association 1965; Society of Polish Internists; Polish Phtisiopulmonological Society; European Academy of Allergy and Clinical Immunology; Advisory Committee, Interasma. *Publications:* 'Bronchial Hyperreactivity and its Estimation', thesis, 1968; 'Prevalence of Chronic non Specific Lung Diseases among 19 Year Old Men in Poland/Analysis of Regional Differences of 576,000 examinees', 1985. *Hobby:* Tourism. *Address:* ul Ludna 10 m 10, 00-414 Warsaw, Poland.

MAY, Wolfgang Werner, b. 12 Sep. 1932, Goerlitz, Germany. Chief, Section of Neurology Clinics; Clinical Instructor of Psychiatry; Psychiatric Consultant. m. Luz Delrosario, 29 Oct. 1976, Ann Arbor, Michigan, USA, 1 son, 1 daughter. *Education:* MD, University of Parana, Brazil, 1958; MSc, University of Michigan, USA, 1966; ECFMG, 1960; American Board of Neurology and Psychiatry, 1971; Graduate Detroit Psychoanalytic Institute, 1983; Resident, Medicine, 1960-63, Neurology, 1963-66, Psychiatry, 1966-69. *Appointments include:* Assistant Chief, Section of Geriatrics and Consultant in Neurology, 1969-70; Chief of Neurology and Gerontology Research, 1970-72; Chief, Section of Neurology Clinics and Gerontology B, 1972-; Clinical Instructor of Psychiatry, University of Michigan; Psychiatric Consultant, Turner Geriatric Clinic. *Memberships:* American Psychiatric Association; Michigan Association of Neuropsychiatric Hospitals and Clinics Physicians, Past President; Associate Member, American Academy of Neurology; Candidate Member, American Academy of Psychoanalysis. *Publications:* Author or Co-Author of numerous papers contributed to: 'Archives of General Psychiatry';

'Acta Neurol Scand'; 'Archives of Neurology', USA; "Progress in Neurogenetics", 1969; "Arquivos de Neuro-psiquiatria'. Numerous papers presented at international conferences. *Address:* 555 East William, 17F, Ann Arbor, MI 48104, USA.

MAYER, Raymond, V J, b. 29 Dec. 1924, Mons, Belgium. University Professor, Chief of Department of Stomatology. m. Yvonne Demaret, 28 Sep. 1952, Ghent, 1 son, 1 daughter. *Education:* Medical Doctor, Licencie en Science Dentaire, Université Libre de Bruxelles; Specialist in General Surgery, stomatology and maxillofacial surgery. *Appointments:* Resident, Surgical Clinic, Ghent, 1951-60; Prospector, Anatomical Institute, Brussels, 1960-62; Assistant, Adjoint, Chef de Clinique, Chef de Service, Service de Stomatologie, Hospital Saint Pierre, Brussels, 1960-85; Professor, Université Libre de Bruxelles, 1963-85; Vice President 1982-85, President 1985-, Faculty of Medicine, Université Libre de Bruxelles. *Memberships:* Former President, Societe Royale Belge de Stomatologie et de Chirurgie Maxillo-Faciale; Founder Member, European Association of Maxillofacial Surgery; Treasurer, Groupement International Pour La Recherche Scientifique en Stomatologie et Odontologie. *Honours:* Honorary Member, Oral Surgery Club of Great Britain; Membre d'Honneur pour le Progres de la Science Stomatologique, France. *Hobbies:* Sculpture; Medical and Dental History. *Address:* Service de Stomatologie, Hopital Universitaire Saint Pierre, Rue Haute 322, 1000 Brussels, Belgium.

MAYNARD, David Stanley, b. 10 Mar. 1937, Sydney, Australia. Consultant Pathologist. m. Natalie Marie Dixon, 12 March 1962, divorced 1982, 2 sons, 2 daughters; (2) Judith Sydney Penn, 8 June 1984. *Education:* BA, 1979, MA, 1983, Sydney; MB, BS, Sydney, 1961; DCP, Sydney, 1967; FRCPA, 1967; MIAC, 1980. *Appointments:* Resident Medical Officer, Sydney Hospital, 1961-62; Fell Path Fairfax Institute of Pathology, Royal Prince Alfred Hospital, 1963; Sen Fell Chemical Pathology, 1967-68; Visiting Histopathologist, Parramatta District Hospital, 1970. *Memberships:* Australian Medical Association; Associate Member, Royal Society of Medicine; International Academy of Pathology; International Academy of Cytology; Fellow, Royal College of Pathologists of Australasia. *Hobby:* Music. *Address:* 26 Killara Ave., Killara, NSW 2071, Australia.

MAYNARD, Frederick M, b. 13 Mar. 1944, Michigan, USA. Associate Professor, Physical Medicine & Rehabilitation, University of Michigan. m. Kathryn Ihver, 21 May 1966, Midland, Michigan, 1 son, 1 daughter. *Education:* AB 1966, MD, 1968, University of Michigan. *Appointments include:* Assistant Chief, Department of Physical Medicine & Rehabilitation, Santa Clara Valley Medical Centre, San Jose, California. *Memberships:* American Academy of PM&R; American Congress of Rehabilitation Medicine; American Spinal Injury Association; American Association of Electromycography & Electrodiagnosis; Michigan State Medical Society; Michigan Academy of PM&R. *Publications*/Presentations include: Numerous papers in scientific journals; Abstracts, published panel discussions, letters etc; Audiovisual & teaching aids; 2 book chapters. *Honours include:* Award, 'Late Effects of Polio Coalition', outstanding contribution to polio research, 1985. *Hobbies:* Gardening; Swimming; Skiing. *Address:* University of Michigan Hospital, Department of Physical Medicine & Rehabilitation, Box 0042-1500 East Medical Centre Drive, Ann Arbor, MI 48109-0042, USA.

MAYNARD, John Hildyard, b. 10 Sep. 1937, Richmond, Victoria, Australia. Director, Pathology, Dandenong and District Hospital. m. Andrea Wightman, 30 Mar. 1963, 2 daughters. *Education:* MB, BS, Melbourne University, 1962; FRCPA; MASM; MASCP; AFAIM. *Appointments:* Assistant Pathologist, 1970-72, Specialist Pathologist, 1972-73, Director, Pathology, 1973-, Dandenong Hospital. *Memberships:* Fellow, Royal College of Pathologists of Australasia; International Academy of Pathology; American Society of Clinical Pathologists; Royal Society of Medicine, London; New York Academy of Sciences. *Publications:* Numerous articles in professional journals including: "Haemochromotosis with Osteogenic Sarcoma in the Liver", 'Medical Journal of Australia', 1969; "Standardization and Evaluation of the Oral Glucose Tolerance Test", 'Medical Journal of Australia', 1971; "Chloral Hydrate Interferes with Radioassay of Vitamin B12", 'Clinical Chemistry', 1981. *Hobbies:* Art; Painting; Sailing. *Address:* Dandenong and District Hospital, David Street, Dandenong, Victoria 3175, Australia.

MAYNE, Lewis Harper, b. 19 Jan. 1926, Ipswich, Queensland, Australia. Director, Oral and Maxillofacial Surgery Unit, South Australian Dental Service. m. Fay Sheldrake, 4 Mar. 1950, Ipswich, Australia, 1 son, 2 daughters. *Education:* BSc; BDSc; MDS; FRACADS; DOS. *Appointments:* Senior Graduate Tutor in Oral Surgery, University of Queensland; Private General Dental Practice; Oral Maxillofacial Surgery Training; Senior Teaching Fellow in Oral Surgery, Senior Lecturer in Oral Surgery, University of Adelaide; Assistant Director, Oral Surgery Unit, Royal Adelaide Hospital; Director, Oral Surgery Unit, Royal Adelaide Hospital; Consultant and Senior Visiting Specialist: Royal Adelaide Hospital; The Queen Elizabeth Hospital; Adelaide Childrens Hospital; Flinders Medical Centre; Modbury Hospital and Lyell McEwin Hospital. *Memberships:* Australian Dental Association; Australian and New Zealand Association of Maxillofacial Oral and Maxillofacial Surgeons; Federation Dentaire Internationale; Adelaide Oral Surgeons Group; Oral Surgery Oral Medicine Study Group; Fellow, International Association of Oral and Maxillofacial Surgeons. *Publications:* 'Xerographic Assessment of craniofacial deformities'; 'Intermaxilliary fixation: How practicable is emergency jaw release', (co author); 'Interferential therapy to promote union in mandibular fractures', (co author). *Hobby:* Bush walking. *Address:* Adelaide Dental Hospital, Frome Road, Adelaide, South Australia.

MAYO, W E Barry, b. 1 Apr. 1930, Ottawa, Canada. Medical Director, Sportopaedics. m. Helene Puskas, 21 June 1958, Detroit, USA. 2 sons, 2 daughters. *Education:* MD, LMCC, FACS, FAAOS, Diplomate of American Board of Orthopaedic Surgeons. *Appointments:* Intern - Surgery Resident, Latter-day Saints Hospital, Salt Lake City; Orthopaedic Surgery Resident, Primary Children's Hospital; Orthopaedic Surgery Resident, Henry Ford Hospital, Detroit; Staff Orthopaedic Surgeon, William Beaumont Hospital, Royal Oak; Staff Orthopaedic Surgeon, St Joseph Hospital, Pontiac; Staff Orthopaedic Surgeon, Madison Community Hospital; Director, Sports Medicine Clinic, William Beaumont Hospital; Director, Haemophilia-Orthopaedic Clinic, William Beaumont Hospital; Medical Director, Sportopaedics. *Memberships:* Fellow, American College of Surgeons; Fellow, American Academy of Orthopaedic Surgeons; Royal Society of Medicine, London; American Medical Association; Mid-West Orthopaedic Association; Michigan Orthopaedic Society etc. *Honours:* Michigan Award, Religious Heritage of America, 1982; District Award of Merit, Boy Scouts of America, 1982; Silver Beaver Award, Boy Scouts of America, 1984 etc. *Hobbies:* Church Committees; Executive Board, Detroit Area, Boy Scouts of America. *Address:* 4387 Barchester Drive, Bloomfield Hills, MI 48013, USA.

MAYOL, Pedro M, b. 22 Jan. 1933, Ciales, Puerto Rico, Professor of Pulmonology, Medical Director of Pediatric Pulmonary Program. m. Nohemi Udraz, 29 Dec. 1957, Arecibo, 1 son, 3 daughters. *Education:* BS, Penn Military College, Widener University, USA, 1954; MD, University of Puerto Rico School of Medicine, Puerto Rico, 1962. *Appointments:* Medical Director, Head Start, 1967-70; Chief of Pediatrics, San Pablo Hospital, Bayamon, 1979-81; Instructor Pediatrics 1967-72, Assistant Professor 1972-77, Associate Professor 1977-84, Medical Director Family Practice

Plan 1982-83, School of Medicine, Medical Director of Pediatric Pulmonary Center 1970-, Special Assistant to the Dean 1982-83, Chief of Respiratory Service - University Pediatric Hospital 1983-, Professor of Pediatrics 1984-, University of Puerto Rico. *Memberships:* American Academy of Pediatrics; American Thoracic Society; American College of Chest Physicians; American Association of University Professors; Puerto Rico Medical Association. *Publications:* "Neumologia Pediatrica", (with J E Sifontes, F Rodriguez and M Valcarcel), 1974; "Prevencion y Manejo de la Tuberculosis en los Ninos", (with J E Sifontes and J F Rivera), 1981. *Honours:* John Genzztlien Chemistry Award, 1954; American Institute of Chemistry Medicine, 1954; Chest Disease Medicine, 1962; Public Health Medicine, 1962; Premio Dist Ped Nestle, 1966. *Hobbies:* Reading; Golf. *Address:* Hospital San Pablo, Bayamon, PR 00619, USA.

MAYOR, Michael Brook, b. 29 Oct. 1937, Bryn Mawr, Pennsylvania, USA. Associate Professor, Clinical Surgery, Orthopaedics. m. Elizabeth Fenner Rowland, 11 June 1960, Rochester, New York, 1 son, 3 daughters. *Education:* BEE, Yale University, 1959; MD, Yale Medical School, 1965; Internship, residency, Cleveland, Ohio, 1965-70. *Appointments include:* Special postdoctorate NIH Fellow, Biomechanics, Case Institute of Technology, Cleveland, Ohio, 1970-71; Instructor, Assistant Professor, Associate Professor, Clinical Surgery in Orthopaedics, Dartmouth-Hitchcock Medical Centre, Hanover, New Hampshire, 1971-; Consultant, US Veterans Association Hospital, White River Junction, Vermont, 1971-. *Memberships:* American Medical Association; Fellow, American Academy of Orthopaedic Surgery, Orthopaedic Research Society; New Hampshire Orthopaedic Society; Grafton County Medical Society. *Publications include:* Numerous contributions to professional journals, presentations, etc. *Honour:* Panel member, New Devices, Orthopaedics & Rehabilitation, FDA, 1985-88. *Hobbies:* Computer Communications; Small woodlot forestry. *Address:* Dartmouth-Hitchcock Medical Centre, 2 Maynard Road, Hanover, NH 03756, USA.

MAYR, Carlos Henrique, b. 5 Aug. 1919. Department Head. Divorced, 2 sons, 1 daughter. *Education:* MD, Faculdade Nacional de Medicina, University of Brazil; Specialist in Surgery, Gynaecology and Obstetrics. *Appointments:* Head, Department of Surgery: Hospital Curuzeiro, Rio do Sul SC; Hospital Timbo, Timbo SC; Hospital Miguel Couto, Ibirama SC; Strangers Hospital, Rio de Janeiro. Consultant; German Hospital, Rio de Janeiro; Casa Saude Sao Jose, Rio; Hospital Sao Lucas, Rio; Casa Saude Santa Lucia. *Memberships:* Fellow: International College of Surgeons; American College of Abdominal Surgeons; Brazilian College of Surgery; Brazilian Society of Obstetrics and Gynaecology. *Publications:* Author of over 50 articles in various medical journals. *Honours:* Latin American Federation Secretary, Vice President, Board of Governors, Executive Council and Committee Member, International College of Surgeons. *Hobbies:* Semi-precious stones and minerals; Coins; Stamps. *Address:* Rua Lacerda Coutinho 49, Copacabana 22041, Rio de Janeiro, Brazil.

MAYWALD, Christoph Alfred Burkat, b. 27 Oct. 1947, Bermuda. Doctor of Chiropractic. m. Lisa Bayard Wood, 1 May 1982, Auburn, Massachusetts, 1 daughter. *Education:* BS Human Biology, Doctor of Chiropractic, Logan College of Chiropractic, St Louis, Missouri; CCTP, National College of Chiropractic. *Appointments:* Private Practice. *Memberships:* New York Academy of Sciences; American Chiropractic Association; Americam Medical Writers Association; Council on Roentgenology, American Chiropractic Association. *Publications:* Nutritional Editor, 'New England Journal of Chiropractic', 1978-79; Editorial review, 'Pangamic Acid and Its Derivatives' by I N Garkina, A N Bakh Institute of Biochemistry, USSR Academy of Sciences; "Dynamic Evaluation of the Sacropelvic Biomechanical Mechanism", 1979; "Hormonal Control of Nutrient Metabolism", 1979; "Hypoglycemia", 1979; "Vitamin C", 1979. *Hobbies:* Writing; Running; Alpine Skiing; Racquet Sports; Biking. *Address:* 484 High Street, Dedham, MA 02026, USA.

MAZUR, Eric Michael, b. 10 July 1949, Connecticut, USA. Assistant Professor. m. Abby Leventhal, 6 Nov. 1972, 2 sons. *Education:* BSE, Princeton University, 1971; MD, Johns Hopkins University School of Medicine, 1975. *Appointments:* Categorical Internal Medicine Internship & Residency, Strong Memorial Hospital, University of Rochester, 1975-77; Postdoctoral Fellow, Haematology, Yale University, 1977-78; Senior Medical Resident, Yale, 1978-79; Postdoctoral Fellow, Yale University, 1979-81; Attending Physician, Medicine, Mary Imogene Bassett Hospital, New York, Assistant Professor, Clinical Medicine, College of Physicians & Surgeons, Columbia University, 1981-83; Assistant Professor, Medicine, Brown University; Director, Haematology, Oncology, The Miriam Hospital. *Memberships:* American College of Physicians; American Society of Haematology; American Federation for Clinical Research; American Society of Clinical Oncology; American Cancer Society; Eastern Cooperative Oncology Group; International Society for Experimental Haematology; American Association for Advancement of Science. *Publications:* Numerous articles in professional journals; book chapters, editorials; etc. *Honours:* Alpha Omega Alpha, 1975, Mosby Scholarship Award, 1975, Henry Strong Denison Scholarship Award for Research, 1975, Johns Hopkins; Nominee, Betsy Winters Housestaff Teaching Award, Yale, 1980; Brown University Nominee, Stratton-Jaffe Haematology Scholar Award, American Society of Haematology, 1984; Brown University Nominee, Life and Health Insurance Medical Research Fund Award, 1984. *Address:* The Miriam Hospital, 164 Summit Avenue, Providence, RI 02906, USA.

MAZUR, Wladyslaw Piotr Bartek, b. 24 Aug. 1921, Poland. Private Practitioner in Psychiatry. m. Kay Emily Smith, 29 May 1961, 3 sons, 3 daughters. *Education:* MB BCh, Edinburgh University, Scotland, 1950. *Appointments:* Assistant Physician, Royal Edinburgh Hospital, Scotland; Assistant Clinical Professor, University of Cincinnati, USA; Associate Clinical Professor, University of Kansas; Faculty Member, Menninger School of Psychiatry; Medical Superintendent, West Central Georgia Regional Hospital; currently in Private Practice, Georgia. *Memberships:* Canadian and American Psychiatric Associations; Medical Association of Georgia. *Publications:* "Problem Oriented System in the Psychiatric Hospital", 1974; 10 articles in British, Canadian, American and Italian Journals. *Honours:* Book of the Year, American Journal of Nursing, 1974. *Hobby:* Sculpture. *Address:* 768 Juniper Street, Atlanta, GA 30308, USA.

MAZZAGLIA, Alfio Joseph, b. 16 Aug. 1932, Lawrence, Massachusetts, USA. Podriatric Surgeon. *Education:* 2-year pre-medical course in Biochemistry, Tufts University; Doctor of Podiatric Medicine, Illinois College of Podiatric Medicine & Surgery, 1955. *Appointments:* Professor of Surgery, Illinois College of Podiatric Medicine, 1955-60; Chief of Surgery, 1955-60; Associate, Henri L DuVries, Columbus & Mother Cabrini Hospitals, 1955-60; Adjunct Clinical Professor, Ohio College of Podiatric Medicine. *Memberships:* American Podiatric Medical Association; First Vice-President, Massachusetts Podiatric Medical Society; Fellow: American Society of Podiatric Medicine, American Society of Laser Surgery, American Academy of Microscopic Surgery, Academy of Ambulatory Foot Surgery; American Association of Hospital Podiatrists; Associate, American College of Foot Surgeons; American Analgesia Society; American Society of Contemporary Medicine & Surgery; Diplomate, International College of Laser Surgery. *Publications:* Author of chapter on Oncology of foot & ankle in Weinstein's "Principles & Practice of Podiatry". *Honours:* Durlacher Scholastic Award, 1955; William Reeda Award for highest proficiency in Clinical Podiatry, 1955. *Address:* Dracut Professional Building, 149 Pleasant Street, Dracut, MA 01826, USA.

MEAD, John Mendenhall, b. 28 Aug. 1930, Cleveland, Ohio, USA. Psychiatrist. m. Nancy Harriman, 28 Nov. 1957, Washington District of Columbia, USA, 1 son. *Education:* BA, Antioch University, USA; MD, Temple University, USA. *Appointments:* Executive and Medical Director, Los Angeles Child Guidance Clinic; Executive and Medical Director, Pasadena Guidance Clinic. *Memberships:* American Psychiatric Association; Academy of Child Psychiatrists; Academy of Psychology and Law; California Medical Society. *Honours:* Diplomate, 1966; FAPA, 1971. *Address:* 2556 Mission Street, San Marino, CA 91108, USA.

MEADOW, Samuel Roy, b. 9 June 1933, Lancashire, England. University Professor and Head of Paediatric Department. m. Marianne Jane Harvey, 7 Aug. 1962, Tunbridge Wells, England, 1 son, 1 daughter. *Education:* BA (Hons Physiology), MA, Oxford University, England, 1953-57; BM, BCh, Guy's Hospital Medical School, London University, 1957-60. *Appointments:* Senior Research Fellow, Medical Research Council, Institute of Child Health, Birmingham, England; Senior Lecturer, Department of Paediatrics and Child Health, Leeds University; Secretary of Academic Board, British Paediatric Association; Secretary of Specialist Advisory Committee for Paediatrics, Joint Higher Committee of Medical Training; Chairman of Association of Child Psychology and Psychiatry; Professor and Head of University Department of Paediatrics, St James' Hospital, Leeds, England. *Memberships:* British Paediatric Association; Royal College of Physicians; Renal Association. *Publications:* "Lecture Notes on Paediatrics", 1973, 5th edition, 1985; co-author "Bladder Control and Enuresis", 1976; co-author "The Child and His Symptoms", 1978; "Help for Bedwetting", 1981; "Recent Advances in Paediatrics", 1984; co-author "Paediatric Kidney Disease", 1986; many papers on renal and urinary tract problems of childhood, Munchhausen's syndrome; medical evaluation. *Honour:* Donald Patterson Prize, British Paediatric Association, 1970. *Hobbies:* Gardening; Hill Walking. *Address:* Department of Paediatrics and Child Health, St James' University Hospital, Leeds, England.

MEAGHER, Ann-Marie, b. 23 Sep. 1931, Portland, Oregon, USA. Psychiatrist, Private practice and in Geriatric Outpatient and Day Treatment Center. m. Donald David Rosenberg, 8 Aug. 1959, San Francisco, California, 1 son. *Education:* BA Summa cum Laude, Dominican College, San Rafael, California, 1953; MD, University of Oregon Medical School, 1957. *Appointments:* Psychiatrist, Private Practice, 1966-; Staff Psychiatrist, Solano County Mental Health Services, 1981-82. Psychiatrist: Adult Day Treatment Center, Solano County, California, 1981-86; Geriatric Outpatient and Day Treatment Center, San Francisco, 1983-. *Memberships:* American Geriatric Society; Marin and Northern California Psychiatric Societies; Marin Medical Society; American Psychiatry Association; California Medical Association. *Honours:* Tuition Scholarship, Dominican College, 1949-53; Highest Honour, 1949-53, President, 1953, Dominican College Honour Society. *Hobbies:* Animals; Music; Nature. *Address:* PO Box 466, Tiburon, CA 94920, USA.

MEAL, Gilbert Marcel, b. 22 Jan. 1948, 56 Questembert, France. Chiropractor. m. Sandra Patricia Meal, 22 Aug. 1970, Bournemouth, England. 2 daughters. *Education:* Doctor of Chiropractic. *Appointments:* Private Practice, Exeter, England, 1970-73; Part Time Lecturer, 1972-73; Full Time Lecturer 1973-80, Clinic Director 1976-80, Part Time Lecturer, Anglo-European College, Chiropractic, Bournemouth, UK, 1981-; Private Practice, Christchurch, England, 1980-. *Memberships:* British Chiropractic Assoc; European Chiropractors' Union; International College of Applied Kinesiology. *Publications:* (Articles) 'Clinical Relevance of Diagnosis in Chiropractic Practice', 1977; 'Radiography vs

Grey-Fog-graphy', 1982; "Analysis of the Joint Crack by simultaneous recording of sound and tension", co-author with R A Scott, DC, 'Journal of Manipulative and Physiological Therapeutics', 1986. *Hobby:* Boardsailing. *Address:* 5 Stour Road, Christchurch, Dorset, BH23 1PL, England.

MEARES, Ainslie Dixon, b. 3 Mar. 1910, Melbourne, Australia. Non-medical Consultant in Mental Relaxation, working on effect of intensive meditation on cancer growth. m. Bonnie Sylvia Byrne, 1934, Melbourne, 1 son, 2 daughters. *Education:* B Agr Sci, 1934, DPM, 1947, MBBS, 1940, MD, 1958, University of Melbourne. *Appointment:* Psychiatrist in Private Practice, 1945-73, 1974-. *Memberships:* Australasian Medical Association; British Medical Association; Foundation Fellow, Australian and New Zealand College of Psychiatrists; Past-President, Medico-Legal Society of Victoria; Foundation President, Australian Society Clinical and Experimental Hypnosis; Past President, International Society Clinical and Experimental Hypnosis. *Publications:* 27 books including: "A System of Medical Hypnosis", 1960; "The Door of Serenity", 1958; "Relief Without Drugs", 1967; "The Introvert", 1958; "Dialogue on Meditation", 1979; "A Way of Doctoring", 1985; 100 scientific papers including: 'What Makes the Patient Better', 'Lancet'; 'The Diagnosis of Prepsychotic Schizophrenia', 'Lancet'; 'Cancer, Psychosomatic Illness and Hysteria', 'Lancet'; 'Stress, Meditation and the Repression of Cancer', 'The Practitioner'; 'The Atavistic Theory of Hypnosis', 'Medical Journal of Australia'; 'A Form of Intensive Meditation association with the Regression of Cancer', 'American Journal of Clinical Hypnosis'. *Hobbies:* Writing; Conversation. *Address:* 99 Spring Street, Melbourne 3000, Australia.

MECH, Arnold Walter, b. 9 Dec. 1952, Chicago, Illinois, USA. Psychiatrist, Private Practice. m. 23 Aug. 1979, Topeka, 1 daughter. *Education:* MD, Loyola University of Chicago, Stritch School of Medicine. *Appointments:* Psychiatric Resident, Loyola University Medical Centre, 1977-78; Psychiatric Resident, Karl Menninger School of Psychiatry, Topeka, 1978-81; Child Fellow, Programme for Career Training in Child Psychiatry, 1980-82, Staff Psychiatrist, Menninger Foundation; Director, Eating Disorders Programme, C F Menninger Memorial Hospital, 1983-. *Memberships:* Shawnee County Medical Society; Kansas Medical Society; American Medical Association; District Branch, American Psychiatric Association; American Academy of Child Psychiatry; American Psychoanalytic Association. *Publications:* Numerous invited papers, addressed, presentations and workshops including: "Consultation liaison work with orthopedically handicapped and mentally retarded children and adolescents: Theoretical and Clinical aspects", Topeka State Hospital, 1982; "Eating Disorders - Theoretical and Clinical Approaches", 1983; Workshop: "Hospital Treatment of Eating Disorders", Air Force Dieticians, 1984; "Diagnosis Understanding and Treatment of Eating Disorders", Annual Meeting of National Association of Social Workers, Kansas chapter, 1984; etc; Articles in 'American Journal of Psychiatry'; 'Bulletin of the Menninger Clinic'; etc. *Honour:* Seeley Fellow, Menninger School of Psychiatry, 1979-80. *Address:* 4100 West 15th Street, Plano, TX 75075, USA.

MEDARIS, Florence I, b. 27 Sep. 1909, Kirksville, Missouri, USA. Retired Osteopathic Physician. *Education:* BA, College of Wooster, 1932; DO, Kirksville College of Osteopathic Medicine, 1939; Graduate Study, Medical School of Wisconsin, Medical College of Marquette, University of Milwaukee, Wisconsin. *Memberships:* Honorary Life Member, Wisconsin Association for Osteopathic Physicians; Life Member, American Osteopathic Association; Academy of Osteopathic Physicians. *Hobbies:* Photography; Golf; Fishing; Hiking in the Mountains. *Address:* 1121 North Waverly Place, Milwaukee, WI 53202, USA.

MEDLICOTT, Reginald Warren, b. 10 Aug. 1913, Waimate, New Zealand. Professor; Consultant Psych-

iatrist. m. Nancy Alice McLaren, 27 Mar. 1940, Wellington, New Zealand, 1 son, 1 daughter. *Education:* MB, ChB, New Zealand; FRACP: FRANZCP: FRC.Psych. Corr. FAPA; F Brit Psychological Society; Fellow, New Zealand Psychological Society. *Appointments include:* Medical Director, Ashburn Hall, Dunedin, New Zealand, 1947-78; Lecturer, Senior Lecturer, Psychological Medicine, Otago University Medical School, 1947-69; Personal Professor of Graduate Studies in Psychological Medicine, Otago University Medical School, 1969-79; Visiting Forensic Psychiatrist, Department of Social Welfare, New Zealand, 1979-; Visiting Psychiatrist and Chairman, Review Panel, Lake Alice Maximum Security Villa, Marton, 1977-82; Visiting Psychiatrist, Porirua Hospital, 1982-85; Professor Emeritus, Otago University Medical School. *Memberships include:* Australian and New Zealand College of Psychiatrists; Hon. Life Member, New Zealand Association of Psychotherapists; American Association for Applied Psychoanalysis; World Psychiatric Association; Trustee, Kathleen Todd Psychiatric Foundation, etc. *Publications include:* Numerous contributions to professional journals including 'The Psychiatric Aspects of Violence' in 'New Zealand Medical Journal', 1980; 'The Akedah' (The Binding of Isaac) in 'Journal of Evolutionary Psychology', 1982; 'Movements Towards a Philosophy of Life' in 'Journal of Evolutionary Psychology', 1983; 'Coming to Terms with Crime' in 'Journal of Evolutionary Psychology', 1985. *Hobbies:* Study of the Western tradition as expressed in Greek and Judaeo-Christian Mythology and Religion; Gardening. *Address:* 11 Key Grove, Raumati, New Zealand.

MEEKIN, Francis Arne, b. 30 Aug. 1932, Rawlins, Wyoming, USA. Director, Radiation Therapy Unit. m. 15 Nov. 1964, Seattle, Washington, 3 sons, 2 daughters. *Education:* BS Chemistry, Carnegie Institute of Technology, Pittsburgh, Pennsylvania, 1954; MD, Marquette University School of Medicine, Milwaukee, Wisconsin, 1958; American Board of Radiology, 1966. *Appointments:* Staff Radiation Oncologist, Tumour Institute of the Swedish Hospital, Seattle, Washington. *Memberships:* American College of Radiology; American Society of Therapeutic Radiology & Oncology; American Medical Association. *Hobbies:* Skiing; Hiking. *Address:* Department of Radiation Therapy, Holy Family Hospital, 5633 Lingerwood, Spokane, WA 99207, USA.

MEESTER, Geert T, b. 9 Mar. 1929. Cardiologist. m. Ilse Roost, 5 Oct. 1961, Barendrecht, 2 sons, 2 daughters. *Education:* MD, University of Utrecht, The Netherlands, 1956; PhD, Erasmus University, Rotterdam, The Netherlands, 1980. *Appointments:* Associate Professor, Cardiology Department, Erasmus University, 1970-73; Chief, Cardiology Department, 1968-70, Consultant, Cardiology Department, 1967-68, Zuiderziekenhuis Institute of Aerospace Medicine; Assistant Professor, Cardiology Department, Utrecht University, 1963-67. *Memberships:* Fellow, American College of Cardiology, 1981. *Publications:* Thesis: "Computer analysis of cardiac catheterization data" 1980. *Hobbies:* Golf; Sailing. *Address:* Erasmus University Rotterdam, Thoraxcenter Bd 412, PO Box 1738, 3000 DR Rotterdam, The Netherlands.

MEFFORD, Dan A, b. 12 Dec. 1950. Doctor of Chiropractic. m. Catherine Ann Hammitt, 2 sons, 1 daughter. *Education:* Doctor of Chiropractic 1976. *Memberships:* American Chiropractic Association; Illinois Chiropractic Society; Council on Roentgenology of American Chiropractic Association; National Health Federation; Palmer College of Chiropractic Alumni Association. *Honours:* Certificate of Registration in Basic Science; Diplomate, National Board of Chiropractic Examiners; President of Local Associatio, National Health Federation. *Hobbies:* Horse riding; Back packing; Hunting; Camping. *Address:* PO Box 64, Pittsfield, IL 62363, USA.

MEIJER, Dirk Klaas Fokke, b. 11 Oct. 1940, Soest, The Netherlands Professor of Pharmacology and Therapeutics. m. Geertje Jacoba Severs, 15 Sep. 1967, 1 son, 1 daughter. *Education:* PhD Medicine, 1973; Research Fellow, State University, 1966-73. *Appointments:* Research Associate, Albert Einstein College of Medicine, New York, USA, 1973-74; Assistant Professor, 1974-79, Professor of Pharmacology, 1979-, State University Groningen, The Netherlands. *Memberships:* Member, European Association for Study the Liver; International Association for Study of the Liver; Dutch Pharmacological Society. *Publications:* Author of numerous articles in professional journals. *Hobbies:* Tennis; Basketball; Music. *Address:* Department of Pharmacology and Pharmacotherapeutics, State University Groningen, Ant Deusinglaan 2, 9713 AW Groningen, The Netherlands.

MEINDERS, Robert L, b. 29 Dec. 1952, St Louis, Missouri, USA. Chiropractic Physician; Clinical Thermographer. m. Pamela Gregory, 9 July 1977, St. Louis, Missouri, 1 son. *Education:* St Louis College of Pharmacy; BS, DC, Logan Chiropractic College; Clinical Internship, Logan Clinic, 2 years; Diplomate, American Board Clinical Thermography. *Appointments:* Diplomate, National Board of Chiropractic Examiners; Acupuncturist, Certified State of Illinois. *Memberships:* Illinois Chiropractic Society; Southern Illinois Chiropractic Society; American Chiropractic Association; Charter Member, International Thermographic Society; Parker Research Foundation; International Academy of Chiropractic Low Back Pain Study. *Publication:* "Monitoring the Acute Accidental Injury Patient", ITS, 1984. *Honours:* X-Ray Award, Logan College Clinic; Civic Awards for Speaking Engagements. *Hobbies:* Golf; Tennis; Swimming. *Address:* 5206 West Main Street, Belleville, IL 62223, USA.

MEINEN, Klaus, b. 9 Dec. 1944, Linz/Rhine, Federal Republic of Germany. Physician in Charge. m. Hannalore Meinen, 29 Aug. 1970, 1 son, 1 daughter. *Education:* Johannes Gutenberg University, Mainz, 1966-72; MD, ibid, 1971, Graduation, 1972, Habilitation, 1981. *Appointments:* Pathology Institute, Federal German Army (under Prof FaBbender), 1973-75; Assistant Physician, since 1979 Senior Physician, Department of Obstetrics & Gynaecology, Rüsselsheim City Hospital, 1975-84; Guest Physician, Women's Clinic, Johannes Gutenberg University, Mainz, 1980; Physician-in-Charge, Department of Obstetrics & Gynaecology, St Lukas Clinic, Solingen, 1984. *Memberships:* German Society for Gynaecology; German Society for Cytology; German Society for Senology; Central Rhineland Society for Obstetrics & Gynaecology. *Publications:* 'Searching for cardiotoxic effects of fenoterol in the new-born infant' (in Beta-mimetic Drugs in Obstetrics & Perinatology), 1982; 'Ultrastrukturelle Befunde am Myokard nach Betamimetikatherapie' 1982; 'Fenoterol-Untersuchungsergebnisse zur Kardiotoxizität', 1982. *Hobbies:* Classical Music; Tennis. *Address:* Gynäkologisch-Geburtshilfliche Abteilung, St Lukas-Klinik, D-5650 Solingen 11, Federal Republic of Germany.

MEISSNER, William Walter, b. 13 Feb. 1931, Buffalo, NY, USA, Clinical Professor of Psychiatry, Harvard Medical School. *Education:* BA, 1956, MA, 1957, PhL, 1957, St Louis University; STL, Woodstock College, 1962; MD, Harvard Medical School, 1967. *Appointments:* Teaching Fellow in Psychiatry, 1968-69, Clinical Fellow in Psychiatry, 1969-71, Clinical Instructor in Psychiatry, 1971-73, Assistant Clinical Professor of Psychiatry, 1973-76, Associate Clinical Professor of Psychiatry, 1976-81, Clinical Professor of Psychiatry, 1981-, Harvard Medical School; Faculty Member, 1971-, Training and Supervising Analyst, 1980-, Boston Psychoanalytic Institute. *Memberships:* Boston Psychoanalytic Institute; Fellow, Massachusetts Psychiatric Society; Fellow, American Psychiatric Association; Member, American Psychoanalytic Association; Fellow, Centre for the Advancement of Psychoanalytic Studies; Member, International Psycho-Analytical Association; Committee on Religion and Psychiatry, American Psychiatric Association.

Publications: "Basic Concepts in Psychoanalytic psychiatry", (with E R Zetzel), 1973; "The Paranoid Process", 1978; "The Borderline Spectrum: Differential Diagnosis and Development Issues", 1984; "Psychoanalysis and Religious Experience", 1984; "Internationalization in Psychoanalysis", 1981; Author of 6 other books and 24 chapters in books; Author of 119 articles. *Honours:* Psi Chi, 1956; Sigma Chi, 1957; Felix and Helene Deutsch Prize, Boston Psychoanalytic Institute, 1969. *Hobbies:* Music; Playing piano. *Address:* 129 Mount Auburn Street, Cambridge, MA 02138, USA.

MEISTER, Steven Gerard, b. 13 Sep. 1937, Boston, Massachusetts, USA. Chief of Cardiology. m. Carol Ross, 26 Jan. 1966, Boston, 2 daughters. *Education:* AB, Bowdoin College, 1958; MD, Tufts University School of Medicine; Internship, University of Indiana Medical Centre; Residency, Boston VA Hospital; Cardiology Fellowship, Boston City Hospital, Tufts Medical School, Peter Bent Brigham Hospital, Harvard Medical School. *Appointments:* Director, Cardiac Catheterization Laboratory, Presbyterian University of Pennsylvania, Medical Centre, 1970-73, Hospital of the Medical College of Pennsylvania, 1973-79; Chief, Cardiology, Hospital of the Medical College of Pennsylvania, 1980-, Professor, Medicine, 1980-. *Memberships:* Fellow, American College of Physicians, American College of Cardiology, American Heart Association, Council on Clinical Cardiology; Board of Governors, American Heart Association, Southeastern Pennsylvania Chapter. *Publications:* Numerous articles in professional journals; Abstracts; Book Review, "Monitoring with the Swan-Ganz Catheter", by Andrew Levy, 1984. *Hobbies:* Skiing; Racketball; Classical Music. *Address:* Medical College of Pennsylvania, 3300 Henry Ave, Philadelphia, PA 19129, USA.

MELGES, Frederick Towne, b. 12 Dec. 1935, Michigan, USA. Vice Chairman, Department of Psychiatry, Duke University, USA. m. Constance Ray Melges, 14 June 1958, 2 sons. *Education:* AB, Princeton University, USA, 1957; MD, Columbia University, USA, 1961. *Appointments:* Research Associate in Neurophysiology and Psychiatry, Stanford University, California, USA, 1965-67, Assistant Professor of Psychiatry, 1967-73; Chairman and Chief of Psychiatry, Santa Clara Valley Medical Centre, 1976; Professor of Psychiatry, Duke University Medical Centre, 1977-, Director of Psychiatry, Durham County General Hospital, 1977-84, Vice Chairman, Director of Clinical Education and Chief, Duke University Psychiatry Service, 1985-. *Memberships:* American Psychiatric Association; American Medical Association; Association for the Advancement of Psychotherapy; International Society for the Study of Time; Marce Society. *Publications:* "Time and the Inner Future: A Temporal Approach to Psychiatric Disorders", 1982. *Honours:* Magna cum Laude, Princeton University, 1957; Phi Beta Kappa, Princeton University, 1957. *Hobbies:* Golf; Creative Writing. *Address:* Duke University Medical Centre, Department of Psychiatry - Box 2995, Durham, NC 27710, USA.

MELLGREN, Svein Ivar, b. 26 Feb. 1943, Kristiansand, Norway. Professor and Chairman, Neurology, University of Tromso. m. Edel Feyling, 30 July 1966, 2 sons, 1 daughter. *Education:* MD, University of Oslo, 1968; Dr Med, University of Bergen, 1973; Certificate, Specialist in Clinical Neurology, 1980. *Appointments:* Lecturer, Anatomy Resident, Neurology, University Hospital of Bergen; Registrar, Lecturer, Neurology, University of Trondheim. *Publications:* "Enzyme histochemical studies in the hippocampal region of the rat", 1973; Publications within the fields of muscle and neurohistochemistry and neurology, particularly neuromuscular diseases. *Hobbies:* Touring; Jogging; Skiing. *Address:* Dept of Neurology, Institute of Clinical Medicine, University of Tromso, N-9012 Regionsykehuset i Tromso, Norway.

MELLINS, Robert B, b. 6 Mar. 1928, New York, USA.

Professor of Pediatrics. m. Sue Mendelsohn, 19 Apr. 1959, New York, 1 son, 1 daughter. *Education:* AB, Columbia College; MD, Johns Hopkins University School of Medicine. *Appointments include:* Part-time Assistant 1957-60, Instructor 1960-65, Associate 1965-66, Assistant 1966-70, Associate Professor 1970-75, Professor 1975-, Pediatrics, Columbia University, College of Physicians and Surgeons; Assistant Resident 1956-57, Assistant Pediatrician 1957-65, Assistant Attending Pediatrician 1965-70, Associate Attending Pediatrician 1970-75, Director Pediatric Medical Intensive Care Unit 1970-75, Director Pediatric Pulmonary Division 1972-, Attending Pediatrician 1975-, Director Cystic Fibrosis Center 1977-, Babies Hospital, Columbia-Presbyterian Medical Center. *Memberships include:* American Academy of Pediatrics; American College of Chest Physicians; American Heart Association; American Federation for Clinical Research; American Pediatric Society; American Physiological Society; American Society for Pharmacology and Experimental Therapeutics; Vice-President 1974-75, President 1982-83, American Thoracic Society; Fleischner Society; Harvey Society; New York Academy of Sciences; Society for Critical Care Medicine; Society for Pediatric Research; Alpha Omega Alpha. *Publications:* Over 100 articles published in scientific journals. *Honours include:* NIH Career Development Award, 1966-71; Career Scientist Award, Health Research Council, New York, 1975; Stevens Triennial Award for Research, Columbia University College of Physicians and Surgeons, 1980. *Hobbies:* Music; Figure Skating; Skiing; Landscaping and Gardening. *Address:* Columbia University College of Physicians and Surgeons, 630 West 168 Street, New York, NY 10032, USA.

MELLORS, Robert C, b. 18 June 1916, USA. Professor and Attending Pathologist. m. Jane Kimball Winternitz, 25 Mar. 1944, New Haven, Connecticut, 3 sons, 1 daughter. *Education:* BA, Western Reserve University, Cleveland, Ohio, 1937; MA, 1938; PhD, 1940; MD, Johns Hopkins University, Maryland, 1944; Fellow, Royal College of Pathology. *Appointments:* Instructor, Biochemistry, Western Reserve University, 1940-42; Research Associate, Poliomyelitis Research Center, Johns Hopkins University, 1942-44; Medical Officer, US Navy, 1944-46; Assistant and Associate, Sloan Kettering Institute for Cancer Research, 1946-58; Assistant and Associate Attending Pathologist, Memorial Hospital for Cancer and Allied Diseases, New York, 1953-58; Assistant and Associate Professor, Pathology, Sloan-Kettering Division, Cornell University, 1952-59; Director of Laboratories, Pathologist in Chief, Hospital for Special Surgery, 1958-84; Director of Research, Hospital for Special Surgery, affiliated to New York Hospital and Cornell Medical Center, 1969-84; currently, Professor and Attending Pathologist, New York Hospital - Cornell Medical Center, New York. *Memberships include:* Medical Society for State and County of New York; American Association of Pathologists; Fellow, Royal College of Pathologists; American Association of Immunologists; American Society of Biological Chemists; American Society of Clinical Pathologists; American Rheumatism Association. *Publications:* "Analytical Cytology", 1955, 59; "Analytical Pathology", 1957; Author over 160 original scientific articles in his field. *Honours:* Appointments to Lung Cancer Research Advisory Committee, American Cancer Society 1957-59, Research Advisory Committee, National Institutes of Health, 1962-66; Council, National Institute of Environmental Health Sciences, 1966-69; Numerous grants and awards. *Address:* 3 Hardscrabble Circle, Armonk, NY 10504, USA.

MELLOTT, Sharon Lee, b. 9 Nov. 1939, Minnesota, USA. Chiropractor. m. Keith D Mellott, 11 August 1962, Seattle, Washington, USA, 1 son. *Education:* Doctor of Chiropractic, Palmer College of Chiropractic-West, Sunnyvale, California, 1982; Diploma, School of Radiologic Technique, University of Oregon Medical School, Portland, Oregon, 1958-60; Diplomate, Roentgenology, Western States Chirop-

ractic College, 1982-85; Certification Programme for Industrial Consultant, Los Angeles Chiropractic College, 1984-85. *Appointments:* Radiological Technologist, hospitals and clinics, Seattle, Washington, Sacramento, California and San Jose, California, 1960-70; Radiological Technologist, for orthopaedic surgeons, Mountain View, California, 1972-78; Insurance Agent and Co-Owner, Keith Mellott Insurance Agency, Sunnyvale, 1968-79; Owner and Operator, The Transcriber, medical transcription secretarial service, Sunnyvale, 1972-83; Chiropractor and owner, Sierra Chiropractic Clinic, Saratoga, 1982-. *Memberships:* International Chiropractors Association; American Chiropractic Association; International Chiropractors Association of California; Council on Roentgenology, American Chiropractic Association; International Academy of Chiropractors Industrial Consultants Christian Chiropractors Association; Community of St Luke. *Honours:* Congressional District Director, International Chiropractic Association, 1984-85; Honorary Doctor of Chiropractic Humanities, 1980. *Hobbies:* Needlework; Travel; Reading. *Address:* Sierra Chiropractic Clinic, 12021 Saratoga-Sunnyvale Rd, Saratoga, CA 95070, USA.

MELSEN, Birte, b. 9 June 1939, Åbenrå) Denmark, Professor & Head, Institute of Orthodontics. m. Flemming Melsen, 3 Apr. 1963, 2 sons. *Education:* DDS, Royal Dental College, Aarhus, 1964; Jus practicandi as dentist, 1971; Orthodontic specialist, 1971; Odontologic doctorate, Royal Dental College, 1974. *Appointments:* Assistant instructor, Royal Dental College, 1964-65; Research associate 1965-67, Associate Professor 1967-75, Professor & Head 1975-, Institute of Orthodontics, Royal Dental College. *Memberships:* Danish Dental Association; Danish Medical Association; Danish Orthodontic Association; Public Health Association; Nordic Odontologic Society; Association of Dental Research; Association of Logopaedia & Phoniatrics. *Publications include:* Thesis: "The Cranial Base", 1974; Numerous papers on growth & development studied on human autopsy material, bone biology, malocclusion, epidemiology, clinical studies by means of implant method. *Honours:* Honorary member, Austrian Dental Society, 1982; Visiting Professor, Padova, Italy, 1983; Strang Award, 1984. *Hobbies:* Surfing; Farming; Opera. *Address:* Svostrupvej 10, 8600 Silkeborg, Denmark.

MELVIN, John Lewis, b. 26 May 1935, Columbus, Ohio, USA. Professor, Chairman, Physical Medicine & Rehabilitation, Medical College of Wisconsin. m. Harriett Elizabeth Warner, 8 June 1957, Delaware, 1 son, 3 daughters. *Education:* BSc, MD, MM Sc, Ohio State University. *Appointments:* Assistant, 1964-65, Demonstrator, 1965-66, Assistant Professor, 1966-69, Associate Professor, 1969-73, Physical Medicine and Rehabilitation. *Memberships include:* Fellow, American Academy for Cerebral Palsy and Developmental Medicine; Fellow, American Academy of Physical Medicine & Rehabilitation; Medical Society of Milwaukee County; Milwaukee Academy of Medicine; Wisconsin State Medical Society; American Heart Association; many other professional organisations. *Publications include:* Numerous articles in professional journals including: 'Archives Physical Medicine Rehabilitation'; 'Wisconsin Medical Journal'; etc. *Honours:* Recipient, various honours & awards including: Ford Foundation Scholarship, 1951-53; Sigma Xi, 1966; Bronze Teaching Award-Scientific Exhibit, Ohio State Medical Association, 1971; various grants etc. *Hobbies:* Tennis; Running; Travel. *Address:* 100 North 92nd St, Milwaukee, WI 53226, USA.

MELVIN, John Wesley, b. 16 July 1957, Duluth, Minnesota, USA. Director/Physician. m. Candace Jane Albon, 21 Nov. 1981, Herrin, Illinois, 1 son, 1 daughter. *Education:* BS, Human Anatomy; Doctor of Chiropractic. *Memberships:* American Chiropractic Assoc; Illinois Chiropractic Assoc; Chi Rho Sigma; Beta Chapter; Diplomate, National Board of Chiro. Exam. *Hobbies:* Fishing; Running; Guitar. *Address:* Rt 1 Box

279A, Duquoin, IL 62832, USA.

MENA, Abelardo, b. 30 July 1927, Merida, Mexico. Chief, Behavior Therapy Unit, Veterans Administration Medical Center, Miami, Florida, USA. m. Jacqueline, 2 Dec. 1983, Miami Beach, 1 son, 2 daughters. *Education:* MD, National University of the Southeast, Merida, Mexico, 1952; PhD, Psychiatry, University of Minnesota, USA, 1963. *Appointments:* Lecturer, University of Minnesota Department of Psychiatry, 1957-58; Psychiatric Research Consultant, Anoka State Hospital, Minnesota, 1958-59; Postdoctoral Research Fellow, Psychiatry, 1958-61; Research Psychiatrist, Early Drug Evaluation Unit, 1961-63; Instructor, Department of Psychiatry, 1963-64; University of Minnesota; Staff, Psychiatrist, VA Hospital, Minneapolis, 1963-64; Clinical Instructor, Department of Psychiatry, UCLA Medical Center, 1964-67; Staff Psychiatrist, Brentwood VA Hospital, Los Angeles, 1964-67; Staff Psychiatrist, VA Hospital, Coral Gable, Florida, 1967-68; Senior Psychiatrist, VA Hospital, Miami, 1968-70. *Memberships:* American Psychiatric Association; American Association for the Advancement of Behavior Therapy; AAAS; South Florida Psychiatric Society. *Publications:* Contributor to professional journals; Presentations. *Honour:* American Board of Psychiatry, 1963. *Hobbies:* Birdwatching; Camping; Hiking; Travel; Mayan Studies; Study of Animal Behaviour; Natural History. *Address:* VA Medical Center 4D, 1201 NW 16th Street, Miami, FL 33125, USA.

MENAHEM, Samuel, b. 17 Jan. 1941, Singapore. Consultant Paediatric Cardiologist and Physician. m. Eva Farkas, 15 Mar. 1964, Melbourne, Australia, 1 son, 2 daughters. *Education:* MB BS, 1963, MD, 1971, MEd, 1983, University of Melbourne; Member, 1968, Fellow, 1974, Royal Australasian College of Physicians; Master of Psychological Medicine, Monash University, 1984. *Appointments:* Junior and Senior Resident Medical Officer, Prince Henry's Hospital, Melbourne, 1964, 65; Resident Medical Officer and Medical Registrar, Royal Childrens Hospital, Melbourne, 1966, 67; Research Fellow, Metabolic Unit, Alfred Hospital, Melbourne, 1968; Cardiac Department, Royal Childrens Hospital, 1969, 70; Assistant Paediatric Physician, Alfred Hospital, Melbourne, 1971-72; Paediatric Physician, Queen Victoria Medical Centre, 1971, 72; Physician, 1972-, Physician Department of Cardiology, 1972-78, Assistant Cardiologist, 1979-83; Cardiologist, 1983-, Royal Childrens Hospital, Melbourne; Consultant Paediatrician, Sandringham and District Memorial Hospital, 1972-, Morabbin Hospital, 1975-. *Memberships:* Australian College of Paediatrics; Cardiac Society of Australian and New Zealand; Australian Society for Ultrasound in Medicine; Australasian and New Zealand Association for Medical Education; Psychotherapy Association of Australia; Australian Perinatal Society; Society for Behavioural Paediatrics. *Publications:* Author or Co-Author of contributions to: 'British Heart Journal'; 'Australian Paediatric Journal'; 'Child Psychiatry and Human Development'; 'Journal of Developmental and Behavioural Medicine'. *Hobbies:* Sailing; Reading. *Address:* 53 Kooyong Road, Caulfield, Victoria 3161, Australia.

MENANTEAU, Bernard Paul, b. 24 Apr. 1939, Angers, France. Professor and Chairman, Department of Diagnostic Radiology. m. Marie-Therese Puig, 30 Dec. 1976, Angers. *Education:* Diploma of Radiology, University of Paris, 1967; MD, University of Rheims, 1969. *Appointments:* Resident, University Hospital, Rheims, 1965-69; Assistant, University of Rheims, 1969-74; Assistant Professor, University of Sherbrooke, Canada, 1974-78; Associate Professor, 1978-83, currently, Professor and Chairman, Department of Diagnostic Radio.logy, University of Rheims, France. *Memberships:* French Society of Radiology; Canadian Association of Radiologists; Radiological Society of North America; Association of University Radiologists; American Institute of Ultrasound in Medicine; International Union of Angiology. *Publications:* 'Angiodysppasie du colon droit' in 'Journal of Radiology', 1980; 'Anatomical basis for tomographic exploration of the suprarenal glands' in 'Anat Clin', 1982; 'Sonography of normal and hypertrophicpylorus' in 'Annals of Radiology', 1983. *Honour:* Vice President, University of Rheims, 1971-74. *Hobbies:* History; Music. *Address:* Department of Radiology, Robert Debre Hospital, 51092 Rheims, France.

MENDELL, David, b. 10 May 1909, New York City, New York, USA. Clinical Professor of Psychiatry; Private Practitioner. m. Miriam Wydra, 27 June 1945, Washington, District of Columbia, 2 sons. *Education:* BS, College of City of New York, 1929; MD, University of Vienna Medical School, 1934. *Appointments:* Commanding Officer, Air Force Medical Department, Camp Pinedale, California, 1943-45; Instructor, Department of Psychiatry, University of California, 1947-48; Assistant Professor, 1950, Associate Professor, 1953-, Baylor Medical School, Houston; Clinical Professor, Psychiatry, University of Texas Medical School, 1976-. *Memberships:* American Medical Association; American Psychiatric Association; AGPA; American Academy of Psychotherapists; Group for Advancement of Psychiatry; International Group Therapy Association; World Psychiatric Association; International Association of Social Psychiatry. *Publications:* Contributor to 'Psychiatry', 1961; Chapters in "Group Therapy", 1976 and "Living Groups, a General System Approach to Group Therapy", 1981. *Honours:* Plaque, honoured as Founder and 1st President, Southwestern Group Therapy Society, 1984; Life Fellow, American Psychiatric Association, 1980. *Hobbies:* Playing the mandolin; Gardening; Travel. *Address:* 7000 Fannin Street, Houston, TX 77030, USA.

MENDELS, Joseph, b. 29 Oct. 1937, Capetown, South Africa. Medical Director, Philadelphia Medical Institute; Professor, Psychiatry & Human Behavior & Pharmacology, Thomas Jefferson University, USA. m. Ora Kark, 10 Jan. 1960, 2 sons, 1 daughter. *Education:* MB, ChB, 1954, The University of Cape Town, South Africa, 1960; MD, University of the Witwatersrand, Johannesburg, South Africa. *Appointments:* Assistant Professor, Associate Professor, University of Pennsylvania, Philadelphia, Pennsylvania, 1967-73; Professor, Psychiatry and Pharmacology, University of Pennsylvania and Veterans Administration Hospital, Philadelphia, 1973-80; Medical Director, Fairmount Institute Philadelphia, 1980-81. *Memberships:* Fellow, International College Neuropsychopharmacology; Member, American Psychiatric Assn; Fellow, American College Neuropsychopharmacology; American College Clinical Pharmacology; and others. *Publications:* Author and Editor: "Concepts of Depression", 1971; "Biological Psychiatry", 1973; "Psychobiology of Affective Disorders", 1981; Author of articles, chapters, letters and abstracts, 1970-85. *Honour:* Lester N Hogheimer Prize, American Psychiatric Association, 1976. *Address:* Philadelphia Medical Institute, 1015 Chestnut street, Suite 1303, Philadelphia, PA 19107, USA.

MENDELSON, Harold L, b. 25 Oct. 1935, New York City, USA. Director, Department of Psychiatry. Married, 2 children. *Education:* BA, Williams College, USA, 1956; MD, State University of New York, (Honours in Paediatrics), 1960; Residency Training, Psychiatry, Kings County Hospital, 1961-64; Fellowship in Child Psychiatry, Hillside Hospital, 1967-69. *Appointments include:* Psychiatric Supervisor in Residency Training Programme, Hillside Hospital, 1969-71; Senior Psychiatric Consultant, Pride of Judee Treatment Centre, 1969-82; Consultant to Brooklyn Home for Children, Forest Hills, 1970-79; Psychiatric Consultant to North Shore Child Guidance Association, 1975-79; Psychiatric Director, Glendale Human Service Centre, 1980-81; Staff Psychiatrist, Flushing Hospital and Medical Centre, 1976-; Director, Department of Psychiatry, Flushing Hospital and Medical Centre, 1981-. *Memberships:* Nassau Psychiatric Society; American Psychiatric Association; Nassau County Medical Society; American Medical Association; New York Council for Child Psychiatry; Society for Adolescent Psychiatry; Explorers' Club. *Publications:* Book review: "The Difficult Child", J Hillside Hospital, 1967; Monthly articles in 'Newsletter of Nassau Psychiatric Society, 1978-79; three presentations to conferences and seminars. *Honours:* Certification, American Board of Psychiatry, 1967; Fellowship in American Psychiatric Association, 1975-. *Hobbies:* Skiing; Horse Riding. *Address:* RR4 Box 294, Salem Road, Pound Ridge, NY 10576, USA.

MENDEZ-BAUER, Carlos, b. 3 Feb. 1930, Montevideo, Uruguay. Professor of Obstetrics and Gynaecology. m. Fiorella B Boffano, 7 June 1968, 2 daughters. *Education:* BSc, Science, 1947; MD, 1955, University of Uruguay Licensure in Medicine; PhD, Medicine, cum laude, Universidad Complutense, Madrid, Spain. *Appointments:* Research Fellow, Rockefeller Foundation; Associate Professor, Pathophysiology; Chief, Service of Obstetrical Physiology in Montevideo, Uruguay; Consultant, WHO/PAHO; Director of Research in Perinatal Medicine, Santa Cristina Hospital, Madrid, Spain, currently; Professor of Obstetrics and Gynaecology, The Chicago Medical School/The University of Medical Sciences and Director of Perinatal Unit, Cook County Hospital, Chicago, Illinois. *Memberships:* Honorary Member of most of the scientific societies related to Obstetrics and Gynaecology in South and Central America, Mexico and Europe; Member of European Perinatal Medicine Society; Sigma Xi. *Publications:* More than 250 papers in European, American and Japanese journals; Several chapters in Books; Presentations of scientific results in more than 100 national and international Congresses and scientific meetings; The Perinatal Unit he organized in Cook County Hospital is a model of prenatal care facility, with computer based survey of clinical diagnosis of fetal condition. 2Honours: Best Scientific Research of the Year, 1955; Prize of Honor, 1964; Luis Calzada Prize, University of Uruguay, 1966. *Hobby:* Classical Music. *Address:* 31 Robinhood Ranch, Oakbrook, IL 60521, USA.

MENDOZA LOPEZ, Arturo, b. 12 Mar. 1948, Mexico City, Mexico. Delegate of the Asociacion Mexicana de Psiquiatria Infantil to the American Academy of Child Psychiatry. m. Anne Macdonald, 15 Sep. 1973, 2 daughters. *Education:* MD with honours, Medical School UNAM, 1973; General, Child, Adolescent and Geriatric Psychiatrist; Adults Psychoanalyst. *Appointments:* Chief Adolescent Department, Mexican National Institute of Mental Health, 1979-81; Professor of Child Psychiatry Training, Universidad Nacional Autonoma de Mexico, 1981-84; Administrator, Grupo Psiquiatrico Infantil de Mexico, 1981-; General Coordinator 1982, Chairman of Scientific Committee 1983-85, National Meeting, Delegate to the American Academy of Child Psychiatry 1982-85, Mexican Association of Child Psychiatry; Professor of Family Therapy, Cento de Integracion Juvenil, 1984; Chairman of Advertising and Press Committee, VI Latino American V National Meeting of Child Psychiatry, 1985; Class representative The XIII Generation of the Instituto De Psychoanalists of the Asociacion Mexicana de Psicoanalisys, 1985. *Memberships:* American Medical Association; American Psychiatric Association; American Academy of Child Psychiatry; Asociacion Mexicana de Psiquiatria Infantil; Asociacion Mexicana de Psiquiatria; Asociacion Psicoanalitica Mexicana; Asociacion For the Study of Multiple Personality; Asociacion Mexicana de Neurologia y Psiquiatria. *Hobbies:* Squash; Travelling; Table Tennis; Karate; Racketball. *Address:* Grupo Psiquiatrico Infantil de Mexico SC, Patricio Sanz 437, Col Del Valle, 03100 Mexico DF, Mexico.

MENG, Dorothy Smith, b. 10 Jan., Oak Creek, Colorado, USA. Registered Nurse, Department of Neurology. m. Ernest Meng, 24 Oct. 1946, 4 sons, 3 daughters. *Education:* BA, Health Care Administration; Associate of Arts Degree, Nursing. *Appointments:* Registered Nurse, Gerontology and Geriatrics; Registered Nurse, Medicine and Psychiatry. *Memberships:* Neurofibromatosis Foundation; Professional Nursing

Staff; Roosevelt University Alumni; International Flying Nurses Association; Daley College Nurses Alumni Association. *Honours:* National Deans List, 1983; Franklin Honor Society, Roosevelt University, 1983; Daley College Deans List, 1976. *Hobbies:* Gardening; Theatre; Decorating; Eastern Philosophy; Real Estate. *Address:* 6039 S Mobile Avenue, Chicago, IL 60638, USA.

MENKES, John Hans, b. 20 Dec. 1928, Vienna, Austria. Professor, Neurology, Pediatrics, University of California, Los Angeles. m. Joan Simon, 28 Sep. 1980, Los Angeles, 2 sons, 1 daughter. *Education:* MS, Chemistry, 1951, AB, Chemistry, 1947, University of Southern California, USA; MD, Johns Hopkins University, 1952. *Appointments:* Assistant Professor, 1960-63, Associate Professor, 1963-66, Pediatrics, Assistant Professor, Neurological Medicine, 1964-66, Head , Pediatric Neurology, 1964-66, Johns Hopkins University; Professor, 1966-74, Head, 1966-70, Pediatric Neurology, Professor, Psychiatry, 1970-74, University of California, Los Angeles; Clinical Professor, Psychiatry, Neurology, Pediatrics, 1974-77, Clinical Professor, Pediatrics and Neurology, 1977,85, Professor, Neurology, Pediatrics, 1985-, University of California, Los Angeles. *Memberships include:* American Academy of Neurology; American Boards of Pediatrics; American Academy of Pediatrics; American Chemical Society; Society for Pediatric Research; American Board of Neurology; Honorary Member, Sociedad Peruana de Neuro-Psiquiatria; American Neurological Association; American Pediatric Society. *Publications:* Contributor of articles to numerous professional journals including: 'Endocrinology'; 'Journal American Chemical Society'; 'Pediatrics'; 'Brain'; 'Journal of Pediatrics'; 'Journal Neurological Sciences'; 'Neurology'; 'Southern Medicine'; 'Clinical Genetics'; etc; (Books) "Textbook of Child Neurology", 1974, 3rd edition 1985; Translated into Spanish, Portugese and Italian; Occasional Reviewer; Editorial Board Member, 'Pediatrics', 1970-76; 'Early Human Development', 1977-80; 'Neuropediatrics', 1969-; 'Bulletin of Clinical Neuroscience', 1983-. *Honours:* Finalist, International Kennedy Award for Research in Mental Retardation, 1975; Hower Award, Child Neurology Society, 1980. *Hobby:* Literature - Professional Writer of Novels, Stage Plays, etc. *Address:* 548 Greencraig Road, Los Angeles, CA 90049, USA.

MENON, Mani, b. 9 July 1948, India. Professor of Surgery; Chairman, Division of Urological and Transplantation Surgery. m. Shameem Ara Begum, 17 Oct. 1972, Pondicherry, India, 1 son, 1 daughter. *Appointments:* Assistant Professor of Urology, Washington University Medical Centre, St Louis, USA, 1980-83; Associate Professor, 1983; Professor of Surgery and Chairman, Division of Urological and Transplantation Surgery, University of Massachusetts Medical Centre, Worcester, Massachusetts, 1983-present. *Memberships:* American Urological Association; American Federation of Clinical Research; American Association for the Advancement of Science; Association of Indian Urologists in North America; Massachusetts Medical Society; Massachusetts Society for Medical Research. *Publications:* Contributions to journals and publications: 'Characterization of the binding of a potent synthetic androgyn, methyltrienolone (R1881) to human tissues' (with others), published in the 'Journal of Clinical Investigation', 1978; co-author of section in "Hormonal Therapy of Prostatic cancer' in 'Cancer' journal, 1979; co-author of 'Ion-Chromatographic measurement of oxalate in unprocessed urine' published in 'Clinical Chemistry', 1983; co-author of 'Oxamate transport by intestinal brush border membrane vesicles', published in the "World Journal of Urology", Volume 1, 1983; co-author of 'Renal tubular acidosis' published in the 'Journal of Urology', 1984. *Hobbies:* Tennis; Rock Climbing; Games and puzzles; Mystery fiction. *Address:* University of Massachusetts Medical Centre, 55 Lake Avenue, North Worcester, MA 01605, USA.

MERA, Jorge Alberto, b. 25 May 1936, Buenos Aires, Argentina. President, National Institute of Welfare Funds, m. Maria Elena Roza, 20 Dec. 1962, 3 sons, 1 daughter. *Education:* MD, 1962, MPH, 1963, Professor of Public Health, 1986, University of Buenos Aires; Postdoctoral Scholar, University of California, Los Angeles, USA, 1970-72. *Appointments:* Director, Student Health Service, University of Buenos Aires, 1965-66; Director, Medicina Administrativa, Bi-monthly, 1967-69; Associate Director, Childrens Hospital, Buenos Aires, 1969-70; Senior Health Officer, National Institute of Welfare Funds, 1975-76; Senior Adviser, Argentine Confederation of Physicians, 1976-77; Associate Editor, 'Medicina y Sociedad', bi-monthly, 1978-83; Director, Health Plan, Italian Hospital of Buenos Aires, 1979-83. *Memberships:* Argentine Medical Association, 1964; Argentine Public Health Association, 1964; Argentine Society of Pediatrics, 1970; American Public Health Association, 1971; Latin American Society for Pediatric Research, 1974; Argentine Society for Medical Audit, 1975. *Publications:* 'Patient dumping and other voluntary agency contributions to public agency problems', 1973; 'The ecology of group medical practice in the USA', 1974; 'Number and distribution of physicians in Argentina', 1978; 'National health insurance and sickness coverage', 1980; 'National health insurance in Argentina', 1983. *Hobbies:* Tennis; Gardening. *Address:* Santa Fe 3508 7o, 1425 Buenos Aires, Argentina.

MERRICK, Malcolm Vivian, b. 13 July 1938, London, England. Hospital Consultant in Nuclear Medicine; University Senior Lecturer in Medicine and Medical Radiology. m. Julia Margaret Stern, 12 June 1966, London, 2 daughters. *Education:* MA, BM, B CL, Oxford and St Mary's, 1959-64; MSc, London; DMRD; Fellow, Royal College of Radiologists; Member, Royal College of Physicians of Edinburgh. *Appointments:* Registrar in Radiodiagnosis, United Oxford Hospitals; Registrar in Diagnosis, Nochand Park Hospital; Research Fellow in Nuclear Medicine, Honorary Senior Registrar in Radiodiagnosis, Royal Postgraduate Medical School and Hammersmith Hospital, London; Currently Consultant in Nuclear Medicine, Western General Hospital, Edinburgh, Scotland; Currently Senior Lecturer in Medicine and Medical Radiology, University of Edinburgh. *Memberships:* British Institute of Radiology; Society of Nuclear Medicine, USA; College of Radiologists; British Nuclear Medicine Society; Scottish Society for Experimental Medicine; Scottish Radiological Society. *Publications include:* "Essentials of Nuclear Medicine", 1984; About 100 papers on various aspects of nuclear medicine. *Hobbies:* Walking; Photography; Winemaking and drinking. *Address:* 10 Sycamore Gardens, Edinburgh EH12 7JJ, Scotland.

MERRIFIELD, Homer H, b. 12 Mar. 1930, Syracuse, New York, USA. Professor and Chairman. Divorced, 1 son, 1 daughter. *Education:* BA, Colgate University; BS, State University of New York, Upstate; MA, Colgate University; PhD, University of Iowa. *Appointments:* Instructor, St Lawrence University; Associate Professor, Ithaca College; Associate Professor, University of California; Professor, Ithaca College; Professor, Texas Tech University Health Sciences Center. *Memberships:* American College of Sports Medicine; American Physical Therapy Association; International Society of Biomechanics; American Congress of Rehabilitation Medicine; New York Academy of Sciences, Sigma Xi; Phi Kappa Phi. *Publications:* 'Influence on Gait Patterns on Hip Rotation and Foot Deviation', 'Journal of the American Podiatry Association', 1970. *Honours:* Fellow, American College of Sports Medicine, 1967; College Marshall, 1969-72. *Hobbies:* Reading; Music; Racquet Sports; Sailing; Skiing. *Address:* Texas Tech University Health Sciences Center, Lubbock, TX 79430, USA.

MERRITT, Doris Honig, b. 16 July 1923, New York City, USA. Research Training and Research Resources Officer; Special Assistant to the Director, NIH, m. A Donald Merritt, 5 May 1953, New York, 2 sons. *Education:* BA cum Laude, Hunter College, UCNY, 1940-44; Premedical Requirements, George Washington University, 1946-48; MD, George Washington University School of Medicine, 1948-52; Paediatric Internship, Duke University Hospital, 1952-53; Teaching and Research Fellow, Department of Paediatrics, George Washington University School of Medicine, 1953-54; Paediatric Resident and Fellow, Duke University Hospital, 1954-56. *Appointments:* Instructor in Paediatrics, Duke University School of Medicine; Director Paediatric Cariorenal Clinic, Duke University Hospital, 1956-57; Executive Secretary, Cardiovascular Study Section and General Medicine Study Section, Division of Research Grants, NIH, 1957-60; Director to Assistant Dean, Medical Research, 1961-65, Assistant to Full Professor of Paediatrics, 1961-78, Indiana University School of Medicine; Assistant Dean to Dean, Research and Sponsored Programs, Indiana University-Purdue University at Indianapolis, 1965-78. *Memberships:* Alpha Omega; Sigma Xi; Phi Beta Kappa; American Academy of Paediatrics, Fellow; American Association for the Advancement of Science; Committee on Institutional Cooperation, Research Administrators Sub-Committee; National Council of University Research Administrators Duke University Medical Society; George Washington University Medical School, Smith Reed Russell Society. *Publications:* Contributor of numerous professional articles to medical journals. *Honours:* Alumni Hall of Fame, Hunter College of the University of the City of New York, 1977; National Institutes of Health Directors Award, 1985. *Hobbies:* Reading; Needlecraft. *Address:* National Institutes of Health, 9000 Rockville Pike, Building 1, Room 209, Bethesda, MD 20892, USA.

MERRITT, George N, b. 10 Nov. 1952, Guadalajara, Mexico. Doctor of Podiatric Medicine. m. Mary Louise Ober, 30 Aug. 1973, Miami, 1 son, 1 daughter. *Education:* BS, Biology, Florida State University; BS, Basic Medical Science, Doctor of Podiatric Medicine, Master of Science, California College of Podiatric Medicine. *Memberships:* Fellow, American College of Foot Surgeons; Diplomate, American Board of Podiatric Surgery; Fellow, American Academy of Podiatric Sports Medicine. *Publication:* 'Medial Plantar Digital Proper Nerve Syndrome (Joplin's Neuroma) - Typical Presentation' Journal of Foot Surgery, 1982. *Hobbies:* Running; Tennis; Hiking; Playing drums. *Address:* 2558 Capital Medical Building, Tallahassee, FL 32308, USA.

MERRITT, John Richard, b. 27 Feb. 1946, London, Ontario, Canada. Dentist; International Dental Consultant. m. Heather R Thomson, 16 Oct. 1976, Grand Bend, Ontario, 1 son, 2 daughters. *Education:* BA 1968, DDS, University of Western Ontario, 1972. *Memberships:* Ontario Dental Assoc; Canadian Dental Assoc; Academy of General Dentistry; International Assoc; of Orthodontics; Ontario Society of Clinical Hypnosis; Ontario Society of Preventive Dentistry. *Publications:* 'Prevention Working', 1972; Journal of Ontario Dental Assoc; (Clinical Papers) 'Advanced Techniques for finishing acid etched Composites, 1978' ODA; 'Posterior Composites, 1982, ODA/CDA. *Hobbies:* Sailing; Skiing; Scuba Diving; Golf. *Address:* 280 Main Street, Parkhill, Ontario, Canada, N0M 2K0.

MERSKEY, Harold, b. 11 Feb. 1929, Sunderland, England. Director of Education and Research; Professor of Psychiatry. m. Susan Jennifer Crann, 21 Feb. 1965, Leeds, 1 son, 2 daughters. *Education:* MA, BM, BCh, 1953, Exeter College, Oxford University; DM, 1965; University College Hospital, Medical School, London, 1950-53. *Appointments:* Assistant Psychiatrist, Senior Hospital Medical Officer, Cherry Knowle Hospital, Sunderland, England; Lecturer in Psychiatry, Sheffield University; Consultant Psychiatrist, Saxondale

Hospital, Nottingham; Consultant Physician in Psychological Medicine, National Hospitals for Nervous Diseases, Maida Vale and Queen Square, London; currently, Director of Education and Research, London Psychiatric Hospital and Professor of Psychiatry, University of Western Ontario, London, Canada. *Memberships include:* EEG Society; American Psychosomatic Society; International Association for the Study of Pain (Chairman of Committee on Taxonomy); Chairman, Scientific Advisory Committee, Gerontology Research Council of Ontario; Canadian and American Psychiatric Associations; Royal Society of Medicine. *Publications:* Co-Author: "Psychiatric Illness", 1965, 3rd edition, 1980; "Pain: Psychological and Psychiatric Aspects", 1967. Author: "The Analysis of Hysteria", 1979; 'Theories of Pain', in "Encyclopaedia Britannica", 1974; about 1907 publications or book chapters in field, 1958-. Co-Editor, "Pain: Meaning and Management", 1980. *Hobbies:* Gardening; Fishing; Hebrew studies. *Address:* Department of Education and Research, London Psychiatric Hospital, PO Box 2532 Terminal A, London, Ontario, Canada N6A 4H1.

MERTICK, Elva Ray, b. 6 Oct. 1943, Calgary, Alberta, Canada. Education and Bereavement Consultant; Private Practitioner. m. Garald Mertick, 10 May 1974, Calgary, 2 sons, 1 daughter. *Education:* Certificate; Instructor, Family Life Education; Instructor, Parent Effectiveness; Human Resource Management; BA; BSW, distinction; MSW; Registered Social Worker. *Appointments:* Youth and Programme Director, Young Womens Christian Association, 1964-67; Casework Supervisor and Staff Development, Alberta Social Services and Community Health, 1968-82; Bereavement Coordinator, 1982-85, Education and Bereavement Consultant, 1985-, Hospice Calgary; Sessional Instructor, Mount Royal College, 1983; University of Calgary, 1983-; Private Practitioner, Clinical Education, 1985-. *Memberships:* Alberta and Canadian Associations of Social Workers. *Publications:* "Grieving Our Time", 1985; Editorial Board, 'Journal of Palliative Care-Canada', 1985. *Hobbies:* Investigation of medical life styles of British Columbia and Alberta indians; Photography of native plants of Eastern British Columbia; Drama; Sewing; Mountain recreation. *Address:* 310 South Heritage Square, 8500 Macleod Trail South East, Calgary, Alberta, Canada T2H 2N1.

MESEC, Donald Francis, b. 29 Aug. 1936, Waukegan, Illinois, USA. Psychiatrist in Private Practice. m. Frances Auditore, 20 June 1964, New York, USA, 1 son. *Education:* BS, University of Notre Dame, Indiana, 1958; MD, New York Medical College, 1963; Rotating Internship, US Public Health Service Hospital, Staten Island, New York, 1963-64; Residencies in Psychiatry, New York Medical College-Metropolitan Hospital, New York, 1964-65, Manhattan State Hospital, 1965-67; Fellow in Child Psychiatry, Mount Sinai Hospital, New York, 1965-66. *Appointments:* Private Practice in General Psychiatry, New York & Englewood, New Jersey, 1967-77; Phoenix, Arizona, 1978-; Chief of Service, Meyer-Manhattan Psychiatric Centre, Ward's Island, New York, 1970-73; Director, Alcoholism Unit, 1975-, other appointments in centre. *Memberships:* American Medical Association; American Psychiatric Association; American Academy of Clinical Psychiatrists; Arizona State & Maricopa County Medical Societies. *Hobbies:* Swimming; Reading. *Address:* St Joseph's Hospital, 350 West Thomas Road, PO Box 2071, Phoenix, AR 85001, USA.

METZGER, Henry, b. 23 Mar. 1932. Mainz, Germany. Chief, Arthritis and Rheumatism Branch, NIADDK, NIH. m. 16 June 1957, Cleveland Heights, USA. 2 sons, 1 daughter. *Education:* AB, University of Rochester, 1953; MD, Columbia University, 1957. *Appointments:* Intern, Internal Medicine, 1957-58, Resident, Internal Medicine, 1958-59, Presbyterian Hospital, New York City; Resident Associate, NIAMD, 1959-61, Helen Hay Whitney Fellow, 1961-63, Senior

Investigator, NIAMDD, 1963-, Chief, Section of Chemical Immunology, 1973-, Chief, Arthritis and Rheumatism Branch, 1983-. *Memberships:* American Association of Immunology, Secretary/Treasurer 1970-; American Society of Biological Chemistry; American Society of Cell Biology; American Rheumatism Association; Fellow, American Academy of Allergy. *Honours:* Phi Beta Kappa 1953; Alpha Omega Alpha 1957; Harvey Lecturer 1984-85. *Address:* Building 10 Room 9N240, NIADDK/NIH, Bethesda, MD 20892, USA.

MEUNIER, Didier Marie Yves, b. 6 June 1944, Brive, France. Microbiologist. m. Annick Vasseur, 19 July 1969, St Julien de Crempse, 3 sons. *Education:* MD, Specialist in Biology; Training in Tropical Medicine, Systematic Microbiology, General Immunology, Haematology, Parasitology. *Appointments:* Medical Biology Laboratory, Laveran Hospital, Marseilles, France; Head of Laboratory, Institut Pasteur, Bangui, Central African Republic. *Memberships:* Société de Pathologie Exotique. *Publications:* Various articles in medical journals. *Honour:* Ordre Nationale de Mérite, France. *Hobbies:* Tennis; Golf; Skiing; Books. *Address:* Institut Pasteur, BP 923 Bangui, Central African Republic.

MEUNIER, Pierre Jean, b. 5 June 1936, Miribel Ain, France. Professor; Consultant; Head, Research Unit. 3 sons. *Education:* Bachelor, Academy of Lyon, 1953; MD, University of Lyon, 1967; Board Certified, Pathology, 1967, Rheumatology, 1971; Associate Professor of Rheumatology, 1971; Professor, 1979. *Appointments:* Resident, Hospices Civils de Lyon, 1963-67; Assistant Professor, 1967-71, Consultant in Rheumatology, 1971-85, Head of Department, 1985-, Hospices Civile de Lyon; Director, INSERM Research Unit 234 on Metabolic Bone Disease, 1979-. *Memberships:* Board of Directors, ICCRH, USA; American Society for Bone and Mineral Research; European Calcified Tissue Society; French Society of Rheumatology; Bone and Tooth Society, UK. *Publications:* 'Bone', Editor, 1978-; Editorial Board member, 'Calcified Tissue International' and 'Journal of Bone and Mineral Research'; Author over 300 articles on bone diseases in International journals on pathophysiology, histomorphometry and treatment of osteopathies. *Honours:* Chevalier dans l'Ordre des Palmes Academiques, 1983. *Hobbies:* Tennis; Music; Hiking. *Address:* INSERM Unit 234, Faculty Alexis Carrel, rue Paradin, 69008 Lyon, France.

MEYER, Bernhardt Heinrich, b. 31 July 1938, Brakpan, South Africa. Head, Hoechst Unit for Clinical Pharmacology, University of Orange Free State. m. Wilhelmina Heslinga, 15 Dec. 1961, Pretoria, 3 sons, 1 daughter. *Education:* BSc; MBA; MB ChB; MMed (Anes); FFA (SA); PhD. *Appointments:* General Medical Practitioner, 1970-75; Registrar, Anesthesiology, 1975-79, Head, Hoechst Clinical Pharmacology Unit, 1979-, Part Time Specialist, Anesthesiologist, 1979-, University of the Orange Free State. *Memberships:* South African Medical Association; South African Pharmacological Society; South African Society of Anesthetists. *Publications:* Numerous articles in professional journals including: 'South African Journal of Science'; 'South African Medical Journals'; etc. *Hobbies:* Photography; Music; Bird Watching & Photography; Hunting. *Address:* Hoechst Clinical Pharmacology Unit, University of Orange Free State, PO Box 339, 9300 Bloemfontein, South Africa.

MEYER, John Stirling, b. 24 Feb. 1924, London, England. Professor of Neurology. m. Wendy Haskell, 20 June 1947, Wellesley, Massachusetts, USA. 5 daughters. *Education:* BS, Trinity College, Hartford, Connecticut; MD, CM, MSc, McGill University, Montreal, Canada. *Appointments:* Instructor Research Associate, Harvard Medical School, 1950-57; Professor, Chairman Neurology Department, Wayne State University, Detroit, Michigan, 1957-69; Professor, Chairman Neurology Department, Baylor College of Medicine, Houston, Texas, 1969-75; Professor of Neurology, Baylor College of Medicine, Director, Cerebral Blood Flow Laboratory, VA Medical Center, Houston, 1975-. *Publications:* Author and editor of 22 books and 700 scientific articles 1950-. *Honours:* Alpha Omega Alpha, Honor Medical Society, 1948; Preisdent, Johnson's Commission (USA) on Heart Disease, Cancer, Stroke, 1964; Harold G Wolff Award, 1977, 1978, 1979; Honorary Member, Japanese and Italian Neurological Societies. *Hobbies:* Golf; Swimming; Walking. *Address:* 2940 Chevy Chase, Houston, TX 77019, USA.

MEYER, Mitchell Dean Molnar, b. 27 May 1957, Regina, Canada. Family Practitioner. m. Patricia R McNaughton, 21 Nov. 1981, Regina, Canada, 1 daughter. *Education:* Medical Doctor; CCFP. *Memberships:* College of Physicians and Surgeons; College of Family Physicians of Canada. *Honour:* Graduate from Medicine with Distinction. *Address:* 200 Scott Block, Moose Jaw, Saskatchewan, Canada.

MEYER, Paul Reims, Jr, b. 2 Nov. 1931, Port Arthur, Texas, USA. Professor of Orthopaedic Surgery; Founder & Director, Midwest Regional Spinal Cord Injury Care System, McGaw Medical Centre, Northwestern University. m. Eileen Carroll, 5 Feb. 1975, 2 sons, 2 daughters. *Education:* BA, Virginia Military Institute, 1954; MD, Tulane University Medical School, 1958. *Appointments include:* Assistant 1961-63, Instructor 1965-67, Orthopaedics, Tulane University Medical School; Associate, Assistant Professor, Associate Professor, 1967-81, Professor 1981-, Department of Orthopaedics, Northwestern University; Associate Professor, Department of Biological Materials, Northwestern University Dental School, 1976-. *Memberships:* American College of Surgeons; American Medical Association; American Academy of Orthopaedic Surgeons; 20th Century Orthopaedic Association; Illinois Medical Society; Chicago Orthopaedic Society. *Publications include:* Numerous papers, professional journals; Reports. Book chapters in "Complications in Orthopaedic Surgery, ed Charles Epps, 1978, 1985; "Current Perspectives in Rehabilitation Nursing", ed Murray & Kijek, 1979; "Manual of the Trauma Systems Development Workshop", 1979; "Radiology in Spinal Cord Injury", ed L Calenoff, 1981; etc. Radio programme, 'Spinal Cord Injury', 1978; various radio talks, interviews, similar subjects. *Honours:* Army Commendation Medal, 1965; Commendation, Vietnamese Government, 1967; Certificate, American Medical Association, 1967; 1st Curtiz P Artz Award, ATS, 1979. *Hobbies:* Photography; Flying; Amateur radio. *Address:* 250 East Superior Street, Room 619, Chicago, IL 60611, USA.

MEYERS, Morton Allen, b. 1 Oct. 1933, Troy, New York, USA. Professor of Radiology. m. Beatrice Applebaum, 1 June 1963, 1 son, 1 daughter. *Education:* MD, Upstate Medical College, State University of New York. *Appointments include:* Associate Radiologist, Bronx-Lebanon Hospital, New York, 1965-68; Assistant Professor of Radiology, 1968-70, Medicine 1969-70, New York Medical College, Metropolitan Hospital Center; Associate Professor of Radiology, 1970-73, Professor of Radiology, 1973-78, Cornell University Medical College; Professor & Chairman, Department of Radiology, School of Medicine, Health Sciences Center, State University of New York at Stony Brook, New York, 1978-. *Memberships include:* American College of Radiology; Association of University Radiologists; Society of Chairmen of Academic Radiology Departments; American Medical Association; American Gastroenterological Association; American Association for the Advancement of Science; New York Academy of Sciences; Long Island, Rocky Mountain, Toronto, Italian, Spanish & Israel Radiological Societies. *Publications:* "Disease of the Adrenal Glands: Radiologic Diagnosis", 1963; "Dynamic Radiology of the Abdomen: Normal & Pathologic Anatomy", 1976; Founding Editor-in-Chief, 'Gastrointestinal Radiology' (international quarterly); General Editor, "Radiology of lat-

rogenic Disorders" (5 volumes), 1981 ff; Editor, international series: "Diagnostic Radiology" (8 volumes so far), 1983 ff; also chapters to textbooks, articles & reviews to medical journals. *Honours:* Fellow, American College of Radiology, 1977; Guest Examiner, Diplomate, American Board of Radiology. *Address:* Department of Radiology, School of Medicine, Health Sciences Center, State University of New York, Stony Brook, NY 11794, USA.

MEZA, César, b. 25 Dec. 1915, Guatemala City, Guatemala. Psychoanalyst in private practice. m. May 1946, divorced, 2 daughters. *Education:* Psychoanalysis graduate, Washington Psychoanalytic Institute, USA, 1959. *Appointments:* Medical Director, Social Security Institute, Guatemala, 1946-48; Associate Professor, Psychiatric Department, University of Maryland, Baltimore, Maryland, USA, 1955-57; Director, Psychiatric Department, University of San Carlos, Guatemala, 1964-66; Professor, Institute of Psychoanalytic Psychotherapy, Mexico City, Mexico, 1972-83; Currently part-time private practice, part-time clinical research. *Membership:* Inactive Fellow, American Psychiatric Association. *Publications:* "Guatemala and The Social Security System", 1947; "El Colérico", (editor J Mortiz) 1970, 2nd edition 1980. *Honours:* MD Dissertation purchased by Government of Guatemala, 1944; 2 Fellowships, 1948 and 1949. *Hobbies:* Golf; Swimming. *Address:* Alcanfores 17, Las Aguilas, Alvaro Obregón, México, DF, 01710.

MEZEI, Györgyi, b. 21 Jan. 1948, Budapest, Hungary. University Assistant. m. Richter Endre, 30 Jan. 1971, 1 son, 1 daughter. *Education:* MD, Pediatrician, Department of Pediatrics, Semmelweis University Medical School. *Memberships:* Hungarian Pediatric Association; EAACI; Interasma EPRS; Hungarian Association for Allergology and Immunology. *Publications:* 'Thorax Deformity and Asthma', 1984; 'Late Prognosis of Bronchial Asthma', 1984; 'Complete Recovery From Paraquat Poisoning', 1985. *Hobbies:* Collecting Stamps; Fine Art. *Address:* 1163 Budapest, Mátrafüred 14, Hungary.

MHOON, Ernest Edward, b. 27 Mar. 1942, Memphis, Tennessee, USA. Associate Professor of Otolaryngology, Assistant Dean of Students. m. Deborah Ann Hoban, 23 July 1977, Chicago. *Education:* BS, Northern Illinois University, 1964; MD 1973, Internship in Surgery 1973-74, Residency in Otolaryngology 1974-77, University of Chicago. *Appointments:* Teacher of High School Biology 1964-67, Chairman of Science Department 1967-69, Hyde Park High School, Chicago; Assistant Professor of Surgery 1977-84, Clinical Director Otolaryngology 1983-84, The University of Chicago. *Memberships:* American Academy Otolaryngology and Head and Neck Surgery; Association of American Medical Colleges; American College of Surgeons; American Medical Association; Centurions of the Deafness Research Foundation; Chicago Foundation for Medical Care; Chicago Laryngological and Otological Society; Chicago Medical Society; Illinois State Medical Society; National Association of Minority Medical Educators; National Society for Medical Research; Pan American Association of Oto-Rhino-Laryngology and Broncho-Esophagology. *Publications:* "Clinical Use of Mechanical Ventilation", contributed with H Taylor and G Matz, 1981; "John Ralston Lindsay 1978-1981", (editor with E Lanzl), 1983; 'Probable Autosomal Dominant Optic Atrophy with Hearing Loss', (with M Mets), 1985. *Hobbies include:* Music; Art. *Address:* The University of Chicago Medical Center, 5841 South Maryland Avenue, Box 412, Chicago IL 60637, USA.

MICHAEL, Donald Joseph, b. 11 Apr. 1947, Detroit, Michigan, USA. Medical Director. m. Nancy Reed, 4 July 1980, Detroit, USA, 1 daughter. *Education:* BSc, Wayne State University, USA, 1969, MD, 1974, Board Eligible Neurology, 1976. *Appointments:* Psychiatric Attendant, Wayne County General Hospital, Michigan, USA, 1966; Research Assistant (Psychology), Wayne State University, 1967-69, Propioceptive

Acuity Research 1969; Comparative Psychology Electrode Implant Study, 1969; Neurological Modelling Electronic Analogs, Lafayette Clinic, Detroit, 1969; Medical Director, Lafayette Clinic, Sleep Centre, 1979; Staff Psychiatrist, North East Michigan Community Mental Health, 1981; Medical Director, North Penn MH/MR, 1983-85; Psychiatrist, Madison Centre, South Bend, Indiana, 1986-present. *Memberships:* American Medical Association; American Psychiatric Society; American MENSA Association; Vice-President Psi Chi (National Honour Society in Psychology), 1969; Phi Beta Kappa Scholar, 1970. *Publications:* Co-author 'Effect of Deprivation Level on Span of Attention' in a Multi Discrimination Task' in "Psychosomatic Science", volume 15 (i), pages 31-32. *Honours:* State of Michigan Competitive Scholarship, 1966; Deans List, Wayne State University, 1967-69; Board of Governors Scholarship, 1967-69; Woodrow Wilson Fellowship Nominee, 1968; Citation of Merit from the Department of Psychology at Wayne State University, 1969; Health Professions Scholarship, 1970-73. *Hobbies:* Gardening; Skiing; Camping; Computers and Electronics. *Address:* 1845 Riverside Place, South Bend, IN 46616, USA.

MICHAEL, John William, b. 28 Aug. 1949, Indianapolis, Indiana, USA. University Professor and Departmental Director. m. Linda Louise Olson, 5 Sep. 1970, Hobart, Indiana, USA, 1 son, 1 daughter. *Education:* BSc, Michigan State University, USA, 1971; CPO, Northwestern University Medical School, 1979; M.E.d. University of Illinois, 1982. *Appointments:* Clinical Prosthetist, Scheck and Siress Inc Illinois, 1976-78; Assistant Director, Prosthetic Education, Northwestern University Medical School, Chicago, 1978-80; Clinical Prosthetist/Orthotist, Scheck and Siress, Inc. Illinois, 1981-82; Director, Prosthetic Services, Northshore Orthopaedics, Illinois, 1982-85; currently Assistant Clinical Professor in Prosthetics and Orthotics, Director Department of P&O, Duke University Medical Centre, USA. *Publications:* Numerous conference papers. *Honours:* Professional Recognition Award, American Academy of Orthotists and Prosthetists, 1981. *Hobbies:* Reading; Personal Computers; Travel. *Address:* Box 3885 Duke University Medical Centre, Durham, NC 27710, USA.

MICHAELS, John Francis, Junior, b. 29 Nov. 1941, Boston, Massachusetts, USA. Assistant Clinical Professor of Psychiatry, University of Pittsburgh Medical Center; Chairman, Department of Psychiatry and Medical Director, Mental Health Center, Conemaugh Valley Memorial Hospital, Johnstown, Pennsylvania. m. Rebecca Anne Lemmel, 30 May 1976, St Louis, Missouri, 1 son, 2 daughters. *Education:* BS, Boston College, 1963; MD, St Louis University School of Medicine, Missouri, 1968. *Appointments:* Rotating Intern, Jackson Memorial Hospital, Miami, Florida, 1968-69; Resident in Psychiatry, St Louis University Hospitals, 1969-72; Chief, Psychiatric Branch, Naval Aerospace Medical Institute, Pensacola, Florida, 1972-74; Assistant Professor and Staff Psychiatrist, St Louis University School of Medicine and Hospitals, 1974-80; Staff Psychiatrist, Veterans Administration Hospital, St Louis, 1974-80. *Memberships:* American Psychiatric Association; Pennsylvania Psychiatric Society; Captain, Medical Corps, US Naval Reserve; Naval Reserve Association; Association of Military Surgeons of the US. *Honours:* Certified in Psychiatry by American Board of Psychiatry and Neurology, 1974; AMA Physician Recognition Award, 1971, 74, 77, 80, 83. *Hobby:* Study of American Civil War. *Address:* 1650 Menoher Boulevard, Johnstown, PA 15905, USA.

MICHAELS, Leslie, b. 24 July 1925, London, England. Professor of Pathology (University of London), Institute of Laryngology and Otology. m. Edith Waldstein, 1951, 2 daughters. *Education:* MB BS, Westminster Hospital School of Medicine; FRCPath; FRCP (C); D Path. *Appointments:* House jobs Westminster Hospital; Registrar and junior university jobs at Bristol, Manchester and St Mary's London; Hospital Pathologist, Northern Ontario, Canada. *Member-ships:* Pathological Society of Great Britain and Ireland; British Medical Association; Association of Clinical Pathologists; British Division of International Academy of Pathology. *Publications:* Editor, "Asbestosis", 1979; "Pathology of the Larynx", 1984. *Hobbies:* Walking; Magic. *Address:* Institute of Laryngology and Otology, 330 Gray's Inn Road, London WC1X 8EE, England.

MICHEL, Christopher Stephan, b. 8 Sep. 1947, Vienna, Austria. Solo Private Practice. m. Sara H Ruddy, 28 Sep. 1974, St Louis, Missouri, USA, 3 sons. *Education:* AB, Oberlin College, Ohio, 1969; MD and Internship, Internal Medicine, University of Maryland School of Medicine, 1973-74; Residency Psychiatry, Herrick Hospital, Berkeley, California, 1974-77. *Appointments:* Associate Chief of Psychiatry, Herrick Hospital, Berkeley, California, 1985; Attending Psychiatrist, Herrick and Alta Bates Hospitals, Berkeley, California. *Memberships:* American Psychiatric Association; California Medical Association; North California Psychiatric Society; Physicians for Social Responsibility. *Publications:* 'The Opiate Receptor: Demonstration in Neural Tissue', (Experimental collaborator, with Candace Pert, Solomon Snyder), Science, 1973. *Hobbies:* Music; Tennis; Photography; Reading; Travel. *Address:* 2515 Milvia Street, Berkeley, CA 94704, USA.

MICHEL, Kathy A, b. 20 July 1952, Scobey, Montana, USA. Private Practitioner. *Education:* BSc, Education; Doctor of Chiropractic. *Appointments:* Private Practice, Chiropractic, 1981-; Instructor, Cleveland Chiropractic College, 1980-82. *Memberships:* American Chiropractic Association; National Back Foundation; Missouri Chiropractic Association. *Hobbies:* Boating; Skiing; Designing; Reading. *Address:* Highway 65 North, Carrollton, MO 64633, USA.

MICHEL, Luc, b. 28 Feb. 1947, Brussels, Belgium. Head of Surgical Unit. m. Marie Kulche, 26 Sep. 1974, Brussels, 1 son, 3 daughters. *Education:* Medical Degree, University of Louvain-Medical School, 1972; FACS; FCCP. *Appointments:* Chief Resident, Section of Intensive Care-Mayo Clinic, 1978; Instructor in Surgery, Harvard Medical School, 1980. *Memberships:* Society of Critical Care Medicine; American Society of Parenteral and Enteral Nutrition; University Association of Emergency Medicine; International Society of Surgery; Belgian Royal Society of Surgery; Fellow, Massachusetts Medical Society of the American College of Chest Physicians; International College of Surgeons; International Academy of Chest Physicians and Surgeons. *Publications:* Br. J. Surgery, 1976; J. Th and CV, Surg., 1979; Chest 74, 1978; 1983; JPEN 7 1983, 1982; Ann. Surg. 1980, 1981; JAMA, 1980, 1981; NEJM, 1981; Am. J. Surg, 1979; Dis. Colon and Rectum, 1981. *Hobbies:* Bicycle; Skiing. *Address:* 10 Aux Quatre Vents, B 5140 - Namur (Naninne) - Belgium.

MICHEL-BRIAND, Yvon, b. 20 May 1934, Besançon, France. Professor of Bacteriology & Virology. *Education:* MD, 1960, Doctor of Physical Sciences, 1967, University of Montpelier. *Appointments:* Chief, Bacteriology Laboratory, Montpellier, 1959- 65; Assistant Bacteriologist, 1965-68; Professor of Bacteriology & Virology, School of Medicine, University of Besançon, 1970; Head of Department of Bacteriology & Virology J Minjoz, Hospital Besançon. *Memberships:* New York Academy of Sciences; French Microbiology Society; International Society for Cell Biology; American Society for Microbiology; British Society for Antimicrobial Chemotherapy; Société de Biologie. *Publications:* Various articles in medical & scientific reviews on Pseudomonas aeruginosa & antibiotic resistance. *Address:* 19 rue de Vittel, 25000 Besançon, France.

MICHELS, Robert, b. 21 Jan. 1936, Chicago, Illinois, USA. University Professor and Chairman, Department of Psychiatry. m. Verena Sterba, 23 Dec. 1962, Detroit, Michigan, 1 son, 1 daughter. *Education:* BA,

University of Chiago; MD, Northwestern University Medical School; Certificate in Psychoanalytic Medicine, Columbia University Psychoanalytic Center. *Appointments:* Psychiatrist, Student Health Service, Columbia University, 1966-74; Instructor to Associate Professor, College of Physicians and Surgeons, Columbia University, 1964-74; Faculty Member, Supervising and Training Analyst, Columbia University Center for Psychoanalytic Training and Research, 1967-; Assistant to Associate Attending Psychiatrist, Vanderbilt Clinic, Presbyterian Hospital, 1964-74; Assistant to Attending Psychiatrist, St Luke's Hospital Center, 1966-80; Honorary Consulting Psychiatrist, 1980-; Professor and Chairman, Department of Psychiatry, Cornell University, Medical College; Psychiatrist in Chief, The New York Hospital. *Memberships include:* Board of Trustees, Association for Research in Nervous and Mental Disease; American Psychiatric Association; Director, American Board of Psychiatry and Neurology; Regent, American College of Psychiatrists; Board on Professional Standards, American Psychoanalytic Association; National Academy of Sciences etc. *Publications:* "The Psychiatric Interview in Clinical Practice" 1971; 125 articles and chapters in edited volumes. *Honours:* George Goldman Award, Columbia University Center for Psychoanalytic Training and Research, 1985; Strecker Award, Institute of Pennsylvania Hospital, 1985. *Address:* 525 East 68th Street, New York, NY 10021, USA.

MICHON, Jacques Lucien Charles, b. 22 Jan. 1921, Nancy, France. Plastic Surgeon. *Education:* MD, 1951; Associate Professor, 1958, Professor, 1970. *Appointments:* Hospital Surgeon, 1953, Chief of Plastic Surgery Unit, 1959; Complete Curriculum in Faculty of Medicine, University of Nancy, University Hospital Centre, Nancy. *Memberships:* Corresponding Member, National French Academy of Medicine; Honorary Member, American Society for Hand Surgery; Founding Member, French Society for Hand Surgery; British Society for Hand Surgery. *Publications:* Numerous articles in field of orthopaedics, plastic surgery, Hand- and Microsurgery. *Hobbies:* Golf; Sailing. *Address:* Hôpital Jeanne d'Arc, BP303, 54201 Toul-Cedex, France.

MICIC, Sava, b. 24 Feb. 1948, Belgrade, Yugoslavia. Urologist; Assistant Professor. m. Miroslava, 6 Nov. 1971, 1 son, 1 daughter. *Education:* MD; ScD. *Appointments:* Urologist; Assistant Professor. *Memberships:* Yugoslav Association of Urology; International Society of Andrology; American Society of Andrology; American Fertility Society. *Publications:* Articles in: 'Progress in Repr Biology & Medicine', 1984; 'Andrologia'; 'Archives of Andrology'; 'Journal of Urology'; 'International Journal of Fertility'. *Hobbies:* Music; Tennis. *Address:* Urologic Clinic, 51 Gen Zdanova, 11000 Belgrade, Yugoslavia.

MIESCHER, Peter Anton, b. 6 Oct. 1923, Zurich, Switzerland. Professor; Head. m. Annatina Lötscher, 1951, 1 son, 1 daughter. *Education:* Medical Degree, Lausanne and Zurich Universities. *Appointments:* Research Fellow, Exp. Pharmacology and Immunology, Basel, 1949; Resident, Pediatric Hospital, Davos, 1950-51; Resident, University Medical Clinic, Lausanne, 1951-54; Chief Resident, University Policlinic, Basel, 1954-59; Visiting Professor, 1959, Professor, New York University, 1959-68. *Memberships:* Société Suisse de Médecine Interne; Société Suisse d'Hématologie; American Society Clinical Investigation; American Society Hematology; American Association Immunologists; International Society Hematology; Society Biology and Experimental Medicine; International Committee Immuno-pathology. *Publications:* "Textbook of Immunopathology", 1968, 2nd edition, 1976; Numerous publications on the immunopathology of systemic lupus erythematosus including 'Discovery of antibodies to nuclear protein', 1957; Numerous contributions to immuno-pathology. *Honours:* Research Award of City of Basel, 1963; Belden Memorial Lecturer, Mayo Clinic, 1976; Blaffer Visiting Professorship, M.D.Anderson Hospital and Tumor

Institute, Houston, Texas, 1979, 1980, 1982; Honorary Professorship Beijing University, 1986. *Hobbies:* Music; Mountains. *Address:* Division of Hematology, Geneva University Hospital, 1211 Geneva 4, Switzerland.

MIJNHEER, Bernard Jochem, b. 18 Oct. 1941, Meppel, The Netherlands. Medical Radiation Physicist. m. Lous Martin, 21 Oct. 1979, Amsterdam, 2 daughters. *Education:* PhD, University of Amsterdam. *Appointments:* Scientific Co-worker, University of Amsterdam, 1965-71; Postdoctoral Fellowship Euratom, Geel, Belgium, 1971-73; Research Fellow, Neutron Therapy Project, 1973-81, Staff Member, Radiotherapy Department, 1981-, The Netherlands Cancer Institute, Amsterdam. *Memberships:* Hospital Physicists Association; European Society for Therapeutic Oncology. *Publications:* 'Progress in Neutron Dosimetry for Biomedical Applications' in "Progress in Medical Radiation Physics" (Co-author of chapter), 1982; "Clinical Neutron Dosimetry", ICRU Report, International Commission on Radiation Units and Measurements, Washington, DC, 1986. *Hobbies:* Photography; Walking. *Address:* The Netherlands Cancer Institute, Plesmanlaan 121, 1066 CX Amsterdam, The Netherlands.

MIKI, Yoshiharu, b. 23 Feb. 1932, Kobe, Japan. Professor and Head of Department of Dermatology. m. Miya Isotani, 13 May 1961, Osaka. *Education:* MD, Medical School, Osaka University; MSc, Postgraduate Medical School, University of Colorado, USA; DMSc, Postgraduate Medical School, Osaka University, Japan. *Appointments:* Lecturer 1963, Assistant Professor 1975, Osaka University Medical School; Currently Professor and Head of Department of Dermatology, University of Ehime School of Medicine. *Memberships:* Delegate, Japanese Dermatological Association; Trustee, Japanese Society of Thermography; American Academy of Dermatology; Society of Investigative Dermatology. *Publications:* "Modern Dermatology", 1976; "Color Atlas of Skin Diseases", 1977; "Case Study in Dermatology", 1978. *Address:* Shitukawa 1303-12, Shigenobucho, Osengun, Ehime 791-02, Japan.

MIKLUSAK, Thomas Alan, b. 25 Mar. 1946, Camp Le Jeune, North Carolina, USA. Assistant Clinical Professor of Child Psychiatry, University of Southern California; Child and Adult Psychiatrist, Private Practice. m. Chris Wolski, 21 June 1969, Notre Dame, Indiana, 1 son, 1 daughter. *Education:* BA, University of Notre Dame, 1968; MD, Indiana University, 1972; Intern, Santa Barbara Cottage and General Hospitals, 1973; Residency, University of California Los Angeles Adult Psychiatry, 1976. *Appointments:* Fellowship, Child Psychiatry, University of California Los Angeles, 1977; Clinical Associate, (Adult and Child), Southern California Psychoanalytic Institute, 1982-. *Memberships:* American Psychiatric Association; Southern California Psychiatric Society. *Honour:* Marie Briehl Child Psychoanalysis Fellowship, 1985. *Address:* 180 S Lake Avenue, Pasadena, CA 91101, USA.

MILGROM, Edwin, b. 6 Dec. 1936. Professor, Faculty of Medicine, Paris; Director INSERM Unit 135. m. Monique Berger, 20 July 1965, 1 son, 1 daughter. *Education:* MD, Faculty of Medicine, Paris, France, 1967; DSc, Faculty of Sciences, Paris, 1972. *Appointments:* Resident, Paris University Hospitals, 1963-67; Attache, Charge de Recherches INSERM, 1968-72; Professor, Faculty of Medicine, Paris-South, 1972-. *Memberships:* Societe d'Endricrinologie, France; Society de Biochemie, France; Endrocrine Society, USA. *Address:* Hopital de Bicetre, 94270 Kremlin-Bicetre, France.

MILLARD, Peter Henry, b. 18 July 1937, Arundel, Sussex, England. Professor of Geriatric Medicine. m. Alys Gillian Thomas, 27 Jan. 1962, Swansea, 3 sons. *Education:* MBBS, Hons, 1960, MRCS, LRCP, 1960, MRCP, 1966, FRCP, 1976, FRIPHH, 1983, University College Hospital, London. *Appointments:* House Surgeon,

University College Hospital; House Physician, North Middlesex Hospital; Medical Officer, Cameroon Development Corporation, 1962-63; SHO, Brighton General Hospital, 1963-64; Registrar in Medicine, National Temperance Hospital, 1964-66; Senior Registrar, University College Hospital, 1966-68; Consultant in Geriatric Medicine, 1968-, Senior Lecturer and Director of Geriatric Teaching and Research Unit, 1976-, Eleanor Peel Professor, 1979-, St George's Hospital, Tooting, London. *Memberships:* British Geriatrics Society; British Society for Research on Ageing; British Association for Service to the Elderly; Governor, Linacre Centre, 1980-. *Publications:* Articles on Attitudes to the Aged, the Care of the Dying and Bone Disease. *Honour:* Fellow, Royal College of Physicians, 1976. *Hobbies:* Golf; Painting; Walking. *Address:* Geriatric Teaching and Research Unit, St George's Hospital Medical School, Cranmer Terrace, Tooting, London SW17 England.

MILES, Sir (Arnold) Ashley, b. 20 Mar. 1904, York, England. Deputy Director, Medical Microbiology, London Hospital Medical College; Honorary Consultant, Microbiology, London Hospital. m. Ellen Marguerite Dahl, 8 Apr. 1930. *Education:* MA, MD, Cambridge; DSc. *Appointments:* Demonstrator, Bacteriology, London School of Hygiene & Tropical Medicine, 1929; University Demonstrator, Bacteriology, Head, Bacteriology, Postgraduate Medical School, 1935-37; Professor, Bacteriology, University of London, 1937-45; Director, Biological Standards, 1946-52, Deputy Director, 1947-52, National Institute for Medical Research, London; Director, Lister Institute of Preventive Medicine, Professor, Experimental Pathology, University of London, 1952-71; Medical Research Council Guest Research Worker, Clinical Investigation, Clinical Research Centre, 1971-76; Lecturer, Deputy Director, Medical Microbiology, London Hospital Medical College, Honorary Consultant, Microbiology, London Hospital, 1976-. *Memberships include:* Fellow: Royal College of Physicians, Royal Society, World Academy of Art & Science; Honorary Fellowships: Royal College of Pathologists, King's College Cambridge, Institute of Biology, Infectious Diseases Society of America, Royal Society of Medicine; Honorary Memberships include: Society for General Microbiology; Foreign Correspondent, Academie Royale de Medicine de Belgique; American Society for Microbiology; British Academy of Forensic Sciences; American Association of Pathologists; Pathological Society of Great Britain & Ireland. *Publications:* "Topley and Wilson's Principles of Bacteriology and Immunity", 4th-7th editions, 7th, 1983-84; Numerous papers in professional journals. *Honours:* Commander, Order of the British Empire, 1953; Knight Bachelor, 1966. *Hobby:* Music. *Address:* Dept. of Medical Microbiology, London Hospital Medical College, London E1 2AD, England.

MILLER, Alexander Lewis, b. 15 Mar. 1943, Glen Cove, New York, USA. Associate Professor. m. Doris Hanson, 1 May 1965, Greenwich, Connecticut, USA, 2 sons. *Education:* BA, Yale University, 1965; MD, Washington University Medical School, St Louis, MO, 1970. *Appointments include:* Staff Associate, Section on Neurochemistry, National Institute of Mental Health, St Elizabeth's Hospital, Washington, DC, 1971-73; Resident in Psychiatry, Massachusetts General Hospital and Clinical Fellow in Psychiatry, 1973-76, Instructor in Psychiatry, 1976-77, Assistant Professor of Psychiatry, 1977-80, Harvard Medical School; Associate Professor of Psychiatry, The University of Texas Health Science Center at San Antonio, 1980. *Memberships:* Society for Neuroscience; American Society for Neurochemistry; American Psychiatric Association; American Association for the Advancement of Science; International Society of Cerebral Circulation and Metabolism. *Publications:* Include numerous papers in professional journals, 'The tricarboxylic acid cycle', in press; 'Carbon dioxide narcosis', 1985; 'Effects of sensory deafferentation on glucose metabolism of muscles during locomotion' (with E Eidelberg), 1985; 'Lithium and imp-

airment of renal concentrating ability' (with C L Bowden, J Plewes), 1985; 'Factors affecting amnesia seizure duration and efficacy in ECT' (with R A Faber, J P Hatch, H E Alexander), 1985. *Honours include:* Alpha Omega Alpha, Washington University Medical School, 1970; Ethel DuPont Warren Fellow, Harvard Medical School, 1975-76; Visiting Faculty Program in Psychiatry, (Sponsored by Mead Johnson Pharmaceutical Division). *Address:* Department of Psychiatry, University of Texas Health Science Center, 7703 Floyd Curl Drive, San Antonio, TX 78284, USA.

MILLER, Barbara Ellen, b. 31 Dec. 1954, Lakewood, New Jersey, USA. Rehabilitation Co-ordinator. m. Joel Behar, 22 Dec. 1985, Great Neck, New York. *Education:* BS, Washington University School of Medicine, St Louis, Missouri, 1977; Columbia University Teachers College. *Appointments:* Staff Therapist, 1977-80, Senior Therapist, 1980-82, Winthrop University Hospital, Nassau; Senior Therapist 1982-86, Rehabilitation Co-ordinator 1986-, Jewish Institute for Geriatric Care, Geriatric Community Health Centre, County, New York, USA; Private Practice, 1977-. *Memberships:* American Physical Therapy Association. *Publications:* 'The Efficacy of HeNe laser use in geriatric patients with skin ulcers'. *Hobbies:* Crafts; Gardening. *Address:* 11 Clement Street, Glen Cove, NY 11542, USA.

MILLER, Barry, b. 25 Dec. 1942, New York, USA. associate Dean for Research. 1 son, 1 daughter. *Education:* BS, Brooklyn College, 1965; MS, Villanova University, 1967; PhD, Medical College of Pennsylvania, 1971. *Appointments:* Assistant Director, Department of Behavioral Science, Eastern Pennsylvania Psychiatric Institute, Philadelphia, 1971-73; Director, Bureau of Research and Training, Office of Mental Health, Harrisburg, Pennsylvania, 1973-81; Associate Dean for Research, Medical College of Pennsylvania, Philadelphia, 1981-. *Memberships:* American Psychological Association; Pennsylvania Psychological Association, Fellow; Eastern Psychological Association; American Association for the Advancement of Science; New York Academy of Sciences; College of Physicians of Philadelphia, Fellow. *Publications:* 50 publications and 50 presentations in Geriatrics, Cross Cultural Psychiatry, Drug Abuse, etc. *Honours:* Maurice Falk Fellowship; Medical College of Pennsylvania Fellowship; 13 Grants worth approximately $5 million. *Hobbies:* Tennis; Classical Music; Civic Affairs. *Address:* Medical College of Pennsylvania, 3200 Henry Avenue, Philadelphia, PA 19129, USA.

MILLER, Bernard Francis, b. 28 July 1907, Neil Harbour, Nova Scotia, Canada. Professor of Surgery (retired). m. Mary Barbara Currie, June 1932, Halifax, 3 sons, 1 daughter. *Education:* BA, St Francis Xavier University, Canada; MD, Master of Surgery, Dalhousie University; Master of Orthopaedic Surgery, University of Liverpool, England; FRCS (Edinburgh); FRCS (Canada). *Appointments:* Lt Col Royal Canadian Army Medical Corps, Europe and SW Pacific, 1939-45; Director, Victorian Order of Nurses, Nova Scotia; Director, Nova Scotia Polio Clinic, March of Dimes; President, Atlantic Provinces, Orthopaedic Society; Concurrent: Chief of Orthopaedic Surgery, Camp Hill Veterans Hospital, Halifax; Chief of Orthopaedic Surgery, Halifax Children's Hospital; Chief of Orthopaedic Surgery, Halifax Infirmary; Chief of Orthopaedic Surgery, Victoria General Hospital, Halifax; Professor of Surgery (Orthopaedic), Dalhousie University, Canada. *Memberships:* Atlantic Provinces Orthopaedic Society; Canadian Medical Association. *Honours:* MBE, 1945; Efficiency Decoration, Canadian Forces, 1945; Liberation of the Philippines Medal, with Three Stars, USA, 1945; Service Star, 1939-45; Canadian Volunteer Service Medal; Defense of Britain Medal; Pacific Star; European Theatre Star; Victory Medal. *Address:* 1526 Lilac Street, Halifax, Nova Scotia, Canada.

MILLER, David Patrick, b. 24 July 1944, Dublin, Ireland. General Practice, Family Medicine. m. Irene Stephanie Coolican, 22 Oct. 1970, St Philip's, Dublin, 3 sons, 2 daughters. *Education:* BA, 1966, MB BCH, BAO, 1968, Trinity College, Dublin; DCH, College of Surgeons, Dublin, 1970; LMMC, Canada, 1974; CCFP, Canada, 1978. *Appointments:* Internship, Royal City of Dublin Hospital, 1968-69; House Officer, Harcourt Street Children's Hospital, Dublin, 1969; House Officer, Rotunda Hospital, Dublin, 1970; Active Staff, Beaverlodge Municipal Hospital, Alberta, Canada, 1970-. *Memberships:* Canadian Medical Association; Irish Medical Association; General Medical Association. *Hobbies:* All Sports; Reading; Gardening; Amateur Theatre (Acting). *Address:* Box 209, Beaverlodge, Alberta, Canada.

MILLER, Elizabeth Louise, b. 5 Dec. 1930, Chattanooga, Tennessee, USA. President, Hypnotism Institute. m. Robert A Miller (deceased), July 1949, Sleepy Eye, Minnesota, 1 daughter. *Education:* Michigan State College, 1948; Graduate, Wms. Institute of Hypnological Science & Research, 1969. *Appointments:* Owner, Mondovi Theatre, Mondovi, Wisconsin; Editor, 'Skyway News', Minneapolis, Woman's Editor, 'La Crosse Tribune', La Crosse, Wisconsin, 'Eau Claire Leader Telegram', Eau Claire, Wisconsin; Promotional Manager, Barberio; Business Consultant, Culler & Associates; Contractor Consultant to Health Field; Teaching professional & lay people in field, Minneapolis Adult Education School System. *Memberships:* Business & Professional Women; Eau Claire Writers' Club. *Publications:* "Just People of the Friendly Valley", 1965; "I am the Mississippi" (co-author), 1975. *Honours:* US Air Force Citation, 1967; Showman of the Year, Allied Theatres, 1964; Citation, Biafran Government, 1967. *Hobbies:* Writing; Creating business philosophies; Reading; Swimming; Theatre; Antiques; and others. *Address:* 4516 58th Avenue North apt 120, Minneapolis, MN 55429, USA.

MILLER, Gary Evan, b. 19 Aug. 1935, Cleveland, Ohio, USA. Commissioner, Texas Department of Mental Health and Retardation. m. Karen Barrett, 16 Sep. 1972, Buffalo, New York, 2 daughters. *Education:* MD, University of Texas Medical Branch, 1956-60; Diplomate in Psychiatry, 1969; Certification in Administrative Psychiatry, 1983. *Appointments include:* Clinical Professor of Psychiatry, University of Texas Health Science Centre, Houston, Tex; Clinical Associate Professor of Psychiatry, University of Texas Health Science Centre, San Antonio, Tex; Chairman, Committee on Patient Care, National Association of State Mental Health Programme Directors, Washington DC; Consultant, Committee on Mental Health and Mental Retardation, Texas Medical Association; Military Service, US Army Medical Corps, 1962-63. *Memberships include:* Board Member, National Association of State Mental Health Programme Directors; Chairman, Committee on Patient Care, National Association of State Mental Health Programme Directors; Fellow, American Psychiatric Association; Texas Psychiatric Society; American Medical Association; Texas Medical Association; American Association of Psychiatric Administrators; American Academy of Psychiatry and the Law; President, 1981-82, New Hampshire Psychiatric Society; Texas Medical Association, 1961-72; Medical Association of Georgia, 1972-75; Medical Association of Atlanta, 1972-75; Mental Health Committee, Medical Association of Georgia, 1972-74. *Publications include:* 'The Unit System, A New Approach in State Hospital Care', 1969; 'Forgotten Addict: The Alcoholic', 1970; 'New Directors in Mental Health', 1974; 'Case Management: The Essential Service', 1983; 'Cost Containment in Public Mental Health Systems', 1984; 'The Public Sector: The State Mental Health Agency', 1985. *Honours include:* Fellow, American Psychiatric Association, 1984; Certificate of Recognition, Georgia Psychological Association, 1973; Certificate of Recognition, Austin Council on Alcoholism, 1966; Charter Fellow, University of Texas-Brookhaven Institute of Nuclear Medicine, Brookhaven National Laboratories, Long Island, NY, 1959. *Address:* 3215 Exposition Boulevard, Austin, TX

78703, USA.

MILLER, George, b. 18 Apr. 1937, Chicago, Illinois, USA. Professor. *Education:* AB cum laude Harvard College, 1958; MD, Harvard Medical School, 1962. *Appointments:* Intern, Assistant Resident, Medicine, University Hospital of Cleveland, 1962-64; Epidemic Intelligence Service Officer, Communicable Disease Centre, Atlanta, US Public Health Service, 1964-66; Chief, Neurotropic Virus Unit, Epidemiology Branch, 1966; Postdoctoral Research Fellow, NIH, 1966-69; Assistant Professor, 1969-72, Associate Professor, 1972-76, Paediatrics & Epidemiology, Yale University School of Medicine; Investigatorship, Howard Hughes Medical Institute, 1972-80; Professor, Paediatrics & Epidemiology, 1976-79; John F Enders Professor, Paediatric Infectious Diseases, Professor, Epidemiology, 1979-83; John F Enders Professor of Paediatric Infectious Diseases, Professor, Epidemiology and Molecular Biophysics and Biochemistry, 1983-. *Memberships include:* Boylston Medical Society; Infectious Disease Society of America; Diplomate, National Board of Medical Examiners, American Board of Internal Medicine; American Association for the Advancement of Science; etc. *Publications:* Editorial Board: 'Infection and Immunity', 1981-83; 'Journal of Virology', 1981-; 'Virology', 1982-; numerous articles in professional journals. *Honours:* Harvard College Scholarship (Honorary), 1955-58; Epidemic Intelligence Service Alumni Association Prize, 1967; Macy Faculty Scholar, 1977; Squibb Award, Infectious Disease Society, 1982. *Address:* New Haven, CT 06510, USA.

MILLER, Glenn Howard, b. 8 Jan. 1942, Chicago, Illinois, USA. Associate Clinical Professor of Psychiatry. m. Michele Prochep, 26 Dec. 1964, Chicago, 1 son, 1 daughter. *Education:* MD, University of Chicago, 1966; Post-doctoral Certificate in Psychiatry, Yale University, 1970; Graduate, Child and Adult Psychoanalytic Programs, Washington Psychoanalytic Institute, 1984. *Appointments:* Resident in Psychiatry, Yale University, 1967-70; Chief, Department of Psychiatry, US Army Hospital, Berlin, Federal Republic of Germany, 1970-73; Associate Clinical Professor of Psychiatry, George Washington University, Washington DC. *Memberships:* American Psychoanalytic Association; International Psychoanalytic Association; American Academy of Psychiatry and Law. *Publications include:* 'Criminal Responsibility: An Action Approach Psychiatry', 1979; 'Goals of Psychoanalysis and Intensive Psychotherapy', (with T M McGlashan), 1982. *Honour:* Co-winner, Gary Morris Research Award, 1980. *Address:* 8213 Tomlinson Avenue, Bethesda, MD 20817, USA.

MILLER, James Douglas, b. 20 July 1937, Glasgow, Scotland. Forbes Professor of Surgical Neurology. University of Edinburgh; Consultant Neurosurgeon, Southeast Scotland. m. Margaret Scott Rainey, 4 Sep. 1965, Melrose, 2 sons. *Education:* MBChB, 1961; MD, 1970; PhD, 1974; Faculty of Medicine, University of Glasgow. *Appointments:* Basic Training in Surgery, Glasgow, 1962-65; Registrar in Neurosurgery, Institute of Neurological Sciences, Glasgow, 1965-67; Medical Council Research Fellow in Surgery, University of Glasgow, 1967-68; Senior Registrar in Neurosurgery, Institute of Neurological Sciences, Glasgow, 1969-70; International Post-doctoral Fellow in Neurosurgery, University of Pennsylvania, Philadelphia, USA, 1970-71; Senior Lecturer, Neurosurgery, Institute of Neurological Sciences, University of Glasgow, 1971-75; Lind Lawrence Professor of Neurological Surgery, Medical College of Virginia, Richmond, USA, 1975-81. *Memberships:* Society of British Neurological Surgeons; Surgical Research Society; Congress of Neurological Surgeons; American College of Surgeons; Canadian Neurosurgical Society; Royal College of Surgeons of Edinburgh; Royal College Physicians Edinburgh; Royal College Physicians and Surgeons Glasgow; British Medical Association. *Publications:* Papers on head injury, intracranial haemodynamics and other neurosurgical topics; Books: "Rehabilitation of the Traumatic Brain Injured Adult", 1983; "Intracranial Pressure'', IV, 1980, VI (in press). *Honour:* Jamieson Medal, Neurosurgical Society of Australasia. *Hobbies:* Hill Walking; Fly Fishing. *Address:* Department of Surgical Neurology, University of Edinburgh, Western General Hospital, Edinburgh EH4 2XU, Scotland.

MILLER, Jacques Francis Albert Pierre, b. 2 Apr. 1931, Nice, France. Head, Thymus Biology Unit, Walter and Eliza Hall Research Institute. m. Margaret Denise Houen, 17 Mar. 1956, Sydney, Australia. *Education:* BSc with honours, 1953, MB, BS, 1955, University of Sydney; PhD, 1960, DSc, 1966, University of London, England; FAA; FRS; AO; Honorary MD. *Appointments:* Junior Resident Medical Officer, Royal Prince Alfred Hospital, Sydney, 1956; Pathological Research, University of Sydney, 1957; Cancer Research, Chester Beatty Research Institute, London, England, 1958-60; Reader, Experimental Pathology, University of London, England, 1965-66. *Memberships:* Foreign Member, US National Academy of Science; Fellow, Royal Society of London; Fellow, Australian Academy of Science; International Agency for Research on Cancer, 1976-80; International Union of Immunological Societies, 1977-83. *Publications:* Contributor of over 280 articles in scientific journals. *Honours:* Esther Langer-Bertha Teplitz Memorial Award for Cancer Research, Chicago, USA, 1965; Gairdner Foundation Annual International Award, Toronto, Canada, 1966; Encyclopaedia Britannica (Australia) Award, Canberra, Australia, 1966; Scientific Medal, Zoological Society of London, 1967; Fellow of the Royal Society, London, 1970; Elected Fellow, The Australian Academy of Science, Canberra, 1970; Burnet Medal, Australian Academy of Science 1971; Paul Ehrlich - Ludwig Darmstaedter Prize, Frankfurt, Federal Republic of Germany, 1974; Sir William Upjohn Medal, University of Melbourne, 1978; Rabbi Shai Shacknai Memorial Prize, Hebrew University, 1978; Appointed Officer of the Order of Australia, 1981; Foreign Associate, US National Academy of Sciences, 1982; Saint-Vincent Prize for Medical Science, Republic of Italy, WHO, UNESCO, 1983; Fellow, Royal Society for the Encouragement of Arts, Manufactures and Commerce, London, 1984; Honorary MD, University of Sydney, 1986. *Hobbies:* Music; Art; Photography; Literature. *Address:* The Walter and Eliza Hall Institute of Medical Research, Post Office Royal Melbourne Hospital, Victoria 2030, Australia.

MILLER, Joe Pete, b. 16 Aug. 1948, Brady, Texas, USA. Registered Nurse; Senior Charge Nurse. *Education:* Diploma in Nursing, Registered Nurse, John Peter Smith Hospital School of Professional Nursing, 1973; BSc, Southwest Texas State University, 1977. *Appointments:* Assistant Head Nurse, St Joseph Hospital, Fort Worth, Texas, 1973; Assistant Charge Nurse, Surgical Intensive Care Unit, Wilford Hall Medical Center, Lackland Air Force Base, 1973-76; Charge Nurse, Emergency Room, Brackenridge Hospital, Austin, 1976-77; Administrator, QMRP, Cresthaven Nursing Center, ICF-MRVI, Austin, 1977-82; Senior Charge Nurse, Texas Rehabilitation Institute, Brackenridge Hospital, Austin, 1982-. *Memberships:* Central Texas District and National Associations of Rehabilitation Nurses; American and Texas Nurses Associations; Austin AIDS Project; Austin AIDS Interfaith Council; Century Club, American Nurses Foundation; Austin Arthritis Foundation. *Publications:* "Rape Care Procedure Manual", 1977; "Policy and Procedure Manual for Emergency Care", 1977. *Honours:* President, Association of Rehabilitation Nurses, Central Texas District, 1985-; Member, Texas State Board of Rehabilitation Nurses, 1985-; Commendation of Merit in Burn Unit, Wilford Hall Medical Center, 1975; Commendation Letter, University of Texas Burn Center, Galveston, 1976. *Hobbies:* Piano playing; Travelling; Collecting American Indian art. *Address:* 900 Hermitage, Austin, TX 78753, USA.

MILLER, John, b. 24 May 1920, Chinley, England. University Professor and Dean of Dental School. m. Mary Kathleen Spiers, 22 May 1948, London, 2 sons. *Education:* BDS, LDS, University of Manchester, 1938-44; MDS, 1951, DDS, 1956, University of Manchester; FDS. RCS, (England) Honorary, 1957. *Appointments:* House Officer, Manchester Dental Hospital, 1944; Surgeon Lt. RNVR, 1945-48; General Practice, 1948-49; Lecturer, 1949-58, Senior Lecturer, 1958-61, Reader, 1961-63, Professor of Dental Surgery, 1963-68, Vice Dean, 1963-66, Professor of Children's Dentistry and Preventive Dentistry, 1968-85 University of Wales. *Memberships:* British Dental Association; International Dental Federation; Organisation for Research into Caries in Europe; International Association for Dental Research; Dental Community of the Medical Defence Union; Member of General Dental Council. *Publications:* Chapter on dental health in "Prevention in Childhood of Health Problems in Adult Life" WHO, 1980; Chapter on Fluoride in Children's Teeth in "Topics in Paediatric Nutrition" 1983; Articles include: "The Relationship between malocclusion oral cleanliness, gingival conditions and dental caries in school children' 1961. Series: "Dentistry for Children" 1962, 1963; "The eruption of teeth" 1965, 1968; "Dental caries and children's weights" 1982. *Hobbies:* Gardening; Golf; Luthier. *Address:* University of Wales College of Medicine, Dental School, Heath Park, Cardiff CF2 5HB, South Wales.

MILLER, John Roy Mackay, b. 26 June 1921, England. Surgeon, Nairobi Hospital. m. Dr Mary Hester Moller, 14 July 1945, Bedford, England, 1 son, 1 daughter. *Education:* King's College London; King's College Hospital Medical School; MB, BS, University of London, 1943; FRCS, England, 1946. *Appointments:* House Surgeon, Surgical Registrar, King's College Hospital, 1943-47; Graded Surgeon, RAMC, 1947-49; Provincial Surgeon, Surgical Specialist, Colonial Service, Kenya; Surgical Specialist, Chief Surgeon, Kenya Government; Honorary Lecturer, Surgery, University of Nairobi. *Memberships:* British and Kenya Medical Associations: Foundation Fellow, Past President, Association of Surgeons of East Africa. *Publications:* Numerous articles in professional journals including: "The Intensive treatment of Tropical Ulcers", 1951, "Five Years' Abdominal Surgery at Kisumu", 1955. "The Pattern of General Surgical Diseases in Nairobi 1960-63", 1964, "The Three Cases of Conjoined Twins of Nairobi 1976-79", co-author, 1981, all in 'East African Medical Journal; "Tropical Coagulopathic ischaemia", 1980, "The Use of streptokinase in tropical coagulopathic ischaemia: a case report", 1980, 'Proceedings of the Association of Surgeons of East Africa'; "The Norfolk Hotel Bomb Disaster", 1982; "Prophylactic Antibiotics", 1982, 'Proceedings of the Association of Surgeons of East Africa'. *Honours:* Hughes Prize for Anatomy, 1941; Entrance Scholarship in Anatomy to King's College Hospital, 1941; OBE, 1975. *Hobbies:* Yacht Racing; Photography. *Address:* PO Box 30026, Nairobi, Kenya.

MILLER, Maurice Geoffrey, b. 13 Nov. 1930, Manchester, England. General Physician, Geriatrician. m. Eileen Patricia Ward, 28 Mar. 1960, Chelsea, London, 2 daughters. *Education:* MB, BS, St Georges Hospital Medical School, London, 1954; LRCP London, MRCS England, 1954; Membership, Royal College of Physicians (London), 1960; Founder Fellow, Australian College of Rehabilitation Medicine, 1980. *Appointments include:* House Physician 1955, Demonstrator in Pathology to London University 1955-56, St George's Hospital; Principal, General Practice, East Brisbane, Queensland, 1963-65; Visiting Physician, Princess Alexandra Hospital, Brisbane, 1963-71; Clinical Examiner, Final degree examination, Queensland University, 1969-71; Private practice as Consultant Physician, Brisbane, 1965-71; Medical Director, National Heart Foundation of Australia (Queensland Division), 1965-71; Specialist Physician in Charge of the Geriatric and Rehabilitation Unit, Health Commission of New South Wales, Northern Metropolitan Region, Ryde, Sydney, 1973-76; Visiting Geriatrician, Lady Davidson Hospital, Sydney, 1977-81; Visiting Physician in Geriatric Medicine, Ryde Hospital Sydney; Consulting Physician in private practice. *Memberships:* Australian Geriatric Society; Associate Member, Cardiac Society of Australia and New Zealand; Australian Association of Physical and Rehabilitation Medicine; Australian Medical Association. *Publications:* "Cardiac Work Assessment in Queensland", 'Medical Journal of Australia', 1967; "Factors Influencing the Rehabilitation of the Patient with Ischaemic Heart Disease", (with J Brewer), 'Medical Journal of Australia', 1969; "The Capacity of the Cardiac Pensioner to Resume Employment", 'Medical Journal of Australia', 1969. *Hobbies:* Naval History 1793-1945; Sailing. *Address:* 134 Cox's Road, North Ryde, New South Wales 2113, Australia.

MILLER, Michael David, b. 12 Feb. 1935, Nyack, New York, USA. Perinatologist, Obstetrician, Gynaecologist. m. Merle J Jablin, 16 Aug. 1959, New York, 1 son, 1 daughter. *Education:* BSc; MD, Albert Einstein College of Medicine, New York, New York; Certified, National Board of Medical Examiners; Certified, American Board of Obstetrics and Gynaecology. *Appointments:* Attending Obstetrician, Gynaecologist and Instructor, Kings County Hospital Center and University Hospital Downstate Medical Center, New York, New York, 1966-67; Obstetrician, Gynaecologist (Major, Medical Corps), United States Army Hospital, Fort Ord, California, 1967-69; Perinatologist, Obstetrician, Gynaecologist, Kaiser Foundation Hospital, San Francisco, California. *Memberships:* American College of Obstetricians and Gynaecologists; Society of Perinatal Obstetricians; California Perinatal Society; Hellman Obstetrical and Gynaecological Society. *Publication:* 'Perinatal Care of Low-Risk Mothers and Infants, Early Discharge with Home Care', 1976. *Hobbies:* Music (harpsichord); Photography; Tennis; Skiing; Hiking; Jogging. *Address:* Department of Obstetrics and Gynaecology, Kaiser Foundation Hospital Medical Center, 2200 O'Farrell Street, San Francisco, CA94115, USA.

MILLER, Phyllis Foreman, b. 1 Aug. 1929, Pittsburgh, Pennsylvania, USA. Director, Nursing Services, University Hospital, Milton S Hershey Medical Centre, Pennsylvania State University. m. Edwin Garvin Miller, 26 Aug. 1950, 2 sons. *Education:* Diploma, School of Nursing, Pennsylvania University Hospital; BSEd 1964, MEd 1968, Millersville State College, Pennsylvania. *Appointments:* Assistant Director of Nursing (Staffing & Staff Development), Ephrata Community Hospital; School Nurse, Manheim Township, Neffisville; Paediatric Supervisor, Lancaster General Hospital. *Memberships include:* American & Pennsylvania Nurses Associations: American Organisation of Nurse Executives; National League of Nurses; Hospital Association of Pennsylvania; ANA Council on Nursing Administration; Executive Committee, ANA Council of Nursing Administration; etc. *Honours:* Pennsylvania Nurses Association 'Distinguished Service' award, 1980; Pomeroy's Salute to Women who Work, outstanding achievement in health services, 1981; Biographical listings; Member, Messiah College Department of Nursing Honour Society, 1985. *Hobbies:* Gourmet cooking; Gardening; Needlework. *Address:* Lancaster, PA 17601, USA.

MILLER, Richard Graham, b. 2 Oct. 1938, St Catherine's, Canada. Professor & Chairman, Department of Immunology, University of Toronto. m. Beverley Joan Barnhouse, 6 Sep. 1963, 2 sons. *Education:* BSc (Honours); MSc; PhD. *Appointments:* Senior Scientist, Ontario Cancer Institute, Toronto, 1967-; Professor & Chairman, Department of Immunology, University of Toronto, 1984-. *Memberships:* American Association of Immunologists; Canadian Society for Immunology; Society for Analytical Cytology. *Publications:* Over 135 research papers, journal articles, etc, including: 'Separation of cells by velocity sedimentation', with R A Phillips, 1969; 'Quantitive analysis of the 51 Cr release assay for cytotoxic lymphocytes', with M Dunkley, 1974; 'Cell separation analysis of B & T lymphocyte differentiation', co-author, 1975; 'An immunological

suppressor cell which inactivates cytotoxic T lymphocyte precursor cells recognizing it', 1980. *Honours:* Governor General's Gold Medal, 1960; Robert Gould Easton Chair of Immunology, 1985. *Address:* Department of Immunology, University of Toronto, Medical Sciences Building, Toronto, Ontario, Canada M5S 1A8.

MILLER, Robert David, b. 4 Sep. 1941, North Carolina, USA. Director of Forensic Training. *Education:* BS Cum Laude, Davidson College, 1964; PhD, 1972, MD, 1973, Duke University; Psychiatry Resident, Duke University, 1973-76. *Appointments:* Staff Psychiatrist, John Unstead Hospital, 1976-78; Clinical Associate, Psychiatry, Duke University, 1976-79; Director, Adult Admissions Unit, 1978-80, Director of Residency Training, 1980-82, John Umstead Hospital; Clinical Assistant Professor, Psychiatry, 1979-81, Clinical Associate Professor, 1981-82, Duke University; Director, Forensic Training, Mendota Mental Health Institute, Madison, Wisconsin, 1982-; Clinical Associate Professor of Psychiatry, Lecturer in Law, University of Wisconsin-Madison, 1982-; Clinical Associate Professor, Psychiatry, Medical College of Wisconsin, 1984-; Diplomate, American Board of Psychiatry and Neurology, 1977; Diplomate, American Board of Forensic Psychiatry, 1983. *Memberships:* American and Wisconsin Psychiatric Associations; American Academy of Psychiatry and the Law; American Academy of Forensic Sciences, International Academy of Law and Mental Health. *Publications:* "Clinical and Legal Aspects of Involuntary Civil Commitment", 1985; "Involuntary Civil Commitment: Clinical versus Legal Paternalism", 1985; "Involuntary Civil Commitment in North Carolina: The Results of the 1979 Statutory Changes", 1981. *Honours:* Fellow, American Academy of Forensic Sciences, 1985. *Hobbies:* Performance of early music; Nature photography. *Address:* 5587 Winsome Way, Oregon, WI 53575, USA.

MILLER, Stephen, H, b. 12 Jan. 1941, New York, New York, USA. Professor of Surgery; Chief and Division Head, Plastic and Reproductive Surgery; Consultant in Plastic Surgery. *Education:* University of Chicago, 1957-58; University of Georgia, 1958-59; University of California, 1959-60; Tulane University Medical School, 1960-61; Cum laude, University of California, 1961-64; Intern, 1964-65, various residencies, 1965-71, University of California; Fellowships, African Medical Research Foundation, 1971-72, Head and Neck Surgery, Roswell Park, 1972. *Appointments include:* Assistant Professor of Surgery, University of California School of Medicine, 1973-74; Associate Professor of Surgery, 1974-78, Associate Chief, Plastic Surgery, 1974-79, Professor of Surgery, 1978-79, Consultant in Plastic Surgery, Good Samaritan Hospital, 1977-79, Pennsylvania State University School of Medicine; Professor of Surgery, 1979-, Chief, Division of Plastic and Reconstructive Surgery, 1979-, Section Head, Veterans Administration Hospital, 1979-, Consultant, Plastic Surgery, Professor of Crippled Childrens Division, 1979-, Shriners Hospital, 1981-, Oregon Health Sciences University. *Memberships include:* Various offices and committees: American Association for the Advancement of Sciences; American Association for Surgery of Trauma; American Association of Plastic Surgery; American Burn Association; Fellow, American College of Surgeons. *Publications:* Author or Co-Author of numerous contributions to professional journals or as book chapters including: "The Hand", 1977; "Operative Surgery Principles and Techniques", 1980; "Pediatric Plastic Surgery", 1984. Totalling 117 papers, 37 abstracts and letters and numerous presentations. Various Associate Editorships. *Honours:* Various. *Address:* Oregon Health Sciences University, 3181 South West Sam Jackson Park Road, Portland, OR 97201, USA.

MILLER, Wallace, E, b. 24 Oct. 1919, USA. Retired University Professor of Orthopaedic Surgery. m. Beverly Dahn Welsh, 28 May 1949, Crawfordsville, Indiana, USA, 1 son, 1 daughter. *Education:* BA, Wabash College, Crawfordsville, 1941; MD, Harvard Medical School, Boston, Massachusetts, 1944; Certified,

American Board of Orthopaedic Surgeons, 1954 and 1982. *Appointments:* Children's Program Resident, Indiana University Medical Faculty, 1951-57; Teacher, Medical School, James Whitcomb Riley Hospital, 1950-57; Continuous Examiner, American Board of Orthopaedic Surgeons, 1956-; Professor of Orthopaedic Surgery, Jackson Memorial Hospital, Variety Hospital and Veterans' Hospital, University of Miami School of Medicine, Florida, 1957-85. *Memberships:* American Academy of Orthopaedic Surgeons; American College of Surgeons; International Arthroscopy Association; Arthroscopy Association of North America; American Orthopaedic Society for Sports Medicine; American Medical Association; President 1979-80, Eastern Orthopaedic Association; President 1984-85, American Orthopaedic Foot and Ankle Society Incorporated. *Publications include:* Numerous contributions to medical journals including: 'Techniques of medical education in orthopaedics', 1970; 'Technics of medical education in orthopaedic residency', 1971; 'Mastery learning and testing orthopaedic transactions', 1981; 'Kinesiology considerations in specific sports activities', 1983; 'Learning Arthroscopy', 1985. *Hobbies:* Scuba diving; Ocean fishing; Interactive video disc authoring for computers. *Address:* PO Box 145353, Coral Gables, FL 33114-5353, USA.

MILLS, William James, Junior, b. 7 July 1918, San Francisco, California, USA. Orthopaedic Surgeon; Director, Center Hi-Latitude Health Research, University of Alaska. m. Elaine Mary Nagelvoort, 23 Aug. 1952, Owosso, Michigan, 3 sons, 4 daughters. *Education:* BA, University California Berkeley, 1942; MD, Stanford Medical School, California, 1950; American Board Orthopaedic Surgery, 1958. *Appointments:* Ensign, US Navy Reserve, 1942; Rear Admiral, Medical Corps, USNR (Retired), 1978; Adjunct Professor, Director, Center for High Latitude Health Research, University of Alaska, Anchorage, 1980-. *Memberships:* American Academy of Orthopaedic Surgery; American Orthopaedic Society; American College of Surgery; Society for Circumpolar Health; Society for Cryo-Biology; American College of Sports Medicine. *Publications:* 'Frostbite, Experience with Rapid Rewarming', 'Alaska Medicine', March 1960; 'Cold, Disturbances due to Current Therapy', 1964; 'Frostbite', "Encyclopaedia Britannica", 1973; 'Hypothermia: Management Approach', 'Alaska Medicine', 1980; 'Thermal Biofeedback in Cold Injuries', 'American Journal of Clinical Biology', 1982. *Honours:* Certificate of Merit, State of Alaska, 1965; Hewitt Memorial Award, State of Alaska, 1982; Fellow, Arctic Institute North American, 1985. *Hobbies:* Wild Life Photography; Fresh Water Angling; Gardening; Winter Sports; Philately. *Address:* 1544 Hidden Lane, Achorage, AK 99501, USA.

MILNER, Morris (Mickey), b. 7 May 1936, Johannesburg, South Africa. Professor and Chairman, Department of Rehabilitation Medicine, University of Toronto; Director, Rehabilitation Engineering and Research, The Hugh MacMillan Medical Centre. m. Maureen Marcia Maltz, 20 Sep. 1959, Johannesburg, 1 son, 2 daughters (1 deceased). *Education:* BSc, Engineering, 1957, PhD, 1968, University of Witwatersrand. *Appointments:* Junior and Senior Lecturer, Electrical Engineering, University of Witwatersrand, 1958-68; Associate Research Officer, National Research Council, Ottawa, Canada, 1969-70; Principal Specialist, Senior Lecturer and Head, Bioengineering and Medicine. Phys. Department, Groote Schuur Hospital and University of Cape Town, 1970-72; Senior Research Associate, Department of Physical Medicine, Emory University, USA and Visiting Associate Professor, School of Electrical Engineering, Georgia Institute of Technology, 1973-74; Associate Professor, Departments of Medicine and Electrical Engineering Program, McMaster University, 1974-78; Director, Biomedical Engineering Department, Chedoke Hospital, Hamilton; Director, Rehabilitation Engineering Department, Hugh McMillan Medical Centre, 1978-; Director, Research Department, Hugh MacMillan Medical

Centre, 1983-; Professor and Chairman, Department of Rehabilitation Medicine, University of Toronto, 1985-; Adjunct Professor, Departments Mechanical Engineering and Surgery, Institute of Biomedical Engineering, University of Toronto. *Memberships:* Director, Canadian Rehabilitation Council for Disabled; Past President, Rehabilitation Engineering Society of North America; Canadian Medical and Biological Engineering Society, Vice-President, 1980-82; IEEE; Chairman, International Committee on Technical Aids, Housing and Transportation, 1984-88 and several other organizations. *Publications:* Co-author: "Understanding the Scientific Bases of Human Movement", 2nd Edition,1980; Numerous papers and presentations in the field. *Honours:* Engineering Medal, Association of Professional Engineers of Ontario, 1982; Isabelle and Leonard Goldenson Award for Technological Research and Development for Disabled Children, 1983; Presidential Citation, Variety Clubs International; Eminent Visiting Speaker, Institute of Engineers, Australia, 1985. *Hobbies:* Swimming; Reading; Photography. *Address:* Department of Rehabilitation Medicine, University of Toronto, 256 McCaul Street, Toronto, Ontario M5T 1W5, Canada.

MILSUM, John H, b. 15 Aug. 1925, Sussex, England. Chairman of Division of Preventive Medicine and Health Promotion and Professor of Health Care and Epidemiology. m. Eileen Mary Moyls, 16 July 1955, 1 son, 1 daughter. *Education:* BSc Engineering, University of London, 1945; SM 1955, ME 1956, ScD Control Engineering 1957, Massachusetts Institute of Technology, USA; Professional Engineer, Province of Quebec, Canada, 1963-72. *Appointments:* Project Engineer 1950-54, Head of Analysis Section 1957-61, Research Council of Canada; Abitibi Professor of Control Engineering 1961-72, Director of Biomedical Engineering Unit 1966-72, McGill University; Imperial Oil Professor of General Systems 1972-77, Director of Division of Health Systems 1972-85, Professor in Department of Health Care and Epidemiology 1972-, Chairman of Division of Preventive Medicine and Health Promotion 1983-, University of British Columbia, Vancouver. *Memberships:* Fellow, American Association for the Advancement of Science; Emeritus Member, Canadian Medical and Bio Engineering Society; Senior Member, Institute of Electrical and Electronics Engineers; Sigma Xi; Physicians for Social Responsibility; Society for General Systems Research; Society of Prospective Medicine; Canadian Public Health Association. *Publications include:* "Biological Control Systems Analysis", 1966, Russian 1968, Japanese 1970; "Positive Feedback", (editor), 1968; "Biomedical Engineering Systems", (edited with M Clynes), 1970; "Health, Stress and Illness: A Systems Approach", 1984; About 100 refereed articles. *Hobbies:* Reading; Cross-country skiing; Microcomputers; Walking. *Address:* Department of Health Care and Epidemiology, University of British Columbia, 5804 Fairview Crescent, Vancouver, British Columbia V6T 1W5, Canada.

MILTON, Anthony Stuart, b. 15 Apr. 1934, London, England. University Professor of Pharmacology. m. Elizabeth Amaret Freeman, 16 June 1962, London, 1 son, 2 daughters. *Education:* MA, D Phil, University of Oxford, 1953-59. *Appointments:* Instructor, Dartmouth Medical School, USA, 1959-60; Research Fellow, Stanford University, 1960-61; Research Fellow, Edinburgh University, Scotland, 1961-63; Lecturer 1966-67, Senior Lecturer 1967-73, The School of Pharmacy, London University, England; Professor of Pharmacology, University of Aberdeen, Scotland, 1973-. *Memberships:* Physiological Society; British Pharmacological Society. *Publication:* "Pyretics and Antipyretics. Handbook of Experimental Pharmacology" volume 60, 1982. *Hobby:* Breeding Border Terrier dogs. *Address:* Department of Pharmacology, University of Aberdeen, Marischal College, Aberdeen, AB9 1AS, Scotland.

MIMS, Albert, b. 28 Feb. 1924, Keyser, Kentucky, USA. Associate Professor of Industrial Safety/Safety and

Health Consultant. m. Margie L Kolbe, 12 Apr. 1985, New London, Wisconsin, 1 son, 1 daughter from previous marriage. *Education:* AB, MS, MBA, PhD. *Appointments:* Assistant Professor, William and Mary, 1953-54; Training Manager, 1953-55, Divisional Safety and Health Engineer, 1955-72, Procter and Gamble. *Memberships:* American Society of Safety Engineers: World Safety Organization; American Industrial Hygiene Association; National Safety Management Society; National Safety Council; Human Factors Engineering; System Safety Society. *Publications include:* 'Chemical Safety Care Histories' 1975; 'Consumer Products Safety' 1975; 'OSHA Regulates Flammable Liquid Storage' 1977; 'Supervisor's Role in Indictrination and Training' 1978; 'Static Electricity, Conduct it to Ground' 1978; 'Charting the Course of Industry and Chemistry in 1980's' 1980. *Hobbies:* Golf; Travel; Tennis; Reading. *Address:* 31 Apache Court, Appleton, WI 54911, USA.

MINIRTH, Franklin Brent, b. 24 Nov. 1946, Leachville, Arkansas, USA. Psychiatrist, Private Practitioner. m. Mary Alice Holt, 28 June 1968, 3 daughters. *Education:* MD, 1972, Internship in Psychiatry, 1972-73, Chief Resident Psychiatry, 1975, University of Arkansas Medical Centre; BS, Arkansas State University, 1968; MABS, Dallas Theological Seminary. *Appointments:* Chairman, Department of Psychiatry, Richardson Medical Centre, 1980-81; Private Practice, Minirth-Meier Clinic PA, 1975-. *Memberships:* Psychiatrist Diplomate, American Board of Psychiatry and Neurology; American Medical Association; Christian Medical Society. *Publications:* "Beating the Clock (Maturing Successfully)"; 'Building a Healthy Self-Concept Study Guide'; "Christian Psychiatry"; "The Christian Sex Manual (maintaining the Honeymoon)"; "Counselling and the Nature of Man"; "Eating Disorders Study Guide"; "Happiness is a Choice"; "Introduction to Psychology and Counselling"; "The Money Diet"; "The Monster Within"; "Sweet Dreams"; "Why be Lonely (A Guide to Meaningful Relationships)"; "The Workaholic and His Family"; "You Can Measure Your Mental Health"; "100 Ways to Live a Happy and Successful Life"; "100 Ways to Obtain Peace"; has also made several videos. *Hobby:* Working guest ranch in Arkansas. *Address:* Minirth-Meier Clinic PA, 2100 N Collins Boulevard, Richardson, TX 75080, USA.

MINJA, Balthazar Mashindano, b. 13 May 1942, Moshi, Tanzania. Senior Lecturer. m. Irene Elianshita Lema, 26 June 1971, 3 sons, 1 daughter. *Education:* MB ChB, Makerere University, Kampala; MMEd, Surgery, University of Dar es Salaam; MSc (ENT), University of Nijmegen/Dar es Salaam. *Appointments:* Medical Officer II; Principal, Medical Assistant Training Centre; Medical Officer I; Lecturer in Surgery; Lecturer in ENT; Senior Lecturer, ENT; Associate Dean, Faculty of Medicine. *Memberships:* Medical Association of Tanzania; Fellow, Association of Surgeons of East Africa; Tanzania Professional Centre. *Publications:* Articles in professional journals including: "Foreign Bodies in the external Ear and Aerodigestive Tracts", 'Proceedings of the Association of Surgeons of East Africa', 1981; "Otitis External: Experience with Quadriderm Cream Therapy", 'Proceedings of the Association of Surgeons of East Africa', 1983. *Memberships:* Medical Association of Tanzania; Fellow, Association of Surgeons of East Africa; Tanzania Professional Centre. *Hobby:* Darts. *Address:* Muhimbili Medical Centre, PO Box 65327, Dar es Salaam, Tanzania.

MINTER, Wayne Robert, b. 18 Apr. 1956, Australia. Director; Governor. m. Susan Kay Minter, 18 Apr. 1981, Melbourne, 2 daughters. *Education:* BEcon, Australian National University; BApp.Sc. (Chiro); Dip App Sc, (Chiro). *Appointments:* President, Chiropractic Students Assoc, 1978; Lecturer, Chiropractic Technique, Phillip Institute of Technology, 1980; Director, Undergraduate Studies, International College of Chiropractic; Governor, Australia Spinal Research Foundation. *Memberships:* Australian Chiropractors

Assoc; Australian Spinal Research Foundation. *Honours:* Chiropractic Science Award, 1981; Meritorious Service Award, Phillip Institute of Technology, 1981. *Hobbies:* Music; Sailing; Camping. *Address:* 41 Wardeen Road, Clareville, NSW, Australia, 2107.

MIRICH, Eleanor Kay, b. East Chicago, Indiana, USA. Health Administrator. m. Ernest C Mirich, 8 Oct. 1960, 2 sons, 3 daughters. *Education:* Registered Nurse, St Elizabeth School of Nursing, Lafayette, Indiana, 1958; BS 1978, MS 1986, Health Service Administration, College of St Francis, Joliet, Illinois. *Appointments:* Chief Executive Officer, Chief Finance Officer, Health Administrator, Mirich Medical Corp, Merrillville, Indiana, 1973-83; Medical Rehabilitation Director/Coordinator, 1982-84; Community Coordinator, Cardiography Laboratory, Merrillville, 1985-. *Memberships include:* American College of Hospital Administrators; Society for Hospital Planning of American Hospital Association; Association of University Programmes in Health Administration; American Health Lawyers Association; National Spinal Cord Injury Association; National Forum of Women Health Care Leaders; American Public Health Association. *Honours include:* Certificate of Appreciation, American Heart Association, 1978; Fellow, Menninger Foundation. *Hobbies:* Classical Piano, Organ; Harvard Classics; Reading; Science; Swimming; Wellness Energy Programmes; Advocate for the Disabled. *Address:* 1000 West 127th Place, Crown Point, IN 46307 - 9204, USA.

MIROW, Susan, b. 15 Feb. 1944, Manhattan, New York, USA. *Education:* BA Biology, Temple University, Philadelphia, Pennsylvania, 1964; PhD Anatomy, New York Medical College, New York, 1970; MD, Medical College of Pennsylvania, Philadelphia, 1973; Certificate, National Board of Medical Examiners, 1973; Certificate, American Board of Psychiatry and Neurology, 1979. *Appointments include:* Research Investigator, Hospital of Joint Diseases, New York, 1969-70; Private practice in Psychiatry, Salt Lake City, 1976-; Clinical Assistant Professor, Department of Psychiatry, University of Utah School of Medicine, Salt Lake City; Active Staff, Holy Cross Hospital, Salt Lake City, 1976-; Courtesy staff, University of Utah Hospital, Salt Lake City, 1977-; Clinical Director, Utah State Hospital, Provo, 1980-82; Psychiatric Consultant, Premenstrual Syndrome Clinic, 1983-; Courtesy staff, LDS Hospital, 1985-. *Memberships:* Secretary, Utah Psychiatric Association, 1985-; American Medical Association; Utah State Medical Association; Salt Lake County Medical Society; American Psychiatric Association; American Association for the Advancement of Sciences; New York Academy of Sciences; Society for Clinical and Experimental Hypnosis; International Society for Clinical Hypnosis; American Society of Clinical Hypnosis. *Publications:* 'An Ultrastructural Study of Early Chondrogenesis in the Chick Wing Bud', (with R Seals and S R Hilfer), 1972; 'Skin Color in the Squids Loligo Pealii and Loligo Opalescens I Chromatophores', 1972; 'An Ultrastructural Study of Osteoarthritic Changes in the Articular Cartilage of Human Knees', (with C Weiss), 1972. *Honours:* National Science Foundation Fellowships, 1965-69; Fellowship Award, Friday Harbor Marine Biology Station, University of Washington, Seattle, 1969; John Polachek Research Foundation Fellowship, New York, 1969-70; Weismann Award for Excellence in Child Psychiatry, Philadelphia, 1973. *Address:* 73 G Street, Salt Lake City, UT 84103, USA.

MIRRA, Joseph Meredith, b. 22 Nov. 1937, New York, USA. Professor of Pathology. m. Carmen Mirra, 20 Aug. 1984, 1 son. 2*Education:* BA, Columbia College; MD Cum Laude, Downstate Medical Centre. *Appointments:* Assistant Professor, Cornell Medical School, 1970-73; Assistant Professor, 1973-76; Associate Professor, 1976-83, Full Professor, 1983-, University of California at Los Angeles Medical Centre. *Memberships:* International Skeletal Society. *Publications:* "Bone Tumors - Diagnosis and Treatment", 1980; 'A New Histologic Approach to the Differentiation of Enchondroma and Chondrosarroma of the Bones', 1985;

'Paget's Disease and Giant Cell Tumor', 1986. *Honours:* Science High School, Arista, 1955; Medical Degree, Cum Laude. *Hobbies:* Competitive sports; Stamps; Writing. *Address:* Department of Pathology, UCLA Medical Centre, Los Angeles, CA 90024, USA.

MIRZA, Mohammad Arshad, b. 7 May 1928, Punjab, India. Professor, Head, Medicine, (Major General); Army Medical College, Rawalpindi; Senior Instructor, Medicine, Armed Forces Medical College, Rawalpindi; Senior Visiting Physician, Military Hospital, Rawalpindi, 1979-. m. Hamida Bano, 9 October 1950, Lahore, 2 sons, 2 daughters. *Education:* MD, Cardiology, Punjab University, 1955; House Physician, Mayo Hospital, Lahore, 1950-51; Medicine Speciality Course, Military Hospital, Rawalpindi, 1952-54; Various other courses; Fellowship and British Council Bursor, Cardiology, Royal Postgraduate Medical School, London, 1971. *Appointments:* Specialist, Medicine, various Defence Hospitals, 1954-78; Visiting Instructor, Pakistan Armed Forces Medical College, Rawalpindi, 1965-72; Chief Physician, Director Eastern Province Armed Forces Hospital, Saudi Arabia, 1972-75; Visiting Instructor, Pakistan Armed Forces Medical College, Rawalpindi, 1965-72; Past Vice President, Pakistan Cardiac Society, also Founder Member; Professor, Head, Medicine, Army Medical College, Rawalpindi, 1979-; Honorary Physician, President of Pakistan. *Memberships:* Fellow, College of Physicians and Surgeons, Pakistan; Fellow, American College of Chest Physicians; Founder Member, Pakistan Cardiac Society. *Publications include:* "Constitution - Study of 5202 Males in Northern Areas of Pakistan", 'Journal Pakistan Army Medical College', 1956; "Innocent Cardiac Murmurs - Study of Young healthy Males", 'Pakistan Armed Forces Medical Journal', 1973; "Prevalence of Hypertension also Comparison with Western Data and Suggestion of a New Classification for Hypertension", 'Pakistan Armed Forces Medical Journal', 1976; "Hypertension in the Elderly", 'Proceedings 16th Annual National Health Conference', 1983. *Honour:* Hilale Imtiaz (Military) 14th August 1983. *Hobbies:* Tennis; Previously Football - Member of North Western India Football Team, 1945, Captain, University of Punjab Football Team, 1948. *Address:* No 74 Race Course Housing Scheme, Rawalpindi Cantt, Pakistan.

MISIASZEK, John, b. 10 Dec. 1948, London, England. Clinical Associate Professor of Psychiatry. m. Jenifer George, 26 Nov. 1983, Tucson, Arizona, USA. *Education:* MD, University of Arizona College of Medicine, 1975; Flexible Internship, Santa Barbara Cottage and General Hospital, 1975-76; Residency, Arizona Health Sciences Centre, Psychiatry Department, 1976-79. *Appointments:* Consulting Psychiatrist to the VA, 1979-80; Attending Physician, Psychiatric Inpatient Services, Arizona Health Sciences Centre, 1979-84; Assistant Professor of Psychiatry, 1979-85; Director of Consultation, Liaison Services, 1979-; Clinical Associate Professor of Psychiatry, 1985-; Consulting Physician, Southern Arizona Mental Health Centre, 1985-. *Memberships:* Tucson Psychiatric Society; Arizona Psychiatric Society; American Psychiatric Association; Association for Academic Psychiatry; Academy of Psychosomatic Medicine. *Publications include:* 'The effect of air pollution and weather on lung function in exercising children and adolescents', (with M Lebowitz, P Bendheim, G Christea, M Markovitz, M Staniec, D Van Wyck), 1974; 'Atypical psychosis is Usher's syndrome', (with M Mangotich), 1983; 'An atypical case of neuroleptic malignant syndrome responsive to conservative management', (with R Potter), 1985; 'Transition from residency training to academia', (with R Potter), 1984; 'Psychiatric morbidity in heart recipients', (with R Novak, R Potter); 'Poor job quality and the decline of public psychiatry', (with K Leehey); 'Diagnostic considerations in deaf patients', (with J Dooling, M Gieseks, H Melman), 1985; Author of several abstracts and book reviews. *Honours:* Diplomate, National Board of Medical Examiners, 1976; Board Certification in Psychiatry; Distinguished Educator, Department of Psychiatry, 1985. *Hobbies:* Athletics; Wood crafting; Painting. *Address:* Arizona Health Sciences Centre, Department of Psychiatry, 1501 North Campbell Avenue, Tucson, AZ 85724, USA.

MISIRLIGIL Aykut, b. 5 May 1949, Ankara, Turkey. University Professor and Consultant in Dentistry. m. Dr Zeynep Misirligil, 1 Oct. 1979, 1 son. *Education:* BDS, 1973, DDS, 1977, Faculty of Dentistry, University of Ankara. *Appointments:* Faculty of Dentistry, University of Ankara 1974-, Senior Lecturer, 1980-82, Assistant Professor, 1982-84, Associate Professor, 1984-. *Memberships:* Turkish Dental Association; Turkish Medical Association; Dental Association of Ankara; Microbiology Society of Ankara. *Publications include:* "Relationship of oral flora with cigarette smoking" 1982; "Syphilis and its importance in dentistry" 1983; "Allergic reactions due to the dental materials" 1984. *Honours:* Best student, University of Ankara Faculty of Dentistry, 1973; British Council Honorary Research Associate, 1976; University of Ankara, Faculty of Dentistry, 1979. *Hobbies:* History; Scuba diving; Fishing; Hunting. *Address:* University of Ankara, Faculty of Dentistry, Besevler - Ankara, Turkey.

MISLIN, Hans, b. 24 May 1909, Basle, Switzerland. Former Director, Institute for Physiological Zoology, Ordinary Comparative Physiology and General Biology. m. Christiane Muhr, 26 Sep. 1956, Liege, Belgium, 1 daughter. *Education:* University of Basle; University of Königsberg; University of Vienna, Austria; University of Prague, Czechoslovakia. *Appointments:* Medical student, Basle, Switzerland; Read in Physiology, Bern; Reader in Comparative Physiology, Basle; Extraordinary Professor, General Biology, Ordinary Professor of Physiology and Zoology, University of Mainz; Director of the Institute, University of Mainz. *Memberships:* Swiss Physiological Society; Swiss Zoological Society; International Society of Lumphology; Swiss Working Party on Immune Research. *Publications include:* "Der Mensch mit den Tieren", 1968; "Handbuch Vergl Pharmakologie", 1968. *Honours:* Honorary Member, German Lymphological Society. *Hobby:* Founder, International Interdisciplinary Journal of Life Science 'Experientia'. *Address:* CH-6914 Carona/Lugano, Switzerland.

MITCH, Paul Steve, b. 3 Oct. 1945, Donora, Pennsylvania, USA. Psychiatrist. m. 2 sons, 1 daughter. *Education:* BS, University of Dayton, Ohio, 1967; MD, Ohio State University, 1971. *Appointments:* Psychiatric Staff, Toledo Mental Health Center, 1975-80; Assistant Professor, Psychiatry, 1976-77, Clinical Assistant Professor, 1977-, Medical College of Ohio, Toledo; Medical Director, Community Mental Health Center West, 1977-85. Psychiatric Consultant: Sunshine Childrens Home, 1978-85; Northwest Ohio Developmental Center, 1978-; Josina Lott Residential, 1979-; Woodlane Residential, 1983-; Bittersweet Farms' 1983-. Medical Adviser, Social Security Administration, 1978-. *Memberships:* American Psychiatric Association; American Medical Association; Biofeedback Society of America. *Publications:* Co-Author: 'Autogenic Feedback Training in Migraine: A Treatment Report', in 'Headache', 1967; 'Effect of Direct Feedback of Systolic Blood Pressure in Essential Hypertension', in 'American Journal of Clinical Biofeedback', 1978. *Honour:* Sandoz Award, 1973. *Hobbies:* Raising cactus and succulents; Motorcycling; Stamp collecting; Stereo and Hi-Fi; Photography; Travel. *Address:* 3171 Republic Boulevard North 101, Toledo, OH 43615, USA.

MITCHELL, Christine I, b. 8 Dec. 1951, Gardner, Massachusetts, USA. Nurse; Clinical Specialist in Ethics. m. Ralph B. Potter, 1985. *Education:* BSN, Boston University School of Nursing; MS, Parent/Child Nursing, Boston University; MTS, Ethics, Harvard Divinity School. *Appointments:* Staff Nurse, VA Hospital, Manchester, New Hampshire; Camp Nurse, Camp Kenwood, New Hampshire; Instructor, Mary Hitchcock Memorial Hospital School of Nursing, Dartmouth Medical Center; Assistant Professor of Nursing, University of Virginia, Charlottesville; Clinical Specialist in Ethics, Children's Hospital, Boston; Lecturer, Boston University School of Nursing Graduate Program. *Memberships:* American and Massachusetts Nurses Associations; Sigma Theta Tau; Hastings Center Institute for Society, Ethics and the Life Sciences; Society for Health and Human Values. *Publications:* Integrity in interprofessional Relationships, 1982; Code Gray: Ethical Dilemmas in Nursing (documentary film with Ben Achtenberg and Joan Sawyer), 1983; Ethical Problems of the Baby Jane Doe Issue: A Nurse's Reaction, 1984; Ethical Issues in Perinatal Nursing, 1985; The Nature of the Nurse-Patient Relationship, 1985. *Honours:* Joseph P Kennedy Jr, Fellowship in Medical Ethics, 1979-81; Award for Excellence in Nursing Practice, Massachusetts Nurses Association, 1984; Code Gray film nominated for Oscar from Academy of Motion Picture Arts & Sciences for best short documentary, 1984. *Hobbies:* Bicycling; Film; Voluntary Cooking. *Address:* 42 Browning Road, Somerville, MA 02145, USA.

MITCHELL, George Patrick, b. 25 Apr. 1917, Insch. m. Hazel Gough, 14 Sep. 1943, Kensington, 2 daughters. *Education:* MB, ChB, University of Aberdeen, 1940; FRCS, 1948. *Appointments:* Senior Registrar, Nuffield Orthopaedic Centre, Oxford, 1949-54; Consultant Surgeon, Princess Margaret Rose Orthopaedic Hospital, Edinburgh, 1954; ABC Travelling Fellowship, 1954; UK National Delegate, Societe International de Chirurgie, 1972-78; Mono-Specialist Section, Orthopaedic Surgery, EUMS, 1972-84; President, British Orthopaedic Association, 1982-83; Vice President, 1980, Executive Committee, 1965-66; Honorary Fellow, Orthopaedic Surgery, University of Edinburgh, 1984. *Memberships:* British Orthopaedic Association; Society International de Chirurgie Orthopedique et de Traumatology. *Publications:* "Deforming Factors in Poliomyelitis", 'Lancet', 1952; "L'elongation du Tibia", 'Revue Chirurgie Orthopedique', 1963; "Arthrography in Congenital Dislocation Hip", 1963; Contributor to various other professional journals. *Honours:* Military Cross, 1944. *Hobbies:* Shooting; Fishing; Sailing. *Address:* 19 Magdala Crescent, Edinburgh EH12 5BD, Scotland.

MITCHELL, Harold Richard, b. 2 Sep. 1940, Charleston, South Carolina, USA. Chairman, Department of Speech Pathology and Audiology; Regional Director, Communicative Skills Consultants. m. Jacqueline Walton, 25 Aug. 1972, Danville, Virginia, 1 daughter. *Education:* BS, South Carolina State College; MS, University of Denver; PhD, Ohio State University. *Appointments:* Speech Therapist: Beaufort Public Schools, 1963; Lincoln State School, 1966; Toledo Hearing and Speech Centre, 1967-69. Hearing and Vision Consultant, 1969-72; Director, Speech and Hearing Programme, 1972-80, Chairman, Department of Speech Pathology and Audiology, 1980-, Tennessee State University; President, Capitol Hill International Communications, 1980-; President to the Executive Director, Eider Care Home Health Agency, currently; Regional Director, Communicative Skills Consultants. *Memberships:* Tennessee Speech and Hearing Association; American Speech and Hearing Association. *Publications:* "Concerns for Minorities in Communication Disorders" Co-Editor, 1985; 'Accountability: A Flipside Purview' in 'The Journal of the Tennessee Speech and Hearing Association'. *Honours:* Maternal and Child Health Travel Grant to study in Europe, 1971; Phelps Stokes Award to study in Caribbeans, 1977; Certificate of Outstanding Service to Upward Bound Programme, 1985. *Hobbies:* Poetry writing; Playwrighting; Tennis. *Address:* 519 Weeping Elm Road, Mount Joliet, TN 37122. USA.

MITCHELL, Malcolm Stuart, b. 6 May 1937, New York, New York, USA. Professor of Medicine and Microbiology. m. June Kan, 14 Aug. 1976, New Haven, Connecticut, 3 sons. *Education:* AB magna cum laude, Harvard, 1957; MD 1962, Fellow in Medical Oncology 1966-68, Yale University School of Medicine; Fulbright Scholar, Sir William Dunn School of Pathology,

University of Oxford, England, 1959-60; Intern in Medicine, University of North Carolina, USA, 1962-63; Resident in Medicine, Boston City Hospital, 1965-66. *Appointments:* Instructor-Associate Professor, Yale University School of Medicine, 1968-78; Chief of Medical Oncology 1978-84, Director for Clinical Investigations 1978-83, University of Southern California Cancer Center; Professor of Medicine and Microbiology, University of Southern California School of Medicine, 1978-. *Memberships:* American Association for Cancer Research; American Federation for Clinical Research; American Society of Clinical Oncology; American Society for Clinical Investigation; American Association of Immunologists; American Radium Society; Western Association of Physicians; Sigma Xi. *Publications:* "Hybridomers in Cancer, Diagnosis and Therapy", (with H F Oettgen), 1982; "Immune Suppression and Modulation", (with J L Fahey), 1984; "The Modulation of Immunity", 1985; "Immunity to Cancer", (with A E Ruf), 1985. *Honours:* Detur Award, 1954; Keese Prize, 1982; Scholar of Leukemia Society of America, 1968-73; Research Career Development Award, 1974-79. *Hobbies:* Tennis; Piano; Skiing. *Address:* University of Southern California Cancer Center, 2025 Zonal Avenue, Los Angeles, CA 90033, USA.

MITCHELL, Marlys Marie, b. 6 Feb. 1931, Hamburg, Minnesota, USA. Professor of Occupational Therapy, University of North Carolina, Chapel Hill. m. Earl Nelson Mitchell, 23 July 1955, Hamburg, Minnesota. *Education:* BS, Occupational Therapy, University of Minnesota, Minneapolis; MS, Special and Elementary Education, University of North Dakota, Grand Forks; PhD, Special Education, University of North Carolina, Chapel Hill. *Appointments:* Assistant Professor, 1968, Associate Professor, 1974, School of Education, University of North Carolina, Chapel Hill; Associate Professor, 1974, Professor, 1978, School of Medicine, University of North Carolina; Director, Occupational Therapy Division, University of North Carolina, Chapel Hill, 1976. *Memberships:* Fellow, American Occupational Therapy Association; North Carolina Occupational Therapy Association; American Association of University Professors; American Association of University Women; Association for Retarded Citizens. *Publications:* Author of 50 articles in professional journals, etc. *Honours:* Terry Sanford Award for Creativity in Teaching, North Carolina, 1966; Peabody Teaching Award, School of Education, University of North Carolina, 1974; Service Award, American Occupational Therapy Association, 1983. *Hobbies:* Sewing; Reading; Vineyard. *Address:* 220 Glenhill Lane, Chapel Hill, NC 27514, USA.

MITCHELL, Paul Robert, b. 25 Jan. 1947, Warren, Ohio, USA. Chiropractic Physician, Physical Therapist. m. Marsha Ann Goodwin, 20 Sep. 1969, Warren, Ohio, 2 sons, 1 daughter. *Education:* BS, College of Medicine, Ohio State University, 1969; DC, Palmer College of Chiropractic, Davenport, Iowa, 1979. *Appointments:* Intern, Rockford Memorial Hospital, Rockford, Illinois, 1969; Institute of Physical Medicine and Rehabilitation, Peoria, Illinois; State Hospital for Crippled Children, Elizabethtown, Pennsylvania; Staff Physical Therapist, Children's Hospital, Columbus, Ohio, 1969; Assistant Chief Physical Therapist, Trumbull Memorial Hospital, Warren, Ohio, 1970-72; Children's Rehabilitation Services, Warren, Ohio, Consulting Physical Therapist, 1970-72; Chief Physical Therapist, Warren General Hospital, Warren, Ohio, 1972-76; Shenango Valley Osteopathic Hospital, Farrell, Penn, 1972-76; Physical Therapist, Illinois Hospital, Siluis, Illinois, 1978-79; Chiropractic Physican, Niles Chiropractic Clinic, Niles, Ohio, 1980-85; Consulting Chiropractor, Health Maintenance Plan of Cortland, Ohio, 1981-; Director, Trumbull Chiropractic and Physical Therapy Rehabilitative Services, 1981-. *Memberships include:* American Physical Therapy Association; Ohio Chapter of the American Physical Therapy Assoc; Chamber of Commerce of the USA. *Honours:* Pi Eta Sigma, 1967; Upsilon Pi Upsilon, 1969; Secretary, Pi Tau Delta, 1979; Sub-Deacon, Orthodox Church of America, 1974. *Hobbies include:*

Reading; Golf; Tennis; Swimming. *Address:* TRI-OP Professional Center, Trumbull Chiropractic and Physical Therapy, Rehabilitation Services, Suite 102, 1552 North Rd. SE, Warren, OH 44484, USA.

MITCHELL, Ross Galbraith, b. 18 Nov. 1920. Emeritus Professor of Child Health. m. June Phylis Butcher, 16 Sep. 1950, 1 son, 3 daughters. *Education:* MB, ChB 1944, MD 1953, University of Edinburgh, Scotland. *Appointments:* Surgeon Lieutenant, Royal Naval Volunteer Reserve, 1944-47; Junior hospital posts, Edinburgh, London, Liverpool, 1947-52; Rockefeller Research Fellow, Mayo Clinic, USA, 1952-53; Lecturer in Child Health, University of St Andrews, Scotland, 1952-55; Consultant Paediatrician Dundee Royal Infirmary, 1955-63; Professor of Child Health, University of Aberdeen, 1963-72; Professor of Child Health 1973-85, Dean of Faculty of Medicine and Dentistry 1977-81, Emeritus Professor of Child Health, University of Dundee. *Memberships:* Chairman of Academic Board 1975-78, British Paediatric Association; Association of Physicians of Great Britain and Ireland; Secretary 1956-63, President 1982-84, Scottish Paediatric Society. *Publications:* "Diseases in Infancy and Childhood", (with R W B Ellis), 7th edition 1973; "Child Health in the Community", 2nd edition 1980; "Low Birth Weight", (with R Illsley), 1984. *Hobbies:* Celtic languages and literature; Fishing. *Address:* Craigard, Abertay Gardens, Barnhill, Dundee DD5 2SQ, Scotland.

MITELMAN, Felix, b. 26 Aug. 1940, Professor and Chairman of University Department of Clinical Genetics. m. Gunnel Lundius, 20 Dec. 1969, Lund, Sweden. 1 son, 1 daughter. *Education:* MD 1969, PhD 1972, DSc 1974, University of Lund, Lund. *Appointments:* Research Assistant in Department of Pathology 1969-72, Professor of Clinical Genetics 1980-, University of Lund; Resident in Department of Medicine 1972-75, Head of Department of Clinical Genetics 1975-, University Hospital, Lund. *Memberships:* Research Council, Swedish Cancer Society; Mendelian Society; Royal Physiographic Society. *Publications:* About 300 scientific publications; "Catalog of Chromosome Aberrations in Cancer", 2nd edition 1985. *Hobby:* Tennis. *Address:* Department of Clinical Genetics, University Hospital, S-221 85 Lund, Sweden.

MITTELMAN, Frederick Stuart, b. 8 Nov. 1945, Sioux City, Iowa, USA. Medical Director. m. Helene Coren, 30 Aug. 1966, Omaha, Nebraska, USA, 2 sons. *Education:* BS, Morningside College, Iowa, USA, 1967; MD, Creighton University Medical School, Omaha, USA, 1970. *Appointments:* Intern, University of Nebraska, Omaha, 1970-71; Psychiatry Resident, Walter Reed Army Hospital, Washington DC, 1971-73; Psychiatrist, Arlington Mental Health Centre, Arlington, Virginia, 1971-73; Psychiatrist, Irvin Army Hospital, Fort Riley, USA, 1973-75; Graduate, Topeka Institute for Psychoanalysis, 1975-85; Certified, American Board of Psychiatry and Neurology in Psychiatry, 1975; Team Leader, CC Menninger Memorial Hospital, Topeka, Kansas, 1975-80, Section Chief ER Admission Unit and Director of Admission Services, 1980-82; Clinical Director of Psychiatry, Menorah Medical Centre, Kansas City, 1982-85; Medical Director, Research Psychiatric Centre, Kansas City. *Memberships:* American Medical Association; Jackson County Medical Society; Missouri Medical Society; American Psychiatric Association; APA, Kansas District; Topeka Psychoanalytic Society. *Publications:* 'Therapeutic Side Effects of Drug Research' in 'Bulletin of the Menninger's Clinic', 1983; 'Effect of Neuroleptic Treatment on Attention, Information Processing and Thought Disorder' in 'The Pharmacology Bulletin', 1985. *Honours:* Alpha Omega Alpha Medical Honorary Society, 1969; Army Commendation Medal, 1975. *Hobbies:* Skiing; Jogging; Travel; Reading. *Address:* 2323E 63rd Street, Kansas City, MO 64130, USA.

MIURA, Shiro-e, b. 11 Sep. 1926, Tokyo, Japan. Professor and Head, Department of Psychiatry. m. Mi-E-Ko Tanaka, 11 Nov. 1952, Tokyo, 2 daughters. *Education:* MD, Tokyo Medical College; DMS, Igaku-Hakushi. *Appointments:* Clinical Assistant, Department of Neuropsychiatry, Instructor, Assistant Professor, Department of Psychiatry, Profess and Head (Currently), Vice Director, Hospital, Tokyo Medical College; past Part-time Medical Staff Member, Tokyo Metropolitan Government. *Memberships:* Japanese Society of Psychiatry and Neurology; Japanese Society of EEG and EMG; Japanese Society of Medical Education; Corresponding Member, Fellow, American Psychiatric Association; Fellow, World Association for Social Psychiatry. *Publications:* In Japanese: "Alcoholism", 1980; "Psychiatric Pocket Dictionary", 1981; "Psychiatric Key Word Dictionary", 1982; "Psychiatry MOOK", no 3, 1982, no 5, 1983; "Illustrated Clinical Medicine", volume 6, Psychiatry 2, 1982; "Clinical Medicine for Nursing", 1983. *Hobbies:* Skiing; Golf; Folk art collecting. *Address:* Department of Psychiatry, Tokyo Medical College Hospital, 6-7-1 Nishishinjuku, Shinjuku-ku, Tokyo, Japan.

MIURA, Yoshiaki, b. 9 Apr. 1915, Tokyo, Japan. Medical Director. m. Reiko Hirata, 27 June 1944, Tokyo, 2 sons. *Education:* BS, Osaka High School, 1937; MD, Tokyo University School of Medicine, 1941; PhD, Graduate School, Tokyo University, 1950. *Appointments:* Associate Professor, Biochemistry, Tokyo University School of Medicine, 1953-60; Professor, Chiba University School of Medicine, 1960-81; Medical Director, Pharmaceutical Division, Suntory Ltd, 1981-. *Memberships:* Honorary Member, Japan Biochemical Society; Japan Association Cancer Society; Japan Association Chemotherapy; French Biochemical Society; Corresponding Member, American Cancer Society. *Publication:* "Textbook of Biochemistry", 1982; "Biomodulation", 1986. *Honours:* Chevalier de l'Ordre National de Merite, French Government, 1969. *Hobby:* Lawn Tennis. *Address:* 1-8-17 Nishikata, Bunkyoku, Tokyo 113, Japan.

MLADENOFF, Evan, b. 16 Nov., 1952, Toronto, Canada. m. Sandra Kathy Phillips, 18 Aug. 1974, Toronto, 1 daughter. *Education:* BSc, Physiology, Biochemistry, University of Toronto, 1974; DC, Canadian Memorial Chiropractic College, 1978; DT, Ontario College of Naturopathy, 1978; FIACA, 1980; DICAK. *Appointments:* Team Doctor, Canadian National Canoe Team, 1978, 1979; Team Doctor, Canadian National Ski Bob, 1980; Chairman, Athletic Advisory Board, International College of Applied Kinesiology, 1984-. *Memberships:* Kansas and Canadian Chiropractic Associations; International College of Applied Kinesiology. *Publications:* Contributing Author 'Sports Chiropractic'', 'American Chiropractor Magazine', 1981-82; Contributing Author, "Kinesiology Korner", 'American Chiropractor Magazine', 1985; other articles in 'American Chiropractor' include "Jumper's Knee", 1982; "Hamstring Injuries", 1982, "Cycler's Neck, 1985; and many others. *Hobbies:* Photography; Bicycling; Canoeing; Weightlifting; Racquetball; Skiing. *Address:* c/o College Blvd, Chiropractic Offices, 11111 Nall Ave, Suite 220, Leawood, KS 66211, USA.

MLADENOVIC, Dragomir, b. 8 Nov. 1919, Leskovac, Yugoslavia. Professor, Gynaecologist. m. Ljiljana, 20 Sep. 1954, Belgrade, 2 daughters. *Education:* Professor of Obstetrics-Gynaecology. *Appointments:* Assistant Professor 1954, Docent 1954-65, Part-time Professor 1965-70, Regular Professor 1970-, Medical Faculty; Director, Midwifery School, 1955-80; Director, 2nd Obstetrics-Gynaecology Clinic, Belgrade, 1969-82. *Memberships:* President 1969-73, Serbian Medical Society; President 1968-72, Gynaecologists of Yugoslavia; Serbian Gynaecologic Doctor's Society; Yugoslav Gynaecologists; Serbian Society of Science; Balkans Society of Doctors; Honorary Member, Science of Gruzia, Gynaecologists of Poland, Hungary, Bulgaria, Czechoslovakia and Romania, etc. *Publications:* "OB-GYN for Students", 12 editions, 1960-; "OB-GYN for Midwifes", 1979; "Atlas For Operations In Gynaecology", 1970; About 200 articles in science editions. *Honours:* Award, Serbian Society for Science, 1973; Award for Life Achievement Yugoslav Award, 1979. *Hobbies:* Golf; Tennis. *Address:* Baba Visnjina 37, Belgrade 11000, Yugoslavia.

MOAT, Albert G(roombridge), b. 23 Apr. 1926, Nyack, New York, USA. Professor and Chairman, Department of Microbiology, Marshall University School of Medicine, Huntington, West Virginia. m. Irene Slattery, 11 June 1949, Ithaca, New York, 1 son, 2 daughters. *Education:* BS, 1949, MS, 1950, Cornell University, Ithaca, New York; PhD, University of Minnesota, Minneapolis, 1953. *Appointments:* Instructor, 1952-53, Assistant Professor, 1953-58, Associate Professor, 1958-65, Professor, 1965-78, Department of Microbiology, Hahnemann University, Philadelphia, Pennsylvania. *Memberships:* American Society of Microbiology, President, Allegheny Branch, 1986-87; Fellow, American Academy of Microbiology; American Association for the Advancement of Science; Genetics Society of America; American Society of Biological Chemists; Sigma Xi; American Society Biological Chemists. *Publications:* "Microbial Physiology", 1979; "Biology of the Lactic, Acetic and Propionic Acid Bacteria", 1985. *Honours:* Lalor Foundation Fellow, Cornell University, 1956; Special Research Fellow, USPHS, with A M Srb, Cornell University, 1971-72. *Hobbies:* Art; Woodworking; Antique restoration. *Address:* Department of Microbiology, Marshall University School of Medicine, 1542 Spring Valley Drive, Huntington, WV 25704, USA.

MODAI, Jacques, b. 21 Oct. 1933, Paris, France. Medical Doctor; Profesor of Infectious Diseases. 1 son, 1 daughter. *Education:* MD, Faculty of Medicine, Paris. *Memberships:* Societe Medicale des Hopitaux de Paris; Societe Francaise de Pathologie Infectius; American Society for Microbiology; International Society of Chemotherapy; Mediterranean Society of Chemotherapy. *Publications:* Contributor to professional journals. *Hobbies:* Golf; Tennis. *Address:* Department of Infectious Diseases, Saint Louis Hospital, 1 av. Claude Vellefaux, 75475 Paris Cedex 10, France.

MODLIN, Herbert Charles, b. 1 Dec. 1913, USA. Noble Professor of Forensic Psychiatry. m. Mildred Thornton, 30 Nov. 1933, Papillion, Nebraska, 1 son. *Education:* MD, 1938; MA, 1940; D.Sc (Honorary), 1985; University of Nebraska; Diplomate, Neurology and Psychiatry, American Board of Neurology and Psychiatry, 1945; Diplomate, American Board of Forensic Psychiatry, 1978. *Appointments:* Staff Psychiatrist, Menninger Foundation, 1949-; Director, Residency Training Program, Menninger Foundation, 1951-55; Director, Department of Preventive Psychiatry, Menninger Foundation, 1956-66; Director, Department of Forensic Psychiatry, Menninger Foundation, 1967-82; Associate Clinical Professor, University of Kansas Medical School, 1949-. *Memberships:* American Medical Association; American Psychiatric Association, Fellow; American College of Psychiatry, Fellow; American College of Psychoanalysts, Fellow; Sigma Xi. *Publications:* Narcotics Addiction in Physicians, American Journal of Psychiatry, 1964; The Physician and the Legal System, Journal of American Medical Association, 1972; Traumatic Neuroses and Other Injuries, Psychiatric Clinics of North America, 1983. *Honours:* Gold Medal, Law-Science Academy; Gold Award, American Academy of Law and Psychiatry; Distinguished Alumnus Award, University of Nebraska. *Hobbies:* Stamp Collecting; Golf; International Travel. *Address:* Menninger Foundation, PO Box 829, Topeka, KS 66601, USA.

MODZELEWSKA, Maria-Irena, b. 3 Aug. 1921, Rzeszów, Poland. Head, Department of Paediatrics. m. 2 Aug. 1942, 1 son, 2 daughters. *Education:* Medical Doctor; PhD. *Appointments:* Assistant, 1952-70, Associate Professor, 1970-82, Professor of Paediatrics, 1982, Institute of Medical Academie, Lublin, Poland. *Memberships:* General Council of Polish Paediatric Association; Immunologic Association; Scientific Association of Lublin. Polish Medical Association. *Publications:* "Jaundice in Newborn"; "Diseases of

Newborn, Vaccinations and Nutrition in Children", etc. 120 articles in Polish and international publications. *Honours:* Several awards of the Rector, Lublin Medical School; Numerous Government decorations. *Hobbies:* Travel. *Address:* 20-045 Lublin, ul Godebskiego 1/60, x-ul Staszica 11, Poland.

MOFFAT, David Burns, b. 3 Oct. 1921, Swansea, Wales. Professor of Anatomy, University College Cardiff. m. Joan Coltman, 21 Oct. 1944, London, England, 2 sons, 1 daughter. *Education:* MRCS, LRCP, MBBS (Lond), MD, FRCS (Eng), St Bartholomew's Hospital Medical College. *Appointments:* House Surgeon, Surgical Registrar, St Bartholomew's Hospital, London; Surgeon Lieutenant, RNVR; Various posts in Anatomy, University College, Cardiff, Wales; Surgeon Captain, Retired, RNR. *Memberships:* Renal Association; International Society of Nephrology; Anatomical Society; Late Secretary, British Association of Clinical Anatomists. *Publications:* "Human Embryology" (joint author), 1985; "Nephrology Illustrated", (co-author), 1982; "Nephro-Urology", (Co-author), 1983; "The Mammalian Kidney", 1975. *Honours:* VRD, 1962; Honorary Surgeon to Her Majesty the Queen, 1970. *Hobbies:* Fell walking; Winemaking; Sailing; Oil painting. *Address:* Department of Anatomy, University College, PO Box 78, Cardiff CF1 1XL, Wales.

MOFFATT, Robert John, b. 23 Nov. 1945, McKeesport, Pennsylvania, USA; Assistant Professor. m. Roberta M Moffatt, 13 June 1975, Louisville, Kentucky, 1 son. *Education:* BS Education, California State University; MS Exercise Physiology, University of Louisville; MPH Nutrition, PhD Kinesiology, University of Michigan. Appointments: Director, Exercise Physiology Laboratory, Department of Physicial Education, Western Washington University; Currently Assistant Professor, Department of Movement Sciences, Florida State University. *Memberships:* American College of Sports Medicine; Sigma Xi; American Alliance for Health, Physical Education, Recreation and Dance. *Publications:* 25 refereed publications in various journals related to exercise sciences. *Honour:* Deans Scholar, University of Louisville, 1974. *Hobbies:* Hiking; Sailing. *Address:* Department of Movement Sciences, Florida State University, Tallahassee, FL 32306, USA.

MOFID, Massoud, b. 1 Apr. 1932, Tehran, Iran. Obstetrician/Gynaecologist. m. Mehrangiz Herandi, 16 Mar. 1967, West Berlin, 1 son, 1 daughter. *Education:* Huron College, South Dakota, 1953-54; Physikum, 1957, MD, 1960, University of Hamburg, Germany; Internship, University Hospital, Hamburg, Germany, 1960-61; Internship, Itzehoe/Holst, Germany, 1961-62; Residency, Obstetrics and Gynaecology, Women's Hospital, Neu-Kolln, West Berlin, 1963-67; Fellowship, West Berlin, 1967-68; Fellowship, UCLA Medical Center, Los Angeles, California, USA, 1971-72. *Appointments include:* Co-Director, Labour and Delivery Area, Co-Director High-Risk Clinic, Cleveland Metropolitan General Hospital, Cleveland, Ohio, 1972-77; Director, Division of Maternal-Fetal Medicine, 1977-82, Active Attending Staff in Obstetrics and Gynaecology, 1977-, White Memorial Medical Center, Los Angeles; Chairman, Department of Obstetrics and Gynaecology, 1984-85, Active Attending Staff in Obstetrics and Gynaecology, 1980-, Verdugo Hills Hospital, Glendale, California; Assistant Professor of Obstetrics and Gynaecology, 1972-77, Case Western Reserve University, Cleveland, Ohio; Associate Clinical Professor of Obstetrics and Gynaecology, Loma Linda University School of Medicine, Loma Linda, California, 1977-. *Memberships:* Cleveland Obstetrics and Gynaecology Society; Cleveland Academy of Medicine; Los Angeles County Medical Association; Los Angeles Obstetrics and Gynaecology Society. *Publications include:* 'Ovarian pregnancy and delivery of a live baby - Case presentation' with M Rhee and M Lankarani, Obstetrics and Gynaecology, 1976; 'Effects of intravenous prostaglandin F2o and oxytocin on mother and fetus in induced labour of near term high risk pregnancies' with J F Roux, L'Union Medicale du Canada, 1976; 'Effect of elective induction of labour with prostaglandins F2o and E2 and oxytocin on uterine contraction and relaxation' with J F Roux, P L Moss and K C Dmytrus, American Journal of Obstetrics and Gynaecology, 1977. *Honour:* Fellow, American College of Obstetricians and Gynaecologists, 1976. *Hobbies:* Swimming; Hiking; Tennis. *Address:* 1808 Verdugo Boulevard 408, Glendale, CA 91208, USA.

MOHAN, Madan, b. 14 May 1929 West Pakistan. University Professor and Adviser on Ophthalmology. m. Dr Shakuntala Bhatnagar, 1 son, 1 daughter. *Education:* MBBS, 1954, MS, 1957, King George's Medical College, Lucknow; FACS, American College of Surgeons, USA, 1963. *Appointments:* Lecturer in Ophthalmology, 1958-60; Assistant Professor of Ophthalmology, 1960-65; Associate Professor of Ophthalmology, 1965-75, Professor of Ophthalmology, 1975-79, Chief and Professor of Ophthalmology, 1979-, AIIMS, New Delhi; Adviser on Ophthalmology, Government of India, 1980-. *Memberships:* Delhi Medical Association; Indian Association for the Advancement of Medical Education; Life Member, All India Ophthalmological Society; Life Member, National Society for the Prevention of Blindness in India; All India Eye Donation Society; National Association for the Blind, Bombay. *Publications include:* Numerous articles in the field of Ophthalmology in medical journals. *Honours:* Fellow, National Academy of Medical Sciences; Fellow, American College of Surgeons; Adenwala Oration and Gold Medal, All India Ophthalmological Society, Vice-President 1986-, President Elect 1987, President 1988; Director, WHO Collaboration Centre on Prevention of Blindness; Honorary Consultant in Ophthalmology, Armed Forces Medical Services; Honorary Surgeon to President of India; Padma Shri National Award by Government of India. *Hobbies:* Badminton; Gardening; Photography. *Address:* Chief and Professor of Ophthalmology, Dr R P Centre for Ophthalmic Sciences, AIIMS, New Delhi, India.

MOHAN RAM, Mamidi, b. 18 Dec. 1936, Hyderabad. Deputy Director, National Institute of Nutrition. m. Dr Kumudini, 24 May 1964, Hyderabad, 1 son, 1 daughter. *Education:* MSc, Biochemistry; PhD Biochemistry; NIH Post-Doctoral Fellow in Nutrition, University of California, Davis, USA, 1974-75; Two-Years Post-Graduate Training in Personnel Management, Osmania University, Hyderabad, 1984-86. *Appointments:* Research Assistant 1963-64, Assistant Research Officer, 1964-69, Research Officer, 1969-72, Senior Research Officer, 1972-78, Assistant Director, 1978-82, Deputy Director, 1982-, National Institute of Nutrition, Hyderabad. *Memberships:* Life Member (Treasurer 1982-) Nutrition Society of India; Life Member and Member of Executive Committee, Society for Biomedical Communicators, India; Fellow, Indian Academy of Social Sciences. *Publications:* 55 original research papers on various aspects of nutrition; Co-editor 'Your Health and Nutrition'. *Honours:* Tuli Memorial Award, 1984; WHO Short-Term Consultant in Nutrition to assess the nutrition training needs in South Eastern Countries, 1981; Temporary Adviser to WHO, Geneva, Switzerland, 1983. *Hobbies:* Reading; Tennis. *Address:* National Institute of Nutrition, Jamai-Osmania PO, Hyderabad-500 007, India.

MOHAPATRA, Lakshmi Narayan, b. 20 Feb. 1925, Balasore, Orissa, India. Director, Regional Medical Research Centre. m. Gouribala, 24 May 1944, Balasore, 4 sons, 1 daughter. *Education:* MB BS, MD, Patna University; Diploma of Bacteriology, London University, England; FAMS. *Appointments:* Civil Assistant Surgeon, College Medical Officer, Government of Orissa; Demonstrator of Pathology, Assistant Professor of Bacteriology, SCB Medical College, Cuttack; Assistant Professor, Associate Professor, Professor and Head, Department of Microbiology, All India Institute of Medical Science, New Delhi; Dean, All India Institute of Medical Science; currently, Director, Regional Med-

ical Research Centre, Bhubaneswar. *Memberships:* Indian Association of Pathologists and Microbiologists; Association of Microbiologists of India. *Publications:* Book Chapters: "Human Infection with fungi, Actinomycetes and Algae", 1971; "Progress in Clinical Medicine", 2nd series, 1978. Published 115 scientific papers. *Honours:* Fellow, Academy of Medical Sciences, 1973; Dr Y S Narayan Rao Oration Award, ICMR, 1976; President, Indian Association of Pathologists and Microbiologists, 1979. *Hobbies:* Photography; Travel. *Address:* Regional Medical Research Centre, PO Sainik School, Bhubaneswar 751005, Orissa, India.

MOHS, Frederic Edward, b. 1 Mar. 1910, Burlington, Wisconsin, USA. Emeritus Clinical Professor of Surgery, School of Medicine; Emeritus Director, Chemosurgery Clinic, University of Wisconsin. m. Mary Ellen Reynolds, 18 June 1934, Madison, Wisconsin, 2 sons, 1 daughter. *Education:* BSc, MD, University of Wisconsin; Intern, Portland, Oregon, 1934-35; Bowman Cancer Research Fellow, 1935-38. *Appointments:* Associate in cancer research, Instructor in Surgery 1939-42, Associate Professor, Chemosurgery 1948-69, Clinical Professor, Surgery 1969-81, Emeritus 1981-, University of Wisconsin Medical School. *Memberships:* Fellow, American Medical Association; President 1959, Dane County Medical Society; American Association for Cancer Research; Founder, President 1967-71, American College of Chemosurgery. *Publications include:* "Chemosurgery: Microscopically Controlled Surgery for Skin Cancer", 1978; 'Chemosurgery: A microscopically controlled method of cancer excision' (Arch Surgery, 1941); 'Chemosurgery for skin cancer: Fixed tissue techniques' (Arch Dermatology, 1976); 'Chemosurgery for melanoma', ibid, 1977. *Honours:* Lila Gruber Award, Cancer Research, 1978; International Facial Plastic Surgery Award, 1979; Honorary memberships, Pacific Dermatologic Association 1969, American Academy of Dermatology 1979, American Dermatological Association 1982. *Hobby:* Reading about inventions & inventors. *Address:* 3616 Lake Mendota Drive, Madison, WI 53705, USA.

MOHYDIN, Mohammad Abu Zafar, b. 1 Sep. 1928, Kasur, Pakistan. Physician. m. Gulshan Ara Begum, 26 Dec. 1954, Lahore, 2 sons, 1 daughter. *Education:* MBBS (PB); FRCP (Edinburgh); FCPS (Pakistan); FACC (USA); MRCP (UK); Advanced Military Medicine Course, (Macolin). *Appointments:* Past: Junior Instructor in Medicine and Medical Specialist, Senior Instructor in Medicine, Director of Medicine GHQ, Head of Department of Medicine, Armed Forces Medical College, Rawalpindi; Senior Physician, Combined Military Hospital, Lahore; Personal Physician to the President and to the Prime Minister of Pakistan; Consulting Physician, Central Government Hospital and Polyclinic, Islamabad; Director, Faculty of Medicine, Postgraduate Medical Institute, Lahore; Examiner, FCPS, College of Physicians and Surgeons; Temporary Advisor, WHO/UNDP Special Programme for Research and Training in Tropical Disease; Present: Dean, Professor & Head Department of Medicine, Postgraduate Medical Institute, Lahore; Chairman, Sheikh Zayed Hospital and National Clinical Research Complex; Chairman, Pakistan Medical Research Council Lt-General, Pakistan Army Medical Corps. *Memberships:* Advisory Committee on Bio-medical Research WHO; Pakistan Academy of Sciences; Pakistan Council for Science and Technology; Pakistan Cardiac Society; Pakistan Medical Association; British Medical Association; Chairman, Board of Editors, Pakistan Medical Research Journal; Board of Editors, Medicine International, The Islamic World Medicine Journal. *Publications:* 'Brucellosis and PUO', 1954; 'Bronchial Asthma and its management', 1961; 'WPW and Quinidine therapy', 1970; 'Study of 100 cases of coronary heart disease; 'Brucellosis in the Punjab', 1973; 'Medical Research in Pakistan', 1976; 'Mitral Valve Prolapse', 1980. *Honours include:* Order of Merit, France; Honorary Physician to the President of Pakistan. *Address:* Sheikh Zayed Hospital, Postgraduate Medical

Institute, National Clinical Research Complex, Lahore 16, Pakistan.

MOLDOFSKY, Harvey, b. 19 Sep. 1934, Toronto, Canada. Professor of Psychiatry and Medicine, University of Toronto; Chief-in-Psychiatry, Toronto Western Hospital. m. Zelda Greenspan, 28 June 1960, Halifax, Nova Scotia, 1 son, 1 daughter. *Education:* MD, 1959; DPsych, 1963; University of Toronto, Faculty of Medicine; Internship: Toronto General Hospital, 1959-60; Shaughnessy Veterans Hospital, Vancouver, 1960-61; Research Assistant, Academic Unit of Psychiatry, Middlesex Hospital, London, England, 1963-64; Resident in Psychiatry, Mount Sinai Hospital, Toronto, 1964-66; Research Fellow, University of California Medical Centre, San Francisco, 1970-71. *Appointments:* Staff Psychiatrist, Clarke Institute of Psychiatry, Toronto, 1966-79; Research Consultant, Gage Research Institute, University of Toronto, 1973-79; Psychiatric Consultant, Workmen's Compensation Board, Ontario, 1976-80; Associate Psychiatrist, Department of Psychiatry, 1978-, Associate Physician, Department of Medicine, 1978-, Toronto General Hospital. Psychiatrist in Chief, Department of Psychiatry, 1979-, Toronto Western Hospital; Various academic teaching appointments at University of Toronto; Visiting Professor, Faculty of Medicine, Technion-Israel Institute of Technology, Haifa, 1982. *Memberships include:* American Psychiatric Association; American Psychosomatic Society; Canadian Medical Association; Canadian Psychiatric Association; Royal College of Physicians and Surgeons of Canada. *Publications:* Contributor to professional journals and chapters in books. *Honours include:* Scholarships and Fellowships; Wellcome Fellowship to Royal Society of Medicine, London England, 1963-64; Schering Travelling Fellowship Award of Canadian Society of Clinical Investigation, 1982. *Hobbies:* Furniture making (cabinet work); Swimming; Tennis. *Address:* Toronto Western Hospital, 399 Bathurst Street, Toronto, Ontario, Canada M5T 2S8.

MOLIDOR, John B, b. 3 July 1951, Des Moines, Iowa, USA. Associate Professor and Assistant Dean. m. Jeanne Marie Doran, 1 May, 1981. *Education:* BA, Psychology, MA, Educational Psychology, PhD, Educational Psychology. *Appointments:* Research Associate, Assistant to Dean, Assistant Dean for Admissions, Assistant Dean for Student Affairs and Admissions, Michigan State University, College of Human Medicine. *Memberships:* Association of American Medical Colleges; AAMC Group on Student Affairs; American Educational Research Association; American Association of Collegiate Registrars and Admissions Officers. *Publications:* "Admissions: Handbook for Interviers" 1982; "Admissions: Handbook for Raters" 1982. *Honours:* Vice-Chair, Group on Student Affairs (AAMC); Chair, National Task Force on Admissions (AAMC). *Hobby:* Photography. *Address:* College of Human Medicine, A-234 Life Sciences, Michigan State University, East Lansing, MI 48824/1317, USA.

MOLINA, Julio Alfredo, b. 28 Mar. 1948, Guatemala. Director, Anxiety Disorders Institute of Atlanta. m. Diana C Montenegro, 18 Dec. 1971, Costa Rica, 1 son, 1 daughter. *Education:* MD, Universidad de San Carlos de Guatemala, 1973; Board Certified, American Board of Psychiatry and Neurology, 1979. *Appointments:* Associate Professor, Department of Neuropsychiatry and Behavioural Sciences, University of South Carolina Medical School, USA, 1979-82; Director, Unit 1, Georgia Mental Health Institute, 1982-83; Assistant Professor, Emory University School of Medicine, 1982-83; Private Practice, Psychiatric Consultants Group of Atlanta, 1983-85; currently, Director, Anxiety Disorders Institute of Atlanta, Georgia. *Memberships:* American Medical Association; American Psychiatric Association; International Society of Hypnosis; Society for Clinical and Experimental Hypnosis; Colegio de Medicos y Cirujanos de Guatemala. *Publications:* 'Understanding the Biopsychosocial Model' in 'International Journal of Psychiatry in Med-

icine', 1983; 'Psychobiosocial Maps', in 'Journal of Clinical Psychiatry', 1982; 'Affective Disorders and Tardive Dyskinesia' in 'Psychiatric Forum', 1982. *Honours:* Annual Teaching Award, William S Hall Psychiatric Institute, 1980; Special Award for Outstanding Service, Medical Staff, W S Hall Psychiatry Institute, 1982. *Hobbies:* Painting; Literature; Music. *Address:* Anxiety Disorders Institute of Atlanta, 1 Dunwoody Park, Suite 112, Atlanta, GA 30338, USA.

MOLINA-CARTES, Ramiro, b. 14 Mar. 1938, Santiago, Chile. Associate Professor, Medicine, University of Chile. m. Sara Saez Suazo, 9 Oct. 1965. Santiago, 1 son, 1 daughter. *Education:* MD, Faculty of Medicine, University of Chile; MPA, Johns Hopkins University, USA. *Appointments:* Regional Advisor, Social Security, Family Planning, Latin America and Caribbean Zone, International Labour Organization UN, San Jose, Costa Rica, 1972-76; Associate Professor, Public Health, Associate Professor, Obstetrics and Gynaecology, Chief, National Maternal and Child Programme, National Health Service, Chile, 1976-80; Chief, Obstetrics, Chairman, Obstetrics & Gynaecology, University of Chile Hospital, 1980-84; Temporal Advisor in MCH of Pan American Health Organization, Lima, 1984-85. *Publications:* Co-Author, "Elementos de Salud Materno y Perinatal: Coleccion temas basicos de Pedistria", 1981; "Aspectos Clinicos en Reproduccion Humana", 1982; Chapters in books including "Aborto", 'Texto docente de Obstetricia y Ginecologia', 1983; Author more than 29 published papers including "Proyecto Regional en Seguridad Social y Planificacion Familiar para Latinoamerica", 'Curso de O.I.T', 1974; "Adolescencia y Embarazo: Resultados de un Modelo de Atencion", 'Revista Medica de Chile', in press. *Memberships include:* Sociedad Chilena de Salubridad; Sociedad Chilena de Obstetricia y Ginecologia; Sociedad Latinoamericana de Perinatologia; Corresponding Member, various other professional organizations. *Honour:* Award Mention for Obstetrics and Gynaecology, Chilean Society for the Paper and Experience in Kidney Transplant and Pregnancy, 1984. *Hobbies:* Coin Collecting. *Address:* Eduardo Castillo Velasco ∅946, Nunoa, Santiago, Chile.

MOLL, Jan Witold, b. 24 Oct. 1912, Poland. Consulting Cardiovascular Surgeon. m. Izabella Staniewski, 18 June 1945, 1 son, 3 daughters. *Education:* Physicians Diploma, 1939; Doctors Degree, 1945; Associate Professor, 1955, Extraordinary Professor, 1961, Professor of Cardiovascular Surgery, 1972. *Appointments:* Assistant, Department of Regular Anatomy, 1934-39; Assistant Surgeon, Municipal Hospital, Radom, 1939-45; Resident, Surgical Clinic, Poznan, 1945-58; Head of Surgical Clinic Medical Academy, 1958-72; Director of Institute of Cardiology, Head of Cardiosurgical Clinic, Medical Academy, Lodz, Poland, 1972-. *Memberships:* European Society of Cardiovascular Surgery; American College of Surgeons; American College of Cardiology; International Society of Angiology; International Society of Surgery. *Publications:* 253 papers published in Polish and international scientific journals. "Technique of Pulmonary Resection" 1957; "Atlas of the Heart Defects" Polish, Russian and Hungarian editions, 1961; 'Arterialisierung des sinus coronarius' Thoraxchirurgie, 1979. *Honours include:* The Officer's Cross of the Order of Polish Resurrection, 1965; Honorary Member: American Medical Society, 1965, Hungarian Surgical Society, 1974, Czechoslovakian Surgical Society, 1977, Bulgarian Surgical Society, 1979; German Surgical Society, 1974; The Commander's Cross of the Order of Polish Resurrection, 1973; Corresponding Member, Germany Academy of Sciences, 1974; First Degree Prize of Polish Academy of Sciences, 1974; Honorary Member, Scandinavian Cardiovascular Society, 1983; Doctor Honoris Causa, Bialystok Medical Academy, 1984. *Hobbies:* Music; Foreign Languages; Skiing. *Address:* Swierczewski str 24a/5, 90-541 Lodz, Poland.

MOLLA, Abdul Majid, b. 7 Jan. 1941, Dhaka, Bangladesh. Paediatric Gastroenterologist. m. Ayesha Molla, 31 Mar. 1967, Dhaka, 1 son, 2 daughters. *Education:* MB BS; MD; DCh; PhD Paediatric Gastroenterology.

Appointments: Medical Officer, Institute of Disease of Chest and Hospital, 1963-65; Research Physician, Cholera Research Laboratory, 1965-69; International Fellow, Saint Rafael Clinic, University Hospital Department of Paediatrics, Catholic University of Leuven, Belgium, 1969-75; Senior Tutor in Paediatrics, Queens University, Belfast, Northern Ireland, 1975-79; Scientist and Paediatric Gastroenterologist, ICDDR- B Visiting Professor, Bangladesh Institute of Child Health, *Memberships:* Belgian Paediatric Society; Ulster Paediatric Society, Northern Ireland; Bangladesh Medical Association; Bangladesh Paediatric Association; Asian Pacific Society of Paediatric Gastroenterology; Bangladesh Association for Advancement of Medical Science; Indian Society of Gastroenterology; International Nutrition Society. *Publications:* 36 articles including: 'Mothers and Family Members Can Prepare and Use Rice ORS in Rural Bangladesh', (with M Rahman, A Rari and W B Greenough); 52 Papers and abstracts including: 'Cereal-based Oral Rehydration Therapy', 1985; 'Nutritional Management of Diarrhoea', 1985. *Honour:* Greatest Distinction for PhD thesis, 1975. *Hobbies:* Gardening; Preservation of wildlife. *Address:* International Centre for Diarrhoeal Disease Research, Bangladesh, GPO Box 128, Dhaka 2, Bangladesh.

MOLLA, Ayesha, b. 27 July 1943, Dhaka, Bangladesh. Associate Scientist. m. Dr Abdul Majid Molla, 31 Mar. 1967, Dhaka, 1 son, 2 daughters. *Education:* BSc, Biochemistry, 1964; MSc, Biochemistry, 1965; University of Dhaka; MS, Clinical Biochemistry, 1975; PhD, Clinical Biochemistry, 1975, University of Leuven, Belgium. *Appointments:* Senior Research Officer, PAK SEATO Cholera Research Laboratory, Dhaka, 1966-69; Research Fellow, University of Leuven, Belgium, 1969-75; Post-doctoral Research Fellow, Queen's University of Belfast, Northern Ireland, 1975-78; Investigator, Cholera Research Laboratory, Dhaka, 1978-80; Associate Scientist, ICDDR B, Dhaka, 1980-85. *Memberships:* Bangladesh Biochemical Society; Bangladesh Association for Women Scientists; Ulster Biochemical Society; Nutrition Society of Bangladesh; Bangladesh Association for Advancement of Science. *Publications:* Contributor to professional journals including: Co-author, 'Zinc deficiency and diarrhoeal disease' in 'Journal of the Bangladesh Agricultural Research Council'; "Evaluation of Vitamin A stores reply" in 'Journal Pediatrics', 1984; Several presentations. *Honours include:* Special award for standing first among the first class students in MSc Examination, 1965; Gold Medal Award for Best Women Scientist of Bangladesh, The Bangladesh Women Scientist Association, 1984. *Hobbies:* Gardening; Reading world journals; Acquiring knowledge of religions especially Islam and Christianity; Praying. *Address:* "Safina", House 9, Rd 15, Sector 1, Uttara Model Town, Dhaka, Bangladesh.

MOLLAN, Raymond Alexander Boyce, b. 10 Aug. 1943, Belfast, Northern Ireland. Professor of Orthopaedic Surgery. m. Patricia Ann Fairbanks Scott, 1 Sep. 1969, Belfast, 3 sons, 1 daughter. *Education:* D Obst, Royal College of Obstetricians and Gynaecologists, 1971; Fellow, Royal College of Surgeons, Edinburgh, 1974; Higher Surgical Training Certificate in Orthopaedic Surgery, 1977; MD, 1981. *Appointments:* Consultant Orthopaedic Surgeon, Ulster and Musgrave Park Hospitals, 1978-79; Consultant and Senior Lecturer in Orthopaedic Surgery, Royal Victoria Hospital, Musgrave Park Hospital and The Queen's University of Belfast, 1979-82; Professor of Orthopaedic Surgery, The Queen's University of Belfast and Consultant, Royal Victoria Hospital, Musgrave Park and Belfast City Hospital, 1982-. *Memberships:* British Medical Association; British Orthopaedic Research Society; British Orthopaedic Association; SICOT; SIROT; Irish Orthopaedic Club. *Honours:* Marion Sims Medal in Obstetrics; Robert Jones Gold Medal; BOA Prize; ABC Travelling Fellowship; Johnson and Johnson Travel Fellowship. *Hobbies:* Gardening; Sailing. *Address:* Department of Orthopaedic Surgery, The Queen's University of Musgrave Park Hospital, Stockman's Lane, Belfast BT9 7JB, Northern Ireland.

MOLLENHAUER, Barry, b. 9 Oct. 1937, Isisford, Queensland, Australia. Specialist Orthodontist; Private Practitioner; Post-Graduate Tutor. m. Margaret Jean Denholm, 14 Apr. 1962, Hobart, Tasmania, 1 son, 2 daughters. *Education:* Master of Dental Science, University of Melbourne; Bachelor of Dental Science, University of Queensland; Licentiate of Dental Surgery, Victoria; Fellow, Royal Australian College of Dental Surgeons. *Appointments:* Currently, Specialist Orthodontist, Royal Dental Hospital of Melbourne; Private practitioner; Post-Graduate Tutor, University of Melbourne. *Memberships:* Chairman, Dental Nurses Training Course Committee, Victorian Branch, Australian Dental Association; Victorian Representative and Agenda Secretary to Certification Board, Australian Dental Assistants Association; Chairman, Australian Begg Orthodontic Study Group; President, Victorian Branch, Federal Vice-President, Chairman of Congress Committee, Australian Society of Orthodontists. *Publications:* Editor: 'Begg Orthodontic Newsletter'; 'Australian Orthodontic Journal'. *Hobby:* Micro-computers. *Address:* 299 Upper Heidelberg Road, Ivanhoe, Victoria 3079, Australia.

MØLLER, Ingolf John, b. 17 Sep. 1928, Chicago, USA. Regional Officer for Oral Health, World Health Organization. m. Aase Johanne Schlosshauer, 5 July 1955, 1 son, 2 daughters. *Education:* DDS, Royal Dental College, Copenhagen, 1955; BS, University of Rochester, New York, USA, 1958; Fellow, Eastman Dental Dispensary, Rochester, New York, 1958; Dr odont, Royal Dental College, Copenhagen, 1965. *Appointments:* Instructor, Royal Dental College, Copenhagen, 1955-57; Dental Officer, Godhavn, Greenland, 1957; Fellow, Eastman Dental Dispensary, Rochester, New York, 1957-58; Research Associate, Royal Dental College, Copenhagen, 1958-65; Professor, Department of Pedodontics, Royal Dental College, Aarhus, 1966-72; Professor, Department of Cariology and Preventive Dentistry, Royal Dental College, Copenhagen, 1972-76; Project Manager, World Health Organization, Geneva, Switzerland, 1976-80; Regional Officer for Oral Health, WHO, Copenhagen, 1980-. *Memberships:* European Organization for Caries Research, Vice-President 1967-71; International Dental Federation, Commission Member, 1977; International Association for Dental Research; Medical-Historical Society, Board Member, 1973-78; Centro de Estudio de Recursos Odontologicos para el Nino, Permanent Advisor, 1974; Indonesian Dental Association, Honorary Member, 1974. *Publications:* "Dental Fluorose og Caries, thesis 1965; More than 150 papers published on dental public health, preventive dentistry and dental epidemiology. *Honours:* Knight Royal Order of Dannebrog (R1), 1975; Benzow Prize, 1975; D-34 Grant, 1965; Fulbright Fellow, 1957. *Hobbies:* Numismatics; Philately; Oriental antiques. *Address:* World Health Organizstion, Regional Office for Europe, Scherfigsvej 8, 2100 Copenhagen 0, Denmark.

MÖLLER, Lars Göran, b. 30 Aug. 1936, Vittangi, Sweden. Professor of Immunology. m. Erna Lindell, 10 June 1960, Stockholm, 1 son, 1 daughter. *Education:* MD, 1963; PhD, 1963. *Appointments:* Research Fellow, Swedish Cancer Society, 1963-67; Associate Professor, 1967-69, Professor, 1969-85, Karolinska Institute; Professor, Stockholm University 1986-. *Memberships:* Honorary Member, American Association of Immunologists; Scandinavian Society of Immunology; British Society of Immunology; Chairman, Publication Committee, International Union of Immunological Societies. *Publications:* Editor of Immunological Reviews since 1969; 350 publications in Immunology; Editor of the 55th Nobel Symposium "Genetics of the Immune Response". *Honours:* Anders Jahres Prize for Medical Research 1976; Vice Chairman the Nobel Assembly, 1984; Member of the Nobel Assembly since 1977, Karolinska Institute. *Hobby:* Sailing. *Address:* Department of Immunology, Stockholm University, 10691 Stockholm, Sweden.

MOMIROV, Dejan, b. 9 Dec. 1943, Zrenjanin, Yugoslavia. Ophthalmologist/Assistant Professor. m. Bozin Ivana MD, 10 Jan. 1971, Belgrade, 1 son. *Education:* MD, Belgrade University Medical School, 1968; MA (MMSci) in Experimental Medicine, 1973-76; Specialisation in Ophthalmology, 1977. *Appointments:* Physician, General Hospital, Zrenjanin, 1968-69; Research Associate, Institute of Physiology, Belgrade University Medical School, 1969-74; Ophthalmologist, Institute for Ophthalmology, City Hospital, Belgrade, 1974-; Assistant Professor, Medical Faculty, Belgrade, 1984-. *Memberships:* Ophthalmology Section, Serbian Medical Association; EEG and Clinical Neurophysiology Section, Serbian Medical Association. *Publications:* Articles in medical journals including: "Draining Implant for Neovascular Glaucoma" with Z Kuljača and V. Ljubojević, in American Journal of Ophthalmology, 1983; "Idiopathic Sectoral Corneal Endothelitis" with Z Kuljaca in American Journal of Ophthalmology, 1985. Presenter of papers to medical conferences. *Hobbies:* Electronics; Astronomy; Diving; Fishing. *Address:* Bulevar AVNOJ-a 86/49, 11070, Belgrade, Yugoslavia.

MOMIROV, Momcilo, b. 5 June 1913, Zrenjanin, Yugoslavia. Doctor of Phthisiology. m. Stojanka Vujanov, 12 July 1940, Zrenjanin, 1 son, 1 daughter. *Education:* Diploma of Faculty of Philosophy, Diploma of Faculty of Medicine, Diploma of Faculty of Medicine specialising in Phthisilogy Belgrade University. *Appointments:* Professor of the Commercial Academy, Zrenjanin, 1941-44; Physician for specialised training in Hospital Zrenjanin, 1952-60; Lecturer of Secondary Medical School, Zrenjanin and of Gymnasium Zrenjanin, 1956-64; Director of Hospital for TBC of Chest, Zrenjanin, 1961-68; Head of Hospital section of Institute for Chest Diseases and TBC, Zrenjanin, 1968-80. *Memberships:* Serbian Medical Association, Beograd; Honorary Member, Pneumophthisiologists Section of Association of Physicians of Vojvodina; Red Cross of Township Committee, Zrenjanin; American College of Chest Physicians. *Publications:* Reports, reviews and contributions on Conferences of Pneumophysiologists of Yugoslavia and on meetings of PneumophthisiologicalSection of Serbian Medical Association. *Honours:* Title of "Primarius" 1971; Diploma with Silver Medallion, Red Cross Assembly of Yugoslavia, 1975; Acknowledgement of Institute for Chest Disease and TBC in Sremska Kamenica, 1980; Acknowledgement of Institute for Chest Disease and TBC in Zrenjanin, 1980; Letter of Thanks of Health Centre in Novi Becej, 1983. *Hobbies:* Painting; Music. *Address:* Manastirska 6, 23000 Zrenjanin, Yugoslavia.

MONEIM, Moheb S, b. 14 May 1941, Cairo, Egypt. Professor of Orthopaedics and Hand Surgery. m. Brigitte Moneim, 14 Nov. 1975, New York City, USA, 1 son, 1 daughter. *Education: MD, Cairo University, 1963; DS, Diploma of Surgery, 1966; Fellow, Royal College of Surgeons, Canada, 1974; Diploma, American Board of Orthopaedic Surgery, 1976. Appointments:* Junior Attending, Orthopaedic Surgery Hospitals for Special Surgery, New York City, New York, USA; Assistant Professor, Associate Professor, Professor of Orthopaedics and Hand Surgery, University of New Mexico Medical School. *Memberships include:* American Academy of Orthopaedic Surgeons; Western and New Mexico Orthopaedic Associations; Royal College of Physicians and Surgeons, Canada; American Society for Surgery of the Hand; Piedmont Orthopaedic Society; Albuquerque-Bernadillo County Medical Association. *Publications:* 'The Tangential Posterioanterior Radiograph to Demonstrate Scapholunate Dissociation', 1981; 'Interfascicular Nerve Grafting', 1982; 'The Effect of Herparin on the Rate of Patency of the Rat Femoral Artery and Vein', 1981; 'Radiocarpal Dislocation-Classification and Rational for Management', 1985; 'Transscaphoid Perilunate Fracture Dislocation', 1984; 'Salvage of Replanted Parts of the Upper Extremity', 1985; 'Volar Dislocation MCP Joint', 1983. *Hobbies:* Swimming; Hiking. *Address:* 2211 Lomas Boulevard North East, Albuquerque, NM 87131, USA.

MONETTE, Francis C, b. 9 Aug. 1941, USA. Professor of Biology and Health Sciences, Boston University, 1982-. m. Yvonne A Belanger, 20 Apr. 1968, Manchester, New Hampshire, 1 son, 1 daughter. *Education:* BA; MS; PhD, 1962. *Appointments:* Postdoctoral Fellow, Tufts University School of Medicine, 1968-71; Assistant Professor of Biology, 1971-77, Associate Professor of Biology, 1978-82, Boston University. *Memberships:* Charter Member, International Society for Experimental Hematology, 1970-; American Society of Hematology, 1970-; American Association for the Advancement of Science, 1968-; Sigma Xi, 1968-. *Publications:* Contributor of over 55 articles and book chapters on professional subjects. *Honours:* Public Health Service Research Career Development Award, 1977-82; Recipient of over 5 competitive research grants from NIH, 1975-; Editorial Board, 'Experimental Hematology'. *Hobbies:* Collector/dealer in antiques. *Address:* Boston University, Department of Biology, 2 Cummington Street, Boston, MA 02215, USA.

MONOD, Hugues, b. 19 Apr. 1929, Paris, France. Professor. m. Jeanine Doucet, 24 Feb. 1953, 2 sons, 1 daughter. *Education:* MD; Agrege Enseignement Superieur; Professor. *Appointments:* Engineer, CNRS, Paris, 1954-60; Professor of Physiology, Amiens, 1961-65, Paris, 1965; Director, Work Physiology Laboratory, CNRS, Paris. *Memberships:* Past General Secretary and President, French Speaking Ergonomics Society; Past Secretary and General Secretary, Association der Physiologistes; National Council for Scientific Research, CNRS, 1969-75, 1980-82; National Council for Universities, 1975-80, 1983-86; Vice President, University Pierre and Marie Curie, 1981. *Publications:* "Le travail musculaire local et la fatique chez l'Humaine", 1960; "How the Muscles are Used in the Body", 1972; "L'Evaluation de la change de travail", 1976; "La validité des mesures de frequence cardiaque en Ergonomie", 1969; "Physiologie du sport", 1985. *Honours:* Laureat de la Faculte de Medecine, Paris, 1956; Laureat de l'Academie de Medecine, France, 1985. *Hobbies:* Roman antiques; Medals in Biology and Medicine. *Address:* 91 Bd de l'Hospital, F-75634 Paris Cedex 13, France.

MONRO, Alastair Macleod, b. 27 Nov. 1934, Cardiff, Wales. Director, Pfizer Laboratories, France. m. Caroline Shaw, 1 son, 1 daughter. *Education:* BA, MA, Oxford University, England, 1956, BSc, Chemistry, 1957, DPhil, 1959; Post-doctoral Fellow, Cornell University, USA, 1960. *Appointments:* Director, Drug Safety Evaluation, Pfizer Central Research, Sandwich, Kent, England; Directeur, Centre de Recherche, Laboratoires Pfizer, Amboise, France. *Memberships:* British Toxicology Society; European Society of Toxicology; Biochemical Society; American Chemical Society. *Publications:* Some 50 papers in 'Journal of Medicinal Chemistry', 'Xenobriotica', 'Archives of Toxicology' and 'Toxicology'. *Hobbies:* Sailing; Skiing. *Address:* Centre de Recherche, Laboratoires Pfizer, 37401 Amboise Cedex, France.

MONROE, Edwin Wall, b. 10 Mar. 1927, Laurinburg, North Carolina, USA. Senior Associate Dean and Professor of Medicine. m. Nancy Laura Gaquerel, 14 Mar. 1953, Fredericksburg, Virginia, 1 daughter. *Education:* BS, Davidson College, 1947; MD, University of Pennsylvania, 1951. *Appointments:* Staff Physician, State Hospital, Butner, North Carolina, 1953-54; Private practice of internal medicine, Greenville, 1956-68; Dean of School of Allied Health Profession and Director of Health Affairs 1968-71, Vice-Chancellor for Health Affairs 1971-79, Professor of Medicine 1971-, Senior Associate Dean of Medical School 1979-, East Carolina University; Executive Director, Eastern Area Health Education Center. *Memberships:* Fellow, American College of Physicians, American Medical Association; Association of Medical Colleges; Sigma Xi; North Carolina Institute of Medicine; North Carolina Health Coordinating Council; Advisory Board, Kate B Reynolds Health Care Trust. *Publications:* Several articles in medical journals. *Honour:* Priestley Prize for Student Research, University of Pennsylvania School of Medicine. *Hobbies:* Golf; Reading. *Address:* East Carolina University, School of Med icine, Greenville, NC 27834, USA.

MONTEFUSCO, Cheryl Marie, b. 14 May 1948, New Kensington, Pennsylvania, USA. Associate Professor in Surgery, Albert Einstein College of Medicine. *Education:* BSc; PhD, Cardiovascular Physiology, College of Medicine and Dentistry, New Jersey, 1975. *Appointments:* Research Associate, Squibb Institute for Medical Research, 1970-71; Editor, Harrison S Martland Medical Center, 1972-73; Instructor, Human Anatomy and Physiology, College of Medicine and Dentistry, New Jersey, 1973-74, Kean College of New Jersey, 1974; Vascular Surgery Research Associate and Director, Scanning Electron Microscopy Laboratory, Newark Beth Israel Medical Center, 1975-76; Technical Sales Representative, W L Gore & Associates Incorporated, 1976-77; Assistant Professor of Surgery, Albert Einstein College of Medicine, New York City, 1977-83; Coordinator of Lung Transplantation, Montefiore Medical Center, New York City, 1977-84; Project Leader USPHS-NHLBI Program Project (Experimental Lung Transplantation), Montefiore Medical Center, 1980-; Coordinator of Lung Transplantation, Montefiore Medical Center, 1984-; Associate Professor of Surgery, Albert Einstein College of Medicine, New York City, 1983-. *Memberships include:* Fellow, International College of Angiology; Fellow, American College of Angiology, etc. *Publications:* Contributor to professional journals; Abstracts; Chapters in Books. *Honour:* Guest Lecturer, Cardiovascular Physiology, University of Utrecht, 1976. *Hobbies:* Breeding and Training German Shepherd Dogs; Gardening; Antique Restoration. *Address:* PO Box 488, Pawling, NY 12564, USA.

MONTEIL, Henri, b. 15 July 1940, Brive, France. Professor of Bacteriology at Strasbourg Faculty of Medicine; Hospital Biologist, Louis Pasteur University. m. Mythese Jochem, 30 July 1963; Colmar, France, 2 sons. *Education:* Doctor of Science; Master of Human Biology; Parmacist; Graduate, Pasteur Institute. *Appointments:* Resident, Strasbourg University Hospital; Assistant, Chief Laboratory, Professor, Strasbourg University Hospital and Faculty of Medicine. *Memberships:* Société Française de Microbiologie; American Society for Microbiology; Société Française de Biologie Clinique; International Society on Toxinology; European Society of Clinical Microbiology. *Publications:* Contributor to professional journals and publications. *Honour:* Prizewinner, French Academy of Medicine, 1979. *Hobbies:* Walking; Mountaineering. *Address:* Institute of Bacteriology, 3 rue Koeberlé, 67000 Strasbourg, France.

MONTES-GALLO, Delia Magdelena Clara, b. 28 Apr. 1932, Buenos Aires, Argentina. Associate Clinical Professor, Psychiatry and Paediatrics; Private Practitioner, Adult and Child Psychiatry; Active Staff Member, numerous hospitals. *Education includes:* BA, 1956, MD, 1958, Fellow, Alberto Peralta Ramos Maternity Hospital, 1956-57, 1959, University of Buenos Aires, Argentina; Attended various Childrens Hospitals, Europe, USA and Argentina; Neonatal Fellowship, Paediatrics, University of Pittsburgh, Pennsylvania, USA, 1963-65; Fellowship in Psychiatry, University of Southern California, 1971. *Appointments include:* Private Practice, Adult and Child Psychiatry, El Paso, Texas, USA, 1972-. Active Staff: Providence Memorial Hospital, El Paso, 1972-; Sierra Medical Center, El Paso, 1972-; Sun Towers Hospital, El Paso, 1972-; Sun Valley Hospital, 1980-. Professional Advisor, St Patricks Cathedral Pro-Life Committee, El Paso, 1981-; Past and Present Consultant to various organisations; Associate Clinical Professor, Paediatrics and Psychiatry, Texas Technical University School of Medicine, 1981- (associated with University since 1977). *Memberships include:* El Paso County Medical Society; Texas Medical Psychiatric Association; American Psychiatric Association; American Society for Adolescent Psychiatry; American Academy of Child Psychiatry; Texas Paediatric Society. *Publica-*

tions: 'Apgar score in newborn infants' in 'Rev Arg de Ped', with E Cerrutti, 1960; 'Acidity and bacterial content of gastric juice during the first day of life' in 'Annal of Paediatric Fenn', 1960. Various presentations and speaker at over 30 professional conferences. *Honours:* Diplomate, American Boards of Psychiatry and Neurology, 1979, American Board of Child Psychiatry, 1981; Physicians Recognition Award, American Medical Association, 1980. *Address:* 6409 Westwind, El Paso, TX 79912. USA.

MONTGOMERY, John Atterbury, b. 29 Mar. 1924, Greenville, USA. Senior Vice President, Laboratory Director. m. Jean Kirkman, 2 sons, 2 daughters. *Education:* AB, 1946; MS, Organic Chemistry, Vanderbilt University, 1947; PhD, Organic Chemistry, University of North Carolina, Chapel Hill, 1951. *Appointments:* Research Assistant, 1943, Teaching Assistant, 1946-47, Vanderbilt University; Teaching Assistant, 1947-49, Teaching Fellow, 1949-50, Postdoctoral Research, 1951-52, University of North Carolina; Adjunct Professor, Birmingham Southern College, 1957-62; Adjunct Senior Scientist, Comprehensive Cancer Centre, University of Alabama, 1978-; Joined, 1952-, Director, Organic Chemistry Research, 1956-, Vice President, 1974-, Senior Vice President, Director, Kettering Meyer Lab, 1981-, Southern Research Institute, Birmingham. *Memberships include:* American Chemical Society; American Association for Cancer Research; Association of American Cancer Institutes; International Society of Heterocyclic Chemistry; American Association for the Advancement of Science; New York Academy of Sciences; Alpha Chi Sigma; Sigma Xi. *Publications:* 350 publications including book chapters, articles in professional journals etc. *Honours:* Herty Medal, 1974; Fellow, New York Academy of Science, 1977; Taito O Soine Memorial Award, 1979; Southern Chemist Award, 1980; Cain Memorial Award, 1982; Alfred Burger Award, Medicinal Chemistry, 1986. *Hobbies:* Boating; Jazz. *Address:* Southern Research Institute, PO Box 55305, Birmingham, AL 35255, USA.

MONTGRAIN, Noel, b. 11 Dec. 1933, Quebec, Canada. Chairman, Psychiatry, Laval University. m. Marcelle Dufour, 8 October 1962, Quebec, 2 daughters. *Education:* MD; FRCP (C); Specialist, Psychiatry; Full Member, Psychoanalysis. *Appointments:* Director, Short Term, Psychoanalytic Psychotherapy Unit, Centre Hospitalier de l'Universite Laval, 1975-; Professor, Laval University, 1984-. *Memberships:* Vice President, Societe Psychoanalytique de Montreal, 1973-77; President, Societe Psychoanalytique de Montreal, 1977-81; Vice-President, Canadian Psychoanalytic Society, 1976-81; International Psychoanalytic Society; Royal College of Physicians and Surgeons of Canada; Canadian and American Psychiatric Associations; Corporation Professionelle des Medecins et Chirurgiens du Quebec. *Publications:* "The Influence of Social Security Systems on the 'Demand' in Medicine", 'Psychosomatic Medicine: Theoretical Clinical and Transcultural Aspects', 1983; "On Female Sexuality: The Difficult Path from Anatomical Destiny to Psychic Representation", 'International Journal of Psychoanalysis', 1983; "Du cote de la psychotherapie analytique breve", 'Psychologie Medicale', 1980. *Honours:* Anatomy Prize, 1954; ACFAS Prize, 1955, 1956; Mosby Scholarship Award, 1957; Foundation Poulenc Prize, 1959; Fellow, de l'American Psychiatric Association, 1981. *Hobbies:* Piano; Skiing; Windsurfing; Squash. *Address:* 2737 Ch St-Louis, Ste-Foy, Canada G1W 1N8.

MONTILEONE, Michael Salvatore, b. 17 Aug. 1953, St Louis, Missouri, USA. Radiologist. *Education:* BSc, Logan College, Missouri, USA; Dr of Chiropractic, Logan College of Chiropractic, USA; Radiology Degree, Phillip Institute, Melbourne, Australia; Board Certified Roentgenologist, American Chiropractic Board of Roentgenology. *Appointments:* Radiographer, Lindell Hospital, Missouri, 1979-80; Private Chiropractic, Melbourne, Australia, 1980-83; Lecturer in Radiology, Phillip Institute, Melbourne; Head Clinician,

Summerhill, Abbotsford and Bulleen Chiropractic Centres, Melbourne; Associate in Roentgenology, Albuquerque, New Mexico, USA, 1983-84. *Memberships:* American Chiropractic Association; Australian Chiropractors' Association; American College of Chiropractic Roentgenology; American Council on Chiropractic Roentgenology; New Mexico Chiropractic Association, (Chairman). *Publications include:* 25 conference papers; Contributions to professional journals including: 'Case of the Missing Pedicle', (case study), published by the American Council on Chiropractic Roentgenology, 1981, with Dr T R Yochum; 'A Solitary Plasmacytoma', case study, in 'Australian Chiropractic Journal', 1982, and in the 'New Zealand Chiropractic Journal', 1983; 'Chordoma of the Sacrum' in 'Journal of Chiropractic', 1983, with Dr T R Yochum and Dr G M Guebert; 'Common Fractures of the Wrist' published by the American Council on Chiropractic Roentgenology, 1983. *Address:* 6921 Montgomery Boulevard NE, Albuquerque, NM 87019, USA.

MOOKERJEE, Guru Charan, b. 1 June 1916, Calcutta, India. Consultant Physician and Cardio-Respiratory Specialist; Diabetologist. m. 29 June 1941, 1 daughter. *Education:* MSc; MB (Cal); FRCP (Edin); FRCP (London); FCCP (USA); FAIID (Bombay). *Appointments:* Past: Senior Adviser, Medicine, Indian Navy & O I/C Medical Division Naval Hospital, Bombay; Professor, Head, Medicine, Armed Forces Medical College, Pune; Present: Principal, Professor, Medicine, NRS Medical College, Calcutta; Extra Mural Professor, Medicine, Calcutta University; Honorary Professor, College of General Practitioners of Indian Medical Association; Honorary Consultant, Professor, Medicine, V.I.M.S. & R.K.M. Hospital; Head, Medicine, Islamia Hospital; Honorary Consultant, Assembly of God Hospital, Calcutta; Governor, East India Chapter, International Academy of Chest Physicians & Surgeons, USA. *Memberships:* Fellow, American College of Chest Physicians and Surgeons; Fellow, All India Institute of Diabetes, Bombay; Indian Medical Association; Calcutta Medical Club and Cardiological Society of India. *Publications:* "Diseases of the Liver", co-author, 1973; "Diagnosis and Management of Common Diseases", Volume I & II, 1979. *Honours:* Colonel, Amirchand Trust Prize; Ati Visit Seva Medal, 1971; Sir Nilratan Sircar Memorial Oration, 1985; etc. *Hobbies:* Writing Popular Articles on Health; Organising Free Dispensaries for the Poor; Music; Travel. *Address:* 14/B Puran Chand Nahar Avenue, Calcutta 700 013, India.

MOONEY, Monica Eucharia Angela. Doctor of Dental Surgery. *Education:* Teaching Licence, New Brunswick, Canada, 1942; University of New Brunswick; Certificate for First Aid, St John's Ambulance; DDS, Dental School, McGill University, 1951; St Thomas University, 1974-75. *Appointments:* Teacher, Canaan Falls, New Brunswick, 1941; Teacher, St John Schools, 1942-46; Dental Division of Nova Scotia Department of Health, 1951-54; Dentist, Municipal Clinic for school children in St John, 1954-71; Dentist at Province Hospital, St John, 1971-78. *Memberships include:* New Brunswick Teachers Association; Nova Scotia Dental Society; Nova Scotia Public Health Association; New Brunswick Dental Society; Canadian Dental Association; International Dental Federation. *Honours:* Certificate from Government on behalf of People of Canada in appreciation for services as a Volunteer Worker for Civil Defence, 1973; Certificate from Canadian Fund for Dental Education in appreciation for special contribution and service to Capital Fund for Dental Education, Dental Research and Oral Health Education in Canada, 1973. *Hobbies:* Collecting Artifacts in own vicinity; insects particularly lava moths.

MOORE, Bruce Warwick, b. 27 Sep. 1950, Perth, Western Australia. Dental Surgeon. m. Carmel Ann Mathieson, 5 Jan. 1974, Sydney, 1 son. *Memberships:* Dental Health Foundation; Australian Dental Association; Federation Dentaire International. *Honour:* University Blue (Golf), 1974. *Hobbies:* Golf; Squash; Travel. *Address:* 3 Ikara Place, St Ives, New South Wales, Australia.

MOORE, Burness Evans, b. 31 Jan. 1914, Clinical Professor of Psychiatry. m. Doris Evelyn Anderson, 5 Aug. 1939, Fitchburg, Massachusetts, USA. 1 son, 1 daughter. *Education:* AB, Emory University, Atlanta, Georgia, 1933; MD, Harvard Medical School, Boston, Massachusetts, 1933. *Appointments:* Physician-in-Charge, Yale Psychiatric Institute, 1944-48; Chief, Consultation Service, Grace New Haven Community Hospital, 1948-49; Instructor, 1943-46, Assistant Professor of Psychiatry, 1946-49, Associate Clinical Professor of Psychiatry, 1949-68, Yale University School of Medicine; Training and Supervising Analyst, New York Psychoanalytic Institute, 1963-; Clinical Professor of Psychiatry, Emory University School of Medicine, 1980-. *Memberships:* New York Psychoanalytic Institute, Past President; American Psychoanalytic Association, Past President; Fellow, American Psychiatric Association; Internation Psycho-Analytical Association Past Treasurer. *Publications:* "A Glossary of Psychoanalytical Terms and Concepts" edited with Bernard D Fine, 1967; "Toward a Clarification of the Concept of Narcissism", 'Psychoanalytic Study of the Child', 1975; "Freud and Female Sexuality: A Current View" in 'International Journal of Psycho-Analysis' 1976; "Psychic Representation and Female Orgasm" in "Female Psychology: Contemporary Psychoanalytic Views" edited by Harold P Blum, 1977. *Address:* 6355 River Overlook Drive, NW Atlanta, GA 30328, USA.

MOORE, Josephine Carroll, b. 20 Sep. 1925, Ann Arbor, Michigan, USA. Professor of Anatomy, University of South Dakota Medical School. *Education:* BA, University of Michigan, 1947; BS, 1954, OTR, 1955, Eastern Michigan University; MS, 1959, PhD, 1964, University of Michigan; DSc (Hons), Eastern Michigan University, 1982. *Appointments:* Instructor, 1955-58, Assistant Professor, 1959-60, Eastern Michigan University; Lecturer, 1962-64, Instructor, 1964-66, University of Michigan; Assistant Professor, 1966-70, Associate Professor, 1970-76, Full Professor, 1976-, University of South Dakota Medical School. *Memberships:* American Association of Anatomists; American Occupational Therapy Association; World Federation of Occupational Therapists; American Association for Advancement of Science; American Women in Science. *Publications:* More than 40 professional publications including: "The Occupational Therapy Glossary", Eastern Michigan University, 1956; "Sensory system's influence on movement and muscle tone", Syllabus, Tenth Annual Sensorimotor Symposium, Office of Continuing Education in the Health Sciences, University of California, San Diego School of Medicine, 1982; "Neuroanatomy Simplified", Spanish Edition, translated by R Benebib, 1985; Book reviews. *Honours include:* Certificate of Appreciation for "expanding the knowledge base of practicing OT's and making a unique contribution to NHOTA continuing education program, 1982; Award of Merit from Quinnipiac College, School of Allied Health and Natural Sciences and Connecticut Occupational Therapy Association, 1982. *Hobbies:* Reading; Illustrating Pen and Ink; Oil Painting; Animal Behavioral Studies. *Address:* Department of Anatomy, University of South Dakota Medical School, Vermillion, SD 57069, USA.

MOORE, Norman Foster, b. 18 Feb. 1947, Belfast, Northern Ireland. Principal Scientific Officer. m. 11 June 1971, Belfast, 2 daughters. *Education:* BSc, Biochemistry, 1969, BSc, Hons, Biochemistry, 1970, Queen's University, Belfast; PhD, Virology, Warwick University, Coventry. *Appointments:* Post-doctoral Fellow, Department of Microbiology, University of Virginia, 1973-76; Post-doctoral Fellow, 1976-77, Senior Scientific Officer, 1977-81, Unit of Invertebrate Virology, Oxford; Principal Scientific Officer, Institute of Virology, Oxford, 1981-85. *Memberships:* American Society of Microbiology; Society for General Microbiology; American Society for Virology and Institute of Biology etc. *Publications:* More than 80 learned articles on Virology. *Hobbies:* Squash; Photography; Fishing; Family. *Address:* N E R C Institute of Virology, Mansfield Road, Oxford OX1 3SR, England.

MOORE, Richard, b. 19 Jan. 1927, Los Angeles, California, USA. Professor of Medical Physics. m. Lillian Elizabeth Hagedorn, 5 Apr. 1969, Washington, 2 sons, 1 daughter. *Education:* BSc Electrical Engineering, University of Missouri, 1947; PhD Biophysics, University of Rochester, New York, 1956; DSc Biomedical Engineering, The George Washington University, Washington DC, 1970. *Appointments:* Commissioned Officer, US Public Health Service, Washington DC, 1955-60; Research Biophysicist, American National Red Cross, Washington DC, 1960-69; Associate Professor, University of Minnesota, Minneapolis, 1969-82; Professor and Head, Department of Medical Physics, University of Witwatersrand, Johannesburg, Republic of South Africa, 1982-. *Memberships:* Royal Society, South Africa; Fellow, American Association for the Advancement of Science; Fellow, Council on Cardiovascular Radiology, American Heart Association; Fellow, Society for Advanced Medical Systems; American Association of Physicists in Medicine; South African Association of Physicists in Medicine and Biology. *Publications:* 110. *Honours:* Scholarship, Deep Springs College, Deep Springs, California, 1944-46; 2 Atomic Energy Commission Fellowships, University of Rochester, 1950-52; President's Award, Society for Radiological Engineering, 1977. *Hobbies:* Computing; Electronic Music. *Address:* Department of Medical Physics, Area 49, Johannesburg Hospital, Private Bag X39, Johannesburg 2000, Republic of South Africa.

MOORE, Sallyann Kelly, b. 28 Aug. 1952, Omaha, Nebraska, USA. Doctor of Chiropractic. Divorced, 2 sons, 1 daughter. *Education:* AA, Parklands College; DC, Palmer College of Chiropractic, Davenport. *Appointments:* Secretary, Illinois Prairie State Chiropractic Association District 5. *Memberships:* American Chiropractic Association; Mississippi Association of Chiropractors. *Hobbies:* Entertaining her Children; Swimming; Hiking; Needlecrafts. *Address:* 1606 South 28th Avenue, Hattiesburg, MS 39401, USA.

MOORHOUSE, Ellen Catherine, b. 13 Feb. 1928, Dublin, Republic of Ireland. Professor of Clinical Microbiology. m. John Richard Moorhouse, 7 Sep. 1963, London, England, 1 son, 1 daughter. *Education:* LRCP & SI, 1952; Diploma in Public Health, National University of Ireland, 1957; Member 1965, Fellow 1975, Royal College of Pathologists; Fellow, Royal College of Physicians in Ireland, 1982. *Appointments:* Intern, 1952-53, Medical Registrar 1953-55, Dr Steeven's Hospital, Dublin; Senior House Officer, Pathology, City General Hospital, Sheffield, England, 1958; Registrar in Bacteriology, Royal Postgraduate Medical School, Hammersmith Hospital, London, 1958-60; Research Member, Medical Research Council Tuberculosis Unit, ibid, 1960-61; Lecturer in Bacteriology, London School of Hygiene & Tropical Medicine, University of London, 1961-64; Reader in Microbiology, Royal College of Surgeons in Dublin, 1964-66; Professor of Clinical Microbiology, Royal College of Surgeons in Dublin, 1966-. *Memberships:* Royal College of Pathologists; Royal College of Physicians, Dublin; British Society for Antimicrobial Chemotherapy; Society of Hospital Infection. *Publications:* Various articles in medical journals, including The Lancet. *Hobbies:* Travel; Collecting. *Address:* 39a Kincora Avenue, Clontarf, Dublin 3, Republic of Ireland.

MOOSSA, A R, b. 10 Oct. 1939, Mauritius. Professor and Chairman, Department of Surgery; Surgeon-in-Chief. m. Denise Elizabeth Willoughby, 28 Dec. 1973, Liverpool, England, 2 sons, 1 daughter. *Education:* BSc; MD; FRCS, England and Edinburgh, Scotland; FACS; University of Chicago, Illinois, USA; Johns Hopkins University, Baltimore, Maryland; University of Liverpool, England. *Appointments:* Assistant Professor, 1974, Associate Professor, 1975, Professor of Surgery, 1977-83, Director of Surgical Research, 1977-83, Chief of General Surgery Service, 1977-83, Vice Chairman, Department of Surgery, 1977-83, University of Chicago, USA; currently, Professor and Chairman, Department of Surgery, Surgeon-in-Chief, Medical Center, University of California, San Diego, California. *Memberships:* Society for Surgery of the Alimentary Tract; Royal College of Surgeons, England and Edinburgh, Scotland; American Society of Clinical Onocology; American College of Surgeons; American Surgical Association; Society of University Surgeons; Society of Surgical Onocology. *Publications:* "Tumors of the Pancreas", 1982; "Essential Surgical Practice", 1983; "Comprehensive Textbook of Oncology", 1986; "Gastrointestinal Emergencies", 1986; Author over 160 articles in major surgical and scientific journals. *Honours:* Hunterian Professor, Royal College of Surgeons, 1977; Litchfield Lecturer, University of Oxford, England, 1978; Praelector in Surgery, Dundee University, Scotland, 1979; Best Medical Specialist in USA, 1984; Best Doctors in USA, 1984. *Hobbies:* Travelling; Soccer. *Address:* Department of Surgery, University of California, 225 Dickinson Street, San Diego, CA 92103, USA.

MORA, George, b. 26 June 1923, Genoa, Italy. Medical Director. M. Marilyn Hall, 3 May, 1958, Providence, Rhode Island, USA, 1 son, 2 daughters. *Education:* MD, University of Genoa, Italy, 1947, training in Paediatrics and Neurology, 1948; Training in Child Psychiatry, University of Zurich, Switzerland, 1949-50. *Appointments:* Resident, Child Psychiatry, Boston, Massachusetts, USA, 1951-52; Resident, Child Psychiatry, Butler Hospital, Providence, Rhode Island, USA, 1953-54; Resident in Psychiatry, University of North Carolina, Chapel Hill, North Carolina, 1955-56; Director, Outpatient Department, Bradley Hospital, Providence, Rhode Island, 1956-60; Research Associate, Yale University, New Haven, 1957-; Lecturer in Psychiatry, New York Medical College, 1965-; Associate Clinical Professor of Psychiatry, Albany Medical College, 1967-; Medical Director, Astor Home for Children, Rhinebeck, New York. *Memberships:* American Medical Association; American Psychiatric Association, Fellow; American Psychopathological Association; American Academy of Child Psychiatry; American Association for the History of Medicine, Member of Council, 1965-68; History of Science Society. *Publications:* Co-editor "Psychiatry and Its History: Methodological Problems in Research", 1970; Co-Editor "Catatonia", 1974; Author of Introduction, "Textbook on Mental Diseases", 1975; Editor "On The Relation Between the Physical and Moral Aspects of Man", 1980. *Honour:* Rockefeller Foundation Fellow, 1951-52. *Address:* 32 Slate Hill Drive, Poughkeepsie, NY 12603, USA.

MORALES, Azorides Rafael, b. 24 Oct. 1933, Cascorro, Cuba. Professor and Chairman, Department of Pathology, University of Miami School of Medicine. m. Mariam Valdes, 27 Dec. 1958, Remedios, Cuba, 1 daughter. *Education:* MD, Madrid Medical School, Spain. *Appointments:* Lieutenant Colonel, Medical Corps, US Army Commanding Officer, 1968-69; Associate in Pathology, Henry Ford Hospital, 1969-71; Associate Professor of Pathology, University of Miami School of Medicine, USA, 1971-74; Acting Director, Division of Anatomic Pathology, Chief, Pathology Services, 1974-, Jackson Memorial Hospital. *Memberships:* College of American Pathologists; American Society of Clinical Pathologists; International Academy of Pathologists; Florida Society of Pathologists; Arthur Purdy Stout Society of Surgical Pathologists; American Medical Association; Association of Pathology Chairmen. *Publications:* "Coronary Artery Disease. Pathologic and Clinical Assessment", (with R J Boucek, R Romamelli, M P Judkins), 1984; "Immunoperoxidase Techniques: A Practical Approach to Tumor Diagnosis", (with M Nadji); Contributor of numerous articles to professional journals. *Address:* Department of Pathology (D-33), University of Miami School of Medicine, PO Box 016960, Miami, FL 33101, USA.

MORA-MORALES, Eric, b. 15 Aug. 1935, Costa Rica.

Head of Endocrine Unit, Calderon Hospital, Guardia, Costa Rica. m. Lylliam Rodriguez Madrigal, 5 Jan. 1963, San José, Costa Rica, 3 daughters. *Education:* Doctoral & Surgical qualifications, Military Medical School, Mexico; Master of Science, Endocrinology, Diabetes & Nutrition, Autonomous University of Mexico, 1966. *Memberships:* American Diabetes Association; International Diabetes Federation; European Association for the Study of Diabetes; Latin-American Diabetes Association. *Publications:* 'Frecuencia de diabetes mellitus en Costa Rica CA' (in Acta Medica Costa, 1969); 'Diabetes Mellitus in Costa Rica' (in IDE Bulletin, 1980); 'Enfermedades de la tiroides y paratiroines' (in Editorial Universidad de Costa Rica). *Honour:* Dr Garcia Parrillo Research Prize, San José, Costa Rica, 1974. *Hobbies:* Tennis; Photography. *Address:* PO Box 25, 2300 Curridabat, Costa Rica, Central America.

MOREAU, Jean-Paul Joseph, b. 16 Oct. 1936, Lorient. Director of the Pasteur Institute of Noumea, New Caledonia. m. Armelle Leguen, 2 July 1959, Port-Louis, France, 3 sons, 1 daughter. *Education:* Medical Doctor; Biologist; Post-graduate of Tropical Medicine, Biochemistry, Microbiology and Immunology (Pasteur Institute of Paris), Parasitology and Haematology. *Appointments:* Laboratory Assistant, Institute of Medical Researches, Tahiti French Polynesia, South Pacific; Laboratory Head, Pasteur Institute, Tananarive, Madagascar; Director of Muraz Center (Medical Researches), Bobo-Dioulasso, Upper Volta, West Africa. *Memberships:* French Army Health Service; French Society of Exotic Pathology; Association of French Speaking Epidemiologists; New Caledonian Medical Association, President. *Publications:* Articles include: Protection trial against schistosomial reinfection by cercarian vaccine, 1966; An epidemic of dengue on Tahiti associated with hemorragic manifestations, 1973; Killed poliovirus antigen titration in humans, 1978. *Honours:* Knight of Honour Legion, 1985; Honour Medal of Army Health Service, 1984; Overseas Medal, 1980; Silver Medal for Scientific Works, Army Health Service, 1977. *Hobbies:* Reading; Classical Music, Opera; Cultural Travels; Snorkel Diving. *Address:* Institut Pasteur, BP 61 Noumea, New Caledonia, South Pacific.

MOREHEAD, Charles David, b. 1936, Pecan Gap, Texas, USA. Professor, Pediatrician. m. Marcia Louise Schmidt, 1959, 4 sons. *Education:* BA, North Texas State University, 1958; MD, University of Texas Health Science Center, Dallas, 1962. *Appointments include:* Instructor, Department of Pediatrics, St Louis University College of Medicine, St Louis, Missouri, 1968-70; Chief, Metabolic Unit, St Louis/Chiang Mai Anemia and Malnutrition Center, Chiang Mai, Thailand, 1968-70; Lecturer 1979-80, Associate Dean 1980-, Professor 1981-, Department of Pediatrics, Student Advisor 1981-, Temple Texas A and M University College of Medicine; Senior Staff Physician 1971-, Director Division of Pediatric Infectious Diseases 1971-, Director Scott and White Neonatal Nurseries 1972-76, Chairman Research and Education Council 1980-, Scott and White Memorial Hospital. *Memberships:* American Academy of Pediatrics; Texas Pediatric Society; American Medical Association; Texas Medical Association. *Publications:* 'Heterotropic Brain in the Nasopharynx and Soft palate', (with H A Zarem, G F Gray and M T Edgerton), 1967; 'Acute Otitis Media: Treatment Results in Relation to Bacterial Etiology', (with B W Wilson, R L Poland, R S Thompson and A Baghdassarian), 1969; 'Why Give Children Penicillin', 1969; 'Epidemiology of Pseudomonas Infections in a Pediatric Intensive Care Unit', (with P W Houck), 1972; 'Pharmacokinetics of Carbenicillin in Neonates of Normal and Low Birth Weight', (with S Shelton, H Kusmiesz and J D Nelson), 1972; 'Basterial Infections in Malnourished Children', (with M Morehead, D M Allen and R E Olson), 1974; 'Carisoprodol Related Death in a Child', (with H R Adams and T Kerzee), 1975; 'What's All The Hollering About?', 1984. *Address:* 2630 Marlandwood Circle, Temple, TX 76502, USA.

MORELL, Franz Wolfgang, b. 24 May 1921, Frankfurt, Germany. Physician. m. Renate Greeff, 5 Oct. 1943, 3 sons, 3 daughters. *Education:* MD, Giessen University, Germany, 1944. *Appointments:* Military Physician, 1944-45; Prisoner of War Physician, (American POW), until 1947; Assistant Physician, Krankenhaus Fischbachau des Krankenhauses rechts der Isar, Munchen, 1947-49; Private medical practice, Ottfingen, Westfalia, Germany, 1949-. *Memberships:* Internationale Gesellschaft fur Elektroakupunktur nach Voll (since 1955); Zentralverband fur Naturheilverfahren; Gesellschaft fur Erfanrungsheilkunde; Internationale Gesellschaft fur Bioelektronik Vincent (SIBEV), (President); Internationale MORA Arzte Gesellschaft (President). *Publications:* Articles: 'Die Pille in Elektroakupunkutur und Nio-Elektronik', in 'Physikalische Medizin und Rehabilitation', 1974; 'Diagnose-und Therapieverfanhren im ultrafeinen Bioenergie-Bereich' in 'MORA Therapie', 1984; 'Das Neue Therapiekonzept. Patientenigene und Farblichtschwingungen' in 'Haug Verlag', 1986. *Hobbies:* Classical Music; Investigations on the human electromagnetic oscillations. *Address:* Doktorgasse 8, D-5963, Wenden 4, Ottfingen, Federal Republic of Germany.

MORENTE CAMPOS, Juan, b. 25 Nov. 1931, Granada, Spain, Jefe de Servicio del Hospital Clinico, S Cecilio. m. Maria Amelia Baena Fernandez, 17 Mar. 1960, 2 sons. *Education:* MD; Professor, Medicine, Grenada. *Appointment:* Cuerpo de Sanidad Militar, E.T. *Memberships:* Fellow, American College of Chest Physicians; Sociedad Espanola de Patologia del Aparato Respiratorio; Sociedad Espanola de Alergia e Imminologia Clinica;-Neumodur S.E.P., S.E. Phys. Clin. Respiratoire. *Publications:* "Tratamiento asma bronquial", 1963; "Terapeutica Respiratoria", 'Pathos', 1984; "Suparaciones broncopulnares", 1984. *Honours:* Presidente, Seccion Broncologia, SEPAR, 1980-; Presidente Neumologos del Sur, NEUMOSUR, 1983. *Address:* Tejeiro 20, Granada 18005, Spain.

MORETZ, Joseph Alfred, b. 4 May 1946, Hickory, North Carolina, USA. Orthopaedic Surgeon. m. 19 Dec. 1971, Orlando, Florida, USA, 3 sons, 1 daughter. *Education:* AB, Duke University; MD, Emory University. *Appointments:* Lieutenant Commander, United States Navy, 1978-80. *Memberships:* American Academy of Orthopaedic Surgery; American Orthopaedic Society for Sports Medicine; American College of Sports Medicine. *Publications:* 'Significance of serum analyse levels in evaluating panceatic trauma', 1975; 'Ligamentous laxity in secondary school athletics', 1978; 'Long-term follow-up of knee injuries in high school football players', 1984. *Hobby:* Sports. *Address:* Hickory Orthopaedic Center, 250 18th Street Circle SE, Hickory, NC 28602, USA.

MORGAN, Brian Patrick, b. 13 July 1926, Sydney, Australia. Consultant Surgeon. m. Jeanette Battye, Sydney, 1 son, 3 daughters. *Education:* MB BS Honours, Sydney, 1953; Fellow, Royal Australian College of Surgeons, 1958. *Appointments:* Surgical Registrar, Broadgreen Hospital, University of Liverpool, England, 1959; Clinical Assistant, St Marks Hospital, London, 1960; Clinical Lecturer in Surgery 1960-, Lecturer in Surgery in Faculty of Dentistry 1966-71, University of Sydney, Sydney, New South Wales, Australia; Honorary Surgeon, Marrickville Hospital, 1966-80; Resident Medical Officer 1953-58, Supervisor Surgical 1960-84, Surgeon 1960-, Royal Prince Alfred Hospital, Sydney; Consultant Surgeon, New South Wales Health Commission, 1979-84; Several visiting lectureships. *Memberships:* Australian Medical Association; Fellow, Councillor 1979-, Chairman Manpower Committee 1979-, Royal Australian College of Surgeons; Gastro-enterological Society of Australia; International Society of Surgery; Honorary Fellow, American Society of Colon and Rectal Surgeons. *Publications:* "Medical Manpower"; "Endometriosis"; "Ano-rectal Disorders"; "Early Detection of Colorectal Carcinoma"; "Squamous Carcinoma of Anus"; "Surgical Treatment of Rectal Prolapse"; "Gastrointestinal Bleeding"; "Criteria for Justification Audit in Appendicectomy"; "An Audit of Appendicectomy in Australia"; Several papers. *Hobbies:* Golf; Medical politics. *Address:* 100 Carillon Ave, Newtown, Sydney 2046, Australia.

MORINO, Yoshimasa, b. 21 Aug. 1931, Tokushima, Japan. Professor of Biochemistry, m. Kiyoko Arita, 14 Nov. 1962, Osaka, Japan, 1 son, 2 daughters. *Education:* MD, 1957, DMS, Postgraduate Course, 1962, Osaka University School of Medicine; National Licence of Clinical Medicine, 1958. *Appointments:* Assistant Professor, 1962, Associate Professor, 1972, Department of Biochemistry, Osaka University Medical School; Professor, Department of Biochemistry, Kumamoto University Medical School, 1974. *Memberships:* Japanese Biochemical Society; Japanese Vitamin Society; Japanese Biophysical Society; American Chemical Society. *Publications:* Author of numerous articles to professional journals. *Honours:* Award for the Promotion of Biochemistry, Japanese Biochemical Society, 1972; Award for Pyridoxal Catalysts, Vitamin Society, 1977. *Hobby:* Watching rugby. *Address:* Department of Biochemistry, Kumamoto University Medical School, 2-2-1 Honjo, Kumamoto, 860 Japan.

MORIO, Michio, b. 19 Apr 1931, Onomichi, Hiroshima, Japan. Professor and Chairman, Department of Anesthesiology, Hiroshima University School of Medicine. m. Akiko Nakatani, 21 Oct. 1957, Hiroshima, 1 daughter. *Education:* MD, Hiroshima Medical College, 1956; Medical License, Japan, 1957; PhD, Kyoto University, 1961; Diploma of Anesthesiologists, Japanese Society of Anesthesiology, 1963. *Appointments:* Instructor, Department of Anesthesiology, Kyoto University Hospital, 1961-62; Lecturer, Department of Surgery, 1962-65; Associate Professor, Division of Anesthesia, 1965-66; Professor and Chairman, Department of Anesthesiology, 1967-; Hiroshima University School of Medicine; Medical Director, Hiroshima University Hospital and Councilor of Hiroshima University, 1980-84; President, Japanese Association for Acute Medicine, 1983-84. *Memberships:* Member, several professional organizations. *Publications:* Over 100 review articles and 200 original publications in various books and journals from 1958; Editor-in-Chief, Hiroshima Journal of Anesthesia, 1965-; Editor, Proceedings of Japanese Symposium on Malignant Hyperthermia, 1977-; Editor, Proceedings of Japanese Symposium on Biotransformation and Hepatotoxicity of Anesthetics, 1980-. *Honours:* Honorary Member of Yugoslav Society of Anesthesiology, Reanimatology and Intensive Therapy, 1983; Honorary Member of Bulgarian Society of Anesthesiology and Resuscitation, 1984. *Hobbies:* Tennis; Travel. *Address:* Midori 2-27-34, Minami-ku, Hiroshima, 734 Japan.

MORIOKA, Tohru, b. 21 Aug. 1928, Japan. Professor, Chairman, Anaesthesiology, Kumamoto University Medical School. m. Mitsuko Katsuya, 18 Oct., 1955, Kumamoto City, 1 son. *Education:* MD; PhD, Kumamoto University Medical School, 1957. *Appointments:* Intern, 1950, Training in Surgery, 1951, Kumamoto University Medical School; Staff, Surgery, National Tokyo Sanatorium, 1955; Fulbright Exchange Scholar, Albert Einstein College of Medicine, New York, USA, 1961; Associate Professor, Anesthesiology, Nihon Medical College, Tokyo, 1963; Professor, Chairman, Anesthesiology, Kumamoto University Medical School, 1965-. *Memberships:* President, Japanese Association of Anesthesiology, 1977; President, Japanese Association for Reanimatology, 1984; Japanese Association for Surgery. *Publications:* "Artificial Respiration", 1959; "Textbook of Anesthesiology", 1977. *Hobby:* Invention of Medical Gadgets. *Address:* Dept. of Anaesthesiology, Kumamoto University, Medical School, Kumamoto, 860 Japan.

MORRELL, David Cameron, b. 6 Nov. 1929, Wimbledon, England. Professor, General Practice, United Medical Schools of Guy's and St Thomas' Hospitals. m. Alison Eaton Taylor, 30 May 1953, Wimbledon, 3

sons, 2 daughters. *Education:* MB BS, 1952; MRCP 1955; DObstRCOG 1957; FRCGP, 1972; FRCP, 1976; MPS (Hon) 1977; St Mary's Hospital Medical School, London University. *Appointments:* Physician to Royal Air Force, 1954-57; Principal, General Practice, 1957-63; Lecturer, General Practice, University of Edinburgh, 1963-67; Senior Lecturer/Reader, Professor, General Practice, United Medical and Dental Schools of St Thomas' & Guy's Hospitals, 1967-. *Memberships:* British Medical Association; Royal College of General Practitioners; Association of University Teachers in General Practice; Royal Society of Medicine; University Grants Committee, Medical Sub-Committee. *Publications:* "Introduction to Primary Medical Care", 2nd edition, 1981; "Teaching General Practice", 1981; Articles in professional journals. *Honours:* OBE, 1982; KSG, 1982. *Hobbies:* Walking; Gardening. *Address:* Dept. of General Practice, United Medical & Dental Schools of St Thomas' and Guy's Hospitals, 80 Kennington Road, London SE11 6 SP, England.

MORRIS, Brian James, b. 14 July 1950, Adelaide, Australia. Senior University Lecturer. *Education:* BSc, University of Adelaide, Australia, 1972; PhD, University of Melbourne and Monash University, 1975. *Appointments:* C J Martin Research Fellow of the National Health and Medical Research Council of Australia, at the University of Missouri, Columbia and the University of California, San Francisco, USA, 1975-78; Senior Lecturer in Physiology and Head of Molecular Biology & Hypertension Laboratory, University of Sydney, Australia. *Memberships:* High Blood Pressure Research Council of Australia; International Society of Hypertension; Australian Biochemical Society; Australian Society for Medical Research; Australian Physiological and Pharmacological Society; Endocrine Society of Australia; Australasian Society of Nephrology; Editorial Board of 'Hypertension', 1980-83. *Publications:* Almost 100 articles on the biochemistry, biosynthesis, gene and protein structure and physiological function of hormones and proteins involved in blood pressure, some of which may be found in: 'Biochim. Biophys. Acta'; 'Endrocrinology'; 'Clin. Exp. Pharmacol. Physiol.'; 'Circ. Res.'; 'J. Clin. Endocr. Metab.'; 'Ann. Rev. Physiol.'; 'Am. J. Physiol.'; 'Eur. J. Pharmacol.'; 'Clin. Sci.'; 'J. Biol. Chem.'; 'DNA'; etc. *Honour:* The Edgeworth David Medal, awarded by the Royal Society of New South Wales, 1985. *Address:* The University of Sydney, New South Wales, 2006, Australia.

MORRIS, Elizabeth Treat, b. 20 Feb. 1936, Hartford, Connecticut, USA. Physical Therapist in Private Practice. m. David Breck Morris, 10 July 1961, 2 sons. *Education:* BS, Physical Therapy, University of Connecticut, 1960. *Appointments:* Crippled Children's Clinic, Northern Virginia, Arlington, 1960-62; Holy Cross Hospital, Salt Lake City, Utah, 1965-68, 1970-73; Shriners Hospital for Crippled Children, Salt Lake City, 1968-70; Valley Therapy Service, Tooele, Provo, Salt Lake City, 1973-75; Elizabeth T Morris RPT, Salt Lake City, 1975-. *Memberships:* American Physical Therapy Association; World Confederation for Physical Therapy; Salt Lake Area Chamber of Commerce. *Publess:* 4177 Mathews Way, Salt Lake City, UT 84124, USA.

MORRIS, Peter, John, b. 17 Apr. 1934, Horsham, Australia. Professor of Surgery, Chairman, Department of Surgery. m. Mary Jocelyn Gorman, 4 Feb. 1960, Melbourne, 3 sons, 2 daughters. *Education:* MB, BS, PhD, Melbourne; MA, Oxford, England. *Appointments:* Assistant Professor of Surgery, Medical College of Virginia, USA; Second Assistant Department of Surgery, Director of Tissue Transplantation Laboratories, University of Melbourne, Australia; Honorary Consultant in Experimental Pathology, Walter and Eliza Hall Institute of Medical Research, Melbourne; Consultant Surgeon, Lymphoma Clinic of Cancer Institute, Melbourne; Nuffield Professor of Surgery, University of Oxford, England; Chairman, Department of Surgery, John Radcliffe Hospital, Oxford. *Memberships:* Fellow, Royal College of Surgeons, England; Fellow, Royal Australasian College of Surgeons; Honorary Fellow, American Surgical Association; Medical Research Council; President, British Transplantation Society; President, International Transplantation Society; National Kidney Research Fund Council. *Publications include:* Editor, 'Transplantation'; "Kidney Transplantation: Principles and Practice" (editor); "Transient Ischaemic Attacks" (editor with C Warlow); "Tissue Transplantation" (editor); "Progress in Transplantation" (editor with N Tilney); Numerous scientific articles. *Hobbies:* Cricket; Golf; Tennis. 2Address: Nuffield Department of Surgery, John Radcliffe Hospital, Headington, Oxford OX3 9DU, England.

MORRIS, Thomas Keith (Chip), b. 31 Dec. 1946, Salinas, California, USA. Podiatric Surgeon. m. Linda Rhae Antram, 7 May 1966, Reno, Nevada, USA, 2 daughters. *Education:* BS, University of California at Irvine, 1974; DPM, Ohio College of Podiatric Medicine, Cleveland, Ohio, 1978; Residency in Foot Surgery, Podiatry Hospital of Pittsburgh, Pennsylvania, 1978-79. *Appointments:* Solo Practice, Laguna Niguel, California, 1980-83; Partnership Practice, Fayette Podiatry Associates, Uniontown, Pennsylvania, 1983-. *Memberships:* Associate, American College of Foot Surgeons; American Podiatric Medical Association; Western Division, Pennsylvania Podiatric Medical Association. *Publication:* 'Podiatric Approach to Russel-Silver Syndrome' (Journal of American Podiatry Association), 1978. *Hobbies:* Running; Skiing. *Address:* 205 Easy Street Suite 106, Uniontown Professional Plaza 1, Uniontown, PA 15401, USA.

MORRISON, Murray Allan, b. 6 Dec. 1939, Columbus, Ohio, USA. Orthopaedic Surgeon. m. Susan Gail Kobren, 30 July 1967, White Plains, New York, USA, 2 daughters. *Education:* AB, Harvard College, USA, 1961; MD, New York University School of Medicine, 1965. *Appointments:* Internship, University of Michigan Medical Centre, 1965-66, Assistant Residency in Surgery, 1966-67; Orthopaedic Resident, Hospital of University of Pennsylvania, 1967-70; Assistant Attending in Orthopaedic Surgery, Bridgeport Hospital, 1970-73, Associate, 1974-78; Orthopaedic Consultant, Fairfield Hills State Hospital, 1970-76; Orthopaedic Surgeon, Bridgeport Hospital, 1978-; Clinical Instructor, Yale University School of Medicine. *Memberships:* American Medical Association; Eastern Orthopaedic Association; Fellow, American Academy of Orthopaedic Surgeons; Fellow, American College of Surgeons. *Publication:* "Thyrocalcitonan Effect on Disease Osteoporosis in Parathyroide Tumired Rats" in "Current Topics in Surgical Research", Volume 2, 1970. *Hobbies:* Photography; Antiques; Travel. *Address:* 325 Reef Road, Fairfield, CT, USA.

MORTON, Oswald, b. 5 Feb. 1928, London, England. Consultant Pharmaceutical Physician. m. Shirley Young, 22 Mar. 1959, London, 1 son, 1 daughter. *Education:* MD, BS honours Pathology, Guy's Hospital Medical School, London; Dip Pharm Med. *Appointments:* House Officer, Dermatology House Physician, Guy's Hospital, London; Trainee Assistant General Practitioner, London; Medical Registrar, St Alban's City Hospital; Principal, General Practice, Romford, Essex; Clinical Assistant, Dermatology, Southend General Hospital; Medical Advisor, World Medical Director and Joint Research Director, British Drug Houses Limited, London; Medical Director, Bristol Laboratories Limited; Director of Research and Head of Marketing, Lloyds Pharmaceuticals Limited, London; Director of Commercial Development, Reckitt and Colman Pharmaceuticals Limited, Hull. *Memberships:* Royal College of Surgeons; Licenciate, Royal College of Physicians; British Medical Association; Royal Society of Medicine; Association of Medical Advisors in the Pharmaceutical Industry; Society of Apothecaries; Royal College of General Practitioners; Society for Drug Research. *Publications include:* "Encyclopaedia of General Practice" (contributor), 1965; Numerous articles on various topics. *Honours:* Freeman of the City of London, 1970; Liveryman of the

Society of Apothecaries, 1970. *Hobbies:* Opera; Theatre; Reading; Television; Good food; Good wine; Good cigars. *Address:* 5 St Hilda's Close, Christchurch Avenue, London NW6 7NY, England.

MOSES, Donald Allen, b. 8 Feb. 1938, Brooklyn, New York, USA. Psychiatrist. m. Sarah Dean, 6 Dec. 1957, 2 sons. *Education:* BS, Bates College; MD, New York Medical College; Internship, Psychiatric Residence, Queens Hospital, Honolulu, Hillside Hospital, Glen Oaks; Psychoanalytic Psychotherapy Fellowship, Hillside Hospital. *Appointments:* Clinical Instructor, Psychiatry, Columbia University Medical College; Psychiatric Consultant, Long Island Jewish-Hillside; Medical Centre Drug Abuse Treatment Centers at Queens Hospital and Manhanet, New York; Senior Assistant Attending, Psychiatry, North Shore University Hospital; Clinical Instructor, Psychiatry, Cornell University Medical College; Staff Psychiatrist, Long Island Jewish Hillside Medical Centre; Psychiatric Consultant, Nassau County Society for Prevention of Cruelty to Children. *Memberships:* American Psychiatric Association; Nassau County Psychiatric Society; American Association of Clinical Psychiatrists. *Publication:* "Are You Driving Your Children to Drink", 1975. *Hobbies:* Skiing; Fishing; Art Collecting; Travel. *Address:* 90 Glen Cove Road, Greenvale, NY 11548, USA.

MOSS, James Percy, b. 29 May 1933, London, England. Professor, Head, Orthodontics. m. 15 June 1963, Watford, 2 sons, 1 daughter. *Education:* BDS, London, 1957; LDSRCS, England, 1956; FDSRCS England, 1959; DOrth RCS (Eng), 1960; PhD, London, 1972. *Appointments:* Treasurer, British Society for Study of Orthodontics, 1970-77, President, 1979-80; President, European Begg Society, 1981-83; Chairman, British Certification Board of Orthodontics, 1984-; Vice Dean, Dental Studies, University College Dental School, London, 1983-; Programme Chairman, Editor, British Society for the Study of Orthodontics, 1982; Elected Member, Board of Faculty of Dental Surgery, Royal College of Surgeons of England, 1984-. *Memberships:* British Dental Association; International Association for Dental Research; International College of Dentists; British Society for the Study of Orthodontics; European Orthodontic Society; United Kingdom Begg Study Group. *Publications:* "Symposium on the Mechanisms of Tooth Support", Contributor, 1965; "Early Treatment of Cleft Lip and Palate", Contributor, 1969; "A Symposium on the prevention of Periodontal Disease", Contributor, 1971. *Honours:* John Mershon Memorial Lecturer, 1974, 1984; William Guy Memorial Lecture, 1984; Charles Tomes Lecturer, 1985. *Hobbies:* Gardening; Squash; Organist. *Address:* Dept. of Orthodontics, University College London Dental School, Mortimer Market, London WC1E 8AU, England.

MOSS, Kathleen Susan, b. 21 Dec. 1950, USA. Patent Attorney, Specialising in Biotechnology, Wegner and Bretschneider, m. Dale Moss, 1 Jan. 1980, USA, 1 son. *Education:* JD, 1978; MS, 1978; BA, 1971. *Appointments:* Patent Examiner, Biotechnology Speciality; Patent Attorney, Bernard and Brown; Attorney, Cotten Day and Doyle; Attorney Adviser, Food and Drug Administration; Law Clerk, National Aeronautics and Space Administration; Research Assistant, Research Fellowship, George Washington University Medical School. *Memberships:* American Bar Association; American Intellectual Patent Association. *Publications:* 'Fertility and Sterility', 1974, 1975; 'FDA decision - DES, Red No 4, Red No 2, X-Otahe plus Benylin Expectorant, Phenformine Hydrochloride'. *Honours:* Fellowship; Letter of Commendation; Acrylonitrite, Copenhagen. *Address:* Wegner and Bretschneider, 2030 M Street NW, Washington DC, 20036, USA.

MOSSOP, Raymond Thomas, b. 25 June 1921, Cape Town, Republic of South Africa. Chairman of University Department of Community Medicine. m. Pamela, 16 Dec. 1950, Cape Town, 3 daughters. *Education:* MB ChB, University of Cape Town, 1950; MCGP (R), 1976; FCGP (R), 1979. *Appointments:* Internships in Medicine, Surgery, Obstetrics and Gynaecology, Grootes-chuhe, Capetown, 1951-52; Government Medical Officer, South Rhodesia and Nyasaland, 1952-55; Private General Practice, Kadoma, Zimbabwe, 1955-75; Chief Medical Officer, Riotinto, Kadoma, 1955-75; Medical Officer of Health, Kadoma, 1955-75; Senior Lecturer, Department of Community Medicine, University of Zimbabwe, 1975-. *Memberships:* President, College of Primary Care Physicians; Past-President of Mashonaland branch, Zimbabwe Medical Association; Direct Member, WOXCA; South African Academy of Family Practice. *Publications include:* "Family Medicine for Students and Teachers", (with G H Jehrsen), 1983; Over 70 contributions to medical journals. *Honours:* Associate Founder, College of Medicine of South Africa, 1976; Honorary Clinical Associate Professor, Emory Medical School, Atlanta, Georgia, USA, 1984. *Hobbies:* Collecting Rhodesiana; Golf. *Address:* 7 Fleetwood Road, Alexandra Park, Harare, Zimbabwe.

MOTLEY, Helen L, b. 18 Dec. 1946, Steamboat Springs, Colorado, USA. Registered Occupational Therapist; Company Owner and President. m. William A Motley, 20 Dec. 1973, Denver, 2 sons. *Education:* BSc; Registered Occupational Therapist. *Appointments:* Staff Occupational Therapist; Colorado Medical Center, Denver, Colorado, 1974-76; Bethany Medical Center, Kansas City, 1977-78. Owner, Private Practice Clinic, Upper Extremity Rehabilitation Incorporated, 1978-. President, Greater Kansas City Physical Therapy. *Memberships:* Kansas Occupational Therapy Association; Associate Member, American Society of Hand Therapists. *Hobbies:* Water and snow sports. *Address:* 6405 Metcalf, Cloverleaf Building 3, Suite 504, Shawnee Mission, KS 66202, USA.

MOTTA, Marcella, b. 16 Nov. 1936, Milan, Italy. Professor of Physiology. *Education:* Degree in Pharmaceutical Chemistry, 1959; Postgraduate degree in Pharmacology, 1962; PhD, Pharmacology. *Appointments:* Assistant Professor, 1963; Associate Professor, 1969; Full Professor of Physiology, 1980. *Memberships:* Council Member, International Society of Neuroendocrinology; Italian Society of Andrology; Italian Society of Endocrinology. *Publications:* Editor: Hypothalamic Hormones, 1975; The Endocrine Function of the Brain, 1980; Pituitary Hormones and Related Peptides, 1982; Opioid Modulation of Endocrine Function, 1984; Sexual Differentiation, 1984. *Honour:* Schoeller-Junkmann Prize of the German Society of Endocrinology, 1968. *Hobbies:* Opera and Symphonic Music; Painting. *Address:* Cso Pta Romana 132, 20122 Milan, Italy.

MOTTO, Jerome Arthur, b. 16 Oct. 1921, Kansas City, USA. University Professor of Psychiatry. *Education:* BA, cum laude, University of California, 1948; MD, University of California, San Francisco School of Medicine, 1951. *Appointments:* Assistant Chief, Psychiatric Service, San Francisco General Hospital, USA, 1956-71; Instructor in Psychiatry, Assistant Professor of Psychiatry, Lecturer in Psychiatry, Associate Clinical Professor of Psychiatry, Associate Professor of Psychiatry, University of California, San Francisco School of Medicine, 1956-73; Director, Psychiatric Emergency Service, San Francisco General Hospital, 1971-74; Director, Psychiatric Consultation Service, 1971-77; Associate Director, Psychiatric Consultation Service, University of California, San Francisco Medical Centre, 1977-. *Memberships:* American Psychiatric Association; Northern California Psychiatric Association; World Psychiatric Association; American Association of Suicidology; International Association for Suicide Prevention. *Publications:* Co-author: 'Suicide and the Medical Community', in 'AMA Archives of Neurology and Psychiatry', 1958; 'Newspaper Influence on Suicide' in 'AMA Archives of General Psychiatry', 1970; Chapter 'Psychiatric Emergencies' in "Current Emergency Diagnosis and Treatment", 1985; 65 articles in professional journals. *Honours:* Phi Beta Kappa, Universtiy of California, Berkeley, 1947; NIMH Grant Awardee,

'Depressive States and Suicide Prevention, 1968-82; Louis I Dublin Award, American Association of Suicidology, 1979, *Hobbies:* Philately; Tennis. *Address:* University of California, San Francisco Medical Centre, Langley Porter Psychiatric Institute, San Francisco, CA 94143, USA.

MOUDREE, Marcia Kay, b. 29 Apr. 1952, Townsend, Montana, USA. Anesthesiologist, Southern California Permanente Medical Group. m. Royal Stapleton Magnus, 25 April 1981, San Diego, 1 son. *Education:* BS, Montana State University, 1974; MD, University of Washington, 1978. *Appointments:* Intern, 1978-79, Resident, 1980-82, US Naval Hospital, San Diego; Staff Anesthesiologist, US Naval Hospital Camp, Pendleton, 1982-84. *Memberships:* American, California, San Diego Societies of Anesthesiologists; American Society of Clinical Hypnosis; San Diego Society of Clinical Hypnosis; American Board of Anesthesiology. *Hobbies:* Wife; Mother; Camping; Music; Philosophy. *Address:* 4647 Zion Avenue, San Diego, CA 92120, USA.

MOUNSEY, John Patrick David, b. 1 Feb. 1914, London, England. Cardiologist, Retired. m. Vera Madeline Sara King, 6 Dec. 1947, London, 1 son, 1 daughter. *Education:* Scholar, King's College, Cambridge; MA, Classics and Modern Languages; MD, (Cantab), King's College Hospital London. *Appointments:* Sherbrook Research Fellow, Cardiac Department, London Hospital, 1951; Lecturer, Royal Postgraduate Medical School, 1960; Senior Lecturer and Sub-Dean, 1962; Consultant Cardiologist, Hammersmith Hospital, 1960; Deputy Director, British Postgraduate Medical Federation, 1967; Provost, Welsh National School of Medicine, 1969-79. *Memberships:* Fellow, Royal College of Physicians; General Medical Council, Member, 1970-79; General Dental Council, 1973-79; South Glamorgan Area Health Authority (Teaching); Council of The British Heart Foundation; Extraordinary Member, British Cardiac Society; Honorary Member, Associations of Physicians and of Society of Physicians, Wales; Corresponding Member, Australasian Cardiac Society; Late Assistant Editor, 'British Heart Journal'. *Publications:* Articles on Cardiology mainly in 'British Heart Journal'. *Honour:* Honorary LL.D, Wales, 1980. *Hobbies:* Gardening; Music; Painting. *Address:* Esk House, Coombe Terrace, Wotton-under-Edge, Gloucestershire GL12 7NA, England.

MOUTQUIN, Jean-Marie, b. 13 Mar. 1945, Belgium. Associate Professor. m. Michelle Gravel, 21 Oct. 1967, Montreal, Canada, 3 sons, 2 daughters. *Education:* BA, University of Montreal, Canada, 1964, MD, 1968; LMCC, 1969; CSPQ; FRCS; FACOG. *Appointments:* Assistant Professor, Department of Obstetrics-Gynaecology, University of Montreal, 1978-83, Associate Professor, 1983-. *Memberships:* Society of Obstetricians and Gynaecologists of Canada; Society for the Study of Hypertension in Pregnancy. *Publications include:* Numerous conference papers and presentations to professional societies; many articles, newsletters for medical journals including: 'Hypertension arterielle et grossese' in 'Clinimed', 1980; 'Les Prostaglandines in obstetrique' in 'Clinimed', 1981; Co-author 'Etude propective de la tension arterielle au cours de la grossesse. Prediction des Complications Hypertensives' in 'Journal Gyn Obst Biol Reprod', 1982; 'Detection precoce de l'hypertension arterielle dyrant la grossesse' in 'Le Courier Medical', 1983; 'Predire la Preeclampsie chez la Femme Enceinte' in 'Actualites Medicales', 1983; Co-author 'A Prospective Study of Blood Pressure in Pregnancy. Prediction of Preeclampsia' in 'American Journal of Obstetricians and Gynaecologists, 1985, etc. *Address:* Department of Obstetrics-Gynaecology, Notre Dame Hospital, 1560 Est, Sherbrooke, Montreal, Quebec, H2L 4K8, Canada.

MOWAT, Alex P, b. 5 Apr. 1935, Scotland. Consultant Paediatrician. m. 2 sons. *Education:* Graduate in Medicine, University of Aberdeen, 1985; Medical and paediatric postgraduate experience in Aberdeen,

Hong Kong, London, England and New York, USA. *Appointments:* Research training, Enzymology Department, The Rowatt Research Institute, Aberdeen, Scotland; 2 year Research Training Fellowship, Department of Medicine, Albert Einstein College of Medicine, Yeshiva University, New York, USA; Consultant Paediatrician, King's College Hospital, London, England, 1978-. *Publications:* "Liver Disorders in Childhood", 1979; Chapter: 'Paediatric Liver Disorders' in "The Liver Annual, 1981'. *Address:* 11 Cator Road, Sydenham SE26, Kent, England.

MRAZEK, David Allen, b. 1 Oct. 1947, USA. Director, Paediatric Psychiatry. m. Patricia J Steinberg, 2 Sep. 1978, Riverside, Illinois, 2 sons, 1 daughter. *Education:* BA cum laude, Cornell University; MD, Wake Forest University. *Appointments:* Lecturer, Child Psychiatry, Institute of Psychiatry, London, England, 1977-79; Assistant Professor, Child Psychiatry, 1979-84, Associate Professor, Child Psychiatry and Paediatrics, 1984-, University of Colorado Medical School, currently, Director, Paediatric Psychiatry, National Jewish Hospital and Research Center, Denver, Colorado. *Memberships:* Fellow, American Academy of Child Psychiatry; American Psychiatric Association; Royal College of Psychiatry, England; Association for Child Psychiatry and Psychology; Society for Research in Child Development. *Publications:* Co-author of contributions to: 'Journal of the American Academy of Child Psychiatry', 1982; "Recent Research in Developmental Psychopathology", 1984; "Child Psychiatry; Modern Approaches", 2nd edition, 1984. *Honours:* 1st Prize, Maurice Levine Essay Award, University of Cincinnati, 1974; Research Scientist Development Award, National Institute of Mental Health, 1983. *Hobby:* Mountain walking. *Address:* National Jewish Center for Immunology and Respiratory Medicine, 1400 Jackson Street, Denver, CO 80206, USA.

MUEGGE, Sarah, b. 12 Jan. 1953, Springfield, Missouri, USA. Registered Nurse; Rehabilitation Educator. m. Frederick David Muegge, 26 Nov. 1977, 1 son, 1 daughter. *Education:* BSN, University of Missouri, 1975. *Appointments:* Staff Nurse, Head Nurse, Rusk Rehabilitation Centre, Columbia, Missouri, 1976-77; Staff Nuse, Memorial Medical Centre, Springfield, 1978-80; Office Nurse, Internist, Springfield, 1980-81; Rehabilitation Educator, L E Cox Medical Centre, Springfield, 1981-. *Memberships:* American Nurses Association; Sigma Theta Tau; Association of Rehabilitation Nurses; National Head Injury Foundation. *Honours:* American Nurses Association Certification in Medicine & Surgery (RNC); Rehabilitation Nurse's Certification (CRRN). *Hobbies:* Reading; Golf; Crafts; Presbyterian church activities. *Address:* 2855 South Versailles, Springfield, MO 65804, USA.

MUELLER, Terrance John, b. 13 Aug. 1953, St Louis, Missouri, USA. Foot Surgeon. m. Barbara, 14 June 1975, 1 son, 1 daughter. *Education:* DPM, Doctor of Podiatric Medicine; BS; BA; Fellow, American College of Foot Surgeons; Diplomate, American Board of Podiatric Surgery. *Appointments:* Clinical Instructor, Podiatric Medicine and Surgery, College of Podiatric Medicine and Surgery, University of Osteopathic Medicine and Health Sciences, Des Moines, Iowa; General Editor, Journal of the American Podiatric Medical Association; President, Quad Cities Podiatric Medical Society; Special Editor, Journal of the American Podiatric Medical Association (current). *Memberships:* American Podiatric Medical Association; American College of Sports Medicine; Illinois Podiatric Medical Society; Fellow, American College of Foot Surgeons; Diplomate, American Board of Podiatric Surgery; American Association of Physicians and Podiatrists. *Publications:* Ruptures and Lacerations of the Tibialis Posterior Tendon, Journal of the American Podiatric Medical Association, 1984; Abductor Hallucis Myocele, Journal of the American Podiatric Medical Association, 1981; The Use of the CO_2 Surgical Laser for the Treatment of Verrucae, Journal of the American Podiatric Medical Associa-

tion, 1980. *Hobbies:* Photography; Biomechanics; Shoe Design; Running; Music; Reading; Anthropology. *Address:* Metropolitan Towers, 1520 Seventh Street, Moline, IL 61265, USA.

MUFTI, Mohammed Hassan, b. 18 June 1952, Jeddah, Saudi Arabia. Assistant Professor, Orthopaedic Surgeon. m. 17 Aug. 1977, 1 son, 1 daughter. *Education:* MBBS 1st degree of honour; MD. *Appointments:* Senior House Officer in Surgery, Riyadh, Saudia Arabia, and London, England; Registrar, General Surgery, Saint James' Hospital, London; Registrar, Orthopaedic Surgery, Saint George's Hospital, London; Senior Registrar, Orthopaedic Surgery, University Hospital, Riyadh, Saudia Arabia; Assistant Proffessor, Consultant Orthopaedic Surgeon, Riyadh Central Hospital, Riyadh. *Memberships:* Royal Society of Medicine; British Orthopaedic Association; American Association for Automotive Medicine; Bahraini Academy for Sports Medicine; FRCMG; FRSS. *Publications:* "Sports Medicine and Sports Injuries", 1983; "First aids in Orthopaedics and Transporting Casualties", 'Road Traffic Accidents as a Public Health Problem', 1984; 'Prime Aetiological Factors of CDH and TEV', 1984. *Honours:* Several awards from the Saudi Royal Family for education and medical services. *Hobbies:* Reading; Swimming; Tennis; Chess. *Address:* PO Box 6557, Riyadh 11452, Saudia Arabia.

MUIR, (Isabella) Helen (Mary), b. 20 Aug. 1920, Naini Tal, UP India. Director; Head of Division. *Education:* MA 1944, DPhil 1947, BSc, Somerville College, Oxford, 1973; FRS. *Appointments:* Research fllow, Sir William Dunn School of Pathology, University of Oxford, 1947-48; Scientific Staff, National Institute for Medical Research, London, 1948-54; Empire Rheumatism Council Fellow, Medical Unit, 1954-58, Pearl Research Fellow, Honorary Lecturer, St Mary's Hospital Medical School, Londo, 1959-66. *Memberships:* Trustee, Wellcome Trust, 1982-; Member, Council of Chelsea College, 1982-85; Member, Council of Royal Society, 1982-83; Editorial Board, Biochemical Journal, 1963-69; Editorial Board, Annals of Rheumatic Diseases, 1971-77; Member, Council of MRC, 1974-77; Member, Board of Governors, Strangeways Research Laboratory, Cambridge, 1978-. *Publications:* Over 300 scientific Papers mainly of biochemistry of connective tissues in relation to arthritis and inherited diseases in scientific journals such as Biochemical Journal; Arthritis and Rheumatism; Nature; etc; Contributor to several specialist books. *Honours:* Fellow, Royal Society, 1977; Feldberg Prize, 1977; Heberden Orator, 1977; Bunim Medal, American Rheumatism Association, 1978; Honorary Fellow, Somerville College, 1979; Steindler Award of the Orthopaedic Research Society (USA), 1982; CBE, 1981; Honorary DSc, Edinburgh, 1982; Strathclyde, 1983; CIBA Medal of Biochemical Society, 1981. *Hobbies:* Gardening; Music; Horses; Natural History; Ballet. *Address:* Kennedy Institute of Rheumatology, Bute Gardens, Hammersmith, London, W6 7DW, England.

MUIRHEAD, Ernest Eric, b. 13 Sep. 1916, Recife, Brazil. Director, Department of Pathology, Baptist Memorial Hospital; Professor Chairman Emeritus, Department of Pathology, College of Medicine, University of Tennessee Memphis. m. Mary Louise Garner, 18 July 1942, Jacksonville, Texas, 2 sons, 3 daughters. *Education:* BA, 1939, MD, 1939 Baylor University Medical School, Texas. *Appointments include:* Consultant in Pathology, US Army Biological Laboratories, Fort Detrick, 1966-71; Professor of Pathology, University of Tennessee Center for Health Sciences, Memphis, 1965-80; Clinical Professor of Medicine, University of Tennessee Center for Health Sciences, 1965-80; Director, Department of Pathology and Blood Bank, Baptist Memorial Hospital, Memphis, 1965-; Professor of Medicine, University of Tennessee, Memphis, 1980-; Professor and Chairman, Department of Pathology, College of Medicine, University of Tennessee, Memphis, 1980-86. *Memberships:* Member and Fellow of numerous professional organizations including:

American Society for Clinical Investigation; Association of American Physicians; American Physiological Society; Diplomate of American Board of Pathology. *Publications:* Contributor to professional journals, books, etc. *Honours:* Emily Cooley Lectureship, AABB, 1963; Arthur C Corcoran Lecture, Council for High BP Research, 1979; Distinguished Service Award, AABB, 1982; Merck, Sharpe and Dohme Award, International Society of Hypertension, 1982. *Hobby:* Fishing. *Address:* Department of Pathology, College of Medicine, University of Tennessee, 858 Madison Avenue, Memphis, TN 38163, USA.

MUKHERJEE, Surath Kumar, b. 1 Mar. 1925, Calcutta, India. Drug Research Scientist. m. Namita Ganguli, 4 Mar. 1960, Calcutta, 2 sons. *Education:* BSc 1944, MSc 1947, MB, BS, 1946 & 1949, D Phil (Science), 1957, University of Calcutta. *Appointments:* Lecturer in Physiology, Vidyasagar College, Calcutta, 1952-53; SMS Medical College, Jaipur, 1953-54; Senior Scientific Officer, 1954-60, Head, 1960-67, Assistant Director & Head, 1967-81, Deputy Director & Head, 1981-85, Emeritus Scientist, 1985-, Central Drug Research Institute, Lucknow. *Memberships:* Diabetic Association of India; Indian Science Congress Association; Physiological Society of India; Society of Toxicology, India; Fellow, Indian National Science Academy, New Delhi, 1984; Fellow, National Academy of Medical Sciences, New Delhi, 1984. *Publications:* Numerous learned articles in medical journals. *Honours:* Visiting Scientist to USA unde Indo-USA Exchange Programme, 1972; P P Surya Kumari Prize, Pharmacological Society of India, 1980. *Hobbies:* Gardening; Tourism. *Address:* 66 S K Deb Road, Calcutta - 48 Pin 700048, India.

MULCAHY, Risteárd, b. 13 July 1922, Dublin, Ireland. Director, Cardiac Dept, Professor, Preventive Cardiology, St Vincent's Hospital & University College, Dublin. m. Aileen Hanton, 30 December 1954, Dublin, 3 sons, 3 daughters. *Education:* MB, BCh, 1945, MD, 1948, University College, Dublin & St Vincent's Hospital. *Appointments:* House Physician, Senior House Officer, St Vincent's Hospital; House Physician, Medical Registrar, Hospital of St John and St Elizabeth, London; Post-doctoral Student, National Heart Hospital, London. *Memberships:* Irish and British Cardiac Societies; American Heart Association; Association of Physicians of Great Britain & Ireland; Royal Academy of Medicine in Ireland; International Society & Federation of Cardiology; European Cardiac Society; Council, Epidemiology & Prevention; International Society & Prevention of Cardiology; etc. *Publications:* "Prevention of Coronary Heart Disease", 1972; "Heart Attack & Lifestyle", 1976; "Beat Heart Disease", 1979; 200 scientific articles, reviews and editorials. *Honour:* President, Medical Section, Royal Academy of Medicine in Ireland, 1958; Founder, President, Irish Heart Foundation, 1966; President, Irish Medical Association, 1970. *Hobbies:* Running; Cycling; Tennis; Silviculture; Gardening; etc. *Address:* Cardiac Dept, St Vincent's Hospital, Dublin 4, Republic of Ireland.

MÜLLER, Christian, b. 11 Aug. 1921, Münsingen, Bern, Switzerland. Professcr of Psychiatry. m. Madeleine Schätti, 1947, 1 son, 2 daughters. *Education:* MD, Bern University. *Appointments:* Assistant in Psychiatric University Clinics of Zürich and Bern, 1947-53; Head Physician 1953-57, Director 1961-, Psychiatric University Clinic, Lausanne; Head Physician, Psychiatric University Clinic, Zürich, 1957-61; Chairman, Psychiatry, Lausanne University, 1961-. *Memberships:* Académie Leopoldina, Halle, Democratic Republic of Germany; German Society of Psychiatry; Italian Society of Psychiatry; Finnish Society of Psychiatry; Swiss Society of Psychiatry. *Publications:* "Lexikon der Psychiatrie", 1973; 'Evolution des maladies mentales', 1981; 'Les institutions psychiatriques', 1982; 'Etudes sur la psychothérapie des psychoses', 1982. *Honours:* Herman-Simon Prize, 1971; Theodore Naegeli Prize, 1978. *Hobbies:* Gardening; Collecting autographs. *Address:* Hôpital de Cery, CH-1008 Prilly-Lausanne, Switzerland.

MÜLLER, Ferdinand A H, b. 28 May 1923, Hamburg, Germany. Director, Division of Immunology of Infectious Diseases, Institute of Hygiene, Hamburg. m. Ingrid Haker, 12 Apr. 1955, 4 sons. *Education:* MD, Professor of Microbiology. *Appointments:* Assistant Professor, Pediatrics, University of Hamburg; Associate Professor, Microbiology and Hygiene, University of Dusseldorf; Professor, Microbiology, University of Hamburg. *Memberships:* WHO Scientific Group on Trepanemal Infections; WHO Expert Advisory Panel on Venereal Diseases, Treponematoses and Neisseria Infections; Corresponding Member, Korean Dermatological Association. *Publications:* Approximately 80 articles on Virus research, 1952-60; more than 100 publications on treponemal research, 1960-85; Textbook on Medical Immunology, 1963. *Address:* Institute of Hygiene, Gorch-Fock-Wall 15/17, D-2000 Hamburg 36, Federal Republic of Germany.

MÜLLER, Hansjakob, b. 23 July 1941, Biel, Switzerland. Human Geneticist. m. Edith Merz, 11 June 1971, Chur. *Education:* University of Basel Faculty of Medicine, 1961-69; Swiss Civil Service examination for MD, 1969; MD, 1971; Baccalaureate, Bünder Kantonsschule, 1981. *Appointments:* Research Fellow in Cytogenetics, University of Basel, 1969; Resident in Pediatrics, University Children's Hospital, Basel, 1970-72; Visiting Scientist, Department of Genetics, Albert Einstein College of Medicine, New York, 1973-74; Human Geneticist, University Children's Hospital, Basel, 1975-; Head of Laboratory of Human Genetics, Department of Research of the University Clinics, Basel, 1979-; Lecturer in Human Genetics, Faculty of Medicine, University of Basel, 1978-. *Memberships include:* Senator, Swiss Academy of Medical Sciences; Senator, Swiss Academy of Natural Sciences. *Publications:* "Cytogenetics of Vertebrates", 1980; "Medizinische Genetik", 1982; "On The Nature of Cancer", 1985; "Familial Cancer", 1985. *Hobbies include:* Sport. *Address:* Department of Human Genetics, University Children's Hospital, CH 4005 Basel, Switzerland.

MULLER, Hans Konrad, b. 16 July 1937, Broken Hill, Australia. Professor of Pathology; Head of Department. m. Margaret Jill Brady, 23 Apr. 1962, Adelaide, 4 sons, 3 daughters. *Education:* BMedSc, 1961; MB, BS, 1963; PhD, 1970; FRCPA, 1971; MRCPath, 1981; Associate, Australasian College of Dermatologists, 1975. *Appointments include:* Commonwealth Medical Fellow, Division of Immunology, Department of Pathology, University of Cambridge, UK, 1972-73; Associate Professor, Pathology & Immunology, Monash University, Australia, 1975-83; Senior Visiting Research Fellow, University of Bristol, UK, 1978-79; Professor of Pathology, University of Tasmania, 1983-; Visiting Pathologist, Royal Hobart Hospital, 1983-; Visiting Pathologist & Immunologist, Repatriation General Hospital, Hobart, 1984-; Chairman, Division of Laboratory Mediicine, Royal Hobart Hospital, 1985-. *Memberships include:* Chair, Board of Censors/Council Member, Royal College of Pathologists of Australasia, 1982-; Chief Examiner, Immunology/Member, Board of Censors, ibid, 1980-82; Member, Joint Specialist Advisory Committees, Royal Australasian College of Physicians, Immunology 1980-, Haematology 1982-; Tasmanian State Committee, Royal College of Pathologists of Australasia, 1983-; Secretary 1977-81, President 1981-83, Australian Society for Experimental Pathology; President 1978, 1981, Victorian Society of Pathology & Experimental Medicine; Numerous other professional organisations. *Publications include:* Over 80 publications on inflammation, immunopathology, immunology, cancer studies. *Honours include:* Commonwealth Medical Fellowship, 1972-73. *Hobbies:* Medical history & biography. *Address:* Department of Pathology, University of Tasmania, GPO Box 252C, Hobart, 7001, Tasmania, Australia.

MULLER, Ralph L J, b. 30 June 1933, London, England. Director, Commonwealth Institute of Parasitology; Honorary Senior Lecturer. m. Annie Badilla, 26

July 1979, 1 son, 1 daughter. *Education:* BSc Honours, 1955, PhD, 1958, London University; Fellow, Institute of Biology, 1976, *Appointments:* Scientific Officer, UK Overseas Development Ministry, 1959-61; Lecturer, Parasitology, University of Ibadan, Nigeria, 1962-65; Senior Lecturer, Medical Helminthology, 1966-80, Honorary Senior Lecturer, 1980-, London School of Hygiene and Tropical Medicine; Director, Commonwealth Institute of Parasitology, St Albans, Hertfordshire. *Memberships:* Treasurer, European Federation of Parasitology; Council, Royal Society of Tropical Medicine and Hygiene; British Society of Parasitology; Secretary, International Filariasis Association. *Publications:* "Worms and Disease", 1975. Chapters contributed: "Tropical Medicine", 1984; "Tropical and Geographical Medicine", 1984; "Infectious Disease", 1983. Over 60 papers contributed to professional journals including 'The Lancet'. Contributing Editor, 'Advances in Parasitology'. *Hobbies:* Photography; Sport. *Address:* Commonwealth Institute of Parasitology, 395A Hatfield Road, St Albans, Hertfordshire AL4 0XU, England.

MULROY, Richard Donovan, b. 6 February 1921, Cambridge, Massachusetts, USA. Orthopaedic Surgeon. m. Anne Elizabeth Carlin, 6 May 1954, Tokyo, Japan, 5 sons, 1 daughter. *Education:* BS, Tufts University, Medford, Massachusetts; MD, Tufts University School of Medicine, Boston, MA; Graduate Medical School, University of Pennsylvania. *Appointments:* Chief of Orthopaedic Surgery, 121st Station Hospital; Assistant Chief of Orthopaedic Surgery, Tokyo Army Hospital; Orthopaedic Consultant, Kennedy Memorial Hospital, Boston; Orthopaedic Surgeon, St Elizabeth's Hospital, Boston; Clinical Professor of Orthopaedic Surgery, Tufts Medical School; Chief of Orthopaedic Surgery, Waltham Hospital, Waltham MA. *Memberships:* Diplomate, American Board of Orthopaedic Surgery; Fellow, American College of Surgeons; Affiliate, Royal Society of Medicine; Governor's Commission on Traffic Safety, MA, Commission on Injuries, American Academy of Orthopaedic Surgeons; Chairman, Executive Committee of Medical Staff, President of Medical Staff, Trustee, Waltham Hospital; Consultant, Boston University Law-Medicine Institute; Councillor, Massachusetts Medical Society; Director, Massachusetts Chapter, American Trauma Society. *Publications:* 'Sub-talar Dislocations' 1955, 'Cyst of the Acromioclavicular Joint' 1962 (in Journal of Bone & Joint Surgery); 'Tetanus at the Rhode Island Hospital' (in Rhode Island Medical Journal), 1950; 'Guillaine-Barre Syndrome' (in New York Journal of Medicine), 1954; 'Iliopsoas Tendon Release' (in Clinical Orthopaedics), 1965. *Honours:* AOA Medical Honour Society, Beta Chapter, Massachusetts, 1947; Commendation Medal, Service in Korea, US Army, 1954. *Hobbies:* Artist; Sailing; Photography. *Address:* 20 Hope Avenue, Waltham, MA 02154, USA.

MUMENTHALER, Marco, b. 23 July 1925, Bern, Switzerland. Head of University Department of Neurology. m. Livia Maria Morandini, 19 Nov. 1949, 3 daughters. *Education:* College at Milan, Italy, 1943; Medical School Zurich, Paris, Amsterdam and Basle, 1943-50; MD Zurich 1951; Intern and Resident, Zurich Medical School, Winterthuv and Munsingen, Switzerland. *Appointments:* Assistant Professor of Neurology, University of Zurich, 1960; Visiting Associate Professor, NIH, USA, 1960-61; Associate Professor of Neurology, 1962-65, Professor 1965- University of Berne, Switzerland; currently Head of Department of Neurology, Berne University. *Memberships:* Swiss Neurological Society, President 1970-72; Corresponding or Honorary Member of the Italian, French, Belgian, German, Polish and American Neurological Societies. Board Member of Academy of Sciences "Peopoldina". *Publications include:* Textbook of Neurology, 8th German edition, Stuttgart 1986, 2nd English edition 1983, Polish, French, Spanish, Portuguese, Italian, Turkish and Japanese editions 1972-83; "Klinische Neurologie" Stuttgart, 1973; "Schulter-Arm-Schmerz" 2nd Ger-

man edition Berm 1982, French edition in preparation; "Neurologische Differential-diagnostik" 2nd German edition 1983, English Spanish and Polish editions 1983; "Atlas der klinischen Neurologie", 2nd edition, Heidelberg, 1987, Japanese edition 1984; "Synkopen" Stuttgart 1984. *Hobby:* Photography. *Address:* Department of Neurology, University Hospital, CH-3010 Bern, Switzerland.

MUNKONGE, Lupando, b. 13 Mar. 1941, Zambia. Head, Paediatric Surgical Centre. m. Theresa Musenge Mole, 27 Aug. 1967, 2 sons, 1 daughter. *Education:* MD, Greisfwald University, Germany, 1968; Diploma in Tropical Medicine and Hygiene, Hamburg, 1969; Fellow, Royal College of Surgeons and Physicians, Scotland, 1978; Diploma in Paediatric Surgery, Juntendo University, Japan, 1981. *Appointments include:* Junior House Officer, 1969-70, Senior House Officer, 1970-71, Registrar in Surgery, 1973-, Lecturer in General Surgery, 1979-82, Senior Lecturer, 1982, Paediatric Surgeon and Head of Paediatric Surgical Centre, 1983-, Acting Head, Department of Surgery, 1983-, Teaching Hospital, University of Zambia. *Publications:* "Infwa Shonse", textbook; "Elementary Organic Chemistry for 6th Forms"; "Orthopaedics for Medical Students", volumes 1 and 2. Contributions to: 'Zambia Medical Journal'; 'Association of Surgeons of East Africa'; Proceedings of Association of Surgeons of East Africa. Various research programmes. *Address:* School of Medicine, University of Zambia, PO Box 50110, Lusaka, Zambia.

MUNOZ, Alvaro, b. 5 Apr. 1951, Medellin, Columbia. Assistant Professor, Epidemiology, School of Hygiene & Public Health, Johns Hopkins University, USA. m. Beatriz Mejia, 7 June 1974, Medellin, 1 son, 1 daughter. *Education:* BS, Honours, Mathematics, Universidad Nacional de Colombia, 1973; MS 1977, PhD 1980, Statistics, Stanford University, USA. *Appointments:* Instructor, Statistics, University de Medellin, Colombia, 1973-75; Teaching Assistant, Statistics, Stanford University, 1977-80; Consultant, Biostatistics, Stanford University Medical Centre, 1978-80; Associate Staff, Medicine, Brigham & Women's Hospital, 1980-82; Instructor in Medicine, Harvard Medical School, 1980-85; Associate Biostatistician, Department of Medicine, Brigham & Women's Hospital, 1982-85; Instructor, Biostatistics, Harvard Medical School, 1982-85; Instructor, Biomedical Introduction to Statistics, Extension Course, Harvard, 1982-85; Associate Professor, Department of Epidemiology, Johns Hopkins University, 1986-. *Memberships:* American Statistical Association; Biometric Society; American Thoracic Society. *Publications include:* Numerous professional research papers, book chapters, etc. *Hobbies:* Cycling; Camping. *Address:* Johns Hopkins University, School of Hygiene & Public Health, 615 North Wolfe Street, Baltimore, MD 21205, USA.

MUNRO, Alistair, b. 6 Apr. 1933, Glasgow, Scotland. Professor of Psychiatry. m. Mary M C Stewart, 26 Mar. 1959, Glasgow, Scotland, 2 daughters. *Education:* MB, ChB, 1950-56, MD, 1965, University of Glasgow; M Psy Med, University of Liverpool, 1981. *Appointments:* Senior Lecturer, First Assistant in Psychiatry, University of Birmingham, 1967-69; Professor and Head, Liverpool University Department of Psychiatry, 1969-75; Psychiatrist in Chief, Toronto General Hospital, Professor of Psychiatry, University of Toronto, 1975-82; Professor and Head, Dalhousie University Department of Psychiatry, Halifax, Nova Scotia, Canada. *Memberships:* Canadian Medical Association; Medical Society of Nova Scotia; Halifax Medical Society; Canadian Psychiatric Association; Nova Scotia Psychiatric Association; Canadian College of Neuropsychopharmacology; Canadian Society for Clinical Pharmacology etc. *Publications:* "Psychiatry for Social Workers" with J W McCulloch, 1969, 1975; "Psychosomatic Medicine" 1973; Editor of series of Psychiatric Texts published by Messrs Macdonald Evans plus chapters in books and approximately 50 scientific articles. *Honour:* Examiner and Visiting Professor, University of Malaya, 1985. *Hobbies:* Reading; Music; Architecture; Travel. *Address:* Dalhousie University Department of Psychiatry, Camp Hill Hospital, 1763 Robie Street, Halifax, Nova Scotia, Canada B3H 3G2.

MUNRO, Donald Sinclair, b. 14 Feb. 1925, London, England. Professor of Medicine and Honorary Consultant Physician. m. Helen Reid Phemister, 28 Dec. 1951, Aberdeen, 2 sons, 2 daughters. *Education:* MB, ChB, 1947, MD Commendation 1957, Aberdeen; Member 1949, Fellow 1967, Royal College of Physicians, London. *Appointments:* House Physician, Royal Infirmary, Aberdeen, 1947; Assistant Lecturer, materia medica, Aberdeen University, 1948-49; Junior Specialist in Medicine, Royal Army Medical Corps, Malaya and Hong Kong, 1949-51; Medical Registrar, Teaching Hospitals, Aberdeen, Scotland 1951-53; Research Fellow, New England Medical Centre, Boston, USA, 1957-58; Lecturer in Therapeutics 1953-59, Senior Lecturer 1959-65, Reader in Clinical Endocrinology 1965-67, Professor of Clinical Endocrinology 1967-73, Sheffield University, England; Currently Professor of Medicine and Honorary Consultant Physician, University Department of Medicine, Clinical Sciences, Centre, Northern General Hospital, Sheffield. *Memberships:* Association of Physicians of Great Britain and Ireland; Royal Society of Medicine; Society for Endocrinology; Associate Member, American Thyroid Association; European Thyroid Association; Medical Research Society. *Publications:* 'Thyroid Stimulating Immunoglobulins', 1984; 'The Role of Thyroid Stimulating Immunoglobulins of Graves's Disease in Neonatal Thyrotoxicosis', (with S M Dirmikis, H Humphries, T Smith and G D Broadhead), 1985. *Address:* University Department of Medicine, Clinical Sciences Centre, Northern General Hospital, Sheffield S5 7AU, South Yorkshire, England.

MUNSEY, William F, b. 24 Aug. 1931, Columbus, Ohio, USA. Doctor of Podiatric Medicine. m. Helen Jarvis, 26 Dec. 1954, Columbus, Ohio, 1 son, 2 daughters. *Education:* Doctor of Podiatric Medicine, Ohio College of Podiatric Medicine, Cleveland, Ohio, USA. *Appointments:* President, Central Academy Ohio Podiatry Association, 1960-61; President, Ohio Podiatry Association, 1963-64; Chairman, Board of Trustees, Ohio Podiatry Association, 1965-66; President, American Podiatry Association, 1979; President of the Fund for Podiatry Education -; President, Podiatry Insurance Co of America -; Private Practice -. *Memberships:* Ohio Podiatric Medical Association; American Podiatric Medical Association; Fellow, American Academy of Practice Administration; Fellow, American College of Foot Surgeons; Honorary Member, American Society of Podiatric Medicine. *Publications:* 'Testing to Find Qualified Office Assistants' in 'Auxiliary Personnel in Podiatry'; 'Podiatry' in "Introduction to Health Professions"; 'Alcohol-Phenal Correction of Nails and Diabetics' in 'Current Podiatry', May 1972. *Honours:* Man of the Year, Ohio Podiatric Association, 1967; Distinguished Alumnus of the Year, Alpha Gamma Kappa Fraternity, 1979; Distinguished Alumnus of the Ohio College of Podiatric Medicine, 1979. Kennison Award, presented by the American Podiatric Medical Students Association, 1983. *Hobbies:* Fishing; Hunting; Woodwork. *Address:* 37 E Wilson Bridge Road, Worthington, OH 43085, USA.

MUNTARBHORN, Smarn, b. 20 Nov. 1914, Bandon, Thailand. Emeritus Professor of Surgery, Mahidol University, Bangkok. m. Niramol Donavanik, 14 Jan. 1949, Bangkok, Thailand, 2 sons, 1 daughter. *Education:* MB, BS, University of London, England; DTM, University of Liverpool, England; FRCS, England; Honorary MD, Songkla, Honorary FRCS, Thailand. *Appointments:* President, International College of Surgeons, 1964-66; President, American College of Chest Physicians, 1959-70; Consultant to Army Medical Department. *Memberships:* British Thoracic Society, 1951; Thai Thoracic Society, Former Vice-President; Member, Cardiac Society of Thailand. *Publications:* "Hippuric Acid Tests, Portal Hypertension &

Port-caval anastomosis", 1951; "Lung Abscess Treatment", 1951; "A Historical Sketch of Commencement of Heart Operations in Thailand". *Honours:* Confined Science Scholarship Guy's Hospital, London, England, 1936; Golding-Bird Gold Medal & Bacteriology Prize, Guy's Hospital, 1939; The first Thai to do: Vascular anastomosis, Lieno-renal anstomosis, 1951; Lung resections; operate on heart closed and open with a heart lung machine 1953, 1959; The first Thai to get FRCS England. *Hobby:* Photography. *Address:* 170 Silom Road, Bangkok, Thailand, 10500.

MURER, Heini, b. 6 Aug. 1944. Professor of Physiology. *Education:* PhD. *Appointments:* Postdoctoral Associate, Institute of Biochemistry, University of Fribourg, 1969-71; Research Associate, Laboratory of Biochemistry, ETH, Zurich, 1972-75; Research Associate, Max-Planck Institute for Biophysics, Frankfurt, 1975-79; Associate Professor, Institute of Biochemistry, University of Fribourg, 1979-80; Professor, Institute of Physiology, 1980-. *Memberships:* Swiss Society for Biochemistry; Mount Desert Island Biological Laboratory, Salsbury Cove, Maine, USA; Swiss Society for Biophysics; American Physiological Society; German Society of Nephrology; German Society of Physiology; New York Academy of Sciences; International Society of Nephrology; Swiss Society of Physiology; European Society for Comparative Physiology and Biochemistry. *Address:* University of Zurich-Irchel, Winterthurerstrasse 190, 8057, Zurich, Switzerland.

MURRAY, James Patrick, b. 17 Jan. 1922, Athenry, Republic of Ireland. Professor of Radiology. m. Irene Lynch, 8 Sep. 1955, Cork, Ireland, 3 sons, 2 daughters. *Education:* MB 1946, MD 1960, University College, Galway; DMR, University of Liverpool, 1955; FRCR, 1958, FFR (RCSI) 1978, Karolinska Sjukuset, Stockholm. *Appointments:* House Surgeon, Central Hospital, Galway, 1946-47; Colonial Medical Service, 1947-53; Registrar, Senior Registrar, Liverpool Teaching Hospitals, 1955-58; Council of Europe Medical Fellow, 1959; Regional Radiologist, Limerick, Ireland, 1959-63; Visiting Professor of Radiology, University of Pittsburgh, USA, 1973-83; Professor of Radiology, University College, Galway; Consultant Radiologist, Regional Hospital, Galway. *Memberships:* Radiological Society of North America; British Institute of Radiology; Royal College of Radiologists, London; Irish Medical Organisation; and others. *Publications:* "Semi-Ortometric Pelvimetry', 1971, 'Deglutition in Myasthenia Gravis', 1962, 'Buscotan in Diagnostic Radiology', 1966, 'Rectilinear Scanning in Myocardial Infarction', 1976, all in 'British Journal of Radiology'; "Galway's Medical History in Galway 1484-1984", 1984. *Hobbies:* Gardening; Historical Research; Travel. *Address:* Aran House, Shangort, Knocknacarra, Co Galway, Republic of Ireland.

MURRAY, Robert, b. 10 Oct. 1916, Scotland. President of International Commission on Occupational Health. m. Noreen Cargill, 3 Apr. 1945, London, England, 1 daughter. *Education:* BSc 1937, MB ChB 1939, Glasgow University, Scotland; Fellow, Royal College of Physicians, Glasgow; DPH 1947, DIH 1949, FFOM 1980, London, England. *Appointments:* House Surgeon, 1939-40; General Practice, 1940-41; Her Majesty's Forces, 1941-46; Her Majesty's Medical Inspector of Factories, 1947-56; International Labour Office, 1956-61; Medical Adviser, Trades Union Congress, 1962-64. *Memberships:* Honorary Treasurer, Royal Society of Medicine; Past President, Society of Occupational Medicine; Past President, British Occupational Hygiene Society; International Health Society; President, International Commission on Occupational Health. *Publications:* "Industrial Health Technology", (co-author), 1956; 'Skin Cancer' chapter in "Cancer"; 'Ethics' article in 'ILO Encyclopaedia"; 'Thackrah Lecture', 1984; Sundry articles. *Honour:* Order of the British Empire, 1978. *Hobbies:* Golf; Piano. *Address:* Department of Occupational Health, London School of Hygiene and Tropical Medicine, Keppel Street, London WC1E 7HT, England.

MURRAY, T J, b. 30 May 1938, Halifax, Nova Scotia, Canada. University Dean of Medicine. m. Janet Kathleen, 27 Aug. 1960, Halifax, 2 sons, 2 daughters. *Education:* St Francis Xavier University; MD, Dalhousie University; FRCP (C); FACP. *Appointments:* Professor of Medicine, Chief of Medicine, Camp Hill Hospital, Head, Division of Neurology; Director, Dalhousie MS Research Unit; President, Canadian Neurological Society; Vice-President, American Academy of Neurology; Governor, American College of Physicians. *Memberships:* Royal Society of Medicine; American Academy of Neurology; American College of Physicians; Canadian Medical Association. *Publications:* "Essential Neurology" textbook, 3rd edition 1986. 112 publications on neurological education, multiple sclerosis and medical history. *Honours:* Alpha Omega Alpha 1961; Commonwealth Scholar, 1967; Professor of the Year Award, 1974; Nuffield Travelling Fellow, 1977; Commonwealth Professor 1985. *Hobbies:* Marathon running; Medical history; Piano; Photography. *Address:* Office of The Dean, Sir Charles Tuppy Medical Building, Dalhousie University, Halifax, Nova Scotia, Canada B3H 4HT.

MUSA, Abdelrahman Mohamed, b. 25 Dec. 1935, Omdurman, Sudan. Dean, Faculty of Medicine, Khartoum, 1983-. m. Nur Hassan, 7 Sep. 1965, Dueim, 5 sons, 1 daughter. *Education:* MB, BS, Khartoum; MRCP, 1967, FRCP, Edinburgh, Scotland. *Appointments:* Lecturer and Consultant Physician, 1968-72; Associate Professor, 1972-78; Professor of Medicine, 1978; Head, Department of Medicine, 1978-82. *Memberships:* Secretary, Sudan Association of Physicians; Vice-President, Nephro-Urological Association. *Publications:* Author of numerous publications. *Honours:* Recipient of prizes from University of Khartoum. *Hobbies:* Photography; Farming. *Address:* PO Box 102, Khartoum, Sudan.

MUSCATELLO, Umberto Guiseppe, b. 5 July 1932, Colonnella, Italy. University Professor of Medicine. *Education:* MD, PhD (General Pathology), PhD (Electron Optics). *Appointments:* Associate Professor, Faculty of Natural and Biological Sciences, University of Modena, 1967-74; Professor, Faculty of Medicine, University of Sassari, 1974-76; Professor, General Pathology, Faculty of Medicine, University of Modena, 1976-78; Vice Chancellor, Modena University, 1978-79; Chairman of Faculty Board of Medical Faculty, University of Modena, 1979-. *Memberships:* Scientific Committee of the Italian National Health Institute, 1979-; Committee for Scientific Activity of the I.R.C.C.S of the Minister of Health, Italy. *Publications:* 'The sarcotubular system of skeletal muscle' 1961; 'The mechanism of muscle fiver relaxation' 1962; 'The differential response of sarcoplasm to denervation' 1965; 'Effect of tonicity of negative stains in electron micro.' 1968; 'Configurational changes in isolated mitochondria' 1972-75; 'Phosphorylating efficiency of mitochondria in state 4' 1984. *Honours:* Fellow, European Molecular Biology Organisation, 1966; Fellow, Collegium Ramazzini, New York, 1982; Fellow, Italian Group of Bioenergetics, 1978. *Address:* Institute of General Pathology, University of Modena, via Campi 287, 4100 Modena, Italy.

MUSIL, Ernst Hans, b. 7 Jan. 1906, Vienna, Austria. Specialist in Obstetrics and Gynaecology. *Education:* Dr Med Univ. *Appointments:* Lecturer, University of Vienna. *Memberships:* Secretary-General, International Federation for Hygiene, Preventive and Social Medicine; President, Austrian Association for Preventive and Social Medicine. *Publications:* "Introduction to Social Medicine"; "Education in Social Medicine". *Honours:* Akfons Fischer Medal, Honorary Member, Baden-Württhembergische Gesellschaft für Sozialhygiene. *Hobby:* Music. *Address:* Mariahilferstrasse 177, 1150 Vienna, Austria.

MUSSENDEN, Maria Elisabeth, b. 4 Oct. 1949, San Juan, Puerto Rico, USA. Pscyhologist; Human Services Counsellor. *Education:* BA, 1971, MA, 1978, University of Puerto Rico; PhD, University of Florida,

1987. *Appointments include:* Lecturer inter American University, Hato Rey, Puerto Rico, 1971-78; Music Teacher, Department of Education, San Juan, Puerto Rico, 1974-79; Teaching Assistant, 1979-80, Undergraduate Psychology Advisor, 1980-81, Counselling Psychology Intern, 1982-83, Counselling Psychology Graduate Assistant, 1983-84, Teaching Assistant, 1984, University of Florida; Counselling Psychology Practica, 1980, Counselling Psychology Practicum, 1981, Veterans Administration Hospital, Gainesville, Florida; Alcohol Specialist, 1983-84, Counsellor I, 1984-, Alcothon House, Gainesville; Rehabilitation Therapist, 1985, Human Services Counsellor III, 1985-, North Florida Evaluation and Treatment Center, Gainesville. *Memberships:* National Alliance for the Mentally Ill; Mental Health Association; Florida Association for Behaviour Analysis; American Psychological Association; Co-Founder, Puerto-Rico Music Therapy Association. *Publications:* Contributor to 'Journal of Counselling and Development', 1986; 'Journal of College Student Personnel', 1985. 'La Musica Funcional y su Aplicacion Terapeutica en Puerto Rico', Masters thesis, 1978; 'The Physiological Effects of Music on Progressive Relaxation Exercises for Alcoholic Patients', PhD dissertation in progress. *Honours include:* Graduate Teaching Assistantships, 1979-80, 1980-81, Graduate Fellowship, 1981-82, Graduate Assistantship, 1983-84, Presidential Award, 1985, University of Florida; Fonalledas Foundation Fellowship, 1982-83; Ford Foundation Fellowship, 1972-73, 1974-75; Angel Ramos Foundation Fellowship, 1973-74, 1979-80; BA Magna cum laude, University of Puerto Rico. *Hobbies:* Music; Reading; Sewing; Cooking. *Address:* 125 South West 40 Terrace, Gainesville, FL 32607, USA.

MUSZBEK, László, b. 25 Feb. 1942, Sárrétudvari, Hungary. Professor of Clinical Chemistry. m. Elisabeth Lindenfeld, 17 Oct. 1972, Debrecen, Hungary, 3 daughters. *Education:* MD, 1966, Specialist in Laboratory Medicine; PhD Medical Biology, 1973, Specialist in Haematology, 1978. *Appointments:* Research Fellow, 1966-68, Assistant Professor, 1968-73, Department of Pathophysiology, University School of Medicine, Debrecen, Hungary; Visiting Associate Professor, National Institute of Health, Bethesda, Maryland, USA, 1973-74; Associate Professor, Department of Pathophysiology, Debrecen, 1974-78; Professor, Chairman, Department of Clinical Chemistry, University Medical School, Debrecen, 1978-. *Memberships:* International Society on Thrombosis & Haemostasis; European Thrombosis Research Organisation; Committee on Biochemistry, National Academy of Science, Hungary; Hungarian Societies on Haematology, Laboratory Medicine, Immunology, Physiology & Biochemistry; Committee on Laboratory Medicine, Hungary. *Publications:* Some 62 publications in professional & international journals of biochemistry and haematology; "Haemostasis & Cancer", 1986. *Honours:* Council Member, European Thrombosis Research Organisation, 1978-; Project Director, National Foundation for Cancer Research, USA, 1979-; International Advisory Committee Member, IXth International Congress on Thrombosis & Haemostasis, 1983; President, International Symposium on Cancer & Haemostasis, 1984; President, Hungarian Society of Haematology, Haemostasis Section. *Hobbies:* Soccer; Tennis; Travel; Fine Art. *Address:* 100 Poroszlay Str. Debrecen, H-4032, Hungary.

MUTHUSWAMY, Petham, b. 12 June 1945, Salem, India. Chairman, Division of Pulmonary Medicine, Cook County Hospital, Chicago, USA. m. Rajeswari Muthuswamy, 14 Nov. 1975, 2 daughters. *Education:* MB, BS; FACP; FRCP (C); FCCP; Member, American Thoracic Society; Critical Care Medicine. *Appointments include:* Attending Physician, Cook County Hospital, 1975; Director of Respiratory Therapy, Hyde Park Hospital, 1976-80; Consulting Physician, Pulmonary Diseases, Mercy Hospital, Hyde Park Hospital, Jackson Park Hospital, South Chicago Community Hospital. *Memberships include:* Fellow: American

College of Physicians, College of Chest Physicians, Royal College of Physicians & Surgeons of Canada; American Medical Association; American Thoracic Society; Society of Critical Care Medicine; etc. *Publications include:* Numerous papers & abstracts in professional & scientific journals. *Hobbies:* Tennis; Travel. *Address:* Pulmonary Division, Cook County Hospital, 1835 W Harrison, Chicago, IL 60612, USA.

MUTI, Musa Mohammed, b. 18 Oct. 1936, Jaffa, Israel. Consultant Radiologist; Physician. m. Dr Widad Qassim Maqsood, 22 June 1966, London, England, 3 sons. *Education:* MB BCh, Cairo, Egypt; MD, Cairo; DMRD, Conjoint Board Diploma of Radiology, UK; Fellow, Royal College of Radiologists, England, International College of Angiology, USA; FFR. *Appointments:* Surgeon, Jordan; Senior Registrar, Central Middlesex Hospital, London, England; Consultant Radiologist, Ministry of Health, Jordan; Consultant, Lebanese Hospitals, Jeddah, Saudi Arabia; Consultant Radiologist and Physician, Private Practice, Saudi Arabia. *Memberships:* Jordan Medical Association; British Institute of Radiology, England; Royal College of Radiologists; International College of Angiology. *Publications:* "Investigation of Subarachnoid Haemorhage by Pan-Cerbral Angiography", 1970; Co-author, 'Jordan Medical Journal, 1974-76. *Honours:* 1st Degree of Honour and Medal, Faculty of Medicine, Cairo, Egypt, 1961. *Hobbies:* Reading; Drawing. *Address:* PO Box 10200, Jeddah 21433, Saudi Arabia.

MUYA, Richard Joseph, b. 29 Apr. 1938, Tanzania. Chief Dental Officer. m. Romana Kindokecha Theobald, 10 Sep. 1960, Moshi, 4 sons, 1 daughter. *Education:* LDS, Royal College of Surgeons, England. *Appointments:* Dental Officer, 1965-70; Senior Dental Officer, 1970-72; Principal Dental Officer, 1972-76; Chief Dental Officer, 1976-. *Memberships:* Medical Association of Tanzania; Tanzania Dental Association; International Federation of Dentists. *Publication:* "Changing and Developing Dental Health Services in Tanzania 1980-2000", (co-author). *Hobbies:* Country walks; Gardening. *Address:* Central Dental Unit, PO Box 273, Dar es Salaam, Tanzania.

MYANT, Nicolas Bruce, b. 26 Oct. 1917, Cardiff, Wales. Retired Medical Practitioner. m. Audrey Palmer, Dec. 1943, 2 sons, 1 daughter. *Education:* BSc, DM, Oxford University, England; FRCP. *Appointments:* Director, MRC Lipid Metabolism Unit, Hammersmith Hospital, London, England, 1969-83. *Membership:* Editor 'Atherosclerosis'. *Publication:* "The Biology of Cholesterol and Related Steroids", 1981. *Address:* 86 Lower Road, Gerrards Cross, Buckinghamshire, England.

MYBURGH, Johannes Albertus, b. 31 May 1928, South Africa. Professor, Head, Surgery, University of Witwatersrand. m. Edith Helen Jacobine Alexander, 8 Dec. 1956, Kroonstad, 1 son, 2 daughters. *Education:* MB, ChB, University of Cape Town; ChM, University of Witwatersrand; FRCS, England. *Appointments:* Surgical Registrar, United Oxford Hospitals & Johannesburg Group of Teaching Hospitals, 1954-60; Surgeon, Senior Surgeon, Principal Surgeon, Johannesburg Hospital, 1960-77; Senior Lecturer, Surgery, 1960-77, Professor, Surgery (ad hominem), 1966-77, Professor, Head, 1977-, University of Witwatersrand. *Memberships:* International Transplantation Society; Surgical Research Society of South Africa, Past President; Southern African Transplantation Society, Past President; Association of Surgeons of South Africa, President, 1984-86; South African Gastroenterological Society. *Publications:* Over 120 articles in professional journals. *Honours:* Rhodes Scholarship, 1952; Claude Harris Leon Award of Merit, 1982; Honorary FACS, 1983; Honorary FRCS, England, 1985. *Hobbies:* Tennis; Music; Reading. *Address:* Dept. of Surgery, University of Witwatersrand Medical School, York Road, Parktown, Johannesburg, South Africa 2193.

MYERS, Allen Richard, b. 14 Jan. 1935, Baltimore, Maryland, USA. Professor of Medicine. m. Ellen Patz, 26 Nov. 1960, Baltimore, Maryland, 3 sons. *Education:* BA, University of Pennsylvania; MD, University of Maryland. *Appointments:* Resident in Internal Medicine, University of Michigan Hospital; Surgeon, United States Public Health Service; Clinical and Research Fellow, Harvard Medical School and Massachusetts General Hospital; Assistant Professor of Medicine, Associate Professor of Medicine, University of Pennsylvania School of Medicine; Professor of Medicine, Temple University School of Medicine. *Memberships:* American Rheumatism Association; American Federation for Clinical Research; Association of Program Directors in Internal Medicine; Association of Professor os Medicine; American College of Physicians, Fellow. *Publications:* Author of 50 Original articles, 9 book chapters and 1 book. *Honours:* Margaret Whitaker Prize, University of Maryland School of Medicine, 1960; Honorary Membership, La Asociocion Colombiana de Rheumatologia, 1973; Lindback Foundation Award for Distinguished Teaching, Temple University, 1981. *Address:* Temple University School of Medicine, Department of Medicine, 3400 North Broad Street, Philadelphia, PA 19140, USA.

MYERS, Carole Robbins, b. 2 July 1937, Hartford, Connecticut, USA. Dialysis Patient/Educator; Editor; Contemporary Dialysis and Neprology. m. Stephen A Myers, 20 June 1959, Stamford, Connecticut, divorced 1975. *Education:* BA, Mathematics, University of Connecticut; Certificate, Medical Systems, Peter Bent Brigham, Boston; Attendance, numerous medical meetings with earned Continuing Education Units. *Memberships:* National Association of Patients on Hemodialysis & Transplantation; National Kidney Foundation; American Association for the Advancement of Science; American Society for Nephrology; American Medical Writers Association; European Dialysis & Transplant Association; International Society of Artificial Organs. *Publications:* Editor, 'Conventions/Conference Contemporary Dialysis'; "Examining Reuse Conference Report", NAPHT-O-Gram', 1982; "Up-Front Opinion - Dialysis & Transplantation', 1982; "Bookshelf - Review of Nephrology Books", 'Napht News', 1983; "Maximizing Rehabilitation in Chronic Renal Disease", 'Dialysis & Transplantation', 1984; "Hepatitis - Avoid it, Understand it, Deal with it", (Renalife), 1986; Contributor to Nephrology Nurse, and many other professional journals. *Honours:* NAPHT Honour Roll, 1980; American Kidney Fund Fellowships, 1979, 1980, 1982. *Hobbies include:* Real Estate; Textiles; Photographer. *Address:* 22 Evergreen Avenue, Hartford, CT 06105, USA.

MYHRE, Hans Olav, b. 19 Oct. 1939, Grimstad, Norway. Professor of Surgery. m. Else Marie, 23 June 1963, 1 son, 2 daughters. *Education:* Graduate of Medical Faculty, University of Oslo, 1964; Specialist in general surgery, 1973; Specialist in thoracic and cardiovascular surgery, 1982; Dr med. *Appointments:* Registrar 1967-73, Senior Registrar 1973-76, Consultant in Vascular Surgery 1977-81, Aker Hospital; Fellow in Cardiovascular Surgery, Baylor College of Medicine, Houston, Texas, USA, 1976-77; Registrar in Cardiac Surgery, Ulleval Sykehus, 1981; Professor of Surgery, Chairman of Department of Surgery, Trondheim University Clinic, Trondheim, 1982-. *Memberships:* European Society for Cardiovascular Surgery; Scandinavian Society for Cardiovascular Surgery; Norwegian Society for Thoracic and Vascular Surgery; Norwegian Surgical Association; Scandinavian Surgical Association; Michael E DeBakey International Surgical Society. *Publications include:* About 250 publications mainly about circulatory physiology, cardiac and vascular surgery including: "Reactive Hyperaemia of the Lower Limbs", 1975; "Surgical Treatment of the Lower Limb Atherosclerosis", 1977; "Ultrasound in the Examination of the Peripheral Circulation", 1979; "Diseases of the Heart and Peripheral Vessels", 1981. *Honour:* His Majesty King Olav V Gold Medal for Medical Research, Oslo, 1979. *Hobbies:* Cross-country running; Painting; Music; Poetry. *Address:* Department of Surgery, Trondheim University Clinic, 7000 Trondheim, Norway.

N

NACE, Edgar P, b. 14 Oct. 1939, Collegeville, Pennsylvania, USA. Chief, Service, Substance Abuse Programmes, Timberlawn Psychiatric Hospital. m. Carol Charlat, 5 June 1965, New York City, 2 sons. *Education:* BS, Muhlenberg College, 1961; MD, University of Pennsylvania School of Medicine, 1965. *Appointments:* Research Psychiatrist, US Army, Major, Walter Reed Army Institute of Research, 1970-73; Director, Strecker Programme, Treatment of Alcoholism, Institute of Pennsylvania Hospital, 1973-81; Assistant Professor, University of Pennsylvania, 1973-81; Associate Professor, Psychiatry, University of Texas Medical Branch, 1981-84; Chief, Service, Substance Abuse Programmes, Timberlawn Psychiatric Hospital, Dallas, 1984-. *Memberships:* American College of Psychiatrists; American Psychiatric Association, Fellow; American Medical Society on Alcoholism; International Society for Clinical and Experimental Hypnosis; American Medical Association. *Publications:* "A Comparison of Borderline and Nonborderline Alcoholic Patients", 'Archives of General Psychiatry', 1983; "Epidemiology of Alcoholism and Prospects for Treatment", 'Annual Review of Medicine', 1984; "Therapeutic Approaches to the Alcoholic Marriage", 'Psychiatric Clinics of North America', 1982; "Depression of Veterans Two Years After Vietnam", 'American Journal of Psychiatry', 1977. *Honours:* Fellow, American Psychiatric Association, 1980; American College of Psychiatry, 1984. *Hobbies:* Rare Books; Racquetball; Bicycling. *Address:* 4701 Samuell Blvd, Suite C, Dallas, TX 75228, USA.

NADA-RAJAH, Shantha Savundaladevi, b. 7 July 1947, London, England. Family Physician. m. Raj Kandiah, 29 Apr., 1972, London, 1 daughter. *Education:* LRCP; MRCS; FLEX. *Appointments:* House Officer, Watford General Hospital, Hertfordshire, England, 1976; House Officer, Whittington Hospital, London, England, 1976-77; Family Physician, Watrous, Saskatchewan, Canada, 1977-; Chief of Staff, Watrous Union Hospital, 1981-. *Memberships:* College of Physicians and Surgeons, Saskatchewan; College of Family Practitioners, Canada; Saskatchewan and Canada Medical Associations; The Federation of Medical Women of Canada; Medical Council of England. *Hobbies:* Reading; Swimming; Music; Travel; Aerobics. *Address:* PO Box 1004, 603 Main Street, Watrous, Saskatchewan, SOK 4T0, Canada.

NADIMINTI, Yallappa, b. 1 Mar. 1949, India. Private Practitioner consulting in Medical Oncology and Haematology, m. Renukadevi, 9 June 1974, Anantapur, India, 3 daughters. *Education:* MB, BS, Government Medical College, Bellary, India, 1973; MD; Diplomate, American Board of Internal Medicine, 1978; Diplomate, Medical Oncology, 1981; Diplomate, Haematology, 1982. *Appointments:* Internship, Unity Hospital, Brooklyn, New York, USA, 1974-75; Residency in Internal Medicine, Kings Brook Jewish Medical Centre, Brooklyn, New York, 1975-77; Fellowship in Medical Oncology, 1977-79, Fellowship in Haematology, 1979-80, Brookdale Medical Centre, Brooklyn, New York. *Memberships:* American College of Physicians; American Medical Association; American Society of Clinical Oncology; American Society of Haematology; Florida Society of Clinical Oncology; Southern Medical Association. *Publications:* 'Lactic acidosis in Hodgekin's Disease: Response to Therapy', 1980. *Hobbies:* Travel; Photography. *Address:* 300 Riverside Drive East, Suite 2800, Bradenton, FL 33508, USA.

NAGAYO, Takeo, b. 25 July 1921, Tokyo, Japan, President, Aichi Cancer Centre. m. Chizuko Iwama, 11 Apr. 1947, Nagoya, Japan, 2 sons. *Education:* Gakushuin Kotoka, 1939-42; MD, Nagoya University School of Medicine, 1942-45. *Appointments:* Assistant, 1945-53, Associate Professor, 1953-56, Professor, 1956-65, Nagoya University School of Medicine, Department of Pathology, Chief, Laboratory of Pathology, 1965-74, Vice Director, 1974-79, Director, 1979-85, President, 1985-, Aichi Cancer Centre. *Memberships:* Japanese Cancer Association; Member of Directors, Japanese Pathological Society; Member of Directors, Japanese Society for Research on Gastric Cancer. *Publications:* 'Recent Changes in the Morphology of gastric cancer in Japan', (with H Yokoyama), 1978; 'Dysplasia of the gastric mucosa and its relation to the precancerous state', 1981. *Honour:* Prize of Chunichi Shimbun, 1978. *Hobbies:* Music; Painting; Driving. *Address:* 81-1159 Kanokoden, Tashiro-cho, Chikusa-ku, Nagoya 464, Japan.

NAGY, Sándor, b. 15 Aug. 1932, Kecskemet, Hungary. Professor and Director, Institute of Experimental Surgery, University Medical School of Szeged, m. Gizella Karacsony, 5 Mar. 1959, Kiskundorozsma, 1 son. *Education:* MD, University Medical School of Szeged, 1957; CmedSc, Hungarian Academy of Sciences, 1971. *Appointments:* Research Associate, Institute of Pathophysiology, 1957-60, Lecturer, Institute of Experimental Surgery, 1961-66, Assistant Professor, 1967-69, 1971-74, Institute of Experimental Surgery, Associate Professor, 1975-84, Professor and Director, 1984-, Institute of Experimental Surgery, University Medical School of Szeged; Visiting Assistant Professor, Department of Physiology, Baylor College of Medicine, Houston, Texas, USA, 1970-71. *Memberships:* Vice President, European Shock Society; Member, Editorial Board, Circulatory Shock; European Society for Surgical Research; International Surgical Society; Hungarian Surgical Society; Hungarian Physiological Society; Neumann Society for Computer Science Division of Biological and Medical Sciences. *Publications:* "Neurohumoral and Metabolic Aspects of Injury", 1973; "Traumatic Shock", (Contributor), 1974; Contributor of over 120 articles in scientific and professional journals. *Hobbies:* Running; Swimming; Music. *Address:* Institute of Experimental Surgery, University Medical School of Szeged, PO Box 464, H-6701, Szeged, Hungary.

NAGY, Thomas Francis, b. 9 June 1945, Newton, Massachusetts, USA. Independent Practice in Psychology; Consultant to Hospitals in Hypnosis, Ethics, Sex Therapy. m. Karen Nani Lingrell, 25 Mar. 1972, Champaign, Illinois, 1 son, 1 daughter. *Education:* BA, Hamilton College, 1967; MEd, 1968, Certificate of Advanced Graduate Study, 1969, University of New Hampshire; PhD, University of Illinois, Champaign-/Urbana, 1972; Registered Psychologist in Illinois, 1973. *Appointments:* Counselor, University High School, Champaign/Urbana, 1969-72; Psychologist, Cleveland State University Counselling Center, Cleveland, Ohio, Summer 1972; Staff Psychologist, Loyola University Counseling Center, Chicago, 1972-78; Independent Practice of Psychology, 1974-; Consultant to Veterans Administration Center, Mt Sinai Hospital and other Chicago area hospitals, regarding hypnosis, sex therapy and ethics. *Memberships:* American Psychological Association; Illinois Psychological Association, Chairperson, Ethics Committee, 1982-; Chicago Psychological Association, President, 1981; Society for Clinical and Experimental Hypnosis; American Society of Clinical Hypnosis; International Society for the Study of Multiple Personality. *Publications:* Co-author, 'Experimental Groups for Teachers', 'Pupil Personnel Services Journal' 2, 1973; Co-author, "Counseling: Preparation, Supervision and Assessment", NH Department of Education, Division of Vocational Rehabilitation, cord, 1971. *Hobbies:* Music (piano); Athletics (squash and swimming). *Address:* 2313 Thayer Street, Evanston, IL 60201, USA.

NAGYLUCSKAY, Sándor, b. 15 Mar. 1932, Debrecen, Hungary. Associate Professor. m. Maria Horváth, 10 Sep. 1969. *Education:* Semmelweis, University of Medicine, 1956; Dr Pharm 1958; Postgraduate Diploma in Hygiene and Epidemiological Laboratory Studies, 1974; Dr med Habil 1975. *Appointments:* Assistant, 1956, Senior Assistant 1962, Associate Professor, 1976-, Institute of Hygiene and Epidemiology, Semmelweis University of Medicine. *Memberships:*

Editorial Board, Acta Pharm, Hungary; Member and Member of Regional Leading Board, Association of Hungarian Hygienists; Hungarian Microbiology Society; Association of Hungarian Oncologists; Hungarian Pharm Association; Hungarian Red Cross Association. *Publications:* Co-author: "Fundamentals in the Field of Hygiene and Epidemiology" edited by Fodor-Vedres, 1981; "Exercises in Hygiene and Epidemiology" edited by Fodor-Vedres, 1978; "The Human Health in the Scientific-Technical Revolution" edited by Soos et al, 1978. 48 scientific articles in the fields of epidemiology, viral hepatitis, AIDS, immunology and the health hazards of smoking. *Address:* Institute of Hygiene and Epidemiology, Semmelweis University of Medicine, VIII Nagyvárad tér 4, Budapest Pf/POB/370 H-1445, Hungary.

NAIR, Vasavan, b. 25 Apr. 1934, India, Director, Douglas Hospital Centre; Professor, McGill University. m. Amma Sreekumari, 17 Jan. 1958, Trivandrum, India, 1 son, 2 daughters. *Education:* DPM, University of Mysore; MBBS; FRCP (C); MRCP; FRCPsych, England. *Appointments:* Director of Research and Education, Saskatchewan Hospital, Weyburn, Saskatchewan, Canada, 1968-69; Director, Research and Education, Saskatchewan Hospital, North Battleford, Saskatchewan, 1969-71; Coordinator, 1972-79, Director, 1979-80, Research Services, Douglas Hospital, Montreal; Director, Douglas Hospital Research Centre, 1980-. *Memberships:* Royal College of Psychiatrists, 1964; Collegium Internationale Neuro-Psychopharmacologium, 1976; American Association for the Advancement of Science, 1976; American Psychiatric Association, 1978; New York Academy of Sciences, 1980. *Publications:* 'Circadian rhythm of plasma melatonin and cortisol in endogenous depression', (with N Hariharasubramanian, C Pilapil), 1985; 'Clinical and neuroendocrine studies with colecystokinin peptides', (with D Bloom, S Lal, G Debonnel, G Swartz, S Mosticyan), 1985. *Honours:* HH Maharajalis Scholarship. *Hobbies:* Chess; Tennis; Philosophy. *Address:* 6875 LaSalle Boulevard, Verdun, Quebec, Canada H4H 1R3.

NAIR, Vatakkepat Parameswaran, b. Malaysia. Consultant Cardiologist. m. Sathy, 18 Aug. 1968, Singapore, 2 sons. *Education:* BSc; MBBS; MRCPI (Dublin); MRCP (London); MRCGP (UK); FCCP; Mi Biol (London). *Appointments:* House Officer and Medical Officer, Singapore General Hospital; Senior House Officer, Middlesex Hospital, London; Registrar, Watford General Hospital, England; Hon Senior Registrar, Regional Cardiothoracic Centre, Freeman Hospital, Newcastle-upon-Tyne, England; Senior Registrar, Singapore General Hospital; Cardiologist and Internist, Alexandra Hospital, Singapore; Cardiologist and Internist, American Hospital, Singapore; Cardiologist, Mount Elizabeth Hospital, Singapore. *Memberships:* Fellow, Royal Society of Medicine; Member, Institute of Biology; Academy of Medicine, Singapore; Royal College of General Practitioners, UK; Fellow, International College of Angiology; Associate Fellow, American College of Angiology; Fellow, American College of Chest Physicians. *Publications:* Cardiac Resuscitation, Medical Digest; The Concept of Mental Health, Singapore Family Physician; Heart Attack: How to Prevent it, Medical Digest, 1982; Several other contributions to professional journals, etc. *Honour:* Medical Advisor to Singapore Civil Defence Force. *Hobbies:* Reading; Teaching; Public Lecturing; Research; Swimming. *Address:* Nair Cardiac & Medical Centre, 3 Mount Elizabeth 16-08, Singapore 0922.

NAKAMURA, Motoomi, b. 5 Mar. 1927, Hiroshima, Japan. Director of Kyushu University Hospital; Professor of Internal Medicine; Chief of Cardiology. m. Sumi Higuchi, 25 Apr. 1954, 2 daughters. *Education:* MD, Kyushu University School of Medicine, 1950; Dr. Med. Sci, Graduate School of Kyushu University, 1956. *Appointments:* Research Fellow, Harvard University School of Public Health, USA, 1956-58; Assistant Professor of Faculty of Medicine, Kyushu University, 1959-63; Professor of Internal Medicine, Cardiol-

ogy, 1963-; Director of Research Institute of Angiocardiology and Cardiovascular Clinic, 1966-; Kyushu University School of Medicine; President, Japanese Circulation Society, 1983-84. *Memberships:* Executive Board, Japanese Circulation Society; Editorial Board: 'Japanese Circulation Journal', 'International Journal of Cardiology', Canadian Journal of Cardiology'; International Fellow, American Heart Association; Member, Basic Science Council, American Heart Association. *Publications:* "Internal Medicine: Section of Cardiology" (in Japanese); 'Our Animal Model of Coronary Vasospasm' in "Stress and Heart Disease" Editors, R E Beamish, P K Singal, N S Dhalla, 1985; About 250 papers in English. *Honours:* Second Prize, Coronary Circulation, Erwin von Baelz, 1964; First Prize, Cerebral Circulation, Erwin von Baelz, 1967; Award for Promotion in Medical Research, Japanese Medical Association, 1972; Mitsukoshi Medical Award, 1975; West Japan Cultural Award, 1984. *Hobbies:* Sports; Tennis; Golf. *Address:* 2-5-18 Muromi, Sawara-ku, Fukuoka, Japan 814.

NAKAO, Makoto, b. 14 Mar. 1924, Japan. Dean, Tokyo Medical and Dental University School of Medicine; Professor. m. Toshiko, 20 Sep. 1954, Tokyo, 1 son. *Education:* Graduated from Faculty of Medicine, The University of Tokyo, 1947; MD, 1958; MSD. *Appointments:* Lecturer, Department of Biological Chemistry and Nutrition, University of Tokyo, 1956-59; Associate Professor, Department of Biochemistry, Gunma University, 1959-61; Professor, Department of Biochemistry, Faculty of Medicine, Yokohama University, 1961-63; Professor, Department of Biochemistry, Tokyo Medical and Dental University School of Medicine, 1963-; Visiting Professor, Department Active Transport, National Institute of Physiology, 1980-83. *Memberships:* Secretary of Japanese Association of Medical Sciences; Council, Japan Biochemical Society; Council, Japanese Association of Haematology; Council, Japanese Association of Blood Transfusion; Member, International Haematology Association. *Publications:* Co-Editor, "Biochemistry of Biological Membranes", 1972; Editor, "Biochemistry of Cell Membrane", 1976; Supervisor, Translation of "Lehninger's Textbook of Biochemistry", 1976; Many original papers on red blood cells and Na, K-AT Pase from brain and kidney. *Honour:* Medical Prize, Japan Medical Association, 1975. *Hobby:* Playing Tennis. *Address:* Royal Garden No 203, Aobadai 1-7-14, Meguro-ku, Tokyo, Japan.

NAMBIAR, P M K, b. 10 Mar. 1943, Kerala, India. Consultant Physician and Cardiologist. m. Premalatha Nambiar, 26 May 1969, 1 son, 2 daughters. *Education:* MB BS, Medical College, Calicut, 1964; MD, Medical College, Trivandrum; MRCP, UK, 1976; FICA, 1975. *Appointments:* Consultant Physician, Kerala Health Services. Consultant Physician and Cardiologist: Keltron; Private sector. *Memberships:* Indian Medical Association; Qualified Medical Practitioners Association; Associate Member, American College of Chest Physicians. *Hobbies:* Reading; Photography. *Address:* Anuraj, Talap, Cannonore 2, Kerala, India.

NÁNÁSI, Pál, b. 17 Sep. 1923, Debrecen, Hungary. Professor of Biochemistry and Chairman of Institute of Biochemistry. m. (1) Eva Nemes, 1 Sep. 1951, Debrecen, 1 son (2) Hajnalka Derzsy, 15 Dec. 1984, Debrecen. *Education:* Chemistry and Physics, University of Debrecen and Budapest, 1941-45; PhD Postgraduate student, University of Debrecen Institute of Organic Chemistry, 1946-48; Fellowship, International Atomic Energy Agency, Rome University Institute of Biochemistry, 1964-65; DSci, 1966. *Appointments:* Lecturer in Chemistry 1948, Senior Lecturer in Chemistry 1952, University Docent 1958, Full Professor of Biochemistry 1966, Dean of Faculty of Science 1981-84, University of Debrecen; Currently Professor of Biochemistry, Chairman of Institute of Biochemistry, Lajos Kossuth University, Debrecen. *Memberships:* Committee of Chemistry of Carbohydrates, Committee of Bioorganis Compounds, Committee of Macromolecular Chemistry, Hungarian Academy of

Sciences; Committee of Biology, Ministry of Education; President of local group, Hungarian Chemical Society, 1969-. *Publications:* 172 scientific papers mainly on the field of carbohydrate chemistry including: 'Stereochemical Aspects of Di and Polysaccharides', (with J Szejtly). *Hobbies:* Archaeology; History of art. *Address:* Institute of Biochemistry, Lajos Kossuth University, Debrecen, Hungary.

NARANJO, Plutarco, b. 18 June 1921, Ambato, Ecuador. President, Ecuadorian Academy of Medicine. m. Enriqueta Banda, 24 July 1946, Quito, 2 sons, 1 daughter. *Education:* MD, Professor of Pharmacology, Faculty of Medicine, University of Quito. *Appointments:* Professor, Pharmacology, 1951-, Head, Pharmacology, 1956-, University of Quito; Director, Medical Services, National Social Security, 1963-65; Vice President, House of Ecuadorian Culture, President, Ecuadorian Academy of Medicine, 1979-83; President, Latin American Association of Academies of Medicine, 1982-84; Director, Centre of Allergy Research, Quito, 1975-. *Memberships:* International Society of Allergology and Clinical Immunology; Society Latinoamericana de Alergologia; Society Ecuatoriana de Alergologia; Society Latinoamericana de Farmacologia; New York Academy of Sciences. *Publications:* "Polinosis: Estudio Clinico y botanico", 1950; "Manual de Farmacologia", 1963; "Timo, Imunicion y alergia", 1969; "Ayahuasca: Etnomedicina y Mitologfa", 1983; About 300 research papers. *Honours:* Universidad Central for Sciencific Research, 1951, 1965, 1972; National Prize of Sciences, 1976. *Hobbies:* Archaeology; Collection of Archaeological Pieces; Botany. *Address:* San Ignacio 851, PO Box 8884, Quito, Ecuador.

NARAYANAPPA, A, b. 3 July 1930, Ayanur, India. Private Consultant. m. Lakshmi Devi, 20 May 1957, Mysore, 2 sons, 2 daughters. *Education:* MB, BS, Mysore, 1956; DCH, Madras, 1961; MD, General Medicine, Bangalore, 1966; Training in Cardiology in USA, 1970-71. *Appointments:* Assistant Surgeon; Lecturer in Pathology; District Pediatrician; Lecturer in Medicine; Physician; Consultant. *Memberships:* National College of Chest Physicians, India; Karnataka Medical Association; Indian Medical Association; Indian Academy of Pediatrics; Association of Physicians of India; Cardiological Society of India; Fellow, American College of Chest Physicians; International College of Angiology; Karnataka Pediatric Association. *Publications:* 'Hyper Abduction Syndrome', 'Vascular Surgery', Jan-Feb 1980; "Thalassemia Major in a Shimoga Family', 'Journal of the Indian Medical Association', Sep. 1963; Mysore University Published books in Kannada: "Pain"; "Child Care"; "Infectious Diseases"; "Congenital Heart Diseases"; "Smoking"; "Alcohol Drinking"; "Obesity"; Karnatak University published: "Diabetes Mellitus". *Honours:* Karnataka State Sahitya Academy Awards, 1974, 77. *Hobbies:* Writing Books; Driving; Reading; Visiting Natural Beauty Spots; Radio; Lecturing; Spending holidays in hill stations. *Address:* Belur Road, Chikmagalur, Karnataka, India.

NARUSE, Gosaku, b. 5 June 1924, Japan. Professor of Psychology. m. Hiroko Amagaya, 17 Dec. 1952, Meikei Kaikan, 2 sons. *Education:* MR Literature, Tokyo Bunrika University, 1950; Dr Med Sc, Niigate University, 1959; Diploma, Clinical Hypnosis, USA, 1962. *Appointments:* Assistant, Psychology Department, Tokyo Bunrika University, 1951; Chairman, Psychological Clinic, Tokyo University of Education, 1953; Associate Professor 1962, Professor 1969, Department of Psychology, Faculty of Education, Kyushu University. *Memberships:* President, Association of Japanese Clinical Psychology, 1982-; President, Japanese Society of Hypnosis, 1970-; President, Japanese Society of Rehabilitation Psychology, 1973-. *Publications include:* "Techniques of Hypnointerview", 1959; "Hypnosis", 1960; "Self Hypnosis", with J H Schultz, 1963; "Jiko-Control", 1969; "Psychological Rehabilitation", 1973; "Theory of

Motor Action Training", 1985. *Honours:* Hayami Award, Japanese Association of Psychology, 1952; Memorial Award, Tokyo Bunrika University, 1953. *Hobbies:* Utai (Noh Song); Skiing; Windsurfing. *Address:* 1-14-14 Ohtake, Higashi, Fukuoka, Japan 811-03.

NASILOWSKI, Vladyslaw Wojciech, b. 8 Apr. 1925, Sosnowiec, Poland. Director of Department of Forensic Medicine. m. Zofia Nasilowska, 6 Dec. 1960, 1 daughter. *Education:* MD, Medical Facultaet, University of Poznan. *Appointments:* Assistant in Department of Anatomo-Pathology, Assistant Professor - Professor and Director, Department of Forensic Medicine, Silesian Medical Academy, Katowice. *Memberships:* Commission of Country Inspection in Legal Medicine; Traumatic Commission, Polish Academy of Science. *Publications:* "Legal Medicine", (with B Popielski and J Kobiela), 1972; "Road Accidents - Legal Medicine, Biology, Reconstruction", (with K Jaegermann), 1975; "Legal Medical Toxicology of Ethyl-Alcohol", (with A Jaklinski and J Markiewicz), 1978; "The Little Encyclopaedia of Medicine", 1979. *Hobbies:* Yachting; Tourism. *Address:* ul Skrzypow 27, Katowice, Poland.

NATHAN, Swami, b. 9 Nov. 1942, India. Assistnt Professor of Psychiatry. m. Girija. 24 Nov. 1969, Madras, 1 son, 1 daughter. *Education:* MB BS; Resident, Psychiatry, Manhattan Psychiatric Center, New York, USA, 1974-77; Candidate in Psychoanalysis, American Institute of Psychoanalysis, Karen Horney Psychoanalytical Institute and Center, New York, 1975-77; Research Fellow, New York State Psychiatric Institute and College of Physicians and Surgeons, Columbia University, 1978-80; Diplomate, American Board of Psychiatry and Neurology, 1980. *Appointments:* Tutor, Microbiology, University of Madras, India, 1968-73; Instructor, Clinical Psychiatry, College of Physicians and Surgeons, 1978-79, Assistant Professor, 1979-80, Columbia University, New York; Assistant Professor, Psychiatry, University of Pittsburgh, Pennsylvania, 1980-. *Memberships:* American Psychiatric Association; American Association for the Advancement of Science; New York Academy of Science; International Society of Psychoneuroendocrinology; International Society of Chronobiology; Endocrine Society. *Publications include:* Co-Author of book chapters in: "Prolactin and Prolactinomas", 1983; "Annual Review of Chronopharmacology", 1984; "Drugs in Psychiatry", Volume III, 1985. Author or Co-Author of numerous papers in professional journals including: 'Psychoneuroendocrinology'; 'Lancet'; 'Psychiatry Research'; 'Psychopharmacology'. *Honours:* Andrew K Bernath Award, for Outstanding Resident Physician, Manhattan Psychiatric Center, New York, 1975, 76. *Hobby:* Tennis. *Address:* Western Psychiatric Institute and Clinic, University of Pittsburgh, 3811 O'Hara Street, Pittsburgh, PA 15213, USA.

NATHWANI, Bharat Narottam, b. 20 Jan. 1945, Bombay, India. Professor of Pathology; Chief of Haematopathology, University of Southern California School of Medicine, USA. m. Mudra Kapadia, 30 Nov. 1970, Bombay. *Education:* MB, BS, Grant Medical College, Bombay; MD, Pathology & Bacteriology, ibid. *Appointments include:* Associate Director/Coordinator, Haematopathology Tutorial, City of Hope National Medical Centre, Duarte, California, 1978-84; Director of Research, Respository Centre/Pathology Panel, Lymphoma Clinical Studies, 1978-84; Professor, Chief of Haematopathology, University of Southern California, 1984-. *Memberships:* American Society of Clinical Oncology; International Academy of Pathology; American College of Pathologists; American Society of Haematology; New York Academy of Sciences; American Association for the Advancement of Science; etc. *Publications:* Numerous contributions to professional journals/conference proceedings etc; Titles include, 'Lymphoblastic lymphoma: A clinicopathologic study of 95 patients' (Cancer, 1981); 'Clinical significance of the morphologic subdivision of diffuse, "histiocytic" lymphoma: Study of 162 patients treated by the Southwest Oncology Group' (Blood, 1982); 'Diagnostic strategies in the hypothesis-directed Pathfinder system' (Proceedings 1st Conf AIA, IEEE, 1984). Co-author. *Hobbies:* Reading; Walking. *Address:* 2232 Golden Meadow, Duarte, CA 91010, USA.

NATORI, Shinsaku, b. 26 Aug. 1923, Tokyo, Japan. Professor, Meiji College of Pharmacy. m. Yoko, 4 Nov. 1951, Tokyo, 1 son, 1 daughter. *Education:* B Pharm, 1946, PhD, 1958, Tokyo University. *Appointments:* Research Associate, 1952, Assistant Professor, 1960, University of Tokyo; Laboratory Chief, 1961, Division Chief, 1967, National Institute of Hygienic Sciences. *Memberships:* Pharmaceutical Society of Japan; The American Society of Pharmacognosy; The Japanese Society of Pharmacognosy; The Royal Society of Chemistry, London. *Publications:* "Natural Products Chemistry" Volumes 1-3, 1974, 1975, 1983; "Advances in Natural Products Chemistry", 1981. *Honours:* Award of Pharmaceutical Society of Japan, 1956. *Address:* 5-1 Otsuka-4-Chome, Bunkyo-ku, Tokyo 112, Japan.

NAYAK, Nabeen Chandra, b. 31 Jan. 1931, Puri, India. Professor and Head of Department of Pathology and Chief. m. Vijoy Laxmi Nayak, 17 Nov. 1957, Cuttack, 2 daughters. *Education:* MBBS, Utkal University, Cuttack; MD, Lucknow University, Lucknow. *Appointments:* Assistant Professor of Pathology, SCB, Medical College, Cuttack, 1957-61; Assistant Professor of Pathology, 1962-65, Associate Professor, 1966-71, Professor of Pathology, 1972-79, Head, Department of Pathology, 1979-, Chief, Cancer Hospital, 1982-, AIIMS, New Delhi. *Memberships:* Ex-Secretary, Indian Association of Pathologists and Microbiologists; President, Liver Study Group of India; Executive Committee Member and Secretary-General, Asian Pacific Association for Study of Liver; International Association for Study of Liver. *Publications:* Contributor of 140 articles in national and international scientific journals; Contributor of chapters in 7 specialised reference books. *Honours:* Expert member in many international bodies including World Health Organisation and cancer organisations. *Hobbies:* Sports; Gardening; Music; Reading. *Address:* Department of Pathology, All-India Institute of Medical Sciences, New Delhi 110029, India.

NAYLOR, Graham John, b. 13 Feb. 1940, England. Reader, Psychiatry, University of Dundee. m. 14 July 1960, Sheffield. *Education:* MB, ChB, 1962, BSc, 1965, MD, 1970, Sheffield University. *Appointments:* Consultant Psychiatrist, Royal Dundee Liff Hospital and Strathmartine Hospital, 1970-71; Senior Lecturer, Psychiatry, University of Dundee, 1971-80. *Memberships:* British Medical Association; Association of University Teachers of Psychiatry; Royal College of Psychiatrists. *Publications:* Various articles in professional journals. *Hobby:* Farming. *Address:* Royal Dundee Liff Hospital, Liff, By Dundee DD2 5NF, Scotland.

NAYLOR, Malcolm Neville, b. 30 Jan. 1926, Wednesbury, Staffordshire, England. Professor of Preventive Dentistry, University London; Head, Department Periodontology and Preventive Dentistry, Guy's Hospital, London. m. Doreen Mary Jackson, 10 Jan. 1956, Edgbaston, 1 son. *Education:* University of Glasgow; BSc, BDS, University of Birmingham; PhD, University of London; FDS RCS (Eng). *Appointments:* House Surgeon, Queen Elizabeth Hospital, Birmingham, 1955; Senior House Officer, Dundee Dental Hospital, 1956; Registrar, Queen Elizabeth Hospital, Birmingham, 1957-59; Research Fellow, 1959-62, Senior Lecturer, 1962-66, Reader, 1966-70, Professor, 1970-, Guy's Hospital Dental School, London. *Memberships:* British Dental Association; International Association for Dental Research; Royal Society of Medicine; British Society for Dental Research. *Publications:* 'Prevention of Dental Disease'; 'Factors underlying decline in caries prevalence', 1985; Contributor to 'Oxford Companion to Medicine'; Author of numer-

ous other articles in scientific and clinical journals. *Honours:* Reserve Decoration, RD, 1967; Honorary Dental Surgeon to Her Majesty the Queen, 1976. *Hobbies:* Off-shore cruising; Music. *Address:* Garrick Lodge, Roehampton, London SW15 5BN, England.

NEANDER, J Michael, b. 25 Nov. 1950, New York, USA. Child Psychiatrist. m. Laurie Graves, 24 June 1978, New York, USA, 1 son. *Education:* BA, 1972; MD, 1976. *Appointments:* Intern, Categorical Medicine, 1976-77; Residency, Adult Psychiatry, 1977-79; Fellowship in Child Psychiatry, 1979-81; Assistant Clinical Professor of Psychiatry and Behavioral Medicine and of Child Health and Development, George Washington University Department of Psychiatry, Childrens' Hospital National Medical Center, Department of Psychiatry; currently Child Psychiatrist in private practice. *Memberships:* Washington Psychiatric Society; American Medical Association; American Psychiatric Association; American Academy of Child Psychiatry; Washington Council of Child Psychiatry. *Honours:* Phi Beta Kappa, University of Rochester, USA, 1972; Board Certification in Adult Psychiatry, 1982. *Hobbies:* Choral Music; Tennis. *Address:* 5410 Connecticut Avenue NW, 110 Washington, DC, USA.

NEATE, Max DeBerry, b. 2 Feb. 1955, Whangareo, New Zealand. General Practitioner. m. Susan Margaret Craig, 26 Mar. 1976, Putaruru, New Zealand, 2 sons. *Education:* BSc; MB, ChB; DRCOG. *Appointments:* House Surgeon, 1976-77, Medical Registrar, 1978-79, Tauranga Hospital; Senior House Officer and study for DRCOG, Portwey Hospital, Weymouth, Dorset, England, 1979-80; General Practitioner, Mount Medical Centre, Mount Maunhanius, New Zealand, 1980-. *Memberships:* Waikato Obstetric and Gynaecological Society; New Zealand General Practitioner Society. *Hobbies:* Sailing; Fishing; Boating; Swimming; Diving; Jogging; Music. *Address:* Mount Medical Centre, PO Box 5176, Mt Maunganuius, New Zealand.

NEDERGAARD, Ove Alfred, b. 18 Feb. 1931, Denmark. Associate Professor. m. Pamela M Lomax, 11 Jan. 1964, Los Angeles, California, USA, 2 daughters. *Education:* BSc, Pharmacy, 1952, MSc, Pharmacy, 1954, Royal Danish School of Pharmacy; MSc, Pharmacology, 1961, PhD, Pharmacology, 1964, University of California Los Angeles School of Medicine, USA. *Appointments:* Research Assistant, University of California Los Angeles, 1954-55; Research Pharmacologist, University of California Los Angeles, 1957-64; Visiting Research Scientist, University of Frankfurt-am-Main and Assistant Professor, University of California Los Angeles, 1964-65; Associate Professor, Odense University, 1969-. *Memberships:* American Society for Pharmacology and Experimental Therapeutics; British Pharmacology Society; Danish Pharmacology Society; Deutsche Pharmakologische Gesellschaft; Western Pharmacology Society. *Publications:* Co-author, "Accumulation of 3H-adrenaline by rabbit aorta', 'Blood Vessels' 22; 32-46, 1985; Co-author, 'Dual inhibitory action of ATP on adrenergic neuroeffector transmission in rabbit pulmonary artery', 'Acta Pharmacol Toxicol', 57, 204-213, 1985. *Honour:* Research Award, Fyns Stiftstidende, 1977. *Address:* Department of Pharmacology, Odense University, J B Winslows Vej 19, DK-5000 Odense C, Denmark.

NEED, Allan Geoffrey, b. 20 May 1945, Adelaide, Australia. Chemical Pathologist. m. Maxine Helen Langeluddecke, 16 Nov. 1973, Adelaide, 1 son, 3 daughters. *Education:* MBBS, University of Adelaide, 1969; MRACP; FRACP; FRCPA. *Appointments:* Resident Medical Officer, Queen Elizabeth Hospital, 1969; Senior Resident Medical Officer, Royal Northern Hospital, London, England, 1970; Hither Green Hospital, London, 1970; Adelaide Childrens Hospital, 1971; Registrar, 1972-74, Senior Registrar, 1975, Adelaide Childrens Hospital; Registrar, Hospital of the Albert Einstein College of Medicine, 1976-77; Chemical Pathologist, Institute of Medical and Veterinary Science, Adelaide, 1977-. *Memberships:* Endocrine Society of Australia; Australian Society for Medical Research. *Publications:* Co-Editor, ''Test Information Book: Clinical Chemistry'', 1981; numerous articles in professional journals including 'American Journal of Clinical Nutrition'; 'Clinica Chimica Acta'; 'Hormone and Metabolic Research'; 'Journal of Chromatography'. *Honour:* Half Blue, University of Adelaide. *Hobby:* Squash Rackets. *Address:* Institute of Medical & Veterinary Science, Frome Road, Adelaide, South Australia 5000.

NEFF, Stephen Howland, b. 30 Oct. 1948, Springfield, Massachusetts, USA. Family Practice Resident Osteopath, Jacuson Park Hospital, Chicago, Illinois. *Education:* BS, Northeastern University; DO, Philadelphia College of Osteopathy. *Appointments include:* General Medical Officer, Martin Army Hospital, Georgia, 1978-82; Family practice, Hohenwald, Tennessee, 1983; Paediatric residency, Oklahoma Osteopathic Hospital, 1983-84; Family practice, Jellico, Tennessee, 1984; Family Practice Resident, Jacuson Park Hospital, 1984-. *Memberships:* Georgia Osteopathic Medical Association; American Medical Association; American Osteopathic Association; Chicago Medical Society; Illinois Medical Association; Academy of Family Practice. *Honour:* Major, US Army Reserve Medical Corps. *Hobbies:* Swimming; Soccer, Racquetball; Singing, church choir. *Address:* Jacuson Park Hospital, 7531 Stony Island Avenue, Chicago, IL 60649, USA.

NEGRONI, Rocardo, b. 11 Mar. 1939, Argentina. University Professor. m. Nidia Elida Rodriguez, 1 Aug. 1964, Buenos Aires, 3 sons. *Education:* MD, Honor Diploma, Associate Professor. *Appointments:* Bacteriologist, Hospital Muniz, 1962; Chief of Workshops in Microbiology, Parasitology, Immunology, 1965-; Professor of Medical Micrology and Veterinary Medicine, 1968-; Associate Professor of Microbiology, Parasitology and Immunology, 1970-; Chief Professor of Medical Micrology, Postgraduate School, 1981-. *Memberships:* Iberoamericanlatin College in Dermatology; International Society for Human and Animal Mycology; Argentine Micrology Society; Honoured Membership of the Spanish Association of Micrologists. *Publications include:* Histoplasmose ''Doengas Infecciosas e Parasitarias'' Ricardo Veronesi 7th edition brasileira, 1982; Capitulo de patogenia en Del Nigro G, Lacaz C, da S, Fiorillo A M Paracoccidioidomicose Ed. Sarvier Sao Paulo, 1982; Pablo Negroni and Ricardo Negroni: Micosis cutaneas y viscerales, September Edition, Lopez Libreros Editores 1980, 8th edition 1984. *Honours:* Gold Medal in Tropical Medicine Course, Sao Paulo, Brazil, 1964; Alois Bachman Award, National Academy of Medicine, 1968; Argentine Society of Allergy and Immunology (Prize for Best Paper of the Year) 1974; Award for 10 Distinctive Juniors of the Year, 1978. *Hobbies:* Swimming; Cycling; Jogging. *Address:* Juncal 3050 3° A C 1425 Capital, Buenos Aires, Argentina.

NEHER, Erwin, b. 20 Mar. 1944, Landsberg, Federal Republic of Germany. Director, Biophysics, Max-Planck Institute for Biophysical Chemistry. m. Eva-Maria Ruhr, 25 Dec. 1978, 3 sons, 1 daughter. *Education:* Dr rer nat; MSc, 1967; Dr habil; Technical University, Munich; University of Wisconsin, USA. *Appointments:* Scientist, Max-Planck Institutes, Munich and Gottingen; Research Associate, Yale University, USA. *Memberships:* Physiological Society; Deutsche Physiological Gesellschaft; Deutsche Gesellschaft fur Biophysik; Bunsengesellschaft fur Physikalische Chemie. *Publications:* Co-Editor, 'Journal Physiology', London; ''Elektronische Messtechnik in der Physiologie'', 1974; ''Single Channel Recording'', Co-editor, 1983. *Honours:* Several awards in Biophysics and Physiology, 1977-84. *Address:* Hirtenweg 3, D 3406 Eddigehausen, Federal Republic of Germany.

NEHRA, Paul, b. 4 Nov. 1949, Nottingham, England.

Director of Intensive Therapy. m. Adrienne Mac-Donell, 20 Sep. 1982, The Pas, Manitoba, Canada, 1 son, 1 daughter. *Education:* MB ChB, Liverpool; LMCC; CCFP (C). *Appointments:* House Officer, Royal Liverpool Teaching Hospitals; Registrar in Medicine, Royal Liverpool Teaching Hospitals; Lecturer in Medicine, University of Manitoba. *Memberships:* British Medical Association; Canadian Medical Association; American Academy of Family Physicians; College of Family Physicians of Canada. *Publications:* Articles on Cirrhosis and Diabetes in North American Indians, 1975-85. *Honour:* Medical Examiner, Province of Manitoba, 1985. *Hobbies:* Philosophy; Comparative Religion; Poetry; Farming. *Address:* Box 4800, The Pas, Manitoba, Canada R9A 1R2.

NEILL, Donald George, b. 2 Mar. 1924, Brisbane, Australia. Retired. *Education:* MRCP, London, England, 1952; FRCPA, 1956; DMRD, RCP&S, London, 1971; MB BS, University of Queensland, Australia, 1946. *Appointments:* Brisbane Hospital, 1946-49; Teaching Fellow, Pathology 1949, Lecturer in Pathology, 1950, University of Queensland; House Physician, Hammersmith Hospital, London, England, 1951; Senior House Officer, Broomfield Hospital, Essex, 1952; Assistant Physician, 1952, Junior Physician, 1956-60, Brisbane Hospital, Australia; Physician to Repatriation Commission, 1954-69; Junior Physician, Princess Alexandra Hospital, 1961-69; Honorary Clinical Assistant, Radiology Department, Hammersmith Hospital, London, England, 1969-71; Private Practitioner, Radiology, Bankstown, 1971-79. *Memberships:* Royal Society of Medicine; British Medical Association; Royal College of Pathologists of Australasia. *Publications:* 'Tuberculosis of the Liver, a Report of 5 Cases', 1951. *Hobbies:* Bridge; Music; Financial and current affairs. *Address:* 25 Birtley Towers, Birtley Place, Elizabeth Bay, New South Wales 2011, Australia.

NEILL, Jimmy Dyke, b. 6 Mar. 1939, Merkel, Texas, USA. Professor and Chairman of Physiology and Biophysics. m. Joan Maxine Byrd, 18 June 1960, Merkel, Texas, 1 son, 1 daughter. *Education:* BS; MS; PhD, University of Missouri, Columbia, 1961-65; Postdoctoral Fellowship, 1965-67. *Appointments:* Instructor, Department of Physiology, University of Pittsburgh, 1967-69; Assistant Professor - Professor of Physiology 1969-76, Endowed William Patterson Timmie Professor of Physiology 1976-79, Emory University, Atlanta, Georgia; Professor and Chairman of Physiology and Biophysics, University of Alabama, Birmingham, Alabama, 1979-. *Memberships:* The Endocrine Society, USA; American Physiological Society; American Association for the Advancement of Science. *Publications include:* ''The Physiology of Reproduction'', (co-editor), 1986; Co-editor, 'Endocrinology'; Editor-in-Chief, 'American Journal of Physiology'; 76 papers in scientific journals. *Hobbies:* Photography; Carpentry. *Address:* Department of Physiology and Biophysics, University of Alabama at Birmingham, University Station, Birmingham, AL 35294, USA.

NEIMS, Allen Howard, b. 24 Oct. 1938, Chicago, Illinois, USA. Professor and Chairman, Pharmacology; Professor of Pediatrics, University of Florida. m. Myrna Gay Robins, 18 June 1961, Chicago, 1 son, 2 daughters. *Education:* BA, BS, University of Chicago, 1953-57; MD, 1957-61, PhD, 1962-66, Pediatric Residency, 1961-62, 1966-68, Johns Hopkins University. *Appointments:* Research Associate, National Institute of Health, 1968-70; Assistant Professor, Pediatrics and Physiological Chemistry, Johns Hopkins University, 1970-72; Associate Professor, Professor, Pharmacology and Pediatrics, Director, Roche Developmental Pharmacology Unit, McGill University, Canada, 1972-78; Professor and Chairman, Pharmacology, Professof Pediatrics, University of Florida, USA, 1978-. *Memberships:* American Pediatric Society; American Society Pharmacology and Experimental Therapy; Association Medical School Pharmacology; AAAS; American Society of Clinical Pharmacology and Therapeutics. *Publications:* Author of numerous publications and articles to professional journals. *Honours:* Royal Children's Hospital, Melbourne, 1974; Member, Human Embryology and Development Study Section, NIH, 1979-83; Scientific Counsellor, NICHD, 1984-. *Hobbies:* Gardening; Racquetball. *Address:* Box J-267, JHMHC, University of Florida, Gainesville, FL 32610, USA.

NEKAM, Kristóf, b. 4 Aug. 1944, Budapest, Hungary. Senior Lecturer. m. Erzsébet Csürös, 17 Mar. 1973, Budapest, 1 son, 2 daughters. *Education:* MD, 1968; PhD, 1979. Specialist: Internal Medicine, 1973; Immunology, 1981; Allergology and Clinical Immunology, 1985. *Appointments:* Assistant Professor, 1970, currently Senior Lecturer, 1981-, 2nd Department of Medicine, Semmelweis University, Budapest, Hungary. *Memberships:* European Academy of Allergology and Clinical Immunology. Hungarian Societies of Allergology and Clinical Immunology, of Immunology, of Hematology, of Internal Medicine, of Pharmacology, of Chemotherapy, of Gerontology, of Gastroenterology. *Publications:* "Immunopathological Syndromes", with Dr P Gergely, 1981; Author or Co-author of 39 publications in Hungarian and 36 in English in International journals. *Hobby:* Tourism. *Address:* 2nd Department of Medicine, Semmelweis University, Szentkirályi utca 46, Budapest H-1088, Hungary.

NELSON, Gloria Lea Bartholomew, b. 13 Feb. 1943, Kansas, USA. Speech Pathologist. m. Stephen D Nelson, 7 May 1966, Alton, Kansas, 1 daughter. *Education:* BA Speech, Kansas State University, 1964; MS Speech Pathology, University of Michigan, 1967; Certification in Neuro-linguistic Programming, 1985. *Appointments:* Speech Pathologist, Topeka, 1964-65, Speech Education Consultant, Stockton, 1965, Kansas Public School; Research Assistant & Clinical Supervisor, Speech Clinic, 1967-68, Clinical Supervisor, Speech & Hearing Sciences Programme, 1968-72, University of Michigan, Ann Arbor; Instructor in Physical Medicine & Rehabilitation, Medical School, Instructor in Speech, Communication & Theatre, College of Literature, Science & the Arts, Lecturer in Education, 1972-74, Private Practice & Consulting in Speech Language Pathology, 1974-78, Ann Arbor; Director, Gloria Bartholomew Nelson Associates, & director, The Nelson Centre, Annandale, Virginia, 1978-. *Memberships:* American Speech Language Hearing Association; Speech & Hearing Association of Virginia; District of Columbia Speech & Hearing Association; Maryland Speech & Hearing Association; Independent Practitioners in Speech Language Pathology & Audiology; Speech & Hearing Discussion Group, Washington Metropolitan Area. *Publications:* Various books & papers on speech difficulties. *Hobbies:* Reading Science Fiction; Flute; Travel; Mountain Climbing; Fire-walking; Public Speaking. *Address:* Gloria Bartholomew Nelson Associates, Springdale Professional Centre, 5103 E Backlick Road, Annandale, VA 22003, USA.

NELSON, Marita Lee, b. 8 Aug. 1934, California, USA. Professor. *Education:* BS 1957, MS, UCLA, 1959; PhD, University of California, Berkeley, 1968, USA. *Appointments:* Instructor, Illinois State University, 1960-64; Lecturer in Optometry and Acting Assistant Professor, 1969, Assistant Professor, University of California, Berkeley, 1972-74; Instructor 1969-70, Assistant Professor, Georgetown University Schools of Medicine-Dentistry, Washington, DC, 1970-72; Assistant Professor, University of Pacific School of Dentistry, San Francisco, 1972-74; Associate Professor 1974-80, Professor, University of Hawaii, John A Burns School of Medicine, 1980-. *Memberships:* American Association of University Professors; American Association of Anatomists; Hawaiian Academy of Science; American Association of Clinical Anatomists; Association for Women in Science; The Endocrine Society; Society of Sigma Xi; Society for Study of Reproduction. *Publications:* Author of major articles in professional journals and books. *Honours:* Science Fellow, 1965-67, Distinguished

Teaching Award, 1983, University of California, Berkeley; Teaching Awards, University of Hawaii, 1977, 1980, 1984. *Hobbies:* Music; Skiing; Swimming; Scuba Diving. *Address:* Department of Anatomy and Reproduction Biology, JAB School of Medicine, 1960 E-W Road, Honolulu, HI 96822, USA.

NELSON, Roy Leslie, b. 3 May 1941, Brooklyn, New York, USA. Attending, Cardiovascular Surgery; Professor, Surgery, Cornell University Medical Centre. m. Ann Judith Sachs, 6 Jan. 1973, New York, 1 son, 2 daughters. *Education:* BA, Lafayette College, 1963; MD, Free University of Brussels, 1971. *Appointments:* Assistant Research Surgeon, Thoracic Surgery, University of California, Los Angeles, 1974-76; Clinical Instructor, Surgery, New York University Medical Centre, 1977-80. *Memberships include:* American College of Surgeons, Candidate; Nassau County Medical Society; Medical Society of State of New York; American Heart Association; International Society for Artificial Organs; New York Academy of Sciences; etc. *Publications:* Over 26 articles in professional journals including: 'Journal of Extracorporeal Technology'; 'Journal Thoracic Cardiovascular Surgery'; etc. *Honours:* Magna Cum Laude, Free University of Brussels, 1971; Barnett Memorial Prize, New York University, 1974. *Hobbies:* Photography; Scuba Diving; Jogging; Tennis. *Address:* North Shore University Hospital, 300 Community Drive, Manhasset, NY 11030, USA.

NEMIR, Rosa Lee, b. 16 July 1905, Texas, USA. Professor of Pediatrics. m. Elias J Audi (deceased) 25 July 1934, New York, 2 sons, 1 daughter. *Education:* BA, University of Texas, 1926, MD, Johns Hopkins University, School of Medicine, 1930; Dr Sc Honoris Causa, Colgate University, 1974. *Appointments:* Instructor of Pediatrics, 1933-39, Assistant Professor of Pediatrics, 1939-50, Associate Professor 1950, New York University Medical School; Associate Professor, 1950-53, Professor 1953-59, New York University Post-Graduate Medical School; Professor of Pediatrics, New York University School of Medicine, 1959-; Visiting Professor of Microbiology, Columbia University College of Physicians and Surgeons, 1958-59; Director of Pediatric Education and Research, New York Infirmary, 1966-73; Director of Continuing Medical Education, American Medical Women's Association, 1978-82; Director of Children's Chest Clinic, Bellevue Hospital, New York City, 1960-85. *Memberships:* American Academy of Pediatrics; American Pediatric Society; Society of Pediatric Research; American College of Chest Physicians; American Thoracic Society; American Medical Association; New York Academy of Medicine; New York Academy of Sciences; Society of Adolescent Medicine; American Medical Women's Association; Medical Women's International Association. *Publications:* Numerous articles in medical journals and chapters in edited medical volumes. *Honours:* Phi Beta Kappa, University of Texas, 1925; Service Award for 35 Years New York University School of Medicine, 1968; Elizabeth Blackwell Award, AMWA 1970; Outstanding Teacher Award, Bellevue Hospital Pediatrics, 1977; Decorated Republic of Lebanon 1968; Outstanding Achievement for Women in Medicine, New York City, 1984. *Hobbies:* Music; Opera; Gardening; Travel; Needlework. *Addresses:* Office: New York University Medical Center, 550 First Avenue, New York, NY 10016, USA; Home: 7 Monroe Place, Brooklyn, NY 11201, USA.

NESER, William Bernard, b. 20 Apr. 1927, USA. Professor of Community & Occupational Health. m. Priscilla J Rose, 26 June 1954, Pittsfield, Massachusetts, 2 sons. *Education:* BA, University of Maryland, 1954; MSSA, Case Western Reserve University, 1956; MS (Public Health), University of Missouri, 1966; Doctor of Public Health, University of North Carolina, 1971. *Appointments:* Case Worker, Supervisor, Instructor, Highland View Hospital, Cleveland, Ohio, 1954-61; Instructor, Assistant Professor, Associate Professor, Community Health & Social Work, University of Missouri, 1961-71; Associate Professor, Family & Community Health, Meharry Medical College, Nashville, Tennessee, 1971-77; Senior Research Associate, Centre for Health Care Research, Meharry Medical College, Nashville, 1971-73; Associate Clinical Professor, Preventive Medicine, Vanderbilt University, Nashville, 1973-; Adjunct Professor, Nursing Education, 1979-, Professor, Community & Occupational Health, Meharry Medical College, Nashville, 1978-. *Publications:* Some 29 articles (author & co-author) in medical journals. *Hobbies:* Hunting; Fishing. *Address:* Division of Community Health Sciences, Meharry Medical College, Box 53-A 1005 D B Todd Boulevard, Nashville, TN 37208, USA.

NESTOROS, Joannis, b. 4 May 1948, Nicosia, Cyprus. Psychiatrist. m. Angeliki Pournara, 12 June 1972. *Education:* Ptychion Iatrikes (Medical Degree) with 'Arista' (Excellent), University of Athens, 1971; ECFMG Degree, 1971; Certification in Psychiatry, American Board of Neurology and Psychiatry, 1977; Specialist's Certificate, Psychiatry, and Fellow, The Royal College of Physicians and Surgeons of Canada, 1977; Diploma in Psychiatry, McGill University, 1978; PhD Neurophysiology, McGill University, 1980. *Appointments:* Rotating Intern, Toronto General Hospital, 1972-73; Resident, Psychiatry, Royal Victoria Hospital, 1973-75; Chief Resident, Psychiatry Douglas Hospital, 1975-76; Post Doctoral Fellow, Neurophysiology, Dept. of Physiology, McGill University, 1976-80; Consultant Psychiatrist, Montreal Neurological Hospital and Institute, 1977-82; Assistant Psychiatrist, Royal Victoria Hospital, 1977-82; Psychiatrist, Chief Co-Ordinator, The Schizophrenia Research Programme, Douglas Hospital Research Centre, 1980-82; Assistant Professor, Psychiatry, McGill University, 1980-82; Consultant Psychiatrist, Consultant Neurophysiologist, Eginition Hospital, Athens University School of Medicine, 1982-84; Psychiatrist-in-Chief and Chief of Research, Athens Tower Institute of Research in Neuropsychology, 1982-; Senior Psychiatrist, 1984-, and Director of Research, 1985-, Centre for Mental Health and Research, Athens. *Publications include:* 3 books; 3 chapters in books; 23 papers in scientific journals; 13 abstracts in proceedings of scientific meetings. *Memberships include:* Society for Neuroscience; American and Canadian Psychiatric Associations; International Academy of Professional Counseling and Psychotherapy. *Honours:* Medical Research Council of Canada Fellowship, 1976-80; Speaker, Gordon Research Conference on Alcohol, California, 1982; The First Five Hundred, The International Director of Distinguished Leadership, and 7 other Who's Who Publications; Life Member, The World Institute of Achievement. *Address:* Department of Research, Centre for Mental Health and Research, Notara 58, GR-106 83 Athens, Greece.

NETTER, Karl Joachim, b. 8 Feb. 1929, Kiel, Germany. Professor; Doctor of Medicine. m. Petra S Munkelt, 23 Aug. 1965, Hamburg. *Education:* MD, University of Kiel, 1953; Internship, Atlantic City Hospital, USA, 1953-54; Licensed Physician, 1954. *Appointments:* Research Fellow, Max-Planck Institute Cell Chemistry, Munich, 1954-57; Research Assistant, Department of Pharmacology, University of Hamburg, 1957-67; Habilitation for Pharmacology & Toxicology, Hamburg, 1963; Visiting Scientist, National Institutes of Health, Bethesda, Maryland, USA, 1960; Professor and Head of Toxicology Division, Department of Pharmacology, University of Mainz, 1967-76; Professor and Chairman, Department of Pharmacology, University of Marburg, 1977-. *Memberships:* Deutsche Pharmacologes, President, 1970, Member of Council, 1970-74; Society of Toxicology, USA; British Pharmacology Society; British Toxicology Society; International Society for Study of Xenobiotics, Member of Council; Ges Deutscher Chemiker; German Ocean Yachting Association. *Publications:* About 100 original publications in professional journals on biochemical pharmacology, drug metabolism, developmental pharmacology, mechanisms of toxicity; Editor various professional journals. *Hobby:*

Blue Water Sailing. *Address:* Department of Pharmacology and Toxicology, Philipps Universität Marburg, Lahnberge, D-3550 Marburg, Federal Republic of Germany.

NEUFELD, Thomas, b. 26 Jan. 1942, Budapest, Hungary. Gynaecologist; Obstetrician; Police Doctor. m. Irma Neufeld, 2 July 1966, 1 son, 1 daughter. *Education:* MD, University of Vienna, Austria, 1970. *Appointments:* General Medicine, 1970-71; Hospital Work, New Zealand, Auckland Public Hospital (General surgery, Urology, Psychiatry) and Obstetrics and Gynaecology, National Womens Hospital; Member, 1st Department of Obstetrics and Gynaecology, 1972, Senior Registrar, 1976-, University of Vienna, Austria; Police Doctor, Police Department of Vienna, 1982-; Chartered and Permanently Sworn Expert to the Court in Gynaecology and Obstetrics, 1984. *Publications:* Author of numerous publications in his field including works on Nystatin, Amphotericin therapy of female genital mycosis, Konisation surgery, Acne and a new Triphasic oral contraceptive. *Honours:* Senior Registrar, 1st Department of Obstetrics and Gynaecology, 1976-; Police Doctor Staff Member, 1982-. *Hobbies:* Skiing; Tennis; Swimming; Theatre; Books. *Address:* Celtesgasse 7, A-1190, Vienna, Austria.

NEUHÄUSER, Gerhard, b. 26 Jan. 1936, Neustadt, Cob. Professor of Paediatrics. m. Dorothea Dimigen, 31 Oct. 1965, 1 son, 1 daughter. *Education:* Universities of Munich and Freiburg, 1954-60; Paediatric Training, Munich, 1962-65; Habilitation in Paediatrics 1971. *Appointments:* Head, Section of Child Neurology and Psychopathology, University of Erlangen, 1971-78; Visiting Professor, University of Wisconsin, 1974-75; Head, Section of Neuropaediatrics, University of Giessen, 1978-. *Memberships:* Gesellschaft für Neuropädiatrie; Gesellschaft für Kinder u Jugendpsych; American Academy of Cerebral Palsy; American Association on Mental Deficiency etc. *Publications:* Author of textbooks and articles in medical journals. *Hobby:* Photography. *Address:* Universitäts-Kinderklinik, Feulgenstrasse 12, 6300 Giessen-Lahn, Federal Republic of Germany.

NEUTZE, John Murray, b. 5 Feb. 1934, Geraldine, New Zealand. Cardiologist in Charge, Green Lane Hospital, Auckland; Clinical Reader, Auckland University School of Medicine. m. Beverly Ann McClure, 4 Jan. 1958, Auckland, 3 sons. *Education:* MB, ChB, Otago University Medical School, 1958; Medical & Cardiological Training, Auckland Hospital Group, & Green Lane Hospital, 1958-64; MRACP, 1963; US Public Health Research Fellowship, 1967; MD, 1968; FRACP. *Appointment:* Cardiologist, Green Lane Hospital, 1965. *Memberships:* Fellow, Royal Australasian College of Physicians; Councillor, Cardiac Society of Australia & New Zealand; Corresponding Member, British Cardiac Society; Scientific Committee, New Zealand Heart Foundation; Scientific Committee, Asian Pacific Society of Cardiology. *Publications:* "Heart Disease in Infancy: Diagnosis & Surgical Treatment", co-author; "Intensive Care of the Heart & Lungs", 3 editions, translated into 4 foreign languages, co-author; 70 book chapters, journal articles; 50 abstracts. *Hobbies:* Music; Visual Arts; Theatre; Cricket; Conservation; Repelling the Nuclear Bomb. *Address:* Dept. of Cardiology, Green Lane Hospital, Green Lane West, Auckland 3, New Zealand.

NEUWIRTH, Peyton Sidney, b. 5 June 1911, New York, New York, USA. Assistant Professor of Operative Dentistry. m. 5 Apr. 1980, Peoria, Illinois, 1 son, 1 daughter. *Education:* University of Florida; BS, DDS, Dental School, Northwestern University. *Appointments:* Associate: B B Rappa Port, 1938-39; S S Ferdinand, 1939-40. Private Practice, 1940-80; Military Service, 1953-57; Assistant Professor of Operative Dentistry, Louisiana State College of Dentistry, 1981-. *Memberships include:* American Illinois and Chicago Dental Societies; New Orleans Dental Association; Peoria District Dental Society; Charter Member, American Association of Endodontics; American Society of Clinical Hypnosis; American Association of State Dental Board of Examiners; Federation Dentaire Internationale; Edgar D Coolidge Endodontic Dental Society of Chicago; New Orleans Dental Society; Louisiana State Association of Endodontists. *Publications:* Author of 4 dental articles and patentee of 3 inventions. *Honours include:* All elective offices including President, Peoria District Dental Society. Fellow: International College of Dentists; American Endodontic Association; American College of Dentists; Pierre Fauchard Academy. Chairman, 1973, 7 year member, Illinois Department of Registration and Education Dental Board of Examiners; Clinical Lecturer at over 75 dental seminars and meetings; Recipient of numerous community honours and awards from Boy Scouts of America, Peoria County Health Department, Council on Responsible Driving, Rotary and various others. *Hobby:* Volunteer work. *Address:* 935 Washington Avenue, New Orleans, LA 70130, USA.

NEWCOMB, Thomas Finley, b. 22 June 1927, Buffalo, New York, USA. Professor of Medicine, Chief of Staff. m. Carol Frances Bielat, 25 Mar. 1978, Cleveland, Ohio, 4 sons, 2 daughters. *Education:* BS magna cum laude 1949, MD 1951, University of Pittsburgh, Pennsylvania. *Appointments:* Intern, Hospital University of Pennsylvania, 1951; Resident and Fellow, University of Washington, 1952-54; Resident and Instructor of Medicine, Peter Bont Brigham Hospital and Harvard University, 1956-58; Howard Hughes Investigator, 1957-59; Assistant, Associate, and Professor of Medicine and Biochemistry, University of Florida, 1959-73; Assistant Chief, Medical Director of Research, Veterans Administration, 1973-78; Chief of Staff, Associate Dean, Professor of Medicine, University of Texas, San Antonio, Texas, 1978-. *Memberships:* Alpha Omega Alpha; American Federation of Clinical Research; Southern Society of Clinical Investigation; International Society of Hematology; Fellow, American College of Physicians. *Publications:* 4 articles in scientific journals, 1959-79. *Honour:* Fulbright Research Scholar, Oslo, Norway, 1955. *Address:* 16030 Doe Lane, San Antonio, TX 78255, USA.

NEWCOMB, Vickie Lee McFall, b. 17 Oct. 1957, Tennessee, USA. Doctor of Chiropractic. m. Thomas Harrison Newcomb, 3 Jan. 1982, Buffalo Trail. *Education:* AA, Secretarial Science, 1977; BS, 1980; DC, 1983. *Appointments:* Doctor of Chiropractic, 1983-; Secretary, Morristown Chiropractic Clinic Incorporated, Tennessee, 1983-. *Memberships:* International and Tennessee Chiropractic Associations. *Publications:* Voice for Health, 'What Chiropractic Really Is', 1984; "Today's Chiropractic, 'Canadida Albicans', 1985. *Honours:* Youngest Female Chiropractor in State of Tennessee. *Hobbies:* Pediatric chiropractic practice; Modelling; Showing Tennessee walking horses; Aerobics; Boating; Reading; Broadway shows; Travelling. *Address:* 714 South Cumberland Street, Morristown, TN 37818, USA.

NEWMARK, Ian H, b. 6 Sep. 1955, New York City, New York, USA. Pulmonary and Critical Care Specialist. m. Joanne Montanaro, 7 Feb. 1981, Long Island. *Education:* BS, Brooklyn College/City University of New York, 1975; MD, Downstate Medical College, 1979. *Appointments:* Clinical Research Fellow, Pulmonary Diseases, NCMC, 1982-84; Currently: Assistant Clinical Instructor in Medicine, State University of New York, Stony Brook; President, Cardiopulmonary Technologies Inc; Associate Director, Respiratory Intensive Care, Nassau County Medical Center, East Meadow. *Memberships:* American Thoracic Society; Fellow, American College of Chest Physicians; Fellow, American College of Angiology; American College of Physicians; New York Trudeau Society; Nassau County Medical Society. *Publications:* 'Intrauterine Contraceptive Devices and Cervical Mucus Lysozyme Levels', 1970; 'Intra-aortic Balloon Pumping and Diastolic Augmentation', 1971-72; 'Psychological and Perceptual Disturbances Among Chronic Drug Abusers', 1976; 'Incidence of Alcohol-

ism Among Emergency Room Patients', 1976; 'Case report: Paraquat Ingestion and Lung Injury', (with O Fulco), 1982; Effects of Thyroid Hormone on Mitochondrial Respiration of Rat Lungs', (with B Raju and V Maddaiah), 1983; 'Effects of Thyroid Hormone on Hemodynamic, Gas Exchange, and Lung Mitochondrial Respiratory Parameters in Dogs', (with B Raju and V Maddaiah), 1984. *Honour:* NCMC Proceedings Medical Writing Award, 1983. *Hobbies:* Racquetball; Literature; Sculpture. *Address:* 175 Jericho Tpke, Syosset, NY 11791, USA.

NEVIN, Norman Cummings, b. 10 June 1935, Belfast, Northern Ireland. Professor, Consultant, Medical Genetics. m. Jean Hamilton, 29 Apr. 1961, 1 son, 1 daughter. *Education:* MB, BCh, BAO (Honours), 1960; BSc., Honours, 1957; MD, 1964; FRCPath., 1981; FFCM, 1981; FRCP (Ed), 1976. *Appointments:* Medical Research Council Fellowship, London/Oxford, 1965-67; Consultant, Senior Lecturer, Human Genetics, 1967-75, Medical Genetics, Professor, Consultant, 1975-, Queen's University of Belfast. *Memberships:* Clinical Genetics Society; Association of Clinical Cytogenticists; Fellow, Ulster Medical Society; Secretary, Clinical Genetics Society. *Publications:* "Illustrated Guide to Malformations of the Central Nervous System", co-author, 1983; Articles in professional journals. *Honours:* Thompson Medal, Medicine, 1960; Sinclair Medal, Surgery, 1960; Gold Medal, Paediatrics, Royal Belfast Hospital for Sick Children, 1960; Medical Research Council Clinical Fellowship, 1965-67; Ninian Falkiner Memorial Medal, Rotunda Hospital, Dublin, 1981. *Hobby:* Oil Painting. *Address:* Dept. of Medical Genetics, Institute of Clinical Science, Grosvenor Road, Belfast BT12 6BJ, Northern Ireland.

NG, Ken Hiu-Ming, b. 4 June 1953, Hong Kong. Education Director. m. Emily 14 Aug. 1982, Toronto, 1 son. *Education:* BSc, University of Toronto, Canada. 1976; MD, CM, McGill University, Canada, 1980. *Appointments:* Education Executive 1983-84; Vice President 1984-85, President, 1985-86, Chinese Canadian Medical Society, Ontario; Education Director, Markham-Stouffville Medical Society, 1985-; Vice President 1984-85, President 1985-86. Federation of Chinese Canadian Professionals; Vice-President, Ontario Medical Association, Scarborough Branch, 1985-87. *Memberships:* Canadian Medical Association; Ontario Medical Association; College of Physicians and Surgeons of Ontario; College of Family Physicians of Canada; Markham-Stouffville Medical Society; Chinese Canadian Medical Society; Federation of Chinese-Canadian Professionals. *Hobbies:* Travel; Gastronomy. *Address:* 11 Wootten Way N, Markham, Ontario, Canada L3P 2Y2.

NICHOLAS, Terence Evan, b. 12 Oct. 1944, Perth, Australia. Associate Professor of Human Physiology. m. Frances Ann Abrunzo, 10 Aug., 1974, Teaneck, New Jersey, USA, 1 son, 1 daughter. *Education:* BSc 1st class honours, Pharmacology, 1966, PhD, 1970, University of Western Australia; Postdoctoral, Cardiovascular Research Institute, University of California, San Francisco, USA, 1970-72. *Appointments:* Assistant Professor, Departments of Physiology and Pharmacology, School of Medicine, University of Hawaii, 1972-74; Lecturer, 1974-76, Senior Lecturer, 1977-81, Associate Professor, 1982-, Human Physiology, School of Medicine, Flinders University of South Australia, Australia. *Memberships:* Australian Physiological and Pharmacological Society; Thoracic Society of Australia; Australian Society for Medical Research; American Physiological Society; American Thoracic Society. *Publications include:* Contributions to 'Journal of Applied Physiology', 1981-84. *Honours:* Fellowship: San Francisco Heart Association, 1970; Fulbright Foundation, 1970. Australian Commonwealth Postgraduate Award, 1967; Robert C Kirkwood Memorial Award, 1971. *Hobbies:* Yacht racing; Woodwork. *Address:* Department of Human Physiology, Flinders Medical Centre, Bedford Park, Adelaide, SA 5042, Australia.

NICHOLS, David Martin, b. 24 Feb. 1951, Aberdeen, Scotland. Active Staff Radiologist; Assistant Professor. m. Gillian Stroud, 3 July 1981, Aberdeen, 1 son. *Education:* MB ChB, DMRD, University of Aberdeen; MRCP; FFR (RCSI); FRCP (C); FRCR; Fellowship, University of British Columbia, Canada. *Appointments:* House Staff, Senior House Officer, Medicine, Registrar, Radiology, Senior Registrar, Radiology, Aberdeen Hospitals; Fellow, Radiology (Abdominal); Staff Radiologist, Assistant Professor, Radiology, Vancouver General Hospital, University of British Columbia. *Memberships:* British and Canadian Medical Associations; British Columbia Radiological Society; Canadian Association of Radiologists. *Publications:* Author, Chapters & papers on Chest, Abdominal and Interventional/Angiographic Radiology, 1982-85. *Hobbies:* Mountaineering; Music. *Address:* 1906 West 44th Ave, Vancouver, British Columbia, Canada V6M 2E7.

NICHOLSON, Bernard Clive, b. 10 Apr. 1904, London, England. Consultant in General Medicine (Retired). m. Frances Rose Burdon-Cooper, 19 Feb. 1938, London, 2 sons, 3 daughters. *Education:* MA, MD, BCh, Cambridge University; MRCP, London; DPH, London; FF Hom; St Bartholemews Hospital, London; London School of Hygiene and Tropical Medicine. *Appointments:* House Physician to Medical Professorial Unit, St Bartholemew's Hospital, London, 1930-31; Assistant Physician, London Homeopathic Hospital, 1937-39; Assistant MOH, City and Port of Bristol, 1940-41; Medical Specialist, RAFVR, 1941-45; Consultant in General Medicine, Royal Bath Hospital, Harrogate and Chapel Allerton Hospital, Leeds, 1952-70. *Memberships:* Life Member, BMA; Past President, Harrogate Medical Society; Fellow, Royal Society of Medicine; Fellow, Faculty of Homeopathy. *Publications:* 'The cardiac arrhythmias of thyrotoxicosis with special reference to prognosis'; 'The Nature of Potency Energy', 1983; 'Placebo Reactors', 1963. *Hobbies:* Music; Violin and viola; Composition. *Address:* Archway House, 24 Swan Road, Harrogate, North Yorkshire HG1 2SA, England.

NICKERSON, H James, b. 7 Dec. 1937, St Ansgar, Iowa, USA. Paediatric Haematologist. m. 17 Sep. 1960, St Ansgar, 1 son, 3 daughters. *Education:* MD, University of Iowa, 1963; Paediatric Residency, Childrens Hospital, & US Naval Hospital, Philadelphia, 1963-66. *Appointments:* Staff Paediatrician, US Naval Hospital, Camp Lejeune, North Carolina, 1966-69; Clinical Assistant Professor, Paediatrics, University of Wisconsin; Paediatric Haematologist, Marshfield Clinic, Wisconsin. *Memberships:* Fellow, American Academy of Paediatrics, 1969; American Society of Clinical Oncology; American Board of Paediatric Haematology and Oncology. *Publications:* "Hepatoblastoma, Thrombocytosis, and Increased Thrombopietin", 'Cancer', 1980; "Comparison of Stage IV and Stage IV-S Neuroblastoma in the First Year of Life", 'Medical and Paediatric Oncology', 1985. *Hobbies:* Golf; Cross Country Skiing; Bicycling. *Address:* Department of Paediatrics, Marshfield Clinic, Marshfield, WI 54449, USA.

NICOLI, René M, b. 16 June 1928, Vermand, France. Professor, Hospital Biologist. m. Mari-Jeanne Cerati, 17 Apr. 1952, 2 sons. *Education:* MD; DSc Physical & Natural Sciences. *Appointments:* Specialist in: Microbiology (bacteriology & parasitology); Relational biology; Sexology (esp human); Thanatology. *Publications:* Over 270 publications, including: "L'Univers de la Sexualité", 1970; "O Universo da sexualidad", 1973; "Elements de biologie relationelle" (4 volumes), 1985. *Address:* Faculté de Medicine secteur nord, F-13015 Marseilles, France.

NICOLLE, Daniel Paul-Eugène, b. 3 Mar. 1949, Paris, France. Doctor of Chiropractic. m. Nicole Millet, Paris, 1 son, 2 daughters. *Education:* Doctor of Chiropractic, Doctor of Naturopathy, Doctor of Medical Science, Palmer College of Chiropractic. *Appointments:* Intern, Palmer College of Chiropractic; First Assistant, International Chiropractic Centre, Paris; Director, Saint Sulpice Chiropractic and Acupuncture International Centre; Chiropractic Counselor, Institute of Diplomatic Relations. *Memberships:* European Chiropractic Union; American Chiropractic Association; International Chiropractic Association; Association Française de Chiropractic; International College of Applied Kinesiology. *Honours:* Doctus Caviatus (H C), Academia Azteca, 1970; Prix Hippocrate, with grand gold medal, 1981; Croix d' Officer d'Academie, Institute of Diplomatic Relations, 1981. *Hobbies:* Tennis; Golf. *Address:* 76 Rue Bonaparte, 75006 Paris, France.

NICOSIA, Joan Elizabeth Wesp, b. New York, USA. Supervisor, Physical Therapy. m. Robert Nicosia, 23 June 1962, New York City. *Education:* BA, Humanities, Hunter College, 1953; Certificate in Physical Therapy, Columbia College of Physicians and Surgeons, School of Physical Therapy, 1954. *Appointments:* Burke Foundation Rehabilitation Department, New York, 1954-56; Burke Foundation Cerebral Palsy Clinic, 1956-59; Chief Physical Therapist, Home Care Incorporated, United Hospital, Port Chester, 1959-60; Supervisor, Physical Therapy, Bronx Municipal Hospital Center/Jacobi Hospital, 1960-; Instructor in Kinesiology, Electrotherapy and Burns, Division of Physical Therapy, Ithaca College, 1960-. *Memberships:* American Physical Therapy Association; American Registry for Physical Therapists; American Burn Association; International Society for the Prevention of Burn Injuries; Founding Member, American Society of Hand Therapists; Association of American Medical Colleges (Avline Reviewer, 1980-82); Association for Burn Care, Yorktown Heights, New York (Educational Chairperson). *Publications:* Numerous articles and papers in professional publications; Lecturers and Presentations; Chapters in books; Co-author: Manual of Burn Care, 1983. *Honour:* Elected to Hall of Fame, Alumni Association of Hunter College, 1984. *Hobbies:* Gardening; Painting; Skiing; Photography; Swimming. *Address:* Rd. 1, Box 184, Colonel Greene Road, Yorktown Heights, NY 10598, USA.

NICU, D Mihail, b. 23 Mar. 1937, Bucharest, Romania. Professor of Biotechnology; Senior Principal, Research Medicine. m. Silvya Nicu, 16 Feb. 1971, Bucharest, 2 daughters. *Education:* MD, Faculty of Medicine, Bucharest; Doctorate in Endocrinology and Radiobiology, 1969; Prof Ass, Bioengineering, Ministry of Education, Romania. *Appointments:* Physician, Hospital, 1960; Specialist in Radiogenetics and Endocrinology, 1963; Scientific Secretary, Medical Section, Academy; Head of Laboratory for Cosmic Medicine; Prof. Ass, Bioengineering Department, Politechnical Institute, Bucharest, 1975; Head, Laboratory of Biotechnology, 1977. *Memberships:* European Society for Radiobiology; International Society for Human Biology; Medical Union of the Balkans. *Publications:* Author of 9 books including: "Radiobiology", 1970; "Biotechnology", 1979; "Bionics and Life", 1984. Author of 155 papers contributed to professional journals including: 'Acta Biotechnologica', Editorial Board, 1983-. *Hobbies:* Rugby; Music. *Address:* Biotechnology Research Department, Institutul Politechnic Bucuresti, Splaiul Independentei 313, 72206 Bucuresti, Romania.

NIEBRÓJ-DOBOSZ, Irena Maria, b. 21 Dec. 1932, Rybnik, Poland. Associate Professor. m. Stanislaw Dobosz, 6 Sep. 1958, 1 daughter. *Education:* MD, summa cum laude, Silesian's Medical School, Katowice, 1957. *Appointments:* Assistant, Department of Biochemistry, Silesian's Medical School, 1953-57; Assistant, Senior Assistant, Assistant Professor, Associate Professor, Department of Neurology, Medical School in Warsaw, 1957-. *Memberships:* Polish Neurological Society; Polish Biochemical Society; Polish Society for Clinical Chemistry; Committee for Neuromuscular Diseases, Polish Academy of Sciences; Committee for Neurochemistry, Polish Academy of Sciences; Committee for Neurochemistry, Polish Neurological Society. *Publications include:*

"Enzymology in Muscle Diseases" (in Polish) 1st and 2nd editions, 1968, 70; "Biochemistry Diagnosis in Muscle Diseases" (in Polish), 1983; Articles in professional journals including: 'Journal of Neurology', 'Neurology', etc. *Honours:* Prizes of Polish Neurological Society, 1966, 74; Prizes of Polish Academy of Sciences, 1973, 75; Prize of Ministry of Health, 1981. *Hobbies:* Travel; Music; Paintings. *Address:* ul Modzelewskiego 65 m. 35, 02-679 Warsaw, Poland.

NIEDERHUBER, John Edward, b. 21 June 1938, Steubenville, Ohio, USA. Professor of Surgery; Professor of Microbiology and Immunology; Head, Division of Surgical Oncology. *Education:* BS, Bethany College, 1960; MD, Ohio State University Medical School, 1964; Graduate Student, Department of Microbiology, University of Michigan, 1969-70. *Appointments:* Assistant Professor of Surgery, 1973-77; Associate Professor, 1977-80; Assistant Professor of Microbiologu and Immunology, 1973-77, 1977-80; Chief, Division of Surgical Oncology and Transplantation, Section of General Surgery, 1979-82; Chief, Division of Surgical Oncology, 1982-; Professor of Surgery; Professor of Microbiology and Immunology, 1980-; University of Michigan; Associate Dean for Research, University of Michigan Medical Center, 1982-; Senior Associate Dean, University of Michigan Medical School, 1983-. *Memberships:* Association for Academic Surgery; American Society of Transplantation Surgeons; Transplantation Society; Transplantation Society of Michigan; American College of Surgeons; American Association of Immunologists; Coller Surgical Society; Society of University Surgeons; Society of Surgical Oncology; Central Surgical Society; American Association for Cancer Research; American Society of Clinical Oncology; Society of Clinical Surgery. *Publications:* Contributor to Books and Professional Journals; Audio-Visual Educational Materials; Books include: "Writing a Successful Grant Application"; Book Reviews. *Honours:* US Public Health Service Research Career Development Award; American Cancer Society Junior Faculty Clinical Fellowship; Distinguished Faculty Service Award, University of Michigan. *Hobbies:* Tennis; Gardening. *Address:* M5812 Medical Science II, Department of Microbiology and Immunology, Ann Arbor, MI 48109, USA.

NIESCHLAG, Eberhard, b. 16 July 1941, Bad Godesberg, Germany. Head of Department and Research Unit. m. Susan Kritz, 23 Nov. 1973, 2 daughters. *Education:* Abitur, 1961; Staatsexamen, 1967; Promotion Dr Med 1967; Habilitation Priv Doz 1975; Specialization in Internal Medicine, 1975; Professor, 1976. *Appointments:* Department of Biochemistry, University College, London, 1967-68; MRC Clinical Research Unit for Reproductive Endocrinology, Edinburgh, 1968; University of Mainz, Department of Medicine, 1968-70; National Institute of Health, Reproduction Research Branch, Bethesda, Maryland, USA, 1971-72; University of Dusseldorf, Department of Internal Medicine, 1972-76; Head, Department of Experimental Endocrinology, University of Munster, 1976- Head, Clinical Research Unit for Reproductive Medicine, Max-Planck Society, Munster, 1980- *Memberships:* American Society of Endocrinology; British Society of Endocrinology; American Society of Andrology; International Society of Andrology, President, 1981-85; European Medical Research Council Advisory Subgroup on Human Reproduction, Chairman, 1982-85; German Society for Endocrinology, Council Member, 1978-81, 1985-. *Publications:* Editor, 2 books; 70 book contributions; Over 200 original publications in scientific journals. *Address:* Max-Planck Clinical Research Unit for Reproductive Medicine, Steinfurter Str 107, D-4400 Munster, Federal Republic of Germany.

NIJS, Piet Alfons Andre, b. 7 June 1937, Tongeren, Belgium. Professor, Medical School, Catholic University, Leuven, Belgium; Psychiatrist; Sexologist. 3 daughters. *Education:* Baccal. Thom. Philosophy, 1959, Candid Psychology, 1960, Lic Family and Sex-

ological Sciences, 1967, MD, 1962, Lic Physical Education, 1962, Catholic University of Leuven. *Appointments:* Associate Chief, University Hospital St Rafael, Leuven, 1968; Associate Professor, 1969, Professor, 1977, Medical School, KUL, Leuven; Chief, University Psychiatric Centre, St Rafael. *Memberships:* American College of Sexologists; Deutsche Gesellschaft fur Sexualforschung; Gesellschaft fur Praktische Sexualmedizin; International Society Psychosomatic Obstetrics & Gynaecology; Flemish Society of Sexologists. *Publications:* 300 articles, 15 books including: "Psychomatische Aspekte der oralen Antikonzeption", 1972; "La pilule et la Sexualité", 1975; "De eenzame Samenspelers", 3 volumes, 1976; "Tegenstromingen in de seksologie Leuven", 1977; etc. *Honours:* Claxo Medical Award, Benelux, 1978. *Hobbies:* Travel; Jogging; Dancing; Poetry; Classical Music; Writing. *Address:* Schrynmaberstrasse 28, B-3000 Leuven, Belgium.

NIKITOVITCH-WINER, Miroslava B, b. 13 May 1929, Kraljevo, Yugoslavia. Professor & Chairman, Department of Anatomy, University of Kentucky, USA. m. Alfred D Winer, 20 Aug. 1955, New Jersey, USA, 1 son, 1 daughter. *Education:* MA, Harvard University 1954; PhD, Duke University, 1957. *Appointments:* Assistant Professor 1961-67, Associate Professor 1967-73, Professor of Anatomy 1973-, University of Kentucky Medical Centre; Chairman & Professor of Anatomy, ibid, 1979-. *Memberships:* New York Academy of Science; American Association of Anatomists; Endocrine Society; Society for the Study of Reproduction; American Association for the Advancement of Science. *Publications include:* 'Effect of hypothalamic deafferentation on hypophysial & other endocrine gland blood flows' in 'Endocrinology', 1986 *Honours:* Golden Podium, outstanding course award, UKMC, 1980, 1979, 1978; Silver Pointer Teaching Award, 1977; SAMA Golden Apple Teaching Award, 1971. *Hobbies:* Tennis; Skiing; Theatre & Concerts; Pottery; Scuba diving. *Address:* Department of Anatomy, University of Kentucky College of Medicine, 800 Rose Street, MN 224 A B Chandler Medical Centre, Lexington, KY 40536-00849, USA.

NIKOLIC, George, b. 7 Feb. 1945, Belgrade, Yugoslavia. Director of Intensive Care Unit; Consultant Physician in Cardiology. m. Annette Coutney Smith, 7 Feb. 1978, Canberra, Australia, 1 son, 1 daughter. *Education:* MB BS 2nd class Honours, University of Sydney, Sydney, 1971; Member 1974, Fellow 1978, Royal Australian College of Physicians; Diploma in Internal Medicine 1980, Diploma in Cardiology 1981, American Boards of Internal Medicine. *Appointments:* Resident Medical Officer, Medical Registrar, Cardiology Registrar, St Vincent's Hospital, Sydney, 1971-75; Fellow in Cardiology, St Vincent's Medical Center, Staten Island, New York, USA, 1979-81; Fellow in Cardiology, St Vincent's Hospital, Worcester, Massachusetts, 1981-82; Medical Cardiology Registrart 1976-77, Director of Intensive Care 1977-78 and 1982-, Woden Valley Hospital, Canberra, Australia. *Memberships:* Royal Australian College of Physicians; Cardiac Society of Australia and New Zealand; Australian New Zealand Intensive Care Society; Critical Care Society, USA; American College of Cardiology; American College of Chest Physicians. *Publications:* 'Sudden Death Recorded During Holter Monitoring', (co-author), 1982; 'Self-Predicting Stress Tests', (co-author), 1982; 'Sudden Death in Aortic Stenosis', (co-author), 1982; 'Lev and Lenegre Diseases', 1983; 'Rationing Intensive Care', 1984; 'Blood Gases in Pulmonary Embolism', 1984. *Address:* PO Box 11, Woden, ACT 2606, Australia.

NIKONOROW, Maksym, b. 19 Aug. 1913, Petersburg. Emeritus Professor; Editor. m. 8 Sep. 1949, 1 son. *Education:* Warsaw University, Poland. 1935. *Appointments:* PhD, Pharm, 1939, Assistant Professor, 1952, Associate Professor, 1954, Professor, 1962; Research Staff, State Institute of Hygiene, Warsaw, Head, Food Research, National Institute of Hygiene, Warsaw; Polish FAO/WHO Expert; Professor, h.c.,

Medical Academy, Lodz, 1985. *Memberships:* Polish Academy Science; Polish Society Pharmacology; Polish Society Pharmacy; Polish Society Toxicology; Polish Society of Hygiene. *Publications:* "Outline of Food Science", 1956; "Food Toxicology", 1979; "Chemical and Biological Contaminations of Food", 1980; "Pesticides in Aspects of Environmental Toxicology", 1979. *Honours:* Decorated Officer Commander with Star Order Polonia Restituta, Order Banner of Labour; Order Merit for Health of People. *Hobbies:* Fishing; Music of Chopin. *Address:* Marszalkowska 28/168 Str, Warsaw, Poland.

NILSSON, Nils Kenneth, b. 8 Aug. 1942, Sunne, Sweden. Professor, Cell Pathology, Uppsala University. m. Karin Edsjo, 22 May 1964, Ed, 1 son, 1 daughter. *Education:* MD; PhD; DrMed.Sci. *Appointments:* Assistant Professor, 1971-76, Associate Professor, 1976-80, Professor, Cell Pathology (Chair), 1980-, Pathology Dept, University of Uppsala. *Memberships:* Swedish Society of Medicine; European Tissue Culture Association; Scandinavian Society for Immunology; Swedish Cancer Society; IACRLRD. *Publications:* 250 papers in professional journals. *Honour:* Hoechst Preis, 1980. *Hobbies:* Photography; Gardening; Mountaineering. *Address:* Rapphonsvagen 11, S-752 52 Uppsala, Sweden.

NILSSON, Sven Erik G, b. 23 Dec. 1931, Sweden. Professor of Opthalmology, University of Linköping. m. Ulla Nilsson, 5 Jan. 1955. *Education:* MD, 1961, PhD, 1964, Karolinska Institute, Stockholm. *Appointments:* Assistant Professor, Cell Biology, University of California, USA, 1962-64; Assistant Professor, Ophthalmology, Karolinska Institute, Stockholm, 1965-71; Professor, Chairman, Ophthalmology, 1972-; Associate Dean, Dean, School of Medicine, 1974-77, University of Linköping, Sweden; Scientific Advisor, Ophthalmology, Swedish National Board of Health and Welfare, 1977-. *Memberships:* International Society for Clinical Electrophysiology of Vision, President; International Society for Contact Lens Research, Council Member; Association for Research in Vision and Ophthalmology; International Society for Eye Research; Association for Eye Research; Swedish Ophthalmological Association. *Publications:* 140 scientific papers, 1963-85, on retinal electrophysiology and ultrastructure, contact lens research. *Honours:* Axel Hirsch Award, Karolinska Institute, Stockholm, 1972; Main Lecture, World Congress of Ophthalmology, Japan, 1978. *Hobby:* Tennis. *Address:* Dept. of Ophthalmology, University of Linköping, S-58185, Linköping, Sweden.

NILSSON-EHLE, Hans Peter Herman, b. 29 May 1944, Lund, Sweden. Assistant Professor and Head of Department of Clinical Chemistry. m. Ingrid Olsson, 21 June 1969, Trollhättan, 1 son, 1 daughter. *Education:* MD, 1967, PhD, 1974. *Appointments:* Research Assistant, Physiological Chemistry, 1965-74; Postdoctoral Fellow, University of California, Los Angeles, 1974-76; Assistant Professor, 1976-, Head of Department of Clinical Chemistry, University Hospital, Lund, Sweden, 1985-. *Memberships:* Swedish Medical Association; Swedish Society of Medicine; The Royal Society of Medicine; European Lipoprotein Club, Committee Member 1983-; Swedish Society for Obesity Research, Committee Member 1983-. *Publications:* Contributor of numerous articles and original papers to medical journals, and chapters to learned books. *Hobbies:* Music; Sailing; Fishing. *Address:* Department of Clinical Chemistry, University Hospital, S-221 85 Lund Sweden.

NISHIDA, Teruo, b. 18 Mar. 1947, Osaka, Japan. Assistant Professor of Ophthalmology. m. Kisako Nanjyo, 4 Oct. 1970, Osaka, Japan, 2 sons, 1 daughter. *Education:* MD, Osaka University Medical School, 1965-71; Research Trainee, Division of Protein Metabolism, Institute for Protein Research, Osaka University, 1971-72; Doctor of Medical Science, Osaka University Medical School, 1972-74. *Appointments:* Research Associate, Department of Biochemistry, Ehime Uni-

versity School of Medicine, Ehime, Japan, 1974-80; Research Associate, Department of Retina Research, Eye Research Institute of Retina Foundation, Boston, Massachusetts, USA, 1977-80; Assistant Professor, Department of Ophthalmology, Osaka University Medical School, 1980-; Assistant Professor, Department of Ophthalmology, Kinki University School of Medicine, Osaka, 1984-. *Memberships:* Societas Ophthalmologica Japonica; American Academy of Ophthalmology; Castroviejo Society; Japan Society for Cell Biology; American Society for Cell Biology; Tissue Culture Association; Association for Research in Vision & Ophthalmology. *Publications:* Various articles, especially in field of Fibronectin. *Address:* 27-14-106 Hinoike-cho, Nishinomiya, Hyogo 662, Japan.

NISHINO, Mizuho, b. 17 Sep. 1940, Osaka, Japan. Professor of Dentistry. *Education:* DDS, DDSc, Osaka University Dental School. *Appointments:* Assistant 1970-72, Lecturer 1973-77, Osaka University Dental School; Professor, Tokushima University School of Dentistry, 1977-. *Memberships:* International Association for Dental Research; International Association of Dentistry for the Handicapped; Academy of Dentistry for the Handicapped; Japanese Society of Pedodontics; Japanese Society of Conservative Dentistry; Japanese Association for Oral Biology; Japanese Society for Dental Health; Japanese Society of Child Health; Japanese Association for Dental Education. *Publications:* "Diammine Silver Fluoride and its Clinical Application", 1978; 'Studies on the Topical Application of Ammoniacal Silver Fluoride for the Arrestment of Dental Caries', 1969; 'Clinico-roentogenographical Study of Iodoform-Calcium Hydroxide Root Canal Filling Material "Vitapex" in Deciduous Teeth', 1980; 'Studies of Dental Health Examination of One and a Half Year Old Infants', 1984. *Address:* Tokushima University School of Dentistry, 3 Kuramoto-cho, Tokushima, Tokushima 770, Japan.

NISSLEK, Peter Christian, b. 13 Apr. 1940, Seattle, USA. Private Practice. Divorced, 2 daughters. *Education:* BA, Zoology, University of California, Santa Barbara, 1963; DDS, Northwestern University Dental School, 1967. *Appointments:* Assistant Professor, Clinical Dentistry, University of Colorado, 1974-79; Board of Trustees, Society for Occlusal Studies, 1982-85; Board of Directors, NGA Associates, 1983-85; Private Practice, Evergreen, Colorado. *Memberships:* American Dental Association; Colorado Dental Association; Society for Occlusal Studies; Colorado Prosthodontic Society; American Equilibration Society; Niles Guichst Associates; Occlusion Associates International. *Hobbies:* Skiing; Trout Fishing; Sailing; Back Packing. *Address:* PO Box 2679 Evergreen, CO 80439, USA.

NOBLE, Mark Ian Munro, b. 6 Sep. 1935, England. Consultant Physician. m. Angela J Drake-Holland, 15 Nov. 1984, Guildford, 2 sons, 1 daughter. *Education:* BSc, 1957, MBBS, St Bartholomews Hospital Medical College, University of London, 1960; PhD, 1965, MD, 1969, DSc, University of London, 1979; MRCP 1969, FRCP Royal College of Physicians, London, 1979. *Appointments:* Research Fellow, 1962-65, Lecturer in Medicine, 1968-71, Senior Lecturer in Medicine, 1971-, Consultant Physician, 1971-, Charing Cross Hospital Medical School; Senior Fellow, Cardiovascular Research Institute, University of California, San Francisco, 1966-68; Consultant Physician, King Edward VII Hospital, Midhurst, 1973; Boerhaave Professor of Medicine, University of Leiden, The Netherlands, 1982. *Memberships:* Physiological Society; Medical Research Society; European Society for Clinical Investigation, Secretary 1972-76; British Cardiac Society; International Society for Heart Research; British Medical Association. *Publications include:* "The Cardiac Cycle", 1979; "Cardiac Metabolism" (with A J Drake-Holland), 1983; Author of book chapters; Numerous scientific papers to journals. *Hobbies:* History; Music. *Address:* Stonywood, Chase Lane, Haslemere, Surrey, GU27 3AG, England.

NOCKS, James Jay, b. 17 Apr. 1943, Brooklyn, New York, USA. Associate Clinical Professor of Psychiatry; Hospital Department Chief. m. Ellen Jane Leblang, 21 June 1964, New York, USA, 2 sons. *Education:* BA, University of Pennsylvania, USA, 1964, MD, 1968. *Appointments:* Internship, Chicago Wesley Memorial Hospital, 1968-69; Resident in Psychiatry, University of Pennsylvania, 1969-73; Staff Psychiatrist, USAF, 1973-75; Clinical Assistant Professor of Psychiatry, University of Texas Health Science Centre, 1973-75; currently, Chief, Alcoholism Programme and Assistant Chief, Psychiatry Service, West Haven, VA Medical Centre and Associate Clinical Professor of Psychiatry, Yale University. *Memberships:* American Psychiatric Association; Connecticut Psychiatric Society; New Haven County Medical Society; American Medical Society on Alcoholism; Association for Medical Education and Research in Substance Abuse; American and World Associations of Social Psychiatry. *Publications:* Chapter 'Alcoholism and Drug Abuse' in "Psychiatry: PreTest, Self-Assessment and Review", 3rd edition, 1984; articles in professional journals including 'Instructing Medical Students on Alcoholism - What to Teach' with limited time' in 'Journal of Medical Education', 1980; 'Biochemical Tests of Alcoholism: A Critical Review' in 'Psychiatric Medicine', 1984, (co-author); 'Alcoholism Treatment of Vietnam Veterans with Post Traumatic Stress Disorder in 'Journal of Substance Abuse', 1984. *Honours:* Phi Beta Kappa, 1963; American Board of Medical Examiners, 1969. *Hobbies:* Cycling; Tennis. *Address:* West Haven VA Medical Centre, West Spring Street, West Haven, CT 06516, USA.

NOH, Kyung-Sun, b. 25 Jan. 1941, Korea. Programme Director, Child Psychiatry Fellowship Programme, Institute for Juvenile Research. m. Joyce Hiew Hahn, 17 June 1972, Philadelphia, Pennsylvania, USA, 2 sons, 1 daughter. *Education includes:* MD, Yonsei University College of Medicine, Seoul, Korea, 1965; Diploma, Psychiatry, McGill University, Canada, 1970. Resident: Philadelphia Psychiatric Center, Pennsylvania University, 1970-72; Child Psychiatry, University of Michigan, 1972-73; College of Physicians and Surgeons, Columbia University, New York, 1973-74; Diplomate: American Board of Psychiatry and Neurology, 1975; American Board of Child Psychiatry, 1977. Family Therapy Programme, Institute for Juvenile Research, Illinois, 1983-84. *Appointments:* Instructor, Psychiatry, College of Physicians and Surgeons, Columbia University, New York, 1974-77; Assistant Professor, Psychiatry, Programme Director, Division of Child and Adolescent Psychiatry, University of Maryland School of Medicine, 1977-79; Assistant Professor, Psychiatry, University of Illinois School of Medicine, 1979-; Programme Director, Child Psychiatry Fellowship Programme, Institute for Juvenile Research, currently. *Memberships:* American Psychiatric Association; Fellow, American Academy of Child Psychiatry; Illinois Psychiatric Society; Illinois Council of Child Psychiatry; American Association of Directors of Psychiatric Residency Training. *Publications:* Contributions to: 'International Journal of Clinical and Experimental Hypnosis', 1984; 'International Journal of Sleep'. *Hobbies:* Tennis; Skiing; Swimming. *Address:* 1785 Willow Road, Winnetka, IL 60093, USA.

NORA, James Jackson, b. 26 June 1928, Chicago, Illinois, USA. Professor of Genetics, Preventive Medicine, Pediatrics; Director, Preventive Cardiology, University of Colorado School of Medicine. m. Audrey Faye Hart, 9 April 1966, Houston, 1 son, 4 daughters. *Education:* AB, Harvard, 1950; MD Yale, 1954; MPH, California, 1978; Diplomate, American Board of Pediatrics; Diplomate, American Sub-Board of Pediatric Cardiology; Diplomate, American Board of Medical Genetics. *Appointments:* Research Fellow, Cardiology, Instructor, Pediatrics, 1962-64; Assistant Professor, 1964, University of Wisconsin; Special NIH Fellow, Genetics, McGill University, and Montreal Children's Hospital, Canada, 1964-65; Head, Human Genetics, Director Birth Defects Centre, Associate Director, Cardiology, Associate Professor, Pediatrics, Baylor College of Medicine, Houston, 1965-71; Director, Pediatric Cardiology, Cardiovascular Training Centre, University of Colorado School of Medicine, 1971-78. *Memberships:* Fellow, American College of Cardiology; Fellow, American Academy of Pediatrics; American Pediatric Society; Teratology Society; European Teratology Society; Society for Pediatric Research; Transplantation Society; American Society for Human Genetics; many other professional organisations. *Publications:* 160 articles, 9 books including: "Medical Genetics Principles and Practice", co-author, 2nd edition, 1981; "Congenital Heart Disease: Causes and Processes", co-author, 1984; "The Whole Heart Book", 1980. *Honours:* World Health Organisation Consultant, Genetic's of Coronary Disease, 1983-; Virginia Apgar Memorial Award, 1976; Various task forces, national commmittees, review boards and editorial boards. *Hobby:* Creative Writing. *Address:* 6135 E 6th Avenue, Denver, CO 80220, USA.

NORBECK, George Philip, b. 15 Jan. 1937, South Dakota, USA. Chief, Psychiatric Outpatient Unit. m. Mary Jeanette Moore, 5 June 1977, Inverness, California, 1 son, 3 daughters. *Education:* BA, St Olaf College, Northfield, Minnesota; BS, MD, University of Minnesota; Psychiatric Residency & MSP, UCLA, Los Angeles, CA. *Appointments:* Staff Psychiatrist, St Johns Hospital, Santa Monica, California; Psychiatric Research Institute, Uppsala, Sweden; Karolinska Hospital, Stockholm, Sweden; Chief, Inpatient Unit, Chief, Outpatient Unit, MPD, Palo Alto V A Medical Center, California; State Air Surgeon; Colonel, USAF-ANG California. *Memberships:* American Psychiatric Association; American College of Physicians; Aerospace Medical Association. *Hobbies:* Music; Horseback Riding. *Address:* V A Medical Center (170A), 3801 Miranda Avenue, Palo Alto, CA 94301, USA.

NORDMAN, Eeva Mirjami, b. 10 Feb. 1931. Viborg, Finland. University Professor of Oncology and Radiotherapy; Head of University Hospital Radiotherapy Clinic. m. Erik Nordman (deceased), 6 October 1956, Helsinki, 1 son, 1 daughter. *Education:* MD, 1957; Specialist in Radiology, 1963; Specialist in Radiotherapy, 1967; Subspecialty in Nuclear Medicine, 1972. *Appointments:* Assistant Chief Physician, Department of Radiotherapy, University Central Hospital, Helsinki, 1966; Chief Physician, Department of Radiotherapy, Middle Finland Central Hospital, Jyväskylä, 1967-72; Consulting Specialist and Assistant Chief Physician 1972-77, Chief Physician 1977-, Department of Radiotherapy, University Central Hospital, Turku; Acting Professor of Oncology and Radiotherapy 1977-79, Professor of Oncology and Radiotherapy 1979-, University of Turku. *Memberships:* Vice-Chairman 1974-77, Finnish Society of Radiology; Chairman 1974-76, Finnish Radiotherapists; Secretary 1975-79, Scandinavian Radiotherapy Club; Chairman 1981, Nordic Society of Medical Radiology; Chairman 1981-82, Turku Medical Society Duodecim; Board Member, Cancer Society of Southwestern Finland, 1975-; New York Academy of Sciences. *Publications:* 150 concerning cancer treatment, immunology and nuclear medicine. *Honour:* Sakari Mustakallio Lecture, 1984. *Address:* Department of Oncology and Radiotherapy, University of Turku, 20520 Turku, Finland.

NORMAN, Harold Glenn, b. 21 June 1937, Birmingham, Alabama, USA. Plastic Surgeon. m. Bonita Todd, 10 Aug. 1958, Tuscaloosa, Alabama, 2 sons, 2 daughters. *Education:* BS, MD, University of Alabama; Certified, American Board of Surgery, American Board of Plastic and Reconstructive Surgery, American Board of Medical Examiners. *Appointments:* Chief Resident General Surgery, St Louis Missouri City Hospital; Chief Resident Plastic Surgery, Barnes Hospital, St Louis; Deputy Hospital Commander, Chief of Surgery, Chief of Professional Services, Reese Air Force Base, Texas; Staff, Doctor's Hospital; Staff, Miami Children's Hospital; Clinical

Assistant Professor, Plastic Surgery Department, University of Miami School of Medicine. *Memberships:* American Society of Plastic and Reconstructive Surgery; American College of Surgeons; American Society of Aesthetic Plastic Surgery; Greater Miami Society of Plastic & Reconstructive Surgeons; Past President, Southeastern Society of Plastic and Reconstructive Surgeons; President, Dade County Medical Association, 1985-86; Past President, Florida Society of Plastic and Reconstructive Surgeons; Royal College of Medicine.*Publications:* On plastic surgery and use of Hypnosis in ambulatory plastic surgery facilities. *Honours:* Air Force Commendation Medal, 1965; Outstanding Alumnus, Miami chapter, University of Alabama, 1979. *Hobbies:* Golf; Art; Orchids. *Address:* 262 Almeria Avenue, PO Box 342098, Coral Gables, FL 33134, USA.

NORMAN, John Nelson, b. 16 May 1932, Paisley, Scotland. Director, Centre for Offshore Health. m. Sarah D Riste, 27 July 1964, Glasgow, 1 daughter. *Education:* MB, ChB 1954, MD 1961, PhD 1964, University of Glasgow; DSc, University of Aberdeen, 1976. *Appointments:* Medical Officer, British Antarctic Survey, 1958-61; Research Fellow in Surgery, University of Glasgow, 1961-64; Lecturer and Senior Lecturer in Surgery 1964-70, Reader in Surgery 1970-76, Professor of Environmental Medicine 1976-82, University of Aberdeen; Director, Centre for Offshore Health, Robert Gordon's Institute of Technology, Aberdeen, 1982-. *Memberships:* Fellow, Royal College of Surgeons, Edinburgh; Fellow, Royal College of Surgeons, Glasgow; Fellow, Institute of Biology; Society of Underwater Technology; Underwater Medical Society; Scottish Society for Environmental Medicine; British Medical Association; Biological Engineering Society; Intensive Care Society. *Publications:* "The Offshore Health Handbook", 1985; 'Action of oxygen on the renal circulation', 1974; 'Management of a complex diving accident', 1979. *Hobbies:* Pipe organ music; Horticulture; Boating. *Address:* Centre for Offshore Health, Robert Gordon's Institute of Technology, Kepplestone Mansion, Viewfield Road, Aberdeen AB9 2PF, Scotland.

NORRBY, Erling Carl Jacob, b. 28 Aug. 1937, Stockholm, Sweden. Professor and Chairman of Department of Virology. m. Annie Margareta Lindqvist, 12 June 1959. *Education:* MD, 1963; Dissertation, 1964; Docent of Medicine, 1964. *Appointments:* Career award, Swedish Cancer Society, 1966-72; Temporary Lecturer in Department of Virus Research 1959-66, Currently Professor and Chairman of Department of Virology, Karolinska Institute, Stockholm. *Memberships:* Advisor, World Health Organisation, 1975-; Board Member 1976-, Chairman of Information Committee 1979-85, Swedish Cancer Society; Grants Committee 1981-85, Chairman of Board for Section of Medical Microbiology 1982-84, Swedish Medical Association; Chairman of Granting Committee 1979-83, National Society for Handicapped Individuals; Chairman of Division of Virology, 1984-, International Union of Microbiological Societies; Member of the Board, King Gustav V Jubilee Fund, 1980-; Board Member, National Bacteriological Laboratory, 1983-; Advisory Committee on Vaccines, National Health Board, 1981-; Grants Committee for Prenatal Research, 1978-; Grants Committee for Microbiology, Swedish Medical Research Council, 1983-; Member 1976-82, Adjunted Member 1973-75 and 1983-, Nobel Committee, Karolinska Institute; Swedish Royal Academy of Sciences. *Publications include:* More than 250 on the structure of viruses, their replication and the mechanism of disease emergence; Editor and author of a textbook of virology; Editor of several journals. *Honours:* Master of Lecturing, Karolinska Institute, 1972; Fernström's Prize for promising young scientists, 1981. *Hobbies:* Sailing; Music; Reading; Cross-country skiing; Jogging. *Address:* Karolinska Institutet, Department of Virology, c/o SBL, S 105 21 Stockholm, Sweden.

NORRE, Marcel Emiel, b. 3 May 1930, St. Stevens Woluwe, Belgium. Head of Department of Otoneurology and Equilibriometry, University Hospital, Leuven. m. Marien Paula, 3 Jan. 1959, 3 sons. *Education:* MD; PhD, Otolaryngology. *Appointments:* ENT Surgeon Mol, Belgium, 1959; Professor and Head of Department of Otoneurology, University of Leuven, 1969. *Memberships:* Barany Society; Neurootological and Equilibriometric Society (NES); International Society of Posturography; Société Française d'Electronystagmographie; Belgische Neus-keel-oorartsen vereniging; Société Française ORL. *Publications:* "Unilateral vestibular Hypofunction Acta Otorhinolar", Belg 32, 421-668; Several articles on vestibular habituation training in medical reviews. *Hobby:* Opera. *Address:* Schotsr 2, B-3020 Herent, Belgium.

NORRIS, Charles Richard, b. 6 Jan. 1949, Danville, Illinois, USA. Director of Adult Outpatient Services. m. Francesca, 18 May 1979, Hartford, Connecticut, 1 son, 1 daughter. *Edcuation:* BS, Chemistry, Bates College; MD, University of Vermont. *Appointments:* Medical Staff, Institute of Living, Connecticut, 1979-80; Director, Alcohol and Substance Abuse, Horizon Hospital, Clearwater, Florida, 1981; Senior Staff, Institute of Living, Connecticut, 1982; Director, Adult Outpatient Services, Institute of Living, Hartford, Connecticut, 1983-. *Memberships:* APA; CPS; HPS; AMA; CMS; Hartford County Medical Society - Committee on Impaired Physicians. *Publications:* "Delayed Carbon Monoxide Encephalopathy: Clinical and Research Implications" in 'Journal of Clinical Psychiatry' 1982. *Honours:* Phi Beta Kappa, 1971; Selected to APA Committee of Residents 1977-80, Chairman 1980. *Hobbies:* Volleyball; Racquetball; Painting. *Address:* 400 Washington Street, Hartford, CT 06106, USA.

NORRIS, Lyle Guy, b. 16 Oct. 1950, Independence, Missouri, USA. Principle, Private Dental Practice. *Education:* Bachelor of Dental Science, University of Queensland, Australia, 1977. *Appointments:* Associate, Hemsley Dental Group, Luton, Bedfordshire, England, 1977-78; Member, British Civil Aviation Disaster Committee, 1977-78; Dentist-in-Charge, Central Burnett Hospital Board, Queensland, Australia, 1978; Principle, Private Practice, Caboolture, Queensland, currently; Secretary, 1981-83, Vice President, 1983-85, Federal (Hon) Secretary, 1985-87, Australian Society for Advancement in Anaesthisa and Sedation in Dentistry. *Memberships:* Federal and Queensland branches, Australian Dental Association; Australian Society for the Advancement of Anaesthesia and Sedation in Dentistry; SAAD, England; American Dental Society of Anesthesiology; Australian Society of Implant Dentistry. *Publications:* 'Eye Complications following Gow-Gates Block technique' in 'Dental Anaesthesiology and Sedation', 1982. *Honours:* Advanced Resuscitation Certificate, Royal Life Saving Society of Australia, 1979; Evaluation Certificate, Australian Society for Advancement of Anaesthesia and Sedation in Dentistry, 1981. *Hobbies:* Research into military history of World War II; Horse back riding; Piano. *Address:* Centrepoint Plaza, 42 King Street, Caboolture, Queensland 4510, Australia.

NORTH, Robert John, b. 22 Aug. 1935, Bathurst, New South Wales, Australia. Director, Trudeau Institute. m. Coralie Fox, 4 Mar. 1961, Sydney, Australia, 1 son, 2 daughters. *Education:* BSc, Biology, University of Sydney, New South Wales, Australia; PhD, Australian National University, John Curtin School of Medical Research. *Appointments:* Technical Officer, Electron Microscope Unit, University of Sydney, 1959-62; Research Assistant, Australian National University, Canberra, 1962-67; Visiting Investigator, Trudeau Institute, 1967-70, Associate Member, 1970-74, Member, 1974-76, Director, 1976-. *Memberships:* American Association of Immunobiologists; American Society for Microbiology; American Association for the Advancement of Science; The Reticuloendothelial Society; Transplantation Society. *Publications:* "Immunology of Human Infection", volume 8, part 1, p 210, 1981; 'Adv Immunology', 35, 89-153, 1984; 'Adv Cancer Res', 45, 1985. *Honours:* President,

Reticuloendothelial Society, 1983; Recipient, Distinguished Human Service Award from State University College of Arts and Sciences, Potsdam, New York, USA, 1984; Recipient, Dr Friedrick-Sasse-Stiftung Prize for Immunology, West Germany, 1984. *Hobby:* Fishing. *Address:* Trudeau Institute Inc, PO Box 59, Saranac Lake, NY 12983, USA.

NORVELL, John Edmondson III, b. 18 Nov. 1929, West Virginia, USA. Professor of Anatomy. m. Rosemary Justice, 2 June 1962, Charleston, West Virginia, 2 sons. *Education:* BSc, Biology, University of Charleston, 1953; MSc, Zoology, University of West Virginia, 1956; PhD, Anatomy, Ohio State University, 1966. *Appointments:* Instructor, Johnstown College, University of Pittsburgh, 1956-60; Assistant Professor, Otterbein College, Ohio, 1960-62; Assistant Instructor, Ohio State University, 1962-65; Assistant Professor, Medical College of Virginia, 1966-69; Associate Professor, Virginia Commonwealth University, Medical College of Virginia, 1969-76; Professor & Chairman, Department of Anatomy, School of Medicine, Oral Roberts University, Tulsa, 1976-; Visiting Professor, University of Nairobi, Kenya, 1982. *Memberships:* Transplantation Society, 1970-; American Association for the Advancement of Science, 1954-, American Association of Anatomists, 1969-; Association of Anatomy Chairman 1976-; Association of American Medical Colleges, 1976-; Oklahoma State Anatomical Board, Chairman 1978-; Sigma Xi, 1967-. *Publications:* "Human Anatomy - A Programme Text", 1968; "Atlas of Neuroanatomy" 4th edition, 1976; "The Inferior Extremity as seen in Crosssection", 1978; "Atlas of Cross-section of the Human Body", 1982; Numerous publications in professional journals, 1968-86. *Hobby:* Scuba Diving. *Address:* Department of Anatomy, School of Medicine, Oral Roberts University, Tulsa, OK 74171, USA.

NOVOTNY, George Milos, b. 7 Mar. 1929, Prague, Czechoslovakia, Professor, Head of Department. m. Elfriede Anna Gruber, 20 Dec. 1952, 2 daughters. *Education:* MD, University of Toronto School of Medicine, 1958; Residency in Otolaryngology, Surgery, Queen's University, Kingston, Ontario, Canada; Otolaryng, McGill University, Montreal, Canada; FRCS (C) Royal College of Physicians and Surgeons, Canada, 1969; FACS, American College of Surgeons, 1971; CD. *Appointments:* Head, Department of Otolaryngology, Canadian Forces Hospital, Halifax, Canada, 1967; Fellow, 1967, Professor, Head, 1974-, Department of Otolaryngology, Residency Programme Director, 1973, Research Associate, Department of Psychology, 1978, Associate Professor, School of Human Communications Disorders, 1977, Darhousie University, Halifax, Canada; Head, Department of Otolaryngology, Victoria General Hospital, 1974; Head, Department of Otolaryngology, Halifax Infirmary, Canada, 1979. *Memberships:* University of Toronto Medical Alumni; Canadian Forces Medical Service Officers Association; American Council of Otolaryngology; Canadian Society of Laryngology; Canadian Society of Aviation Medicine; Society of Academic Chairman of Otolar; Royal Society of Medicine; Eastern Canada Otolaryngology Society; Canadian Medical Association; American Academy of Otolaryngology; Nova Scotia Medical Society; Halifax Medical Society; Dartmouth Medical Society. *Publications:* 'Tumours of Major Salivary Glands', 1968; 'Synovial Sarcoma of the Tongue', 1971; 'Gustatory Sweating and Related Syndromes', 1976; 'Cochlear Densis', 1980. *Honours:* Canadian Decoration, 1969; Clasp, 1979; Queen's Silver Jubilee Medal, 1977; President, Eastern Canada Otolaryngology Society, 1978-79; President, Canadian Society Otolaryngology, 1983-84; Honour Award, Canadian Society of Otolaryngology, Head and Neck Surgery, 1985. *Hobbies:* Skiing; Golf; Sailing; Gardening; Painting; Art appreciation. *Address:* Department of Otolaryngology, Dalhousie University, c/o Halifax Infirmary, Halifax, Nova Scotia, Canada B3J 2H6.

NOWOSLAWSKI, Adam, b. 30 Apr. 1925, Rzeszow,

Poland. Head of Department of Immunopathology. m. Wieslawa Grzegorzewska, 31 Aug. 1959, Warszawa. *Education:* Graduate, Medical Academy of Warsaw, 1951; Diplomate, Polish Board of Anatomic Pathology, 1959; MD, Medical Academy of Warsaw, 1963; Doctor Habilitatus of Medicine, National Institute of Hygiene, Warsaw, 1966. *Appointments:* Assistant Professor, Department of Anatomic Pathology, Medical Academy, Warsaw, 1952-64; Research Fellow, Laboratory of Pathology, Hospital for Special Surgery, Cornell University Medical Center, New York City, 1960; currently Head of Department of Immunopathology, National Institute of Hygiene, Warsaw. *Memberships:* Polish Society of Pathologists; Polish Society of Immunology; International Cell Research Organization; Polish Academy of Sciences. *Publications include:* "Immunopathological aspects of hepatitis type B" in American Journal of Medical Science, 1975; "Hepatitis B virus-induced immune complex disease" in "Progress on Liver Diseases" 1979. *Honours:* Polish National Prize, 1966; Polish Academy of Sciences Award, 1969. *Hobby:* Collecting old microscopes. *Address:* Department of Immunopathology, Microbiology and Epidemiology Division, National Institute of Hygiene, ul Chocimska 24, 00-791 Warsaw, Poland.

NOWAK, Stanislaw Zygmunt, b. 28 Jan. 1917, Wielgomlyny, Poland. Professor and Head. Paediatric Clinic. m. 18 Nov. 1944, Niedospielin, 3 sons, 1 daughter. *Education includes:* Graduate Diploma, 1948, Diploma of Specialist, 1954, University of Poznan; MD, Medical Academy of Poznan, 1954; Diploma of Habilitation, Lecturer Diploma, 1963. *Appointments:* Member, 1948, Paediatric Department, University of Poznan, 1948-65; Assistant Adjunct, Lecturer, Medical Academy in Poznan, 1950-; Head, 1965-, Professor, 1978, 11 Pediatric Clinic, Medical Academy of Lodz. *Memberships:* Polish Paediatric Association; Polish Diabetologic Association; Societas Scientiarum Lodzensis; International Diabetes Federation; European Association for the Study of Diabetes; Polish Physicians Association. *Publications:* "Focal infection and its influence on adrenal glands", 1963; "Serological incompatibility in neonates", Handbook, 1966; "Propaedeutics in paediatrics", textbook for students, 6th edition, 1984; "Epidemiology of Diabetes in Children", 1985; "Blood platelets aggregation and retinopathy in children", 1981. *Hobbies:* Music; Chess; Mountain trips. *Address:* ul Brzezna 14 m, 90-303 Lodz, Poland.

NOZAKI, Mitsuhiro, b. 11 Nov. 1931, Osaka, Japan. Professor. m. 3 Feb. 1963, Osaka, 2 daughters. *Education:* BS, Department of Biology, 1954, PhD, Department of Biochemistry, 1958, Faculty of Science, Osaka University. *Appointments:* Research Biochemist, Department of Plant Physiology, University of California, Berkeley, California, USA, 1958-62; Assistant Professor, Department of Biochemistry, Osaka University School of Medicine, Osaka, Japan, 1962-63; Assistant Professor 1963-64, Associate Professor 1964-75, Department of Medical Chemistry, Kyoto University Faculty of Medicine, Kyoto; Professor, Department of Biochemistry, Shiga University of Medical Science, Ohtsu, Shiga, 1975-. *Memberships:* Japanese Biochemical Society; Japanese Society of Clinical Chemistry. *Publications:* "Oxygenases and dioxygenases' in "Topics in Current Chemistry", 1979; "Oxygenases and Oxygen Metabolism" (coeditor), 1982; 'Dioxygenases and Monooxygenases' in "The Biology and Chemistry of Active Oxygen", 1984. *Hobby:* Tennis. *Address:* Department of Biochemistry, Shiga University of Medical Science, Seta, Ohtsu, Shiga 520-21, Japan.

NSEYO, Unyime, b. 30 Oct. 1948, Nigeria. Oncologic Research Clinician; Clinical Co-ordinator. Photodynamic Therapy Center. m. Grace Utuk, 16 June 1984, Buffalo, New York, USA. 1 daughter. *Education:* BS, University of Oregon, 1972; MD, University of Missouri, 1976; Postgraduate training: Ellis Fischel Cancer Hospital, University of Missouri Columbia Medical Center; University of Michigan Hospitals;

Roswell Park Memorial Institute, Buffalo; Albany Medical College. *Appointments:* Teaching Assistantship, Anatomy, University of Missouri Medical School, Columbia, 1973-75; Assistant Instructor, Urology, 1980-81, Instructor, Urology, 1981-82, Albany Medical College, New York. *Memberships:* American Medical Association; American Association for the Advancement of Science; American Society for Laser Medicine and Surgery; National Medical Association; New York Academy of Sciences; New York State Urological Association; Western Biolaser Institute. 2Publications include: Scientific and Clinical Papers presented at Meetings; Contributor to professional Journals including 'Urology Times'; 'Journal of Urology'; 'Lasers in Medicine and Surgery'. *Honours include:* Roswell Park Memorial Institute Resident Award for Outstanding Contributions to Clinical and Basic Science, 1984. *Hobbies:* Running (long distance races); Tennis; Art; Jazz and Traditional Music. *Address:* Roswell Park Memorial Institute, 666 Elm Street, Buffalo, NY 14263, USA.

NUCHPRAYOON, Chaivej, b. 3 Apr. 1938, Thailand. Associate Professor, Medicine, Chulalongkorn University; Director, Anti-TB Hospital, Bangkok; President, Thai Chapter, American College of Chest Physicians. m. Thassanee Pornpiboon, 22 June 1966, Washington DC, USA, 1 son, 1 daughter. *Education:* MD, cum laude, University of Medical Sciences, Bangkok, 1962; MS, University of Chicago, 1966; Certificate of Proficience, Chest Diseases, Thai Medical Council, 1973. *Appointments:* Instructor, 1967-70, Lecturer, 1970-75, Assistant Professor, 1975-78, Associate Professor, 1978-, Associate Dean, 1981-85, Medicine, Chulalongkorn University, Bangkok. *Memberships:* Medical Association of Thailand; Thai Medical Council; American Thoracic Society; American College of Chest Physicians. *Publications:* Text Book, "Fiberoptic Bronchoscopy", 1984; Contributor to numerous professional journals including 'American Review of Respiratory Diseases'; 'Journal of the Medical Association of Thailand'; 'Siriraj Medical Gazette'; etc. *Honours:* Fulbright Travel Grant for Postgraduate Study in USA, 1964; Eudowood Fellowship, ACCP, 1965-66; Visiting Associate Professor, University of Iowa, USA, 1978. *Hobbies:* Swimming; Thai Classical Music. *Address:* Dept. of Medicine, Chulalongkorn Hospital, Bangkok 10500, Thailand.

NUSS, Robert Conrad, b. 11 Sep. 1937, Boyertown, Pennsylvania, USA. Associate Professor, University of Florida College of Medicine, Department of Obstetrics & Gynaecology; Director, Division of Gynaecology. m. Ann L Harwood, MD, 21 Sep. 1984, Jacksonville, 3 daughters. *Education:* BS, Muhlenberg College, Allentown, Pennsylvania; MD, Thomas Jefferson Medical School, Philadelphia. *Appointments include:* Chief, Department of Obstetrics & Gynaecology, Cherry Point Naval Hospital, North Carolina, 1967-69, Jacksonville Naval Hospital, Florida, 1969-70; Associate Professor, Hahnemann Medical College, Philadelphia, 1970-72. *Memberships:* Fellow, American College of Obstetricians & Gynaecologists; American Association of Gynaecological Laparoscopists; American Society of Colposcopy & Cervical Pathology; South Atlantic Association of Obstetricians & Gynaecologists; Society of Gynaecologic Oncologists; American Radium Society; Various state, local, military associations. *Publications include:* Contributions to professional journals; Abstracts; Presentations to medical conferences. *Honours:* Award, Florida Medical Association; Award, American Medical Association, Physician's Recognition; JHEP, OB/GYN Alumni Association, outstanding teaching award. *Hobbies:* Sport; Travel; Reading;

Woodwork. *Address:* University Hospital of Jacksonville, 655 West 8th Street, Jacksonville, FL 32209, USA.

NUSSDORFER, Gastone Giovanni, b. 28 Nov. 1943, Venice. Professor of Anatomy. *Education:* MD, Padua University, 1967. *Appointments:* Assistant Professor, 1967-70, Assistant Professor with Annual Teaching Contract, 1971-74, Full Professor of Anatomy, 1975, University of Padua. *Publications:* "International Review of Cytology" 1978, 1980; "Cytophysiology of the Adrenal Cortex" 1986. *Honour:* Angelo Minich Prize for Medicine, 1971. *Hobby:* Baroque chamber music. *Address:* Istituto di Anatomia Umana Normale, University of Padova, Via Gabelli 65, I-35100 Padova, Italy.

NUTIK, Gordon Philip, b. 22 Jan. 1948, Montreal, Canada. Orthopaedic Surgeon. m. Rickie, 1971, 1 son, 2 daughters. *Education:* BSc, 1969; MSCM, 1973; MSc, 1975. *Appointment:* Practice of Orthopaedic Surgery, New Orleans, 1978-85. *Memberships:* American Medical Association; American Academy of Orthopaedic Surgeons. *Honour:* Assistant Professor, Tulane University, Department of Orthopaedics. *Hobbies:* Clock Repairing; Architecture; Model Railroading. *Address:* 3525 Prytania Street, New Orleans, LA 70115, USA.

NUTTALL, Richard Norris, b. 7 Feb. 1940, Canada. President, Rutland Consulting Group Ltd. m. E Jane Pickering, 9 July 1977, Ottawa, 2 sons. *Education:* MPA, MB BS, CMC (Certified Management Consultant, Canadian Institutes of Management Consultants); FACPM (Fellow, American College of Preventive Medicine). *Appointments:* Regional Director, Alberta Region, Department of National Health and Welfare; President, Rutland Consulting Group Ltd. *Memberships:* Canadian Medical Association; Canadian College of Health Service Executives; American College of Healthcare Executives. *Address:* 3220, 666 Burrard Street, Vancouver, British Columbia, Canada V6C 2X8.

NYGREN, Lars Åke, b. 10 Nov. 1937, Grundsunda, Sweden. Medical Expert at Research and Development Division, Folksam Insurance Company. m. Elin Carin Birgitta Nylander, 8 July 1961, Själevad, 1 son, 1 daughter. *Education:* DDS, 1963; MD, 1973; Karolinska Institute; Licentiat in Medicine and Surgery, University of Barcelona, 1978; Dr Med Sc, Karolinska Institute, 1984. *Appointments:* Private Practice, Dentistry, Stockholm, 1963-73; Clinical training in traumatology, Karolinska Hospital, Huddings Hospital and Sodersjukhuset, 1973-78; Consultant, The National Board of Health and Welfare, Stockholm, Sweden, 1976-; Medical Expert, Folksam Insurance Company, Traffic Medicine, 1978-85, Folksam Research and Development Division, 1985-; Associate Professor, Karolinska Institute, Stockholm, 1985-; Adjunct Professor, Chalmers University of Technology, Göteborg, 1986. *Memberships:* Member of Board of Swedish Association of Traffic Medicin belonging to The Swedish Society on Medical Sciences, Stockholm, 1978-; American Association for Automotive Medicine; Member, Scientific Committee, OECO, Paris. *Publications:* 'Injuries to Car Occupants: Some Aspects of the Interior Safety of Cars', 'Acta Otolaryngol'. Stockholm Supplement 395, 1984; 'The Protective Effect of a Special Designed Suit for Motorcyclists' in Proceedings of Tenth ESV Conference, 1985. *Hobbies:* Outdoor Life; Language Studies. *Address:* Research and Development Division, Folksam Insurance Company, Box 20500 S-10460 Stockholm, Sweden.

O

O'BANNION, Mindy Martha, b. 19 Aug. 1953, Cushing, Oklahoma, USA. Registered Nurse. m. William Neal O'Bannion, 9 Oct. 1976, Cushing, Oklahoma, 1 son, 1 daughter. *Education:* Oklahoma State University, 1971-72; Oscar Rose Junior College, 1972; Diploma, Professional Nursing, St Anthony Hospital School of Nursing, Oklahoma City, 1972-75. *Appointments:* Charge Nurse, 1975-76, Staff Nurse, 1978-79, Team Leader, 1982-83, Cushing Regional Hospital; Staff, Medical-Surgical Unit, Metropolitan Hospital, Dallas, 1985-; Staff, Medical Unit, Mesquite Community Hospital, Texas, 1985-. *Memberships:* American, Texas and Oklahoma Nurses Associations. *Hobbies:* Gardening; Dish Collection; Antiques. *Address:* 6631 Day, Dallas, TX 75227, USA.

O'CONNELL, Barbara Eustace, b. 25 June 1926, Boston, Massachusetts, USA. Psychiatrist, Private Practice. m. George J Halpern, MD, 19 Dec. 1981, Rye, 1 son, 3 daughters. *Education:* BA, Cornell University, 1947; MD, Columbia University, 1951; Internship, Strong Memorial Hospital, 1951-53; Residency, Psychiatry, Bronx Municipal Hospital Centre, 1958-61; Diplomate, National Board of Medical Examiners, 1952; American Board of Psychiatry & Neurology (P) 1978; American Psychiatric Association, Fellow, 1978. *Appointments:* General Practice, Medicine, Bergenfield and Cresskill, New Jersey, 1953-56; Assistant to Chairman of Dept. of Anthropology, American Museum of Natural History, 1954-55; General Practice, Psychiatry, Mamaroneck-Rye, 1961-85; Clinical Instructor, Psychiatry, Albert Einstein College of Medicine, 1961-66; Clinical Assistant Professor, Cornell University Medical College, 1976-85; Visiting Physician: Englewood Hospital, 1954-56, Holy Name Hospital, Teaneck, 1954-56; Psychiatrist, Bronx Municipal Hospital Centre, 1961-66; Courtesy Staff, United Hospital, Port Chester, 1966-75; Assistant Attending Psychiatrist, Cornell Medical Centre, New York Hospital, (Westchester Division), White Plains, 1976-85. *Memberships:* American Medical Association; Westchester County Medical Society; American Psychiatric Association; Society of Adolescent Psychiatry; Medical Society of the State of New York; many other professional organisations. *Publications:* "Viewpoints: Is There a Need for Men's Liberation?", 'Medical Aspects of Human Sexuality', Volume 10, No 7, 1976; "The Evolution of a Professional Support System for Women Physicians", 'Psychiatric Annals', volume 7, No 4, co-author, 1977; "Women's Reactions to 'Wolf Whistles' and Lewd Remarks", 'Medical Aspects of Human Sexuality', Volume 11, No 10, co-author, 1977. *Hobbies:* Sailing; Gardening; Tennis; Photography; Bridge; Chess. *Address:* 240 Brevoort Lane, Rye, NY 10580, USA.

O'CONNELL, Ralph Anthony, b. 26 Jan. 1938, New York, USA. Associate Director, Psychiatry, St Vincent's Hospital & Medical Centre, New York; Clinical Professor, Psychiatry, New York Medical College; Editor-in-Chief, 'Comprehensive Psychiatry'. m. Jane Burke, 15 June 1963, New York, 2 sons, 1 daughter. *Education:* AB, cum laude, College of the Holy Cross, Worcester, 1959; MD, Cornell University Medical College, 1963. *Appointments:* Chief, Inpatient Service, Psychiatry, St Vincent's Hospital & Medical Centre, 1971-76. *Memberships:* Fellow, American Psychiatric Association; New York Academy of Medicine, American Psychopathological Association; Examiner, American Board of Psychiatry & Neurology Inc; Secretary, American Committee for the Prevention and Treatment of Depression; American Medical Association; New York Psychiatric Society; World Psychiatric Society. *Publications:* "Depression: Bipolar or Unipolar? Directions in Psychiatry", 1983; Editorial, Editor-in-Chief, Comprehensive Psychiatry, Volume 24, 1983; "Commentary on Characterological Manifestations of Affective Disorder" by Akiskal, HS, 'Intergrative Psychiatry', 1984; "Time-limited treatment: The DRG challenge in Common Treatment Problems in Depression", Schatzberg AF (ed), Washington, Dc, "American Psychiatric Press Inc, 1985; Co-author, "Social support and long-term lithium outcome", 'British J Psychiatry, 1985. *Address:* 144 West 12th Street, New York, NY 10011, USA.

ODA, Teiichi, b. 22 Sep. 1928, Seoul, Korea. Professor, Chairman, Pediatrics, School of Medicine, Fukuoka University. m. Sachiko Kano, 5 May 1954, Fukuoka, 1 son, 2 daughters. *Education:* MD, 1953; DMSc, 1958, Kyushu University; Fellow, American College of Chest Physicians. *Appointments:* Resident, Kyushu University Hospital; Pediatric Staff, Kyushu Welfare Penaion Hospital; Lecturer, Kyushu University; Research Fellow, Cardiovascular Research Institute, University of California, San Francisco; Associate Professor, Kyushu University. *Memberships:* New York Academy of Sciences; Executive Member, Japanese Society of Pediatrics; Japan Society of Pediatric Cardiology; Japanese Society of Pediatric Pulmonology; Japanese Society of Rheumatology; Japanese Society of Biological Interface for Medicine. *Publications:* "Rheumatic Fever", 1964; "Pediatric Cardiology", 1973; "Pediatric Pulmonary Function", 1977; Co-author, 24 Textbooks, 270 papers on pediatric cardiology, pulmonology and rheumatology, coenzyme q10 and mitral valve prolapse. *Honours:* Honorary Member, National Society for Prevention of Heart Disease, India. *Hobby:* Recorded Music. *Address:* 2-9-24 Heiwa, Minamiku, Fukuoka 815, Japan.

ØDEGAARD, Kristian, b. 26 Mar. 1913, Norway. Bacteriologist. m. Ingebøorg Andrup, 23 June 1945, 2 sons, 1 daughter. *Education:* Approved Specialist in Dermatology & Venereology and Medical Microbiology, 1950; Academic Postgraduate Certificate in Applied Parasitology & Entomology, University of London, 1960. *Appointments:* Resident, Department of Microbiology & Dermatology, Rikshospitalet, Oslo; Resident, Department of Dermatology, Ulleval Hospital, Oslo; Deputy Chief, Department of Bacteriology, National Institute of Public Health, Oslo, 1957-83. *Memberships:* International Society of Tropical Dermatology; Norwegian Society of Dermatology (President 1955-57); Norwegian Society of Medical Microbiology. *Publications:* Various articles in field in medical journals. *Hobby:* Gardening. *Address:* Svenstuveien 4 B, 0389 Oslo 3, Norway.

ODELL, William D, b. 11 June 1929, California, USA. Professor, Chairman, Internal Medicine, University of Utah School of Medicine. m. Margaret F Reilly, 19 Aug. 1950, Orinda, 4 sons, 1 daughter. *Education:* AB, University of California, Berkeley, 1952; MD, University of Chicago, 1956; PhD, George Washington University, 1965. *Appointments:* Resident, Chief Resident, Internal Medicine, Postdoctoral Fellow, Endocrinology, University of Washington, 1956-60; Senior Investigator, National Cancer Institute, 1960-65; Chief, Endocrine Service, National Institute Child Health & Human Development, 1965-66; Chief, Endocrinology and Metabolism, Harbor UCLA Medical Centre, 1960-72; Professor, Chairman, Internal Medicine, Harbor UCLA Medical Centre, 1972-79; Visiting Professor, University of Auckland, New Zealand, 1979-80; Professor, Chairman, Internal Medicine, University of Utah Medical School, 1980-. *Memberships:* American College of Physicians; American Society for Clinical Investigation; Association of American Physicians; American Physiological Society; Endocrine Society, Vice President, 1972-73; Western Association of Physicians, President, 1986-87; American Andrology Society, President, 1986-87; Pacific Coast Fertility Society, President, 1977-78. *Publications:* Over 250 scientific articles including 5 books. *Honours:* Distinguished Service Award, University of Chicago, 1973; First Pharmacia Award, 1977; Squibb Research Awards, 1978, 1982; Member, American Board Internal Medicine, 1982-83, Chairman Subsection on Endocrinology and Metabolism. *Hobbies:* Golf; Backpacking; Trout Fishing; Running; Woodwork. *Address:* University of Utah Medical School, Dept. of Internal Medicine, 50 North Medical Drive, Salt Lake City, UT 84132, USA.

OECKERMAN, Per-Arne, b. 31 Aug. 1933, Göteborg, Sweden. Professor. *Education:* MD 1960; PhD 1965. *Appointments:* Assistant, Physiological Chemistry, Uppsala, 1957-60; Physician, Clinical Chemistry, Eskilstuna, 1960-65; Boden, 1965-66; Assistant Professor, Chemistry, 1966-69, Professor, Chemistry, 1969-. *Memberships:* Swedish Society of Clinical Chemistry (Chairman, retired); Biochemical Society (London); World Association Societies of Pathology (Swedish Representative). *Publications:* About 200 papers in clinical chemistry, nutrition and pediatrics. *Honour:* Royal Order of North Star, 1975. *Hobbies:* Ocean Sailing; Skiing; Stamps. *Address:* Department Clinical Chemistry, University Hospital S-22185 Lund, Sweden.

OEDING, Per, b. 5 Feb. 1916, Oslo, Norway. Professor of Medical Microbiology. University of Bergen. m. Birit Ottersland, 10 May 1941, Arendal, 1 son, 1 daughter. *Education:* MD, University of Oslo, 1949. *Appointments:* Resident, Microbiology, Internal Medicine, Surgery, Rikshospitalet, Oslo, 1945-48, Dermatology, 1948-49; Professor, Medical Microbiology, 1949, Vice-Dean, Medical Faculty, 1961-66, Dean, 1967-70, Prorector, 1969-70, University of Bergen; Medical Board and Senate, Norwegian Research Council, 1966-73. *Memberships:* Norwegian Academy of Science; American Association for the Advancement of Science; American Society of Microbiology. *Publications:* Approximately 230 articles on Bacteriology, Immunology, 1940-; Co-author several scientific books. *Address:* Professorvei 4, 5032 Minde, Norway.

OFFENKRANTZ, William Charles, b. 2 Sep. 1924, Newark, New Jersey, USA. Professor of Psychoanalysis & Psychiatry. m. Sandra Topp, 15 Nov. 1982, Milwaukee, 2 sons. *Education:* BS, Biological Science, Rutgers University, 1945; MD, Columbia University College of Physicians & Surgeons, New York, 1947; Certification, American Board of Psychiatry & Neurology, 1954; Certificate in Psychoanalysis, William Alanson White Institute, New York, 1957; Certificate in Psychoanalysis, Chicago Institute for Psychoanalysis, 1966. *Appointments:* Assistant Clinical Professor of Psychiatry, University of Southern California School of Medicine, 1957; Director of Residency Training in Psychiatry, University of Chicago School of Medicine, 1958-69; Professor, Department of Psychiatry, University of Chicago School of Medicine, 1957-79; Professor of Psychoanalysis & Psychiatry, Medical College of Wisconsin, 1979-. *Memberships:* Life Fellow, American Psychiatric Association, 1985; Certified Member, American Psychoanalytic Association, 1968; Group for the Advancement of Psychiatry, 1962. *Publications:* Various articles in Psychoanactic & psychiatric journals. *Hobbies:* Tennis; Jazz. *Address:* 2321 E Stratford Court, Milwaukee, WI 53211, USA.

OGBORNE, Warren Lambert. *Education:* MB, BS, Sydney University Faculty of Medicine, Australia, 1953-59; MRCP Ed, 1959; FRACGP, 1969; FRCP Ed, 1983. *Appointments:* JRMO, 1959, SRMO, 1960, Honorary Associate Physician, 1963-69, Honorary Physician, 1969-74, Parramatta District Hospital, New South Wales, Australia; RMO, Chase Farm Hospital, Enfield, Middlesex, England, 1961; Medical Registrar, Bolinbroke Hospital, London, 1962; Outpatients Registrar, Edgware General Hospital, London, 1962; Locum in General Practice, Middlesex, 1963; Locum in General Practice, Blacktown, New South Wales, Australia, 1963; Group General Practice, Ermington, New South Wales, 1964-74; Honorary Medical Officer, Yallambi Home for the Aged, Carlingford, 1966-74; Honorary Medical Officer, Burnside Children's Homes, North Parramatta, 1970-74; Medical Educator/Associate State Director, Family Medicine Programme, RACGP, 1974-; Part-Time Consulting Medical Practice, Parramatta, New South Wales, 1975-; Member, Medical Education Committee, NSW Faculty, RACGP, 1969-; Examiner for Fellowship, RACGP, 1959-; Chairman of Panel of Examiners, 1972-73, Faculty Censor, 1972-73, NSW Faculty, RACGP; Clinical Lecturer, Department of Community Medicine, University of New South Wales, 1973-; Part-time Clinical Lecturer, Department of Community Medicine, University of Sydney, 1975-; Member, NSW Co-ordinating Committee in Family Planning Education, 1978-; Member, National Education Advisory Committee, AFFPA, 1979-; Visiting Lecturer, School of Nursing, Royal North Shore Hospital, St Leonards, 1978-; Chairman, Medical and Academic Staff Association Family Medicine Programme, 1980-, Chairman, 1983 Examination Review Working Party, 1983, RACGP. *Publications:* "Take Care of Yourself", (with Donald M Vickery, James F Fries, Lou Goldman, Doug Killer, June Raine), 1981; "Choices - a patient booklet about family planning", (with Audrie Wray, Wendy McCarthy, Rodney Shearman), 1980; 'RACGP Handbook for Candidates on Fellowship by Examination and Assessment", 1978. *Address:* Family Medicine Programme, 48 Albany Street, St Leonard, NSW 2065, Australia.

OGNYANOV, Karl Ivanov, b. 28 Feb. 1916, Sofia, Bulgaria. Professor, Director, I Clinic of Obstetrics and Gynaecology, T Korkowa; Consultant, Research Institute of Obstetrics and Gynaecology, Medical Academy. m. Angelina Grigorowa Wassilewa, 27 Feb. 1944. *Education:* MD, Medical Faculty, Sofia, 1942; DSc, 1976. *Appointments:* Assistant Professor, University Clinic Obstetrics and Gynaecology, 1945-50; Chief, Department of Obstetrics and Gynaecology, District Hospital, Burgas, 1950-52; Head, Department, I and II Clinic, Sofia, 1953-72; Senior Research Worker, Higher Medical Institute, Sofia, 1972-77; Professor, Head of Chair, Institute Obstetrics and Gynaecology, Medical Academy Sofia, 1977-82; Director, I Clinic, Obstetrics and Gynaecology T Korkowa and Consultant Professor, Medical Academy, Sofia, 1982-. *Memberships include:* European Association of Perinatal Medicine; International Society of Immunology and Reproduction. *Publications:* Diagnostic Difficulties in Obstetrics and Gynaecology, 1966; Surgery of the Abdominal Wall and Intestines in Gynaecological Operation, 1967; Haemolytic Disease of the Newborn, 1969, 78; Physiology of the Foetus in The Foetus at Risk, 1973; Factors for Premature Labour in the Big City, 1975; Pregnancy Zone Protein in Normal and Pathological Pregnancies, 1979. *Honours include:* Medal for Contribution in Scientific and Technical Progress, 1978; Award and Medal for Discovery, State Committee Science, 1983. *Hobbies:* Hiking; Reading; Mountaineering. *Address:* Director I Clinic of Obstetrics and Gynaecology T Kirkowa, 2 Mihalaki Tashev Street, 1330 Sofia, Bulgaria.

OGSTON, Derek, b. 31 May 1932, Aberdeen, Scotland. Professor of Medicine, Dean. m. Cecilia Marie Clark, 19 July 1963, Aberdeen, 1 son, 2 daughters. *Education:* MA 1952, MB, CHB, 1957, PhD, 1962, MD, 1969, DSc, 1975, University of Aberdeen; DTM & H, University of Edinburgh, 1959. *Appointments:* Lecturer, Senior Lecturer, Reader in Medicine, University of Aberdeen, 1962-76; Regius Professor of Physiology, University of Aberdeen, 1977-83; Professor of Medicine, Dean, Faculty of Medicine, 1983-. *Memberships:* Association of Physicians of Great Britain; General Medical Council. *Publications:* (Co-editor) "Haemostasis: Biochemistry, Physiology & Pathology", 1977; "The Physiology of Haemostasis", 1983; "Antifibrinolytic Drugs: Chemistry, Pharmacology & Clinical Usage", 1984. *Address:* Department of Medicine, Phase II Building, Aberdeen Royal Infirmary, Foresterhill, Aberdeen, Scotland.

OH, Jang Ok, b. 15 Jan. 1927, Seoul, Korea. Associate Director, Francis I Proctor Foundation. m. Won Y Hyun, 16 June 1955, Erie, Pennsylvania, USA, 1 son. *Education:* MD, Yonsei University College of Medicine, Seoul, Korea, 1944-48; Resident Doctor, Pathology, Hamot Hospital, Erie, Pennsylvania, USA, 1953-55; PhD, University of Washington School of

Medicine, 1956-60. *Appointments:* Pathologist, Carle Clinic Hospital, Urbana, Illinois, USA, 1955-56; Instructor, University of Washington, Seattle, 1956-61; Assistant Professor of Pathology, University of British Columbia, Vancouver, Canada, 1961-66; Associate Research Microbiologist, 1967-70; Research Microbiologist, 1970-, Associate Director, 1984-, Francis I Proctor Foundation, San Francisco, California; Consultant, National Institutes of Health, US Public Health Service, Washington DC, 1979-83. *Memberships:* Member, Programme Committee Chairman, Association for Research In Vision & Ophthalmology USA; American Association for Pathologists; American Society of Microbiology; Society for Experimental Biology & Medicine. *Publications:* Editor, Monograph on Herpetic Eye Infections, 1976; Over 70 scientific & medical articles in various medical journals, many chapters in medical monographs & textbooks. *Honours:* Lederle Medical Faculty Award, 1963; Honorable Mention, Medical Exhibit, American Medical Association; Research Grant Awards, US Public Health Service, 1970-. *Hobbies:* English Literature; Carpentry; Gardening. *Address:* Francis I Proctor Foundation, University of California, San Francisco, CA 94143, USA.

OH, Suk-Whan, b. 20 Oct. 1926, Seoul, Republic of Korea. Professor: Chairman. m. Jung-Sook Lee, 6 Sep. 1961, Seoul, 1 son, 1 daughter. *Education:* MD, College of Medicine Seoul National University, Seoul, Korea; PhD, Graduate School, Pusan National University. *Appointments:* Professor; Chairman, Department of Neuropsychiatry, Dean, College of Medicine, Pusan National University; President, Chairman, Korean Neuropsychiatric Association. *Memberships:* Korean Neuropsychiatric Association; Korean Neurological Association; Korean Social Psychiatric Association; American Psychiatric Association; International College of Psychosomatic Medicine. *Publications:* 'The Etiological Significance of Interpersonal Environment of Korean Mental Patients', 1963; 'The Study on the Maternal Attitude by PARI', 1967; 'Sociopsychiatric Study of Epilepsy', 1971; 'Perceptions of Illness Etiology by Psychiatric Patients', 1976; 'A Study on the Diagnosis of Schizophrenia', 1977. *Hobbies:* Music; Hiking. *Address:* Inje College Paik Hospital, 85, 2-Ka, Jurdong, Chung-Ku, Seoul, Korea.

OHBA, Hidekazu, b. 9 Dec. 1915, Tokyo, Japan. Director, Dental Clinic. m. Anita Marie Lococo, 16 Jan. 1981, Honolulu, Hawaii, 1 son, 2 daughters. *Education:* Doctor of Dental Surgery, Nihon University Dental College, 1938; MD, Hokkaido University, Japan; School of Dentistry, Washington University, USA, 1961-65; Postgraduate study, University of California at Los Angeles, Oregon University, 1970. *Appointments:* Director, 808 Dispensary, Major, National Safety Forces, 1951; Committee Member, Japan Dental Association, 1967; Director-General, World Council Academies of General Dentistry, Professor, Toho Dental College, 1969; Director, Olympia Ohba Dental Clinic, Tokyo, Japan; President, Aloha Orchid Inc. *Memberships:* Academy of General Dentistry 1965-; Seabornia Mens Club, Japan. *Publications:* "Ceramco Restoration", 1969; "English Conversation for Clinical Dentistry", 1973; "How to Practise Modern Dentistry through English Conversation", 1979. *Honours:* Honorary Citizen of Portland, Oregon, 1965, Honorary Sheriff, Texas, 1969, Honorary Citizen, Los Angeles, 1970; Letter of Appreciation, Japan Dental Association, 1973. *Hobbies:* Yachting; Power-boat Cruising; Water-skiing; Ice-skating; Shooting; Dancing; Jazz. *Address:* Olympia Ohba Dental Clinic, 203 Olympia Annex 6-chome, Jingu-mae, Shibuya-ku, Tokyo 150, Japan.

OHNESORGE, Friedrich Karl Hans Erich, b. 20 Nov. 1925, Prenzlau, Germany. Professor. m. Ursula Kempf, 1 July 1955, 2 sons, 1 daughter. *Education:* Civil Service Examination in Medicine, MD, 1955, Habilitation, Pharmacology & Toxicology, 1960, University of Kiel, Federal Republic of Germany. *Appointments:* Assistant, 1957-64, Senior Assistant, 1964-67, Professor, 1967-74, Institute of Pharmacology, University of Kiel; Head, Department of Toxicology, University of Kiel, 1969-74; Professor, Director, Institute for Toxicology, Faculty of Medicine, University of Düsseldorf, 1974-. *Memberships:* German Pharmacological Society; European Association of Poison Control Centres; Scientific Commission of Pesticides, CEC; Federal Drinking Water Commission; and others. *Publications:* Various, in fields of pesticides, heavy metals & risk assessment. *Hobbies:* Classical Music; Nature. *Address:* G Hauptmann-Weg 5. D-4021 Mettmann, Federal Republic of Germany.

OHTA, Yasuyuki, b. 5 Nov. 1929, Osaka, Japan. Professor of Medicine. m. Tsuneko Yokata, 20 May 1958, 1 son. *Education:* Dr Med Sci, Okayama University, 1960. *Appointments:* Intern, Shikoku Railway Road Hospital, 1953-54; Resident 1954-57, Assistant Professor, 1957-61, 1963-75, Okayama University Medical School; Professor, Ehime University Medical School, 1976-. *Memberships:* New York Academy of Science; International Association for the Study of Liver Diseases; Asian Pacific Association for the Study of the Liver. *Publications include:* Books: "Handbook of Internal Medicine", 1961; "Hepatocellular Carcinoma", 1976; "Etiology of Liver Cirrhosis in Japan", 1984. Articles: "Fatty cirrhosis in the rat" (American Journal of Pathology, 1963); 'Gastroenterology: Intranuclear virus-like particles in an asymptomatic HBsAg carrier', 1975. *Honour:* President, 27th Annual Meeting, Japanese Society of Gastroenterology, 1985. *Hobby:* Listening to music. *Address:* Department of Internal Medicine, Ehime University, Shigenobu-cho, Onsen-gun, Ehime 791-02, Japan.

OKASHA, Ahmed Mahmoud, b. 2 Feb. 1935, Cairo, Egypt. Professor & Chairman, Department of Psychiatry. m. Jennifer Helen Peckham, 16 Jan. 1964, Cairo, 2 sons. *Education:* MD; FRCP; FRCPsych; DPM (London). Fellow, American Psychiatric Association. *Appointments include:* Clinical Assistant, Institute of Psychiatry, Maudsley & Bethlem Royal Hospital, London, UK; Lecturer, Assistant Professor, Psychiatry, Ain Shams University, Cairo; Visiting Professor, Physiological Psychology, Cairo University; Consultant, Forensic Psychiatry, to HE Minister of Justice; Consultant, Armed Forces of Egypt; Member, World Health Organisation Panel & Advisory Committee of Mental Health. *Memberships include:* Chief Editor, 'Egyptian Journal of Psychiatry'; Committee, World Psychiatric Association; Treasurer, Clinical Psychopathology Committee, ibid; President, Biological Psychiatry Section, Egyptian Psychiatric Association; French Medical Psychological Association. *Publications include:* "Textbook of Psychiatry (Clinical), English, 1977; "Contemporary Psychiatry", Arabic, 1984; "Guide to Psychiatry", 1983; "Essentials of Psychology", 1983; "Physiological Psychology", Arabic, 1984. Approximately 90 published papers including: 'Cortical & Central Atrophy in Chronic Schizophrenia", 1981; 'Academic difficulty in university students', 1985; 'Mental disorders in Pharoanic Egypt', 1978; 'Attempted suicide in Egypt', 1979; 'Problems of schizo-affective disorders', 1983. *Honours include:* Fellowships: Royal College of Physicians, 1973; Royal College of Psychiatrists, 1973; American Psychiatric Association, 1982; International Academy of Psychotherapy, 1982; Representative, International Association for Suicidal Prevention. *Hobbies:* Reading; Music; Squash. *Address:* 3 Shawarby Street, Kars-el-Nil, Cairo, Egypt.

O'KEEFE, Declan, b. 18 Feb. 1922, London, England. Consultant Surgeon. m. Isabella Margaret McNeill, 18 Aug. 1947, Hampstead, London, England, 3 sons, 1 daughter. *Education:* MB, BS Guy's Hospital Medical School, London; FRCS (England); DTM&H (London); MRCSLRCP, 1945. *Appointments:* Squadron Leader, Royal Air Force Flying Training Command, 1946-48; Demonstrator and Lecturer in Anatomy, Guy's Hospital Medical School, London, 1948-50; Registrar, Guy's and St John's Hospital, 1950-52; Provincial Surgeon Rift, Colonial Medical Service, Kenya, 1952-58. *Mem-*

berships: Fellow, Association of Surgeons, East Africa; Chairman, Mombasa Medical Advisory Board; Member of Committee, Mombasa Hospital Association. *Hobbies:* Golf; Tennis; Photography. *Address:* PO Box 83987, Mombasa, Kenya.

O'KEEFFE, Daniel, b. 13 Oct. 1947, Garden City, New York, USA. Director of Maternity and Fetal Medicine. m. Mary Helen Aspland, 21 Aug. 1971, Glens Falls, New York, 2 daughters. *Education:* BA, Holy Cross College, 1969; University Autonoma of Guadalajara, 1970-74; Internship, Dalhousie University, Halifax, Nova Scotia, Canada; Residency, University of California Irving Medical Center; Fellowship, University of California Irving Medical Center and Long Beach Memorial Hospital. *Memberships:* Fellow, American College of Obstetricians and Gynaecologists; Society of Perinatal Obstetricians; Fetal Medicine and Surgery Society; March of Dimes, Professional Advisory Committee; Phoenix Obstetrics and Gynaecology Society. *Publications:* 'The Accuracy of Estimated Gestational Age Based on Ultrasound Measurement of Biparietal Diameter in Preterm Premature Rupture of Membranes' (with T J Garite, J P Elliott and others) in American Journal of Obstetrics and Gynaecology, 1985; 'Intrapartum Evaluation of the High-Risk Pregnancy' (with R K Freeman) chapter 12 in "Principles and Practice of Perinatal Medicine" 1983. *Hobbies:* Snow and water skiing; Golf; Racquet ball; Fishing; Hunting; Kyacking. *Address:* 1111 E McDowell Road, Phoenix, AZ 85006, USA.

OKOISOR, Adebola Taiwo Oyindamola, b. 8 May 1934, Lagos, Nigeria. Chief Consultant and Medical Director. m. Frank E Okoisor, 26 June 1965, London, England, 1 son, 2 daughters. *Education:* Queens College, Lagos; Royal Free Hospital, London; MRCS, LRCP; MB, BS, 1964; DRCOG; MRCOG; FRCOG; FWACS; FMCOG. *Appointments:* House Officer, Royal Free Hospital, London, England, 1964-65; Senior House Officer, Registrar, Hillingdon Hospital Middlesex, England, 1971-73; Senior House Officer, Registrar, 1968-70, Senior Registrar, 1973-77, Consultant Obstetrician, 1977-78, Lagos University Teaching Hospital, Nigeria; Chief Consultant and Medical Director, Bonheur Maternity Hospital, Lagos, 1978-. *Memberships:* Nigerian Medical Association; Association of Women Doctors; Society of Gynaecologists and Obstetricians. *Publications:* "Maternal Maternity", 1975; "Vacuum Extraction", 1976. *Honours:* Treasurer, Association of Women Doctors. *Hobbies:* Reading; Travel; Swimming. *Address:* House D2B, Oritshejolomi Crescent, University of Lagos Campus, Yaba, Nigeria.

OKOISOR, Frank Etumiwe, b. 14 July 1933, Ibadan, Nigeria, Professor and Head of Department of Preventive Dentistry, University of Lagos. m. Adebola Taiwo Adesanya, 26 June 1965, London, England, 1 son, 2 daughters. *Education:* St Gregory's College, Lagos; LDS, Leeds; FDS RCPS, Glasgow, Scotland; FWACS; FMCDS, Nigeria. *Appointments:* School Dental Officer, West Riding of Yorkshire County Council, England, 1965-67; Clinical Demonstrator (1968-70), Professor and Head, Department of Preventive Dentistry, University of Lagos, Nigeria; Clinical Assistant, Eastman Dental Clinic, London, England, 1970-73; Consultant Dental Surgeon, Lagos University Teaching Hospital, Nigeria, 1973-. *Memberships:* Nigerian Dental Association; Secretary-General, Federation of African Dental Association; Nigeria Medical Association; Nigeria Medical Council; Federation Dentaire Internationale. *Publications:* 'Pattern and Causes of Tooth Loss in Nigerians', 1975; 'Demand and need for dental care in Nigerians', 1982; 'Utilisation of dental auxiliaries', 1983; 'Oral Health Status and treatment needs of children with sickle cell anaemia', 1984; 'Dental disease as an indication of nutritional problems', 1985. *Honours:* Vice-President of the Nigerian Union (UK), 1964. *Hobbies:* Reading; Travel. *Address:* Umuagehe Village, Ogboli, Ibusa, Nigeria.

O'LEARY, Patricia Ann, b. 15 May 1949, Steubenville,

Ohio, USA. Assistant Professor, East Carolina University School of Nursing, Greenville, North Carolina. *Education:* LPN, Belmont County Joint Vocational School of Practical Nursing, Ballaire, Ohio, 1969-70; RN, Diploma in Nursing, Mercy Hospital School of Nursing, Pittsburgh, Pennsylvania, 1971-73; BSN, West Liberty State College, West Liberty, West Virginia, 1976-78; MSN, Vanderbilt University, Nashville, Tennessee, 1979-80; Post-graduate studies, West Virginia University, Morgantown, 1982-84. *Appointments:* LPN, Ohio Valley Hospital, General Medicine, Steubenville, Ohio, 1970-73; Staff Nurse, Team Leader, Charge Nurse, Cleveland Clinic, Intermediate Cardiovascular Unit, Cleveland, Ohio, 1973-75; Staff Nurse, Team Leader, Charge Nurse, Ohio Valley Hospital, General Medicine, Steubenville, Ohio, 1975-79; Assistant Head Nurse, Supervisor, Royal Pavilion Extended Care Facility, Steubenville, Ohio, 1979; Instructor, West Liberty State College, Upper Level RN only Programme, West Liberty, West Virginia, 1980-84. *Memberships:* American Nurses Association; North Carolina Nurses Association, District 30; Vanderbilt University Alumni Association; Vanderbilt University Nursing Alumni Association; Vanderbilt University School of Nursing Continuing Education Alumni Association; West Liberty State College Alumni Association; West Liberty State College Nursing Alumni Association. *Publications:* Contributor to various professional journals. *Honours:* Bueleh Boyd Scholarship, American Society of University Women, Wheeling Branch. *Hobbies:* Music; Record Collecting; Photography; Ceramics; Sports. *Address:* 1149 Mulberry Lane 35C, Greenville, NC 27834, USA.

OLIECH, Joseph Samuel, b. 22 Nov. 1945, Kisumu, Kenya. Senior Lecturer; Consultant Urological Surgeon. m. Risper Anyango, 18 Dec. 1984, Kisumu, 1 son, 1 daughter. *Education:* MB ChB, FRCS (i); FICA (NY). *Appointments:* Medical Officer, Ministry of Health, 1971-74; Senior House Officer, Derby Royal Infirmary, 1974-76; Lecturer, University of Nairobi Medical School, 1976-80; Postgraduate, Institute of Urology, London University, 1980-81; Senior Lecturer, Urological Surgeon, Kenya, 1981-85; Kidney Transplant Surgeon, 1985. 2Memberships: Kenya Medical Association; Association of Surgeons East Africa; Kenya Hospital Association. *Publications:* Many papers on Thyroid Diseases in East African Medical Journals. *Honours:* Best Postgraduate Master of Medicine, Surgery, Nairobi, 1974; Best Postgraduate Student, Institute of Urology, London, 1981. *Hobbies:* Mountain Climbing; Music; Films; Travel. *Address:* PO Box 48961, Nairobi, Kenya.

OLIVE, Georges, b. 2 Feb. 1931, Paris, France. Professor, Pharmacology, Head, Clinical Pharmacology, Faculty of Medicine Cochin, University Paris V. m. A Lalanne, 21 Oct. 1958, Paris, 1 son, 2 daughters. *Education:* Pharmacist, Paris, 1954; MD, Paris, 1963; BSc, Paris, 1960. *Appointments:* Assistant Pharmacologist, 1962-65, Associate Professor, 1966-69, Professor, Pharmacology, 1970-. *Memberships:* Society of Clinical Pharmacology; Society of Pharmacologists; Society of Clinical Biology. *Publications:* "Developmental Pharmacology and Therapeutics", 'Proceedings of the 4th International Colloq. of Develop. Pharmacol.', 1984; several articles in field of placental transfer, etc. *Honours:* Expert in Pharmacology and Toxicology, Health Ministry, 1980; Member, National Adverse Effects of Drugs Commission, 1983; Member, Working Group, Safety of Drug EEC Brussels, 1975. *Hobby:* Drawing. *Address:* Dept. of Clinical Pharmacology, Hopital St Vincent de Paul, 74 Av. Denfert Rochereau, 75674 Paris Cedex 14, France.

OLIVERIO, Alberto, b. 1 Dec. 1938, Catania, Italy. University Professor of Psychobiology. m. Anna Ferraris, 3 Oct. 1970, Biella, 1 daughter. *Education:* MD, University of Rome, 1962. *Appointments:* Assistant Research Pharmacologist, UCLA School of Medicine, Los Angeles, California, USA, 1964-65; Research Director, Laboratory Psychobiology and Psychopharmacology, National Research Council,

Italy, 1967-70; Director, Institute Psychobiology and Psychopharmacology, National Research Council, 1975-; Professor of Psychobiology, Faculty of Biological Sciences, University of Rome, 1978-. *Publications:* "Genetics, Environment and Intelligence", 1977; "Biology and Behavior", 1982; 'Genes and Behavior', 1983; "The Natural History of the Brain", 1984; 'Psychobiology of Opioids', 1984. *Address:* Via Reno 1, 00198 Rome, Italy.

OLLERICH, Dwayne A, b. 30 June 1934, South Dakota, USA. Associate Dean. 3 sons, 1 daughter. *Education:* BA, Augustana College, Sioux Falls, SD, 1960; MS, 1962, PhD, University of ND, Grand Forks, ND, 1964. *Appointments:* Postdoctoral Fellow, 1964-65; Assistant Professor, Anatomy, University of Alberta, Edmonton, Alberta, Canada, 1965-66; Assistant Professor, 1966-70, Associate Professor, 1970-72, Associate Professor and Chairman, 1972-76, Professor and Chairman, Anatomy, 1976-79, Associate Dean for Academic and Research Affairs, School of Medicine, University of ND, 1979-. *Memberships:* American Association of Anatomists; Association of Anatomy Chairman; American Society for Cell Biology; ND Academy of Science. *Publications:* Author of numerous scientific papers in professional journals including 'Morphology of cartilage canals in chick epiphyseal plate: A light and electron microscopic study', 1976; (co-author); 'Some observations on hypertrophic chondrocytes of chick tibial epiphyseal growth plate', 1977, (co-author); 'Effects of postnatal zinc deficiency on cerebellar and hippocampal development in the rat', 1977 (co-author); 'Morphology of the perforating cartilage canals in the proximal tibial growth plate of the chick', 1978 (co-author); 'Lamellar structures in Purkinji cell dendrites of rat cerebellum', 1978 (co-author); 'Alterations in the postnatal development of Cerebellar Cortex due to Zinc deficiency. 1. Impaired Acquisition of Granule Cells', 1982, (co-author). *Honour:* Golden Apple Award, Outstanding Professor, Student American Medical Assn., 1970. *Hobbies:* Oil and Water Colours; Fishing; Hunting. *Address:* 407 Hamline, Grand Forks, ND 58201, USA.

OLOFSSON, Jan-Gunnar Vilhelm (Jan), b. 28 Mar. 1940, Malmoe, Sweden. Associate Professor of Otolaryngology. m. Margareta, 7 Dec. 1963, 3 daughters. *Education:* MD, University of Lund, 1967; Resident, Fellowship Training, Department of Otolaryngology, Linköping University Hospital; Fellow, Department of Otolaryngology, University of Toronto, Canada, 1970-72; PhD, Linköping University, 1973. *Appointments:* Assistant Professor 1973-75, Associate Professor, 1975-, Department of Laryngology, Linköping University Hospital, in charge of Head & Neck Surgery & Laryngology. *Memberships:* Swedish Medical Association; Swedish Otorhinolaryngological Association; Swedish Otorhinolaryngological Society; Canadian Society of Otolaryngology - Head & Neck Surgery; Danish Society for Head & Nech Oncology; Association of Head & Neck Oncologists of Great Britain; European Society of Surgical Oncology; Royal Society of Medicine (England); International Bronchoesophagological Society. *Publications:* More than 150 publications mainly in Laryngology and Head & Neck Oncology (including textbook chapters etc). *Honours:* Charlie Conacher Memorial Lecturer, Vancouver, Canada, 1980; Honorary Member, La Societa di Scienze Mediche di Conegliano, Vittorio Veneto e del quartier del Piave, 1984. *Address:* Department of Otolaryngology, University Hospital, S-581 85 Linköping, Sweden.

OLSON, Randall J, b. 12 Apr. 1947, Glendale, California, USA. Professor and Chairman of Ophthalmology. m. Ruth Louise, 3 sons, 2 daughters. *Education:* BA, Medical Biology, University of Utah; MD, University of Utah College of Medicine. *Appointments:* Instructor in Ophthalmology, University of Florida; Assistant Professor, Louisiana State University; Associate Professor, University of Utah School of Medicine; Medical Director, King Khaled Eye Specialist Hospital,

Riyadh, Saudi Arabia; Professor and Chairman, University of Utah, Department of Ophthalmology. *Memberships:* Served on Scientific Advisory Board, American Intra-Ocular Implant Society; Board of Councilors, American Academy of Ophthalmology; Served as Secretary-Treasurer, Association of University Professors of Ophthalmology. *Publications:* Author of over 100 different publications. *Honour:* Nominated Phi Kappa Phi; University of Utah, 1970. *Address:* University of Utah School of Medicine, Department of Ophthalmology, 50 No. Medical Drive, Salt Lake City, UT 84132, USA.

O'MALLEY, Eoin, b. 5 Apr. 1919, Galway, Ireland. Professor, Surgery. m. Una Mary O'Higgins, 4 Oct. 1952, Howth, 5 sons, 1 daughter. *Education:* MB; BCh; BAO; MCH; FRCSI. *Appointments:* Surgical Resident: Southend General Hospital, 1944-45; Royal National Orthopaedic Hospital, London, 1944-45; Chief Surgical Resident, Mater Mis Hospital, Dublin, 1945-48; Surgical Fellow, Lahey Clinic, Boston, 1948-49; Assistant Surgeon, Mater Mis Hospital, 1950; Consultant Surgeon: Cedars Sanatorium, Dublin, Peamount Sanatorium, Dublin, National Maternity Hospital, St Luke's Hospital, Dublin; Chairman, Medical Research Co, Ireland, 1968-76; President, Royal College Surgeons in Ireland, 1982-84; Professor, Surgery, University College, Dublin, Mater Misericordiael Hospital. *Memberships:* Association of Surgeons of Great Britain & Ireland; Society of Thoracic Surgeons Great Britain & Ireland; International Society of Surgery; International Cardiac Society; etc. *Publications:* Articles in numerous journals. *Honours:* A Murat Willis Lecturer, Richmond, Virginia, USA, 1972; Colles Medal, RCSI, 1973; Guest Lecturer, South California Chapter, American College of Surgeons, 1975; Guest Lecturer, Honorary Memberships, American Association for Thoracic Surgeons, 1981; Honorary MD (NUI); Honorary DSc, (QUB), 1984; Deryl Hart Lecture, Duke University, South Carolina, 1985. *Hobbies:* Plants; Fishing. *Address:* Dunamase, Cross Avenue, Booterstown, Dublin, Republic of Ireland.

OMELCHUK, Alex, b. 24 July 1935, Bloomsbury, Alberta, Canada. Private Practice Edmonton, Alberta and Associate Chief of General Practice, Royal Alex Hospital, Edmonton, Alberta. m. Audrey Orissa Paley, 10 Aug. 1985, Edmonton, 1 son, 1 daughter (Previous Marriage). *Education:* Certification in Education and Industrial Arts, 1956; MD, 1962, University of Alberta; LMCC, 1962; CCFP, 1970; FCFP, 1979. *Appointments:* Active Medical Staff: Royal Alexandra Hospital, Edmonton; Glenrose Provincial Hospital, Edmonton; Norwood Auxiliary Hospital, Edmonton; Dr Angus McGugan Nursing Home, Edmonton; Dickensfield Auxiliary Hospital, Edmonton; Clinical Lecturer, Department of Family Medicine, Faculty of Medicine, University of Alberta, 1967-76; Examiner for Certification Examinations of College of Family Physicians of Canada, 1971-76. *Memberships:* Canadian and Alberta Medical Associations; College of Physicians and Surgeons of Alberta; College of Family Physicians of Canada; Edmonton Academy of Medicine; Aerospace Medical Association, USA; Canadian Society of Aviation Medicine; Edmonton Medical-Legal Society; Ukrainian Professional Businessmen's Club of Edmonton; Kingsway Emergency Service (President, 1972-75); Founding Member, World Organization of National Colleges and Academies of Family Medicine, 1976; Vice-President, 1981 and President, 1982, Royal Alexandra Hospital, etc. *Hobbies:* Automechanics; Woodworking; Racquetball; Hunting. *Address:* 221 10106 - 111 Avenue, Edmonton, Alberta, T5G 0B4, Canada.

O'MOORE, Rory Robert, b. 20 Dec. 1940, Dublin, Republic of Ireland. Consultant Chemical Pathologist. m. Astrid Mona Dahl, 15 May 1969, Dublin University, 3 sons. *Education:* BA Natural Sciences, 1962, MSc Steroid Biochemistry, 1966, MD, BCh, BAO, 1968, University of Dublin; C. Chem, Fellow, Royal Institute of Chemistry, 1974; Member, Royal College of Pathologists, 1974; Fellow, Faculty of Pathology,

Royal College of Physicians of Ireland, 1982. *Appointments:* Lecturer in Clinical Chemistry, University of Edinburgh, Scotland, 1969-73; Senior Registrar in Chemical Pathology, St Mary's Hospital, London, England, 1973-75; Consultant Chemical Pathologist to the Federated Dublin Voluntary Hospitals, 1975-. *Memberships:* Association of Clinical Biochemists (Ireland & Great Britain); Royal Society of Chemistry; Royal Academy of Medicine in Ireland. *Publications:* Editor & Co-editor of 'Lecture Notes in Medical Informatics' Volumes 16, 24 & 25; Author & Co-author of over 40 scientific papers on Biochemical aspects of infertility, Medical Computing, Lipid Absorption. *Honours:* Secretary, Faculty of Pathology, RCPI, 1982-85; Secretary 1983-86, Vice President 1986-87, President 1987-90, European Federation for Medical Informatics, 1983-86. *Hobbies:* Music; Theatre; Gardening; Squash. *Address:* Ebb Tide, Breffni Road, Sandycove, Co Dublin, Republic of Ireland.

O'NEILL, Richard P, b. 7 Jan., 1930, Dublin, Republic of Ireland. Doctor of Internal Medicine. m. Caroline Martin, 10 June 1960, New York, USA, 3 sons, 1 daughter. *Education:* MB, BCh, University of Dublin, Republic of Ireland; MD, Internal Medicine, USA; Fellow, American College of Chest Physicians (Pulmonary Medicine). *Appointments:* Internships & Residences in Dublin, United Kingdom & Boston, USA; Research Fellow, National Heart & Lung Institute, Harvard University, University of Pittsburgh, 1958-64; Professor of Medicine, University of Kentucky, 1964-80; Private Practitioner, Internal Medicine, Pulmonary & Occupational Lung Diseases, 1980-. *Memberships:* American College of Chest Physicians; American Thoracic Society; Kentucky Thoracic Society; Southern Medical Association. *Publications:* "Intracellular Acid-base Relations of Dog-brain with Reference to Extracellular Volume', Journal of Chest Infections 1964; 'Recognition & Management of Complications of Coal Workers' Pneumoconosis', Annals of the New York Academy of Sciences, 1972; "Fungal Diseases of the Lung: Pulmonary Thromboembolism", 1975; "Pulmonary Medicine", 1982; and others. *Honours:* Research Fellowship, National Heart & Lung Institute, 1958-64; Governor, American College of Chest Physicians, 1979-85; President, Kentucky Thoracic Society 1975. *Hobbies:* Swimming; Music; Antique & Art Collecting; Reading; Rugby. *Address:* Richmond East III, St Margaret Drive, Lexington, KY 40502, USA.

ONESTI, Silvio J, b. 3 Jan. 1926, San Francisco, USA. Director of Child Psychiatry. m. Jean Thomas, 12 Apr. 1956, New Haven, Connecticut, USA, 1 son, 1 daughter. *Education:* BSc, Stanford University, USA, 1947; MDCM, McGill University Medical School, 1951; Certified, Adult Psychoanalysis, Boston Psychoanalytic Society and Institute, 1970; Certification in Child Psychiatry, 1977. *Appointments:* Instructor in Paediatrics, Yale Medical School, 1956-58; Director, Paediatric Outpatient Department, Yale-New Haven Hospital, 1957-58; Director, Child Psychiatric-Liaison Service, Beth Israel Hospital, Boston, 1963-65, Head, Child Psychiatry Unit, 1965-73; Director of Child Psychiatry and the Hall-Mercer Children's Centre, McLean Hospital, Belmont, Massachusetts, 1973-; Clinical Director, McLean Hospital, 1981-83. *Memberships:* American Psychiatric Association; American Association of Psychiatric Services for Children; Boston Psychoanalytic Society and Institute Inc; Group for the Advancement of Psychiatry; Association for Academic Psychiatry; Massachusetts Medical Society. *Publications:* 'Plague, Press and Politics' in 'Stanford Medical Bulletin', 1955; co-author 'Comprehensive Child Psychiatry Through a Team Approach' in 'Children', 1969; Editor "Annual Progress in Child Psychiatry and Child Development", 1970. *Honours:* Alpha Omega Alpha, 1951; Sol Ginsburg Fellow, Group for the Advancement of Psychiatry, 1959-61; Fellow, American Psychiatric Association, 1975; Fellow, American Academy of Child Psychiatry, 1977. *Hobbies:* Reading; Swimming. *Address:* Hall-Mercer Children's Centre, McLean Hospital, 115 Mill Street,

Belmont, MA 02178, USA.

ONKEY, Richard G, b. 29 Feb. 1932, Bridgeport, Connecticut, USA. Orthopaedic Surgeon. m. Margaret Gorrie, 26 Nov. 1969, Naples, Florida, 1 son, 3 daughters. *Education:* MD, University of Tennessee, 1957; Internships, residencies, US Army hospitals, 1957-62. *Appointments include:* Assistant Chief, Orthopaedics, US Air Force Base, Tachikawa, Japan, 1962-65; Chief, Orthopaedics/Chief, Professional Services, US Air Force Hospital, Homestead AFB, 1965-67; Staff, former Chief, Department of Surgery, Naples Community Hospital. *Memberships:* President 1984-85, numerous offices, Florida Orthopaedic Society; Complications Committee 1982-85, Arthroscopy Association of North America; Board of Councillors, 1982-85, American Academy of Orthopaedic Surgeons; Site Committee 1983-86, International Society for the Study of Lumbar Spine; Former Member, American College of Sports Medicine; International Arthroscopy Association; Local & State Medical Societies. *Publications include:* 'The Displaced Intrascapular Fracture of the Neck of the Femur' in 'Journal of Bone & Joint Surgery', 1970; 'Anterior Thigh Syndrome', published as audiovisual presentation, also in library, American Academy of Orthopaedic Surgeons; 'Lumbar Spinal Stenosis' in "Instructional Course Lectures" Volume 28, co-authors M Tile MD & William Kirkaldy-Willis MD, 1979. *Honours:* Team physician, US Track & Field team, Eight-Nation Meeting, Japan/China, 1980; Team physician, US Olympic Cycling team, Summer Olympics, Los Angeles, 1984. Biographical listings. *Hobbies:* Snow skiing; Wind surfing. *Address:* 101 8th Street South, Naples, FL 33940, USA.

OOSTEROM, Adriaan Van, b. 15 Mar. 1942, Abcoude, The Netherlands. Professor, Medical Physics. m. Judith Irene Pooley, 4 Oct. 1968, Abcoude, 1 son, 2 daughters. *Education:* Electronics Engineer, 1962; Physics Degree, 1971, Doctor, Physics, 1978, University of Amsterdam. *Appointments:* Medical Physics, University of Amsterdam, 1971-81; Laboratory of Medical Physics & Biophysics, Kastholieke University of Nijmegen, 1981-. *Publications:* Articles in numerous professional journals. *Hobbies:* Music; Sports. *Address:* Laboratory of Medical Physics & Biophysics, Geert, Groot Plein N 21, 6525 EZ Nijmegen, Netherlands.

OOTA, Kunio, b. 23 Feb. 1913, Kobe, Japan. President, Japanese Association of Medical Sciences. m. Chizu Yanagita, 12 Oct. 1940, 1 son, 1 daughter. *Education:* MD; D Med Sci; Tokyo Imperial University Medical School, 1937. *Appointments:* Assistant of Pathology, 1937, Lecturer, 1941, Tokyo Imperial University; Head, Pathology Department, Cancer Institute, Tokyo, 1947; Professor of Pathology, Tokyo Medical and Dental College, 1948; Professor of Pathology, University of Tokyo, 1963-73; Director, Tokyo Metropolitan Institute of Gerontology, 1972-81; Vice President, 1976-84, President, 1984-, Japanese Association of Medical Sciences. *Memberships:* President, Japanese Society of Biomedical Gerontology; Honorary Member, Japanese Pathological Society; Honorary Member, Japanese Society of Cancer Research; Honorary Member, Japanese Society of Clinical Cytology; Honorary Member, Gastric Cancer Research; Honorary Member, Colonic Cancer Research; Honorary Member, Pulmonary Cancer Research. *Publications:* "Recent Knowledges of Cancer", 1954; "Carcinoma of Stomach in Early Phase", 1967; "Histological Classification of Esophagel and Gastric Tumours", 1977; "Aging Phenoma", 1979; "Science of Cancer", 1981; "Handbook of Gerontology", 20 Volumes, 1984; "Introduction to Pathology", 1984. *Hobbies:* Music; History. *Address:* Hakusan 2-31-2, Bunkyoky, Tokyo, Japan 112.

OPPENHEIM, Joost J, b. 11 Aug. 1934, Venlo, Netherlands. m. 4 children. *Education:* AB, 1956, MD, 1960, Columbia College, USA; NIH Postgraduate Programme, Bethesda, 1962-65, 1966-. *Appointments*

include: Various Positions, Hospitals, Laboratories, 1960-76; Internist, Mobile Medical Care, Montgomery County Free Clinics, 1977-81; Immunology Lecturer, Zoology, 1977-, Adjunct Professor, Zoology, 1979-, University of Maryland; Co-Organizer, 3rd International Lymphokine Workshop, 1982; Chief, Laboratory of Molecular Immunoregulation, Biological Response Modifiers Programme, National Cancer Institute, Frederick, 1983-. *Memberships:* American Federation for Clinical Research; American Association for Immunologists; American Society for Clinical Investigations; Reticuloendothelial Society. *Publications:* Over 250 articles in professional journals including: 'Cancer Research'; 'New England Journal of Medicine', 'British Medical Journal'; 'Nature'; 'Journal of Immunology'; 'Journal of Experimental Medicine'; 'Cellular Immunology'; etc. *Honours include:* New York State College Scholarships, 1952-56; Columbia University Scholarships, 1957-60; Alpha Omega Alpha; Diplomate, National Board of Medical Examiners, 1961; Editorial Board, 'Cellular Immunology', 1970-; Member, Organizing Committee, International Leukocyte Culture Conferences, 1970-; Associate Editor, 'Journal of Immunology', 1973-79; Meritorious Service Medal, 1978; Ferdin and Von-Hebra Prize for Dermatological Research, 1982. *Address:* NCI-NIH, Biol Response Modifiers Programme, Lab. Molecular Immunoregulation, Bldg. 560, Frederick, MD 21701, USA.

ORBECK, Kenneth William, b. 28 Nov. 1940, Edmonton, Alberta, Canada. Private Practitioner, Department of General Practice, Riverside Hospital of Ottawa and Childrens Hospital of Eastern Ontario, m. Beverley Rae Bradstock, Ottawa, 1 son, 1 daughter.*Education:* MD, CCFP; Postgraduate, Medicine for 1 year; Postgraduate, Surgery for 1 year.*Appointments:* Casualty Officer, Ottawa Civic Hospital, 1968-70; Flight Surgeon, Royal Canadian Air Force, 1965-68; Casualty Emergency Physician, Riverside Hospital of Ottawa, 1967-76; Chief, Department of General Practice, Childrens Hospital of Eastern Ontario, 1979-84. *Memberships:* Canadian Medical Association; Ontario Medical Association; Association of Independent Physicians; Ottawa Academy of Medicine; District 8 Alternate Representative, Ontario Medical Association. *Hobby:* Electronics. *Address:* 190 Main street, Suite 100, Ottawa, Ontario, Canada K1S 1C2.

ORDOG, Gary Joseph, b. 2 June 1954, Canada. Assistant Professor. m. Cindy Solodki, 2 June 1979, Maple Ridge. *Education:* BA; BSc; MD, University of British Columbia; Fellow, American College of Emergency Medicine; Fellow, American Academy of Clinical Toxicology; Diplomate: American Board of Emergency Medicine, American Board of Medical Toxicology, National Board of Medical Examiners.*Appointments:* Assistant Professor, Drew University of California, Los Angeles School of Medicine, and The Charles R Drew University of California, Los Angeles Postgraduate School of Medicine; Assistant Professor, University of California, Los Angeles School of Medicine. *Memberships:* Society of Teachers of Emergency Medicine; British Columbia Medical Association; College of Family Physicians of Canada; Society of Clinical Research, USA; Examinee, American Board of Medical Toxicology. *Publications:* "Gunshot Wounds - A Textbook", 1985; "Outpatient Management of 357 Gunshot Wounds to the Chest", 1983; "110 Gunshot Wounds to the Neck", 'Journal of Trauma', 1985. *Honour:* Award of Merit, Canada, 1971. *Hobbies:* Medical Research; Medical Toxicology Research; Scuba Diving; Medical Conference Lecturer; Writer. *Address:* Box 219-12021 So. Wilmington Avenue, Los Angeles, CA 90059, USA.

ORDWAY, Craig Bradford, b. 27 June 1945, Southbridge, Massachusetts, USA. Orthopaedic Surgeon. m. Sandra, 1 son, 1 daughter. *Education:* BA, Dartmouth College; MD, Boston University School of Medicine. *Appointments include:* Chief of Orthopaedic Services, Patterson Army Hospital; Director, Division of Trauma, Department of Orthopaedic Surgery, Nassau County Medical Centre; Chairman, ibid; Assistant Professor of Orthopaedic Surgery, State University of New York, Stony Brook; Private Orthopaedic Practice. *Memberships include:* Numerous committees, Nassau County, Huntington Hospital, SUNY School of Medicine; Consultant, American Arbitration Board. *Publications include:* Contributions to national & international medical journals, book chapters, videotapes, etc. Basic research interest, physiology of fracture healing. *Honours include:* A-O International Fellowship in Polytrauma, University of Basle; National Institutes of Health Student Fellowship Research Grant, Dartmouth College; Translation prize for pamphlet, ibid, 1967. *Hobbies:* Skiing; Sailing; Powerboat racing. *Address:* East Huntington Orthopaedic Group, 166 East Main Street, Huntington NY 11743, USA.

ORELAND, Lars, b. 29 Sep. 1939, Umea, Sweden. Professor of Biochemical Pharmacology. m. Anita Jonsson, 16 May 1964, Hammerdal, Sweden, 1 son. *Appointments:* Lecturer in Clinical Pharmacology, 1969-75, Professor of Pharmacology, 1975-82, University of Umea; Professor of Pharmacology, University of Gothenburg, 1982-84; Professor of Biochemical Pharmacology, University of Uppsala, 1984-. *Membership:* Swedish Society of Medicine. *Publications:* Various, in the field of enzyme monoamine oxidase. *Address:* Department of Biochemical Pharmacology, BMC, PO Box 591, 75124 Uppsala, Sweden.

ORELLANA, Juan, b. 22 Jan. 1951, Assistant Professor/Assistant Director, Department of Ophthalmology. m. Jeanne Orellana, 11 May 1974, New York, USA. 2 sons, 2 daughters. *Education:* BA, New York University, 1973; MD, Mount Sinai School of Medicine, 1978. *Memberships:* American Medical Association; Fellow of the American Academy of Ophthalmology; Pan-American Association of Ophthalmology; Association of Research in Vision and Ophthalmology; Heed Society. *Publications:* 'Ocular manifestations of multiple myeloma, waldenstrom's macroglobulinemia and benign monoclonal gammopathy' 1981; 'Topical steroid therapy in malignant atrophic papulosis' 1983; 'Cytomegalovirus retinitis: A manifestation of the acquired immunodeficiency syndrome (AIDS), 1983; 'Medulloephithelioma diagnosed by ultrasound and vitreous aspirate' 1983. *Honour:* New York State Physician Shortage Award. *Address:* Department of Ophthalmology, Beth Israel Medical Center, 1st Avenue and 16th Street, New York, NY 10003, USA.

ORFANOS, Constantin Emmanuel, b. 28 June 1936, Neapolis, Crete. University Professor. m. Vera-Marina Thommeck, 1978, 2 daughters. *Education:* MD, University of Dusseldorf, 1961; Docent 1969, Professor 1972, University of Cologne; Max Kade Foundation Stipend, Tufts University, Boston, USA; Armed Forces Institute of Pathology, Washington, DC, USA. *Appointments:* Assistant, Institute of Biophysics and Electron Microscopy, Dusseldorf, 1960-61; Assistant, Departments of Dermatology, Dusseldorf and Cologne, 1963-69; Lecturer/Research Fellow, Department of Dermatology, Cologne, 1969-72; Research Associate, Tufts University Boston, AFIP, Washington DC, 1971-72; Associate Professor, University of Cologne Medical School, 1972; Full Professor and Chairman, Department of Dermatology, University Medical Centre, Steglitz, The Free University of Berlin, 1978-. *Memberships:* Honorary and Corresponding Member of numerous National and International Medical Societies; Ex-officio Member, International Committee of Dermatology; General Secretary of 17th World Congress of Dermatology. *Publications:* Over 300 publications in national and international scientific journals. Books: "Haar und Haarkrankheiten" 1979; "Retinoids: Advances in Basic Research and Therapy" 1981; "Hair Research Status and Future Aspects" 1981; "Recent Developments in Clinical Research" 1985. *Honours:* Hans Schwarzkorf Prize in Hair Research, 1970; Oscar Gans Prize of the German

Dermatological Society, 1977. *Address:* Department of Dermatology, University Medical Center, Steglitz, The Free University of Berlin, 1 Berlin 45, Federal Republic of Germany.

ORLOWSKI, Tadeusz, b. 25 Jan. 1927, Czartoria, Poland. Head, Centre of Postgraduate Medical Education. m. 2) Halina Witek, 22 Feb. 1975, Warsaw, 2 sons, 1 daughter. *Education:* MD; PhD; Professor. *Appointments:* Head, Surgical Department, Wroclaw Hospital; Head, Surgical Clinic, Medical Academy, Lodz; Head, Surgical Clinic, Centre of Postgraduate Medical Education, MMA, Warsaw. *Memberships:* Polish Society of Surgeons; Societe Internationale de Chirurgie; New York Academy of Sciences, USA; Emergency and Disaster Medical Association. *Publications:* "Postoperative Biliary Shock and Its Treatment", 1963; "General and Local Hypothermy in Renal Hypoxia", 1965; contributions to 'American Journal of Surgery', 1974, 75; "Lasers in Surgical Practice", 1979. *Honour:* Award, Ministry of National Defence, 1980, 83. *Hobbies:* Stamp collecting; Tourism; Gardening. *Address:* Belwederska 36/38 m 118, 00 594 Warsaw, Poland.

ORNE, Martin Theodore, b. 16 Oct. 1927, Vienna, Austria. Professor, University of Pennsylvania; Director, Unit for Experimental Psychiatry, Institute of Pennsylvania Hospital. m. Emily Farrell Carota, 3 Feb. 1962, Boston, USA, 1 son, 1 daughter. *Education:* AB, 1948, AM, 1951, PhD, 1958, Harvard University; MD, Tufts University Medical School, 1955; Honorary DSc, John F Kennedy University, 1980. *Appointments:* Lecturer, Graduate School of Arts & Sciences, Harvard University, 1958-59; Instructor, 1959-62, Associate, Psychiatry, 1962-64, Harvard Medical School; Associate Professor, Psychiatry, 1964-67, Professor, 1967-, University of Pennsylvania; Director, Studies in Hypnosis Project, Massachusetts Mental Health Centre, 1960-64; Director, Unit for Experimental Psychiatry, Institute of Pennsylvania Hospital, 1964-. *Memberships:* Fellow, AAAS, American Medical Association, American Psychiatric Association, American Psychological Association, American Society Clinical Hypnosis, New York Academy of Sciences, Society Clinical & Experimental Hypnosis (President 1971-73); Member: American Psychopathological Society; American Psychosomatic Society; Association for Psychophysiology Study of Sleep; etc. *Publications:* (With R E Shor): "The Nature of Hypnosis: Selected Basic Readings", 1965; (with others): "Psychiatry: Areas of Promise and Advancement", 1977; "Psychotherapy in Contemporary America: Its Development and Context, in American Handbook of Psychiatry", Volume 5, 1975; (with G Hammer) "Hypnosis", 'Encyclopaedia Britannica', 15th edition, 1974; "The Use and Misuse of Hypnosis in Court, in Crime and Justice", Volume 888, 1981; some 100 other chapters and articles in scientific publications; Editor-in-Chief, International Journal of Clinical Exp. Hypnosis, 1961-. *Honours:* Rantoul Scholar, 1949-50; Fulbright Scholar, 1960; American Psychiatric Association Hofheimer Prize (honorable mention), 1966; International Society of Hypnosis Benjamin Franklin Gold Medal, 1982. *Address:* 111 North 49th Street, Philadelphia, PA 19139, USA.

ORMOS, Jenó, b. 21 Dec. 1922, Hódmezóvasarhely. Professor; Chairman, Department of Pathology. m. Judit Lantos, Kiskundorozsma, 27 Dec. 1960, 2 sons, 1 daughter. *Education:* Doctor of Medicine, University of Szeged, Hungary. *Appointment:* Chairman, Department of Pathology, University of Medicine, Kossuth Lajos sgt 40, H-6720 Szeged, Hungary. *Memberships:* Hungarian Pathological Society; German Pathological Society; European Pathological Society; International Academy of Pathology. *Honours:* Distinguished Person of Higher Education, 1971; Honorary Member, Polish Pathological Society, 1975; Distinguished Physician, 1980. *Address:* Department of Pathology, University of Medicine, Kossuth Lajos sgt 40, H-6720, Szeged, Hungary.

OROSZ, László, b. 1 Aug. 1943, Kotlina. Professor. m.

Zsuzsanna Buzas, 1 son, 2 daughters. *Education:* MSc, 1966; PhD, Genetics & Biochemistry, Eotvos University, Budapest, 1969; Candidate of Sciences, 1973, DSc, 1983, Hungarian Academy of Science; PhD. *Appointments:* Research Fellow, 1966-69, Research Associate, 1969-74, Academy of Sciences, Hungary; Reader, Genetics, 1974-85, Professor, Genetics, 1985-, Attila Jozsef University, Szeged. *Memberships:* Genetic Society of Hungary, Secretary, 1975-; Society for Microbiology of Hungary; Society for Biochemistry of Hungary; Eotvos Lorand Society for Physics. *Publications:* "Classic and Molecular Genetics", 1980; "Genetic Analysis, Examples and Resolutions", 1981; articles in scientific journals. *Honour:* Young Scientist of the Year, Hungary, 1973. *Hobbies:* River Boating; Watching Red & Fallow Deer. *Address:* Department of Genetics, Attila Jozsef University, Közepfasor 52, 6726 Szeged, Hungary.

ORR, James Cameron, b. 10 Aug. 1930, Paisley, Scotland. Professor of Biochemistry and Chemistry, Memorial University, St John's Newfoundland, Canada. m. Robin Denise Moore, 22 Nov. 1958, Ames, Iowa, USA, 2 sons, 2 daughters. *Education:* PhD, Glasgow University, 1957; ARCS, Royal College of Science, London, England, 1954; BSc, Honours, Imperial College, London, 1954. *Appointments:* Research Chemist, Syntex, SA, Mexico City, Mexico, 1959-63; Assistant Professor of Biological Chemistry, 1969-72, Associate Professor of Biological Chemistry, 1972-75, Harvard Medical School, Boston, Massachusetts, USA; Chairman, Board of Tutors in Biochemical Sciences, Harvard College, Boston, 1970-72; Associate Dean for Basic Sciences, Faculty of Medicine, University of Newfoundland, St John's, Newfoundland, Canada, 1975-79. *Memberships:* Fellowships Committee, Medical Research Council, Ottawa. *Publications:* 'Biological applications of mass spectrometry'; Contributor of articles on professional subjects in scientific and medical journals. *Hobbies:* Sailing; Swimming; Tennis; Sculpting; Scottish country dancing. *Address:* 360 Hamilton Avenue, St John's, Newfoundland, Canada A1E 1K2.

ORR, W. Robert, b. 30 Apr. 1909, Portland, Indiana, USA. Retired Medical Practitioner. m. Mary M. Kochanowski, 6 Aug. 1937, Naugatuck, Connecticut, USA, 1 son. *Education:* BS, Indiana University, USA, 1933, MD, 1935. *Memberships:* St. Joseph County Medical Society, South Bend, Indiana; Indiana State Medical Association; American Medical Association; Indiana Orthopaedic Society; American Academy of Orthopaedic Surgery; Indiana Bone and Joint Club. *Hobbies:* Golf; Swimming; Cycling. *Address:* 12388 East Jefferson Road, Mishawaka, IN 46545, USA.

ORTONNE, Jean Paul, b. 25 Sep. 1943, Yzeure, France. Professor of Dermatology. m. 26 July 1979, Moulins, 2 sons, 1 daughter. *Education:* MD. *Appointments:* Resident in Dermatology, Lyon, 1970-74; Assistant Professor, Department of Dermatology, University Medical School, Lyon, 1975-79; Research Fellow, Harvard Medical School, Department of Dermatology, Massachusetts General Hospital, Boston, Massachusetts, USA, 1976; Professor of Dermatology, University Medical School, Nice, France, 1980-; Chief, Department of Dermatology, University Hospital, Nice, 1983-. *Memberships:* International Pigment Cell Society; Board Member, European Society for Dermatological Research; Society for Cutaneous Ultrastructure Research; Comite de Direction, Société Française de Dermatologie; President 1984-85, Société de Recherche Dermatologique. *Publication:* "Vitiligo and Other Hypomelanoses of Hair and Skin" (with D B Mosher and T B Fitzpatrick), 1983. *Address:* Service de Dermatologie, Hôpital Pasteur, BP 69, 30 Avenue de la Voie-Romaine, Nice 06002, France.

ORVIN, George Henry, b. 6 Aug. 1922, South Carolina, USA. Professor of Child Psychiatry. m. Rosalie Greer Salvo, 16 Sep. 1944, Charleston, 1 son, 3 daughters. *Education:* BS, MD; Diplomate, American Board of Psychiatry and Neurology. *Appointments:* Private

Practice, General Medicine, 1948-57; Resident in Psychiatry, Medical University of South Carolina, 1957-60; Clinical Clerk, Maudsley, Hospital, University of London, England, 1960-61; Instructor, 1961, Chief Adolescent Psychiatrist, 1967, Professor, 1977-, Acting Chairman, Department of Psychiatry, 1982-83, Medical University of South Carolina, Charleston, South Carolina, USA. *Memberships:* American and South Carolina Medical Associations; American and Southern Psychiatric Associations; American Society of Adolescent Psychiatry; Royal Society of Medicine, England. *Publications:* 'Treatment of the Phobic Obsessive Compulsive Patient with Oxazepam, Improved Benzodiazepine Compound', in 'Psychosomatics', 1967; 'Intensive Treatment of the Adolescent and His Family' in 'Archives of General Psychiatry', 1974. *Honours:* Fellow: American Psychiatric Association, 1970; Southern Psychiatric Association, 1970; American Society of Adolescent Psychiatry, 1981. *Hobbies:* Running; Reading. *Address:* Medical University of South Carolina, 171 Ashley Avenue, Charleston, SC 29425, USA.

ORZECHOWSKA-JUZWENKO, Krystyna, b. 18 Apr. 1933, Lodz, Poland. Head of Department of Clinical Pharmacology. m. 14 June 1969, 1 son. *Education:* MD, Medical Academy of Wroclaw, 1957; Habilitation, 1976; Associate Professor, 1976. *Appointments:* Assistant in Department of Pharmacology and Physician at the bedside 1957-79, Head of Department of Clinical Pharmacology 1979-, Medical Academy, Wroclaw. *Memberships:* President of Wroclaw Section of Clinical Pharmacology 1979-, Wroclaw Secretary 1965-69, General Secretary of Executive Committee 1977-80, Polish Pharmacological Society; Polish Medical Society; Polish Society of Internal Medicine; Polish Hematological Society; Vice-President of Committee of Clinical Pharmacology 1985-, Polish Academy of Sciences. *Publications:* 2 chapters in "Pharmacodynamics", 1985; 4 chapters in "Clinical Pharmacology", in press; Editor and author, "The Basis of Clinical Pharmacokinetics", in press; 20 learned articles. *Honour:* Golden Cross of Merit, 1981. *Hobbies:* Skiing; Skating; Horseback riding; Swimming; Theatre; Belleslettres. *Address:* Department of Clinical Pharmacology, Medical Academy, ul Mikulicza-Radeckiego 2, 50-368 Wroclaw, Poland.

OSBORN, Gerald Guy, b. 6 Nov. 1947, Cincinnati, Ohio, USA. Professor of Psychiatry. m. Sue Ellen Granger, 9 July 1983, East Lansing, Michigan, USA, 1 son, 2 daughters. *Education:* BA, Wilmington College, Ohio, 1969; Schiller-University, Klein-Ingersheim, Federal Republic of Germany, 1968-69; DO, Kirksville College of Osteopathic Medicine, Missouri, 1973; Residency in Psychiatry, Michigan State University, Diplomate, 1977; MPhil, University of Cambridge, England, 1985. *Appointments:* Instructor in Psychiatry, Michigan State University, 1974-77; Assistant Professor of Psychiatry, 1977-82, Dean of Academic Affairs, 1982-83, College of Osteopathic Medicine, Michigan State University. *Memberships:* American Osteopathic Association; American Psychiatric Association; American College of Neuropsychiatrists (Senior Member); Board of Examiners, American Board of Osteopathic Neurology & Psychiatry. *Publications:* "Interaction of Body & Mind", 1972, 'A Psychiatric Elective in Great Britain', 1973, The Osteopathic Physician; 'Stevens-Johnson Syndrome', The DO: Precepts & Practice, 1974; 'Psychoactive Drugs in the Treatment of the Aged', Practical Psychology for Physicians, 1977. *Honours:* Charles F Kettering Science Foundation Scholarship, 1968, Michigan Osteopathic College Foundation Writing Award, 1976; Sigma Sigma Phi (National Osteopathic Honors Fraternity), 1982. *Hobbies:* Distance Running; Sailing; Flying; Stained Glass Art. *Address:* 1313 Basswood Circle, East Lansing, MI 48823, USA.

OSBORNE, Neville N, b. 15 Nov. 1942, University Lecturer. m. Janet Susan, 3 July 1970, Monifieth, Dundee, Scotland, 2 sons, 1 daughter. *Education:* MA, Oxford University, 1983; BSc, London University, 1966; PhD, St Andrews University, 1970; DSc, St Andrews University, 1982. *Appointments:* Research Scientist, Max-Planck Institute for Experimental Medicine, Gottingen, Germany, 1972-79; Oxford University, 1979-. *Memberships:* Bio-chemical Society of Great Britain; International Society of Neurochemistry; International Society of Eye Research; The Association for Research in Vision and Ophthalmology; European Society for Neurochemistry. *Publications:* Over 150 scientific papers; Books: Microchemical Analysis of Nervous Tissue, 1974; Microchemical Analysis of Nervous Tissue (in Russian), 1978; Biochemistry of Characterised Neurones, 1978; Biology of Serotonergic Neurones, 1982; Dale's Principle and Communication Between Neurones, 1983; Chief Editor, Neurochemistry International; Co-Chief Editor, Progress in Retinal Research; Editorial Board, three journals. *Hobbies:* Squash; Running; Cricket; Reading. *Address:* Nuffield Laboratory of Ophthalmology, University of Oxford, Walton Street, Oxford OX2 6AW, England.

O'SHANICK, Gregory John, b. 22 Nov. 1953, Akron, Ohio, USA. Assistant Professor of Psychiatry; Director, Medical/Psychiatry Service. m. Alison Marshall, 4 June 1977, Galveston, Texas, 1 daughter. *Education:* MD, University of Texas Medical Branch, 1977; Fellow, 1980-81, Chief Resident, 1980-81, Resident, 1978-80, Intern, 1977-78, Duke University. *Appointments include:* Assistant Staff Psychiatrist, Memorial Southwest Hospital, Houston, Texas, 1981-84; Associate in Private Practice, Houston, 1981-82; Clinical Assistant Professor of Psychiatry, Clinical Instructor of Family Practice, 1981-82, Coordinator, PGY-1 Resident Education, 1982-83, Assistant Professor of Psychiatry, Associate Director, Consultation-Liaison Service, 1982-84, University of Texas Health Science Center, Houston; Assistant Professor of Psychiatry, Director of "Medical Psychiatry Service, Consultation" Liaison Psychiatry, Medical College of Virginia, Richmond, 1984-. *Memberships:* Neuropsychiatric Society of Virginia; Association for Academic Psychiatry; American Psychoomatic Society; Academy of Psychososmatic Medicine; American Psychiatric Association. *Publications:* Editor, "Psychiatric Aspects of Trauma", volume 1, 1986. Contributions to: 'MMPI 168 Codebook', 1984; 'Psychiatric Medicine'. *Honours:* Hamilton Ford Award for Excellence in Study of Psychiatry, Medical Branch, 1977, Mu Delta Honorary Medical Service Society, 1976-77, Texas University. *Hobbies:* Racquetball; Reading. *Address:* Division of Consultation Liaison Psychiatry, Medical College of Virginia, Box 268, MCV Station, Richmond, VA 23298, USA.

O'SHEA, Barbara Jean, b. 13 May 1937, Hastings, Ontario, Canada. Director, School of Occupational Therapy. *Education:* MS, Colorado State University, USA; BSc, Queens University, Kingston, Ontario, Canada; Diploma in Physical and Occupational Therapy, University of Toronto. *Appointments:* Senior Staff Occupational Therapist, Ontario Crippled Children Centre, Toronto; Research Associate, Bio-Engineering Institute, University of New Brunswick; Associate Professor, Division of Occupational Therapy, School of Rehabilitation Therapy, Faculty of Medicine, Queens University, Kingston; currently, Director, School of Occupational Therapy, Dalhousie University, Halifax, Nova Scotia. *Memberships:* World Federation of Occupational Therapists; Canadian and Nova Scotia Associations of Occupational Therapists; Nova Scotia Society of Occupational Therapists. *Publications:* "Independence Through EnvirOnmental Control Systems", co-author, 1980; "Proceedings, Symposium on Occupational Therapy Service Delivery Patterns and Manpower Planning", Editor, 1979; contributions to 'Journal of Occupational Therapy', USA and Canada, 'Archives of Physical Medicine and Rehabilitation', 1983. *Honours:* W T MacClement Prize for highest standing in biology, Queens University, Kingston, Ontario, 1970; Phi Kappa Phi, 1977; Muriel Driver Memorial Lectureship,

Canadian Association of Occupational Therapists, 1977. *Hobbies:* Hiking; Nature Study; Cross Country Skiing; Photography. *Address:* School of Occupational Therapy, Faculty of Health Professions, Dalhousie University, Halifax, Nova Scotia, B3H 3J5, Canada.

OSSOFSKY, Helen Johns, b. Philadelphia, Pennsylvania, USA. Physician, Private Practice. m. Eli Ossofsky, 8 Aug. 1950, Havre de Grace, deceased. *Education:* AB, Honours, Mount Holyoke College; MD, Johns Hopkins University School of Medicine. *Appointments:* Fellow, Research Associate, Johns Hopkins University, 1956-59; Assistant Professor, Associate Professor, Pediatrics, Georgetown University School of Medicine, 1959-79; Consultant, NICHHD, NIH, Bethesda, 1962; Consultant, Medical Training, USPHS, 1963-64; Consultant, Attending Staff, Psychiatric Institute of Washington DC, 1968-. *Memberships:* American Medical Association; American Psychiatric Association; MEDICO Alumni; Northern Virginia Pediatric Society; Washington Psychiatric Society; Phi Beta Kappa. *Publications:* "Drug Therapy of Anorexia Nervosa", 'Current Psychiatric Therapies', 1984; "Affective and atopic disorders and cyclic AMP", 'Comprehensive Psychiatry', 1974. *Honours:* International Rescue Committee's Award for Outstanding Service in the Near East, 1959; Honoured by President Lyndon Johnson as Outstanding Women in Government, 1964. *Hobbies:* Swimming, Ice Skating; Piano. *Address:* 1333 Merrie Ridge Road, McLean, VA 22101, USA.

OSTERBALLE, Ole, b. 3 Aug. 1942, Denmark. Physician in Chief. m. Dida, 17 Dec. 1966, 2 sons. *Education:* MD. *Memberships:* Danish Paediatric Society; Danish Society of Allergologi. *Publications:* 'Immunotherapy with purified grass pollen extracts', 1983. *Hobbies:* Flyfishing. *Address:* Paediatric Department, Viborg County Hospital, DK-8800 Viborg, Denmark.

ÖSTÖR, Andrew George, b. 28 July 1943, Hungary. Pathologist. m. Elizabeth Ryan, 6 Sep. 1968, Melbourne, Australia, 1 son, 1 daughter. *Education:* MBBS; FRCPA. *Appointments:* Junior Resident Medical Officer, St Vincent's Hospital, Melbourne, Australia, 1968; Trainee in Pathology, Alfred and Fairfield Hospitals, Melbourne; Pathologist, Royal Women's Hospital, Melbourne-. *Memberships:* Royal College of Pathologists of Australasia; Australian Medical Association; International Society of Gynaecological Pathologists. *Publications:* 'The Medical Complications of Narcotic Addiction' in 'Medical Journal of Australia', 1977; 'Congenital Cystic Adenomatoid Malformation of Lung' in 'American Journal of Clinical Pathology', 1978; 'Benign and Low Grade Variants of Mixed Mullerian Tumour of Uterus' in 'Histopath', 1980; 'Site and Origin of Squamous Cervical Cancer' in 'Obstetrics and Gynaecology', 1983; Co-author "Colposcopy, Cervical Pathology" (textbook), 1984; 'Adenocarcinoma in Situ of Cervix' in 'International Journal of Gynaecology and Pathology', 1984; 'Mixed Mullerian Tumours of Uterus', chapter in "Gynaecological and Obstetrical Pathology", 1986. *Honours:* Velma Stanley Award, 1976; Olive Hewitt Scholarship, 1979. *Hobbies:* Classical Music; Literature; Languages; Tennis; Travel. *Address:* Department of Pathology, The Royal Women's Hospital, Melbourne, Victoria, Australia.

OSTROWSKI, Kazimierz, b. 24 Oct. 1921, Lwow, Poland. Head of Department of Histology. m. Leontyna Celewicz, 25 July 1945. *Education:* MD, Medical Faculty, Warsaw University; PhD. *Appointments:* Assistant, Associate Professor, Currently Head, Department of Histology, Medical School, Warsaw. *Memberships:* Vice-President, Federation of European Cell Biology Organizations; Specialist, World Health Organisation, 1964-80. *Publications:* 'Accuracy, Sensitivity and Specificity of Electron Spin Resonance Analysis of Mineral Constituents of Irradiated Tissues', 1974; 'ESR Spectrometry in Investiga-

tion of Mineralized Tissues' in "The Biochemistry and Physiology of Bone" (editor G H Bourne), 1976; 'Radiation Induced Paramagnetic Entities in Tissue Mineral' in "Free Radicals in Biology", (editor W Pryor), 1980; 'Crystallinity of Tissue Mineral Deposited in the Course of Biomineralization Process' in "International Cell Biology", (editor H G Schweiger), 1981. *Honour:* Doctor honoris causa, University of Orleans, France, 1984. *Hobbies:* Skiing; Tennis; Sailing. *Address:* Department of Histology, Medical School, ul Chalubinskiego 5, 02-004 Warsaw, Poland.

OSVATH, Pål, b. 18 June 1928, Kisvarda, Hungary, Chief of Hospital Pediatric Department. m. (1) Judit Lehrner, 3 Aug. 1957, Szekesfehervat, divorced 1982, 1 son, 1 daughter, (2) Gizella Karoliny, 12 Jan. 1985, Budapest. *Education:* Specialization in Laboratory Works, 1955; Specialization in Pediatrics, 1961; Specialization in Infectious Diseases, 1964; Candidate of Sciences, 1970; Specialization in Immunology, 1979; Doctor of Sciences, 1982; Docent Titulaire, University of Budapest, 1984; Specialization in Allergology, 1985. *Appointments:* Intern, Laboratory of Hospital of Szekesfehervar, 1952-54; Research Worker, Institute of Public Health, Budapest, 1954-57; Intern, Laszlo Hospital for Infectious Diseases, Budapest, 1957-63; First Assistant, Department of Pediatrics, University of Szeged, 1964-74; Chief of Pediatric and Allergologic Department, Children's Hospital of Buda, Budapest, 1974-. *Memberships:* Vice-President 1983-, Hungarian Society of Allergology and Clinical Immunology; Member of the Board and of Executive Committee, Foundation of Allergy Research in Europe, 1983-; European Academy of Allergology and Clinical Immunology; Interasma; Advisory panel on Pediatric Allergy, 1985, International Pediatric Association. *Publications include:* 125 publications including: 'Cross Reaction of Cow's Hair and Milk Antigen', 1972; 'Pediatric Allergy in Central Europe' in "Allergy in Childhood" by F Speer and R J Dockhorn, 1973; "Pediatric Allergology" in Hungarian 1976, Russian 1983; 'Allergic Diseases of Childhood' chapter in "Immunological Aspects of Allerga" by Rajka and Korossy, 1976. *Honour:* For excellent work, 1985. *Hobbies:* Tourism; Walking in mountains; History; Geography; Botany. *Address:* Budapest Szolo u 37, H-1034, Hungary.

OSWALD, Neville Christopher, b. 1 Aug. 1910, Barnet, Hertfordshire, England. Retired. m. Marjorie Mary Sinclair, 1948, Marylebone, 1 son, 2 daughters. *Education:* MRCS (Eng), LRCP (London), 1934; MB. BCh (Cantab), 1935; MD (Cantab), 1947; MRCP (London), 1935; FRCP (London), 1947; TD. *Appointments:* House Surgeon, House Physician, Charing Cross Hospital, 1934-35; House Physician, Brompton Hospital, 1935; Medical Registrar, Charing Cross Hospital, 1936-38; Dorothy Temple Cross Research Fellow, New York, USA, 1938-39; RAMC, 1939-45; Physician, St Bartholomew's Hospital, London, 1946-75, Brompton Hospital, 1948-75, King Edward VII Hospital for Officers, London, 1955-75, King Edward VII Hospital, Midhurst, 1965-75. *Memberships:* Thoracic Society, President, 1974; British Tuberculosis Association, President 1971-72; Association of Physicians. *Publications:* "Honeycomb Lungs", 1948; "Recent Trends in Chronic Bronchitis", 1960; "Diseases of the Respiratory System", 1962. *Honours:* Honorary Physician to H.M. The Queen, 1956-58; Deputy Lieutenant, Greater London, 1973-78; Honorary Colonel, (late RAMC). *Hobbies:* Golf; Local History. *Address:* The Old Rectory, Thurlestone, South Devon TQ7 3NJ, England.

OTSUKA, Yasuo, b. 29 Jan. 1930, Kochi, Japan. Vice President, Oriental Medicine Research Center. m. Yasuko Kobayashi, 23 Nov. 1960, Tokyo, 2 daughters. *Education:* MD, PhD, Tokyo University Medical School. *Appointments:* Director: Kitasato Institute, 1976; Oriental Medicine Research Center, Kitasato Institute, 1976-82. Professor, Kitasato University, 1981-; Vice President, Oriental Medicine Research Centre, Tokyo, 1982-. *Memberships:* Vice President, Japan Society of Oriental Medicine; Executive Director, Japan Society of History of Medicine. *Publications:* 'Chinese Traditional Medicine in Japan', in 'Asian Medical Systems", 1976; "Kanpo, Geschichte, Theorie und Praxis der Chinesisch-Japanischen Medizin', 1976; "Toyoigaku Nyumon", in Japanese, Introduction to Traditional Sino-Japanese Medicine, 1983. *Address:* Oriental Medicine Research Center, Kitasato Institute, 5-9-1 Shirokane, Minato-ku, Tokyo 108, Japan.

OTT, John Edward, b. 2 Nov. 1936, Washington, Pennsylvania, USA. University Professor and Department Chairman. m. Louise Sprajcar, 17 Nov. 1962, Pittsburgh, Pennsylvania, 1 son. *Education:* BS, Psychology, MD, University of Pittsburgh. *Appointments:* Assistant Professor, 1969-76, Associate Professor 1976-77, Department of Paediatrics, University of Colorado; Professor and Chairman, Department of Health Care Sciences, George Washington University, 1977-. *Memberships include:* American Academy of Paediatrics; American Academy of Clinical Toxicology; American Association of Poison Control Center; Ambulatory Paediatric Association; American College of Clinical Pharmacology; American Public Health Association; Medical Directors Division of Group Health Association of America; American Academy of Medical Directors; American College of Physician Executives. *Publications:* Contributor of numerous articles to medical journals and presenter of papers to medical conferences. *Honours:* Alpha Epsilon Delta; Kappa Delta Award, 1970; President, American Academy of Clinical Toxicology, 1975-78. *Hobbies:* Stamp collecting; Antiques collecting; Hiking; Swimming; Tennis. *Address:* 1229 25th Street NW, Washington, DC 20037, USA.

OVERSTREET, David Harold, b. 4 Aug. 1943, Martinez, California, USA. Associate Professor of Psychobiology. m. Judith Ann Zito, 20 May 1972, Firebaugh, California, 1 son, 4 daughters. *Education:* BA, 1965, Graduate Student, 1965-66, University of California; PhD, 1972. *Appointments:* Secondary School Teacher, Dos Palos High School, USA, 1966-69; Research Assistant, 1969-72, Research Associate, 1972-73, Department of Psychobiology, University of California; Lecturer, 1973-75, Senior Lecturer, 1976-78, School of Biology, Flinders University, Australia; Visiting Associate Professor, University of Arizona, USA, 1979; Senior Lecturer, 1980-83, Associate Professor, 1984, 1985-, School of Biology, Flinders University, Australia; Visiting Associate Professor, Department of Psychiatry, San Diego, 1984-85, Department of Pharmacology, Los Angeles, 1984-85, University of California, USA. *Memberships:* Collegium International Neuropsychopharmacologicum; Australasian Society for Clinical and Experimental Pharmacology; Australia Society of Neuroscience; Western Pharmacology Society; Society for Neuroscience; International Society for Neurochemistry. *Publications:* Author or co-author of contributions to: 'Brain Research'; 'Biological Psychiatry'; "Animal Models of Psychopathology", 1984; 'Behavioural and Neural Biology'; "Basal Ganglia: Structure and Function", 1984. *Honours:* Phi Beta Kappa, 1964; Medal in Psychology, 1965; Predoctoral Fellowship, National Institute of Mental Health, 1970-72. *Hobbies:* Duplicate bridge; Baseball; Jigsaw puzzles; Squash. *Address:* School of Biological Sciences, Flinders University of South Australia, Bedford Park, SA5042, Australia.

OWOR, Raphael, b. 7 July 1934, Tororo, Uganda. Professor and Dean, Faculty of Medicine, Makerere University. m. Mary Francis Nyakecho, 2 Jan. 1965, Tororo, 1 son, 4 daughters. *Education:* MB ChB, Makerere University College, 1962; MRCPath, Royal Infirmary, Glasgow, Scotland, 1968; MD, University of East Africa, 1970. *Appointments:* Internship, Mulago Hospital, Kampala, 1962-63; Demonstrator in Pathology, Makerere University, 1963-65; Registrar in Pathology, Glasgow Royal Infirmary, Scotland, 1965-69; Senior Lecturer, 1969-71; Reader in Pathology, 1971-72; Professor of Pathology, 1972-; Maker-

ere University; Dean, Faculty of Medicine, Makerere University, 1981-. *Memberships:* Fellow, Royal College of Pathologists; Fellow, East and Central African Association of Surgeons; East and Central African Association of Physicians; Uganda Medical Council. *Publications:* Contributor to professional journals including: Co-author, 'The Diagnosis of Primary Carcinoma of the Liver', 'East African Medical Journal', 1960; 'Aortic Embolism in endomyocardial fibrosis', 'African Journal Medical Science', 1973; Chapters in books include: 'Cancer Patterns in African Populations' in "Geographical Pathology in Cancer Epidemiology", 1982. *Honour:* Given Benemerenti by Pope John XXIII, 1961. *Hobby:* Gardening. *Address:* Makerere University Medical School, PO Box 7072, Kampala, Uganda.

OXLADE, Zena Elsie, b. 26 Apr. 1929, London, England. Regional Nursing Officer, East Anglia. *Education:* State Registered Nurse, 1950; Sister Tutor's Diploma, London, 1956. *Appointments:* Ward Sister, 1951-52; Theatre Sister, 1952-53; Night Sister, 1953-54; Sister Tutor, 1956-63; Principal Tutor, 1963-69; Principal Nursing Officer, 1969-73; District Nursing Officer, 1973-78; Area Nursing Officer, 1978-81; Regional Nursing Officer, 1981-, East Anglian Regional Health Authority. *Memberships:* Chairman 1977-83, General Nursing Council, England & Wales; UK Central Council for Nurses, Midwives & Health Visitors. *Publication:* "Ear, Nose & Throat Nursing". *Honour:* Commander, Order of the British Empire (CBE), 1984. *Hobbies:* Motoring; Travel; Homecrafts. *Address:* 5 Morgan Court, Old Ipswich Road, Claydon, Suffolk IP6 0AB, England.

OXLEY, Jolyon, b. 27 Nov. 1946, London, England. Senior Physician, National Society for Epilepsy. *Education:* BA, MB, B Chir, MA, University of Cambridge, England; St Bartholomew's Hospital, London; Member, Royal College of Physicians. *Appointments:* House Surgeon; Whipps Cross Hospital; House Physician, St Bartholomew's Hospital; Senior House Officer, Whittington Hospital; Senior House Officer, National Hospital for Nervous Diseases; Registrar, Department of Neurology & Psychiatry, St Thomas's Hospital, London; Medical Research Council Research Fellow & Honorary Senior Registrar, St Bartholomew's Hospital; Honorary Clinical Assistant, National Hospital for Nervous Diseases, London; Registrar, National Hospital; Senior Physician, National Society for Epilepsy, Chalfont St Peter. *Memberships:* Royal College of Physicians; Academic Board, Institute of Neurology; International League against Epilepsy; National Advisory Council for the Employment of Disabled People; Council of Management, British Epilepsy Association; Research Sub-Committee, British Epilepsy Research Foundation. *Publications:* "Chronic Toxicity of Antiepileptic Drugs" (co-editor), 1983; "A Textbook of Epilepsy" (co-editor) in press. *Hobbies:* Theatre; Gardening. *Address:* National Society for Epilepsy, Chalfont Centre for Epilepsy, Chalfont St Peter, Buckinghamshire, SL9 0RJ, England.

OYSTRAGH, Philip, b. 22 Aug. 1930, Harbin, China. Clinical Lecturer, Department of Community Medicine, University of Sydney, Australia; Visiting GP Obstetrician, Royal Hospital for Women; General Practitioner. m. Anne-Louise Singer, 17 July 1976, Sydney, 3 sons, 2 daughters. *Education:* MB, BS; FRACGP, 1974; D(Obs)RCOG, 1971; DipRACOG, 1980. *Appointments include:* Honorary clinical assistant, Royal Alexandra Hospital for Children, 1960-63, Sydney Hospital (Gynaecology), Womens Hospital, Crown Street (Obstetrics). *Memberships:* Australian Medical Association; Australian Society of Hypnosis; International Society of Hypnosis; American Society of Clinical Hypnosis; Australian Society of Psychosomatic Medicine & Obstetrics. *Publications include:* Contributions to various professional journals, 'Pregnancy in Uterus Didelphys', 'Use of Hypnosis in General Practice', 'Hypnosis & Frigidity', 'A Clinically Useful Induction Technique', etc. Contributor to: "Application of Hypnosis in Sex Therapy", Biegel & Johnson, USA; Symposium, 'Psychological Influences & Illness', Hypnosis & Medicine, Royal Society of Medicine, London, 1982. *Address:* 177-179 Glenayr Avenue, Bondi, NSW 2026, Australia.

OZEK, Metin, b. 29 June 1930, Istanbul, Turkey. Ex-Professor, Psychiatry & Medical Psychology. m. Sevim Pakalin Cözek, 21 Apr. 1955, Istanbul, 1 son, 1 daughter. *Education:* Prof Dr Med, University of Istanbul. *Appointments:* Resident, Psychiatric Clinics, Universities of Freiburg, 1955, University of Tubingen, 1956-58; Chief Resident, Fellow, Psychiatric University Clinic, Zurich, Switzerland, 1958-60; Head, State Hospital, Istanbul, 1961-66; Professor, Psychiatry, Head, Psychotherapy, University of Istanbul, 1967-82. *Memberships:* Committee Member, World Psychiatric Association; Corresponding Member, Deutsche Gesellschaft fur Psychiatore und Nervenherlkunde; International Federation for Medical Psychotherapy; International Federation for Mental Health; etc. *Publications:* Over 200 scientific articles in various journals. *Honours:* Professor, University Heidelberg, 1973; Alexander von Humboldt Foundation, 1955-58, 1971-72. *Hobbies:* Photography; Literature; Translation from German into Turkish. *Address:* Tesvikiye Pk 23, 80212 Istanbul, Turkey.

OZER, Mark Norman, b. 17 Jan. 1932, Cambridge, Massachusetts, USA. Associate Professor. m. (2) Martha Ross Redden, 14 Aug. 1979, Washington, District of Columbia, 1 son, 4 daughters. *Education:* AB, Harvard University; MD, Boston University School of Medicine. *Appointments:* Director, Program for Learning Studies, Childrens Hospital National Medical Center, Washington, District of Columbia; Assistant Professor, Neurology, Associate Professor, Child Health and Development, George Washington School of Medicine; Associate Professor, Neurology, Medical College of Virginia, Richmond, Virginia; Assistant Chief, Spinal Cord Injury Service, McGuire Veterans Administration Medical Center, Richmond, Virginia. *Memberships:* American Academy of Neurology; American Academy of Aphasia; American Society for Cybernetics; Congress of Rehabilitation Medicine; American Paraplegia Society; International Medical Society of Paraplegia. *Publications:* "A Cybernetic Approach to the Assessment of Children", 1979; "Solving Learning and Behavioral Problems of Children", 1981; "The Ozer Method", 1983; about 60 articles in professional journals. *Address:* 1919 Stuart Avenue, Richmond, VA 23220, USA.

ÖZGÜNEN, Tuncay, b. 17 June 1942, Antakya, Turkey. Chairman and Associate Professor, Department of Physiology and Biophysics; Chief, Clinical Pathology Laboratories, Department of Experimental Surgery, University Cukurova, Faculty of Medicine. m. Dr Fatma Tuncay Özgünen, 11 Nov. 1967, Ankara, 2 sons. *Education:* MD; Diploma Flight Surgeon; PhD, Biochemistry and Clinical Pathology. *Appointment:* Assistant Professor, Gulhane Military Medical Academy, 1972-78. *Memberships:* Turkish Medical Association; Turkish Society of Biochemistry; International Union of Physiological Sciences; New York Academy of Science; Aerospace Medical Association. *Publications:* 10 Books and 36 Articles, in Turkish, on Physiology and Clinical Pathology. *Honours:* Turkish Scientific and Technical Research Council Grant, 1965; Distinguished Medical Officer, Turkish Air Force, 1978. *Hobbies:* Literature; Music. *Address:* Cukurova Üniversitesi, Tip Fakültesi, Fizyoloji ve Biofizik Anabilim Dali Baskani, Adana, Turkey.

P

PAARFUS, Barbara Diane Leidholdt, b. 29 Apr. 1936, Hartford, Connecticut, USA. Licensed Psychologist. *Education:* BA (Psychology), Gettysburg College, Philadelphia, USA, 1957; MA (Clinical Psychology), Temple University, Philadelphia, 1959. *Appointments:* Teacher, Overbrook School for the Blind, Philadelphia, 1958-60; Guidance Counsellor, Henrico County, Virginia, 1960-61; Staff Psychologist, Medical College of Virginia, 1961-64; Instructor in Psychiatry/{ Psychologist, 1964-67, Clinical Instructor in Psychiatry, 1968-73; School Psychologist, Richmond Public Schools, 1973-79; Psychology Assistant, Westbrook Psychiatric Hospital, Richmond, Virginia, 1982-83; School Psychologist, Diagnostic Centre, Mecklenburg County School Board, Boydton, Virginia, 1984-. *Memberships:* National Association of School Psychologists; American Psychological Association; Virginia Psychological Association; Virginia Association for School Psychologists; American Group Psychotherapy Society; Mid-Atlantic Group Psychotherapy Society; Richmond Area Psychological Association. *Honours:* Psi Chi, 1957; Alpha Psi Omega, 1957; Temple University Phi Delta Gamma Award, 1959; Community Actors Playhouse Best Actress Award, 1963; Rehabilitation Action Programme Certificate of Appreciation, 1975. *Hobbies:* Little theatre acting; Production; Make-up; Bridge; Gardening; Roller Skating; Swimming; Boating; Animals; Church and Charity volunteer work. *Address:* 803 West Street, Clarksville, VA 23927, USA.

PADILLA, Geraldine, b. 28 Feb. 1940, Manila, Philippines. Research Scientist. m. Gilbert J Padilla, 30 June 1966 (deceased), 2 sons. *Education:* BA, Assumption College, Manila; MA, Ateneo University, Manila; PhD, University of California, Los Angeles, USA. *Appointments:* Research Assistant, Psychology Department, University of California, Los Angeles, 1967-68; Instructor, Department of Nursing, California State University, Los Angeles, 1981-; Director of Nursing Research, 1970-85, Research Scientist, 1985-, City of Hope National Medical Center. *Memberships:* Sigma Theta Tau; American Association for the Advancement of Science; American Psychological Association; Western Society for Research in Nursing. *Publications:* 'Quality of Life as a Cancer Nursing Outcome Variable', 'Advances in Nursing Science', 1985; 'Psychosocial Aspects of Artificial Feeding', 'Cancer', 1985. *Honours:* US East-West Fellow, University of Hawaii and University of California, 1965-67; USPHS Traineeship, University of California, Los Angeles, 1968-70. *Address:* City of Hope National Medical Center, Department of Nursing Research and Education, 1500 E Duarte Road, Duarte, CA 91010, USA.

PAHLAJANI, Devikishan Bherumal, b. 4 Dec. 1938, Bombay, India. Consulting Cardiologist. m. Dr Pramode V Kamath, 23 Feb. 1968, 1 son, 1 daughter. *Education:* MD, FACC, FCCP (USA); FISE; FIMSA. *Appointments:* Post-doctoral Fellow in Paediatric cardiology, Cook County Hospital, Chicago, Illinois, USA; Honorary Assistant Professor of Cardiology, ITM Medical College, Bombay, India; Honorary Cardiologist, Narasah Hospital; Consultant Cardiologist, Breach County Hospital. *Memberships:* Association of Physicians of India; Cardiological Society of India; American College of Cardiology; International Academy of Chest Physicians. *Publications:* More than 50 articles, one book on electrocardiology, section editor on cardiology in textbook of API in medicine. *Honour:* Order of Merit, MD examination, University of Bombay, 1967. *Hobbies:* Music; Travel. *Address:* Bherumal Bhavan, Mogul Lane, Mehin, Bombay 400016, India.

PAIN, Roger Harry, b. 21 May 1927, London, England. Professor of Physical Biochemistry. m. Beryl Jones, 5

Dec. 1964, Beckenham, Kent, 1 son, 1 daughter. *Education:* BA 1953, BSc 1954, Chemistry, University of Oxford; PhD, Chester Beatty Cancer Research Institute, London, 1956. *Appointments:* Gordon Jacobs Research Fellow, 1953-56; Wellcome Research Laboratories, 1956-60; Research Associate, Wright Fleming Institute, Department of Immunology, 1960-66; R A Department of Biochemistry, Duke University, North Carolina, 1963-64; Lecturer, Professor, Department of Biochemistry, University of Newcastle-upon-Tyne, England, 1966-. *Memberships:* British Biophysical Society (Meetings Secretary, Secretary & Chairman); Biochemical Society; British Society for Immunology. *Publications:* Various papers in professional & scientific journals. *Honour:* Medal of the Josef Stefan Institute, Ljubljana, Yugoslavia, 1983. *Hobbies:* Singing; Sailing; Walking. *Address:* Department of Biochemistry, University of Newcastle-upon-Tyne, Newcastle, NE1 7RU, England.

PALACIO, Alfredo, b. 22 Jan. 1939, Ecuador. Institute Director. m. Maria Beatriz Paret, 5 Sep. 1969, Guayaquil, 1 son, 3 daughters. *Education:* Doctor in Medicine and Surgery; Medical School, University of Guayaquil; Intern in Medicine, Mount Sinai Hospital, Ohio, USA; Medical Residencies, Veterans Hospitals, Case Western Reserve University; Cardiology Fellowship, Barnes Hospital, University of St Louis, Missouri, USA. *Appointments:* Professor of Internal Medicine, University of Guayaquil, 1975; Cardiologist-Haemodynaist, Hospital Regional del IESS, 1974-76, Hospital Luis Vernaza, 1977-78; Director, Instituto Nacional de Cardiologia, Guayaquil, 1980-; Scientific Director, Boletin Ecuatoriano de Cardiologia, 1981-; Editorial Committee, Ultrasonidos Revista de Ecografia en Medicina. *Memberships:* Fellow: American College of Cardiology; American College of Chest Physicians, New York Academy of Sciences; Council of Ecuadorean Institute of Science. *Publications:* "Atlas de Ecocardiografia Bidimensional", 1981; English edition, 1983; "Cardiopatia Isquemica. Prueba de Esfuerzo y Prescripcion de ejercicio". Author of 32 scientific abstracts, 15 other publications. Participant in 16 international congresses. *Honours:* Recognition Award, American Medical Association, 1973-76; Ilustre Consejo Cantonal de Guayaquil Award (City award for best scientist of the year); Eugenio Espejo Award for best book published by Ecuadorean, 1983. *Hobbies:* Reading; Swimming; Music. *Address:* PO Box 5681, Guayaquil, Ecuador.

PALLADINO, Michael, Angelo, b. 21 Dec. 1948, Jersey City, New Jersey, USA. Scientist, Genentech; Associate Professor, University of California San Francisco Medical Center. m. 17 July 1976, New York, 1 son. *Education:* MS, Biochemistry, Fairleigh Dickenson University School of Dentistry, 1973; PhD, Immunology, Pathology, New York University, 1978. *Appointments:* NIH Postdoctoral Fellowship, Sloan-Kettering Cancer Center, 1978-80; Research Associate, Sloan-Kettering Cancer Center, 1981-83; Scientist II, 1983-84, Scientist I, 1984-, Genentech Incorporated; Associate Professor, University of California at San Francisco, 1985-. *Memberships:* American Association of Cancer Researchers; American Association of Immunologists; New York Academy of Sciences; Reticuolendothelial Society; American Association for the Advancement of Science. *Publications:* Contributor to professional journals, books, etc; Abstracts; Presentations. *Honours include:* American Cancer Society Junior Faculty Research Award, 1980-83; American Cancer Society Study Section, 1985-; NIH Predoctoral Fellowship; numerous other awards, grants, etc. *Address:* Genentech Incorporated, 460 Point San Bruni Boulevard, South San Francisco, CA 94080, USA.

PALLIE, Wazir, b. 12 Mar. 1922, Colombo, Ceylon. Professor of Anatomy. m. Wenche Elisabeth Michelsen, June 1955, 3 sons. *Education:* MB, BS, Faculty of Medicine, University of Ceylon, 1945; Primary Fellow,

Royal College of Surgeons (England), 1950; D. Phil, Oriel College, University of Oxford, England, 1955; Postgraduate training, Electron Microscopy, University of California at Los Angeles, 1957-58. *Appointments:* House Surgeon, House Physician, Colombo General Hospital, Ceylon, 1946-47; District Medical Officer, Medical Officer of Health, 1950; Lecturer in Anatomy, Faculty of Medicine, University of Ceylon, 1950, 1955-56; Tutor & Demonstrator in Anatomy, University of Oxford, 1951-55; Head, Department of Anatomy, Peradeniya, University of Ceylon, 1961-62; Foundation Professor & Head, Department of Anatomy, University of Malaya, 1962-69; Professor of Anatomy, 1969-75, Professor & Chairman of Anatomy, 1975-, McMaster University, Hamilton, Ontario, Canada. *Memberships:* Life Member, Ceylon Medical Association; Affiliate, Royal Society of Medicine; Canadian Association of Anatomists; American Association of Anatomists; External Examiner, Faculty of Medicine, Universities of Penang & Malaysia. *Publications:* More than 50 articles in professional journals. *Honours:* Research Fellow, University of California at Los Angeles Medical Centre, 1957-58; Smith-Mundt & Fulbright Award Scholarships, 1957-58; 'Sida' (Swedish) Fellowship, Karolinska Institute, Stockholm, Sweden, 1966. *Hobbies:* Tennis; Golf; Chamber & Orchestral Music (violinist). *Address:* Faculty of Health Sciences, McMaster University, 1280 Main Street West, Hamilton, Ontario, L8S 4K1, Canada.

PALLONE, Francesco, b. 1 Aug. 1945, Camerino, Italy. Senior Research Officer, University of Rome. m. F I Habib, 21 May 1972, Rome, 2 sons, 1 daughter. *Education:* MD; Specialist in Gastroenterology. *Appointments:* Honorary Research Assistant, Royal Postgraduate Medical School, University of London, England, 1974-75; Research Fellow, University of Rome, Italy, 1975-81; NATO Senior Research Fellow, The Radcliffe Infirmary, Oxford, England, 1982. *Memberships:* The Italian Society of Gastroenterology; The New York Academy of Science. *Publications:* Contributor of articles to various medical journals. *Hobbies:* Music; Soccer. *Address:* Viale Regina Margherita 93, 00198 Rome, Italy.

PALMA-CARLOS, Antero Manuel, b. 21 Mar. 1933, Lisbon, Portugal. Professor, Clinical Director. m. Dra Maria Laura A de Almeida da Palma-Carlos, 22 Dec. 1956, Lisbon, Portugal. *Education:* MD, Lisbon School of Medicine; PhD, University of Lisbon; Internship, Residency, Lisbon University Hospital. *Appointments:* Assistant Professor, Associate Professor, Titular Professor of Clinical Immunology, Lisbon School of Medicine; Director, Centre for Allergology & Clinical Immunology. *Memberships:* IAACI; Vice-President, EAACI; General Secretary Interasma, UE Allergist (Secretary-General); President, Portuguese Society of Allergology. *Publications:* Some 300 papers; also books: "Bronchial Asthma", 1973; "Respiratory Allergy", 1981; "Clinical Immunology", 1981. *Honour:* Chevalier de l'Ordre National de Mérite, France. *Hobbies:* Opera; Concerts; Reading; Art; etc. *Address:* Centro Alergologia e Imunologia Clinica, Rua Sampaio e Pina, 16-40, 1000 Lisbon, Portugal.

PALMER, Patrick Michael, b. 30 June 1948, San Antonio, Texas, USA. Clinical Assistant Professor, Orthopaedics, University of Texas Health Science Centre, San Antonio. m. Kathy B Kelly, 16 June 1973, San Antonio, 1 son, 1 daughter. *Education:* BA, Special Honours, Psychology, 1969, MD 1973, University of Texas; Residency, University of California, San Francisco, 1978; Fellowship, Paediatric Orthopaedic Surgery, Alfred I, du Pont Institute, Delaware, 1982. *Appointments include:* Assistant Professor of Orthopaedics, University of Missouri, 1982-85. *Memberships:* American Academy of Orthopaedic Surgery; Le Roy C Abbott Orthopaedic Society; Paediatric Orthopaedic Society of North America. *Honour:* Diplomate, American Board of Orthopaedic Surgery, 1980. *Address:* Village Oaks Orthopaedics, 12709 Toepperwein Road, Suite 102, San Antonio, TX 78233, USA.

PALMER, Wilfred H, b. 3 Apr. 1929, Montreal, Quebec, Canada. Professor of Family and Community Medicine, Family Physician-in-Chief. m. Joanne, 16 June 1955, Montreal, 2 sons, 1 daughter. *Education:* BSc 1952, MDCM 1954, McGill University; Diploma Internal Medicine, 1959; FRCP (C), 1959; CSPQ; Internal Medicine 1959, Cardiology 1961; FACP, 1968; CCFP, 1975. *Appointments:* Clinical Assistant 1960, Assistant Physician 1962, Associate Physician 1968, Royal Victoria Hospital, Montreal; Physician-in-Chief, 1971-75, Director Family Medicine Unit 1975-78, Queen Elizabeth Hospital, Montreal; Affiliated Physician 1979-80, Senior Physician 1980-81, Montreal General Hospital; Professor and Chairman, Department of Family and Community Medicine, University of Toronto, 1982-; Family Physician-in-Chief, Toronto General Hospital, 1982-. *Memberships:* Advisory Committee, University of Toronto Gerontology Program; Editorial Board, Journal Canadian Family Physicians; Chairman of Board of Examiners, Certification Process Committee, Canadian representative, Ontario Chapter Board of Representatives, CFPC; Membership Committee, Society of Teachers of Family Medicine. *Publications:* 19 on cardiology, 13 in health care delivery. *Address:* Department of Family and Community Medicine, University of Toronto, c/o Toronto General Hospital, Charlie Connacher Research Wing, CCRW 4-800, 200 Elizabeth Street, Toronto, Ontario, M5G 2C4, Canada.

PALO, John, b. 27 Feb. 1920, New York, USA, Chiropractic Orthopaedist. *Education:* BS, Queens College; DC, National College of Chiropractic; Diplomate, American Board Chiropractic Orthopedists; Fellow, Academy of Chiropractic Orthopedists; Certified Team Physician, ACA Council on Sports Injuries and Physical Fitness. *Appointments:* Assistant Director, New York City Department of Health, Chiropractic Division; Chiropractic Orthopedist; Faculty Member, Postgraduate Division, New York Chiropractic College for Diplomate Course in Chiropractic Orthopedics. *Memberships:* American Chiropractic Association; Council of Chiropractic Orthopedists; Fellow, Academy of Chiropractic Orthopedists; ACA Council on Sports Injuries and Physical Fitness; New York State Chiropractic Association. *Publications:* "While Passing Through", 1954; "New World Mystics", 1980; 'Quality Health Care', 1977; 'Neurological Diagnosis', 1975; 'Look at Yourself - Keys to Good Posture', 1981; 'No Fault Arbitration', 1982; 'Running Smart', 1982; 'I Love Boxing, But . . .', 1983; 'Trochanteric Bursitis', 1983. *Honours:* Fellow, American College of Chiropractors; Member, International Research Council of Rose-Croix University, University of Rosicrucian Order. *Hobbies:* Writing; Sport. *Address:* 50 East 42nd Street, New York, NY 10017, USA.

PANAYI, Gabriel Stavros, b. 9 Nov. 1940, Cyprus, Professor of Rheumatology. m. Alexandra Ourrou, 13 Mar. 1973, 2 sons. *Education:* Gonville and Caius College, Cambridge, England; St Marys Hospital Medical School, London; MD; FRCP. *Appointments:* House Physician, Queen Elizabeth II Hospital, Welwyn Garden City, 1965-66; House Surgeon, St Marys Hospital, London, 1966; Senior House Officer, Medicine, General Hospital, Nottingham, 1966; Senior House Officer, Pathology, Central Middlesex, London, 1967; MRC Junior Research Fellow, St Marys Hospital Medical School, London, Kennedy Institute of Rheumatology, Bute Gardens, London, 1967-69; Clinical Research Fellow, Rheumatic Diseases, Northern General Hospital, Edinburgh, Scotland, 1970-73; Lecturer in Rheumatology, Department of Medicine, 1973-76, ARC Senior Lecturer, Consultant in Rheumatology, 1976-80, Professor, ARC Chair of Rheumatology, 1980-, Guy's Hospital, London. *Memberships:* Heberden Society; Honorary Secretary, Section of Medicine, Experimental Medicine and Therapeutics, 1977-79, Royal Society of Medicine; British Society of Immunology; Editorial Board, Clinical and Experimental Immunology, 1984. *Publications:* Author of numerous articles on medical subjects especially rheumatoid arthritis. *Honours:* Max-Bonn Prize, Gold

Medal in Pathology; Sir Lionel Whitby Medal, University of Cambridge, 1970-71; Margaret Holroyde Prize, The Heberden Society, 1975; Allesandro Robecci Prize, European League against Rheumatism, 1979. *Address:* Rheumatology Unit, Division of Medicine, Guy's Hospital, London, England.

PANCER, Jeffrey Paul, b. 6 Jan. 1943, Toronto, Ontario, Canada. Private Practice, Orthodontics. m. 7 Aug. 1966, Toronto, Ontario, 1 son, 1 daughter. *Education:* DDS, University of Toronto. *Appointments:* Private Practice, Toronto, Ontario. *Memberships:* Canadian and Ontario Dental Associations; Associate Member, Atlantic Coast Dental Research Clinic; Toronto Crown and Bridge Study Club. *Hobbies:* Tennis; Swimming; Board sailing. *Address:* 1709 Bloor Street West, Toronto, Ontario, Canada M6P 1B2.

PANCONESI, Emiliano, b. 20 June 1923, Pistoia, Italy. Professor and Chairman, Department of Dermatology, University of Florence, Italy. m. Diana Sears, New York City, USA. 2 sons, 1 daughter. *Education:* MD, 1947; Specialist in Dermatology, 1949; Libera Docenza in Dermatology, 1956. *Memberships:* Italian Society of Dermatology and Venereology; Italian Society of Allergology and Clinical Immunology; Italian Society of Psychosomatics; French Society of Dermatology; Polish Society of Dermatology (Honorary); American Academy of Dermatology; College of Physicians of Philadelphia; International Society of Dermatology; Colegio Ibero-Latino-Americano de Dermatologie. *Publications:* Approximately 200 publications including 3 books: "Immunopatologia Cutanea", 1981; "Manuale di Dermatologia", 1982; "Stress and Skin Diseases: Psychosomatic Dermatology", 1984. *Address:* Istituto di Clinica Dermosifilopatica, Via degli Alfani 37, 50121, Florence, Italy.

PANDEYA, Nirmalendu Kumar, b. 9 Feb. 1940, Bihar, India. Plastic Surgeon. *Education:* BSc, Bihar University, India, 1958; MS, University of Nebraska, USA, 1962; DO, University of Osteopathic Medicine, Des Moines, USA, 1969. *Appointments:* Private Practice, 1975-present. *Memberships:* Association of Plastic Surgeons of India; Association of Surgeons of India; Association of Military Surgeons of the United States; Aerospace Medical Association; Americal Medical Association; American Osteopathic Association; American College of Osteopathic Surgeons; Aerospace Medical Association; Society of United States Air Force Clinical Surgeons; ANG Alliance of Flight Surgeons, etc. *Publications include:* Numerous conference papers, articles in professional journals and book reviews, including: 'Secondary Burn Reconstruction' in "The American Surgeon", 1982, (with others); "Male Aesthetic Surgery", 1983 (book review); "Hair Transplantation", 1984 (book review); "Aesthetic and Reconstructive Breast Surgery", 1985 (book review). *Honours:* Life Member, Science Society, MS College, Bihar, India; Regents Fellow, University of Nebraska, 1961-62; Membership of Scientific Register, Council of India; Included in 'Men of Sciences and Technology', India, 1964. *Hobby:* Air National Guard. *Address:* 1000 73rd Street, Suite 21, Des Moines, IA, USA 50311.

PANIDIS, Dimitrios, b. 10 Oct. 1942, Greece. Assistant Professor in Endocrinology. m. Katerina, 13 Nov. 1971, Greece, 2 daughters. *Education:* MD; PhD, Reproductive Endocrinology; Member, Royal College of Medicine, London, England. *Appointments:* Registrar in Endocrinology, Evangelismus Medical Centre, Athens, Greece; Registrar, Fertility Unit, University College Hospital, London, England; Assistant Professor, Fertility Unit, 2nd Department of Obstetrics and Gynaecology, Aristotelian University of Thessaloniki, Greece. *Memberships:* Endocrinological Society of Greece; Fellow, Greek Society of Fertility and Sterility; Royal Society of Medicine, London. *Publications:* "Modern Trend in Semen Analysis", editor, 1980; "Infertile Couple", editor, 1982; 'Semen Parameters in 114 Fertile Men', 1984; 'CK Activity and isoenzyme

Analysis in Thtroid Disorders', 1984. *Hobbies:* Gardening; Painting. *Address:* Mitropoleos 119, Thessaloniki, Greece.

PANSU, Danielle Fernande Josette née Esclangon, b. 8 Oct. 1932, Paris, France. Laboratory Director. m. Claude Pansu, 17 May 1956, Lyon, France, 3 sons, 1 daughter. *Education:* BS, University of Grenoble, 1949; MD, Lyon, 1961; Graduate in Paediatrics, 1960; Diploma for use of Radioisotopes in Medicine, 1965; Validation of 1st year in Radiology, 1978. *Appointments:* External Medical Student, 1952-55, Internist, 1955-59, Attaché, 1961-78, Civil Hospices of Lyon; Assistant, Lyons School of Medicine, 1975; Acting Director, 1970-78, Director, 1978-, Practical School of Higher Studies, Lyons. *Memberships:* French Society of Rheumatology; French Society of Endocrinology; French Antirheumatism Association; French Association of Nutrition; Study Group on Epithelial Digestive Cells; European Transport Group; American Society for Bone & Mineral Research; Study Group on Biorhythms. *Publications:* (With others) "Physiologie Comparée des Echanges Calciques", 1974; (with P Meunier J L Vauzelle) chapter on "Classification des décalcifications primitives du sujet âgé" in "Symposium: Problèmes de Gériatrie", 1968; Various articles in 'Digestion', 'Journal of Nutrition', 'American Journal of Physiology', 'Diabète et Métabolisme', and others. *Honours:* Clin Comar Prize of Medical Studies, 1957; Visiting Professor, University of Connecticut Health Centre, 1982-. *Hobbies:* Fostering; Piano; Chorus. *Address:* Laboratoire de Physiologie des Echanges Minéraux, Ecole Pratique des Hautes Etudes, Pavilion H Bis, Hôpital E Herriot, 69374 Lyon Cedex 08, France.

PAOLETTI, Rodolfo, b. 23 Aug. 1931, Milan, Italy. Dean, Pharmacy. *Education:* MD 1955; Pharmacology, 1967; Honorary MD Karolinska, 1983. *Appointments:* Assistant Professor, 1955-62, Associate Professor, 1962-67, Professor, Chairman, 1970-, Pharmacology, Chairman, Council on Postgraduate Education, 1976-, Dean, School of Pharmacy, 1982-, University of Milan; Professor, Pharmacology, Chairman, Pharmacology, University of Cagliari, Sardinia, 1967-70; Italian Representative NATO Scientific Council, Brussels, Belgium, 1981-. *Memberships:* American Academy for the Advancement of Science; American Heart Association; Council on Atherosclerosis; American Oil Chemists Society; Biochemical Society, London; British Pharmacology Society; European Neuroscience Association; European Society Clinical Investment; European Society Study of Drug Toxicity; French Society Ather. Research; International Ather. Society; International Cardiology Foundation; International Reticuloendotherlial Society; International Society Neurochemistry. *Address:* Institute of Pharmacology and Pharmacognosy, Via Andrea del Sarto 21, 20129 Milan, Italy.

PAPAKOSTAS, Yiannia, b. 14 Apr. 1941, Greece. Senior Lecturer, Psychiatry, University of Athens. m. Areti Mougias, 4 July 1971, 1 son, 1 daughter. *Education:* MD, University of Athens Medical School; Diplomat, Psychiatry, American Board of Psychiatry and Neurology; Certification, Behaviour-Cognitive Psychotherapies, Behaviour Therapy Institute, White Plains, New York. *Appointments:* 1st, 2nd, 3rd year Resident, Psychiatry, State University of New York, Stony Brook, 1975-78; Research Assistant Professor, Psychiatry, State University of New York, 1978-81; Senior Lecturer, Psychiatry, University of Athens, Greece, 1981-. *Memberships:* American Psychiatric Association; Greek Psychiatric and Neurological Society. *Publications:* Co-author, "Neuroendocrine measures in psychiatric patients: course and outcome with ECT", 'Psychiatry Research', 1981; "Increases in prolactin levels following bilateral and Unilateral ECT", 'American Journal of Psychiatry', 1973. *Honours:* Physicians' Recognition Awards, in Continuous Medical Education, 1978-81, 1981-84. *Hobby:* Literature. *Address:* Kyprou 49, Glyfada, Athens, Greece.

PAPANASTASSIOU, Anocstocssios, b. 15 May 1934, Xanthi, Greece. Assistant Clinical Professor, Psychiatry, University of Illinois; Private Practice; Staff, Chicago Read Mental Health Centre, Ravenswood Hospital, Maine Township Mental Health Centre. m. Margaret Reukauf, 8 June 1963, Buffalo, USA, 1 son, 2 daughters. *Education:* MD, Athens University School of Medicine, Greece, 1959; Deaconess Hospital, Buffalo New York, USA; Residency, Psychiatry, Rollman Psychiatric Institute, University of Cinconnati, Ohio, Mount Sinai Hospital, Chicago Medical School, Illinois; Residency, Neurology, University of Louisville, Kentucky, Louisville General Hospital, Hines VA Hospital, Hines, Illinois. *Appointments:* Assistant Medical Director, Daphni State Hospital, Athens, Greece, 1967-69. *Memberships:* American Psychiatric Association; Illinois Psychiatric Society. *Publications:* "A Three Years Longitudinal Study of the Effect of Neuroleptics in Schizophrenia", 1974. *Honours:* Award, Ravenswood Hospital, as main contributor and organizer of continuing medical edication, 1980; Awards, American Medical Association for continuing medical education. *Hobby:* Painting. *Address:* 730 South Greenwood, Park Ridge, IL 60068, USA.

PAPAPANAGIOTOU, John, b. 14 Sep. 1921, Patras, Greece. Professor, Microbiology, Medical School, University of Thessaloniki. m. Clea Countouris, 27 Apr. 1957, Athens, 1 son, 1 daughter. *Education:* Bachelor of Medicine, MD, University of Athens. *Appointments:* Director, Microbiology Laboratory, Seamens Hospital, Athens, 1956-65, I.K.A. General Hospital, Penteli, Athens, 1965-67; Professor, Microbiology, Medical School, University of Thessaloniki, 1967-. *Memberships:* Greek Society for Microbiology; Medical Society of Thessaloniki; Society for General Microbiology; Society of Applied Bacteriology, England; International Association of Biological Standardisation; New York Academy of Sciences. *Publications:* "Medical Microbiology and Immunology", 2 volumes; many articles in Greek and Foreign Journals. *Honours:* WHO Fellow, London, England, 1954; Greek State Scholarships, 1958; Distinguished Service Medal, Greek Army. *Address:* 5 Mitropolitou Iossif Str. 546, 22 Thessaloniki, Greece.

PAPERNY, David Mark, b. 26 Feb. 1951, Los Angeles, USA. Director of Hawaii Kaiser Adolescent Clinic. *Education:* BS, Biochemistry, 1973, MD, 1977, University of California at Los Angeles. *Appointments:* Staff, Hawaii Sexual Abuse Treatment Center, Honolulu, 1978; Kapiolani Children's Medical Center, Honolulu, 1979; Children's Orthopaedic Medical Center, Seattle, 1980; Kaiser Foundation Hospital, Honolulu, Director Adolescent Clinic 1981-; Director, March of Dimes Teen Health Computer Programs, 1985. *Memberships:* American Academy of Paediatrics; Fellow; American Board of Paediatrics, Diplomat; Society for Adolescent Medicine; American Society for Clinical Hypnosis; Hawaii Academy of Hypnosis, Founder. *Publications include:* 'Chlamydial Pelvic Inflammatory Disease in Adolescents', 1981, 'Adolescent Sexual Offense Behavior, 1982, both in Journal of Adolescent Health Care; 'Variations in Sexual Behavior of Adolescents' in "Practice of Pediatrics" 1983; 'Maltreatment of Adolescents' in Adolescence, 1983. *Honours:* Court-qualified expert child sexual abuse, 1980; March of Dimes Grantee on Computer-Assisted Instruction, 1985; Magna Cum Laude, UCLA, 1973. *Hobbies:* Hawaiian dance; Electronics; Computer science. *Address:* 1697 Ala Moana Boulevard, Honolulu, HI 96813, USA.

PAPPAS, George, b. 1 Aug. 1933, Pennsylvania, USA. Associate Professor of Surgery. m. Gail Houston, 1 son, 2 daughters. *Education:* BS, Davis & Elkins College; MS University of Minnesota; Jefferson Medical School. *Appointments:* Chief, Cardiothoracic Surgery, VA Hospital, Denver, Colorado, 1967-76; Chief, Cardiovascular & Thoracic Surgery, The Children's Hospital, Denver, 1976-85; Associate Professor of Surgery, University of Colorado. *Memberships:* Society of Thoracic Surgeons; American Association of Thoracic Surgery; Western Thoracic Surgical Society; American College of Surgeons; American Heart Association; Mayo Alumni Association; International Cardiovascular Surgical Society; Society for Vascular Surgery; Denver & Colorado Medical Societies; Rocky Mountain Cardiac Surgical Society; Society of Academic Surgeons. *Publications:* Author & Co-author of more than 70 articles in medical & surgical journals. *Honours:* Distinguished Alumni Award, Davis & Elkins College, 1980; Allen Welkind Award, Mayo Graduate School of Medicine, 1966. *Hobby:* Hunting. *Address:* 1056 East 19th Avenue, Denver, CO 80218, USA.

PAPPAS, George Demetrios, b. 26 Nov. 1926, Portland, Maine, USA. Professor and Head. m. Bernice Levine, 2 daughters. *Education:* AB, Bowdoin College, 1947; MSc, 1948, PhD, 1952, Ohio State University. *Appointments:* Visiting Investigator, The Rockefeller Institute, New York, 1952-54; Associate to Associate Professor of Anatomy, College of Physicians and Surgeons, Columbia University, 1956-66; Professor of Anatomy, 1967-77, Professor of Neuroscience, 1974-77, Albert Einstein College of Medicine, New York; Professor and Head, Department of Anatomy, University of Illinois, College of Medicine, Chicago, Illinois, 1977-. *Memberships:* Fellow, American Association for the Advancement of Science; Chairman of Public Policy Committee, 1981-84, American Association of Anatomists; President, 1974-75, American Society for Cell Biology; President, 1981-82, Association of Anatomy Chairmen; Program Chairman, 1984-85, Electron Microscopy Society of America; Harvey Society; International Brain Research Organisation (UNESCO); Board of Trustees, 1975-81, Marine Biological Laboratory, Woods Hole, Massachusetts, Corporation Member; Fellow, New York Academy of Science; President, 1967-68, New York Society of Electron Microscopy; Sigma Xi; President, 1985-86, Society for Neuroscience, Chicago Chapter. *Publications:* Over 140 original articles on professional subjects in medical and scientific journals. *Honours:* Career Development Award, Public Health Service, NIH, 1964-66. *Address:* Department of Anatomy/University of Illinois at Chicago, 808 South Wood Street, Chicago, IL 60612, USA.

PAQUET, Karl-Joseph, b. 25 Aug. 1937, Aachen, Germany. Professor of Surgery. m. Dietlinde Grunwald, 15 July 1975, 3 sons, 1 daughter. *Education:* Einhard-Gymnasium, Aachen, 1958; Studies of Human Medicine & Psychology, Medical & Philosophical Faculties, Universities of Cologne, Free University, Berlin; Study of Human Medicine, Rheinische Friedrich-Wilhelms-University, Bonn, 1959-64. *Appointments:* Registrar, Department of Anaesthesiology, University of Bonn, 1964-66; Registrar, Department of Medicine, University of Heidelberg, 1966-67; Registrar, Department of Surgery, University of Bonn, 1967-72; Associate Professor, Faculty of Medicine, 1972, Consultant Surgeon, Department of Surgery, 1972-75, Chief Surgeon, Department of Surgery, 1975-81, Professor of Surgery, 1977, University of Bonn; Director, Department of Surgery & Vascular Surgery, Heinz Kalk-Klinik, Bad Kissingen, 1981-. *Memberships:* Fellow, American College of Surgeons; Fellow, International College of Surgeons; Société Internationale de Chirurgie; Collegium Internationale Chirurgicae Digestivae; International Society for Diseases of the Oesophagus; European Society of Diseases of the Oesophagus; European Society of Gastroenterology & Gastrointestinal Endoscopy; German Societies of Surgery, Gastroenterology, Gastroenterology & Endoscopy; German Association for the Study of the Liver; German Societies of Surgery in North-West Germany, Westfalia, Bavaria. *Publications:* "Das Schrittmacher-EKG" (co-editor), 1968; "Allgemeine Chirurgie für Zahnmediziner" (co-editor); "Septische Chirurgie" (co-author), 1980; "Portale Hypertension" (co-editor), 1982; "Therapie-Handbuch", Innere Medizin und Allgemeinmedizin", 1983; "DieOOsophagusvarizenblutung", 1984; Various contributions to German medical journals. *Honour:* Grand Crosse al Merito della Academia Italiana, 1981. *Hobbies:* Antiquities; Tennis; Golf. *Address:* P.O. Box 2180, D-8730 Bad Kissingen, Federal Republic of Germany.

PARDO, Waldo e, b. 17 Sep. 1932, New York City, USA. Medical Doctor. Private Practice. m. Thais Gonzalez, 20 May 1963, San Jose, Costa Rica, 1 son, 3 daughters. *Education:* MD, Universidad Nacional de Cordoba, Argentina, 1959; Internship, Psychiatry, Chapui Psychiatric Hospital, San Jose, Costa Rica, 1962; Psychiatry Residence, Missouri Institute of Psychiatry, USA, 1964-65; Psychiatric Residence, Washington University, St Louis, 1965-66; Child Psychiatry Residency, Washington University, 1966-68. *Appointments:* Director, Sanitary Unit, Parrita, Costa Rica, 1959-62; Staff Psychiatrist, Youth Centre, St Louis, Missouri, USA, 1968-69; Clinical Instructor, New York Medical College, 1969-70; Private Practice, 1970-; Assistant Attending, Presbyterian Hospital, New York City, 1974-80; Assistant Attending, New York Psychiatric Institute, 1974-80; Associate, Psychiatry, Columbia University, New York City, 1974-80; Attending, St Joseph's Hospital, Paterson, New Jersey, 1974-. *Memberships:* Colegio de Medicos y Cirujanos de Costa Rica; American Psychiatric Association; American Association of General Hospital Psychiatrics. *Hobby:* Violin Player. *Address:* 704 Howard Road, Ridgewood, NJ 07450, USA.

PARHAD, Salwa Elias, b. 25 Sep. 1942, Iraq. Psychiatrist. m. Harvey M Parhad, 5 Dec. 1968, Baghdad, Iraq, 2 sons, 1 daughter. *Education:* MB, ChB; Diploma of Psychological Medicine, Joint Board of Royal College of Physicians & Surgeons (UK), 1974; Member, Royal College of Psychiatrists (UK), 1974; Diplomate, American Board of Psychiatry & Neurology, 1982. *Appointments:* Psychiatry, Goodmayes Hospital, London, England, 1975-76; Staff Psychiatrist, Fairfield Hospital, Newtown, Connecticut, USA, 1977-78; Staff Psychiatrist, VA Medical Centre, North Chicago, Illinois, USA, 1979-. *Memberships:* Royal College of Psychiatrists (UK); American Psychiatric Association; American Geriatric Society. *Address:* 404 Aurora Court, Vernon Hills, IL 60061, USA.

PARIENTE, Rene Guillaume, b. 1 Sep. 1929, La-Maisa, Tunisia. Professor of Medicine; Director of INSERM. m. Dominique Savary, 26 Dec. 1971, 3 sons. *Education:* Lycée Carnot; Faculté de Médecine et des Sciences, Paris, France; MD; Certificate of General Chemistry; Certificate of General Physiology; Specialist of Cardiology and Pneumology. *Appointments:* Hospital Intern, 1956; Chief of Clinic, 1962; Professor Agrege, Medicine, Hospitals of Paris, 1966; Chief of Service Pneumology and Reanimation, 1970; Professor of Pneumology, 1977; Head of Department, Lung Diseases and Intensive Care, Hospital A Beclere 1970, Hospital Beaujon Paris VII 1977; Director, INSERM (U226), 1978. *Memberships:* 1st Secretary, French Thoracic Society; European Society of Respiratory Physiopathology; American Chest Association; French Society of Respiratory Pathology; French Society of Cardiology; French Society of Epidemiology. *Publications:* Over 300 works; 50 works in international reviews. *Hobby:* History. *Address:* 12 Rue de la Neva, 75008 Paris, France.

PARIS ROMEU, Francisco, b. 1 Aug. 1932, Valencia, Spain. Professor, Thoracic Surgeon. m. Maria Bueno Altabella, 4 Oct. 1961, Valencia, 3 sons, 1 daughter. *Education:* Graduate Licence in Medicine & Surgery, Valencia Medical School, 1955; Internship at University Hospital (by competitive examination); Doctorate, University of Valencia, 1959, extraordinary prize for doctoral thesis; Training in General Thoracic Surgery (under Prof C Carbonell & F Gomar), University Hospital 1955-60; Assistant Professor of Surgical Pathology 1960-63, Associate Professor of Surgery, 1963, Titular Professor, University of Valencia. *Appointments:* Chief of Clinic, General Surgery Services, University Hospital, Valencia, 1960-; Head of Thoracic Surgery

Service, Tuberculosis Hospital 'La Magdalena', Castellon, Spain, 1967; Head of Horacic Surgery Service, Hospital 'La Fé', National Head Service, Valencia, Spain, 1969. *Memberships:* Society of Thoracic Surgeons of Great Britain; Societé de Chirurgie Thoracique et Cardiovasculaire de la langue Française; Society of Thoracic Surgeons of America; International Society of Surgeons; Sociedad de Cirugia Espanola; Royal Academy of Medicine (UK). *Publications:* 'Haemodynamic alterations in bronchiectasis', 1963; 'Diffuse esophageal spasm', 1975; 'Surgical fixation of traumatic flail chest', 1977; 'Advances in esophageal surgery', 1978; 'Advances in tracheal surgery', 1979; 'Total sternectomy for malignant disease', 1980; 'Motor activity after colon replacement of esophagus', 1981; 'Gastroplasty with partial or total plication', 1982; 'Hilioscopy in lung carcinoma', 1985. *Honours:* President, Thoracic Surgery Section (SEPAR), 1974; President, National Commission of Thoracic Surgery, 1978; Member, National Council of National Specialities, 1978. *Hobbies:* Sailing; Photography. *Address:* Almirante Cadarso 6, Valencia 46005, Spain.

PARK, Jason Shinho, b. 8 May 1930, Seoul, Korea. Supervising Psychiatrist; Acupuncturist. m. Naomi S Park, 9 Sep. 1953, Seoul, Korea, 1 son, 2 daughters. *Education:* BMOS, Yonsei University College of Music; MD, Korea University School of Medicine. *Appointments:* Chief of Paediatric Department, Korea Adventist Hospital; currently Supervising Psychiatrist and Acupuncturist, USA. *Memberships:* American Psychiatric Association; Medical Society of State of New York; New York Society of Acupuncture for Physicians and Dentists. *Hobbies:* Piano; Golf; Fishing. *Address:* 121 South Highland Avenue, Pearl River, NY 10965, USA.

PARKER, Malcolm Spencer, b. 31 Aug. 1931, Grangetown, England. Dean, Faculty of Natural and Life Sciences. m. Lorna Hudson, 10 Aug. 1956, Manchester, 2 daughters. *Education:* BSc Honours Pharmacy 1951, MSc, 1962, University of Manchester; PhD, University of Strathclyde, Scotland, 1968. *Appointments:* Head of Chemistry, Eston Grammar School, Yorkshire, England, 1956-59; Lecturer, Pharmacy, Liverpool Polytechnic, 1959-64; Lecturer in Pharmacy 1959-64, Senior Lecturer in Pharmacy 1970-75, University of Strathclyde, Glasgow, Scotland; Head, Department of Pharmacy 1975-82, Dean, Faculty of Natural and Life Sciences 1982-, Brighton Polytechnic, Brighton, England. *Memberships:* Institute of Biology; Fellow, Pharmaceutical Society of Great Britain; Institute of Pharmacy Management; College of Pharmacy Practice; Society of Applied Bacteriology. *Publications:* Contributions to: "Practice of Pharmacy", 1962; "Principles and Practice of Distinfection, Preservation and Sterilisation", 1982; "Cosmetic and Drug Sterilisation", 1984; "Microbial Biodeterioration of Pharmaceutical Preparations", 1984. *Honour:* Brindle Prize, University of Manchester, 1962. *Hobbies:* Walking; Gardening. *Address:* 56 Rowan Way, Rottingdean, Brighton BN2 7FP, England.

PARKER, Lucy T, b. 21 Jan. 1933, Vienna, Austria. Academy Director. m. Dr Robert A Parker, 1 Feb. 1980, Boston, Massachusetts, USA, 1 son, 3 daughters. *Education:* BS, 1958, EdM, 1974, Boston University, Massachusetts, USA; PhD, Heed University, Hollywood, Florida, 1973. *Appointments include:* Private Practice in Psychotherapy, Waban, Massachusetts, 1965-72; Consulting Psychologist, Walker Home for Children, Needham, 1968-72; Sensitivity Group Trainer and Human Relations Consultant, National Training Laboratories, 1968-80; Professor in Psychology and Education, Heed University, Hollywood, Florida, 1972-78; Vice President, Universal Freedom Incorporated, Chestnut Hill, Massachusetts, 1970-85; Clinical Director and Senior Staff Psychologist, Chestnut Hill Psychotherapy Association, Medical Center, Chestnut Hill, 1970-85; Senior Consultant, Parker Associates, Chestnut Hill, 1977-85; Director,

The Parker Academy, Sudbury, 1985-; various guest lectureships. *Memberships include:* American Psychological Association; American Association of University Professors; American Society of Clinical Hypnosis; American Personnel and Guidance Association; American Orthopsychiatric Association. *Publications:* Author of various contributions to professional journals: 'New England Journal of Optometry'; 'Needham Teachers Newsletter' and others. 2Honours include: Numerous professional certificates; various biographical entries. Diplomate: International Association of Professional Counseling and Psychotherapy, 1983; American Academy of Behavioral Medicine, 1982. Fellow: American Academy of Optometry, 1974; International Council for Sex Education and Parenthood, 1980; International Biographical Association, 1981; International Hypnotherapy Society, 1983. *Hobbies include:* Painting; Travel; Gardening. *Address:* The Parker Academy, 248 Concord Road, Sudbury, MA 01776, USA.

PARKER, Neville Edward, b. 1 Feb. 1928, Brisbane, Australia. Consultant Forensic Psychiatrist. m. Joyce Helen Greenwood, 6 Feb. 1954, Brisbane, 3 sons, 4 daughters. *Education:* MD, University of Queensland; DPM, University of Melbourne; Genetics, University of London, England; Statistics, School of Hygiene and Tropical Medicine, London. *Appointments:* Visiting Lecturer, Psychiatry, Psychology and Genetics, University of Queensland, 1957-73; Research Fellow, MRC Psych. Genetics Research Unit, Maudsley Hospital, London, England, 1962-63; Liaison Psychiatrist, St Vincents Hospital, Melbourne, Australia, 1977-82; Consultant, Western Pacific Region, World Health Organisation, 1979-83. *Memberships:* Foundation Fellow, Royal College of Psychiatrists; Corresponding Fellow, American Psychiatric Association. Fellow: International College of Psychosomatic Medicine; Royal Australia and New Zealand College of Psychiatrists. Foundation Member, Australian Psychological Society. *Publications:* In 'Medical Journal of Australia'; 'Murderers, A Personal Series', 1979; "Twins. A Psychiatric Study of a Neurotic Group', 1964. 'Personality Change following Accidents', in 'British Journal of Psychiatry', 1980; 'Hereditary Whispering Dysphonia', in 'Journal of Neurology, Neurosurgery and Psychiatry', 1985; 'The Moustache' in 'Journal of Australia and New Zealand College of Psychiatrists', 1980. *Honours:* Nuffield Dominion Travelling Fellowship, 1962; Jackson Lecturer, Australian Medical Association, Queensland, 1984. *Hobbies:* Lecturing; Australian history. *Address:* Temple Court, 422 Collins Street, Melbourne, Australia 3000.

PARKER, Robert Alan, b. 22 June 1944, New York City, USA. Associate Director; Educator; Psychologist. m. Lucy T Parker, 1 Feb. 1980, 1 son, 3 daughters. *Education:* BS, Westminster College, 1968; MEd, University of Missouri, 1969; ScD, Boston University, 1977. *Appointments:* Counselor, University of Missouri, 1968-69; Rehabilitation Specialist, Fulton State Hospital, Missouri, 1969-72; Director of Rehabilitation Services, 1972-74, Staff Psychologist, Ward Administrator, 1974-77, Solomon Carter Fuller Mental Health Center, Boston, Massachusetts; Staff Psychotherapist, Crossroads Counseling Center, Massachusetts, 1976-77; Senior Staff Psychologist, 1977-80, Board of Directors, Associate Clinical Director, 1980-85, Chestnut Hill Psychotherapy Associates, Massachusetts; Board of Directors, Senior Development Specialist, 1982-85, The Parker Associates; Associate Director, 1985-, The Parker Academy, Sudbury, Massachusetts. *Memberships:* American Orthopsychiatric Association; American Psychological Association; American Association for Marriage and Family Therapy; American Group Psychotherapy Association; Association for Humanistic Psychology; American Association for the Advancement of Science. *Publications:* Contributor to 'Journal of Applied Rehabilitation Counseling'; "Social Prestige and Helpfulness of Psychiatric Staff as Perceived by Patients and Staff" (publication pending); "Diagnosis and Treatment of the Borderline Patient" (in preparation); several presentations to

learned societies. *Hobbies:* Woodworking; Travel; Swimming; Reading. *Address:* The Parker Academy, 248 Concord Road, Sudbury, MA 01776, USA.

PARKER, William Arthur, b. 23 May 1949, Tacoma, Washington, USA. Associate Professor and Coordinator of Clinical Pharmacy. m. Lynda Ann Kline, 14 Aug. 1970, St Paul, Minnesota, USA, 2 daughters. *Education:* BSc Pharm, with distinction, 1971, Pharm D, 1973, University of Minnesota; MBA, Dalhousie University, 1979; PhC. *Appointments:* Research Assistant, College of Pharmacy, 1971-72, Teaching Assistant, College of Pharmacy, 1972-73, Instructor of Clinical Pharmacy, 1973-74, University of Minnesota; Assistant Professor of Clinical Pharmacy, Dalhousie University, 1974-79; Clinical Pharmacist Consultant/Instructor, Departments of Pharmacy and Family Medicine, Halifax Infirmary, Nova Scotia, Canada, 1975-85. *Memberships:* Rho Chi; Sigma Xi; Canadian Pharmaceutical Association; Canadian Society of Hospital Pharmacists; Association of Faculties of Pharmacy of Canada; American College of Clinical Pharmacy; American Society of Consulting Pharmacists; Nova Scotia Pharmaceutical Society; Pharmacy Association of Nova Scotia. *Publications:* 'Effects of pregnancy on pharmacokinetics', 1984; 'Epilepsy', 1984. *Honours:* Rho Chi, 1971; Sigma Xi, 1972; Eli Lilly Achievement Award, 1972; CSHP Burroughs Wellcome Award, 1978, 1985; E R Squibb Award for Teaching Excellence, 1985. *Hobbies:* Jogging; Cycling; Writing; Travel. *Address:* Dalhousie University, College of Pharmacy, Halifax, Nova Scotia, Canada B3H 3J5.

PARKHOUSE, James, b. 30 Mar. 1927, Southport, England. Director, Medical Careers Research Group. m. Hilda Florence Rimmer, 23 July 1952, Liverpool, 3 sons, 2 daughters. *Education:* MB ChB 1950, MD 1955, Liverpool University; DA, England, 1952; FFARCS, 1953; MA, Oxford University, 1960; MSc, Manchester University, 1974. *Appointments:* Professor of Anaesthetics, University of Manchester, 1970-80; Postgraduate Dean, Director, Regional Postgraduate Institute for Medicine and Dentistry, Newcastle, 1980-84; Professor, Postgraduate Medical Education, University of Newcastle-upon-Tyne, 1980-84. *Memberships:* Central Medical Council; Association for the Study of Medical Education; Association for Medical Education in Europe. *Publications:* "A New Look at Anaesthetics", 1965; "Medical Manpower in Britain", 1978; "Analgesic Drugs", (with B J Pleuvry, J M H Rees), 1979; 'Medical Manpower Information', 1983; 'Summary of Proceedings of Working Groups', 1984; Author of numerous publications on medical education and manpower planning. *Honours:* Frederick Hewitt Lectureship, Royal College of Surgeons, 1979. *Hobbies:* Music; Golf. *Address:* Medical Careers Research Group, The Churchill Hospital, Headington, Oxford OX3 7LJ, England.

PARMEGGIANI, Luigi, b. 9 Feb. 1918, Turin, Italy. Occupational Health Consultant. m. Renata Bossi, 12 Dec. 1949, Milan, Italy, 1 son, 3 daughters. *Education:* MD; Diploma in Occupational Health; Libera Docenza in Occupational Health and in Preventive Medicine & Psychotechnic. *Appointments:* Assistant Professor in Occupational Health, University of Milan, Italy, 1945-62; Chief, Occupational Safety & Health Division, International Labour Office, Geneva, Switzerland, 1962-72; Corporate Medical Director, FIAT SA, Turin, Italy, 1973-75; Teacher of Industrial Hygiene, Catholic University, Rome, Italy, 1976-; Counsellor, World Health Organisation, Geneva, 1976-77; Counsellor, LLO, Geneva, 1978-84; Visiting Professor, University of Geneva, 1982-85; Secretary-Treasurer, International Commission on Occupational Health, Geneva, 1981-. *Memberships:* Fellow, Royal Society of Medicine, UK; American Conference of Governmental Industrial Hygienists; Corresponding Member, American Academy of Occupational Medicine; Honorary Member, Italian Society of Occupational Health; Honorary Member, Sociedad Esponola de Seguridad y higiene del Trabajo; and others. *Publications:* Editor, ILO Encyclopaedia on Occupational Health & Safety, 1971, 1983; "Igiene del Lavoro industriale", 1961; More than 250 scientific papers. *Honours:* 10 University Awards, Italy, 1937-52; Ardeshil Dalal, Bombay, India, 1965; Zastitu na Radu, Nis, Yugoslavia, 1970; Honorary Fellowship, Royal College of Physicians of Ireland, Dublin, 1984. *Hobbies:* Walking; Skiing; Gardening. *Address:* 10 Avenue Jules Crosnier, 1206 Geneva, Switzerland.

PARMLEY, Loren Francis, b. 19 Sep. 1921, El Paso, Texas, USA. Professor of Medicine/Chief Division of Cardiology. m. Dorothy Louise Turner, 4 Apr. 1942, Culpepper, Virginia, 2 sons, 1 daughter. *Education:* BA, University of Virginia College of Arts, 1941; MD, University of Virginia College of Medicine, 1943; Fellowship, Walter Reed Medical Center, 1957. *Appointments include:* Chief, Department of Medicine, Walter Reed Medical Center, 1965-68; Clinical Associate Professor of Medicine, Georgetown University, 1967-68; Professor of Medicine, Assistant Dean, Medical College of South Carolina, 1968-75; Clinical Professor of Medicine, Medical College of Georgia, 1969-75; Professor of Medicine, Chief Division of Cardiology, University of South Alabama College of Medicine, 1975-. *Memberships:* Fellow, American College of Physicians; Fellow, American College of Cardiology, Fellow, American College of Chest Physicians; Fellow, Council of Cardiology, American Heart Association. *Publications:* Contributor of chapters to edited medical textbooks. *Honours:* Gold Award, Annual Scientific Exhibit, American Society of Clinical Pathologists and College of American Pathologists, 1959; Certificate of Achievement, Cardiovascular Disease, Surgeon Generals Department, US Army, 1962; Legion of Merit, US Army 1968. *Hobby:* Swimming. *Address:* Department of Internal Medicine, University of South Alabama College of Medicine, 2451 Fillingim Street, Mobile, AL 36617, USA.

PARR, Susan, E, b. 9 Feb. 1935, Baltimore, Maryland, USA. Assistant Director of Nursing. *Education:* Maryland General Hospital School of Nursing, Baltimore, 1953-56; University of Maryland; Community College of Baltimore; BS, General Studies and Certificate in Gerontology, 1984; Registered Nurse, 1956-85; Certification Nursing Administration, ANA. *Appointments:* Student Aide, Head Nurse, Staff Nurse, Maryland General Hospital, 1953-63; LPN Instructor, Baltimore Board of Education, 1963-66; Nursing Supervisor, Sinai Hospital Incorporated, Baltimore, 1966-82; Assistant Director of Nursing, Levindale Geriatric Hospital, Baltimore, 1980-82; Assistant Director of Nursing, Pimlico Manor, Baltimore, current position; Assistant Director of Nursing, Eastpoint Nursing Home, Baltimore, 1984-. *Memberships:* American and Maryland Nurses Association; Levindale Geriatric Hospital (Audit Committee, In-service program, Procedure Committee); Sinai Hospital (Chairman, Red Cross Blood Drive, 3 years; Chairman, United Wat Committee 3 years); Chairman Medical Audit Committee; Chairman, Patient Teaching Committee; Diabetic Instructor). *Address:* 3209 Brendan Avenue, Baltimore, MD 21213, USA.

PARREIRA, Francisco, b. 7 July 1921, Lisbon, Portugal. Professor, Clinical Pathology. m. Maria de Jesus, 26 July 1944, Lisbon, 2 sons. *Education:* MD, 1944; Generalist Resident, 1945, 1946; International Medicine Resident, 1947, 1948. *Appointments:* Lecturer, Istituto di Pat Medica University Siena, Italy, 1950-51; Lecturer, Institute Med Trop-Haematol, Lisbon University Hospital, 1954-70; Graduated Lecturer, Italian University, 1955; Doctoral Degree, Lisbon University, 1961; Associate Professor, Medical School of Lisbon, 1970; Professor, Lisbon Medical School, 1979-. *Memberships:* Society Cienc Medicas Lisboa; Society Portug Medica Interna; Society Portug Pediatria; Society Portug Bioguimica; Society Portug Clinical Pathology; Society Portug Hematology; many other professional organisations. *Publications:* "Diateses Hemore de

causa plasm", Editor, 1957; "Trombelas tografia", 'Anal Exper e Semiol', Editor, 1961; "Propedutica Med-Hematol", Editor, 1st Edition 1966, 3rd edition 1975; over 150 articles in professional journals. *Honours:* Dean, Lisbon Medical School, 1978, 1979, 1982, 1983, 1984; President, Portug Society of Clinical Pathology, 1970-; Portugal Counselor of the International Society of Haematology, 1980-85. *Address:* R. ECA De Queiroz, 17-1°, 1000 Lisbon, Portugal.

PARRISH, W Keith, b. 28 Oct. 1951, Beaver Falls, Pennsylvania, USA. Chiropractor. m. Victoria Ann Wood, 15 Aug. 1982, Erie, 2 daughters. *Education:* BS, Pre-Medicine, Pennsylvania State University, 1973; DC, Logan College of Chiropractic, St Louis, 1977; Board Qualified, Certified Orthopedics, American Chiropractic Association, 1985. *Appointments:* Board of Directors, Northeastern Erie County Kiwanis Club, 1983-84; President, District 7, Pennsylvania Chiropractic Society, 1985; President, Erie County Chiropractic Society 1985; Board of Directors, Methodist Towers, 1984-85; Board of Directors, Kiwanis Club, Erie, 1984-85; Industrial Consultant, 1984-85. *Memberships:* American Chiropractic Association; Pennsylvania Chiropractic Society; Erie County Chiropractic Society. *Honours:* Recognition for Dedication to the Basic Science Division, Logan College of Chiropractic, 1975; Past President, Erie County Chiropractic Society. *Hobbies:* Woodwork; Decoy Carving; Camping; Singing; Handbell Playing. *Address:* 4932 Iroquois Avenue, Erie, PA 16511, USA.

PARTANEN, Juhani V S, b. 17 Nov. 1945, Helsinki, Finland. Chief of Department of Clinical Neurophysiology. m. Kaarina Partanen, 1972, Helsinki, 2 sons. *Education:* Physician in Clinical Neurophysiology; MD. *Appointments:* Assistant Physician, Laboratory of Clinical Neurophysiology, University Central Hospital, Turku, 1974-77; Currently Chief, Department of Clinical Neurophysiology, University Central Hospital of Kuopio, Kuopio. *Membership:* Chairman, Society of Clinical Neurophysiology. *Publications:* 'Time-Locked Phenomena of Human Motor Unit Potentials', dissertation, 1979; 'End-Plate Spikes in EMG Are Fusimotor Unit Potentials', 1983. *Address:* University Central Hospital of Kuopio, Department of Clinical Neurophysiology, SF-70210 Kuopio, Finland.

PARTSCH, Hugo, b. 28 Sep. 1938, Vienna, Austria. Professor of Dermatology, Head of Vascular Service. m. Eva Grech, 8 May 1965, Vienna, 2 sons, 1 daughter. *Education:* MD, 1962; University Dozent, 1979; University Professor, 1985. *Appointments:* Community Hospital, Lieienfeld, 1962-65; Wilhelminen Hospital, Vienna, 1965-79; Head of Vascular Service, Hanusch-Hospital, 1980-. *Memberships:* Austrian Society for Dermatology; Austrian, German, Swiss Society of Angiology; German and Swiss Society of Phlebology; Austrian Nuclear Medical Society; French Union de Phlebologie; ADF; Society Thermology. *Publications:* 250 publications including: "Ulcero-mutiliating Neuropathies", 1979; "Perforating Veins", (with R May and J Staubesand), 1981; "Initial Lymphatics", (with A Bollinger), 1984. *Honours:* First Award, Swiss Phlebologice Society, 1980, 1982 and 1984; Wiener Hochschuljubilavmstipendium, Mayor of the City of Vienna, Theodor Korner Award. *Hobbies:* Mountain Climbing; Skiing. *Address:* Hanusch-Hospital, H Collin-Strasse 30, A 1140 Vienna, Austria.

PARYANI, Shyam B, b. 19 July 1954, India. Radiation Oncologist. m. Sharon Goldman, 12 May 1979, Jacksonville, Florida, USA, 1 daughter. *Education:* BS, Electrical Engineering; MS, Nuclear Engineering and Radiation Physics; MD. *Appointments:* Director, C J Williams Cancer Centre, Baptist Medical Centre, Jacksonville, Florida, USA. *Memberships:* American Society of Therapeutic Radiologists and Oncologists; American Society of Clinical Oncology; American College of Radiology; American Medical Association. *Publications:* 'Analysis of Non-Hodgkins Lymphomos' in 'Cancer', 1983; 'Cranial Nerve Involvement' in 'Journal of Clinical Oncology', 1983; 'Extralymphatic Involvement' in 'Journal of Clinical Oncology', 1983; 'Iodine - 125 Suture Implants' in 'Journal of Clinical Oncology', 1985. *Honours:* Summa Cum Laude, 1975; Alpha Omega Alpha, 1979. *Hobbies:* Golf; Cycling. *Address:* 800 Prudential Drive, Jacksonville, FL 32207, USA.

PASCHKE, Lois Ruth née Kroeker, b. 6 May 1953, Winnipeg, Manitoba, Canada. Occupational Therapist. m. Reginald E Paschke, 23 July 1983, Winnipeg, 1 daughter. *Education:* Diploma in Occupational Therapy, 1977; Bachelor of Occupational Therapy, 1980. *Appointments:* Staff Occupational Therapist, Health Sciences Centre, Burns Unit, Winnipeg, Manitoba, 1977; Staff Occupational Therapist, Rehabilitation Centre, Neurology Service, Winnipeg, 1978; Sole Charge Occupational Therapist, Canadian National Institute for the Blind, Manitoba Division, 1979- (working with paediatric blind, multihandicapped). *Memberships:* Canadian Association of Occupational Therapists; Manitoba Society of Occupational Therapists; Association of Occupational Therapists in Manitoba; Paediatric Interest Group. *Honour:* Dr J D Adamson Medal 1977 for highest standing final year diploma course in OT. *Hobbies:* Reading; Cross-Country Skiing; Hiking; Canoeing; Windsurfing. *Address:* 972 McLeod Avenue, Winnipeg, Manitoba, R2G 2K9, Canada.

PASSOW, Hermann, b. 18 Dec. 1925, Tubingen, Germany. Director, Max-Planck-Institute for Biophysics. m. Inge Jentschura, 1957, Hamburg. *Education:* PhD, Physiology, Universities of Gottingen and Hamburg, 1946-51. *Appointments:* Post Doctoral/Dozent, University of Hamburg, 1951-62; Professor, Chairman, Physiology, University of Saarland, 1962-70; Director, Physiology, Max-Planck-Institute, 1970-. *Memberships:* Deutsche Biophysikalische Gesellschaft; American Physiological Society; others. *Publications:* Articles in professional journals & monographs. *Address:* Max-Planck-Institut fur Biophysik, Heinrich-Hoffman Str 7, D-6000 Frankfurt/M 71, Federal Republic of Germany.

PASTEELS, Jean-Lambert, b. 30 Jan. 1934, Uccle, Belgium. Professor, University of Brussels School of Medicine; Director, Laboratory of Histology. m. Aline Godding, 22 July 1957, Brussels, 2 daughters. *Education:* MD, University of Brussels School of Medicine, 1951-58; Research Fellow, College de France, Paris, France, 1960; Agrege de L'Enseignement, Superieur, University of Brussels, 1964. *Appointments:* Assistant Professor, 1958, Charge de Cours (Agrege), 1964, Professor, Histology, 1970, Professor and Director, Laboratory of Histology, 1977, Vice Dean, 1976-79, Dean, 1979-82, Commissaire General, 1983-86, University of Brussels, School of Medicine; Consulting Pathologist. *Memberships:* President, 1985-86, Belgian Society of Endocrinology; Corresponding Member, Belgian Royal Academy of Medicine, 1977-; Member of Council, 1980-84, International Society of Neuroendocrinology. *Publications:* 'Recherches Morphologiques et Experimentales sur la Secretion de Prolactine', 1963; 'Human Prolactin', (Co-Editor), 1973; 'Rat brain synthesizes two vitamin dependent calcium binding proteins', (with Pochet, Parmentier, Lawson), 1985. *Honours:* Prix Kleefeld, 1958; Laureat du Concours Universitaire, Belgium, 1956; Prix Empain, Sciences Naturelles et Medicales, Belgium, 1961; Laureat, Belgian Royal Academy of Medicine, 1967; Laureat de L'Institut, French Academy of Sciences, 1974. *Hobbies:* Gardening; Orchid collection. *Address:* Laboratory Histology, University of Brussels School of Medicine, 2 Rue Evers, B1000 Brussels, Belgium.

PÁSZTOR, Emil, b. 18 Apr. 1926, Budapest, Hungary. Neurosurgeon. m. Esther Pásztor, 29 June 1949, Budapest. *Education:* Semmelweis Medical University, Budapest. *Appointments:* Chief of Department, 1956-70, Vice-Director, 1970-74, Director, 1975-, National Institute of Neurosurgery; Corresponding

Member, Hungarian Academy of Sciences, 1979-. *Memberships:* Vice-President, World Federation of Neurosurgical Societies; Administrative Council, Hungarian Neurosurgical Society; Corresponding Member, American Association of Neurological Surgeons, also of Scandinavian, Italian, Bulgarian & Cuban Neurosurgical Societies. *Publications:* Various articles in Journal of Neurosurgery; "Concise Neurosurgery", 1980. *Hobby:* Ceramic Art. *Address:* Amerikai ut 57, H-1145, Budapest, Hungary.

PATCHEN, Myra Louise, b. 15 May 1952, Norwalk, Ohio, USA. Research Physiologist. The Armed Forces Radiobiology Research Institute, Bethesda, Maryland, 1982-. *Education:* PhD, University of Texas Graduate School of Biomedical Sciences, Houston, Texas, 1980; MS, 1975, BS, 1973, Bowling Green State University, Ohio. *Appointments:* Research Specialist, Department of Haematology and Oncology, Ohio State University Hospitals, Columbus, Ohio, 1975-76; Senior Research Assistant, Haematology Department, MD Anderson Hospital and Tumour Institute, Houston, Texas, 1976-80; National Research Council Resident Research Associate, The Armed Forces Radiobiology Research Institute, Bethesda, Maryland, 1980-82. *Memberships:* International Society for Experimental Haematology; National and International Reticuloendothelial Society; International Society for Immunopharmacology; Association of Women in Science. *Publications:* 'Glucan-induced hemopoietic and immune stimulation: Therapeutic effects in sublethally and lethally irradiated mice', (with T J MacVittie); 'Soluble polyglycans enhance recovery from cobalt-60 induced hemopoietic injury', (co-author), 1985; 'Immunomodulation and Hemopoiesis', 1983. *Honours:* National Research Council Research Associateship, 1980, 1981. *Hobbies:* Travel; Meeting people. *Address:* Department of Haematology, The Armed Forces Radiobiology Research Institute, Bethesda, MD 20814-5145, USA.

PATEL, Atilkumar Manubhai, b. 9 Sep. 1947, Baroda. Family Physician. m. Krishna, 4 Dec. 1973, Baroda, 2 daughters. *Education:* MB; MCFP; MCGP. *Appointments:* Senior General Practitioner, Principal, Medical Clinic Centre, Lusaka, Zambia; Family Physician, Harare, Zimbabwe. *Memberships:* College of Family Physicians of Canada; College of General Practice of Zimbabwe; Associate Member, Royal College of General Practitioners, London; Member, American College of Chest Physicians, USA; American Medical Society; Royal Society of Health, London. *Hobbies:* Playing Bridge; Playing Cricket. *Address:* PO Box 665, Harare, Zimbabwe.

PATEL, Mehmood Moosa, b. 25 May 1945, India. Cardiologist. m. Audrey Madray, 13 July 1977, Lafayette, Louisiana, USA, 1 son. *Education:* MB BS, Baroda University College of Medicine, India, 1970; FRCP (C); FACC; FACP; Certified: American Board of Internal Medicine, American Board of Cardiology, Royal College of Canada, Internal Medicine. *Appointments:* Director of Heart Station, 1977-78; Chief of Cardiology, University Medical Center, 1977-78; Assistant Professor of Medicine, Louisiana State University, 1977-; Private Practice Cardiology, 1978-. *Memberships:* Fellow, American College of Cardiology; Fellow, Royal College of Physicians and Surgeons of Canada; Louisiana State Medical Society; American Medical Association; American Society of Echocardiography. *Publications include:* Contributor to professional journals; Chapters in books; Abstracts; Presentations including: Dissertation on "Anaemia in Pregnancy" and Public Health Important, at Graduate Level, in 'Public Health', 1968; Lectures. *Honours:* Higher Education Scholarship from Gujarat State Government, 1963-68; Physicians Recognition Award from American Medical Association, 1977. *Hobbies:* Tennis; Jogging; Cricket. *Address:* 101B St Thomas Street, Lafayette, LA 70506, USA.

PATEL, Shashi Chhotabhai, b. 30 June 1936, Mombasa, Kenya. Consultant Surgeon. m. Sudha Patel, 15 Apr. 1967, Kampala, 2 sons. *Education:* MBBS, Gujarat University, India, 1961; FRCS, Edinburgh, 1968; FICS, Hon, 1972. *Appointments:* Senior House Officer and Registrar in Orthopaedics, 1965-70, Senior Registrar in Surgery (General) 1970-72, Aga Khan Hospital, Nairobi, Kenya; Consultant Surgeon, Aga Khan Hospital, Nairobi and M P Shah Hospital, Nairobi, 1982-. *Memberships:* Medical Protection Society, UK; Kenya Medical Association, Nairobi; AO International, Switzerland; World Orthopaedic Concern, Singapore. *Publications:* 'Retroperitoneal Fibrosis' in E A Surgeons Association Journal 1974; 'Role of Synovectomy' in R A Surgeons Association Journal, 1975. *Honour:* AO International Scholarship in Surgery, 1979. *Hobbies:* Swimming; Travel. *Address:* Box 46256, Nairobi, Kenya.

PATEL, Sumany Rai, b. 21 Dec. 1933, India. Consultant Obstetrician/Gynaecologist. m. Rama Amin, 24 June 1961, Dar es Salaam, 1 son, 1 daughter. *Education:* MBBS, King's College Medical School, Newcastle-upon-Tyne, England, 1958; MRCOG, 1966, FRCOG, 1979, Royal College of Obstetricians and Gynaecologists, London; FRCS, Royal College of Surgeons of Edinburgh, 1972. *Appointments:* Medical Officer of Health, Taita District, Kenya, 1960-63; Resident Medical Officer, Women's Hospital, Paddington, Sydney, 1963-66; Provincial Gynaecologist, Nyanza Province, Kenya 1966-68; Consultant Gynaecologist, Kenyatta National Hospital Nairobi, Kenya, 1968-74; Senior Consultant, Kenyatta National Hospital, 1975-80; Private Consultant in Gynaecology, Nairobi, Kenya, 1980-; Honorary Lecturer, University of Nairobi, 1968-80. *Memberships:* Kenya Medical Association; Kenya Obstetric and Gynaecology Society; East African Association of Surgeons. *Publications:* 'Post menopausal bleeding' in "Australian Journal of Medicine" 1967; 'Practice of Obstetrics and Gynaecology in Kenya' "East African Medical Journal", 1980. *Honours:* Daniel Farm Prize in Physiology, Royal College of Surgeons of Edinburgh, 1969. *Hobbies:* Swimming; Golf. *Address:* PO Box 49808, Nairobi, Kenya.

PATERSON, Janet Martha, b. 26 Apr. 1935, Boston, Massachusetts, USA. Director, Rehabilitation Services/Administrative Director, Scoliosis Centre. *Education:* BSc, Physical Therapy; Certificate, Biofeedback. *Appointments:* Physical therapist, Rancho Los Amigos Hospital, Downey, California, 1958-61; PT consultant, Visiting Nurse Association of Los Angeles, 1961-64; Presbyterian Intercommunity Hospital, Whittier/Advisory Board, Cerritos College, 1964-. *Memberships:* Administration & Geriatric Sections, American Physical Therapy Association; Biofeedback Association of America. *Honour:* Scholarship, National Foundation for Infantile Paralysis, 1956. *Hobbies:* Philately; Leaded glass; Hiking; Dog training. *Address:* 10104 Grayling Avenue, Whittier, CA 90603, USA.

PATHAN, Abdullah Jan, b. 1 Sep. 1935, Junagadh, Pakistan. Director, Ojha Institute of Chest Diseases. m. Amna Abdullah, 13 June 1954, Hyderabad, 3 sons, 4 daughters. *Education:* MBBS; TDD (PB); DTM & H (England); DTCD (Wales); MRIT (Japan); FCCP (USA). *Appointments:* Bacteriologist 1960, Deputy Medical Superintendent 1961-64, Government Tuberculosis Sanatorium, Kotri; Medical Officer in Charge, Government Tuberculosis Clinic, Sanhar, 1964-67; Regional Tuberculosis Control Officer, 1967-70; District Health Officer, Tharparker, 1970-72; Provincial Tuberculosis Control Officer, Sind, 1979-82; Deputy Director, Health Services, 1982-84; Director, Ojha Institute of Chest Diseases, Karachi, 1984-. *Memberships:* Pakistan Medical Association; Pakistan National Tuberculosis Association; Pakistan Red Crescent Society; Pakistan Family Planning Association. *Publications:* "Castor Oil Seed Poisoning", 1959; "Study of Myocardial Infarction Cases in Liaquat Medical College, Hyderabad", 1959; Various papers at provincial and national conferences. *Honours:* Silver Medal, ENT &

Eye, 1959; CENTO Fellowship, 1963; WHO Fellowship 1970, Member Expert Advisory Panel on Tuberculosis and Respiratory Diseases, 1981, World Health Organisation. *Hobbies:* Tennis; Books. *Address:* Dilkusha, 165-D, Unit 7, Latifabad, Hyderabad, Pakistan.

PATIL, Jaywant Joachim P, b. 30 Sep. 1942, Bombay, India. Assistant Professor of Medicine. m. Helen, 5 Oct. 1974, 2 sons. *Education:* MB BS, University of Bangalore, India. *Appointments:* Clinical Instructor in Physical Medicine & Rehabilitation, Temple University, Philadelphia, USA, 1975-76; Lecturer in Medicine, 1978-84, Assistant Professor of Medicine, 1984-, Dalhousie University, Halifax, Nova Scotia, Canada. *Memberships:* Fellow, Royal College of Physicians & Surgeons of Canada; Fellow, American Academy of Physical Medicine & Rehabilitation. *Hobbies:* Tennis; Short-Wave Radio; Painting. *Address:* 1341 Summer Street, Halifax, Nova Scotia, B3H 4K4, Canada.

PATTERSON, Earl Stewart, b. 31 Aug. 1927, USA. Psychiatrist, Private Practice. m. 31 Dec. 1971, Middletown, Connecticut, 1 daughter. *Education:* BA, Columbia University, 1950; MD, University of Iowa, 1954. *Appointments:* Intern, Middlesex Memorial Hospital, Middletown, Connecticut, 1954-55; Psychiatric Resident, Connecticut State Hospital, 1955-58; Private Practice, Meriden, 1958-; Consultant, Psychiatry, 1959-62, Assistant Superintendent, 1962-65, Undercliffe Hospital, Meriden; Consultant, Psychiatry, Connecticut School for Boys, Meriden, 1966-71; Director, Professional Service for Youth Incorporated, Meriden, 1969-80; Member, National Forum on Children in Trouble, White House Conference on Children, 1970; Medical Director, The Center, Collinsville, currently; Biofeedback Therapy, Meriden; Clinical Director, Altobello Center for Children and Youth, Meriden, 1979-82. *Memberships:* Fellow; American Psychiatric Association; American Geriatrics Association. American Medical Association; Society of Biologic Psychiatry; New York Academy of Sciences; Biofeedback Research Association; Biofeedback Society of America; American Association of Biofeedback Clinicians. *Publications:* "Case Books from Hell: Psychiatry and the Occult", 10 volumes; "Tool Children"; contributions to 'Journal of Nervous and Mental Disease', 'Medical Science', 'American Medical Association Archives of Neurology and Psychiatry'. Various reviews of research and professional work. *Honours:* Diplomate: Clinical Biofeedback, American Association of Biofeedback Clinicians, 1979; Biofeedback Certification Institute of America, 1981. *Hobbies:* Writing; Sketching; Gardening; Philately; Sailing; Travel. *Address:* 234 Hobart Street, Meriden, CT 06450, USA.

PATTERSON, Roy, b. 26 Apr. 1926, Ironwood, Michigan, USA. Chairman, Department of Medicine, Northwestern University Medical School. m. Elaine Gustafson, 28 July 1948, 2 sons. *Education:* MD, cum laude, University of Michigan, Ann Arbor. *Appointments include:* University of Pittsburgh; Assistant Professor of Medicine, University of Michigan, 1953-57; Consultant in Allergy, US Air Force. Current: Member, Council for the National Institute of Allergy & Infectious Diseases; Professor of Medicine/Chairman, Department of Medicine/Chief, Outpatient Allergy Clinics, Northwestern University. *Memberships:* President 1975-76, American Academy of Allergy; President 1978-79, Central Society for Clinical Research; Fellow, American College of Physicians; American Association of Immunologists; American Society for Clinical Investigation; Fellow, American College of Allergy; Association of Professors of Medicine; Emeritus, American Association of Physicians. *Publications:* Over 400. *Honours:* Distinguished service award, AAA, 1982; 1st Allergist of the Year Award, editorial board, 'Journal of Dermatology & Allergy', 1982; Technical Excellence Award, 1st Place, University of Atlanta, Georgia; Master, American College of Physicians; Award, International Academy of Chest Physicians & Surgeons; ACCP Medalist. *Address:* 3109 Country Lane, Wilmette, IL 60091, USA.

PATTISON, E Mansell, b. 23 June 1933, Portland, Oregon, USA. Professor and Chairman, Department of Psychiatry and Health Behaviour, Medical College of Georgia, 1979-, m. Myrna Loy Mischke, 22 June 1956, Salem, Oregon, 2 sons, 1 daughter. *Education:* BA, Reed College, 1956; MD, 1958, Intern, 1958-59, University of Oregon Medical School; Resident Psychiatrist, University Cincinnati, 1961-64. *Appointments:* Professor of Psychiatry, University of California, Irvine, 1970-79; Assistant Professor of Psychiatry, University of Washington, 1965-70; Senior Psychiatrist and Assistant Clinical Director, Clinical Neuropsychopharmacology Research Centre, National Institute of Mental Health, 1964-65. *Memberships:* Fellow, American Psychiatric Association; Fellow, American College of Psychiatrists; Fellow, American Group Psychotherapy Association; Fellow, Vice-President, American Association of Social Psychiatry; Fellow, American Anthropological Association. *Publications:* "Clinical Psychiatry and Religion", 1969; "Pastor and Parish", 1977; "Emerging Concepts of Alcohol Dependence", 1977; "Clinical Applications of Social Network Theory", 1981; "Encyclopaedia Handbook of Alcoholism", 1982; "Advances in the Psychosocial Treatment of Alcoholism", 1984; Contributor of over 400 scientific articles. *Honours:* Career Development Award, NIMH, 1961-65; Sigma Xi, 1964; Man of the Month in Pastoral Psychology, 1969; Significant Program Achievement Award, APA, 1977; VA Special Performance Award, 1982. *Hobbies:* Skiing; Camping; Art; Music. *Address:* Department of Psychiatry and Health Behaviour, Medical College of Georgia, Augusta, GA 30912, USA.

PATTON, Walter William, b. 23 Dec. 1948, Sapulpa, Oklahoma, USA. Private Practitioner. m. Dorcas Schoneweis, 10 Aug. 1968, Honolulu, Hawaii, 5 sons. *Education:* DC, Palmer College of Chiropractic; Undergraduate, Tulsa Junior College, Northwestern Oklahoma State University; Postgraduate, National College of Chiropractic, Lombard, Illinois; University of Bridgeport, Connecticut; Oklahoma City College; Certified Medical Examiner; Certified Acupuncturist. *Appointments:* President, Iowa Association of Concerned Veterans; President, Veteran's Association of Palmer College of Chiropractic; Vice-President, Public Relations, Iowa Association of Concerned Veterans; Board of Directors, Chiropractic Association of Oklahoma; Adjunct Professor, Texas Chiropractic College; Board of Oklahoma Reserve Law Officers Association. *Honours:* President's Honour Roll, Tulsa Junior College; Dean's Honour Roll, Northeastern State University; Magna cum Laude Grad, Palmer College of Chiropractic. *Hobbies:* Scuba diving; Martial arts; Private pilot. *Address:* 5304 S Western , Oklahoma City, OK 73109, USA.

PAULSON, George W, b. 27 July 1930, Raleigh, North Carolina, USA. Professor and Chairman of University Department of Neurology, m. Ruta B Paulson, 4 sons, 1 daughter. *Education:* BS Zoology, Yale University, 1952; MD, Duke University, 1956. *Appointments include:* Resident in Neurology, 1957-59, Instructor 1963-64, Assistant Professor 1964-66, Neurology, Duke University; Resident in Psychiatry 1959-60, Research Neurologist 1962-66, Dorothea Dix Hospital, Raleigh, North Carolina; Associate Professor of Neurology, Ohio State Medical School, 1967-71; Consultant, Ohio Department of Mental Hygiene and Corrections, 1967-; Veterans Administration, Harding Hospital, 1967-; Private practice, Neurological Associates Incorporated, 1971-82; Program Director of Neurology 1971-82, Director of EEG Laboratory 1975-82, Co-Director of Vascular Laboratory 1975-82, Riverside Methodist Hospital; Clinical Associate Professor Paediatrics 1968-81, Clinical Professor of Medicine 1971-82, Professor 1982-, Director of Division of Neurology 1982, Acting Chairman 1982-83, Kurtz Professor 1983-, Chairman 1983-, Department of Neurology, Ohio State University. *Memberships include:* American Electroencephalographic Society; American Neurological Association; Fellow, First Vice-President, American Academy of Neurology; American Geriatrics Association; World Federation of Neurology; Emeritus Member, Central Society for Neurological Research; Board, National Tuberous Sclerosis Association; American Epilepsy Society; Board, United Parkinson Foundation; Association of University Professor of Neurology; Alpha Omega Alpha. *Publications include:* Contributor and co-editor with A Barbeau and T N Chase, "Advances in Neurology", 1973; 168 articles and chapters in books. *Honours include:* Teacher of the Year, Ohio State University, 1971; Special Teaching Award, Riverside Hospital, 1982; Kurtz Chair of Neurology, 1983-. *Address:* 1655 Upham Drive, Columbus, OH 43210, USA.

PAUMGARTNER, Gustav, b. 23 Nov. 1933, Neumarkt/A Chairman, Medicine. m. Dagmar Paumgartner, MD, 6 June 1963, Graz. *Education:* MD, Princeton University, USA, University of Graz, University of Vienna. *Appointments:* Postdoctoral Training, Pharmacology, Resident, University of Vienna; Fellow, Medicine, New Jersey College of Medicine; Attending & Consulting Physician, New Jersey VA Hospital; Resident, Internal Medicine, Gastroenterology, University of Vienna; Consultant, Associate Professor, Clinical Pharmacology and Hepatology, Vice Director, University of Berne; Chairman, Medicine II, University of Munich, 1979-. *Memberships:* AASLD; AGA; European Society for Clinical Investigation; IASL; Reticuloendothelial Society; German Society for Gastroenterology; German Society for Internal Medicine; Swiss Society for Gastroenterology; Swiss Society for Pharmacology; Austrian Society for Gastroenterology. *Publications:* Over 200 in scientific journals. *Honour:* Forderpreis fur die Europaische Wissenschaft, Korber Foundation, 1985. *Address:* Department of Medicine II, Klinikum Grosshadern, University of Munich, D-8000 Munich 70, Federal Republic of Germany.

PAUSTIAN, Frderick Franz, b. 24 Nov. 1926, Grand Island, Nebraska, USA. Professor Internal Medicine and Physiology. m. Mary Ann Mohrman, 20 June 1953, Lincoln, Nebraska, 2 sons, 2 daughters. *Education:* BSc, University of Nebraska, Lincoln, 1952; MD, University of Nebraska College of Medicine, Omaha, 1953. *Appointments include:* Gastroenterology Fellowship, University of Pennsylvania, 1956-59; Fellowship Tropical Medicine and Parasitology, Central America, Panama and Mexico, Louisiana State University Medical School, 1960; Faculty 1958-, Dean for Continuing and Graduate Medical Education, Division Head Digestive Diseases and Nutrition 1959-84, Professor 1967-, Internal Medicine and Physiology, University of Nebraska College of Medicine; Vice President and Medical Director, Share Health Plan Nebraska. *Memberships:* Fellow, American College of Physicians; American Gastroenterology Association; American Medical Association; Board of Directors 1972-74, American Society of Internal Medicine; American Society for Gastrointestinal Endoscopy; Board of Directors 1979-83, Bockus International Society of Gastroenterology; Board of Directors 1978-83, Nebraska State Medical Association; House of Delegates 1973-, Executive Committee 1977-, Secretary-Treasurer 1982-, Metropolitan Omaha Medical Society; Alpha Omega Alpha; Sigma Xi. *Publications:* 'Importance of the Brief Trial of Rigid Medical Management in the Diagnosis of Benign Versus Malignant Gastric Ulcer', 1960; 'Accuracy of X-Ray Diagnosis of Ulcerating Gastric lesions', 1961; 'Tuberculosis of the Intestine', 1963, 1975 and 1984; 'Tuberculous Enteritis', 1983. *Honour:* Best Clinical Teacher, 1972. *Hobbies:* Hunting; Fishing; Canoeing; Camping; Golf; Tennis. *Address:* Section of Digestive Diseases and Nutrition, University of Nebraska Medical Center, 42 Street and Dewey Avenue, Omaha, NE 68105, USA.

PAVRI, Mehli Kavasji, b. 7 Oct. 1923, Bombay, India. Honorary Physician to His Excellency the Governor of Maharashtra and to B D Petit Parsee General Hospital. m. Ratu Dalal, 7 Feb. 1960, Bombay, 2 daughters. *Education:* MD, Bombay; Fellow, College of Physicians and Surgeons, Bombay and American College of Chest Physicians. *Appointments:* Honorary Assistant Physician, St George's Hospital, Bombay, 1959-66; currently, Honorary Physician to His Excellency the Governor of Maharashtra, Bombay and B D Petit Parsee General Hospital, Bombay. *Memberships:* Fellow: College of Physicians and Surgeons, Bombay; American College of Chest Physicians. Member, New York Academy of Sciences, USA. *Publications:* Contributor to: "Text Book of Medicine", 1st and 2nd editions; "Diagnosis and Management of Medical Emergencies". *Honours:* Gold Medal for all round excellence during school career. *Hobbies:* Riding; Music. *Address:* Northcote Nursing Home, Best Marg, Apollo, Opp Taj Mahal Hotel, Bombay 400 039, India.

PAYNE, Lloyd Dale, b. 11 Sep., 1946, Tucumcari, New Mexico, USA. Chiropractic Physician, 2 daughters. *Education:* AD, Eastern New Mexico University; BS, DC, Palmer College of Chiropractic; MT, RT, Trigg Memorial Hospital School of Technology. *Appointments:* President, New Mexico Society of Medical Technologists; President, New Mexico Society of Radiological Technologists; Associate Instructor, Palmer College of Chiropractic. *Memberships:* Palmer College Alumni; American Chiropractic Association; New Mexico Chiropractic Association; International Thermographic Society; Parker Foundation for Chiropractic Education. *Publications:* 'Evaluation of Brain Dysfunction', Journal of the American Chiropractic Association, 1977. *Honours:* American Chiropractic Association Scientific Journal Award, 1977. *Hobby:* Breeding Racehorses. *Address:* 1500 North Washington, Roswell, NM 88201, USA.

PEAK, Howard John, b. 17 May 1926, Sydney, Australia. Cardiologist. m. Judith Peak, 29 Nov. 1969, Sydney, 2 sons, 1 daughter. *Education:* MB, BS (Sydney); FRACP, 1972; FACC, 1975; DDU, 1977. *Appointments include:* Fellow in Medicine, Johns Hopkins Hospital, Baltimore, USA, 1965-66; Honorary Assistant Physician 1966-70, Honorary Assistant Cardiologist 1970-71, Royal Prince Alfred Hospital, Sydney; Consulting Cardiologist, National Heart Foundation of Australia, 1966-70; Consulting Cardiologist, Royal Canberra Hospital, 1971-75; Director of Cardiology, ibid, 1975-; President, ACT Division, National Heart Foundation of Australia, 1980-85. *Memberships:* Cardiac Society of Australia & New Zealand; Fellow, Royal Society of Medicine; New York Academy of Sciences; Corresponding Member, British Cardiac Society; Australian Institute for Ultrasound in Medicine. *Publications include:* 'The treatment of hypercholesterolaemic by MER-29', co-author, 1961 (Med J Austr); 'A two-year evaluation of 'Atromid' for the control of abnormal blood lipid levels', co-author, 1965 (ibid); 'Rheumatic heart disease 1970: A brief review for the General Practitioner', co-author, 1971; 'Clinical profile of hypertrophic cardiomyopathy' co-author, 1977. *Hobbies:* Music; Languages; Walking; Fishing. *Address:* Department of Cardiology, Royal Canberra Hospital, Canberra, ACT 2601, Australia.

PEARSON, Eric John Philippe, b. 12 Jan. 1955, Orleans, France. Doctor of Veterinary Medicine. *Education:* BSc, Animal Science, University of Hawaii, 1977; DVM, University of the Philippines, 1982. *Appointments:* Kaneohe Veterinary Clinic, Surgical Intern; Chief Surgeon, Kapalama Veterinary Hospital; Veterinary Medical Officer, Department of Agriculture, State of Hawaii; Director, Animal Emergency Clinic, Relief Veterinary Practice (current). *Memberships:* Wildlife Disease Association; American Veterinary Medical Association; University of the Philippines Alumni Association; Hawaii Veterinary Medical Association; Honolulu Veterinary Society. *Publication:* "The Efficacy of the Mare Immunological Pregnancy (MIP) Test", 1982. *Honour:* Outstanding International University of the Philippines Student, 1981. *Hobbies:* Horse-riding; Cycling; Surfing; Running; Scuba Diving; Skiing; Foreign Languages; Reading Journals. *Address:* 635 Onaha Street, Honolulu, HI 96816, USA.

PEARSON, David Allen, b. 21 Jan. 1935, Jamestown, New York, USA. Associate Dean for Public Health, Yale University School of Medicine, Department of Epidemiology and Public Health. m. Jo-Ann Louise Darrow, 9 Aug. 1958, Ithaca, New York, 1 son, 1 daughter. *Education:* BS, State University of New York, Cortland, 1956; MPH, University of Michigan, 1961; PhD Yale University, 1970. *Appointments:* Public Health Analyst, US Public Health Service, Department of Health, Education and Welfare, 1966-67; Acting Director, Health Economics Analysis Program, National Center for Health Services Research and Development; Director, Office of Regional Activities, 1968-69; Research Associate, Department of Epidemiology and Public Health, 1969-70; Assistant Professor, 1970-75; Associate Professor, 1975-80; Associate Dean for Public Health, 1980-, Yale University School of Medicine. *Memberships:* Chairman, Board of Directors, The Hospital Fund; Councilor, Council on Education for Public Health; Member, Executive Committee, Association of Schools of Public Health; Fellow, American Public Health Association; Gerontological Society of America; Association of Teachers of Preventive Medicine; Connecticut Public Health Association. *Publications:* Co-author, "The Dynamics of Health and Disease", 1973; 'The Concept of Regionalized Personal Health Services in the United States 1920-55' in E W Saward, Editor, "The Regionalization of Personal Health Services", 1975; Co-author: "Regulating Hospital Costs: The Development of Public Policy", 1979; Co-author, 'Long-Term Care' in S Jonas, Editor, "Health Care Delivery in the United States", 1981; Book Review Editor, 'Inquiry'; Contributor to professional journals. *Honours:* Superior Work Performance, US Department of Health, Education and Welfare, 1967, 69; Distinguished Alumnus Award, State University of New York, Cortland, 1983. *Hobbies:* Sailing; Walking. *Address:* 25 Thimble Farms Road, Branford, CT 06405, USA.

PEARSON, Warren Thomas, b. 8 Dec. 1929, Iowa, USA. Surgeon. m. Margaret, 5 Sep. 1965, San Diego, California, 2 sons. *Education:* MD, University of Iowa, 1955. *Memberships:* American College of Cardiology; American Thoracic Society; New York County Medical Society; New York Trudeau Society; Los Angeles Trudeau Society; American College of Angiology; International Union Against Tuberculosis; Royal College of Medicine; American Medical Association; American College of Surgeons; Society of Thoracic Surgeons; American Association for the Advancement of Science; New York Academy of Science; New York Academy of Medicine; American College of Chest Physicians; International Society of Transplantation; International Society for the Study of Lung Cancer. *Address:* PO Box 8490, Calabasas, CA 91302, USA.

PEAT, Malcolm, b. 4 Apr. 1932, Dundee, Scotland. Associate Dean, Faculty of Medicine (Rehabilitation) and Professor and Director, School of Rehabilitation Therapy. m. Enid Lucy Lyons, 6 July 1954, Bristol, England, 1 daughter. *Education:* BPT, MSc, PhD, University of Manitoba; Diploma, Teacher of Physiotherapy; Member, Chartered Society of Physiotherapy. *Appointments:* Physiotherapist, Royal Air Force, 1953-56; Lecturer, Physiotherapy; Royal Infirmary Glasgow, 1956-59; United Kingdom Colombo Plan Advisor, South East Asia, 1960-70; Assistant Professor, School of Medical Rehabilitation, University of Manitoba, Canada, 1971-76; Associate Professor and Director, Programme in Physical Therapy, University of Western Ontario, 1976-84; Professor and Director, School of Rehabilitation Therapy, Associate Professor of Anatomy and Associate Dean, Faculty of Medicine, Queens University, Kingston, 1984-. *Memberships:* Chartered Society of Physiotherapy; Canadian Physiotherapy Association; Canadian Association of Anatomists; International Society of Electrophysiological Kinesiology. *Publications:* Author or co-author of numerous papers contributed to professional journals: 'Physiotherapy Canada'; 'Archives of Physical

Medicine'; 'Journal of Biomechanics'; 'American Journal of Physical Medicine'; 'Anat Anz Jen'; Various contributions to international congresses. *Honours:* Award of Appreciation, Foundation for Welfare of Crippled, Thailand, 1964; MBE, 1967; Presidents Award, University of the Philippines, 1970; British Council Fellowship, 1983; Honorary Member, Jamaican Physiotherapy Association, 1983; Robins Memorial Lecturer, 1983, Convocation Speaker, 1983, University of Southern California, 1983; Fellow, Lincoln Institute for Health Sciences, 1983; Special Award, Ontario Physiotherapy Association, 1984 and others. *Hobbies:* Music; Theatre; Travel. *Address:* Louise Acton Building, George Street, Queens University, Kingston, Ontario, Canada K7L 3N6.

PECORARI, Domenico, b. 19 Sep. 1934, Milan, Italy. Professor of Obstetrics and Gynaecology. m. Mariateresa Ferrata, 3 Sep. 1983, Brescia. *Education:* MD. *Appointments:* Research Fellow, Department of Obstetrics and Gynaecology, Boston University School of Medicine, Boston, Massachusetts, USA; Assistant Professor, Department of Obstetrics and Gynaecology, University of Parma School of Medicine, Parma, Italy; Associate Professor, Department of Obstetrics and Gynaecology, University of Genoa School of Medicine, Genoa; Professor, Chairman, Department of Obstetrics and Gynaecology, University of Trieste School of Medicine, Trieste. *Memberships:* American Medical Association; Royal Society of Medicine; Societa Italiana di Ginecologia e Obstetricia. *Publications:* "Manuale di Clinica Ostetrica e Ginecologica", 2 volumes, 1977; "Puericultura Prenatale", 1980. *Address:* Viale XX Settembre 1, 1 34125 Trieste, Italy.

PEDERICK, Frank Oliver, b. 30 Oct. 1931, Kyabram, Victoria, Australia. Chiropractor in Private Practice. m. Mary Alexander MacKenzie, 24 Mar. 1956, Deepdene, 2 sons, 2 daughters. *Education:* Bachelor of Applied Science, Chiropractic; Diplomate, National Board oif Chiropractic Examiners, USA; Fellow, RMTC, Communications Engineering; PSC, Royal Australian Air Force. *Appointments:* Communications Engineer, Royal Australian Air Force, 1954-78 (retired as Wing Commander); Private Practice, Chiropractic, 1982-. *Memberships:* Australian and American Chiropractic Associations; Chiropractic Alumni Association. *Publications:* Contributions to: 'Pacific Defence Reporter'; 'Army Journal'; 'Australian Defence Force Journal'; 'Journal of Australian Chiropractors Association'; "Pederick Family in Australia", book, 1974. *Honours:* National Medal, 1984; Defence Force Service Medal, 1977. *Hobbies:* Swimming; Writing. *Address:* 120 Balwyn Riad, Balwyn, Victoria 3103, Australia.

PEDICORD, Ronald Harold, b. 15 Feb. 1927. Battle Creek, Michigan, USA. Doctor of Chiropractic. m. Janet Alice Earnhart, 12 Sep. 1947, Dayton, Ohio, 1 son, 1 daughter. *Education:* Miami University, Oxford, Ohio, Pre-Chiropractic; DC, International Chiropractic College; DM, Great Lakes College; Certificate in Acupuncture, Columbia Institute of Chiropractic. *Appointments:* Faculty of International Chiropractic College; President, Dayton School of Massage; Vice-President, Miami Valley Chiropractic Society; President, Ohio Academy of Chiropractic Neurology; Board of Directors, Ohio State Chiropractic Association. *Memberships:* American, Ohio State, South Central Chiropractic Associations; Council on Roentgenology, American Chiropractic Association; Council on Neurology, ibid; Foundation for Chiropractic Education & Research. *Publications:* Various articles in chiropractic journals. *Hobbies:* Farming; Raising Cattle; Photography; Fishing. *Address:* 129 West Main Street, West Union, OH 45693, USA.

PEGINGTON, Anne, b. 2 Oct. 1936, Swansea, Wales. Chief Executive Officer to Wales; Secretary to the Board. 1 son. *Education:* State Registered Nurse, North Middlesex Hospital, London, England. *Appointments:* Staff Nurse and Ward Sister, 1958-64; Nurs-

ing Officer, 1965-70; Senior Nursing Officer, 1970-75; Divisional Nursing Officer, 1975-78; Chief Executive Officer, Secretary to the Board, Royal College of Nursing. *Membership:* Fellow, British Institute of Management; Chairman, Joint Staff, Consultative Council of Wales. *Publications:* Various contributions to media and nursing journals. *Hobbies:* Travel; Visiting nurses in other countries. *Address:* Royal College of Nursing, Ty Maeth, King George V Drive East, Cardiff, Wales.

PELIKAN, Zdenek, b. 18 Sep. 1938, Prezsburg. Director, Department of Allergology and Immunology. m. Dr M Pelikan-Filipek. *Education:* Doctor of Medicine, MD, Medical Faculty of Masarykis, University of Brno, 1961; Specialisation: Internal Medicine, Ophthalmology, Hygiene & Immunology, Allergology; Palacky University, Olomouc, 1961-66; Masaryk's University, Brno, 1966-69; Studied allergology, State University Hospital, Groningen, 1969-74. *Appointments:* Student, Masaryk's University, Brno, 1961; Fellow in Training, Palacky's University, Olomouc, 1969, Masaryk's University, Brno. 1967; Junior Lecturer, Masaryk University, 1967-69; Fellow in Training, State University, Groningen, 1969-74; Director, Department of Allergology and Immunology, Institute of Medical Sciences De Klokkenberg, Breda, The Netherlands, 1974-. *Memberships:* European Academy of Allergology and Clinical Immunology; Royal Dutch and Royal British Societies of Medicine; Dutch and British Societies of Allergology; Dutch and British Societies of Immunology; British Society of Allergology and Immunology; American Academy of Allergology; American Association of Clinical Immunology and Allergology; American Association of Immunology; American College of Allergists; American Aerospace Medical Association; Swiss Society of Allergology; Interosma Belgian Society of Allergology; German Society of Space Medicine; International Association of Immunopharmacology; Canadian Society of Allergology; New York Academy of Science. *Publications:* Author of more than 100 papers in field. *Honours:* Student Scientific Award, 1960. Fellow: American College of Allergists, 1978; American Academy of Allergy, 1984. *Hobbies:* Science; Sports; Music. *Address:* Effenseweg 42, 4838 BB Breda, The Netherlands.

PELIKAN-FILIPEK, Marta, b. 28 Jan. 1941, Rakwitz, Pediatrician-Allergologist; Chief of Clinic. m. Dr Zdenek Pelikan. *Education:* Dr med, MD, Masaryk's University, Brno, 1964; Affiliated District Hospital, Specialising in pediatrics, Masaryk's University, 1964-67; Trained in allergology, 1967. *Appointments:* Medical student, 1964, Fellow in Training, 1964-67, Senior Pediatrician, 1967-69; Masaryk's University, Brno; Pediatrician Consultant, Municipal Health Service, Groningen, 1969-73; Pediatrician, State University, Groningen, 1974; Pediatric Consultant, Dutch State Teaching Programme for nutrition and general medicine education, 1974-76, Municipal Health Services, North Brabant, 1976-78; Pediatric Allergologist, Chief of Clinic, Department of Allergology and Immunology, Institute of Medical Sciences De Klokkenberg, Breda, The Netherlands, 1978-. *Memberships:* Dutch Society of Pediatrics; Society of Northern Pediatrics; Dutch Society of Allergology and Clinical Immunology; European Academy of Allergology and Clinical Immunology; American Academy of Allergy; Dutch Society of Clinical Immunology. *Publications:* Author of some 27 papers on clinical and experimental aspects of allergy and pediatrics. *Hobbies:* Literature; Sport; Music. *Address:* Effenseweg 42, 4838 BB Breda, The Netherlands.

PELLEGRINO, Rand J, b. 31 Dec. 1948, New York, USA. Clinic Director, President, Chiropractic Arts Centre Inc. m. Ruth M Uemura, 22 Dec. 1983, Honolulu. *Education:* BS, Physiology, Health & Psychology, California State University; DC, University of Pasadena, 1977. *Appointments:* Treasurer, Hawaii Chiropractic Association, Examiner, Hawaii Chiropractic Board of Examiners. *Memberships:* Hawaii State Chiropractic Association; Partners in Health;

Foundation for Chiropractic Education & Research. *Publication:* "Balance: Your Key to Health", 1984. *Hobbies:* Water Skiing; Skiing; Racquetball; Sports Cars. *Address:* 615 Piikoi Street, 2002, Honolulu, HI 96814, USA.

PELOSOF, Henri Vidal, b. 9 Apr. 1934, France. Physician, Specialist Physical Medicine & Rehabilitation. m. Anne Gelfand, 7 Nov. 1969, New York City, 2 daughters. *Education:* MD, University of Paris, 1960. *Appointments include:* Attending Physician & Chief, Amputee Service, Texas Institute for Rehabilitation & Research, USA, 1970-73; Assistant Professor, Department of Physical Medicine & Rehabilitation, Baylor College of Medicine, Houston, Texas, 1970-73; Attending Physician, St Paul Medical Center, Dallas, 1974-. *Memberships:* American Academy of Physical Medicine & Rehabilitation; American Association of Electromyography & Electrodiagnosis; American Congress of Rehabilitation Medicine; International Medical Society for Paraplegia. *Publications include:* 'Hydronephrosis: Silent Hazard of Intermittent Catheterization' (J Urol), 1973; 'Progressive Quadriplegia in a Paraplegic Patient: Stabilization with the Harrington Technique' (Arch Phys Med), 1973; 'Endoskeletal Prosthesis: Use in Patient with Insilateral Fore-and-Hund Quarter Amputations' (Arch Phys Med), 1974; etc. *Honour:* President, Dallas Metroplex Physical Medicine & Rehabilitation Society, 1984. *Hobby:* 19th & 20th century military history. *Address:* 5959 Harry Hines Blvd, 306, Dallas, TX 75235, USA.

PENA, Saúl K, b. 23 Aug. 1932, Jauja, Peru. Psychiatrist; Psychotherapist; Adult and Child Psychoanalyst. m. Luise Boettcher, 17 Mar. 1971, Lima Peru, 4 sons. *Education:* Bachelor of Medicine, 1962, MD, 1962, Universidad Nacional Mayor de San Marcos, Lima; PhD, Department of Psychiatry, Hospital Obrero, Lima, 1963; PhD Studies: The Institute of Psychiatry, London University, Maudsley Hospital, Bethlem Royal Hospital, 1964-69; The British Psychoanalytical Society, Institute of Psycho-Analysis, 1965-69. *Appointments include:* Pioneer, Psychoanalysis in Peru; Professor of Psychoanalysis, Universidad Nacional Mayor de San Marcos, Lima, 1982-86; Director of Institute of Psychoanalysis of Peru, 1983-87; Founder, President and Professor of the Peruvian Institute of Psychotherapy Research and Interdisciplinary Application of the Psychoanalysis Sigmund Freud, 1983-89; Assessor of Psychological Affairs of the Foreign Office of Peru, 1984-86. *Memberships:* Founder Member, Royal College of Psychiatrists, 1973; Peruvian and Latin American Psychiatric Associations; Peruvian (Founder and Pasy President) and British Psychoanalytical Societies; Latin American and European Psychoanalytical Federations; International Psychoanalytical Association; President, Latin American Association of Psychotherapy; International Association of Medical Psychotherapy. *Publications:* "A Psycho-Analytical Contribution to the Study of the Couple" 1978; "Psycho-Analytical Contribution to the Study of Agression" 1980; "Eros and Thanatos", 1980; Preventive Psychotherapy, Psychoanalytical Oriented" 1982; "Development of Psycho-Analysis in Peru. Reflections from a Pioneer Experience" 1985; "Sexuality and Psycho-Analysis" II Peruvian Congress of Sexology, Lima, Peru, 1986. *Hobbies:* Art; Archaeology and Philosophy; Collector of paintings, sculptures and archaeological pieces; Chess. *Address:* Av Salaverry 3463, San Isidro, Lima, Peru.

PENDLETON, Olga Jean, b. 28 Mar. 1948, Naples, Italy. Manager, Statistical Analysis and Research Programme. m. Ronald R Hocking, 6 June 1980, 1 son. *Education:* BS, University of South Alabama, 1970; MS, 1973, PhD, 1976, Emory University, USA. *Appointments:* Assistant Professor: Statistics, Mississippi State University, 1976-79; University of Georgia, 1979-80. Biometrician, Southwest Oncology Group, M D Anderson Hospital, Houston, Texas, 1980-81; Associate Research Statistician, Texas Transportation

Institute (Manager, Statistical Analysis and Research Programme), College Station, 1981-. *Memberships:* American Association of Automotive Medicine; Traffic Research Board; American Statistical Association; Biometric Society; American Society of Quality Control. *Publications:* Author or co-author of contributions to professional publications including: "Contributions to Survey Sampling and Applied Statistics", 1978; "New Expressions for Variance Component Estimates", 1985; 'Journal of American Statistical Association'; 'Communications in Statistics'; 'American Journal of Clinical Oncology'; 'American Journal of Surgical Oncology'; 'Medical and Paediatric Oncology Supplement'. *Address:* Texas Transportation Institute, Texas A&M University System, College Station, TX 77843, USA.

PENG, Ming-Tsung, b. 28 Nov. 1917, Taiwan, Republic of China. Professor of Physiology. m. Sen-Chin Yuan, 3 Oct. 1946, 3 sons, 1 daughter. *Education:* MD, PhD, Taihoku Imperial University. *Appointments:* Director of Studies, Chairman of Physiology Department, Dean, College of Medicine, National Taiwan University. *Memberships:* Endocrine Society USA; International Brain Research Organization; Controller, Endocrine Society, Republic of China; Controller, Neurological Society, Republic of China; Controller, Geriatric Society, Republic of China; President, Chinese Physiological Society. *Publications:* Contributor "Neuroendocrinology of Aging", (editor J Meites), 1983; 76 original papers on Endocrinology, Gerontology, Neuroscience; 8 review articles. *Honours:* Best Medical Research, Ministry of Education, Republic of China; Member, Academia Sinica. *Hobby:* Music. *Address:* 30 Jen-ai Road, Taipei 100, Taiwan, Republic of China.

PEPYS, Jacob (Jack), b. 15 May 1914, Johannesburg, Republic of South Africa. Emeritus Professor of Clinical Immunology. m. Rhoda Gertrude Kussel, 6 Dec. 1938, Port Elizabeth, 1 son, 1 daughter. *Education:* MB ChB, University of Witwatersrand, 1935; MD, University of Cape Town, 1939; Fellow, Royal College of Physicians, Edinburgh and London; Fellow, Royal College of Pathologists. *Appointments include:* General Medical Practice, Republic of South Africa, 1938-48; Clinical Assistant 1951-55, Honorary Consultant in Clinical Immunology 1960-79, Brompton Hospital, London, England; Scientific Staff, Tuberculosis Research Unit, Medical Research Council, 1956-60; Senior Lecturer and Head of Department of Clinical Immunology 1955-79, Director of MRC Research Group in Clinical Immunology 1960-67, Institute of Diseases of the Chest (now Cardiothoracic Institute), Professor of Clinical Immunology 1967-79, Emeritus Professor of Clinical Immunology 1979, University of London; Honorary Professor in Clinical Immunology, Guy's Hospital, London, 1979; Distinguished Visitor in Clinical Immunology, Royal Free School of Medicine, London, 1981. *Memberships include:* British and International Societies for Allergology and Clinical Immunology; British Society for Immunology; Royal Society of Medicine; Society for Experimental Pathology; British Thoracic and Tuberculosis Association; Medical Research Society; British Medical Association. *Publications:* "Hypersensitivity Diseases of the Lungs due to Fungi and Organic Dusts", 1969; "The Mast Cell", 1979; "Occupational Respiratory Allergy Clinics in Immunology and Allergy", 1984. *Honour:* Docteur Medecine honoris causa, University of Clermont Ferrand, France, 1973. *Hobby:* Art. *Address:* 34 Ferncroft Avenue, Hampstead, London NW3 7PE, England.

PERALES, Albertò, b. 12 July 1932, Lima, Peru. Director of Research, Professor of Psychiatry. m. Isabel Reyes, 1 June 1963, 3 sons, 4 daughters. *Education:* BSc, MD, Universidad Nacional Mayor de San Marcos, 1959; Diploma in Psychiatry, McGill University, Canada, 1966; CRCP (C), The Royal College of Physicians and Surgeons of Canada, 1967. *Appointments:* Psychiatric Institut de Recherche, Hôpital St Charles de Joliette, Quebec, Canada, 1966-68; Directeur Clinique et de Recherche, Centre Medico-Social des Monts, P Q, 1968-69; Medical and Research Director, Clinica San Antonio, Anexo Psiquiatria, 1969-75; Professor of Psychiatry, University of San Marcos, Lima, 1969-; Director of Research, Instituto Nacional de Salud Mental Honorio Delgado, Hideyo Noguchi, Lima; Professor of Psychiatry, Universidad Nacional Mayor de San Marcos, Lima. *Memberships:* Colegio Medico del Perú; Asociación Psiquiátrica Peruana; Sociedad Peruana de Psicoterapia; American Psychiatric Association; American Society of Hispanic Psychiatrists. *Publications include:* "Comunidad Terapéutica en el Perú", 1971; "Psicoterapia: Coencia o Arte?", 1981; 'Relación Madre-Hijo en una población marginal de Lima Estudio Piloto', 1984; 30 other articles. *Honour:* Lelio Zeno Prize - best research work on psychosomatics, 1959. *Hobbies:* Music; Soccer. *Address:* Av Javier Prado Este 2372, San Borja, Lima 41, Peru.

PERCIACCANTE, Ronald George, b. 26 Mar. 1938, New York City, USA. Director, Cystic Fibrosis Clinic and House of Good Samaritan, Watertown, New York; Private Practice. m. Celia Fay, 25 May 1963, New York City, 2 sons, 4 daughters. *Education:* BS, Georgetown University College of Arts and Sciences, 1959; MD, Georgetown University College of Medicine, 1963. *Memberships:* American Medical Association; Medical Society of the State of New York; Medical Society of Jefferson County; American Academy of Pediatrics; American Thoracic Society; American College of Chest Physicians; New York Trudeau Society. *Publications:* "D/G Translocation Mongolism: A Family Study" presented at Resident's Night, New York Academy of Medicine, April 1965; 'Ulm's Tumor and Associated Anomalies", 'American Journal Dis. Child', May 1965; 'Recurrence Risk of D/G Translocation Mongolism', 'The California Bulletin', 1968-69; 'Anophthalmia and other Anomalies Associated with a Ring Chromosome', 'Cytologia' 40, 1975. *Honours:* Physicians Recognition Awards, American Medical Association, 1975-78, 1978-81, 1981-84, 1984-87. *Hobby:* Flying. *Address:* 145 Clinton Street, Watertown, NY 13601, USA.

PERDIKIS, Phoebus, b. 1 July 1933, South Africa. General Surgeon. m. Francine Elizabeth Braam, 3 Mar. 1962, Johannesburg, 1 son, 1 daughter. *Education:* MB, BCh, University of the Witwatersrand, 1957; Fellow, College of Surgeons (SA), 1966; Fellow, Royal College of Surgeons (Edinburgh, Scotland), 1968; Fellow, Royal College of Surgeons (London, England), 1968. *Appointments:* Assistant Lecturer, Department of Anatomy, University of Witwatersrand, 1961; Surgical Registrar, Johannesburg General Hospital, 1962-66; Surgical Registrar, Orpington Hospital, England, 1966-69; Consultant Surgeon, Baragwanam Hospital, SA, 1970; Part-time Surgeon, Department of Paediatric Surgery, 1971-82, Department of Surgery, 1971-, University of Witwatersrand; Part-time Surgeon, New Johannesburg General Hospital. *Memberships:* National Executive of the Association of Surgeons of SA, 1978-80, Honorary Secretary, 1980-84, Vice-Chairman, 1984-; Medical Association of South Africa; British Medical Association; Medical Advisor, Board of General Purposes, Transvaal District, SA. *Publications:* (In SA Journal of Surgery): 'Incidence of Supracondyloid Process', 1962; 'Idiopathic Neuropathic Feet in Bantu', 1969; 'Non-operating Removal of Gall-stones', 1969; 'Intestinal Obstruction produced by cenema of small bowel, 1971; 'Lip-load operation in facial palsy', 1973; 'Transcutaneous Nerve Stimulation in treatment of Ileus', 1977; 'The Acute N on Surgical Abdomen' (in Surgery Annual), 1982; 'An effective local treatment for auxiliary Hyperhidrosis', 1983. *Hobbies:* Philately (Great Britain, also forgeries of GB & South Africa); Golf. *Address:* Kenridge Hospital, 19 Eton Road, Parktown 2193, Johannesburg, Republic of South Africa.

PEREDA, Francisco E, b. 4 Mar. 1923, Havana, Cuba.

Private Practitioner, Neurology and Psychiatry. m. (1) 2 May 1953, Havana, Cuba, 1 son, 1 daughter, (2) 11 Sep. 1980, New York City, New York, USA. *Education:* MD, University of Havana, Cuba. *Appointments:* Private Practice, Owner and Administrator, Medical Center, Queens, New York, USA; Neurology Consultant, Boulevard Hospital, Astoria, Queens, New York. *Memberships:* American Psychiatric Association; American Medical Association; Queens County Medical Association; Cuban Medical Association in Exile; Royal Academy of Medicine. *Hobby:* Philately. *Address:* 40-38 75th Street, Elmhurst, NY 11373, USA.

PERERA, Lalith Michael, b. 5 Sep. 1935, Colombo, Sri Lanka. Consultant Urologist, General Hospital, Colombo. m. Dr Charlotte Salvamanie Perera nee Salvanayagan, 2 Dec. 1961, Colombo, 4 daughters. *Education:* MBBS (Ceylon); Master of Surgery (Sri Lanka); Fellow, Royal College of Surgeons of England. *Appointments:* Consultant Surgeon, District Hospital, Panadura; Consultant Urologist, General Hospital, Galle; Consultant Urologist, Colombo North Hospital. *Membership:* Full Member, British Association of Urological Surgeons. *Hobbies:* Flautist, Ceylon Symphony Orchestra; Sings Bass in Colombo Philharmonic Choir; Organist. *Address:* 69/31 Green Path, Colombo 7, Sri Lanka.

PEREZ, Josephine, b. 10 Feb. 1941, Tijuana, Mexico. Private Practitioner; Psychotherapist; Educator; Clinical Instructor of Psychiatry. *Education:* BS, Los Angeles City College; MD, University of Santiago de Compostela, Spain, 1975; Resident in General Psychiatry, University of Miami, Jackson Memorial Hospital and Veterans Administration Hospital, USA, 1978. *Appointments:* Attending Staff Psychiatrist, Assistant Director of Adolescent Unit, 1979-82, Jackson Memorial Hospital; Clinical Instructor, Psychiatry, University of Miami Medical School, 1979-; Private Practice of Individual, Marriage and Family Psychotherapy, 1979-; Consultant, Juvenile Court System, Health and Rehabilitation Service, School System. *Memberships:* American Psychiatric Association; South Florida Psychiatric Society; American Association of Marriage and Family Therapy; American Medical Women Association; Clinical Faculty, University of Miami School of Medicine; Treasurer and President Elect, Dade Association for Marriage and Family Therapy. *Publications:* Numerous. *Honours:* Physicians Recognition Award, American Medical Association, 1980, 1983, 1985. *Hobbies:* Sailing; Fishing; Gardening; Music. *Address:* 921 South West 27th Avenue, Suite 2-A, Miami, FL 33135, USA.

PERIČIĆ, Danka, b. 27 Oct. 1943, Zagreb, Yugoslavia. Head, Laboratory of Neuropharmacology. m. Duško Peričić, 29 Nov. 1967, Zagreb, 1 son, 1 daughter. *Education:* MD, PhD, Medical Faculty; MSc, Faculty of Sciences; Research Training as a Public Health Service International Research Fellow, USA. *Appointments:* Postgraduate, 1967; Research Assistant, 1969; Senior Research Assistant, 1973; Research Associate, 1979; Senior Research Associate, 1982; Scientific Adviser, 1985. *Memberships:* Yugoslav Physiological Society; Yugoslav Pharmacological Society; Medical Association of Croatia; European Society for Neurochemistry. *Publications:* Contributor of articles to numerous professional journals. *Hobbies:* Gardening; Swimming. *Address:* Department of Experimental Biology and Medicine, "Rudjer Bošković" Institute, Bijenička 54, 41000 Zagreb, Yugoslavia.

PERKIN, Reginald Lewis, b. 16 Oct. 1930, Toronto, Canada. Executive Director, College of Family Physicians of Canada. m. Alison Beverly Hyde Smith, 5 June 1954, Toronto, 2 sons, 2 daughters. *Education:* MD, University of Toronto, 1954; Certification, College of Family Physicians of Canada, 1970. *Appointments:* Senior Partner, Dixie Road Medical Associates in Mississauga, Ontario, 1962-85; Head, Family Practice, Mississauga Hospital, 1967-75; Professor, Family & Community Medicine, University of Toronto, 1969-85; Consultant, Family Medicine, Credit Valley Hospital, Mississauga, 1984-85. *Memberships:* College of Family Physicians of Canada; Ontario Medical Association; Canadian Medical Association. *Publications include:* "Medical Manpower in General Practice", 'Canadian Medical Association Journal', 1967; "Medical Ethics", 1969; "Tonsillectomy and Adenoidectomy", 'Primary Care', Volume 5, 1978. *Honours:* Alpha Omega Alpha, 1954; Fellowship, College of Family Physicians of Canada 1970; Honorary Fellowship, Royal College of General Practitioners; Visiting Professor, Royal Australian College of General Practitioners, 1982. *Hobbies:* Golf; Skiing; Choral Music. *Address:* College of Family Physicians of Canada, 4000 Leslie Street, Willowdale, Ontario, Canada M2K 2R9.

PERLMAN, Robert Louis, b. 15 Aug. 1938, Chicago, Illinois, USA. Professor & Head, Physiology & Biophysics, University of Illinois College of Medicine. m. Caryle Geier, 22 Mar. 1964, New York, 1 son, 1 daughter. *Education:* AB 1957, SB 1958, MD 1961, PhD 1963, University of Chicago. *Appointments include:* Associate Professor, Physiology, Harvard Medical School, 1971-81; Professor & Head, Department of Physiology & Biophysics, University of Illinois, 1981-. *Memberships:* American Society of Biological Chemists; American Physiological Society; American Society for Neurochemistry; Society for Neuroscience; Endocrine Society. *Address:* Department of Physiology & Biophysics m/c 901, University of Illinois College of Medicine, Box 6998, Chicago, IL 60680, USA.

PERRI, Vincent L, b. 6 Feb. 1953, New York, New York, USA. Chiropractic Physician. m. Susan Oldham, 5 Aug. 1972, 1 son, 1 daughter. *Education:* Pre-Medical Degree, Thomas A Edison College, Princeton, New Jersey, 1976; DC, Life Chiropractic College, Georgia, 1981; Certified Psychotherapist, American Institute of Psychotherapy and Behavioural Medicine, 1985. *Appointments:* Watertown Chiropractic Office, Connecticut, 1981-84; Private Practice, Waterbury, 1984-. *Memberships:* American International and Connecticut Chiropractic Associations; Council on Diagnosis and Internal Disorders; Council on Paediatrics; Board of Examiners, Connecticut Department of Health; Christian Chiropractors Association; Past Chairman, State of the Art Committee, Connecticut Chiropractic Association. *Publications:* 'Exogenous Hypertrighlyceridemia', 1983, 'Diagnosis/Management of Duodernal Bulb Ulceration', 1983, 'Evaluation of the Sick Child', 1984, 'Oral Hyperalimentation of the Sick Child', 1984, 'The Dying Patient', 1984, 'Death of a Child Living Beyond the Grief', 1985, all contributed to 'Journal of American Chiropractic Association'. *Honours:* Graduated Magna cum laude, Life Chiropractic College, 1981; Pi Tau Delta, 1981; Recipient of "Distinguished Leadership" Award, 1986, American Biographical Society. *Hobby:* Reading important data of related academic significance. *Address:* 34 Quail Run Road, Woodbury, CT 06798, USA.

PERRIN, Louis Francois Marie, b. 22 Mar. 1921, Lyon, France. Deputy Physician, Cardiovascular and Pneumological Hospital. m. Dr Michele Labry, 20 Apr. 1963, Ormes, 1 son. *Education:* MD, 1950; Certification as Professor, 1962. *Appointments:* Intern, Lyons Hospital, 1946-50; Clinical Chief of Faculty, 1954-56; Head, Respirator Physiopathology Laboratory, 1959-63; Certified Professor, Faculty of Medicine, 1962; Lecturer, Catholic Faculty of Sciences, 1975; Clinical Expert for Trials of New Drugs, Ministry of Health, 1966; Member, College des Trois Medecins, specialising in pneumoconioses, 1966; currently, Deputy Physician, Cardiovascular and Pneumological Hospital, Lyon. *Memberships:* American Academy of Allergy and Clinical Immunology; French-Speaking Society of Pneumology; French Society of Allergology and Clin-

ical Immunology; European Academy of Allergology and Clinical Immunology. *Publications:* "Allergologie Pratique", volume 1, 1984; "Les Essais therapeutiques chez l'homme", 1980; "Radiologie Clinique", volume 2, 1974; "Physiologie et Physiopathologie de la Respiration", 1962; "Traite de Radiodiagnostic", 1957. *Honours:* Chevalier, French National Order of Merit, 1974. *Hobbies:* Skiing; Windsurfing. *Address:* 2 rue Alphonse-Fochier, 69002 Lyon, France.

PERROT, Linda J, b. 4 Feb. 1952, Jefferson City, Missouri, Assistant Professor of Pathology and Paediatrics. *Education:* BSc cum laude Biology, Lincoln University, Jefferson City, Missouri, 1974; MD honours in Pathology, Missouri School of Medicine, Columbia, Missouri, 1978; Board Eligible, Anatomic and Clinical Pathology. *Appointments:* Resident 1978-82, Chief Resident 1982, University of Missouri Health Science Center, Columbia, Missouri; Anatomic Pathology Fellow 1982-83, Clinical Assistant, Pathology Department, Research Associate, Hematology/Oncology section 1983-84, Department of Medicine, University of Arizona Health Science Center, Tucson, Arizona; Assistant Professor of Pathology, Department of Pathology, University of Arkansas for Medical Sciences and Arkansas Children's Hospita, Little Rock, Arkansas 1984-; Assistant Professor of Pediatrics, Arkansas Children's Hospital, 1984-. *Memberships include:* American Society of Clinical Pathologists; College of American Pathologists; American Medical Women's Association; American Medical Association; Arizona Society of Pathologists; Arkansas Cadusus Society; Arkansas Society of Pathologists. *Publications include:* 'Feasibility of a prospective randomised correlative trial of advanced non-small lung cancer using the human tumor clonogenic assay' (co-author), 1984; 'Benign mediastinal teratoma with immature elements exhibits clonal growth and motility in human tumor clonogenic assay' (co-author), 1985; 'Bone marrow emboli versus fat emboli as the cause of unexpected death' (with R C Froede), 1985. *Hobbies include:* Backpacking; White water canoeing; Reading; Horseback riding; Cooking; Knitting; Painting; Marshall arts; Diving. *Address:* 701 Green Mountain Drive, Little Rock, AR 72211, USA.

PERRY, Michael Clinton, b. 27 Jan. 1945, Michigan, USA. Professor and Chairman, Department of Medicine. m. Nancy Kaluzny, 22 June 1968, Detroit, Michigan, 2 daughters. *Education:* BA, 1966, MD, 1970, Wayne State University; MS, University of Minnesota, 1975; Internship, 1970-71, Residency, 1971-72, Haematology Fellowship, 1972-74, Oncology Fellowship, 1974-75, Mayo Graduate School of Medicine. *Appointments:* Instructor, Mayo Medical School, 1974-75; Assistant Professor, 1975-80, Associate Professor, 1980-85, Chairman, 1983-, Professor, 1985, University of Missouri School of Medicine. *Memberships:* American Society of Haematology; American Society of Clinical Oncology; American College of Physicians; American Federation for Clinical Research; American Society of Internal Medicine; American Medical Association; Association of Professors of Medicine; Cancer and Leukemia Group B. *Publications:* "Toxicity of Chemotherapy", (Co-Editor with J W Yarbro), 1984. *Honours:* McKenzie Honour Society, 1966; Omicron Delta Kappa, 1966; Sigma Xi, 1980; Alpha Omega Alpha Faculty Award, 1980; American Society of Internal Medicine, Young Internist of the Year, 1981; Missouri Society of Internal Medicine, Young Internist of the Year, 1981; University of Missouri Faculty/Alumni Award, 1985. *Address:* Department of Medicine, University of Missouri Health Sciences Center, MA 406D Medical Science Building, Columbia, MO 65212, USA.

PERRY, Seymour Monroe, b. 26 May 1921, New York City, USA. Senior Fellow and Deputy Director, Institute for Health Policy Analysis, Georgetown University Medical Center. m. Judith Carol Kaplan, 18 Mar. 1951, Los Angeles, California, 2 sons, 1 daughter. *Education:* BA (Hons), University of California, Los

Angeles; MD (Hons), University of Southern California, Los Angeles; Fellow in Hematology, University of California, Los Angeles. *Appointments:* Senior Investigator, Medicine Branch, National Cancer Institute, NIH, 1961-65; Chief, Medicine Branch, 1965-68; Associate Scientific Director for Clinical Trials NCI (concurrent), 1966-71; Associate Director for Program Planning, Division of Cancer Treatment, NCI, 1971-74; Special Assistant to Director, NIH, 1974-78; Associate Director (Medical Application of Research), NIH, 1978-80; Director, National Center for Health Care Technology, US Department of Health and Human Services, 1980-82; Assistant Surgeon General, US Public Health Service, 1980-82. *Memberships:* American Federation for Clinical Research; American Society of Hematology; International Society of Hematology; American Association for Cancer Research; American Society of Clinical Oncology; International Society for Technology Assessment in Health Care. *Publications:* Numerous articles on studies of tumor cell growth and biochemistry and in the last 10 years on medical technology assessment and health public policy. *Honours:* Fellow, American College of Physicians; Public Health Service Commendation Medal, 1967; Award from Government of Peru, Comendador Orden Al Merito per Servicios Distinguidos, 1971; Public Health Service Meritorious Medal, 1980; Award from Government of Peru, Condecoracion, Orden Hipolito Unanue en el Grado de Oficial, 1984; Member, Institute of Medicine, National Academy of Science; President, International Society of Technology Assessment in Health Care, 1985-. *Hobbies:* Gardening; Photography; Squash. *Address:* Institute for Health Policy Analysis, Georgetown University Medical Center, 2121 Wisconsin Avenue NW, Suite 220, Washington, DC 20007, USA.

PERRY, Thomas Lockwood, b. 10 Aug. 1916, Asheville, North Carolina, USA. Professor. m. Claire Joan Lippman, 3 June 1941, New York, 2 sons, 2 daughters. *Education:* AB 1937, MD, 1942, Harvard University; BA, Oxford University, 1939. *Appointments:* Instructor, Paediatrics, University of Southern California, 1948-52; Medical Research Consultant, California Institute of Technology, 1956-62; Associate Professor, 1962-65, Professor, 1965-, Pharmacology & Therapeutics, University of British Columbia, Canada. *Memberships:* World Federation of Neurology's Huntington's Chorea Research Group; Scientific Advisory Council, Huntington Society of Canada; Canadian Society for Clinical Investigation; Society for the Study of Unborn Errors of Metabolism; Physicians for Social Responsibility, Canada. *Publications:* 218 articles in professional journals; Editor, 'Nuclear War: The Search for Solutions', 1985. *Address:* Department of Pharmacology & Therapeutics, University of British Columbia, Vancouver, Canada V6T 1W5.

PERSKY, Bruce, b. 12 Mar. 1953, West Point, New York, USA. Assistant Professor of Anatomy. m. Karen P. Asche, 3 June 1978, Grand Forks, North Dakota, 2 sons, 1 daughter. *Education:* BA, University of Colorado, 1975; MA 1977, PhD 1980, Anatomy, University of North Dakota. *Appointments:* Postdoctoral Cancer Research Training Fellowships: Department of Internal Medicine 1981-82, Department of Anatomy 1982-83, University of Arizona College of Medicine; Assistant Professor of Anatomy, full-time teaching & research, Loyola University of Chicago, 1983-. *Memberships:* American Society for Cell Biology; American Association of Anatomists; Sigma Xi. *Publications include:* Research articles, professional journals: 'Diagnostic electron microscopy for amelanotic melanoma', 1983; 'Amyloid production in human myeloma stem cell cultures', 1982; etc. *Honours:* 1st place, Chicago Laryngological Lederer-Pierce Award (with J P Leonetti), 1985; Award of merit, graduate scientific research, Sigma Xi, 1980. *Hobbies:* Scuba diving; Backpacking; Swimming; Basketball; Racquetball. *Address:* Loyola University of Chicago, Stritch School of Medicine, 2160 South First Avenue, Maywood, IL 60153, USA.

PÉTER, Ferenc, b. 1 Aug. 1934, Debrecen, Hungary. Director, Buda Children's Hospital. m. Fleur Mailath, 14 Mar. 1959, Debrecen, 1 son, 1 daughter. *Education:* MD, 1958; Paediatrician, 1962; Clinical Chemist/Laboratorian, 1968; PhD, 1971; Associate Professor, 1975; One year scholarship: Department of Paediatrics, University of Oxford, John Radcliffe Hospital, Oxford, 1980-81; Endocrinologist, 1985. *Appointments:* Demonstrator, University Institute for Clinical Chemistry, 1956-57; University Institute for Public Hygiene, 1957-59; Clinician, 1959-64, Department Head, Assistant, First Assistant, 1964-73, University Paediatric Department, Debrecen; Head, 2nd Paediatric Department and Endocrine Unit, Radioisotopic Laboratory, 1973-76; Director of the Institute, Buda Children's Hospital and Polyclinic, Budapest, 1976-. *Memberships:* Council Member, Hungarian Paediatric Association; Council Member, Hungarian Society for Endocrinology and Metabolism; Secretary, Common Endocrine Committee, Hungarian Academy of Science and Ministry of Health; Chairman, National Growth Hormone Committee; President, Hungarian Section for Paediatrics Endocrinology; European Thyroid Association; European Society for Paediatric Endocrinology. *Publications:* Contributor of numerous articles and chapters in professional and medical journals and books. *Honours:* Bokay Medallion, Hungarian Paediatric Association, 1974; Copernicus Medallion, University of Cracow, Poland, 1975. *Hobbies:* Tennis; Modern history. *Address:* Buda Children's Hospital and Polyclinic, PO Box 14, 1277 Budapest, 23, Hungary.

PETER. Joshua, b. 1 Jan. 1942, Bangalore. Reader in Reproductive Physiology and Human Cytogenetics, Bangalore University. m. Vasantha, 18 May 1970, Bangalore, 1 son, 1 daughter. *Education:* BSc; MSc; PhD. *Appointments:* Senior Research Officer, Head, Unit of Medical Genetics, Institute for Research in Reproduction, Bombay, 1971-85; Reader in Reproductive Physiology and Human Cytogenetics, Bangalore University, 1985-; Programme Director, IVF-ET (Invitro Fertilisation and Embryo Transfer, in charge of Human Cytogenetics Laboratories and Human Reproductive Laboratories. *Memberships:* Indian Society of Human Genetics; Society of Fertility and Sterility of India; Endocrine Society of India; Adviser, World Health Organisation Temporary adviser on Zona Free hamster oocyte Penetration test. *Publications include:* 'Leukocyte culture for chromosome preparation using Eagle's Minimym Essential Medium (MEM), Eagle's Modified Medium (EM) and Eagle's Basal Medium (EM)', 1971; 'Hot aceto orcein for staining human chromosomes', 1974; 'In vitro fertilization of human Oocyters and embryo transfer. An alternative to tubal recanalization', 1984; Co-authored various articles in professional journals. *Honours:* Ford Foundation Fellowship, to visit University of Hawaii, Honolulu, 1978-79; World Health Organisation Temporary Adviser, 1985. *Hobbies:* Stamp Collecting; Photography. *Address:* Associate Professor, Centre for Applied Genetics, Central College, Bangalore University, Bangalore 560001, India.

PETERS, Alan, b. 6 Dec. 1929, Nottingham, England. Chairman and Professor of Anatomy. m. Verona Muriel Shipman, 30 Sep. 1955, Nottingham, 3 sons. *Education:* BSc 1951, PhD 1954, Bristol University. *Appointments:* Lecturer in Anatomy, Edinburgh University, Scotland, 1958-66; Visiting Lecturer, Harvard University, USA, 1963-64; Professor of Anatomy, Boston University, 1966-. *Memberships:* American Anatomical Association; Society for Neuroscience; American Society for Cell Biology. *Publications:* "The Fine Structure of the Nervous System", (with S L Palay and H de F Webster), 1970 and 1976; "Myelination", (with A N Davidson), 1970; "Cerebral Cortex", (with E G Jones), 1984. *Honour:* Symington Prize in Anatomy, Anatomical Association of Great Britain and Ireland, 1962. *Address:* Department of Anatomy, Boston University School of Medicine, 80 East Concord Street, Boston, MA 02118, USA.

PETERS, David Keith, b. 26 July 1938, Neath, Glamorgan. Professor of Medicine, Royal Postgraduate Medical School, London. m. (1) Jean Mair Garfield, 1961 (diss 1978), 1 son, 1 daughter. (2) Pamela Wilson Ewan, 1979, 1 son, 1 daughter. *Education:* MB ChB (Wales), 1961; MRCP (London), 1964. *Appointments include:* Research Fellow, Experimental Pathology, University of Birmingham/NIMR London, 1965-68; Lecturer, Medicine, Welsh National School of Medicine, 1968-69; Lecturer/Senior Lecturer, Medicine, Royal Postgraduate Medical School, London, 1969-75; Reader in Medicine, ibid, 1975-77. *Memberships:* Renal Association; Medical Research Society; British Society for Immunology; Association of Physicians of Great Britain & Ireland; Association of American Physicians (Hon); Scandinavian Society for Immunology (Hon); International Society of Nephrology. *Publications include:* Co-editor: "Clinical Aspects of Immunology", 4th edition, 1982; "Recent Advances in Renal Medicine", 2nd edition, 1983. Publications, various journals, immunology of renal disease. *Hobbies:* Music; Tennis; Chess. *Address:* 3 St Ann's Villas, London W11 4RU, England.

PETERS, Harold Olu, b. 19 Sep. 1942, Aba, Nigeria. Director and Physician, Family Clinic. m. Catherine Doherty, 10 Dec. 1970, Dublin, Eire, 2 sons, 1 daughter. *Education:* BA, 1968, MA, 1970, Dublin, Eire; MB BCh, BAO Trinity College, Dublin, 1970; Barrister at Law, called to English Bar, Middle Temple, London, England, 1965. *Appointments:* Physician, Kelvington Union Hospital, Saskatchewan, Canada, 1974-78; Physician, Chief of Staff, Preeveville Union Hospital, Saskatchewan, 1978-83; currently, Director and Physician, Family Clinic, Portage la Prairie, Manitoba. *Memberships:* Medical Defence Union, England. *Hobbies:* Woodworking; Astronomy; Reading; Jogging; Outdoor camping. *Address:* 864 Holly Avenue, Fort Garry, Winnipeg, Manitoba, Canada R3T 1W4.

PETERS, Margaret Helen, b. 5 Nov. 1936, Australia. Deputy Director of Nursing. *Education:* Registered General Nurse; Registered Midwife; Infant Welfare Nurse; Diploma Nursing Administration. *Appointments:* Staff Nurse, Charge Nurse, West Gippsland Hospital, Victoria, Australia, 1958-61; Agency Nurse, London, England, 1961-62; Staff Nurse, Bush Nursing Hospital, Mirboo North, Victoria, Australia, 1963; Staff Nurse, Charge Nurse, Night Supervisor Midwifery, Supervisory Nurse Administrator, Assistant Director of Nursing, Deputy Director of Nursing 1978, The Royal Women's Hospital, Melbourne, Victoria, 1964-. *Memberships:* Inaugural President 1978-83, National Widwives' Association, Australia; President 1981-84, International Confederation of Midwives; Deputy Director Board of Management, International Confederation of Midwives, 1984-; Maternal Health Committee, National Health, Medical and Research Council, Australia, 1985-, Midwives Association of Victoria; Victorian Branch, Royal Australian Nursing Federation; College of Nursing Australia; Perinatal Society of Australia; Sterilization and Disinfection Society-Victoria. *Honour:* Medal of the Order of Australia, 1985. *Hobbies:* Opera; Gardening. *Address:* c/o The Royal Women's Hospital, 132 Grattan Street, Carlton, Victoria 3053, Australia.

PETERS, Timothy John, b. 10 May 1939, Manchester, England. Head, Division Clinical Cell Biology; Consultant Physician. m. Judith Mary Bacon, 25 Sep. 1965, 1 son, 2 daughters. *Education:* BSc, MB, ChB (Hons), MSc, University of St Andrews, Scotland; PhD, University of London, England. *Appointments:* MRC Research Student, University of St Andrews, Scotland, 1966-67; MRC Clinical Research Fellow, Royal Postgraduate Medical School, University of London, England, 1967-70; MRC Travelling Fellow, The Rockefeller University, New York City, USA, 1970-72; Successively Lecturer, Senior Lecturer, Reader, Department of Medicine, Royal Postgraduate Medical School, University of London, England, 1972-79. *Memberships:* Association of Physicians; Biochemical Society; Medical Research Society; European Society for Clinical Investigation. *Publications:* Author of over 500 scientific medical publications in Clinical Science, Gastroenterology, biochemistry and cell biology. *Honours:* Visiting Professor of Biochemistry, Chelsea and Kings Colleges, University of London, 1980-; Mack Forster Award European Society of Clinical Investigation; Visiting Professor of Biochemistry, School of Pharmacy, University of London, 1984-; Visiting Professor of Biochemistry University of West London, Brunel, 1986-. *Hobby:* Member, Society of Recorder Players. *Address:* Division of Clinical Cell Biology, MRC Clinical Research Centre, Watford Road, Harrow, Middlesex HA1 3UJ, England.

PETERS, Wallace, b. 1 Apr. 1924, London, England. Professor of Medical Protozoology. m. Ruth Scheidegger-Frehner, 18 Sep. 1954, Geneva, Switzerland. *Education:* MD, London; FRCP, England; DTM&H, London. *Appointments:* Intern, Tilbury Seaman's Hospital, 1947-48; Medical Officer, RAMC, 1948-50; Physician, Colonial Development Corp, Tanganyika, Africa, 1950-53; Malariologist-Entomologist, WHO, Liberia, Nepal, 1953-55; Assistant Director, Malaria, Papua New Guinea, 1956-61; Research Associate, CIBA, Basle, Switzerland, 1961-66; Professor of Parasitology, 1966-79, Dean School of Tropical Medicine, 1977-79, Liverpool, England; Professor of Medical Protozoology, London School of Hygiene and Tropical Medicine, 1979-. *Memberships:* Vice President, Royal Society Tropical Medicine Hygiene; Royal Ent Society London; BMA; Ex-President, British Society Parasitology; Ex-President, British Section Society Protozoology. *Publications:* "Chemotherapy and Drug Resistance in Malaria", 1970; "Rodent Malaria", (Co-editor, Killick-Kendrick, Co-author); 1978; "Antimalarials", 2 volumes, (Senior editor, Co-author), 1984; "Atlas of Tropical Medicine and Parasitology", (with H M Gilles), 1977, 1981; Author of numerous chapters, articles on medical parasitology, entomology and chemotherapy. *Honours:* King Faisal International Prize in Medicine, Malaria, 1983. *Hobbies:* Entomology; Photography. *Address:* London School of Hygiene and Tropical Medicine, Keppel Street, London WC1E 7HT, England.

PETERSEN, Paul Christian, b. 3 July 1948, New York City USA. Assistant Professor, Elizabethtown College; Professional Privileges, US Naval Hospital, Philadelphia. m. Carol Jean Evans, 5 Aug. 1972, Wantagh, New York, 2 sons. *Education:* BS, Syracuse University; MA, Occupational Therapy, New York University; PhD, Psychology, University of Nebraska. *Appointments:* Director, Occupational Therapy, Boston Naval Hospital, 1972-74; Supervisor, Neuropsychiatric Occupational Therapy, Naval Regional Medical Centre, 1974-76; Fellowship, Meyer Children's Rehabilitation Institute, University of Nebraska Medical Centre, 1976-79; Consultant, Beatrice State Developmental Centre, 1979-81; Instructor, University of Nebraska, Omaha, 1980-81; Consultant Psychologist, RFDF Inc, Madison, Wisconsin, 1981-82; Assistant Professor, University of Wisconsin, 1981-84. *Memberships:* Fellow, American Academy of Cerebral Palsy and Developmental Medicine; American Psychological Association; American Congress of Rehabilitation Medicine; American Occupational Therapy Association; Association for the Severely Handicapped; US Naval Institute. *Publications:* Co-Author, Chapter, "Vestibular Processing Dysfunction in Children", 1985; articles in 'Psychosomatic Research'; 'Clinical Paediatrics'; 'American Journal of Occupational Therapy'; etc. *Honours:* Phi Kappa Phi; Psi Chi. *Hobbies:* Photography; Woodwork; Hiking; Children's Sports & Scouting; Keyboard Instruments. *Address:* Elizabethtown College, 368 B Esbenshade Hall, Elizabethtown, PA 17022, USA.

PETERSON, Edward Nohl, b. 13 Feb. 1930, Tulsa, Oklahoma, USA. Associate Dean. m. Karen Thune Sturgeon (divorced), 2 sons. *Education:* Associate in Arts, University of Wisconsin, 1950; BS 1952, MD 1954,

University of Minnesota. *Appointments:* Clinical Instructor 1961-65, Assistant Professor 1965-68, University of Oregon Medical School, Portland, Oregon; Assistant Professor 1968-73, Assistant Dean 1971-80, Associate Professor 1973-, Associate Dean 1980-, University of Pittsburg School of Medicine, Pittsburg, Pennsylvania. *Memberships:* Fellow, American College of Obstetrics and Gynaecology; Society for Gynaecological Investigation; Association of American Medical Colleges; American Medical Association; Pennsylvania Medical Society. *Publications:* 18scientific articles in various medical journals, on maternal and foetal physiology and related topics; 5 book chapters and accounts of proceedings. *Honours:* Special Research Fellow, National Institutes of Health, 1966-68; Fellow in Academic Administration, American Council in Education. *Hobbies:* Golf; Tennis; Swimming; Sailing; Hiking. *Address:* 4610 Sykvonia Avenue, Toledo, OH 43623, USA.

PETERSON-FALZONE, Sally, b. 22 Feb. 1942, Paxton, Illinois, USA. Associate Professor, University of California, San Francisco. m. Nicholas R Falzone, 17 May 1975, Chicago. *Education:* BSc 1964, MA 1965, University of Illinois; PhD, University of Iowa, 1971. *Appointments:* Research Associate, Otolaryngology, University of Illinois, 1965-67; Chief, Speech Pathology, Institute of Physical Medicine & Rehabilitation, Peoria, Illinois, 1970-71; Associate Professor, Department of Otolaryngology, University of Illinois, Chicago, 1971-. *Memberships:* American Speech-Language-Hearing Association; American Association for the Advancement of Science; Sigma Xi; California Speech & Hearing Association; Society for Ear, Nose & Throat Advances in Children; International Association of Logopaedics & Phoniatrics; President, American Cleft Palate Association. *Publications include:* Research papers, professional journals: 'Speech pathology in craniofacial malformation other than cleft lip & palate', 1973; 'Velopharyngeal inadequacy in the absence of overt cleft palate', 1985. *Honours:* Phi Beta Kappa, 1963; Alpha Lambda Delta, 1962; Zeta Phi Eta, 1963; Bronze Tablet, University of Illinois, 1964; Fellow, American Speech-Language-Hearing Association, 1983. *Address:* Centre for Craniofacial Anomalies, 747 Medical Sciences, University of California, San Francisco, CA 94143, USA.

PETERSON, Hans Erik, b. 9 Oct. 1928, Sweden. Director, Health Care Information System. m. Berit, 13 Feb. 1950, 2 sons. *Education:* Certified Physician, 1958; MD, 1966; Fellow, Royal Carolinian Institute, Medical Faculty, Stockholm University, 1968. *Appointments:* Physician, Ophthalmology, 1959-68, Assistant Professor, 1968-71, Karolinska sjukhuset; Director, Health Care Information Systems, Stockholm County, 1971-. *Memberships:* President, International Medical Informatics Association, 1983-; Board Member, Association pour promotion de l'informatique de sante, 1981-; Chairman, Swedish Society for Medical Information Processing, 1976-78. *Publications:* "The Normal B-Poetential in the single-flash Electroretinogram" thesis, 1968; "Communication Networks in Health Care", Editor, 1982; "Human-Computer Communications in Health Care", Editor, 1985; "Datorer i vården Esselte", 1985. *Address:* Hälso-och sjukvåardsnämnden, Box 9099, S-102 72 Stockholm, Sweden.

PETERSON, Michael Robert, b. 10 Feb. 1943, Seattle, Washington, USA. Priest; Doctor. *Education:* MD, University of California, San Francisco, 1968; Ordained, St Matthew's Cathedral, Washington DC, 1978; Intern, University of Washington Hospital; Commissioned Officer, US Public Health Service. *Appointment:* Private Medical Practice; St Bernadine's Rectory, St Luke's Institute, Founder. *Memberships:* Numerous professional organisations. *Honours:* Bank of America Award for Science, 1960; Career Development Award, National Institute of Mental Health, 1971-74; University of California Laughlin Award for Merit, 1974; Langley Porter Neuropsychiatric Institute Award for Creative Achievement,

1974. *Address:* Saint Luke Institute, 2420 Brooks Drive, Suitland, MD 20746, USA.

PETITE, Elizabeth Ann, b. 21 June 1939, Youngstown, Ohio, USA. Laboratory Manager; Haematology. *Education:* BA, Biology, Mercyhurst College, Erie, Pennsylvania, 1961; Medical Technologist Internship, George Washington University School of Medicine, Washington, DC, 1962. *Appointments:* Medical Technologist, Haematology, George Washington University Hospital, Washington, DC, 1962-64; Senior Medical Technologist, Special Haematology, Georgetown University Hospital, Washington, DC, 1964-70; Chief Medical Technologist, Haematology and Urinalysis, 1970-77. *Memberships:* American Society for Medical Technologists; Clinical Labotatory Management Association National and DC Chapter. *Publications:* Technical Consultant for US Medical Services Haematology Procedure Manual, 1975; Technical Consultant and Assistant on special platelet research projects dealing with kidney and cardiac patients, 1966-70, 79; Technical Consultant for Health Care Movie, "No Not Another Lab Test", in script writing and production, 1980; 1st Illustrated Editor, The American Biographical Institute Inc, Raleigh, North Carolina, USA. *Hobbies:* Gourmet Cooking; Fashion Design; Art; Music; Football; Reading. *Address:* 4545 MacArthur Boulevard NW, Washington, DC 20007, USA.

PETKOVIC, Dragoljub, b. 3 Sep. 1920, Belgrade, Yugoslavia. Professor of Physiology. m. Radojka Pavlović, 9 May 1952, Belgrade, 2 daughters. *Education:* MD, Faculty of Medicine, University of Belgrade, 1949; Post-graduate Fellow, Western Reserve University, Cleveland, Ohio, USA, 1956-57; PhD Habil, Belgrade, 1961; DMSci, Belgrade, 1977. *Appointments:* Assistant Physiologist, Medical Faculty, Belgrade, 1949-53, Assistant Professor, 1953-61; Visiting Assistant Professor, Skopje, 1958-60; Associate Professor, 1961-69; Visiting Associate Professor, Nis, 1961-64; Visiting Professor, Medical Faculty, University of Khartoum, Sudan, 1969-82; Visiting Professor, Medical Faculty, El Fateh University, Tripoli, Libya, 1983-. *Memberships:* Yugoslav Society of Physiology; Yugoslav Society of Biochemistry. *Publications:* Some 60 research papers on Physiology of Vision, Heart & Circulation, Biochemistry & Toxicology of snake venoms in medical journals. *Hobbies:* Music; Sport; Travel; Philately. *Address:* M Tita 19, 11 000 Belgrad, Yugoslavia.

PETRUCELLI, Elaine Wodzin, b. 30 Sep. 1942, Chicago, Illinois, USA. Executive Director, American Association for Automotive Medicine. m. Robert Charles, 3 July 1965, Chicago, Illinois. *Education:* PhD, Northwestern University, Chicago; Research Assistant, University of Illinois School of Public Health, Chicago. *Appointments:* American Medical Association; Administrative Assistant for Program Development in Environmental and Occupant Health, 1962-67; Staff Associate, Safety Education, 1967-80; Assistant Director, Safety Education, 1980-81; Founder of New York Safety Belt Coalition which was instrumental in enactment of first safety belt use law in USA. *Memberships:* American Association for Automotive Medicine, Life Member; International Association for Accident and Traffic Medicine; Transportation Research Board; American Public Health Association; Highway Users Federation for Safety and Mobility; National Child Passenger Safety Association; Illinois Child Passenger Safety Association, Founding Member. *Publications:* Articles: The Abbreviated Injury Scale: Evolution, Usage and Future Adaptability, 1981; Medical Consequences of Motorcycle Helmet Nonusage, 1984; The USA and Safety Belt Use: A Prognosis for the Remainder of the 80's, 1984 and several other papers and articles in professional journals, etc. *Honours:* International Association for Accident and Traffic Medicine Award for Outstanding Achievement in field of traffic medicine, 1983; Award for Public Service, US Department of Transportation, 1984. *Hobby:* Bicycling. *Address:* 40 2nd Avenue, Arlington Heights, IL 60005, USA.

PETTIGREW, Clinton Gary, b. 4 Oct. 1946, Baton Rouge, Louisiana, USA. Mental Health Director, Hunt Correctional Center, St Gabriel, Louisiana. *Education:* BA, 1968; MA, 1974; PhD, 1977; Louisiana State University; Internship, Southwest Medical School, Dallas, Texas, 1977. *Appointments:* Staff Psychologist: East Louisiana State Hospital, Jackson; Margaret Duman Mental Health Center, Baton Rouge; Mental Health Director: Louisiana Department of Corrections, Baton Rouge; Louisiana State Penitentiary, Angola; Clinical Psychologist (Private Practice), Dawson Psychological Associates, Baton Rouge. *Memberships:* Phi Eta Sigma; Phi Kappa Phi; American Psychological Association; Southeastern Psychological Association; Louisiana Psychological Association; Baton Rouge Area Society of Psychologists, Past President. *Publications:* "Death Anxiety: 'State' or 'Trait'", 1979; "Sexual Expression of Seminarians on Projective Techniques", 1982; "Seasonality and Lunacy of Inate Behavior", 1985. *Honours:* Fellowship, National Institute of Mental Health; American Legion Award, 1964; Outstanding Correctional Leadership Certificate, 1982. *Hobbies:* Reading; Writing; Computer Programming; Cycling. *Address:* 7510 Highland Road, Baton Rouge, LA 70808, USA.

PETZOLDT, Detlef, b. 21 Apr. 1936, Sommerfeld, Germany. Head, Department of Dermatology, Ruprecht-Karls-Universität, Heidelberg, Germany. *Education:* Prof Dr Med. *Appointment:* Head, Department of Dermatology and Venerology, Medical University, Lübeck, Germany. *Memberships:* Hon Member, Polish Dermatological Society; Corresponding Member, Swedish Dermatological Society; Member, Executive Committee, IUVDT; Chairman, Deutsche Gesellschaft zur Bekämpfung der Geschlechtskrankheiten. *Address:* Department of Dermatology, Voss strasse 2, D-6900 Heidelberg, Federal Republic of Germany.

PFALTZGRAFF, Royal Edward, b. 13 Sep. 1917, York, Pennsylvania, USA. Consultant, American Leprosy Missions. m. Violet Hackman, 10 Apr. 1942, 4 sons, 1 daughter. *Education:* BS, Elizabethtown College, Pennsylvania; MD, Temple University Medical School; Surgical Residency, Episcopal Hospital, Philadelphia, Pennsylvania. *Appointments:* Medical Officer i/c Lassa Hospital, Nigeria; Medical Officer i/c Garkida Leprosarium, Nigeria; Chief of Rehabilitation, US Public Health Service Hospital Carville, Louisiana, USA; Tutor in Leprosy, Ahmadu Bello University, Zaria, Nigeria; Medical Officer i/c State Leprosy Hospital, Gongola State, Nigeria; Chief Consultant, Leprologist, Gongola State, Nigeria; Consultant, Planning and Training, American Leprosy Missions Inc, USA. *Memberships:* American Medical Association; International Leprosy Association; Christian Medical Society; Fellow, Nigerian Medical Council. *Publications:* "Leprosy for Students of Medicine", 1973, "Leprosy" 1979 (both with A Bryceson). *Honour:* Doctor of Science, Ahmadu Bello University, Zaria, Nigeria, 1982. *Hobbies:* Gardening; Photography. *Address:* 76 Florence Place, Elmwood Park, NJ 07407, USA.

PHADKE, Kiran Prabhakar, b. 26 Dec. 1948, Kampala, Uganda. Medical Oncologist, St George & Sutherland Hospitals, Sydney, Australia. m. Linda Sykes, 21 May 1977, Sydney, 1 daughter. *Education:* MB, ChB, Honours, Makerere University, Uganda; FRACP, FRCPA. *Appointments include:* CRC Research Fellow, Department of Oncology, Manchester University, UK, 1980; Consultant Physician, Sydney Hospital, Australia, 1981-82. *Memberships:* Haematology Society of Australia; Clinical Oncology Society of Australia. *Publications:* Co-author, numerous articles in professional journals, including 'Prostaglandins in induction of labour & therapeutic abortion' (Mak Med J, 1971); 'Platelet dysfunction in the myeloproliferative syndromes' (American Journal of Haematology, 1981); 'Controlled clinical trial of adjuvant chemotherapy in operable cancer of the breast', in "Adjuvant Therapy of Cancer, III", eds. Salmon & Jones, 1981; etc. *Hob-*

bies: Squash; Gardening. *Address:* 2/22 Belgrave Street, Kogarah, Sydney, NSW 2257, Australia.

PHAROAH, Peter Oswald Derrick, b. 19 May 1934, Ranchi, India. University Professor of Community Health. m. Margaret McMinn, 17 May 1960, 3 sons, 1 daughter. *Education:* MD 1972, MSc 1974, University of London, England; FFCM. *Appointments:* District Medical Officer, Papua New Guinea; Senior Lecturer, London School of Hygiene and Tropical Medicine, London, England; Currently Professor of Community Health, University of Liverpool, Liverpool. *Memberships:* British Paediatric Association; Society for Social Medicine. *Publications:* "Endemic Cretinism", 1971; Various articles on the effects of nutritional iodine deficiency. *Hobbies:* Fell walking; Philately. *Address:* 11 Fawley Road, Liverpool L18 9TE, England.

PHILLIPS, Calbert Inglis, b. 20 Mar. 1925, Glasgow, Scotland. Professor of Ophthalmology, University of Edinburgh. m. C Anne Fulton, 29 Dec. 1962, 1 son. *Education:* MB, ChB, MD, University of Aberdeen; PhD, University of Bristol, England; DPH; DO; FRCS Edinburgh and England; FBOA. *Appointments:* Resident Registrar, Moorfields Eye Hospital, London; Senior Registrar, St Thomas' Hospital; Research Assistant, Institute of Ophthalmology; Consultant Surgeon, Bristol Eye Hospital; Consultant Eye Surgeon, St George's Hospital; Professor of Ophthalmology, University of Manchester. *Memberships:* Member of various medical and ophthalmological societies. *Publications:* Author of numerous articles to medical and ophthalmic journals. *Address:* Princess Alexandra Eye Pavilion, Chalmers Street, Edinburgh EH3 9HA, Scotland.

PHILLIPS, Ian, b. 10 Apr. 1936, England. Professor of Medical Microbiology; Civil Consultant in Microbiology, Royal Air Force. *Education:* BA, 1958, MA, 1961, MB BChir, 1961, MD (Cantab) 1966, FRCP 1982, FRCPath 1981, St Johns College, Cambridge University; St Thomas's Hospital Medical School, London. *Appointments:* House Officer, 1961-62, Resident Pathologist, 1962-63, Lecturer Medical Microbiology, 1963-66, Senior Lecturer, 1969-72, Reader, 1972-74, Professor, 1974-, St Thomas's Hospital Medical School, London; Lecturer, Microbiology, Makerere University, Uganda, 1966-69; currently Civil Consultant, Microbiology, Royal Air Force; Visiting Professor, University Complytensis and Hospital Ramion y Cayal, Madrid, 1985-86. *Memberships:* Former Chairman and Journal Editor, British Society for Antimicrobial Chemotherapy; Hospital Infection Society; Pathological Society; Former Council Member, Pathology Section, Royal Society of Medicine; Former Council Member, Royal College of Pathologists; Senior Examiner in Microbiology, Royal College of Pathologists 1985-. *Publications:* Co-Editor: "Laboratory Methods in Antimicrobial Chemotherapy", 1978; "Microbial Disease", 1979. Author of numerous papers in professional journals. *Honours:* Corresponding Fellow, Infectious Diseases Society of America, USA. *Hobbies:* Botany; Classical music. *Address:* Department of Microbiology, St Thomas' Hospital, London SE1 7EH, England.

PHILLIPS, Peter Alexander, b. 30 June 1934, Perth, Western Australia. Virologist. m. Kerry Ann Stokes, 17 May 1980, Perth, 2 sons, 1 daughter. *Education:* BSc, 1967, PhD, 1971, University of Western Australia; Research Training Fellowship, IARC, 1971. *Appointments:* Technologist in Virology, State Health Laboratory Services of Western Australia, 1970-71; IARC Research Training Fellow, Houghton Poutry Research Station, Hungtindon, England, 1971-72; Microbiologist in virology laboratory, 1972-82, Virologist, 1985-, State Health Laboratory Services of Western Australia; Virologist, Papua New Guinea Institute of Medical Research, Goroka, Papua New Guinea, 1983-85. *Memberships:* Australian Society for Microbiology. *Publications:* 'Chronic obstructive jaundice', 1969;

'Hydrocephalus', 1970; 'Granuloma inguinale', 1980; 'Adenovirus genital infection', 1984; 'Influenza in Papua New Guinea', 1984, 1985; Contributor to professional journals. *Honours:* Convocation Prize, 1964, Lady James Prize in Natural Science, 1965, University of Western Australia; Laboratory Consultant visiting Papua New Guinea with South Pacific Commission and Institute of Medical Research, 1978, 1981. *Hobbies:* Identification, cultivation and protection of Western Australian flora; Natural history; Cycling; Squash; Bushwalking. *Address:* Virology Laboratory, State Health Laboratory Services, Queen Elizabeth II Medical Centre, PO Box F312, GPO Perth 6001, Western Australia.

PHILPOTT, Richard Lee, b. 22 July 1937, Chicago, Illinois, USA. Physician (Obstetrician and Gynaecologist). m. Anita Claire Wehmer, 3 Aug. 1963, Wilmette, Illinois, 2 sons, 2 daughters. *Education:* BSc, Loyola University, Chicago, 1959; MD, Stritch School of Medicine, Loyola University, 1963; Internship, 1963-64, Residency Obstetrics and Gynaecology, 1964-67, St. Francis Hospital, Evanston, Illinois. *Appointments:* Chief OB Service, David Grant USAF Hospital, Travis AFB, California, 1968-69; Chairman, GYN Department, Alvarado Hospital, San Diego, 1973-74, 1981-82, Vice-Chairman, 1979-80; Vice-Chairman, OB-GYN Department, Grossmont Hospital, La Mesa, 1974-76, 1979-80, Chairman, 1981-83; Teaching Staff, Mercy Hospital, San Diego, 1972-. *Memberships:* Chicago Medical Society, 1963; San Diego Medical Society; California Medical Association; San Diego Gynaecological Society, Secretary-Treasurer, 1975-76, Vice-President, 1976-77, President, 1977-78; American College of OB-GYN; American College of Surgeons; San Diego Surgical Society. *Honour:* Board Certified OB-GYN by American Board of OB-GYN, 1969, Recertification, 1985. *Hobbies:* Gardening; Jogging. *Address:* 6367 Alvarado Court, San Diego, CA 92120, USA.

PICARD-AMI, Luis Alberto, b. 27 Jan. 1927, Colon, Republic of Panama. Chief, Department of Psychiatry, Paitilla Medical Center; Professor, Medical Ethics and History of Medicine, University of Panama; Clinical Professor, Psychiatry, University of Panama. m. M. Patricia, 26 Dec. 1951, Omaha, Nebraska, USA, 1 son, 2 daughters. *Education:* BSc, Biology, Iowa Wesleyan College, Iowa, USA; MD, Creighton University, Nebraska; Fully approved Residency by American Board of Psychiatry, State of Connecticut, 1956-59, based at Fairfield Hospital in affiliation with Yale University. *Appointments include:* Chief, Psychiatric Section, Santo Tomas Hospital, Panama, 1961-70; Chief, Mental Health Division, Ministry of Health, Panama, 1970-71; Chief, In-Patient Service, Social Security Hospital, Panama, 1973-82; Teaching experience includes: Assistant Professor, Psychiatry, University of Panama, 1962-66. *Memberships:* Panamanian Medical Association; Panamanian Psychiatric Association; American Psychiatric Association; World Psychiatric Association; Panamanian Academy of Medicine and Surgery; Panamanian Academy of Psychology. *Publications:* The Bio-Psico-Social Medical Model and Comprehensive Medical Care. Revista Medico-Cientifica, Asociacion de Estudiantes de Medicina, University of Panama, Aug. 1982; Serotonin Content of the Pineal Gland of Man and Monkey, Nature. (Coauthor), 1960; Numerous papers, presentations and contributions to professional publications. *Honour:* Elected Panamanian Academy of Medicine and Surgery (limited to 40 physicians in the country), 1977. *Hobbies:* History; Theatre; Musical Golf. *Address:* Apartado 2144, Balboa, Ancon, Panama, Republic of Panama.

PICK, Robert Yehuda, b. 24 Dec. 1945, Israel. Orthopaedic Surgeon. m. Roni L. Kestenbaum, New York City, USA. 2 sons, 1 daughter. *Education:* BA, BHL, Yeshiva University, 1967; MD, Albert Einstein College of Medicine, 1971; MPH, Harvard School of Public Health, 1979. *Appointments:* L.Cdr, US Public Health Service, 1975-78; Assistant Professor, Touro College, New York, 1976-78; Assistant Chief, Orthopaedic Surgery, USPHS Hospital, Boston, 1977-78; Orthopaedic Consultant, Int. Ladies Garment Workers' Union, 1978-79; Director, Spinal Screening Programme, Health and Hospitals, Boston, 1979-82; Instructor, Orthopaedic Surgery, Boston University School of Medicine, 1980-82; Associate Director, Orthopaedic Surgery, Boston City Hospital, 1980-84; Assistant Professor, Orthopaedic Surgery, Boston University School of Medicine, 1982-; Medical Adviser, Boston Retirement Board, 1983-84; Medical Adviser, US Department of Labour, 1983-; Orthopaedic Consultant, New England Telephone Company, 1985-. *Memberships:* Diplomate, National Board of Medical Examiners, 1972; Diplomate, American Board of Orthopaedic Surgery, 1983; American Academy of Orthopaedic Surgeons; American Association of Anatomists; Boston Orthopaedic Club; Massachusetts Orthopaedic Association; American Physicians Fellowship for Medicine in Israel. *Publications:* 25 contributions to professional journals including: 'Quadricepsplasty' in "Clinical Orthopaedics", 1976; 'Today's Automobile Driver', Editorial in "Journal of Trauma", 1981; The Chapter 'Ankle Arthrodesis' in The Book "Ankle Injuries", 1983, etc. *Honours:* Traineeship, National Institute for Occupational Safety and Health, Harvard University, 1978-79; Member of MENSA. *Address:* 25 Boylston Street, Chestnut Hill, MA 02167, USA.

PICKERING, Donald Everett, b. 12 June 1923, Sacramento, California, USA. Paediatric Medical Consultant, Endocrinology and Metabolism. *Education includes:* BA cum laude, Whitman College, Washington, 1945; MA, 1948, MD, 1949, Intern, Paediatrics, Hospital, 1949-50, Assistant Resident, 1951-52, University of California, Berkeley and San Francisco; Licensed, California, 1949, Oregon, 1956, Washington, 1956, Nevada, 1964, Alaska, 1980. Diplomate, 1954, Fellow, American Board and Academy of Paediatrics. *Appointments include:* Instructor, 1951-53, Assistant Professor, 1953-56, Director, Paediatric Andocrine and Metabolic Laboratory, 1952-56, University of California School of Medicine; Assistant Professor, 1956-58, Professor, 1958-63, Director, Endocrine and Metabolic Laboratories, 1956-63, Research Associate, 1956-63, Acting Chairman, Department of Paediatrics, 1960-61, University of Oregon Medical School; President, Health Facilities Incorporated, 1967-, Director, Microlaboratories, Portland, 1967-, Oregon Regional Private Research Center; Professor, Developmental Biology, 1964-67, Adjunct Professor, Bio-Engineering, 1969-, Professor of Paediatrics, 1977-, Professor, Department of Physiology, 1977-, University of Nevada; Clinical Professor of Medical Sciences, University of Alaska, 1983-. *Memberships include:* Society and Western Society for Paediatric Research; American and North Pacific Paediatric Societies; American Institute of Nutrition; Nevada State, Washoe County, Alaska and Anchorage Medical Societies. *Publications include:* "Fluid and Electrolyte Therapy: A Unified Approach", co-author also Metalyte Calculator used in conjunction with book, 1959; Editor, "Research with Primates", 1963; author of some 64 articles including pamphlets and contributions to professional journals, several book chapters. *Honours include:* Honour societies; Ross Laboratories International Award, 1958; E Mead Johnson International Award, 1961. *Address:* 2841 DeBarr Road, Suite 33, Anchorage, AK 99504, USA.

PICKERING, Trevor George, b. 30 Apr. 1934, Adelaide, South Australia. President, Australian Medical Association; Senior Visiting Surgeon, The Queen Elizabeth Hospital, Adelaide. m. Marilyn Elsie Chartres, 25 May 1957, Adelaide, 1 son, 1 daughter. *Education:* BS BS, University of Adelaide, 1958; FRCS (England), 1964; FRACS, 1965. *Appointments:* RMO, Royal Adelaide Hospital, 1958; RMO, Public Hospital, Ashburton, New Zealand, 1959-60; House Surgeon, Warwick Hospital, England, 1961; Casualty Officer, Royal Buckinghamshire Hospital, Aylesbury, England, 1961-62; Senior House Officer, Cuckfield Hospital, Sussex, England, 1962-63; Surgical Registrar, West Suffolk General Hospital, Bury St Edmunds, England, 1963-64; Senior Surgical Registrar, 1964-66, Honorary Assistant Surgeon, 1966-68, The Queen Elizabeth Hospital, Adelaide; Vascular Surgeon, The Queen Elizabeth Hospital, 1968-72; Consultant Vascular Surgeon, Modbury Hospital, Adelaide, 1973-80; Senior Visiting Surgeon, The Queen Elizabeth Hospital, 1973-; Clinical Lecturer in Surgery, University of Adelaide, 1973-. *Memberships:* Australian Medical Association, President, South Australian Branch, Member, Federal Council, 1978-, Federal Treasurer, 1980-82, Federal Vice-President, 1982-85, Fellow, 1979. *Hobbies:* Music; Art; Golf. *Address:* Hunter House, 42 Walter Street, North Adelaide, South Australia 5006.

PICÓ-ARACIL, Francisco, b. 4 May 1947, Alicante, Spain. Head of Haemodynamic Unit. m. Anne Marie Odermatt, 4 Aug. 1973, Solothurn, 1 son. *Education:* MD; Specialist in Cardiology. *Appointments:* Resident, Cardiovascular Hospital 1971, Military Hospital 1972, Alicante; Resident, Cardiology Department 1973-75, Cardiologist, Department of Internal Medicine 1976, Head, Haemodynamic Unit 1977-, Arrixaca Hospital, Murcia; Training, Cardiology Department 1973, Assistant, Cardiovascular Unit of the Radiological Department 1977, University Hospital, Lausanne, Switzerland; Training, Cardiology Department, Bicetre Paediatric Hospital, Paris, France, 1975. *Memberships:* Spanish Cardiology Society; Fellow, American College of Chest Physicians. *Publications:* 'Introduction to the hemodynamic study of acquired cardiopathies', 1975; 'Bradycardias', 1983; 'Quadrivalvular heart stenosis', 1983; 'Hemodynamic study comparing sequential pacing and ventricular stimulation', 1983; 'Syncope' in "Cardiac Pacing" (editor: G Rouz), 1985. *Hobby:* Music. *Address:* Plaza de la Ensenanza, Edificio Geminis Rojo, E-2, B-2, 30011, Murcia, Spain.

PIERCE, Ralph Wendell, b. 5 November 1944, Waco, Texas, Orthopaedic Surgeon. m. Linda Lee Kenyon, 31 May 1970, Boston, Massachusetts, 2 daughters. *Education:* BA, summa cum laude, 1966, MD, cum laude, 1970, Harvard University. *Appointments:* Instructor in Orthopaedics, Massachusetts General Hospital, 1976; Major, US Army, Leonard Wood Army Hospital, 1976-78; Orthopaedic Surgeon, Harvard University, 1978-; Chief of Orthopaedics, Winchester Hospital, Massachusetts; Orthopaedic Consultant to New England Rehabilitation Hospital. *Memberships:* American Academy of Orthopaedic Surgeons; Arthoscopy Association of North America; American Orthopaedic Society for Sports Medicine. *Publications:* Author of numerous publications. *Honours:* Detur Award, 1963, Summa Cum Laude, 1966, Harvard University; Cum Laude, Harvard Medical School, 1970. *Hobbies:* Japanese Gardens; Multiple sports and outdoor activities. *Address:* Russell Hill, 955 Main Street, Winchester, MA 01890, USA.

PIERCE, Raymond O, b. 17 May 1931, Monroe, Louisiana, USA. Director of Orthopaedic Surgery, Wishard Hospital; Professor of Orthopaedic Surgery, Indiana University. m. Geraldine Brundidge, 18 June 1955, 2 sons, 3 daughters. *Education:* BA, Fisk University, Nashville, Tennessee, 1951; MD, Meharry Medical College, Nashville, Tennessee, 1955; Graduate, VA Hospital, Des Moines, Iowa, University of Iowa, Iowa City, 1958-63. *Appointments:* Private Practice Orthopaedic Surgery, Indianapolis, Indiana, 1963-69; Instructor in Orthopaedic Surgery, 1963-69; Associate in Orthopaedic Surgery, 1967-70; Assistant Professor of Orthopaedic Surgery, 1970-76; Associate Professor of Orthopaedic Surgery, 1976-80; Professor of Orthopaedic Surgery, 1981-. *Memberships include:* American Academy of Orthopaedic Surgery; American Association for the Advancement of Science; American Association for the Surgery of Trauma; Examiner for Certification, American Board of Orthopaedic Surgery; Credentials Committee, 1983-84, American Col-

lege of Surgeons; Charter Member, American Trauma Society; President, 1973-75, Secretary, 1968-70, Hoosier State Medical Association; International College of Surgeons; Orthopaedic Trauma Hospitals Association Incorporated; Pan-Pacific Surgical Society; Sigma Xi; Tri-State Orthopaedic Society. *Publications include:* 'Soft Tissue Chondrosarcoma of the Hand', 1979; 'Aseptic Necrosis of the Hip in Sickle Cell Disease', 1979; 'Bone Changes in Alcoholics', 1979; 'Degenerative Ankle Conditions', 1981; 'A Study of Bone Density in Black Women with Hip Fractures', 1982; 'The Functional Treatment of Fractures of the Proximal End of the Humerus', 1985. *Honours include:* Physicians Recognition Award, AMA, 1977-80, 1981-83; Physicians Recognition Award, NMA, 1981-83; Governors Award, Council of the Sagamore of the Wabash, 1984; Summer Furness Award for Outstanding Community Service, 1977. *Address:* 960 Locke Street, Indianapolis, IN 46202, USA.

PIERIS, Ernest Victor, b. 16 Jan. 1926, Badulla, Sri Lanka. Consultant Physician. m. Philine Theophila Pieris, 31 May 1952, Colombo, 4 daughters. *Education:* MB. BS, MD, University of Ceylon; MRCP, Edinburgh; MRCP London. *Appointments:* House Surgeon: Orthopaedics, General Hospital, Colombo, De Soysa Maternity Hospital, Surgery, General Hospital; House Physician, General Hospital, Colombo; Research Assistant, Professor, Paediatrics, Registrar, Professor, Medicine, University of Ceylon; Physician, General Hospital, Ragama, OPD General Hospital, Colombo, Consultant Physician, General Hospital, Colombo, 1961-72; Private Practice, 1972-. *Memberships:* Sri Lanka Medical Association; Ceylon College of Physicians; Royal College of Physicians, London; Royal College of Physicians, Edinburgh. *Publications:* "Successful Pregnancy in Patient with Eisenmenger's Syndrome", 'Post Graduate Medical Journal', 1964; "Myelomatosis", 'Ceylon Medical Journal', 1966; "Refsum's Syndrome", 'Ceylon Medical Journal', 1968; "Spontaneous Mediastinal emphysema", 'Ceylon Medical Journal', 1972. *Honours:* Fellowships, Royal College of Physicians, Edinburgh, 1972, London, 1975; Fellow, Ceylon College of Physicians, 1979. *Hobbies:* Photography; Writing Short Stories. *Address:* 51/3 Norris Canal Road, Colombo 10 Sri Lanka.

PIERREPOINT, Colin Geoffrey, b. 26 Aug. 1934, Nottingham, England. Senior Lecturer; Deputy Director. m. 30 May 1964, Ilkeston, 2 sons, 1 daughter. *Education:* BVSc, MRCVS, Liverpool University, 1963; PhD, Glasgow University, Scotland, 1967; Fellow, Royal College of Veterinary Surgeons, 1977; DVSc, Liverpool University, England, 1983. *Appointments:* Small Animal House Surgeon, Glasgow University, Scotland, 1963-64; Post-Doctoral Research Assistant, Royal Infirmary, Glasgow, 1967-68; Wellcome Trust Senior Research Fellow, Cardiff, 1968-72; Tenovus Senior Research Fellow, 1972-75; currently, Senior Lecturer, University of Wales College of Medicine and Deputy Director, Tenovus Institute for Cancer Research, University of Wales. *Memberships:* Society for Endocrinology; Society for the Study of Fertility; British Veterinary Association; European Society for Urological Oncology and Endocrinology. *Publications:* Editor of 4 books; Author of over 100 papers in leading scientific journals. *Honours:* Visiting Professor, New York Branch, American Urological Association, 1980; Royal Society European Programme Award Winner, 1967. *Hobbies:* Sports; Good food, especially shell fish; Travelling; Opera. *Address:* Tenovus Institute for Cancer Research, University of Wales College of Medicine, Heath Park, Cardiff, Wales.

PIESSENS, Jan Hendrik, b. 25 July 1941, Ruisbroek, Antwerpen, Belgium. Professor of Cardiology, Catholic University of Leuven. m. Maria-Christina LePoutre, 3 Aug. 1968, Mol, 2 sons, 1 daughter. *Education:* MD, 1965; Fellow, Cardiac Laboratory and Cardiovascular Diseases, Cleveland Clinic, Ohio, USA, 1969-70; Doctor in Cardiology, 1975. *Memberships:*

Belgian Society of Cardiology; Fellow, Society for Cardiac Angiography. *Publications:* Many cardiological papers in different scientific journals. *Address:* Galgebergstraat 45, 3000 Leuven, Belgium.

PIETERSE, Arnoldus Stephanus, b. 22 Aug. 1949, Republic of South Africa, Specialist Pathologist. m. Alison Rowe, 6 Dec. 1975, Pretoria, 2 sons. *Education:* MB, ChB, Pretoria; FRCPA; MRC Path; Diploma, Microbiology; Diploma, Medical Technology. *Appointments:* Medical Technologist, 1966-71; Intern, 1977; Registrar in anatomical pathology, 1978-83; Consultant pathologist. *Memberships:* International Academy of Pathology; Gastroentrological Society of Australasia. *Publications:* 'Myocardial fibre calcification', 1981; 'Collagenous colitis', 1982; 'Fibroma of tendon sheath', 1982; 'Colonic angiodysplasia', 1982; 'Osteoid osteoma transforming to aggressive (low grade malignant) osteoblastoma', 1983; 'Focal rheumatoid-like prostatic granulomas', 1984; 'The mucosal changes and pathogenesis of pneumatosis cystoides intestinalis', 1985. *Hobby:* Stamps. *Address:* 197 Old Mt Barker Road, Aldgate, South Australia 5154.

PIKE, Gary D, b. 15 Mar. 1954, England. Clinic Director. m. Laura Sue Coy, 7 Aug. 1982, South Carolina, USA. *Education:* Doctor of Chiropractic; Board Certification, American National Board, Canadian National Board. *Appointments:* Private Practice, 1977-85, Geonoa, Italy; Medical Consultant, Computerised Dietological Therapy to Medicalc Dea, V Malta, Genoa, Italy, 1984-. *Memberships:* American Chiropractic Association; Council on Roentogenology, American Chiropractic Association. *Publications:* "Effects of Chiropractic on Immunocompetence", 'Journal of American Chiropractic Association', Volume 18, No 3; "The Synovial Jack", Volume 15, 1981, "Journal of American Chiropractic Association", "Trigeminal Neuralgia", volume 21, 1984, 'Journal of the American Chiropractic Association'; "L'Artrosi", 'Naturopatia E Omeopatia", 1983. *Hobbies:* Skiing; Outdoor Sports; Squash; Photography; Computers. *Address:* Vle B Bisagno No 4/6, Genoa, Italy.

PILLAI, Narayana G N, b. 22 Jan. 1951, India, Assistant Professor of Medicine. m. Priya Pillai, 30 Nov. 1975, Mavelikara, India, 2 daughters. *Education:* MB, BS, University of Kerala, 1974; MRCP (UK), 1978; MRCP (I), 1978; Diplomate, American Board of Internal Medicine, 1983. *Appointments:* Chief, Section of Medical Oncology, VA Medical Centre, Amarillo, Texas; Assistant Clinical Professor, Department of Medicine, Texas Technical University Medical School, Amarillo. *Memberships:* Royal College of Physicians, UK; Royal College of Physicians of Ireland; American College of Physicians; American Society of Clinical Oncology; M D Anderson Associates, Houston, Texas. *Publications include:* 'Localized Lymphomas of the Female Genital Organs' ('Blood'), 1982; 'Prognostic Factors for Stage IV Hodgkins's Disease Treated with MOPP, with or without Bleomycin' ('Cancer'), 1985; 'Relapsing Hodgkins's Disease: The Importance of Original Stage & Sites of Extranodal Disease when Treating with MOPP' ('Blood'), 1984. *Honours:* Gold Medal, Internal Medicine, University of Kerala, 1973; Resident of the Year, Texas Tech University Medical School, 1983. *Hobby:* Travel. *Address:* 1901 Medi Park Place, Suite 1050, Amarillo, TX 79106, USA.

PINELLI, Paolo Aurelio, b. 16 Dec. 1921, Italy. Professor, Neurology, Consultant Scientist, Neurological Rehabilitation. m. Maria Luisa Lanzoni, 18 Apr. 1949, Milan. *Education:* Dr, Neuropsychiatry, Rome, 1955; MEd. Candidatus, 1939-45. *Appointments:* Professor, Psychiatry and Neurology, 1965, Professor, Neurology, 1972, Pavia; Professor, Neuropsychiatry, Rome, 1966; Professor, Neurology, Milan, 1981; Consultant Neurologist, Neurological Rehabilitation, Research Centre, University of Paris, 1980-. *Memberships:* Italian Society of Neurology, Scientific Committee; International Society of Electrical Kinesiology; etc. *Publications:* "Advances in EMG", 1962; "Prognosis of C Vascular Diseases", 1965; "Behavioural Neurol-

ogy", 1977; Restorative Neurology", 1980; "Italian Handbook of Neurology", 1985. *Honours:* Honorary Member: Polish Society of Neurology, 1969, Spanish Society of Neurology, 1970, British Society of Neurology, 1985, Czechoslovakian Society of Neurology, 1985. *Hobby:* Classical Music. *Address:* University Studi Milano, Clinical Neurologica la, 8 Via Di Rudini, 20142 Milan, Italy.

PINEYRO, José Ricardo, b. 13 Dec. 1928, Buenos Aires, Argentina. Paediatric Surgeon. m. Marcela Rocca, 3 sons, 1 daughter. *Education:* MD. *Appointments:* Professor of Surgery; President of Fundacion Hospitalaria, Buenos Aires; Director, Head of Surgery Department of Mother & Child Centre, Buenos Aires. *Memberships:* Vice-President, World Federation of Associations of Paediatric Surgeons; Past President, Pan-American Association of Paediatric Surgery, 1982-84. *Publications:* 'Tisular Ph Monitoring in Paediatric Surgery'; 'Treatment of Mediastinal Neuroblastomas'; 'Surgical Treatment of Abdominal non-Hodgkin Lymphomas'; 'Surgical Treatment of Hiatus Hernia in Children'; 'Surgical Treatment of Diaphragmatic Hernia in Children'; and others. *Address:* Crámer 4601, 1429 Buenos Aires, Argentina.

PINO y TORRES, Jose Luis, b. 14 Dec. 1944, Arequipa, Peru. Staff Member, Radiation Medicine Department, Florida Hospital, USA. m. Maria Luisa Gutierrez Rexach, 6 Sep. 1967, Madrid, Spain, 2 sons, 1 daughter. *Education:* Lic med, University of Madrid, Spain, 1967; Internship, Tucson Hospitals, Arizona, USA, 1967-68; Residency, Internal Medicine, University of Minnesota affiliated hospitals, 1968-70; Certificates, American Board of Internal Medicine, 1972, 1973, 1976, American Board of Radiology 1981; Fellowship. Haematology-Oncology, Wisconsin, 1970-72; Assistant, Johns Hopkins University, 1978-80. *Appointments include:* Sterling-Rock Falls Clinic, Illinois, 1972-77; Loyola Stritch School of Medicine, 1975-77; Johns Hopkins University 1977-78; Assistant Professor, Oncology & Radiological Sciences, Johns Hopkins University School of Medicine, 1980-82; Staff Member, Radiation Medicine, Florida Hospital, Orlando, 1982-. *Memberships:* American Medical Association; Florida State Medical Society; American Society of Therapeutic Radiology; American Society of Clinical Oncology. *Publications:* Contributions to 'American Journal of Hematology', 'American Journal of Pathology', 'International Journal of Radiologic Oncology', 'Cancer Treatment Reports', etc. *Address:* 918 Versailles Circle, Maitland, FL 32751, USA.

PINOTTI, Oreste, b. 24 Feb. 1912, Padova, Italy. Head, Human Physiology, University of Turin; Head, A. Mosso Height Altitude Laboratories, Monte Rosa. m. Bianca Zorzan. *Education:* MD, PhD, Physiology. *Appointments:* Professor, Head, Physiology, University of Turin; Director, Postgraduate School of Sports Medicine, University of Turin. *Membership:* Accademia Nazionale dei Lincei. *Hobbies:* Mountaineering, Former Director, Alpine Rescue Corp. *Address:* Universita Di Torino, Istituto Di Fisiologia Umana, C.so Raffaello 30, 10125 Torino, Italy.

PINZUR, Michael, b. 26 June 1949, Chicago, Illinois, USA. Associate Professor. m. Debora Pinzur, 24 June 1978, 2 sons. *Education:* BS, University of Illinois; MD, Rush Medical College; Residency, Orthopaedic Surgery, Northwestern University. *Appointments:* Instructor, Orthopaedic Surgery, Northwestern University, 1979; Assistant Professor, Surgery, University of Health Sciences, Chicago Medical School, 1980; Assistant Professor, Orthopaedics and Rehabilitation, Loyola University Stritch School of Medicine, 1982; Associate Professor, Orthopaedics and Rehabilitation, Loyola University Stritch School of Medicine, 1986. *Memberships:* American Academy of Orthopaedic Surgeons; Orthopaedic Research Society; Association of Veteran's Administration Surgeons; AMA;

Illinois and Chicago Medical Societies; Chicago Orthopaedic Society; American College of Surgeons; etc. *Publications include:* Articles in professional journals including 'Orthopaedics'; 'Journal of Bone and Joint Surgery'; 'Illinois Medical Journal'; 'Iowa Orthopaedic Journal'; 'Orthopaedic Review'; 'Journal of Hand Surgery'; etc.*Honours:* Fellow, American Board of Orthopaedic Surgeons, 1980; Fellow, American Academy of Orthopaedic Surgeons, 1983; Edmond J James Scholar, University of Illinois. *Hobby:* Tennis. *Address:* Dept. of Orthopaedics and Rehabilitation, 216 S First Ave, Maywood, IL 60153, USA.

PISETSKY, Myron Matthew, b. 12 July 1935, Hartford, Connecticut, USA. Director, Group Therapy Programme; Associate Clinical Professor of Psychiatry. m. Rita Baker, 20 Aug. 1960, Connecticut, 1 daughter. *Education:* BS, Trinity College, 1957; MD, Tufts Medical School, Boston, Massachusetts, 1961; Intern, St Francis Hospital, Hartford, Connecticut, 1962; Resident in Psychiatry, Institute of Living, Hartford, 1962-65. *Appointments:* Medical State, 1967-, currently Director of Group Therapy Training Programme, Institute of Living, Hartford; Assistant Chief of Section, Institute of Living, 1967-; currently, Associate Clinical Professor of Psychiatry, University of Connecticut Medical School. *Memberships:* American Medical Association; American Psychiatric Association; American Group Psychotherapy Association; Hartford County Medical Association. *Honour:* Fellow, American Psychiatric Association, 1977. *Hobbies:* Music; Clarinet.*Address:* 173 West Ridge Drive, West Hartford, CT 06117, USA.

PITOT, Henry Clement, b. 12 May 1930, New York, NY, USA. Professor, Oncology, Pathology, University of Wisconsin. m. Julie Sybil Schutten, 29 July 1954, New Orleans, 1 son, 7 daughters. *Education:* BS, Chemistry, Virginia Military Institute, 1951; MD, 1955, PhD, Biochemistry, 1959, Tulane University. *Appointments:* Assistant Professor, 1960-63, Associate Professor, 1963-66, Professor, 1966-, Oncology and Pathology, Chairman, Pathology, 1968-71, Acting Dean, Medical School, 1971-73, Director, McArdle Laboratory for Cancer Research, Medical School, 1973-, University of Wisconsin.*Memberships include:* AAAS, Fellow; American Chemical Society; American Association for Cancer Research, Board of Directors, 1969-72; American Association of Pathologists, Co-President, 1976-77; American Society of Cell Biology; American Society of Biological Chemists; New York Academy of Sciences, Fellow; American Society of Preventive Oncology; etc. *Publications:* Numerous articles in scientific journals including: 'Cancer Research'; 'Journal of Biological Chemistry'; 'Science'; 'Radiation Research'; 'Journal of Nutrition'; etc. *Honours include:* Distinguished Graduate, Virginia Military Institute, 1951; Borden Award for Undergraduate Research, 1955; American Society of Clinical Pathology, Student Prize, Pathology, 1955; Diplomat, American College of Pathology, 1968; Lederle Medical Faculty Award, 1962-65; Career Development Awardee, National Cancer Institute, 1965-68; Parke-Davis Award, 1968; Lucy Wortham James Laboratory Research Award, Society of Surgical Oncology, 1981; Noble Foundation Research Recognition Award, 1983; Esther Langer Award, Cancer Research, University of Chicago, 1984; Honorary Membership, Japanese Cancer Association, 1985. *Hobbies:* Bicycling; Fishing; Philately. *Address:* 1812 Van Hise Avenue, Madison, WI 53705, USA.

PLASCHKES, Jack, b. 13 Apr. 1932, Czechoslovakia, Oberarzt, Department Paediatric Surgery, University Childrens Hospital, Berne, Switzerland. *Education:* MD, Berne University, 1958; FRCS, England, 1978; Higher Specialist Certificate in Paediatric Surgery, Royal College of Surgeons, 1979; Certificate in Paediatric Surgery, Swiss Medical Specialist Board, 1977; Specialist Certificate in Paediatrics, 1965, and General Surgery, 1970, Israel Medical Association. *Appointments:* Houseman and Registrar, Paediatrics, Hadas-sah University Hospital, Israel, 1958-63; Houseman, Paediatric Surgery, Alder Hey Children's Hospital, Liverpool, England, 1964-65; Assistant, 1965-67, Oberarzt, 1972-74, Paediatric Surgery, University Children's Hospital, Zürich, Switzerland; Senior Registrar, General Surgery, Hadassah University Hospital, Israel, 1967-70; Registrar, 1971-72, Senior Registrar, 1974-76, Hospital for Sick Children, London, England; Associate Paediatric Surgeon, Emma Children's Hospital, Amsterdam, The Netherlands, 1977-78; Consultant Paediatric Surgery, Medical Centre, University of Nottingham, England, 1979-80.*Memberships:* British Association of Paediatric Surgeons; Swiss Association of Paediatric Surgeons; International Society of Paediatric Oncology; British Association of Surgical Oncology; European Association of Surgical Oncology; Member, Chairman, Scientific Committee, International Society of Paediatric Oncology; Member, Surgical Principal Co-Investigator, Paediatric Oncology Group, USA; Member, Surgical Co-ordinator, Swiss Paediatric Oncology Group.*Publications:* 'Surgical Oncology in Children', 1986; 'Surgical Strategies in the diverse management of atypical liver tumors', 1984; 'Limb saving operations for malignant tumours of the shoulder', 1982; 'Congenital Fibromatosis', 1974. *Address:* Department of Paediatric Surgery, University Children's Hospital, Freiburgstrasse, CH-3010 Berne, Switzerland.

PLASSCHAERT, Alphons Johannes Marie, b. 3 Jan. 1942, Helmond, Netherlands. Professor of Cariology & Endodontology. m. Pauline Louise van Lommel, 4 June 1966, Laren, Netherlands, 1 son, 3 daughters. *Education:* DDS, 1966, University of Utrecht; PhD, 1972, University of Mijmegen.*Appointments:* Private Practice (part-time) in Dentistry, 1967-70; Instructor, Research Prosthetic Dentistry, 1966-69; Chief of Clinic, Department of Preventive & Community Dentistry, 1969-75; Curriculum Coordinator, 1973-75; Coordinator, Health Education Project, 1970-75; Chairman, Professor, Department of Cariology & Endodontology, University of Nijmegen, 1976-; Assistant Editor, 'Caries Research', 1983-. *Memberships:* President, Health Education Project - Nijmegen, Foundation; European Organisation for Caries Research (Board Member); Foundation of the Dutch Dental Journal (Board Member); Member, Editorial Board, International Endodontic Journal; International Association for Dental Research; Fédération Dentaire Internationale; Academy of Operative Dentistry; American Association for Endodontics. *Publications:* Various articles and books in field. *Honour:* Fulbright Award, 1985. *Hobbies:* Violinist, Concertmaster, Nijmegen Chamber Orchestra; Leader, Animato String Quartet. *Address:* Witsenburgselaan 56, 6524 TL Nijmegen, Netherlands.

PLATT, Henry, b. 6 Aug. 1916, Boston, Massachusetts, USA. Chief Clinical Psychologist; Director of Clinical Training and Research, Devereux Foundation, Devon, Pennsylvania; Attending Psychologist, Philadelphia Psychiatric Center; Clinical Associate Professor, Hahnemann University; Private Clinical Practice of Psychology. m. Carolyn Louise Lindner, 5 June 1949, Boston, 2 sons. *Education:* BS, Boston University, 1937; MEd, Boston University Graduate School of Education, 1938; MA, Columbia University, 1950; PhD, Yeshiva University Graduate School of Education, New York, 1952. *Appointments:* Director, Westinghouse Junior Hall of Science, New York World's Fair, 1939-40; Director, American Institute Gifted Childrens Research Laboratory, AM Institute, New York, 1940-42; Psychologist, Classifications and Selection Office, US Maritime Service, 1943-46; Clinical Psychologist, US Veterans Administration Hospital, New York, 1947-50; Chief Psychologist, Children and Family Service, Boston, 1950-55; Research Consultant, American Public Health Association, Prof Exam Serv New York, 1960-63. *Memberships:* Fellow: American Psychological Association; American Orthopsychiatric Association; American Association on Mental Deficiency; American Rehabilitation Counseling Association; Pennsylvania Psychological Association; Royal Society of Health. *Publications include:* "Inventory of Family Life and Attitudes", Devereux Foundation, 1968; "A Multidisciplinary Training Program for Houseparents", Devereux Foundation, 1969; "The AIRS-Applicant Interview Rating Scale", Devereux Foundation, 1970. *Honour:* American Psychological Association, Division of Counseling Psychology, Distinguished Senior Contributor to Counseling Psychology, August 1985. *Hobby:* Photography. *Address:* 05 Eisenhower Drive, Malvern, PA 19355, USA.

PLAWECKI, Henry Martin, b. 7 Feb. 1941, East Chicago, Indiana, USA. Associate Professor of Nursing. m. Judith Ann Curosh, 10 June 1967, Whiting, Indiana, 2 sons. *Education:* BS Biology, Illinois Benedictine College; BSN Nursing, Creighton University; MA Education, EdS, PhD Educational Administration, University of Iowa; MSN Community Health Nursing, Lewis University. *Appointments:* Primary Nurse, Veterans Administration Medical Center, Minneapolis, Minnesota; Assistant Professor, Project Director, Gustavus Adolphus College, Saint Paul, Minnesota; Clinical Associate Professor, Acting Director of Graduate Studies, University of North Dakota, Grand Forks, North Dakota; Associate Professor of Nursing, Purdue University - Calumet, Hammond, Indiana. *Memberships:* Phi Delta Kappa; Sigma Theta Tau; Sigma Phi Omega; New York Academy of Sciences; Midwest Nursing Research Society; American Holistic Nurses Association; American Assembly for Men in Nursing; American Association of Nephrology Nurses and Technicians; Association of Rehabilitation Nurses. *Publications:* "Normal Aging: Dimensions of Wellness" (co-editor and contributor), scheduled for publications 1986; various articles and book reviews on nursing topics. *Hobbies:* Gardening; Fishing. *Address:* Purdue University - Calumet, Department of Nursing, 2233-171st Street, Hammond, IN 46323, USA.

PLESNICAR, Stojan, b. 5 Feb. 1925, Gorica, Yugoslavia. Professor, Oncology; Director, Institute of Oncology. m. Ljudmila Gec, 15 Sep. 1957, Sezana, 2 sons. *Education:* Faculty of Medicine, Ljubljana; Specialisation, Radiotherapy, Oncology, Ljubljana; Research Fellow, Royal Marsden Hospital, London, England; Postgraduate Study, Radiumhemmet, Karolinska Sjukhuset, Stockholm, Sweden. *Appointments:* Internship, General Hospital, Koper, Yugoslavia; Specialist, Radiotherapy, Oncology, Ljubljana, Yugoslavia; Head, Radiotherapy, Senior Investigator, Clinical Cancer Immunology, Institute of Oncology; Director, Institute of Oncology. *Memberships:* British Society for Immunology; American Association for Research on Cancer; European Society of Medical Oncology; New York Academy of Sciences. *Publications:* "Textbook of Radiotherapy and Oncology", in Slovenian, 1977; "Treatment of Skin Metastases with BCG and Irradiation", 'Cancer', 1982; "Metastasi in "Manuale di Oncologia'", 1982; etc. *Honours:* Editor in Chief, 'Radiologia Yugoslavica'; Visiting Professor, Eppley Cancer Institute, University of Nebraska, USA, 1979-80. *Hobby:* History of Medicine. *Address:* Institute of Oncology, Vrazov trg 4, 61000 Ljubljana, Yugoslavia.

PLOTZ, Charles M, b. 6 Dec. 1921, New York City, USA. Professor of Medicine. *Education:* BA, Columbia College, 1941; MD, Long Island College of Medicine, 1944; Med Sc D, Columbia University College of Physicians & Surgeons, 1951. *Appointments include:* Consultant: Rheumatology, Veterans Administration Hospital, Brooklyn, 1970-; Medicine, Long Island College Hospital, 1985-; Family Practice, Jamaica Hospital, 1978-; Family Practice, Lutheran Medical Centre, 1973-; Medicine, Peninsula General Hospital, 1970-; Internal Medicine, Avecenna Hospital & Waxir Akbar Hospital, Kabul, Afghanistan, 1965. Fellow, World Health Organization, Ben-Gurion University, Israel, 1974; Fulbright Visiting Professor & Lecturer, University of Paris, 1984. Current: Professor of Medicine, State University of New York, Downstate Medical Centre; Director, Continuing Education/Chairman, Department of Family Practice, ibid. *Memberships include:* Fellow, American College of Physicians; Offices in: American Medical Association, Medical Society of State of New York, Medical Society of County of Kings, New York State Society of Internal Medicine, New York Academy of Medicine (Fellow), Associated Medical School of New York, etc. *Honours include:* Distinguished Service awards, Arthritis Foundation, 1971, 1974, 1982; Honorary memberships, medical societies in Yugoslavia, Mexico, Brazil, France. *Hobbies:* Trustee, Brooklyn Institute of Arts & Sciences, 1974-80, Trustee Governor, Brooklyn Botanic Garden, 1974-; Active member, Mystery Writers of America, 1974-85; Member, Advisory Board, Police Athletic League, Brooklyn, 1985. *Address:* 184 Columbia Heights, Brooklyn, NY 11201, USA.

PLUECKHAHN, Vernon Douglas, b. 25 Mar. 1921, Riverton, South Australia. Director, Pathology, Geelong Hospital. m. Ann Norma Roark, 7 Dec. 1953, Melbourne, 2 sons, 2 daughters. *Education:* MBBS, 1949; FRCPA, 1956; MD, University of Adelaide, 1961; FRACP; FRC Path; FAACB; FAMA; FACP; MJAC. *Appointments:* Assistant Pathologist, Royal Melbourne Hospital, 1953-54; Tutor, Pathology, Trinity College, Melbourne, 1952-63; Senior Lecturer, Dental Pathology, University of Melbourne, 1952-74; Senior Lecturer, Forensic Medicine, 1975-86, Senior Associate, Pathology, 1980-86, University of Melbourne; Senior Associate, Pathology & Immunology, 1975-83, Associate Professor, 1983-86, Monash University; Director of Medical Services, 1970-72, Director & Chairman, Pathology, 1954-86, Geelong Hospital. *Memberships:* Australian Medical Association, President, Victorian Branch, 1968; Royal College of Pathologists of Australasia, Vice President 1973-77, President, 1977-79; British Academy of Forensic Sciences; International Academy of Pathology; Royal Society of Medicine; Australian Academy of Forensic Sciences; British Medical Association; etc. *Publications:* "Lectures on Forensic Medicine & Pathology", 5 editions 1977-83; "Ethics Legal Medicine & Forensic Pathology", 1983; Two Chapters: "Recent Advances in Forensic Medicine", 1969; more tha, 100 original papers in Australian & World Medical Scientific Journals. *Honours:* OBE 1979; ED, 1962. *Hobbies:* Tennis; Skiing. *Address:* 15 Culzean Crescent, Highton, Victoria, Australia 3216.

PODLESKI, Wojciech Konstanty, b. 10 Dec. 1941, Chorzow, Poland. President, Clinical Immunopharmacology, Allergy and Asthma. m. Winnifred Moll, 7 July 1982, Denver, Colorado, USA, 1 daughter. *Education:* MD, Medical School, Wroclaw, Poland, 1965; Fellowship, World Health Organisation, International Center for Immunoglubuins, Switzerland, 1970; Summer School in Immunology, British Society for Immunology, Edinburgh, Scotland, 1971; PhD, University of Lausanne, Switzerland, 1972. *Appointments:* Full Staff Member, Internal Medicine Clinic, Wroclaw, Poland; Clinical Research Assistant, Medical Clinic, University of Lausanne, Switzerland; Research Assistant Professor, Center for Immunology, Medical School, State University of New York, USA; Assistant Professor, Medicine, Medical School, University of Colorado; Head, Department of Immunology Assessment Laboratory, National Jewish Hospital and Research Center, Denver; currently, President, Clinical Immunopharmacology, Allergy and Asthma, Denver. *Memberships:* Fellow: American Academy of Allergy and Immunology; American College of Allergists; American Association for Clinical Immunology and Allergy. *Publications:* Contributor to: "Allergy Problems", 1981; 'Clinical Experimental Immunology'; 'Nature'; 'American Journal of Medicine'; 'Annals of Allergy'; 'New England Journal of Medicine'; 'Allergy'. *Honour:* Buffalo Collegium of Immunology. *Hobbies:* Undersea exploration; Hiking; Skiing. *Address:* The Podleski Foundation, 11750 West Colfax Avenue, Denver, CO 80215, USA.

PODURI, Kanakadurga Rao, b. 21 Jan. 1944, Attili, India. Attending Physician. m. S R S Rao Poduri, 22 Aug. 1970, Hyderabad, India, 1 son 1 daughter. *Education:* Pre University, 1961; Pre Medical Degree, 1964; MBBS, 1970; MD, 1984; Diplomate, American Board of Physical Medicine and Rehabilitation, 1985. *Appointments:* Internship in Medicine, St Mary's Hospital, New York, USA, 1972-73; Residency in Physical Medicine and Rehabilitation 1976-78, Attending Physician in Physical Medicine, Strong Memorial Hospital, Rochester; Fellowship in Geriatric Rehabilitation, Monroe Community Hospital, 1979-80; Clinical Instructor in Physical Medicine and Rehabilitation, University of Rochester Medical Center, 1981-. *Memberships:* American Academy of Physical Medicine and Rehabilitation; Medical Women's Association of Rochester; American Medical Association. *Publication:* 'Medical Management of Spinal Cord Injured Patients', booklet, (with C J Gibson), 1984. *Honours:* Physicians Recognition Awards, American Medical Association, 1980 and 1983. *Hobbies:* Tennis; Reading; Stamp Collecting. *Address:* 66 Irving Road, Rochester, NY 14618, USA.

POGSON, Christopher Ian, b. 28 June 1942, Bury, Lancashire, England. Head, Biochemistry Department. m. Elizabeth Helen Schofield, 18 July 1964, Oxshott, Surrey, England, 1 son, 1 daughter. *Education:* BA, 1963, PhD, 1967, University of Cambridge. *Appointments:* Assistant Lecturer in Biochemistry, 1966-68, Research Associate in Biochemistry 1968-72, University of Bristol; Lecturer in Biochemistry, University of Kent, Canterbury, Kent, 1972-79; Professor of Biochemistry, 1979-84, Head of Department, 1981-84, University of Manchester; Head, Biochemistry Department, Wellcome Research Laboratories, Beckenham, Kent, 1984-. *Memberships:* Member, Editorial Board, 'Biochemical Journal', 1975-79, Deputy Chairman, 1979-82, Chairman, 1982-, Biochemical Society. *Publications:* Contributor of 110 papers in various journals. *Hobby:* Wild flower photography. *Address:* Biochemistry Department, Wellcome Research Laboratories, Langley Court, Beckenham, Kent BR3 3BS, England.

POHLIT, Wolfgang, b. 26 Jan. 1928, Grünberg, Federal Republic of Germany. University Professor. *Education:* Diploma, Physics; Doctor, Biophysics and Physiology; Professor, Biophysics and medical physics. *Appointments:* Scientist, Max Planck Institute for Biophysics. *Memberships:* German Radiation Protection Board; German Board for Civil Defence. *Publications:* "Biophysik Vol I, II"; "Lehrbuch Biophysik". *Address:* Paul Ehrlich Strasse 20, D6000 Frankfurt am Main, Federal Republic of Germany.

POLAN, Simon, b. 24 Dec. 1912, Philadelphia, Pennsylvania, USA. Senior Consultant, Philadelphia Psychiatric Centre. m. Gertrude Muroff, 24 Nov. 1949, 1 son, 1 daughter. *Education:* BS, Temple University College of Liberal Arts, 1933; MD, Temple University School of Medicine, 1937. *Appointments:* Senior Physician, VA Hospital Coatsville; Chief, Neuropsychiatric Service, VA Hospital, Oteen; Senior Attending, Albert Einstein Medical Centre, Philadelphia; Major, MC, AUS, World War II; Past President, Philadelphia Psychiatric Centre. *Memberships:* American Medical Association; Pennsylvania Medical Society; Philadelphia County Medical Society; American Psychiatric Association; Pennsylvania Psychiatric Society; Philadelphia Psychiatric Society; American Psychoanalystic Association; Philadelphia Association for Psychoanalysis; International Psychoanalytic Association. *Publications:* "Group Psychotherapy of Schizophrenics in an Outpatient Clinic", 'American Journal Orthopsychiatry', co-author, 1950; "Cutis Verticis Gyrata", 'American Journal of Mental Deficiency', co-author, 1953; "Mental Disorders with Organic Diseases of the Brain", Chapter, 'Psychoanalytic Psychiatry for Lawyers", 1982. *Honours:* Diplomate, American Board of Psychiatry and Neurology, 1946; Certified, Psychoan-

alysis, American Psychoanalytic Association, 1977; Fellow, American Psychiatric Association, 1947; Fellow, College of Physicians of Philadelphia, 1985. *Address:* 286 N Highland Ave, Merion, PA 19066, USA.

POLLEY, Theodore Zane, b. 22 Feb. 1915, Joliet, Illinois, USA. Cardiologist. m. Catherine Cordogan, 18 June 1942, Aurora, Illinois, 2 sons, 1 daughter. *Education:* BS, 1937; MB, 1940; MD, University of Illinois College of Medicine, 1941; Diplomate, American Board of Internal Medicine. *Appointments:* Teaching Fellow, Marquette University School of Medicine, 1941-44; Instructor, St Joseph and Silver Cross Hospitals Schools of Nursing, 1946-52; Clinical Assistant and Instructor 1946-52, Clinical Assistant Professor 1952-60, Clinical Associate Professor of Medicine 1960-84, University of Illinois College of Medicine; Director of Medical Education, Silver Cross Hospital, 1968-83; Clinical Associate Professor of Medicine, Abraham Lincoln School of Medicine. *Memberships include:* Fellow, American College of Physicians; Fellow, American College of Chest Physicians; Fellow, American College of Cardiology, American Heart Association; Secretary 1957, President 1958, Illinois Heart Association; Honorary Fellow, Royal Society of Medicine, England; Illinois State Medical Society; American Medical Association. *Publications:* 12 articles including: 'Cardiac Involvement in Trichinosis' (co-author), 1944; 'The Role of the Liver in Renal Sulfonamide Complications', 1947; 'Clinical Use of Nitrogen Mustard', 1951; 'The Nature and Development of Focal Glomerulonephritis' (with J F Kuzma), 1953; 'Management of Acute Myocardial Infarction', 1960; 'Plasmodium Malariae Imported From Vietnam' (with D Willerson), 1972; 'Lutemacher's Syndrome', under review. *Honours:* Physicians Recognition Award, American Medical Association, 1983; T Z Polley Educational Conference Room in honour of Dr T Z Polley, 1983. *Hobbies:* Photography; Gardening; Coin, gun and old watch collecting; Old books on Abraham Lincoln; The Civil War and Carl Sandburg. *Address:* 1301 Copperfield Court, Suite 103, Joliet, IL 60432, USA.

POLLIACK, Mendel Rafael, b. 7 Aug. 1929, Poland. Chairman, Family medicine. m. Shirley Futerman, 21 Mar. 1954, Cape Town, South Africa, 3 sons, 1 daughter. *Education:* MB ChB, South Africa; Specialist, Family Medicine, Israel; Specialist, Public Health, Israel; Fellow, Royal College of General Practitioners, UK. *Appointments:* Medical Director, Preventive and Public Health, Kupat Holim Health Insurance Institution, Israel, 1968-70; Chief Editor, 'The Family Physician', Israel, 1973; Medical Director, Herzlia Medical Clinic, 1970-85; Chairman, Family Medicine, Sackler School of Medicine, Tel-Aviv University, Israel. *Memberships:* National Advisory Councils to Ministries of Social Welfare, Education, Health, 1970-74; Chairman, Israel Association of Family Physicians, 1977-79; World Executive of World Organization of National College & Academies of Family Medicine/{ General Practice; Chairman, Specialty Board of Examiners, Family Medicine Israel, 1985; etc. *Publications:* Articles in professional journals: "National Perspectives in Israel", 'Primary Health Care 2000', 1985; "Case Reports from General Practice", 'Nature of General Family Practice'; "Teamwork in Family Practice", 'Family Medicine', 1978; etc. *Honours:* Work Merit Prize, Kupat Holim Health Insurance Institution, Israel, 1974; Visiting Scholarship, Update Foundation, UK. *Hobbies:* Photography; Hiking. *Address:* Dept. of Family Medicine, Building 130, Sheba Medical Centre, Tel Hashomer, Israel.

POLSON, James Bernard, b. 29 Apr. 1938, Kansas City, Missouri, USA. Professor of Pharmacology and Therapeutics. m. Nancy Ellen Keith, 2 Oct. 1959, Columbia, Missouri, USA, 1 son, 1 daughter. *Education:* BA, Zoology, University of Missouri, Columbia, USA, 1961, MS, Physiology and Pharmacology, 1966, PhD, Pharmacology, 1968; Postdoctoral training, Pharmacology, University of Minnesota, USA. *Appointments:* Assistant Professor, University of South Florida, USA, 1971-75, Associate Professor, 1975-83,

Professor, 1983-, Assistant Dean, Graduate Affairs and Research, 1982-85, Associate Dean, 1985-. *Membership:* American Society for Pharmacology and Therapeutics. *Publications:* More than 30 scientific articles; 7 book chapters. *Address:* University of South Florida, Department of Pharmacology and Therapeutics, 12901 North 30th Street, Box 9, Tampa, FL, USA.

POOL, Jan, b. 2 Nov. 1931, Amsterdam, The Netherlands. Professor in Cardiology. m. 15 Jan. 1959, Amstelveen, 4 sons. *Education:* HBS B, 1949, Med brs, 1956, Physician, 1958, Amsterdam; Cardiologist, 1966, Med Dr Thesis, 1969, Leiden. *Appointments:* Research Assistant, 1960-62, Fellow in Cardiology, 1962-66, Leiden; Cardiologist, Scientist, 1966-71, Leiden; Cardiologist, Scientist, 1971-76, Lecturer in Cardiology, 1976-80, Professor in Cardiology, 1980-, Rotterdam. *Memberships:* Dutch Society of Cardiology; European Society of Cardiology; Dutch Society of Sports Medicine; President, Scientific Council Sports Medicine, Netherlands. *Publications:* 'Maximum Oxygen Uptake of Lung Patients', 1969; 'Maximum Oxygen Uptake in Healthy non-athletic Males', (Co-author), 1966; 'Acute Coronary Events in General Practice', (with Lubsen, Van der Does), 1976; 'Sudden Death Outside Hospital', 1978; 'Risk of Sudden Death in Sports', 1982. *Hobbies:* Politics; Athletics; Cycling; Swimming. *Address:* Thorax Centre, Erasmus University, PO 1738, 3000 DR Rotterdam, The Netherlands.

POOLE, Alfred Philip, b. 15 Jan. 1922, Invercargill, New Zealand. Consultant/Physician/Cardiologist. m. Nancye Irwin Brown, 2 Feb. 1948, Oamaru, 2 daughters. *Education:* MB ChB, New Zealand; FRACP; FRCP ED; DA; Dip Obst. *Appointments:* Junior Medical Staff, Southland Hospital, Invercargill, New Zealand, 1946-58; Junior-Registrar Staff, Western General Hospital and Deachoness Hospital, Edinburgh, 1954-57; Consultant, Physician/Cardiologist and Chairman Department of Medicine, Southland Hospital, Invercargill, New Zealand. *Memberships:* Fellow, Royal Australasian College of Physicians; Fellow, Royal College of Physicians, Edinburgh; Australia and New Zealand Cardiac Society. *Hobbies:* Several regional Art Societies; Chairman, Southland Branch of Historic Places Trust; Chairman, Southland Museum Art Gallery Trust Board; Artist - Member Jade and Stone Sculpture. *Address:* 77 Layard Street, Invercargill, New Zealand.

POORTMANS, Jacques, R, b. 3 Sep. 1933, Brussels, Belgium. Professor, Biochemistry. m. Christen Jo, 26 June 1954, Brussels, 3 sons. *Education:* Graduate, 1960, PhD, 1964, Physical Education, Brussels. *Appointments:* Professor, Physical Education, Brussels, 1954-56; Postdoctoral Research Fellow, Biological Chemistry, Harvard Medical School, USA, 1965-67; Research Assistant, Physiology, Brussels, 1967-72; Assistant Professor, 1972-79, Associate Professor, 1979-84, Biochemistry; Professor, Biochemistry and Physiology, 1984-, Université Libre de Bruxelles; Professor of Biology of Exercise, Université Paris, 1978-. *Memberships:* Fellow: American College of Sports Medicine, Human Biology Council; Société Belge de Biochimie; Société Belge de Médecine et des Sciences du Sport; Chairman, Research Group, Biochemistry of Exercise, UNESCO. *Publications:* Editor, Co-editor, 6 books on biochemistry of exercise, 1969-84; 143 papers, 3 reviews on protein metabolism, 3 reviews on renal physiology. *Honours:* Philip Noel Baker Research Prize, UNESCO. *Hobbies:* Romanesque Art; Jogging. *Address:* Chimie Physiologique, Institut Supérieur d'Education Physique et de Kinésithérapie, Université Libre de Bruxelles, Brussels, Belgium.

POPESCU, Nicolae Constantin, b. 4 Mar. 1940, Bucharest, Romania. Microbiologist. m. Susan Eleanor Armiger, 27 May 1977, 1 daughter. *Education:* BS 1964, PhD 1971, University of Bucharest, Romania. *Appointments:* Head, Cellular Biology Department,

Oncological Institute, Bucharest, 1967-71; Visiting Scientist, Somatic Cell Genetics, 1972-77, Staff Fellow, 1981-84, Microbiologist, 1984-, Laboratory of Biology, National Cancer Institute, Bethesda, Maryland. *Memberships:* American Association for Cancer Research, 1984; New York Academy of Sciences, 1985. *Publications:* Various articles in cancer research publications. *Honours:* Cancer Research Fellow, International Agency of Cancer Research, Lyon, France, 1971. Editorial Board, Cancer Genetics & Cytogenetics, 1984. *Hobbies:* Politics; Sport. *Address:* National Cancer Institute, 9000 Rockville Pike, Bldg 37, Rm 2A15, Bethesda, MD 20892, USA.

POPIELA, Tadeusz, b. 23 May 1933, Nowy Sacz, Poland. Head of the I Department of General Surgery and Clinic of Gastroenterology, Medical Academy, Krakow. m. 28 Oct. 1955, 1 son, 1 daughter. *Education:* MD, 1955; PhD, 1961, Medical Academy of Nicolaus Copernicus, Krakow; Assistant Professor, 1965-72; Professor of Surgery, 1972. *Appointments:* Research Assistant, 1955-65; Associate Professor, 1965-71; Head of Unit of Gastroenterological Surgery, 1971-76, III Department and Clinic of General Surgery, Nicolaus Copernicus Medical Academy, Krakow; Head of I Department of General Surgery and Clinic of Gastroenterology, Nicolaus Copernicus Medical Academy, Krakow, 1976-. *Memberships:* Polish Association of Surgery; Polish Association of Gastroenterology; Polish Academy of Sciences; Scientific Committee of Ministry of Health and Social Welfare, Poland; American Gastroenterological Association; New York Academy of Science; CICO; West German Association of Endoscopy; Czech Association of Surgery. *Publications:* Author of numerous papers and books including: Clinical Chemistry (co-author), 1982; Clinical and Operative Surgery (co-author), 1983; Internal Diseases (co-author), 1983; Gastric Cancer, 1985. *Honours:* Recipient of many honours and awards including: Honorary Diploma, Distinguished Achievement Award of Polish Medical Aliance in USA, 1976. *Hobby:* Travel. *Address:* ul. Zulawskiego 5/8, 31-145 Krakow, Poland.

POPOWICH, Kenneth Robert, b. 25 Jan. 1956, Regina, Saskatchewan, Canada. Family Practitioner; Clinical Preceptor. m. Nicola Cruse, 3 July 1979, Calgary, Alberta, Canada, 3 sons. *Education:* BSc; MD; LMCC; CCFP; DNBME. *Appointments:* Chief Resident, Holy Cross Hospital, Calgary, Family Medicine Programme, 1982-83; Active staff, Holy Cross Hospital and Grace Hospital; Chairman, Library Committee; Medical Executive Representative; Courtesy staff, Rockyview Hospital; Clinical Preceptor, Family Medicine Residency Programme, Holy Cross Hospital. *Memberships:* Alberta Medical Association; Canadian Medical Association; College of Family Physicians of Canada. *Address:* 4020 17th Avenue SW, Calgary, Alberta, Canada.

PORTER, Kenneth, b. 24 Jan. 1943, USA. Assistant Clinical Professor of Psychiatry. *Education:* BA cum laude, Harvard College; MD, Albert Einstein College of Medicine, 1969; Residency in Psychiatry, 1973. *Appointments:* Clinical Instructor in Psychiatry, Albert Einstein College of Medicine, 1975-78; Director of Group and Family Therapy, St Luke's Hospital, 1976-81; currently, Assistant Clinical Professor of Psychiatry, Columbia College of Physicians and Surgeons. *Memberships:* American Psychiatric Association; American Group Psychotherapy Association; American Orthopsychiatric Association; Physicians for Social Responsibility. *Publications:* Co-Author: 'Combined experiential and didactic aspects of a new group therapy training approach' in 'International Journal of Group Psychotherapy', 1978; 'Group therapy combined with individual therapy', chapter in "Special Techniques in Individual Psychotherapy", 1979. *Address:* 125 East 87th Street, New York, NY 10128, USA.

PORTER, Richard Maxwell, b. 28 Feb. 1916, Narrogin, Western Australia. Medical Officer, Queenslea Hospice (part-time). m. Anne Elizabeth Paterson, 5 June 1946, Perth, 3 sons, 2 daughters. *Education:* Bachelor of Medicine; Bachelor of Surgery. *Appointments:* Senior Medical Officer, Wooroloo Sanatorium; Public Health Dept, Western Australia, Assistant Tuberculosis Physician, Tuberculosis Physician, Director-Chest & Tuberculosis Services; Director, Alcohol & Drug Authority of Western Australia; Medical Officer, Queenslea Hospice. *Memberships:* Australian Medical Association; Australian Thoracic Society; International Academy of Chest Physicians& Surgeons; International Union Against Tuberculosis. *Publications:* "Endogenous Tuberculosis" Medical Journal Australia, 1967; Co-Author, "Geographic Variations in the Prevalence of Sensitivity to PPD-S and PPD-B in Western Australia", 'Tubercle', London. *Hobbies:* Reading; Rotary. *Address:* 38 Broome Street, Mosman Park, WA 6012, Australia.

PORTIN, Petter Erik, b. 12 Dec. 1940, Kruunupyy, Finland. Professor of Genetics. m. Raija Inkeri Mettälä, 26 Dec. 1965, 1 son, 1 daughter. *Education:* MSc, 1965, Licentiate of Sciences, 1968, PhD, 1972, University of Turku. *Appointments:* Assistant Teacher of Genetics, 1969, Lecturer in Genetics, 1975, Professor of Genetics, 1980, University of Turku. *Publications:* Some 60 scientific publications in field of gametogenesis & gene action in Drosophila, dental genetics in man. *Address:* Laboratory of Genetics, Department of Biology, University of Turku, SF-20500 Turku 50, Finland.

POSNER, Joel David, b. 9 Feb. 1942, Brooklyn, New York, USA. Director, Geriatric Centre. Divorced, 3 daughters. *Education:* BA, University of Vermont, 1962; Honours, Programme of Natural Sciences, Trinity College, Dublin, Ireland, 1964-65; MD, University of Montpellier, France, 1970. *Appointments:* Director, Pulmonary Diagnostic Services, Lankenau Hospital, Philadelphia, USA, 1975-80; Chief, Department of Pulmonary Diseases, Haverford Community Hospital, 1979-80; Medical Director, Philadelphia Geriatric Centre, 1980-present. *Memberships:* Gerontological Society of America; American Geriatrics Society; American College of Chest Physicians (Fellow); American College of Physicians (Fellow); Philadelphia College of Physicians (Fellow). *Publications include:* Conference papers; articles in medical and current affairs journals and magazines including: 'Chronic Respiratory Failure and Physical Reconditioning: Case Study of an Elderly Obese Woman' in 'British Journal of Sports Medicine', 1979 (co-author); 'Particular Problems on Antibiotic Use in the Elderly', in "Geriatrics", volume 37, 1982; 'Healthier Aging', weekly column for the 'Philadelphia Bulletin', 1981/82; 'The Heart of the Problem' in 'Inside' magazine, 1982; 'How to Live Forever' in 'Playboy' magazine, 1982; 'Dementia is Forever' in 'Inside' magazine, 1983; 'Maybe Herpes isn't Forever' in 'Inside' magazine, 1983. *Honours:* Elected to the Governing Board of the five county Health Systems Agency of Southeastern Pennsylvania, 1979; Chairman, Mayor's Committee on Health Services for the Elderly and Chronic Care, 1982. *Address:* 532 College Avenue, Haverford, PA 19041, USA.

POSNEY, Kazimierz, b. 4 Feb. 1924. Consultant Clinical Pathologist. m. 1949, Sydney, Australia, 1 daughter. *Education:* MB, BS, Sydney; D Path (RCP&S), FRCPath; FRCPA. *Appointments include:* Staff Pathologist, Liverpool District Hospital, 1960-63; Honorary Pathologist, Backtoon Hospital; Honorary Pathologist, Fairfield Hospital. *Memberships:* Australian Medical Association; Haematology Society of Australia; etc. *Hobby:* Collecting Australian bookplates. *Address:* 49 Greens Avenue, Dundas, New South Wales, 2117, Australia.

POSPISCHIL, Vladimir Viktor, b. 23 May 1913, Opatovice, Czechoslovakia. Team Work Researcher. m.

Margherita Dallabetta, 2 Feb. 1971, Augsburg, Federal Republic of Germany, 1 son, 1 daughter. *Education:* MD, 1938; Specialist in Pneumology, 1941. *Appointments:* Chief of Lung Hospitals, Bohemia, 1943-55; Contract Surgeon, 7th Army, USA in Europe, 1957-78. *Memberships:* European Academy of Allergology and Clinical Immunology; German Society of Allergology and Clinical Immunology. *Publications:* "Physician and Tuberculosis", 1945; Author of numerous articles in numerous magazines on fthiseology, medical history, deontology, allergy and psychosomatic medicine, 1943-84. *Honours:* Commended for Outstanding Performance, International Conference for Allergists, 1977; Officially Commended for unique sensitivity to problems of patients, 1978. *Hobbies:* Travelling to South East Asia, pursuing interest in Hindu ceremonies from psychosomatic point of view. *Address:* August-Vetter-Str 42, D-8900 Augsburg, Federal Republic of Germany.

POSTEL, Jacques Albert, b. 1 Jan. 1927, Clermont-Ferrand, France. Chief Physician, St Anne Hospital, Paris, m. Madeleine Bernuy, 7 Mar. 1957, Nuits St Georges, 2 sons, 2 daughters. *Education:* MD, 1955; DES, Diploma of Higher Studies in Philosophy, 1960; PhD, 1967; Assistant in Psychopathology, Sorbonne, 1968-70; Associate Professor, Psychopathology, University of Paris VII, 1971-78. *Appointments:* Chief Physician, Nice Psychiatric Hospital, 1956-62; Assistant Physician, La Seine Psychiatric Hospitals, 1962-65; Chief Physician, La Seine Psychiatric Hospital, 1965; Maison Blanche Hospital, 1965-72; Esquirol Hospital, Charenton, 1973-82; St Anne Hospital, 1982-. *Memberships:* Evolution Psychiatrique; French Society of Psychosomatic Medicine; French Association of Psychiatry; French Society of History of Medicine; International Society of History of Psychiatry and Psychoanalysis, Chairman. *Publications:* "L'Evolution Psychique de l'enfant", 1970; "Genese de la Psychiatrie", 1981; "Nouvelle Histoire de la Psychiatrie", (with C Quetel), 1983; Editor of "L'Evolution Psychiatrique". *Address:* Centre Hospitalier Sainte-Anne, 1 rue Cabanis, 75674 Paris Cedex 14, France.

POTASH, Marlin S, b. 23 Oct. 1951, USA. Psychotherapist, Educator, Psychologist. m. Frederick Howard Fruitman, 19 Dec. 1981, 1 daughter. *Education:* BS, Jackson College, Tufts University; MEd 1975, Ed.D, 1977, Humanistic & Behavioural Studies, University of Boston. *Appointments:* Organisational Consultant, Private Practice in Psychotherapy, 1979-; Psychological Consultant, Middlesex Family & Probate Court, Cambridge, Massachusetts, 1980-; Instructor, Radcliffe Seminars Certificate of Management Programme, 1983-; Consulting Psychologist, Children's All-Day School, New York, 1984-; Adjunct Assistant Professor, Fordham University Graduate School of Social Service, New York. *Memberships:* Commissioner, Human Relations - Youth Resources Commission of Brookline, Chair, Budget Committee, 1982-84; Board of Trustees, Boston Ballet Society, 1981-83. *Publications:* Various papers and invited addresses. *Address:* 1133 Park Avenue, New York, NY 10128, USA.

POTTER, Rebecca Lynn, b. 10 June 1951, Kingman, Arizona, USA. Assistant Professor, Psychiatry, University of Arizona College of Medicine; Consultant, Tucson VA Medical Centre. m. Sterling J Torrance, 26 May 1979, Tucson. *Education:* MD, University of Arizona, College of Medicine, 1978. *Appointments:* Psychiatry Internship, University of Arizona, Health Sciences Centre, 1978-79; Neurology Internal Medicine Internship, University of California, San Diego, 1979-80; Resident, Psychiatry, University of Arizona, 1980-83. *Memberships include:* American Association for Social Psychiatry; American Association of University Professors; American Medical Women's Association, President, Tucson Branch, 1983-85; American Psychiatric Association; American Medical Association; Arizona District Branch, American Psychiatric Association, Executive Council 1983-; Association for Academic Psychiatry, Fellowship Committee, 1984-; Group for the Advancement of Psychiatry; Physicians for Social Responsibility; Tucson Psychiatric Association; World Association for Social Psychiatry; etc. *Publications include:* Articles in numerous professional journals including 'experientia'; 'American Journal of Social Psychiatry'; 'Psychiatric Medicine'; 'Psychosomatics'; etc. *Honours:* Phi Beta Kappa, 1973; Arizona Medical Association Scholarship, 1975; Joseph Goldberger Scholarship, Clinical Nutrition, Columbia University, 1978; James L Grobe Award, Outstanding Senior Planning to enter a Family Practice Residency, 1978; Ginsburg Fellow, Group for the Advancement of Psychiatry; Falk Fellow, American Psychiatric Association; Fellow, Association for Academic Psychiatry. *Address:* Dept. of Psychiatry, Arizona Health Sciences Centre, Tucson, AZ 35724, USA.

POULSEN, Knud, b. 25 Jan. 1936, Copenhagen, Denmark. Professor of Biochemistry. m. Lise Lotte Svane, 5 Sep. 1964. *Education:* MD. *Appointments:* Lecturer, Institute for Experimental Medicine, University of Copenhagen, 1964-78; Research Fellow and Instructor in Medicine, Massachusetts General Hospital, Harvard Medical School, Boston, USA, 1971-73; Currently Professor of Biochemistry, Institute for Biochemistry, The Royal Dental College, Copenhagen, Denmark. *Publications:* Articles including: 'Kinetics of the Renin System', 1973. *Address:* Institute for Biochemistry, The Royal Dental College, Panum Institute, Blegdamsvej 3c, 2200 Copenhagen, Denmark.

POWELL, Frank Conor, b. 18 Jan. 1950, Dublin, Ireland. Consultant Dermatologist, Mater Hospital, Dublin. m. Maria Regan, 3 Jan. 1975, Dublin, 1 son, 1 daughter. *Education:* MB, BCh, BAO, University College, Dublin; MRCPI, Mater Hospital; Board Certified, Dermatology, Mayo Clinic, USA. *Appointments:* House Officer, Medicine, Consultant Dermatologist, Mater Hospital; Registrar, Dermatology, Consultant Dermatologist, Federated Dublin Hospitals; Resident, Senior Associate, Instructor, Dermatology, Mayo Clinic, USA. *Memberships:* Society of Investigative Dermatology; Royal College of Physicians of Ireland; Fellow, Royal Academy of Medicine of Ireland; Fellow, American Academy of Dermatology; Sigma Xi; Royal Society of Medicine; International Society of Dermatologists. *Publications:* 37 articles in professional journals including: Co-Author, "Genital Pagets Disease and Urinary Tract Malignancy", 'Journal American Academy of Dermatology', 1985; "HLA DR and MT Typing in Lichen Planus", 'British Journal of Dermatology', in press; "Cancer de la prostate Metastasique se Manifestant Par des nodules peniens", 'JAMA', France, 1985; "Oral Mucosal Diseases", 'Journal American Academy of Dermatology'. *Honours:* Outstanding Resident Award, Mayo Clinic, 1983; Gold Award, American Academy of Dermatology, 1983. *Hobbies:* Fishing; Golf. *Address:* Dept. of Dermatology, Mater Hospital, Eccles Street, Dublin 7, Ireland.

POWELL, Robin Dale, b. 19 Apr. 1934, Indianapolis, Indiana, USA. Vice Chancellor, Dean. m. Gwen Julie Van Lieshout, 28 Dec. 1957, Baraboo, Wisconsin, 2 sons, 1 daughter. *Education:* Johns Hopkins University, 1951-53; MD honours Medicine, University of Chicago School of Medicine, 1957. *Appointments:* Instructor 1963-65, Assistant Professor of Medicine 1965-69, University of Chicago; Associate Professor 1969-72, Professor of Internal Medicine 1972-78, University of Iowa; Associate Chief of Staff for Research and Education, Assistant Chief, Medical Service, Iowa City Veterans Administration Hospital, 1970-78; Professor of Medicine, Associate Dean for Academic Affairs, Northwestern University, 1978-84; Professor, Dean, Vice Chancellor for Clinical Professional Services, University of Kentucky College of Medicine, 1984-. *Memberships include:* Alpha Omega Alpha; American Society of Tropical Medicine and Hygiene; American Federation for Clinical Research; Fellow,

Royal Society of Tropical Medicine and Hygiene; New York Academy of Sciences; American Association for the Advancement of Science. *Publications include:* Over 60 articles in scientific journals; various book chapters, book reviews and abstracts. *Honours include:* Certificate of Achievement, Walter Reed Army Medical Center, 1963; Outstanding Educator of America, 1971. *Hobby:* Collector of political memorabilia. *Address:* University of Kentucky College of Medicine, Albert B Chandler Medical Center, MN 150, Lexington, KY 40536-0084, USA.

POYANIL, Mathew Mathew, b. 10 Jan. 1930, Kerala, India. Clinical Director, Psycho-Geriatrics. m. Molly, 30 Dec. 1954, 3 daughters. *Education:* MB. BS; Certified by the American Board of Psychiatry and Neurology. *Appointments:* Intern, 1954-55; Resident in Psychiatry, 1971-74; Physician, Kerala Medical Service, India, 1955-58; General Physician, Ministry of Health, Malaysia, 1958-61; Psychiatrist, Division of Mental Health, Ministry of Health, Malaysia, 1961-70; Psychiatrist, I, II & III, St Louis State Hospital, St Louis, Missouri, USA, 1974-78; Clinical Director, Psycho-Geriatrics, St Louis State Hospital, 1978-; President, Medical Staff, St Louis State Hospital, 1974-75; Clinical Assistant Professor, St Louis University School of Medicine, 1984. *Memberships:* Eastern Missouri Psychiatric Society; American Psychiatric Association; American Geriatrics Society; Academy of Psychosomatic Medicine; Fellow of the Masters & Johnson Institute; Master Mason Lodge Angus No 1529 on the Rolls of the Grand Lodge of Scotland. *Publications:* Contributions to professional journals including Journal of the American Geriatric Society. *Honour:* Plaque and Award for Best Resident, Sandoz Wander, 1973-74. *Hobbies:* Photography; Fishing; Tennis; Stamps. *Address:* 1816 Mannington Court, Chesterfield, MO 63017, USA.

PRÁGAI, Géza, b. Aug. 1923, Szeged, Hungary. Assistant Professor. m. Ilona Császa Putti, 29 June 1947, Szeged, 1 son, 2 daughters. *Education:* MD; CM Sc. *Appointments:* Licensed Dental Technician; Physician; Surgeon; Dentist; Assistant Professor, Department of Dentistry and Oral Surgery, University Medical School, Szeged. *Memberships:* Federation Dentaire Internationale; Hungarian Medical Association (Magyar Orvosok Egyesulete); Association of Hungarian Dentists (Magyar Fogorvosok Egyesulete). *Publications:* "Bevezeto fogpotlastanba", 1972; "Introduction to Pental Prosthetics"; "Study of Muscle Masseter", 1976; "The Height of the Mandibular Ridge", 1983; "Anatomy of the Retromolar Region", 1983; "Geronto-Anatomical Aspects of the Buccinator Muscle", 1985. *Hobbies:* Gerontostomato Anatomy; Sports. *Address:* Department of Dentistry and Oral Surgery, University Medical School Szeged, H-6720 Szeged, Lenin krt. 64, Hungary.

PRAMBERGER, Peter Anton, b. 18 Feb. 1953, New York City, USA. Director, Hillside Chiropractic Centre. m. Julie Rose Manno, 9 Aug. 1980. *Education:* BS, Honours, Physiological Psychology; DC. *Memberships:* International Chiropractic Association; American Chiropractic Association; New York State Chiropractic Association. *Honours:* BS, Honours, 1977. *Hobbies:* Skiing; Golf; Tennis. *Address:* 6 Tuxedo Avenue, New Hyde Park, NY 11577, USA.

PRANATA, Widya, b. 14 Dec. 1943, Pekalongan. Instructor, Fixed Prosthodontic. m. Wirya Pranata, 23 June 1974, Jakarta, 1 son, 1 daughter. *Education:* Graduate, Dentistry, Trisakti University; English Course, USIS; Continuing Education, Technical Prosthodontics, Ivoclar, Liechtenstein, Biobon, Japan. *Appointments:* Guidance, Counselling, Student Affairs, Dentistry, Trisakty University; Secretary, Indonesian Prosthodontics Society, Jakarta Branch. *Memberships:* International Dental Federation; Indonesian Dental Association; Indonesian Prosthodontics Society. *Hobbies:* Music; Gardening; Knowledge Exchange in Dental Prosthetic. *Address:* Jl. Gedung Hijau 1 No 22, Pondok Indah, Jakarta Selatan, Indonesia.

PRANKERD, Thomas Arthur John, b. 11 Sep. 1924, England. Retired Professor. m. Margaret Vera Harrison Cripps, 18 Feb. 1950, England, 3 sons, 1 daughter (1 son, 1 daughter deceased). *Education:* MB BS, London, 1947; MRCS LRCP, 1947; MD, London, 1949; MRCP, London, 1951; FRCP, 1962. *Appointments:* House Physician, St Bartholomew's Hospital, 1947; Major, RAMC, 1949-50; Postgraduate Travelling Fellow, USA, 1953-54; First Assistant, Medical Unit, University College Hospital Medical School, 1954-60; Sec NRC Committee on Blood Transfusion, 1956-60; Consultant and Physician, University College Hospital, 1960-65; Professor, Clinical Haematology, University College Hospital Medical School, 1965-82; Honorary Physician, Whittington Hospital, 1974-80; Dean, University College Hospital Medical School, 1972-79; Member, Board of Governors, University College Hospital, 1971-73; Member, N E Thames, RHA, 1976-79; Examiner, Royal College of Physicians, MRCP, 1963-71, various other universities, 1963-80; Visiting Professor: University of Western Australia, 1972, University of Cape Town, 1978. *Memberships:* Physiological Society; Medical Research Society; Association of Physicians. *Publications:* Many medical and scientific papers; "The Red Cell", 1961; "Clinical Physiology", 1963; "Haematology in Diagnosis and Treatment", 1968; "French's Index of Differential Diagnosis", 1973. *Honours:* MD Gold Medal, 1949; Goulstonian Lecturer, Royal College of Physicians, 1963. *Hobbies:* Painting; Gardening; Fishing. *Address:* Milton Lake, Milton Abbas, Blandford, Dorset, England.

PRATHAP, Gopal, b. 3 May 1935, Malaysia. Director, National Tuberculosis Centre. m. Vasanthakumari, 16 May 1965, India, 1 son, 1 daughter. *Education:* MB BS, University of Singapore; MRCP, London, England, 1968; Diploma in Control of Tuberculosis, Prague, Czechoslovakia, 1973; Fellow, American College of Chest Physicians. *Appointments:* Registrar, Internal Medicine, 1963; Chest Consultant, General Hospital, Seremban, Malaysia, 1969; Senior Chest Physician, 1972, Director, 1983-, National Tuberculosis Centre, Jalan Pahang, Kuala Lumpur. *Memberships:* Malaysian Medical Association; College of Physicians, Malaysia; Academy of Medicine, Malaysia; American College of Chest Physicians. *Publications:* Contributor of papers to: 'Medical Progress', 1976; 'Bulletin of the IUAT', Proceedings of 23rd Conference, 1975; 'Journal of Malaysian Society of Health', 1984. *Honours:* Honorary Consultant, University Hospital, 1977; Member, Treatment Committee, IUAT, 1973-79. *Hobbies:* Electronics; Listening to classical music. *Address:* c/o National Tuberculosis Centre, Jalan Pahang, Kuala Lumpur, Malaysia.

PRENTICE, Neil Gorman, b. 24 May 1923, Riverton, New Zealand. Senior Pathologist, Southland Hospital, Invercargill, New Zealand. m. Christine Doris Taylor, 3 Feb. 1948, Invercargill, 1 son, 3 daughters. *Education:* MD, ChB, Otago University; MRACP; FRACP; FRCPA. *Appointments:* General Practitioner; Junior Lecturer, Pathology, University of Otago Medical School. *Memberships:* Past President, New Zealand Society of Pathologists; New Zealand Health Department Laboratory Advisory Committee; National Hormone Committee; President, New Zealand Medical Association, 1984; Southland Medical Foundation. *Honours:* New Zealand Red Cross Society Award of Merit; Queens Silver Jubilee Medal. *Hobbies:* Horticulture; Sport. *Address:* 119 Don Street, Invercargill, New Zealand.

PRESANT, Cary Arnet, b. 16 Dec. 1942, Buffalo, New York, USA. Professor of Medicine. m. Shiela Lassman, 11 June 1966, Buffalo, 3 sons, 1 daughter. *Education:* MD, New York State University, USA, 1966. *Appointments:* Staff Associate, National Cancer Institute, Bethesda, USA, 1967-69; Assistant Professor of Medicine, Washington University, 1973-79; Director Medical Oncology, City of Hope, 1979-82; Professor of Medicine, University of Southern California, 1982-;

Staff Physician, Wilshire Oncology Medical Group. Los Angeles, 1982-. *Memberships:* Fellow, American College of Physicians; American Society of Clinical Oncology; American Society of Haematology; American Association for Cancer Research; International Society of Haematology. *Publications:* Author of over 200 book chapters, scientific manuscripts and scientific communications on cancer research, treatment, biochemistry, Lipsome research, supportive care of cancer patients, pharmacology and immunotherapy. *Honours:* James Gibson Anatomical Society, 1963; Alpha Omega Alpha, 1965; Phi Beta Kappa, 1965; Sklarlow Memorial, Miamonedes Society, 1981; Board of Directors, American Cancer Society, 1985-. *Hobbies:* Skiing; Tennis; Boy Scouts. *Address:* 935 South Sunset Avenue, West Covina, CA 91790, USA.

PRESCOTT, Laurence Francis, b. 13 May 1934, London, England. Professor of Clinical Pharmacology, Consultant Physician. m. Jennifer Ann, 6 Sep. 1980, 1 son, 3 daughters. *Education:* Downing College, University of Cambridge, MA, 1954-57; MD, Middlesex Hospital Medical School, London, 1957-60. *Appointments:* House Officer, The Middlesex Hospital, London, The Royal Northern Hospital, London; Senior House Officer, New End Hospital, London; Resident (Registrar), Boston City Hospital, Boston, Massachusetts, USA; Research Fellow, Division of Clinical Pharmacology, Department of Medicine, Johns Hopkins Hospital, Baltimore, Maryland, USA; Lecturer in Therapeutics, Department of Therapeutics & Pharmacology, University of Aberdeen; Senior Lecturer, Reader, Professor of Clinical Pharmacology, Consultant Physician, Royal Infirmary & University of Edinburgh, Scotland. *Memberships:* Association of Physicians of Great Britain & Ireland; Scottish Society of Physicians; Scottish Society for Experimental Medicine; British Pharmacological Society; European Society of Toxicology; and others. *Publications:* Numerous publications in general medical, clinical, pharmacological & toxicological journals; numerous contributions to books, including "Drug Absorption" 1981, "Rate Control in Drug Therapy", 1985. *Honours:* American Therapeutics Society Prize Essay Award, 1966; Lilly Prize, British Pharmacological Society 1978; W N Creasy Visiting Professor, Baylor Medical College, Houston, Texas, USA, 1980. *Hobbies:* Gardening; Music; Sailing. *Address:* "Redfern", 24 Colinton Road, Edinburgh, EH10 5EQ, Scotland.

PRESS, Stephen J, b. 20 Oct. 1947, New York City, USA. Chief-of-Staff, Allied Chiro-Medical Institute. m. Janice S Feldman, 16 January 1983, Union, New Jersey, 1 son. *Education:* Biochemistry, Farleigh Dickinson University; BA, Biological Sciences, Thomas Edison College; DC, Palmer College of Chiropractic; CCTP, National Lincoln School of Postgraduate Education. *Appointment:* Chief-of-Staff, Allied Chiro-Medical Institute, Englewood, New Jersey. *Memberships:* Fellow, American College of Sports Medicine (only DC to be so honoured); American Chiropractic Association; New Jersey Chiropractic Society; New York Academy of Science; Bergen-Passaic Chiropractic Society; various US Olympic Committees; Bergen County Health and Fitness Council, Chairman, 1984-85; American Red Cross, Safety Services Committees; Northern Valley Chapter. *Publication:* Balance in Skates, Professional Skates Guild Journal, November 1978. *Hobbies:* Dance Skating; Fencing; Shooting. *Address:* Allied Chiro-Medical Institute, 291 S. Van Brunt Street, Englewood, NJ 07631, USA.

PRESSMAN, Alan H, b. 17 Sep. 1942, New York City, USA. Chairman, Department of Nutrition, New York Chiropractic College, 1 son, 1 daughter. *Education:* Doctor of Chiropractic, Chiropractic Institute of New York, 1963; MS, Human Biology, University of Bridgeport, Connecticut, 1978; Certificate in Nutrition, Harvard Medical School, 1981. *Appointments:* Director of Public Affairs, Council on Nutrition, American Chiropractic Association, 1974; Vice-President, 1976; President, 1978, 79; Chairman, Department of Nutrition,

New York Chiropractic College, 1979; Associate Professor, Biology-Nutrition, University of Bridgeport, Connecticut, 1980. *Memberships:* Diplomate, American Chiropractic Board of Nutrition; Fellow: International College of Chiropractors; American College of Chiropractic; International Academy of Preventive Medicine; Member, NY Academy of Sciences; US Congressional Council; Academy of Sciences of Rome, Italy; American Public Health Association; International College of Applied Nutrition; International Academy of Preventive Medicine; Nutrition Today Society. *Publications:* Mediators of the Mind, 1979; C.inical Assessment of Nutritional Status and over 70 papers. *Honours:* 12 Meritorious and Testimonial Awards including Testimonial Award, Board of Trustees, University of Bridgeport. *Address:* 7 East 9th Street, New York, NY 10003, USA.

PRICE, C Gordon, b. 27 Nov. 1924, Morwell, Victoria, Australia. Chest Physician. Married in Heidelberg, 3 sons, 2 daughters. *Education:* MB BS, University of Melbourne; FRACMA; FCCP. *Appointments:* Senior Resident Medical Officer, 1st Assistant, Medical Officer in Charge, Thoracic Physician, Thoracic Unit, Austin Hospital, Heidelberg; Senior Medical Officer, Tuberculosis Branch, Austin Hospital; Member, Pharmaceutical Advisory Council, Austin. *Memberships:* Melbourne University Medical Society; Australian Medical Association; British Medical Association; Australian Thoracic Society; Foundation Member, Laennec Society, Australia; Fellow, American College of Chest Physicians; Fellow, Royal Australasian College of Medical Administrators; International Union Against Tuberculosis. *Publications:* Various articles in medical journals and papers in proceedings, esp. in field of Sarcoidosis. *Hobbies:* Old Cars; Photography; Hiking. *Address:* Austin Hospital, Heidelberg, Victoria 3084, Australia.

PRICE, Christopher Philip, b. 28 Feb. 1945, Cheltenham, England. Consultant Clinical Biochemist; Associate Lecturer. m. Elizabeth Ann Dix, 13 July 1968, Southport, 2 daughters. *Education:* BSc, London University; MA; PhD, University of Birmingham; MCB; FRSC; Chem. *Appointments:* Principal Biochemist, East Birmingham Hospital; Top Grade Biochemist, Honorary Senior Lecturer, Southampton General Hospital; currently, Consultant Clinical Biochemist and Associate Lecturer, Department of Clinical Biochemistry, Addenbrooke's Hospital, Cambridge. *Memberships:* Association of Clinical Biochemists; American Association of Clinical Chemists; Royal Society of Chemistry; International Society for Clinical Enzymology. *Publications:* Co-Editor, "Centrifugal Analysers in Clinical Chemistry", 1980. Contributor to Volume 2, 1981 and Co-Editor, Volumes 2 and 3 "Recent Advances in Clinical Biochemistry". Author or Co-Author of contributions to: 'Annals of Clinical Biochemistry'; 'Transactions of Royal Society', London. *Hobbies:* Running; Gardening; Walking. *Address:* Department of Clinical Biochemistry, Addenbrooke's Hospital, Hills Road, Cambridge CB2 2QR, England.

PRICE, Leonard Anthony, b. 28 Nov. 1935, London, England. Private Practice, Consultant Physician & Medical Oncologist; UK Representative, International Advisory Council, New York Chemotherapy Foundation, USA. m. Valerie Frances Whiteman, 1 Feb. 1964, Leatherhead, 1 son, 1 daughter. *Education:* MBBS, 1962, MD, 1980, University of London; MRCP (UK) Collegiate Member, Royal College of Physicians of London, 1972; Approved Certificate, Joint Committee of Higher Medical Training - Medical Oncology, 1981. *Appointments:* House Physician, Brook Hospital Group, London, 1962; House Surgeon, Greenwich District Hospital, London, 1963; Senior House Officer, St John's Hospital, London, 1964-65; Medical Registrar, Westminster Hospital, 1965-67, Royal Marsden Hospital, 1967-69; MRC Clinical Research Scientist, Institute of Cancer Research, Honorary Senior Registrar, Royal Marsden Hospital, 1970-73; Senior Lecturer, Medicine, Institute of Cancer Research, Honor-

ary Consultant Physician, Royal Marsden Hospital, 1973-80. *Memberships:* New York Academy of Sciences; International Society of Internal Medicine; American Society of Clinical Oncology; British Medical Association. *Publications:* Co-Author, "Safer Cancer Chemotherapy using a kinetically-based approach: Implications for the Next Decade", 'Safe Cancer Chemotherapy', 1981, "Safer Cancer Chemotherapy using a kinetically-based experimental approach", 'Mount Sinai Journal of Medicine', 1985, "An Experimentally-based safe Method of Administering Intensive Cancer Chemotherapy: Prospects for Increased Survival in Patients with 'solid' tumours in the next Decade", 'South African Medical Journal', 1983, "An Experimental Biological basis for increasing the therapeutic index of clinical cancer Therapy", 'Annals of the New York Academy of Sciences', 1982; etc. *Honours:* Gordon Jacobs Research Fellow, Clinical Research, Royal Marsden Hospital, 1969-70; Recognised Teacher, University of London, 1977-80. *Hobbies:* Music; Philosophy; Rugby Football; Cricket. *Address:* 111 Harley Street, London W1N 1DG, England.

PRICE, Margaret Fraser, b. 20 Sep. 1950, Scotland. Research Associate/Director, Special Infectious Disease Laboratory, St Luke's Episcopal Hospital, Houston, Texas, USA. *Education:* BSc 1971, MIBiol 1972, Paisley College of Technology; PhD, University of London. Postdoctoral work, Temple University, Baylor College of Medicine, USA. *Appointments include:* Research Assistant, Guys Hospital, London 1972-74; Medical Research Council Studentship, ibid, 1974-77; Research Associate, Temple University School of Medicine, 1978-79; Fellow, Department of Microbiology, Baylor College of Medicine, Texas, 1979-82. *Memberships:* Institute for Biology; British Society for Mycopathology; Medical Mycology Society fo the Americas; International Society for Human & Animal Mycology; American Society for Microbiology. *Publications include:* Thesis, "Aspects of Phospholipase Activity in 'Candida Albicans'" 1977; Contributions to various professional journals, book "Urinary & Genital Tract Infection in Candidiasis", ed G P Bodey & V Fainstein, 1985. *Hobbies:* Sailing; Photography; Reading. *Address:* Infectious Diseases, Department of Medicine, Baylor College of Medicine, Houston, TX 77030, USA.

PRICE, Michael Rawling, b. 7 Dec. 1947, Wisbech, Cambridgeshire, England. Research Officer, Head of Biochemistry. m. Frances Margaret Scalbert, 22 Mar. 1980, Shaftesbury, Dorset, England. *Education:* BSc, 1969, PhD, 1972, University of Nottingham. *Appointments:* Research Assistant, Cancer Research Campaign Laboratories, 1969-72. *Memberships:* Biochemical Society; British Association for Cancer Research; European Association for Cancer Research. *Publications:* Author of over 150 research papers, review articles, meeting proceedings and abstracts, 1971-. *Honours:* Elected General Secretary, European Association for Cancer Research, 1977; Elected Executive Committee Member, British Association for Cancer Research, 1979-82; Co-Editor, European Journal of Cancer and Clinical Oncology, 1983. *Hobbies:* Skiing; 20th Century literature; Music; Visual arts; Travel; Angling; Gardening; French wines; Home brewing. *Address:* Cancer Research Campaign Laboratories, University of Nottingham, University Park, Nottingham NG7 2RD, England.

PRICE, Nicholas Charles, b. 12 Aug. 1946, Stafford, England. Senior Lecturer in Biological Science. m. Margaret Hazel Millen, 4 Aug. 1973, Oxford, 1 son, 2 daughters. *Education:* Merton College, Oxford, 1964-69; St John's College, Oxford, 1969-74; School of Medicine, University of Pennsylvania, Philadelphia, USA, 1971-72; BA 1st Class Honours Chemistry 1968, MA and DPhil 1971, Oxford University, England. *Appointments:* Fereday Research Fellow, St John's College, Oxford, 1969-74; Harkness Fellow, University of Pennsylvania, USA, 1971-72; Departmental Demonstrator, Department of Biochemistry, University of Oxford, England, 1973-74; Lectureship in Biochemistry 1974-77, Senior Lectureship in Biological Sciences 1977-, University of Stirling, Scotland; Alexander von Humboldt Fellow, University of Regensburg, Federal Republic of Germany, 1982. *Memberships:* Biochemical Society. *Publications include:* "Principles and Problems in Physical Chemistry for Biochemists", (with R A Dwek), 1974 and 1979; "Fundamentals of Enzymology" (with L Stevens), 1982; Numerous articles in journals. *Honour:* Gibbs Prize in Chemistry, Oxford University, 1967. *Hobbies:* Running; Fund raising. *Address:* Department of Biological Science, University of Stirling, Stirling FK9 4LA, Scotland.

PRICE, Trevor Robert Pryce, b. 29 Nov. 1943, Concord, New Hampshire, USA. Associate Professor, Psychiatry, University of Pennsylvania School of Medicine. Director, Psychiatric Inpatient Services, Hospital of the University of Pennsylvania. m. Barbara Cynthia Lerner, 5 June 1965, New Haven, Connecticut, 1 son, 1 daughter. *Education:* BA, Yale College, New Haven, Connecticut, 1965; MD, Columbia University College of Physicians and Surgeons, New York City, New York, 1969. *Appointments:* Medical Intern, 1969-70, Resident in Internal Medicine, 1972-74, University of California, San Francisco; Medical Officer, US Public Health Service, Indian Health Service, 1970-72; Resident, Psychiatry, Dartmouth Hitchcock Medical Center, 1974-77; Instructor, Clinical Psychiatry, 1976-77, Assistant Professor, Psychiatry and Medicine, 1977-81, Associate Professor, Psychiatry and Assistant Professor of Medicine, 1981-83, Associate Professor of Psychiatry and Medicine, 1983-85, Dartmouth Medical School, Hanover, New Hampshire; Staff Psychiatrist and Co-Director, Dartmouth-Hitchcock Mental Health Center Inpatient Unit, Hanover, 1977-85. *Memberships:* New Hampshire and American Psychiatric Associations. *Publications:* Author or Co-author of papers contributed to journals: 'Archives of General Psychiatry'; 'Journal of Nervous and Mental Disease'; 'The Journal of Death and Dying'; 'American Journal of Psychiatry'; 'Psychopaharm Bulletin'; 'Journal of Clinical Psychiatry', 'Convulsive Therapy'. Editorial Board, 'Convulsive Therapy' 1984-. *Honours:* William C Meninger Award, Central Neuropsychiatrists Association, 1977; Faculty Teaching Award, Department of Psychiatry, Dartmouth Medical School, 1983-84. *Hobbies:* Fly fishing and Fly tying; Running; Tennis; Guitar; Piano. *Address:* 717 W Mt Ainy Ave, Philadelphia, PA 19119, USA.

PRICHARD, John Franklin, b. 16 Apr. 1907, Texas, USA. Periodontist, Private Practice. m. Edna Crabtree, 6 Nov. 1928, Dallas, Texas, 1 daughter. *Education:* DDS. *Appointments:* Senior Consultant, Periodontia, University of Washington, Seattle; Visiting Lecturer, Periodontia, University of Pennsylvania, Graduate Periodontics, Baylor University; Former Consultant, Carswell and Lackland Air Force Bases and US Public Health Service Hospital of Fort Worth; Postgraduate Lecturer, Courses, USA, Canada, Europe. *Memberships:* American Society of Periodontists, President 1964-65; Southwestern Society of Dental Medicine, past President; Texas Dental Association, Past Vice President; Good Fellow, Texas Dental Association; Vice-Chairman, American Board of Periodontology, 1975-76; Executive Committee, American Academy of Esthetic Dentistry, 1975-78. *Publications:* More than 50 scientific papers and chapters for textbooks; "Advanced Periodontal Disease: Surgical and Prosthetic Management", 1965; Editor, "Dental Clinics of North America", 1969; "Glossary of Terms", American Academy of Periodontology, 1977; "The Diagnosis and Treatment of Periodontal Disease", 1979; Consultant to various periodontal books. *Honours:* Recipient, numerous honours and awards including: William J Gies Award for Achievements in Periodontology, 1977; Honorary Member, Texas Academy of General Dentistry, 1962; Omicron Kappa Upsilon; Fellow, American College of Dentists, 1944, Southwest Society of Periodontists; Distinguished Service Award, Fort Worth District Dental Society;

Life Member, American Dental Association; Fellow, Academia Internationali Lex et Scientiae, 1964; Trustee, Baylor University College of Dentistry, 1986. *Address:* 3833 Camp Bowie Blvd, Fort Worth, TX 76107, USA.

PRIETO, Jesus, b. 6 Apr. 1944, Oviedo, Spain. Professor of Medicine. *Education:* MB, University of Valladolid, Spain, 1967, MD, 1969. *Appointments:* Assistant Professor, University Hospital, Valladolid, Spain, 1969-72; Research Fellow and Clinical Assistant, Royal Free Hospital, London, England, 1972-73; Associate Professor, University Hospital, Valladolid, 1973-76; Professor of Medicine and Head of Department of Medicine, University Santiago de Compostela, 1977-79; Professor of Medicine, Head of Department of Medicine, Clinica Universitaria, Pamplona, Spain-. *Memberships:* Spanish Society of Internal Medicine and Digestive Diseases; Vice President, Spanish Association for the Study of the Liver; European and International Association for the Study of the Liver. *Publications:* "Temas de Hepatologia", 1978; 'Serum ferritin in acute and chronic liver diseases' in 'Gastroenterology', 1975; 'Serum antibodies against Porphyric Hepatocytes in PCT in 'Gastroenterology', 1983; 'Sistemic prostacyclin synthesis in cirrhosis:' 'Gastroenterology', 1985; 'Liver cell cytoprotection by prostaglandins' in 'Liver', 1985. *Honour:* British Council Scholarship, 1972. *Hobby:* Tennis. *Address:* Department of Medicine, Clinica Universitaria, Pamplona, Spain.

PRIEST, Robert George, b. 28 Sep. 1933, London, England. Professor of Psychiatry. m. Marilyn Baker, 24 June 1955, Westcliff-on-Sea, 2 sons. *Education:* MB BS 1956, MD 1970, University of London; DPM, Royal Colleges of England, 1963; MRCP, Edinburgh, 1964; MRCPsych, 1971. *Appointments:* Lecturer in Psychiatry, University of Edinburgh, Scotland, 1964-67; Exchange Lecturer, University of Chicago, USA, 1966-67; Consultant, Illinois State Psychiatric Institute, 1966-67; Senior Lecturer, St George's Hospital Medical School, London, England, 1967-73; Honorary Consultant, St George's Hospital and Springfield Hospital, London, 1967-73; Currently Professor of Psychiatry, University of London at St Mary's Hospital Medical School. *Memberships:* Fellow, Registrar, Royal College of Psychiatrists; Fellow, Vice-President, International College of Psychosomatic Medicine; Past President, Society for Psychosomatic Research; Central Committee, World Psychiatric Association. *Publications:* "Insanity: A Study of Major Psychiatric Disorder", 1977; "Handbook of Psychiatry for Students" 8th edition, (with G Woolfson), 1986; "Sleep Research", (editor with A Pletscher and J Ward), 1979; "Benzodiazepines Today and Tomorrow", (editor with U Vianna Filho, R Amrein and M Skreta), 1980; "Psychiatry in Medical Practice", editor, 1982; "Anxiety and Depression", 1983; "Sleep: An International Monograph", 1984; "Psychological Disorders in Obstetrics and Gynaecology", (editor, 1985; Over 100 learned articles. *Honours:* A E Bennett Award (jointly), Society for Biological Psychiatry, USA, 1965; Doris Odlum Prize, British Medical Association, 1968; Gutheil Von Domarus Award, Association for the Advancement of Psychotherapy and American Journal of Psychotherapy, New York, 1970. *Hobbies:* Squash; Tennis; Swimming; Foreign Languages. *Address:* Academic Department of Psychiatry, St Mary's Hospital, Praed Street, London W2 1NY, England.

PRINCE, Raymond Harold, b. 27 Sep. 1925, Barrie, Ontario, Canada. Professor of Psychiatry. Married, 3 sons, 7 daughters. *Education:* MD 1950, BA 1951, MSc (Anatomy) 1952, University of Western Ontario; Fellow, Royal College of Physicians & Surgeons (Canada), 1955. *Appointments:* Medical Officer (Psychiatric), Government of Nigeria, 1957-59; Psychiatrist, Royal Victoria Hospital, Montreal, Canada, 1957-; World Health Organisation Consultant, Kingston, Jamaica, 1967-69; Director of Resident Training, Department of Psychiatry, McGill University, 1973-84;

Associate Dean (Postgraduate Education), Faculty of Medicine, McGill University, 1977-80; Editor, 'Transcultural Psychiatric Research Review', 1982-; Director, Division of Social & Transcultural Psychiatry, McGill University, 1981-. *Memberships:* Canadian Psychiatric Association; Society of Psychological Anthropology; President, R M Bucke Memorial Society for the Study of Religious Experiences. *Publications:* Some 100 publications in scientific journals; Editor, "Trance and Possession States", 1968; Editor, "Configurations: Biological & Cultural Factors in Sexuality & Family Life", 1974. *Address:* Department of Psychiatry, McGill University, 1033 Pine Avenue West, Montreal, H3A 1A1, Canada.

PRITCHARD, Robert Hugh, b. 25 Jan. 1930, London, England. Professor Emeritus. m. Susan Beth Rosenberg, 3 Nov. 1973, Leicester, 2 sons, 1 daughter. *Education:* BSc, Botany, King's College, London; PhD, Genetics, Glasgow University; Fl Biol. *Appointments:* Lecturer, Genetics, Glasgow University, 1956-59; Scientific Staff, Medical Research Council, 1959-64; Professor, Genetics, Leicester University, 1964-. *Membership:* Fellow, Institute of Biology; American Society for Microbiology; Society for General Microbiology; Genetical Society. *Publications:* Articles in professional journals; Editor, "Basic Cloning Techniques", 1985. *Hobbies:* Politics; Squash; Landscape Gardening. *Address:* Department of Genetics, University of Leicester, University Road, Leicester LE2 2LE, England.

PROCKOP, Darwin Johnson, b. 31 Aug. 1929, USA. Professor & Chairman, Biochemistry, UMDNJ-Rutgers Medical School; Director, Jefferson Institute of Molecular Medicine, Thomas Jefferson University. m. Elinor Sacks, 15 Apr. 1961, Bethesda, Maryland, 1 son, 1 daughter. *Education:* AB, Haverford College; Honours BA, Oxford University, UK; MD, University of Pennsylvania; PhD, Biochemistry, George Washington University. *Appointments include:* Director, Clinical Research Centre, Philadelphia General Hospital, 1966-72; Professor/Chairman of Biochemistry, University of Medicine & Dentistry, New Jersey, Rutgers Medical School, 1972-86; Professor of Medicine, ibid, 1974-86; Director, Centre for Human Molecular Genetics, ibid, 1983-86; Chairman of Biochemistry, Jefferson Medical School, Thomas Jefferson University, 1986-; Director, Jefferson Institute of Molecular Medicine, 1986-. *Memberships:* Phi Beta Kappa; Alpha Omega Alpha; American Society for Clinical Investigation; American Society for Biological Chemists. *Publications:* Over 200 in review journals, including 'Journal of Biological Chemistry', 'Biochemistry', etc. *Honours:* Honorary doctorate, University of Oulu, 1984; Elected Fellow, American Association for the Advancement of Science 1985, Association of American Physicians 1981. *Hobbies:* Running; Tennis. *Address:* Jefferson Institute of Molecular Medicine, Thomas Jefferson University, 11th & Locust Streets, Philadelphia, PA 19607, USA.

PROCTOR, Arthur Laurence, b. 18 Oct. 1927, Queensland, Australia. Consultant Psychiatrist. m. Elaine McQuie, 25 Nov. 1950, Brisbane, Australia, 3 sons. *Education:* MB BS, Queensland, 1950; DPM, Melbourne, 1963; MRANZCP, 1964; FRANZCP, 1972; MRCPsych, 1973; FRCPsych, 1980. *Appointments:* RMO, 1950-52, Surgical Registrar and Acting Superintendent, 1953, Townsville General Hospital, Queensland; General Practice, 1953-60; Medical Officer, Sunbury Mental Hospital, Victoria, 1960-61; Medical Officer, Royal Park Psychiatric Hospital, Melbourne, 1961-62; Private Psychiatric Practice, 1962-; Junior Psychiatrist, 1964-67, Junior and then Senior Psychiatrist, Department of Repatriation, 1964-70, Psychiatrist-in-Charge, Day Hospital, 1967-72, Senior Psychiatrist, 1972-76; Clinical Supervisor in Psychiatry, 1976-78, Royal Brisbane Hospital; Command Consultant Psychiatrist, 1 Military District, Australian Army, Lt Col Retired, RAAMC, 1972-76; Federal Councillor, Royal Australian and New Zealand College of Psychiatrists, 1972-80; Psychiatrist-in-Charge, Sex

Dysfunction Clinic, Princess Alexandra Hospital, 1981-84. *Memberships:* Australian Medical Association; Australian and New Zealand College of Psychiatrists; Royal College of Psychiatrists; Australian Society Sex Educators, Researchers and Therapists; Society for the Scientific Study of Sex. *Publications:* 'Stress', 'Annals of General Practice', 1965; 'Adolescent Problems', 'Annals of General Practice', 1965; 'Common Errors in Psychiatric Diagnosis and Management', 'Australian Family Physician', Vol 2, 1973; 'Diagnosis and Treatment of Frigidity and Impotence', 'Australian New Zealand Journal Obstetrics and Gynaecology', 1975. *Hobbies:* Boating; Fishing. *Address:* Morris Towers, 149 Wickham Terrace, Brisbane, Australia, 4000.

PROCTOR, Richard Culpepper, b. 4 Apr. 1921, Raleigh, North Carolina, USA. Professor & Chairman, Department of Psychiatry & Behavioural Medicine. m. Dixie Proctor, 1 Jan. 1948, Bennettsville, South Carolina, 1 son, 1 daughter. *Education:* BS, Wake Forest University, 1942; MD, Bowman Gray School of Medicine, 1945; LFAPA. *Appointments:* Instructor 1950-52, Assistant Profess 1952-60, Associate Professor 1960-62, Professor of Psychiatry 1962-, Bowman Gray School of Medicine. *Memberships include:* American & Southern Psychiatric Associations; American College of Psychiatrists; Academy of Psychosomatic Medicine; Academy of Psychiatry & Law; North Carolina Foundation for Mental Health Research; etc. *Publications include:* Monographs, Book chapters & reviews, articles in professional journals. *Honours:* Biographical listings; Charter Fellow & Founder, American College of Psychiatrists; Life Fellow, American Psychiatric Association; Fellow, Southern Psychiatric Association. *Hobby:* Golf. *Address:* Department of Psychiatry & Behavioural Medicine, Bowman Gray School of Medicine, 300 S Hawthorne Road, Winston-Salem, NC 27103, USA.

PROKOPOWICZ, Jan, b. 31 July 1931, Jaworowka, Poland. Director, Institute of Laboratory Diagnostics. m. Danuta-Anna Szostak, 18 June 1958, 1 daughter. *Education:* Physician, Medical School, Bialystok, 1960; MD, 1963; PhD, 1968; Associate Professor, 1976; Professor, 1983. *Appointments:* Assistant, 1960-62, Senior Assistant, 1962-64, Lecturer, 1964-69, Assistant Professor, 1969-76, Associate Professor, 1976-83, Professor, 1983-, Director, Institute of Laboratory Diagnostics, Medical School, Bialystok. *Memberships:* Deputy President, Polish Society of Laboratory Diagnostics; National Board for Laboratory Diagnostics; President, Counsel Education for Medical Analytics of Ministry of Health; National Representative, IFCC; Committee, Clinical Pathophysiology of Polish Academy of Science. *Publications:* Articles in professional journals including: 'Polish Medical Journal'; 'Experientia'; 'Coagulation'; etc. *Hobbies:* Music; Jogging; Allotment. *Address:* Lubienieckiego 5 B m6, 15-304 Bialystok, Poland.

PROMINSKA, Elzbieta Maria, b. 3 Apr. 1941, Warsaw, Poland. Professor, Polish Academy of Sciences. m. Tadeusz Dzierzykray-Rogalski, 8 Dec. 1968, Warsaw, 1 daughter. *Education:* Physician's Diploma, 1964, MD, 1968, Habilitation, 1973, Professor, 1983, Faculty of Medicine, Warsaw. *Appointments:* Assistant, Laboratory of Human Ecology and Palepathology, Institute of Mediterranean Archaeology, 1962-68, Assistant Professor, 1968-73, Docent, 1973-83, Professor, Centre for Studies of Non-European Countries, 1983-, Vice Director, 1986, Head of Department of Functional Anatomy, Academy of Physical Education, 1981, Polish Academy of Sciences. *Memberships:* International Association of Human Biologists; International Paleopathological Association; Society for Nubian Studies; International Egyptological Association; Societe des Africanistes a Paris; Yugoslav Association of Science and Society. *Publications:* "Natural Population Movement in the Faiyum Oasis", 1971; "Investigation on the Population of Muslim Alexandria", 1972; 'Variations de taille des habitants d'Alexandrie au cours des siecles', 1985. *Honours:* Honorary Memberships, Slavo-baltiska Sällskapet vid Lunds Universitet, 1966; Golden Cross of Merit, 1980; Medal of National Education Commission, 1981. *Hobbies:* Modern Literature. *Address:* Kasprowicza 91, 01-823 Warsaw, Poland.

PRUITT, Basil Arthur Jr., b. 21 Aug. 1930, Nyack, New York, USA. Commander and Director, US Army Institute of Surgical Research. m. Mary Sessions Gibson, 4 Sep. 1954, Lakewood, Ohio, 2 sons, 1 daughter. *Education:* AB, Harvard College, USA, 1952, MD, Tufts University School of Medicine, 1957. *Appointments:* Intern, Boston City Hospital, 1957-58; Resident in Surgery, 1958-59; Resident in Surgery, Brooke Army Medical Centre, 1961-64; Chief, Burn Study Branch, US Army Surgical Research Unit, Chief, Clinical Division; Chief, Professional Svc, 12th Evac Hospital, 67th Med Gp, Vietnam; Chief, Trauma Study Section, US Army Medical Research Team, Walter Reed Army Institute of Research, Vietnam; Commander and Director, US Army Institute of Surgical Research. *Memberships:* American Board of Surgery; American Surgical Association; American Association for the Surgery of Trauma; American Burn Association; American College of Surgeons Board of Governors; ACS Committee on Trauma; American Trauma Society Board of Directors; International Society for Burn Injuries; Co-Chairman, Disaster Planning Committee; Social Infection Society; Societe Internationale de Chirurgie; Society of University Surgeons; Surgical Biology Club III; Shock Society; Southern, Texas and Western Surgical Associations; International Surgical Group. *Publications:* Author and co-author of 7 medical books; Author and co-author of 69 chapters in medical textbooks; Author and co-author of 260 articles in medical journals. *Honours include:* Metcalfe Award, 1965; Sustaining Membership Award, Society of Military Surgeons, 1972; Harvey Stuart Allen Distinguished Service Award, American Burn Association, 1984; Dominique Larrey Award for Surgical Excellence, 1985. *Hobbies:* Reading; Tennis. *Address:* US Army Institute of Surgical Research, Fort Sam Houston, TX 78234-6200, USA.

PRUSOFF, William Herman, b. 25 June 1920, USA. Professor. m. Brigitte Averbach, 19 June 1948, 1 son, 1 daughter. *Education:* BS, University of Miami, 1941; MS, 1947, PhD, 1949, Columbia University. *Appointments:* Ordinance Inspector, War Dept, 1941-43; Assistant Chemist, Miami Beach, 1943-44; Research Assistant, Columbia University, 1944-49; Research Associate, Instructor, Pharmacology, Western Reserve University School of Medicine, Yale University School of Medicine, 1949-53; Assistant Professor, 1954-59, Associate Professor, 1959-66, Professor, 1966-, Acting Chairman, 1968-69, Yale University School of Medicine. *Memberships:* American Association for Cancer Research; American Society for Pharmacology and Experimental Therapeutics; American Society of Biological Chemists; American Chemical Society; Sigma Xi; etc. *Publications:* Over 200 research articles. *Honours:* Recipient, 1982 ASPET Award, Experimental Therapeutics. *Hobbies:* Walking; Swimming; Travel. *Address:* Department of Pharmacology, Yale University School of Medicine, New Haven, CT 06510, USA.

PRUYN, Stephen Charles, b. 28 Mar. 1939, Baton Rouge, Louisiana, USA. Chairman, Department of Obstetrics and Gynaecology, Naval Hospital, San Diego, California. m. Carolyn Sue Tribble, 8 June 1963, Gueydan, Louisiana, 2 sons, 1 daughter. *Education:* MD, Louisiana State University; Internship, Naval Hospital, Great Lakes, Ill; Residency, Naval Hospital, San Diego, California; Microsurgery, AAGL; FACOG. *Appointments:* General Medical Practice, US Naval Dispensary, Taichung, Taiwan, ROC, 1965-67; Chief of Obstetrics and Gynaecology, 1970-74, Executive Officer, 1971-74, US Naval Dispensary, Sasebo, Japan; Staff, Head of Gynaecologic Division, 1974-80,

Director, Endocrine and Infertility Service, 1975-80, Director of Resident Education, 1976-80, Naval Regional Medical Centre, Portsmouth, VA, USA; Chairman, Department of Obstetrics and Gynaecology, Naval Regional Medical Centre, San Diego, California, 1980-. *Memberships:* Fellow, American College of Obstetrics and Gynaecologists; Member, Alpha Omega Alpha; Member, American Association of Gynaecologic Laparoscopists; Member, American Fertility Society; Member, Association of Professors in Gynaecology and Obstetrics; Associate Member, San Diego Gynaecological Society. *Honours:* Navy Commendation Medal, 1974; Navy Commendation Medal with Gold Star, 1977; Unit Commendation Medal, 1977. *Publications include:* 'Microsurgery in Gynaecologic Residency Training', 1980; 'Proposed modification of Uchida technique', (with R J Stock), 1980; 'Salpingitis Isthmica Nodosa Revisited', (with R Stock), 1983; 'Management of Ureteral Endometriosis', (with V Ellis), 1983; 'Tubal Reanastomosis', 1984; 'Acute Necrotizing Fasciitis of the Endopelvic Fascia', 1978; 'Long Term Propranol Therapy in Pregnancy: Maternal and Fetal Outcome', (with J P Phelan, G C Buchanan), 1979; 'Vaginal Evisceration During Coitus', (with B D Hall, J P Phelan, D G Gallup), 1978; 'Prophylactic Antibiotics in Cesarean Section', (with J P Phelan), 1979. *Address:* 2067 Manzanita Drive, Oakland, CA 94611, USA.

PRYDZ, Hans Peter, b. 6 Sep. 1933, Oslo, Norway. Professor of Medicine. m. (1) Reidunn Svensen, 4 Aug. 1954, 2 sons, 1 daughter. (2) Anne-Brit Kolstø) 11 July 1985. *Education:* MD, 1957; PhD, 1965. *Appointments:* Internships, Department of Medicine, Department of Surgery, Drammen Hospital, 1958; Resident, Medical Department A, University Clinic, University of Oslo, 1960; Research Fellow, Norwegian Council Cardiovascular Diseases, 1961; Assistant Professor, Department of Microbiology, Dental Faculty, University of Oslo, 1965; Fogarty International Research Fellow, McArdle Laboratories, University of Wisconsin, Madison, Wisconsin, USA, 1967-68; Professor and Chairman, Department of Biochemistry, University of Tromsø) Norway, 1971; Honorary Guest Researcher, Medical Research Council Clinical Research Centre, Northwick Park, London, England, 1976-77; Professor and Head, Research Institute for Internal Medicine, University of Oslo, Norway, 1980-; Visiting Professor, Brunel University 1985-; Visiting Worker, National Institute for Medical Research, London, 1985-86. *Memberships:* Biochemical Society UK; Norwegian Biochemical Society; International Committee for Thrombosis and Haemostasis; Member of Board, Norwegian Cancer Society; Member of Board, Norwegian Council for Cardiovascular Diseases. *Publications:* 160 scientific papers; Editor or Contributor to 6 books; Editorial Board 'Haemostasis Scandinavian Journal of Clinical and Laboratory Investigation', Editorial Adviser 'Biochemical Journal'. *Address:* Research Institute for Internal Medicine, University of Oslo, Rikshospitalet, Oslo 1, Norway.

PRZBYLSKI, Jerzy Antoni, b. 1 Sep. 1930, Lille, France. Director of Regional Orthopedy and Rehabilitation Hospital for Children. m. 3 Aug. 1959, Wroclaw, 1 son, 1 daughter. *Education:* Medical Academy, 1950-55; Specialist in Orthopedy and Traumatology, 1963; MD, 1964; Specialist in Rehabilitation, 1969; Habilitation, 1971; Professor Assistant/Docent in Poland, 1976. *Appointments:* Assistant Orthopedy and Rehabilitation Centre, Wroclaw, 1955-58; Assistant, Orthopedy Clinic, Wroclaw, 1957-63; Chief of Postural Disfunctions Ambulatory Service, 1958-63; Director, Regional Orthopedy-Rehabilitation Hospital for Children, 1963-; Professor Assistant, Wroclaw Physical Culture Academy, 1976-77; Consultant, Rehabilitation for Jelenia Gora District, 1977-. *Memberships:* Polish Orthopedy and Traumatology Association; World Federation of Spine Surgeons; Polish Society for Preventing and Combatting Disability. *Publications:* 11 articles on operative orthopedy; 13 original primal works; 58 articles on rehabilitation. *Honours:* Silver Merit Cross,

1970; Smile Order, 1975; Perfect Worker of Polish Health Service, 1976; Dr H Jordan's Medal, 1980. *Hobby:* Gardening. *Address:* ul. Kolbuszewska 48, 53-404 Wroclaw, Poland.

PUECH, Pierre-Francois Flavien, b. 16 Oct. 1941, Amiens, France. Dental Surgeon; Paleoanthropologist; Master of Research attached to Institute of Legal Medicine and Occupational Medicine, Marseilles. m. Eva Robert, 26 June 1976, Paris, 2 daughters. *Education:* Dental Surgeon, Dentistry School of Paris, 1967; Doctorate, Periodontist, University Montpellier, 1973; Doctor of Odontological Sciences, University of Marseilles, 1976; DEA, Diploma of Advanced Studies in Geology, 1980; DSc, Paleontology, University Provence, 1983. *Appointments:* Researcher attached to Anthropology Laboratory, Marseilles, 1976-80; Researcher, Laboratory No 184 of National Center of Scientific Research, 1980-; Laboratory of Prehistory, National History Museum and Museum of Man, Paris, 1980-. *Memberships:* Institute of Human Palaeontology, Paris; Consultant, International Dentistry Federation; American Association Physical Anthropologists; European Paleopathology Association; European Association Anthropologists; Consultant, French Association Normalisation. *Publications:* Contributor to professional journals including: 'American Journal Physical Anthropology'; 'Journal Human Evolution'; 'Current Anthropology'; 'Archeologia', etc. *Honour:* Prize, International French-Speaking Association of Odontological Research, 1976. *Address:* Musée de l'Homme, Paris, BP 191, 30008 Nimes, France.

PUGA MENDILAHARZU, Horacio José, b. 16 Apr. 1935, Argentina. Professor of Public Health and of Microbiology. m. Elvira Nougués, 28 Dec. 1977, Argentina, 2 sons, 3 daughters. *Education:* MD, Licenciado en Salubridad; Diplomado en Public Health; Doctor en Medicine; MPH. *Appointments:* Professor of Public Health, Professor of Microbiology, Academy Secretary, National University of Tucuman, Tucuman; Medical Officer Consultant, PAHO; Director of Department of Health Promotion. *Memberships:* Honourable Council of the Medical School, National University of Tucuman; Founding Member, Medical Association of Public Health; Harvard Alumni Association. *Publications:* "Epidemiology of Leprosy", 1969; "Siphyllisa Attacked Secundary", 1970. *Honours:* Diploma and Gold Medal for the Ambulatory Treatment of Infectious Diseases, 1968; Award for the Best Thesis of the Year, 1969. *Hobbies:* Golf; Rugby. *Address:* C Alvarez 66, 4000 Tucuman, Argentina.

PUJOL, Rémy Jean-Louis, b. 12 Mar. 1939, Florensac, Hérault, France. Professor; Research Unit Director. m. Maryse Bouniol, 28 Nov. 1961, Florensac, 1 son, 1 daughter. *Education:* Lic sci nat, Montpellier, 1959; Ag sci, Toulouse, 1963; Dr sci, Montpellier, 1971. *Appointments:* Assistant 1963-66, Maître-assistant, 1966-71, Montpellier; Research Associate, Yale University School of Medicine, 1971-72; Professor, University of Aix-Marseille 1972-81, University of Montpellier II 1981-. *Memberships:* International Brain Research Organisation; Association des Physiologistes; European Neuroscience Association; International Society for Developmental Neurosciences; American Acoustical Society; Association for Research in Otolaryngology; Collegium Oto-Rhino-Laryngologicum. *Publications include:* Bibliography, mainly on auditory phsyiology & physiopathology (neurobiology & development); 50 main articles in scientific journals such as 'Brain Research', 'Journal of comp.Neurology', 'Hearing Research', 'Neuroscience', etc; 9 book chapters; 74 abstracts. *Honour:* Philips Prize, 1982. *Hobbies:* Rugby;Bowling; Scrabble; Opera. *Address:* INSERM U.254, Lab.Neurobiologie de L'Audition, Hôpital St Charles, 34059 Montpellier, Cedex, France.

PUMAROLA, Agustin, b. 15 Mar. 1920, Barcelona, Spain. Professor of Microbiology & Parasitology, Health Officer, Administrator. m. Maria Rosa Suné, 6

Dec. 1956, Barcelona, Spain, 2 sons. *Education:* MB, MD, Faculty of Medicine, University of Barcelona; National School of Public Health (Officer Health); Stages at: Statens Seruminstitut, Copenhagen, Denarmk, Karolinska Institutet, Stockholm, Sweden, Institut Pasteur, Paris, France, Tropical Medicine Institute, Lisbon, Portugal. *Appointments:* Health Officer, Provincial Health Service, Barcelona, Spain, 1954; Professor of Microbiology, Parasitology, Hygiene & Public Health, Faculty of Medicine, University of Salamanca, 1958; Director, Instituto Municipal de Higiene, Barcelona, 1963; Professor of Microbiology & Parasitology, Faculty of Medicine, University of Barcelona, 1963; Chief, Haemoparasitology Section, Consejo Superior de Investigaciones Cientificas, 1965; Vice-Dean, Faculty of Medicine, Barcelona, 1968; currently: Professor of Microbiology & Parasitology, Chairman, Faculty of Medicine, Barcelona, Chief, Microbiology Department, Clinic & Provincial Hospital, Barcelona, Director, WHO National Influenza Centre, Barcelona. *Memberships:* Sociedad Espanola de Microbiologia, Madrid, Spain; Associacion Nacional de Biopatologia, Madrid; American Society for Microbiology, Washington, USA; Société Française de Microbiologie, Paris, France; Society for General Microbiology, London, England; International Epidemiological Association, London; Royal Society of Health, London. *Publications:* "Higiene Medicina Preventiva y Social" (2 volumes 7 editions) 1964; "Microbiologia y Parasitologia" (6 editions), 1967, 1968; "Microbiologia y Parasitologia médica", 1984; More than 100 articles, mainly on leptospires, respiratory viruses, enterobacteria and vaccines. *Honours:* Cross of Merit (2nd class), Sovereign Order of San Juan de Malta, 1954; Civil Order of Health, 1968; 'Narciso Monturiol' medal of the Generalidad de Cataluna for Scientific Merit, 1983; Various awards. *Hobbies:* Skiing; Swimming; Music; Reading. *Address:* Department of Microbiology & Parasitology, Faculty of Medicine, University of Barcelona, Casanova 143, 08036, Barcelona, Spain.

PUNWAR, Alice Johnson, b. 9 Sep. 1932, Wisconsin, USA. Professor. m. J K Punwar, 15 Jan. 1955, Madison, 2 sons. *Education:* BS, Occupational Therapy, 1954, MS, Behavioral Disabilities, 1969, University of Wisconsin; OTR. *Appointments:* Staff, Occupational Therapist, Mendota St. Hospital, 1957-59; Learning Disabilities Teacher, 1965-69; Assistant Professor, 1969-73, Associate Professor, 1973-79, Professor, Dept Chair, Occupational Therapy Programme, 1980-84, University of Wisconsin; Sabbatical Leave, 1985-86. *Memberships:* Pi Lambda Theta; American Occupational Therapy Association; Wisconsin Occupational Therapy Association; World Federation of Occupational Therapists; American Association for Mental Deficiency. *Publications:* Articles in professional journals. *Honours:* Roster of Expert Advisors, World Federation of Occupational Therapy, 1975; Fellow, American Occupational Therapy Association, 1979. *Hobbies:* Music; Travel; Needlework; Writing. *Address:* Medical Sciences Centre, 1300 University Ave, Madison, WI 53706, USA.

PUPELLO, Dennis Frank, b. 31 May 1939, Tampa, Florida, USA. Chief, Department of Cardiac Surgery. Divorced, 2 sons, 1 daughter. *Education:* BS, University of Tampa, 1961; Graduate Studies, Zoology, 1962, MD, College of Medicine, 1967, University of Florida; Member, Stanford University Cardiac Transplant Team, 1970-72. *Appointments:* Director, Cardiac Surgical Programme: Tampa General Hospital, Tampa, Florida, 1972-82; St Joseph Hospital, Tampa, 1983-84. Chief Department of Cardiac Surgery, St Josephs Hospital, 1984-. *Memberships:* International Association for Cardiac Biological Implants; Florida Society of Thoracic and Cardiovascular Surgeons; American and Florida Medical Associations; Hillsborough County Medical Association. *Publications:* Co-Author of over 24 papers published in professional works including: 'Annals of Thoracic Surgery'; 'California Medicine'; 'Journal of American Medical Association'; 'Journal of Florida Medical Association';

'Annals of Surgery'; 'American Journal of Cardiology'; 'Medical World News'; 'Journal of American College of Emergency Physicians'; 'Journal of Cardiovascular Surgery'. Numerous papers presented at International conferences. *Honours:* 1st Award, San Jose Surgical Society Annual Surgical Symposium, 1969; Service to Mankind Award, Sertoma Club, 1974; Distinguished Service Award, American Heart Association, 1978. *Hobbies:* Piano; Diving; Boating. *Address:* 2727 West Buffalo Avenue, Suite 70, Tampa, FL 33607, USA.

PURI, Prem, b. 23 Sep. 1944, India. Consultant Paediatric Surgeon, National Children's Hospital; Associate Paediatric Surgeon, Our Lady's Hospital for Sick Children, Dublin. m. Veena, 18 Feb. 1982, New Delhi, 2 sons, 1 daughter. *Education:* MBBS; LRCP; LRCS; MS; DCH. *Appointments:* House Physician, All India Institute of Medical Sciences, New Delhi, 1967; Senior Resident, 1968-70; Tutor, 1969-70, Maulana Azad Medical College, New Delhi; Senior House Officer, Paediatric Surgery, Fleming Memorial Hospital for Sick Children, UK, 1971-72, Royal Manchester Children's Hospital, UK, 1972; Senior Registrar, Our Lady's Hospital for Sick Children, Dublin, 1972-74; Research Fellow, Paediatric Surgery, 1974-75, Registrar, Paediatric Surgery, 1975-76, Hospital for Sick Children, Great Ormond Street, UK. *Memberships:* British Association of Paediatric Surgeons & Irish Paediatric Association; Asian Association of Paediatric Surgeons; British Society of Immunology; Royal Society of Medicine; United Kingdom & European Society of Paediatric Research; Irish Society of Immunology. *Publications:* Volume Editor, "Modern Problems in Paediatrics", 'Surgery and Support of the Premature Infant', 1985; 70 articles in professional journals; Editorial Board, 'Journal of Paediatric Surgery', 'Paediatric Surgery International', 'Annals of Paediatric Surgery'. *Honours:* Travelling Fellowship, Excerpta Medica Foundation, 1981; People of the Year Award in Science and Technology, 1984. *Hobbies:* Cooking; Chess. *Address:* Children's Research Centre, Our Lady's Hospital for Sick Children, Crumlin, Dublin 12, Ireland.

PURKERSON, Mabel Louise, b. 3 Apr. 1931, South Carolina, USA. Associate Professor of Medicine and Associate Dean for Curriculum, Washington University School of Medicine. *Education:* AB, Erskine College, Due West, South Carolina, 1951; MD, Medical University of South Carolina, Charleston, 1956. *Appointments:* Washington University School of Medicine: Instructor in Pediatrics, 1961-67; Instructor in Medicine, 1966-67; Assistant Professor of Pediatrics, 1967-; Assistant Professor of Medicine, 1967-76; Associate Professor of Medicine, 1976-; Assistant Dean for Curriculum, 1976-78; Associate Dean for Curriculum, 1978-; Visiting Assistant Professor, Department of Anatomy, Columbia University College of Physicians and Surgeons, 1971-72. *Memberships include:* Sigma Xi; American Physiological Society; American and International Societies of Nephrology; New York Academy of Science; American Association for the Advancement of Science; American Society for Internal Medicine; National Kidney Foundation; Central Society for Clinical Research. *Publications:* Papers, presentations and contributions to professional journals including Journal of Clinical Investigation, Kidney International; American Journal of Physiology; Science. *Honour:* Service recognition by American Heart Association Council on the Kidney in Cardiovascular Disease, November 1979. *Hobbies:* Photography; Gardening; Travel. *Address:* Renal Division, Department of Medicine, Washington University School of Medicine, Box 8126, 660 S Euclid Avenue, St Louis, MO 63110, USA.

PYKE, David Alan, b. 16 May 1921, London, England. Physician, Diabetic Department; Registrar, Royal College of Physicians. m. Janet Stewart, 19 Mar. 1948, London, 1 son, 2 daughters. *Education:* BA, Cambridge University, 1942; University College Hospital Medical School, London; MB BChir, 1945, MD, 1956, Cambridge; FRCP, 1964. *Appointments include:* Junior Medical appointments; Senior Medical Registrar, Radcliffe Infirmary, Oxford, 1952-57; Medical Tutor, University of Oxford, 1957-59 currently, Physician, Diabetic Department, King's College Hospital, London; Registrar, Royal College of Physicians. *Memberships:* British Diabetic Association; Association of Physicians; Royal Society of Medicine; British Medical Association. *Publications:* "Clinical Diabetes and Its Biochemical Basis", Joint Editor, 1968; "Diabetes: The Genetic Connection, Diabetologia", 1979. *Honour:* Claude Bernard Medal European Association for the Study of Diabetes, 1979. *Hobbies:* Opera; Golf. *Address:* 17 College Road, London SE21 7BG, England.

Q

QADIR, Ghulam, b. 18 Aug. 1947, Pakistan. Chief, Department of Psychiatry, Oakwood Hospital, Dearborn, Michigan, USA. m. Shirlin Qadir, 4 Jan. 1979, Multan, Pakistan, 2 sons, 1 daughter. *Education:* MB, BS, Pakistan; MD, USA. *Appointments include:* Pakistan Army Medical Corps, 1971-74; Health Ministry of Pakistan, 1974-75; VA Medical Centre, Allen Park, Michigan, USA, 1978-81. *Memberships:* (American) Psychiatric Association; Academy of Clinical Psychiatrists; Academy of Behavioural Medicine; Academy of Psychosomatic Medicine; Association of Psychiatric Administrators. *Publications include:* 'Liaison Psychiatry & Conspiracy of Silence', 1978; 'An Assessment of After Hours Visits to a Community Mental Health Center', 1979; 'Violence in an Open Psychiatric Ward', 1982. *Address:* 2038 Monroe, Dearborn, MI 48124, USA.

QUADROS, Peter Anthony Canuto de, b. 10 Oct. 1915, Raia, Goa. Consulting General Physician. m. Jean Anne Coelho, 3 Sep. 1949, Bombay, 1 son, 2 daughters. *Education:* MB BS, Bombay; Emeritus Fellow, American College of Chest Physicians. *Appointments:* House Surgeon, B J Hospital for Children, JJ Group of Hospitals, Bombay; House Physician, J J Hospital, Bombay; House-Surgeon, Obstetrics and Gynaecology, Mottibai and Petit Hospitals of J J Group of Hospitals; Lecturer in Physiology, Grant Medical College, Bombay; Administrator and Consulting Physician, Watumuh Hospital for Chest Diseases, Mahim, Bombay. *Memberships:* British Medical Association, London; Fellow Emeritus, American College of Chest Physicians. *Hobbies:* Reading; Music. *Address:* Scheherazade, near Strand Cinema, Colaba, Bombay 400005, India.

QUIGLEY, John Howden, b. 21 Apr. 1925, Halifax, Nova Scotia, Canada. Associate Professor of Ophthalmology. m. Gloria Lorraine Monseur, 11 June 1951, 2 sons, 1 daughter. *Education includes:* BSc 1946, MD 1951, Dalhousie University; Fellowship in Ophthalmology, Royal College of Physicians and Surgeons of Canada, 1972; Diplomate, American Board of Ophthalmology, 1956. *Appointments include:* Staff, Ophthalmology and Otolaryngology, Victoria General Hospital, Halifax Children's Hospital, Halifax Infirmary, 1956-62; Instructor 1959-61, Lecturer 1961-66, Assistant Professor 1966-69, Associate Professor of Ophthalmology 1970-, Dalhousie University Medical School; Consulting Ophthalmologist, Nova Scotia Rehabilitation Centre, 1959-; Head, Department of Ophthalmology 1964-79, Associate Ophthalmologist, 1979-, Halifax Infirmary; Associate Ophthalmologist 1970-80, Consulting Ophthalmologist 1980-, Victoria General Hospital; Active Staff, Ophthalmology, Izaak Walton Killam Hospital for Children, 1970-80. *Memberships include:* Fellow, Royal College of Surgeons of Canada; Canadian Medical Association; American Academy of Ophthalmology; The Society of Eye Surgeons. *Publications include:* 'Testing Higher Visual Functions', 1959; 'Prevention of Blindness in Canada'; 'The Role of the General Physician', (with B Steinberg)', 1858; 'Eye Injuries', 1959; 'Recent Advances in Ophthalmic Investigation', 1968; 'Intraocular Pressure under Cataract Extraction: Effects of Alpha Chymotrypsin', (with J M Lantz), 1973; 'Immunoglobulins in Aqueous Humor and Iris From Patients with Endogenous Uveitis and Cataract', (with T Ghose, P L Landrigan and A Asif), 1973; 'Immunological Studies of Human Anterior Uveitis', (with V P Audain, S Vethamany and T Ghose), 1977; 'An Experimental Model of Acute Immune-Complex Uveitis', (with V P Audain, V G Vethamany and T Ghose), 1978. *Address:* 1674 Oxford Street, Halifax, Nova Scotia, B3H 3Z4, Canada.

QUINN, Brian Francis William, b. 19 Jan. 1934, Melbourne, Victoria, Australia. Clinical Pathologist, Private Practice. m. Anne Adele Lakeland, 14 July 1962, Sydney, 3 daughters. *Education:* MB, BS, 1959, DCP, 1964, University of Sydney; FRCPA, 1966. *Appointments:* RMO, St Vincent's Hospital, Sydney, 1959-60; Registrar, 1961-64, Director, 1969-83, Visiting Pathologist, 1984-86, Mater Hospital, Sydney; Staff Pathologist, St George Hospital, Sydney, 1964-67; RAAF Consultant Pathologist, Visiting Pathologist, No 3 RAAF Hospital, Richmond, NSW, Wing Commander RAAF Reserve, 1967-86; Visiting Part-time Lecturer, Pathology, University of Sydney, 1969-84. *Memberships:* Australian Medical Association; International Academy of Pathology; Haematology Society of Australia; International Society of Haematology. *Publications:* "Listeria Monocytogenes in Neonate", 1964, "Argentaffin Carcinoma in Ovary", 1965; "Homozygous Thalassaemia - a in Australia", 1974, all in 'Medical Journal of Australia'; "Immune Red Cell Aplasia", 'Proceedings Haematology Society of Australia', 1978. *Hobbies:* Music; Theatre; Skiing. *Address:* 9 Noonbinna Crescent, Northbridge, NSW 2063, Australia.

QUINN, Wade G, b. 9 Mar. 1952, New Jersey, USA. Doctor of Chiropractic. m. Dawn Quinn, 25 Mar. 1975, 2 sons. *Education:* BS Business Administration, Monmouth College, New Jersey; BS Human Biology, National College of Chiropractic, Lombard, Illinois; DC Doctor of Chiropractic, National College of Chiropractic. *Appointments:* Past President, International Professional Fraternity Chi Rho Sigma; Chairman, Board Big Brothers/Big Sisters of Williamsburg, 1985-86. *Memberships:* American Chiropractic Association; Virginia Chiropractic Association; American Council of Chiropractic Orthopaedists; American Council of Chiropractic Roentgenologists; National Association of Nutritional Consultants; Certified, Post-graduate study in Acupuncture. *Hobbies:* Racquetball; Woodworking; Model Railways. *Address:* 1675 Richmond Road, Williamsburg, VA 23185, USA.

QURESHI, Bashir, b. 25 Sep. 1935, Rohtak, India. General Practitioner & Community Medical Officer. *Education:* MB, BS; DCH; Fellow, Royal Society of Health; Fellow, Royal College of General Practitioners, Academic Award: Silver Medal, Preventive Medicine, Punjab University, Lahre, 1959. *Appointments:* Medical Officer, Nishtar Medical College Hospital, Multan, Pakistan, 1961-64; Hospital Doctor in London Hospitals, 1964-70; Community Medical Officer & General Practitioner, 1970-. *Memberships:* Communications Executive and Publications Committee, Royal College of General Practitioners; Editor 'Faculty News', newspaper of the RCGP; Member of Council, Royal Society of Health; London Local Advisory Committee (Radio) of the Independent Broadcasting Authority. *Publications:* Over 20 published articles in professional journals. *Hobbies:* Lecturing, Writing & Broadcasting on Transcultural Medicine; Dancing; Cinema; Sightseeing; Dining Out. *Address:* 'Al-Bashir', 32 Legrace Avenue, Hounslow West, Middlesex, TW4 7RS, England.

R

RAAB, Wolfgang Paul Emanuel Franz, b. 22 Dec. 1934, Vienna, Austria. Chairman, Allergy Clinic 'Innere Stadt', Vienna. m. Gertrud, 28 Aug. 1961, Vienna, Austria, 1 son, 1 daughter. *Education:* MD Vienna University Medical School, Austria, 1958. *Appointments:* Assistant, University, Skin Clinic, Vienna, Austria; Research Fellow, Columbia University, New York, USA. Assistant,University Clinic Internal Medicine; University Dozent, Department of Medical Chemistry, Vienna University. *Memberships:* Austrian Dermatological Society; Austrian Immunological Society; Fellow, American Academy of Dermatology; Founding Member, International Society of Cosmetic Dermatology. *Publications:* 13 books; 300 scientific publications. *Honours:* Innitzer Award, 1968; Renner Award, 1968, Hoechst Award, 1969. *Hobby:* Farming. *Address:* 3 Walfischgasse, A-1010 Vienna, Austria.

RABINOWITZ, Michael Jeffrey, b. 30 Sep. 1945, Boston, Massachusetts, USA. President, Healthcare Dynamics Incorporated. m. Kathleen Coulman, 13 Mar. 1971, Dothan, Alabama, 2 daughters. *Education:* BA, Middlebury College; MBA, New York University. *Appointments:* Assistant Chief, Facilities Division, USAMC, Europe; Senior Health Planner, Office of State Health Planning, Massachusetts DPH; Manager, Healthcare Industries Division, Laventhol and Horwath; President, Health Care Dynamics Incorporated. *Memberships:* American Association of Healthcare Consultants; American Association of Medical Administrators; American Hospital Association; American Management Association; American Marketing Association. *Publications:* Practice Profile, Product-Line Differentiation and Customer Targeting: A Road Out of the Tar Pits?, Advances in Health Care Research, Brigham Young University, 1985; Energy Executive See Swing Towards Private Sector, Health Facilities Energy Report, 1985; One and Five-Year Plan for Hospitals in Massachusetts, DPH, 1977; Guidelines for the Appropriate Utilization and Distribution of CT Scanners in Massachusetts, DPH, 1977; The National Guidelines of Health, DPH, 1977; Tertiary Care Planning in Massachusetts, DPH, 1977 and contributions to professional journals, etc.*Honours:* Pforzheimer Foundation Fellow, 1969-70; Harvard University Associate Professor, 1982. *Hobbies:* Travel; Golf. *Address:* 4 Maddison Lane, Lynnfield, MA 01940, USA.

RABSON, Arthur Ronald, b. 31 Aug. 1940, Johannesburg. Republic of South Africa, Professor, Head of Department. m. Valerie Berelowitz, 5 Jan. 1965, Cape Town, 1 son, 1 daughter. *Education:* MB, BCh, Witwatersrand, RSA, 1962; DCP, London, England, 1969; DPath, Royal College Physicians and Surgeons, 1969; MRCPath, Royal College Pathologists, 1978. *Appointments:* Pathologist, South African Institute for Medical Research, 1969-76; Professor of Immunology, SAIMR, 1976-. *Memberships:* British Immunological Society; American Association of Immunologists; Royal College of Pathologists. *Publications:* Author of 75 major works. *Hobby:* Growing cacti and succulents. *Address:* South African Institute for Medical Research, PO Box 1038, Johannesburg, Republic of South Africa.

RABY, Justin Bernard, b. 25 Nov. 1932, Murrumburrah, New South Wales, Australia. Director of Microbiology, ACT Health Authority Laboratories, Canberra. m. Beverley Anne Brady, 28 Dec. 1957, Sydney, 4 sons, 2 daughters. *Education:* BSc (Med); MB, BS; FRCPA; MASM. *Appointments:* RMO Trainee Pathologist, 1958-65, Director of Microbiology, 1970-75, St Vincent's Hospital, Sydney; Assistant Director, National Biological Standards Laboratory, Canberra, 1965-70. *Memberships:* Royal Australasian College of Pathologists; Australian Society for Microbiology. *Hobbies:* Fishing; Gardening. *Address:* 49 Arndell Street, Macquarie, ACT 2614, Australia.

RACHMILEWITZ, Eliezer Akiva, b. 23 Mar. 1935, Jerusalem, Israel. Head, Haematology. m. Bracha Rachmilewitz, 2 sons, 1 daughter. *Education:* MD, 1961. *Appointments:* Residency: Internal Medicine, B Hadassah University Hospital, 1961-64, Haematology & Internal Medicine, 1964-66; Haematology Dept, Tufts University, Boston, USA, 1966-67; Lecturer, Internal Medicine, 1966; Research Fellow, Albert Einstein Medical School, New York, USA, 1967-68; Chief Physician, Haematology, 1970, Senior Lecturer, 1970, Associate Professor, 1974, Internal Medicine, Acting Head, Haematology Service, University Hospital, 1976, Head, Haematology Service, 1978, Professor, Medicine, 1978, Head, Haematology, Hadassah Medical Organization, Hadassah Medical School. *Memberships:* Israeli Medical Association; Israeli Society of Haematology; International Society of Haematology; American Society of Haematology; International Society of Experimental Haematology; Honorary Member, Burmese Medical Association; Chairman, Prize Committee, 1983; Chairman, Admission Committee, 1980-84, Chairman, Teaching Division, Internal Medicine, 1983-; Hebrew University Hadassah Medical School. *Hobby:* Tennis. *Address:* Department of Haematology, Hadassah University Hospital Jerusalem, Israel.

RÁCZ, István, b. 14 Apr. 1924, Budapest, Hungary. Professor, Director of Clinic of Dermatology of State Institute of Dermatovenerology. m. Agnes Szebehelyi, 27 Dec. 1968, Budapest, 2 daughters. *Education:* MD, Pazmany Peter University Budapest, Speciality Dermato-venerology and cosmetology, Budapest; CSci. *Appointments:* Assistant, University Clinic of Dermatology; Medical Officer, Military Hospital, Budapest; Director of Dermato-Venerologic Dispensaries; Associate Professor, University Clinic of Dermatology. *Memberships:* President, College of State Institute for Dermato-Venerology; President, Hungarian Society of Dermatology; Vice-President, Hungarian Society of Allergology and Clinical Immunology; Honorary Member of Austrian, German, Bulgarian, North American Clinical, Polish and Yugoslavian Dermatological Societies. *Hobbies:* Archaeology; Collecting Records; Gardening. *Address:* Pasaréti ut 153/a, H-1026, Budapest, Hungary.

RADDSEVICH, Michael Scott, b. 21 Nov. 1950, Elyria, Ohio, USA. Private Chiropractic Practitioner. m. Terri Jean Lance, 17 Mar. 1973, 1 daughter. *Education:* BS, University of Akron, 1973; DC, National College of Chiropractic, 1978; 108 hours of post-graduate clinical education. *Memberships:* American Chiropractic Association; Ohio State Chiropractic Association; North Eastern Ohio Academy of Chiropractic. *Honour:* Dr Wayland McLane Memorial for Outstanding Fraternal Award, 1978. *Hobbies:* Fishing; Sailing; Skeet Shooting; Cross-country Skiing. *Address:* 304 E Broad Street, Elyria, OH 44035, USA.

RADEMEYER, Adrian Werendly Roux, b. 29 June 1939, Bulawayo, Zimbabwe (Rhodesia). General Dental Practitioner. m. Patricia Edmund Nightingale, 23 May 1964, London, England, 1 son, 2 daughters. *Education:* BChD (Pret).*Appointments:* General Dental Practice, 1962-77; Senior Lecturer, Department of Restorative Dentistry, University of Stellenbosch, Republic of South Africa, 1977-83; General Dental Practice, 1983-. *Memberships:* Dental Association of South Africa; South African Division of IADR; IOFOS; Federal Council of Dental Association of South Africa; President, Cape Western Branch (1984-85), DASA. *Hobbies:* Painting (Watercolours); Hiking; Gardening. *Address:* 24 Grove Avenue, Claremont, 7700 Cape Town, Republic of South Africa.

RADFORD, Dorothy Jane, b. 10 Jan. 1943, Nambour, Australia. Cardiologist. *Education:* MB, BS, University of Queensland, Australia; MRCP (UK); FRACP; DDU. *Appointments:* Resident Medical Officer, Medical Registrar, Princess Alexandra Hospital, Brisbane, Australia; Medical Registrar, Prince Charles Hospital, Brisbane; Senior House Officer, National Heart Hospital, London, England; Registrar in Cardiology and Medicine, Royal Infirmary, Edinburgh, Scotland; Cardiology Fellow, Hospital for Sick Children, Toronto, Canada, Staff Cardiologist, Assistant Professor of Paediatrics; Cardiologist, Paediatric and Adult, The Prince Charles Hospital, Brisbane, Australia. *Memberships:* Cardiac Society of Australia and New Zealand; Australian College of Paediatrics. *Publications:* 'Oral Contraceptives and Myocardial Infarction' in 'British Medical Journal', 1973; 'The Sick Sinus Syndrome' in 'British Medical Journal', 1974; 'Echocardiac Assessment of Bicupsid Aortic Valves' in 'Circulation', 1976; 'Atrial Fibrillation in Children' in 'Paediatrics', 1976; 'Evaluation of Ventricular Arrhythmias in Children' in 'Arch Dis Choldhood', 1977; 'Truncus Arteriosus and Facial Dysmorphism' in 'Australian Paediatric Journal', 1985; 'Diagnosis and Natural History of Ebstein's Anomaly' in 'British Heart Journal', 1985. *Hobbies:* Windsurfing; Walking. *Address:* The Prince Charles Hospital, Chermside 4032, Brisbane, Australia.

RADIC, Alicja, b. 19 July 1933, Poland. Senior Researcher, Epidemiology. m. Drago, 12 Dec. 1959, Dublin, Ireland, 2 sons, 1 daughter. *Education:* BA, 1957, MB, BCh, BAO, 1959, MA, 1962, Trinity College, Dublin. *Appointments:* Houseman, Senior Houseman, Royal City of Dublin Hospital; Project Supervisor, WHO Collaborative Study on Heart Attacks, Medico-Social Research Board; Project Supervisor, WHO Collaborator Study on Strokes, Medico-Social Research Board, Registry Leader, EEC Concerted Action Project on Registration of Congenital Malformation (EUROCAT). *Memberships:* Fellow, Faculty of Community Medicine, Royal College of Physicians of Ireland; Council on Epidemiology and Prevention; International Society and Federation of Cardiology; Associate Member, Faculty of Homeopathy, London. *Publications:* "Incidence of Heart Attacks in Dublin", 1974; "Incidence of Strokes in Dublin", 1977; "Functional Recovery after Stroke", 1979; "Post Neonatal Mortality in Dublin", 1983; "Surveillance of Congenital Malformation in Dublin", 1985. *Hobbies:* Stamp Collecting; Reading; Gardening; Travel. *Address:* 12 Taney Avenue, Dublin 14, Republic of Ireland.

RADZIKOWSKI, Czeslaw Marian, b. 17 July 1929, Bydgoszcz, Poland. Professor, Head of Department of Tumor Immunology. m. Jytte Topp, 21 Sep. 1969, 1 son, 1 daughter. *Education:* MD, Medical Faculty Gdansk, 1959; PhD, Polish Academy of Sciences, Institute of Immunology and Experimental Therapy, Wroclaw, 1965; Professor, 1972; Fulbright Fellowship for post-doctoral studies at National Cancer Institute, NIH, Bethesda, USA, 1962-63. *Appointments:* Department of Morbid Anatomy, Medical Academy, Gdansk, 1951-65; Department of Drug Technology and Chemistry, Polytechnic University, Gdansk, 1960-68; Head, Department of Tumor Immunology, Institute of Immunology and Experimental Therapy, Wroclaw, 1968; Member, Coordination Committee responsible for research projects in tumor immunology and subcommittee for research projects in experimental cancer chemotherapy-pre-clinical level. *Memberships:* Scientific Board, Institute of Immunology and Experimental Therapy, Wroclaw; Institute of Haematology, Warsaw; Institute of Genetics, Poznan, etc. *Publications include:* 'The Cytostatic Drugs' chapter in "Experimental Methods in Drug Testing", 1981; "Research on Cytostatic Drugs in Poland" (monograph), in press; 'Current Problems in Tumor Immunology' chapter in "Progess in Immunology" (in Polish), 1984. *Honours:* From Ministry of Health and Social Welfare, 1959, 81; From Secretary of Polish Academy of Sciences, 1972, 79; Golden Cross of Merit, 1979. *Hobbies:* Theatre; Mountain Climbing; Swimming; Cross-country Skiing. *Address:* Zaporoskastr 26/35, 53-520, Wroclaw, Poland.

RAE-GRANT, Quentin Alexander F, b. 5 Apr. 1929, Aberdeen, Scotland. Professor and Chairman, Department of Behavioral Science; Professor and Head, Division of Child Psychiatry, University of Toronto; Psychiatrist-in-Chief, The Hospital for Sick Children, Toronto. m. Naomi, 7 Sep. 1955, 2 sons. *Education:* Robert Gordon's College, Aberdeen, 1940-46; MB, ChB (Hons), University of Aberdeen School of Medicine, 1951; Diploma, Psychological Medicine, University of London, 1958; Certification in Psychiatry, Royal College of Physicians and Surgeons of Canada, 1969; FRCP (C), 1973. *Appointments:* Director of Child Psychiatry, Jewish Hospital, St Louis, 1958-60; Assistant Director, Child Psychiatry, Johns Hopkins Hospital, 1960-62; Director, Mental Health, St Louis County, 1962-64; Director, Social Psychiatry, 1965; Director, Mental Health Study Centre, National Institute of Mental Health, 1966-68; Psychiatrist-in-Chief, The Hospital for Sick Children, 1968; Professor and Vice-Chairman, Department of Psychiatry, University of Toronto, 1971; Consultant: Clarke Institute of Psychiatry, St Michael's Hospital, Family Court Clinic, Thistletown Regional Centre; Consultant, Addiction Research Foundation, 1982. *Memberships:* Canadian Psychiatric Association, Chairman, Board of Directors, Past-President and Member; Canadian Academy of Child Psychiatry, President; American Psychiatric Association; Ontario Psychiatric Association, Past-President and Member; Life Member, American Orthopsychiatric Association, etc. *Publications:* Contributor to professional journals; Book Reviews; Presidentations; Books and Chapters in Books including: 'Childhood and Adolescent Disorders' in "A Method of Psychiatry", 1980; Co-editor, "Psychological Problems of the Child in his Family", 1st Edition, 1977, 2nd Edition, 1982. *Honours:* Sheppherd Gold Medal in Surgery, University of Aberdeen, Ogston Prize in Surgery, Wyllie Prize in Mental Disorders, 1946-51. *Hobbies:* Sailing; Cross Country Skiing. *Address:* The Hospital for Sick Children, 555 University Avenue, Toronto, Ontario M5G 1X8, Canada.

RAEKALLIO, Jyrki, b. 27 Mar. 1929, Raahe, Finland. Professor and Head, Department of Forensic Medicine, University of Turku, Finland. m. Eeva Mustakallio, 12 Dec. 1953, 2 sons, 1 daughter. *Education:* MD, 1954; ScD, 1961; University of Helsinki; Postgraduate studies: Medizinische Akademie, Dusseldorf, 1958-59; Fulbright Fellow, Johns Hopkins University, Baltimore, Maryland, USA, 1963. *Appointments:* Junior Forensic Pathologist, 1956-61; Senior Lecturer, Forensic Medicine, University of Helsinki, 1962; Associate Professor, 1962; Professor and Head, Department of Forensic Medicine, 1963-; Dean of Medical Faculty, 1969-70, University of Turku, Finland; Scientific Councillor, Finnish National Board of Health, 1962-. *Memberships:* Hon Member, Italian Society of Legal Medicine; International Academy of Legal Medicine, Vice-President, 1970-73; Corresponding Member: American Academy of Forensic Sciences and Deutsche Gesellschaft fur Rechtsmedizin; Fellow: Royal Microscopical Society, Oxford, England; Histochemical Society, USA; INFORM, Vice-President for Finland; Representative of Finland, Collegium Europaeum for the Evaluation of Injuries. *Publications include:* Histochemical Studies on Vital and Postmortem Skin Wounds, 1961; Enzyme Histochemistry of Wound Healing, 1970; Oikeuslaaketiede (Finnish textbook of Forensic Medicine, Editor-in-Chief), 1981; Editor, Medicolegal Postmortems, 1985. *Honours:* Thomasius Plakette, University of Halle, 1978; Honorary Diplomat, INFORM, 1979. *Hobbies:* Amnesty International; Medical Ethics; Travelling. *Address:* Department of Forensic Medicine, University of Turku Kiinamyllynkatu 10, 20520 Turku 52, Finland.

RAFAELSEN, Ole Jørgen, b. 13 Apr. 1930, Denmark. Head of Department of Psychiatry, Rigshospitalet, Copenhagen; Director, Psychochemistry Institute, Copenhagen University. m. Lise Hylén, 22 May 1963, 1 son, 1 daughter. *Education:* MD, University of Copenhagen, Denmark, 1953; Doctorate Thesis, University of Aarhus, 1961. *Appointments:* Intern, Kolding Hospital, Denmark, 1953-54; Resident in Psychiatry, Aarhus University, 1956-60; Research Fellow, Harvard University, USA, 1961-62; Resident in Internal Medicine, Glostrup Hospital, Denmark, 1962-65;

Head, Psychochemistry Institute, University Hospital, Rigshospitalet, Copenhagen, 1965-; Professor, Biol. Psychiatry and Head of Department of Psychiatry, 1972-; Head, two WHO national reference centres. *Memberships:* CINP, President, 1984-86; AAAS; American College of Neuropsychopharmacology; American Psychiatric Association. *Publications:* Psychotherapeutic Drugs: An Ultra-short Practice (several translations), 1979; Depression/Melancholia/Mania: A Book for Patients and their Relatives (several translations), 1981. *Address:* Department of Psychiatry, Rigshospitalet, 9 Blegdamsvej, DK-2100 Copenhagen 0, Denmark.

RAFF, Moses Jacob, b. 1 Dec. 1900, Montreal, Canada. Retired Medical Practitioner. m. Sylvia Schwartz, 26 Sep. 1929, Montreal, Canada, 1 daughter. *Education:* MD, CM McGill University, Canada, 1923. *Appointment:* Chief Resident Intern, Troy General Hospital, New York, USA, 1924. *Memberships:* Association of Medical Groups from America in Vienna; Quebec Association of Laryngologists. *Honours:* Honorary Diploma from Jewish General Hospital, Montreal, Canada; Gold key from the College in Vienna, Austria for three years; Post Graduate Studies in Laryngology. *Hobbies:* Painting; Art Collecting. *Address:* 3720 The Boulevard, Westmount, Quebec, Canada.

RAHAMAN, Mohammad Mujibur, b. 3 Dec. 1936, Rangpur, Bangladesh. Associate Director and Senior Scientist, International Centre for Diarrhoeal Disease Research, Bangladesh. m. Marzina Begum, 23 Apr. 1955, Rangpur, 1 son, 3 daughters. *Education:* MB BS, Dhaka Medical College, 1959; MSc, Nutrition, Columbia University, New York, USA, 1962; PhD, Medicine, University of Glasgow, Scotland, 1966. *Appointments:* Housemanship, Dhaka Medical College, 1960; Research Fellow, Pakistan Council of Scientific and Industrial Research, Central Laboratories, Karachi, 1961; Fellowship of National Institutes of Health at Institute of Human Nutrition, Columbia University, New York, USA, 1961-62; Visiting Fellow in Nutrition, American University in Beirut, Lebanon, 1962; Research Associate, Institute of Physiology, University of Glasgow, Scotland, 1963-66; Clinical Investigator, Head of Clinical Division, Acting Director, Cholera Research Laboratory, Dhaka, Bangladesh, 1967-78; Associate Director and Senior Scientist, International Centre for Diarrhoeal Disease Research, Bangladesh, 1978-. *Memberships:* Bangladesh Medical Association; Bangladesh Nutrition Society; International Union of Nutrition Sciences; British Nutrition Society. *Publications:* Over 50 scientific papers; Editor, three proceedings of international conferences, 1965-85. *Honours:* Director of Health Services Scholarship, 1955; District Board (Rangpur) Scholarship, 1957. *Hobby:* Photography. *Address:* 30 D Banani Model Town, Road 10, Dhaka-13, Bangladesh.

RAINE, George Edward Thompson, b. 1 Aug. 1934, Corbridge, England. Consultant Orthopaedic Surgeon. m. Ena Josephine Noble, 11 June 1960, Longstowe, Cambridgeshire, 1 daughter. *Education:* MA Natural Sciences Tripos, Emmanuel College, Cambridge, 1955; MB, BChir (Cantab), Saint Thomas' Hospital Medical School, 1958. *Appointments:* Chairman, Division of Surgery, Senior Consultant Orthopaedic Surgeon, West Middlesex University Hospital; Associate Surgeon, Royal Masonic Hospital, London; Medical Adviser, Ballet Rambert School, various Sports Clubs. *Memberships:* Fellow, Royal College of Surgeons; Fellow, British Orthopaedic Association; Member of Council, Back Pain Association; Examiner, Chartered Society of Physiotherapists. *Publications:* Papers and reviews on various orthopaedic subjects. *Honours:* Lord Riddell Surgical Scholarship, 1957; Bhatia Medallist, 1959. *Hobby:* Travel. *Address:* 144 Harley Street, London W1N 1AH, England.

RAISMAN, Geoffrey, b. 28 June 1939, Leeds, England.

Head of Laboratory of Neurobiology and Development. *Education:* BA, 1960; MA, DPhil, 1964; BM; BCh, 1965; DM, 1974. *Appointments:* University Lecturer, Oxford, England, 1966-74; Medical Tutor, Oriel College, Oxford, 1970-74; Harvard Research Fellow, 1968-69. *Publications:* 'Neuronal Plasticity' in 'Brain Research', 1969; 'Sexual Dimorphism' in 'Brain Research', 1973. *Honour:* Wakeman Award for Research in Neurosciences, 1980. *Hobbies:* Languages; History. *Address:* National Institute for Medical Research, Mill Hill, London, NW7 1AA, England.

RAKOFF, Vivian Morris, b. 28 Apr. 1928, Cape Town, South Africa. Professor, Chairman, Psychiatry, University of Toronto, Canada; Director, Psychiatrist-in-Chief, Clarke Institute of Psychiatry. m. Gina Shochat, 29 Nov., 1959, Cape Town, 2 sons, 1 daughter. *Education:* MA; MB.BS; MRCS; LRCP; D.Psych (McGill); FRCP (C); FAPA; FACP. *Appointments:* Director, Research, Psychiatry, Jewish General Hospital, Montreal, Canada, 1967; Associate Professor, Psychiatry, 1968-71, Professor, Director, Postgraduate Education, 1971-74, Professor, Psychiatric Education, 1974, University of Toronto; Co-Ordinator, Education, Clarke Institute, Toronto, 1977-78; Psychiatrist-in-Chief, Psychiatry, Sunnybrook Medical Centre, Toronto, 1978-80. *Memberships:* Canadian Medical and Psychiatric Associations; Canadian Association of Professors of Psychiatry; American Psychiatric Association; American College of Psychiatrists; etc. *Publications:* Contributor, "Dictionary of Psychiatry"; Chapters in "A Method of Psychiatry", 2nd edition; articles in professional journals. *Hobbies:* Writing; Painting. *Address:* Clarke Institute of Psychiatry, 250 College Street, Toronto, Ontario, Canada M5T 1R8.

RAMAN, Leela, b. 15 Nov. 1939, Khandwa. Deputy Director. m. B V Raman, 6 Nov. 1974, 1 son, 1 daughter. *Education:* MBBS, 1960, MD, 1964, Nagpur University. *Appointments:* Assistant Director, 1974-77, Deputy Director, 1977-, National Institute of Nutrition, Hyderabad. *Memberships:* Nutrition Society of India; India Women Scientists Association; International Society for Study in Hypertension in Pregnancy. *Publications:* Cahpters: "Anaemia in Pregnancy", 'Post Graduate Obstetrics & Gynaecology', 1982; "Nutrition in Pregnancy", 1982; "Nutrition in Pregnancy in 'Material & Child Health Around the World", 1981. *Honours:* Palwandhar Prize, for Work on Anaemia in Pregnancy, 1976. *Hobbies:* Music; Photography. *Address:* National Institute of Nutrition, Jamai Osmania, Hyderabad, 500007 AP, India.

RAND, Robert Wheeler, b. 28 Jan. 1923, Los Angeles, California, USA. Professor of Neurosurgery. m. Helen Pierce Rand, 17 Dec. 1949, New Jersey, USA, 2 sons. *Education:* MD, University of Southern California, 1947; MS, 1951, PhD, 1952, University of Michigan; JD, University of West Los Angeles, 1974. *Appointments include:* Instructor in Surgery, University of Michigan, 1950-52; Instructor in Surgery, Neurological, 1953-56, Assistant Professor of Neurosurgery, 1956-61, Associate Professor of Neurosurgery, 1961-68, Professor of Neurosurgery, 1968-, University of California at Los Angeles; Attending Neurosurgeon, Wadsworth VA Hospital, 1953-. *Memberships include:* American Medical Association; Californian Medical Association; American College of Surgeons; International College of Surgeons; American Surgical Association; American Association of Neurological Surgeons; Society of Neurological Surgeons; Western Neurosurgical Society; Southern California Neurosurgical Society; Frederick A Coller Surgical Society; Bay Surgical Society; International Surgical Society; Society of Surgical Oncology; Bioelectromagnetic Society; Pan Pacific Surgical Association; Society for Neurovascular Surgery; Laser Association of Neurological Surgeons International. *Publications include:* "Microneurosurgery", 1969, 3rd Edition, 1985; "Intraspinal Tumors in Childhood", 1960; "Microsurgical Neuroanatomy Atlas", 1967; "Cryosurgery", 1968; 'Hypothermis anaesthesia in the sitting position. Report of two cases of acoustic neurinoma', 1957; 'A new intervertebral spreader and special angled curettes for lumbar disc surgery', 1958; 'Further observations on Lissauer tractolysis', 1960; 'Spinal cord injuries', 1966; 'Hypophysectomy in endocrine disorders', 1970; 'Endocrine disorders', 1970; 'Surgery of acoustic tumor', 1970; 'Suboccipital transmeatal microneurosurgical resection of acoustic tumors', 1971; 'Microsurgical treatment for the ischemic cerebral vascular accident', 1980; 'Stereotactic Treatment of Pituitary Tumor', 1983. *Honours:* Recipient of numerous honours. *Address:* UCLA School of Medicine, NP1 17-382, 760 Westwood Plaza, Los Angeles, CA 90024, USA.

RANDERATH, Kurt, b. 2 Aug. 1929, Dusseldorf, Germany. Professor, Pharmacology, Baylor College of Medicine. m. Erika Ehrhardt, 19 Dec. 1962. *Education:* MD, 1955, Dipl.Chem., 1959, University of Heidelberg. *Appointments:* Assistant Professor, Harvard Medical School, 1968; Associate Professor, 1971, Professor, 1974, Baylor College of Medicine, USA. *Memberships:* American Chemical Society; American Association for the Advancement of Science; American Association Cancer Research; American Society Biological Chemists. *Publications:* 130 articles in scientific journals; (Book) "Thin-Layer Chromatography", 2nd edition 1966. *Honours:* US National Institute of Health Research Career Development Award, 1968-71; American Cancer Society Faculty Research Award, 1972-77. *Hobbies:* Music; Literature. *Address:* Dept. of Pharmacology, Baylor College of Medicine, Houston, TX 77030, USA.

RANDLE, (Sir) Philip (John), b. 16 July 1926, Nuneaton, England. Professor of Clinical Biochemistry, Oxford University. m. Elizabeth Ann Harrison, 27 Sep. 1952, 3 daughters. *Education:* MA; PhD; MD; FRCP, 1964; FRS, 1983; Sidney Sussex College, Cambridge; University College Hospital Medical School. *Appointments:* Research Fellow, Sidney Sussex College, Cambridge, 1954-57; Lecturer in Biochemistry, Cambridge, 1955-64; Fellow and Director, Medical Studies, Trinity Hall, 1957-64; Professor and Head of Department of Biochemistry, University of Bristol, 1964-75. *Memberships:* Biochemical Society; Society for Endocrinology. *Honours:* Banting Lecturer, British Diabetic Association, 1965; Minkowski Prize, European Association for Study of Diabetes, 1966; Copp Lecture, La Jolla, 1972; Humphry Davy Rolleston Lecture, Royal College of Physicians, London, 1983; CIBA Medal, Biochemical Society, 1984; Knight Bachelor, 1985. *Hobbies:* Travel; Books; Swimming. *Address:* Department of Clinical Biochemistry, John Radcliffe Hospital, Oxford, OX3 9DU, England.

RAPHAEL, Paul Stephen, b. 26 June 1939, New York City, USA. Physiatrist. m. Ann, 30 Jan. 1972, Philadelphia, USA, 2 sons. *Education:* AB, Cornell University, New York, USA, 1961; MD, University of Bologna Medical School, Italy, 1969. *Appointments:* Director, Department PM&R, Sacred Heart Hospital, Allentown, Pennsylvania, USA, 1978-; Attending Physiatrist, Good Shepherd Rehabilitation Hospital, Allentown, Pennsylvania, 1979-. *Memberships:* LeHigh County Medical Society; Pennsylvania Medical Society; American Medical Association; American Congress of Rehabilitation Medicine; American Academy of Phys Med and Rehab; American Association of Electromyography and Electrodiagnosis; Pennsylvania Academy of Phys Med and Rehab; American Geriatrics Society; International Rehabilitation Medicine Association; American Society for Clinical Evoked Potentials; Philadelphia Society of Phys Med and Rehab; Vice President and President Elect, Pennsylvania Academy PM&R, 1985-; Secretary and Treasurer, 1983-85. *Hobbies:* Hiking; Tennis; Swimming. *Address:* Department PM&R, Sacred Heart Hospital, 421 Chew Street, Allentown, PA 18102, USA.

RAPP, Fred, b. 13 Mar. 1929, Fulda, Germany. University Professor and Chairman of Microbiology Department. *Education:* BS, Brooklyn College, New York,

USA, 1951; MS, Albany Medical College, Union University, USA 1956; PhD, University of Southern California, 1958. *Appointments:* Junior Bacteriologist, New York State Department of Health, 1952-55; Teaching Assistant to Instructor, University of Southern California, 1956-59; Consulting Supervisory Microbiologist and Virologist, Hospital of Special Surgery, New York City, 1959-62; Assistant Professor, Department of Microbiology and Immunology, Cornell University Medical College, New York, 1961-62; Associate Professor, Virology and Epidemiology, Baylor College of Medicine, Houston, Texas, 1962-66, Professor, 1966-69; Professor and Chairman, Microbiology, College of Medicine, Pennsylvania State University, Hershey, Pennsylvania, 1969-. *Memberships:* Sigma XI; American Society for Microbiology; American Society for the Advancement of Science; American Association for Immunologists; Harvey Society; Society for Experimental Biology and Medicine; American Association for Cancer Research; The Royal Society of Medicine; Society for General Microbiology; The American Society for Virology; American Association of University Professors. *Publications:* 320, from 1955-85; Book Chapters - 105 from 1960-85; Editor of 6 books from 1969-85. *Honours:* American Cancer Society Professor of Virology, 1966-69, 1977; Ciba-Geigy Drew Award for Biomedical Research, 1977. *Hobby:* Sailing. *Address:* 2 Laurel Ridge Road, Hershey, PA 17033, USA.

RAPPAPORT, Richard Gerald, b. 10 Aug. 1936, Philadelphia, Pennsylvania, USA. Psychiatrist (private practice). m. Nancy Rappaport, 6 July 1969, Louisville, Kentucky, 1 son, 2 daughters. *Education:* BA, University of Pennsylvania, 1958; MD, Chicago Medical School, 1963. *Appointments:* Consultant, Illinois Department of Correction (Group therapy in prison), 1967-72, House of Good Shepherd (Home for delinquent girls), 1970-73, Jewish Federation Drug Response Committee, 1970-74; American Psychiatric Association Representative to American College of Sports Medcine 1984, President's Council on Physical Fitness & Sports 1984. *Memberships:* American Psychiatric Association; American Academy of Psychiatry & Law; Illinois Psychiatric Society; American College of Sports Medicine. *Publications:* "Follow-up of Therapeutic Abortion' (in Archives of General Psychiatry) 1969; 'Group Therapy in Prison' (in International Journal of Group Therapy) 1971; 'Crisis in Confidentiality, Ethics & Legality for a Psychiatrist', 1977, 'The Psychiatrist on Trial', 1979 (both in Journal of Psychiatry & Law); 'Group Therapy in Prison - a Strategic Approacj' (chapter in book on group counselling by Seligmann) 1977. *Honours:* 1st Prize, Michael Reese Medical Research Institute Council Award, 1968, 1969 (twice); Michael Reese Hospital Residents' Prize, 1968, 1969; Illinois Psychiatric Society Research Prize, 1969, 1970; American Medical Association Physicians Recognition Award, 1978. *Hobbies:* Sport; Photography. *Address:* 1990 St John's (200), Highland Park, IL 60035, USA.

RAPPOPORT, William Joseph, b. 28 Aug. 1932, Baltimore, Maryland, USA. Cardiologist. m. Tula Challas, 11 Feb. 1973, Phoenix, Arizona, 2 sons, 1 daughter. *Education:* BA, Johns Hopkins University, Baltimore, 1953; MD, University of Maryland School of Medicine, 1957; Internship, 1957-58, Resident, 1958-59, Sinai Hospital of Baltimore; Resident, University of Colorado Medical Centre, 1959-60; Specialist Cardiovascular training as Fellow, University of Colorado, 1960-62. *Appointments:* Lieutenant-Commander, US Armed Forces, 1962-64; Cardiovascular practice, Denver, Colorado, 1964-72, Phoenix, 1972-84, own practice, Phoenix, 1984-; Teaching Appointments, Maricopa County Hospital, Phoenix, 1962-64, Clinical Instructor in Medicine, University of Colorado Medical Centre, 1964-70, Assistant Clinical Professor of Medicine, University of Colorado, 1970-72; Cardiovascular Training of Residents in Internal Medicine, St Joseph's Hospital, Denver, 1964-72, Cardiology Training of Family Practice Residents, Phoenix Baptist Hospital & Medical Centre, Phoenix, 1979-. *Member-*

ships: Alpha Omega Alpha; American Medical Association; Fellow, American College of Cardiology; Fellow, American College of Chest Physicians; American Heart Association; Arizona, Colorado, Denver Medical Societies. *Publications:* Various articles on cardiovascular surgery. *Address:* 6036 North 19th Avenue Suite 506, Phoenix, AR 85015, USA.

RASK, Michael Raymond, b. 24 Oct. 1930, Butte, Montana, USA. Professor of Orthopaedic Surgery. m. Elizabeth Ann Shannon-Rask, 21 Mar. 1984, Las Vegas, Nevada, 2 sons, 2 daughters. *Education:* BS, Oregon State College, 1951; MD, University of Oregon Medical School, 1955; PhD, American Academy of Neurological & Orthopaedic Surgery, 1979; PhD, University for Humanistic Studies, 1985; Resident, Orthopaedic Surgery, University of Oregon Medical School, 1959-63. *Appointments:* Clinical Instructor in Orthopaedics, University of Oregon Medical School, 1964-71; Neurological & Orthopaedic Surgeon, New York, 1971-76; Private Practice, Neurological & Orthopaedic Surgery, Las Vegas, Nevada, 1976-. *Memberships:* American Medical Association, 1958-76; American Academy of Neurological & Orthopaedic Surgeons, 1977-; American Federation for Medical Accreditation, 1978-; Neurological & Orthopaedic Institute, 1978-; Institute for Bloodless Medicine & Surgery, 1982-; American Academy for Medical Specialists, 1982-; American Back Society, 1982-; American Academy for Sports Physicians, 1985-. *Publications:* Over 300 articles, papers & books in field. *Honours:* Honorary Member, Cuban Medical Society; Nevada State Pharmaceutical Society; Editor-in-Chief, 'Journal of Neurological & Orthopaedic Medicine & Surgery'; Editor, 'Journal of Bloodless Medicine & Surgery'. *Hobbies:* Editorial Reviewer; Medical Writing; Oil-painting; Production of Musical Phonograph records (owner of Pianissimo Record Company). *Address:* 2320 Rancho Drive, Suite 108, Las Vegas, NV 89102-4592, USA.

RASMUSSEN, Knut, b. 27 July 1938, Oslo, Norway. Professor of Cardiology. m. Sigrun Aarbakke, 26 June 1961, 1 son, 2 daughters. *Education:* MD, Bergen University, 1962; Dr Med, Oslo, 1976. *Appointments:* Fellowship, Residency, Medical Department B, Rikshospitalet, Oslo, Norway, 1965-69, University Lecturer, 1970-71, Research Fellow, 1971-73; Professor of Internal Medicine, University Hospital of Tromsø) Head, Section of Cardiology, 1974-; Visiting Professor, Stanford Medical Centre Division of Cardiology, USA, 1980-81. *Membership:* European Society of Cardiology. *Publications:* 60 papers in international journals on clinical cardiology. *Hobbies:* Outdoor sports - skiing, mountaineering, etc; Literature. *Address:* Department of Internal Medicine, Section of Cardiology, University Hospital of Tromsø) Norway.

RASTOGI, Indra, b. 20 June 1938, India. Consultant Obstetrician-Gynaecologist. m. Dr Hirsch Rastogi, 11 Dec. 1963, Lucknow, 1 son, 1 daughter. *Education:* MD, OBS.GYN, Lucknow, 1963; FRCS (C), OBS.GYN, Canada, 1967; FACOG. OBS.GYN, America. *Appointments:* Active Staff, St Joseph's Hospital, Hamilton, Ontario, Canada, 1968-; Consultant, Planned Parenthood Clinic, Hamilton, 1968-81; Consultant, Obstetrics, Gynaecology, Hamilton Civic Hospital, 1968-; Assistant Clinical Professor, Obstetrics, Gynaecology, McMaster University, Hamilton, 1973-. *Memberships:* Fellow, American College Obstetricians and Gynaecologists; Fellow, American Fertility Society; American Society for Colposcopy and Cervical Pathology; Society of Obstetricians and Gynaecologists of Canada; Hamilton Academy of Medicine; Niagara Society of Obstetricians and Gynaecologists; Hamilton Chapter, Federation of Women Physicians. *Hobbies:* Swimming; Music; Arts and Crafts; Outdoor Activities; Community Work. *Address:* 25 Charlton E 307, Hamilton, Ontario, Canada L8N 1Y2.

RATNER, Jerald, b. 15 Dec. 1944, Philadelphia, Pennsylvania, USA. Psychiatrist. m. Eileen, 18 July 1982, Ft.

Lauderdale, 2 sons. *Education:* BA, Temple University, 1966; MD, Hahnemann Medical College, 1970; Internship, Bridgeport Hospital; Residency, Philadelphia Psychiatric Centre; Diplomate, American Board of Psychiatry & Neurology. *Appointments:* Private Practice, Psychiatry, 1975-; Vice Chairman, Psychiatry, Imperial Point Medical Centre. *Memberships:* Alpha Omega Alpha; American Psychiatric Association; Florida Medical Association; Broward County Medical Association. *Honours:* Diplomate, National Board of Medical Examiners, 1971; Diplomate, American Board of Psychiatry & Neurology, 1980. *Hobbies:* Music; Tropical Fish. *Address:* 9600 West Sample Road, Suite 500, Coral Springs, FL 33065, USA.

RATSEY, David Hugh Kerr, b. 7 June 1944, Birmingham, England. Consulting Homeopathic Physician. m. Christin Tutt-Harris, 6 Sep. 1969, Stourpaine, Dorset, 3 sons, 1 daughter. *Education:* MB, BS (London), 1967; MRCS, LRCP (UK), 1967; MFHom, 1980. *Appointments include:* Anaesthetist, London hospitals, 1969-75; General Practice, 1975-80; Consultant Homeopath, 1980-. *Memberships:* Faculty of Homeopathy; British Medical Association. *Honours:* Council, Faculty of Homeopathy, 1983-, Executive Committee, External Examiner, ibid, 1984-. *Hobby:* Sailing. *Address:* 18 Thurloe Street, South Kensington, London SW7 2SU, England.

RAUCH, Harry Ben, b. 29 May 1954, Tulsa, Oklahoma, USA. Staff Psychiatrist. m. Lenore G Rauch Greenberg, 23 June 1981, San Antonio, Texas, 1 daughter. *Education:* BS Pharmacy, Southwestern Oklahoma State University, 1977; MD, Oklahoma University, 1981; Residency in Psychiatry, Wilford Hall USAF Medical Center. *Appointments:* Pharmacist, 1977-78; Medical/Psychiatric Intern, 1981-82; Psychiatric Resident, 1982-85; Chief Psychiatric Resident, Administrative, 1984; Staff Psychiatrist, Chief of Inpatient and Consultant Psychiatrist, Clark Air Base, Philippines, 1985; Captain, US Air Force Medical Corps. *Memberships:* Bexar County Medical Society; Texas Medical Association; American Medical Association; American Psychiatric Association; American Society of Clinical Hypnosis. *Publication:* 'Competency Issues in Psychiatric Consultation'. *Hobbies:* Violin; Chess; Tae Kwon Di; Sailing; Scuba Diving; Computers; Local Gifted Children Coordinator and active member, MENSA. *Address:* Department of Mental Health, USAF Regional Medical Center Clark (PACAF), (Republic of the Philippines), APO San Francisco, CA 96274, USA.

RAUS, Jef C M, b. 12 Oct. 1940, Turnhout, Belgium. Director, Dr L Willems Instituut; Professor, Limburgs Universitair Centrum. m. Agnes M E L Vossen, 13 Aug., 1966, Hasselt, 3 sons, 1 daughter. *Education:* MD, Catholic University of Leuven, 1966; PhD, Pure Sciences, Columbia University, New York, USA, 1971. *Memberships:* American Society of Clinical Pathologists; World Federation of Neurology, Research Group of Multiple Sclerosis; Hoge Raad voor Anthropogenetica; Hoge Gezondheidsraad. *Publications:* "Cytotoxic Estrogens in Hormone Receptive Tumors", 1980; "Immunoregulatory Processes in Experimental Allergic Encephalomyelitis and Multiple Sclerosis", 'Res. Monographs in Immunology', Volume 7, 1984. *Hobbies:* Chess; Tennis; Cycling. *Address:* Reinpadstraat 170, B-3600 Genk, Belgium.

RAUSCHER, Gregory, b. 18 Sep. 1946, New Jersey, USA. Chairman, Plastic Surgery, University Medicine and Dentistry, New Jersey. m. Irene Boucher, 22 Aug. 1970, Maine, 2 sons. *Education:* BS, Fairchild University, Connecticut, 1968; MD, Downstate Medical Centre, Brooklyn, New York, 1972; Board Certified in general surgery; Board certified in plastic surgery; Diplomate, American College of Surgeons; FACS; FICS. *Appointments:* Instructor, Surgery, 1972-76, Instructor, Plastic Surgery, 1976-82, Downstate Medical Centre, Brooklyn New York; Director, Clinical Replantation, Hackensack Medical Centre, New Jersey, 1982-85; Assistant Professor Plastic Surgery, University Medicine and Dentistry, New Jersey, 1983-. *Memberships:* American Burn Association; Diplomate, American Society of Plastic Reconstructive Surgeons; American Society of Hand Surgery; NJ Society of Plastic Surgeons; NY Region, Society of Plastic Surgeons. *Publications:* 'Surgical treatment of fiber implanted scalps', (with V R DiGregario), 1981; 'Plastic Surgery of Head and Neck', 1986. *Hobbies:* Skiing; Windsurfing. *Address:* 321 Essex Street, Hackensack, NJ 07670, USA.

RAVEN, Clara, b. 9 Apr. 1907, Consultant Forensic Pathologist; Emeritus. *Education:* BA, University of Michigan; MS, BM, Northwestern University Medical School; MD Diplomate, American Board of Pathology. *Appointments:* Research Bacteriologist, University of Michigan, University of Chicago, Northwestern University Medical School, 1928-37; John W. Garrett, International Fellow, University of Liverpool, 1938-39; Teacher, Women's Medical College of Pennsylvania, 1941; Chief Laboratory Services, Scranton, PA General Hospital, 1941-43; US Army Medical Corps, WWII, France and Germany, 1943-45; Japan and Korea, Korean War, 1951-54; Captain to Colonel, Chief Laboratory Services, Veterans Adm. Hospital, Dayton, Ohio, 1948-51; Chief Laboratory Services, US General Army Hospitals, 1954-59, Armed Forces Institute of Pathology, Washington, DC; Deputy Chief Medical Examiner, Wayne County, Detroit, Michigan, 1959-73. *Memberships include:* American Society Pathology and Bacteriology; American Academy of Forensic Sciences; International Academy of Pathology; Association of Military Surgeons; National Association of Military Surgeons. *Publications:* "Japanese Textbook of Histopathology", (co-author), 1956, 2nd edition, 1980; 'Studies of the Gonococcus', 1934; 'Studies of the Leptospirosis', 1941-42; 'Water Analysis', 1940; 'Epidemic Hemorrhagic Fever', 1951-52; Pioneer, 'Studies of Crib Deaths' or the 'Sudden Infant Death Syndrome' or SIDS, 1959-85. *Honours:* WWII and Korean Service Ribbons; Alumnae Award for Exhibit on SIDS, ASCP, Chicago, 1962; Horizon Recognition for Exhibit SIDS, Bicentenary, 1976; Flag Award, Michigan Medical Society, 1982; Elizabeth Blackwell Medal, 1983; Fellow, American Writers Association (Medical). *Hobbies:* Sports; Travel; Gardening. *Address:* 1419 Nicolet Place, Detroit, MI 48207, USA.

RAVENTOS, Antolin, b. 3 June 1925, Wilmette, Illinois, USA. Professor of Radiology, University of California, Davis. m. Anne Patricia Gray, 23 July 1976, San Francisco. *Education:* SB 1945, MD 1947, University of Chicago; MSc, University of Pennsylvania, 1955. *Appointments include:* Assistant Professor to Professor, University of Pennsylvania, 1950-70; Professor 1970-, Chairman of Department 1970-77, University of California, Davis. *Memberships:* Fellow, Chancellor 1964-70, American College of Radiology; President 1974, American Radium Society; President, N California Chapter 1984-85, American Medical Writers Association; American Medical Association; American Society for Cancer Education; Radium Research Society; etc. *Publications include:* 89 scientific journal articles. *Address:* University of California Davis, 150 Muir Road 114B, Martinez, CA 94553, USA.

RAZZOLI DELLA MADDALENA VON ALLESTEIN, Guy, b. 25 Mar. 1925, Genoa, Italy. Associate Professor, Experimental Medicine, University La Timone. m. Paola C Gonella, 28 Mar. 1973, Monte Carlo, 4 sons, 2 daughters. *Education:* Specialist, Science of Nutrition, Paris, France, 1958, Modena, Italy, 1968; Specialist, Psychosomatics and Clinical Psychology, Milan, 1973; MD, University of Pavia, Italy. *Appointments:* Medical Assistant, Medical Service, Vatican City; Vice-Director, Clinic La Tour de Baousset of Mentone, France; Technical Manager, Biological Research Centre, Nice, France; Technical Manager, Institute for the Scientific Nutrition Spreading of Nice; Committee Member, Dietetique et Nutrition,

Paris; Human Nutrition Research Lab, Hôpital Bichart, Paris; Technical Adviser, Microalgae Research Lab of Bologna, Italy; Director, Centre de Medicine Psychosomatique, Cannes, France; Technical Advisor, Juridic International Association, Vienna, Austria; Technical Adviser, Radio TV Suisse for programmes on Nutrition. *Memberships include:* Italian and French Medical Associations; Association for Fighting against Obesity, Rome. *Publications:* "A New Proteic Source: Chlorella", 1966; "A Physician in a Kitchen - A Dietetic Guide", 1976; "An Alimentary Guide to Aesthetics", 1975; "Food Biochemistry", 1965; "The Italian Gourmet Diet", 1983; "Een Neuw Sportman Voeding", 1979. *Honours:* Borromini Prize for Dietetics, 1970; Accademia Teatina per le Scienze, 1971; Seville City Prize, 1972; Academia Gentium Pro Pace, 1976; Lacan Prize, 1983. *Hobbies include:* Music; Archaeology; Foreign Languages. *Address:* Chateau Amiral, 42 Boulevard d'Italie, MC 98000 Monte Carlo.

READER, George Gordon, b. 8 Feb. 1919, New York, New York, USA. Professor and Chairman of Department of Public Health. m. Helen Charlotte Brown, 23 May 1942, Rye, New York, 4 sons. *Education:* BA 1940, MD 1943, Cornell University; Certified, American Board of Internal Medicine, 1951. *Appointments:* Intern, Fellow, Assistant Resident Physician, 1944-47; Physician to OPD, Assistant, Associate, Attending Physician, The New York Hospital, 1947-56; Instructor, Assistant Professor, Associate and Full Professor of Medicine 1947-56, Livingston Farrand Professor of Public Health 1972-, Cornell University Medical College; Member Medical Board 1972-, Secretary 1985-, New York Hospital. *Memberships:* Fellow and Life Member, American College of Physicians; Fellow, American Public Health Association; Fellow, New York Academy of Medicine; American Sociological Association; International Sociological Association; International Epidemiological Association. *Publications:* "Comprehensive Medical Care and Teaching", (with Goss); "Welfare Medical Care", (with Goodrich and Olendzki); "Student Physician", (with Merton and Kendall). *Honour:* Elected Senior Member, Institute of Medicine of National Academy of Sciences, 1985. *Hobbies:* Gardening; Fishing; Travel. *Address:* 1300 York Avenue, New York, NY 10021, USA.

REARDON, Gerald Peter, b. 10 Feb. 1951, Halifax, Nova Scotia, Canada. m. Catherine Maclennan Moffatt, 1 May 1976, Sydney, Nova Scotia, 2 daughters. *Education:* MD 1974, Orthopaedic Surgery 1977-81, Dalhousie University. *Appointments:* Active Staff, Sydney City and St Rita's Hospitals, Sydney, Nova Scotia, 1975-77; Clinical Fellow, St Michael's Hospital, University of Toronto, 1981-82; Assistant Professor, Department of Surgery, Dalhousie University, 1985; Chief, Orthopaedic Surgery, Halifax Infirmary. *Memberships:* Canadian Orthopaedic Association; American Academy of Orthopaedic Surgeons. *Hobbies:* Sports; Philately. *Address:* 5595 Fenwick Street, Halifax, Nova Scotia, B3H 4M2, Canada.

REARDON, John V, b. 2 June 1936, Cork, Ireland. Director, Department of Radiology, The Valley Hospital; President, Radiology Association of Ridgewood, PA, USA. m. Frances P, MD, 29 July 1960, 1 daughter (deceased). *Education:* Matriculated, Presentation Brothers College, Cork, Ireland, 1953; MD, BCh, BAO, University of Ireland, 1959; Internship, So Charitable Infirmary, 1959-60; Internship, St Charles Hospital, Toledo, Ohio, USA, 1960-61; Chief Resident in Family Practice; Internship, St Mary's Hospital, Waterbury, Connecticut, 1961; Family Practice, Nechells Green Health Center, Birmingham, England, 1961-62; Birmingham University Hospital, England, 1962-65; Asst Attend, Yale New Haven Hospital, 1965-67; Assoc Attend Yale New Haven Hospital. *Appointments:* Diplomat, Medical Radiological Diagnosis, Royal College of Physicians and Surgeons, London, 1965; Diplomat of American Board of Radiology, 1968; The Valley Hospital, Ridgewood, New Jersey, USA, 1967-68; Director, Valley Hospital School of Radiography, 1971-; Secretary-Treasurer, 1977-78, Vice-President, Medical Staff, 1978, President, 1980-82, The Valley Hospital. *Memberships:* American Medical Association; Fellow, American College of Radiology; Radiological Society of North America; Radiological Society of New Jersey; Society of Medicine of New Jersey; Society for Magnetic Resonance Imaging; New Jersey State Medical Society; Bergen County Medical Society; Academy of Medicine of New Jersey; British Institute of Radiology; Faculty of Radiologists, London. *Publications:* 'Massive Hernation of the Bladder, The Roentgen Findings', 'Journal of Urology', Vol 97, June 1967; 'Role of Pulmonary Angiography in Pulmonary Embolism', 'Angiology', Vol 18, May 1967; 'Carbon Dioxide Pneumoencephalography', 'Radiology', Vol 89 July 1967. *Address:* The Valley Hospital, Department of Radiology, Linwood and Van Dien Avenues, Ridgewood, NJ 07451, USA.

RECHENMANN, Roger Victor, b. 2 May 1927, Strasbourg, France. Director of Research. m. Elisabeth Wittendorp, 28 Sep. 1978, Eckbolsheim. *Education:* Licence es-Sciences Physiques; Doctorat d'Etat es-Sciences Physiques. *Appointments:* Scientist, Centre National de la Recherche Scientifique (CNRS), 1952-62; Science Research Officer of the European Communities (EURATOM), Head of Research Team Association EURATOM-ITAL, Wageningen, The Netherlands, 1962-70; Director of Research of Institut National de la Santé et de la Recherche Médicale (INSERM), Director of Laboratoire de Biophysiques des Rayonnements et de Méthodologie, Université Louis Pasteur - INSERM Research Unit 220, Strasbourg, France, 1970-. *Memberships:* European Radiation Dosimetry Group; French Society for Electron Microscopy; French Physics Society. *Publications:* Scientific articles in various periodicals. *Hobbies:* Photography; Art and Antiques; Philosophy; Sports. *Address:* LBRM-INSERM U. 220, Université Louis Pasteur, Faculté de Médecine, 11 rue Humann 67085 Strasbourg-Cedex, France.

REDDING, Marshall Sims, b. 14 Oct. 1934, Greensboro, North Carolina, USA. Ophthalmologist. *Education:* AB, Duke University, USA, 1958; MD, Duke Medical School, 1966. *Appointments:* Rotating Internship, US Naval Hospital, Portsmouth, Virginia, USA, 1966-70; Residency in Ophthalmology, US Naval Hospital, Philadelphia, 1967-69; Staff Ophthalmologist, US Navy Medical Corps, Long Beach, California, 1970-71; Staff Ophthalmologist, Albemarle Hospital, Elizabeth City, North Carolina, 1971-; Staff Ophthalmologist, Chowan Hospital Inc. Edenton, North Carolina, 1971-; Associate Staff Ophthalmologist, Medical Center Hospital, Norfolk, Virginia, 1984; Assistant Professor, Eastern Virginia Medical School, Norfolk, Virginia, 1975-. *Memberships:* Fellow, American Academy of Ophthalmology; Fellow, American College of Surgeons; American Medical Association; American Intra-Ocular Implant Society; American Society of Clinical Hypnosis; North Carolina Medical Society (president 1982-83); North Carolina Society of Ophthalmology (president, 1981-82); Pasquotank-Camden-Durrituck-Dare Medical Society (past president and past secretary); Seaboard Medical Association; Southern Medical Association; Tidewater Ophthalmology and Otolaryngology Society. *Honour:* American Medical Association Physician's Recognition Award, 1985. *Address:* Albemarle Eye Care Center Limited, 1142 North Road Street, Elizabeth City, NC 27909, USA.

REDDY, Danda Jayapal, b. 20 Jan. 1942, India. Professor of Cardiothoracic Surgery/Cardiothoracic Surgeon. m. Sujana, May 1966, India, 1 son, 1 daughter. *Education:* MBBS, 1965, ECFMG, 1966, MS, General Surgery, 1970, Osmania Medical College; MCh, Cardiothoracic Surgery, Post-graduate Institute of Medical Education and Research, Chandigarh, 1974. *Appointments:* Most recently include: Civil Surgeon and Lecturer in Cardiothoracic Surgery, Kurnool General Hospital and TB Sanitorium, 1975-78; Commonw-

ealth Medical Fellowship to study techniques of Open Heart Surgery, Harefield Hospital, Middlesex Centre, London, 1978-79; Resident in Cardiothoracic and Vascular Surgery, University of Alberta Hospital, Edmonton, Canada, 1979-80; Assistant Professor, Cardiothoracic Surgery, Gandhi Medical College, 1980-82; Professor of Cardiothoracic Surgery and Cardiothoracic Surgeon, Guntur Medical College, Guntur, India, 1982-. *Membership:* Associate Member, American College of Chest Physicians and Surgeons. *Publications:* Dissertation: 'Carcinoma oesophagus' submitted to Osmania University, 1696; 'Surgical aspect of closed mitral volvotomy' read in Academy of Medical Sciences, Guntur, AP, India. *Honours:* Gold Medal in MBBS Examination, 1965; Commonwealth Medical Fellowship, 1978. *Hobby:* Shuttlecocks. *Address:* 16-9-817/7 Old Malakpet, Hyderabad, AP, India.

REDEBAUGH, John Charles, b. 14 Apr. 1948, Kewanee, Illinois, USA. Doctor of Chiropractic. m. Mary Sue Blachinsky, 18 Dec. 1976, Kewanee, Illinois, 1 son, 2 daughters. *Education:* BA (Pre-med), Bemidji State University, 1970; Doctor of Chiropractic, Palmer College of Chiropractic, 1978; Certified Team Physician, Northwestern College of Chiropractic, 1984; Diplomate, American Board of Chiropractic Examiners. *Memberships:* Minnesota Chiropractic Association; American Chiropractic Association; ACA Council on Roentgenology; ACA Council on Sports Injuries; Delta Delta Pi - Professional Chiropractic Fraternity; Vice-President, Treasurer, Palmer Alumni Association of Minnesota. *Publication:* Nationwide Lecturer on Sports Chiropractic. *Honours:* NAIA All-American Football 1968-69; Pi Tau Delta; National Chiropractic Honour Society. *Hobbies:* Many competitive Athletics; Outdoor Sport; Hunting; Fishing. *Address:* Redebaugh Chiropractic Office, PO Box 689, Nisswa, MN 56468, USA.

REECE, Robert Denton, b. 25 Oct. 1939, Bonham, Texas, USA. Associate Professor and Chairman of Department of Medicine in Society. m. Donna Walters, 5 June 1965, Louisville, Kentucky, USA, 2 sons, 2 daughters. *Education:* BA, Baylor University, 1961; BD, Southern Baptist Theological Seminary, 1964; MA 1968, MPhil 1968, PhD 1969, Yale University. *Appointments:* Assistant Professor 1969-73, Associate Professor 1974-, Department of Religion, Associate Professor and Chair 1975-, Department of Medicine in Society, School of Medicine, Wright State University, Dayton, Ohio. *Memberships:* Society for Health and Human Values; Society for Values in Higher Education; American Academy of Religion; Society of Christian Ethics. *Publications:* 'Christian ethics and human experimentation' in "A Matter of Life and Death: Christian Perspectives", 1978; 'The use of placebo and deception', (with F A Saber), 1979; "Studying People: A Primer in the Ethics of Social Research", (with Harvey A Siegal), 1986. *Honour:* Danforth Fellow, 1964-68. *Hobby:* Tennis. *Address:* Department of Medicine in Society, School of Medicine, Wright State University, PO Box 927, Dayton, OH 45401, USA.

REED, Barbara, b. 12 Dec. 1931, Waterville, Maine, USA. Administrative Director, Rehabilitation Services. m. Malcolm Reed, 30 Jan. 1954, Boston, Massachusetts, 2 sons, 1 daughter. *Education:* BS, Physical Therapy, Simmons College, 1953; MEd, Rehabilitation Administration, Northeastern University, 1976. *Appointments:* Staff Physical Therapist, Easter Seal Society, Bridgeport, Connecticut, 1954-55; Staff Physical Therapist, Lynn VNA, Lynn, Massachusetts, 1965-67; Staff Physical Therapist, Winchester Hospital, Winchester, Massachusetts, 1967-70; Administrative Director, Rehabilitation Services, Winchester, 1970-. *Memberships:* American Physical Therapy Association; Massachusetts Society for Cardiac Rehabilitation. *Publications:* 'The Quality Quandary: Physical Therapy and PRSOs/PROs 1984' in "Clinical Management" vol 4 No 3. *Hobbies:* Nautilus; Aerobics; Hiking; Swimming; Cross-country skiing; Reading; Knitting; Grandchild. *Address:* 62 Scotland

Road, Reading, MA 01867, USA.

REEDER, Oscar Samuel, b. 9 Oct. 1906, Spartanburg, USA. Retired. m. Dorothy Leonide Speissegger, 20 Feb. 1931, Appling, 1 son, 2 daughters. *Education:* BS, Citadel, 1928; MD, Medical College of South Carolina, 1933; Graduate, Medical School, US Army, 1938; Graduate Medical Field Service School, US Army, 1937; Graduate, Command and General Staff School, US Army, 1941. *Appointments:* Hospital Assignments, Medical Services, Army Hospitals, 1935-38, Surgical Services, Army Hospitals, 1938-41; Medical Evacuation and Hospitalisation Officer, Mediterranean Theatre, 1942-44; Chief Surgeon, 6th Army Group, 1944-45; Resident, Orthopaedic Surgery, Walter Reed General Hospital, 1946-49; Chief, Orthopaedic Service, Valley Forge General Hospital, 1949-50; Consultant, Orthopaedic Surgery, Surgeon General, US Air Force, 1950-54; Member, Surgery Study, Division of Research Grants and Fellowships, National Institute of Health, Washington DC, 1951-54; Associate Member, Medical Sciences, National Research Council, 1953-54; Member, Military Affairs Committee, Academy of Orthopaedic Surgeons, 1953-54; Consultant, Orthopaedic Surgery, Chief Surgeon of USAF, Europe, 1954-55. *Memberships include:* Diplomate, American Board of Orthopaedic Surgery; Fellow: American Academy of Orthopaedic Surgeons, American College of Surgeons; South Carolina Medical Association; South Carolina Medical Society. *Publications:* Articles in professional journals including, 'Journal of Bone and Joint Surgery'; 'Abstracts of Orthopaedic Surgery'; Chapter on "Wounds of the Hand", "Surgery of Trauma', 1953. *Honours:* Award of Legion of Merit, 1943; Bronze Star Medal, 1945; Croix de Guerre de Corps, 1945. *Hobbies:* Skeet Shooting; Golf. *Address:* 5 Johnson Road, Charleston, SC 29407, USA.

REES, Richard John William, b. 11 Aug. 1917, Wimbledon, Surrey, England. Grant Holder, Division of Communicable Diseases, Clinical Research Centre. m. Kathleen Harris, 25 Aug. 1942, Dartford, Kent, 3 daughters. *Education:* Guy's Hospital Medical School, 1935-41, BSc, 1939, MB BS, 1942, London University; LRCP, MRCS, 1941; MRCPath, 1963; FRCPath, 1964; FRCP, 1983. *Appointments:* House Surgeon and Physician, Southern Hospital, Kent, 1941-42; Captain, Bloodtransfusion Service, Royal Army Medical Corps, North Africa and Italy, 1942-46; Assistant Clinical Pathologist and Demonstrator, Morbid Pathology, Guy's Hospital, London, England, 1948-49; Scientific Staff, National Institute for Medical Research, London, 1949-69; Head, Laboratory for Leprosy and Mycobacterial Research and World Health Organisation Centre for Research, National Institute for Medical Research, London, 1969-82; currently, Grant Holder, Division of Communicable Diseases, Clinical Research Centre, Harrow, Middlesex. *Memberships:* Fellow and Honorary Member, Past President, Royal Society of Medicine (Section of Comparative Medicine); Chairman, Medical Advisory Board, Executive Committee Member, LEPRA (British Leprosy Relief Association); Expert Advisory Panel on Leprosy, World Health Organisation. *Publications:* Author of numerous scientific papers on basic and applied studies in animals and man relevant to the pathogenesis, immunology and chemotherapy of leprosy and tuberculosis. *Honours:* Erich Hoffman Lecturer, 1968; Almoth Wright Lecturer, 1971; Erasmus Wilson Demonstration, Royal College of Surgeons, London, 1973; British Medical Association, Film Silver Medal, Leprosy, 1974; CMG, 1979; Manson Medal, 1982. *Hobbies:* Gardening; Travelling. *Address:* Clinical Research Centre, Division of Communicable Diseases, Watford Road, Harrow, Middlesex HA1 3UJ, England.

REFSHAUGE, John George Hamilton, b. 28 Apr. 1919, Melbourne, Australia. Consultant, Ear, Nose and Throat, Williamstown Hospital. m. Diana Bindon Stoney, 7 Dec. 1949, Melbourne, 1 son, 3 daughters. *Education:* MB BS, Melbourne University, 1951; FRACS,

1983; FRACGP (Hon), 1983; Fellow, American College Sports Medicine, 1983; Foundation Fellow, Australian Sports Medicine Federation, 1984. *Appointments:* Self-employed Ear, Nose and Throat Specialist; Assistant, Ear, Nose and Throat Surgeon, Alfred Hospital, Melbourne, 1972-80; Consultant, Ear, Nose and Throat Surgeon, Williamstown Hospital, 1957-85. *Memberships:* Australian Sports Medicine Federation (Past President); International Sports Medicine Federation, Vice-President, 1982-; Chairman, Sports Federation of Victoria; Member, Sports Council of Victoria; Chairman, State Branch Menzies Foundation; Foundation Member of and Present Chairman of Physical Education Advisory Board, Member, Nurse Training Advisory Board; and several other professional and civic organizations. *Publications:* Sports Medicine as a Discipline, World Health Organization Publication, 1978; Contributor to professional journals, etc. *Honours:* OBE, 1978; Bronze Medal, FIMS, 1978. *Hobbies:* Golf; Renovations of Old Houses; Gardening. *Address:* 40/225 Beaconsfield Parade Middle Park, 3206 Melbourne, Victoria, Australia.

REGNIER, Claude, b. 26 Apr. 1931, La Rochelle, France. Hospital Doctor; Head of Service; Professor of Paediatrics. m. Rolande Regnier, 18 Apr. 1960, 2 sons, 1 daughter. *Education:* MD, Certified Professor. *Appointments:* Faculty Head of Clinic; Hospital Doctor, Certified Professor; Hospital Doctor, Head of Service; Titular Professor, Paediatrics. *Memberships:* National Federation of Study Groups in Neo Natology, France; French Society of Paediatrics; French Society of Perinatal Medicine; European Society of Paediatrics; International Society of Paediatrics. *Publications:* Works concerning paediatrics in infantile nephrology, infantile haematology & neo natology. *Hobbies:* Skiing; Tennis; Music; Reading. *Address:* Service de Médecin Infantile B, Centre Hospitalier et Universitaire de Purpan, 31059 Toulouse Cedex, France.

REHAK, Svatopluk, b. 20 Jan. 1926, Cesky Brod, Czechoslavakia. Ophthalmologist; University Professor. m. Jirina Svobodova, 1 Dec. 1951, 2 sons. *Education:* MD; DSc. *Appointments:* Professor of Ophthalmology, Charles University, Hradec Kralove, 1967, Dean, Medical Faculty, 1963; Regional Expert for Ophthalmology, 1957, Member, Medal Medical Faculty, 1970; Corresponding Member, Czechoslovak Academy of Sciences, 1984. *Memberships:* Czechoslovak Ophthalmological Society; Member, Committee of European Glaucoma Society; International Board of Governors International Glaucoma Congress; Czechoslovak Writers Association; Corresponding Member, Cuban Ophthalmological Society; Member, Committee of European Ophthalmological Society, 1980. *Publications:* Editor-in-Chief: "Recent Advances in Glaucoma"; Editor-in-Chief, "Textbook of Ophthalmology"; 6 books of poetry; 180 scientific papers in ophthalmology. *Honours:* State Honour for Excellent Work, 1967; Bronze Medal Charles University, Prague, 1975; Memorial Medal, Palacky University Olomouc Czechoslovakia, 1976; State Order of Labour. *Hobby:* Writing poetry. *Address:* Jungmannova 1390, 500 02 Hradec Kralove, Czechoslovakia.

REHM, Nancy Evans, b. 20 Sep. 1944, Louisville, Kentucky, USA, Perinatal Specialist, Nurse Midwifery Program. m. Ed Moss, 21 Dec. 1984, 2 sons, 2 daughters. *Education:* RN, University of Pittsburgh; CNM, University of Kentucky; University of Montpelier, France; University of Georgetown, Kentucky, USA; Norton Memorial Infirmary School of Nursing, Louisville, Kentucky; University of Louisville, Louisville, Kentucky; BRN; MRN. *Appointments:* Chairman, Utah Section, NAACOG, 1981-84; Chairman of Communications Committee, 1980, Program Committee, 1979-80, UPA; Secretary, Regiono, Chapter 2, American College of Nurse-Midwives, 1980; MAA-COG Representative to American Academy of Paediatrics Section on Perinatal Paediatrics of District VIII, 1982. *Memberships:* American College of Nurse Midwives; Nurses Association of the American College of Obstetricians and Gynaecologists; National Perinatal Association; Kentucky Perinatal Association; Utah Perinatal Association. *Publications:* 'Antpartum diagnosis and intrapartum management of Potter's Syndrome', (with R W Allen and J R Scott). *Address:* Department of Obstetrics and Gynaecology, University of Utah School of Medicine, 50 North Medical Drive, SLC, Utah 84132, USA.

REHMAN, Naeem-ur-, b. 18 Aug. 1940, Bihar, India. Physician. m. Asifa Begum, 11 Dec. 1966, Karachi, Pakistan, 3 sons, 2 daughters. *Education:* MB, BS, University of Karachi, 1964; Diploma in Tuberculosis & Chest Diseases, University of Karachi, 1980. *Appointments:* Project Medical Officer, TB Centre, Rawalpindi, Pakistan; Medical Officer in Charge, Central Government Dispensary, Karachi, Pakistan; Medical Officer in Charge, Bilharzia Control Project, Sebha, Libya; Consultant Chest Physician, Family Services Hospital, Karachi; Consultant Chest Physician, Izhar Hospital, Karachi. *Members:* Life Member, American Medical Society, Vienna, Austria; Member, College of Chest Physicians, USA. *Hobbies:* Cricket; Chess; Table-tennis; Bridge. *Address:* A-19 Block Q, North Nazimabad, Karachi, Pakistan.

REHNQVIST-AHLBERG, Nina Anna Kristina, b. 6 Apr. 1944, Tehran, Iran. Associate Professor. m. Staffan Ahlberg, 4 Apr. 1970, Stockholm, 2 sons, 1 daughter. *Education:* MD; PhD. *Appointments:* Dept. of Rheumatology, Strangnas; Dept. of Medicine, Serafimer Hospital. *Memberships:* Swedish Societies of Cardiology, Internal Medicine and Medical Sciences; American Heart Association; European Society of Cardiology. *Publications:* "Ventricular arrhythmias after acute myocardial infaction. Natural History, Prognostic Weight", 1978; More than 100 papers in various medical and cardiological journals. *Hobbies:* Golf; Sailing; Skiing; Family. *Address:* Dept. of Medicine, Danderyd Hospital, S-182 88 Danderyd, Sweden.

REICH, Laurence Alan, b. 17 Oct. 1945, USA. Physician and Surgeon. m. Carole Ching, 4 daughters. *Education:* BS, 1967; DO, 1971; Residency, Obstetrics and Gynaecology, 1971-75; Ortho Fellow, 1971; US State Department Visiting Scholar, 1972. *Appointments:* Assistant Professor, Department of Obstetrics and Gynaecology, 1975-77, Assistant Clinical Professor, 1977; Director, Maternal Infant Care Project, 1977; Director of Medical Education, Women's Centre, 1978-79. *Memberships:* American College of Obstetricians and Gynaecologists; American Public Health Association; American Fertility Society; American Association of Gynaecological Laparoscopists; American Perinatal Association. *Publications include:* Chapter 'Vag Admin Prostag' in "Clin Applic Future Hum Repro", 1972; 'Intra-amniot Prost w/Lamin Contrac', 1974; 'Office Mgmt Sex Prob' in 'Journal Repro Med' invited Symposium, 1975; Chapter 'Emer Ob/Gyn' in "Emergency Medicine", 1977; 'Mgmt Sex Disord' in 'Journal Repro Med', 1978; 'Enab Sex Health in 'Cur Prob OB/Gyn', 1978; 'Management of Obesity' in 'Journal Reprod Med', editor, invited symposium, 1979; 2 book reviews in 'New England Journal of Medicine', 1984. *Honours:* Ortho Fellowship, 1971; Upjohn Fellowship, 1972; US State Department Visiting Scholar, Uganda, 1972. *Address:* 11 Welina Place, Kula 200, Maui, Hawaii 96788, USA.

REICH, Nathaniel E, b. 19 May 1907, New York City, USA. Clinical Professor of Medicine (Emeritus). m. Joan, New York City, 23 May 1943, 2 sons. *Education:* BS, MD; Diplomate, American Board of Internal Medicine. *Appointments:* Past President, New York State Chapter, American College of Chest Physicians; Consultant to 7 State & Federal organisations& hospitals; Visiting Professor to San Marcos University (Peru), Universities of Indonesia, Afghanistan, Sri Lanka; Consultant at 5 major hospitals. *Memberships:* Fellow, American College of Physicians; Fellow, American College of Cardiology; Fellow, American College of Chest Physicians; Fellow, American College of Ang-

iology; Fellow, Royal Society of Medicine (UK); Past President & Member, New York Cardiological Society. *Publications:* "Diseases of the Aorta", 1949; "The Uncommon Heart Disease", 1954; "Chest Pain: Differential Diagnosis & Treatment" (with R E Fremont) 1961; more than 50 research articles. *Honours:* Honour Award (twice), American College of Angiology. *Hobbies:* Art - 13 one-man shows, represented in 4 museums & important collections; Tennis; Member, Explorers Club. *Address:* 135 Eastern Parkway, Brooklyn, NY 11238, USA.

REICHMISTER, Jerome Paul, b. 13 Apr. 1940, Baltimore, Maryland, USA. Orthopaedic Surgeon and Private Practitioner. m. Susan Baer, 3 July 1962, Baltimore, 2 daughters. *Education:* BA, Johns Hopkins University, 1960; MD, University of Maryland School of Medicine, 1964; Completed Orthopaedic training, 1969; Board certified, 1971. *Appointments:* Instructor, Orthopaedic Surgery, University of Maryland and Johns Hopkins School of Medicine; Assistant and Associate Professor of Orthopaedic Surgery, University of Maryland School of Medicine; Assistant Chief Orthopaedic Surgery, Sinai Hospital, Baltimore, Maryland. *Memberships:* American Academy of Orthopaedic Surgery; American College of Surgeons; Eastern Orthopaedic Association; Maryland Orthopaedic Society; American Medical Association. *Publications:* 'Injection of the deep infrepatellar bursar for Osgood-Schlatter Disease', 1969; 'Homocystinuria', 1971; 'Seat Belt Spinal Fractures', 1969; 'Monocycling Hyperpigmentation: Skin, Nail, Tooth and Bone Involvement', 1984; 'The Painful Os Intermetatarsum', 1980; 'Differential Diagnosis of Neck and Shoulder Pain', 1982. *Honours:* Golden Apple Award for Outstanding Teaching, 1974. *Hobbies:* Tennis; Golf. *Address:* 6080 Falls Road, Suite 203, Baltimore, MD 21209, USA.

REID, Robert L, b. 4 Apr. 1930, Livia, Kentucky, USA. Hand Surgeon. m. Bettye Sue Cobb, 25 Jan. 1951, Calhoun, Kentucky, USA, 1 son, 1 daughter. *Education:* BS, Chemistry, Biology, Murray State College, 1952; MD, University of Louisville School of Medicine, 1956. *Appointments:* Chief Orthopaedic Hand Surgeon, Walter Reed Army Medical Centre, Washington DC, Consultant to Army Surgeon General, 1976-78; Chairman, Orthopaedic Division, Uniformed Services University of Health Sciences, Bethesda, Maryland, 1978; Clinical Professor of Surgery, Uniformed Services University, 1978-. *Memberships:* American Medical Association; American Academy of Orthopaedics; American College of Surgeons; Diplomate, American Board of Orthopaedics; Active Member, American Society for Surgeons of the Hand; Founding Member, Society of Military Orthopaedic Surgeons. *Publications:* 60 articles in American & British medical journals. *Honours:* Robert Skelton Award for Outstanding Resident, Letterman Army Medical Centre, 1965; "A" Award, Army Surgeon General for Outstanding Orthopaedic Surgery, 1976. *Hobby:* Farming. *Address:* 1504, College Drive, Owensboro, KY 42301, USA.

REIF, Arnold Eugene, b. 15 July 1924, Vienna, Austria. Research Professor of Pathology. m. (1) 3 sons, (2) Katherine E Hume, 7 July 1979, Wellesley, Massachusetts, USA. *Education:* BA 1945, MA 1949, Cambridge University, England: BSc (external studies), London University, 1946; MS 1949, DSc 1950, Carnegie-Mellon University, Pittsburgh, Pennsylvania, USA. *Appointments:* Postdoctoral Fellow in McArdle Laboratory for Cancer Research 1950-52, Research Associate in Department of Physiological Chemistry 1953, University of Wisconsin Medical School; Research Associate, Department of Biochemistry, Lovelace Foundation for Medical Education and Research, Albuquerque; Assistant Professor of Surgery (Biochemistry) 1957-68, Assistant Professor of Surgery (Oncology) 1968-69, Associate Professor of Surgery (Immunology) 1969-71, Associate Professor of Surgery 1971-75, Part-time Lecturer in Surgery 1975-, Tufts University School of Medicine; Research

Pathologist 1973-, Chief of Experimental Cancer Immunotherapy Laboratory 1979-, Mallory Institute of Pathology, Boston City Hospital; Research Professor of Pathology, Boston University School of Medicine, 1975-. *Memberships include:* American Association for Cancer Research Incorporated; American Association of Immunologists; Health Physics Society; Sigma Xi; New York Academy of Sciences. *Publications include:* "Immunity and Cancer in Man", (editor), 1975; "Immunity to Cancer", (edited with M S Mitchell), 1985; 103 papers; 57 abstracts and letters. *Honours include:* American Cancer Society Faculty Research Associate, 1967-68. *Address:* Boston City Hospital, Boston, MA 02118, USA.

REIFLER, Clifford Bruce, b. 28 Dec. 1931, Chicago, Illinois, USA. Professor of Health Services; Psychiatry; Preventive, Family and Rehabilitation Medicine; Director, University Health Service. m. Barbara Karnuth, 11 Sep. 1954, Chicago, 3 daughters. *Education:* BA, University of Chicago, 1951; BS, Northwestern University, 1953; MD, Yale University, 1956; Intern, University Hospital, Ann Arbor, Michigan, 1957-58; Resident, Strong Memorial Hospital, Rochester, New York, 1958-61; MPH, University of North Carolina, 1967. *Appointments:* Instructor, Assistant Professor, Associate Professor, Psychiatry, School of Medicine, 1963-70, Assistant Professor, Associate Professor, Mental Health, School of Public Health, 1967-70, University of North Carolina; Interim Vice President, Student Affairs, 1980-81, Medical Director, Acting Chairman, Department of Health Services, Strong Memorial Hospital, Senior Associate Dean for Clinical Affairs, 1983-85; Professor of Health Services etc, Director, University Health Services, 1970-, University of Rochester, New York. *Memberships:* Fellow and Past President, American College Health Association; Fellow, American Psychiatric Association; American Academy of Medical Directros; American College of Physician Executives. *Publications:* Co-Author: "Mental Health on the Campus: A Field Study", 1973; "The Alternative Services: Their Role in Mental Health", 1975; "Old Folks at Homes - A Field Study of Nursing and Board-and-Care Homes", 1976. Author or co-author of over 51 papers contributed to professional journals. *Honours include:* Edward Hitchcock Award, 1981, Journal Executive Editor, 1983-. American College Health Association; Elected, American College of Physicians Executives. *Hobbies:* Various collections. *Address:* University Health Service, Box 617, 250 Crittenden Boulevard, Rochester, NY 14642, USA.

REILLY, Peter Lawrence, b. 15 Apr. 1941, Adelaide, South Australia. Director of Neurosurgical Research. m. Helen Margaret McKenzie, 25 Jan. 1967, Norwood, South Australia, 3 sons, 1 daughter. *Education:* BMed.Sc (Hons), Adelaide, 1963, MB, BS, 1966, FRACS (Neurosurgery), 1972; MD, Adelaide, 1980. *Appointments:* Honorary Neurosurgeon, Adelaide Children's Hospital, 1976-; Head of Neurosurgery, Flinders Medical Centre, South Australia, 1976-80; Senior Staff Specialist, Department of Neurosurgery, Royal Adelaide Hospital, 1980-85, Director, Neurosurgical Research, 1985-; Senior Lecturer in Neurosurgery, University of Adelaide, 1980-. *Memberships:* Neurosurgical Society of Australasia; Royal Australasian College of Surgeons; Congress of Neurological Surgery; International Society of Pituitary Surgeons. *Hobbies:* Tennis; Sailing; Music. *Address:* Department of Neurosurgery, Royal Adelaide Hospital, Adelaide, South Australia 5000.

REINHERZ, Richard Phillip, b. 30 Aug. 1951, Kenosha, Wisconsin, USA. Podiatrist. m. 16 July 1978. Detroit. 2 sons. *Education:* BA, Biology, cum laude, Washington University, St Louis, 1973; DPM, California College of Podiatric Medicine, 1976; Postgraduate Residency, Foot Surgery, Kern Hospital, Warren, Michigan, 1976-78. *Appointments:* Chief Resident, Foot Surgery, Kern Hospital, 1977-78; Editor in Chief, 'Journal of Foot Surgery, American College of Foot Surgeons, 1980-; Director, Postgraduate Residency Programme,

American International Hospital, 1979-; Family Practice, Medical Programme, Medical College of Wisconsin/St Catherine's Hospital, Keosha, 1983-; Chairman, City of Kenosha Board of Health, Kenosha, 1983-85. *Memberships:* Fellow, American College of Foot Surgeons; Diplomate, American Board of Podiatric Surgery; Staff Affiliations: American International, Kenosha Memorial, St Catherine's Hospitals; American Medical Writers Association; American Podiatric Medicwl and Wisconsin Society of Podiatric Medicine Associations. *Publications:* Numerous articles in professional journals, most recent include: "Garre's Osteomyelitis in the Foot", 'Wisconsin State Podiatry Journal', 1983; "Bone Regenration Following Podiatric Surgery", 'Journal of Foot Surgery', co-author, 1984; "Prostheses Following Limb Amputations", Chapter, 'A Textbook of Foot Surgery', 1986; "Management of Flexor Hallucis Longus Tendon Injuries", 'Journal of Foor Surgery", 1984. *Honours:* Journal Award, Wisconsin Scoiety of Podiatric Medicine, 1982, 1984. *Hobbies:* Swimming; Camping; Former Scout Master; American Red Cross water safety Instructor (Certified for the Handicapped). *Address:* 6801 Sheridan Road, Kenosha, WI 53140, USA.

REINKER, Dale Leo, b. 17 Feb. 1943, St Louis, Missouri, USA. President Elect, American Association of Osteopathic Specialists. m. Joan Ann Brehm, 1 July 1967, Troy, 1 son, 2 daughters. *Education:* BS, North East Missouri State University, 1965; DO, University of Health Sciences, Kansas City, 1969; Intern, Bay View Hospital, Cleveland, Ohio, 1969-70; Resident, General Surgery, CCH Lutheran Hospital, Burlington, 1970-75; Diplomate, Board of Surgery, Board Certified, American Association of Osteopathic Specialists. *Appointments:* Attending and DME, Coffey County Hospital, 1975-85; KAOM Executive Committee, 1976-84; Adjunct Professor, University of Health Sciences College of Osteopathic Medicine, Kansas City, 1977-83; President, Kansas Association of Osteopathic Medicine, 1982-83; Medical Advisory Committee, Kansas Blue-Cross-Blue Shield, 1984-85; Board of Governors, American Academy of Osteopathic Surgeons, 1980-85; Chief of Surgery, Coffey County Hospital, 1977-. *Memberships:* American Osteopathic Association; American Association of Osteopathic Specialists; American Academy of Osteopathic Surgeons; Kansas Association of Osteopathic Medicine; American College of Osteopathic Obstetricians and Gynaecologists. *Publications:* 'Benign Ovarian Neoplasms', Thesis, 1976; 'Ovarian neoplasms: An indication for laparotomy' in 'The Osteopathic Physician', 1976; 'Colonoscopy for the general surgeon', paper presented to Kansas Association of Osteopathic Medicine, 1977; "Endoscopic evaluation of colon disease", in 'Kansas Association of Osteopathic Medicine Journal', 1978. *Honours:* Fellow, American Academy of Osteopathic Surgeons, 1981; Surgeon of the Year, American Association of Osteopathic Specialists, 1984. *Hobbies:* Horseback riding; Downhill skiing; Water sports. *Address:* 43 Metz Court, Lake St Louis, MO 63367, USA.

REISER, Morton Francis, b. 22 Aug. 1919, Cincinnati, Ohio, USA. Chairman and Professor, Psychiatry, Yale University School of Medicine. m. Lynn Whisnant, 19 Dec. 1976, New Haven, Connecticut, 3 sons. *Education:* BS, MD, University of Cincinnati, Ohio, 1940-43; New York Psychoanalytic Institute, 1960. *Appointments:* Internship, Internal Medicine, Long Island Medical College Division, Kings County Hospital, Brooklyn, 1944; Junior and Senior Assistant Resident, Internal Medicine, Cincinnati General Hospital, 1944-46; Various positions including Assistant Professor of Psychiatry and Internal Medicine, 1950-52, Cincinnati General Hospital, 1946-52; Associate Staff, Jewish Hospital, Cincinnati, 1952; Research Psychiatrist, Walter Reed Army Medical Center, Washington, DC, 1952-54, 1954-55; Visiting Psychiatrist, Bronx Municipal Hospital Center, New York, 1954-69; Various positions including Professor of Psychiatry, Albert Einstein College of Medicine, New York, 1955-69; Professorial Lecturer in Psychiatry, State University of New

York, Downstate Medical Center, 1959-65; Chief, Division of Psychiatry, 1965-69, Attending Psychiatrist, 1965-69, Montefiore Hospital and Medical Center, New York; Assistant Lecturer, New York Psychoanalytic Institute, 1967-68; Fellow, Davenport College, Yale University, 1969-; Faculty, Western New England Institute for Psychoanalysis, New Haven, 1969-; Attending Psychiatrist, Yale New Haven Hospital, 1969-; Training and Superivising Psychoanalyst, Western New England Institute for Psychoanalysis, 1972-; Professor and Chairman, Department of Psychiatry, Yale University School of Medicine, New Haven, 1969-. *Memberships:* American Psychoanalytic Association; American Psychiatric Association; Benjamin Rush Society; American College of Psychiatrist. *Publications include:* "Mind, Brain, Body: Toward a Convergence of Psychoanalysis and Neurobiology", 1984; Co-author: "The Patient: Biological, Psychological and Social Dimensions of Medical Practice", 2nd Edition, 1985; Contributor to professional journals; Presentations; Chapters in Books, etc. *Address:* Department of Psychiatry, Yale University School of Medicine, 25 Park Street, New Haven, CT 06519, USA.

REISNER, Ronald Morton, b. 2 May 1929, Buffalo, New York, USA. Professor; Chief of Division. m. Ellen Sue Mosko, 29 Jan. 1972, 2 sons. *Education:* BA 1952, MD, University of California, Los Angeles, 1956. *Appointments include:* Professor of Medicine-/Dermatology, 1972-, Chief, Division of Dermatology, UCLA School of Medicine, Los Angeles, 1973-; Chief, Dermatology Service, Wadsworth VA Hospital, Los Angeles, 1977-; Director, Dermatology Resident Training, 1977-, Director, Combined UCLA-VA Wadsworth Dermatology Program, 1977-. *Memberships include:* Alpha Omega Alpha; Phi Beta Kappa; Pi Gamma Mu; Phi Eta Sigma; Alpha Mu Gamma; Fellow, American Academy of Dermatology; American Dermatologic Association; Society for Pediatric Dermatology. *Publications include:* Editorial Services to numerous scholarly publications; Producer of Audiovisual Teaching Materials; Case Presentations at Regional, National and International Meetings; Presentations to Professional Groups; Lectures to Professional Groups, General Public; Reviews; Book Chapters; Original Papers to Scientific journals including: 'Introduction to special issue on acne', (co-author), 1982; 'A clinical and bacteriologic evaluation of topical erythromycin in the treatment of acne vularis' (co-author), 1982; 'Hairless mice as models for chloracne: A study of cutaneous changes induced by topical application of established chloracnegens' (co-author), 1982; 'A prospective longitudinal study of the development of acne in children, I Preliminary Observations' (co-author), 1982. *Address:* Division of Dermatology, UCLA School of Medicine, Los Angeles, CA 90024, USA.

REITAN, Ralph M, b. 29 Aug. 1922, Beresford, USA. Professor; Clinical Neuropsychologist; Publisher. m. Ann Kirsch, 15 Feb. 1952, Rossville, 3 sons, 2 daughters. *Education:* PhD, Psychology, University of Chicago, 1950. *Appointments:* Assistant Professor to Professor & Director, Neuropsychology, Indiana University Medical Centre, 1951-70; Professor, Psychology & Neurological Surgery, University of Washington, 1970-79; Professor, Psychology, University of Arizona, 1977-; President, Reitan Neuropsychology Labs Inc, 1982-; President, Neuropsychology Press, 1984-. *Memberships:* American Psychological Association; American Neurological Association; American Academy of Neurology; American Board of Examiners in Professional Psychology (Clinical Psychology). *Publications:* Co-Author: "Clinical Neuropsychology", 1974, "The Halstead-Reitan Neuropsychological Test Battery", 1985; "Neuroanatomy and Neuropathology", 1985; Author, "Aphasia and Sensory Perceptual Deficits in Adults", 1984; "Aphasia and Senory Perceptual Deficits in Children", 1985; 200 scientific articles in professional journals. *Honours:* Gordon Barrow Memorial Award; Arizona Psychological Association Research Award. *Address:* Neuropsych-

ology Lab., 1338 E Edison Street, Tucson, AZ 85719, USA.

REMACLE, José, b. 31 Aug. 1946, Belgium. Professor of Biochemistry. m. 3 Apr. 1982, Kaduvamakhal, 2 sons. *Education:* Licence in Science, MD Major cum laude; Doctorat in Science, PhD, major cum laude. *Appointments:* Fellowship, Fonds National de la Recherche Scientifique, Belgium, 1970-71; Graduate Student, University of Louvan Medical School, 1971-74; Postdoctoral Research, University of California, USA, 1973-74; Associate Professor, Medical School, 1974-76, Assistant Professor, 1976-80, Professor, Science Faculty, 1980-, University of Namur, Belgium. *Memberships:* Belgian Society of Biochemistry; Belgian Society of Cell Biology; Belgian Society of Gerontology and Geriatry. *Publications:* Author or Co-Author of book chapters: "Biological and Clinical Aspects of Superoxide and Superoxide Dismutase", 1980; "Cancer Cell Organellas", 1982; "New Trends on Atheroschlerosis", 1984. Co-Author, "Evolution, platicite et modifications des cellules au cours du vieillissement cellulaire", 1982. Author or Co-Author of over 48 papers contributed to professional journals including: 'European Journal of Cell Biology'; 'Archives of Biology'; 'Probio'; 'Experimental Gerontology'; 'Mechanism of Ageing and Development' and numerous others. *Honours:* Award, Union Carbide European Research Associates, 1968; Fellow, William Hallan Tuck, sponsored by Foundation Francqui, 1973; Award, Andre Vander Stricht, 1984. *Hobbies:* Gardening; Animal farming. *Address:* Facultes Universitaires, Rue de Bruxelles 61, 5000 Namur, Belgium.

REMIC, Milos, b. 12 Mar. 1919, Ljubljana, Yugoslavia. Neurosurgeon. m. 26 Dec. 1952, 1 daughter. *Education:* Primarius, 1969; Doctor of Medicine; General Surgeon; Neurosurgeon, Faculty of Medicine. *Appointments include:* Physician, General Practice, 1945-52; General Surgeon, 1952-60; Neurosurgeon, 1960-. *Memberships:* Slovenian Medical Society; Society for Clinical & Experimental Hypnosis, USA; American Society for Psychical Research. *Publications include:* 'Hypnotic Exploration of Amnesia after Cerebral Injuries' (International Journal of Clinical & Experimental Hypnosis, 1975); 'Physiological Aspects of Hypnosis' (9th International Congress on Hypnosis, Glasgow, 1982). *Hobbies:* Chess, representative, University Clinical Centre, Ljubljana. *Address:* Ilirska 4, Ljubljana, Yugoslavia.

RENAUD, Serge Charles, b. 21 Nov. 1927, Cartelegue, France. Director, INSERM, Research Unit on Nutrition and Vascular Physiopathology. m. Helena Kogut, 29 Mar. 1984, 1 daughter. *Education:* VMD, University of Montreal, Canada, 1957; PhD, Faculty of Medicine, University of Montreal, 1960; PhD, Hematology, University of Lyon, France, 1978. *Appointments:* Research Assistant, Institute of Experimental Medicine and Surgery, 1957-60; Research Assistant, Montreal Heart Institute, 1960-65; Director, Laboratory Experimental Pathology, Montreal Heart Institute, 1965-72; Associate Professor, Faculty of Medicine, 1967-72; Full Professor, 1972; Professor and Chairman, Department of Nutrition, 1957-81; University of Montreal; Visiting Professor, Faculty of Medicine, Boston University, USA, 1970-71; Director, INSERM Research Unit No 63, Nutrition and Vascular Physiopathology, Lyon-Bron, 1972-. *Memberships:* Member of Canadian, American and European professional organizations. *Publications:* 140 scientific publications in field of atherosclerosis, thrombosis and coronary heart disease in relation to nutrition and other environmental factors, 1957-85. *Honours include:* Several Fellowships; Borden's Award of Canadian Society of Nutrition, 1967; Award of Fondation Francaise de Nutrition, 1983. *Address:* INSERM, Unit 63, 22 av du Doyen Lepine, Case 18, 69675 Bron Cedex, France.

RENIERI, Alberto, b. 22 June 1943, Latina, Italy. Coordinator for Health Statistics and O R. m. Eva Celotti, 2 Jan. 1969, Pisa, 3 daughters. *Education:* Engineering Degree. *Apppointments:* Research Worker, University of Pisa; Operation Research Unit Coordinator, Italsider SpA and Dalmine SpA; Coordinator, Health Statistics and OR, Health Services Research Institute, SAGO, Florence, Italy. *Memberships:* Italian Statistics Society; Italian Association of Epidemiology; Euro working Group OR applied to Health Services, EWGORAHS; Centro Nazionale Edilizia e tecnica Ospedaliera. *Publications:* Co-Author: "Il medico generico nella medicina di base", 1982; "Factors affecting list size of general practitioners and number of drugs prescribed" in 'Social Science and Medicine'; 'Nursing Team Organisation' in '3rd International Conference of System Science in Health Care', 1984. *Address:* c/o SAGO, Viale Gramsci 22, 50132 Florence, Italy.

RENNER, Stephen F, b. 27 Mar. 1959, Spokane, Washington, USA. Chiropractic, Clinical practitioner. m. Sherilyn D Nordhagen, 12 May 1979, Spokane, Washington. *Education:* Washington State University; Gonzaga College; Palmer Junior College; BS, DC, Palmer College of Chiropractic; Diplomat, National Board of Chiropractic Examiners. *Memberships:* Chiropractic Society of Washington; International Chiropractors Association; Congress of Chiropractic State Associations. *Homour:* 3 Special Service Awards, 1978-80. *Hobbies:* Piano and percussion music; Snow and water skiing; Racquetball. *Address:* Tapio Office Center, Suite 212, South 104 Freya, Spokane, WA 99202, USA.

RENNIE, Michael John, b. 28 July 1946, Wallsend-on-Tyne, England. Symers Professor and Head of Department of Physiology, University of Dundee. m. Anne Macgregor Gill, 1975, St Louis, Missouri, USA, 1 son, 2 daughters. *Education:* MSc, University of Manchester, 1970; PhD, University of Glasgow, 1973. *Appointments:* Research Assistant, Department of Neurology, Glasgow University, 1970-74; MRC Travelling Fellow and Instructor, Washington State University, St Louis, USA, 1974-76; Muscular Dystrophy Association of America, Fellow and Instructor, 1976-77; Lecturer in Human Metabolism, 1977-79; Wellcome Senior Lecturer, 1979-83, Department of Medicine, University College London Medical School. *Memberships:* Medical Research Society; The Physiological Society; The Biochemical Society; The European Society for Clinical Investigation; The Scottish Society for Experimental Medicine. *Publications:* Contributor of articles and papers to professional journals including: 'Science'; 'Clinical Science'; 'Metabolism'; 'British Medical Journal'. *Honour:* Arvind Wretland Lecturer, European Society Parenteral and Enteral Nutrition, 1985. *Hobbies:* Modern Literature; Rock and Roll; Jazz; Cooking and Eating; Talking; Outdoor Life; Working with Hands; Practical Jokes. *Address:* Department of Physiology, The University, Dundee DD1 4HN, Scotland.

RENSHAW, Domeena C, b. 20 July 1929, Republic of South Africa. Psychiatrist-Physician. m. Robert Harris Renshaw, 13 June 1965. *Education:* MB; ChB; MD. *Appointments:* Medical Officer, St Mary's Hospital, Republic of South Africa, 1964-65; Faculty of Medical School 1968-, Director Outpatient Clinic 1968-78, Director Child Programme 1969-78, Assistant Chariman 1970-, Director Sexual Dysfunction Clinic 1972-, Professor of Psychiatry 1977-, Loyola University, Maywood, Illinois, USA. *Memberships:* Fellow, American Psychiatric Association; Fellow, American College of Psychiatry; American Medical Society; Illinois and DuPage Medical Society; Illinois Psychiatric Society; American Association Sex Therapists and Educators; Society for Sex Therapy and Research. *Publications:* "The Hyperactive Child", 1974 and 1976; "El Ninos Hyperactivo", Mexico, 1976; "Incest-Understanding and Treatment", 1982; "Sex Talk For A Safe Child", 1984. *Honours:* Aescalupian Award for Medical Student Teaching, University of Ottawa, Canada, 1978; Honorary Citizen of New Orleans, 1978; Special Teacher Award, Oregon Academy Family Physicians,

1978. *Hobbies:* Photography; Gardening; Hiking. *Address:* Loyola University of Chicago, 2160 South First Avenue, Maywood, IL 60153, USA.

RENSING, Ludger, b. 23 Oct. 1932, Munster, Germany. Professor of Cell Biology, University of Bremen. m. Roswitha Holberg, 11 Feb. 1963, New York, USA, 1 son, 1 daughter. *Education:* PhD, Goettingen, 1960; Habilitation, Goettingen, 1966. *Appointments:* Research Fellow, Princeton University, USA, 1962-64; Assistant Professor, Zoology, Goettingen University, 1960-75; Professor of Cell Biology, University of Bremen, 1976-. *Memberships:* International Society for Chronobiology; German Society for Cell Biology; German Zoological Society; Society for Biological Chemistry. *Publications:* "Biologische Rhythmen und Regulation", 1973; "Allgemeine Biologie", 2nd Edition, 1984; "Temporal Order", Editor, 1985. *Address:* Fachbereich 2 (Biologie/Chemie), Zellbiologie, Leobener Strasse NW 2, D-2800 Bremen 33, Federal Republic of Germany.

RENSON, Cecil Edward, b. 12 Oct. 1925, London, England. Professor of Conservative Dentistry, University of Hong Kong. m. Hilary Berry née Pitts, 5 July 1979, Hong Kong, 1 daughter. *Education:* BDS, London Hospital Medical College, London; LDS, RCS, England, 1958; PhD, University of London, 1970; DDPH, 1973. *Appointments:* House Officer, 1957-58, part-time Lecturer, General Dental Practitioner, 1958-66, London Hospital; Lecturer, Conservative Dentistry, 1966-67, Senior Lecturer, 1967-76, London Hospital Medical College; Honorary Consultant Dental Surgeon, London Hospital, 1970-78; Reader, Conservative Dentistry, University of London, 1976-78; Professor of Conservative Dentistry, Head of Department, University of Hong Kong, 1978-; Consultant Dental Surgeon, Hong Kong Government, 1980-; Member, Board of Governors, The Prince Philip Dental Hospital, Hong Kong, 1981-. *Memberships:* Life Member, British Dental Association; Fédération Dentaire Internationale; Fellow, Royal Society of Medicine; British Society for Dental Research; British Society for Restorative Dentistry (Founder-Member); International Association for Dental Research; Founder-Member, British Association for Study of Community Dentistry; Hong Kong Dental Association. *Publications:* (co-author) "Dental Public Health" (edited G L Slack), 1973; (editor) "Oral Disease", 1978; More than 60 papers, some 140 leading articles in professional journals. *Honours:* Freeman, Liveryman, City of London, 1971; Fellow, International College of Dentists, 1981; Elected Life Member, British Dental Association, 1983; Elected Honorary Member, American Dental Association, 1985; Visiting Lecturer/Professor in 15 countries. *Hobbies:* Reading; Writing; Travel. *Address:* The Prince Philip Dental Hospital, Hospital Road, Hong Kong.

RETSAS, Spyros, b. 4 Dec. 1942, Thessaloniki, Greece. Consultant Physician in Medical Oncology. m. Diana Gillian Rees, 8 July 1972, London, England, 1 son. *Education:* Aristotle University Medical School, Thessaloniki Greece; Doctoral Thesis, University of Athens, Greece. *Appointments:* Lieutenant of the Hellenic Army Medical Corps, 1967-69; Senior House Physician in Oncology, Royal Marsden Hospital, 1971-72; Registrar in General Medicine & Gastroenterology, Whipps Cross Hospital, 1973-75; Lecturer in Medical Oncology & Honorary Senior Registrar, Westminster Hospital, 1975-78; Senior Lecturer in Medical Oncology & Honorary Consultant Physician, Westminster Hospital, 1978-85. *Memberships:* Fellow, Royal Society of Medicine, London; British Association of Cancer Research; European Society of Medical Oncology; American Society of Clinical Oncology; Founding Member, Melanoma Study Group in Britain. *Publications:* Various articles on Cancer research in professional journals. *Hobbies:* Riding; Skiing; Travel; History of Medicine. *Address:* Medical Oncology Unit, Westminster Hospital, London, SW1P 2AP, England.

RENTSCHLER, Gary J, b. 9 June 1947, Buffalo, New York, USA. Executive Director, Portland Center for Hearing and Speech. *Education:* BA, Baldwin-Wallace College; MA, Speech Pathology, PhD, Speech Pathology, State University of New York, Buffalo. *Appointments:* Speech Pathologist, Glen Falls Hospital; Professor, Mississippi University for Women; Professor, University of Michigan; Director, Sandy Trails Camp; Executive Director, Portland Center for Hearing and Speech. *Membership:* American Speech-Language-Hearing Association. *Publications:* Contributor of articles and papers to professional journals including: Co-author, 'Language Impaired Children's Use of Language across three conversational situations', 'Australian Journal of Human Communication Disorders', 1983; 'The Onset of Stuttering Following Drug Overdose', 'Journal of Fluency Disorders', 1984; 'Effects of subgrouping in Stuttering Research', 'Journal of Fluency Disorders', 1984; Presentations include: Co-author, "Auditory processing skills of language-impaired children', MSHA Convention, Traverse City, 1985; "Computer Synthesized Speech: Intelligibility and the Language Impaired Child", ASHA Convention, Washington, DC, 1985. *Hobby:* Computing. *Address:* 3515 SW Veterans Hospital Road, Portland, OR 97201, USA.

RENZULLI, Raymond Mario, b. 8 Dec. 1927, Newark, New Jersey, USA. Anaesthesiologist (retired). m. Carmela Avorio, 25 Aug. 1956, Rome, Divorced 1 son, 1 daughter. *Education:* Medicine & Surgery Degree, 1954; Speciality in Anaesthesiology, 1957; Pneumology, 1975 *Appointments:* Associate Anaesthesiologist, St Joseph's Hospital, Paterson, New Jersey, 1957-58; St Elizabeth's Hospital, Elizabeth, New Jersey, 1958-60; Chief Anaesthesiologist, Riverside Hospital, Boonton, New Jersey, 1960-61; Associate Anaesthesiologist, Newark Beth Israel Hospital, Newark, 1961-65; Since retirement helping with handicapped children. *Memberships:* American Medical Association; New Jersey Medical Association; American Society of Anaesthesiology; New Jersey State Society of Anesthesiology; American College of Chest Physicians; Italian Medical Society; Ordine dei Medici of Avellin Province. *Address:* Via Donato Anzani 16, Ariano Irpino (AV) 83031, Italy.

RESCALDINA, Guiseppe, b. 10 Oct. 1957, Magenta, Milan, Italy. Psychotherapist. m. Nadia Scioscia, 29 October 1983, S Stefano, Ticino, Italy. *Education:* Laurea in Psychology; Corso di formazione in Analisi Transazionale; Diploma in Medical Psychomatics; Diploma in Hypnotherapy. *Appointments:* Psicologo presso il centro Tossico-dipendenze di Magenta; Psicologo presso la divisione di Ostetricia e Finecologia dell'Ospedle di Magenta; Docente di Training Autogeno presso la libera Post. University internazionale della Nuova Medicina; Direttore del Centro di Psicoprofiossi Ostetrica di Magenta; Consultente presso il Centro Studi Coppia di Milano; Consulente presso il Centro di Terapie Naturali Integrate di Milano; Svolge livera professione presso il proprio studio sito in Magenta. *Memberships:* European Association for Transactional Analysis; International Centre of Medical and Psychological hypnosis; Societa italiano di Biofeedback. *Publications:* "Un approccio non ideologico alla situazione tossicomanica", 1981; "Modello di Analisi della personalita tossicomanica", 1983; "Analisis Psicosociale dell'isterectomia sia su un campione di 103 casi", 1984; "Dubbi e paure della contraccezione in rapporto con la richiesta di l.v.g", 1985. *Hobbies:* Sport; Fencing; Travel. *Address:* Via Ticino 28/A, S Stefano Ticino, Milan 20010, Italy.

RÉVÉSZ, Laszlo, b. 31 Mar. 1926, Nagkaroly, Sweden. Professor of Tumor Biology; Head of Department of Tumor Biology II, Karolinska Institute, Stockholm, Sweden. m. Shizuko Fukushima, 26 Mar. 1974, Tokyo, Japan, 1 son. *Education:* Dr med univ, University of Innsbruck, Austria, 1950; Medicinae licenciate, 1955, MD, 1958, Karolinska Institute, Stockholm. *Appointments:* Assistant Physician, hospitals in Sto-

ckholm, 1950-52; Research Associate, Institute of Cell Research, 1952-57, Associate Professor of Tumor Biology, 1958-68, Professor of Tumor Biology, 1969-; Head of Department of Tumor Biology II, 1978-, Karolinska Institute. Visiting Professor: Stanford University Medical School, California, USA, 1960-61; Kyoto University Medical School, Japan, 1971-72. *Memberships:* Member of several national and international professional societies concerned with cancer and radiology research. *Publications:* Over 200 scientific articles on cancer and radiology research. *Address:* Department of Tumor Biology II, Karolinska Institute, Box 60400, 104 01 Stockholm, Sweden.

REVILLARD, Jean-Pierre, b. 12 Jan. 1938, Suresnes (92), France. Professor of Immunology, University Claude Bernard, Lyon. m. Mariel Cuilleret, 18 March 1961, Lyon, 2 daughters. *Education:* MD, 1964. *Appointments:* Post-doctoral Research Fellow, New York University, USA, 1966-67; Assistant Professor in Nephrology, Lyon, 1968-71; Maitre de Conferences Immunology, 1973-81; Professor of Immunology, University Lyon II, 1982-; Dean of Human Biology Faculty, 1977-84; Medecin des Hopitaux, 1971-. *Memberships:* American Association of Immunologists; Transplantation Society; British Society for Immunology; Societe Francaise d'Immunologie; Appointed by several government research agencies (grant committees) and by Ministry of Education as consultant for biology and medicine. *Publications:* 350 scientific articles; 3 books on Proteinuria, 1971, Delayed Hypersensitivity, 1972 and Local Immunity, 1985. *Hobbies:* Skiing; Sailing. *Address:* Hopital E Herriot, Pavillon P, 69374 Lyon Cedex 08, France.

REVOLTELLA, Roberto Paolo, b. 10 Jan. 1939, Rome, Italy. Chief, Division of Immunobiology. m. Fanchin Bruna Maria, 2 July 1967, Arcugnano, Vicenza, Italy, 1 son, 2 daughters. *Education:* MD, University of Padua, Padua, Italy; PhD, Graduate School of Arts and Sciences, New York University, USA. *Appointments include:* Staff Member, Researcher and Co-ordinator, Division of Immunobiology, Institute of Cell Biology, CNR, Rome, Italy, 1972-; Professore Incaricato, School of Medicine, Chair of Immunology, University of Trieste, Italy, 1974-77; Visiting Professor, CUNY, New York, USA, 1977; Professore a Contratto (Immunobiology) State University, Rome, Italy, 1982-85. *Memberships include:* American Association for Cancer Research; American Association of Immunologists; New York Academy of Sciences; American Society for Cell Biology; European Association for Cancer Research; Gruppo Cooperazione di Immunologia. *Publications:* "Expression of differentiated functions in cancer cells" co-author, 1982; Articles in medical journals. *Honours:* NYU Founders Day Award, 1972; CNR, PF Oncology, Genetic Engineering 1979-86. *Hobbies:* Painting; Archaeology; Music. *Address:* Via G Pecci 12 - 00165 Rome, Italy.

REY, Paule Yvonne, b. 15 Jan. 1929, Geneva, Switzerland. Professor, University of Geneva. *Education:* Federal diploma, Medicine, Geneva, 1953; Master's degree, Public Health, Harvard University, USA, 1955; MD (thesis), Geneva, 1958. *Appointments:* Research Fellow, Department of Physiology, Geneva, 1958-69, University of California, Los Angeles, USA, 1964-65; Full Professor/Vice Director, Institute of Social & Preventive Medicine, 1970-; Head, University Centre for Work Ecology, 1981-; Invited Professor, Kansas State University, USA, 1971. *Memberships:* International Commission on Occupational Health; International Ergonomical Association; International Epidemiological Association; Human Factors Society. *Publications include:* Book chapter, 'Visual Impairments & Their Objective Correlate' in "Ergonomic Aspects of Visual Terminals", Milan, 1980; 'Ambiances Lumineuses' in "Encyclopédie Médicine du Travail", 1986; 'Vision et Éclairage' in "Précis de Physiologie du Travail", Scherrer, 1981; Several reports, World Health Organisation, ILO. *Honours:* Prix Tissot, Geneva; Chairman, Ergonomics Scientific Committee, ICOH. *Hobbies:* Music (piano); Carpentry. *Address:* Institute of Social & Preventive Medicine, Unit of Occupational Health & Ergonomics, 10 rue Jules-Grosnier, 1206 Geneva, Switzerland.

REYES-DÁVILA, José Manuel, b. 17 Aug. 1923, Gurabo, Puerto Rico. Psychiatrist in Private Practice. m. Ida M Laborde, 14 Aug. 1952, Humacao, Puerto Rico, 2 sons, 3 daughters. *Education:* University of Puerto Rico, 1943-45; AA, City College of Los Angeles, California, USA, 1946-49; Doctor of Medicine & Surgery, Temple University of School of Medicine, Philadelphia, Pennsylvania, 1949-53; Resident in General Psychiatry, Norristown State Hospital, 1965-68, Diploma, 1968. *Appointments:* Rotating Internship, Bayamón District Hospital, Puerto Rico, 1953-54; General Practice, Las Piedras, PR, 1954-55; US Air Force, Flight Surgeon, 1955-57, Discharged as Major; Medical Director, Las Piedras Medical Centre PR, 1957-62; Medical Director, Humacao University College & Private Practice, 1962-65, Professor of Science, Humacao University; Resident in Psychiatry, Norristown State Hospital, Pennsylvania, 1965-68; Staff Psychiatrist, Norristown, also Pottstown Mental Health Centre, 1968-69; Private Practitioner in Psychiatry, Humacao, PR, 1969-. *Memberships:* Puerto Rico Medical Association; American Psychiatric Association; American Medical Association; Puerto Rico Psychiatric Association; Fellow, Inter-American College of Physicians & Surgeons. *Honours:* Physicians' Recognition Award, American Medical Association, 1982; Psychiatry Certification, Puerto Rico Board of Medical Examiners, 1983. *Hobbies:* Reading; Music; Sport; Travel. *Address:* PO Box F, Humacao, PR 00661, USA.

REYES, HERNAN M, b. 5 Apr. 1933, Philippines. Professor, Surgery, Chief, Pediatric Surgery, University of Illinois, USA; Surgeon-in-Chief, Cook County Children's Hospital. m. Dolores C, 27 Feb. 1960, Chicago, 1 son, 4 daughters. *Education:* MD, 1957. *Appointments:* Clinical Assistant, Surgery, Stritch School of Medicine, 1964-65, Clinical Assistant, 1968, 1969, Loyola University; Instructor, Surgery, Chief, Pediatric Surgery, University of Santo Tomas College of Medicine, Manila, 1966-67; Assistant Professor, 1969-73, Acting Chief, Pediatric Surgery, 1973-74, Associate Professor, 1973-76, Pritzker School of Medicine, University of Chicago; Professor, Surgery, University of Illinois College of Medicine at Chicago, 1976-; Professor, Clinical Pediatrics, University of Illinois College of Medicine, 1982-. *Memberships include:* American College of Surgeons, Chicago Committee on Trauma; American Academy of Pediatrics, Section on Surgery, Section on Oncology-Hematology; American Association for the Surgery of Trauma; American Association of University Professors; American Pediatric Surgical Association; Association for Academic Surgery; Central Surgical, Western Surgical, Chicago Surgical and Illinois Pediatric Surgical Association. *Publications:* Author, numerous articles in professional journals; Numerous chapters in books including: "Management of Trauma in the Pediatric Patient", 'Neonatal and Pediatric Intensive Care', 1985. *Honours include:* Gregorio T Singian Lecturer, Philippine College of Surgeons, 1979; Luis Guerrero Memorial Lecture, University of Santo Tomas, 1979. *Hobby:* Tennis. *Address:* Cook County Children's Hospital, 700 South Wood Street, Room B-40, Chicago, IL 60612, USA.

REYS, Philip, b. 5 Dec. 1928, Strasbourg, France. Professor of Surgery. m. Kathreen Fabry, 19 Sep. 1964, Strasbourg, France, 1 son, 3 daughters. *Education:* MD; Professor, General Surgery. *Appointments:* Professor of General Surgery, Medical School, University of Kabul, Afghanistan, 1966-70; Chief, Department of Surgery, Colmar General Hospital, France; Professor of Surgery, Faculty of Medicine, University of Strasbourg, France. *Memberships:* President, Departmental Committee of the Haut-Rhin National League against Cancer. *Publications:* Numerous articles on visceral, thoracic & vascular surgery. *Hobbies:* Piano; Skiing. *Address:* 7a rue Bartholdi, Colmar 68000, France.

REYNOLDS, Paul E, b. 17 Feb. 1942, Dublin, Ireland. Associate Professor of Psychiatry, Dalhousie University. m. Frances, 6 July 1968, 2 sons, 2 daughters. *Appointments include:* Associate Professor, University of Calgary, Canada. *Memberships:* Canadian & American Psychiatric Associations; Canadian Medical Association; American Group Psychotherapy Association. *Publications include:* Articles, professional journals: 'Suicide attempt in Emergency Department', 1985; 'Multiple suicide attempt in Emergency Department', 1985; 'Psychiatric education of family practice residents', 1982; Also presentations to medical conferences, etc. *Honour:* Fellow, American Psychiatric Association, 1982. *Address:* 5763 Inglis Street, Halifax, Nova Scotia, Canada B3H 1K5.

RHODE, Jeffrey Charles, b. 28 Jan. 1942, USA. Neuropathologist. m. Deborah Mary Braithwaite, 18 Dec. 1970, Roxwell, England, 2 daughters. *Education:* BA, Princeton University, USA, 1963; MD, Temple University, 1968. *Appointments:* Flight Surgeon, NAS Agana Guam, 1970-73; Anatomical Pathologist, Christchurch Hospital, New Zealand, 1979-83. *Memberships:* Fellow, RCPA; Diplomat, American Board of Pathology. *Hobbies:* Sailing; Swimming; Cycling; Running; Farming. *Address:* Department of Pathology, Christchurch Hospital, CHB Private Bag, Christchurch, New Zealand.

RHODES, Elaine, b. 17 Apr. 1943, Hamilton, Ontario, Canada. Assistant Registrar, Health Sciences, 1 son. *Education:* Certificate, Life Officers Management Association; Ontario Teacher's Certificate; BA; MA, Teaching, inprogress. *Appointments:* Self-employed, 1960; Purchaser, food freezer company, 1962; Assistant Administrator, Food Freezer Company, 1963; Agency Administrator, Life Insurance Company; Teacher, Primary Education, 1973; President, Day Care Centre, 1976; Assistant Registrar, Health Sciences, 1975-. *Memberships:* Burlington Chamber of Commerce; Association for Bright Children; Association of Canadian Medical Colleges; Ontario Universities Registrar's Association. *Hobbies:* Art; Photography; Skiing; Travel. *Address:* Faculty of Health Sciences, McMaster University, 1200 Main Street West, Hamilton, Ontario, Canada L8N 3Z5.

RHOTON, Albert Loren, Junior, b. 18 Nov. 1932, Parvin, Kentucky, USA. R D Keene Family Professor and Chairman, Department of Neurosurgery, University of Florida College of Medicine. m. Joyce L Moldenhauer, 23 June 1957, 2 sons, 2 daughters. *Education:* BS, Ohio State University, 1954; MD, cum laude (highest academic standing in class of 1959), Washington University School of Medicine, 1959. *Appointments:* Intern, Columbia Presbyterian Medical Center, New York City, 1959; Resident in Neurological Surgery, Barnes Hospital, St Louis, Missouri, 1961-65; Consultant in Neurological Surgery, The Mayo Clinic, Rochester, Minnesota, 1965-72; Chief, Division of Neurological Surgery, 1972-80; R D Keene Family Professor and Chairman, Department of Neurological Surgery, 1980-, University of Florida College of Medicine, Gainesville. *Memberships:* Congress of Neurological Surgeons, President, 1978; Florida Neurosurgical Society, President, 1978; American College of Surgeons, Board of Governors, 1978-; American Association of Neurological Surgeons, Chairman, Vascular Section, 1983-86, Treasurer, 1983-86; Society of Neurological Surgeons, Treasurer, 1975-81; Southern Neurological Society, Vice-President, 1976; Alachua County Medical Society, Executive Committee, 1978; American and Florida Medical Associations; American Surgical Association; Society of University Neurosurgeons; American Heart Association Stroke Council; Neurosurgical Society of America. *Publications:* Author of over 100 scientific papers and one monograph on neurological surgery, mainly in 'Journal of Neurosurgery', 'Neurosurgery' and 'Surgical Neurology'. *Honours:* Recipient of numerous honours and awards including honoured guest and lecturer of neurosurgical societies in Switzerland, Japan, Venezuela, Brazil,

France, Columbia and Middle East; Honorary membership in six state neurosurgical societies. *Address:* Department of Neurological Surgery, Box J265, University of Florida Health Center, Gainesville, FL 32610, USA.

RHYNE, Linda Dean, b. 20 Feb. 1946, Dallas, North Carolina, USA. Chief Psychologist. m. Christopher Watts, 19 Sep. 1976, Dallas. *Education:* BA, University of North Carolina, Greensboro, 1968; PhD, 1975, MA, 1970, University of Illinois, Champaign. *Appointments:* Clinical Counsellor, University of Illinois, 1974-75; Inpatient Psychiatry Staff Psychologist, 1975-83; Staff Psychologist, Alcohol Admissions Unit, 1983-84, VA Medical Centre, Danville; Adjunct Associate Professor, Psychology, Purdue University, 1981-83; Chief Psychologist, Mental Health Clinic, VA medical Centre, Cincinnati, 1984-. *Memberships:* American Psychological Association; American Society of Clinical Hypnosis. *Publications:* Articles in scientific journals including: 'Journal of Counselling Psychology'; 'Psychological Record', etc. *Honours:* Phi Beta Kappa, 1968; Hands and Heart Award (VA), 1983; Quality Increase (VA), 1982. *Hobbies:* Photography; Cooking; Running. *Address:* Psychology Service (116B), VA Medical Centre, 3200 Vine Street, Cincinnati, OH 45220, USA.

RIBARI, Otto, b. 26 Feb. 1932, Budapest, Hungary. Otolaryngologist. m. Judit Reök, 20 Dec. 1960, Budapest, 1 son, 1 daughter. *Education:* MD, University Medical School, Budapest, 1956; DSc, Hungarian Academy of Science, 1969; Specialist in Otorhinolaryngology, Budapest, ENT Clinic, 1959. *Appointments:* Resident, 1956, Assistant Professor, 1964, Associate Professor, 1970, Budapest, Director and Professor, 1977-85, Szeged, University ENT Clinic; Director and Professor, State Institute of Otorhinolaryngology and Department of Otorhinolaryngology, Head and Neck Surgery, Semmelweis University Medical School, Budapest, 1985. *Memberships:* Past General Secretary, Past Representative at IFOS, Hungarian ORL Society; Past Vice President, 12th World Congress of ORL, Budapest; Past President, Danubian Symposium of ORL; Fellow, World Health Organisation; Collegium ORL Amicitiae Sacrum; International Audiology Society; West German ENT Society; Politzer Society; Pro-Rector, Szeged University; Past President, Hungarian ORL Society. *Publications:* "Otolaryncology Textbook", 1977; author of 19 book chapters in English, German and Hungarian, 130 scientific publications in English, German, Russian and Hungarian journals. *Honours:* Honorary Memberships: German ORL Society, 1979; Austrian ORL Society, 1981, Czechoslovakian ORL Society, 1982; State Honour and Prize, Eminient Physician, 1982. *Hobbies:* Tennis; Swimming. *Address:* Semmelweis University Medical School, Department of Otorhinolaryngology - Head and Neck Surgery, Szigony u 36, Budapest, H-1083 Hungary.

RICCI, Mario, b. 10 June 1925, Stia (AR), Italy. University Professor. m. Dina Eugenia, 30 Apr. 1951. *Education:* MD, 1950; Habilitation, Medical Pathology, 1960, Internal Medicine, 1965, Clinical Immunology, 1969. *Appointments:* Acting Professor, Clinical Immunology, 1970, Director, Postgraduate School of Allergology and Clinical Immunology, 1971-, Professor, 1980-, University of Florence; Elected Expert Member, International Consulting Committee, Immunology, WHO, Geneva, 1981; President, Italian Society of Allergology and Clinical Immunology, Executive Committee Member, International Society of Allergology and Clinical Immunology, 1985. *Memberships:* Ordine dei Medici, Florence. *Publications:* 290 Papers in professional journals including: 'Journal of Immunology', 'Journal of Clinical Investigation'; etc; Co-author, 2 books, 1970-72, 1978. *Honours:* Achievement Award, International Association of Allergology and Clinical Immunology, 1973. *Hobbies:* Cinema; Theatre; Music. *Address:* Cattedra di Allergologia e Immunologia Clinica, Universita di Firenze, Policlinico di Careggi, Viale Morgagni 85, 50134 Firenze, Italy.

RICE, Dale H, b. 23 June 1943, USA. Professor and Chairman, Department of Otolaryngology. m. Barbara L Ballash, 19 Apr. 1969, Ann Arbor, Michigan, 1 son. *Education:* MD, University of Michigan. *Appointments:* Currently, Professor and Chairman, Department of Otolaryngology, School of Medicine, University of Southern California, Los Angeles, California. *Memberships:* Fellow: American College of Surgeons; American Academy of Otolaryngology - Head and Neck Surgery; American Academy of Facial Plastic and Reconstructive Surgery. Society of University Otolaryngologists; Association of Academic Departments of Otolaryngology - Head and Neck Surgery. *Publications:* Author of over 70 scientific works. *Honour:* Outstanding Teacher Award, University of California, Los Angeles, 1979-80, 1981-82. *Hobbies:* Running; Skiing; Karate. *Address:* Department of Otolaryngology - Head and Neck Surgery, University of Southern California, Box 795, 1200 North State Street, Los Angeles, CA 90033, USA.

RICE, Margaret Anne Fiske, b. 2 Jan. 1945, New York City, USA, Nursing Administrator; Adjunct Professor of Nursing. m. Gerald William Rice, 4 June 1966, Manchester, New Hampshire, 1 son, 1 daughter. *Education:* BSN, St Anselm College, 1967; MSN, Boston University 1973. *Appointments:* Staff Nurse, The Hospital of Albert Einstein, College of Medicine; Public Health Nurse, Maternal Infant Care Project; Nursing Instructor, Lawrence General Hospital; Family Planning Consultant, Maternal Child Health Nursing Consultant, NH Health Department; Health and Social Service Co-ordinator, Community Guidance Center; Human Sexuality Teacher, Trinity High School, Instructor of Nursing, Lowell University ; Assistant Professor of Nursing, University of New Hampshire; Co-ordinator of Staff Development, Elliot Hospital. *Memberships:* President, Northern New England, ASHET; Sigma Theta Tau, Nursing Honor Society; Coalition for Action in Nursing; American Nurses Association; New Hampshire Hospital Association; New England Hospital Assembly; New Hampshire Nurses Association. *Publications:* 'Identifying the Adolescent Substance Abuser', (with P Kibbel), 1983; 'Hospital Consortia', (with S Citarella), 1981. *Honours:* State Representative Extension Committee NEHA, 1985; Regional Network Facilitator, ASHET, 1984; Citation of Service, American Diabetic Association, New Hampshire Affiliate, 1984; National Institute of Mental Health, Traineeship, 1971. *Hobbies:* Swimming; Cross Country Skiing; Bird Watching; Wild Life Activities; Theatre; Travelling. *Address:* 14 Cedar Street, Derry, NH 03038, USA.

RICHARDS, Marcia Jean Stahmann, b. 14 Sep. 1945, Boston, Massachusetts, USA. Radiation Oncologist. m. Donald R Whitaker, 6 June 1974, 1 daughter. *Education:* MD, University of Wisconsin School of Medicine, 1970. *Appointments:* Assistant Professor, Departments of Radiology and Human Oncology, 1974-77; Director, Department of Radiation Oncology, Trinity Memorial Hospital, Milwaukee, 1980-; Co-Medical Director, Women's Health Institute, Good Samaritan Medical Center, 1984-; Director, Department of Radiation Oncology, Good Samaritan Medical Center, Milwaukee, 1985-; Radiation Oncologist, St Luke's Hospital, Milwaukee, 1984-. *Memberships include:* Radiological Society of North America; American Society of Therapeutic Radiology and Oncology; American College of Radiology; American Medical Association. *Publications:* Contributor of numerous articles to medical journals. *Honours:* Evan and Marian Helfaer Award, 1968; Sigma Sigma, 1968; Alpha Omega Alpha, 1969; Cora M and Edward J Van Liere Award, 1970; Janet M Glasgow Award, American Medical Womens Association, 1970. *Hobby:* Black and white fine art photography. *Address:* St Luke's Hospital, 2900 W Oklahoma Avenue, Milwaukee, WI 53215, USA.

RICHARDS, Victor, b. 4 June 1918, Fort Worth. Texas,

USA. Chief of Surgery; Clinical Professor of Surgery. m. Jennette O'Keefe, 7 June 1941, San Diego, California, 2 sons, 2 daughters. *Education:* AB 1935, MD 1939, Stanford University. *Appointments:* Instructor - Professor of Surgery 1941-52, Professor and Chairman of Department of Surgery 1952-58, Clinical Professor of Surgery 1958-, Stanford University; Clinical Professor of Surgery, University of California, 1958-; Chief of Surgery, Pacific Medical Center, 1958-68; Chief of Surgery, Children's Hospital, San Francisco, 1968-. *Memberships:* American Medical Association; California Medical Association; Society of University Surgeons; American Surgical Association; American Thoracic Association; International Surgical Society; Pan-Pacific Surgical; Pacific Coast Surgical; Western Thoracic Association; American College of Surgeons; International Surgical Society; Sigma Xi; Alpha Omega Alpha. *Publications include:* "Surgery for General Practice", 1955; "Cancer, The Wayward Cell", 1977; Over 150 major articles in surgical journals. *Honour:* Commonwealth Research Scholar, Harvard University, 1950. *Hobbies:* Photography; Skiing; Horseback Riding; Tennis; Hiking; Stereoscopic Photography. *Address:* 2714 Broadway, San Francisco, CA 94115, USA.

RICHARDSON, (Sir) John Eric, b. 30 June 1905, Woodchurch, England. President, Association of Optical Practitioners. m. Alice May Wilson, 26 Dec. 1941, Hull, 1 son, 3 daughters (1 deceased). *Education:* B.Eng., 1st Class Honours; PhD; DSc (Honorary); Kt.; CBE. *Appointments:* Head, Engineering, Hull Municipal Technical College, 1937-41; Principal: Oldham Technical College, 1941-44, Royal Technical College, Salford, 1944-47, Northampton Polytechnic, London, 1947-56; Director, National College of Horology, London, 1947-56; Director, the Polytechnica, Central London, 1956-70; Member: General Optical Council, 1959-78, Chairman, 1975-78; Member, The Leprosy Mission, 1970-84, International Chairman, 1974-84. *Memberships:* Fellow, Institition of Electrical Engineers; Member, Instituvugn of Mechanical Engineers; Fellow, British Optical Association. *Publications:* Paper, 'Journal of IEE', 1933; various papers on Higher Technical Education, UK & Nigeria, 1950-65. *Honours:* CBE, 1962; Kt., 1967; DSc (Honorary) City University, London. *Address:* 73 Delamere Road, Ealing, London W5 3JP, England.

RICHMAN, Jack, b. 24 June 1941, Toronto, Ontario, Canada. Director Occupational Medical Services. m. Editt Davidovich, 28 May 1967, Tel Aviv, Israel, 2 sons, 1 daughter. *Education:* MD; Certificant, College of Family Physicians, Canada; Certificant, Canadian Board of Occupational Medicine; Diploma of Occupational Health and Safety, Oakville Trafalgar Memorial Hospital. *Appointments:* Family practice 1968-; Former Medical Consultant, Canadian Admiral Company; Medical Consultant, St Lawrence Cement Company, 1969-; Medical Consultant, Canadian General Electric, 1972-; Medical Consultant, Ratcliffs Canada, 1978-; Medical Director, BP Canada Limited, Trafalgar Refinery; Director Medical Services, Goodyear Canada. *Memberships:* Canadian Medical Association; Ontario Medical Association; Board of Directors, American Occupational Medical Association; Occupational Medical Association of Canada; Society of Occupational Medicine of Great Britain; International Association for Study of Pain; Medichem; President, Acupuncture Foundation of Canada. *Publication:* 'Value of Medical Monitoring including Legal, Ethical and Human Rights Considerations' in 'Canadian Occupational Health and Safety News', 1984. *Hobbies:* Skiing; Squash. *Address:* 264 Elton Park Road, Oakville, Ontario L6J 4C1, Canada.

RICHMAN, Lynn Charles, b. 4 June 1945, Montezuma, Iowa, USA. Professor & Chair, Paediatric Psychology. m. 1973, Iowa City, 1 son. *Education:* BA, Grinnel College, Iowa, 1967; MA 1970, PhD, Paediatric Psychology 1973, University of Iowa. *Appointments:* Psychological consultant, Iowa State Services for Crippled Children, 1970; Assistant Professor 1973, Associate Professor 1978, Professor 1983, Department of Paediatrics, College of Medicine, University of Iowa. *Memberships:* Fellow, American Psychological Association; Society of Paediatric Research; American Cleft Palate Association; Sigma Xi. *Publications include:* 'Cross National Comparisons of Developmental Dyslexia' in "Child Development", 1985; 'Type of Reading Disability Related to Cleft Type & Neuropsychological Patterns' in "Cleft Palate Journal", 1984; 'Verbal Mediation Deficits: Relation to Behaviour & Achievement in Children' in 'Journal of Abnormal Psychology', 1986; 'Hyperlexia as a Variant of Developmental Language Disorder' in 'Brain & Language', 1981; etc. Total, 28 articles, 4 book chapters. *Honours:* Fellow, American Psychological Association, 1983; Sigma Xi, 1983; Society of Paediatric Research, 1983. *Hobbies:* Travel; Photography. *Address:* 220 1st Avenue, Iowa City, IA 52240, USA.

RICHMOND, David Robin, b. 29 Aug. 1939, Leeds, Yorkshire, England. Cardiologist. m. Robyn Lesley Adelstein, 17 Apr. 1966, Sydney, 1 son, 2 daughters. *Education:* BSc (Hons), 1959; MB ChB (hon 1st class), University of Leeds, England, 1961; MRCP, London, 1964; MRACP, 1966; MS, Physiology, University of Minnesota, USA, 1970; FRACP, 1971; FACC, 1979; FRCP, London, 1980. *Appointments:* Several positions as Hospital Resident, 1962-64; Registrar, 1965-68; Research Fellow, Mayo Clinic, Minnesota, USA, 1968-70; Staff Cardiologist, Hall strom Institute of Cardiology, Royal Prince Alfred Hospital, Sydney, 1970-72; Cardiologist, 1972-. *Memberships:* Fellow: Royal Society of Medicine, London; Royal College of Physicians, London; Royal Australian College of Physicians; American College of Cardiologists; American Heart Association; Member: Australian Medical Association; British Medical Association; Cardiac Society of Australasia; 1972-84. *Publications:* Author or co-author of 34 publications. *Honours:* State Scholarship; Senior City Scholarship and Exhibition; University Prizes; Fellowship: Lederle International Fellow, 1968-69; Minnesota Heart Association Fellowship, 1969-70; Grant-in-Aid, American Heart Association, 1969-70. *Hobbies:* Tennis; Reading; Theatre. *Address:* 141 Macquarie Street, Sydney, New South Wales 2000, Australia.

RICHMOND, Shirley Jean, b. 14 July 1934, Sheffield, England. Senior Lecturer in Virology; Honorary Consultant in Virology. m. Marcus Henry Richmond, 15 Feb. 1958, Bristol. *Education:* BA, MB BChir, MD, Cambridge University; University College Hospital, London. *Appointments:* Medical Microbiologist, Public Health Laboratory Service, Bristol; Senior Medical Microbiologist, Public Health Laboratory Service, Manchester. *Memberships:* Society for General Microbiology; Medical Society for the Study of Venereal Diseases; Association of Medical Microbiologists; Manchester Medical Society. *Publications:* Publications on genus Chlamydia. *Address:* North Manchester Regional Virus Laboratory, Booth Hall Children's Hospital, Manchester M9 2AA, England.

RIDDELL, Rees James, b. 12 May 1912, Melbourne, Australia. Retired Pathology Practice. m. Ursula Jean Gray, 19 Oct. 1943, Melbourne. *Education:* MB BS, Melbourne, 1935; Diploma in Tropical Medicine & Hygiene, 1939, London. *Appointments:* Medical Officer, RAAF; Pathologist, Ballarat, Victoria; Pathologist, Austin Hospital, Melbourne; Demonstrator in Anatomy, University of Melbourne; Relief Pathologist (part-time). *Memberships:* College of Pathologists; Australian Medical Association. *Honour:* Duncan Medal, School of Hygiene & Tropical Medicine, London, 1939. *Hobbies:* Woodwork; Golf. *Address:* 13 Carmichael Street, East Ivanhoe, Victoria 3079, Australia.

RIDING, Keuth Howard, b. 6 Oct. 1943, Oxford, England. Clinical Associate Professor in Department of Surgery. m. Margaret Mary Webb, 1 Oct. 1966, Scorton, Lancashire, 1 son, 1 daughter. *Education:* MB BS (London), 1967; LRCP MRCS (England), 1967; Primary FRCS (England), 1970; LMCC (Canada), 1975; FLEX (USA), 1976; FRCS (Canada), 1976. *Appointments include:* Head, Department of Otolaryngology, Children's Hospital, 1979-; Clinical Associate Professor, Division of Otolaryngology, University of British Columbia, 1983-. *Memberships:* Canadian and British Columbia Otolaryngology Societies; British Columbia Medical Association; Editorial Board, 'Canadian Journal of Otolaryngology'', 1983-; Advisory Board, Vancouver Oral Centre for Deaf Children, 1983-. *Publications:* Contributor to professional journals including 'Journal of Otolaryngology'; Chapters in books; Presentations. *Honour:* I B Holubitsky Award, University of British Columbia. *Hobbies:* Sailing; Ornithology. *Address:* Otolaryngology Department, Children's Hospital, 4480 Oak Street, Vancouver, British Columbia V6H 3V4, Canada.

RIDLEY, Charles L, b. 26 Dec. 1953, Mobile, Alabama, USA. Doctor of Chiropractic. m. Mary Alice, 28 Apr. 1976, 2 sons, 1 daughter. *Education:* AS, Biology; DC, Chiropractic; FACACN, Clinical Nutrition. *Appointments:* Principal Doctor, Manhatten Chiropractic Centre; Founder, Whole Life Medical Centre; Founder, Self Care Systems; Columnist for 'Whole Life Times'; Columnist 'Dance Times' magazine. *Memberships:* New York State Chiropractic Association; International Craniopathic Society; Founder, Self Care Systems (President). *Publications:* "Integrating Self Help into your Practice" - cover story in 'Digest of Chiropractic Economics', June 1985; "Free from Pain: A Comprehensive Guide to Treatment of Chronic Anxiety, Stress, Tension and Pain". *Honour:* Key speaker at the Whole Life Exposition, Boston and New York. *Hobbies:* Cycling; Hiking; Music. *Address:* 11 ½ Twin Lakes Drive, Monsey, NY 10952, USA.

RIEKMAN, George Allan, b. 25 Oct. 1931, Rosthern, Saskatchewan, Canada. Associate Dean, College of Dentistry. m. Edith Bergman, 5 Nov. 1955, Saskatoon, Canada, 4 sons. *Education:* DDS, McGill University; Diploma in Paedodontics, University of Toronto. *Appointments:* Head, Department of Paediatric Dentistry, University of Saskatchewan; Council, College of Dental Sureons of Saskatchewan; President, Saskatoon & District Dental Society; President, College of Dental Surgeons of Saskatchewan. *Memberships:* Canadian Dental Association; Canadian Academy of Paedodontics; American Society of Dentistry for Children; American Academy of Dentistry for the Handicapped. *Publications:* 'A Sedation Technique for the Younger Child' (with A S Ross), 1981; 'Waste Nitrous Oxide Exposure' (with A S Ross & B Carley), 1984; 'Oral findings of foetal alcohol syndrome Patients', 1984 (all in Journal of Canadian Dental Association). *Honour:* Fellowship, Academy of Dentistry for the Handicapped. *Hobbies:* Woodwork; Fishing; Skiing; Gardening. *Address:* Dental Clinic, University of Saskatchewan, Saskatoon, Saskatchewan, S7N 0W0, Canada.

RIENUS, Rienk, b. 15 Aug. 1954, Amsterdam, Netherlands. Resident in Cardiology. m. Elisabeth de Vroom, 28 Dec. 1978, Amsterdam, 1 son, 1 daughter. *Education:* Physician, Free University, Amsterdam, 1981. *Appointments:* Assistant, Department of Physiology, Free University, Amsterdam, The Netherlands, 1978-81; Resident, Internal Medicine, St Elisabeth Hospital, Curacao, Netherlands Antilles, 1981-83; Resident, Cardiology, specialising in Lasers in Cardiology, University Hospital, Utrecht, Netherlands, 1983-. *Memberships:* Dutch College of Cardiology; American Society for Laser Medicine and Surgery; European Laser Association. *Publications:* 'Possible Uses of Laser Radiation in the Treatment of Coronary Artery Disease', in 'Netherlands Journal of Medicine'; contributions to Proceedings of 6th Congress of International Society for Laser Medicine and Surgery, 1985. *Hobby:* Piano playing. *Address:* University Hospital, Department of Cardiology, Catherynesingel 101, 3511 GV Utrecht, The Netherlands.

RILEY, Colin Douglas, b. 16 Oct. 1957, Melbourne, Australia. Dental Officer. *Education:* Bachelor of Dental Science, University of Melbourne; Licentiate of Dental Surgery, Victoria. *Appointments:* Dental Officer; Royal Dental Hospital of Melbourne, 1981; Sunshine Hospitals and Health Services Complex, Victoria, 1982-. *Memberships:* Australian Dental Association. *Hobbies:* Public transport; Philately. *Address:* 176 Furlong Road, St Albans, Victoria 3021, Australia.

RILEY, Paul David, b. 14 Aug. 1938, Indiana, USA. Medical Director. m. Helena Storey, 28 June 1969, Elizabeth City, USA, 2 daughters. *Education:* AB, Chemistry; MD, Medicine; MPH, Public Health; MRS, Religious Sciences. *Appointments:* Medical Director, Kiamosi Hospital, Tiriki, Kenya; Director of Paediatrics, Norfolk Hospital, Virginia, USA; Staff Psychiatrist, VA Hospital, Indianapolis, USA; Medical Director, St Vincents Hospital, Indianapolis; Associate Professor, Psychiatry, Indiana University, Indianapolis; Medical Director, St Vincents Street Clinic-. *Memberships:* American Medical Association; American Academy of Medical Directors; American Psychiatric Association; American Academy of Child Psychiatry; American Academy of Paediatrics. *Publications:* 'Stress in American Society' in 'Quaker Life', December 1984; 'Response to Ecumenical Union' in 'Quaker Life', June 1985. *Honour:* Outstanding Teacher, Indiana University, 1976-81. *Address:* 8401 Harcourt Road, Indianapolis, IN 46260, USA.

RILEY, Stancel Martin, Junior, b. 16 July 1947, Birmingham, Alabama, USA. Cardiac Surgeon. m. Linda Phillips, 17 Mar. 1975, Birmingham, Alabama, 2 sons, 2 daughters. *Education:* BS, University of Alabama, 1968; MD, University of Alabama in Birmingham, 1972. *Appointments:* Intern, Resident, General Surgery, University of Alabama, Birmingham, 1972-77; Senior Registrar, Cardiothoracic Surgery, Guy's Hospital, London, England, 1977-78; Resident, Thoracic and Cardiovascular Surgery, University of Alabama, Birmingham, 1978-80. *Memberships:* Southeastern Association for Academic Surgery; Fellow, American College of Cardiology; Fellow, American College of Chest Physicians; Fellow, American College of Surgeons. *Publications:* 'Role of Splenectomy in Felty's Syndrome', 'American Journal of Surgery', 1975; 'Left Ventricular Pressure-Volume Relations in Patients with Mitral Valve Disease', 'Surgical Forum', 1975; 'Echocardiographic Assessment of Cardiac Performance in Patients with Arterio-Venous Fistulae', 'Surgery, Gynaecology and Obstetrics', 1978. *Hobbies:* Skiing; Sailing. *Address:* 520 Madison Street, Suite B, Huntsville, AL 35801, USA.

RILEY, William James, b. 30 Mar. 1947, USA. Assistant Professor of Pathology and Paediatrics. m. Rebecca, 27 Sep. 1969, Crestwood, 2 sons. *Education:* BS, Xavier University; MD, University of Kentucky. *Appointment:* Chief of Paediatric Service, US Army Hospital, Okinawa, Japan. *Memberships:* American Diabetes Association; Society of Pediatric Research; Lawson Wilkins Pediatric Endocrine Society; American Academy of Pediatrics; College of American Pathologists. *Publications:* Co-author: "Adrenal Autoantibodies and Addison's Disease in Insulin Requiring Diabetes', 'Journal of Pediatrics', 1980; 'The Diabetogenic Effects of Streptozotocin in Mice are Prolonged and Inversely Related to Age", "Diabetes", 1981; 'Thyroid Autoimmunity in Insulin Dependent Diabetes Mellitus: The Case for Routine Screening', 'Journal of Pediatrics', 1981; "Predictive Value of Gastric Parietal Cell Autoantibodies as a Marker for Gastric and Hematologic Abnormalities Associated with Insulin Dependent Diabetes", 'Diabetes', 1982; 'Autoimmune Adrenal Diseases' in "Pediatric and Adolescent Endocrinology: Adrenal Diseases in Childhood", 1984. *Honour:* Kokomoor Award, 1980. *Hobbies:* Swimming; Bridge. *Address:* Box J-275 JHMHC, Gainesville, FL 32610, USA.

RIMAWI, Mohammad Mujahed Abdul Ghani, b. 29 May 1954, Zerka, Jordan. Anaesthesiologist. m. Hana

Said Al-Dajani, 21 June 1985, Amman, Jordan. *Education:* High School Certificate, Zerka, Jordan, 1973; MD, University of Cairo, Egypt, 1980; Studying for Master's Degree in Anaesthesia, University of Alexandria, Egypt. *Appointments:* Resident Anaesthesiologist, Bashir Government Hospital, Amman, 1980-82, 1983-84, Hussein Medical Centre, 1982-83, Zerka Government Hospital, 1984-. *Memberships:* Jordanian Medical Association; Jordanian Anaesthesia Association. *Hobbies:* Painting; Tennis; Squash; Reading. *Address:* P.O. Box 93, Amman, Jordan.

RIMON, Ranan Hilel, b. 3 Apr. 1938, Turku, Finland. Professor of Psychiatry. m. Anni Helena Laakso, 16 June 1967, Turku, 2 sons, 2 daughters. *Education:* Candidate in Medicine, 1958, Licentiate of Medicine, 1963, University of Turku School of Medicine; DMS, 1969; Consultant's Course in Hospital Administration, London, England, 1969; Special Fellowship to University of California, National Institutes of Health, USA, 1970-71. *Appointments:* Assistant Clinical Chief Physician, Psychiatric Clinic, 1967-70, Assistant Professor of Psychiatry, 1969-72, University of Turku; Assistant Professor of Psychiatry, University of Helsinki, 1971-72; Assistant Clinical Professor of Psychiatry, University of California, San Diego Medical School, USA, 1971; University of Helsinki, Finland, 1972-74; Professor and Chairman, Department of Psychiatry, University of Kuopio, 1974-75; Visiting Professor and Senior Scientist, Hebrew University, Israel, 1975-79; Professor of Psychiatry, University of Helsinki, Finland, 1980-. *Memberships:* Finnish and Israel Medical Associations; Finnish Psychiatric Association; Association of Military Surgeons of Finland; Association of the Scandinavian Military Surgeons; Scandinavian Association of Psychopharmacologists. *Publications:* Academic dissertation and 141 other publications in field of psychosomatic medicine, biological psychiatry and psychopharmacology. *Honours:* Badge of Merit, Finnish Amateur Athletics Association, 1980. *Hobby:* Bridge. *Address:* Department of Psychiatry, University of Helsinki, Lapinlahdentie, SF-00180 Helsinki, Finland.

RINDAL, Roar, b. 19 Aug. 1932, Meldal, Norway. Consultant Plastic Surgeon, Det Norske Radium Hospital. m. Målfrid Pauline R, 17 Aug. 1957, Oslo, 2 sons, 1 daughter. *Education:* MD, Bergen University, 1958. *Appointments:* Registrar, 1963-64, Senior Registrar, 1964-68, Surgery, Narvik Sylelius; Registrar, 1968-71, Senior Registrar, 1971-75, Plastic Surgery, Rileshoupitalet; Consultant, Plastic Surgery, Wergelandsun Klinikle, 1975-78, Det Norske Radium Hospital, 1978-. *Memberships:* Norwegian, Scandinavian and International Association of Plastic Surgeons; Norwegian Association for Plastic Cosmetic Surgery. *Hobby:* Cabin, South Coast of Norway. *Address:* Gabels Gt 27, 0272 Oslo 2, Norway.

RINDI, Gianguido, b. 2 Oct. 1920, Palazzolo s/Oglio, Italy. Professor of Human Physiology. m. Bruna May, 1 Aug. 1950, Pavia, 2 sons, 1 daughter. *Education:* Doctor of Chemistry, MD, Pavia; PhD, Human Physiology and Biochemistry. *Appointments include:* Currently, Professor of Human Physiology, University of Pavia. *Memberships:* Italian Society of Experimental Biology; Italian Society of Physiology; Society of Physiologists; New York Academy of Sciences. *Publications:* "Fisiologia umana", 2 volumes, 1980, 83; Author of 157 scientific papers in Italian and International journals of Physiology and Biochemistry. *Hobbies:* Literature; Mountains. *Address:* Viale Liberta 18, 27100 Pavia, Italy.

RINGERTZ, Hans Gösta, b. 3 Aug., 1939, Stockholm, Sweden. Professor of Diagnostic Radiology. m. Brittmarie Kristina Molin, 23 Nov. 1963, Uppsala, 3 daughters. *Education:* MD 1964, PhD Biophysics 1969, Karolinska Institute, Stockholm. *Appointments:* Research Assistant, Biophysics 1960-69, Resident, Radiology 1969-73, Assistant Head, Paediatric Radiology, 1973-77, Karolinska Institute, Stockholm, Chairman, Paediatric Radiology, Sachs Paediatric Hospital, Stoc-

kholm, 1978-84; Chairman, Professor of Diagnostic Radiology, Huddinge University Hospital, Huddinge. *Memberships:* Honorary Member, Swedish Society of Medical Radiology; Board Member, Swedish Society of Medicine; Board Member, Scandinavian Society of Medical Radiology; Swedish Society of Paediatric Radiology; European Society of Paediatric Radiology; Society of Paediatric Radiology. *Publications include:* "Stereochemical Aspects of Purine Degradation", 1969; about 125 articles on biophysics, general radiology, paediatric radiology, and related topics. *Honours:* Alvarenga Prize, Swedish Society of Medicine, 1976; The first Jaques Lefebvre Memorial Award, European Society of Paediatric Radiology, 1976. *Hobbies:* Philately (Iceland Official); Tennis; Orienteering. *Address:* Department of Diagnostic Radiology, Huddinge University Hospital, S-141 86 Huddinge, Sweden.

RINGOIR, Severin Maria Ghislenus, b. 17 June 1931, Aalst, Belgium. Professor of Medicine. 2 sons. *Education:* MD, University of Ghent, 1956; PhD, University of Ghent, 1967. *Appointments:* Resident, 1958; Instructor, 1961; Associate Professor, 1971; Professor of Medicine, 1975; University of Ghent, Belgium; Head, Renal Division, 1971-; Co-Chairman of Medicine, 1975-; University Hospital, Ghent. *Memberships:* Royal Academy of Medicine of Belgium; General Secretary, International Society of Artificial Organs; Congress President, European Dialysis and Transplant Association, Brussels, 1985; Member of Dutch, German, French, Swiss Societies of Nephrology; American Society of Artificial Internal Organs. *Publications:* More than 230 publications. *Honour:* Joseph Lemaire Prize, 1970. *Address:* Renal Division, University Hospital, De Pintelaan 185, B-9000 Ghent, Belgium.

RIORDAN, Hugh Desaix, b. 7 May 1932, Milwaukee, Wisconsin, USA. Centre and Institute Director. m. 4 Apr. 1956, Iowa, 4 sons, 2 daughters. *Education:* BS 1954, MD 1957, University of Wisconsin. *Appointments:* Professional Advisory Board, La Leche League International; Electroencephalographer, St Francis Medical Center, Wichita, Kansas; Consultant, EVP American Medical Association and to Sunflower Mental Health Center; Director and President, Oliver W Garvey Center for the Improvement of Human Functioning; President, Biomedical Synergistic Institute. *Memberships:* American Holistic Medical Association; American Holistic Institute/Foundation; American Medical Association; American Psychiatric Association; Academy of Psychosomatic Medicine. *Publication:* 'Proceedings of International Conferences on Human Functioning', 1979-82, Editor; 'Clinical Correlations Between Serum Glucose Variance and Reported Symptoms in Human Subjects', 1984; 'Blood Histamine Level As a Factor in Skin Conductance and Response', 1980. *Honours:* President, American Holistic Medical Association, 1984-86; Silver Award, as Executive Producer of Television Health Series 'One of a Kind', International Film Festival of New York, 1982. *Hobbies:* Reading; Writing; Creative design; Travel; Photography; Kirlian photography; Walking; Wood working. *Address:* 3100 North Hillside Street, Wichita, KS 67219, USA.

RIOUX, Jacques-Emile, b. 13 Nov. 1935, Ste-Anne des Monts, Quebec, Canada. Professor of Obstetrics & Gynaecology. m. Juanita Bongartz, 22 Jan. 1966, Baltimore, USA, 2 sons, 1 daughter. *Education:* BA, University of Montreal, 1955; MD, Laval University, 1960; Post-doctoral training in Obstetrics & Gynaecology, Union Memorial Hospital, Hospital for Women of Maryland, Johns Hopkins Hospital, Baltimore, Maryland, USA, 1963-67; Master of Public Health, University of California at Berkeley, 1976. *Appointments:* Assistant Professor of Obstetrics & Gynaecology, Faculty of Medicine, Laval University, 1968-75; Director, Department of Gynaecology, Le Centre Hospitalier de l'Université Laval, 1972-76; Associate Professor, 1973-78; Professor of Obstetrics & Gynaecology, Faculty of Medicine, Laval University, 1978-; Director, Family Planning Clinic, 1979-. *Memberships:* Society of Onstetricians & Gynaecologists of Canada; Canadian Fertility Society; Canadian Committee on Fertility Research; American College of Obstetricians & Gynaecologists; American Fertility Society; American Association of Gynaecological Laparoscopists. *Publications:* "A Manual of Laparoscopy", 1972; "A Practical Manual on Reproduction", 1973; "An Atlas of Hysterosalpingography", 1977; "Endoscopy in Gynaecology", 1978; "Artificial Insemination", 1983; "More than 80 scientific publications & book-chapters since 1969. *Honours:* President, Canadian Fertility Socoety, 1973-74; President, American Association of Gynaecological Laparoscopists, 1978; Vice-President, Canadian Committee on Fertility Research, 1976-82. *Hobbies:* Swimming; Scuba-diving; Tennis; Skiing. *Address:* 2776 Sasseville, Ste-Foy, Quebec, G1W 1A2, Canada.

RIPPIE, Edward Grant, b. 29 May 1931, Beloit, Wisconsin, USA. Professor of Pharmaceutics, College of Pharmacy, University of Minnesota, Minneapolis. m. Dorothy Ruth Tegtmeyer, 24 Sep., 1955, Chicago, Illinois, 1 son. *Education:* BS, Pharmacy, University of Wisconsin, 1953; MS, Pharmacy, University of Wisconsin, 1956; PhD, Physical Pharmacy and Pharmaceuticals, University of Wisconsin, 1959. *Appointments:* College of Pharmacy, University of Minnesota: Assistant Professor of Pharmaceutical Technology, 1959-62; Associate Professor of Pharmaceutics, 1962-66; Professor and Head, Department of Pharmaceutics, 1966-74; Professor and Director, Department of Graduate Studies in Pharmaceutics, 1974-80; Professor, Department of Pharmaceutics, 1980-; Upjohn Visiting Summer Research Professor, The Upjohn Company, Kalamazoo, Michigan, 1962. *Memberships:* Rho Chi; Phi Kappa Phi; Sigma Xi; Kappa Psi; Academy of Pharmaceutical Sciences and several professional organizations in USA. *Publications:* Chapters in Remington's Pharmaceutical Sciences, 1970, 75, 80, 85; Chapters in Industrial Pharmaceutical Technology, 1970, 75, 85; Research papers in areas of mass transport kinetics in liposome systems, particulate solids mass transport, thermodynamics of drug - protein binding, hydrodynamics of drug dissolution and viscoelasticity of pharmaceutical compressed tablets. *Honours:* Elected Fellow; Academy of Pharmaceutical Sciences, 1975 and American Institute of Chemists, 1972; The Ebert Prize, Academy of Pharmaceutical Sciences, 1982. *Hobbies:* Mechanical and Instrument Design; Hunting; Camping. *Address:* 2 North Mallard Road, North Oaks, MN 55110, USA.

RISQUEZ, Fernando, b. 14 May 1925, Caracas, Venezuela. Professor of Psychiatry & Psychology. m. Estrella Parra, 10 Dec. 1955, Caracas, 2 sons, 3 daughters. *Education:* BPh, 1941, Diploma in Medicine & Surgery, 1947, MD, 1947, Central University of Venezuela; Diploma in Psychiatry, McGill University, Canada; Diploma in Homeopathy, 1961; Diploma in Analytical Psychology, 1983. *Appointments:* Extern & Intern of the Vargas, Military, Leprocomy Hospitals, Venezuela, Royal Victoria Hospital, Canada, 1944-49; Resident, Verdun Protestant Hospital, Canada, 1949-50; Senior House Officer, Maudsley Hospital, England, 1950-51; Chief of Service, Psychiatric Hospital, Venezuela, 1952-59; Psychiatric Consultant, Vargas Hospital, Venezuela, 1953-55; Chief of Service in Neuropsychiatry, Military Hospital, Venezuela, 1952-76; Titular Member, Psychiatry Service, Central University of Venezuela, Chief of Service (Psychiatry), Central University Hospital, Venezuela, 1984-; Director of Psychiatric Post-graduate courses, 1966-. *Memberships:* Venezuelan Psychiatric & Neurological Association, Caracas, 1952; American Psychiatric Association; American Psychological Association; Venezuelan Psychological Association, 1959; Liga Medicorum Homeopathic Internationalis, Bloomendaal, 1961 (President 1985); Venezuelan Society of Homeopathic Medicine, 1970; International Association of Analytical Psychology, Zurich, Switzerland, 1983; Venezuelan Society of Gynaecology & Obstetrics, 1979; Venezuelan Academy of Medicine; Zulian Academy of

Medicine, Maracaibo, 1985. *Publications:* 'Feminine Delinquency in Venezuela" (bi-lingual edition), 1960; 'Psiocolgía Profunda y Transformismo", 1969; "Convulsion y Agresión", 1972; "Conceptos de Psicodinamia", 1975; "Aproximacion a la Feminidad", 1983; More than 100 Scientific articles in Spanish, English, French, German, more than 100 lectures on scientific matters. *Hobbies:* Mountaineering; Sub-aqua fishing; Tennis; Painting; Chess; Dominoes. *Address:* Apartado Postal 60143, Caracas 1060, Venezuela.

RITCHIE, Alexander Charles, b. 2 Apr. 1921, Auckland, New Zealand. Professor. m. Susan Liszauer, 10 Oct. 1956. *Education:* MB, ChB, University of Otago; D Phil, University of Oxford; Massachusetts General Hospital. *Appointments:* Visiting Fellow, Chicago Medical School; Assistant, and Associate Professor, McGill University; Head, Pathology, University of Toronto; Pathologist in Chief, Toronto General Hospital. *Memberships:* American Association for Cancer Research; American Association of Pathologists; Canadian Association of Pathologists, President, 1966-67; Royal College of Physicians and Surgeons of Canada, Chairman, various Pathology Committees, Chief Examiner, Pathology; President, World Association of Societies Pathology, 1980-85; President, World Pathology Foundation, 1979-84. *Publications:* Articles in various medical journals. *Honours:* Centennial Medal of Canada, 1967; Jubilee Medal, Canada, 1977; Honorary Memberships, various bodies; Admiral, Texas Navy. *Address:* Department of Pathology, Toronto General Hospital, EN 4-305, 200 Elizabeth Street, Toronto, Ontario M5G 2C4, Canada.

RIVA, Alessandro, b. 25 Aug. 1939, Milan, Italy. Professor & Chairman of Department. m. Francesca Testa, 8 Oct. 1969, Cagliari, 2 daughters. *Education:* MD, Collegio Ghislieri, University of Pavia, 1964; LD Anatomy, University of Cagliari, 1970. *Appointments:* Fellow in Anatomy, Collegio Ghislieri Pavia, 1964-65; Research Fellow, in Anatomy, Department of Anatomy, St Thomas' Hospital Medical School, London, England, 1965-66; Assistant Lecturer in Anatomy, 1966-71, Professor of Topographical Anatomy, 1968, Professor of Histology, 1969-71, Professor of Anatomy & Chairman of the Department, 1971-75, Professor of Anatomy in the Medical School & Chairman of the Anatomy Department, 1975-, Medical School, University of Cagliari; Professor of Oral Anatomy in the Dental School, 1979-86; Member, Board of Governors, University of Caglieri. *Memberships:* Italian Society of Anatomists; Italian Histochemical Society; Electron Microscopy Society of Italy; Italian Society of Andrology; Anatomical Society of Great Britain & Ireland; Histochemical Society; American Association of Anatomists; American Society of Andrology. *Publications:* Various articles in medical journals. *Hobby:* History of Medicine. *Address:* Vico Regina Margherita n.l, 09100 Cagliari, Italy.

ROBBIN-COKER, Daniel Josephus Olubunmi, b. 15 July 1934, Freetown, Sierra Leone. Chief Consultant, Ministry of Health, Sierra Leone; Paediatrician in Charge, Children's Hospital, Freetown. m. Clara Edmina Asgill, 12 Mar. 1966, Durham, England, 2 sons, 2 daughters. *Education:* BSc Hons, MB BS, Durham University, England; Diploma in Child Health, London; MRCP, London; Fellow, West African College of Physicians. *Appointments:* House Officer, Royal Victoria Infirmary, Newcastle upon Tyne, England, 1961-62; Medical Officer, 1962-64, Senior Registrar, 1969-71, Consultant, 1971, Children's Hospital, Sierra Leone; Registrar, Preston Hospital, North Shields, England, 1965-67; Paediatric Registrar, Liverpool Maternity Hospital, England, 1967-68; Paediatric Registrar, Royal Liverpool Children's Hospital, 1968-69; Chief Consultant, Ministry of Health, Sierra Leone, 1981-. *Memberships:* Sierra Leone Medical and Dental Association; Founder President, 1977-79, Nutrition Society of Sierra Leone; Board Member, 1982-85, Union of National African Medical Associations; Vice-President, 1980-82, Commonwealth Medical Association; Examiner, 1979-83, West African College of Physicians; Chairman, Faculty Board of Paediatrics, 1985, Council Member, 1977-85, West African College of Physicians. *Publications:* "Manual of Maternal and Childhealth for Sierra Leone", (with B Williams), 1976; 'Our Children, Our most valuable natural resources', 1979; 'Infant Feeding and PCM in Freetown', 1975. *Hobbies:* Freemasonry; Lionism. *Address:* PO Box 447, Freetown, Sierra Leone, West Africa.

ROBBINS, Carey Angelyn May, b. 24 Feb. 1952, Fayette, Alabama, USA. Registered Nurse in Emergency Department. m. Berlin Jackson Robbins Junior, 5 June 1980, 3 sons. *Education:* Athens College, 1970-72; BSN, University of Alabama, Birmingham 1974. *Appointments:* BS Supervisor, Bryee Hospital, Tuscaloosa, Alabama, 1974-75, 1976-78; Nurse Recruiting, Bryee Hospital, 1975-76; Psychiatric Charge Nurse, Huntsville Hospital, 1978-80; Nurse, Emergency Department, Huntsville Hospital, 1980-. *Memberships:* Huntsville Civic Ballet Association; Huntsville Historic Society. *Honours:* International Platform Association, Member, 1985-; Featured in numerous biographical publications. *Hobbies:* Scuba diving; Travel. *Address:* 6100 University Drive, Huntsville, AL 35806, USA.

ROBBOY, Stanley, J, b. 5 Jan. 1941, Cleveland, Ohio, USA. Pathologist, Professor fo Pathology. m. Anita Henrietta Wyzanski, 23 July 1968, Cambridge, Massachusetts, 2 daughters. *Education:* MD, University of Michigan, Ann Arbor, 1965. *Appointments include:* Chief, Pathology Department, Ireland Army Hospital, Fort Knox, Kentucky, 1970-72; Pathologist, DES Clear Cell Adenocarcinoma Registry, 1972-83; Pathologist and principal investigator, National Collaborative Diethylstilbestrol (DESAD) Project, 1974-; Visiting Scientist, New England Regional Primate Center, 1973-84; Visiting Professor, University of Shiraz Medical School, Iran, 1976; Assistant Professor of Pathology 1972-76, Associate Professor 1976-84, Harvard Medical School; Assistant Pathologist 1972-76, Associate Pathologist 1976-84, Massachusetts General Hospital; Professor and Chairman of Pathology, New Jersey Medical School of the University of Medicine and Dentistry of New Jersey, 1984-; Pathologist-in-Chief, University Hospital, 1984-. *Memberships include:* American Society of Clinical Pathologists; International Academy of Pathology; College of American Pathologists; International Society of Gynaecologic Pathologists; American Pathology Foundation. *Publications include:* 170 publications including: 'A Hypnothetic Mechanism of Diethylstilbestrol (DES) - induced Anomalies in Prenatally Exposed Women', 1983; 'Insular Carcinoids of Ovary Associated with Malignant Mucinous Tumors', 1984; 'An Atlas of Findings in the Human Female After Intrauterine Exposure to Diethylstilbestrol', (co-author), 1984. *Honours:* Commendation Award for Research, US Army, 1972; Junior Faculty Fellow, American Cancer Society, 1972-75; Foundation Prize, American College of Obstetricians and Gynaecologists, 1973. *Hobby:* Skiing. *Address:* Department of Pathology, UMDNJ-New Jersey Medical School, Newark, NJ 07103-2484, USA.

ROBERT, Jacques-Michel, b. 8 Feb. 1928, France. Head, Medical Genetic Department. m. 12 July 1952, 3 sons. *Education:* MD, 1958; Intern, Maitre de Conferences, 1963; Human Geneticist, Professor, 1970. *Appointments:* Head, Faculty of Medicine, Lyon Sud, 1974; President, Scientific Council of Institute Europeen des Genomutations, 1978; currently, Head, Medical Genetic Department, Lyons University. *Memberships:* Founder-President, European Club of Genetic Counselling; Editor in Chief, Journal de Genetique Humaine, Switzerland; Neurogenetic group, World Federation of Neurology. *Publications:* "Elements de Genetique medicale", 1968; "Genetique et cytogenetique cliniques", 1977; "L'Heredite raconte aux parents", 1978; "Comprendre notre nerveau", 1982; "Genetique: de la biologie a la clinique", 1983. *Honours:* Chevalier, Legion of Honour, 1977; Past President, Rotary Club, Lyon-Est, 1971-72. *Hobby:* Classi-

cal music. *Address:* Hotel Dieu, 1 place de l'Hopital, 69002 Lyon, France.

ROBERTS, Derek Frank, b. 20 July 1925, London, England. Professor of Human Genetics. m. 6 children. *Education:* ScD, MA, Cambridge University; DPhil, Oxford University. *Appointments:* Demonstrator, University of Oxford, England. *Memberships:* Secretary-General, International Association of Human Biologists; Treasurer, International Union of Biological Sciences; Chairman, Society for the Study of Human Biology; Clinical Genetics Society; Eugenics Society; Institute of Biology. *Publications:* Author of 300 publications on professional subjects. *Honours:* ScD, Cambridge, 1975; FRSSA, 1984; FRSE, 1985. *Address:* Department of Human Genetics, 19 Claremont Place, Newcastle upon Tyne NE2 4AA, England.

ROBERTS, Jay, b. 15 July 1927, New York, USA. Professor and Chairman, Pharmacology Department. m. Marian Camenson, 18 June 1950, 1 son, 1 daughter. *Education:* BS, Long Island University, 1949; PhD, Cornell University, New York, 1953. *Appointments:* Associate Professor of Pharmacology, Cornell University, New York, 1962-66; Programme Director, 1966-70, Graduate Faculty, 1966-70, Professor of Pharmacology, 1966-70, University of Pittsburgh School of Medicine; Professor and Chairman, Medical College of Pennsylvania, Philadelphia, 1970-; Research Associate on Consultant Staff, Philadelphia Geriatric Center, 1975-. *Memberships:* College of Physicians; Chairman, Section of Biological Sciences, Gerontological Society of America; Nominating Committee, American Society for Pharmacology and Experimental Therapeutics. *Publications:* Editorial Board: 'Journal of Gerontology', 1980-; 'Journal of Cardiovascular Pharmacology', 1979-. Reviewer, "Experimental Aging Research", 1978-. "The Encyclopedia of Aging". *Honours:* Postdoctoral Fellow: US Public Health, 1953-55; New York Heart Association, 1955-57. 7th Annual Science Writers Forum, American Heart Association, 1980; Linkback Award for Distinguished Teaching, 1973. *Address:* Department of Pharmacology 305C, Medical College of Pennsylvania, 3300 Henry Avenue, Philadelphia, PA 19129, USA.

ROBERTS, John Charles, b. 28 Sep. 1938, Wollongong, New South Wales, Australia. Director of Pathology. m. Jennifer Mary Haynes, 14 Dec. 1962, Hunters Hill, 1 daughter. *Education:* MB, BS, University of Sydney; PhD, Australian National University; FRCPA; FRCS (Edinburgh, written); ECFMG. *Appointments include:* Surgical Registrar, Australia & London, UK; Research Scholar, John Curtin School, Australian National University; Pathology Registrar, Melbourne & Sydney; Pathologist, St Vincent's Hospital, Sydney. *Memberships:* Royal College of Pathologists of Australia; Australian Society for Experimental Pathology. *Publications include:* Thesis, "Lymph After Injury", 1969; Journal articles, 'Protein. . . Thermal Injury", 1969; 'Traumatic Pancreatitis' 1975; etc. *Hobbies:* Jazz music; Skiing; Riley Cars; Gliding. *Address:* 32 Farnell Street, Gladesville, NSW 2111, Australia.

ROBERTS, Newell Orville, b. 7 Aug. 1955; Psychiatry, Baylor University College of Medicine, 1959. *Appointments:* Fighter Pilot, US Air Force, 1940-45; Atomic Energy Research Commission, University of California at Los Angeles, 1948-49; Internship, Wadsworth Hospital, 1955-56; Chief, Veterans Administration Department of Psychiatry, 1960-. *Memberships:* American Medical Association; American Psychiatric Association, Texas Medical Association; Masonic Lodge 329; Eastern Star no 856; Scottish Rite, Los Angeles; Noble Shriner Arabia Temple, Houston, Texas; American Fighter Aces Association. *Honour:* Distinguished Flying Cross, 1943. *Address:* 7111 Spring Leaf, San Antonio, TX 78249, USA.

ROBERTS, Richard Noel, b. 4 June 1943, Wales. Optomotrist. m. Susan Margaret Deere, 23 Aug. 1969, Cardiff, Wales, 1 son, 1 daughter. *Education:* BSc (Hons) University of Cardiff; FBCO; FAAO. *Appointments:* S/E Optomotrist, 1967-present. Examiner, British Optical Association, 1970-78; Visiting Lecturer in Optomotry, 1970-80; Examiner, British College of Ophthalmic Opticians, 1978-present; Senior Examiner, British College of Ophthalmic Opticians, 1981-present. *Memberships:* Secretary of Local Optical Committee, South Glamorgan, 1968-78; Chairman South Glamorgan Optical Committee since 1978; Chairman, Welsh Optical Committee since 1980; General Optical Council; Fellow, British College of Ophthalmic Opticians; Fellow, American Academy of Optometry. *Hobbies:* Opera; Classical Music; Pianist; Organist; Walking; Badminton. *Address:* 56 Daw y Cold Road, Cyncold, Cardiff CF2 6ME, Wales.

ROBERTSON, James Ian Summers, b. 5 Mar. 1928, Welbeck, England. Physician, Blood Pressure Unit, Western Infirmary, Glasgow. m. Maureen Patricia Doherty, 10 Sep. 1955, Cuddington, Surrey, 1 son, 2 daughters. *Education:* BSc 1949, MB BS, 1952, London; Fellow, Royal College of Physicians, London, 1970, Glasgow, Scotland, 1984. *Appointments:* Senior Lecturer in Therapeutics, St Mary's Hospital Medical School, London, 1963-67; President, International Society of Hypertension, 1976-78; Chairman, Scientific Council on Hypertension, International Society and Federation of Cardiology, 1976-78; President, British Hypertension Society, 1981-83; Currently, Physician, Blood Pressure Unit, Medical Research Council, Western Infirmary, Glasgow, Scotland. *Memberships:* Fellow, Medical Advisory Board, High Blood Pressure Council, American Heart Association; Honorary Fellow, Cardiac Society of Australia and New Zealand; Portuguese Cardiac Society; Mexican Hypertension Society; Southern African Hypertension Society. *Publications:* Author or co-author over 300 papers on clinical and experimental hypertension, cardiac failure, coronary artery disease and endocrinology; Editor 'Clinical Aspects of Essential Hypertension", 1983, "Clinical Aspects of Secondary Hypertension", 1983 and others. *Honours:* A C Corcoran Lectureship, American Heart Association, 1978; Jodh Gold Medal, 1979; MSD International Award, 1980; Scott Heron Medal, 1982. *Hobbies:* Cricket; Travel; Opera; Literature. *Address:* Elmbank, Manse Road, Bowling, Glasgow, Scotland G60 5AA.

ROBINSON, Arvin E, b. 29 Jan. 1939, Richmond, Virginia, USA. Professor of Radiology. m. Beverly Morgan, 19 June 1960, Richmond, Virginia, 1 son, 3 daughters. *Education:* AB, University of Pennsylvania; MD, Medical College of Virginia. *Appointments:* Instructor in Radiology, Duke University Medical Centre, Durham, North Carolina, 1968-69; Staff Radiologist, Fitzsimmons General Hospital, Denver, Colorado, 1969-71; Assistant Professor, 1971-74, Director, Division of Diagnostic Radiology, 1972-75, Duke University Medical Centre; Consultant in Radiology, Womack Army Hospital, Fort Bragg, North Carolina, 1972-75; Associate Professor, Duke University Medical Centre, 1974-75; Professor & Chairman, Department of Radiology, University of South Alabama Medical Centre, Mobile, Alabama, 1975-85. *Memberships:* Publications: Honours: James Picker Foundation Advanced Fellow in Radiology, 1968-69, 1971-74. *Hobby:* Tennis. *Address:* Department of Radiology, University of South Alabama Medical Centre, 2451 Fillingim Street, Mobile, AL 36617, USA.

ROBINSON, David Errol, b. 6 Mar. 1939, Brisbane, Australia. Ultrasonic Physicist. m. Helen Gordon, 6 Jan. 1962, Sydney, Australia, 1 son, 2 daughters. *Education:* BEng, 1960, MEng, 1967, DSc, 1982, University of New South Wales. *Appointments:* Physicist, National Acoustics Laboratories; Physicist, Ultrasonics Institute; Head, Advanced Techniques Section, Ultrasonics Institute. *Memberships:* Fellow, Australian Institute of Physics; Fellow, Australasian College of Physical Scientists in Medicine; Honorary Fellow, Royal Australasian College of Radiologists;

Honorary Fellow, American Institute of Ultrasound in Medicine. *Publications:* 77 papers & 8 patents on Ultrasound in Medical Diagnosis. *Hobbies:* Sailing; Hobby Farming; Scouting Association. *Address:* c/o Ultrasonics Institute, 126 Greville Street, Chatswood, New South Wales 2000, Australia.

ROBINSON, Patricia Ann Gordon, b. 7 Dec. 1920, Oakland, California, USA. Medical Clinical Social Worker. m. Geo B. Robinson, 20 June 1941, deceased, 1 son. *Education:* BA, Social Work, MSW, Social Work, University of Michigan; American Red Cross Grey Lady, American Army Hospitals, Germany & France, 1949-55. *Appointments:* Head Start Social Worker, 1968; Project Director, Project FIND, 1972; Instructor, Extension Division, University of California, Davis; Activities Director, Geriatric Convalescent Home, 1973-74; VA Medical Centre, 1975-. *Memberships:* National Association of Social Workers; Society for Clinical Social Workers; American Orthopsychiatric Association; Association of Military Surgeons of the USA; Captain, Medical Service Corps, 101st Medical Group; 1st Medical Brigade; California State Military Reserve. *Honours:* Certificate of Merit, 3rd Army HQ for Army Relief Society Representative, 1957; citation for Project FIND, White House, 1972; Nominated for Samuel Rose Award, Virginia, 1979; Virginia Achievement Award, 1982; Citation from the Ex Prisoners of War, 1984. *Hobbies:* Golf; Swimming; Reading; Painting. *Address:* 9907 Balboa Way, Cypress, CA 90630, USA.

RÖCKERT, Hans Otto Ernst, b. 10 Jan. 1932, Sundsvall, Sweden. Professor, Chief Medical Diving Officer, Swedish Navy. m. Lise Lotte, 31 Oct. 1958, Göteborg, 2 sons, 1 daughter. *Education:* PhD, 1958; MD, 1961. *Appointments:* Assistant Professor, 1959-65, Associate Professor, 1965-79, Professor of Histology, 1979-, University of Göteborg. *Memberships:* Undersea Medical Society; European Undersea Biomedical Society. *Publications:* Some 100 scientific papers on X-ray microscopy & Diving Medicine; 4 monographs. *Honours:* American Academy of Dental Medicine, 1961; Örlogsmannasällskapet (Royal Academy of Sea Warfares), 1983. *Hobbies:* Golf; Yachting; Skiing. *Address:* Department of Histology, University of Göteborg, P.O. Box 33031, S-400 33 Göteborg, Sweden.

ROCKWELL, Sara Campbell, b. 8 Sep. 1943, Somerset, Pennsylvania, USA. Professor. m. Charles Rockwell, 2 sons. *Education:* BS, Distinction, Pennsylvania State University, 1965; PhD, Physics, Stanford University, 1971. *Appointments:* Engineering & Technical Assistant, H EB Singer Inc, 1963-64; Graduate Research Assistant, 1967-70, Postdoctoral Fellow, 1971, 1972, 1974, Stanford University; Attache de Recherche, Institut de Recherche de Radiobiologie Clinique, Institut Gustavus Roussy, Villejuif, France, 1973; Assistant Professor, 1974-78, Associate Professor, 1978-84, Professor, 1984-, Therapeutic Radiology, Yale School of Medicine. *Memberships:* Radiation Research Society, Councillor, 1985-; Cell Kinetics Society, President 1982-83; Tissue Culture Association; Bioelectromagnetics Society; American Association for Cancer Research; American Association for the Advancement of Science; American Society for Therapeutic Radiology and Oncology; American Association of University Women. *Publications:* Author, over 60 articles in the field of experimental cancer research. *Honours:* Outstanding Senior, Pennsylvania State University, 1965; Francis Lou Kellman Award for Outstanding PhD Candidate in Biological Science, Stanford University, 1971; Elected to various honour societies including Mortarboard, 1964; Member, Experimental Therapeutics Study Section, NIH, 1982-. *Hobbies:* Cooking; Fishing; Needlework. *Address:* Department of Therapeutic Radiology, Yale School of Medicine, 333 Cedar St, New Haven, CT 06510, USA.

ROCMANS, Pierre Arthur, b. 15 Mar. 1937, Uccle, Belgium. Associate Professor of Thoracic Surgery.

m. Christiane Borrey, 7 May 1975, Brussels, 2 sons, 1 daughter. *Education:* MD, PhD, University Libre, Brussels, 1962, 77. *Appointment:* Research Fellow, Harvard University and Massachusetts Institute of Technology, Boston, USA, 1966-68. *Memberships:* International Association Study of Lung Cancer; European Society of Pneumology; European Thyroid Association; Societe Royale Belge de Chirurgie. *Hobbies:* Family; Sailing. *Address:* Department of Thoracic Surgery, Hospital Erasme, 1070 Brussels, Belgium.

RODDIE, Ian Campbell, b. 1 Dec. 1928, Portadown, Northern Ireland. Dunville Professor of Physiology; Pro-Vice-Chancellor. m. Elizabeth A G Honeyman, deceased, 1 son, 3 daughters. *Education:* BSc, 1st class honours, 1950; MB BS, Bachelor of Obstetrics, 1953; MD, Gold Medal, 1957; DSc, 1962; Fellow, Royal College of Physicians, Ireland, 1965. *Appointments:* Resident Medical Officer, Royal Victoria Hospital, Belfast, 1953-54; Lecturer, Physiology, Queen's University, Belfast, 1954-60; Harkness Fellow, University of Washington, Seattle, Washington, USA, 1960-61; Senior Lecturer, Physiology, 1961-62, Reader, 1962-64, Dunville Professor of Physiology, 1964-, Dean of Medicine, 1976-81, Pro-Vice-Chancellor, 1982-, Queen's University, Belfast, Northern Ireland. *Memberships:* Fellow and Past President, Royal Academy of Medicine, Ireland; Past Council Member, Physiological Society; Past President, Belfast Branch, Association of University Teachers; Medical Research Society; Pharmacological Society; Past President, Ulster Biomedical Engineering Society. *Publications:* "The Physiology of Disease", 1975; "Physiology for Practitioners", 1971; "Multiple Choice Questions in Human Physiology", 1971. *Honours:* Beit Memorial Research Fellowship, 1957; Harkness Fellow, Commonwealth Fund of New York, USA, 1960; Member, Royal Irish Academy, 1978; Conway Review Lectureship and Bronze Medallist, 1977; Japan Society for the Promotion of Science Research Fellowship, 1983. *Hobbies:* Gardening; Carpentry. *Address:* Department of Physiology, Queen's University of Belfast, Medical Biology Centre, 97 Lisburn Road, Belfast BT9 7BL, Northern Ireland.

RODGER, Alan, b. 9 June 1946, Kirkcaldy, Fife, Scotland. Consultant Radiation Oncologist. *Education:* BSc Medical Sciences, Physiology, 1968, MB ChB, 1971, University of Edinburgh; Fellow, Royal College of Surgeons of Edinburgh, 1975; Diploma in Medical Radiology (Therapy), University of Edinburgh, 1977; Fellow, Royal College of Radiologists, 1979. *Appointments:* House Officer, Edinburgh Royal Infirmary, 1971-72; House Officer, Victoria Hospital, Kirkcaldy, 1972; Senior House Officer in Radiotherapy, Edinburgh, 1972-73; Senior House Officer, Professional Surgical Unit, Edinburgh Royal Infirmary, 1973-74; Surgical Registrar, Edinburgh Surgical Training Scheme, Edinburgh Royal Infirmary, 1974-75; Radiotherapy Registrar, Western General Hospital, Edinburgh, 1975-77; Lecturer in Radiotherapy, University of Edinburgh & Medical Research Council Cyclotron Unit, 1977-80; Project Investigator, M D Anderson Hospital & Tumour Institute, University of Texas, Houston, USA, 1980-81; Consultant Radiation Oncologist to the Edinburgh Royal Infirmary & Western General Hospital, Edinburgh, 1981-. *Memberships:* British Institute of Radiology; G H Fletcher Society; European Society of Therapeutic Radiation Oncology; Scottish Radiological Society; UK Childrens Cancer Study Group; Rad Society. *Publications:* Various articles in medical journals in field of festicular tumours & breast cancer. *Hobbies:* Cooking & eating good food; Restoring a Georgian House. *Address:* 1 Laverockbank Road, Trinity, Edinburgh, EH5 3DG, Scotland.

RODIN, Alvin Eli, b. 25 Mar. 1926, Winnepeg, Canada. Professor of Pathology. m. Jean Callady, 8 Feb. 1974, Galveston, Texas, USA, 4 daughters. *Education:* MD 1950, MSc 1960, University of Manitoba; Fellow, Royal College of Physicians (Canada), 1959. *Appoin-

tments: Associate Pathologist, Royal Alexandre Hospital, Edmonton, Canada, 1959-60; Director of Laboratories, Misericordia Hospital, Edmonton, Canada, 1960-63; Professor of Pathology, University of Texas Medical Branch at Galveston, Texas, 1963-75; Professor & Chairman, Department of Postgraduate Medicine & Continuing Education, Wright State University School of Medicine, Dayton, Ohio, 1975-. *Memberships:* International Academy of Pathology; Society for Paediatric Pathology; American Medical Association; Society for Health & Human Values; American Medical Colleges Association; American Osler Society; and others. *Publications:* "Oslerian Pathology", 1981; "Pathology Objectives for Medical Student Education", 1984; "Medical Case Book of Dr Arthur Conan Doyle", 1984; Various articles in medical journals. *Honours:* Various awards for teaching, Community Service & Medical Education. *Hobbies:* Community Theatre; History of Medicine. *Address:* Wright State University School of Medicine, PO Box 927, Dayton, OH 45401, USA.

RODRIGUEZ, Maria P, b. 26 Nov. 1957, Bogota, Colombia. Dentist. *Education:* BA, Biology, Queens College, 1980; DDS, New York University Dental School, 1984. *Memberships:* American Dental Association; Association of Women Dentists of New York; Academy of General Dentistry; Alumni Association of New York University; Alumni Association of Queens College. *Hobbies:* Oil Painting; Photography. *Address:* 154-08 64th Avenue, Flushing, NY 11367, USA.

ROE, Francis John Caldwell, b. 16 Aug. 1924, London, England. Independent Consultant in Experimental Pathology and Toxicology; Honorary Member, Institute of Cancer Research, London. m. Brenda Joan Beckett, 26 August 1948, Oxford, 2 sons, 2 daughters. *Education:* BM, BCh, 1948; MA, 1950; DM, 1957, Oxford University; DSc London University, 1965; FRCPath, London, 1967. *Appointments:* House Physician/Surgeon, London Hospital, 1948-49; Graded Pathologist, Royal Army Medical Corps, England, Austria and Germany, 1949-51; Lecturer, Cancer Research, London Hospital Medical College, 1951-62; Reader in Experimental Pathology, Chester Beatty Research Institute, Institute of Cancer Research, London, 1961-71; Research Coordinator, Tobacco Research Council, London, 1971-73; Independent Consultant in Experimental Pathology and Toxicology, 1973-. *Memberships:* World Health Organization: Department of Health and Social Security, Committee on Toxicology and Committee on Carcinogenicity; British Association for Cancer Research; British Toxicology Society; British Occupational Hygiene Society; Royal College of Pathologists; Society of Toxicology; Royal Society of Medicine; British Medical Association. *Publications:* Author of over 650 articles in medical and scientific journals; Editor-/Contributor: "The Biology of Cancer", 1966; "The Prevention of Cancer", 1967; "The Pathology of Laboiratory Rats and Mice", 1967; Editor: "Metabolic Aspects of Food Safety", 1970; "The Chemical Industry and Health of the Community", 1985; "Microbiological Standardisation of Laboratory Animals", 1985. *Honours:* Price University Scholarship, London Hospital Medical College; Lord Kitchener Scholarship; Gold Medal, Centro Sociale Studio Precencerosi of Rome; The Ver Heyden de Lancey Prize for Medicine and Art, Royal Society of Medicine, London. *Hobby:* Portrait Sculpture. *Address:* 19 Marryat Road, Wimbledon Common, London SW19 5BB, England.

ROGER, Francis Henri, b. 24 July 1941, Etterbeek, Belgium. Head, Medical Records Department; Vice President, Department of Hospital and Medico-Social Sciences. m. Anne-Marie Wouters, 12 July 1967, Brussels, 2 sons, 1 daughter. *Education:* MD, 1967, Board Certified in Internal Medicine, 1972, Agrege de l'Enseignement Superieur en Medecine, 1982, University of Louvain; MSc, University of Minnesota, USA, 1972. *Appointments:* Post Doctoral Graduate Fellow in Medicine and Laboratory Medicine, Health Computer Sciences, 1970-72; Attache to Medical Director, University Hospital of Louvain, 1972-; Chef de Clinique Associe, Department of Internal Medicine, 1981-; Scientific Expert: Commission of European Communities, 1973-85; Council of Europe, 1985-; World Health Organisation, 1985-89. Currently: Head Medical Records Department, St Luc Hospital; Adjunct to the Director of the Center for Medical Informatics, University of Louvain. *Memberships:* President: European Federation for Medical Informatics; Belgian Society for Medical Informatics. International Society of Biometry; Belgian Society of Internal Medicine; American Association for Medical Systems and Informatics. *Publications:* "Recherches sur les conditions sociales de la medecine", 1965; "Medecine et Informatique", 1979; "The Minimum Basic Data Set for hospital statistics in the EEC", 1981; "Le sume du dossier medical, indicateur informatise de performance et de qualite des soins", thesis, 1982; "Hospital Statistics in Europe", 1982; 'MIE', 1982, 84, 85. *Honours:* Social Medical Award, 1965; CRB Fellow, Belgian American Education Foundation, 1970; Laureat du Concours de Bourses de Voyage, 1974; Van Beneden Award, 1982. *Hobbies:* Jogging; Windsurfing. *Address:* Cliniques Universitaires St Luc, Centre d'Informatique Medicale, Av Hippocrate 10, B-1200 Brussels, Belgium.

ROGERS, Lesley Joy, b. 31 July 1943, Australia. Physiologist. *Education:* BSc 1st Class Honours, University of Adelaide, Australia, 1964; D.Phil, University of Sussex, England, 1972. *Appointments:* Teaching Fellow, Harvard University USA, 1965-66; Research Assistant, Tufts New England Medical Centre, Boston, 1967; Tutor for the Open University, England, 1969-71; Senior Tutor in Physiology, Monash University, Australia, 1972-75; Senior Research Fellow, Australian National University, 1976; Senior Tutor in Pharmacology, Monash University, 1977; Australian Research Grants Research Fellow, Monash University, 1978-81; Lecturer in Pharmacology, Monash University, 1981-85; Lecturer in Physiology, University of New England, 1985-. *Memberships:* British & Australian Societies for the Study of Animal Behaviour; International Neuroethology Society; Australian Neuroscience Society; Australian Physiological & Pharmacological Society; Dialectics in Biology Group. *Publications:* Some 85 papers mainly on research in brain and behaviour, and some on social & sexual matters. *Honours:* Bursary to Adelaide University; Commonwealth Scholarship; George Murray Scholarship; Commonwealth Postgraduate Scholarship. *Hobbies:* Music; Playing the 'cello; Stained Glass Craft; Writing in areas of sexuality & feminism. *Address:* c/o Department of Pharmacology, Monash University, Clayton, Victoria 3168, Australia.

ROGERS, Olbert William, b. 21 Aug. 1930, Australia. Dental Research. m. Dorathee Muriel Pye, 10 Dec. 1969, Sydney, Australia, 1 son, 2 daughters. *Education:* BDS, DDSc, University of Sydney; FADM. *Appointments:* Teaching Fellow, University of Sydney; Clinical Adviser, Australian Dental Standards Laboratory; Research Director, Electro-ceram Pty Ltd; Research Director, Electrodent Pty Ltd; National Secretary, Australian Society of Implant Dentistry. *Memberships:* Australian Dental Association; Fédération Dentaire; International; Australian Society of Implant Dentistry; International College of Oral Implantology; Australian Prosthodontic Society; Society for the Advancement of Anaesthesia & Sedation in Dentistry; International Precious Metal Institute; Dental Aesthetics & Ceramic Society. *Publications:* "An Investigation of Metal-to-Metal unions used in dentistry with special reference to electrodeposition procedures" (doctoral thesis), 1974; "Dental Application of electroformed pure gold" (in 3 parts), 1980. *Honours:* Various research grants, Fellow, American Academy of Dental Materials, 1984. *Hobbies:* Skin-diving; Farming. *Address:* 70 Gymea Bay Road, Gymea, New South Wales 2227, Australia.

ROGERS, R Claude, b. 3 June 1923, Paris, France. Assistant Professor; Chief, Rehabilitation Consultations, University of Pennsylvania. m. F Antoinette, 17

Nov. 1954, 1 son. *Education:* MD, 1951. *Appointments:* Medical Director, General Hospital; Chief Education, Rheumatol Gick Institute. *Memberships:* American Medical Association; American Congress of PMR; American Academy of PMR. *Publications:* "Chronic Brain Syndrome Reconsidered" Proceedings, New Frontiers That Influence Disease and Rehabilitation, IRMA 4 International Congress, Puerto Rico, 1982; Monograph: "Prevention and Management of Heterotopic Ossification in Severe Head Injuries", 1985. *Honour:* American Physician Award, 1973, 77, 81, 85. *Hobby:* Painting. *Address:* 161 Highland Circle, Baia-Cynwyd, PA 19004, USA.

ROHDE, Charles A, b. 7 Apr. 1937, Baltimore, Maryland, USA. Professor and Chairman, Department of Biostatistics. m. Savilla, 10 July 1981, Silver Run, Maryland. *Education:* BS, Case Institute of Technology, 1959; PhD, North Carolina State University, 1964. *Appointments:* Assistant Professor 1965-68, Associate Professor 1968-79, Professor, 1979-81, Professor and Chairman, 1981-, Department of Biostatics, The Johns Hopkins University, Baltimore. *Memberships:* American Statistical Association; Biometric Society; Institute of Mathematical Statistics; Royal Statistical Society. *Publications include:* 'Batch, bulk and composite sampling' in "Satellite Program in Statistical Ecology" edited by R M Cormack, G P Patil and D S Robson, 1978; 'Hereditary Polyposis Coli. III. Genetic and evolutionary fitness' with E A Murphy, A J Krush and M Dietz, in American Journal of Human Genetics, 1980; 'The bingo model of survivorship: 1. Probabilistic Aspects WITH E A Murphy, J E Trojak and W Hou, in American Journal of Medical Genetics, 1981; 'Statistical Considerations and Protocol Using Small Numbers of Animals. Acute Toxicity Testing Alternative Approach' edited by Alan M Goldberg, Mary Ann Liebert Inc.' 1984. *Honours:* Sigma Xi; Phi Kappa Phi; Delta Omega. *Address:* Department of Biostatistics, The Johns Hopkins University, School of Hygiene and Public Health, 615N Wolfe Street, Baltimore, MD 21205, USA.

ROHDE, Jon Eliot, b. 22 Oct. 1941, USA. Advisor in Child Survival Management Sciences for Health/New Delhi, India. m. Cornelia, 8 Aug. 1964, Ohio, 2 daughters. *Education:* BA (Magna), Amherst, 1963; MD (Magna), Harvard University, 1967. *Appointments:* United States Public Health Service Cholera Research Laboratory, East Pakistan; Instructor, Harvard Medical School Paediatrics; Medical Advisor, UNICEF, Calcutta; Paediatrician, Albert Schweitzer Hospital, Haiti; Field Staff, Rockefeller Foundation; Professor of Paediatrics, Yogyakarta, Indonesia; Representative Management Sciences for Health, Rural Health Advisor, Government of Haiti; Children Survival Advisor, India. *Memberships:* Fellow, American Academy Paediatrics; Fellow, American College Preventive Medicine; Sigma Xi; Phi Beta Kappa; Alpha Omega Alpha. *Publications:* 100 published articles on Child Health Infectious Disease, Nutrition, Medical Education, Management of Primary Health Care Services. *Honours:* Ten Outstanding Young Men of America, 1972; Leonard Parsons Lecture, Birmingham England, 1982; Honorary DSc, Amherst, 1983; Irving Johnson Lecture, Amherst, 1985. *Hobbies:* Sailing; Scuba; Tennis; Mountain Climbing. *Address:* c/o Management Sciences for Health, 165 Allandale Road, Boston, MA 02130, USA.

ROHE, Daniel E., Clinical Psychologist. *Education:* BA, Honours, Ohio State University, 1973; MA, 1980, PhD, 1980, Psychology, University of Minnesota. *Appointments:* Vocational Rehabilitation Counsellor, Ohio Bureau of Vocational Rehabilitation, Cincinnati, 1973-75; Research Associate, Spinal Cord Injury Project, University of Minnesota Hospitals, 1977-78; Assistant Professor, Psychology, Mayo Medical School; Consultant, Mayo Clinic, Psychiatry & Psychology. *Memberships:* American Psychological Association; American Congress of Rehabilitation Medicine; Minnesota Psychological Association. *Publications:* Articles in professional journals including 'Journal of

Counselling Psychology'; 'Rehabilitation Psychology'; 'Archives of Physical Medicine & Rehabilitation'; Book Chapter, "Rehabilitation Psychology: Current Status and Future Trends", in press. *Honours:* Dissertation Received Award for Outstanding Research in Service to the Handicapped, 1981; Graduate School Doctoral Dissertation Grant; Phi Beta Kappa, 1973; etc. *Address:* Mayo Clinic, Clinical Psychology, Rochester, MN 55901, USA.

RÖHLICH, Pál, b. 9 Nov. 1929, Miskolc, Hungary. Professor. m. Márta Sóskuti, 4 July 1981. *Education:* MD, Budapest, 1954; C Med Sci, 1968. *Appointments:* Assistant Professor, 1954-60, Scientific Researcher, 1961-63, Department of Histology, Semmelweis University, Budapest; Chief Scientific Researcher, 1963-68, Head of Department, 1968-, Laboratory I of Electronmicroscopy, Semmelweis University; Professor, 1983-. *Memberships:* European Cell Biology Organisation; Member of Executive Committee; Hungarian Group for Cell Biology (Secretary); Society of Hungarian Anatomists, Histologists & Embryologists (member of the Board of Governors); Hungarian Group for Electronmicroscopy (member of Board of Governors); Hungarian Biophysical Society. *Publications:* Various articles in medical & scientific journals. *Honour:* Award of the Hungarian Academy of Sciences, 1975. *Hobbies:* Painting; Tourism. *Address:* Laboratory I of Electronmicroscopy, Semmelweis University of Medicine, H-1450 Budapest, Tüzoltó u. 58, Hungary.

ROLLAND, Jennifer May, b. 1 Mar. 1946, Melbourne, Australia. Senior Lecturer in Immunology, Monash University, Australia. *Education:* BSc, Melbourne University, 1966; PhD, Monash University, 1971. *Appointments:* Senior Tutor, Monash University, 1971-74; Lecturer, 1975-81; Senior Lecturer, 1982-. *Memberships:* Australian Society for Immunology; Australian Society for Immunology, Clinical Immunology Group; Victorian Society of Pathology and Experimental Medicine, President; Australian Society for Experimental Pathology; Royal Australian Ornithologists Union. *Publications:* Author of 37 publications in international scientific journals; Assistant Editor, Fluorescent Protein Tracing by R C Nairn, 4th Edition, 1976. *Hobbies:* Ornithology; Bushwalking; Reading. *Address:* Department of Pathology and Immunology, Monash Medical School, Commercial Road, Prahran, Victoria, Australia 3181.

ROLLAND, John Steven, b. 4 Feb. 1948, Perth Amboy, New Jersey, USA. Medical Director; Clinical Assistant Professor. *Education:* BA, University of Pennsylvania, 1969; MD, University of Michigan, 1973; MC, Harvard University School of Public Health, 1974; Resident, Psychiatry, Yale University School of Medicine, 1974-77; Board Certified in Psychiatry and Neurology, 1980; Post-Doctoral Fellow, Yale University, Institute for Social and Policy Studies, 1982-84; Ackerman Institute for Family Therapy, Advanced Training, New York City, New York, 1982-83. *Appointments:* Associate Medical Director, Division of Psychiatry, Meriden-Wallingford Hospital, Meriden, Connecticut, 1977-82; Lecturer, 1977-84, currently, Clinical Assistant Professor, Department of Psychiatry, Yale University School of Medicine; Medical Director, Center for Illness in Families, New Haven, Connecticut. *Memberships:* American Psychiatric Association; Connecticut Psychiatric Society; Physicians for Social Responsibility; Programme Committee, Family Section, American Orthopsychiatric Association; American Family Therapy Association. *Publications:* Author or Co-Author: 'With Patient in Mind: A Study of the Eric Lindemann Mental Health Center' in 'Environmental Design Research Association Annual Proceedings', 1975; Chapter in "Further Explorations in Social Psychiatry", 1976; 'Toward a Psychosocial Typology of Chronic and Life Threatening Illness' in 'Family Systems Medicine', 1984. *Honour:* Post Doctoral Fellowship, National Institute of Mental Health, 1982-84. *Address:* 165 Alden Avenue, New Haven, CT 96515, USA.

ROLSTON, Kenneth Vijaykumar Isaac, b. 23 Apr. 1951, India. Assistant Professor, Medicine. m. Mariam R Cracko, 6 May 1984, Baltimore, USA. *Education:* MB, BS, Christian Medical College, Punjab University, India, 1972; Fellow, Infectious Diseases, Hahnemann University, Philadelphia, USA, 1981-83; Residency, Internal Medicine, Franklin Square Hospital, 1976-77. *Appointments:* Staff Physician, Internal Medicine, North Charles General Hospital, Baltimore, 1979-81; Assistant Internist, Assistant Professor, Medicine, Infectious Diseases, University of Texas System Cancer Centre, MD Anderson Hospital and Tumour Institute, Houston, 1983-. *Memberships include:* American College of Physicians; American Society of Microbiology; American Venereal Disease Association; Association for Gnotobiotics; American Federation for Clinical Research; Harris County, Texas and American Medical Associations. *Publications include:* Numerous articles in scientific journals: Co-Author, "Antimicrobial Agents in the Immunocompromised Host", "Antimicrobial Agents and Immunity', in press; "Methicillin-resistant staphylococci", 1982; "Medical Update - AIDS: New Advances in Treatment", 1985. *Honours:* Award, Anatomy, 1969, Award, Eye and ENT, 1972, Alumni Prize, Best All Round Student, 1972, Christian Medical College, Punjab University, India. *Hobbies:* Travel; Philately; Photography; Cricket; Cooking. *Address:* Section of Infectious Diseases, M. D. Anderson Hospital & Tumour Institute, 6723 Bertner Ave, Houston, TX 77030, USA.

ROMAN, Donato, b. 20 Jan. 1939, Moca, Puerto Rico. Psychiatrist, Medical Director. m. Dulce M, 1 Aug. 1964, 3 daughters. *Education:* BSc, University of Puerto Rico, 1960; MD, University of Puerto Rico Medical School, 1964; Rotating Internship, San Juan City Hospital, PR, 1964-65; Psychiatric Residence, Jackson Memorial Hospital, University of Miami, Florida, USA, 1967-70; Diplomate, American Board of Psychiatry & Neurology, 1982; Fellow, Inter-American College of Physicians & Surgeons, 1982. *Appointments:* Chief of Aerospace Medicine, Flight Surgeon, Captain, US Air Force, 1965-67; Clinical Instructor, University of Miami Medical School, 1965-82; Clinical Director, Horizon Hospital, Clearwater, Florida, 1980-85; President of Medical Staff, Horizon Hospital, 1981, 1984; President, Dr Roman & Associates PA, 1980-82. *Memberships:* American Medical Association; American Psychiatric Association; American Geriatric Society; American Association for Geriatric Psychiatry; Florida Medical Association; Florida Psychiatric Society; Chairman, Credentials Committee, Horizon Hospital, 1981-84; Consultant to Florida Health & Rehabilitation Services, 1980-84; Member, Florida Psychiatric Society Insurance & Plans Committee, 1984; Member of Clinical Task Force to review Baker Act in Florida, 1984. *Honours:* Meritorious Service Award, USAF; Consultant ot South Central Community Mental Health Services, Alabama. *Hobbies:* Cycling; Racquetball; Softball; Tennis; Jogging; Reading; Family activities; Listening to Music; Pursuit of Spiritual Matters. *Address:* Brantley Highway, PO Box 161, Luverne, AL 36049-0161, USA.

ROMANO, Michael Charles, b. 8 Feb. 1951, Fort Lauderdale, Florida, USA. Pulmonary Internist; Associate Director, Pulmonary Department. m. Melinda Dalby Hayes, 7 June 1977, Miami, Florida, 1 son, 1 daughter. *Education:* BSc cum laude, University of Florida, 1973; MD, University of Miami, 1977; Fellow, American College of Chest Physicians. *Appointments:* Residency, Georgetown University Hospital, 1977-80; Pulmonary Fellowship, University of Miami, 1980-82; Pulmonary Internal Medicine & Critical Care, North Broward Medical Center, Pompano Beach, Florida, 1982-. *Memberships:* American College of Physicians; Society of Critical Care Medicine; Fellow, American College of Chest Physicians; American Thoracic Society; Broward County Medical Association; American Society of Internal Medicine. *Publications include:* Co-author, paper, 'American Review of Respiratory Disease', 1980. *Honours:* Alpha Omega

Alpha, 1977; Diplomate, American Board of Internal Medicine 1980, Pulmonary Disease, 1982. *Hobbies:* Boating; Fishing; Hiking; Camping; Outdoor activities; 19th century art & music; Community & environmental issues; Performing arts; Photography. *Address:* North Broward Medical Center, Pulmonary Department, 201 East Sample Road, Pompano Beach. FL 33064, USA.

ROMENSKI, Kathryn B, b. 13 Aug. 1948, Pawtucket, Rhode Island, USA. Director of Physical Therapy, Allied Services for the Handicapped, Scranton, Pennsylvania, USA. *Education:* BS, Physical Therapy, Boston University, 1970. *Appointments:* Staff Physical Therapist, Allied Services for the Handicapped, 1970-71; Assistant Chief Physical Therapist, 1971-74; Chief Physical Therapist, 1974-77; Director of Patient Services, 1977-79; Director of Physical Therapy, 1979-. *Memberships:* American Physical Therapy Association; Pennsylvania Physical Therapy Association; American Management Association; National Rehabilitation Association; Prosthetics and Orthotics American Academy of Orthotics and Prosthetics; National Rehabilitation Administrators Association; International Rehabilitation Institute; National Association for Female Executives; National Association for Management. *Address:* 208 Barry Drive, RD 5 Box 546, Clarke Summit, PA 18411, USA.

ROMEO, Aurelio, b. 29 Mar. 1923, Calabria, Italy. University Professor. m. Gabriella De Carli, 7 Feb. 1953, Rome, Italy, 2 sons, 2 daughters. *Education:* Chemistry, Pharmacy degrees, Rome University, Italy. *Appointments:* Professor, University of Rome, 1958-; Director of CNR Medicinal Chemistry Centre, Rome, 1969-. *Memberships:* Royal Society of Chemistry; Group of Experts of European Pharmacopoeia Commission. Several papers in organic and medicinal Chemistry. *Address:* Instituto di Chimica Farmaceutica e Tossicologica, P le Aldo Moro, 5 Universita 'La Sapienza', Rome, Italy.

ROMINGER, C Jules, b. 10 May 1925, Philadelphia, Pennsylvania, USA. Chairman, Radiation Oncology. m. Martina Henry, 14 June 1948, Philadelphia, 3 sons, 2 daughters. *Education:* MD, Jefferson Medical College, Philadelphia, Pennsylvania, 1948. Certification: American Board of Radiology, 1954; American Board of Therapeutic Radiology, 1952; American Board of Nuclear Medicine, 1972. *Appointments:* Assistant Radiologist, Madison Army Hospital, Tacoma, Washington, 1952-54; Associate Radiologist, Misericordia Hospital, Philadelphia, Pennsylvania, 1954-59; Chairman Department of Radiology, 1959-75, Department of Radiation Therapy and Nuclear Medicine, 1972-81, Department of Radiation Oncology, 1981-, Mercy Catholic Medical Center, Philadelphia; Associate Professor, Radiology, Thomas Jefferson University, Philadelphia, 1970-. *Memberships:* Radiation Therapy Oncology Group; Fellow, American College of Radiology; American Society of Therapeutic Radiologists and Oncologists; American Radium Society; Pennsylvania Radiological Society; Philadelphia Roentgen Ray Society; Keystone Area Society of Radiation Oncologists; Honorary Life Member, Philadelphia Division, American Cancer Society; Past President, Philadelphia Division, American Cancer Society. *Publications:* Numerous in field. *Honour:* National Bronze Medal, Divisional, American Cancer Society, 1982. *Hobbies:* Gardening; Fishing; Philately; Travel. *Address:* Misericordia Division, Mercy Catholic Medical Center, 5301 Cedar Avenue, Philadelphia, PA 19143, USA.

ROOS, Dirk, b. 16 Nov. 1941, The Hague, The Netherlands. Head, Department of Blood Cell Chemistry. m. Lily Roorda, 20 Apr. 1968, Amsterdam, 1 son. *Education:* MSc, Biochemistry, PhD, Biochemistry, University of Amsterdam. *Appointments:* Staff Member, Netherlands Red Cross Laboratory; Currently: Head of Department of Blood Cell Chemistry, Staff Member, Laboratory for Experimental and Clinical Immunology, University of Amsterdam. *Memberships:* Ameri-

can Association of Clinical Investigation; Netherlands Society for Immunology; Netherlands Society for Biochemistry; Netherlands Society for Hematology; Netherlands Society for Cell Biology. *Publications:* 'The Oxidative metabolism of monocytes' in "The Reticuloendothelial System" 1980 (with A J Balm); 'The metabolic response to phagocytosis' in "Handbook of Inflammation" 1980; Co-author: 'Functional activity of neutrophil cytoplasts' Journal Cell Biology, 1983. *Hobbies:* Sailing; Gardening. *Address:* Central Laboratory of the Netherlands Red Cross Blood Transfusion Service, PO Box 9190, 1006 AD Amsterdam, The Netherlands.

ROOSE, Paul Eugene, b. 22 Aug. 1947, Hart, Michigan, USA. Orthopedic Surgeon. m. Linda Leone Asplund, 12 May 1984, Cadillac, Michigan. *Education:* BS, Wayne State University, Detroit, Michigan, 1969; DO, Kirksville College of Osteopathic Medicine, Kirksville, Missouri, 1973; Internship, Mt Clemens General Hospital, Mt Clemens, Michigan, 1974; Residency in Orthopedic Surgery, Doctor's Hospital, Massillon, Ohio, 1978. *Appointments:* Practicing in Massillon, Ohio, 1978-79; Practicing in Cadillac, Michigan, 1979-; Hospital Staff: Cadillac Mercy Hospital, Clare Oseopathic Hospital, Reed City Hospital. *Memberships:* American Osteopathic Association; American College of Osteopathic Surgeons; American Osteopathic Academy of Orthopedic Surgeons; Board Certified in Orthopedic Surgery, Hand Surgery section, AOAO; Michigan Association of Osteopathic Physicians and Surgeons, Wexford-Missauke County Medical Society. *Publications:* 'Proximal Femoral Replacement Total Hip Arthroplasty', 1979; 'Open Reduction for Congenital Dislocation of the Hip Using the Ferguson Procedure, A Review of 6 Cases', 1977. *Honour:* Geigy Award, 1977. *Hobbies:* Travel; Fly Fishing. *Address:* 302 Hobart, Cadillac, MI 49601, USA.

ROOTH, Gosta, b. 17 Dec. 1918, Stockholm, Sweden. Professor Emeritus of Perinatal Medicine. m. Anna Birgitta Waldermarson, 16 Aug. 1942, Angelholm, 1 son, 2 daughters. *Education:* Candidate of Medicine 1940, Licentiate of Medicine 1945, MD, 1949, University of Lund. *Appointments:* Department of Pathology 1945, Department of Infectious Diseases 1947, Assistant Professor 1957, Research Professor 1966, Department of Internal Medicine 1948-72, University of Lund; Personal Chair, Professor Emeritus, Perinatal Medicine, University of Uppsala, 1973-85. *Memberships include:* Swedish Society of Physicians; Swedish Society of Paediatricians; Swedish Society of Obstetricians; Swedish Society of Internal Medicine; Scandinavian Society of Perinatal Medicine; European Society of Perinatal Medicine; Neontal Society; Honorary Member, Italian Society of Perinatal Medicine, Finnish Society of Perinatal Medicine. *Publications include:* Books: "The Onset of Respiration", 1966; "Acid-Base and Electrolyte Balance" (many reprints in 10 languages), 1966; "Oxygen Cardiorespiragram", 1983; papers: 'Dysmaturity', 1957; 'Clinical value of ketone body determination in brittle diabetes', 1972; 'Time factor in fetal distress', 1973; 'Continuous monitoring of fetal oxygen tension during labour', 1977. *Honour:* Honorary Symposium, Zurich, Switzerland, 1984. *Hobbies:* Country life; Skiing; Skating; Reading. *Address:* ofre Slottsgatan 14 C, 752 35 Uppsala, Sweden.

ROPER, Stephen David, b. 30 May 1945, Rock Island, USA. Professor of Anatomy and Physiology. m. Nirupa Chaudhari, May 1985, Denver, Colorado, USA, 1 son, 1 daughter. *Education:* BA, Harvard College, USA, 1967; PhD, University College, London, England, 1970; Postdoctoral Fellow, Harvard Medical School, USA, 1970-73. *Appointments:* Instructor, Harvard Medical School, USA, 1971-73; Assistant Professor of Anatomy, University of Colorado Medical School, 1973-79, Assistant Professor of Physiology, 1976-79, Associate Professor of Anatomy and Physiology, 1979-85, Professor of Anatomy and Physiology, 1985-; Chairman of Anatomy, 1985-; Associate Director of Neurobiology, Colorado State University. *Memberships:* Society for Neuroscience; American Association of Anatomists; Association for Chemoreception Sciences; American Physiological Society; Rocky Mountain Region Neuroscience Group. *Publications:* Numerous articles in scientific journals. *Honours:* Fulbright Fellow, 1967-69; NSF and NIH Postdoctoral Fellow, 1970-73; Research and Career Development Award, NIH, 1978-82. *Hobbies:* Music performance; Musicology; Skiing; Reading; Gardening. *Address:* Department of Anatomy, Colorado State University, Fort Collins, CO 80523, USA.

ROSE, Noel Richard, b. 3 Dec. 1927, Stamford, Connecticut, USA. Immunologist; Microbiologist. m. Deborah Harber Rose, 2 sons, 2 daughters. *Education:* BS, Yale University, 1948; AM, 1949, PhD, 1951, University of Pennsylvania; MD, State University of New York, Buffalo, 1964. *Appointments:* Instructor to Professor, University of Buffalo, 1951-73; Associate Director to Director, Erie County Labs, Buffalo, 1964-70; Professor, Chairman, Wayne State University School of Medicine, 1963-82; Professor, Chairman, 1982-, Department of Immunology and Infectious Diseases, The Johns Hopkins University School of Hygiene and Public Health; Professor, Medicine, 1982-, Johns Hopkins University School of Medicine, Baltimore; Expert Consultant, WHO, Geneva, Switzerland, 1964-. *Memberships include:* Fellow, American Academy Allergy; American Academy Microbiology, Emeritus Fellow; American Association Advanced Science, Fellow; American Association Immunologists; American Public Health Association, Fellow; etc. *Publications:* 11 Books, 3 second editions, 1 third edition; 360 articles and chapters in scientific books and journals. *Honours:* Commonwealth Fellow, Pasteur Institute, Paris, 1958, Institute of Biochemistry, Lausanne, 1966-67; Buswell Fellow, University of Oxford, England, 1972-73; Macy Fellow, Walter & Eliza Hall Institute Medical Research, Melbourne, 1979-80. *Address:* Johns Hopkins University School of Hygiene and Public Health, 615 North Wolfe Street, Baltimore, MD 21205, USA.

ROSEN, David B, b. 17 Apr. 1949, Boston, Massachusetts, USA. Private Practitioner, Periodontics. *Education:* BS, Syracuse University; MEd, Boston College; MBA, Northeastern University; DMD, Certificate, Advanced Dental Studies, Tufts University. *Appointment:* Assistant Professor, Periodontology, Tufts University School of Dental Medicine. *Memberships:* American Dental Association, Academy of Periodontology, Academy of Dental Science; Greater Boston Dental Society; Alpha Omega; American Society of Clinical Hypnosis. *Honours:* Fellow, American Academy of Dental Science, Academy of International Dental Studies, Academy of General Dentistry. *Hobbies:* Golf; Skiing; Sailing; Flying. *Address:* 1 Wallis Court, Lexington, MA 02173, USA.

ROSENBAUM, Maurice, b. 25 June 1936, Australia. Consutaltant Cardiologist. m. Zelda, 16 Dec. 1958, Melbourne, 1 son, 2 daughters. *Education:* MB BS; MD; FRACP. *Appointments:* Resident Medical Officer, Prince Henry's Hospital, Melbourne; Research Worker, Baker Institute, Melbourne; National Heart Foundation Fellow, Bockus Institute, Philadelphia, Pennsylvania, USA; Director of Cardiology, currently Consultant Cardiologist, Austin Hospital, Heidelburg, Victoria, Australia. *Membership:* Cardiac Society of Australia. *Publications:* Author of various papers. *Address:* 17 George Street, East Melbourne, Victoria, Australia.

ROSENBERG, Ian, b. 12 Feb. 1939, South Africa. Private Practice, Oral & Maxillo-Facial Surgery; Consultant, Perth School of Dentistry, Princess Margaret Hospital for Children(part-time). m. Renee Rachbind, 12 July 1965, Johannesburg, 1 son, 2 daughters. *Education:* BDS; H Dip Dent; DIP MFOS; FDSRCS (Ed); FFDRCS (Ir); M Dent. *Appointments:* General Dental Practice, London, 1962-64; General Dental Practice, Johannesburg, 1964-73; Medical Officer, Maxillo-Facial & Oral Surgery, Johannesburg General Hospi-

tal, University of the Witwatersrand, 1976-80; Private Practice, Maxillo-Facial & Oral Surgery, Western Australia, 1980-; Part-time Consultant, Oral Surgery, School of Dentistry, University of Western Australia, 1981-; Consultant, Oral & Maxillo-Facial Surgeon, Princess Margaret Hospital, Western Australia, 1983-. *Memberships:* Dental Association of South Africa; Federation of Dentaire Internationale; Fellow, Dental Surgery, Royal College of Surgeons of Edinburgh; Fellow, Faculty of Dentistry, Royal College of Surgeons; International Association of Oral Surgeons; etc. *Publications:* "Aneurysmal Bone Cyst of the Mandible", 'Journal of Dental Association of South Africa', 1975; "A Survey on Factures of the Mandible", 'Journal of the Dental Association of South Africa"; other articles in professional journals. *Honours:* Recipient, various honours and awards including Rousseau Viljoen Memorial Prize, Oral Medicine, 1962; Merit Certificate of the American Academy of Dental Medicine, 1962. *Hobbies:* Golf; Music. *Address:* 7 Malcolm Court, Noranda, Perth, WA 6062, Australia.

ROSENBERG, Leon, b. 3 Mar. 1933, Madison, Wisconsin, USA. Dean, Yale University School of Medicine. m. Diane Drobnis, 2 sons, 2 daughters. *Education:* BA, 1954; MD, 1957; University of Wisconsin. *Appointments:* Assistant Professor of Medicine, 1965-68; Associate Professor, Pediatrics and Medicine, 1968-72; Chairman and Professor, Human Genetics, 1972-84; CNH Long Professor, 1980-; Dean, 1984-; Yale School of Medicine, New Haven, Connecticut. *Memberships:* Fellow, American Association for Advancement of Science; Institute of Medicine, NAS, 1982; Fellow, American Academy of Arts and Sciences; National Academy of Sciences, 1984; American Society for Clinical Investigation, Vice-President, 1978-79; American Society for Human Genetics, President, 1980-81; Association of American Physicians; American Pediatric Society; American Society of Biological Chemists. *Publications:* Author, "Amino Acid Metabolism and its Disorders", 1974; Editor, "Metabolic Control and Disease", 1981. *Honour:* Distinguished Alumni Citation, University of Wisconsin, 1982. *Hobbies:* Tennis; Skiing; Jogging. *Address:* Yale University School of Medicine, 333 Cedar Street, New Haven, CT 06510, USA.

ROSENFELD, Alvin, b. 9 May 1945, New York, USA. Director of Psychiatric Services. m. Dorothy Levine, MD, 8 Sep. 1985, NJ, USA. *Education:* BA, Cornell University; MD, Harvard University. *Appointments:* Faculty, Harvard Medical School, 1975-77; Director, Child Psychiatry Training, Stanford University Medical School, 1977-83; Associate Professor, Adjunct, 1984-85, Senior Research Scholar, Columbia University Teachers College, 1985. *Memberships:* American Psychiatric Association; American Academy Child Psychiatry. *Publications include:* "Decision-making in child abuse and neglect", Vulletin of the American Academy of Psychiatry and the Law, Volume 13, 1985; "Incidence of child sexual abuse", Medical Aspects of Human Sexuality, Volume 19, 1985; "Parents Who Nag", Medical Aspects of Human Sexuality, 1985; "Somatization Disorders in Children", with Dr Elsa Shapiro, 1986. *Honours:* Rose Sergal Award, Harvard University, 1970; Outstanding Teacher Award, Child Psychiatry, Stanford University, 1981; Scholar, Rockefeller Foundation, Bellagio Study Center, 1985. *Address:* Jewish Child Care Association of New York, 575 Lexington Avenue, NY 10022, USA.

ROSENFELDT, Franklin Lawrence, b. 15 May 1941, Albury, New South Wales, Australia. Senior Research Fellow and Head of Cardiac Surgical Research Laboratory, Baker Institute, Melbourne. m. Anne Lewis, 12 June 1971, 1 son, 2 daughters. *Education:* St Ignatius College, Adelaide; University of Adelaide; Duke University, North Carolina, USA. *Appointments:* Kleinwort Research Fellow and Honorary Lecturer in Surgery, St Thomas' Hospital, London, England; Senior Registrar, Cardiac Surgery, Research Senior Registrar, Killingbeck Hospital, Leeds; Registrar, Cardiac Surgery, National Heart Hospital, London; Registrar, Cardiac Surgery, Royal Alexandra Hospital for Children and St Vincent's Hospital, Sydney, Australia; Research Fellow, Department of Surgery, Duke University Medical Centre, Furham, North Carolina, USA. *Memberships:* Fellow, Royal Australasian College of Surgeons; Fellow, Royal College of Surgeons of Edinburgh; Member, International Society for Heart Research; Member, Society of Thoracic and Cardiovascular Surgeons of Great Britain and Northern Ireland. *Publications:* Author of numerous articles in surgical and scientific journals. *Hobbies:* Music; Tennis; Gardening. *Address:* Baker Medical Research Institute, PO Box 348, Prahran, Australia 3181.

ROSENFIELD, Allan, b. 28 Apr. 1933, Cambridge, Massachusetts, USA. University Professor/Director of Center for Population and Family Health. m. 31 July 1966, Boston, 1 son, 1 daughter. *Education:* MD, College of Physicians and Surgeons, Columbia University. *Appointments include:* Senior Registrar, University of Lagos Medical School, Nigeria; 1966-67; Representative, The Population Council, Thailand, 1967-73; Associate Director, The Population Council, New York, 1973-75; Director of Center for Population and Family Health and Professor of Obstetrics and Gynaecology and Public Health, Columbia University, New York, 1975-; Acting Chairman, Department of Obstetrics and Gynaecology, Faculty of Medicine, Columbia University and Acting Director, Obstetrics and Gynaecology Presbyterian Hospital, 1983-85. *Memberships:* Fellow, American College of Obstetrics and Gynaecology; Fellow, American Public Health Association; Fellow, American Fertility Society; Member, International Union for the Scientific Study of Population; Member, Association of Planned Parenthood Physicians; Member, Population Association of America. *Hobbies:* Skiing; Tennis. *Address:* Center for Population and Family Health, Columbia University, 60 Haven Avenue, New York, NY 10032, USA.

ROSENFIELD, Robert Cee, b. 16 Dec. 1934, USA. Professor of Paediatrics and Medicine. m. Sandra McVicker, 12 Apr. 1983, Chicago, Illinois, 3 sons. *Education:* BA, Northwestern University, 1956; MD, Northwestern University Medical School, 1960. *Appointments:* Assistant, Associate Professor of Paediatrics, 1968-78; Professor of Paediatrics and Medicine, 1978-. *Memberships:* Endocrine Society; American Paediatric Society; Society for Gynaecology Research. *Publications include:* About 100 scientific articles; textbook chapters, including: 'Somatic Growth' in De Groot's "Endocrinology", 1979; 'The Ovary and Female Sexual Maturation' in Kaplan's "Pediatric Endocrinology", 1983. *Honours:* ADA, 1960; Fogarty Senior International Fellow, 1978. *Hobbies:* Photography; Racquetball. *Address:* Wyler Children's Hospital, 5841 South Maryland, Chicago, IL 60637, USA.

ROSENKRANZ, Bruce Richard, b. 24 Feb. 1954, Brooklyn, New York, USA. Director of Miami Beach Rehabilitation Center; Chiropractic Physician. m. Toni Ann Leon, 7 Aug. 1976, Lauderhill, Florida, 1 son, 1 daughter. *Education:* BA, Florida Atlantic University; DC, New York Chiropractic College; Certified by National-Lincoln College of Chiropractic in Acupuncture and Impairment Rating; Diplomate of National Board of Chiropractic Examiners. *Memberships:* Phi Chi Omega; Florida Chiropractic Association; Dade County Chiropractic Society; FCA Council on Orthopaedics; Foundation for Chiropractic Education and Research. *Honours:* National Dean's List; Distinguished Service to American Chiropractic Association. *Hobbies:* Racquetball; Tennis. *Address:* 337 Lincoln Road, Miami Beach, FL 33139, USA.

ROSENTHAL, Robert, b. 2 Mar. 1933, Giessen, Federal German Republic. Professor of Social Psychology, Harvard University, USA. m. MaryLu Clayton, 20 Apr. 1951, Los Angeles, 1 son, 2 daughters. *Education:* AB, 1953; PhD, 1956; University of California,

Los Angeles. *Appointments:* Clinical Psychology Trainee, Los Angeles Area VA, 1954-57; Lecturer, University of Southern California, 1956-57; Acting Instructor, UCLA, 1957; Assistant to Associate Professor and Coordinator, Clinical Training, University of North Dakota, 1957-62; Visiting Associate Professor, Ohio State University, 1960-61; Lecturer, Boston University, 1965-66; Lecturer, Clinical Psychology, 1962-67; Professor of Social Psychology, 1967-; Harvard University. *Memberships:* Fellow, American Psychological Association; Fellow, Eastern Psychological Association; Midwestern Psychological Association; North Dakota Psychological Association, Past President; Fellow, Massachusetts Psychological Association; Society for Projective Techniques; American Association for the Advancement of Science, Fellow; Society of Experimental Social Psychology; Society for Social Studies of Science. *Publication:* Author, Co-author or Editor, 18 books including: 'Experimenter effects in behavioral research", 1966; "Pygmalion in the classroom: Teacher expectation and pupils' intellectual development", 1968; Co-author: "Contrast Analysis: Focused Comparisons in the Anlysis of Variance", 1985; Co-editor: "Nonverbal Communication in the Clinical Context", 1986; Co-author: "BASIC Mete-analysis: Procedures and Programs", 1985. *Honour include:* Guggenheim Fellowship, 1973-74; Wiener Award, University of Manitoba, 1979; Distinguished Lecturer APA Div. 26, 1982; Lansdowne Visitor, University of Victoria, 1982. *Hobbies:* Squash Racquets; Travel. *Address:* Department of Psychology and Social Relations, Harvard University, 33 Kirkland Street, Cambridge, MA 02138, USA.

ROSENTHAL, Robert, b. 6 Dec. 1946, Paterson, New Jersey, USA. Cardiologist. m. Janet M Harnick, 9 June 1974, Queens, New York, 2 sons. *Education:* BA, Rutgers University, 1967; MD, Albany Medical College, 1974. *Appointments include:* Fellow, Cardiology, Montefiore Hospital, Bronx, New York; Attending Cardiologist & Internal Medicine, Greenwich Hospital, Connecticut; Attending Cardiologist, Westchester County Medical Centre; Clinical Instructor, Medicine, Yale University School of Medicine. *Memberships:* Fellow: American College of Physicians, American College of Cardiology, American College of Chest Physicians, American Heart Association; Member, American Society of Echocardiography; North American Society of Pacing & Electrophysiology. *Publications include:* Research papers, cardiology, various professional journals. *Honour:* Alpha Kappa Delta, 1969. *Hobbies:* Cycling; Jogging; Reading. *Address:* 49 Lake Avenue, Greenwich, CT 06830, USA.

ROSIVAL, Ladislav, b. 19 Aug. 1924, V Polana, Czechoslovakia. Director, Centre for Hygiene; Deputy Director, Research Institute for Preventive Medicine. m. Ann Rosival, 22 Dec. 1967, 1 daughter. *Education:* Medical Faculty, Bratislava, 1951; PhD, 1957; Assistant Professor, 1961; DMS, 1977. *Appointments:* Assistant, Medical Faculty, Bratislava, 1951-67; Director, Research Institute of Hygiene, Bratislava, 1968-78; Director, Research Institute of Occupational Medicine, Bratislava, 1971-73; currently, Director, Centre of Hygiene, Research Institute of Preventive Medicine, and Deputy Director, Research Institute of Preventive Medicine, Bratislava. *Memberships:* Vice Chairman, Scientific Council of Ministry of Health, Slovak Socialist Republic; Council of Government of Slovak Socialist Republic for fight against Cancer; Chairman, Editorial Board, Osveta Publishing House; International Academy for Protection of Environment; Expert Advisory Panel Member, World Health Organisation; Chairman, Scientific committee on pesticides, International Commission on Occupational Health; Secretary, Commission on Toxicology, International Association of Agricultural Medicine and Rural Health; Editorial Boards, Regulatory Toxicology and Pharmacology and others; Coordinator, Research on Pesticides in COMECON countries from the health point of view. *Honours:* MD of Merit, 1974; Medal of J E Purkyne, 1976. *Publications:* "Toxicology and Pharmacobiodynamics of OPI Compounds", 1959; "Foreign Compounds in Food", 1969, German edition, 1979, Russian Edition, 1982, Revised, 1984; Author of 3 other books and 200 scientific articles in field of environmental health and 200 presentations at congresses and symposium. *Hobby:* Sport. *Address:* Research Institute of Preventive Medicine, Limbova 14, 833 01 Bratislava, Czechoslovakia.

ROSNER, Laurie, b. 3 Feb. 1948, New York City, USA. Public Relations, Medical Accounts. *Education:* BA, Barnard College, 1969; MPA, New York University, 1977 (Health Care Administration). *Appointments:* Administrator, New York City Health & Hospitals Corporation; Public Relations Director, Coopers Lybrand; Media Relations Director, National Multiple Sclerosis Society; Vice-President, Robert Marston & Associates; Vice-President, Account Director, Carl Byoir & Associates. *Memberships:* American Medical Writers Association; Women in Communications. *Honour:* Governor's Citation, 1979. *Hobbies:* Travel; Foreign Languages (French & Italian). *Address:* 80 Central Park West, New York, NY 10023, USA.

ROSS, Clive Bentley, b. 19 Oct. 1937, New Zealand. Dentist. m. Wendy Shieff, 31 Jan. 1963, 2 sons, 1 daughter. *Education:* BDS (with Distinction); Fellow, Dental Surgery Royal College of Surgeons (England); Fellow, Royal Australian College of Dental Surgeons. *Appointments:* Eastman Dental Hospital, London, England; Royal Dental Hospital, London; External Examiner, Otago University Dental School, New Zealand; Chairman, Fédération Dentaire Internationale (WHO) Manpower Committee; WHO Consultant; Council Member FDI. *Memberships:* New Zealand Dental Association; Australasian College of Dental Surgeons. *Publications:* 'Future Needs in Periodontology in New Zealand' (in NZ Dental Journal), 1983; 'Oral Health Status & Tradition in New Zealand' (in International Dental Journal), 1984. *Hobby:* Sailing. *Address:* Quay Towers (12th Floor), 29 Customs Street, Auckland, New Zealand.

ROSS, Deborah Ann, b. 5 Dec. 1953, Davenport, Iowa, USA. Chiropractic Physician. *Education:* BS, Biology, Zoology, Marshall University, 1971-72, 1974-76; Dean's List, World Campus Afloat, 1973; DC, Texas Chiropractic College, 1981. *Memberships:* National Female Executives; American and West Virginia Chiropractic Associations; Council on Nutrition; Council on Sports Injuries and Physical Fitness; Council of Women Chiropractors; Council of Internal Disorders & Diagnosis. *Hobbies:* Tennis; Waterskiing; Skiing; Scuba Diving; Photography; Gymnastics. *Address:* 1229 6th Avenue, Huntington, WV 25701, USA.

ROSS, Dolores, b. 4 Apr. 1952, Brooklyn, New York, USA. Assistant Director of Nursing, Rusk Institute of Rehabilitation Medicine, New York University Medical Centre. *Education:* MA, Nursing Administration 1982, Certificate, Health Care Administration 1984, New York University. *Appointments include:* Head Nurse, Rusk Institute of Rehabilitation Medicine. *Memberships:* Association of Rehabilitation Nurses; American Nurses Association. *Honour:* Certified Rehabilitation Registered Nurse (CRRN). *Hobby:* Snow skiing. *Address:* Rusk Institute of Rehabilitation Medicine, 400 East 34th Street, New York University Medical Centre, New York, NY 10016, USA.

ROSS, Philip Drew, b. 4 Sep. 1952, Abington, Pennsylvania, USA. Associate Director, Kuakini Osteoporosis Center; Assistant Researcher, Cancer Research Center of Hawaii. *Education:* BS, 1973, MS, 1977, PhD, 1979, Pennsylvania State University. *Appointments:* Research Associate, Duke University Medical Center, Department of Pharmacology, 1979-80. *Memberships:* American Association for the Advancement of Science. *Publications:* 'Prediction of post-menopausal fracture risk with bone mineral measurements', (with R D Wasnich, L K Heilbrun, J M Vogel), 1985; 'Differential effects of thiazide and estrogen upon bone mineral content and fracture preva-

lence', (with R D Wasnich, L K Heilbrun, J M Vogel), 1986. *Honours:* Individual National Research Service Award, US Public Health Service, 1980-82. *Hobbies:* Aikido; Bonsai. *Address:* Kuakini Medical Center, 347 North Kuakini Street, Honolulu, HI 96817, USA.

ROSS, Russell, b. 25 May 1929, St Augustine, Florida, USA. Professor and Chairman, Department of Pathology, University of Washington. m. Jean Long Teller, 22 Feb. 1956, 1 son, 1 daughter. *Education:* AB, Cornell University, Ithaca, New York, 1947-51; DDS, Columbia University, New York, 1951-55; PhD, University of Washington, Seattle, Washington, 1958-62. *Appointments:* Intern, Presbyterian Hospital, New York, 1955-56; Staff Member in Charge, US Public Health Service Hospital, Seattle, Washington, 1956-58; Special Research Fellow, Department of Pathology, School of Medicine, 1958-62, Assistant Professor, Departments of Pathology and Oral Biology, Schools of Medicine and Dentistry, 1962-65, Member of Graduate Faculty, 1964-, Associate Professor, Department of Pathology, School of Medicine, 1965-69, Professor of Pathology, School of Medicine, 1969-, Associate Dean for Scientific Affairs, School of Medicine, 1971-78, Chairman, Department of Pathology, 1982-, University of Washington, Seattle; Visiting Scientist, Strangeways Research Laboratory, Cambridge, England, 1966-68. *Memberships:* American Society for Cell Biology; Sigma Xi; American Association for the Advancement of Science; Fellow, Royal Microscopical Society; International Academy of Pathology; Electron Microscope Society of America; American Association of Pathologists; American Association of University Professors; International Society for Cell Biology; Fellow, Council on Arteriosclerosis, American Heart Association; Gerontological Society; The Tissue Culture Association; Honorary Member, Harvey Society; Member of Council, Society for Experimental Biology and Medicine; Association of Pathology Chairmen; Member of numerous committees, Washington University; Member of numerous committees and Advisory Boards of professional societies and Universities. *Publications:* Contributor of over 300 articles, chapters in books and publications in professional and scientific journals. *Honours include:* Birnberg Research Medal, Columbia University School of Dental and Oral Surgery, 1975; Gordon Wilson Medal, American Clinical and Climatological Association, Ponte Vedra Beach, Florida, 1981. *Address:* Department of Pathology SM-30, University of Washington School of Medicine, Seattle, WA 98195, USA.

ROSS, William Felton, b. 9 May 1927, England. Medical Director, American Leprosy Missions. m. Una Dickenson, 2 May 1959, Bermondsey, London, 4 sons, 1 daughter. *Education:* MD, BS; DPH. *Appointments:* Area Superintendent, Oji River, Enugu, Eastern Nigeria; Director of Training, Alert, Addis Ababa, Ethiopa. *Membership:* Treasurer, International Leprosy Association. *Publications:* "A Guide to Leprosy For Field Staff", 1975; "A Self-Instruction Module on Self Instruction", (with Charles R Ausherman), 1983; Contributor: "On Being In Charge", 1980. *Hobbies:* Family; Bible Study; Walking. *Address:* 14 Lincoln Street, Glen Ridge, NJ 07028, USA.

ROSS, William Mackie, b. 14 Dec. 1922, Glasgow, Scotland. Consultant in Radiotherapy; Lecturer in Radiotherapy, University of Newcastle. m. Mary Burt, 17 Apr. 1948, Durham, 1 son, 2 daughters. *Education:* MB BS, University of Durham, 1945; UMRT, London, 1948; MD, University of Durham, 1953; FRCS, Royal College of Surgeons, England, 1956; FRCR, Royal College of Radiologists, 1961. *Appointments:* Trainee in Radiotherapy, Newcastle-upon-Tyne, 1946-51; National Service in RAMC, specializing in Radiology, 1951-53; Service in RAMC(TA) reaching rank of Colonel, 1953-70. *Memberships:* Royal Society of Medicine; President of Section of Radiology, 1979; British Institute of Radiology, President, 1980; Royal College of Radiologists, Treasurer, 1978-83, President, 1983-. *Honours:* Territorial Decoration, 1968; Deputy Lieutenant, 1972. *Address:* 62 Archery Rise, Durham City DH1 4LA, England.

ROSSANO, Carlo, b. 8 Nov. 1923, Scafati, Italy. Professor of Anaesthesiology. m. Maria Celentano, 1 Oct. 1964, Scafati, Italy, 1 son, 1 daughter. *Education:* BS, University of Naples, 1948; Teaching Anaesthesiology, University of Modena, 1958; Specialist in Rheumatology, University of Rome, 1961; Specialist in Physiokinesitherapy, University of Bologna, 1964; Specialist in Hydrology, University of Rome, 1967. *Appointments:* Assistant Professor of Anaesthesiology, University Surgical Clinic, Turin, 1949-50; Chief, Anaesthesiology, Ancona Regional Hospital, 1950-80; Teacher of Analgesia, University of Rome, 1966-77; Director, Department of Pain Therapy, Ancona Hospital, 1980-; Professor of Anaesthesiology, Special School of Anaesthesiology, University of Ancona, 1980-. *Memberships:* Italian Society of Anaesthesiology; IASP; Italian Society for the Study of Pain; European Society of Regional Anaesthesia; Society of Surgical Medicine, Modena; Medical Society of Piceno; International Society of Medical Hypnosis & Psychology, Milan; Brazilian Society of Anaesthesiology; Pain Control Institute of Kyoto. *Publications:* 3 books, 4 monographs, 165 papers on anaesthesiology, Intensive care, Physiopathology & pain therapy, in Italian, French, Portuguese & American medical journals. *Honours:* Invited Lecturer/Teacher to China, Switzerland, Germany; Honorary Member, Academia Tiberina, 1975; Founder, International Phitotherapic Society. *Hobbies:* Stamp-collecting; Collecting modern paintings; Travel; Sport. *Address:* Via Santa Margherita 11, 60124, Ancona, Italy.

ROTBART, Abraham, b. 30 Sep. 1944, Cuba. Physician; Chief of Pulmonary Medicine, St Francis Hospital, Miami Beach, Florida, USA. m. Shelly Sharpe, 18 June 1970, 1 son, 1 daughter. *Education:* BA, Liberal Arts; MD; Diplomate, American Board of Internal Medicine; Fellow, American College of Chest Physicians, Academy of Chest Physicians. *Memberships:* Council of Critical Care; Society of American Inventors; American Thoracic Society; American Board of Internal Medicine. *Publications:* "Asthma, Kaposi's Sarcoma, & Nodular Pulmonary Infiltrates"; "Contralateral Effusions Secondary to Subclavan Venous Catheters". *Honours:* Awards: Sociedad Cubana de Medicina Internal; American Medical Association; Florida Medical Association; Freedom from Smoking. *Hobbies:* Tennis; Boating; Travel. *Address:* 1680 Michigan Avenue, Suite 1012, Miami Beach, FL 33139, USA.

ROTH, Barry Howard, b. 22 Oct. 1947, Rochester, New York, USA. Private Practice. *Education:* BA, Cornell University, 1969; MD, University of Rochester School of Medicine and Dentistry, 1973. *Appointments:* Clinical Instructor, Ambulatory and Community Medicine, University of California, San Francisco, 1975; Clinical and Research Fellow, 1975-79; Clinical Instructor and Instructor, 1978-, Harvard Medical School; Clinical Assistant Professor of Psychiatry, University of California, San Francisco, 1984-85. *Memberships:* American Psychiatric Association; Physicians for Social Responsibility; International Physicians for the Prevention of Nuclear War. *Hobbies:* Photography; Dance. *Address:* Harvard Medical School, PO Box 1000, Cambridge, MA 02140, USA.

ROTH, Harold Philmore, b. 2 Aug. 1915, Cleveland, Ohio, USA. Director, Division of Digestive Diseases and Nutrition, National Institute of Arthritis, Diabetes and Digestive and Kidney Diseases, National Institutes of Health. m. Kelly Cecile Rabinovitch, 9 Dec. 1952, New York City, 1 son, 1 daughter. *Education:* BA, Adelbert College, Western Reserve University, Ohio, 1936; MD, School of Medicine, Western Reserve University, 1939; MS, Hygiene: Biostatistics and Epidemiology, Harvard University, 1967; Certification: American Board of Internal Medicine, 1946; Gastroenterology, 1956. *Appointments:* Associate Physician, University Hospitals, Cleveland, Ohio, 1969-74; Associate Professor of Medicine, 1963-;

Associate Professor, Department of Community Health, 1971-74; Case Western Reserve University; Chief, Gastroenterological Service, Veterans Administration Hospital, Cleveland, Ohio, 1963-74; Director, Gastroenterology Training Program, University Hospitals and Veterans Aministration Hospital, Cleveland, 1963-74; Association Director, Division of Digestive Diseases and Nutrition, National Institutes of Health, Bethesda, Maryland, 1974-. *Memberships:* American Gastroenterological Association; American Association for the Study of Liver Disease; Central Society for Clinical Research; Fellow, American College of Physicians; Society for Clinical Trials, President, 1978-80; Phi Beta Kappa. *Publications:* Papers, chapters and monographs on peptic ulcers, gallstone formation, esophageal motility, patients' understanding and compliance with medical regimens, and clinical trials, 1952-86. *Honours:* Special Fellow, US Public Health Service, Harvard School of Public Health, 1966-67; Award of Special Recognition, American Gastroenterological Association, 1984; Award for extraordinary and conscientious administration of research and education programs, Coalition of Digestive Disease Organizations, 1984. *Address:* National Institutes of Health, Building 31, Room 9A23, 9000 Rickville Pike, Bethesda, MY 20205, USA.

ROTH, Loren, H, b. 9 May 1939, USA. Psychiatrist. m. Ellen A Roth, PhD, MFA, ATR, 19 May 1974, Cleveland, Ohio, USA, 1 son, 2 daughters. *Education:* BA, Cornell University, USA, 1961; MD, Harvard Medical School, 1966. *Appointments:* Staff Psychiatrist, National Institute of Mental Health, 1969-74; Assistant Professor of Psychiatry, University of Pittsburgh, 1974-78, Associate Professor, 1978-82, Professor, 1982-; Chief, Adult Clinical Services, Western Psychiatric Institute and Clinic, 1983-; Medical Staff, Presbyterian University Hospital, Pittsburgh, 1983-. *Memberships:* Cleveland Heart Association; American Psychiatric Association; American Medical Association; American Academy of Psychiatry and the Law; American Society of Law and Medicine; American Society of Criminology; Fellow, American College of Psychiatrists. *Publications include:* 43 articles in professional journals; 33 symposium presentations; 18 chapters, monographs and book reviews including: "Psychiatry and the Law" (book review), 1975; Co-author chapter 'What we do and do not know about treatment refusals in mental institutions' in "Refusing Treatment in Mental Institutions: Values in Conflict", 1982; "Taking Care of Strangers", (book review), 1982. Books: "Informed Consent: A Study of Decisionmaking", (co-author), 1984; "Clinical Treatment of the Violent Person", (in press). *Honours:* Phi Beta Kappa, 1961; Outstanding Teacher Award, WPIC Psychiatric Residents, 1966 and 1983; William E Schumaker Distinguished Lecturer, Maine Department of Mental Health, 1982; Co-recipient, Nellie Westerman Prize for Research in Medical Ethics, 1984; John MarryDay Lecturer, Saint Elizabeth Hospital, Washington, 1985. *Hobby:* Golf. *Address:* Western Psychiatric Institute and Clinic, 3811 O'Hara Street, Pittsburgh, PA 15213, USA.

ROTH, (Sir) Martin, b. 6 Nov. 1917, Budapest. Professor of Psychiatry. m. Constance Heller, 14 Aug. 1945, London, 3 daughters. *Education:* MB, BS, MD (Lond) MD (Cantab) FRCP (Lond) FRCPsych (Foundation Fellow) Hon FRCP & S (Glasgow); ScD (Hon) University of Dublin, Trinity College; Distinguished Fellow, American Psych Association; Honorary Fellow, Royal College of Physicians and Surgeons, Glasgow; Honorary Fellow, Canadian Psychiatric Association; Honorary Fellow, American College of Neuropsychopharmacology; Honorary Fellow, Royal Society of Medicine; Foundation Member (CINP). *Appointments:* Visiting Assistant Professor, McGill University, Montreal, 1954-55; Director of Clinical Research, Graylingwell Hospital, Chichester (Later MRC Unit) 1950-55; Professor, Head of Department of Psychological Medicine, University of Newcastle upon Tyne and Durham, 1976-77; Honorary Director of Medical Research Council Group, University of Newcastle upon Tyne, 1962-68. *Memberships:* Scientific Member, Medical Research Council, 1964-68; Chairman, Advisory Committee for Joint MRC and DHSS Research Unit on Drug Dependance, 1970-75; Consultant, WHO International Project on Senile Dementia, 1981-; First President and Chairman, Court of Electors, Royal College of Psychiatrists, 1971-75. *Publications:* "Clinical Psychiatry" with Eliot Slater, 3rd edition 1977, translations into Italian, Spanish, Portuguese, Chinese and Japanese; "Psychiatry, Genetics and Pathology" with V Cowle; "Psychiatry, Human Rights and the Law" with R Bluglass, 1985; "The Reality of Mental Illness" with J Kroll, 1986; "Alzheimer's Disease and Related Disorders" with L Iversen, 1986. *Honours include:* Gold Medal, Society of Biological Psychiatry, USA, 1980; Erik Strömgren Medal, University of Aarhus, Denmark, 1982; Kesten Award, University of Southern California, 1983; Linacre Lecturer, St John's College, Cambridge, 1984; Sandoz Research Prize for Gerontological Research of the International Association of Gerontology, 1985; Kraepelin Gold Medal for Psychiatric Research, 1986. *Hobbies:* Music; Literature; Travel; Swimming. *Address:* 270 Hills Road, Cambridge, England.

ROTHBERG, June Simmonds, b. Philadelphia, Pennsylvania, USA. Vice Provost, Dean and Professor. m. Jack Rothberg, 2 sons. *Education:* BS, MA, PhD, New York University, New York. *Appointments:* Instructor 1964-65, Assistant Professor 1965-68, Director of Graduation Program in Rehabilitation Nursing 1965-69, Associate Professor 1968-69, New York University Division of Nursing, New York; Vice Provost for Academic Administration, Dean, Professor, Adelphi University, Garden City, New York, 1969-. *Memberships:* President 1974-76, Chairman, Governmental Affairs Committee, American Association of Colleges of Nursing; Fellow, American Academy of Nursing; President 1977-78, Chairman, Continuing Education Committee 1979-, American Congress of Rehabilitation Medicine; Health Advisory Council, New York State Health Planning Commission. *Publications:* 'Leadership in Rehabilitation Nursing', 1979; 'The Rehabilitation Team: Future Direction', 1981; 'The Inter-disciplinary Process: Is It a Chimera for Clinical Practice and for the ACRM?', 1985; 'Rehabilitation Team Practice' in "Interdisciplinary Team Practice: Issues and Trends", in press. *Honours include:* Gold Key Award, American Congress of Rehabilitation Medicine, 1984. *Hobby:* Needlepoint. *Address:* Adelphi University, Garden City, NY 11530, USA.

ROTHMAN, Nathan Ira, b. 9 Mar. 1950, Bronx, New York, USA. Chief of Hospital Pulmonary Division. m. Joan Warburg, 8 June 1971, 2 sons, 1 daughter. *Education:* BA, Yeshiva University, 1971; MD, Albert Einstein College of Medicine, 1974. *Appointments:* Internship, Hahnemann Hospital, 1974-75; Junior Medical Resident 1975-76, Senior Medical Resident 1976-77, Fellow in Pulmonary Medicine, 1977, Montefiore Hospital; Assistant Director of Medicine and Chief of Pulmonary Division, St John's Episcopal Hospital, 1981-. *Memberships:* American College of Physicians, Associate, American Thoracic Society; Fellow, American College of Chest. *Publications:* 'Fiberbronchoscopic Retrieval of Latrogenically Introduced Endobronchial Foreign Body', with S L Kamholz and P S Underwood, 1979; 'Actinomycotic Cervical Abscess: A Complication of Transtracheal Aspiration', (with K L Pinsker and S L Kamholz), 1979. *Hobbies:* Tennis; Basketball. *Address:* 360 Central Avenue, Lawrence, NY 11559, USA.

ROTHWEILER, Theresa Marie, b. 18 Feb. 1929, Neola, Iowa, USA. Assistant Professor. m. George A Rothweiler, 12 Sep. 1953, Denver, 3 sons, 2 daughters. *Education:* BS, Nursing, Loretto Heights College, Denver, 1951; MS, Nursing, 1972, PhD, Education 1980, University of Minnesota. *Appointments:* Staff Nursing; Night Supervisor; Nurse Educator; Founder, Professional Stress Management Programme Inc, 1985. *Memberships:* American Institute of Stress, Fellow; Sigma Theta Tau; American Nurses Association;

Minnesota Nurses Association; Sigma Xi; Oncology Nursing Society; Midwestern Nurse Research Society. *Publications:* "Coping with Complications of Cancer", 'RN', 1965; "Assessments in Nursing Education", 'Nurse Educator', 3; "Stress and Cancer", 'Inner Urban', 1984. *Honours:* Sigma Xi; Sigma Theta Tau, Faculty advisor, 1983-85; Horace T Amoco Outstanding Teacher Nominee, 1983. *Hobbies:* Cross Country Skiing; Biking; Walking; Travel. *Address:* 8707 Grosspoint Av. S, Cottage Grove, MN 55016, USA.

ROUGHAN, Simon Christopher, b. 26 Nov. 1951, Masterton, New Zealand. Director of Chiropractic Clinic. m. Maria Theresia Brandt, 5 July 1975, Dublin, Eire, 2 sons, 2 daughters. *Education:* BA Psychology (incomplete), Victoria University, Wellington, New Zealand; Diploma of Community Development (Hons), Institute for Community Development, Dublin; Doctor of Chiropractic; Diploma in Roentgenology, Anglo European College of Chiropractic, Bournemouth, England. *Appointments:* Youth Worker, Counsellor and National Co-ordinator, for IBO; Dublin; Intern, Anglo-European College of Chiropractic Clinic, Bournemouth, England; Preceptorship Programme, Phillip Institute School of Chiropractic. *Memberships:* New Zealand Chiropractors Association; NZCA Council; British Chiropractors Association; American Chiropractic Association; ACA Council on Roentgenology. *Publications:* 'Maintaining the Functional Lumbar Curve in Sitting Posture' - 'Bulletin of ECU, volume 29, No 1, 1981; 'Psychological Aspects of Patient Care' - 'New Zealand Chiropractic Journal', 1984. *Honours:* European Chiropractor Union Award for best AECC Research Thesis, 1980; New Zealand Agfa-Geveart Award for the best New Zealand Chiropractic paper, 1984. *Hobbies:* Gymnastics; Cycling; Hiking; Photography; Stamp Collecting. *Address:* 13 Heaphy Street, Greymouth 7800, Westland, New Zealand.

ROUNTREE, George Denton, b. 14 Mar. 1937, Houston, Texas, USA. President. *Education:* BSc, Lamar University, Beaumont, Texas, 1960; Master of Hospital Administration, Washington University, St Louis, Missouri, 1963; Advanced Continuing Education Program in Health Systems Management, Graduate School of Business and Public Health, Harvard University, 1976. *Appointment:* Vice-President, The Methodist Hospital, Houston, Texas, Tenure July 1963 - Dec. 1975. *Memberships:* Rotary International; The Mental Health Association of Houston and Harris County, Professional Advisory Committee; Boy Scouts of America, Advisory and Institutional Representative; Houston Chamber of Commerce; Chairman, Art Committee, Ronald McDonald House; Fellow, American College of Hospital Administrators; Member; American Association of Hospital Planning; American Hospital Association; Texas Hospital Association; Greater Houston Hospital Council; National Council for International Health; Association of University Programs in Health Administration. *Publications:* Contributions to professional journals including: Texas Hospitals; Hospitals; The Physician and Sportsmedicine. *Honour:* Fellowship Award, American College of Hospital Administrators, 1976. *Hobbies:* Travel; Skiing (Downhill and Crosscountry); Swimming; Photography; Reading. *Address:* 3401 Louisiana §230, Houston, TX 77002, USA.

ROUSH, Robert Ellis, b. 15 July 1942, Baytown, Texas, USA. Director of Center for Allied Health Professions. m. Carole Ann King, 29 May 1965, Baytown, Texas, 1 son, 1 daughter. *Education:* AA, Lee College, Baytown, Texas, 1962; BSc 1964, MEd 1966, Sam Houston State University, Huntsville; EdD University of Houston, 1969; MPH, University of Texas School of Public Health, Houston, 1979. *Appointments:* Teacher, Clear Creek School District, League City, Texas, 1964p66; Assistant Director and Director, Teacher Corps, University of Houston, Texas, 1966-69; Post-Doctoral Fellow, US Department of Health Education and Welfare, Washington DC, 1969-70; Post-Doctoral Fellow, University of Southern California Medical School, Los

Angeles, California, 1970-71; Director, Center for Allied Health Professions, Baylor College of Medicine, Houston, 1971-; Visiting Graduate Faculty, University of Houston and Texas A and M University, 1972-. *Memberships:* Association of American Medical Colleges; American Society of Allied Health Professions; Phi Kappa Phi; American Public Health Association; American Association of University Professor. *Publications include:* 'Interdisciplinary Education in the Health Professions: A Caveat from Research', 1973; 'Potential Pattersn: The Houston High School for Health Professions', 1973; "Basic Rehabilitation Techniques", (with R D Sine, S E Liss and J D Holcomb), also Spanish, German and Japanese translations, 1977; 'The Development of Midwifery - Male and Female, Yesterday and Today', 1979; 'Cardiovascular Disease and Diet: Research Findings for Health Education and Science Teachers' Use in the Classroom', 1980. *Honours:* 2 competitive post-doctoral Fellowships, 1969-71. *Hobbies:* Jogging; Racquetball. *Address:* Center for Allied Health Professions, Baylor College of Medicine, One Baylor Plaza, Houston, TX 77030, USA.

ROUZ BAYANI, Parviz, b. 26 June 1942, Khamion, Iran. Psychologist, Psychotherapist, Hypnotherapist. *Education:* BS, Social Work; MA, PhD, Clinical Psychology. *Appointments:* Head, Social Work, Rouzheh Hospital, 1970-78; Instructor, College of Social Work, 1970-78; Trainee Supervisor, College of Social Work. *Publications:* "Psychiatry Social Work", 'Psychiatry Journal', 1975. *Honours:* Attended Symposiums. *Hobbies:* Reading; Tennis. *Address:* PO Box 17185-436 Ava 17, Tehran, Iran.

ROWE, Lindsay John, b. 11 Oct. 1955, Sydney, New South Wales, Australia. Associate Professor. *Education:* BSc; Diplomate, American Chiropractic Board of Roentgenology; Fellow, Chiropractic College of Roentgenologists, Canada. *Appointments include:* Locum, Australia, 1979-81; Assistant Clinician, Consultant, Phillip Institute of Technology, Melbourne, 1979-81; Chairman Department of Radiology, Canadian Memorial Chiropractic College, 1981-83; Guest Lecturer, various Chiropractic Colleges, 1981-; Associate Professor, Department of Radiology, Northwestern Chiropractic College, Bloomington, Minnesota, USA, 1984-. *Memberships:* Australian and American Chiropractic Associations; American Chiropractic College of Roentgenology; Canadian Chiropractic Association. *Publications:* "Essentials of Skeletal Radiology", 1985. Contributions to: 'American Chiropractic Association Journal'; 'Australian Chiropractic Association Journal'; 'Journal of the Canadian Chiropractic Association'; various others. *Honours:* Russell Clarke Memorial Scholarship, Phillip Institute of Technology, Melbourne, Australia, 1978, Clinical Proficiency lence Award, New Zealand Chiropractors Association, 1979; Scientific Article Award, American Chiropractic Association, 1981; Fellow, American and Canadian Colleges of Roentgenology; Various Chiropractic licences, Australia and Canada. *Hobbies:* Outdoor photography; Sailing; Travel. *Address:* 30 Norman Avenue, Auburn, NSW 2144, Australia.

ROY, Richard, b. 2 Aug. 1953, Lachine, Quebec, Canada. Doctor of Chiropractic, Private Practice; Faculty Member. m. Claire Deland, 30 Sep. 1978, Napierville, 1 son, 1 daughter. *Education:* Diplome a Etudes Collegiale; Doctor of Chiropractic; Diplomate, International College of Applied Kinesiology; Certified Proficiency, Motion Palpation Institute. *Appointments:* Medical Team Member, Montreal Alouettes, Professional football team, 1981; Certified Teacher, International College of Applied Kinesiology, 1981-83; Head of Medical Team, Les Ligues Colombiennes de ballon sur Glace du Quebec, 1983-85; Faculty, Motion Palpation Institute, 1984-. *Memberships:* Ordre des Chiropraciciens de Quebec; Association des Chiropracticiens du Quebec; Association Chiropractique Canadienne; American Chiropractic Association. *Honours:* Graduate Summa cum Laude, 1977; Pi Tau Delta, 1977. *Hobbies:* Golf; Tennis; Ice

Hockey; Skiing. *Address:* 1191 90e Avenue, LaSalle, Quebec, Canada H8R 3A6.

ROY, Somnath, b. 19 Jan. 1929, Raghunathganj, India. Director, National Institute of Health and Family Medicine. m. Meenakshee, 12 Dec. 1964, 2 sons. *Education:* MB BS, 1952, PhD, 1958, DSc, 1981, Calcutta University. *Appointments:* Assistant Resident Professor of Endocrinology, Medical College, Georgia, Augusta, USA, 1961-63; Pool Officer and Resident Associate, All India Institute of Medical Sciences, New Delhi, India, 1964-66; Deputy Director and Head, Biomedical Division, 1966-76, Director, 1976-77, National Institute of Family Planning, New Delhi; Professor and Head, Department of Reproductive Biomedicine, National Institute of Health and Family Medicine, New Delhi, 1977-79; Consultant, World Health Organisation in Family Health in Sri Lanka, 1979-80; currently, Director, National Institute of Health and Family Medicine, New Delhi. *Memberships:* Fellow, National Academy of Medical Sciences, India. Life Member: Endocrine Society, India (Past President); Indian Public Health Association. Honorary Member, Indian Society of Human Genetics; Endocrine Society, USA (Past Member). *Publications:* Author over 200 research and scientific papers; Published and Editor 12 monographs; Co-Author of 3 books; Chief Editor, 2 journals. *Honours:* Rubin Award of Merit, American Society for the Study of Sterility, 1962; Certificate of Merit, American Medical Association, 1963; Dr S Mitra Memorial Oration Award, Bengal Obstetrics and Gynaecological Society, 1969; Annual Oration, Endocrine Society of India, 1971; Laximipathi Oration Award, National Academy of Medical Sciences, 1983; Dr B Mukherjee Oration Award, Indian Pharmacological Society, 1983. *Hobbies:* Swimming; Jogging; Photograph; Travelling. *Address:* National Institute of Health and Family Welfare, New Mehrauli Road, Munirka, New Delhi 110067, India.

ROYCE, Paul C, b. 2 July 1928, Minneapolis, Minnesota, USA. University Dean. m. Jacqueline S. Marofsky, 5 June 1956, Cambridge, Massachusetts, USA, 1 son, 2 daughters. *Education:* PhD, Case-Western Reserve University; MD, University of Minnesota. *Appointments:* Assistant Professor of Medicine, The Albert Einstein College of Medicine, New York, 1961-70; Associate Professor of Medicine, Hahnemann Medical College, Philadelphia, 1973-81; Clinical Professor of Medicine, Upstate Medical Center, State University of New York, Syracuse, 1979-81; Dean and Professor of Physiology and Clinical Sciences, University of Minnesota, Duluth School of Medicine, 1981-. *Memberships:* American Medical Association; American Physiological Society; Harvey Society. *Publication:* Most recent: 'Value of postirradiation screening for thyroid nodules' JAMA 1979. *Honours:* Alpha Omega Alpha 1952; National Science Foundation Fellow 1953, 1956-58. *Address:* School of Medicine, University of Minnesota, Duluth, MN 55812, USA.

ROZEE, Kenneth Roy, b. 7 Feb. 1931, Halifax, Nova Scotia, Canada. Professor of Microbiology. m. Patricia M Reyno, 11 Aug. 1973, Halifax, Nova Scotia, Canada, 2 sons, 3 daughters. *Education:* BSc, Hons, 1953, MSc, 1955, Dalhousie University; D Bact University of Toronto, 1958; PhD, Dalhousie University, 1958. *Appointments:* Assistant Professor of Microbiology, Dalhousie University, 1959-61; Associate Professor of Microbiology, University of Toronto, 1962-67; Professor of Microbiology, Dalhousie University, 1968-; Director, Infectious Diseases Research Laboratory, IWK Hospital, 1974-78; Head of Department of Microbiology, Dalhousie University, 1973-84; Head of Department of Microbiology, Victoria General Hospital, Halifax, Nova Scotia, 1973-. *Memberships:* Canadian Public Health Association; Canadian Society of Microbiologists; American Society of Microbiologists; Infectious Disease Society of America; Canadian College of Microbiologists. *Publications:* "Plasmids and Transposons" with C Stuttard, 1980; 'The etiologic significance of a Compromised Interferon Response in Reyes Syndrome' in Journal of National Reyes Syndrome Foundation, 1984 co-author. *Hobbies:* Fishing; Sailing; Canoeing. *Address:* Department of Microbiology, Faculty of Medicine, Dalhousie University, Halifax, Nova Scotia, Canada B3H 4H7.

ROZENBERG, Maurice Charles, b. 19 Dec. 1931, Brussels, Belgium. Chairman, Clinical Haematology, 1967-. m. Gillian Livermore, 15 May 1976, Sydney, Australia, 1 son, 1 daughter (from previous marriage). *Education:* MB BS, 1956, MD, 1967, University of Sydney, Australia; FRACP; FRCPA. *Appointments:* Resident Medical Officer, 1957-63, Research Fellow, Clinical Research, 1963-65, Royal Prince Alfred Hospital; Research Fellow, Institute for Thrombosis Research, Oslo, Norway, 1965-67. *Memberships:* Chairman, NSW State Committee, Royal Australasian College of Physicians; Secretary General, Asian Pacific Division, International Society of Haematology. *Hobbies:* Australian Paintings;·Cooking; Wines. *Address:* Division of Haematology, Prince Henry Hospital, PO Box 233, Matraville, NSW 2036, Australia.

ROZENGURT, Juan Enrique, b. 20 Nov. 1942, Buenos Aires, Argentina. Staff Scientist, Cancer Research. m. Nora Fretz, 19 July 1969, Buenos Aires, 1 son. *Education:* Doctor of Veterinary Medicine, School of Agronomy & Veterinary, 1965; PhD Biological Chemistry, School of Sciences, 1971, University of Buenos Aires; Post-doctoral training, Department of Biological Sciences, Princeton University, USA, 1972. *Appointments:* Instructor 1963-66, Chief Instructor 1966-68, Physiology, School of Agronomy & Veterinary, University of Buenos Aires; Research Staff, Department of Biological Chemistry, University of Buenos Aires, 1968-71; Research Associate, Department of Biological Sciences, Princeton University, 1971-72; Visiting Scientist 1972-73, Research Fellow 1973-74, Research Scientist 1974-77, Senior Research Scientist, 1977-80, Special Appointment (University Chair), Head of Laboratory of Membrane Physiology & Growth Regulation, 1980-, Imperial Cancer Research Fund, London, England. *Memberships:* British Society of Cell Biology; American Society of Physiologists. *Publications:* Numerous articles in medical journals & proceedings. *Honour:* M Kamen Prize in Biochemistry. *Hobbies:* Music; Opera. *Address:* Imperial Cancer Research Fund, PO Box 123, Lincoln's Inn Fields, London, WC2A 3PX, England.

ROZNIECKA-ROSCISZEWSKA, Danuta Helena, b. 14 Apr. 1926, Lwow, Poland. Vice Head, Department of Neurology; Head, Epilepsy Outpatient Clinic. m. Lech Michal Rosciszewski, 18 Oct. 1956, 2 daughters. *Education:* Physicians Diploma, 1950, MD, 1951, Habilitation, 1975, Medical Faculty of Jagiellon University, Krakow; Degrees of Specialisation in Neurology, 1958, 61. *Appointments:* Assistant, Senior Assistant, Department of Microbiology, Senior Assistant, Tutor, 1956-75, Assostant Professor, Department of Neurology, 1976-, Silesian Medical Academy; Head, Epilepsy Outpatient Clinic, Regional Epilepsy Centre, 1956-. *Memberships:* President, Regional Branch, Polish Neurological Association; Committee of Neurology, Section for Researches in Epilepsy, Polish Academy of Science; Polish Chapter of International League Against Epilepsy. *Publications:* 'Certain Clinical and Social Aspects of Post-traumatic Epilepsy in Women', 1979; 'Analysis of Seizure dispersion during Menstrual Cycle in Women with Epilepsy', 1980; 'Problems in Children Upbringing in Women with Epilepsy', 1985; 'Ovarian Hormones anticonvulsant drugs and seizures during menstrual cycle in women with epilepsy', 1985; 'Analysis of Changes in Frequency of seizures during pregnancy in 65 epileptic women', 1979; 'Epilepsy and menstruation', book chapter, 1986. Has carried out complex studies on clinical and psychosocial aspects of epilepsy in women, presenting results at various international congresses and symposiums. *Honour:* Golden Cross of Merit, 1980. *Hobbies:* Gardening; Travelling. *Address:* Department of Neurology, 3-go Maja 15, 41-800

Zabrze, Poland.

ROZNIECKI, Jerzy Kazimierz, b. 3 Sep. 1929, Piekary, Poland. Professor of Medicine; Head, Department of Pneumology and Allergology. m. 15 Apr. 1958, 1 son, 1 daughter. *Education: Graduate Medical Diploma, 1954, MD, 1962, Habilitation Associate Professor, 1968, Professor, 1975, Ord. Professor, 1985, Medical Faculty, Lodz. Appointments:* Assistant, 1954, Docent, 1968, Head of Clinic of Penumology and Allergology, Medical Academy, Lodz, Poland. *Memberships include:* Fellow: President Polish Society of Penumology; Polish Society of Allergology; Polish Society of Internal Medicine. Committee Member, Polish Academy of Sciences; European Academy of Allergology and Clinical Immunology; European Pneumonoligical Society. *Publications:* Author of some 280 original papers contributed to national and international professional journals. *Honours:* Professional and civic honours. *Hobbies:* Literature; Poetry. Various others. *Address:* Al Kopciuszki 98 im 15, 90-442 Lodz, Poland.

ROZSOS, István, b. 28 Aug. 1932, Nagykanizsa, Hungary. Associate Professor of Surgery. m. Magdalen Máté, 15 Feb. 1958, 2 sons. *Education:* MD, University of Pécs Medical School, 1957; Candidate of Medical Science (PhD), Hungarian Academy of Sciences, 1974. *Appointments:* Demonstrator, Department of Anatomy, Histology & Embriology, University Medical School, Pécs, 1953-57; Junior Assistant in Surgery, City Hospital of Keszthely, 1957-61; Adjunct in Surgery, County Council Hospital, Kaposvár, 1961-70; Vascular Surgical Clinic, University of Utrecht, Netherlands, 1970-71; Chief Surgeon, 1971-81, Chief Surgeon & Head of Surgery Department, County Council Teaching Hospital, Kaposvár, 1981-; Surgical Supervisor, Somogy County; Titular Associate Professor, University Medical School, Pécs. *Memberships:* Hungarian Surgical Society; Hungarian Gastroenterological Society; European Society of Surgical Oncology. *Publications:* More than 100 papers in surgical field in medical journals. *Hobbies:* History; Moral Philosophy; Angling. *Address:* Kaposvár, Bajcsy Zs ut 35, Kórház, Sebészet, 7400 Hungary.

RUBENSTEIN, Arthur Harold, b. 28 Dec. 1937, Germiston, Republic of South Africa. Professor and Chairman, Department of Medicine, Lowell T Coggeshall Professor of Medical Sciences. m. Denise Hack, 19 Aug. 1962, Pretoria, Republic of South Africa, 2 sons. *Education:* MBBCh; FCP; MRCP; FACP; Diplomat, American Board of Internal Medicine; Diplomat, Endocrinology-Metabolism Subspecialty Board. *Appointments:* Part time Lecturer, Department of Physiology, University of Witwatersrand, Republic of South Africa, 1964-65; Research Assistant, Section of Endocrinology, Department of Medicine, 1965-66; Tutorial Registrar in Medicine to Professional Unit, Johannesburg General Hospital, 1966-67; Assistant in Medicine, OSPHS Research Fellow, 1967-68, Assistant Professor, Department of Medicine, 1968-70; Associate Professor, Department of Medicine, 1970-74, Professor and Associate Chairman, Department of Medicine, 1974-81, University of Chicago, Chicago, Illinois, USA. *Memberships:* American Society for Clinical Investigation; Endocrine Society; Member, Midwest Council, 1976-, Midwest Program Committee, 1976, National Program Committee, 1977, American Federation for Clinical Research; Association of American Physicians; Member, Research Committee, 1976-78, Chairman, Program Committee, Annual Scientific Meeting, 1979, Chairman, Coordinating Committee for Scientific Affairs, 1979-80, American Diabetes Association; Scientific Advisory Board, 1973-76, 1978-81, Chairman, MSAB, 1979-81, Juvenile Diabetes Foundation; President, Subspeciality Section (Endocrinology/Metabolism), 1980-82, Member of Council, 1982-, Central Society for Clinical Research; American Board of Internal Medicine, 1986; Treasurer, Association of American Physicians, 1984-. *Publications:* Contributor of articles to numerous medical and professional journals.

Honours: Merit Award, University of Witwatersrand Council, 1957; Bronze Medal for most distinguished graduate, 1960; Schweppe Fellowship Award, 1970; Lilly Award, American Diabetes Association, 1973; Juvenile Diabetes Association Scientific Award, 1977; Banting Medal, American Diabetes Association, 1983; Solomon Berson Lecturer, American Diabetes Association, 1985. *Address:* University of Chicago, 5841 South Maryland Avenue, Chicago, IL 60637, USA.

RUBIN, David Howard, b. 29 Dec. 1950, New York, USA. Assistant Professor of Paediatrics, Albert Einstein College of Medicine, Bronx, New York. m. Ea Jensen, 30 June 1979, Copenhagen, Denmark, 2 sons, 1 daughter. *Education:* BA, 1973, MD, 1978, Case Western Reserve University, Cleveland, Ohio, USA. *Appointments:* Paediatric Intern, Resident, University of California, San Francisco, 1978-81; Chief Resident in Paediatrics, San Francisco General Hospital, 1981-82; Robert Wood Johnson Fellow in General Paediatrics, Department of Paediatrics, Yale University School of Medicine, New Haven, Connecticut. *Memberships:* Ambulatory Paediatric Association, 1982. *Publications:* 'Chronic INH poisoning: Case report and recommendations for usage of the drug' (with others), 1983; 'Risk Factors for hearing loss in the high risk premature infant', (with L C Mayes), 1985; 'Educational intervention by computer in childhood asthma', (with J M Leventhal, R T Sadock, E Letovsky, P Schottland, I Clemente, P McCarthy), 1986; 'The relationship between cigarette smoking and alcohol consumption during pregnancy by Danish women', (with P A Krasilnikoff, J M Leventhal, A Berger); Contributor of various chapters in books, abstracts and presentations). *Honours:* Fulbright Fellowship, Denmark, 1984-85. *Hobbies:* Photography; Rock concerts. *Address:* Bronx Municipal Hospital Centre, Albert Einstein College of Medicine, Jacobi BS19, Pelham Parkway South and Eastchester Road, Bronx, NY 10461, USA.

RUBIN, Karen Ann Brown, b. 2 Aug. 1951, Chicago, Illinois, USA. Clinical Psychologist. m. Hardin Edward Rubin, 8 Sep. 1973, Knoxville, Tennessee, 1 son. *Education:* BA with Honours, Florida State University, 1973; MA 1975, PhD 1977, Development Psychology, Ohio State University; Fellow in Clinical Psychology, University of Kansas Medical Center. *Appointments:* Clinical Psychologist, Tri-County Mental Health Complex, Child and Youth Division, 1978-79; Part-time Instructor, Sacred Heart Night College, 1979-80; Consultant for Mental Retardation and Developmental Disabilities Services, Gaston-Lincoln Mental Health, 1980; Instructor, University of North Carolina, Charlotte, 1982; Consultant, Gaston County Residential Services, 1982-. *Memberships:* American Psychological Association; North Carolina Psychological Association; American Society of Clinical Hypnosis; American and North Carolina Associations on Mental Deficiency; American Association of Marriage and Family Therapy; Phi Beta Kappa. *Publication:* 'Special problems faced by elderly victims of crime' (with J D Hirschel), 1982. *Hobbies:* Modern and Jazz Dance. *Address:* 209 W 2nd Avenue, Gastonia, NC 28052, USA.

RUBIO, Juanito Adiarte, b. 29 May 1939, Philippines. Chief of Hospital, Slocos Regional Hospital. *Education:* MD, cum Laude, University of Sto Tomas, Philippines, 1962; Certificate in Hospital Administration, Masters in Hospital Administration. *Appointments:* Rotating Intern & Surgical Resident, Frankford Hospital, Philadelphia, USA; OB-Gyne, 1st Year, St Vincent's Hospital, Bridgeport, Connecticut, 2nd Year, Sinai Hospital of Baltimore; Chief Resident, Obstetrics Gynaecology, Sinai Hospital of Baltimore; Fellow, grantee, US Public Health Service, Ellis Fischel State Cancer Hospital, Columbia; Obstetrician, Gynaecologist, Private Practice, Philippines; Medical Specialist I, Medical Specialist II, Ilocos Norte Provincial Hospital; Officer in Charge, Gabriela Silang General Hospital. *Memberships:* Fellow: American College of Obst-

etrics & Gynaecology, Philippine College of Surgeons; Philippine Obstetrical & Gynaecologic Society; Life Member, Maternal and Child Health Association of the Philippines; Ilocos Norte Medical Society; Philippine Medical Association. *Honours:* Certificate of Appreciation, Scientific Speaker, La Union Medical Society, 1972; Plaque of Appreciation, Lecturer, Philippine Society of Anaesthesiologists Postgraduate Course, 1977; Resolution of Adoption, As Adopted Son of Il cos Sur, 1985; Certificate of Appreciation, Town Fiesta, Municipality of San Fernando, La Union, 1985; many other honours and awards. *Hobbies:* Tennis; Swimming. *Address:* 33 Gen Segundo St, Laoag City, Philippines.

RUDERT, Heinrich, b. 5 July 1935, München, Germany. Head of ENT Department, University of Kiel. m. Anneliese Thiele, 26 Dec. 1960, 1 son, 1 daughter. *Education:* Promotion Dr Med, 1961; Habilitation, 1968; apl Professor, 1971; o Professor, 1976. *Appointments:* Assistant, ENT Department, University of Munich, 1962-68; Oberarzt, ENT Department, University of Cologne, 1969-76; Head, ENT Department, University of Kiel, 1976-. *Membership:* Deutsche Gesellschaft f HNO-Heilkunde, Kopf und Halschirurgie. *Publications:* "Experimentelle Untersuchungen zur Resorption der Endolymphe in Innenohrdes Meerschweinchens", Arch klin exp Ohr, Nas-u Kehlk-Heilk 193, 138-170, 201-235, 1969; "Die Oropharynx-Tumoren", In Berendes, Link u Zollner: HNO-Heilkinde, Bd 4, Teil 2, Georg-Thieme Verl, Stuttgart, New York, 1983. *Hobbies:* Hunting; Golf. *Address:* Klinik und Poliklinik für HNO-Krankheiten der Universität Kiel Hospitalstr 20, 2300 Kiel, Federal Republic of Germany.

RUDIN, Edward, b. 9 Sep. 1922, Philadelphia, Pennsylvania, USA. Private Consultation Practitioner; Associate Clinical Professor, University of California, Davis, California, USA. m. Anna Noto, 6 June 1948, Philadelphia, Pennsylvania, 1 son, 3 daughters. *Education:* MD, AB, Temple University; Fellow, American Psychiatric Association; Fellow, American Public Health Association; Certified in Psychiatry, American Board of Psychiatry and Neurology. *Appointments:* Medical Intern, Cedars of Lebanon Hospital, Hollywood, California; Psychiatric Resident, Veterans Administration Hospital, Palm Alto, California; Captain, US Air Force Medical Corps; Director, State of California Mental Hygiene Clinic, Riverside, California; Deputy Director, Department of Mental Hygiene, Community Services, Sacramento, California; Director, Sutter Hospitals Diagnostic and Treatment Centre, Sacramento, California; Director, Sutter Community Hospitals Mental Health Centre, Sacramento, California. *Memberships:* American Medical Association; American Public Health Association; American Psychiatric Association; California Medical Association; Central California Psychiatric Society; Sacramento-El Dorado Medical Society; Physicians for Social Responsibility; Phi Delta Epsilon Medical Fraternity. *Publications:* 'Psychiatric Inpatient Services in General Hospitals', 1960; 'A Philosophy of State Government participation in an overall mental health program', 1961; 'A Long Range Plan for Mental Health Services in California', 1963; 'Comprehensive Centers for the Mentally Retarded', 1964; 'Psychiatric Treatment: General Implications and Lessons from Recent Court Decisions in California', 1978. *Honours:* Certificate of Appreciation, Southern California Psychiatric Society, 1977; Outstanding Mental Health Staff, Sacramento Chapter, Mental Health Association, 1978; Friend of the Family Award, Sacramento Family Service Agency, 1985. *Hobbies:* Reading; Music. *Address: Sacramento, CA 95822, USA.*

RUDOWSKI, Witold Janusz, b. 1918, Piotrkow, Trybunalski, Poland. Director of Research Institute of Haematology and Blood Transfusion, Warsaw, 1964-. *Education:* MB, 1943; Clandestine Medical Faculty, MD, 1947, Medical Faculty, Warsaw University; Docent, 1954; Professor of Surgery, Warsaw Medical Academy, 1961. *Appointments:* Surgeon, Child

Jesus Hospital, Warsaw, 1943; Senior Surgeon, First Department of Surgery, Faculty of Medicine, Warsaw University; Surgeon, Research Investigator, Marie Curie Cancer Institute; Head, Department of Surgery, Institute of Haematology and Blood Transfusion, Warsaw, 1964-. *Memberships:* Honorary Member, American College of Surgeons; Honorary Member, Royal Colleges of Surgeons of Edinburgh and England; Royal College of Surgeons Ireland; Royal College of Physicians and Surgeons of Canada; International Surgical Society; International Society for Burn Injury; Honorary Fellow, Association of Surgeons of Great Britain and Ireland; Corresponding Fellow, Surgical Associations of the Netherlands, Sweden and West Germany; President, 1975-78, International Federation of Surgical Colleges; Member of the Executive Board of the World Health Organisation, 1985-. *Publications:* Author of over 400 original papers, 40 critical reviews, 60 reports and book reviews; A member of Editorial Boards of many Polish and International surgical and medical journals. *Address:* Research Institute of Haematology and Blood Transfusion, Chocimska 5, 00957 Warsaw, Poland.

RUDY, David Robert, b. 19 Oct. 1934, Columbia, Ohio, USA. Director, Family Practice. m. Rosemary Sims, 23 Oct. 1981, Delaware, Ohio, 3 sons and 1 daughter by previous marriage. *Education:* BSc, 1956, MD, 1960, Ohio State University; Certified, American Board of Family Practice, 1971, 77, 83. *Appointments:* Intern, Northwestern Memorial Hospital, Chicago, Illinois, 1960-61; Flight Surgeon, US Air Force (Captain), 1961-63; Resident, Internal Medicine, 1963-64, Paediatrics, 1964, Ohio State University; Private Practice, Upper Arlington, Ohio, 1964-75; Director, Family Practice Programme, Riverside Methodist Hospital, Columbus, Ohio, 1975-85; Clinical Associate Professor, Ohio State University, Department of Family Medicine, 1980-; currently, Director, Family Practice, Monsour Medical Center, Jeannette, Pennsylvania. *Memberships:* American Academy of Family Physicians; Ohio and Pennsylvania State Academies of Family Physicians; American and Ohio State Medical Associations; American MENSA Society. *Publications:* Author and Co-Author of 19 papers contributed to professional journals including: 'Journal of Ohio State Medical Association'; 'American Family Physician'; 'Family Practice Research Journal'. *Honours:* President: Central Ohio Academy of Family Physicians, 1979; Board of Directors, Pennsyl £nia Academy of Family Physicians; Medical Symposium, 1980. *Hobbies:* Languages; Classical piano; History; Writing and publishing essays. *Address:* 1633 Timberlake Drive, Delaware, OH 43015, USA.

RUDY, Lester H, b. 6 Mar. 1918, Chicago, Illinois, USA. Professor of Psychiatry. m. Ruth Jean Schmidt, 20 Nov. 1950, Menominee, Michigan, USA, 1 daughter. *Education:* MD, University of Illinois, USA, 1941; MSHA, Northwestern University, 1957; Diplomate, American Board of Psychiatry and Neurology, 1951, certified Hospital Administration, American Psychiatric Association, 1957. *Appointments:* US Army, 1940-46; US Army Reserve. 1946-61, retired, US Army, 1961; Chief, Acute Intensive Treatment Services, Veterans Hospital, Downey, 1948-54; Superintendent, Galesburg State Research Hospital, 1954-58; Director, Illinois State Psychiatric Institute, 1958-75; Acting Director, Illinois State Paediatric Institute, 1961-72; Professor and Head, Department of Psychiatry, University of Illinois College of Medicine, 1975-; Acting Director, Univesity of Illinois Hospital, University of Illinois at Chicago, 1981-82. *Memberships:* Academy of Psychoanalysis; American Association of Chairmen of Departments of Psychiatry; American Psychiatric Association; Chicago Medical Society; Illinois Psychiatric Society; Illinois State Medical Society. *Publication:* 'American Board of Psychiatry and Neurology' in "Comprehensive Textbook of Psychiatry", 4th edition, chapter 45.1, pp 1910-1917, 1984; 46 other articles and chapters. *Honours:* Bowis Award for Outstanding Achievement and Leadership in the field of Psychiatry, 1979; University of Illinois Medi-

cal Alumni Association Annual Outstanding Achievement Award, 1980. *Address:* University of Illinois, Department of Psychiatry, 912 South Wood Street, Chicago, IL 60612, USA.

RÜEGG, Johann Caspar, b. 28 Jan. 1930, Zurich, Switzerland. Professor of Physiology. m. Elvira Cullman, 26 Aug. 1967, Zurich, 1 son, 1 daughter. *Education:* MD Medicine, Zurich; PhD Biochemistry, Cambridge, England. *Appointments:* Research Associate 1960-67, Professor of Cell Physiology 1967-72; Bochum, Federal Republic of Germany; Professor of Physiology, Head of Department, II, Physiologisches Institut, University of Heidelberg, 1973-. *Memberships:* German Physiological Society; German Biochemical Society; Swiss Physiological Society; American Physiological Society. *Publication:* 'Smooth Muscle Tone', 1971. *Honour:* Adolf Fick Award, Merits in Physiology, 1974. *Hobbies:* Painting; Skiing. *Address:* II, Physiologisches Institute, Universitat Heidelberg, Im Neuenheimer Feld 326, D-6900 Heildeberg, Federal Republic of Germany.

RUFF, Tibor, b. 9 May 1942, Hungary. Director, Division of Otolaryngology. m. Cynthia Alexandra Cardwell, 27 Dec. 1969, Montreal, Canada, 1 son, 1 daughter. *Education:* BA, University of Western Ontario, Canada; MD, University of Ottawa; Fellow, Royal College of Physicians and Surgeons of Canada, American College of Surgeons. *Appointments:* Resident, University of Toronto Hospitals, Canada; Registrar, Radcliffe Infirmary, Oxford, England; Private Practice, Affiliate Staff, McMaster University, Hamilton, Canada; ENT Consultant, Director, Division of Otolaryngology (currently), Scott and White Clinic, Temple, Texas, USA; Professor of Surgery, Texas A&M University. *Memberships:* Fellow: American Academy of Otolaryngology, Head and Neck Surgery; Royal College of Physicians and Surgeons, Canada; American College of Surgeons; American Society for Head and Neck Surgery; Society of Ear, Nose and Throat Advances for Children. *Publications:* Co-author of papers contributed to: 'Annals of Otology, Rhonology and Laryngology', 1974; 'Archives of Otolaryngology', 1985; 'Geriatric Clinics of North America', 1985. *Hobbies:* Reading; Travel; Personal computing; Swimming; Fishing. *Address:* Division of Otolaryngology, Scott and White Clinic, Temple, TX 76508, USA.

RUH, Dennis Robert, b. 24 Oct. 1957, Buffalo, New York, USA. President & Chief Administrator, Southtowns Physical Therapy. *Education:* BSc. *Appointments:* Staff Physical Therapist, Our Lady of Victory Hospital, Lackawanna, New York, Visiting Nursing Association, Buffalo. *Memberships:* Recording Secretary, local chapter, Council of Licensed Physiotherapists, New York State; American Physical Therapy Association. *Hobbies:* Skiing; Cycling; Golf; Fishing. *Address:* 300 Center Road, West Seneca, NY 14224, USA.

RUSDIDJAS, Rusdidjas, b. 4 May 1937, Padang, Indonesia. Staff Department of Child Health, Medical School, North Sumatera University, Indonesia. m. Rafita Ramayati, MD, 17 Jan. 1968, Medan, 1 son, 1 daughter. *Education:* Postgraduate course in Institute of Medical Microbiology, University of Copenhagen, Denmark, 1971-72; Bacteriologist, Medical School, North Sumatera University, Medan, Indonesia, 1974; Pediatrician, 1979; MD. *Appointments:* Staff Department of Microbiology, Medical School, North Sumatera University, 1965-74; Staff Department of Child Health, Medical School University of North Sumatera, Medan, 1975-. *Memberships:* Indonesian Medical Association; Indonesian Pediatrics Association; Indonesian Nephrologist Association; International Society of Nephrology; Indonesian Rheumatism Association. *Publication:* "Nephrotic Syndrome in Children at Medan", 1982. *Hobbies:* Radio (amateur); Orchids Plantations; Swimming. *Address:* Department of Child Health, Pirngadi Hospital, Medan, Indonesia.

RUSH, Augustus John Jr, b. 15 Dec. 1942, New Jersey, USA. Professor of Psychiatry. m. Susan Meyer, 5 Dec. 1970, Nurnberg, Germany, 1 son. *Education:* AB, biochemistry, Princeton University, 1964; MD, Columbia College, 1968. *Appointments include:* Assistant Professor, Department of Psychiatry & Behavioural Sciences, University of Oklahoma, 1975-78; Associate Professor/Director of Affective Disorders Unit, 1978-83, Betty Jo Hay Professor of Mental Health/Director, Affective Disorders Unit, Department of Psychiatry, 1983-, Southwestern Medical School, Dallas, Texas. *Memberships include:* American College of Psychiatry; Psychiatric Research Society; Society for Biological Psychiatry; American Psychopathological Association; American College of Neuropsychopharmacology; etc. *Publications include:* Books: 'Cognitive Therapy of Depression", co-author, 1979; "Short-term Psychotherapies for Depression", editor, 1982; "Beating Depression", London, 1983; "Recent Advances in the Diagnosis & Treatment of Depression", co-editor, in press. Numerous papers in professional journals. *Honours include:* Fellow, American Psychiatric Association, 1986. *Hobbies:* Boy Scouts; Boating. *Address:* Department of Psychiatry, Southwestern Medical School, 5323 Harry Hines Blvd, Dallas, TX 75235, USA.

RUSH, Robert Archer, b. 16 Dec. 1944, Melbourne, Australia. Lecturer in Physiology. m. Vivienne Dorothy June Gardner, 3 Feb. 1968, Malvern, 2 sons, 1 daughter. *Education:* BSc, PhD, Monash University. *Appointment:* Senior Lecturer in Human Physiology, School of Medicine, Flinders University. *Memberships:* New York Academy of Sciences; Australian Neurosciences Society; Australian Physiological & Pharmacological Society. *Publications:* 56 learned articles, including: 'Immunohistochemical localisation of protein components of catecholamine storage vesicles' (with L B Geffen & B G Livett), 'Journal of Physiology', 1969; 'Mechanism of transmitter release from sympathetic neurons!' (doctoral thesis), 1973; 'Dipamine-B-hydroxylase in Health & Disease' (with L B Geffen), Critical Reviews in Clinical Laboratory Sciences, 1980; 'Neuronal regulation of mascarine receptors in the chick expansor secundariorum muscle', Nature, 1982; (with M F Crouch, C P Morris & B J Gannon); 'Dopamine-B-hydroxylase Immunohistorchemistry and Immunocytochemistry', Methods in Neuroscience, 1983; 'Immunohistochemical Localization of endogenous Nerve Growth Factor', Nature, 1984. *Hobbies:* Music; Various Sports. *Address:* School of Medicine, Flinders University, Bedford Park, South Australia 5042, Australia.

RUSKIN, Asa Paul, b. 26 Sep. 1929, New York City, New York, USA. Attending Physician in Neurology; Professor of Rehabilitation Medicine. m. Francine Klein, 6 July 1953, Buenos Aires, Argentina, 2 sons, 1 daughter. *Education:* BA, Emory University, Atlanta, Georgia, USA, 1951; MD, University of Paris-Sorbonne, France, 1957; American Board of Physical Medicine and Rehabilitation, 1966. *Appointments include:* Assistant Neurologist, Montefiore Hospital, Bronx, New York, USA, 1961-64; Director of Chemotherapy Programme, Alcoholic Clinic, Domestic Relations Court of City of New York, 1962-66; Attending Neurologist, Mahattan Eye, Ear and Throat Hospital, New York City, 1965-73; Associate Attending-Neurology, Director of Neuroelectrodiagnostic Laboratories, French-Polyclinic Medical School and Health Center, New York City, 1962-73; Associate Attending-Neurology 1964-72, Director of Physical Medicine and Rehabilitation 1968-70, Trafalgar Hospital, New York City; Adjunct Attending-Neurology, Lenox Hill Hospital, New York City, 1963-; Director of Department of Rehabilitation Medicine 1973-, Attending Physician-Neurology 1975-, Kingsbrook Jewish Medical Center, Brooklyn, New York; Associate Clinical Professor of Rehabilitation Medicine, Albert Einstein College of Medicine of Yeshiva University, New York, 1975-. *Memberships include:* Board of Directors 1985, Secretary 1985, Rehabilitation International USA; Secretary 1983-85, American Congress of Rehabilitation Medicine; Fellow, American College of

Physicians; Fellow, American Academy of Physical Medicine and Rehabilitation; Fellow, Royal Society of Health; Fellow, American Academy for Cerebral Palsy. *Publications include:* "Current Therapy in Physiatry: Physical Medicine and Rehabilitation", (editor), 1983; Numerous articles, essays, editorials and chapters in books; 8 USA Patents. *Honour:* Chevalier Dans L'Ordre des Palmes Academiques, France, 1972. *Address:* 262 Central Park West, New York, NY 10024, USA.

RUSSELL, Bonnie Faye, b. 20 June 1939, Fort Edward, New York, USA. Manager; Researcher. *Education:* BA, Chemistry; Postgraduate, University of Southern California School of Medicine, California State University, School of Business Administration; Licensed: State of Florida, Clinical Laboratory Technologist; State of California, General Laboratory Supervisor, Radiation Safety Officer. *Appointments:* Medical Technologist, Glensfalls Hospital; Vice President, Williams Ceramic Lab; Manager, Orlando Plasma Centre; Supervisor, Houston Plasma Centre; Vice President, Medical Affairs, Lopapa Institute Inc; Owner, Fashion Dynamics. *Memberships:* California Business Women's Network; Summit Organization; American Management Association; National Association of Female Executives; New York Academy of Science; etc. *Honours:* Certificate of Appreciation, City of Los Angeles, 1984. *Hobbies:* Swimming; Sewing; Piano; Flute; Chess; Reading; Knitting; Hiking; Riding; Skiing; Golf. *Address:* 722 S Ardmore 36, Los Angeles, CA90005, USA.

RUSSELL, Gerald Francis Morris, b. 12 Jan. 1928, Granmont, Belgium. Professor of Psychiatry. m. Margaret Euphemia Taylor, 8 Sep. 1950, Edinburgh, Scotland, 3 sons. *Education:* MB, ChB, MD, Edinburgh; Registrar in Neurology, Northern General Hospital, Edinburgh, 1954-56; Medical Research Council Clinical Research Fellowship, National Hospital and Maudsley Hospital, 1956-58. *Appointments:* Dean, Institute of Psychiatry, University of London, 1966-70; Senior Lecturer and Consultant Psychiatrist, Institute of Psychiatry and the Bethlem Royal and Maudsley Hospital, 1960-70; Professor of Psychiatry, Royal Free Hospital Medical School, University of London, 1971-79; Currently Professor of Psychiatry, Institute of Psychiatry, University of London and Maudsley Hospital. *Memberships:* Fellow, Royal College of Physicians of Edinburgh; Fellow, Royal College of Physicians of London; Fellow, Royal College of Psychiatrists; Fellow, Royal Society of Medicine, London; 1942 Club. *Hobbies:* Photography; Language. *Address:* Institute of Psychiatry, de Crespigny Park, Denmark Hill, London SE5 8AF, England.

RUSSELL, John Gordon, b. 21 Aug. 1928, Northern Ireland. Professor and Head, Department of Dental Surgery, University College, Cork. m. Mary Ferguson, 12 Aug. 1964, Dumfries, 6 sons, 3 daughters. *Education:* MB BCh; BAO; BDS; (NUI); LAH (Ireland); FDSRCS (England); FFDRCSI (with examination). *Appointments:* House Surgeon, Dental Department, Royal Hospital, Sheffield, 1952; Registrar, Dental Department, Central Middlesex Hospital, London, 1952-53; Demonstrator in Anatomy, University College, Cork, 1953-55; House Officer (Medicine), St Finbans Hospitals, Cork, 1957; House Surgeon, Birmingham and Midland Ear and Throat Hospital, 1957-58; Registrar, Dental Department, University College Hospital, London, 1958-59; Clinical Tutor, Cork Dental Hospital, 1959-64; Lecturer in Periodontology, University College, Cork, 1959-66. *Memberships:* Member of Council of Directors, Association Stomatologique Internationale; National Secretary for Ireland; British Medical Association; British Society for Oral Medicine; Irish Medical Organisation. *Publications:* Contributor to professional journals including: 'Irish Medical Times'; 'Journal of Dental Education'; 'Australian Dental Journal'; 'Journal of Oral Surgery'; 'British Dental Journal'; 'Public Health'; 'Acta Stomatologica Internationalia'. *Hobbies:* Sailing; Hill Track Walking; Folk Dancing. *Address:* 5 Alta Terrace, Monkstown, County Cork, Republic of Ireland.

RUSSELL, Peter, b. 7 June 1944, Sydney, New South Wales, Australia. Head of Gynaecological Pathology. m. Gail Stevens, 2 Dec. 1967, Kingsgrove, 2 sons. *Education:* MB, BS; BSc Medicine; Fellow, Royal College of Pathologists of Australasia. *Appointments:* Resident Medical Officer 1968, Fellow in Pathology 1969-73, Specialist Histopathologist 1975-, Royal Prince Alfred Hospital, Camperdown, New South Wales; Instructor in Pathology, University of Cincinnati, Ohio, USA, 1974; Assistant Director, Fels Feto-Placental Unit, 1974; Assistant Director, NIH Breast Cancer Detection Center, 1974; Clinical Lecturer, University of Sydney, New South Wales, Australia, 1975-; Examiner, Royal Australian College of Obstetrics and Gynaecology, 1979-; Consultant Pathologist, Commonwealth Department of Health, 1982-; Member of Maternal and Perinatal Committee, New South Wales Department of Health, 1984-. *Memberships:* Fellow, Royal College of Pathologists of Australasia; Australasian Division, International Academy of Pathology; Executive Councillor 1982-86, International Society of Gynaecological Pathologists. *Publications:* "Pigment Cell Volume I - Mechanisms in Pigmentation", (edited with V J McGovern), 1973; 'Human placental villitides. A review of chronic intrauterine infection', 1975; "Surgical Pathology of the Ovary", 1986. *Hobbies:* Australian Wine; Stamps; Classical Music. *Address:* 3 Avon Close, Pymble, NSW 2073, Australia.

RUSSELL, Richard Olney Jr, b. 9 July 1932, Birmingham, Alabama, USA. Professor of Medicine; Private Practitioner, Cardiology. m. Phyllis Hutchinson, 15 June 1963, Birmingham, 2 sons, 2 daughters. *Education:* AB 1953, MD 1956, Vanderbilt University, Nashville, Tennessee. *Appointments include:* Instructor 1962-65, Assistant Professor 1965-70, Associate Professor 1970-73, Professor 1973-80, Clinical Professor of Medicine 1981-, University of Alabama, Birmingham. *Memberships include:* American Heart Association (Fellow, Council of Clinical Cardiology); American College of Cardiology (Fellow); American College of Chest Physicians (Fellow); American College of Physicians (Fellow); American Federation for Clinical Research; Southern Society of Investigation. *Publications include:* Books: "Hemodynamic Monitoring in a Coronary Intensive Care Unit", 2 editions, with C E Rackley MD; "Radiographic Anatomy of the Coronary Arteries: An Atlas" with B Soto MD & R E Moraski MD; "Coronary Artery Disease, Recognition & Management", with C E Rackley MD. *Honours:* President, Alabama Heart Association, 1975-76; President, Jefferson County Medical Society, 1984. *Hobbies:* Golf; Camping; Hiking; Reading. *Address:* Cardiovascular Associates, 1320 19th Street South, Birmingham, AL 35205, USA.

RUSSO FRATTASI, Carlo A, b. 5 July 1947, Italy. Registrar of Orthopaedics and Traumatology. m. Isa R. Bozzolini, 22 Dec. 1978, Torre Pellice, Italy, 1 son, 1 daughter. *Education:* Laurea in Medicina e Chirurgia, Turin, Italy, 1973; Specialist in Orthopaedics and Traumatology, Turin, 1976; Specialist in Medicine of Sport. *Appointments:* Assistant C/O, Hospital Maria Adelaide, Turin, 1974-75; Assistant C/O, Hospital Civico di Chivasso, 1982-83; Consultant, Ministry of Transport. *Memberships:* Federazione Medico Sportiva Italiana; Collegiè Consulenti Tecnici del Tribunale di Torino; Comitato Regionale Periti e Consulenti del Piemonte; Societa Italiana di Ortopedia e Traumatologia; Club Italiano di Chirurgia del Ginocchio; Societa Italiana di Traumatologia dello Sport; Societa Italiana di Medicine e Chirurgia del Piede; Societa Italiana di Traumatologia Pediatrica; College International de Medicine et Chirurgie du Pied; American Association for Automotive Medicine; Societa Italiana di Traumatologia della Strada. *Publications include:* Over 58 articles and sections of books. *Hobbies:* Tennis; Holidays; Jogging. *Address:* Via Cibrario 68-10144, Turin, Italy.

RUTHERFORD, John Douglas, b. 12 Jan. 1946, New Zealand. Assistant Professor. m. Cynthia J Kerr, 23 Nov. 1968, Wellington, 1 son, 1 daughter. *Education:* MBChB, 1969; MRACP, 1974; FRACP, 1977; American Board of Internal Medicine, 1980; FACC, 1984. *Appointments:* Research Fellow, Medicine, Harvard Medical School, & Peter Bent Brigham Hospital, 1976-78; Instructor, Medicine, Harvard Medical School, 1978-81; Co-Director, Samuel A Levine Cardiac Unit, Brigham and Womens Hospital, 1980-81; Cardiologist, Green Lane Hospital, Auckland, New Zealand, 1981-84; Co-Director, Clinical Cardiology Services, Brigham and Womens Hospital; Assistant Professor, Medicine, Harvard Medical School. *Memberships:* Scientific Committee, Publicity and Promotions Committee, Health Education Committee, 1982-84, National Heart Foundation of New Zealand; Cardiac Society of Australia & New Zealand; Honorary Secretary-Treasurer, Cardiac Society of Australia & New Zealand; International Fellow, Council on Clinical Cardiology, American Heart Association. *Publications:* Sub Editor, Australian and New Zealand Journal of Medicine, 1982-84; 27 articles in scientific journals; "Coronary Care Medicine: A Practical Approach", 1986. *Honours:* Ivan and Maud St Romain Travelling Fellowship, National Heart Foundation of New Zealand, 1976-77; New Zealand Medical Research Council Overseas Fellowship, 1977-78. *Hobby:* Photography. *Address:* Cardiovascular Division, Brigham and Womens Hospital, 75 Francis St, Boston, MA 02115, USA.

RUTLEDGE, Felix Noah, b. 20 Nov. 1917, Anniston, Alabama, USA. Surgeon and Professor of Gynaecology. m. Dorothy Wood, 16 July 1983, Houston, Texas, 1 son. *Education:* BS, The University of Alabama, 1935-39; MD, Johns Hopkins University School of Medicine, 1939-43; Internship, 1943-44, Resident, 1944-45, Resident, Gynaecology and Female Urology, 1946-47, Johns Hopkins Hospital; Resident, Obstetrics and Gynaecology, Hospital for the Women of Maryland, 1945-46. *Appointments include:* Assistant Gynaecologist, 1948-54, Head of Department of Gynaecology 1954-, The Texas University System Cancer Centre, M D Anderson Hospital and Tumour Institute; Professor of Gynaecology, The University of Texas M D Anderson Hospital, Houston, Texas, 1954-; Consultant, American Journal of Obstetrics and Gynaecology Clinical Problems, 1962-; Professor, Department of Obstetrics and Gynaecology, The University of Texas Health Science Centre, Houston, 1979-. *Memberships include:* American Association of Obstetricians and Gynaecologists; American Association for the Advancement of Science; American College of Obstetricians and Gynaecologists; American Gynaecological Society; American Medical Society; President, 1976, American Radium Society; British Association for Surgical Oncology; Central Association of Obstetricians and Gynaecologists; Continental Gynaecological Society; Houston Gynaecological and Obstetrical Society; International Society for the Study of Vulvar Disease; Italian Society of Obstetrics and Gynaecology; New York Academy of Sciences; President, 1979, Society of Pelvic Surgeons; President, 1975, Society of Gynaecologic Oncologists. *Publications:* Author and Contributor to over 200 books, journals and meetings. *Hobbies:* Fishing; Jogging; Woodworking. *Address:* University of Texas System Cancer Centre, M D Anderson Hospital and Tumour Institute, Department of Gynaecology, 6723 Bertner Avenue, Houston, TX 77030, USA.

RUTTER, Philip E H, b. 2 Mar. 1924, Hampshire, England. General Practitioner; Chief of Medical Staff, Valleyview General Hospital, Alberta. m. Diana Louise Crosdale, 18 Dec. 1948, London, 1 son, 2 daughters. *Education:* BSc, Reading University, 1944; St Mary's Hospital, London; MRCS; LRCP, 1951; MB, BS, 1952; D.ObstRCOG, 1953; LMCC, 1971; CCFPC, 1972; FCFPC, 1981. *Appointments:* General Practitioner, Nottinghamshire, 1953-65; General Practitioner and Chief of Staff, High Prairie, Alberta, Canada, 1965-80; Clinical Lecturer, University of Alberta, Family Practice Department, 1975-. *Memberships:* Royal College of General Practitioners; Canadian College of Family

Physicians. *Publications:* Myocardial Infarction in a Canadian Rural Practice, Canadian Family Physician, 1974; Domiciliary Midwifery: Is It Justifiable?, Lancet, 1964. *Honour:* President, Alberta Chapter of College of Family Physicians, Canada, 1985-86. *Hobbies:* Music; Square Dancing; Badminton. *Address:* Box 1628, Valleyview, Alberta, Canada T0H 3N0.

RYAN, Kenneth John, b. 26 Aug. 1926 New York, USA. Professor and Chairman, Department of Obstetrics and Gynaecology, Harvard Medical School. m. Marion Kinney, 8 June 1948, Evanston, Illinois, 2 sons, 1 daughter. *Education:* Northwestern University, 1946-48; MD, Harvard Medical School, 1952. *Appointments:* Professor and Chairman, Obstetrics and Gynaecology, Case Western Reserve University, Cleveland, Ohio, 1961-70; Professor and Chairman, Obstetrics and Gynaecology, University of California, San Diego, 1970-72. *Memberships:* American Academy of Arts and Sciences; Institute of Medicine, National Academy of Science; American Society Clinical Investigation; Endocrine Society. *Publications:* 'Steriod 21-Hydroxylation', (with L Engel), 1957; 'Biological Aromatization', 1959; 'Biogenesis of steroid hormones in the ovary', (with O W Smith), 1965. *Honours:* Schering Award, 1951; Soma Weiss Award, 1951; Borden Award, 1952; Ernst Openheimer, 1964; Daggett Harvet, 1983. *Hobby:* Photography. *Address:* Brigham and Women's Hospital, 75 Francis Street, Boston, MA 02115, USA.

RYAN, Maximilian John, b. 17 June 1927, Dublin, Republic of Ireland. Consultant Radiologist. m. Valerie Coffey, 9 Sep. 1961, Dublin, 3 sons, 3 daughters. *Education:* Fellow, Royal College of Radiologists, London; Fellow, Faculty of Radiologists, RCSI, Ireland; Diploma in Medical Radiodiagnosis, London. *Appointments:* House Surgeon, House Physician, St Laurence's Hospital, Dublin; Senior House Officer & Registrar, Manchester Royal Infirmary; Lecturer in Radiology, New England Medical Centre, Boston; Senior Registrar, Manchester Royal Infirmary & Christie Hospital and Holt Radium Institute; External Examiner & Visiting Professor, University of Baghdad; Senior Consultant Radiologist, St Laurence's & Jervis Street Hospitals; Chairman, Medical Board, St Laurence's Hospital; Senior Lecturer in Radiology, Royal College of Surgeons in Ireland. *Memberships:* Vice President, Section of Radiology, Royal Society of Medicine, 1979-82; Royal College of Radiologists; British Institute of Radiology; Royal Academy of Medicine in Ireland; Irish Medical Organisation; Irish Society of Gastroenterology; Irish Thoracic Society; Biological Club; Co. Physician Club; 25 Radiology Visiting Club (Founder). *Publications:* "Moments in Diagnostic Radiology"; "The Abdomen: A Short Text-book for Medical Students", 1969; 'The Challenge of Radiology' (presidential address, JRCSI), 1973; "The Value of the Lateral Stooping Position in the Demonstration of the Cardia & Fundus of the Stomach', in 'British Journal of Radiology', 1968; 'Mucocoele of the Sphenoidal Sinus' in 'New England Journal of Medicine', 1958; 'Radiological manifestations of Ectopic Salivary Adenomas', in 'Proceedings of the RSM', 1957; 'Low Back Pain' in IJMS, 1964; 'Computerised Tomographic Scanning', in JIMA, 1976; 'Changes in Diagnostic Radiology' in JIMA, 1978; 'Up-date in Gastro-intestinal Imaging' in JIMA, 1983. *Honours:* Dean, Faculty of Radiologists, 1979-81; President, Biological Society, RCSI, 1973; President, Section of Radiology, Royal Academy of Medicine, 1977-80; International Commission on Radiological Education, 1979-82; Scientific Committee, International Congress of Radiology, Hawaii, 1985; Leader, Irish delegation to International Congress of Radiology, Rio de Janeiro, 1977, Brussels, 1981, Hawaii, 1985; Post-graduate Medical & Dental Board, Ireland, 1980-83; Council of Europe Scandinavian Fellowship, 1960; WHO Fellowships, 1964, 1975 (both in US). *Hobbies:* Sailing; Horse-Riding; Photography; Travel; President, Dublin Hospitals Rugby Club, 1985-86. *Address:* "Annacreevy", Brennanstown Road, Dublin 18, Republic of Ireland.

RYAN, William Francis, b. 17 July 1942, Melbourne, Australia. Director, Coronary Care Unit, Box Hill Hospital, Melbourne. m. Christine Mullen, 12 July 1980, Melbourne, 2 daughters. *Education:* MBBS; FRACP; MRCP (UK). *Appointments:* Junior Resident Medical Officer, Senior Resident Medical Officer, Registrar, General Medicine, University of Melbourne, St Vincents Hospital, 1967-71; Registrar, Medicine, Chest Disease & Cardiology, United Oxford Hospitals, England, 1972-73; Senior Registrar, Cardiology, Liverpool Regional Cardiac Centre, England, 1973-76; Research Cardiologist, Myocardial Infaction Research Unit, School of Medicine, University of California, San Diego, USA, 1976-78; Part-time Senior Lecturer, Medicine, University of Melbourne, 1978; Sessional Cardiologist, National Heart Foundation of Australia, Victorian Division, 1980-82; Visiting Physician, Cardiac Investigation Unit, St Vincents Hospital, Melbourne, 1978-82. *Memberships:* Royal College of Physicians, UK; Fellow, Royal Australian College of Physicians; Cardiac Society of Australia. *Publications:* Articles in professional journals including: 'American Journal Cardiology'; 'British Heart Journal'; 'Thorax'; 'Circulation'; 'Clinical Cardiology'; 'British Medical Journal'; 'Australian and New Zealand Journal of Medicine'. *Address:* 19 Chaucer Crescent, Canterbury 3126, Victoria, Australia.

RYCKEN, Jan-Mathỹs, b. 7 May 1941, Kerkrade, The Netherlands. Surgical Specialist. m. Marietje Willems, 16 July 1966, Amstenrade, 2 sons. *Education:* MB BS, MD, State University of Groningen, The Netherlands, 1959-67; Diploma of Tropical Medicine and Hygiene, Amsterdam, 1979. *Appointments:* Houseman, Elisabeth Hospital, Willemstrad, 1969-72; Registrar, Surgery, Catherina Hospital, Eindhoven, Netherlands, 1972-79; Surgical Specialist, Queen Elisabeth Central Hospital, Blaufyre, Malawi, 1979-. *Memberships:* Royal Dutch Medical Association; Dutch College of Surgeons; Medical Association of Malawi; Fellow, Association of Surgeons of East Africa. *Publications:* 'Spontanous Bladder Ruptures', in 'Proceedings of Association of Surgeons of East Africa', 1983; Paper in preparation for Proceedings. *Hobbies:* Tennis; Squash; Horse-riding; Walking; Mountaineering; Photography. *Address:* c/o PO Box 95, Blaufyre, Malawi.

RYDER, Elena M, b. 22 May 1940, Maracaibo, Venezuela. Director, Institute of Clinical Research. *Education:* MD, University of Zulia, 1962; Philosophus scientiarum, Venezuelan Institute for Scientific Research, 1970. *Appointments:* Head, Biochemistry Section, 1969-80, Director, Institute of Clinical Research, 1980-83, 1983-, Faculty of Medicine, University of Zulia, Maracaibo. *Memberships:* Venezuelan Association for the Advancement of Sciences; Venezuelan Association of Biochemists; Venezuelan Association of Physiological Sciences; American Association of Biological Chemists, USA; Biochemical Society, England; American Diabetes Association. *Publications:* Contributions to: 'Proceedings of National Academy of Sciences'; 'Biochemistry Journal'; 'Journal of Neurochemistry'; 'Journal of Medical Virology'. *Honour:* Orden Andres Bello 2nd class, 1980. *Address:* Inst Invest Clin, Faculty of Medicine, University of Zulia, Apartado 1151, Maracaibo, Venezuela.

RYHÄNEN, Pauli Taavetti, b. 19 Oct. 1939, Kajaani, Finland. Chief Anaesthetist. m. Elsi Kaarina Kalaja, 24 June 1962, Kajaani, 2 sons. *Education:* Doctoral Thesis, University of Oulu, 1977; Docent (Associate Professor) of Anaesthesiology, University of Oulu, 1979; MD. *Appointments:* Finnihs Board Examination in Anaesthesia, 1972; Lecturer, Anaesthesia, University of Oulu, 1972-74; Research Assistant, Medical Research Council of Academy of Finland, 1974-77; Special in Anaesthesia, University Central Hospital of Oulu, 1977-81; Chief Anaesthetist, Children's Hospital, University Central Hospital of Oulu, 1982-. *Memberships:* Finnish Society for Intensive Care; Finnish Society of Anaesthesiologists, Member of Board, 1973-75; Finnish Society for Immunology; The Association of Paediatric Anaesthetists of Great Britain and Ireland. *Publication:* "Effects of Anaesthesia and Operative Surgery on the Immune Response of Patients of Different Ages", Thesis, University of Oulu, 1977. *Hobby:* Farming. *Address:* Uistintie 3, 90550 Oulu 55, Finland.

RZEPECKI, Wit Maciej, b. 30 Apr. 1909, Wolanka, Poland. Professor Emeritus. m. (1) Apolonia Tyszkowska, Zakopane, 1936 (divorced) (2) Janina Suchecka, 1950, 4 sons, 2 daughters. *Education:* MB, MD, Medical Department, John Casimir University of Lwów, Poland. *Appointments:* Assistant, Surgical Clinic, University of Lwów; Surgeon, 1st Polish Rifle Brigade, Scotland; Travelling Scholarship in Thoracic Surgery, Great Britain; House Physician, Southfield Sanatorium, Edinburgh, Scotland; House Surgeon, Poole Sanatorium, Nunthorpe, Newcastle, England; Head Surgeon, Thoracic Unit of Teachers' Sanatorium, Zakopane, Poland; Professor, Thoracic Clinic Postgraduate Medical School, Warsaw & Zakopane, Tuberculosis Institute, Warsaw-ZZakopane. *Memberships:* Polish Medical Association; Polish Phtisio-Pneumonological Association; Polish Surgeons Association; Czechoslovak Medical Association of J E Purkanê, Prague; American College of Chest Physicians. *Publications:* "Surgical Treatment of Purulent Thoracic Disease", 1972; "Thoracic Surgery" 1979 (two editions); Articles: 'Results & Complications of Pulmonary Resection in Tuberculosis' (in British Journal of Diseases of the Chest) 1961; 'The Effect of Thymus Fragments Transplants on Leukemia' (in Acta Medica Polonia) 1975; 'Appreciation du traitement de las Myasthenie par la Thymectomie' (in Ann Chir) Paris, 1981. *Honours:* Honorary Membership, Polish Surgeons Association; Polish State Awards, Polonia Restituta; Order of Labour 2nd Class. *Hobbies:* Writing Memoirs "A-Double- edged Scalpel"; Hunting; Trout-fishing; Caricature-drawing; Photography; Ready-made artistry in wood; Essays & Memoirs. *Address:* 34 Zeromski Street, Zakopane, 34-500 Poland.

S

SABINE, John Robert, b. 29 Jan. 1934, Melbourne, Australia. Reader, Animal Physiology. m. Mary Ann Schneider, 28 Nov. 1964, Cairo, Illinois, USA, 2 sons, 4 daughters. *Education:* MAgr.Sc, University of Melbourne, 1959; PhD, University of Illinois, USA, 1962. *Appointments include:* Visiting Professor, Brandais University 1970, University of Stockholm 1976, University of Oklahoma 1977, University of Kuwait 1984; Visiting Scholar, Oxford University 1983, Harvard University 1983, Lecturer 1967-70, Senior Lecturer 1971-78, Reader 1979-, University of Adelaide. *Memberships:* Australian Biochemical Society; Australian & New Zealand Association for the Advancement of Science; Australian Physiological & Pharmacological Society; Nutrition Society of Australia. *Publications include:* Book: "Cholestral", 1977; Editor, "3-Hydroxy-3-Methylglutaryl Co-Enzyme A Reductase", 1983; Articles in professional journals include: 'Susceptibility to cancer & the influence of nutrition'; 'The use of macro-organisms for the recovery of protein from agricultural food wates'; 'Lipids in cancer - a functional or a fictional association?'; 'The error rate in biological publication: a preliminary survey'. *Honours include:* Fulbright Travel Grant, 1959; Research Fellowship, Damon Runyon Memorial Fund for Cancer Research, 1965; Distinguished Visiting Lecturer, Memphis Regional Cancer Center, Tennessee, 1976; 12th Patricia Chomley Orator, Australian College of Nursing, 1979. *Hobbies:* Bioethics; Gardening; Amateur theatricals; Consulting on biological waste management; Amateur athletics; Travel; Public speaking. *Address:* University of Adelaide, Waite Agricultural Research Institute, Glen Osmond, SA 5064, Australia.

SADEK, Adel, b. 9 Oct. 1943, Cairo, Egypt. Professor of Psychiatry. m. Zeinab Labib, 8 July 1970, Cairo, 1 son, 1 daughter. *Education:* DPM&N, Cairo; DM, Cairo; MD, Cairo; DPM, London; MRCPsych, London. *Appointments:* Consultant Psychiatrist, Glasgow, Scotland; Assistant Professor, Professor 1982-, Ain-Shams University, Cairo, Egypt. *Memberships:* Biological Psychiatry, Psychosomatic Medicine; Egyptian Psychiatric Association; Fellow, American Psychiatric Association; Fellow, Royal College of Psychiatrists. *Publications:* "Psychiatry"; "Psychiatry for Lay People", 4 parts; "Descriptive Psychopathology"; "Psychiatry for Physicians". *Address:* 25 Sharif Street, City Centre, Cairo, Egypt.

SAFAR, Michel Emile, b. 17 Mar. 1937. Professor of Internal Medicine. m. Anne May, 14 Dec. 1967, 1 son, 2 daughters. *Appointments:* Physician, 1966, Associate Professor, 1972, Professor of Internal Medicine, Chief of Department, Diagnostic Centre, Hôpital Broussais, Paris, France. *Membership:* Internal Society of Hypertension. *Publications:* On haemodynamic mechanisms & clinical pharmacology of hypertension. *Address:* Centre de Diagnostic, Hôpital Broussais, 96 rue Didot, 75674 Paris Cedex 14, France.

SAGER, Clifford J, b. 28 Sep. 1916, New York, USA. Clinical Professor of Psychiatry. m. Anne, 2 Sep. 1978, 2 sons, 2 daughters by previous marriage. *Education:* BS, Pennsylvania State University, 1937; MD, New York University, 1941; Rotating Internship, Montefiore Hospital, New York City, 1941-42; Psychiatry, Bellevue Hospital, New York City, 1942; US Army Hospitals, 1942-46; Fellow in Psychiatry, Bellevue Hospital, 1946-48; Certificate in Psychoanalysis, New York Medical College, 1949. *Appointments:* Associate Dean, Director, Therapeutic Services, Postgraduate Centre for Mental Health, 1948-60; Associate Professor, 1960-66, Professor of Psychiatry, 1966-70, Department of Psychiatry, New York Medical College; Chief, Family Treatment & Study Unit, Beth Israel Medical Centre, 1970-74; Director of Psychiatry, Gouverneur Hospital, 1971-74; Associate Director, Family & Group Therapies, Department of Psychiatry, Beth Israel Medical Centre, 1971-74; Clinical Professor of Psychiatry, Attending Psychiatrist, Mount Sinai Medical Centre, 1970-80; Clinical Professor of Psychiatry, Attending Psychiatrist, New York Hospital, Cornell Medical Centre, 1980-; Director of Family Psychiatry, Jewish Board of Family & Children's Services, 1974-. *Memberships:* Life Fellow, American Psychiatric Association; Fellow, Academy of Psychoanalysis; Past President, American Group Psychotherapy Association; Fellow, Society of Medical Psychoanalysts; Life Fellow, American Orthopsychiatric Association; Diplomate, American Board of Psychiatry & Neurology; Fellow, American Medical Association. *Publications:* More than 85 articles in professional journals; Author 6 professional books. *Honours:* Various awards for contributions to Family Therapy. *Hobbies:* Sailing; Scuba-diving; Windsurfing. *Address:* 65 East 76th Street, New York, NY 10021, USA.

SAHANDY, Parviz, b. 14 Sep. 1934, Iran. Psychiatrist. m. Jaleh Sahandy, 18 Dec. 1976, Teheran, 3 daughters. *Education:* MD, University of Teheran, Iran, 1960; Diplomate, American Board of Psychiatry, USA, 1979, American Board of Child and Adolescent Psychiatry, 1981. *Appointments:* Staff Psychiatrist, 1964-70; Fellow, Child Psychiatry, University of Maryland, Baltimore, Maryland, USA, 1970-72; Staff Psychiatrist, 1972-74; Assistant Professor, Psychiatry, University of Teheran, Iran, 1974-76; Director, Youth Services, South West Community Mental Health Center, Baltimore, Maryland, USA, 1976-; Private Practitioner, Psychiatry, 1979-. *Memberships:* American Psychiatric Association; Maryland Psychiatric Society. *Hobbies:* Music; Water sports; Traveling. *Address:* 133 East Bay View Drive, Annapolis, MD 21403, USA.

SAKINOFSKY, Isaac, b. 28 Dec. 1931, Cape Town, South Africa. Professor of Psychiatry. m. Blume Oddes, 15 Feb. 1959, Cape Town, 1 son, 1 daughter. *Education:* MB, ChB 1955, MD 1961, University of Cape Town; Academic Diploma, Psychological Medicine, University of London, UK, 1964; FRCPsych, 1977; FRCP (C), 1973. *Appointments include:* Senior Lecturer/Senior Consultant Pscyhiatrist, University of Cape Town, 1965-68; Associate Professor, McMaster University, 1968-70; Professor, Department of Psychiatry, ibid, 1971-84; Professor, Department of Psychiatry, University of Toronto, 1984-. *Memberships include:* Canadian, World Psychiatric Associations; Royal College of Psychiatrists; International Association for Suicide Prevention; American Association for Suididology; Society for Psychotherapy Research. *Publications include:* 'Depression & Suicide in the Disabled' in "Behavioural Problems & the Disabled", ed D S Bishop, 1984; Articles, suicide & parasuicide, evaluating psychotherapy. *Honours:* Charles & Margaret Bell Travelling Fellowship, South African College of Physicians, 1961; Crowhurst Archer Bronze Medal, 1966; Ontario Ministry of Health Travelling Fellowship, 1979-80. *Hobbies:* Walking; Reading; Swimming. *Address:* St Michael's Hospital, 30 Bond Street, Toronto, Ontario, Canada M5B 1W8.

SALAS CENICEROS, Salvador, b. 22 Dec. 1939, Durango Dgo, Mexico. Professor of Obstetrics & Gynaecology. m. Guadalupe Almanza Terrazas, 23 Nov. 1968, Durango, 1 son, 1 daughter. *Education:* MD, School of Medicine, Universidad Juarez Estado de Durango; Postgraduate Obstetrics & Gynaecology, Universidad Nacional Autonoma de Mexico. *Appointments:* Specialist in Obstetrics & Gynaecology, Hospital Seguro Social Durango-Dgo; Professor, School of Medicine, Universidad Juarez Estado de Durango, Head of Department, Member of Council for Research. *Memberships:* American College of Obstetricians & Gynaecologists; Mexican Council of Gynaecology; Mexican Association of Ultrasonography; Associacion Mexicana Para est Fert.; President, Associacion Duranguense de Ginecologia & Obst; Medical College of Durango; Associacion de Egresados de la Faculdad de Medicina Durango. *Publications:* Presentation of picture of non-compressure torceps to correct asinclitism-rotation of the foetal head. *Hobbies:* Designing Surgical appliances; Music. *Address:* Av Chihuahua 120 Y del Valle, Fraccionamiento lomas del Guadiana, Apartado Postal 86 Bm Durango, Dgo, Mexico.

SALEM, Hatem Hassan, b. 11 Sep. 1951, Alexandria, Egypt. Lecturer in Medicine. m. Frances Marion Melody, 27 Aug. 1977, Birmingham, England, 1 son, 1 daughter. *Education:* MB, ChB, Mosul, Iraq, 1974; MRCP, UK, 1976, LRCP, 1977; FRACP, 1980; FRCPA, 1981; MD, Monash, 1984. *Appointments:* Senior Tutor in Medicine, Monash University, Victoria, Australia, 1977-78, Lecturer in Medicine, 1978-82; Research Fellow, Washington University School of Medicine, St. Louis, Missouri, USA, 1982-84; Senior Lecturer in Medicine, Monash, University, Victoria, Australia, 1984-. *Memberships:* Royal College of Physicians; Royal Australasian College of Physicians; Royal Australasian College of Pathologists; Australasian Society for Medical Research. *Publications:* 'Human Coagulation Factor Va as a co-factor for the Activation of Protein C' in 'Proceedings of the National Academy of Sciences', USA, 1983; 'Isolation and Characterisation of Thrombomodulin from Human Placenta' in 'Journal of Biological Chemistry', 1984. *Honours:* Edward Wilson Memorial Travelling Fellowship, 1982; Fullbright Fellowship, 1982; G.J. Coles Fellowship, 1982; R.T. Hall Prize, 1985. *Hobbies:* Tennis; Swimming. *Address:* Department of Medicine, Monash Medical School, Alfred Hospital, Commercial Road, Zprahran, Victoria 3181, Australia.

SALERNO, Alphonse, b. 4 Mar. 1923, Newark, New Jersey, USA. Osteopathic Surgeon, 1 son, 1 daughter. *Education:* Louisiana State University, New York University, Seton Hall University, Philadelphia; BS, 1944; DO, College of Osteopathic Medicine, 1958. *Appointments:* Fellowship in General Surgery, 1966; Member & certified in surgery (Fellowship), 1967; Chief of Staff, West Essex General Hospital, 1967; President, Essex County Osteopathic Society, 1966; Board of Governors, American Academy of Osteopathic Surgeons, 1966-70; Chief of Surgery, West Essex General Hospital, 1975-; International College of General Practitioners, 1982. *Memberships:* President, American Academy of Surgeons, 1975-76; Certifying Committee of Board of Surgery, 1985; Vice-President of Hospital Staff, West Essex General Hospital, 1980; Secretary, Treasurer of Staff, 1983; Essex County, New Jersey State 9 National Osteopathic Societies; Life Member, American Medical Society of Vienna; New York Academy of Sciences; American Academy of Osteopathic Specialists. *Publications:* 'Pseudo-Hermaphroditism', Journal of American Osteopathic Association, 1967; 'Different Phases of Placenta Accreta', New Jersey OPS, 1981. *Hobbies:* Music; Opera; Rennaissance Art; Tennis; Reading Biographies & Classics. *Address:* 613 Park Avenue, East Orange, NJ 07017, USA.

SALFELDER, Karlhanns, b. 27 Jan. 1919, Germany. Director, Research Laboratory of Pathology, m. 25 Aug. 1952, Caracas, Venezuela, 1 son, 3 daughters. *Education:* MD, 1943, Postgraduate Course, Anatomical Pathology, Frankfurt, FRG, 1945-50. *Appointments:* Chief of Department, Pathology, Medical School, Universidad de los Andes, Merida, Venezuela; Director, Research Laboratory of Pathology, University Merida, Venezuela. *Memberships:* German Society of Pathology; International Academy of Pathology; International Society of Human and Animal Mycoses; Member of societies of pathology and mycolosy in several countries. *Publications:* "Histopatologia, Guia Trabajos Practicos", 1967; "Farbatlas Tiefer Mykosen beim Menschen", 1979; "Las Protozoonosis en el Hombre Atlas en Color", 1985. *Address:* Apartado de Correos No 681, 5101-A Merida, Venezuela.

SALKELD, Lesley, Joan, b. 12 Aug. 1952, New Zealand. Paediatric Otolaryngologist. *Education:*

MBChB; FRCS (C); FRACS; Diplomate of American Board of Otolaryngology. *Appointments:* Consultant, Paediatric Otolaryngology Children's Hospital, Vancouver, BC, Canada; Clinical Instructor, University of BC. *Memberships:* BC Otolaryngological Society; Canadian Otolaryngological Society; Member, American Academy of Otolaryngology. *Address:* Department of Otolaryngology, Children's Hospital of British Columbia, 4480 Oak Street, Vancouver, BC, Canada.

SALLE, Bernard, b. 18 Feb. 1931, Tangier. Professor, Neonatology & Paediatrics. m. Regine Philip de Laborie, 6 July 1960, Rabat, Morocco, 2 sons, 1 daughter. *Education:* Medical degree, 1963; Board of Paediatrics, 1964; National Diploma, Pathology. *Appointments include:* Associate Professor, Paediatrics, 1970; Dean of Faculty, Lyon, 1975, 1980; Full Professor, Neonatology & Paediatrics, 1982; Chief, Department of Neonatology, 1976, Hôpital, E Herriot, Lyon, France. *Memberships:* British Neonatal Society; French Paediatric Association; Expert, International Congress of Paediatrics. *Publications include:* "Intensive Care of the Newborn", with Leo Stern; Major papers on Calcium Metabolism of the Premature & Newborn, American & European journals. *Hobbies:* Tennis; Skiing. *Address:* 15 Cours Lafayette, Lyon, 69006, France.

SALLICK, Richard M, b. 3 Sep, 1936, New York, USA. Chairman, Department of Psychiatry and Clinical Associate Professor. m. Lucy E Riley, 25 June 1960, New York City, USA, 1 son, 2 daughters. *Education:* AB, Harvard University, USA, 1958; MD, Cornell University Medical College, 1962. *Appointments:* Internship, Vanderbilt University Hospital, 1962; Residency, Payne Whitney Clinic, New York Hospital, 1963-66; Special Assistant to Director, National Institute of Mental Health, 1966-67; Deputy Director, Division of Special Mental Health Problems, NIMH, 1967-68; Director, Outpatient Department, Payne Whitney Clinic, 1970-72; Chairman, Department of Psychiatry, Norwalk Hospital, 1972-; Chairman, Department of Psychiatry and Clinical Associate Professor, Yale School of Medicine, New Haven, Connecticut. *Memberships:* American Psychiatric Association; Connecticut Psychiatric Society; Fairfield County Medical Association; American Association of General Hospital Psychiatrists. *Honour:* President, Connecticut Psychiatric Society. *Address:* Norwalk Hospital, Norwalk, CT 06856, USA.

SALMON, Peter Alexander, b. 5 Aug. 1929, Victoria, British Columbia, Canada. Professor of Surgery. m. Janet Nancy, 28 Dec. 1953, Seattle, Washington, USA, 3 sons. *Education:* BSc 1947-51, MD 1951-55, University of Washington; MSc Physiology 1961, PhD Surgery 1962, University of Minnesota. *Appointments:* Assistant Professor, Department of Surgery, University of Minnesota, 1962-63; Director of Surgical Education and Research, Mount Sinai Hospital, Minnesota, 1963-66; Associate Professor 1966-73, Professor 1973-, Department of Surgery, University of Alberta, Edmonton, Alberta, Canada. *Memberships include:* American Association for the Advancement of Science; American College of Angiology; American College of Surgeons; Association for Academic Surgery; Canadian Association for Gastroenterology; Canadian Association of Clinical Surgeons; Canadian Society for Cell Biology; Pan-Pacific Surgical Association; Royal College of Physicians and Surgeons of Canada; Sigma Xi; Society for Experimental Biology and Medicine; Society of University Surgeons; Transplantation Society. *Publications include:* 72 contributions to learned journals including: 'The Digitus Quintus, Rigid Stoma, 4-5 Position Gastroplasty', 1983; 'Incarceration of Gastric Fundus in a Paraesophageal Hernia After Gastroplasty', (with W S Kendal), 1983; 'Weight Loss Following Horizontal Gastroplasty with Rigid Stoma and Variable Pouch Size: Comparison With Intestinal Bypass', 1984; 'Small Bowel Varices', 1984; 'A Technique For Banding Vertical Gastroplasties'. *Honours:* University of

Washington Hall of Fame; British Columbia Sports Hall of Fame. *Hobbies:* Golf; Swimming. *Address:* 84 Quesnell Crescent, Edmonton, Alberta, Canada.

SALO, Matti Sakari, b. 18 Sep. 1938, Turku, Finland. Assistant Chief Anaesthetist, Turku University Central Hospital. m. Annikki Kettunen, 23 Aug. 1964, 1 son, 3 daughters. *Education:* MD, 1963; Certified Anaesthetist, 1969; Medical Dissertation, 1978; Docent in Anaesthesiology, 1979. *Appointments:* Resident in Surgery, 1963-65; Resident in Anaesthesiology, 1966-69; Anaesthetist in Chief, Central Hospital of North Carelia, 1969-70; Anaesthetist in Chief, Loimaa Regional Hospital, 1970-75; Anaesthetist, 1975-76, Assistant Chief Anaesthetist, 1977-, Turku University Central Hospital. *Memberships:* Board Member, Finnish Society of Anaesthesiologists, 1983-; Chairman, Postgraduate Education Committee of Finnish Society of Anaesthesiologists, 1984-. *Publications:* Co-author: "Stress and Immunity in Anaesthesia and Surgery", 1982; 'Immune Response to Shock' in "Treatment of Shock", 2nd edition, by J A Barrett and L M Nyhus, 1985; Professional articles on "Immune response during Anaesthesia, Surgery and Accidental Trauma" in various journals. *Hobby:* Summer House. *Address:* Department of Anaesthesiology, University of Turku, SF-20520 Turku 52, Finland.

SALOMON, Lucy, b. 25 Jan. 1925, Yugoslavia. Clinical Instructor, Psychiatry, Harvard Medical School, USA; Psychiatrist, Associate Attending Psychiatrist, McLean Hospital, Belmont, Massachusetts; Attending Psychiatrist, Beth Israel Hospital, Boston, Massachusetts. m. Salomon M Salomon, 4 Feb. 1950, 2 sons, 1 daughter. *Appointments:* Intern, Madison General Hospital, Wisconsin, 1968-69; Resident, Psychiatry, McLean Hospital, Belmont, 1969-71, Beth Israel Hospital, Boston, 1971-72; Assistant Psychiatrist, Beth Israel Hospital, 1972-; Assistant Attending Psychiatrist, 1972-80, Associate Attending Psychiatrist, 1980-, McLean Hospital; Clinical Instructor, Psychiatry, Harvard Medical School, 1972-; Certified Psychiatry and Neurology, 1978. *Memberships:* American Medical Association; American Psychiatric Association; American Association for the Advancement of Science. *Address:* 219 Buckminster Road, Brookline, MA 02146, USA.

SALVIDIO, Emanuele Pietro, b. 25 May 1922, Acri, Italy. Professor of Haematology. m. Maria Vittoria Tilli dell'Orso, 3 June 1954, Sienna, 2 sons, 1 daughter. *Education:* MD, University of Rome. *Appointments:* Associate Professor of Medicine, Sienna; Associate Professor of Medicine, Head, Department of Haematology, University of Genoa. *Memberships:* German Society of Haematology; Swiss Society of Haematology; Accademia Ligure Scienze e Lettere. *Publication:* "Haematology, Pathophysiology and Clinic", 1982. *Hobbies:* Music; Shell Collection. *Address:* Instituta di Sinatologia, Universita di Genova, Italy.

SALVOSA-LOYOLA, Carmencita, b. 21 July 1932, Manila, Philippines. Associate Professor and Chairman of Department of Nutrition. m. Crispin A Loyola, 3 Apr. 1976, Manila, 1 daughter. *Education:* MS, Utah State University, USA, 1964; PhD, London School of Hygiene and Tropical Medicine, University of London, England, 1972. *Appointments:* Research Assistant, University of the Philippines-Philippine General Hospital Medical Centre, Philippines, 1953-54; Statistician, Food and Nutrition Research Institute, National Science and Technology Authority, 1954-58; Faculty Member 1964-, Currently Associate Professor and Chairman of Department of Nutrition of Institute of Public Health, University of the Philippines. *Memberships:* Committee V5, Schools of Public Health, IUNS; Phi Sigma; National Research Council of the Philippines; Philippine Association of Nutrition; Philippine Association for the Advancement of Science. *Publications:* 'Environmental Conditions and Body Temperatures of Elderly Women

Living Alone or in Local Authority Home', (with P R Payne and E F Wheeler), 1971; 'Typical Daily Energy Expenditure in Jamacan Farmers as Determined by the Pulse Rate Method', (with A Ashworth, G J Miller and P R Payne), 1974; 'The Individual Dietary Intake of Some Children Living in a Children's Home in Quezon City, Philippines', (with G R Wadsworth and S B Bibera), 1979; Contributor, "The Health Aspects of Food and Nutrition", 3rd edition 1979. *Honours:* Awardee, Study grants, PhD programme 1969-72, Nutrition programme 1975-76 and 1984, World Health Organisation; Awardee, Diamond Jubilee Faculty Grant, University of the Philippines, 1983-85. *Address:* Institute of Public Health, University of the Philippines, Manila, 625 Pedro Gil, Ermita, Manila, Philippines.

SALZANO, Francisco Mauro, b. 27 July 1928, Cachoeira do Sul, RS, Brazil, Professor of Genetics. m. Thereza Torres Salzano, 20 Mar. 1952, Porto Alegre, Brazil, 2 sons. *Education:* BSc, 1950, Private Docent, 1960, Federal University Rio Grande do Sul; PhD, University of Sao Paulo, 1955. *Appointments:* Instructor, 1952, Assistant Professor, 1960, Associate Professor, 1967, Professor, 1981, Federal University of Rio Grande Do Sul; Head, Genetics Section, 1963-68, Director, 1968-71, Natural Sciences Institute; Head, Genetics Department, 1973-75, Biosciences Institute. *Memberships:* General Secretary, International Association Human Biologists, 1974-80; Vice-President, International Union of Anthrop Ethnol Sciences, 1978-88; Member, Brazilian Academy of Sciences, 1973-. *Publications:* Author, Co-author of over 460 contributions to scientific literature; Author of 7 books. *Honours:* Silver Jubilee Medal, Brazilian Association Advancement of Science, 1973; Honorary Member, Genetical Society, Chile, 1983; Honorary Member, Venezuelan Society Biological Anthropology, 1984. *Address:* Departamento de Genética, Instituto de Biociências, Universidade Federal do Rio Grande do Sul, Caixa Postal 1953, 90001 Porto Alegre, RS, Brazil.

SALZMAN, Barnett Seymour, b. 15 Feb. 1939, New York City, USA. Specialist in Health & Beauty, Longevity Medicine. m. Dianna Olivia Toney, 31 Dec. 1980, 1 son, 3 daughters. *Education:* BA, Hunter College, 1960; Biochemistry Research Fellowship, Northeastern University, Boston, 1961; MD, University of Buffalo, 1965; Internship, Good Samaritan Hospital, Los Angeles, California, 1966; Residency, Psychiatry, Cedars Sinai Medical Centre, 1968; Chief Resident Psychiatrist, Cedars Sinai Medical Centre, 1969; Ethical Hypnosis Institute Graduate, S Orange, New Jersey, 1973. *Appointments:* Clinical Associate, Southern, California Psychoanalytic Institute, 1968; US Navy Medical Corps, 1962-73 with hon. discharge as Lieutenant-Commander; Senior Psychiatrist attending Physician in various hospitals, 1969-85; Private Practice, Health & Beauty, Life Extension Medicine, Forensic Medicine, Environmental Medicine, 1974-; President, Private Medical Investigations Medical Group Inc, 1984-. *Memberships:* New York Academy of Sciences; Academy of Orthomolecular Psychiatry; National Forensic Centre of Distinguished Experts; World Association for Social Psychiatry; World Medical Association; World Academy of Holopsychiatry. *Publications:* 'The Anti-Human Personality Disorder' in Proceedings of the VIIth World Congress of Psychiatry, Vienna, 1983; "Biogeomagnetic Medicine", 1982; "Forensic Psychiatry", 1984. *Honours:* Wurlitzer Prize for Medicine, 1964; Fellow, Royal Society of Health, 1974; FWASP, 1983; FAASP, 1983. *Hobbies:* Stained Glass Crafting; Poetry; Videophotography; Beachcombing. *Address:* Private Medical Investigations Inc, 8728 Sherry Drive, O-Vale, CA 95662, USA.

SAMARRAE, Faik Abdul Jabbar Al, b. 1 July 1932, Amarah, Iraq. Chief Radiotherapist. m. Dr Siham T Al-Suhaily, 29 May 1959, Baghdad, 1 son, 2 daughters. *Edcuation:* Diploma in Radiotherapy, Royal College of Radiologists, London. *Appointments:* Doctor in charge of DXT in Basrah Hospital, Iraq; General Practitioner; Registrar, Radiotherapy Department, The Royal Free Hospital; Doctor in charge of Radiotherapy Department, Institute of Radiooogy and Nuclear Medicine, Baghdad, Iraq; Chief Radiotherapist and Oncologist, Institute of Radiology and Nuclear Medicine, Baghdad, Iraq. *Memberships:* Royal College of Radiologists, UK; The British Institute of Radiologists; Member of Executive Board, Iraqi Cancer Society. *Hobbies:* History; Music; General Education. *Address:* Radiotherapy Department, Institute of Radiology and Nuclear Medicine, Baghdad, Iraq.

SAMBO, Delia Manga, b. 13 Aug. 1941, Philippines. Gynaecologist and Obstetrician. *Education:* Doctor of Medicine. *Appointments:* Obstetrician/Gynaecologist, Health Alliance of Northern California, 1978-79; Obstetrician/Gynaecologist, Family Health Foundation of Alviso, 1979-84; Obstetrician/Gynaecologist, Chaboya Clinic of Valley Medical Center, 1984-85; Private practice in Obstetrics and Gynaecology, 1985-. *Memberships:* California Medical Association; Santa Clara County Medical Society, California. *Address:* 14651 South Bascom Avenue, Suite 250, Los Gatos, CA 95030, USA.

SAMMEL, Neville Leonard, b. 6 Jan. 1945, South Africa. Cardiologist. m. Ingrid Carol Ann Stiles, 23 Mar. 1975, 1 son, 1 daughter. *Education:* MB, ChB, University of Witwatersrand, South Africa; MRACP 1975, FRACP 1978, Royal Australasian College of Physicians; DDU, Australian Society of Ultrasound in Medicine. *Appointments include:* Medical Registrar, Sydney, 1972-74; Cardiology Registrar, Royal Prince Alfred Hospital, Sydney, 1975, St Vincent's Hospital, 1976-77; Research Fellow, Green Lane Hospital, Auckland, New Zealand, 1978-79; Fellow in Cardiology, St Vincent's Hospital, Sydney, Australia, 1979-80; Cardiologist, ibid, 1980-. *Memberships:* Cardiac Society of Australia & New Zealand; New South Wales State Committee, Royal Australasian College of Physicians; Medical Advisory Board, NSW Ambulance Service. *Publications:* Co-author, 17 abstracts including: 'Failure of ejection fraction to rise with exercise in the recently transplanted heart'; 'Evaluation of recurrent suncope using signla-averaged electrocardiography'; 'High dose furosemide in heart failure'. Co-author, 18 contributions to medical journals including 'Medical Journal of Australia'; 'British Heart Journal'; 'American Journal of Cardiology'; etc. 4 review articles including editorials, 'Medical Journal of Australia'. *Hobbies:* Sailing; Skiing. *Address:* 376 Victoria Street, Darlinghurst, New South Wales 2010, Australia.

SAMUELSON, Edwin Arthur, b. 24 July 1939, Richmond Hill, New York, USA. Chiropractor. Divorced, 1 son. *Education:* DC, Chiropractic Institute, 1965; DABCO, American Board of Chiropractic Orthopedists, 1980; Post Graduate, Chiropractic Roengenology, 1972-75; Chiropractic Orthopaedics, National College Chiropractic, 1975-78; International Academy, Clinical Acupuncture, 1985. *Appointments:* Past President, District 1, NY State Chiropractic Association, 1981-83; Delegate, District 1, NY State Chiropractic Association, 1984-85; Secretary, Ancient Order of Hibernians; Local Trustee, Academy of Chiropractic, 1986-. *Memberships:* American Chiropractic Association; NY State Chiropractic Association; Academy of Chiropractic; NY Academy of Sciences; Ancient Order of Hibernians, 1981; New York Council of Chiropractic Orthopaedics, 1986. *Publications:* 'Mind over Matter'; 'Health and Diet'. *Honours:* Award of Merit, NY State Chiropractic Association, 1986; President's Award, NY State, Chiropractic Association, 1981-83; Notable Americans American Biographical Institute, 1978-79. *Hobbies:* Walking; Yoga; Swimming. *Address:* 133 East 58th Street, New York, NY 10022, USA.

SAMUELSSON, Bengt Ingemar, b. 21 May 1934, Halmstad, Sweden. President/Vice Chancellor, Karolinska Institute. m. Karin Bergstein, 1958, 1 son, 2 daughters. *Education:* D Med Sci, 1960; MD 1961. *Appointments:* Assistant Professor, Medical Chemistry, Karolinska Institute, 1961-66; Professor of Medical Chemistry Royal Veterinary College, Stockholm, 1967-72; Professor of Medical and Physiological Chemistry, 1973-, Chairman, Department of Physiological Chemistry, 1973-83, Karolinska Institute, Stockholm; Visiting Professor in Chemistry, Harvard University, Cambridge, Massachusetts, USA, Spring term 1976; Dean of Medical Faculty, 1978-83, President 1983- Karolinska Institute, Stockholm. *Memberships:* Honorary Member, American Society of Biological Chemists; Member, Royal Swedish Academy of Sciences; Honorary Member, Association of American Physicians; Mediterranean Academy; Foreign Honorary Member, American Academy of Arts and Sciences; Honorary Member, Swedish Medical Association; Foreign Associate, US National Academy of Sciences. *Publications:* Publications on biochemistry of prostaglandins, thromboxanes and leukotrienes. *Honours include:* Gairdner Foundation Award, Toronto, 1981; Heinrich Wieland Prize, Munich, 1981; American Chemical Association, Division of Medicinal Chemistry Award, 1982; Waterford Bio-Medical Science Award, La Jolla, 1982; International Association of Allergology and Clinical Immunology Award, London, 1982; Nobel Prize in Physiology or Medicine, Stockholm, 1982; Honorary Doctor of Science, University of Illinois, 1983; Abraham White Sciento Achievement Award, George Washington University, 1984. *Address:* Karolinska Institutet, Box 60400, S-104 ol Stockholm, Sweden.

SANCES, Anthony Jnr, b. 13 July 1932, Chicago, Illinois, USA. Professor and Chairman of Department of Neurosurgery. m. Starr Lockhart, 18 Feb. 1965, 2 sons, 1 daughter. *Education:* BS, Electrical Engineering, American Institute of Technology; MS, Physics, DePaul University; PhD, Biomedical Engineering, Northwestern University. *Appointments:* Assistant Professor, American Institute of Technology, 1959-60; Advanced Research Manager, Sunbeam Corporation, 1959-61; Resident Engineer, Surgical and Biomedical Engineering Department, Northwestern University, 1960-64; Associate Professor and Director, 1964-67, Professor and Chairman, 1967-, Marquette University and Medical College of Wisconsin. *Memberships:* Past President, Executive Committee, Alliance for Engineering in Medicine and Biology; Founding Member, Board of Directors, Biomedical Engineering Society; Board of Governors, International Institute for Medical Electrical and Biological Engineering; Vice President, International Society for Electrostimulation; President, Neuroelectric Society; Fellow, Institute of Electrical and Electronic Engineers. *Publications:* "Impact Injury of the Head and Spine" editor, 1983; "Neural Stimulation" editor, 1985; "Mechanisms of Head and Spine Trauma" editor, in Press; 'The biomechanics of spinal injuries' CRC Cit Rev Bioeng, 1984. *Honours:* DePaul University Award for Achievement, College of Graduate School, Chicago, 1972; IEEE Milwaukee Section Memorial Award for Research Contributions in Biomedical Engineering, 1977. *Address:* Department of Neurosurgery, The Medical College of Wisconsin, 8700 W Wisconsin Avenue, Milwaukee, WI 53226, USA.

SANCHEZ, Nestor P, b. 30 June 1949, Aibonito, Puerto Rico, USA. Assistant Professor. m. Nelly, 24 Dec. 1972, 1 son, 1 daughter. *Education:* BS, University of Puerto Rico, 1970; MD, Albert Einstein College of Medicine and University of Puerto Rico, 1975. Resident in Dermatology, New York University Medical Center, USA, 1976-78, Massachusetts General Hospital, 1978-79; Clinical Fellow, Dermatology, 1978-79, Dermapathology, 1979-80, Research Fellow, 1979-80, Harvard University Medical School; Dermatopathology Fellow, Mayo Graduate School of Medicine, 1980-81. *Appointments:* Currently, Assistant Professor, University of Puerto Rico Medical School. *Memberships:* American Medical Association; American

Academy of Dermatology; American Society of Dermatologists. *Publications:* Co-Author over 40 papers including 5 abstracts contributed to professional journals such as: 'Acta Dermtovener'; 'British Journal of Dermatology'; 'Journal of Dermatology'; 'International Journal of Dermatology'; 'American Journal of Surgical Pathology'; 'Cancer'; 'Journal of Gynaecological Oncology'; 'Clinical Research'. *Honours:* Certified, American Board of Dermatology, 1980; Sigma Xi, 1981. *Hobby:* Basketball. *Address:* 43 Concordia Street, 405, Ponce, PR 00731, USA.

SANDBERG, Finn, b. 11 Apr. 1920, Randers, Sweden. Professor of Pharmacognosy. m. Ilse Grebe, 16 May 1985, Skokloster. *Education:* MPharm, 1948; MD, 1957. *Appointments:* Assistant 1952, Associate Professor of Pharmacology Karolinska Institutet, Stockholm; Professor of Pharmacognosy, University of Uppsala, 1954-; Special Technical Advisor, UNIDO, Vienna, 1979-; Member, Scientific Advisory Board, International Foundation for Science, Stockholm. *Memberships:* Swedish Medical Society; Swedish Pharmaceutical Society; Swedish Botanical Society. *Publications include:* "Textbook in Pharmacology", Part I 1958, Part II 1962; "Textbook in Phytopharmacy", 1983; "Medicinal Plants", 1982; Approximately 150 scientific publications in pharmacognosy, phytochemistry, pharmacology. *Honours:* PhD honoris causa, Abo Akdemi, Finland, 1978; Member, Real Accademia de Pharmacia, Barcelona, Spain. *Hobbies:* Gardening; Travel; History of Romanov family. *Address:* Bultarbo Estate, Skokloster, S-19800 Bålsta, Sweden.

SANDERS, Roger Cobban, b. 17 June 1936, England. Doctor of Medicine. m. Angelita Mascardo, 28 Dec. 1975, Maryland, USA, 2 sons, 1 daughter. *Education:* BM, BCh, MA, Oxford University, England, 1964; FRCR, 1971; MD (FLEX) Maryland, USA, 1972. *Appointments:* Assistant Professor of Radiology, Johns Hopkins Hospital, Baltimore, Maryland, USA, 1971-76, Assistant Professor of Urology, 1976-80, Associate Professor of Radiology, 1976-, Associate Professor, Urology, 1980-, Associate Professor, Obstetrics/Gynaecology, 1985-; Professor Radiology, 1986. *Memberships:* AIUM; Chairman of Education Committee, 1981-84, Central Programme Committee, 1981-84, Legal Committee, 1982-present, Secretary 1984-, Chairman Memberships Committee, 1984, Executive Committee, 1984-. *Publications:* "Ultrasound in Urology", 1984; "Ultrasound in OB/GYN", 1984; "Ultrasound Annual", 1984-85; "Clinical Sonography", 1984; "Atlas of Normal Variants", 1985. *Honours:* Medical Prize, Oxford University, 1963; Surgical Prize, Oxford University, 1963; President's Award, AIUM, 1982; Fellow, AIUM, 1984; Fellow, College of Radiologists, 1985. *Hobbies:* Skiing; Racquetball; Dancing. *Address:* Johns Hopkins Hospital, 600 North Wolfe Street, Baltimore, MD 21205, USA.

SANDFORD, John R, b. 6 May 1930, Saltash, Cornwall, England. m. Dabney Thompson Crawford, 15 Mar. 1975, NYC, 2 sons, 1 daughter. *Education:* BA 1953; Bachelor of Surgery, 1956; Bachelor of Medicine 1957, MA, Cambridge University, 1958; MRCS 1956, LRCP, London University, 1956; LMCC, Canada, 1958; ECFMG 1964; FRCS (C) 1965. *Appointments:* House Physician, Dean of Middlesex Hospital, 1956-57; House Surgeon, Department of Obstetrics and Gynaecology, Middlesex Hospital, 1957; Senior House Officer, Emergency Department, Hampstead General Hospital, London, 1957-58; Resident, Department of Paediatrics, War Memorial Hospital, London, Ontario, 1958; Family Practice, Deep River Ontario, Atomic Energy of Canada Limited, 1958-60; Nassau, Bahamas, 1960-61; (Speciality Training-Otolaryngology) Junior Assistant Resident, General Surgery, Vancouver General Hospital, BC, Canada, 1961-62; Residency Programme, Otolaryngology, McGill University, Montreal, 1962-65; Chief, Resident, Otolaryngology, University of Colorado, Medical Center, Denver, CO, 1965-66; (Speciality Practice) Consultant Otolaryngologist, Oakville-Trafalgar

Memorial Hospital, 1966-; Consultant (Courtesy) Otolaryngology, Queensway General Hospital; Milton District Hospital. *Memberships:* American Academy of Ophthalmology and Otolaryngology; Canadian Medical Association Academy of Medicine, Toronto; American Society of Ophthalmology and OTL Allergists. *Address:* 213 Church Street, Oakville, Ontario L6J 1N4, Canada.

SANDMAN, Kathleen B, b. 4 June 1949, Warren, Ohio, USA. Medical Writer; Chiropractor; Owner, Sandman Clinics, 1 son, 2 daughters. *Education:* DC, Chiropractic National College, 1977; BS, Human Biology, 1973; Journalism Study, Geneva College; Private Pilot's Licence, 1981. *Appointments:* Associate Chiropractic Physician, Rehabilitation Associates, Denver, 1978-79; Faculty Department of Diagnosis Clinician, 1979-82; Medical Writer, National College, 1982; Director, Owner, Sandman Chiropractic Clinics, 1982-. *Memberships include:* American Medical Writers Association; American Chiropractic Association; Delta Tau Alpha; National College Chiropractic Alumni, Reunion Chairman, 1982; American Council of Women Chiropractors, President, Student Chapter, 1976-77; etc. *Publications include:* "Myofascial Pain Syndromes: Their Mechanism, Diagnosis and Treatment", 1981, "Rheumatoid Arthritis of the Cervical Spine: Examination Prior to Chiropractise Manipulative Therapy Procedure", 1981; "Psychophysiological Aspects of Myofascial Pain", 1984, all in 'Journal of Manipulative Physiological Therapy'. *Honours:* Recipient, various honours and awards. *Hobbies:* Flying; Sailing. *Address:* 233 East Ontario, Chicago, IL 60610, USA.

SANDOR, Stefan, b. 16 May 1927, Oradea, Romania. Head of Laboratory of Embryology Center of Hygiene and Public Health, Timisoara. m. Livia, 3 May 1956, 1 son, 1 daughter. *Education:* MD, 1951; DMSc, 1956; Doctor Docent in Medical Sciences, 1974. *Appointments:* Assistant Professor, Department of Pathology, Medical School Tg. Mures; Assistant Professor, Department of Pathology, Medical School, Timisoara; Senior Research Fellow; Head of Section, Center of Embryology, Timisoara. *Memberships:* European Teratology Society; International Society for Developmental Biology; Member, Editorial Board, 'Romanian Journal of Morphology, Embryology and Physiology'. *Publications:* "Malformations and Monsters" (in Romanian), 1969; "Prenatal Life" (in Romanian), 1974; "Experimental Embryology and Teratology in Laboratory Mammals" (in Romanian), 1984. *Hobbies:* Travel; Photography; Literature. *Address:* Laboratory of Embryology, Center of Hygiene and Public Health, Timisoara, BV.V Babes 16-18 1900, Romania.

SANDRIK, James Leslie, b. 7 July 1938, Chicago, Illinois, USA. Professor and Chairman, Department of Dental Materials. m. Joan Kaye, 17 June 1967, Highland Park, 1 son, 1 daughter. *Education:* PhB, 1967, MS, 1968, PhD, 1972, Northwestern University. *Appointments include:* Research Apparatus Glassblower, 1959-66, Graduate Student, 1967-72, Northwestern University, Evanston, Illinois; Assistant Professor, Dental Materials, 1972-77, Coordinator of Conjoint Courses, 1974-, Associate Professor, 1977-82, Chairman, Department of Dental Materials, 1977-, Professor of Dental Materials, 1982-, Loyola University School of Dentistry, Maywood. *Memberships:* International and American Associations for Dental Research; Academy of Dental Materials; American Dental Association; American Society of Metals. *Publications:* Co-Author of contributions to: "Research in Dental and Medical Materials", 1969; "Encyclopedia of Materials Science and Engineering"; "Tylman's Theory and Practice of Fixed Prothodontics", 1978; "Textbook of Crown and Bridge", 1986. Author or Co-Author of 32 papers contributed to professional journals, 71 presentations and invited lectures, 13 ancilliary lectures. Member of various journal manuscript review boards. *Honours:* Omicron Kappa Epsilon, 1975; Sigma Xi, 1977; Fellow,

Academy of Dental Materials, 1985. *Hobbies:* Orchid horticulture; Cycling. *Address:* Loyola University School of Dentistry, 2160 South 1st Avenue, Maywood, IL 60153, USA.

SANFORD, Edward F, b. 26 July 1925, Botosani, Romania. Physician, Clinical Director, Taylor Manor Hospital. m. Claire A Stainberg, 16 Sep. 1948, Botosani, Romania, 2 sons, 1 daughter. *Education:* MD, Iasi Medical Institute, Romania, 1951; Diplomate in Psychiatry; Certified by American Board of Psychiatry & Neurology, 1972. *Appointments:* Instructor, Department of Psychiatry, University of Missouri Medical School, USA, 1969-70; Assistant Professor of Psychiatry, Department of Neurology & Psychiatry, St Louis University Medical School, 1970-72; Chief Psychiatrist, St Vincent Hospital Mental Health Centre, Erie, Pennsylvania, 1972-75; Chairman, Department of Psychiatry, St Vincent Hospital, 1974-75; Consultant in Psychiatry, Erie VA Hospital, Child Study Clinic, Erie, PA, 1973-74; Private Practice, General Psychiatry, Erie, PA, 1972-75. *Memberships:* American Medical Association; American Psychiatric Association; Medical & Chirurgical Faculty of Maryland; Maryland Psychiatric Society; Southern Medical Association; New York Academy of Sciences; American Association for the Advancement of Science; Association for the Advancement of Psychotherapy. *Publications:* 'An Acoustic Mirror in Psychotherapy' (in American Journal of Psychotherapy, 1969); 'Acoustic Perception of Human Emotion' (in Proc. WPA, 1981); 'The Active Search for Relevance in the Systematic Feedback of Videotherapy' (in Proc. of 78th Annual Scientific Ass. Southern Medical Assoc. 1984). *Honour:* Physicians Recognition Award, American Medical Association, 1974-1985. *Hobbies:* Travel; Writing. *Address:* Taylor Manor Hospital, PO Box 396, Ellicott City, MD 21043, USA.

SANGHI, Harishankar Lal, b. 15 Jan. 1937, Hyderabad, Andha-Pradesh, India. Psychiatrist. m. Vijay Kumari Sanghi, 4 Dec. 1961, Hyderabad, India, 1 son, 3 daughters. *Education:* MB, BS, Osmania, 1964; DPM, England, Member, Royal College of Psychiatrists (UK), 1973; Psychotherapy Training, Tavistock Clinic, London, England, 1972-74; ABPN, Psychiatry, 1981; Clinical Hypnosis in Treatment at Institute of Pennsylvania Hospital, 1982. Licensed, Hyderabad, India; General Medical Council of England; North Carolina, Virginia & New York States, USA. *Appointments:* Assistant Surgeon, Government of Andhra-Pradesh, India, 1965-69; Registrar in Psychiatry, Winterton Hospital, England, 1969-71, Horton Hospital, Epsom, Surrey, England, 1971-72, Whitchurch Hospital, Cardiff, Wales, 1972, Holloway Sanatorium, Virginia Water, Surrey, England, 1972-74; Staff Psychiatrist, Cherry Hospital, Goldsboro, North Carolina, USA, 1974-77, Veteran's Medical Center, Salem, Virginia, 1977-84; Assistant Professor in Psychiatry, University of Virginia Medical School, USA, 1977-84; Staff Psychiatrist, Veteran's Medical Center, Montrose, New York, 1984; Veteran's Medical Center, Lebanon, Pennsylvania, USA, 1984-. *Memberships:* American Medical Association; American Psychiatric Association; Royal College of Psychiatrists, UK; Indian Psychiatric Society. *Hobbies:* Reading; Travel; Anthropology, Cultural Studies. *Address:* 650 Aspen Lane, Lebanon, PA 17042, USA.

SANGSTER, John Fraser, b. 21 Jan. 1942, Adelaide, Australia. Senior Visiting Cardiologist. m. Verity Elix, 8 Jan. 1964, Adelaide, 2 sons, 1 daughter. *Education:* MB, BS, Adelaide University, 1965; Member 1969, Fellow 1974, Royal Australasian College of Physicians. *Appointments:* Resident Medical Officer, Repatriation General Hospital, Adelaide, 1967; National Heart Foundation Overseas Clinical Fellow, Hammersmith Hospital, London, England, 1972-73; Resident Medical Officer 1966, Registrar - Senior Registrar 1968-71, Visiting Cardiologist 1974-75, Senior Visiting Cardiologist 1976-, Royal Adelaide Hospital, Adelaide, Australia. *Memberships:* Australian Medical Association; Royal Australasian

College of Physicians; Cardiac Society of Australia and New Zealand. *Publications:* 'A No-smoking Ward', 1967; 'Endocardial Pacing in Acute Myocardial Infarction', 1970; 'Diastolic Murmur of Coronary Stenosis', 1973; 'Ephedrine-induced Cardiomyopathy', 1980. *Honour:* National Heart Foundation of Australia Overseas Clinical Fellowship, 1972. *Hobbies:* Golf; Tennis; Music; Reading. *Address:* 327 South Terrace, Adelaide, South Australia 5062, Australia.

SANT, Grannum Remy, b. 23 Oct. 1948, Trinidad. Assistant Professor, Urology, Tufts University School of Medicine, Boston, USA. m. Kathleen Mary Farrelly, 2 Jan. 1972, Couva, Trinidad, 1 son, 1 daughter. *Education:* BA, Dublin University, Ireland, 1969; MB, BCh, BAO (Hons), Dublin University, 1971; FRCS (E), 1976; MD, Dublin University, 1978; FICS, 1979. *Appointments:* Intern, Meath Hospital, Dublin; Research Fellow, Department of Pathology, Dublin University; Resident Surgery, Albert Einstein College of Medicine, New York, USA; Senior Registrar, Consultant in Surgery, Ministry of Health, Port-of-Spain, Trinidad; Reisdent in Urology, Assistant Professor of Urology, Tufts University School of Medicine, Boston, USA. *Memberships:* British Association Urological Surgeons; Irish Society of Urology; American Urological Association; Association for Academic Surgery; American Medical Association. *Publications include:* Co-author: 'Disorders of the male external genitalia', chapter in "Clinical Pediatric Urology", 1984; "Computed tomographic findings in renal angiomyolipoma: histologic correlation', 'Urology', 1984; 'Congenital ureteral valve: abnormality of ureteral embryogenesis?', 'Journal of Urology', 1985; 'Intravesical dimethyl sulfoxide (DMSO) in the treatment of early interstitial cystitis', 'Journal of Urology', 1985. *Honours include:* Edward Hallaran Bennett Medal in Postgraduate Surgery, Dublin University, 1976; Postgraduate Travelling Scholarship in Surgery, Dublin University, 1976. *Hobbies:* Horseback Riding; Golf; Cricket. *Address:* 171 Harrison Avenue, Boston, MA 02111, USA.

SANTANGELO, Anthony Joseph, b. June 1909, Gretna, Louisiana, USA. Deceased. Consultant; Prviate practitioner. m. Natalie Williams, 3 Mar. 1946, Leland, Mississippi, 1 son, 5 daughters. *Education:* BSc, Loyola University, 1935; MD, Royal University, Rome, Italy, 1944. *Appointments include:* Director, East Mississippi State Hospital; Assistant Clinical Professor, Psychiatry, University of Mississippi Medical Centre; Consultant, East Mississippi State Hospital, 1980-; Private practice, 1960-. *Memberships:* Life Member, Mississippi & American Medical Associations, Psychiatric Associations; East Mississippi Medical Society; Southern Medical Association. *Publication:* Graduation thesis. *Honour:* Past President, Mississippi Psychiatric Association. *Hobbies:* Collecting guns & coins.

SANTIAGO-Lugo, Haydée, b. 3 July 1936, Mayaguez, Puerto Rico. Director of Medicine; Psychiatrist. m. Francisco J. Buxo, 25 May 1957-71, Mayaguezz, 3 sons, 1 daughter. *Education:* BSc; Medical Technologist; MD; Diplomate, American Psychiatric Association. *Appointments include:* Medical Technologist, Puerto Rico, USA, Pakistan; Medical Director, State Government Diagnostic Centre, 1977; Assistant Medical Director, State Hospital, Psychiatry, 1978; Emergency Room Group Director, Hospital Hnos Melendez, 1979; Ward Psychiatrist, Hato Rey Psychiatric Hospital, 1983, Centre Medico Psiquiatrico del Caribe, 1985-. *Memberships include:* American Psychiatric Association, American Medical Association; Puerto Rico Medical Association; American Society of Clinical Pathologists; Registry, American Society of Medical Technologists; Puerto Rico & American College of Emergency Physicians. *Honours:* Honour grade, School of Medicine, 1976; Women's honour society. *Hobbies:* Tennis; Instrumental music; Gardening. *Address:* Calle San Joaquin 1878, San Juan Gardens, Rio Piedra, PR 00926, USA.

SANTIĆ, Ante, b. 12 Nov. 1928, Novi Sad, Yugoslavia. University Professor. m. Nada Saks, 14 Mar. 1953, Karlovac, 1 daughter. *Education:* Diploma in Engineering, 1953; DSc, 1966, University of Zagreb. *Appointments:* Research Engineer, 1954, Director of Electronics Laboratory, 1959, Institute of Electrical Engineering; Professor of Electrical Engineering, 1970-, Dean, Faculty of Electrical Engineering, 1978, 81, University of Zagreb; Fulbright Hays Fellow, 1975-76; Visiting Professor, Case Western Reserve University, Cleveland, Ohio, ISA, 1982-84. *Memberships:* Past Chairman, Yugoslav Society of Medical and Biological Engineering; Institute of Electrical and Electronics Engineers, USA; Yugoslav Association of Electrical Engineers. *Publications:* "Electronic Measurement Instrumentation", 1974; "Electronic Instrumentation Skolska knjiga", 1982; "Dictionary of Biomedical Engineering", Editor, 1983. *Honours:* Nikola Tesla Award of Yugoslavia, 1980; Fulbright Hays Award, 1975-76; Holder of 2 patents, Yugoslavia. *Hobbies:* Photography (Cinema); Boating; Personal computers; Carpeting. *Address:* Elektrotehnicki fakultet, Unska 3, Zagreb 41000, Yugoslavia.

SANTORO, Samuel Jay, b. 29 Jan. 1955, Hillsboro, Oregon, USA. Staff Obstetrician; Gynaecologist. m. Junee Deborah Avers, 14 June 1981, Oakland, California, 1 son, 1 daughter. *Education:* BA, University of Washington; Doctor of Osteopathy, Chicago College of Osteopathic Medicine; Residency in Obstetrics/Gynaecology, David Grant Medical Center, US Air Force. *Memberships:* American Medical Association; American Osteopathic Association; California Osteopathic Association; Association of American Gynaecologic Laparoscopists; American College of Obstetricians and Gynaecologists; American Osteopathic Association of Obstetricians and Gynaecologists; Military Association of Osteopathic Physicians and Surgeons. *Honours:* Outstanding Resident in Laparoscopy, 1985; Outstanding Student in Obstetrics/Gynaecology, 1981; Sigma Sigma Phi Honorary Society, 1977; McClauglin Scholarship Recipient, 1978; Graduated Cum Lata, University Washington, 1977. *Hobbies:* Reading; Sports; Racketball; Snow Skiing; Jogging. *Address:* 5641 South 4050 West Roy, UT 84067, USA.

SANTOS, Alberto B, b. 18 Jan. 1951, Havana, Cuba. Director of Residency Training; Associate Professor of Psychiatry. *Education:* BS, MA, Psychology, University of South Carolina, USA; MD, Medical University of South Carolina; NIMH Medical Student Training appointment in Psychiatry. *Appointments:* Categorical Internship, Residency in Psychiatry, Medical University of South Carolina; Staff Psychiatrist, NIMH Psychiatry Education Branch, 1979-80; Attending Psychiatrist, Adult Inpatient Unit, Medical University of South Carolina, 1980-85, Assistant Professor of Psychiatry, 1980-86, Director of Residency Training, 1982-, Director Community Psychiatry Section, 1985-, Associate Professor, 1986-, Chief Inpatient and Emergency Psychiatry Service, Charleston Memorial Hospital, South Carolina, 1985-. *Memberships:* American Psychiatric Association; American Association of Directors of Psychiatry, Residency Training (Treasurer 1986); South Carolina Psychiatric Association; Association for Academic Psychiatry; Charleston County Medical Society; American Medical Association. *Publications:* Co-author 'Delirium or Psychosis? The Use of Sodium Amobarbital Interview' in 'Psychosomatics', 1980; Co-author 'Behaviour Therapy', section in "The Psychiatry Learning System", 1982; Co-author 'Atypical Somatoform Disorder Following Infection in Children - A Depressive Equivalent?' in 'Clinical Psychiatry', 1984. *Honours:* APA/NIMH Fellowship, 1977-80; Southern Medical Association Research Project Grant, 1979; Examiner, American Board of Psychiatry and Neurology, 1983-. *Hobbies:* Percussion; Saltwater Sports Fishing. *Address:* Medical University of South Carolina, Department of Psychiatry and Behavioural Sciences, 171 Ashley Avenue, Charleston, SC 29425, USA.

SANTOS GARCIA, Juan Matias, b. 14 May 1964, Salamanca, Spain. Medical Student. *Education:* Third Year, Salamanca Medical School, Spain. *Appointments:* None. *Memberships:* Aerospace Medical Association; Aerospace Physiologist Society; Space Medicine Branch. *Publication:* 'Que es la Medicina Aereospacial' in 'El Adelanto', 1983. *Honours:* 'A' with distinction, Biochemistry, 1983; 'A' with distinction, Human and Medical Physiology, 1984; 'A' with distinction Medical Psychology, 1984. *Hobbies:* Beautiful women; Reading; Aircraft and Aerospace Technology. *Address:* Paseo de St Vicente, 32.34, 6oD, Salamanca, Spain.

SANYAL, Suhas Chandra, b. 1 Jan. 1942, Mymensingh. Professor, microbiology. m. Kalyani Sanyal, 8 May 1970, Calcutta, 1 son, 1 daughter. *Education:* MS, BS, 1966, PhD, 1969, Calcutta University; MD, Banaras Hindu University, 1974. *Appointments:* Senior Research Fellow, Calcutta, 1966-69; Research Officer, NICED, Calcutta, 1969-70; Lecturer, 1970-73; Reader, 1973-79, Professor, 1979-, Banaras Hindu University; Visiting Professor, ICDDR, B Dhaka, 1981-83. *Memberships:* Life Member, Indian Society of Microbiology; Indian Association of Medical Microbiologists; Indian Association of Pathologists and Microbiologists; Indian Society of Gastroenterology; Indian Society of Basic and Applied Microbiology; Bangladesh Society of Pathologists; International Society of Toxicology; American Society of Microbiology. *Publications:* 118 Original Research articles on Diarrhoea Diseases in 'Journal Medical Microbiology'; 'Journal of Hygiene'; 'Bull WHO'; 'Experientia'; 'Journal of Infectious Disease'; 'Infection Immunity'; 'Journal Applied Environmental Microbiology'; 'Lancet'; 'British Medical Journal'; 'Indian Journal of Medical Research'; etc. *Honours:* Shakuntala-Amirchand Award, ICMR, 1970; Nominated, Member, International Subcommittee, Taxonomy of Vibrios, 1974; Member Advisory Board, International Centre for Diarrhoea Diseases International & Docymentation 1982-; Temporary Advisor, WHO CDD Program; Expert, Indian Council of Medical Research; Advisor CDD Program, Government of India; Invited, Visiting Professor, many countries, 1978-84. *Hobby:* Study of History. *Address:* Dept. of Microbiology, Institute of Medical Sciences, Banaras Hindu University, Varanasi 221005, India.

SAPHIRE, Gary Steven, b. 10 July 1952, Brooklyn, New York, USA. Private Practice. m. Helene Koolik, 12 Sep. 1982, Brooklyn. *Education:* BS, Health Science, Brooklyn College; BS, Biological Science, Illinois College Podiatric Medicine; DPM, Illinois College Podiatric Medicine. *Appointments:* Resident Podiatric Medicine & Surgery, 1978, Chief Resident, 1979, Coney Island Hospital; Attending, Coney Island Hospital, Caledonian Hospital, Maimonides Medical Centre, 1979, Community Hospital, 1984, Brooklyn. *Memberships:* American College of Foot Surgery; American Podiatric Medical Association; New York Academy of Science. *Publications:* Contributing Author, "Podiatric Care of Diabetic or Ischemic Foot", 'Vascular Diseases', 1982. *Honour:* Durlacher Honour Society, 1978. *Hobbies:* Tennis; Woodwork; Music; Birding. *Address:* 7516 Bay Pkwy, Brooklyn, NY 11214, USA.

SARAI, Keisuke, b. 30 Mar. 1929, Kurashiki, Japan. Professor & Chairman, Neurology & Psychiatry. m. Hideko Sarai, 23 May 1959, 2 daughters. *Education:* MD, PhD (Igakuhakushi), Okayama University. *Appointments:* Assistant, Neuropsychiatry, Okayama University Medical School, 1955; Lecturer 1958, Assistant Professor 1960, Neuropsychiatry, Tottori University Medical School; Professor, Department of Neurology & Psychiatry, Hiroshima University Medical School, 1970-. *Memberships:* Fellow, International College of Psychosomatic Medicine, Pacific Rim College of Psychiatrists; Member, International Society of Psychoneuroendocrinology. *Publications include:* 'Biological factors of affective disorders' in "Studies on Pathogenesis of Mental Disorders", ed. Toru,

1980. *Honour:* Kawasaki Prize, biological study of manic-depressive illness, 1967. *Hobbies:* Sports; Shogi; Igo; Golf. *Address:* Koiohsako 2-9-7, Nishikum, Hiroshima City 733 Japan.

SARAN, Shabd, b. 22 Nov. 1931, Gwalior, Madhya Pradesh, India. Principal of Health and Family Welfare Training Centre. m. Manorama, 14 May 1952, Morena, 1 daughter. *Education:* Diploma in Psychological Medicine; MB; DPM; FIPS; MAPA; FAGS. *Appointments:* Medical Officer, General Jail Hospital; Medical Officer, Civil Hospital; Superintendent, Mental Hospital; Specialist in Psychiatry, ESI Scheme; Lecturer in Psychiatry, GR Medical College; Superintendent, ESI Hospital; Superintendent, DK Hospital; District Health Officer; Currently Principal, Health and Family Welfare Training Centre, Gwalior. *Memberships:* Indian Medical Association; Life Member, Indian Red Cross Society; Life Member, Society for Prevention of Blindness; Fellow, Indian Psychiatric Society; Fellow, American Geriatric Society; American Psychiatric Association. *Hobbies:* Music; Reading. *Address:* Shabd Pratap Ashram, Gwalior 474012 Madhya Pradesh, India.

SARGENT, Jeffrey John, b. 19 Nov. 1958, Melbourne, Australia. Dentist. *Education:* BDSc, Melbourne. *Appointments:* Dental Officer, Royal Australian Air Force Base, Wagga, 1982-84; Senior Dental Officer, RAAF Support Unit, Melbourne, 1984-. *Membership:* Victorian Branch, Australian Dental Association. *Hobby:* Athletics. *Address:* 265 Rathmines Street, Fairfield, Victoria 3078, Australia.

SARIS, Nils-Erik Leo, b. 2 Nov. 1928, Helsinki, Finland. Professor of Medical Chemistry, University of Helsinki. m. (1) Eva M Wollitz, 2 Aug. 1953; (2) Margita S Lund, 23 Apr. 1981, 2 sons, 1 daughter. *Education:* MSc, Biochemistry, 1953; PhD, Biochemistry, University of Helsinki. *Appointments:* Research Assistant, Biochemical Research Institute, Helsinki; Clinical Biochemist, Aurora Hospital, Helsinki; Research Fellow, Johnson Foundation, University of Pennsylvania, USA; Principal Clinical Biochemist, Meilahti Hospital, Helsinki; Visiting Professor: University of Trieste, Italy; University of Munich, Germany. *Memberships:* New York Academy of Science; American Association of Clinical Chemists; International Society Clinical Enzymology; Bioelectrochemical Society; IUPAP-IUPAC Bioenergetics Groups; Science Society of Finland; Finnish Society Clinical Chemistry; Society Biochemical Biophysical Microbiology, Finland; Finnish Society Nuclear Medicine; Finnish Society Haematology; Finnish Medical Society; Finnish Chemical Society. *Publications:* Co-editor "Manual in Clinical Laboratory Methods" (in Finnish), 1965; "Clinical Laboratory Methods", 1972; Editor, 'Journal Clinical Chem. Clin. Biochem', 'Clin. Chim. Acta'; Coordinator of Publications in 'Intern. Fed. Clin. Chem.'; Editor, "IFCC Recommendations and Related Documents 1978-83", 1984. *Honours:* Harry Sobotka Lecturer, American Association of Clinical Chemists, 1968; Invited Lecturer by Academy of Science, USSR, 1974; Commemorate Medal of Finnish Winter War, 1939-40. *Hobbies:* Entomology; Fishing; Boating. *Address:* Department of Medical Chemistry, University of Helsinki, Siltavuorenpenger 10, SF-00170 Helsinki 17, Finland.

SARMA, Ravi Pudipeddi, b, 4 Jan. 1950, Chittoor, India. Staff Physician; Assistant Professor. m. Seshu Sarma, 1974, 1 son, 1 daughter. *Edcuation:* MD; MBBS, 1973; Diplomat, American Boards of Internal Medicine, 1976, Haematology, 1978, Oncology, 1979. *Appointments:* Resident, Internal Medicine, 1973-76; Fellow, Haematology, Medical Oncology, 1976-79; Staff Physician, VA Medical Centre, 1979-; Assistant Professor, Medicine, Emory University School of Medicine. *Memberships:* Secretary, Georgia Society of Clinical Oncology; American College of Physicians; American Society of Clinical Oncology; American Association for Medical Decision Making; South Eastern Cancer Study Group. *Hobbies:* Literature;

Classical Music. *Address:* 1670 Clairmont Road, Decator, GA 30033, USA.

SARMA, Tenneti Venkata Anantha Subrahmanya, b. 29 June 1942, Vijayawada, India. Consultant Physician & Cardiologist. m. Suseela, 9 June 1973, Vijayawada, India, 1 son, 1 daughter. *Education:* MB, BS, Andhra Medical College, Vizag, India; MD General Medicine (including Tropical Medicine), Guntur Medical College, Guntur, 1971; Cardio-Thoracic Institute, London, England, 1976. *Appointments:* House Surgeon, King George Hospital, Vizag, India, 1966-67; Senior House Surgeon & Post-graduate student, Government General Hospital, Guntur, 1967-71; Consultant Physician & Cardiologist, Dr T V S Clinic, 1971-; Gifford Memorial Hospital, Nuzvid, 1982-83; Various industrial & commercial consultancies. *Memberships:* Fellow, American College of Chest Physicians; Fellow, American College of Angiology; Life Member, Cardiological Society of India; Life Member, Association of Physicians of India; Life Member, Diabetic Association of India; Indian Medical Association; Bezwada Medical Association; various honorary secretaryships of local and state branches. *Publications:* 'Role of S-T segment in intensive coronary care', 1982; 'Parasympathetic Overactivity in Coronary Care', 1982; 'Ambulation after myocardial infarction', 1982; 'A Study of the significance of treadmill exercise testing for predicting future coronary events', 1983; 'Acute combined myocardial infarction', 1983; 'Complete heart block in acute myocardial infarction', 1983; various other articles and congress papers. *Honours:* First place, Andhra University in Physiology, 1962; also Social & Preventive Medicine, 1965; Delegate to IX World Congress of Cardiology, Moscow, USSR, 1982, British Cardiac Society Meeting, 1976. *Hobby:* Cricket. *Address:* Dr T V S Clinic, Dr Mallikharjunarao Street, Hanumanlupeta, Vijayawada-530 003, Andhra Pradesh, India.

SAROSI, George A, b. 15 Jan. 1938, Budapest, Hungary. Professor and Vice-Chairman, Department of Internal Medicine and Director, Division of General Medicine. 2 sons. *Education:* BA, University of North Dakota, USA; MD, Harvard Medical School. *Appointments:* Assistant Professor of Medicine, 1970-73, Associate Professor of Medicine, 1973-77, Professor of Medicine, 1977-83, University of Minnesota Medical School; Professor of Medicine, University of Texas Medical School at Houston, 1983-. *Memberships:* Fellow, American College of Physicians; Fellow, American College of Chest Physicians; Member, American Thoracic Society; Infectious Diseases Society of America; American Federation for Clinical Research; Central Society for Clinical Research. *Publications:* Author of numerous articles including, 'Action of Choline on Lipid Phosphorylation in the Kidney, Heart and Aorta', (with W D Cornatzer and J Newland Jr), 1961; 'Sporotrichosis in children: Report of an epidemic', (with B A Dahl, P M Silberfarb, R J Weeks and F E Tosh), 1982; 'Cryptococcosis and pregnancy', (with P M Silberfarb and F E Tosh), 1972; 'Management of Blastomycosis', 1982. *Honours:* Recipient of numerous honours for professional services. *Hobbies:* Tennis; Opera; Classical music; Philately. *Address:* University of Texas Medical School, Department of Internal Medicine, PO Box 20708, Houston, TX 77225, USA.

SARRA-CARBONELL, Salvador, b. 24 July 1939, Barcelona, Spain. Professor of Internal Medicine. m. Rosa Ester Aravena Lazo, Feb. 1980, Santiago, Chile. *Education:* MD, University of Chile, 1963; Fellowship in Clinical Hospital, University of Barcelona, Spain; Metabolic diseases & Nuclear Medicine, 1975-76; Training Programme, School of Medicine, University of Miami USA, at Jackson Memorial Hospital & Veterans Administration Hospital, active in Internal Medicine Department (with Prof J Maxwell McKenzie), Teaching Methodology & Curriculum; WHO Fellowship in Medical Education, (with Prof Stephen Abrahmson PhD), Training Programme in Internal Medicine, (with Prof John Bethune), School of Medicine,

University of Southern California at Los Angeles, County Medical Center. *Appointments:* Internship, José Joaquin Aguirre Hospital, Santiago, University of Chile, 1963; Residency, Barros Luco Trudeau Hospital, 1964-66, Attendant, 1966-75; Faculty Member, Catholic University, 1966-67; Faculty Member, Barros Luco Trudeau Hospital, 1964-85; Chief of Intensive Care Unit, 1967; Clinical Chief, 1970-77; Faculty Secretary, University of Chile, Santiago; Chairman of Clinical Department 1977-80, Chairman of Internal Medicine Department, 1980-86, School of Medicine, University of Chile (South Division), 1977-80. *Memberships:* Internal Medicine Society of Santiago; Medical Faculty of Chile; International School of Medical Sophrology; Fellow, American College of Physicians. *Publications:* Numerous articles, including: 'Plasmatic & Urinary Electrolytes in the Elderly'; 'Gaucher's Disease'; 'Primary Heart Tumor'; 'Pleural effusion & hepatic Cirrhosis'; 'Intestinal Tuberculosis'; 'Heterogeneity of Ehlers-Danlos Syndrome'. *Honour:* Premio Juan Grandulfo 1967, Chilean Surgeons Society for paper on Chronic relapsed Pancreatites. *Hobbies:* Philosophy; Poetry; Gardening; Walking; Sea Recreation. *Address:* Universidad de Chile, Facultad de Medicina, Casilla 10-D, Correo 13, San Miguel, Santiago, Chile.

SARUNGI, Philemon Mikol, b. 23 Mar. 1936, Tarime, Tanzania. Professor of Orthopaedics and Trauma; Director General, Muhimbili Medical Centre. m. 30 Oct. 1970, Miskolc, Hungary, 1 son, 3 daughters. *Education:* MD cum laude, MS, University of Szeged, Hungary; Postgraduate, Orthopaedics and Trauma Surgery, University of Vienna, Austria; Advanced course of study in replantation of severed limbs, Peoples Republic of China. *Appointments:* Lecturer; Senior Lecturer; Associate Professor; Full Professor; External Examiner, University of Nairobi, Kenya; currently, Professor of Orthopaedic/Trauma, Director General, Muhimbili Medical Centre, Dar Es Salaam, Tanzania. *Memberships:* Founder, World Orthopaedic Concern, 1975; Member and Zonal Chairman, Eastern and Central Africa, World Orthopaedic Concern, 1977-83; Past President, MAT; Director General, MMC. *Publications:* 'Trauma Posterior dislocation of the hip in a child' in 'East African Medical Journal', 1974; 'Role of Orthopaedic/Trauma Surgery in Developing Countries, Tanzania Experience' in 'Proceedings of the 2nd International Conference of World Orthopaedic Concern Association', Singapore, 1975. *Hobbies:* Badminton; Yoga. *Address:* Muhimbili Medical Centre, PO Box 65000, Dar Es Salaam, Tanzania.

SASLAW, Leonard David, b. 27 Aug. 1927, Brooklyn, New York, USA. Physiologist. *Education:* BS, CCNY, 1949; MS, Biochemistry, 1954, PhD, Chemistry, 1963, Georgetown Univesity. *Appointments:* Chemist, National Cancer Institute, NIH, 1951-57; Biophysics, Sloan-Kettering Institute, 1957-58; Biochemistry, Armed Forces Institute of Pathology, 1958-65; Director, Biochemistry, Pharmacology of Cancer Chemotherapy Dept, Microbiological Association Inc, 1965-68; Senior Biochemist, National Drug Co, 1968-69; Chief, Cellular Biochemistry, Albert Einstein Medical Centre, 1969-70; Clinical Laboratory Director, Medical Diagnostic Centres Inc, 1970-71; Laboratory Director, Research Associate, Renal Laboratory, New York Medical College, 1971-73; Manager, Biochemistry, Bio/Dynamics Inc, New Jersey, 1973-74; Professional Associate, Smithsonian Scientific Information Exchange, 1975-77; Consultant, Burton Parsons Co Inc, Seat Pleasant, Maryland, 1977-78; Physiologist, Toxicology, Vet Medicine, FDA, Washington and Rockville, Maryland, 1978-. *Memberships:* American Chemical Society; American Society Pharmacology and Experimental Therapeutics; Clinical Ligand Assay Society; American Association Cancer Research; American College Toxicology; etc. *Publications:* 50 scientific articles in professional journals. *Honours:* Meritorious Achievement Award, Armed Forces Institute of Pathology, 1964. *Hobbies:* Art Print Collecting; American Anti-

que Furniture. *Address:* 425 G St SW, Washington DC 20024, USA.

SATO, Takumi, b. 2 Mar. 1932, Japan. Professor of Surgery. m. Shizu Sato, 1 Nov. 1963, Kyoto, Japan, 1 son. *Education:* Graduate School of Medicine, Kyoto University, Japan. *Appointments:* Assistant of Medical Faculty, Kyoto University, 1961; Lecturer, Kyoto University, 1968; Professor, Department of Oral & Maxillo-facial Surgery, Shiga University of Medical Science, Japan, 1979. *Memberships:* Councillor, Japanese Stomatological Society; Councillor, Japanese Society of Oral & Maxillo-facial Surgery; Councillor, Japanese Society for Dental Health; Japanese Society of Plastic & Reconstructive Surgery. IADR; IAOS. *Publications:* (Co-author) "Surgery: an itemized Discussion", 1979; (co-author) "Illustrated Handbook of Internal Medicine Volume 17", 1981; 'Mechanism of Fluoride Absorption from the Gastrointestinal Tract' (in Bull. Stom. Kyoto Univ), 1978; "Modern Oral Surgery" (co-author), 1982. *Hobbies:* Fine Arts, especially pictures. *Address:* Yosai, Momoyama-cho, Fushimi-ku, Kyoto, 612 Japan.

SATORI, Odon, b. 7 Apr. 1926, Budapest, Hungary. Surgeon. m. Edit Ilona Szatmari, 2 Oct. 1982, Budapest, 3 daughters. *Education:* MD, 1951, Master of Surgery, 1954, Candidate of Medical Sciences, 1981. *Appointments include:* Resident Doctor, 1955-61, Assistant Professor and Research Worker, 1961-64, Deputy Head of Surgical Department, 1964-77, Tetenyi Street Medical Centre, Budapest; Head of Surgery, County Hospital, Gyula, 1977-. *Memberships:* Society of Hungarian Surgeons; Society of Hungarian Physiologists; Association of Hungarian Angiologists; Koranyi Sandor Society of the Hungarian Academy of Sciences; Executive Board Member, Southern Section of Hungarian Surgeons. *Publications include:* 'Arterial Hypotension-induced Cytoplasmic NADH Fluorescence Changes in the Cat Brain Cortex-Effect of Dexamethasone' 1980; 'Protection of Myocardial Function in Hemorrhagic Shock' 1980; 'The Effect of Dexamethasone in Clinical and Experimental Shock' 1981. *Honours:* North Korean 'Order of the Flag' 1954; 'Memorial Medal for Chinese Volunteers' 1954; 'Order of Socialist Work' 1954; Distinguished Service Award, 1984. *Hobbies:* Rowing; Waterside camping; Tennis; Skiing. *Address:* Latinka S.u.82.IX.96, 1116 Budapest, Hungary.

SATYAVATI, Gowdagere Vedanti Prasad, b. 25 Aug. 1937, Megaravalli, India. Senior Deputy Director-General. m. Dr D N Pradad, 27 Aug. 1972, Brindavan, Uttar Pradash, 2 adopted sons. *Education:* MB BS; Kayachikitsa and MD, Pharmacology. *Appointments:* Senior Research Officer, in charge of research on indigenous drugs, 1969, Officer-in-Charge, Non-Communicable Diseases, 1973, Chief, Division of Basic Medical Sciences and PL-480 Programmes, 1974, Deputy Director-General and Chief, Division of Publication and Information, 1976; Senior Deputy Director-General and Chief, Division of Publication and Information and Traditional Medicine Research, 1982-, Indian Council of Medical Research, New Delhi, India; Officer-in-Charge, Monograph on Medicinal Plants of India, 1970. *Memberships:* Indian Pharmacological Society; Indian Association of Traditional Asian Medicine, Regional Secretary; Founder, Fellow, National Academy of Indian Medicine; International Federation of Scientific Editors Association; Secretary, Society for Biomedical Communication, India. *Publications:* "Monograph on Medicinal Plants of India", 3 volumes, 1976-86; "Indian Journal of Medical Research - Editor-in-Chief, 1976-; Over 100 oroginal research publications and reviews. *Honours:* Editorial Boards: Indian Journal of Pharmacology; Indian Journal of Medical Education; International Journal of Science of Life. Member, Expert Panel on Traditional Medicine, World Health Organisation; Technical Consultant, Herbal Medicine, UNICEF; WHO Consultant for Health Publications; Research Advisory Committees, Regional Research Laboratory Jammu and Centre for Indian Medicinal and

Aromatic Plants. *Hobbies:* Music; Literature; Theatre. *Address:* Indian Council of Medical Research, PO Box 4508, Ansari Nagar, New Delhi 110029, India.

SAUER, Rolf, b. 19 Sep. 1939, Hamburg, Federal Republic of Germany. Professor of Radiotherapy. m. Martina Sauer, 20 May 1966, 2 sons, 1 daughter. *Education:* State examinations in Medicine, 1963, MD, 1964, University of Hamburg; Specialist in Radiology, Basel, Switzerland, 1972; PhD, Radiology, venia legendi, Basel, 1976; Professor & Chairman of Department of Radiotherapy, University Hospital of Erlangen/Nuremberg, Federal Republic of Germany, 1977. *Appointments:* Resident, Physiology, University of Basel, 1967; Resident of Radiology, University of Basel, 1968; Consultant of Radiotherapy, University of Basel, 1972; Chairman of the German Group of Radiotherapy, 1982; Director, University Hospital of Erlangen, 1985. *Memberships:* Swiss Society for Radiology & Nuclear Medicine; Swiss Society for Oncology; German Roentgen Society; German Cancer Society; American Society of Therapeutic Radiology & Oncology; European Society of Therapeutic Radiology & Oncology. *Publications:* "Strahlentherapy" (Radiotherapy), (Handbook for technologists), 1984; 120 publications in nation & international journals. *Honour:* Jubilee prize of the Swiss Society for Radiology & Nuclear Medicine, 1977. *Hobbies:* Music (singing, playing 'cello). *Address:* Strahlentherapeutische Klinik und Poliklinik der Universitat, D-8520 Erlangen, Universitatsstrasse 27, Federal Republic of Germany.

SAUTER, Willi Friedrich, b. 21 July 1928, Loerrach. Director, Myoelectric Prosthetics. m. Elizabeth Bulling, 28 Aug. 1948, 3 sons. *Education:* Certified in Prosthetics, 1968; Certified in Orthotics, 1968; FCBC. *Appointments:* Chief Prothetist, Znahl Orthopedics, Basel, Switzerland, 1952-61; Chief Orthotist, Orthopedic Appliance Research, Toronto, 1961-64; Research Teaching Prosthetist, Ontario Crippled Childrens Centre; Co-Ordinator, Administrator, Powered Upper Extremity Prosthetic Dept, Hugh MacMillan Medical Centre. *Memberships:* Canadian Association Prosthetist and Orthotist. *Publications:* "Prostheses for the Child Amputee", 1972; "Flexible Sockets for Short Below Elbow Amputee", 1975; "Application of 3 state myoelectric control system", 1977; "Myoelectric and switch controlled upper extremity prosthese, Amputation Surgery and Rehabilitation The Toronto Experience", 1980; "A Prosthesis with an Electric Elbow for a Severely Handicapped 3 year old Patient". *Honours:* Canadian Board for Prosthetist Orthotist Fellowship, 1981. *Hobbies:* Bee Keeping; Canoeing. *Address:* R.R. 1, Claremont, Ontario, Canada L0H 1E0.

SAUTTER, Richard Daniel, b. 30 Dec. 1926, Ord, Nebraska, USA. Executive Director, Marshfield Medical Foundation; Director of Medical Education, Marshfield Clinic. m. Rosemary Graham, 4 Aug. 1952, Lincoln, Nebraska, 3 sons, 1 daughter. *Education:* BSc, Science and Medicine; MD; University of Nebraska. *Appointments:* Internship, Highland Alameda County, Oakland, California, 1953-54; State University of Iowa, Iowa City, 1954-58; Instructor, General Surgery, 1959-61; Resident, Thoracic Surgery, 1959-61; Department of Cardiovascular and Thoracic Surgery, Marshfield Clinic, Wisconsin, 1961-; Assistant Dean, Clinical Affairs, University of Wisconsin Medical School; Associate Editor, Wisconsin Medical Journal. *Memberships:* American Association of Thoracic Surgery; The Society of Thoracic Surgeons, Founding Member; Central Surgical Association; Fellow, American College of Surgeons; Wisconsin Surgical Society; Wisconsin Chapter, American College of Surgeons; Wisconsin Heart Club; Wood County Medical Society; Council on Thrombosis, American Heart Association; State Medical Society; Western Surgical Association; Society for Clinical Trials Incorporated. *Publications:* 130 Contributions to professional journals; Chapters in Books include: "The Effectiveness of Thrombolytic Therapy' in "Con-

troversy in Internal Medicine II", 1974; 'The treatment of life-threatening massive pulmonary embolism' in "Controversy in Surgery", 1976; Book in progress: "Pulmonary Embolism: All You Really Need to Know". *Hobbies:* Fishing; Gardening; Cooking. *Address:* 510 North St Joseph Avenue, Marshfield, WI 54449, USA.

SAUVAGE, Dominique, b. 10 Sep. 1942. Graduate Professor. m. Odile Gaslais, 1 Sep. 1966, Tours, France, 2 sons. *Education:* MD, 1972; Paediatrician, 1972; Psychiatrist & Child Psychiatrist, 1976. *Appointments:* Resident, 1967-72, Clinical Head, 1972-76, Assistant, 1976-80, Graduate Senior Lecturer, 1980-84, Head of the University Hospital Service of Child Psychiatry, 1984-, All Tours Hospital. *Memberships:* French Society of Child & Adolescent Psychiatry; French-speaking Congress on Psychiatry & Neurology. *Publications:* "Autisme du Nourrisson et du jeune Enfant", 1984; Various contributions to professional journals. *Address:* Service de Pédopsychiatrie, Chu Bretonneau, 37044 Tours Cedex, France.

SAVARY, Paul, b. 7 Apr. 1932, Metabetchouen, Quebec, Canada. Professor of Medicine. m. Denyse Boberge, 15 May 1957, Quebec, 2 sons, 2 daughters. *Education:* BA; MD; Specialist in Ear, Nose and Throat, Quebec and Canada; FRCS, Canada. *Appointments:* Professor, Faculty of Medicine, Laval University, 1964-; Director and Head, Department of Ear, Nose and Throat, Laval, 1980-84; President, Portmanns Foundation, 1983-. *Memberships:* Vice President, Pan American Association of ORL and Head and Neck Surgery; Past President, Association of ORL and Head and Neck Surgery, Province of Quebec; Royal College of Physicians and Surgeons of Canada; Canadian Society of Ear, Nose and Throat; Pan American Association of Ear, Nose and Throat; Societe Francaise d'ORL; Royal Society of Medicine, England; Politzer Society. *Publications:* Author of 88 publications and communications in North and South America, Europe and Central America on Vertigo, ENG and surgical treatment, cancer of head and neck and surgery of deafness. *Honours:* Honours, College of Physicians and Surgeons of Province of Quebec, 1955; Medal, City of Marseille, 1978; Medal, City of Bordeaux, 1980; Honours, Pan American Association of ORL, 1984. *Hobbies:* Sports such as windsurfing, tennis, skiing and swimming. *Address:* 44 Cole du Palais, Quebec, Canada G1R 4H8.

SAVIC, Dragoslav, b. 18 July 1927, Kanjiza, Yugoslavia. Director, Research Department. m. Leposava Todorovic, 6 May 1952. *Education:* Medical Faculty, 1946-52; Specialisation, Clinic of Otorhinolaryngology, 1952-55; MS, 1959, PhD, DMS, 1974, Medical School, University of Belgrade. *Appointments:* Assistant, 1955, Assistant Professor, 1960, Professor, 1968, Director, Clinic, 1969, Full Professor, 1975-, Otorhinolaryngology, University of Belgrade. *Memberships:* Yugoslavian, French and Austrian Otorhinolaryngologic Societies. *Publications:* "Otorhinolaryngology", 1983; "Laryngomicroscopy", 1975; "Otosclerosis", 1980; "Frontal and Ethmoidal Sinuses", 1982; "Appreciation of the working ability of otorhinolaryngologic diseases", 1985. Author over 250 published articles. *Address:* Clinic of Otorhinolaryngology, University of Belgrade Medical School, Pasterova 2, 11000 Belgrade, Yugoslavia.

SAW, Daisy, b. 13 Aug. 1940, Burma, Consultant Pathologist. m. Derrick Tin Nyunt, 4 June 1966, 1 son, 1 daughter. *Education:* MB, BS, Rangoon Medical College, Burma, 1964; MRCP, England, 1975; FRC Path, Australia, 1977; FCAP, 1980. *Appointments:* Rangoon General Hospital, Burma, 1964-65; Institute of Medicine I, Rangoon, Burma, 1965-68; Medical Officer, Kwong Wah Hospital, Kowloon, Hong Kong, 1970-72; Medical Officer, 1972-78, Consultant Pathologist, 1978-, Queen Elizabeth Hospital, Kowloon, Hong Kong. *Memberships:* Royal College of Pathologists of United Kingdom; Fellow, Royal College of Pathologists of Australia; Fellow, College of

American Pathologists; Treasurer, Medical and Health Department Consultants Group; Council Member, Government Doctors' Association; Hong Kong Pathology Society; Hong Kong Anti-Cancer Society; Hong Kong Medical Association; Hong Kong Chinese Medical Association. *Publications:* Contributor of numerous articles in professional journals. *Honours:* Col Min Sein Gold Medal, 1961; Prize in Pathology, 1963. *Hobbies:* Reading; Walking; Golf; Swimming. *Address:* Institute of Pathology, Queen Elizabeth Hospital, Kowloon, Hong Kong.

SAWHNEY, Om Prakash, b. 15 Oct. 1937, India. Plastic Surgeon. m. Veena Bhandari, 28 Oct. 1968, Delhi, 1 son, 1 daughter. *Education:* MBBS, Amritsar Medical College, India, 1962; Fellow, Royal College of Surgeons, Edinburgh, 1967; Certified American Board of Plastic and Reconstructive Surgery, 1975. *Appointments:* Resident, Irwin Hospital, Delhi, 1963; Methodist Hospital, Central Illinois, USA, 1964; District and General Hospital, Mansfield, 1965; Englewood Hospital, 1966-68; St Barnabas Medical Centre, 1968-71; Instructor, Plastic Surgery, Kings County Hospital, 1971-72; Clinical Professor, Rutgers Medical School, 1973-; Senior Attending, Muhlenberg Hospital, Plainfield, 1973-. *Memberships:* American Society of Plastic and Reconstructive Surgeons; Union County Medical Society; New Jersey Medical Society; American Medical Association. *Publications:* "Free Composite Lip Craft", 1974. *Honours:* Professional Examination; Bronze Medal, Anatomy & Surgery; etc. *Hobbies:* Photography; Tennis; Boating. *Address:* 421 West 7th Street, Plainfield, NJ 07060, USA.

SAWIAK, Oksana Maria, b. 12 May 1942, Poland, Dental Surgeon. m. Alexander James Black, 5 Sep. 1981, Toronto, 2 daughters. *Education:* DDS, University of Toronto Faculty of Dentistry; LD, Pakey Institute; Fellow, Academy of General Dentistry. *Appointments:* Intern, Toronto General - Toronto Western Hospital; Associate in Dentistry, Mississauga; Solo practice, Mississauga, 1968-; Demonstrator-Instructor, Department of Oral Anatomy, University of Toronto. *Memberships:* Ontario Dental Association; Ontario Women Dentists Association; Canadian Dental Association; International Association for Orthodontics; Academy of General Dentistry; Ontario Society of Clinical Hypnosis; American Society of Clinical Hypnosis; Ontario Society of Preventive Dentistry; Applied Kinesiology Canada; Academy of Stress and Chronic Disease; Royal College of Dental Surgeons of Ontario. *Honour:* Fellow, Academy of Dentistry, 1979. *Hobbies:* Reading; Embroidery; Knitting; Skiing; Camping; Travelling. *Address:* 2274 Courrier Lane, Mississauga, Ontario L5C 1U2, Canada.

SAXEN, Arno Erik (Erkki), b. 23 Aug. 1921, Helsinki, Finland. Professor and Head, Department of Pathology. m. Eva Paula Margareta Ryti, 1947, 4 daughters. *Education:* MD, Medicine and Surgery. *Appointments:* Chief Pathologist, Central Institute for Radiotherapy, Helsinki, 1949-59; Director, Finnish Cancer Registry, Helsinki, 1952-; Professor and currently Head, Department of Pathology, University of Helsinki. *Memberships:* Past President, International Academy of Pathology; President, International Council of Societies of Pathology; Royal Scientific Academy of Sweden; Finnish Academy of Science. *Publications:* Author of 200 scientific papers on tumor pathology and cancer epidemiology. *Honours:* Liberty Cross IV, 1942; Commander, Order of the Lion of Finland, 1969; Honorary Award, Finnish Academy of Science, 1978; Maude Abbott Lecturer, USA, 1978. *Hobbies:* Agriculture; Fishing; Hunting. *Address:* Department of Pathology, University of Helsinki, Haartmaninkatu 3, SF-00290 Helsinki, Finland.

SAYEED, Abul Fatah Akram, b. 23 Nov. 1935, Bangladesh. Senior Principal, General Practitioner in Medicine. m. Hosne-Ara Ali, 11 Oct. 1958, Dhaka, 2 sons, 1 daughter. *Education:* MB BS, University of Dhaka.

Appointments: House Officer, Dhaka Medical College Hospital, 1958-59; Senior House Officer, Dhaka Medical College Hospital, 1959-60; Rotating Internship, Monmouth Medical Centre, Long Beach, New Jersey, USA, 1960-61; Medical Director, Pinehill Scout Reservation, Camden, New Jersey, 1961; Senior House Officer, Ophthalmology, Leicester Royal Infirmary, England, 1961-63; Assistantship in General Practice, Leicester, 1963; Principal General Practitioner, 1964-. *Memberships:* British Medical Association; Bangladesh Medical Association in UK; Life Member, Overseas Doctors Association in UK; Life Member, Pakistan Medical Society in UK; Fellow, Royal Society of Medicine. *Publications:* Editor (Literary Secretary), 'Dhaka Medical College Journal' and Magazine, 1957-58; Editorial Advisor, 'Asian Observer'; Member, Editorial Board, 'ODA News Review'; Author of many articles on current medico-political issues. *Honours:* OBE, 1976; Fellowship of Overseas Doctors' Association, 1985. *Hobbies:* Stamp and Coin Collections; Photography; Reading; Gardening; Walking. *Address:* "Ramna", 2 Mickleton Drive, Leicester LE5 6GD, England.

SAZ, Arthur Kenneth, b. 2 Dec. 1917, New York, USA. Professor of Microbiology. m. Ruth Marjorie Lieb, 31 Oct. 1945, New York, 1 daughter. *Education:* BS, City College of New York, 1938; MA, University of Missouri, 1939; PhD, Duke University, 1943. *Appointments:* Associate, Rockefeller Institute for Medical Research, New York, 1947-48; Assistant Chief, Laboratory of Infectious Disease, Chief, Section on Medical and Physiological Bacteria, NIADD NIH, 1957-64; Environmental Health Scientist, USA EPA, 1977-78; Professor and Chairman, Department of Microbiology, 1964-84, Professor of Microbiology, 1984-, Georgetown University Schools of Medicine and Dentistry. *Memberships:* American Society of Microbiology; American Academy of Microbiology; American Board of Microbiology. *Publications:* 'Effect aromatic l2 on tubercle bacillus' in American Review of Tuberculosis, 1943; 'An Introspective Compound View of Penicillinase' in Journal of Cell. Physiol, 1970; 'Transfer Plasmid-Borne B-Lactamase in "Neisseria gonorrhoeae" 1977; 'Do B-Lactamases have a biological function' in "Beta-Lactamases" edited by J H T Hamilton-Miller. *Honours:* Phi Beta Kappa 1943; Post Doctoral Fellow, NIH, 1949-50; American Board of Microbiology, 1972; Member, Marine Biology Laboratory, 1969-; Editorial Board, Antimicrobial Agents - Chemotherapy, 1971-82. *Hobby:* Raising Beagle hounds. *Address:* Georgetown University Schools of Medicine and Dentistry, Washington, DC 20007, USA.

SAZIMA, Henry John, b. 25 Dec. 1927, Cleveland, Ohio, USA. Rear Admiral, Dental Corps, US Navy. m. Carol Ann Watson, 10 Sep. 1955, Cleveland, Ohio, 1 daughter. *Education:* BS Chemistry, 1948, DDS, School of Dentistry, 1953, Case Western Reserve University, Cleveland, Ohio; Certification, Graduate School of Medicine, University of Pennsylvania, Philadelphia, 1956; Certification, Graduate School of Education, Chapman College, Orange, California, 1969. *Appointments:* Chief, Oral Surgery, Naval Dental School, Bethesda, Maryland, Naval Hospital, Camp Pendleton, California; Chief, Oral & Maxillo-facial Surgery, Naval Hospital, Philadelphia, Pennsylvania, Naval Hospital, San Diego, California; Consultant Staff Oral & Maxillo-facial Surgery, Naval Hospital, Bethesda, Maryland; Associate Professor of Surgery, Hahnemann Medical College, Philadelphia. *Memberships:* American Dental Association; American Association of Oral & Maxillo-facial Surgeons; Diplomate, American Board of Oral & Maxillo-facial Surgery; Federation Dentaire International; Association of Military Surgeons of the US; American & International Association for Dental Research; American Association for the Advancement of Science. *Publications:* "Management of War Injuries to Jaws", 1977; "Life Threatening Infection", 1980; 'Medical Evaluation of Dental Patients', 1981; 'Trans-oral Open Reduction of Mandibular Fractures', 1970.

Honours: Fellow, International College of Dentists, 1963; Fellow, American College of Dentists, 1974; Margetis Award of AMSUS, 1971. *Hobbies:* Tennis; Sport; Music; Travel; Gardening. *Address:* Deputy Commander for Readiness & Logistics, Naval Medical Command, Washington, DC 20372-5120, USA.

SCHACHT, Mervyn, b. 28 Sep. 1915, New York, NY, USA. Director, Department of Psychiatry, New Rochelle Hospital Medical Centre, USA. m. Leatrice, 11 Feb. 1951, 2 sons, 2 daughters. *Edducation:* AB, New York University, 1936; MD, Creighton University School of Medicine, 1940; Certificate in Psychoanalysis, New York Medical College, 1952. *Appointments:* Medical Doctor, High Point Hospital, Port Houston, NY, 1952-58; Assistant Clinical Professor, 1960-74, Associate Clinical Professor, 1974-85, Albert Einstein Medical College. *Memberships:* Fellow, American Academy of Psychoanalysis; Life Fellow, American Psychiatric Association; Fellow, Westchester Academy of Medicine. *Hobbies:* Fly fishing; Print collecting. *Address:* 3 Oak Way, Scarsdale, NY 10583, USA.

SCHACHTER, Joseph, b. 26 Aug. 1925, New York City, USA. Research Associate Professor of Epidemiology. m. Judith A Spector, 12 June 1949, New York City, 1 son, 2 daughters. *Education:* MD, New York University Bellevue College of Medicine, 1952; PhD, Social Relations, Harvard University, 1955; Certificate of Psychoanalytic Training, Columbia University Psychoanalytic Clinic for Training and Research, 1957. *Appointments:* Research Associate, 1956-68, Assistant Clinical Professor, 1960-68, Department of Psychiatry, College of Physicians and Surgeons, Columbia University; Director, Post-Doctoral Research Training Program in the Biological Sciences in Relation to Mental Health, 1965-68; Chief of Psychiatric Research in Child Development, New York State Psychiatric Institute, 1967-68; Associate Professor of Psychiatry, 1968-75, Research Associate Professor of Psychiatry, 1976-79, Clinical Associate Professor of Psychiatry, 1979-, University of Pittsburgh School of Medicine; Research Associate Professor of Epidemiology, Graduate School of Public Health, University of Pittsburgh, 1979-85; Associate Professor of Epidemiology, Graduate School of Public Health, University of Pittsburgh, 1985-. *Memberships:* American Psychiatric Association; American Psychoanalytic Association; Fellow, Council on Epidemiology, American Heart Association; Society for Psychophysiological Research. *Publications:* 'Pain, fear and anger in hypertensives and normotensives' Psychosomatic Medicine, 1957; 'Blood volume expension among blacks: An hypothesis' Medical Hypotheses 1984, with L H Kuller; 'Blood pressure during the first five years of life: Relation to ethnic group (black or white) and to parental hypertension' American Journal of Epidemiology, 1984 with L H Kuller and C Perfetti. *Honours:* AB Summa Cum Laude, Dartmouth College, 1946; J B Richardson Fellowship for Postgraduate Study, Dartmouth College, 1948; Research Training Grant, Foundations Fund for Research in Psychiatry, 1960. *Address:* 5400 Darlington Road, Pittsburgh, PA 15217, USA.

SCHACHTER, Melville, b. 22 Sep. 1920, Montreal, Canada. Professor of Physiology, University of Alberta. m. Ruth Nisse, 23 July 1944, Montreal, 2 sons, 1 daughter. *Education:* BSc, 1941, MSc, 1942, MD, CM, 1945-46, McGill University. *Appointments:* Assistant Professor of Physiology, Dalhousie University, Canada, 1947-50; Member of Staff, National Institute for Medical Research, London, England, 1950-53; Member of Staff, Lister Institute for Preventive Medicine, London, 1953-54; Reader, Physiology, University College London, 1954-65; Consultant, Parke-Davis Ltd, England and USA, 1959-65; Professor and Head, Physiology, University of Alberta, Canada, 1965-85; Honorary Professor, Stanford University, California, USA, 1970-72. *Memberships:* Physiology Society, Great Britain; Pharmacological Society, Great Britain; Physiological Society, Canada; Pharmacological Society, Canada. *Publications:* 'Endogenous substances capable of producing some features of the acute inflammatory reaction', 1960; 'Polypeptides which affect vessels and smooth muscles', 1960; 'Inflammation, immunity and hypersensitivity', 1960. *Honours:* Outstanding Contributions Award, International Congress on Kallikreins and Kinins, Savannah, USA, 1984. *Hobbies:* Gardening. *Address:* Department of Physiology, University of Alberta, Edmonton, Alberta, Canada.

SCHAFER, Donald William, b. 18 Oct. 1919, Argos, Indiana, USA. Clinical Professor, Psychiatry. m . Viola (Begley) Wald 24 Oct., 1942, Cincinnati, Ohio, 1 son, 1 daughter. *Education:* BS 1940, MD 1943, University of Cincinnati. Life Fellow, American Psychiatric Association. *Appointments include:* Medical Officer, US Army, 1944-46; General Practice, Indiana, 1946-52; Private Practice, Psychiatry, California, 1954-70; Assistant Clinical Professor, University of Southern California, 1958-68; Staff Psychiatrict, 1970-84, Clinical Professor, Department of Psychiatry & Human Behaviour, 1984-, University of California, Irvine. *Memberships include:* America, California & Orange County Medical Associations; American, Southern California, Orange County Psychiatric Associations; Society for Clinical & Experimental Hypnosis (Fellow, past President); American Society of Clinical Hypnosis (Fellow); International Society of Hypnosis; American Pain Society. *Publications include:* 'AS.IF Electroschock Therapy', 1960; 'Lithium Treatment of Mania', 1966 (in "Diseases of the Nervous System"); 'T Group Sensitivity Training & Group Therapy', 1971; 'Hypnosis Use on a Burn Unit', 1975; 'Psychological Profile of a Gynaecologic Microsurgeon', 1977 (in "Microsurgery in Gynaecology"); 25 other research articles, various medical journals. *Honours:* Fellowships: (Life Fellow 1984) APA 1972, SCEH 1973, ASCH 1978; Many awards, SCEH; American Board of Medical Hypnosis. *Hobbies:* Reading; Writing; Travel. *Address:* 50 Emerald Bay, Laguna Beach, California 92651, USA.

SCHAIN, Ronald Burton, b. 13 Dec. 1934, Los Angeles, California, USA. Chiropractic Doctor. m. Kimberly Schain, 17 Nov. 1976, Granada Hills, California, USA, 1 son, 1 daughter. *Education:* Medical Specialist Certificate, Brooks Army Medical Corps, Houston, Texas, 1953-55; Doctor of Chiropractic, Cleveland Chiropractic College, Los Angeles, 1973-76; Postgraduate work, Los Angeles College of Chiropractic, 1976-77. *Appointments:* Instructor, Cleveland Chiropractic College, Los Angeles, 1975-76; Associate, Encino-Tarzana Chiropractic Offices; Chiropractic offices, Canoga Park, California, 1979-; Holistic Chiropractic Clinic, Canoga Park, 1983-. *Memberships:* International Chiropractic Association of California; American Chiropractic Association Council on Roentgenology; California Chiropractic Association; American Association of Nutritional Consultants; Sigma Chi Psi National Honorary Proffessional Society; Cleveland Chiropractic College Alumni Association, Founding Member. *Publications:* 'An Amazzing Profile of America's Most Effective Drugless Healers', Chiropractic Doctors, 1981; also articles in California Chiropractic Association Journal, professional newsletter 'Boning Up'. *Honours:* Doctor of the Year, California Chiropractic Association, 1982-83, 1984-85; 'Best of Best', Council of Society Presidents, California Chiropractic Association. *Hobbies:* Music; Archery; Travel. *Address:* 8231-3 Canoga Avenue, Canoga Park, CA 91304, USA.

SCHALM, Solko Walle, b. 14 July 1940, Arnhem, The Netherlands, Staff Physician. 2 sons, 1 daughter. *Education:* Arts-Examen (MD equivalent) 1968, MD cum laude (by thesis) 1968, University of Leyden; Specialist in Internal Medicine, 1973; ECFMG, 1973. *Appointments:* Resident in Internal Medicine, University Hospital, Leyden 1968-74; Research Assistant, Gastroenterology Unit, Mayo Clinic, Rochester, Minnesota, USA, 1974-76; Instructor in Medicine, Mayo Medical School, Rochester, Minnesota, 1975; Resident in Internal Medicine 1968-74, Staff Physician in Internal Medicine and Gastroenterology, University Hospital, Rotterdam, The Netherlands, 1976-. *Memberships:* Secretary 1978-83, Dutch Society of Gastroenterology; Chairman 1981-84, FUNGO-Liver Research Group; European Association for the Study of the Liver; American Gastroenterological Association; International Association for the Study of the Liver; American Association for the Study of the Liver. *Publications:* 56 original articles. *Honours:* Fulbright Scholar, 1959; Eli Lilly International Fellowship, 1973; Bargen Award for Gastroenterology, Mayo Clinic, 1976. *Hobbies:* Tennis; Cooking. *Address:* Department of Internal Medicine II & Hepatogastroenterology, University Hospital Dijkzigt, Dr Molewaterplein 40, 3015 GD Rotterdam, The Netherlands.

SCHAPER, Wolfgang, b. 11 Jan. 1934, Oschersleben, Federal Republic of Germany. Director, Head, Department of Experimental Cardiology. m. Jutta Pflaume, 1958, 2 sons, 1 daughter. *Education:* Martin-Luther University School of Medicine, Halle/Saale, 1952-57; Catholic University of Louvain, Belgium, 1965-67. *Appointments:* Intern 1958-59, Resident 1959-60, City Hospital of Magdeburg, Federal Republic of Germany; Research Associate 1960-63, Director 1963-72, Department of Cardiovascular Research, Janssen Pharmaceutica, Beerse, Belgium; Director, Head of Department of Experimental Cardiology, Max-Planck-Institute, Bad Nauheim, Federal Republic of Germant, 1972-. *Memberships:* German Physiological Society; German Pharmacological Society; German Cardiac Society; Council of Basic Sciences, Council of Circulation, American Heart Association. *Publications:* "The Colateral Circulation of the Heart", 1971; "The Pathophysiology of Myocardial Perfusion", 1979; 380 publications in journals; Chief Editor, Basic Research in Cardiology; Editorial board of 11 journals. *Honour:* Arthur-Weber-Price, German Cardiac Society, 1972. *Hobbies:* Sports. *Address:* Max-Planck-Institute, Department of Experimental Cardiology, Benekestrasse 2, D 6350 Bad Nauheim, Federal Republic of Germany.

SCHATTEN, Gerald Phillip, b. 1 Nov. 1949, New York, USA. Professor. m. Dr Heide Bloh, 15 Apr. 1977, Heidelberg. *Education:* AB, 1971, PhD, 1975, University of California, Berkeley; Rockefeller Postdoctoral Fellow, 1976, 1977; NIH Research Career Development Award, 1980-86. *Appointments:* Instructor, University of California, Berkeley, 1975; Assistant Professor, 1977-80, Associate Professor, 1981-85, Professor, 1986-, Florida State University. *Memberships:* American Society of Cell Biology; American Society for Developmental Biology; AAAS; Society for Study of Reproduction; American Society of Zoologists; British Society for Developmental Biology. *Publications:* Articles in professional journals. *Honours:* Guest Researcher, Cancer Centre, Heidelberg, 1977, 1984; UNESCO Professor, Palermo, 1984; Boehringer-Ingelheim-Fonds Professor, 1984. *Hobby:* Apiarist. *Address:* Department of Biological Science, Florida State University, Tallahassee, FL 32306, USA.

SCHAUMANN, Wolfgang, b. 20 Nov. 1926, Wiesbaden, Germany. Professor of Pharmacology. m. Dr Med Elisabeth Schaumann, 27 Aug. 1955, Innsbruck, Austria, 2 sons, 1 daughter. *Education:* MD 1952; Lecturer (Privatdozent) in Pharmacology, 1959; Professor of Pharmacology, 1965. *Appointments:* Head of Medical Research Department, Boehringer, Manneheim GmbH. *Memberships:* German Society of Pharmacology. *Publications:* Some 100 publications in various fields of pharmacology. *Hobbies:* Tennis; Recorder. *Address:* Mönchhofstrasse 58, D-6900 Heidelberg, Federal Republic of Germany.

SCHEIN, Philip Samuel, b. 10 May 1939, USA. Professor, Medicine & Pharmacology; Vice President, Clinical Research & Development, Smith, Kline & French Laboratories. m. Dorothy Rosenfeld, 17 May 1967, 1 son, 1 daughter. *Education:* AB, Rutgers University; MD, State University of New York. FRCP; FRCP (Gla-

sgow); FACP. *Appointments include:* Senior Investigator/Head, Clinical Pharmacology, National Cancer Institute; Professor, Medicine & Pharmacology, University of Pennsylvania; Scientific Director, Lombardi Cancer Research Centre, Georgetown University. *Memberships:* Past President, American Society of Clinical Oncology; American Association for Cancer Research; American Society of Clinical Investigation; Association of American Physicians; Royal Society of Medicine; American College of Physicians. *Publications include:* Books: "Medical Oncology: Basic Principles & Clinical Management of Cancer", 1985. Articles: 'Streptozotocin Diabetes: Correlation with Extent of Depression of Pancreatic Islet Nicotinamide Adenine Dinocleotide', (J Clin Invest, 1974); '5-Fluorouracil, Doxorubicin & Mitomycin (FAM) Combination Chemotherapy for Advanced Gastric Cancer' (Ann Int Med, 1980). *Honours:* Alpha Omega Alpha; Sigma Xi; Honorary Doctorate, National University, Argentina; Harvey W Wiley Medal, FDA. *Hobbies:* Music; Cycling. *Address:* Research & Development, Smith, Klein & French Laboratories, PO Box 7929, Philadelphia, PA 19101, USA.

SCHEJA, Johann Wolfgang, b. 1 Mar. 1940, Kattowitz, Upper Silesia. Head of Protein Labour & Plasma Fractionation Department. m. Wilhelmine Scheja MD, 23 Dec. 1965, 1 son, 1 daughter. *Education:* Master of Clinical Analytic, Master of Pharmacy, Medical School, Danzig, 1964 and Humboldt University, Berlin 1971; Qualified as II0 Specialist in clinical analysis, Medical School, Warsaw, 1974; DSc, Silesian Medical School, 1975. *Appointments:* Assistant, Institute of Drugs, 1964-67; Assistant, Institute of Occupational Medicine, 1967-74; Chief, Clinical Laboratory, Burns & Surgical Hospital, 1967-77; Senior Consultant, Clinical Chemistry Department, Institute of Pharmacodynamics & Medical Analytics, Silesian Medical School, 1974-77; Head, Protein Labour & Plasma Fractionation Department, Institute of Thrombosis & Transfusion Medicine, University of Düsseldorf, Federal Republic of Germant, 1977-. *Memberships:* Deutsche Gesellschaft für Klinische Chemie; Computer Club Deutschland. *Publications:* Some 60 publications in occupational medicine (polycyclic aromatic hydrocarbons), clinical chemistry (enzyme assay), blood products (factionation and purity control), haematology (haemoglobinopathie & thalassemias), therapeutic drug monitoring (determination of drugs and computer programming). *Honour:* Prize of Medicine, Warsaw, 1972. *Hobby:* Swimming. *Address:* Institute of Thrombosis & Transfusion Medicine, Universität Düsseldorf, Morrenstrasse 5, D-4000 Düsseldorf, Federal Republic of Germany.

SCHELER, Werner, b. 12 Sep. 1923, Coburg, Democratic Republic of Germany. President, German Democratic Republic Academy of Sciences. m. Ingeborg Fischbach, 31 Dec. 1960, 3 daughters. *Education:* Dr med, Friedrich-Schiller University, Jena, 1951; Dr sc med, Humboldt University, Berlin, 1956. *Appointments:* Assistant, Senior Assistant, Humboldt University, 1951-54; Senior Assistant, Academy of Sciences, Institute of Medicine and Biology, 1954-59; Director of Institute of Pharmacology 1959-71, Rector 1966-70, University of Greifswald; Director, Academy of Sciences, Research Centre of Molecular Biology and Medicine,1 1971-79; President, Academy of Sciences of German Democratic Republic, 1979-. *Memberships:* Academy of Sciences of German Democratic Republic; Deutsche Akademie der Naturforscher Leopoldina; Foreign Member, Academies of Sciences of USSR, Czechoslovakia, Bulgaria and USSR Academy of Medical Sciences. *Publications:* "Grundlagen der Allgemeinen Pharmakologie", 1969 and 1980; Chief editor, Biomedica Niochimica Acta, 1958-. *Honours:* National prize for Science and Technology, 1970; Doctor of Medicine honoris causa, University of Vilnius, USSR, 1979; Doctor of Medicine honoris causa, University of Griefswald, 1981. *Address:* Lienhardweg 47, DDR 1170 Berlin, Democratic Republic of Germany.

SCEMAMA-ITTAH, Florence, b. 10 Mar. 1951, Tunis.

Allergologist. m. Alain Ittah, 6 Apr. 1978, Paris, France, 1 son, 1 daughter. *Education:* Studies of immunology & allergology, experimental cancerology. *Appoint:* Attache to Paris Hospitals. *Memberships:* European Association of Allergology. *Publications:* "Utilisation des theophyllines dans l'asthme", 1980; "Asthme professionnel", 1981. *Hobbies:* Sports. *Address:* 112 Boulevard de Courcelles, 75017 Paris, France.

SCHENK, Roy U, b. 18 Nov. 1929, Indiana, USA. President, Bioenergetics Incorporated. m. Martha Wathen, Indiana, USA, 7 sons, 3 daughters. *Education:* PhD, 1954, MS, 1953, Cornell University; BS, Purdue University, 1951. *Appointments:* Chemist, Northern Regional Research Laboratories; Associate Professor of Pharm (Bio-) Chemistry, University of Cincinnati, Cincinnati, Ohio; Senior Researcher, Bjorksten Research Foundation for Longevity Research. *Memberships:* American Chemical Society; Sigma Xi; American Academy of Forensic Sciences. *Publications:* "The Other Side of the Coin"; 4 patents; Contributor of over 30 articles to technical journals. *Honours:* Wisconsin Peace Prize, 1973. *Hobbies:* Hiking; Gardening; Biking; Reading. *Address:* 1129 Drake Street, Madison, WI 53715, USA.

SCHERL, Donald J, b. 1 Oct. 1935, New York, USA. Medical Centre President. *Education:* BA, Yale University, 1957; MD, Harvard University, 1961; Certified Psychiatrist, American Board of Psychiatry and Neurology; Licensed, Massachusetts, California and New York. *Appointments include:* Deputy Director of Health Affairs, Chief of Clinical Service, Office of Economic Opportunity, Washington, 1966-67; Director, Community Mental Health Service, Massachusetts Mental Health Centre, Harvard Medical School, 1967-71; Under Secretary, Human Services, Commonwealth of Massachusetts, Boston, 1971-75; Associate Professor of Psychiatry, Acting Chairman, Department of Psychiatry and Psychiatrist in Chief, Childrens Hospital Medical Center, Harvard Medical School, 1975-81; President, SUNY Health Science Center, Brooklyn, and Professor of Psychiatry, State University of New York, New York, 1981-. *Memberships:* Fellow: American College of Psychiatrists; New York Academy of Medicine; American Psychiatric Association (Committee Chairman). Member: Harvey Society of Rockefeller University; Hospital Society of New York. *Publications:* Co-Author: "Mental Health Technical Supplement, Job Corps Health Program Manual", 1967; "Overcoming Systems Barriers to Improved Mental Health Services", 1977; "Joint Study of Mental Health Services", 1978. Author or co-author of numerous book chapters and papers contributed to professional journals. Co-Editor, "Neighbourhood Psychiatry", 1977. Various committee reports. *Honours:* Sigma Xi, 1957; Phi Beta Kappa, 1956; Yale Club of New York Award, 1954; Summa cum laude, Yale, 1957; Diplomate, National Board of Medical Examiners. *Address:* Box 1, 450 Clarkson Avenue, Brooklyn, NY 11203, USA.

SCHERRER, Klaus Dominik, b. 10 Dec. 1931, Schaffhausen, Switzerland. Director of Research. m. Maria-Tereza Imaizumi, 3 May 1978, Schaffhausen, 1 daughter. *Education:* Graduate Chemical Engineer, 1956, Doctor of Scientific Technology, 1961, ETH, Zurich, Switzerland. *Appointments:* Assistant, Biochemistry Department, ETH, Zurich; Research Associate, Massachusetts General Hospital, Boston and Massachusetts Institute of Technology, Cambridge, Massachusetts, USA; In charge of Research project, Institute of Physico-Chemical Biology, French National Centre for Scientific Research, Paris, France; Head, Molecular Biology Department, ISREC, Swiss Institute for Experimental Cancer Research, Lausanne, Switzerland; Associate Professor, University of Paris; Master of Research and currently Director of Research, CNRS, French National Center for Scientific Research, Paris. *Memberships:* Union of Swiss Societies of Experimental Biology; French Society of Biochemistry; Society of Cell Biology of

France; International Society of Development Biologists; International Society of Differentiation; New York Academy of Sciences. *Publications:* Author of some 150 articles in major journals of molecular and cell biology including: 'Cascade Regulation' in "Eucaryotic Gene Regulation", 1980; 'A Unified Matrix Hypothesis' in "The Nuclear Matrix", 1986. *Hobbies:* Reading; Sailing; Swimming. *Address:* 9 rue Larrey, F-75005 Paris, France.

SCHERRMANN, Jean-Michel Georges Louis, b. 1 June 1948, Sarre-Union, Bas-Rhin, France. Associate Professor; Biologist. m. Marie-Christine Coulomb, 9 Oct. 1976, Soreze, Tarn, France, 2 daughters. *Education:* Pharmacist, School of Pharmacy, Paris, France, 1973; Diplomas in Analytical Chemistry, 1974, Nuclear Medicine and Pharmacy, 1975, Organic Chemistry, 1979; PhD, 1978. *Appointments:* Assistant Professor, Analytical Chemistry, School of Pharmacy, Paris, France, 1975; Assistant Biologist, Fernand Widal Hospital, Paris, 1975; Associate Professor, School of Pharmacy, Paris, 1980; Biologist, Fernand Widal Hospital, 1980; Research Member, National Institute of Medical Research, Department of Experimental Toxicology-, Head of Immunotherapy Group-. *Memberships:* French Pharmacologists Association; French Nuclear Medicine Association; Clinical Ligand Assay Society. *Publications:* Contributions to "Cannabinoid Analysis" 1979; Contributions in "Toxicological Aspects", 1980. 50 publications in 'Clinical Chemistry', 'Toxicology', 'Pharmacokinetics' and 'Nuclear Pharmacy' 1975-85. *Honours:* First Prize, School of Pharmacy, Paris, 1974; Henri Moisson Prize, 1974; First Prize Chemical and Physical Thesis, 1979. *Hobbies:* Painting; Tennis. *Address:* Experimental Toxicology Department, Institut National de le Recherche Medicale, Hôpital Fernand Widal, 200 Rue du Faubourg Saint-Denis, 75475 Paris Cedex 10, France.

SCHEUER, Peter Joseph, b. 15 Nov. 1928, Hamburg. Professor of Histopathology, Royal Free Hospital School of Medicine, University of London. m. Dr Louise Withington, 12 Mar. 1960, London, 2 sons. *Education:* MB, BS, Honours, Royal Free Hospital School of Medicine, 1949-54; British Postgraduate Medical Federation Travelling Fellow, 1962-63, Mount Sinai Hospital, New York; DSc (Med), MD, FRC Path. *Appointments:* House Surgeon, Physician Posts in London and Newfoundland, 1954-55; Officer, Royal Army Medical Corps, Far East, 1955-57; Pathologist, Royal Free Hospital, 1958-, Senior House Officer, Reader 1970, Professor, Clinical Histopathology, 1975, Head of Department, 1983-; Administrator, Electron Microscopy Unit, Royal Free Hospital School of Medicine; Sub-Dean for Admissions, 1978-82. *Memberships:* British Medical Association; British Society of Gastroenterology; Association of Clinical Pathologists; European Association for the Study of the Liver, excommittee member; International Academy of Pathology; International Association for the Study of Liver; British Association for the Study of the Liver, ex Committee Member; American Association for the Study of Liver Diseases; Pathological Society. *Publications:* "Liver Biopsy Interpretation", 1968, 3rd edition 1980, Spanish & Japanese translations; "Pathology of the Liver", joint editor; many papers in professional journals; Editorial or Advisory Boards of various journals. *Hobbies:* Playing the Cello; Fellwalking. *Address:* Dept. of Histopathology, Royal Free Hospital, Pond Street, London NW3 2QG, England.

SCHICK, Harry Benjamin, b. 27 Dec. 1952, Elizabeth, New Jersey, USA. Chiropractor. m. Kellee Irene Dederick, 22 Feb. 1981, Union, New Jersey, 2 daughters. *Education:* BA Psychology, Rutgers University; DC, Western States Chiropractic College. *Appointments:* Consultant, New Jersey Association for Children With Learning Disabilities; Guidance Counselor, Township of East Brunswick; Director, Tall Pines Chiropractic Center. *Memberships:* American Chiropractic Association; National Academy of Research Biochemists; New Jersey State Chiropractic Society. *Pub-*

lications: "Nonstructured Environments for Learning Disables Children", 1972; 'The Social Programming of the Handicapped'. *Honour:* Diplomate, National Board of Chiropractic Examiners, 1980. *Hobbies:* Baseball; Running; Guitar; Philosophy; Reading. *Address:* 15 Cedar Grove Lane Suite 1, Somerset, NJ 08873, USA.

SCHIFFER, Irvine, b. 8 Feb. 1917, Toronto, Canada. Retired Professor, Psychoanalyst. m. Ellen Elizabeth Morgan, 22 Apr. 1949, Waltham, 2 sons, 2 daughters. *Education:* MD, University of Toronto, 1941; Fellow, Montreal Neurological Institute; Graduate, Boston Psychoanalytic Institute. *Appointments:* Director, Toronto Institute of Psychoanalysis; Professor, Psychoanalysis, University of Toronto; Associate Professor, Psychiatry, University of Toronto. *Memberships:* Canadian, American, International Psychoanalytic Associations; Canadian Medical Association; etc. *Publications:* "Charisma", 1973; "The Trauma of Time", 1978. *Honours:* African & Italian Stars, World War II. *Hobbies:* Music; TV Performer, Canadian TV series. *Address:* 40 Delisle Ave, Toronto M4V ØS6, Canada.

SCHILDBERG, Friedrich-Wilhelm, b. 6 Mar. 1934, Essen, Germany. Director of Surgical Clinic, University of Lübeck. m. Christa Denz, 21 Oct. 1967, Freiburg, 2 sons. *Education:* Abitur, 1954; State exams, Freiburg in Breisgau, 1960; Graduation, Freiburg in Breisgau, 1962; Habilitation, Cologne, 1972. *Appointments:* Pathology Institute, Munich-Schwabing Hospital, 1961-62; Physiology Institute, University of Freiburg, 1962-64; Surgical University Clinic, Cologne, 1964-73; Surgical University Clinic, Munich, 1973-78; Surgical University Clinic, Lübeck, 1978-. *Memberships:* Society of German Natural Scientists and Doctors; Association of Bavarian Surgeons, Munich; Medical Society of Lübeck; German Society for Surgery, Munich; International Society of Surgery; German Society for Accident Treatment, Berlin; Berlin Surgical Society; Society for Advancement of Biomedical Research, Munich, etc. *Publications:* 154 scientific publications and 6 books including: Co-author, "Aktuelle Probleme des Colon und Rektumcarcinoms", 1977; Co-author, "Atemstorungen beim Polytrauma - praeklinische Aspekta", 1984; Co-author, "Chirurgische Intensivmedizin", 1985; Co-author, Volume VI/I "Die Eingriffe an der Brust und in der Brusthohle", 1986. *Address:* Klinik fur Chirurgie, Medizinische Universität Lübeck, Ratzeburger Allee 100, D-2400 Lübeck 1, Germany.

SCHIMELFENIG, Arthur C, b. 7 Apr. 1948, North Dakota, USA. Certified Psychologist/Neuropsychologist. 1 son. *Education:* BA, Psychology, 1972; MA, Educational Psychology, 1978; PhD, Educational Psychology, 1980; 2 year Post Doctoral Study Neuropsychology. *Appointments:* Mental Health Technician, 1971-73; Play Therapist, 1973; Counselor, 1974-75; Graduate Research Assistant, Graduate Teaching Assistant, Psychological Consultant, Arizona State University, Tempe, 1976-77; Teacher Therapist, Psychological Consultant, Graduate Teaching Associate, Arizona State University, 1978-79; Psychology Intern, Payson Mental Health Center, 1979-80; Psychologist, Jane Wayland Center, 1980; Psychologist Consultant, Albery Headache Clinic, 1981-82; Psychologist Consultant, The Meta Group, 1982; Psychologist Consultant, Deer Valley Unified School District, 1980-83; Psychologist, Private Practice, Phoenix, 1980-83; Director, Institute for Neurodevelopmental Training, Phoenix, 1983-. *Memberships:* American Society of Clinical Hypnosis; National Academy of Neuropsychologists; Council for the National Register of Health Service Providers in Psychology. *Publications:* Manuscripts; Papers presented at professional meetings. *Hobbies:* Playing Guitar; Dance; Judo. *Address:* 926 E McDowell, Suite 21, Phoenix, AZ 85006, USA.

SCHIMMELBUSCH, Werner Helmut Joachim, b. 16 Nov. 1937, Austria. Clinical Professor of Psychiatry. m. Jeanette Ramona Dyal, 26 Mar. 1971, Seattle, Washington, USA, 1 son, 1 daughter. *Education:* MD, University of Washington, 1962; Psychiatric training, Yale University, 1965-68; Graduate, Seattle Psychoanalytic Institute, 1976; Board Certification, Psychoanalysis, 1980. *Appointments include:* Instructor, Clinical Assistant/Associate Professor, Clinical Professor, Department of Psychiatry, University of Washington, 1968-; President, Seattle Psychoanalytic Society, 1977-80; Head, Psychopathology Division, Seattle Psychoanalytic Institute, 1976-; Trustee, ibid, 1976-79; President, Faculty Organisation, Psychoanalytical Association of Seattle, 1985-. *Memberships:* American Medical, Psychiatric, Psychoanalytic Associations; Center for Advanced Psychoanalytic Studies. *Publications include:* Co-author, 'The Positive Correlation between Insulin Resistance & Duration of Hospitalization in Untreated Schizophrenia' (British Journal of Psychiatry, 1971). *Honours:* Memberships, National Mathematics, Pre-med, Medical Honorary Societies. *Hobbies:* Skiing; Travel; Horse riding; Hiking. *Address:* 1436 86th Avenue, NE, Bellevue, WA 98004, USA.

SCHINDLER, Adolf Eduard, b. 7 June 1936, Asch, Germany. Professor, Obstetrics & Gynaecology. *Education:* Dr med, Frankfurt, 1962; ECFMG 1963; AmericanBoard, Obstetrics & Gynaecology, 1969; German Board, Obstetrics & Gynaecology, 1969; Privatdozent 1971; Associate Professor 1974; Professor 1979. *Appointments include:* Senior Ford Foundation Research Fellow, Seattle, USA, 1964-66; Resident, Obstetrics & Gynaecology, Southwestern Medical School, Dallas, Texas, 1966-69; University of Tübingen, Germany, 1969-71; Oberarzt, 1971-76, Geschäftsführender Oberarzt 1976-, University Women's Clinic, Tübingen. *Memberships include:* American College of Obstetrics & Gynaecology; American Fertility Society; International Menopause Society; International Society of Psychoneuroendocrinology; Deutsche Gesellschaft Gynäkologie & Geburtshilfe; Various other medical associations. *Publications include:* Over 300 scientific publications; "Hormones in Human Amniotic Fluid" (Monographs on Endocrinology, Berlin, 1982). *Honours:* Lynch Memorial Award, 1965; Frederik Purdue Award, 1967; Honorable Mention, Student American Medical Association, 1968; 3rd Prize, 1st Annual Meeting, District VII, Junior Fellow Division, American College of Obstetrics & Gynaecology, 1968; Vesalius Medal, City of Augsburg, 1978; Guest Professor, Greece 1971, Romania 1974, Republic of China 1981. *Hobbies:* Playing violin & trumpet; Skiing; Hiking. *Address:* Universitäts Frauenklinik, D-7400 Tübingen, Schleichstrasse 4, Federal Public of Germany.

SCHINDLER, Sepp, b. 14 Dec. 1922, Vienna, Austria. Head, Department of Psychology, University of Salzburg, Austria. m. Elfriede Onder, 28 Aug. 1964, Klagenfurt, Austria, 2 sons, 1 daughter. *Education:* Gymnasium, Vienna-Döbling, 1941; Dr phil, University of Vienna, Austria, 1949; University Professor, Salzburg University, 1969. *Appointments:* Child Psychoanalyst, Institut für Eeziehungshilfe, Vienna; Founder and Head, Austrian Probation Service; Clinical Psychologist, Vienna; Professor, Institute of Psychology, Salzburg University-. *Memberships:* Österreiche Arbeitskreise für Tiefenpsychologie; Society for Prenatal Psychology, past president; International Society for Research on Aggression; International Society for Behavioural Development. *Publications:* "Juvenile Delinquency", 1963; "Aggressive Actions of Juveniles", 1964; "Birth Entering a New World", 1982; Joint editor "Pre and Prenatal Psychosomatosis", 1982; Joint editor "Ecology of Perinatal Time", 1983. *Honour:* Goldenes Ehrenzeichen der Republik Österreich", 1983. *Hobbies:* Cycling; Hiking. *Address:* Institut für Psychologie, Universität Salzburg, A-5020 Salzburg, Austria.

SCHLESSINGER, Nathan, b. 31 Oct. 1924, Ciechanow, Poland. Psychoanalyst/University Professor. m. Alice Wiley, 7 Sep. 1947, Cincinnati, Ohio, 4 sons, 1 daughter. *Education:* MD, College of Medicine, University of Cincinnati, 1949; Certificate, Institute for Psychoanalysis, Chicago, 1962. *Appointments:* Instructor, Billings Hospital, University of Chicago, 1954; Attending Physician, Michael Reese, 1957-; Faculty, Institute for Psychoanalysis, Chicago, 1964-; Training and Supervising Analyst, 1969-; Clinical Professor, University of Illinois, 1965-. *Memberships:* Alpha Omega Alpha; American Medical Associatoin; American Psychiatric Association; American Psychoanalytic Association. *Publications:* "A Developmental View of the Psychoanalytic Process: Follow-up Studies and Their Consequences" with F Robbins, 1983; Contributor of several chapters to "Freud: The Fusion of Science and Humanism" edited by J Gedo and G Pollock, 1976; Contributor of chapter in "Methods and Research in Psychotherapy" edited by L Gottschalk and A Auerbach, 1966; Number of scientific articles in journals. *Honours:* Fellow, American Psychiatric Association, 1976; Fleming Award for Teaching, Institute for Psychoanalysis, 1978. *Address:* 230 North Michigan Avenue, Chicago, IL 60601, USA.

SCHLICHTER, Jakub G, b. 10 Aug. 1912, Austria (now Poland). Emeritus Professor; Senior Attending Physician; Private Practitioner. m. Lois Newman, 3 Oct. 1965, Chicago, USA, 1 son. *Education:* BM 1938, Switzerland; MD 1940, Certified, Medicine, 1950, Recertified 1980; Certified, Cardiovascular Disease, 1953. *Appointments include:* Senior Attending Physician, Michael Reese Hospital, Chicago, 1969-, Weiss Memorial Hospital 1977-; Associate Professor 1952, Clinical Associate Professor of Medicine & Emeritus Professor 1980-, Northwestern Medical School, Northwestern University, Chicago; Various hospital appointments. *Memberships include:* Fellow, Council of Clinical Cardiology, American Heart Association; Fellow, American College of Physicians; Fellow, American College of Chest Physicians; New York Academy of Sciences; Emeritus Member, American Medical Association, Chicago & Illinois Medical Societies; Various other medical associations. *Publications include:* Lectures, presentations, research papers in professional journals. *Honours include:* Award, Northwestern Medical School, 25 years' teaching, 1977; Award, Michael Reese Hospital, 30 years' service, 1977; American Medical Association Physician Recognition Awards. *Hobby:* Photography. *Address:* 55 East Washington Street, Chicago, IL 60602, USA.

SCHMALZ, Gretchen Marie, b. 22 Jan. 1936, Minneapolis, Minnesota, USA. Professor and Associate Chairman, University Department of Occupational Therapy. *Education:* Valparaiso University, 1953-54; BS, University of Minnesota, 1954-57; Roosevelt University 1968; MA, University of Southern California, 1968-69, University of Houston, 1982-. *Appointments:* Staff Occupational Therapist, Cleveland City Hospital, 1957-58; Assistant Supervisor, Occupational Therapy, University of Illinois, Research and Education Hospital, 1958-61; Supervisor, Occupational Therapy, Hines VA Hospital, 1961-68; Assistant Professor, Department of Occupational Therapy, University of Alabama in Birmingham, 1969-73; Professor and Associate Chairman, Department of Occupational Therapy, The University of Texas School of Allied Health Sciences at Galveston, 1973-. *Memberships:* American Occupational Therapy Association; World Federation of Occupational Therapists; Texas Occupational Therapy Association; American Society of Allied Health Professions. *Honour:* Allied Health Traineeship Grant 1968-69. *Hobbies:* Music; Hiking; Birdwatching; Needlework. *Address:* Department of Occupational Therapy, School of Allied Health Sciences, The University of Texas Medical Branch, Galveston, TX 77550, USA.

SCHMEER, Arline Catherine, b. 14 Nov. 1929, Rochester, New York, USA. Director, Mercenene Cancer Research Institute. *Education:* BA, College of St Mary of the Springs, Columbus, Ohio, 1951; MS, University of Notre Dame, Indiana, 1961; PhD, Cellular & Molecular Biomedicine, University of Colorado, 1969. *Appointments include:* Chair, Biology, Ohio Dominican College; Senior Investigator, Marine Biological Laboratory, Woods Hole, Massachusetts, 1963-71; Director, St Thomas Institute/Tenured Professor of Biology, Ohio Dominical College, Columbus, Ohio, 1964-72; Consultant, National & International Medical Institutions; Director, Anticancer Agents of Marine Origin, AMC Cancer Research Centre & Hospital, Denver, Colorado, 1972-82. *Memberships:* American Society for Cell Biology; New York Academy of Sciences; Fellow, Royal Microscopical Society; Sigma Xi; American Chemical Society. *Publications:* Contributions to: 'Science'; 'Annals, New York Academy of Science'; 'International Journal of Cancer'; 'Journal of Cell Biology'; 'National Cancer Institute Monography No 31'; 'Life Sciences'; 'Cell & Tissue Kinetics'; etc. *Honours:* Fellowships &/or Scholarships from: National Cancer Institute; National Institutes of Science; National Science Foundation; Schmitt Foundation; German Government; Medical School, University of Colorado (teaching/research awards). President's Medal, University of Detroit; Honorary DSc; etc. *Hobby:* Photography. *Address:* Mercenene Cancer Research Institute, Hospital of St Raphael, New Haven, CT 06511, USA.

SCHMETZER, Alan David, b. 3 Sep. 1946, Louisville, Kentucky, USA. Assistant Professor, Psychiatry, Indiana University School of Medicine; Medical Director, Emergency Psychiatric Services, Midtown Mental Health Centre. m. Janet Lynn Royce, 25 Aug. 1968, LaGrange, Illinois, 2 daughters. *Education:* MD, Indiana University, 1972; FAPA; Diplomate, American Board of Psychiatry. *Appointments include:* Director, Psychiatric Clinics of Indiana, Inc, 1975-78; Founding Chairman, St Francis Hospital Centre, Beech Grove, Indiana, Department of Psychiatry, 1980-81; Attending Psychiatrist, Roudebush VA Medical Centre, 1982-84; Psychiatric Consultant, Fairbanks Hospital, Indianapolis, 1982-85. *Memberships:* Fellow, American Psychiatric Association; Treasurer, Indiana Psychiatric Society; World & American Medical Associations, & state & local affiliates; American Orthopsychiatric Association; American Academy of Clinical Psychiatry; American Association of Community Mental Health Centre Psychiatrists. *Publications include:* "Crisis Intervention", with Levy & Thoresen, videotape series, No 1, 'The Psychotic Assaultive Patient', No 2, 'The Suicidal Patient', 1981; "Rape Survival Resource Manual", with Stewart & Korbly-Shepard, 1983. *Honours:* Alpha Epsilon Delta Psi Chi, 1968; Certificate of appreciation, American Academy of Family Practice, 1976; Certificate of Merit, LaRue D Carter Memorial Hospital, 1975. *Hobbies:* Reading; Collecting (almost anything); Woodwork. *Address:* Crisis Intervention Unit, Midtown Mental Health Centre, 1001 W 10th Street, Indianapolis, IN 46202, USA.

SCHMIDHOFER, Ernst Siegfried, b. 8 Mar. 1911, Minneapolis, Minnesota, USA. Director, Cerebral Training Institute. m. Genevieve Reichert, 11 Nov. 1942, Waukegan, Illinois, 2 sons 2 daughters. *Education:* MD, University of Illinois College of Medicine, 1936. *Appointments:* Superintendent, State Hospital, Jamestown, North Dakota; Medical Director, Milwaukee County Asylum, Milwaukee, Wisconsin; Deputy Commissioner for Professional Standards and Services, Department of Mental Hygiene for the State of New York; Assistant Commissioner for Research and Program Development in the Division of Psychiatric Criminology, State of Ohio; Director of Professional Education and Training, Perkins State Hospital, Jessup, Maryland; Assistant Medical Director for Planning and Evaluation, Ancora Hospital, Hammonton, New Jersey. *Memberships:* Fellow, Southern Psychiatric Association; Fellow, American Association for the Advancement of Science; Life Fellow, American Psychiatric Association. *Publications:* "Cerebral Training: An Application of Clinical Neurophysiology" 1968; Monograph: "North Carolina's 1984 Plan For Education Has An Achilles Heel" 1984; More than 25 articles in scientific literature since 1946. *Honours:* Awarded honours by the Society of Sigma XI for work in Cerebral Training. *Hobbies:* Teaching; Self-defence; Disco dancing. *Address:* 2113 Forest Hills Drive §1057, Arlington, TX 76011, USA.

SCHMIDT, John Donald, b. 22 Mar. 1936, New York City, USA. Coordinator of Rehabilitation Medicine. m. Mary R. Beresford, 23 Oct. 1976, N Babylon, New York. *Education:* BA; MPA. *Appointments:* Administrator, Psychiatry, Bronx Lebanon Hospital Centre, New York City, 1974; Co-ordinator, Rehabilitation Medicine, North Central Bronx Hospital, 1977-80; Co-ordinator, Rehabilitation Medicine, New York Medical College Affiliation, New York Medical College, Coler Memorial Hospital, New York City, 1980-. *Memberships:* President, Association for Medical Rehabilitation Directors & Co-ordinators, 1985-86; American Hospital Association. *Hobby:* Philately. *Address:* Lakeview Drive, PO Box 405, Shen o Rock, NY 10587, USA.

SCHMIDT, Katalin, b. 14 Aug. 1930, Budapest, Hungary, Director of Paediatric Psychopharmacology, Clinical Assistant Professor of Psychiatry. m. George Schmidt, 29 June 1955, 2 sons. *Education:* MD, Budapest, Hungary, 1954; American Board of Psychiatry and Neurology, 1981. *Appointments:* Attending Physician, National Rehabilitation Centre, Budapest, Hungary, 1954-56; Attending Physician, Mental Hospital, Haifa, Israel, 1957-59; Post doctoral Research Fellow, Neonatal Psychophys, 1967-70; Clinical Instructor, Psychiatry, 1970-72; Resident in Psychiatry, Co-Investigator in Psychophys Research, 1972-77; Child Psychiatry Fellow, 1977-79; Director, Pediatric Psychopharmacology, Albert Einstein College of Medicine, NY, USA, 1980-. *Memberships:* Member, American Psychiatric Association, 1982; Fellow, Royal Society for the Promotion of Health, 1971. *Publications:* 'Effect of heartbeat sound on the cardiac and behavioral responsiveness to tactual stimulation in sleeping pretern infants', 1980; 'The effect of stimulant medication in childhood-onset pervasive development disorder', 1982; 'The effect of stimulant medication on academic performance in the context of multimodal treatment, in attention deficit disorder with hyperactivity', 1984; 'Electrodermal activity of undersocialized aggressive children', 1985. *Honours:* Sandoz Award of Excellence in Psychiatry, 1978. *Hobby:* Chess. *Address:* Albert Einstein College of Medicine, 1300 Morris Park Avenue, Bronx, NY 10461, USA.

SCHMIDT-NIELSEN, Knut, b. 24 Sep. 1915, Trondheim, Norway. James B Duke Professor of Physiology, Duke University, USA. *Education:* University of Oslo, 1933-37; Mag Sci, 1941, Dr Phil 1946, University of Copenhagen, Denmark; Dr Med hc, University of Lund, Sweden, 1985. *Appointments:* Research Associate, Swarthmore College, 1946-48; Research Associate, Stanford University, USA, 1948-49; Docent, University of Oslo, Norway, 1947-49; Assistant Professor, College of Medicine, University of Cincinnati, USA, 1949-52; Professor of Physiology, 1952-63, James B Duke Professor of Physiology, 1963-, Department of Zoology, Duke University; Professor of Physiology, Department of Physiology, Duke Medical Centre, 1980-. *Memberships:* American Physiological Society; President, International Union of Physiological Sciences, 1980-; American Society of Zoologists; Society of Experimental Biology; Sigma Xi; The Physiological Society, United Kingdom; The Royal Society, London. *Publications:* "Animal Physiology", 1975, 3rd Edition, 1983; 'Desert Animals. Physiological problems of heat and water', 1964;

'How Animals Work', 1972; 'Scaling. Why is Animal Size so Important?', 1984. *Honours:* Poteat Award, North Carolina Academy of Sciences, 1957; Brody Memorial Lecturer, University of Missouri, 1962; Honorary Member, Harvey Society Lecturer, 1962; Regents Lecturer, University of California at Davis, 1963; Elected, National Academy of Sciences, 1963; NIH Research Career Award, 1964-; Hans Gadow Lecturer, University of Cambridge, 1971; Visiting Agassiz Professor, Harvard University, 1972; Elected, Royal Norwegian Society of Arts and Sciences, 1973; Elected, Royal Danish Academy, 1975; Visiting Professor, University of Nairobi, 1977; Foreign Associated Elected, Academie des Sciences, France, 1978; Elected Norwegian Academy of Science, 1979; American Academy of Arts and Sciences, 1963; Elected Associated Member, The Physiological Society, United Kingdom, 1983; Foreign Member, Elected, The Royal Society, London, 1985; Honorary Doctor of Medicine, University of Lund, Sweden, 1985. *Address:* Department of Zoology, Duke University, Durham, NC 27706, USA.

SCHMITT, Laura Marie, b. 6 Apr. 1958, Bath, Maine, USA. Dentist. m. Steven Barry Schwartzberg, 4 Sep., 1983, Columbia University. *Education:* BS cum laude, St John's University, New York, 1979; DDS, New York University, 1983. *Appointments:* Junior Associate, Corona Dental Care, New York, 1983-84; Senior Partner, Jackson Heights, New York, 1985. *Memberships:* Academy of General Dentistry; American Dental Association; New York State Dental Society; Queens County Dental Society; American Medical Association Auxiliary; New York University College of Dentistry Alumni Association. *Honours:* New York State Regents Scholarship, 1975-79; St John's University Scholastic Excellence Scholarship, 1975-79. *Hobbies:* Skiing; Painting; Poetry; Ballooning; Swimming; Playing piano; Travel. *Address:* 185-03 80th Road, Jamaica Estates, NY 11432, USA.

SCHNAAS, Francisco Javier, b. 9 Jan. 1947, Mexico City, University Professor. m. Lilia M Groues, 25 Jan. 1969, Mexico City, 1 son, 1 daughter. *Education:* BSc, Colegio Aleman AC, 1964; MD, School of Medicine, National University of Mexico, 1971; Psychiatrist, The Johns Hopkins Hospital, 1976; Psychoanalyst, Mexican Psychoanalytical Association, 1982. *Appointments:* Chief Resident in Psychiatry, The Johns Hopkins Hospita, 1975-76; Director, Treatment and Rehabilitation Programs, National Institute of Drug Abuse, 1976; Consultant, Private National Television Network, 1983-. *Memberships:* Mexican Society for Neurology and Psychiatry; American Psychiatric Association; International Psychoanalytic Association; American Association for the Advancement of Science; The Johns Hopkins Medical and Surgical Association. *Publications:* 'Contemporary Marriage and Divorce' Cuader. Ps An Mexico, 1979; 'Family Constellation and Development of Identity' Mexico, 1982. *Honours:* Cum Laude, 1971, National University of Mexico; American Board of Psychiatry and Neurology, 1976. *Hobbies:* Cross-country riding; Wind-surfing; Fox and staghunting. *Address:* Homero 527-202, Mexico DF 11560, Mexico.

SCHNEIDER, Dennis Charles, b. 23 Nov. 1945, Grosse Pointe, Michigan, USA. University Professor. m. Sharon L. Harris, 17 Feb. 1976, Monterey, California, USA, 1 son, 2 daughters. *Education:* BS, Wayne State University, USA, 1968; MS, University of California, 1976; PhD, 1982. *Appointments:* Research Associate, Wayne State University, USA, 1964-67; Staff Engineer, Automobile Manufacturers Association 1967-68; Associate Senior Research Engineer, General Motors Research Laboratories, 1968-80, Engineering Analysis Consultant, 1980-82; Assistant Adjunct Professor, University of California, 1983-present. *Memberships:* Society of Automotive Engineers; American Association of Automotive Medicine. *Publications:* 21 scientific articles, theses and conference presentations; chapters in: "Human Impact Response", 1973; "4th International Symposium on Plastic and Reconstructive Surgery of the Head and Neck", 1984; "Biomechanics of Trauma", 1984. *Address:* 8758 La Jolla Scenic Drive North, La Jolla, CA 92037, USA.

SCHNEIDER, Jean-Gabriel, b. 5 Jan. 1936, France. Doctor of Dental Surgery. m. 4 July 1970, Cahtenois, 1 son, 1 daughter. *Education:* Doctor in Dental Surgery. *Appointments:* Member, Department Council, 1972, Member, Regional Council, 1972, Order of Dental Surgeons of France; Regional Delegate, UFSBD, French Union of Dental and Oral Health, 1975; Department Treasurer, Syndicate of Dental Surgeons of the Haut-Rhin, 1978; Vice President, Ondonto-Stomatological Society, 1982; Member, Council of Administration, UFSBD, French Union of Dental and Oral Health, 1984. *Honours:* Chevalier, Award of Rank, French National Order of Merit, 1983. *Hobbies:* Mathematics; Chess. *Address:* 18 Grand'rue, F-68720 Zillisheim, France.

SCHNEIDERMAN, Mark I, b. 22 May 1951, Bronx, New York, USA. Self employed, All County Chiropractic Centre. m. Joan Merskey, 24 Dec. 1972, NJ, USA, 2 daughters. *Education:* BA, Long Island University; DC, New York Chiropractic College, NY. *Appointments:* Vice President, Chiropractic Society of Hunterdon County, 1984-85. *Memberships:* New Jersey Chiropractic Society; American Chiropractic Society; Council on Nutrition; Council on Roentgenology; Council on Sports. *Honours:* Outstanding Young Men of America, 1980; Phi Chi Omega; Deans List for Academic Excellence. *Hobbies:* Tennis; Running. *Address:* All County Chiropractic Centre, 77 Church Street, Flemington, NJ 08822, USA.

SCHNEIDERMAN, William L, b. 19 June 1944, Brooklyn, New York, USA. Obstetrician & Gynaecologist. m. Michele H Weiss, 1972, Long Island, New York, 2 sons. *Education:* BA, Franklin Marshall College, Pennsylvania; MD, New York Medical College. *Appointments include:* Clinical Instructor, University of Connecticut, 1977-78; Permanent Medical Group, Santa Clara, California, 1978-. *Memberships:* American Medical Association; American College of Obstetricians & Gynaecologists; Schufelt Gynaecologic Society. *Honours:* All-American, 1965-66; Past Treasurer & President, Porter Scientific Society. *Hobbies:* Swimming; Gardening. *Address:* 1068 Queensbridge Court, San Jose, CA 95120, USA.

SCHNELL, Richard Dale, b. 17 Feb. 1930, Edgeley, North Dakota, USA. Mental Health Doctor. m. Nancy Lee Tompkins, 19 June 1965, Anaheim, California, USA, 2 sons. *Education:* BS Education, 1952; MS Zoology, 1957; MD Medicine, 1961. *Appointments:* Superintendent of Elementary Schools, West Fargo, North Dakota; Instructor of Anatomy & Physiology, North Dakota State University; Assistant Director, State Easter Seal Camp, Wisconsin; Director, Day Treatment Centre, USC Metropolitan Hospital, Norwalk, California; Chief, Aftercare Facility, Assistant Superintendent, USC Metropolitan Hospital, Norwalk; Medical Director, Chief, Rio Hondo Community Mental Health Centre, Cerritos, California. *Memberships:* Kappa Delta Pi Honour Society in Education; American Medical Association; California Medical Association; American Psychiatric Association; California Psychiatric Association; Los Angeles County Mental Health Association; American Scientific Affiliation. *Publications:* "Embryological Studies of Air Sacs in Melopsittacus Undulatus", 1957; 'Postpartum Psychosis', 1958; 'Magnesium Sulphate in sudden Coronary Occlusion', 1959; 'Biophysical Correlates of levels of hypnosis', 1960; 'Studies of Suicide in Children & Adults', 1961; 'Suicide & the Mental Hospital', 1963; 'Some aspects of the Countertransference', 1964; 'The Therapeutic Community in

Day-Centres', 1965. *Hobbies:* Reading; Ornithology; Piano & Organ; Fishing; Skiing; Hiking. *Address:* Suite 290, Rio Hondo Community Mental Health Center, 17707 Studebaker Road, Cerritos, CA 90701, USA.

SCHÖCH, Gerhard Konrad, b. 31 Dec. 1936, Sarata. Professor of Paediatrics. m. Gesa Heller-Schöch, 18 Dec. 1970, Hamburg, 1 son, 1 daughter. *Education:* MD, 1967; Habilitation 1976; Professor of Paediatrics and Clinical Molecular Biology, 1981. *Appointments:* Max-Planck-Institute for Experimental Medicine, Göttingen, 1966-67; University of Ulm, 1968-69; Children's Hospital of University of Hamburg, 1970-81; Forschungsinstitut für Kinderernährung, Dortmund, 1981-. *Memberships:* Deutsche Gesellschaft für Ernährung (Board Member); Deutsche Gesellschaft für Kinderheilkunde (Committee on Nutrition); Deutsche Gesellschaft für Sozialpädiatrie (Scientific Advisory Board Member); European Society for Paediatric Research; New York Academy of Sciences. *Publications:* 'Molekularbiologie und klinische Bedeutung des Stoffwechsels normaler und modifizierter Nucleobasen' Helv. Paediatr. Act. Suppl 1977 with G Heller-Schöch. *Honours:* Adalbert Czerny-Preis, Deutsche Gesellschaft für Kinderheilkunde, 1977; Jürgen und Margarete Voss-Preis, Werner Otto-Stiftung Hamburg. *Address:* Forschungsinstitut für Kinderernährung, Heinstück 11, D-4600 Dortmund 50, Federal Republic of Germany.

SCHOENFELD, Myron Royal, b. 10 Nov. 1928, New York City, USA. Cardiologist. m. Gloria T Edis, 14 June 1959, New York City, 2 sons, 2 daughters. *Education:* BA, University College, New York University, 1948; MA, Cellular Physiology, Columbia University, 1949; MD, Chicago Medical School, 1953; Physiological Chemistry, University of Illinois, 1951-52; Internship, Kings County Hospital, Brooklyn, 1953-54; Residency, Kingsbridge VA Hospital, Bronx, 1954-55; 1958-59; Cardiology, Mt. Sinai Hospital, New York City, 1959-60; USAF School of Aviation Medicine, 1956. *Appointments:* Former Assistant Clinical Professor of Medicine, The Albert Einstein College of Medicine, New York City; Senior Partner, Schoenfeld-Edis Medical Associates, 1960-; Founder and President, Life-line Special Medical Services, 1977-; Hospital affiliations include: Attending Cardiologist, Lawrence Hospital, Bronxville; Courtesy Staff, Dobbs Ferry Hospital, NY; Special Staff Member, Department of Medicine, Cabrini Medical Center, NY; Attending Physician, Westchester County Medical Center; Assistant Attending Physician, St. Agnes Hospital, White Plains; Assistant Attending Cardiologist, White Plains Hospital Medical Center. *Memberships include:* Phi Beta Kappa; Fellow, American College of Physicians; Fellow, Westchester Academy of Medicine; Fellow, American College of Cardiology; Fellow, American College of Chest Physicians; Fellow, New York Cardiological Society; Fellow, American Association for the Advancement of Science. *Publications:* "Behind Closed Doors: How Doctors Make Decisions" (in preparation). Contributor to professional journals; Editor-in-Chief, 'Journal of Cardiovascular Ultrasonography'; Member of Editorial Board, 'Indian Journal of Medical Ultrasound'. Inventor of The Infusion Monitor. *Honours include:* Distinguished Alumnus Award, The Chicago Medical School, 1974; Finalist for Mitchell Prize, 1979. *Hobbies:* Goldsmithing; Writing Essays and Short Stories. *Address:* 2 Overhill Road, Suite 200-201, Scarsdale, NY 10583, USA.

SCHOKNECHT, Guenter, b. 10 Mar. 1930, Berlin, Germany. Director and Professor. m. Denita von Knobloch, 10 May 1967, Berlin, Germany. *Education:* Physics, Mathematics, Freie Universität, Berlin, Germany; Technische Universität, Berlin; Dipl Phys; Dr rer nat; Professor. *Appointments:* Fritz-Haber Institute of Max-Planck Society; Auguste Viktoria Hospital, Berlin; Bundesgesundheitsamt, Berlin; Institute for Social Medicine and Epidemiology, Medical Physics and Medical Technology Unit. *Memberships:*

Deutsche Gesellschaft für Medizinische Physik; Deutsche Physikalische Gesellschaft; Deutsche Röntgengesellschaft; Fachverband für Strahlenschutz. *Publications:* Various publications on Crystallography, Dosimetry, Computers in Medicine, Ultrasonics, Medical Physics, Epidemiology. *Hobbies:* Electronics; Photography. *Address:* Muehlenstrasse 5, D-1000 Berlin 37, Federal Republic of Germany.

SCHOKNECHT, Jean Donze, b. 31 Oct. 1943, Urbana, Illinois, USA. Associate Professor. *Education:* BS, 1965, MS, 1967, Biology, PhD, Botany & Zoology, University of Illinois. *Appointments:* Research & Teaching Assistant, 1965-72, Research Associate, 1972-73, University of Illinois; Visiting Assistant Professor, Electron Microscopist, Indiana State University, 1973-74; Assistant Professor, Life Sciences, Adjunct Assistant Professor, 1974-78, Indiana State University; Visiting Lecturer, University of Illinois Veterinary School, 1984; Associate Professor, Indiana State University, Affiliate Mycologist, Illinois Natural History Survey. *Memberships:* British Mycological Society; Mycological Society of America; Medical Mycology Society of the Americas; British Lichen Society; Electron Microscopy Society; American Microscopical Society; Botanical Society of America; Sigma Xi. *Publications:* "Biology and Taxonomy of Whetzelinia", 1972; "Scanning Electron Microscopy of the acellular slime molds. . .", 1972; Articles in professional journals. *Honours:* National Science Foundation Grant for Major Equipment, 1980; Outstanding Young Women of America Citation, 1979; Mathew Arnold Scholarship, 1961-63; University of Illinois Teaching and Research Assistantships. *Hobbies:* Photography; Biking; Hiking; International Platform Association. *Address:* Life Sciences Department, Indiana State University, Terre Haute, IN 47809, USA.

SCHÖPF, Josef, b. 2 Oct. 1945, Lans, Austria. Assistant at Division of Clinical Neurophysiology, Geneva Cantonal University Hospital. *Education:* Medical Studies, University of Innsbruck, Austria, 1963-70; Doctorate, ibid; Assistant, Institute of Pharmacology, University of Innsbruck (participation in research programme on protein metabolism & catecholamines of juxtamedulla cells), 1970-71; Clinical training, Hall Regional Hospital, Tyrol, 1971-72 (3 months surgery, 10 months internal medicine). *Appointments:* Assistant, Zürich University Psychiatric Clinic in Clinical Department (under Prof. K Ernst), 1972-74; Assistant at same clinic in Research Department (under Prof. J Angst), 1974-75; Assistant & Psychiatric Polyclinic, Zürich University Hospital, 1975-76; Assistant, Consultation Centre, Department of Clinical Psychology, University of Zürich, 1976-78; Assistant, Psychotherapy Unit, Hohenegg Psychiatric Clinic, Meilen, 1978-79; Deputy Clinical Director, Psychopathological Research Centre, Lausanne University Psychiatric Clinic, 1979-80, Clinical Director, 1980-84; Freudian Psychoanalyst, 1974-79; Assistant, Clinical Neurophysiology Centre, Geneva Cantonal Hospital, 1984-. *Membership:* Swiss Society of Biological Psychiatry. *Publications:* Author & co-author of some 35 articles in medical journals. *Address:* Hôpital de Cery, CH-1008 Prilly, Switzerland.

SCHRAMM, Lee Clyde, b. 20 July 1934, Portsmouth, Ohio, USA. Senior Regional Medical Associate. m. Linda Christine Schade, 29 Oct. 1964, St Paul, Minnesota, 2 sons, 1 daughter. *Education:* BS, Pharmacy, Ohio State University, 1957; MS, Pharmacognosy, 1959, PhD, Pharmacognosy, 1962, University of Connecticut. *Appointments:* Assistant Professor of Pharmacognosy, University of Minnesota, 1961-67; Associate Professor of Pharmacognosy, 1967-81, Head, Department of Pharmacognosy, 1968-81, University of Georgia; Regional Medical Associate, 1981-82, Senior Regional Medical Associate, 1982-, Smith Kline and French Laboratories. *Memberships:* American Society of Pharmacognosy; American Pharmaceutical Association; American Society of Microbiology; Georgia Pharmaceutical Association; Georgia Society of Hospital Pharmacists; German Society for

Medicinal Plant Research. *Publications:* Various scientific publications between 1957 and 1981. *Honours:* Kilmer Prize, American Pharmaceutical Association, 1957; Fellow, American Foundation for Pharmaceutical Education, 1959; Oersted Bronze Medallion, Royal Danish School of Pharmacy, 1973. *Hobbies:* Amateur radio; Model railroading. *Address:* 290 Kings Road, Athens, GA 30606, USA.

SCHRENK, Otto Jozsef Imre Pal von, b. 21 Apr. 1934, Budapest, Hungary. Dental Surgeon. m. Anne-Margreth Strömberg, 1 Aug. 1964, Stockholm, Sweden, 1 son, 2 daughters. *Education:* DDSC. *Memberships:* Dental Board of Victoria, Australia; Dental Board of Sweden. *Honour:* Honorary doctorate, Swedish Academy, Stockholm, 1973. *Hobby:* Squash. *Address:* 510 Kooyong Road, Caulfield South, Victoria 3162, Australia.

SCHREVEL, Joseph, b. 11 Dec. 1939, Bailleul, France. Professor, Cell Biology. m. Genevieve Debersee, 6 Sep. 1962, Lille, 3 daughters. *Education:* Dr of Natural Sciences, Lille University. *Appointments:* Assistant, Zoology, Lille University, 1960-68; Assistant Master, Lille University, 1968-69; Master of Conferences, 1969-72; Professor, 1972-, Poitiers University. *Memberships:* President, French Protozoology Association, 1984-87; Board Member, Societe Francaise de Microscopie Electronique; American Association for Advancement of Science, Washington, USA. *Publications:* Co-Editor, "Membrane glycoconjugates", 'Biologie Cellulaire', 1979; Co-author, "Cytochemistry of Cell glycoconjugates", 'Progr Histochem Cytochem', 1981; "Cell Motility & Microtubules", Film, co-author. *Honours:* Chevalier Palmes Academiques, 1979. *Hobbies:* Sky; Music. *Address:* Laboratoire de Biologie Cellulaire, U.A. CNRS No 290, 40 Avenue du Recteur Pineau, 86022 Poitiers, France.

SCHROEDER, Mathias J., b. 12 Oct. 1928, Ettelbruck, Luxemburg. Head, Odonto-Stomatology Department, Luxembourg Army. m. Charlotte Kerschen, 23 Oct. 1969, Luxembourg. *Education:* Medical School, Paris, France; Dental School, Bonn, Germany; Royal Dental Hospital, London, England; Medical School Hospitals, Clinics, Portland, Oregon, USA; Doctor, Dental Medicine; Diplomate, Oral-Maxillar Surgery. *Appointments:* Private Practice until 1975. *Memberships:* Dental Examination Board of Luxembourg; Medical Council of Luxembourg. *Publications:* "La Tumeur de Burkitt et ses rapports avec la Medecine Buccale", 'Revue Francaise d'Odonto-Stomatologie', 1969; "Tumeur de Burkitt", 'Pratique Odonto-Stomatologique', 1972. *Honours:* Officier de l'Ordre de Mérite Civil et Mérite et Militaire d'Adolphe de Nassau; Chevalier de l'Ordre de Mérite du Grand-Duché de Luxembourg; Appointed to the Court. *Hobbies:* Music; Philosophy; Animal Defense; Horse Riding; Golf; Hiking. *Address:* Head Section Odonto-Stomatologie, Service de Sante de l'Armee, Luxembourgeoise.

SCHROEDER, Steven A, b. 26 July 1939, New York, USA. Professor of Medicine. m. Sally Rose, 21 Oct. 1967, New York, 2 sons. *Education:* BA, Stanford University, 1960; MD, Harvard Medical School, 1964. *Appointments:* Intern & Resident, Harvard Medical Service, Boston City Hospital, 1964-66, 1968-69; Epidemic Intelligence Officer, Centre for Disease Control, Atlanta, Georgia, 1966-68; Fellow & Instructor in Medicine, Harvard Medical School, 1969-71; Assistant Professor, Associate Professor, Departments of Medicine & Health Care Sciences; Medical Director, George Washington University Health Plan, 1971-76; Professor of Medicine, Chief, Division of General Internal Medicine, Member, Institute for Health Policy Studies, University of California at San Francisco, 1976-; Visiting Professor, Department of Community Medicine, St Thomas's Medical School, London, England, 1982-83. *Memberships:* American College of Physicians; American Federation for Clinical Research; American Public Health Association; Society for Research & Education in Primary Care Internal

Medicine (President); Editorial Board, Annals of Internal Medicine. *Publications:* Over 80 articles in medical journals, in fields of the epidemiology of health services, medical economics, health manpower, use of technology. *Honours:* Member, US Prospective Payment Assessment Commission, 1983-; Alpha Omega Alpha, 1964; Phi Beta Kappa, 1960; Member, Institute of Medicine, National Academy of Sciences, 1982. *Hobbies:* Tennis; Travel; Rose Gardening; Reading History. *Address:* 400 Parnassus Avenue, A-405, San Francisco, CA 94143, USA.

SCHROEDER, Sydney Owen, b. 5 Feb. 1918, Beatrice, Nebraska, USA. Emeritus, Head of Mental Health Clinic, Student Health Service, University of Kansas. m. Margaret W Loomis, 30 July 1939, Wichita, Kansas, USA, 1 son, 3 daughters. *Education:* AB, University of Wichita, Kansas, 1938; MD, University of Kansas, Lawrence, Kansas, 1944. *Appointments:* Intern, Kansas City General Hospital, Kansas City, Missouri, USA, 1944-45; Captain, MC, AUS, 1945-46; General Practitioner of Medicine, Liberty, Missouri, USA, 1947-60; Preceptor in Medicine, University of Kansas School of Medicine, 1954-60; Preceptor in Medicine, University of Missouri School of Medicine, 1959-60; Fellow, Faculty, Menninger School of Psychiatry, 1965-83; Resident, Topeka State Hospital, Topeka, Kansas, 1960-63; Head, Mental Health Clinic, University of Kansas, Lawrence, Kansa, 1963-83. *Memberships:* Douglas County and Kansas Medical Society; Kansas Psychiatric Association; American Psychiatric Association; Mid-Continent Psychiatric Society. *Publications:* 'Psychosomatic Illness (Emotional Factors in Illness - Frequency in General Practice', 1964; 'Destructive Group Dynamics', 1966. *Honours:* President, Clay County Medical Society, Missouri, USA, 1955; President, Douglas County Medical Society, 1970; President-elect, Mid-Continent Psychiatric Society, 1985-86. *Hobbies:* Travel; Golf; Theatre. *Address:* 902 W 25th, Lawrence, KS 66046, USA.

SCHUBERT, Frederick, b. 23 May 1926, Brisbane, Australia. Senior Partner, large private radiology practice, Brisbane. m. Joan Margaret, 31 Oct. 1953, Brisbane, 2 sons, 4 daughters. *Education:* BSc 1947, MB, BS 1951, BA 1974, University of Queensland, Diploma 1956, Member 1957, Fellow 1969, Royal Australasian College of Radiologists; Fellow, Royal College of Radiologists, UK, 1969; Diploma, Diagnostic Ultrasound, Australian Society for Ultrasound in Medicine, 1980. *Appointments include:* Various positions, hospitals in Brisbane & Melbourne, 1951-83, hospitals in UK, 1970-71. Current positions include: Visiting Radiologist, Mater Misericordiae Public Hospitals (all sections), Brisbane, & Princess Alexandra Hospital, Brisbane; Honorary Consultant Radiologist, Mount Olivet Hospital for the Incurable Sick & Ill, Brisbane; Member, Medical Board (Chest Diseases), Queensland; Foundation Member, Radiological Services Advisory Committee, Queensland Department of Health; Representative, Queensland Branch, Royal Australasian College of Radiologists to Queensland Department of Health, on radiological appointments to government hospitals. *Memberships:* President 1985-86, numerous offices, 1959-, Royal Australasian College of Radiologists; Offices, Australian Medical Association; British Medical Association; Teaching faculty, University of Queensland, College of Nursing of Australia (Queensland branch). *Publications include:* Journal contributions, radiological subjects; Biography, Dr Valentine McDowell, for College Roll, Royal Australasian College of Physicians, 1985. *Honour:* Harold Plant Prize, University of Queensland, 1951. *Hobbies:* Reading; History; Philately; Music; Walking. *Address:* 27 Seventh Avenue, St Lucia 4067, Brisbane, Queensland, Australia.

SCHUBERT, William Kuenneth, b. 12 July 1926, Hamilton County, Ohio. University Professor/President and Chief Executive Officer, Children's Hospital Medical Center. m. Mary Jane Pamperin, 5 June 1948, 4 daughters. *Education:* BS, University of Cincinnati College of Liberal Arts, 1949; MD, University of Cincinnati College of Medicine, 1952; Internship, Indiana University Medical Center, Indianapolis, 1952-53; Residency, 1953-55, Fellow 1955-56, Children's Hospital Medical Center, Cincinnati. *Appointments:* Private practice of Pediatrics, Cincinnati, Ohio, 1956-63; Director, Clinical Research Center, Children's Hospital Medical Center, Cincinnati, 1963-76; Director, Division of Gastroenterology, Children's Hospital Medical Center, 1968-79; Professor of Pediatrics, University of Cincinnati, 1969-; Chief of Staff, Children's Hospital Medical Center, Cincinnati, 1972-; Chairman Department of Pediatrics, University of Cincinnati, 1979-; Director, Children's Hospital Research Foundation, 1979-; President and Chief Executive Officer, Children's Hospital Medical Center, Cincinnati, 1983-. *Memberships include:* American Medical Association; Diplomate, American Board of Pediatrics; Fellow, American Academy of Pediatrics; American Pediatric Society; Society of Pediatric Research; American Gastroenterological Association; American Association for the Study of Liver Disease. *Publications:* Contributor of numerous articles in medical journals and of chapters to edited volumes. *Honours:* Phi Beta Kappa; Alpha Omega Alpha. *Hobbies:* Reading; Tennis. *Address:* Children's Hospital Medical Center, Elland and Bethesda Avenue, Cincinnati, OH 45229, USA.

SCHUCKIT, Marc Allan, b. 5 Mar. 1944, Milwaukee, Wisconsin, USA. Professor of Psychiatry; Director, Alcohol Research Centre. m. Judith Schrinsky, 2 July 1967, Milwaukee, Wisconsin, 1 son, 1 daughter. *Education:* BSc, University of Wisconsin, USA, 1964; MD, Washington University Medical School, St Louis, Missouri, USA, 1968. *Appointments:* Director, Consultation-Liaison Psychiatric Service, San Diego Veterans Administration Medical Centre; Director, Alcohol and Drug Abuse Institute, University of Washington; Professor of Psychiatry, University of Washington; Professor of Psychiatry, University of California, San Diego Medical School-; Director, Alcohol Research Centre, San Diego Veterans Administration Medical Centre-. *Memberships:* American College of Neuropsychopharmacology; International Society for the Biological Research in Alcoholism; Research Society on Alcoholism; Behaviour Genetics Association; Psychiatric Research Society; Society of Biological Psychiatry; American College of Clinical Psychiatry. *Publications:* "Drug and Alcohol Abuse: A Clinical Guide to Diagnosis and Treatment" 1984; "Alcohol Patterns and Problems, Series in Psychosocial Epidemiology"; volume 5, 1985; Articles include 'Ethanol Induced Changes in Body Sway in Men at High Alcoholism Risk' in 'Archives of General Psychiatry', 1985; 'Studies of populations at High Risk for Alcoholism' in 'Psychiatric Developments', 1985. *Honours:* Hofheimer Award, American Psychiatric Association, 1972; San Diego's Black Thorn Award (Young Man of the Year), 1982. *Hobbies:* Squash Racquetball; Walking; Travel; Reading. *Address:* UCSD School of Medicine, Director, Alcohol Research Centre, Department of Psychiatry (116A), VA Medical Centre, 3350 La Jolla Village Drive, San Diego, CA 92161, USA.

SCHUFFEL, Wolfram Dieter, b. 18 Aug. 1938, Pirna, Saxony, Germany. m. The Hon Janet Edmund-Davies, 28 Feb. 1964, Heidelberg, Federal Republic of Germany, 1 son, 1 daughter. *Education:* Undergraduate Medical Training, Schools of Hamburg, Berlin, Heidelberg; MD, University of Heidelberg, 1965; Internist, Psychotherapist, Ulm Medical School, 1967-74; PhD, Ulm Medical School, 1975. *Appointments:* Physician, Department of Internal Medicine, University of Ulm, 1968; Lecturer in Internal Medicine, Psychosomatic Medicine, Ulm, 1975; Professor, Head of Division of Psychosomatic Medicine, University of Marburg, 1976-; Secretary, German College of Psychosomatic Medicine since Foundation in 1974; Chairman, Education Committee, International College of Psychosomatic Medicine, 1980-; Advisory Board, 'Journal of Psychosomatic Research'; 'Psychiatry in

General Hospitals'; 'Zeitschrift Allgemeinmedizin'. *Memberships:* German College of Psychsosmatic Medicine; German College of Internal Medicine; German College of Practitioners (Corresponding Member); International College of Psychosomatic Medicine. *Publications:* 'Can Medical Students acquire Patient-centred Attitudes at Medical Schools?', 1983; 'Sprechen mit Kranken - Student. Anamnesegruppen', 1983; ''Erkennen in der Medizin'', 1986. *Honour:* Corresponding Member, General Practitioners. *Hobbies:* Cross-country Skiing; Swimming. *Address:* Abteilung Psychosomatik, Zentrum Innere Medizin, BaldingerstraBe, D-3550 Marburg, Federal Republic of Germany.

SCHULLER, Diane Ethel, b. 27 Nov. 1943, New York, New York, USA. Director, Department of Paediatric Allergy, Immunology and Pulmonary Disease, Associate Clinical Professor of Paediatrics. *Education:* AB cum laude with honours Biology, Bryn Mawr College; MD, State University of New York, Downstate Medical College; Pediatric Residency, Roosevelt Hospital, Columbia University, New York City, 1970-72; Fellowship, Allergy and Immunology Cooke Institute, 1972-74; Certified, National Board of Medical Examiners 1971, American Board of Pediatrics 1975 and 1981, American Board of Allergy and Immunology. *Appointments include:* Associate, Department of Pediatrics 1974-78, Director, Department of Pediatric Cardiopulmonary, Allergic and Infectious Diseases 1979-84, Director, Department of Pediatric Allergy, Immunology and Pulmonary Disease 1985-, Geisinger Medical Center, Danville, Pennsylvania; Assistant 1975-81, Associate 1981-, Clinical Professor of Paediatrics, Pennsylvania State University, Milton S Hershey Medical College. *Memberships include:* Fellow, American Academy of Allergy and Immunology; Fellow, American College of Allergy; Fellow and Regional Director (Northeast), American Association for Clinical Immunology and Allergy; Fellow, American Academy of Pediatrics; American Medical Association; New York Academy of Sciences; American Association for the Advancement of Science; Association for the Care of Asthma; Board of Directors 1981-, Pennsylvania State Lung Association; Executive Committee 1983, American Lung Association of Pennsylvania. *Publications include:* 19 articles and 33 presentations including: 'Acute Urticaria with Streptococcal Infection', 1980; 'Prophylaxis of Otitis Media in Asthmatic Children', 1983; 'Adverse Effects of Brompheniramine on Pulmonary Function in a Subset of Asthmatic Children', 1983; 'Skin Tests at Cessation of Immunotherapy', 1985; 'Remission of Hereditary Angioedema at Puberty', 1985. *Hobbies:* Numismatics; Travel. *Address:* Geisinger Medical Center, Danville, PA 17821, USA.

SCHULMAN, André, b. 3 Dec. 1936, Berlin, Germany. Senior Specialist and Senior Lecturer, Radiology Department, Tygerberg Hospital and University of Stellenbosch. m. Dorthy Pead, 18 Sep., 1965, London, England, 1 son, 1 daughter. *Education:* MB (London); FRCR; MRCP (London); University College Hospital Medical School, London, Graduated 1961. *Appointments:* Senior Registrar, Leeds General Infirmary; Assistant Professor, Los Angeles County, University of Southern California Medical Center; Principal Specialist, Groote Schuur Hospital and University of Cape Town. *Publications:* 'Urinary Tract Dilation in Pregnancy', 'British Journal of Radiology', 1975; 'Lymphographic Anatomy of Thylothorax', 'British Journal of Radiology', 1951; 'Extrinsic stretching, narrowing and arterior indentation of rectorgmond junction', 'Clinical Radiology', 1979; 'Some causes and ramifications of pneumomediartiava', 'Clinical Radiology', 1982; 'Sonograph diagnosis of biliary ascariasis', American Journal of Roentology', 1982, and others. *Hobby:* Reading. *Address:* 5 Alster Avenue, Newlands, Cape Town 7700, South Africa.

SCHULMAN, Claude Charles, b. 30 Apr. 1943, Brussels. University Professor. m. Mireille Weinstein, 22 Aug. 1970, Brussels, 1 son, 1 daughter. *Education:*

MD; PhD. *Appointments:* Assistant 1968-72, Associate Chief 1972-76, Department of Urology, University of Brussels; Chief of Urology, University Clinics of Brussels, 1976-. *Memberships:* Member of 20 International Scientific Societies, all major International Urological Societies and Pediatric Urological Societies. *Publications:* 250 scientific papers approximately, among them several books like: ''Advances in Diagnostic Urology'' 1981; ''Urologie Pediatrique'' 1985. *Honour:* Alken Prize for scientific research in Urology. *Address:* Department of Urology - University Clinics of Brussels, 808 route de Lennik, 1070 Brussels, Belgium.

SCHULTZ, Robert Jordan, b. 29 June 1930, Brooklyn, New York, USA. Professor and Chairman, Department of Orthopaedic Surgery. m. Marcie, 13 July 1958, 1 daughter. *Education:* BS, Brooklyn College, 1952; MD, Chicago Medical School, 1957. *Appointments include:* Intern, Meadowbrook Hospital, 1957-58; Resident, Mount Sinai Hospital, 1958-59, Charity Hospital, 1959-62; Fellowship, Columbia Presby Medical Center, 1968; Various appointments and currently, Visiting Member, Department of History of Medicine, Albert Einstein College of Medicine; Professor and Chairman, Department of Orthopaedic Surgery, 1977-, Director, Sylvester J Carter Hand Service, 1980-, Director, Sports Medicine, New York Medical College. Attending Orthopaedic Surgeon: Metropolitan Hospital; Lincoln Hospital; Bird S Coler Hospital; Lenox Hill Hospital and others. Director Orthopaedic Surgery, Westchester County Medical Center, 1977-. *Memberships include:* Diplomate, American Board of Orthopaedic Surgery. Fellow: American Academy of Orthopaedic Surgeons; American College of Surgeons; American Society for Laser Medicine and Surgery; New York Academy of Medicine. President, New York Society for Surgery of the Hand; Honorary Member, Sociedad de Cirugia de la Mano del Caribe and Amicale International de Chirurgie de la Main. *Publications:* The Language of Fractures'', 1972, Author of 3 book chapters, numerous papers in professional journals, invited lectures and presentations. *Honours:* Emanuel Kaplan Award, Outstanding Paper in Anatomy, American Society for Surgery of the Hand, 1983; Various honorary positions in professional associations; Consultant and advisor to numerous community, national and international organisations. *Hobbies:* Skiing; Guitar. *Address:* Department of Orthopaedic Surgery, New York Medical College, Valhalla, NY 10595, USA.

SCHMAN, Daniel C, b. 13 Aug. 1941, New York, USA. Director of Psychiatry. *Education:* BS, City University of New York, USA, 1962; MD, Tufts University School of Medicine, Boston, 1966. *Appointments:* Internship in Mixed Medicine, Mount Zion Hospital, San Francisco, 1966-67; Residency Training in Psychiatry, Tufts Medical Centre, Boston, 1967-68, 1970-72; Psychiatrist, US Marines 2nd Division, 1968-70; Correctional Centre Rehabilitation Programme Psychiatrist, Naval Station, Boston, 1970-73; Private Practice, 1972-; Director of Psychiatry, Norfolk County Probate and Family Court, Dedham, Massachisetts, 1972-; Assistant Clinical Professor, Psychiatry Tufts Medical School, 1973; Lecturer in Psychiatry Harvard Medical School, 1974-77; Forensic Consultant, Department of Child Psychiatry, Tufts University School of Medicine, 1985-. *Memberships:* American Psychiatric Association; Fellow, American Orthopsychiatric Association; American Academy of Psychiatry and the Law; Massachusetts Psychiatric Society; New England Council for Child Psychiatry. *Publications:* ''Beyond the Best Interests of the Child'' (book review), 1974; Chapter: 'Psychodynamics of Custody Loss' in ''Children of Separation and Divorce'', 1981; 'Potential Complications in Adoption', in 'Med Asp Hum Sex', 1983; 'The Unreliability of Childrens' Expression of Preference in Domestic Relations Litigation: A Psychiatric Approach' in 'Mass Law Rev' 1984; 'False Accusations of Sexual Abuse', in Bulletin of American Academy of Psychiatry and the Law, 1986. *Honour:* Diplomate, American Board of Psychiatry and Neurology, 1973. *Hobbies:* Family Psychiatry and the Law. *Address:* 16

Harcourt Street, Boston, MA 02116, USA.

SCHWANGER, Michael Larry, b. 27 Mar. 1945, Toledo, Ohio, USA. Chiropractic Physician. m. Cheryl Dearth, 25 Sep. 1970, Toledo, 3 sons. *Education:* Doctor of Chiropractic, Palmer College of Chiropractic, Iowa, 1972; University of Michigan Medical School, 1982; Department of Postgraduate Medical Education and Orthopaedics, Loyola University of Chicago, 1982; Logan College of Chiropractic, St Louis, 1982; Medical Evaluation for Disability Claims, The Medical-Legal Involvement, University of Michigan Medical School Department of Postgraduate Medicine and Health Professions Education, 1982; John A Burns School of Medicine, University of Hawaii, 1983. *Appointments:* Faculty, Life Chiropractic College, Atlanta, Georgia, 1982, 83; Claims Examiner, Aetna Life and Casualty, Toledo, Ohio, 1984; Grand Rapids, Michigan, 1984; Columbus, Ohio, 1984; Reading, Pennsylvania, 1984; Green Bay, Wisconsin, 1984. *Memberships include:* National Association of Disability Evaluating Physicians, Charter Member, 1982; American Chiropractic Association; International Chiropractic Association; Michigan State Chiropractic Association; Foundation for Chiropractic Education and Research; American Public Health Association; Michigan Association of Public Health. *Publications:* Contributor to professional journals including: 'Ergonomics: A New Factor in the Evaluation of Disabilities' in 'Journal of Manipulative and Physiological Therapeutics, June 1983. *Address:* 6588 Secor Road, Lambertville, MI 48144, USA.

SCHWARTZ, Bernard, b. 12 Nov. 1927, Toronto, Canada. Professor and Chairman Department of Ophthalmology. *Education:* MD, University of Toronto, 1951; MS, 1953, PhD, 1959, University of Iowa. *Appointments:* Associate Professor, State University of New York, Downstate Medical Center, 1958-69; Professor of Ophthalmology and Chairman of Department of Ophthalmology, Tufts University School of Medicine. *Memberships:* American Academy of Ophthalmology; Fellow, American College of Surgeons; New York; Academy of Medicine; Societe Francaise d'Ophthalmologies; Association for Research in Vision and Ophthalmology; American Society for Clinical Pharmacology and Therapeutics. *Publications:* "Corticosteroids and the Eye"; "Decision Making in the Diagnosis and Therapy of the Glaucomas"; "Primary Open Angle Glaucoma". *Address:* Tufts - New England Medical Center, 171 Harrison Avenue, Boston, MA 02111, USA.

SCHWARTZ, Ceryl Ann, b. 4 Sep. 1949, Cincinnati, Ohio, USA. Women's Health Lecturer. *Education:* AS A, Business Administration, University of Cincinnati, 1972; Los Angeles College (Biology), 1977-79; California State University, (Cell and Molecular Biology) 1979-80; Pierce College, (Media) 1981-83. *Appointment:* Founder and Director of the International Toxic-Shock Syndrom Network. *Memberships:* Consultant, American Society for Testing and Materials; Consultant, Empire State Consumer Association; National Consumers League; Consultant, National Women's Health Network; California Womens Health Network; Women's Health International. *Publications:* Editor: "The Well Woman" (Toxic-Shock Newsletter) 1980-; "Jaw Surgery - How to Have a Comfortable and Creative Recovery" 1980. *Honour:* Commendation from Mayor Tom Bradley, Los Angeles, California, 1984. *Hobbies:* Polo; Private Pilot; Pistol Shooting; Swimming; Backgammon; Horseback Riding; Films; Reading. *Address:* PO Box 1248, Beverly Hills, CA 90213, USA.

SCHWARTZ, Gordon Francis, b. 29 Apr. 1935, Plainfield, New Jersey, USA. Professor of Surgery. m. Rochelle Gail DeG Krantz, 5 Sep. 1959, Philadelphia, Pennsylvania, 1 son, 1 daughter. *Education:* AB, Princeton University, 1956; MD, Harvard Medical School, 1960; Intern, Surgery, New York Hospital-Cornell Medical Center, 1960-61; Resident, Surgery, Columbia-Presbyterian Medical Center, 1963-68; Fel-

low in Cancer Control, University of Pennsylvania, 1968-69. *Appointments include:* Assistant in Surgery, 1966-68, Instructor, 1968, College of Physicians and Surgeons of Columbia University, New York; Associate, Surgery, University of Pennsylvania School of Medicine, 1968-70; Assistant Professor in Surgery, 1970-71, Associate Professor of Surgery, 1971-78, Professor of Surgery, 1978-, Director of Surgical Academic Programmes, 1970-80, Director of Clinical Services, Breast Diagnostic Center, 1973-, Jefferson Medical College, Philadelphia. Consulting Surgeon: Bryn Mawr Hospital, 1972-; Chestnut Hill Hospital, 1972; Wilmington Veterans Administration Center, Delaware, 1974-. *Memberships include:* American Association for Advancement of Science; Association for Academic Surgery; American Medical Association; New York Academy of Sciences; Fellow, American College of Surgeons; American Association of University Professors; American Society of Transplant Surgeons; Society of Surgical Oncology. *Publications:* Author or co-author over 101 papers contributed to professional publications including: "Yearbook of General Surgery", 1969; "Yearbook of Orthopaedic and Traumatic Surgery", 1974; "Women and Health", 1978; "Breast Disease", 1979; "Yearbook of Diagnostic Radiology", 1981; "Current Emergency Therapy", 1984. *Honours:* Phi Beta Kappa; Sigma Xi; Alpha Omega Kappa. *Hobbies:* Travel; Photography. *Address:* 1015 Chestnut Street, Suite 510, Philadelphia, PA 19107, USA.

SCHWARTZ, Michael Alan, b. 13 Dec. 1944, New York City, USA. Psychiatrist. m. Joan Clayton, 12 Jan. 1980, 1 son, 2 daughters. *Education:* AB, Princeton University, USA; MD, Cornell Medical College. *Appointments:* Clinical Associate, National Institute of Mental Health, 1972-74; New York Hospital, Cornell University Medical College, 1974-79. *Memberships:* American Psychiatric Association; Association for Academic Psychiatry; American Association of Directors of Psychiatric Residency Training. *Publications:* Co-Author "Science, Humanism and the Nature of Medical Practice: A Phenomeulogical View"; "Perspectives in Biology and Medicine", 1985. *Address:* 17 Crooked Mile Road, Westport, CT 06880, USA.

SCHWARTZ, Peter Edward, b. 28 Mar. 1941, New York City, USA. Professor, Obstetrics & Gynaecology. m. 13 Aug. 1966. *Education:* BS, Union College, Schenectady, New York, 1958; MD, Albert Einstein College of Medicine, Yeshiva University, 1966. *Appointments include:* Assistant Professor 1975-80, Associate Professor 1980-85, Professor, Obstetrics & Gynaecology 1985-, Yale University School of Medicine; Director, Gynaecologic Oncology, ibid, 1979-. *Memberships:* Fellow, American College of Obstetrics & Gynaecology; Felix Rutledge Society; Sigma Xi; Society of Gynaecologic Oncologists; American Society of Clinical Oncologists; New York Academy of Sciences; State & Local Medical Associations. *Publications include:* Numerous contributions to professional journals, reviews, book chapters, etc. *Honour:* Clinical Fellowship, American Cancer Society, 1973-74. *Address:* 1001 Pleasant Hill Road, Orange, CT 06477, USA.

SCHWARTZBERG, Steven Barry, b. 3 Oct. 1958, Brooklyn, New York, USA. Pediatric Resident. m. Laura M Schmitt, 4 Sep. 1983, New York. *Education:* BA, New York University College of Arts and Science, 1979; MD with honours in pharmacology, New York University School of Medicine, 1983. *Memberships:* American Academy of Pediatrics; Phi Beta Kappa; American Medical Association; New York State Medical Society; Queens County Medical Society; New York Academy of Science. *Publications:* 'The Organic Chemistry Problem Solver', 1978; 'The Biology Problem Solver', 1979; Abstract, Eleventh International Congress of Biochemistry, 1979; 'Prostaglandins Leukotrienes and Medicine', 1983. *Honours:* Founders Day Award, New York University, 1979; Honors Program Research Fellowship, 1979-83. *Hobbies:* Skiing; Travelling; Football; Water Skiing; Tenis.

Address: 185-03 80th Road, Jamaica Estates, NY 11432, USA.

SCHWARZ, Berthold Eric, b. 20 Oct. 1924, Jersey City, New Jersey, USA. Psychiatrist, private practice; Research, psi & ufology. m. 22 Jan. 1955, Minneapolis, 1 son, 1 daughter. *Education:* AB, Dartmouth College, New Hampshire; MD, New York University; MS, May0 Graduate School of Medicine; Diplomate, American Board of Psychiatry & Neurology; Certified, American Board of Electroencephalography. *Memberships:* Fellow, American Psychiatric Association; American Geriatrics Society; American Association for Advancement of Science; American Society for Psychical Research. Member, American Medical Association; International Psychosomatics Institute. *Publications:* 8 books, 98 professional articles. Books include: "Parent/Child Tensions", co-author, 1958; "Psychic-Dynamics", 1965; "The Jacques Romano Story", 1968; "Parent-Child Telepathy", 1971; "You Can Raise Decent Children", co-author, 1971; "Psychic Nexus: Psychic Phenomena in Psychiatry & Everyday Life", 1980; "UFO-Dynamics: Psychiatric & Psychic Dimensions of the UFO Syndrome", 1983. *Address:* 642 Azalea Lane, Vero Beach, FL 32963, USA.

SCHWARZ, M(erle) Roy, b. 30 July 1936, American Falls, Idaho, USA. Assistant Executive Vice-President, Medical Education & Science, American Medical Association. m. Thelma Constance Nygaard, 9 June 1957, Stanwood, 1 son, 1 daughter. *Education:* BA, Pacific Lutheran University; MD, University of Washington School of Medicine. *Appointments:* Instructor, 1963-64, Assistant Professor, 1965-68, Associate Professor, 1968-73, Biological Structure, Assistant Dean, Medicine, 1968-70, Professor, Biological Structure, 1973-79, Director, WAMI, 1970-79, Associate Dean, Academic Affairs, 1973-79, University of Washington School of Medicine; Dean, Professor, Anatomy, 1979-83, Vice Chancellor, Academic Affairs, 1983-84, University Colorado; Assistant Executive, Vice President, Medical Education & Science Policy, American Medical Association, 1984-. *Memberships:* American Association Advancement of Science; American Medical Association; Colorado & Denver Medical Associations; Alpha Omega Alpha; American Association of Anatomists; American Association of Immunologists; etc. *Publications:* Author, 138 articles & Abstracts. *Honours:* Outstanding Graduate, University of Washington School of Medicine; Alpha Omega Alpha, 1962; Alumnus of the Year, Pacific Lutheran University, Tacoma, 1969; Danforth Associate, 1971- etc. *Hobbies:* Fishing; Woodwork; Reading. *Address:* American Medical Association, 535 North Dearborn Street, Chicago, IL 60610, USA.

SCHWEMMLE, Konrad Erwin Hildebrand, b. 25 Dec. 1934, Erlangen, Germany. Professor of Surgery; Chief, Surgical Clinic, University of Giessen. m. Irmgard Opp, 17 Feb. 1961, Forchheim, 1 son, 2 daughters. *Education:* Abitur, 1953; Staatsexamen, 1959; MD. *Appointments:* Intern, Resident, Surgical Clinic, Bayreuth, 1961-67; Resident, Senior Resident, Surgical Clinic, University of Erlangen, 1967-76. *Memberships:* International Society of Surgery; International College of Surgeons; Deutsche Gesellschaft für Chirurgie. *Publications include:* "Allgemeinchirurgische Operationen am Hals", 1980; "Akutdiagnostik & Akuttherapie", editor, 1981; "Vascular Perfusion in Cancer Therapy", co-editor, 1983. *Hobbies:* History; Music. *Address:* Leihgestern, Finkenweg 30, D-6307 Linden, Federal Republic of Germany.

SCOLA, David A, b. 9 Sep. 1953, Philadelphia, Pennsylvania, USA. Staff Psychiatrist, Coatesville VA Medical Centre. m. Mariellyn Meehan, 19 June 1983, Philadelphia, 1 son, 4 daughters. *Education:* BS, St Joseph's College, 1975; MD, Temple University, 1980. *Appointments include:* Resident, Psychiatry, Thomas Jefferson University Hospital, 1980-84. *Memberships:* American Medical Association; American

Psychiatric Association; Pennsylvania Psychiatric Society. *Publications include:* 'The Hemispheric Specialization of the Human Brain & its Application to Psychoanalytic Principles' (Jefferson Journal of Psychiatry, 1984). *Honours:* Kenneth Appel Award, Philadelphia County Medical Society, 1984); Lieberman Award, Thomas Jefferson University Hospital, 1984; Menninger Award, Central Neuropsychiatric Association (nattional), 1984. *Hobbies:* Jogging; Swimming. *Address:* 179 Hughes Road, Gulph Mills, PA 19406, USA.

SCOTT, Anne Hiller, b. 10 Jan. 1946, New York City, USA. Assistant Professor, Occupational Therapy. m. Richard Scott, 19 Sep. 1976. *Education:* BA 1969, MA 1982, New York University; PhD in process. *Appointments:* Assistant Chief, Occupational Therapy, St Vincent's Hospital & Medical Centre, Department of Psychiatry, New York City, 1969-82; Assistant Professor, Occupational Therapy, College of Health Related Professions, State University of New York Downstate Medical Centre, 1982-. *Memberships:* World Federation of Occupational Therapy; American Occupational Therapy Association; American Association of Partial Hospitalisation; American Society of Allied Health Professionals. *Publications include:* 2 book chapters: 'Documentation & Research', with B Neuhaus, in "Physical Disabilities Manual", ed B Abreu, 1981; 'Present Resources as a Basis for Group Dynamics in Occupational Therapy', with M Ross, in "Group Practice in an Occupational Therapy Activity Group", ed M Ross & C B Slack, in press. Various articles in professional journals. *Hobbies:* Photography; Travel. *Address:* State University of New York, Downstate Medical Centre, Occupational Therapy Programme, Box 81, 450 Clarkson Avenue, Brooklyn, NY 11203, USA.

SCOTT, Byron C, b. 3 Nov. 1948, Mobile, Alabama, USA. Dentist. m. Sharon Marie Russell, 1 July 1978, Mobile, AL, 2 sons, 1 daughter. *Education:* BA, Samford University, DMD, University of Alabama, Birmingham, Alabama. *Memberships:* American Dental Association; American Academy of Implant Dentistry; Fellow & Master, Academy of General Dentistry; Fellow, International Congress of Oral Implantologists; Fellow, Academy of Implants & Transplants; Academy of Reconstructive & Cosmetic Dentistry; International Association of Orthodontics; International Analgaesia Society; Staff Member, University of South Alabama, Medical Centre; American Endodontic Society; Alumnus, L D Pankey Institute for Advanced Dental Studies; Staff, Mobile Surgical Center; Fellow, Academy of Dentistry International. *Honour:* Master, Academy of General Dentistry, 1985. *Address:* 4620 Springhill Avenue, Mobile, AL 36608, USA.

SCOTT, Gerald William, b. 12 Jan. 1931, London, England. Professor of Surgery. m. Beryl Elizabeth Hubbard, 14 May 1955, Kingsbury, London, 3 sons, 2 daughters. *Education:* MB, BS, London, 1955; MS (minn), Mayo Clinic & Graduate School of Medicine, USA, 1964. FRCS (C); FACS. *Appointments include:* Fellow, Surgery, Mayo Clinic, 1960-64; Teaching Fellow, University of Alberta, 1964-65; Associate Professor, University of Calgary, 1967-73; Professor of Surgery, University of Alberta, Canada, 1973-. *Memberships include:* Fellow: American College of Surgeons; Royal College of Physicians & Surgeons, Canada. Member: Western Surgical Association; Canadian Associations of Clinical Surgeons, General Surgeons; British Pharmacological Society; American Motility Society; Canadian Medical Association. *Publications include:* Research papers, 'Resistance to flow through the common bile duct in man', 1963; 'Flow through the bile duct after cholecystectomy', 1975; 'Flow through the canine sphincter of Oddi', 1975; 'Resistance & sphincter-like properties of the cystic duct', 1979; 'Biliary tract: anatomy & pathophysiology' (in "Scientific Foundations of Gastroenterology", ed. Sircus & Smith, 1980. *Honours:* Fulbright Scholarship, 1960; E Starr Judd Award, Mayo Foundation, 1964; Sir Peter Freyer Lecturer, University College, Galway, 1983. *Hobby:* Landscape painting. *Address:* Department of Surgery, University of Alberta, Edmonton, Alberta, Canada.

SCOTT, James Thomas, b. 10 Nov. 1926, London, England. Consultant Physician. m. Faith Margaret Smith, 26 Oct. 1956, Baltimore, USA, 3 sons. *Education:* MD, London; FRCP. *Appointments include:* Research Fellow, Johns Hopkins Hospital, Baltimore, USA, 1956-58; Senior Registrar, Royal Postgraduate Medical School & Canadian Red Cross Memorial Hospital, Taplow, 1958-61; Lecturer & Consultant Physician (Rheumatology), Royal Postgraduate Medical School, London, 1961-66; Consultant Physician, Charing Cross Hospital, London & Honorary Physician, Kennedy Institute of Rheumatology, London, 1966-. *Memberships include:* Association of Physicians of Great Britain; Former Secretary & President, Heberden Society; Council, British Society for Rheumatology; Former Chairman, Committee on Rheumatology, Royal College of Physicians; Honorary Physician (Rheumatology), Royal Navy; President, Rheumatology Section, Royal Society of Medicine; Executive Committee, Arthritis & Rheumatism Council. *Publications include:* Numerous papers, rheumatic diseases, gout. Editor, 5th & 6th editions, "Copeman's Textbook of the Rheumatic Diseases"; former editor, 'Annals of the Rheumatic Diseases'. *Honours:* Heberden Roundsman & Medallist, 1970; Van Breeman Orator & Medallist (Amsterdam), 1978; Visiting Professor, Mayo Clinic, USA, 1977, Dalhousie University, Nova Scotia, Canada 1983. *Hobbies:* Ancient Coins; Fishing. *Address:* 4 Northumberland Place, Petersham Road, Richmond-upon-Thames, Surrey, TW10 6TS, England.

SEAGREN, Stephen Linner, b. 13 Mar. 1941, USA. Associate Professor of Radiology and Medicine. m. Jill Garrie, 27 May 1976, Los Angeles, California, USA, 1 son. *Education:* AB, Harvard University, USA; MD, Northwestern University, USA. *Appointment:* Assistant Professor, University of California, San Diego, USA, 1977-84. *Memberships:* American College of Physicians; American Society of Clinical Oncology; American Society of Therapeutic Radiology and Oncology. *Publications:* 'Combined Therapy for Head and Neck Cancer' in 'International Journal of Radiology', 1983; 'Endubronchiac Irradiation' in 'Chest', 1985. *Honour:* Fellow, American College of Physicians, 1983. *Hobby:* Physical Fitness. *Address:* UCSD Medical Centre, 225 West Dickinson, San Diego, CA 52103, USA.

SEARLE, Jeffrey Wolstenholme, b. 12 Apr. 1943, Maryborough, Queensland, Australia. Hospital Senior Anatomical Pathologist. m. Marjorie Shackleton, 23 May 1966, Brisbane, 1 daughter. *Education:* BSc 1965, MBBS 1967, MD 1975, University of Queensland, 1961-67; Fellow, Royal College of Pathologists of Australasia. *Appointments:* Resident Medical Officer and Registrar 1968-71, Consultant Pathologist 1977-, Royal Brisbane Hospital; National Health and Medical Research Council Scholar, 1971-72; Lecturer 1972-74, Senior Lecturer 1976-77, Pathology Department, University of Queensland; Nuffield Commonwealth Travelling Fellow, 1975. *Memberships:* Australasian Society for Experimental Pathology; Australian Dermatopathology Society; Gastroenterological Society of Queensland. *Publications:* 'A suggested explanation for the paradoxically slow growth rate of basal-cell carcinomas that contain numerous mitotic figures', 1972; 'Necrosis and apoptosis: distinct modes of cell death with fundamentally different significance', 1982. *Hobbies:* Music; Reading; Driving. *Address:* Pathology Department, Royal Brisbane Hospital, Herston 4029, Australia.

SEARS, Victoria Conason, b. 3 Nov. 1929, USA. Medical Director, Chief of Section of Psychiatry and Neurology. m. Sam Wade Sears, 13 Feb. 1954, Geneva, Switzerland, 1 son. *Education:* BA, New York University Washington Square College; MD, University of Geneva Faculty of Medicine, Switzerland; Medical

Psychotherapy, New York School of Psychiatry, USA. *Appointments:* Rotating Internship, St Johns Episcopal Hospital, Brooklyn, New York; Staff Psychiatrist, Nassau County Family Court, Westbury, New York; Director of Treatment, Nassau County Department of Drug and Alcohol Abuse; Medical Director, Chief of Section of Psychiatry, Long Beach Memorial Hospital Mental Health Clinic. *Memberships:* American Psychiatric Association; Nassau Psychiatric Society; New York State Medical Society; Fellow, Nassau Academy of Medicine; Academy of Psychosomatic Medicine. *Publications:* "EKG in the Elderly", 1958; "Methadone Maintenance Program in a Suburban Community", 1970. *Honour:* Diplomate, ABPN-Psychiatry, 1975. *Hobbies:* Tennis; Skiing; Boating; Reading. *Address:* 17 Kings Place, Great Neck, NY 11024, USA.

SEBASTIAN, Peter, Founder and Hon Secretary, Institute of Sports Medicine. m. Pegitha Saunders, 27 May 1946, 2 sons. *Education:* BA; BCom; JP; FCP. *Memberships:* British Academy of Forensic Sciences; FSCA; MBIM. *Publications:* Numerous articles and Broadcasts. *Honour:* Stella Della Soliderieta Italiana. *Hobbies:* Foreign travel; Walking; Solving other people's problems. *Address:* Institute of Sports Medicine, c/o Faculty of Engineering and Science, The Polytechnic of Central London, 115 New Cavendish Street, London, W1M 8JS, England.

SECORD, David Cartwright, b. 6 June 1933, Canada. Professor of Surgery. m. Joan B Williamson, 6 Sep. 1957, Edmonton, 1 son, 3 daughters. *Education:* DVM, 1958, MVSc, University of Toronto; VS, Ontario Veterinary College, 1958; Fellow, Academy of Surgical Research, 1985. *Appointments:* Assistant Professor, 1961, Associate Professor, 1964, Professor, 1973-, Honorary Professor of Physical Education, 1984, University of Alberta. *Memberships:* Academy of Surgical Research; New York Academy of Sciences; Canadian Association of Laboratory Medicine; Alberta Veterinary Medical Association; American Association of Laboratory Animal Science; Canadian Association of Sports Medicine. *Publications:* 60 articles in professional journals. *Honours:* Veterinarian of the Year, Canadian Veterinary Medical Association, 1974; Quill Award, Best Publication, Canadian Physiotherapy Association, 1984; Veterinarian of the Year, Alberta Veterinary Medical Association, 1985. *Hobbies:* Camping; Hunting; Fishing; Writing Poetry. *Address:* Dept. of Surgery, University of Alberta, Edmonton, Alberta T6G 2N8, Canada.

SEDVALL, Carl Göran, b. 4 Jan. 1936, Professor of Psychiatry. m. Marie Billing, 1 son, 3 daughters. *Education:* MD; PhD. *Appointments:* NIH Postdoctoral Fellow, Laboratory Clinical Science, NIMH, Bethesda, Maryland, USA; Assistant Professor of Pharmacology, Associate Professor of Psychiatry, Associate Professor of Neuropsychopharmacology, Karolinska Institute, Stockholm, Sweden; Associate Professor and Head of Laboratory of Experimental Psychiatry, Professor of Psychiatry and Chairman of Department of Psychiatry and Psychology, Karolinska Hospital, Stockholm. *Memberships:* Scandinavian Society for Neuropsychopharmacology; Scandinavian Society for Biological Psychiatry; Foreign Corresponding Member, American College of Neuropsychopharmacology. *Address:* Department of Psychiatry and Psychology, Karolinska Institute, Karolinska Hospital, PO Box 60500, S-104 01 Stockholm, Sweden.

SEEBOHM, Paul Minor, b. 13 Jan. 1916, Cincinnati, Ohio, USA. Executive Associate Dean; Professor. m. Dorothy Jane Eberhart, 13 July 1942, Cleveland, Ohio, USA, 1 daughter. *Education:* BA, University of Cincinnati Liberal Arts College, 1938, MD, College of Medicine, 1941. *Appointments:* Internship, Wisconsin General Hospital, Madison, Wisconsin, 1941-42; Flight Surgeon, Major, USAAF, 1942-46; Resident, Internal Medicine, Cincinnati General Hospital, 1946-48; Fellow, R A Cooke Institute of Allergy, Roosevelt Hospital, New York City, 1948-49; Associate, Internal Medicine, University of Iowa College of Medicine, 1949-51; Assistant Professor, 1951-54, Associate Professor, 1954-59, Professor, 1959-; Director, Allergy Section, University of Iowa Hospital, 1949-70; Executive Associate Dean, University of Iowa College of Medicine, 1970-. *Memberships:* American Academy of Allergy and Immunology, President, 1966; Speciality Delegate to American Medical Association House of Delegates; Iowa Medical Society, President, 1979-80; Central Society for Clinical Research; Fellow, American College of Physicians; FDA Advisor, Panel on Allergenic Extracts, Chairman, 1974-84. *Publications:* 'Passive Transfer of Cold Urticaria' in 'Journal of Allergy', 1950; 'A Method for Measuring Nasal Resistance' in 'Journal of Allergy', 1958; 'Delayed Type Hypersensitivity to Alcohol' in 'Journal of Allergy', 1961; 'Primary Pulmonary Emphysema in Young Adults', in 'American Review of Respiratory Diseases', 1963; 'Nasal Airway Response to Exercise' in 'Journal of Allergy', 1968; Chapter 'Allergic and non-Allergic Rhinitis' in "Allergy: Principles and Practice", 1978. *Honours:* Alpha Omega Alpha', 1942; Distinguished Service Award, American Academy of Allergy, 1974, etc. *Hobbies:* Golf; Furniture Refinishing. *Address:* 1908 Glendale Road, Iowa City, IA 52240, USA.

SEGAL, Bernard Louis, b. 13 Feb. 1929, Montreal, Canada. Professor of Medicine, Director, Likoff Cardiovascular Institute. m. Idajane Fischman, 18 Feb. 1963, Philadelphia, USA. 1 daughter. *Education:* BSc 1950, Physiology 1951, MD CM 1955, McGill University, Montreal, Canada; Internship in Medicine, Jewish General Hospital, Montreal, 1955-56; Resident in Medicine, Johns Hopkins Division, Baltimore City Hospital, Baltimore, Maryland, USA, 1956-57, Harvard Medical School Service, Beth Israel Hospital, Boston, 1957-58. *Appointments:* Assistant in Medicine, Johns Hopkins Medical School, Baltimore, 1956-57; Teaching Fellow, Harvard Medical School, Boston, 1957-58, Georgetown Medical School Washington DC, 1958-59; Honorary Clinical Assistant, Department of Cardiology, St George's Hospital, London, England, 1959-60; Associate in Medicine, 1961-62, Assistant Professor of Medicine, Head of Auscultation Unit, 1962, Assistant Head of Cardiovascular Division, 1963-68, Associate Professor of Medicine, 1965-68, Clinical Associate Professor of Medicine, 1968-72, Professor of Medicine, Director, Postgraduate Education Division of Cardiology, 1973-75, Professor, Director of Services, Likoff Cardiovascular Institute, 1975-78, Professor, Director, Likoff Institute, 1978-, Hahnemann University Medical College & Hospital, Philadelphia. *Memberships:* American Medical Association; New York Academy of Sciences; Fellow, American Heart Association; Fellow, American College of Cardiology; Fellow, American College of Chest Physicians; Fellow, American College of Physicians; American Federation for Clinical Research; President, Hahnemann University Medical Staff; and others. *Publications:* Some 350 articles, papers and publications in medical journals. *Honours:* Various visiting professorships in USA & abroad. *Address:* Likoff Cardiovascular Institute, Broad & Vine Streets, Philadelphia, PA 19102, USA.

SEGHERS, Karel C.F.M., b. 1 June 1922, Buggenhout, Belgium. Surgeon; Medical Director, Imeldaziekenhuis, Bonheiden. 6 sons, 1 daughter. *Education:* MD, University of Leuven, Belgium, 1946; MD, State University of Groningen, The Netherlands, 1953; Degree of Tropical Medicine, Tropical Institute, Antwerp, Belgium, 1954. *Appointment: Professor of Surgery, Lovanium University, Kinshasa, Zaire, 1954-61.* *Memberships:* Fellow, American College of Chest Physicians; Member, Belgian Society of Surgery; Belgian Society of Tropical Medicine; Dutch Society of Thoracic Surgery. *Publication:* "Segmentresectie von de Long", 1953. *Hobbies:* Reading; Sports (Swimming, Skating, Skiing, Cycling). *Address:* Beukenlaan 9, 2830 Rijmenam, Belgium.

SEGUCHI, Harumichi, b. 19 Feb. 1940, Amagasaki,

Japan. Professor of Kochi Medical School. m. Toshiko Senoh, 7 Mar. 1965, 1 son, 2 daughters. *Education:* MD, Kobe University School of Medicine, 1965; License to Practice Medicine, No 189916, 1966; DMS, PhD, Kobe University School of Medicine, 1970. *Appointments:* Assistant, Kobe University, 1970; Lecturer, Basle University, Switzerland, 1971; Assistant Professor, Kobe University, 1974; Assistant Professor, Kyoto University, 1976; Professor of Kochi Medical School, 1979. *Memberships:* Council of Japanese Association of Anatomists; Council of Japanese Society of Histochem. Cytochem.; Director, Japanese Society for Electron Microsc.; Anatomische Gesellschaft; American Society of Cell Biology. *Publications:* "Anatomical Dictionary", 1984; "Histochemistry and Cytochemistry", 1985; "Ultracytochemical study of the stria vascularis of the Guinea Pig cocholea", 1985. *Hobbies:* Music; Golf. *Address:* B-202, 1823-1, Takasu, Kochi 780, Japan.

SEIFERT, Alvin Ronald, b. 22 Oct. 1941, Wheatland, Iowa, USA. Staff Psychologist, James A Haley Veterans Hospital, Tampa, Florida and Department of Neurology, College of Medicine, University of South Florida. *Education:* BA, Psychology, Iowa Wesleyan College, 1967; PhD, Physiological Psychology, University of Tennessee, 1975. *Appointments:* James A Haley Veterans Hospital, Tampa, Florida, 1974-; University of South Florida, Department of Psychiatry, Tampa, 1974-84; Sidney J Merin, PhD and Associates, Tampa, 1975-79; University of South Florida, Department of Neurology, Tampa, 1985-. *Memberships:* American Psychological Association; Biofeedback Society of America; Society for Psychophysiological Research; Society of Behavioral Medicine; New York Academy of Science; American Association for the Advancement of Science. *Publications:* Books include: Contributor to "Encyclopaedia of Sociology", 1975; Contributor to "Therapies for Psychosomatic Disorders in Children", 1979; Editor, Proceedings of 14th Annual Meeting, The Biofeedback Society of America, 1983; Contributor to professional journals, etc; Symposia presented: "Efficacy of Biofeedback: EEG" sponsored by the Biofeedback Society of Florida, May, 1979; "Computer Assisted Biofeedback: State-of-the-Art", The Biofeedback Society of America, 25 March 1984. Discussant; Dissertation: "Reduction in Seizures in Refractory Epileptic Patients Through EEG Biofeedback Training". *Honours:* Graduate Research Assistantship, Drake University, 1968-70; Graduate Assistantship, The University of Tennessee, 1970-74; Distinguished Service Plaque, The Gulf Coast Epilepsy Foundation, 1978; Certificate of Appreciation, Veterans Administration, 1983, 84. *Hobbies:* Scuba Diving; Snow Skiing; Fishing. *Address:* Psychology Service, Veterans Administration Medical Center, 13000 North 30th Street, Tampa, FL 33612, USA.

SEIFERT, Gerhard Johannes, b. 9 Sep. 1921, Leipzig, Germany. Chairman, Institute of Pathology, University of Hamburg. m. Leonore Sallmann, 16 Sep. 1950, 2 sons. *Education:* MD 1949, Universities of Leipzig & Münster; o.Prof. *Appointments include:* Institute of Pathology, University of Leipzig, 1951-58 (Habilitation 1955); Institute of Pathology, University of Münster, 1958-65 (Prof 1961); Institute of Pathology, University of Hamburg, 1965-. *Memberships:* Leopoldina; International Academy of Pathology; President 1985-87, European Society of Pathology; President 1985-86, Deutsche Gesellschaft für Pathologie; Deutsche Gesellschaft Naturforscher & Artze; International Association of Oral Pathologists; etc. *Publications include:* "Pathol. kindl. Pankreas", 1956; "Cytomegalie", 1957; "Oral Pathology", 1966; "Salivary Gland Diseases", 1984; "Pancreatic Pathology", 1984; etc. *Honours:* Lisec-Artz Arize, 1979; Honorary member: Société Anatomique, Paris; Hungarian Society of Pathology; Deutsch Gesellschaft Hals-Nasen-Ohren; etc. *Hobbies:* Music; Theatre. *Address:* Schwarzdornweg 18a, D-2000 Hamburg 65, Federal Republic of Germany.

SEKHON, Awatar, S, b. 15 Jan. 1941, Punjab, India,

Mycologist. m. Jasbir K Sidhu, 12 May 1965, Daudpur, Punjab, 1 son, 2 daughters. *Education:* BSc 1961, MSc 1963, Agra University, India; PhD 1969, University of Alberta, Canada; CLD. *Appointments include:* Research Assistant 1963-64, Senior Scientific Assistant, 1964-65, Graduate Research Assistant 1965-69, Postdoctorate Fellow, 1969-70, 1970-73, Assistant Mycologist 1973-77, Mycologist 1977-, University of Alberta. Advisor, Pan-American Health Organisation, Brazil, June 1977. *Memberships include:* American Society for Microbiology; Medical Mycological Society of the Americas; American Mycological Society; International Society for Human & Animal Mycology; Canadian Public Health Association; Canadian Association of Clinical Microbiology & Infectious Diseases; Canadian Society of Tropical Medicine & International Health; American Board of Bioanalysis. *Publications include:* Contributions to numerous professional journals. *Honours:* Research Grant, Medical Research Council of Canada, 1974-77; Visiting Speakers Award, Alberta Heritage Foundation for Medical Research, Sept. & Nov. 1982, Nov. 1984. *Hobbies:* Reading; Jogging; Photography; Nautilis; etc. *Address:* National Reference Centre for Human Mycotic Diseases, Provincial Laboratory of Public Health, University of Alberta, Edmonton, Alberta, Canada T6G 2J2.

SEKIYA, Tohru, b. 24 Oct. 1949, Gifu, Japan. Associate Professor of Radiology. m. Hiroko Imai, 13 Aug. 1972, Gifu, 1 son, 1 daughter. *Education:* MD; Fellow, Japanese College of Radiology. *Appointments:* Staff, Department of Radiology, Jikei University School of Medicine, Tokyo, 1979 and 1983; Visiting Fellow, Department of Nuclear Medicine and Ultrasound, Royal Marsden Hospital, Sutton, Surrey, England, 1980; Clinical Research Fellow, Department of Diagnostic Radiology, University of Manchester, 1981; Associate Professor, Department of Radiology, Ryukyu University Hospital, Okinawa, Japan, 1985-. *Memberships:* Japan Radiological Society; Japanese College of Radiology; British Institute of Radiology; British Medical Ultrasound Society; American Institute of Ultrasound in Medicine; Japan Society of Ultrasonics in Medicine. *Publications:* 'Clinical application of computer tomography in thyroid disease', 1979; 'Ultrasonographic evaluation of hepatic metastases in testicular tumour', 1982; 'Ultrasonography of Hodgkin's Diseases in the liver and spleen', 1982. *Honour:* British Council Award, 1980. *Hobby:* Golf. *Address:* Department of Radiology, Ryukyu University Hospital, 207 Uehara, Hishihara-cho, Okinawa 903-01, Japan.

SELBY, George, b. 21 Mar. 1922, Vienna, Austria. Chairman, Section of Neurology, Royal North Shore Hospital, Sydney; Visiting Neurologist, Royal North Shore Hospital. m. Deirdre Ann, 26 Oct. 1973, 2 sons, 1 daughter. *Edcuation:* MB, BS, University of Sydney, 1946; MD, 1968; FRCP (London), 1970; FRCP (Edinburgh), 1962; FRACP, 1965; Several visits to major neurological centres in USA and Europe for postgraduate studies. *Appointments:* Clinical Clerk and later Supernumerary Registrar at National Hospital for Nervous Diseases, London; Honorary Assistant Physician in Charge of Neurology Clinic, Royal North Shore Hospital, Sydney, 1953-64; Part-time Lecturer in Medicine and Therapeutics (Neurology), University of Sydney, 1959-; Honorary and later Visiting Neurologist, Royal North Shore Hospital, 1964-; Honorary Consultant Neurologist, Mater Misericordiae Hospital and Hornsby and District Hospital, Sydney. *Memberships:* Australian Association of Neurologists; President, 1974-78; Research Group on Extrapyramidal Diseases of World Federation of Neurology, 1973-; Association of British Neurologists, Honorary Member; Director, Australian Brain Foundation, Chairman, Scientific Advisory Committee, 1973-84. *Publications:* 'Stereotactic Surgery for the Relief of Parkinson's Disease', 'Journal of Neurological Science', 1967; 'Cerebral Atrophy in Parkinsonism', 'Journal of Neurological Science', 1968; Parkinson's Disease in "Handbook of Clinical

Neurology", 1968; Fifth Cranial Nerve in "Peripheral Neuropathy", 1973, 84; "Migraine and Its Variants", 1983. *Hobbies:* Trout Fishing; Golf; Skiing. *Address:* North Shore Medical Centre, 66-80 Pacific Highway, St Leonards, New South Wales 2065, Australia.

SELDON, William Anthony, b. 1 Nov. 1915, Sydney, Australia. Honorary Consultant Cardiologist, St Vincent's Hospital, Sydney. m. Hilda Muriel Laborde, 14 Sep. 1946, London, England, 2 sons. *Education:* MB, BS, Sydney; FRCP, London; FRACP; FACC; FACRM. *Appointments include:* Medical Officer, Royal Australian Air Force, 1940-46; Consultant Physician, RAAF, 1952-70; Cardiologist, St Vincent's Hospital, 1952-80; Consultant Physician, Manly District Hospital, 1962-82; Medical Director, Cardiac Rehabilitation Unit, National Heart Foundation of Australia, New South Wales Division, 1962-70. *Memberships:* Foundation Member, Sciencific Council on Cardiac Rehabilitation; International Society & Federation of Cardiology; Life Member, Past President, Cardiac Society of Australia & New Zealand; Aviation Medicine Society of Australia & New ZZealand. *Publications include:* Contributions to various professional journals: 'The Prognosis of Myocardia Infarction', 1955; 'Cardiac Rehabilitation: Experience with 1000 Cases', 1967; 'Planning Cardiac Rehabilitation', 1971; 'Pros & Cons of Rehabilitation in Sanatoria', 1977. *Hobbies:* Gliding; Sailing; Skiing; Trout fishing. *Address:* 376 Victoria Street, Darlinghurst, NSW 2010, Australia.

SELIGMAN, Roslyn, b. 1 July 1935, Augusta, Georgia, USA. Associate Professor of Child Psychiatry. *Education:* BS, University of Georgia; MD, Medical College of Georgia; Certification, The American Board of General Psychiatry Certification 1973, Child Psychiatry, The American Board of Psychiatry and Neurology, 1975. *Appointments:* Instructor Child Psychiatry, 1966-69; Assistant Professor of Child and Adolescent Psychiatry 1969-74, Associate Professor of Child and Adolescent Psychiatry 1974-, Department of Psychiatry, University of Cincinnati. *Memberships:* Fellow, American Psychiatric Association; Fellow, American Academy of Child Psychiatry; President 1975, Ohio Psychiatric Association; President 1974, Cincinnati Psychiatric Society; Ohio State Medical Association. *Publications:* 'A Psychiatric Classification System for Burned Children', 1974; 'The Effect of Earlier Parental Loss in Adolescence', (with G Gleser, J Rauh et al), 1974; 'Mental Health Care in an Adolescent Medical Setting', (with G Glaser, J Rauh and C Winget), 1980. *Address:* University of Cincinnati, Department of Psychiatry, 231 Bethesda Avenue, Cincinnati, OH 45267-0559, USA.

SELIGMANN, Maxime Gérard, b. 14 Mar. 1927, Paris, France. Head of Department of Immunohematology, Hôpital St Louis, Paris; Professor of Immunology, University of Paris VII. m. Francoise Brolliet, 11 Mar. 1953, Paris, 2 sons, 1 daughter. *Education:* MD, School of Medicine, University of Paris. *Appointments:* Scientist of Centre National de la Recherche Scientifique (Institut Pasteur, Paris), 1957-61; Associate Professor, School of Medicine, 1961-71, Professor, Immunology, 1971-, University of Paris; Head, INSERM Unit on Immunochemistry and Immunopathology, 1966-86. *Membership:* President, French Society for Immunology. *Publications:* More than 400 publications in the fields of human immunology and hematology. *Address:* Hôpital Saint-Louis, 75475 Paris Cedex 10, France.

SELLA, Gabriel Eugen, b. 10 May 1948, Bucarest, Romania. Chief of Staff, Midale Union Hospital, Canada. m. Nicoletta Villa, Montreal, 1 son. *Education:* BSc., St George Williams University; MSc., McGill University; MPH, Johns Hopkins University; MD, University of Pavia. *Appointments:* Research/Clinical Fellow, Royal Victoria Hospital, McGill University, 1978-79; Associate, International Health, Johns Hopkins School of Hygiene and Public Health, 1983-84; Family Physician, Midale Diagnostic Clinic, 1984-; Staff Physician, Souris Valley Regional Care

Centre, 1985-. *Memberships:* American Medical Association; Canadian Medical Association; International Health Society; American College of Nutrition; American Society of Clinical Hypnosis; New York Academy of Sciences; etc. *Honours:* Sir George Williams Best Students Award, 1969; Can. Cystic Fibrosis Foundation Scholarship, 1973; Johns Hopkins Best Students Fellowship, 1982; McNamara Fellowship, 1984. *Hobbies:* Chess; Dancing; Reading; Classical Music; Spending Time With His Family. *Address:* Osgood Community Medical Center, State, Route 7165, Osgood, OH 45351, USA.

SELTZER, Joseph Louis, b. 25 May, 1945, Darby, Pennsylvania, USA. Professor and Chairman of Anaesthesiology. m. Suzanne Frankhouser, 30 May 1970, Philadelphia, USA, 2 sons, 2 daughters. *Education:* BS, St. Joseph's College, Philadelphia, 1967; MD Jefferson Medical College, Philadelphia, 1971. *Appointments:* Intern in Surgery, Albert B. Chandler Medical Centre, USA, 1971-72; Resident in General Surgery, Geisinger Medical Centre, 1972-73; Resident in Anaesthesiology, Thomas Jefferson University Hospital, 1973-75; Staff Anaesthesiologist, USAF Medical Centre, Ohio, 1975-77; Assistant Clinical Professor, Wright State University, 1976-77; Assistant Professor of Anaesthesiology, SUNY Upstate Medical Centre, 1977-80; Associate Professor of Anaesthesiology, Jefferson Medical College, 1980-84, Professor and Chairman, 1984-present. *Memberships:* American Society of Anaesthesiologists; International Anaesthesia Research Society; American Society of Regional Anaesthesia; Association of Anaesthetists of Great Britain and Ireland; Society of Cardiovascular Anaesthesiologists; American Medical Association; College of Physicians of Philadelphia. *Publication:* Co-Author "Anaesthesia", 2nd edition, 1983. *Hobbies:* Golf; Sailing; Windsurfing; Cross Country Skiing. *Address:* Department of Anaesthesiology, Jefferson Medical College, Philadelphia, PA 19107, USA.

SELTZER, Ronni Lee, b. 24 Apr. 1952, New York, New York, USA. Physician, Psychiatrist. m. Gary Broder, 20 Jan. 1980, New York. *Education:* BA, Syracuse University, New York, 1973; MD, Chicago Medical School, 1977. *Appointments:* Resident, Psychiatry, New York University Medical Center, Bellevue Hospital, New York, 1977-81; Private Practice, Psychiatry, 1980-; Teaching Assistant, Psychiatry, New York Medical Center, New York, New York, 1980-; Medical Staff, Englewood Hospital, New Jersey, 1980-; Contributing Editor, Ophthalmology Management Magazine, 1983-; Medical Staff, Holy Name Hospital, 1984-. *Memberships:* Corresponding Secretary 1985-, The North Jersey Psychiatric Association; American Psychiatric Association; New Jersey Psychiatric Association; Eastern Psychiatric Research Association; American Medical Association; Bergen County Medical Society; American Medical Women's Association; Alumni Association, Chicago Medical School. *Publications:* 'Monoamine-Oxidase-Inhibitor-Induced Rapid Cycling Bipolar Affective Disorder in an Adolescent', 1981; 'Lithium Carbonate and Gastric Ulcers', 1981; 'Spotting Problable Contact Lens Failures', 1983; 'Coping with Patient's Pre-Op Fears', 1983; 'Dealing with Psychiatric Problems After Eye Surgery', 1984; 'Coping with Career Stress', 1984; 'Happy Retirement!', 1984. *Hobbies:* Skiing; Golf; Gourmet Cooking. *Address:* 200 Engle Street, Englewood, NJ 07631, USA.

SELTZER, Vicki Lynn, b. 6 Feb. 1949, USA. President, Medical Board; Director, Department of Obstetrics & Gynaecology, Queens Hospital Centre, Jamaica, New York. m. Richard Brach, 2 Sep. 1973, New York City, 1 son, 1 daughter. *Education:* BS, Rensselaer Polytechnic Institute, 1969; MD, New York University School of Medicine, 1973. *Appointments include:* Associate Director, Gynaecologic Oncology, Assistant Professor, Obstetrics & Gynaecology, Albert Einstein College of Medicine; Assistant Attending, North Central Bronx Hospital, Bronx Municipal Hospital Centre; Attending Physician, Albert Einstein College; Consultant, Jewish Institute for Geriatric Care; Director of Obstetrics & Gynaecology, President of Medical Board, Queens Hospital Centre; Associate Professor, State University of New York, Stony Brook. *Memberships include:* 2nd Vice President, Womens Medical Association, NYC; Alpha Omega Alpha; Gynaecological Practice Committee, American College of Obstetricians & Gynaecologists; Chair, Publicity & Public Relations, American Medical Womens Association; Scientific Advisory Panel, Gyneco Surgical Instrument Company; Obstetric Advisory Committee, Commissioner of Health, NYC; etc. *Publications include:* Various contributions to professional journals. *Honours:* Biographical listings; Young Woman Achiever Award, National Council of Women; New York University Alumni Award; Citation, American Medical Womens Association. *Hobbies:* Water skiing; Tennis. *Address:* Queens Hospital Centre, 82-68 164th Street, Jamaica, NY 11432, USA.

SELWYN, Donald, b. 31 Jan. 1936, New York City, New York, USA. Director and Executive Vice President, The National Institute for Rehabilitation Engineering. m. (1) Delia Nemec, 11 Mar. 1956, Madison, Wisconsin, divorced 1983, 1 son, 2 daughters; (2) Myra Rowman Markoff, 17 Mar. 1986. Paterson, New Jersey. *Education:* BA, Thomas A Edison College, New Jersey, 1976. *Appointments:* Service Engineer, Bendix Aviation, Teterboro, New Jersey, 1956-59; Service Manager, Bigue Electric Manufacturing Company, Paterson, 1959; Proposal Engineer Advanced Design Group, Curtiss-Wright Corporation, East Paterson, 1960-64; Independent Bioengineer, Rehabilitation Engineering Consultant, New York City, 1964-67; Consultant, New York State Office Vocational Rehabilitation, 1964-; President's Committee on Employment of Handicapped, 1966-; President of Board of Trustees, Executive Technical and Training Director, National Institute for Rehabilitation Engineering, Butler, New Jersey, 1967-; Numerous state rehabilitation agencies, health departments, voluntary groups and agencies for the handicapped in foreign countries. *Memberships:* American Academy of Consultants; Senior, Institute of Electrical and Electronic Engineers; Senior, Society of Technical Writers and Publishers; National Rehabilitation Association; New York Academy of Sciences, MENSA. *Publications:* Articles on amateur radio and rehabilitation of severely and totally disabled to professional and general magazines; Developer or co-developer of inventions including: Field-expander glasses for hemainopsia, tunnel and monocular vision; Electronic speech clarifiers; Electrically guided wheelchairs; Off-road vehicles and cars for quadriplegics; Patentee of industrial, military and handicapped rehabilitation inventions. *Honours:* Humanitarian Award, USA House of Representatives, 1972; Knight of Malta, 1973; Bicentennial Public Service Award, 1975. *Address:* c/o The National Institute for Rehabilitation Engineering, 97 Decker Road, Butler, NJ 07405, USA.

SENEVIRATNE, Hilarian Sarath Kumar, b. 21 Oct. 1943, Sri-Lanka. Consultant Pathologist. *Education:* MB.BS; FRCPA. *Appointments:* Intern, Sri Lanka, 1969-70; Rotating Intern, USA, 1970-71; Medical Officer, Alice Springs, Australia, 1971-72; Registrar: Royal Alexandra Hospital for Children, Sydney, Australia, 1972-73, Royal Prince Alfred Hospital, Sydney, 1974-77, Port Moresby General Hospital, Papua New Guinea, 1975; Specialist Pathologist, Commonwealth Health Dept., Australia, 1978-81; Senior Resident, Pathology, USA, 1981-82; Specialist Pathologist, Commonwealth Health Dept., Australia, 1982-84; SMO, 1984-85, Consultant, 1985-, Pathology, Medical & Health Dept., Hong Kong. *Memberships:* Fellow, Royal College of Pathologists of Australasia; Affiliate Member, Royal Society of Medicine; International Academy of Pathology. *Hobbies:* Horticulture; Travel. *Address:* Institute of Pathology, Kowloon Hospital, Kowloon, Hong Kong.

SENIOR, Steven Lee, b. 12 Mar. 1948, Montreal, Canada. Family Physician. m. Colleen Walsh, 19 June

1976, Toronto, 1 son, 2 daughters. *Education:* MD; CCFP. *Appointments:* Resident in Family Medicine, Ottawa Civic Hospital, 1973-75; Family Practice, Moosonee, Ontario, 1975-77; Medical Registrar, Gisborne, New Zealand, 1978; Family Practice, Lakefield, Ontario, Canada, 1979-. *Memberships:* Ontario and Canadian Medical Associations; College of Family Physicians of Canada; Society of Orthopedic Medicine; Peterborough County Medical Society; Physicians For Social Responsibility. *Publication:* 'Study of smoking in hospital and attitudes of medical staff towards smoking', 1982. *Hobbies:* Sports. *Address:* 18 Queens Street, Lakefield, Ontario K0L 2H0, Canada.

SENTERRE, Jacques, b. 4 Mar. 1938, Longueville, Belgium. Professor, Neonatology. *Education:* MD, 1962; Paediatrician, 1967; Agrege de l'Enseignement Superieur, 1976. *Appointments:* Research Worker, National Belgian Fund for Scientific Research, 1964-81; Professor, Neonatology, Paediatrics, State University of Liege. *Memberships:* European Society of Paediatric Gastroenterology and Nutrition; European Society of Perinatal Medicine; Expert Committee, Hec M Perinatology of the International Paediatric Association. *Publications:* 180 articles in journals. *Honours:* Prix Specia, 1962; Laureat du Concours Universitaire, 1964; Laureat de la Fondation Universitaire, 1967; Prix International de e'Alimentation Moderne, Switzerland. *Address:* Dept. of Paediatrics, University of Liege, Hopital de la Citadelle, B-4000 Liege, Belgium.

SEPPÄLÄ, Markku Tapio, b. 16 May 1936, Helsinki, Finland. Professor of Obstetrics & Gynaecology, Clinical Chairman. m. Maija-Leena née Peltonen, 28 Aug. 1961, Mänttä, Finland, 2 sons. *Education:* MD 1964, Doctor of Medical Science, 1965, University of Helsinki; MFOG, 1969; Associate Professor, 1976, Professor of Obstetrics & Gynaecology, University of Helsinki, 1979. *Appointments:* Resident, 1966-69, Lecturer, Senior Lecturer, 1970-75, Associate Professor, 1976-78, Department of Obstetrics & Gynaecology, University Central Hospital, Helsinki; Research Professor, The Academy of Finland, 1978-80; Visiting Professor, St Bartholomew's Hospital Medical College, London, England, 1979-80; Professor & Chairman of Department, Helsinki, 1980-; Associate Editor Obstetrical & Gynaecological Survey, 1981-; Editor, Acta Endocrinologica (KBH), 1980-85; Editor, Acta Obstetricia et Gynecologica Scandinavica, 1984-; President, III World Congress of In Vitro Fertilization & Embryo Transfer, Helsinki, 1984. *Memberships:* Finnish Gynaecological Association, 1967; Scandinavian Society for Obstetricians & Gynaecologists, 1970; American Fertility Society, 1984; New York Academy of Sciences, 1973; American Association for Cancer Research, 1976; International Society for Oncodevelopmental Biology & Medicine, 1973; Secretary-General, European Association of Gynaecologists & Obstetricians, 1985; International Society of Gynaecological Pathologists, 1985. *Publications:* 290 peer-reviewed original articles; Books: "Placental Proteins: Biochemistry, Biology & Clinical Application" (edited J G Grudzinskas, B Teisner & M T Seppälä), 1982; "In Vitro Fertilization & Embryo Transfer" (edited M T Seppälä & R G Edwards), 1985. *Honours:* Science Prize, Lucerne, Switzerland, 1971; Matti Äyräpää Prize, Helsinki, 1981; Fellow, New York Academy of Sciences, 1974. *Hobby:* Music. *Address:* Department I of Obstetrics & Gynaecology, Helsinki University Central Hospital, SF-00290 Helsinki, Finland.

SERLUPI CRESCENZI, Giovanni, b. 14 Feb. 1925, Rome, Italy. Director, Laboratory of Metabolism and Pathological Biochemistry. m. Bellardo Luisa, 29 Oct. 1951, Torino, 4 sons, 2 daughters. *Education:* Doctor in Chemistry. *Appointments:* Researcher: University of Rome, Italy, 1950; Instituto Superiore di Sanita, Rome, 1951-66. Administrator, Scientific Aff Division, North Atlantic Treaty Organisation, Bussels, Belgium, 1967-70; Director, Research Laboratory Pierrel

Spa, Milan, Italy, 1971-73; Director, Laboratory of Metabolism and Pathological Biochemistry, Instituto Superiore di Sanita, Rome, 1973-. *Memberships:* Italian Biochemical Society; International Society of Neurochemistry; Italian Society of Metabolism and Pathologic Biochemistry; Italian Society of Nutrition. *Honours:* Libero Docente in Biochimica Applicata; Official of Merit, Italian Republic and of DBR; Commendor, El Merito Civil Espana. *Hobby:* Agriculture. *Address:* Instituto Superiore di Sanita, Viale Regina Elena 299, 00161 Rome, Italy.

SERRA, Jody Lawrence, b. 1 Sep. 1957, Staten Island, New York, USA. Chiropractor, Applied Kinesiology, Accuressturist. m. Lori Taeger, 30 June 1984, Oldwick, New Jersey. *Education:* West Virginia University; DC, Palmer College of Chiropractic; International Academy of Clinical Acupuncture; Parker Chiropractic Research Foundation. *Appointments:* Associate, Berkeley Heights Chiropractic Center; Currently Director, Cokesbury Chiropractic Center. *Memberships:* International College of Applied Kinesiology; American Chiropractic Association; New Jersey Chiropractic Society; Parker Chiropractic Research Foundation; Pi Kappa Chi; ACA Council on Sports Injuries/{ ACA Council on Nutrition. *Honour:* Outstanding Service Award, Pi Kappa Chi, 1982. *Hobbies:* Skiing; Weight Training; Rugby Football; Racquetball; Hunting; Fishing. *Address:* Route 22 West Box 332, Lebanon, NJ 08833, USA.

SERRANO, Salvatore, b. 27 May 1925, Catania, Italy. Head, Department of Thoracic Surgery, S Martino Hospital, Genoa. m. Matilde Parona, 8 May 1950, Carella, near Milan, 4 daughters. *Education:* MD; Specialist, General Surgery, Thoracic Surgery, Vascular & Cardiac Surgery. *Appointments include:* Training, University School of Medicine, Parma & Genoa, 1950-56, 1957-64. *Memberships:* Secretary, Italian Society of Thoracic Surgery; Secretary, Italian Society of Thoracic Endoscopy; Fellow, American College of Chest Physicians; Fellow, International College of Surgeons. *Publications include:* 'Critical assessment of the employment of 192 Ir in the management of broncopulmonary tumours', 1971; 'Dix années d'experience du traitement chirurgical du cancer du poumon', 1977; 'Immunologia del cancro del polmone', 1980; 'Staging nel cancro del polmone', 1981; 'Staging of operable pulmonary tumors and organization', 1984. *Hobby:* Sea sports. *Address:* Via Polanesi 59, 16036 Recco (Ge), Italy.

SERRATRICE, Georges T, b. 1927. President, Université d'Aix-Marseille II, France. *Education:* MD, Université d'Aix-Marseille. *Memberships:* World Federation of Neurology; French Society of Neurology; French Society of Rheumatology. *Publications:* 12 books, including "Advances in Neuromuscular Disease", 1971; "Peroneal Atrophies", 1979; "Muscular Dieases", 1982. *Honour:* Chevalier de la Legion d'Honneur, 1986. *Address:* Université d'Aix-Marseille, Jardin Emile Duclaux, 58 Boulevard Charles Livon, F-13007, Marseille, France.

SERVADIO, Ciro, b. 1931. Director and Head of Urology Department, Beilinson Medical Centre, Israel. *Education:* MD, Hebrew University of Jerusalem. *Appointments:* Director, Central Emek Hospital, Afula, 1964-74; Chief, Urology and Renal Transplantation Department, Beilinson Medical Centre, Petah Tikva, 1975-. *Memberships:* Israel Surgical Society; Israel Urological Society; Israel Nephrology Society; European Dialysis and Transplantation Association; American College of Surgeons; American Urological Association. *Address:* Beilinson Medical Centre, Petah Tikva 49100, Israel.

SETTIPANE, Guy A, b. 19 July 1930, Middletown, Connecticut, USA. Clinical Associate Professor. 4 sons. *Education:* BA, Brown University; MD, New York Medical College. *Appointments include:* Clinical Associate Professor, Brown University Medical School, Providence, Rhode Island. *Memberships:* President, New England Society of Allergy; Past Chairman, Council of Regional and State Allergy Society Presidents; American Medical Association; American Academy of Allergy and Immunology. *Publications:* Editor, "Rhinitis", 1984, Author or Co-Author over 70 papers contributed to professional journals including: 'Archives of Internal Medicine'; 'New England Society of Allergy Proceedings'; 'Journal of the American Academy of Dermatology'; 'Journal of Allergy Clinical Immunology'; 'American Journal of Medicine'; 'New England and Region Allergy Proceedings'. *Honours:* New York Allergy Round Table. *Hobbies:* Swimming; Writing. *Address:* 95 Pitman Street, Providence, RI 02906, USA.

SEVERIN, Matthew Joseph, b. 7 Aug. 1933, Omaha, Nebraska, USA. Professor of Microbiology; Dean of Students. m. Catherine Sullivan, 27 Dec. 1958, Chicago, Illinois, USA, 2 sons, 2 daughters. *Education:* BS, 1955; MS, 1960; PhD, 1968; JD, 1986; Registered Specialist, Microbiology. *Appointments:* Bacteriologist, Immanuel Hospital, Omaha, Nebraska, USA, 1958-60; Chief of Laboratories, Douglas County Health Department, Omaha, 1962-76; Infectious Diseases Officer, Douglas County, Nebraska, 1970-72; Chief of Microbiology Laboratories, St Joseph's Hospital, 1972-75; Assistant Dean, Creighton University School of Medicine, 1975-80, Associate Dean, 1980-85, Dean -. *Memberships:* American Society of Microbiologists; Infectious Disease Society of America; American Society of Epidermiologists; American Association of Medical Education; Association of Clinical Scientists. *Publications include:* 'The Neurol Transmission of Herpes Simplex' in 'American Journal of Pathology', 1967, etc. *Honour:* Distinguished Teacher, Golden Apples, 1983, 1984, 1985. *Hobby:* Golf. *Address:* Creighton University School of Medicine, Omaha, NE 68178, USA.

SEYMOUR, Anthony Elliot, b. 3 Sep. 1939, Adelaide, Australia. Pathologist. m. Wendy Sue MacRae, 22 Dec. 1962, Adelaide, separated, 2 daughters. *Education:* MD, 1981; MBBS, 1963; FRCPA; Fellow, Royal College of Pathologists of Australia, 1968. *Appointments:* Resident Medical Officer, Royal Adelaide Hospital, 1963; Registrar, Pathology, Queen Elisabeth Hospital, Adelaide, 1964-68; Assistant Professor, University of Chicago, USA, 1968-72; Senior Morbid Anatomist, Royal Brisbane Hospital, 1973; Senior Specialist, Pathology, Head of Renal Pathology, Institute of Medical & Veterinary Science, 1974-80; Consultant, Renal Pathology, Royal Adelaide Hospital, 1974-80; Senior Director, Queen Elizabeth Hospital, 1981-83; Associate Pathologist, Renal, Adelaide Childrens Hospital, 1978-; Consultant, Renal Pathology, Queen Elizabeth Hospital, 1983-. *Memberships:* Royal College of Pathologists of Australia; Australian Medical Association; International Academy of Pathology; etc. *Publications:* Co-Author, "Renal Biopsy Pathology with diagnostic and therapeutic implications", 1980; numerous articles in professional journals. *Hobbies:* Reading; Gardening. *Address:* 1 Goodwood Road, Wayville, South Australia 5034.

SEYMOUR, Gregory John, b. 29 Nov. 1948, Sydney, Australia. Associate Professor of Periodontology. m. Mary Patricia Cullinan, 3 Aug. 1974, Sydney, 1 son, 2 daughters. *Education:* BDS, Honours, 1971; MDSc 1974, University of Sydney; PhD, University of London, UK, 1978; MRCPath, Royal College of Pathologists, London, 1984. *Appointments:* Teaching Fellow, Department of Preventive Dentistry, University of Sydney, 1971-73; Lecturer, Periodontology, Royal Dental Hospital, University of London, & Research Assistant, Pathology, 1974-78. *Memberships:* Australian Dental Association; Australian Society of Periodontology; British Society for Immunology; Australian Society for Immunology; Australian Society for Microbiology. *Publications include:* Co-author, 60 papers in various professional journals: 'The Immunopathogenesis of Chronic Inflammatory Periodontal Disease'; 'Conversion of a Stable T-Cell lesion to a

progressive B-cell lesion in the Pathogenesis Periodontal Disease'; 'Analysis of Lymphocyte populations extracted from human Periodontal tissues'. *Honours:* Sir Wilfred Fish Research Prize, British Society for Periodontology, 1977; Ray Williams Prize, Australian Society of Periodontology, 1980. *Hobbies:* Surfing; Skiing. *Address:* Department of Social & Preventive Dentistry, University of Queensland Dental School, Turbot Street, Brisbane, Queensland 4000, Australia.

SHADER, Richard Irwin, b. 27 May 1935, Mount Vernon, New York, USA. Professor and Chairman, Tufts University School of Medicine. m. Aline Brown, 21 Sep. 1958, Cleveland Ohio, USA, 1 son, 2 daughters. *Education:* AB, Harvard University, USA, 1956; MD, New York University, School of Medicine, 1960; Diploma in Psychoanalysis, Boston Psychoanalytic Institute, 1970. *Appointments include:* Associate in Psychiatry, Harvard Medical School, USA, 1967-68; Director, Psychopharmacology Research Laboratory, Massachusetts Mental Health Centre, 1968-79; Chairman, Department of Psychiatry, Tufts University School of Medicine, 1979-; Assistant Professor, Associate Professor, Harvard Medical School. *Memberships include:* American Medical Association; American Psychiatric Association; Massachusetts Psychiatric Society; Massachusetts Medical Society; Group for the Advancement of Psychiatry; American College of Neuropsychopharmacology; Boston Psychoanalytic Society; Association for Academic Psychiatry; American Association of Chairmen of Departments of Psychiatry, etc. *Publications include:* Co-author "Psychotropic Drug Side Effects", 1970; "Clinical Handbook of Psychopharmacology", 1973; Co-author "Schizophrenia: Pharmacotherapy and Psychotherapy", 1977; Editor "Manual of Psychiatric Therapeutics", 1975; Co-author "Pharmacokinetics in Clinical Practice", 1985; 373 articles in learned journals. *Honours include:* Career Teacher Award, National Institute of Mental Health, 1965-67; House Staff Teaching Cup, Massachusetts Mental Health Centre, 1977; The Taylor Manor Hospital Psychiatric Award, 1980; Kentucky Colonel (Honorable Order of Kentucky Colonels), 1985. *Hobby:* Gardening. *Address:* 132 Homer Street, Newton Centre, MA 02159, USA.

SHAH, Amil, b. 27 Nov. 1949, Guyana. Medical Oncologist, Cancer Control Agency of British Columbia, Canada. m. Colleen Horner, 15 June 1975, Montreal, Canada, 1 son, 2 daughters. *Education:* BSc, Honours, 1971, MD, CM, 1975, McGill University; Fellow, Royal College of Physicians (Canada), 1979. *Current Appointment:* Assistant Professor of Medicine, University of British Columbia. *Memberships:* Canadian Oncological Society; American College of Physicians; Royal College of Physicians & Surgeons (Canada). *Publications include:* Various research papers in medical journals; Book, "Cancer: An Act of Evolution", in preparation. *Honours:* Scholar, McGill University; E D G Murray Prize, Microbiology & Immunology, McGill, 1971. *Hobby:* Judo. *Address:* 600 West 10th Avenue, Vancouver BC, Canada V5Z 4E6.

SHAH, Kamla Jiven, b. 23 May 1928, Seychelles. Medical & Administrative Director; Professor, Chief of Radiation Oncology. *Education:* MB, BS, Bombay University; MRCP; FRCR; ABR. *Appointments:* Radiation Oncologist, Ontario Cancer Foundation; Assistant Professor, Queen's University, Kingston, Canada; Assistant Professor, University of Texas Medical Branch, Galveston, USA; Professor, Medical & Administrative Director, Georgia Radiation Therapy Centre, College of Georgia, Augusta. *Memberships:* American Medical Association; Radiologic Society of North America; American Society for Therapeutic Radiology and Oncology; American College of Radiology. *Publications:* Articles in professional journals. *Hobbies:* Painting; Travel; Literature; Politics. *Address:* Georgia Radiation Therapy Centre, Medical College of Georgia, Bldg HK, Augusta, GA 30912, USA.

SHAH, Lalit, b. 22 Apr. 1936, Bombay, India. Professor of Psychiatry. m. Bombay, India, 1965. *Education:* MB; DPM; MRC Psych, England; FIPS; FAPA (USA). *Memberships:* Fellow, Indian Psychiatry Society; Indian Neurological Society; Indian Medical Association; Seth G S Medical College of KEM Hospital; Staff Society and Research Society; Royal College of Psychiatry; Fellow, APA. *Publications:* "A Handbook of Psychiatry", 2nd edition; 90 published papers. *Honours:* Gold Medal for best paper, IVth Annual Conference of IPS, West Zone Branch; Hon General Secretary, IPS for 3 terms of 2 years; President, Bombay Psychiatric Society; President, IPS, WZ Branch. *Hobbies:* Dramatics; Music; Literature. *Address:* Kailash Darshan, 5th Floor, Flat No 19, Kennedy Bridge, Nana's Chowk, Bombay 400 007 India.

SHAH, Mahesh H, b. 12 July 1946, Dhamtari, MP, India. Consultant Cardiologist. m. Lata M Shah, 26 Jan. 1973, Bhopal MP, 2 sons, 1 daughter. *Education:* MB, BS; MD. *Appointments:* Resident Medical Officer, M Y Hospital, Indose India; Tutor, Department of Internal Medicine, Lecturer, Ratdiputsa Medical College, Dhanbad, Bihar, India; Consultant in Cardiology running (privately) Intensive Coronary Care Unit. *Memberships:* Fellow, American College of Chest Physicians; Fellow, International Academy of Chest Physicians; Association of Physicians of India; Cardiological Society of India; Indian Medical Association. *Hobbies:* Reading Medical Journals; Music; Conema & Films. *Address:* Jawahar Nagar, Raipur (MP), India.

SHAHEEN, Priscilla Pauline, b. 8 Apr. 1928m Lawrence, Massachusetts, USA. Nurse. m. Joseph Richard Shaheen, 3 Feb. 1951, Lawrence, Massachusetts, 1 son, 1 daughter. now widowed. *Education:* Nursing Diploma, St John's Hospital School of Nursing, 1948; BS, St Anselm's College School of Nursing, 1973; MS, School of Nursing, Boston University, 1975. *Appointments:* Staff Nurse, 1948-50; Public Health Nursing, 1950-52; Private Duty Nursing, 1952-56; Staff Nurse, 1956-60; Head Nurse, 1960-71; Assistant Director (Nursing), 1973; Hospital Supervisor, 1976-77; Assistant Professor, 1977-81; Currently part-time Gerontological Nursing, full-time student, Doctoral Programme in Sociology & Consultant Nursing Service Administration, Biston University. *Memberships:* St John's Nurses Alumni; Massachusetts Nurses Association; American Nurses Association; National League of Nursing; Sigma Theta Tau, Theta Chapter, Boston (National Honour Society of Nursing). *Publications:* Critique of: 'Effects of Structured Preparation for Transfer on Patient Anxiety on Leaving Coronary Care Unit', Nursing Research, 1980; 'Nationalizing Health Care: A Humanitarian Approach', Nursing Outlook, 1981; 'Staffing & Scheduling Reconcile Practical Means with the Real Goal', 1985. Nursing Management. *Hobbies:* Singing; Painting; Drawing. *Address:* 10 Perley Street, Methuen, MA 01844, USA.

SHALACK, Joan Helen, b. 6 Mar. 1932, New Jersey, USA. Physician. *Education:* BA, New York University, Washington Square College, USA; MD, Women's Medical College of Pennsylvania, USA. *Appointments:* President, Chairman of Board, Totizo Inc, USA, 1969-71; Medical Practitioner-. *Memberships:* American Medical Association; American Psychiatric Association; American Association for Social Psychiatry. *Honour:* Phi Beta Kappa, 1958. *Hobbies:* Tennis; Cycling; Hiking; Gardening; Archaeology. *Address:* 2080 Century Park East, Suite 1403, Los Angeles, CA 90067, USA.

SHALEV, Moshe, b. 27 Oct. 1946, Galilee, Israel. Director, Division of Laboratory Animal Medicine. m. Dorothy McCormick, 14 Oct. 1978, Newport, Rhode Island, USA, 4 daughters. *Education:* BSc Microbiology, 1969, MSc Genetics, 1971, Hebrew University of Jerusalem, Israel; Veterinary Medical Doctor, School of Veterinary Medicine, University of Pennsylvania, USA, 1975. *Appointments include:* Staff Veterinarian

& Cardiologist, Women's SPCA Hospital for Small Animals, Philadelphia, 1975-76; Clinical Veterinarian, Division of Laboratory Animal Medicine, Massachusetts Institute of Technology, 1976-80; Director, Division of Laboratory Animal Medicine, School of Medicine, University of Pennsylvania, Philadelphia, 1980-; Assistant Clinical Professor, Department of Human Genetics, University of Pennsylvania, 1984-. *Memberships:* Diplomate, American College of Laboratory Animal Medicine; American Association for the Accreditation of Laboratory Animal Care; American Veterinary Medical Association; American Association for Laboratory Animal Science; American Association for the Advancement of Science. *Publications:* Various publications and abstracts in professional journals. *Honours:* Financial Awards for Scholastic Achievements, 1967, 1969, 1971. *Hobbies:* Piano; Flute; Photography; Swimming. *Address:* 406 Pembroke Road, Bala Cynwyd, PA 19004, USA.

SHAMOIAN, Charles A, b. 5 Oct. 1931, Worcester, Massachusetts, USA. Professor of Clinical Psychiatry. m. Paula, 8 Oct. 1961, 1 son, 1 daughter. *Education:* AB, Clark University, USA, 1954, MA, 1956; PhD, Tufts University, 1960, MD, 1966. *Appointments:* Fellow, Physiology, Tufts University, USA, 1960, Instructor, 1960-62; Instructor, Psychiatry, Cornell University, 1967-70, Assistant Professor, 1970-75, Associate Professor, Clinical Psychiatry, 1979-84, Professor, 1984-, Director, Geriatric Services, New York Hospital, White Plains, New York-. *Memberships:* American Psychiatric Association; American Association of Geriatric Psychiatry; Society of Biological Psychiatry; Gerontological Society of America; American Geriatric Society. *Publications:* "Psychogeriatrics - Medical Clinics of North America", 1984; Editor, "Dementia in the Elderly", 1984; Editor "Treatment of Affective Disorders in the Elderly", 1985. *Honours:* Charlton Fellowship, 1956-60; US AMS Post Doctorate Fellow, 1960-61. *Hobbies:* Baseball; Coin Collecting; Hiking. *Address:* New York Hospital, Cornell Medical Centre, 21 Bloomingdale Road, White Plains, NY 10605, USA.

SHANFIELD, Stephen B, b. 14 Aug. 1939, Toronto, Canada. Professor of Psychiatry. m. Carmen Kight, 15 Aug. 1971, San Antonio, Texas, USA, 1 son. *Education:* BA, University of California at Los Angeles, 1961; MD, University of Southern California, 1965; Intern, Montefiore Hospital & Medical Centre, New York, 1965-66; Resident in Psychiatry, Yale University School of Medicine, 1966-69. *Appointments:* Assistant Clinical Professor of Psychiatry, Yale School of Medicine, 1971-73; Assistant Superintendent, Undercliff Mental Health Centre, Meriden, Connecticut, 1971-73; Director, Outpatient Psychiatric Services, University of Arizona Health Sciences Centre, Tucson, Arizona, 1973-85; Assistant to Full Professor of Psychiatry, University of Arizona, 1973-85. *Memberships:* American Psychiatric Association; Group for the Advancement of Psychiatry; American College of Psychiatrists; Houston Committee on Foreign Relations. *Publications:* Over 50 articles, abstracts & book chapters. *Address:* Departmentof Psychiatry, University of Texas Health Sciences Centre, 7703 Floyd Curl Drive, San Antonio, TX 78284, USA.

SHANKAR, Patil S, b. 1 Jan. 1936, Halgeri, India. Professor; Head of Department. m. Ambika Shankar, 25 Nov. 1965, Davangere, 1 son, 1 daughter. *Education:* MBBS, Mysore; MD, Delhi; FCCP, USA; FIMSA; FNCCP. *Appointments:* Lecturer in Medicine, Medical College, Bangalore, 1962-64; Assistant Professor of Medicine, Karnatak Medical College, Hubli, 1964-66; Reader, Head of Department of Medicine, 1966-67, Professor, Head of Department of Medicine, Medical College, Gulbarga, 1967-; Dean, Faculty of Medical Sciences, Gulbarga University, 1981-84. *Memberships:* Member, Association of Physicians of India; Cardiological Society of India; Indian Chest Society; Indian Medical Association; Fellow, American College of Chest Physicians; International Medical Sciences Academy; National College of Chest Physicians (India). *Publications:* "Chest Medicine",

1971, 2nd edition, 1979; "Side Room Investigations and Instrumentation", 1975, 2nd edition, 1980; "Manual of Clinical Methods", 1976; "Pulmonary Tuberculosis", 1982; "Your Body in Health and Sickness", 1982; 142 articles in scientific journals; 6 monograms; 14 books and 12 booklets in Kannada. *Honours:* Soviet Land Nehru Award, 1977; Mrs Jal Vakil Lecturer in Cardiopulmonary diseases, 1981; Sri. Krishnaji and Mrs Premalabai Bhate Lecturer in Asthma and Bronchitis, 1982; Karnataka State Award, 1984; Dr B C Roy Awardee, Eminent Medical Teacher, 1985. *Hobbies:* Travel; Writing. *Address:* Deepti, Behind District Court, J. P. Extension, Gulbarga 585 102, Karnataka, India.

SHANLEY, David Francis, b. 17 May 1943, Dublin, Ireland. Consultant Psychiatrist. m. Elizabeth Macguinness, 8 Jan. 1971, 2 sons, 1 daughter. *Education:* MB; BCH, BAO (NUI) Honours Degree, 1967; DPM, Trinity College, Dublin, 1972; MRCPsych (UK), 1975; FRCP (C), 1976. *Appointments:* Tutor, Psychiatry, University College, Dublin, 1973-75; Chief Resident, Wellesley Hospital, Toronto, Canada, 1976; Teaching Fellowship, University of Toronto, 1977; Assistant Professor, Consultant Psychiatrist, 1977; Consultant Psychiatrist, St Patrick's Hospital, Dublin, 1978-, and Sir Patrick Dun's Hospital, Dublin, St James's Hospital, Dublin. *Memberships:* Irish Division, Royal College of Psychiatrists; Irish Psychiatric Association. *Publications:* "A Case of Cutaneous Tuberculosis", 'Journal of Irish Medical Association', 1967; "Personality and Performances in Psychiatric Education", 'Medical Education', 1982; "Psychiatric Interviewing and Clinical Skills", 'Canadian Journal of Psychiatry', 1985. *Honours:* Honorary Secretary, Irish Division, Royal College Psychiatrists, 1979-84; Council Member, Royal College Psychiatrists, 1983-. *Hobbies:* Music; Fishing; Reading; Golf; Tennis. *Address:* Percy Lodge, Killiney, Co Dublin, Ireland.

SHANKS, John Alexander, b. 10 Aug. 1926, Glasgow, Scotland. Consulting Obstetrician/Gynaecologist. m. Sheila Stewart Smith, 27 Nov. 1950, Bahrain, 4 sons, 1 daughter. *Education:* MB, ChB, University of Aberdeen, 1948; Memberships, 1962, Fellowship, 1974, Royal College of Obstetricians and Gynaecologists; Fellowship, Royal College of Physicians and Surgeons of Canada, 1964. *Appointments:* Lecturer, Pathology, Obstetrics & Gynaecology, University of Aberdeen; Private Practice, Brockville, Ontario, Canada. *Memberships:* Canadian Medical Association; Ontario Medical Association; Ontario Society of Clinical Hypnosis; American Society of Clinical Phynosis; Fellow, American College of Obstetricians & Gynaecologists. *Hobbies:* Sailing; Photography; Drama. *Address:* Glenwood Medical Centre, Suite 207, 6 Glenwood Pl, Brockville, Ontario, Canada.

SHANKS, Michael Kevin, b. 27 Nov. 1956, Augusta, Georgia, USA. Chiropractor. *Education:* BSc, St Ambrose College; Doctor of Chiropractic, Palmer College of Chiropractic. *Appointments:* Director, Research, Parker Chiropractic Research Foundation; Chiropractor, Static Bologna, Italy. *Memberships:* American Chiropractic Association; International Chiropractic Association; Associazione Italiana Chiropractici; European Chiropractor's Union; Foundation for Athletic Research and Education; Gonstead Clinical Studie Society. *Honours:* Quill and Scroll, 1974; Gold Seal Gold Award, Southwestern College, 1974. *Hobbies:* Tennis; Jogging; Swimming; Photography. *Address:* 3825 South Drive, Fort Worth, TX 76109, USA.

SHANNON, William Francis Eugene, b. 13 Feb.Republic of Ireland, General Practitioner, Director of Vocational Training in General Practice. m. Clodagh Magner, 15 Aug. 1967, Cork, 2 sons, 3 daughters. *Education:* MB, BCh, BAO (NUI), DCH, D Obst, MD. *Appointments include:* House Officer, Selly Oak Hospital, Birmingham, England, 1966; Senior House Officer, National Maternity Hospital, Dublin, Republic of Ireland, 1967, Our Lady's Hospital for Sick Children, Dublin 1967-68; General Practice Trainee, Departm-

ent of General Practice, University of Edinburgh, Scotland, 1968-69; Principal in General Practice, Bishopstown, Cork, Republic of Ireland, 1969-; Course Organiser, Director, Vocational Training in General Practice, Cork University, 1976-. *Memberships:* Foundation Member, Irish College of General Practitioners; Fellow, Royal College of General Practitioners; Association of University Teachers of General Practice; Diplomate, Royal College of Obstetricians and Gynaecologists. *Publications include:* 'Vulvo-Vaginitis and Vaginal Discharge in General Practice', 1975; 'The General Practitioner in Ireland', 1976; 'A Case of Right Iliac Fossa Pain' (various authors), 1977; 'A Review of the Factors affecting Consultations in General Practice', 1984. *Honour:* Dr John Sheppard Memorial Prize, 1980. *Hobbies:* Reading; Music; Fishing; Gaelic Games. *Address:* Ballavone House, Farrenlea Road, Cork, Republic of Ireland.

SHAPIRO, Arthur K, b. 1 Nov. 1923, New York, USA. Clinical Professor of Psychiatry, Director, Tourette and Tic Laboratory and Clinic, Mount Sinai School of Medicine, New York, USA. m. Elaine Shapiro, 23 Jan. 1949, New York, 1 son, 2 daughters. *Education:* MD, University of Chicago Medical School, 1955. *Appointments:* Clinical Professor Psychiatry and Pharmacology, Director, Special Studies Laboratory, Cornell University College of Medicine, 1967-77. *Memberships:* American Psychiatric Association; American Psychopathological Association; AMA. *Publications:* Author of over 150 articles, chapters and books on professional subjects. *Honours:* Summa cum Laude; Phi Beta Kappa. *Hobby:* Research. *Address:* 17 Colvin Road, Scarsdale, NY 10583, USA.

SHAPIRO, Barry A, b. 8 May 1937, Detroit, Michigan, USA. Professor of Anaesthesia. 2 sons. *Education:* BA 1959, MD 1963, University of Michigan; Fellow, American College of Anaesthesiology, 1971; Fellow, American College of Chest Physicians, 1972; Diplomate, American Board of Anaesthesiology, 1968. *Appointments:* Professor of Clinical Anaesthesia & Physical Medicine, Northwestern University Medical School. *Memberships:* Chairman, Respiratory Care Committee, American Society of Anaesthesiology; Society of Critical Care Medicine, Council, 1977-83; President, National Association of Medical Directors of Respiratory Care, 1982--84; Board of Medical Advisors of American Association of Respiratory Care, Chairman, 1980; American Medical Association; American College of Chest Physicians; ATS. *Publications:* "Clinical Application of Blood Gases", 3rd edition 1982; "Clinical Application of Respiratory Care", 3rd edition 1985; "Case Studies in Critical Care Medicine", 1985. *Honours:* Bird Literary Award, 1977; Jimmy Young Distinguished Service Award, 1981. *Hobby:* Sailing. *Address:* Suite 678, 250 East Superior Street, Chicago, IL 60611, USA.

SHAPIRO, Larry Jay, b. 6 July 1946, Chicago, Illinois, USA. Professor of Pediatrics and Biological Chemistry. m. Carolyn Kirk, 3 June 1968, St Louis, Missouri, 1 son, 2 daughters. *Education:* AB, MD, Washington University, St Louis. *Appointments:* Intern and Assistant Resident, St Louis Children's Hospital and Washington University School of Medicine, 1971-73; Research Associate in Biochemical Genetics, National Institutes of Health, 1973-75; Assistant Professor, Associate Professor, Professor, University of California at Los Angeles School of Medicine, 1975-. *Memberships include:* Council Member, Society for Pediatric Research; AFCR; American Pediatric Society; American Society for Clinical Investigation; Board of Directors, American Society of Human Genetics; Council, Western SPR; Fellow, American Academy of Pediatrics; President elect, Society for Inherited Metabolic Disease; Chairman, Genetic Basis of Disease Study Section, NIH. *Publications:* Many articles and book chapters. *Honours:* Ross Award, Western Society for Pediatric Research, 1981; E Mead Johnson Award, American Academy of Pediatrics, 1982; NIH Research Career Development Award, 1980-85. *Address:* Division of Medical Genetics, Harbor/UCLA

Medical Center, 1000 W Carson Street, Torrance, CA 90509, USA.

SHAPIRO, Robert Stephen, b. 6 Dec. 1945, Montreal, Canada. Associate Professor, McGill University. m. Tina Schleifer, 22 Dec. 1968, Montreal, 1 son, 2 daughters. *Education:* BSc, 1967, MD, CM, McGill University, 1969. *Memberships:* The Association of Otolaryngologists of the Province of Quebec; Canadian Medical Association; Quebec Medical Association; Canadian Society of Otolaryngology, Head and Neck Surgery; American Academy of Otolaryngology, Head and Neck Surgery; Society for Ear, Nose and Throat Advances in Children; Fellow, American College of Surgeons; Canadian Craniofacial Society; American Cleft Palate Association; American Society of Pediatric Otolaryngology. *Publications:* Several publications to professional journals including 'Partial Adenoidectomy', 1982; 'Computed Tomography in the Evaluation of An Osteoma of the Ethmoid Sinus', (with EM Azouz, RA Daou), 1982; 'Foreign Bodies in the Nose', 1983; 'Epignathus: A Report of Two Cases', (with JE Pavlin, A O'Gorman, HB Williams, RJ Crepeau), 1984. *Address:* The Montreal Children's Hospital, 2300 Tupper Street, Montreal, Quebec H3H 1P3, Canada.

SHARMA, Shiv R, b. 14 June 1937, Jammu, India. Clinic Medical Director. m. Shashi, 6 Feb. 1963, Nairobi, Kenya, 2 sons. *Education:* MBBS, Agra; LMCC; FLEX; Certificant in Family Medicine, CCFP (C); Diplomate, American Board of Family Practice. *Appointments:* Resident Intern, Mulago Hospital, Kampala, Uganda, 1963-64; Rotating Intern, St Boniface General Hospital, Manitoba, Canada, 1965-66; Family Medicine, Canada, 1966-. *Memberships:* Canadian Medical Association; American Academy of Family Practice; College of Family Physicians of Canada; American Society of Clinical Hypnosis. *Hobbies:* Photography; Travelling. *Address:* Albro Lake Medical Clinic, 107 Albro Lake Road, Dartmouth, Nova Scotia B3A 3Y7, Canada.

SHAVER, David Paul, b. 24 Oct. 1949, Bradenton, Florida, USA. Psychologist. m. Jessica Ann Connavino, 1 June 1985, Lake Charles, Louisiana. *Education:* BA English and Philosophy, Arkansas State University, 1973; MEd 1977, EdD 1980, Mental Health Counseling, University of Arkansas. *Appointments:* Private Practice, Houston, Texas, and Little Rock, Arkansas. *Memberships:* American Society of Clinical Hypnosis; International Society of Hypnosis; National Academy of Certified Clinical Mental Health Counselors. *Hobbies:* Aviation (private pilot); Photography. *Address:* Associate in Psychology, Counseling and Education, 650 South Shackleford Road, Suite 202, Little Rock, AR 72211, USA.

SHAW, Anthony, b. 31 Oct. 1929, Shanghai, China. Paediatric Surgeon. m. Iris Azian, 12 Mar. 1955, Boston, Massachusetts, USA, 2 sons, 1 daughter. *Education:* BA, Harvard College, 1950; MD, New York University, 1954. *Appointments include:* Professor of Surgery & Paediatrics, University of Virginia Medical School, 1973-80; Clinical Professor of Surgery, University of California, Los Angeles (UCLA) School of Medicine, 1981-; Director, Department of Paediatric Surgery/Surgeon-in-Chief, Familian Children's Hospital, City of Hope National Medical Centre, 1981-. *Memberships include:* Fellow, American College of Surgeons; Surgical Fellow, American Academy of Paediatrics; Association of Harvard Chemists; American Medical Association; Founder Member, New York Society for Paediatric Surgery; Founder Member, American Paediatric Surgical Association; Fellow, New York Academy of Medicine; American Association for the Advancement of Science; Physicians for Automotive Safety; Institute of Society, Ethics & the Life Science; Founding Member, American Trauma Society; Paediatric Oncology Group; British Association of Paediatric Surgeons; etc. *Publications include:* Numerous contributions, refereed professional journals; Book chapters. *Honours include:* Alpha Omega Alpha; Commissioners Award, Virginia Department of Welfare; Various offices, professional organisations; Consultant, American Academy of Paediatrics Bioethics Committee, 1983; Visiting Professor of Surgery, Yale University School of Medicine, 1985; Invited guest speaker, opening Virginia Conference, Child Abuse/Neglect, 1985; Visiting Professor, People's Republic of China, 1985. *Hobby:* Writing. *Address:* City of Hope National Medical Centre, Department of Paediatric Surgery, 1500 East Duarte Road, Duarte, CA 91010, USA.

SHAW, Gavin Brown, b. 24 May 1919, Glasgow, Scotland. Retired Consultant Physician. m. Margaret Mabon Henderson, 25 May 1943, Edinburgh, 1 son, deceased, 2 daughters. *Education:* BSc; MB ChB; FRCP, Glasgow, 1964, Edinburgh, 1965, London, 1965. *Appointments:* House Physician, Sir J W McNee, West Inf, Glasgow; T/Surg. Lieut. RNVR; Clinical Assistant, Sir J W McNee, West Inf, Glasgow; Senior Registrar, South General Hospital, Glasgow; Consultant Physician & Cardiologist, South General Hospital, Glasgow; Acting Post-graduate Dean, Glasgow University. *Memberships:* Association of Physicians UK & Ireland; Scottish Society of Physicians; British Cardiac Society; Scottish Society of Experimental Medicine. *Publications:* Articles in professional journals; Editor, "Resuscitation & Cardiac Pacing", 1965. *Honours:* CBE, 1981; President, Royal College of Physicians & Surgeons of Glasgow, 1978-80; Honorary FACP, 1979 FRCP (I) 1979, FRCPsych, 1980, FRCGP, 1980. *Hobbies:* Walking; Gardening; Painting; Reading; Music. *Address:* 4 Horseshoe Road, Bearsden, Glasgow G61 2ST, Scotland.

SHAW, Henry Jagoe, b. 16 Mar. 1922, Stafford, England, Consultant Surgeon, Head and Neck/ENT, Royal Marsden Hospital, London. *Education:* BM, BCh, 1945, MA, 1946, Oxford University; FRCS England, 1950; VRD. *Appointments:* Consultant Ear, Nose and Throat Surgeon, Royal National Throat Nose and Ear Hospital, London; Civilian Consultant Ear Nose and Throat Surgeon, Royal Navy; Consultant Ear Nose and Throat Surgeon, St Mary's Hospital, Praed Street, London. *Memberships:* Member, Association of Head and Neck Surgeons of Great Britain; Member, British Association of Surgical Oncology; Corresponding Member, Association of Head and Neck Surgeons of the USA; Fellow, Royal Society of Medicine, London; Member, British Association of Otolaryngologists; Honorary Member, American Laryngological Association; Honorary Member, Otolaryngological Association of Australia; Member, Société Francaise d'Otorhinolaryngologie. *Publications:* 'Partial Laryngectomy after irradiation', 1978; 'Malignant disease of the Oropharynx', 1980; 'Conservation and Repair in Cancer Surgery of the Head and Neck', 1980. *Honours:* Hunterian Professor, Royal College Surgeons, 1957; W J Harrison Prize, Royal Society of Medicine, 1980; President, Section of Laryngology, Royal Society of Medicine, 1979-80; Semon Lecturer, University of London, 1984; Ernest Miles Lecturer, Royal Marsden Hospital, 1985. *Hobbies:* Walking; Sailing; Swimming. *Address:* 106 Harley Street, London W1, England.

SHEARS, Arthur Howard, b. 27 July 1924, Glace Bay, Nova Scotia, Canada. Professor & Head, Division of Physical Medicine & Rehabilitation, Dalhousie University Medical School; Medical Director, Physiatrist-in-Chief, Nova Scotia Rehabilitation Centre. m. Dorothy Claire Bulmer, 2 September 1950, Chester, Nova Scotia, 1 son, 4 daughters. *Education:* MD, CM, Dalhousie University; Certification, PM&R, Royal College of Physicians & Surgeons of Canada, 1956; Fellow, ibid, 1972. *Appointments:* Family & industrial practice, Glace Bay, Nova Scotia, 1950-52; Resident, Fellow, Dalhousie University, Toronto/Harvard University, 1952-56; Consulting Physician/Teacher of Medicine, 1956-. *Memberships:* Royal College of Physicians & Surgeons of Canada; Canadian Medical Association; American Academy of Physical Medicine & Rehabilitation; American Congress of PM&R; American Academy of Academic Phyiatrists.

Publications include: 'New Drugs & Hypertension', with S Speller & Steeves, Treatment Services Bulletin, 1953; 'Symposium on Medical Education & Practice, Medicine in the University & Community of the Future', Dalhousie Medical School Centennial, 1969; 'Preliminary Clinical Observations on the Therapeutic Effect of Clonidine in Spinal Cord Injury', co-author, 'Canadian Medical Association Journal', 1985; 'Gonadal Regulation in Men with Flaccid Paraplegia', co-author, 'Archives of Physical Medicine & Rehabilitation', 1985. *Honour:* Plaque, Rehabilitation, Province of Nova Scotia, 1977. *Hobbies:* Racquet sports; Skiing; Sailing; Golf; Photography; Men's choir. *Address:* Nova Scotia Rehabilitation Centre, 1341 Summer Street, Halifax, Nova Scotia, Canada B3H 4K4.

SHEEHY, James Luhn, b. 21 Dec. 1926, USA. Otologist; Medical Director of Otologic Medical Group. m. 3 Feb. 1951, San Francisco, 3 sons. *Education:* AB, Stanford University, 1947; MD, Stanford University Medical School, 1950. *Appointment:* Otologist, Otologic Medical Group, Los Angeles, 1958-. *Memberships:* Fellow, American Medical Association; California Medical Association; Los Angeles County Medical Association; Diplomat, American Board of Otolaryngology; Fellow, American Academy of Otolaryngology-Head and Neck Surgery; Pacific Coast Oto-Ophthalmological Society, Scientific Program Chairman, 1964-68, President, 1983-84; Los Angeles Society of Otolaryngology, President, 1978-79; Alpha Omega Alpha; Otosclerosis Study Group, President, 1979-80; Fellow, American Laryngological, Rhinological and Otological Society; Fellow, American Otological Society, Council Member, 1979-81; Association of Otolaryngologists of India, Honorary Member; Australian Otolaryngology Society, Honorary Member; American Medical Writers Association; Medical Group Management Association. *Honours:* J. MacKenzie Brown Award (most outstanding paper), 1964; Recipient of Professor Doctor Ignacio Barraquer Memorial Award, in recognition of important contributions to medicine and surgery through cinematography, 1966. *Address:* Otologic Medical Group Incorporated, 2122 West Third Street, Los Angeles, CA 90057, USA.

SHEEN, Alan Edward, 1 May 1950, New Orleans, Louisiana, USA. Private Practitioner. m. Joan Carolyn Kessler, 10 Jan. 1981, New Orleans, 2 daughters. *Education:* Tulane University, New Orleans, 1968-71; MD, Louisiana State University School of Medicine, New Orleans, 1974. *Appointments:* Intern, Oschner Foundation Hospital, New Orleans, 1975-76; Resident, Pediatrics, Charity Hospital in New Orleans (Tulane Divion), New Orleans, 1976-78; Fellow, Pediatric Allergy Charity Hospital in New Orleans (Louisiana State University Division), New Orleans, 1978; Fellow, Pediatric Allergy, Children's Hospital, National Medical Center, Washington, District of Columbia, 1978-80; Staff, Pediatric Allergy, Children's Hospital New Orleans, East Jefferson General Hospital, Metairie, Louisiana, 1980-; Private Practice. *Memberships:* Alpha Epsilon Delta; Orleans Parish Medical; Louisiana State Medical Society; American Medical Association; American Academy of Pediatrics; American Academy of Allergy and Immunology; American College of Allergy; American College of Chest Physicians. *Publications include:* 'Serum Theoplylline Concentrations in Asthmatic Children' (with R M Sly), 1978; 'Comparison of Theolair SR and Theodur Tablets' (co-author), 1979; 'Evaluation of Calibration of Spirometers' (with R M Sly), 1980; 'Status Asthmaticus and Bleeding Duodenal Ulcer Disease' (co-author), 1980. *Honours:* Gold Medal Scholastic Award, 1964-68; Physics Award, 1968; Valedictorian, 1968. *Hobbies include:* Collecting antique music boxes; Construction; Travel; Amateur Dramatics; History of Art; Sailing; Fishing; Golf; Tennis. *Address:* 3701 Houma Boulevard 101, Metairie, LA 70002, USA.

SHELDAHL, Lennie Diane McCord, b. 6 Oct. 1947,

Iowa, USA. Psychology Instructor. Married, 1 son. *Education:* BS Psychology & History, Iowa State University, 1969; MS Counselling Psychology, Drake University, 1976; (Candidate) PhD Social Psychology, Iowa State University. *Appointments:* Counsellor, Lincoln High School, Des Moines, Iowa; Counsellor, Psychological Testing Services, West Des Moines, Iowa; Psychology Instructor, Grandview College, Urbandale High School, Des Moines Area Community College. *Memberships:* American Psychological Association; American Sociological Association; American Society for Training & Development; Iowa Personnel & Guidance Association; Intra-family Sexual Abuse Council; Smithsonian Associate; and others. *Publications:* "Anorexia Nervosa: A Teaching Manual", 1980; Various articles in field of adolescent psychology. *Honours:* Phi Delta Kappa, 1977; Phi Kappa Phi, 1985; ASTD Regional Award for Community Service, 1984. *Hobbies:* Riding; Scubadiving; Geology. *Address:* 923 42nd Street, West Des Moines, IA 50265, USA.

SHELDON, Stephen Howard, b. 4 Nov. 1947, Florida, USA. Associate Professor and Chairman, Department of Paediatrics. m. Eugenia Korona, 5 Dec. 1976, Chicago, Illinois, 1 son, 1 daughter. *Education:* BS, University of Florida; DO, Chicago College of Osteopathic Medicine; FAAP. *Appointments:* Assistant, 1975-78, Instructor, 1978-80, Department of Paediatrics, Rush Medical College; Adjunct Attending Pediatrician, 1978-80, Assistant Professor and Programme Director, Attending Paediatrician, 1980-83, Rush Pres St Lukes Medical Center; Visiting Assistant Professor, Department of Paediatric Dentistry, University of Illinois College of Dentistry, 1981; Assistant Professor, Rush Medical Center; Medical Director of Educational Research, Mount Sinai Hospital Medical Center, 1983-85; Associate Professor and Chairman, Department of Paediatrics, Chicago College of Osteopathic Medicine, 1985-; Attending Physician, Chicago Osteopathic Center and Olympia Fields Osteopathic Medicine Center, 1985-. *Memberships include:* International Society for Prevention of Child Abuse and Neglect; American Medical Association; Illinois State and Chicago Medical Societies; Chicago Paediatric Society; American Osteopathic Association; American Academy of Paediatrics. *Publications:* "Pediatric Differential Diagnosis", 1979 & 85; "Manual of Practical Pediatrics", 1981; "Diagnosis and Management of the Hospitalized Child", 1984; "Airplane Travel and Child Safety", 1980; "Hospitals Response to Increased Incidence of Child Abuse and Neglect", 1984. *Honour:* Citation of Merit, American Academy of Pediatrics, 1984. *Hobbies:* Golf; Painting; Photography; Ship building; Book collecting; Creative writing. *Address:* Department of Paediatrics, Chicago College of Osteopathic Medicine, 5200 South Ellis Avenue, Chicago, IL 60615, USA.

SHEMEN, Larry Judah, b. 19 Feb. 1954, Toronto, Canada. Program Director and Attending Surgeon, Manhattan Eye, Ear and Throat Hospital; Attending Surgeon, St. Vincent's Hospital. m. Sherri Deborah Rochwerg, 22 June 1980, Hamilton, Ontario. *Education:* MD, University of Toronto, 1978; Residency: Otolaryngology, Head and Neck Surgery, University of Toronto, 1983; General Surgery, Cedars Sinai Medical Center, Los Angeles, California, 1982; Fellowship, Head and Neck Surgery, Memorial Sloan-Kettering Cancer Center, New York, 1984. *Memberships:* American Academy of Otolaryngology, Head and Neck Surgery; American Academy of Facial Plastic and Reconstructive Surgery; Society for Head and Neck Surgeons. *Publications include:* Co-author, "Distribution of High Affinity Sodium-Independent (3/H) - Gamma Amino Acid H-GABA Binding in the Human Brain", 'Brain Research', 1977; Co-author: "Melanosis Coli: Changes in Appearance when Associated with Colonic Neoplasia', 'Arch Surg', 1983; Co-author: 'Cockayne Syndrome. An audiologic and Temporal Bone Analysis', 'American Journal of Otolaryngology', 1984; Co-author,

"Selecting Variants in Pharyngeal Reconstruction', 'Ann. Oto. Rhon. Laryn', 1984; Co-author: "Increased Incidence of Oral Tongue Cancers in Young Males", 'Journal of American Medical Association', 1984; Presentations. *Hobbies:* Scuba Diving; Photography; Tennis; Sailing. *Address:* Manhattan Ear, Eye and Throat Hospital, 210 East 64th Street, New York, NY 10021, USA.

SHEMISA, Othman, b. 24 July 1941, Libya. Director General, Centre for Health and Drug Research; Consultant Obstetrician Gynaecologist. m. Tahani M Kablan, 17 Aug. 1981, Benghazi, 3 sons, 2 daughters. *Education:* BSc, Pharmacy, Honours; MSc, Pharmacology; PhD, Pharmacology; Post Doctoral Fellow, Pharmacology; MD; NBD; JFACOG. *Appointments:* Assistant Professor, Chairman, Pharmacology, University of Garyounis Medical Faculty, Benghazi; Acting Dean, Chairman, Popular Committee, Medicine, Garyounis University; Associate Professor, Chairman, Pharmacology, University of Al-Fateh, Medical Faculty, Tripoli; Consultant Gynaecologist Obstetrician, 11th June Clinics and Hospital, Tripoli; Director General, Centre for Health and Drug Research, Tripoli. *Memberships:* American Pharmaceutical and Medical Associations; Sigma Xi; Royal Chemical Society of Great Britain; American College of Obstetrics and Gynaecology; Libyan Pharmaceutical Association. *Publications:* Author, numerous articles in professional journals including: 'Molecular Pharmacology'; 'Journal Biological Chemistry'; 'The Pharmacologist'; 'Garyounis Medical Journal'; 'Al-Fateh Medical Journal'; etc. *Honours:* Rho Chi; Phi Kappa Phi; Phi Lambda Epsilon; Honoured by Libyan Medical Sydnicate and Libyan Pharmaceutical Association. *Hobby:* Travel. *Address:* PO Box 4091, Tripoli OR 2670 Benghazi, Libya.

SHEMO, John Palmer David, b. 20 Oct. 1948, Waterford, New York, USA. Associate Professor, Behavioral Medicine & Psychiatry; Associate Professor, Internal Medicine. m. Mary Carroll Shemo, 20 May 1972, Silver Spring, 1 daughter. *Education:* BSc, Wheeling College, 1970; MD, West Virginia University, 1975; Residencies, various hospitals. *Appointments:* Assistant Professor, Behavioral Medicine & Psychiatry, 1978-79, Assistant Professor, Internal Medicine, 1978-79, Director, Inpatient Psychiatry and Emergency Psychiatric Services, 1978-79, Chief, Behavioral Medicine, Inpatient Service, 1979-82, Director, Psychiatric Emergency Service, 1982-, Chief, Behavioral Medicine & Psychiatry Consulta-Virginia. *Memberships:* American Psychiatric Association; Virginia Neuropsychiatric Association; Guest, Group for the Advancement of Psychiatry. *Publications:* Numerous articles in scientific journals. *Honours:* Alpha Sigma Nu; Alpha Omega Alpha; Ginsburg Fellow, Group for the Advancement of Psychiatry. *Hobbies:* Sports Participation; Landscaping; Woodwork; Reading; Art Collecting. *Address:* Box 203 Dept. of Behavioral Medicine & Psychiatry, University of Virginia Medical Centre, Charlotteville, VA 22908, USA.

SHENKOYA, Kayode Adeleye, b. 29 Nov. 1943, Lagos, Nigeria. Director of Medical Services. m. Folashade Adetoun Neye, 29 Nov. 1971, Lagos, Nigeria, 1 son, 3 daughters. *Education:* MB, BS, Lagos, 1969 (Distinctions in Pathology, Physiology & Medicine); Fellow, American College of Chest Physicians, 1980; Fellow, International Academy of Chest Physicians & Surgeons, 1982. *Appointments:* House Officer (Professorial Units), 1960-70, Senior House Officer in Medicine, 1970-71, Lagos University Teaching Hospital; Resident in Internal Medicine, 1971-73; Fellow in Cardiology, 1973-75, Clinical Instructor in Medicine (Faculty) 1975, University of Chicago, USA; Supernumerary Registrar (Cardio-Pulmonary Unit), Lagos University Teaching Hospital, 1976-78; Part-time Consultant Physician/Cardiologist, Central Bank of Nigeria, 1976-78; Head, Health Department, 1978, Chief Medical Officer, Chief Consultant Physician, 1982, Nigerian National Petroleum Corporation.

Memberships: First President, Federation of African Medical Student Associations, 1967-68; Executive Council Member, Nigerian Medical Association, 1976-79; American Heart Association; American Thoracic Society; International Society of Occupational Health Physicians. *Publications:* 'Mitral Valve Prolapse in Sacoid Heart Disease', Illinois Medical Journal, 1976; 'Aortic Arch Dissection - Medical v Surgical Therapy', American Journal of Cardiology, 1977; 'Medical Hazards of Oil Pollution', Nigerian Medical Journal, 1983; 'Tetra-Ethyl Lead in Nigerian Oil Industry Workers - Clinical & Laboratory Studies' (in press). *Honour:* Provost's Award for Best Student in Medicine, College of Medicine, University of Lagos, 1969. *Hobbies:* Classical Music; Light Reading; Lawn Tennis. *Address:* Health Department, Nigerian National Petroleum Corporation, Falomo Office Complex, PMB 12701, Ikoyi, Lagos, Nigeria.

SHEPHERD, John Henry, b. 11 July 1948, London, England. Consultant Gynaecological Surgeon; Gynaecological Oncologist. m. Alison Sheila Brandom-Adams, 27 May 1972, London, 1 son, 1 daughter. *Education:* MB, BS, St Bartholomew's Hospital Medical College, London University, 1971; FRCS; MRCOG; FACOG. *Appointments:* House Officer, St Bartholomew's Hospital, 1971-72; Lecturer, Human Morphology, Southampton University, 1973; Surgical Registrar, Royal Hampshire County Hospital, Winchester, 1974; Resident Surgical Officer, Queen Charlotte's Hospital, 1975, Samaritan Hospital, 1976; Gynaecological Registrar, Kingston Hospital, & Westminster Hospital, 1977-78; Lecturer, Senior Registrar, Queen Charlotte's Hospital, & Chelsea Hospital, 1978-79; Gynaecological Oncology Fellow, University of South Florida, Tampa, USA, 1979-81. *Memberships:* Royal College of Obstetricians and Gynaecologists, Council Member, 1984-; Fellow, Royal College of Surgeons of England; Fellow, American College of Obstetricians and Gynaecologists; Fellow, Royal Society of Medicine, Council, 1984-; Member, British Gynaecological Cancer Society. *Publications:* "Gynaecological Oncology", Co-Editor, 1985; Various Chapters & Scientific articles in numerous professional books and journals. *Honours:* Gold Medal, RCOG, 1978; Fulbright-Hays Scholarship, 1979. *Hobbies:* Travel; Skiing; Sailing; Squash; Cricket; Classical Music; Ballet. *Address:* 40 Harley Street, London W1N 1AS, England.

SHEPHERD, Ross William, b. 8 June 1947, Australia. Senior Lecturer, Child Health, University of Queensland; Paediatric Gastroenterologist, Royal Childrens Hospital. m. Karin Radcliffe, 28 Dec. 1968, Brisbane, 2 sons, 1 daughter. *Education:* MBBS, University of Queensland, 1970; MRCP, Paediatrics, England, 1974; FRACP, 1978; MD, Queensland, 1979. *Appointments:* Resident Medical Officer, Rockhampton General Hospital, Royal Childrens Hospital; Registrar, Paediatrics, Royal Childrens Hospital, Brisbane; Senior Resident, Queen Elizabeth Hospital for Children; Senior House Physician, The Hospital for Sick Children, London; Fellow, Gastroenterology, The Hospital for Sick Children, Toronto, Canada. *Memberships:* Gastroenterological Society of Australia; Australian College of Paediatrics; Australian Society for Medical Research; Paediatric Research Society; etc. *Publications:* Numerous articles, in professional journals. *Honours:* Recipient various honours and awards. *Hobbies:* Music; Travel. *Address:* Department of Child Health, Royal Childrens Hospital, Brisbane, Australia 04029.

SHEPPARD, Ronald Gene, b. 8 Apr. 1954, Logansport, Indiana. Chiropractic Physician. *Education:* BS, DC, Palmer College; Biochemistry Major, Purdue University, 1972-. *Appointments:* Owner of Glendale & Castleton Chiropractic Clinics, Indianapolis. *Memberships:* American Chiropractic Association, Councils on Neurology, Athletics & Physical Fitness; American Medical Joggers Association; American Biomagnetic Society; American Holistic Medical Institute; Holistic Health Care Association; Lambda Chi Alpha. *Address:* 8208 Allisonville Road, Indianapolis, IN 46250, USA.

SHEPSTONE, Basil John, b. 4 Aug. 1935, Bloemfontein, South Africa. University Lecturer, Radiology, Head of Department, Deputy Director, Clinical Studies, University of Oxford, England; Hon. Consultant, Nuclear Medicine & Radiology, Oxfordshire Health Authority; Fellow, Wolfson College, Oxford. m. Brenda Victoria Alen, 23 Sep. 1961, Cambridge, England, 1 son, 1 daughter. *Education:* BSc, BSc, Honours, 1958, MSc, 1960, DSc, Physics, University of the Orange Free State; F. Inst. P, 1960; D Phil, Radiobiology, 1964, BMBCh, 1968, Oxon; DMRD (RCPS); MD, University of Capetown, 1977; MA, Oxon, 1978; BA Econ, University of South Africa, 1982; FRCR, 1984. *Appointments:* House Officer, United Oxford Hospitals, 1969; Senior Medical Officer, Later Acting Head, Bio-Engineering & Medical Physics, Groote Schuur Hospital, 1970-71, Head, Senior Lecturer, Nuclear Medicine, Groote Schuur Hospital, 1972-78, University of Capetown; Clinical Lecturer, Radiology, 1978-81, Lecturer, Radiology, 1981-, University of Oxford, England. *Memberships:* Fellow, Royal College of Radiologists; British Nuclear Medicine Society; British Institute of Radiology; Fellow, Institute of Physics. *Publications:* Numerous articles in professional journals. *Honours:* Alan Nicholls Memorial Lecturer, University of Oxford, 1977; Oxford Clinical Student Award for Best Clinical Teacher, 1979, 1980. *Hobbies:* Legal & Theological Studies; Travel; Art; Swimming; Philately. *Address:* 464 Banbury Road, Oxford OX2 7RC, England.

SHERIDAN, Brian Leslie, b. 6 Apr. 1945, Liverpool, England. Director of Haematology Laboratory and Assistant Professor of Pathology. m. Jennifer Dunderdale, 9 June 1967, Liverpool, 2 sons, 1 daughter. *Edcuation:* MB, BS, Newcastle upon Tyne; MRCP (UK); MRC (Path); FRCP (C); MRC Research Assistant, NW Cancer Research Fellowship. *Appointments:* Registrar in Pathology, 1969-71; Registrar in Medicine, 1972-73, Liverpool; Research Positions, Haematology, University of Liverpool, 1973-75; Resident, Haematology, University of Toronto, Canada, 1975-77; Assistant Haematologist, 1978-82, Director, Division of Haematology, 1982-, Dalhousie University, Halifax, Nova Scotia, Canada. *Memberships:* Member, Royal College of Pathologists; Member, Royal College of Physicians, England; Member, Royal College of Physicians and Surgeons of Canada; Member, Canadian Association of Pathologists; Member, International Society of Experimental Haematology. *Publications:* 'Patterns of foetal laemoglobin production in leukaemia', 1976; 'Vitamin B12 Assays', 1985. *Hobbies:* Masters swimming; Soccer; Modern jazz. *Address:* 521 Tower Road, Halifax, Nova Scotia, Canada.

SHERIDAN, Edward Patrick, b. 2 December 1937, USA. Professor and Chairman, Division of Psychology, Department of Psychology and Behavioral Sciences, Northwestern University Medical School. m. Kathleen, JD, PhD, 3 June 1963, St Louis, Missouri. *Education:* BA, University of Windsor, Ontario, 1961; MA, University of Detroit, 1964; PhD, Loyola University, Chicago, 1968. *Appointments:* Assistant Professor, University of Windsor, Ontario, 1966-67; Chief Psychologist, Oakland County Mental Health Services, 1967-68; Assistant Professor and Director of Clinical Training, University of Illinois, Counseling Center, 1968-73; Associate Professor to Professor and Director of Psychiatry Outpatient Services, Northwestern University Medical School, 1973-81; Adjunct Professor of Law, Northwestern University, 1981-. *Memberships:* American Psychological Association; American Association of University Professors; International Association of Psycho Social Rehabilitation Agencies; International Association of Applied Psychology; Mid-Western Psychological Association. *Publications include:* Co-author, 'Police referred psychiatric emergencies: Advantages of community treatment', 'Journal of Community Psychology', 1981; Co-author, 'Evolution of an emergency room psychiatric staffing', 'American Journal of Orthopsychiatry', 1982; Co-author, 'Task group on health

policy', 'Health Psychology', 1983; Co-author, 'Management of burnout: Training psychologists in professional life-span perspectives', 'Professional Psychology: Research and Practice', 1985. *Hobbies:* Tennis; Travel; Novels; Movies. *Address:* Division of Psychology Ward 12-138, Northwestern University Medical School, 303 East Chicago Avenue, Chicago, IL 60611, USA.

SHERIDAN, Susan Nager, b. 19 Apr. 1953, New York City, New York, USA. Private Practitioner; Director of Summer Programming and Staff Member. m. Richard M Sheridan, 24 May 1981, New York City. *Education:* BA, Magna cum laude, Radcliffe College, Harvard University, 1974; MSW, Smith College School for Social Work, 1977; Licensed Clinical Social Worker. *Appointments:* Family Counselling and Guidance Centers Incorporated, Mashfield, Massachusetts, 1977-81; Westchester Community Health Plan, White Plains, New York, 1981-82; Private Practice, 1982-; Director of Summer Programming, Staff Member, Wilkins Center for Eating Disorders, Greenwich, Connecticut, 1983-. *Memberships:* National Association of Social Workers; Association for Clinical Social Workers; Westchester Chapter, New York Society for Clinical Social Workers. *Publications:* 'A Thematic Analysis of Short-Term Group Psychotherapy with Bulimic Young Women' in 'Bulima Anorexia Self Help Newsletter', 1985. *Hobbies:* Choral Singing; Interior decorating; Gardening; Reading. *Address:* c/o Wilkins Center for Eating Disorders, 7 Riversville Road, Greenwich, CT 06830, USA.

SHERMAN, Fred, b. 21 May 1932, Minneapolis, Minnesota, USA. Professor. m. Revina Freeman, 25 July 1958, 2 sons, 1 daughter. *Education:* BA, University of Minnesota, 1953; PhD, University of California, Berkeley, 1958. *Appointments:* Senior Instructor 1961-62, Assistant Professor 1962-66, Associate Professor 1966-71, Professor 1971-, Chairman, Biochemistry, 1982-, University of Rochester. *Memberships:* Genetic Society of America; Environmental Mutagen Society; American Association for the Advancement of Science; American Society of Microbiology; Biophysical Society. *Publications include:* "Cold Spring Harbor Manual on Yeast Genetics & Molecular Biology", co-author, annually 1970-85; 'Methionine or not methionine at the beginning of a protein' in "Bioessays", 1985, co-author; etc. *Honours:* Magna cum laude, 1953; Fellow, National Institutes of Health, 1959-61; Wander Memorial Lecturer, 1975; National Academy of Sciences, 1985; National Institutes of Health grants, 1963-. *Address:* Department of Radiation Biology & Biophysics, University of Rochester Medical School, 575 Elmwood Avenue, Rochester, NY 14642, USA.

SHERMAN, Robert Lee, b. 3 Mar. 1929, New York City, USA. Chairman, Department of Psychiatry, Holmes Regional Medical Center, Melbourne, Florida. m. Claudine Martin-de Lorme, 21 June 1974, Huntington, New York, 1 son, 2 daughters. *Education:* MD; MS, Medicine; BA, Chemistry; ABPN, Psychiatry; Certificate in Neurology, Pilgrim Psychiatric Center, 1970; Certified in CPR, ALS, Diplomat, Behavioral Medicine Techniques, Medical Hypnosis, American Society Clinical Hypnosis. *Appointments:* Chief, Girls' Adolescent Unit, Northeast Nassau Psychiatric Hospital, 1967; Chief, Psychiatric Services, Suffolk Development Center, Melville, New York, 1970; Unit Chief, Adolescent Unit, Pilgrim Psychiatric Center, West Islip, New York, 1975; Chief Medical Officer, Pilgrim Psychiatric Center, 1977; Private Practice, Vero Beach, Florida, 1978-79; Chairman, Department of Psychiatry, Holmes Regional Medical Center, 1980-; Chief Psychiatric Consultant, Brevard County Mental Health Center and Hospital, Florida, 1982-; Lecturer, University of Central Florida, Florida Institute of Technology and Brevard Community College, 1982-. *Memberships:* American Medical Association; Florida Medical Association; American Psychiatric Association; Florida Psychiatric Society; American Society of Clinical Hypnosis; Florida Society of Clinical Hypnosis; American Association of Clinical Psychiatry; American Association of Adolescent Psychiatrists; Royal Society of Health, etc. *Publications include:* "Factors influencing the incorporation on 1131 into thyroid protein of the rat", thesis presented at Hahnemann Medical College, Philadelphia, 1955; "Graphics aid in computer programs for teaching Learning Disabled Children: 1) Multiplication Aid TRS-80', 'Microcomputer News', October 1981; 'Comparative Review of Automated MMPI Services', 'Computers in Psychiatry/Psychology' (in press); Contributor to professional journals; Presentations. *Honours:* American Medical Association's Physician's Recognition Award, yearly 1963-; Citizen's Award, Huntington Township, 1964. *Hobbies:* Sailing; Music; Reading; Swimming; Computer Programming. *Address:* 664 Tallwood Circle, Melbourne, FL 32904, USA.

SHETH, Anil, b. 5 Aug. 1933, Ahmedabad, India. Deputy Director. m. Dr Nandini, 15 May 1958, Bombay, India, 1 daughter. *Education:* MSc; PhD; Worc Fdn Expt Biol, USA, 1963; University Wisconsin, USA, 1964; University Ann Arbor, USA, 1970; Ben May Cancer Research Centre, Chicago, USA, 1971; The Salk Institute, USA, 1978; The Karolinska Institute, Sweden, 1983. *Memberships:* Endocrine Society of India. *Publications:* Author of over 350 research papers in national and international journals. *Honours:* Prize by Indian Council of Medical Research, 1963. *Hobby:* Music. *Address:* Indian Council of Medical Research, Institute for Research in Reproduction, J M Street, Parel, Bombay 400 012, India.

SHETTY, Prakash Sarvotham, b. 28 Sep. 1943, India. Professor and Chairman. m. Nandini Pathak, 25 June 1980, Bangalore, 1 son, 1 daughter. *Education:* MB BS; MD; Madras University; PhD, Cambridge University. *Appointments:* Assistant Professor; Commonwealth Medical Scholar; Associate Professor; Department of Physiology, St. John's Medical College, Bangalore. *Memberships:* Nutrition Society, UK; Association of Physiologists and Pharmacologists, India; Indian Society of Gastroenterology; Ethological Society of India; Indian Society for Chronobiology. *Publications:* Con tributor to: 'Lancet', 1979; 'Clinical Science', Editorial Review, 1980; 'Clinical Nutrition-Human Nutrition', Editorial, 1983; Editor, "Studies in Animal Behaviour". *Hobbies:* Study of Indian Sculptures and Art. *Address:* ICMR Nutrition Research Centre, Department of Physiology, St. John's Medical College, Bangalore 560 034, India.

SHIFFMAN, Melvin Arthur, b. 23 Aug. 1931, Brooklyn, New York, USA. General Surgeon, Oncology; Medical-Legal Consultant. m. Pearl Asher, 28 Aug. 1955, Chicago, Illinois, 1 son, 2 daughters. *Education:* BS, 1953; MD, Northwestern School of Medicine, Chicago, 1957; JD, Western State University, Fullerton, California, 1976. *Appointments include:* Assistant Clinical Professor of Surgery, University of California, Irvine, 1968-83. *Memberships include:* President 1984-2, Orange County Loca, Union of American Physicians & Dentists; Board, California Federation, Union of American Physicians & Dentists; Society of Head & Neck Surgeons; American Society of Clinical Oncology; American Society of Abdominal Surgeons. *Publications:* Various scientific papers including: 'Parathyroid Disease' (Oral Surgery, Medicine & Pathology, 1964); 'Multiple Phlebectasia' (Archives of Surgery, 1967); 'Evaluation of Recurrence Following Vagotomy & Pyroplasty' (International Surgery, 1967); etc. *Honours:* Fellow, International College of Surgeons, 1965; Fellow, American College of Legal Medicine; Life Fellow, International Biographical Association. *Hobbies:* Antiques; Stamp collecting; Guns. *Address:* 1076 E First Street, Suite D, Tustin, CA 92680, USA.

SHIFTAN, Thomas André, b. 3 May 1946, New York City, USA. Staff Physician, Scripps Clinic. m. Maureen Clancey, 19 July 1969, Lynn, Massachusetts, 2 sons. *Education:* BA, Distinction; MD; Diplomate, American

Board of Internal Medicine, American Board of Haematology, American Board of Medical Oncology. *Appointments include:* Fellow, Division of Haematology & Oncology, University of California, San Diego, 1975-77; Clinical Instructor, Medicine, ibid, 1976-77; Assistant Professor of Medicine, ibid, 1978-79; Visiting Physician, University of Innsbruck, Austria, 1977-78; Assistant Clinical Professor, University of California, San Diego (UCSD), 1979-; Physician, San Diego Internal Medicine Group Medical Clinic, Inc, San Diego, 1979-83; Medical Director, Scripps Clinic, San Diego, 1983-. *Memberships:* American Society of Haematology; American Society of Clinical Oncology. *Publications include:* Numerous contributions to professional journals, conference presentations, etc. *Honours:* Alpha Epsilon Delta, 1966; BA, Distinction, University of Virginia, 1968; Irwin S Markel Award, Alpha Epsilon Pi, 1968. *Hobbies:* Skiing; Cycling; Opera. *Address:* Scripps Clinic San Diego, 2020 Genesee Avenue, San Diego, CA 92123, USA.

SHILKIN, Keith Brian, b. 23 Dec. 1938, Perth, Western Australia, Australia. Head, Department of Histopathology. m. Sarah Goldner, 12 Mar. 1972, London, England, 1 son, 1 daughter. *Education:* MB, BS (Western Australia). *Appointments:* Lecturer, Pathology, University of Western Australia, Australia, 1965; Registrar, Pathology, Royal Perth Hospital, Western Australia, 1966-67; Lecturer, Pathology, University of Singapore, Malaysia, 1968-70; Senior Lecturer, Department of Morbid Anatomy, Kings College Hospital, University of London, London, England, 1970-73; Head, Department of Histopathology, Sir Charles Gairdner Hospital, Nedlands, Western Australia, Australia, 1973-; Visiting Associate Professor, Department of Pathology, Albert Einstein College of Medicine, Yeshiva University, New York, USA, 1982. **Memberships:** Fellow, Royal College of Pathologists of Australasia; Fellow, Royal College of Pathologists; President 1984-85, Western Australia Branch, Australian Medical Association; President Elect, Australasian Division, International Academy of Pathology; Pathological Society of Great Britain and Ireland; Asian Pacific Association for the Study of the Liver; GastroEnterological Society of Australia; Australian Society of Cytology. *Honour:* Elected Fellow, Australian Medical Association, 1986. *Publications:* Author and co-author of many papers on various aspects of pathology; "Histopathology", (Member of Editorial Advisory Board). *Address:* Department of Histopathology, Sir Charles Gairdner Hospital, Nedlands, Western Australia 6009, Australia.

SHIMOJI, Koki, b. 21 Nov. 1935, Japan. University Professor/Chairman. m. Yoko 9 Jan. 1972, Japan, 2 daughters. *Education:* MD, Kumamoto University School of Medicine, 1960; Dr Med Science, Kyoto University, 1965; Mayo Graduate School of Medicine, 1967. *Appointments:* Lecturer, Kyoto University, 1965-66; Associate Professor, Kumamoto University, 1968-73; Associate Professor, Tokyo Medical and Dental University, 1973-74; Professor, Chairman, Anaesthesiology, Niigata University, 1974-. *Memberships:* Japan Society of Anesthesiology; Japan Society Resuscitation; Japan Society EEG & EMG; Japan Society Pain Clinic; Japan Society Critical Medicine; Japan Society Physiology; Japan Society CBF & Metabolism. *Honours:* Most Distinguished Paper, Japan Society Anesthesiology Research, 1965; Medical Research Award, Japan Medical Association, 1983. *Publications:* "Neuroanesthesia", (Japanese), 1972; "Electroanesthesia", 1975; "Neurophysilogical Basis of Anesthesia", 1975; "Practice of Emergency Medicine", (Japanese), 1980; "Atlas Anesthesia", (Japanese), 1986. *Hobbies:* Painting; Photography; Sports. *Address:* Department of Anesthesiology, Niigata University School of Medicine, Asahi-Machi, Niigata 951, Japan.

SHIN, Kyu Ho, b. 9 May 1944, Korea. Professor. m. Won Yong Shin, 8 Sep. 1980, Seoul, 2 sons, 1 daughter. *Education:* MD, Seoul National University; DMR (T), CRCP (I); FRCP (C), University of Toronto, Canada.

Appointments: Lecturer, Queen's University, Kingston, 1974-76; Assistant Professor, McGill University, Montreal, 1976-78; Associate Professor, 1978-85, Professor, 1985-, University of Calgary. *Memberships:* ASTR; CUS; RTUG. *Publications:* 30 articles. *Hobby:* Music. *Address:* 1331 29 St NW, Calgary, Alberta, Canada T2N 4N2.

SHIPPEY, Brian George, b. 2 May 1949, Middlesborough, England. Dental Surgeon. m. Moira Jennifer Bushe, 10 Apr. 1981, Gretna, Scotland. *Education:* BChD, Leeds, 1968-73. *Appointments:* Assistant, Group Practice, Leeds, 1973; Associate, Group Practice, Bradford, 1974; Assistant, Group Practice, Lerwick, 1975; Principal, General Practice, Stornoway, 1976-81; Private Dental Practitioner, Calowndra, Australia, 1982-. *Memberships:* Australian Dental Association; Associate Member, Australian Society of Orthodontists; Overseas Member, British Dental Association. *Hobbies:* Music; Swimming; Astronomy. *Address:* 82 Bulcock St, Caloundra, Queensland 4551, Australia.

SHOCHAT, Stephen Jay, b. 17 Dec. 1938, Baltimore, Maryland, USA. Associate Professor. m. Carla, 27 Jan. 1980, 2 daughters. *Education:* MD, Medical College of Virginia, 1959-63; Internship, Barnes Hospital, St Louis, 1963-64; Resident, Barnes Hospital, 1964-68; Children's Hospital Medical Centre, Boston, 1968-70; Fellow, Surgical Research, Children's Hospital Medical Centre, Boston, 1970; Fulbright Scholar, Thoracic Surgery, Queen Elizabeth Hospital, Birmingham, England, 1970-71; Senior Registrar, Thoracic Surgery, Queen Elizabeth Hospital, Birmingham, 1971; Fellow, Thoracic Surgery, George Washington University, USA, 1973-74. *Appointments:* Chief, Paediatric Surgery, USAF, 1973-74; Assistant Professor, Surgery and Paediatrics, Chief, Paediatric Surgery, Milton S Hershey Medical Centre, Penn State University School of Medicine, 1974-77; Assistant Professor, Surgery & Paediatrics, 1977-83; Associate Professor, Surgery and Paediatrics, 1983-, Stanford University School of Medicine. *Memberships include:* American Academy of Paediatrics; American Association of Tissue Banks; American College of Surgeons; American Medical Association; American Society for Parenteral and Enteral Nutrition; New York Academy of Sciences; American Association for Thoracic Surgery; etc. *Publications:* Articles in scientific journals including: 'American Surgeon'; 'Radiology'; 'Surgery'; 'Paediatrics'; 'European Journal of Paediatrics', etc. *Honours:* Alpha Omega Alpha, 1963; William M Hume Faculty Scholar, 1979, 1980, 1981. *Address:* Department of Surgery, Division of Paediatric Surgery, Stanford University Medical Centre, Stanford, CA 94305, USA.

SHOCKMAN, Gerald D, b. 22 Dec. 1925, Mount Clemens, Michigan, USA. Professor of Microbiology & Immunology. m. Arlyne Taub, 2 June 1949, Ithaca, New York, 1 son, 2 daughters. *Education:* BS, Cornell University, 1947; PhD, Rutgers University, 1950. *Appointments:* Predoctoral Fellow, Rutgers University, 1947-50; Research Associate, University of Pennsylvania, 1950-51; Research Fellow, Institute for Cancer Research, Philadelphia, 1951-60; Associate Professor 1960-66, Professor 1966-77, Professor & Chairman, Department of Microbiology & Immunology, School of Medicine, Temple University. *Memberships:* American Society of Biological Chemists; American Academy of Microbiology; American Society for Microbiology; American Association for the Advancement of Science; Sigma Xi; Theobald Smith Society; Philadelphia Biochemists Club; Society for General Microbiology. *Publications:* Author & Co-author of some 139 articles, abstracts & papers in medical journals. *Address:* Temple University School of Medicine, Department of Microbiology & Immunology, 3400 North Broad Street, Philadelphia, PA 19140, USA.

SHOKEIR, Mohamed H K, b. 2 July 1938, Mansoura, Egypt. Professor, Head of Department. m. Donna Jean Nugent, 27 Feb. 1968, St Claire, Michigan, USA, 1 son, 1 daughter. *Education:* MB, Bch, Faculty of Medicine, 1954-60, DCh (Ortho), Postgraduate School of Medicine, 1960-64, Cairo University, Egypt; MS, 1964-65, PhD, 1965-69, University of Michigan, Ann Arbor, USA; FCCMG, Canadian College of Medical Geneticists, 1975. *Appointments:* Intern, Resident, Cairo University Hospitals, 1960-64; Fulbright Research Scholar, University of Michigan, Ann Arbor, USA, 1964-69; Queen Elizabeth II Scientist, Assistant and Associate Professor, Department of Paediatrics, 1969-73, Director, Division of Medical Genetics, 1975-, Professor and Head, Department of Paediatrics, 1979-, University of Saskatchewan, Canada; Head, Section of Clinical Genetics, Health Sciences Centre, Winnipeg, Manitoba, Canada, 1972-75. *Memberships:* Canadian College of Medical Geneticists; Chairman, Canadian Paediatric Department; Association of Medical Schools Department of Paediatrics Chairmen Incorporated; Canadian Paediatric Society; American Board of Medical Genetics National Board of Medical Examiners; Academic Freedomnand Tenure Committee of the Canadian Association of University Teachers; Canadian Society of Andrology. *Publications:* Author of numerous professional articles for medical journals. *Honours:* Medical Basic Sciences Award, 1957; Solomon Award for Internal Medicine, 1960; Day Award for Medicine, 1960; John Phillips Award for Contribution to Internal Medicine, 1960; Fulbright Scholar, 1964-69; Queen Elizabeth II Scientist Award, 1960-75; Issa Hamdy Award for Distinguished Contribution to Medicine. *Hobbies:* Music; Canoeing. *Address:* Department of Paediatrics, University Hospital, Saskatoon, Saskatchewan S7N 0X0, Canada.

SHOLEVAR, Bahman, b. 6 Feb. 1941, Tehran, Iran. Clinical Associate Professor of Psychiatry. *Education:* BS, MD, University of Tehran, 1957-67; Diploma of English Studies, Cambridge University, 1964; BA, English, North Texas State University, Denton, Texas, 1968; MFA, 1970, MA, English, 1971, PhD, English and Modern Letters, 1973, University of Iowa; MD, Hahnemann Medical College, Philadelphia, 1976. *Appointments:* Assistant Economic Secretary, Diplomatic Corps, Central Treaty Organisation (CENTO), Ankara, Turkey, 1965-67; Clinical Assistant Professor of Psychiatry, Thomas Jefferson University, Philadelphia, 1979-82; Assistant Chief of Psychiatry, 1982-84, Associate Chief of Staff for Geriatrics and Extended Care, 1984-85, Acting Chief of Staff, VA Medical Center, Coatsville, Pennsylvania; Clinical Associate Professor of Psychiatry, Thomas Jefferson University, Philadelphia. *Memberships:* American Psychiatric Association; PENNA Psychiatric Association; Philadelphia Psychiatric Association; Charter Member, American Physicians' Poetry Association; Charter Member, Board of Directors, International Arts-Medicine Association. *Publications:* Persian: Translation of W Faulkner's "The Sound and Fury" 1960; Translation of T S Eliot's "The Waste Land" in Aresh Journal, Tehran, 1963; "Epic of Life, Epic of Death" (poetry) 1961; "The Night's Journey" 1967. English: "Making Connection: Poems of Exile" 1979; "Odysseus' Homecoming", "The New Adam", "The Angel with Bushbaby Eyes", "Lovesong of Achilles" (poems) 1982; Editor and co-author with William G Niederland "The Creative Process: A Psychoanalytical Discussion" 1982; "The Night's Journey" 1982; "The Coming of the Messiah" 1982. *Hobbies:* Swimming; Hiking; Mountain climbing; Classical music; Theatre. *Address:* 825 Bowman Avenue, Wynnewood, PA 19096, USA.

SHOTWELL, Thomas Knight, b. 31 May 1934, Hillsboro, Texas, USA. President, Shotwell & Carr Inc. m. Shirley Imogene Plunkett, 29 Dec. 1955, Hillsboro, 1 daughter. *Education:* BSc, 1955, MEd, 1959, Texas A & M University; PhD, Louisiana State University, 1965. *Appointments:* County Extension Agent, Van Zandt County, Texas, 1955; Biology Teacher, 1958, Head, Biological Sciences, 1960, Allen Academy & Junior College, Bryan, Texas; Agricultural Teacher, Public Schools, Charleston, 1965; Regulatory Manager, Salsbury Labs, Charles City, 1966; Director, Regulatory Affairs, Zoecon Corp, Dallas, 1971; President, Shotwell & Carr Inc, Dallas, 1973-; President, Comparative Religion Research Center Inc, Dallas, 1984-. *Memberships:* United States Animal Health Association; American Association of Industrial Veterinarians; American Society of Agricultural Consultants; American Association for the Advancement of Science; New York Academy of Sciences. *Publications:* "The World of Plants", 1964; "The Ecology of Antibiotic Usage", 1967; "Handbook of Approved New Animal Drug Applications", 1980; Numerous professional papers published; Member, Editorial Board, 'Journal Clinical Research Practices and Drug Regulatory Affairs'. *Honour:* President, American Society of Agricultural Consultants, 1980-81. *Hobby:* Collection 19th Century Science Books. *Address:* 2925 LBJ Freeway 251, Dallas, TX 75234, USA.

SHOWALTER, Carl Robert, b. 12 July 1938, Broadway, Virginia, USA. Psychiatrist. m. Charity Shank, 14 Sep. 1963, Charlottesville, 2 daughters. *Education:* BSc, Eastern Mennonite College; MD, University of Virginia. *Appointments:* Psychiatrist, National Institute of Mental Health; Medical Director, Shenandoah Lodge Treatment Center; Assistant Director, Forensic Clinic, Lecturer in Law, School of Law, Associate Medical Director, Institute of Law, Psychiatry and Public Policy, Clinical Associate Professor of Psychiatry and Behavioural Medicine, Department of Psychiatry, University of Virginia; Consulting Psychiatrist, James Madison University. *Memberships:* American Medical Association; American Psychiatric Association; American Academy of Psychiatry and the Law; Psychiatric Society of Virginia Incorporated; American Society of Law and Mecicine Incorporated. *Publications:* Author and Co-Author of contributions to: 'Psychiatric Quarterly', 1968; 'Journal of Psychiatry and Law', 1974; 'Virginia Weekly', 1975; 'Virginia Medical Monthly', 1975; 'International Journal of Law and Psychiatry', 1980, 84; 'American Journal of Psychiatry and The Law', 1984; 'Law and Human Behavior', 1984; 'Judicature', 1985; 'Medicine and Law', 1985. *Honours:* Adolph Meyer Award, Department of Psychiatry, University of Virginia, 1967. Diplomate: American Board of Psychiatry and Neurology, 1970; American Board of Forensic Psychiatry, 1981. Fellow, American Psychiatric Association, 1982. *Address:* Medical Arts Building 17, 1031, South Main Street, Harrisonburg, VA 22801, USA.

SHROFF, Fali Jamsedji, b. 25 Nov. 1934, Hong Kong. Consultant Neurosurgeon. Private Practitioner. m. Thrity J Baria, 29 Nov. 1960, Bombay, India. *Education:* MB; BS; FRCS (ED); FICS. *Appointments:* Registrar, Neurosurgery, Newcastle upon Tyne, England; Medical Officer, Queen Elizabeth Hospital, Hong Kong. *Memberships:* Council, British Medical Association; Council, Hong Kong Neurosurgical Society. *Publication:* 'A Case of Thalamic Pain' in 'Journal of Grant', Medical College, Bombay, India, 1961. *Hobbies:* Classical Music; Hi-Fi; Golf. *Address:* Suite 818-819 Holland House, 9 Ice House St, Hong Kong.

SHULTZ, Susan Kay, b. 24 Apr. 1954, Reading, Pennsylvania, USA. Doctor of Chiropractic, Lecturer and Clinic Director. m. Michael D Craig, 31 Dec. 1985, Reading, Pennsylvania. *Education:* DC, Western States Chiropractic College, Portland, Oregon. *Appointments:* Doctor of Chiropractic, Vancouver, Washington; Lecturer and Clinic Director, Western States Chiropractic College, Portland. *Memberships:* Phi Beta Kappa; International Chiropractic Association. *Publication:* "Extremity Orthopedic Tests", 1982 (2nd edition 1983). *Address:* 10536, North East San Rafael, Portland, OR 97220, USA.

SHURLEY, Jay Talmadge, b. 20 Dec. 1917, Sonora, Texas, USA. Emeritus Professor, Psychiatry, Behavioural Sciences, University of Oklahoma; Private Practice. m. Emily Alexander Jackson, 4 Jan. 1964, Austin, Texas, 5 sons. *Education:* MD, University of Texas, 1942; Rockefeller Fellow Neuropsychiatry, Pennsylvania Hospital, 1943-47; Hall-Mercer Resea-

rch Fellow, Pennsylvania Hospital, 1950; Graduate Institute of Philadelphia Association for Psychoanalysisis, 1951. *Appointments:* Attending Psychiatrist, Institute of Pennsylvania Hospital, Philadelphia, 1947-51; Clinical Director, Oak Ridge San, Austin, 1951-52; Instructor, Military Neuropsychiatry, Medical Field Service School, Fort Sam Houston, 1952-54; Chief, Adult Psychiatry, Clinical Investigations, National Institute Mental Health, National Institute of Health, Bethesda, 1955-57; Professor, Psychiatry 9 Behavioural Science, Oklahoma University, College of Medicine, Chief Psychiatrist, Service and Mental Hygiene Clinics, VA Hospital, Oklahoma, 1957-63; Senior Medical Investigator, Veterans Administration, 1963-76; Medical Director, Outpatient Psychiatry Clinics, Oklahoma Teaching Hospital, 1977-71; Medical Director, Willow View Hospital, Oklahoma City, 1985-. *Memberships include:* Oklahoma County, Oklahoma State and American Medical Associations; Life Fellow, American Psychiatric Association; Charter Fellow, American College Psychiatrists; Foundation Fellow, Royal College of Psychiatrists, UK. *Publications:* Editor, "Relating Mental Health to Environment", 1979; "Man on South Polar Plateau", 1980; Author, "Insulin Shock Treatment of Schizophrenia Experimental Sensory Isolation", 'American Journal Psychiatry', 1960; etc. *Honours include:* Alpha Omega Alpha; Sigma Xi; Antarctic Service Medal, 1969; Shurley Ridge, Pensacola Mountains, Antartica named in his honour, 1970. *Hobbies:* Photography; Exploration; Travel. *Address:* PO Box 18526, Oklahoma City, OK 73118, USA.

SHUTE, Wallace Beresford, b. 4 June 1911, Canada. *Education:* BA, Honours, Science, 1933, MD, 1936, University of Western Ontario; Diplomate, American Board of Obstetrics and Gynaecology, 1942; MRCOG; FRCS (C); FACS; FACOG. *Appointments:* Internship, Harper Hospital, Detroit, USA, 1936-37; Intern, Royal Victoria Hospital, Montreal, 1937-38; Senior, Gynaecology, Montreal General, 1938-39; Assistant Resident, Chicago Maternity Centre, 1939-40; Fellowship, Pathology, Cook County Hospital, Chicago, 1940; Personal Assistant, to Dr N Sproat, Rush Medical School, Chicago, 1940-41; Resident, Obstetrics, Cook County Hospital, 1941-42; Gynaecologist, Army, Navy, Air Force, Special Services, Women's Division Overseas, 1945-46. *Memberships:* Numerous professional organisations including: Ontario and Canadian Medical Associations; Society of Obstetricians and Gynaecologists of Canada; Canadian Society for the Study of Fertility; American College of Surgeons; American Society of Abdominal Surgeons. *Publications include:* Articles in professional journals including: 'Journal of Obstetrics & Gynaecology''; "Virginia Obstetrics & Gynaecology'; (Current Medical Digest'; 'British Journal of Clinical Practice'; 'Gynaecology and Obstetrics'; etc. *Honours:* Recipient, various honours and awards. *Address:* 340 McLeod Street, Suite B4, Ottawa, Canada K2P 1A4.

SICILIANO, Ann P, b. 20 Dec. 1930, New Jersey, USA. *Education:* Wilson College, 1947-48; Cytology, Parkway Hospital, 1949; BS, Northwestern University, 1962. *Appointments:* Parkway Hospital, 1949-53; Highland Park Hospital, 1954-60; University of Illinois Medical School, 1960-61; Edgewater Hospital, 1961-68; Northsuburban Clinic, Skokie, Illinois, 1964-. *Memberships:* American Society of Cytology; Past Treasurer, Illinois Society of Cytology; American Society of Cytotechnologists; International Academy of Cytology; American Society of Clinical Pathologists. *Publications:* 'Necrotizing Herpes Simplex Viral Infection of the Cervix During Pregnancy', Co-author (1st paper on subject in Chicago area and only 2nd paper published in USA and Internationally), 1964. *Honours:* Committee Member, American Society of Cytology; Founder, Illinois Society of Cytology. *Hobbies:* Sports; Music. *Address:* PO Box 609, Evanston, IL 60204, USA.

SIDDIQUE, Mohammad Aqeel, b. 7 Jan. 1935, Baraut,

India. Surgeon. m. Nayyar, 26 Feb. 1960, Meerut, 1 son, 1 daughter. *Education:* BSc, Jal Vedie Degree College, Baraut, 1953; MBBS, King George's Medical College, Lucknow, India, 1958; Fellow, Royal College of Surgeons, England, 1965; Fellow, International College of Surgeons, 1973. *Appointments:* Rotating Intern, Ottawa General Hospital, Canada; Senior House Officer, Royal Infirmary, Hull, England; Registrar, Bury General Hospital, Lancashire; Head, Surgery, Queen Elizabeth II Hospital, Maseru, Lesotho, 1969-. *Memberships:* British Medical Association; South African Medical Association; Lesotho Medical Association; Chairman, Workman Compensation Board, Chairman, Medical Board, Government of Lesotho; Moderator, Nursing Examination Board, Botswana, Lesotho and Swaziland. *Honours:* OBE, 1973; Commander of Mohlomi; Moshoeshoe of Lesotho. *Address:* QE II Hospital, PO Box 122, Maseru, Lesotho, Southern Africa.

SIDES, Ricky Reich, b. 31 Dec. 1948, Winston Salem, Forsyth County, North Carolina, USA. Doctor of Chiropractic. m. Kathleen Fay Anastasoff, 2 May 1981, Wheaton, Illinois. *Education:* BA Accounting, Catawba College, 1971; BA Anatomy 1979, DC 1981, National College of Chiropractic. *Appointments:* Accountant, Ernst and Whinney, San Juan, Puerto Rico, 1971-73; Controller, Mandala Psychiatric Hospital, Winston Salem, North Carolina, 1975-77; Founder, Sides Center of Chiropractic, 1981-. *Memberships:* American Chiropractic Association; North Carolina Chiropractic Association; Forsyth County Chiropractic Association; Central District Chiropractic Association; Diplomate, National Board of Chiropractic Examiners; North Carolina Child Passenger Safety Association; President, Kiwanis Club, Winston Salem Stratford; Home Moravian Church. *Honours:* Certificate of Appreciation, Davidson County Board of Education, 1971; Honor Award, San Juan Jaycees, Puerto Rico, 1973; Outstanding Senior Award, National College of Chiropractic, 1981. *Hobbies:* Travel; Playing Piano. *Address:* 1427 Peters Creek Parkway, Winston Salem, NC 27103, USA.

SIDHU, Sher Singh, b. 10 Oct. 1933, Gabbe Majra, India. Professor and Head of Department of Dental Surgery. m. Swarn Bains, 22 Oct. 1959, Mahilpur, 2 sons. *Education:* BDS; MDS; DFR; FICD; FAMS. *Appointments:* House Surgeon, 1956; Demonstrator, Dental Wing, Madras Medical College, Madras, 1956-57; Demonstrator, Government Dental College and Hospital, 1957-58; Chief Dental Surgeon, E Rly, Calcutta, 1958-60, Lecturer, 1960-69; Assistant Professor 1969-76, Associate Professor 1976-82, Professor and Head 1983-, AIIMS. *Memberships:* International College of Dentists, India section; Indian Orthodontic Society; Indian Society of Oncology; Indian Dental Association. *Publications:* 105. *Honours:* Medal, International College of Oral Implantologists, 1975; Fellowship, International College of Dentists. *Address:* Department of Dental Surgery, AIIMS, New Delhi 110029, India.

SIEBERTH, Heinz-Guenter, b. 6 May 1960, Wasungen/Thurigen, Germany. Director, International Clinic II, Medical Faculty, RWTH Aachen. m. Gudrun Richter, 17 Sep. 1960, 1 son, 1 daughter. *Education:* Professor Doctor of Medicine, Humboldt University, Berlin. *Appointments:* Akademie d Wisserschaften, Berlin, 1958-59; Medical University Klinik, Rostock, 1959-61; Medical University Poliklinik, Freiburg, 1962-64; Medical Universitatsklinik, Koln, 1974-81; Habilitation, 1969, Professor Doctor of Medicine, 1971, Medical UnivKlinik, Koln; Director, Department Internal Medicine II, Medical Faculty, Aachen, 1981-. *Memberships:* Deutsche Ges fur Innere Medizin; Deutschesprachige Society of Nephrology; European Dialysis and Transplant Association; American Society of Artificial Internal Organs; International Society of Artificial Organs. *Publications:* "Plasma Exchange", 1980; 'Erkrankungen der Niere' in "Lehrbuch d Inneren Medizin 2", 1982; 'Akutes Nierenversagen' in "Klinische Nephrologie",

1982; "Der internistische Notfall", 1973. *Address:* Abt Innere Medizin II der RWTH Aachen, Pauwelsstrasse, D-5100 Aachen, Federal Republic of Germany.

SIEGLER, Ilene C, b. 17 July 1946, Syracuse, New York, USA. Associate Professor of Medical Psychology. m. Charles D Edelman, 7 June 1975, Durham, North Carolina, USA. *Education:* PhD, MA, Syracuse University, Syracuse, NY, 1972-73; AB, University of Michigan, Ann Arbor, Michigan, 1968. *Appointments:* Postdoctoral Fellow, Duke Centre for Aging, 1972-74; Assistant Professor of Medical Psychology, 1974-79, Associate Professor, 1980-, Department of Psychiatry, Duke University School of Medicine. *Memberships:* American Psychological Association; Division 20, Adult Development and Aging, 1984-85; Gerontological Society of America. *Publications:* 'Health Behavior Relationships', (with P T Costa Jr), 1985; 'Federal Age Discrimination in Employment Law', (with C D Edelman), 1978, 1979, 1980. *Honours:* Sigma Xi. *Address:* Box 2969, Duke University Medical Centre, Durham, NC 27710, USA.

SIEVER, Larry Joseph, b. 2 Sep. 1947, Chicago, Illinois, USA. Director, Outpatient Psychiatry Clinic, Bronx Veterans Administration Medical Center; Associate Professor, Mt Sinai School of Medicine. *Education:* BA, Harvard College, 1969; MD, Stanford University Medical School, 1975. *Appointments:* Medical Intern, Mary's Help Hospital, Daley City, California, 1975; Resident in Psychiatry, McLean Hospital, Belmont, Massachusetts, Fellow, Department of Psychiatry, Harvard Medical School, 1975-78; Staff Psychiatrist, Clinical Neuropharmacology Branch, 1978-82; Ward Administrator, 1979; Chief, Unit on Biological Correlates of Behavior, CNB, 1980-82; National Institute of Mental Health, Bethesda, Maryland; Director, Psychiatry Outpatient Clinic, Bronx Veterans Administration Medical Center, Bronx, Associate Professor of Psychiatry, Mt Sinai Medical School, New York City, 1982-. *Memberships:* Phi Beta Kappa; Sigma Xi; American Psychiatric Association; New York Psychiatric Association; American Association for the Advancement of Science; Society of Biologic Psychiatry. *Publications:* Contributor to professional journals; Books including: Co-editor, "Biologic Response Styles: Clinical Implications" (in press); "Biological Markers in Schizotypal Personality Disorder" Schizophrenia Bulletin (in press); Presentations. *Honours:* Magna cum laude, Harvard University, 1969; Diplomate, American Board of Psychiatry and Neurology, 1980; A E Bennett Clinical Science Research Award, 1983. *Address:* Bronx Veterans Administration Center, 130 W Kingsbridge Road, Bronx, NY 10468, USA.

SIGNORINI, Lorenzo Federico, b. 30 July 1923, Genoa, Italy. Institute Director. m. Fiorella Kircheis, 2 Dec. 1954, Florence, 2 sons, 1 daughter. *Education:* MD; Professor of Hygiene. *Appointments:* Assistant Professor, University of Florence, 1948-56. Director: Institute of Hygiene, University of Camerino, 1957-68; Institute of Hygiene, University of Florence, 1969-; Post Graduate School of Hygiene and Preventive Medicine, 1971-. *Memberships:* President, Tuscany Section, Italian Society of Hygiene; Italian Society of Epidemiology; International Union ag. Tuberculosis; Association Francais pur l'Etude des Eaux. *Publications:* Author of about 150 publications on epidemiology, infectious diseases, preventive medicine, tuberculosis, vital and health statistics, environmental hygiene. *Honour:* Gold Medal, Ministry of Education, Italy, 1982. *Hobby:* Renaissance art. *Address:* Institute of Hygiene, University of Florence, viale G B Morgagni 48, 50134 Florence, Italy.

SIGÜENZA, Carlos Humberto, b. 6 Apr. 1941, El Salvador. Psychiatrist. Divorced, 1 daughter. *Education:* MD, University of El Salvador School of Medicine; Psychiatrist, New York University, Bellevue Medical Centre, USA. *Appointments:* President, University of El Salvador; Private Practice. *Memberships:* American Medical Association; American Psychiatric Association; Canadian Psychiatric Association; Salvadorian Psychiatric Association. *Publications:* "The Management of Large Educational Organisations"; "Design of Curricula for Medical Schools". *Hobbies:* Tennis; Golf; Windsurfing; Polo. *Address:* 220 East 57 St, New York, NY 10022, USA.

SIKDAR, Brajendra Mohan Deb, b. 1 Oct. 1929, Tugaldia, Bangaldesh. Founder, Director, Kripamayee Institute for Mental Health. m. Meera, 29 June 1959, Bilaspur, 2 sons, 3 daughters. *Education:* DPM, 1958; Member, Royal College of Psychiatrists, 1973; Fellowship, American Psychiatric Association, 1974; Fellowship, Indian Psychiatric Society, 1959. *Appointments:* Psychiatrist, 1954-; Resident, Psychiatry, Hospital for Mental Diseases, Ranchi; All India Institute for Mental Health, Bangalore, 1956-58; Assistant Psychiatrist, Kishore Nursing Home; Head, Psychiatry, Wanless Hospital, 1960-63; Part-time Lecturer, Psycho Government Medical College, Miraj, 1962-76; Founder, Director, Kripamayee Institute for Mental Health. *Memberships:* Indian Medical Association, Miraj Branch, President, 1972-73, 1973-74; Indian Psychiatric Society, Vice President, 1972-73; President, IPS, 1973-74; IPS West Zone President, 1978-79; Art Circle President, 1970-81; etc. *Publications:* Book Chapter, "Psychiatry in India"; Articles include: "Glimpses of Medico-Psychological Practices in Ancient India"; etc. *Honours:* Recipient various honours and awards. *Hobbies:* Agriculture; Spiritual Study; Founder, Secretary, Society for the Rehabilitation of the Handicapped, 1966-. *Address:* Kripamayee Institute for Mental Health, Miraj, PO Wanlesswadi Dist, Sangli Pin, 416 414, Maharashtra, India.

SILBERBERG, Alexander, b. 24 Feb. 1923, Vienna, Austria. Professor. m. Leah Abrahams, 30 Mar. 1948, Johannesburg, South Africa, 1 son, 1 daughter. *Education:* BSc, Engineering, University of the Witwatersrand, South Africa, 1944; PhD, summa cum laude, University of Basel, Switzerland, 1952. *Appointments include:* Research Associate 1952-59, Senior Scientist 1959-63, Associate Professor 1963-70, Professor 1970-, Head, Department of Polymer Research 1978-84, Weitmann Institute of Science, Rehovot, Israel; Editor-in-Chief, 'Journal of Biorheology', 1978-; Director, Aharon Katzir-Katehalsky Centre, Weitmann Institute, 1972-. *Memberships include:* Royal Society of Chemistry, UK; Council for Thrombosis, American Heart Association; International Association of Colloid & Interface Scientists; International Committee on Rheology; President 1980-82, European Microcirculation Society; President 1972-78, International Society of Biorheology; Chairman, Israel Microcirculation Society; etc. *Publications:* Numerous contributions to scientific literature. *Honours include:* Visiting Fellow, American Heart Association, University of Washington, 1968-69; Visiting Professor, University of Copenhagen, Denmark, 1972; Unilever Professor, University of Bristol, UK, 1975; Fairchild Distinguished Scholar, California Institute of Technology, USA, 1977; Royal Society Visiting Professor, Imperial College, London, UK, 1983; Poiseuille Gold Medal, International Society of Biorheology, 1981. *Hobbies:* History; Swimming. *Address:* Weitmann Institute of Science, Rehovot 76100, Israel.

SILBERBERG, Donald H, b. 2 Mar. 1934, Washington District of Columbia, USA. University Professor and Department Chairman. m. Marilyn Alice Damsky, 7 June 1969, 2 sons. *Education:* MD, University of Michigan, USA, 1958; Honorary MA, University of Pennsylvania, 1971. *Appointments include:* Associate, Department of Neurology, University of Pennsylvania School of Medicine, 1963-65, Assistant Professor, 1965-67, Associate Professor, 1967-71, Professor, 1971-73, Acting Chairman, 1974-82, Professor and Chairman, 1982-present. *Memberships include:* Alpha Omega Alpha; American Neurological Association; International Brain Research Organisation; New York Academy of Sciences; Tissue Culture Association; Society for Neuroscience; American Association

for Neuropathologists; American Society for Neurochemistry; Association of University Professors of Neurology. *Publications include:* Some 200 learned articles, abstracts and contributions to professional journals, conference papers and chapters of books including "Scientific Approaches to Clinical Neurology", 1977; "Infection, Immunity and Genetics", 1978; "Humoral Immunity in Neurological Diseases", 1979; "Progress in Multiple Sclerosis Research", 1980; "Current Neurology", 1981; "Cecil Textbook of Medicine", 1982; "Advances in Neurochemistry", 1984' "The Diagnosis of Multiple Sclerosis", 1984, etc. *Honours:* Alpha Omega Alpha Medical Honour Society, 1957; US Public Health Service, 1959-61; Fulbright Scholar, London, 1961-62; NINDB Special Fellow in Neuro-Ophthalmology, St Louis, USA, 1962-63. *Address:* Department of Neurology, Hospital of the University of Pennsylvania, 3400 Spruce Street, Philadelphia, PA 19104, USA.

SILBURN, Peter Allen, b. 9 Oct. 1957, Sydney, Australia. Hospital Scientist. m. Sue-Ellen Jane Budge, 10 Dec. 1983, Brisbane, Australia. *Education:* BSc Hons, Newcastle, New South Wales; PhD, Queensland University; 4th Year Student, MB BS. *Appointments:* Hospital Scientist, Royal Brisbane Hospital, Queensland. *Memberships:* Australian Society Immunology; Australia Society Reproductive Biology. *Publications:* 'Mobius DNA', (with B Daunker, R Hill), 1981; 'Immunoglobins reactive with carcinoembryonic antigen and their relationship to the antigen in malignant ascitic fluid of ovarian carcinoma', (with R Hill, S K Khoo, B Daunker, E V Mackay), 1982; 'Affinity chromatography separation of tumour associated antigens from ascitic fluid of ovarian cancer patients', (with R Hill, B Daunker, S K Khoo, E V Mackay), 1983; 'The Types of immune complexes in the ascitic fluid from women with carcinoma of the ovary', (Co-author), 1983; 'Immun complexes in ovarian cancer: Association between IgM class complexes and antinuclear autoantibodies', (Co-author), 1984; 'Demonstration of tumour associated immunoglobin G isolated from immune complexes in ascitic fluid of ovarian cancer', (Co-author), 1984; 'Characterization of immune complexes from women with ovarian cancer', 1983. *Hobbies:* Surfing; Cricket; Soccer. *Address:* 78 Butterfield Street, Herston, Queensland, Australia.

SILLENCE, David Owen, b. 31 Aug. 1944, Sydney, New South Wales, Australia. Professor of Public Health Biology. m. Dr Jennifer Elsie Ault, 3 sons. *Education:* MB BS Honours, University of Sydney, 1969; MD, University of Melbourne, 1978; Fellow, Royal Australasian College of Physicians, 1977, Royal College of Pathologists of Australasia, 1982. *Appointments:* Assistant Professor of Paediatrics, University of California at Los Angeles, USA, 1978-80; Senior Lecturer, 1980-82, Associate Professor, 1982, Human Genetics, University of Sydney, New South Wales, Australia; Professor of Public Health Biology, 1983-85; Visiting Physician, Clinical Genetics, 1980-, Head, Medical Genetics Unit, 1984-, Children's Hospital, Camperdown, New South Wales. *Memberships:* American Society of Human Genetics; Australian Teratology Society; Australian Society for Infectious Disease; Australian Medical Association; Human Genetics Society of Australasia; Genetics Society of Australia; Royal Australasian College of Physicians; Royal College of Pathologists of Australasia. *Publications:* "Bone Dysplasias: Genetic and Ultrasound Aspects with Special Reference to Osteogenesis Inperfecta", with revised preface; "Osteogenesis Imperfecta: A Handbook for Medical Practitioners and Health Care Professionals", Editor and major contributor, 1981. Author or Co-Author of contributions to professional journals including: 'Journal of Medical Genetics'; 'American Journal of Pathology'; 'American Journal of Medical Genetics'. *Honours:* Fulbright-Hays Fellowship, 1977; Uncle Bobs Club Travelling Fellowship, 1977. *Hobbies:* Music; Reading; Gardening. *Address:* Medical Genetics Unit, Children's Hospital, Camperdown, NSW 2050,

Australia.

SILLERO, Antonio, b. 13 Jan. 1938, Rute, Spain. University Professor. m. Maria Antonia Gunther, 17 Dec. 1966, Madrid, 2 sons. *Education:* PhD, Chemistry, University Complutense, Madrid, 1967; MD, University of Granada, 1967. *Appointments:* Investigador, Spanish Research Council, 1973-75; Associate Professor, Valladolid Medical School, 1975-78; Chairman, Department of Biochemistry, Badajoz Medical School, 1979-; Director, Instituto Ciencias Educacion, U Extremadura, 1981-82; Vicerrector, U Extremadura, 1982-84; Professor and Chairman Department of Biochemistry, Faculty of Medicine, Badajoz, Spain. *Memberships:* Spanish Society of Biochemistry; Portuguese Society of Biochemistry; American Society of Microbiology; Spanish Federal Society of Experimental Biology. *Publications:* "Biologia" 1978; Contributor of articles to scientific journals. *Honours:* Gregorio Maranon Prize 1968; Recipient of Grants from several agencies. *Hobbies:* Tennis; Music. *Address:* Departamento de Bioquimica, Facultad de Medicina, Badajoz, Spain.

SILOBRĆIĆ, Vlatko, b. 18 Apr. 1935, Split, Yugoslavia. Professor; Chief of Research Unit. m. Mira Potocki, 30 Apr. 1959, Zagreb, Yugoslavia, 1 son. *Education:* MD, Medical School, Zagreb, 1959, DSc, 1963; Postdoctoral Fellow, Baylor Medical School, Houston, Texas, USA, 1963-65. *Appointments:* Research Assistant, Institute R Boskovic, Zagreb, Yugoslavia, 1959-63; Project Investigator, M D Anderson Hospital and Tumour Institute, Houston, Texas, USA, 1965-66; Research Associate, Institute R Boskovic, Zagreb, Yugoslavia, 1966-69; Research Associate and Assistant Professor, Institute of Immunology, Zagreb, 1969-75; Visiting Scientist, Massachusetts General Hospital, Harvard Medical School, Boston, USA, 1975-76; Research Consultant, Associate Professor, Institute of Immunology, Zagreb, Yugoslavia, 1976-84; Research Consultant, Professor, 1984-. *Memberships:* Yugoslav Immunological Society, Secretary, Vice President, President; International Union of Immunological Societies, Vice President, Commn. for Europe, Symposium Comm; Transplantation Society, Founding Member, Committee for Immunological Monitoring; Editor in Chief 'Period Biol.'; Editorial Board 'European Journal of Immunology', 'Fol. Biol.' and several Yugoslav journals. *Publications:* 1 book; 125 scientific and professional articles 1958-85. *Honours:* Annual Award for Scientific Research of SR Croatia, 1974; Member, Medical Academy SR Croatia, 1974; Associate Member, Yugoslavian Academy of Sciences and Arts, 1977; Annual Award of the City of Zagreb, 1981. *Hobbies:* Music; Theatre; Films; Tennis. *Address:* Tomašičeva 11, 41 000 Zagreb, Yugoslavia.

SILVANI, Stephen Henry, b. 23 July 1953, San Francisco, California, USA. Staff Podiatrist. *Education:* BS, University of California at Davis, 1974; DPM, California College of Podiatric Medicine, 1977; Resident, Levine General Hospital, 1978; Surgical Resident, Kaiser Foundation Hospital, 1979. *Appointments:* Clinical Assistant Professor in Surgery, California College of Podiatric Medicine, 1979-; Examiner, Podiatric Examining Committee of the Board of Medical Quality Assurance, State of California, 1982-. *Memberships:* American Podiatric Medical Association; California Podiatric Medical Association; American Public Health Association. *Publications:* Numerous articles in 'Journal of the American Podiatric Association', 'Journal of Foot Surgery', 'The Hospital Podiatrist', numerous lectures. *Honour:* Pi Delta Honour Society, 1977. *Hobbies:* Running; Skiing; Windsurfing. *Address:* Permante Medical Group, 27400 Hesperian Boulevard, Hayward, CA 94545, USA.

SILVEIRA, Guiomar, b. 30 Sep. 1909, Brazil. Private Practitioner. *Education:* Teacher's Certificate, Brazil, 1925; MD, Rio de Janeiro, Brazil, Medical School, 1942; Medical Licences, New Hampshire, Massachusetts, Rhode Island, USA; Board Certification, Psychiatry & Neurology, USA. *Appointments:* Rotating Int-

ernships in Obstetrics, Gynaecology, Paediatrics, Emergency Hospital, Rio de Janeiro; Chief, Paediatric Service, St Francis of Assisi Hospital, Rio de Janeiro until 1955; Private Practice in Rio de Janeiro, State of Goias; Rotating Internships in Massachusetts, Residencies in Orthopaedics & Surgery, Illinois, Internist in Psychiatry, Massachusetts, Residency in Psychiatry, Rhode Island & Massachusetts; Training, Columbia University, New York, Harvard University, Boston, USA. *Memberships:* American Medical Association; American Psychiatric Association; International College of Surgeons. *Honour:* Physicians Recognition Award for Continuing Medical Education. *Hobbies:* Choral Singing; Dancing; Swimming; Gardening; Crafts. *Address:* 1524 Atwood Avenue, Johnston, RI 02919, USA.

SILVER, George Albert, b. 23 Dec. 1913, USA. Emeritus Professor of Public Health. m. Mitzi Blieden, 5 June 1937, USA, 1 son, 2 daughters. *Education:* BA, University of Pennsylvania; MD, Jefferson Medical College; MPH, Johns Hopkins University. *Appointments:* Assistant Demonstrator, Bacteriology, Jefferson Medical College; Assistant Professor, Health Administration, Johns Hopkins University; Associate Professor, Health Administration, Columbia University; Professor of Social Medicine, Albert Einstein Medical College; Professor of Public Health, Yale University; Health Officer, Eastern Health District, Baltimore; Chief, Division of Social Medicine, Montefiore, New York City; Deputy Assistant Secretary Health, HEW, Washington DC. *Memberships:* APHA, New York Academy of Medicine. *Publications:* "Family Medical Care" 1963; "A Spy in the House of Medicine" 1974; "Child Health: America's Future" 1978. Over 100 articles to professional journals. *Honours:* Superior Service Award, HEW, 1966; Institute of Medicine, 1980. *Address:* 590 Ellsworth Avenue, New Haven, CT 06511, USA.

SILVER, Ian Adair, b. 28 Dec. 1927, Poona, India. Professor, Chairman, Pathology, Medical School, Bristol, England. m. Marian Scrase, 30 June 1950, London, 2 sons, 2 daughters. *Education:* BA, Corpus Christi College, Cambridge, 1948; MRCVS, Royal Veterinary College, London, 1952; MA, Cambridge, 1952. *Appointments:* Demonstrator, Zoology, 1952, Lecturer, Anatomy, 1957, Director of Studies, St Catherines College, 1957, University of Cambridge; Fellow, Lecturer, Anatomy, Director Medical/Veterinary Studies, 1965, Senior Tutor, Graduate Students, 1966, Churchill College, Cambridge; Professor, Comparative Pathology, Medical School, Bristol University, 1970; Visiting Professor, Louisiana Technical University, USA, 1973; Royal Society, Professor, Federal University, Rio de Janeiro, Brazil, 1977; Adjunct Professor, Neurology, Medical School, University of Pennsylvania, USA, 1978; Chairman, Professor, Pathology, Medical School, Bristol University, 1982. *Memberships:* Anatomical Society; Pathological Society; Royal College of Veterinary Surgeons; International Society for Study of 02 Transport to Tissue; etc. *Publications:* More than 170 in scientific journals. *Honours:* Royal Agricultural Society Silver Medal, 1952; Sir Frederick Hobday Medal, 1978; Dalrymple Champrys Medal, 1984; President, Royal College of Veterinary Surgeons. *Hobbies:* Farming; Fishing; Mountain Climbing. *Address:* Dept. of Pathology, Medical School, University Walk, Bristol BS8 1TD, England.

SILVERMAN, Joel Jeremy, b. 23 May 1943, Battle Creek, Michigan, USA. Professor of Psychiatry. m. Phyllis, 12 July 1970, Wichita, Kansas, USA, 3 sons. *Education:* BA, Washington University, St Louis Missouri, 1965; MD, University of Kansas Medical School, Kansas City, 1969. *Appointments:* Chief, Psychiatry Service, US Army Hospital, Camp Zama, Japan, 1973-75; Psychiatric Consultant and Member of Division of Plastic and Reconstructive Surgery, 1975-; Director, Undergraduate Psychiatric Education, Department of Psychiatry, 1976-78; Chairman, Division of Consultation/Liaison Psychiatry, Department of Psychiatry, 1978-, Assistant Professor of Psychiatry and Surgery, 1978-79, Associate Professor of

Psychiatry and Surgery, 1979-85, Interim Chairman, Department of Psychiatry, 1984-, Professor and Interim Chairman, Department of Psychiatry, 1985-, Medical College of Virginia. *Memberships:* American Association for the Advancement of Science; Academy of Psychosomatic Medicine; Alpha Omega Alpha; American Psychiatric Association; American Psychosomatic Society; Association for Academic Psychiatry; Association of General Hospital Psychiatrists; Medical Society of Virginia; Psychiatric Society of Virginia; PSRO, Richmond, Virginia; Richmond Academy of Medicine; Richmond Psychiatric Society. *Publications:* 22 publications including 'Surgical staff recognition of psychopathology in trauma patients' with others in 'Journal of Trauma' 1985; 'Post Traumatic Stress Syndrome: A Neuropsychiatric Appraisal' in "Psychosomatic Aspects of Trauma, Advances in Psychosomatics" edited by L M Peterson and G O'Shanick, 1984. *Honours:* Medical College of Virginia Psychiatry Resident Award, 1985; Departmental Nominee, University Distinguished Faculty Award for Teaching, VCU, 1984; Examiner, ABP&N 1980; Teacher of the Year, Medical College of Virginia Class of 1978, 1975-76; AOA 1969. *Hobbies:* Camping; Fishing; Skiing; Gardening. *Address:* Department of Psychiatry, Medical College of Virginia, Virginia Commonwealth University, Box 710, Richmond, VA 23298, USA.

SILVERMAN, Morton Mayer, b. 15 Aug. 1947, Utica, New York, USA. Associate Administrator for Prevention. m. Kineret S Jaffe, 5 July 1970, South Orange, 1 son, 1 daughter. *Education:* BA, University of Pennsylvania, 1969; MD, Northwestern University Medical School, Chicago, 1974. *Appointments:* Assistant Professor, Psychiatry, University of Chicago Pritzker School of Medicine, 1978-80; Assistant to Chief Editor, 'Archives of General Psychiatry', 1978-80; Temporary Advisor, World Health Organization, 1979-80; Staff Psychiatrist, 1980-82, Chief, Centre for Prevention Research, 1982-85, National Institute of Mental Health; Associate Administrator for Prevention, Alcohol, Drug Abuse and Mental Health Administration 1985-. *Memberships:* American Psychiatric Association; Washington (DC) Psychiatric Society; American Public Health Association; National Conference of Community Health Centre. *Publications:* Co-Author, "Dietary and Nutritional Interventions in Preventive Mental Health"; Book Chapters: "Preventive Interventions in Psychiatry: Issues and Research Goals", 'Preventive Intervention Research: A New Beginning'; Co-Author, "Diet, Nutrition, and the Prevention of Mental Illness", 'Research on the Prevention of Psychological Disorders of Infancy: A Federal Perspective'; Articles in many professional journals including: 'Public Health Reports', 1985; 'Phi Delta Kappa', 1983; 'American Journal of Psychiatry', 1983; 'WHO Chronicle', 1980; 'Psychiatry Research', 1979; etc. *Honours:* US Public Health Service Special Recognition Award, 1985; Alcohol, Drug Abuse and Mental Health Administration Meritorious Achievement Award, 1983. *Hobbies:* Photography; Collecting Old Medical Texts. *Address:* 5600 Fishers Lane - Room 13C-05, Rockville, MD 20857, USA.

SIM, Cho-Boon, b. 17 Sep. 1935, Canton, China. Psychiatrist. m. Ai-Chiu Chen, 20 May 1956, 1 son, 1 daughter. *Education:* National Defence Medical Centre, Taipei, MD 1964. *Appointments:* Psychiatrist 1, Utica Psychiatric Centre, New York, USA; Staff Psychiatrist, Head of Acupuncture Research Committee, Tri-Service Hospital, Taipei, Taiwan; Associate Professor of Psychiatry, National Defence Medical Centre, Taipei, Taiwan; Associate Professor, Department of Applied Psychology, Fu-Jen Catholic University, Taipei; Associate Professor, Department of Psychology, Cheng-Che University; Head of Department of Psychiatry, Veterans General Hospital, Taipei; Clinical Professor, National Yang-Ming Medical College. *Memberships:* Chinese Society of Neurology & Psychiatry; Neurological Society of ROC (Taiwan); Chinese Medical Association (ROC Taiwan); American Psychiatric Association. *Publications:* "Patterns of Drug Abuse among Psychiatric Inpatients", 1979;

"The Role of Psychiatric Practice in General Hospital - A VGH Model", 1985; "Overview of General Hospital Psychiatry", 1985. *Hobbies:* Reading; Swimming; Travel. *Address:* 320 9F-2 Shih-Pai Road Sec II, Taipei, Taiwan, Republic of China, 112.

SIMBURG, Earl Joseph, b. 21 Mar. 1915, Canada. Private medical practitioner; President, Hospital medical staff. m. Virginia Roman, 10 Feb. 1957, Santa Barbara, California, USA, 2 sons, 1 daughter. *Education:* BSc, Certificate in Medicine, University of Saskatchewan, Canada, 1935; MD, CM, McGill University, Canada, 1938; Diplomate, Psychiatry, American Board of Psychiatry/Neurology, 1946, Psychoanalysis, 1962. *Appointments:* Post-Graduate Internship, Internal Medicine, Royal Victoria Hospital, Montreal, Canada, 1938-39; Junior Physician, Brandon Hospital, Brandon, Manitoba, Canada, 1939-41; Resident in Psychiatry, Grace, New Haven Hospital, USA, Instructor, Psychiatry, Yale University School of Medicine, 1941-43; Major, Medical Corps, USAF, 1943-47; Private Practice, Psychiatry, Berkeley, California, USA, 1947-. *Memberships:* American Medical Association; American Psychiatric Association; American Psychoanalytic Association; President, Medical Staffs, Berkeley, California, 1985. *Publications:* 'Must our Children be Neurotic' in 'Mental Hygiene', 1951; 'The Misuse and Abuse of Certain Mental Health Concepts' in 'Mental Hygiene', 1952; 'The Physician in Private Adoptions' in 'Psychiatric Studies and Projects', 1963; 'Psychoanalysis of the Older Patient', in 'Journal of the American Psychoanalytic Association', 1985. *Hobby:* Tennis. *Address:* 2006, Dwight Way, Berkeley, CA 94704, USA.

SIMKIN, Ruth Joy, b. 18 March 1944, Winnipeg, Canada. Physician and Assistant Professor. *Education:* BA cum laude Chemistry, Trinity College, Washington DC, USA, 1966-69; MD, LMCC, University of Calgary Medical School, Alberta, Canada, 1970-73; CCFP. *Appointments include:* Self-employed Family Physician, Calgary, 1975-83; Chief Medical Officer, Alberta Vocational Centre, Calgary, 1977-78; Lecturer 1977-81, Assistant Professor 1981-, Division of Family Practice, Faculty of Medicine, University of Calgary; Physician, Alexandra Community Health Centre, Calgary, 1983-. *Memberships:* Physicians for Social Responsibility; Doctors for The Repeal of the Abortion Law; Section of General Practice, Alberta Medical Association; Founding Member Calgary branch, The Federation of Medical Women of Canada; Canadian Medical Association; Certified Member, College of Family Physicians of Canada. *Publications include:* 'Methanolysis of 2-Nitrophenyl Acetate, (with A Kirkien-Konasiewicz and R Murphy), 1968; 'Basal Cell Epithelioma of the Vulva', (with Benjamin K Fisher), 1977; "Political Involvement Handbook for Alberta Women", co-editor, 1978; 'The Inadequacy of Health Care of Women', 1979; 'Alternative Birthing', 1981; Numerous papers. *Honours:* Hillebrand Jr Awards, The Chemical Society of Washington, 1968; co-recipient, YWCA Woman Of The Year Award in Health and Fitness, Calgary, 1981. *Address:* Box 12, Site 14, SS3, Calgary, Alberta T3C 3N9, Canada.

SIMMONDS, Wilfred John, b. 29 Nov. 1918, Queensland, Australia. University Professor of Physiology. m. Natalie Baker, 11 Dec. 1946, Adelaide, Australia, 1 son, 1 daughter. *Education:* BSc, University of Queensland, Australia, 1940, MB, BS, 1942; D. Phil, Oxford University, England, 1949; FRACP, 1969; FAA, 1982. *Appointments:* Lecturer in Pathology, University of Queensland, Australia, 1946; Nuffield Dominions Demonstrator, Physiology, Oxford University, England, 1947-50; Senior Research Fellow, Kanematsu Memorial Institute of Pathology, Sydney Hospital, Australia, 1950-57; Foundation Professor of Physiology, University of Western Australia, 1957-83. *Memberships:* Physiological Society of Great Britain; Physiological Society of Australia, President 1984; Royal Australasian College of Physicians. *Publications:* About 50 research papers and invited reviews on lympathic and gastrointestinal physiology, e.g.

'The role of micellar solubilization in lipid absorption' in 'The Australian Journal of Exp Biol Sci', 1972; Chapter 'Absorption of Lipids' in "Gastrointestinal Physiology", 1974. *Honours:* Nuffield Dominions Fellow in Physiology, Oxford, 1947-50; Fulbright Fellowship, 1965; Commonwealth Fund of New York, 1965; Visiting Faculty Member, Mayo Foundation, Graduate School of Medicine; Visiting Professor of Medicine, University of California at San Diego. *Hobbies:* Tennis; Reading; Research. *Address:* Department of Physiology, University of Western Australia, Nedlands, Western Australia 6009, Australia.

SIMPSON, Charles David, b. 16 Sep. 1951, Ottawa, Ontario, Canada. Assistant Chief of Medicine. m. Catherine Tait, 8 June 1974, Kingston, Ontario, 1 son, 2 daughters. *Education:* BSc, Maths and Physics, Hons, 1973, Royal Military College of Canada; MD, Queen's University, Kingston, Ontario, 1977. *Appointments:* Medical Officer, CFB Borden, Ontario, 1978-80; Resident, Internal Medicine, National Defence Medical Center, Ottawa, Ontario, Canada, 1980-81; Resident, Internal Medicine, Dalhousie University, 1981-83; Chief Resident, Medicine, Dalhousie University, 1983-84. *Memberships:* Fellow, Royal College of Physicians and Surgeons of Canada; Member, Canadian Medical Association; Nova Scotia Medical Society; Alpha Omega Alpha Honor Medical Society. *Publications:* 'Malignant Histiocytosis Associated with Siadh and Retinal Haemorrhages' in "Canadian Medical Association Journal" 1982 with S L Aitken. *Honour:* Governor General's Gold Medal, Royal Military College, 1973. *Hobbies:* Collecting swords and militaria. *Address:* Archie McCallum Hospital, CFB Halifax, Halifax, Nova Scotia, Canada.

SIMPSON, Claire Rittmeyer, b. 31 May 1923, Cincinnati, Ohio, USA. Speech and Language Pathologist. m. Lawrence A Simpson (deceased), 27 June 1945, 2 sons, 4 daughters. *Education:* BA, University of Cincinnati, 1945; MS, University of Vermont, 1973. *Appointments:* Remedial Reading Specialist, Saint Albans-Fairfield Supervisory Union, Saint Albans City Elementary School System, Vermont, 1966-68; Adult Basic Education Teacher 1967-68, Speech and Language Pathologist 1968-, Coordinator, Communication Services 1976-, Adjunct Professor, Department of Communication Science and Disorders 1979-, University of Vermont; Consultant, Franklin County Home Health Agency, 1974-; Saint Mary's Parish Lectors Association, 1974-; Franklin County Vocational Rehabilitation Division, State Agency for Human Services, 1974-. *Memberships include:* Delta Kappa Gamma; Zeta Tau Alpha; American Speech Language and Hearing Association; National Council for Exceptional Children; National Education Association; Vermont Association of Mental Health; National Association for Retarded Citizens; Vermont Children's Aid Society; American Council on Rural Special Education; Director 1975-, Saint Mary's Senior Choir. *Public tions:* "Let's Talk Speech! A Handbook for Parents", 1969; 'Desensitization With and Without Biofeedback', 1973. *Honours include:* ARC Gray Lady, 1951-61. *Address:* 96 Bank Street, Saint Albans, VI 05478, USA.

SIMPSON, George M, b. 28 Sep. 1926, USA. Director, Clinical Psychopharmacology; Professor, Psychiatry. m. Inger M Lilja, 23 Mar. 1961. *Education:* BSc, Glasgow University, Scotland, 1948; MB, Ch.B Liverpool University, England, 1955. *Appointments include:* Internships, Residencies, various hospitals, 1955-59; Associate Director, Rockland County Mental Health Association, USA, 1958-62; Senior Psychiatrist, 1959-61, Supervising Psychiatrist, 1961-68, Research Centre, Rockland State Hospital, Orangeburg; Assistant, Psychiatry, Columbia University, 1959-77; Visiting Professor, Menninger Clinic, Topeka, 1968; Associate Director, 1968-75, Principal Research Psychiatrist, 1968-77, Rockland Psychiatric Centre; Unit Chief, Yonkers-Hudson Shore Unit, 1971-75; Associate Clinical Professor, New York Medical College, 1974-77; Research Consultant, Bergen Pines County Hospital, 1975-77; Director, USC/Metro

Psycho pharmacology Services, Norwalk, 1977-80; Professor, Psychiatry, University of Southern California, 1977-83; Director, Adult Psychiatric Centre, Los Angeles, 1980-83; Professor, Psychiatry, Director, Clinical Psychopharmacology, Medical College of Pennsylvania, 1983-. *Memberships include:* American Psychiatric Association; American College of Neuropsychopharmacology; American Therapy Society; British Medical Association; etc. *Publications:* Numerous articles in professional journals; Advisory Editor: 'Psychopharmacology'; 'Hillside Journal of Clinical Psychiatry'. *Hobby:* Golf. *Address:* Dept. of Psychiatry, Medical College of Pennsylvania, 3200 Henry Avenue, Philadelphia, PA 19129, USA.

SIMPSON, William Stewart, b. 11 Apr. 1924, Edmonton, Alberta, Canada. Associate Director Medical Services. m. Eleanor Elizabeth Whitbread, 17 June 1950, Edmonton, Alberta, 4 sons. *Education:* BSc 1946, MD 1948, University of Alberta, Edmonton; Certified, American Board of Psychiatry and Neurology in Psychiatry, 1955; Topeka Institute of Psychoanalysis, USA, 1965; Certified, Board of Professional Standards of American Psychoanalytic Association, 1976; Certified Sex Counselor and Sex Therapist, American Association of Sex Educators, Counselors and Therapists. *Appointments:* Fellowship 1950-53, Associate Director 1966-68, Menninger School of Psychiatry; Residency in Psychiatry 1950-53, Assistant Section Chief 1953-54, Clinical Director 1954-59 and 1968-72, Topeka State Hospital; Section Chief, C F Menninger Memorial Hospital, 1959-66; Chief, Psychiatry service and Director of Psychiatric Residency Training, Topeka VA Hospital, 1974-77; Director Field Services 1972-74, Senior Psychiatrist 1977-84, Associate Director Medical Services 1984-, Adult Outpatient Department, Menninger Foundation. *Memberships include:* American Medical Association; Fellow, American Psychiatric Association; Kansas Psychiatric Society; American and International Psychoanalytic Associations; Kansas Medical Society; American Association of Sex Educators, Counselors and Therapists; Society for the Scientific Study of Sex. *Publications:* Contributor to "A Field Program in the Treatment of Alcoholics", 1982; "Selection of Treatment for Alcoholics"; 'Kopel and Othmer Discuss Anxiety', 1983; 'Psychoanalysis and Sex Therapy', 1985. *Honours:* Outstanding Achievement Award, Medical Alumni Association of University of Alberta, 1975; Silver Key Award 1975, Bronze Key Award 1976, National Council on Alcoholism. *Hobbies:* Reading; Classical Music; Swimming; Photography. *Address:* 834 Buchanan, Topeka, KS 66608, USA.

SIMS, Andrew Charles Petter, b. 5 Nov. 1938, Exeter, England. Professor of Psychiatry. m. Ruth Marie Harvey, 25 Apr. 1964, Birmingham, 2 sons, 2 daughters. *Education:* Cambridge 1960; MB, BChir, 1963; MRCS, LRCP (England), 1963; MA (Cambridge), 1964; Dip Obs RCOG, 1965; DPM (Manchester), 1969; MRCPsy, 1971; MD (Cambridge) 1974; FRC Psych, 1979. *Appointments:* Consultant Psychiatrist, All Saints Hospital, Birmingham 1971-76; Senior Lecturer, University of Birmingham, 1976-79. *Memberships:* Royal Society of Medicine; British Medical Association; Society of Clinical Psychiatrists; Association of University Teachers of Psychiatry. *Publications:* "Neurosis in Society"; "Psychiatry" (Concise Medical Textbooks with Sir William Trethowan); Lecture Notes Behavioral Sciences with W I Hume; Over 80 articles on Epidemiology of Neuroses, Psychopathology; Social Psychiatry, etc. *Hobbies:* Gardening; Music; Walking; Squash. *Address:* Department of Psychiatry, St James's University Hospital, Leeds, England.

SIMS, Francis Harding, b. 27 Jan. 1913, Auckland, New Zealand. Honorary Research Fellow, (retired). m. (1) Gertrude Jean Millar, 10 June 1946, Auckland, 1 son, 1 daughter, (2) Philippa Ethel Anderson, 4 May 1973, Toronto, Canada. *Education:* MSc 1st Class Honours Physics, Auckland University College, New Zealand, 1934; MB ChB, University of Otago, 1941;

PhD Pathology, University of Edinburgh, Scotland, 1950; Member 1964, Fellow 1968, Royal College of Pathologists of Australasia; Fellow, Australian Association of Clinical Biochemists. *Appointments:* Assistant Pathologist, Wellington Hospital, New Zealand, 1946-48; Lecturer in Clinical Chemistry, University of Edinburgh, Scotland, 1949-51; Chemical Pathologist, Auckland Hospital Board's Region, New Zealand, 1951-64; Pathologist in Charge, Green Lane Hospital, Auckland, 1964-70; Associate Professor, Departments of Clinical Biochemistry and Pathology, University of Toronto, Canada, 1970-78; Clinical Biochemist, Women's College Hospital, 1970-78; Honorary Turot in Pathology, School of Medicine, Suva, Fiji, 1979-81; Honorary Research Fellow, Pathology Department, School of Medicine, University of Auckland, New Zealand, 1981-. *Memberships:* Senior Member, Pathology Society of Great Britain and Ireland; Australian College of Pathologists; Australian Association of Clinical Biochemists; British Medical Association, New Zealand Branch; Emeritus Member, Canadian Society of Clinical Chemistry. *Publications:* The machanism of intimal thickening in arteriosclerosis', 1978; 'The arterial wall in malignant disease', 1979; 'A comparison of coronary and internal mammary arteries and implications of the results in the etiology of arteriosclerosis', 1983; 'Discontinuities in the internal elastic lamina: a comparison of coronary and internal mammary arteries', 1986. *Hobbies:* Sailing; Music. *Address:* 13 Endymion Place, Half Moon Bay, Bucklands Beach, Auckland, New Zealand.

SINCLAIR, Warren Keith, b. 9 Mar. 1924, Dunedin, New Zealand. President, National Council on Radiation Protection and Measurements; Professor (Emeritus), University of Chicago, USA. m. Elizabeth Joy Edwards, 19 Mar. 1948, London, England, 1 son, 1 daughter. *Education:* BSc, 1944, MSc, Physics (1st class hons), 1945, University of New Zealand; PhD, Physics, University of London, 1950; Also courses in biological sciences and biophysics. *Appointments:* Physicist, Dunedin Public Hospital, New Zealand and Demonstrator in Physics, University of Otago, New Zealand, 1945-47; Physicist, Royal Marsden Hospital, London and Lecturer, Extramural Program in Physics, University of London, 1947-54; Chairman, Department of Physics, University of Texas M D Anderson Hospital, Houston, Texas, USA, 1954-60; Professor of Physics, University of Texas, 1957-60; Senior Biophysicist, 1960-, Division Director, Biology Division, 1970-74; Associate Laboratory Director, 1971-81, Argonne National Laboratory; Professor of Radiology (Emeritus), University of Chicago, 1985-; President, National Council on Radiation Protection and Measurements, 1981-; (Part-time 1977-81). *Memberships:* American Association of Physicists in Medicine, President, 1961-62; Bioelectromagnetics Society; Biophysical Society; British Institute of Radiology; Faculty of Radiologists; Health Physics Society; Hospital Physicists Association; Institute of Physics, Fellow; Physical Society, Fellow; Radiation Research Society, President, 1978-79; Radiological Society of North America; Society of Nuclear Medicine. *Publications:* More than 130 original peer reviewed articles; Contribution to various books on radiation biophysics; Author, "Radiation Research, Physical, Chemical and Biomedical Perspectives", 1975; Contributor to many reports of the National Council on Radiation Protection and Measurements, the International Commission on Radiation Units and Measurements, the International Commission on Radiological Protection and the United Nations Scientific Committee on Effects of Atomic Radiation. *Honours:* Special University Lecturer, London, 1971; Secretary-General, 5th International Congress, Radiation Research, Seattle, 1974; Curie Lecturer, Buffalo, New York, 1979; Failla Lecturer, New York, 1981. *Hobbies:* Tennis; Golf; Swimming; Hunting; Reading. *Address:* National Council on Radiation Protection and Measurements, 7910 Woodmont Avenue, Suite 1016, Bethesda, MD 20814, USA.

SINGER, Jack Wolfe, b. 11 Sep. 1942, New York, USA.

Professor of Medicine. m. Celestia S Higano, 15 Dec. 1984, Seattle, Washington, 1 son. *Education:* BA, Columbia College of Columbia University, 1964; MD, State University of New York Downstate Medical College, 1968; Intern and Resident in Medicine, University of Chicago Hospitals, 1968-70; Fellowship in Haematology and Oncology, University of Washington, Seattle, 1972-75. *Appointments:* Chief Medical Oncology, VA Medical Centre, 1975-; Assistant Professor of Medicine, 1975-78, Associate Professor of Medicine, 1979-85, Professor of Medicine, 1986-, University of Washington; Assistant Member, Fred Hutchinson Cancer Research Centre, 1975-. *Memberships:* American Society of Haematology; American Society of Clinical Oncology; American Federation for Clinical Research; International Society for Experimental Haematology; Western Society for Clinical Research. *Publications:* "Cancer Care, A Personal Guide", 1979; Contributor of over 90 articles in major scientific journals. *Honours:* Alpha Omega Alpha, 1967; New York State Regents Scholar, 1964. *Hobbies:* Classical piano; Squash; Skiing. *Address:* VA Medical Centre, 1660 South Columbian Way, Seattle, WA 98108, USA.

SINGH, Bawa Prehlad, b. 22 Feb. 1923, Lucknow, India. Obstetrician, Gynaecologist. m. Renate Maria Trawniczek, 20 Jan. 1962, Vienna, Austria, 1 son. *Education:* BSc, Lucknow University, 1941; MBBS, University of Punjab, 1946; FACS, 1960; FACOG, 1952; FICS, 1957; Diplomate, American Board of Obstetrics-Gynaecology, 1965. *Appointments:* Teaching Fellow in Oncologic Surgery, City of Hope Medical Center, Duarte, California, USA, 1956-57; Instructor 1952-56, Assostant Clinical Professor 1962-70, Associate Clinical Professor 1970-, Obstetrics-Gynaecology, University of California Medical School, Los Angeles; Private practice Obstetrics-Gynaecology. *Memberships:* American, California and Los Angeles County Medical Associations; Life Fellow, Los Angeles Obstetrical and Gynaecological Society; Life Member, American Medical Society of Vienna; Diplomate, American Board of Obstetrics and Gynaecology; Fellow: American College of Surgeons; American College of Obstetricians and Gynaecologists; International College of Surgeons. *Publications include:* 'Leiomyosarcoma of the uterus', 1958; 'Intra-aortic Nitrogen Mustard Therapy in Advanced Pelvic Malignancies', 1959. *Honour:* Outstanding Teacher Award-Obstetrics/Gynaecology, University of California at Los Angeles Medical Centre, Torrance, 1971. *Hobbies:* Photography; Tennis; Travel. *Address:* 1300 West 155 Street, Suite 102, Gardena, CA 90247, USA.

SINGH SEKHON, Arjinderpal, b. 10 Jan. 1949, Punjab, India. Private Practitioner; Associate Professor. m. Dr Daljit Kaur, 8 April 1973, Punjab, 2 sons, 2 daughters. *Education:* MD Fellow: American College of Angiology; College of Chest Physicians. Diplomate: American Board of Internal Medicine; American Board of Pulmonary Medicine; American Board of Tropical Medicine. *Appointments:* Medical Director, Respiratory Department: Good Samaritan Hospital, Mount Vernon, Illinois, USA; Cross Road Community Hospita, Mount Vernon; currently, Associate Professor, Southern Illinois University. *Memberships:* Fellow: American College of Chest Physicians; American College of Angiology, American College of Physicians. *Hobbies:* Flying; Gardening. *Address:* 4207 Fox Creek Drive, Mount Vernon, IL 62864, USA.

SINHA, Amarendra Kumar, b. 9 Oct. 1948, Bhagalpur, India. Physician, Cardiologist. m. Prativa Sinha, 27 June 1971, Morghyr, India, 2 sons. *Education:* MB, BS (Honours), Gold Medallist, PAT; MD, New Jersey State Board, USA; Doctor of Tropical Medicine & Hygiene, England; Diplomate, National Board of Medicine, India. *Appointments:* Internship & Houseemanship, PMCH, Patna; Resident in Medicine & Cardiology, Medical Centre, Jersey City, New Jersey, USA; Consultant Physician, in charge of Cardiopulmonary laboratory, KK Nursing Home & Research

Centre, Bhagalpur, India. *Memberships:* School of Tropical Medicine, Liverpool, England; American College of Chest Physicians; National College of Chest Physicians (India); Cardiological Society of India; Indian Medical Association; Austrian Medical Society. *Publications:* 'Intractable Heart Failure' (in Patna Journal of Medicine, 1981; Lightning Induced Myocardial Injury' in Angiology USA, 1985. *Honours:* Awards in Anatomy, Gold Medals in Anatomy, Pathology, Clinico-pathological Society; University Merit Scholarship, 1967-69. *Hobbies:* Photography; Travel. *Address:* KK Nursing Home 9 Research Centre, Raja S N Road, Bhagalpur 812001, India.

SINNATAMBY, Arthur Sothyrajan, b. 15 June 1932, Colombo. Personal Physician, to His Royal Highness Paduka Seri Begawan, Sultan of Brunei Darussalam. m. Christobelle Sarojini Hunt, 8 Sep. 1960, Colombo, 1 daughter. *Education:* DCH (Eng); FRCP (Glasgow); MRCP (London); AM (Singapore); FCCP (USA). *Appointments:* Consultant Geriatrician, Wakefield, England, 1967-69; Senior Lecturer, Physiology, University of Sri Lanka, 1969-74; Senior Registrar, Internal Medicine, Singapore, 1974-78; Specialist Physician, Head, Medical Units, Raja Isteri, Pengiran Anak Saleha Hospital, Bandar Seri Begawan, 1978-. *Memberships:* British Medical Association. *Publications:* Senior Author, "Pulmonary Candidiasis: An Unusual Presentation with Immunological Implications", Annals of the Academy of Medicine, Singapore, 1977; "A Case of Thrombotic Thrombocytopaenic Purpura Surviving for 4 Years", 'Singapore Medical Journal', 1980. *Honours:* DPMB, Knight of the Royal Order of the Crown of Brunei, 1982. *Hobbies:* Poetry; Art; Photography; Reading; Palaentology; History of Cricket; Squash. *Address:* Ripas Hospital, Bandar Seri Begawan, Brunei Darussalam.

SINNIAH, Rajalingam, b. 19 Feb. 1937, Malaysia. Professor of Pathology. m. Madhavi Krishnan, 26 June 1980, Singapore, 1 daughter. *Education:* MB BCh BAO, 1961, MA, 1964, MD, 1967, Trinity College, University of Dublin, Republic of Ireland; PhD, Queen's University, Belfast, Northern Ireland, 1969; Member, Royal College of Physicians in Ireland, 1964, Fellow, 1976; Member, Royal College of Pathologists, 1971, Fellow, 1983; Fellow, Royal College of Physicians of Australasia, 1977. *Appointments:* Medical Registrar & Clinical Tutor, Meath Hospital, Trinity College, Dublin, 1962-65; Registrar & Tutor in Pathology & Clinical Medicine, 1965-68, Senior Registrar & Lecturer in Pathology, 1968-70, 1970-72, Royal Victoria Hospital, Queen's University, Belfast; Senior Lecturer in Pathology, 1972-74, Associate Professor in Pathology, 1974-79, University of Singapore; Professor of Pathology, National University of Singapore, 1980-; Visiting Professor in Pathology & Nephrology, Harbor, University of California at Los Angeles Medical Centre, USA, 1983. *Memberships:* International Society of Nephrology; International Academy of Pathology; Pathological Society of Great Britain & Ireland; Founder President, Singapore Society of Pathology, 1976-78; Singapore Academy of Medicine; WHO committee for Classification of Tropical Kidnet Diseases, 1984. *Publications:* Various articles & publications in field of renal disease & nephropathology. *Honours:* 1st Prize Silver Medal in Internal Medicine, Meath Hospital, Dublin, 1961; Stewart-Fry Scholarship, Queen's University, Belfast, 1965; Adrian Stokes Memorial Fellowship, Trinity College, Dublin, 1966; Gold Medal Prize, Nihon University, 1981. *Hobbies:* Music; Collecting Art Works (painting & sculptures); Reading; Travel; Photography; Cinema; Theatre & Dance. *Address:* Department of Pathology, National University of Singapore, National University Hospital, Lower Kent Ridge Road, Singapore 0511.

SIRAGUSA, Joseph S, b. 24 Apr. 1958, Buffalo, New York, USA, President, Monroe Chiropractic Clinic. *Education:* DC, Palmer College of Chiropractic, 1982; Buffalo State University, New York. *Appointments:* Assistant Clinic Intern Director, Public Clinic, Palmer College of Chiropractic, Davenport, Iowa; Associate,

Cararrus Chiropractic Clinic, Indianapolis, North Carolina; President, Monroe Chiropractic Clinic. *Memberships:* Council on Orthopedics, Council on Roentgenology, American Chiropractic Association; North Carolina Chiropractic Association; Pi Tau Delta. *Publication:* 'Anatomical and Biomechanical Basis for Motion Palpation of the Sacro-Iliac Joint', 1985. *Honour:* National Dean's List, 1980. *Hobbies:* Golf; Music. *Address:* 2202-C W Roosevelt Boulevard, Monroe, NC 28110, USA.

SJOHOLM, Ingvar Gösta Holger, b. 23 Mar. 1933, Stockholm, Sweden. Professor, Department of Drugs, Swedish National Board of Health and Welfare, 1982-. m. 1960, 2 sons, 1 daughter. *Education:* Pharmacist, 1960; Licentiate, 1964; DrPharm Sci, Docent in Pharmaceutical Biochemistry, 1967. *Appointments:* Assistant, 1960-64, Research Assistant, 1964-67, Docent, 1967-68, Royal Pharmaceutical Institute; Research Fellow, Hormone Research Laboratory, University of California, USA, 1968-69; University Lecturer, University of Uppsala, 1969-80; Head, Academic Pharmacy, Uppsala, Sweden, 1980-82. *Memberships:* Swedish Academy of Pharmacy; American Chemical Society. *Publications:* Contributor of over 120 scientific papers and patents. *Honours:* The Scheele Prize, 1965. *Address:* Department of Drugs, Swedish National Board of Health and Welfare, Box 607, S-75125 Uppsala, Sweden.

SKALOVA, Radmila, b. 10 Jan. 1923, Skopje, Yugoslavia. University Professor; Head of Staphylococcus Phage Typing Laboratory. *Education:* MD; Diploma in Bacteriology 1948, Specialisation in Microbiology 1951, Belgrade; Dr Sc, Zagreb, 1961. *Appointments:* Institute of Microbiology, Medical School, University of Skopje, 1949-54; Staff 1954-, Professor, Andrija Stampar School of Public Health, Medical School, University of Zagreb; Head, National Reference Laboratory for Staphylococcus Phage Typing. *Memberships:* International Subcommittee for Staphylococcus Phage Typing; American Public Health Association; Council of the International Congress for Infectious Diseases; Associationof Microbiological Societies of Yugoslavia; Editorial Board, 'Infection'. *Publications include:* 'Interaction of moxalactam and gentamicin: in-vitro study with strains of S aureus and P seruginosa' (co-author), Journal of Antimicrobial Chemotherapy' 1982; 'Epidemiology of Meningococcal Mengingitis in Sahel a. Mongolia', 'For the second: Infection', 1984. *Honours:* Diploma, Medical School University of Zagreb, 1967; Appreciation, Council of the International Congress for Infectious Diseases, 1985. *Hobbies:* History of Art; Music. *Address:* Andrija Stampar School of Public Health, Medical School, University of Zagreb, Rockefellerova 4, 41000 Zagreb, Yugoslavia.

SKELTON, Lana S, b. 9 Mar. 1941, Groveland, Florida, USA. Cardiologist. m. Marvin Skelton, 5 Apr. 1981, Glynn County, USA. *Education:* Emory University, Atlanta, Georgia, 1959-60; BA, Winthrop, Rockhill, South Carolina, 1960-62; MD, Medical College of Georgia, Augusta, 1962-66; Internship, Charity Hospital, New Orleans, 1966-67; Internal Medicine Residency, 1967-70; Cardiology Fellow 1970-72, Gullentine Fellow 1972-73, Tulane Medical School. *Appointments:* Instructor of Medicine, Charity Hospital, Tulane, 1967-70; Supervisor, Charity Hospital Emergency Room, 1970-72; Cardiology Consultant, VA Hospital, New Orleans, 1971-75; Crippled Children's Hospital, New Orleans & Alexandria, 1971-75; Director of Tulane CCU, Charity Hospital of New Oreleans, 1970-75; Director of Physical Diagnosis, 1972-75, Assistant Professor of Medicine, 1972-75, Associate Professor of Medicine, 1975-76, Tulane Medical School; Cardiologist, Glyy Brunswick Memorial Hospital, Brunswick, Georgia, 1976-. *Memberships include:* American Medical Association; American College of Physicians; American College of Chest Physicians; American College of Cardiology; American Heart Association; American Association of University Professors. *Publications:* Various articles in medical journals. *Honours:* AMA Physician's Recognition Award, 1970. *Hobby:* Photography. *Address:* 3212 Shrine Road, Brunswick, GA 31520 - 4389, USA.

SKETRIS, Ingrida Selga, b. 24 May 1955, London, Canada. Associate Professor. *Education:* BSc, Pharmacy, University of Toronto, 1977; Doctor, Pharmacy, University of Minnesota, USA, 1979. *Memberships:* Canadian Society of Hospital Pharmacists; Canadian Pharmaceutical Association; Canadian Society of Clinical Pharmacology; American College of Clinical Pharmacy; Canadian Foundation for the Advancement of Pharmacy; Northeast Canadian American Health Council. *Publications:* Various contributions to medical journals, including 'Plasmapheresis: Its effect on toxic agents & drugs', 1984; 'Is there a problem with benzodiazepine prescribing in Maritime Canada?', 1985; 'A poison education program for primary schools', 1984; etc. (Co-author). *Honours:* B Trevor Pugsley Lecturer, Pharmacy Education, 1984; Visiting Pharmacy Professor, University of British Columbia, Medical Research Council of Canada, 1985. *Hobbies:* Skiing; Skating; Tennis; Squash; Swimming; Canoeing; Bridge. *Address:* College of Pharmacy, Dalhousie University, Halifax, Nova Scotia, Canada B3H 3J5.

SKOLNIKOFF, Alan Z, b. 25 Sep. 1932, New York City, USA. Associate Clinical Professor, University of California, San Francisco. m. Suzanne Chevalier, 22 Aug. 1965, Stinson Beach, California, 2 sons. *Education:* BA, Columbia College, NY, 1953; University of Basel, Switzerland Faculty of Medicine, 1953-57; MD, State University of New York, Downstate Medical Center, 1959; Internship, Madigan General Hospital, 1960; Psychiatry Residency, Langley Porter Psychiatric Institute, 1963-66. *Appointments:* Captain, General Medical Officer, US Army, 1960-63; Psychiatric Resident, 1963-66; Private Practice of Psychiatry and Psychoanalysis, 1966-; Faculty, Center for Training in Community Psychiatry, Berkeley, 1968-70; Faculty, San Francisco Psychoanalytic Institute, 1975-; Consulting Editor, 'Psychoanalytic Inquiry', Analytic Press, New Jersey, 1980-. *Memberships:* American Psychoanalytic Association; Fellow, American Psychiatric Association; Member, San Francisco Psychoanalytic Society; Member, Northern California Psychiatric Society. *Publications:* Coauthor, "Psychosocial Function in Epilepsy", 1970; 'Cinfigurational Analysis: A Method to Measure Change in Psychotherapy' in "Cures by Psychotherapy", Ed. J. Martin Myers, 1984; 'Analysis of the Transference: Implications for Theory and Research' in 'Psychoanalytic Inquiry', 1985; 'Consensual Analysis: Introduction and Case Presentation' co-authored with Emanuel Windholz in "New Ideas in Psychoanalysis: The Process of Change in a Humanistic Science", Eds. C. F. Settlage and R. Brockbank, 1985. *Address:* 205 Edgewood Avenue, San Francisco, CA 94117, USA.

SKORNICK, Yehuda Gabriel, b. 26 Jan. 1945, Jerusalem, Israel. Deputy Chief of Surgery. m. Esther, 9 Oct. 1969, Tel Aviv, 2 sons, 2 daughters. *Education:* MD, The Hebrew University, Jerusalem, 1973. *Memberships:* Israel Medical Association; Israel Surgical Society; Israel Gastroenterological Society; American Society of Clinical Oncology, USA; American Association of Cancer Research, USA; American Society of Surgical Oncology; European Society of Surgical Oncology. *Publications:* 'Effective tumor immunization induced by cells of elevated membrane microviscosity', (Co-author), 1979; 'Positive skin tests with antologus tumor cells or increased membrane microviscosity', 1981; 'Active immunization of hamsters against pancreatic carcinoma cells with lipid treated cells or their shed antigens', 1984; 'Inhibition of growth and metastasis of lung tumor in mice by immunization with cholesteryl-hemisuccinate enriched tumor cells', 1984; 'Active immunotherapy of human solid tumor with autologous cells treated with cholesteryl-hemisuccinate'; 'Regulation of tumor growth by lipids. Possible clinical applications', (with M Shinitzky), 1982. *Hobbies:* Sport; Music.

Address: Surgery Department, Rokach Hospital, Tel Aviv Medical Centre, 8 Balfour Street, Tel Aviv, Israel.

SKORYNA, Stanley Constantine, b. 4 Sep. 1920, Warsaw, Poland. Associate Professor, Surgery & Biology. m. Jane Marie Polud, 8 Aug. 1970, Montreal, Canada, 2 sons, 1 daughter. *Education:* MD, University of Vienna, Austria, 1943; MSc, McGill University, Montreal, Canada, 1950; PhD, University of Vienna, 1962. *Appointments:* Research Fellow, National Cancer Institute of Canada, 1950-53; Research Director, Department of Experimental Surgery, McGill University, 1954-59; Director, Gastroint Research Laboratory, McGill University, 1959-; Director, Clinical Investigation Service, Surgery, St Mary's Hospital Centre, Montreal, 1976-; Director, Groupe de Cherche Biomedical, University of Montreal, 1984-; Associate Professor of Surgery, McGill University; Associate Professor of Biology, University of Montreal. *Memberships:* American Association for Cancer Research; American College of Surgeons; American Physiological Society; American Gastroenterological Association; Canadian Physiological Society; Canadian Society for Nutritional Sciences; International Society for Trace Element Research in Humans. *Publications:* Over 150 publications on carcinogenesis, gastrointestinal physiology & trace elements; Books: "Pathophysiology of Peptic Ulcer", 1963; "Guidelines to Radiological Health", 1967; "Intestinal Absorption of Trace Elements", 1970; "Handbook of Stable Strontium", 1981. *Honours:* Gold Medalist, Surgery, Royal College of Physicians & Surgeons of Canada, 1959; Director, Medical Expedition to Easter Island (WHO), 1964-65; Outstanding Achievement Award, McGill Graduate Society, 1966; Outstanding Citizenship Award, Montreal Citizenship Council, 1967. *Address:* 4773 Sherbrooke Street West, Westmount, Quebec, H3Z 1G5, Canada.

SKOSEY, John L, b. 19 Jan. 1936, USA. Professor of Medicine and Chief, Section of Rheumatology, University of Illinois College of Medicine. m. Conseula Lira, 18 June 1960, Chicago, 2 sons, 1 daughter. *Education:* BA, Southern Illinois University, Carbondale, 1957; MD, 1961, PhD, 1964, University of Chicago. *Appointments:* Instructor, Department of Medicine, University of Chicago, 1967-69; Assistant Professor of Medicine, University of Chicago Pritzker School of Medicine and Franklin McLean Memorial Research Institute, Chicago, 1969-74; Associate Professor of Medicine, University of Chicago Pritzker School of Medicine and Franklin McLean Memorial Research Institute, 1974-77; Associate Professor, Cook County Graduate School of Medicine, 1974-82; Associate Professor of Medicine, Chief Section of Rheumatology, Department of Medicine, Abraham Lincoln School of Medicine, The University of Illinois at the Medical Centre, Chicago, 1978-82; Member of the Graduate College, Department of Microbiology, 1981-. *Memberships:* American Federation for Clinical Research; American Physiological Society; American Rheumatism Association; Arthritis Foundation; Illinois Chapter; Arthritis Foundation, National Central Society for Clinical Research; Chicago Rheumatism Society; New York Academy of Sciences; Sigma Xi. *Publications:* Contributor of numerous articles in professional journals. *Honours:* Ginsberg Award in Physiology, 1961; Fellow, The Arthritis Foundation, 1968-71. *Hobbies:* Travel; Music; Swimming; Tennis. *Address:* University of Illinois College of Medicine at Chicago, Department of Medicine/Rheumatology, 840 South Wood Street, Room 1006 CSB, Chicago, IL 60612, USA.

SLADE, Walter R, b. 11 Nov. 1911, Raleigh, North Carolina, USA. Neurology Chief. m. Ruth Sims, 2 Feb. 1947. *Education:* BS, St Augustine's College, Raleigh, 1939; MD, Meharry Medical College, Nashville, Tennessee, 1947. *Appointments:* Teacher, Brunswick Georgia High School, 1939; Teacher, Edenton Public Schools, North Carolina, 1940-44; Resident, Internal Medicine and Neurology, K JM C Brooklyn, New York, 1948-52; Resident Psychiatrist 1952-54, Staff Neurologist and Psychiatrist 1954-69, Chief of Neurology 1969-, Brooklyn VAMC; Adjunct Professor Health Sciences, LICU Brooklyn, New York; Clinical Professor Neurology, State University New York, Downstate Medical Center. *Memberships include:* International Society of Psychoendocrinology; American Association of Hospital Medical Education; American Psychiatric Association; Fellow: American College of Angiology; American Academy of Neurology; American Geriatric Society; International College of Angiology. *Publications:* "Physiological Functioning of the Ageing Brain Lex et Scientia", 1975; "Approaching the Clinical Problems of Patients with Cerebrovascular Disease Angiology", 1978; 'Sarcoid of the Nervous System', 1979; Editor, Geriatric Neurology, 1980. *Honours:* Doctor of the Year Award, Tan Magazine, 1952; William B Moss Distinguished Award, 1979; Family of the Year Award, Brooklyn Council of Churches, 1982. *Hobbies:* Tennis; Music; Photography; Electronics. *Address:* 1344 E 22nd Street, Brooklyn, NY 11210, USA.

SLADEK, John Richard Jr, b. 6 Feb. 1943, Chicago, Illinois, USA. Professor and Chairman of Neurobiology and Anatomy. m. Celia Davis Sladek, 2 sons, 1 daughter. *Education:* BA, Carthage College, 1965; MS, Northwestern University, 1968; PhD, University Health Sciences/The Chicago Medical School, 1971. *Appointments:* Teaching Assistant, Anatomy, 1968-70, Assistant Professor of Anatomy, 1971-73; Chicago Medical School; Assistant Professor of Anatomy, 1973-77, Associate Professor of Anatomy, 1977-82, Associate Professor, Centre for Brain Research, 1979-82, Professor of Brain Research, 1982-85, University of Rochester School of Medicine, New York. *Memberships:* American Association of Anatomists; The Histochemical Society; The New York Academy of Sciences; American Association of Anatomy Chairmen; The Society of Sigma Xi; The Society for Neuroscience; Gerontological Society. *Publications:* 'Fluorescence-immunocytochemistry: Simultaneous localization of catecholamines and gonadotropin-releasing hormone', (with T H McNeill), 1978; 'Functional Development of grafted peptidergic neurons', (with D M Gash, C D Sladek), 1980; 'Monoamine distribution in primate brain V Primate monoaminergic nuclei: Anatomy, projections and local organization', (with D L Felten), 1983; 'Morphological and functional properties of transplanted vasopressin neurons', (with D M Gash), 1984. *Honours:* Outstanding Young Men of America, 1972; American Men and Women of Science, 1981; Distinguished Alumnus, Carthage College, 1983; Grass Visiting Scientist, Society of Neuroscience, 1984; Burton Baker Memorial Lecturer, University of Michigan, 1985. *Address:* Department of Neurobiology and Anatomy, Box 603, University of Rochester School of Medicine, 601 Elmwood Avenue, Rochester, NY 14642, USA.

SLAVIN, Laverne A, b. 23 May 1957, New York City, USA. Director of Private Speech Pathology Practice. *Education:* BA, Magna cum laude, City University of New York; MA, Magna cum laude, University of Houston. *Current appointments:* Director of Speech Pathology, St Vincent's Medical Centre, Los Angeles. *Memberships:* California Board of Medical Quality Assurance; National & California Speech-Language-Hearing Associations; Voice Foundation. *Publications:* 'Optimal Pitch', in 'Los Angeles City Press', 1984; 'Components of Voice' in 'Asian American News', 1984. *Hobbies:* Sailing; Running; Horseback riding. *Address:* The Professional Voice, 3550 Wilshire Boulevard, Suite 1406, Los Angeles, CA 90010-2521, USA.

SLEEPER, Harold George, b. 11 Oct. 1921, Wagoner, Oklahoma, USA. Psychiatrist. m. Dolores R Wiggins, 26 Sep. 1983, Oklahoma City, 2 sons, 1 daughter. *Education:* BA, Baylor University, 1942; MD, Texas University Medical Branch, Galveston, 1945; Residency, Psychiatry, John Sealy Hospital, Galveston, 1955-56; Certified, Psychiatry, American Board of Psychiatry & Neurology, 1956. *Appointments:* Chief, Medical Staff, Coyne Campbell Hospital, 1957-64;

Chairman, Psychiatry, St Anthony Hospital, 1959-61; President, Oklahoma Psychiatric Foundation, 1963-65, 1971-84; Chairman, Oklahoma Psychiatric Foundation Board of Trustees, 1963-65, 1971-84; President, Oklahoma Psychiatric Foundation Authority, 1973-84; Chief, Medical Staff, Medical Director, Willow View Hospital, 1976-84; Established, 1st Department, Electroencephalography, St Anthony Hospital, 1960; Chairman, Committee for Evaluation of Quality Assurance, Willow View, 1979-84; Chairman, Peer Review Committee, District Branch, American Psychiatric Association, 1980-81. *Memberships:* American Psychiatric Association; American Medical Association; Oklahoma State & County Medical Associations; International Psychiatric Association for Advancement of ECT; American Medical Electroencephalographic Association. *Honours:* Fellow, American Psychiatric Association, 1956, Life Fellow, 1979. *Hobby:* Photography. *Address:* 2801 Parklawn Drive, Suite 505, Midwest City, OK 73110, USA.

SLOCUM, Eleanor English, b. 5 Sep. 1922, Ridge Mills, New York, USA. Boarding Home Owner and Operator. m. Floyd Oliver Slocum, 17 June 1951, Syracuse, 1 son, 1 daughter. *Education:* Pre-Nursing, 1942-43, Nursing Diploma, 1948, Union College School of Nursing; BS, 1949; Colorado University, 1950; Licensed Nursing Home Administration, New York State, 1972; Corresponding Student, George Washington University, 1973-75. *Appointments:* Head Nurse, Hospital Supervisor, Medical Desk Nurse, Boulder Memorial Hospital, Colorado, 1948, 1949-50; Supervisor, Alex Nursing Home, 1950-51; Charge Nurse, Syracuses University Hospital, New York, 1951-56; Administrator, Sunnyside Nursing Home, East Syracuse, 1956-58; Administrator, Scott Nursing Home, 1959; Founder and Administrator, Maple Law Nursing Home, 1958-81; Founder and Operator, Maple Lawn of Manlius Residential Care Facility, 1981-85; Owner and Operator, Maple Lawn of Manlius Boarding Home, 1985-. *Memberships:* Past Memberships: Fellow, American College of Nursing Home Administrators; American Academy of Medical Administrators; National Fire Protection Association; American Health Care Association; New York State Health Care Association; New York State Nursing Home Association; National Federation Professional Business and Chamber of Commerce. *Honours:* Honorable Convocation in Graduate Studies, Unwin College, Lincoln, Nebraska, 1949. *Hobbies:* Music; Sewing; Writing. *Address:* PO Box 237, Farley Lane, Manlius, NY 13104, USA.

SLOMAN, John Graeme, b. 1 Feb. 1927, Australia. Consultant Cardiologist; Director of Cardiology. m. Isabel Mary Sloman, 6 Aug. 1952, 3 sons, 1 daughter. *Education:* BSc, 1950, MBBS, 1953, Melbourne; MRCP, Edinburgh, Scotland, 1957; MRCP, London, England, 1958; MRACP, 1960; FRACP, 1967; FACC, 1968; FRCP, Edinburgh, 1968; FRCP, London, 1977. *Appointments:* Director of Cardiology, Royal Melbourne Hospital, 1976-80; Director of Cardiology, Epworth Hospital, 1980-. *Memberships:* World Health Organisation; Cardiac Society of Australia and New Zealand; North American Society of Pacing and Electrophysiology; American College of Cardiology. *Publications:* Author of numerous publications including, 'Recent concepts in the management of Ischaemic Cardiac Syndromes', (with P A Valentine and L D Sutton), 1982; 'The First Pacemaker', (with H G Mond and R H Edwards), 1982. *Honours:* Leverhulme Research Fellowship, 1958; Royal College of Physicians, London, Efficiency Decoration. *Hobbies:* Bush walking; Mountain climbing; Canoeing; Skiing; Cycling. *Address:* Cardiovascular Unit, Clinical Sciences Building, 62 Erin Street, Richmond, 3121 Victoria, Australia.

SLOMIC, Ahmet, b. 5 Feb. 1925, Brcko. Head, X-Ray Department. *Education:* MD, Sarajevo, Yugoslavia; X-Ray Speciality, Paris, France; PhD, Paris. *Appointments:* Head, X-Ray Department, Mekues; Assoc iate Professor, Radiology, CHUL, Quebec, Canada; Head, X-Ray Department, Highland View Regional Hospital,

Amherst, Nova Scotia. *Memberships:* Fellow, Royal College of Physicians, Canada; Societe Francaise de Radiologie; Societe d'Anthropologie de Paris, France. *Publications:* Author or co-author over 40 publications. Main Publications: 'Staircase Phenomenon in Myasthenia gravis, (Brain Research 1968) and 'Crainology of Quebec' (Societe d'Anthropologie de Paris 6 Papers). *Honour:* Prix d'Ansouvall d'electrologie, Paris, France, 1962. *Hobbies:* Skiing. *Address:* Highland View Regional Hospital, Amherst, Nova Scotia, Canada B46 1N6.

SLOMSKI, Ryszard, b. 21 Jan. 1950, Poznan, Poland. Associate Professor. m. Magdalena Skapska, 2 Apr. 1972, Poznan, 1 son, 1 daughter. *Education:* MS, Biochemistry, University of Poznan, 1973; PhD, Human Genetics, Institute of Human Genetics, Polish Academy of Sciences, Poznan, 1976. *Appointments:* Research Associate 1973-76, Assistant Professor, 1976-82, Associate Professor, 1983-, Institute of Human Genetics, Polish Academy of Sciences, Poznan, Poland; Visiting Professor, Department of Microbiology and Immunology, University of Chicago, 1978; Visiting Professor, Department of Microbiology and Immunology, University of Illinois, Chicago, 1979, 1981, 1983, 1985. *Memberships:* Polish Biochemical Society; Polish Society for Genetics. *Publications:* 32 publications in major scientific journals. *Honours:* Award from Polish Society for Biochemistry, 1975; Award from Scientific Secretary of Polish Academy of Sciences, 1975, 1976; Awards from Medical Section, Polish Academy of Sciences 1979, 1982. *Hobby:* Sailing. *Address:* Szeherezady 100, 60-159 Poznan, Poland.

SLONECKER, Charles Edward, b. 11 Nov. 1938, Gig Harbor, Washington, USA. Professor, Head, Anatomy, University of British Columbia, Canada. m. Jan Hunter, 24 Apr. 1961, Bremerton, 3 sons. *Education:* DDS, 1965, PhD, 1967, University of Washington. *Appointments:* Scientific Assistant, Institute of Pathology, University of Bern, Switzerland, 1967-68; Assistant Professor, 1968-71, Associate Professor, 1971-76, Professor, 1976-, Head, Anatomy, 1981, University of British Columbia. *Memberships:* American & Canadian Association s of Anatomists; Sigma Xi; Omicron Kappa Upsilon. *Publications:* Numerous articles in professional journals including: 'American Journal of Anatomy'; 'Journal of Research'; Nature; etc. *Honours:* Omicron Kappa Upsilon; American Academy of Dental Medicine Award of Merit, University of Washington, 1965; Washington State Dental Association Certificate of Merit, 1965; Dennis P Duskin Memorial Award, University of Washington, 1965; Certificate of Merit, Master Teaching Award, University of British Columbia, 1975-76. *Hobbies:* Travel; Reading; Golf; Baseball Coach. *Address:* Department of Anatomy, University of British Columbia, 2177 Wesbrook Mall, Vancouver, BC, Canada V6T 1W5.

SLONIM, Leon, b. 11 July 1935, Melbourne, Australia. Consultant Radiologist. m. Frances Simmons, 8 Dec. 1957, Melbourne, 1 son, 2 daughters. *Education:* MBBS, Melbourne, 1957; MRACR, 1967; FRCR, 1969; FRACR, 1973; DDU 1978. *Appointments:* Assistant Radiologist, 1968, Honorary Clinical Assistant to Radiologist, 1969-72, Sessional Radiologist, RCH, 1969-70, Senior Radiologist, 1972-79, R.M.H; Senior Associate, University of Melbourne, 1972-79; Federal Councillor, 1972-84; RACR Examiner Physics Part 1, 1973-76; RACR Chairman, Victorian Branch, 1976-79; RACR Examiner Radiodiagnosis, 1977-. *Memberships:* Royal Australasian College of Radiologists; Royal College of Radiologists, London; Australian Ultrasound Society; British Institute of Radiology; Roentgenological Society of North America; Australian Medical Association. *Publications:* "Good Pasture's Syndrome", 1968, "Duodenal Haematoma", 1971, "The Folded Brest Prosthesis", 1972, all in 'Australian Radiology'; "High Resolution CT Scanning of the Lumbar Spine", 'MJA', 1983; "DT Appearance of a Prosthetic Methyl Methacrylate Mass Mistaken for Abscess", 'Radiology', 1984. *Honours:*

Path/3rd C. H. Prizewinner Part II, MCRA, 1967; Thomas Baker Memorial Fellow, College of Radiologists of Australasia, 1971. *Hobbies:* Sailing; Tennis; Music. *Address:* 376 Albert St., East Melbourne, Victoria, Australia.

SLOPER, John Chaplin, b. 2 Mar. 1922, Singapore. Professor; Head of Department. m. Susan Chappel, 26 Sep. 1946, 3 daughters. *Education:* MA, MB BChir, MD, University of Cambridge, England. *Appointments:* Member, Dermatological Research Team, Royal Army Medical Corps; Lecturer, Senior Lecturer, London Hospital Medical College; University of London Postgraduate Research Fellow, Kiel University, Federal Republic of Germany, and AFIP, Washington, USA; Reader, Professor, Head of Department of Experimental Pathology, Charing Cross Medical School, London, England; Professor, Head of Department of Histopathology, Charing Cross Hospital Medical School, London; Professor, Head of Department of Histopathology, Charing Cross and Westminster Medical School, London. *Memberships:* Fellow, Royal College of Physicians; Fellow, Royal College of Pathologists; Pathological Society; Association of Clinical Pathologists; Society for Endocrinology. *Publications:* 'Experimental and epidemiological study of dermatomycoses' 1953 and 1954; 'Diabetes insipidus: the complexity of the syndrome', 1969; 'Nephritis in interferon-treated neonatal mice', 1978; 'Skeletal muscle: regeneration and transplantation studies', 1980; 'The Hypothalamo-neurohypophysial System' in "Cytology and Cytopathology of the Nervous System", 1982. *Address:* Department of Histopathology, Charing Cross and Westminster Medical School, Fulham Palace Road, London W6 8RF, England.

SLUYSER, Mels, b. 12 Nov. 1930, Amsterdam, The Netherlands. Senior Scientist, Research Department, The Netherlands Cancer Institute, Amsterdam, The Netherlands. m. Erica Bennewitz, 24 Apr. 1934, Delft, The Netherlands, 2 daughters. *Memberships:* Member, Board of Governors, International Association for Breast Cancer Research; Editor-in-Chief, 'Netherlands Cancer Journal'. *Publications:* 'Sex hormone receptors in mammary tumours of GR mice', (co-author), 1976; 'Mammary Tumours in the Mouse', (Co-editors), 1981; 'Interaction of steroid hormone receptors with DNA', (Editor), 1985. *Hobbies:* Painting; Writing Science Fiction. *Address:* The Netherlands Cancer Institute, Plesmanlaan 121, 1066 CX Amsterdam, The Netherlands.

SMAJE, Laurence Hetherington, b. 13 Aug. 1936, London, England. Professor and Head of Department of Physiology. m. Joan Allanach, 11 June 1960, 2 sons. *Education:* BSc 1958, PhD 1967, University College London; MB BS, University College Hospital Medical School, 1961. *Appointments:* House Surgeon and Physician, University College Hospital, London, 1961-62; Research Assistant 1962-65, Lecturer in Physiology 1965-74, Senior Lecturer in Physiology 1974-78, University College London; Professor of Physiology and Head of Department, Charing Cross and Westminster Medical School, London, 1978-. *Memberships:* Committee 1981-85, Physiological Society; Editorial Board 1975-82, 'Journal of Physiology'; Honorary Secretary 1979-84, British Microcirculation Society; Executive Committee 1979-, General Secretary 1984-, European Society for Microcirculation; Member 1982-, Microcirculatory Society Incorporated. *Publications include:* "Multiple Choice Questions in Physiology" (with L J Bindman and B R Jewell), 1978; "Microcirculation of the Alimentary Tract" (with A Koo and S K Lam), 1983; Articles in 'Journal of Physiology' and 'Microvascular Research'. *Hobbies:* Walking and scrambling; Classical music. *Address:* Department of Physiology, Charing Cross and Westminster Medical School, Fulham Palace Road, London W6 8RF, England.

SMATKO, Andrew John, b. 14 June 1917, Fort Edward, New York, USA. Gynaecologist; Obstetrician. m. Shirley Jean Robertson, 7 Dec. 1957, Santa Monica, 1 son. *Education:* BA, Columbia University, 1938; MD, New York University College of Medicine; 2 year Rotating Internship, City Hospital, New York; 3 year Residency, Obstetrics & Gynaecology, Detroit. *Memberships:* California, Los Angeles County, Medical Associations; American Board of Obstetrics & Gynaecology; Fellow, American College of Obstetricians & Gynaecologists; Pacific Surgical Society; Los Angeles Obstetrical & Gynaecological Society. *Publications:* Editor, "Mountaineer's Guide to the High Sierra", 1972; Several articles in professional journals; "Physiology of Muscular Exercise", 'Summit Magazine', 1976. *Honour:* Past President, Bay Gynecic Society. *Hobbies:* Mountain Climbing; Photography - Outdoor Scenes; General Science; Astronomy. *Address:* 2021 Santa Monica Blvd, Santa Monica, CA 90404, USA.

SMATHERS, James Burton, b. 26 Aug. 1935, Prairie du Chien, Wisconsin, USA. Professor, Medical Physics & Radiation Oncology. m. Sylvia Lee Rath, 20 Apr. 1957, 2 sons. *Education:* BNE 1957, MS 1959, North Carolina State College; PhD, University of Maryland, 1967. *Appointments:* US Army Officer, 1st Lieutenant, 1959-61; Nuclear Engineer, Walter Reed Army Institute of Research, 1961-67; Professor, Nuclear Engineering, Professor & Director BioEngineering, Texas A&M University, 1967-80; Professor, Radiation Oncology, University of California, Los Angeles, 1980-. *Memberships include:* American College of Medical Physics; American Association of Physicists in Medicine; Radiation Research Society; Health Physicists Society; Chairman, Divisions for Education, Technical Group for Biology & Medicine, Isotopes & Radiation (Secretary), American Nuclear Society. *Publications include:* Over 50 technical papers & reports; Contributions to 4 books. *Honours:* Research award, 1976, teaching award 1972, Texas A&M University; Teaching award, Nuclear Engineering Division, American Society of Engineering, 1973. *Hobbies:* Photography; Gardening. *Address:* Department of Radiation Oncology, B3-109 CHS UCLA, Los Angeles, CA 90024, USA.

SMITH, Alexander Tait, b. 20 Oct. 1915, Inglewood, Victoria, Australia. Surgical Pathologist, St Frances Xavier Cabrini Hospital, Malvern, Victoria, 1976-. m. Margaret Eva Graham, 9 July 1949, London, England, 3 sons. *Education:* MB, BS, 1940, MD, 1946, Trinity College, Melbourne University; MTACP, 1946, FRACP, 1966, St Vincent's Hospital Clinical School, Melbourne. *Appointments:* Resident MO, St Vincents Hospital, 1941-46; Beany Scholar Pathology, University of Melbourne, 1944; Assistant Pathologist, St Vincent's Hospital, 1944-46; Assistant Curator of Shattock Museum, St Thomas' Hospital Medical School, London, England, 1948-51; Anatomical Pathologist, St Vincent's Hospital, 1951-56; Assistant Physician, St George Hospital, Sydney, 1958-62; Associate Professor, School of Pathology, University of New South Wales and Associate Director, Anatomical Pathology, University Hospitals, 1962-76. *Memberships:* Fellow, Royal Society of Medicine, London; Pathological Society of Great Britain and Ireland; International Academy of Pathology; Australian Medical Association. *Publications:* Contributor of numerous articles to professional journals. *Hobbies:* Playing chamber music; Gardening. *Address:* Pathology Department, St Francis Xavier Cabrini Hospital, Malvern 3144, Australia.

SMITH, Anthony David, b. 16 Sep. 1938, Kunming, China. Professor of Pharmacology and Honorary Director, MRC Anatomical Neuropharmacology Unit. m. Dr Ingegerd Östman, 15 Aug. 1975, Arvika, Sweden, 1 son, 1 daughter from previous marriage. *Education:* BA, Hons, Biochemistry, 1963, MA, 1966, DPhil, 1966, University of Oxford. *Appointments:* Royal Society Stothert Research Fellow; University Lecturer in Pharmacology and Student of Christ Church, Oxford; Professor of Pharmacology and Honorary Director, MRC Anatomical Neuropharmacology Unit, Oxford University. *Memberships:* Physiological Society; British Pharmacological Society. *Publications:* Editor: "Handbook of Physiology Section 7, vol 6 'The Adrenal Gland'", "Neuroscience", IBRO Handbook Series: "Methods in the Neurosciences". *Honour:* Gaddum Prize, British Pharmacological Society, 1979. *Hobbies:* Opera; Music; Reading. *Address:* University Department of Pharmacology, South Parks Road, Oxford OX1 3QT, England.

SMITH, Colin John, b. 7 June 1938, Croydon, Surrey, England. Professor of Oral Pathology. m. Mary Margaret Kathrine MacMahon, 24 Feb. 1962, Purley, Surrey, 3 daughters. *Education:* LDS Royal College of Surgeons, BDS, Royal Dental Hospital, School of Dental Surgery, University of London, 1956-60; PhD, Institute of Basic Medical Sciences, University of London, 1964-68; MRCPath, Royal Postgraduate Medical School, London, 1969-71; Elected Fellow, Royal College of Pathologists, 1982. *Appointments:* House Surgeon, Royal Dental Hospital, London, 1961-62; Medical Research Council Scientific Assistant & Prophit Cancer Research Student, Department of Dental Science, Royal College of Surgeons of England, London, 1962-68; Wellcome Travelling Research Fellow, Department of Oral Pathology, Royal Dental College, Copenhagen, Denmark, 1968-69; Nuffield Dental Research Fellow, Department of Morbid Anatomy, Royal Postgraduate Medical School, London, 1969-71; Senior Lecturer & Research Fellow, Department of Oral Medicine & Pathology, Guy's Hospital Dental School, London, 1971-72; Professor of Oral Pathology, University of Sheffield & Honorary Consultant, Sheffield Health Authority, 1972-. *Memberships:* British Society for Oral Pathology; International Association of Oral Pathologists; International Academy of Pathology; International Association for Dental Research; Pathological Society of Great Britain & Ireland; Royal Society of Medicine. *Publications:* Various articles in field of Oral Pathology in dental jounals in USA & Britain. *Honour:* Colgate Prize, British Division IADR, 1964. *Hobbies:* Tennis; Gardening; Reading; Walking; Listen to Classical Music. *Address:* Department of Oral Pathology, University of Sheffield, 31 Claremont Crescent, Sheffield, S10 2TA, England.

SMITH, Colin McPherson, b. 14 Mar. 1927, Edinburgh, Scotland. Clinical Professor, Psychiatry; Director of Srvices to the Elderly. m. Eva Mae Eloise Stephens, 24 Mar. 1962, Regina, 2 daughters. *Education:* MB, ChB, 1949, MD, 1959, University of Glasgow, Scotland; MD, University of Saskatchewan, 1962; FRCP (C): FRCPsych; DPM; FAPA; FA Geriatric Society. *Appointments:* Director, Psychiatric Services for Saskatchewan, 1967-76; Member, Lt Governor's Board of Review, Saskatchewan, 1979-; Clinical Professor, Psychiatry, University of Saskatchewan; Director, Services to Elderly, Saskatchewan Department of Health Education; Editor, Canadian Psychiatric Association Bulletin. *Memberships:* Founding Board Member, Saskatchewan Alcoholism & Drug Addiction Commission, 1968-78; Past President, Saskatchewan Gerontology Association, 1982-84; Treasurer, Canadian Association of Gerontology, 1983-; Fellow, Royal College of Physicians & Surgeons, Canada; Fellow, Royal College of Psychiatrists, UK; Fellow, American Psychiatric Association; Fellow, American Geriatric Society; Honorary Fellow, North Pacific Society of Neurology & Psychiatry; etc. *Publications:* Over 100 scientific papers, reports etc, including "The Family Doctor in a Programme of Comprehensive Psychiatric Care", 'New Abstracts of the Mental Health Service'; "You Only Die Twice"; "Retirement in Canada", 1978. *Honours:* Federal Provincial Government Scholarship for Postgraduate Studies, University of London, England, 1958-59; Canadian Mental Health Association Research Award, 1962; etc. *Hobbies:* Chess; Swimming; Show Jumping. *Address:* 4437 Castle Road, Regina, Saskatchewan, Canada S4S 4W4.

SMITH, Edward John, b. 29 Dec. 1911, Shediac,

Canada. Honorary Consultant, Mont General Hospital. m. Marjory MacKenzie Gilpin, 31 Mar. 1944, Canada, 1 son, 1 daughter. *Education:* BSc, MD, CM, LMCC, Dalhousie University, Halifax, Canada; FRCS (Canada); Fellow, American Academy of OJL. *Appointments:* Senior Surgeon, Mont General Hospital, Canada; Associate Professor, Department of OTL, McGill University ; Hon Consultant, Royal Victoria Hospital, Mont Childrens' Hospital, Queen Elizabeth Hospital, St Mary's Hospital, Montreal, Canada. *Memberships:* Past President, Canada OTL Society; Fellow, American Academy of OTL; National Defence Board, Consultant. *Publications:* Various. *Hobbies:* Hunting; Fishing; Golf; Painting. *Address:* 179 Country Club Drive, Kingston, Ontario, Canada K7M 7G8.

SMITH, Gayle Green, b. 21 Oct. 1949, Seattle, Washington, USA. Chief of Occupational Therapy. m. Richard Bruce Smith, 18 Mar. 1972, Seattle, Washington, USA, 1 son, 1 daughter. *Education:* BSc, Occupational Therapy, University of Washington, Seattle, 1973; MEd, Counseling, University of Puget Sound, Tacoma, Washington, 1982. *Appointments:* Sole Occupational Therapist, The Mason Clinic, Virginia Mason Hospital, Seattle, Washington, 1973-79; Faculty, University of Puget Sound School of Occupational and Physical Therapy, Tacoma, Washington, 1979-81; American Lake Veterans' Administration Center Tacoma, Washington, 1983-85; Seattle Veterans Administration Medical Center, 1985-. *Memberships:* American Occupational Therapy Association; Washingtion Occupational Therapy Association; American Congress of Rehabilitation; Arthritis Health Professions Association. *Publications:* Contributor of section on Joint Protection in "Methods to Protect Joints in Patients with Arthritis" by K Wilske et al. *Honours:* Kiwanis Spade Scholarship, 1967; Rehabilitation Traineeship 1970 and 1971; May Dunn Ward Scholarship, 1972. *Hobbies:* Tropical Fish; Philately. *Address:* RMS 117, Seattle VAMC 1660 So Columbian Way, Seattle, WA 98108, USA.

SMITH, Hamilton, b. 27 Apr. 1934, Stirling, Scotland. Reader in Forensic Medicine. m. Jacqueline Ann Spittal, 14 May 1962, Glasgow. *Education:* BSc, PhD, University of Glasgow; Fellow, Royal Society of Chemists; Fellow, Royal College of Pathologists. *Appointments:* Research Assistant, Glasgow Health Board, Department of Clinical Physics, Regional Physics Department, 1956; Research Fellow, Medical Research Council, held at Regional Physics Department, 1960; Senior Research Fellow, 1963, Lecturer, 1964, Senior Lecturer, 1973, Department of Forensic Medicine, University of Glasgow. *Memberships:* Forensic Science Society; International Association of Forensic Toxicologists; Souvenir Napoleonien, Canada. *Publications:* Numerous papers & book chapters, 1 book. *Hobbies:* Garden & Greenhouse (Specialist collections); Stamps; Model Railways; Woodworking; Photography; Electronics; Golf. *Address:* Department of Forensic Medicine & Science, University of Glasgow, Glasgow G12 8QQ, Scotland.

SMITH, Jaime Alfred, b. 18 Nov. 1933, Appleton, Wisconsin, USA. Clinical Assistant Professor, Psychiatry. m. Cathleen Benson, 24 Aug. 1956, Montevideo, Uruguay, 3 daughters. *Education:* BA, 1954; MSc, 1966, University of Minnesota; MD, University of British Columbia, 1976; Psychiatric Residency, University of British Columbia, 1976-80; Fellow, Royal College of Physicians of Canada, 1980. *Appointments:* Clinical Assistant Professor, Psychiatry, University of British Columbia; Active Staff, Psychiatry, St Paul's Hospital, Vancouver, 1982-. *Memberships:* Canadian Medical and Psychiatric Associations; American Association of Physicians for Human Rights; Physicians for Social Responsibility. *Publications:* "Ego-dystonic Homosexuality", 'Comprehensive Psychiatry', volume 21, 1980; "Treatment of Ego-Dystonic Homosexuality: Individual and Group Psychotherapies", 'Journal of American Academy of Psychoanalysis', Volume 13, 1985. *Hobbies:* Opera;

Photography; Modern Languages; Railway Travel. *Address:* Dept. of Psychiatry, University of British Columbia, 2075 Wesbrook Mall, Vancouver, BC, Canada V6T 1W5.

SMITH, Linda Wheatland, b. 13 June 1954, Washington, District of Columbia, USA. Clinic Director, Logan College; Private Practice. *Education:* BA, 1976; Doctor of Chiropractic, 1982. *Appointment:* Clinic Director, Logan College of Chiropractic, 1983-. *Memberships:* American Chiropractic Association; Foundation for Chiropractic Education and Research; Connecticut Chiropractic Association. *Honour:* Dean's List, Chiropractic College, 1980-82. *Hobbies:* Guitar; Sailing; Swimming; Running. *Address:* Suite 208, 225 South Meramec Avenue, Clayton, MD 63105, USA.

SMITH, Paul Francis, b. 3 Apr. 1927, Brookville, Pennsylvania, USA. Professor; Department Chairman. m. Marie D Rymshaw, 1 July 1951, 1 son, 3 daughters. *Education:* BS, Bacteriology, Pennsylvania State University, 1949; MS, 1950, PhD, 1951, University of Pennsylvania. *Appointments:* Research Microbiologist, Merck & Co, Rahway, 1951-52; Instructor to Assistant Professor, University of Pennsylvania School of Medicine, 1952-61; Professor, Chairman, Microbiology, University of South Dakota School of Medicine, 1961-; Visiting Scientist, State University, Utrecht, The Netherlands, 1970; Co-ordinator, Basic Medical Sciences, University of South Dakota, 1982-. *Memberships:* American Society for Microbiology; American Chemical Society; American Academy Microbiology, Fellow; American Association for Advancement of Science, Fellow; International Organization of Mycoplasmology. *Publications:* "Biology of Mycoplasmas", 1971; 130 articles in scientific journals & books. *Honours:* Lederle Medical Faculty Award, 1960; Foundation for Microbiology National Lecturer, 1967; Divisional Lecturer, American Society Microbiology, 1981; Waksman Fellowship of Japan, 1982. *Hobbies:* Travel; Camping; Woodwork. *Address:* Department of Microbiology, School of Medicine, University of South Dakota, Vermillion, SD 57069, USA.

SMITH, Stanley George, b. 11 Aug. 1939, Muskegon, Michigan, USA. Adjunct Professor. m. Toreen E Smith, 9 Apr. 1979, Panama City, 1 son, 6 daughters. *Education:* BA, Michigan State University, 1966; MA, Western Michigan University, 1967; PhD, University of Mississippi, 1977. *Appointments:* Research Scientist, Psychology, 1968-72; Pharmacology, 1972-78, University of Mississippi; President, CTC Inc, Oxford, 1977-80; Mental Health Specialist, Choctaw Health Center, 1981-; Director, Choctaw Community Mental Health Centre, 1981-; Professor, Psychology, Mississippi State University, 1983-; Instructor/Consultant, US Department of Justice DEA, 1973-. *Memberships:* American Psychological Association; American Society of Clinical Hypnosis; National Society of Hypnotherapists; Society for Neuroscience; Mississippi Psychological Association; Mississippi Academy of Science; American Association for the Advancement of Science; Mississippi Association for Christian Counselor. *Publications:* Over 150 scientific works in 20 different science journals; Author, Co-Author, 10 books or chapters in books. *Honours:* National Police Instructors Awards US Dept. of Justice DEA, 1973, 1974, 1975, 1978; Honours British Brain Research Association, European Brain and Behaviour Society for Brain Research. *Address:* 1206 Kosciusko Road, Philadelphia, MS 39350, USA.

SMITH, Theodore Roosevelt Jr, b. 20 Apr. 1943, Wheeler County, Georgia, USA, Consultant Psychologist. m. Bernice Swiggett, 19 Aug. 1966, Ramstein, Federal Republic of Germany, 4 sons, 1 daughter. *Education:* BS, Hampton Institute, Virginia, USA; MS Education, Eastern Illinois University, Illinois; Ed S, Ball State University, Indiana; Psy D, Wright State University, Ohio; Certificate, Beratung in der Erziehung, Funkolleg, Sudwestfunk, Deutches Institut fur Fernstudien an der Universität Tübingen, Federal

Republic of Germany, 1976. *Appointments:* Resident, Clinical Psychology, Wilford Hall United States Air Force Medical Center, USA; Aircraft Mechanic, Aircraft Maintenance Officer, Aircraft Maintenance Branch Chief for Maintenance Training, Clinical Psychologist, United State Air Force; Chief Psychologist, Psychiatric Associates of Middle Georgia; Consulting Psychologist, Private Practice. *Memberships:* American Society of Clinical Hypnosis; American Psychological Association; International Society in Hypnosis. *Hobbies:* Electronic and small engine repair; Flying small aircraft and gliders; Camping; Foreign languages; Special interest in 'Gerontology'. *Address:* 1417 South Houston Lake Road, Kathleen, GA 31047, USA.

SMITH, Trevor, b. 13 Sep. 1934. Consulting Homoeopathic Physician. *Education:* Cambridge, England. *Appointments:* Senior Registrar, Tavistock Clinic; Consultant, Belmont Hospital; Consultant, Surrey & Cambridge County Councils. *Memberships:* British Homoeopathic Association; British Acupuncture Association; Hahnemann Society. *Publications:* Homoeopathic Medicine'', 1982; ''The Homoeopathic Treatment of Emotional Illness'', 1983; ''A Woman's Guide to Homoeopathic Medicine'', 1984; ''Understanding Homoeopathy'', 1984; ''An Encyclopaedic of Homoeopathy'', 1984; ''The Principles, Art & Practice of Homoeopathy'', 1985; ''Emotional Health'', 1986; ''Personal Growth and Creativity'', 1986; ''Talking about Homoeopathy'', 1986. *Address:* The Winchester Clinic, Bereweeke Road, Winchester, Hampshire, England.

SMITH, William John, b. 21 Nov. 1936, De Smet, South Dakota, USA. Doctor of Chiropractic. m. Gloria Dell Patterson, 12 Mar. 1958, Watertown, South Dakota, 2 daughters. *Education:* Pre-professional College, South Dakota State University; Doctor of Chiropractic, National College of Chiropractic, Chicago, Illinois; Diplomate, American Board of Chiropractic Orthopaedists, Northwestern College of Chiropractic, St Paul, Minnesota; Licentiate of Acupuncture, College of Traditional Acupuncture, UK; Bachelor of Acupuncture, ibid. *Appointments:* Doctor of Chiropractic, Owner, Traditional Acupuncture & Chiropractic Centre, Webster, S Dakota. *Memberships:* South Dakota Chiropractic Association; American Chiropractic Association; Council on Chiropractic Orthopaedists; Academy of Chiropractic Orthopaedists; Traditional Acupuncture Society; British Acupuncture Association; Diplomate of the Examination Board of the National Commission for the Certification of Acupuncturists. *Hobbies:* Fishing; Hunting. *Address:* 511 Main Street, Webster, SD 57274, USA.

SMODLAKA, Vojin, b. 14 Nov. 1912, Belgrade, Yugoslavia. Clinical Professor of Rehabilitation Medicine. m. Melanie Janković, 26 May 1962, Philadelphia, Pennsylvania, USA, 1 son, 3 daughters. *Education:* MD, University of Belgrade, Yugoslavia, 1936; Speciality Board of Rehabilitation Medicine, Belgrade, 1958; D Med Sc, University of Berlin, Federal Public of Germany, 1960; Speciality Board of Rehabilitation Medicine, 1969. *Appointments:* Lecturer in Sports Medicine, Faculty of Medicine, Belgrade, 1940; Lecturer on Sports Medicine, Military Medical Academy, Belgrade, 1946-59; Director, Sports Medicine Institute, Belgrade, 1950; Clinical Assistant - Associate - Full Professor of Rehabilitation Medicine, State University of New York, New York, USA, 1967-; Director, Department of Rehabilitation, Methodist Hospital of Brooklyn, New York, 1967-82; Adjunct Professor of Sports Medicine, Department of Physical Education, Long Island University, 1970-. *Memberships:* Serbian Medical Society; German Medical Society, Berlin; American College of Sports Medicine; American Academy of Physical Medical Rehabilitation; American Congress of Rehabilitation Medicine; Honorary Member, Yugoslav Society of Sport Physicians; Honorary Member, International Federation of Sports Medicine, 1974. *Publications include:* 'Anthropometric Technique. Handbook for Physicians'', 1948; ''Introduction in Sports Medicine Practice'',

1951; ''Ergometry: Basics of Medical Exercise Testing'', (edited with Harald Mellerowicz'', 1981; ''Sport Massage and Selfmassage'', 1984; Numerous articles. *Honours include:* Citation, College of Sports Medicine, USA, 1975. *Hobbies:* Mountaineering; Skiing; Swimming. *Address:* 16 Signal Hill Road, Staten Island, NY 10301, USA.

SMYTH, Derek George, b. 24 Apr. 1927, England. Head, Laboratory of Peptide Chemistry, National Institute for Medical Research. m. Elizabeth J Robb, Nov. 1973, 2 daughters. *Education:* BSc; PhD. *Appointments:* Assistant Lecturer in Chemistry, Assistant Lecturer in Biochemistry, St Bartholomew's Hospital, London; Research Associate, Department of Biochemistry, Yale University, USA; Research Associate, Rockefeller University, USA; Member of Scientific Staff, National Institute for Medical Research. *Memberships:* Chemical Society; Biochemical Society; International Narcotics Research Conference; British Opioid Colloquium. *Publications:* 'The Sequence of amino acid residues in bovine pancreatic ribonuclease: revisions and confirmations', (with W H Stein, S Moore), 1963; 'Carbamylation of amino and tyrosine hydroxyl groups; preparation of an inhibitor of oxytocin with no intrinsic activity on the isolation uterus', 1967; 'C-Fragment of lipotropin - an endogenous potent analgesic peptide', (with W Feldberg), 1977; 'Mechanism of C-Terminal amide formation by pituitary enzymes', (with A F Bradbury, M D A Finnie), 1982; 'B-Endorphin and related peptides in pituitary, brain, pancreas and antrum', 1983. *Hobbies:* Tennis; Music. *Address:* National Institute for Medical Research, The Ridgeway, Mill Hill, London NW7 1AA, England.

SNELL, Richard Saxon, b. 3 May 1925, Richmond, Surrey, England. Professor and Chairman of Anatomy, George Washington University Medical Center, Washington, District of Columbia, USA. m. Maureen Cashin, 4 June 1949, London, England, 2 sons, 3 daughters. *Education:* MB BS, 1949; PhD, 1955; MD, 1961; University of London, King's College Hospital Medical School, England; MRCS Eng, 1948; LRCP, London, 1948. *Appointments include:* House Surgeon, Lecturer, Anatomy, Hospitals and Universities, England, 1948-63; Assistant Professor, Anatomy & Medicine, Yale University, USA, 1963-65; Associate Professor, 1965-67; Chairman, Department of Anatomy, New Jersey College of Medicine and Dentistry, Jersey City, 1967-69; Visiting Professor, Yale University and Harvard University, 1969-71; Professor of Anatomy, College of Medicine, University of Arizona, Tucson, 1970; Professor and Chairman, Department of Anatomy, George Washington University Medical Center, 1972-; Visiting Professor, Stanford Medical School and Harvard University, 1974, 1979-86. *Memberships:* Anatomical Society of Great Britain and Ireland; American Association of Anatomists; Alpha Omega Alpha. *Publications:* ''Clinical Embryology for Medical Students'', 3rd Edition, 1983; ''Clinical Anatomy for Medical Students'' 3rd Edition, 1986; ''Atlas of Normal Radiographic Anatomy'', 1976; ''Atlas of Clinical Anatomy'', 1978; ''Cross Anatomy Dissector'', 1978; ''Clinical Neuroanatomy for Medical Students'', 1980; Numerous articles on the female reproductive tract, the distribution of cholinesterase in the nervous system and pigmentation of the skin in medical and scientific journals. *Hobbies:* Sailing; Gardening. *Address:* Department of Anatomy, The George Washington University Medical Center, 2300 Eye Street, NW, Washington, DC 20037, USA.

SNOW, Harold Dale, b. 6 Nov. 1920, San Francisco, California, USA. Professor of Radiology. m. Susie Wall, 28 Sep. 1975, Santa Barbara, California. *Education:* BS Zoology; Doctor of Veterinary Medicine. *Appointments:* Private Practice in Surgery & Clinics, 1946-66; Lecturer, Department of Surgery, School of Medicine, University of California at Los Angeles, 1966; Chief, Surgery & Clinics, Division of Laboratory Animal Medicine, 1969; Associate Director, Rigler

Centre for Radiological Sciences; Assistant Professor 1970, Associate Professor 1975, Professor of Radiology, 1976-; Director of Animal Tumour Project, 1976-, Department of Radiology, School of Medicine, University of California at Los Angeles. *Memberships:* American Association of University Professors; American Veterinary Medical Association; Association of University Radiologists; California Academy of Veterinary Medicine; Jonson Comprehensive Cancer Centre, School of Medicine, UCLA. *Publications:* Chapter on 'Nuclear Medicine' in "Veterinary Cancer Medicine" (edited Theilen & Macewell), 1979; 'Importance in Radiological & Interdisciplinary Medical Research'; Contributor to 'Annual Tumour Registries' (edited E Milne) 1983, 'Old Dog Encephalitis - A Clinical & Seriological Study' (with J Adams) 1979. *Hobbies:* Golf; Farming. *Address:* 2720 Long Canyon Road, Santa Ynez. CA 93460, USA.

SNOW, Herman Bernard, b. 6 Mar. 1909, New York City USA. Physician; Consulting Psychiatrist. m. Reta Mae Gullackson, 12 Dec. 1982, 1 son. *Education:* BA, Syracuse University, 1929; MD, 1933; Diplomate, American Board of Psychiatry and Neurology. *Appointments:* Intern, University Hospital, Syracuse 1933-34; Residency, Psychiatry, Binghamton (NY) State Hospital, 1934-36; Senior Psychiatrist, 1936-39; Supervising Psychiatrist, 1939; Practice Medicine specializing in consultant Psychiatry, Binghamton, 1946-48, Utica, 1948-54, Ogdensburg, NY, 1954-62; Poughkeepsie, NY, 1962-79; Assistant Director, Utica State Hospital, 1948; Medical Inspector, Department of Mental Hygiene, Albany, 1949-51; Director, St Lawrence State Hospital, Ogdensburg, 1954-62; Psychiatric Consultant, VA Hospital, Sunmount, NY, 1957-62; Potsdam, NY, Hospital, 1959-62; Director, Hudson River State Hospital, Poughkeepsie, 1962-79; Psychiatric Consultant, Vassar Bros, St Francis Hospitals; Member, Governor's Prison Commission, 1963-; Consultant, Hudson River Psychiatric Center; Member, New York State Board of Medicine, 1963-75 *Memberships:* Fellow, American Psychiatric Association; American College of Psychiatry; Life Member, Medical Society State of New York; American Medical Association; Medical Superintendents Mental Hospitals; Dutchess County Medical Society; 50 Year Club American Medicine. *Publications:* Contributor of articles to professional journals. *Honours:* Citations from St Lawrence University, 1958, Congregation Anshe Zophen, 1958; Adolf Meyer Award for Distinguished Service on behalf of improved care and treatment of mentally ill, 1959; Named Kentucky Colonel, 1963. *Address:* PO Box 514, Hyde Park, NY 12538, USA.

SOBRINHO-SIMOES, Manuel, b. 8 Sep. 1947, Porto, Portugal. Professor of Pathology. m. Maria Augusta Areias, 31 May 1972, Porto, Portugal, 2 sons, 1 daughter. *Education:* MD and PhD, University of Porto, Portugal, 1971; Board certified specialist in anatomic pathology, Portugal, 1976; Degree in Medical Statistics, University of Paris, France, 1977. *Appointments:* Assistant of Pathology, Medical Faculty of Porto, Portugal, 1972-79; Visiting Professor, Radium Hospital, Oslo, Norway, 1979-80; Consultant Pathologist, Hospital S. Joao, Porto, Portugal, 1979-present; Head, Unit of Immunocytochemistry and Electron Microscopy, 1981-present; Assistant Professor of Pathology, Medical Faculty of Porto, 1980-82, Associate Professor, 1982-85, Professor, 1985-present. *Memberships:* European Society of Pathology; International Academy of Pathology; Portuguese Society of Anatomic Patholyg. EORTC Thyroid Study Group. *Publications:* 82 scientific papers; 8 book chapters, mainly in the series "Electron Microscopy in Human Medicine"; 2 books "Occult Thyroid Carcinoma", "Diagnostic Electron Microscopy"; various articles on electron microscopic techniques, thyroid pathology, soft tissue tumours and application of electron microscopy and immunocytochemistry to the diagnosis of human neoplasms. *Honours:* National Prize, High School, 1964; National Prize, MD, 1971; Pfizer Research Award, 1976. *Hobbies:* Jogging; Table Tennis; Tennis; Antiques. *Address:* Rua Damiao de Gois

329 4oDto, 4000 Porto, Portugal.

SOBUE, Itsuro, b. 19 Mar. 1921, Aichi, Japan. Professor Emeritus. m. 17 May 1949, 1 son, 1 daughter. *Education:* MB, Nagoya University School of Medicine, 1943; Licenced, 1943; Post-graduate course, Doctor's Degree, Nagoya University School of Medicine, 1951. *Appointments:* Assistant Professor, 1952-67, Associate Professor 1967-75, Professor, 1975-84, Nagoya University School of Medicine; Director, Nagoya University Hospital, 1976-78, 1980-82; Dean, Nagoya University School of Medicine, 1978-80; Professor Emeritus, Nagoya University, 1984; President, National Chubu Hospital, 1984-. *Memberships:* Trustee & Councillor of: Japan Society of Neurology 1960-, Japan Society of Psychosomatic Medicine 1960-, Japan Society of Internal Medicine 1975-; Councillor, Japan Society of Rehabilitation Medicine, 1963-. *Publications:* 'Spinocerebeller Degenerations', 1980; 'Peripheral Neuropathy', 1984; 'Clinical Aspects of Subacute myelo-opticoneuropathy' (in Handbook of Clinical Neurology vol. 37), 1979; "Neurological Diseases" (Japanese), 1979. *Honours:* Morimura Prize, Japan Association of Neurology & Psychiatry 1950; Chu-nichi Bunka Prize, Chu-nichi Press, 1979. *Hobbies:* Reading; Driving; Tennis; Travel. *Address:* 4-118 Umemorizaka, Ueda, Tenpaku-cho Meito-ku, Nagoya 465, Japan.

SODDY, Kenneth, b. 27 July 1911. Coventry, England. Consulting Physician, University College Hospital, London. m. (1) Emmeline Johnson, 23 Apr. 1936 (deceased May 1972); (2) Mary Kidson, 9 Sep. 1972, Hampstead, 1 son, 2 daughters. *Education:* MRCS, LRCP, 1934; MB BS, 1934; DPM, 1937; MD, 1938, FRCPsych, 1971; University College London; University College Hospital Medical School. *Appointments:* Psychiatrist, London Child Guidance Clinic; War Service in RAMC India Command (Colonel); Medical Director, National Association for Mental Health; Psychiatrist, Tavistock Clinic; Psychiatrist, Medical Director, Child Guidance Training Centre; Physician-in-Charge, Children's and Adolescent Department, University College Hospitals; Lecturer, Recognised Teacher, University of London; Scientific Director and Assistant Director, World Federation for Mental Health; Member, Expert Panel on Mental Health, World Health Organisation; Consultant to: WHO, UKAKEA, National Spastics Society; Chairman and President, Institute of Religion and Medicine; Member, General Synod Marriage Commission; Member, St Lawrence's Hospital, Caterham Management Committee; Honorary Consultant in Child Psychiatry, Royal Free Hospital, London. *Memberships:* Royal College of Psychiatrists; American Psychiatric Association; Association for Child Psychology and Psychiatry; Royal Society of Medicine; British Psychological Society. *Publications:* "Clinical Child Psychiatry", 1960; Co-author, "Mental Retardation", 11th Edition, 1970; Co-author, "Men in Middle Life", 1967; Editor: "Mental Health and Infant Development" 2 volumes, 1955; "Identity Mental Health and Value Systems", 1961; (with R H Ahrenfeldt) "Mental Health in a Changing World", 1965, "Mental Health and Contemporary Thought", 1967; "Mental Health in the Service of the Community", 1967; Many articles in British, American and International medical and social journals. *Honours:* Commonwealth Fund Fellowship in Child Guidance, 1938; Honorary Membership, American Psychiatric Association, 1951; Fellow, University College, London, 1978. *Hobbies:* Organ Playing; Chamber Music; Moor and Mountain Walking. *Address:* The Manor Cottage, Doccombe, Moretonhampstead, Devon TQ13 8SS, England.

SOEPRONO, Raden, b. 14 Apr. 1924, Wonogiri, Indonesia. Senior Lecturer. m. Mastinah Soeprono, 4 Apr. 1951, Yogyakarta, 2 sons. *Education:* MD, Universitas Gadjah Mada, Yogyakarta, 1957; Certification, Specialist Training, Obstetrics Gynaecology, 1962; NCH Training as WHO Fellow, Uk, Sweden, Denmark, Holland, 1969-70; Advanced Fertility Control Techniques Course, Johns Hopkins University, USA, 1973;

etc. *Appointments:* Teaching Staff, 1957-, Vice Chief, Hospital, Obstetrics Gynaecology, 1962-67, Chief, Obstetrics Gynaecology, 1967-82, Dean, Faculty of Medicine, 1979-85, Universitas Gadjah Mada; Chief, School for Midwifery, Universitas Gadjah Mada Hospital, 1960-74; Chief, Obstetrics, Gynaecology, Chief of School for Midwifery, Panti Rapih Hospital, Yogyakarta, 1958-59, 1979-, Senior Visiting Obstetrician and Gynaecologist. *Memberships:* Indonesian Medical Association; Indonesian Society for Obstetrics and Gynaecology, Vice President 1976-79, Chairman, Yogyakarta Chapter, 1971-79; Indonesian Society for Secure Contraception, Member, National Board, Chairman Yogyakarta Chapter, 1974-78; Society for the Advancement of Contraception, etc. *Publications:* Author of more than 40 articles on education, clinical and social obstetrics-gynaecology, medical ethics, medical philosophy in Bahasa, Indonesian and English; Presented papers in National and International Congresses and Seminars. *Hobbies:* Reading; Travel; Sports; Light Classical Music. *Address:* Dept. of Obstetrics-Gynaecology, Faculty of Medicine, Universitas Gadjah Mada, Sekip Utara, Yogyakarta, Indonesia.

SOKOL, Gerald H, b. 21 Oct. 1943, New York City, USA. Chief, William W Trice Radiation Oncology Centre, Tampa General Hospital, Florida. m. Katharine Cristol, 24 June 1973, Philadelphia, 2 daughters. *Education:* MS 1968, MD 1970, Indiana University; Board certification, Internal Medicine 1973, Therapeutic Radiology 1976, Internal Medicine (Oncology) 1977. *Appointments include:* Adviser, Janssen Research Council, Janssen Pharmaceutica, 1985-; Medical Director, Hillsborough Community College, Radiation Oncology Technical Programme, 1981-; Programme Coordinator/Director, University Cancer Study Group Update, Tampa, 1981-; Director, Radiation Oncology, Town & Country Hospital, 1981-; Consultant in Radiation Therapy & Oncology, University Hospital, Tampa, 1980-; Assistant Professor of Medicine, Pharmacology & Therapeutics, University of South Florida School of Medicine, 1977-. *Memberships include:* Sigma Xi; American Medical Association; New York Academy of Science; American Society of Clinical Oncology; American Society of Therapeutic Radiology; American Society of Internal Medicine; American Society of Clinical Pharmacology; National Association for the Advancement of Science; Liaison Fellow, American College of Surgery; etc. *Publications include:* "Radiation Drug Interactions in Cancer Management", ed with R P Maickel, 1980; 'Radiation Effects on the Physiological Disposition of Drugs' in "Radiation Drug Interactions in Cancer Management", co-editor, 1980; 'The Rationale of Combined Modality Treatment of Cancer' in "Radiation Drug Interactions", co-editor, 1980; Numerous papers in professional journals, submissions, abstracts. *Honours:* Upper 130, medical class; Pitman-Moore Fellow; Little '500' Scholar; Health Professions Scholar; AEO Honorary Premedical Fraternity; Fellow, American Cancer Society; National Scientific Advisory Board, Janssen Pharmaceutica. *Hobbies:* Amateur radio; Boating. *Address:* William W Trice Radiation Oncology Centre, Tampa General Hospital, Tampa, FL 33606, USA.

SOLIMAN, Mohamed Diaa Eldin Soliman, b. 10 Jan. 1939, Cairo, Egypt. Professor. m. Fatma Kamed Abdel-Motaal, 7 Sep. 1972, 2 daughters. *Education:* MBBcH 1960, DM 1964, MD, Ain-Shams faculty of Medicine, Ain Shams University, Cairo, 1967; FACA, FCCP, USA, 1983. *Appointments:* Clinical Demonstrator of Medicine, 1964-67; Teacher, Medicine and Allergy, 1967-74; Assistant Professor, Medicine and Allergy, 1974-79; Professor, Medicine and Allergy, 1979-; Consultant Physician, Allergist, Public Security Hospital, Cairo. *Memberships:* Ain-Shams Medical Society; Egyptian Society of Allergy and Clinical Immunology; International Society of Allergy; American College of Allergists. *Publications:* Papers and articles on allergy and medicine in various English medical and allergy journals; articles on allergy in Arabic Journals; Papers on Allergy, local and international conferences and symposia; Supervisor, MD and MS theses. *Hobbies:* Violin; Tennis; Swimming; Do-It-Yourself. *Address:* Ain-Shams Faculty of Medicine, Cairo, Egypt.

SOLIMANDO, Dominic Anthony, b. 4 Apr. 1950, Brooklyn, New York, USA. Pharmacist. *Education:* BSc, Pharmacy, Philadelphia College of Pharmacy & Science, 1976; MA, Management & Supervision, Central Michigan University, 1980. *Appointments:* Pharmacist, Pharmacy Service, Walter Reed Army Medical Centre, Washington DC, 1977; Chief, Pharmacy Service, Andrew Rader Army Health Clinic, Fort Myer, 1977-79; Clinical Pharmacist, Hematology-Oncology Service, Walter Reed Army Medical Centre, Washington DC, 1979-82; Chief, Oncology Pharmacy Section, Tripler Army Medical Centre, Honolulu. *Memberships:* American Pharmaceutical Association; American Society of Hospital Pharmacists; Hawaii Pharmaceutical Association, Vice President, 1983-84, President 1984-86; Hawaii Society of Hospital Pharmacists, Vice-President, 1984, President, 1985; Association of Military Surgeons of the US; American Institute of the History of Pharmacy; Federation Internationale de Pharmaceutique; International Pharmaceutical Students Federation; American Association for the Advancement of Science; New York Academy of Science. *Publications include:* Articles and Abstracts to professional journals including: "Preparation of Antineoplastic Drugs - A Review", 'American Journal of IV Therapy and Clinical Nutrition', 1983; "Doxorubicin-Induced Hypersensitivity Reactions", 'Drug Intelligence and Clinical Pharmacy', 1984. *Honours:* Bristol Award, Philadelphia College of Pharmacy & Science, 1976; Hawaii Pharmaceutical Association, President 1984-86; Hawaii Society of Hospital Pharmacists, Vice President 1984, President, 1985. *Hobbies:* History; Chess; Cycling; Cooking. *Address:* PO Box 220, Tripler US Army Medical Center, Honolulu, HI 96859, USA.

SOLL, David Benjamin, b. 9 Aug. 1930, New York City, USA. Ophthalmologist. m. Jean Shtasel, 23 Dec. 1956, 3 sons, 1 daughter. *Education:* BA, New York University, 1951; MD, Chicago Medical School, 1955; Certification, American Board of Ophthalmology, 1960; MS in Ophthalmology, New York University Postgraduate Medical School, 1963. *Appointments include:* Director, Department of Ophthalmology, Frankford Hospital, Philadelphia, 1965-; Associate Assistant, 1961-65, Consultant, Ophthalmology, 1975-77, Philadelphia General Hospital; Attending in Ophthalmology, Veterans Administration Hospital, Philadelphia, 1961-; Clinical Affiliate, Department of Surgery, The Children's Hospital, Division of Ophthalmology, Philadelphia, 1961-; Director, Philadelphia Geriatric Center, Department of Ophthalmology, Philadelphia, 1965-; Instructor 1961, Associate 1962-68, Assistant Professor 1968-72, Associate Professor, 1972-75, Department of Ophthalmology, University of Pennsylvania; Director, Rolling Hill Hospital, and Diagnostic Center, Department of Ophthalmology, Elkins Park, Pennsylvania, 1969-; Visiting Professor in Ophthalmology, University of Puerto Rico, San Juan, Puerto Rico, 1982-; Professor and Chairman, Hahnemann Medical College and Hospital, Department of Ophthalmology, Philadelphia, 1974-; Consultant in Ophthalmology, Magee Memorial Rehabilitation Center, Philadelphia, 1980-. *Memberships include:* Fellow, American College of Surgeons; Fellow, American Academy of Ophthalmology and Otolaryngology; Charter Fellow, The American Society of Ophthalmic Plastic and Reconstructive Surgery; American Medical Association; American Association of Cosmetic Surgeons; American Association of Ophthalmology. *Publications:* Contributor of numerous articles to medical journals and numerous chapters to edited medical textbooks. *Honours:* Honor Award, American Academy of Ophthalmology, 1977; Distinguished Alumni Award, Chicago Medical School, 1979; Legion of Merit Award, Chapel of Four Chaplains, 1979. *Address:* 1127 Devon Road, Rydal, PA 19046, USA.

SOLOMON, Louis, b. 31 Dec. 1928, Republic of South Africa. Professor of Orthopaedic Surgery, University of Bristol, England. m. 1 July 1951, Johannesburg, Republic of South Africa, 1 son, 2 daughters. *Education:* MB, ChB, MD, University of Cape Town; FRCS. *Appointments:* Registrar, Royal National Orthopaedic Hospital, London, England, 1958-62; Senior Orthopaedic Surgeon, Johannesburg Hospital, Johannesburg, Republic of South Africa, 1963-66; Professor of Orthopaedic Surgery, University of the Witwatersrand, Johannesburg, 1967-85. *Memberships:* South African Orthopaedic Association; British Orthopaedic Association; British Rheumatological Society; International Skeletel Society; International Hip Society. *Publications:* "Apley's System of Orthopaedics and Fractures", (with A G Apley); Author of 87 publications on professional subjects. *Honours:* Robert Jones Prize, Royal College of Surgeons, 1966; President's Medal, South African Orthopaedic Association, 1968; Robert Jones Lectureship, Royal College of Surgeons, 1982. *Hobbies:* Sculpture; Tennis; Cycling. *Address:* Department of Orthopaedic Surgery, Bristol Royal Infirmary, Bristol BS2 8HW, England.

SOLOMONOW, Moshe, b. 24 Oct. 1944, Tel-Aviv, Israel. Professor of Orthopaedic Surgery; Director of Bioengineering. m. Susanne E Nickerson, 29 May 1982, Santa Monica, California, USA, 2 daughters. *Education:* BSc, 1970, MSc 1972, Electrical Engineering, California State University; PhD, Systems Engineering & Neurosciences, University of California, Los Angeles, 1976. *Appointments:* Research Associate, 1973-76, Assistant Research Professor 1976-80, University of California, Los Angeles; Associate Professor, Tulane University, New Orleans, 1980-83; Professor of Orthopaedic Surgery/Director of Bioengineering, Louisiana State University Medical Centre, 1983-. *Memberships:* Senior Member, Institute of Electrical & Electronics Engineers, Biomedical Engineering Society; Active Member, American Congress of Rehabilitation Medicine; Member, Orthopaedic Research Society, International Society of Electrophysiological Kinesiology. *Publications:* Over 80 articles in medical & bioengineering, 1973-. *Honours:* Crump Award, Medical Engineering, UCLA, 1977; Sigma Xi, 1977. *Hobby:* Sailing. *Address:* Department of Orthopaedics, LSU Medical Centre, New Orleans, LA 70112, USA.

SOLOMONS, Gerald, b. 22 Feb. 1921, London, England. Emeritus Professor of Pediatrics. m. Hope C. Solomons, 12 June 1955, 2 daughters. *Education:* American Board of Paediatrics; LRCP & S, Royal College of Physicians and Surgeons, Edinburgh, Scotland. *Appointments:* Assistant Superintendent, Charles V Chapin Hospital, Providence, Rhode Island, 1952-59; Deputy Director of Pediatrics, Brown University, Providence, Rhode Island, 1959-62; Assistant Professor 1962-65, Associate Professor, 1965-69, Professor of Pediatrics, 1969-85, University of Iowa, Iowa City; Director, Child Development Clinic, University of Iowa, 1963-85; Acting Director, Institute of Child Behavior and Development, University of Iowa, 1975; Program Director, Region VII Child Abuse and Neglect Resource Center, University of Iowa, 1975. *Memberships:* American Acacemy of Pediatrics; American Academy for Cerebral Palsy and Developmental Medicine; American Association on Mental Deficiency; State of Iowa Medical Society; American Medical Society. *Publications:* "Encyclopedia of Pediatric Psychology" with L Wright and A Schaefer, 1979; 'The physician and psychological appraisal' in 'Devel. Med. Child. Neurol.' 1973; 'Motor development in Yucatecan Infants' in 'Devel. Med. Child. Neurol.' 1975; 'Child Abuse and Developmental Disabilities' in 'Devel. Med. Child. Neurol.' 1980. *Honours:* Sigma Xi; Senior Student Award for Outstanding Instructor, 1963. *Hobbies:* Interest in Yucatan Peninsula, Mexico - Long time member of the Iowa-Yucatan Exchange Program; Woodworking. *Address:* 319 Mullin Avenue, Iowa City, IA 52240, USA.

SOLTYSIAK, Adam, b. 24 May 1933, Chrzan, Poland.

Director, Institute of Surgery. m. 31 Jan. 1959, 1 son. *Education:* Diploma, Medical Academy Lodz, 1958; MD, 1965; Docent, 1973; Professor, 1983. *Appointments:* House Officer, 1959-62, Senior House Officer, 1963-68, 2nd Surgical Clinic; Senior House Officer, Registrar, Royal Hospital, Wolverhampton, England, 1968-69; Registrar, 1970-76, Docent, 1977-83, 2nd Surgical Clinical Medical Academy Lodz; Professor, Director, Institute of Surgery, Medical Academy Lodz, 1983-. *Memberships:* Polish Surgical Association; Polish Gastroenterological Association; Collegium Internationale Chirurgiae Digestivae. *Publications:* "Vagotomy in the Surgical Treatment of Gastric and Duodenal Ulcer", co-author, 1978; "Highly Selective Vagotomy in the Treatment of Duodenal Ulcer", co-author, 1980; "Surgery of the Stomach", co-author, 1985. *Honours:* Golden Cross, 1980. *Hobbies:* Classical Music; Films. *Address:* Al Michiewicza 11, M 20, 90-438 Lodz, Poland.

SOMMER, Marc Lloyd, b. 16 May 1948, New York, USA. Director, Back Care Centres. m. Goldie DeBlasio, 26 May 1973, Maplewood. *Education:* BA, University of Hartford; Doctor of Chiropractic, New York Chiropractic College, 1978. *Appointments:* Founder, Main St. Chiropractic Clinic, Lincoln Park, 1979; Founder, Broadway Chiropractic Clinic, Paterson, 1982; Founder, Teaneck Chiropractic Group, 1985, united all to form Back Care Centers, 1985-. *Memberships:* American Chiropractic Association, Councils on Radiology, Nutrition, Sports Medicine; New Jersey Chiropractic Society, Chairman, Ethics Committee. *Publication:* "Effective Practice Management Systems", 1985. *Honour:* N J Chiropractic Society Distinguished Service Award, 1984. *Hobbies:* Football; Tennis; Skiing; Reading. *Address:* 4 Beaverbrook Road, Lincoln Park, NJ 07035, USA.

SOMMERS, Frank G, b. in Hungary. Psychiatrist. *Education:* MD, University of Toronto, Canada, 1970; Fellow, Royal College of Physicians (Canada), 1975. *Appointments:* Lecturer, Department of Psychiatry, University of Toronto, 1976; Private Practice of Psychiatry, specialising in sexology, 1976; Lecturer, course in Human Sexuality, Faculty of Medicine, University of Toronto, 1980; Consultant Psychiatrist, East York Board of Education, Toronto, 1981; Member, Canadian Pugwash Delegation, 1981-82. *Memberships:* Fellow, American College of Sexologists, 1980; Founding Chairman, Section of Sexology, Canadian & Ontario Psychiatric Associations, 1980, 1979; Founding President, Physicians for Social Responsibility Inc, Canada, 1979-84; Councillor, International Physicians for the Prevention of Nuclear War, 1984. *Publications:* Numerous publications in field of sexology & psychiatry; Producer of internationally recognised instructional films in human sexuality (Finalist, American Film Festival, 1978); Author (with Tana Dinnen PhD) of "Curing Nuclear Madness", Methuen, Toronto, 1984. *Address:* Suite 406, 360 Bloor Street West, Toronto, Ontario, M5S 1X1, Canada.

SONDEREGGER, Morris Arthur, b. 21 Feb. 1912, Beatrice, Nebraska, USA. General Practice. m. Edwina Madeline Adams, 24 July 1942, Toronto, Canada, 2 sons, 1 daughter. *Education:* MD, BSc, University of Nebraska. *Memberships:* American Medical Association; Washoe Medical Society; Nevada State Medical Society; American Academy of Family Practice; American Society of Bariatrics; American Society of Clinical Hypnosis. *Hobbies:* Skiing; Golf; Travel. *Address:* 2660 Lakeridge Shores West, Reno, NV 89509, USA.

SOO, Yoi-Sun, b. 16 Apr. 1933, Hong Kong. Neuroradiologist. m. Shirley Lam, 9 Apr. 1960, Hong Kong, 1 son, 3 daughters. *Education:* MB, BS, Hong Kong, 1957; DMRD, England, 1966; FRACR, 1973. *Appointments:* Professorial Registrar in Obstetrics and Gynaecology, Queen Mary Hospital, Hong Kong, 1958-59; Registrar in Diagnostic Radiology, Royal Free Hospital, London, 1964-66; Clinical Assistant, Lysholm Department of Radiology, Queens Square,

London, 1967; Staff Radiologist, University Hospital, Kuala Lumpur, Malaya, 1967-68; Director of Radiology, 1969-71; Staff Radiologist, Repatriation General Hospital, Concord, Australia, 1971-78; Senior Staff Radiologist, Westmead Hospital, Westmead, Australia, 1978-present. *Memberships:* European Society of Neuroradiology; Australian Association of Neurologists; Neurosurgical Society of Australasia; British Institute of Radiology; Royal College of Radiologists. *Publications:* 'CT in Management of Normal Pressure Hydrocephalus' in 'Australasian Radiology', 1979; 'Suprasellar Metrizamide Cisternography' in 'Australasian Radiology', 1982; 'The Narrow Cervical Canal' in 'Australasian Radiology', 1983. *Hobbies:* Jazz; Chinese Martial Arts; History of Second World War; Test Cricket. *Address:* 77 Felton Road, Carlingford, New South Wales 2118, Australia.

SORBIE, Janet, b. 15 Feb. 1931, Montreal, Canada. Associate Professor, Family Medicine, Queen's University, Kingston. m. Charles Sorbie, 27 Apr. 1957, Aberdeen, Scotland. 3 daughters. *Education:* MB, ChB, Aberdeen University, 1955; MSc, Queen's University, 1969; MD, Aberdeen University, 1975; CCFP, 1977. *Appointments:* Resident, Medicine, Royal Infirmary, Aberdeen, 1955-56, Paediatrics, Royal Hospital for Sick Children, Glasgow, 1956-57; Locum Medical Officer, Child Welfare, Glasgow, 1957-65; Research Fellow, Medicine, Queen's University, 1966-69; MRC Professional Assistant, Medicine, 1969-75, Instructor, Physiology, 1969-70, Clinical Assistant, 1696-74, Lecturer, 1974-75, Assistant Professor, 1977-84, Queen's University. *Memberships:* College of Family Physicians of Canada; Canadian Medical Association; Canadian Public Health Association; North American Primary Care Research Group; Attending Staff: Kingston General Hospital, Hotel Dieu Hospital. *Publications include:* Most recent "Prostaglandin Inhibitors: Rational Therapy for Dysmenorrhea", 'Canadian Family Physician', 1982; co-author, "Chlamydia Trachomatic in Women with Urogenital Symptoms", 'Canadian Medical Association Journal', 1982; "Chlamydial Infection: A Common Sexually Transmitted Disease", 'Canadian Family Physician', 1982; Co-author, "Efficacy of Ketoprofen in Treating Primary Dysmenorrhea", 'Canadian Medical Association Journal', 1983; "Clinical Aspects of Chlamydial Infections", 'Canada Diseases Weekly Reports", 1985. *Honours:* John Alexander Stewart Fellowship, Queen's University, 1966-67; Henry Albert Beatty Fellowship, Queen's University, 1967-69; Ortho Literary Award, College of Family Physicians of Canada, 1983. *Hobbies:* Skiing; Tennis; Swimming; Sailing. *Address:* 208 Alwington Place, Kingston, Ontario K7L 4P8, Canada.

SOREL, Eliot, b. 2 Oct. 1940, Romania, Assistant Professor of Psychiatry; Consultant, World Health Organization. m. Christiane E M Doerwaldt, 19 Aug. 1979, Alexandria, Virginia, 1 son, 1 daughter. *Education:* BA, New York University, 1966; MD, State University of New York, New York, 1971; Psychiatry, Yale University, 1975. *Appointments:* Clinical Director, East End Mental Health Clinic, St Thomas, Virgin Islands, 1975-77; Chairman, Advisory Board, Operation Sister United National Council of Negro Women, St Thomas, 1976-77; Board of Directors, Council of International Programs, Howard University, 1979-84; Director, Family Studies Center, Psychiatric Institute Foundation, Washington, DC, 1979-83; Director, Open Adult Unit, Psychiatric Institute, Washington, DC, 1980-82; National Advisory Committee on Marital and Family Therapy Education, 1981-83; Director, Intensive Care Unit, Psychiatric Institute, Washington, DC, 1982-83. *Memberships:* American Medical Association; American Psychiatric Association; American Association for the Advancement of Science; World Association for Social Psychiatry; American Anthropological Association; Society for the Study of Psychiatry and Culture. *Publications:* Contributor to professional journals; Reflections on Afro-West Indian Families in Family Therapy in Psychiatry-State of the Art (in press). *Honours:* University Scholarship, NYU, 1962-66; Health Professions

Scholarship, SUNY, 1967-71. *Hobbies:* Photography; Music; Film; Theatre; Sports; Nature. *Address:* Suite 810, 2020 K Street, NW, Washington, DC 20006, USA.

SØRENSEN, Bent, b. 8 Mar. 1924, Fredericia, Denmark. Consultant Plastic Surgeon/Chief of Staff, Department of Plastic Surgery & Burns Unit, Københavns Kommunes Hvidovre Hospital. m. Kirsten Ammentorp, MD, 29 July 1949, 2 sons. *Education:* MD, 1949; Specialist of Surgery 1960; Specialist of Plastic Surgery 1964; Professor of Surgery 1971, University of Copenhagen. *Appointments include:* Chief of Staff, Department of Plastic Surgery & Burns Unit, Københavns Kommunehospital, 1965-75, Københavns Kommunes Hvidovre Hospital, 1976-; Vice Dean, Faculty of Medicine 1971-73, Dean 1974-75, University of Copenhagen; Chairman, Board of Medical Education, 1980-82; Member, Danish Medical Research Council, 1976-84; Chairman, Medical Research Council, EEC (Comité de Recherchere en Médecine et en Santé Publique), 1981-83; Member 1975-85, Chairman 1975-81, Advisory Committee on Medical Training, EEC; Chairman, Rehabilitation Centre for Torture Victims, 1985-. *Memberships:* Co-founder, International Society for Burn Injuries; Chairman, Disaster Planning Committee, ibid, 1978-; Co-founder, Danish Society for Plastic & Reconstructive Surgery; Co-founder, Organisation of Danish Plastic Surgeons (Chairman 1984-). *Publications* include: Thesis, "Late Results of Radium Therapy in Cervical Carcinoma", 1958; Over 100 publications on burns, especially prevention & controlled trials on treatment of burns. *Honours:* Knight, Order of Dannebrog, 1978; Honorary Member, American Burn Association 1975, British Burn Association 1981, Indian Burn Association 1984, Hungarian Burns Association 1985; Honorary Citizen, town of Fredericia, 1979; Memorial Medal, Congo, Red Cross Committee, 1961; Everett Evan's Award, 1975; A B Wallace Award, 1981; Whitaker International Burn Prize, Italy, 1983. *Hobbies:* Music; Literature; Art. *Address:* 12 Toftholm Allé, DK 2900 Hellerup, Denmark.

SOROWORA, Ezekiel Abayomi, b. 16 May 1941, Lagos, Nigeria. University Professor. m. Florence Oluwajemite Orangun, 15 July 1967, London, England. 2 sons, 2 daughters. *Education:* B Pharm, Hons, 1964, PhD, 1967, University of Nottingham. *Appointments:* Lecturer in Pharmacognosy, 1969-70, Senior Lecturer in Pharmacognosy, 1970-75, Acting Head of Pharmacognosy and of Drug Research Unit, 1972-82, Acting Dean, Faculty of Pharmacy, 1974-76, Reader in Pharmacognosy, 1975-79, Professor in Pharmacognosy, 1979-, Dean, Faculty of Pharmacy, University of Ife, 1982-85. *Memberships:* Pharmaceutical Society of Nigeria; Nigerian Society of Pharmacognosy, President; Society for Public Analysts of Nigeria. *Publications:* "Medicinal Plants and Traditional Medicine in Africa" 1982; "Man, Plants and Medicine in Africa: Some Fundamental Perspectives" 1982. *Honours:* Senior Research Fellowship of Tropical Products Institute, London, 1971-72 (Bath, England); Western Nigeria Scholarship 1964 (Nottingham, England); German DAAD Award, 1976 (Munster); African Universities' Staff Exchange Programme, 1985 (Dakar, Senegal). *Hobbies:* Badminton; Squash. *Address:* Faculty of Pharmacy, University of Ife, Ile-Ife, Nigeria.

SORREL, William Edwin, b. 27 May 1913, USA. Psychiatrist and Professor of Human Behaviour. m. Rita Marcus, 1 July 1950, New York City, New York, 3 daughters. *Education:* BS 1933, PhD 1963, New York University; MA, Columbia University, 1935; MD, 1939; Qualified Psychiatrist Certificate, New York State, 1946. *Appointments:* Chief, Clinical Psychiatry, Jewish Memorial Hospital, New York City; Chief, Child Psychiatry, Lebanon Hospital, New York City; Chief, Mental Hygiene Service, Beth David Hospital, New York City; Chief Psychiatrist of Psychiatric Clinic, Professor Psychiatry, Yeshiva University, New York City; Visiting Professor of Psychiatry, Hebrew University, Israel, Tokyo University School of Medicine, Japan; Professor of Human Behaviour, Touro College, New York City, New York, USA; Attending Psychiatrist, Saint Clares Hospital, New York City; Consulting Psychiatrist, Bronx-Lebanon Hospital, New York City. *Memberships:* Past President, American Association of Psychoanalytic Physicians, District Branch of American Psychiatric Association, Bronx Society of Neurology and Psychiatry; President of Section on Suicidology, Trustee, Pan-American Medical Association; American Medical Association; American Academy of Psychotherapy; American Association of University Professors; New York State Society of Clinical Research Psychiatry. *Publications:* 'Neurosis in a Child', 1949; 'A Psychiatric Viewpoint on Child Adoption', 1957; 'Shock Therapy in Private Practice', 1958; 'The Genesis of Neurosis', 1958; 'Prognosis with Electroshock Therapy', 1963; 'Psychodynamic Effects of Abortion', 1967; 'Violence Towards Self', 1971; 'Transference in Psychoanalysis', 1973; 'Cults and Cult Suicide', 1979. *Honours include:* Gold Medal, Sir William Osler Honor Medical Society 1939, American Psychiatric Association, 1974. *Hobbies:* Oil painting; Bowling. *Address:* 263 West End Avenue, New York, NY 10023, USA.

SOTTO, Luciano, S J, b. 6 Oct. 1925, Philippines. Professor, Gynaecology, Obstetrics, University of the Philippines College of Medicine. m. Norma Labrador, 19 Aug. 1962, Manila, 3 sons, 1 daughter. *Education:* AA, 1946, MD, 1951, University of the Philippines. *Appointments:* Instructor, 1961, Assistant Professor, 1964, Gynaecology, Associate Professor, 1966, Professor, 1975, Chairman, 1973-76, Gynaecology & Obstetrics, Chief, Gynaecology Oncology, 1961-73, University of the Philippines College of Medicine. *Memberships:* Philippine Medical Association; Philippine Obstetrical & Gynaecological Society; Philippine College of Surgeons; American College of Obstetricians & Gynaecologists; Society of Pelvic Surgeons; International Society for the Study of Vulvar Disease; Gynaecologic Oncology Society of the Philippines. *Publications:* Book - "Carcinoma of the Cervix", 1962; Author, numerous articles (54) in professional journals. *Honours:* Baldomero Roxas Memorial Lecturer, Annual Convention, Philippine Obstetrical and Gynaecological Society; Elena Paez Tan Professorial Chair Award, 1983; Golden Jubilee Award, 1983; James Platt White Memorial Lecture, Buffalo Gynaecologic & Obstetric Society, 1985; etc. *Address:* Dept. of Obstetrics & Gynaecology, College of Medicine, University of the Philippines, Manila, Philippines.

SOUCACOS, Panayotis, b. 27 Apr. 1941, Athens, Greece. Professor and Chairman, Orthopaedic Department, University of Ioannina, Greece. m. Dorina Papaeconomou, Mar. 1975, England, 1 son, 1 daughter. *Education:* MD; FICS; Clinical and Research Fellow, Orthopaedic Department, Duke University Medical Center, Durham, North Carolina, USA. *Appointments:* Clinical and Research Fellow, Orthopaedic Department, Duke University, Medical Center, Durham, North Carolina, 1971-74; Assistant Professor, Orthopaedic Department, University of Athens, Greece, 1975-80; Professor and Chairman, Orthopaedic Department, University of Ioannina Medical School, Greece, 1985-. *Memberships:* Greek Society Orthopaedic Surgery and Traumatology; International College of Surgeons; International Medical Society of Paraplegia; International Society for Reconstructive Microsurgery, Sicot. Contributions to Professional Journals, etc. *Hobby:* Athletics. *Address:* Professor and Chairman, Orthopaedic Department, University of Ioannina, Medical School, Ioannina, Greece.

SOUTER, Brian Heylen, b. 13 May 1934, Adelaide, Australia. Dental Surgeon. m. 10 Aug. 1957, Adelaide, 2 sons, 1 daughter. *Education:* BDS, Adelaide, 1956. *Appointments:* Private Practice; President, Royal Flying Doctor Service, Dental Panel, 1970-80; Organiser, Dental Service to Aboriginal People of NW Reserve of South Australia in an Honorary capacity, 1968-82; Part-time Tutor, University of Adelaide

Dental School, 1965-74. *Memberships:* Australian Dental Association, Councillor, 15 years, Treasurer 3 years, Vice President 2 years, President, South Australian Branch, 1977, Federal Councillor, 4 years, Chairman, Pain Control Study Group 1975-; FDI; Periodontal Society; General Practice Study Branch, Delta Sigma Delta; etc. *Honour:* Queen's Medal, 1977. 2Hobbies: Sailing; Golf; Fishing; Reading. *Address:* 1st Floor, ANZ Bld, 148 Rundle Mall, Adelaide, South Australia 5000.

SOUTO, Jose C, b. 9 Sep. 1920, La Guardia, Spain. Professor and Department Chairman. m. Maria Dolores, 1 Oct. 1946, Madrid, 1 son, 2 daughters. *Education:* MD; PhD. *Appointments:* Assistant Professor, Institute for Medical Research, Madrid, Spain; Department of Physiology, University of Halle a S, Germany. Professor and Chairman, Department of Physiology, University Los Andes, Merida, Venezuela and Medical School, Central University, Caracas; Associate Professor, Physiology, Atomic Energy Commission, University of Tennessee, USA; Professor and Chairman, University of Tennessee; Professor of Physiology, University of Caribe, Puerto Rico, USA; Professor and Chairman, Physiology, Ponce School of Medicine, Ponce, Puerto Rico, currently. *Memberships:* New York Academy of Sciences, USA; American Association for the Advancement of Science; Radiation Research Society, USA; Association for Muscle Research, Uruguay. *Publications:* "Textbook of Physiology", 1958; "Blood Gylcolysis", 1950; "Method for Insulin Evaluation", 1950; Author of over 50 published papers. *Honours:* Prize, Institute of Experimental Medicine, Spain, 1940; Department of Physiology Award, Spain, 1939; Award, Medical Students, Ponce School of Medicine, 1978; Award by Medical Students, Ponce, 1980. *Address:* Ponce School of Medicine, Department of Physiology, PO Box 7004, Ponce, PR 00732, USA.

SOVALENI, Pisila, b. 9 Mar. 1934, Tonga. Senior Public Health Nursing Sister. *Education:* Diploma of Nursing, New Zealand; Certificate of Nutrition, London, England, Badan, Nigeria. *Appointments:* War Sister, Child Welfare Nursing Sister, Public Health Tutor Sister, Ministry of Health, Tonga. *Memberships:* President, Tonga Nurses Association; Vice-President, Commonwealth Nurses Federation, 1984-86. *Publications:* 'Status of Breast-feeding in Tonga', 1981; 'The Desirability of Uniform Contingency Planning to mitigate proerty damage & human suffering in the event of natural disasters' (Report of Commonwealth Foundation Seminar), 1982. *Hobbies:* Weaving (Handicraft); Sewing. *Address:* Ministry of Health, PO Box 59, Nuku'alofa, Tonga.

SOVNER, Robert, b. 9 Nov. 1943, New York City, USA. Psychiatrist; Editor. m. 1 son, 1 daughter. *Education:* BS cum laude, Allegheny College, USA, 1965; MD, State Univesity of New York, Upstate Medical Centre, 1969. *Appointments:* Research Psychiatrist, Boston State Hospital, 1973-78; Director, Acute Psychiatric Inpatient Service, Dorchester Mental Health Centre, Boston, Massachusetts, 1974-76; Medical Director, Drug Intake, Management and Evaluation System Inc, Watertown, Massachusetts, 1979-84; Staff Psychiatrist, Mount Auburn Hospital, Cambridge, Massachusetts-; Co-Editor 'Psychiatric Aspects of Mental Retardation Reviews' -. *Memberships:* American Psychiatric Association; American Association for Mental Deficiency; National Association for the Dually Diagnosed. *Publications:* "Psychopharmacology: A Generation of Progress", 1978; contributor; 'Do the Mentally Retarded Suffer from Affective Illness?' in 'Archives of General Psychiatry', 1983; 'Is Mania Incompatible with Down's Syndrome?' in 'British Journal of Psychiatry', 1985. *Hobbies:* Oriental Cooking; Horticulture; Swimming. *Address:* Suite 101, 697 Cambridge Street, Brighton, MA 02135, USA.

SPAGNOLO, Samuel Vincent, b. 3 Sep. 1939, Pittsburgh, Pennsylvania, USA. Professor of Medicine; Director of Pulmonary Medicine Divisions. m. Lucy Weyandt, 21 June 1961, Winchester, Virginia, 3 sons.

Education: BA, Washington and Jefferson College, Washington, Pennsylvania, 1961; MD, Temple University School of Medicine, Philadelphia, 1965; Diplomate 1971, Recertification 1977, American Board of Internal Medicine; Diplomate, Subspeciality Board in Pulmonary Diseases, 1972. *Appointments include:* Senior Resident 1969-70, Chief Resident 1970-71, Medicine, Veterans Administration Hospital, Boston, Massachusetts; Assistant Chief 1972-75, Acting Chief 1975-76, Medical Service, Chief of Pulmonary Diseases Section 1976-, Veterans Administration Medical Center, Washington, District of Columbia; Assistant Professor 1972-75, Associate Professor 1975-81, Professor 1981; Medicine, George Washington University School of Medicine and Health Services, Washington; Acting Director 1976-78, Director 1978-, Division of Pulmonary Diseases and Allergy, George Washington University Medical Center, Washington. *Memberships include:* Fellow, American College of Physicians; Fellow, Council of Critical Care 1981-, American College of Chest Physicians; American Thoracic Society; American Association for the Advancement of Science. *Publications include:* 'The medical intensive care unit: mortality experience in a large teaching hospital', (with P Hershberg and H J Zimmerman), 1973; 'Cyanosis of cirrhosis', 1975; 'Nine month chemotherapy for pulmonary tuberculosis', (with J M Raver), 1982; 'Speaking out - legacy of life', 1982. *Honours:* Babcock Honorary Society, Dean's Letter of Commendation for Achievement, Temple University School of Medicine, 1965; Consultant to President Reagan, 1981; Cavaliere, Order of Merit, Republic of Italy, 1983. *Hobbies:* Swimming; Biking; Auto restoration; Philatelist. *Address:* George Washington University School of Medicine, 2150 Pennsylvania Avenue, Fourth Floor NW, Washington DC 20037, USA.

SPARRIUS, Otto, b. 27 May 1951, Bloemfontein, Republic of South Africa. Dental Surgeon. m. Sandra Karin Hutty, 24 Sep. 1977, Johannesburg, 1 son, 1 daughter. *Education:* BDS, currently completing MSc, University of the Witwatersrand. *Appointments:* Private practice, 1978-; Part-time Lecturer in Dental Materials 1983-84, Staff of Dental Research Unit 1984, University of the Witwatersrand. *Memberships:* South African Dental Association; International Association of Dental Research. *Publication:* 'Experimental marginal leakage', (with A Jodaiken), 1980 and 1981. *Hobbies:* Fencing; Computer programming. *Address:* PO Box 2215, Beacon Bay, 5205, Republic of South Africa.

SPECTOR, Roy Geoffrey, b. 27 Aug. 1931, Leeds, England. Professor of Applied Pharmacology. m. Evie Freeman, 27 Mar. 1960 (divorced 1979), 2 sons, 1 daughter. *Education:* MB; ChB; MD; Leeds University; PhD, London University; FRCP; FRCPath. *Appointments:* Senior Lecturer, Experimental Biology, Paediatric Research Unit, Guy's Hospital, London, 1961-67; Reader then Professor of Applied Pharmacology, Guy's Hospital Medical School, 1968-. *Memberships:* British Medical Association; Royal Society of Medicine. *Publications:* "Textbook of Clinical Pharmacology", 1986; "Psychiatry: Common Drug Treatments", 1985; "The Nerve Cell", 1986; "Clinical Pharmacology in Dentistry", 1985; "Aids to Pharmacology", 1986. *Hobbies:* Walking; Music. *Address:* 60 Crescent Drive, Orpington, Kent BR5 1BD, England.

SPECTOR, Sheldon L, b. 13 Feb. 1939, Detroit, Michigan, USA. Clinical Professor of Medicine. m. Judith Lukacs, 7 Aug. 1966, 1 son, 2 daughters. *Education:* University of Michigan, 1956-59; MD, Wayne State University, Detroit, 1964; Internship, 1964-65, Residency, Internal Medicine, 1965-66, Mount Sinai Hospital, New York; Residency, Research Investigator, Laboratory of Virology & Rickettsiology, DBS, National Institutes of Health, 1966-68; Internal Medicine, Resident II, University of California, Los Angeles, 1968-69; Fellowship, Allergy & Clinical Immunology, National Jewish Hospital, Denver, 1969-71. *Appoin-*

tments include: Officer, US Public Health Service, Bethesda, 1966-68; Various Positions, National Jewish Hospital, Denver, 1971-79; Assistant Professor, 1971-77, Associate Professor, 1977-81, University of Colorado; Associate Clinical Professor, 1981-82, Clinical Professor, 1982-, Medicine, University of California, Los Angeles, California. *Memberships include:* American Association for the Advancement of Science; American Academy of Allergy & Immunology, Fellow, 1974, Various other positions; American College of Allergists, Fellow, 1980, Scientific & Education Council, 1985-86; American College of Chest Physicians, Fellow, 1976, Various positions; American College of Physicians, Fellow, 1976; American Society of Internal Medicine, 1972; American Thoracic Society; Colorado Allergy Society; Colorado Medical Society, Senior Member 1974; Denver Medical Society, Senior Member, 1974; Los Angeles Society of Allergy; California Medical Association; California Society for Allergy/Clinical Immunology. *Publications:* Author, numerous papers, articles, reviews, letters, and essays in professional journals, newspapers & magazines. *Honours:* Lady Davis Postdoctoral Fellow, Allergy, Hebrew University, Israel, 1977-78; Original Research Award, William Beaumont Society, Wayne State University School of Medicine; President, William Beaumont Society; L E Smith, Lecturer, 1980. *Hobby:* Tennis. *Address:* 11645 Wilshire Blvd, Suite 600, Los Angeles, CA 90025, USA.

SPEED, Isobel Ethel, b. 6 Mar. 1931, Adelaide, Australia. Deputy Director, Haematology, A.C.H. m. Norman Clarence Koch, 9 Mar. 1968, Adelaide. *Education:* MBBS, University of Adelaide, 1957; FRCPA, Royal College of Pathologists of Australasia, 1974. *Appointments:* Resident Medical Officer, Royal Adelaide Hospital, 1957; Lecturer, Anatomy, University of Adelaide, 1958; Registrar, Anaesthetics, Royal Adelaide Hospital, 1959-61; Registrar, Clinical Pathology, IMVS, Adelaide, 1961-62; Medical Officer, School Medical Services, Adelaide, 1963-64; Senior Registrar, Haematology, 1965-68, Assistant Haematologist, 1968-75, Senior Specialist Haematologist, 1975-78, Deputy Director, Haematology, 1978-, Adelaide Children's Hospital; Honorary Consultant Haematologist, Queen Victoria Maternity Hospital, Adelaide, 1983-. *Memberships:* Australian and British Medical Associations; Haematology Society of Australia; International Society of Haematology; Haemophilia Society of South Australia, etc. *Publications:* Articles in professional journals including: 'Australian Paediatric Journal'; 'Medical Journal of Australia'. *Honours:* Life Member, Adelaide Childrens Hospital Inc. *Hobbies:* Reading; Music; Medical Adviser, South Australian Variety Club; Photograph; Travel. *Address:* Department of Haematology, Adelaide Childrens Hospital, 72 King William Road, North Adelaide, South Australia 5006.

SPENCE, David Stephen, b. 22 Dec. 1945, Bristol, England. Consultant, Homoeopathic Medicine. m. Denise Burnup, 6 May 1972, East Dean, 1 son, 1 daughter. *Education:* Kings College, London; St George's Hospital Medical School, London; MBBS, London; MF.Hom; MRCS; LRCP; DRCOG. *Appointments:* Dean's House Physician, St George's Hospital, London; Medical Registrar, Mount Vernon Hospital, London; Consultant, Homoeopathic Medicine, Bristol Homoeopathic Hospital. *Memberships:* Faculty of Homoeopathy, Vice President and Executive Dean; Fellow, Royal Society of Medicine. *Hobbies:* Climbing; Cricket; Swimming; Surfing; Travel; Philately; Ornithology; Photography. *Address:* Bristol Homoeopathic Hospital, Cotham Hill, Bristol BS6 6JU, England.

SPENCER, Richard Paul, b. 7 June 1929, New York City, USA. Professor & Chairman, Department of Nuclear Medicine, University of Connecticut Health Centre. m. Gwendolyn Enid Williams, Garden City, New York, 7 Apr. 1956, 3 daughters. *Education:* AB, Dartmouth College, 1951; MD, University of Southern California, 1954; MA 1958, PhD 1961, Biochemistry, Harvard University. *Appointments:* Medical Officer,

US Navy, 1955-57; Helen Hay Whitney & National Science Foundation Fellowships, Harvard University, 1957-60; Assistant, Associate Professor, Biophysics, University of Buffalo School of Medicine, 1961-63; Assocuate Professor, Professor, Nuclear Medicine, Yale University School of Medicine, 1963-74. *Memberships:* Biophysical Society; American Physiological Society; National Trustee 6 years, President, Greater New York chapter 1971-72, Society of Nuclear Medicine; President, New England chapter, ibid, 1982-84. *Publications include:* Over 640 scientific articles & books. *Honour:* Honorary MA, Yale University, 1968. *Address:* Department of Nuclear Medicine, University of Connecticut Health Centre, Farmington, CT 06032, USA.

SPENGLER, Dan M, b. 25 Feb. 1941, Defiance, Ohio, USA. Professor, Chairman, Orthopaedics and Rehabilitation. m. Cynthia Niswonger, 2 Oct. 1965, 1 son, 1 daughter. *Education:* BS, Baldwin Wallace College; MD, University of Michigan Medical School; Internship, King City Hospital, Seattle; Residency, University of Washington; Fellowship, Biomechanics, Case Western Reserve University. *Appointments:* Assistant Professor, 1974-78, Associate Professor, 1978-83, Orthopaedics, University of Washington; Professor, Chairman, Orthopaedics and Rehabilitation, Vanderbilt University Medical Centre, Nashville, 1983-. *Memberships:* American Board of Orthopaedic Surgeons; Association of Bone and Joint Surgeons; North American Lumbar Spine Association; Interuban Orthopaedic Society; American Academy of Orthopaedic Surgeons, Member at Large, Board of Directors. *Honours:* American Orthopaedic Association, ABC Exchange, Great Britain, 1981; Resident, Teaching Award, University of Washington, 1983; Kosmos Achievement Award, NASA, 1975. *Hobbies:* Flying; Back Packing; Tennis; Golf. *Address:* D-4219 Vanderbilt University Medical Centre North, 21st Avenue and Garland Street, Nashville, TN 37232, USA.

SPENSLEY, James, b. 19 May 1938, Detroit, Michigan, USA. Psychiatrist; Associate Clinical Professor, University of California. m. Jeanette A. Mattern, 17 Feb. 1962, Menasha, 2 sons, 2 daughters. *Education:* MD, University of Michigan, 1963. *Appointments:* Instructor, 1969-71, Assistant Clinical Professor, 1971-73, Assistant Professor, 1973-76, Associate Professor, 1976-80, University of California, Davis; Adjunct Professor, Pacific Graduate School of Psychology, 1982-. *Memberships:* Central California Psychiatric Society; American Psychiatric Association; Sacramento Medical Society; California Medical Association; American Society for Clinical Hypnosis. *Publications:* Approximately 38 Scientific publications. *Honours:* Sigma Xi, 1977; Fellow, American Psychiatric Association, 1974; Diplomate, American Board Psychiatry & Neurology. *Hobbies:* Tennis; Skiing; Woodwork. *Address:* 2650-21st St., Sacramento, CA 95818, USA.

SPERBER, Geoffrey Hilliard, b. 26 December 1933, Bloemfontein, South Africa. Professor of Oral Biology, University of Alberta, Canada. m. Robyn Carol Fox, 24 June 1963, Edmonton, Canada, 1 son, 2 daughters. *Education:* BSc, 1954, BDS, 1956, BSc (Hons), 1958, University of Witwatersrand; MSc, University of Rochester, 1962; PhD, University of Witwatersrand, 1974. *Appointments:* Junior Lecturer, Anatomy, University of Witwatersrand, 1957-58; General Dental Practice, London, England, 1958-59; Research Fellow, Eastman Dental Center, Rochester, New York, USA, 1959-61; Assistant Professor, Dentistry, University of Alberta, Canada, 1961-66; Associate Professor, 1966-72; Senior Research Fellow, Anatomy, University of Witwatersrand, 1969-70; Curator, University of Alberta Dental Museum, 1970-; Professor of Oral Biology, University of Alberta, 1972-; Visiting Research Associate Palaeoanthropology, Research Group, University of Witwatersrand, 1980. *Memberships:* International Association for Dental Research; Federation Dentaire International; American Association for Advancement of Science;

American Association of Anatomists; Canadian Association of Anatomists; Canadian Dental Association; Association of Canadian Faculties of Dentistry; Canadian Museums Association; Alberta Dental Association; Edmonton Dental Society. *Publications:* "Demineralization Lesions of Intact Enamel", University of Rochester, 1962; "Craniofacial Embryology", 1st Edition, 1973, 2nd Edition, 1975, 3rd Edition, 1980; "The Morthology of the Cheek Teeth of Early South African Hominids", Xerox University Microfilms, 1975; Co-author, "Atlas of Radiographs of Early Man", 1982; "Embryology of the Head and Neck", 1986; Editor, Association Con. Fac. Dentistry News, 1972-. *Honours include:* Research Fellowship, Eastman Dental Center, 1959-61; Frank Ritter Memorial Award for Dentists, Rochester Academy of Medicine, 1960; Seventh District of New York State Dental Society Prize Award, 1961; Several Fellowships. *Hobbies:* Classical Music; Philately; Dental History. *Address:* Department of Oral Biology, Faculty of Dentistry, University of Alberta, Edmonton, Alberta, T6G 2N8, Canada.

SPIECHOWICZ, Eugeniusz Aleksander, b. 10 June 1929, Marki, Poland. Head of Prosthetic Dentistry, Warsaw Medical University. m. Leokadia Zmyslowska, 15 September 1951, 2 daughters. *Education:* DS, Faculty of Odontology, Medical University, Warsaw, 1952; DMD, 1963; MDS, 1968; Professor of Prosthetic Dentistry, 1975. *Appointments:* Teacher, Research Worker, Department of Prosthetic Dentistry, 1951-70; Head, Department of Propaedeutic a Prophylaxis Dentistry, 1970-73; Head, Department of Prosthetic Dentistry, 1973-; Deputy Rector, Warsaw Medical University, 1972-78; Deputy Editor, 1965-75; Editor, Polish Prosthetic Journal, 1975-; President, Country Specialist Group in field of Prosthetic Dentistry, 1975-. *Memberships:* Polish Dental Association; British Society for the Study of Prosthetic Dentistry; European Prosthodontic Association (former President); Expert of World Health Organization; Consultant of International Dental Federation; Corresponding Member GDR Prosthetic Association. *Publications:* Allergy to Acrylic Resin, 1961; The Immediate Complete Lower Denture, 1966; Laboratory Prosthetic Dentistry, 1977; Oral Microflora in Patients with Denture Stomatitis, 1978; Allergy to Chrom and Nickel in Prosthetic Dentistry, 1981. *Honours:* Golden Cross of Merit, 1970; Polonia Restituta, 1976; Medal, University of Lund, 1977; Honorary Teacher of Poland, 1982. *Hobbies:* Hunting; Fishing. *Address:* Starej Basni 12 ap. 40, 01 853 Warsaw, Poland.

SPIEGEL, David, b. 11 Dec. 1945, New York City, USA. Associate Professor, Psychiatry & Behavioral Sciences, Stanford University School of Medicine; Director, Adult Psychiatric Outpatient Clinic, Stanford University. m. Helen Margaret Blau, 25 July 1976, Palo Alto, 1 son, 1 daughter. *Education:* BA, Yale College, 1967; MD, Harvard Medical School, 1971; Fellow, Laboratory of Community Psychiatry, Harvard, 1973-74; Residencies, various Harvard Hospitals, 1971-74. *Appointments:* Staff Psychiatrist, San Mateo County Mental Health Services, 1974-75; Assistant Professor, Psychiatry and Behavioral Sciences, Stanford School of Medicine, 1975-82; Associate Professor, Clinical, 1983-, Chief, Brief Treatment Unit, 1974-76, Director, Social Psychiatry, Community Services, Palo Alto VA Medical Centre, 1976-80; Director, Stanford Adult Psychiatry Outpatient Clinic, 1980-. *Memberships:* Numerous professional organisations. *Publications:* Co-Author, "Trance & Treatment: Clinical Uses of Hypnosis", 1978; 45 articles in professional journals; Reviewer, 8 major journals; Editor, 'Progress in Psychiatry Series', 'American Psychiatric Press', 1984-; Associate Editor, 'Journal of Psychosocial Oncology', 1983-, 'American Journal of Clinical Hypnosis', 1985-; Examiner, American Board of Psychiatry and Neurology. *Honours:* Recipient, various honours & awards. *Hobbies:* Folk Music; Hiking; Travel. *Address:* Dept. of Psychiatry & Behavioral Science, Stanford University School of Medicine, Stanford University Medical Centre, Stanford, CA 94305,

USA.

SPIELMAN, Gerri (Geraldine) McGinnis, b. 11 Apr. 1944, Philadelphia, Pennsylvania, USA. Neurosurgical Clinical Specialist. m. 1 son, 2 daughters. *Education:* Registered Nurse, Misericordia Hospital School of Nursing, Philadelphia, Pennsylvania; BA Psychology, BS Nursing, Neumann College; MS Nursing, University of Pennsylvania; Certified Neurosurgical Registered Nurse, American Board of Neurosurgical Nursing. *Appointments:* Neurosurgical Clinical Specialist, Clinical Coordinator, Head Injury Center, University of Pennsylvania. *Memberships:* American Association of Critical Care Nurses; American Association of Neurosurgical Nurses; National Head Injury Foundation; American Association of Automotive Medicine; American Trauma Society. *Publications:* 5 articles in scientific journals, 1979-85; book chapter in "Trauma Nursing", 1984. *Honours:* Occupant Protection Citation, National Safety Council; Outstanding Nursing Leader, Neumann College. *Hobbies:* Sailing; Hiking. *Address:* Philadelphia, Pennsylvania, USA.

SPIELMEYER, Ruth, b. 31 May 1922, Munich, Germany. Private Practitioner; Attending Physician. *Education:* BA, Oberlin College; MD, Yale University School of Medicine. *Appointments:* Clinical Assistant, Mount Sinai Hospital; Clinical Instructor, Albert Einstein Hospital, New York College of Medicine; Bureau of Child Guidance; New York Criminal Court; Clinical Director, Methodist Maintenance Centers; Fordham-Tremont Community Mental Health Centre; Assistant Attending, Lutheran Hospital. *Memberships:* New York County Medical Society; American Psychiatric Society; Fellow, American Association of Psychoanalytic Physicians; American Association of Sex Educators and Therapists. *Publications:* "The Epic of Gilgamesh: Resolution of Concepts of Evil and Death in Ancient Babylon". *Hobby:* Music. *Address:* 4 East 89th Street, New York, NY 10128, USA.

SPIESS, Heinz, b. 13 Apr. 1920. Head of Department of Paediatrics, Poliklinik, University of Munchen, Federal Republic of Germany. m. 1944, Göttingen (divorced), 1 daughter. *Education:* Dr Med, 1945; Prof, 1957. *Appointments:* Assistant, Uni-Children Hospital, Gottingen, 1945; Research Fellow, Medical Research Council, London, 1950; Exchange Professor of 'Deutsche Forschungsgemeinschaft' in USA, 1958; Professor of Paediatrics, University of Munich, 1968-. *Publications:* "Schutzimpfungen" 1st Edition, 1958, 2nd Edition, 1985; "Impfkompendium", 2nd Edition, 1976; "Viruslebendimpfungen", 1975; "Virusdiagnostik f. Klinik u Praxis", 1979; "Immunglobuline in Prophylaxe und Therapie", 1977; "Der praenatale und perinatale Virusinfekt", 1981. *Honours:* Honorary Member, Children Society Paediatrics, 1960; Honorary Member, Institute Tub. Research, Bahia, Brasil, 1961; Redecker Prize, 1964. *Hobby:* Horseback riding. *Address:* Kinderpoliklinik der Unversität München, Pettenkoferstr 8a, 8000 Munich, Federal Republic of Germany.

SPITZER, John J, b. 9 Mar. 1927, Baja, Hungary. Professor & Head, Department of Physiology. 1 son, 1 daughter. *Education:* Medical Schools of the Universities of Budapest, Vienna, Munich; Physician's Diploma 1950, MD 1950, University of Munich, Federal Republic of Germany. *Appointments:* Lecturer, Department of Physiology, School of Medicine, Dalhousie University, Halifax, Nova Scotia, Canada, 1951-52; Assistant Professor of Physiology, Florida State University, 1952-54; Research Scientist, New York State Department of Health, Albany, New York, 1954-57; Assistant Professor of Physiology & Biophysiology, 1957-58, Associate Professor, 1958-61, Hahnemann Medical College; Visiting Scientist, Laboratory of Physiology, University of Oxford, England, 1963-64; Professor, Department of Physiology & Biophysiology, Hahnemann Medical College, 1961-73; Professor & Head of Department of Physiology, Louisiana State University Medical Centre, 1973-.

Memberships: American Physiology Society; American Heart Association; New York Academy of Sciences; Society for Experimental Biology & Medicine; American Association for the Advancement of Science; Sigma Xi; International Society of Cardiology; International Society for Heart Research; International Society of Neurochemistry; Shock Society; Association of Chairmen of Departments of Physiology. *Publications:* Over 165 publications in 'American Journal of Physiology' and other journals. *Honours:* Various positions in professional associations. *Address:* Department of Physiology, Louisiana State University Medical Centre, 1901 Paerdido Street, New Orleans, LA 70112, USA.

SPIZIZEN, John, b. 7 Feb. 1917, Winnipeg, Canada. Professor of Microbiology. m. Louise Myers, 26 Apr. 1967, San Francisco, California, USA, 1 son. *Education:* BA, University of Toronto, Canada, 1939; PhD, California Institute of Technology, USA, 1942; Postdoctoral studies, Vanderbilt University, 1942-43. *Appointments:* Instructor in Bacteriology, Loyola University Medical School, Chicago, USA, 1943; Bacteriologist and Chief of Virology, US Army 1944-46; Associate in Virus Research, Merck, Sharp and Dohme Inc 1946-54; Assistant, Associate Professor of Microbiology, Western Reserve University School of Medicine, 1954-61; Professor and Head Department of Microbiology, University of Minnesota, 1961-65; Member and Chairman, Department of Microbiology, Scripps Clinic and Research Foundation, 1965-79; Professor and Head Department of Microbiology/Immunology, University of Arizona, 1979-. *Memberships:* American Society for Microbiology; American Society of Biological Chemists; American Association for the Advancement of Science; American Association of University Professors. *Publications:* Co-author: "Medical Microbiology", 1984; More than 50 papers in various scientific journals, 1940-85. *Honours:* National Research Council Fellowship, 1942-43; Research Career Development Award, National Institutes of Health, 1956-61. *Address:* 2540 Camino la Zorrela, Tucson, AZ 85718, USA.

SPODAK, Michael Kenneth, b. 5 Nov. 1944, Brooklyn, New York, USA. Forensic Psychiatrist. 1 son, 1 daughter. *Education:* BS, Union College, 1966; MD, State University of New York, Buffalo, 1970; Diplomate: National Board Medical Examiners, American Board Neurology and Psychiatry; Intern, Mary Imogene Bassett Hospital, Cooperstown, New York, 1970-71; Resident, Johns Hopkins Hospital, Baltimore, 1974-77. *Appointments:* Practice Medicine specializing in civil and criminal forensic psychiatry, Towson, Maryland, 1977-; Chief, Psychiatry, Baltimore County General Hospital, Randallstown, 1978-85; Member, Staff, Clifton T Perkins Hospital, Centre, Jessup, 1977; Clinical Assistant Professor, Psychiatry, University of Maryland Hospital, 1983-; Psychiatrist, Consultant, Bur. Disability Insurance Social Security Administration, Workmen's Compensation Commission, Baltimore, 1981-; Director, Community Forensic Services, Mental Hygiene Administration, Baltimore, 1982-; Member, Task Force on Somatic Therapies. 2Memberships: American Academy Psychiatrists and Law; American Psychiatrist Association; Maryland Psychiatric Society; Maryland Medical Society, Chairman Occupational Health Committee, 1983-; Baltimore County Medical Society. *Publications:* Contributor, numerous articles on forensic psychiatry to professional journals, chapter to book. *Address:* 1018 Dulaney Valley Road, Towson, MD 21204, USA.

SPOTO, Peter John, b. 30 July 1926, Tampa, Florida, USA. Private Practitioner of Psychiatry. m. 30 June 1962, Georgia, 2 sons, 1 daughter. *Education:* Tulane University, 1951, Intern, Tampa Municipal Hospital, Florida, 1951-52; Resident, Southeast Louisiana Hospital, 1952-55; Training, Tulane University, 1952-55. *Appointments include:* Assistant, 1952-53, Instructor, 1953-56, Tulane University; Staff Psychiatrist, Southeast Louisiana Hospital, 1955-56; Clinical Director,

1956-59, Director of Training, 1959-61, Consultant, 1961-, Anclote Manor, Tarpon Springs, Florida; Consultant, Criminal Court, Pinellas County, 1956-; Private Practitioner, 1957-; Consultant, Department of Vocational Rehabilitation, 1958-, Department of Disability, 1958-, US Army, 1970-, Center for Human Development, University of Southern Florida, 1971-; Psychology Lecturer, St Petersburg Junior College, 1971-; Active Staff, Morton Plant Hospital, Mease Hospital; Courtesy Staff, Clearwater Community Hospital. *Memberships:* Fellow, Southern Psychiatric Association; American, Southern, Pan American Medical Associations; American Group Psychotherapy Incorporated; Pinellas County and Florida Medical Societies; Past President, Pinellas County Psychiatric Association; Florida and American Psychiatric Associations. *Hobbies:* Travel; Music; Reading; Swimming. *Address:* 611 Druid Road, East Suite 301, Clearwater, FL 33516, USA.

SPRATT, John Stricklin, b. 3 Jan. 1929, San Angelo, Texas, USA. Professor of Surgery and Community Health. m. Beverley Jane Winfiele, 27 Dec. 1951, Dequincy, Louisiana, 2 sons, 1 daughter. *Education:* AS, University of Texas, Arlington, Texas, 1945-47; BS, Southern Methodist University, Dallas, Texas, 1947-48; MD, University of Texas, Southwestern Medical School, Dallas, Texas, 1948-52; MSPH, University of Missouri School of Medicine, 1968-70; FACS; Diplomate, American Board of Surgery. *Appointments include:* Medical Director, Department of Surgery, Ellis Fischel State Cancer Hospital, Columbia, Miss, 1961-76; American Cancer Society Professor of Clinical Oncology in Surgery, 1976-81, Deputy Director, Cancer Centre, 1976-79, University of Louisville School of Medicine, Louisville, KY; Member, Graduate Faculty, University of Louisville, KY, 1976-; Member, Executive Faculty, School of Medicine, University of Louisville, KY, 1976-. *Memberships:* American College of Surgeons; American Surgical Association; Society of Surgical Oncology and numerous others. *Publications:* "Anatomy and surgical technique of groin dissection", (with W Shieber, B M Dillard), 1965; "Cancer of the Breast", (with W L Donegan), 1967; "Extenterative Surgery of the Pelvis", (with J R Butcher, E M Bricker), 1973; "Epidemiology of screening for cancer", 1982; "Neoplasms of the colon, rectum and anus", 1984; Author of over 198 papers and numerous chapters in books dealing mainly with cancer, surgery and medical education. *Honours:* Citation Classic, Citation Index, 1983; Conspicuous Service Medal, Governor of Missouri, 1984. *Hobby:* Naval Reserve. *Address:* James Graham Brown Cancer Centre, 529 South Jackson, Louisville, KY 40202, USA.

SPURGEON, Andra Lon, b. 15 June 1953, Sevierville, Tennessee, USA. Doctor of Chiropractic. m. Lucy Lovell, 16 Mar. 1974, Knoxville, Tennessee, 2 sons. *Education:* AA Horticulture, University of Tennessee, 1973; BS, Lincoln Memorial University, Harrogate, Tennessee, 1975; DC, Life Chiropractic College, Marietta, Georgia, 1978. *Appointments:* Associate Doctor, Williams Clinic, Austell, Georgia, 1978-79; Private Practitioner, Chiropractic, Knoxville, 1979-; On staff at Northwest General Hospital, Knoxville. *Memberships:* American, International, Tennessee, Georgia and Florida Chiropractic Associations; National Board of Roentgenology; Foundation for Chiropractic Education & Research. *Honours:* Pi Tau Delta, 1978; Alpha Chi Honor Society; 32nd Degree Mason; Life Member, Board of Trustees, Chiropractic College, 1984-; Life Fellowship, President of Alumni, Life College, 1983-84. *Hobbies:* Fishing; Hunting; Golf; Swimming; Racquetball. *Address:* 6313 Chapman Highway, Knoxville, TN 37920, USA.

SPUŽIĆ, Ivan, b. 2 Sep. 1928, Beograd. University Professor. m. Milica Spuzic, 4 Aug. 1957, Beograd. *Education:* MD, PhD. *Appointments:* Professor of Physiology, Medical Faculty of Beograd; Chief of Department for Experimental and Clinical Pathology, Institute for Medical Research, Belgrade; Chief of Department for Experimental and Clinical Oncology, Institute for Oncology and Radiology, Belgrade. *Memberships:* Yugoslav Society of Physiology; Yugoslav Society of Immunology; Yugoslav Society for Allergology and Clinical Immunology; Yugoslav Society of Oncology; Union of Medical Society of Yugoslavia; Interasma; European Society of Allergology and Clinical Immunology. *Publications:* "Immunological Explanations of Allergology: findings in Yugoslavia" Book 2, 1977; Numerous articles in medical journals. *Address:* Mose Pijade 19, Beograde, Yugoslavia.

SPYER, Kenneth Michael, b. 15 Sep. 1943, London, England. Head of Department of Physiology; Sophia Jex-Blake Professor of Physiology. m. Christine E Spalton, 26 Aug. 1971, Derby, 2 sons. *Education:* BSc, First Class Honours, University of Sheffield, 1966; PhD, 1969, DSc, 1979, University of Birmingham. *Appointments:* Royal Society European Programme Fellow, University of Pisa, Italy, 1972-73; Research Fellow, Department of Physiology, 1969-72, Research Fellow, Department of Physiology, 1973-78, Senior Research Fellow, Department of Physiology, 1978-80, The Medical School, University of Birmingham. *Memberships:* The Physiological Society; Deutsche Physiologische Gesellschaft; Brain Research Association; European Neurosciences Association; International Brain Research Organisation. *Publications:* Contributor of articles in scientific and medical journals. *Hobbies:* Fly-fishing; Country pursuits; Cinema; Theatre. *Address:* Department of Physiology, Royal Free Hospital, School of Medicine, Rowland Hill Street, London NW3 2PF, England.

SREEBNY, Leo M, b. 8 Jan. 1922, USA. Professor of Dental Medicine. m. Mathilda Sternfield, 9 Mar. 1945, 2 sons. *Education:* AB, Chemistry, 1942; DDS Dentistry, 1945; MS Therapeutics, 1950; PhD Pathology, 1954. *Appointments:* Director, Division of Periodontics, University of Illinois, 1945-57; Associate Professor 1957-61, Professor 1961-75, Pathology, Chairman of Department of Oral Pathology 1957-61, Chairman of Department of Oral Biology 1961-75, Director of Center for Research in Oral Biology 1967-75, University of Washington, Seattle; Dean of School of Dental Medicine 1975-79, Professor of Department of Oral Biology and Pathology 1979-, State University of New York, Stony Brook, New York. *Memberships:* Federation Dentaire Internationale; American Dental Association; International Association for Dental Research; Fellow, American Association for Advancement of Science. *Publications:* "Salivary Glands and Their Secretions", (with J Meyer), 1964; "Mechanisms of Exocrine Secretions", (with Han and Suddick), 1973; "Dental Plaque and Its Relation to Oral Disease", (with Rabinovitch), 1974; "The Salivary System", "Sugar and Human Dental Caries", (monograph), 1982; Over 100 articles in scientific learned journals. *Honours:* Fulbright Award, University Lectureship and Advanced Research, 1963; Anatomical Science Award, International Association for Dental Research, 1968; Science Award, City of Paris, France, 1979. *Hobbies:* Gardening; Music. *Address:* School of Dental Medicine, State University of New York, Stony Brook, NY 11792-8702, USA.

SRINIVASAN, Samuel Vethanayagam, b. 17 July 1936, India. Private Practitioner. m. Victoria Sathianathan, 8 June 1960, India, 2 sons. *Education:* MB BS, Fellow, Royal College of Surgeons, Edinburgh, Scotland; Diplomate, American Academy of Physical Medicine and Rehabilitation. *Appointments:* Rotating Intern, Erskine Hospital, Madurai, South India, 1960-61; Orthopaedic Surgery, Royal Lancaster Infirmary, Lancaster, England, 1966-68; Trauma/Orthopaedic Surgeon, Queen Victoria Hospital, Morecombe, 1970-73; Selly Oak Hospital, Birmingham, 1973-74; Resident, Physical Medicine and Rehabilitation, University of Michigan Hospital, Ann Arbor, Michigan, USA, 1976-79; Director, Rehabilitation Medicine, Rhode Island Hospital, Providence, Rhode Island, 1979-84; Assistant Professor, Programme in Medicine, Brown University, Rhode Island, 1979-84;

currently, Private Practitioner, Saginaw, Michigan. *Memberships:* American Association of Electromyography and Electrodiagnosis; American Society for Clinical Evoked Potentials; American Academy of Thermology. *Hobbies:* Tennis; Travel; Music. *Address:* 830 South Jefferson, Saginaw, MI 48601, USA.

SRISOPARK, Mongkol M, b. 5 Feb. 1931, Thailand. Medical Director, Acute Unit. m. Rampaipan Suwarnasarn, 9 May 1965, Vienna, Austria, 3 daughters. *Education:* Pre-medical degree, Chulalongkorn University, Bangkok, Thailand, 1949-51; MD, Mahidol University Siriraj Hospital School of Medicine, Thailand, 1952-56; Internship, Phra Mongkut Kleo & Somdet Chao Praya Hospitals, Thailand, 1956-57; Psychiatric Residency, Somdet Chao Praya Hospital, 1958-62; Psychiatrisch-Neurologische Universität Wien, Austria, 1963-65; Diploma in Neurology & Psychiatry, Vienna; Psychiatry Residency, Indiana University, Indianapolis, USA, 1979-80. *Appointments:* Staff Psychiatrist, Phrasrimahabhodi Hospital, Thailand, 1958-64; Assistant Director, Psychiatric Rehabilitation Unit, Srithunya Hospital, Thailand, 1965-69; Staff Psychiatrist & Instructor, Psychiatric Teaching Service, Somdet Chao Praya Hospital, 1970-73; Staff Psychiatrist & Section Chief, Larned State Hospital, Kansas, USA, 1974-76; Staff Physician, Grafton State School, Grafton, North Dakota, USA, 1977-80; Unit Clinical Director, WDB Region, N Dak St Hospital, Jamestown, North Dakota, USA, 1980-84; Medical Director, Acute Unit, Jamestown, 1984-. *Memberships:* American Psychiatric Association of Vienna; Thai Psychiatric Association; Thai Medical Association; American Psychiatric Association; North Dakota Medical Association; Seventh District Medical Society. *Publications:* "Schizophrenia" (in Thai textbook of Psychiatry), 1977; Various articles in professional & medical journals in English, German & Thai. *Hobbies:* Classical Music; Playing Violin. *Address:* 714 9th Street NW, Jamestown, ND 58401, USA.

STAFFEN, Alfred, b. 23 July 1935, Vienna, Austria. Surgeon. m. Gudrun, 2 May 1959, 1 son. *Education:* MD, University of Vienna; University of Dozent, Hofrat. *Appointments:* Department Head, II Surgical Klinik, University of Vienna. *Memberships:* Austrian Society of Surgeons; Austrian Society of Gastroenterology; Austrian Society of Senologie; Medical Committee, FISA. *Publications:* About 90 *Hobbies:* Motorsport; Tennis; Skiing. *Address:* 1090 Vienna, II Surgical Klinik, Spitalgasse 23, Austria.

STAFL, Adolf, b. 5 May 1931, Prague, Czechoslovakia. Professor of Gynaecology & Obstetrics. m. Jaroslava Bumanova-Stafl, 2 June 1955, 2 sons. *Education:* MD, PhD, Charles University, Prague. *Appointments:* Assistant Professor of Gynaecology & Obstetrics, Charles University, Plzen, Czechoslovakia, 1962-68; Instructor in Gynaecology & Obstetrics, Johns Hopkins University, Baltimore, Maryland, USA, 1968-69; Assistant Professor 1969-75, Associate Professor 1975-85, Professor of Gynarcology & Obstetrics, Medical College of Wisconsin, 1985-; President, International Federation for Cervical Pathology & Colposcopy, 1975-78; American Society for Colposcopy & Cervical Pathology, President 1982-84. *Memberships:* American Association of Obstetricians & Gynaecologists; Society of Gynaecological Oncologists; American Association of Obstetricians & Gynaecologists; Wisconsin Obstetrical-Gynaecological Society; Milwaukee Gynaecological Society. *Publication:* "Atlas of Colposcopy" (with P Kolstad), 1972, revised 1977, 1982, translated into Italian, German, Japanese. *Honours:* Gerald P Lamberd Award for organisation of Cancer Detection programme in state of Wisconsin; Distinguished Scientific Achievement Award, American Society for Colposcopy & Cervical Pathology, 1984. *Address:* 17305 Holly Lane, Brookfield, WI 53005, USA.

STAHL, Jan Steven, b. 28 Jan. 1948, New York, USA. Dentist. m. Geri Weinstein, 21 Nov. 1973, New York, USA, 1 son, 1 daughter. *Education:* BA Art History 1970, BS Biological Sciences, Rutgers University;

DDS, New York University Dental School, 1973. *Appointments:* Dentist, 1973-82; President, Chief Executive Officer, PJS Scientific Ltd, 1982-84; Vice-President, Advanced Bio Systems, 1985-. *Membership:* American Dental Association, 1973-. *Honour:* Dean's List, Rutgers University, 1970. *Hobbies:* Tennis, Photography; Boating; Travel. *Address:* 3141 Ann Street, Baldwin Harbor, NY 11510, USA.

STAHL, Stephen Michael, b. 14 Sep. 1951, Wauseon, Ohio, USA. Executive Director. m. Cynthia Davis, 1973, 2 daughters. *Education:* BS, MD, Northwestern University; PhD, Neuropharmacology, University of Chicago. *Appointments:* Assistant Director, Stanford Mental Health Clinical Research Centre, Stanford University Medical Centre, 1981-85; Instructor, Assistant Professor, Psychiatry, Stanford University Medical School; Guest Research Physician, Donner Lab, California; Director, Movement Disorders, Research Clinic, California; Medical Director, Schizophrenia Biological Research Centre, California; Ward Chief, Staff Physician, Psychiatry Service, California; Director, Laboratory of Neuropsychopharmacology, California; Neuroscience Consultant, Merck Sharp & Dohme, Pennsylvania & New Jersey; Neuropsychopharmacology Consultant, Merrell Dow Research Laboratory, Ohio; Director, Clinical Sciences, Associate Medical Director, Principal Scientist, Alza Corporation, California; Executive Director, 1985-, Clinical Neuroscience, Director, Laboratory of Clinical Neuropharmacology, Merck Sharp & Dohme Research Laboratories, Harlow, England; Honorary Consultant, Visiting Clinical Investigator, Institute of Psychiatry & Maudsley Hospital. *Memberships:* American Academy of Child Psychiatry; American Academy of Neurology; American College of Neuropsychopharmacology, various offices; American Psychiatric Association; etc. *Honours:* French Ministry Visiting Professor of Psychiatry & Neurology, Lyon, France, 1984; Merrell Dow Visiting Professor, Psychiatry & Pharmacology, Chicago, 1983; etc. *Address:* Neuroscience Research Centre, Merck Sharp and Dohme Research Labs, Terlings Park, Eastwick Road, Harlow, Essex CM20 2QR, England.

STAHLE, Jan, b. 28 Sep. 1924, Eksjo, Sweden. Professor; Chairman. m. Ulla Hillman, 12 June 1948, Ljungskile, 2 sons, 1 daughter. *Education:* MD, 1950, PhD, 1958, Uppsala University. *Appointments:* Assistant Professor, 1960-78, Professor, Chairman, 1979-, Otorhino-laryngology, Uppsala University; Naval Medical Officer, Lieutenant Commander, Reserve, 1950-79. *Memberships:* Fellow, Swedish Society of Medicine; President, Barany Society, 1978-. *Publications:* "Electro-nystagmography in the Caloric and Rotatory Tests", 1958; "Vestibular function on earth and in space", 1970; "Frontiers in vestibular and oculomotor Research", 1979; "The Vestibular System: Fundamental and Clinical Observations", 1984. *Honours:* Honorary Member, Oto-Rhino-Laryngological Society of Japan, 1978. *Address:* Department of Otolaryngology, Akademiska Sjukhuset, Uppsala University, S-751 85 Uppsala, Sweden.

STAINES, Norman Allyn, b. 3 Aug. 1942, Solihull, England. Reader, Immunology, King's College, London. m. Anne S. Hamblin, 13 July 1984. *Education:* BSc, Zoology, 1966, PhD, Immunology, 1971, Edinburgh University. *Appointments:* Head, Transplantation Immunology, Searle Research Laboratories, High Wycombe, until 1977; Head, Immunogenetics Laboratory, Kennedy Institute of Rheumatology, Hammersmith, London, 1977-81. *Memberships:* British Society for Immunology; British Transplantation Society; Royal Society of Medicine; Transplantation Society, USA. *Publications:* Co-Author, "Introducing Immunology", 1985; articles in professional journals including 'Immunology'; 'European Journal of Immunology'; etc. *Address:* Immunology Section, King's College London, Chelsea Campus, Manresa Road, London SW3 6LX, England.

STALPORT, Jean Arthur Ernest, b. 18 July 1920, Tihange, Belgium. Medical Doctor; Certified Teacher in Higher Education. m. Suzanne Antoine Moussiaux, 20 Apr. 1948, 7 sons, 2 daughters. *Education:* MD, University of Liege; Certified Teacher in Higher Education, University Louvain. *Appointments:* Chief of Queen Astrid Surgical Clinic, Huy, Belgium; Course Teacher, Lecturer, Catholic University of Louvain. *Memberships:* Past President, Belgian Society of Gastroenterology; Past President, Belgian Society of Surgery; International Society of Surgery; North Lotharingian Society of Gastroenterology; Past Member, International College of Surgeons; Member, Societe d'evaluation des dommages corporels; Member, International College of Digestive Surgery. *Publications:* 105 publications mostly on biliary physiology. *Honours:* President, Professor, Lucien Dautrebande Foundation; Commander, Belgian Order of Leopold. *Address:* 3 Avenue Batta, a 5200 Huy, Belgium.

STALSBERG, Helge, b. 7 Oct. 1932, Oslo, Norway. Professor, Morphology. m. Else-Marie Paulsen, 14 Jan. 1961, 1 son, 2 daughters. *Education:* Cand. Med., Oslo, 1957; MD, 1965. *Appointments:* Research Fellow, 1960-61, Assistant Professor, Anatomy, 1962-65, Assistant Professor, Pathology, 1966-70, University of Oslo; Resident, Pathology, Oslo City Hospital, 1965-66; US Public Health Service Fellow, Embryology, Carnegie Institute, 1966-67; Consultant, Cancer Registry, Norway, 1970-71; Professor, Morphology, 1972-, Pro-Rector, 1974-75, Rector, 1981-85, University of Tromso; Head, Pathology, Tromso Regional Hospital, 1972-; Consultant Special Adviser, WHO, 1978-. *Memberships:* Chairman: Norwegian University Council, 1982, 1984, Council of Higher Education in North Norway, 1982-85; Board Member, Norway Cancer Society, 1972-82; Research Foundation, University of Tromso, 1984-; Norwegian Medical Association; Norwegian Pathology Society; International Academy of Pathology. *Publications:* Articles in professional journals; "Effects of the Extirpation of the Epiphysis cerebri in 6 day chick embryos", Doctoral Thesis, 1965. *Hobbies:* Skiing; Mountain Hiking; Gardening; Piano Music. *Address:* Institute of Medical Biology, University of Tromso, N 9001 Tromso, Norway.

STANKIEWICZ, Andrzej, b. 14 Oct. 1942, Warsaw, Poland. Chief, Ophthalmological Clinic. m. Maria Hetman, 15 June 1975, 1 son, 1 daughter. *Education:* MD, Military Academy of Lodz, 1971; Dr. Hab., Ophthalmology, 1975. *Appointments:* Assistant to Senior Assistant Ophthalmological Clinic, Medical Academy of Lodz, 1965-77; Chief, Ophthalmology, Child Health Centre, Warsaw, 1977-79; Chief, Ophthalmological Clinic, Academy of Bialystock, 1979-. *Memberships:* Polish Ophthalmological Society, Presidium Member. *Publications:* "Orbital Surgery", 'Surgery in Ophthalmology', 1985. *Honour:* Gold Medal of Awards, 1979. *Hobbies:* Hunting; Fishing; Bridge; Chess; Classical Music-Bach. *Address:* ul. Szpitaina 35A M11, Bialystok 15-276, Poland.

STAPLES, Eugene Leo, b. 26 Aug. 1926, Walker, Minnesota, USA. Vice-Chancellor for Hospital Administration. m. Noreen Janice Henry, 23 June 1951, 1 daughter. *Education:* BA, 1950; MHA, 1952; The University of Minnesota. *Appointments:* Assistant Director and Assistant Professor, The University of Minnesota Hospitals, 1955-60; Administrator of West Virginia University Hospital, Associate Professor, Departments of Medicine and Psychiatry, 1960-82; Hospital Administrator, The University of Kansas Medical Center, 1982-. *Memberships:* American Hospital Association; American College of Hospital Administrators; Kansas City Area Hospital Association; American Medical Association. *Hobbies:* Gardening; Swimming. *Address:* The University of Kansas Medical Center, 39th and Rainbow, Kansas City, KS 66103, USA.

STARAJ, Sergio, b. 29 July 1946, Yugoslavia. Forensic Pathologist. m. Elizabeth Anne Stanyer, 6 Dec. 1964, Sydney, New South Wales, 1 son. *Education:* MB BS, Sydney University, 1971; Diploma in Criminology, 1984. *Appointments:* Forensic Pathologist, 1979-84; 1985-; Director of Pathology, Manly Hospital, 1984-85. *Memberships:* Fellow, The Royal College of Pathologists of Australia, 1976; Australian Association of Clinical Biochemists; Endocrine Society of Australia; Australian Diabetes Society; The Forensic Science Society; The Forensic Society of Australia; The Australian Society of Microbiology. *Publication:* "Testicolar Size: The Effects of Aging, Malnutrition and Illness", 'Journal of Andrology', 1985 (co-author). *Hobby:* Marathoning. *Address:* 6 Cambourne Avenue, St Ives, New South Wales, Australia 2075.

STARCICH, Riccardo, b. 14 Jan. 1925, Buye, Italy. Chief of Institute of Medical Pathology, University of Parma. m. Dott. Solassi Carla, 20 Dec. 1952, Parma, 1 son, 1 daughter. *Education:* Degree in Medicine and Surgery, University of Parma. *Appointments:* Assistant, Medical Clinic; Vice-Chief of Medical Clinic; Chief of Post-degree School in Clinical Haematology and Laboratory; Chief of Institute of Medical Pathology; University of Parma. *Memberships:* Fellow, International Academy of Chest Physicians and Surgeons; Italian Society of Internal Medicine, Pharmacology, Cardiology, etc. *Publications:* 'Terminal Deoxynucleotidyl transferase in human fetal tissues' in "Terminal transferase in immunology and leukemia" (co-author), 1982; "AMA Drug Evaluations", 5th edition (co-author) (a translation of some chapters), 1985; "Angina Pectoris: An Isolated Syndrome of Coronary Cardiopathy", Il Pensiero Scientifico Ed. (In Press). *Address:* Institute of Medical Pathology, University of Parma, Via Gramsci 14, 43100 Parma, Italy.

STEELE, Richard Donald, b. 12 Jan. 1943, Modesto, California, USA. Research Health Scientist. m. Karen Moxness Dorn, 4 July 1983, Spokane, Washington, 2 stepdaughters. *Edcuation:* BS, Physics, Stanford University, Palo Alto, 1964; MA, 1966, PhD, Slavic Linguistics, 1973, Harvard University; Certificate, US-USSR Exchange Language Study Program, Moscow State University, USSR, 1973. *Appointments:* Assistant Professor, Cornell University, Department of Modern Languages and Linguistics, Ithaca, New York, 1973-74; Lecturer, Harvard University and Massachusetts Institute of Technology, Modern Language Department, Cambridge, Massachusetts, 1974-76; Assistant Professor, Grinnell College, Russian Department, Iowa, 1976-80; Research Health Scientist, Rehabilitation Research and Development Center, Veterans Administration Medical Center, Palo Alto, California, 1982-. *Memberships:* Phi Beta Kappa; IEEE; EMBS Technical Interest Committee on Rehabilitation Engineering; IEEE Engineering in Medicine and Biology Society; IEEE Social Implications of Technology Society; IEEE Computer Society; International Society for Alternative and Augmentative Communication. *Publications:* "A Microprocessor-Driven Optacon Interface to a Reading Aid for the Blind", ICRE Proceedings, 1984; "Use of Solid State Imaging Components in a Reading Aid for the Blind", RESNA Proceedings, 1985; 'Towards Computer-Aided Visual Communications for Amphasics, RESNA Proceedings, 1985; "An Implementation of Computer-Assisted Visual Communication for Aphasics" ANA Proceedings, 1985. *Honours:* Graduation with Distinction, Stanford University, 1964; Maud E Warwick and NDEA Graduate Fellowship, Harvard University, 1964-68. *Hobbies:* Travel to Foreign Countries; Environmental Activities; Racquet Sports; Numismatics. *Address:* Rehabilitation Research and Development Center (153), Veterans Administration Medical Center, 3801 Miranda Avenue, Palo Alto, CA 94304, USA.

STEELE, Stuart James, b. 13 Jan. 1930, London, England. Consultant in Obstetrics and Gynaecology, The Middlesex Hospital, The Hospital for Women, The Margaret Pyke Centre; Reader in Obstetrics and Gynaecology, Middlesex Hospital Medical School. m. Jill Westgate Smith, 23 Oct. 1965, 2 sons. *Education:* MA, MB BChir (Cantab); D Obs RCOG; MRCOG.

Appointments: House Surgeon, Casualty Officer, The Middlesex Hospital; House Officer, Gastroenterology, Central Middlesex Hospital; Surgical Registrar, The Middlesex Hospital; RMO Queen Charlotte's Maternity Hospital; RSO The Hospital for Women, Soho Square; Senior House Officer, Canadian Red Cross Memorial Hospital, Taplow; Registrar, The Middlesex Hospital and The Hospital for Women; Senior Registrar, The Whittington Hospital; Senior Registrar, Senior Lecturer, The Middlesex Hospital. *Memberships:* British Medical Association; Fellow, Royal Society of Medicine; Blair Bell Research Society; British Medical Laser Association; British Fertility Society; British Society for Colposcopy and Cervical Pathology. *Publications:* Chapter on Reproductive Endocrinology in "Essentials of Endocrinology", 1982; Natural History of Cervical Intraepithelial Neoplasia', 'Acta Cytologica', 1983; Author, 'Gynaecology, Obstetrics and the Neonate", 1985. *Honours:* WHO Fellow, 1969; Fellow of The Royal College of Obstetricians and Gynaecologists, 1975. *Hobbies:* Opera; Ballet; Theatre; Gardening. *Address:* Middlesex Hospital, Mortimer Street, London W1N 8AA, England.

STEEN, Bertil, b. 15 Apr. 1938, Stockholm, Sweden. Professor of Geriatric Medicine, Physician-in-Chief. m. Gunilla Hörnstein, 1 June 1968, Fru Alstad, 1 son. *Education:* MD, 1964; MD, PhD, 1977. *Appointments:* Assistant in Department of Anatomy 1958-64, Assistant Professor 1978-80, University of Göteborg; Resident, Sahlgren's Hospital, Göteborg, 1964-66; Resident and Physician-in-Chief 1966-80, Deputy Chairman 1968-77, Vasa Hospital, Göteborg; Professor, University of Umeå) 1980-81; Consultant to World Health Organisation, Swedish Board of Health and Welfare, Swedish National Food Administration Board and Swedish Medical Research Council. *Memberships:* Board Member 1978-, Chairman 1985-, Swedish Geriatric Association; Scientific Secretary 1978-83, Deputy President 1983-, Swedish Society for Research on Ageing; International Psychogeriatric Association; International Union of Nutirional Sciences Committee on Nutrition and Ageing; Scientific Council of Federation Internale des Associations de Personnes Agées. *Publications:* Author or coauthor of several international and Swedish textbooks on geriatric medicine; Author or co-author of about 300 scientific publications in fields including geriatric medicine. *Hobby:* Music. *Address:* Varnhem Hospital, S-212 16 Malmö, Sweden.

STEENBERGHE, Daniel van, b. 21 May 1947, Zottegem, Belgium. Professor of Periodontology. m. Baroness K van Hovell tot Westerflier, 8 June 1974, Ohé en Laak, Netherlands, 2 sons, 1 daughter. *Education:* MD 1971, Dental Licence 1972, Catholic University, Leuven, Belgium; Specialist in oral & maxillofacial surgery, ibid, 1976; Specialist in Periodontology, University of Amsterdam, 1975-79; PhD, Catholic University, Leuven, 1979. *Appointments:* Assistant, Department of General Surgery, Municipal Hospital, Diest, 1972-73; Assistant, Department of Oral & Maxillofacial Surgery, University Clinic St Rafael, Leuven, 1973-75; Researcher, Assistant Professor, Department of Periodontology, University of Amsterdam, 1975-79; Professor, Faculty of Medicine, Catholic University, Leuven, Head of Department of Periodontology (School of Dentistry, oral pathology & oral surgery), Guest Professor, University of Amsterdam, University of Limburg (Belgium), 1979-. *Memberships:* Founding President, Belgian Society of Periodontology; Board Member, Dutch Society for Oral Biology; International Society for Oral Physiology; British, Dutch Societies of Periodontology; Founding Member, European Society of Maxillofacial Bone Pathology. *Publications:* More than 100 articles & abstracts on the neurophysiology of the trigeminal system in man, periodontology, oral pathology; Mainly in 'Journal of Periodontal Research', 'Archives of Oral Biology', 'Brain Research', 'Pflügers Archiv', and others. *Hobbies:* Art; Politics. *Address:* Department of Periodontology, Catholic University Leuven, Kapucijnenvoer 7, B-3000 Leuven, Belgium.

STEEVES, Roy Alexander, b. 19 Apr. 1955, Moncton, New Brunswick, Canada. Clinical Pharmacy Co-ordinator; Residency Programme Director. *Education:* BSc, Pharm, 1977; Pharm.D, 1981. *Appointments:* Staff Pharmacist, Waite's Drug Mart, Summerside, 1977; Staff Pharmacist, 1977-79, Clinical Pharmacy Co-ordinator, Residency Programme Director, 1981-, Saint John Regional Hospital, Saint John, New Brunswick. *Memberships:* New Brunswick Pharmaceutical Society; New Brunswick Pharmacists' Association; Nova Scotia Pharmaceutical Society; Canadian Pharmaceutical Association; Canadian Society and American Society of Hospital Pharmacists; Canadian Foundation for Pharmacy; Registrant, Pharmacy Examining Board of Canada. *Publications:* Co-Author, "EMIT theophylline assay at reduced cost", 'Ther Drug Monit.', 1982; "Effects of metoclopramide on the pharmacokinetics of a slow-release theophylline product", 'Clinical Pharmacy', 1982; "A Comparison of various types of patient instruction in the proper administration of metered dose inhalers", 'Drug Intell. Clin. Pharm.' 1982. *Honours:* Kenneth F Finger Award, 1981; O'Brien Fellowship, 1979. *Hobbies:* Cooking; Photography; Golf. *Address:* Pharmacy Dept, Saint John Regional Hospital, PO Box 2100, Saint John, New Brunswick, Canada E2L 4L2.

STEFANOVIĆ, Petar, b. 11 May 1924, Požarevac, Yugoslavia. Medical Surgeon. m. Andja, 10 Sep. 1954, 2 sons. *Education:* Dr sci Otorhinolaryngology Surgery, Faculty of Medicine, Belgrade, 1952. *Appointments:* Assistant in Clinic of Otorhinolaryngology, 1956, Chief of Department ENT Clinic 1956, Assistant Professor Otorhinolaryngology, 1960, Professor 1965, Honorary Professor of Faculty of Stomatology, Medical Faculty, Belgrade. *Memberships:* Academy Medicine Societe Sebian, Belgrade; President 1972-74, General Secretary 1968-72, Serbian Medical Society; Société d'Oto-Rhono-Laryngologie et de Pathologie Cervico-Faciale, France. *Publications include:* Co-author of handbook of medicine; "Papilomes of Laryngis", habilitacia; "Faculte Medicine in Belgrade", 1975; "Premalignant lesion of the larynx', monograph; "A Textbook of Otorhinolaryngology", 1984; About 250 articles. *Hobby:* Photography. *Address:* University ENT Clinic, Medical Faculty, Pasterova 2, Belgrade, Yugoslavia.

STEFANU, Constantine, b. 1 June 1930, Patras, Greece. Medical School Administrator. m. Mary L Pate, 4 Jan. 1975, Memphis, Tennessee, USA, 1 son, 2 daughters. *Education:* AB, Jacksonville State, Ala, 1957; MS, Alabama Medical College, 1969; PhD, University of Alabama, 1972. *Appointments:* Computer Specialist, Heart Research, Veterans Hospital, Birmingham, Ala, 1964-67; Epidemiologist, Medical College of Alabama, 1967-72; Director of Management and Planning, University of Tennessee Medical School, 1972-75; Director of Planning and Institutional Studies, 1975-, Associate Professor, Chairman, Division of Health Planning and Epidemiology, University of Texas Health Science Centre, Dallas, Texas. *Memberships:* National Chairman, Planning Group, Association of American Medical Colleges; Assistant Secretary, American Medical Association; Member, American College of Epidemiology; American Public Health Association; Society for Colleges and University Planning; Phi Delta Kappa; Alpha Mu Gammin Language Club. *Publications:* 'Patient Acuity: An Important Factor Contributing to Laboratory Costs in a Teaching Hospital', 1984; 'MBO: An Effective Mechanism to Improve Productivity in a Teaching Hospital', 1983; 'Impact of a Family Practice Residency Program on Physician Location in Small Communities', 1980. *Honours:* Hope Chest Award, National Multiple Sclerosis Society, 1969. *Hobbies:* Hiking; Fishing; Music. *Address:* 7140 Baxtershire Drive, Dallas, TX 75230, USA.

STEFFEL, Patricia E Steadman, b. 21 Apr. 1924, Youngstown, Ohio, USA. Director of Hospital Nursing Service and Clinical Professor of Medical and Surgical Nursing. m. George L Steffel, 30 April 1949, Youngstown, Ohio, 4 daughters (1 deceased). *Education:* Diploma, RN St Elizabeth Hospital School of Nursing, Youngstown, Ohio, 1945; Certificate in Public Health, Case Western Reserve University, Cleveland, 1946; BSN, 1948, MSN, 1964, Case Western Reserve University; Certified Nursing Administration Advanced, American Nurses Association, 1984. *Appointments:* Medical Supervisor, University Hospital, Cleveland, Ohio, 1964-67; Director of Nursing, Health Hill Hospital, Cleveland, Ohio, 1967-70; Director of Nursing, Highland View Hospital, Sunny Acres Skilled Nursing Facility, 1975-81; Acting Director of School of Nursing, Cleveland Metropolitan General Hospital, School of Nursing and Highland View Hospital, Sunny Acres Skilled Facility, 1976-. *Memberships include:* American Nursing Association; Ohio Nursing Association; American Hospital Association; American Organisation of Nursing Executives; Cleveland League of Nursing, National Rehabilitation Association etc. *Publications:* Co-author: 'Reducing Devices for Pressure Sores with Respect to Nursing Care Procedures' "Research" vol 29 1980; Editor: "Facing Spinal Cord Injury" 1982; Co-author: chapter on 'Skin Integrity' in "Neurological and Neurosurgical Nursing" edited by Mariah Snyder, 1982. *Honours:* Greater Cleveland Nursing Association Award of Recognition as Nurse Administrator, 1980; American Society of Nursing Administrators, Nominee 1984. *Hobbies:* Hiking; Swimming. *Address:* 910 Colony Drive, Highland Heights, OH 44143, USA.

STEFFEN, Jan Andrzej, b. 17 July 1936, Poznan, Poland. Associate Director for Research Coordination; Head, Department of Immunology, The M Sklowowska-Curie Memorial Center of Oncology, Warsaw. m. Alicja Grabowska, 8 December 1978. *Education:* Graduate from Medical School, Poznan, 1958; MD, 1960; Dr habil of Medicine, 1965. *Appointments:* Research Fellow, Department of Pathophysiology, Medical School Poznan, 1958-61; Rockefeller Foundation Fellow, Medical Center, Denver, Colorado, USA, 1961-62; Research Associate, Department Hum. Genetics, Medical School Poznan, 1963-69; Associate Professor, Department of Radiobiology, 1970-74, Head, Department of Immunology, 1974-, Associate Director, 1976-, The M Sklodowska-Curie Memorial Institute, Center of Oncology, Warsaw. *Memberships:* Coordinating Committee, Programme for Fight Against Cancer in Poland, President, Section for Basic Research on Cancer; Scientific Council, Ministry of Health; Member. several committees of Polish Academy of Sciences; Member, Council of Europe Association for Cancer Research. *Publications:* "An Introduction to Human Genetics", 1965 (in Polish); Co-author and Editor, "Medical Genetics", 1970 (in Polish and Russian); Articles include: 'Life Cycle Analysis of Mammalian Cells', 1963 (Co-author); 'In Vitro Kinetics of Human Lymphocytes Activated by Mitogens', 1978, etc. *Honours:* Several scientific awards from the Polish Academy of Sciences, Minister of Health, Award of City of Poznan, Golden Cross of Merit. *Hobbies:* Photography; Swimming. *Address:* Maklakiewicza 17, 02-642 Warsaw, Poland.

STEHELIN, Dominique, b. 4 Sep. 1943, Thoisy, France. Head of the INSERM-CNRS Research Unit of Molecular Oncology, Pasteur Institute, Lille, France. divorced, 1 daughter. *Education:* PhD, Organic Chemistry, 1969; PhD, Biochemistry, 1972; Strasbourg. *Appointments:* Assistant then Associate Researcher, CNRS (Centre National de la Recherche Scientifique), Strasbourg, 1969, Villejuif, Paris, 1976; Post-doctoral Fellow, University of California, San Francisco Medical Center, 1972-75; Laboratory Chief of INSERM (Institut National de la Sante et de la recherche Medicale) Unite 186, Pasteur Institute, Ille, 1979; Professor at Pasteur Institute, 1984; Director of Research, CNRS, 1985. *Memberships:* American Society of Microbiology, 1983-; European Molecular Biology Organization, 1983-. *Publications:* Contributor to professional journals and publications, including: "Discovery of the first viral/cellular oncogene', 'Journal of Molecular Biology', 'Nature', 1976. *Honours:* Grand

Prix of the Academy of Science, Paris, 1975; Prix Rosen, 1980; Prix Griffuel, 1982; Prix Lacassagne, 1984; Chevalier de l'Ordre National du Merite, 1982. *Hobbies:* Skiing; Scuba Diving; Sailboarding. *Address:* Institut Pasteur, 1 Rue Calmette, 59019, Lille, France.

STEIDLER, Nandor Edward, b. 13 Oct. 1951, Melbourne, Australia. Private Practice of Oral and Maxillofacial Surgery 1986-; Senior, Research Associate, Department of Dental Medicine& Surgery, University of Melbourne. m. Chee Chen, 7 July 1973, Melbourne, Australia. *Education:* LDS, Dental Board of Victoria, 1974; BDSc 1975, MDSc 1978, PhD, 1981, University of Melbourne; Fellow, Royal Australasian College of Dental Surgeons, 1978. *Appointments include:* Various appointments as demonstrator, University of Melbourne, 1975-1980; Research Fellow, Department of Dental Medicine & Surgery, University of Melbourne, 1981-83; Various residencies & registrarships, 1975-77; Assistant, Oral Pathology Diagnostic Service, University of Melbourne, 1978-83; Faciomaxillary Dental Surgeon, Western General Hospital, 1980-84; Senior Lecturer, Department of Dental Medicine & Surgery, University of Melbourne, 1983-86; parallel appointments at Austin, Royal Melbourne & Royal Dental Hospitals, Melbourne, 1983-. *Memberships:* International Association for Dental Research, 1975-; Australian Dental Association, 1975-; Clinical Oncological Society of Australia, 1976-; Australian & New Zealand Association of Oral & Maxillofacial Surgeons, 1979-; International Association of Oral Pathologists, 1977-. *Publications:* Numerous papers in scientific & professional journals. *Hobbies:* Motor Cars; Stamp & Coin collecting; Aquaria; Gardening. *Address:* 62 Normanby Road, Kew, Victoria 3101, Australia.

STEIN, Valerie T, b. 22 May 1951, St Louis, Missouri, USA. Counseling Psychologist, North Arizona University. *Education:* BA, Sociology, Education (magna cum laude), 1972, MA, Counseling, 1976, St Louis University; EdD, Educational Psychology, Texas Tec University, 1981. *Appointments:* Career Counselor, St Louis University, 1973-76; Career Counselor, University of Wisconsin, Eau Claire, 1976-78; Instructor, College of Education, Texas Tech University, 1981; Therapist, Private Practice, Silver City, New Mexico, 1982; Counselor and Assistant Professor, Western New Mexico University, 1981-82. *Memberships:* American Psychological Association; American Society of Clinical Hypnosis; American Association for Counseling and Development; Society for Clinical and Experimental Hypnosis; Arizona Counseling Association. *Publications:* 'Counselor Burnout', 'Arizona Counseling Journal' (in press); 'Hypnotherapy of Involuntary Movements', 'American Journal of Clinical Hypnosis', 23(2), 128-131; Co-author, 'Cognitive Expansion, Relaxation and Music in a Recognition Task', 'Journal of Suggestive-Accelerative Learning and Teaching', 5 (2), 99-105. *Honours:* Jones Leadership Fellow in Education, Texas Tech University, 1978-79; Speaker, Presenter at 12 different conferences/workshops. *Hobbies:* Metaphysics; Spiritual Healing. *Address:* 115 E Terrace, Suite 18, Flagstaff, AZ 86001, USA.

STEINBERG, Melvyn Arthur, b. 8 July 1941, Long Island, New York, USA. Associate Professor, Fixed Restorative Dentistry, University of Maryland Dental School. m. Susan Niles, 3 May 1980, Miami, Florida, 1 son, 1 daughter. *Education:* BS, DDS, University of Maryland. *Appointments include:* Private practice, Moodus, Connecticut; Director of Education, L D Pankey Institute for Advanced Dental Education. *Memberships:* American Dental Association; American Equilibration Society. *Publications include:* "The Functionally Generated Path Technique: Laboratory Procedures", with J Snyder; "The Functionally Generated Path Technique: Variations", with J P Potts. Instructional media, including numerous audiovisual productions. Inventor, Electronic Centric Relation Simulator. *Honours:* Numerous certificates of appreciation, recognition; 'Boss of the Year', South

Dade Dental Assistants Society, 1980; 'Golden Pencil Award', drawings, International College of Dentists. *Hobbies:* Skiing; Scuba diving; Running. *Address:* University of Maryland Dental School, Department of Fixed Restorative Dentistry, 666 West Baltimore Street, Baltimore, MD 21201, USA.

STENBÄCK, Frej Gustav, b. 11 Apr. 1941, Vöyri, Finland. Associate Professor, Department of Pathology, m. Leena Lustig, 7 Aug. 1982, Äanekoski, 1 son, 1 daughter. *Education:* BSc, 1962; MD, 1966; Licensed to practice medicine, 1966; PhD, 1970; Diploma in Pathology, 1973. *Appointments:* Resident, University of Oulu, 1963-69; Assistant Professor, 1970-73, Associate Professor, 1974, University of Nebraska, USA; Associate Professor, University of Oulu, 1975-. *Memberships:* Finnish Physicians Society; Finnish Medical Society; International Society of Pathology; International Society of Dermatopathology; American Association for Cancer Research; European Association for Cancer Research; International Society of Gynaecological Pathologists. *Publications:* "Promotion in the Morphogenesis of chemically inducible skin tumors: A histological and histochemical study", 1969; "Morphology of experimentally induced respiratory tumors in Syrian Golden hamster", 1977; "Life history and histopathology of ultraviolet light-induced skin tumors", 1978; Environmental health criteria 14. ultraviolet radiation", 1979; "Initiation and promotion at different ages and doses in 2,200 mice", 1981; "Ovarian tumors in Atlas of Human Reproduction", 1982. *Honours:* University of Oulu Fellowship, 1968; Finnish Cancer Society Fellowship, 1978; Nordic Council Fellowship, 1985. *Address:* Department of Pathology, University of Oulu, Kajaanintie 52D, 90220 Oulu 22, Finland.

STENHOUSE, Diane Rosina, b. 31 Oct. 1939, Wellington, New Zealand. Dentist. *Education:* BDS, Melbourne University, 1964; LDS, Victoria, 1964. *Appointments:* Dental Officer, Royal Melbourne Dental Hospital, 1964-78; Civilian Dental Officer, Defence Department, Australian Army Dental Corps, 1979-83; Private practice (2 practices), 1984-. *Memberships:* Fédération Dentaire Internationale; Australian Dental Association; Melbourne University (Women) Graduates Association. *Hobbies:* Travel; Reading; Photography; Music. *Address:* 233 Balwyn Road, North Balwyn, Melbourne, Victoria 3104, Australia.

STENRAM, Unne, b. 29 Dec. 1926, Malmö, Sweden. Professor and Head of Department of Pathology, University of Lund, University Hospital, Lund. 4 daughters. *Education:* MD; PhD. *Appointments:* Assistant Professor of Pathology, Lund, 1958; Associate Professor of Pathology, Uppsala, 1962; Professor of Pathology, University of Lund, 1973-. *Memberships:* Royal Physiographic Society, Lund; European Association for Cancer Research; Swedish Society of Medicine; European Society of Pathology. *Publications:* "Relationships between essential amino acids in the diet and nucleolar size in the liver of rat", thesis, Lund, 1956; "Cytological, radioautographic and ultrastructural studies on the effect of 5-fluorouracil on rat liver", Z. Zellforsch, 71, 207, 1966. *Address:* Department of Pathology, University of Lund, University Hospital, S-221 85 Lund, Sweden.

STEPANIK, Joseph, b. 22 Oct. 1922, Vienna, Austria. Ophthalmologist; Eye Surgeon. m. (1) Hanna Safar, 25 Mar. 1948, Vienna, 2 sons, 1 daughter, (2) Louise Wolf, 21 June 1980. *Education:* Dr. Med; Medical School, University of Vienna, 1940-42, 1945-47; Internship, City Hospital, Vienna, 1947-48; Resident, 2nd University Eye Clinic, Vienna, 1949-60, Eye Dept., University of Cincinnati, Ohio, USA, 1952-53; Research Fellow, Wilmer Institute, Columbia University, New York, 1953-54. *Appointments:* Head, Eye Dept., City Hospital, Vienna, 1960; Assistant Professor, 1961, Associate Professor, 1970, Ophthalmology, University of Vienna. *Memberships:* Ophthal. Ges. Wien; Öster Biophysikal Ges.; European Glaucoma Society; Association Eye Research. *Publications:* 119

scientific articles; Monography: "Die Tonographie", 1961. *Honour:* 1st Class Austrian Honorary Cross for Arts and Science. *Hobby:* Chamber Music (Piano). *Address:* Schloessel Grasse 22, A-1080 Vienna, Austria.

STEPHENS, Simon Dafydd Glyn, b. 2 July 1942, Caerfyrddyn, Wales. Physician-in-Charge, Welsh Institute of Hearing Research, Cardiff. m. Janig Bodiou, 21 July 1970, Brittany, France, 1 son, 2 daughters. *Education:* BSc, Physiology, 1962; MB, BS 1965, Charing Cross Hospital Medical School, University of London. *Appointments include:* Scientific staff, MRC Applied Psychology Unit, Cambridge/Acoustics Section, National Physical Laboratory, Teddington, 1967-71; Clinical Research Fellow, Institute of Sound & Vibration Research, Southampton University, 1971-76; Consultant, Audiological Medicine, Royal National Throat, Nose & Ear Hospital, London, 1976-85. *Memberships:* International Association of Physicians in Audiology; International Society of Audiology; European Association of Audiophonological Centres; Royal Socoety of Medicine; Medical Disability Society. *Publications include:* Editor: "Disorders of Auditory Function 2", 1976, "Disorders with Defective Hearing", 1985; Author, 'Audiological Rehabilitation: Management Model I' in 'Audiology', 1981; 'Subjective & Electrophysiologic Tests in Brainstem Lesions' in 'Archives of Otolaryngology', 1976. *Honours:* T. S. Littler Prize, British Society of Audiology, 1972; Inserm/CIBA Anglo-French Exchange bursary, 1973. *Hobbies:* Celtic languages & culture; Smallholding; Cycling; Running. *Address:* Welsh Institute of Hearing Research, University Hospital of Wales, Heath Park, Cardiff, Wales.

STEPHENSON, Hugh Edward, b. 1 June 1922, Columbia, Missouri, USA. Professor; Associate Dean. m. Sarah N. Dickinson, 15 Aug. 1969, Georgetown, 1 son, 1 daughter. *Education:* AB, BS, University of Missouri; MD, Washington University School of Medicine, St Louis. *Appointments:* Assistant, Surgery, Washington and New York Universities; Chairman, Surgery, UMMC; Professor, Chief, General Surgery, Chief of Staff, University of Missouri Hospital and Clinics; Associate Dean, Clinical Affairs, University of Missouri Medical School. *Memberships:* American Association for Surgery of Trauma; American College of Chest Physicians; James IV Association of Surgeons Inc; American Medical Association; American College of Surgeons; American Association of Thoracic Surgeons; Southern Thoracic Surgery Association; International Society for Heart Transplantation; American College of Cardiology; Central Surgical Association; Society for Vascular Surgery. *Publications:* 4 editions, "Cardiac Arrest and Resuscitation"; 2 editions, "Immediate Care of the Acutely Ill and Injured"; 123 scientific articles; 17 contributing chapters. *Honours:* Markle Scholar, Academic Medicine, 1954-59; TOYM Award, 1956; 1st Surgical Traveller, James IV Association of Surgeons Inc, to British Isles, 1962; University of Missouri Citation of Merit Award, 1973; Recipient, Alumni Achievement Award, University of Missouri, 1982. *Hobbies:* Drop Kicking; Tennis; Golf; History; Civil War. *Address:* One Hospital Drive, Columbia, MO 65212, USA.

STERKOWICZ, Stanislaw, b. 14 Mar. 1923, Pinsk, Poland. Chief, Cardiology, County Hospital, Wloclawek. m. Janina Jane Marczewska, 1 Jan. 1948, 2 sons. *Education:* Diploma, Physician, 1951; Doctorate of Medicine, 1951; Habilitation, 1979. *Appointments:* Assistant, 1951-56, Chief, 1956-75, Internal Department, District Hospital, Lebork; Chief, Cardiology, County Hospital, Wlocklawek, 1975-; Junior Lecturer, Medical Academy, Lodz, 1979-; County Specialist, Internal Diseases, Chairman, County Specialists Team, Wloclawek; Clinical Team, Medical Education, Wloclawek. *Memberships include:* Chairman, Polish Internist Society Section, Wloclawek; Chairman, National Department of Scientific Society of Wloclawek; Polish Union of Physicians Writers; Council, Polish Internist Society; Committee, Investigations of the Nazi Crimes in Poland. *Publications:* "Tadeusz Boy - Zelenski, Lekarz, Pisarz, Spolecznik", 1959, 2nd edition 1974; "Interpretacja bana biochemicznych", 1964; "Zbrodnicze eKsperymenty medyczne w obozach Koncentracyjnych III Rzeszy", 1981; numerous articles in professional journals. *Honours:* Cross, Cavalier, Polonia Restituta, Silver Cross of Merit, Auschwitz Cross, etc. *Hobby:* Medical Journalism. *Address:* ul Hoza 8 M 32, Wloclawek, 97 800, Poland.

STERN, Myra, b. 25 Sep. 1939, Philadelphia, Pennsylvania, USA. Management, Marketing Consultant. *Education:* MS, Management/Human Resource Development, National College of Education, 1985; RN, Albert Einstein School of Nursing; BA, Temple University. *Appointments:* Head Nurse, Michael Reese Hospital Medical Center, Chicago, 1965-68; Dialysis Coordinator, 1968-73; Corporate Manager, North Central Dialysis Centers, Chicago, 1973-79; Director of Development, 1979-81; Consultant, Myra Stern & Associates, Chicago, 1982-; Consultant, Department of Health and Human Services, 1979-81; Lecturer, Northwestern University School of Nursing, 1978-81. *Memberships:* American Hospital Association; American Management Association; American Nurses Association; Women in Health Care; Jewish United Fund; National Kidney Foundation; Founder, North Central Dialysis & Transplant Society, 1969. *Honours:* Kidney Foundation of Illinois: Volunteer of the Year, 1970; Community Education, 1976. *Hobbies:* Tennis; Swimming; Biking; Theatre; Music; Collecting Art, Sculpture and Antiques. *Address:* 5445 N Sheridan Road, Suite 812, Chicago, IL 60640, USA.

STERN, Stephen L, b. 13 Apr. 1946, New York, New York, USA. Associate Professor of Psychiatry; Director, Depression Treatment Programme. m. Marion B Goertzel, 2 Jan. 1972, White Plains, New York, 1 son. *Education:* BA cum laude, Columbia College, New York, 1967; MD, New York University, New York, 1971. *Appointments:* Intern, Medicine and Psychiatry, Philadelphia General Hospital, Philadelphia, Pennsylvania, 1971-72; Residency in Psychiatry, Hospital of the University of Pennsylvania, Philadelphia, 1972-75; Instructor, Clinical Psychiatry, Washington University School of Medicine, St Louis, Missouri, 1976-77; Assistant Professor of Psychiatry 1977-79, Assistant Professor of Clinical Psychiatry 1979-80, University of Pennsylvania School of Medicine; Associate Professor of Psychiatry, Director, Depression Treatment Programme, The Ohio State University College of Medicine, Columbus, Ohio, 1980-. *Memberships:* Phi Beta Kappa; American Psychiatric Association; Ohio Psychiatric Association; Neuropsychiatric Society of Central Ohio; Ohio State Medical Association; Academy of Medicine of Columbus and Franklin County. *Publications:* 'Towards a rational pharmacotherapy of depression' (with A J Rush and J Mendels), 1980; 'Drug combinations in the treatment of refractory depression: a review' (with J Mendels), 1981; 'Affective disorder in the families of women with normal weight bulimia' (co-author), 1984. *Hobbies:* Camping; Guitar. *Address:* Department of Psychiatry, The Ohio State University Hospitals, 473 West 12th Avenue, Columbus, OH 43210, USA.

STERNBERG, David Edward, b. 1 Jan. 1946, Norfolk, Virginia, USA. Medical Director of Falkirk Hospital, Central Valley, New York; Lecturer in Psychiatry, Yale University School of Medicine. m. 23 Aug. 1970, Belle Harbour, New York, 2 sons. *Education:* BA, University of Chicago, 1967; MD, Tufts University School of Medicine, 1971; Residency in Psychiatry, Yale University School of Medicine, 1972-75. *Appointments:* Chief, Clinical Research Unit and Associate Professor of Psychiatry, Yale University, 1979-84; Research Coordinator, Section on Neuropsychopharmacology, Biological Psychiatry Branch, National Institute of Mental Health, Bethesda, Maryland, 1975-79. *Memberships:* American Psychiatric Association; Society of Biological Psychiatry; American Association for the Advancement of Science; Society for Neuroscience. *Publications:* Contributor to professional journals including 'Science'; 'British Journal of Psychiatry';

Chapters in Books. *Honours:* Tufts Medical School, Research Honors, 1971; Seymour Lustman Research Award, Department of Psychiatry, Yale University, 1975. *Hobbies:* Tennis; Windsurfing. *Address:* Falkirk Hospital, Central Valley, NY 10917, USA.

STEVENSON, David John Douglas, b. 6 Jan. 1933, Glasgow, Scotland. Senior Lecturer in International Community Health, Liverpool School of Tropical Medicine, England. m. Anna Marie Skadegaard, 29 July 1967, Hørsholm, Denmark, 2 sons, 1 daughter. *Education:* BA, 1954, MA, 1958, Cambridge; MB ChB, 1957, MD, 1965, DPH, 1964, Glasgow, Scotland; DTM&H, Liverpool, England, 1961. *Appointments:* Medical Officer, Diocese of Malawi, 1958-63; Medical Officer, Government of Malawi, 1965-66; Lecturer in Tropical Diseases, University of Edinburgh, Scotland, 1966-72; Adviser, Tribhuwan University, Kathmandu, Nepal, 1974-75. *Memberships:* Faculty of Community Medicine; Member of Committee of Patronage of Médecine d'Afrique Noire; Member, Society for Scientific Exploration; The American Society of Phychical Research; The Freshwater Biological Association; Fellow, The Royal Society of Tropical Medicine and Hygiene. *Publications:* "A Short Scots-Norwegian Wordlist", 1963; "Scotland's Responsibility in International Aid and Cooperation", 1977; 'Primary Health Care-Therapeutic Aspects', 1985. *Honours:* Knight of the Order of Saint Lazarus of Jerusalem, 1984. *Hobbies:* Politics; Aquatic biology; Psychical Research; Bagpipes and Ethnic music; Language and communication. *Address:* 22 Blacket Place, Edinburgh EH9 1RL, Scotland.

STEVENSON, Eugene Davis, b. 21 May 1953, Murfreesboro, Tennessee, USA. Supervisor, Dental Clinic; Clinician. m. Stephanie Lolita Anderson, MD, 9 July 1985, Dallas, 3 sons by previous marriage. *Education:* University of California, Davis, 1973-74; BA, California State University, 1977; DDS, Meharry Medical College School of Dentistry, 1981. *Appointments:* US Public Health Service, Commission Corps; Captain, Dentist, 1981-83; University of Texas Health Science Center, Dallas, Clinic Supervisor - Unclassified Faculty, 1983-; Clinic Supervisory Position, 1984-, Dental Clinician, 1981-84; Navy Ready Reserves, Dental Officer, Lieutenant, 1985-. *Memberships:* Academy of Dentistry International; Association of Military Surgeons of the USA; MC Cooper Dental Society, Dallas. *Honours:* Office of President, Soph Dental Class, 1979; President, Ewell Niell Dental Society, 1980; US Public Health Scholarships Recipient; Certificate of Merit, American Society of Dentistry for Children; Acceptee, Baylor School of Dentistry, Division of Pedodontics. *Hobbies:* Basketball; Camping. *Address:* 9447 Culberson St., Dallas, TX 75227, USA.

STEVENSON, Jean Christine, b. 25 Dec. 1930, Birmingham, England. Dental Surgeon. m. Peter Charles Stevenson, 19 May 1956, Birmingham, 1 son, 1 daughter. *Education:* BDS, Final Year Prize for Prosthetics. *Appointments:* House Surgeon, Dudley Road Hospital, Birmingham; Dentist, Clinic, Doha, Qatar, Arabian Gulf; Clinical Teacher, Baghdad Dental School, Iraq; Assistant, Private Practice, Near Iver, Buckinghamshire, England; Dentist, School Clinic, Carlton, Nottingham; School Clinic, Hobart, Tasmania; Assistant, Private Practice, Hobart; Private Practice, Hobart, Tasmania. *Memberships:* Australian Dental Association; British Dental Association; Tasmanian Medical Womens Association. *Publication:* "Dental Work in the Persian Gulf", 'British Dental Journal', 1958. *Hobbies:* Training & Showing St Bernard Dog; Geneology; Sailing; Gardening. *Address:* 111 King Street, Sandy Bay, Hobart, Tasmania 7005, Australia.

STEVKO, Annette M, b. 11 Oct. 1957, Castro Valley, California, USA. Chiropractor. m. Timothy J . Frary, 13 Aug. 1983, Castro Valley. *Education:* AA, Chabot College; Doctor of Chiropractic, Western States Chiropractic College. *Memberships:* World Wide Christian Chiropractic Association; Christian Medical Society;

Oregon Chiropractic Physicians Association; Gonstead Clinical Studies Society. *Publication:* "The Treatment of Psoriasis Using Aloe Vera", 1985. *Honours:* Christian Chiropractic Student Scholarship, 1981; Womens Auxillary of the International Chiropractic Association Scholarship, 1980. *Hobbies:* Racquetball; Fishing; Outdoor Recreation; Cross Country Skiing. *Address:* 4037 NE Tillamook, Portland, OR 97212, USA.

STEWARD, Edward George, b. London, England. Professor of Molecular Medicine. m. Dorothy Mary Turner (deceased 1984), 1 son, 1 daughter. *Education:* BSc, King's College, London University; PhD, DSc, London University. *Appointments:* Senior Principal Scientific Staff, General Electric Company Laboratories; Reader, Professor of Molecular Medicine, The City University, London, 1960-. *Memberships:* Institute of Physics; Chairman of X-ray Analysis Group 1966-69; FInstP, C Phys; Past member of various commissions, International Union of Crystallography. *Publications include:* "Fourier Optics: An Introduction", 1983; about 100 papers including: 'Molecular flexibility and drug action' (with D Warner and R B Player), 1973; 'Conformational adaptability at GABA-sensitive inhibtory synapses' (with G R Clarke), 1975; 'Structure-activity relationships in inhibitory processes involving the GABA-nergic system' (with R H Lowe) in "Iontophoresis and Transmitter Mechanisms in the Mammalian Central Nervous System" (editors: R W Ryall and J S Kelly), 1978; 'The theoretical design of drugs; some progress, problems and prognoses', 1981; 'An examination of the solution conformation of bicuculline using NMR and theoretical methods' (with G W Pooler), 1985. *Hobbies:* Music; Theatre; Painting; Swimming; Skiing. *Address:* The City University, Northampton Square, London EC1V 0HB, England.

STEWART, David James, b. 15 May 1950, Ottawa, Canada. Medical Oncologist and Associate Professor of Medicine. m. Nancy I M Hall, 26 July 1975, Toronto, Canada. 1 son, 1 daughter. *Education:* MD, Queen's University, Kingston, Ontario, 1974; Internship, 1974-75, Residency, 1975-76, Royal Victoria Hospital, McGill University; Medical Oncology Fellowship, University of Texas Cancer Centre, M D Anderson Hospital and Tumour Institute, USA, 1976-78; FRCP (C) Internal Medicine, 1978; Medical Oncology, 1985; Certification in Medical Oncology, American Board of Internal Medicine, 1979. *Appointments:* Faculty Associate and Instructor, 1978-79, Assistant Professor and Assistant Internist, 1979-80, Department of Developmental Therapeutics, M D Anderson Hospital and Tumour Institute, Houston, Texas, USA; Staff, Ontario Cancer Treatment and Research Foundation, Ottawa General Hospital, Ottawa, Ontario, Canda, 1980-; Clinical Assistant Professor of Medicine, University of Ottawa, 1980-84; Associate Professor of Medicine, University of Ottawa, 1984-. *Memberships:* Ontario Medical Association; Canadian Oncology Society; Canadian Medical Protective Association; American Society of Clinical Oncology; American Association for Cancer Research; Royal College of Physicians and Surgeons of Canada. *Publications:* Author of over 66 publications including, 'Human Central Nervous System Distribution of Cis-Diamminedichloroplatinum and Use as a radiosentitizer in Malignant Brain Tumors', (Co-author), 1982; 'Introcarotid artery infusion of cis-diamminedichloroplatinum, Phase 1 study in patients with recurrent malignant intracerebral tumors', (Co-author), 1982; 'Intracarotid Chemotherapy with a combination of BCNU, cisplatin and VM-26 in the treatment of primary and metatastic brain tumors', (Co-author), 1984. *Honours:* Queen's University Provincial Scholarship for Ontario, 1968; WW Near and Susan Near Scholarship, 1969; Roberta McCulloch Scholarship, 1969; Isaac Cohn Scholarship, 1972; WW Near and Susan Near Scholarship, 1972; Reuben Wells Leonard Scholarship, 1973; Plunkett Prize, 1974. *Address:* Ontario Cancer Treatment and Research Foundation, Ottawa Regional Cancer Centre, General Hospital Division, 501 Smyth Road, Ottawa, Ontario, Canada K1H 8L6.

STEWART, John Hamlyn, b. 15 Sep. 1922, New Zealand. Radiologist; Clinical Teacher. m. Marjorie, 16 Jan. 1957, Mawera, New Zealand, 1 son, 1 daughter. *Education:* MB, ChB, University of Otago, 1945; DMRD (London), 1954; FFR (London) (now FRCR), 1957; MRACR, 1957; FRACR, 1968. *Appointments:* Assistant Lecturer, Otago Medical School, 1948-49; House Surgeon, Auckland hospitals, 1946, 1950; Registrar, United Oxford Hospitals, UK, 1952-55; Radiologist, Green Lane Hospital, Auckland, 1955; Radiologist, National Women's Hospital, Auckland, 1956-. *Memberships:* New Zealand Medical Association; British Institute of Radiology; Royal Australasian College of Radiologists; Australian Society for Ultrasound in Medicine. *Hobbies:* Politics; Travel. *Address:* 19 St Vincent Avenue, Remuera, Auckland, New Zealand.

STEWART, William Edgar II, b. 17 July 1940, USA, Professor of Medical Microbiology and Immunology. m. (1) Marilyn Mays, 1961; (2) Teresa H Shirley, 1968; (3) Marzenna Wiranowska, 1976; (4) Julia L Ungstad, 1984, 2 sons, 2 daughters. *Education:* BS, Texas Technological University, 1964; MS 1967, PhD 1969, University of Texas Medical School. *Appointments:* Research Fellow, DuPont Experimental Station, Wilmington, Delaware, 1969-71; Assistant Professor, University of Leuven, Belgium, 1971-74; Visiting Professor, Rega Institute, Leuven, 1974-75; Associate Professor, Institut Recherches Scientifiques Sur le Cancer, Villejuif, France, 1975-76; Associate Member, Sloan-Kettering Institute for Cancer Research, New York, USA, 1976-81; Associate Professor, Genetics and Molecular Biology, Cornell University School of Medicine, New York, 1978-81; Professor of Microbiology, University South Florida, Tampa, 1982-85. *Memberships:* President 1983, International Society for Interferon Research; European Molecular Biology Organization; American Society for Microbiology. *Publications:* "Interferons and Their Actions", editor, 1977; "The Interferon System", 1979 and 1981; "The Lymphokines", editor, 1982. *Honours:* O B Williams Research Award, 1976-81; Senior Research Fellow, EMBO, 1975-76. *Hobbies:* Comic Art; Chasing and catching women; Fishing; Playing with his children. *Address:* Department of Medical Microbiology and Immunology, University of South Florida College of Medicine, Tampa, FL 33612, USA.

STIEHL, Walter Leoncio, b. 13 Dec. 1926, Puerto Rico. Professor of Anatomy. m. Carmen E Cabrera Chico, 3 May 1972, San Juan, PR, 3 sons, 1 daughter. *Education:* BSc 1951, MD 1955; Internship, St Luke's Hospital, Pittsburgh, Massachusetts, USA, 1955-56; Fellow in Psychiatry, MGH, 1970-71; Resident in Radiology, Rio Piedras Medical Centre, 1981-82. *Appointments:* Associate in Anatomy, 1956-59, Assistant Professor, 1959-63, Associate Professor, 1963-68, Professor of Anatomy, Head of Department of Anatomy, 1968-78, University of Puerto Rico School of Medicine; Visiting Scientist, NINDB Perinatal Physiology Laboratory, San Juan, PR, 1962-63, Consultant, 1963-66; Co-Founder & President, San Juan Bautista School of Medicine, 1978-80; Professor of Anatomy (part-time), UPR School of Medicine, 1978-80; Professor of Anatomy (part-time), 1980-83, Present Professor, Head of Department of Anatomy, Ponce School of Medicine, 1983-. *Memberships:* Sociedad de Médicos Graduados Escuela de Medicina UPR; American Medical Association; Society for Neuroscience; New York Academy of Sciences. *Publications:* 'A Condition resembling 'Cerebral Palsy' in young Macaca Mulatta surviving asphyxia neonatorum, 1959; 'Pulmonary Angiography - Gross Anatomy Chapter XV, Vascular Roentgenology, Arteriography/Phlebography-Lymphangiography', 1964; 'Innervation of components of velopharyngeal musculature in the Cat (felix domestica), 1983. *Honours:* Alpha Omega Alpha, 1977; Omicron Kappa Upsilon (dental); 1965; Fellow, Royal Society of Health (England), 1971. *Hobbies:* Photography; Electronics; Poetry; Literature.

Address: LL 8 Urb. Dorado del Mar, Dorado, PR 00646, USA.

STILLNER, Verner, b. 7 Dec. 1940, Porto Allegro, Brazil. Medical Director; Professor of Psychiatry. m. Marianne Koch, 30 June 1967, Munich, West Germany, 1 son, 2 daughters. *Education:* MD, Wayne St University, Detroit, Michigan, USA; MD, Johns Hopkins University, Baltimore, USA; Mixed Medical Internship, Presbyterian Medical Centre, San Francisco, California; Psychiatric Residency, Harvard Medical School. *Appointments:* Senior Surgeon, Psychiatry, US Public Health Service, Bethel, Alaska; Medical Staff, Alaska Psych. Int., Anchorage, Alaska; Director, Div. Mental Health and Dev. Disabilities, State of Alaska; Medical Director, Charter Ridge Hospital, Lexington, Kentucky; Professor, Department of Psychiatry, University of Kentucky College of Medicine, Lexington. *Memberships:* American Association for the Advancement of Science; American Psychiatric Association (Fellow); Antarctic Society; American Psychiatric Association; Kentucky Psychiatric Association; American Psychosomatic Society; American College of Sports Medicine; American Society for Circumpolar Health; American Association of Psychiatric Hospital Administrators; American Orthopsychiatric Association; American Medical Society on Alcohol; National Council on Alc; American Association for Social Psychiatry. *Hobbies:* Choral Music; Gardening; Running. *Address:* Charter Ridge Hospital, 3050 Rio Dosa Drive, Lexington, KY 40509, USA.

STILLWATER, Richard Bernard, b. 15 Jan. 1933, Winnipeg, Canada. Active Teaching Staff, St Boniface Hospital and Children's Center; Assistant Professor, Department of Otolaryngology, University of Manitoba, Winnipeg, Canada. m. Jacqueline Soltzman, 24 May 1956, Winnipeg, 3 sons. *Education:* MD, 1957; Certificate, Royal College of Surgeons of Canada in Otolaryngology. *Appointments:* Head, Department of Otolaryngology, Victoria General Hospital, Winnipeg, Canada, 1962-84; Active Private Practice, Otolaryngology, 1960-. *Memberships:* Fellow, Royal College of Surgeons of Canada; Canadian Otolaryngology Society; Canadian Medical Association; Manitoba Medical Association; Canadian Division of Israeli Medical Association; Fellow, International College of Surgeons. *Hobbies:* Electronics; Photography; Travel; Weekend Golf Duffer. *Address:* 701-388 Portage Avenue, Winnipeg, Manitoba, Canada R3C 0C8.

STJERNSWARD, Jan, b. 2 June 1936, Copenhagen, Denmark. Chief, Cancer, WHO HQ. m. Gunilla Dinkelspiel, 12 Apr. 1962, Stockholm, 1 son, 4 daughters. *Education:* Qualified Physician, 1962, MD, 1967, Docent, Tumorbiology, 1967, Karolinska Institute; Specialist, Radiotherapy and Oncology, Sweden, 1972. *Appointments:* Research Fellow, Assistant, Associate, Tumor Biology, Karolinska Institute, 1962-67; Doctor, Kenyatta National Hospital, Nairobi, 1967-68; Physician, Radiumhemmet, Karolinska Hospital, Stockholm, 1968-78; Professeur Associe, Medicine, University of Lausanne, 1975; Director, Ludwig Institute for Cancer Research, Inselspital, Bern, 1972-80; Chief, Cancer, Headquarters, World Health Organization, Geneva, 1980-. *Memberships:* Numerous professional organisations. *Publications:* Approximately 200 articles in professional journals. *Address:* Cancer, WHO, CH-1211 Geneva 27, Switzerland.

STOCK, Barbara Morris, b. 4 May 1943, Pittsburgh, Pennsylvania, USA. Psychologist, Paediatric Ecology Programme, Mount Sinai Hospital, Chicago. m. E Lee Stock, 21 June 1964, Pittsburgh, 3 sons; divorced 1984. *Education:* BA English, Chatham College, Pittsburgh, 1964; MS Psychology, University of Michigan, Ann Arbor, 1967; PhD Psychology & Education, University of Michigan, 1972. *Appointments:* Psychologist, San Francisco Public Schools, California, 1968; Consultant, Kentucky Infant Pre-school Project, 1972; Assistant Professor of Psychology, Eastern Kentucky University, 1972-73; Parent Effectiveness

Training, London, England, 1974; Various psychology appointments, 1979-; Psychotherapy, Ravenswood Hospital Medical Centre, Chicago, 1981-83; Psychologist, Lake County Mental Health, Round Lake Park, Illinois, 1983-85; Psychologist, Paediatric Ecology Programme, Mount Sinai Hospital, Chicago, 1985-. *Memberships:* American Psychological Association; American Orthopsychiatric Association; International Transactional Analysis Association. *Hobbies:* Writing; Parenting; Walking; Travel. *Address:* Mount Sinai Hospital, Paediatric Ecology Programme, 15th and California, Chicago, IL 60608, USA.

STÖGER, Richard Hubert, b. 14 Nov. 1912, Braunau am Inn, Austria. Specialist in Internal Diseases, Oncologist. m. 25 Mar. 1953, Vienna, 1 daughter. *Education:* MD, University of Innsbruck, Austria, 1937; Habilitation, University of Vienna, 1944. *Appointments:* Resident, University Hospital, Innsbruck, 1937-38, Assistant Doctor, 2. University Hospital for Internal Diseases, Vienna, 1938-40; Hospital work & Military Service, 1940-45; Liberal Practice in Vienna. *Memberships:* Society of Physicians in Vienna; Austrian Cancer Society; Association for the furtherance of an active remediable cancer prophylaxis and prevention of relapse. *Publications:* "Proposal for an easily practicable Cancer Prophylaxis", 1949; "Growing Older without Cancer", 1981; 65 scientific publications. *Honours:* Prize of the Society for pre and postoperative tumour therapy, Germany, 1969. *Hobbies:* Sport; Tennis; Skiing; Swimming; Landscape painting. *Address:* Walfischgasse 10, A-1010 Vienna, Austria.

STOJANOVIC, Bozidar, b. 15 Nov. 1927, Krusevac, Yugoslavia. Mentor of General Hospital. m. Dusica, 25 Apr. 1974, 1 son. *Education:* Primarijus, Pulmonologist. *Appointments:* Chief of Radiology Department; Chief, Pulmonary Disease Department. *Memberships:* American College of Chest Physicians; Serbian Medical Association. *Publications:* 'Experiences in Diagnostic treatment of primary benign & malignant tuberculosis', 1958; 'X-ray diagnostic carcinoma of the Stomach', 1963; 'Pneumoconiosis', 1969; 'Pathophysiology of Respiration', 1969; 'Restrictive Syndrome of Pulmonary Ventilation', 1972; 'Pathophysiology & clinic of Chronic Bronchitis', 1974; 'Mucodyne in COPD Treatment', 1982. *Honours:* Letter of Thanks, Serbian Medical Association, 1972; Medallion, Serbian Medical Association, 1985. *Hobbies:* Beletristic Literature; Physics & Philosophy; History; Walking. *Address:* Trg Stubalskih Junaka 6, 37000 Krusevac, Yugoslavia.

STOLLER, Alan, b. 26 May 1911, London, England. Consultant Psychiatrist. m. Joan Leneveu, 6 Aug. 1948, Melbourne, Australia, 2 sons, 1 daughter. *Education:* University College Hospital, London University, England, 1929-35; MRCS, LRCP, 1935; DPM (RCP&S), 1938; Foundation Fellow, FRAMZCP, 1963; FRACMA, 1968, FRCPsych, 1972. *Appointments:* Senior Medical Officer and Acting Superintendent, 1939-41, Claremont Mental Hospital, Western Australia; Major, Australian Imperial Forces, 1941-45; Research Assistant, Institute of Psychiatry, London University, England, 1946-47; Consultant, Veterans Administration, Australia, 1947-53; Chief Clinical Officer and Director, Mental Health Research Institute, Victoria, 1953-59; Chairman, Mental Health Authority, Victoria, 1969-75; Senior Lecturer, Political Science, Monash University, 1969-76; Chairman, Victorian State Council of Special Education, Victoria, 1976-82; Consultant, Alcoholism, Drug and Forensic Services, Victoria, 1983-85; Consultant, Psychogeriatrics, Mount Eliza Geriatric Centre, Victoria, 1985-. *Memberships include:* Past Member, Expert Advisory Panel, Mental Health, World Health Organisation; Distinguished Fellow, American Psychiatric Association; Past President: World Federation for Mental Health; Australian and New Zealand College of Psychiatrists; Victoria Council for Mental Health; Marriage Guidance Council, Victoria; Australian Committee on Prevention of Alcoholism, and Drug Addiction. *Publi-*

cations: "Report of Juvenile Delinquency Advisory Committee", 1955; "Mental Health Facilities and Needs of Australia", 1955; "Growing Old", 1966; "Family Today", 1962; "New Faces, Immigration and Family Life", 1966; "Health of a Metropolis", 1972; "Family in Australia", 1974; author of over 150 papers. *Honours include:* CBE, 1976; Queens Jubilee Medal, 1977. *Address:* 71 Glen Shian Lane, Mount Eliza, Vic 3930, Australia.

STOLZMANN, Wlodzimierz Maciej, b. 3 Apr. 1940, Czestochowa, Poland. Head of Cytogenetics Group. m. Maria Piorunska, 19 Feb. 1976, Poznan, 2 sons. *Education:* Diploma of the Physician 1963, MD 1969, Medical Faculty, Medical Academy of Poznan. *Appointments:* Assistant 1964-66, Senior Assistant 1966-74, Department of Human Genetics, Medical Academy of Poznan; Adjunct 1974-, Head of the Cytogenetic Group, Institute of Human Genetics, Polish Academy of Sciences, Poznan. *Memberships:* Polish Genetical Society; Member of the Poznan Section Board 1983-, Polish Biochemical Society. *Publications:* "Replication variants of the human inactive X chromosome" (with M Schmidt), part I 1982, part II 1984; "Handbook on Physiopathology for Medical Students" in Polish (co-author), 1985. *Hobbies:* History of Art; Music; Tourism. *Address:* Slowackiegc 29/8, 60-824, Poznan, Poland.

STONE, Janet H, b. 24 Oct. 1948, Mountain Lake, Minnesota, USA. Hand Therapist. m. (divorced), 2 daughters. *Education:* BS summa cum laude Occupational Therapy, State University of New York, Downstate Medical Center, New York, 1972; Diploma, Surgical Technology, American College of Paramedical Arts and Sciences, 1980. *Appointments:* Pediatric Occupational Therapist, Petersburg Training School and Hospital, Petersburg, Virginia, 1973-74; Hand Therapist: Hand Therapy Services, Office of Dr Charles McDowell, Richmond, Virginia 1975-77, Office of Dr John O'Hara, Torrance, California 1978-82; Hand Therapy Department, California Hospital Medical Center, Los Angeles, California, 1978; Private Practice, Lomita, California, 1982-; Surgical Assistant to Dr John O'Hara, Torrance, California, 1982. *Memberships:* Associate Founding Member, 1978, Active Member, 1979, American Society of Hand Therapists; Association of Surgical Technologists; California Occupational Therapy Association; American Occupational Therapy Association. *Hobbies:* Skiing; Tennis; Attending musical plays; Reading; Classical music; Dining out. *Address:* 26116-K Narbonne Avenue, Lomita, CA 90717, USA.

STONE, Marvin Jules, b. 3 Aug. 1937, Columbus, Ohio, USA. Director of Immunology Department, Chief of Oncology. m. Jill Feinstein, 29 June 1958, 1 son, 1 daughter. *Education includes:* Ohio State University, 1955-58; SM Pathology 1962, MD with honours 1963, University of Chicago; Clinical Associate arthritis and rheumatism, National Institute Arthritis and Metabolic Diseases, NIH, Bethesda, Maryland, 1965-68; Fellow in Hematology, Department of Internal Medicine, University of Texas Southwestern Medical School, Dallas, 1969-70. *Appointments include:* Instructor in Department of Internal Medicine 1970-71, Assistant Professor 1971-73, Associate Professor 1974-76, Clinical Professor 1976-, Chairman Bioethics Committee 1979-81, Director Charles A Sammons Cancer Center 1976-, Chief of Oncology 1976-, Director of Immunology 1976-, Co-Director of Division of Hematology-Oncology 1976-, Baylor University Medical Center, Dallas; Faculty, Immunology Graduate Programme, University of Texas Health Science Center, Dallas, 1975-; Adjunct Professor Biology, Southern Methodist University, Dallas, 1977-. *Memberships include:* American Rheumatism Association; Reticuloendothelial Society; American Association of Immunologists; American Federation Clinical Research; American Society of Hematology; International Society of Hematology; New York Academy of Science; American Association of Cancer Education; American Medical Association; American Heart Association; American Association for the

Advancement of Science; American Association for Cancer Research; Phi Beta Kappa; Sigma Xi; Alpha Omega Alpha; Medical Vice-President Dallas 1977-78, President 1978-80, American Cancer Society. *Publications:* Chapters in books and articles in professional journals. *Honour:* Established Investigator, American Head Association. *Address: Charles A Sammons Cancer Center, 3500 Gaston Avenue, Dallas, TX 75246, USA.*

STOPCZYK, Marius Jan, b. 23 Aug. 1935, Warsaw, Poland. Professor, Cardiology & Biomedical Engineering. m. Christine, 8 Sep. 1957, Warsaw, 1 son, 1 daughter (deceased). *Education:* MD, 1958, PhD, 1966, Warsaw Medical University; Doctor Habilitation, 1979; Professor, Medicine & Biomedical Engineering, Polish Academy of Science, 1986. *Appointments:* Assistant, Research Assistant, Assistant Professor, Medical University, 1958-66; Assistant Professor, Medicine, Medical University, 1966-74; Assistant Professor, Medicine, Head, Scientific Director, Professor, Medicine & Biomedical Engineering, 1975-. *Memberships:* Board of Directors, International Society of Cardiac Pacing, 1979-; Vice President, Polish Society of Cardiology, 1978-82; Editor in Chief, Polish Cardiac Journal; Board Member, Polish Society of Cardiology, Polish Society of Medical Physics; etc. *Publications:* Numerous articles in professional journals. *Honours:* Several Awards, Polish Ministry of Health, & Ministry of Machinery, 1972; 2 Awards, Polish Academy of Science; Honorary Citizenship, Nice, France. *Hobbies:* Insect's Macyophotography; Children's Gardening. *Address:* National Institute of Cardiology, Alpejska Str. 42, 02-637, Warsaw, Poland.

STORER, Roy, b. 21 Feb. 1928. Professor of Prosthodontics; Dean of Dentistry. m. Kathleen Mary Frances Pitman, 1953, 1 son, 2 daughters. *Education:* LDS, University of Liverpool, England, 1950; FDSRCS, 1954; MSc, Liverpool, 1960; DRD, RCS Ed. 1978. *Appointments:* House Surgeon, United Liverpool Hospitals, England, 1950, Registrar, 1952-54; Lieutenant, Captain, Royal Army Dental Corps, 1950-52; Lecturer, Dental Prosthetics, University of Liverpool, 1954-61; Visiting Associate Professor, Northwestern University, Chicago, USA, 1961-62; Senior Lecturer, Dental Prosthetics, University of Liverpool, 1962-67; Honorary Consultant, United Liverpool Hospitals, 1962-67; United Newcastle Hospitals (now Newcastle Health Authority), 1968-. *Memberships:* British Society for the Study of Prosthetic Dentistry, 1960-69 (President, 1968-69); Board of Faculty, RCS; Medical Rugby Football Club (President, 1968-82); Northern Sports Council, 1972-; Chairman Division of Dentistry, Newcastle University Hospitals, 1972-75; External Examiner in Dental Subjects, Universities of Belfast, Birmingham, Bristol, Dublin, Dundee, Leeds, London, Newcastle upon Tyne and Royal College of Surgeons, England. *Publications:* "A Laboratory Course in Dental Materials for Dental Hygienists" (with D. C. Smith), 1963; "Immediate and Replacement Dentures" (with J. N. Anderson), 3rd edition, 1981; papers on science and clinical subjects in dental and medical journals. *Hobbies:* Rugby; Cricket; Squash; Gardening. *Address:* University of Newcastle upon Tyne, The Dental School, Framlingtam Place, Newcastle upon Tyne NE2 4BW, England.

STORMS, William Wallace, b. 18 May 1942, Racine, Wisconsin, USA. Private Practice; Assistant Clinical Professor. m. Bette Bear, 14 Aug. 1965, Saginaw, 3 daughters. *Education:* BS, Northwestern University, 1964; MD, University of Wisconsin, 1968; Internship, San Francisco General Hospital, 1969; Internal Medicine, 1969-70, 1972-73, Allergy & Immunology, 1973-75, University of Wisconsin Hospitals. *Appointments:* Private Practice, Allergy Associates; PC; Assistant Clinical Professor, School of Medicine, University of Colorado Health Sciences Centre. *Memberships:* American Board of Internal Medicine; American Board of Allergy & Immunology; Fellow, American College of Physicians; Fellow, American Academy of Allergy; American Thoracic Society;

West Coast Society of Allergy and Immunology. *Publications include:* "Aerosol Sch 1000: An Anticholinergic Bronchodilator", 'American Review of Respiratory Disease, 1975; "Alternaria IgG Precipitins and Adverse Reactions", 'Journal Allergy Clinical Immunology', 1976; "Miller Moth Asthma", 'Clinical Allergy', 1981; "Allergenicity of Cotton of the Cottonwood Tree", 'Annals of Allergy', 1984. *Honours:* Fellow: American College of Physicians, 1979, American Academy of Allergists, 1981, American College of Allergists, 1981; Fellow, American College of Chest Physicians, 1984. *Hobbies:* Tennis; Golf; Squash; Skiing; Hunting; Fishing. *Address:* 2709 North Tejon Street, Colorado Springs, CO 80907, USA.

STORY, Michael John, b. 5 Nov. 1940, Adelaide, South Australia. Divisional Manager, Technical, Research and Development. m. Marie Louise Hann, 29 Jan. 1982, Adelaide, 1 son, 2 daughters. *Education:* BE (Hons), University of Adelaide; PhD, University of Cambridge. *Appointments:* Lecturer, Department of Chemical Engineering, University of Adelaide, 1967-70; Assistant to Manager, Combustion Engineering, Broken Hill Proprietary Co Ltd, 1970-73; F H Faulding & Co Ltd: Development Engineer, 1973-74; Project Manager, 1974-75; Product Manager, Enteric Release Systems, 1975-79; Manufacturing Manager, Medical Products, 1979-80; Divisional Manager, Technical, Research and Development, 1980-. *Memberships:* MIChE; ARACI; Associate APhA. *Hobbies:* Squash; Bridge. *Address:* F H Faulding & Company Limited, 129 Dew Street, Thebarton, South Australia 5031.

STOUDEMIRE, G. Alan, b. 24 Nov. 1950, Gastonia, North Carolina, USA. Assistant Professor of Psychiatry, Emory University School of Medicine. m. Sue Joyner Sprunt, 28 Nov. 1975, Raleigh, 1 son, 1 daughter. *Education:* AB, cum laude, 1973; MD, 1977, University of North Carolina; Internship/Residency, University of Colorado, 1977-81. *Appointments:* Assistant Professor, Psychiatry, Duke University Medical Center, 1981-83; Assistant Professor, Psychiatry, Emory University School of Medicine, 1983-; Director, Medical-Psychiatry Unit, Emory University Hospital. *Memberships:* American Psychiatric Association; American Medical Association; American Psychosomatic Society; Academy of Psychosomatic Medicine; Association for Academic Psychiatry. *Publications:* 'Synergism between prolactin and ovarian hormones on DNA synthesis in rat mammary gland', Proc. Soc. Exp. Biol. Med, 1975; 'When the Doctor needs a doctor: Special considerations for the physician-patient', 'Ann. Inter. Med', 1983; 'The onset and adaptation to cancer: Psychodynamics of an ill physician', 'Psychiatry', 1983. *Honours:* Morehead Scholar; Phi Beta Kappa. *Address:* Section of Psychiatry, Emory University Clinic, 1365 Clifton Road, NE, Atlanta, GA 30322, USA.

STOVER, Diane Elizabeth, b. 17 Sep. 1945, New York. Associate Professor of Medicine. m. Anthony J Pepe, 7 June 1970, New York, 1 daughter. *Education:* BS (Magna Cum Laude), St John's University, Jamaica, New York, 1966; MD, The Albert Einstein College of Medicine, Bronx, New York, 1970. *Appointments:* Clinical Assistant Physician, Cardiopulmonary Service, Department of Medicine, 1977-79, Clinical Assistant Attending, Thoracic Service, Department of Surgery, 1977-, Memorial Hospital for Cancer and Allied Diseases; Assistant Professor, Cornell University Medical College, 1977-; Assistant Attending Physician, Cardiopulmonary Service, Department of Medicine, Memorial Hospital for Cancer and Allied Diseases, 1979-84; Assistant Physician, Rockefeller University Hospital, 1979-81; Medical Director, Pulmonary Function Laboratory, 1979-, Assistant Attending Critical Care Physician, Department of Critical Care, 1980-, Associate Attending Physician, Cardiopulmonary Service, Department of Medicine, 1984-, Memorial Hospital for Cancer and Allied Diseases. *Memberships:* Fellow, American College of Chest Physicians; Trudeau Society; American Thoracic Society; New York State Lung Association

etc. *Publications:* Contributor of numerous original reports, reviews and abstracts to professional journals and conferences. *Honours:* Physicians Recognition Award; Biomedical Research Grant; Ancell Clinical Studies Fund; American Medical Association. *Address:* 1275 York Avenue, New York, NY 10021, USA.

STRATAS, Nicholas E, b. 9 Aug. 1932, Toronto, Canada. Professor of Psychiatry. m. Rene, 14 Dec. 1955, Toronto, 3 sons. *Education:* MD, Faculty of Medicine, University of Toronto; Resident in Psychiatry, Eastern Street Hospital, Williamsburg, Virginia; Chief Resident in Psychiatry, Dorothea Dix Hospital, Raleigh, North Carolina. *Appointments:* Director, Residency Training, Dorothea Dix Hospital, Raleigh, NC, 1961-68; Director, Professional Education & Training, 1963-66, Director, Research, 1965-66, Deputy Commission, 1966-73, Department of Mental Health, State of North Carolina; Private Practice in Psychiatry; Associate Clinical Professor of Psychiatry, Duke University Medical Centre; Clinical Professor of Psychiatry, University of North Carolina. *Memberships:* American Medical Association; American Psychiatric Association; American Public Health Association; Academy of Psychosomatic Medicine; American Academy of Behavioural Medicine; American Society of Clinical Hypnosis. *Publications:* Over 130 papers & articles & 12 books. *Honours:* Fellow, Royal Society of Health, London, England. *Address:* 3900 Browning Place, Suite 201, Raleigh, NC 27609, USA.

STRAUBER, Grace Frances, b. 24 Oct. 1927, USA, President, Chief Executive Officer, Saint Mary Hospital, Hoboken, New Jersey. *Education:* BBA Siena College, New York, 1963; MHA, Saint Louis University, Saint Louis, Missouri. *Appointments include:* Business Manager, Saint Francis Hospital, Bronx, New York, 1954-56; Assistant Administrator, Saint Clare Hospital, Schenectady, New York 1956-59 and 1962-65, Saint Michael's Medical Center, Newark, New Jersey 1960-61; Provincial Treasurer for Eastern Province 1966-68, General Treasurer for Congregation 1969-70, Franciscan Sisters of the Poor; President, Chief Executive Officer, Saint Mary Hospital, Hoboken, New Jersey, 1971-; Board of Trustees: President 1980-84, Saint Anthony Community Hospital, Warwick, New York, 1966-; Saint Francis Community Health Center, Jersey City, New Jersey, 1981-. *Memberships include:* American College of Hospital Administrators; American Hospital Association; Catholic Health Association; Hudson Hospital Council; Charter Member, Northeastern New York Chapter, Hospital Financial Management Association; National Association for Female Executives; Academy for Catholic Health Care Leadership; International Health Economics and Management Institute. *Honours:* Hudson County Health Hall of Fame, 1975; Jersey Journal Women of Achievement, 1977. *Hobbies:* Music; Art; Reading. *Address:* 380 Mount Road, Union City, NJ 07087, USA.

STRAZNICKY, Charles, b. 28 June 1935, Budapest, Hungary. Associate Professor of Neuroanatomy. m. Georgette E Szabo, 1 Feb. 1958, Budapest, 1 son, 1 daughter. *Education:* BSc honours Zoology 1957, PhD Neuroembryology 1961, Budapest University; Cand Bio Sci, Hungarian Academy of Sciences, 1971; DSc, Flinders University of South Australia, Australia, 1982. *Appointments:* Tutor, Lecturer, Senior Lecturer, Department of Anatomy, University Medical School, Pecs, Hungary, 1957-70; Wellcome Research Fellow, Department of Physiology, Edinburgh University, Edinburgh, Scotland, 1969; Senior Lecturer, Department of Anatomy, University of Zambia, Lusaka, Zambia, 1971-74; Senior Research Fellow, National Institute for Medical Research, Mill Hill, London, England, 1974; Associate Professor, Department of Anatomy and Histology, School of Medicine, Flinders University of South Australia, Australia, 1974-. *Memberships:* Australian Neuroscience Society; Society for Neuroscience, USA; European Neuroscience Association; British Brain Research Association;

Australian and New Zealand Anatomical Societies; Australian Physiological and Pharmacological Society. *Publications include:* 3 books; over 60 articles, including: 'The Development of the tectum in Xenopus: an autoradiographic study' (with R M Gaze), 1971; 'Stable programming for map orientation in fused eye fragments in Xenopus' (with R M Gaze), 1980; 'Function of heterotopic spinal cord segments investigated in the chick', 1983; 'Nerve growth factor treatment does not prevent dorsal root ganglion cell death induced by target removal in chick embryos' (with R A Rush), 1985. *Honours include:* Wellcome Research Fellowship, 1969 and 1978-79. *Hobbies:* Gardening; Carpentry; Water skiing; Snorkelling; Chess. *Address:* Department of Anatomy and Histology, Flinders University of South Australia, Bedford Park, South Australia 5042, Australia.

STREULI, Rolf Alfred, b. 18 Jan. 1944, Bern, Switzerland. Doctor of Medicine. m. Barbara Langenbacher, 14 Aug. 1971, Bern, 1 son, 2 daughters. *Education:* MD, University of Bern, 1970. *Appointments:* Oberarzt, Regionalspital, Interlaken; Research Associate, Medicine, Hematology/Oncology, University of Chicago; Leitender Arzt, Universitatsspital, Zurich. *Memberships:* Swiss Society of Internal Medicine; American Society of Clinical Oncology; International Society of Internal Medicine, Secretary General. *Publications:* 64 publications. *Address:* Regionalspital, 4900 Langenthal, Switzerland.

STRICKLAND, Daniel Stephen, b. 23 Oct. 1931, Atlanta, Georgia, USA. Medical Center President. m. Mary Elizabeth Zondca, 15 Oct. 1960, Kansas City, Missouri, 1 son, 1 daughter. *Education:* Pre-Medical: Duke University; University of Georgia. DO, University of Health Sciences; Rotating Intern, University Hospitals, Kansas City, Missouri; Anesthesia Preceptorship, Doctors Hospital, Tucker, Georgia. *Appointments:* Medical Director, Wellington Medical Center, Wellington, Missouri, 1961-65; President, Chief Executive Officer, Tucker Medical Center, Tucker, Georgia, 1965-; Founder, Chairman and Medical Director, Respiratory Technology Department, 1974-79; Founder, Director, Family Residency Programme, 1979-81, Doctors Hospital, Tucker. *Memberships:* American Medical Technologists; American College of General Practice; American College of Osteopathic Anesthesiologists; American Society of Anesthesiologists; American College of Emergency Physicians; American College of Sports Medicine; American Medical Association; American Association of Osteopathic Specialists; Southeastern Osteopathic Anesthesiologists Association; Georgia Osteopathic Association; Medical Association of Georgia; American Osteopathic Association. *Publications:* Numerous nationally published articles on osteopathic medicine, anesthesiology and pulmonary medicine. *Honours:* Award of Merit, American Medical Technologists; Physician of the Year, Georgia Osteopathic Association, 1983-84; Outstanding Anesthesiologist of Nationa, American Association of Osteopathic Specialists, 1983-84. Fellow: American College of Medical Technologists; American College of General Practice; American College of Osteopathic Anesthesiologists. *Address:* 4445 Cowan Road, Tucker, GA 30084, USA.

STRIDE, Brian David, b. 6 July 1955, Vancouver, British Columbia, Canada. Computer Centre Director. m. Guylaine Lavoie, 17 Mar. 1983, Vancouver. *Education:* BSR (OT/PT). *Appointments:* Staff Occupational Therapist, Pearson Hospital; currently, Director, Pearson Computer Centre, Vancouver British Columbia. *Memberships:* Canadian Association of Occupational Therapists; Canadian Physiotherapy Association; Canadian Association of Rehabilitation Personnel; Rehabilitation Engineering Society of North America. *Publications:* 'Computers and the Severely Handicapped: A Pilot Project at Pearson Hospital', 1982; 'Assessment of Computer Skills at the Pearson Computer Centre', 1984; 'Computer Vocations for Severely Physically Disabled Persons: Survey Results', 1985. *Hobbies:* Wildlife preservation; Gardening; Brass bands. *Address:* Pearson Computer Centre, 700 West 57th, Vancouver, British Columbia, Canada V6P 1S1.

STRINGER, David Alexander, b. 10 Mar. 1947, England. Head, Division of General Radiology & Assistant Professor, University of Toronto, Canada. m. L. Judith Malbon, 3 Nov. 1973, Portsmouth, 2 sons, 1 daughter. *Education:* BSc., London, 1968; MRCS LRCP, 1971; MBBS, 1972; DRCOG, 1974; LMCC, 1976; DMRD 1978; FRCR, 1980; FRCP (C), 1982. *Appointments:* House Officer, various Hospitals, England, 1972-74; Former Acting Consultant, Hospital for Sick Children, London, England. *Memberships:* British Institute of Radiology; Royal College of Radiologists; Society of Paediatric Radiology; Radiological Society of North America; Canadian Association of Radiologists; Society of Gastro-Intestinal Radiologists; American Institute of Ultrasound in Medicine. *Publications:* "Multiple Choice Questions in Diagnostic Radiology", 1983; Co-author, "Clinical Gastro-Intestinal Imaging in Paediatrics", in press; Co-author, "Manual of Procedures in Gastro-Intestinal Radiology", in press; Numerous papers in professional journals including: 'Clinical Radiology'; 'British Journal of Radiology'; 'Journal Paediatric Surgery'; 'Radiology'; 'Paediatric Radiology and American Journal of Roentgenology; etc. *Honours:* Invited Member, International Advisory Council, Foundation for Craniofacial Deformities, Dallas, 1983; Invited Member and Abstract Editor, North American Working Group on Cleft Palate and Craniofacial anomalies, 1986; Faculty Member, Society of Gastrointestinal Radiologists, Acapulco, 1986. *Hobbies:* Collecting Antique Furniture and Clocks; Participating in Sherlock Holmes Societies (The Bootmakers); Skiing. *Address:* Hospital for Sick Children, Dept. of Radiology, 555 University Avenue, Toronto, Ontario, Canada M5G 1X8.

STRITTER, Frank Thomas, b. 4 June 1937, Syracuse, New York, USA. Professor and Director, Office of Research and Development for Education in the Health Professions. *Education:* PhD, Syracuse University, Syracuse, New York, 1968; AM, Colgate University, Hamilton, New York, 1961; AB, St Lawrence University, Canton, New York, 1959. *Appointments:* Assistant Professor, 1971-75, Associate Professor, 1975-82, Professor, 1982-, Schools of Medicine and Education, University of North Carolina, Chapel Hill, North Carolina. *Memberships:* American Educational Research Association; Association of American Medical Colleges; Phi Delta Kappa. *Publication:* 'Faculty Evaluation and Development' in 'Handbook of Health Professions Education', 1983; 'Professional Education', (with Dinham) in 'AERA Handbook of Research on Teaching', 1985; 'Clinical Instruction', (with others) in 'Handbook for the Academic Physician', 1986. *Honours:* Visiting Scholar, Stanford University, Stanford, California supported by Kenan Award from the University of North Carolina, 1983; Distinguished Alumnus Citation, St Lawrence University, 1982. *Hobbies:* Running; Skiing; Wrestling. *Address:* Office of Research and Development for Education in the Health Professions, 322 Macnider Building, 202-H University of North Carolina, Chapel Hill, NC 27514, USA.

STRÖMBECK, Jan Olof, b. 4 June 1925, Stockholm, Sweden, Head of the Department of Plastic Surgery, Sabbatsberg Hospital, Stockholm. m. Margareta Martin, 22 June 1951, Stockholm, 3 sons, 2 daughters. *Education:* MD, 1951, Assistant Professor of Plastic Surgery, 1967, Karolinska Institute, Stockholm. *Appointments:* Resident in General Surgery and Anaesthesiology, Karolinska Sjukhuset, 1951-55; Resident in Plastic Surgery, St Goerans Sjukhus, 1956-60; Karolinska Sjukhuiset, 1960-66; Assistant Chief, Department of Plastic Surgery, St Goerans Sjukhus, 1966-71. *Memberships:* Swedish Society Plastic Surgeons; Scandinavian Association of Plastic Surgeons; Corresponding Member, Italian Association of Plastic Surgeons; Corresponding Member,

American Society of Plastic Reconstruction Surgery. *Publications:* Contributor of numerous articles on professional subjects to medical journals. *Address:* Appelviksvägen 21, 16136 Bromma, Sweden.

STROUD, Charles Eric, b. 15 May 1924, Cardiff, Wales. Professor, Director, Child Health, Kings College Hospital, London. m. June Mary Neep, 15 Apr. 1950, Wales, 1 son, 2 daughters. *Education:* BSc., MB., BCh., Welsh National School of Medicine; DCH (London); FRCP (London). *Appointments:* House Physician, Welsh National School of Medicine, 1948; Senior House Physician, East Glamorgan Hospital, 1949-50; Squadron Leader, RAF Medical Branch, 1950-52; Pathology Registrar, 1952-53, Paediatric Registrar, 1953-55, Welsh National School of Medicine; Paediatric Registrar, 1955-57, Senior Registrar, 1957-61, Great Ormond Street; Paediatrician, Makerere University, Uganda, 1958-61; Assistant to Director, Guy's Hospital, 1961-62; Consultant Paediatrician, 1962-68, Director, 1968-, Kings College Hospital; Civil Consultant Advisor in Paediatrics, Royal Air Force; Honorary Physician, Adelaide Children's Hospital, South Australia. *Memberships:* BPA; British Medical Association; Royal Society Medicine; Medical Adviser, Eastern Hemisphere Variety Club International. *Publications:* Articles in professional journals. *Hobbies:* Fishing; Tortuous Following of Golf Balls; Good Fishing; Cheap Antiques. *Address:* 84 Copse Hill, Wimbledon, London SW20 OEF, England.

STUART, Hubert James, b. 21 Oct. 1930, Brownsboro, Texas, USA. Psychiatrist. m. Eva Jean Judy, 24 Aug. 1952, Kilgore, 1 daughter. *Education:* BS, North Texas State University, 1952; MD, University of Texas Medical Branch, 1959; Intern, Rotating, Parkland Memorial Hospital, 1960; Resident, Department of Psychiatry, University of Texas Medical Branch, 1963. *Appointments include:* Chief, Inpatient Psychiatry, 1963-65, Director, Consultation and Liaison Service, Hospital, Oklahoma City, 1965, Instructor, Medical Center, 1963-64, Assistant Professor, 1964-65, University of Oklahoma; Coordinator, Programme for Psychiatric Residency Training, 1969-71, Vice Chairman, Department of Psychiatry, 1969-71, Assistant Professor, 1965-69, Associate Professor, 1969-71, University of Texas Southwest Medical School; Private Practice, Houston, 1971-; Clinical Associate Professor, Baylor University College of Medicine, 1971-; Clinical Associate Professor, 1972-75, Director, Psychiatric Residency Training, 1972-78, Clinical Professor, 1975-, Director, Clinical Services, Department of Psychiatry, 1984-, University of Texas, Medical School, Houston. *Memberships include:* Fellow, American Psychiatry Association; American and Southern, Texas Medical Associations; American Medical EEG Association; Pan American Medical Association; Royal Society for Health; American Association for the Advancement of Science; Sigma Xi; Fellow, Southern Psychiatric Association. *Publications:* Co-Author of papers contributed to: 'Proceedings of AMS 7th National Conference on Medical Aspects of Sports'; 'Journal of Family Practice'; 'Journal of Clinical Psychology'; 'MMPI-168 Code Book'. *Honours include:* Recognition Awards: American Medical Association, 1978, 80, 83; American Psychiatric Association, 1978, 80, 83. Recognition Certificate, American Board of Psychiatry and Neurology, 1978. *Hobbies:* Fishing; Hunting. *Address:* 7777 Southwest Freeway 1036, Houston, TX 77074, USA.

STURM, Walter Donald, b. 23 Nov. 1944, Guelph, Ontario, Canada. Board Chairman of Research Institute. m. Carolyn Louise Winsor, 18 Feb. 1975, Las Vegas, Nevada, USA. *Education:* Standard A Teaching Certificate, University of Saskatchewan, 1969; Master of Acupuncture, Bernadean, Nevada, 1973; MD Homeopathy, Metropolitan, London, England, 1977; PhD Chinese Studies, Academy of Oriental Heritage, Vancouver, 1981; Qualified in Naturopathy, Federal Republic of Germany, 1985. *Appointments:* Private Practice in Acupuncture, Alberta, Canada, 1970-72; Director, Acupuncture Training, Occidental

Institute of Chinese Studies, Toronto, 1972-74; Executive Director, OICS Alumni Association, Miami, Florida, USA, 1977-79; President, OICS Alumni Association (under ULC), San Francisco, California, USA, 1980-83; Chairman of Board, Chief Executive Officer, Occidental Institute Research Foundation, Delta, British Columbia, Canada, 1984-. *Memberships:* National Centre for Homeopathy, Washington DC, USA, 1977-; International Research Society for Bioelectronic Functions Diagnosis, Federal Republic of Germany, 1979-; Research Associate, OIR Foundation, Canada, 1984-; and others. *Publications:* "Modern & Traditional Acupuncture: An Extension Training Programme" (major author), 1972, 1979; "German Electro-Acupuncture Manual" parts I-II, 1979, 1981 (co-author & editor); Editor, OICSAA & OIRF Newsletters, 1978-85. *Honours:* Honorary Member, Nevada Association for Chinese Medicine, 1975-; Most Outstanding Teacher in traditional Chinese medicine, Chinese Foundations of Natural Health, 1981. *Hobbies:* Electronics; German Language Translation; Travel (mostly in Germany). *Address:* 5180 Whitworth Crescent, (Ladner) Delta, British Columbia, V4K 1A9, Canada.

SUAREZ-TORRES, Jose Rogerio, b. 26 Mar. 1947, Ambato, Ecuador. Head, Division of Socio Medical Research, Health Ministry of Ecuador. m. Dolores, 17 Oct. 1971, Quito, Ecuador, 2 sons. *Education:* MD, School of Medicine, Quito, 1973; MPH, University of Minnesota, USA, 1978; PhD, Epidemiology, University of Minnesota, 1984. *Appointments:* Director, Tocachi Health Center, Pichincha, Ecuador, 1973-76: Research Associate, Massachusetts Institute of Technology, USA, 1975-76; Professor of Epidemiology and Research Methods, School of Medicine, Quito, Ecuador, 1979-. *Memberships:* Federacion Medica Ecuatoriana; Colegio Medico de Quito; Sociedad de Amigos de la Ciencia y la Cultura; Sociedad Latinoamericana de Medicina Social. *Publications:* Effect of Iodine Correction Early on Fetal Life on Intelligence Quotiente in Human Development and the Thyroid Gland, Editor, J B Stanbury, 1972; Evaluacion de los Programas de Atencion Primaria por Organizaciones no Gibernamentales, ININMS, Quito, 1981; Evaluacion del Plan Nacional de Salud Rural, ININMS, Quito, 1982; Health Needs Assessment of Specific Population Groups in the Cayambe Region, Pichincha Province, Ecuador. An Epidemiological Study of the Impact of Agricultural Development on Health Status, PhD Thesis, University of Minnesota, 1984. *Hobbies:* Painting; Sculpture. *Address:* Calle Ambato 366, Quito, Ecuador.

SUBRAHMANYAM, Devaguptapu, b. 25 Dec. 1932, India. Research Director, Hindustan Ciba-Geigy. m. D Savitri Devi, 6 July 1961, India, 1 son, 2 daughters. *Education:* BSc, Chemistry, 1950, MSc, Chemistry of Food Nutrition, 1952, Andhra University, Waltair; PhD, Biochemistry, Northwestern University, Illinois, USA, 1957. *Appointments:* Research Associate, University of Pittsburg, USA, 1957-59; Research Associate, University of Western Ontario, London, Ontario, Canada, 1959-60; Senior Research Officer, V P Chest Institute, University of Delhi, India, 1960-65; Dy Director, National Institute of Communicable Diseases, Delhi, 1965-70; Professor of Biochemistry, Postgraduate Institute of Medical Research, Chandigarh' India, 1970-80; Research Director, Hindustan Ciba-Geigy, Bombay. *Memberships:* Expert Committee on Parasitic Diseases, WHO, Geneva; Indian Institute of Chemical Biology and Scientific Advisory Committee, Calcutta; National Institute of Cholera and Enteric Diseases, Calcutta; New York Academy of Sciences, USA. *Publications:* Publications in the field of Research in Biochemistry, Immunology, Communicable Diseases, Vector Control. *Honours:* Member, Advisory Group, International Atomic Energy Agency on Parasitic Diseases, 1982; Yodh Memorial Oration, India, 1973; Sinha Memorial Oration, India, 1983. *Hobbies:* Tennis; Cricket; Indoor Games. *Address:* Hindustan Ciba-Geigy Research Centre, Goregaon East, Bombay 400 063, India.

SUGAHARA, Tsutomu, b. 5 Feb. 1921, Kyoto, Japan. Director, Health Research Foundation. m. Akiko Fujita, 6 Apr. 1957, Takarazuka, 2 sons, 1 daughter. *Education:* BSc, Faculty of Science, Osaka University, 1950; MD, Faculty of Medicine, Kyoto University, 1944. *Appointments:* Assistant Professor, Mie Medical College, Yokkaichi, Japan, 1950; Laboratory Head, National Institute of Genetics, Mishima, 1956, National Institute of Radiological Sciences, Chiba, 1960; Professor, Experimental Radiology, Faculty of Medicine, 1961, Dean, 1975-79, Director, Radiation Biology Center, 1976-80, Kyoto University; Director, Kyoto National Hospital, 1980-84, Health Research Foundation, Kyoto, 1984-. *Memberships:* New York (USA) and Indian Academies of Science; Radiation Research Society; Japanese Society of Hyperthermic Oncology; Japan Radiological Society; Japan Health Physics Society; Japanese Society of Biomedical Gerontology. *Publications:* "Modification of Radiosensitivity in Cancer Treatment", 1984; "Fraction Size in Radiobiology and Radiotherapy", 1973; "Hyperthermia", in Japanese, 1985. *Honours:* Emeritus Professor, Kyoto University. *Hobbies:* Classical music; Tennis. *Address:* 14-46 Zushioku, Onoe-cyo, Yamashina-ku, Kyoto 607, Japan.

SUGERMAN, David Alexander, b. 22 Feb. 1929, Sydney, Australia. Private Practice, Pathology; Honorary Consultant Pathologist, Sutherland Hospital. m. Esmae Frances Tudor Carver, 20 July 1956, Sydney, 2 sons, 2 daughters. *Education:* BSc, Medicine, MB BS, University of Sydney; DCP, University of London. *Appointments:* JRMO, RPAH, Sydney; Senior House Physician & Surgeon, Clinical Pathology Registrar, RMH, Melbourne; Senior Assistant Resident, Mallory Institute of Pathology, Boston City Hospital; Visiting Pathologist: Royal South Sydney Hospital, Sutherland Hospital. *Memberships:* Fellow, Royal College of Pathologists of Australasia, former Honorary Treasurer, Council Member, Executive; Founder Fellow, Royal College of Pathologists of England; Fellow, College of American Pathologists. *Publications:* "The Bone Marrow in Ischaemia", 'Medical Journal of Australia', 1956; "Haemoglobin and Plasma Protein Values in the Puerperium", co-author, 'Medical Journal of Australia', 1955; etc. *Hobbies:* Music; Tennis; Skiing. *Address:* PO Box 297, Hurstville, NSW 2220, Australia.

SUGIHARA, Hitohiko, b. 13 June 1900, Yamaguchi-ken, Japan. Director, International Hospital. m. Kyono Dogen, 28 Mar. 1926, Izumo, Japan, 3 sons, 3 daughters. *Education:* School of Medicine, Tokyo Imperial University, Graduate 1925; MD, 1934. *Appointments:* Professor, Toho Women's Medical University, 1935-51; Professor, Showa Medical University, 1952-59; Director of International Jinyu Hospital, 1959-. *Memberships:* Interasma; International Association of Allergology & Clinical Immunology; Japanese Society of Allergology; Japan Society of Chest Diseases. *Publications:* "The Best Therapy of Bronchial Asthma", 1961; "Non-specific Therapy of Asthma with Gold Preparation & Insulin", 1981. *Hobby:* Oriental Antiques. *Address:* Suite 425, 1-9-25 Kasuga, Bunkyo-ku, Tolyo, Japan.

SUKUMARAN, P K, b. 10 Apr. 1943, Perinnanam, India. Consultant Psychiatrist and Medical Superintendent. m. K C Ratnaually, 3 Dec. 1967, Kodungallure, 2 sons. *Education:* MBBS; Post Graduate Qualification in Psychiatry and General Practice; MAPA; DPM; FCGP. *Appointments:* Assistant Surgeon, Government Health Services; Resident, Psychiatry, Central Institute of Psychiatry, Ranchi; Consultant Psychiatrist, Government Health Services; Consultant Psychiatrist and Medical Superintendent, Prasanthi Hospital, Trichur. *Memberships:* KGMOA; PGSA; Indian Medical Association; Indian Psychiatry Society; American Psychoatric Association. *Publications:* Author of various case reports and numerous general articles. *Hobbies:* Reading; Table tennis; Literary pursuits. *Address:* XX/352 Prasanthi, Sankarayya Road, Trichur 4 680004, India.

SULLIVAN, John Joseph, b. 29 Aug. 1925, Southport, Australia. Founder, Senior Partner, Drs Sullivan, Nicolaides & Partners. m. Helen Grace Guinn, 10 July 1954, Mackay, 1 son, 2 daughters. *Education:* MB, BS, 1st Class Honours, William Nathaniel Robertson Medal; FRACP; FRCPA. *Appointments:* Resident Medical Officer, 1949-51, Registrar, Pathology, 1953-55, Senior Pathologist, 1955-84; Royal Brisbane Hospital; Teacher, University of Queensland, Pathology Dept., 1952-53; Tutor, Pathology, University of Queensland, 1970-84. *Memberships:* American Society of Dermatopathology; Fellow, American Academy of Dermatology; Past President, Australian Society of Dermatopathology; Associate Member, Australasian College of Dermatologists; Past Vice President, Australian Society of Haematology. *Publications:* "Dissecting Aneurysm of the Aorta associated with Marfan's Syndrome", 1954; "Localized Submucosal Mucous Cysts of the Rectum", 1968; "Inverted Papilloma of the Urinary Bladder", 1971; "Fibrin-Bound Tumour Cells on a Sclerosed Mitral Valve", 1977; "Secretory (Juvenile) Carcinoma of the Breast", 1977; "Keratoacanthoma in a sub-tropical climate", 1979; "Multiple Keratoacanthomas", 1980; "Pathology of Keratoacanthoma in Malignant Skin Tumours", 1982. *Hobbies:* Golf; Member, Rose and Camellia Societies. *Address:* 112 Sherwood Road, Toowong, Brisbane 4066, Queensland, Australia.

SULOVIC, Vojin, b. 18 May 1923, Kursumlija, Yugoslavia. Deputy Rector; Director, Clinic of Obstetrics and Gynaecology. m. Dr Ljiljana Milojević, 29 Aug. 1964, Beograd, 2 daughters. *Education:* Faculty of Medicine, University of Belgrade; Specialist in Gynaecology and Obstetrics; MD; DSc. *Appointments:* Assistant, Associate Professor, President of the Assembly, currently Deputy Rector and Director of Clinic of Obstetrics and Gynaecology, Belgrade University. *Memberships:* Honorary Member, French Society of Perinatal Medicine; Serbian Academy of Sciences; Honorary Member, Roumanian Medical Academy. *Publications:* Author of 12 books on gynaecology and obstetrics, specialising in perinatal medicine, 280 papers in Yugoslav journals and 65 in foreign publications. *Honours:* Le Chevalier dans National Order of Merit, France, 1974; 3 Yugoslav medals, 1972, 77, 85. *Hobbies:* Swimming; Football; Climbing. *Address:* Dzordza Vasingtona 32-a, 11000 Beograde, Yugoslavia.

SUMMERS, Roger James, b. 11 Apr. 1943, Coventry, England. Senior Lecturer. m. Elizabeth Anne Gadd, 12 Apr. 1969, Coventry, 3 daughters. *Education:* B Pharm, University of London, 1965; PhD, National Institute for Medical Research Mill Hill, 1968. *Appointments:* Lecturer in Pharmacology, Glasgow University, 1969-77; Visiting Research Fellow, University of Melbourne, 1977-78; Lecturer in Pharmacology, Glasgow University, 1978-19; NH & MRC Research Fellow, 1979-80, NH & MRC Senior Research Fellow, 1980-84, Senior Lecturer, Department of Pharmacology, 1984-, University of Melbourne. *Memberships:* British Pharmacological Society; Physiological Society; Australian Society of Clinical and Experimental Pharmacologists; Australian Physiological and Pharmacological Society; Australian Neuroscience Society. *Publications:* More than 60 papers in scientific journals mainly British Journal of Pharmacology, European Journal of Pharmacology and Biochemical Pharmacology. *Hobbies:* Trout fishing; Computing. *Address:* Department of Pharmacology, University of Melbourne, Parkville, Victoria 3052, Australia.

SUMMERS, Stephen Lynn, b. 14 Nov. 1953, Lubbock, Texas, USA. Clinic Director, Administrator, Chief of Staff Clinician. m. Susan Elizabeth Stover, 10 Mar. 1984, Austin, 1 daughter. *Education:* Doctor of Chiropractic; Basic Science Certificate; National Board Certified; Doctorate, Texas Chiropractic College; Post graduate certification from: Motion Palpation Institute, Brickley Physical Therapeutics, Yoakum Radiological Association, International College of

Applied Kinesiology. *Appointments:* Chief of Medical Technology, Pasadena Memorial Hospital; Intern, Texas, Chiropractic College Public Clinic, Pasadena, Texas; Associate Doctor, Family Chiropractic Center, Austin. *Memberships:* American Chiropractic Association; Texas Chiropractic Association; Whole Health Institute; Renaissance Business Associates. *Honour:* Ordained as Server by Mother Church of Emissaries of Divine Light, 1983. *Hobbies:* Writing; Drama; Songwriting; Singing; Dance choreography; Long distance bicycling; Swimming; Racquetball. *Address:* 3405 Westside Cove, Austin, TX 78730, USA.

SUMMITT, Robert Layman, b. 23 Dec. 1932, Knoxville, Tennessee, USA. Dean, University of Tennessee College of Medicine. m. 23 Dec. 1955, LaFollette, Tennessee, 2 sons, 1 daughter. *Education:* Davidson College, North Carolina, 1950-51; University of Tennessee, 1951-52; MD, University of Tennessee College of Medicine, 1955; MS, Pediatrics, University of Tennessee Graduate School of Medical Sciences, 1962; Internship, University of Tennessee Memorial Hospital, 1956; Residency in Pediatrics, 1959-61; Fellowship in Pediatric Endocrinology and Metabolism, 1961-62; University of Tennessee College of Medicine; Fellowship in Medical Genetics, University of Wisconsin School of Medicine, 1963. *Appointments include:* US Navy Flight Surgeon, 1957-59; Assistant, Associate and Professor of Pediatrics and Anatomy, University of Tennessee College of Medicine, Memphis, 1971-; Dean, University of Tennessee College of Medicine, Memphis, 1981-; President and Chairman, Board of Directors, University Physicians Foundation, Memphis, 1983-; Rear Admiral, Medical Corps, US Naval Reserve, 1985-. *Memberships include:* Fellow, American Academy of Pediatrics; American Pediatric Society; American Society of Human Genetics; Official Oral Examiner for American Board of Pediatrics, Chairman of Written Examination Committee, 1984-85; Board of Directors, American Board of Medical Genetics, 1985-; American Medical Association, Consultant to Judicial Council, etc. *Publications:* 72 contributions to books; 66 publications in professional journals. *Honours include:* Award as Outstanding Alumnus of University of Tennessee College of Medicine presented by College of Medicine Alumni Association, 1984. *Hobbies:* Photography; Philately; Collection of Models of US Naval Aircraft. *Address:* University of Tennessee College of Medicine, 800 Madison Avenue, Memphis, TN 38163, USA.

SUN, Anthony Mien-Fang, b. 10 Apr. 1935, Nanking, China. Senior Research Scientist, Connaught Research Institute; Adjunct Professor, University of Toronto. m. Irene Ma, 20 June 1964, Toronto, Canada, 1 son, 1 daughter. *Education:* BSc, National Taiwan University, Taipei; MSc, PhD, University of Toronto, Ontario, Canada. *Appointments:* Lecturer, Assistant Professor, University of Toronto, 1965-68; Research Scientist, Research Consultant, Toronto Hospital for Sick Children, 1972-78; Research Scientist, Head of Islet and Hormone Research, Senior Research Scientist, Connaught Research Institute, Connaught Laboratories Limited, 1974-; Adjunct Professor, Department of Physiology, University of Toronto, 1978-; Honorary Professor of Medicine, Shanghai Medical University, China, 1984-. *Memberships:* International Society for Artificial Organs; Canadian Physiological Society; International Controlled Release Society; American Diabetes Association; Canadian Diabetes Association; Toronto Diabetes Association; Banting and Best Diabetic Centre; American Society of Artificial Internal Organs. *Publications:* Co-author, 'Encapsulated cells as long-term hormone delivery systems', 'Journal Critical Reviews' in 'Therapeutic Drug Carrier Systems'; 'Method in the Medical Applications of Microencapsulated Pancreatic Islets', 'Method in Enzymology'. *Hobbies:* Tennis; Art. *Address:* Connaught Research Institute, 1755 Steeles Avenue West, Willowdale, Toronto, Ontario, Canada M2R 3T4.

SUN, Mehmet Sadi, b. 27 July 1922, Istanbul, Turkey. Professor; Director. *Education:* MD, Specialist of Anaesthesiology; Anaesthesiologist. *Appointments:* Director, Department of Anaesthesia and Reanimation, Medical Faculty of Istanbul, Director, Department of Anaesthesia and Reanimation, Medical Faculty of Cerrahpasa. *Memberships:* Turkish Society of Anaesthesiology and Reanimation; Founder, Former Senator, European Academy of Anaesthesiology; Turkish Society of Intensive Care. *Publications:* 'Anaesthesia in intrathorasic surgery without CO2, absorption', 1955; 'Ketamine anaesthesia without dreams', 1973; 'The effects of nitrous oxide on pulmonary arterial pressure', 1974. *Hobbies:* Electronics. *Address:* Department of Anaesthesiology, Medical Faculty of Cerrahpasa, Istanbul, Turkey.

SUN, Yan, b. 1 Feb. 1929, China. Professor, Head of Department of Medical Oncology. m. Dr Mei-fang Cui, 12 Aug. 1954, Beijing, China, 1 son, 1 daughter. *Education:* MS, Yenching University, Beijing; MD, Peking Union Medical College; Visiting Professor, M D Anderson Hospital & Tumour Institute. *Appointments:* Resident, Peking Union Medical College Hospital, Beijing; Medical Oncologist, Cancer Institute & Hospital, Chinese Academy of Medical Sciences, Beijing; Head of Department, Professor of Medical Oncology, Chinese Academy of Medical Sciences, Beijing. *Memberships:* International Association for the Study of Lung Cancer; American Society of Clinical Oncology; Chinese Association of Oncology; Chinese Association for Integration of TCM and Western Medicine; Chinese Cancer Research Foundation; Evaluation Committee of New Drugs, Ministry of Public Health, Beijing. *Publications:* More than 100 articles & 15 books in field of medical oncology, malignant lymphomas & lung cancer; Chinese Medical Herbs as BRMs, 1983, 1984. Lung Cancer, 1983. *Hobbies:* Music; Photography. *Address:* 1-4-6 Cancer Institute & Hospital, Chinese Academy of Medical Sciences, Beijing, Republic of China.

SUNDBLAD, Lars Karl Magnus, b. 14 July 1921, Nederluleå) Sweden. Head Department of Clinical Chemistry. m. Görel Margareta Wikström, 4 Apr. 1950, 1 son, 2 daughters. *Education:* MD, University of Uppsala, 1953. *Appointments:* Assistant in Medical Chemistry, University of Uppsala; Research Fellow, Department of Connective Tissue Research, Retina Foundation, Boston, Massachusetts, USA; Laboratory Physician, Central Clinical Laboratory of Södersjukhuset, Stockholm, Sweden; Assistant Professor in Medical Chemistry, Uppsala University, 1953; Assistant Professor in Clinical Chemistry, Karolinska Institute, Stockholm, 1967-; Head of Department of Clinical Chemistry, Karolinska Institute. *Memberships:* Member of various biochemical and medical associations in Stockholm. *Publications:* 'Studies in Hyaluronic Acid in Synovial Fluid' thesis, Uppsala University, 1953; About 100 articles in Biochemistry and Clinical Chemistry. *Honour:* Knight 1st class of The Royal Order of the Northern Star, 1972. *Hobbies:* Tennis; Angling. *Address:* Department of Clinical Chemistry, Södersjukhuset, Stockholm, Sweden.

SUNDELL, Börje W, b. 2 Nov. 1927, Turku, Finland. Head, Division of Plastic Surgery. m. Birgit Soderstrom, 18 July 1953, Helsinki, 1 son, 1 daughter. *Education:* MD, 1953; DMS, 1958; Assistant Professor of Plastic Surgery, 1965; Professor of Plastic Surgery, University of Bergen, Norway, 1982. *Appointments:* Resident, General Surgery, Maria Municipal Hospital, Finnish Red Cross Hospital and University Hospital Helsinki, 1955-60; Resident, Plastic Surgery, Finnish Red Cross Hospital, 1960-62, 65, 66; Consultant, Plastic Surgeon, Orthopaedic Hospital Invalid Foundation, 1963-65; Roswell Park Memorial Institute, Head and Neck Service, Buffalo, New York, USA, 1962-63; Head, Division of Plastic Surgery, University Hospital Helsinki, 1966-. *Memberships:* Finnish Medical Association; Finnish Surgical Society; Chirurgi Plastici Fenniae; Scandinavian Society of Plastic

Surgeons; British Association of Plastic Surgery; American Association of Plastic and Reconstructive Surgery. *Publications:* Author of textbook on traumatology in Swedish and Finnish and 120 scientific publications on research on reconstructive plastic surgery, microsurgery and burns. *Honours:* Postdoctoral Fellowship, 1962-63, Returning Fellowship, 1964-66, National Institute of Health, Bethesda, Maryland, USA. *Hobbies:* Sports; Photography; Literature. *Address:* Division of Plastic Surgery, University Hospital Helsinki, Toolo Hospital, Topeliuksenkatu 5, 00260, Helsinki 26, Finland.

SUNDERMAN, F(rederick) William, Junior, b. 23 June 1931, Philadelphia, Pennsylvania, USA. Professor of Laboratory Medicine and Pharmacology. m. Carolyn Reynolds, MD, 24 Aug. 1963, Chestertown, Maryland, 1 son, 2 daughters. *Education:* BS, Emory University, Atlanta, 1952; MD, Jefferson Medical School, Philadelphia, 1955; Diplomate in Clinical Chemistry, American Board of Clinical Chemistry, 1960; Diplomate in Clinical Pathology, American Board of Pathology, 1961. *Appointments:* Instructor in Medicine, Thomas Jefferson University, Philadelphia, 1961-64; Associate Professor of Pathology, 1964-67, Professor of Pathology, 1967-68, University of Florida, Gainesville; Professor and Chairman, Department of Laboratory Medicine, 1965-, Professor of Pharmacology, 1979-, University of Connecticut, Farmington. *Memberships:* American Association for Cancer Research; American Association for Clinical Chemistry; American Association of Pathologists; College of American Pathologists; Association of Clinical Scientists; American Society for Pharmacology and Experimental Therapeutics; Endocrine Society; Society of Experimental Biology and Medicine; Society of Toxicology. *Publications:* Editor of 16 books and author of 236 scientific papers, primarily in the areas of trace metal metabolism, toxicology, cancer research and clinical laboratory methods. *Honours:* Clinical Scientist of the Year, Association of Clinical Scientists, 1977; Ames Award for Research, American Association for Clinical Chemistry, 1978. *Hobby:* Chamber Music (viola). *Address:* University of Connecticut School of Medicine, 263 Farmington Avenue, Farmington, CT 06032, USA.

SUNDWALL, Dale, b. 5 Dec. 1947, Miami, Arizona, USA. Obstetrician; Gynaecologist. m. Susan Adamson, 28 May 1971, Salt Lake City, 1 son, 3 daughters. *Education:* BS, Brigham Young University, 1972; MD, University of Oregon Medical School, 1978; Residency, Obstetrics, Gynaecology, Madigan Army Medical Centre, 1978-82; ABOG Board Certification, 1984. *Appointments:* Assistant Chief, OB-GYN Dept, US Army Hospital, Fort Ord, California, 1982-84; Group Practice, Eugene, Oregon. *Memberships:* American College of Obstetricians & Gynaecologists; American Medical Association; Oregon Medical Association; Lane County Medical Society; American Fertility Society; American Association Gynec. Laparoscopists. *Publications:* Author, "Reye Syndrome Associated with Hemophilus Influezal Inflection", 'Clinical Pediatric', 1980; "Unusual Hypersensitivity Reaction Association with Bromocriptine Mesylate", Presented at 19th Annual Armed Forces District ACOG Meeting, 1981; etc. *Honours:* Clinical Professor, University of California, San Francisco, 1982-; Clinical Faculty, University of Oregon Medical School, 1984-. *Hobbies:* Flying; Wind Surfing; Fishing; Hiking; Skiing. *Address:* 1490 Flintridge Ave, Eugene, OR 97401, USA.

SUPPAN, Raymond J, b. 26 Jan. 1931, Pennsylvania, USA. Podiatric Surgeon; University Professor. m. Donna J Suppan, 7 sons, 3 daughters. *Education:* DPM; Kent State University; Ohio College of Podiatric Medicine. *Appointments:* Chairman, Surgery, 1956-70, Professor, Surgery, 1956-, Ohio College of Podiatric Medicine; Director, Residence Programme, Cleveland Foot Clinic, 1956-70; Chairman, Podiatry Division, Wayne General Hospital, 1956-75. *Memberships:* Diplomate, American Board of Podiatric

Surgery; Founder, American College of Podopediatrics; Fellow, American College of Foot Surgeons; Past President, Ohio Podiatric Medical Association; Past President, Alumni Association, Ohio College of Podiatric Medicine. *Publications:* "Clinic in Podiatry (Podopediatrics)", 1985, "Podiatric Surgery", 1964, both in 'Text'; numerous articles in medical journals, 1956-85. *Honours:* Outstanding Alumnus, Ohio College of Podiatric Medicine, 1983; Year Book Dedication, Ohio College of Podiatric Medicine, 1960; Outstanding Young Men of America, 1956; Outstanding Teacher, Ohio College of Podiatric Medicine, 1979. *Hobby:* Running. *Address:* 1720 Paradise Road, Orrville, OH 44667, USA.

SUREAU, Claude Guy Robert, b. 27 Sep. 1927, Paris, France. Professor, Chairman, Clinique Universitaire Baudelocque. m. Janine Murset, 2 Oct. 1956, 1 son, 2 daughters. *Education:* MD, University of Paris, 1955; Visiting Fellow, Columbia Presbyterian Medical Centre, New York, USA, 1955-56; Specialization in Obstetrics and Gynaecology. *Appointments:* Assistant Professor, University of Paris, Assistant Attending, Hospital St Vincent de Paul, 1956-61; Associate Professor, Associate Attending, Hospital St Vincent de Paul and Clinique Baudelocque, 1961-74; Professor, Chairman, Obstetrics & Gynaecology, Hospital St Vincent de Paul, 1974-76; Professor, Chairman, University Clinique Baudelocque, 1976-; Director, Unit 262, National Institute of Health and Medical Research, 1983-. *Memberships:* National Academy of Medicine, France; International Federation of Obstetrics and Gynaecology, President, 1982-85; President, Standing Committee, Study of Ethical Problems in Human Reproduction; Federation, French Speaking Gynaecologists and Obstetricians, Secretary General, 1968-84, Vice President, 1984-86; National Society of Obstetrics and Gynaecology of France, Executive Board, 1971-; French Society of Perinatal Medicine, President, 1975-77. *Publications:* "Le Danger de Naitre", 1978; "Clinical Perinatology", co-author, 1980; "Immunologie de la Reproduction Humaine", co-author, 1983. *Honours:* Chevalier de la Legion d'Honneur, 1977. *Address:* Clinique Universitaire Baudelocque, 123 Boulevard de Port Royal, 75674 Paris Cedex 14, France.

SURMELI, Suphi, b. 18 Jan. 1931, Turkey. Assistant Clinical Director; Assistant Professor. m. Guner Erdal, 13 June 1965, Mersin, Turkey, 2 sons, 1 daughter. *Education:* BA 1951, MD, University of Istanbul, Turkey, 1954. *Appointments:* Internship, St Francis Hospital, Poughkeepsie, New York, 1958-59; Resident, Harlem Valley State Hospital, Wingdale, New York, 1959-60; Hudson River State Hospital, Poughkeepsie, New York, 1961-64; Training, New York State Psychiatric Institute, 1959; Vanderbilt Clinic Columbia Presbyterian Hospital, 1964; House Staff, Kingston General Hospital, Kingston, New York, 1966-67; Senior Psychiatrist, Harlem Valley State Hospital, Wingdale, New York, 1967-68; Acting Medical Director, Southeast Nassau Guidance Clinic, Seaford, New York, 1969-70; Staff Psychiatrist, Brunswick Hospital Center, Amityville, New York, 1969-71; Attending Staff Psychiatrist, Mercy Hospital, Rockville Center, New York, 1970-71; Senior Psychiatrist, 1970-72, Assistant Clinical Director, 1972-86, Clinical Director, 1986-, South Oaks Hospital, Amityville, New York, 1972-; Associate Attending Psychiatrist, Good Samaritan Hospital, West Islip, 1972-; Attending Psychiatrist, Lakeside Hospital, Copiague, New York, 1972-77; Attending Staff Psychiatrist, Syosset Hospital, Syosset, New York, 1976-78; Southside Hospital, Bay Shore, New York, 1979-83; Central General Hospital, Plainview, New York, 1981-82. *Memberships:* Nassau County Medical Society; NY State Medical Society; American Psychiatric Association; Turkish American Physician Association; Turkish American Neuropsychiatric Society; Suffolk County Psychiatric Society. *Honour:* Recipient, Good Citizenship Award, Department of Education, Ministry of Education, Turkey, 1974. *Hobbies:* Playing Cards; Tennis; Swimming. *Address:* 400 Sunrise Highway, Amityville, NY 11701, USA.

SURYANTORO, Purnomo, b. 18 Apr. 1942, Pati Central, Java. Lecturer, Pediatric Faculty of Medicine, Gadjah Mada University. m. Inda Suprati, 2 Aug. 1970, 2 sons. *Education:* Pediatrician, Gadjah Mada University, 1975; Diploma, Tropical Medicine & Hygiene, Mahidol University, Banbkok, 1976. *Memberships:* Indonesian Medical Association; Indonesian Pediatric Association; International Club of Physicians. *Publications:* "Five Years follow up of Nephrotic Syndrome on Children in Jogyakarta, Indonesia", 1974; "One Year Follow up on LBW Infants in Jogyakarta", 1980. *Hobby:* Tennis. *Address:* Child Health Dept, Faculty of Medicine, Gadjah Mada University, Jogyakarta, Indonesia.

SUSSMAN, Michael David, b. 20 Feb. 1943, Baltimore, Maryland, USA. Associate Professor, Orthopaedic Surgery & Rehabilitation; Associate Professor, Orthopaedic Surgery, Division of Paediatric Orthopaedics. m. Nancy Whiteley, 13 Aug. 1971, 1 son, 1 daughter. *Education:* MD, University of Maryland School of Medicine, 1967. *Appointments:* Instructor, Orthopaedic Surgery, Children's Hospital, Harvard Medical School, 1976; Assistant Professor, University of Virginia, 1976-81; Assistant Professor, Paediatrics, University of Virginia, 1977-81. *Memberships:* American Academy Cerebral Palsy and Development Medicine; Fellow, American Academy Pediatrics; Paediatric Orthopaedic Society; Fellow, American Academy of Orthopaedic Surgeons; Fellow, Scoliosis Research Society; etc. *Publications include:* Numerous articles in professional journals including: 'Journal Pediatric Orthopaedics'; 'Journal Orthopaedic Research'; 'American Journal Physiology'; 'Journal Experimental Medicine'; 'American Journal of Roentgenology'; etc. *Honours:* Robert B. Lovett Fellow, Paediatric Orthopaedics, 1976; Orthopaedic Research and Education Foundation, Gianestras-Schmerge Travelling Fellowship to Germany & Finland, 1977. *Address:* Children's Rehabilitation Centre, 2270 Ivy Road, Charlottesville, VA 22901, USA.

SUTHERLAND, Ian, b. 30 June 1921, London, England. Director, Biostatistics Unit, Medical Research Council, Cambridge, 1969-. m. Susanne Lederer, 30 Mar. 1946, Cambridge, 2 sons. *Education:* MA, Cambridge University; DPhil, Oxford University. *Appointments:* Assistant in Statistics, Institute of Social Medicine, Oxford, 1945; Member, Scientific Staff, Statistical Research Unit, Medical Research Council, London, 1952. *Memberships:* Royal Statistical Society; Biometric Society; Honorary Member, British Thoracic Society. *Publications:* "Stillbirths", 1949; 'Recent studies in the epidemiology of tuberculosis', 1976. *Honours:* Silver Jubilee Medal, 1977; Weber-Parkes Prize, Royal College of Physicians, 1984. *Address:* MRC Biostatistics Unit, 5 Shaftesbury Road, Cambridge CB2 2BW, England.

SUTTER, Morley Carman, b. 18 May 1933, Redvers, Saskatchewan, Canada. Professor. m. Virginia F M Laidlaw, 29 June 1957, Winnipeg, 2 sons, 1 daughter. *Education:* MD, BSc (Med), 1957, PhD, Pharmacology, 1963, University of Manitoba; LMCC, 1957. *Appointments:* General Medical Practice, Souris, 1957-58; Medical Resident, Winnipeg General Hospital, 1958-59; Medical Research Council Fellow, University of Manitoba, 1959-63; Imperial Chemical Industries, Fellow, Cambridge University, 1963-65; Supervisor, Member, Downing College, Cambridge, England, 1963-65; Assistant Professor, Pharmacology, University of Toronto, 1965-66; Medical Research Council Scholar, 1966-71, Associate Professor, 1968-71, Professor, Head of Dept, 1971-, University of British Columbia. *Memberships:* Pharmacological Society of Canada; British Pharmacological Society; American Society Pharmacology & Therapeutics; Canadian Society for Clinical Investigation; Canadian Medical Association; New York Academy of Sciences. *Publications:* Author, various articles in scientific journals. *Honours:* Governor General's Medal, 1950; Isbister Scholarship, 1952; Gold Medal, Physiology, 1954;

Powse Prize for Research, 1961. *Hobbies:* Gardening; Baseball; Jazz. *Address:* University of British Columbia, Department of Pharmacology & Therapeutics, 2176 Health Science Mall, Vancouver, BC, V6T 1W5, Canada.

SUTTON, Jere G, b. 9 Oct. 1932, Fairview, Oklahoma, USA. Orthopaedic Surgeon. m. Margaret A McConnell, 12 June 1954, Cherokee, Oklahoma, 2 sons, 1 daughter. *Education:* BS, Central State University, Edmond, Oklahoma, 1954; DO, Kirksville College of Osteopathic Medicine, 1959. *Appointments:* Resident, Rocky Mountain Hospital, Denver, Colo5ado, 1970-71 and 1973-74, Detroit Osteopathic Hospital, Detroit, Michigan, 1971-73; Flight Surgeon, United States Air Force, Medical Corps; Medical Board, Lapeer County General Hospital, Lapeer, Michigan; Vice-Chief of Staff, Craig County General Hospital, Vinita, Oklahoma; Orthopaedic Surgeon, Lieutenant Colonel, Medical Corps, United States Air Force Reserves. *Memberships include:* Board of Trustees, Oklahoma Osteopathic Association; Northeast Oklahoma Osteopathic Association; American Academy of Osteopathic Surgeons; Christian Medical Society; American Osteopathic Association; American Academy of Osteopathic Specialists; American Osteopathic Academy of Orthopedics; American Osteopathic Academy of Sports Medicine; Aerospace Medical Association; Association of Military Osteopathic Physicians and Surgeons; Society of USAF Flight Surgeons; Association of Military Surgeons of the United State; National Association of Disability Evaluation Physicians. *Publications:* 'Factors Affecting Wound Healing: A Scientific Review', 1972; 'Immediate Fitting of a Plaster Cast and Prosthetic Pylon Following a Below the Knee Amputation: A Case Report', 1973; 'Pulmonary Embolism', 1974. *Hobbies:* Travel; Sightseeing; Cooking; Bowling; Fishing; Hunting; Skiing; Photography. *Address:* 3100 North Hillside, Wichita, KS 67219, USA.

SVEDMYR, Nils Lennart Walter, b. 13 Nov. 1927, Göteborg, Sweden. Professor of Clinical Pharmacology. m. (1) Siv Andersson, 1949, 2 sons; (2) Karin Wilkström, 1974. *Education:* MD, 1957, PhD, Assistant Professor, 1966; Professor, Clinical Pharmacology, 1981. *Appointments:* Lecturer, University of Göteborg, 1953-67, Assistant Professor, Clinical Pharmacology, 1969-81, Professor, 1981-. *Memberships:* Swedish Society for Clinical Pharmacology; Swedish Society of Pneumology; European Society of Pneumology; European Society of Allergology and Immunology. *Publications:* 'Studies on the relationships between some metabolic effects of thyroid hormones and catecholamines in animal and man' in 'Acta Physiol. Scand.', (thesis), 1966; Scandinavian Symposium on Chronic Obstructive Airways Disease, 1978; 'Long term theophylline therapy' in 'Eur J Respir Dis Suppl'; 'Drugs in the treatment of asthma' in 'Respiratory Pharmacology'; 'Airway hyperreactivity' in 'Eur J Respir Dis', 1983; 'Asthma - pathophysiology and treatment' in 'Eur J Respir Dis suppl', 1984; 'Is beta adrenoceptor sensitivity a limiting factor in asthma therapy?' in 'Beta-adrenoceptors in asthma', 1984. *Hobby:* Sailing. *Address:* Department of Clinical Pharmacology, Sahlgren's Hospital, S-413 45 Göteborg, Sweden.

SWAN, William Russell, b. 27 Nov. 1943, Fort Smith, Arkansas, USA. Doctor. m. Janet Ruth Morgan, 19 Sep. 1969, Pryor, 2 sons. *Education:* MD, Oklahoma University School of Medicine, 1969; Rotating Internship, US Naval Hospital, 1969-70; Flight Surgeon's School, Naval Aerospace Medical Institute, Pensacola, 1970-71; Fellowship, Tropical Medicine, Macau, China, 1980-84; Diplomate, Tropical Medicine and Public Health, Macau, China, 1985. *Appointments include:* Lecturer, Eastern Virginia School of Medicine, 1974; Asia Consultant, World Concern, 1979-; Asia Consultant, Baylor Medical School, 1983-, Bowman Gray School of Medicine, 1983-; Medical Consultant, Realife Ranch Juvenile Rehabilitation Center, Rogers, Arkansas, 1974-; Medical Examiner, Mayes County, 1974-76; Director, Hope Medical

Group, Macau, China, 1979-; Director, Refugee Nutrition Project, Macau, 1983-85; Director, Health Education Project for Vietnamese Refugees, Macau, 1983-84; Staff Physician, Kiang Wu Chinese Hospital, 1985-; Private Practice. *Memberships include:* Oklahoma, Texas, Virginia, and American Medical Associations; Medical Association of Manitoba, Canada; British Medical Association; World Medical Association; Ordem dos Medicos, Macau, Portugal; American College of Chest Physicians; American College of Physicians; New York Academy of Sciences; Christian Medical Society, etc. *Publications:* "Effect of BCG Vaccination received at Birth on Later PPD Evaluation", in press; "Effect of BCG at Birth with Booster at School Entrance on Later PPD Evaluation", in press; "Effect of adequate Bacteriocidal Treatment of TBC on later PPD Evaluation", in press. *Honours:* Recipient, various honours and awards. *Hobbies:* Bluegrass Banjo; Guitar; Home Computers; Squash Racquets. *Address:* 12 Calcado Do Monte, Macao, China.

SWENSON, Rand Stephen, b. 14 Nov. 1953, Mineola, New York, USA. Doctor of Chiropractic; Professor. m. Mardrey Ellen Fish, 23 Apr. 1977, Norwalk, Connecticut, 1 son, 1 daughter. *Education:* BS 1974, DC, National College of Chiropractic, 1976; PhD, Loyola University of Chicago, 1981. *Appointments:* Instructor 1977-79, Assistant Professor 1979-81, Associate Professor 1981-85, Professor, National College of Chiropractic, 1985-, Research Associate, Loyola University Medical School, 1981-82; Visiting Professor, Tokyo Metropolitan Institute of Gerontology, 1983, 1984. *Memberships:* Sigma Xi; National Scientific Honor Fraternity; American Association for the Advancement of Science. *Publications:* 15 papers, in the field of cerebellar motor systems neuroanatomy and autonomic neurophysiology, in such journals as, Neuroscience; Brain Research; Neuroscience Letters; American Journal of Anatomy; Journal of the Autonomic Nervous System; Neuroscience Research, 1979-85. *Honour:* Summa Cum Laude Graduate of National College of Chiropractic, 1976. *Hobbies:* Soccer; Golf; Computers. *Address:* 200 East Roosevelt Road, Lombard, IL 60148, USA.

SWIFT, Ronnie Elaine Gorman, b. 13 Sep. 1948, New York, USA. Private Practitioner; Clinical Assistant Professor of Psychiatry. m. Michael Ronald Swift, 27 Nov. 1971, New York, New York, 3 daughters. *Education:* BS, City College of New York, New York, 1969; MD, University of North Carolina, 1975. *Appointments:* Resident Psychiatry, North Carolina Memorial Hospital, 1976-78; Clinical Assistant Professor, Duke University, 1981-82, University of North Carolina, 1982-. *Memberships:* Alpha Omega Alpha; American Psychiatric Association; North Carolina Neuropsychiatric Association; North Carolina Psychoanalytic Association. *Publications:* Co-author of contributions to: 'Nature', 1972; 'Annals Rev Med', 1972. *Honours:* Honours in Chemistry, City College of New York, 1969; Alpha Omega Alpha, 1975; George C Thrasher Award, 1976; Falk Fellowship, 1977. *Hobbies:* Cooking; Gardening; Travelling; Hiking. *Address:* Route 7 Box 284, Chapel Hill, NC 27514, USA.

SWINBURN, Malcolm John, b. 16 Nov. 1937, Canungra, Queensland, Australia. Consultant Physician and Cardiologist; Visiting Medical Officer. m. Meryl Elizabeth Evans, 7 Aug. 1965, Concord, Sydney, New South Wales, 2 sons, 1 daughter. *Education:* BA, Oxford University, England; BSc, MB BS, Sydney University; Diploma of Physical Anthropology, Oxford; FRACP; New South Wales Rhodes Scholar, 1960. *Appointments:* Tutor, Physiology, St Pauls College, Sydney, 1964; Resident Medical Officer, Bankstown Hospital, 1966; Resident Medical Officer, Pathology Registrar, Medical Registrar, Fellow in Cardiology, Sydney Hospital, 1967-71; Fellow in Cardiology, Prince Henry Hospital, 1972-74; Visiting Lecturer, Queen Mary Hospital, Hong Kong, 1974; Physician, Randwick Chest Hospital, 1974-75; Relieving Honorary Consultant Physician, Western Suburbs Hospital, 1974-82; currently, Consultant Physician and Cardiologist, Visiting Medical Officer, Prince Henry and Prince of Wales Hospital; Visiting Staff, Institute of Sports Medicine, Lewisham. *Memberships:* Fellow, Royal Australasian College of Physicians; Cardiac Society of Australia and New Zealand. *Honour:* Haswell Prize in Zoology, Sydney University, 1956. *Hobbies:* Family; School sports; Church. *Address:* 6 Carlotta Street, Greenwich, NSW 2065, Australia.

SYLVESTER, Robert Louis Joseph, b. 25 Oct. 1956. Chiropractor. *Education:* BA, Biology; Doctor of Chiropractic. *Memberships:* American Chiropractic Association; Bergen-Passaic Chiropractic Society; New Jersey Chiropractic Association; 1st Vice President, Palisades Park Chapter, Unico. *Hobbies:* Music; Fishing; Softball; Racketball; Recreational sport; Reading. *Address:* 130 Kinderkamack Road, Suite 207, River Edge, NJ 07661, USA.

SYMINGTON, David Cambridge, b. 12 Sep. 1928, Glasgow, Scotland. Professor of Rehabilitation Medicine. m. Evelyn Prizzell, 19 Dec. 1950, Williamwood, 2 sons, 4 daughters. *Education:* MB, ChB, Glasgow, 1951; D Phys Med, Royal College of Physicians and Surgeons - England, 1955; American Board of Physical Medicine and Rehabilitation, 1963; FRCP (C) Physical Medicine and Rehabilitation, 1972. *Appointments:* Senior Medical Officer, RAF Medical Rehabilitation Centre, Headley Court, Surrey, 1955-57; Assistant Medical Director, G F Strong Rehabilitation Centre and Greater Vancouver Cerebral Palsy Clinic, Canada, 1957-62; Lecturer-Assistant Professor, Department of Physical Medicine and Rehabilitation, University of Washington, Seattle, USA, 1962-66; Director of School of Rehabilitation Therapy 1966-73, Professor and Head of Department of Rehabilitation Medicine 1966-82, Professor of Rehabilitation Medicine 1982-, Queen's University, Kingston, Ontario, Canada; Director of Regional Rehabilitation Centre, Kingston General Hospital, 1966-82; Senior Consultant in Rehabilitation Medicine, Ministry of Community and Social Services, Ontario, 1982-. *Memberships:* World Health Organisation Expert Advisory Panel on Rehabilitation; Chairman, Medical Commission, Rehabilitation International; Chairman, National Research Council Associate Committee on Research and Development for Benefit of Disabled Persons; President 1983-85, Canadian Association of Physical Medicine and Rehabilitation; Honorary Member, Section of PMR, BCMA; Honorary Member, Canadian Association of Rehabilitation Personnel. *Publications:* "Independence Through Environmental Controls", 1980; 'The Goals of Rehabilitation', 1984. *Honours:* Bronze Medal, American Congress PMR, 1963; Queen's Jubilee Medal, 1977; Coulter Lecturer, American Congress of PMR, 1983. *Hobbies:* Photography; Poetry; Travel. *Address:* Department of Rehabilitation Medicine, Queens University, Kingston, Ontario K7L 3N6, Canada.

SYMMANS, William Ashley, b. 19 Oct. 1929, Manaia, New Zealand. Haematologist, Waikato Hospital & Hamilton Medical Laboratory. m. Mary Forbes Whimster, 3 June 1961, Auckland, 1 son, 3 daughters. *Education:* MB, ChB; FRCPA. *Appointments:* Pathology Registrar, Princess Alexandra Hospital, Brisbane, Australia; Pathologist, Waikato Hospital, Hamilton, New Zealand; Haematologist, Hamilton Medical Laboratory. *Memberships:* New Zealand Society of Pathologists; Haematology Society of Australia; New York Academy of Sciences; New Zealand Society for Haematology; International Society of Haematology. *Publications:* "Hereditary Acanthocytosis Associated with McLeod Phenotype of the Kell Blood Group System", 'British Journal of Haematology', 1979; "Elevated Serum Creatine Phosphokinase in Subjects with McLeod Syndrome", 'Vox Sanguinis', 1981; "Two Unstable Hemoglobins in One Individual: Hb Atalnta and Hb Coventry", 'Hemoglobin', 1983; "Cyclic Eosinophilic Myositis and Hyperimmunoglobulin-E", 'Annals of Internal Medicine', 1986. *Hobbies:* Honorary Surgeon, New Zealand Rugby League; Trout Fishing; Commodore, Auckland Grammar School Rowing. *Address:* Hamilton Medical Laboratory, PO Box 52 Hamilton, New Zealand.

SZADAY, Barbara Ann, b. 18 Nov. 1956, Melbourne, Australia. Officer Commanding, 18 Dental Unit. *Education:* BDSc, University of Melbourne; LDS, State of Victoria. *Appointments:* Captain, Dental Officer, Melbourne, 1980-82, Bandiana 1983; Major, Officer Commanding 18 Dental Unit, Singleton, NSW, 1984-. *Memberships:* Australian Dental Association. *Honour:* First female ARA RAADC, 1984. *Hobbies:* Classical Guitar; Singing; Athletics; Swimming; Tennis; Reading. *Address:* c/o 28 Park Road, Mount Waverly, Victoria, Australia.

SZCZEPANIAK, Stanislaw, b. 10 Apr. 1929, Syry, Poland. Professor and Chief of Department of Toxicological Chemistry. m. Julitta Hentel, 27 July 1958, 1 son, 1 daughter. *Education:* Master of Chemistry, Maria Curie-Sklodowska University, Lublin, 1952; Doctor of Chemistry, Adam Mickiewicz University, Poznan, 1964. *Appointments:* Assistant 1952-55, Assistant Lecturer 1955-64, Adjunct/Lecturer 1964-73, Department of General Chemistry, Medical Academy, Lublin; Assistant Professor 1974-82, Professor and Chief 1982-, Department of Toxicological Chemistry, Medical Academy, Lublin. *Memberships:* Polish Toxicological Society; Polish Biochemical Society; Polish Pharmaceutical Society. *Publications include:* 'Gaschromatographische Bestimmung von Athanol neben anderen flüchtigen Stoffen in frischem und konserviertem Blut', 1978; 'The influence of carbaryl on biochemical processes of the organism', 1979; 'Body amino acid balance in acute poisoning with chlorfenvinphos', 1981; 'Brain free amino acid levels in rats following the acute intoxication with chlorfenvinphos', 1984. *Honours:* The Golden Cross of Merit, 1974; Order of Knight, 1984. *Hobbies:* Motor car touring; Chess. *Address:* Department of Toxicological Chemistry, ul Dymitrowa 5, 20-080 Lublin, Poland.

SZECHY, Miklos, b. 15 July 1928, Török St Miklos, Hungary, Head Surgeon, County Hospital, Tatabanya, Hungary. Surgical Inspector, County Komarom, Hungary. m. Susanna Machatsek, 21 Mar. 1952, Budapest, 2 sons. *Education:* MD, Medical University, Budapest, 1952; Special Exam in Surgery, Medical University, Debrecen, 1956; Habilitation for Candidate of Medical Sciences, Budapest, 1973. *Appointments:* Medical University, Budapest, 1946-52; Internship, Apponyi Poliklinika, Budapest, 1948-52; Residentship, County Hospital, Satoraljaujhely, 1952-56; Surgeon, Koranyi Hospital, Budapest, 1956-60; Adjunct, Uzsoki Hospital, Budapest, 1960-65. *Memberships:* Hungarian Medical Association; Member of Board, Hungarian Surgical Society. *Publications:* 'Hidrogen-ion deficiency in surgery', 1973; Author of over 60 medical and surgical articles. *Honours:* Excellent worker of Health, 1977; Order for Labour, Silver Grade, 1979. *Hobbies:* Music; Literature. *Address:* 30 Uri Street, Budapest 1, H-1014, Hungary.

SZILAGYI, Tibor, b. 13 Aug. 1921, Debrecen, Hungary. Professor of Pathophysiology. m. Hajnalka Hegyesi, 17 Aug. 1962, Budapest, Hungary. *Education:* C Sci, 1961, D Sci, 1974, Hungarian Academy of Sciences; MD, University of Debrecen, 1944. *Appointments:* Assistant, Institute of Physiology, 1943-49, First Assistant, Institute of Pathophysiology, 1949-54, Assistant Professor, Institute of Pathophysiology, 1954-69, Professor, Institute of Pathophysiology, 1969-, Medical University, Debrecen. *Memberships:* Hungarian Physiology Society; Hungarian Allergol, Clinical Immunology Society; European Academy of Allergology; Hungarian Intercosmos Committee; Hungarian Immunology, Pharmacology, Microbiology Society; President, Section of Sportbiology, Debrecen Academic Committee; President, Astronaut Section, Debrecen. *Publica-*

tions: 'Antigens, Shwartzman-reaction' in "Immunological Aspects of Allergy and Allergic Disease", editor Rajka-Korossy, 1974; 150 articles in the field of anaphylaxis, allergy, hypothermia, endotoxin, space biology. *Honours:* Eminent Worker of Higher Education, 1964 and 1982; Eminent Worker of Sport, 1978; Medal of Merits for Socialist Culture, 1983. *Hobbies:* Philatelist; Numismatist. *Address:* Institute of Pathophysiology, Medical University, 4012 Debrecen, P.O.B. 23, Hungary.

SZMITKOWSKI, Maciej, b. 8 May 1946, Czeremcha, Poland. Head of Department of Biochemical Diagnostics. m. 6 July 1968, 2 daughters. *Education:* Physician 1970, MD 1973, Specialist in Laboratory Diagnostics 1976, PhD 1979, Medical Faculty, Medical School, Bialystok. *Appointments:* Assistant 1970-74, Senior Researcher 1974-79, Assistant Professor 1979-84, Department of Clinical Biochemistry, Vice-Dean 1984-, Faculty of Medical Analytics, Head 1985-, Department of Biochemical Diagnostics, Medical Faculty, Medical School, Bialystok. *Memberships:* International Federation of Clinical Chemistry; Executive Council, Polish Society of Laboratory Diagnostics; Polish Biochemical Society; Polish Physicians Society. *Publications:* 'Colony Stimulating Factor and its role in the regulation of granulopoiesis', 1978; 'The Inhibitors of Granulopoiesis', 1979; 'Haematopoietic Stem Cells', 1984. *Honours:* Awards of the Polish Minister of Health and Welfare for scientific research on Pathophysiology of Leucocytes 1978, and Protein's Stimulators of Granulopoiesis 1979. *Hobby:* Tourism. *Address:* Department of Biochemical Diagnostics, Institute of Laboratory Diagnostics, Medical School, Sklodowska-Curie 24 A, 15-276 Bialystok, Poland.

SZOCSKA, János Adám, b. 15 May 1926, Nagyszöllös, Hungary. Ear, Nose & Throat Specialist. m. Irén Szócska, 17 Jan. 1953, Budapest, 1 son, 1 daughter. *Education:* MD, 1950, ENT Specialist, 1953, Budapest. *Appointments:* Assistant Doctor 1951-57, Resident Physician 1957-62, First Assistant to Professor Krepuska 1962-69; Chief of ENT Department of County Hospital; ENT Inspector of Szabolcs-Szatmar County, Nyiregyháza. *Memberships:* Motesz; Board of Hungarian ENT Society. *Publications:* Various articles in international journals & proceedings, especially on tympanoplasty. *Honours:* Ministerial Award document, 1969; Outstanding Worker of Public Health Document, 1976. *Hobbies:* Hungarian Language & History. *Address:* H-1024 Budapest, Fény-u 2, Hungary.

SZOCSKA, Miklos, b. 15 July 1924, Nagyszöllös, Hungary. Head of Respiratory and Allergy Unit. m. Kornelia Szeniczey, 22 May 1958, 3 sons, 2 daughters. *Education:* Diploma 1950, Specialisation in Pediatrics 1954, Specialisation in Pneumology 1958, Medical University, Budapest. *Appointments:* Physician 1950-, Head of Respirator and Allergy Unit 1968-, Paediatric Institute of Szabadsaghegt and I, Paediatric Clinic, Budapest. *Memberships:* European Academy of Allergology and Clinical Immunology; European Society of Pneumology; Hungarian Paediatric Society; Hungarian Society of Allergology and Clinical Immunology; Hungarian Society of Pneumology and Paediatric Pneumology; Secretary, Hungarian Society of Pediatric Pneumology. *Publications:* "Die Nichttuberkulösen Lungenkrankheiten im Kindesalter", (with O Görgenyi-Göttche, 1979; Publications and lectures on asthma bronchiale, allergy, pediatric pneumology and Lungfunction-diagnostics. *Hobbies:* Tourism; Fine Art; Sports; Ancient Cultures. *Address:* Paediatric Institute of Szabadsaghegy, Diana 26.1.2, H-1125 Budapest XII, Hungary.

SZTANYIK, László Bálint, b. 9 Oct. 1926, Endrod, Hungary. Director-General, National Research Institute. m. Margit Orszigeti, 12 Aug., 1956, Budapest, 1 son, 1 daughter. *Education:* Medical Doctor; Specialist: Nuclear Medicine, Radiobiology and Radiohygiene. *Appointments:* Junior Scientist,

1951-56, Head of Division, 1956-66, Deputy Director, 1966-69, Director, 1974-81, Director-General, 1981-, Frederic Joliot-Curie National Research Institute, Budapest; Head of Section, International Atomic Energy Agency, Vienna, Austria, 1969-74. *Memberships:* Hungarian Societies of Physicists, Biophysicists, Biologists, Haematologists, Specialists in Nuclear Medicine, Oncologists, Radiologists; European Society for Radiation Biology; International Radiation Protection Association; International Commission on Radiological Protection. *Publications:* "Radiobiology", 1963; "Strahlenbiologie", 1966; "Application of Ionizing Radiation for Sterilization", 1974; "Late Radiobiological Effects of A-bombing in Japan", 1978; "Neutrons in Biology and Medicine", 1980. *Honours:* Order of Labour, Gold 1976; Order of Liberation, 1985; Memorial Medal of J. E. Purkyn., 1985. *Hobbies:* Horticulture; Viniculture. *Address:* Frederic Joliot-Curie National Research Institute for Radiobiology and Radiohygiene, H-1221 Budapest,

Pentz Karoly u.5, Hungary.

SZULC-KUBERSKA, Janina Irma, b. 30 Jan. 1929, Warszawa, Poland. Docent/Assistant Professor. m. Zdzislaw Kuberski (dec), 14 Feb. 1959, 1 daughter. *Education:* MD 1963; Doctor Habilitowany-Assistant Professor 1973. *Appointments:* Junior Assistant, 1953, Assistant Lecturer, 1957, Tutor Lecturer, Adiunkt in Poland, 1966, Docent in Poland, Assistant Professor, 1973, Department of Neurology, AM Loodz. *Memberships:* Member, Polish Neurological Society, 1954-; Society of War Concentration Labour Camp. *Publications:* 'The plantar reflex in normal children and in certain distinguishing neurogical problems', 1967; 'The disturbances of histidine metabolism in hereditary stammering', 1969. *Honour:* Gold Cross of Merit, 1984. *Hobbies:* Painting; Hiking. *Address:* Department of Neurology, Akademia Medyczna w Lodzi, Kopcinskiego 22, Szpital Barlickiego, Poland.

T

TABBARA, Abdul Ghany, b. 11 Sep. 1938, Syria. Chief, Obstetrics-Gynaecology. m. 2 Aug. 1968, 3 sons. *Education:* Medical School, Damascus, 1957-64; Residency, Obstetrics, Gynaecology, Cook County Hospital, Chicago, USA, 1972-76; American Board Certification, 1977. *Appointments:* Attending, Obstetrics, Gynaecology, Cook County Hospital, Chicago, 1972-76; Attending, Military Maternity Hospital, Damascus, 1978-80; Chief, Obstetrics, Gynaecology, Tal Hospital, Damascus, 1980-82; Chief, Obstetrics, Gynaecology, Techrin Hospital, Damascus, 1982-. *Memberships:* Fellow, American College of Obstetricians and Gynaecologists; Syrian Society of Obstetricians and Gynaecologists; American Medical Association. *Hobbies:* Reading; Travel. *Address:* Jeser Alabaid, Basatneh Building, Damascus, Syria.

TADROSS, Emmanuel H, b. 28 Oct. 1940, Cairo, Egypt. Consultant Psychiatrist & Adjunct Professor of Clinical Psychology. m. Mary E Aldridge, Hornchurch, London, England, 1 son, 1 daughter. *Education:* Diploma in Psychological Medicine, London; Member, Royal College of Psychiatrists; Fellow, Royal College of Physicians, Canada; DPM&N; DABP&N; CRCP(C); IAPCP. *Appointments:* Registrar in Psychiatry, Warley Hospital, Essex, England; Registrar, Central Middlesex Hospital, London; Senior Registrar in Psychiatry, Cell Barnes Hospital, St Albans, Herts, England; Staff Psychiatrist, Queen Street Mental Health Centre, Toronto, Canada; Lecturer, Department of Psychiatry, University of Toronto; Consultant Psychiatrist, Psychiatrist-in-Chief, Kitchener-Waterloo Hospital, Kitchener, Ontario; Adjunct Professor of Clinical Psychology, University of Waterloo, Canada. *Memberships:* Royal College of Psychiatrists, England; Canadian Psychiatric Association; American Psychiatric Association; Canadian Medical Association; Ontario Medical Association; International Academy of Psychotherapy; Association for Academic Psychiatry (USA). *Hobbies:* Photography; Music; Electronics. *Address:* 40 Green Street, Kitchener, Ontario, N2G 4K9, Canada.

TAI, Vivienne Veronica, b. 27 Dec. 1944, Jamaica, West Indies. Family Physician. *Education:* BA English, St Bonaventure University, New York, USA, 1968; MB, BS, University of the West Indies, Jamaica, 1977; Member, College of Family Physicians, Family Medicine Residency, University of Saskatchewan, Canada, 1980-82. *Appointments:* Administrative Officer & Assistant to the Minister of State for Youth & Community Development, Kingston, Jamaica, 1969-71; Medical Intern, Port of Spain General Hospital, Trinidad, West Indies, 1977-78; House Officer, Caribbean Medical Centre, Trinidad, 1979-80; Family Physician, Prince Albert Community Clinic, Canada, 1980-. *Memberships:* College of Family Physicians of Canada; Saskatchewan Medical Association; Canadian Medical Association; Prince Albert District Medical Association; Medical Advisory Committee, Victoria Union Hospital, 1984-85; Prince Albert Level of Care & Assessment Committee; Board Member, Prince Albert Community Clinic. *Honour:* Upjohn Postgraduate Award, 1985. *Hobbies:* Dancing; Reading; Tennis; Travel; Theatre, Photography. *Address:* 409-33 River Street East, Prince Albert, Saskatchewan S6V 6C1, Canada.

TAKAHAMA, Yasuhide, b. 7 Mar. 1928, Nobeoka, Japan. Professor and Chairman of Department of Orthodontics. m. Masako Tamaki, 18 Oct. 1958, 2 sons, 1 daughter. *Education:* Doctor of Dental Surgery, Tokyo Medical and Dental University, Faculty of Dentistry, 1953; Degree in Medical Science, Tokyo Medical and Dental University, 1958. *Appointments:* Chairman of Orthodontic Department, University Gadjah Mada, Faculty of Dentistry, Yogyakarta, Indonesia, 1961-63; Chairman and Professor, Department of Orthodontics Kanagawa Dental College, 1964-70; Chairman and Professor, Department of Orthodontics Kyushu University Faculty of Dentistry, 1970-; Dean, Faculty of Dentistry, Kyushu University 1973-75; Visiting Professor, University of Chicago, 1976-77. *Memberships:* Councillor, Japan Orthodontic Society; Councillor, Stomatological Society; Member, Japan Anthropological Society and International Dental Research. *Publications:* "Homo Sapiens Americana" 1982; "Orthodontic Treatment in New Concept" 1983. *Hobbies:* Wood-cut printing. *Address:* Matuyama 2-31-29, Fukuoka 814-01, Japan.

TAKASHIMA, Hiroshi, b. 27 Feb. 1912, Tokyo, Japan. Director, Psychosomatic Medicine; Cardiologist. m. Kimiko Kimura, 30 May 1953, Tokyo, 1 daughter. *Education:* MD, 1935; PhD, Pharmacology, 1945; Counsellor, Trainer, 1982, Diplomate, Fellow, 1983, Institute of Logotherapy, Berkeley, USA; Jury Member, Examiner, Doctrat d'Etat es Lettres, Sorbonne, France, 1983. *Appointments:* Assistant, Internal Medicine, St Luke's Hospital, Tokyo, 1935-40; Director, Takashima Hospital, Honorary Physician, Italian Embassy, Tokyo, 1938-45; Pharmacological Researcher, Keio University, Tokyo, 1936-40; Lecturer, Internal Medicine, Nihon University Hospital, 1940-46; Psychosomatologist, General Hospital of Health Insurance, Tokyo, 1953-; Cardiologist, Maruzen Clinic, Tokyo, 1953-; Professor, Existential Psychology, Tokyo Rissho Women's College, 1970-75; Visiting Lecturer, Universities of Melbourne, Queensland, Australia, 1981, University of Alaska-Fairbanks, 1985; etc. *Memberships:* Institute of Logotherapy, USA, Regional Director, Trainer of Counsellors; Institute of Humanistic Anthropology, Tokyo, Executive Director; Society of Humanistic Psychosomatic Medicine, Tokyo, President. *Publications:* "Psychosomatic Medicine and Logotherapy", 1977; "Logotherapy in Action" (Living with Disease), 1978; "Humanistic Psychosomatic Medicine", 1984; 21 other books. *Hobby:* Gourmet. *Address:* No 103, 9-25-2 Chome, Minami-Aoyama, Minato-ku, Tokyo, Japan.

TAKAYANAGI, Tetsuya, b. 18 Apr. 1933, Nagoya, Japan. Professor of Neurology. m. Yasuye Takayanagi, 11 Jan. 1959, Nagoya, 2 daughters. *Education:* MD, Nagoya University School of Medicine. *Appointments:* Research Associate, Department of Neurology, University of Maryland, USA, 1969; Instructor, First Department of Internal Medicine 1972, Associate Professor 1981, Nagoya University School of Medicine, Japan; Professor of Neurology, Department of Neurology, Nara Medical University. *Memberships include:* Councillor, Japanese Society of Neurology; Councillor, Japanese Society of Internal Medicine; Japanese Society of Neuropathology; Japanese Society of EEG and EMG; Japanese Society of Electromicroscopy; Japanese Society of Neurovegetative Research. *Publications:* 'An electromicroscopic study of intimal cushions in the intracranial artery of the cat', 1972; 'Serum enzyme activities and clinical course' in "Duchenne Muscular Dystrophy" (editor: S Ebashi), 1982; 'Immunological aspects of polymyositis', 1983. *Hobby:* Baseball. *Address:* Skyheights 406, 38 Mise-cho, Kashihara, Nara 634, Japan.

TALA, Eero Otto Juhani, b. 26 Sep. 1931, Kiika, Finland. Professor of Dieseases of the Chest. m. Maija-Leena Teinilä, 4 Dec. 1955, 1 son, 3 daughters. *Education:* Certified Physician, 1957; Doctor of Medical Science, 1967; Specialist in Chest Diseases, 1968; Professor, 1970. *Appointments:* Research Fellow in Pharmacology, 1958-61; Resident in Chest Diseases and Medicine, 1962-67; Associate Chief Physician, 1968; Chief Physician, 1968-; Professor, University of Turku, 1970-; Editor, 'European Journal of Respiratory Diseases', 1975-. *Memberships:* British Thoracic Society; American College of Chest Physicians; European Society of Pneumology; Vice-President Europe Region, International Union Against Tuberculosis; President, XXVII Nordic Congress on Chest Diseases; Honorary Member, Hungarian Lung

Association. *Publications include:* "Carcinoma of the Lung", 1967; "Tuberculosis", 1985; About 150 publications in pharmacology, medicine and chest diseases. *Hobby:* Fine Arts. *Address:* Department of Diseases of the Chest, University of Turku, SF 21540 Preitilä, Finland.

TALLEY, Joseph Eugene, b. 27 May 1949, Springfield, Massachusetts, USA. Staff Psychologist and Coordinator of Research. m. Vibeke Absalon, 3 Jan. 1981, Ronne, Denmark, 1 daughter, 1 son. *Education:* BA, University of Richmond, Virginia, USA; MA, Radford College, Radford, Virginia; PhD, University of Virginia, Charlottesville, Virginia. *Appointments:* Currently Staff Psychologist and Coordinator of Research, Programme Evaluation and Testing, Counseling and Psychological Services, Clinical Faculty, Department of Psychiatry, Duke University. *Memberships:* American Psychological Association; American Society of Clinical Hypnosis; Association for the Advancement of Psychology; Southeastern Psychological Association; North Carolina Psychological Association; Phi Kappa Phi; Omicron Delta Kappa; Psi Chi. *Publications:* "Study Skills: A Comprehensive Program For Colleges and Universities", 1981; "Counselling and Psychotherapy Services for University Students", 1985; "Counseling and Psychotherapy with College Students: A Guide to Treatment", 1986; 'The Use of Imagery in Psychotherapy' in "Baker's Encyclopedia of Psychology", editor David Benner, 1985. *Hobbies:* Music; Genealogical Research. *Address:* Counseling and Psychological Services, Suite 214 Old Chemistry Building, Duke University, Durham, NC 27706, USA.

TAN, Chee Khuan, b. 5 Aug. 1948, Muar, Johore. Consultant Psychiatrist. m. Khor Siau Bian, 28 Apr. 1973, Penang, 1 son, 1 daughter. *Education:* MBBS; MPM; FRANZCP; AM. *Appointments:* Lecturer, Psychological Medicine, University of Malaya, 1979-81; Consultant Psychiatrist, Klinik Serene, 1981-83; Consultant Psychiatrist, Lam Wah Ee Hospital, Penang, 1983-. *Memberships:* Immediate Past President, Penang Medical Practitioners' Society; Chairman, Malaysian Medical Association, Penang Branch; President, Rotary Club of Bayan Baru, Penang, 1986-87; Life Member, Malaysian Medical Association, Malaysian Psychiatric Association, Malaysian Mental Health Association, Malaysian Nature Society. *Publications:* "Stress and Mental Health in Malaysian Society", 1985; Editor, "Emergencies and First Aid", 1985; Medical Articles in professional journals. *Honours:* Modern Medicine of Asia Writing Award, 1981; PJK Award, Penang Governor, 1984. *Hobbies:* Squash; Bonsai Cultivation; Philately. *Address:* Lam Wah Ee Hospital, Batu Lanchang Road, Penang, Malaysia.

TAN, Eng-Seong, b. 10 Mar. 1934, Penang, Malaysia. Senior Psychiatrist; Professorial Associate. m. Harriet Teh, 9 Aug. 1958, Penang, 2 sons, 2 daughters. *Education:* MB, BS, University of Malaya, Singapore, 1957; DPM, Institute of Psychiatry, London University, England, 1962; Research Fellow, Psychological Medicine, Edinburgh University, Scotland, 1967; Teaching Fellow, Harvard University, USA, 1967-68. *Appointments:* Specialist Psychiatrist, Tampoi Mental Hospital, Johore, Malaysia, 1962-66; Foundation Professor, Psychological Medicine, University of Malaya, 1968-76; Consultant Psychiatrist, Deputy Psychiatrist Superintendent, Larundel Hospital, Bundoora, Australia, 1977-78; Psychiatrist, St Vincent's Hospital, Fitzroy Senior Association, Psychiatry, University of Melbourne, Australia, 1978-84. *Memberships:* Fellow: Royal College of Psychiatrists, Royal Australian & New Zealand College of Psychiatrists; Corresponding Fellow, American Psychiatric Association: Member, Expert Advisory Panel, Mental Health, World Health Organisation. *Publications:* Co-Author, "Attempted Suicide in Social Networks", 'British Journal Preventive Medicine', 1969; Co-Editor, 'Psychological Problems & Treatment in Malaysia", 1971; Co-Author, "Psychiatric Sequelae to a

Civil Disturbance", 'British Journal of Psychiatry', 1973; "Culture-Bound Syndromes among Overseas Chinese", 'Normal & Abnormal Behavior in Chinese Culture'; etc. *Honour:* Recipient, Johan Setia Diraja, Malaysian Government. *Hobbies:* Reading in English, Chinese, Malay; Music; Sailing; Tai-Chi. *Address:* Dept. of Psychiatry, University of Melbourne, St Vincent's Hospital, Fitzroy, Victoria 3065, Australia.

TANAGHO, Emil, b. 8 Dec. 1929, Egypt. Professor, Urology. m. Mona Armanious, 21 Nov. 1957, Egypt, 1 son, 2 daughters. *Education:* PCN, 1946, MB, ChB, 1952, Faculty of Medicine, Alexandria University; House Officer, Alexandria University Hospitals, 1952-53; Diploma, Surgery, Resident, 1954, Diploma, Urology, Resident, 1955, Master of Surgery, Urology, 1957, Alexandria University. *Appointments:* Clinical Demonstrator, 1957-59, Lecturer, 1959, 62, Assistant Professor, 1962-66, Urology, University of Alexandria; Research Urologist, Institute of Urology, University of London, England, 1962-63, University of California, San Francisco, USA, 1963-64; Assistant Professor, 1967-70, Associate Professor, 1970-72, Professor, 1972-, Chairman, 1977-, Urology Dept, University of California. *Memberships include:* Egyptian and American Medical Associations; Fellow, American College of Surgeons; California Medical Association; San Francisco Medical Society; Western Section, American Urological Association Inc; American Academy of Paediatrics; Societe Internationale d'Urologie; California Academy of Medicine; International Continence Society; Arab American Medical Association; Urological Research Society. *Publications:* Co-Author, "Urodynamics: Hydrodynamics of the Urete and Renal Pelvis", 1971; Co-Author, "Surgery of Female Incontinence", 1980; Numerous articles in professional journals, book chapters, symposia, etc. *Honours include:* Recipient, numerous prizes and awards most recent being: 1st Prize, Laboratory Research, American Urological Association Meeting, Las Vegas, 1983; 1st Prize, Joseph F. McCarthy Essay Contest, Western Section, American Urological Association, Vancouver, 1983; Honorary Member, Urological Society of Australasia, 1984; Jacob K. Javits Neurosciences Award, 1985. *Address:* University of California Room U 518, Department of Urology, San Francisco, CA 94143, USA.

TANCREDI, Laurence R, b. 15 Oct. 1940, Hershey, Pennsylvania, USA. Kraft Eidman Professor of Medicine and Law; Director, Health Law Program at University of Texas Health Science Center, Houston. *Education:* AB, English, Franklin & Marshall College, Pennsylvania, 1962; MD, University of Pennsylvania School of Medicine, 1966; JD, Yale Law School, 1972; Psychiatric Resident, Columbia University Department of Psychiatry, 1974-75; Psychiatric Post-Doctoral Fellow, Yale University Department of Psychiatry, 1975-77; Straight Medicine Intern, Presbyterian University Pennsylvania Medical Centre, 1966-67. *Appointments:* Lieutenant Commander, US Public Health Service, 1967-69; Senior Professional Associate, Institute of Medicine, National Academy of Sciences, 1972-74; Associate Professor of Psychiatry and Law, New York University School of Medicine; Adjunct Professor of Law, New York University School of Law, 1977-84; Kraft Eidman Professor, Medicine and the Law; Director, Health Law Program, University of Texas Health Science Center, Houston, 1984-. *Memberships:* American Psychiatric Association; International Academy of Law and Psychiatry; American Society of Law and Medicine; American Public Health Association. *Publications:* Author or Co-author in law, medicine and psychiatry 9 books, over 35 articles and chapters in 12 books. *Hobbies:* Walking; Reading Novels; Art Galleries. *Address:* Health Law Program UTHSCH, School of Public Health Building, Suite 901, 1200 Herman Pressler Drive, Houston, TX 77030, USA.

TAPPAN, James Gregory, b. 27 Nov. 1943, New York, USA. Obstetrician; Gynaecologist. m. Rhonda Rhenea Phillips, 29 Sep. 1984, Portola Valley, California, USA, 1 son. *Education:* BA, University of California, Berkeley, 1965, MD, San Francisco, 1969. *Appointments:* Chairman, Department of Gynaecology, USAF Regional Hospital, March AFB, California, 1974-76; Chairman, Department of Obstetrics and Gynaecology, Mills Memorial Hospital, San Mateo, California, 1980-84, Member Executive Committee, 1980-84. *Memberships:* San Mateo County Medical Society; California Medical Association; American College of Obstetricians and Gynaecologists; American College of Surgeons. *Publication:* 'Kroener Tubal Libation in Perspective' in 'American Journal of Obstetrics and Gynaecology', April, 1973. *Honours:* Regional Consultant, USAF, 1974-76; President Elect, Peninsula Gynaecologic Society, 1985; President, Peninsula Gynaecologic Society, 1986. *Hobbies:* Ski; Scuba Diving; Jogging. *Address:* 1040 Macadamia Drive, Hillsborough, CA 94010, USA.

TARANTA, Angelo, b. 18 Apr. 1927, Rome, Italy. Director and Professor of Medicine. m. Bruna Taranta, 2 daughters. *Education:* MD, University of Rome, Italy, 1949. *Appointments include:* Director, Medicine, Cabrini Health Care Center, New York City, USA. 1973-; Professor. 1979-85, Chief. Humanition and Ethics Division, 1985, Medicine, Chief Rheumatology and Immunology Division, New York Medical College, 1979-; Co-Chairman, Study group on heart diseases in the young, Inter-Society Commn, on Heart Diseases resources, 1972-; Vice-President, Comite Panamericano de Estudio y Prevencion de las Fiebre Reumatica, 1974-; Board Directors, American Heart Associatin, 1975-77; Chairman, Council on Cardiovascular Disease in the Young, 1975-77; Consultant in field. *Memberships:* American Society for Clinical Investigation: American Rheumatism Association; American Association of Immunologists. *Publications:* Co-author of a book; Co-editor of a monograph; 9 chapters in multi-authored books; 145 articles in medical and scientific journals including Nature, Science, The New England Journal of Medicine, The Annals of Internal Medicine. *Honours:* Terence Cardinal Cooke Medal for Distinguished Service in Health Care awarded by NYMC, 1985. *Hobbies:* Writing; Photography. *Address:* Cabrini Medical Center, 227 East 19th Street, Department of Medicine, New York, NY 10003, USA.

TARJAN, George, b. 18 June 1912, Zsolna, Hungary. Professor, Psychiatry. m. Helen E Blome, 11 June 1941, Janesville, Wisconsin, USA, 2 sons. *Education:* Tisza Istvan University, Hungary, 1929-32; Peter Pazmany University, Budapest, 1935, MD; Intern, General Hospitals, Budapest, 1934-35; Menorah Hospital Kansas City, USA, 1939-40; Resident, Jewish Hospital, Budapest, 1935-39; Mercy Hospital, Janesville, USA, 1940-41; Utah State Hospital, Provo, 1941-43; US Army Medical Corps, 1943-46; Diplomate, National Board of Medical Examiners; American Board of Psychiatry & Neurology, Psychiatry & Child Psychiatry. *Appointments:* Clinical Director, Peoria State Hospital, Illinois, 1946-47; Director, Clinical Service, Superintendent Medical Director, Pacific State Hospital, Pomona, 1947-65; Assistant Clinical Professor, 1953-57; Associate Clinical Professor, 1957-60, Clinical Professor, 1960-65, Professor, 1965-, Director, Mental Retardation & Child Psychiatry, 1965-82, University of California, Los Angeles. *Memberships:* American Psychiatric Association, President, 1983-84; American Academy of Child Psychiatry, President 1977-79; Group for the Advance of Psychiatry, President 1971-73; American College of Psychiatry; American Medical Association; California Medical Association; Benjamin Rush Society; etc. *Publications:* "The Natural History of Mental Deficiency in a State Hospital", 'AMA Journal Dis. of Child', 1958; "Prevention a Program Goal in Mental Deficiency", 'AMJD', 1959; "Mental Retardation: A Handbook for the Primary Physician", 'AMA', 1965, 1974; "Classification 9 Mental Retardation", 'AJP Supplement', 1972; "The Physician and the Mental Health of Child", 'AMA', 1979, 1980, 1981; "American

Psych: A Dynamic Mosaic", 'AJP', 1984; etc. *Honours:* Leadership Award, AAMD, 1970; Kennedy Foundation International Award, 1970; Distinguished Service Award, APA, 1973; Seymour D Vestermark, 1978; Agnes Purcell McGavin, 1978; Andres Bellow, Venezuela, 1976; Salmon Medal, New York Academy of Medicine, 1979; William Schonfeld Memorial, ASAP, 1980; etc. *Hobbies:* Bridge; Tennis. *Address:* NPI/UCLA, 760 Westwood Plaza, Los Angeles, CA 90024, USA.

TARJAN, Imre, b. 26 July 1912, Szabadka. Emeritus Professor/Scientific Adviser. m. (1) Magda Kincsek, 23 Apr. 1940, Debrecen, (2) Margit Kardos, 7 Sep. 1955, Budapest, 3 daughters. *Education:* Dr rer nat 1939; Doctor of Physical Science, 1966. *Appointments:* University Assistant 1936-40; High School Teacher 1940-49; University Professor, Director of Institute of Biophysics, 1950-82, Dean of Faculty of General Medicine, 1959-63, Scientific Vice-Rector, 1970-73, Semmelweis University of Medicine; Deputy Secretary 1964-70, Vice President 1970-76, President of Mathematics and Physical Science Section, 1976-, Hungarian Academy of Sciences. *Memberships:* Regular Member of Hungarian Academy of Sciences; Individual Ordinary Member, European Physical Society; Member of the Presidium of the Eötvös Physical Society of Hungary; Member of the Presidium of the Hungarian Biophysical Society. *Publications:* "Fizika Orvosok es Biológusok zamára" (Physics for Physicians and Biologists) 1964, 1969, 1971, in Russian 1969, in Polish 1975; "A Biofizika Alapjai" (An Introduction to Biophysics) 1977, 1981. "Laboratory Manual for Crystal Growth" 1972. About 160 papers in international and Hungarian scientific journals. *Honours:* Golden Order of Labour 1960, 1964; Kossuth Prize 1961; State Prize 1985. *Hobbies:* Sport; Tourism; Travel; Literature; Fine arts. *Address:* Institute of Biophysics, Semmelweis Medical University, Puskin u 9 POB 263, H-1444 Budapest VIII, Hungary.

TARKOWSKA, Anna, b. 11 Oct. 1931, Lublin, Poland. Associate Professor, Head of Department of Nuclear Medicine. *Education:* Medical Diploma; Doctor of Medicine; Habilitated Doctor of Medicine; 1 and 2 Specialist in Internal Medicine; Specialist in Nuclear Medicine. *Appointments:* Assistant and Senior Assistant, Clinic of Internal Medicine, Head of Radioisotope Department of Institute of Radiology, Medical Academy in Lublin; Regional Consultant in Nuclear Medicine. *Memberships:* Vice President, Committee of Medical Physics, Polish Academy of Sciences; President, Polish Society of Nuclear Medicine; European Society of Nuclear Medicine; Polish Society of Radiology; Polish Society of Endocrinology; Society Scientiarum Lublinensis. *Publications:* 'Equilibrium/Gated/Radiouclide Ventriculography', 1979; 'Regional Evaluation of the Left Ventricular Wall Motion by Radionuclide Ventriculography', 1982; 'Phase Analysis in Diagnosing Left Ventricular Aneurysm' in "Nuklearmedizin, Darstellung von Metabolismen und Organ-Funktionen", 1984. *Honours:* Fellowship, A V Humboldt Foundation, 1972-73, 1978-79 and 1983; Golden Order of Merit, 1979; Award of the Ministry of Health and Social Care, 1983. *Hobbies:* Collecting books; Tourism; Swimming. *Address:* Department of Nuclear Medicine, Medical Academy in Lublin, ul Jaczewskiego 8, 20-090 Lublin, Poland.

TASHEV, Tasho Anghelov, b. 14 Feb. 1909, Dulbok Izvor, Bulgaria. University Professor (retired). m. Srebra Rodopska, 18 July 1935, 1 son, 1 daughter. *Education:* Professor Dr Med, Sofia University, 1935; Gastroenterology and Dietetics, France, 1947-48; Nutrition Sciences, USSR, 1949. *Appointments:* Assistant Professor, Medical Faculty, Sofia University, 1937-44; Director, Red Cross Hospital, Sofia, 1944-46; Associate Professor, Medical Faculty, 1946-49; Professor, 1949; Head, Department of Internal Medicine with Gastroenterology and Clinical Nutrition at Postgraduate Medical Institute, Sofia,

1950-72; Rector, Postgraduate Medical Institute, 1952-55; Director, Nutrition Institute of Bulgarian Academy of Sciences, 1960-72; Director, Centre of Hygiene and Nutrition, Sofia, 1973-77; Director, Nutrition Institute of Medical Academy, Sofia, 1978-79. *Memberships:* Member, Officer and Corresponding Member of numerous professional organizations in USSR, Poland, Germany, Hungary, Slovakia, Europe, etc. *Publications:* Over 350 scientific publications in Bulgarian, Russian, English, French, German, Italia, Czech and other languages; 16 manuals, monographs and other books. Major Books include: Gastroenterology, 3 volumes; Stomach Diseases; Clinical Dietetics; Dietetic Nutrition; Diseases of the Liver; Textbook of Internal Medicine. *Honours include:* Merited Scientist of Bulgaria, 1969; Gold Medal of Bulgarian Red Cross, 1946; Gold Medal of Labour, 1958; Red Banner of Labour, 1960; People's Republic of Bulgaria I cl, 1969. *Hobbies:* Fishing; Travel. *Address:* San Stefano 15, 1504 Sofia, Bulgaria

TATPATI, Daniel A, b. 8 Aug. 1944, Dharwar, India. Cardiovascular Thoracic Surgeon. m. Olga A Lobo, 27 Mar. 1970, Cleveland, 1 son, 2 daughters. *Education:* MB, BS, Karnatak Medical College; FACS (Thor); FCCP. *Appointments:* Rotating Internship, KMC Hospital, Hubli, India, 1967-68; House Officer, Church of South India Hospital, 1968-70; Internship, Medicine, Lutheran Hospital, Cleveland, USA, 1970, Surgery, University of Connecticut Health Centre, 1970-71; Surgical Resident, St Francis Hospital, Hartford, 1971-72, University of Connecticut Affiliated Hospitals, 1972-75; Thoracic Surgery Resident, State University of New York, 1975-77; Private Practice, 1977-78; Group Practice, Cardiovascular and Thoracic Surgery, Wichita, 1978-. *Memberships:* Fellow, American College of Surgeons; Fellow, American College of Chest Physicians; Society of Thoracic Surgeons; American Board of Surgery; American Board of Thoracic Surgery. *Hobbies:* Photography; Aviation; Collecting Art Works. *Address:* 1461 Caddy Ct, Wichita, KS 67212, USA.

TAUC Ladislav, b. 28 May 1926, Brno, Czechoslovakia. Director of Laboratory of Cellular and Molecular Neurobiology. m. Henriette Dejean, 22 Oct. 1949, 2 sons. *Education:* PhD, University of Brno, Czechoslovakia, 1949; PhD, University of Paris, France, 1950. *Appointments:* Member of the Centre National de la Recherche Scientifique, Research Director CNRS, 1968-, Director of Laboratory Cellular and Molecular Neurobiology, CNRS, 1972-. *Memberships:* Association des Physiologistes; Société de Biologie; European Neuroscience Association; Society for Experimental Biology; Sigma Xi, etc. *Publications:* Numerous publications and reviews in scientific journal related to Life Sciences. *Honours:* Prix Lallemand de l'Académie des Sciences, 1964; Medaille d'Argent du CNRS, 1966. *Address:* Laboratoire de Neurobiologie Cellulaire et Moleculaire, CNRS, 91190 Gif sur Yvette, France.

TAUSSIG, Helen Brooke, b. 24 May 1898, Cambridge, Mass, USA. Professor Emeritus, JHU School of Medicine, 1983. *Education:* BA, University of California, 1921; Postgraduate, Harvard University School of Medicine, 1921; Postgraduate, Boston University School of Medicine, 1922-24; MD, Johns Hopkins University School of Medicine, 1927; Archibald Fellow in Medicine, 1927-28; Intern, Paediatrics, Harriet Lane Home, Johns Hopkins University School of Medicine. *Appointments:* Physician in Charge, Cardiac Clinic, Harriet Lane Home, 1930-63, Instructor, Paediatrics, 1930-41, Assistant Professor, 1941-46, Associate Professor, 1946-59, Professor of Paediatrics, 1959-63, Professor Emeritus, 1963, Johns Hopkins University School of Medicine; Thomas Rivers Memorial Distinguished Research Fellow, 1963-68; Professor, Georgetown University School of Medicine, 1969-; Clinical Care, Teaching and Research, Patients with rheumatic fever, chorea, congenital heart disease, 1930-42; Member, Pres Commission Heart Disease, Stroke and Cancer, 1964;

Alt USA del XX International Conference of Red Cross Vienna, 1965; Member, International Cardiac Foundation, 1969; Member, Commission of Social Responsibility for war-injured Vietnamese Children, 1969; Member, Board of Managers, Harriet Lane Home, 1972-; Research on Evolutionary Origin of Common Cardiac Malformations, 1977-. *Memberships include:* President, 1952-54, Maryland Heart Association; President, 1965-66, American Heart Association; Paediatric Research; American Paediatric Society; President, 1969-70, Maryland Society for Medical Research; European Paediatric Society; Master, 1954, American College of Physicians. *Publications include:* 'Surgical Treatment of Congenital Pulmonary Stenosis and Artesia', (with Alfred Blalock), 1945; 'German Outbreak of phocomelia: The Thalidomide Syndrome', 1962; 'World Survey of Common Cardiac Malformations', 1982; 'Further Studies on Origin of Cardiac Malformations', 1986; Author of numerous other scientific papers. *Honours:* Recipient of numerous honours including, Chevalier Legion d'Honneur, 1947; Award of Merit, Gold Heart Award, 1963, American Heart Association; Medal of Freedom presented by President Johnson, 1964; Carl Ludvig Medal of Honour, 1967; Milton Stover Eisenhower Gold Medal, 1967; Howland Award, 1971, American Paediatric Society. *Address:* Crosslands Apt 158, Kennett Square, PA 19348, USA.

TAWADROSE, Victor Anis, b. 7 June 1931, Egypt. Otorhinolaryngologist. *Education:* MB BCh, Cairo, 1950-57; DLO, London, 1963-64; MCh.OTOL, Liverpool, 1967-70; LMCC, Canada, 1972; ECFMG, USA, 1972; Board Eligible in Otorhinolaryngology. *Appointments include:* Private General Practice, Cairo, Egypt, 1959-61; General Surgery, Central Hospital, Riyadh, 1961-63; House Surgeon, St Mary Abbots Hospital, London, England, 1964-65; ENT Specialist, Students' Hospital, Riyadh, 1965-67; Internship and Residency, Canada, 1970-72; ENT Specialist, Chaleur General Hospital and Private Practice, Bathurst, New Brunswick, Canada, 1973-76; Private Practice, Otalryngology, Padadena, Texas, USA, 1976-. *Memberships include:* Fellow, American Academy of Otalaryngology, Head and Neck Surgery; Fellow, American Academy of Otalaryngic Allergy; Fellow, American Society for Laser Medicine and Surgery; Member of International Correspondence Society of Allergists. *Honours:* American Medical Association-Physician's Recognition Award. *Hobbies:* Art; Handicrafts (work with hands); Chess. *Address:* 901 E Curtis 36, Pasadena, TX 77502, USA.

TAYLOR, Aubrey E., b. 4 June 1933, El Paso, Texas, USA. Professor, Chairman, Physiology. m. Mary Jane Davis, 4 Apr. 1953, 3 daughters. *Education:* BA, Texas Christian University, 1960; PhD, Physiology, University of Mississippi College of Medicine, 1964; Postdoctoral Fellow, Harvard School of Medicine, 1965-67. *Appointments:* Assistant Professor, 1965, Associate Professor, 1967-72, Professor, 1972-77, Physiology, University of Mississippi; Professor, Chairman, Physiology, University of South Alabama College of Medicine, 1977-. *Memberships:* American Physiological Society, Councillor, 1984-87; AAAS; Microcirculatory Society, President, 1981-83; American Heart Association, Circulation and Cardiopulmonary Executive Council; Biophysical Society; International Lymphology Society; New York Academy of Sciences; Sigma Xi; Mississippi and Alabama Academy of Science. *Publications:* "Circulatory Physiology", 1975; "Edema", 1984; "Oxygen Radicals in Physiology", 1986; etc. *Honours:* Dean's List, Texas Christian University; Pi Mu Epsilon; Lederle Medical Faculty Award, 1968-71; Landis Award, Microcirculatory Society, 1985. *Hobbies:* Fishing; Bird Watching. *Address:* 11 Audubon Place, Mobile, AL 36606, USA.

TAYLOR, Brian Oscar Treweek, b. 26 Nov. 1921, Upminster, Essex, England. Private Practitioner of Homeopathy/Osteopathy; Locum Consultant Physician, Royal London Homeopathic Hospital. m. Patricia, 26 Nov. 1955, Sutton Coldfield, England, 2 sons, 1 daughter. *Education:* MRCG; LRCP; NRCGP; MF Hom. *Appointment:* Principal, General Practice, Earls Colne, Essex, England, 1948-82. *Memberships:* Medical Defence Union; British Medical Association. *Hobbies:* Gardening; Small Livestock; Bridge. *Address:* Elmstead House, 23 Coggeshall Road, Earls Colne, Colchester CO6 2RR, Essex, England.

TAYLOR, Bruce Terry, b. 22 Apr. 1950, Baltimore, Maryland, USA. Director; Vice-President. m. 15 June 1975, Baltimore, Maryland, 2 sons. *Education:* BA, Haverford College, 1971; MD, Johns Hopkins School of Medicine, 1975. *Appointments:* Instructor, 1977-78, Supervisor, Mental Health Counselors, Social Workers, Nurses-Outpatients, Phipps Clinic, 1980; Supervisor, Staff Psychiatrists, Resident, Medical Students, Psychologists, Psychology Interns and Externs, Social Workers, Nursing Staff, Physician Assistants, General Staff, Taylor Manor Hospital; Lecturer, University of Maryland, for Psychiatric residents, on ECT, new antidepressants and the management of affective disorders, parts I and II; Clinical Assistant Professor, University of Maryland, 1984-. *Memberships:* American Medical Assn.; American Psychiatric Assn.; Maryland Psychiatric Society; Chairman, Committee on Addictions; Mental Health Liaison Committee and Insurance and Professional Practice Committee; Central Maryland Health Systems Agency; Member, Governing Body; American Society of Law and Medicine; Howard County Medical Society; Maryland State Medical Society; Co-Chairman, Alcoholism and Chemical Dependency Committee. *Publications:* (Symposiums) 'New Antidepressants', 1983; 'The Psychiatric Hospital: Multimodal Treatment or Restrictive Environment?', 1980; (paper) 'Clinical Applications of the Dexamethasone Suppression Test, with Case Report', 1981. *Hobbies:* Waterskiing; Boating. *Address:* Director of Admissions, Taylor Manor Hospital, PO Box 396, College Avenue, Ellicott City, MD 21043, USA.

TAYLOR, Carl Thomas, b. 9 Oct. 1926, Pouce Coupe, British Columbia, Canada. Medical Doctor; Certified Hypnotherapist. m. 22 Dec. 1950, Edmonton, Alberta, 2 sons, 2 daughters. *Education:* BSc, Civil Engineering; MD; LMCC. *Appointments:* With Secret Service, World War II; Established, Northern Canadian Loran and Shoran (Long and short range aerial navigation systems, now, early warning network for North America); Built Canada's largest complete Treatment plant. *Memberships:* Canadian College of Family Physicians; Engineering Institute of Canada. *Hobbies:* Scuba Diving, Past Club President; Metal work; Big game hunting; Public speaking on health and fitness. *Address:* Box 27 Site 4 RR2, Stony Plain, Alberta, Canada T0E 2G0.

TAYLOR, Clive Roy, b. 24 July 1944, Littleport, England. Professor; Chairman. m. Susan Hoyland, 29 July 1967, Ely, Cambs, England, 3 sons, 1 daughter. *Education:* BA, Natural Sciences, Cambridge (1st Class Honours), 1966; MBBChir., Cambridge, 1969; MA, 1972; MD, Cambridge, 1978; D.Phil, Oxford, 1975. *Appointments:* Lecturer, Pathology, University of Oxford, 1970-75; Medical Resident Council Fellow in Cancer Research, 1975-76; Chief of Immunology, Associate Professor, University of Southern California, 1976-82; Chairman, Pathology, 1983-, Director, Laboratories, Los Angeles County Medical Centre, 1983-, University of Southern California. *Memberships:* British Medical Association; Royal College of Pathologists; Histochemistry Society; American Society of Chemical Pathologists. *Publications:* Over 200 papers in medical journals; 10 books including: "Lymph Node Biopsy", 1982; "Lymph Proliferative Diseases", 1985; "Basic Pathology", 1986. *Honours:* Distinction in Pharmacology, University of Cambridge, 1969; Karger Prize for Research, 1978. *Hobbies:* Soccer; Racquetball; Skiing; Writing; Collecting Neckties. *Address:* 1601 Marengo Avenue, South Pasadena, CA 91030, USA.

TAYLOR, Della Brewer, b. 15 Apr. 1932, Johnson City, Tennessee, USA. Registered Nurse. m. John R Taylor, 12 Feb. 1955, Johnson City, 2 daughters. *Education:* Registered Nurse, Memorial Hospital School of Nursing, Johnson City, 1953; Diploma, Newspaper Institute of America, 1968; BS Management, Steed College, Johnson City, 1978. *Appointments:* Head Nurse, Poliomyelitis, 1953; Staff Nurse, VA Centre, Tennessee, 1954-55; Staff Nurse, Memorial Hospital, Clarksville, Tennessee, 1955; Paediatric Nurse, US Army Hospital, Augsburg, Federal Republic of Germany, 1957-61; Private Duty (part-time), 1964-78; Farm Bureau Life Insurance Exams, 1978-86. *Memberships:* National Association for Female Executives; Christian Nurses Fellowships; Chairman: 1st Dr Charles T R Underwood MD Scholarship Fund, 1984; Mothers March of Dimes; Neighborhood Cancer Drive; Tennessee Lung Association Road Block Fund Drive. *Publications:* 'Weddings & the Handicapped' in 'Brides Magazine', 1980; Recipes, 'Southern Living Magazine'. *Hobbies:* Swimming; Gardening; Raising Hybrid Roses; Cooking. *Address:* RFD 8 Taylor Road, Jonesborough, TN 37659, USA.

TAYLOR, Irving, b. 7 Jan. 1945, Leeds, England. Professor. m. Berenice Penelope Brunner, 31 July 1969, London, 3 daughters. *Education:* MB ChB, University of Sheffield, 1968; MD, Distinction, 1973; ChM 1978. *Appointments:* Senior Registrar, Honorary Clinical Tutor, Sheffield, 1973-77; Senior Lecturer, Surgery, University of Liverpool, 1977-81; Professor of Surgery, University of Southampton, 1981-. *Memberships:* Honorary Secretary, Surgical Research Society; British Society of Gastroenterology; Committee Member, Association of Surgical Oncology; Royal Society of Medicine; European Society for Surgical Research; Association of Surgeons of England; Fellow, Royal College of Surgeons. *Publications:* "Progress is Surgery", 1985; "Complications of Lower Gastrointestinal Surgery", 1985; Many publications related to surgical gastroenterology and oncology. *Honours:* Hunterian Professorship, 1981; Hingston Memorial Lecture, McGill University, Montreal, 1985. *Hobbies:* Squash; Swimming; Gardening. *Address:* University Surgical Unit, F Level, Centre Block, Southampton General Hospital, Tremona Road, Southampton, Hampshire, England.

TAYLOR, Michael Alan, b. 6 Mar. 1940, New York City, USA. Doctor of Medicine. m. Ellen Schoenfield, 28 June 1963, New York, 2 sons. *Education:* MD, New York Medical College, New York City, 1965; Rotating Internship, Lenox Hill Hospital, New York City, 1966; Psychiatry Residency, New York Medical College, 1969. *Appointments:* Staff Psychiatrist, US Naval Hospital, Oakland, California, 1969-71; Research Psychiatrist and Lecturer in Biological Psychiatry, 1971-72, Instructor, 1971-72, Chief, Acute Treatment Unit, 1972-73, Assistant Professor, 1972-73, New York Medical College; Associate Professor and Director of Residency Training, Department of Psychiatry, State University of New York at Stony Brook, 1973-76. *Memberships:* Behavioral Neurology Association; Behavioral Genetics Association; Psychiatric Research Society; Association for Academic Psychiatry; American Psychiatric Association; American Psychopathological Association; International Neuropsychology Society; American Association for the Advancement of Science; Illinois Psychiatric Association; Society of Biological Psychiatry; Alpha Omega Alpha. *Publications:* "The Neuropsychiatric Mental Status Examination", 1981; Co-author, "General Hospital Psychiatry", 1985; 94 articles and chapters in books. *Honours:* First Prize Clinical Research, New York Academy of Medicine, 1969; A E Bennett Clinical Research Award, Society for Biological Psychiatry, 1969; The Morris L Parker Award for Outstanding Intramural Research, Chicago Medical School, 1978. *Address:* UHS/The Chicago Medical School, 3333 Green Bay Road, North Chicago, IL 60064, USA.

TAYLOR, Peyton T, b. 21 July 1941, Alabama, USA. Director, Gynaecologic Oncology, University of Virginia. m. Helena Ström, 27 Sep. 1967, Sweden, 3 daughters. *Education:* BS, University of Alabama, Tuscaloosa; MS, University of Alabama, Birmingham, University of Uppsala, Sweden; MD, Medical College of Alabama; Residency, University of Virginia; Fellowship Training, Surgery, National Cancer Institute, Gynaecologic Oncology, University of Virginia. *Appointments:* Clinical Associate, Surgery, National Cancer Institute, 1970-72; Assistant Professor, University of Virginia, 1977-79; Associatr Professor, (OB-GYN), University of Alabama, 1979-81; Associate Professor, Director, Gynaecologic Oncology, Ambulatory Cancer Centre, University of Virginia, 1981-. *Memberships:* American College Obstetricians and Gynaecologists; American College of Surgeons; Society of Gynaecologic Oncologists; Society of Surgical Oncologists; American Society Clinical Oncologists. *Publications:* Numerous articles in scientific journals. *Honours:* Alpha Omega Alpha; Junior Faculty Fellow, American Cancer Society, 1979. *Hobbies:* Waterfowling; Wildlife. *Address:* Division of Gynaecologic Oncology, University of Virginia, Charlottesville, VA 22908, USA.

TAYLOR, Roger Ralph, b. 27 May 1935, Tenterfield, New South Wales, Australia. Professor of Cardiology, University of Western Australia, 1974-. m. Lorraine McGlynn, 29 July 1961, Sydney, 2 sons, 1 daughter. *Education:* MB, BS, University of Sydney, 1952-57; FRACP. *Appointments:* Fellow in Cardiology, Hallstrom Institute, 1962-64; Research Fellow, 1965-67, Visiting Scientist, 1967, National Heart Foundation in NHI, Bethesda, USA; Associate Professor, Cardiology and Cardiovascular Research, University of Western Australia, 1968-74. *Memberships:* Royal Australasian College of Physicians; Cardiac Society of Australia and New Zealand; International Society for Heart Research; Medical and Scientific Advisory Committee of National Heart Foundation of Australia, WA Division. *Publications:* Author of numerous publications on medical subjects. *Honours:* R T Hall Prize, 1974. *Hobbies:* Fishing; Gardening. *Address:* Department of Cardiology, Royal Perth Hospital, PO Box X2213, Perth, Western Australia, 6001.

TAYLOR, William Paxton, b. 1 Nov. 1955, Winnipeg, Manitoba, Canada. Active Staff, Medicine Hat Regional Hospital. m. Margaret Elizabeth McNutt, 16 June 1984, Blairmore, Alberta, 1 son. *Education:* BMS, University of Alberta, 1977; CCFP; Diplomate, NBME. *Appointments:* Intern, Family Medicine, 1979-80; Resident, Family Medicine, 1980-81; Family Physician: Locum, Canada and USA, 1981-82; President, Medical Staff, Mayerthorpe General Hospital, Alberta, 1982-85; Medical Staff Member, Medicine Hat Regional Hospital, Alberta, 1985-. *Memberships:* Active Member, Section of General Practice, Alberta Medical Association; Canadian Medical Association; College of Family Physicians of Canada; Diplomate, National Board of Medical Examiners, USA; Licentiate, Medical Council of Canada; Canadian Medical Protective Association. *Honours:* Scholarship, Geriatric Medicine, Youville Wing, Edmonton General Hospital; Robert Hartley Fellowship. *Hobbies:* Chess; Curling; Saxophone; Numismatics; Philately; Photography; Racquet sports; Swimming. *Address:* 56 Red Deer Drive South West, Medicine Hat, Alberta, Canada T1A 4A4.

TAYLOR-PAPADIMITRIOU, Joyce, b. 11 Nov. 1932, Burnley, England. Staff Scientist, Imperial Cancer Research Fund. m. Spyros Papadimitriou, 14 Mar. 1964, Burnley, 2 daughters. *Education:* MA, Biochemistry, Cambridge University, 1956; MA, Biochemistry, 1957, PhD, Microbiology, 1962, Toronto University. *Appointments:* Research Assistant, Connaught Medical Research Laboratories; Fellow MRC Mill Hill; Research Associate, University of Athens, Department of Organic Chemistry; Head of Laboratory, Theagenion Cancer Institute, Salonica, Greece; Head of Laboratory of Epithelial Cell Growth Regulation, Imperial Cancer Research Fund. *Memberships:* European Association for Cancer Research; International Society for Interferon Research; President, International Association for Breast Cancer; International Society for Differentiation; British Society of Cell Biology. *Publications:* Numerous articles in medical journals, in the field of Cancer Research. *Honours:* Newnham College Scholarship, 1952-55; Canadian Medical Research Council Fellow, 1962-64; Eleanor Roosevelt Fellow, 1969-70. *Hobbies:* Gardening; Cooking. *Address:* 9 Cedar Road, Berkhamstead, Hertfordshire, England.

TEFFT, Melvin, b. 15 Dec. 1932, Boston, Massachusetts, USA. Chairman, Department of Radiation Therapy; Professor of Radiation Medicine. *Education:* BA, Harvard College, 1954; MD, Boston University, 1958; FACR. *Appointments:* Radiotherapist, Childrens Hospital Medical Center, Boston Massachusetts; Associate Radiologist, Peter Bent Brigham Hospital, Boston; Consultant Radiologist, Boston Lying-in-Hospital, Boston; Chief Radiotherapy and Nuclear Medicine, Childrens Hospital, Boston; Consultant Radiotherapy, Tufts Medical Center, Boston; Associate Attending Radiotherapist, Memorial Sloan-Kettering Cancer Center, New York City, New York; Associate Radiotherapist, Massachusetts General Hospital, Boston; Consultant Radiotherapy, Attending Radiotherapist, Memorial Sloan-Kettering Cancer Center, New York; Attending Radiologist, New York Hospital; Director, Medical Education and Radiation Therapy, Memorial Sloan-Kettering Cancer Center, New York; Associate Member, Paediatrics, Rhode Island Hospital; currently, Chairman, Department of Radion Therapy, Rhode Island Hospital and Professor, Radiation Medicine, Brown University. *Memberships include:* Apollo Applications Programme; American Association for the Advancement of Science; Association for Advancement of Civil Rights; American Board of Radiology; American College of Surgeons; American Medical Association; Air Space Travel Research Organisation; Institute of Space Sciences; Radiation Research Society; Royal Society of Medicine; Society of Nuclear Medicine. *Publications:* Author of 10 books and 133 papers in his field. *Honours:* Bronze Medal, American Roentgen Ray Society, 1968; Commendation, American Academy of Paediatrics, 1983; Travelling Oncology Consultant, American Cancer Society, 1981. *Hobby:* Art Collecting. *Address:* Rhode Island Hospital, Department of Radiation Therapy, 593 Eddy Street, Providence, RI 02902, USA.

TEITELBAUM, Mark Lewis, b. 22 Oct. 1941, Bronx, New York, USA. Assistant Professor. *Education:* AB, cum laude, Williams College, 1963; MD, Cornell University Medical College, 1967. *Appointments:* Assistant Professor, Department of Psychiatry and Behavioral Sciences, Assistant Professor, Department of Medicine, The Johns Hopkins University School of Medicine. *Memberships:* APA; American Association General Hospital Psychiatrists; American Psychosomatic Society; Academy of Psychosomatic Medium. *Address:* Osler 320, The Johns Hopkins Hospital, Baltimore, MD 21205, USA.

TEJADA REATEGUI, Francisco, b. 25 July 1942, Moyobamba, Peru. Clinical Associate Professor, Oncology, University of Miami School of Medicine, USA. m. Barbara Ann Kotowski, 1 Feb. 1970, Baltimore, Maryland, 2 sons, 3 daughters. *Education:* BS, Universitas Nacional Mayor San Marcos, Lima, Peru, 1961; MD, Peruvian Universitas Cayetano Heredia, 1968; Fellow, Medical Haematology, Johns Hopkins University, USA, 1972; Fellow, Oncology, National Institutes of Health, Maryland, USA, 1974. *Appointments include:* Associate Professor, Oncology, University of Miami, 1980-; Oncologist, Miami Cancer Institute, 1980-, Oncology Association of Miami, 1980-. *Memberships:* American College of Physicians; American Association for Cancer Research; American Society of Haematology; American Society of Clinical Oncology; Peruvian College of Physicians; Chilean Cancer Society. *Publications include:* Contributions to various professional journals. *Honours:* Hipolito Unanere Award, Lima, Peru, 1969; Fellow, American College of Physicians, 1976. *Hobbies:* Travel; Photography. *Address:* 1321 NW 14th Street, Suite 401, Miami, FL 33136, USA.

TELEGDY, Gyula, b. 5 June 1935, Nagyszeben, Hungary. Institute Director; Dean of Medical Faculty. m. 1960, 1 son, 2 daughters. *Education:* MD, 1959; PhD, 1964; DSc, 1974. *Appointments:* Assistant Professor 1961-70, Adjunct 1970-72, Docent 1972-75, Professor 1975-, Dean of Medical Faculty, Director, Institute of Pathophysiology, University Medical School, Szeged. *Memberships:* International Neuroendocrinology Society; International Reproductive Society; Brain Behaviour Society; International Brain Research Organisation; European Pineal Study Group; New York Academy of Sciences; Hungarian Physiological Society; Hungarian Endocrinology Society. *Publications:* About 300 articles. *Hobby:* Tennis. *Address:* Institute of Pathophysiology, University Medical School, PO Box 531, Szeged, Hungary.

TELIVUO, Leila Marjatta, b. 10 Aug. 1929, Juankoski, Finland. Dentist. m. Leo Johannes Telivuo, 27 June 1953, Juankoski, 3 sons. *Education:* DDS, 1953; Specialist in Endodontics, 1981. *Appointments:* School Dentist, 1953-57; Private Practitioner, Helsinki, 1957-; various appointments in the Finnish Dental Association, 1964-; Consultant for various groups, Commission on Dental Practice, 1974-; Editorial Board, Finnish Journal of Dentistry, 1977-; Vice-Chairman, State Committee on Dental Health; Vice-Chairman, Organisation Committee, Helsinki Congress, 1984. *Memberships include:* Vice-President 1972-75, Chairman, Private Practitioners' Committee 1973-75, Chairman, Executive Committee 1976-83, President 1976-84, Chairman of the Council, Chairman, Finance Committee, Finnish Dental Association; National Treasurer 1967-75, President 1975, Finnish National Committee, Federation Dentaire Internationale; Council Member 1982-, Vice-President 1984, Federation Dentaire Internationale; Fellow, International Academy of Dentistry. *Publications:* Various articles on endodontics and dental health politics. *Honours:* Silver 1968, Gold, 1972, Badge of Merit, Finnish Dental Association; Silver Badge of Merit, Central Organisation of Professional Associations in Finland; Knight, first class, Order of the Lion of Finland, 1982. *Hobbies:* Music; Slalom skiing. *Address:* Johanneksentie 8 C 36, Helsinki 12, Finland.

TEMPELIS, Laurence Douglas, b. 18 Apr. 1948, Superior, Wisconsin, USA. Assistant Professor. m. Jane Larson, 3 July 1970, Superior, 2 sons, 1 daughter. *Education:* BA, High Honours, 1970, MD, 1974, University of Wisconsin. *Appointments:* Resident, Internal Medicine, University of Wisconsin Medical School, 1974-77; Haematology Clinical and Research Fellowship, Tufts University School of Medicine, 1977-80; Assistant Professor, Medicine, University of Wisconsin Medical School. *Memberships:* American College of Physicians; American Society of Haematology; International Association for Comparative Research on Leukemia and Related Diseases. *Publications:* Articles in professional journals. *Honours:* Milheim Foundation Cancer Award, 1981; Elsa Y Pardee Foundation Cancer Research Award, 1982; New Investigator Research Award, National Cancer Institute, National Institutes of Health, 1984. *Address:* 950 North 12th Street, Milwaukee, WI 53201, USA.

TEMPLETON, Lillian Richeson, b. 28 Sep. 1943, Ohio, USA. Chief Speech-Language Pathologist, St Mary Medical Center. m. J Charles Templeton, 26 Aug. 1967, Fredericksburg, Ohio, 2 daughters. *Education:* BA, The College of Wooster; MA, Michigan State University. *Appointment:* Clinical Director, Cerebral Palsy Clinic, Michigan State University. *Memberships:* Phi Beta Kappa; American Speech, Language and Hearing Association; Washington Speech and Hearing Association. *Hobby:* Skiing. *Address:* 925 Alvarado Terrace, Walla Walla, WA 99362, USA.

TERNBERG, Jessie Lamoin, b. 28 May 1924, Corning, California, USA. Professor of Surgery and Paediatrics; Chief of Division of Paediatric Surgery. *Education:* AB, 1946; PhD, 1950; MD, 1953. *Appointments:* Instructor and Trainee in Surgery 1959-62, Assistant Professor of Surgery 1962-65, Associate Professor of Surgery 1965-71, Associate Professor of Surgery in Paediatrics 1971-75, Professor of Surgery 1971-, Chief of Division of Paediatric Surgery 1972-, Professor of Surgery in Paediatrics 1975-, St Louis Children's Hospital at the Washington University Medical Center, St Louis, Missouri. *Memberships:* American Academy of Paediatrics; American Association for the Advancement of Science; American College of Surgeons; American Paediatric Surgical Association; Pan American Medical Association; Society of Pelvic Surgeons; Society for Surgery of the Alimentary Tract; Western Surgical Association. *Publications include:* "A Handbook for Pediatric Surgery", (with M J Bell and R J Bower), 1980; Chapters in: "Clinical Pediatric Oncology", (editors W W Sutow, T J Vietti and D J Fernbach), 1973, 1977 and 1983; "Manual of Surgical Nutrition", (editors W F Ballinger, J A Collins, W R Drucker and S J Dudrick), 1975; "Swenson's Pediatric Surgery", 1979; 6 abstracts; 79 papers in journals. *Honours:* Alumni Award 1966, Honorary DSc 1972, Grinnell College; International Women's Year Award for Health Care, Region VII, 1975; Globe-Democrat Woman of Achievement, 1976; Horatio Alger Award, 1977; Honorary DSc, University of Missouri, St Louis, 1981. *Hobbies:* Travelling; Skiing; Reading. *Address:* St Louis Children's Hospital at Washington University Medical Center, 400 S Kingshighway, Suite 5W12, St Louis, MO 63110, USA.

TERRENI, Anne A, b. 18 Aug. 1924, Columbia, South Carolina, USA. Microbiologist IV; Mycology Supervisor. m. Renato G Terreni, 18 Aug. 1955, Bergamo, Italy, 1 son. *Education:* BA, University of South Carolina, 1944; MA, Duke University, 1948. *Appointments:* Medical Technologist, Supervisor, Mycology, University of Virginia Medical School, 1949-50; Associate in Bacteriology, Supervisor, Mycology Section, Medical University of South Carolina, 1950-55; Instructor in Bacteriology, Supervisor Mycology Section, 1959-60; Bureau of Laboratories, South Carolina Department of Health and Environmental Control, 1975-78; Supervisor, Mycology Section, Bureau of Laboratories, South Carolina Department of Health and Environmental Control, 1978-. *Memberships:* American Society for Microbiology; South Carolina Public Health Association; Southern Health Association; Medical Mycological Society of the Americas; International Society for Human and Animal Mycoses. *Publications:* Co-author, "Tinea Capitis: A Report of One Hundred Cases', 'Journal of the South Carolina Medical Association', June 1954; Co-author: 'Systemic and Subcutaneous Mycoses in South Carolina: A Five Year Review', 'Journal of the South Carolina Medical Association', 1980; Co-author: 'Evaluation of Commercial Reagents to Identify the Exoantigens of Blastomyces dermatitidis, Coccidioides immitis and Histoplasma Special Culture', 'American Journal of Clinical Pathology' (in press); Co-author: 'Epidermophyton floccosum infection in a dog from the United States. Sabouraudia', 'Journal of Medical and Veterinary Mycology', 1985. *Address:* 3901 MacGregor Drive, Columbia, SC 29206, USA.

TERRY, Stephen, b. 3 Jan. 1936, New York, USA. Gynaecologist, Obstetrician. m. Barbara Anne Brown, 3 Sep. 1960, Gravenhurst, Ontario, Canada, 2 sons, 1 daughter. *Education:* BA, Chemistry, BS Zoology, University of Arizona, 1957; Columbia College of Physicians & Surgeons, 1961; MD. *Appointments:* Intern, Belleview Hospital, New York, 1961-62; Resident, New York Lying-In Hospital,

1962-65; Clinical Assistant, Cornell Medical School, 1962-65; Major USAR, US Army Hospital, Neuremberg, 1965-68; Obstetrician, Gynaecologist, Oklahoma City Clinic, 1968-69; Assistant Instructor, University of Oklahoma Medical School, 1968-69; Fellow, Gynaecological Oncology, M D Anderson Hospital,Tumor Instructor, University of Texas, 1969-70; Chief, Obstetrics, Pima County Hospital, Instructor, University of Arizona, 1970; Private Practice, Consultant, Obstetrics and Gynaecology, Tucson; Active Staff, Tucson Medical Centre and El Dorado; Hospital Courtesy Staff, St Josephs Hospital; Consultant Staff, Da-Monthan Air Force Hospital. *Memberships:* American College of Obstetricians and Gynaecologists, Fellow; American Fertility Society, Fellow; Tucson Obstetrical Society; American Medical Association; Southwest OB-GYN Society; American Association of Gynaecological Laparoscopists; American Society for Colposcopy and Cervical Pathology; Gynaecologurology Society; Felix-Rutlege Society; Medical Society of US and Mexico; Past President, Tucson Obstetrical & Gynaecological Society. *Honours:* American Field Service International Scholarship, 1953; Phi Lamba Upsilon, 1956; Phi Beta Kappa, 1957; Beta Beta Beta, 1957; Army Commendation Medal, 1967; American Cancer Fellowship, 1969. *Hobbies:* Philately; Music; Skiing. *Address:* 5295, East Knight, Tucson Medical Park West, Tucson, AZ 85712, USA.

TERZIC, Milorad, b. 30 Jan. 1932, Pirot, Yugoslavia. Professor of Pharmacology. m. Elisabeth Macri, 5 Feb. 1961, 1 son. *Education:* MD; PhD. *Appointments:* Assistant, Faculty of Medicine, University of Belgrade, Yugoslavia, 1959, Associate Professor, Faculty of Stomatology, 1969, Professor and Head, Institute of Pharmacology, 1975-. *Memberships:* Societe Francaise de Therapeutique et de Pharmacologie Clinique, Paris, France; Yugoslav Societies of Pharmacology and Toxicology; Groupement International de Recherche en Odontologie et Stomatologie. *Publications:* "Prescription Writing", 1972, 1984; "General Pharmacology for Dentistry", 1980. Numerous articles.*Hobbies:* Violin; Chess. *Address:* Department of Pharmacology, Faculty of Stomatology, D-Subotica 8, 11000 Belgrade, Yugoslavia.

TEWFIK, T Louli, b. 29 Aug. 1946, Egypt. Assistant Professor, Otolaryngology, McGill University, Montreal, Canada. m. Viviane Habib, 25 Mar. 1979, Alexandria, Egypt, 1 son, 1 daughter. *Education:* MB, B Surgery, Diploma of Surgery, Alexandria University, Egypt, 1969-72; FICS; FRCSC; FAAP; Diploma, American Board of Otolaryngology, 1982. *Appointments:* Resident, Alexandria University Hospitals, 1969-70; Resident, Public Health Hospitals, Egypt, 1970-83; Teaching Fellow, Department of Anatomy, University of Saskatchewan, Canada, 1973-74; Resident, General Surgery, 1974-76, Intern, 1976-77, St John's NFLD, Canada; Resident, Otolaryngology, McGill Hospital, Montreal, Canada, 1978-81; Clinical Fellow, University of Cincinnati, USA, 1981. *MEMBERSHIPS:* Fellow, Royal College of Surgeons of Canada; Fellow, American Academy of Otolaryngology; Fellow, American Academy of Pediatrics; Fellow, International College of Surgeons. *Publications:* 'Corrosive Lye Ingestion', 1981; 'Hemangiopericytoma of the Temporal bone', 1982; 'Adenoidcystic Carcinoma of Larynx', 1983; 'Lymphangioma in Children', 1985. *Honours:* Med-Chi Resident Award in Otolaryngology, 1979-81. *Hobbies:* Swimming; Biking; Collecting stamps. *Address:* 2300 Tupper Street, Montreal, Quebec, Canada H3H 1P3.

THACKER, Bettye Bennett Drake, b. 25 Sep. 1930, Isle of Wight County, Virginia, USA. Registered Nurse Co-ordinator. m. Thomas Eugene Drake Sr, 11 Jan. 1953, Smithfield, Virginia, 1 son, 4 daughters, one deceased. *Education:* Diploma, Louise Obici School of Nursing, 1952; BSc Nursing, 1972; Candidate, MSc Nursing, 1985. *Appointments:* Various Nursing posts in Virginia, Alabama & Georgia, 1952-65; Head Nurse, 1966-68, Supervisor, 1968-69, Student Nurse Instructor, 1969-78, Nurse Coordinator, 1978-80, Unit Administrator, Medical/Surgical Unit, 1978-80, Acting Director Nursing, Psychiatric Division, 1980-81, Director of Nursing, 1981-85, Nurse Coordinator, Community Liaison Team, 1986-, all Eastern State Hospital, Williamsburg, Virginia. *Memberships:* American Nurses' Association; Cardiovascular Nursing Committee of American Heart Association; York County Social Services Board, 1986. *Honour:* Outstanding Nurse, Virginia Nurses' Association, 1975; Sigma Theta Tau, 1984.*Hobbies:* Sewing; Collecting Pitchers & Shells; Aerobics; Tennis. *Address:* 115 Quaker Meeting House Road, Williamsburg, VA 23185, USA.

THALER, Arnulf Richard Gunnar, b. 22 Aug. 1942, Klagenfurt, Austria. Head Physician. *Education:* MD, 1967; University Dozent, 1978; University Professor, 1984. *Appointments:* Resident, Institute for General and Comparative Physiology, 1968-70, 2nd Department of Ophthalmology, 1970-, currently, Head Physician, 2nd Department of Ophthalmology, University of Vienna; Research Fellow, Department of Ophthalmology, Iowa University, USA, 1977. *Memberships:* International Society for Clinical Electrophysiology of Vision; Ophthalmology Society of Vienna; Austrian Ophthalmology Society. *Publications:* Author over 80 publications mainly on electrophysiology of the eye. *Address:* 2nd Department of Ophthalmology, University of Vienna, Alserstrasse 4, A-1090 Vienna, Austria.

THANG, Ming-Nguy, b. 9 Jan. 1929, Canton, China. Director of Research. *Education:* DSc, Paris Faculty of Sciences, France, 1960. *Appointments:* In charge of Research Project, 1960, Master of Research, 1966, Director, ER 238, CNRS, 1980-85, currently, Director of Research, CNRS, Paris (French National Centre for Scientific Research); Director, U 245, INSERM, France, currently. *Memberships:* Scientific Adviser, Zhong Shan University, Canton, China; Vice President, Franco-Chinese Association for Research in Biology and Medicine.*Publications:* 100s of research articles on nucleic acids and enzymology in major international journals including: 'Proceedings National Academy of Sciences', USA; 'Journal of Biological Chemistry'; 'Journal of Molecular Biology'; 'European Journal of Biochemistry'; 'Nucleic Acids Research'; 'Cancer Research'; 'Biochimca'; Biophysics Acta' and others. *Honours:* P Doisteau and E Blutal Prize, Academy of Sciences, 1977. *Hobbies:* Arts and beauty; Cooking; Dreaming.*Address:* Centre INSERM, Hôpital St Antoine, rue du Faubourg, St Antoine, 75012 Paris, France.

THANGARAJ, Roy Handel, b. 21 Mar. 1930, Salur, AP, India. Director, The Leprosy Mission Southern Asia Consultant WHO; Secretary, International Leprosy Association. m. Esther Sarojini, 7 June 1957, Vellore, 2 sons, 1 daughter. *Education:* MB BS; FACS; FICS; FIMSA. *Appointments:* Registrar in Orthopaedics and Plastic Surgery, England, 1961-65; Surgeon and Superintendent, Philadelphia Leprosy Hospital, Salur, India, 1965-77; Director, The Leprosy Mission Southern Asia, 1978-. *Memberships:* International Leprosy Association; International Plastic and Reconstructive Surgery Association; International Orthopaedic Association; International Hand Surgery Association; Indian Association of Leprologists; Hing Kusht Nivaran Sangh (Indian Leprosy Association); Indian Medical Association. *Publications:* 'Indian Journal of Leprosy'; 'Christian Medical Association of India Journal'; Editor, "A Manual of Leprosy", 4th edition under print; Several articles in 'Leprosy Review'. *Honours:* FACS, 1974; FICS, 1973. *Hobbies:* Photography; Music.*Address:* The Leprosy Mission, 5 Amrita Shergill Marg, New Delhi, 110003, India.

THASE, Michael Edward, b. 24 Aug. 1952, Dayton, Ohio, USA. Assistant Professor of Psychiatry. m.

Linda L Soifer, 28 May 1976, Dayton, Ohio, 2 sons, 1 daughter. *Education:* BA, Wright State University, Dayton, Ohio, 1970-75; MD, Ohio State University, Columbus, Ohio, 1976-79; Internship, Residency, Postdoctoral Fellowship, Western Psychiatric Institute & Clinic, Pittsburgh, PA, 1979-84. *Appointments:* Mental Health Therapist, Good Samaritan Mental Health Centre, Dayton, Ohio, 1974-76; Staff Psychiatrist, Mayview State Hospital, Bridgeville, Pennsylvania, 1980-; Staff Psychiatrist, Allegheny East MH/MR Centre, Wilkinsburg PA, 1981-83; also Allegheny Valley MH/MR Centre, New Kensington PA, 1981-83; Assistant Professor, Department of Psychiatry, University of Pittsburgh School of Medicine, 1983-. *Memberships:* American Medical Association, 1978; Association for the Advancement of Behaviour Therapy, 1980; American Psychiatric Association, 1980; Society for Psychotherapy Research, 1984; American Association for the Advancement of Science, 1984. *Publications:* (With D J Kupfer) 'The Use of the Sleep Laboratory in the diagnosis of affective disorders' (in Psychiatric Clinics of N America 1983); (co-author) 'Age-related neuropsychological deficits in Down's Syndrome' (in Biological Psychiatry, 1984); 'Cognitive & Behavioural treatments for depression' (chapter in Affective Disorders Reassessed (edited Fayd, I & B Taylor) 1983. *Honours:* Alpha Omega Alpha, 1978; Samuel Roessler Research Foundation Scholarship, 1978; Falk Fellowship, American Psychiatric Association, 1981; Laughlin Fellowship, American College of Psychiatrists, 1983; Marie Eldridge Award, American Psychiatric Association, 1984. *Hobbies:* Baseball; Basketball; Gardening. *Address:* Western Psychiatric Institute & Clinic, 3811 O'Hara Street, Pittsburgh, PA 15213, USA.

THAW, Marsha Roslyn, b. 31 Dec. 1946, Texas, USA. Private Practice Clinical Social Worker; Director. Marsha Thaw, Licensed Clinical Social Worker Inc. m. Thomas J Henderson, 14 July 1976, Orange County, California. *Education:* AA, San Antonio Junior College; BA, MSW, University of Houston. *Appointments:* Teacher, Workshops in Art Therapy for California State and University of California; Comprehensive Intake Worker, 1968-69; Caseworker II, 1969-71; With Dr J F Kleen, Houston, Texas, 1971-73; Children's Mental Health Services, Houston, Texas, 1971-72; Texas Research Institute of Mental Sciences, Houston, 1972; Texas Institute of Child Psychiatry, Houston, 1972-73; Psychiatric Social Worker, Intercommunity Child Guidance Center, Hawaiian Gardens, California, 1974-75; Licensed Clinical Social Worker (part-time), Family Guidance Center, Buena Park, California, 1975-77; California Licensed Clinical Social Worker, Private Practice, Garden Grove and Dana Point, California, 1976-. *Memberships:* National Association of Social Workers; Society for Clinical Social Work; Forensic Mental Health Association of California; NASW Register of Clinical Social Workers. *Hobbies:* Sailing; Tennis; Oil Painting; Knitting; Gardening; Cooking. *Address:* 26932 Oso Parkway, Suite 200, Mission Viejo, CA 92691, USA.

THEILADE, Jørgen, b. 23 May 1929, Copenhagen, Denmark. Reader in Periodontology and Public Health. m. Else Agnete Vorbeck, 21 Nov. 1958, Toronto, Canada, 2 daughters. *Education:* DDS, Royal Dental College, Copenhagen, Denmark, 1952; BSc Dentistry, University of Toronto, Canada, 1958; Certificate in Periodontology, Eastman Dental Center, Rochester, New York, 1960; MS, School of Medicine and Dentistry, University of Rochester, New York, 1961. *Appointments include:* Instructor 1954-57, External Examiner of Department of Periodontology 1982-, Royal Dental College, Copenhagen, Denmark; District Dental Officer in Greenland, Ministry of Greenland, Danish Government, 1956 and 1957; Visiting Associate, Laboratory of Histology and Pathology, National Institute of Dental Research, Bethesda, Maryland, USA, 1960-61; Associate Professor 1961-67, Acting Head 1966-67, Department of Periodontology, Head 1964-85, Associate Professor 1967-85, Department of Electron

Microscopy, Senior Lecturer, School of Dental Auxiliaries, 1982-85, Royal Dental College, Aarhus, Denmark; Reader, Department of Periodontology and Public Health, Faculty of Dentistry, University of Hong Kong, The Prince Philip Dental Hospital, Hong Kong, 1985-. *Memberships include:* International Association for Dental Research; Scandinavian Association for Dental Research; Danish Dental Association; Jysk-Fynsk Society of Periodontology; Scandinavian Society for Electron Microscopy; Scandinavian Society of Periodontology; Charter Member, International Academy of Periodontology; Honorary Member, Indian Society of Periodontology. *Publications include:* Over 70 publications including: 'Role of plaque in the etiology of peridontal disease and caries' (with E Theilade), 1976; 'Dental plaque and dental calculus' in "Textbook of Clinical Periodontology" (editor: J Lindhe), 1983-84. *Honour:* John O Butler Prize, 1984. *Hobbies:* Violin; Rowing. *Address:* Department of Periodontology and Public Health, Faculty of Dentistry, University of Hong Kong, The Prince Philip Dental Hospital, 34 Hospital Road, Hong Kong.

THERBAULT, Pierre, b. 20 Dec. 1951, Paris, France. Chiropractor. m. Brigitte Therbault, 22 June 1981, Versailles. *Education:* State Registered Physiotherapist, Necker Hospital, Paris, 1975; DC, Palmer College of Chiropractic, Davenport, USA, 1979. *Appointments:* Physical Therapist, 1975; Faculty Member, Palmer College of Chiropractic, USA, 1977-79; Private Practitioner of Chiropractics, Versailles, France, 1979-. *Memberships:* American and French Chiropractic Associations; Palmer College of Chiropractic Alumnis Association. *Hobbies:* Music; Snow skiing competitions; Guitar; Reading. *Address:* 98 Boulevard de la Reine, 78000 Versailles, France.

THEUMA, Marianne, b. 19 Feb. 1950, Malta, Childbirth Educator. m. Lawrence, 21 July 1973, Vittoriosa, Malta, 1 son, 1 daughter. *Education:* Teachers Training College; Attended 2 conventions in USA; Attended 2 symposiums in London, England. *Appointments:* School teacher. *Memberships:* International Childbirth Education Association, USA; National Childbirth Trust, United Kingdom; La Leche Keague International; International Breastfeeding Affiliation. *Publications:* 'Mill-Benniena', (Editor); Author of articles to various magazines and journals. *Hobbies:* Tennis; Swimming; Reading. *Address:* 5 Trafalgar Flats, Cardinal Street, Vittoriosa, Malta.

THIE, John Francis, b. 25 Jan. 1933, Detroit, Michigan, USA. Doctor of Chiropractic. m. Clara Pauline Wright, 27 Dec. 1952, El Cajon, California, USA, 3 sons. *Education:* AA, Pasadena City College, USA, 1952; BS, University of Southern California, 1954; DC, Los Angeles College of Chiropractic, 1957; Diplomate, International College of Applied Kinesiology, 1976. *Appointments:* Faculty, Los Angeles College of Chiropractic, 1957-58; Chairman, Adult Advisory Board, Pasadena Area Youth Council, 1960-64; Associate Lecturer, Parker Chiropractic Research Foundation, 1967-81; Director/Owner, Thie Chiropractic Clinic. *Memberships include:* American Association for Nutritional Consultants; International College of Applied Kiniesology; Board of Christian Education; California Chiropractic Association; American Chiropractic Association; National Chiropractic Association Committee on Nutrition; American Association for the Advancement of Science. *Publications:* Author "Touch for Health", 1973, revised, 1980; 'Touch for Health' reference chart; 'Touch for Health' Acupuncture Reference Chart; articles in 'Healthways' magazine; 'National Chiropractic Journal'; 'Share' Magazine; 'Journal of the American Chiropractic Association'; 'European Chiropractic Journal'; (Science of Mind magazine; 'New Reality'; Annual papers of International College of Applied Kinesiology. *Honours include:* Doctor of the Year, San Gabriel Valley Chiropractic Society, 1960; Chiropractor of the Year Distinguished Service Award, Parker Chiropractic Research Foundation,

1967; Robert Botterman Outstanding Education Service Award, 1977; Super 20 Seminar Chairman for the International College of AK, 1984. *Hobby:* Photography. *Address:* 1192 North Lake Avenue, Pasadena, CA 91104, USA.

THIERY, Michel, b. 14 Nov. 1924, Gent, Belgium. Professor and Chairman of Department of Obstetrics. m. Huguette Descheemaker, 28 Aug. 1957, Gent, 1 daughter. *Education:* MD 1949, PhD 1962, Faculty of Medicine, University of Gent. *Appointments:* Assistant and Chef de Clinique in Department of Obstetrics-Gynaecology 1949-63, Assistant Professor 1963-64, Professor and Chairman 1964-, Department of Obstetrics, Lecturer in Sexuology of Faculties of Psychology and of Philsophy 1980-, Gent University. *Memberships:* Royal Belgian Society of Gynaecology and Obstetrics; European Society of Perinatal Medicine; Deutsche Gesellschaft für Perinatalogie; American Society of Cytology; Societas Belgica Medicinae Historiae; Royal Academy of Medicine; Past-President, Belgian Royal Society of Gynaecologists and Obstetricians; Past Medical Director, Belgian Society of Family Planning; Expert, State Committee for Control of Drugs; President 8th European Congress, Perinatal Medicine, 1982; President, State Subcommittee on Contraceptives; Royal Commissar, Committee for the Study of Ethical Problems; Past-President, Concerted Action Project Perinatal Medicine, European Economic Community. *Publications:* Books on abortion, contraception, fetal pharmacology, induction and preinduction of labour; Co-editor, loose-leaf textbook on fertility regulation; Chapters in textbooks; Author or co-author of approximately 850 scientific papers on obstetrical/gynaecological subjects. *Hobbies:* History of Medicine; Hiking. *Address:* Department of Obstetrics, Academic Hospital, De Pintelaan 185, 9000 Gent, Belgium.

THIMMEL, William F, b. 12 Feb. 1960, Hackensack, USA. Doctor of Chiropractic. *Education:* Rutgers College, Rutgers University; Doctorate, Palmer College of Chiropractic. *Memberships:* International Chiropractic Association; American Chiropractic Association; New Jersey Chiropractic Society. *Honour:* Pi Tau Delta Chiropractic Honour Society, 1983. *Hobbies:* Swimming; Aerobic Conditioning. *Address:* 15-01 Broadway, Fair Lawn, NJ 07410, USA.

THOFERN, Edgar, b. 6 May 1925, Bovenden/Göttingen, Germany. Director, Institute of Medical Hygiene, University of Bonn. m. Traute Kuhlmann, 2 sons, 1 daughter. *Education:* Staatsaxamen and Promotion, 1950; Habilitation, 1959; Apl. Professor, 1965; O. Professor, Director, Institute of Medical Hygiene, University of Bonn, 1971. *Memberships:* DGHM, President, 1983-85; Frontinus-Gesellschaft; ÖGHM; German Society for History of Medicine, Natural Science and Technology. *Publications:* 140 articles in professional journals; Book Chapters; (Book) "Hygiene und Infektionen im Krankenhaus", co-author. *Address:* Hygiene Institut der Universität Bonn, Sigmund-Freuds Strasse 25, Klinikgelände 35, D-5300 Bonn 1-Venusberg.

THOMAS, Irene Manorama, b. 12 Oct. 1935, Mangalore, India. Professor. m. Dr John Arthur Thomas, 27 Jan. 1962, Vellore, 1 son. *Education:* BSc, 1956; MBBS, 1960; MS, 1969. *Appointments:* Demonstrator, Tutor, Anatomy, Christian Medical College, Vellore, 1963-66; Tutor, 1966-71, Assistant Professor, 1971-75, Associate Professor, 1971-75, Associate Professor, 1975-84, Professor, Head, Anatomy, 1984-, St John's Medical College, Bangalore. *Memberships:* Life Member, Anatomical Society of India, Executive Committee Member; American Association of Anatomists; Life Member, Indian Society of Human Genetics, Society of History of Medicine; Genetic Association of India; Expert Committee, Genetics, Dept of Science & Technology; etc. *Publications:* "Medical Genetics in India", 1978; "Modi's Medical Jurisprudence and Toxicology", 18th Edition, 1972;

THOMAS, James Enos, b. 7 May 1922, Flint, Michigan, USA. Diplomate and Fellow in Orthopaedics. m. Marilyn Louise Phillips, 10 Feb. 1945, Flint, Michigan, USA. 2 daughters. *Education:* Chiropractic Physician, Lincoln Chiropractic College, 1949; Diplomate, Orthopaedics, National College 1973; Chiropractic Internist, American College of Chiropractic, 1972. *Appointments:* President, Michigan Orthopaedic Society, 1967-71; Chairman, Michigan Peer Review Board, 1967-71; Lecturer, National College Extension Division Orthopaedic, 1968-73; Writer of questions on diagnosis for Michigan State Licensing Board, 1968-71. *Memberships:* American Chiropractic Association; Council on Chiropractic Orthopaedists; Florida Chiropractic Association; Florida Council of Chiropractic Orthopaedics. *Publications:* Booklet: "Instructions for Constructing Removable Body Caste", 1972 (donated to National Chiropractic College); Awaiting publication: "Classification and Charting of Low Back/Leg Pain Syndrome", 1984. *Honour:* Certificate of Merit, Michigan State Chiropractic Association, 1974. *Hobbies:* Golf; Boating. *Address:* 3129 F Tamiami Trail, Port Charlotte, FL 33952, USA.

THOMAS, Jesse James, b. 13 Nov. 1933, Greenfield, Indiana, USA. Psychotherapist. m. Bonnie Jean Grihalva, 29 Oct. 1983, San Diego, 2 sons, 6 daughters, by previous marriages. *Education:* BA, Taylor University; MTh, Garrett Theological Seminary; PhD, Northwestern University; Post-graduate Diploma, Gestalt Institute of Cleveland, Ohio. *Appointments:* Assistant Professor to Associate Professor, Saginaw Valley State College, Michigan, 1967-77; Staff, Gestalt Institute, San Diego, 1977-79; Private Practice, 1977-; Adjunct Faculty, California School of Professional Psychology, 1979-; Adjunct Faculty, San Diego State University, 1978-. *Memberships:* American Society for Clinical Hypnosis; American Academy of Psychotherapists; California Association of Marriage & Family Therapists; San Diego Society of Sex Therapists & Educators; San Diego Society for Clinical Hypnosis. *Publications:* "The Youniverse & Gestalt Therapy & Non Western Religions", 1978; "Hypnosis & Psychotherapy", 'Clinical Hypnosis Primer', 1983; "The Return of Marriage", 1986. *Hobby:* American Indian Rock Art. *Address:* Doctors Bldg, Scripps Hospital, 9834 Genesee Ave, 427, La Jolla, CA 92037, USA.

THOMAS, Joseph E, b. 11 Feb. 1937, India. Assistant Professor of Psychiatry and Behavioural Sciences. m. Chinnamma Thomas, 23 Nov. 1964, Piravom, 2 sons, 1 daughter. *Education:* MA; PhD, University of Kerala, India, 1969; Post-Doctoral Fellowship, Northwestern University Medical School, Chicago, Illinois, USA, 1971-72. *Appointments:* Lecturer in Psychology, University of Kerala, 1966-70; Psychologist, Department of Psychiatry, University of Chicago, Illinois, USA, 1972-74; Psychologist, North Western Memorial Hospital, 1974-76; Psychologist, Rehabilitation Institute of Chicago, 1976-80; Private Practice of Behavioural Medicine, 1980-; Assistant Professor, Department of Psychiatry and Behavioural Sciences, Northwestern University Medical School, Chicago, Illinois; Editor, Kerala Christian Times, Illinois. *Memberships:* President 1985, Biofeedback Society of Illinois; American Psychological Assoc iation; Society for Behavioural Medicine. *Publications include:* 'Personality' in "Vijnanam" (editor: P T B Panikaar), 1972; 'Management of pain in sickle-cell disease using biofeedback therapy - A preliminary study', 1984. *Honours:* University Grants Commission Research Fellowship (India), 1961-62; Commonwealth Fellowship, 1970-72. *Hobbies:* Travel; Literature; Painting. *Address:* 16 W, 731-89th Place, Hinsdale, IL 60521, USA.

THOMAS, Klaus Johannes, b. 31 Jan. 1915, Berlin, Federal Republic of Germany. Director, I H Schultz Institute and Director of the Medical Suicide Prevention Centre, Berlin. *Education:* Theological Studies, Instructorship, Berlin, 1934-35; Ordained as Lutheran

Minister, 1940; PhD, 1940; Qualifying examinations for teaching, Berlin University, 1941-42; MD, Marburg University, 1947; DD, New York, USA, 1964. *Appointments include:* Founder and Chaplain, German Branch of the International Order of Saint Luke the Physician, 1950-; Founder, Chairman, German Telephone Counselling Service, Berlin, 1956-; Professor, Pastoral Care and Psychology, Lutheran Seminary 'Paulinum' and Priests Seminary, Roman Catholic Church, Berlin, 1950-; Practicing Physician and Psychiatrist, 1947-; Physician, Child Guidance Clinic and Home for Juvenile Delinquents, 1950-53; Staff Psychiatrist, St Elizabeth's Hospital, Washington DC, USA, 1964-65; Professor, Psychotherapy, German Academy for Medical Training, 1966-; Chairman, Postgraduate Psychiatric Training Seminary, Freiburg/Bad Bellingen, Federal Republic of Germany, 1969-; President, European Society of Medical Hypnosis, 1980-; Professor, Psychology, Lessing-Hochschule, Berlin, 1966-; Co-editor, 'Archivesdfor Psychology and Religion, Member of Board of Directors, International Society for Psychology of Religion, 1959-. *Memberships:* International Association for Suicide Prevention; The German Society of Psychotherapy; President, European Society of Hypnosis; Honorary Member, American Society of Clinical Hypnosis; Member, International Society of Hypnosis; Member, British Society of Medical Hypnosis. *Publications:* 'Wege zum Menschen', (Founder and editor), 1949-57; "Handbook for Prevention of Suicide", 1964; "Practice of Autogenic Training", (7th edition, 1986); "Medical Suicide Prevention", 1969, 2nd Edition, 1969; "Sexual Education", 1969; "Men in Front of the Precipice", 1970; "The Manipulated Soul", 1970; Contributor of over 800 articles in national and international scientific journals, 1949-; "Handbook on Youth - Anthropology", (Co-author), 1964. *Hobbies:* Piloting; World travel. *Address:* Glockenstrasse 17, 1000 Berlin 37, Federal Republic of Germany.

THOMAS, Michael, b. 20 June 1935, Loughborough, England. Consultant Cardiac Physician. m. Barbara Anne Lockley, 16 June 1962, Stoke on Trent, 1 son, 1 daughter. *Education:* MA, Jesus College, Cambridge; MD, St Mary's Hospital, London; Fellow, Royal College of Physicians. *Appointments:* Consultant Physician, Lecturer in Medicine, Royal Postgraduate Medical School, London; Scientific Staff, Medical Research Council, Hammersmith Hospital, London; Currently Consultant Cardiac Physician, King Edward VIIth Hospital, Midhurst, Brompton Hospital, London. *Memberships:* Fellow, College of Physicians of London; Fellow, Royal Society of Medicine, London. *Publications:* 'Haemodynamic changes in patients with acute myocardial infarction', (with R Malmcrona and J P Shillingford), 1965; 'Free noradrenaline and adrenaline urinary excretion in relation to clinical syndromes following myocardial infarction', (with C Valori and J P Shillingford), 1967; 'Does beta blockade directly reduce myocardial oxygen consumption?', (with I T Gabe, H Kimber, C J Mills and T K Sweeting), 1981. *Hobbies:* Photography; Life in the Scottish Western Isles. *Address:* 'Copsen', Knoll Road, Frith Hill, Godalming, Surrey, England.

THOMASON, Harry, b. 29 Feb. 1940, Preston, England. Professor, Head, PE & Sport Science, Loughborough University of Technology, 1977-; Pro-Vice-Chancellor, 1985-. m. Marion Flintoff, 3 Aug. 1966, Hoole, 1 son. *Education:* Teacher's Certificate, Chester College; Supplementary Certificate, Education, DLC, Loughborough Training College; MSc, Human Biology, Salford University; PhD, Human Science, Loughborough University of Technology. *Appointments:* Lecturer, 1963-75, Senior Lecturer, 1975-77, Salford University. *Memberships:* Fellow, Royal Society of Medicine; Ergonomics Society; New York Academy of Sciences; British Association of Sport and Medicine; British Olympic Committee, Medical Sub-Committee. *Publications:* "Sports Medicine", 1975; "Basic Book of Sports Medicine", 1977; "Science and Sporting Performance", 1983. *Honours:*

Churchill Travelling Fellowship, 1976. *Hobbies:* Sailing; Skiing; Walking the Dog. *Address:* Loughborough University of Technology, Loughborough, Leicestershire LE11 3TU, England.

THOMASSON, Björn Henrik, b. 22 May 1931, Tammerfors, Finland. Professor of Paediatric Surgery. m. Karin E E Solin, 27 June 1964, Abo, 3 sons. *Education:* MD 1955, Dr Med Sci 1959, Abo University; Board Certified; Surgery 1964; Paediatric Surgery 1967; Orthopaedics and Traumatology 1983; Diploma, Scandinavian Federation Medical Education, 1977. *Appointments:* Resident, Consultant, Faculty Member, Surgery and Paediatric Surgery, Abo University, Finland, 1956-76; Fellow in Surgery, Johns Hopkins University, Baltimore, Maryland, USA, 1959-61; Resident in Paediatric Surgery, Zürich University, Switzerland, 1965; Resident Associate, Assistant Professor, Pediatric Surgery, University of Chicago, Chicago, Illinois, USA, 1968-69; Professor of Paediatric Surgery, Karolinska Institute, Stockholm, Sweden. *Memberships:* Swedish, Finnish, British, and Greek (honorary) Association of Paediatric Surgeons; General Secretary, Scandinavian Association of Paediatric Surgeons; Finnish Association of Paediatricians (Correspondant). *Publications:* Several publications on surgical, paediatric surgical and experimental topics. *Honours:* Rotary International Fellowship, 1959; Medal, Academia Wratislaviensis Polonia, 1979. *Hobbies:* Choir singing; Boating. *Address:* Karolinska Institute, Saint Göran's Hospital, S-112 81 Stockholm, Sweden.

THOMPSON, Dennis Scott, b. 18 June 1943, Detroit, Michigan, USA. Medical Director, Hamilton Centre, Terre Haute, Indiana. *Education:* BS, University of Michigan; DO, Chicago College Osteo Medicine; Fellow AACP; Medical Internship, Cook County Hospital, 1970-71; Psychiatric Residency, University of Illinois, 1971-74; Child Psychiatry Fellowship, Institute for Juvenile Research, Chicago, 1973-75. *Appointments:* Assistant Professor, Psychiatry, University of Illinois, 1976-83; Staff Psychiatrist, Institute for Juvenile Research, 1976-83; Medical Director, Elmhurst Memorial Hospital Guidance Centre, 1981-84; Private Practice, Chicago, Palos, Illinois, 1981-84; Psychiatric Consultant, Barrington School District, 1982-84; Psychiatric Consultant, Ada McKinley Therapeutic Day School, 1983-84; Assistant Professor, Psychiatry, Chicago College of Osteopathic Medicine, 1983-84. *Memberships:* American Psychiatric Association; Indiana Psychiatric Society; American Academy of Child Psychiatry; American Society for Adolescent Psychiatry; American Osteopathic Association; American Association for the Advancement of Science. *Publication:* "Childhood Psychoses", Medical Student Manual and Videotape, 1982. *Honours:* Diplomate, American Board of Psychiatry and Neurology, 1978, American Board in Child Psychiatry, 1979; Fellow, American Academy of Child Psychiatry, 1983. *Hobbies:* Nature; Swimming; Hiking. *Address:* 620 8th Ave., PO Box 4323, Terre Haute, IN 47804, USA.

THOMPSON, Peter Lindsay, b. 26 December 1941, Perth, Australia. Cardiologist. m. Andrea Jane Stimson, 16 Aug. 1967, Perth, Australia, 2 sons, 1 daughter. *Education:* MBBS, FRACP, FACP, FACC. *Appointments:* Resident Medical Officer, Royal Perth Hospital, 1965; Research Fellow, Pathology Department, University of Western Australia, 1966; Medical Resident, Royal Perth Hospital, 1967; Medical Registrar, Royal Melbourne Hospital, 1968; Cardiology Registrar, Royal Melbourne Hospital, 1969; Fellow in Cardiology, Peter Bent Brigham Hospital and Harvard School of Public Health, 1970-72; Cardiologist, Sir Charles Gardner Hospital, 1972-. *Memberships:* Australian Medical Association; Royal Australasian College of Physicians; Cardiac Society of Australia and New Zealand; Council on Epidemiology; American Heart Association; American College of Physicians; American College of Cardiology. *Publications:* 80 articles on coronary heart disease, 1970-85. *Hon-*

ours: National Heart Foundation, Overseas Clinical Fellow, 1970-72; M D Silberberg Lecturer 1976; Visiting Fellow, University of Gothenburg, 1977, Harvard School of Public Health, 1978. *Hobbies:* Boating; Music; Tennis. *Address:* 168 Hampden Road, Nedlands, Australia.

THOMPSON, Richard Paul Hepworth, b. 14 Apr. 1940, Esher, Surrey, England. Consultant Physician. m. Eleanor Mary, 11 May 1974, Dublin, Ireland. *Education:* MA, BM, DM, Oxford University, England. *Appointments:* Clinical Research Fellow, Medical Research Council, Liver Unit, King's College Hospital, London, 1967-69; Fellow, Gastroenterology Unit, Mayo Clinic, USA, 1969-71; Honorary Senior Registrar and Lecturer, Liver Unit, King's College Hospital, London, 1971-72; Consultant Physician, St Thomas' Hospital, London. *Memberships:* Fellow, Royal College of Physicians; Association of Physicians; Royal Society of Medicine; British Society of Gastroenterology, etc. *Publications:* Many articles in Medical/Scientific journals; "Lecture Notes on the Liver", 1985; "Physical Signs in Medicine", 1981. *Hobby:* Work. *Address:* 36 Dealtry Road, London, SW15, England.

THOMPSON, William Moreau, b. 20 Oct. 1943, Philadelphia, Pennsylvania, USA. Physician Radiologist. m. Judy Anne Seel, 28 July 1968, 2 sons. *Education:* BA, Colgate University, 1965; MD, University of Pennsylvania School of Medicine, 1969. *Appointments:* Internship, Case Western Reserve, 1969-70; USPHS, Anchorage, Alaska, 1970-72; Radiology Residency, Duke University, 1972-75; Chief Resident, 1975, Assistant Professor, 1975-77, Associate Professor, 1977-81, Professor of Radiology, 1981-, Duke University Medical Center; Chief of Radiology, Durham VA Hospital, 1979-86; Professor and Chairman, Department of Radiology University of Minnesota, Minneapolis, 1986-. *Memberships:* AMA; Association of University Radiologists; American College of Radiology; RSNA; Sigma Xi; American Roentgen Ray Society. *Publications:* Contributor of over 110 articles, 11 book chapters and 30 abstracts. *Honours:* Fellow, ACR; James Picken Scholar, 1975-79; Teacher of the Year, 1980; Recipient of 11 prizes for exhibits. *Hobbies:* Tennis; Fishing; Hunting. *Address:* Department of Radiology, Box 292, Mayo Memorial Building, 420 Delaware Street, SE Minneapolis, MN 55455, USA.

THOMSON, (Sir) Evan Rees Whitaker, b. 14 July 1919, Brisbane, Australia. Honorary Consultant Surgeon, Princess Alexandra Hospital, Brisbane. m. Mary Kennedy, 18 June 1955, Brisbane. *Education:* University of Queensland; MB BS; FRCS (Eng); FRACS; FACS. *Appointments:* Resident Medical Officer; Surgical Registrar, Brisbane General Hospital, 1942-48; Junior Surgeon, 1950-56; Senior Surgeon, Princess Alexandra Hospital, 1956-71; Clinical Lecturer in Surgery, University of Queensland, 1950-71. *Memberships:* Australian Medical Association; British Medical Association; Medical Board of Queensland; Medico-Legal Society of Queensland, Vice-Patron; Society for Health and Human Values. *Publications:* "Indications for Surgery in Peptic Ulcer", 1957; "Your Way of Life", 1958; "The Difficult Appendix", 1960; "On the Classification of Toxic Goitre", 1964; "Hazards of the Commonplace in Surgery", 1965; "Some Aspects of Non-toxic Goitre", 1966; "Medical Ethics", 1967; "Of Change and Constancy", 1968; "Medicine Scientific and Otherwise", 1968; "The Christian in Surgical Practice", 1969; "Training in Surgery", 1969; "The Coat of Arms of the Princess Alexandra Hospital", 1972; "Future Needs for Medical Education in Queensland", 1981; Part author and editor: "The Thomson Report". *Honours include:* Government Medal for Outstanding Merit, 1942; Honorary Surgeon to Her Majesty and Members of the Royal Family; Knight Bachelor, 1977; Queen's Silver Jubilee Medal, 1977. *Hobbies:* Reading; Theology; History; Archaeology. *Address:* 10-104 Station Road, Indooroopiley, Brisbane, Queensland 4068, Australia.

THOMSON, Julian George, b. 1 June 1927, London, England. Assistant Professor. m. Eileen Yarker, 30 Mar. 1959, Kirby Bedon, Norfolk, 2 sons, 1 daughter. *Education:* MB, BS, London; Doctor of Anaesthesiology. *Appointments:* Captain, Royal Army Medical Corps; Anaesthetist, BMH, Berlin, Federal Republic of Germany; Senior Resident Anaesthetist, Leicester Royal Infirmary, England; Anaesthetic Registrar, Thoracic Surgical Unit, Harefield Hospital, Middlesex; Staff Anaesthetist, Grace General Hospital, Winnepeg, Manitoba, Canada; Assistant Professor, Faculty of Medicine, Dalhousie University, Halifax, Nova Scotia. *Memberships:* Licenciate, Royal College of Physicians, London; Royal College of Surgeons, England; Fellow, Royal College of Physicians, Canada; Canadian Anaesthetists Society; Canadian Medical Association; Royal Society of Medicine. *Publications:* Various articles, 1979-. *Hobbies:* Music; Walking; Railway history. *Address:* Department of Anaesthesia, Dalhousie University, Halifax, Nova Scotia, Canada.

THOMSON, Kenneth Robert, b. 3 April 1945, Christchurch, New Zealand. Cardiovascular Radiologist. m. Barbara Thompson, 9 Dec. 1967, Sumner, 2 sons, 1 daughter. *Education:* MB ChB (Otago); Diploma, Royal Australasian College of Radiologists, 1974; Certified, American Board of Radiology, 1978. *Appointments:* Teaching Fellow, Radiology, University of British Columbia, Vancouver, Canada, 1974; Chest Fellow, Radiology, Royal Victoria Hospital, Montreal, 1975; Cardiovascular Fellow 1976, Assistant professor of Radiology, 1977, Strong Memorial Hospital, Rochester, New York, USA; Director of Angiography, Flinder Medical Centre, South Australia, Australia, 1978-80; Cardiovascular Radiologist, Royal Melbourne Hospital, Victoria. *Memberships:* Licenciate, Medical Council of Canada; Fellow, Royal Australasian College of Radiologists; American College of Radiology; Cardiac Society of Australia and New Zealand. *Publications:* 'Discrimination of normal and overinflated lungs and prediction of TLC based on chest film measurements', 1976; 'Reliability of echocardiography in the diagnosis of infective endocarditis', 1977; 'Contrast media in coronary arteriography', 1978; 'Symposium on Interventional Radiology', 1979. *Honour:* Rouse Travelling Fellow, Royal Australasian College of Radiologists, 1983. *Hobbies:* Computers; Sailing; Skiing; Woodworking. 2Address: 5 Wellington Street, Brighton, Victoria 3186, Australia.

THORNE, Napier, b. 26 Dec. 1920, London, England. Consulting Dermatologist. m. Pamela Joan Houchin, 16 May 1953, London, 1 son, 3 daughters. *Education:* MB BS 1945, MD 1949, London; Member, Royal College of Surgeons, 1945; Licentiate 1945, Member 1949, Fellow 1972, Royal College of Physicians. *Appointments:* Senior Registrar, Medical Department, Whipps Cross Hospital, London; Senior Registrar, Skin Department, The London Hospital; Consultant Dermatologist, St Andrews Hospital, Bow; Consultant Dermatologist, Prince of Wales's General Hospital, Tottenham, London; Currently Consulting Dermatologist the London Hospital. *Memberships:* St Johns Hospital Dermatological Society; British Medical Association; Fellow: Royal Society of Medicine; Medical Society of London; Hunterian Society; Chelsea Clinical Society; Hampstead Medical Society; Royal Society of Arts. *Publications:* 'Cosmetics and the Dermatologists', series, 1963-65; 'Topical Steroids - Their Use and Abuse', 1970. *Honours:* Liveryman, Worshipful Company of Farriers; Liveryman, Worshipful Society of Apothecaries. *Hobbies:* Yacht sailing; Swimming; Gardening. *Address:* 96 Harley Street, London W1N 1AF, England.

THORNE, Michael Charles, b. 7 Oct. 1950, Stalham, Norfolk, England. Scientific Secretary, International Commission on Radiological Protection. m. Susan Eldershaw, 7 Aug. 1971, Sprowston, 2 daughters. *Education:* BSc., Physics, PhD, Experimental High Energy Physics, University of Sheffield. *Appoint-*

ments: Research Scientist, Medical Research Council, Radiobiology Unit; Principal Scientist, Associated Nuclear Services, Epsom. *Membership:* Society for Radiation Protection. *Publications:* "Radionuclide Distribution and Transport in Terrestrial and Aquatic Ecosystems", co-author, Volumes 1-6, 1983-85. *Hobbies:* Cycling; English Poetry. *Address:* International Commission on Radiological Protection, Clifton Avenue, Sutton, Surrey SM2 5PU, England.

THORWARD, Sul Ross Olen, b. 15 Sep. 1947, Cleveland, Ohio, USA. Psychiatrist/Associate University Professor. m. Frances, 28 Dec. 1972, San Marcos, Texas, 1 son, 1 daughter. *Education:* BA, Psychology, University of Texas at Austin; MD, University of Texas Medical School at San Antonio. *Appointments:* Psychiatric Residency, Northwestern University, 1974-77; War Director, Staff Psychiatrist, Arnold Hall, San Antonio State Hospital, 1977-78; Staff Psychiatrist, Director, South Berkeley Short Term Evaluation Unit, Director, Outpatient/Emergency Services, 1978-; Clinical Associate Professor, The Ohio State University School of Medicine, 1978-. *Memberships:* Neuropsychiatric Society of Central Ohio, Past President; Ohio State Psychiatric Society, Council Member; American Psychiatric Association; American Medical Association; Ohio Medical Association; Fellow, Franklin County Academy of Medicine; Harding Hospital Medical Staff, Past President; Central Neuropsychiatric Hospital Association; University of Texas Health Science Center at San Antonio; St Ann's Hospital Staff; America Orthopsychiatry Association; Internation Society Study of Multiple Personality Disorder. *Publications:* "Characteristics of Borderline Patients Admitted to CNPHA Hospitals" co-authored by CNPHA Research Collaborative; Presented at CNPHA Annual Meeting, Stockbridge, Massachusetts, 1984; "Case Study" in The Harding Report, Harding Hospital, Worthington, Ohio, 1982; "Inpatient Family Therapy Approaches" in the Psychiatric Hospital, 1985 (with James Lantz). *Honours:* Jules Masserman Award for Outstanding Resident, 1977; Outstanding Achievement Award, Harding Hospital, 1980; Outstanding Leadership Award, Neuropsychiatric Society, 1984. *Hobbies:* Camping; Photography. *Address:* 445 E Granville Road, Worthington, OH 43085, USA.

TIBBS, (Geoffrey) Michael (Graydon), b. 1921, Ewell, Surrey, England. Secretary of the Royal College of Physicians. m. Anne Rosemary Wortley, 6 October 1951, 2 sons. *Education:* BA (Hons), Geography, 1948, MA, 1952, St Peter's Hall, Oxford University. *Appointments:* Royal Navy, 1940-45; Sudan Political Service, 1949-55; The Automobile Association, 1955-68. *Memberships:* Fellow, Royal Geographical Society; Fellow, Institute of Administrative Management; Member, Institute of Personnel Management. *Hobbies:* Producing pantomimes; Parish Affairs; Making Bonfires. *Address:* Welkin, Lynchmere Ridge, Haslemere, Surrey GU27 3PP, England.

TIDEMAN, Henk, b. 29 May 1942, Malang, Indonesia. Professor, Oral & Maxillofacial Surgery. m. Marion, 27 Aug. 1966, The Hague, 1 daughter. *Education:* DDS, 1967; MD, 1977; PhD, 1973. *Appointments:* Consultant, Oral & Maxillofacial Surgery, Gemeente Ziekenhuis, Arnheim, The Netherlands, 1973-83; Professor, Oral & Maxillofacial Surgery, University of Adelaide, Australia, 1983-. *Memberships:* Nederlands Vereniging van Mondziekten en Kaakchirurgie; International Association of Oral Surgeons; Deutsche Gesellschaft fur Mund-Kiefer und Gesichtschirurgie; European Association for Maxillofacial Surgery; British Association of Oral Surgeons, Associate Member; American Association of Oral and Maxillofacial Surgeons; Australian Medical and Dental Associations; Australian & New Zealand Society of Oral and Maxillofacial Surgeons, Vice President; Adelaide Oral Surgeon's Group; Member, Surgeon's Executive Committee, Royal Adelaide Hospital; Medical Staff Society, Royal Adelaide Hospital; Dental Advancement Society. *Publications:* Articles in numerous professional journals including: "N.T.v.T"; 'International Journal of Oral Surgery'; 'Journal of Oral Surgery'; etc. Numerous Audio-visual contributions, most recent being "Correction of Orofacial Deformity", 24th Australian Dental Congress, Brisbane, 18985; "The Transmandibular Implant of Bosker", 1st International Congress on Pre-Prosthetic Surgery, Palm Springs, USA, 1985. *Hobbies:* Music; Golf; Tennis; Sportflying; Underwater Diving. *Address:* Oral and Maxillofacial Surgery, University of Adelaide, GPO Box 498, Adelaide, South Australia 5001.

TIENARI, Pekka Johannes, b. 27 May 1931, Perniö. Professor. m. Helena Rauhala, 29 Apr. 1954, Helsinki, 2 sons. *Education:* MD, 1957; MD, Dissertation, 1964. *Appointments:* Resident, 1959-61, Chief Consultant, 1961-65, Professor, Psychiatry, 1965-, Psychiatry, Professor, Neurologia and Psychiatry, 1965-69; Dean, Medical Faculty, 1971-75, University of Oulu. 2Memberships: Finnish Psychiatric Association, President, 1970-76; Joint Scandinavian Committee of Psychiatry, President, 1979-82. *Publications:* "Psychiatric Illnesses in Identical Twins", 1963; "Intrapair Differences in Twins", 1966, 'Acta Psychiatrica Scandinavica'; "Textbook of Psychiatry", 4th Edition, 1-11, 1981. *Hobbies:* Music; Golf. *Address:* Department of Psychiatry, University of Oulu, 90210, Oulu, Finland.

TINGVALL, Claes, b. 2 Nov. 1953, Karlstad, Sweden. Statistician. m. Ewa, 24 Apr. 1976, Leksand, 1 son, 1 daughter. *Education:* BSc., Statistician; Medical Studies, Karolinska Institute; Submitted to Doctoral Examination, Karolinska Institute, 1985. *Appointment:* Statistician, Swedish Road Traffic Safety Office (TSV). *Membership:* Swedish Society of Medicine, Traffic Medicine Section. *Publications:* 60 papers in professional journals; Rating System for Serious Consequences - Risk of Death and Permanent Disability, 10th International Conference ESV, 1985; "Children in Cars", OECD Seminar, Road Traffic Safety, Washington, 1985. *Address:* Folksam R/D Division, PO Box 20500, S-104 60 Stockholm, Sweden.

TIPPIT, David Harlow, b. 2 July 1948, Denver, Colorado, USA. Researcher. m. Eve Shere, 28 Nov. 1972, Denver, Colorado. *Education:* BS, PhD, University of Colorado. *Appointments:* Researcher, 1973-79, Research Assistant, 1979-83, Research Associate, 1983-, University of Colorado. *Membership:* American Society of Cell Biology. *Publications:* Various articles in field. *Address:* Department of Molecular Cellular Developmental Biology, Box 347, University of Colorado, Boulder, CO 80309, USA.

TIRADO, Orthon Manuel, b. 5 June 1939, Mexico City, Mexico. Head, Adolescent Medicine & Laboratory of Puberty's Physiology. m. Patricia Corella, 28 July 1979, Mexico City, 2 sons, 1 daughter. *Education:* MD, National Autonomous University, Mexico City, 1964; Pathology, Penrose Cancer Hospital, Colorado, USA, 1965; Internal Medicine, Mercy Hospital, Colorado, 1965; Psychiatry, Menninger School of Psychiatry, Kansas, 3 years; Neurology, Georgetown University Medical Centre, 6 months. *Appointments:* Assistant Physician, Johns Hopkins Hospital, Maryland, 1970; Staff Physician, 1971, Head, 1971-76, Adolescent Dept, Iman University Hospital, Mexico City; Assistant Professor, 1981-84, Psychological Medicine, Professor, 1982-, Psychosomatic Medicine, National Autonomous University, Mexico City; Head, Adolescent Medicine, Laboratory of Puberty's Physiology, Children's Hospital, Mexico, 1984-. *Memberships:* Medical Association of the Children's Hospital; Medical Association of the American British Cowdray Hospital, Mexico City; New York Academy of Sciences; American Association for the Advancement of Science. *Publications:* Co-Author: "Manual de Procedimientos del Servicio de Adolescentes del Hospital Infantil de la Institucion Mexicana de Asistencia a la Ninez", 'Acta Ped. Latinoamer.', 1970;

"Neoplasms and Mental Disorders: An Expression of the Body-mind Dichotomy", 'Neurologia, Neurocirugia, Psiquiatria', 1971. *Honours:* American Medical Association, Physicians Recognition Awards, 1-VII, 1969, 1-VII, 1982; American Psychiatric Association: Continuing Medical Education Standards, 3 years, VI, 1986. *Hobbies:* Baroque Music; Swimming; Tennis. *Address:* Ave Fuente de Piramides 1, Suite 201, Lomas de Tecamachalco, Naucalpan, Edo de Mexico 53950, Mexico.

TISLOW, Richard Frederick, b. 6 Mar. 1906, Czernowitz, Austria. Psychiatrist. m. Sybil Ray Hungerford-Jones, 28 June 1946, New York City, USA, 1 son. *Education:* MD, University of Vienna Medical School, 1931; Med. Sci. D., University of Warsaw Medical School, Poland, 1936. *Appointments:* Senior Assistant, University of Warsaw Medical School, 1934-38; Fellow, University of Amsterdam, Department of Pharmacotherapy, Holland, 1937-38; Assistant, Paediatrics, Endrocrinology, Johns Hopkins University Medical School, USA, 1938-39; Assistant, Peter Brent Brigham Hospital, Harvard Medical School, Boston, USA, 1940-43; Director, Biological Research Laboratories, Schering Corporation, Bloomfield, New Jersey, USA, 1943-53; Chief Pharmacologist, Wyeth Laboratories, Pennsylvania, 1953-70; Resident, Psychiatry, Temple University Medical School, 1968-70; Fellow, Psychiatry, University of Pennsylvania, 1969-70; Director, Psychiatric Emergency Services, West Philadelphia Consortium, 1970-75; Clinical Associate, Department of Psychiatry, University of Pennsylvania, 1970-84; Staff Psychiatrist, Haverford and Philadelphia State Hospitals, 1974-. *Memberships:* American Psychiatric Association; American Society of Pharmacology and Exp. Therapeutics; American Society of Physiology; American College of Neuropsychopharmacology. *Publications:* 'Megadoses of Vitamins C and A in dogs, vitamin C in man' in 'Klin. Woschen Schr.', 1934-37; 'Antithyroid Effects of Thiouracil', 1940-43; 'Extraction of Corticotropin (ACTH) and Demonstration of its small molecular size (Science)', 1946; 'Pharmacology of Chlortrimeton', 1955; Publications on Psychiatry, Autokinesis, delayed psychosomatic reactions, 1960-. *Honours:* Dazian Fellowship, 1940-43; Fellow, American College Neuropsychopharmacology, 1965; Fellow, American Psychiatric Association, 1975. *Hobby:* Music. *Address:* 2512 Pine Street, Philadelphia, PA 19103, USA.

TODD, Ian Pelham, b. 23 Mar. 1921, London, England. Honorary Consulting Surgeon, St Bartholomew's Hospital; Consulting Surgeon, St Mark's Hospital and King Edward VII Hospital for Officers, London; Consulting Surgeon (Procol) to RN. m. Jean Audrey Ann Noble, 25 July 1946, London, 2 sons, 3 daughters. *Education:* MD, Toronto, 1945; MS, 1956; FRCS, England, 1949; DCH, England, 1947; St Bartholomew's and University of Toronto, Canada. *Appointments:* Hunt Prof RCS, England, 1953; Arris and Gale Lecturer, 1957-58; Past President, Section of Proctology, Royal Society of Medicine and the Medical Society of London; Zachary Cope Memorial Lecture, 1986. *Memberships:* Member of Council: Royal College of Surgeons, England; Imperial Cancer Research Fund; Royal Society of Medicine; African Medical and Research Foundation, UK. *Publications:* Chapters in Selwyn Taylor's "Recent Advances in Surgery", 1980; Editor, volume 'Colon, Rectum and Anus' in Rob and Smith's "Operative Surgery", 4th edition, 1982; Editor, volume 'Stomas', "Clinics in Gastroenterology", 1982; Co-author, "Inflammatory Bowel Disease", 1983. *Honour:* Lister Prize in Surgery, Toronto, 1956. *Hobbies:* Skiing; Gardening; Travel; Music; Philately. *Address:* 149 Harley Street, London W1N 2DE, England.

TOFLER, Oswald Boaz, b. 21 Dec. 1926, Sydney, Australia, Senior Physician, Cardiology Department. m. Tamara Atlas, 28 Mar. 1951, Perth, Australia, 3 sons, 1 daughter. *Education:* Graduate in Medicine, Sydney University; FRACP. *Appointments:* RMO,

Sydney Hospital; RMO, Princess Alexandra Hospital for Children; RMO, Royal Newcastle Hospital; Registrar, National Heart Hospital, London, England, 1957-58; Head of Department, Paediatric Cardiology, Princess Margaret Hospital for Children, 1960-82; Head of Cardiology Department, Royal Perth Hospital, Australia, 1962-73. *Memberships:* FRACP; Cardiac Society of Australia and New Zealand. *Publications:* "The Heart of the Social Drinker", 1985. *Hobbies:* Squash. *Address:* 4 Walker Avenue, West Perth, Australia.

TOFT, Lloyd Arthur, b. 14 Feb. 1938, Brisbane, Queensland, Australia. Orthopaedic Surgeon. m. Carol O'Connor, 10 Dec. 1974, Brisbane, 3 daughters. *Education:* MB BS, Queensland, 1961; FRCS (Edinburgh), 1967; FRACS, 1971; FACRM, 1980. *Appointments:* Resident Medical Officer and Surgical Registrar, Brisbane General Hospital, 1962-65; Orthopaedic Registrar, Notley Hospital, Essex, 1967-69; Orthopaedic Registrar, Centre for Hip Surgery, Wrightington, 1970; Orthopaedic Supervisor, Royal Brisbane Hospital, 1973-74; Visiting Orthopaedic Surgeon, Royal Brisbane Hospital and Royal Children's Hospital. *Memberships:* Australian Medical Association; Australian Orthopaedic Association. *Hobby:* Royal Australian Naval Reserve. *Address:* Watkins Medical Centre, 225 Wickham Terrace, Brisbane, Queensland 4000, Australia.

TOH, Ban-Hock, b. 5 July 1940, Malaysia. Clinical Associate Professor. m. Wan-Her Seet, 31 July 1965, Singapore, 1 son, 1 daughter. *Education:* MBBS, Singapore; DSc, Monash Medical School; FRACP; FRCPA. *Appointments:* Postgraduate Fellow, Singapore University, 1966; Lecturer, Department of Medicine, University of Malaya, 1969; Registrar, Royal Melbourne Hospital, Australia, 1971; Commonwealth Medical Fellow, London Hospital, England, 1978; Visiting Scientist, NIH, Bethesda, USA, 1984. *Memberships:* Fellow, Royal Australian College of Physicians; Fellow, Royal College of Pathologists of Australia. *Publications:* 'On actin localization in synapses', 1976; 'Co-distribution with surface receptors', 1977; 'Neuropeptide localization in ovaries', 1984; 'Autoantibody to gastrin receptors', 1985. *Hobbies:* Reading; Music; Hiking. *Address:* Department of Pathology and Immunology, Monash Medical School, Commercial Road, Prahran, Victoria 3181, Australia.

TOKI, Satoshi, b. 8 Feb. 1929, Fukuoka, Japan. Professor. m. Keiko, 8 Nov. 1959, Fukuoka, 2 sons, 1 daughter. *Education:* BSc, Pharmacy, Kyushu University, Faculty of Medicine, Institutes of Pharmaceutical Sciences, 1953; PhD, Pharmacy, Kyushu University, Faculty of Pharmaceutical Sciences, 1961. *Appointments:* Research Assistant, Kyushu University, 1953-62; Assistant Professor, 1962-66; Professor, 1966-; Dean of Pharmaceutical Sciences, 1979-83; Director of Central Institute, 1985-, Fukuoka University. *Memberships:* Pharmaceutical Society of Japan; The Japanese Biochemical Society; The International Association of Forensic Toxicologists. *Publication:* 'Purification and Characterization of Guinea Pig Liver Morphine 6-Dehydrogenase', 'Journal of Biological Chemistry', 1985. *Honour:* Miyata Prize, 1978. *Hobbies:* Pottery (collection); Gardening. *Address:* Faculty of Pharmaceutical Sciences, Fukuoka University, 8-19-1 Nankuma, Jonanku, Fukuoka 814-01, Japan.

TONDERA, Harold Boyd, b. 8 July 1938, Waco, Texas, USA. Doctor of Chiropractic in Private Practice. m. Patricia Joan Lewis, 5 June 1959, Waco, 2 sons, 1 daughter. *Education:* DC; Board Certified, American Board of Chiropractic Orthopaedists. *Appointments:* Secretary, District 11, Texas Chiropractic Association; Director, Vice President and President (2 terms), Texas Chiropractic College Alumni Association; Chairman, Board of Regents, Texas Chiropractic College. *Memberships:* Deacon, Second Baptist Church, Houston, Texas; Southwest Houston Chamber of

Commerce; Masonic Lodge; American Chiropractic Association; Texas Chiropractic College Alumni Association; American Chiropractic Association Council of Chiropractic Orthopaedics. *Publication:* 'It's About Time' in 'Healthways', 1972. *Honours:* Doctor of the Year, District 11, Texas Chiropractic Association, 1985; Student of the Year, 1970, Omega Psi Honor Society, Class President, 1967, 69, 70, Texas Chiropractic College. *Hobbies:* Music; Fishing; Horticulture; Oil painting. *Address:* 3510 Robinson Road, Missouri City, TX 77459, USA.

TONG, Yit Chow, b. 19 Aug. 1948, Hong Kong. Senior Research Fellow. m. Kim Kheng Toh, 19 Dec. 1976, Melbourne, Australia, 1 son. *Education:* BSc, Mechanical Engineering, PhD, Otolaryngology, University of Melbourne, Australia. *Appointments:* Research Officer, Department of Otolaryngology, University of Melbourne, Australia, 1976-78, Senior Research Officer, 1979-82, Research Fellow, 1982-84, Senior Research Fellow, 1985-. *Membership:* Australian Physiological and Pharmacological Society. *Publications include:* Co-author of the following articles: 'Speech Processing for a multiple-electrode cochlear implant hearing prosthesis' in 'Journal of the Acoustical Society of America', 1980; 'A multiple-channel cochlear implant and wearable speech processor: An audiological evaluation' in 'Acta Otolaryngol', 1981; 'Psychophysical studies for two multiple-channel cochlear implant patients' in 'Journal of the Acoustic Society of America', 1982; 'Two-component hearing sensations produced by two-electrode stimulation in the cochlea of a totally deaf patient' in 'Science', 1983. *Hobbies:* Personal Computers; Sports. *Address:* Department of Otolaryngology, University of Melbourne, Parkville 3052, Australia.

TONKIN, Andrew Maxwell, b. 20 Feb. 1944, Melbourne, Australia. Director of Cardiology, Flinders Medical Centre. m. Denise Helen, 18 Jan. 1970, Melbourne, 1 son, 2 daughters. *Education:* MB; BS; MD, Royal Melbourne Hospital, 1971; Royal Prince Alfred Hospital, Sydney, 1972-73; Duke University Medical Centre, North Carolina, USA, 1973-75. *Appointment:* Senior Specialist in Cardiovascular Medicine, Flinders Medical Centre, South Australia. *Memberships:* Fellow, Royal Australasian College of Physicians; The Cardiac Society of Australia and New Zealand, Council; Australian Physiological and Pharmacological Society; Australian Society of Medical Research. *Publications:* 'Management of arrhythmias due to accessory conduction pathways', 'Pacing and Clinical Electrophysiology', 1978; 'Electrophysiological testing of sinus node function', 'Pacing and Clinical Electrophysiology', 1984. *Honours:* Lindsay White Award of National Heart Foundation of Australia, 1973; R. T. Hall Prize of Cardiac Society of Australia and New Zealand, 1979. *Hobbies:* Sports; Antiquarian Books. *Address:* Department of Medicine, Flinders Medical Centre, Bedford Park, 5042 South Australia, Australia.

TOPHAM, Lawrence Garth, b. 14 Nov. 1914, Bradford, Yorkshire, England. Retired Surgeon Captain, Royal Navy and Consultant Physician. m. Olive Barbara Marshall, 8 May 1943, Ewell, Surrey, 1 son, 1 daughter. *Education:* MB ChB, Leeds, 1937; MRCP, Edinburgh, Scotland, 1957, London, England, 1969; MD, 1946; FRCP, £967. *Appointments:* Medical Officer, Royal Navy, 1938-71; Flight Surgeons Wings, US Navy, 1943; Pilots Wings, Fleet Air Arm, 1944; Medical Specialist and Consultant in Medicine, Royal Naval Hospitals, Trincomalee, Plymouth and Haslar; Professor of Medicine, Royal Navy and Royal College of Physicians London, 1966-71; House Governor and Medical Superintendent, King Edward VII Convalescent Home for Officers, Osborne House, Isle of Wight; Consultant Physician, Winchester and Andover Hospitals, Winchester District Health Authority, Hampshire, 1974-82. *Memberships:* British Geriatric Society; Wessex Physicians Club. *Publications:* 'Chest Complications of the Influenza Epidemic' in 'Journal of Royal Naval Medical Service',

1957; 'Insulinoma presenting with Episodic attacks of Unconsciousness', in 'Proceedings of Royal Society of Medicine', 1969. *Honours:* Officer Brother, Order of St John; Queens Honorary Physician, 1969-71. *Hobbies:* Oriental cooking; Photography. *Address:* Tilings, Holt Close, Wickham, Hampshire PO ŒY, England.

TORBERGSEN, Torberg, b. 31 Mar. 1937, Alta, Norway. m. Brith Karoline, 18 Apr. 1962, 1 son, 3 daughters. *Education:* MD, University of Oslo, 1963; Certificate as Specialist in Clinical Neurology, 1974. *Appointments:* Registrar, Department of Neurology, Ullevål University Hospital, Oslo. *Publications:* 'A Family with dominant hereditary myotonia, muscular hypertrophy, and increased muscular irritability, distinct from myotonia congenita', 1975; Author of numerous publications on medical subjects. *Hobbies:* Skiing; Skating; Fishing. *Address:* Department of Neurology, University Hospital, N-9012 Tromsø) Norway.

TOREMALM, Nils Gunnar, b. 14 Feb. 1923, Torekov, Sweden. Professor, Ear, Nose and Throat Diseases, University of Lund, Malmo General Hospital, Malmö, Sweden. m. Greta Walander, 23 June 1947, 1 son, 2 daughters. *Education:* Doctor of Medical Sciences. *Appointments:* Naval Medical Officer, Swedish Navy; Associate Professor, Lund University, 1961; Ordinary Professor, Ear, Nose and Throat Diseases, Lund University, Malmö General Hospital, 1981. *Memberships:* Collegium Oto-rhino-laryngologicicum; Royal Physiographic Society, Lund; Swedish Medical Society, Delegation of Medical Ethics. *Publications:* Functional Changes in the Respirator Tract after Tracheotomy, 1960; Studies on the Physiology of the Trachea I-V, 1965-68; The Noise Dosimeter for Measuring Personal Noise Exposure, 1970; The Management of Laryngo-Tracheal Injuries (colour film), 1973. *Hobby:* Medical Ethics. *Address:* University of Lund, Department of Oto-Rhino-Laryngology, Malmö General Hospital, S-214 01 Malmö, Sweden.

TÖRÖK, Bela, b. 25 Nov. 1925, Gige, Hungary. Professor of Experimental Surgery. m. Dr Therese Erdelyi, 14 Nov. 1953, Pécs, 2 sons. *Education:* Diploma in Medicine, 1953; Specialist in Surgery, Diploma 1957; DSc, Hungarian Academy of Sciences, 1970. *Appointments:* Associate Professor, Department of Experimental Surgery, University of Medicine, Pecs, 1963-72; Professor and Head, Department of Experimental Surgery, 1972-; Prorector in Charge of Education, 1976-79; Prorector in Charge of Science and Research, 1979-82. *Memberships:* Hungarian Society of Surgeons, Executive Board, 1972-; Editorial Board of 'Magyar Sebeszet' (Hungarian Periodical of Surgery); President, Science Committee Section, Pecs of Hungarian Academy of Sciences, 1976-; Honorary Member, Czechoslovakia Society of Surgeons, 1976. *Publications:* 148 Scientific Papers in different experimental, surgical and cardiological journals and chapters in books. *Honour:* Gold Medal of Labour, 1982. *Hobbies:* Tourism; Belles-lettres; Athletics. *Address:* Department of Experimental Surgery, University of Medicine, Pécs, Hungary.

TOSHKOV, Assen Stavrev, b. 7 Aug. 1915, Tran, Bulgaria. Professor; Deputy Director, Institute of Microbiology. m. Tanja Harizanova, 31 Dec. 1948, 2 sons. *Education:* MD, Faculty of Medicine, University of Sofia, Bulgaria, 1940. *Appointments:* Deputy Director, Institute of Infectious and Parasitic Diseases, Medical Academy, 1943-60; Scientific Director of Institute of Microbiology, Bulgarian Academy of Sciences, 1960-83; Professor of Immunology, Department of Microbiology Medical Academy, 1963-75; Professor of Immunology, Department of Microbiology, University of Sofia, 1976-85. *Memberships:* Union of Scientific Workers in Bulgaria; Bulgarian Microbiological Society; Bulgarian Society of Immunology; Illinois State Academy of Sciences; Union Medical Balkanique; Societe Francaise de Microbiologie. *Publications:* "Antibiotics and Immunity", 1962; "Microbiology of Septicemias", 1973; "Immunology", 1975, 1981, 1985; "Antibiotics, Micro-organisms, Macro-organism", 1979; "Chronic and Persistant Infections", 1982. *Honours:* 9 awards from Bulgarian Government; 2 scientific awards of Union of Scientific Workers in Bulgaria. *Hobby:* Bibliophylia. *Address:* Department of Immunology, Institute of Microbiology, Bulgarian Academy of Sciences, 26 G Bonchev Street, Sofia 1113, Bulgaria.

TOTH-MARTINEZ, Bela Laszlo, b. 15 Mar. 1931, Gyongyos, Hungary. Chief of Pharmacobiochemistry Laboratories. m. Gabriella Katharina Cserép, 9 July 1960, Debrecen, 2 daughters. *Education:* Diploma in Chemistry, Kossuth Lajos University, Debrecen, 1950-55; Preclinical Researcher Course, Debrecen Medical University, 1956-58; PhD, Debrecen; Dr. *Appointments:* Assistant Professor of Biochemistry Department 1953-66, Senior Research Fellow of Pharmacology Department 1966-, Debrecen Medical University; World Health Organisation Professor of Biochemistry, The Dar es Salaam University, Tanzania, 1967-70; World Health Organisation Professor of Biochemistry, CUSS, Yaounde, Cameroon, 1970-71. *Memberships:* Hungarian Biochemistry, Physiology, Pharmacology and Chemotherapy Societies; International Society of Biochemistry, Milan, 1966; Royal Society of Chemistry, London, 1968; International Society of Quantumbiology, New Orleans, 1974. *Publications:* Contributions to: 'Biosystems', 1975; 'Biochemical Pharmacology', 1977; 'Pharmacological Research Communication', 1978; 'Journal Chromatography', 1983, 1984 and 1985. *Hobbies:* Skiing; Climbing; Stamps; Hunting. *Address:* Institute of Pharmacology, The Debrecen Medical University, H 4012 Debrecen, Hungary.

TOURAINE, Jean-Louis, Didier, b. 8 Oct. 1945, Lyon, France. Professor in Medicine; Medical Doctor; Scientist. m. Francoise Moulin, 7 Sep. 1968, 2 daughters. *Education:* MD, 1972; Professor of Medicine, 1979; Certificates in Nephrology, Immunology, Genetics and Haematology. *Appointments:* Resident, Lyon Hospitals; Research Fellow, Edinburgh, Scotland; Research Fellow, Minneapolis and New York, USA; Assistant Professor, Professor, Claude Bernard University, Lyon, France. *Memberships:* President of various associations including: ARTMO, CEDIC, GERMI; Member of various international societies Transplantation, Immunology, Nephrology, Immunopharmacology, Bone Marrow Transplantation. *Publications:* "Human Renal Allotransplantation and Antilymphocyte Globulin"; "Bone Marrow Transplantation in Europe" volume 1, 1979, volume 2, 1981; "Transplantation and Clinical Immunology", yearly since 1975; "Hors de la Bulle", 1985. Editor in Chief of the journal "Thymus". Author of 450 medical and scientific articles.*Main contributions:* Discovery of the "Bare Lymphocyte Syndrome" a disease which demonstrates the crucial role of histocompatibility HLA antigens in the normal immunity; Development of fetal thymus and liver transplantation in immunodeficiency diseases and inborn errors of metabolism; Participation to the development of kidney, pancreas and bone marrow transplantation; Investigation of immunodeficiencies, analysis of T-cell differentiation and immunopharmacological studies. *Honours:* Prize of Alexis Carrel Foundation, 1969; Delahautemaison Prize, 1982; MEDEC Prize of Medical Information for the book "Hors de la Bulle" on psychological, ethical and legal aspects of fetal tissues transplantation, 1985 (Flammarion Publ.) *Hobbies:* Skiing; Swimming. *Address:* Pavillon P, Hôpital E. Herriot, 69374 Lyon Cedex 08, France.

TOW, Tony W Y, b. 23 Feb. 1950, The People's Republic of China. Private practice in pulmonary medicine. m. Lai K Foong, 22 Aug. 1979, New York City, USA, 1 son, 1 daughter. *Education:* BS 1972, Master of Engineering 1973, College of Engineering, Cornell University, New York; MD, Cornell Medical College, 1979. *Appointments:* Technical Staff, Bell Telephone Laboratories, 1973-75; Internship 1979-80, Residency 1980-82, Internal Medicine, New York Hospital - Cornell Medical Center; Fellowship in Pulmonary Medicine, Mount Sinai Medical Center, New York City, 1982-84; Private practice in pulmonary medicine, 1982-. *Memberships:* New York County Medical Society; American College of Physicians; American College of Chest Physicians; Diplomates, American Board of Internal Medicine and Pulmonary Disease; Eta Kappa Nu; Tau Beta Pi; Phi Kappa Pi; Alpha Omega Alpha. *Publications:* 'Normal Chest Roentgenogram as a Prognostic Factor in Pneumocystic Carcinii Pneumonia in Patients with Acquired Immunodeficiency Syndrome', 1984; 'DLCO in Screening For Pneumocystitic Carcinii Pneumonia in Patients With Acquired Immunodeficiency Syndrome', 1984; 'Diagnosis of Pulmonary Complications of the Acquired Immunodeficiency Syndrome'. *Honours:* Mosby Award in Medicine, 1977; ENT Award, Cornell Medical College, 1979. *Address:* 375 East Main Street Suite 27, Bay Shore, NY 11706-8472, USA.

TOWNSEND, Jocelyn F, b. 7 Nov. 1932, Louisiana, USA. Service Director of Mental Health Rehabilitation Therapy. 1 son, 1 daughter. *Education:* BSN, MPH, PhD; Certified Mental Health Consultant, 1985; Certified Insurance Rehabilitation Specialist. *Appointments include:* Staff, Head Nurse and Supervisory Positions, Alameda County Health Department, Parkland Hospital, Dallas, Texas, Methodist Hospital, Dallas and Confederate Memorial Medical Center, 1955-62; Assistant Professor, Louisiana State University Department of Psychiatry, 1965-; Medical Center, 1965-75; G Pierce Wood Memorial Hospital Director, Mental Health Rehabilitation Therapy Services, Arcadia, Florida, 1983-. *Memberships:* National Rehabilitation Association; National Rehabilitation Association of Administrators; Florida Public Health Association. *Publications:* Author or co-author of 7 papers contributed to: 'Information Bulletin: Day Treatment Centers'; 'Pelican News Buletin'; "Partial Hospitalisation: Problems, Purposes and Changing Objectives", 1969; "Great Contemporary Poems Anthology", 1978; "Whoistic Living'; Pulse' columnist. *Honours:* Fellow, American Public Health Association; Royal Society of Health, England. *Hobbies:* Music; Writing poetry; Sailing. *Address:* PO Box 2031, Arcadia, FL 33821, USA.

TOWNSEND, Nancy Jean Germond, b. 8 Oct. 1949, Utica, New York, USA. Continuing Education Consultant. m. Jackson Townsend, 9 Apr. 1977, New Orleans, Louisiana, 3 sons. *Education:* Associate in Applied Science, State University of New York, Mohawk Valley Community College, 1970; BS Nursing, William Carey College, 1979; Certified Critical Care Nursing, 1979; MN, Louisiana State University, 1981; Certified Clinical Specialist, 1983. *Appointments:* Staff Nurse Cardiopulmonary ICU and Recovery Room 1973, Orientation-Inservice Coordinator Cardiopulmonary ICU 1974, Staff/Charge Nurse Orthopaedics and Cardiopulmonary, 1970, State University of New York, Upstate Medical Center; Unit Director, Coronary Care, Touro Infirmary, 1975; Staff Development Instructor, Ochsner Foundation Hospital, 1977; Clinical Education Coordinator, Critical Care, East Jefferson General Hospital, 1978; Continuing Education Consultant/Programme Director, Nursing Knowledge Incorporated, 1979-. *Memberships:* Society of Critical Care Medicine; American Association of Critical Care Nurses; Greater New Orleans chapter, AACN; American Nurses Association; Epsilon Nu chapter, Sigma Theta Tau. *Honour:* Research Award, LSUMC, 1981. *Hobbies:* Reading; Swimming; Fishing. *Address:* 1037 Sena Drive, Metairie, LA 70005, USA.

TRACZYK, Wladyslaw Zygmunt, b. 27 June 1928, Warsaw. Professor of Physiology. m. Zdzislawa Andrysik, 7 Dec. 1954, 1 son. *Education:* MD, School of Medicine Warsaw, 1951; PhD, First School of Medicine, Moscow, USSR, 1955; D Med Sci, School of

Medicine, Warsaw, 1962; Postdoctoral study in Neurophysiology, University of California at Los Angeles, 1967. *Appointments:* Assistant to Head of Laboratory of Physiology, Polish Academy of Sciences, Warsaw, 1956-62; Associate Professor of Physiology, School of Medicine, Warsaw, 1963; Professor and Head of Department of Physiology, School of Medicine, Lodz, 1963-; Director, Institute of Physiology and Biochemistry, School of Medicine in Lodz, 1973-. *Memberships:* Member of Council of Ministry of Health and Social Welfare, Warsaw; Member of Committee of Physiological Sciences of the Polish Academy of Sciences, Warsaw; International Brain Research Organization; International Neuroendocrinological Society. *Publications:* Books: "Neurohormones" in Polish 1970; "Outline of Human Physiology" in Polish, 1973, 1976, 1982; Co-author and editor: "Human Physiology" in Polish 1980; "Neuropeptides and Neural Transmission" IBRO Monograph Series vol 7, 1980; "The Vasopress in Content in Perfusion Fluid from the Hypothalamus in Conscious Chronic Dogs" 1966. *Honours:* Chevalier Order Polonia Restituta, 1974; Officer, Order Polonia Restituta, 1985; Awards Ministry of Health 1971. *Hobbies:* Canoeing; Oil painting. *Address:* Department of Physiology, Institute of Physiology and Biochemistry, School of Medicine in Lodz, ul Lindleya 3, 90-131 Lodz, Poland.

TRAEGER, Jules E C, b. 12 Mar. 1920, Lyon, France. Professor of Nephrology and Metabolic Diseases. m. 3 Apr. 1953. *Education:* MD; PhD; Directeur Scientifique, INSERM, 1980. *Appointments:* Chief, Clinic of Nephrology and Metabolic Diseases; Head of Transplant Unit. *Memberships:* Societe Internationale de Transplantation; European Societe Transplantation Dialysis (Past President); President, Rhone Mediteranee Transplant; Vice President, France Transplant. *Publications:* 'Transplantation and Clinical Immunology', annuall, 1978- and others. *Honours:* Legion d'Honneur, Chevalier; Officier, Order of Merit. Honorary Doctor: University of Liege; University of Asuncion; University of Cordoba. *Hobby:* Sailing. *Address:* 37 Boulevard des Belges, F-69006 Lyon, France.

TRAUGOTT, Frans Maurice, b. 24 Sep. 1952, Sydney, New South Wales, Australia. Hospital Research Scientist. m. Deborah Jane Foote, 12 Nov. 1983, Seaforth, Sydney, New South Wales. *Education:* BSc, 1975, BSc, Honours, 1976, Diploma in Education, University of New England, Armidale, New South Wales, 1977; PhD, Faculty of Medicine, University of Newcastle, 1984. *Appointments:* Technical Officer, Human Physiology, Faculty of Medicine, University of Newcastle and Research Fellow, Department of Anaesthesia and Intensive Care, Royal Newcastle Hospital, 1977-80; NH&MRC Research Officer, Faculty of Medicine, University of Newcastle, 1980-82; Project Manager, Clinical Research and Regulatory Affairs, Sandoz Australia, North Ryde, 1983; Senior Scientific Officer, 1984, currently, Department of Anaesthetics, Royal North Shore Hospital, St Leonards, New South Wales. *Memberships:* Australian Physiological and Pharmacological Society; Australian Neuroscience Society; Australasian Society for Clinical and Experimental Pharmacology; Australian Sports Medicine Federation. *Publications:* Author of 35 publications in International journals. *Honours:* Minor scholarships and awards. *Hobbies:* Sailing; Scuba Diving; Surfing; Photography; Bushwalking; Tae Kwon Do. *Address:* 5 St Pauls Road, North Balgowlah, NSW 2093, Australia.

TRAUTMAN, Paul Douglas, b. 18 May 1949, Buffalo, New York, USA. Assistant Professor of Clinical Psychiatry, Columbia University College of Physicians and Surgeons. m. Kristin Ellen Dietz, 5 Dec. 1979, New York City. *Education:* MD, State University of New York at Buffalo, 1975. *Memberships:* American Academy of Child Psychiatry; American Psychiatric Association; Association for Child

Psychology and Psychiatry. *Honours:* National Institute of Mental Health Faculty Development Award, 1983-84; Diplomate, American Board of Psychiatry and Neurology, General Psychiatry, 1981, Child Psychiatry, 1984. *Address:* New York State Psychiatric Institute, 722 W 168th Street, New York, NY 10032, USA.

TRIMBLE, George Alan, b. 29 May 1940, Wewoka, Oklahoma, USA. Psychiatrist. m. Beverly Jean Comp, 8 Sep. 1962, Arlington, Virginia, USA, 1 son, 1 daughter. *Education:* BA, Biology and Chemistry, Houston Baptist University, 1972; MD, University of Texas Medical Branch, 1976. *Appointments:* Co-Founder, Galveston Psychiatric Services, Galveston, Texas; Medical and Psychiatric Director, Gulf Coast Regional MHMR, Galveston, Texas; President, Pain and Stress Center, Galveston, Texas; Consultant, Permian Basin MHMR, Odessa, Texas; President, Midland Psychiatric Services, Texas. *Memberships:* American Society of Clinical Hypnosis; Academy of Psychosomatic Medicine; The Titus Harris Society. *Hobbies:* Guitarist; Impressionist; Photography. *Address:* Midland Psychiatric Services, 2910 La Force, Midland, TX 79711, USA.

TROWBRIDGE, Ben C, b. 27 Feb. 1952, Midland, Texas, USA. Doctor of Chiropractic. m. Janie M Elrod, 12 June 1971, Odessa, Texas, 2 sons. *Education:* Associate of Science, Degree in Nursing, Angelo State University, San Angelo, Texas; Doctor of Chiropractic, Life Chiropractic College, Marietta, Georgia. *Appointments:* Supervisor of Nursing, Shannon West Texas Memorial Hospital, San Angelo, 1973-78; Laboratory Technician, Life Chiropractic College, Marietta, Georgia, 1978-80; RN, Stanton, Texas, 1981; RN, West Coke County Hospital, 1982-83; Doctor of Chiropractic, Cleere Chiropractic Clinic, San Angelo, 1983; Doctor of Chiropractic, Trowbridge Chiropractic Center, San Angelo, 1983-. *Memberships:* Texas Chiropractic Association; International Chiropractic Association; Clinic Masters. *Honour:* Diplomate, National Board of Chiropractic Examiners, 1980. *Hobbies:* Hunting; Fishing; Skiing; Camping; Golf; Tennis; Swimming. *Address:* 3180 Executive Drive, Suite 102, San Angelo, TX 76904, USA.

TRUJILLO, Jaime, b. 26 Sep. 1941, Colombia, South America. Chairperson, Adolescent Psychiatry. m. Yolanda, 16 Dec. 1967, Colombia, South America, 1 son, 1 daughter. *Education:* MD, Caldas University, 1966; American Board of Psychiatry and Neurology, 1975. *Appointments:* Chief, Adolescent Unit, Illinois State Psychiatric Institute, USA, 1974-81; Chairperson, Adolescent Division, Department of Psychiatry, Cook County Hospital, 1981-. *Memberships:* Illinois State Psychiatric Society; American Psychiatric Association; Chicago Society for Adolescent Psychiatry; American Association for the Advancement of Science. *Publications:* 'Four Psychodynamic Types of Hospitalised Juvenile Delinquents' in "Adolescent Psychiatry", volume VII, 1979; 'Measuring Delinquent Behaviour in Inpatient Treatment Settings: Review and Validation of the Adolescent Antisocial Behavior Checklist' in 'Journal of the American Academy of Child Psychiatry', 1983. *Honour:* Best Medical Student, 1962. *Hobby:* Travel. *Address:* 2501 Cobblewood Drive, Northbrook, IL 60062, USA.

TRUNK, Gary, b. 7 Dec. 1941, Detroit, Michigan, USA. Medical Director; Liberty Care HMO. m. Virginia, 2 sons, 1 daughter. *Education:* BA, University of California, Los Angeles, 1963; MD, University of California, Irvine, 1967. *Appointments:* Chief, Internal Medicine, USAF Regional Hospital, March AFB, California, 1974; Chief of Staff, Parkview Community Hospital, Riverside, California, 1982-. *Memberships:* American Medical Association; American Academy of Medical Directors; American College of Physicians; American College of Chest Physicians; American Society of Internal Medicine; American Society of Law and Medicine. *Publication:* "Management and Evaluation of the Solitary Pulmonary Nodule", 'Chest', volume 66, 1974. *Address:* 8777 East Via De Ventura, Scottsdale, AZ 85358, USA.

TRUNKEY, Donald Dean, b. 23 June 1937, Oakesdale, Washington, USA. Professor and Vice-Chairman, Department of Surgery, University of California, San Francisco; Chief of Surgery, San Francisco General Hospital. m. Jane Mary Henry, 26 Sep. 1958, Colfax, 1 son, 1 daughter. *Education:* BS, Washington State University, 1959; MD, University of Washington, 1963; Internship, University of Oregon Medical School, 1963-64; Residency, Surgery, University of California Hospitals, 1966-68, 1969-70. *Appointments:* Assistant Research Professor of Surgery, University of Texas South Western Medical School, 1971-72; Vascular Consultant, Lagunda Honda Hospital, 1972-; University of California School of Medicine: Assistant Professor, Department of Surgery, 1972-76; Associate Professor, 1976-78; Director of Surgery, Mission Emergency Hospital, 1973-76; Chief of Surgery, San Francisco General Hospital, 1978-; Vice-Chairman, Department of Surgery, University of California San Francisco, 1978-; Professor of Surgery, 1979-. *Memberships include:* American College of Surgeons; San Francisco Medical Society; California Medical Association; American Burn Association; American Medical Association; American Board of Surgery; Society of University Surgeons. *Publications:* Contributor to professional journals, etc; Books include: Co-author: "Current Therapy of Trauma 1984-85", 1984; "Trauma Management", Volume II: "Urogenital Trauma", 1985; Presentations; Monographs. *Honours:* UCSF Teacher of the Year, 1975; James IV Surgical Traveller, 1981; University of Washington Distinguished Alumnus, 1983. *Hobby:* Wine Making. *Address:* Department of Surgery, Ward 3A, San Francisco General Hospital, 1001 Potrero Avenue, San Francisco, CA 94110, USA.

TRUPIN, Suzanne R, b. 10 July 1953, New York City, New York, USA. Acting Head of University Department of Obstetrics-Gynaecology. m. Stanley Ross Johnson, 1 son, 1 daughter. *Education:* MD; Certified, National Board of Medical Examiners, 1978; Residency in Obstetrics and Gynaecology, University of Southern California, Women's Hospital, 1977-81; Certified, American College of Obstetrics and Gynaecology, 1984. *Appointments include:* Joint private practice, 1981-; Physician, Women's Hospital Emergency Room, Los Angeles County General Hospital, 1978-81; Physician, 3 Planned Parenthood Clinics, Los Angeles, 1978-81; Clinical Faculty 1981-, Clinical Assistant Professor 1983-, College of Medicine, Director of Department of Obstetrics and Gynaecology of Medical School 1982-; Coordinator of Continuing Medical Education and Acting Head of Department of Obstetrics and Gynaecology of School of Clinical Medicine 1985-, University of Illinois, Urbana-Champaign, Illinois; Active Staff, Burnham City Hospital, Cole Hospital, Champaign and Mercy Hospital, Urbana. *Memberships include:* American Institute of Ultrasound in Medicine; American Medical Association; American Fertility Society; American Women's Medical Association; National Women's Health Network; National Organization of Women; International Correspondence Society of Obstetricians and Gynaecologists. *Publications include:* "Introductory Handbook for Medical Students - Obstetrical and Gynaecologic Residency Training", (co-author), 1983; "Coping With Premenstrual Syndrome, A Personal Workbook for Premenstrual Syndrome Patients", 1984 and 1985; "The Handbook of Sexually Transmitted Diseases: Recognition, Prevention and Treatment", (with Ray Fish), 1985; "Changing Without Aging, A Woman Doctor Discusses Menopause", 1986; Chapters in books, papers and articles. *Honours include:* Award for Feminism, National Organization of Women. *Hobbies:* Swimming; Skiing; Scuba Diving; Painting; Reading; Art collecting. *Address:* 301 East Springfield Avenue, Champaign, IL 61820, USA.

TRZEBIATOWSKI, Gregory L., b. 19 May 1937, Buena Vista, Wisconsin, USA. Associate Dean. m. 18 June 1960, Glidden, Wisconsin, USA., 3 daughters. *Education:* BS, University of Wisconsin-Stout, Menomonie, WI, 1959; PhD, Michigan State University, East Lansing, MI, 1967. *Appointments include:* (Administrative Associate Dean, 1978-, Assistant Dean, Medical and Graduate Education, 1973-77, Director, Office of Geriatrics and Gerontology, 1985-, Director, Cancer Education, Comprehensive Cancer Center, 1982-, Assistant Dean, Medical Education, 1970-73, College of Medicine, Ohio State University; (Academic) Professor of Education, Educational Policy and Leadership, College of Education, 1974-, Professor, Department of Preventive Medicine, College of Medicine, 1981-, Professor, School of Allied Medical Professions, College of Medicine, 1974-, Ohio State University. *Memberships include:* Phi Delta Kappa; The National Council on the Aging, 1984-; The Academy of Political Science, 1984-. *Publications include:* 'Medical Student Performance: A Comparison of Independent Study and Traditional Programs' (co-author); 'A Crisis in Medical Education: Thoughts on Listening to a Conference on Medical Education for the 21st Century' (co-author), 1985; 'Community-Based Practitioners as Medical Student Preceptors - Dispelling an Old Myth', (co-author), 1979; 'A Study of Faculty Attitudes towards a Three-Year Medical Program and Three-Year Medical Students', (co-author); 'Independent Study Programs in Medical Education: The State of the Art', 1976; 'Multitrack Instructional Systems for the Basic Sciences', 1976; (editor) 'Independent Medical Studies: Their Potential Impact on the Health Care System', 1976. *Honours include:* Epsilon Pi Tau National Honor Society; Recipient, Honorary Professorship, School of Medicine University of Comcepcion, Chile, 1981. *Address:* 1890 Tremont Road, Columbus, OH 43212, USA.

TRZEBSKI, Andrzej Marian, b. 2 Feb. 1928, Warsaw, Poland. Professor of Physiology. m. Hanka Torun, 26 June 1959, Warsaw, 1 son. *Education:* Medical Diploma 1952, Doctor's Degree 1958, Habilitation 1961, Medical Academy Warsaw; Extraordinary Professor, 1971; Ordinary Professor, 1981. *Appointments:* Assistant and Associate Professor 1952-64, Chairman 1967-, Department of Physiology, Dean of Medical Faculty 1972-75, Director of Institute of Physiological Sciences 1974-84, Deputy Rector 1981-84, Professor 1981-, Medical Academy, Warsaw; World Health Organisation Visiting Professor, 1964-67. *Memberships:* Deputy Chairman of Committee of Physiological Sciences, Polish Academy of Sciences; Council Member, Chairman of Commission on Autonomic Nervous System, International Union of Physiological Sciences; Polish Physiological Society; Correspondent Member, American Physiological Society. *Publications:* "Central Interaction Between Respiratory and Cardiovascular Control Systems", (co-author and co-editor), 1980; "Human and Clinical Physiology", academic textbook, in Polish, (co-editor and co-author), 1980; "Physiology of the Peripheral Arterial Chemoreceptors", (co-author), 1983; "Control of Respiration", (co-author), 1983. *Honours:* Awards of the Secretary of the Polish Academy of Sciences, 1976, 1978 and 1983. *Address:* Department of Physiology, Institute of Physiological Sciences, Medical Academy, Krakowskie Przedmiescie 26/28, Warsaw 00-927, Poland.

TSAI, Albert Y M, b. 3 Apr. 1941, China. Consultant Obstetrician & Gynaecologist. m. Suzanna, 16 July 1968, Chicago, Illinois, USA, 1 son, 1 daughter. *Education:* MD, University of Chicago, 1968; Diplomate, American Board of Obstetrics & Gynaecology, 1974; Diploma of special competence in reproductive endocrinology, American Board of Obstetrics & Gynaecology, 1978. *Appointments:* Assistant Professor, School of Medicine, University of Chicago, 1973-75; Associate Professor, Abraham Lincoln School of Medicine, University of Illinois, 1975-78. *Memberships:* Fellow, American College of Obstetricians & gynaecologists, 1974; Fellow, American College of Surgeons; American Diabetes Association; College of Physicians & Surgeons, Manitoba, Canada; American Medical Association; Illinois State Medical Association; Chicago Medical Society; Chicago Gynaecological Society; Chicago Endocrine Club. *Publications:* 12 learned articles in field of Obstetrics & Gynaecology, 1966-78. *Hobbies:* Swimming; Chinese Art; Antiques. *Address:* Suite 1005, Takshing House, 20 Des Voeux Road Central, Hong Kong.

TSANG, Jeffrey Y. S., b. 1932, Hong Kong. Orthodontist, Private Practice; Part-time Lecturer, Dental Faculty, University of Hong Kong. m. Loretta Tsang, 28 Jan., 1961, Hong Kong, 2 sons. *Education:* BDS, Hong Kong Government Dental Scholarship; D. Orth. RCS (Eng), Commonwealth Scholarship. *Appointments:* Dental Officer, Hong Kong Government; Senior Dental Officer, Orthodontist, Hong Kong Government; Orthodontist, private practice. *Memberships:* Consultative Committee, Basic Law of Hong Kong; Vice President, Asian Pacific Dental Federation; Dental Council of Hong Kong; Chairman, Preliminary Investigation Committee, Dental Council of Hong Kong; President, Hong Kong Dental Association, 1972-73, Honorary Life Member; President, Hong Kong Society of Orthodontists; Regent, International College of Dentists; Honorary Fellow, Academy Dentistry International; Chairman, Organizing Committee, 11th Asian Pacific Dental Congress, Hong Kong, 1984. *Hobbies:* Sports; Photography. *Address:* 218 Holland House, 9 Ice House Street, Hong Kong.

TSOU, Kang, b. 1 Jan. 1932, Shanghai, China. Professor; Department Chairman. m. 1 Jan. 1958, 1 son, 1 daughter. *Education:* MD, Shanghai First Medical College, 1954; PhD, Shanghai Institute of Materia, 1957-61. *Appointments:* Teaching Assistant, Pharmacology, Shanghai Second Medical College, 1954-57; Research Associate, Pharmacology, Shanghai Institute of Materia Medica, 1961-78; Associate Professor, Pharmacology, Shanghai Institute of Material Medica, 1978-83; Visiting Research Scientist: University of California, San Francisco, 1979-80, University of Michigan, 1980, 1985, Yale University, 1981-82. *Memberships:* Academia Sinica; Chinese Pharmacology Society, Vice President; Chinese Physiology Society; Chinese Biochemistry Society; International Brain Research Organization; Society for Neuroscience, USA. *Publications:* Articles in professional journals. *Honours:* Elected Member, Academia Sinica, 1980; Second Prize, Natural Sciences, China, 1982. *Hobby:* Photography. *Address:* Shanghai Institute of Materia Medica, Academia Sinica, 319 Yu-Yang Road, Shanghai, 200031, China.

TSOUTSOURIS, George Vlasios, b. 3 Apr. 1944, Gary, Indiana, USA. Podiatrist. m. Charlene Isaacson, Gary, Indiana, 17 Aug. 1969, 2 sons. *Education:* AB, Chemistry, Indiana University, USA, 1966; Doctor of Podiatric Medicine, cum laude, Illinois College of Podiatric Medicine, 1974. *Appointments:* Podiatric Surgical Residency, 1975; Chemistry Teacher, Valparaiso High School, Indiana, USA; Clinical Instructor, Illinois College of Podiatric Medicine; Chief of Podiatry, Methodist Hospitals -; Assistant Professor of Anatomy, Indiana University -. *Memberships:* American Podiatric Medical Association; Indiana Podiatric Medical Association; Lake County, Indiana, Podiatric Medical Society; Former President, American Cancer Society, Lake County Division. *Publications:* 'Journal of the American Podiatric Medical Association', 1975; 'Journal of Foot Surgery', 1982. *Honours:* Fellow, American College of Foot Surgeons; Diplomate, American Board of Podiatric Surgery. *Hobbies:* Music; Reading. *Address:* 7127 Indianapolis Boulevard, Hammond, IN 46324, USA.

TSUJIMOTO, Akira, b. 3 Apr. 1927, Japan. Professor, Pharmacology, Hiroshima University School of Dentistry. m. Norikom 16 May 1957, Japan, 2 sons, 2 daughters. *Education:* Graduated, Nara Medical University, 1952. *Appointments:* Associate Professor, Pharmacology, 1960-68, Research Associate, Internal

Medicine I, 1958-60, Instructor, 1954-58, Research Associate, 1953-54, Pharmacology, Nara Medical University; Intern, Nara Medical University Hospital, 1952-53. *Memberships:* Japanese Pharmacological Society; Japanese Association for Oral Biology; Japanese Society of Toxicological Sciences. *Publication:* "Dental Pharmacology", Editor, Author, Japanese, 2nd edition 1979. *Hobbies:* Go; Golf. *Address:* Dept. of Pharmacology, Hiroshima University, School of Dentistry, 1-2-3 Kasumi, Minami-ku, Hiroshima City 734, Japan.

TSUKAMOTO, Naoki, b. 6 Oct. 1940, Kobe, Japan. Associate Professor of Obstetrics & Gynaecology. m. Shizuko Tsukamoto, 18 Sep. 1969, 1 son, 1 daughter. *Education:* MD, Faculty of Medicine, Kyushu University, Fukuoka, Japan, 1965; Diplomate, American Board of Obstetrics & Gynaecology, Diplomate, Division of Gynaecological Oncology, American Board of Obstetrics & Gynaecology. *Appointments:* Internship, Buffalo General Hospital, New York, USA, 1967-68; Resident, Obstetrics & Gynaecology, University Hospitals of Cleveland, Ohio, 1968-72; Instructor, Department of Obstetrics & Gynaecology, Faculty of Medicine, Kyushu University, 1972-76; Fellowship, Gynaecology Service, Memorial Sloan-Kettering Cancer Centre, New York, USA, 1976-78; Assistant Professor, Department of Obstetrics & Gynaecology, Faculty of Medicine, Kyushu University, Fukuoka, Japan, 1979-83, Associate Professor, 1983-. *Memberships:* Society of Gynaecological Oncologists; Society of Memorial Gynaecological Oncologists; American College of Obstetricians & Gynaecologists; Japan Society of Obstetrics & Gynaecology; Japan Society for Cancer Therapy; Japanese Society of Clinical Cytology; Japan Society for Laser Medicine; International Society for Gynaecological Pathologists. *Publications:* 'Choriocarcinoma occurring within the Normal Placenta with Breast Metastasis' (in Gynaecological Oncology, 1981); 'Cytological Presentation of Ovarian Adenosquamous Carcinoma in Ascitic Fluid: A Case Report' (in Acta Cytologica, 1984); 'Gestational Trophoblastic Disease in Women aged 50 or more' (in Gynaecological Oncology, 1985). *Address:* Department of Obstetrics & Gynaecology, Kyushu University Hospital, Maidashi 3-1-1, Higashi-ku, Fukuoka 912, Japan.

TU, Gui-yi, b. 12 Jan. 1928, Shanghai, China. Deputy Director, Cancer Hospital. m. Hong Yunlin, 1 son. *Education:* MD, Medical College, St John's University, Shanghai. *Appointments:* Resident, Peking Union Medical College, 1953; Senior Surgeon, Surgery, Cancer Hospital, Chinese Academy of Medical Sciences, Beijing, 1963; Deputy Head, Surgery, Cancer Hospital, 1979; Head, Division of Head and Neck Surgery, Cancer Hospital, 1982; Head, Department of Head and Neck Surgery, Cancer Hospital, Chinese Academy of Medical Sciences, Beijing, 1985-; Deputy Director, Cancer Hospital, CAMS, Beijing. *Memberships:* Chinese Medical Association; Editorial Board, 'Chinese Journal Otolaryngology'; Council Member, Chinese Society of Oncology. *Publications:* Articles in professional journals including: 'Chinese Journal of Oncology'; 'Chinese Journal Otolaryngology'; 'Arch. Otolaryngology'. *Hobby:* Reading. *Address:* Cancer Hospital, CAMS, Chaoyangqu, Beijing, China.

TUCKER, Sheridan Gregory, b. 26 Feb. 1950, USA. Director, Child & Adolescent Services; Clinical Assistant Professor; Private Practitioner USA. m. Jaylene D Lambert, 30 Dec. 1977, Winfield, 1 son, 1 daughter. *Education:* BSc, Biology, University of Missouri, Kansas City, 1972; MD, University of Kansas, 1975. *Appointments:* Chief, Psychiatry, Ft Polk; Consultant, Army Drug Abuse & Prevention Programme, Ft. Polk; Clinical Assistant Professor, Kansas University Medical Centre; Director, Child and Adolescent Services, Kansas Institute. *Memberships:* American Medical Association; American Psychiatric Association; American Academy of Clinical Psychiatrists; American Academy of Child Psychiatrists; Association for Child Psychology & Psychiatry. *Honour:* Army

Commendation Medal, 1980. *Hobbies:* Reading; Wood Carving. *Address:* 4121 W 83rd Street, Suite 150, Prairie Village, KS 66208, USA.

TUCKER, William Eldon, CVO 1954; MBE, 1944; TD, 1951; FRCS. Formerly Honorary Orthopaedic Surgeon, Royal London Homoeopathic Hospital; Director and Surgeon, The Clinic Park Street, 1936-80. b. 6 Aug. 1903. m. (1) Jean Stella, 1931, divorced 1953, 2 sons; (2) Mary Beatrice Castle, 1956. *Education:* Sherborne; Gonville and Caius College, Cambridge, MA 1931; FRCS 1930; MB, BCh, 1946, St George's Hospital, 1925-34. *Appointments:* Lieutenant, RAMC, TA 1930-34; Major RAMC, Orthopaedic Specialist, 1939-45; Lt Col, RAMC TA, 1946-51; Colonel and Honorary Colonel, 17th General Hospital, TA, 1951-63; Surgeon, St John's Hospital, Lewisham, 1931-37; Registrar, Royal National Orthopaedic Hospital, 1933-34; Orthopaedic Consultant, Horsham Hospital, 1945, Dorking Hospital, 1956; Hunterian Professor, RCS, Oct. 1958. *Address:* West Dunes, 4£ South Road, Paget West, Bermuda.

TUGWELL, Peter, b. 30 Mar. 1944, Egypt. University Professor and Department Chairman. m. Jane Katherine Tugwell, 26 June 1971, Southport, England. 1 son, 1 daughter. *Education:* MBBS, London, 1969; MRCP, UK, 1971; MD, London, 1976; FRCPC, 1976; FACP, 1984. *Appointments:* Montreal Register, Ahmadu Bello University Hospital, Nigeria, 1971-74; Chief Resident and Fellow in Rheumatology, McMaster University, Ontario, Canada, 1975-77; Assistant Professor, Associate Professor then Professor, Department of Clinical Epidemiology and Department of Medicine, McMaster University, Ontario, Canada, 1977-; Chairman, Department of Clinical Epidemiology and Biostatistics, McMaster University, 1979-; Visiting Professor, University of Sydney, Australia, 1984-85. *Memberships:* Society for Epidemiologic Research; International Epidemiological Association; American Federation for Clinical Research; American Rheumatology Association; Canadian Rheumatism Association; Sydenham Society; Canadian Society for Clinical Investigation; Society for Medical Decision Making; American College of Physicians; The Canadian Public Health Association; The Canadian Society for Tropical Medicine and International Health. *Publications:* Book: Sackett DL, Haynes RB, Tugwell P: "Clinical Epidemiology: A Basic Science for Clinical Medicine" 1985; 73 published learned articles. *Honours:* Ontario Health Scientist, 1978-79; National Health and Welfare Visiting National Health Scientist, 1984-85. *Hobby:* Tennis. *Address:* Department of Clinical Epidemiology and Biostatistics, Room 2C16, McMaster University, 1200 Main Street, West, Hamilton, Ontario, Canada L8N 3Z5.

TUPIN, Joe Paul, b. 17 Feb. 1934, Comanche, Texas, USA. Medical Director, Davis Medical Center. *Education includes:* BS, 1955, MD, Medical Branch, 1959, University of California; Intern, University of California Hospitals, 1959-60; Resident, University of Texas Medical Branch, 1960-62, National Institute of Mental Health, 1963-64. *Appointments include:* Assistant Professor, Psychiatry, 1964-68, Associate Professor, 1968-69, Director, Psychiatric Research, 1965-69, Assistant Dean, Medicine, 1967-68, Associate Dean, 1968-69, University of Texas Medical Branch, Galveston, Texas; Associate Professor, Psychiatry, 1969-71, Professor, 1971-, Director, Psychiatric Consultation Service, 1969-74, Co-Director, 1974-77, Vice Chairman, Department of Psychiatry, 1970-76, Chief, Division of Mental Health, 1977-, University of California; various hospital appointments and consultancies. *Memberships include:* Fellow: American Psychiatric Association; American College of Psychiatrists. American, Texas, Galveston County, California and Southern Medical Associations; American Association for Advancement of Science; Sigma Xi. *Publications:* Author or Co-Author of some 76 papers contributed to professional journals and as book chapters including: "Beneficent Euthansis", 1975; "Manual of Psychiatric Therapeutics", 1975, "Behavioral Science in Family Practice", 1980; "The Treatment of

Antisocial Syndromes", 1981; "Digestive Diseases", 1983; "Manual of Psychotropic Drugs", 1983; "Origins and Future Developments", 1984. Numerous professional journals internationally and nationally. *Honours include:* Rho Chi; Alpha Omega Alpha; Fellow, National Foundation of Infantile Paralysis, 1957; Principle Investigator in various topics; Friars Society, 1954, Mosby Scholarship Award, 1959, University of Texas. *Address:* Department of Psychiatry, University of California, Davis, CA 95616, USA.

TURCO, Ronald, b. 11 Apr. 1940, Philadelphia, Pennsylvania, USA. Psychiatrist; Clinical Associate Professor. m. Joanne Labezius, Delaware County, 2 daughters. *Education:* BS, Pennsylvania State University; MD, Jefferson Medical College. *Appointments:* Director, Cedar Hills Hospital, 1973-75; Major, USAF, 1970-73; Specialist Consultant, Impaired Phys. Committee, Good Samaritan Hospital; Consultant, Law Enforcement, Portland Police and Newberg Police; Diplomate, American Board of Psychiatry and Neurology. *Memberships:* President, Portland Psychiatrists in Private Practice; Oregon Medical Association; American Society of Clinical Hypnosis; Portland Academy of Clinical Hypnosis; Flying Doctors Society of Africa; Worls Psychiatric Association; Undersea Medical Society; Board of Directors, Oregon Psychoanalytic Foundation, 1973-; Founding Member, NW Association for Professional Treatment of Offenders, (President 1979); MAZAMAS; Underwater Society of America. *Publications:* 35 Publications including: "Culture and Conflict: Eskimo Youth", 'Journal Past. Couns.', 1974; "Regrief Treatment Facilitated by Hypnosis", 'American Journal Clinical Hypnosis', 1981; "Treat. Unresolved Grief Following Infant Loss", 'American Journal of Obstetrics and Gynaecology', 1981; multiple articles on law enforcement, grief and loss and pain and disability. *Honours:* Diplomate, American Board of Psychiatry and Neurology, 1973; AMA Outstanding Physician Awards, 1970-. *Hobbies include:* Nordic and Alpine Skiing; Scuba Diving; Mountain Survival; Oil Painting; Contemporary Japanese Literature; Photography; Swimming; Many Community Interests. *Address:* 1220 SW Morrison, Suite 606, Portland, OR 97205, USA.

TURINA, Marko, b. 23 Jan. 1937, Zagreb, Yugoslavia. University Professor. m. Helga Seidel, Sindelfingen, Germany, 26 Nov. 1966, 2 sons. *Education:* MD, University of Zagreb; Spezialarzt FMH fur Chirurgie. *Appointments:* Residence, University Hospital Zurich, Switzerland; Research Assistant, Institute of Pharmacology, University of Zurich; Assistant Research Surgeon, University of California, San Diego, USA; Staff Member, Surgical Clinic A, Assistant Professor for Cardiac Surgery, Professor of Cardiovascular Surgery, University of Zurich; Professor of Surgery and Director, Clinic for Cardiovascular Surgery, University Hospital, Zurich. *Memberships:* Swiss Medical Association; Medical Society of Canton, Zurich; Swiss Surgical Association; German Surgical Association; Society of Thoracic Surgeons; German Society for Thoracic & Cardiovascular Surgery; Swiss Bioengineering Society; German Bioengineering Society; American Society for Artificial Internal Organs; International College of Angiology. *Publications:* 227 articles in various Biomedical Journals; 202 Abstracts. *Honour:* Goetz-Preis, University of Zurich, 1977. *Address:* Direktor, Klinik für Herzgefässchirurgie, Universitätsspital, 8091 Zürich, Switzerland.

TURK, Vito, b. 27 June 1937, Osijek, Yugoslavia. Professor and Head of Biochemistry Department. m. Breda Turk, 9 May 1959, 2 sons. *Education:* Diploma Engineer of Chemistry, 1961; PhD Biochemistry, 1966. *Appointments:* Assistant 1961-69, Research Associate 1969-74, Assistant Professor 1974-79, Associate Professor 1979-85, Professor and Head of Department of Biochemistry 1985-, J Stefan Institute, Ljubljana. *Memberships:* International Society for Radiobiology; International Committee on Proteolysis. *Publica-

tions include: "Intracellular Protein Catabolism II" (with N Marks), 1977; "Proteinases and their Inhibitors" (with L Vitale), 1981; 142 publications, 1963-85. *Honours:* Boris Kidric Foundation, 1979; Boris Kidric Prize, 1984. *Hobbies:* Jogging; Surfing. *Address:* Department of Biochemistry, J Stefan Institute, Jamova 39, 61000 Ljubljana, Yugoslavia.

TURNBERG, Leslie Arnold, b. 22 Mar. 1934, Manchester, England. Dean of Medical School. m. Edna Barme, 30 Jan. 1968, Dallas, Texas, USA, 1 son, 1 daughter. *Education:* MB, ChB, 1957, MD, 1966, University of Manchester, England; MRCP (London), 1961; FRCP (London), 1973. *Appointments:* Manchester Northern Hospital, 1958; Manchester Jewish Hospital, 1958; Senior House Officer, Medical, Ancoats Hospital, 1959-61; Senior House Officer, 1959-61, Senior Registrar, 1964-66, Manchester Royal Infirmary; Registrar, University College Hospital, 1961-64; Lecturer, Medical, Royal Free Hospital, 1966-67; Research Fellow, Dallas, Texas, USA, 1967-68; Lecturer, Medicine, 1968-70, Senior Lecturer, Medicine, 1970-73, University of Manchester, England; Professor of Medicine, 1973, Dean of Medical School, 1986, University of Manchester; Honorary Consultant Physician, Salford Health Authority, 1973. *Memberships:* American Gastroenterology Association; European Society of Clinical Investigations; British Society of Gastroenterology; Association of Physicians of Great Britain and Ireland; Medical Research Society. *Publications:* "Intestinal Secretion", 1983; "Mechanisms of mucosal protection in the upper gastro-intestinal tract", 1984; 'Electrolyte transport across gastrointestinal epithelia', 1982. *Honours:* Sir Arthur Hurst Lecturer of British Society Gastroenterology, 1984; Franz Barani Lecturer, 1983; Sir Frances Avery Jones Lecturer, 1981; Fellows Visiting Professor, Mayo Clinic, 1984; Visiting Professor, Jerusalem, 1981; Visiting Professor, Brisbane, 1980; Visiting Professor, Calgary, 1984. *Hobbies:* Reading; Walking. *Address:* 5 Broadway Avenue, Cheadle, Cheshire SK8 1NN, England.

TURNDORF, Herman, b. 22 Dec. 1930, Paterson, New Jersey, USA. Professor and Chairman, Department of Anaesthesiology, New York University. m. Sietske Huisman, 27 Nov. 1957, New York City, 2 sons. *Education:* BA, Oberlin College, Ohio, 1952. *Appointments:* Instructor in Anaesthesiology, Hospital of the University of Pennsylvania, 1957-59; Assistant Attending, Harvard Medical School, 1961-63; Clinical Professor of Anaesthesiology, The Mount Sinai Medical School, 1966-70; Professor and Chairman, Department of Anaesthesiology, West Virginia University Medical Center and Hospital, 1970-74; Professor and Chairman, Department of Anaesthesiology, New York University Medical Center, 1974-. *Memberships include:* New York State Society of Anaesthesiologists; American Society of Anaesthesiologists; American College of Anaesthesiologists; New York County Medical Society; American College of Chest Physicians; Society of Academic Anaesthesia Chairman; Fellow, New York Academy of Medicine; International Anaesthesia Research Society; International Society for the Study of Pain and many other organizations. *Publications:* Books: Co-author: "Anaesthesia and Neurosurgery', 1980; "Humidification of Anaesthetic Gases", 1981; Chapters in books; Contributor to professional journals; Presentations; Scientific exhibits; Twitch Box, a New Device to Monitor Neuromuscular Blockage (with Azar I). *Address:* 560 1st Avenue, New York, NY 10016, USA.

TURNER, David Avery, b. 8 May 1940, USA. Private Practice of Psychoanalysis and Psychiatry. m. Carol E Ferguson, 17 Sep. 1966, Atlanta, Georgia, 1 son, 1 daughter. *Education:* BA, Wesleyan University, Middletown, Connecticut, 1962; MD, University of Chicago, Chicago, Illinois, 1966. *Appointments:* Assistant Professor of Psychiatry, University of Chicago, Pritzker School of Medicine, 1972-74; Psychiatrist, United States Veterans Administration, Portland, Oregon 1974-82, Portland State University Health Service,

Portland, Oregon, 1975-78; Private Practice, Psychiatry 1974-, Psychoanalysis 1983-, Portland, Oregon. *Memberships:* Multnomah County Medical Society; Oregon Medical Association; American Psychiatric Association; Associate, American Psychoanalytic Association. *Address:* 2250 North West Flanders Street 306, Portland, OR 97210, USA.

TURNER, Keven James, b. 24 Nov. 1930, Adelaide, Australia. Associate Professor. m. Margaret Fay Conley, 6 Jan. 1956, 1 son, 3 daughters. *Education:* BSc, Honours, 1953, PhD, 1956, Adelaide; FRCPath (UK), 1981. *Appointments include:* Post Doctoral Fellowship, National Research Council of Canada, 1956-57; Assistant Section Controller, Research, Commonwealth Serum Laboratories, Victoria, 1958-61; Research Fellow, University of Adelaide, 1962-68; Associate Professor, Johns Hopkins University, USA, 1968; Senior Research Fellow, 1969-77, Associate Professor, 1978-, Microbiology, University of Western Australia, Australia; 1969-, Consultant, 1977-, Princess Margaret Hospital for Children. *Memberships include:* Australian Society for Immunology; Australian College of Allergy; British Society for Immunology; British Society for Allergy & Clinical Immunology; Executive, International Association of Allergology and Clinical Immunology; American Academy of Allergy & Immunology; American Association of Immunologists. *Publications:* 135 articles in professional journals including: 'Nature'; 'Immunology'; 'The Lancet'; 'Journal Immunology'; 'South African Medical Journal'; 'Clinical Immunology'; 'Journal Experimental Biology'; etc. *Honours:* Fellow: Royal College of Pathologists, UK, 1981; Fellow, Australian College of Allergy, 1982; Corresponding Fellowship, American Academy of Allergy & Immunology, 1984; Fellow, Royal Society of Tropical Medicine & Hygiene, UK. *Hobbies:* Music; Golf; Tennis; Fishing; Gardening. *Address:* Dept. of Microbiology, University of Western Australia, Nedlands, WA 6009, Australia.

TURNER, Michael Rex, b. 31 July 1934, England. Consultant Nutritionist. *Education:* BSc, MSc, PhD, London University. *Appointments:* National Health Service, 1959-60; Medical Research Council, 1960-66; University of Southampton 1966-78, Senior Lecturer 1974-78; British Nutrition Foundation, Director General 1978-82; Consultant in Nutrition and Health Affairs, 1982-. *Memberships:* Fellow, Royal Society of Medicine; Fellow, Royal Society of Health; Fellow, Institute of Food Science and Technology; Fellow, Institute of Biology. *Publications:* Editor: "Nutrition and Life Styles" 1979; "Problems in Nutrition Research Today" 1981; "Preventive Nutrition and Society" 1981; "Nutrition and Diabetes" 1981; "Nutrition and Health" 1982; "Food and People" 1983; Also 6 chapters in books and numerous scientific papers and articles in newspapers. *Hobby:* Bridge. *Address:* 119 Thomas More House, Barbican, London WC2Y 8BU.

TURNER, Paul, b. 16 Apr. 1933, London, England. Professor of Clinical Pharmacology; Consultant Physician, St Bartholomew's Hospital, London. m. Kathleen Weaver, 21 Mar. 1968, Guildford, 2 daughters. *Education:* BSc, 1954; MB, BS, 1958; MRCP, 1962; MD, 1965; FRCP, 1973. *Appointments:* Home Officer, Middlesex Hospital, 1959; Senior House Officer, Royal Free Hospital, 1969; Registrar, Edgware General Hospital, 1961-62; Lecturer in Pharmacology, Medical College, 1963-64, Lecturer in Clinical Pharmacology, 1964-65, Senior Lecturer in Clinical Pharmacology, 1965-67, Reader in Clinical Pharmacology, 1967-72, St Bartholomew's Hospital, London. *Memberships:* Fellow, Royal Society of Medicine; Society of Apothecaries of London; Fellow, Institute of Biology; British Pharmacological Society; British Toxicology Society; Society for Drug Research. *Publications:* "Clinical aspects of autonomic pharmacology"; "Clinical Pharmacology", (Co-author); "Drug Treatment in Psychiatry", (Co-author); "Drugs Handbook", (Co-author); "Recent Advances in Clinical Pharmacology", (Co-author). *Honours:* Dixon Lecturer, Royal

Society of Medicine, 1975; Honorary Memberships of Pharmaceutical Society of Great Britain, 1976; Lettsomian Lecturer, Medical Society of London, 1978; Royal Society of Medicine Visiting Lecturer to USA, 1984. *Hobbies:* Music; Literature; Travel. *Address:* Department of Clinical Pharmacology, St Bartholomew's Hospital, London EC1A 7BE, England.

TURNER-WARWICK, Margaret Elizabeth, b. 19 Nov. 1924, London, England. Dean of Cardiothoracic Institute and Professor of Medicine. m. Richard Turner-Warwick, 21 Jan. 1950, London, 2 daughters. *Education:* MA, DM, Oxford University; PhD, London University; DSc (Hon) New York; FRCP; FRACP; FFOM. *Appointments:* House Physician and Registrar, University College and Brompton Hospitals, 1950-56; Senior Registrar and Chief Medical Assistant, Brompton Hospital, 1956-61; Consultant Physician, Elizabeth Garrett Anderson Hospital, 1961-67; Senior Lecturer, Department of Medicine, Cardiothoracic Institute, 1962-72; Consultant Physician, London Chest and Brompton Hospitals, 1967-72; Currently: Dean of Cardiothoracic Institute and Professor of Medicine. *Memberships:* Association of Physicians of Great Britain; British Thoracic Society; American Thoracic Society; Australian Thoracic Society etc. *Publications:* "Immunology of the Lung"; "Occupational Lung Diseases Research Approaches and Methods" co-editor with Hans Weill. Publications on Immunology, Respiratory Medicine especially Interstitial Diseases and Asthma. *Honours:* Honorary DSc, New York City University, 1984; Fellow, Royal College of Australasian Physicians, 1984; Fellow of Faculty of Occupational Medicine, Royal College of Physicians, London, 1983. *Hobbies:* Watercolour painting; Classical music; Gardening; Family. *Address:* 55 Fitzroy Park, Highgate, London N6, England.

TURNS, Danielle M, b. 26 Dec. 1936, Toulouse, France. Chief, Psychiatry Service, Veterans Administration Medical Center, Louisville, Kentucky, USA; Professor, Department of Psychiatry and Behavioral Sciences, University of Louisville School of Medicine. Divorced, 1 son, 1 daughter. *Education:* BA, Lycee de Toulouse, France, 1953; Graduate, 1954-60; MD, 1963. *Appointments:* Psychiatric Residency, France, Lyon and New York, USA, 1959-65; Associate Research Scientist, Psychiatrist II, Manhattan St Hospital, 1965-69; Research Psychiatrist II, then Deputy Director, Psychiatric Epidemiology, Research Unit, Hudson River State Hospital, Poughkeepsie, NY, 1969-76; Board Certified, 1973; Associate then Full Professor, University of Louisville, 1976-; Assistant Chief, then Chief, Psychiatry Service, Louisville Veterans Administration Medical Center, 1976-. *Memberships:* Fellow, APA; KMA; AMWA; Central Neuropsychiatric Association; International Epidemiological Association; American Society of Physician Analysts; NAVAP; NAVACOP. *Publications:* Co-Author: 'Epidemiology' in "Comprehensive Textbook of Psychiatry" II Volume 1, 2nd Edition, 1975; Co-author: 'The Measurement of Health Status' chapter in "Assessing Health and Human Service Needs: Concepts, Methods and Applications", 1983. Contributor to books, journals, etc. *Address:* 3611 Cascade Road, Louisville, KY 40222, USA.

TURSI, Alfredo, b. 30 Mar. 1935, Sante Marie (Aq). Full Professor of Allergy and Clinical Immunology, University of Bari Medical School, Italy. m. Maria Rosaria Ciancio, 6 Feb. 1963, Bari, 1 son, 1 daughter. *Education:* Diploma of Specialist in Internal Medicine, 1966; Diploma of Libero Docente in Rheumatology, 1969; MD. *Appointments:* Research Fellow, University of Bari Medical School, 1960-66; Assistant Professor of Internal Medicine, 1966-71; Associate Professor, Clinical Immunology, 1971-73; Full Professor of Clinical Immunology, 1975-83. *Memberships:* Vice-President, Italian Association of Aerobiology; British Society of Immunology; British Society Transplantation; European Academy Allergol. Clinical Immunology; Vice-Presient Italian Society of Allergology Clin. Immunology Italian Society of Immun-

ology and Immunopatology; Italian Society Rheumatology. *Publications:* Contributor of papers and articles to professional journals. *Hobbies:* Gastronomy; Photography. *Address:* Cattedra di Allergologia ed Immunologia Clinica, Policlinco, 70124 Bari, Italy.

TYLDESLEY, William Randolph, b. 21 July 1927, Lancashire, England. Director of Dental Education, University of Liverpool. *Education:* DDS; MSc; PhD; FDSRCS (Edinburgh). *Publications:* "Oral Diagnosis", 1969, 3rd Edition, 1987; "Oral Medicine", 1974, 3rd Edition, 1986; "Colour Atlas of Oral Medicine", 1978. *Address:* School of Dental Surgery, Pembroke Place, Liverpool L69 3BX, England.

TYLER, Varro Eugene, b. 19 Dec. 1926, Auburn, Nebrasks, USA. University Professor and Dean. m. Virginia May Demel, 20 Aug. 1947, Nebraska, 1 son, 1 daughter. *Education:* BS, Pharmacy, University of Nebraska, 1949; MS, 1951, PhD, 1953, University of Connecticut. *Appointments:* Associate Professor, University of Nebraska, Lincoln, 1953-57; Associate Professor, University of Washington, Seattle, 1957-61; Professor, University of Washington, Seattle, 1961-66; Professor and Dean, School of Pharmacy and Pharmacal Sciences, 1966-, Professor and Dean, Schools of Pharmacy, Nursing, and Health Sciences, 1979- Purdue University, West Lafayette, Indiana. *Memberships:* American Society of Pharmacognosy, President 1959-61; American Association of Colleges of Pharmacy, President, 1970-71; Gesellschaft für Arzneipflanzenforschung; Rho Chi - Lecture Award 1983; Phi Kappa Phi. *Publications:* "Pharmacognosy" 8th edition, 1981; "The Honest Herbal" 1982; More than 190 scientific and educational articles in professional journals. *Honours:* Outstanding Service Award, Indiana Pharmacists Association, 1971; Distinguished Service Award, University of Connecticut, 1973; Merit Award, Wayne State University, 1978; Fellow, Academy of Pharmaceutical Sciences (Research Achievement Award 1966). *Hobby:* Philately. *Address:* Schools of Pharmacy, Nursing and Health Sciences, Purdue University, West Lafayette, IN 47907, USA.

TYO, Diane Marie Schomers, b. 28 Oct. 1954, Lockport, New York, USA. Certified Orthotist. m. James Tyo, 5 May 1984, East Aurora, New York. *Education:* BS, Occupational Therapy, State University of New York at Buffalo; Certificate in Orthotics, Northwestern University Postgraduate Medical School. *Appointments:* OTR, Braintree Intensive Rehabilitation Facility, Braintree, Massachusetts, 1976-78; Clinical Instructor, Medical Training Centre, Nairobi, Kenya (as volunteer in US Peace Corps), 1978-80; Residency, Orthotics Certification, Green Bay, Wisconsin, 1980-81 (established Therapeutic Services Upjohn Home Health); Director, Occupational Therapy & Orthotics, St Vincent Hospital, Green Bay, WI, 1981-84; Owner, Tyo & Tyo Ltd, Orthotics Practice, Green Bay WI, Hand Therapy Consultant, Bellin Memorial Hospital, 1984-. *Memberships:* American Academy of Orthotists & Prosthetists; American Orthotics & Prosthetics Association; American Occupational Therapy Association. *Honour:* Dean's Award, University of New York at Buffalo, 1976. *Hobbies:* English Riding; Fox-hunting; Cross-country skiing; Restoring Carousel Horses; Restoring old Houses; Canoeing. *Address:* 633 East Walnut Street, Green Bay, WI 54301, USA.

TYRRELL, David Arthur John, b. 19 June 1925, Ashford, Middlesex, England. Director of Common Cold Unit. m. Moyra Wylie, 15 Apr. 1950, Woodlands, Doncaster, 1 son, 2 daughters. *Education:* MB ChB Honours, MD Distinction, Sheffield University; Fellow, Royal College of Physicians; Fellow, Royal College of Pathologists; Fellow, Royal Society. *Appointments:* Junior Medical Posts, Sheffield United Hospitals; Assistant Physician and Assistant in the Institute, Rockefeller Institute, New York, USA; External Scientific Staff, Medical Research Council, England; Head of Division of Communicable Diseases and Deputy Director of Clinical Research Centre, Harrow, Middlesex; Currently Director, Common Cold Unit, Salisbury. *Memberships:* Association of Physicians; Society of General Microbiology; British Medical Association; American Society of Infectious Diseases; American Association of Physicians. *Publications:* "Common Colds and Related Diseases", 1965; "The Abolition of Infection - Hope or Illusion?", 1982. *Honours:* Commander of the Order of the British Empire; Honorary DSc, Sheffield. *Hobbies:* Gardening; Music. *Address:* Common Cold Unit, Coombe Road, Salisbury, SP2 8BW, England.

TZARTOS, Socrates J, b. 13 July 1945, Athens, Greece. Head, Biochemistry Dept. m. Elisabeth Perdiki, 12 Sep. 1971, Athens, 1 son. *Education:* BSc, Natural Sciences, 1971, PhD, Biochemistry, 1976, University of Athens. *Appointments:* Postdoctoral Fellow, Cambridge University, England, 1976-78; Postdoctoral Fellow, Salk Institute, San Diego, USA, 1978-81; Research Associate, Institut Pasteur, Paris, France, 1981-83; Head, Biochemistry, Hellenic Pasteur Institute, Athens, 1983-. *Memberships:* Society for Neuroscience, USA; European Neurscience Association; British Society for Developmental Biology; Hellenic Biochemical and Biophysical Society. *Publications:* "Monoclonal Antibodies to probe acetylcholine receptor structure: Localization of the Main Immunogenic Region", 1980; 'PNAS'; "Specificities of antibodies to acetylcholine receptors in sera from myasthenia gravis patients measured by monoclonal antibodies", 'PNAS', 1982; "Role of the main Immunogenic Region of Acetylcholine Receptor in Myasthenia Gravis", 'Journal of Immunology', 1985; 32 original papers. *Honours:* 4 EMBO Long Term Postdoctoral Fellowships, 1976-78, 1981-83; 2 Muscular Distrophy Association of America Fellowships, 1979-81. *Address:* Hellenic Pasteur Institute, 127 Vas Sofias Avenue, 115 21 Athens, Greece.

U

UHDE, Thomas Whitley, b. 6 Jan. 1948, Louisville, Kentucky, USA. Chief, Unit on Anxiety and Affective Disorders, Biological Psychiatry Branch, National Institute of Mental Health; Associate Clinical Professor, Psychiatry, Uniformed Services, University of the Health Sciences. m. Marlene Kraus, 22 Oct. 1977, New Haven, 1 son, 1 daughter. *Education:* BS, Duke University, 1971; MD, University of Louisville, 1975. *Appointments:* Director, Opiate Antagonist Programme, Substance Abuse Treatment Unit, Yale University, 1977-79; Consultant Methadone Maintenance Programme, Yale University, Consultant, Whiting Forensic Institute, Middletown, 1979; Chief Resident, Clinical Research Unit, Yale University, 1979; Ward Administrator, Section on Psychobiology Biological Psychiatry Branch, National Institute of Mental Health, Bethesda, 1979-80; Unit Chief, 3-West Clinical Research Unit, NIMH, 1980-; Chief, Anxiety and Affective Disorders, NIMH, 1982-; Attending Staff, National Institutes of Health, 1982-; Assistant Clinical Professor, 1982-85, Associate Clinical Professor, 1985-, Uniformed Services, University of the Health Sciences. *Memberships:* American Psychiatric Association; Society of Biological Psychiatry; Washington Psychiatric Association; American Association for the Advancement of Science.*Publications:* "Longitudinal Course of panic disorder: Clinical and Biological Considerations", 'Prog. Neuropsychopharmacol. Biol. Psychiatry', co-author, 1985; "Fear and Anxiety: Evidence for the role of the noradrenergic system", 'Psychopathology', co-author, 1984; "Caffeine: Relationship to human anxiety, plasma MHPG and Cortisol", 'Psychopharmacological Bulletin', 1984, co-author. *Honours:* Cleveland Achievement Award, 1975; Ackerly Award, 1975; National Research Service Award, 1979; American College of Neuropsychopharmacology Travel Fellowship, 1981; A E Bennett Neuropsychiatric Research Foundation Award, 1984; Commendation Medal, USA Public Health Service, 1984. *Address:* National Institute of Mental Health, 9000 Rockville Pike, Bld. 10, 3-2 239, Bethesda, MD 20205, USA.

ULLMAN, Uwe, b. 10 Nov. 1939, Ludwigshafen, Germany. Head of the Department of Medical Microbiology, University of Kiel. m. Anneliese, 2 sons. *Education:* Professor for Medical Microbiology. *Memberships:* American Society for Microbiology; British Society for Antimicrobial and Chemotherapy; The American Venereal Disease Association; International Society for Human and Animal Mycology; Campylon. Society; German Society for Hygiene and Microbiology; Paul Ehrlich-Gesellschaft; Paul Ehrlich Institut, WHO Expert Advisory Panel on Acute Bacterial Disease.*Publications:* Author of 140 papers in professional journals, etc. *Address:* Brunswiker Str. 2-6, 2300 Kiel 1, Federal Republic of Germany.

UMAKANTHA, Kaggal V, b. 6 Jan. 1943, Bellary, India. Chief, Rehabilitation Medicine Service; Director, Physical Medicine and Rehabilitation Unit; Assistant Clinical Professor. m. Kamala, 18 Sep. 1974, Trinidad, West Indies, 1 daughter. *Education:* MB BS, Karnatak Medical College, 1965; MS, King Georges Medical College, 1969; Diplomate, American Board of Physical Medicine and Rehabilitation. Residency: Northwestern University, Rehabilitation Institute of Chicago, USA, 1975-78.*Appointments:* Registrar in Orthopaedics, Acting Consultant, General Hospitals, Port of Spain and San Fernando, Government of Trinidad and Tobago; Lecturer in Orthopaedics, Orthopaedic Surgeon, Government Medical College and Hospital, Bellary, India; currently, Chief, Rehabilitation Medicine Service, Veterans Administration Medical Center, Tuscaloosa, Alabama, USA; Director, Physical Medicine and Rehabilitation, DCH Regional Medical Center, Tuscaloosa; Assistant Clinical Professor, Medicine and Orthopaedics, University of Alabama. *Memberships:* American Academy of Physical Medicine and Rehabilitation; American Congress of Rehabilitation Medicine; International Rehabilitation Medicine Association; Southern Society of Physical Medicine and Rehabilitation; American Association of Electromyography and Electrodiagnosis. *Publications:* Contributor to: 'Karnatak Medical College Magazine'; 'Journal of Christian Medical Association of India'; 'Caribbean Medical Journal'; 'Archives of Physical Medicine and Rehabilitation'.*Hobbies:* Golf; Tennis; Photography.*Address:* Veterans Administration Medical Center, Tuscaloosa, AL 35404, USA.

UNDERHILL, Michael Lyle, b. 19 March 1958, Tokyo, Japan. Chiropractic Physician in private practice. *Education:* DC; AA Psychology. *Appointments:* Research, Western States Chiropractic College, 1980-81; Private Practitioner, Beaverton Clinic of Chiropractic, 1981-. *Memberships:* International Chiropractors Association; Oregon Chiropractic Physicians Association; Western States Chiropractic College Alumni Association. *Hobbies:* Snow and water skiing; Karate; Boating. *Address:* 12801 SW Jenkins Road, Suite "B", Beaverton, OR 97005, USA.

UPADHYAYA, Purushottam, b. 1 May 1928, Gokul, India. Professor; Head, Department of Paediatric Surgery. m. Indu, 4 May 1954, Dehradun, India, 1 son, 1 daughter. *Education:* MS, 1955; FRCS (Eng), 1959; FAMS, 1977. *Appointments:* Surgical Registrar, Brighton General and Royal Alexandra Hospital for Sick Children, Brighton, England, 1959-60; Lecturer, Medical College, Kanpur, India. Assistant Professor of Surgery, All-India Institute of Medical Sciences, New Delhi, India, 1961-68; Associate Professor and Department Head, 1968-76, Professor and Department Head, 1976-. *Memberships:* Indian Association of Paediatric Surgeons, President, 1980-82; Fellow, National Academy of Medical Sciences; British Association of Paediatric Surgeons; Society for Research into Hydrocephalus and Spina Bifida, England; Asian Association for Paediatric Surgeons, President; Hon Member, Greek Association of Paediatric Surgeons. *Publications:* 'Experimental Study of Splenic Trauma in Monkeys' in 'Journal of Paediatric Surgery', 1971; 'Pathogenesis of Trypan Blue Induced Experimental Hydrocephalus in Rats' in 'Indian Journal of Medical Research', 1972; 'Results of VA Shunt Surgery for Hydrocephalus using Indian Shunt Valve' in "Progressive Paediatric Surgery", volume 15, 1982; 'Hydrocephalus Caused by Tuberculous Meningitis' in 'Journal Kinderchir', 1983. *Honours:* National Awards from: Medical Council of India, 1974, National Research Development Corporation of India, 1974 and 1977, Association of Surgeons of India, 1978, Indian Council of Medical Research, 1982. *Hobbies:* Painting; Photography; Theatre. *Address:* Professor and Head, Department of Paediatric Surgery, All-India Institute of Medical Sciences, New Delhi 110 029, India.

UPTON, Authur Canfield, b. 27 Feb. 1923, Ann Arbor, Michigan, USA. Professor of Environmental Medicine. m. Elizabeth Perry, 1 Mar. 1946, Ann Arbor, 1 son, 2 daughters. *Education:* BA 1944, MD 1946, University of Michigan, Ann Arbor; Intern, 1947, Resident in Pathology, 1948-50, University Hospital, University of Michigan. *Appointments:* Instructor in Pathology, University of Michigan, 1950-51; Pathologist, Biology Division, Oak Ridge National Laboratory, 1951-54; Chief, Pathology-Physiology Section, ibid, 1954-59; Professor of Pathology, 1969-77, Chairman, Department of Pathology, 1969-70, Dean, School of Basic Health Science, 1970-75, State University of New York at Stony Brook; Associate Pathologist, Medical Department, Brookhaven National Laboratory, 1969-77; Director, National Cancer Institute, 1977-79; Director, Institute of Environmental Medicine, 1980-, Professor & Chairman, Department of Environmental Medicine, New York University School of Medicine, 1980-. *Memberships include:* American Association for the Advancement of Science; American Association for Cancer Research; American Association of Pathologists & Bacteriologists; American College of Toxicology; American Society for Experimental Pathology;

International Academy of Pathology; Radiation Research Society; and others. *Publications:* Over 250 publications in medical journals, especially in field of cancer research. *Honours include:* Alpha Omega Alpha; Phi Beta Kappa; Comfort Crookshank Award for Cancer Research, 1978; Institute of Medicine, National Academy of Sciences, 1979. *Address:* Institute of Environmental Medicine, New York University Medical Centre, 550 First Avenue, New York, NY 10016, USA.

URBONT, Allan Lawrence, b. 12 Apr. 1942, Brooklyn, New York, USA. Attending Ophthalmologist. Bayley Seton Hospital, Staten Island and Woodhull Medical Center, Brooklyn; Medical Specialist in Ophthalmology, New York City Department of Health, Richmond County. *Education:* AB, Zoology, Indiana University, Bloomington; MD, Faculty of Medicine and Surgery, Bologna, Italy; Straight Internal Medicine Internship, Radiology 1sr Year Residency, Complete Ophthalmology Residency, US Public Health Service, Marine Hospital, Staten Island; Basic Science Course, Ophthalmology, Harvard University. *Appointments include:* Chief Resident, Ophthalmology, 1979, Assistant Chief, Department of Ophthalmology 1979-81, US Public Health Service Marine Hospital, Staten Island; Medical Director, Bayley Seton Hospitals Physician Assistant Training Program, Staten Island, 1981-84; Adjunct Clinical Instructor, St John's University, Queens, for Department of Allied Health Division, Staten Island, 1981-; Instructor in Clinical Ophthalmology, Bayley Seton Hospital for Physician Assistant Training Program, 1976-; Member, Staten Island Lighthouse Advisory Board, 1984-; Member, Richmond County Speaker's Bureau for New York Eye Bank for Sight Restoration, 1983-. *Memberships:* American Medical Association; New York State and Richmond County Medical Society; New York Academy of Science, etc. *Publications:* Contributor to professional journals. *Honours:* Service with Distinction Award, US Public Head Service Marine Hospital, Staten Island, 1981. *Hobbies:* Archaeology, Anthropology (American Indian); Photography; Collecting rare Medical Books and Articles; History of Medicine; Choral and Classical Music. *Address:* 1288 Victory Boulevard, Staten Island, NY 10301, USA.

URIEL, Guevara, b. 29 Apr. 1928, Managua, Nicaragua. Head of Department of Pathology. m. Nubia Pacheo, 5 Mar. 1982, Leon, Nicaragua, 1 daughter. *Education:* BSc; BA; MD; Anatomic Pathologist and Clinical Pathologist. *Appointments:* Head, Pathology Department, Dean of Medical School, National Chief of Speciality of Pathology, Sub-Director, Medical Service, University Hospital; National Adviser, Ministry of Health; Secretary-Treasurer, Asociacion Nicaraguense de Pat; Secretary-Treasurer, Asociacion Centroamericana de

Patlogia; Professor of Pathology. *Memberships:* American Society of Clinical Pathologists; College of American Pathologists; International Academy of Pathology; Latin American Society of Cytology; Sociedad Latinoamericana de Patologia; Asociacion Centroamericana de Patologia; Asociacion Nicaraguens de Patologia. *Publications:* "Cardiac Arrest and Resuscitation", (with H E Stephenson Jr), 1964; 'Traumatic Damage to the Heart from Cardiac Massage Anesthesiology', 1962; 'Abdominal Angiostrongyliasis in Nicaragua', (with Z Muarte, P Morera). *Honours:* Gold Medal, Outstanding Student in College; Gold Medal, Outstanding Student in Medical School; Gold Medal, Intern and Senior Resident in Pathology; President Gold Medal, Best Professor. *Hobby:* Photography. *Address:* Apartado Postal No 178, Leon, Nicaragua, Central America.

USTIANOWSKI, Peter Andrew, b. 29 Mar. 1941, Biala, Poland. Private Consulting Physician in Homeopathic Medicine. m. Katharine Klein, 16 Jan. 1965, London, England. 2 sons. *Education:* Guy's Hospital, University of London; MB; BS; MRCS; LRCP; D.Obst; RCOG; Faculty of Homeopathy, London; MFHom. *Appointments:* House Physician and House Surgeon, Coventry Group of Hospitals, 1963-64; Resident Obstetrician and Gynaecologist, Gulson Hospital, Coventry, 1964-65; Principal in General Practice in Coventry, 1965-70; Medical Registrar and Clinical Assistant, Royal London Homeopathic Hospital, 1970-78; Medical Director, Birth Control and Pregnancy Counselling and Family Planning Association, London, 1971-76; Medical Officer, Brooke Bond, Oxo Limited, 1972-74; Private Practice, London and Chislehurst, 1969-. *Memberships:* Faculty of Homeopathy; British Society for Medical and Dental Hypnosis; Assurance Medical Society; Family Planning Association; Medical Defence Union. *Publications:* Contributions to British Homeopathic Journal and Journal of Osteopathy and Guy's Hospital Gazette. *Honour:* Study Fellowship of Faculty of Homeopathy in London, 1971-75. *Hobbies:* Collecting Dogs; Ancient History; Cars; Travel; Art Appreciation. *Address:* St Nicholas Lodge, St Pauls Cray Road, Chislehurst, Kent BR7 6QA, England.

UY, Jameson T, b. 3 Oct. 1956, Manila, Philippines. Doctor of Chiropractic. m. Audrey Wong, 21 Jan. 1983, Wheaton, Illinois, USA. *Education:* BS Human Biology, National College; BS Zoology, University of the Philippines, 1977; DC, National College of Chiropractic, Lombard, Illinois, USA, 1983. *Appointments:* Internship, Chicago Health Service, 1982-83; Private Chiropractic, Manila, Philippines, 1983-. *Memberships:* International College of Applied Kinesiology; Sacro-occipital Technique Organisation; American Chiropractic Association; International Chiropractor's Association. *Hobbies:* Shooting; Sports; Golf; Physical Fitness. *Address:* 6 Molave Street, Forbes Park, Makati, Metro-Manila, Philippines.

V

VACCAREZZA, Jorge Raul, b. 14 July 1929, Buenos Aires, Argentina. University Professor; Society Adviser. m. Maria Ines Pena, Buenos Aires, 3 daughters. *Education:* MD, 1954; DMS, 1959; Professor of Neumotisiology, 1967. Fellow: University Madrid, Spain, 1954-55; C Forlanini Institute, University of Rome, Italy, 1955; University of Paris, France, 1959-61; Board certified, Phthisioneumonology and Allergology, 1964. *Appointments:* Head of Asthma and Respiratory Diseases Service, 1957-80, Laboratory Chief, Physiopathology Research, Department of Phthisiology, 1962-80, Professor of Neumotisiology, 1967-, University of Buenos Aires. *Memberships include:* President: Sociedad Argentina de Alergia; Argentine Chapter, American College of Respiratory Dieases; American College of Chest Physicians, Secretary, International Congress of Allergology; International Society of Allergy. *Publications:* "Blood Proteins and Electrolytes in Allergic Asthma", 1959; "Adrenal Function in Asthma", 1960; "Historia del Pueblo Vaccarezza", 1966; "A New Test for Presuntive Diagnosis of Cancer", 1966; author of 82 scientific articles published in professional journals, North and South America, Europe. *Honours:* Llanos Prize, National Academy of Medicine, 1961-65; Muniz Hospital Prize, 1959; E Tornu Prize, National Academy of Medicine, 1965; Prize, Argentine Anticancer League, 1966; Essex Prize, Sociedad Argentina de Alergia, 1974; Archivo Historico Prize, Province of Buenos Aires, 1966; J V Gonzalez Prize, 1982. *Hobbies:* Horsemanship; History. *Address:* Av Callao 1382, 1923 Buenos Aires, Argentina.

VACHHER, Prehlad S, b. 30 Nov. 1933, Pakistan. Staff, Mercywood Hospital, USA. m. Margaret M. Begley, 9 Oct. 1963, Rochester, 2 sons, 3 daughters. *Education:* FSc., Khalsa College, India; MBBS (MD), Medical College, Panjab University, India. *Appointments:* Postgraduate Medicine, King Edward Memorial Hospital, Bombay, 1956-59; Lecturer, Pharmacology, Gandhi Medical College, Bhopal, 1959-60; Staff Psychiatrist, New Jersey State Hospital, USA, 1965-66, Wayne County General Hospital, Michigan, 1966-68; Director, Community Psychiatry, Northville State Hospital, Michigan, 1968-71; Private Practice, Psychiatry, 1966-; Active Staff Psychiatrist, Mercywood Hospital, Ann Arbor, 1970-; Consulting Psychiatrist, Kingswood Hospital, 1966; Annapolis Hospital, 1967, St Joseph Mercy Hospital, 1975. *Memberships:* American Medical Association; American Psychiatric Association; Michigan Psychiatric Society. *Publication:* "Acute Intermittant Hepatic Coma", 'Journal of Association of Physicians of India', 1959. *Hobbies:* Reading; Photography; Travel. *Address:* 32300 Schoolcraft, Livonia, MI 48150, USA.

VAGUE, Jean Marie, b. 25 Nov. 1911, Draguignan, France. Professor of Clinical Endocrinology. m. Denise Marie Jouve, 3 Sep. 1936, 3 sons, 1 daughter. *Education:* Baccalauret, Catholic College, Aix-en-Provence, 1928; MD, Marseilles University, 1935. *Appointments:* Intern, Hotel Dieu Conception, Marseilles, 1930; Resident, 1932-39; Practice Medicine specializing in Endocrinology, Marseilles, 1943-; Associate Professor, Marseilles University, 1946-57; Professor, Clinical Endocrinology, 1957-; Director, Center Alimentary Hygiene and Prophylaxis Nutrition Diseases, National Railways, Mediterranean region, 1958-; Expert, Chronic Degenerative Dieases (Diabetes), WHO, 1962-; Served to Lieutenant French Army, 1939-40. Work: Demonstration of Diabetogenic and Atherogenic Power of Obesity with Topographic distribution fat in upper part of body, evolution of android diabetogenic obesity from 1st stage of efficacious hyperinsulinism to less efficacious hyperinsulinism and hyponinsulinism. *Memberships:* Endocrine Society, USA; American Diabetes Association; Royal Society of Medicine (London); European Association for Study Diabetes; Spanish, Italian, French (Past President) Societies Endocrinology; French Academy of Medicine; Spanish Academy of Medicine; French Language Diabetes Association (Past President). *Publications:* Author of Human Sexual Differentiation, 1953; Notions of Endocrinology, 1965, etc. *Honours:* Decorated Cross, Legion Honor; Acad. Palms; Knight Public Health; Knight, Military Merit; War Cross. *Address:* 411 Ave du Prado, 13008 Marseilles, France.

VAGUE, Philippe, b. 18 Feb. 1938, Marseille, France. Professor of Internal Medicine and Nutrition, Faculte de Medecine de Marseille. m. Veronique Lassmann, 16 Dec. 1982, Marseille, 4 sons, 1 daughter. *Education:* Licence Degree in Biochemistry; DSc; MD; PhD. *Memberships:* French Speaking Association for Study of Diabetes; French Society of Endocrinology; European Association for Study of Diabetes; American Diabetes Association; Endocrine Society. *Publications:* Author of over 250 papers on pathophysiology of non-insulin; 'Etiology of Insulin Dependent Diabetes'; 'Hemorheology and Diabetes'. *Hobby:* Sailing. *Address:* 90 Traverse Fort Fouque, 13012 Marseille, France.

VAILLANT, Jean-Marie, b. 25 July 1927, Paris, France. Head of Department; Professor, Paris Medical School (Maxillofacial Surgery). m. Colette Idoux-Cattoen, 19 Feb., 1955. Viroflay, 2 sons. *Education:* MD; Intern, Paris Hospitals; Certified Professor, Faculty of Medicine, Paris. *Memberships:* French Society of Reconstructive Plastic Surgery; French Society of Cervico-Facial Carcinology, Secretary General; French Society of Stomatology and Maxillofacial Surgery. *Publications:* Numerous papers and contributions on major topics in maxillofacial surgery. *Honours:* Commander, Order of Merit of Republic of the Ivory Coast, 1978; Chevalier, French National Order of Merit, 1982. *Hobby:* Skiing. *Address:* 7 Av de Bretteville, F-92200 Neuilly s/Seine, France.

VAINIO, Harri Uolevi, b. 2 July 1947, Finland. Unit Chief, International Agency for Cancer Research. m. 7 Dec. 1968, Finland, 3 daughters. *Education:* MD, University of Turku, PhD, Finland. *Appointments:* Research Associate, University of Turku, 1969-75; Director of Department, Institute of Occupational Health, Helsinki, Finland, 1975-83. *Memberships:* Society of Toxicology; European Society of Toxicology; European Environmental Mutagen Society. *Publications:* About 200 original articles in the field of toxicology and epidemiology. *Hobbies:* Tennis; Skiing. *Address:* IARC/WHO, 150 Cours Albert Thomas, F-69372 Lyon, Cedex 08, France.

VAJARADUL, Yongyudh, b. 18 Aug. 1940, Chiangmai, Thailand. Orthopaedic Surgeon; Associate Professor, Director, Bangkok Biomaterial Centre. m. Dr Chirasri, 11 Nov. 1968, Bangkok, 1 son, 1 daughter. *Education:* MB, Dr. Med., Freie University, Berlin, 1974; Facharzt fur Orthopaedie, (Berliner Arzte Kammer), 1974; FICS; FIMS; FRCST; Fellow Royal Institute. *Appointments:* Instructor, 1968-76; Assistant professor, 1976-79; Associate Professor, 1979-. *Memberships:* Thai Orthopaedic Association; German & French Orthopaedic Associations; German Sportanzt Federations. *Publications:* "Double Blind Clinical Evaluation of Intra-articular Glucosamine in OPD Patient with Gonerthsoris", 'Clinical Therapeutics', 1981; Author, "Fractures Around the Ankle Joints", 'Journal of the Medical Association of Thailand', 1981. *Honours:* National Award, Inventional Discovery, National Research Council, 1980, 1982, 1983, 1984; Mahidol University Award, 1985. *Hobby:* Antiques. *Address:* Orthopaedic Dept., Siriraj Hospital, Mahidol University, Bangkok 10700, Thailand.

VALADEZ, Stephen Kent, b. 28 July 1950, Chattanooga, Tennessee, USA. General & Cosmetic Dentist. m. Susan Dabney James, 16 June 1973,

Chattanooga, 2 sons. 2Education: BA, Economics, DDS, University of Tennessee. *Appointments:* Instructor, University of Tennessee College of Dentistry, Department of Periodontics, 1976-78; Private Practice. *Memberships:* Founding Member, American Academy of Cosmetic Dentistry; American Dental Association; Tennessee Dental Society; American Society of Clinical Hypnosis; International Society of Hypnosis; Academy of General Dentistry. *Publication:* "Isobutyleyanoacrylate as a Cavity Liner", 'Journal of Prosthetic Dentistry', 1978. *Honours:* Fellow, Charter Member, Academy of Scientific Hypnotherapy. *Hobbies:* Aerobics; Jogging; Golf. *Address:* 5742 Brainerd Road, Cattanooga, TN 37411, USA.

VALENCA, Laericoa Moreira, b. 22 Jan 193, Brazil, Chief of Pulmonology Service. m. Maria Aurea Marcelino Valenca, 31 May 1967, 2 daughters. *Education:* MD, Faculdade de Medicina da Universidade Federal de Pernambuco, Brazil. *Appointments:* Resident in Internal Medicine, Hospital dos Servidores do Estado, Rio de Janeiro, Brazil, Physician, Pulmonary Service, Rio; Fellow (Clinical & Research) in Internal Medicine, Massachusetts General Hospital & Harvard Medical School, Boston, Massachusetts, USA. *Memberships:* Fellow, International Academy of Chest Physicians & Surgeons; American Thoracic Society; Sociedade Brasileira de Pneumologia e Tisiologia. *Publications:* (Co-author) 'Abnormalities of lung function in malignant lymphoma' (in Cancer, 1970); (co-author) 'Pulmonary vascular response of the reimplanted dog lung to hypoxia' (in Journal of Thoracic & Cardiovascular Surgery), 1971. *Hobbies:* Cycling; Tennis. *Address:* Centro Médico de Brasilia, SHLS Q. 716 Bloco E Sala 305, 70.390 - Brasilia, DF, Brazil.

VALENTINE, Anthony Douglas, b. 24 Feb. 1928, Manchester, England. University Professor and Head of Department of Paediatric and Preventive Dentistry. m. Surya Dalla, 11 Aug. 1958, London, 2 daughters. *Education:* MDS, BDS, University of London; LDS, DDPH, Royal College of Surgeons of England. *Appointments:* Principal in General Practice 1958-69; Clinical Lecturer, Royal Dental Hospital, 1961-69; Senior Lecturer, College of Dental Medicine, Rangoon, 1969-72; Lecturer, Sheffield University, 1973-79; Senior Lecturer, Queen's University, Belfast, 1979-82; Consultant Dental Surgeon, Royal Belfast Hospital for Sick Children; Professor and Head of Department of Paediatric and Preventive Dentistry, Queen's University of Belfast; Regional Postgraduate Dental Tutor for Northern Ireland. *Memberships:* Past President, British Paedodontic Society; British Dental Association; British Association for the Study of Community Dentistry; Federation Dentaire Internationale; International Association of Dentistry in Children. *Publications:* Articles on Paediatric and Preventive and Community Dentistry including: "Planning for Dental Health for Developing Nations using a Treatment Need Index" 1980; "Dental Health for a Developing Nationa, Dental Update", 1979; "Geography and Dental Caries" British Dental Journal, 1982. *Honours:* Wisdom Award, 1976, Preventive Dentistry; International Research Prize, World Congress, Hamburg, 1982. *Hobbies:* Sailing; Painting; Photography; Gardening; Walking my dogs; Music; Reading; Cooking. *Address:* The Queen's University of Belfast, Belfast, Northern Ireland.

VÄLIMÄKI, Ilkka Aimo Tapio, b. 21 Mar 1939, Pori, Finland. Associate Professor of Paediatrics. m. (1) Marja-Leena Sävelkoski, 1962, (2) Tuula Aärimaa, 1974, 2 sons, 1 daughter. *Education:* MD, 1965, DMS, 1969, University of Turku, Finland; MSc, Dalhousie University, Halifax, Nova Scotia, Canada, 1971. *Appointments:* House Officer, University Childrens Hospital, Turku, Finland, 1965-69; Canadian Heart Foundation Research Fellow, Dalhousie University, Canada, 1969-71; Lecturer, Physiology and Paediatrics, University of Turku, Finland, 1971-72; Consultant, Neonatology, University Childrens Hospital,

Turku, 1972-73; Associate Professor, Paediatrics, University of Turku, 1974-; British Council Research Fellow, Bioengineering Unit, University of Oxford, John Radcliffe Hospital, Oxford, England, 1985-. *Memberships:* Finnish Medical Society Duodecim; Finnish Medical Association; Past Vice Chairman, Finnish Paediatric Society; Finnish Medical Engineering Society; Past Chairman, Finnish Perinatal Society; European Society for Paediatric Research; Société Francaise de Pédiatrie; Co-Editor, Journal: Gynecol Obstet Investigation. *Publications:* "Special Problems of Electrocardiology", 1971; "Data Processing in Electrocardiology", 1974; "Children and Sports", with J Ilmarinen, 1984; "Respiratory Distress Syndrome", co-author, 1984; contributor to various professional conferences. *Honours:* Research Grants: Academy of Finland, 1972-73, 1981-85; Sigrid Juselius Foundation, 1982-85; J Vainio Foundation, 1978-85. *Hobbies:* Surrealist art; Gastronomy; Sailing. *Address:* Department of Paediatrics, University of Turku, 20520 Turku, Finland.

VALIQUETTE, Jean, b. 5 Oct. 1938, Canada. Chief of Psychiatry, Community Hospital of Western Suffolk. m. Huguette Monty, 25 Aug. 1962, Montreal, 1 son, 1 daughter. *Education:* BA; MD; DPN(P); CRCP(C); FRCP(C). *Appointments:* Chief of Service, Kingspark Psychiatric Center, 1970-72; Active Statt Psychiatry, Community Hospital Western Suffolk, St John's, Smithtown, 1971-85; Chief of Service, Psychiatry, Community Hospital Western Suffolk, 1980-85. *Memberships:* American Psychiatric Association; American Medical Association; Canadian Medical Association; Canadian Psychiatric Association. *Hobbies:* Travel; Skiing; Tennis; Jogging; Fishing; Golf. *Address:* 9 Brooksite Drive, Smithtown, NY 11787, USA.

VALLI, Ragna Marjaleena, b. 1 July 1940, Pori, Finland. Chiropractor. m. Simo Sulo Valli, 22 Feb. 1976, Pori, 2 sons. *Education:* Business College, 1963; DC, Palmer College of Chiropractic, Davenport, Iowa, USA, 1968. *Appointments:* Private practice (2nd DC and 1st female) chiropractor, Pori, Finland. *Memberships:* Founding member, President 1977-83, Finnish Chiropractic Union; International Chiropractic Association; European Chiropractic Union. *Hobbies:* Wintersports; Sailing; Art. *Address:* Paanakedonkatu 12, 28100 Pori, Finland.

VALVO, Barbara-Ann V, b. 7 June 1949, Elizabeth, New Jersey, USA. General Surgeon. *Education:* BA, Hofstra University, New York, 1971; MD, MS, Hershey College of Medicine, Pennsylvania, 1975; Chief Surgical Resident, Allentown-Sacred Heart Hospital Center, Allentown, Pennsylvania, 1980; Certified, American Board of Surgery, 1981; Fellow, American College of Surgeons, 1984. *Appointments:* Assistant Chief of Surgery, US Public Health Service Hospital, New Orleans, Louisiana, 1980; General Surgeon in solo private practice. *Memberships:* Louisiana State Medical Society; Jefferson Parish Medical Society, New Orleans. *Honour:* Upjohn Award 1975 for Creative Scholarship (Research paper). *Hobbies:* Reading; Dog-raising. *Address:* St Jude Medical Centre, 200 West Esplanade Avenue, Suite 610, Kenner, LA 70065, USA.

VAN ASSCHE, Frans-Andre, b. 17 Dec. 1937, Liezele. Professor, Chairman, Obstetrics & Gynaecology. m. Liddy Tierens, 16 Aug. 1964, Breendonk, 3 sons, 1 daughter. *Education:* MD, 1963, PhD, 1970, magna cum laude. *Appointments:* Resident, Obstetrics & Gynaecology, Leuven, 1963-68; Resident, Belfast-/Liverpool, 1968-69; Lecturer, 1970-74, Associate Professor, 1974-78, Professor, 1977-83, Professor, Chairman, 1983-, Obstetrics & Gynaecology, University Leuven. *Memberships:* Chairman, Belgian Society of Obstetrics & Gynaecology; Chairman, European Diabetic Pregnancy Study Group; Nominating Committee, FIGO; European Perinatal Society; Blair Bell Research Society. *Publications:* "The Fetal Endocrine Pancreas: A Quantitative Morfological

Approach", 1970; "Pregnancy and Delivery", 1982; "Contraception", 1984; Co-Author, "Menselijke vruchtbaarheid en geboortenplanning", 1976; "Fetal Growth Retardation", 1982; Author, numerous articles in professional journals & book chapters. *Honours:* Special Prize, 1963; Special Award, Young Researchers, Belgian Research Foundation, 1965. *Hobby:* Gardening. *Address:* University Hospitals, Herestraat 49, 3000 Leuven, Belgium.

VAN CAMP, Koenraad Oktaaf Walter, b. 3 Mar. 1928, Antwerp, Belgium. Ordinary Professor of Urology, University of Antwerp; Head of the Urological Department, University Hospital, Antwerp, 1972-. m. Annie Van Mierlo, 16 Oct. 1954, Hove, 2 sons, 1 daughter. *Education:* MD, 1954, Lic Criminology, 1954, PhD, 1968, State University Genth. *Appointments:* Dean, Faculty of Medicine, University of Antwerp, 1976-84. *Memberships:* President, 1980-82, Vice-President, 1978-80, Belgian Society of Urology; New York Academy of Sciences; European Society of Urology. *Publications:* "Biochemical examinations on human prostate tissue (normal and pathological)", 1968. *Honours:* Officer Order of the Crown, 1976; Officer Order of Leopold, 1979. *Address:* Lovelingstraat 70, B-2008 Antwerp, Belgium.

VAN CAUWENBERGE, Paul Basiel, b. 2 Apr 1949, Zottegem, Belgium. Senior Lecturer in Otorhinolaryngology. m. Lieve Maudens, 17 July 1971, Wetteren, 1 son, 2 daughters. *Education:* BMS, Pre-Med School, 1969, MD, Medical School, 1973, State University of Ghent; Resident in Otorhinolaryngology, University Hospital, Ghent, 1973-78; PhD candidate, Universities of Ghent and Pittsburgh, USA. *Appointments:* Junior Assistant Human Anatomy, 1969-72, Assistant, Department of Otolaryngology, 1973-78, Lecturer, 1979-84, Senior Lecturer, 1985-, State University, Ghent; Visiting Professor, Childrens Hospital, University of Pittsburgh, USA, 1985. *Memberships:* Societies of Otolaryngology, Head and Neck Surgery, Belgium, The Netherlands and France; Belgian, Netherlands Societies of Allergology and Clinical Immunology; European Academy of Facial Surgery; European Academy of Allergology and Clinical Immunology; Proper Meniere Society; Infectious Diseases Society of the Netherlands. *Publications:* Author of 12 books including: "L'Equilibre et ses Problems", 1981; "Otitis Media with Effusion Functional Morphology and Physiopathology of the Structures Involved", 1982; Co-author, Editor and Co-Editor of various other works; Author of 14 monographs. 150 Papers contributed to professional publications including: 'Rhinology'; 'Archives of Otolaryngology'; 'International Journal of Paediatric Otorhonolaryngology'; 'American Journal of Otolaryngology'. Book contributions including: "Surgery and Pathology of the Middle Ear", 1985. *Honours:* President, ISIAN, 1979-82; Vice President, 1985-89, President Elect, 1989, President, 1993, International Rhinologic Society; Secretary General, Belgian Society for Allergology and Clinical Immunology; North Atlantic Treaty Organisation Fellow, 1985. *Hobbies:* Music, folk songs and negro spirituals; Passive practitioner of track and field events, cycling. *Address:* University Hospital, ENT Dept., De Pintelaan 185, B-9000 Ghent, Belgium.

VANCE, Dennis E, b. 14 July 1942, Idaho, USA. Professor, Biochemistry. m. Jean Eaton, 10 June 1967, Bramhall, 1 son, 1 daughter. *Education:* BS, Dickinson College, 1964; PhD, University of Pittsburgh, 1968. *Appointments:* Assistant Professor, 1972-77, Associate Professor, 1977-82, Professor, 1982-86, Head, 1982-86, Biochemistry, Associate Dean, Medicine, 1978-81, University of British Columbia, Canada; Director, Lipid and Lipoprotein Research Group, 1986-; Professor of Biochemistry, 1986-, University of Alberta, Canada. *Memberships:* Canadian and British Biochemical Societies; American Society Biological Chemists. *Publication:* "Biochemistry of Lipids and Membranes", with Jean Vance, 1985.

Honours: NIH Postdoctoral Fellowship, 1968-70; British Heart Foundation-American Heart Association Fellowship, 1972-73; Established Investigator, American Heart Association, 1973-78; Bristol Lipoprotein Research Award, with Jean Vance, 1985. *Hobbies:* Wine-Making; Fishing; Skiing. *Address:* Lipid and Lipoprotein Research Group, University of Alberta, Edmonton, Alberta, Canada, T6G 2R7.

VANCEA, Petre, b. 27 June 1902, Rudari, Romania. Academician. m. Silvia Aurora Simon, 15 Aug 1926, Cluj, 2 sons, 1 daughter. *Education:* Faculty of Medicine, Cluj; MD, University Professor; Corresponding Member, Academia Republicii Socialiste Romania, 1963; Academia Romana de Stiinte Medicale, 1968; Professor Emeritus, University of Bucharest. *Appointments include:* Professor, Head of Chair, Institute of Medicine and Pharmacy, Jassy; Professor, Head of Chair, Ophthalmologic Clinic, Institute of Medicine and Pharmacy, Bucharest. *Memberships:* Society of Biology, France; Institute J Barraquer, Spain; Council of European Society of Ophthalmology; German Academy of Scientists Leopoldana; Vice President, Honorary Member, International Society of Ergophthalmology; Titular Member, Italian Society of Ophthalmology; Local Secretary, International Society of Geographical Ophthalmology. *Publications:* Author of over 700 works including monographs, studies, notes and memories. Books including: "Trachoma Biology"; "The Role of Sympathicus in Eye Physiology"; "On the Tumours of Eye and Its Annexes"; "Glaucoma, Light Again"; "Moving Pictures"; "Permanences"; "Travelling in the Light and Shade"; "Travels"; "Ocular Affections of a Virotic Nature". *Honours:* Laureate, International League Against Trachoma, with Trachoma Gold Medal, 1969. *Hobbies:* Normal social life; Writing. *Address:* Bd Schitu Magureanu nr 3, Sector 5, Bucharest, Romania.

VANDAMME, Jean-Pierre, b. 30 Mar. 1941, Kruishoutem, Belgium. Chief, Hospital Department of Surgery. m. Bernadette Decuypere, 28 Oct. 1970, Knokke, 2 sons, 1 daughter. *Education:* Doctor of Medicine (magna cum laude) 1965, Doctor of Anatomy (summa cum laude) 1971, Catholic University, Louvain, Belgium; Graduation as Surgeon, 1971. *Appointments:* Prosector, Department of Anatomy, Vesalius Institute Louvain, Belgium; Chief, Department of Surgery, Elisabeth Hospital, B-8340 Sijsele-Damme, Belgium. *Memberships:* Fellow, American College of Surgeons; Intern, College of Surgeons; Fellow, Royal College of Surgeons, Belgium; Deutsche Anatomische Gesellschaft; Dutch Anatomic Society; Belgian Society of Digestive Endoscopy; Flemish Association of Gastroenterology; Cancer Center and Cancer Register, Western Flanders. *Publications:* 29 publications including: 'The branches of the celiac trunk' Acta Anat 1922, 1985 with J Bonte; 'One-stage resection and reanatomosis for urgencies upon the left colon and rectum' in Dutch, T Gastro-ent 12, 1985 with T Timmermans; 'A preperitoneal approach in the prosthetic repair of inguinal hernia' Int Surg 70, 1985. *Honour:* Laureate of the Bursary competition of the Secretary of State, 1966. *Hobbies:* Stamp collecting; Antiques. *Address:* Elisabeth Hospital, B-8340 Sijsele-Damme, Belgium.

VANDERBURGH, George Albert, b. 28 Mar. 1946, Toronto, Canada. Family Physician. m. Patricia Anne Faulkner, 9 Aug. 1969, Brighton, Ontario, Canada. *Education:* MD, University of Toronto, 1971; College of Family Physicians of Canada, 1977. *Appointments:* Divisionul Surgeon, St. John's Ambulance Brigade; Ontario Coroner; Family Physician, Shelburne, Ontario-. *Membership:* President, Ontario Lung Association. *Honour:* Canadian Decoration (CD), 1981. *Hobby:* Philately. *Address:* 420 Owen Sound Street, PO Box 204, Shelburne, Ontario, Canada, L0N 1S0.

VANDENBROUCKE, Jan Paul, b. 8 Mar 1950, Leuven,

Belgium. Scientific Collaborator, m. Christina MJE grauls, 7 Sep 1974, 3 daughters. *Education:* Bachelor Philosophy, 1970, MD, 1974, Specialist, Internal Medicine, 1979, University Leuven, Belgium, MSc, Epidemiology, Harvard School of Public Health, USA, 1979; PhD, Epidemiology, Erasmus University, Rotterdam, Netherlands, 1983. *Appointments:* Resident, Internal Medicine, University Leuven, 1974-78; Head, Epidemiology, Netherlands Heart Foundation, 1979-81; Scientific Collaborator, Erasmus University, 1981-; Lecturer, part-time, Epidemiology, Tropical and Public Health, Agricultural University, Wageningen, 1982-; Honorary Consultant, Rheumatology, Leyden University, 1983-. *Memberships:* Society for Epidemiologic Research; American Public Health Association; International Epidemiologic Association. *Publications:* "Oral Contraceptives and Rheumatoid Arthritis", co-author, 'Lancet', 1982; "Parental Survival, an independent predictor of mortality in middle-aged persons", 'American Journal Epidemiology', co-author, 1984. *Hobby:* Medical History. *Address:* c/o Professor L Fuchslaan, 10, 3571 HC Utrecht, The Netherlands.

VAN DER KLOOT, William G, b. 18 Feb. 1927, Chicago, Illinois, USA. Professor and Chairman, Department Physiology and Biophysics, State University of New York, Stony Brook. m. Teresa M C McOustra, 30 Nov. 1984, New York, 2 sons. *Education:* SB cum laude, 1948, AM, 1950, PhD, 1952, Harvard University; Post doctoral Fellow, Jesus College, Cambridge University, England, 1953. *Appointments:* Instructor in Biology, Harvard University, 1953-56; Assistant Professor, Zoology, 1956-67, Associate Professor, Zoology, 1957-58, Cornell University; Professor and Chairman, Pharmacology, 1958-61, Professor and Chairman, Physiology, 1961-71, New York University; Professor of Pharmacological Science, SUBB, 1985-. *Memberships:* Physiological Society; American Physiological Society; IBRO; Society of Neuroscience; Fellow, AAAS; Sigma Xi. *Publications:* "Behavior", 1968. *Honours:* Lalor Fellow, 1950-52; Fellow of the NRC, 1952-53; Fellow, AAAS, 1982; Fogarty Fellow, 1980. *Hobby:* Music. *Address:* Department of Physiology and Biophysics, HSC, SUNY, Stony Brook, NY 11794, USA.

VANDERSCHUEREN, Roland Gaston Jules Robert Antoine, b. 23 June 1943, Gerardsbergen, Belgium. Doctor of Medicine, Head of Department of Pulmonary Medicine. m. Annie de Clercq, 11 July 1943, Geraardsbergen, Belgium, 1 son, 1 daughter. *Education:* MD, University of Leuven, Belgium, 1968; Pulmonary Medicine, St Antonius Hospital, Utrecht, 1968-73; thesis, University of Leiden, 1981. *Appointments:* Staff Member, Department of Pulmonary Medicine, 1973; Head of Department of Pulmonary Diseases, 1977. *Memberships:* Vice-President, Dutch Society for Pulmonology; Fellow, American College of Chest Physicians; European Academy of Allergology & Clinical Immunology; World Association for Bronchology; Foundation of Biophysics; Dutch Society for Immunology. *Publications:* 17 publications in medical journals in the field of pulmonary medicine. *Hobbies:* Tennis. *Address:* Saint Antonius Hospital, Koekoekslaan 1, 3435 CM Nieuwegeln, Netherlands.

VANDERSCHUEREN-LODEWEYCKX, Magda A A, b. 4 May 1943, Antwerp, Belgium. Head, Department of Paediatric and Adolescent Endocrinology; Professor of Paediatrics. m. P Vanderschueren, 29 July 1967, 1 son, 1 daughter. *Education:* MD, summa cum laude; Diploma in School Medicine, cum magna laude; Geaggregeerde van het hoger onderwijs, Faculty of Medicine, Department of Paediatrics. *Appointments:* House Officer, Department of Paediatrics, University of Leuven; Research Associate, National Fonds voor Wetenschappelijk Onderzoek, University of Leuven; British Council Scholar; Senior Registrar, Department of Chemical Pathology, Great Ormond Street Hospital for Sick Children and Department of Growth

and Development, Institute of Child Health, London, England; Qualified Researcher, Department of Paediatrics, Reader in Paediatrics, Professor of Paediatrics, University of Leuven, Belgium; Editorial Board, Acta Paediatrica Belgica. *Memberships:* European Society for Paediatric Endocrinology; Belgian and Dutch Societies for Paediatrics; Belgian Society for Endocrinology; Belgian Study Group for Paediatric Endocrinology; International Study Group for Diabetes in Children and Adolescents. *Publications:* Author or co-author of numerous book chapters contributed to works including: "Neonatal Thyroid Screening", 1980; "Diabetic Angiography in Children", 1981; "Clinical Paediatric Endocrinology", 1981; "Human Growth and Development", 1984. Numerous contributions to national and international journals including: 'Lancet'; 'Pediatric Research'; 'Acta Paediatr Scand'; 'Helv Paediatr Acta'; 'Clinical Endocrinology'; 'Annals of Human Biology'; 'Hormone Research'; 'Annales d'Endocrinologie'; 'Acta Paediatr Belg'. *Hobbies:* Reading; Music; Gardening; Sports. *Address:* U Z Gasthuisberg, Herestraat 49, B-3000 Leuven, Belgium.

VAN DER WEYDEN, Martin Bernard, b. 17 May 1942, Bussum, Netherlands. Director; Professor. m. Enid Merle Donovan, 14 July 1967, Sydney, 1 son, 2 daughters. *Education:* MB BS, Sydney University, 1966; MD, Monash University, 1978; FRACP, 1974; FRCPA, 1980. *Appointments:* Junior Resident Medical Officer, 1966, Senior Resident Medical Officer, 1967, Medical Registrar, 1968, Sydney Hospital; Research Fellow, Monash University, Alfred Hospital, 1970-72; Research Fellow, Duke University, Durham, USA, 1972-75; NH & MRC Research Fellow, 1975-77, Senior Lecturer, 1977-80, Clinical Associate Professor, 1980-84, Professor, 1984-, Haematology, Monash University; Director, Haematology, Alfred Hospital, Prahran, Australia. *Memberships:* Royal Australasian College of Physicians; Royal College of Pathologists of Australia; American Federation of Clinical Research; Haematology Society of Australia, President, 1985-; American Society of Haematology. *Publications:* Over 75 in Haematology and Biochemical journals. *Honours:* Merk Sharpe and Dohme International Fellowship, Clinical Pharmacology, 1972; Eric Susman Prize for Medical Research, RCAP, 1981. *Hobbies:* Squash; Gardening; Reading. *Address:* Haematology Department, Alfred Hospital, Prahran, Victoria, Australia.

VAN RENSBURG, L C J, b. 20 Aug. 1925, Republic of South Africa. University Professor and Head of Department of Surgery. m. Elizabeth Graham-Wolfaardt, 18 Dec. 1966, Republic of South Africa, 1 son. *Education:* MB ChB, 1949, M Med (Surg) 1961, University of Cape Town; FCS (SA) College of Medicine, Republic of South Africa, 1961; FRCS (Eng) Royal College of Surgeons, 1962. *Appointments:* Private Practice, Mombassa, Kenya; Mine Medical Officer, Luanshya, Zambia; RSO, Pontefract General Infirmary, Pontefract, Yorkshire, England; Senior Registrar, St Mary's Hospital, Paddington, London; First Senior Surgeon, Department of Surgery, University of Stellenbosch, Republic of South Africa; Registrar King Edward VII Hospital, Durban, RSA; Private Surgical Practice, Port Elizabeth, RSA; Senior Surgeon, Department of Surgery, University of Stellenbosch, RSA; Professor and Head of Department of Surgery, University of Stellenbosch, RSA. *Memberships:* Medical Association of South Africa; Surgical Research Society of SA; Association of Surgeons of SA; College of Medicine of SA; SA Gastroenterology Society; SA Society of Vascular Surgeons; SA Society of Trauma; University Lecturers Society; SA Association for Medical Education; SA Astronomical Society; Friends of the SA Library Association; Senate Faculty of Medical University of Stellenbosch. *Publications:* 35 published works. *Honours:* Adams Travelling Fellowship, 1962. *Hobbies:* Astronomy; Marathon running; Golf; Tennis; Squash; Mountaineering. *Address:* Department of Surgery, University of Stellenbosch, Medical School, PO Box 63,

Tygerberg 7505, Republic of South Africa.

VAN SELM, Justin Leander, b. 6 Mar 1918, Bloemfontein, Republic of South Africa. Consultant Ophthalmic Surgeon. m. Cherry Ida Drew, 16 Aug 1938, Somerset West, 1 son, 2 daughters. *Education:* MB ChB, University of Cape Town, 1936-42; Diploma in Ophthalmic Medicine and Surgery, Royal College of Surgeons, England; Fellow, American College of Surgeons; Fellow, American Academy of Ophthalmology. *Appointments include:* Registrar 1945-46, Ophthalmic Surgeon 1946-48, Senior Surgeon 1955-78, Groote Schwur Hospital; Private practice of Ophthalmology, 1948-78; Ophthalmic Surgeon in Charge, Red Cross Children's Hospital, 1956-78; Ophthalmology Tutor 1948-52, Senior Lecturer 1955-78, Professor of Ophthalmology and Chairman 1979-84, University of Cape Town. *Memberships include:* South African Medical Association; Ophthalmological Society of United Kingdom; South African Society of Surgeons; President 1972-73, Ophthalmological Society of South Africa; South African Association of Paediatric Surgeons; American Association of Paediatric Ophthalmology and Strabismus; International Paediatric Ophthalmology Society; International Association of Cular Surgeons. *Publications include:* 'Cataract Surgery With General Anaesthesia', 1962; 'Vertical Ocular Deviations in Children', 1962; 'Management of Lacrimal Obstruction in Infants', 1964; 'Cataract and The Pre-Diabetic State', 1965; 'Surgery For Retinal Dysplasia and Hyperplasia of the Persistant Primary Vitreous', 1969; 'Results of Early Surgery in the Management of the Squinting Child', 1973; 'Why Intracapsular Lens Extraction?', 1973; 'Infantile Squint, Its Etiology and Management', 1973; 'Classification of Glaucoma in Children', 1977; 'Some Aspects of Learning Disabilities in Children', 1975. *Honours include:* 1st D J Wood Memorial Lectureship, 1973. *Hobbies:* Golf; Hockey. *Address:* 08 Vincent Pallotti Medical Centre, Pinelands 7405, Republic of South Africa.

VANWAGONER, Wayne Thomas, b. 18 Jan. 1941, Dallas, Texas, USA. President, Wayne T VanWagoner & Associates Inc. m. Patricia Ross, 7 July 1973, Ann Arbor, Michigan, 1 son, 1 daughter. *Education:* Duke University, 1958-61; BS, Michigan Technological University, 1963; MS, ibid, 1965; MS, University of Michigan, 1966; PhD, being completed, University of Utah. *Appointments:* Graduate Research Assistant; Consultant in Environmental Safety Research; Legal Consultant, Expert Witness in field of Highway Safety & Collision reconstruction; Project Leader of US Department of Transport contract for University of California at Los Angeles Trauma Research Group; Partner & Director of Transportation Studies of STEP; Transportation Specialist with Accident Investigation Division of NHTSA; Assistant Professor of Civil Engineering; President & Founder, Wayne T VanWagoner & Associates Inc, Consulting Engineers. *Memberships:* National Safety Council; American Society of Civil Engineers; Institute of Transportation Engineers; American Association of Automotive Medicine; Society of Automotive Engineers; Phi Kappa Phi; Tau Beta Phi; Chi Epsilon. *Publications:* "Investigating the Roadway Environment", 1977; "In-Service Failure of Highway Safety Systems", 1978; "This is the Way it can be", 1980; "Safety: Highway & Air", 1983; "Highways Safety Appurtenances - Successes & Failures", 1983. *Honours:* University of Michigan Highway Safety Research Institute Fellow, 1966; National Highway Traffic Safety Administration Certificate of Recognition, 1973; Institute of Transportation Engineers Intermountain Annual Meetings, 1974-76 outstanding papers. *Hobbies:* Sailing; Skiing; Hiking. *Address:* Wayen T VanWagoner & Associates Inc, 3808 South West Temple, Salt Lake City, UT 84115, USA.

VARBANOVA, Ana, b. 25 July 1922, Strelets, Bulgaria. Director, Institute for Brain Research. m. Nikolai Todorov Todorov, 1 son, 2 daughters. *Educa-*

tion: DMS, Kliment of Ohrid University of Sofia, Faculty of Medicine, 1947; Post Graduate Study, I P Pavlov Institute of Physiology, Leningrad, USSR, 1952-55; Candidate in Medical Sciences, 1955. *Appointments:* Research Scientist, Institute of Experimental Medicine, 1949-52, Senior Research Scientist, 1960, Head of Laboratory, PHD, 1969, Professor of Interoception, Central Laboratory for Brain Research, 1971, currently, Director of Institute for Brain Research, Bulgarian Academy of Sciences, Sofia, Bulgaria. *Memberships:* Fellow; Bulgarian Academy of Sciences; Union of Bulgarian Scientists. *Publications:* "Interoceptive Signalization", 1967; "Interoception and Rhythms in the Nervous System", 1982. Author of some 125 papers published in professional works. *Honours:* Order for Participation in the Resistence, World War II, 1956; Order Cyril and Methodius, 1st Class, 1973; Merited Scientist, 1981. *Address:* 15 San Stefano, Sofia, Bulgaria.

VARENNE, André Georges, b. 27 Nov. 1926, Cabrespine, Aude, France. Consultant Cardiologist. m. Huguette Comes, 11 Dec. 1954, 1 son, 3 daughters. *Education:* MD; National Certification in Cardiology. *Appointments:* Consultant Cardiologist, Department of Cardiology Hôpital Pasteur, Nice; Assistant Professor, Director of the Laboratory of Cardiology (CRECEC), University of Nice. *Memberships:* French Society of Cardiology; Society of Electrics & Electronics; Society of Engineers & Scientists of France; Honorary Member, Italian Institute of Cardio-surgery. *Publications:* Various articles on internal Medicine, Cardiology, Cardiac pacing, Cardiac electrophsyiology; publications in various collective books; Editor of 'High Amplification Electrocardiography'. *Honours:* Patents in Electronics & Cardiac signal processing systems; Research grants from the French Government 1977-79, 1981-82. *Address:* 6 rue Spitaliéri, 06000 Nice, France.

VARIA, Mahesh, b. 7 Oct. 1943, Kampala, Uganda. Associate Professor, Division of Radiation Oncology, Department of Radiology. *Education:* MB ChB, Obstetrics and Gynaecology, Liverpool Medical School, 1967; Residency, Radiation Oncology, Hahnemann Medical College, Philadelphia, USA, 1973-76. *Appointments:* Medical Officer, Ministry of Health, Uganda, 1968-72; Residency Program, Hahnemann Medical College, Philadelphia, USA, 1973-76; Assistant Professor, Division Radiation Oncology, University of North Carolina, Chapel Hill, 1977-83; Associate Professor, 1983-. *Memberships:* American Society of Therapeutic Radiologists and Oncologists; American College of Radiology; American Medical Association; American Association for Cancer Education. *Publications:* Contributor to professional journals including: Co-author, 'Small Cell Carcinoma of the Lung: Results of Combination Chemotherapy and Radiation Therapy', 'North Carolina Medical Journal', 1983; Co-author, 'Chemotherapy and Radiation Therapy of Human Medulloblastoma in Athymic Nude Mice', 'Cancer Research', 1983. *Address:* Division of Radiation Oncology, University of North Carolina, North Carolina Memorial Hospital, Chapel Hill, NC 27514, USA.

VARMA, Vijoy K, b. 6 Nov 1937, Maur, Bihar, India. University Professor. m. Nirmala, 23 June 1958, 1 son, 1 daughter. *Education:* MBBS, Patna University, India, 1959; MSc, Psychiatry, University of Michigan, USA, 1965; Diploma, American Board of Psychiatry and Neurology, 1966; Diploma, Psychological Medicine (England) 1967; Fellow, Royal College of Psychiatrists, UK, 1978; Fellow, National Academy of Medical Sciences (India), 1982. *Appointments:* House Physician, Patna Medical College Hospital, India; Residency in Internal Medicine, Aultman Hospital, Canton, Ohio, USA; Residency in Psychiatry, Columbus State Hospital, Columbus Ohio and Ypsilanti State Hospital, Ypsilanti, Michigan, USA; Medical Assistant in Psychiatry, Abergavenny and Bradford, UK; Assistant Professor, Associate Professor of Psychiatry, PGIMER, Chandigarh, India; WHO

Short-term Consultant, Professor and Head of Department of Psychiatry, PGIMER and Program Director, WHO Collaborating Centre, Postgraduate Institute of Medical Education and Research, Chandigarh, India. *Memberships:* Corresponding Fellow, American Psychiatric Association; Fellow, Indian Psychiatric Society; Member, Indian Medical Association; Fellow, Indian Association for Social Psychiatry. *Honours:* Marfatia Award 1974 and 1985 and Dr D L N Murti Rao Oration Award, 1986, Indian Psychiatric Society; Dr B C Roy National Award, 1984. *Hobbies:* Chess; Poetry; World History. *Address:* Department of Psychiatry, PGIMER, Chandigarh-160012, India.

VARNAI, Ferenc, b. 24 Jan 1928, Budapest, Hungary. Institute Director. m. Dr Agnes Forro, 22 Feb 1974. *Education:* MD; DID; DPH; DTM and H Scientific Degrees, Academy; Specialist in Internal Medicine, Infectious Diseases, Public Health, Tropical Medicine and Hygiene. *Appointments:* Lecturer, 1952, Senior Lecturer, 1962, Associate Professor, 1976, Professor and Head, 1979, Director General, 1981-, Postgraduate Medical School, Budapest; currently, Director, Hungarian Tropical Health Institute, Budapest. *Memberships:* Executive Council, IFIPD; Temporary Advisor, World Health Organisation Malaria Action Programme; Council of Directors, Past President, Tropmedeurop; President, Hungarian Society of Infectology; President, Executive Board, Infectious Diseases; Executive Board, Education Council and Examinations Board of Postgraduate Medical School. *Publications:* Author of 106 works including: "Tropical Diseases"; "Handbook of Tropical Health"; "Tropical Climate - Travel - Health". *Honours:* Honour for Excellent work, 1979, 83; Honour of Excellent Physician, 1984; Professor and Head, 1979. *Address:* Postgraduate Medical School, Chair of Tropical Medicine, H1389 Budapest, Szabolcs u 35, Hungary.

VARON, Silvio S, b. 25 July 1924, Milan, Italy. Professor. m. Ingrid E Brantl, 24 May 1967, Monterey, 1 son, 1 daughter. *Education:* BS, 1941; Chemical Engin D, Federal Polytechnical School of Lausanne, Switzerland, 1945; BA, Classical Lyceum, Milan, Italy; MD, Medical School, University of Milan, 1959. *Appointments:* Research Associate, Biochemistry, City of Hope Medical Centre, Duarte, California, USA, 1962-63; Associate Professor, Biology, Washington University, St Louis, 1964-66; Visiting Associate Professor, Genetics, Stanford University, 1964-67; Associate Professor, 1967-72, Professor, 1972-, Biology & School of Medicine, University of California, San Diego. *Memberships:* Society for Neuroscience; International Society for Neurochemistry; American Society for Neurochemistry; American Society for Cell Biology; International Brain Research Organization. *Publications:* Articles in professional journals. *Honours:* Medical Degree, Summa Cum Laude; 1981 Appointment to the White House, US President's Council on Spinal Cord Injury. *Hobbies:* Skiing; Swimming; Tennis; Golf; Music. *Address:* University of California, Department of Biology, School of Medicine, M-001, La Jolla, CA 92093, USA.

VARONIER, Hubert Silvio, b. 14 Sep 1932, Geneva, Switzerland. Specialist in Allergy and Clinical Immunology; Private Docent at University of Geneva. m. Berta Brucker, 3 Jan 1973, Zermatt, Switzerland, 3 sons, 1 daughter. *Education:* Universities of Geneva and Paris, Certified Physician, 1956, Certification in Paediatrics, 1961, Certification in Allergy and Clinical Immunology, 1979. *Appointments:* Resident in Dermatology, Internal Medicine, Paediatrics, 1957-62; Chief Resident, Paediatrics, 1962-64; Post Doctoral Fellow, Allergy, Johns Hopkins Hospital and University, Baltimore, USA, 1964-65; Children's Research Institute and Hospital, Denver, 1964-66; Assistant Director, Youth Health Service, Geneva, 1966-70; Judge, Geneva Juvenile Court, 1974-present. *Memberships:* Secretary, Swiss Paediatric Society; Swiss Allergy and Immunology Society; Interasma; European Academy of Allergology; Corresponding Fellow, American Academy of

Allergy and Clinical Immunology. *Publications:* Contributions to professional publications including: 'Médecine et Hygiène'; 'Acta Allergologica'; 'Respiration'; 'Rêvue Suisse de médecine'; 'Helvetica Paediatrica'; 'International Archives of Allergy'; 'Rêvue Thérapeutique'; etc. *Hobbies:* Travel; Cross-country skiing; Hiking. *Address:* 11, Rue Emile Yung, CH-1205, Geneva, Switzerland.

VASCONEZ, Luis Oswaldo, b. 17 July 1937, Ambato, Ecuador. Professor and Chief, Division of Plastic Surgery. m. Diane Vasconez, 3 daughters. *Education:* BA magna cum laude, University of Miami, Miami, Florida, USA, 1958; MD, Washington University, Saint Louis, Missouri, 1962; Diplomate, National Board of Medical Examiners, 1963; Board Certified, American Board of Surgery, 1970, American Board of Plastic and Reconstructive Surgeons, 1971. *Appointments include:* Assistant Professor, Division of Plastic and Reconstructive Surgery, Gainesville, Florida, 1969-71, Emory University School of Medicine, Atlanta, Georgia, 1972-78; Professor of Surgery, Division of Plastic and Reconstructive Surgery, University of California at San Francisco , San Francisco, California, 1978-85; Professor and Chief, Division of Plastic Surgery, University of Alabama at Birmingham, Birmingham, Alabama. *Memberships:* American Association of Plastic Surgeons; American Burn Association; Fellow, American College of Surgeons; American Medical Association; American Society of Aesthetic Plastic Surgery; California Society of Plastic Surgeons; Plastic Surgery Research Council; Society of Head and Neck Surgeons; Honorary Member, Argentinian, Costa Rican, Ecuadorian and Chilean Societies of Plastic Surgeons. *Publications include:* 'Comparative Study of Fascicular Nerve Repair and Interfascicular Nerve Grafting in Rhesus Monkeys', 1973; 'Breast Reconstruction After a Radical Mastectomy', 1978; 'Studies of the Blood Supply to the Breast', 1980; 'Blood Supply to the Breast', 1981. *Honours include:* Honor Achievement Award, Pharmacology, Washington University School of Medicine, 1959; James Barrett Brown Award, 1978; James A Valone Distinguished Visiting Professor, 1982; Thuss, Visiting Professor, 1986. *Hobbies:* Reading: Music appreciation; Skiing; Tennis. *Address:* University of Alabama at Birmingham, Division of Plastic Surgery, University Station, Birmingham, AL 35294, USA.

VAUGHN, David Warren, b. 7 Nov 1952, Kingsport, Tennessee, USA. President, Prosthetic Treatment Center Incorporated, Kingsport, Tennessee. Divorced, 1 daughter. *Education:* Certified Prosthetic and Orthotist; BS, State University of New York, 1978; AA, Prosthetics & Orthotics, Carritos College, California, 1976; Postgraduate Prosthetics, Northwestern University, 1978; Postgraduate Prosthetics and Orthotics, UCLA, 1976-77; Internship, Clinical Orthotics, University of Southern California, 1976; Internship, Clinical Prosthetics, Loma Linda University Medical Center, 1976. *Appointments:* US Army, 1976-78; Instructor, Incarnate Word College & US Army Academy of Health Sciences, Fort Sam Houston; Clinical Director, US Army Orthotic Specialist Course; Director and Developer, Prosthetics & Orthotics Department, Thom's Rehabilitation Hospital, Ashville, North Carolina, 1978-79; Clinical Assistant Professor and Director, Duke University Medical Center, 1978-84; President and Founder, Prosthetic Treatment Center Incorporated, Kingsport, Tennessee, 1984-. *Memberships:* American Academy of Orthotists and Prosthetists; American Orthotics and Prosthetics Association; International Society for Prosthetics and Orthotics; Society of Plastic Engineers; Prescription Footwear Association. *Publications:* Author of pamphlets, articles, papers, etc. *Honours include:* Professional Recognition Award, American Academy of Orthotists and Prosthetists, 1979; Several other awards etc, from US Army, University, etc. *Hobbies include:* Hunting; Fishing; Boating; Free Masons; Scottish Rite; Loyal Order of Moose; Girl Scout Volunteer. *Address:* 449 East Market Street, Kingsport, TN 37660, USA.

VAYDA, Eugene, b. 1 Aug. 1925, Ohio, USA. Associate Dean, Community Health. m. Elaine, 2 sons. *Education:* MD; FRCP (C); FACP; FACPM. *Appointments:* Active Staff, University Hospitals, Cleveland, Ohio, 1955-70; Clinical Associate, The Yale-New Haven Hospital, Connecticut, 1969-70; Active Consulting Staff, St Joseph's Hospital, Hamilton, 1970-76; Active Staff, Department of Medicine, McMaster University Medical Centre, Hamilton, 1972-76; Active Staff, Department of Medicine, Toronto Western Hospital, Toronto, Canada, 1976-; Professor, Part-time Department of Clinical Epidemiology and Biostatistics, McMaster University, Hamilton, 1976; Associate Professor, Part-time, Department of Medicine, Faculty of Medicine, 1977, Professor and Chairman, Department of Health Administration, 1976-81, Associate Dean, Division of Community Health, 1981-, Chairman, Graduate Department of Community Health, 1981-, University of Toronto. *Memberships:* Fellow, American College of Physicians; Fellow, American College of Preventive Medicine; Fellow, American Public Health Association; Fellow, Royal College of Physicians and Surgeons (Canada); Royal Society for Health. *Publications:* 'Health Policy in Canada: The Lalonde Report and Emerging Patterns', 1978; 'Five Year Study of Surgical Rates in Ontario's counties', (with J Barnsley, W R Mindell, B Cardillo), 1984. *Honours:* Faculty Fellowship, The Millbank Memorial Fund, 1966-73. *Hobby:* Theatre. *Address:* Division of Community Health, Faculty of Medicine, Medical Science Building, University of Toronto, Toronto, Ontario, Canada M5S 1A8.

VEENSTRA, Emma, b. 1 June 1922, Michigan, USA. Massage Therapist and Instructor. m. 7 Nov. 1952. *Education:* Detroit Institute of Technology, 1941; Spa School of Swedish Massage, 1942; Waddington School of Physical Therapy, 1943; Mid-Western University 1961. *Appointment:* Detroit School of Swedish Massage, 1949-. *Memberships:* American Massage Therapy Association, Education Director 1963-65; National Health Federation, Michigan President. *Honour:* Certificate of Award, AMTA, 1974. *Hobbies:* Reading; Cycling. *Address:* 15139 Grand River, Detroit, MI 48227, USA.

VEKEMANS, Michel Jean-Jacques, b. 1 Dec. 1948. Anvers, Belgium. Associate Professor of Pathology, Paediatrics, Human Genetics and Biology. m. Nicole Leurquin, 2 May 1970, Namur, 1 son, 1 daughter. *Education:* BSc, Namur, Belgium, 1970; MD, cum laude, Louvain, 1974; PhD summar cum laude, McGill University, Canada, 1981; FCCMG, 1983. *Memberships:* American Society of Human Genetics; Genetics Society of Canada; Teratology Society. *Publications:* Contributions to learned journals. *Hobbies:* Baroque music; Sailing. *Address:* The Montreal Children's Hospital, Department of Pathology, 2300 Tupper, Montreal H3H 1P3, Canada.

VELASCO, Xavier George, b. 11 Nov 1954, Los Angeles, California, USA. Chiropractic Office President and Owner. *Education:* AA, Mount San Antonio Community College, 1975; BA, New College of California, 1977; Diplomate, National Board of Chiropractic Examiners, 1977; DC, Cleveland College of Chiropractic, 1977; Licensed, California State Board of Chiropractic Examiners, 1978; Certified X-Ray Supervisor and Operator, 1978; Graduate, Erhardt Radiologic Studies, 1978; Recognised Disability Evaluator, California Chiropractic Association, 1980. *Appointments:* President, Owner, La Mirada Chiropractic Officer, La Mirada, California. *Memberships:* American and California Chiropractic Associations; Sigma Chi Psi; American Chiropractic Association Council on Roentgenology. *Honours:* Graduated Summa Cum Laude, 1977; Valedictorian of Graduating Class, 1977. *Hobbies:* Basketball; Football; Baseball; Aerobics; Weightlifting; Cycling. *Address:* La Mirada Chiropractic Office, 15020 Imperial High-

way, La Mirada, CA 90638, USA.

VENDITTI, Patrick Peter, b. 16 June 1949, Rome, New York, USA. Chiropractic Physician; Instructor; Consultant. *Education:* BA, Psychology; BS, Human Biology; DC. *Appointments:* Chiropractic Physician, Private Practice, 1978-; Industrial Consultant, 1982-; Author, 1983-; Lecturer, 1982-; Post-graduate Instructor, 1985. *Memberships:* American Chiropractic Association; American Public Health Association; American College of Sports Medicine; American Medical Writer's Association. *Publications:* "It's Your Body", video training programme, 1984; "Discerning the Legitimacy of soft-tissue injuries", 'Proceedings of the American Society of Safety Engineers', 1983. *Hobbies:* Racquetball; Skiing; Sailing; Photography. *Address:* 22 East Avenue, New Canaan, CT 06840, USA.

VERCO, Peter Joseph Willis, b. 15 May 1947, Adelaide, Australia. Paediatric Dental Surgeon. m. Phillippa Margaret Burnett, 17 August 1973, Adelaide, 1 son, 2 daughters. *Education:* BDS; BSc.Dent. (Hons); LDS; MDS; FAAPD. *Appointments:* President, Australian Society of Dentistry for Children (SA) 82, 83; President, Australian Dental Association (SA Branch) 85; Part-time Tutor, Children's Dentistry, The University of Adelaide. *Memberships:* Australian Dental Association; Australian Society of Dentistry for Children; Australian Society of Endodontology. *Publications:* "Formocresol Pulpotomies in Primary Teeth", 'International Association of Dental Research', 1975; "Formocresol Pulpotomies in Primary Teech", 'International Association of Dentistry for Children', 1984; "Microbiological Effectiveness of a Reduced Concentration of Buckley's Formocresol", 'Paediatric Dentistry', 1985. *Honours:* Baillieu Medical Research Grant, 1974, 1975; G O Lawrence Scholarship, 1974, 1975; Australian Society of Endodontology Travel Grant, 1975. *Hobbies:* Flying; Water Skiing; Snow-Skiing; Golf. *Address:* 11 Pridmore Road, Glen Osmond SA 5064, Australia.

VERHEY, Lynn James, b. 13 Apr. 1940, Michigan, USA. Associate Radiation Biophysicist, Massachusetts General Hospital. m. Marilyn Paul, 23 Dec. 1967, Waterloo, Iowa, 1 son. *Education:* AB, Kalamazoo College, 1962; MS, 1964, PhD, 1968, University of Illinois, Urbana, Illinois. *Appointments:* Assistant Professor in Residence, University of California, Los Angeles, 1968-70; Lecturer, 1970-72; Assistant Professor of Physics, 1972-75, Assistant Professor of Radiation Therapy, 1975-, Harvard University Medical School, Cambridge, Massachusetts. *Memberships:* Phi Delta Kappa; American Physical Society; Sigma Pi Sigma; American Association of Physics Teachers; American Association of Physicists in Medicine; American Society of Therapeutic Radiologists; Radiation Research Society. *Publications:* 'Experimental investigation of CP violation in K^3c^o decays', (co-author), 1966; 'The determination of absorbed dose in a proton beam for purposes of charged particle radiation therapy', 1979; 'Precise positioning of patients for radiation therapy', 1982; 'Proton beam therapy', (with Munzenkider), 1982. *Honours:* Phi Beta Kappa, 1962; John Wesley Hornbeck Prize in Physics, 1962. *Hobby:* Running. *Address:* Department of Radiation Medicine; Massachusetts General Hospital, Boston, MA 02114, USA.

VERNICK, David Murray, b. 18 Oct. 1951, Cocoa, Florida, USA. *Education:* BA, University of Kansas, 1973; MD, Johns Hopkins Medical School, 1977. *Appointments:* Surgical Intern, 1977-79, Assistant Resident, Surgery, 1978-79, George Washington Hospital; Resident, Otolaryngology, Massachusetts Eye and Ear Infirmary, Boston, 1979-82; Fellow, Otology, Neurotology, Skull Base Surgery, University of Michigan, 1982; Fellow, Otology, Providence Hospital, 1983; Instructor, Otolaryngology, Harvard Medical School, 1983; Assistant, Otolaryngology,

Massachusetts Eye & Ear Infirmary, 1983; Assistant Surgeon, Beth Israel Hospital, 1983; Associate Surgeon, Brigham & Women's Hospital, 1983. *Memberships:* American and Massachusetts Medical Associations; Fellow, American Society for Laser Medicine & Surgery; Fellow, American Academy of Otolaryngology; Fellow, American Neurotology Society; etc. *Publications:* Co-author, "Manual in Otolaryngology", 1985; "Otologic Complications of Laser Surgery", in 'Complications of Laser Surgery of the Head and Neck' in press; "The Painfully Discharging Ear", in 'Office Practice in Medicine', in press; numerous journal articles. *Address:* 29 Garfield Street, Quincy, MA 02169, USA.

VERNON-ROBERTS Barrie, b. 22 Mar. 1935, North Wales. Professor of Pathology. m. 1960, 2 sons, 2 daughters. *Appointments:* House Surgeon and House Physician, Charing Cross Hospital, London, 1960-61; Lecturer in Anatomy, King's College, University of London, 1962-68; Lecturer in Morbid Anatomy, 1969-70, Senior Lecturer in Morbid Anatomy, 1970-76, The London Hospital Medical College; Honorary Consultant Pathologist, The London Hospital, 1972-76; Co-Director, Bone and Joint Research Unit, The London Hospital Medical College, 1972-76; Professor of Pathology, University of Adelaide and Head of Division of Tissue Pathology, Institute of Medical and Veterinary Science, and Senior Visiting Pathologist, Royal Adelaide Hospital, 1976-. *Memberships:* British Rheumatism Association; Australian Rheumatism Association; Pathological Society (UK). *Publications:* "The Macrophage" 1972; Numerous articles on clinical and experimental pathology of muskulo-skeletal disease. *Honours:* Association Prize, British Association of Physical Medicine and Rheumatology, 1971; Margaret Holroyde Prize, Heberden Society, 1972. *Hobbies:* Music; Natural History, Bush walking. *Address:* Department of Pathology, The University of Adelaide, South Australia 5001.

VERTUA, Rodolfo, b. 17 July 1932, Milan, Italy. Professor of Pharmacology and Pharmacognosy. m. Alda Boeuf, 14 Oct. 1964, Milan, 2 sons, 1 daughter. *Education:* MD, 1957, LD in Pharmacology, 1964, University of Milan. *Appointments:* Visiting Assistant Professor, University of Detroit, Michigan, USA, 1960; Assistant Professor, 1965-69, Associate Professor 1969-73, Professor 1973-, University of Trieste. *Memberships:* New York Academy of Sciences; Societa Italia di Farmacologia; International Association of Radiopharmacology; American Society of Hospital Pharmacists; Associazione Biologi di Farmacia; European Neuroscience Association. *Publications:* Numerous publications in the field of Pharmacology. *Honour:* President of Associazione Biologi di Farmacia. *Address:* Istituto di Farmacologia e Farmacognosia, Universita degli Studi, Via A Valerio 32, 1-34100 Trieste, Italy.

VESENJAK-HIRJAN, Jelka, b. 2 Feb 1913, Ljubljana, Yugoslavia. Professor (Emeritus) of Microbiology. m. Franjo Hirjan, 5 Mar 1958, Zagreb, Yugoslavia. *Education:* MD, Postgraduate courses in virology in Denmark, England, USA; Study tours as Fellow of World Health Organisation. *Appointments:* Clinical Practice, General Hospital, Varazdin, Yugoslavia, 1942; Physician, Liberation Army, 1943-45; Assistant, Assistant Professor, Professor, Medical Faculty, University of Zagreb, 1945-, President, Chair of Microbiology, Head of Department of Virology of 'Andrija Stampar' School of Public Health, Medical Faculty, University of Zagreb; Founder of Medical Virology in Croatia. *Memberships:* Microbiological Society of Croatia, President 1969-75; Yugoslav Microbiological Association, President 1971-76; Federal Research Council; World Health Organisation Panel of Virus Diseases; Fellow, European Microbiological Society, 1974-; New York Academy of Sciences, 1974-. *Publications:* 'Tick-borne Encephalitis in Croatia', 1976; 'Arbo Viruses in the Mediterranean Countries', 1980; 'Virus Meningo-Encephalitis in

Slovenia', Bulletin of the WHO, 1955; 'Isolation of Bhanja Virus', American Journal of Tropical Medicine & Hygiene, 1977; over 100 other scientific papers. *Honours:* Partisan Memorial Medal, 1941; Award for Life Work, 1982; Various Decorations & Distinctions; Honorary Member, Microbiological Society of Croatia, 1979; Honorary Member, American Society of Tropical Medicine & Hygiene, 1980. *Hobbies:* Travel; Swimming. *Address:* Jabukovac 27, 41000 Zagreb, Yugoslavia.

VIBY-MOGENSEN, Jørgen, b. 13 May 1938, Denmark. Associate Professor. m. Grethe Funder, 17 Mar. 1962, 3 sons. *Education:* MD, Århus University, Denmark, 1966; Diploma of Anaesthesia, World Health Organisation, Copenhagen, Denmark, 1971; Specialist in Anaesthesia, Denmark, 1974; Doctor of Medicine, PhD, Copenhagen University, 1983. *Appointments:* Assistant Professor, Department of Anaesthesia, Gentofte Hospital, Copenhagen University, Denmark, 1975-76; Associate Professor, Department of Anaesthesia, Herlev University Hospital, Copenhagen, Denmark, 1976-. *Memberships:* Danish Society of Anaesthesiologists; Scandinavian Society of Anaesthesiologists; American Society of Anaesthesiologists; European Academy of Anaesthesiology. *Publications:* 'A Danish Cholinesterase Research Unit', (with H K Hanel), 1977; 'Residual Curarization in the Recovery Room' (with Bent Chraemmer Jørgensen MD, Helle Ørding MD), 1979; 'Correlation of Succinylcholine Duration of Action with Plasma Cholinesterase Activity in Subjects with the Genotypically Normal Enzyme', 1980; 'Succinylcholine Neuromuscular Blockade in Subjects Heterozygous for Abnormal Plasma Cholinesterase', 1981; 'Succinylcholine Neuromuscular Blockade in Subjects Homozygous for Atypical Plasma Cholinesterase', 1981; 'Clinical Assessment of Neuromuscular Transmission', 1982; 'Cholinesterase and succinylcholine', 1983; 'Interaction of Other Drugs with Muscle Relaxants', 1985; 'Clinical Measurement of Neuromuscular Function: An Update', 1985; 'Posttetanic Count (PTC): A New Method of Evaluation an intense Nondepolarizing Neuromuscular Blockade', (with Paul Howardy-Hansen MD, Bent Chraemmer-Jørgensen MD), 1981. *Hobby:* Tennis. *Address:* Department of Anaesthesia, Herlev University Hospital, Herlev Ringvej, 2730 Herlev, Denmark.

VICE, Marvin Clark, b. 13 July 1946, Mount Sterling, Kentucky, USA. Orthopaedic Surgeon. m. Pamela Sue, 22 Dec 1979, 2 sons, 1 daughter. *Education:* BS University of Dayton, 1970; DO, Kansas City College of Osteopathic Medicine 1975. *Appointments:* Clinical Professor, Ohio University College of Osteopathic Medicine; Clinical Professor in Orthopaedics, Pacific College of Osteopathic Medicine. *Memberships:* American Osteopathic Association; American Osteopathic Academy of Orthopaedics. *Publications:* 'Piso-Homate Hiatus Syndrome' (in Journal of Hand Surgery 1983); 'Dupuytren's Contracture' (in DO Journal 1982). *Hobbies:* Scuba Diving; Camping; Cars. *Address:* 1130 N Monroe Drive, Xenia, OH 45385, USA.

VICKERS, Tony, b. 6 July 1932, Denton, Lancashire, England. United Kingdom Administrator, Ludwig Institute for Cancer Research. *Education:* BA, 1953, MA, 1957, PhD, 1958, Sidney Sussex College, Cambridge. *Appointments:* Fellow, Sidney Sussex College, Cambridge, 1956-70; Lecturer, Physiological Laboratory, University of Cambridge, 1956-71; Member of Headquarters Staff, United Kingdom Medical Research Council, 1972-84; Head of Medical Division, 1980-84. *Address:* Ludwig Institute, Haddon Laboratories, Clifton Avenue, Belmont, Sutton, Surrey, England.

VICTORIN, John Lars Hugo, b. 19 July 1931, Sweden. Professor, Chairman, Kuwait University. m. Inger Lindberg, 20 May 1956, Goteborg, 2 sons, 2 daughters. *Education:* MD, 1958; PhD, University of Goteborg, 1970. *Appointments:* Paediatrician, Boras,

1958-62, University of Goteborg, 1962-68; Consultant Neonatologist, 1968-74, Associate Professor, 1971-, University of Goteborg; Research Lecturer, Vanderbilt University, Nashville, USA, 1971-72; Chairman, Paediatrics, Uddevalla, 1974-82; Senior Consultant, Ministry of Health, Qatar, 1979-80; Professor, Chairman, Paediatrics, Kuwait University, 1982-. *Memberships:* Swedish Medical Association; Swedish Society of Medicine; Swedish Paediatric Association; Royal Society of Medicine; International College of Paediatricians, Fellow; Kuwait Medical Association. *Publications:* 70 articles; Book chapters, etc. *Hobby:* Sailing. *Address:* Central Hospital, 45180 Uddevalla, Sweden.

VIGDOR, Robert Charles, b. 27 Apr. 1947, New York City, USA. Assistant Professor, New York Medical College. *Education:* BA, Southampton College of Long Island University, 1969; MD, Universidad Autonoma de Guadalajara, 1973. *Appointments:* Consultant, Veterans Administration Hospital, New York; Attending Physician, Westchester County Medical Center, Valhalla, New York. *Memberships:* Medical Society of the State of New York; American Psychiatric Association. *Address:* RR5, Box 133, Putnam Valley, NY 10579, USA.

VILARDELL, Francisco, b. 1 Apr. 1926, Barcelona, Spain. Professor of Medicine. m. Leonor March, 18 May 1958, 1 son, 2 daughters. *Education:* MD, University of Barcelona; DSc (Med), University of Pennsylvania, USA. *Appointments:* Instructor in Medicine, University of Pennsylvania, USA; Fellow in Gastroenterology, Graduate Hospital, Philadelphia; Head, Gastroenterology Service, Hospital Santa Cruz y San Pablo, Barcelona, Spain; Director, Professional School of Gastroenterology, Universidad Autonoma, Barcelona; Director General, Health Planning, Ministry of Health, Madrid. *Memberships:* Fellow, American College of Physicians; American Gastroenterological Association; American College of Gastroenterology; British Society of Gastroenterology; President 1970-74, European Society for Gastrointestinal Endocopy; President 1975, European Society for the Study of the Liver; President, World Organisation of Gastroenterology, 1982-; Swiss, French, Spanish, Portuguese, Venezuelan, Colombian, Argentinian, Polish and Hungarian Societies of Gastroenterology. *Publications:* 2 books; 20 chapters of books; 150 papers. *Honours include:* Doctor honoris causa, University of Toulouse, France. *Hobby:* Music. *Address:* Juan Sebastian Bach II, 08021 Barcelona, Spain.

VILJOEN, Charles Eugene Marais, b. 20 May 1930. Secretary General, Medical Association of South Africa. m. Retha Roux, 17 Dec. 1952, Pretoria, 1 son, 2 daughters. *Education:* MB ChB. *Appointments:* General Practice, Heidelberg, Transvaal, 1955-65; Captain, Witwatersrand Commando, SA Defence Force; Medical Officer of Health, Heidelberg, Railway Medical Officer, Heidelberg, Hospital Board, Heidelberg; Assistant Secretary, 1965-67, Associate Secretary, 1967-71, Secretary General, 1971-, Medical Association of South Africa. *Memberships:* Medical Association of South Africa, 1965; South African Academy for Arts and Science; Council Member, World Medical Association. *Publications:* Numerous. *Honours:* Bronze Medal, Medical Association, South Africa for signal service, 1981. *Hobbies:* Golf; Swimming; Photography. *Address:* PO Box 29272, Alkantrant, 0005 Republic of South Africa.

VILLALBA, Abdon Enrique, b. 26 May 1929, Argentina. Psychiatrist in Private Practice. m. Francisca, 23 July 1955, Rosario, Argentina, 1 son, 3 daughters. *Education:* BA, Teacher's National School, Manuel Belgrano, Sgo. del Estero, Argentina, 1946; BS, National College, Sgo. del Estero, 1947; MD, University of Litoral, Rosario, 1954. *Appointments include:* Teaching Staff, St Thomas Hospital; Senior Staff, Akron City Hospital; Courtesy Staff: Akron General Medical Center, Barberton City Hospital, Children's Hospital; Assistant Clinical Professor, Northeastern

Ohio University College of Medicine; Credential Committee and Program Committee, Summit County Medical Society, 1980; History and Ad Hoc Committees, Ohio Psychiatric Association, 1980-81; Program and Continuing Education Committees, OPA, 1980; Medical Records and Medical Quality Care Audit Committees, St Thomas Hospital, 1980; OPA Peer Review Committee and Membership Committee, 1982-85; Electoral Committee and Mediation Committee, of SCMS, 1982; Assistant Professor of Psychiatry at NEOUCOM, 1982. *Memberships:* Member and Officer of numerous professional organizations. *Publications:* "Long Live the King, Mar. 1985"; The Search for Excellence, Apr. 1985; Project May: Physician Physical Examination Month, May 1985; The Politics of Nutrition, June 1985; Transplantation: A Changing World View, July 1985. All published in The Bulletin, Summit County Medical Society. *Honours include:* Fellowship Award from American Psychiatric Association, 1983. *Hobbies:* Swimming; Skiing; Photography; Travel. *Address:* 2341 Oakwood Drive, Cuyahoga Falls, OH 44221, USA.

VILLANUEVA, Thelma Guilas, b. 3 Apr 1931, Philippines. Director, Cytopathology & Surgical Pathology; Acting Chief, Laboratory Service. m. Francisco S Villanueva, 12 Aug 1963, Media, USA, 3 sons, 3 daughters. *Education:* BA, Biology; MD; FCAP; MIAC. *Appointments:* Instructor, Staff Pathologist, Hahnemann University & Hospital; Director, Cytopathology Division of Analytical Pathology, Philadelphia General Hospital; Staff Pathologist, VA Medical Centre; Acting Chief, Laboratory Service, VA Medical Centre; Assistant Professor, Medical College of Pennsylvania. *Memberships:* Delaware Valley Society of Cytology; Metropolitan Washington Society of Cytology; American Society of Cytology; International Academy of Cytology; Pathologic Society of Philadelphia; College of American Pathologists. *Publications:* At least 10 with various authors, 2 most recent: "Autopsy Study Correlating Degree of Osteoarthritis, Synovitis and Evidence of Articular Caldification", 1984; "Respiratory Cryptosporidosis in Aids", 1984; "Medical Advice to Sexual Freedom (Sexually Transmitted Diseases)", in Press. *Honours:* Pathology Award, Research Studies on Veratrum Viride, 1954; Marquis Award, 1985; Legion of Honour 1977; American Cancer Society, 1962; AMA Physician's Award and Pathology Continuing Medical Education Award, every 3 years, 1977-. *Hobbies:* Music; Tennis; Swimming. *Address:* VA Medical Centre, Philadelphia, PA 19104, USA.

VILLENEUVE, Andre, b. 17 Sep. 1932, Chicoutimi, Canada. Professor, Department of Psychiatry, Laval University, Quebec; Psychiatrist-in-Chief, Clinique Roy-Rousseau. m. Gisele Bellefeuille, 16 June 1958, 1 daughter. *Education:* MD, Laval University, Quebec; Graduate, New York School of Psychiatry, USA; MSc, McGill University, Montreal; Fellow, Royal College of Physicians and Surgeons of Canada. *Appointment:* Consultant Emeritus, Neuropsychopharmacology Unit, Centre Hospitalier Robert Giffard, Quebec, Canada. *Memberships:* American Psychiatric Association, Fellow; Canadian Psychiatric Association; Royal College of Psychiatrists, Fellow; Collegium Internationale Neuropsychopharmacologicum, Fellow; American College of Forensic Psychiatry, Fellow; also member or fellow of several other professional organizations. *Publications:* Around 150 various scientific publications; 5 Books including: Editor, Lithium in Psychiatry, 1976; Co-Editor, NeuroPsychopharmacology, 1978; Editor, Brain Neurotransmitters and Psychiatry, 1985. *Hobbies:* Tennis; Alpine Skiing. *Address:* 1536 Parc Beauvoir, Quebec G1T 2M4, Canada.

VINCENT, Anne-Marie Claire, b. 14 Feb. 1958, Melbourne, Australia. Private Practitioner in Restricted Practice, Orthodontics. *Education:* Bachelor of Dental Science; Candidate, Master in Dental Science, Melbourne University. *Appointments:* Private Practice,

General Practice, Dental. *Memberships:* Australian Society of Orthodontists; Australian Society of Dentistry for Children; International Association of Dentistry for Children; American Society of Dentistry for Children; Australian Dental Association. *Hobbies:* Philately; Handicrafts; Tennis. *Address:* 11 Flora Grove, East Ivanhoe, Victoria 3079, Australia.

VINCENT, Jean-Louis, b. 20 May 1949, Schaerbeek, Belgium. Specialist in Intensive Care. m. Cong-Huyen-Ton-Nu Bach Hac, 29 Sep 1979, Brussels, 1 daughter. *Education:* MD, 1973; Internal Medicine, 1978; PhD (Agrégé), 1982. *Appointments:* Internal Medicine, St Pierre University Hospital, Brussels, Belgium; Critical Care Medicine, Centre for the Critically Ill, University of Southern California at Los Angeles, USA. *Memberships:* Society of Critical Care Medicine; Council Member, European Society of Intensive Care; American College of Chest Physicians; Vice-President, European Shock Society. *Publications:* Over 100, including: "Circulation", 1980, 1981; "American Journal of Surgery", 1981; "American Review Respiratory Diseases", 1981; "Chest", 1981, 1984, 1985; "Critical Care Medicine", 1983, 85; 2 books on "Update" in "Intensive Care and Emergency Medicine", 1984, 86, 86. *Address:* Erasme University Hospital, Department of Intensive Care, Route de Lennik 808, 1070, Brussels, Belgium.

VIRTAMA, Pekka Eero Juhani, b. 23 June 1922, Helsinki, Finland. Professor of Radiology. m. Sinikka Nivala, 27 June 1948, Lapua, Finland, 3 daughters. *Education:* Med. Sci. Dr. 1958; ECFMG, USA, 1970; FLEX (MO), 1984. *Appointments:* Director, Radiological Department, Internal Medicine Department, University Hospital, Helsinki, Finland; Chairman and Professor, Radiological Department, Turku University Hospital; Visiting Professor, University of Rochester, New York, USA currently. *Memberships:* Finnish Medical Association; Finnish Radiological Society; Swedish Radiological Society; Hungarian Radiological Society (Honorary Member); Sigma Xi (USA); Skeletan Society (International); New York Academy of Science. *Publications:* "Cortical Thickness of Finger Bones", 1967; "Bone Radiology" (University textbook), 1980, 1983; approximately 200 articles in professional journals dealing with medical radiology. *Honours:* The British Council Scholarship, 1957; ASLA-Fulbright Scholarship, 1964; Commander of the Finnish Lion Order, 1976. *Hobbies:* Viola music; Hiking in Lappland. *Address:* Radiology Department, PO Box 648, The University of Rochester Medical Centre, Rochester, NY 14642, USA.

VIRTANEN, Simo Kasper, b. 4 Nov. 1925, Varkaus, Finland. Head of Finnish National Public Health Institute. m. Raili Virtanen MD, 4 Sep. 1960. *Education:* MD; DM Sci; Professor. *Appointments:* Acting Professor of Microbiology, University of Oulu, Finland; Acting Professor of Medical Microbiology, Acting Professor of Hygiene, Universit, of Turku, Finland; Head, National Public Health Institute, Turku, Finland. *Memberships:* Society for General Microbiology; American Public Health Association; International Society for Human and Animal Mycology; International Union against Tuberculosis. *Publications:* 90 publications on medical microbiology and immunology. *Hobbies:* Foreign languages; Gardening. *Address:* National Public Health Institute, Box 57, 20521 Turku, Finland.

VISOTSKY, Harold Meryle, b. 25 May 1924, Chicago, USA. University Professor and Chairman, Department of Psychiatry. m. Gladys Mavrich, 18 Dec. 1955, Chicago, 1 son, 1 daughter. *Education:* Baylor University, Waco, Texas, 1944-45; Sorbonne University, Paris, 1945-46; BS, University of Illinois, Urbana, 1947; MD, University of Illinois College of Medicine, 1947-51. *Appointments:* Psychiatric Consultant Fellow to National Federation for Infantile Paralysis and University of Illinois, Polio Respiratory Center, 1955-59; Acting Head, Inpt. Division, University of Illinois, Neuropsychiatric Institute, 1957-58; Director

of Psychiatric Residency Education and Training, University of Illinois, 1955-59; Chief of Female Psychiatric Section, Chicago State Hospital, State of Illinois Department of Mental Health, 1955-59; Director of Mental Health, Chicago Board of Health, 1959-63; Director, State of Illinois Department of Mental Health, 1963-69; Chief of Service, Department of Psychiatry, Wesley and Passavant Memorial Hospitals, 1969-74; Owen L Coon Professor and Chairman, Department of Psychiatry and Behavioral Sciences, Northwestern University Medical School, Director, Institute of Psychiatry, Northwestern Memorial Hospital, 1974-. *Memberships include:* American Association of Psychoanalytic Physicians; American Bar Association; American Board of Psychiatry and Neurology (Emeritus Director and Examiner); American College of Mental Health Administration; American Hospital Association (Consultant, Ctr for Mental Health and Psychiatric Services 1979-) American Orthopsychiatric Association; American Psychiatric Association. *Publications:* "First US Mission on Mental Health Services to the USSR" 1969; Contributions to medical journals and edited scientific volumes. *Honours:* The Institute of Pennsylvania Hospital Strecker Award, 1969; Anti-Defamation League, B'nai B'rith - Distinguished Service Award, 1978; American College of Psychiatrists' Bowis Award, 1981; American Psychiatric Association, Administrative Psychiatry Award, 1985. *Hobby:* Tennis. *Address:* Institute of Psychiatry, 320 East Huron, Chicago, IL 60611, USA.

VISSER, Harry John, b. 22 Sep 1952, Huntsburg, Ohio, USA. Podiatric Physician & Surgeon. m. Katharine Sackett Baxter, 26 June 1976, Cooperstown, New York, USA, 2 sons. *Education:* BA, Chemistry, Hiram College, 1974; DPM, Ohio College of Podiatric Medicine, 1978. *Appointments:* Resident, Podiatric Medicine & Surgery, Lindel Hospital, St Louis, Missouri, 1978-81; Director, Residency Training, Podiatric Medicine and Surgery, Mineral Area Osteopathic Hospital, 1984-; Private Practice, Midwest Podiatry Inc, 1981-. *Memberships:* Diplomate, American Board of Ambulatory Foot Surgery, 1982; American Podiatric Medical Association; Missouri Podiatric Medical Association, President, 1985; St Louis Podiatric Medical Society, President, 1983-85; American College of Foot Orthopedists, Fellow; American College of Foot Surgeons, Fellow; American Board of Podiatric Surgery, Diplomate. *Publications:* "Lateral Ankle Stabilization Procedures: Criteria and Classification", 'Journal of Foot Surgery', 1980; "Calcaneal Osteotomy in the diagnosis and management of Flexible and Non-flexible Flatfoot Deformity: A Preliminary Report", 'Journal of Foot Surgery', 1981; "The Use of Differential Scintigraphy in the Diagnosis and Management of the Diabetic Foot", 'Journal of Foot Surgery', 1984. *Honours:* Pi Delta Honor Fraternity 1978; Hall of Science Award, 1st Place, American Podiatric Medical Association Meeting, 1980; Bruce Landry Memorial Award, Alpha Gamma Kappa Fraternity, 1978. *Hobbies:* Reading; Historical Biographies; Baseball; Football; Weightlifting; Classical Music; Masonry. *Address:* 1455 Westbrooke Meadows Lane, Manchester, MO 63021, USA.

VISWESWARARAO, Kakaraparti, b. 1 July 1938, India. Assistant Director. m. Kakaraparti Sita, June 1962, 1 son, 2 daughters. *Education:* BA, Andhra University; MA, Delhi University; MS, Harvard University, USA; PhD, Osmania University, India; Fellow, Institute of Statisticians, England. *Appointments:* Research Associate/Scholar, Assistant Research Officer, Research Officer, Senior Research Officer, Assistant Director, 1984-, National Institute of Nutrition, Hyderabad, India; World Health Organisation Consultant; 1983, 85. *Memberships:* Institute of Statisticians, England; Nutrition Society of India; Indian Society for Medical Statistics; Computer Society of India; Harvard Alumni Association; Association of Harvard Chemists. *Publications:* "Diet Atlas of India", 1969, 72. Author of over 73 learned articles including: 'Growth Retardation and Malnutrition'; 'Growth Retardation and Mental Function'; 'Nutritional Statistics, Availability and Needs'; 'Experimental Designs - Nutrition Contents of Foods'; 'Growth Modelling and Nutritional Status'; 'Calorie Co-Efficients: Validity'; 'Nutrition and Family Planning'. *Honours:* Award as Best BA Student of Professor Rangachar, Gold Medalist; Harvard Fellowship; Merit Fellowships and Ranks, College and University; Fellow, Institute of Statisticians, England. *Hobbies:* Development of approaches for data utilisation and inference; Modelling in nutrition; Bridge; Discussion on nutritional topics. *Address:* Department of Statistics, National Institute of Nutrition, Indian Council of Medical Research, Jamai Osmania, Hyderabad 500007, India.

VITTONE, Bernard John, b. 5 Oct 1951, Latrobe, USA. Director, National Centre for Treatment of Phobias, Anxiety and Depression; Guest Researcher, NIMH. m. Laurie Denton Vittone, 26 Aug 1979, New York State, 1 son. *Education:* BS, Georgetown University, 1973; MD, Georgetown University Medical School, 1977; Internship, St Vincent's Hospital and Medical Centre of New York, 1977-78; Ophthalmology Residency, Wills Eye Hospital, 1978-79; Psychiatric Residency, St Vincent's Hospital and Medical Centre of New York, 1979-82; Medical Staff Fellow, National Institute of Mental Health, 1982-84. *Appointments:* Staff Psychiatrist, Roundhouse Square Psychiatric Centre, 1983-85, Philadelphia State Hospital, 1979. *Memberships:* Alpha Omega Alpha; American Medical Association; American Psychiatric Association; Washington Psychiatric Society; Phobia Society of America; Washington Phobia Society. *Publications:* Contributor of articles to professional journals including 'Australian and New Zealand Journal of Psychiatry'; 'American Journal of Psychiatry'; 'The Lancet'; 'Clinical Insights: Biology of Agrophobia'; 'Psychopathology'; 'Psychiatry Research'; etc. *Honours:* Board Certificate as Diplomate, American Board of Psychiatry and Neurology, 1983; Chief Resident, St Vincent's Hospital, 1981; Outstanding Achievement in Microbiology, Georgetown Medical School, 1977; Alpha Omega Alpha 1976; Psi Chi, 1973. *Hobbies:* Tennis; Table Tennis; Chess. *Address:* 1801 18th St, NW, Washington DC 20009, USA.

VOCALAN, Leopoldo Unidad, b. 11 Nov 1943, Philippines. Psychiatrist. *Education:* Diplomate, American Board of Psychiatry and Neurology, 1982; Psychiatry Residency Training, New York Medical College. *Appointments:* Unit Director, Acute Admissions, Cherry Hospital, Goldsboro, North Carolina, 1981-83; Private Practice of Psychiatric Medicine, Jacksonville, Florida, 1978-81; Psychiatric Consultant, Wayne Mental Health Clinic, Goldboro, North Carolina, 1984-. Assistant Clinical Professor, East Carolina University School of Medicine, Department of Psychiatric Medicine. *Memberships:* American Psychiatric Association; Cherry Hospital Medical Staff Organisation. *Hobbies:* Tennis; Swimming; Boating; Fishing. *Address:* 203 Stratford Road, Goldsboro, NC 27530, USA.

VOET, Richard Leo, b. 17 Apr 1949, Cincinnati, Ohio, USA. Pathologist. m. Kathleen Cole, 26 Dec 1970, Cincinnati, Ohio, 2 daughters. *Education:* BS Chemistry, University of Cincinnati College of Arts & Sciences; MD, University of Cincinnati College of Medicine. *Appointments:* Assistant Professor of Pathology and Obstetrics & Gynaecology, Medical Centre, University of California at Los Angeles, 1979-81; Assistant Professor of Pathology, Obstetrics & Gynaecology, University of Texas Southwestern Medical Centre, Dallas, Texas, 1981-85; Pathologist, Presbyterian Medical Centre, Dalls. *Memberships:* International Society of Gynaecological Pathologists; International Academy of Pathology; Arthur Purdy Stout Society of Surgical Pathologists; College of American Pathologists; American Society of Cytol-

ogy. *Publications:* (With S Lifsaitz) 'Clear Cell Adenocarcinoma of the Fallopian Tube' (in Int. J of Gynae. Pathology, 1982). *Honour:* Alpha Omega Alpha, 1975. *Hobbies:* Computers; Bible Study. *Address:* Department of Pathology, Presbyterian Medical Centre, 8200 Walnut Hill Lane, Dallas, TX 75231, USA.

VOGT, Walther, b. 5 July 1918, Dessau. MD/Honorary Professor of Pharmacology. m. Heidi Pfersdorff, 1 Dec. 1946, Gross-Umstadt, 2 sons. *Education:* MD, Universities of Munich and Marburg. *Appointment:* Currently Director, Department of Biochemical Pharmacology, Max Planck Institute for Experimental Medicine, University of Gottingen. *Memberships:* Deutsche Pharmakol. Gesellschaft; Gesellschaft f. Biol. Chemie; Immunologische Gesellschaft; Immunological Society of Great Britain; American Association of Immunologists; British Physiological Society; Collegium Int. Allergolocicum. *Publications:* About 300 publications on amines, prostaglandin formation, kallikrein-kinin system; complement activation, anaphylatoxins. *Address:* Max Planck Institute for Experimental Medicine, Herman Rein-Str 3, 3400 Göttingen, Federal Republic of Germany.

VOIPIO, Niilo, b. 10 May 1921, Viipuri, Finland. Secretary General, Cancer Society of Finland. m. Synnöve Eleonora Nordberg, 10 May 1943, Helsinki, 1 son, 2 daughters. *Education:* MA, Helsinki Finland University, 1946. *Appointments:* Information Officer, Finland Relief, 1947-48; Director, Finnish National Chest, 1949; Secretary General, Cancer Society of Finland, 1949-, Finnish Cancer Foundation, 1950-, Secretary: Finnish Foundation for Cancer Research, 1969-; Republic President J K Passikivi Foundation for Cancer Research, 1950. President, Council for Volunteer Health and Social Agencies, Finland, 1972-76; Board of Directors, Scandinavian Cancer Union. *Memberships:* Finnish Slot Machine Association (Past Board of Directors). *Honour:* Decorated SVR 4, SVR 4th class. *Address:* The Cancer Society of Finland, Liisankatu 21 B, 00170 Helsinki, Finland.

VON EIFF, August Wilhelm, b. 15 Aug. 1921, Darmstadt. Director of Medical Clinic. m. Rita Maria Kercher, 6 May 1950, 3 sons, 2 daughters. *Education:* Studies of Medicine, Marburg, 1939, Frankfurt, 1940, Heidelberg, 1943-44, Tubingen, 1945; Dr med, Professor. *Appointments:* Assistant Doctor; Medical Clinic, University of Frankfurt, 1945, 1947, Hospital Seligenstadt, 1948, Institute of Physiology, University of Heidelberg, 1949-52; Associate Professor, 1953-72, Director, 1973-, Medical Clinic, Bonn University. *Memberships:* International Society of Hypertension; New York Academy of Sciences; Interdisciplinary Institute Gorres-Gesellschaft; Consultant of Federal & Environmental Agency; German Society of Internal Medicine. *Publications:* "Essential Hypertension", 1967, Japanese edition 1970; "Aircraft Noise Effect", 1974; "Stress", 1976, 3rd edition 1980; "Science and Ethos", 1982, 2nd edition 1984; "Death, Dying and the Aporia of Medicine", 1984; "Anthropologische Grundlagen einer interdisziplinaren Diskussion Uber menschliche Sexualitat", 1985; "The Protective Mechanism of Estrogen on High Blood Pressure", 1985; "School Stress", 1985. *Hobbies:* Music; Literature. *Address:* Medical Clinic of University, 5300 Bonn 1, Federal Republic of Germany.

VON GIERKE, Henning Edgar, b. 22 May 1917, Karlsruhe, Germany. Director, Biodynamics and Bioengineering, Aerospace Medical Research Laboratory. m. Hanlo Weil, 22 Oct. 1950, Doylestown, 2 daughters. *Education:* Dipl Ing., Dr. Ing., Technical University Karlsruhe, Germany. *Appointments:* Research Assistant, Lecturer, Technical University, Karlsruhe, 1944-47; Consultant, 1947-50, Research Physicist, 1950-54, Chief Biocoustics, 1954-63, Director, Biodynamics, Bionics, Bioengineering, 1963-, Aerospace Medical Research Laboratory, Ohio; Clinical

Professor, Community Medicine, Wright State University, 1980-. *Memberships:* Fellow, Aerospace Medical Association, Past Vice-President; Fellow, Acoustical Society of America, Past President; Honorary Fellow, Institute of Environmental Sciences; International Academy of Aviation and Space Medicine; International Academy of Astronautics; National Academy of Engineering; Biomedical Engineering Society. *Publications:* "Criteria for Noise and Vibration Exposure", in 'Handbook of Noise Control', co-author, 1979; "Sound, Vibration and Impact", with D. E. Parker, in 'Environmental Physiology', 1974; over 150 scientific articles, book chapters, government reports, etc. *Honours:* Dept. of Defence Distinguished Service Medal, 1963; E. Liljencrantz Award, 1966; A. D. Tuttle Award, 1974; Hubertus Strughold Medal, 1980; H. R. Lissner Award, ASME, 1983; National Academy of Engineering. *Address:* 1325 Meadow Lane, Yellow Springs, OH 45387, USA.

VON HOFF, Daniel Douglas, b. 29 Apr. 1947, Wisconsin, USA. Professor, Department of Medicine, Division of Oncology; Head, Section of Drug Development. m. Ann, 1 son, 2 daughters. *Education:* BS, Carroll College, Waukesha, Wisconsin, 1969; MD, Columbia College of Physicians and Surgeons, New York City, 1973. *Appointments:* Internship, Moffitt Hospital University of California, 1973-74; Medical Residency, University of California, San Francisco, 1974-75; Staff Associate, Cancer Therapy Evaluation Program, 1975-77, Clinical Associate, Medicine Branch, 1977-79, National Cancer Institute, Bethesda, Maryland; Assistant Professor, 1979-80; Associate Professor, 1980-85; Professor, 1985-; Department of Medicine, University of Texas Health Science Center, San Antonio, Texas; Head, Section of Drug Development, Division of Oncology, Department of Medicine, University of Texas Health Science Center, San Antonio, 1985-. *Memberships:* American College of Physicians; American Society for Clinical Oncology; American Association for Cancer Research; Texas Medical Association; American Medical Association; Southwest Oncology Group; Bexar County Medical Society; American Federation for Clinical Research; Alpha Omega Alpha. *Publications:* Abstracts; Proceedings; Contributor to professional journals, national and international; Research Papers; Editor, IND: Investigational New Drugs, 'The Journal of New Anticancer Agents'; Associate Editor, 'Cancer Research'; Member of several Editorial Boards. *Honours:* Tri Beta Award for Excellence in Biology, 1969; Scholarship Awards, Columbia College of Physicians and Surgeons; Clinical Teacher of the Year, Department of Medicine, 1980-81; Bruce K. Wiseman Memorial Lectureship, Ohio State University, 1985; Corrine Rosenberg Research Prize, 1985. *Address:* Department of Medicine/Oncology, UT Health Science Center at San Antonio, 770? Floyd Curl Drive, San Antonio, TX 78284, USA.

VON OLDENBURG, Albert Elimar, b. 8 Aug 1930, Germany. Private Practice; Director, Clinical Services, New Hampshire Air National Guard, m. Chantal Cousson, 8 Feb 1961, Woluwe, Belgium, 4 sons, 1 daughter. *Education:* Pre-Med, Sorbonne, Paris, France; MD, Catholic University, Louvain, Belgium; Post-Doctoral Fellow, Yale University, USA. *Appointments:* Senior Psychiatrist, New Hampshire Hospital, 1970; Founder, President, Psychiatry, 1973, Vice President, Medical Staff, 1982, President, Medical Staff, 1983, St Joseph Hospital, Nashua; Delegate from Nashua to New Hampshire Medical Society, 1975-85; Director, Clinical Services, 157th Air National Guard, 1984; Advisory Board, World Medical Society, 1985. *Memberships:* New Hampshire Medical Association; The New York Academy of Sciences; American Medical Association; World Medical Society. *Publication:* Tested and Evaluated of Alprazolam, published the results. *Honour:* Award, American Academy of Human Services, 1974-75. *Hobbies:* Archaeology; History. *Address:* 38 Berkeley Street, Nashua, NH 03060, USA.

VOSS, Carlyle Bradley, b. 27 Mar. 1940, Orange, New Jersey, USA. Director, Outpatient Psychiatry and Research. m. Patricia Ann Zurcher, 19 Aug. 1961, Ridgewood, New Jersey, 2 sons. *Education:* BA, Colgate University, 1961; MD, Baylor College of Medicine, 1965. Resident in Psychiatry: Mary Imogene Bassett Hospital, New York, 1968-69; New York State Psychiatric Institute, 1969-71. *Appointments include:* Ward Physician, US Public Health Service, Fort Worth Clinical Research Center, 1966-68; Director, Adult Out-Patient Psychiatric Service, 1971-, Director, Psychiatric Research, 1979-, Maine Medical Center, Portland, Maine; Privaye Practice, 1971-; Assistant Clinical Professor, Tufts University School of Medicine, 1976-80; Associate Clinical Professor, Vermont University Medical School, 1980-; Attending House Staff, Mercy Hospital, Portland, Maine, 1983-; Examiner, American Board of Psychiatry and Neurology, 1982, 84. *Memberships:* Fellow, American Psychiatric Association; Past President, Maine Psychiatric Association; Maine Medical Association. *Publications:* Co-Author of papers contributed to: 'Psychopharmacology Bulletin'; 'Archives of General Psychiatry'; 'Cardiovascular Bulletin'. Book Review in 'Hospital and Community Psychiatry'. *Honour:* Fellow, American Psychiatric Association. *Hobbies:* Golf; Hunting; Fishing; Photography. *Address:* 216 Vaughan Street, Portland, ME 04102, USA.

VREELAND, Kurt Arthur, b. 8 July 1952, New Jersey, USA. Chiropractor. 2 sons. *Education:* Diplomate, International College of Applied Kinesiology; Temple University, Philadelphia, Pennsylvania; Doctor of Chiropractic, Logan College of Chiropractic, St Louis, Missouri. *Memberships:* American Chiropractic Association; New Jersey Chiropractic Society; Southern New Jersey Chiropractic Society; Council on Chiropractic Roentgenology; Council on Chiropractic Orthopedics; Diplomate, International College of Applied Kinesiology; Diplomate, National Board of Medical Examiners; Council Sports Injuries. *Hobbies:* Sailing; Jogging; Skiing. *Address:* 9002 D Greentree Commons, Marlton, NJ 08053, USA.

VUKADINOVIC, Sreto, b. 8 June 1924, Nasice, Yugoslavia. Professor and Chairman, Department of Paediatrics, University of Zagreb Medical Faculty. m. Marija Pindulic, 25 Mar 1948, Zagreb, 1 daughter. *Education:* MD, 1949; Assistant, Medical Faculty, Zagreb, 1951; Assistant Professor of Paediatrics, 1965; Associate Professor of Paediatrics, 1975; Professor of Paediatrics, 1977. *Appointments:* Chief, Section of Paediatric Cardiology and Rheumatology, Paediatric Department, Zagreb, 1957; Head, Paediatric Department, "Rebro", University Hospital Centre, Zagreb, 1979-84. *Memberships:* Croatian and Yugoslav Medical Associations; Academy of Medical Association of Croatia; International Paediatric Association; International Society of Cardiology. *Publications:* Rheumatic Carditis in Preschool Children and Its Evolution (Doctorate Dissertation), 1964; Heart Diseases in Children, Medicinska Enciklopedija, 1964; Evaluation of Some Electro- and Phonocardiographic Characteristics of the Newborns (co-author), 1971. *Honours:* Yugoslav President Orders of Work, 1961, of Merit, 1968, of Fraternity and Unity, 1974, of Republic, 1982. *Hobbies:* History; Chess. *Address:* Pedijatrijska klinika "Rebro", Kispatićeva 12, 41000 Zagreb, Yugoslavia.

VUYLSTEKE, Jacques P E G, b. 4 Sep. 1922, Lochristi, Belgium. Professor and Head of Nutrition Unit. m. Pauline Charpentier MD, 27 Dec. 1956, Brussels, 2 sons, 2 daughters. *Education:* Medical Officer, University Leuven 1947; Doctor of Tropical Medicine and Hygiene I T M Antwerp, 1955; Paediatric Board Paris, recognised in 1961 for Belgium; MSc, Nutrition, Columbia University New York, 1968. *Appointments:* District Medical Officer, Paediatric Ward in Zaire 1953-55; District Medical Officer and MCH Officer, Rwanda-Burundi 1957-60; Senior MCH Advisor

WHO, Turkey-Gabon 1961-65; Senior Nutrition Advisor, WHO, Zaire 1965-68; Assistant Nutritionist Royal Tropical Institute, Amsterdam, 1972-74; Head of Department of Nutrition, Institute of Tropical Medicine, Antwerp, 1975-. *Memberships:* Association of Tropical Medicine, Belgium; Association Tropical Medicine, Netherlands; Association of Paediatricians, Belgium; Association of Auxology (International); Association of Anthropologists, Netherlands. *Publications:* Contributor of articles in the field of Nutrition to medical journals, and presenter of papers to scientific conferences. *Honours:* Medaille de Bronze, Academie de Medecine de Paris, au titre de l'Hygiene; Life Member of British Commandos 1940-45; Knight of the Leopold's Order. *Hobbies:* Art; Photography. *Address:* Institute of Tropical Medicine - Nutrition, Nationale Street 155, 2000 - Antwerp, Belgium.

W

WACKENHEIM, Auguste Ernest, b. 19 July 1925, Haguenau, France. University Professor of Radiology. m. Marie Terese Claudepierre, 3 Oct. 1953, Strasbourg, France, 1 son, 1 daughter. *Education:* MD, 1955. *Appointments:* Neurologist prior to 1966; Radiologist 1966; Professor and Chairman of Radiology, Strasbourg, 1979-. *Memberships:* Past President, French Society of Neuroradiology; Past President, European Society of Neuroradiology; Vice-President, CEPUR. *Publications:* 32 books in the professional field of Radiology; 429 scientific articles on Radiology; 10 books on Alsatian literature. *Honours:* Bretzel d'or, 1979; Palmes academiques, 1981. *Hobbies:* Painting; Poetry. *Address:* 4 rue Dotzinger, 67000 Strasbourg, France.

WADE, Adelbert Elton, b. 29 Apr. 1926, Hilliard, Florida, USA. Professor and Head, Department of Pharmacology and Toxicology. m. Mary L Cooper, 20 Jan. 1950, Fernandina Beach, Florida, 2 sons. *Education:* BS, 1954, MS, 1956, PhD, 1959, University of Florida. *Appointments:* Assistant Professor, School of Pharmacy, 1959-62, Associate Professor, 1962-67, Professor, College of Pharmacy, 1967-, currently Head, Department of Pharmacology and Toxicology, University of Georgia, Athens, Georgia. *Memberships:* American Association of Colleges of Pharmacy; American Society of Pharmacology and Experimental Therapeutics; International Society for Biochemical Pharmacology; Society of Experimental Biology and Medicine. *Publications:* Author of over 70 research papers in refereed journals including: 'Journal of Pharmacology and Experimental Therapeutics'; 'Biochemical Pharmacology'; 'Journal of Environmental Pathology and Toxicology'; 'Pharmacology'; 'Drug-Nutrient Interactions'; 'Drug Metabolism and Disposition'; 'Mutation Research'; 'Carcinogensis', 1954-. *Honours:* Rho Chi, 1953; Gamma Sigma Epsilon, 1953; Phi Kappa Phi, 1954; Sigma Xi, 1958; Award for Excellence in Research and Creativity, University of Georgia, 1981. *Hobbies:* Gardening; Fishing; Music; Stamp collecting. *Address:* College of Pharmacy, Department of Pharmacology and Toxicology, University of Georgia, Athens, GA 30602, USA.

WADE, Barbara Elizabeth, b. 5 Nov. 1932, Wakefield, Yorkshire, England. Director, Daphne Heald Research and Development Unit. m. John Norman Selwyn Wade, 14 Aug. 1954, St Michaels, Wakefield, 1 son, 2 daughters. *Education:* SRN; BEd, University of Lancaster; PhD, Educational Research, University of Lancaster. *Appointments:* Staff Nurse/Sister, Royal Infirmary, Bradford, 1951-57; Research Officer, Educational Research, University of Lancaster, 1973-78; Research Fellow, Health Services Research Centre, University of Birmingham, 1978-79; Research Fellow, London School of Economics, 1980-82; Director, Daphne Heald Research & Development Unit, Royal College of Nursing, 1982-. *Memberships:* Royal College of Nursing, UK. *Publications:* Co-author, "Pupil Personality and Classroom Behaviour", 'Teaching Styles and Pupil Progress', 1976; Articles in professional journals including: 'Op Cit'; 'British Journal Educational Psychology'; 'International Journal Nursing Studies'; 'Nursing Research'; 'Nursing Focus'; 'Acta Psychiatr. Scand'. *Hobbies:* Painting; Swimming; Sailing. *Address:* 38 Knolly's House, Tavistock Place, London WC1H 9SA, England.

WADHAWAN, Devinder Nath, b. 2 Jna. 1931, India. Head of Medicine. m. Sunita, 4 Mar. 1965, New Delhi, 2 sons. *Education:* MBBS, 1955, MD, 1958, Agra, India; MRCP, Glasgow, Scotland, 1963; MRCP, Edinburgh, Scotland, 1964. *Appointments:* Senior Physician, Central Health Service, Government of India, Delhi, 1965-75; Consultant Physician, Government of Zambia, 1975-79; Senior Lecturer, 1979-82, Head of Medicine, 1982-, University of Zambia. *Memberships:* Association of Physicians of India; Zambia Cardiac Society; Association of Physicians of Central and East Africa; Medical Association of Zambia. *Publications:* Numerous articles in professional journals. 2Hobbies: Photography; Yoga. *Address:* Box 50743, Lusaka, Zambia.

WADUD, Abdul, b. 4 Nov. 1935, Peshawar City, Pakistan. Clinical Assistant Professor of Psychiatry. *Education:* MB BS, University of Peshawar, 1960; DPM, Royal College of Physicians, London, England, Royal College of Surgeons, England, 1966; Fellow, Royal College of Physicians and Surgeons, Canada, 1977; MD, USA, 1972, 74. *Appointments include:* Demonstrator, Pathology, Khyber Medical College, Pakistan, 1961-63; General Practitioner, 1961-63; Clinical Assistant, Institute of Psychiatry, Maudsley Hospital, London, England, 1963-65; Assistant Psychiatrist, Netherene Hospital, Surrey, 1966-69; Instructor, Psychiatry, University of Missouri, USA, 1970-73; Assistant to Chief of Child Psychiatry Section, Missouri Institute of Psychiatry, 1974; Consultant, St Louis County Hospital, 1972-75, St Louis State Hospital Complex, 1972-75; Assistant Professor, University of Missouri, 1973-75; Clinical Assistant Professor, Psychiatry, University of Kansas Medical School, Wichita, Kansas, 1975-. *Memberships:* American Psychiatric Association; Royal College of Psychiatrists; Royal College of Physicians and Surgeons of Canada; American Medical Association; Medical Society of Sedgwick County; Kansas Medičal Society. *Publications:* Co-Author of contributions to: 'Journal of Nervous and Mental Disease'; 'Hospital and Community Psychiatry'; 'Current Therapy Research'. Various conference presentations and workshops. *Honours:* Merit Scholarship, Khyber Medical College, University of Peshawar, 1955; MB BS with Distinction of being 3rd on University Pass List; Physicians Recognition Award, American Medical Association, 1972. *Address:* 1543 South Hillside, Wichita, KS 67211, USA.

WAGA, Shiro, b. 1 Jan. 1935, Japan. Professor, Chairman, Neurosurgery. m. Takako, 15 May 1963, Kyoto, 1 son. *Education:* MD, DMSc, Kyoto University Medical School. *Appointments:* Instructor, 1967, Associate Professor, 1972, Kyoto University Medical School; Associate Professor, 1977, Professor, Chairman, 1978-, Mie University Medical School. *Memberships:* Japan Neurosurgical Society; Asian-Australasian Neurological Society; World Federation Neurological Surgery; Congress of Neurological Surgeons. *Hobbies:* Baseball; Swimming; Reading; Classical Music. *Address:* 770-139 Shibumi-cho, Tsu, Mie 514, Japan.

WAGNER, Aleksander Andrzej, b. 3 Aug. 1935, Grudziadz, Poland. Surgeon in Chief, Department of Paediatric Surgery. m. Aleksandra Kawalkowska, 6 Oct. 1956, Warsaw. *Education:* Medical Academy, Warsaw, 1959; Degrees of Surgery, 1965, 68; Medical Doctor, Medical Academy, 1972. *Appointments:* Assistant, Department of Urology, Warsaw, 1960-62, Assistant, Department of Paediatric Surgery, Senior Assistant, Professor, 1962-77, Medical Academy, Warsaw; Surgeon in Chief, Department of Paediatric Surgery, Medical Academy, Bialystok, 1977-. *Memberships:* National Council for Paediatric Surgery; Council Member and Branch Chairman, Polish Association of Paediatric Surgeons; British Association of Paediatric Surgeons; American Institute of Ultrasound in Medicine. *Publications:* "Encyclopedia of Health", contributor, 1986; "Ultrasonic Doppler's Method in the Evaluation of Shock', 1985; "Modern Problems in Pediatrics"; "Ultrasound Doppler's Technique in Children", Polish, German and English, 1978-85; "Peripheral Circulation, Portal Hypertension", Polish and German. *Hobbies:* Skiing; Sailing. *Address:* Department of Paediatric Surgery, Medical Academy, Wolodyjowskiego 2/1, 15 287 Bialystok, Poland.

WAGNER, Gustav Alfred, b. 10 Jan. 1918, Hanover, Federal Republic of Germany. Director of German

Cancer Research Centre. m. Inge Combiuiquz, 6 Dec. 1941, Berlin, 1 son. *Education:* Studied medicine at Leopzig and Berlin Universities; Professor of Medical Documentation, Information and Statistics, University of Kiel. *Appointments:* Dermatological Hospital, University of Kiel; Assistant Professor, Associate Professor, Professor of Medical Documentation, Data Processing and Statistics, University of Heidelberg; Director, Institute of Documentation, Information and Statistics, German Cancer Research Center, Heidelberg. *Memberships:* Member of more than 30 scientific bodies. *Publications:* Handbook of Medical Data Processing 1975; "Atlas of Cancer Mortality in the Federal Republic of Germany" 1984. *Honours:* Advisor to WHO; Corresponding Member of Danish and Finnish Dermatological Societies; Honorary Member of German Society for Medical Documentation, Information and Statistics. *Hobbies:* Philately; Gardening. *Address:* 64 Blütenweg, D-6905 Schrieshaim, Federal Republic of Germany.

WAGNER, Henry Nicholas Jr, b. 12 May 1927, Baltimore, Maryland, USA. Director, Divisions of Nuclear Medicine and Radiation Health Sciences, Johns Hopkins Medical Institutions. m. Feb. 1951, Baltimore, Maryland, 2 sons, 2 daughters. *Education:* AB, 1948, MD, 1952, The Johns Hopkins University and Medical School, Baltimore, Maryland. *Appointments:* Intern, Department of Medicine, 1952-53, Assistant Resident, Osler Medical Service, 1953-55, The Johns Hopkins Medical Service; Clinical Associate, National Institutes of Health, Bethesda, Maryland, 1955-57; Special Fellow, Postgraduate Medical School of London, Hammersmith Hospital, London, England, 1957-58; Chief Medical Resident, Osler Medical Service, Instructor of Medicine, 1958-59, Assistant Professor of Medicine, 1959-64, Associate Professor, Medicine, Radiology and Radiological Science, 1964-67, Professor of Medicine, Radiology and Radiological Sciences, Professor of Environmental Health Sciences, 1967-, Director of Nuclear Medicine and Radiation Health Science, 1965-, The Johns Hopkins Medical Institutions, Baltimore. 2Memberships: Past President, Baltimore City Medical Society; Past President, The Johns Hopkins Medical Society; Past President, World Federation of Nuclear Medicine and Biology; Founding Member, American Board of Nuclear Medicine; Past President, Research Societies Council; Past President, Eastern Section, American Federation for Clinical Research; Past President, American Federation for Clinical Research; Past President, Society of Nuclear Medicine; Member, The Fleischner Society; Endocrine Society; American Society for Clinical Investigation. *Publications:* Author of over 500 publications. *Honours:* Phi Beta Kappa, 1948; Alpha Omega Alpha, 1952, Fellow, American College of Physicians, 1961; Sigma Xi, 1962; Recipient, 1st Vikram Surhabel Gold Medal, 1972; Georg von Hevesy Medalist, 1976. *Address:* 5607 Wildwood Lane, Baltimore, MD 21209, USA.

WAHBY, Victor Samuel, b. 8 July 1945, Alexandria, Egypt. Professor. m. Susan T, 8 Dec. 1984, Kingston, Rhode Island, USA. *Education:* MD, PhD. *Appointments:* Associate Director, Psychoendocrine Laboratory, VA Medical Centre, Yale University, West Haven, Connecticut, 1981-85; Assistant Clinical Professor of Psychiatry, Yale Medical School, 1981-85; Associate Chief of Staff for Education, VA Medical Centre, North Chicago; Associate Professor of Medicine, Chicago Medical School. *Memberships:* American Medical Association; International Society of Psychoneuroendocrinology; American Association for the Advancement of Science; Society of Neuroscience; American Diabetes Association; North American Association of the Study of Obesity; New York Academy of Sciences; Society of Biological Psychiatry; Chairman, Programme Committee of the 1st International Symposium of Adolescent Obesity, Cairo, Egypt, 1986. *Publications:* Over 35 articles & abstracts (author & co-author) in fields of neuroendocrinology, psychoendocrinology & obesity and eat-

ing disorders. *Honour:* Merit Research Grant Award, Veterans Administration, 1982. *Hobbies:* Tennis; Swimming; Music. *Address:* ACOS/E (141), VA Medical Centre, North Chicago, IL 60064, USA.

WAHI, Purshottam Lal, b. 4 Dec. 1928, Sargodha, Pakistan. Professor of Cardiology. m. Dr. Pushpa Wahi, 1 son, 1 daughter. *Education:* MBBS, Panjab University, Pakistan, 1951; MD, 1956; FCCP; FICA; FAMS; FACC. *Appointments:* Assistant Registrar, Medical Colleges of Amritsar and Patiala, 1956-57; Registrar in Clinical Medicine, Medical College, Patiala, 1957-60; Assistant Professor and visiting Consultant, Medical College, Amritsar, 1960-62; Assistant Professor of Medicine and Cardiologist, PGI, Chandigarh, 1962-64, Associate Professor and Cardiologist, 1964-68, Professor and Senior College, 1968-73, Professor and Head Department of Cardiology, Chairman Department of Medicine, Chief Cardiologist, 1973-. *Memberships include:* British Medical Association; Indian Academy of Medical Science; Fellow, Royal Society of Medicine; Association of Physicians of India; Cardiology Society of India; Indian Association for Chest Diseases; American College of Chest Diseases; American College of Cardiology; American Heart Association, etc. *Publications include:* Over 200 contributions to international journals and publications including 'Journal of the Indian Medical Association'; 'Antiseptic'; "The Indian Year Book of Medical Sciences"; 'Indian Heart Journal'; 'Indian Journal of Surgery'; 'Indian Paediatrics'; 'Indian Journal of Chest Diseases and Allied Sciences'; Numerous conference papers and book chapters. *Honours:* Amalnanda Das Gold Medal at the Oration, 1976; Padam Shri, 1983. *Hobbies:* Reading; Painting; Table Tennis. *Address:* Department of Cardiology, Postgraduate Institute of Medical Education and Research, Chandigarh, India.

WAHLGREN, Sven Erik, b. 18 Dec. 1934, Umea, Sweden. Vice-President of pharmacy operations, Stockholm, m. Ingegard Nyqvist, 27 Dec. 1957, Stockholm, 3 daughters. *Education:* MSc, Pharmacy, Stockholm, 1961; PhD, Saarbrucken, West Germany, 1971. *Appointments:* Research Pharmacist, AB Bofors, Research Department, Karlskoga, 1962-64; Research Pharmacist, 1964-68, Department Manager, 1968-72, Apotekens Centrallab, Solna; Vice-President, Research and Development, ACO Lakemedel AB, Solna, 1972-82; Regional Manager, Apoteksbolaget (The Association of Swedish Pharmacies), Uppsala, 1982; Vice-President, Pharmacy Operations, Apoteksbolaget, Stockholm, 1983-. *Membership:* Swedish Academy of Pharmaceutical Sciences. *Publications:* Untersuchungen uber Lufteinschlusse in Salben (Doctor's thesis), 1961; About 50 articles, basically on pharmaceutical technology. *Honour:* The Royal Swedish Academy of Sciences, Scheele Scholarship, 1960. *Address:* Apoteksbolaget AB, S-105 14 Stockholm, Sweden.

WAHLIN, Anders Carl Engelbrekt, b. 15 Dec. 1944, Skellefteå) Head, Haematology; Associate Professor. m. Ylva Britt Wahlin, 31 July 1971, Ytterhogdal, 2 sons. *Education:* MD, 1971; Specialist Diplomas in: Nephrology, 1978, Internal Medicine, 1979, Haematology, 1981; PhD (Dissertation); 1978; Associate Professor, 1980. *Appointments:* Head, Haematology, Associate Professor, University Hospital of Umea. *Membership:* Swedish Society of Physicians. *Publications:* "Differential County of Urinary Granuloctytes, Mononuclear Leukocytes and Rental Epithelial Cells", 1978; Scientific articles in professional journals. 2Honours: Associate Professorship, Medical Faculty, University of Umea, 1980. *Hobbies:* Hunting; Fishing. *Address:* Rödhakevägen 25 B, 90237 Umeå) Sweden.

WAKIL, Salih Jawad, b. 16 Aug. 1927, Kerballa, Iraq. Educator; Biochemist. m. Fawzia Bahrani, 29 Nov. 1952, Madison, Wisconsin, USA, 2 sons, 2 daughters. *Education:* BSc, American University of Beirut, Beirut, Lebanon, 1948; PhD, University of Washington, Seattle, Washington, USA, 1952. *Appointments:* Research Fellow, University of Washington, Seattle, Washington, 1949-52; Research Fellow, 1952-56, Assistant Professor, 1956-59, University of Wisconsin, Madison, Wisconsin; Assistant Professor, 1959-60, Associate Professor, 1960-65, Professor, 1965-71, Duke University, Durham, North Carolina; Professor and Chairman, Baylor College of Medicine, Houston, Texas, 1971-. *Memberships:* American Society of Biological Chemists; American Society for Neurochemistry; American Society for Microbiology; American Chemical Society. *Publications:* "Lipid Metabolism", (Editor), 1971; 'The Enzymes', (with Stoops), 1983; 'The Enzymes of Biological Membranes', (with Joshi), 1983; Contributor of 157 published articles. *Honours:* The Paul Lewis Award in Enzyme Chemistry, 1967; John Simon Guggenheim Fellowship, 1968-69; Distinguished Duke Medical Alumnus Award, 1973. *Address:* Department of Biochemistry, Baylor College of Medicine, 1 Baylor Plaza, Houston, TX 77030, USA.

WAKISAKA, Gyoichi, b. 24 Mar. 1914, Shiga Prefecture, Japan. President, Shiga University of Medical Science. m. Tomi Ochiai, 12 Sep. 1939, 1 son, 2 daughters. *Education:* Graduate, Faculty of Medicine, 1937, DMS, 1947, Kyoto University; Student, Nuffield Department of Internal Medicine, Radcliffe Infirmary, Oxford, England, 1952-54. *Appointments:* Assistant Professor, Department of Internal Medicine, Faculty of Medicine, 1946, Professor of Internal Medicine, 1957, Professor Emeritus, 1975, Kyoto University; President, Shiga University of Medical Science, 1974. *Memberships:* Honorary Member, Japanese Society of Internal Medicine; Honorary Member, Japan Society of Haematology; Member, International Society of Haematology. *Publications:* "Pathophysiological Haematology", 1977; "Clinical Nuclear Medicine", 1981. *Honours:* Award from the Vitamin Society of Japan, 1947. *Address:* Shiga University of Medical Science, Setatsukinowacho, Ohtsu, Shiga Prefecture, 520-21 Japan.

WAITE, John Graham, b. 3 Nov. 1943, Khartoum, Sudan, North Africa. Medical Director, County Mental Health Services. m. Edith Rose, 2 sons. *Education:* MB BS, University of London, England, 1967; MRCS; LRCP, 1968; DPM, 1972; MRCPsych, 1973; Postdoctoral Fellow, Missouri Institute of Psychiatry, St Louis, USA, 1975-78; Diplomat of American Board of Psychiatry and Neurology, 1979. *Appointments:* House Surgeon, House Physician, Senior House Officer and Registrar, Kings College Hospital, London, England, 1963-73; Senior Registrar in Psychiatry, Goodmayes Hospital, Essex, England, 1973-75; Postdoctoral Fellow, Missouri Institute of Psychiatry, St Louis, USA, 1975-78; Practicing Student, Family Psychicenter, St Louis, 1979-81. *Memberships:* Royal College of Psychiatrists; American Psychiatric Association; Eastern Missouri Psychiatric Association; St Louis Metropolitan Medical Society. *Publications:* Lithium Effects on Leucocytosis and Lymphopenia in Lithium in Medical Practice, 1977 (co-author); Volunteer Effectiveness in Counseling Chronically Depressed Women Outpatients, Resources in Education (co-author), 1978; Admission Decisions in the Psychiatric Emergency Room, Comprehensive Psychiatry (co-author), 1983. *Honour:* Associate of Kings College, 1967. *Hobbies:* Private Pilot since 1983; Boating on Mississippi; Photography and Film-making; Playing Guitar and Singing. *Address:* County Mental Health Services, 77 Westport Plaza Medical Center, Suite 368, St Louis, MO 63146, USA.

WAITKUS, John P, b. 19 Aug. 1918, Cicero, Illinois, USA. Assistant Clinical Professor of Surgery. m. Shirley U Underwood, 22 Oct. 1958, Gilman, Illinois, 1 son, 2 daughters. *Education:* BS, Central YMCA College, 1940; MD, Loyola Medical School, Stritch School of Medicine. *Appointments include:* Assistant Clinical

Professor of Surgery, Loyola University, Stritch School of Medicine. *Memberships:* Diplomat, American Board of Surgery, 1951; Fellow, American College of Surgeons, 1952; Fellow, International College of Surgeons, 1953; Fellow, American College of Gastroenterology, 1955; Fellow, American College of Chest Physicians, 1959; Fellow, International Academy of Proctology, 1956; Board of Proctology, American Board of Abdominal Surgery. *Hobbies:* Skeet and trap shooting; Boating; Skiing. *Address:* 2700 West 43rd Street, Chicago, IL 60632, USA.

WAKEFIELD, Denis, b. 11 Mar. 1950, Sydney, Australia. Consultant Immunologist. m. Jennifer Aileen, 10 June 1977, Sydney, Australia, 2 sons, 1 daughter. *Education:* MB BS, MD, University of New South Wales; Fellow, Royal Australian College of Physicians; Fellow, Royal College of Pathologists of Australasia. *Appointments:* Registrar, The Prince Henry & Prince of Wales Hospitals, Sydney; Research Fellow, St Vincent's Hospital, Sydney; Staff Specialist in Immunology, St Vincent's Hospital, Sydney; Senior Lecturer in Pathology, University of New South Wales; Consultant Physician in Immunology, The Prince Henry & Prince of Wales Hospitals, also Sydney Eye Hospital. *Memberships:* Fellow, Royal Society of NSW. *Publications:* "Examination Medicine" (with Z Endre), 1982; various articles in medical journals. *Honours:* University Medal for Medicine, University of New South Wales, 1976; Edgeworth David Medal for Medical Research, Royal Society of NSW, 1984. *Hobbies:* Reading; Golf; Swimming; Art. *Address:* School of Pathology, University of New South Wales, P.O. Box 1, Kensington, New South Wales, Australia.

WAKIM, Paul E, b. 31 Mar. 1945, Dlebta, Lebanon. Orthopaedic Surgeon; DME. m. Constance J Coles, 10 June 1968, Selma, California, USA, 2 sons, 1 daughter. *Education:* DO; DME; DCC; FAAOS; FAANaOs; University of Health Sciences, Kansas City, Missouri, USA; St Francis Hospital, Kansas; Duke University (workshop). *Appointments:* Various residencies and workshops, Duke University and Chicago; Vice President, President, Sedjwick County Osteopathic Society; Vice President, Kansas Osteopathic Board of Trustees; President, Texas Osteopathic Medical Association, District 8. *Memberships:* American Academy of Orthopaedic and Neurologic Surgeons; American Academy of Osteopathic Specialists; American Osteopathic Association; Texas Osteopathic Association; American Academy of Sports Medicine. *Publications:* Author of various works on knee replacement, reimplantation of extremities and sports injuries. *Honours:* Honorable Mention, Determination of Sex of Offspring research, American Osteopathic Association. *Hobbies:* Fishing; Sailing; Golf; Tennis; Travelling; Jogging. *Address:* 100 Markham, Portland, TX 78374, USA.

WALACH, Natalio Noah, b. 19 June 1942, Buenos Aires, Argentina. Deputy Director, Department of Oncology, Assaf Harofeh Medical Centre, Zerifin, Israel. m. Naomi, 22 Dec. 1970, Tel Aviv, 2 sons, 2 daughters. *Education:* MD, University of Buenos Aires Medical School, Argentina, 1967; Residence, Department of Oncology, Hadassah University Hospital, Jerusalem, Israel, 1970-77; Certificate of Radiation Therapist (Oncologist), 1977. *Appointments:* Senior Physician, Department of Oncology, Assaf Hardeh Medical Centre Affiliated to Sackler School of Medicine, Tel Aviv University, Zerifin, 1978-; Visiting Professor, Department of Radiation Therapy, Beth Israel Hospital, New York, USA, 1982. *Memberships:* American Society of Clinical Oncology; European Society for Therapeutic Radiology and Oncology. *Publications:* 'Male Breast Cancer', (with A Hochman), 1974; 'Leucocyte alkline phosphatase in cancer patients', (with S Kaufman and V Horn), 1981. *Honours:* Department of Radiotherapy, The Royal Marsden Hospital, London and Surrey, England granted by the Lewis Fellowship Fund, 1982. *Hobbies:* Music; Painting. *Address:* Department of Oncology, Assaf

Harofeh Medical Centre, Zerifin 70300, Israel.

WALD, Ignacy, b. 21 Jan. 1923, Warsaw, Poland. Professor of Neurology and Genetics, Head of Department. m. Janina Prot, 4 Jan. 1956, Warsaw, 1 son, 1 daughter. *Education:* Physician Medical Academy, Wrocaw, 1950; MD, Institute of Neurology, Academy of Medical Sciences of USSR, 1956; DSc, Medical Academy, Lodz, 1962. *Appointments:* Assistant, Military Hospital, Warsaw, 1950-52; Research Fellow, Institute of Neurology, Academy of Medical Sciences, Moscow, USSR, 1953-56; Senior Lecturer, 1956-62, Director for Research, 1961, Head of Department of Genetics, Reader, 1962, Professor, 1978-, Psychoneurological Institute, Warsaw, Poland. *Memberships:* Polish Neurological Society; Polish Genetical Society; Polish Sociological Society; Polish Biometrical Society; European Society of Human Genetics; International Association for the Scientific Studies of Mental Deficiency; International Council on Alcohol and Addictions. *Publications:* "Clinical Neurology II", (Co-editor), 1980; "Report on Alcohol Policy", 1981; "Outline of Medical Genetics", (co-author), 1985. *Hobby:* Theatre. *Address:* Czarnieckiego 5/2, 01-511 Warsaw, Poland.

WALDOW, Stephen Michael, b. 19 Aug. 1959, Buffalo, New York, USA. Assistant Director and Associate Research Coordinator. m. Kathleen A Donnelly, 29 Dec. 1984, Queens, 1 daughter. *Education:* BS, BA, Niagara University, 1981; PhD, State University of New York, Roswell Park Graduate Division, 1984. *Appointments:* Laboratory and Teaching Assistant, Physics Department, 1979-80, Radiation Field Monitor, Biology Department, 1980-81, Niagara University, New York; Research Affiliate, Division of Radiation Biology, Department of Radiation Medicine, Roswell Park Memorial Institute, Buffalo, 1981-84; Professional Health Staff, Assistant Director and Associate Research Coordinator, Wenske Laser Center, Department of Surgery, Ravenswood Hospital Medical Center, Chicago, Illinois, 1985-. *Memberships:* American Association for Advancement of Science; American Society for Lasers in Medicine and Surgery; American Society for Photobiology; North American Hyperthermia Group; Laser Institute of America; New York Academy of Sciences; Midwest Bio-Laser Institute; Radiation Research Society. *Publications:* Author of photodynamic therapy and hyperthermia for cancer articles in: 'Radiation Research'; 'Lasers in Surgery and Medicine'; 'Cancer Research' and other professional publications. *Honours:* Student Travel Award, Radiation Research Society, 1984; Deans List, 1979-81, Academic Scholarship, 1977-81, Niagara University; Stephen H Jamieson Memorial Scholarship, 1977; New York State Science Supervisors Association Chemistry Award, 1976. *Hobbies:* Baseball; Football; Tennis; Basketball; Golf. *Address:* Wenske Laser Center Suite 5503, Ravenswood Hospital Medical Center, 4550 North Winchester Avenue, Chicago, IL 60640, USA.

WALDRON, Joseph Anthony, b. 3 Oct. 1943, Batavia, New York, USA. Associate Professor of Department of Criminal Justice; Director of Forensic Research Laboratory. m. 31 Oct. 1967, Fort Erie, Canada, 3 daughters. *Education:* BA Psychology magna cum laude, State University of New York College, Buffalo, New York, 1972; MA 1973, PhD 1975, Psychology, Ohio State University. *Appointments include:* Head, Department of Psychology, Buckeye Youth Center, Ohio Youth Commission, 1976-77; Chief Psychologist, Diagnosis and Evaluation Clinic, Mahoning County, Ohio, 1977-78; Owner, Towne Square Psychiatric Services Incorporated, 1977-; Assistant Professor 1978-84, Associate Professor 1984-, Department of Criminal Justice, Senior Member Graduate Faculty 1980-, Director of Forensic Research Laboratory 1984-, Youngstown State University, Youngstown, Ohio. *Memberships:* Kappa Delta Pi; Sigma Xi; American Association for the Advancement of Science; American Society of Criminology; Academy of Criminal Justice Sciences. *Publications include:*

"Manual for the Audio Presentation of the Personality Research Form - E for Use With Adolescent Delinquenta", (with G Kreuchauf and C Sutton), 1981; "A Framework for Developing an Early Warning System for Business Retention", (with T Buss), 1981; "Computer Applications in Criminal Justice", (with C Sutton and T Buss), 1983; "Manual for Interpreting the Medical and Mental Health MMPI Reports", (with C Sutton), 1983; "The Automated Social History", 1984; "Using the ASH in Practice, Teaching, Research and on Various Computers", 1984; "Contemporary Issues in the Use of Microcomputers", (with W Archambault, B Archambault, J Conser, E Hernandez and C Sutton), 1986; MMPI Computer Program; Numerous contributions to journals; Copyrighted Psychometric Software. *Honour:* Graduated magna cum laude, 1972. *Hobbies:* Chess; Reading; Swimming; Microcomputers. *Address:* Forensic Research Laboratory, Youngstown State University, Youngstown, OH 44555, USA.

WALDSTEIN, Gail, b. 9 Apr. 1942, Brooklyn, New York, USA. Paediatric Pathologist. m. Mark Levine, 1965, divorced 1976, 1 son, 2 daughters. *Education:* AB, Douglass, College, 1964; MD, Temple University School of Medicine, 1968. *Appointment:* Paediatric Pathologist, Children's Hospital, Denver, Colorado, USA, 1972-. *Memberships:* Society for Paediatric Pathology; Physicians for Social Responsibility; Colorado Society for Clinical Pathology. *Publications:* "Pre-Leukaemia in Childhood" Pemediatric Oncology, Reviews, 1985; Fragile Syndrome: Skin Elastin Abnormalities; March of Dimes Birth Defects, Original Article Series, in press, 1986. *Honour:* Clinical Fellow, American Cancer Society, 1972-75. *Hobbies:* Bird Watching; Cooking; Crocheting; Fencing. *Address:* Department of Pathology, The Children's Hospital, 1056 East 19th Avenue, Denver, CO 80218, USA.

WALES, Raymond George, b. 24 Aug. 1931, Melbourne, Australia. University Professor of Physiology. m. Margaret Anne Mitchell, 15 Aug. 1959, Sydney, Australia, 1 son, 2 daughters. *Education:* BVSc, 1955, PhD, 1961, DVSc, 1970, University of Sydney. *Appointments:* Lecturer/Senior Lecturer/Associate Professor, University of Sydney, 1960-75; Visiting Associate Professor, University of Pennsylvania, 1966; Visiting Associate Professor, Washington University, St Louis, 1973; Visiting Scientist, MRC Laboratories, Carshalton, UK, 1984; Professor of Physiology, School of Veterinary Studies, Murdoch University, Murdoch, Western Australia. *Memberships:* Australian College of Veterinary Scientists; Society for the Study of Fertility; Australian Society for Reproductive Biology; Australian Biochemical Society; Australian Physiological and Pharmacological Society. *Publications:* Author of some 100 scientific articles since 1960. *Honours:* Population Council Fellow, 1966; Senior Hays Fulbright Scholar, 1973. *Hobbies:* Gardening; Art. *Address:* School of Veterinary Studies, Murdoch University, Murdoch, WA 6150, Australia.

WALKER, Colin Heriot Macdonald, b. 15 May 1923, Edinburgh, Scotland. Consultant Paediatrician. m. Anne Eddie Gillieson, 19 Dec. 1949, Edinburgh, 1 son, 1 daughter. *Education:* MB ChB, 1946, MD, 1952, University of Edinburgh; Fellow, Royal College of Physicians, 1963; Diploma, Child Health, Royal College Physicians, London, 1951; Diplomat, American Board of Paediatrics, 1960. *Appointments:* Registrar, Senior Registrar, Hospital for Sick Children, Great Ormond Street, London, 1952-57; Senior Hospital Medical Officer, Princess Margaret Hospital, Perth, Australia, 1957-58; Instructor, Assistant Professor, University of Colorado Medical Centre, Paediatrics, 1958-64; Consultant Paediatrician, Honorary Reader, Child Health University of Dundee, 1964-. *Memberships:* British Medical Association; British Paediatric Association; Society of Paediatric Research, USA; American College of Cardiology. *Publications:* Over 120 articles, chapters for books, editorials and book reviews. *Honours:* Creighton Research Scholar,

1949; Fellow, American College of Cardiology, 1964. *Hobbies:* Swimming; Gardening; Golf; Curling; Writing. *Address:* 2 The Stables, Pitfour Castle, Glencarse, Perthshire, Scotland.

WALKER, Donald Murray, b. 5 July 1939, Cardiff. Reader; Honorary Consultant; Head, Department of Oral Medicine & Oral Pathology, Dental School, University of Wales College of Medicine, Cardiff. m. Susan Mary Peacock, 7 Sep. 1966, Dorset, 1 son, 1 daughter. *Education:* BDS, University of Bristol; MB, ChB, Welsh National School of Medicine. *Appointments include:* Dental House Officer, University of Bristol Dental Hospital, 1962-63; Medical/Surgical House Officer, Cardiff Royal Infirmary, 1969-70; Resident, SHO, Oral Surgery/Registrar, University of Wales Dental Hospital, 1971; Lecturer 1971, Senior Lecturer, 1977, Reader 1984, University of Wales College of Medicine. *Memberships:* British Dental Association; Royal Society of Medicine; Royal College of Pathologists; Royal College of Surgeons of England; British Society for Immunology; International Association for Dental Research. *Publications include:* "The Oral Mucosa in Health & Disease", ed A. E. Dolby, 1975; "Introduction to Oral Immunology", 1981; Chapter 5, "Immunology of Oral Diseases", 1985; Journal contributions. *Honours:* Distinction, Social Medicine; Distinction, Surgery; Willie Seager Prize in Surgery, University of Wales College of Medicine. *Hobbies:* Playing the piano; Golf; Visiting English country houses. *Address:* Department of Oral Medicine & Oral Pathology, Dental School, University of Wales College of Medicine, Heath Park, Cardiff CF4 4XY, Wales.

WALKER, Marian Cooper, b. 13 Apr. 1928, New York, USA. Director of Physical Therapy. Divorced, 2 daughters. *Education:* BS, PT, University of Pittsburgh, USA; MPA, Middle Tennessee State University, USA. *Appointments:* Industrial Home for Crippled Children, Pittsburgh, Knoxville Cerebral Palsy Centre, USA; Tennessee Department of Public Health; Veterans Administration Hospital; Clover Bottom Developmental Centre. *Memberships:* American Physical Therapy Association; American MENSA. *Hobbies:* Reading; Music. *Address:* 1203 Taylor Place, Murfreesboro, TN 37130, USA.

WALKER, Marilyn Louise, b. 21 Mar. 1951, Toronto, Ontario, Canada. Medical Doctor. m. James D Walker, 17 Aug. 1974, Beaconsfield, Quebec, 1 son, 1 daughter. *Education:* BSc, MD, University of Toronto; Certificate, College of Family Practice, Canada. *Memberships:* Ontario Medical Association; Canadian Medical Association; Canadian Academy of Sports Medicine; Physicians for a Smoke Free Canada. *Honour:* Kathleen Chambers Memorial Award, 4th year medicine. *Hobbies:* Sports (previous Olympic team member, track & field, Canada, 1972, 1976); Sewing. *Address:* Sports Medicine Clinic, Carleton University, Colonel By Drive, Ottawa, Ontario, Canada K1S 5B6.

WALKER, Wayne Edward, b. 18 July 1956, Niagara Falls, Canada. Vice-President, College of Chiropractic Sports Sciences, Canada. m. Dr Fiona P Weetman, 14 May 1983, Queenston, Ontario. *Education:* BSc Honours, Zoology; DC Honours. *Appointments:* Advisor, Sports Advisory Committee of Greater Niagara; Executive Director, Southern Vancouver Island Chiropractic Society; British Columbia Director, Council of Chiropractic Sports Sciences, Canada; President, B C Chiropractic Sports Academy. *Memberships:* Canadian, American Chiropractic Associations; British Columbia, Southern Vancouver Island Chiropractic Societies; College of Chiropractic Sports Sciences, Canada. *Publication:* Editor, British Columbia Chiropractic Sports Academy Journal. *Hobbies:* Head Coach, B C Chiropractors' Running Club; Photography; Athletics; Astronomy. *Address:* 401 - 3939 Quadra Street, Victoria, British Columbia, Canada.

WALL, Patrick David, b. 5 Apr. 1925, Nottingham, England. Professor; Director. *Education:* BM, BCH 1948, MA 1950, DM Oxford, 1960, FRCP, 1984. *Appointments:* Instructor, Physiology, Yale, 1948-50; Assistant Professor, Anatomy, University of Chicago, 1950-53; Instructor, Harvard, Physiology, 1953-55; Associate Professor 1958-60, Professor, Biology, M.I.T., 1960-67; Visiting Professor, Biology, Hebrew University, 1975-. *Memberships:* Physiology Society; International Association Study Pain; Brain Research Association. *Publications:* "The Challenge of Pain" (with R. Melzack), 1983; "The Textbook of Pain" (with R Melzack), 1984; 250 papers on sensory nervous system. *Honours:* Forbes Lecturer, 1972; Beecher Lecturer, 1974; Founding Editor "Pain", 1975; Bonica Lecturer, 1979; Honorary FRCP, 1984; Sherrington Medal, 1986; Founding Chairman, Brain Research Association, 1970. *Hobby:* Filling Out Questionnaires. *Address:* Department Anatomy, University College, Gower Street, London, WC1E 6BT, England.

WALLACE, Edwin Ruthven IV, b. 10 Mar. 1950, Portsmouth, Virginia, USA. Professor of Psychiatry. m. Laura Martin Elmore, 13 May 1972, Wilmington, North Carolina, 1 son, 1 daughter. *Education:* BS, BA, University of South Carolina, 1970; MD, Medical University of South Carolina, 1973; MA, Johns Hopkins University, 1979; Residency in Psychiatry, William S Hall Psychiatric Institute; Fellowship in Psychiatry, Yale University School of Medicine. *Appointments:* Assistant Professor of Neuropsychiatry, University of South Carolina School of Medicine, 1978-80; Asisstant Professor of Psychiatry, Yale University, 1980-82; Associate Professor of Psychiatry, Medical College of Georgia, 1982-. *Memberships:* American Psychiatric Association; American Medical Association; American Association for the History of Medicine. *Publications:* "Essays in the History of Psychiatry", 1980; "Freud & Anthropology", 1983; "Dynamic Psychiatry in Theory & Practice", 1983; "Historiography & Causation in Psychoanalysis", 1985. *Honour:* Phi Beta Kappa. *Hobbies:* Archaeology; Hiking; Travel. *Address:* Department of Psychiatry, Medical College of Georgia, Augusta, GA 30912, USA.

WALLERSTEIN, Ralph O, b. 7 Mar. 1922, Dusseldorf, Germany. Clinical Professor. m. Betty Ane Christensen, 21 June 1952, 2 sons, 1 daughter. *Education:* MD, University of California School of Medicine, 1949; AB, University of California, Berkeley, 1943. *Appointments:* Intern, San Francisco Hospital, UC Service, 1945-46, Resident, 1948-49; Resident, University of California Hospital, 1949-50; Research Fellow, Thorndike Memorial Lab, Boston City Hospital, 1950-52; Clinical Professor of Medicine & Laboratory Medicine, University of California, San Francisco, 1969-. *Memberships:* American Board of Internal Medicine, Board of Governors, 1975-83, Chairman Elect, 1981-82, Chairman, 1982-83, 1974-77; American College of Physicians, Governor-elect Northern California, 1976, Governor, 1977-81, Chairman Board of Governors, 1980-81, Regent, 1981-; Federated Council for Internal Medicine. *Publications:* Numerous articles in professional journals; Book Chapter, "Using the Clinical Laboratory in Medical Decision Making", 'Anemia', 1983. *Honours:* Outstanding Civilian Service Medal, Army, 1981; Selected as one of 120 Best Doctors in America by Good Housekeeping Nationwide Survey of Departmental Heads in 87 Medical Schools, 1984. *Hobbies:* Photography; Travel. *Address:* 3838 California St, Suite 707, San Francisco, CA 94118, USA.

WALSH, Donal A, b. 17 Aug. 1939, London, England. Professor, Biological Chemistry. 1 son, 1 daughter. *Education:* BSc, 1959, MSc, 1961, SW Essex Technical College, London University, England; PhD, University of Wisconsin, USA, 1965. *Appointments:* Postdoctoral Fellow, Biochemistry, University of Washington, 1966-68; Visiting Research Fellow, Biochemistry, University of Bristol, England, 1974-75; Assistant Professor, 1968-73, Associate Professor, 1973-78, Professor, 1978-, Biological Chemistry, University of California, Davis. *Memberships:* American Society of Biological Chemists; Biochemical Society, UK. *Publications:* Numerous articles in scientific journals including: 'Journal Biological Chemistry'; 'Biochemistry'; 'European Journal Biochemistry'; 'Access'; Abstracts; etc. *Honours:* Established Investigator, American Heart Association, 1970-75; Postdoctoral Fellow, American Cancer Society, 1966-68; The 1000 Contemporary Scientists Most Cited 1965-78, 1981. *Address:* Department of Biological Chemistry, School of Medicine, University of California, Davis, CA 95616, USA.

WALTER, George S, b. 4 Apr. 1934, Vom, Nigeria. Medical Training Coordinator. m. (1) Barbara W Herlihy (deceased), 11 June 1955, Denver, Colorado, USA, 2 sons, 2 daughters, (2) Bonnie R Lockhart, 16 Aug. 1980, Felton, California, 1 step-son, 1 step-daughter. *Education:* BS, Chemistry, University of Denver; MD, University of Colorado; MPH, University of California, Berkeley. *Appointments:* Medical Officer in Charge, Native Health Service Hospital, Point Barrow, Alaska, 1959-60; Medical Officer in Charge, Indian Health Service Hospital, Ohyhee, Nevada, 1960-62; Chief, Obstetrics and Gynaecology, Indian Health Service Hospital, Fort Defiance, Arizona, 1965-69; Maternal and Child Health Consultant, Navajo Area Indian Health Service, Window Rock, 1970-71; Field coordinator, African Maternal and Child Health Project, University of California, Cotonou, Benin, West Africa, 1971-75; Medical Training Coordinator, International Health programs, University of California, San Francisco, USA, 1975-. *Memberships include:* Fellow, American College of Obstetricians and Gynaecologists; American Public Health Association; American Association of Planned Parenthood Professionals; American Association of Sex Educators, Counselors and Therapists. *Publication:* 'Psychological and Emotional Consequences of Elective Abortion', 1970. *Hobbies:* Reading; Writing; Music; Hiking; Travel. *Address:* International Health Programs, 210 High Street, Santa Cruz, CA 95060, USA.

WALTER, Tadeusz Mieczyslaw, b. 26 Feb. 1921, Lwow, Poland. Epidemiologist. m. Zofia Wojcikiewics, 28 Sep. 1946, 1 son. *Education:* MD, University of Jagiellonica, Krakow, Poland, 1964, Assistant Professor, 1976. *Appointments:* Surgeon, 1948-50; Military Service, 1950-52; Epidemiologist, Sanitary Station, 1952-57; Head, Epidemiology, Dep. Academy of Medicine, 1972-. *Memberships:* Polish Society of Epidem. and Infec. Dis. Physicians; Corresponding Member, Society of Hygiene, DDR. *Honour:* Golden Medaille of Merit, 1967. *Hobbies:* Philately; Basketball. *Address:* Marcelinska Str 52, 60-354, Poznan, Poland.

WALTHER, David Sidney, b. 19 Marh 1937, Pueblo, Colorado, USA. Director of Chiropractic Health Center, P C and Director of Walther Applied Kinesiology Seminars. m. Jeanne Beach, 22 June 1963, Pueblo, Colorado. *Education:* Doctor of Chiropractic, Palmer College of Chiropractic, 1959; Postgraduate: National College of Chiropractic; American Chiropractic Association Qualified Orthopedist; Diplomate, International College of Applied Kinesiology. *Memberships:* International College of Applied Kinesiology; American Chiropractic Association; Colorado Chiropractic Association, Past President; Council of Chiropractic Orthopedists; Council of Chiropractic Roentgenologists. *Publications:* Applied Kinesiology: The Advanced Approach in Chiropractic, 1976; Applied Kinesiology, Volume I Basic Procedures and Muscle Testing, 1981; Applied Kinesiology, Volume II Head, Neck and Jaw Pain and Dysfunction: The Stomatognathic System, 1983. *Honours:* Outstanding Service, Colorado Chiropractic Association, 1967; Distinguished Service Award, Colorado Chiropractic Association, 1968; Chiropractor of the Year, Colorado Chiropractic Association, 1973; Outstanding Service Award, Colorado Chiropractic Association, 1976; Outstanding Paper Award, International Col-

lege of Applied Kinesiology, 1982. *Hobbies:* Photography; Machine Shop. *Address:* 255 West Abriendo Avenue, Pueblo, CO 81004, USA.

WALTON, John Nicholas, b. 16 Sep. 1922, Rowlands Gill, County Durham, England. University College Warden. m. Mary Elizabeth Harrison, 31 Aug. 1946, Newcastle-upon-Tyne, 1 son, 2 daughters. *Education:* MB BS 1st class honours, Medical School, King's College, Newcastle-upon-Tyne, 1945; MD, Durham, 1952; DSc, Newcastle-upon-Tyne, 1972. *Appointments include:* Medical Registrar, Department of Medicine, Newcastle-upon-Tyne, 1951-56; Nuffield Foundation Fellow in Neurology, Massachusetts General Hospital, Boston, Massachusetts, USA, 1953-54; King's College Travelling Fellow, Neurological Unit, National Hospital, Queen Square, London, England, 1954-55; 1st Assistant in Neurology, Newcastle-upon-Tyne; Consultant Neurologist, Newcastle General Hospital, and Physician in Neurology, Royal Victoria Infirmary, Newcastle-upon-Tyne, 1958-63; Professor of Neurology 1968-83, Dean of Medicine 1971-81, University of Newcastle-upon-Tyne; Warden, Green College, University of Oxford, 1983-. *Memberships include:* Fellow 1963, Royal College of Physicians, London; President 1982-, General Medical Council; President 1984-86, Royal Society of Medicine; President 1980-82, British Medical Association; 1st Vice-President 1981-, World Federation of Neurology; Chairman 1971-, Muscular Dystrophy Group of Great Britain. *Publications include:* "Subarachnoid Haemorrhage", 1956; "Polymyositis" (with R D Adams), 1956; "Essentials of Neurology", 5th edition 1982; "Disorders of Voluntary Muscle" (editor), 4th edition 1981; "Skeletal Muscle Pathology" (editor with F L Mastaglia), 1982; "Brain's Diseases of the Nervous System", 9th edition 1985; "Oxford Companion to Medicine" (with P B Beeson and R Bodley Scott), 1986. *Honours include:* Knight Bachelor, 1979; Honorary Doctor of the University, Aix-Marseilles, 1975; Honorary DSc, Leeds 1979, and Leicester 1980; Honorary Fellow and Member of Royal Colleges and many national neurological societies. *Hobbies:* Golf; Cricket; Reading; Music. *Address:* Green College, Radcliffe Observatory, Oxford OX2 6HG, England.

WALZ, Felix H, b. 29 Oct. 1948, Zurich, Switzerland. Deputy Medical Examiner; Professor in Forensic Biomechanics; Lecturer on Forensic Medicine. m. Beatrice Kurt, 5 Apr. 1980, Zurich, Switzerland. *Education:* MD. *Appointments:* M General Motora Research Laboratory, Warren, USA; Institute of Forensic Medicine, St Gallen Switzerland; Cantonal Hospital, Winterthur, Switzerland; Lecturer, Forensic Medicine, University of Zurich -. *Memberships:* American Association of Automotive Medicine; IRCOBI Steering Committee; Swiss Society of Forensic Medicine. *Publications include:* Numerous conference proceedings including 'The Influence of Protection Helmets in Motorcycle Accidents' (Co-author), 1976; 'Adverse Effects of Seat Belts and Causes of Belt Failures on Severe Car Accidents in Switzerland During 1976', 1977; 'Severely and Fatally Injured Rear Seat Passengers in Switzerland During 1976' (Co-author); 'Lower Abdomen and Pelvis: Anatomy and Types of Injury' in "The Biomedics of Impact Trauma", 1984; 'Head Injuries in Moped and Bicycle Collisions: Implications for Bicycle Helmet Design', (co-author), 1985; 'Car-Pedestrian Collision: Injury Reduction, Accident Reconstruction, Mathematical and Experimental Simulation. Head Injuries to Two Wheelers', Report Interdisciplinary Working Group for Accident Mechanics, University and Swiss Federal Institute of Technology, 1985. *Honours:* Award on Traffic Medicine, Swiss Automobile Club, 1972; Georg Friedrich Götz Award, 1982; Technical Award, Swiss Automobile Club 1984. *Hobbies:* Home Improvements; Skiing; Family Sport. *Address:* Institute of Forensic Medicine, University of Zurich, Zurichbergstrasse 8, 8028 Zurich, Switzerland.

WAMBEBE, Charles Nima, b. 8 Sep. 1946, Emi-Tsado,

Nigeria. Dean, Faculty of Pharmaceutical Sciences. m. Victoria, 26 Dec. 1973, Ecewu, 1 son, 4 daughters. *Education:* BPharm, University of Ife, 1972; PhD, Neuropharmacology, Ahmadu Bello University, 1979; MPSN. *Appointments:* Intern Pharmacist, General Hospital, Lokoja, 1972; Assistant Lecturer, Pharmacology, 1973-75; Lecturer II, 1975; Lecturer I, 1978; Senior Lecturer, 1980; Reader, 1983; Dean, Faculty of Pharmaceutical Sciences, Ahmadu Bello University, Zaria, 1982-86. *Memberships:* Society of Biological Psychiatry; British Society of Pharmacology; Academy of Pharmaceutical Sciences; Pharmaceutical Society of Nigeria. *Publications:* Over 25 articles in learned journals. *Honours:* Pfizer Travel Fellowship, 1978; Young Pharmacologist Fellowship, IUPHAR, 1981; CIBA-Geigy Award, 1982. *Hobbies:* Swimming; Reading. *Address:* Department of Pharmacology, Faculty of Pharmaceutical Sciences, Ahmadu Bello University, Zaria, Nigeria.

WANERMAN, Leon Ralph, b. 12 July 1935, Philadelphia, Pennsylvania, USA. Chief, Mental Health Department. m. Paddy Laura Moore, 4 Aug. 1962, San Anselmo, California, 2 sons, 1 daughter. *Education:* AB, University of Chicago, USA, 1954; MD, Albany Medical College, New York, 1960. *Appointments include:* Director, Consultation Service, Department of Psychiatry, Mount Zion Hospital and Medical Centre, 1970-73; Consultant, Alameda County Mental Health Services, Residency Training Programme, 1975-77; Director, UCB-UCSF, Doctor of Mental Health Programme, 1975-80; Consultant, The Poplar Centre, San Mateo, California, 1980-; Chief, Mental Health Department, Health America Rockridge, Oakland, California -. *Memberships:* American Academy of Child Psychiatry; American Psychiatric Association, Northern California; American Orthopsychiatric Association; American Association of Psychiatric Services for Children; Fellow, American College of Mental Health Administration. *Publications include:* Co-author 'Ventricular Fibrillation Successfully Treated by External Electric Countershock' in 'American Journal of Cardiology', 1962; "A Study of Mental Health Services for Children in the Westside Catchment Area of San Francisco" prepared for the Westside Community Mental Health Centre, 1969; Co-author "children in Treatment - A Primer for Beginning Child Psychotherapists", 1977; 'The Psychosocial Impact of Cranio-Facial Anomalies', workshop and seminar, 1981, 1983; Co-author "A Child Psychiatry Casebook: Strategies and Technique", 1984. *Honours:* Numerous community and professional service activities. *Address:* Health America Rockridge, 420 40th Street, Oakland, CA 94609, USA.

WANG, Jie, b. 26 Jan. 1926, Jinan, China. Associate Professor. *Education:* Graduate, Medical College, Tongji University, Shanghai, 1952. *Appointments:* Research Fellow under practice, Dept of Protozoology, National Institute of Health, 1952-55 Assistant Research Fellow, Kalaazar, Institute of Parasitic Disease, Chinese Academy of Medical Sciences, 1956-78; Chief, Diagnosis & Immunology, Institute of Parasitic Diseases, Chinese Academy of Medical Sciences, 1980-. *Memberships:* Chinese Medical Association; Manager, Chinese Protozoological Society. *Publications:* Articles in professional journals. *Address:* Department of Diagnosis & Immunology, Chinese Academy of Preventive Medicine, 207 Rui Jin Er Lu, Shanghai, Peoples Republic of China.

WANG, Pei-yen, b. 1 Feb. 1926, Honan, China. Chief, Surgery, Veterans General Hospital, Taichung. m. Chu Shu-Mei, 8 Oct. 1954, Taichung, 2 sons, 1 daughter. *Education:* MB, National Defense Medical Centre, China. *Appointments:* Surgical Resident, Thoracic Surgeon, First Army General Hospital, China, 1952-65; Surgical Resident, Special Fellow, Memorial Cancer Centre, New York, 1965-68; Instructor, Assistant Professor, Professor, Surgery, National Defence Medical Centre, 1970-84; Chief, Thoracic Surgery, 1968-74; Chief, Experimental Surgery, 1974-82, Veterans General Hospital, Taipei; Chief, Surgery, Vete-

rans General Hospital, Taichung, 1982-. *Memberships:* Chinese Medical Association; Surgical Association, China; Association of Surgeons of South Wast Asia; Association of Thoracic and Cardiovascular Surgeons of Asia; Fellow, International College of Surgeons; International College of Chest Physicians. *Publications:* "Vascular Implantation of the Liver"; "Total Parenteral Alimentation with a Combination of Carbohydrates in Surgical Patients with Carcioma of the Esophagus"; "Surgical Treatment of the Esophagus and Cardia Among the Chinese"; "A Spiral Grooved Endoesophageal Tube for Management of Malignant Esophageal Obstruction", "Annals of Thoracic Surgery", 1985. *Hobbies:* Go Go Chess; Mountain Climbing; Tennis. *Address:* 10B, 321 Fu-Hsing South Road, Section 1, Taipei, Republic of China 106.

WARAMBO, Malaki Wilson, b. 28 Aug. 1932, Gem, Kenya. Consultant Surgeon. m. Edwina Odera Omulo, 14 Apr. 1956, Kisumu, 1 son, 6 daughters. *Education:* LMS, 1958, MB ChB, 1963, Makerere University; Fellow, Royal College of Surgeons, Edinburgh, Scotland, 1963. *Appointments:* Senior Consultant Surgeon, Kenyatta National Hospital, Nairobi, Kenya; Honorary Lecturer in Surgery; Consultant Surgeon, Aga Khan Hospital, Nairobi and Nairobi Hospital. *Memberships:* Fellow, Association of Surgeons of East Africa; President, East Africa Section, International College of Surgeons; Past Chairman, Association of Surgeons of East Africa. *Hobby:* Chairman, Nairobi Club. *Address:* PO Box 162, Sawagongo, Kenya.

WARA-WASOWSKI, Janusz Bogumil, b. 8 Feb. 1935, Lodz, Poland. Assistant Professor, Head of Department, Anaesthesia and Intensive Therapy. m. Anna Chmielewska, 11 February 1961, 1 son, 1 daughter. *Education:* Graduate 1958, MD 1968, Assistant Professor 1981, Medical Academy of Lodz. *Appointments:* Houseman 1962-64, Registrar 1964-69, of Anaesthesia in Neurosurgery Clinic, Registrar 1969-70, Senior Registrar 1970-74, Consultant 1974-82, Head 1982-, Department of Anaesthesia, Medical Academy of Lodz. *Memberships:* Committee Member, Polish Academy of Science; Board Member, Polish Society of Anaesthesia; National Board, Polish Society of Anaesthesia and Intensive Therapy; Expert, Health Committee, Council of Mutual Economic Aid; Associate Member, European Academy of Anaesthesiology. *Publications:* Book chapters: in "Intensive Therapy", 1978; "Clinical Toxicology" in press; "Emergency Treatment in Health Diseases" (3 chapters) in press; 96 articles in medical journals and assembly proceedings. 2Honours: Award, Ministry of Health, 1974; Honorable Award, City Council of Lodz 1978, Polish Red Cross 1983; Golden Order of Merit, 1983. *Hobbies:* Travel; Fishing; Bridge. *Address:* ul. Lubeckiego 19 m 6, 91-403 Lodz, Poland.

WARD, Carley C, b. 14 Mar. 1933, Detroit, USA. President, Biodynamics Engineering Inc. m. John F Ward, 1 Dec. 1961, Las Vegas, 1 son. *Education:* BSc, Mechanical Engineering, 1955, MSc, Engineering Mechanics 1959, University of Michigan; PhD, Biomechanics & Dynamics, University of California, Los Angeles, 1974. *Appointments include:* Director of Research Grant, University of Southern California, 1985-86; Various appointments, University of California San Diego, Medical School, 1975-; Deputy Coroner, Los Angeles County Medical Examiners Office, 1980-85. *Memberships:* Society of Automotive Engineers; American Association of Automotive Medicine; Society of Experimental Stress Analysis; American Academy of Forensic Sciences; American Trauma Society. *Publications:* Over 40, including: Book chapter, 'Mathematical Models: Animal & Human Models' (Biomechanics of Trauma, 1985); Book chapter, 'Finite Element Modeling of the Head & Neck' (Impact Injury of the Head & Spine, 1982). *Honours:* Outstanding Achievement Award, US Navy, 1974; Sigma Xi, 1973-80; Amelia Earhart Fellowship, 1968-69; Citation, McDonnell-Douglas Corporation, 1966. *Hobbies:* Hiking; Skiing. *Address:* 705 Hampden Place, Pacific Palisades, CA 90272, USA.

WARD, Harold William Cowper, b. 24 Nov. 1925, Southend-on-Sea, England. Associate Clinical Professor of Radiation Therapy. m. Barbara Mary Sanderson, 6 Oct. 1962, Stanhope, 1 son, 2 daughters. *Education:* Kings College, London; MB, BS, Charing Cross Hospital Medical School; Fellow, Royal College of Radiology, United Kingdom; Member, Royal College of Physicians, London. *Appointments:* House Physician, Royal Postgraduate Medical School, London, 1954; Radiotherapy Registrar, Charing Cross Hospital, London, 1955-57; Radiotherapy Senior Registrar, Royal Infirmary, Edinburgh, Scotland, 1958-59; Research Fellow, Saint Bartholomew's Hospital, London, England, 1959-65; Consultant Radiotherapist, United Birmingham Hospitals, 1966-75; Full Professor and Director of Radiation Oncology, University of Texas Southwestern Medical School, Dallas, USA, 1976-78; Clinical Professor of Radiology and Associate Clinical Professor of Medicine, University of Cincinnati, Ohio, 1978-82; Associate Clinical Professor of Radiation Therapy, University of Texas Medical Branch, Galveston, 1982-. *Memberships:* Fellow, Royal College of Radiology; British Society of Radiology; British Medical Association; Royal College of Physicians; International Society for Pediatric Oncology; American Society of Therapeutic Radiology and Oncology; American Medical Association. *Publications:* 'Electron therapy at 15MeV', 1964; 'Disordered Vertebral growth following irradiation', 1965; 'Anti-oestrogen therapy for breast cancer', 1973. *Hobbies:* Music; Theological studies; Horticulture. *Address:* 2601 Hospital Boulevard, Suite 215, Corpus Christi, TX 78405, USA.

WARD, Helen Anne, b. 27 Nov. 1943, Bathurst, New South Wales, Australia. Medical Director. *Education:* ECFMG, 1970; LRCP MRCS, London, 1973; BSc Honours Physics 1976, MSc Physics 1980, PhD Electrical Engineering 1986, University of New South Wales. *Appointments:* Research Doctor, Microsurgery Foundation, Sydney, 1976-79; Tutor in Physics, University of New South Wales, 1977-79; Medical Director, Clinical Practice and Research Capacity, Medical Health and Research Centre, Sydney, 1979-. *Memberships:* Fellow, American Society for Laser Medicine and Surgery; Laser Institute of America; The Society of Photo-Optical Instrumentation Engineers. *Publications:* 'Advanced Fuel Reaction Feasibility Using Laser Compression 11', (with R Castillo et al), 1977; 'Nonlinear Forces, Solutions and Self-Focusing in Laser Irradiation Plasmas for optimised Fusion', (with H Hora et al), 1978; 'An Irreversible Effect at Intensive Radiations', (with S Hinckley et al), 1980; 'Interference with Electrical Conduction Due To Laser Induction of Electric Fields in Heart Muscle', 1982; 'Destructive, Nonclassical 'Beating' of Acoustic Waves and Electric Field Generation in Lased Heart Muscle', 1983; 'Laser Recannalization of Atheromatous Vessels Using Fiber Optics', 1984. *Hobbies:* High Technology Inventions; Swimming; Dancing; Skiing. *Address:* Medical Health and Research Centre, 152-154 Avoca Street, Randwick 2031, New South Wales, Australia.

WARD, Henry Arthur, b. 5 Dec. 1925, Melbourne, Australia. Senior Lecturer, Department of Pathology and Immunology. m. Noelleen Toussaint, 14 May 1955, Melbourne, 1 son, 2 daughters. *Education:* BSc, MSc, Melbourne University; PhD, Monash University. *Appointments:* Research Chemist, Department of Supply, Australian Government Research Laboratories; Research Biochemist, Baker Medical Research Institute; Research Fellow, Department of Pathology, Lecturer, currently Senior Lecturer, Department of Pathology and Immunology, Monash University, Prahran, Victoria, Australia. *Memberships:* Australian Society for Immunology; Australian Biochemical Society; Australian Society for Experimental Pathology; British Society for Immunology. *Publications:* Co-Author and Author in: 'Clinical

Experimental Immunology', 1972; "Fluorochromes and Their Conjugation with Proteins" in 'Fluorescent Protein Tracing', 1976; 'Pathology', 1979; 'European Journal of Biochemistry', 1982. *Hobbies:* Music; History of Science; Languages. *Address:* Department of Pathology and Immunology, Monash University Medical School, Commercial Road, Prahran, Victoria 3181, Australia.

WARD, John Robert, b. 23 Nov. 1923, Utah, USA. Professor of Medicine; Chief of Division of Rheumatology. m. Norma Harris, 5 Nov. 1948, Salt Lake City, 3 sons, 1 daughter. *Education:* BS 1944, MD 1946, University of Utah, Salt Lake City; MPH, University of California School of Public Health, Berkeley, 1967. *Appointments:* Internship 1947-48, Residency 1949-51, Salt Lake County General Hospital, Utah; Research Fellow in Physiology 1948-49, Instructor in Medicine 1954-58, Chief of Rheumatology Division 1957-, Assistant Professor of Medicine 1958-63, Associate Professor of Medicine 1963-69, Professor of Medicine 1969-, University of Utah College of Medicine; Active Duty, United States Army Medical Corps, Edgewood, Maryland, 1951-53; Research Fellow in Medicine 1953-54, Chairman of Department of Preventive Medicine 1966-70, University of Utah; Research Fellow in Medicine, Harvard Medical School, 1955-57; Clinical Fellow in Medicine, Massachusetts General Hospital, 1955-57. *Memberships:* Diplomate, American Board of Internal Medicine, 1956; Fellow, Governor for Utah 1979, American College of Physicians; American Rheumatism Association; Western Association of Physicians; New York Academy of Science; Utah State Medical Society; Society of Sigma Xi; American Society for Experimental Pathology; Western Society for Clinical Research; Salt Lake County Medical Society. *Publications include:* 164 articles on experimental models of arthritis, controlled clinical trials of antrheumatic treatments, and mycoplasmal physiology and pathogenesis; 21 book chapters on experimental arthritis and treatment of arthritis. *Honours:* Outstanding Professor 1970, Professor of the Year 1974, University of Utah College of Medicine; Honorary Faculty Member, AOA, 1976; Man of the Year, Arthritis Foundation, 1983; Distinguished Physician, Salt Lake County Medical Society, 1984; Modern Medical Monograph Award, 1985. *Hobbies:* Fishing; Writing. *Address:* University of Utah Medical Center, 50 North Medical Drive, Salt Lake City, UT 84132, USA.

WARD, Wallace Dixon, b. 30 June 1924, Pierre, South Dakota, USA. Professor. m. Edith Marion Bystrom, 29 Dec. 1949, Minneapolis, Minnesota, 4 daughters. *Education:* BS, South Dakota School of Mines and Technology, Rapid City, South Dakota, 1944; PhD, Harvard University, Cambridge, Massachusetts, 1953. *Appointments:* Research Associate, Central Institute for the Deaf, St Louis, Missouri, 1954-57; Associate Director of Research, Research Center, Subcommittee on Noise, American Academy Ophthalomology and Otolaryngology, Los Angeles, California, 1957-62; Professor, Departments of Otolaryngology, Communication Disorders, Environmental Health and Psychology, University of Minnesota, Minneapolis, 1962-. *Memberships:* Acoustical Society of America; American Speech, Language and Hearing Association; American Otological Society; American Academy of Otolaryngology; International Society of Audiology; American Auditory Society; International Commission on Biological Effects of Noise; Association for Research in Otolaryngology; American Industrial Hygiene Association; Society for research in Psychology of Music and Music Education. *Publications:* 162 publications including, "Adaptation and Fatigue", 1973; "Noise-induced Hearing Loss", 1984; Editor, "Proceedings of the International Congress on Noise as a Public Health Problem', 1974. *Honours:* Honorary ScD, South Dakota Mines and Technology, 1971; Fellow, Acoustical Society of America, 1961; American Speech and Hearing Association, 1966; President, International Society of Audiology,

1978-80; President, American Auditory Society, 1976; Vice President, Acoustical Society of America, 1986. *Hobbies:* Piano Playing; Singing; Hunting; Fishing; Golf. *Address:* 246 Maple Hill Road, Hopkins, MN 55343, USA.

WARNER, James Keith, b. 11 Sep. 1954, Eugene, Oregon, USA. Chiropractic Office President. m. Linda Diane Leaton, 27 July 1975, Eugene, Oregon. *Education:* Associate of Science; DC, Western States Chiropractic College, 1979; Certificate in Sports Injuries, 1979; Diplomate, in Toftness Post Graduate Chiropractic, 1985, Foundation for the Advancement of Chiropractic Research. *Appointments:* Lecturer, Mountain Medicine, Search and Rescue, Field Trainer, International Wilderness Club, 1973-75; Associate Clinic Director, Western States Chiropractic College, 1978; Director, Oregon Nordic Club, Wilderness/Snow Survival School, 1979; Faculty Member, Clinical Sciences and Chiropractic Sciences Departments, Western States Chiropractic College, 1979-80; Clinical Private Practice, 1980-; Clinical Advisor, EMCO Health Sciences, 1983-; Clinical Advisor, American Running and Fitness Association, 1985; Guest Lecture Chair, Anglo-European College of Chiropractic, Bournemouth, England, 1985; currently, President, Warner Chiropractic Office. *Memberships:* American Public Health Association; American College of Sports Medicine; American Running and Fitness Association; International Chiropractic Association; Foundation for the Advancement of Chiropractic Research; Renaissance International. *Publications:* "Cross Country Skiing Exercises for Injury Prevention", 1984; "A Practitioners Guide to the Injured Knee", 1986. *Honours:* Diplomate, National Board of Chiropractic Examiners, 1979; Accredited Instructor, Renaissance International (Scientific communications), 1985. *Hobbies:* Cross country skiing; Ski Mountaineering; White water canoeing; Shooting sports; Mountaineering Medicine. *Address:* 4163 Cherry Avenue, Keizer, OR 97303, USA.

WARREN, John Robin, b. 11 June 1937, Adelaide, South Australia. Pathologist. m. Winifred Teresa Williams, 5 May 1962, Adelaide, 4 sons, 1 daughter. *Education:* MB, BS, University of Adelaide, 1961; Fellow, Royal College of Pathologists of Australasia. *Appointments:* Pathology Registrar, Institute of Medical & Veterinary Science, Royal Adelaide Hospital; Lecturer in Pathology, University of Adelaide; Pathology Registrar, Royal Melbourne Hospital. *Memberships:* Royal College of Pathologists of Australasia; International Academy of Pathology; Australian Society of Cytology; Australian Medical Association; British Medical Association. *Publications:* Various articles in medical journals. *Hobbies:* Target rifle-shooting; Photography; Computer Programming. *Address:* Department of Pathology, Royal Perth Hospital, PO Box X2213, Perth, Western Australia 6001, Australia.

WÄSSLE, Heinz, b. 11 Oct. 1943, Salzburg. Director of Department of Neuroanatomy. m. Gisela Wässle, 28 Aug. 1970, Bad Pyrmont, 1 son, 1 daughter. *Education:* Master of Physics, PhD in Physics; Habilitation in Physiology; Professor of Biology. *Appointments:* Post doctoral position, Department of Biophysics, Kings College, London; Post doctoral position, Department of Physiology, Australian National University, Canberra; Research Fellow, University of Constance; Senior Research Fellow, Max-Planck-Institut, Tubingen; Head of Department, Max-Planck-Institut, Frankfurt. *Publications:* Articles in Journal of Physiolofy and papers presented to Proceedings to Royal Society of Biology. *Hobbies:* Classical music; History of art; Skiing; Bicycling; Gardening. *Address:* Max-Planck-Institut für Hirnforschung, Deutschordenstr 46, D-6000 Frankfurt/M 71, Federal Republic of Germany.

WASSERMAN, Martin, b. 19 Jan. 1938, New York, USA. Psychiatrist; Child Psychiatrist; Psychoanalyst. m. Francine Bartfield, 27 June 1976, San Marino,

California, 1 son. *Education:* AB, Columbia College, 1959; MD, State University of New York, Downstate Medical Center, 1963; Intern, Union University, Albany Medical Center, 1964; Residency, King County Hospital, New York City, 1964-67; Child Fellow, University of Michigan Child Psychiatric Hospital, 1969-70; Los Angeles Psychoanalytic Institute, 1970-75. *Appointments:* Instructor, State University of New York, Downstate Center, 1966; Assistant Professor of Psychology, Long Island University, Southampton College, 1966; Chief Psychiatrist, USN, Camp Pendleton, California, 1967-69; Assistant Professor of Psychiatry and Child Psychiatry, 1970-73, Associate Professor, 1970-, University of Southern California, School of Medicine; Faculty, Los Angeles Psychoanalytic Institute, 1975-; Guest Lecturer in Psychiatry, UCLA, 1974, 85; Examiner, National Board of Neurology and Psychiatry in Psychiatry and Child Psychiatry. *Memberships:* Fellow, American Psychiatric Association; American Psychoanalytic Association; American Academy of Child Psychiatry; Southern California Psychiatry Association; Los Angeles Psychoanalytic Society and Institute. *Honours:* Research Fellowship, 1966, Career Teacher, 1973, National Institute of Mental Health; Senior Examiner, Board of Neurology and Psychiatry. *Hobbies:* Swimming; Jogging; Poetry; Film; Skiing; Photography. *Address:* 510 E Channel Road, Santa Monica, CA 90402, USA.

WASYLENKI, Donald, b. 18 Dec. 1946, Regina, Saskatchewan, Canada. Associate Professor of Psychiatry. m. Lesley Monette, 16 Aug. 1968, Regina, 1 daughter. *Education:* BA, University of Manitoba, 1967; MD, University of Saskatchewan, 1971; Fellow, Royal College of Physicians & Surgeons of Canada (Psychiatry), 1976; MSc, University of Toronto, 1980; Graduate, Canadian Institute of Psychoanalysis, 1981. *Appointments:* Consultant Psychiatrist, Clark Institute of Psychiatry, Toronto; Director of Continuing Education and Associate Professor, Department of Psychiatry, University of Toronto; Psychiatrist-in-Chief & Clinical Director, Whitby Psychiatric Hospital. *Memberships:* Canadian Medical Association; Ontario Medical Association; Canadian Psychiatric Association; Ontario Psychiatric Association; American Psychiatric Association; Canadian Psychoanalytic Society; International Psychoanalytic Association. *Publications:* More than 25 articles in scientific & medical journals. *Honours:* Lt Governor's Gold Medal, University of Manitoba, 1967; William Osler Award, Canadian Medical Association, 1976. *Hobbies:* Golf; Tennis; Skiing. *Address:* 17 Woodlawn Avenue, Toronto, Ontario, M4T 1B9, Canada.

WATANABE, Mamoru, b. 15 Mar. 1933, Vancouver, Canada. Dean, Faculty of Medicine, University of Calgary. m. Marie Katie Bryndzak, 1 June 1974, 1 son. *Education:* BSc, 1955, MDCM, 1957, PhD, 1963, McGill University; FRCP (C), 1963. *Appointments:* Professor, Medicine, University of Alberta, 1970-74; Professor, Head, Medicine, Director, Medicine, Foothills Hospital, 1974-76, Associate Dean, Education, 1976-80, Associate Dean, Research, 1980-81, Acting Dean, 1981-82, Dean, 1982-, Medicine, University of Calgary. *Memberships include:* American Society for Microbiology; Canadian Medical Association; Royal College of Physicians and Surgeons; Canadian Arthritis Society; Canadian Hypertension Society; etc. *Publications:* Numerous articles in professional journals including: 'Journal Steroid Biochemistry'; 'Canadian Journal Biochemistry'; etc. *Address:* Faculty of Medicine, University of Calgary, 3330 Hospital Drive N.W., Calgary, Alberta T2N 4N1, Canada.

WATANABE. Kazoi, b. 1 Jan. 1910, Ibaraki, Japan. Hospital Director, Physician. m. 17 Oct. 1939, 2 sons, 3 daughters. *Education:* MD, School of Medicine, Jikeikai University, Tokyo; Doctor of Medical Science. *Appointments:* Lecturer, School of Medicine, Jikeikai University, Tokyo, 1944; Chief, Medical Department, Tochigi National Sanatorium, 1945;

Director of Kawasaki Rinko General Hospital. *Memberships:* Fellow, Japanese Society of Internal Medicine; Councillor, Japanese College of Angiology; Fellow, International College of Angiology; Emeritus Fellow, International Academy of Chest Physicians & Surgeons. *Publications:* "Kabuto no Homare", 1968; "Lied von Mor Joy", 1978; "Recent Advances in the Treatment of ischemic hear disease", 1978; "The Nittas History", 1980. *Honours:* Order of the Sacred Treasure, 1981; District Governor of Rotary International, 1981; Honours awards from General Chairman of International College of Angiology, 1978, 1983. *Hobbies:* Travel; Japanese Fencing (5th Grade). *Address:* 8-5 Osonedai, Kohoku-ku, Yokohama, Japan.

WATERS, William Estlin, b. 6 Nov. 1934, Toronto, Canada. Professor of Community Medicine. m. Judith Lloyd, 14 Mar. 1964, 2 sons. *Education:* MB BS, London, England, 1958; DIH St Andrew's, Scotland, 1965. *Appointments:* Scientific Staff, Medical Research Council's Epidemiology Unit, Cardiff, Wales, 1965-70; Senior Lecturer 1970-75, Reader 1975, in Clinical Epidemiology and Community Medicine, Professor of Community Medicine, University of Southampton, England. *Memberships:* Member 1972, Fellow 1976, Faculty of Community Medicine; Council 1971-77 and 1981-84, Executive Committee 1974-77, International Epidemiological Association; Society for Social Medicine; Medical Section, Royal Statistical Society; British Medical Association. *Publications include:* "The Elderly in Eleven Countries: A Sociomedical Survey" (editor with E Heikkinen and Z J Brzezinski), 1983; "Community Medicine: A Textbook for Nurses and Health Visitors" (with K S Cliff), 1963; Over 100 papers on epidemiology and community medicine. *Hobbies:* Ornithology; Island-going; Collecting books. *Address:* Department of Community Medicine and Medical Statistics, Southampton General Hospital, Southampton SO9 4XY, England.

WATSON, Donald Charles. Jr, b. 15 Mar. 1945, Fairfield, Ohio, USA. Associate Professor of Surgery & Paediatrics, Cardiothoracic Surgeon. m. Susan Robertson Prince, 23 June 1973, Durham, North Carolina, 3 daughters. *Education:* BA Applied Science, BS Mechanical Engineering, 1968, Lehigh University; MS Mechanical Engineering, Stanford University, 1969; MD, Duke University School of Medicine, 1972; Intern, Surgery, 1972-73, Resident, Cardiovascular Surgery, 1973-74, Stanford University Medical College; Clinical Associate, 1974-76, Acting Senior Surgeon, 1976, Surgery Branch, NHLI; Resident, Surgery, 1976-78. Chief Resident, Heart Transplants, 1978-79, Chief Resident, Cardiovascular & General Surgery, 1978-80, Stanford University Medical College. *Appointments:* Associate Cardiovascular Surgeon, Department of Child Health & Development; Attending Cardiovascular Surgeon, ibid, 1983-84; Assistant Professor of Surgery & of Child Health & Development, George Washington University, 1980-84; Associate Professor of Surgery & of Paediatrics, University of Tennessee at Memphis, 1984-; Chairman, Cardiothoracic Surgery, ibid, 1984-; Chairman, Cardiothoracic Surgery, Le Bonheur Children's Medical Centre, 1984-. *Memberships include:* Fellow, American College of Cardiology; Fellow, American College of Chest Physicians; Fellow, American Academy of Paediatrics; American Association for Thoracic Surgery; Association for Academic Surgery; International Society for Heart Transplantation; American Federation for Clinical Research; American Association for the Advancement of Science; New York Academy of Science; American Medical Association. *Publications:* Over 40 original contributions, over 50 major presentations, over 150 reviews. *Honours include:* Various scholarships, fraternities, certifications. *Hobbies include:* Flying; Sailing; Racquets; Alumni activities. *Address:* 956 Court Avenue, 230, Memphis, TN 38163, USA.

WATSON, James Patrick, b. 14 May 1936, London.

Professor of Psychiatry. m. Christine Mary Colley, 4 Apr. 1962, Teignmouth, Devon, 4 sons. *Education:* MA, Trinity College, Cambridge, 1957; MD, King's College Hospital Medical School, 1960; FRCP; FRCPsych; DPM; DCH. *Appointments:* House Physician and Surgeon, Senior House Officer and Registrar in Neurosurgery and Medicine, 1960-64; Trainee Psychiatrist, Bethlem Royal and Maudsley Hospitals and Institute of Psychiatry, London 1964-71; Senior Lecturer in Psychiatry and Honorary Consultant, St George's Hospital Medical School, 1971-74; Professor of Psychiatry, United Medical and Dental Schools of Guy's and St Thomas's Hospitals, London, 1974-. *Memberships:* Member, British Psychological Society; Member, Society for Psychotherapy Research; Fellow, Royal College of Physicians of London; Fellow, Royal College of Psychiatrists. *Publications:* Papers on various aspects of Psychotherapy in British Journal of Psychiatry (1970), Behaviour Research and Therapy (1972), British Journal of Medical Psychology (1970-76); Editor: "Personal Meanings" 1983. *Honours:* Senior Scholar, Trinity College, Cambridge, 1956; Visiting Professor, University of Toronto, 1972. *Hobbies:* Music (Mozart); Gardening; Travel; Sport. *Address:* 36 Alleyn Road, London SE21 8AL, England.

WATTS, Richard William Ernest, b. 6 Sep. 1923, Peterborough, England. Assistant Director; Honorary Consultant Physician. m. Joan Ellen Maude Lambert, 6 May 1948, 1 son. *Education:* MB BS, PhD, MD, DSc, University of London; MRCP; FRCP. *Appointments:* Resident: St Bartholomew's Hospital, London, 1946-47; Royal Army Medical Corps, 1947-49; Demonstrator, Lecturer, Physiology, St Bartholomew's Hospital Medical College, 1949-54; Travelling Fellow, British Postgraduate Medical Federation, 1954-55; Senior Lecturer, Medicine, St Bartholomew's Hospital Medical College, 1956-66; Reader, University of London, Consultant Physician, St Bartholomew's Hospital, 1966-69; Clinical Scientific Staff, Medical Research Council, 1970-; Head, Inherited Metabolic Diseases, 1972-; Assistant Director, Clinical Research Centre, 1982-; Consultant Physician, Northwick Park Hospital, 1970-. *Memberships:* Fellow, Royal College of Physicians of London, Royal Society of Chemistry; Association of Physicians of Great Britain & Ireland; Biochemical Society; Medical Research Society; European Society for Clinical Investigation. *Publications:* Editor: "Clinical Science", 1970-74, "Advances in the Treatment of Inborn Errors of Metabolism", 1982; Author, 350 scientific papers. *Honours:* Travelling Fellowship, British Postgraduate Medical Federation, University of California, Berkeley, USA, 1954-55; Columbia University, New York, Visiting Associate, US Public Health Services, NIH Bethesda, Maryland, USA, 1963. *Hobby:* Music. *Address:* Clinical Research Centre, Watford Road, Harrow, Middlesex HA1 3UJ, England.

WATTS, Theresa Elizabeth Ellen, b. 26 Dec. 1930, Leicestershire, England. Associate Professor and Head of Community Medicine. m. Edward Ronald Watts, 18 June 1959, 1 son, 2 daughters. *Education:* MB BS, London, 1956; Certificate of Family Planning, 1961; DPH, East Africa, 1969; MFCM, England, 1977. *Appointments:* House Officer, Mulago Hospital, Uganda, 1956-57; Senior House Officer, Watford and High Wycombe, England, 1957-59; Started health centre, Serowe, Botswana, 1959-61; Kaimosi Friends Hospital, Kenya, 1962-65; Medical Officer, Embu Hospital, 1965-67; Lecturer in Community Medicine, Makerere, Uganda, 1967-72; Special Tuberculosis Doctor, Mulago, 1967-72; Registrar in Community Medicine, In-service Training, West Glamorgan, Wales, 1972-77; Senior Lecturer 1977-85, Associate Professor 1985-, Community Medicine, University of Zambia, Lusaka. *Memberships include:* Action on Smoking and Health; International Epidemiological Association; International Union Against Tuberculosis; International Association of Cancer Registries; International Physicians for Prevention of Nuclear War; Medical Association for Prevention of War. *Publications include:* 'Thymus weights in malnourished children', 1968; 'Tuberculosis infections in Zambia', 1982; 'A case study of still births in Zambia 1978-80, serological investigations', (co-author), 1984. *Hobbies:* Choral music; Squash; Walking; Hard work. *Address:* Department of Community Medicine, School of Medicine, Box 50110, Lusaka, Zambia.

WAYNE, Victor Samuel, b. 7 Jan. 1953, Melbourne, Australia. Physician-Cardiologist; Private Consultant Practice. m. Karen Susan Eisinger, 21 Dec. 1976, Melbourne, 1 daughter. *Education:* MBBS (Hons), Monash University, 1976; Training, Alfred Hospital, Melbourne, St Vincent Hospital, University of Massachusetts Medical School, USA; FCCP, 1983, FACC 1985, DDU 1985. *Appointments:* Intern, 1977, Junior Resident Medical Officer, 1978, Senior Resident Medical Officer and Professorial Registrar, Monash University, 1979, Medical Registrar, Cardiology, 1980-81, Alfred Hospital; Instructor, Medicine, University of Massachusetts Medical School, USA, 1982-83; Advanced Cardiology Fellow, St Vincent Hospital, Worcester, USA, 1982-83; Visiting Physician, Monash University Department of Medicine; Cardiology Service, Alfred Hospital; Private Consultant, Cardiology. *Memberships:* Fellow, Royal Australasian College of Physicians; Fellow, American College of Chest Physicians; Fellow, International Academy of Chest Physicians and Surgeons; Fellow, American College of Cardiology; Member, Cardiac Society of Australia and New Zealand; Fellow, New York Academy of Sciences; Diplomate, Australian Society for Ultrasound in Medicine; Australasian Society of Echocardiography. *Publications:* Author, Co-Author, numerous articles in professional journals including: 'American Journal of Cardiology'; 'Journal American College of Cardiology'; 'Chest'; 'Australian and New Zealand Medical Journal'; 'Cardiomyopathy'; etc. *Honours:* Honours, every subject, Monash University Medical Course; Alfred Hospital Travelling Scholarship, 1982; Graduated MBBS Honours; National Heart Foundation Overseas Travel Grant, 1982. *Hobbies:* Travel; Music; Theatre; Reading; Tennis. *Address:* 16 Dunraven Ave, Toorak, Victoria 3142, Australia.

WAYOFF, Michel Robert Pierre, b. 24 Apr. 1927, Chateau Roux, France. Head of ENT Department. m. Marie-Colette Dupin, 11 Apr. 1950, Mirecourt, France, 2 sons, 1 daughter. *Education:* MD, 1953, Professor of Otorhinolaryngology. *Appointments:* Resident 1949; Assistant ENT, 1953; Associate Professor 1961; Clinical Professor ENT, 1970; Head of ENT Department and Director of School of Logopedics, 1974-. *Memberships:* French ENT Society; Belgian ENT Society; European Rhinologic Society; New York Academy of Sciences; German ENT Society, etc. *Publications:* "Allergies in ENT Field" 1967; "Functional Rhinplasty" 1970; "Chronic Otitis Media" 1966; "Vasomotor Rhinitis" 1978 etc. *Honours:* President of Society of Functional Medicine, 1975; President of European Rhinologic Society, 1984; President of French ENT Society, 1985; Decoration of the Education Ministry, 1983. *Hobbies:* Golf; Fencing; Walking; Philosophy; Ethology. *Address:* ENT Department, Hospital Central, 54000 Nancy, France.

WEBER, Genevieve Elaine, b. 15 Mar. 1953, Minot, North Dakota, USA. Chiropractor. m. Robert C Meager, 15 Dec. 1984, Harvey, North Dakota. *Education:* Bachelor of Science, Doctor of Chiropractic, Diplomate status in Chiropractic Orthopaedics. *Memberships:* North Dakota Chiropractic Association; American Chiropractic Association; International Chiropractic Association. *Hobbies:* Gardening; Raising Riding-Horses. *Address:* 900 Adams Avenue, Harvey, ND 58341, USA.

WEBER, Jeffrey Eric, b. 14 Dec. 1950, Haifa, Israel. Director, Council on Nutrition; Secretary, Kings County State Chiropractic Association USA. 2 sons. *Education:* BA, City University of New York, 1971; MA, Teachers College, Columbia University, 1972;

DC, New York Chiropractic College, 1978; Diplomate of the American Chiropractic Board of Nutrition, 1985. *Memberships:* American Chiropractic Association; International College of Applied Kinescology; New York Academy of Science; Council on Nutritio, Council on Roentgenology, American Chiropractic Association, National Academy of Research Biochemists. *Publications:* "Temperomandibular, Joint Dysfunction", 1981; "Applied Kinescology in Dental Practice", 1982. *Hobbies:* Cinema; Skiing; Racquetball; Swimming. *Address:* 2037 Ocean Avenue, Brooklyn, NY 11230, USA.

WEBER, Theodor (Teddy) Hugo Holgersson, b. 24 July 1939, Helsinki, Finland. Head of Clinical Laboratory, Aurora Hospital; Director, Strategic Research, Medix Biochemica. m. Aslög Mari-Louise Domars, 29 Dec. 1973, Jakobstad. *Education:* MD; Specialised in Chemical Pathology and Haematology; Assistant Professor in Clinical Chemistry. *Appointments:* Director, Medix Clinical Laboratories; Assistant Professor, Medical Genetics, University of Uppsala, Sweden; Research Fellow, San Francisco Medical Centre, University of California, USA. *Memberships:* Finnish Medical Association; Finska Läkaresällskapet; Finnish Association Clinical Chemistry; Finnish Association Haematology; Finnish Association Immunology. *Publications:* 'Isolation and characterization of a lymphocyte-stimulating leukoagglutinin from red kidney beans', 1969; Author of over 100 papers and abstracts on scientific subjects. *Honours:* 1st Class Medal, Finnish Yacht Racing Union, 1960 *Hobbies:* Off shore sailing and racing; Downhill skiing. *Address:* Medix Biochemica, PO Box 819, SF 00101 Helsinki 10, Finland.

WEBSTER, Keith Edward, b. 18 June 1935, England. Professor and Head of Department of Anatomy and Human Biology. m. Felicity Grainger, 2 Mar. 1984, London, 2 sons from previous marriage. *Education:* BSc, 1957, PhD, 1960, University College, London; MB BS, 1962, University College Hospital Medical School. *Appointments:* Lecturer, 1962-66, Senior Lecturer 1966-74, Reader 1974-75, Department of Anatomy, University College London; Honorary Research Associate, Centre for Neuroscience, 1975-, University College, London; Professor and Head of Department of Anatomy, 1975-85, Professor and Head of Department of Anatomy and Human Biology, 1985-, King's College, London. *Memberships:* Anatomical Society of Great Britain and Ireland; Royal Society of Medicine; International Brain Research Organisation. *Publications:* "The Central Nervous System" 1967; Numerous articles on Brain Research in Journal of Comparative Neurology, Neuroscience etc, 1961-. *Honour:* Symington Prize, British Anatomical Society, 1966. *Hobbies:* Music of Richard Wagner; Watching television wearing headphones. *Address:* Department of Anatomy and Human Biology, King's College (KQC), Strand, London WC2R 2LS, England.

WEEKE, Bent, b. 10 Feb. 1936, Copenhagen, Denmark. Medical Doctor; Head, Allergy Unit, University Hospital of Copenhagen, Rigshospitalet, 1978-. m. Eva Weeke, 18 June 1960, Copenhagen, 1 son, 3 daughters. *Education:* MD; Specialist in internal medicine and allergology; Assistant Professor. *Appointments:* Medical Diploma in Internal Medicine, 1961; Thesis on serumprotein, University Hospital, 1971. *Memberships:* President, Danish Society for Allergology; Member of the Board, European Academy of Allergy and Clinical Immunology; Member, Nominating Committee for the International Association of Allergology and Clinical Immunology; Member of the Board, Nordic Allergen Standarisation Committee. *Publications:* Author of over 150 publications on professional subjects. *Honours:* Gold Medal for research work, EAACI Meeting, London, England, 1974. *Hobbies:* Jazz pianist; Playing Football. *Address:* Medical Department for Allergy 7551, University Hospital, Rigshospitalet, Tagensvej 20, DK-2200 Copenhagen N, Denmark.

WEEKES, Leroy R, b. 17 Jan. 1913, Atlantic City, New Jersey, USA. Medical Doctor. m. Sylvia M Weekes, 2 sons, 3 daughters. *Education:* BS, Howard University College of Liberal Arts, 1931-35; MD, Howard University Medical School, 1935-39; Internship, Provident Hospital, Chicago, Illinois, 1939-40. *Appointments:* Residency, General-Burrell Memorial Hospital, Roanoake, Virginia, 1940-41; Major, Medical Corps, United States Army, Air Force, 1941-46; Residency, Obstetrics and Gynaecology, Washington DC, 1940-41, 1946-48; Medical Practice, 1948-; Senior Attending and Consultant, Queen of Angels Hospital, Chairman of Obstetrics and Gynaecology; Senior and Attending Consultant, West Adams Hospital; Senior Attending Staff, Los Angeles County-University of Southern California Medical Centre; Attending, Martin Luther King Jr Hospital; Clinical Professor of Obstetrics and Gynaecology, Emeritus Professor, University of Southern California Medical School; Professor of Obstetrics and Gynaecology, Charles R Drew Postgraduate Medical School; Courtesy Staff, Cedars-Sinai Medical Centre; Courtesy Staff, Kaiser-Permanente Hospital; Courtesy Staff, Ross-Loos Medical Centre. *Memberships include:* Los Angeles County Medical Society; California Medical Association; American Medical Association; Charles Drew Medical Society; National Medical Association; Los Angeles Obstetrical and Gynaecological Society; Former Member, Executive Board, Former Member, Executive Committee, American Red Cross; American Society of Clinical Oncology; Board of Directors, Charles Drew Postgraduate Medical School; Alpha Omega Alpha; Life Member, NAACP; Former Member, Board of Trustees, Howard University Washington DC; American Board of Obstetrics and Gynaecology, 1950; American College of Surgeons, 1951; Founding Member, American College of Obstetrics and Gynaecology. *Publications:* Author of 49 professional and medical publications in medical journals. *Honours:* Recipient of numerous awards and honours for professional services. *Address:* Julian W Ross Medical Centre, Los Angeles, California, USA.

WEI, Hon-Yin Stephen, b. 17 Sep. 1937, China. Professor and Head of Department. m. Gladys Li, 3 Aug. 1985, 2 daughters. *Education:* BDS (Hons), 1962, MDS, 1965, University of Adelaide, Australia; MS, University of Illinois, Chicago, USA, 1967; DDS, University of Iowa, 1971; FRACDS, 1965; FICD, 1979; FACD, 1985. *Appointments:* Associate Professor, 1970-74, Professor, 1974-76, Professor and Head, Department of Pedondontics, 1976-83, University of Iowa; Professor and Chairman, Division of Pedodontics; Vice-Chair, Department of Growth and Development, University of California, San Francisco, 1983-84; Professor and Head, Department of Children's Dentistry and Orthodontic, University of Hong Kong, 1984-. *Memberships:* Association of American Board of Pedodontics Diplomates; American Academy of Pediatric Dentistry; American Association of Dental Schools; American Dental Association; Royal Australasian College of Dental Surgeons; Hong Kong Dental Association, Clinical Member; International Association for Dental Research; International College of Dentists; Federation Dentaire Internationale. *Publications:* Co-author, "Pediatric Dentistry", 1981; Co-author, "Clinical Uses of Fluorides", 1985; Co-author, "Needs and Implementation of Preventive Dentistry in China", Comm. Dental Oral Epid., 1986. *Honours:* Member, California Statewide Task Force on Dental Health, 1983-84; Member, Expert Advisory Panel on Oral Health, WHO; Award of Excellence, American Society of Dentistry for Children. *Hobbies:* Tennis; Travel. *Address:* Department of Children's Dentistry and Orthodontics, Prince Philip Dental Hospital, 34 Hospital, Sai Ying Pun, Hong Kong.

WEIGAND, Dennis Allen, b. 17 Mar. 1939, Alva, Oklahoma, USA. Professor and Vice-Head, Department of Dermatology, Chief, Dermatology Service. m. Janet Deann White, 7 July 1961, Dacoma, Oklahoma, 1 son, 1 daughter. *Education:* BS, Northwestern (Oklahoma) State College, 1960; MD, Uni-

versity of Oklahoma School of Medicine, 1963. *Appointments:* Rotating Intern, St Francis Hospital, Witchita, Kansas, 1963-64; Resident in Dermatology 1964-67, Instructor 1967-70, Assistant Professor 1970-73, Associate Professor 1974-77, Adjunct Associate Professor of Pathology 1977-, Professor and Vice-Head, Department of Dermatology, University of Oklahoma Health Sciences Center, Oklahoma City; Currently Chief Dermatology Service, Veterans Administration Medical Center, Oklahoma City. *Memberships:* Fellow, American Academy of Dermatology; Fellow, American Society of Dermatopathology; Certified, American Boards of Dermatology and Dermatopathology; American Medical Association; American Dermatological Association; Alpha Omega Alpha; Sigma Xi. *Publications include:* "Medical Examination Review Book" Volume 21 dermatology, 1983; "Atopic Dermatitis, Current Therapy"; Numerous articles. *Honour:* Army Commendation Medal, 1970. *Hobbies:* Music - performance and composition. *Address:* 619 N E 13, Oklahoma City, OK 73104, USA.

WEIL, Max Harry, b. 7 Feb. 1927, Baden, Switzerland. Professor of Medicine. m. Marianne Judith Posner, Apr. 1955, 2 daughters. *Education:* AB, University of Michigan, Ann Arbor, 1948; MD, State University of New York College of Medicine, 1952; Rotating Internship, Internal Medicine, Cincinnati General Hospital, Ohio, 1952-53; Residency, Internal Medicine, University Hospital, Minnesota, 1953-55; PhD Physiology, University of Minnesota, 1957. *Appointments include:* Assistant Clinical Professor of Medicine, 1957-59, Assistant Professor of Medicine, 1959-63, Associate Professor of Medicine, 1963-71, Professor of Clinical Medicine, 1971-81, Adjunct Professor of Medicine, 1981-, University of Southern California School of Medicine; Professor & Chairman, Department of Medicine, University of Health Sciences, Chicago Medical School. *Memberships include:* Fellow, American College of Cardiology; American College of Physicians; American College of Chest Physicians; American Heart Association; American Medical Association; American Physiological Society; American Thoracic Society; Association of Professors of Medicine; Fellow, New York Academy of Science. *Honours:* Alpha Omega Alpha; Sigma Xi; Various Visiting Professorships. *Publications:* Over 500 publications papers & monographs. *Hobbies:* Swimming; Tennis. *Address:* Department of Medicine, University of Health Sciences, The Chicago Medical School, 3333 Green Bay Road, North Chicago, IL 60064, USA.

WEINBERG, Simon, b. 26 Sep. 1935, Toronto, Canada. Associate Professor of Oral & Maxillofacial Surgery. m. Roselyn née Dolman, 5 July 1959, Toronto, 2 sons, 1 daughter. *Education:* DDS, 1959, Diploma in Oral & Maxillofacial Surgery, 1963, University of Toronto; Diplomate, American Board of Oral & Maxillofacial Surgery, 1965; Fellow, Royal College of Dentists of Canada, 1967; Fellow, International College of Dentists, 1984. *Appointments:* Chairman, Examinations Committee, Royal College of Dentists of Canada; Examiner-in-Chief, Section of Oral & Maxillofacial Surgery, Royal College of Dentists of Canada; Past President, Ontario Society, Canadian Association of Oral & Maxillofacial Surgeons; Councillor, Great Lakes Society of Oral & Maxillofacial Surgeons; Associate Professor, Oral & Maxillofacial Surgery, Faculty of Dentistry, University of Toronto. *Memberships:* Canadian, American Associations, Great Lakes, Ontario Societies of Oral & Maxillofacial Surgeons; Chalmers J Lyons Academy of Oral Surgery; International Association for the Study of Dentofacial Deformities; Canadian Dental Association; Ontario Dental Association. *Publications:* Midline Cleft of the Mandible' 1975, 'Osteoma of the Mandibular Condyle' 1977 (in J. of Oral Surgery); 'Eminectomy and Meniscorrhaphy for Internal Derangements of the TMJ' (in Oral Surgery, Oral Medicine, Oral Pathology 1984); 'Surgical Correction of Jaw Fractures' (in Dental Clinics of North America 1982); 'Treatment of Facial Fractures' (in

Clinical Problems in Dental Practice 1985); 'Surgical Treatment of Internal Derangements of the Temporomandibular Joint' (in Facial Pain Textbook 1985). *Honour:* OKU Honour Dental Society, 1959. *Hobbies:* Squash Racquets; Reading; Pen Collecting. *Address:* 35 Bayhampton Court, Downsview, Ontario M3H 5L5, Canada.

WEINER, Allen Lewis, b. 29 Dec. 1943, Everett, Massachusetts, USA. Dentist. m. Georgene S Ganezer, 15 April 1967, Meriden, Connecticut, USA, 1 son, 2 daughters. *Education:* BA, Yeshiva University, New York, 1965; DMD, Harvard University School of Dental Medicine, Boston, Massachusetts, 1969. *Appointments:* General Dentist, Dover Air Force Base, Delaware, 1969-71; Clinical Instructor, Harvard School of Dental Medicine, 1971-76; General Dental Practice, Medfield Massachusetts, 1971-. *Memberships:* American Dental Association; Massachusetts Dental Society; American Prosthodontic Society; Harvard Odontological Society; American Society of Clinical Hypnosis. *Publications:* Presentation before 1969 International Association of Dental Research Weiner A L, Ofner P, Sweeney E: 'Metabolism of Testosterone-4-C14 by the Canine Submaxillary Gland' Journal of Endocrinology, 1970; 'A Nonparallel Cast Post Core Technique for Teeth with Divergent Canals' Journal of Prosthetic Dentistry, 1981; Clinical Presentation: Academy of General Dentistry, 1982. *Honours:* Nesbitt Award for Excellence in Clinical Dentistry, Harvard Dental Alumni Association, 1969; President, Norfolk County Dental Society, 1976; Fellow, Academy of General Dentistry, 1982. *Hobby:* Photography. *Address:* Park Street, Professional Building, 16 Park Street, PO Box 276, Medfield, MA 02052, USA.

WEIR, Bryce Keith Alexander, b. 29 Apr. 1936, Edinburgh, Scotland. Director, Division of Neurosurgery. m. Marylou Lauber, 25 Feb. 1976, Edmonton, 1 son, 2 daughters. *Education:* MSc; MDCM; FRCS (C); FACS; McGill University, Canada. *Appointments:* Chief, Neurosurgery, Royal Alexandra Hospital, Edmonton. *Memberships:* Royal College of Physicians & Surgeons of Canada; American College of Surgeons; Canadian Neurosurgical Society; American Association of Neurological Surgeons; Society of Neurological Surgeons; Western Neurosurgical Society; American Academy of Neurological Surgery. *Publications:* 100 articles; "Aneurysms Affecting the Nervous System", 1986. *Honours:* Wood Gold Medal, McGill University, 1960; Clinical Research Award, Edmonton Academy of Medicine, 1983; Hans Berger Prize of American EEC Society, 1963. *Hobby:* Painting. *Address:* Division of Neurosurgery, University of Alberta Hospitals, Edmonton, Alberta, Canada.

WEISBARD, Marvin, b. 10 Aug. 1928, New York, New York, USA. Director, Center for Marital Sexual and Emotional Problems. m. Eileen Helene Goldsmith, 21 Mar. 1953, New York City, 3 sons, 1 daughter. *Education:* BS, Columbia University, 1947; MD, University of Oklahoma, 1965. *Appointments:* Out-Patient Director, Southern Arizona Mental Health Center, Tucson, Arizona, 1969-70; Director, 1970, Consultant to Paediatric Unit, 1971-72, Southern Arizona Mental Health Center; Individual Practice of Psychiatry, Tucson, 1970-; currently, Director-Center for Marital Sexual and Emotional Problems. *Memberships:* American and Arizona Psychiatric Associations; Tucson Psychiatric Society; Alpha Omega Alpha. *Hobbies:* Computer programming; Astronomy; Stamp collecting. *Address:* 601 North Wilmot, Suite 236, Tucson, AZ 85711, USA.

WEISBERG, Paul Stephen, b. 9 Mar. 1932, Superior, Wisconsin, USA. Physician. m. (1) Tamara Levin, 21 May 1958, Tel Aviv, Israel, 2 sons, 1 daughter; (2) Gabrielle Grunau, 9 Jan. 1980, Washington, DC, USA, 1 daughter. *Education:* Harvard College, 1948-52; AB, Harvard Law School, 1953; MD, Marquette University School of Medicine, 1958; Internship: Mount

Zion Hospital, San Francisco, 1958-59; Residency in Psychiatry, Cincinnati General Hospital, 1959-62. *Appointments:* Lieutenant Commander, Medical Corps, USNR, 1962-64; Assistant Professor of Psychiatry, Department of Psychiatry, George Washington University School of Medicine, Washington, DC, 1964-67; Associate Professor of Psychiatry, 1967-69; Associate Clinical Professor of Psychiatry, 1969-; Director, Group Therapy Center of Washington, 1969-73. *Memberships:* American Society for Adolescent Psychiatry (Fellow); American Psychiatric Association; American Medical Association; American Group Psychotherapy Association. *Publications:* Editor, Critical Issues in Adolescent Mental Health, 1978; The Changing Nature of Adolescence and Group Therapy with Adolescents in A Short Course in Adolescent Psychiatry, Brunner, Mazel, 1979. Contributor to professional journals. *Honours:* Founding President, Metropolitan Washington Society for Adolescent Psychiatry, 1972-74; President, American Society for Adolescent Psychiatry, 1979-80. *Address:* 3261 Prospect Street, NW, Washington, DC 20007, USA.

WEISS, Arthur J, b. 11 Apr. 1925, Philadelphia, Pennsylvania, USA. Assistant Professor of Medicine. m. Lillian Alexander, 24 Feb. 1952, 2 sons, 1 daughter. *Education:* BS, Pennsylvania State University, 1945; MD, University of Pennsylvania, 1950; Certified, American Board of Internal Medicine, 1958; Certified, American Board of Medical Oncology, 1973. *Appointments:* Director, Division of Medical Oncology, Department of Medicine, 1959-69, Assistant Professor of Medicine, 1958-, Thomas Jefferson University Hospital; Staff, US Naval Research Institute, 1956-57; Fellow, National Foundation of Medicine (Hematology) Jefferson Medical College, 1954-55; Resident, Internal Medicine, Hospital University of Pennsylvania, 1951-52. M*Memberships:* New York Academy of Sciences; International Society of Blood Transfusion; American Society of Hematology; Founding Member, American Society of Clinical Oncology; American Association of University Professors; Society of Experimental Pharmacology and Therapeutics; American Association for Clinical Research; American Association for Cancer Research; Fellow, American College of Physicians. *Publications:* Author of over 70 medical articles including 'Factors in the Variation and Regulation of Coronary Blood Flow in Intact Anesthatized Dogs', (with E L Foltz, D M Aviado), 1950; 'An Ion Exchange Resin Kidney for use on Human Patients', (with J L Sandler, J E Clark, T F Nealon Jr), 1961; 'Evaluation of the Combination of Hexamethylemelamine and Methotrexate in Carcinoma of the Lung', (with W L Wilson), 1971); 'Adsorption and Metabolism of Dibromodulcitol in Patients with Advanced Cancer' (with M A Belej, W M Troetel, J E Stambaugh, R W Manthei), 1972; 'A Pharmacologic Study of Yoshi 864', 1975; 'The Myocardial Toxicity of Adriamycin Administered Weekly', 1983; "Effects of Daunorubicin, Actinomycin, Verapamil and Trifluoperazine on Doxorubicin Uptake by Calcium-Resistant Cardiac Myocytes from Adult Rats', (with V K Kheterpal, J J Kocsis), 1985. *Address:* 1265 Old Ford Road, Huntingdon Valley, PA 19006, USA.

WEISS, George Arthur, b. 1 Feb. 1921, Brooklyn, New York, USA. Orthodontist, Private Practice; Director, Orthodontics, Samaica Hospital; Assistant Professor, Stonybrook College of Dentistry. m. Jacqueline H Weiss, 28 Jan. 1944, New York, 2 daughters. *Education:* BA, Brooklyn College, 1941; DDS, Columbia College of Dental Surgery, 1944; Certificate, Orthodontics, Columbia College, 1954; American Board of Orthodontics, 1962; Fellow, American College of Dentistry, 1974. *Appointments:* Chief, Dental Surgery, Nagoya, Japan, 1946; Chief, Dental Surgeon, Kobe Base, Japan, 1947; Chief Dental Surgeon, Olmstead Airforce Base, Pennyslvania, 1948; Chief Orthodontist, Community Service Society, 1954-58; Chief, Administrator, 1962-72, President, 1973, Queens College; Board of Governors,

Dental Society of State of New York, 1975-85. *Memberships:* American Dental Association; American Association of Orthodontists; Diplomate, American Board of Orthodontics; Fellow, American College of Dentists; Strang Tweed Study Clubs. *Publications:* "Peridontal Conditions Related to Class I, II, III", 1962; "How to Become Financially Independent of your Practice", 1982. *Honours:* Honorary Medal, American Chemical Society, 1941; Proplae Honorary Society of Brooklyn College, 1940; Wm. Jaquie Society, 1943; etc. *Hobbies:* Travel; Bridge; Golf. *Address:* 5901 Springfield Blvd, Bayside, NY 11364, USA.

WEISS, Joseph F (Francis), b. 26 Jan. 1940, Taylor, Pennsylvania, USA. Chief, Physiological Chemistry Division, Armed Forces Radiobiology Research Institute, Bethesda, Maryland, 1976-. m. Elvira S de Castro, 7 Sep. 1968, Milan, Italy, 2 sons. *Education:* BS, 1961, University of Scranton, Pennsylvania, USA; MS, 1963, PhD, The Ohio State University, Columbus, Ohio, 1966. *Appointments:* Postdoctoral Fellow, Institute of Pharmacology, University of Milan, Italy, 1966-68; Instructor in Neurosurgery, 1968-72; Assistant Professor of Experimental Neurosurgery, Department of Neurosurgery, New York University Medical Centre, New York, USA, 1972-74; Research Chemist, Radiation Biology Department, 1974-76. *Memberships:* American Chemical Society; Phi Lambda Upsilon; Sigma Xi; American Oil Chemists' Society; Radiation Research Society; American Association for Cancer Research; American Society of Clinical Oncology; International Society of Immunopharmacology. *Publications:* 'Acute-phase proteins and systemic immunity', (with P B Chretien), 1985; 'Sterols and other lipids in tumors of the nervous system', 1975; 'Serum acute-phase proteins and immunoglobulins in patients with gliomas', 1979, (Co-author); 'Suppression of delayed-type hypersensitivity to oxazolone in whole-body irradiated mice and protection by WR-2721', (with V Srinivasan), 1984. *Address:* Biochemistry Department, Armed Forces Radiobiology Research Institute, Bethesda, MD 20814-5145, USA.

WEISS, Pauline, b. 23 Nov. 1931, Assistant Clinical Psychiatry, Columbia University College of Physicians and Surgeons. m. Aaron Weiss, 26 Nov. 1964. *Education:* BA, 1952; MSc, 1958; MD, Auton University of Guad, 1977; Senior Candidate, American Institute for Psychoanalysis, 1978-. *Appointments:* Teacher, Intelligent Gifted Children; Resident Psychiatry, Chief Resident, Staff Psychiatrist, Assistant Clinical Psychiatry, Columbia University, College of Physicians and Surgeons, USA; Psychoanalyst, Private Practitioner, Karen Horney Institute. *Memberships:* American Psychiatric Association; American Medical Women's Association; American Institute for Psychoanalysis. *Honours:* NYC Board of Education Certificate of Excellence, 1973. *Hobbies:* Theatre; Art collecting. *Address:* 435 West 57 Street, New York City, NY 10019, USA.

WEISS, Robert Jerome, b. 9 Dec. 1917, West New York, New Jersey, USA. De Lemar Professor of Public Health Practice. m. Minnie Thompson Moore, 21 Apr. 1945, New York, 2 sons, 1 daughter. *Education:* The Johns Hopkins University, 1934-37; AB, The George Washington University, 1946-47; MD, Columbia University College of Physicians and Surgeons, 1947-51. *Appointments:* Professor and Chair, Department of Psychiatry, Dartmouth Medical School; Associate Dean for Health Care Planning, Harvard Medical School; Associate Director, Harvard Centre for Community Health and Medical Care; Associate, 1954-59, Professor of Psychiatry and Social Medicine, Director, Centre for Community Health, De Lemar Professor of Public Health Practice, Dean of School of Public Health, Columbia University. *Memberships:* Life Fellow, American Psychiatric Association; American Public Health Association; Fellow, New York Academy of Medicine; Herman Biggs Society. *Publications:* 'Epidemiology of emotional disturbances in a mens' college, 1965; 'Social supports

and the reduction of psychiatric disability', 1968; 'Trends in health insurance operating expenses', 1972; 'Foreign medical graduates and the medical underground', 1974; 'The effect of importing physicians', 1974. *Honours:* Honorary MA, Dartmouth College, 1964; Silver BiCentennial Medal, Columbia University, 1967. *Hobbies:* Woodcarving; Walking; Sailing. *Address:* 51 Hickory Hill Road, Tappan, NY 10983, USA.

WEISSBERG, Josef H, b. 25 Oct. 1928, New York, New York, USA. Associate Clinical Professor of Psychiatry. m. Ann Elizabeth Klein, 15 June 1958, New York City, 1 son, 2 daughters. *Education:* MD, Albany Medical College, Albany, New York, 1952; Certificate in Psychoanalytic Medicine, Columbia University, New York, 1962. *Appointments:* Director, Training and Education, Catholic Medical Center of Brooklyn and Queens New York, 1970-72; Collaborating Psychoanalyst, Columbia University Psychoanalytic Center, 1971-; Director, Association for Short-Term Psychotherapy, 1982-; Psychiatry Consultant, Metropolitan Life Insurance Company, 1983-. *Memberships:* Fellow: American Psychiatric Association; American Academy of Psychoanalysis. Association for Psychoanalytic Medicine; New York City and New York State Medical Societies. *Publications:* 'Short Term Dynamic Psychotherapy: An Application of Psychoanalytic Personality Theory' in 'Journal of the American Academy of Psychoanalysis', 1984. *Honour:* Alpha Omega Alpha, 1952. *Hobbies:* Music; Opera; Tennis. *Address:* 4 East 89th Street, New York, NY 10028, USA.

WELCH, Gary William, b. 4 Jan. 1943, Buffalo, New York, USA. Chairman, Department of Anaesthesiology, UMass Medical Centre. *Education:* BA, 1964, MD, 1970, PhD, 1970, University of Virginia. *Appointments:* Staff Surgeon, USAISR, Fort Sam Houston, Texas, 1971-72; Chief of Anaesthesiology Section, USAISR, Fort Sam Houston, 1974-76; Chief of Pulmonary Section, USAISR, Fort Sam Houston, 1975-76; Staff Anaesthesiologist, Assistant Professor, 1977-78, Associate Professor of Anaesthesiology, 1978-83, Vice-Chairman, Anaesthesiology, 1980-81, Acting Chairman, Anaesthesiology, 1981-82, UMass Medical Centre, Worcester, Massachusetts. *Memberships:* Member of numerous professional societies. *Publications include:* 'Anaesthesia for thermally injured patients', 1978; 'Deep vein thrombosis and pulmonary embolism', 1981; 'Anaesthesia for the patient with thermal injury', 1983; 'Airway management and endotracheal intubation', 1985; 'Burn management in the intensive care unit', 1985; 'Recovery Room Management of the Postoperative Patient', 1985; 'Anaesthesia and the Geriatric patient', 1985; Contributor to scientific exhibits, lectures and symposia. *Address:* Department of Anaesthesiology, UMass Medical Centre, Worcester, MA 01605, USA.

WELDON, Virginia Verral, b. 9 Aug. 1935, Toronto, Canada. University Vice Chancellor for Medical Affairs, Professor of Paediatrics, Vice President of Medical Center. 2 daughters. *Education:* AB, cum laude, Smith College, 1957; MD, State University of New York at Buffalo, 1962; Doctor of Humane Letters (Hon) Rush University, 1985; Intern, Resident and Fellow, The Johns Hopkins University School of Medicine and The Johns Hopkins Hospital, 1962-67. *Appointments:* Instructor in Paediatrics, Johns Hopkins University, 1967-68; Instructor in Paediatrics, 1968-69, Assistant Professor of Paediatrics, 1969-73, Associate Professor of Paediatrics, 1973-79, Professor of Paediatrics, 1979-, Assistant Vice Chancellor for Medical Affairs, 1975-81, Deputy Vice Chancellor for Medical Affairs, 1983-, Washington University School of Medicine; Vice President, Washington University Medical Center, 1980-. *Memberships:* Commissioner, St Louis, Zoological Park; Board of Directors, Centerre Trust Co, of St Louis; Board of Directors, St Louis Regional Commerce and Growth Association; Board of Directors, United Way of Greater St Louis; Endocrine Society; Society of Pediatric

Research; American Paediatric Society; Paediatric Endocrine Society; American Association for the Advancement of Science; Institute of Medicine of National Academy of Sciences; Association of American Medical Colleges; Chairman 1986; Council of Academic Societies, Chair 1984-85; Commonwealth Fund Task Force on Academic Health Centers; Board of Directors National Association for Biomedical Research. *Publications:* Numerous articles in medical journals and chapters in edited medical volumes; numerous papers presented to medical conferences and symposia. *Honours:* Sigma Xi 1957; Alpha Omega Alpha 1962; Smith College Medal, 1984; Fellow, American Association for the Advancement of Science, 1984. *Address:* Washington University School of Medicine, Box 8106, 660 South Euclid Avenue, St Louis, MO 63110, USA.

WELLER, Elizabeth Boghossian, b. 7 Aug. 1949, Lebanon. Professor of Psychiatry. m. Ronald A Weller, MD, 18 Feb. 1978, Granite City, Illinois, USA, 1 son. *Education:* MD, 1975; Board Certified in Psychiatry, 1981; Board Certified in Child Psychiatry, 1982. *Appointments:* Staff Psychiatrist, Division of Child Psychiatry, University of Kansas Medical Centre, 1979-; Director, Inpatient Children's Unit, 1982-, Director of Training, Child Psychiatry Fellows, 1984-, Director of Consultation and Liaison in Child Psychiatry, 1984-, Co-ordinator of Psychiatry Grand Rounds, 1984-. *Memberships:* American Psychiatric Association; Kansas Psychiatric Association; American Medical Association; Kansas Medical Society; Wyandotte County Medical Society; American Academy of Child Psychiatry; American Academy of Clinical Pharmacology and Therapeutics; Childhood Affective Disorders Consortium. *Publications:* "Current Perspectives on Major Depressive Disorders in Children", editor, 1984; Articles: 'Dexamethasone Suppression Test in Prepubertal Depressed Children' in 'American Journal of Psychiatry', 1984; 'Diagnosing Depression in Children' in 'Psychiatric Annals', 1985. *Honours:* National Valedictorian Honour Scholarship, 1962-67; National Valedictorian Honour Scholarship, 1968-74; Dean's Honour List, 1968-72; Alpha Omega Alpha, 1975; Academy of Clinical Psychiatry Clinical Research Award, 1982; Outstanding Young Women of America, 1985; American Academy of Clinical Psychiatry Clinical Research Award, 1984. *Hobbies:* Cooking; Reading; Study of different cultures; Antique collecting. *Address:* Department of Psychiatry, Ohio State University, Upham Hall, 473 W. 12th Avenue, Columbus, OH 43210, USA.

WELLER, Ronald Alan, b. 14 July 1948, Bowling Green, Ohio, USA. Professor. m. Elizabeth Boghossian, 18 Feb. 1978, Granite City, Illinois, 1 son. *Education:* BA, Wabash College, Crawfordville, Indiana, 1970; MD, Washington University, St Louis, Missouri, 1974. *Appointments:* Assistant Instructor, Washington University Medical School, 1974-78; Assistant Professor, 1978-83, Associate Professor, 1983-85, University of Kansas Medical Centre; Professor, Ohio State University Hospitals, 1986. *Memberships:* Kansas Medical Society; American Medical Association; Kansas Psychiatric Association; American Psychiatric Association; American Academy of Clinical Psychiatrists. *Publications:* "Major Depressive Disorders in Children", 1984; "Objective Criteria for Diagnosis of Marijuana Abuse", 1980; "Adult Psychiatric Disorders in Psychiatrically Ill Young Adolescents", 1983; "Psychotropic Drugs & Alcohol", 1984; "Agreement Between Two Structured Diagnostic Interviews", 1985; "Marijuana Use & Psychiatric Illness", 1985. *Honours:* Norman Treeves Award in Science, Wabash College, 1970; Co-recipient, Clinical Research Award, American Academy of Clinical Psychiatrists, 1982, 1984. *Hobbies:* Reading; Gardening. *Address:* Ohio State University Hospitals, 473 West 12th Avenue, Columbus, OH 43210, USA.

WELLER, Roy Oliver, b. 27 May 1938, London, England. Professor, Neuropathology; Consultant Neuropathologist. m. Francine Michelle Cranley, 22

Dec. 1960, St Albans, 1 son, 1 daughter. *Education:* BSc; LRCP; NRCS; MB; BS; PhD; MD; FRCPath. *Appointments:* House Officer, 1961-62, Junior Lecturer, Anatomy, 1963-64, Lecturer, Pathology, 1964-67, Guy's Hospital; USPHS Postdoctoral Fellow, Albert Einstein College of Medicine, New York, USA, 1967-68; Lecturer, Senior Lecturer, Pathology, 1968-72, Consultant Neuropathologist, Guy's and Maudsley Hospitals, 1971-72; Senior Lecturer, Professor, Neuropathology, Southampton University Medical School, 1973-. *Memberships:* British Neuropathological Society; Pathological Society; Society for Research in Hydrocephalus and Spina Bifida; Developmental Biology Society; Brain Research Association. *Publications:* "A Colour Atlas of Neuropathology", 1984; "Clinical Neuropathology", jointly, 1983; "MacAlpine's Multiple Sclerosis", jointly, 1985; "Pathology of Peripheral Nerves", jointly, 1977; numerous articles in major journals. *Honours:* Payling Wright Travelling Fellowship, 1967; US PHS International Postdoctoral Research Fellowship, 1967-68; Virginia Kneeland Franz Prize, 1968; British Council Travelling Fellowship, 1971. *Hobbies:* Squash; Music; Literature; Walking. *Address:* Dept. of Pathology (Neuropathology), Southampton University Medical School, Southampton General Hospital, Southampton SO9 4XY, England.

WELLISCH, Robert, b. 24 Aug. 1938, Budapest, Hungary. Chiropractor; Clinical Nutritionist; Residency Supervisor. *Education:* Diploma in Podiatry and Chiropody; Diploma in Psychology; BA, Literature and Philosophy; Doctorate in Chiropractic Philosophy; Postgraduate Diploma, Orthomolecular Nutrition; Postgraduate Diploma in Clinical Nutrition. *Appointments:* Associate Clinician; Private Practice. *Memberships:* Australian and American Chiropractic Associations; International Academy of Nutrition. *Publications:* 'Farrago', Melbourne University; 'Rabelais', La Trobe University; 'Learning Exchange'; 'New Voices'; 'Educational Magazine'; 'Art Look'. *Hobbies:* Chess; Walking; Pushbike riding; Swimming. *Address:* 12/66 Alma Road, St Kilda, Victoria 3182, Australia.

WELSCH, Clifford William, b. 10 Sep. 1935, St Louis, Missouri, USA. Professor. m. Margaret, 1 June 1958, 3 sons. *Education:* BS, Chemistry; MS, PhD, Physiological Chemistry. *Appointments:* Assistant Professor, Natural Science, 1965, Research Associate, Physiology, 1966, Assistant Professor, Anatomy, 1968, Associate Professor, 1971, Professor, 1974-, Anatomy, Michigan State University. *Memberships:* American Association for Cancer Research; American Physiological Society; Society for Experimental Biology and Medicine; American Association for the Advancement of Science. *Publications:* 130 articles in the field of breast cancer research. *Honours:* NIH-NCI Research Career Development Award, 1971-76; Associate Editor, 'Cancer Research', 1980-1990. *Hobbies:* Fishing; Hunting. *Address:* 11408 Forest Hill Road, DeWitt, MI 48820, USA.

WENDELL SMITH, Colin Peter. University Deputy Vice-Chancellor and Professor of Anatomy. m. Pamela Joy Eustace, 10 Mar. 1951, 2 sons. *Education:* MB BS, St Bartholomew's Hospital Medical College, 1951; D Obst, RCOG, 1953; PhD, University of London, 1967; Fellow, Australian College of Education, 1972; Fellow, Royal Australian College of Obstetricians and Gynaecologists, 1983. *Appointments:* Lecturer in Anatomy, Guy's Hospital Medical School, London 1956-61; Associate Professor of Anatomy, University of New South Wales, 1961-68; Professor of Anatomy, 1968-, Pro-Vice-Chancellor, 1975-76, 1982-85, Deputy Vice-Chancellor, Dean, Faculty of Medicine, 1983, University of Tasmania; Honorary Anatomist, Royal Hobart Hospital, Tasmania, 1968-. *Memberships:* Australian representative on Members' Assembly and Regional Council for East and South East Asia and Oceania, and Regional representative on Central Council, International Planned Parenthood Federation; Patron, Australian

Federation of Family Planning Associations Incorporated; Founder President, Family Planning Association of Tasmania Incorporated; Member, National Population Council; Member, Tasmanian Council of Advanced Education. *Publications:* Contributor to "Systemic Pathology" 1976; "Scientific Foundations of Obstetrics and Gynaecology" 1985 and numerous scientific papers. Co-author: "Basic Human Embryology" 1984. *Honours:* Commonwealth Fellowship, 1967. *Hobbies:* Philately; Bush walking. *Address:* University of Tasmania, PO Box 252C, GPO Hobart,· Tasmania 7001, Australia.

WENGER, Don S, b. 18 Dec. 1911, Monroe, Wisconsin, USA. Physician (retired); Attorney (retired). m. Mary Vancho Hoornstra, 24 Aug. 1974, Annapolis, Maryland, 1 son, 1 daughter. *Education:* AB, University of Wisconsin, 1934; MD, Marquette University 1937; MS, Georgetown University, 1956; George Washington University, 1962. *Appointments include:* Resident in Surgery, Assistant to Chief of Surgery, Regional Surgical Consultant for Army, Oliver General Hospital, Augusta, Georgia, 1947-49; Chief of Surgery, 1949-50, Commander and Chief of Surgery, 1950-53; Chanute Air Force Base Hospital; Chief, Consultants Group, Deputy Director, Office of USAF Surgeon-General, 1953-57; Chair, Department of Surgery and Deputy Hospital Commander, Lackland Air Force Base Hospital, 1957-59; Chief Professional Consultant for USAF, 1959-63, Director of Professional Services, Office of USAF Surgeon General, 1959-65; Deputy Chief of Staff, Bioastronautics and Medicine, HQ AF Systems (Research) Command, 1965-67; Retired as Major-General 1967. *Memberships:* Society of Air Force Clinical Surgeons, Founder-Member; Fellow, International College of Surgeons; American Bar Association; American College of Legal Medicine; Fellow, American College of Emergency Medicine; National Lawyers Club; Cosmos Club. *Publications include:* Pilonidal Cyst: Their Origin and Treatment, American Journal of Surgery, 1950; This One Came Back, Flying Safety, 1951 and numerous other professional papers. *Honours include:* Air Force Commendation Medal; Legion of Merit; Distinguished Service Medal. *Hobbies:* Jazz Pianist (professional); Organist; Tennis. *Address:* 9409 Falls Bridge Lane, Potomac, MD 20854, USA.

WENGER, Franz, b. 11 June 1913, Vienna, Austria. University Professor. m. Maria Bohorquez, 7 May 1954, 3 sons, 1 daughter. *Education:* MD, University of Vienna. *Appointments:* Professor of Pathology, Sucre, Bolivia, 1939-45; Professor of Pathology, Maracaibo, Venezuela, 1946-57; Chief of Pathology Department, Clinice Falcon, 1960-; Chief of Pathology Department, Centro Medico Paraiso, 1984-. *Memberships:* Academie de Medicina del Zulia; Sociedad Latino Americana de Patologia; Sociedad Venezolana de Patologia. *Publications:* Some 100 scientific papers in Journals of Pathology and General Medicine. *Honours:* Premio Adolfo D'Empaire, 1961; Premio Marciel Hernandez, 1968. *Hobbies:* Piano music: music critic, organiser of concerts. *Address:* Edificio El Saman - 8o, C73A, No-2B-45, Maracaibo, Venezuela.

WENGER, Rudolf, b. 4 Sep. 1915, Linz, Donau, Austria. Specialist in Internal Medicine. m. Gisela Rieger, 24 Dec. 1943, Frankfurt am Main, Federal Republic of Germany, 1 son, 2 daughters. *Education:* MD, 1938, University Dozent, 1955, University of Vienna; University Professor, Internal Medicine, 1965. *Appointments:* Military Service, 1939-45; Assistant, Associate Professor, Head of Cardiology Department, 1st Medical University Clinic, Vienna, 1945-67; Medical Department, Krankenanstalt Rudolfstiftung Vienna, 1967-80. *Memberships include:* Past President: Austrian Cardiology Society; Austrian Society of Internal Intensive Medicine; Austrian Society for Tropical Medicine. President, Austrian Society for Nutrition Research. *Publications:* "Dietetics", 1955, 64; "Klin Vektorkardiographie", 1956, 68; "Endokard-fibrosen", 1964; "Aktuelle Probleme der Vektorkar-

diographie", 1968; Handbuchbeiträge, Author over 300 articles. *Honours:* Grosses Ehrenzeichen für Verdienste um die Republik Osterreich, 1973; Goldenes Ehrenzeichen Land Wien, 1982. *Hobbies:* Archaeology; Hunting; Travelling. *Address:* Esteplatz 5, A-1030 Vienna, Austria.

WENZ, Werner Simon, b. 18 Mar. 1926, Limburg/1, Germany. Professor, Radiology; Department Chairman. m. Hannelore Protz, 5 Oct. 1956, Limburg, 1 son, 6 daughters. *Education:* University of Giessen; MD, University of Mainz; University of Zurich, Switzerland; Professor, Radiology, University of Heidelberg. *Appointments:* Internship, Pathology, 1952, Resident Radiology, 1953, Institute, University of Zurich; Resident, Surgery, University Clinic, Heidelberg, 1955; Head, Radiology, Surgical University Clinic, Heidelberg, 1958; Chairman, Radiology Diagnosis, University of Freiburg, 1972; Doyen, Medical Faculty, 1976-77, Vice President, 1983-85, University of Freiburg. *Memberships:* Deutsche Rontgengesellschaft; Sudwestdeutsche Radiologenvereinigung; Deutsche Ges fur Angiologie; European College of Angiography; Ges Deutscher Naturforscher und Arzte; etc. *Publications:* "Abdominal Angiographie", 1972; "Extremitatenangiographie", 1974; "Studienbuch Radiologie", 1978; "Rontgenologische Differentialdiagnostik", 1978; "Taschenbuch Radiologie", 1976/1980; "Kursus Radiologie", co-author, 1972, 1976, 1981; "Radiologie in Freiburg", 1981. *Honours:* Verdienstkreuz, 1944; Holthusenring der Dtsch Rontgengesellschaft, 1972; Ritter Ordo equestr Jerusolim, 1983; Corresponding Member, Schweiz Rontgengesellschaft, 1983; Honorary Member, Franzosische Ro. Ges., 1985. *Hobbies:* Classical Music; History. *Address:* Riedbergstrasse 6, D-7800 Freiburg, Federal Republic of Germany.

WERBLOWSKY, Joshua H, b. 25 May 1942, Brooklyn, New York, USA. University Professor. m. Joan, 17 Marh 1968, 1 son, 2 daughters. *Education:* BA, Yeshiva College; MD, Einstein College of Medicine; Psychiatric Residency, Philadelphia Psychiatric Center; Certificate, Board of Psychiatry and Forensic Psychiatry. *Appointments:* Director, Community Mental Health Inpatient Department, Philadelphia Psychiatric Center; Director of Psychiatry, Downtown Home for the Aged. *Memberships:* American Psychiatric Association; American Academy of Psychiatry and Law; American Academy of Forensic Sciences; Center for Psychology and Judaism. *Publications:* 'Amoxapine and Imipramine in Depressed Patients' American Journal of Psychiatry, 1981; 'Insanity Defense: Comparative Analyses Anglo-Saxon and Jewish Law' Springer-Verlag Press - Chapter, 1984. *Hobby: Sport. Address:* 509 Waldron Terrace, Merion, PA 19066, USA.

WERNER, Ivar, b. 30 Jan. 1923, Karlstad, Sweden. Physician, Professor. m. Margareta Johnsén, 1968, 1 son, 1 daughter. *Education:* MB 1944, MD 1950, PhD 1953, Uppsala University, Sweden. *Appointments:* Reader, Physical Chemistry, 1950-53, Assistant Professor, 1953-58, Associate Professor, Internal Medicine, 1958-74, Professor & Director, Institute & Department of Geriatrics, 1974-, all University of Uppsala. *Memberships:* Swedish Medical Association; Swedish Medical Society; Royal Society of Scientists, Uppsala; Royal Society of Medicine, London; Swedish Society for Geriatric Research, President 1976-; Royal Society of Sciences, Uppsala. *Hobbies:* Tennis; Fishing. *Address:* Department of Geriatrics, PO Box 12042, S-750 12 Uppsala, Sweden.

WERTHEIM, Raymond Benedict, b. 30 Oct. 1942, Philadelphia, Pennsylvania, USA. Clinical Assistant Professor, (Child) Psychiatry. *Education:* BS, Trinity College, Hartford, Connecticut; MD, Temple University, Philadelphia, Pennsylvania. *Appointments include:* Post Doctoral Fellowship, Philadelphia Child Guidance Clinic, 1978-80; Associate, University of Pennsylvania School of Medicine, 1980-81; Clinical Assistant Professor, Pediatric Health Sciences and

Child Psychiatry, George Washington University School of Medicine, 1981-; Family Therapy Supervisor, National Childrens Hospital, Washington, District of Columbia, 1981-; Instructor and Supervisor, Family Therapy Training, Family Therapy Institute of Alexandria, 1981-; Private Practice, Psychiatry, 1981-. *Memberships:* American Psychiatric Association; Virginia Medical Society; Alexandria Medical Society; American Academy of Pediatrics; American Association of Marriage and Family Therapy; American Orthopsychiatric Association; Washington Psychiatric Society, various others. Participant in numerous workshops as Presenter, Invited presenter, Speaker and Leader. *Honours:* BS cum laude, 1964; Diplomate, National Board of Medical Examiners, 1970, American Board of Pediatrics, 1975, American Board of Psychiatry and Neurology, 1984. *Hobbies:* Tennis; Bicycling; Music; Pianist. *Address:* Family Therapy Institute of Alexandria, 220 South Washington Street, Alexandria, VA 22314, USA.

WERTLIEB, Donald, b. 22 Feb. 1952, Washington, District of Columbia, USA. Assistant Professor of Child Study, Tufts University. m. 2 children. *Education:* BS, Department of Psychology, 1974, MA, Eliot-Pearson Department of Child Study, 1975, Tufts University; MA, Psychology, 1976, PhD, Clinical Community Psychology, 1978, Boston University. *Appointments include:* Teaching Assistant, Clinical Fellow in Psychology, Instructor, various colleges, university, hospitals, etc, 1973-; Staff Psychologist, Judge Baker Guidance Center, Boston, 1978-81; Consulting Psychologist, Massachusetts Department of Youth Services, Lakeville, 1978-80; Lecturer, Eliot-Pearson Department of Child Study, Tufts University, 1978-79; Instructor, Psychiatry, Harvard Medical School, 1978-81; Assistant Professor, Eliot-Pearson Department of Child Study, Tufts University, 1979-; Senior Research Associate, Principal Investigator, Child Stress and Coping Project, Harvard Community Health Plan, Boston, 1981-; Faculty, Institute for Health Research, Harvard Community Health Plan and Harvard University, Boston, 1983-; Lecturer, Department of Social Medicine and Health Policy, Harvard Medical School, 1984-. *Memberships:* American Association of University Professors; American Orthopsychiatric Association, Fellow; American Psychological Association; Association for the Advancement of Psychology; Massachusetts Psychological Association, Board of Directors, 1982-84; National Council on Family Relations; Society for Research in Child Development; Society of Pediatric Psychology; Phi Beta Kappa; Psy Chi, etc. *Publications:* Numerous papers and presentations; Contributor to professional journals; Editor or Consulting Editor several professional journals. *Honours:* Research and Training Grants; Carmichael Prize, 1973; NIMH Training Fellow in Clinical Psychology, Boston University, 1974-76. *Address:* 308 Prince Street, West Newton, MA 02165, USA.

WESSLER, Stanford, b. 20 Apr. 1917, New York USA. Professor of Medicine. m. Margaret Barnet Muhlfelder, 17 Dec. 1942, Albany, New York, 3 sons. *Education:* BA, Harvard University; MD, New York University School of Medicine. *Appointments:* Research Fellow to Assistant Professor of Medicine, Harvard Medical School, 1946-64; Professor of Medicine, Washington University School of Medicine, 1964-74; Professor of Medicine and Associate Dean of Postgraduate Programs, New York University School of Medicine, 1974-. *Memberships:* Alpha Omega Alpha; Fellow AAAS; American Physiological Society; American Society for Clinical Investigation; Association of American Physicians. *Publications:* 11 books and pamphlets and over 160 articles in the area of Vascular Disease. *Honours:* James F Mitchell Award for Heart and Vascular Research, 1972; Award of Merit, American Heart Association, 1978. *Address:* 550 First Avenue, New York NY 10016, USA.

WEST, Bob, b. 7 March 1931, Ellenville, New York, USA. Drug Company Executive. m. (1) Betty Parker, 9 May 1957 (divorced), 3 daughters; (2) Jacqueline Cutler, 3 March 1982. *Education:* BS, Union University, 1952; MS, Purdue University, 1954; PhD, 1956; Postgrad Graduate, Management Seminar, University of Chicago, 1972. *Appointments:* Research Pharmacologist, American Cyanamid Co, Stamford, Connecticut, 1958-60; Vice President, Rosner-Hixson Laboratories, Chicago, 1960-68; Director, Scientific and Regulatory Affairs, Vick Chemical Co, Mount Vernon, New York, 1968-75; President, Bob West Associates Inc, Stamford, Connecticut, 1975-. *Memberships:* American Society of Pharmacology and Experimental Therapeutics; Society of Toxicology; Academy of Pharm. Scientists; Rotary Club. *Publications:* Numerous articles in professional journals. *Address:* 54 Ledge Brook Road, Stamford, CT 06903, USA.

WEST, Dorothy, b. 27 Apr. 1935, England. Principal in Private Practice. m. Dr E C Hamlyn, 27 June 1970, Plymouth, 1 son, 2 daughters. *Education:* MRCS (Eng); LRCP (London); MF Hom. *Appointments:* Principal in General Practice, 1967-72; Honorary Clinical Assistant, Royal London Homoeopathic Hospital, 1977. *Memberships:* British Medical Association; British Society for Nutritional Medicine; British Society for Allergy and Environmental Medicine. *Hobbies:* Music (piano); Photography; Windsurfing; Tennis. *Address:* Rutt House, Ivybridge, Devon PL21 0DQ, England.

WEST, Richard John, b. 8 May 1939, London. Consultant Paediatrician/Dean of Medical School. m. Jenny Winn Hawkins, 1962, 1 son, 2 daughters. *Education:* MBBS, 1962; MRCP 1967; DCH 1968; MD (London); FRCP. *Appointments:* Lecturer, Institute of Child Health, London 1974-75; Senior Lecturer 1975-, Consultant Paediatrician 1975-, Dean 1982-, St George's Hospital and Medical School, London. *Membership:* British Paediatric Association. *Publications:* "Family Guide to Children's Ailments" 1983; Research articles on "Metabolic Diseases. *Hobbies:* Medical History, Philosophy and Ethics. *Address:* St George's Hospital Medical School, London SW17, England.

WESTERHOLM, Barbro, b. 16 June 1933, Stockholm, Sweden. Medical Director; Professor. m. Peter 20 Feb. 1959, 3 sons, 1 daughter. *Education:* MD, 1959, PhD, 1964, Professor in Drug Epidemiology, Karolinska Institute, Stockholm. *Appointments:* Teaching Appointments, Research, Department of Pharmacology, Karolinska Institute, Stockholm, 1956-65; Secretary, Adverse Drug Reaction Committee, National Board of Health and Welfare, Stockholm, 1965-66, 1967-70; Research Scholar, Toxicology Research Unit, British Medical Research Council, Carshalton, Surrey, England, 1966-67; Senior Medical Officer, 1971-74, Director General, 1979-85, National Board of Health and Welfare, Stockholm; Medical Expert, National Corporation of Pharmacies, Stockholm, 1974-79; Member, Date Inspection Board, 1974-79; Member, Drug Damage Insurance Board, 1978-79; Member, Nordic Council on Medicines, 1978-79; Member Swedish Medical Research Council, 1976-85; Director General, Member of a number of boards within the area of Health and Social Welfare Sector, 1979-85; Medical Director, National Corporation of Pharmacies, 1985-. *Publications:* Author of over 150 publications on: professional and scientific subjects; general and political matters. *Hobbies:* Sailing; Skiing; Classical music; Theatre; Bicycling. *Address:* National Corporation of Pharmacies, S10514 Stockholm, Sweden.

WESTERMEYER, Joseph, b. 8 Apr. 1937, Chicago, Illinois, USA. Psychiatrist. m. 2 children. *Education:* BS Biology-Chemistry, 1959, MD 1961, MA Anthropology 1969, MPH 1970, PhD Psychiatry 1970, University of Minnesota. *Appointments include:* General Practice, Payne Avenue Medical Clinic, St Paul, 1962-65; Deputy Chief, Director of Public Health, Agency for International Development, Laos, 1965-67; Resident in Psychiatry 1967-70, Psychiatry

Staff 1970-, Consultant to Primary Care Clinic 1970-83, Outpatient Psychiatric Practice 1970-, Director Drug Programme 1982-, International Clinic in Department of Psychiatry 1984-, University of Minnesota Hospitals and Clinics. *Memberships include:* Fellow, American Anthropological Association; Fellow, American Association of Family Practice; Fellow, American Psychiatry Association; Association for Medical Research and Education in Substance Abuse; American Medical Society of Alcoholism; Society for Study of Psychiatry and Culture; American Board of Psychiatry; World Psychiatric Association; American Public Health Association. *Publications include:* "A Primer on Chemical Dependency: A Clinical Guide to Alcohol and Drug Problems", 1976; "Anthropology and Mental Health", editor, 1976; "Transcultural Psychiatry", (edited with E Foulks, R Wintrob and A Favazza), 1977; "Poppies, Pipes and People: A Study of Opium and Its Use in Laos", 1983; "A Manual For Substance Abuse Education", (with A Arif), 1984; "An Update on Methadone", (with A Arif); "Refugees and Mental Health" (with C Williams), 1985; "A Clinical Guide to Diagnosis and Management of Substance Abuse", 1985; 102 contributions to journals; 29 book chapters and monographs. *Honours include:* Numerous grants; Meritorious Service Award, United States Agency for International Development, 1967. *Address:* 1935 Summit Avenue, St Paul, MN 55105, USA.

WESTHAUSE, Cary, b. 9 Feb. 1932, Birmingham, Alabama, USA. Occupational Therapist. m. Erwin C Westhause, 19 July 1974, Houston, Texas, 4 sons, 2 daughters. *Education:* BS, Occupational Therapy. *Appointments:* Rehabilitation Director, Austin State Hospital, Texas, Portsmouth Area Rehabilitation Centre, Virginia, Director, Occupational Therapy Holy Cross Mental Health Centre, Director, Rehabilitation, St Joseph's Mental Health Centre, Houston, Texas; Occupational Therapy Director, Bellaire General Hospital, Texas, Director of Clinical Programs, Medical Branch, Galveston, Texas; Mental Retardation Consultant, State of Rhode Island; Executive Director, Texas Advisory Board of Occupational Therapy. *Memberships:* American Occupational Therapy Association; Texas Occupational Therapy Association; National Rehabilitation Association. *Hobbies:* Sailing; Water-colours; Music; Reading. *Address:* Star Route 1 Box 422, Spring Branch, TX 78070, USA.

WESTMAN, Jack Conrad, b. 28 Oct. 1927, USA. Professor of Psychiatry. m. Nancy K Baehre, 17 July 1953, Grand Rapids, Michigan, 3 sons. *Education:* BS, College of Liberal Arts, 1949, MD, Medical School, 1952, MS, Graduate School, 1959, University of Michigan. *Appointments:* Director, Outpatients and Day Care Services, Childrens Psychiatric Hospital, University of Michigan, 1961-65; Director, Child Psychiatry Division, Hospitals, 1965-73, Coordinator, Diagnostic and Treatment Unit, Center for Mental Retardation, 1966-74, Director, Psychiatric Section, Learning Disabilities Service, 1975-, University of Wisconsin. *Memberships:* Fellow: American Psychiatric Association; American Academy of Child Psychiatry; American Orthopsychiatric Association (Board of Directors); Past President, American Association of Psychiatric Services for Children; Society of Professor of Child Psychiatry. *Publications:* "Individual Differences in Children", 1973; "Child Advocacy", 1979; "Barriers to Learning in School", 1986; author of 70 articles and book chapters. *Honours:* Phi Beta Kappa, 1948; Sigma Xi, 1970; Public Service Award, 1974, Citizens of the Year, 1976, Wisconsin Association for Mental Health; Teaching Recognition Award, Wisconsin Law College, 1984. *Hobbies:* Running; Philately. *Address:* 600 Highland Avenue, Madison, WI 53792, USA.

WESTON, William Alan, b. 9 Dec. 1922, Liverpool, England. Clinical Director, Forensic Assessment and Out-Patients Service; Associate Professor, University of Calgary, Canada. m. Glenys. *Education:* MB ChB, University of Liverpool, 1952; Diploma, Psychological Medicine, University of Manchester, 1963; Fellow, Royal College of Psychiatrists, England, 1977. *Appointments:* Consultant Forensic Psychiatrist to Home Office and Yorkshire Regional Health Authority, 1967-78; Director, Regional Psychiatric Center; Clinical Professor of Psychiatry, University of Saskatchewan, 1978-80; Director, Medium Service, Royal Ottawa Hospital, Associate Professor of Psychiatry, University of Ottawa, 1980-82. *Memberships:* Fellow, Royal College of Psychiatrists, UK; Canadian Psychiatric Association; International Society for Criminology; American Psychiatric Association; American Academy of Psychiatry and Law. *Publications:* Contributor of paper and articles to professional journals and books. *Honours:* Council of Europe Fellowship, 1970; Member of Committee of Mentally Abnormal Offenders. *Address:* 318 26th Avenue SW, 1502, Calgary, T2S 2TG, Alberta, Canada.

WESTON, Windsor John, b. 4 Aug. 1920, New Plymouth, New Zealand. Private Radiological Practitioner, Lower Hutt. m. Elizabeth McKnight, 2 Sep. 1946, Wanganui, 3 daughters. *Education:* MB ChB, Otago, 1943; MRCP, Edinburgh, 1949; DMRD, University of Edinburgh, 1951; FRCP, Edinburgh, 1959; MCRA, 1960; FCRA now FRCRA, 1965; MD, Otago, 1979; FRACP, 1981. *Appointments:* Demonstrator, Department of Anatomy, Otago University, 1944; Italy and Japan 5th Field Ambulance, 1944-46; OC 102 NZ Venereal Disease Treatment Centre; Department of Radiology, Royal Infirmary, Edinburgh, 1949-51; Radiologist, Hutt Hospital, 1951-58; Visiting Radiologist, Hutt Hospital, 1958-81; Visiting Professor, University of Manitoba, Canada, 1970; Visiting Lecturer, University of Washington, Seattle, USA, 1973; Visiting Professor of Skeletal Radiology, University of California, Los Angeles, 1979 one month. *Memberships:* New Zealand Medical Association; New Zealand Rheumatism Association; Foundation Member, International Skeletal Society; New Zealand Branch, Australasian College of Radiologists; Wellington Medical Research Foundation; Australasian College of Physicians. *Publications:* 71 published papers; Co-author: "Soft Tissues of the Extremities", 1977; Chapter in "Rheumatoid Arthritis in the Finger", 1979. *Honours:* War Medal 1939-45; New Zealand War Service Medal; Rouse Travelling Fellowship, 1966. *Hobbies:* Building in Concrete and Wood; Sea Water Fishing; Books; Music. *Address:* 229-231 Rosetta Road, Raumati Beach, New Zealand.

WESTRIN, Claes-Göran, b. 10 Mar. 1929, Örebro, Sweden. Professor in Social Medicine, University of Uppsala. m. Karin Bergholz, 2 sons, 1 daughter. *Education:* MA, 1956; PhD, 1970; Specialist in Psychiatry, 1964, in Social Medicine, 1974; Associate Professor in Social Medicine, University of Gothenburg, 1971. *Appointments:* District Doctor, Vindeln, 1956-60; Training in Psychiatry and Social Medicine, 1960-70; Head, Health Centre of Skara, 1972-73; Medical Social Officer, Gothenburg, 1971; Head, Psychiatric Services, Skaraborg County, 1973-81; Professor and Chairman, Department of Social Medicine, University Hospital, Uppsala, 1981-. *Memberships:* Swedish Psychiatric Association, President, 1974-79; Swedish Association for Social Medicine, Vice-President, 1981-; Swedish Medical Association; Swedish Academy of Medical Sciences. *Publications:* "Low Back Sick Listing", 1970; Some hundreds of articles on Psychiatry and Social Medicine in various publications. *Address:* Ymergatan 30 c, 753 25 Uppsala, Sweden.

WEXLER, Bruce Edward, b. 20 May 1947, Baltimore, Maryland, USA. Associate Professor of Psychiatry. m. Laura Kaplan, 21 June 1971, Newton, Massachusetts, 1 son 1 daughter. *Education:* BA American Government magna cum laude, Harvard College, 1969; MD, Albert Einstein College of Medicine, 1973. *Appointments:* Intern in Medicine, Bronx Municipal Hospital Center, Albert Einstein College of Medicine; Post Doctoral Fellow and Resident in Psychiatry, Assistant Professor of Psychiatry, Currently Associate Professor of Psychiatry, Yale University; Associate Chief, Clinical Research Unit, Connecticut Mental

Health Center; Chief, Mental Hygiene Clinic, Veterans Administration Medical Center, West Haven, Connecticut; Research Associate, Veterans Administration Career Development Program. *Membership:* American Psychiatric Association. *Publications:* 'Alterations in Cerebral Laterality During Acute Psychotic Illness', 1979; 'Dichotic Listening Tests in Studying Brain-Behaviour Relationships', (with T Halwest), 1985; 'A Model of Brain Function and Its Implications for Psychiatric Research', 1986. *Honours:* National Honor Society National Scholarship, 1965; Seymour Lustman Research Award, Yale University, 1977; Research Training Award, National Institute of Mental Health, 1977 and 1978. *Hobbies:* Parenting; Gardening; Hiking; Jogging; Swimming. *Address:* Veterans Administration Medical Center, 116A/1, West Spring Street, West Haven, CT 06516, USA.

WHARTON, Ralph Nathanial, b. 15 June 1932, Boston, Massachusetts, USA. Clinical Professor. m. Elinor Walden, 15 Aug. 1955, Boston, 1 son, 2 daughters. *Education:* AB, Biology, Harvard College; MD, Columbia University; Certificate, Psychoanalysis, Columbia University. *Appointments:* Senior Research Psychiatrist, NYSPI, 1964-70; Assistant Professor, 1968-73; Associate Professor, 1974-83, Columbia University; President, Society of Practitioners, Columbia Presbyterian Medical Centre, 1980-82; Chairman, Committee on Biological Psychiatry, NYCDB, 1980-84; Member, Board of Trustees, Presbyterian Hospital, New York City, 1980-82. *Memberships:* American Psychiatric Association; New York Academy of Medicine; American Psychoanalystic Association; Society of Biological Psychiatry; Association for Research in Nervous and Mental Diseases. *Publications:* Most Recent Book Chapters: "Management of Depression", in 'Psychiatric Management for Medical Practitioners', 1982; "Uses of Antidepressants", 'Advances in Consult-Liaison Psychiatry', 1983; 28 articles. *Honours:* Fellow, American Psychiatric Association, 1970; Fellow, New York Academy of Medicine, 1970; Fellow, American College of Psychoanalysts, 1983. *Hobbies:* Sailing; Skiing; Windsurfing; Tennis. *Address:* 1070 Park Avenue, Office 1 D, New York, NY 10028, USA.

WHEELER, John Howard, b. 2 Sep. 1939, London, England. General Surgeon. m. Janet Stephanie Earnshaw, 1 son, 1 daughter. *Education:* MB, BS, London, 1963; FRCS Edinburgh, 1967; FRCS England, 1970; LMCC, 1985. *Appointments:* House Surgeon, House Physician, Harrow Hospital; Senior House Officer, Accident & Emergency, Obstetrics and Gynaecology, Charing Cross Hospital; Senior House Officer, Royal National Orthopaedic Hospital, Stanmore; Junior Registrar, Surgery, St George's Hospital, London; Registrar, Surgery, Nottingham General Hospital; Registrar, General Surgery, St Mary Abbot's Hospital, London; First Assistant, Urology, Registrar, Professorial Dept of Surgery, Charing Cross Hospital; Senior Registrar, Lecturer, Surgery, St Bartholomew's Hospital Medical College; Consultant, General Surgery, St Nicholas Hospital, Plumstead, London; Consultant, General & Urological Surgery, G R Baker Memorial Hospital, British Columbia, Canada. *Memberships:* Vice President, Hospital Doctors Association; British Medical Association. *Publications:* Articles in professional journals including: 'British Journal of Pharmaceutical Practice'; 'Spectrum'; 'Annals of the Royal College of Surgeons of England'; 'Hospital Doctor'. *Honours:* Vice President, Hospital Doctors Association, 1970. *Hobbies:* Writing; Cycling; Photography; Computers. *Address:* 8 Little Brownings, Sydenham Rise, London SE23 3XJ, England.

WHEELER, John Ingraham Junior, b. 27 Nov. 1925, St Louis, Missouri, USA. Corporation President; Professor of Psychiatry and Paediatrics. m. Marion Huffman, 21 Jan. 1956, Mexia, Texas, USA, 2 sons, 2 daughters. *Education:* BS, St. Louis University, Missouri, USA, 1949; MS, 1951; PhD, University of Texas, 1955.

Appointments: Assistant Medical Psychologist, 1955-56, University of Texas M. D. Anderson Hospital and Turner Institute, Associate, 1956-58, Psychologist, 1976-85; Clinical Professor, University of Texas System Cancer Centre, Houston, Texas, 1976-85; Clinical Associate Professor, Departments of Psychiatry and Pediatrics, Baylor College of Medicine. *Memberships:* American Psychological Association; South Western Psychological Association; Texas Psychological Association; Texas Board of Psychological Examiners; American Academy of Psychotherapists; American Society of Clinical Hypnosis; American Society of Psychologists in private practice. *Publications:* "The J W Sentence Completion Test", 1955. *Honours:* Combat Infantryman's Badge, US Army, 1944; Army Commendation Medal, 1944; Distinguished Psychologist Award, Texas Psychological Association, 1979; The Roger C. Smith Memorial Award, American Association of State Psychology Boards, 1982. *Hobbies:* Cattle Farming; Historical Preservation. *Address:* 4550 Post Oak Place Drive, Suite 320, Houston, TX 77027, USA.

WHEELWRIGHT, Joseph Balch, b. 6 June 1906, Hardwick, Massachusetts, USA. Semi-retired Psychiatrist; Jungian Analyst; Clinical Professor of Psychiatry Emeritus, University of California Medical School. m. Jane Byers Hollister, 16 Sep. 1929, Santa Maria, California, 1 son, 1 daughter. *Education:* MRCS (Eng.); LRCP (London); Licensed as MD in California, USA, 1940; St. Bartholomew's Medical College, 1932-38; Graduate work: Harvard University, Cambridge, Mass, 1928. *Appointments:* University of California Medical School, Department of Psychiatry, 1941-; Clinical Instructor; Assistant Clinical Professor; Associate Clinical Professor; Professor. Retired in 1973 at age of 65 years. *Memberships:* British Medical Association; Life Fellow, American Psychiatric Association; Life Fellow, American Academy of Psychoanalysis; Contributing Member of Group for the Advancement of Psychiatry; Past President, International Association of Analytical Psychology. *Publications:* Sex and the College Student (co-author); St. George and the Dandelion, 1982; The Reality of the Psyche, Editor, 1968; The Analytic Process, Editor, 1971 Chapter on Termination in Jungian Analysis, 1982. *Honour:* Plaque for Outstanding Achievement from the Northern California Psychiatric Society, 1982. *Hobbies:* Music (piano, guitar, etc.); Norman Churches; Malacology; Birds and Wild Flowers. *Address:* 8 Live Oak Way, Kentfield, CA 94904, USA.

WHITE, Allen Collier, b. 9 Feb. 1940, Los Angeles, California, USA. Child and Adolescent and Family Psychiatrist. *Education:* BA, Occidental College, Los Angeles, 1961; MD, George Washington University School of Medicine, Washington, DC, 1965. *Appointments:* Private Practice, Child, Adolescent, Adult Psychiatry, Cupertino, California; Consultant, Child Psychiatry, The Chamberlain's Childrens Centers, San Martin and Hollister; Consultant, Psychiatry, Beacon School, San Jose; Assistant Professor, Clinical Faculty, Department of Psychiatry and Behavioral Sciences, Stanford University Medical Center; Consultant, Special Problems Clinic, Santa Clara Valley Medical Center, San Jose; Consultant, Special Schools, Santa Clara County; Consultant, C Thomas Foundation, Cupertino. *Memberships:* American Psychiatric Association; American Academy of Psychiatry and the Law; American Orthopsychiatric Association (Fellow); Clinical Faculty Association Stanford University Medical School. *Hobbies:* Backpacking; Amateur Radio; Cooking. *Address:* 20396 Town Center Lane, Suite 9E, Cupertino, CA 95014, USA.

WHITE, Harvey Douglas, b. 19 Nov. 1947, Te Awamutu, New Zealand. Cardiologist. m. Janette Frances Venus, 3 Feb. 1973, Invercargill, New Zealand, 1 son, 1 daughter. *Education:* MB ChB; Fellow, Royal Australasian College of Physicians. *Appointments:* Acting Specialist, Cardiology, Green Lane Hospital, Auckland, 1980; Clinical Lecturer, School of Medicine,

University of Auckland, 1981; Research Fellow in Medicine, Harvard Medical School, Research/Clinical Fellow in Medicine, 1981-84, Associate Physician, 1983-84, Brigham & Women's Hospital, Boston, Massachusetts, USA; Senior Fellow, National Heart Foundation of New Zealand, 1984-; Part-time Specialist Cardiologist, Green Lane Hospital, Auckland, New Zealand, 1985-. *Memberships:* New Zealand Medical Association; Associate Member, Cardiac Society of Australia & New Zealand. *Publications:* 16 papers in medical journals in Australia & USA. *Honours:* American Field Service Scholarship, Tenafly, New Jersey, USA, 1965; Overseas Clinical Fellow, National Heart Foundation of New Zealand, 1980-81; Odlin Research Fellowship, RACP, 1981. *Hobbies:* Reading; Tennis; Camping; Windsurfing. *Address:* Green Lane Hospital, Green Lane, Auckland, New Zealand.

WHITE, Philip Anthony, b. 20 Aug., 1945, Bristol, England. Chief of Staff, Kelowna General Hospital, British Columbia, Canada. m. Zandra Gwendoline Duly, 10 Apr. 1968, Hayling Island, 2 sons. *Education:* MB, King's College, London, 1966; MB, BS, St George's Hospital Medical School, London University, 1969; LMCC, CCFP, Canada, 1980. *Appointments:* House Surgeon, St George's Hospital, London, 1969; House Physician, Ashford Hospital, Middlesex, 1970; Senior House Officer, 1970, Medical Registrar, 1970-72, Ashford, Middlesex; Family Practice, Staines, 1972-75; Family Practice, Moose Jaw Saskatchewan, Canada, 1975-80; Medical Staff Member, Moose Jaw Union Hospitals, 1975-80; President, Medical Staff, Moose Jaw, Providence Hospital, 1978; President, Moose Jaw and District Medical Society, 1978; Active Medical Staff, Kelowna General Hospital, 1981-. *Memberships:* Canadian Medical Association; British Columbia Medical Association. *Hobbies:* Pilot; Fly Fishing; Automobiles. *Address:* 205 Rutland Road, Kelowna, BC, Canada V1X 2B1.

WHITE, Roger James, b. 10 Apr. 1939, Luton, England. Consultant Physician. m. Christine Pike, 10 Feb. 1962, London, 2 sons. *Education:* MA, MD, Cambridge University; MB BChir, St Bartholomew's Hospital, London. *Appointments:* Senior Medical Registrar, St Bartholomew's Hospital; Consultant Physician, Frenchay Hospital, Bristol. *Memberships:* British Thoracic Society; British Society of Allergy & Clinical Immunology. *Publications:* "Respiratory Infections & Tumours", 1981; "Respiratory Disorders", 1984. *Hobby:* Ornithology. *Address:* 4 Church Avenue, Stoke Bishop, Bristol BS9 1LD, England.

WHITTET, Thomas Douglas, b. 4 Jan. 1915, Hartlepool, England. Pharmacist (retired). m. Doreen Mary Bowes, 20 June 1942, Hartlepool, 2 sons. *Education:* Rosebank School, Hartlepool; PhC (now FPS) Sunderland Polytechnic, 1935-38, Diploma in Biochemical Analysis 1942; BSc Physiology, University College, London, 1948-53; PhD Medicine (non-clinical), University College Hospital Medical School, 1958. *Appointments:* Chief Chemist, Numol Ltd, Newcastle-upon-Tyne, 1939-41; Pharmacist, Chesterfield & N Derbyshire Royal Hospital, 1941-42; Chief Pharmacist, Baguley Infirmary & Emergency Hospital, Manchester, 1942-43; Chief Pharmacist & Lecturer in Pharmacy, Charing Cross Hospital, 1943-47, University College Hospital, Medical & Dental Schools, 1947-65; Deputy Chief Pharmacist, Ministry of Health, 1965-67; Chief Pharmacist, Department of Health & Social Security, 1967-78. *Memberships:* Fellow, Pharmaceutical Society; Fellow, Royal Society of Chemistry; Fellow, Royal Society of Medicine; Member, College of Pharmacy Practice; British Pharmacological Society. *Publications:* "Hormones", 1946; "Diagnostic Agents", 1947; "Sterilisation & Disinfection", 1965; "The Apothecaries in the Great Plague of 1665", 1971; "Clerks, Bedels & Chemical Operators of the Society of Apothecaries", 1980; "Apothecaries & their Lodgers", 1980; Chapters in "Handbook of Water Purification", 1981, "Oxford Companion to Medicine", 1985; Numerous papers on

medical & pharmaceutical history; articles in medical journals. *Honours:* CBE, 1977; Honorary DSc, Universities of Bath (1968), Aston (1974); Fellow, University College, London, 1979; Honorary Fellow, Sunderland Polytechnic, 1980; Honorary Licentiate in Medicine & Surgery of the Society of Apothecaries, 1984; Master, Worshipful Society of Apothecaries of London, 1982-83; President, History of Medicine Section, Royal Society of Medicine, 1981-83; Chairman, Faculty of the History & Philosophy of Medicine & Pharmacy, Society of Apothecaries, 1975-78; President, British Society for the History of Pharmacy, 1972-74. *Hobbies:* Medical History; Travel; Heraldry; Sport (cricket, Rugby football, Tennis). *Address:* Woburn Lodge, 8 Lyndhurst Drive, Harpenden, Herts. AL5 5QN, England.

WHYBROW, Peter Charles, b. 13 June 1939, England. Professor of Psychiatry. m. Margaret Ruth Steele, 8 Dec. 1962, Hatfield, Hertfordshire, 2 daughters. *Education:* University College London, 1959-62; MB, BS, University College Hospital Medical School, London, 1962; Diploma, Psychological Medicine, 1968; MA, Dartmouth College, USA 1974, University of Pennsylvania 1984. *Appointments:* House Physician, University College Hospital, London, 1962-64; House Surgeon, Saint Helier Hospital, Surrey, 1963; House Paediatrician, Prince of Wales Hospital, London; Resident in Psychiatry 1965-67, Instructor, Research Fellow 1967-68, University of North Carolina, USA; Scientific Staff, Medical Research Council, England, 1968-69; Associate Professor 1970, Chairman, Department of Psychiatry 1971-78, Professor 1971-84, Executive Dean 1980-82, Dartmouth Medical School, USA; Professor and Chairman, Department of Psychiatry, University of Pennsylvania, Philadelphia, Pennsylvania, 1984-. *Memberships include:* Licenciate, Royal College of Physicians; Royal College of Surgeons; American Association for the Advancement of Science; American College of Psychiatrists; American Psychiatric Society; Fellow, Royal College of Psychiatrists; Society for Neuroscience; American Psychopathological Association. *Publications:* Over 70 published articles and 2 books including: 'Thyroid-Catecholamine-Receptor Interaction' (with A J Prange); "Mood Disorders, Towards a New Psychology" (with H Akiskal, W McKinney), 1984; 'Thyroid State and Human Behaviour' in "Thyroid Axis Drugs and Behaviour" (editor: A J Prange), 1986. *Honours:* Anclote Manor Award for Psychiatric Research, 1967; Josiah Macy Junior, Foundation Faculty Scholar, 1978-79. *Hobbies:* Squash; Sailing; Running; Chess; Music; Farming. *Address:* Department of Psychiatry, University of Pennsylvania, Philadelphia, PA 19104, USA.

WICHLINSKI, Leslaw Marek, b. 1 Sep. 1925, Podz, Poland. Head of Institute, Medical Centre of Postgraduate Education. m. Janina Kaus, 8 Jan. 1952, Szczecin, 1 son. *Education:* Master of Pharmacy, 1952, Assistant Professor, 1970, Professor, 1982, Medical Academy Lodz; Doctor of Pharmacy, Medical Academy, Krakow, 1961. *Appointments:* Pharmacist and Head of Pharmacy, 1951-56; Scientific Worker, Research Laboratory, Pharmaceutical Industry, 1956-73; Head, Institute of Pharmacy, Head of Department of Biopharmaceutics, Medical Centre of Postgraduate Education, Bydgoszcz, 1973. *Memberships:* President, Subcommittee, Drug Bioavailability, Polish Academy of Science; Vice-President, Polish Pharmaceutical Association; Member, Board of National Specialists in Pharmacy; Member, Editorial Advisory Board, Drug Intelligence and Clinical Pharmacy. *Publications:* "Alcaloids of Ergot", 1968; "Fundamentals of Biopharmaceutics", 1978; "Clinical Pharmacokinetics of Antiepileptic Drugs", 1983; "Clinical Data of Drugs", 1985; Author of 120 publications and 10 patents. *Honours:* Awarde of I Degree, Ministry of Health, 1984. *Hobbies:* Tourism. *Address:* Medical Centre of Postgraduate Education, 3 Debowa Street, 85-626 Bydgoszcz, Poland.

WICK, Erika Elisabeth, b. 31 July 1937, Basel, Switzerland. Professor. *Education:* Baccalaureate, Mädchergymnasium, Basel; MA, PhD, 1964, University of Basel. *Appointments:* Assistant Professor, Manhattan College, New York, USA, 1965-66; Assistant Professor, 1966-69, Associate Professor, 1969-75, Professor, 1975-, St John's University, New York. *Memberships:* Academy Psychosomatic Medicine; Society for Clinical and Experimental Hypnosis; New York Academy of Science; American Psychological Association. *Publications:* "Zur Psychologie der Reue", 1971; "Obesity", co-author; articles in professional journals. *Honours:* Fellow, Academy of Psychosomatic Medicine; Fellow, Society of Clinical and Experimental Hypnosis. *Hobbies:* Swimming; Jogging; Volleyball. *Address:* 3076 Riverside Drive, Wantagh, NY 11793, USA.

WICKSTRÖM, Gustav, b. 8 Sep. 1941, Helsinki, Finland. Professor of Occupational Health. *Education:* MD. *Appointments:* Docent, Professor in Occupational Health, Director, Turku Regional Institute of Occupational Health. *Memberships:* Finnish Medical Association; International Commission on Occupational Health. *Publications:* Various articles in medical journals. *Address:* Turku Regional Institute of Occupational Health, Hämeenkatu 10, 20500 Turku, Finland.

WIDHOLM, Olof Eric Bernhard, b. 30 June 1923, Helsinki, Finland. Professor. m. Kerstin Stadigh, 1952, 2 sons. *Education:* MD, 1950, MD, PhD, 1953, University of Helsinki; Specialist, 1957, Serobacteriology, Specialist, Obstetrics & Gynaecology, 1957, University of Helsinki. *Appointments:* Resident, Maria Hospital, Institute of Serobacteriology, Helsinki, 1949-58; Senior Lecturer, 1959-63, Assistant Professor, 1963-69, Associate Professor, 1969-75, Helsinki University Centre Hospital; Professor, Chairman, Helsinki University Centre Hospital, 1975-. *Memberships:* President, Association of Scandinavian Professors of Obstetrics & Gynaecology; President, Finnish Gynaecological Association, 1978-80; President, Scandinavian Association of Obstetricians & Gynaecologists, 1980-82; Finnish Cancer Association, 1977-; Board of Finnish Cancer Foundation, 1979-; Society of Adolescent Medicine, 1970-. *Publications:* Over 200 scientific articles. *Honours:* Commander, Order of the Lion of Finland, 1981; Civil Service Medal of Merit, 1982; Commander of the Order of Swedish North Star. *Address:* Westendintie 11, 02160 Espoo, Finland.

WIEBE, Richard Herbert, b. 28 Dec. 1937, Saskatchewan, Canada. Professor of Obstetrics & Gynaecology. m. Jacquelyn Dee Yancy, 30 Aug. 1975, 1 son. *Education:* PreMed, 1956-58; MD 1958-62; Internship, Vancouver General Hospital, Vancouver, 1962-63; Graduate Programme in Obstetrics & Gynaecology, Ontario, 1967-71; Fellow in Gynaecological Endocrinology, Queen's University, Ontario, 1972-73. *Appointments:* General Practice, Estevan, Saskatchewan, Canada, 1964-67; Faculty Associate, 1972-73, Assistant Professor, 1973-78, Associate Professor 1978-81, Duke University, Durham, North Carolina; Director, Medical Student Education, Duke University, 1978-81; Associate Professor 1982-85, Director of Ambulatory Care 1982-, Professor 1985, all Department of Obstetrics & Gynaecology, University of South Alabama. *Memberships:* F B Carter Society of Obstetricians & Gynaecologists; American Fertility Society; Royal College of Physicians & Surgeons of Canada; Piedmont Reproduction Colloquium; Canadian Medical Association; American Society of Andrology; American College of Obstetricians & Gynaecologists; Association of Professors of Gynaecology & Obstetrics; Society for the Study of Reproduction; Endocrine Society; American Society of Primatologists. *Publications:* Some 78 papers, abstracts & papers in field. *Address:* University of South Alabama, Department of Obstetrics & Gynaecology, Division of Reproductive Endocrinology, Rm 324 Clinical Services Building, Mobile, AL 36688, USA.

WIEDERHOLT, Wigbert C, b. 22 Apr. 1931, Germany. Professor of Neurosciences. 1 son, 2 daughters. *Education:* Attended Universities of Wuerzbug, Bonn, Berlin and Freiburg, 1950-55; MD, University of Freiburg 1956. *Appointments include:* Chief of Neurology, VA Medical Center, San Diego, 1972-79; Neurologist-in-Chief, UCSD Medical Center 1972-83; Chairman, Department of Neurosciences, UCSD, 1978-83; Chairman, Group in Neurosciences, UCSD, 1978-83; Chairman, Executive Committee, UCSD Medical Center, 1980-82; NIH Fellowship in Epidemiology, Mayo Clinic, 1983-84; Current positions include: Professor of Neurosciences, UCSD, 1972-; Attending Physician, UCSD Medical Center, 1972-; Attending Physician, VA Medical Center San Diego, 1972-; Visiting Senior Scientist, Mayo Clinic, 1983-. *Memberships include:* Fellow, American Academy of Neurology; American Association for the Advancement of Science; American Association of Electromyography and Electrodiagnosis; Secretary- Treasurer 1971-76, President 1977-78; American Association of University Professors of Neurology; Fellow, American Electroencephalographic Society. *Publications:* Contributor of numerous articles, papers, book reviews etc to medical journals in the field of Neurology. *Honours:* Medical School Scholarship, Free University of Berlin, 1952-53; Fulbright Scholarship, 1956-58; S Weir Mitchell Award, American Academy of Neurology, 1956; NIH Senior Scientist Fellowship, 1983-84; Department of Neurology Award for Outstanding Teaching, UCSD, 1984-85. *Address:* 6683 La Jolla Senic Dr. South, La Jolla, CA 92067, USA.

WIEGAND, Herbert, b. 27 June 1941, Wuppertal Germany. Head, Toxicology, Medical Institute of Environmental Hygiene, University of Düsseldorf. m. Ortrud Paul, 1 Aug. 1964, Wuppertal, 1 son, 1 daughter. *Education:* Dr med; Privatdozent. *Appointments:* Scientist, Rudolf Buchheim Institute of Pharmacology, Justus Liebig University Giessen. *Membership:* German Pharmacological Society. *Publications:* Articles in, 'Naunyn-Schmiedeberg's Arch. Pharmacology'; 'Arch Toxicology'. *Hobbies:* Squash; Tennis. *Address:* Medical Institute of Enviromental Hygiene, Auf'M Hennekamp 50, D-4000 Dusseldorf, Federal Republic of Germany.

WIEMAN, Thomas Jeffrey, b. 25 Sep. 1947, USA. Assistant Professor, Surgery. m. Gayle Marie Lannert, 10 May 1974, Louisville, 2 sons, 1 daughter. *Education:* BS, University of Southern California, 1969; MD, University of Louisville, 1974; MS, University of Louisville, 1978. *Appointments:* Research Assistant, Middlesex Hospital, Dept of Surgical Studies, London, England, 1984-85; Research Fellow, Roswell Park Memorial Institute, Division of Radiation Biology, Buffalo, New York, 1985; Assistant Professor, Surgery, University of Louisville. *Memberships:* American Medical Association; Kentucky and Jefferson County and Taylor County Medical Associations; Kentucky Society for Gastrointestinal Endoscopy; American Society for Gastrointestinal Endoscopy; Hiram C. Polk Junior Surgical Society; Westlake Cumberland Medical Society. *Publications:* Articles in professional journals including: 'Journal Kentucky Medical Association'; 'Surgical Forum'; etc. *Honours:* Alpha Omega Alpha; Phi Kappa Phi. *Address:* Department of Surgery, University of Louisville, 550 South Jackson Street, Louisville, KY 40292, USA.

WIENER, Sondra Madoff, b. 16 June 1934, New York City, USA. Senior Rehabilitation Nurse. m. Dr Marvin M Wiener, 1955, 2 sons, 2 daughters. *Education:* MS, Health Science Education, State University of New York, Stony Brook; BS, St Joseph's College, Patchoque, New York; RN, Beth Israel Hospital, New York City. *Appointments:* Staff Nurse, Beth Israel Hospital, New York City, 1955; Office Manager for Private Practitioner, 1960; Senior Rehabilitation Nurse, Liberty Mutual Insurance Co, 1977-; Freelance Research Journalist; Consultant Insurance Rehabilitation Specialist. *Memberships:* American Association of Rehabilitation Nurses; Professional Rehabilitation Association. *Publications:* Articles in professional journals on Rehabilitation Nursing. *Honours:* Barsky Award, 1955; Distinguished Scholarship, St Joseph's College, Dean's List, 1981; Highest Honours in Graduate Studies, SUNY, Stony Brook, 1983. *Hobbies:* Travel; Boating; Water Sports. *Address:* Liberty Mutual Insurance Company, 260 Middle Country Road, Smithtown, NY 11787, USA.

WIERZBICKA, Maria Helena, b. 7 Dec. 1933, Poznan, Poland. Head, Conservative Dentistry and Periodontology, Vice-Dean, Medical Faculty. m. Janusz Wierzbicki, 25 July 1953, 1 son, 1 daughter. *Education:* MD, 1965; Dr Hab Med, 1976; Assistant Professor, 1978, Postgraduate Training: Periodontology, University of Gothenburg, 1973, Royal Dental College, Copenhagen, 1980; Preventive Dentistry, University of Bern, 1982. *Appointments:* Academy of Medicine, Poznan, 1956-79; Academy of Medicine, Warsaw, 1979-. *Membership:* Polish Dental Association. *Publication:* "The Effect of Metronidazole in the Treatment of Some Periodontal Diseases", 1973; "Morphology of Dental Pulp in Experimental Periodontitis in Dogs", 1966; "Electron Microscopic Study of Sulcus Bottom Area in Gingivitis", 1979; "Beurteilung der Behandlungsbedurftigkeit bei Peredontalerkrankungen mit dem Bellini System", 1977. *Honour:* Award of Cieszynski, 1984. *Hobby:* Travel. *Address:* ul. Dworkowa 2m.20, Warsaw, Poland.

WIESER, Heinz-Gregor, b. 25 Mar. 1943, Reddemitz, Poland. Head of Department of EEG and Clinical Neurophysiology. m. Rita Bernhard, 10 May 1975, Switzerland, 2 sons. *Education:* MD; Postdoctoral Education in Neurology, Neurosurgery and Clinical Neurophysiology; Diploma as Specialist in Neurology and Psychiatry; Habilitation, Neurology with special emphasis on Epileptology and Electroencephalography; Private Dozent. *Appointments:* Assistant, Neurological Clinic, University Graz; Assistant, Neurological Clinic, "Risenhügel", Vienna, Austria; Assistant, Psychiatric Clinic, Beverin, Graubunden; Assistant, Neurological and Neurosurgical Department, Assistant, Department of Stereo-Electroencephalography and Functional Neurosurgery, Oberarzt, Institute for Electroencephalography, Oberarzt Department of Neurology, University Hospital, Zürich, Switzerland; Assistant, Internal Medicine, Oberarzt, Neurological Department, Cantonal Hospital, Aarau, Switzerland; Research Fellow, Department of Functional Neurosurgery, St Anne's Hospital, Paris, France. *Memberships:* Member, German and Swiss Branches, International League Against Epilepsy; Member, Swiss, German and French Associations for EEG and Clinical Neurophysiology; Member, European Society for Sterotactic and Functional Neurosurgery; Member, Austrian Society for Biomedical Techniques; Member, International Study Group on Psychosis with Epilepsy; Member, International Temporal Lobe Club; Member, Herbert von Karajan Society. *Publications:* Author of numerous articles and chapters in books on medical and professional subjects. *Honours:* Friedrich von Bodelschwingh Prize, 1979-80. *Hobbies:* Music; Hiking; Skiing. *Address:* University Hospital Zürich, Department of Neurology, CH-8091 Zürich, Switzerland.

WIG, Narendra N, b. 1 Oct. 1930, Gujranwala. Regional Adviser Mental Health, World Health Organization, Eastern Mediterranean Region. m. Veena, 24 May 1963, Delhi, India, 2 sons. *Education:* MB BS, 1953, MD, 1957, King George's Medical College, Lucknow; DPM, Conjoint Board of Royal Colleges of Scotland, 1962; DPM, Conjoint Board of Royal Colleges of England, 1962; FRC Psych, Royal College of Psychiatrists, London, 1972; FAMS, Indian Academy of Medical Sciences, 1974. *Appointments:* Lecturer, Neuro Psychiatry, King George's Medical College, Lucknow, 1958-63; Assistant Professor of Psychiatry, 1963-68, Professor and Head of Department of Psychiatry, 1968-80, Postgraduate Institute of Medical Education and Research, Chandigarh; Professor and Head of Department of Psychiatry, All India Institute of Medical Sciences, New Delhi, 1980-84; Regional Adviser on Mental Health, World Health Organization, EMRO, 1984-. *Memberships:* Fellow, Indian Psychiatric Society; Foundation Fellow, Royal College of Psychiatrists, UK; Fellow, Indian Academy of Medical Sciences; Corresponding Fellow, American Psychiatric Association; Member, Central Committee of World Psychiatric Association; Member WHO Advisory Panel on Mental Health. *Publications:* Over 200 scientific papers in different journals; Chapters in books, etc. *Honours:* Dr Marfatia Award, Indian Psychiatric Society, 1972, 80; Dr Murthyrao Oration Award, Indian Psychiatric Society, 1979; Dr Seshadhari Award, Indian Council Medical Research, 1981; Dr Vidyasagar Award, Indian Council Medical Research, 1986. *Address:* World Health Organization, PO Box 1517, Alexandria, Egypt.

WILBANKS, George Dewey Junior, b. 24 Feb. 1931, Gainesville, Georgia, USA. Professor and Chairman, Obstetrics and Gynaecology. m. Evelyn Rivers, 31 July 1954, New Orleans, Louisiana, 2 sons. *Education:* AB, 1953, MD, 1956, Duke University School of Medicine. *Appointments:* Clinical Instructor, Obstetrics and Gynaecology, University of Oklahoma, 1963-64; Assistant Professor, 1964-69, Associate Professor, 1970, Duke University Medical Center; Professor, Obstetrics and Gynaecology, Rush Medical College, 1970-. *Memberships:* American College of Obstetrics and Gynaecology; American College of Surgeons; Society Gynaecologic Oncologists; American Association Obstetrics and Gynaecology; American Society Clinical Oncology; American Association Cancer Research; Society Pelvic Surgeons; American Society Colposcopy and Cervical Pathology; International Federation Cervical Pathology and Coposcopy. *Publications:* Contributor to professional journals, etc. *Honour:* NIH Fellow Obstetrics and Gynaecology Pathology, Columbia University, 1964-65. *Hobbies:* Sailing; Tennis; Swimming. *Address:* Rush Presbyterian St Luke's Medical Center, 1753 West Congress Parkway, Chicago, IL 60612, USA.

WILCOX, Benson Reid, b. 26 May 1932, Charlotte, North Carolina, USA. Professor of Surgery; Chief, Division of Cardiothoracic Surgery. m. Lucinda Holderness, 25 July 1959, Greensboro, 1 son, 3 daughters. *Education:* MD, University of North Carolina, 1957. *Appointments:* Currently, Professor of Surgery, Chief Division of Cardiothoracic Surgery, University of North Carolina, Chapel Hill. *Memberships:* American Association of Thoracic Surgery; American College of Cardiology; American College of Chest Physicians; American College of Surgeons; American Heart Association; American Society of Clinical Anatomists; American Surgical Association; American Academy of Surgery; Halsted Society; International Cardiovascular Society; Society of Thoracic Surgeons; Society of University Surgeons; Thoracic Surgery Directors Association. *Publications:* "Surgical Anatomy of the Heart", with R H Anderson, 1985; 'The Role of surgery in the management of infective endocarditis' in "Difficult Problems in Adult Cardiac Surgery", 1985; contributor to 'JTCS', 1981. *Honours:* Markle Scholar in Academic Medicine, 1967; President's Award for Best Scientific Paper, Southern Thoracic Surgical Association, 1977 and 84 as co-author. *Address:* Division of Cardiothoracic Surgery, University of North Carolina, Chapel Hill, NC 27514, USA.

WILDY, Peter, b. 31 Mar. 1920, Tunbridge Wells, Kent, England. Professor of Pathology. m. Joan Audrey Kenion, Brompton, London, 3 Feb. 1945, 1 son, 2 daughters. *Education:* BA, MA, MB BChir, Gonville & Caius College, University of Cambridge & St Thomas's Hospital Medical School. *Appointments:* House Surgeon, St Thomas's Hospital, 1944-45; Served in India, Egypt, West Africa with Army 1945-47; Senior House Physician, Plymouth, 1948; Michael & Sidney Herbert & Leonard Dudgeon Research Fellow, 1949-51, Lecturer in Bacteriology, 1952-57, St Thomas's Hospital Medical School, London; British Memorial Fellow in Virology, Walter & Eliza Hall Institute, Melbourne, Australia, 1953-54;

Senior Lecturer in Bacteriology, St Thomas's, 1957-58; Assistant Director, Medical Research Council Experimental Virus Research Unit, Glasgow, 1959-63; Professor of Virology, University of Birmingham, 1967-75; Professor of Pathology, University of Cambridge, 1975-. *Memberships:* Member, Past Chairman, Society of General Microbiology; Pathological Society of Gt Britain & Ireland; Chairman, International Committee on Nomenclature of Viruses; Vice-Chairman, Chairman, Virology Section, IAMS. *Publications:* "Andrewes Viruses of Vertebrates"; Numerous articles, mostly on herpes. *Hobbies:* Spinning, Weaving, Dyeing. *Address:* Department of Pathology, Tennis Court Road, Cambridge CB2 1QJ, England.

WILKES, Eric, b. 12 Jan. 1920, Gateshead, Co Durham, England. Emeritus Professor of Community Care. m. Jessica Grant, 17 Aug. 1953, Crawley Down, 2 sons, 1 daughter. *Education:* MA; MB BCh; Fellow, Royal College of Physicians; Fellow, Royal College of General Practitioners; Fellow, Royal College of Psychiatrists; Diplomate of Obstetrics & Gynaecology (Royal College). *Appointments:* House Physician, Senior House Officer, St Thomas's Hospital, London; Principal in General Practice, Baslow, Derbyshire; Professor of Community Care & General Practice, Sheffield Medical School; Emeritus Professor & President, St Luke's Nursing Home, Sheffield; Co-Chairman, Help the Hospices. *Memberships:* National Cancer Sub-Committee; Trinity Day-Care Trust; Association of University Teachers of General Practice; Royal Society of Medicine. *Publications:* "Long-Term Prescribing", 1982; "The Dying Patient", 1982; Various papers on Primary Care & Chronic Disease Management. *Honours:* MBE (Military Division), 1944; OBE (Civil Division), 1973; Deputy Lieutenant for the County of Derbyshire, 1984; Honorary MD, Sheffield University, 1986. *Hobbies:* Gardening; Natural History; The Arts; Good food & wine. *Address:* Grislow Field, Curbar, Sheffield, S30 1XF, England.

WILKES, Mahlon McGregor, b. 15 July 1949, Deland, Florida, USA. Biomedical Consultant, Hygeia Associates. m. Roberta J Navickis, 15 Jan. 1983, La Jolla, California, USA. *Education:* JM, Stanford University; PhD, California Institute of Technology. *Appointments:* Assistant Professor, School of Medicine, University of California, San Diego. *Memberships:* American Chemical Society; American Association for the Advancement of Science. *Publications:* Contributor to numerous professional and scientific journals. *Honours:* Purdue Frederick Award, American College of Obstetricians and Gynaecologists, 1980; National Institutes of Health, USA, Research Grant, 1979. *Hobbies:* Shotokan karate. *Address:* Hygeia Associates, 1740 Hygeia Avenue, Leucadia, CA 92024, USA.

WILKIE, Douglas Robert, b. 2 Oct. 1922, London, England. Jodrell Research Professor, Physiology, University College, London. m. June R Hill, 18 Mar. 1949, Folkestone, divorced 1982, 1 son. *Education:* FRS; FRCP; MD (Yale); MRCP (London); MB, BS (London). *Appointments:* House Physician, Medical Unit, University College Hospital, London, 1944-45; Joined Physiology Dept., 1945, Reader, 1954, Professor, 1965, Jodrell Professor, Head of Dept, 1969, Jodrell Research Professor, Physiology, 1979, Medicine, 1981, University College, London; National Service RAF, Institute Aviation Medicine, 1948-51. *Memberships:* Physiological Society; Physiological Reviews; Chairman, European Board, 1969-74; Society of Magnetic Resonance in Medicine, Editorial Board. *Publications:* Over 100 articles in scientific journals, 1948-. *Honours:* State Scholarship, Intercollegiate Scholarship, 1940; Physiology Gold Medal, 1942; Rockefleer School Locke Research Fellowships, 1951; Senior Research Fellowship, SERC, 1979; etc. *Hobbies:* Sailing Small Cruising Boats; Company of Friends; Photography. *Address:* Dept. of Physiology, University College London, Gower Street, London

WC1E 6BT, England.

WILKINSON, Doris Y, b. Lexington, Kentucky, USA. Professor. *Education:* MPH, Johns Hopkins University, 1985; MA, 1960, PhD, 1968, Case Western Reserve University. *Appointments:* Associate, Full, Professor, Macalester College, St Paul, Minnesota, 1970-77; Executive Associate, American Sociological Association, 1977-80; Professor, Howard University, 1980-84; Visiting Professor, University of Virginia, 1984-85; Professor, University of Kentucky, 1985-. *Memberships:* American Orthopsychiatric Association; The New York Academy of Sciences; Eastern Soliological Association; Society for the Study of Social Problems; American Sociological Association; Sociologists for Women in Society. *Publications:* "Alternative Health Maintenance and Healing Systems", (Co-editor, M Sussman), 1986; 'Politics and sickle cell', 1974; 'Minority Women: Social-cultural issues', 1980; 'Ethnic diversity, Dietary customs and cardiovascular risks', 1984. *Honours:* Valedictorian, 1954; Woodrow Wilson Fellow, 1959-61; Outstanding Graduate Student, 1964; Outstanding Faculty Award, 1969; Phi Beta Kappa, 1978; President, DCSS, 1982-83; Vice President, Society for the Study of Social Problems, 1984-85. *Hobbies:* Piano; Swimming. *Address:* Department of Sociology, University of Kentucky, Lexington, KY 40506-0027, USA.

WILKINSON, Hei Sook, b. 11 Oct. 1947, Seoul, Korea. Clinical Psychologist. m. Todd Scripps Wilkinson, MD, 7 Mar. 1973, Nashville, Tennessee, USA, 1 son, 1 daughter. *Edcuation:* BA, Ewha Womens' University, Seoul, Korea, 1969; MA, George Peabody College of Vanderbilt University, Nashville, Tennessee, 1973; Post-MA Certificate, Merrill-Palmer Institute, Detroit, Michigan, 1978; PhD, Saybrook Institute, San Francisco, California, 1981. *Appointments:* Consultant to Peace Corps, Washington DC, 1971-72; Liaison Specialist, Metro Davidson Co School System, 1973-75; Educational Therapist, Childrens' Day Treatment Programme, Detroit, Michigan, 1975-76; Cross-Cultural and Psychological Consultant, Intercountry Adoptions, Michigan Department of Social Services, 1978-82; Psychotherapist, Lee M. Shulman & Associates, Royal Oak, Michigan, 1978-84; Adjunct Faculty Member, Union Graduate School, Cincinnati, Ohio, 1982-; Cross-Cultural and Psychological Consultant to Americans for International Aid and Adoption, Birmingham, Missouri, 1982-; Cross-Cultural and Psychological Consultant to Bethany International Adoptions, Michigan, 1982-; Faculty, Institute for Advanced Pastoral Studies, Detroit, 1984-. Clinical Psychologist, The Birmingham Clinic, Birmingham, Michigan, 1985-. *Memberships:* American Psychological Association; Association for Humanistic Psychology; Michigan Psychological Association. *Publications:* 'Play Therapy' in 'Researches on Children', Ewha Womens' University, 1979; "Birth is More Than Once", 1985. *Honours:* Summa cum laude, 1969; Korean Youth Representative to World Youth Assembly, United Nations, 1970. *Hobbies:* Tennis; Cross-Country; Ski-ing. *Address:* 802 S Worth, Birmingham, MI 48011, USA.

WILKINSON, Warwick James, b. 26 Jan. 1931, Killara, Australia. Pharmacist. m. Janet Mary Fisher, 12 Apr. 1958, Bathurst, 2 sons, 1 daughter. *Education:* Qualified, University of Sydney, 1952; Fellow, Pharmaceutical Society of Australia, 1981. *Appointments:* National President, Pharmaceutical Society of Australia; Chairman, Pharmacy Practice Foundation, University of Sydney; Consultant Medical Equipment, Lieutenant Colonel, Royal Australian Army Medical Corp; Director, External Affairs, Merck Sharp & Dohme (Australia) Pty Ltd; President, NSW Council of Professions; Chairman, Council of Australian College of Pharmacy Practice; Treasurer, Australian Council of Professions; Director, Health Services, Pharmacy Guild of Australia, NSW, 1970-73; Pharmaceutical Services Advisory Committee of Health Commission of NSW, Western Metropolitan Region, 1973-79; President, Pharmacy Board of NSW, 1975-80; President, Pharmaceutical Society of NSW,

1979-81; Councillor, Association of Health Professions, 1978-83; Chairman, Australian Council of Coeliac Societies, 1978-85. *Honours:* Reserve Forces Declaration with Bar, 1968; Efficiency Declaration with Bar, 1985. *Hobbies:* Skiing; Opera; Ballet; Horse Racing; Rugby; Politics. *Address:* 18 Robvic Avenue, Sylvania, NSW 2224, Australia.

WILLIAMS, Akinwole Olufemi, b. 3 Oct. 1935, Lagos, Nigeria. Executive Secretary, OAU/STRC, Lagos. m. Abimbola, 2 sons, 1 daughter. *Education:* BA; MB BCh; BAO, 1961; MA; MD, 1964; Trinity College, Dublin, Ireland; MRCP, 1964; FRCP, 1975; London; MRCP, 1964; FRCP, 1971; Royal College of Physicians: Ireland, MRCPath, 1966; FRCPath, 1978, Royal College of Pathologists, London. *Appointments:* Executive Secretary, Scientific Technical Research Commission of OAU; Research Fellow and Tutor in Pathology, Queens University, Belfast; Lecturer in Pathology, Trinity College, Dublin; Lecturer, Senior Lecturer, Pathology; Professor and Head of Department of Pathology, University of Ibadan; Provost, University of Calabar Medical School, Nigeria. *Memberships:* Vice-President, International Academy of Pathology; President, International Association for the Study of the Liver. *Publications:* "Atherosclerosis in the Nigerian"; "Ultrastructure of Liver in Jaundice Pneumonia and C6PD G Deficiency". *Honours:* Sir James Craig Memorial Prize, 1961; Adrian Stokes Memorial Fellowship, 1962. *Hobbies:* Music; Photography. *Address:* OAU/STRC Office, 26-28 Marina, PMB 2359, Marina, Lagos, Nigeria.

WILLIAMS, Christopher Beverley, b. 8 June 1938, Norwich, England. Consultant Physician. m. Christina Janet Seymour Lawrie, 25 Apr. 1970, 1 son, 1 daughter. *Education:* BA, Honours, Physiology, Oxon, 1950; MA, 1961; BM BCh, 1964; LRCP, MRCS, 1965; MRCP, 1968; FRCP, 1979. *Appointments:* House Physician, Surgeon & Registrar, University College Hospital, London; Consultant Physician Gastrointestinal Endoscopy, St Marks Hospital for Diseases of Rectum & Colon, London, St Bartholomews Hospital, London, London Clinic; Honorary Physician: King Edward VIIth Hospital for Officers, Hospital for Sick Children, Great Ormond Street, St Lukes for the Clergy. *Memberships:* British Medical Association; British Society of Gastroenterology; Fellow, Royal Society of Medicine; Liveryman, Society of Apothecaries. *Publications:* "Practical Gastrointestinal Endoscopy", with P. B. Cotton, 1981, 2nd edition, 1983 (Italian, German & French Editions); "Colorectal Disease", jointly, 1981; Chapters & papers on Colonoscopy and Colonic Diseases. *Hobbies:* Fine Wines & Good Food; Travel; Speaking French; Skiing. *Address:* St Marks Hospital, City Road, London EC1V 2PS, England.

WILLIAMS, Darryl Marlowe, b. 3 Apr. 1938, Denver, Colorado, USA. Acting Dean. m. Susan Arlene Moore, 24 June 1966, Fort Worth, Texas, 1 son, 2 daughters. *Education:* MS, Baylor University, Waco, Texas; MD, Baylor College of Medicine, Houston, Texas. *Appointments:* Assistant Professor, University of Utah, 1973-77; Associate Professor and Chief of Haematology 1977-80, Professor of Internal Medicine 1980-, Associate Dean for Academic Affairs, 1981-85, Acting Dean 1985-, Louisiana State University Medical Center in Shreveport, Shreveport, Louisiana. *Memberships:* American Society for Clinical Nutrition; American Institute of Nutrition; American Society of Hematology; Fellow, American College of Physicians. *Publications:* 'Drug Induced Aplastic Anemia', 1973; 'Wilsons Disease' in "Diseases of the Liver" (editor: Powell), 1978; 'Drug Induced Aplastic Anemia' in "Aplastic Anemia" (editor: Gearry), 1979; 'Cooper Deficiency in Humans', 1983. *Address:* Louisiana State University Medical Center in Shreveport, PO Box 33932, Shreveport, LA 71130, USA.

WILLIAMS, Gerald Vincent John, b. 28 Apr. 1948, Sydney, Australia. Staff Microbiologist, Liverpool Hospital. m. Colleen Marea, 14 Dec, 1974, Camperdown, 1 daughter. *Education:* MB, BS (Hons), 1972; BSc (Med); FRACP; FRCPA. *Appointments:* Resident Medical Officer, 1972, 1975, 1976, Microbiology Registrar, 1977, 1978, 1980, Royal Prince Alfred Hospital, Sydney, Australia; Medical Registrar, Prince Henry Hospital, Sydney, 1979; Research Fellow, Faculty of Medicine, University of Sydney, 1972, 1973, 1980-83. *Memberships:* Australian Medical Association; Royal Australasian College of Physicians; Royal College of Pathologists of Australasia. *Publications:* 'Delta Associated Hepatitis in Australia', (with Y E Cossart), 1983; 'Campylobacter: Common Cause of Enteritis in an Infectious Diseases Hosital', (with G J Deacon), 1980; 'Severe Anaemia in Port Moresby, PNG8, (with S Narari), 1979. *Honours:* Harold John Ritchie Prize in Clinical Medicine, University of Sydney, 1972. *Hobbies:* Squash; Swimming. *Address:* 25 Abbotsford Road, Homebush, New South Wales 2140, Australia.

WILLIAMS, (Sir) David Innes, b. 12 June 1919. Director, British Postgraduate Medical Federation. m. Margaret Eileen Harding, 1944, 2 sons. *Education:* MB. BCh., 1942, MA, 1943, MChir., 1945, MD, 1952, Trinity Hall, Cambridge, England; University College Hospital Medical School, London. *Appointments:* Urological Surgeon, St Peter's Hospital, London, 1950-78; Urologist, Hospital for Sick Children, Gt. Ormond Street, 1952-78; Civilian Consultant Urologist, Royal Navy, 1971-78; Senior Lecturer, Institute of Child Health, 1952-; Dean, Institute of Urology, 1972-78; Vice President, Royal College of Surgeons of England, 1983-85; Chairman, Council for Postgraduate Medical Education, England and Wales, 1985-; Pro-Vice Chancellor, University of London, 1985-. *Memberships:* Council, Royal College of Surgeons of England, 1974-; General Medical Council, 1979-; Chairman, Imperial Cancer Research Fund, 1982-; Board of Governors, The Hospitals for Sick Children, 1961-72, 1980-. *Publications:* "Urology of Childhood", Volume XV 'Encyclopedia of Urology', 1958, Supplement, "Paediatric Urology", 1968, 2nd edition 1982; Editor, Author, "Operative Surgery" (Urology), 1975; Joint Editor, "Scientific Foundations of Urology", 1976, 2nd edition, 1982. *Honours:* St Peter's Medal, British Association of Urological Surgeons, 1968; Denis Browne Gold Medal, British Association Paediatric Surgeons, 1975; Fellow, American College Surgeons (Hon) 1983; Fellow RCSI (Hon), 1984; Hon FDSRCS, 1986; Hon. Fellow, University College London, 1986. *Hobby:* Gardening. *Address:* British Postgraduate Medical Federation, 33 Millman Street, London WC1N 3EJ, England.

WILLIAMS, Lester F, Jr, b. 28 June 1930, Brockton, Massachusetts, USA. Professor of Surgery. *Education:* AB, Brown University, 1952; MD, Boston University School of Medicine, 1956. *Appointments:* Chief, Peripheral Vascular Surgery, Assistant Chief, General Surgery, USAF Medical Center, Wilford Hall; Assistant Professor of Surgery, Boston University School of Medicine, 1965-67; Associate Director, Boston University Surgical Service & Research Laboratory, Boston City Hospital, 1965-71; Associate Professor of Surgery, Boston University School of Medicine, 1967-71; Director, Surgical Internship & Residency Programme, BU Affiliated Hospitals, 1969-75; Professor of Surgery, BU School of Medicine, 1971-85; Associate Director, Surgical Service Boston VA Hospital, 1972-73; Executive Director, Medical & Dental Staffs, Department of Health & Hospitals, City of Boston, 1975-81; Director, Division of Surgery, Boston City Hospitals, 1973-85; James Utley Professor & Chairman, Division of Surgery, Boston University School of Medicine, 1977-84; Chief, Surgical Service, VA Medical Centre, Nashville, Professor of Surgery, Vanderbilt University School of Medicine, Nashville, Tennessee, 1985-. *Memberships include:* Alpha Omega Alpha; American Association for the Advancement of Science; American Association for the Surgery of Trauma; American College of Surgeons; American Gastroenterological Association; American Surgical Association; New York Academy of Sciences; Sigma Xi; Société Internationale de Chirurgie; Society for Surgery of the Alimentary Tract; Society of University Surgeons. *Publications:* "Fundamental Approach to Surgical Problems", 1961; "Vascular Disorders of the Intestinal Tract", 1971; "Core Textbook of Surgery", 1972; Over 100 scientific publications, 1954-84. *Address:* VA Medical Center, 1310, 24th Avenue South, Nashville, TN 37203, USA.

WILLIAMS, Norman Stanley, b. 15 Mar. 1947, Leeds, England. Professor of Surgery. m. Linda Feldman, LLB, 20 Feb. 1977, London, England, 1 son, 1 daughter. *Education:* MB, BS, London, 1970; FRCS (Eng.) 1975; MS, London, 1982. *Appointments:* House Officer, London Hospital, 1970-71, Surgical Senior House Officer and Registrar, 1971-76; Registrar, Bristol Royal Infirmary, 1976-77; Research Fellow, University of Leeds, 1977-78; Lecturer/Senior Registrar, Leeds General Infirmary, 1978-80; Research Fellow, UCLA, Los Angeles, USA, 1980-82; Senior Lecturer/{ Consultant Surgeon, Leeds General Infirmary, England, 1982-86. *Memberships:* Surgical Research Society; Fellow, Association of Surgeons; British Society of Gastroenterology; International Society of Surgeons; British Journal Surgery Society. *Publications:* Various papers and review articles on colorectal disease and Gastrointestinal motility. *Honours:* Patey Prize, Surgical Research Society, 1978; British Journal of Surgery Travelling Scholarship, 1979; Ethicon Foundation Travelling Fellowship, 1980; Fulbright Scholar, 1980-81; Moynihan Fellowship, 1985. *Hobbies:* Marathon Swimming; Cinema and Theatre. *Address:* Surgical Unit, The London Hospital, Whitechapel, London, E1 1B8, England.

WILLIAMS, Sir Robert Evan Owen, b., 30 June 1916, London, England. Professor (retired). m. Margaret Lumsden, 30 Dec. 1944, Birmingham, 1 son, 2 daughters. *Education:* BSc, MD, University College & Hospital, University of London; Fellow, Royal College of Physicians; Fellow, Royal College of Pathologists; FFCH. *Appointments:* Director, Streptococcus Staphylococcus & Air Hygiene Reference Laboratory; Professor of Bacteriology, University of London at St Mary's Hospital Medical School; Director, Public Health Laboratory Service. *Publications:* Numerous articles on hospital infection, bacteriology & epidemiology. *Honours:* Knight Bachelor, 1976; Honorary degrees of MD, Uppsala 1970, FRCPA 1977, DSc Bath, 1977. *Hobbies:* Horticulture; Photography. *Address:* Little Platt, Plush, Dorchester, Dorset, DT2 7RQ, England.

WILLIAMS, Thomas Arthur, b. 11 May 1936, Kenosha, Wisconsin, USA. Clinical Professor; Private Practitioner of Psychiatric Medicine. *Education:* BA, Harvard University, 1958; MD, Columbia University, 1963; Intern and Resident in Psychiatry, Presbyterian Hospital and New York State Psychiatric Institute, 1963-67. *Appointments include:* Various Clinical and Administrative appointments, 1968-83; various positions, Universities of Pittsburgh, Utah, Columbia University, Veterans Administration Hospitals, 1959-; Reviewer, American Journal of Psychiatry, 1979-; Chief, Psychiatry Service, James A Haley Veterans Hospital, Tampa, Florida, 1981-83; Private practice, Tampa, 1983-; Clinical Professor of Psychiatry, University of South Florida, College of Medicine, Tampa, 1983-; Editorial Reviewer, Archives of Internal Medicine, 1983. *Memberships:* American Medical Association; American Psychiatric Association; American Psychopathological Association; Society for Psychophysiological Research; Hillsborough County Medical Society, Tampa, Florida; Florida Medical Association; Tampa Psychiatric Society. *Publications:* Author or co-author of numerous papers contributed to professional journals including: 'American Journal of Psychiatry'; 'Psychophysiology'; 'Archives of General Psychiatry'; 'American Psychologist'; 'Behaviour Research Methods and Instrumentation'. Contributing Editor; "Recent

Advances in the Psychobiology of the Depressive Illnesses"; "Psychobiology of Convulsive Therapy". *Honours:* Predoctoral Fellowship, National Institute of Mental Health, Columbia University, 1960-61; Resident Research Prize, Alumni Association of New York State Psychiatric Institute, 1965; Member, Veterans Administration Mental Health Mission to USSR, 1974; Various awards, American Psychiatric Association, 1975; Examiner, American Board of Psychiatry and Neurology. *Address:* Lincoln Pointe, Suite 855, 2502 Rocky Point Drive, Tampa, FL 33607, USA.

WILLIAMSON, Patrick L, b. 15 Apr. 1948, Dickinson, North Dakota, USA. Associate Professor of Biology. m. Anne Kirkpatrick, 18 Apr. 1970, Lake Bluff, Illinois, 1 son. *Education:* BA, Beloit College; MS, PhD, Harvard University. *Appointments:* Staff Fellow, National Institutes of Health, Bethesda, Maryland, 1974-77; Department of Biology, Amherst College, 1977-. *Membership:* American Society for Cell Biology. *Publications:* Over 730 contributions to scientific journals. *Address:* Department of Biology, Amherst College, Amherst, MA 01002, USA.

WILLIAMSON, Robin Charles Noel, b. 19 Dec. 1942, Hove, Sussex, England. Professor of Surgery and Hon Consultant Surgeon. m. Judith Marjorie Bull, 21 Oct. 1967, London, England, 3 sons. *Education:* BA, Cambridge University, England, 1964; BChir 1967, MA, 1968, MB, 1968, MChir 1978, MD 1983; FRCS, 1972. *Appointments:* House Surgeon, St BartholomewʼS Hospital, London, England, 1968; Surgical Registrar, Reading, 1971-73; Senior Surgical Registrar, Bristol, 1973-75; Research Fellow, Massachusetts General Hospital, Harvard Medical School, 1975-76; Lecturer in Surgery, University of Bristol, England, 1977, Consultant Senior Lecturer, 1977-79; Professor of Surgery and Honorary Consultant Surgeon, Bristol Royal Infirmary, 1979-. *Memberships:* Association of Surgeons; Pancreatic Society; Surgical Research Society; British Society of Gastroenterology; British and American Associations for Cancer Research, etc. *Publications:* Co-author "Colonic Carcinogenesis", 1982; Co-author "General Surgical Operations", 1986; Numerous articles in intestinal adaptation and carcinogenesis, etc. *Honours:* Arris and Gale Lecturer, 1978; Hunterian Professor, Royal College of Surgeons, 1982; Moynihan Fellow, Association of Surgeons, 1979; Research Medal, British Society of Gastroenterology, 1982. *Hobbies:* Travel; Military History and Uniform. *Address:* Department of Surgery, Bristol Royal Infirmary, Bristol BS2 8HW, England.

WILLS, Brian Alan, b. 17 Feb. 1927, England. Chief Pharmacist of United Kingdom Department of Health and Social Security. m. Barbara Joan Oggelsby, 20 Aug. 1955, London, 1 son. *Education:* B Pharm, University of Nottingham; PhD, University of London; Fellow, Pharmaceutical Society; Fellow, Royal Society of Chemists. *Appointments:* Lecturer in Pharmaceutics, School of Pharmacy, University of London, 1951-57; Head of Research and Control Division, Allen and Hanbury's (Africa) Limited, 1957-62; Head of Control Division, Allen and Hanbury's Limited, 1962-78; Chief Pharmacist, United Kingdom Department of Health and Social Security, 1978-; Visiting Professor, University of Bath, 1979-83; Visiting Professor, University of Bradford, 1983-. *Memberships:* Fellow, Pharmaceutical Society of Great Britain; Fellow, Royal Society of Chemistry; British and European Pharmacopoeia Commissions. *Publications include:* Numerous articles on sterilisation and disinfection, preservation and quality control of pharmaceutical products. *Address:* 8 Graces Maltings, Akeman Street, Tring, Hertfordshire HP23 6DL, England.

WILLSON, Robert Dale, b. 12 July 1943, Houston, Texas, USA. President of Beta Associates, Occupational Health Consulting Organization. m.

Mary Susan Bear, 20 Apr. 1968, Columbus, Ohio, 1 son, 1 daughter. *Education:* BS, Electrical Engineering, Ohio State University, Columbus, 1966; MS, Industrial Hygiene, University of Cincinnati, 1972; Certified in Comprehensive Practice of Industrial Hygiene by American Board of Industrial Hygiene, 1976. *Appointments:* Industrial Hygienist, Senior Santiary Engineer, National Institute for Occupational Safety and Health, Cincinnati, 1972-76; Manager, Industrial Hygiene, Pedco Environmental Incorporated, Cincinnati, 1976-81; President, Beta Associates, Cincinnati, 1981-. *Memberships:* Acoustical Society of America; American Board of Industrial Hygiene; American Industrial Hygiene Association; American Foundrymen's Society. *Hobbies:* Fishing; Hiking. *Address:* Beta Associates, 7916 Christine Avenue, Cincinnati, OH 45241, USA.

WILSON, Alan Donald, b. 21 Mar. 1928, London, England. Head, Dental Materials Research, Laboratory of the Government Chemist. m. Margaret Hendley, 4 Aug. 1951. *Education:* BSc 1949, DSc, London University, 1976; D Tech 1981; C Chem 1976; FRSC (FRIC) 1965. *Appointments:* Scientific Officer, Alcohol Control, Laboratory of the Government Chemist, 1949-52; Senior Scientific Officer, Geological Museum 1952-62; Senior Scientific Officer, Fluoridation Research, Laboratory of the Government Chemist, 1962-64; Chairman, Dental Conservation Materials, British Standards Institute, 1969-. *Memberships:* Member, British Dental Association; Fellow, Royal Chemical Society; Consultant, International Dental Federation. *Publications:* 'Dental silicate cements', 1972; 'A new translucent cement for dentistry', 1972; 'Organolithic macromolecular materials', 1977; 'Clinical development of the glass ionomer cement', 1977; 'The chemistry of dental cements', 1978; 'Developments in Ionic Polymers', 1983. *Honours:* Wilmer Souder Award for Dental Research, 1976; International Association of Dental Research; Holliday Prize, Materials Science Club, 1978. *Hobbies:* Creative Writing; Architecture; Chess. *Address:* Laboratory of the Government Chemist, Cornwall House, Waterloo Road, London, SE18XY, England.

WILSON, Archie Fredric, b. 7 May 1931, Los Angeles, California, USA. University Professor of Medicine and Physiology. m. Tamar Braverman, 17 Oct. 1966, 2 sons. *Education:* AB, UCLA, 1953; MD, UCSF, 1957; PhD, UCLA, 1967. *Appointments:* Assistant Professor, UCLA, 1967-70; Assistant Professor, 1970-73, Associate Professor, 1973-79, Professor of Medicine and Phsyiology, University of California, Irvine. *Memberships:* Fellow, American College of Physicians, 1971; Fellow, American College of Chest Physicians, 1972; American Federation of Clinical Research; Western Society of Clinical Research. *Publications:* Contributor of numerous articles to medical journals and chapters to edited medical volumes. *Hobbies:* Tennis; Gardening; Jogging. *Address:* University of California, Irvine Medical Center, Orange, CA 92668, USA.

WILSON, Frances Helen, b. 17 Oct. 1929, Pittsburgh, Pennsylvania, USA. Occupational Therapist, retired. *Education:* BA, Connecticut College for Women, 1951; Advanced Standing Certificate, Columbia University School of Occupational Therapy, 1953. *Appointments:* Therapist, Washington County Society for Crippled Children & Adults, Washington, Pennsylvania, 1953-54; Staff Therapist, Oakland Veterans Administration Hospital, Pittsburgh, 1955-66; Supervisor, Occupational Therapy, Aspinwall Veterans Administration Hospital, Pittsburgh, 1966-74; Oakland VA Hospital, 1974-80; Aspinwall VA Hospital, 1980-85. *Memberships:* American Occupational Therapy Association; Pennsylvania Occupational Therapy Association. *Community Memberships:* Connecticut College Club of Pittsburgh; Junior League of Pittsburgh; 20th Century Club, Pittsburgh. *Address:* 14 Devon Lane, Ben Avon Heights, Pittsburgh, PA 15202, USA.

WILSON, Harry Gilmore, b. 3 Apr. 1917, Ipswich, Queensland, Australia. Physician, Private Practitioner. m. Elisabeth Stephens, 10 Mar. 1945, Brisbane, 4 sons, 1 daughter. *Education:* MA, MB BS, Queensland University; Diplomas in Agricultural Science, Elementary and Industrial Electronics; MRCP, London; FRACP. *Appointments:* Resident Medical Officer, Royal Brisbane Hospital, 1940-41; Assistant Physician, 1948-51, Junior Physician, 1952-53, Junior Cardiologist, 1953-56, Royal Brisbane Hospital; Senior Physician, 1956-77, Senior Cardiologist, 1958-77, Princess Alexandra Hospital; Private Practitioner, 1977. *Memberships:* Royal Australasian College of Physicians; Cardiac Society of Australia and New Zealand. *Publications:* Contributor of papers: 'Medical Journal of Australia'; 'Gerontological Society'; 'Circulation'; 'Bulletin of Princess Alexandra Hospital'. *Honours:* W N Robertson Memorial Medal, 1st in final year, Medical, Queensland University, 1940. *Hobbies:* Tennis; Surfing; English literature; Gardening. *Address:* 8 Milford Street, Ipswich, Queensland, Australia.

WILSON, James Leslie, b. 10 Aug. 1944, Wichita, Kansas, USA. Chiropractor. m. Vivien Fairlie Dawson, 21 Mar. 1984, Stratford, 1 son and 1 daughter. *Education:* BA, 1968, MA, 1971, Wichita State University; DC Canadian Memorial Chiropractic College, 1978; ND, Ontario College of Naturopathic Medicine, 1981; MSc, Biology, Nutrition, University of Bridgeport, 1985. *Appointments:* Research Co-ordinator, University College, Wichita State University, 1969-71; Counsellor, University of Lethbridge, Alberta, Canada, 1972-73; Director, Federal Research Grant, Non-Medical Use of Drugs, Saskatchewan, 1973-74; Private Clinical Practice, Fergus, Ontario, 1978-; Visiting Lecturer, Ontario College of Naturopathic Medicine, 1981-. *Memberships:* International Academy for Preventive Medicine; American Chiropractic Association; Occidental Institute Research Association; Canadian Naturopathic Association; Ontario Naturopathic Association. *Honours:* Fellow, International Association of Clinical Acupuncture, 1981-84; Board of Governors, Ontario College of Naturopathic Medicine; Diplomate, American Board of Chiropractic Examiners. *Hobbies:* Public Speaking; Skiing; Sailing; Windsurfing; Swimming; Reading; Private Research. *Address:* Box 902, Elora, Ontario, Canada N0B 1S0.

WILSON, Kathleen, b. 14 Dec. 1946, Brisbane, Queensland, Australia. Cardiac Scientist. *Education:* Bachelor of Veterinary Science, 1970, Bachelor of Science, 1970, University of Queensland; Master of Veterinary Science, University of Liverpool, England, 1975. *Appointments:* Private Practitioner, Biloela, Queensland, Australia, 1971; Government Veterinary Officer, Honiara, Solomon Islands, 1971-73; Research Officer, Department of Physiology and Pharmacology, University of Queensland, Australia, 1978-80; Cardiac Scientist, Prince Charles Hospital, Brisbane, 1980-. *Membership:* Royal College of Veterinary Surgeons. *Publications:* Numerous communications to learned societies including: Australian Physiological and Pharmacological Society, 1969, 77, 78, 79, 80; Australian Society for Medical Research, 1978; Australian Society of Clinical and Experimental Pharmacology, 1978; Cardiac Society of Australia and New Zealand, 1983. Articles in: 'Australian Journal of Experimental Biology and Medical Science'; 'Quarterly Journal of Experimental Physiology', 1980. *Honour:* Commonwealth Post-Graduate Award, 1977-78. *Hobbies:* Fishing; Swimming; Solar power generation; Computing. *Address:* The Prince Charles Hospital, Rode Road, Chermside, Brisbane, Qld 4032, Australia.

WILSON, Michael Bernard Howitt, b. 17 Aug. 1938, Walton-on-Thames, England. Private Practice Specialist in Manipulative Medicine (Chiropractic). m. Christine Ann Lindsey, 28 Aug. 1965, Godalming, 5 sons. *Education:* DOBSTRCOG, 1964; MB, BS, LRCS, LRCP, Kings College, London and Westminster

Medical School; DC, Anglo-European College of Chiropractic. *Appointments:* House Physician, St Charles' Hospital, London, 1962; House Surgeon, Hospital of St John and St Elizabeth, London, 1963; House Surgeon Obstetrics and Gynaecology, Farnborough Hospital, Kent, 1963; Trainee General Practitioner, London, 1964-65; General Practitioner, Woking, 1965-74; Specialist in Manipulative Medicine (Chiropractic), 1975-. *Memberships:* British Chiropractic Association; British Association of Manipulative Medicine, Fellow, Royal Society of Medicine; British Medical Association; Vice-Chairman 1985, British Section, World Federation of Doctors Who respect Human Life; Committee Member Southwark Branch, Build of Catholic Doctors. *Publication:* 'Chiropractic', 1984. *Hobbies:* Tennis; Voluntary work; Teacher of Natural Family Planning. *Address:* Dormans, Hollybank Road, Hook Heath, Woking, Surrey GU22 0JN, England.

WILSON, Michael J, b. 3 June 1942, Iowa City, USA. Research Biochemist; Associate Professor. m. Martha Swartzwelter, 7 June 1969, Richland, 1 son. *Education:* BA, Biology, St Ambrose College; MS, 1967, PhD, 1971, Zoology, University of Iowa. *Appointments:* Postdoctoral Fellow, Harvard University, 1971-73; Research Associate, Medicine & Pathology, 1973-75, Assistant Professor, Medicine & Pathology, 1975-82, Associate Professor, Medicine & Pathology, 1982-, University of Minnesota; Research Biochemist, VA Medical Centre, Minneapolis, 1976-. *Memberships:* American Physiological Society; Endocrine Society; American Society for Cell Biology; American Society of Zoologists. *Publications:* Co-author, "Studies of Human Seminal Fluid: Presence of Protein phosphokinase activities", in 'Male Reproduction and Fertility', 1983; "Melanin Pigment Production", in 'Advanced Cell Biology'; etc. *Hobbies:* Scuba Diving; Cross Country Skiing; Travel. *Address:* Research Service, VA Medical Centre, Minneapolis, MN 55417, USA.

WILSON, Noble Mowat, b. 15 May 1928, Perth. Broadcasting Consultant. m. Judith Ann Hill, 14 Feb. 1970, London, England, 1 daughter, 1 son, 1 daughter by previous marriage. *Education:* MA, Honours, Modern Languages, Corpus Christi College, Oxford, 1951. *Appointments:* Stage Manager, TV, Glasgow, 1952-54, Producer, TV, Glasgow, 1954-56, Lonson, 1956-61; BBC Representative, Paris, 1962-65, Chief Assistant, Current Affairs, 1965-68, Assistant Head, Features Group, TV, 1968-74, Controller, International Relations, 1974-83, Chief Assistant, International Developments TV, 1983-85, Early Retirement, 1986, BBC. *Publications:* Various articles in EBU Review, 1974-85; Articles in 'The Listener', 1985. *Hobby:* Photography. *Address:* 12 The Roystons, Berrylands, Surbiton, Surrey, England.

WILSON, Nairn Hutchinson Fulton, b. 26 Apr. 1950, Kilmarnock, Scotland. Senior Lecturer in Conservative Dentistry and Honorary Consultant in Restorative Dentistry, University Dental Hospital of Manchester. m. Margaret Alexandra Jones, 12 Apr. 1982, Cheadle, Cheshire, 1 son, 3 daughters. *Education:* University of Edinburgh, 1968-73; BDS, 1973; FDS RCS (Edinburgh), 1977; MSc, University of Manchester, 1979; DRD RCS (Edinburgh), 1980; PhD, University of Manchester, 1985. *Appointments:* House Officer, Edinburgh Dental Hospital, 1973-74; Lecturer in Restorative Dentistry, University of Edinburgh, 1974-75; Lecturer in Conservative Dentistry, 1975-, Senior Lecturer in Conservative Dentistry, 1981, University of Manchester; Honorary Consultant in Restorative Dentistry, Central Manchester Health Authority, 1982-. *Memberships:* British Dental Association; British Dental Editors Forum; British Society for Dental Research; British Society for the Study of Prosthetic Dentistry; British Society for Restorative Dentistry; International Association for Dental Research; Honorary Secretary of Odontology, Manchester Medical Society, 1981-85. *Publications:* Contributor to professional

journals, etc. including: Co-author, "A comparison of methods for contouring the occlusal surfaces of posterior composites', 'Journal of Dentistry', 1985; Co-author, 'The use of a new splint bridge system for cross pinning', British Dental Journal', 1985; Editor, 'Journal of Dentistry', 1986. *Hobbies:* Gardening; Squash. *Address:* Department of Conservative Dentistry, University Dental Hospital, Manchester M15 6FH, England.

WILSON, Peter G, b. 1 Jan. 1932. Associate Professor of Clinical Psychiatry, Cornell University Medical College; Director of Psychiatric Services, Rogosin Kidney Center, New York Hospital, 2 sons, 1 daughter. *Education:* AB, Columbia College, 1953; MD, College of Physicians and Surgeons, Columbia University, 1957; Internship and Residency, St. Luke's Hospital and Payne Whitney Clinic, 1957-61; Certificate in Psychoanalysis, 1967; Diplomate, American Board of Neurology and Psychiatry, 1965. *Appointments include:* Assistant in Psychiatry; Director of Admissions; Clinical Instructor in Psychiatry; Private Practice (part-time), 1961-68; Clinical Assistant Professor of Psychiatry, Cornell University Medical Center; Director of Residency Training and Coordinator of Inpatient Units, PWC, 1969-75; Associate Attending Psychiatrist, New York Hospital, 1970; Associate Professor of Clinical Psychiatry, Cornell University Medical Center, 1975-; Director of Psychiatric Services, Rogosin Kidney Center, New York Hospital, currently. *Memberships:* Fellow, American Psychiatric Association; American Association of Directors of Psychiatric Residency Training Program; Association for Psychoanalytic Medicine; New York Society for Clinical Psychiatry; American Medical Association, etc. *Publications:* Contributor to professional journals; Chapters in books include: 'Psychological factors in lower limb amputations' (Co-author) in "Psychological Experience of Surgery" by R Blacher (in press). *Address:* 525 East 68th Street, New York, NY 10021, USA.

WILSON, Thomas, b. 5 Nov. 1905, Belfast Northern Ireland. University Professor. m. Annie Cooley, 10 July 1930, Wallasey, England, 2 sons, 1 daughter. *Education:* MB, BCh, BAO, Queens University, Belfast, Northern Ireland, 1927, DPH, 1929, MD, 1952. DTM, DTH, Liverpool School of Tropical Medicine, 1930. *Appointments:* Health Officer, Senior Malaria Research Officer, Director, Institute for Medical Research, Malayan Medical Service, Kuala Lumpur; Senior Lecturer, Professor, Tropical Hygiene, Liverpool School of Tropical Medicine, University of Liverpool, England. *Memberships:* British Medical Association; Fellow, Royal Society of Tropical Medicine and Hygiene. *Publications:* Co-author "Davey and Lightbody's Control of Disease in the Tropics", 4th edition, 1971; Chapter: 'Worm Infections' in "Hobson's Theory and Practice of Public Health", 5th edition, 1979; numerous articles on malaria and filariasis in medical journals. *Honour:* CBE, 1959. *Hobbies:* Golf; Photography. *Address:* 77 Strand Road, Portstewart, County Londonderry BT55 7LX, Northern Ireland.

WILSON, William Rosser, b. 3 Apr. 1938, Tuxedo, New York, USA. Professor of Surgery; Chief Division of Otolaryngology and Head and Neck Surgery, George Washington University, Washington DC. *Education:* BA, Yale University, 1960; Columbia University Medical School, 1964; MD; FACS. *Appointments:* Instructor in Otolaryngology, 1968-69, Clinical Instructor, 1973-74, Assistant Professor, 1974-81, Associate Professor, 1981-84, Otolaryngology, Harvard Medical School; Assistant Professor of Surgery, Division of Otolaryngology, University of Connecticut School of Medicine, 1971-73; Professor of Surgery, (Otolaryngology), 1984-, Chief, Division of Otolaryngology/Head and Neck Surgery, 1984-, George Washington University Medical Centre. *Memberships:* AMA; American College of Surgeons, Fellow; DC Medical Society; American Council of Otolaryngology; American

Rhinologic Society; Fellow, American Academy of Otolaryngology; Society of University Otolaryngologists; American Neurotology Association; Association for Research in Otolaryngology; American Society of Head and Neck Surgeons. *Publications:* "Quick Reference to Ear, Nose and Throat Disorders", (with J B Nadol Jr), 1982; 'Histopathology of the Ear and Its Clinical Implications', (with J B Nadol Jr), 1984. *Address:* 2150 Pennsylvania Avenue NW, Division of Otolaryngology/Head and Neck Surgery, GWUMC, Washington, DC 20037, USA.

WIMAN, Lars-Gösta, b. 22 Sep. 1926, Norberg, Sweden. Chief, Lung Medicine, Karolinska Instituet, Huddinge University Hospital, Sweden. m. Elisabeth Rosengren, 21 Aug. 1955, Goethenburg, 3 sons. *Education:* BM, Uppsala University, 1951; MD, Clinical, Uppsala University, 1956; Specialist Competence for Pulmonary Diseases, 1963; PhD, Uppsala University, 1964; Postgraduate Courses, Chicago, Vancouver, Brussels, Marseilles. *Appointments:* Instructor, Pathology, Uppsala University, 1962; Consultant, Tuberculosis, Ulleraker Mental Hospital, Uppsala, 1964; Associate Professor, Lung Diseases, Uppsala University, 1965; Chief, Lung Medicine, Umea University, 1965; Dean, Physical Examination, Umea University, 1972; Chief, Lung Medicine, 1975; Lecturer, Pulmonary Medicine, Mentor, Research Instructor, 1975, Karolinska Institutet, Huddinge University. *Memberships:* Swedish Medical Association; Swedish Society of Lung Medicine; World Association for Bronchology; International Association for the Study of Lung Cancer; American College of Chest Physicians; Governor of Sweden, 1985. *Publications:* "Cytological examination of sputum and bronchial washings in carcinoma of the lung", 1959; "Proteinbound sulfydryl groups in pulmonary cytodiagnosis", 1964; "Fysikalisk diagnostik", 1972; "Familial occurrence of sarcoidosis", 1972; "Scanning electron microscopy of the bronchial mucosa", 1976; "Nuclear DNA in Histological sections of Carcinoma of the Lung", 1985; "Ciliary beat frequency in tracheal mucosa studied by dynamic laser light scattering", 1986; etc. *Hobbies:* Poetry; Fiction; Music; Tennis. *Address:* Dept. of Lung Medicine, Karolinska Institutet, Huddinge University Hospital, Huddinge, Sweden.

WIMBERLEY, Jerral Bruce, b. 29 Apr. 1938, Cuba Township, Illinois, USA. Owner, Physician, Magic Valley Chiropractic Clinic. m. Janet Aline Rogers, 20 Sep. 1969, Portland, Oregon, 1 son, 3 daughters. *Education:* BS, Physics, Wheaton College, 1968; DC, Western States Chiropractic College, 1977; Postgraduate Board Qualifying Certificate, Chiropractic Orthopedics, Los Angeles Chiropractic College, 1983; DABCO, Diplomate, American Board of Chiropractic Orthopedists, 1985. *Appointments:* Intern, WSCC Outpatient Clinic, Portland, 1976-77; Staff Physician, Southeast Chiropractic Clinic, Portland, 1977-78; WSCC Alumni Board Member, 1977-78; Board Member, Idaho Association of Chiropractic Physicians, 1985-87; Secretary Treasurer, IACP Physiotherapy Council, 1984-86, Central District 1984-86. *Memberships:* American Chiropractic Association; IACP; IACP Central District; Oregon Chiropractic Physicians Association; ACA Orthopedics Council; American College of Chiropractic Orthopedists; Fellow, Academy of Chiropractic Orthopedists; Foundation for Athletic Research and Education; Christian Chiropractic Association; American Scientific Affiliation, Fellow; National Academy of Research Biochemists. *Honours:* Certificate of Appreciation, Distributive Education Clubs of America, 1979; Partner in Progress Award, Foundation for Chiropractic Education & Research, 1983. *Hobbies:* Running; Hunting; Hiking; Camping; Wood Cutting; Photography; Reading. *Address:* 800 Main Street, Buhl, ID 83316, USA.

WIMMER, Eckard, b. 22 May 1936, Berlin, Germany. Professor. m. Astrid Brose, 4 Sep. 1965, 1 son, 1 daughter. *Education:* Vordiplom, Diplom, Chemistry, Dr rerum. Naturalis, Organic Chemistry, University of Gottingen. *Appointments:* Research Associate, Biochemistry, University of British Columbia, Canada, 1964-66; Research Associate, Botany, University of Illinois, Urbana, USA, 1966-68; Assistant Professor, Microbiology, St Louis University School of Medicine, 1968-73; Associate Professor, 1974-79, Professor, 1979-, Chairman, 1984-, Microbiology State University of New York, Stony Brook. *Memberships:* American Association for the Advancement of Science; American Society for Microbiology; American Society for Virology. *Publications:* "Primary Structure, gene organization and polypeptide expression of poliovirus RNA", 'Nature', 1981. *Honours:* Josiah Macy Junior Foundation Faculty Scholar Award, 1980-81; NATO Lecturer, 1980-81; M R Hilleman Lecture, University of Chicago School of Medicine, 1984. *Hobbies:* Music; Sports. *Address:* Department of Microbiology, State University of New York, Stony Brook, NY 11794, USA.

WINBERG, Jan, b. 11 Apr. 1923, Bollnäs Sweden. Professor of Paediatrics; Physician in Ordinary to the children of the King Carl Gustaf XVI and Queen Silvia of Sweden. *Appointments:* Associate Professor, University of Göteborg, 1959-67; Karolinska Institute, 1968-71; Professor & Chairman, Department of Paediatrics, University of Umea, 1972-74; Professor & Chairman, Department of Paediatrics, Karolinska Institute, Stockholm, 1974-. *Memberships:* European Society of Paediatric Research; European Society for Paediatric Nephrology; International Paediatric Nephrology Association. *Publications:* About 250 scientific publications on various paediatric topics. *Address:* Department of Paediatrics, Karolinska Hospital, 104 01 Stockholm, Sweden.

WINBLAD, Bengt Göran, b. 17 Mar. 1943, Falun, Sweden. Professor. m. 1967, Stockholm, 1 son, 2 daughters. *Education:* MD, 1971; PhD, 1975; Assistant Professor, 1977; Professor, 1981. *Appointments:* Professor of Geriatric Medicine, University of Umea, 1981-. *Publications:* Author of publications mainly in the field of Alzheimer's disease. *Address:* Department of Geriatric Medicine, University of Umea, S-901 87, Umeå) Sweden.

WINCHESTER, William J, b. 23 Mar. 1923, Tulsa, Oklahoma, USA. Director of Veterinary Medicine; Assistant Dean. m. Betty Winchester, 4 sons. *Education:* DVM, Kansas State University School of Veterinary Medicine; Graduate Studies, University of Wisconsin; Licensed by States of Kansa, Oklahoma and Wisconsin; Federal Accreditation. *Appointments include:* Director, Owner, Veterinary Hospital, San Gabriel, California, 1947-66; Division of Comparative Veterinary Medicine, Los Angeles County Veterinary Hospital, 1966-71; Director, Animal Resource Facility, College of Medicine, 1972-, Assistant Dean, College of Medicine and School of Veterinary Medicine, 1974-, Director of Veterinary Medicine, 1977-, University of California. *Memberships include:* American Association for Accreditation of Laboratory Animal Care; American Association for Laboratory Animals; American Society of Laboratory Animal Practitioners; American Animal Hospital Association; American Veterinary Medical Association; Association of American Veterinary Medical Colleges, Council of Educators. *Publications:* Co-Author of book contributions: "Microsurgery in Gynaecology", 1977, 79; "Clinical Obstetrics and Gynaecology", volume 23, 1980; "Models and Techniques in Medical Imaging Research", 1983. 'Teaching Microsurgery to Gynaecologists' in 'Journal of Microsurgery', 1979. *Honours:* Honorary Member, Elected, International Medical Teaching Team to Peoples Republic of China, 1984; Continuing Veterinary Educator of the Year Award, 1984. *Hobbies:* Reading; Travelling. *Address:* Assistant Dean, California College of Medicine, University of California, Irvine, CA 92717, USA.

WINFIELD, John Buckner, b. 19 Mar. 1942, Kentfield. California, USA. Professor of Medicine. m. Teresa McGrath, 22 Mar. 1969, New York, 1 son, 2 daughters. *Education:* BA, Biology, Williams College, Williamstown, Massachusetts, 1964; MD, Cornell University Medical College, New York, 1968. *Appointments:* Intern, Internal Medicine, New York Hospital, 1968-69; Staff Associate, Laboratory of Immunology, NIAID, NIH, Bethesda, Maryland, 1969-71; Residency in Medicine, Fellowship in Rheumatology, University of Virginia, Charlottesville, Virginia, 1971-73; Postdoctoral Fellow, Rockefeller University, New York, 1973-75; Assistant Professor, Associate Professor of Medicine, 1978-80, Professor of Medicine 1980-. Chief, Division of Rheumatology and Immunology, Director Multipurpose Arthritis Center, 1978-, University of North Carolina, Chapel Hill. *Memberships:* American Rheumatism Association, Executive Committee 1978-84, Chairman Education Committee, 1980-84; American Association of Immunologists; American Society for Clinical Investigation. *Publications:* More than 100 scientific articles published in professional journals. *Honours:* Borden Prize, Cornell University, 1968; Senior Investigator Award of the Arthritis Foundation, 1976. *Hobbies:* Motorcycling; Golf. *Address:* Division of Rheumatology and Immunology, 932 FLOB 231H, University of North Carolina, Chapel Hill, NC 22514, USA.

WINK, Michael John, b. 16 Mar. 1950, London, England. Family Physician. m. Jill Mason, 23 Aug. 1985, Edmonton, Canada. *Education:* BSc; LRCP; MRCS; MB; BS; MD; Family Planning Certificate. *Appointments:* House Physician, St. Helen's Hospital, Hastings, England, 1975; House Surgeon, Royal East Sussex Hospital, Hastings, 1975-76; Senior House Officer, Charing Cross Hospital, London, 1976; Senior House Officer, Guy's Hospital, London, 1976-77; Chief Medical Officer, Port Saunders Hospital, Canada, 1978; Family Physician, Brookfield Hospital, Canada, 1979; Chief of Staff, Lampman Hospital, Saskatchewan, Canada, 1979-81; Resident, University Alta O & G, Canada, 1981-83; Family Physician and Surgeon, Radwater General Hospital, Canada, 1983-present. *Memberships:* British Medical Association; Medical Defence Union; General Medical Council; Canadian Medical Protective Association; Canadian Medical Association, Alberta Chapter. *Publications:* 'Postcoital Contraception' in 'British Medical Journal', 1977; 'Air Traffic Control' in 'CIBA Review' 1982. *Honour:* Wooldridge Prize in Physiology, Guy's Hospital, University of London, 1971. *Hobbies:* Hunting; Fishing; Music; Skiing; Psychology; Oil Painting. *Address:* Box 930, Gibbons, Alberta T0A 1N0, Canada.

WINKELHAKE, Jeffrey Lee, b. 5 Oct. 1945, Champaign, Illinois, USA. Senior Scientist/Director, Department of Pharmacology. *Education:* BS, Chemistry/Physics/Zoology, 1967, MS, Microbiology 1969, PhD, Immunochemistry 1974, University of Illinois. *Appointments include:* Assistant, Associate, Professor, Department of Microbiology, Medical College of Wisconsin, 1976-84; Adjunct Professor, Department of Microbiology & Immunology, University of California, Berkeley, 1984-; Senior Scientist, Director of Pharmacology, Cetus Corporation, Emeryville, California, 1984-. *Memberships:* American Association of Immunology; American Society of Biological Chemistry; American Society for Pharmacological & Experimental Therapy; American Association for Cancer Research; American Chemical Society; Biochemical Society, UK. *Publications include:* Over 80 published papers in professional journals, books & reviews. *Honours:* US Public Health Service Fellow, 1972-74; Postdoctoral Fellow, Jane Coffin Child Memorial Fund for Medical Research, 1974-76; Fulbright-Hayes International Scholar, Oxford University, UK, 1982. *Hobbies:* Tennis; Sailing; Skiing. *Address:* Department of Pharmacology, Cetus Corporation, 1400 53rd Street, Emeryville, CA 94608, USA.

WINKLER, Cuno G, b. 30 Sep. 1919, Koenigsberg,

Federal Republic of Germany. Professor of Nuclear Medicine; Institute Director. *Education:* MD; PhD honours. *Appointments:* Professor, Director, Institute of Nuclear Medicine, Bonn. *Memberships:* A von Humboldt Foundation; European Society of Nuclear Medicine. *Publications:* "Nuclear Medicine in Clinical Oncology"; "Datenverarbeitung in der Nuklearmedizin"; "Neue Aspekte in Diagnose und Therapie des Schilddrüsenkarzinoms". *Honour:* Grand Cross for Distinguished Service of the Federal Republic of Germany. *Hobby:* Viola player with String Quartet. *Address:* Institute of Nuclear Medicine, 5300 Bonn, Federal Republic of Germany.

WINSLOW, Walter William, b. 23 Nov. 1925, Canada. University Professor and Department Chairman. *Education:* BS, La Sierra College, Arlington, California, USA, 1949; MD, Loma Linda University, California, 1951; Diplomate, American Board of Psychiatry and Neurology (P), 1964. *Appointments:* Instructor, Department of Psychiatry, University of Cincinnati College of Medicine, Ohio, USA, 1960-66; Assistant Professor, Department of Psychiatry, University of New Mexico School of Medicine, Albuquerque, New Mexico, USA, 1966-68, Associate Professor, 1969-74, Professor and Chairman Department of Psychiatry, 1974-; Associate Professor, Department of Psychiatry, Georgetown University, Washington DC, 1968-69; Director, University of New Mexico Mental Health Programmes, 1978-. *Memberships:* American Medical Association; American Psychiatric Association; American Academy of Psychiatry and the Law. *Publications:* "Changing Trends in CMHC's: Keys to Survival in the Eighties" in 'Hospital Community Psychiatry', 1982; Co-author 'Hypochondriacal Beliefs and Attitudes in Family Practice and Psychiatric Patients' in 'International Journal of Psychiatry in Medicine', 1983; Co-author 'The Relationship of Hypochondriacal Fears and Beliefs to Anxiety and Depression' in 'Psychiatric Medicine', 1984. *Honour:* Warren Williams Award, American Psychiatric Association, Washington DC Area VII, 1984. *Address:* University of New Mexico, Department of Psychiatry, 2400 Tucker NE, Albuquerque, NM 87131, USA.

WINTER, Gerald Bernard, b. 24 Nov. 1928, London, England. Director of Studies, Children's Dentistry. m. Brigitte Eva Fleischhacker, 24 Apr. 1960, London, 1 son, 1 daughter. *Education:* BDS, MB, BS, DCH, London Hospital Medical College; FDS, RCS, Royal Dental Hospital. *Appointments:* House Surgeon, House Physician, London Hospital Medical College, 1955-59; Lecturer in Children's Dentistry, Royal Dental Hospital, London, 1959-62; Dean & Director of Studies, Head of Department of Children's Dentistry, Eastman Dental Hospital, London. *Memberships:* British Dental Association; British Medical Association; British Paedodontic Society; British Paediatric Association; International Association of Dentistry for Children. *Publications:* "A Colour Atlas of Clinical Conditions in Paedodontics" (with R Rapp), 1979; Various papers in dental & medical journals. *Hobbies:* Do-It-Yourself; Gardening; Music; Theatre. *Address:* Institute of Dental Surgery, Eastman Dental Hospital, Gray's Inn Road, London, WC1X 8LD, England.

WINTER, James, b. 1947, New York City, USA. *Education:* BS, Pennsylvania State University, 1967; MD, Jefferson Medical College, 1969; MS, 1972, PhD, 1978, University of California, Los Angeles. *Appointments:* Intern, University of Chicago, 1969-70; Radiology Resident, 1970-74, Neuroradiology Fellow, 1973-75, University of California; Instructor, Radiological Sciences, 1973-74, Assistant Professor, 1974-83, Associate Professor, 1983-, Diagnostic Radiology and Biomedical Physics, University of California; various hospital positions including: Olive View Medical Centre, Los Angeles County, 1980; Chief Scientist, Founder, Information Appliance Inc, Palo Alto, 1982-. *Memberships:* Committee, Computers, American College of Radiology, 1971-82; American Institute of Ultrasound in Medicine; Senior Member, American Society of Neuroradiology; Association of University Radiologists; Radiologic Society of North America; Society for Magnetic Resonance Imaging; Society of Nuclear Medicine; many other professional organisations. *Publications:* Numerous articles, papers, etc, in professional journals. *Honours:* National Science Foundation Fellow, 1962; NIH Fellow, 1966, 1967; US Public Health Service Fellow, 1970-74; James Picker Foundation Fellow, 1974-77; Alpha Omega Alpha; Hare Medical Honour Society; Phi Eta Sigma; Sigma Xi; BSc, Summa Cum Laude; James T Case Memorial Prize, 1972; American Society of Neuroradiology Exhibit, Summa Cum Laude, 1980. *Address:* Department of Radiological Sciences, Los Angeles, CA 90024, USA.

WINTHER, Jens Erik, b. 16 Jan. 1933, Aarhus, Denmark. Director. m. Anne Elisabeth Jacobsen, 1 Apr. 1961, Gentofte, 1 son, 1 daughter. *Education:* DDS, 1957; Specialist, Oral Surgery, 1967. *Appointments:* Assistant Professor, 1961-67, Associate Professor, 1967-75, Oral Surgery, Director, Dental Auxiliary Training, 1975-, Royal Dental College, Aarhus; Senior Lecturer, Public Health, Dental Assistants, Uganda, 1972. *Memberships:* Danish Dental Association; Scandinavian Association of Oral and Maxillofacial Surgeons; Dental Advisory Board, Danida. *Publications:* "Manual of Minor Oral Surgery", 1982; "Facial Asymmetries Following Unilateral Condylar Replacement", 'International Journal Oral Surgery', 1979; 'Mycotic Infection in Oral Leucoplakia'', 'Acta Odont.', 1965; "Evaluation of Carticaine, a new local Analgesic", 'International Journal Oral Surgery', 1974; "Periapical Granulomas and Cysts", 'Scandinavian Journal Dental Research", 1970; "Antimicrobial effect of anesthetic sprays", 'Acta Odont. Scand.', 1969; etc. *Honours:* Knight, Order of Dannebrog, 1986. *Hobbies:* Bridge; Tennis; Windsurfing; Hunting. *Address:* Royal Dental College, 8000 Århus C, Denmark.

WIRASUGENA, Solihin, b. 23 June 1932, Rajagaluh, West Jawa, Indonesia. Pathologist. m. Dr Wuryarin, 25 May 1961, Yogyakarta, Indonesia, 1 son, 2 daughters. *Education:* MD, Faculty of Medicine, University of Gajah Mada, Yogyakarta, 1961; Pathologist & Forensic Pathologist. *Appointments:* High School Teacher (part-time) Faculty of Pedagogy, University of Gajah Mada, 1953-58; Assistant, Department of Pathology, University of Gajah Mada, 1958-61; Head of Department of Pathology & Forensic Pathology, University of Hasanuddin Ujung Pandang, 1961-; Deputy III, Dean of Faculty of Medicine, 1963-66, Dean of Faculty, 1974-80, University of Hasanuddin. *Memberships:* Indonesian Medical Association; Indonesian Pathologists Association. *Publications:* 'Diagnostic of lymph nodes enlargement by fine needle aspiration biopsies' (research project, University of Hasanuddin, 1982); 'Cytological Presentation of Mammary tumours on Fine needle aspiration smears' (research project, 1983). *Hobbies:* Tennis; Photography. *Address:* Jalan Kartini 1 C, Ujung Pandang, Indonesia.

WISSINGER, H Andrew, b. 14 Sep. 1930, Pittsburgh, Pennsylvania, USA. Orthopaedic Surgeon; Clinical Professor. m. Patricia A Bik, 2 sons. *Education:* MD, University of Pittsburgh, 1956. *Appointments:* Currently Clinical Professor, University of Pittsburgh School of Medicine. *Memberships:* American Academy of Orthopaedic Surgeons; American College of Surgeons; American Society for Surgery of the Head. *Publications include:* Author or co-author of 20 refereed articles including: 'Incidence of cutaneous eruption due to sulphamenthoxpyridazine', 1963; 'Gouty arthritis of the hip joints', 1963; 'Digital flexor lag in rheumatoid arthritis', 1971; 'Total knee replacement prosthesis', 1971; 'Prophylactic anticoagulation in total hip replacement surgery', 1975; 'Resection of the hook of the hamate, its place in the treatment of median and ulnar nerve en-

trapment in the hand', 1975; 'Chondromalacia: a nonoperative treatment program', 1982. *Hobby:* Tree farming. *Address:* 5820 Centre Avenue, Pittsburgh, PA 15206, USA.

WITHERS, H. Rodney, b. 21 Sep. 1932, Queensland, Australia. Professor, Radiation Oncology; Director, Experimental Radiation Oncology. m. Janet E. Macfie, 9 Oct. 1959, 1 daughters. *Education:* MBBS, University of Queensland, 1956; MRACR, 1961; FRACR, 1977; PhD, 1965, DSc., 1982, University of London, England; various Hospitals, 1958-63; Gray Laboratory, Northwood, Middlesex, 1963-65. *Appointments:* Radiotherapist, Prince of Wales Hospital, Sydney, 1966; Visiting Research Scientist, Physiology, National Cancer Institute, Maryland, USA, 1966-68; Associate Radiotherapist, Associate Professor, University of Texas System Cancer Centre, 1968-71; Associate Graduate Faculty, University of Texas Graduate School of Biomedical Sciences, Houston, 1969-73, Member 1973-80; Radiotherapist, Professor, Radiotherapy, Chief of Section, University of Texas System Cancer Centre, 1971-80, Professor, Medical School, Radiotherapy, 1975-80; Professor, Director, Experimental Radiation Oncology, Centre for Health Sciences, University of California, Los Angeles, 1980-. *Memberships include:* American College of Radiology; American Radium Society; American Society Therapeutic Radiology and Oncology; British Institute of Radiology; Radiation Research Society; etc. *Publications include:* Numerous articles in professional journals; book chapters; etc. *Honours:* Gaggin Fellowship for Cancer Research, University of Queensland, 1963-66; Finzi Bequest Prize, British Institute of Radiology, 1974; Commemorative Medal of Achievement, University of Texas System Cancer Centre, 1981. *Address:* Dept. of Radiation Oncology, UCLA Centre for Health Sciences, Los Angeles, CA 90024, USA.

WITHERSPOON, Edward William, b. 19 Dec. 1925, Liverpool, England. m. Jean McKellar, 10 June 1964, Edinburgh, Scotland. *Education:* DTM & H; Royal College of Physicians, London; Royal College of Surgeons, England; Fellow, Royal Society of Health. *Appointments:* Major, RAMC, Suez Canal Zone, Egypt, and Cyprus; Assistant Government Medical Officer, Sydney, Australia; Medical Director, Wellcome Group, Australasia; Medical Director, Warner/Parke Davis, Europe & Africa; Pharmacovigilance & Medical Services, Roussel Laboratories, Uxbridge, Middlesex, England. *Memberships:* Vice-Chairman, BMA/MAPI Committee; Fellow, Royal Society of Medicine; Fellow, Royal Society of Tropical Medicine; Fellow, Hunterian Society; Society of Apothecaries of London. *Publications:* "Toxocaral Infection in Man", 1965; "Menopausal Syndrome", 1975; "Chemotherapy Malaria', 1976; 'Nephropathy', 1981. *Honour:* UK Trade Mission to Japan, 1968. *Hobby:* National Trust for Scotland. *Address:* Brook Cottage, 4 Manor Road, Oakley, Nr Aylesbury, Buckinghamshire, HP18 9QD, England.

WOGAN, Gerald Norman, b. 11 Jan. 1930, Altoona, Pennsylvania, USA. Professor of Toxicology and Department Head, Department of Applied Biological Sciences, Massachusetts Institute of Technology. m. Henrietta E Hoenicke, 24 Aug. 1957, 1 son, 1 daughter. *Education:* BS, Juniata College, 1951; MS, 1953, PhD, 1957, University of Illinois. *Appointments:* Assistant Professor, Physiology, Rutgers University, New Brunswick, New Jersey, 1957-61; Assistant Professor of Toxicology, 1962-65, Associate Professor, 1965-69, Professor, 1969-, Massachusetts Institute of Technology, Cambridge, Massachusetts. *Memberships:* American Association for Cancer Research; American Society of Pharmacology and Experimental Therapeutics; American Society for Microbiology; Society of Toxicology; American Society for Preventive Oncology; AACS; Sigma Xi. *Publications:* Contributor of articles and reviews to professional journals. *Honours:* Elected to the National Academy of Sciences of the USA, 1977. *Address:*

Building 16, Room 333, Department of Applied Biological Sciences, Massachusetts Institute of Technology, Cambridge, MA 02139, USA.

WOJTOWICZ, Jerzy Stanislaw, b. 9 Dec. 1932, Poznan, Poland. Professor of Radiology. m. Maria Pasek, 13 Sep. 1955, Poznan, 1 son, 1 daughter. *Education:* MB, Faculty of Medicine, University Medical School, Poznan, 1957; Specialisation in Radiology, 1962; MD, 1962; Further Study in Radiology at Oxford, England, Stockholm, Sweden, Tübingen, Federal Republic of Germany. *Appointments:* House Officer, Senior House Officer, Department of Radiology, 1957-66, Docent in Radiology, 1966-75, Professor of Radiology, 1975-81, University Medical School, Karol Marcinkowski, Poznan; Rector, University Medical School, 1981-; Scientific Adviser, World Health Organisation, 1978; Director, Department of General Diagnostic Radiology, University Medical School, Poznan. *Memberships:* International Society of Radiology, 1965; European Association of Radiology, 1975; European College of Angiography, 1976; European Society of Thermography, 1978; Cardiovascular & Interventional Society of Europe, 1985; International Physicians for Prevention of Nuclear War, 1985; President, Polskie Lekarskie Towarzy stwo Radiologiczne, 1974-77; Corresponding Member, Society of Radiology of the German Democrat Republic, 1977; Honorary Member, Radiological Society of Czechoslovakia, 1985; Slovak Medical Society, 1985. *Publications:* Editor-in-Chief, 'Polski Przeglad Radiologii', 1978-; Over 200 scientific papers & books on efficacy of Radiological methods, Medical Radiology, Angiography, computer tomography, ultrasonography. *Honours:* Several Awards for research, 1966-. *Hobby:* Cycling. *Address:* Zaklad Radiologii Ogolnej, Instytut Radiologii AM, ul. Szkolna 8/12, 61-833 Poznan, Poland.

WOLF, Alexander, b. 16 Apr. 1907, New York City, USA. Senior Training Psychoanalyst. *Education:* BA, Columbia University, New York, 1928; MD, Cornell University Medical College, 1932. Internship, 1932-33, Resident Neurologist, 1933-34, Bellevue Hospital, New York City. Numerous posts in USA, US Armed Forces and abroad; Finally Faculty Senior Supervisor, Training Psychoanalyst, Postgraduate Center for Mental Health, New York. *Memberships:* Life Fellow, American Psychiatric Association; Life Fellow, American Academy of Psychoanalysis; Distinguished Fellow, American Group Psychotherapy Association; Diplomate, Board of Psychiatry & Neurology; Fellow, The Menninger Foundation. *Publications:* "Psychoanalysis in Groups", 1962; "Beyond the Couch", 1970; Over 115 papers in medical and professional journals. *Honours:* Various awards and honours. *Hobbies:* Reading; Walking; Clinical Research. *Address:* 11 East 68th Street, New York, NY 10021, USA.

WOLF, Augustin, b. 28 May 1921, Prague, Czechoslovakia. Professor of Food Hygiene and Nutrition, Faculty of Hygiene, Universita Karlova, Prague. m. Jarmila Kubenová, 26 Aug. 1949, 1 daughter. *Education:* MD; DSc; Specialisation in Hygiene; Professor. *Appointments:* Chemist; Assistant, Chair of Hygiene, Medical Faculty; Hygienist, State Sanitary Institute; Chief of Department of Food Hygiene and Nutrition, Research Institute of Hygiene; Chief of Research Centre Food Hygiene and Nutrition, Institute of Hygiene and Epidemiology. *Memberships:* Czechoslovak Medical Society J E Purkyne; Czechoslovak Technical Scientific Society; Hygiene Society of German Democratic Republic; Adviser, WHO and Food Additives; Codex Alimentarious Committee for Food Additives. *Publications:* 'Changes in Food irradiated by ionising Radiation', 1957; "Food Hygiene and Nutrition", 1960; 'Nutritive Value of Irradiated Food', 1961; 'Food Additives in CSSR', 1965; "Community Catering", 1970; "Toxicology of Sweeternes", 1979; 'Sanitary Safety of irradiated Food', 1973, 1983. *Honours:* Medal of Li-

beration, 1965; Honorary Member, Czechoslovak Medical Society, 1981; Honorary Member, Hygienic Society, GDR, 1978. *Hobbies:* Playing chess; Tourism. *Address:* 5-Smichov, Kirovova 27, 150-00 Praha, Czechoslovakia.

WOLFE, George Arthur, b. 9 Jan. 1947, Oceanside, California, USA. Associate Professor, School of Physicial Therapy, Children's Hospital, Los Angeles. m. Nancy Sue Kiefer, 29 March 1969, Polos Verdes Est, California, 1 son, 2 daughters. *Education:* BA, University of California, Los Angeles, 1968; MA, Certificate in Physical Therapy, 1973, PhD 1984, University of Southern California. *Appointments:* Staff physical therapist, Supervising physical therapist, LAC/USC Medical Centre, 1973-76; Instructor, Department of Physical Therapy, University of Southern California, 1976-81; Consultant, California State Department of Rehabilitation, 1979-81; Lecturer, Department of Physical Therapy, Mount St Mary's College, 1981; Adjunct Instructor, Department of Physical Therapy, University of Southern California, 1981-84; Associate Professor, School of Physical Therapy, Children's Hospital, Los Angeles, 1984-. *Memberships:* Sections on Research/Cardiopulmonary disorders, American Physical Therapy Association; American College of Sports Medicine. *Publications include:* 'Influence of Floor Surface on the Energy Cost of Wheelchair Propulsion', co-author, 1977; 'Burnout of Therapists: Inevitable or Preventable?', 1981; 'Aerobic Capacity of Patients' Dependence on Haemodialysis', 1983; 'Effects of Exercise Training and Patients Dependent on Haemodialysis', co-author, 1984. *Honour:* Research Award, California Chapter APTA, 1977. *Hobbies:* Hiking; Guitar; Boy Scout, Girl Scout leader. *Address:* 28018 Charles Drive, Saugus, CA 91350, USA.

WOLFF, Klaus, b. 4 Dec. 1935, Hermannstadt, Austria. Chairman, Department of Dermatology. m. Elizabeth C Schreiner, 9 July 1971, Weston, Massachusetts, USA, 1 son, 2 daughters. *Education:* MD, University of Vienna, Austria, 1962. *Appointments:* Chief, Division of Experimental Dermatology, University of Vienna, 1973; Chairman, Department of Dermatology, University of Innsbruck, 1976, University of Vienna 1981. *Memberships include:* 14 Medical and Scientific Associations; Honorary Member of 13 International Medical Associations; Board and Executive Committee 1970-78, European Society for Dermatological Research; President 1975-76, Scientific Council CIRO Executive Committee, Association Internationale de Photbiologie; Member 1977-82, International Committee of Dermatology. *Publications include:* "Dermatology in General Medicine" (with T B Fitzpatrick, A Z Eisen, I M Freedberg and K F Austen), 1979; "Vasculitis" (with R K Winkelmann), 1980; Over 290 articles in scientific journals. *Honours include:* 14 Scientific Awards including: Taub International Psoriasis Research Award, 1979; Alexander Besredka Award, 1981; Dohi Memorial Lecture, 1983; Carl Truman Nelson Memorial Lecture, 1984; Pillsbury Lecture, 1985. *Hobbies:* Music; Reading; Sports. *Address:* Department of Dermatology, Alserstrasse 4, A-1090 Vienna, Austria.

WOLFF, Mark M, b. 16 Mar. 1956, Denver, Colorado USA. Director, Green Mountain Chiropractic Clinic. m Debra K. Murphy, 15 Feb., Pasadena, Texas, 2 sons *Education:* University of Colorado; Doctor of Chiropractic, Texas Chiropractic College; Postgraduate; National Chiropractic College, Los Angeles Chiropractic College; Achieved Board Qualified Status in Orthopaedics. *Appointments:* Staff Head in Charge of Biofeedback Department, Texas Chiropractic College Outpatient Clinic; Staff Doctor, Pearl Street, Chiropractic Clinic. *Memberships:* American College of Chiropractic Orthopaedists; American Chiropractic Association, Council on Chiropractic Orthopaedics and Council on Roentgenology; Colorado Chiropractic Council, Board Member, Peer Review Committee Member; Colorado State Chiropractic Society, Board

Member, Chairman of Membership Committee; Colorado Chiropractic Association, Legislative Committee Member, Past Alternate Board Member; Jefferson County Chiropractic Society, President; Member of Foundation for Chiropractic Education and Research. *Hobby:* Skiing. *Address:* 345 S Union Boulevard §106, Lakewood, CO 80228, USA.

WOLFF, William I, b. 24 Oct. 1916, USA. President, Wm. I. Wolff MD PC. m. Rita Smith, 15 Feb. 1972, New York City, 5 sons, 4 daughters (by previous marriage). *Education:* BS, New York University; MD, University of Maryland, School of Medicine. *Appointments:* Director of Surgery, Beth Israel Medical Center; Professor of Clinical Surgery, Mount Sinai School of Medicine. Pioneered the use of colonscopes techniques at Beth Israel Hospital, NY. *Memberships:* Society International de Chirur; International Cardiovascular Society; American College of Surgeons; American College of Gastroenterology; American College of Chest Physicians; American Gastroenterological Assoc.; American Assoc. for Thoracic Surgery; Society Thoracic Surgeons; Society for Surgical Alimentary Tract; SAGES; American Society GI Endoscopy; NY Surgical Society. *Publications:* Over 100 publications. *Honours:* University Prize Gold Medalist, University of Maryland School of Medicine, 1940; President, NY Surgical Society. *Address:* 44 Gramercy Park North, New York, NY 10010, USA.

WOLFFE, Gordon Nicholas, b. 30 Aug. 1948, London, England. Former Head, Department of Periodontology, University of Utrecht, Netherlands. *Education:* Diploma in Periodontology, University of Pennsylvania, USA; MSc; BDS (Lond); FDS; RCS (Eng). *Appointment:* Lecturer, Department of Periodontology, Eastman Dental Hospital, London, Enggland; Former Head, Department of Periodontology, University of Utrecht, Netherlands-. *Memberships:* British Dental Association; British Society of Periodontology; American Dental Association; American Academy of Periodontology; Dutch Society of Periodontology. *Publications:* 'An evaluation of proximal surface cleansing agents' in 'Journal of Clin Perio.', 1976; 'Gingival inflammation and bone loss in periodontal dissect.' in 'J. Clin. Perio.', 1979; 'Migrated upper anterior teeth in patients with chronic periodontis' in 'Ned. Tijd voor Tand.', 1985. *Hobbies:* Music; Horticulture. *Address:* Burgemeester van de Weijerstraat 6, 3981 Ek Bunnik, Netherlands.

WOLFLEY, Vern A, b. 4 Aug. 1912, Etna, Wyoming, USA. Life Member, American Dental Association and Arizona State Dental Association. m. Bernice Michaelson, 12 June 1936, Salt Lake City, Utah, 2 sons, 2 daughters. *Education:* BS, University of Wyoming, 1934; BSD, 1947, DDS, 1947, University of Nebraska. *Former Appointments:* President: Idaho Falls Dental Society; Upper Snake River District Dental Society; Arizona State Childrens Dental Society. *Memberships:* American and Arizona State Dental Associations; Life Member, American Society of Dentistry for Children; Central Arizona District Society; Academy of General Dentistry; International Association for Orthodontics; American Association of Functional Orthodontists; Federation Dentaire International; American Society of Dentistry for Children. *Honours:* 19th Annual Honors Convoacation, High Scholastic Achievement, University of Nebraska, 1947; Scholastic Proficiency in Gold Foil, Woodbury Study Club, 1947; Omicron Kappa Upsilon, 1947. *Hobbies:* Deep sea fishing; Painting; Jewellery casting and design; Computer science. *Address:* 2837 West Northern Avenue, Phoenix, AZ 85051, USA.

WOLFSON, Hyman William, b. 1 Feb. 1957, Montreal, Canada. Doctor of Chiropractic. m. Deborah S Tannenbaum, 3 Aug. 1980, South Huntington, New York, USA, 1 son. *Education:* BA, Cum Laude, SUNY at Buffalo; DC, Dean's List, New York Chiropractic College; Disability Evaluation Certificate, National College of Chiropractic, Postgraduate Division; Diplomate, National Board of Chiropractic Examiners. *Memberships:* New York State Chiropractic Association, Suffolk County; American Chiropractic Association; Foundation for Chiropractic Education and Research; American Public Health Association. *Honour:* Outstanding Young Men of America, 1982. *Hobbies:* Swimming; Racquetball; Tennis; Gardening; Walking. *Address:* 131, Parkway Drive North, Commack, NY 11725, USA.

WOLKOV, Harvey B., b. 8 Feb. 1953, Cleveland, Ohio, USA. Radiation Oncologist, Sutter Memorial Hospital. *Education:* BS, Microbiology, Honours Programme, MS, Bionuclear Physics, Purdue University; MD, Medical College, Ohio. *Appointments:* Teaching Assistant, Purdue University, 1975-76; Chief Resident, Radiation Therapy, Stanford University Medical Centre, 1982; Research Assistant, Radiation Biology, Stanford University Medical Centre, 1982-83; Assistant Clinical Professor, Radiology, School of Medicine, University of California, Davis, 1983-. *Memberships include:* American Society for Therapeutic Radiology and Oncology; American Endocurietherapy Society; American College of Radiology; Sacramento-El Dorado Medical Society; California Radiologic Society; Northern California Radiation Therapy Association; Children's Cancer Study Group; New York Academy of Science; etc. *Publications:* Articles in various professional journals including: 'Intraoperative Radiation Therapy', 1986. *Honours:* BS, Honours, Microbiology, Purdue University, 1975; Phi Eta Sigma; American Cancer Society Clinical Fellowship; Eta Sigma Gamma; Phi Kappa Phi. *Hobbies:* Skiing; Sculpting; Fishing. *Address:* Radiation Oncology Centre, Sutter Memorial Hospital, 5271 F Street, Sacramento, CA 95819, USA.

WOLLENBERGER, Albert, b. 21 May 1912, Freiburg. Professor. m. Gertrud Basse, 14 Nov. 1951, Copenhagen, 1 son, 6 daughters. *Education:* Medical Student, University of Berlin, 1931-33; BS, Physical Education, Springfield College 1939; AM, Biology, 1942, Pharmacotherapy, 1946, PhD, Harvard University, USA. *Appointments:* Research Assistant, 1945-48, Research Associate, 1948-51, Harvard Medical School; Guest Investigator, Carlesberg Laboratory, Copenhagen Institute of Biochemistry, University of Uppsala; Institute of Psychiatry, University of London, England; Institute of Neurophysiology, University of Copenhagen, 1951-54; Associate Professor, Pharmacology, Humboldt University, Berlin, 1954-55; Chief, Laboratory of Circulation Research, German Academy of Sciences, Berlin, 1956-64; Director, Institute of Circulation Research, German Academy of Sciences, 1964-72; Director, Cellular and Molecular Cardiology, Central Institute of Heart and Circulatory Regulation Research, 1972-77; Chief, Cellular Pharmacology Group, Academy of Science, Berlin. *Memberships include:* Gesellschaft fur Pharmakologie und Toxikologie der DDR; Biochemische Gesellschaft der DDR; International Society for Heart Research; American Association for the Advancement of Science; Sigma Xi; Gesellschaft fur Kardiologie und Angiologie der DDR; Royal Society of Medicine, London; etc. *Publications:* Articles in scientific journals. *Honours:* Honorary Member, Cardiac Muscle Society, USA, 1970; Gesellschaft fur Kardiologie und Angiologie der DDER, 1973; Hungarian Pharmacological Society, 1985; Distinguished Alumnus Award, Springfield College, 1976. *Hobbies:* Music; Mountain Climbing; Athletics. *Address:* Zentralinstitut für Herz-Kreislauf-Forschung der Akademie der Wissenschaften der DDR, Wiltbergstrasse 50, 1115 Berlin-Buch, Democratic Republic of Germany.

WOLLMAN, Leo, b. 14 Mar. 1914, New York, USA. Physician. m. Eleanor Rakow, 16 Aug. 1936, (deceased 1953), 2 sons; m. Charlotte Kornberg Seidman, 6 Oct. 1954 (divorced 1969); m. Ellen Han, 25 Mar. 1985. *Education:* BS, Columbia University, USA, 1934; MS, New York University, 1948; MD, Royal College, Edinburgh, Scotland, 1942; PhD, Rochdale, 1972; DSc, (Hon), University of Michigan, USA. *Appointments:* Intern, Cumberland Hospital, Brooklyn, New York, 1942-43; Resident, Leith General Hospital, 1942; Medical practice specialising in Obstetrics and Gynaecology, Brooklyn, 1944-; Specialising in Psychiatry, 1961-. *Memberships:* Diplomate, American Board of Obstetrics and Gynaecology; National Board of Acupuncture Medicine; American Board of Psychiatry and Neurology; Fellow, American Geriatrics Society; New York Academy of Sciences; Academy of Psychosomatic Medicine; American Society of Clinical Hypnosis; American Society of Psychical Research; American Academy of Dental Medicine; American Society of Abdominal Surgeons; American Medical Writers Association; Royal Medico-Psychological Association, England; Society for Medical Jurisprudence, etc. *Publications include:* "Write Yourself Slim", 1976; "Eating Your Way to a Better Sex Life", 1983; Numerous articles in professional journals; Editor in chief, 'American Society of Psychosomatic Dentistry and Medicine Journal'; Films: 'I am Not This Body', 1970; "Strange Her", 1971; "Let me Die a Woman", 1978. *Honour:* Jules Weinstein Ann Pioneer in Modern Hypnosis Award, 1964. *Address:* 3817 Poplar Avenue, Brooklyn, NY 11224, USA.

WOLOSOWICZ, Nina, b. 28 Feb. 1931, Ryboly, Poland. Head of Department of Hematological Diagnostics. m. Wsiewolod, 16 Nov. 1957, 2 sons. *Education:* MSc, Chemistry; PhD, Biological Sciences. *Appointments:* Assistant, 1956, Senior Assistant, 1961; Lecturer, 1968, Medical School Bialystok, Department of Biochemistry; Senior Lecturer, 1974, Assistant Professor, 1978, Department of Clinical Biochemistry, Medical School Bialystok; Head, Department of Hematological Diagnostics, 1985. *Memberships:* Polish Society of Chemistry; Polish Society of Biochemistry; Polish Society of Laboratory Diagnostics. *Publications:* Over 55 publications including: Co-author, 'The Inhibitory Effect of Heparin on Trypsinogen Activation with Enterokinase', 'Acta Hepato-Gastroenterology', 1977; Co-author, 'The Count of Blood Platelets and Sex in Humans', 'Experientia', 1978. *Honours:* Two Scientific Awards from Ministry of Health 11°. *Hobby:* Gardening. *Address:* Institute of Laboratory Diagnostics, Akademia Medyczna, ul. M Sklodowskiej-Curie 24A, 15-276 Bialystok, Poland.

WOLSTENHOLME, Gordon (Ethelbert Ward) Sir, b. 28 May 1913, Sheffield, England. Harveian Librarian, Royal College of Physicians. m. (1) Mary Elizabeth Spackman, 1939, 1 son, 2 daughters. (2) Dushanka Messinger, 1948, 2 daughters. *Education:* MRCS, LRCP, 1939; MA, 1940; MB BChir, 1948; Member, 1959, Royal College of Physicians; Fellow, 1964. *Appointments:* RAMC, 1940-47, Lieutenant Colonel, Advisor in Resuscitation and Transfusion; Registrar, Dematology, Middlesex Hospital, 1947-49; Director, The Ciba Foundation, 1949-78; currently Harvian Librarian, Royal College of Physicians. *Memberships:* Honorary Fellow: Royal Society of Medicine (former President); American College of Physicians, 1979; Royal Academy of Medicine in Ireland, 1976. Honorary Foreign Member, American Academy of Arts and Sciences, 1981. Honorary Member, International Association for Dental Research, 1984. *Publications:* Editor: "Ciba Foundation Symposia", 1950-78; "Royal College of Physicians: Portraits", volume 1, 1963, volume 2, 1977; "Royal College of Physicians: Munk's Roll", Volume 6, 1982, volume 7, 1984; Author of numerous papers on world health, medical ethics and other topics. *Honours:* Honorary LLD, Cambridge University, 1968; Honorary DTech, Brunel University, 1981; Honorar6 MD, Grenada University, 1982; OBE, 1944; Knight, 1976. *Hobbies:* Non-technical photography; Music; Hill walking. *Address:* 10 Wimpole Mews, London W1M 7Tf, England.

WONG, Henry Yick Tung, b. 7 May 1937, China. Radiotherapist. m. Sylvia S S Ho, 17 May 1969, Hamilton, 3 sons. *Education:* BA, Honours, 1958, MASc, 1960, University of Toronto; MD, McMaster University, Canada, 1973; PhD Candidate, Princeton University, 1960-61; Diploma, American Board of Radiology, 1977. *Appointments:* Internship, LAC, USC Medical Centre, Los Angeles, 1973-74; Residency, Radiation Medicine, LAC USC Medical Centre, 1974-77; Radiotherapist, 1977-. Chief, Radiotherapy, 1983-84, St Joseph's Hospital, Stockton, USA. *Memberships:* American Society of Therapeutic Radiology and Oncology; American Endocupictherapy Society; American Medical Association; California Medical Association; Northern Radiation Oncologist Association. *Hobbies:* Swimming; Jogging. *Address:* 1800 N California St, Stockton, CA 95204, USA.

WONG, Richard Cheun Hoong, b. Kuala Lumpur, Malaysia. Dental Surgeon. m. June Ann Ansell, Sep. 1982, Tom Price, Western Australia. *Education:* BDS Honours; LDS; RCS, England. *Appointments:* Dental Officer, Perth Dental Hospital, Western Australia; Mobile Dental Officer, serving remote areas and country towns, Dental Health Services, Western Australia; Private Practice, Tom Price, Western Australia. *Memberships:* Australian Dental Association. *Honours:* In Surgery, Medicine, Paedodontics and Orthodontics, University College Dental School, 1976. *Hobbies:* Tae Kwon Do, 1st Dan black belt; Jogging; Swimming; Gardening. *Address:* 1706 Milpera Street, Tom Price, WA 6751, Australia.

WONG, Tung-Lau Anne, b. 1 Nov. 1939, Mauca, The People's Republic of China. Chiropractor, Acupuncturist. *Education:* Chinese Traditional MD, Canton Chinese Medical College, Canton, 1962; Registered Nurse, Midwife, Kwong Wah Nursing School, 1963-67; Registered Mental Nurse, Long Grove Hospital Nursing School, England, 1970-72; Doctor of Chiropractic, Logan College of Chiropractic, 1976-79. *Appointments:* Traditional Chinese Medical Doctor, 1963-70; Registered Nurse, 1973-76; Doctor of Chiropractic, Acupuncturist, 1980-. *Memberships:* American Chiropractic Association; Logan Alumni Association; American Acupuncturist Association. *Honours:* 2nd Award of Graduation, Long Grove Nursing School, 1972; Dean's List, Logan College, 1978. *Hobbies:* Reading; Music Analysis; Calligraphy; Painting. *Address:* 440 E Shields Avenue, Fresno, CA 93704, USA.

WONG, William Wing-Bill, b. 17 June 1937, Guangdong, China. Dental Surgeon. *Education:* BSc, University of British Columbia, Canada, 1959; DDS, University of Toronto, Canada, 1963; LDS, Royal College of Dental Surgeons of Ontario, Canada, 1963; FICD. *Appointments:* Dental Surgeon. *Memberships:* Honary Life Member Past President, Hong Kong Dental Association; Former Member, Dental Council of Hong Kong; Past Regent, Executive Council Member, International College of Dentists; Past 4th, 3rd and 2nd Vice President, Past Senior Vice President, Past President, Asian Pacific Dental Federation; American Dental Association; Pierre Fauchard Academy; Federation Dentaire Internationale; Honorary Member, Korean Dental Association; Fellow, International College of Dentists. *Honours:* Fellowship, International College of Dentists, 1968; Honorary Citizen, State of Texas, USA, 1969; Honorary Member, Korean Dental Association, 1978. *Hobbies:* Sports; Travelling. *Address:* Suite 208, 9 Ice House Street, Hong Kong.

WOOD, Christopher Harald, b. 5 June 1924, Richmond, Surrey, England. Director-General, African Medical & Research Foundation. m. Elizabeth Cope Collins, 25 Sep. 1953, Shipbourne, Kent, England, 2 sons, 2 daughters. *Education:* Member, Royal College of Surgeons, Licentiate, Royal College of Physicians, Middlesex Hospital Medical School, 1947; MB BS, 1950; MD, 1965, University of London; DPH 1953, DIH 1959, London School of Hygiene & Tropical Medicine; SM in Hygiene, Harvard School of

Public Health, 1956. *Appointments:* Rotating Internship, Singapore General Hospital; House Physician, Central Middlesex Hospital; Lecturer, Senior Lecturer, Occupational Health, London School of Hygiene & Tropical Medicine; Adviser in Public Health, Ministry of Health, Tanganyika; Professor of Community Health, Dar es Salaam Medical School; Head of Training Department, 1973-82, Medical Director, 1982-85, African Medical & Research Foundation, Nairobi, Kenya. *Memberships:* Society for Social Medicine; Society for Occupational Medicine; Association for the Study of Medical Education; International Epidemiological Association; American Public Health Association. *Publications:* "Occupational Health Services in Smaller Work Places in Britain", 1960; "Common Sense about Smoking", 1962; "The Health Services of Tanganyika: A Report to the Government", 1964; "The Epidemiology of Continuing Ignorance", 1979; "The Selection, Training & Support of Primary Health Care Workers", 1981; "Community Health", 1981; "The Role of Education in Development", 1985. *Honours:* Adrian Graves Exhibition, 1942-45; Eliston Scholarship, 1953; Commonwealth Fund Fellowship, 1955-56. *Hobbies:* Mountaineering; Sailing. *Address:* PO Box 30125, Nairobi, Kenya.

WOOD, Ian Jeffreys, b. 5 Feb. 1903, Melbourne, Australia. Consultant Physician, Royal Melbourne Hospital. m. Edith Mary Cooke, 23 Oct. 1935, Melbourne, 1 son, 1 daughter. *Education:* MD, University of Melbourne, 1931; Fellow, Royal Australasian College of Physicians, 1937; Fellow, Royal College of Physicians, London, 1942. *Appointments:* Medical Superintendent, Royal Children's Hospital, Melbourne, 1928; House Physician, Hospital for Sick Children, Great Ormond Street, London, England, 1932; Australian Imperial Force, 1939-45; Physician, Royal Melbourne Hospital, 1946-63; Assistant Director, Walter and Eliza Hall Institute of Research, 1946-63. *Memberships:* Honorary Fellow, British Society Gastroenterology, 1970; Honorary Fellow, Royal Society of Medicine, London, 1984. *Publications:* Co-author, "Diffuse Lesions of Stomach", 1958; "Discovery and Healing in Peace and War" (an autobiography), 1984. *Honours:* MBE, 1942; Neil Hamilton Fairley Medal, 1974; Stowell Medal, 1975; Knight, 1976; RACP Medal, 1985. *Hobbies:* Reading; Writing. *Address:* 1/27 Tintern Avenue, Toorak, Victoria 3142, Australia.

WOOD, Jackie D, b. 16 Feb. 1937, Oklahoma, USA. Professor and Chairman of University Department of Physiology. *Education:* BS; MS; PhD, University of Illinois, 1969. *Appointments:* Assistant-Associate-Professor of Physiology, University of Kansas Medical School, Kansas City, Kansas, 1971-79; Professor and Chairman, Department of Physiology, School of Medicine, University of Nevada, Reno, Nevada, 1979-85; Professor and Chairman, Department of Physiology, College of Medicine, Ohio State University, Columbus, Ohio, 1985-. *Memberships:* American Physiological Society; American Federation of Clinical Research; Society for Neuroscience; American Gastroenterological Association; International Union of Physiological Sciences. *Publications:* 'Intrinsic neural regulation of intestinal motility', 1981; 'Enteric neurophysiology', 1984. *Honours:* Chancellor's Award for Excellence in Teaching, University of Kansas, 1975; Alexander von Humboldt Fellowship, Federal Republic of Germany, 1976. *Hobbies:* Tennis; Alpine skiing. *Address:* Department of Physiology, Ohio State University, College of Medicine, 4196 Graves Hall, 333 West 10th Avenue, Columbus, OH 43210, USA.

WOOD, Joe George, b. 8 Dec. 1928, Victoria, Texas, USA. Professor, Department of Neurobiology & Anatomy. m. Jane L Andrews, 4 Dec. 1982, Houston, Texas, 1 daughter. *Education:* BS 1953, MS 1958, University of Houston; PhD, University of Texas, 1962. *Appointments:* Assistant/Associate Professor, Anatomy, Universities of Arkansas & Texas,

1963-70; Assistant Dean, Academic Development, University of Texas Medical School, San Antonio, 1967-79; Professor & Chairman, Department of Neurobiology & Anatomy, University of Texas Health Science Centre, Houston, 1970-84; Professor, ibid, 1984-. *Memberships:* American Association of Anatomists; Histochemical Society; Cajal Club; Society for Neuroscience; American Society for Cell Biology; Sigma Xi; Electron Microscope Society of America; Society for Neurochemistry. *Publications include:* Over 100 articles & abstracts; Co-author, Volume I, "Anatomy & Physiology" in "The Nervous System", 1983. *Honours:* Sigma Xi Research Award, 1962; Golden Apple (SAMA) teaching award, 1963; Best teacher awards, 1973, 1975; Alpha Omega Alpha, 1975. *Hobbies:* Photography; Travel. *Address:* University of Texas Health Science Centre at Houston, Department of Neurobiology & Anatomy, 6431 Fannin Street, Houston, TX 77030, USA.

WOODHOUSE, Stanley Peter, b. 9 Oct. 1936, Delhi, India. Director of Cardiology. 3 sons, 1 daughter. *Education:* MB, ChB (Otago); FRACP. *Appointments:* Research Fellow, McGill University, Johns Hopkins University; Research Visitor, Mayo Clinic; Senior Lecturer, Clinical Science, Otago; Director, Cardiology, Princess Alexandra Hospital, Brisbane, Australia, 1983-. *Memberships:* Royal Australasian College of Physicians; Cardiac Society of Australia and New Zealand; International Society for Heart Research; International Society of Epidemiology; New Zealand Sports Medicine Federation; Australian Sports Medicine Federation. *Publications:* Numerous articles in professional journals including: 'New Zealand Medical Journal'; 'Clinical Physiology'; 'Atherosclerosis'; 'Metabolism'; 'American Heart Journal'; "The Use of Computers in the Operational Handling of Data from an Intensive Care Area", 1976; Co-Author, "Reducing Diets for the Overweight", 1972; "Your Food and Your Heart", 1972; "Eating for Health", 1975; "Eating for Health", 1982; Book Reviews; etc. *Honours:* Emily Johnson Research Fellow, University of Otago, 1967-68; Fellow, Maryland Heart Association, 1970; Postgraduate Fellowship, Pacific Island Teaching, 1975; Wolfson Foundation Fellowship, 1977; Fellow, International Federation of Epidemiology, 1978. *Hobbies:* Winter Sports; Running; Martial Arts; Sailboard. *Address:* Department of Cardiology, Princess Alexandra Hospital, Brisbane, Queensland 4102, Australia.

WOODLE, Alan Stuart, b. 31 July 1953, Vancouver, Washington, USA. Physician & Surgeon of Foot & Ankle. m. Roslyn Louise Knodel, 9 Oct. 1983, Seattle, Washington, USA. *Education:* BS Molecular Biology, 1975; BS Neurophysiology, 1976; BS Basic Medical Sciences, 1978; Doctor of Podiatric Medicine, 1979. *Appointments:* Sports Medicine Fellowship, Seattle, Washington, 1979; Resident, Foot & Ankle Surgery, Valley West General Hospital, Los Gatos, California, 1980-81; Private Practice, Foot & Ankle Surgery, Sports Medicine, Seattle, 1981; Clinical Assistant Professor, Foot & Ankle Surgery, Des Moines College of Podiatric Medicine, 1984; VA Medical Center, Foot & Ankle Surgery Residency Training Faculty, 1984. *Memberships:* American College of Foot Surgeons; Washington State Podiatric Medical Association; American College of Sports Medicine; American Academy of Podiatric Sports Medicine. *Publications:* Various articles on Sports Medicine and camera use. *Honours:* House Staff Officer, Waldo General Hospital, 1985. *Hobbies:* Skiing; Running. *Address:* 9730 3rd NE Suite 208, Seattle, WA 98115, USA.

WOODLIFF, Hugh Jackson, b. 16 Oct. 1927, England. Consultant Physician. m. Mary Isabel Oglethorpe, 17 Feb. 1951, Keswick, Cumbria, 2 sons. *Education:* DCP, London University; DPath, Royal Colleges of Surgeons of England and Physicians of London; Fellow, Royal College of Physicians, Edinburgh and Australasia; Fellow, Royal College of Pathologists, London; MD, University of Western Australia; PhD

Cantab. *Appointments:* House Surgeon & Physician, Edinburgh Teaching Hospitals, 1950-51; Lecturer, Pathology, Bacteriology, Edinburgh University, Scotland, 1951-54; Junior Specialist, Pathology, RAMC, 1954-56; Elmore Research Student, Cambridge University, England, 1956-58; Research Fellow, Children's Cancer Research Foundation, Boston, USA, 1959-60; Lecturer, Haematology, Oxford, 1960-62; Head, Haematology, Royal Perth Hospital, Australia, 1962-72; Professor, Haematology, Makerere University Medical School, Kampala, Uganda, 1972-74; Senior Haematology, Royal Perth Hospital, Australia, 1974-75; Professor, Pathology, University of Papua New Guinea, and Consultant Haematologist, Port Moresby General Hospital, 1976-79; Consultant Physician, Haematology. *Memberships:* Australasian and International Haematology Societies. *Publications:* "Blood and Bone Marrow Cell Culture", 1964; "Leukemia Cytogenetics", 1971; "Concise Practical Haematology", 1972; "Concise Haematology", co-author, 2nd edition, 1979; "Practical Haematology Notes", 1979, 2nd edition 1984; numerous articles in medical literature. *Honour:* Efficiency Decoration. *Hobbies:* Vigneron; Oenophile. *Address:* 97 Hardy St, Nedlands 6009, Western Australia.

WOODS, Stephen James, b. 28 Jan. 1950, Sydney, Australia. Clinical Psychologist. m. Antoinette Patricia, 3 Jan. 1976, Sydney, 2 daughters. *Education:* Dip T; MA; MA; MEd; DCH. *Appointments:* Teacher, 1974-75; Hospital work, 1976-79; University, 1979; School and Educational Psychology; Private Practitioner, 1980-; Consultant, Child Development, Government Organisations; Consultant Clinical Psychology in Community Health, 1980-82. *Memberships:* Australian Psychological Society; Australian College of Private Consulting Psychologists; Australian Society of Clinical Hypnotherapists. *Publications:* "Cognitive Self-Talk and Behaviour"; "Academic Anxiety and Cognitions - An Alternative Approach to a Problem"; "The Psychology of Long Distance Runners"; "The Psychology of Children's Play"; "The Use of Play Therapy in School Settings". *Hobbies:* Snow skiing; Mountain and rock climbing; Sailing; Collecting vintage wine. *Address:* 15 Cavell Avenue, Rhodes 2138, New South Wales, Australia.

WOODWARD, Edwin Geoffrey, b. 19 Sep. 1934, Leamington Spa, England. Principal Ophthalmic Optician. m. Elizabeth Ann Gilian Marsden, 7 Sep. 1957, 2 daughters. *Education:* PhD, Department of Optometry and Visual Science, City University, London, England; Health Services Management Centre, University of Birmingham; FBCO; DCLP. *Appointment:* Principal Ophthalmic Optician, Moorfields Eye Hospital, London. *Publications:* 'Keratoconus: Material Age and Social Class', 1981; Author of numerous articles on contact lenses and corneal measurement. *Hobby:* Narrow boats. *Address;* Department of Contact Lens and Prosthesis, Moorfields Eye Hospital, City Road, London EC1 2PP, England.

WOOLSTON-CATLIN, Marian. b. 20 Jan. 1931, Seattle, Washington, USA. Private Practice; Courtesy Medical Staff, Childrens Unit, Massachusetts Mental Health Centre. m. Randolph Catlin, 5 July 1959, Seattle, 1 son, 2 daughters. *Education:* BA, Vassar College, 1951; MD, Harvard, 1955. *Appointments:* Intern, Assistant Resident, Paediatric Medicine, Childrens Hospital Medical Centre, Boston, 1956; Harvard Clinical Fellow, Psychiatry, Massachusetts Mental Health Centre, 1957-59; Clinical Fellow, Psychiatry, Tufts University, 1957-59; Visiting Fellow, Child Psychiatry, Tavistock Clinic, London, England, 1960; Clinical Instructor, Psychiatry, Commonwealth Fellow, Child Psychiatry, Harvard, 1975-78; Staff, Childrens Unit, Massachusetts Mental Health Centre, 1979-82; Board: Parents and Children's Services, Boston, 1986-. *Memberships:* American Academy of Child Psychiatry; New England Council of Child Psychiatry; American Psychiatric Association; Massachusetts

Psychiatric Society; American Medical Association; Massachusetts Medical Society. *Honours:* Speaker, Rhodes House, Oxford University, "Women in the Professions", 1960. *Hobbies:* Landscape Design - Garden Design; Sculpture. *Address:* 316 Washington Street, Wellesley Hills, MA 02181, USA.

WORM-PETERSEN, jørgen, b. 10 Aug. 1930, Maribo, Denmark. Head, University Department of Medical Neurology, Gentofts Hospital, University of Copenhagen. 1 son, 1 daughter.*Education:* Graduated as Physician, University of Copenhagen, 1957; MD, 1963; Diploma, Public Health, 1968; Registered Specialist in Neurology, 1966. *Appointments:* Research Fellow, Institute of Biochemistry, University of Copenhagen, 1959-62; Specialist Training, Neurology, Copenhagen and National Hospital, London, England, 1962-68; Medical Advisor to Director General of Health, 1965-74; Senior Neurologist, Department of Medical Neurology, Glostrup Hospital, Copenhagen, 1969-72; Special Advisor, Neurology, National Board of Health, 1974-; Chief, University Department of Medical Neurology, Gentofts Hospital, Copenhagen, 1972. *Memberships:* Executive Committee, Junior Doctors Association, 1957, President, 1963-64; President, Medical Society of Copenhagen, 1969-72; Executive Committee Danish Medical Association, 1961-63. *Publications:* Biochemical Studies on Vitamin B12 in the Central Nervous System, 1963; Publications on Clinical Neurology, Public Health Administration, Accident Prevention. *Address:* University Department of Medical Neurology, Gentofts Hospital, DK-2900 Hellerup, Copenhagen, Denmark.

WOROWSKI, Krzysztof, b. 30 Jan. 1936, Wierzbica, Poland. Professor, Chief of Department of Instrumental Analysis, Medical Academy, Bialystok, Poland. m. 11 Jan. 1958, 1 daughter. *Education:* MD, 1961, PhD, 1964, ScD, 1975, Medical Academy, Bialystok. *Appointments:* Associate Professor, Department of Biochemistry, Medical Academy, Bialystok, Poland. *Memberships:* Member, Polish Biochemical Society; Member, Polish Chemical Society. *Publications:* 'Investigation of specificity of proteolytic enzymes on oxidised bovine insulin B chain', 1974; 'The biological significance of limited proteolysis', 1975; 'Molecular mechanism of blood coagulation and fibrinolysis activation', 1980. *Honours:* Award, Polish Haematological Society, 1966; Award from Ministry of Health and Social Welfare, 1968. *Address:* Department of Instrumental Analysis, Medical Academy, ul Mickiewicza 2, 15-230 Bialystok 8, Poland.

WORTH, Peter H L, b. 17 Nov. 1935, London, England. Consultant Urologist. m. Judith Girling, 8 Feb. 1969, Langham, Essex, 1 son, 1 daughter. *Education:* MA, MB BChir, Trinity Hall, University of Cambridge; The Middlesex Hospital Medical School. *Appointments:* Senior Urological Registrar, Middlesex Hospital and St Paul's Hospital, London; Consultant Urologist, North Middlesex Hospital, London; Currently, Consultant Urologist, University College Hospital and St Peter's Hospitals, London. *Memberships:* Fellow, Royal College of Surgeons; Royal Society of Medicine; British Association of Urological Surgeons; International Continence Society. *Publications include:* "Operative Urology", 1984; "Textbook of Genito-Urinary Surgery", 1985; Articles on enuresis and bladder trauma, and cecocystophasty; 'Post-prostatectomy incontinence and urodynamics', 1984; 'Urethrotomy in female stress incontinence'. *Hobbies:* Music; Gardening; Foreign travel. *Address:* 34 Wimpole Street, London W1, England.

WREN, William Stephen, b. 21 July 1929, Dublin, Ireland. Consultant Anaesthetist. m. Maev-Ann Isabel McGrath, 12 Sep. 1955, Dover, 1 son, 4 daughters. *Education:* MB, BCh, BAO (NUI), 1952; FFARCSI; FFARCS; DA (RCS). *Appointments:* Dean, Anaesthetists, Royal College of Surgeons, Ireland,

1973-76; Founder, Chairman, Irish National Anaesthetic Training Programme, 1974-. *Memberships:* Board, Faculty of Anaesthetists, 1968-82; Vice Chairman, Joint Committee, Higher Training of Anaesthetists, 1973-80; Founder, Chairman, Irish National Anaesthetic Training Programme; Vice President, Association of Anaesthetists of Great Britain and Ireland, 1976-77; Founding Secretary and Member, Senate and Executive European Academy of Anaesthesiology, 1978-84; Fellow: Faculty of Anaesthetists of Royal College of Surgeons, Ireland, Faculty of Anaesthetists, Royal College of Surgeons, England; Senate, European Academy of Anaesthesiology; Council, Association of Anaesthetists, Great Britain and Ireland; etc. *Publications:* Articles in professional journals including: 'Irish Medical Journal'; 'British Journal of Anaesthesiology'; 'Acta Anaesthesiologia Scand'; etc. *Honours:* Honorary Member, Societe Francaise d'Anaesthesie et Reanimation. *Hobbies:* Music; Art; History. *Address:* Department of Anaesthetics, Our Lady's Hospital for Sick Children, Dublin 12, Republic of Ireland.

WRIGHT, Peter Henry, b. 18 Feb. 1945, Reading, England. Senior Lecturer; Consultant Physician. *Education:* MB, BS, (London), University College London and University College Hospital; LRCP; MRCS; MRCP (UK), 1971; MSc, London School of Hygiene, 1982. *Appointments:* Registrar, King's College Hospital, UCH, London Chest Hospital; Senior Registrar, London Chest and St Thomas's Hospital; Consultant Physician, Sandwell. *Memberships:* Thoracic Society; American Thoracic Society; American College of Chest Physicians. *Publications:* Articles on respiratory medicine and industrial lung disease. *Address:* London School of Hygiene and Tropical Medicine, Keppel Street, London, WC1E 7HT, England.

WRIGHT, Robert Gordon, b. 11 Feb. 1953, Dumfries. Director of Pathology. m. Naomi Elizabeth Wright, 12 Aug. 1978, Brisbane, 3 sons. *Education:* BSc, Honours 1st Class, 1974, MB, ChB, 1977, University of Edinburgh; FRCPA. *Appointments:* House Officer, Surgery, Eastern General Hospital, Edinburgh, 1977; House Officer, Medicine, Royal Infirmary Edinburgh, 1978; Lecturer, Pathology, University of Edinburgh, 1978-80; Lecturer, Pathology, University of Queensland, 1980, 1982; Registrar, Pathology, Royal Brisbane Hospital, 1981-82; Director, Pathology, Royal Women's Hospital, Brisbane. *Memberships:* Fellow, Royal College of Pathologists of Australasia; Associate, Royal College of Pathologists of London; Australian Society for Cytology; Australian Society for Experimental Pathology; Australian Paediatric Pathology Group. *Publications:* Articles in: 'Medical Journal of Australia'; 'Journal Clinical Pathology'. *Hobby:* Photography. *Address:* Royal Women's Hospital Laboratory, Department of Pathology, Royal Brisbane Hospital, Brisbane, Queensland, 4029, Australia.

WRIGHT-HECKER, Eleanore Reidell, b. 17 June 1915, Mattoon, Illinois, USA. Retired. m. (1) Curtis Wright, 21 Mar. 1941, Chicago, Illinois, (2) Arthur O Hecker, 14 Feb. 1956, Elkton, Maryland, 1 son, 1 daughter. *Education:* BS, BM, MD, University of Illinois; University of Michigan; FACN. *Appointments:* Intern, Augustana Hospital, Chicago; Private Practitioner; Resident, Psychiatry; Guest Lecturer, University of Illinois Law School; Guest Lecturer, University of Michigan Law School; Director, Out-Patient Department, Friends Hospital, Philadelphia; Faculty Womens Medical School, Philadelphia; Clinical Director, Embreeville State Hospital, Embreeville, PA; Regional Director, Mental Health Programme for Eastern PA; Superintendent, Embreeville State Hospital, Retired, 1971. *Memberships:* Illinois Medical Society; Americal Medical Society; Champaign County Medical Society; Michigan Medical Society; American Psychiatric Association; Pennsylvania Medical Society; Chester County Medical Society.

Publications: "Family Physician After Care - Mental Hospitals", 1960; 'Forced Motivation', 1962; 'The Employment of Patients as Full Time', 1962; 'Comparative Clinical Experience with Five Antidepressants', 1960; 'Clinical Evaluation of Fluphenazine-Diseases of Nervous System', 1961; 'Preliminary Results with Fluphenazine', 1960; 'Open Doors (totally unlocked hospital), 1959, 1960; 'A Study of PerDiem Cost for Three Catagories'; 'Alcoholism: A Need for Diagnostic Classification', 1966; 'Reassessing Hospital Treatment Practices', 1968. *Honours:* Honorary Award of FACN, 1965; National Register of Prominant Americans, 1967. *Hobbies:* Crafts; Bridge; Politics. *Address:* 1657 Elk Forest, Elkton, MD 21921, USA.

WRIGLEY, Peter Francis Martyn, b. 13 May 1939, Manchester, England. Consultant Cancer Physician, St Bartholomew's Hospital and Hackney Hospital. m. Sally Walker, 28 Feb. 1968, Chelsea, 1 son, 1 daughter. *Education:* BSc Hons, University College, London; BM, BCh, Magdalen College, Oxford University; PhD, St Bartholomew's Hospital Medical College; FRCP, London. *Appointments:* House Physician, House Surgeon, Nuffield Departments of Medicine and Surgery, Radcliffe Infirmary, Oxford; Senior House Officer, Department of Neurology, Churchill Hospital, Oxford; Lecturer in Clinical Medicine, Cancer Research Campaign Fellow, Senior Lecturer and Honorary Consultant Physician, OCRF Department of Medical Oncology, St Bartholomew's Hospital, London. *Memberships:* British Medical Association; British Stomach Cancer Group; Medical Research Council; Chairman, Working Party Group on Gastric Cancer; Member, Working Party Group on Rectal Cancer. *Publications:* Author of articles on medical oncology. *Honours:* Brian Johnson Prize, 1962; Maccabaean Prize, 1963. *Hobbies:* Canals; Shooting. *Address:* 134 Harley Street, London W1N 1DJ, England.

WRONG, Oliver Murray, b. 7 Feb. 1925, Oxford, England. Professor of Medicine (Research). m. Marilda Musacchio, 8 June 1956, Aosta, Italy, 3 daughters. *Education:* MA, DM, University of Oxford & Clinical Medical School; Fellow, Royal College of Physicians; Fellow, Royal College of Physicians of Edinburgh. *Appointments:* Junior Hospital Posts, Oxford Teaching Hospitals & Toronto General Hospital, Canada, 1947-48, 1950-52; Medical Officer, Royal Army Medical Corps, Singapore & Malaya, 1948-50; Clinical & Research Fellow, Massachusetts General Hospital, Boston, USA, 1952-53; Medical Tutor, University of Manchester, England, 1954-58; Lecturer in Medicine, University College Hospital Medical School, London, 1959-61; Senior Lecturer in Medicine, Consultant Physician, Royal Postgraduate Medical School, London, 1961-69; Professor of Medicine, University of Dundee, Scotland, 1969-72; Professor of Medicine, Head of Department of Medicine, University College, London, 1972-82. *Memberships:* Renal Association (Former Honorary Secretary); Medical Research Society (Former Honorary Treasurer); Royal Society of Medicine; International Society of Nephrology; Zoological Society. *Publications:* "The Large Intestine" (with C J Edmonds & V S Chadwick), 1981; Numerous articles & book chapters on Renal Disease, Electrolyte, Water & Renal Metabolism & intestinal function. *Honour:* DEMY, Magdalen College, University of Oxford, 1943-47. *Hobbies:* Music; Gardening; Travel. *Address:* Flat 8, 96-100 New Cavendish Street, London, W1M 7FA, England.

WU, Chung-Hsiu, b. 10 Oct. 1936, Taiwan, Republic of China. Professor and Director of Division of Reproductive Endocrinology and Infertility. m. Fang-Rong Chen, 20 Oct. 1963, Taiwan, 1 son, 2 daughters. *Education:* MD, National Taiwan University School of Medicine, Taipei, 1962; Postdoctoral Fellow in Reproductive Endocrinology, Department of Obstetrics-Gynaecology, University of Pennsylvania School of Medicine, Philadelphia, Pennsylvania, USA, 1965-67. *Appointments:* Assistant Professor

1972-77, Associate Professor 1977-79, Obstetrics-Gynaecology, University of Pennsylvania School of Medicine, Philadelphia; Professor of Obstetrics and Gynaecology, Director of Division of Reproductive Endocrinology and Infertility, Jefferson Medical College of Thomas Jefferson University, Philadelphia, 1980-. *Memberships:* Endocrine Society; American Fertility Society; American College of Obstetrics and Gynaecologists; Society of Gynaecologic Investigation; International Society of Reproductive Medicine; New York Academy of Science. *Publications:* 'Radioimmunoassay of plasma estrogens', (with L E Mundy), 1971; 'Estrogen/androgen balance in hirsutism', 1979; 'Estrogen/androgen balance in anovulation', (co-author), 1981; 'A rational and practical approach to clomiphene therapy', 1984; 'Free and protein bound E2 during the menstrual cycle', (co-author), 1986. *Hobbies:* Tennis; Classical music; Oil painting. *Address:* Department of Obstetrics and Gynaecology, Jefferson Medical College, 1025 Walnut Street Room 310, Philadelphia, PA 19107, USA.

WU, Francis Ying-Wai, b. 25 June 1936, China. Obstetrician, Gynaecologist. m. Amy C M Hu, 24 Aug. 1965, Hong Kong, 2 sons, 1 daughter. *Education:* MB; BS; Certificate, Board of Medical Examiners of State of California, USA, 1970; Certificate of Chinese Basic Acupuncture, 1973; Diploma 1974, Fellow 1975, American Board of Obstetrics-Gynaecology. *Appointments:* Intern, Queen Mary Hospital, Hong Kong; Resident, Tsau Yuk Hospital, Hong Kong; Resident, Bronx Lebanon Hospital, New York, USA; Full time partner Obstetrics-Gynaecology practice, South California Permanente Medical Group, Bellflower, California; Assistant Clinical Professor, Department of Obstetrics-Gynaecology, University of California at Los Angeles School of Medicine; Professional Staff, Member of Research and Education Institute, Harbor/UCLA Medical Center. *Publication:* 'Recurrent Hydatidiform Mole', 1972. *Hobbies:* Swimming; Travelling. *Address:* 9400 E Rosecrans Avenue, Bellflower, CA 90706, USA.

WU, Min, b. 16 Dec. 1925, Peking, China. Professor. m. Renling Peng, 21 July 1956, Beijing, 2 daughters. *Education:* Tongji University Medical College, 1943-50; Candidate of Medical Sciences, Doctor of Medical Sciences, Institute of Experimental and Clinical Oncology, Academy of Medical Sciences, Moscow, USSR, 1957-61. *Appointments:* Assistant, Institute of Pathology, Tongji University Medical College, Research Associate, Lecturer: Pathology, Inst. Epidemiol., Research Associate, Lecturer, Head, Genetics Group, Institute of Experimental Medicine, CAMS, Beijing, 1961-69; Village Doctor, Xiariha Commune, Dulan County, Qinghai Province, 1973; Research Associate, 1978, Associate Professor, 1979, Professor, Chairman, Cell Biology, Cancer Institute, CAMS, Beijing. *Memberships:* Genetics Society of China, Deputy Secretary General, 1978-82; Vice President, 1983-; Population Association of China, Director, Board of Directors, 1982-; Chinese Cancer Association, Director, 1980-. *Publications:* "Cloning of human cells in vitro and their cytogenetic characters", Chinese Medical Journal', 1963; "Malignant transformation of baby hamster lung fibroblasts induced in vitro by a new nitrosamine compound", 'Scientia Sinica (Series B)', 1982; etc. *Honour:* National Award for the Advancement of Technology, 1985. *Hobby:* Swimming. *Address:* Department of Cell Biology, Cancer Institute, Chinese Academy of Medical Sciences, Peking Union Medical College, Beijing, PO Box 2258, China.

WURTELE, Paul, b. 3 July 1947, Ste. Therese de Blainville, Canada. Oto-rhino-laryngologist in Solo Practice. m. Diane Tremblay, MD, 24 June 1972, Montreal, 1 son, 2 daughters. *Education:* Baccalauréat es arts; Doctorat en Medecine, University of Montreal; Diplôme d'études spécialisées en chirurgie, University of Montreal; Licenciate of Medical Council of Canada, 1973; Diplomate, National Board of Medical Examin-

ers of USA; Diplomate of American Board of Otolaryngology, 1977. *Appointment:* Regular Staff, Department of Otolaryngology, Centre Hospitalier Honoré Mercier. *Memberships:* Canadian Medical Association; Association d'otorhinolaryngologie du Quebec; Canadian Otolaryngological Society; Fellow, American Academy of Otolaryngology. *Publications:* 'Traumatic rupture of the eardrum with round window fistula', 'Journal of Otolaryngology', Vol. 13 No. 4, 1981; 'Ulcerative Tuberculous Tonsillitis: An Un common Entity', 'Journal of Otolaryngology', March 1983; 'Nasotracheal Intubation: A Modality in the Management of Acute Epiglottitis in Adults', 'Journal of Otolaryngology', Vol. 13 No. 2, 1984; 'The Pale Epiglottitis: A Misnomer or Not?', 'Journal of Otolaryngology', Vol. 13 No. 6, 1984. *Hobbies:* Reading (mostly historical essays); Listening to Classical Music; Swimming; Woodcraft. *Address:* 2780 Raymond Street, St. Hyacinthe, Province of Quebec, Canada J2S 5W7.

WYATT, Richard Jed, b. 5 June 1939, Los Angeles, California, USA. Chief, Neuropsychiatry Branch, Intramural Research Program, National Institute of Mental Health. m. 3 children. *Education:* BA, 1961, MD, 1964, Johns Hopkins University, Baltimore. *Appointments:* Paediatric Intern, Western Reserve University Hospital, Cleveland, 1964-65; Psychiatric Resident and Teaching Assistant, Massachusetts Mental Health Center and Harvard University Medical School, Boston, 1965-67; Clinical Associate, Laboratory of Clinical Psychobiology, Intramural Research, NIMH, 1967-69; Research Psychiatrist, Laboratory of Clinical Psychopharmacology, Intramural Research, NIMH, 1967-71; Chief, Neuropsychiatry Branch, Intramural Research Program, NIMH, 1972-; Consulting Associate Professor of Psychiatry, Stanford Medical Center, Palo Alto, 1973-74; Clinical Professor of Psychiatry, Duke University, 1975-; Associate Director for Research, St Elizabeth's Hospital (Previously Director, Division of Special Mental Health Research), Intramural Research Program, NIMH, St Elizabeth's Hospital, 1977-; Adjunct Professor of Psychiatry, Uniformed Services University School of Medicine, Bethesda, 1980-. *Memberships:* American Association for Geriatric Psychiatry; American College of Neuropsychopharmacology, Fellow; American Medical Association; American Psychiatric Association, Fellow; Association for Clinical Psychosocial Research; International Psychogeriatric Association; Psychiatric Research Society; Society for Biological Psychiatry; Washington Psychiatric Society. *Publications:* Contributor to professional journals; Presentations; Chapters in Books, etc. *Honours include:* Honorary Degree of Medicine, Universidad Central de Venezuela, 1977; Daniel Efron Award, American College of Neuropsychopharmacology, 1983; Senior Executive Service/Senior Scientific Service Outstanding Performance Award, 1983; Margaret Byrd Rawson Award, Tri-Service Incorporated, Washington, DC, 1985. *Address:* Neuropsychiatry Branch, NIMH, William A White Building, Room 536, Saint Elizabeths Hospital, Washington, DC 20032, USA.

WYNEN, André J P, b. 8 Dec. 1923, Uccle, Belgium. Physician. m. Nicole Musche, 1 son, 3 daughters. *Education:* MD, University of Brussels, 1950; Postgraduate study in General & Thoracic Surgery, 1954. *Appointments:* Chairman & Medical Director, Hôpital de Braine-l'Alleud, Waterloo, Brussels, 1954; Chairman & Medical Director, Edith Cavell Hospital, Brussels, 1983; Chairman of the Belgian Medical Association, 1963; Secretary-General of the World Medical Association, 1976. *Memberships:* Honorary Member, American Medical Association. *Publications:* Traumatologie de la Route", 1962; "La Médicine sans Médecin", 1972; various articles. *Honour:* Belgian Military Cross. *Hobby:* Drawing. *Address:* Hôpital de Braine-l'Alleud-Waterloo, Rue Wayez 35, B-1420 Braine-l'Alleud, Belgium.

WYNGAARDEN, James Barnes, b. 19 Oct. 1924, East Grand Rapids, Michigan, USA. Director, National Institutes of Health. m. Ethel Vredevoogd, 20 June 1946, Grand Rapids, Michigan (divorced 1977), 1 son, 4 daughters. *Education:* Calvin College, Grand Rapids, 1942-43; Western Michigan University, Kalamazoo, 1943-44; MD, University of Michigan Medical School, 1948; DSc (Hon Michigan, Ohio, Illinois); FACP; FRCP (London). *Appointments:* Intern in Medicine, 1948-49, Assistant Resident, 1949-50, Resident, 1951-52, Massachusetts General Hospital; Visiting Investigator, Public Health Research Institute of City of New York, 1952-53; Research Associate, National Heart Institute, Bethesda, 1953-54; Clinical Associate, National Institute of Arthritis and Metabolic Diseases, NIH, 1954-56; Associate Professor, 1956-59, Associate Professor of Medicine and Biochemistry, 1959-61, Professor of Medicine and Associate Professor of Biochemistry, 1961-65, Duke University Medical Center; Frank Wistar Thomas Professor and Chairman, Department of Medicine, University of Pennsylvania School of Medicine, Philadelphia, 1965-67; Frederic M Hanes Professor and Chairman, Department of Medicine, Duke University School of Medicine and Physician-in-Chief, Medical Service, Duke University Hospital, 1967-82; Chief of Staff, Duke University Hospital, 1981-82. *Memberships include:* American Board of Internal Medicine; American Clinical and Climatological Association; American College of Physicians; American Rheumatism Association; Endocrine Society; Institute of Medicine; National Academy of Sciences. *Publications:* Co-Editor: "The Metabolic Basis of Inherited Disease", 1960, 66, 72, 78, 93; Co-author, "Purine Metabolism in Man", 1974; "Gout and Hyperuricemia", 1976 (with W N Kelley); "Cecil Textbook of Medicine", 16th edition, 1982 (with L H Smith Junior), 17 edition, 1985. *Honours include:* Recipient of numerous honours and awards including: Distinguished Alumnus Award, Western Michigan University, 1984; Robert H Williams Distinguished Chairman of Medicine Award, Association of Professors of Medicine, 1985. *Hobbies:* Tennis; Skiing; Painting. *Address:* National Institutes of Health, Building 1 Room 124, Bethesda, MD 20892, USA.

WYSOCKI, Glenn Roman, b. 5 Feb. 1954, Milwaukee, Wisconsin, USA. Doctor of Chiropractic. m. Marilyn Jeanne Franko, 16 Oct. 1976, Northbrook, Illinois, 2 daughters. *Education:* Certified Tam Physician University of Wisconsin, Parkside, Whitewear and Milwaukee; DC, Palmer College of Chiropractic, 1979; National Lincoln School of Postgraduate Education; Diplomate, American Board of Chiropractic Orthopedists. *Memberships:* American and Wisconsin Chiropractic Associations; Council on Sports Injuries and Physical Fitness, Council on Orthopaedics, American Chiropractic Association (and Council on Roentgenology); Pi Tau Delta; Fellow, American College of Chiropractic Orthopaedists; Diplomate, American Board of Chiropractic Orthopaedists; Fellow, The Academy of Chiropractic Orthopedsts. *Honours:* Deans List, 1971; Certificate of Merit, Clinical, 1979; Certificate of Merit, 1979; Summa Cum Laude Honours, 1979; Salutatorian of Graduating Class, 1979; Pi Tau Delta, 1979; Diplomate, American Board of Chiropractic Orthopaedists, 1985. *Hobbies:* Reading; Travel; Bicycling. *Address:* 7537 22nd Avenue, Kenosha, WI 53140, USA.

WYSOCKI, Miroslav Jan, b. 6 May 1941, Warsaw, Poland. Head, Medical Statistics, National Institute of Hygiene, Warsaw. m. Hanna Lewicka, 25 Dec. 1963, Warsaw, 1 son, 1 daughter. *Education:* MD, Medical Academy, Warsaw, 1964; Associate Professor, Epidemiology. *Appointments:* Senior Research Fellow, Social Medicine, St Thomas's Hospital Medical School, London, England, 1971-72; Head, Laboratory of Epidemiology of Chronic Diseases, National Institute of Hygiene, Warsaw, 1973-79; Head, Medical Statistics, National Institute of Hygiene, Warsaw, 1980-. *Memberships:* International Epidemiological Association; Scientific Council, National Institute of Hygiene, Warsaw. *Publications:* About 40 articles in professional journals including: 'Gruzlica'; 'British Journal Preventive Social Medicine'; 'Diabete and Metebolisme' 'IDF Bulletin'; 'Scandinavian Journal Rheumatology'. *Hobbies:* Travel; Sports. *Address:* National Institute of Hygiene, Chocimske 24, 00-791 Warsaw, Poland.

X

XIAO, Peigen, b. 2 Feb. 1932, Shanghai, China. Professor, Director, Institute of Medicinal Plant Development. m. 1956, 2 daughters. *Education:* BSc, Biology, Amoy University, 1953. *Appointments:* Research Assistant, Central Institute of Health, 1953-62; Lecturer, 1962-78, Associate Professor, 1978-85, Professor 1985-, Chinese Academy of Medical Sciences/Director Institute of Medicinal Plant Development. *Memberships:* Society of Medicinal Plant Development; Chinese Pharmaceutical Society; Consultant in Traditional Medicine, World Health Organization. *Publications:* "Chinese Materia Medica I-IV", 1959-61, new edition I, 1979, II 1982, III 1985; "Flora Reipublicae Popularis Sinicae" 1979; Total of 85 scientific papers. *Address:* Institute of Medicinal Plant Development (IMPLAD), Chinese Academy of Medical Sciences, Hai Dian District, Dong Bei Wang, Beijing, People's Republic of China.

Y

YAKUBU, Alhassan Mela, b. 10 Nov. 1943, Nigeria. Consultant Paediatrician. m. Keshiya, 15 Dec. 1973, Zaria, 2 sons, 3 daughters. *Education:* FMC Paed; FWACP; National Postgraduate College of Nigeria; MB BS (ABU). *Appointments:* House Physician, 1973-74; Registrar, 1975-77; Senior Registrar, 1977-80; Lecturer, Consultant, 1980-82, Senior Lecturer, Consultant, 1982-86, ABU Teaching Hospital, Zaria. *Memberships:* Paediatric Association of Nigeria; Nigerian Cancer Society; International Paediatric Association. *Publications:* Author of numerous publications including: 'Sickle cell disease in Pregnancy', 1972; 'Secretory IgA in gastroenteritis and Kwaskiokor', 1982; 'Congenital abnormalities of genitourinary system in Northern Nigeria', (with M B Abdurrahman, S K Garg, O A Mabogunje, J T Momoh, J H Lawrie), 1982; 'Wilm's tumour in Northern Nigeria', (with M B Abdurrahman, J T Momoh, S S Ango and P Narayana), 1984; 'Neurological disturbances in Sickle cell disease', (with B Werblinska), 1985; 'Congenital hepatic fibrosis', 1985; 'Aetiology of cerebral palsy in Zaria', (with M Sathiakumar), 1984. *Honours:* UNICEF Consultant on ORT, 1985; Member, International Paediatric Association, 1984. *Hobbies: Gardening. Address:* Department of Paediatrics, ABU Teaching Hospital, Zaria, Nigeria.

YAMAGATA, Shoichi, b. 27 Feb 1913, Ishinomaki, Miyagi-Pref, Japan.University Professor/Medical Adviser. m. 13 Oct 1936 at Sendai, Miyagi-Pref, Japan, 4 sons, 1 daughter. *Education:* Machelor of Medicine, 1936, Doctor of Medicine, 1942, Medical School of Tohoku Imperial University. *Appointments:* Assistant, 1936-42, Associate Professor, 1942-57, Professor, 1957-76, Emeritus Professor, 1976-, Tohoku Imperial University; Medical Adviser of Tohoku Rosai Hospital, 1976-. *Memberships:* Science Council of Japan, Chairman of 7th Division, 1975-85, Chairman National Committee for CIOMS, 1976-; President, Miyagi Cancer Society, 1978-. *Publications:* 'Clinical and Experimental Studies in Gastroenterology and Hematology' Supplement of Tohoku Journal of Experimental Medicine, 1976; 'Recent Advances in Cancer Control' Ecerpla Medica, 1983. *Honours:* Prize of Japan Invention Society, 1964; Prize of Japan Cancer Society, 1976. *Hobbies:* Medical History of Japan; Japanese verse. *Address:* 3-5 Kamisugi 2 chome, Sendai, Miyagi 980, Japan.

YAMAGUCHI, Nobuo, b. 27 Apr 1937, Japan. Professor of Virology. m. Nanami Shigenobu, 21 Nov 1965, Tokyo, 2 sons, 1 daughter. *Education:* MD, The University of Tokyo, School of Medicine, 1963; PhD Microbiology, The University of Tokyo, 1968. *Appointments:* Intern, The Tokyo University Hospital, 1963-64; Research Associate 1968-72 and 1974-78, Associate Professor 1979-82, Professor, Department of Virology, 1983-, Institute of Medical Science, The University of Tokyo; Research Associate, Institute of Cancer Research, Columbia University, USA, 1972-74. *Memberships:* Japanese Cancer Society; Society of Japanese Virologists. *Publications:* 'Characterization of T antigen in cells infected with a temperature-sensitive mutant of simian virus 40', 1975; 'Two classes of transformation-defective, immortalization-positive simian virus 40 mutants constructed by making three-base insertions in the T antigen gene', 1984. *Hobbies:* Mountain skiing; Go. *Address:* The Institute of Medical Science, The University of Tokyo, 1-22-1, Shirokanedai, Minato-ku, Tokyo 108, Japan.

YAMASHITA, Hisao, b. 19 Sep 1910, Tokyo. Director of Keio Cancer Center. m. 5 Mar 1943, Tokyo, Japan, 2 sons, 1 daughter. *Education:* MD, Keio University School of Medicine, 1934; Degree in Medical Science, Keio University, 1938. *Appointments:* Staff Doctor, 1935-41, Chief, Department of Radiology, 1941-45, Japan Cancer Institute Hospital; Professor,

Department of Radiology, Keio Medical College, 1945-48; Chief, Department of Radiology, Tokyo 2nd National Hospital, 1948-58; Director, Department of Radiology, Japan Cancer Institute Hospital, 1958-63; Professor, Department of Radiology, Keio University School of Medicine, 1963-75; Chairman, Radiation Effects Research Foundation, Hiroshima, 1975-78; Director, Keio Cancer Center, 1978-. *Memberships:* Board of Directors, Japan Radioisotope Association, Tokyo; Councillor, Japan Cancer Society; Honorary Member: American College of Radiology; American Radium Society; Japan Radiology Society; Japan Society of Cancer Therapy; Japan Society of Nuclear Medicine. *Publications:* "Medical Use of Radioisotopes" 1960; "Practice of Radiation Therapy" 1960; "Practice of Clinical Radiology" 1974; 'High LET Radiation Therapy' in "Encyclopedia of Surgery" 1977; "Nursing of Radiology" 1982. *Honours:* Prize of Sanshikai, Keio University School of Medicine, 1948; Testimonial of Japan Medical Association, 1968; Purple Ribbon Medal, Ministry of International Trading and Industry, 1974; Bonus of Ministry of Health and Welfare, 1977. *Hobbies:* Photography; Golf. *Address:* Keio Cancer Center, 35 Shinanomachi, Shinjuku, Tokyo 160, Japan.

YANG, Sze-Piao, b. 4 June 1920, Taiwan. Professor of Internal Medicine. m. Yun-Kuang Chang, 21 Feb. 1945, Taiwan, 3 sons, 1 daughter. *Education:* MB, Imperial Taihoku University, Faculty of Medicine, 1942; Doctor of Medical Science, Niigata University, School of Medicine, Japan. *Appointments:* Instructor, 1951-54, Associate Professor, 1954-57, Professor, 1957-, National Taiwan University, College of Medicine, Department of Internal Medicine; Professor and Director, National Taiwan University, School of Medical Technology and Department of Clinical Pathology, 1958-72; Visiting Professor, State University of New York, Downstate Medical Center, Jan-June 1965; Superintendent, National Taiwan University Hospital, 1978-84; Dean, College of Medicine, National Taiwan University, 1983-85. *Memberships:* Fellow, American College of Chest Physicians; Governor, Regent, American College of Chest Physicians; Standing Board Member, Formosan Medical Association; Standing Board Member, Chinese Medical Association. *Publications include:* 'Lymphangitic Carcinomatosis of the Lung - The Clinical Significance of its Roentgenolgic Classification' Chest 62, 1972; 'Short-term Intensive Initial Chemotherapy for Pulmonary Tuberculosis - Preliminary Report: Can the Duration of TB Treatment be even Shorter?' KEKKAKU 1978; 'Chronological Observation of Epidemiological Consideration - a 30-year Consecutive Study' Japanese Journal of Clinical Oncology, 1984. *Address:* No 6 Long 7 Lane, 183 Ho-Ping E Road, Section 1, Taipei, Taiwan, Republic of China.

YANIV, Moshe, b. 7 Nov. 1938, Israel. Head of Tumor Virus Unit, Pasteur Institute, France. m. Dr. Rouviere-Yaniv Josette, Sep. 68, Paris, 1 son, 1 daughter. *Education:* MSc, Chemistry, Hebrew University, Jerusalem, 1961; DSc, University of Paris, 1969. *Appointments:* Postdoctoral Fellow, Stanford University, 1969-72; Scientist CNRS and Institut Pasteur, 1972-; Director of Research CNRS 1982-; Head of Tumor Virus Unit, Department of Molecular Biology, Pasteur Institute, France. *Memberships:* American Society of Microbiology; European Molecular Biology Organization. *Publications:* About 110 publications in various journals in the fields of Molecular Biology and Virology. *Honour:* Rosen prize for cancer research, 1984. *Hobbies:* Hiking; Swimming; Jogging. *Address:* Department of Molecular Biology, Pasteur Institute, 25 rue du Dr Roux, 75724 Paris Cedex 15, France.

YANKEE, Ronald August, b. 24 May 1934, Franklin, Massachusetts, USA. Director of Rhode Island Blood Center. *Education:* BS, Tufts University, 1956; MD, Yale University, 1960. *Appointments:* Senior Investigator, National Cancer Institute, Bethesda, Maryland; Associate Professor in Medicine, Harvard Medical School, Boston, Massachusetts; Chief, Division of Supportive Care and Blood Bank Director, Sidney Farber Cancer Institute, Boston, Massachusetts; Professor of Medicine, Brown University, Providence, Rhode Island; Director, Rhode Island Blood Center, Providence. *Memberships:* Medical Adviser, National Hemophilia Foundation; Board, American Red Cross; Council of Community Blood Centers; American Association Blood Banks. *Publications:* 2 contributions to 'New England Journal of Medicine', 1969 and 1973; "Platelets, Production, Function, Transfusion and Storage", contributor, 1974. *Honour:* Morten Grove Rasmussen Award, Massachusetts Association of Blood Banks, 1984. *Hobby:* Gardening. *Address:* 551 North Main Street, Providence, RI 02904, USA.

YARZAGARAY, Everildes Polo, b. 3 Dec. 1935, Colombia, South America. Director of Medical Education; Director of Hospital Pulmonary Department. m. Dr Luis Yarzagaray, 1 Apr. 1962, 5 daughters. *Education:* MD, University of Cartagena College and Medical School, Colombia, South America, 1962. *Appointments:* Internship, Baptist Clinic, Barranquilla, Colombia, 1962; Residency, Illinois Masonic Hospital, USA, 1963-66; Currently Director of Medical Education, Director of Pulmonary Department, Norwegian-American Hospital, Chicago, USA. *Memberships:* Alumni Association, Colombia; American Medical Association; Chicago Medical Society; Illinois Medical Society; American College of Chest Physicians; American Thoracic Society; American Society of Internal Medicine; American College of Physicians; International College of Physicians and Surgeons; Associate Founder of Cartamedas (University of Cartagena), 1969; Founder and 1st President, Ladies Auxiliary of Cartamedas, 1976; Associate Founder of Colombia Cultural Centre, 1978; President of the Scientific Committee of Cartamedas, 1981; Member of the Chicago Board of Health TB Advisory Committee; Student Advisor for the University of Illinois. *Publications include:* Medical Screening Articles for 'Pulmonary Function outline'; 'Pulmonary Emergencies'; many articles in medical publications and journals; 'The Role of Women in Science', awarded article in 'The Herald' newspaper, Barranquilla; Co-author: "Cook with Us", 1982. *Honours:* Woman of the Year, Cartamedas University, 1976-77; Couple of the Year (with husband, Dr L Yarzagaray, 1983-84. *Hobbies:* Dancing; Opera Music; Travel; her children. *Address:* Norwegian-American Hospital, 1044 North Francisco Street, Chicago, IL 60622, USA.

YASUDA, Mineo, b. 8 July 1937, Kyoto, Japan. Professor of Anatomy. m. Iku Yasuda, 25 Aug 1968, Kyoto, 2 daughters. *Education:* MD, Kyoto University, 1962; Dr Med Sci. *Appointments:* Instructor, Anatomy, Faculty of Medicine, Kyoto University, 1963-71; Lecturer, 1971-75, Associate Professor, 1975, Kyoto Prefectural University of Medicine; Head, Perinatology, Institute for Developmental Research, Aichi Prefectural Colony, 1975-77; Professor, Anatomy, Hiroshima University School of Medicine, 1977-. *Memberships:* Teratology Society; International Society of Developmental Biologists; Japanese Teratology Society; Japanese Association of Anatomists; Japanese Society of Developmental Biologists; Japanese Society of Toxicological Sciences; Japan Society of Human Genetics; Environ Mutagen Society of Japan; Japan Society of Neonatology; Japan Society of Medical Education. *Publications:* "Congenital Malformations", 1974; "Modern Trends in Human Genetics-2", 1975; "Gene-Environment Interaction in Common Diseases", 1977; "Clinical Human Embryology", 1983. *Hobbies:* Skiing; Classical Music. *Address:* Dept. of Anatomy, Hiroshima University School of Medicine, Kasumi 1-2-3, Minami-ku, Hiroshima 734, Japan.

YEATES, W(illiam) Keith, b. 10 Mar. 1920, Helensburgh, Scotland. Honorary Consultant Urologist. m. Jozy McIntyre Fairweather, 3 Apr. 1946, 1 son, 1 daughter. *Education:* MB BS 1942, MS 1945, MD 1950, Medical School, University of Newcastle upon Tyne; Fellow, Royal College of Surgeons of England, 1945. *Appointments:* House Surgeon 1942, Surgical Registrar, Royal Victoria Infirmary, Newcastle upon Tyne; Demonstrator of Anatomy, Medical School, Newcastle, 1944; Resident Surgical Officer, Tynemouth Infirmary, 1945-47; Assistant Surgeon 1948-49, Senior Registrar 1951, Department of Urology, Newcastle General Hospital; Senior Registrar, St Pauls Hospital, London, 1950; Consultant Urologist, Newcastle University Hospitals, 1952-; Honorary Senior Lecturer, Institute of Urology, University of London, 1981-; Honorary Editor 1973-78, Chairman of Editorial Committee 1979-84, Honorary Consulting Editor 1985-, 'British Journal of Urology'; Chairman, Specialist Advisory Committee in Urology 1984-86, Intercollegiate Speciality Advisory Board 1984-, Royal Surgical Colleges. *Memberships:* President 1980-82, Honorary Member, British Association of Urological Surgeons; European Association of Urology; British Andrology Society; Honorary Member, Urological Society of Australasia; Honorary Member, Canadian Urological Association. *Publications include:* 'A new tissue drain', 1962; 'Transaction of the bladder in enureas', 1973; 'Male infertility' in "Urology" (editor Blandy), 1976; 'Uretero-vaginal fistula' in "Surgery of Female Incontinence", (editors Stanton and Tanagh), 1980; 'Coordination in bladder function' in "Benign Prostate Hypertuphy", (editor Hinman), 1983. *Honours:* St Peters Medal, British Association of Urological Surgeons, 1983; Fellow - without examination, Royal College of Surgeons, 1985. *Hobby:* Expansion of urological services in the United Kingdom. *Address:* 22 Castleton Grove, Newcastle upon Tyne, NE2 2HD, England.

YEH, Sze-ya, b. 12 Feb. 1937, Taipei, Taiwan. Chairman of Obstetrics and Gynaecology. m. Grace, 31 Oct. 1964, Taipei, Taiwan, 1 son, 1 daughter. *Education:* BS, National Taiwan University College of Science, 1957, MD, 1962. *Appointments:* Instructor, Obstetrics and Gynaecology, University of Southern California School of Medicine, Los Angeles, USA, 1971-74; Assistant Professor, College of Physicians and Surgeons, Columbia University, New York, 1976-78; Assistant Professor, University of Southern California School of Medicine, Los Angeles, 1979-82, Associate Professor, 1982-84; Chairman, Department of Obstetrics and Gynaecology, The Allentown Hospital, Allentown, Pennsylvania, 1984-. *Memberships include:* Fellow, American College of Obstetricians and Gynaecologists; New York Academy of Sciences; Society for Gynaecologic Investigation; Society of Perinatal Obstetricians; California Perinatal Association; Metropolitan Perinatal Society; APPLE Medical Users Group; Fellow, Los Angeles Obstetrician and Gynaecological Society. *Publications include:* 73 articles in professional journals including 'Computer Diagnosis of Fetal Heart Rate Patterns' in 'Am. J. Obstet.', 1970; co-author 'Computer Diagnosis of Fetal Heart Rate Patterns', in 'Am. J. Obstet.', 1972; "Quantification of Fetal Heart Rate Beat-to-Beat Internal Differences' in 'Obstet Gynaecol' 1973; 'A Study of Diazepam During Labor' in 'Obstet Gynaecol, 1974; Co-author 'Continuing Role of the Nonstress Test in the Management of Postdates Pregnancy' in 'Obstet Gynaecol', 1984. *Honours:* 1st Prize, Purdue-Frederick Award, 1975; 3rd Prize, 29th ACOG Presentation. *Hobbies:* Personal Computers; Classical Music; Photography. *Address:* The Allentown Hospital, 17th and Chew Street, Allentown, PA 18102, USA.

YEMM, Robert, b. 31 Jan. 1939, Bristol, England. Head of Department. m. Glenys Margaret Oliver, 1 May 1962, Colwyn Bay, Wales, 1 son, 1 daughter. *Education:* BDS, 1961, BSc (Hons) Physiology, 1965; PhD, 1969, University of Bristol. *Appointments:* Lecturer in Dental Surgery (Prosthetics), Lecturer in Dental Medicine (Oral Biology), University of Bristol; Associate Professor, Department of Oral Biology, University of Alberta, Canada; Senior Lecturer, Honorary Consultant, Department of Dental Prosthetics and Gerontology, Personal Chair and Head of

Department, University of Dundee, Scotland. *Memberships:* British Society for the Study of Prosthetic Dentistry; British Society for Dental Research; Royal Odonto-churgical Society, Edinburgh; British Association for Service to the Elderly. *Publications:* 'Neurophysiologic studies of temporomandibular joint dysfunction', 1979; 'An alternative method for recording the occlusion of the edentulous patient during construction of replacement dentures', (with N Duthie), 1985. *Honours:* Nuffield Fellowship, 1963-65. *Hobbies:* Gardening; Sailing. *Address:* 10 Birkhill Avenue, Wormit, Newport-on-Tay, Fife DD6 8PX, Scotland.

YERNAULT, Jean-Claude, b. 1 Jan 1943, Bassilly, Belgium. Head, Chest Department, Cliniques Universitaires de Bruxelles. m. Beatrice Mahaux, 15 Dec 1967, Brussels, 1 son. *Education:* MD, Universite Libre de Bruxelles, 1966; PhD, 1978. *Appointment:* Assistant, Chest Department, Hospital Universitaire Saint Pierre, Brussels, 1967-77. *Memberships:* European Society of Clinical Respiratory Physiology; Societe de Pneumologie de Langue Francaise; International Association Against Tuberculosis; Societe Belge de Pneumologie; Societe de Pathologie Thoracique du Nord; Fellow, American College of Chest Physicians. *Publications:* More than a hundred articles published in international medical journals. *Honours:* Secretary of Belgian Society of Pneumology, 1983-; Editor-in-Chief of Bulletin Europeen de Physiopathologie Respiratoire (Clinical Respiratory Physiology), 1984. *Address:* Chest Department, Hopital Erasme, Route de Lennik 808, B-1070 Brussels, Belgium.

YEUNG, Chap-Yung, b. 29 Dec. 1936, Hong Kong. Professor, Paediatrics, University of Hong Kong. m. Helen Kwan-sik Chiu, 18 Aug. 1963, 2 daughters. *Education:* MB BS; MRCP and DCH; FRCP (Canada); FRCP (Edinburgh, Glasgow); CRCP (Canada); Diplomate American Pediatric Board. *Appointments:* Consultant, Paediatrician, Paediatric B Unit, QEH Hospital, Hong Kong, 1970-72; Assistant Professor, Paediatrics, McMaster University, Canada, 1972-76; Consultant Paediatrician, Scarborough Centre Hospital, Ontario, 1977-80; Professor, Chairman, Paediatrics, University of Hong Kong, 1980-. *Memberships:* Past President, Canadian Chinese Medical Association; Past President, Honorary Member, Honorary Advisor, Federation of Chinese Canadian Professionals; Honorary Advisor, Hong Kong Society for Child Health & Development Ltd; President, Maternal & Infant Health Association. *Publications:* "rG globulin levels in newborn", 'Lancet', 1968; "Phenobarbitone for neonatal jaundice", 'Lancet', 1969, 'Pediatrics', 1971; "Hypolgycemia in neonatal sepsis", 'Journal Pediatrics', 1970, 1973; "Neonatal hyperbilirubinaemia in Chinese", 'Tropical Geographic Medicine', 1973; "Prevention of Hepatitis B in Newborn", 'Lancet', 1984. *Honours:* Commonwealth Medical Scholar, Institute of Child Health and Hammersmith Hospital, London, England, 1966-68; Commonwealth Foundation Travelling Fellow, Royal Children's Hospital, Melbourne, Australia, 1970; Honorary Consultant, Guangdong People's Hospital, 1984; Visiting Professor, Peking Union Medical College, 1985. *Address:* Dept. of Paediatrics, Queen Mary Hospital, University of Hong Kong, Hong Kong.

YEW, Wing Wai, b. 7 Oct 1950, Hong Kong. Consultant Physician, Pulmonary Medicine. m. Mary Lai-Yung Lee, 30 Sep 1980, Hong Kong, 1 son. *Education:* MB, BS, Distinction, Pathology, Hong Kong; MRCP, United Kingdom. *Appointments:* Medical Officer, General Outpatients Clinic, 1975; Registrar, Medicine, University of Hong Kong (Professorial Unit), 1975-78; Medical Officer, Hong Kong Tuberculosis & Chest Services, 1978-81; Senior Medical Officer, 1981-84, Consultant, Chest Physician, 1984-, Hong Kong Tuberculosis & Chest Services. *Membership:* American College of Chest Physicians. *Publications:* "Amikacin Treatment of Pulmonary Tuberculosis", 'Tubercle', 1983; "An Intensive Short Course Programme for Drug Addicts & Prisoners with Pulmonary Tuberculosis", 'Proceedings VIII Asia-Pacific Congress Chest Diseases', 1983. *Honours:* Ng Li Hing Prize, 1st Place Anatomy, 1970; Ho Fook Prize, 1st Place, Anatomy, Physiology, Biochemistry, 1970; Distinctions, Pathology, Microbiology, Pharmacology, 1971; Li Shu Fan Clinical Scholarship, 1971-74; Morse Scholarship, 1971-74. *Hobbies:* Music; Reading; Design. *Address:* 62A, Leighton Road, 5th Floor, Hong Kong.

YIN, Wei-bo, b. 5 Dec. 1931, Tianjin, China. Professor, Director of Department of Radiotherapy, Cancer Institute, Chinese Academy of Medical Sciences, Beijing. m. Ying-chi Tsui, 20 Sep. 1957, 1 son, 1 daughter. *Education:* Delhi College, Delhi University, India, 1949-51; Yenching University 1951-52; MD, Peking Union Medical College, 1952-57. *Appointments:* Resident, Department of Radiology, Peking Union Hospital, 1957-58; Resident, Department of Radiation Oncology, 1958-64; Attending Doctor, Cancer Institute (Hospital), 1964-73; Deputy Director of Department, 1973-85, Associate Professor, 1981-85, Professor and Director of Department, 1985-, Chinese Academy of Medical Sciences. *Memberships:* Committee of Academic Degree, State Council; Academic Committee of Chinese Academy of Medical Sciences; Chinese Society of Ionization Dosimetry; Chinese Medical Association; Board of Directors, China Cancer Research Fund. *Publications:* "Textbook of Radiation Oncology", (Co-author), 1983; Contributor of numerous articles to professional journals. *Hobby:* Classical music. *Address:* Department of Radiation Oncology, Cancer Institute (Hospital), Chinese Academy of Medical Sciences, Zuo An Men Wai, Beijing, China.

YOCHUM, Terry Robert, b. 23 Feb. 1947, St Louis, Missouri, USA. Director. m. Inge Geiselhart, 4 June 1972, St Louis, Missouri, 1 son, 2 daughters. *Education:* BS, Illinois Department of Education, 1972; DC, cum laude, National College of Chiropractic, Chicago, IL, 1972; DACBR; FCCR (Canada); FICC (Honors). *Appointments include:* Assistant Professor, Radiology, National College of Chiropractic, Chicago, IL, 1974-76; Private Practice, Chiropractic, St Louis, MO, 1976-78; Private Practice, Radiology, St Louis, 1976-78; Professor and Chairman, Department of Radiology, Logan College of Chiropractic, St Louis, 1976-78; Professor and Chairman, Department of Radiology, Senior Lecturer, Department of Diagnostic Sciences, Phillip Institute of Technology, International College of Chiropractic, Melbourne, Australia, 1978-83. *Memberships include:* American Chiropractic Assn.; Australian Chiropractors' Assn.; New Zealand Chiropractors' Assn.; American College of Chiropractic Roentgenology; American Council on Chiropractic Roentgenology. *Publications include:* "Radiology of the Arthritides", 1978; "The Seven Wonders of the Spine", 1983; "Radiology of Trauma", 1984; Numerous publications in professional journals; Contributor to Lectures, Conferences and Presentations. *Honours:* Outstanding Graduate National College of Chiropractic, 1972. *Address:* 9464 North Federal Boulevard, Denver, CO 80221, USA.

YOON, Bong-Hyun, b. 11 Apr. 1939, South Korea. Associate Professor. m. Chung-Ja Suh, 8 May 1968, South Korea, 1 son, 1 daughter. *Education:* BA, College of Liberal Arts and Sciences, 1962, MD, Chonnam Medical School, 1964, Chonnam National University, Korea. *Appointments include:* Assistant Professor, Associate Professor, Department of Radiology, University of Health Sciences and the Chicago Medical School, North Chicago, Illinois, USA. *Memberships:* American College of Radiology; Radiological Society of North America; Association of University Radiologists; American Institution of Ultrasound Medicine. *Publications:* 'Pulmonary Scan Carcinoma, A Clinical Pathological Analysis' in 'Cancer', 1983; 'Elephantiosis-like Appearance in Upper and Lower Extremities in Grave's Disease', in 'American Journal of Medical Sciences', 1985. *Hobby:* Classical music. *Address:* 823 Whitman Court, Libertyville, IL 60048, USA.

YOSHIHASHI, Masahiro, b. 1 Aug 1943, Sapporo, Japan. Chiropractor; Teacher. m. 10 Oct 1972, 1 son. *Education:* BSc, Toho University, 1968; Bone Setter, Hokkaido Bone Setter School, Sapporo, 1972; DC, National College of Chiropractic, USA, 1980. *Appointments:* Clinical Laboratory Technician, Physical Therapist, Sapporo Daiichi Hospital; Committee, Hakkaido Ryojitu Association; Teacher, Hokkaido Ryojitu Association; Board of Education, Japan Chiropractic Association; Standing Committee, Hokkaido Ryojitu Association, Council Member; etc. *Memberships:* American Chiropractic Association, Council on Roentgendegy; Japan Chiropractic Association; Hokkaido Ryojitu Association; National College of Chiropractic Alumni Association. *Publications:* "Essential of Chiropractic", volume 1, 1982, volume 11, 1983; "Chiropractic (Definition and Clinical Practice)", 1981; "Chiropractic (Biomechanics and Clinical Practice)", 1982; "Clinical Lab. for Chiropracten", 1981. *Hobbies:* Music; Skiing; Bowling; Hiking; Painting. *Address:* 5 Chome Higashi Odori, Sapporo, Hokkaido, Japan 060.

YOSHIMURA, Hidetoshi, b. 4 May 1927, Fukuoka, Japan. Professor of Hygienic and Forensic Chemistry. m. Kyoko Hakamata, 20 Oct. 1951, Fukuoka, 1 son, 1 daughter. *Education:* BS, Faculty of Pharmaceutical Sciences, 1950, PhD, 1959, University of Tokyo, Japan. *Appointments:* Instructor of Faculty of Pharmaceutical Sciences, 1951-60, Associate Professor, 1960-68, Professor, 1968-, Dean, 1982-84, Kyushu University. *Memberships:* Pharmaceutical Society of Japan; Japanese Biochemical Society; Japanese Society of Toxicological Sciences; Japanese Association of Forensic Toxicology; International Society for the Study of Xenobiotics. *Publications:* Editor and Co-Author: "Newer Aspects of Hygienic Chemistry", 1980. Various other works. *Honours:* Abbott Award, 1967; Miyata Award, 1973; Pharmaceutical Society of Japan Award, 1985. *Hobbies:* Travelling; Gardening. *Address:* 1-11-23 Heiwa, Minami-ku, Fukuoka 815, Japan.

YOUNATHAN, Margaret Juanita Tims, b. 25 Apr. 1926, Clinton, Miss, USA. Professor, Human Nutrition and Food. m. Ezzat S Younathan, 11 Aug. 1958, Tallahassee, Florida, 2 daughters. *Education:* PhD, Florida State University, 1958; MS, University of Tennessee, 1951; BS, University of Southern Mississippi, 1950. *Appointments:* Instructor, Food and Nutrition, Oregon State University, 1951-55; Postdoctoral Research Associate, Florida State University, 1958-59; Senior Nutritional Consultant, Arkansas State Health Department, 1962-68; Instructor, Pediatrics, 1962-65, Assistant Professor, Pediatrics, 1965-68, University of Arkansas School of Medicine; Associate Professor, Human Nutrition and Food, Louisiana State University, 1971-79. *Memberships:* Institute of Food Technologists; American Dietetic Association; American Home Economics Association. *Publications:* "Nutritional Requirements of Infants and Children", (with T C Panos), 1966; "Hematological status of rats fed oxidized beef lipids', (with Deborah G McWilliams), 1985; Author of chapters in books. *Honours:* Phi Kappa Phi, 1958; Sigma Xi, 1958. *Hobbies:* Gardening; Art. *Address:* Human Nutrition and Food, School of Home Economics, Louisiana State University, Baton Rouge, LA 70803-4300, USA.

YOUNG, David Albin, b. 10 Nov. 1955, Newton, Massachusetts, USA. Doctoral Candidate, Department of Biometrics, UCHSC. *Education:* AS, Newton Junior College, Massachusetts; BS, University of Massachusetts, Boston; MS, UCHSC, Physiology, Denver, Colorado. *Appointments:* Consultant, AAAS, Office of Opportunities in Science, Washington, DC, 1976-; Research Assistant, Boston Biomedical Research Institute, 1977-79; Research Assistant,

UCHSC, Physiology, 1981-85. *Memberships:* American Association for Advancement in Science; Rocky Mountain Region Neurosciences Group; Foundation for Science and the Handicapped. *Publications:* "Turnover and Migration of Teste Bud Cells", Masters Thesis, UCHSC, Denver, 1985; 'Access to Science', AAAS, Editor-in-Chief of Newsletter, 1976-77. *Honours:* Salutatorian, 1975, AS with distinction, 1975, Newton Junior College; Magna Cum Laude, 1979, Senior Honors in Chemistry, 1979, University of Massachusetts, Boston. *Hobbies:* Camping; Travel; Chess; Scrabble; Conversation. *Address:* 2658 Garfield Street, Denver, CO 80205, USA.

YOUNG, Donald Stirling, b. 17 Dec., 1933, Belfast, Northern Ireland. Professor of Pathology. m. Silja Meret, 3 sons. *Education:* MB ChB 1957; PhD 1962. *Appointments:* Lecturer in Materia Medica, University of Aberdeen, Scotland, 1958-59; Fellow, 1959-62, Registrar, 1962-64, Royal Postgraduate Medical School, London; Visiting Scientist, National Institutes of Health, 1965-66; Chief, Clinical Chemistry Service, ibid, 1966-67; Head, Section of Clinical Chemistry, Mayo Clinic, Rochester, Minnesota, 1977-84; Professor, Department of Pathology & Laboratory Medicine, University of Pennsylvania, 1985-. *Memberships:* Association of Clinical Biochemists; American Association for Clinical Chemistry; Academy of Clinical Laboratory Physicians & Scientists. *Publications:* Co-author of: "The Neonate: Clinical Biochemistry, Physiology & Pathology", 1976; "Drug Interferences & Drug Measurement in Clinical Chemistry", 1976; "Chemical Diagnosis of Disease", 1979; "Drug Measurement & Drug Effects in Laboratory Health Science", 1980. *Honours:* AACC Award for outstanding contributions to Clinical Chemistry, 1977; President, American Association for Clinical Chemistry, 1980; President, International Federation of Clinical Chemists, 1985. *Address:* Department of Pathology & Laboratory Medicine, University of Pennsylvania, 3400 Spruce Street, Philadelphia, PA 19104, USA.

YOUNG, James Edward Massey, b. 23 July 1943, Toronto, Canada. Associate Clinical Professor of Surgery, McMaster University. m. Linda Joyce Minnes, 28 Aug. 1965, Toronto, 1 son, 1 daughter. *Education:* BSc, McMaster University, 1965; MD, University of Toronto, 1969; Fellow, Royal College of Surgeons, 1974; Fellow, American College of Surgeons, 1978. *Appointments include:* Head, Head & Neck Service, St Joseph's Hospital/McMaster University, 1978-; Surgical Consultant/Head, Surgical Oncology, Ontario Cancer Treatment & Research Foundation, Henderson Hospital Clinic, 1984-; Associate Clinical Professor of Surgery, McMaster University, 1982-; Chairman, Subcommittee on Head & Neck Surgery, Canadian Association of General Surgeons, 1982-; President, Eastern Great Lakes Head & Neck Oncology Association, 1980, 1981. *Memberships:* American College of Surgeons; Canadian Association of General Surgeons; Canadian Association of Clinical Surgeons; Canadian Oncology Association; Society of Head & Neck Surgeons; Royal College of Physicians & Surgeons of Canada; Various regional associations. *Publications include:* Book, "Head & Neck Cancer: Management of the Unknown Primary" (2 chapters); Book, "Needle Aspiration Cytology of Head & Neck Masses", with Dr. A. Qizilbash; Numerous contributions to professional journals, conference proceedings, etc. *Hobbies:* Archaeology (Egyptology); Gardening. *Address:* Suite 204, 25 Charlton Avenue East, Hamilton, Ontario, Canada L8N 1Y2.

YOUNG, Jay A, b. 8 Sep. 1920, USA. Consultant in Chemical Safety and Health. m. Anne Elizabeth Neff, 29 June 1942, 6 sons, 6 daughters. *Education:* BS, Indiana University, 1939; AM, Oberlin College, 1940; PhD, University of Notre Dame, 1950. *Appointments:* Chief Chemist, Asbestos Manufacturing Company; Ordnance Engineer, US Department of Defense; Professor of Chemistry, King's College, Carleton University, Auburn University, Florida State University;

Manager of Technical Publications, Chemical Manufacturers Association; Consultant, Chemical Health and Safety. *Memberships:* American Chemical Society; American Association for the Advancement of Science; American Conference on Chemical Labelling. *Publications:* "The OSHA 'Right to Know' Regulations", 1984; "Handbook of Chemical Industry Labelling", contributor, (editors O'Connor and Lirtzman), 1984. *Honours:* University of Notre Dame Centennial Award of Honor for Excellence in the Teaching of Chemistry, 1965; Manufacturing Chemists Association National Award for Contribution to the Teaching of Chemistry, 1971. *Hobbies:* Furniture design and construction; Pastel sketching. *Address:* 12916 Allerton Lane, Silver Spring, MD 20904, USA.

YOUNG, Paul Andrew, b. 3 Oct. 1926, St. Louis, Missouri, USA. Professor & Chairman, Department of Anatomy, St. Louis University School of Medicine. m. Catherine Ann Hofmeister, 14 May 1949, St. Louis, 8 sons, 2 daughters. *Education:* BS 1947, MS (R) 1953, St. Louis University; PhD, University of Buffalo, 1957. *Appointments:* Assistant, Instructor in Anatomy, 1953, 1957; Assistant Professor, Associate Professor, Professor of Anatomy, St. Louis University, 1957, 1966, 1972. *Memberships:* American Association for the Advancement of Science; American Association of Anatomists; Cajal Club; Sigma Xi; Society for Neuroscience. *Publications include:* Book, "Fundamentals of Visceral Innervation", co-author, 1977; Numerous neuroanatomical research articles, teaching guides, atlases. *Honours:* Alpha Omega Alpha, 1972; Golden Apple Award, teaching, 1974; Teaching awards, dedication & academic excellence, 1981, 1985. *Hobbies:* Photography: Tennis; Golf. *Address:* Department of Anatomy, St. Louis University School of Medicine, 1402 South Grand Boulevard, St. Louis, MO 63104, USA.

YOUNG, Rosie Tse Tse, b. 23 Oct. 1931, Hong Kong. Professor of Medicine. *Education:* MB BS, 1953; MD 1956, University of Hong Kong; Member 1959, Fellow 1968, Royal College of Physicians of Edinburgh; Member 1959, Fellow 1972, Royal College of Physicians, London; Fellow 1985, Royal College of Physicians, Glasgow; Fellow 1976, Royal Australasian College of Physicians. *Appointments:* Clinical Assistant, Assistant Lecturer, Lecturer, Senior Lecturer, Reader, Department of Medicine, 1954-74; Titular Professor, Department of Medicine, 1974-79, Professor of Medicine, 1979-; Sub-Dean, 1978-83, Dean 1983-84, Pro-Vice-Chancellor, 1985, Faculty of Medicine, University of Hong Kong; Consultant, Queen Mary Hospital, Hong Kong. *Memberships:* Association of Physicians of Great Britain & Ireland; American Diabetes Association; American Endocrine Society; Vice-President, Society for the Study of Endocrinology. Metabolism & Reproduction, Hong Kong. *Publications:* Various articles in medical journals. *Honours:* Justice of the Peace, Hong Kong, 1971-. *Address:* Department of Medicine, University of Hong Kong, Hong Kong.

YOUNGSWICK, Fred Donald, b. 28 Oct. 1949, New York, New York, USA. Associate Clinical Professor, Podiatric Surgery; Director of Residency Training. m. Catherine Kal Haas, 27 Jan. 1971, Shreveport, Louisiana, 2 daughters. *Education includes:* BA, Richmond College, City University of New York, 1971; BS, DPM, California College of Podiatric Medicine; Resident, Podiatric Surgery, California Podiatry Hospital, San Francisco, California, 1975-77; MS, California College of Podiatric Medicine, 1981, Diplomate, 1979, American Board of Podiatric Surgery, 1979; Fellow, American College of Foot Surgeons, 1980; Oral Examiner, Certification Exam, American Board of Podiatric Surgery, Illinois, 1980-83. *Appointments include:* Associate Clinical Professor, Department of Podiatric Surgery, 1977-, Coordinator of Clinical Affairs, 1980-82, California College of Podiatric Medicine, San Francisco; Director, Residency Training, 1978-, Chief of Staff,

1980-84, California Podiatry Hospital, San Francisco. Hospital Affiliations: California Podiatry Hospital, 1977-; St Mary's Hospital, 1979-; St Francis Memorial Hospital, 1978-; Children's Hospital, San Francisco, 1978-. *Memberships include:* Various committees and currently Vice President, Board of Directors, California Podiatric Medical Association; Residency Alumni Association, California College of Podiatric Medicine; American Podiatric Medical Association; Past President, 2 terms, San Francisco/San Mateo Counties Podiatry Association. *Publications:* "Textbook of Bunion Surgery", Co-Author, 1979; 'Journal of the American Podiatry Association'; 'Journal of the American College of Foot Surgeons'. Presenter of numerous lectures. *Hobbies:* Biking; Weight training; Tennis. *Address:* 96 San Domingo Way, Novato, CA 94947, USA.

YOUSSEF, Nazih Rizk, b. 24 Feb. 1931, United Arab Republic. Director, Oncology Centre, Wheeling Hospital Medical Park. m. Heather Ann Swain, 8 Nov. 1967, London, England, 2 sons, 1 daughter. *Education:* DMRT, 1964, FFR, 1971, London University; CRCP(C), FRCP(C), Dalhousie University, Canada, 1970, 1974; FRCR, London University, 1975; MB; BCh. *Appointments:* Registrar, Royal Free Hospital, London, 1964-66; Senior Registrar, Christie Hospital, Manchester, 1967; Assistant, Associate Radiotherapist, Fellow Lecturer, Assistant Professor, Victoria General Hospital & Dalhousie University, Halifax, Canada, 1967-77; Director, Oncology Centre, Wheeling Hospital, West Virginia, USA, 1977-. *Memberships:* Medical Society of West Virginia; American College of Radiology; American Society of Therapeutic Radiologists; Fellow, Royal College of Physicians of Canada; Fellow, Royal College of Radiologists. *Publications:* "Adenosine Phosphates as Radioprotectors", 1973; "3 Split Course for Ovarian Carcinoma", 1977; "Benzydamine HCL Oral Rinse", 1978. *Hobbies:* Sports (Tennis, Swimming); Travel; Reading. *Address:* Oncology Centre, Wheeling Hospital Medical Park, Wheeling, WV 26003, USA.

YOZAWITZ, Allan, b. 8 Jan. 1949, Brooklyn, New York, USA. Director, Neuropsychology, Hutchings Psychiatric Center. m. Arlene Susan Greenfield, 20 Jan. 1973, 1 son, 1 daughter. *Education:* MA, Psychology, Queens College, CUNY, 1973; PhD, Psychology, City University of New York, 1977; Diplomate, Clinical Neuropsychology, 1984; American Board of Professional Psychology and American Board of Clinical Neuropsychology. *Appointments:* Research Scientist, New York State Psychiatric Institute, 1970-77; Director, Neuropsychology, Hutchings Psychiatric Center, Syracuse, 1977-; Consultant, Neuropsychology, Syracuse Developmental Center, 1979-83; Assistant Professor, SUNY Upstate Medical Center, 1979-; Private Practice, 1979-. *Memberships:* American Association for the Advancement of Science; American Psychological Association; International Neuropsychological Society; New York Academy of Sciences; Society for Neuroscience. *Publication:* "Dichotic Perception: Evidence for Right Hemisphere Dysfunction in Affective Psychosis", 'British Journal of Psychiatry', 1979. *Address:* Neuropsychology Unit, 625 Madison Street, Syracuse, NY 13210, USA.

YU, Henry Chung-hoa, b. 2 Mar. 1950, Hong Kong. Certified Specialist & Clinical Instructor in Endodontics. m. Karen S Siu, 12 June 1976, Chicago, USA, 1 son, 1 daughter. *Education:* BA, Indiana State University, 1972; DDS, Northwestern University, 1976; CAGS, MScD, Endodontics, 1983, DScD 1984, Boston University School of Graduate Dentistry; MRCD Endodontics 1984, FAGD General Dentistry 1985, Royal College of Dentists of Canada. *Appointments include:* Practitioner, General Dentistry, 1976-81; Teaching Fellow, Endodontics, Henry M Goldman School of Graduate Dentistry, Boston University, 1983-84; Clinical Instructor, Graduate Endodontics, Boston University, 1984-; Research Associate, University of Alberta, 1984-; Vice President, Alberta

Academy of General Dentistry, 1984-; Chairman of Continuing Education, ibid, 1985; Representative, Alberta Endodontic Society in Peer Review to Alberta Dental Association. *Memberships:* American Dental Association; Canadian Dental Association; American Association of Endodontists; Society of Occulsal Study Club, Pulp Biology Group, International Association of Dental Research; Interdisciplinary Dental Study Club; Academy of General Dentistry; etc. *Publications include:* Thesis, "To study the cutting efficiency of small files on dentin under different irrigating medium", 1983; Dissertation, "To study the cutting action of file tip on dentin (to disprove the Washington Monument shape of canal preparation theory)", 1984. *Hobbies:* Fishing; Model building. *Address:* Suite 1201, Baker Centre, 10025-106 Street, Edmonton, Alberta, Canada T5J 1G4.

YUDILEVICH, David L, b. 15 June 1930, Santiago, Chile. Professor of Physiology. m. dissolved, 1 son, 1 daughter. *Education:* MD, University of Chile, 1957. *Appointments:* Lecturer in Physiology, School of Medicine, 1962-67, Principal Investigator, Faculty of Sciences, 1967-73, University of Chile; Professor of Physiology, Head of Department of Physiology, Queen Elizabeth College, University of London, 1974-85. *Memberships:* Physiological Society; Biophysical Society; Microcirculatory Societies, Great Britain, USA & Europe. *Publications:* (Editor) "Carrier Mediated Transport of Solutes from Blood to Tissue", 1985; Various articles in physiological journals. *Hobbies:* Music; Reading; Walking. *Address:* King's College, University of London, Campden Hill Road, London W8 7AH, England.

YUE, Paul Cheung Kong, b. 28 Nov. 1934, Hong Kong. Consultant Paediatric Surgeon. m. Catherine Mei Oie Ng, 18 Nov. 1962, 1 son, 1 daughter. *Education:* MB, BS, Hong Kong; FRCS, England; FRCS, Edinburgh, Scotland; FRACS; FACS; DCH, London. *Appointments:* Honorary Surgical Registrar, Hospital for Sick Children, Great Ormond Street, London, England, 1966-67; Senior Lecturer in Surgery, 1970-75, Reader in Surgery, 1975-77, University of Hong Kong; Currently, Honorary Consultant Paediatric Surgeon, Alice Ho Miu Ling Nethersole Hospital, Hong Kong, Hong Kong Sanitorium and Hospital and British Military Hospital, Hong Kong. *Memberships:* British Association of Paediatric Surgeons; Pacific Association of Paediatric Surgeons; Asian Association of Paediatric Surgeons. *Publications:* 'Glucose-6-Phosphate-Dehydrogenase deficiency and neonatal jaundice in Chinese male infants in Hong Kong', 1965; 'Recurrent pyogenic cholangitis in children', 1974; 'Ectopic ureter in girls as a cause of wetting', 1974; 'Choledochal cyst: a review of 18 cases', 1974; 'Indirect immunofluorescence assay for antibody to germ tube of candida albicans - a new diagnostic test', 1976; 'Histochemical criteria for the diagnosis of Hirschsprung's Disease in rectal suction biopsies by acetylcholinesterase activity', 1977. *Hobbies:* Swimming; Fishing. *Address:* 712 Melbourne Plaza, 33 Queen's Road Central, Hong Kong.

Z

ZACHAU-CHRISTIANSEN, Bengt Niels, b. 7 July 1927, Copenhagen, Denmark. Professor of Paediatrics. m. Kirsten Rolighed, 12 May 1951, 2 sons, 2 daughters. *Education:* MD, University of Copenhagen, 1953; DPH 1958; Specialist in Paediatrics, 1962; PhD 1972; Specialist in Community Medicine, 1984. *Appointments:* Registrar, Copenhagen Municipality Hospitals, 1953-62; Research Fellow, Senior Registrar, State University Hospital, 1962-68; District Medical Officer, Elsinore, 1968-73; Consultant, State University Hospital, 1973-; Senior Lecturer in Paediatrics, 1970-77; Professor of Paediatrics, University of Copenhagen 1977-. *Memberships:* Former President, Danish Paediatricians Association; Danish School Doctors Association; Confederation of European Paediatric Association; Vice-President, International Academy of Transdiscipline Paediatric Education; Danish Medical Research Council, 1976-84. *Publications:* "Development in the First Year of Life", 1972; "Babies", 1975; 153 papers in internal medicine, paediatrics and community medicine. *Address:* Carl Johans Gade 1, DK-2100 Copenhagen Ø, Denmark.

ZAMAN, Khandaker Shahiduz, b. 1 Feb. 1931, Tangail, Bangladesh. Professor of Special Radiology. *Education:* MB, BS, Dhaka Medical College, 1961; DMRD, Queen's University, Kingston, Ontario, Canada. *Appointments:* Assistant Radiologist, Dhaka Medical College, Dhaka; Resident Radiologist, Kingston General Hospital, Kingston, Ontario; Assistant Professor of Radiology, Institute of Postgraduate Research in Medicine; Associate Professor of Special Radiology, I Pemar; Consultant Radiologist, Bengazi Hospital; Professor of Special Radiology, Dhaka Medical College. *Memberships:* British Institute of Radiology; Society of Radiologists, Bangladesh. *Hobbies:* Reading; Travel. *Address:* 51 Juginagar, PO Wari, Dhaka, Bangladesh.

ZAPATER, Ricardo Carlos, b. 4 Nov. 1917, Buenos Aires, Argentina. Ophthalmologist. m. Lucia Bruzzone, 29 Dec. 1956, Buenos Aires, 2 sons. *Education:* Doctor of Pharmacy and Biochemistry, 1947; University teaching qualification in Microbiology, Immunology, University of Buenos Aires, Argentina, 1957; Attendee, International Congress of Human and Animal Mycology, Paris, 1971, Tokyo, 1977, Jerusalem, 1979, New Zealand, 1982. *Appointments:* Head, Mycological and Bacteriological Section, Army Allergy Centre, 1947-55; Head, Bacteriology Section, Institute for Haematological studies of the National Academy of Medicine, 1956-62; Head, Santa Lucia Ophthalmological Laboratory, Buenos Aires, 1973-. *Memberships:* Argentine Biochemical Association; Argentine Medical Association; International Society for Human and Animal Mycology; Societas Internationalis Dermatologise Tropicae; Honorary Academy of Doctors of Madrid, Spain. *Publications:* "Micologia alergogena", editorial, 'El Ateneo', 1953; "Introduccion a la micologia medica", 1970; "Micologia Medica", editorial, 'El Ateneo', 1981; Co-editor "La infeccion ocular", 1985; 60 papers in national and international journals. *Honours:* Dr Antonio Cetrangolo Prize for a study presented to the Vte Lopez Hospital specialising in acute and chronic chest complaints, Buenos Aires, 1975. *Hobbies:* Rowing. *Address:* Rawson 2246, 1636 Olivos, Buenos Aires, Argentina.

ZARUR, Claudio Mallet, b. 5 July 1954, Rio de Janeiro, Brazil. Head of Internal Medicine and Pulmonology at Hospital Geral da Santa Casa; Professor, Chief of Internal Medicine and Pulmonology. m. Carla Palmieri, 8 Dec. 1983, Rio de Janeiro. *Education:* MD; Associate Member of The American College of Chest Physicians; Professor of Medicine. *Appointments:* Assistant, Pulmonology Department;

Assistant, Internal Medicine, Hospital Geral da Santa Casa; Assistant, Intensive Care Unit, Hospital Geral da Santa Casa; Doctor of Public Health Department, Rio de Janeiro; Professor Assistant, Gama Filho University and Souza Marques University; Head, Internal Medicine, Hospital Nossa Senhora do Socorro; Chief Substitute, Pulmonology Department, Hospital Geral da Santa Casa; Director of Hospital Nossa Senhora do Socorro. *Memberships:* Brazilian Society of Tisiology and Pulmonology; French Brazilian Society of Medicine; Representative Doctor of Hospital Geral Santa Casa at XXII Brazilian Congress of Pneumology and Tisiology; Associate Member, American College of Chest Physicians. *Publications:* Chromatography and Electrophoresis in Medicine, 1975; A Suggested New Treatment in Patients with Bad Prognosis in Tuberculosis, 1984; New Management of Hemoptysis (in process). *Honour:* Invited to be guest speaker at post graduation course, Carlos Chagas Foundation. *Hobbies:* Breeding Dogs; Classical Pianist; Tennis. *Address:* Avenida Ataulfo de Paiva, 935 salas 703/704, 22440 Leblon, Rio de Janeiro, Brazil.

ZEE-CHEN, Eunice Ling-Fong, b. 2 Jan. 1948, China. District Motor Development Team Occupational Therapist. m. Alfread H Chen, July 1977, Ventura, California, USA. *Education:* BS, San Jose, California, 1972; MS, University of Utah, 1980; Certified in Administration of Southern California Sensory Integration Tests and Neurodevelopmental Treatment. *Appointments:* Staff Occupational Therapist, City of Hope National Medical Center, Duarte, California, USA, 1973-75; Special Needs Coordinator, Ventura County Head Start/State Preschool Programme, Ventura, 1976-77; Pediatric Occupational Therapist, Jordan Valley Child Development Center, Midvale, Utah, 1977-80; District Motor Development Team Occupational Therapist, Jordan School District, Sandy, Utah, 1980-; Adjunct Instructor, Special Education Department, University of Utah, 1985-. *Memberships:* American and Utah Occupational Therapy Associations; Sensory Integration International; Council for Exceptional Children; Phi Kappa Phi. *Publications:* 'Motion Economy', Chairperson for booklet, 1975; 'Postrotary Nystagmus Responses in Down's Syndrome Children' in 'American Journal of Occupational Therapy', 1983. *Honours:* Tuition Grant, Department of Health, Education and Welfare, 1976, 78, 80; Special Educator of the Year, Council for Exceptional Children, Snowbird Chapter, 1981. *Hobbies:* Sculpture; Stamp collecting; Acupuncture study. *Address:* c/o Jordan Valley School, 7501 South 1000 East, Midvale, UT 84047, USA.

ZEIBARTS, Imants Robert, b. 17 Feb 1953, Adelaide, South Australia. Dental Surgeon. m. Ilze Sandra, 20 Dec 1975, Wayville, 1 son, 1 daughter. *Education:* BDS. *Appointments:* Private Practice, Morphett Vale, 1978-80; Visiting Dental Surgeon, Royal Adelaide Hospital, Gilles Plains Clinic, 1980-85; Private Practice, Ingle Farm and Para Hills, 1981-. *Membership:* Australian Dental Association. *Hobbies:* Fishing; Aviation History. *Address:* Suite 18, Ingle Farm Shopping Centre, Corner of Walkley's and Montague Roads, Ingle Farm, SA 5098, Australia.

ZEIN, Zein Ahmed, b. 13 Aug. 1947, Goba, Ethiopia. Associate Professor of Public Health; Assistant Dean. m. Yewegnesh Azeze, 24 Jan. 1979, Gondar, 1 son, 1 daughter. *Education:* BSc, Haile Seillase I University; MPH, American University of Beirut; Dr Med, Leipzig. *Appointments:* Health Officer, Ministry of Health, Ethiopia, 1969-71; Health Education Specialist, Ministry of Health, Ethiopia, 1974-75; Epidemiologist, Ministry of Health, Ethiopia, 1976; Lecturer, Gondar Public Health College, 1976-79; Assistant Professor, 1979-85, Associate Professor, 1985; Assistant Dean, 1981-85, Associate Dean, 1986-, Gondar College of Medical Sciences. *Memberships:* Ethiopian Medical Association; International Union for Health Education; International Epidemiological Association; Fellow, Royal Society of Health, UK; Member,

Advisory Panel on Cigarette Smoking, World Health Organization; Member, Ethiopian Delegation to the World Health Assembly, Geneva, 1984. *Publications:* Co-author: 'A Household Morbidity Survey in Northwestern Ethiopian Town", 1986; "The Epidemiology of Onchocerciases in Northwestern Ethiopia" (in press); Contributor to professional journals including: Co-author: "The Pattern of Cigarette Smoking among Ethiopian Medical and Paramedical Students', 'Ethiopian Medical Journal', 21, 1983; Co-author: "Birth weight of hospital delivered neonates in Northwestern Ethiopia', 'Ethiopian Medical Journal', Apr. 1985; 'Cigarette Smoking among Ethiopian School teachers', African Medical Journal', 1986, Proceedings. *Hobbies:* Reading; Radio; Listening to Music. *Address:* Addis Ababa University, Gondar College of Medical Sciences, PO Box 196, Gondar, Ethiopia.

ZEITER, Walter Jacob, b. 1 Jan. 1908, Danville, Illinois, USA. Emeritus Consultant. m. Gertrude Paul, 15 Sep. 1934, Cicero, Illinois, 2 daughters. *Education:* MD, University of Illinois College of Medicine, 1934. *Appointments:* Head of Department of Physical Medicine and Rehabilitation 1937-54, Assistant to the Executive Director 1948-55, Executive Secretary of Board of Governors 1956-63, Cleveland Clinic; Director of Education, Cleveland Clinic Educational Foundation, 1962-72; Emeritus Consultant, Cleveland Clinic Foundation, 1973-. *Memberships:* American Medical Association; Ohio State Medical Association; Cleveland Academy of Medicine; Fellow, American College of Physicians; Fellow, American Academy of Physical Medicine and Rehabilitation; American Congress on Physical Medicine and Rehabilitation. *Publications:* 27 scientific papers. *Honours:* Gold Key Award, American Congress of Rehabilitation Medicine, 1951; Annual 'Walter J Zeiter' lecture established by American Academy of Physical Medicine and Rehabilitation, 1968. *Hobbies:* Classical music; Golf; Photography. *Address:* Cleveland Clinic Foundation, 9500 Euclid Avenue, Cleveland, OH 44120, USA.

ZELDIS, Steven M, b. 11 June 1946, Brooklyn, New York, USA. Chief of Cardiology. m. Roberta L Weiss, 8 June 1974, New York, 1 son, 1 daughter. *Education:* BA, Rochester University, 1968; MD, Yale University School of Medicine, 1972; FACC; FCCP, FCCC. *Appointments:* Intern and Resident, Yale-New Haven Hospital, 1972-75; Fellow in Cardiology, University of Pennsylvania, 1975-77; Section Chief Noninvasive Cardiology, Long Island Jewish Medical Center, 1977-81; Acting Chief of Cardiology, 1981-84, Chief of Cardiology, 1984-, Nassau Hospital; Chief of Cardiology, Winthrop-University Hospital, 1984-. *Memberships:* Fellow: American College of Cardiology; American College of Chest Physicians; Clinical Council of Cardiology; American Heart Association. *Publications:* Co-author of papers contributed to: 'Journal of the American College of Cardiology'; 'New England Journal of Medicine'. *Honours:* Outstanding Teacher Award, Long Island Jewish Hillside Medical Center 1980; Leadership Award, Nassau Heart Association, 1984. *Hobbies:* Computers; Photography; Camping; Hiking. *Address:* Division of Cardiology, Winthrop University Hospital, Mineola, NY 11501, USA.

ZELLE, Raeone, b. 8 Feb. 1934, Torrey, Utah, USA. Consultant, High Risk/Developmentally disabled infants. m. Michael J Zelle, 6 Dec. 1958, Salt Lake City, Utah, 1 daughter. *Education:* BSc, University of Utah, Salt Lake City, 1956; Master of Nursing, University of Washington, Seattle, 1969. *Appointments:* Consultant, Developmental Disabilities, Alta California Regional Centre, Sacramento, CA, 1970-80; Instructor in Child Development, Paediatric Practitioner Course, University of California, Davis, 1971-78; Consultant High Risk/Developmentally Disabled Infants & Maternal Child Health (private practice), 1981-. *Memberships:* American Nurses Association; American Public Health Association. *Publica-*

tions: 'Early Intervention: Panacea or Experiment?' in 'Maternal Child Nursing', 1976; "The Developmentally Disabled Child & the Family" in "Family Health Care" edited D P Hymovich & M Barnard, 1979; "Developmentally Disabled Infants & Toddlers: Assessment & Intervention", 1983; Profeile of Interactional & Environmental Risks - Assessment Instrument & Training Manual", 1984. *Honours:* American Journal of Nursing Book of the Year Award, 1984; Outstanding Community Service, Sacramento Association of the Retarded, 1974, 1977. *Hobbies:* Gourmet Cooking; Wellness & Fitness Activities. *Address:* 1756 Olympus Drive, Sacramento, CA 95864, USA.

ZERNICKI, Boguslaw, b. 10 Apr. 1931, Dabrowa Gornicza. Head, Neurophysiology. m. Danuta Szulc, 16 Apr. 1960, 1 daughter. *Education:* MD, University of Lodz, 1954; PhD, 1959, Docent, 1966, Nencki Institute. *Appointments:* Junior Scientific Worker, 1953-66; Senior Scientific Worker, 1966-72; Associate Professor, 1972-80, Professor, 1980, Head, 1973-, Neurophysiology, Nencki Institute of Experimental Biology. *Memberships:* IBRO; European Training Programme in Brain and Behaviour Research, International Scientific Committee, 1981-84. *Publications:* Editor in Chief, 'Acta Neurobiol. Exp.', 1973; Articles in professional journals. *Honours:* Sociedad de Biologia de Santiago, 1965; State Prize, 1983. *Hobby:* Tennis. *Address:* Department of Neurophysiology, Nencki Institute of Experimental Biology, Pasteura 3, 02-093 Warsaw, Poland.

ZERVAS, Nicholas T, b. 9 Mar. 1929, Massachusetts, USA. Chief, Neurosurgical Service; Professor. m. Thalia Poleway, 15 Feb. 1959, 2 sons, 1 daughter. *Education:* MD, Honours, University of Chicago Medical School, 1954; AB, Harvard University, 1950. *Appointments:* Resident, Neurology, Neuropathology, Montreal Neurological Institute, 1955-56; Resident, Neurosurgery, Massachusetts General Hospital, 1958-62; Fellow, Stereotactic Surgery, University of Paris, 1960-61; Associate, Neurosurgery, Jefferson Medical College, Assistant Neurosurgeon, Wills Eye Hospital, Philadelphia, 1962-67; Assistant Professor, Surgery, Beth Israel Hospital, Harvard Medical School, 1967-71; Chief, Neurosurgery, Beth Israel Hospital, Boston, 1968-77; Professor, Surgery, Harvard Medical School, Chief, Neurosurgery, Massachusetts General Hospital, 1977-. *Memberships:* American College of Surgeons; American Association of Neurological Surgeons; American Medical Association; Society of Neurological Surgeons; World Society of Stereotaxic and Functional Surgery. *Publications:* Numerous articles in professional journals. *Hobbies:* Board of Trustees, New England Conservatory, Boston; Board of Directors, Museum of African Art, Washington DC; Board of Directors, Hellenic College, Brookline; Advisory Board, Regis College. *Address:* Massachusetts General Hospital, Boston, MA 02114, USA.

ZETTERSTRÖM, Rolf Olof Fredrik, b. 24 Aug. 1920, Stockholm, Sweden. Professor of Paediatrics. m. Jelena Renner, 17 Oct. 1959, 1 son, 5 daughters. *Education:* MD, Karolinska Institute, Stockholm, 1944; PhD Biochemistry, 1951; Post-graduate Training, Biochemistry Biophysics, 1949-51, in Paediatrics 1944-48; Research Fellow, Wennergren Institute, Experimental Biology, University of Stockholm, 1948-50. *Appointments:* Assistant Professor of Biochemistry & Pediatrics, Karolinska Institute, 1952-57; Professor of Paediatrics, Chairman of Department, University of Gothenburg, 1958-62; Professor of Paediatrics, Chairman of Department, Karolinska Institute, 1963-; Medical Director, Children's Hospital, Gothenburg, 1958-62, Crown Princess Lovisa's Children's Hospital, Stockholm, 1963-69, St Göran's Children's Hospital, Stockholm, 1970-. *Memberships:* Royal Swedish Academy of Sciences; Royal Norwegian Society of Sciences; Swedish Board of Postgraduate Medical Training, 1969-82; Nobel Committee for Medicine & Physiology, 1965-82; Honorary Member of some 10 foreign national paediatric societies. *Publications:* Some 270 scientific papers in biochemistry, biophysics & paediatrics, 1948-85. *Honours:* Lennander Award, Swedish Medical Society, 1959; Vice-President, Royal Swedish Academy of Sciences, 1982-83; Editor-in-Chief, Acta Paediatrica Scandinavica, 1964-. *Address:* St Göran's Children's Hospital, S-112 81 Stockholm, Sweden.

ZHOU, Fuzhen, b. 1 Aug. 1938, Peoples Republic of China. Senior Lecturer. m. Jing Wang, 24 Jan. 1963, Peoples Republic of China, 2 daughters. *Education:* PhD. *Appointments:* Resident, 1961-78, Lecturer, 1979-, Department of Obstetrics and Gynaecology, Ob/Gyn Hospital affiliated to Zhejiang Medical University, Hangzhou, Zhejiang, Peoples Republic of China; Postdoctoral Fellow, Department of Obstetrics and Gynaecology, University of British Columbia, Vancouver, Canada, 1985-86. *Membership:* Chinese Obstetrical and Gynaecological Association. *Publications:* Co-author, "Textbook of Obstetrics and Gynaecology", 1973; "The Influence of Female Reproductive System with Intrauterine DES Exposure", 'Overseas Medicine', 1982. *Honour:* World Health Organization Fellowship, Department of Obstetrics and Gynaecology, University of British Columbia, Vancouver, Canada, 1985-86. *Address:* Obstetrics and Gynaecology Hospital Affiliated to Zhejiang Medical University, Hangzhou, Zhejiang, People's Republic of China.

ZHOU, Tong-Hui, b. 8 Nov. 1924, Beijing, China. Professor of Analytical Chemistry. m. Xu-qing Wang, 20 Apr. 1957, Beijing, China, 2 daughters. *Education:* BS, Peking University, Beijing, China, 1944; MS, University of Washington, Seattle, USA, 1952, PhD, 1952. *Appointments:* Assistant Professor, Department of Chemistry, University of Kansas, Lawrence, USA, 1952-53; Research Analytical Chemist, Burroughs Wellcome Co, Tuckahoe, New York, USA, 1953-55; Associate Professor, Department of Analytical Chemistry, Institute of Materia Medica, Chinese Academy of Medical Sciences, Beijing, China, 1955-79, Professor and Head, -. *Memberships:* Chinese Pharmacopoeia Committee; Chinese Chemical Society; Associate Editor in Chief, 'Acta Pharmaceutica Sinica'; Associate Editor in Chief 'Chinese Journal of Pharmaceutical Analysis'; Editorial Board Member 'Analytical Chemistry', China; Editorial Board Member 'Water, Air and Soil Pollution'. *Publications:* 'Polarographic Determination of Nitrate in Sea Water' in 'Journal Marine Res.', 1953; 'Chromatographic studies of ergot alkaloids' in 'Acta Pharm. Sinica', 1957, 1958, 1960, 1963; Co-editor and contributor "Instrumental Analysis", volumes 1 and 2, 1965, volume 3, 1975; 'Amperometric titration of alkaloids', 1965; 'Chromatographic analysis of digitalis leaves', 1966; 'Studies on the components of essential oils', 1980, 1983; 'Study on ion-selective electrodes', 1983; 'Polarographic study of gossypol', 1984. *Honours:* National Award for Study in Ergot, 1978; Ministry of Health Award for Study in Santonin Analysis, 1958. *Hobbies:* Photography; Beijing Opera; Bridge; Sports. *Address:* Institute of Materia Medica, 1 Xian Nong Tan Street, Beijing 100050, China.

ZICH, Sue Schaab, b. 18 Oct. 1946, Buffalo, New York, USA. Director of Nursing Service. m. Timothy J Zich, 25 Nov. 1976, Buffalo, 2 sons. *Education:* BS Nursing, Villa Maria College, Erie, Pennsylvania, 1968; Licensed Registered Professional Nurse, New York State 1968-, Virginia 1976-. *Appointments:* Staff Nurse, Charge Nurse, Team Leader, Children's Hospital, 1968-71; Staff Nurse, Plasmapheres Unit, Roswell Park Memorial Institute, 1971-72 and 1973-75; Camp Nurse and Health and Safety Officer, Boy Scouts of American Summer Camp Ti-wa-ya-ee, Summers, 1971 and 1973-75; Staff Development Coordinator, Episcopal Church Home, 1975-77; Pediatric Charge Nurse, Loudoun Memorial Hospital, 1977; Nursing Instructor, Northern Virginia Mental Health Institute, 1977-78; Director, Nursing Service, Bancroft Institute, 1978-. *Memberships:* Secretary/{ Treasurer 1979-80, Vice President 1981-, Northern Virginia Directors of Nursing Association; Long Term Care Enducators Group of Northern Virginia. *Honours:* Den Leader Training Award, 1982; Key Leader Award of Prince William District 1982, District Award of Merit 1985, Boy Scouts of America; Den Leader Coach Training Award, 1985. *Hobbies:* Adult Leader, Boy Scouts of America; Sewing; Macrame; Soccer Referee; Reading. *Address:* 9709 Evans Ford Road, Manassas, VA 22111-2633, USA.

ZIEGLER, Dewey Kiper, b. 31 May 1920, Omaha, Nebraska, USA. Professor of Neurology. m. Gertrude Benjamin, 30 Mar. 1954, Kansas City, Missouri, 3 daughters. *Education:* BA, Harvard College, Cambridge, Massachusetts; MD, Harvard Medical School, Cambridge. *Appointments:* Adjunct Attending Physician, Acting Chief of the Division of Neurology and Psychiatry, Montefiore, Hospital, New York, NY, 1953-55; Assistant Professor, Division of Neurology, University of Minnesota Medical School, Minneapolis, Minnesota, 1955-56; Assistant Clinical Professor of Neurology 1956-58, Associate Professor of Neurology, 1958-64, Professor of Neurology, Chairman of Neurology, 1974-85, Professor of Neurology, Kansas University Medical School, Kansas City, Kansas, 1985-. *Memberships:* American Neurological Association; American Academy of Neurology; American EEG Society; American Pain Society. *Publications:* 'Headache Syndromes: Problems of Definition', 1979; 'Prolonged Relief of Dystonic Movements with Diazepam', 1981; 'Headache Syndromes suggested by Statistical Analysis of Headache Symptoms', 1982; "Genetics of Migraine", (Handbook), 1985; "Epidemiology of Migraine", (Handbook), 1985. *Honours:* President, American Academy of Neurology, 1979-81; Secretary, American Board of Psychiatry and Neurology, 1980-81. *Hobbies:* Gardening; Bonsai. *Address:* Department of Neurology, Kansas University Medical School, 39th and Rainbow Blvd., Kansas City, KS 66103, USA.

ZIEGLER, Reinhard, b. 8 Dec. 1935, Leipzig. Head, Endocrinology. m. Uta, 18 July 1959, Rothenbach, 1 son, 2 daughters. *Education:* Dr Med, University of Frankfurt, 1963; Privatdozent, University of Ulm, 1972. *Appointments:* Assistant Professor, University of Ulm, 1975-79; Head, Internal Medicine, Endocrinology, University of Heidelberg, 1979-. *Memberships:* Arzneimittelkommission der Deutchen Azteschaft; Deutsche Gesellschaft fur Innere Medizin, Endokrinologie; American Society for Bone and Mineral Research; Calcified Tissues Societies. *Publications:* "Calcitonin", 1974; "Endokrinologie", 1976; "EHDP", 1982; 200 articles in professional journals. *Honours:* Scientific Prize, City of Ulm, 1977. *Hobbies:* Clocks; Music. *Address:* Department of Internal Medicine I, Endocrinology and Metabolism, University of Heidelberg, Bergheimer Str 58, D-6900 Heidelberg, Federal Republic of Germany.

ZIELINSKI, Jerzy, b. 6 May 1914, Ruda, Poland. Professor Emeritus. m. Maria Magdalena Grzymalska, 31 Dec. 1941, Lwos, 3 daughters. *Education:* Diploma, Medical Faculty, University of Lwos, 1937; Doctor of Medicine, Medical Faculty University of Wroclaw, 1949; Doctor habilil med, Medical School, Katowice, 1963; Assistant Professor, 1963; Professor, 1972. *Appointments:* General Hospital Internship, 1937-38; Resident in Surgical and Urological Departments, Municipal Hospitals, Lwos, Krakow, Warsaw, Bytom, Zabrze, Katowice, 1938-41; Diverse professions and occupations, 1941-45; Senior Resident, I Surgical Clinic, Silesian Medical School, Zabrze and Katowice, 1954-64; Head, I Urological Clinic, Silesian Medical School, Katowice, 1964-84. *Memberships:* Executive Committee Member, European Association of Urology; Deutsche Urologische Gesellschaft; Honorary Member, Czechoslovakian Urological Association; President 1974-78, Honorary Member, Polish

Urological Association; French Urological Association; International Urological Association; Honorary Member, Polish Medical Association. *Publications include:* "Urological Radiology", (co-author), 1977; "Urological Oncology", (editor and co-author), 1978 and 1981; "Urology for General Practitioners", (co-author), 1982; Consulting editor, 'European Urology', 1975; Co-editor, 'Urologia Polska', 1975; Articles in Polish and international journals. *Hobbies:* Music; Tourism; History of 20th Century. *Address:* 30 Sklodowska-Curie Str app 9, 40058 Katowice, Poland.

ZILBERBERG, Barbara Zysman, b. 15 Sep. 1943, Kenya. School Psychologist. m. Charles Zilberberg, 2 Sep. 1965, New York, USA, 1 daughter. *Education:* BA Cum Laude; MA; Certification, School Psychologist. *Appointments:* Intern Psychologist; Senior Clinical Psychologist; Psychologist; School Psychologist. *Memberships:* National Association of School Psychologists; New Jersey Association of School Psychologists; American Psychological Association. *Publications:* Contributor to MENSA. *Honours:* Psi Chi, 1981; Exemption MA Thesis, 1966. *Hobbies:* Mensa; Sewing; Yoga; Charitable Work. *Address:* 469 Stratford Road, Union, NJ 07083, USA.

ZILKO, Paul John, b. 8 June 1944, Perth, Western Australia. Clinical Immunologist, Rheumatologist. m. Julia Mary Roberts, 19 July 1969, Kidderminster, England, 2 sons, 1 daughter. *Education:* MB, BS, university of Western Australia, 1967; Member, Royal College of Physicians, London, England, 1972; Fellow, Royal Australasian College of Physicians, 1974; Fellow, Royal College of Pathologists of Australasia, 1978. *Appointments:* Clinical Immunologist, Sir Charles Garrdner Hospital & Royal Perth Hospital, 1977-84; Sessional Clinical Immunologist, Sir Charles Gairdner Hospital & Fremantle Hospital, 1984-; Sessional Rheumatologist, Repatriation Hospital, Hollywood, 1984-. *Memberships:* Australian Rheumatism Association; Australian Society for Immunology; American Rheumatism Association; Heberden Society. *Publications:* Various articles in medical journals. *Honour:* P F Sobotka Overseas Travelling Fellowship, 1976. *Hobbies:* Tennis; Photography. *Address:* 30 Ventnor Avenue, West Perth, Western Australia 6005, Australia.

ZIMMER, Jens Rasmussen, b. 18 Apr. 1947, Hinge, Denmark. Lektor (Associate Professor). m. Kirsten Rasmussen, MD, 29 June 1968, Aarhus, 1 son, 2 daughters. *Education:* MD 1975, Dr med (PhD) 1976, Aarhus University Medical School. *Appointments:* Scholarship in Neuroanatomy 1969, Research Assistant 1970, Assistant Professor (Adjunkt) 1970, Associate Professor (Lektor) 1976-, Institute of Anatomy B; Leave of absence/senior research scholarship, Laboratory of Neurobiology, NIMR, Mill Hill, London, UK, 1977-78. *Memberships:* Medical School Study Board, Aarhus University, 1976-77; Medical School Faculty Council, ibid, 1980-85; Administrative Head, Institute of Anatomy B, 1982-84; Board Member, Danish Society of Neuroscience, 1984-. *Publications include:* Research papers, hippocampal anatomy, lesion-induced growth, plasticity of central nervous connections, 1971-; Transplantations of central nervous tissue, 1978-. *Hobbies:* Medical history; Tennis; Surrealistic paintings. *Address:* Institute of Anatomy B, University of Aarhus, DK 8000 Aarhus C, Denmark.

ZIMMERMAN, Daniel Lee, b. 12 Apr. 1954, Loma Linda, California, USA. Clinical Professor of Obstetrics-Gynaecology. m. (2) Susan B Tate, July 1985, San Bernadino, 1 son. *Education:* BS Biology magna cum laude, 1976; MD, 1979; Pediatric Residency, 1980-81; Obstetrics-Gynaecology Residency, 1981-84. *Appointments:* Clinical Professor of Obstetrics-Gynaecology, Loma Linda University Medical Center; Private practice, Obstetrics-Gynaecology, 1985-. *Memberships:* California Medical Association; American Medical Association; Junior Fellow, American College of Obstetrics and Gynaecology; San Bernadino County Medical Society; International Association of Gynaecological Laparoscopists. *Hobbies:* Water skiing; Motorcycles; Tennis; Stamp Collecting; Woodworking. *Address:* 3737 Lone Tree Way, Antioch, CA 94509, USA.

ZIMMERMAN, Manfred, b. 5 Nov. 1933, Herzheim, Germany. Professor of Physiology, University of Heidelberg. 2 sons. *Education:* Studies in Physics, Diplom-Physiker, 1953-59; Dr. ing; Dr. med. habil. *Appointments:* Assistant Professor, University of Karlsruhe, 1959-64; Assistant Professor, 1964-69, Universitatsdozent, 1969-73, University of Heidelberg; Visiting Professor, Monash University, Melbourne, Australia, 1973-74; Professor of Physiology, University of Heidelberg, 1973-. *Memberships:* Council Member, International Association for the Study of Pain; Gesellschaft zum Studium des Schmerzes fur Deutschland, Osterreich und die Schweiz. *Publications:* Co-author, "Phantom and Stump Pain", 1981; Co-author, "Pain in the Cancer Patient", 1984; Co-author, "Schmerz", 1984; Editor-in-Chief, 'Journal Neuroscience Letters'. *Honours:* Pischinger Award, Vienna, Austria, 1978; René Lériche Award, Speyer, Federal Republic of Germany, 1985. *Hobbies:* Performing Barock Recorder; Mountain Climbing. *Address:* II Physiologisches Institut der Universität, Im Neuenheimer Feld 326, D-6900 Heidelberg, Federal Republic of Germany.

ZINBERG, Scott David, b. 29 Mar. 1953, Rahway, New Jersey, USA. Doctor of Chiropractic. m. Laurie Klein, 3 Aug., 1980, Fairlawn, New Jersey, 1 son, 1 daughter. *Education:* BA, Curry College, 1975; DC, New York Chiropractic College, 1980. *Appointments:* Chief of Staff, Forster Chiropractic, Brooklyn; Staff Member, Parsons Hospital, New York. *Memberships:* American and New York Chiropractic Associations; Council on Nutrition; Council on Sports Injuries; Acupuncture Society of America. *Honours:* Diplomate, National Board of Chiropractic Examiners. *Hobbies:* Tennis; Skiing; Racquetball; Sailing. *Address:* 448 Marlborough Road, Brooklyn, NY 11226, USA.

ZOON, Kathryn Christine, b. 6 Nov. 1948, Yonkers, New York, USA. Chief of Immunology Laboratory. m. Robert Z Zoon, 22 Aug. 1970, Yonkers, 1 daughter. *Education:* BS Chemistry cum laude, Rensselaer Polytechnic Institute, Troy, New York, 1970; PhD Biochemistry, Johns Hopkins University, Baltimore, Maryland, 1975. *Appointments:* NIH Postdoctoral Fellow 1975-77, NIH Staff Fellow 1977-79, NIH Senior Staff Fellow 1979-80, Laboratory of Chemical Biology, NIAMDD, National Institutes of Health, Bethesda, Maryland; FDA Senior Staff Fellow 1980-83, Research Chemist in Cell Biology Branch of Division of Biochemistry and Biophysics 1983, Research Chemist and Chief of Immunology Laboratory in Division of Virology 1984-, Office of Biologics Research and Review, Center for Drugs and Biologics, Food and Drug Administration. *Memberships:* International Society of Interferon Research; Alpha chapter, Phi Lambda Upsilon. *Publications include:* 'The comparative structures of mammalian interferons' (with R Wetzel) in "Interferons and Their Applications Handbook of Experimental Pharmacology", (editors P Came and W Carter), 1983; 'Receptor-mediated binding and internalization of human interferon alpha by bovine kidney cells' (with H Arnheiter and D zur Nedden) in "Frontiers in Biochemical and Biophysical Studies of Proteins and Membrances" (editor T Y Liu and K Yasunobo), 1983; "Interferon: Research, Clinical Application and Regulatory Consideration", (co-contributor and co-editor), 1984; Numerous papers in journals and chapters in books. *Honours include:* William Pitt Mason Prize in Chemistry, 1970; Johns Hopkins University Fellowship, 1970-75. *Address:* Building 29A Room 2A17, 8800 Rockville Pike, Bethesda, MD 20205, USA.

ZRUBEK, Henryk Walerian, b. 28 Jan. 1929, Turobin, Poland. Director, Institute of Obstetrics and Gynaecology; Head, of Operative Gynaecology Clinic. m. Natalia Ann Dudka, 15 May 1950, Lublin, 2 daughters. *Education:* MD, 1953; PhD, 1962; Assistant Professor, 1972; Professor, 1980. *Appointments:* Assistant, Clinic of Obstetrics and Gynaecology, Head, 1 Clinic of Operative Gynaecology, 1973-; Director, Institute of Obstetrics and Gynaecology, Academy of Medicine, Lublin, 1974-. *Memberships:* Regional Consultant, Obstetrics and Gynaecology; National Body for Obstetrics and Gynaecology; General Board of Polish Gynaecological Society; Chairman, Regional Polish Gynaecological Society. *Publications:* Author over 100 publications on oncological surgery, fertility and biochemical examinations of human placenta perfounded in vitro; "Operative Treatment in Obstetrics and Gynaecology", book, 1984. *Honours:* For Exemplary Work in Health Service, 1970; Gold Cross of Merit, 1974; Chivalrous Cross, Order of Poland's Rebirth, 1979. *Hobbies:* Hunting; Sailing; Skiing. *Address:* ul Staszica 16, 20-081 Lublin, Poland.

ZUBERI, Sarwar Jehan, b. 1 Jan. 1934. Research Director, PMRC Research Centre, Karachi, Pakistan. *Education:* Intermediate Science, Gordon College, Rawalpindi; MB, BS, Dow Medical College, Karachi; various postgraduate courses. *Appointments include:* House Physician, Jinnah Central Hospital, Karachi, 1957-58; Various Medical Positions, Hospitals in England, 1958-1965; Resident, Gastroenterology, Bergen Pines Country Hospital, USA, 1965-66; Resident, Gastroenterology, 1966-67, Research Fellow, 1967-68, Lahey Clinic Foundation, Boston, USA; Research Officer, Pakistan Medical Research Council, 1968-73, Senior Research Officer, 1973-76, Principal Research Officer, 1976-77, Research Director, 1977-, Jinnah Postgraduate Medical Centre; Acting Director, Pakistan Medical Research Council, 1978, 1979. *Memberships include:* American Federation for Clinical Research; British Association of Surgical Oncology; Pakistan Cancer Society; Asian Pacific Association of Gastroenterology; Pakistan Medical Association; Pakistan Society of Gastroenterology and G. I. Endoscopy, Founder Member, Member, Executive Committee. *Publications:* Numerous Articles in professional journals, including: 'Journal of Pakistan Medical Association'; 'Pakistan Journal of Medical Research'; etc; Editor, 'Journal of the Pakistan Medical Association', 1974-; Editor, 'Regional Bulletin of Asian Pacific Association for the Study of Liver', 1982; Editor, 'Pakistan Journal of Medical Research', 1983-; Chief Editor, 'News Bulletin of the Pakistan Society of Gastro-Enterology and G I Endoscopy', 1984; etc. *Honours:* MSc, MPhil, University of Karachi, 1977. *Hobbies:* Photography; Travel; Reading. *Address:* PMRC Research Centre, Jinnah Postgraduate Medical Centre, Karachi, Pakistan.

ZUK, Tomasz, b. 12 Nov. 1921, Poland. Head of Department and Chair of Orthopaedics & Traumatology. m. (1) Stanislawa Krawiec, 29 June 1946, 3 sons, 1 daughter, (2) Barbara Borowska, 22 Dec. 1973. *Education:* MD, 1957; Habilitation, 1965; Professor, 1976; Specialisation in Orthopaedics and Traumatology, 1955. *Appointments:* Resident in Hospitals; Myslowice, Szczecin, Gliwice, 1948-49; Medical Corps, Military Service, 1949-57; Assistant, 1957, Adjunct, 1960, Docent, 1965, Organizer and Head, 1966-, Orthopaedics and Traumatology, Medical Academy, Warsaw, Szczecin; Consultant of Province and Member, State Consultants Board, Orthopaedics and Traumatology, 1965-82; Organiser, Head, Sanatorial Rehabilitations Centre in Orthopaedics, Kamien Pomorski, 1967-85. *Memberships:* Pomeranian Section, Polish Society of Orthopaedics and Traumatology; "Szczecinian Section, Crippled Rehabilitation, Supervision Board Member"; International Society of Orthopaedic Surgery and Traumatology; EULAR; ISFR; WFSS; ESSD. *Publications:* "Fundamentals of Orthopaedics", 1970, 4 editions; "Propedeutic of Orthopaedics", 1972, 2 edi-

tions; "Joint and Long Bones Lesions", 1983; "Pathological Fractures", Chapter in 'Traumatology', 1985; 120 papers in professional journals. *Honours:* Prize, Polish Academy of Sciences, 1962; Golden Cross of Merits, 1978; Order of Polonia Restituta, 1980; Teacher of Merit, 1982; Guerilla Cross, 1982; Medaille of Victory and Freedom, 1980. *Hobby:* Roses & Other Decorative Plants. *Address:* ul. Boh. Warszawy 105 m 3, 70373 Szczecin, Poland.

ZUKIWSKY, Ted Michael, b. 10 Jan 1954, Smoky Lake, Alberta, Canada. General Practitioner. m. Susan Jayne Birse, 26 Aug 1978, Calgary, Alberta, Canada. *Education:* BSc, DDS, Clinical Foundation for Orthopaedics/Orthodontics Certificate, Philadelphia College of Osteopathic Medicine; Postdoctoral course, Maxillo-temporomandibular Dysfunction. *Appointments:* Captain, Canadian Armed Forces attached to Special Service Force; General Practice. *Memberships:* Northeastern Alberta District Dental Society; Alberta Dental Association; British Columbia College of Dental Surgeons; Western Canada Dental Society; Canadian Dental Association; Fédération Dentaire Internationale; Academy of General Dentistry; International Association for Orthodontics. *Honours:* International College of Dentists (Canadian Section) Prize, 1977; Certificate of Merit, American Academy of Oral Medicine, 1978; Dean McCutcheons Honour Award, 1978; Certificate of Appreciation, Canadian Dental Association, 1982; 1983. *Hobbies:* Squash; Running. *Address:* PO Box 3069, St Paul, Alberta, T0A 3A0, Canada.

ZUMBRO, George Lionel, b. 11 Nov 1938, Murfreesboro, Tennessee, USA. Cardiothoracic Surgeon. m. Pennis Drinkard, 5 Oct 1984, Augusta, Georgia, 3 sons, 2 daughters. *Education:* BS, Mathematics, Middle Tennessee State University; University of Tennessee College of Medicine; Internship, Walter Reed General Hospital, 1965-66; Residencies: General Surgery, Tripler General Hospital, 1966-70; Thoracic Surgery, Walter Reed General Hospital, 1970-72. *Appointments:* Commanding Officer, 43rd Surgical Hospital (MA), Korea, 1972-73; Assistant Chief Cardiothoracic Surgery Service, Brooke Army Medical Center, 1973-75; Chief of Thoracic Surgery, University Hospital, 1980; Assistant Clinical Professor of Surgery, Medical College of Georgia; Consultant, Cardiac Surgery, Eisenhower Medical Center, Ft Gordon, Georgia. *Memberships:* Fellow, American College of Surgeons; Society of Thoracic Surgeons; Fellow, American College of Cardiology; Fellow, American College of Chest Physicians; International Society of Heart Transplantations; American Heart Association; Alpha Omega Alpha. *Publications:* Contributor to professional journals. *Hobbies:* Hunting; Fishing; Deep Sea Diving. *Address:* Cardiothoracic Surgical Associates of Augusta, PA, 820 St Sebastian Way, Suite 20, Augusta, GA 30901, USA.

ZVETINA, James Raymond, b. 14 Oct. 1913, Chicago, Illinois, USA. Section Chief Tuberculosis. m. Florence C Courtney, 4 Feb. 1944. *Education:* BS, Loyola University, 1940; MD, University of Illinois College of Medicine, 1943; Intern Certificate, 1944, Resident Certificate, 1945, West Suburban Hospital, Oak Park, Illinois; Veterans Administration Assistant Ward Medical Officer, USNR. *Appointments:* Medical Officer, USS Southampton, US Navy, 1945-46; Staff Physician, TB Service, 1946-54; Chief, Tuberculosis Section, Illinois, 1946-; Representative of Research Conference in Pulmonary Disease, VA Armed Forces; Clinical Instructor, University of Illinois, 1954-62; Clinical Assistant Professor, 1971-73, Clinical Associate Professor, 1973-78, Clinical Professor, 1978-, Medicine, University of Illinois; Attending Physician, 1984-. *Memberships:* American Medical Association; Illinois State and Chicago Medical Societies; American Thoracic Society; American College of Chest Physicians; American and Chicago Heart Associations. *Publications:* Contributor of papers to professional publications including: 'American Review of Respiratory Disease'; 'AJR'; 'Journal of Bone and

Joint Surgery'; 'Tubercle'. *Honours:* Fellow, American College of Chest Physicians; President, Catholic Physicians Guild, Chicago; Commondore, USNR ML Retired, 1973. *Hobbies:* Travel; Cruising. *Address:* 96 Forest Avenue, Riverside, IL 60546, USA.

ZWI, Saul, b. 7 July 1930, Johannesburg, South Africa. Professor of Pulmonology, Chief Physician, Johannesburg Hospital. m. Helga Charlotte Getz, 16 Dec 1953, Johannesburg, 2 sons, 2 daughters. *Education:* BSc, 1950, Bachelor of Medicine and Surgery, 1953, Witwatersrand University; US Public Health Service International Postdoctorate Fellowship, Cardiovascular Research Institute, University of California, San Francisco, 1963-64. *Appointments include:* House Physician, Johannesburg Hospital, 1954; Senior Research Bursar and Senior Research Officer, Physiology Division, SACSIR, 1956-59; Tutorial Registrar, Department of Medicine, Witwatersrand University and Johannesburg Hospital, 1959-60; Same institutions: Physician, Thoracic Surgery Unit, 1961-66; Physician in charge of Respiratory ICU, 1966-68; Principal Physician and Head, Respiratory Unit, 1968-85; Ad hominem Professor of Respiratory Medicine, 1973-85; Deputy Dean, Faculty of Medicine, 1981, 82; Dean, 1983; Visiting Professor, University of Chicago, 1971 and 1980. *Memberships:* Member and Officer of South African British and USA Medical Associations. *Publications:* Over 90 publications in medical journals and books from 1957-. *Honours include:* Medical Graduates Association Prize for Medicine, 1953; USPHS International Postdoctorate Fellow, 1963; Ethical Drug Association Award, 1968; FRCP, 1975; FCCP, 1976. *Hobbies:* Golf; Photography. *Address:* 15 St Andrews Avenue, Senderwood, Bedfordview 2008, South Africa.

ZYGULSKA-MACH, Helena Elzbieta, b. 7 Jan. 1926, Lwow, Poland. Professor. m. Zdzislaw Mach, 15 Mar. 1952, 2 sons. *Education:* MD, Jagiellonian University, 1951; M of Philosophy, Chemistry, 1952. *Appointments:* Assistant, Senior Assistant Lecturer, 1950-59; Assistant Ophthalmology Clinic, 1959-61, Senior Assistant, Lecturer, 1961-68, Professor, 1973-, Ophthalmological Clinic, Medical Academy, Cracow. *Memberships:* Vice President, Polish Ophthalmological Society; French Ophthalmological Society; Polish Ecological Club; Polish Society for Radiation Research. *Publications:* Numerous papers in professional journals, chapters in books; "Okulistyka wspolczesna"; "Kliniczna farmakologia ubocznych dziakan lekow", 1982. *Honours:* Recipient, Cross of Polonia Restituta, 1974; Medal, National Education. *Hobbies:* History of Fine Arts; Travel. *Address:* Rynek Kleparski 6/2, 31-150 Krakow, Poland.